TABLE OF CONTENTS

This edition of the MOTOR Auto Repair Manual, Vol. 1, covers specifications and service procedures on 2001-2005 Daimler-Chrysler Corporation, Ford Motor Company and General Motors Corporation models available at time of publication. Volume 2 covers Dash Gauges, Speed Controls, Wiper Systems, Passive Restraints, Dash Panel Service, Anti-Lock Brakes, Tire Pressure Monitoring System and Active Suspension Systems. The remaining vehicle information is located in Volume 1.

This manual is divided into four sections using three tabs. The section before Tab 1 covers Vehicle Identification, Air Bag System Precautions, Computer Relearn Procedures, Service Reminder & Warning Lamp Reset Procedures, Vehicle Lift Points, Non-Standard Tire & Wheel Size Adjustment To Ride Height Specifications & Tire Size Adjustment Charts, Electrical Symbol & Wire Color Code Identification and Vehicle Maintenance Schedules. Tab 1 covers DaimlerChrysler Corp. Tab 2 covers Ford Motor Company vehicles. Tab 3 covers General Motors Corporation vehicles. Each tabbed section reported in this manual is subject to change.

D1093755

DAIMLERCHRYSLER CORP.—TAB 1

Page No.

Page No.

FORD MOTOR COMPANY—TAB 2

TABLE OF CONTENTS-Continued

GENERAL MOTORS CORP.—TAB 3

VEHICLE IDENTIFICATION
INDEX

DIGIT 1   Country Of Origin
1 = USA
1 = USA
2 = Canada
2 = Canada
3 = Mexico
3 = Mexico
4 = USA
4 = USA

DIGIT 2   Manufacturer
G = General Motors
G = General Motors

DIGIT 3   Make
4 = Buick
4 = Buick

DIGIT 4   Restraint System
A = Manual Belts
B = Automatic Belts
C = Passive/Inflatable

DIGIT 4-5   Carline/Series
AG = Century Special
AG = Century Special & Wagon
AG = Century Special
AG = Century T-Type
AG = Century Special & Wagon
AG = Century
AG = Century
AH = Century Custom
AH = Century Custom
AL = Century Limited
AL = Century Estate Wagon
AL = Century Limited
BN = Roadmaster
BN = LeSabre Custom
BN = Roadmaster
BP = LeSabre Limited
BR = LeSabre Estate Wagon
BR = Roadmaster Estate Wagon
BR = Roadmaster Estate Wagon
BT = Roadmaster Limited
BT = Roadmaster Limited
BV = Electra Estate Wagon
CF = Electra T-Type
CU = Park Avenue Ultra
CU = Park Avenue Ultra
CU = Electra Park Avenue Ultra
CW = Park Avenue
CW = Electra Park Avenue
CW = Park Avenue
CX = Electra
CX = Electra Limited
EC = Reatta
EC = Reatta
EY = Riviera T-Type
EZ = Riviera
EZ = Riviera
GD = Riviera
GD = Riviera
GJ = Regal
GK = Regal T-Type
GM = Regal Limited
HH = LeSabre
HP = LeSabre Custom
HP = LeSabre Custom
HR = LeSabre Limited
HR = LeSabre Limited
JE = Skyhawk T-Type
JS = Skyhawk
JS = Skyhawk Custom
JT = Skyhawk Limited

DIGIT 4-5   Carline/Series
NC = Skylark 4D Custom
NC = Skylark 4D Custom
ND = Skylark 4D Luxury
ND = Skylark 4D Luxury
ND = Skylark Limited
NJ = Skylark Custom
NJ = Skylark 2D Custom
NJ = Skylark
NJ = Skylark 2D Custom
NJ = Skylark Limited
NJ = Skylark Limited
NJ = Somerset
NJ = Skylark
NJ = Skylark Custom
NK = Somerset T-Type
NM = Skylark Gran Sport
NM = Skylark 2D Limited
NM = Skylark Gran Sport
NM = Somerset Limited
NM = Skylark Limited
NV = Skylark
NV = Skylark Custom
NV = Skylark Custom
NV = Skylark
WB = Regal 2D Gran Sport
WB = Regal 2D Gran Sport
WB = Regal Custom
WB = Regal LS
WB = Regal Custom
WB = Regal LS
WC = LaCrosse CX
WD = Regal Limited
WD = Regal Limited
WD = LaCrosse CXL
WE = LaCrosse CXS
WF = Regal GS
WF = Regal Gran Sport
WF = Regal GS
WF = Regal Gran Sport
WF = Regal 4D Gran Sport
WF = Regal 4D Gran Sport
WS = Century Custom
WS = Century Custom
WY = Century Limited
WY = Century Limited
XB = Skylark Custom
XC = Skylark Limited

DIGIT 5   Carline/Series
B = Skylark Custom
B = Skylark
C = Skylark Limited
D = Skylark Sport
D = Skylark T-Type
E = Century Wagon
E = Skyhawk T-Type
G = Century T-Type
H = Century Custom
H = Century
J = Regal
K = Regal Sport
K = Regal T-Type
L = Century Limited
M = Regal Limited
N = LeSabre Custom
N = LeSabre
P = LeSabre Limited
R = LeSabre Estate Wagon
R = Electra Limited
S = Skyhawk Custom
S = Skyhawk
T = Skyhawk Limited

ARM0400000000642

Fig. 1   VIN Identification (Part 1 of 3). Buick

DIGIT 5 — Carline/Series

Code	Carline/Series
U	Electra Park Avenue
V	Electra Estate Wagon
W	Electra Park Avenue
X	Electra Limited
Y	Riviera T-Type
Z	Riviera

DIGIT 6 — Body Style

Code	Body Style
1	2D Coupe
1	2D Coupe
2	2D Hatchback
2	2D Coupe
3	2D Convertible
3	2D Convertible
5	4D Sedan
5	4D Sedan
8	4D Wagon
8	4D Wagon
8	4D Station Wagon
8	4D Station Wagon

DIGIT 6-7 — Body Style

Code	Body Style
11	2D Coupe
11	2D Sedan
19	4D Sedan
27	2D Coupe
35	4D Wagon
37	2D Coupe
47	2D Coupe
57	2D Convertible
67	2D Convertible
69	4D Sedan
77	2D Hatchback

DIGIT 7 — Restraint System

Code	Restraint System
1	Manual Belts
2	Dual Front Airbags w/Manual Belts
3	Driverside Airbag w/Manual Belts
3	Driverside Airbag w/Manual Belts
4	Automatic Belts
4	2nd Generation Dual Front & Side Airbags w/Manual Belts
4	Dual Front & Side Airbags w/Manual Belts
4	Automatic Belts
4	2nd Generation Dual Front & Side Airbags w/Manual Belts
5	Driverside Airbag w/Automatic Belts
5	Dual Front & Side Airbags w/Manual Belts
5	Driverside Airbag w/Automatic Belts
5	Dual Front & Driver's Side Airbags w/Manual Belts

DIGIT 8 — Engine

Code	Engine
0	1.8L L-4 EFI
1	3.8L V6 MPI S/C
1	2.0L L-4 EFI
1	3.8L V6 SFI S/C
3	3.8L V6 SFI
3	3.8L V6 SFI
3	2.3L L-4 EFI OHC
3	3.8L V6 4BBL T/C
3	2.3L L-4 EFI OHC
3	3.8L V6 FI TBO
3	3.8L V6 2BBL
4	4.1L V6 4BBL
4	2.2L L-4 MPI
4	2.2L L-4 MPI
5	2.5L L-4 2BBL
7	3.6L V6 SFI
7	3.8L V6 SFI

Fig. 1 VIN Identification (Part 2 of 3). Buick

ARM040000000643

DIGIT 8 — Engine

Code	Engine
7	5.7L V8 TBI
7	5.7L V8 TBI
8	3.8L V6 2BBL
9	3.8L V6 SFI
A	3.8L V6 2BBL
B	2.0L L-4 2BBL
C	3.8L V6 MPI
C	3.8L V6 MPI
D	2.3L L-4 EFI Quad
D	2.3L L-4 EFI Quad
E	3.0L V6 2BBL
E	5.0L V8 TBI
E	5.0L V8 TBI
G	1.8L L-4 2BBL
H	5.0L V8 4BBL
J	1.8L L-4 MPI
J	3.1L V6 SFI
J	3.8L V6 MPI
K	3.8L V6 SFI
K	3.8L V6 SFI
K	3.8L V6 SFI
L	2.0L L-4 EFI
L	3.8L V6 MPI
L	3.8L V6 MPI
L	3.0L V6 MPI
M	3.1L V6 MPI
M	2.0L L-4 EFI
M	3.1L V6 SFI
M	3.1L V6 SFI
N	5.7L V8 4BBL Dsl
N	3.3L V6 MPI
N	5.7L V8 Dsl
P	2.0L L-4 EFI
P	5.7L V8 MPI
P	5.7L V8 MPI
R	2.5L L-4 TBI
R	2.5L L-4 TBI
S	4.3L V8 2BBL
T	2.4L L-4 SFI DOHC
T	3.1L V6 MPI
T	2.4L L-4 SFI DOHC
T	4.3L V6 Dsl
U	3.1L V6 MPI
U	2.5L L-4 TBI
V	4.3L V6 Dsl
W	3.1L V6 MPI
X	2.8L V6 2BBL
Y	5.0L V8 4BBL
Z	2.8L V6 2BBL HO

DIGIT 10 — Model Year

Code	Model Year
1	2001
1	2001
2	2002
2	2002
3	2003
3	2003
4	2004
4	2004
5	2005
5	2005
B	1981
C	1982
D	1983
E	1984
F	1985

DIGIT 10 — Model Year

Code	Model Year
G	1986
H	1987
J	1988
K	1989
L	1990
M	1991
M	1991
N	1992
N	1992
P	1993
P	1993
R	1994
R	1994
S	1995
S	1995
T	1996
T	1996
V	1997
V	1997
W	1998
W	1998
X	1999
X	1999
Y	2000
Y	2000

DIGIT 11 — Assembly Plant Location

Code	Assembly Plant Location
1	Wentzville, MO, USA
1	Oshawa #2, ON, Canada
1	Oshawa #2, ON, Canada
1	Wentzville, MO, USA
2	Ste. Therese, PQ, Canada
4	Orion, MI, USA
4	Orion, MI, USA
6	Oklahoma City, OK, USA
6	Oklahoma City, OK, USA
A	Lakewood, GA, USA
B	Lansing, MI, USA
B	Lansing, MI, USA
C	Lansing, MI, USA
C	Lansing, MI, USA
D	Doraville, GA, USA
D	Doraville, GA, USA
E	Linden, NJ, USA
G	Framingham, MA, USA
H	Flint, MI, USA
H	Flint, MI, USA
J	Janesville, WI, USA
K	Linden, NJ, USA
K	Leeds, MO, USA
M	Lansing, MI, USA
M	Lansing, MI, USA
P	Pontiac, MI, USA
R	Arlington, TX, USA
R	Arlington, TX, USA
S	Ramos Arizpe, Mexico
S	Ramos Arizpe, Mexico
T	Tarrytown, NY, USA
U	Hamtramck, MI, USA
U	Hamtramck, MI, USA
W	Willow Run, MI, USA
W	Willow Run, MI, USA
X	Fairfax, KS, USA
Z	Fremont, CA, USA

Fig. 1 VIN Identification (Part 3 of 3). Buick

ARM040000000644

DIGIT 11 Assembly Plant Location

Code	Location
E	Pontiac East, MI, USA
E	Linden, NJ, USA
J	Janesville, WI, USA
K	Leeds, MO, USA
N	Russelsheim, Germany
R	Arlington, TX, USA
R	Russelsheim, Germany
R	Arlington, TX, USA
U	Hamtramck, MI, USA
U	Hamtramck, MI, USA

DIGIT 8 Engine

Code	Engine
B	4.9L V8 MPI
B	4.9L V8 MPI
E	5.0L V8 TBI
G	1.8L L4 2BBL
N	3.2L V6 SFI DOHC
N	3.2L V6 SFI DOHC
N	5.7L V8 Dsl
P	5.7L V8 MPI
P	5.7L V8 MPI
P	2.0L L4 EFI
R	3.0L V6 MPI
R	3.0L V6 MPI
S	5.7L V8 SFI HO
S	5.7L V8 SFI HO
T	4.3L V6 Dsl
W	2.8L V6 MPI
Y	4.6L V8 SFI DOHC
Y	4.6L V8 MPI DOHC
Y	4.6L V8 MPI DOHC
Y	5.0L V8 4BBL
Y	4.6L V8 SFI DOHC

DIGIT 10 Model Year

Code	Year
1	2001
1	2001
2	2002
2	2002
3	2003
3	2003
4	2004
4	2004
5	2005
5	2005
B	1981
C	1982
D	1983
E	1984
F	1985
G	1986
H	1987
J	1988
K	1989
L	1990
M	1991
M	1991
N	1992
N	1992
P	1993
P	1993
R	1994
R	1994
S	1995
S	1995
T	1996
T	1996
V	1997
V	1997
W	1998
W	1998
X	1999
X	1999
Y	2000
Y	2000

DIGIT 11 Assembly Plant Location

Code	Location
0	Lansing, MI, USA
0	Lansing, MI, USA
4	Orion, MI, USA
4	Orion, MI, USA
5	Bowling Green, KY, USA
9	Detroit, MI, USA
C	Southgate, CA, USA

Fig. 2 VIN Identification (Part 2 of 2). Cadillac

DIGIT 1 Country Of Origin

Code	Country
1	USA
1	USA
W	Germany
W	Germany

DIGIT 2 Manufacturer

Code	Manufacturer
0	Opel
0	Opel
G	General Motors
G	General Motors

DIGIT 3 Make

Code	Make
6	Cadillac
6	Cadillac

DIGIT 4 Restraint System

Code	Restraint System
A	Manual Belts

DIGIT 4-5 Carline/Series

Code	Carline/Series
CB	DeVille Sixty Special
CB	Fleetwood
CB	Fleetwood
CD	DeVille Sixty Special
CD	DeVille
CG	Fleetwood Sixty Special
CG	Fleetwood Sixty Special
CS	Fleetwood Sixty Special
CT	DeVille Touring
DC	DeVille Touring
DG	STS-V8
DG	CTS
DM	CTS
DN	CTS
DN	CTS-V
DN	CTS-V
DP	CTS
DW	Brougham RWD
DW	Fleetwood Brougham RWD
DW	STS
DW	Fleetwood RWD
DW	Fleetwood RWD
EC	Eldorado ETC Collector's Edition
EC	Eldorado ETC Collector's Edition
EL	Eldorado ESC
EL	Eldorado
EL	Eldorado ESC
ET	Eldorado ETC
ET	Eldorado ETC
ET	Eldorado Touring
ET	Eldorado Touring
JG	Cimarron
KD	DeVille
KD	DeVille
KE	DeVille D'Elegance
KE	DeVille D'Elegance
KE	DeVille DHS
KF	DeVille DHS
KF	DeVille Concours
KF	DeVille Concours
KF	DeVille Concours
KF	DeVille DTS
KS	Seville SLS
KS	Seville SLS
KS	Seville
KS	Seville
KY	Seville Touring
KY	Seville STS
KY	Seville STS
KY	Seville STS
KY	Seville Touring
VR	Catera

DIGIT 4-5 Carline/Series

Code	Carline/Series
VR	Allante
VR	Allante Convertible w/Hardtop
VR	Catera
VR	Allante Convertible w/Hardtop
VS	Allante Convertible
VS	Allante Convertible
YV	XLR

DIGIT 5 Carline/Series

Code	Carline/Series
B	Fleetwood, Brougham
B	Fleetwood
D	DeVille
F	Fleetwood Limousine
G	Cimarron
L	Eldorado
M	DeVille RWD
S	Seville

DIGIT 6 Body Style

Code	Body Style
1	2D Coupe
1	2D Coupe
3	2D Convertible
3	2D Coupe/Convertible
3	2D Convertible
5	4D Sedan
6	4D Sedan

DIGIT 6-7 Body Style

Code	Body Style
23	4D Sedan Limousine
33	4D Sedan Limousine
47	2D Coupe
57	2D Coupe
67	2D Convertible
69	4D Sedan

DIGIT 7 Restraint System

Code	Restraint System
1	Manual Belts
2	Dual Front Airbags w/Manual Belts
2	Dual Front Airbags w/Manual Belts
3	Driverside Airbag w/Manual Belts
3	Driverside Airbag w/Manual Belts
4	Dual Front & Side Airbags w/Manual Belts
4	Dual Front & Side Airbags w/Manual Belts
4	Automatic Belts
5	Dual Front & Side Airbags w/Manual Belts
5	Dual Front & Side Airbags w/Manual Belts
5	Dual Front & Front Side Airbags, Front-to-Rear Head Curtai
7	Dual Front & Front Side Airbags & Manual Belts
7	Dual Front & Rear Side Airbags & Manual Belts
7	Dual Front & Rear Side Airbags & Manual Belts

DIGIT 8 Engine

Code	Engine
1	2.0L L4 EFI
3	4.5L V8 DFI
4	4.1L V6 4BBL
5	4.5L V8 DFI
6	6.0L V8 4BBL
7	4.1L V8 SFI
7	3.6L V6 SFI
7	5.7L V8 TBI
7	5.7L V8 MPI
7	3.6L V6 SFI
8	4.5L V8 MPI
8	4.1L V8 TBI
8	4.1L V8 DFI
9	4.6L V8 MPI
9	4.6L V8 MPI
9	6.0L V8 MPI
9	5.0L V8 4BBL
A	4.6L V6 SFI DOHC
A	4.6L V8 SFI

Fig. 2 VIN Identification (Part 1 of 2). Cadillac

ARM040000000646

ARM040000000645

DIGIT 1	Country Of Origin
1	= USA
1	= USA
2	= Canada
2	= Canada
3	= Mexico
3	= Mexico
4	= USA
4	= USA
J	= Japan
K	= Korea

DIGIT 2	Manufacturer
8	= Isuzu
C	= Cami
C	= Cami
G	= General Motors
G	= General Motors
L	= General Motors
Y	= Nummi

DIGIT 3	Make
1	= Chevrolet
1	= Chevrolet

DIGIT 4	Restraint System
A	= Manual Belts

DIGIT 4-5	Carline/Series
AW	= Celebrity
BL	= Impala SS
BL	= Caprice
BL	= Caprice Classic
BL	= Impala
BL	= Caprice
BL	= Impala SS
BL	= Caprice Classic
BN	= Caprice Classic
BN	= Caprice Classic
BN	= Caprice Classic LS
BN	= Impala SS
BN	= Impala SS
BN	= Caprice Classic LS
BU	= Caprice Brougham
FP	= Camaro
FP	= Camaro
FS	= Camaro Berlinetta
GZ	= Monte Carlo
J*	= LS
J*	= LT
J*	= Base
J*	= SS
JC	= Cavalier Base
JC	= Cavalier VL
JC	= Cavalier Base
JC	= Cavalier RS
JC	= Cavalier RS
JC	= Cavalier VL
JD	= Cavalier CS
JE	= Cavalier RS
JE	= Cavalier Type 10 & Conv
JF	= Cavalier RS
JF	= Cavalier LS Sedan
JF	= Cavalier LS
JF	= Cavalier Z24
JF	= Cavalier Z24
JF	= Cavalier LS
JF	= Cavalier RS
JF	= Cavalier LS Sedan
JH	= Cavalier LS Sport
JH	= Cavalier LS Sport
JS	= Cavalier LS Coupe
JS	= Cavalier LS Coupe
LD	= Corsica

DIGIT 4-5	Carline/Series
LD	= Corsica
LS	= Malibu LS
LT	= Corsica LT
LT	= Corsica
LT	= Malibu LT
LT	= Corsica LT
LV	= Beretta
LV	= Beretta
LW	= Beretta Z26
LW	= Beretta GT
LW	= Beretta Z26
LW	= Beretta GT
LZ	= Beretta GTZ
LZ	= Beretta GTZ
LZ	= Corsica LTZ
MR	= Metro
MR	= Metro
MR	= Sprint
MS	= Sprint ER
ND	= Malibu
ND	= Malibu Classic
ND	= Malibu
ND	= Malibu Classic
NE	= Malibu LS
NE	= Malibu LS
RF	= Spectrum
RF	= Spectrum Coupe
RG	= Spectrum Sedan
SK	= Nova
SK	= Prizm
TB	= Chevette CS
TD	= Aveo Base & LS
TD	= Aveo Base
TG	= Aveo LT
TJ	= Aveo LS & LT
WF	= Impala
WF	= Impala
WH	= Impala LS
WH	= Impala LS
WL	= Lumina LS
WL	= Lumina
WL	= Lumina
WL	= Lumina LS
WN	= Lumina Euro
WN	= Lumina LTZ
WN	= Lumina Euro
WN	= Lumina LS
WN	= Lumina LS
WN	= Lumina LTZ
WP	= Impala SS
WP	= Impala SS
WP	= Lumina Z34
WP	= Lumina Z34
WW	= Monte Carlo LS
WW	= Monte Carlo LS
WX	= Monte Carlo Z34
WX	= Monte Carlo SS
WX	= Monte Carlo SS
WX	= Monte Carlo Z34
WZ	= Monte Carlo SS S/C
WZ	= Monte Carlo SS S/C
XX	= Citation II
YY	= Corvette
YY	= Corvette
YZ	= Corvette ZR1
YZ	= Corvette ZR1
ZL	= Lumina LS
ZS	= Malibu
ZS	= Malibu
ZT	= Malibu LS
ZU	= Malibu LT

ARM0400000000647

Fig. 3 VIN Identification (Part 1 of 4). Chevrolet

DIGIT 5	Carline/Series
B	= Chevette
B	= Chevette CS
C	= Cavalier
D	= Cavalier CS
D	= Cavalier
E	= Cavalier Type 10
H	= Citation Coupe
J	= Chevette Scooter
J	= Chevette
L	= Impala
N	= Caprice Classic
P	= Camaro Sport Coupe
S	= Camaro Berlinetta
T	= Malibu
W	= Malibu
W	= Malibu Classic
W	= Celebrity
X	= Citation
Y	= Corvette
Z	= Monte Carlo

DIGIT 6	Body Style
1	= 2D Coupe
1	= 2D Coupe/Sedan
1	= 2D Coupe
1	= 2D Coupe/Sedan
2	= 2D Coupe Liftback
2	= 2D Hatchback/Liftback
2	= 2D Hatchback
2	= 2D Coupe Liftback
2	= 2D Liftback
2	= 2D Hatchback/Liftback
2	= 2D Hatchback
2	= 2D Liftback
3	= 2D Convertible
3	= 2D Convertible
5	= 4D Sedan
5	= 4D Sedan
6	= 4D Hatchback
6	= 4D Sedan Maxx
6	= 4D Sedan Maxx
6	= 4D Hatchback
6	= 4D Hatchback, Sedan
8	= 4D Station Wagon
8	= 4D Station Wagon

DIGIT 6-7	Body Type
07	= 2D Coupe
08	= 2D Hatchback
11	= 2D Coupe
19	= 4D Sedan/Hatchback
27	= 2D Coupe/Hatchback
27	= 2D Coupe
35	= 4D 2-Seat Wagon
37	= 2D Coupe/Hatchback
47	= 2D Hatchback Sport
67	= 2D Convertible
68	= 4D Hatchback
68	= 4D Sedan/Hatchback
69	= 4D Seadn/Hatchback
69	= 4D Sedan
77	= 2D Coupe/Hatchback
77	= 2D Hatchback
87	= 2D Sedan/Hatchback
87	= 2D Hatchback

DIGIT 7	Restraint System
1	= Manual Belts
1	= Manual Belts
2	= Dual Front Airbags w/Active Seat Belt Restraints
2	= Dual Front Airbags w/Manual Belts
2	= Dual Front Airbags w/Manual Belts
3	= Driverside Airbag w/Manual Belts

DIGIT 7	Restraint System
3	= Driverside Airbag w/Manual Belts
4	= Dual Front & Side Airbags w/Manual Belts
4	= Dual Front & Side Airbags w/Manual Belts
4	= Passive Automatic Belts
4	= Passive Automatic Belts
4	= Automatic Belts
5	= Dual Front & Driver's Side Airbags w/Manual Belts
5	= Driverside Airbag w/Automatic Belts
5	= Dual Front & Driver's Side Airbags w/Manual Belts
5	= Driverside Airbag w/Automatic Belts
7	= Dual Front, Side & Head Curtain Airbags, w/Manual Belts
7	= Dual Front, Side & Head Curtain Airbags w/Manual Belts

DIGIT 8	Engine
1	= 2.8L V6 2BBL
1	= 3.8L V6 SFI S/C
1	= 3.8L V6 SFI S/C
1	= 2.0L I-4 EFI
2	= 1.3L I-4 EFI SOHC
2	= 1.3L I-4 EFI SOHC
2	= 1.0L I-3 Turbo
2	= 2.5L I-4 EFI
2	= 2.5L I-4 TBI
3	= 3.8L V6 2BBL
4	= 2.2L I-4 MPI
4	= 2.2L I-4 MPI
4	= 1.6L I-4 2BBL
5	= 5.7L V8 SFI DOHC
5	= 5.7L V8 SFI DOHC
5	= 1.6L I-4 MPI
5	= 1.0L I-3 2V
5	= 2.5L I-4 2BBL
6	= 2.2L I-4 MPI DOHC Flex Fuel
6	= 1.6L I-4 MPI DOHC
6	= 5.7L V8 4BBL
6	= 1.0L I-3 EFI SOHC
6	= 1.0L I-3 EFI SOHC
7	= 5.7L V8 TBI
7	= 1.5L I-4 2BBL
7	= 5.0L V8 CPI
7	= 5.7L V8 TBI
7	= 5.7L V8 EFI
7	= 5.7L V8 EFI
8	= 3.5L V6 SFI
8	= 1.8L I-4 SFI DOHC
8	= 3.5L V6 SFI
8	= 5.7L V8 TPI
8	= 5.7L V8 TPI
9	= 1.5L I-4 FI TBO
9	= 1.3L I-4 EFI
9	= 1.3L I-4 EFI
9	= 3.8L V6 2BBL
9	= 1.6L I-4 2BBL
A	= 2.3L I-4 MPI
A	= 2.3L I-4 MPI
A	= 3.8L V6 2BBL
C	= 1.6L I-4 2BBL
D	= 2.3L I-4 MFI
D	= 1.8L I-4 Dsl
D	= 2.3L I-4 MFI
D	= 1.6L I-4 MPI DOHC
E	= 3.4L V6 SFI
E	= 5.0L V8 TBI
E	= 3.4L V6 SFI
E	= 5.0L V8 TBI
F	= 5.0L V8 MPI
F	= 2.2L I4 MPI DOHC
F	= 2.2L I4 MPI DOHC
F	= 2.5L I-4 2BBL
F	= 2.2L I-4 MPI DOHC
F	= 2.2L I-4 MPI DOHC
F	= 5.0L V8 MPI

ARM0400000000648

Fig. 3 VIN Identification (Part 2 of 4). Chevrolet

DIGIT 8	Engine
G	= 2.2L I-4 TBI
G	= 5.7L V8 SFI
G	= 5.7L V8 MPI
G	= 2.2L I-4 TBI
G	= 1.8L I-4 2BBL
G	= 5.7L V8 MPI
G	= 5.7L V8 SFI
G	= 5.0L V8 4BBL
H	= 5.0L V8 4BBL
J	= 5.7L V8 MFI
J	= 3.1L V6 SFI
J	= 3.1L V6 SFI
J	= 5.7L V8 MPI
J	= 5.7L V8 SFI
J	= 5.7L V8 MPI
J	= 5.7L V8 MFI
J	= 5.7L V8 SFI
J	= 4.4L V8 2BBL
K	= 3.8L V6 SFI
K	= 3.8L V6 SFI
K	= 1.5L I-4 2BBL
K	= 3.8L V6 2BBL
L	= 2.8L V6 2BBL
L	= 5.7L V8 4BBL
M	= 1.0L I-3 2BBL
M	= 3.1L V6 SFI
M	= 3.1L V6 SFI
N	= 5.7L V8 Dsl
N	= 5.7L V8 FI Dsl
P	= 5.7L V8 SFI
P	= 5.7L V8 SFI
P	= 5.7L V8 MPI
P	= 5.7L V8 MPI
P	= 2.0L I-4 EFI
R	= 2.5L I-4 TBI
R	= 2.5L I-4 TBI
S	= 5.7L V8 SFI HO
S	= 3.4L V6 MPI
S	= 3.4L V6 MPI
S	= 2.8L V6 EFI
S	= 5.0L V8 TBI
S	= 5.7L V8 SFI HO
T	= 3.1L V6 MPI
T	= 4.3L V6 EFI
T	= 2.4L I-4 SFI DOHC
T	= 2.4L I-4 SFI DOHC
T	= 3.1L V6 MPI
T	= 4.3L V6 DSL
V	= 4.3L V6 FI Dsl
V	= 4.3L V6 Dsl
W	= 2.8L V6 MPI
W	= 4.3L V8 SFI
W	= 4.3L V8 SFI
W	= 3.1L V6 MPI
W	= 3.1L V6 MPI
X	= 3.4L V6 SFI DOHC
X	= 3.4L V6 SFI DOHC
X	= 2.8L V6 2BBL
Y	= 5.0L V8 4BBL
Z	= 2.8L V6 2BBL HO
Z	= 4.3L V6 EFI

DIGIT 10	Model Year
1	= 2001
1	= 2001
2	= 2002
2	= 2002
3	= 2003
3	= 2003
4	= 2004
4	= 2004
5	= 2005

DIGIT 10	Model Year
5	= 2005
B	= 1981
C	= 1982
D	= 1983
E	= 1984
F	= 1985
G	= 1986
H	= 1987
J	= 1988
K	= 1989
L	= 1990
M	= 1991
M	= 1991
N	= 1992
N	= 1992
P	= 1993
P	= 1993
R	= 1994
R	= 1994
S	= 1995
S	= 1995
T	= 1996
T	= 1996
V	= 1997
V	= 1997
W	= 1998
W	= 1998
X	= 1999
X	= 1999
Y	= 2000
Y	= 2000

DIGIT 11	Assembly Plant Location
0	= Lansing, MI, USA
0	= Lansing, MI, USA
1	= Oshawa #2, ON, Canada
1	= Oshawa #2, ON, Canada
1	= Oshawa, ON, Canada
2	= Ste. Therese, PQ, Canada
2	= Ste. Therese, PQ, Canada
3	= Kawasaki, Japan
5	= Bowling Green, KY, USA
5	= Bowling Green, KY, USA
6	= Oklahoma City, OK, USA
6	= Ingersoll, ON, Canada
6	= Oklahoma City, OK, USA
6	= Ingersoll, ON, Canada
7	= Fujisawa, Japan
7	= Lordstown, OH, USA
7	= Lordstown, OH, USA
8	= Fujisawa, Japan
9	= Detroit, MI, USA
9	= Oshawa #1, ON, Canada
9	= Oshawa #1, ON, Canada
A	= Lakewood, GA, USA
B	= Lansing, MI, USA - Craft Center
B	= Baltimore, MD, USA
B	= Lansing, MI, USA - Craft Center
B	= Lansing, MI, USA
B	= Lansing, MI, USA
C	= Lansing, MI, USA - South Plant
C	= Lansing, MI, USA - South Plant
C	= South Gate, CA, USA
D	= Doraville, GA, USA
E	= Linden, NJ, USA
E	= Linden, NJ, USA
F	= Fairfax, KS, USA
F	= Fairfax, KS, USA
G	= Framingham, MA, USA
H	= Flint, MI, USA
J	= Janesville, WI, USA
J	= Janesville, WI, USA

ARM0400000000649

Fig. 3 VIN Identification (Part 3 of 4). Chevrolet

DIGIT 11	Assembly Plant Location
K	= Kosai, Japan
K	= Leeds, MO, USA
L	= Van Nuys, CA, USA
L	= Van Nuys, CA, USA
M	= Toluca, Mexico
M	= Lansing, MI, USA
M	= Lansing, MI, USA
N	= Norwood, OH, USA
P	= Pontiac, MI, USA
R	= Arlington, TX, USA
R	= Arlington, TX, USA
S	= Ramos Arizpe, Mexico
S	= Ramos Arizpe, Mexico
T	= Tarrytown, NY, USA
W	= Willow Run, MI, USA
W	= Willow Run, MI, USA
W	= Iwata, Japan
X	= Fairfax, KS, USA
Y	= Wilminton, DE, USA
Y	= Wilminton, DE, USA
Y	= Wilmington, DE, USA
Z	= Fremont, CA, USA

ARM0400000000650

Fig. 3 VIN Identification (Part 4 of 4). Chevrolet

DIGIT 1	Country Of Origin
1	= USA
1	= USA
2	= Canada
2	= Canada
3	= Mexico
3	= Mexico
4	= USA - MMMA
4	= USA - MMMA
J	= Japan
W	= Germany

DIGIT 2	Manufacturer
A	= Imperial
B	= Dodge
C	= Chrysler
C	= Chrysler
J	= Chrysler

DIGIT 3	Vehicle Type
3	= Passenger Car
3	= Passenger Car
4	= Multipurpose Passenger Vehicle
4	= Multipurpose Passenger Vehicle
8	= Multipurpose Passenger Vehicle w/Side Airbags
8	= Multipurpose Passenger Vehicle w/Side Airbags
A	= PT Cruiser w/Side Airbags
A	= PT Cruiser w/Side Airbags

DIGIT 4	Restraint System
A	= Active Front & Side Airbags
A	= Dual Front Airbags w/Manual Belts
A	= Dual Airbags w/Manual Belts
A	= Dual Front Airbags w/Manual Belts
A	= Driverside Airbag w/Motorized Passenger Belt
A	= Active Front & Side Airbags
B	= Manual Seat Belts
C	= Automatic Seat Belts
E	= Dual Front Airbags w/Manual Belts
E	= Dual Airbags w/Manual Belts
E	= Dual Front Airbags w/Manual Belts
H	= Dual Airbags w/Manual Belts
H	= Dual Front Airbags w/Manual Belts
H	= Dual Front Airbags w/Manual Belts
H	= Hybrid Airbags
J	= Front, Next Generation, MultiStage Airbags
J	= Dual Front Next Generation Multi Stage Airbags
J	= Dual Front Airbags w/Manual Belts
X	= Driverside Airbag w/Manual Seat Belts
X	= Driverside Airbag w/Manual Belts
Y	= Driverside Airbag w/Automatic Passenger Belt

DIGIT 4*	Restraint System
A	= Active Front & Side Airbags
A	= Dual Front Airbags w/Manual Belts
A	= Dual Airbags w/Manual Belts
A	= Driverside Airbag w/Motorized Passenger Belt
C	= Automatic Seat Belts
C	= Automatic Seat Belts
E	= Dual Airbags w/Manual Belts
E	= Dual Front Airbags w/Manual Belts
E	= 3001-4000 Lbs
E	= 3001-4000 Lbs
F	= 4001-5000 Lbs
F	= 4001-5000 Lbs
H	= Dual Front Airbags w/Manual Belts
H	= Hybrid Airbags
X	= Driverside Airbag w/Manual Belts

DIGIT 4+	GVWR
E	= 3001-4000 Lbs
F	= 4001-5000 Lbs

DIGIT 5	Carline
A	= Lebaron 4D
A	= Lebaron 4D
A	= Laser
A	= 300
C	= New Yorker
C	= Conquest
C	= LHS
C	= Lebaron
C	= Dynasty
C	= New Yorker
C	= Lebaron 4D
C	= LHS
D	= New Yorker
D	= Concorde
D	= New Yorker
D	= LHS
D	= LHS
D	= Concorde
D	= Intrepid
E	= 300M
E	= 300M
F	= Fifth Avenue
F	= New Yorker
G	= Sebring Coupe
G	= Daytona
G	= Sebring Coupe
H	= Lebaron GTS
J	= Lebaron 2D
J	= Lebaron 2D
J	= Cirrus
J	= Cordoba
J	= Cirrus
L	= Concorde
L	= Sebring Convertible
L	= Sebring
L	= Sebring
L	= Concorde
M	= Fifth Avenue
M	= Lebaron
N	= Crossfire
R	= New Yorker
R	= Newport
S	= Cordoba
S	= Neon
T	= E Class
T	= New Yorker
T	= New Yorker Turbo
U	= New Yorker
U	= Sebring
U	= Lebaron 2D
U	= Sebring
U	= Lebaron 2D
V	= Fifth Avenue
V	= Imperial
V	= Imperial
V	= Fifth Avenue
W	= Daytona
W	= Prowler
Y	= PT Cruiser
Y	= Imperial
Y	= Fifth Avenue
Y	= Fifth Avenue
Y	= Imperial
Y	= PT Cruiser

DIGIT 6	Series
2	= Base
3	= Concorde LXi
3	= Medium
3	= Concorde LXi
3	= Medium
4	= ES
4	= Sebring LX

ARM0400000000651

Fig. 4 VIN Identification (Part 1 of 3). Chrysler

DIGIT 6	Series
4	= Base
4	= Concorde LX
4	= Base
4	= SE
4	= Sebring LX
4	= High
4	= High Line
4	= Concorde LX
4	= High Line
4	= High
5	= Premium
5	= Sebring LXi
5	= Premium
5	= Sebring LXi
5	= Premium Line
5	= Comcorde Limited
5	= Touring
5	= Premium Line
5	= Base
5	= Base/Touring/Limited
5	= ES
5	= ES/SXT
5	= Comcorde Limited
5	= Touring
6	= Base
6	= Sebring Limited
6	= Limited
6	= ACR
6	= Special
6	= Sebring Limited
6	= IROC R/T
6	= Special
6	= Fifth Avenue
6	= 300C
6	= Base
6	= Crossfire
6	= Limited
7	= GT
7	= Sebring GTC
7	= R/T
7	= X Series
7	= IROC
7	= Sebring GTC
7	= Performance
7	= Special
7	= X Series
7	= Performance
7	= Special
7	= GT

DIGIT 7	Body Style
1	= 2D Coupe
1	= 2D Sedan
1	= 2D Coupe
1	= 2D Sedan
2	= 2D Specialty Hardtop
2	= 2D Pillared Hardtop
2	= 2D Hardtop
2	= 2D Pillared Hardtop
3	= 2D Specialty Hardtop
4	= 2D Hatchback
4	= 2D Hatchback
5	= 2D Convertible
5	= 2D Convertible/Open Body
5	= 2D Convertible
6	= 4D Sedan
6	= 4D Sedan
7	= 4D Pillared Hardtop
8	= 4D Hatchback
9	= 2D Coupe
9	= 4D Wagon

DIGIT 7*	Body
5	= 2D Convertible
8	= Hatchback
8	= Hatchback
B	= Hatchback
B	= Hatchback

DIGIT 8	Engine
3	= 3.0L V6 TBI
3	= 3.0L V6 MPI
3	= 3.0L V6 MPI
8	= 2.4L I-4 DOHC TURBO
8	= 2.4L I-4 DOHC TURBO
A	= 2.2L I-4 Turbo
A	= 2.2L I-4 Turbo
B	= 2.4L I-4 MPI
B	= 2.4L I-4 DOHC SMPI
B	= 2.4L I-4 DOHC SMPI
B	= 2.2L I-4 2BBL
B	= 2.4L I-4 MPI
C	= 2.2L I-4
C	= 2.0L I-4 SFI SOHC
C	= 2.2L I-4 2BBL
C	= 2.2L I-4 EFI Turbo
C	= 2.0L I-4 SFI SOHC
D	= 2.2L I-4 Turbo
D	= 2.2L I-4 EFI
D	= 2.6L I-4 2BBL
D	= 2.2L I-4 TBI
E	= 2.2L I-4 Turbo
E	= 2.2L I-4 FI Turbo
E	= 3.7L I-6 1BBL
E	= 2.4L I-4 DOHC TURBO
F	= 3.7L I-6 1BBL
F	= 2.0L I-4 SFI SOHC HP
F	= 3.5L V6 MPI
F	= 2.0L I-4 SFI SOHC
F	= 3.5L V6 MPI
G	= 3.5L V6 MPI SOHC HO
G	= 2.4L I-4 DOHC HO TURBO
G	= 3.5L V6 EFI SOHC HO
G	= 2.4L I-4 EFI DOHC
G	= 3.5L V6 MPI HO
G	= 3.5L V6 MPI SOHC HO
G	= 3.5L V6 MPI HO
G	= 3.5L V6 EFI HO SOHC
G	= 2.6L I-4 2BBL
G	= 2.6L I-4
G	= 2.4L I-4 DOHC HO TURBO
G	= 2.4L I-4 EFI DOHC
G	= 3.5L V6 EFI SOHC HO
G	= 3.5L V6 EFI HO SOHC
H	= 2.5L V6 SFI SOHC
H	= 3.7L I-6 1BBL
H	= 2.5L V6 SFI SOHC
H	= 3.0L V6 MPI SOHC
H	= 5.7L V8 SFI
H	= 3.0L V6 MPI SOHC
H	= 2.5L I-4 EFI
J	= 2.5L I-4 FI Turbo
J	= 3.2L V6 EFI SOHC
J	= 2.5L I-4 FI Tbo
J	= 3.2L V6 EFI SOHC
J	= 3.2L V6 SFI SOHC
J	= 5.2L V8 EFI
J	= 2.5L I-4 FI Tbo
K	= 3.5L V6 MPI HO
K	= 3.5L V6 MPI HO
K	= 2.5L I-4 TBI
K	= 5.2L V8 2BBL
K	= 2.5L I-4 TBI
L	= 3.8L V6 MPI
L	= 5.2L V8 2BBL HD

ARM0400000000652

Fig. 4 VIN Identification (Part 2 of 3). Chrysler

Fig. 4 VIN Identification (Part 3 of 3). Chrysler

DIGIT 8 — Engine

Code	Description
L	5.2L V8 EFI
L	5.2L V8 2BBL
L	3.2L V6 MPI SOHC
L	3.8L V6 MPI
M	5.2L V8 4BBL
M	5.2L V8 MPI
M	3.5L V6 MPI
M	3.5L V6 MPI SOHC
M	3.5L V6 MPI SOHC
N	2.6L I-4 T/C I/C
N	5.2L V8 2BBL
N	2.5L V6 SFI SOHC
N	5.2L V8 4BBL HD
N	5.2L V8 4BBL
P	5.2L V8 2BBL
R	3.3L V6 EFI
R	3.3L V6 EFI
R	2.7L V6 MPI DOHC
R	3.3L V6 MPI
R	2.7L V6 MPI DOHC
S	2.4L I-4 DOHC HO TURBO
S	3.3L V6 MPI
T	3.3L V6 MPI
T	2.7L V6 MPI FFV
T	2.7L V6 MPI FFV
U	3.0L V6 MPI
U	2.7L V6 MPI DOHC
U	2.7L V6 SFI DOHC
V	3.3L V6 EFI SFlex
V	2.7L V6 MPI DOHC
V	2.7L V6 SFI DOHC
V	2.7L V6 SFI DOHC
W	3.5L V6 MPI SOHC
X	3.5L V6 SFI DOHC
X	3.5L V6 EFI SOHC
X	2.4L I-4 EFI DOHC
X	2.4L I-4 EFI DOHC
X	2.4L I-4 SFI DOHC
Y	2.0L I-4 DOHC SMPI
Y	2.0L I-4 SFI DOHC
Y	2.0L I-4 SFI DOHC
N	2.0L I-4 DOHC

DIGIT 10 — Model Year

Code	Year
1	2001
1	2001
2	2002
2	2002
3	2003
3	2003
4	2004
5	2005
1	1981
2	1982
3	1983
C	1982
D	1983
E	1984
F	1985
G	1986
H	1987
J	1988
K	1989
L	1990
M	1991
N	1992

DIGIT 10 — Model Year

Code	Year
N	1992
P	1993
P	1993
R	1994
R	1994
S	1995
T	1996
T	1996
V	1997
V	1997
W	1998
W	1998
X	1999
X	1999
Y	2000
Y	2000

DIGIT 11 — Assembly Plant Location

Code	Description
A	Auburn Hills, MI, USA
A	Lynch RD, USA
C	Jefferson, MI, USA
D	Belvidere, IL, USA
D	Belvidere, IL, USA
E	Normal, IL, USA
E	Normal, IL, USA
F	Newark, DE, USA
F	Newark, NJ, USA
F	Newark, DE, USA
G	St. Louis #1, MO, USA
G	St. Louis #1, MO, USA
H	Bramalea, ON, Canada
H	Brampton, ON, Canada
H	Bramalea, ON, Canada
N	Sterling Heights, MI, USA
N	Sterling Heights, MI, USA
R	Windsor, Canada
T	Toluca, Mexico
T	Toluca, Mexico
U	Mizushima, Japan
V	Conner Ave, Detroit, MI, USA
W	Kenosha #1, USA
X	Osnabruck, Germany
X	St. Louis #2, MO, USA
Y	Nagoya 1, Japan
Y	Kenosha #2, USA
Z	Okazaki, Japan

DIGIT 1 — Country Of Origin

Code	Description
1	USA
1	USA
2	Canada
3	Mexico
3	Mexico
4	USA - MMMA
4	USA - MMMA
J	Japan
J	Japan

DIGIT 2 — Manufacturer

Code	Description
B	Dodge
B	Dodge

DIGIT 3 — Vehicle Type

Code	Description
3	Passenger Car
3	Passenger Car
4	Multi-Purpose Passenger Vehicle
8	Multi-Purpose Passenger Vehicle w/Side Airbags

DIGIT 4 — Restraint

Code	Description
A	Dual Front Airbags w/Manual Belts
A	Active Front & Side Airbags
A	Dual Airbags w/Manual Belts
A	Driverside Airbag w/Motorized Passenger Belt
A	Dual Airbags w/Manual Belts
B	Driverside Airbag w/Motorized Passenger Belt
B	Manual Seat Belts
B	Manual Seat Belts
C	Automatic Belts
C	Automatic Seat Belt
C	Automatic Seat Belts
C	Automatic Seat Belts
E	Active Driver & Passenger Airbags
E	Driverside Airbag
E	Dual Front Airbags w/Manual Belts
E	Dual Airbags w/Manual Belts
E	Driverside Airbag
H	Dual Airbags, Passenger Hybrid w/Manual Belts
H	Dual Front Airbags w/Manual Belts
H	Dual Front Airbags w/Manual Belts
J	Dual Front Next Generation Multi Stage Airbags
J	Dual Front Airbags Next Generation Multi Stage
X	Driverside Airbag w/Manual Seat Belts
X	Dual Front Airbags w/Manual Belts
X	Driverside Airbag w/Manual Passenger Belt
Y	Driverside Airbag w/Automatic Passenger Belt

DIGIT 4* — GVWR/Brake System

Code	Description
F	4001-5000 Lbs, Hydraulic
G	5001-6000 Lbs, Hydraulic

DIGIT 5 — Carline

Code	Description
A	Spirit
A	Spirit
A	Colt
A	Daytona
A	Colt
B	Monaco
C	Conquest
C	Dynasty
D	Stealth
D	Stealth
D	Aries
D	Challenger
D	Intrepid
E	Colt
E	600
E	Stealth
E	Stealth
F	Daytona
G	Stratus Coupe

Fig. 5 VIN Identification (Part 1 of 3). Dodge

DIGIT 5 — Carline

Code	Description
G	Diplomat
G	Colt Wagon
H	Colt Wagon AWD
H	Lancer
J	Stratus
J	Stratus
J	Mirada
J	Stratus Sedan
K	Stratus
L	Aries
L	Stratus Sedan
L	024 Omni
L	Omni
M	Stealth FWD
M	Stealth FWD
M	Stealth
M	Diplomat
N	Stealth Turbo
N	Stealth AWD
N	Stealth AWD
P	Shadow
P	Shadow
R	Viper
R	St. Regis
S	Neon
S	Shadow
S	Shadow
U	Colt
U	Dynasty
U	Avenger
U	Colt
V	Avenger
V	Colt Wagon
V	Avenger
V	600 2D Coupe/Convertible
V	400
W	Daytona
W	Colt Wagon AWD
X	Lancer
X	Mirada
Z	Omni
Z	Viper

DIGIT 5* — Line

Code	Description
V	Magnum RWD
Z	Magnum AWD

DIGIT 6 — Series

Code	Description
1	Economy
1	Economy
2	SE
2	Low
2	Base
2	Low
3	Medium
3	High
3	SE
4	Medium
4	Medium Base
4	Magnum SXT
4	SXT
4	SE
4	SE
4	High
4	High
5	Base
5	Premium
5	SXT
5	ES/SXT
5	Premium
5	Pacifica
5	Magnum R/T
5	ES
6	Special

ARM040000000654

ARM040000000653

DIGIT 6 — Series

Code	Series
6	IROC R/T
6	SRT-4
6	ACR
6	SRT-10
6	Special
6	Turbo
6	Turbo Z
6	Shelby Z
6	ES Turbo
7	Performance
7	R/T
7	IROC
7	Shelby
8	R/T Turbo
8	R/T Turbo

DIGIT 7 — Body Style

Code	Body Style
1	2D Coupe
2	2D Coupe
2	2D Pillared Hardtop
2	2D Pillared Hardtop
2	2D Hatchback
3	2D Hatchback
4	2D Convertible / Open Body
4	2D Convertible
5	2D Convertible/Open Body
5	2D Convertible
6	4D Sedan
6	4D Sedan
7	4D Pillared Hardtop
7	4D Pillared Hardtop
8	4D Hatchback
8	4D Hatchback
8	4D Hatchback Tall
9	2D Specialty Coupe
9	4D Wagon

DIGIT 7* — Body Type

Code	Body Type
1	2D Sedan
1	4D Wagon
1	4D Wagon AWD
2	2D Coupe
3	2D Hatchback
4	4D Sedan
4	4D Hatchback
8	4D Wagon
8	4D Wagon

DIGIT 8 — Engine

Code	Engine
2	5.7L V8 SFI
2	1.4L I-4 2BBL
2	1.6L I-4 2BBL
3	3.0L V6 MPI
3	5.2L V8 2BBL
4	5.2L V8 EFI
4	2.6L I-4
A	1.7L I-4 2BBL
A	2.2L I-4 MPI Turbo
A	1.5L I-4 MPI
A	2.2L I-4 FI Turbo
A	2.2L I-4 MPI Turbo
A	1.6L I-4 2BBL
A	1.4L I-4 2BBL
A	1.7L I-4 2BBL
B	1.8L I-4 MPI
B	1.8L I-4 MPI

DIGIT 8 — Engine

Code	Engine
B	1.6L I-4 2BBL
B	3.0L V6 MPI
C	1.8L I-4 MPI
C	2.2L I-4 EFI Turbo
C	2.2L I-4
C	3.0L V6 MPI Turbo
C	1.8L I-4 MPI
C	2.0L I-4 SFI SOHC
C	2.2L I-4 2BBL
C	3.0L V6 MPI Turbo
D	2.0L I-4 SFI SOHC
D	2.2L I-4 FI Turbo
D	2.6L I-4
D	2.2L I-4 EFI
D	2.0L I-4 MPI
D	2.2L I-4 EFI
E	8.0L V10 SFI
E	3.2L I-4 Turbo
F	3.7L I-6
F	2.0L I-4 SFI SOHC
F	3.5L MPI
F	3.7L I-6 HD
F	2.2L I-4 2BBL HO
F	2.0L I-4 SFI SOHC HP
F	3.7L I-6
G	1.6L I-4 Turbo
G	3.5L V6 MPI SOHC HO
G	2.4L I-4 MPI SOHC
G	3.5L V6 EFI SOHC HO
G	2.6L I-4
H	2.5L V6 SFI
H	2.5L V6 SFI
H	3.7L I-6
H	2.5L I-4 EFI
H	3.0L V6 MPI SOHC
H	2.5L V6 SFI SOHC
H	3.0L V6 MPI SOHC
J	2.6L I-4 Tbo
J	2.5L V6 MPI DOHC
J	3.0L V6 MPI DOHC
J	3.0L V6 SFI SOHC
J	2.5L I-4 MPI Turbo
J	2.5L I-4 FI Turbo
K	2.5L I-4 MPI Turbo
K	2.5L I-4 TBI
K	5.2L V8 2BBL
K	1.5L I-4
K	2.5L I-4 TBI
K	3.0L V6 MPI Tbo DOHC
K	3.5L V6 MPI Tbo DOHC
M	2.5L V6 MPI SOHC
M	5.2L V8
N	5.2L V8
N	5.2L V8 HD
N	5.2L V8 2BBL
P	5.2L V8 2BBL
R	2.7L V6 MPI
R	5.2L V8 4BBL
R	3.3L V6 MPI
R	3.0L V6 MPI
S	2.7L V6 SFI DOHC
S	2.7L V6 MPI FFV
S	2.7L V6 MPI DOHC
S	3.0L V6 MPI
S	2.4L 4 SFI DOHC TURBO

Fig. 5 VIN Identification (Part 2 of 3). Dodge

DIGIT 8 — Engine

Code	Engine
S	2.4L I-4 SFI DOHC HOT
S	3.0L V6 MPI
S	3.3L V6 MPI
T	1.8L I-4 MPI
T	2.7L V6 MPI FFV
U	2.7L V6 MPI
U	3.0L V6 MPI
U	2.7L V6 SFI DOHC
U	3.3L V6 SFI Flex
V	3.5L V6 MPI SOHC
V	3.5L H/O V6 MPI
V	3.5L V6 EFI SOHC HO
V	3.5L V6 EFI SOHC HOT
V	2.0L I-4 MPI
X	2.5L I-4 TBI Flex Fuel
X	2.4L I-4 SFI DOHC
X	1.5L I-4 MPI
X	2.4L I-4 SFI DOHC
X	2.4L I-4 SFI DOHC HOT
Y	2.0L I-4 SFI DOHC
Y	2.0L I-4 SFI DOHC
Z	1.6L I-4 Turbo
Z	1.5L I-4 MPI
Z	8.3L V10 SFI

DIGIT 10 — Model Year

Code	Model Year
1	2001
2	2002
3	2003
4	2004
5	2005
B	1981
C	1982
D	1983
E	1984
F	1985
G	1986
H	1987
J	1988
K	1989
L	1990
M	1991
N	1991
N	1992
P	1992
P	1993
R	1993
R	1994
R	1994
S	1995
S	1995
T	1995
T	1996
V	1996
V	1997
V	1997
W	1998
W	1998
X	1999
X	1999
Y	2000

DIGIT 11 — Assembly Plant

Code	Assembly Plant
A	Mizushima 2, Japan
B	St. Louis South, MO, USA
C	Jefferson North Assembly, Detroit, MI, USA
D	Belvidere, IL, USA
D	Belvidere, IL, USA
E	Normal, IL, USA
E	Normal, IL, USA
F	Newark, NJ, USA
F	Newark, NJ, USA
G	St. Louis #1, MO, USA

Fig. 5 VIN Identification (Part 2 of 3). Dodge

DIGIT 11 — Assembly Plant Location

Code	Assembly Plant Location
H	Bramalea, ON, Canada
J	Nagoya 3, Japan
J	Nagoya 3, Japan
N	Sterling Heights, MI, USA
N	Sterling Heights, MI, USA
P	Nagoya 2, Japan
P	Nagoya 2, Japan
R	Windsor, On, Canada
T	Toluca, Mexico
T	Toluca, Mexico
U	Mizushima 1, Japan
U	Mizushima 1, Japan
V	Detroit, MI, USA
W	Kenosha #1, WI, USA
X	St. Louis, MO, USA
X	Kenosha #2, WI, USA
Y	Nagoya 1, Japan
Y	Nagoya 1, Japan
Z	Okazaki, Japan
Z	Okazaki, Japan

Fig. 5 VIN Identification (Part 3 of 3). Dodge

Fig. 6 VIN Identification (Part 1 of 5). Ford

DIGIT 1-3 — World Manufacturer Identifier

Code	Description
1FA	Ford Motor Company, USA
1FA	Ford Motor Company, USA
1ZV	AutoAlliance International
1ZV	AutoAlliance International
2FA	Ford Motor Company of Canada
2FA	Ford Motor Company of Canada
2FD	Ford Motor Company of Canada
2FD	Ford Motor Company of Canada
3FA	Ford Motor Company of Mexico
3FA	Ford Motor Company of Mexico
3FA	Ford Motor Company, USA
3FA	Ford Motor Company, USA
KNJ	Kia Motors Inc., Korea
KNJ	Kia Motors Inc., Korea

DIGIT 4 — Restraint System

Code	Description
A	Driverside Airbag w/Driver & Rear Manual Belts & Front Pas
A	Driverside Airbag w/Driver & Rear Manual Belts & Front Pat
B	Manual Belts
C	Driverside Airbag w/Manual Belts
C	Driverside Airbag w/Manual Belts
F	2nd Generation Dual Airbags w/Manual Belts
F	2nd Generation Dual Airbags w/Manual Belts
F	Active Belts, Dual Front Airbags
H	Dual Front & Front Side Airbags w/Manual Belts
H	2nd Generation Front & Side Airbags w/Manual Belts
H	2nd Generation Front & Side Airbags w/Manual Belts
K	Dual Front & Front Side Airbags w/Manual Belts
K	Dual Front Airbags w/Manual Belts
L	Dual Front Airbags w/Manual Belts
P	Front Automatic Belts & Rear Manual Belts
P	Front Automatic Belts & Rear Manual Belts
R	Driverside Airbag w/Front Automatic Belts & Rear Manual Belts E
R	Dual Airbags w/Front Automatic Belts & Rear Manual Belts E
S	Dual Airbags w/Front Automatic Belts & Rear Manual Belts

DIGIT 5 — Designation

Code	Description
P	Passenger Car - Ford Make
P	Passenger Car - Ford Make
T	Passenger Car
T	Passenger Car

DIGIT 6-7 — Carline/Series/Body Style

Code	Description
01	EXP 2D Hatchback
04	Escort L 2D Hatchback
04	Escort Base 2D Hatchback
05	Escort Hatchback
05	Escort GL 2D Hatchback
05	Aspire 2D Hatchback
05	Festiva L 2D Hatchback
05	Festiva L 2D Hatchback
06	Aspire 4D Sedan
06	Escort GLX 4D Hatchback
06	Festiva GL 2D Hatchback
06	Festiva L Plus 2D Hatchback
06	Festiva L 2D Hatchback
06	Escort GL 2D Hatchback
07	Festiva GL 4D Sedan
07	Festiva LX 2D Hatchback
07	Escort GT 2D Hatchback
07	Aspire SE 2D Hatchback
07	Aspire SE 2D Hatchback
08	Escort 4D Wagon
09	Escort 4D Wagon
10	Escort Base LX 4D Sedan
10	Escort LX 4D Sedan
10	Escort Base 4D Sedan
10	Escort LX 4D Sedan
11	Escort LX 4D Wagon
11	Escort Base LX 4D Sedan
11	Escort LX 2D Hatchback
11	Escort ZX2 2D Coupe
12	Escort GT 2D Hatchback
12	Escort LX 2D Hatchback
12	Escort ZX2 2D Coupe
13	Escort LX 2D Hatchback
13	Escort LX 4D Wagon
13	Escort GT 2D Hatchback
13	Escort GT 2D Hatchback
13	Mustang GLX 2D Coupe
13	Mustang Ghia 2D Coupe
13	Escort L 4D Hatchback
13	Escort Base 4D Hatchback
13	Mustang GLX 2D Hatchback
13	Escort SE 4D Sedan
13	Escort 4D Sedan
14	Escort LX 4D Hatchback
14	Escort GL 4D Hatchback
15	Escort SE 4D Sedan
15	Escort SE 4D Wagon
15	Escort SE 4D Wagon
15	Escort LX 4D Wagon
15	Mustang 2D Hatchback
15	Escort GLX 4D Hatchback
16	Escort LX 4D Hatchback
16	Mustang GL 2D Hatchback
16	Escort LX-E 4D Sedan
17	Escort Exp Luxury 2D Coupe
18	Tempo L 2D Coupe
19	Escort Exp Sport 2D Coupe
20	Tempo GL 2D Coupe
20	Probe SE 2D Hatchback
20	Tempo GLX 2D Coupe
20	Probe SE 2D Hatchback
20	Fairmont 2D Coupe
20	Tempo SE 2D Hatchback
20	Probe Base 2D Hatchback
20	Probe Base 2D Hatchback
21	Fairmont Futura 4D Sedan
21	Probe GL 2D Hatchback
21	Tempo GL 4D Sedan
21	Fairmont Futura 2D Sedan
21	Tempo L 4D Sedan
22	Escort GL 2D Hatchback
22	Escort GT 2D Hatchback
22	Tempo GL 4D Sedan
23	Fairmont Futura 4D Sedan
23	Tempo LX 4D Sedan
23	Fairmont 4D Sedan

Fig. 6 VIN Identification (Part 1 of 5). Ford (continued)

DIGIT 6-7 — Carline/Series/Body Style

Code	Description
23	Tempo GLX 4D Sedan
23	Five Hundred 4D Sedan SE FWD
24	Five Hundred 4D Sedan SEL FWD
25	Escort GL 4D Hatchback
25	Escort LX 4D Hatchback
25	Five Hundred 4D Sedan Limited FWD
26	Mustang L 2D Coupe
26	Mustang 2D Coupe
26	Five Hundred 4D Sedan SE AWD
26	Granada 2D Sedan
27	Mustang LX 2D Coupe
27	Granada 4D Sedan
27	Mustang GT 2D Convertible
27	Five Hundred 4D Sedan SEL AWD
27	Mustang LX 2D Hatchback
27	Mustang 2D Convertible
28	Mustang GT 2D Hatchback
28	Mustang LX 2D Hatchback
28	Mustang SVO 2D Hatchback
28	Mustang L 2D Hatchback
28	Mustang Ghia 2D Hatchback
28	Five Hundred 4D Sedan Limited AWD
28	Escort GL 4D Wagon
28	Escort LX 4D Sedan
28	Granada 4D Wagon
29	Taurus 4D Sedan
30	Focus SVT 4D Hatchback
30	Tempo L 2D Coupe
30	Taurus 4D Wagon
30	Focus SVT 4D Hatchback
31	Tempo L 2D Coupe
31	Focus ZX3 2D Hatchback
31	Escort Base 2D Hatchback
31	Escort L 2D Hatchback
31	Tempo GL 2D Coupe
31	Focus ZX3 2D Hatchback
31	LTD S 4D Sedan
31	Tempo GL 2D Coupe
31	Escort Pony 2D Hatchback
32	Tempo LX 2D Coupe
32	Escort GL 2D Hatchback
32	LTD 2D Sedan
33	Escort LX 4D Sedan
33	Focus LX 4D Sedan
33	LTD 4D Sedan
33	Tempo Sport GL 2D Coupe
33	Focus LX 4D Sedan
33	Escort GT 2D Hatchback
33	Tempo GLS 2D Coupe
34	Focus SE 4D Sedan
34	Escort SE 4D Sedan
34	Escort L 4D Wagon
34	Tempo AWD 2D Coupe
34	LTD Crown Victoria 2D Sedan
35	Fairmont Futura 2D Sedan
35	Tempo L 4D Sedan
35	Focus ZTW 4D Wagon
35	Focus L 4D Sedan
35	LTD Crown Victoria 4D Sedan
35	Escort GL 4D Wagon
36	Focus ZTW 4D Wagon
36	Escort GL 2D Hatchback
36	Fairmont Futura 4D Sedan
36	Focus SE 4D Sedan
36	Escort Base 4D Hatchback
36	Tempo GL 4D Sedan
36	Fairmont 4D Sedan

Fig. 6 VIN Identification (Part 2 of 5). Ford

DIGIT 6-7 — Carline/Series/Body Style

Code	Description
36	Tempo GL 4D Sedan
36	Escort L 4D Wagon
37	Tempo LX 4D Sedan
37	Escort LX 4D Hatchback
37	Focus ZX5 4D Hatchback
37	Focus ZX5 4D Hatchback
37	Escort LX 4D Sedan
37	LTD S 4D Wagon
37	Fairmont Futura 2D Coupe
37	LTD S 4D Sedan
37	Escort GL 4D Hatchback
38	Focus ZTS 4D Sedan
38	Focus GLS 4D Sedan
38	Focus ZTS 4D Sedan
38	Tempo GLS 4D Sedan
38	Tempo Sport GL 4D Sedan
38	LTD 4D Sedan
39	Tempo AWD 4D Sedan
39	LTD 4D Sedan
39	Focus SVT 2D Hatchback
39	LTD 4D Squire Wagon
39	Focus SVT 2D Hatchback
39	Tempo AWD 4D Sedan
40	Mustang Base 2D Coupe
40	Mustang LX 2D Coupe
40	Mustang Base 2D Coupe
40	Mustang LX 2D Coupe
40	LTD 4D Wagon
41	Mustang LX 2D Hatchback
41	Mustang LX 2D Hatchback
42	LTD Crown Victoria 2D Sedan
42	Mustang GT 2D Coupe
42	Mustang GT 2D Coupe
42	Mustang Cobra 2D Hatchback
42	Mustang GT 2D Hatchback
42	Mustang Cobra 2D Hatchback
42	Mustang GT 2D Hatchback
42	Mustang GTS 2D Coupe
42	Mustang GTS 2D Coupe
42	Thunderbird 2D Coupe
43	LTD Crown Victoria 4D Sedan
44	LTD Crown Victoria 4D Squire Wagon
44	Mustang Base 2D Convertible
44	Mustang LX Limited Edition 2D Convertible
44	Mustang LX 2D Convertible
44	Mustang LX 2D Convertible
44	Mustang LX 2D Sedan
45	Mustang GT 2D Convertible
45	Mustang GLS 2D Coupe
45	Mustang SE 4D Sedan
45	Mustang Cobra 2D Convertible
45	Mustang Cobra 2D Convertible
46	Mustang Cobra 2D Convertible
46	Mustang Cobra 2D Convertible
46	Thunderbird 2D Coupe
47	LTD Crown Victoria 2D Sedan
47	Mustang Cobra 2D Coupe
48	Mustang Cobra 2D Coupe
48	Mustang Cobra 2D Coupe
49	Mustang Cobra 2D Convertible
49	Mustang Cobra 2D Convertible
50	Taurus L 4D Sedan
51	Taurus L 4D Sedan
51	Taurus MT5 4D Sedan
51	Taurus G 4D Sedan
52	Taurus G 4D Sedan
52	Taurus SE 4D Sedan
52	Taurus LX 4D Sedan
52	Taurus GL 4D Sedan

DIGIT 6-7	Carline/Series/Body Style
52	= Taurus LX 4D Sedan
52	= Taurus GL 4D Sedan
53	= Taurus SE Comfort 4D Sedan
53	= Taurus LX 4D Sedan
53	= Taurus LX 4D Sedan
53	= Taurus SE 4D Sedan
53	= Taurus SE 4D Sedan
53	= Taurus SE 4D Sedan - 2V
53	= Taurus SE 4D Sedan - 2V
53	= Taurus SE Comfort 4D Sedan
54	= Taurus SE 4D Sedan - 4V
54	= Taurus SHO 4D Sedan
54	= Taurus SE 4D Sedan - 4V
54	= Taurus SHO 4D Sedan
55	= Taurus L 4D Wagon
55	= Taurus L 4D Wagon
55	= Taurus SES 4D Sedan
55	= Taurus SES 4D Sedan
56	= Taurus SEL 4D Sedan
56	= Taurus MT5 Wagon
56	= Taurus SEL 4D Sedan
57	= Taurus SE 4D Wagon
57	= Taurus GL 4D Wagon
57	= Taurus SE 4D Wagon
57	= Taurus GL 4D Wagon
58	= Taurus LX 4D Wagon
58	= Taurus SE 4D Wagon
58	= Taurus SE Comfort 4D Wagon
58	= Taurus SE 4D Wagon
58	= Taurus SE Comfort 4D Wagon
58	= Taurus LX 4D Wagon
59	= Taurus SEL 4D Wagon
59	= Taurus SEL 4D Wagon
60	= Thunderbird 2D Coupe
60	= Thunderbird 2D Coupe
60	= Thunderbird 2D Sport Coupe
60	= Thunderbird Base 2D Coupe
60	= Thunderbird 2D Sport Coupe
60	= Thunderbird 2D Convertible
60	= Thunderbird 2D Convertible
60	= Thunderbird Base 2D Coupe
60	= Thunderbird Sport 2D Coupe
61	= Thunderbird Sport 2D Coupe
62	= Thunderbird 2D Convertible
62	= Thunderbird LX 2D Coupe
62	= Thunderbird 2D Convertible
62	= Thunderbird LX 2D Coupe
63	= Thunderbird Pacific Coast Roadster
63	= Thunderbird Pacific Coast Roadster
64	= Thunderbird Super Coupe
64	= Thunderbird 2D Super Coupe
64	= Thunderbird Super Coupe
64	= Thunderbird Turbo 2D Coupe
64	= Thunderbird 2D Convertible Neiman Marcus
64	= Thunderbird 2D Super Coupe
64	= Thunderbird 2D Convertible Neiman Marcus
65	= Contour Base 4D Sedan - Early Production
65	= Contour Base 4D Sedan
65	= Contour GL 4D Sedan
65	= Contour GL 4D Sedan
65	= Contour GL 4D Sedan - Early Production
65	= Contour Base 4D Sedan
65	= Contour GL 4D Sedan - Early Production
65	= Contour Base 4D Sedan - Early Production
65	= Contour LX 4D Sedan
65	= Contour LX 4D Sedan
66	= Contour SE 4D Sedan
66	= Contour LX 4D Sedan - Early Production
66	= Contour LX 4D Sedan - Early Production
66	= Contour SE 4D Sedan
66	= Contour LX 4D Sedan
66	= Contour Sport 4D Sedan

DIGIT 6-7	Carline/Series/Body Style
66	= Contour LX 4D Sedan
67	= Contour SE 4D Sedan
67	= Contour SE V6 4D Sedan - Early Production
67	= Contour SE 4D Sedan
67	= Contour SE V6 4D Sedan - Early Production
68	= Contour SVT 4D Sedan
68	= Contour SVT 4D Sedan
69	= 50th Anniversary Feature Car
70	= Crown Victoria 4D Sedan LWB - Fleet
70	= LTD Crown Victoria 2D Coupe
70	= Crown Victoria 4D Sedan LWB - Fleet
71	= LTD Crown Victoria LX 2D Coupe
71	= Crown Victoria 4D Sedan w/Police Interceptor Package
71	= Crown Victoria 4D Sedan w/Police Interceptor Package
72	= LTD Crown Victoria S 4D Sedan
72	= LTD Crown Victoria S 4D Sedan
72	= Crown Victoria 4D Sedan - Fleet
72	= Crown Victoria 4D Sedan - Fleet
72	= LTD Crown Victoria Base 4D Sedan
73	= Crown Victoria 4D Sedan
73	= LTD Crown Victoria Base 4D Sedan
73	= Crown Victoria 4D Sedan
73	= LTD Crown Victoria Base 4D Sedan
74	= LTD Crown Victoria LX 4D Sedan
74	= Crown Victoria LX 4D Sedan
74	= LTD Crown Victoria LX 4D Sedan
74	= Crown Victoria LX 4D Sedan
75	= Crown Victoria Touring 4D Sedan
75	= Crown Victoria Touring 4D Sedan
76	= LTD Crown Victoria Base 4D Wagon
76	= LTD Crown Victoria Base 4D Wagon
77	= LTD Crown Victoria LX 4D Wagon
77	= LTD Crown Victoria LX 4D Wagon
78	= LTD Crown Victoria Country Squire 4D Wagon
78	= LTD Crown Victoria Country Squire 4D Wagon
79	= LTD Crown Victoria Country Squire LX 4D Wagon
79	= LTD Crown Victoria Country Squire LX 4D Wagon
90	= GT
90	= Escort Pony 2D Hatchback
91	= Escort LX 2D Hatchback
93	= Escort GT 2D Hatchback
95	= Escort LX 4D Hatchback
98	= Escort LX 4D Wagon

DIGIT 8	Engine
1	= 3.0L V6 Duratec
1	= 3.0L V6 SFI FFV - Methanol
1	= 3.0L V6 SFI FFV - Methanol
2	= 3.0L V6 EFI FFV
2	= 3.0L V6 SFI FFV - Ethanol
2	= 3.0L V6 SFI FFV - Ethanol
2	= 3.0L V6 EFI FFV
2	= 1.6L I-4 2BBL
3	= 3.8L V6 CFI
3	= 2.0L I-4 SFI DOHC
3	= 2.0L I-4 EFI DOHC
3	= 3.8L V6 2BBL
3	= 2.0L I-4 DOHC
3	= 2.0L I-4 SFI DOHC
3	= 2.0L I-4 EFI DOHC
4	= 3.8L V6 EFI
4	= 1.6L I-4 2BBL HO
4	= 3.8L V6 EFI
5	= 2.0L I-4 SFI HO
5	= 2.0L I-4 SFI HO
5	= 1.6L I-4 EFI
6	= 2.3L I-4 1BBL OHC LPG
6	= 4.6L V8 EFI SOHC
6	= 4.6L V8 EFI SOHC
6	= 3.9L V6 EFI
8	= 1.8L I-4 EFI DOHC
8	= 1.8L I-4 EFI DOHC

ARM0400000000659

Fig. 6 VIN Identification (Part 3 of 5). Ford

DIGIT 8	Engine
8	= 1.6L I-4 EFI Tbo
8	= 1.6L I-4 FI Turbo
9	= 4.6L V8 EFI SOHC CNG
9	= 1.9L I-4 2BBL
9	= 1.9L I-4 CFI
9	= 4.6L V8 EFI SOHC CNG
A	= 3.9L V8 EFI DOHC
A	= 2.0L I-4 EFI DOHC
A	= 2.3L I-4 2BBL
A	= 2.3L I-4 1BBL
A	= 2.0L I-4 EFI DOHC
A	= 2.3L I-4 1BBL OHC
A	= 2.3L I-4 EFI SOHC
A	= 3.9L V8 EFI DOHC
B	= 3.3L I-6 1BBL
B	= 3.3L V6 1BBL
B	= 2.5L V6 EFI DOHC
B	= 2.5L V6 EFI DOHC
C	= 2.2L I-4 EFI
C	= 3.8L V6 EFI S/C
C	= 2.2L I-4 EFI
D	= 5.0L V8 EFI SHP
D	= 2.5L I-4 CFI HSC
D	= 4.2L V8 2BBL
D	= 5.0L V8 EFI SHP
E	= 5.0L V8 EFI HO
E	= 5.0L V8 EFI HO
F	= 5.0L V8 EFI
F	= 5.0L V8 4BBL
F	= 5.0L V8 EFI
F	= 5.0L V8 2BBL
G	= 2.5L V6 EFI DOHC HO
G	= 2.5L V6 EFI DOHC HO
G	= 5.8L V8 2BBL HO
H	= 1.3L I-4 EFI
H	= 1.3L I-4 EFI
H	= 1.3L I-4 EFI SOHC
H	= 2.0L I-4 FI Dsl
H	= 1.3L I-4 EFI SOHC
J	= 1.9L I-4 EFI
J	= 1.9L I-4 EFI
J	= 1.9L I-4 EFI HO
K	= 1.3L I-4 2BBL
L	= 2.5L V6 EFI DOHC
L	= 2.5L V6 EFI DOHC
L	= 2.2L I-4 EFI T/C I/C
L	= 2.2L I-4 EFI T/C I/C
M	= 2.3L I-4 EFI
M	= 2.3L I-4 EFI
M	= 5.0L V8 EFI HO
N	= 2.5L I-4 EFI
N	= 3.4L V8 EFI DOHC SHO
N	= 2.5L I-4 EFI
N	= 3.4L V8 EFI DOHC SHO
P	= 2.0L I-4 DOHC PZEV
P	= 2.0L I-4 SPI
P	= 3.2L V6 EFI DOHC SHO
P	= 2.0L I-4 SPI
P	= 3.2L V6 EFI DOHC SHO
R	= 4.6L V8 EFI DOHC Ram Air
R	= 3.8L V6 EFI S/C
R	= 3.8L V6 EFI S/C
R	= 2.3L I-4 1BBL HSC
R	= 4.6L V8 EFI DOHC Ram Air
S	= 3.0L V6 EFI DOHC
S	= 3.0L V6 EFI DOHC
S	= 2.3L I-4 EFI HSO
S	= 5.4L V8 SC DOHC
S	= 2.3L I-4 CFI HSC+
S	= 2.3L I-4 EFI HSO
T	= 2.3L I-4 EFI T/C I/C
T	= 5.0L V8 EFI HO

DIGIT 8	Engine
T	= 5.0L V8 EFI HO
U	= 3.0L V6 EFI
U	= 3.0L V6 EFI
V	= 4.6L V8 EFI DOHC
V	= 4.6L V8 EFI DOHC
W	= 4.6L V8 EFI SOHC
W	= 4.6L V8 EFI SOHC
W	= 2.3L I-4 EFI SOHC Turbo
W	= 2.3L I-4 EFI SOHC T/C
X	= 2.3L I-4 EFI HSC
X	= 4.6L V8 EFI SOHC
X	= 2.3L I-4 CFI HSC
X	= 4.6L V8 EFI SOHC
X	= 3.3L I-6 1BBL
X	= 2.3L I-4 EFI HSC
Y	= 3.0L V6 EFI DOHC SHO
Y	= 4.6L V8 EFI DOHC SC
Y	= 3.0L V6 EFI DOHC SHO
Y	= 4.6L V8 EFI DOHC SC
Z	= 2.0L I-4 DOHC PZEV
Z	= 2.3L I-4 DOHC
Z	= 2.0L I-4 DOHC PZEV
Z	= 2.0L I-4 EFI DOHC GFP
Z	= 2.0L I-4 EFI DOHC GFP

DIGIT 10	Model Year
1	= 2001
1	= 2001
2	= 2002
2	= 2002
3	= 2003
3	= 2003
4	= 2004
4	= 2004
5	= 2005
5	= 2005
B	= 1981
C	= 1982
D	= 1983
E	= 1984
F	= 1985
G	= 1986
H	= 1987
J	= 1988
K	= 1989
L	= 1990
M	= 1991
M	= 1991
N	= 1992
N	= 1992
P	= 1993
P	= 1993
R	= 1994
R	= 1994
S	= 1995
S	= 1995
T	= 1996
T	= 1996
V	= 1997
V	= 1997
W	= 1998
W	= 1998
X	= 1999
X	= 1999
Y	= 2000
Y	= 2000

DIGIT 11	Assembly Plant Location
5	= AAI - Flat Rock, MI, USA
5	= AAI - Flat Rock, MI, USA
6	= Mazda-Kia, Korea
6	= Mazda-Kia, Korea

ARM0400000000660

Fig. 6 VIN Identification (Part 4 of 5). Ford

DIGIT 11	Assembly Plant Location
A	= Atlanta, GA, USA
A	= Atlanta, GA, USA
B	= Oakville, ON, Canada
B	= Oakville, ON, Canada
F	= Dearborn, MI, USA
F	= Dearborn, MI, USA
G	= Chicago, Illinois, USA
G	= Chicago, IL, USA
G	= Chicago, IL, USA
H	= Lorain, OH, USA
H	= Lorain, OH, USA
K	= Kansas City, MO, USA
K	= Kansas City, MO, USA
M	= Cuautitlan, Mexico
M	= Cuautitlan, Mexico
R	= Hermosillo, Mexico
R	= San Jose, CA, USA
R	= Hermosillo, Mexico
R	= San Jose, CA, USA
T	= Edison, NJ, USA
U	= Louisville, KY, USA
W	= Wayne, MI, USA
W	= Wayne, MI, USA
X	= St. Thomas, ON, Canada
X	= St. Thomas, ON, Canada
Y	= Wixom, MI, USA
Y	= Wixom, MI, USA
Z	= St. Louis, MO, USA

ARM0400000000661

Fig. 6 VIN Identification (Part 5 of 5). Ford

DIGIT 1-3	World Manufacturer Identifier
1L1	= Ford Motor Company, USA - Lincoln, Limousine
1L1	= Ford Motor Company, USA - Lincoln, Limousine
1LJ	= Ford Motor Company, USA - Lincoln, Hearse
1LJ	= Ford Motor Company, USA - Lincoln, Hearse
1LN	= Ford Motor Company, USA - Lincoln
1LN	= Ford Motor Company, USA - Lincoln
1MR	= Ford Motor Company, USA - Continental

DIGIT 4	Restraint System
B	= Manual Belts
C	= Driverside Airbag w/Manual Belts
C	= Driverside Airbag w/Manual Belts
F	= 2nd Generation Dual Front Airbags w/Manual Belts
F	= 2nd Generation Dual Front Airbags w/Manual Belts
H	= 2nd Generation Front & Side Airbags w/Manual Belts
H	= 2nd Generation Front & Side Airbags w/Manual Belts
L	= Dual Front Airbags w/Manual Belts
L	= Dual Front Airbags w/Manual Belts

DIGIT 5	Designation
L	= Passenger Car - Lincoln Make
L	= Passenger Car - Lincoln Make
M	= Passenger Car - Lincoln Make
M	= Passenger Car - Lincoln Make
P	= Passenger Car

DIGIT 6-7	Carline/Body Style
81	= Town Car Executive 4D Sedan
81	= Town Car Signature 4D Sedan
81	= Town Car 4D Sedan
81	= Town Car 4D Sedan
81	= Town Car Executive 4D Sedan
82	= Town Car Signature 4D Sedan
82	= Town Car Signature Limited
82	= Town Car Signature 4D Sedan
83	= Town Car Cartier 4D Sedan
83	= Town Car Ultimate 4D Sedan
83	= Town Car Cartier 4D Sedan
83	= Town Car Ultimate 4D Sedan
84	= Town Car Executive L 4D Sedan
84	= Town Car Executive L 4D Sedan
84	= Town Car Signature Special Edition 4D Sedan
85	= Town Car Signature L 4D Sedan
85	= Town Car Cartier L 4D Sedan
85	= Town Car Ultimate L 4D Sedan
85	= Town Car Cartier L 4D Sedan
85	= Town Car Ultimate L 4D Sedan
86	= LS V6
86	= LS V6
87	= LS V8
87	= LS V8
88	= Town Car Executive 4D Sedan
91	= Mark VII Base 2D Coupe
91	= Mark VIII Base 2D Coupe
91	= Mark VIII Base 2D Coupe
92	= Mark VII Bill Blass Designer 2D Coupe
92	= Mark VII Bill Blass Designer 2D Coupe
92	= Mark VIII LSC 2D Coupe
92	= Mark VIII LSC 2D Coupe
93	= Town Car 2D Sedan
93	= Mark VII LSC 2D Coupe
93	= Mark VII LSC 2D Coupe
94	= Town Car 4D Sedan
95	= Mark VI 2D Coupe
96	= Mark VI 4D Sedan
96	= Town Car 4D Sedan
97	= Continental 4D Sedan
97	= Continental 4D Sedan
98	= Mark VI 2D Coupe
98	= Continental Signature 4D Sedan
98	= Continental Givenchy Designer 4D Sedan
98	= Continental Signature 4D Sedan
98	= Mark VII 2D Coupe

DIGIT 6-7	Carline/Body Style
99	= Mark VI 4D Sedan

DIGIT 8	Engine
3	= 3.8L V6 EFI
4	= 3.8L V6 EFI
4	= 3.8L V6 EFI
A	= 3.9L V8 EFI DOHC
A	= 3.9L V8 EFI DOHC
E	= 5.0L V8 EFI HO
E	= 5.0L V8 EFI HO
F	= 5.0L V8 EFI
L	= 2.4L I-6 FI TDsl
M	= 5.0L V8 SFI HO
S	= 3.0L V6 EFI DOHC
S	= 3.0L V6 EFI DOHC
V	= 4.6L V8 EFI DOHC
V	= 4.6L V8 EFI DOHC
W	= 4.6L V8 EFI SOHC
W	= 4.6L V8 EFI SOHC

DIGIT 10	Model Year
1	= 2001
1	= 2001
2	= 2002
2	= 2002
3	= 2003
3	= 2003
4	= 2004
4	= 2004
5	= 2005
5	= 2005
B	= 1981
C	= 1982
D	= 1983
E	= 1984
F	= 1985
G	= 1986
H	= 1987
J	= 1988
K	= 1989
L	= 1990
M	= 1991
M	= 1991
N	= 1992
N	= 1992
P	= 1993
P	= 1993
R	= 1994
R	= 1994
S	= 1995
S	= 1995
T	= 1996
T	= 1996
V	= 1997
V	= 1997
W	= 1998
W	= 1998
X	= 1999
X	= 1999
Y	= 2000
Y	= 2000

DIGIT 11	Assembly Plant Location
Y	= Wixom, MI, USA
Y	= Wixom, MI, USA

ARM0400000000662

Fig. 7 VIN Identification. Lincoln

DIGIT 1-3	World Manufacturer Identifier
1ME	= Ford Motor Company, USA - Mercury
1ME	= Ford Motor Company, USA - Mercury
1ZW	= Auto Alliance International, Inc
1ZW	= Auto Alliance International, Inc
2ME	= Ford Motor Company of Canada - Mercury
2ME	= Ford Motor Company of Canada - Mercury
3MA	= Ford Motor Company of Mexico - Mercury
3MA	= Ford Motor Company of Mexico - Mercury
3ME	= Ford Motor Company of Mexico - Mercury
3ME	= Ford Motor Company of Mexico - Mercury
6MP	= Ford Motor Company of Australia, Ltd.
WF1	= Merkur

DIGIT 4	Restraint System
A	= Driverside Airbag w/Manual Driver & Rear Belts & Automati
A	= Driverside Airbag w/Manual Driver & Rear Belts & Automati
B	= Manual Belts
C	= Driverside Airbag w/Manual Belts
C	= Driverside Airbag w/Manual Belts
F	= 2nd Generation Dual Front Airbags w/Manual Belts
F	= 2nd Generation Dual Front Airbags w/Manual Belts
H	= 2nd Generation Dual Front & Side Airbags w/Manual Belts
H	= 2nd Generation Dual Front & Side Airbags w/Manual Belts
H	= Dual Front & Front Side Airbags w/Manual Belts
H	= Dual Front & Front Side Airbags w/Manual Belts
L	= Dual Front Airbags w/Manual Belts
L	= Dual Front Airbags w/Manual Belts
P	= Automatic Front Belts & Manual Rear Belts
P	= Automatic Front Belts & Manual Rear Belts
R	= Driverside Airbag w/Automatic Front Belts & Manual Rear E
S	= Dual Front Airbags w/Automatic Front Belts and Manual Re

DIGIT 5	Designation
M	= Passenger Car - Mercury Make
M	= Passenger Car - Mercury Make
P	= Passenger Car
P	= Ford Make
T	= Ford Import
T	= Ford Import

DIGIT 6-7	Carline/Body Style
01	= Capri Base 2D Convertible
03	= Capri XR2 2D Convertible
10	= Tracer Base 4D Sedan
10	= Tracer Base 4D Sedan
10	= Tracer GS 4D Sedan
11	= Tracer Base 2D Hatchback
12	= Tracer Base 4D Hatchback
13	= Tracer Base 4D Wagon
13	= Tracer LS 4D Sedan
14	= Tracer LTS 4D Sedan
14	= Tracer LTS 4D Sedan
15	= Tracer Base 4D Wagon
15	= Tracer Base 4D Wagon
15	= Tracer LS 4D Wagon
20	= Lynx L 2D Hatchback
21	= Lynx GS 2D Hatchback
23	= Lynx XR3 2D Hatchback
25	= Lynx GS 4D Hatchback
28	= Lynx GS 4D Wagon
31	= Topaz GS 2D Coupe
31	= Topaz GS 2D Coupe
33	= Topaz XR5 2D Coupe
33	= Topaz GS Sport 2D Coupe
33	= Topaz XR5 2D Coupe
36	= Topaz GS 4D Sedan
36	= Topaz GS 4D Sedan
37	= Topaz LS 4D Sedan
37	= Topaz LS 4D Sedan
38	= Topaz LTS 4D Sedan
38	= Topaz LTS 4D Sedan
38	= Topaz GS Sport 4D Sedan
40	= Montego 4D Sedan Luxury FWD

DIGIT 6-7	Carline/Body Style
41	= Montego 4D Sedan Luxury AWD
42	= Montego 4D Sedan Premier FWD
43	= Montego 4D Sedan Premier AWD
50	= Sable LS 4D Sedan
50	= Sable GS 4D Sedan
50	= Sable GS 4D Sedan
50	= Sable LS 4D Sedan
51	= Sable G 4D Sedan
51	= LN7 2D Hatchback
51	= Lynx L 2D Hatchback
51	= Sable G 4D Sedan
51	= Lynx Base 2D Hatchback
52	= Lynx GS 2D Hatchback
53	= Sable LS Premium 4D Sedan
53	= Lynx XR3 2D Hatchback
53	= Sable LS 4D Sedan
53	= Sable LS Premium 4D Sedan
53	= Sable LS 4D Sedan
54	= Lynx Base 2D Hatchback
54	= Lynx L 2D Hatchback
55	= Sable GS 4D Wagon
55	= Sable GS 4D Wagon
55	= Lynx GS 2D Hatchback
55	= Sable LS 4D Sedan
55	= Sable LS 4D Wagon
55	= Sable LS 4D Wagon
55	= Sable LS Premium 4D Sedan
57	= Lynx RS 2D Hatchback
58	= Sable LS Premium 4D Wagon
58	= Lynx L 4D Wagon
58	= Sable LS 4D Wagon
58	= Sable LS Premium 4D Wagon
58	= Lynx LS 2D Hatchback
58	= Sable GS 4D Wagon
58	= Sable LS 4D Wagon
59	= Lynx GS 4D Wagon
59	= Sable LS Premium 4D Wagon
59	= Sable LS 4D Wagon
60	= Cougar LS 2D Coupe
60	= Cougar I-4 2D Coupe
60	= Lynx L 4D Wagon
60	= Cougar I-4 2D Coupe
60	= Cougar LS 2D Coupe
61	= Lynx GS 4D Wagon
61	= Cougar V6 2D Coupe
61	= Cougar V6 2D Coupe
61	= LN7 2D Hatchback
62	= Cougar XR-7 2D Coupe
62	= Cougar V6 2D Coupe
62	= Cougar XR-7 2D Coupe
62	= Cougar S 2D Coupe
62	= Cougar V6 2D Coupe
62	= Cougar S 2D Coupe
63	= Lynx LS 4D Wagon
63	= Lynx L 4D Hatchback
63	= Lynx 2D Hatchback
64	= Lynx 4D Hatchback
64	= Lynx GS 4D Hatchback
65	= Mystique Base 4D Sedan
65	= Lynx 4D Wagon
65	= Mystique Base 4D Sedan
65	= Lynx L 4D Hatchback
65	= Mystique GS 4D Sedan
65	= Mystique GS 4D Sedan
65	= Lynx Base 4D Hatchback
65	= Lynx 4D Liftgate
66	= Mystique LS 4D Sedan
66	= Lynx GS 4D Hatchback
66	= Mystique LS 4D Sedan
67	= Capri 2D Hatchback
68	= Lynx LTS 4D Hatchback
68	= Capri GS 2D Hatchback

ARM0400000000663

Fig. 8 VIN Identification (Part 1 of 3). Mercury

DIGIT 6-7	Carline/Body Style
70	= Zephyr 2D Sedan
71	= Zephyr 4D Sedan
72	= Zephyr Z-7 2D Sedan
72	= Topaz GS 2D Coupe
72	= Grand Marquis LS 2D Sedan
73	= Zephyr 4D Wagon
73	= Topaz LS 2D Coupe
74	= Grand Marquis GS 4D Sedan
74	= Grand Marquis GS 4D Sedan
75	= Grand Marquis LSE 4D Sedan
75	= Grand Marquis Marauder 4D Sedan
75	= Grand Marquis Marauder 4D Sedan
75	= Grand Marquis LSE 4D Sedan
75	= Grand Marquis LS 4D Sedan
75	= Grand Marquis LS 4D Sedan
75	= Topaz GS 4D Sedan
76	= Cougar 2D Coupe
76	= Topaz LS 4D Sedan
77	= Cougar 4D Sedan
78	= Cougar GS 4D Wagon
78	= Grand Marquis Colony Park GS 4D Wagon
78	= Grand Marquis Colony Park GS 4D Wagon
79	= Grand Marquis Colony Park LS 4D Wagon
79	= Grand Marquis Colony Park LS 4D Wagon
79	= Capri 2D Hatchback
81	= Marquis 4D Sedan
82	= Marquis Brougham 2D Sedan
83	= Marquis Brougham 4D Sedan
84	= Grand Marquis 2D Sedan
85	= Grand Marquis 4D Sedan
86	= Zephyr 4D Sedan
87	= Sable 4D Sedan
87	= Zephyr Z 2D Coupe
87	= Marquis 4D Wagon
87	= Zephyr Z-7 2D Sedan
88	= Marquis Colony Park 4D Wagon
88	= Sable 4D Wagon
89	= Marquis 4D Sedan
90	= Marquis 4D Wagon
90	= Cougar XR-7 2D Coupe
92	= Cougar 2D Coupe
93	= Grand Marquis 2D Sedan
94	= Grand Marquis Colony Park 4D Wagon
95	= Grand Marquis 4D Sedan

DIGIT 8	Engine
2	= 3.0L V6 EFI FFV
2	= 1.6L I-4 2BBL
2	= 3.0L V6 Duratec
3	= 2.0L I-4 EFI DOHC
3	= 2.0L I-4 EFI DOHC
3	= 3.8L V6 EFI
3	= 3.8L V6 2BBL
4	= 3.8L V6 EFI
4	= 3.8L V6 EFI
4	= 1.6L I-4 2BBL HO
5	= 1.6L I-4 EFI
6	= 1.6L I-4 EFI Turbo
6	= 4.6L V8 EFI SOHC
6	= 4.6L V8 EFI SOHC
6	= 2.3L I-4 1BBL LPG
8	= 1.8L I-4 EFI DOHC
8	= 1.8L I-4 EFI DOHC
9	= 1.9L I-4 EFI
9	= 1.9L I-4 2BBL
A	= 2.3L I-4 1BBL SOHC
A	= 2.3L I-4 2BBL
B	= 3.3L I-6 1BBL
D	= 2.5L I-4 EFI HSC
D	= 4.2L V8 1BBL
D	= 4.2L V8 2BBL
F	= 5.0L V8 EFI

DIGIT 8	Engine
F	= 5.0L V8 EFI
F	= 5.0L V8 4BBL HO
F	= 5.0L V8 2BBL
G	= 2.5L V6 EFI DOHC HO
G	= 2.5L V6 EFI DOHC HO
G	= 5.8L V8 2BBL HO
H	= 2.0L I-4 Dsl
J	= 1.9L I-4 EFI
J	= 1.9L I-4 EFI
J	= 1.9L I-4 EFI HO
L	= 2.5L V6 EFI DOHC
L	= 2.5L V6 EFI DOHC
M	= 5.0L V8 4BBL
M	= 5.0L V8 EFI HO
P	= 2.0L I-4 SPI
R	= 3.8L V6 EFI S/C
R	= 2.3L I-4 1BBL HSC
S	= 3.0L V6 EFI DOHC
S	= 3.0L V6 EFI DOHC
S	= 2.3L I-4 EFI HSO
S	= 2.3L I-4 EFI HSO
T	= 5.0L V8 EFI HO
T	= 5.0L V8 EFI HO
U	= 3.0L V6 EFI
U	= 3.0L V6 EFI
V	= 4.6L V8 EFI DOHC
V	= 4.6L V8 EFI DOHC
V	= 2.9L V6 EFI
W	= 4.6L V8 EFI
W	= 4.6L V8 EFI SOHC
W	= 2.3L I-4 EFI T/C I/C
W	= 4.6L V8 EFI SOHC
W	= 2.3L I-4 EFI Turbo
W	= 4.6L V8 EFI
X	= 2.3L I-4 EFI HSC
X	= 3.3L I-6 1BBL
X	= 2.3L I-4 EFI HSC
Z	= 1.6L I-4 EFI DOHC

DIGIT 10	Model Year
1	= 2001
1	= 2001
2	= 2002
2	= 2002
3	= 2003
3	= 2003
4	= 2004
4	= 2004
5	= 2005
5	= 2005
B	= 1981
C	= 1982
D	= 1983
E	= 1984
F	= 1985
G	= 1986
H	= 1987
J	= 1988
K	= 1989
L	= 1990
M	= 1991
M	= 1991
N	= 1992
N	= 1992
P	= 1993
P	= 1993
R	= 1994
R	= 1994
S	= 1995
S	= 1995
T	= 1996
T	= 1996

ARM0400000000664

Fig. 8 VIN Identification (Part 2 of 3). Mercury

DIGIT 10 — Model Year

Code	Year
V	1997
V	1997
W	1998
W	1998
X	1999
X	1999
Y	2000
Y	2000

DIGIT 11 — Assembly Plant Location

Code	Location
5	AAI: Flat Rock, MI, USA
5	AAI: Flat Rock, MI, USA
8	Broadmeadows: Campbellfield, Australia
A	Atlanta, GA, USA
A	Atlanta, GA, USA
B	Oakville, ON, Canada
B	Oakville, ON, Canada
F	Dearborn, MI, USA
G	Chicago, IL, USA
G	Chicago, IL, USA
H	Lorain, OH, USA
H	Lorain, OH, USA
K	Kansas City, MO, USA
K	Kansas City, MO, USA
M	Cuautitlan, Mexico
M	Cuautitlan, Mexico
R	San Jose, CA, USA
R	Hermosillo, Mexico
R	Hermosillo, Mexico
T	Metuchen, NJ, USA
T	Edison, NJ, USA
W	Wayne, MI, USA
X	St. Thomas, ON, Canada
X	St. Thomas, ON, Canada
Z	St. Louis, MO, USA

Fig. 8 VIN Identification (Part 3 of 3). Mercury

ARM0400000000665

DIGIT 1 — Country Of Origin

Code	Origin
1	USA
1	USA
2	Canada
2	Canada
3	Mexico
3	Mexico

DIGIT 2 — Manufacturer

Code	Manufacturer
G	General Motors
G	General Motors

DIGIT 3 — Make

Code	Make
3	Oldsmobile
3	Oldsmobile

DIGIT 4 — Restraint System

Code	System
A	Manual Belts

DIGIT 4-5 — Carline/Series

Code	Carline/Series
6K	Cutlass Salon 442
AG	Cutlass Ciera S
AG	Cutlass Ciera S
AJ	Cutlass Ciera SL
AJ	Cutlass Ciera S Cruiser Wagon
AJ	Cutlass Ciera S
AJ	Cutlass Ciera Base
AJ	Cutlass Ciera SL
AJ	Cutlass Ciera S Cruiser Wagon
AJ	Cutlass Ciera S
AL	Cutlass Ciera LS
AL	Cutlass Ciera Base
AL	Cutlass Ciera S
AL	Cutlass Ciera S
AM	Cutlass Ciera Base
AM	Cutlass Ciera SL
AS	Cutlass Ciera Brougham
BN	Cutlass Ciera International
BP	Eighty Eight Royale
BY	Eighty Eight Custom Cruiser
CV	Eighty Eight Brougham
CV	Ninety Eight Touring Sedan
CW	Ninety Eight Touring Sedan
CW	Ninety Eight Regency Elite
CX	Ninety Eight Regency Brougham
CX	Ninety Eight Regency Elite
CX	Ninety Eight Regency
EV	Ninety Eight Regency
EV	Ninety Eight Regency Elite
EZ	Toronado Trofeo
EZ	Toronado Trofeo
GK	Toronado
GM	Toronado
GR	Cutlass Salon Coupe
GR	Cutlass Supreme Brougham RWD
GR	Aurora
GR	Cutlass Salon 442
GS	Cutlass Supreme RWD
GS	Aurora
HC	Aurora
HC	Aurora
HN	Eighty Eight Anniversary Edition
HN	Eighty Eight Anniversary Edition
HN	Regency
HN	Eighty Eight Base
HN	Eighty Eight Royale
HN	Eighty Eight LS
HY	Eighty Eight LS
HY	Eighty Eight Royale
	Eighty Eight Royale
	Eighty Eight Royale LSS
	Eighty Eight Brougham

DIGIT 4-5 — Carline/Series

Code	Carline/Series
HY	Eighty Eight Royale Brougham
HY	Eighty Eight LSS
HY	Eighty Eight LSS
HY	Eighty Eight Royale LSS Brougham
HY	Eighty Eight Royale LS
JC	Firenza S
JC	Firenza Base
JD	Firenza LX
JD	Firenza LC
JD	Firenza SX
JD	Firenza GT
NB	Cutlass GL
NF	Cutlass Calais S
NF	Cutlass Calais S
NF	Achieva SL
NF	Achieva SL
NF	Alero GLS
NF	Achieva SC
NF	Alero GLS
NF	Achieva SC
NG	Calais
NK	Cutlass GLS
NK	Cutlass Calais International
NK	Alero GX
NK	Cutlass Calais International
NL	Alero GX
NL	Achieva
NL	Achieva
NL	Alero GL
NL	Cutlass Calais
NL	Cutlass Calais
NL	Achieva S
NL	Alero GL
NT	Achieva S
NT	Cutlass Calais Supreme
NT	Calais Supreme
WH	Cutlass Calais Supreme
WH	Cutlass Supreme SL
WH	Cutlass Supreme SL
WH	Cutlass Supreme SL
WH	Intrigue
WH	Cutlass Supreme S
WH	Cutlass Supreme Base
WH	Intrigue GX
WR	Intrigue
WR	Cutlass Supreme S
WR	Cutlass Supreme Base
WS	Intrigue GX
WS	Cutlass Supreme International
WS	Cutlass Supreme International
WS	Cutlass Supreme SL
WT	Intrigue GL
WT	Cutlass Supreme SL
WX	Intrigue GL
WX	Cutlass Supreme Convertible
	Cutlass Supreme Convertible
	Intrigue GLS
	Intrigue GLS

DIGIT 5 — Carline

Code	Carline
B	Omega
C	Firenza
D	Firenza LX
D	Firenza SX
E	Firenza Brougham
E	Omega Brougham
G	Ninety Eight Regency
G	Cutlass Ciera
G	Cutlass
H	Ninety Eight Brougham

Fig. 9 VIN Identification (Part 1 of 3). Oldsmobile

ARM0400000000678

Fig. 9 VIN Identification (Part 2 of 3). Oldsmobile

DIGIT 5 — Carline

Code	Carline
H	Cutlass Cruiser
J	Cutlass Ciera LS
K	Cutlass Calais
L	Delta Eighty Eight
M	Cutlass Supreme Brougham
M	Cutlass Ciera Brougham
N	Ninety Eight Brougham
P	Delta Eighty Eight Royale
P	Eighty Eight Custom Cruiser
R	Cutlass LS
R	Cutlass Supreme
V	Ninety Eight Luxury
V	Ninety Eight Regency
W	Delta Eighty Eight Royale Brougham LS
W	Ninety Eight Regency Brougham
X	Ninety Eight Regency
X	Delta Eighty Eight Royale Brougham
Z	Toranado Brougham

DIGIT 6 — Body Style

Code	Body Style
1	2D Coupe
1	2D Coupe/Sedan
1	2D Sedan
1	2D Sedan
2	2D Coupe/Sedan
2	2D Hatchback
3	2D Convertible
3	2D Convertible
5	4D Sedan
6	4D Sedan
6	4D Sedan
8	4D Station Wagon
8	4D Station Wagon

DIGIT 6-7 — Body Type

Code	Body Type
11	2D Notchback Sedan
19	4D Sedan
27	2D Coupe
35	4D 2-Seat Wagon
37	2D Notchback Special Coupe
47	2D Notchback Special Coupe
47	2D Coupe
57	2D Notchback Special Coupe
69	4D Sedan
69	4D Notchback Sedan
77	2D Coupe

DIGIT 7 — Restraint System

Code	Restraint System
1	Manual Belts
1	Manual Belts
2	Dual Front Airbags w/Manual Belts
2	Dual Front Airbags w/Manual Belts
3	Driverside Airbag w/Manual Belts
3	Driverside Airbag w/Manual Belts
4	Automatic Belts
4	Automatic Belts
4	Dual Front & Side Airbags w/Manual Belts
4	Dual Front & Side Airbags w/Manual Belts
4	Dual Front Airbags w/Automatic Belts
5	Driverside Airbag w/Automatic Belts
5	Dual Front & Side Airbags w/Automatic Belts
6	Driverside Airbag w/Automatic Belts
6	Dual Front & Side Airbags, Auto Passenger Sensor w/Manu
6	Dual Front & Side Airbags, Auto Passenger Sensor w/Manu

DIGIT 8 — Engine

Code	Engine
0	1.8L I-4 TBI
1	3.8L V6 MPI
1	2.0L I-4 EFI
1	3.8L V6 SFI S/C
1	3.8L V6 MPI
1	3.8L V6 SFI S/C
3	3.8L V6 MPI
3	2.3L I-4 MPI

DIGIT 10 — Model Year

Code	Model Year
1	2001
2	2002
2	2002
3	2003
3	2003
4	2004
B	1981
C	1982

Fig. 9 VIN Identification (Part 2 of 3). Oldsmobile

ARM040000000667

Fig. 9 VIN Identification (Part 3 of 3). Oldsmobile

DIGIT 8 — Engine

Code	Engine
3	2.3L I-4 MPI
4	2.2L I-4 MPI
4	2.2L I-4 MPI
4	4.1L V6 4BBL
5	2.5L I-4 2BBL
7	5.7L V8 TBI
8	4.3L V8 2BBL
9	5.0L V8 4BBL
A	2.3L I-4 HO Quad 4
A	2.3L I-4 HO Quad 4
B	2.0L I-4 EFI
B	3.8L V6 SFI
C	3.8L V6 MPI
C	4.0L V8 SFI
C	3.8L V6 MPI
C	4.0L V8 SFI
D	2.3L I-4 Quad 4
D	2.3L I-4 Quad 4
E	3.0L V6 2BBL
E	5.0L V8 TBI
E	3.4L V6 SFI
F	2.0L I-4 MPI DOHC
F	2.0L I-4 MPI DOHC
F	4.3L V8 2BBL
G	1.8L I-4 2BBL
H	3.5L V6 MPI
H	5.0L V8 4BBL
H	3.5L V6 MPI
J	3.1L V6 MPI
K	2.0L I-4 EFI
K	3.8L V6 MPI S/C
K	3.8L V6 MPI S/C
L	3.0L V6 MPI
L	3.8L V6 MPI
M	3.1L V6 MPI
M	2.0L I-4 EFI
N	3.3L V6 MPI
N	3.3L V6 MPI
P	5.7L V8 Dsl
P	2.0L I-4 EFI
R	2.5L I-4 TBI
R	2.5L I-4 TBI
T	2.4L I-4 MPI
T	2.4L I-4 MPI
T	4.3L V6 Dsl
T	3.1L V6 MPI
U	2.5L I-4 TBI
U	2.5L I-4 TBI
V	4.3L V6 MPI
W	2.8L V6 MPI
X	3.8L V6 2BBL
X	3.4L V6 MPI
X	3.4L V6 MPI
Y	5.0L V8 4BBL
Z	2.8L V6 2BBL HO

DIGIT 10 — Model Year

Code	Model Year
D	1983
E	1984
F	1985
G	1986
H	1987
J	1988
K	1989
L	1990
M	1991
M	1991
N	1992
P	1992
P	1993
R	1993
R	1994
S	1994
S	1995
T	1995
T	1996
V	1996
V	1997
W	1997
W	1998
X	1998
X	1999
Y	1999
Y	2000
	2000

DIGIT 11 — Assembly Plant Location

Code	Assembly Plant Location
1	Wentzville, MO, USA
1	Wentzville, MO, USA
2	Ste. Therese, PQ, Canada
2	Ste. Therese, PQ, Canada
4	Orion, MI, USA
4	Orion, MI, USA
6	Oklahoma City, OK, USA
6	Oklahoma City, OK, USA
9	Detroit, MI, USA
9	Oshawa #1, ON, Canada
9	Oshawa #1, ON, Canada
9	Detroit, MI, USA
B	Lansing, MI, USA
B	Lansing, MI, USA
C	Lansing, MI, USA
C	Lansing, MI, USA
D	Doraville, GA, USA
D	Doraville, GA, USA
E	Linden, NJ, USA
F	Fairfax II, KS, USA
F	Fairfax II, KS, USA
G	Framingham, MA, USA
H	Flint, MI, USA
H	Flint, MI, USA
K	Linden, NJ, USA
K	Leeds, MO, USA
M	Lansing, MI, USA
M	Lansing, MI, USA
P	Pontiac, MI, USA
R	Arlington, TX, USA
R	Arlington, TX, USA
S	Ramos Arizpe, Mexico
S	Ramos Arizpe, Mexico
U	Hamtramck, MI, USA
U	Hamtramck, MI, USA
W	Willow Run, MI, USA
W	Willow Run, MI, USA
X	Fairfax, KS, USA
X	Fairfax, KS, USA
Y	Wilmington, DE, USA
Y	Wilmington, DE, USA

Fig. 9 VIN Identification (Part 3 of 3). Oldsmobile

ARM040000000668

Fig. 10 VIN Identification (Part 1 of 3). Plymouth

DIGIT 1 — Country Of Origin

Code	Description
1	= USA
1	= USA
2	= Canada
3	= Mexico
3	= Mexico
4	= USA - MMMA
4	= USA - MMMA
J	= Japan
J	= Japan

DIGIT 2 — Make

Code	Description
P	= Plymouth
P	= Plymouth

DIGIT 3 — Vehicle Type

Code	Description
3	= Passenger Car
3	= Passenger Car
4	= Multi-Purpose Passenger Vehicle
4	= Multi-Purpose Passenger Vehicle

DIGIT 4 — Restraint

Code	Description
A	= Dual Front & Side Airbags w/Manual Belts
A	= Driverside Airbag w/Automatic Passenger Belt
B	= Manual Belts
B	= Manual Seat Belts
C	= Automatic Seat Belts
C	= Driverside Airbag
E	= Dual Airbags w/Manual Belts
E	= 4001-5000 Lbs, Hydraulic Brakes
H	= Dual Airbags w/Manual Belts
X	= Driverside Airbag w/Manual Belts
Y	= Driverside Airbag w/Automatic Passenger Belt

DIGIT 4* — Restraint

Code	Description
A	= Driverside Airbag w/Automatic Passenger Belt
B	= Manual Seat Belts
B	= Manual Seat Belts
C	= Automatic Seat Belts
C	= Driverside Airbag
E	= Dual Airbags w/Manual Belts
E	= 3001-4000 Lbs, Hydraulic
E	= Dual Airbags w/Manual Belts
F	= 3001-4000 Lbs, Hydraulic
F	= 4001-5000 Lbs, Hydraulic Brakes
P	= Manual Seat Belts
P	= Manual Seat Belts
X	= Driverside Airbag w/Manual Belts

DIGIT 5 — Carline

Code	Description
A	= Colt
B	= Gran Fury Salon
C	= Conquest
D	= Sapporo
G	= Colt
G	= Colt Vista
J	= Caravelle
K	= Reliant
L	= Horizon
M	= Horizon
P	= Reliant

DIGIT 5* — Model

Code	Description
E	= Champ

DIGIT 5-6 — Carline

Code	Description
A4	= Acclaim
A4	= Acclaim
A5	= Acclaim LE
A5	= Acclaim LE
A7	= Acclaim LX
A7	= Acclaim LX
B1	= Gran Fury Special
B2	= Gran Fury Salon
F3	= Laser
F3	= Laser
F4	= Laser RS & RS Turbo FWD
F4	= Laser RS & RS Turbo FWD
G4	= Laser RS Turbo AWD
G4	= Laser RS Turbo AWD
J3	= Caravelle
J4	= Caravelle SE
J4	= Breeze
K4	= Breeze
L1	= Reliant
M1	= Horizon
M1	= Horizon
M2	= Gran Fury Salon
M3	= Gran Fury Special
M4	= Horizon Turismo
P2	= Sundance America
P2	= Sundance America
P2	= Sundance
P4	= Sundance
P4	= Sundance Highline
P4	= Sundance Highline
P6	= Sundance Duster
P6	= Sundance RS
P6	= Sundance RS
S2	= Sundance Duster
S2	= Neon Base
S2	= Neon Competition
S2	= Neon Competition
S2	= Neon Base
S3	= Laser
S3	= Laser
S4	= Laser RS 2WD
S4	= Laser RS 2WD
S4	= Sundance
S4	= Neon Highline
S4	= Neon Highline
S6	= Neon Sport
S6	= Neon Sport
T4	= Laser RS AWD
T4	= Laser RS AWD
W6	= Prowler

DIGIT 6 — Series

Code	Description
1	= Miser
2	= Base
2	= Base
2	= Low
3	= DLX
3	= High
3	= Medium
4	= High
4	= DLX
4	= Base
4	= Custom
4	= Turismo
4	= SE
5	= Premium
5	= Euro
5	= Turismo
5	= Turismo 2.2
5	= Custom

DIGIT 7 — Body Style

Code	Description
1	= 2D Sedan
2	= 2D Pillared Hardtop
2	= 2D Pillared Hardtop
3	= 2D Hardtop
4	= 2D Hatchback

ARM0400000000669

Fig. 10 VIN Identification (Part 1 of 3). Plymouth

Fig. 10 VIN Identification (Part 2 of 3). Plymouth

DIGIT 7 — Body Style

Code	Description
4	= 2D Hatchback
5	= 2D Convertible
6	= 4D Sedan
6	= 4D Pillared Hardtop
7	= 4D Pillared Hardtop
7	= 4D Sedan
8	= 4D Hatchback
8	= 4D Hatchback
9	= 4D Wagon

DIGIT 7* — Body Type

Code	Description
0	= Wagon
1	= Wagon
1	= 2D Sedan
1	= Wagon
1	= 2D Hatchback
4	= 2D Hatchback
6	= 4D Sedan
6	= 4D Hatchback
8	= Wagon
9	= Wagon
9	= Wagon

DIGIT 8 — Engine

Code	Description
2	= 1.4L I-4 2BBL
3	= 3.0L V6 MPI
3	= 1.6L I-4 2BBL
3	= 3.0L V6 MPI
4	= 5.2L V8 2BBL
7	= 2.6L I-4 2BBL
A	= 1.5L I-4 MPI
A	= 1.6L I-4 MPI
A	= 1.5L I-4 MPI
A	= 1.7L I-4 2BBL
B	= 1.8L I-4 MPI
B	= 1.6L I-4 2BBL
B	= 1.8L I-4 MPI
B	= 1.7L I-4 2BBL
C	= 1.8L I-4 MPI
C	= 2.0L I-4 SFI SOHC
C	= 1.8L I-4 MPI
C	= 2.0L I-4 SFI SOHC
D	= 2.2L I-4 Turbo
D	= 2.2L I-4 TBI
D	= 1.8L I-4 MPI
D	= 2.0L I-4
D	= 2.0L I-4 MPI
D	= 2.6L I-4 2BBL
E	= 2.0L I-4 MPI DOHC
E	= 2.2L I-4 2BBL
E	= 2.0L I-4 MPI DOHC
F	= 3.7L 6 Cyl 1BBL
F	= 3.5L V6 MPI
F	= 3.7L 6 Cyl 1BBL
F	= 2.2L I-4 Turbo
G	= 2.0L I-4 DOHC T/C I/C
G	= 2.0L I-4 DOHC T/C I/C
G	= 2.4L I-4 MPI
G	= 2.4L I-4 MPI SOHC
G	= 2.6L I-4 2BBL
G	= 2.0L I-4 MPI SOHC
G	= 3.5L V6 MPI SOHC HO
H	= 3.7L 6 Cyl 1BBL

DIGIT 8 — Engine (continued)

Code	Description
H	= 2.6L I-4 Tbo
H	= 2.5L I-4 EFI
H	= 2.5L I-4 EFI
J	= 2.5L I-4 Turbo
J	= 2.5L I-4 Turbo
K	= 1.5L I-4
K	= 2.5L I-4 TBI
K	= 2.5L I-4 TBI
L	= 5.2L V8 2BBL
L	= 5.2L V8 2BBL
M	= 5.2L V8 4BBL
N	= 2.6L I-4 Tbo
N	= 5.2L V8 2BBL
P	= 5.2L V8 4BBL
R	= 2.0L I-4 MPI DOHC
R	= 2.0L I-4 MPI DOHC
S	= 5.2L V8 4BBL
T	= 1.8L I-4 MPI
T	= 1.8L I-4 MPI
U	= 2.0L I-4 MPI DOHC Turbo
U	= 2.0L I-4 MPI DOHC Turbo
U	= 2.5L I-4 TBI Flex Fuel
V	= 2.5L I-4 TBI Flex Fuel
V	= 2.0L I-4 MPI
V	= 2.0L I-4 MPI
W	= 2.0L I-4 MPI
W	= 2.4L I-4 MPI
X	= 2.4L I-4 SFI
X	= 2.4L I-4 SFI
X	= 1.5L I-4 MPI
Y	= 2.0L I-4 SFI DOHC
Y	= 2.0L I-4 SFI DOHC
Z	= 1.5L I-4 MPI
Z	= 1.6L I-4 Turbo

DIGIT 10 — Model Year

Code	Description
1	= 2001
B	= 1981
C	= 1982
D	= 1983
E	= 1984
F	= 1985
G	= 1986
H	= 1987
J	= 1988
K	= 1989
L	= 1990
M	= 1991
N	= 1991
N	= 1992
P	= 1992
P	= 1993
R	= 1994
R	= 1994
S	= 1995
S	= 1995
T	= 1996
T	= 1996
V	= 1997
V	= 1997
W	= 1998
W	= 1998
X	= 1999
X	= 1999
Y	= 2000

DIGIT 11 — Assembly Plant Location

Code	Description
D	= Belvidere, IL, USA
E	= Bloomington - Normal, IL, USA
F	= Newark, NJ, USA

ARM0400000000670

Fig. 10 VIN Identification (Part 2 of 3). Plymouth

DIGIT 11   Assembly Plant Location

J	= Nagoya 3, Japan
N	= Sterling Heights, MI, USA
P	= Nagoya 2, Japan
T	= Toluca, Mexico
U	= Mizushima 1, Japan
U	= Mizushima, Japan
Y	= Nagoya 1, Japan
Y	= Nagoya, Japan
Z	= Okazaki, Japan
Z	= Okazaki, Japan

DIGIT 12   Transmission

4	= 5-Speed Manual - Federal
5	= 5-Speed Manual - California
7	= Automatic - Federal
8	= Automatic - California

Fig. 10 VIN Identification (Part 3 of 3). Plymouth

DIGIT 1   Country Of Origin

1	= USA
1	= USA
2	= Canada
2	= Canada
3	= Mexico
3	= Mexico
4	= USA
4	= USA
K	= Korea
K	= Korea

DIGIT 1-3   Manufacturer Identification

5Y2	= Pontiac, Nummi
5Y2	= Pontiac, Nummi
6G2	= Pontiac, Australia

DIGIT 2   Manufacturer

G	= General Motors
G	= General Motors
L	= Daewoo
L	= Daewoo

DIGIT 3   Make

2	= Pontiac
2	= Pontiac

DIGIT 4   Restraint System

A	= Manual Belts

DIGIT 4-5   Carline/Series

AE	= 6000 SE
AF	= 6000
AF	= 6000 LE
AG	= 6000 LE
AH	= 6000 STE
AJ	= 6000 SE
AJ	= 6000 SE
BL	= Parisienne
BT	= Parisienne Brougham
FS	= Firebird
FS	= Firebird
FV	= Formula
FV	= Formula
FV	= Trans AM
FV	= Trans AM
FW	= Trans AM
FW	= Trans AM GTA
FW	= Trans AM
FW	= Trans AM GTA
FX	= Firebird SE
GJ	= Grand Prix
GK	= Grand Prix LE
GN	= Bonneville
GP	= Grand Prix Brougham
GR	= Grand Prix Brougham
GS	= Bonneville LE
HX	= Bonneville SLE
HX	= Bonneville LE
HX	= Bonneville SLE
HX	= Bonneville SE
HX	= Bonneville SE
HX	= Bonneville LE
HY	= Bonneville
HY	= Bonneville SSE
HY	= Bonneville SSE
HY	= Bonneville SLE
HY	= Bonneville SSEi
HY	= Bonneville SE
HY	= Bonneville SSEi
HZ	= Bonneville LE
HZ	= Bonneville SSEi
HZ	= Bonneville SSE

DIGIT 4-5   Carline/Series

HZ	= Bonneville SE
HZ	= Bonneville SSE
HZ	= Bonneville SE
HZ	= Bonneville GXP
HZ	= Bonneville SSEi
JB	= Sunfire SE Convertible
JB	= Sunfire SE Convertible
JB	= Sunfire GT Convertible
JB	= Sunfire LE
JB	= Sunfire SE
JB	= Sunfire GT Convertible
JB	= Sunbird SE & Convertible
JB	= Sunbird LE & Convertible
JB	= Sunbird SE & Convertible
JB	= Sunfire SE
JB	= Sunbird LE
JB	= Sunbird LE & Convertible
JB	= Sunbird
JC	= Sunbird LE
JC	= Sunbird LE
JC	= Sunbird
JD	= Sunfire GT
JD	= Sunbird SE
JD	= Sunbird GT
JD	= Sunbird GT
JD	= Sunfire GT
JL	= Sunbird SE
JL	= Sunbird SE
JU	= Sunbird GT
JU	= Sunbird GT
NE	= Grand AM LE
NE	= Grand AM LE
NE	= Grand AM SE
NE	= Grand AM
NF	= Grand AM SE1
NF	= Grand AM SE1
NG	= Grand AM
NG	= Grand AM
NG	= Grand AM SE2
NG	= Grand Am SE2
NV	= Grand AM LE
NV	= Grand AM GT1
NV	= Grand AM GT1
NW	= Grand AM SE
NW	= Grand AM SE
NW	= Grand AM GT
PE	= Fiero Coupe
PE	= Fiero Formula
PF	= Fiero SE Coupe
PG	= Fiero GT Coupe
PM	= Fiero Sport Coupe
TL	= 1000
TN	= Lemans SE
TN	= Lemans LE
TN	= Lemans SE
TN	= Lemans
TR	= Lemans SE
TS	= Lemans GSE
TX	= Lemans Coupe
TX	= Lemans Aerocoupe
WH	= Grand Prix LE
WH	= Grand Prix SE
WJ	= Grand Prix LE
WJ	= Grand Prix SE
WJ	= Grand Prix
WJ	= Grand Prix SE

Fig. 11 VIN Identification (Part 1 of 4). Pontiac

ARM040000000671

ARM040000000672

DIGIT 4-5	Carline/Series
WK	= Grand Prix SE1
WK	= Grand Prix SE1
WK	= Grand Prix LE
WP	= Grand Prix GT
WP	= Grand Prix Base
WP	= Grand Prix GT
WP	= Grand Prix SE
WR	= Grand Prix GTP
WR	= Grand Prix GTP
WS	= Grand Prix GT
WS	= Grand Prix GT2
WS	= Grand Prix GT2
WT	= Grand Prix STE
WT	= Grand Prix STE
ZG	= G6 Base
ZH	= G6 GT

DIGIT 5	Carline
B	= J2000
B	= Sunbird 2000
C	= Sunbird 2000 LE
C	= J2000 LE
D	= Lemans
D	= Sunbird 2000 SE
D	= J2000 SE
E	= J2000 S
E	= Fiero Coupe
F	= Grand Lemans
F	= 6000
F	= Fiero SE Coupe
G	= 6000 LE
H	= 6000 STE
J	= Grand Prix
K	= Grand Prix LE
K	= Grand Prix LJ
L	= Parisienne
L	= 1000
L	= Catalina
M	= 1000
M	= Fiero Sport Coupe
N	= Bonneville
P	= Grand Prix Brougham
R	= Bonneville Brougham
S	= Bonneville LE
S	= Firebird
T	= Phoenix SE
T	= Firebird Esprit
T	= Parisienne Brougham
T	= Phoenix SJ
V	= Formula
W	= Trans AM
X	= Firebird SE
X	= Trans AM Turbo Special
Y	= Phoenix
Z	= Phoenix LE
Z	= Phoenix LJ

DIGIT 6	Body Style
1	= 2D Coupe/Sedan
1	= 2D Coupe, Notchback Special
1	= 2D Coupe
1	= 2D Coupe
1	= 2D Coupe/Sedan
2	= 2D Hatchback/Liftback
2	= 2D Hatchback/Liftback
2	= 2D Hatchback
3	= 2D Convertible
3	= 2D Convertible
5	= 4D Sedan
5	= 4D Sedan
6	= 4D All Purpose w/Liftgate
6	= 4D All Purpose w/Liftgate

DIGIT 6	Body Style
6	= 4D Hatchback
8	= Station Wagon
8	= Station Wagon

DIGIT 6-7	Body Type
08	= 2D Hatchback
19	= 4D Notchback Sedan
27	= 2D Notchback Coupe
35	= 4D Wagon
37	= 2D Notchback Special Coupe
67	= 2D Convertible
68	= 4D Hatchback
69	= 4D Notchback Sedan
77	= 2D Hatchback
87	= 2D Coupe
97	= 2D Notchback Sport Coupe

DIGIT 7	Restraint System
1	= Manual Belts
1	= Manual Belts
1	= Active Belts
2	= Dual Front Airbags w/Manual Belts
2	= Dual Front Airbags w/Manual Belts
3	= Driverside Airbag w/Manual Belts
3	= Driverside Airbag w/Manual Belts
3	= Dual Front Airbags w/Manual Belts
3	= Dual Front Airbags w/Manual Belts
4	= Automatic Belts
4	= Dual Front & Side Airbags w/Manual Belts
4	= Dual Front & Front Side Airbags w/Manual Belts
4	= Dual Front & Side Airbags w/Manual Belts
4	= Dual Front & Front Side Airbags w/Manual Belts
4	= Automatic Belts
5	= Dual Front & Driver's Side Airbags w/Manual Belts
5	= Dual Front & Driver's Side Airbags w/Manual Belts
5	= Driverside Airbag w/Automatic Belts
5	= Driverside Airbag w/Automatic Belts
6	= Dual Front Airbags w/Automatic Belts
6	= Dual Front Airbags w/Automatic Belts
7	= Dual Front, Front & Rear Side Airbags & Manual Belts
7	= Dual Front, Front & Rear Side Airbags & Manual Belts

DIGIT 7*	Restraint
2	= Dual Front Airbags w/Manual Belts
2	= Dual Front Airbags w/Manual Belts
4	= Dual Front & Front Side Airbags w/Manual Belts
4	= Dual Front & Front Side Airbags w/Manual Belts

DIGIT 8	Engine
0	= 1.8L I-4 TBI
1	= 3.8L V6 SFI S/C
1	= 2.8L V6 2BBL
1	= 3.8L V6 SFI S/C
2	= 2.5L I-4 TBI
2	= 3.8L V6 SFI
2	= 3.8L V6 SFI
3	= 2.3L I-4 MPI
3	= 3.8L V6 SFI
3	= 2.3L I-4 MPI
4	= 2.2L I-4 MPI SOHC
4	= 3.8L V6 SFI S/C
4	= 3.8L V6 SFI S/C
4	= 4.1L V6 4BBL
4	= 2.2L I-4 MPI SOHC
5	= 2.5L I-4 2BBL
6	= 1.6L I-4 TBI
6	= 1.6L I-4 TBI
7	= 5.0L V8 CPI
8	= 1.8L I-4 MPI
8	= 2.5L I-4 EFI
8	= 5.7L V8 MPI
8	= 3.5L V6 SFI
8	= 1.8L I-4 MPI

ARM0400000000673

Fig. 11 VIN Identification (Part 2 of 4). Pontiac

DIGIT 8	Engine
8	= 5.7L V8 MPI
9	= 2.8L V6 MPI
A	= 2.3L I-4 MPI Quad HO
A	= 2.3L I-4 MPI Quad HO
A	= 3.8L V6 2BBL
C	= 3.8L V6 MPI
C	= 3.8L V6 MPI
C	= 1.6L I-4 2BBL
D	= 2.3L I-4 MPI Quad 4
D	= 2.3L I-4 EFI Quad 4
D	= 2.3L I-4 MPI Quad 4
D	= 2.3L I-4 EFI Quad 4
D	= 2.3L I-4 MPI DOHC
D	= 2.3L I-4 MPI DOHC
E	= 5.0L V8 TBI
E	= 5.0L V8 TBI
E	= 3.4L V6 SFI
E	= 3.4L V6 SFI
F	= 2.2L I-4 MPI DOHC
F	= 2.2L I-4 MPI DOHC
F	= 5.0L V8 MPI
F	= 2.5L I-4 2BBL
F	= 5.0L V8 MPI
G	= 5.7L V8 MPI
G	= 5.7L V8 MPI
G	= 5.7L SFI V8
G	= 5.0L V8 4BBL
G	= 2.5L I-4 EFI
G	= 1.8L I-4 2BBL
H	= 2.0L I-4 MPI
H	= 5.0L V8 4BBL
H	= 2.0L I-4 MPI
J	= 1.8L I-4 FI Turbo
J	= 3.1L V6 SFI
J	= 3.1L V6 SFI
J	= 1.8L I-4 Turbo
K	= 3.8L V6 2BBL
K	= 3.8L V6 MPI
K	= 2.0L I-4 TBI
K	= 3.8L V6 EFI
K	= 3.8L V6 MPI
K	= 3.8L V6 EFI
K	= 3.8L V6 SFI
K	= 2.0L I-4 TBI
K	= 3.8L V6 SFI
L	= 1.8L I-4 SFI DOHC
L	= 1.8L I-4 SFI DOHC
L	= 3.8L V6 MPI
L	= 3.8L V6 MPI
L	= 2.8L V6 2BBL
L	= 3.0L V6 EFI
M	= 3.1L V6 SFI
M	= 2.0L I-4 Turbo
M	= 2.0L I-4 FI Turbo
M	= 3.1L V6 SFI
M	= 2.0L I-4 MPI
N	= 5.7L V8 Dsl
N	= 3.3L V6 MPI
N	= 3.3L V6 MPI
P	= 5.7L V8 EFI
P	= 5.7L V8 MPI
P	= 2.0L I-4 TBI
P	= 5.7L V8 MPI
P	= 2.8L V6 MPI
P	= 5.7L V8 EFI
P	= 2.0L I-4 EFI
R	= 2.5L I-4 TBI
R	= 2.5L I-4 TBI
S	= 2.8L V6 MPI
S	= 3.4L V6 SFI HO
S	= 4.3L V8 2BBL
S	= 3.4L V6 SFI HO

DIGIT 8	Engine
T	= 3.1L V6 MPI
T	= 4.9L V8 4BBL
T	= 2.4L I-4 EFI DOHC
T	= 2.4L I-4 MPI DOHC
T	= 4.3L V6 Dsl
T	= 2.4L I-4 EFI DOHC
T	= 2.4L I-4 MPI DOHC
T	= 3.1L V6 MPI
U	= 2.5L I-4 TBI
U	= 2.5L I-4 TBI
V	= 3.0L V6 TBI
V	= 3.1L V6 EFI
W	= 4.9L V8 4BBL
W	= 2.8L V6 MPI
X	= 3.4L V6 EFI DOHC
X	= 2.8L V6 2BBL
X	= 3.4L V6 EFI DOHC
Y	= 5.0L V8 4BBL
Y	= 4.6L V8 MPI
Y	= 4.6L V8 MPI
Z	= 2.8L V6 2BBL
Z	= 4.3L V6 EFI

DIGIT 10	Model Year
1	= 2001
1	= 2001
2	= 2002
2	= 2002
3	= 2003
3	= 2003
4	= 2004
4	= 2004
5	= 2005
5	= 2005
B	= 1981
C	= 1982
D	= 1983
E	= 1984
F	= 1985
G	= 1986
H	= 1987
J	= 1988
K	= 1989
L	= 1990
M	= 1991
M	= 1991
N	= 1992
N	= 1992
P	= 1993
P	= 1993
R	= 1994
R	= 1994
S	= 1995
S	= 1995
T	= 1996
T	= 1996
V	= 1997
V	= 1997
W	= 1998
W	= 1998
X	= 1999
X	= 1999
Y	= 2000
Y	= 2000

DIGIT 11	Assembly Plant Location
1	= Wentzville, MO, USA
1	= Oshawa # 2, ON, Canada
1	= Oshawa # 2, ON, Canada
1	= Oshawa, ON, Canada
1	= Oshawa #2, ON, Canada
1	= Wentzville, MO, USA

ARM0400000000674

Fig. 11 VIN Identification (Part 3 of 4). Pontiac

Fig. 11 — VIN Identification (Part 4 of 4). Pontiac

DIGIT 11   Assembly Plant Location

Code	Location
2	Ste. Therese, PQ, Canada
2	Ste. Therese, PQ, Canada
4	Orion, MI, USA
4	Orion, MI, USA
6	Oklahoma City, OK, USA
6	Oklahoma City, OK, USA
7	Lordstown, OH, USA
7	Lordstown, OH, USA
9	Oshawa # 1, ON, Canada
9	Oshawa #1, ON, Canada
9	Oshawa # 1, ON, Canada
A	Lakewood, GA, USA
B	Pupyong, Korea
B	Lansing, MI, USA
B	Baltimore, MD, USA
B	Lansing, MI, USA
B	Pupyong, Korea
C	Lansing, MI, USA
C	Lansing, MI, USA
F	Fairfax II, KS, USA
F	Fairfax II, KS, USA
G	Framingham, MA, USA
H	Flint, MI, USA
H	Flint, MI, USA
J	Janesville, WI, USA
K	Leeds, MO, USA
L	Van Nuys, CA, USA
L	Van Nuys, CA, USA
M	Lansing, MI, USA
M	Lansing, MI, USA
N	Norwood, Oh, USA
P	Pontiac, MI, USA
S	Ramos Arizpe, Mexico
S	Ramos Arizpe, Mexico
T	Tarrytown, NY, USA
U	Hamtramck, MI, USA
U	Hamtramck, MI, USA
W	Willow Run, MI, USA
X	Fairfax, KS, USA
X	Fairfax I, KS, USA
Y	Wilmington, DE, USA

Fig. 11   VIN Identification (Part 4 of 4). Pontiac

ARM040000000675

Fig. 12 — VIN Identification (Part 1 of 2). Saturn

DIGIT 1   Country Of Origin

Code	
1	USA
1	USA

DIGIT 2   Manufacturer

Code	
G	General Motors
G	General Motors

DIGIT 3   Make

Code	
8	Saturn
8	Saturn

DIGIT 4-5   Carline/Series

Code	
AF	Level 1 Sedan 5sp
AF	Level 1 Sedan 5sp
AG	Level 1 Sedan at
AG	Level 1 Sedan at
AJ	Level 2 Sedan 5sp
AJ	Level 2 Sedan at
AK	Level 3 Sedan 5sp
AK	Level 3 Sedan 5sp
AL	Level 3 Sedan at
AL	Level 3 Sedan at
AM	Level 2 Quad Coupe 5sp
AM	Level 2 Quad Coupe 5sp
AN	Level 2 Quad Coupe at
AN	Level 2 Quad Coupe at
AV	Level 3 Quad Coupe 5sp
AV	Level 3 Quad Coupe 5sp
AW	Level 3 Quad Coupe at
AW	Level 3 Quad Coupe at
AZ	Level 2 Sedan 5sp
AZ	Level 2 Sedan 5sp
JC	L300 Base
JC	L300 Base
JD	L300 Mid-level
JD	L300 Mid-level
JL	L300 Up-level
JL	L300 Up-level
JR	LS 5sp
JR	L100 5sp
JR	LS 5sp
JS	LS at
JS	L100 at
JS	LS at
JT	L200 5sp
JT	LS1 5sp
JT	L200 5sp
JT	LS1 5sp
JU	LW200 5sp
JU	L200 5sp
JU	LW200 at
JU	L200 at
JU	LW300 at
JU	L300 at
JU	LW300 at
JU	L200 at
JW	LS1 at
JW	LW1 at
JW	L200 at
JW	LS2 at
JW	LW2 at
JW	L300 at
JW	LW300 at
JW	LW2 at
ZE	SC1 5sp
ZE	SC1 at
ZF	SL 5sp
ZF	SC1 at

DIGIT 4-5   Carline/Series (continued)

Code	
ZF	SL 5sp
ZG	SC 5sp
ZG	SL1 5sp
ZG	SC2 5sp
ZG	SW1 5sp
ZG	SW1 5sp
ZG	SC 5sp
ZG	SL1 5sp
ZH	SC2 5sp
ZH	SW1 at
ZH	SC2 at
ZH	SL1 at
ZH	SC at
ZH	SW1 at
ZH	SC at
ZJ	SL2 5sp
ZJ	SW2 5sp
ZJ	SW2 5sp
ZJ	SL2 5sp
ZK	SL2 at
ZK	SW2 at
ZK	SW2 at
ZK	SL2 at
ZN	SC1 5sp
ZN	SW2 at
ZN	SW2 at
ZP	SC1 at
ZP	SC1 at
ZR	SC2 5sp
ZR	SC2 5sp
ZS	SL 5sp Spring Special
ZS	SL 5sp Spring Special
ZY	SC2 at
ZY	SC2 at

DIGIT 6   Body Style

Code	
1	2D Coupe
1	4D Quad Coupe
1	2D Coupe
5	4D Sedan
5	4D Sedan
8	4D Wagon
8	4D Wagon

DIGIT 7   Restraint System

Code	
2	Dual Front Airbags w/Manual Belts
2	Dual Front Airbags w/Manual Belts
4	Automatic Belts
4	Dual Front & Side Airbags w/Manual Belts
4	Dual Front & Side Airbags w/Manual Belts
4	Automatic Belts
5	Driverside Airbag w/Automatic Belts
5	Driverside Airbag w/Automatic Belts

DIGIT 8   Engine

Code	
7	1.9L L4 MPI DOHC
7	1.9L L4 MPI DOHC
8	1.9L L4 TBI
8	1.9L L4 TBI
9	1.9L L4 TBI
9	1.9L L4 TBI
F	2.2L L4 SFI DOHC
F	2.2L L4 SFI DOHC
R	3.0L V6 SFI DOHC
R	3.0L V6 SFI DOHC

DIGIT 10   Model Year

Code	
1	2001
1	2001

Fig. 12   VIN Identification (Part 1 of 2). Saturn

ARM040000000676

DIGIT 10   Model Year

2	= 2002
2	= 2002
3	= 2003
3	= 2003
4	= 2004
4	= 2004
5	= 2005
M	= 1991
N	= 1992
N	= 1992
P	= 1993
P	= 1993
R	= 1994
R	= 1994
S	= 1995
S	= 1995
T	= 1996
T	= 1996
V	= 1997
V	= 1997
W	= 1998
W	= 1998
X	= 1999
X	= 1999
Y	= 2000
Y	= 2000

DIGIT 11   Assembly Plant Location

Y	= Wilmington, DE, USA
Y	= Wilmington, DE, USA
Z	= Spring Hill, TN, USA
Z	= Spring Hill, TN, USA

ARM0400000000677

Fig. 12   VIN Identification (Part 2 of 2). Saturn

DAIMLERCHRYSLER

Disarming

It may be required to access and record Diagnostic Trouble Codes (DTCs) prior to disarming the air bag system.

1. Place ignition switch in Lock position.
2. **On Avenger, Breeze, Cirrus, Crossfire, Magnum, Neon, Sebring, Stratus and 2005 300 models,** disconnect and isolate battery ground cable.
3. **On Concorde, Intrepid, LHS and 300M models,** disconnect and isolate battery ground cable remote terminal at remote battery post, **Fig. 1.**
4. **On all models except Sebring and Stratus Coupe,** wait at least two minutes after disconnection before doing any further work on vehicle. The air bag system is designed to retain enough voltage to deploy air bags for short time even after battery has been disconnected.
5. **On Sebring and Stratus Coupe,** wait at least sixty seconds after disconnection before doing any further work on vehicle. The air bag system is designed to retain enough voltage to deploy air bags for short time even after battery has been disconnected.

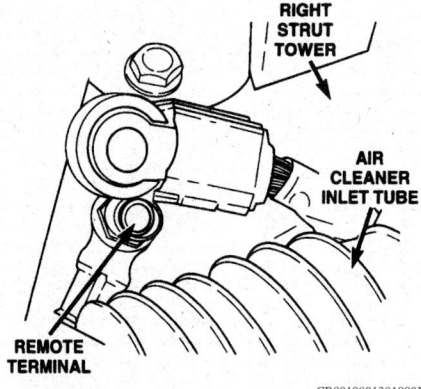

CR8019801381000X

Fig. 1 Battery ground remote terminal. Concorde, Intrepid, LHS & 300M

Arming

1. **Ensure no one is inside vehicle and ignition switch is in Lock position.**
2. Connect battery ground or negative remote cable or terminal.
3. **From safe location at sides or below air bag modules,** turn ignition switch to On position.
4. SRS lamp should light for 7–10 seconds and remain off for at least 45 seconds to indicate SRS is functioning properly.

FORD MOTOR CO.

Disarming

CONTINENTAL

1. Disconnect and isolate battery ground cable.
2. **On models equipped with auxiliary batteries and power supplies,** disconnect and isolate these items.
3. **On all models,** wait one minute for back-up power supply to deplete.
4. Remove two steering wheel spoke bolt covers, if equipped.
5. Remove two air bag module to steering wheel mounting bolts.
6. Lift air bag module away from steering wheel, then disconnect air bag module and horn to clockspring electrical connectors. **When carrying live air bag module, ensure bag and trim cover are pointed away from your body. Place module on bench with trim cover facing upward.**
7. Remove driver's air bag module.
8. Attach Rotunda air bag simulator tool No. 105-R0012, or equivalent, to vehicle harness connector at top of steering column.

9. Open glove compartment, push tabs in and turn door downward past stops.
10. Disconnect passenger air bag module electrical connector.
11. Attach Rotunda air bag simulator tool No. 105-R0012, or equivalent, to passenger air bag module electrical connector on vehicle wiring harness side.
12. Disconnect side impact air bag module electrical connector located beneath driver's seat.
13. Attach Rotunda air bag simulator tool No. 105-R0012, or equivalent, to side impact air bag connector under driver's seat on vehicle wiring harness side
14. Disconnect side impact air bag module electrical connector located beneath passenger seat.
15. Attach Rotunda air bag simulator tool No. 105-R0012, or equivalent, to side impact air bag connector under passenger seat on vehicle wiring harness side
16. If side impact air bag diagnosis or service is to be performed, remove front seats as follows:
    a. Move front seat all way rearward, then remove covers and seat track front bolts.
    b. Move front seat all way forward, then remove covers and seat track rear bolts.
    c. Disconnect front seat electrical connectors and remove front seats.
17. Connect battery ground cable.

COUGAR

Prior to disconnecting battery, record preset radio frequencies.
1. Disconnect and isolate battery ground cable, then the positive cable.
2. **On models equipped with auxiliary batteries and power supplies,** disconnect and isolate these items.
3. **On all models,** allow at least one minute for back-up power supply to deplete.
4. Remove two driver's air bag module Torx mounting screws at rear of steering wheel.
5. Lift driver's air bag module upward and disconnect air bag module electrical connector.
6. Remove air bag module. **When carrying live air bag module, ensure bag and trim cover are pointed away from your body. Place module on bench with trim cover facing upward.**
7. Connect Rotunda air bag simulator tool No. 105-R0012, or equivalent, to vehicle harness at top of steering column.
8. Remove three glove compartment Torx mounting screws.
9. Open glove compartment and depress side stops to detach sides.
10. Remove four Torx screws and glove compartment finish panel.
11. Remove passenger air register duct.
12. Disconnect passenger air bag module electrical connector.
13. Remove two passenger air bag module to crossbeam mounting bolts.
14. Lower front edge of passenger air bag

module, roll air bag module around crossbeam. Lower air bag module to passenger foot well and remove it. **When carrying live air bag module, ensure bag and trim cover are pointed away from your body. Place module on bench with trim cover facing upward.**
15. Connect second Rotunda air bag simulator tool No. 105-R0012, or equivalent, to wiring harness in place of passenger air bag.
16. **On models equipped with side impact air bags,** proceed as follows:
    a. From driver's and passenger seats, remove seat back rest, cover and pad.
    b. Depress retaining tang at each side and disconnect side impact air bag module electrical connector at driver's and passenger seats.
    c. Remove side impact air bag module mounting nuts from driver's and passenger seats.
17. **On all models,** connect battery ground cable.

CROWN VICTORIA & GRAND MARQUIS

2001-04

1. Disconnect battery ground cable.
2. Wait at least one minute for back-up power supply in restraints control module (RCM) to deplete its' stored energy.
3. Remove two steering wheel back cover plugs and two air bag module bolts.
4. Release two air bag retaining tabs. Label driver's air bag squib number on air bag module connector before disconnecting.
5. Remove wire harness from holder.
6. Disconnect horn switch electrical connector.
7. Remove air bag module.
8. Attach restraint system diagnostic tools 418-F395, or equivalent, to clockspring side of driver's air bag module electrical connectors.
9. Disconnect rear window defroster switch, clock and air bag deactivation lamp electrical connectors, then remove trim panel.
10. Open glove compartment and disconnect glove compartment isolator.
11. While pushing in on two glove compartment door tabs, lower glove compartment door.
12. Remove air bag module bolts through glove compartment opening,
13. Place one hand in glove compartment opening and push air bag module out from instrument panel. **Do not handle passenger air bag module by grabbing edges of deployment doors.**
14. Attach restraint system diagnostic tools 418-F395, or equivalent, to vehicle harness side of passenger air bag module electrical connectors.
15. Remove front seats.
16. Access passenger safety belt retractor and pretensioner located behind passenger side B-pillar.
17. Disconnect passenger safety belt retractor and pretensioner electrical connector.

18. Attach restraint system diagnostic tool 418-F088, or equivalent, to passenger safety belt retractor and pretensioner electrical connector.
19. Access driver's safety belt retractor and pretensioner located behind driver's side B-pillar.
20. Disconnect driver's safety belt retractor and pretensioner electrical connector.
21. Attach restraint system diagnostic tool 418-F088, or equivalent, to driver's safety belt retractor and pretensioner electrical connector.
22. Connect battery ground cable.

2005

1. Turn all vehicle accessories OFF.
2. Turn ignition switch to OFF position.
3. Remove restraints control module (RCM) fuse F2.22 (10A) from central junction box (CJB).
4. Turn ignition ON and visually monitor air bag indicator for 30 seconds. The air bag indicator will remain lit continuously if correct RCM is removed.
5. Turn ignition switch to OFF position.
6. Disconnect battery ground cable and wait at least 60 seconds for power to deplete.
7. Remove driver's side air bag module from steering wheel.
8. Disconnect driver's side air bag module electrical connectors from module.
9. Attach restraint system diagnostic tool to clockspring electrical connectors the top of steering column.
10. Separate trim panel pulling out to release retaining clips.
11. Slide trim panel to the righthand side aligning the keyway and pullout trim panel from instrument panel.
12. Disconnect rear window defrost switch, clock connector, passenger side air bag deactivation (PAD) indicator then remove trim panel.
13. Open glove compartment and disconnect glove compartment isolator.
14. Pushing in glove compartment tabs, lower door.
15. Separate passenger side air bag module electrical connector and pin-type retainer from bracket, disconnect passenger side air bag electrical connector.
16. Remove passenger side air bag module bolts, then the passenger side air bag module.
17. Separate locking insert from passenger side air bag module jumper harness electrical connector.
18. Disconnect passenger side air bag module electrical connector tabs.
19. Attach two restraint system diagnostic tools to two passenger side air bag module jumper harness electrical connectors and align and install locking inserts to electrical connectors.
20. Connect passenger side air bag module jumper harness to passenger side air bag module electrical connector on vehicle wiring harness.
21. **On models less side impact air bag modules,** if side air bag bridge resistor is removed, an open circuit fault will be

generated by the restraints control module.

22. **On models less side impact air bag modules,** if a restraint system diagnostic tool is installed at the side air bag floor electrical connector, a low resistance fault will be generated by RCM.

23. **On models equipped with side impact air bag modules,** proceed as follows:
    a. Disconnect passenger seat side air bag module electrical connector.
    b. Attach restraint system diagnostic tool to seat harness side of passenger seat side air bag module electrical connector.
    c. Disconnect driver's seat side air bag module electrical connector.
    d. Attach restraint system diagnostic tool to seat harness side of driver's seat side air bag module electrical connector.

24. **On all models,** install RCM fuse F2.22 (10A) to CJB.

25. Connect battery ground cable as required.

ESCORT & ZX2

1. Disconnect and isolate battery ground cable. Allow at least one minute for back-up power supply to deplete.

2. **On models equipped with auxiliary batteries and power supplies,** disconnect and isolate these items also.

3. **On all models,** remove two air bag module mounting bolts, then disconnect air bag and horn electrical connectors.

4. Remove driver's air bag module from steering wheel. **When carrying live air bag module, ensure bag and trim cover are pointed away from your body. Place module on bench with trim cover facing upward.**

5. Connect air bag simulator tool No. 105–00012, or equivalent, to air bag wiring harness at top steering column.

6. Open glove compartment, push in on two door tabs and roll door downward.

7. Remove four passenger air bag module mounting bolts.

8. Pull passenger air bag module from instrument panel and disconnect electrical connector. **When carrying live air bag module, ensure bag and trim cover are pointed away from your body. Place module on bench with trim cover facing upward.**

9. Connect Rotunda air bag simulator tool No. 105-R00010, or equivalent, to wiring harness in place of passenger air bag module.

10. Connect battery ground cable.

FOCUS

2001-04

1. Disconnect and isolate battery ground cable.

2. **On models equipped with auxiliary batteries and power supplies,** disconnect and isolate these items also.

3. **On all models,** wait one minute for

back-up power supply to deplete.

4. Remove two air bag module mounting bolts, then disconnect air bag and horn electrical connectors.

5. Remove driver's air bag module from steering wheel. **When carrying live air bag module, ensure bag and trim cover are pointed away from your body. Place module on bench with trim cover facing upward.**

6. Connect air bag simulator tool No. 418-037, or equivalent, to air bag wiring harness at top steering column.

7. Remove mounting screws and glove compartment.

8. Disconnect passenger air bag module electrical connector.

9. Connect Rotunda air bag simulator tool 418-138, or equivalent, to wiring harness in place of passenger air bag module.

10. From beneath driver's seat, disconnect side impact air bag module electrical connector. Connect Rotunda air bag simulator tool 418-139, or equivalent, to connector on wiring harness side of side impact air bag harness.

11. From beneath passenger seat, disconnect side impact air bag module electrical connector. Connect Rotunda air bag simulator tool 418-139, or equivalent, to connector on wiring harness side of side impact air bag harness.

12. Disconnect driver's seat belt pretensioner electrical connector. Connect Rotunda air bag simulator tool 418-139, or equivalent, to connector on wiring harness side of seat belt pretensioner harness.

13. Disconnect passenger seat belt pretensioner electrical connector. Connect Rotunda air bag simulator tool 418-139, or equivalent, to connector on wiring harness side of seat belt pretensioner harness.

14. Connect battery ground cable.

2005

1. Turn all vehicle accessories to OFF position.

2. Turn ignition switch to OFF position.

3. Remove restraints control module (RCM) fuse F2.60 (7.5A) from central junction box (CJB).

4. Turn ignition ON and visually monitor air bag indicator for 30 seconds. Air bag indicator will remain lit continuously if correct RCM fuse removed.

5. Turn ignition switch to OFF position.

6. Disconnect battery ground cable and wait at least 60 seconds for power to deplete.

7. Remove driver's side air bag module bolts and retaining clips then the air bag module.

8. Disconnect driver's side air bag module electrical connector.

9. Connect restraint system diagnostic tool to driver's air bag module electrical connector on clockspring.

10. Open glove compartment.

11. Remove ventilation pipe and detach defroster pipe from heater housing and defrost vent.

12. Remove passenger air bag module trim cover retaining bolts, detach passenger air bag module trim cover from instrument panel.

13. Remove passenger side air bag module trim cover.

14. Remove passenger air bag module and reinforcement bracket from instrument panel.

15. Remove passenger side air bag module, disconnecting electrical connectors.

16. Connect restraint system diagnostic tools to vehicle harness side of passenger side air bag module electrical connectors.

17. **On models equipped with side impact air bag modules,** disconnect passenger seat electrical connector from under seat.

18. **On models equipped with side impact air bag modules,** connect restraint system diagnostic tool to vehicle harness side of passenger seat side air bag module electrical connector.

19. **On models equipped with side impact air bag modules,** disconnect driver's seat electrical connector from under seat.

20. **On models equipped with side impact air bag modules,** connect restraint system diagnostic tool to vehicle harness side of driver's seat side air bag module electrical connector.

21. **On all models,** install RCM fuse F2.60 (7.5A) to CJB.

22. Connect battery ground cable.

LS

2001-04

1. Disconnect and isolate battery ground cable.

2. **On models equipped with auxiliary batteries and power supplies,** disconnect and isolate these items.

3. **On all models,** wait one minute for back-up power supply to deplete.

4. Remove two rear cover plugs from steering wheel in order to access air bag module screws.

5. Remove driver's air bag module mounting bolts and disconnect electrical connector.

6. Remove air bag module. **When carrying live air bag module, ensure bag and trim cover are pointed away from your body. Place module on bench with trim cover facing upward.**

7. Connect Rotunda air bag simulator tool No. 418-F395, or equivalent, to air bag wiring harness at top steering column.

8. Remove glove compartment.

9. Reaching over cross-car beam, slide passenger air bag connector lock downward. Squeeze connector lock tabs and pull connector from air bag.

10. Connect Rotunda air bag simulator tool No. 418-F395, or equivalent, to vehicle side of passenger air bag wiring

harness connector.

11. From beneath driver's seat, disconnect side impact air bag module electrical connector. Connect Rotunda air bag simulator tool 418–133, or equivalent, to connector on wiring harness side of side impact air bag harness.

12. From beneath passenger seat, disconnect side impact air bag module electrical connector. Connect Rotunda air bag simulator tool 418–133, or equivalent, to connector on wiring harness side of side impact air bag harness.

13. Remove driver's side B-pillar pillar trim.

14. Access and disconnect driver's side seat belt pretensioner electrical connector. Connect Rotunda seat belt pretensioner simulator tool 105-R0012, or equivalent, to seat belt pretensioner electrical connector.

15. Remove passenger side B-pillar pillar trim.

16. Access and disconnect passenger side seat belt pretensioner electrical connector. Connect Rotunda seat belt pretensioner simulator tool 105-R0012, or equivalent, to seat belt pretensioner electrical connector.

17. Connect battery ground cable.

2005

1. Turn all vehicle accessories to OFF position.

2. Turn ignition switch to OFF position.

3. Remove restraints control module (RCM) fuse F2.05 (10A) from central junction box (CJB).

4. Turn ignition switch to ON position and visually monitor air bag indicator for 30 seconds. Air bag indicator will remain lit continuously if correct RCM fuse has been removed.

5. Turn ignition switch to OFF position.

6. Disconnect battery ground cable and wait 60 seconds for power to deplete.

7. Remove two steering wheel plugs, then the driver's side air bag module bolts.

8. Disconnect and remove driver's side air bag module.

9. Attach restraint system diagnostic tools to clockspring electrical connectors at top of steering column.

10. **On models equipped with roof panel air bag modules,** remove A-pillar trim panel.

11. **On models equipped with roof panel air bag modules,** disconnect driver's side roof panel air bag module electrical connectors.

12. **On models equipped with roof panel air bag modules,** attach restraint system diagnostic tool to vehicle harness side of driver's side roof panel air bag module electrical connector.

13. **On all models,** remove glove compartment.

14. Locate passenger side air bag module electrical connector, then disconnect passenger air bag module electrical connector.

15. Attach restraint system diagnostic tool to vehicle harness side of passenger

side air bag module electrical connector.

16. **On models equipped with side impact air bag modules,** remove A-pillar trim panel.

17. **On models equipped with roof panel air bag modules,** disconnect passenger side roof panel air bag module electrical connector.

18. **On models equipped with roof panel air bag modules,** attach restraint system diagnostic tool to vehicle harness side of passenger side roof panel air bag module electrical connector.

19. **On all models,** release tab and disconnect passenger seat side impact air bag or passenger seat side impact thorax air bag electrical connector.

20. **On models less roof panel air bag modules,** attach restraint system diagnostic tool to vehicle harness side of passenger seat side impact air bag electrical connector.

21. **On models equipped with roof panel air bag modules,** attach restraint system diagnostic tool to vehicle harness side of passenger seat side thorax air bag electrical connector.

22. **On all models,** from under driver's seat, release tab and disconnect driver's seat side impact air bag or driver's seat side thorax air bag electrical connectors.

23. **On models less roof panel air bag modules,** attach restraint system diagnostic tool to vehicle harness side of driver's seat side impact air bag electrical connector.

24. **On models equipped with roof panel air bag modules,** attach restraint system diagnostic tool to vehicle harness side of driver's seat side thorax air bag electrical connector.

25. **On all models,** install RCM fuse F2.05 to CJB.

26. Connect battery ground cable.

MUSTANG

1. Turn all vehicle accessories to OFF position.

2. Turn ignition switch to OFF position.

3. Remove restraints control module (RCM) fuse F2.17 (10A) from smart junction box (SJB).

4. Turn ignition ON and visually monitor air bag indicator for 30 seconds. Air bag indicator will remain lit continuously if correct RCM fuse is removed.

5. Turn ignition switch to OFF position.

6. Disconnect battery ground cable.

7. Allow at least one minute for back-up power supply to deplete.

8. **On models equipped with auxiliary batteries and power supplies,** disconnect and isolate these items also.

9. **On all models,** remove two rear cover plugs from steering wheel in order to access air bag module screws.

10. Remove driver's air bag module mounting screws and washers, then disconnect electrical connector.

11. Remove air bag module. **Place module on bench with trim cover facing upward.**

12. Connect Rotunda air bag simulator tool, or equivalent, to air bag wiring at top of steering column.

13. Open glove compartment, press sides inward to release it from instrument panel and lower glove compartment to floor.

14. Remove righthand air conditioning duct and passenger air bag mounting bolts from instrument panel steel reinforcement.

15. Disconnect electrical connector at lower lefthand corner of passenger air bag module and remove connector from instrument panel reinforcement.

16. Gently pull upon each corner of air bag cover to disconnect from instrument panel and push air bag module out from behind instrument panel. **Place module on bench with trim cover facing upward.**

17. Install second air bag simulator Rotunda air bag simulator tool, or equivalent, on passenger air bag harness.

18. **On models equipped with side impact air bag module,** release red locking tab and disconnect passenger side impact air bag module electrical connector.

19. **On models equipped with side impact air bag module,** attach restraint system diagnostic tool to vehicle harness side of passenger side impact air bag module electrical connector.

20. **On models equipped with side impact air bag module,** release red locking tab and disconnect driver's side impact air bag module electrical connector.

21. **On models equipped with side impact air bag module,** attach restraint system diagnostic tool to vehicle harness side of driver's side impact air bag module electrical connector.

22. **On all models,** install RCM fuse 2.17 (10A) to SJB.

23. Connect battery ground cable.

SABLE & TAURUS

2001-04

1. Move front seat to full rear and highest position.

2. Disconnect and isolate battery ground cable.

3. **On models equipped with auxiliary batteries and power supplies,** disconnect and isolate these items also.

4. **On all models,** wait one minute for back-up power supply to deplete.

5. Remove mounting screws and pull out release clips, then remove lower steering column cover with reinforcement.

6. Disconnect driver's air bag sliding contact electrical connect at base of steering column.

7. Connect driver's air bag restraint system diagnostic tool 418-F403, or equivalent, to vehicle side of driver's air bag sliding contact four-pin electrical connector.

8. Open glove compartment, push in on tabs and release glove compartment.

9. Through glove compartment opening,

remove two passenger air bag module mounting bolts.

10. Pull lefthand corner of passenger air bag trim cover away from instrument panel.

11. From left to right, slide across seam between instrument panel and trim cover to release trim cover retaining clips.

12. Pull passenger air bag module and trim cover away from instrument panel.

13. Disconnect passenger air bag module electrical connector and remove harness retainer from air bag module.

14. Remove passenger air bag module. **When carrying live air bag module, ensure bag and trim cover are pointed away from your body. Place module on bench with trim cover facing upward.**

15. Connect passenger air bag restraint system diagnostic tool 418-F403, or equivalent, to vehicle side of passenger air bag electrical connector.

16. **On models equipped with side impact air bags,** disconnect passenger seat air bag electrical connector and attach side impact air bag restraint system diagnostic tool 418-133, or equivalent, to side impact air bag floor electrical connector on passenger side.

17. **On all models,** disconnect passenger seat belt pretensioner electrical connector.

18. Attach passenger seat belt pretensioner restraint system diagnostic tool 418-F407, or equivalent, to floor electrical connector.

19. **On models equipped with side impact air bags,** disconnect driver's seat air bag electrical connector and attach side impact air bag restraint system diagnostic tool 418-133, or equivalent, to side impact air bag floor electrical connector on driver's side.

20. **On all models,** disconnect driver's seat belt pretensioner electrical connector.

21. Attach driver's seat belt pretensioner restraint system diagnostic tool 418-F405, or equivalent, to floor electrical connector.

22. Connect battery ground cable.

2005

1. Turn all vehicle accessories to OFF position.

2. Turn ignition switch to OFF position.

3. Remove restraints control module (RCM) fuse F2.20 (10A) from smart junction box (SJB).

4. Turn ignition ON and visually monitor air bag indicator for 30 seconds. Air bag indicator will remain lit continuously if correct RCM fuse has been removed.

5. Turn ignition switch to OFF position.

6. Disconnect battery ground cable and wait 60 seconds for power to deplete.

7. Remove driver's side air bag module cover plugs, then the bolts and air bag module.

8. Release two retaining tabs and disconnect driver's side air bag module electrical connector. **Label squib number**

on module electrical connector before disconnecting for installation.

9. Attach restraint system diagnostic tools to clockspring electrical connectors at top of steering column.

10. Open and release glove compartment to lowest position.

11. Remove passenger side air bag module retaining bolts.

12. Separate passenger side air bag module and trim cover from instrument panel.

13. Remove passenger side air bag module and trim cover, disconnecting electrical connectors as required.

14. Attach restraint system diagnostic tool to vehicle harness side of passenger side air bag module electrical connector.

15. **On models equipped with side impact air bag modules,** proceed as follows:
   a. Disconnect passenger seat side impact air bag module electrical connector.
   b. Attach restraint system diagnostic tool to vehicle harness side of passenger seat side impact air bag module electrical connector.
   c. Disconnect driver's seat side impact air bag module electrical connector.
   d. Attach restraint system diagnostic tool to vehicle harness side of driver's seat side impact air bag module electrical connector.

16. **On all models,** install RCM fuse F2.20 (10A) to SJB.

17. Connect battery ground cable.

THUNDERBIRD

2002-04

1. Disconnect battery ground cable and wait at least one minute for back-up power supply to deplete.

2. Remove two pin-type retainers from lower steering column opening finish panel, pull out on finish panel far enough to access and disconnect electrical connectors.

3. Remove lower steering column finish panel.

4. Remove two pin-type retainers from driver's side lower insulator panel.

5. Remove light socket from insulator panel and panel from instrument panel.

6. Remove mounting screws and disconnect hood latch from steering column reinforcement.

7. Remove mounting screw and heater duct.

8. Position carpet aside and loosen two driver's side instrument panel tunnel brace bolts.

9. Remove mounting screws and lower steering column reinforcement from instrument panel.

10. Disconnect clockspring electrical connector located at base of steering column.

11. Attach restraint system diagnostic tool No. 418-F088, or equivalent, to clockspring electrical connector.

12. Remove glove compartment and door.

13. Locate passenger air bag module electrical connector by reaching through glove compartment opening towards center of instrument panel and above cross-car beam. **Passenger air bag module connector is not visible because of its mounting position in instrument panel.**

14. Disconnect passenger air bag module electrical connector.

15. Attach restraint system diagnostic tool No. 418-F395, or equivalent, to vehicle harness side of passenger air bag electrical connector.

16. Connect battery ground cable and move front seats to highest and most forward positions.

17. Disconnect battery ground cable and wait at least one minute for back-up power supply to deplete.

18. Disconnect passenger seat side impact air bag electrical connector located under passenger seat.

19. Attach restraint system diagnostic tool No. 418-F133, or equivalent, to passenger seat side impact air bag electrical connector.

20. Remove passenger side door scuff plate and weather stripping.

21. Remove safety belt from passenger seat guide.

22. Remove speaker grille from passenger side rear trim panel.

23. Remove snap screws and passenger side rear trim panel.

24. Disconnect passenger safety belt retractor pretensioner electrical connector.

25. Attach restraint system diagnostic tool No. 418-F395, or equivalent, to passenger safety belt retractor pretensioner electrical connector.

26. Disconnect driver's seat side impact air bag electrical connector located under driver's seat.

27. Attach restraint system diagnostic tool No. 418-F133, or equivalent, to driver's seat side impact air bag electrical connector.

28. Remove driver's side door scuff plate and weather stripping.

29. Remove safety belt from driver's seat guide.

30. Remove speaker grille from driver's side rear trim panel.

31. Remove snap screws and driver's side rear trim panel.

32. Disconnect driver's safety belt retractor pretensioner electrical connector.

33. Attach restraint system diagnostic tool No. 418-F395, or equivalent, to driver's safety belt retractor pretensioner electrical connector.

34. Connect battery ground cable.

2005

1. Disconnect battery ground cable and isolate as required. **Wait at least 60 seconds for power supply to deplete.**

2. Remove two steering wheel back cover plugs & two driver's side air bag module bolts.

3. Remove driver's side air bag module,

disconnecting electrical connectors as required.

4. Attach a restraint system diagnostic tool to clockspring electrical connector at top of steering wheel.

5. Remove glove compartment and door as required.

6. Disconnect passenger side air bag module electrical connector locking clip. **This is a blind operation due to electrical connector mounting location.**

7. Attach a restraint system diagnostic tool to vehicle harness side of passenger side air bag module electrical connector.

8. Connect battery ground cable.

9. Place front seats to highest and most forward position.

10. Disconnect battery ground cable and isolate as required. **Wait at least 60 seconds for power supply to deplete.**

11. Disconnect passenger seat side impact air bag module electrical connector from under seat.

12. Attach a restraint system diagnostic tool to side impact air bag module electrical connector.

13. Remove passenger side door scuff plate and weatherstripping.

14. Remove safety belt from passenger seat guide.

15. Separate passenger side rear trim panel.

16. Disconnect passenger side safety belt retractor pretensioner electrical connector.

17. Attach a restraint system diagnostic tool to passenger side safety belt retractor pretensioner electrical connector.

18. Disconnect driver's seat side impact air bag module electrical connector from under seat.

19. Attach a restraint system diagnostic tool to side impact air bag module electrical connector.

20. Remove driver's side door scuff plate and weatherstripping.

21. Remove safety belt from driver's seat guide.

22. Remove driver's side rear trim panel.

23. Disconnect driver's side safety belt retractor pretensioner electrical connector.

24. Attach a restraint system diagnostic tool to driver's side safety belt retractor pretensioner electrical connector.

25. Connect battery ground cable.

26. With restraint system diagnostic tools connected at all devices, prove out system as required.

27. Disconnect battery ground cable and isolate as required. **Wait at least 60 seconds for power supply to deplete.**

TOWN CAR

2001-04

1. Disconnect and isolate battery ground cable.

2. **On models equipped with auxiliary batteries and power supplies,** disconnect and isolate these items, too.

3. **On all models,** wait one minute for back-up power supply to deplete.

4. Remove steering column opening lower finish panel by removing parking brake release then pulling out at top of panel to release retaining clips.

5. Remove mounting bolts and steering column lower reinforcement.

6. Remove lefthand lower instrument panel insulator.

7. Pushing in on release tab, disconnect clockspring electrical connector at base of steering column.

8. Attach restraint system diagnostic tool No. 418-F403, or equivalent to vehicle harness side of clockspring electrical connector.

9. Remove audio unit.

10. Remove instrument panel cluster finish panel from instrument panel.

11. Open glove compartment and disconnect glove compartment isolator.

12. While pushing in on two glove compartment door tabs, position glove compartment downward.

13. Through glove compartment opening, remove passenger air bag module wire harness pin type fasteners from instrument panel.

14. Through glove box opening, remove passenger air bag module bolts.

15. Placing one hand in glove compartment opening, push passenger air bag module out from instrument panel. **Do not handle air bag module by grabbing edges of deployment doors.**

16. Disconnect passenger air bag module electrical connector and remove air bag module.

17. Attach restraint system diagnostic tool No. 418-F403, or equivalent, to vehicle harness side of passenger side impact air bag module electrical connector.

18. Connect battery ground cable.

19. Move and tilt front seats to highest and most forward position.

20. Disconnect battery ground cable and wait at least one minute for back-up power supply to deplete.

21. **On models equipped less side impact air bags,** proceed as follows:

a. **Do not deactivate side impact air bags module circuit by removing side impact air bag bridge resistor from side impact air bag floor electrical connector.**

b. If side impact air bag bridge resistor is removed, an open circuit fault will be generated by restraints control module (RCM)

c. If restraint system diagnostic tool is installed at side impact air bag floor electrical connector, low resistance fault will be generated by RCM.

22. **On models equipped with side impact air bags,** proceed as follows:

a. From under front passenger seat, release tab and disconnect passenger seat side impact air bag electrical connector.

b. Attach restraint system diagnostic tool No. 418-FO88, or equivalent, to vehicle harness side of passenger seat side impact air bag electrical connector.

23. **On all models,** remove passenger side B-pillar lower trim panel.

24. Push in on release tab and disconnect passenger safety belt retractor pretensioner electrical connector.

25. Attach restraint system diagnostic tool No. 418-FO88, or equivalent, to vehicle harness side of passenger safety belt retractor pretensioner electrical connector

26. **On models equipped with side impact air bags,** proceed as follows:

a. From under driver's seat, release tab and disconnect driver's seat side impact air bag electrical connector.

b. Attach restraint system diagnostic tool No. 418-FO88, or equivalent, to vehicle harness side of driver's seat side air bag electrical connector.

27. **On all models,** remove driver's side B-pillar lower trim panel.

28. Push in on release tab and disconnect driver's safety belt retractor pretensioner electrical connector.

29. Attach restraint system diagnostic tool to vehicle harness side of driver's side safety belt retractor pretensioner electrical connector.

30. Connect battery ground cable.

31. With restraint system diagnostic tools installed on all deployable devices, prove out supplemental restraint system.

32. Turn ignition switch from Off to Run position and visually monitor air bag indicator with air bag modules and pretensioners or restraint system diagnostic tools installed.

33. Air bag lamp will illuminate for approximately six seconds and turn off.

34. If air bag supplemental restraint system fault is present, air bag indicator will either fail to illuminate, remain illuminate continuously or flash.

35. Disconnect battery ground cable and wait for at least one minute for back-up power supply to deplete.

2005

1. Turn all vehicle accessories to OFF position.

2. Turn ignition switch to OFF position.

3. Remove restraints control module (RCM) fuse F2.2 (10A) from central junction box (CJB).

4. Turn ignition ON and visually monitor air bag indicator for 30 seconds. Air bag indicator will remain lit continuously if correct fuse has been removed.

5. Turn ignition switch to OFF position.

6. Disconnect battery ground cable and isolate as required. **Wait at least 60 seconds for power supply to deplete.**

7. Remove driver's side air bag module using a suitable flatbladed screwdriver's placed through one of four holes to disengage spring clips and locking pins.

8. Disconnect and remove driver's side air bag module, disconnecting electrical connectors as required.

9. Attach a restraint system diagnostic tool to clockspring electrical connectors at top of steering wheel.

10. Open glove compartment, disconnect glove compartment isolator.

11. Position glove compartment door

downward while pushing inward on door tabs.

12. Disconnect passenger side air bag module electrical connector.

13. Remove passenger side air bag module bolts, pushing air bag module out from instrument panel.

14. Disconnect electrical connectors from passenger side air bag module jumper harness.

15. Depress two locking tabs on side of passenger side air bag module jumper harness electrical connector and disconnect.

16. Attach two restraint system diagnostic tools to two passenger side air bag module jumper harness electrical connectors, install locking inserts to connectors.

17. Connect passenger side air bag module jumper harness to passenger side air bag module electrical connector at vehicle wiring harness.

18. Connect battery ground cable.

19. Place front seats to their highest and most forward position.

20. Disconnect battery ground cable and isolate as required. **Wait at least 60 seconds for power supply to deplete.**

21. Disconnect passenger seat side impact air bag module electrical connector.

22. Attach a restraint system diagnostic tool to seat harness side of passenger seat side impact air bag module electrical connector.

23. Disconnect driver's seat side impact air bag module electrical connector.

24. Attach a restraint system diagnostic tool to seat harness side of driver's seat side impact air bag module electrical connector.

25. Install RCM fuse F2.2 (10A) to CJB.

26. Connect battery ground cable.

FIVE-HUNDRED, FREESTYLE & MONTEGO

1. Turn all vehicle accessories to OFF position.

2. Turn ignition switch to OFF position.

3. Remove restraints control module (RCM) fuse F2.21 (7.5A) from smart junction box (SJB).

4. Turn ignition switch ON and visually monitor air bag indicator for 30 seconds. Air bag indicator will remain continuous if correct fuse has been removed.

5. Turn ignition switch to OFF position.

6. Disconnect battery ground cable and isolate as required. **Wait at least 60 seconds for power supply to deplete.**

7. Remove steering wheel access cover to release driver's side air bag module wire clips.

8. Release horn and using suitable tool, lift end of wire clip over post.

9. Release other side of module wire clip.

10. Release horn and with a suitable tool, lift end of wire clip over post causing both ends of wire clip to overlap.

11. Actuate horn at upper section of air bag cover, then push on both ends of wire

clip inward to release driver's air bag module from steering wheel.

12. Release two retaining tabs on driver's side air bag module electrical connector and disconnect connectors.

13. Disconnect horn and electrical accessories connectors.

14. Remove driver's side air bag module.

15. Attach a restraint system diagnostic tools to clockspring electrical connectors at top of steering column.

16. Open glove compartment and release dampening strut form lefthand side and lower door fully.

17. Disconnect two passenger side air bag module electrical connectors through glove compartment.

18. Attach a restraint system diagnostic tool to passenger side air bag module electrical connector.

19. **On models equipped with side impact air bag modules,** proceed as follows:

   a. Slide and disengage passenger seat side impact air bag module electrical connector locking clip and release tab, then the electrical connector.

   b. Attach a restraint system diagnostic tool to vehicle harness side of passenger seat side imacpt air bag module electrical connector.

   c. Slide and disengage driver's seat side impact air bag module electrical connector locking clip and release tab, then the electrical connector.

   d. Attach a restraint system diagnostic tool to vehicle harness side of driver's seat side imacpt air bag module electrical connector.

20. **On models less roof panel air bag modules,** if safety canopy bridge resistor is removed, an open circuit fault will be generated by RCM.

21. **On models equipped with roof panel air bag modules,** proceed as follows:

   a. Release and position aside driver's and passenger side D-pillar trim panel.

   b. Disconnect driver's and passenger side roof panel air bag module electrical connector.

   c. Attach a restraint system diagnostic tool to vehicle harness side of roof panel air bag module electrical connector.

   d. Remove C-pillar trim panels, then disconnect driver's and passenger side roof panel air bag module electrical connector.

   e. Attach restraint system diagnostic tool to vehicle harness side of driver's and passenger side roof panel air bag module electrical connector.

22. **On all vehicles,** install RCM fuse F2.21 (7.5A) to SJB.

23. Connect battery ground cable.

Arming

CONTINENTAL

1. Disconnect and isolate battery ground cable.

2. **On models equipped with auxiliary batteries and power supplies,** disconnect and isolate these items.

3. **On all models,** wait one minute for back-up power supply to deplete.

4. Remove air bag simulator harness connector at top of steering column.

5. **When carrying live air bag module, ensure bag and trim cover are pointed away from your body. Place module on bench with trim cover facing upward.**

6. Connect driver's air bag module and horn to clockspring electrical connectors.

7. Position driver's air bag module to steering wheel.

8. Install two driver's air bag module to steering wheel mounting bolts.

9. **Torque** mounting bolts to 108 inch lbs.

10. Install two steering wheel spoke bolt covers, if equipped.

11. Remove air bag simulator at passenger air bag connector.

12. Connect passenger air bag electrical connector and close glove compartment.

13. Remove air bag simulator from side impact air bag connector located beneath driver's seat and connect side impact air bag electrical connector.

14. Remove air bag simulator from side impact air bag connector located beneath passenger seat and connect side impact air bag electrical connector.

15. If front seats were removed, install as follows:

   a. Disconnect side air simulator tools from side impact air bag module floor connectors at driver's and passenger sides.

   b. Position front seat in vehicle.

   c. Move front seat all way forward, then install seat track rear bolts and covers.

   d. Move front seat all way rearward, then install seat track front bolts and covers.

   e. Disconnect side air simulator tools from side impact air bag module floor connectors at driver's and passenger sides.

   f. Connect driver's and passenger front seat electrical connectors.

16. Connect battery ground cable.

17. **From safe location at sides or below air bag modules,** place ignition switch in Run position and observe air bag warning lamp operating. Indicator lamp should light for approximately six seconds and turn off.

COUGAR

1. Disconnect and isolate battery ground cable.

2. Allow at least one minute for back-up power supply to deplete.

3. Remove air bag simulator tool from driver's air bag sliding contact connector.
4. Connect driver's air bag module electrical connector.
5. Position driver's air bag module to steering wheel.
6. Install driver's air bag module Torx mounting screws.
7. **Torque** mounting screws to 44 inch lbs.
8. Remove air bag simulator tool from passenger air bag wiring harness.
9. From passenger foot well, roll passenger air bag module around crossbeam.
10. Position air bag module and install two air bag module to crossbeam mounting bolts.
11. **Torque** mounting bolts/nuts to 12 ft. lbs.
12. Connect passenger air bag module electrical connector.
13. Install passenger air register duct.
14. Install glove compartment finish panel and secure with four Torx mounting screws.
15. Depress side stops to attach glove compartment sides and close glove compartment.
16. Install three glove compartment Torx mounting screws.
17. **On models equipped with side impact air bags,** proceed as follows:
    a. Install side impact air bag module.
    b. **Torque** side impact air bag module mounting bolts/nuts to 12 ft. lbs.
    c. Connect side impact air bag module electrical connector at driver's and passenger seats.
    d. Install seat pads, covers and back rests.
18. **On all models,** connect battery ground cable.
19. **From safe location at sides or below air bag modules,** place ignition switch in Run position and observe air bag warning lamp operating. Indicator lamp should light for approximately three seconds and turn off.

CROWN VICTORIA & GRAND MARQUIS

2001-04

1. Disconnect battery ground cable.
2. Wait at least one minute for back-up power supply to deplete.
3. Remove restraint system diagnostic tool from driver's safety belt retractor and pretensioner electrical connector.
4. Connect driver's safety belt retractor and pretensioner electrical connectors.
5. Remove restraint system diagnostic tool from passenger safety belt retractor and pretensioner electrical connectors.
6. Connect passenger safety belt retractor and pretensioner electrical connectors.
7. Install front seats.
8. Remove restraint system diagnostic tools from passenger air bag module electrical connectors.

9. Install passenger air bag module electrical connector.
10. Remove restraint system diagnostic tools from driver's air bag module electrical connectors.
11. Install driver's air bag module electrical connector.
12. Connect battery ground cable.
13. Turn ignition switch from OFF to RUN position and visually monitor air bag indicator with air bag modules and safety belt pretensioners or restraint system diagnostic tools installed.
14. Air bag indicator will light continuously for approximately six seconds and then turn off.
15. If air bag supplemental restraint system (SRS) fault is present, air bag indicator will either fail to light, remain lit continuously, or flash.
16. Flashing might not occur until approximately 30 seconds after ignition switch has been turned from OFF to RUN position. This is time required for restraints control module (RCM) to complete testing of SRS.
17. If air bag indicator is inoperative and SRS fault exists, chime will sound in pattern of five sets of five beeps. If this occurs, air bag indicator will need to be repaired before diagnosis can continue.

2005

1. Remove RCM fuse F2.22 (10A) from CJB.
2. Disconnect battery ground cable and isolate as required. **Wait at least 60 seconds for power supply to deplete.**
3. **On models equipped with side impact air bag modules,** proceed as follows:
    a. Remove restraint system diagnostic tool from driver's seat side impact air bag module electrical connector.
    b. Connect driver's seat side impact air bag module electrical connector at lower rear of seat cushion pan.
    c. Remove restraint diagnostic tool from passenger seat side impact air bag module electrical connector.
    d. Connect passenger seat side impact air bag module electrical connector at lower rear of seat cushion pan.
4. **On all models,** disconnect passenger side air bag module electrical connector on vehicle wiring harness.
5. Separate locking inserts and disconnect two restraint diagnostic tools from passenger side air bag module jumper harness electrical connectors.
6. Align and connect passenger side air bag module jumper harness electrical connectors to passenger side air bag module and install locking inserts.
7. Ensure that J-nuts on passenger side air bag module are fully attached into slots as required.
8. Install passenger side air bag module into instrument panel, then the bolts.
9. Connect passenger side air bag mod-

ule electrical connector and attach retainer to bracket.
10. Install trim panel and connect glove compartment isolator.
11. Remove restraint system diagnostic tools from clockspring electrical connectors from steering column.
12. **There are two steering wheels for these models, if installing a new steering wheel, ensure that correct wheel is being installed.**
13. Identify and install correct driver's side air bag module, connect horn electrical connector and air bag module electrical connectors.
14. Align driver's side air bag module locking pins to openings in steering wheel and position driver's side air bag module on steering wheel.
15. With locking pins aligned, push inward seating four locking pins to spring clips.
16. **Ensure that all restraint system diagnostic tools from vehicle and all SRS components are connected.**
17. Turn ignition switch to ON position.
18. Install RCM fuse F2.22 (10A) to CJB and replace cover.
19. Connect battery ground cable.
20. Prove out system as follows:
    a. Turn ignition key to OFF position.
    b. Wait 10 seconds, then turn key to ON position and visually monitor air bag indicator.
    c. Air bag indicator will be lit continuously for 6 seconds then turn Off.
    d. If air bag system fault is present, air bag indicator will fail to light, remain lit continuously or flash.
    e. Flashing will occur up to 30 seconds after ignition switch has been turned from the OFF to ON position.
    f. If fault occurs, a chime will sound.

ESCORT & ZX2

1. Disconnect battery ground cable. Allow one minute for back-up power supply to deplete.
2. **On models equipped with auxiliary batteries and power supplies,** disconnect and isolate these items also.
3. **On all models,** remove air bag simulator from harness on top of steering column.
4. Connect driver's air bag connector.
5. Position driver's air bag on steering wheel and secure with two bolts.
6. **Torque** mounting bolts to 70–86 inch lbs.
7. Remove air bag simulator from passenger air bag harness connector.
8. Connect air bag module electrical connector and position module in instrument panel.
9. Install four air bag module bolts.
10. **Torque** air bag module mounting bolts to 72–103 inch lbs.
11. Push glove compartment door back into instrument panel.
12. Connect battery ground cable.
13. **From safe location at sides or below air bag modules,** place ignition switch in Run position and observe air bag

AIR BAG SYSTEM PRECAUTIONS

warning lamp operating. Indicator lamp should light for approximately six seconds and turn off. If air bag indicator is inoperative and SRS fault exists, chime will sound in pattern of five sets of beeps. If this occurs, air bag indicator will need to be repaired before diagnosis can continue

14. Reset radio stations and clock.

FOCUS

2001-04

1. Disconnect and isolate battery ground cable.
2. **On models equipped with auxiliary batteries and power supplies,** disconnect and isolate these items, too.
3. **On all models,** wait one minute for back-up power supply to deplete.
4. Remove air bag simulator from harness on top of steering column.
5. Connect driver's air bag connector.
6. Position driver's air bag on steering wheel and secure with two bolts. **When carrying live air bag module, ensure bag and trim cover are pointed away from your body. Place module on bench with trim cover facing upward.**
7. **Torque** mounting screws to 44 inch lbs.
8. Remove air bag simulator from passenger air bag harness connector.
9. Connect passenger air bag module electrical connector.
10. Remove air bag simulator from driver's side seat belt pretensioner connector.
11. Connect driver's side seat belt pretensioner electrical connector.
12. Remove air bag simulator from driver's side impact air bag connector.
13. Connect driver's side impact air bag electrical connector.
14. Remove air bag simulator from passenger side seat belt pretensioner connector.
15. Connect passenger side seat belt pretensioner electrical connector.
16. Remove air bag simulator from passenger side impact air bag connector.
17. Connect passenger side impact air bag electrical connector.
18. Install glove compartment.
19. Connect battery ground cable.
20. **From safe location at sides or below air bag modules,** place ignition switch in Run position and observe air bag warning lamp operating. Indicator lamp should light for approximately six seconds and turn off.
21. Reset radio stations and clock.

2005

1. Remove RCM fuse F2.60 (7.5A) from CJB.
2. Disconnect battery ground cable and isolate as required. **Wait at least 60 seconds for power supply to deplete.**
3. **On models equipped with side impact air bag modules,** remove restraint system diagnostic tool from vehicle harness side of driver's seat side impact air bag modules electrical connectors, then install driver's seat

electrical connector.
4. **On models equipped with side impact air bag modules,** remove restraint system diagnostic tool from vehicle harness side of passenger seat side impact air bag modules electrical connectors, then install passenger seat electrical connector.
5. **On all models,** loosen passenger side air bag module floating bracket nuts, remove restraint system diagnostic tools, then install passenger side air bag module and connect electrical connectors.
6. Attach passenger side air bag module and reinforcement bracket to instrument panel.
7. Install passenger side air bag module trim cover.
8. Install passenger side air bag module trim cover bolts, do not tighten bolts at this time.
9. **Torque** passenger side air bag module floating bracket bolts to 104 inch lbs.
10. **Torque** passenger side air bag module trim cover bolts to 104 inch lbs.
11. Install defroster pipe to heater housing and defroster vent.
12. Install ventilation pipe and retaining clip.
13. Close glove compartment door.
14. Remove restraint system diagnostic tool from driver's side air bag module electrical connector at clockspring.
15. Install driver's side air bag module electrical connector, then the air bag module to steering wheel connecting clips and bolts.
16. Ensure all restraint system diagnostic tools from SRS system and all SRS components are connected.
17. Turn ignition switch from OFF to ON position.
18. Instal RCM fuse F2.60 (7.5A) to CJB.
19. Connect battery ground cable.
20. Prove out system as follows:
    a. Turn ignition key to OFF position.
    b. Wait 10 seconds, then turn key to ON position and visually monitor air bag indicator.
    c. Air bag indicator will be lit continuously for 6 seconds then turn Off.
    d. If air bag system fault is present, air bag indicator will fail to light, remain lit continuously or flash.
    e. Flashing will occur up to 30 seconds after ignition switch has been turned from the OFF to ON position.
    f. If fault occurs, a chime will sound.

LS

2001-04

1. Disconnect and isolate battery ground cable.
2. **On models equipped with auxiliary batteries and power supplies,** disconnect and isolate these items also.
3. **On all models,** wait one minute for back-up power supply to deplete.
4. Remove seat belt pretensioner simulator tool from passenger seat belt pretensioner harness connector.
5. Connect passenger seat belt pretensioner electrical connector.

6. Install passenger side B-pillar pillar trim.
7. Remove seat belt pretensioner simulator tool from driver's seat belt pretensioner harness connector.
8. Connect driver's seat belt pretensioner electrical connector.
9. Install driver's side B-pillar pillar trim.
10. Remove air bag simulator tool from harness connector at top of steering column.
11. Connect driver's air bag electrical connector.
12. Position driver's air bag on steering wheel and secure with its bolts. **When carrying live air bag module, ensure bag and trim cover are pointed away from your body. Place module on bench with trim cover facing upward.**
13. **Torque** mounting bolts to 108 inch lbs.
14. Remove air bag simulator from passenger air bag harness connector.
15. Connect passenger air bag module electrical connector.
16. Install glove compartment.
17. Remove air bag simulator from passenger side impact air bag connector.
18. Connect passenger side impact air bag electrical connector.
19. Remove air bag simulator from driver's side impact air bag connector.
20. Connect driver's side impact air bag electrical connector.
21. Connect battery ground cable.
22. **From safe location at sides or below air bag modules,** place ignition switch in Run position and observe air bag warning lamp operating. Indicator lamp should light for approximately six seconds and turn off.
23. Reset radio stations and clock.

2005

1. Remove RCM fuse F2.05 (10A) from CJB.
2. Disconnect battery ground cable and isolate as required. **Wait at least 60 seconds for power supply to deplete.**
3. **On models less side impact air bag modules,** remove restraint system diagnostic tool from vehicle harness side of driver's seat side impact air bag electrical connectors.
4. **On models equipped with side impact air bag modules,** remove restraint system diagnostic tool from vehicle harness side of driver's seat side thorax impact air bag module electrical connector.
5. **On all models,** connect driver's seat side impact air bag module or driver's seat side thorax impact air bag module electrical connector.
6. **On models less roof panel air bag modules,** remove restraint system diagnostic tool from vehicle side harness side of passenger seat side impact air bag module electrical connector.
7. **On models equipped with side impact air bag modules,** remove restraint system diagnostic tool from vehicle harness side of passenger

seat side thorax air bag electrical connector.

8. **On all models,** connect passenger seat side thorax or passenger seat side impact air bag module electrical connectors.
9. **On models equipped with roof panel air bag modules,** remove restraint system diagnostic tool from vehicle harness side of passenger side roof panel air bag module electrical connector.
10. **On models equipped with roof panel air bag modules,** connect passenger side roof panel air bag module electrical connector, then install A-pillar trim panel.
11. **On all models,** remove restraint system diagnostic tool from vehicle harness side of passenger side air bag module electrical connector, then connect passenger side air bag module electrical connectors.
12. Install glove compartment.
13. **On models equipped with roof panel air bag modules,** remove restraint system diagnostic tool from vehicle harness side of driver's side roof panel air bag module electrical connector, then connect module electrical connectors and install A-pillar trim panel.
14. **On all models,** remove restraint system diagnostic tool from clockspring electrical connectors at steering column.
15. Install driver's side air bag module electrical connectors, then the module to steering wheel.
16. Install driver's side air bag module bolts and plugs and **torque** to 108 inch lbs.
17. Turn ignition switch from OFF to ON position.
18. Install RCM fuse F2.05 (10A) to CJB and replace cover.
19. Prove out system as follows:
    a. Turn ignition key to OFF position.
    b. Wait 10 seconds, then turn key to ON position and visually monitor air bag indicator.
    c. Air bag indicator will be lit continuously for 6 seconds then turn Off.
    d. If air bag system fault is present, air bag indicator will fail to light, remain lit continuously or flash.
    e. Flashing will occur up to 30 seconds after ignition switch has been turned from the OFF to ON position.
    f. If fault occurs, a chime will sound.

MUSTANG

1. Disconnect battery ground cable.
2. **On models equipped with auxiliary batteries and power supplies,** disconnect and isolate these items also.
3. **On all models,** allow at least one minute for back-up power supply to deplete.
4. **On models equipped with side impact air bag modules,** proceed as follows:
    a. Remove restraint system diagnostic tool from vehicle harness side of driver's side impact air bag module electrical connector.

b. Connect driver's side air bag module electrical connector and reset red locking tab.
c. Remove restraint system diagnostic tool from vehicle harness side of passenger side air bag module electrical connector.
d. Connect passenger side air bag module electrical connector and reset red locking tab.

5. **On all models,** remove air bag simulator tool from harness connector at top of steering column.
6. Connect driver's air bag connector.
7. Position driver's air bag on steering wheel and secure with four nut and bolt assemblies.
8. **Torque** driver's air bag module mounting bolts/nuts to 80 inch lbs.
9. Remove air bag simulator tool from passenger air bag module harness then position module in instrument panel.
10. Attach connector to instrument panel reinforcement and wiring harness.
11. Install passenger air bag mounting bolt.
12. **Torque** passenger air bag module mounting bolts to 80 inch lbs.
13. Press gently on air bag module corners to engage with instrument panel trim and install righthand side air conditioning duct.
14. Press sides of glove compartment together and lift into position in instrument panel. Close glove compartment door.
15. Turn ignition switch from OFF to ON position.
16. Install RCM fuse F2.17 (10A) to SJB and replace cover.
17. Connect battery ground cable.
18. Prove out system as follows:
    a. Turn ignition key to OFF position.
    b. Wait 10 seconds, then turn key to ON position and visually monitor air bag indicator.
    c. Air bag indicator will be lit continuously for 6 seconds then turn Off.
    d. If air bag system fault is present, air bag indicator will fail to light, remain lit continuously or flash.
    e. Flashing will occur up to 30 seconds after ignition switch has been turned from the OFF to ON position.
    f. If fault occurs, a chime will sound.

SABLE & TAURUS

2001–04

1. Disconnect and isolate battery ground cable.
2. **On models equipped with auxiliary batteries and power supplies,** disconnect and isolate these items also.
3. **On all models,** wait one minute for back-up power supply to deplete.
4. Disconnect driver's air bag restraint system diagnostic tool from vehicle side of driver's air bag sliding contact electrical connector.
5. Connect driver's air bag sliding contact electrical connector.
6. Install steering column lower cover and reinforcement.
7. Disconnect passenger air bag restraint

system diagnostic tool from vehicle side of passenger air bag electrical connector.
8. Inspect position of passenger air bag module J-nuts.
9. Position air bag module and trim cover to instrument panel. **When carrying live air bag module, ensure bag and trim cover are pointed away from your body. Place module on bench with trim cover facing upward.**
10. Install wiring harness pin retaining to air bag module.
11. Connect passenger air bag module electrical connector.
12. Align air bag module channels with instrument panel rails.
13. Starting at lefthand side of air bag module trim cover, install upper and lower alignment pins into instrument panel.
14. Working from left to right, install trim cover alignment pins and retainers into instrument panel. When all channels and rails are aligned, gap around perimeter of air bag module trim cover will be even.
15. Through glove compartment opening, install passengers air bag module mounting bolts.
16. **Torque** mounting bolts to 71 inch lbs.
17. Close glove compartment.
18. Disconnect passenger seat belt pretensioner restraint system diagnostic tool from 10 pin floor electrical connector.
19. Connect passenger seat belt pretensioner electrical connector.
20. **On models equipped with side impact air bags,** disconnect side impact air bag restraint system diagnostic tool from side impact air bag floor electrical connector on passenger side. Connect side impact air bag electrical connector on passenger side.
21. **On all models,** disconnect driver's seat belt pretensioner restraint system diagnostic tool from 10 pin floor electrical connector.
22. Connect driver's seat belt pretensioner electrical connector.
23. **On models equipped with side impact air bags,** disconnect side impact air bag restraint system diagnostic tool from side impact air bag floor electrical connector on driver's side.
24. **On models equipped with side impact air bags,** connect side impact air bag electrical connector on driver's side.
25. **On all models,** connect battery ground cable.
26. **From safe location at sides or below air bag modules,** place ignition switch in Run position and observe air bag warning lamp operating. Indicator lamp should light for approximately six seconds and turn off.

2005

1. Remove RCM fuse F2.20 (10A) from SJB.
2. Disconnect battery ground cable and

isolate as required. **Wait at least 60 seconds for power supply to deplete.**

3. **On models equipped with side impact air bag modules,** remove restraint system diagnostic tool from vehicle harness side of driver's seat side impact air bag module electrical connector.

4. **On models equipped with side impact air bag modules,** connect driver's seat side impact air bag module electrical connector.

5. **On models equipped with side impact air bag modules,** remove restraint system diagnostic tool from vehicle harness side of passenger seat side impact air bag module electrical connector.

6. **On models equipped with side impact air bag modules,** connect passenger seat side impact air bag module electrical connector.

7. **On all models,** remove restraint system diagnostic tool from vehicle harness side of passenger seat side air bag module electrical connector.

8. Install passenger side air bag module electrical connector, position air bag module in alignment channels and install module and trim cover to instrument panel.

9. Install trim cover tabs and alignment pins into instrument panel moving from lefthand to righthand side.

10. Install passenger side air bag module bolts, **torque** to 80 inch lbs.

11. Close glove compartment.

12. Remove restraint system diagnostic tools from clockspring electrical connectors at steering column.

13. Connect driver's side air bag module electrical connectors and place module to steering wheel.

14. Install two driver's side air bag module bolts, **torque** to 80 inch lbs.

15. Install two driver's side air bag module back cover nuts.

16. Turn ignition switch from OFF to ON position.

17. Install RCM fuse F2.20 (10A) to SJB and install cover.

18. Connect battery ground cable.

19. Prove out system as follows:
   a. Turn ignition key to OFF position.
   b. Wait 10 seconds, then turn key to ON position and visually monitor air bag indicator.
   c. Air bag indicator will be lit continuously for 6 seconds then turn Off.
   d. If air bag system fault is present, air bag indicator will fail to light, remain lit continuously or flash.
   e. Flashing will occur up to 30 seconds after ignition switch has been turned from the OFF to ON position.
   f. If fault occurs, a chime will sound.

THUNDERBIRD

2001-04

1. Disconnect battery ground cable and

wait at least one minute for back-up power supply to deplete.

2. Remove diagnostic tool No. 418-F395, or equivalent, from driver's side safety belt retractor pretensioner electrical connector.

3. Connect driver's side safety belt retractor pretensioner electrical connector.

4. Install driver's side rear trim panel and speaker grille.

5. Position safety belt back into driver's seat guide, then install driver's side door weather stripping and scuff plate.

6. Remove diagnostic tool No. 418-F133, or equivalent, from driver's seat side impact air bag module electrical connector located under driver's seat.

7. Connect driver's seat side impact air bag module electrical connector.

8. Remove diagnostic tool No. 418-F395, or equivalent, from passenger side safety belt retractor pretensioner electrical connector.

9. Connect passenger side safety belt retractor pretensioner electrical connector.

10. Install passenger side rear trim panel and speaker grille.

11. Position safety belt back into passenger seat guide, then install passenger side door weatherstripping and scuff plate.

12. Remove diagnostic tool No. 418-F133, or equivalent, from passenger seat side impact air bag module electrical connector located under passenger seat.

13. Connect passenger seat side impact air bag module electrical connector.

14. Connect battery ground cable and move seats as far rearward as possible.

15. Disconnect battery ground cable and wait at least one minute for back-up power supply to deplete.

16. Reach through glove compartment opening and remove diagnostic tool No. 418-F395, or equivalent, from passenger air bag module electrical connector located behind center of instrument panel, above cross-car brace.

17. Connect passenger air bag module electrical connector, then install glove compartment and door.

18. Remove diagnostic tool No. 418-F088, or equivalent, from clockspring electrical connector located at base of steering column.

19. Connect clockspring electrical connector and install steering column reinforcement.

20. Tighten two driver's side instrument panel tunnel brace bolts and position carpet back in place.

21. Install heater duct and hood latch.

22. Install driver's side insulator panel and light socket.

23. Connect electrical connectors and install lower steering column opening finish panel.

24. Connect battery ground cable.

25. **From safe location at sides or below air bag modules,** place ignition switch in RUN position and observe air bag warning lamp operating. Indicator lamp should light for approximately six seconds and turn off.

2005

1. Disconnect battery ground cable and isolate as required. **Wait at least 60 seconds for power supply to deplete.**

2. Remove restraint system diagnostic tool from driver's side safety belt retractor pretensioner electrical connector.

3. Install driver's side safety belt retractor pretensioner electrical connector.

4. Install driver's side rear trim panel and speaker grille.

5. Place safety belt into driver's seat guide.

6. Install driver's side door weatherstripping and scuff plate.

7. Remove restraint system diagnostic tool from under driver's seat side impact air bag module floor electrical connector.

8. Connect driver's seat side impact air bag module electrical connector.

9. Remove restraint system diagnostic tool from passenger side safety belt retractor pretensioner electrical connector.

10. Install passenger side safety belt retractor pretensioner electrical connector.

11. Install passenger side rear trim panel and speaker grille.

12. Place safety belt into passenger seat guide.

13. Install passenger side door weatherstripping and scuff plate.

14. Remove restraint system diagnostic tool from under passenger seat side impact air bag module floor electrical connector.

15. Connect passenger seat side impact air bag module electrical connector.

16. Connect battery ground cable.

17. Place front seats in rearward position.

18. Disconnect battery ground cable and isolate as required. **Wait at least 60 seconds for power supply to deplete.**

19. Remove restraint system diagnostic tool from vehicle harness side of passenger side air bag module electrical connector.

20. Connect passenger side air bag module electrical connector.

21. Install glove compartment and door.

22. Remove restraint system diagnostic tool from top of steering column.

23. Install driver's side air bag module to steering wheel, connecting electrical connectors as required.

24. Install two module bolts, **torque** to 108 inch lbs.

25. Install two back cover plugs.

26. Connect battery ground cable.
27. Prove out system as follows:
    a. Turn ignition key to OFF position.
    b. Wait 10 seconds, then turn key to ON position and visually monitor air bag indicator.
    c. Air bag indicator will be lit continuously for 6 seconds then turn Off.
    d. If air bag system fault is present, air bag indicator will fail to light, remain lit continuously or flash.
    e. Flashing will occur up to 30 seconds after ignition switch has been turned from the OFF to ON position.
    f. If fault occurs, a chime will sound.

TOWN CAR

2001–04

1. Disconnect and isolate battery ground cable.
2. **On models equipped with auxiliary batteries and power supplies,** disconnect and isolate these items also.
3. **On all models,** wait one minute for back-up power supply to deplete.
4. Remove air bag simulator from harness connector at top of steering column.
5. Connect driver's air bag module and horn to clockspring electrical connectors. **When carrying live air bag module, ensure bag and trim cover are pointed away from your body. Place module on bench with trim cover facing upward.**
6. Position driver's air bag module to steering wheel.
7. Install two driver's air bag module to steering wheel mounting bolts, **torque** to 108 inch lbs.
8. Install two steering wheel spoke bolt covers, if equipped.
9. Remove air bag simulator at passenger air bag connector.
10. Connect passenger air bag electrical connector and close glove compartment.
11. Remove air bag simulator from side impact air bag connector located beneath driver's seat and connect side impact air bag electrical connector.
12. Remove air bag simulator from side impact air bag connector located beneath passenger seat and connect side impact air bag electrical connector.
13. If front seats were removed, install as follows:
    a. Position front seat in vehicle.
    b. Move front seat all way forward, then install seat track rear bolts and covers.
    c. Move front seat all way rearward, then install seat track front bolts and covers.
    d. Disconnect side air simulator tools from side impact air bag module floor connectors at driver's and passenger sides.
    e. Connect driver's and passenger

front seat electrical connectors.
14. Connect battery ground cable.
15. **From safe location at sides or below air bag modules,** place ignition switch in Run position and observe air bag warning lamp operating. Indicator lamp should light for approximately six seconds and turn off.

2005

1. Remove RCM fuse F2.2 (10A) from CJB.
2. Disconnect battery ground cable and isolate as required. **Wait at least 60 seconds for power supply to deplete.**
3. Remove restraint system diagnostic tool from driver's seat side impact air bag electrical connector.
4. Connect driver's seat side impact air bag module electrical connector from under rear of seat cushion pan.
5. Remove restraint system diagnostic tool from passenger seat side impact air bag module electrical connector.
6. Connect passenger seat side impact air bag module electrical connector from under rear of seat cushion.
7. Disconnect passenger side air bag module jumper harness from passenger side air bag electrical connector on vehicle wiring harness.
8. Separate locking inserts and disconnect two restraint system diagnostic tools from passenger side air bag module jumper harness electrical connectors.
9. Align and connect passenger side air bag module jumper harness electrical connectors to module, install locking inserts and attach passenger side air bag module electrical connector pintype retainer to passenger air bag module.
10. Ensure J-clips on back of passenger side air bag module are locked into slots.
11. Ensure retaining clips on back of passenger side air bag module are locked onto ears.
12. Install passenger side air bag module into instrument panel.
13. Install passenger side air bag module bolts, **torque** to 80 inch lbs.
14. Connect passenger side air bag module electrical connector.
15. Connect glove compartment isolator, close glove compartment.
16. Remove restraint system diagnostic tools from clockspring electrical connectors at top of steering column.
17. Ensure that if new steering wheel is being installed, it is the same OEM that came off. **On early build models, tower is on lefthand side, on later built models, tower is on righthand side.**
18. Install driver's side air bag module, connect electrical connectors and align locking pins to openings in steer-

ing wheel and position air bag module in place.
19. Ensure that all restraint system diagnostic tools have been removed and all SRS components connected.
20. Turn ignition switch from OFF to ON position.
21. Install RCM fuse F2.2 (10A) to CJB and replace cover.
22. Connect battery ground cable.
23. Prove out system as follows:
    a. Turn ignition key to OFF position.
    b. Wait 10 seconds, then turn key to ON position and visually monitor air bag indicator.
    c. Air bag indicator will be lit continuously for 6 seconds then turn Off.
    d. If air bag system fault is present, air bag indicator will fail to light, remain lit continuously or flash.
    e. Flashing will occur up to 30 seconds after ignition switch has been turned from the OFF to ON position.
    f. If fault occurs, a chime will sound.

FIVE-HUNDRED, FREESTYLE & MONTEGO

1. Remove RCM fuse F2.21 (7.5A) from SJB.
2. Disconnect battery ground cable and isolate as required. **Wait at least 60 seconds for power supply to deplete.**
3. **On Five-Hundred and Montego models equipped with roof panel air bag modules,** proceed as follows:
    a. Remove restraint system diagnostic tool from vehicle harness side of passenger side roof panel air bag module electrical connector.
    b. Connect passenger side roof panel air bag module electrical connector.
    c. Remove restraint system diagnostic tool from vehicle harness side of driver's side roof panel air bag module electrical connector.
    d. Connect driver's side roof panel air bag module electrical connector.
    e. Install C-pillar trim panels using suitable tool.
4. **On Freestyle models equipped with roof panel air bag modules,** proceed as follows:
    a. Remove restraint system diagnostic tool from vehicle harness side of passenger side roof panel air bag module electrical connector.
    b. Connect passenger side roof panel air bag module electrical connector.
    c. Install passenger side D-pillar trim panel.
    d. Remove restraint system diagnostic tool from vehicle harness side of driver's side roof panel air bag module electrical connector.
    e. Connect driver's side roof panel air bag module electrical connector.
    f. Install driver's side D-pillar trim panel.

14. **On models equipped with side impact air bag modules,** remove restraint system diagnostic tool from vehicle harness side of driver's seat side impact air bag module electrical connector.
15. **On Freestyle models equipped with roof panel air bag modules,** proceed as follows:
    a. Connect driver's seat side impact air bag module electrical connector, then slide and engage seat side impact air bag module electrical connector locking clip.
    b. Remove restraint system diagnostic tool from vehicle harness side of passenger seat side impact air bag module electrical connector.
    c. Connect passenger seat side impact air bag module electrical connector, then slide and engage seat side impact air bag module electrical connector locking clip.
16. **On all models,** remove restraint system diagnostic tools to vehicle harness side of passenger side air bag module electrical connectors.
17. Connect two passenger side air bag module electrical connectors.
18. Attach dampening strut to lefthand side of glove compartment door.
19. Close glove compartment door.
20. Remove restraint system diagnostic tools from clockspring electrical connectors at top of steering column.
21. Push driver's side air bag module wire clip fully back on six tabs on top of module.
22. **Ensure that wire clip stays fully seated on six tabs on top of module using a suitable tool to reset end of wire clip that is on top.** Carefully lift one end of wire clip over post, pull wire clip outward to reset.
23. **Ensure that wire clip stays fully seated on six tabs on top of module using a suitable tool to reset end of wire clip that is on top.** Carefully lift other end of wire clip over post, pull wire clip outward to reset.
24. When wire clip is reset correctly, wire clip hook ends are evenly spaced from center post.
25. Ensure that driver's side air bag module wire clip is fully seated on all of the tabs and guides.
26. Connect horn and accessories electrical connectors.
27. Connect driver's side air bag module electrical connectors.
28. Attach driver's side air bag module to steering wheel, align and press into steering wheel until module wire clip is fully engaged to steering wheel.
29. Install steering wheel access cover.
30. Turn ignition switch from OFF to ON position.
31. Install RCM fuse F2.21 (7.5A) to SJB and replace cover.
32. Connect battery ground cable.
33. Prove out system as follows:
    a. Turn ignition key to OFF position.
    b. Wait 10 seconds, then turn key to ON position and visually monitor air bag indicator.
    c. Air bag indicator will be lit continuously for 6 seconds then turn Off.
    d. If air bag system fault is present, air bag indicator will fail to light, remain lit continuously or flash.
    e. Flashing will occur up to 30 seconds after ignition switch has been turned from the OFF to ON position.
    f. If fault occurs, a chime will sound.

GENERAL MOTORS

Disconnect battery ground cable. The Diagnostic Energy Reserve Module or Sensing and Diagnostic Module (DERM/SDM) can maintain enough voltage to cause air bag deployment for up to 10 minutes after the ignition is turned Off and the battery is disconnected. Servicing the SIR system during this period may result in accidental deployment and personal injury.

Disarming

ALERO, GRAND AM, MALIBU & MALIBU MAXX

2001-02

1. Ensure front wheels are pointed straight-ahead.
2. Ensure ignition switch is in Off or Lock position. Remove key.
3. Remove lefthand instrument panel wiring harness junction block access panel.
4. Remove AIR BAG fuse from lefthand instrument panel fuse junction block.
5. Disconnect Connector Position Assurance (CPA) located above lefthand instrument panel wiring harness junction block.
6. Disconnect steering wheel module coil connector.
7. Remove righthand instrument panel wiring harness junction block access panel.
8. Disconnect CPA located above righthand instrument panel wiring harness junction block.
9. Disconnect passenger air bag module connector.

2003-04

Zone 3

1. Ensure front wheels are pointed straight-ahead.
2. Turn ignition key off and remove ignition key from switch.
3. Remove access panel from lefthand instrument panel wiring harness junction block.
4. Remove AIR BAG fuse from junction block.
5. Remove Connector Position Assurance (CPA) cover from steering wheel module coil connector. Connector is located above lefthand instrument panel wiring harness junction block.
6. Disconnect steering wheel module coil connector.

Zone 5

1. Ensure front wheels are pointed straight-ahead.
2. Turn ignition key off and remove ignition key from switch.
3. Remove access panel from lefthand instrument panel wiring harness junction block.
4. Remove AIR BAG fuse from junction block.
5. Remove access panel from righthand instrument panel wiring harness junction block.
6. Remove Connector Position Assurance (CPA) cover from instrument panel module connector. Connector is located above righthand instrument panel wiring harness junction block.
7. Disconnect instrument panel module electrical connector.

2005

Zone 1

1. Ensure steering wheel is in straight ahead position.
2. Ensure ignition switch is in OFF position and key is removed.
3. Remove AIR BAG (IGN) and AIR BAG (BATT) fuses from body control module (BCM) fuse center.
4. Remove connector position assistance (CPA) from lefthand and righthand side front end sensor connector.
5. Remove lefthand and righthand side front end sensor connectors from sensor.

Zone 2

1. Ensure steering wheel is in straight ahead position.
2. Ensure ignition switch is in OFF position and key is removed.
3. Remove AIR BAG (IGN) and AIR BAG (BATT) fuses from body control module (BCM) fuse center.
4. Disable roof panel air bag module as outlined under "Zone 8."
5. Remove fastener from seat belt D-ring, then the D-ring.
6. Remove adjustable shoulder belt knob.
7. Remove center pillar upper trim molding by pulling forward.
8. Remove front and rear carpet retainers.
9. Remove lower center pillar trim molding.
10. Remove connector position assurance (CPA) from lefthand side seat belt pretensioner connector.
11. Disconnect lefthand side seat belt pretensioner connector from vehicle harness connector.
12. Remove upper lock pillar trim panel.
13. Remove CPA from lefthand side roof panel air bag module vehicle harness connector.
14. Remove lefthand side door trim panel using suitable screwdriver's.

15. Remove CPA from lefthand side SIS connector.
16. Remove lefthand side SIS connector from SIS.

Zone 3

"2005 Grand Am" models, refer to "Zone 3" in "2003–04" year coverage for procedure.
1. Ensure steering wheel is in straight ahead position.
2. Ensure ignition switch is in OFF position and key is removed.
3. Remove AIR BAG (IGN) and AIR BAG (BATT) fuses from body control module (BCM) fuse center.
4. Remove driver's side outer trim cover from instrument panel.
5. Remove connector position assurance (CPA) from steering wheel coil connector.

Zone 5

2005 Grand Am models, refer to "Zone 5" in "2003–04" year coverage for procedure.
1. Ensure steering wheel is in straight ahead position.
2. Ensure ignition switch is in OFF position and key is removed.
3. Remove AIR BAG (IGN) and AIR BAG (BATT) fuses from body control module (BCM) fuse center.
4. Remove passenger side outer trim panel from instrument panel.
5. Remove connector position assurance (CPA) from vehicle harness connector.

Zone 6

1. Ensure steering wheel is in straight ahead position.
2. Ensure ignition switch is in OFF position and key is removed.
3. Remove AIR BAG (IGN) and AIR BAG (BATT) fuses from body control module (BCM) fuse center.
4. Disable roof panel air bag module system as outlined under "Zone 8."
5. Remove upper center trim molding.
6. Remove front and rear carpet retainers.
7. Remove lower center pillar trim panel using suitable flatbladed tool.
8. Remove connector position assurance (CPA) from righthand front seat belt pretensioner connector.
9. Disconnect righthand front seat belt pretensioner connector from vehicle harness connector.
10. Disable roof panel air bag module system as outlined under "Zone 8."
11. Remove upper lock pillar trim molding at rear corner upper trim.
12. Disconnect CPA from roof panel air bag module connector.
13. Remove righthand door trim panel using suitable flat bladed tool.
14. Remove CPA from righthand side SIS connector.
15. Remove righthand SIS connector from SIS.

Zone 7

1. Ensure steering wheel is in straight

ahead position.
2. Ensure ignition switch is in OFF position and key is removed.
3. Remove AIR BAG (IGN) and AIR BAG (BATT) fuses from body control module (BCM) fuse center.
4. Remove connector position assurance (CPA) from lefthand side impact module yellow connector from under driver's seat.
5. Disconnect vehicle harness yellow connector from lefthand side impact module yellow connector.

Zone 8

1. Ensure steering wheel is in straight ahead position.
2. Ensure ignition switch is in OFF position and key is removed.
3. Remove AIR BAG (IGN) and AIR BAG (BATT) fuses from body control module (BCM) fuse center.
4. Remove righthand side upper lock pillar trim molding using suitable flatbladed tool.
5. Remove connector position assurance (CPA) from roof panel air bag module righthand side connector.
6. Disconnect roof panel air bag module righthand connector from vehicle harness connector.
7. Remove upper trim panel molding, then the front and rear carpet retainers.
8. Remove CPA from righthand front seat belt pretensioner connector.
9. Disconnect righthand front seat belt pretensioner connector from vehicle harness connector.
10. Remove passenger side outer trim panel cover from instrument panel.
11. Remove CPA from instrument panel connector.
12. Disconnect instrument panel module connector from vehicle harness connector.
13. Remove driver's side outer trim panel from instrument panel.
14. Remove CPA from steering wheel module coil connector.
15. Disconnect steering wheel module coil connector from vehicle harness connector.
16. Remove lefthand side lower center pillar trim.
17. Remove CPA from lefthand side front seat belt pretensioner connector.
18. Disconnect lefthand side seat belt pretensioner connector from vehicle harness connector.
19. Remove lefthand side upper lock pillar trim panel.
20. Remove CPA from lefthand side roof panel air bag module connector.
21. Disconnect lefthand side roof panel air bag module connector from vehicle harness connector.

Zone 9

1. Ensure steering wheel is in straight ahead position.
2. Ensure ignition switch is in OFF position and key is removed.
3. Remove AIR BAG (IGN) and AIR BAG (BATT) fuses from body control mod-

ule (BCM) fuse center.
4. Remove connector position assurance (CPA) from passenger side impact module yellow connector located under passenger seat.
5. Disconnect vehicle harness yellow connector from passenger side impact module yellow connector.

AURORA

2001-02

1. Ensure front wheels are pointing straight ahead.
2. Turn ignition switch to Off position and remove key.
3. Remove SIR fuse from rear fuse block located under rear seat.
4. Remove instrument panel lefthand side sound insulator.
5. Remove Connector Position Assurance (CPA) from driver's air bag module yellow connector located next to steering column.
6. Disconnect driver's air bag module yellow connector from harness yellow connector.
7. Remove instrument panel righthand side sound insulator.
8. Remove CPA from passenger air bag module yellow connector located above instrument panel righthand side sound insulator.
9. Disconnect passenger air bag module yellow connector from harness yellow connector.
10. Remove CPA from lefthand side impact air bag module yellow connector located under driver's seat.
11. Disconnect lefthand side impact air bag module yellow connector from harness yellow connector.
12. Remove CPA from righthand side impact air bag module yellow connector located under righthand front seat.
13. Disconnect righthand side impact air bag module yellow connector from harness yellow connector.

2003

Zone 1

1. Position steering wheel in straight ahead position.
2. Turn ignition switch to Off position and remove key.
3. Remove rear seat lower cushion.
4. Remove SIR fuse from rear fuse center.
5. Remove Connector Position Assurance (CPA) lock from Electronic Frontal Sensor (EFS) connector. EFS is located on front lefthand side of engine compartment.
6. Disconnect EFS connector.

Zone 2

1. Position steering wheel in straight ahead position.
2. Remove rear seat lower cushion.
3. Remove SIR fuse from rear fuse center.
4. Remove front and rear carpet retainers from lefthand center pillar trim panel.
5. Remove lefthand center pillar trim panel from pillar.

6. Remove Connector Position Assurance (CPA) lock from lefthand Side Impact Sensor (SIS) connector.
7. Disconnect SIS connector.

Zone 3

1. Position steering wheel in straight ahead position.
2. Turn ignition switch to Off position and remove key.
3. Remove rear seat lower cushion.
4. Remove SIR fuse from rear fuse center.
5. Remove lefthand closeout/insulator panel from under lefthand side of instrument panel.
6. Remove Connector Position Assurance (CPA) lock from steering wheel module yellow connector.
7. Disconnect steering wheel module connector from yellow harness connector.

Zone 5

1. Position steering wheel in straight ahead position.
2. Turn ignition switch to Off position and remove key.
3. Remove rear seat lower cushion.
4. Remove SIR fuse from rear fuse center.
5. Remove righthand closeout/insulator panel from under righthand side of instrument panel.
6. Remove Connector Position Assurance (CPA) lock from instrument panel module yellow connector.
7. Disconnect instrument panel module connector from yellow harness connector.

Zone 6

1. Position steering wheel in straight ahead position.
2. Turn ignition switch to Off position and remove key.
3. Remove rear seat lower cushion.
4. Remove SIR fuse from rear fuse center.
5. Remove front and rear carpet retainers from righthand center pillar trim panel.
6. Remove righthand center pillar trim panel from pillar.
7. Remove Connector Position Assurance (CPA) lock from righthand Side Impact Sensor (SIS) connector.
8. Disconnect SIS connector.

Zone 7

1. Turn steering wheel to straight-ahead position.
2. Turn ignition switch to Off position and remove key.
3. Remove steering column upper and lower covers.
4. Disconnect inflatable restraint steering wheel module coil connector from inflatable restraint steering wheel module coil.
5. Remove passenger air bag module cover.
6. Disconnect Connector Position Assurance (CPA) from passenger air bag module electrical connector.
7. Disconnect passenger air bag module

electrical connector.
8. Remove driver's outer seat track cover.
9. Disconnect driver's seat belt pretensioner two-way electrical connector from inline connector C315.
10. Disconnect CPA from lefthand side impact air bag module electrical connector.
11. Disconnect lefthand side impact air bag module electrical connector.
12. Remove righthand front outer seat track cover.
13. Disconnect passenger seat belt pretensioner two-way electrical connector from inline connector C316.
14. Remove CPA from righthand side impact air bag module electrical connector.
15. Disconnect righthand side impact air bag module electrical connector.
16. Remove rear seat lower cushion.
17. Remove SIR fuse from rear fuse center.
18. Remove Connector Position Assurance (CPA) lock from lefthand driver's side impact module and seat belt pretensioner yellow connector. Connector is located under driver's seat.
19. Disconnect lefthand driver's side impact module and seat belt pretensioner yellow connector from harness connector.

Zone 8

1. Position steering wheel in straight ahead position.
2. Turn ignition switch to Off position and remove key.
3. Remove steering column upper and lower covers.
4. Disconnect inflatable restraint steering wheel module coil connector from inflatable restraint steering wheel module coil.
5. Remove passenger air bag module cover.
6. Disconnect Connector Position Assurance (CPA) from passenger air bag module electrical connector.
7. Disconnect passenger air bag module electrical connector.
8. Remove driver's outer seat track cover.
9. Disconnect driver's seat belt pretensioner two-way electrical connector from inline connector C315.
10. Disconnect CPA from lefthand side impact air bag module electrical connector.
11. Disconnect lefthand side impact air bag module electrical connector.
12. Remove righthand front outer seat track cover.
13. Disconnect passenger seat belt pretensioner two-way electrical connector from inline connector C316.
14. Remove CPA from righthand side impact air bag module electrical connector.
15. Disconnect righthand side impact air bag module electrical connector.
16. Remove rear seat lower cushion.
17. Remove SIR fuse from rear fuse center.
18. Remove Connector Position Assur-

ance (CPA) lock from righthand side impact module and seat belt pretensioner yellow connector. Connector is located under passenger front seat.
19. Disconnect righthand side impact module and seat belt pretensioner yellow connector from harness connector.
20. Remove righthand closeout/insulator panel from under righthand side of instrument panel.
21. Remove CPA lock from instrument panel module yellow connector.
22. Disconnect instrument panel module connector from yellow harness connector.
23. Remove lefthand closeout/insulator panel from under lefthand side of instrument panel.
24. Remove CPA lock from steering wheel module yellow connector.
25. Disconnect steering wheel module connector from yellow harness connector.
26. Remove CPA lock from lefthand driver's side impact module and seat belt pretensioner yellow connector. Connector is located under driver's seat.
27. Disconnect lefthand driver's side impact module and seat belt pretensioner yellow connector from harness connector.

Zone 9

1. Position steering wheel in straight ahead position.
2. Remove rear seat lower cushion.
3. Remove SIR fuse from rear fuse center.
4. Remove Connector Position Assurance (CPA) lock from righthand passenger side impact module and seat belt pretensioner yellow connector. Connector is located under passenger seat.
5. Disconnect righthand side impact module and seat belt pretensioner yellow connector to vehicle harness connector.

BONNEVILLE & LESABRE

2001-02

1. Ensure front wheels are pointed straight-ahead.
2. Turn ignition switch to Off position and remove key.
3. Remove SIR fuse from rear fuse block located under rear seat.
4. Remove instrument panel lefthand sound insulator.
5. Disconnect Connector Position Assurance (CPA) from driver's air bag module yellow two-way connector at base of steering column.
6. Disconnect driver's air bag module yellow two-way connector from harness yellow connector.
7. Remove righthand sound insulator.
8. Disconnect CPA and yellow two-way connector from passenger air bag module yellow connector located above righthand sound insulator.
9. Disconnect passenger air bag module yellow connector from harness yellow connector.

10. Disconnect CPA from lefthand side impact air bag module yellow electrical connector located under driver's seat.
11. Disconnect lefthand side impact air bag module yellow electrical connector from harness yellow connector.
12. Remove CPA from righthand side impact air bag module electrical connector located under righthand front seat.
13. Disconnect righthand side impact air bag module yellow electrical connector from harness yellow connector.

2003–05

For disarming procedures on these models, refer to "2003" in "Aurora."

CAMARO & FIREBIRD

1. Ensure front wheels are pointed straight-ahead.
2. Turn ignition switch to Off position and remove key.
3. Remove instrument panel fuse block access door.
4. Remove AIR BAG fuse from instrument panel fuse box.
5. Remove lefthand instrument panel insulator.
6. Disconnect Connector Position Assurance (CPA) from inflatable restraint steering wheel module coil connector located at base of steering column.
7. Disconnect steering wheel module coil connector located at base of steering column.
8. Remove righthand instrument panel insulator.
9. Disconnect CPA from passenger air bag module connector located behind instrument panel compartment door.
10. Disconnect yellow two-way connector from passenger air bag module located behind glove compartment.

CATERA

1. Turn steering wheel to straight-ahead position.
2. Turn ignition switch to Off position and remove key.
3. Remove steering column upper and lower covers.
4. Disconnect inflatable restraint steering wheel module coil connector from inflatable restraint steering wheel module coil.
5. Remove passenger air bag module cover.
6. Disconnect Connector Position Assurance (CPA) from passenger air bag module electrical connector.
7. Disconnect passenger air bag module electrical connector.
8. Remove driver's outer seat track cover.
9. Disconnect driver's seat belt pretensioner two-way electrical connector from inline connector C315.
10. Disconnect CPA from lefthand side impact air bag module electrical connector.
11. Disconnect lefthand side impact air bag module electrical connector.
12. Remove righthand front outer seat track cover.
13. Disconnect passenger seat belt pretensioner two-way electrical connector

from inline connector C316.
14. Remove CPA from righthand side impact air bag module electrical connector.
15. Disconnect righthand side impact air bag module electrical connector.

CAVALIER & SUNFIRE

2001–02

1. Ensure front wheels are pointed straight-ahead.
2. Turn ignition switch to Off position and remove key.
3. Remove lefthand instrument panel junction block access panel.
4. Remove SIR or AIR BAG fuse from lefthand instrument panel fuse block.
5. Disconnect Connector Position Assurance (CPA) from driver's air bag module coil connector located above lefthand instrument panel wiring harness junction block.
6. Disconnect steering wheel module coil connector.
7. Remove righthand instrument panel wiring harness junction block access panel.
8. Disconnect CPA from passenger air bag module connector located above righthand instrument panel wiring harness junction block.
9. Disconnect passenger air bag module connector.

2003–05
Zone 1

1. Position steering wheel in straight ahead position.
2. Ensure ignition switch is Off and key is removed.
3. Remove lefthand instrument panel outer trim cover.
4. Remove AIR BAG fuse from lefthand instrument panel junction block.
5. Remove hood closeout filler panel from front of engine compartment.
6. Remove Connector Position Assurance (CPA) cover from inflatable restraint Electronic Front Sensor (EFS) connector.
7. Disconnect connector from EFS.

Zone 2, Coupe

1. Position steering wheel in straight ahead position.
2. Ensure ignition switch is Off and key is removed.
3. Remove lefthand instrument panel outer trim cover.
4. Remove AIR BAG fuse from lefthand instrument panel junction block.
5. Remove window regulator handle from lefthand door trim panel.
6. **On models equipped with power door locks,** remove power door lock switch from lefthand door trim panel.
7. **On all models,** remove lefthand door trim panel mounting screws and pull trim panel away from door.
8. Remove inflatable restraint Side Impact Sensor (SIS) from door.
9. Remove Connector Position Assurance (CPA) cover from SIS connector.
10. Disconnect SIS connector.

Zone 2, Sedan

1. Position steering wheel in straight ahead position.
2. Ensure ignition switch is Off and key is removed.
3. Remove lefthand instrument panel outer trim cover.
4. Remove AIR BAG fuse from lefthand instrument panel junction block.
5. Remove upper trim from lefthand center pillar.
6. Remove inflatable restraint Side Impact Sensor (SIS) from center pillar.
7. Remove Connector Position Assurance (CPA) cover from SIS connector.
8. Disconnect SIS connector.

Zone 3

1. Position steering wheel in straight ahead position.
2. Ensure ignition switch is Off and key is removed.
3. Remove lefthand instrument panel outer trim cover.
4. Remove AIR BAG fuse from lefthand instrument panel junction block.
5. Remove Connector Position Assurance (CPA) cover from inflatable restraint steering wheel module coil connector. Connector is located under lefthand side of instrument panel, left of steering column.
6. Disconnect steering wheel module coil connector.

Zone 5

1. Position steering wheel in straight ahead position.
2. Ensure ignition switch is Off and key is removed.
3. Remove lefthand instrument panel outer trim cover.
4. Remove AIR BAG fuse from lefthand instrument panel junction block.
5. Remove Connector Position Assurance (CPA) cover from inflatable restraint instrument panel module inline connector. Connector is located under lefthand side of instrument panel, left of steering column.
6. Disconnect instrument panel module inline connector.

Zone 6, Coupe

1. Position steering wheel in straight ahead position.
2. Ensure ignition switch is Off and key is removed.
3. Remove lefthand instrument panel outer trim cover.
4. Remove AIR BAG fuse from lefthand instrument panel junction block.
5. Remove window regulator handle from righthand door trim panel.
6. **On models equipped with power door locks,** remove power door lock switch from righthand door trim panel.
7. **On all models,** remove righthand door trim panel mounting screws and pull trim panel away from door.
8. Remove inflatable restraint Side Impact Sensor (SIS) from door.
9. Remove Connector Position Assurance (CPA) cover from SIS connector.
10. Disconnect SIS connector.

AIR BAG SYSTEM PRECAUTIONS

Zone 6, Sedan

1. Position steering wheel in straight ahead position.
2. Ensure ignition switch is Off and key is removed.
3. Remove lefthand instrument panel outer trim cover.
4. Remove AIR BAG fuse from lefthand instrument panel junction block.
5. Remove upper trim from righthand center pillar.
6. Remove inflatable restraint Side Impact Sensor (SIS) from center pillar.
7. Remove Connector Position Assurance (CPA) cover from SIS connector.
8. Disconnect SIS connector.

Zone 7

1. Position steering wheel in straight ahead position.
2. Ensure ignition switch is Off and key is removed.
3. Remove lefthand instrument panel outer trim cover.
4. Remove AIR BAG fuse from lefthand instrument panel junction block.
5. Remove Connector Position Assurance (CPA) cover from inflatable restraint side impact module connector. Connector is located under driver's seat.
6. Disconnect side impact module connector.

Zone 9

1. Position steering wheel in straight ahead position.
2. Ensure ignition switch is Off and key is removed.
3. Remove lefthand instrument panel outer trim cover.
4. Remove AIR BAG fuse from lefthand instrument panel junction block.
5. Remove Connector Position Assurance (CPA) cover from inflatable restraint side impact module connector. Connector is located under passenger front seat.
6. Disconnect side impact module connector.

CENTURY & REGAL

2001-02

1. Ensure front wheels are pointed straight-ahead.
2. Turn ignition to Off position and remove ignition key.
3. Remove instrument panel fuse block access door.
4. Remove AIR BAG fuse from instrument panel fuse block.
5. Remove lefthand underdash trim panel.
6. Disconnect Connector Position Assurance (CPA) from driver's air bag module coil connector located at base of steering column.
7. Disconnect driver's air bag module coil connector.
8. Disconnect passenger air bag module CPA located to right of steering column.
9. Disconnect passenger air bag module yellow air bag module connector.

10. **On models equipped with side impact air bag modules,** proceed as follows:
    a. Remove CPA from lefthand side impact air bag module impact module.
    b. Disconnect lefthand side impact air bag module.

2003-05

Zone 2

1. Position steering wheel in straight ahead position.
2. Ensure ignition switch is Off and key is removed.
3. Remove instrument panel fuse block cover.
4. Remove SIR fuse from fuse block.
5. Remove lefthand center pillar trim panel.
6. Remove Side Impact Sensor (SIS) from center pillar.
7. Remove Connector Position Assurance (CPA) cover from SIS connector.
8. Disconnect SIS connector.

Zone 3

1. Position steering wheel in straight ahead position.
2. Ensure ignition switch is Off and key is removed.
3. Remove instrument panel fuse block cover.
4. Remove SIR fuse from fuse block.
5. Remove insulator panel from under lefthand side of instrument panel.
6. Remove Connector Position Assurance (CPA) cover from inflatable restraint steering wheel module coil connector. Connector is located at base of steering column.
7. Disconnect steering wheel module coil connector.

Zone 5

1. Position steering wheel in straight ahead position.
2. Ensure ignition switch is Off and key is removed.
3. Remove instrument panel fuse block cover.
4. Remove SIR fuse from fuse block.
5. Remove insulator panel from under lefthand side of instrument panel.
6. Remove Connector Position Assurance (CPA) cover from inflatable restraint instrument panel module connector. Connector is located on righthand side of steering column.
7. Disconnect instrument panel module connector.

Zone 7

1. Position steering wheel in straight ahead position.
2. Ensure ignition switch is Off and key is removed.
3. Remove instrument panel fuse block cover.
4. Remove SIR fuse from fuse block.
5. Remove Connector Position Assurance (CPA) cover from lefthand side impact module connector. Connector is located under driver's seat.

6. Disconnect side impact module connector.

Zone 9

1. Position steering wheel in straight ahead position.
2. Ensure ignition switch is Off and key is removed.
3. Remove instrument panel fuse block cover.
4. Remove SIR fuse from fuse block.
5. Remove insulator panel from under lefthand side of instrument panel.
6. Remove Connector Position Assurance (CPA) cover from inflatable restraint steering wheel module coil connector. Connector is located at base of steering column.
7. Disconnect steering wheel module coil connector.
8. Remove CPA cover from inflatable restraint instrument panel module connector. Connector is located on righthand side of steering column.
9. Disconnect instrument panel module connector.
10. Remove lefthand center pillar trim panel.
11. Remove Side Impact Sensor (SIS) from center pillar.
12. Remove CPA cover from SIS connector.
13. Disconnect SIS connector.

CORVETTE

2001-02

1. Place front wheels in straight-ahead position.
2. Turn ignition switch to Off position and remove key.
3. Remove front floor kick-up panel.
4. Remove SDM fuse from instrument panel fuse block.
5. Remove lefthand sound insulator.
6. Disconnect Connector Position Assurance (CPA) from driver's air bag module coil connector located at base of steering column.
7. Disconnect driver's air bag module coil yellow two-way SIR electrical connector at base of steering column.
8. Disconnect CPA from passenger air bag module coil connector located at base of steering column.
9. Disconnect passenger air bag module coil yellow two-way SIR electrical connector at base of steering column.

2003-04

Zone 3

1. Position steering wheel in straight ahead position.
2. Ensure ignition switch is Off and key is removed.
3. Remove kick-up panel from under instrument panel.
4. Remove SDM fuse from instrument panel fuse block.
5. Remove sound insulator panel from under lefthand side of instrument panel.
6. Remove Connector Position Assurance (CPA) cover from inflatable restraint steering wheel module coil

connector. Connector is located at base of steering column.

7. Disconnect steering wheel module coil connector.

Zone 4

1. Position steering wheel in straight ahead position.
2. Ensure ignition switch is Off and key is removed.
3. Remove kick-up panel from under instrument panel.
4. Remove SDM fuse from instrument panel fuse block.
5. Remove sound insulator panel from under lefthand side of instrument panel.
6. Remove Connector Position Assurance (CPA) cover from inflatable restraint steering wheel module coil connector. Connector is located at base of steering column.
7. Disconnect steering wheel module coil connector.
8. Remove CPA cover from inflatable restraint instrument panel module connector. Connector is located near base of steering column.
9. Disconnect instrument panel module connector.

Zone 5

1. Position steering wheel in straight ahead position.
2. Ensure ignition switch is Off and key is removed.
3. Remove kick-up panel from under instrument panel.
4. Remove SDM fuse from instrument panel fuse block.
5. Remove sound insulator panel from under lefthand side of instrument panel.
6. Remove Connector Position Assurance (CPA) cover from inflatable restraint instrument panel module connector. Connector is located near base of steering column.
7. Disconnect instrument panel module connector.

2005

Zone 1

1. Ensure steering wheel is in straight ahead position.
2. Ensure ignition switch is in OFF position.
3. Remove kick-up panel then the instrument panel fuse block cover.
4. Remove sensing and diagnostic module (SDM) from instrument panel fuse block.
5. Remove splash shield from vehicle.
6. Disconnect electrical connector for mass air flow/intake air temperature sensor (MAF/IAT).
7. Remove connection for IAT sensor and loosen clamps.
8. Remove air intake duct, MAF/IAT sensor then the air cleaner assembly.
9. Remove both front end sensor connectors from lefthand and righthand sensors.

Zone 2

1. Ensure steering wheel is in straight ahead position.
2. Ensure ignition switch is in OFF position.
3. Remove kick-up panel then the instrument panel fuse block cover.
4. Remove sensing and diagnostic module (SDM) from instrument panel fuse block.
5. Remove driver's side door trim panel using suitable flatbladed tool.
6. Remove connector position assurance (CPA) from SIS connector.
7. Remove SIS connector from SIS.

Zone 3

1. Ensure steering wheel is in straight ahead position.
2. Ensure ignition switch is in OFF position.
3. Remove kick-up panel then the instrument panel fuse block cover.
4. Remove sensing and diagnostic module (SDM) from instrument panel fuse block.
5. Remove driver's side sound insulator from instrument panel.
6. Remove connector position assurance (CPA) from vehicle harness yellow connector.
7. Disconnect steering wheel module coil yellow connector from vehicle harness yellow connector.

Zone 4

1. Ensure steering wheel is in straight ahead position.
2. Ensure ignition switch is in OFF position.
3. Remove kick-up panel then the instrument panel fuse block cover.
4. Remove sensing and diagnostic module (SDM) from instrument panel fuse block.
5. Remove passenger side sound insulator from instrument panel.
6. Disconnect passenger side air bag module yellow connector from vehicle harness yellow connector.
7. Remove both CPA's from passenger side impact air bag module and seat belt pretensioner yellow connector from under passenger seat.
8. Disconnect vehicle harness yellow connector from passenger side impact module and pretensioner yellow connector.
9. Remove driver's side sound insulator from instrument panel.
10. Remove CPA from vehicle harness yellow connector.
11. Disconnect steering wheel coil yellow connector from vehicle harness yellow connector.
12. Remove both CPA's from driver's side impact air bag module and seat belt pretensioner.

Zone 5

1. Ensure steering wheel is in straight ahead position.
2. Ensure ignition switch is in OFF position.
3. Remove kick-up panel then the instru-

ment panel fuse block cover.
4. Remove sensing and diagnostic module (SDM) from instrument panel fuse block.
5. Remove passenger side sound insulator from instrument panel.
6. Disconnect passenger side air bag module yellow connector from vehicle harness yellow connector.

Zone 6

1. Ensure steering wheel is in straight ahead position.
2. Ensure ignition switch is in OFF position.
3. Remove kick-up panel then the instrument panel fuse block cover.
4. Remove sensing and diagnostic module (SDM) from instrument panel fuse block.
5. Remove passenger side door trim panel using suitable flatbladed tool.
6. Remove connector position assurance (CPA) from SIS connector.
7. Remove SIS connector from SIS.

Zone 7

1. Ensure steering wheel is in straight ahead position.
2. Ensure ignition switch is in OFF position.
3. Remove kick-up panel then the instrument panel fuse block cover.
4. Remove sensing and diagnostic module (SDM) from instrument panel fuse block.
5. Remove both connector position assurance (CPA) from driver's side impact air bag module and pretensioner yellow connector from under driver's seat.
6. Disconnect vehicle harness yellow connector from driver's side impact air bag module and pretensioner yellow connector.

Zone 9

1. Ensure steering wheel is in straight ahead position.
2. Ensure ignition switch is in OFF position.
3. Remove kick-up panel then the instrument panel fuse block cover.
4. Remove sensing and diagnostic module (SDM) from instrument panel fuse block.
5. Remove both connector position assurance (CPA) from passenger side impact air bag module and seat belt pretensioner yellow connector from under passenger seat.
6. Disconnect vehicle harness yellow connector from passenger side impact air bag module and pretensioner yellow connector.

CTS

ZONE 1

1. Position steering wheel in straight ahead position.
2. Turn ignition to Off position and remove key.
3. Remove rear seat lower cushion.
4. Remove SIR fuse from righthand rear fuse center.

5. Remove Connector Position Assurance (CPA) lock from Electronic Frontal Sensor (EFS) connector. EFS is located on front lefthand side of engine compartment.
6. Disconnect EFS connector.

ZONE 2

1. Position steering wheel in straight ahead position.
2. Turn ignition to Off position and remove key.
3. Remove rear seat lower cushion.
4. Remove SIR fuse from righthand rear fuse center.
5. Release lefthand rear sail panel retaining clips.
6. Remove lefthand rear sail panel from lefthand side of rear window.
7. Remove Connector Position Assurance (CPA) lock from lefthand roof rail module yellow electrical connector.
8. Disconnect lefthand roof rail module connector.
9. Remove front and rear carpet retainers from lefthand center pillar trim panel.
10. Remove lefthand center pillar trim panel from pillar.
11. Remove Connector Position Assurance (CPA) lock from lefthand Side Impact Sensor (SIS) connector.
12. Disconnect SIS connector.

ZONE 3

1. Position steering wheel in straight ahead position.
2. Turn ignition to Off position and remove key.
3. Remove rear seat lower cushion.
4. Remove SIR fuse from righthand rear fuse center.
5. Remove lefthand closeout/insulator panel from far lefthand side of instrument panel.
6. Remove Connector Position Assurance (CPA) lock from steering wheel module yellow connector.
7. Disconnect steering wheel module connector from yellow harness connector.

ZONE 5

1. Position steering wheel in straight ahead position.
2. Turn ignition to Off position and remove key.
3. Remove rear seat lower cushion.
4. Remove SIR fuse from righthand rear fuse center.
5. Remove righthand closeout/insulator panel from far righthand side of instrument panel.
6. Remove Connector Position Assurance (CPA) lock from instrument panel module yellow connector.
7. Disconnect instrument panel module connector from yellow harness connector.

ZONE 6

1. Position steering wheel in straight ahead position.
2. Turn ignition to Off position and remove key.
3. Remove rear seat lower cushion.

4. Remove SIR fuse from righthand rear fuse center.
5. Release righthand rear sail panel retaining clips.
6. Remove righthand rear sail panel from righthand side of rear window.
7. Remove Connector Position Assurance (CPA) lock from righthand roof rail module yellow electrical connector.
8. Disconnect righthand roof rail module connector.
9. Remove front and rear carpet retainers from righthand center pillar trim panel.
10. Remove righthand center pillar trim panel from pillar.
11. Remove Connector Position Assurance (CPA) lock from righthand Side Impact Sensor (SIS) connector.
12. Disconnect SIS connector.

ZONE 7

1. Position steering wheel in straight ahead position.
2. Turn ignition to Off position and remove key.
3. Remove rear seat lower cushion.
4. Remove SIR fuse from righthand rear fuse center.
5. Remove Connector Position Assurance (CPA) lock from lefthand driver's side impact module and seat belt pretensioner yellow connector. Connector is located under driver's seat.
6. Disconnect lefthand driver's side impact module and seat belt pretensioner yellow connector from harness connector.

ZONE 8

1. Position steering wheel in straight ahead position.
2. Turn ignition to Off position and remove key.
3. Remove rear seat lower cushion.
4. Remove SIR fuse from righthand rear fuse center.
5. Release righthand rear sail panel retaining clips.
6. Remove righthand rear sail panel from righthand side of rear window.
7. Remove Connector Position Assurance (CPA) lock from righthand roof rail module yellow electrical connector.
8. Disconnect righthand roof rail module connector.
9. Remove righthand closeout/insulator panel from far righthand side of instrument panel.
10. Remove Connector Position Assurance (CPA) lock from instrument panel module yellow connector.
11. Disconnect instrument panel module connector from yellow harness connector.
12. Remove Connector Position Assurance (CPA) lock from righthand driver's side impact module and seat belt pretensioner yellow connector. Connector is located under passenger front seat.
13. Disconnect righthand driver's side impact module and seat belt pretensioner yellow connector from harness connector.
14. Remove lefthand closeout/insulator

panel from far lefthand side of instrument panel.
15. Remove Connector Position Assurance (CPA) lock from steering wheel module yellow connector.
16. Disconnect steering wheel module connector from yellow harness connector.
17. Remove Connector Position Assurance (CPA) lock from lefthand driver's side impact module and seat belt pretensioner yellow connector. Connector is located under driver's seat.
18. Disconnect lefthand driver's side impact module and seat belt pretensioner yellow connector from harness connector.
19. Release lefthand rear sail panel retaining clips.
20. Remove lefthand rear sail panel from lefthand side of rear window.
21. Remove Connector Position Assurance (CPA) lock from lefthand roof rail module yellow electrical connector.
22. Disconnect lefthand roof rail module connector.

ZONE 9

1. Position steering wheel in straight ahead position.
2. Turn ignition to Off position and remove key.
3. Remove rear seat lower cushion.
4. Remove SIR fuse from righthand rear fuse center.
5. Remove Connector Position Assurance (CPA) lock from righthand passenger side impact module and seat belt pretensioner yellow connector. Connector is located under passenger seat.
6. Disconnect righthand driver's side impact module and seat belt pretensioner yellow connector to vehicle harness connector.

DEVILLE

2001–02

1. Place front wheels in straight-ahead position.
2. Turn ignition to Off position and remove key.
3. Remove rear seat cushion.
4. Remove SIR fuse from fuse block under rear seat.
5. Remove instrument panel lefthand sound insulator.
6. Disconnect Connector Position Assurance (CPA) from driver's air bag module yellow connector located next to steering column.
7. Disconnect driver's air bag module connector from harness yellow connector.
8. Remove instrument panel righthand sound insulator.
9. Disconnect CPA from passenger air bag module yellow connector located above righthand sound insulator.
10. Disconnect passenger air bag module yellow connector from harness yellow connector.
11. Remove both CPAs locks from lefthand side impact air bag module and

pretensioner yellow electrical connectors located under seat.

12. Disconnect lefthand side impact air bag module and pretensioner yellow electrical connectors from harness yellow connector.

13. Disconnect both CPAs from righthand side impact air bag module and pretensioner yellow electrical connectors located under seat.

14. Disconnect righthand side impact air bag module and pretensioner yellow electrical connectors.

15. **On models equipped with rear side impact air bag modules,** proceed as follows:
    a. Remove rear seatback.
    b. Disconnect CPA from righthand rear side impact air bag module yellow electrical connector.
    c. Disconnect righthand rear impact air bag module yellow electrical connector.
    d. Disconnect CPA from lefthand rear side impact air bag module yellow electrical connector.
    e. Disconnect lefthand rear side impact air bag module yellow electrical connector.

2003–05
Zone 1

1. Position steering wheel in straight ahead position.
2. Turn ignition to Off position and remove key.
3. Remove rear seat lower cushion.
4. Remove SIR fuse from rear fuse center.
5. Remove Connector Position Assurance (CPA) lock from Electronic Frontal Sensor (EFS) connector. EFS is located on front lefthand side of engine compartment.
6. Disconnect EFS connector.

Zone 2

1. Position steering wheel in straight ahead position.
2. Turn ignition to Off position and remove key.
3. Remove rear seat lower cushion.
4. Remove SIR fuse from rear fuse center.
5. Remove front and rear carpet retainers from lefthand center pillar trim panel.
6. Remove lefthand center pillar trim panel from pillar.
7. Remove Connector Position Assurance (CPA) lock from lefthand Side Impact Sensor (SIS) connector.
8. Disconnect SIS connector.

Zone 3

1. Position steering wheel in straight ahead position.
2. Turn ignition to Off position and remove key.
3. Remove rear seat lower cushion.
4. Remove SIR fuse from rear fuse center.
5. Remove lefthand closeout/insulator panel from under lefthand side of instrument panel.
6. Remove Connector Position Assur-

ance (CPA) lock from steering wheel module yellow connector. Connector is located near steering column.
7. Disconnect steering wheel module connector from yellow harness connector.

Zone 5

1. Position steering wheel in straight ahead position.
2. Turn ignition to Off position and remove key.
3. Remove rear seat lower cushion.
4. Remove SIR fuse from rear fuse center.
5. Remove righthand closeout/insulator panel from under righthand side of instrument panel.
6. Remove Connector Position Assurance (CPA) lock from instrument panel module yellow connector. Connector is located under righthand side of instrument panel.
7. Disconnect instrument panel module connector from yellow harness connector.

Zone 6

1. Position steering wheel in straight ahead position.
2. Turn ignition to Off position and remove key.
3. Remove rear seat lower cushion.
4. Remove SIR fuse from rear fuse center.
5. Remove front and rear carpet retainers from righthand center pillar trim panel.
6. Remove righthand center pillar trim panel from pillar.
7. Remove Connector Position Assurance (CPA) lock from righthand Side Impact Sensor (SIS) connector.
8. Disconnect SIS connector.

Zone 7

1. Position steering wheel in straight ahead position.
2. Turn ignition to Off position and remove key.
3. Remove rear seat lower cushion.
4. Remove SIR fuse from rear fuse center.
5. Remove Connector Position Assurance (CPA) lock from lefthand driver's side impact module and seat belt pretensioner yellow connector. Connector is located under driver's seat.
6. Disconnect lefthand driver's side impact module and seat belt pretensioner yellow connector from harness connector.

Zone 8

1. Position steering wheel in straight ahead position.
2. Turn ignition to Off position and remove key.
3. Remove rear seat lower cushion.
4. Remove SIR fuse from rear fuse center.
5. Remove righthand rear passenger seat back.
6. Remove Connector Position Assurance (CPA) lock from rear righthand side impact module and seat belt pre-

tensioner yellow connector. Connector is located near righthand rear door jamb.
7. Disconnect rear righthand side impact module connector.
8. Remove CPA lock from righthand front side impact module yellow connector. Connector is located under passenger front seat.
9. Disconnect righthand side impact module and seat belt pretensioner yellow connector from harness connector.
10. Remove righthand closeout/insulator panel from under righthand side of instrument panel.
11. Remove CPA lock from instrument panel module yellow connector.
12. Disconnect instrument panel module connector from yellow harness connector.
13. Remove lefthand closeout/insulator panel from under lefthand side of instrument panel.
14. Remove CPA lock from steering wheel module yellow connector.
15. Disconnect steering wheel module connector from yellow harness connector.
16. Remove CPA lock from lefthand driver's side impact module and seat belt pretensioner yellow connector. Connector is located under driver's seat.
17. Disconnect lefthand driver's side impact module and seat belt pretensioner yellow connector from harness connector.
18. Remove lefthand rear passenger seat back.
19. Remove Connector Position Assurance (CPA) lock from rear lefthand side impact module and seat belt pretensioner yellow connector. Connector is located near lefthand rear door jamb.
20. Disconnect rear lefthand side impact module connector.

Zone 9

1. Position steering wheel in straight ahead position.
2. Turn ignition to Off position and remove key.
3. Remove rear seat lower cushion.
4. Remove SIR fuse from rear fuse center.
5. Remove Connector Position Assurance (CPA) lock from righthand passenger side impact module and seat belt pretensioner yellow connector. Connector is located under passenger seat.
6. Disconnect righthand side impact module and seat belt pretensioner yellow connector to vehicle harness connector.

Zone 10

1. Position steering wheel in straight ahead position.
2. Turn ignition to Off position and remove key.
3. Remove rear seat lower cushion.
4. Remove SIR fuse from rear fuse center.

5. Remove lefthand rear passenger seat back.
6. Remove Connector Position Assurance (CPA) lock from rear lefthand side impact module and seat belt pretensioner yellow connector. Connector is located near lefthand rear door jamb.
7. Disconnect rear lefthand side impact module connector.

Zone 12

1. Position steering wheel in straight ahead position.
2. Turn ignition to Off position and remove key.
3. Remove rear seat lower cushion.
4. Remove SIR fuse from rear fuse center.
5. Remove righthand rear passenger seat back.
6. Remove Connector Position Assurance (CPA) lock from rear righthand side impact module and seat belt pretensioner yellow connector. Connector is located near righthand rear door jamb.
7. Disconnect rear righthand side impact module connector.

ELDORADO

1. Place front wheels in straight-ahead position.
2. Turn ignition to Lock position and remove key.
3. Remove SIR fuse from trunk compartment fuse block.
4. Remove instrument panel lefthand sound insulator.
5. Disconnect CPA and both yellow two-way SIR electrical connectors at base of steering column.
6. Remove glove compartment.
7. Disconnect CPA and yellow two-way connector from passenger air bag module pigtail behind instrument panel.

GRAND PRIX & INTRIGUE

2001-02

1. Ensure front wheels are pointed straight-ahead.
2. Turn ignition switch to Lock position and remove ignition key.
3. Remove AIR BAG or SIR system fuse from instrument panel fuse block.
4. Remove lefthand underdash trim panel.
5. Disconnect Connector Position Assurance (CPA) and yellow air bag module connectors at base of steering column.
6. Disconnect passenger air bag module CPA and yellow air bag module connectors located to right of steering column.

2003-04

Zone 3

1. Position steering wheel in straight ahead position.
2. Turn ignition Off and remove key from ignition switch.
3. Remove instrument panel fuse block cover.

4. Remove SIR fuse from instrument panel fuse block.
5. Remove lefthand insulator panel from under lefthand side of instrument panel.
6. Remove Connector Position Assurance (CPA) cover from inflatable restraint steering wheel module coil connector. Connector is located at base of steering column.
7. Disconnect steering wheel module coil connector.

Zone 5

1. Position steering wheel in straight ahead position.
2. Turn ignition Off and remove key from ignition switch.
3. Remove instrument panel fuse block cover.
4. Remove SIR fuse from instrument panel fuse block.
5. Remove lefthand insulator panel from under lefthand side of instrument panel.
6. Remove Connector Position Assurance (CPA) cover from inflatable restraint instrument panel module connector. Connector is located on righthand side of steering column.
7. Disconnect instrument panel module connector.

Zone 9

1. Position steering wheel in straight ahead position.
2. Turn ignition Off and remove key from ignition switch.
3. Remove instrument panel fuse block cover.
4. Remove SIR fuse from instrument panel fuse block.
5. Remove lefthand insulator panel from under lefthand side of instrument panel.
6. Remove Connector Position Assurance (CPA) cover from inflatable restraint steering wheel module coil connector. Connector is located at base of steering column.
7. Disconnect steering wheel module coil connector.
8. Remove CPA cover from inflatable restraint instrument panel module connector. Connector is located on righthand side of steering column.
9. Disconnect instrument panel module connector.
10. Remove CPA cover from Sensing and Diagnostic Module (SDM). Connector is located under front righthand seat.
11. Disconnect SDM wiring harness connector.

2005

Zone 1

1. Ensure steering wheel is in straight ahead position.
2. Ensure ignition switch is in OFF position.
3. Remove key from ignition switch.
4. Remove SIR fuse from underhood fuse box.
5. Remove radiator upper air baffle and deflector.

6. Remove connector position assurance (CPA) from front end sensor connector.
7. Remove front end sensor connector from front end sensor.

Zone 2

1. Ensure steering wheel is in straight ahead position.
2. Ensure ignition switch is in OFF position.
3. Remove key from ignition switch.
4. Remove SIR fuse from underhood fuse box.
5. Remove rear door weatherstrip from pinchweld flange as required.
6. Remove screw button cover from sail panel.
7. Remove retaining screw using a flat-bladed tool, then the trim panel from vehicle.
8. Remove driver's door trim panel using suitable flatbladed tool.
9. Remove water deflector to access SIS, then the SIS CPA from lefthand side SIS connector.
10. Remove SIS connector from SIS.

Zone 3

1. Ensure steering wheel is in straight ahead position.
2. Ensure ignition switch is in OFF position.
3. Remove key from ignition switch.
4. Remove SIR fuse from underhood fuse box.
5. Remove driver's side sound insulator from instrument panel.
6. Remove connector position assurance (CPA) from steering wheel module coil yellow connector.
7. Disconnect steering wheel module coil yellow connector from vehicle harness yellow connector.

Zone 5

1. Ensure steering wheel is in straight ahead position.
2. Ensure ignition switch is in OFF position.
3. Remove key from ignition switch.
4. Remove SIR fuse from underhood fuse box.
5. Remove passenger side sound insulator from instrument panel.
6. Remove connector position assurance (CPA) from instrument panel.
7. Disconnect passenger side air bag module yellow connector from vehicle harness yellow connector.

Zone 6

1. Ensure steering wheel is in straight ahead position.
2. Ensure ignition switch is in OFF position.
3. Remove key from ignition switch.
4. Remove SIR fuse from underhood fuse box.
5. Remove righthand side rear sail panel using suitable flat bladed tool.
6. Remove connector position assurance (CPA) from passenger side roof panel air bag module connector.
7. Disconnect passenger side air bag

module wiring harness yellow connector from roof panel air bag module.

Zone 7

1. Ensure steering wheel is in straight ahead position.
2. Ensure ignition switch is in OFF position.
3. Remove key from ignition switch.
4. Remove SIR fuse from underhood fuse box.
5. Remove connector position assurance (CPA) from driver's side seat belt pretensioner connector from under driver's seat.
6. Disconnect driver's side seat belt pretensioner connector from vehicle harness connector.

Zone 9

1. Ensure steering wheel is in straight ahead position.
2. Ensure ignition switch is in OFF position.
3. Remove key from ignition switch.
4. Remove SIR fuse from underhood fuse box.
5. Remove righthand side rear sail trim panel using a suitable flatbladed tool.
6. Remove connector position assurance (CPA) from passenger side roof panel air bag module.
7. Disconnect passenger side air bag module wiring harness yellow connector from module.
8. Remove passenger side sound insulator from instrument panel.
9. Remove CPA from instrument panel yellow connector.
10. Disconnect passenger side air bag module yellow connector from vehicle harness yellow connector.
11. Remove driver's side sound insulator from instrument panel.
12. Remove CPA from driver's side air bag module coil yellow connector.
13. Disconnect driver's side air bag module coil yellow connector from vehicle harness yellow connector.
14. Remove CPA from driver's side seat belt pretensioner connector from under driver's seat.
15. Disconnect driver's side seat belt pretensioner connector from vehicle wiring harness connector.
16. Remove lefthand side rear sail panel using suitable flatbladed tool.
17. Remove CPA from driver's side roof panel air bag module connector.
18. Disconnect driver's side roof panel air bag module wiring harness yellow connector from module.
19. Remove CPA from passenger side seat belt pretensioner connector from under passenger seat.
20. Disconnect passenger side seat belt pretensioner connector from vehicle wiring harness connector.

GTO

ZONE 3

1. Ensure steering wheel is in straight ahead position.
2. Ensure ignition switch is in OFF position.

3. Remove SIR fuse from instrument panel fuse panel located near base of steering column.
4. Disconnect battery ground cable.
5. Remove upper steering column trim cover.
6. Release inflatable restraint steering wheel module coil connector locking tab.
7. Disconnect inflatable restraint steering wheel module coil connector.

ZONE 5

1. Ensure steering wheel is in straight ahead position.
2. Ensure ignition switch is in OFF position.
3. Remove SIR fuse from instrument panel fuse panel located near base of steering column.
4. Disconnect battery ground cable.
5. Remove glove compartment door.
6. Disconnect instrument panel module connector.

ZONE 8

1. Ensure steering wheel is in straight ahead position.
2. Ensure ignition switch is in OFF position.
3. Remove SIR fuse from instrument panel fuse panel located near base of steering column.
4. Disconnect battery ground cable.
5. Remove upper steering column trim cover.
6. Disconnect inflatable restraint steering wheel module coil connector locking tab.
7. Remove glove compartment door.
8. Disconnect passenger side air bag module connector.

G6

Refer to "2005" under "Alero, Grand Am, Malibu & Malibu Maxx" for disarming procedures.

IMPALA & MONTE CARLO

2001–02

1. Ensure front wheels are pointed straight-ahead.
2. Turn ignition switch to Off position and remove ignition key.
3. Remove lefthand instrument panel fuse access cover.
4. Remove SRS fuse from fuse block.
5. Disconnect Connector Position Assurance (CPA) from driver's air bag module coil connector, located at lefthand side of instrument panel.
6. Disconnect driver's air bag module coil connector.
7. Remove instrument panel righthand access hole cover.
8. Unclip driver's and passenger air bag modules' yellow four-way electrical connector from metal rail.
9. Disconnect CPA from passenger air bag module connector, located at righthand side if instrument panel.
10. Disconnect passenger air bag module connector.
11. Disconnect CPA from side impact air

bag module, located under driver's seat.
12. Disconnect side impact module.

2003–05

Zone 1

1. Position steering wheel in straight ahead position.
2. Turn ignition Off and remove key from ignition switch.
3. Remove instrument panel fuse block cover.
4. Remove SIR fuse from instrument panel fuse block.
5. Remove upper air baffle and deflector from radiator.
6. Remove orange Connector Position Assurance (CPA) cover from yellow sensor harness.
7. Disconnect sensor harness from sensor.

Zone 2, Impala

1. Position steering wheel in straight ahead position.
2. Turn ignition Off and remove key from ignition switch.
3. Remove instrument panel fuse block cover.
4. Remove SIR fuse from instrument panel fuse block.
5. Remove trim panel from lefthand center pillar.
6. Remove Side Impact Sensor (SIS) from center pillar.
7. Remove Connector Position Assurance (CPA) cover from SIS connector.
8. Disconnect SIS connector.

Zone 2, Monte Carlo

1. Position steering wheel in straight ahead position.
2. Turn ignition Off and remove key from ignition switch.
3. Remove instrument panel fuse block cover.
4. Remove SIR fuse from instrument panel fuse block.
5. Remove door handle trim bezel from lefthand front door trim panel.
6. Remove door trim panel to door mounting screws.
7. Pry trim panel away from door and disconnect power door lock and power window switch electrical connectors.
8. Remove trim panel from door.
9. Remove Side Impact Sensor (SIS) from mounting bracket on door impact beam.
10. Remove Connector Position Assurance (CPA) cover from SIS connector.
11. Disconnect SIS connector.

Zone 3

1. Position steering wheel in straight ahead position.
2. Turn ignition Off and remove key from ignition switch.
3. Remove instrument panel fuse block cover.
4. Remove SIR fuse from instrument panel fuse block.
5. Remove insulator panel from under lefthand side of instrument panel.

AIR BAG SYSTEM PRECAUTIONS

6. Remove Connector Position Assurance (CPA) cover from inflatable restraint steering wheel module coil connector. Connector is located at base of steering column.
7. Disconnect steering wheel module coil connector.

Zone 5

1. Position steering wheel in straight ahead position.
2. Turn ignition Off and remove key from ignition switch.
3. Remove instrument panel fuse block cover.
4. Remove SIR fuse from instrument panel fuse block.
5. Remove access panel from far righthand side of instrument panel.
6. Remove Connector Position Assurance (CPA) cover from instrument panel module connector.
7. Disconnect instrument panel module connector.

Zone 7

1. Position steering wheel in straight ahead position.
2. Turn ignition Off and remove key from ignition switch.
3. Remove instrument panel fuse block cover.
4. Remove SIR fuse from instrument panel fuse block.
5. Remove Connector Position Assurance (CPA) cover from lefthand side impact module connector. Connector is located under driver's seat.
6. Disconnect side impact module connector.

Zone 9

1. Position steering wheel in straight ahead position.
2. Turn ignition Off and remove key from ignition switch.
3. Remove instrument panel fuse block cover.
4. Remove SIR fuse from instrument panel fuse block.
5. Remove insulator panel from under lefthand side of instrument panel.
6. Remove Connector Position Assurance (CPA) cover from inflatable restraint steering wheel module coil connector. Connector is located at base of steering column.
7. Disconnect steering wheel module coil connector.
8. Remove access panel from far righthand side of instrument panel.
9. Remove Connector Position Assurance (CPA) cover from instrument panel module connector.
10. Disconnect instrument panel module connector.
11. Remove Connector Position Assurance (CPA) cover from lefthand side impact module connector. Connector is located under driver's seat.
12. Disconnect side impact module connector.

LACROSSE

ZONE 1

1. Ensure steering wheel is in straight ahead position.
2. Ensure ignition switch is in OFF position.
3. Remove ignition key from ignition switch.
4. Remove SIR fuse from underhood fuse box.
5. Remove radiator upper air baffle and deflector.
6. Remove connector position assurance (CPA) from both front end sensor connectors.
7. Remove both front end sensor connectors from front end sensors.

ZONE 2

1. Ensure steering wheel is in straight ahead position.
2. Ensure ignition switch is in OFF position.
3. Remove ignition key from ignition switch.
4. Remove SIR fuse from underhood fuse box.
5. Remove driver's side rear quarter upper panel using suitable flat bladed tool.
6. Remove connector position assurance (CPA) from driver's side roof panel air bag module connector.
7. Disconnect driver's side roof panel air bag module wiring harness yellow connector from module.
8. Remove driver's side door trim panel using suitable flatbladed tool.
9. Remove water deflector to access SIS unit.
10. Remove SIS CPA from driver's side SIS connector.
11. Remove SIS connector from SIS unit.

ZONE 3

1. Ensure steering wheel is in straight ahead position.
2. Ensure ignition switch is in OFF position.
3. Remove ignition key from ignition switch.
4. Remove SIR fuse from underhood fuse box.
5. Remove driver's side sound insulator from instrument panel.
6. Remove connector position assurance (CPA) from steering wheel module coil yellow connector.
7. Disconnect steering wheel module coil yellow connector from vehicle harness yellow connector.

ZONE 5

1. Ensure steering wheel is in straight ahead position.
2. Ensure ignition switch is in OFF position.
3. Remove ignition key from ignition switch.
4. Remove SIR fuse from underhood fuse box.
5. Remove passenger side sound insulator from instrument panel using suitable flat-bladed tool.
6. Remove CPA from instrument panel

module yellow connector.
7. Disconnect instrument panel yellow connector from vehicle harness connector.

ZONE 6

1. Ensure steering wheel is in straight ahead position.
2. Ensure ignition switch is in OFF position.
3. Remove ignition key from ignition switch.
4. Remove SIR fuse from underhood fuse box.
5. Remove righthand rear trim panel.
6. Remove CPA from passenger side roof panel air bag module connector.
7. Disconnect passenger side roof panel air bag module wiring harness yellow connector from passenger side roof panel air bag module.
8. Remove passenger side door trim panel.
9. Remove water deflector to locate side impact sensor.
10. Remove side impact sensor CPA from passenger side impact sensor.
11. Remove side impact sensor connector from side impact sensor.

ZONE 7

1. Ensure steering wheel is in straight ahead position.
2. Ensure ignition switch is in OFF position.
3. Remove ignition key from ignition switch.
4. Remove SIR fuse from underhood fuse box.
5. Remove CPA from driver's side seat belt pretensioner connector located under seat bottom.
6. Disconnect driver's seat belt pretensioner connector from vehicle wiring harness connector.

ZONE 9

1. Ensure steering wheel is in straight ahead position.
2. Ensure ignition switch is in OFF position.
3. Remove ignition key from ignition switch.
4. Remove SIR fuse from underhood fuse box.
5. Remove CPA from driver's seat belt pretensioner connector located under driver's seat bottom.
6. Disconnect seat belt pretensioner driver's side connector from vehicle wiring harness connector.
7. Remove righthand side rear trim panel.
8. Remove CPA from passenger side roof panel air bag module connector.
9. Disconnect passenger side roof panel module wiring harness yellow connector from module.
10. Remove passenger side sound insulator from instrument panel.
11. Remove CPA from instrument panel module yellow connector.
12. Disconnect instrument panel module yellow connector from vehicle harness yellow connector.
13. Remove driver's side sound insulator

from instrument panel.
14. Remove CPA from steering wheel module coil yellow connector.
15. Disconnect coil yellow connector from vehicle harness yellow connector.
16. Remove CPA from driver's side seat belt pretensioner connector located under driver's seat bottom.
17. Disconnect seat belt pretensioner connector from vehicle wiring harness connector.
18. Remove lefthand side rear trim panel.
19. Remove CPA from driver's side roof panel air bag module connector.
20. Disconnect driver's side roof panel air bag module wiring harness yellow connector from module.

LUMINA

1. Ensure front wheels are pointed straight-ahead.
2. Turn ignition to Lock position and remove ignition key.
3. Remove instrument panel fuse block door.
4. Remove Fuse 21 from fuse block.
5. Remove instrument panel lefthand sound insulator.
6. Disconnect CPA and yellow air bag module electrical connectors at base of steering column.
7. Remove instrument panel righthand sound insulator.
8. Open glove compartment door.
9. Disconnect passenger air bag module CPA and yellow electrical connector.

METRO

1. Ensure front wheels are pointed straight-ahead.
2. Turn ignition to Lock position.
3. Remove AIR BAG fuse from fuse block near steering wheel base.
4. Remove steering wheel side cap.
5. Remove Connector Position Assurance (CPA) and disconnect yellow two-way electrical connector for driver's air bag module.
6. Pull glove compartment out while pushing inward on left and righthand stoppers.
7. Remove CPA and disconnect passenger air bag module electrical connector.

PARK AVENUE

2001-02

1. Ensure front wheels are pointed straight-ahead.
2. Turn ignition to Lock position and remove key.
3. Remove SIR fuse from underhood fuse block.
4. Remove lefthand sound insulator.
5. Disconnect Connector Position Assurance (CPA) and driver's air bag module yellow two-way connector at base of steering column.
6. Remove righthand sound insulator.
7. Disconnect CPA and yellow two-way connector from passenger air bag module wiring.
8. Disconnect CPA and yellow two-way connector from righthand side impact air bag module electrical connector

under front seat.

2003-05

Zone 2

1. Position steering wheel in straight ahead position.
2. Turn ignition Off and remove key from ignition switch.
3. Remove SIR fuse from underhood fuse center.
4. Remove trim panel from lefthand center pillar.
5. Remove Connector Position Assurance (CPA) cover from Side Impact Sensor (SIS) connector.
6. Disconnect SIS connector.

Zone 3

1. Position steering wheel in straight ahead position.
2. Turn ignition Off and remove key from ignition switch.
3. Remove SIR fuse from underhood fuse center.
4. Remove insulator panel from under lefthand side of instrument panel.
5. Remove Connector Position Assurance (CPA) cover from steering wheel module coil yellow connector. Connector is located near steering column.
6. Disconnect steering wheel module coil yellow connector.

Zone 5

1. Position steering wheel in straight ahead position.
2. Turn ignition Off and remove key from ignition switch.
3. Remove SIR fuse from underhood fuse center.
4. Remove insulator panel from under righthand side of instrument panel.
5. Remove Connector Position Assurance (CPA) cover from instrument panel module connector. Connector is located under righthand side of instrument panel.
6. Disconnect instrument panel module connector.

Zone 6

1. Position steering wheel in straight ahead position.
2. Turn ignition Off and remove key from ignition switch.
3. Remove SIR fuse from underhood fuse center.
4. Remove trim panel from righthand center pillar.
5. Remove Connector Position Assurance (CPA) cover from Side Impact Sensor (SIS) connector.
6. Disconnect SIS connector.

Zone 7

1. Position steering wheel in straight ahead position.
2. Turn ignition Off and remove key from ignition switch.
3. Remove SIR fuse from underhood fuse center.
4. Remove Connector Position Assurance (CPA) cover from driver's side impact module connector. Connector

is located under driver's seat.
5. Disconnect driver's side impact module connector.

Zone 9

1. Position steering wheel in straight ahead position.
2. Turn ignition Off and remove key from ignition switch.
3. Remove SIR fuse from underhood fuse center.
4. Remove Connector Position Assurance (CPA) cover from passenger side impact module connector. Connector is located under passenger front seat.
5. Disconnect passenger side impact module connector.
6. Remove insulator panel from under righthand side of instrument panel.
7. Remove CPA cover from instrument panel module connector. Connector is located under righthand side of instrument panel.
8. Disconnect instrument panel module connector.
9. Remove insulator panel from under lefthand side of instrument panel.
10. Remove CPA cover from steering wheel module coil yellow connector. Connector is located near steering column.
11. Disconnect steering wheel module coil yellow connector.
12. Remove CPA cover from driver's side impact module connector. Connector is located under driver's seat.
13. Disconnect driver's side impact module connector.

PRIZM

1. Ensure front wheels are pointed straight-ahead.
2. Turn ignition to Lock position.
3. Remove IGN and CIG fuses from junction block No. 1 near base of steering column.
4. Remove steering column lower trim cover.
5. Remove Connector Position Assurance (CPA) and disconnect yellow two-way electrical connector at base of steering column.
6. Remove glove compartment from instrument panel.
7. Remove CPA and disconnect yellow two-way connector from passenger air bag module.
8. Release, unlock and disconnect side impact air bag modules' electrical connectors.

SEVILLE

2001-02

Refer to "2001–02" under "DeVille" for disarming procedure.

2003-04

Zone 2

1. Position steering wheel in straight ahead position.
2. Turn ignition switch to Off position and remove key.

3. Remove rear seat lower cushion.
4. Remove SIR fuse from rear fuse center.
5. Remove trim panel front lefthand center pillar.
6. Remove Connector Position Assurance (CPA) cover from Side Impact Sensor (SIS) connector.
7. Disconnect SIS connector.

Zone 3

1. Position steering wheel in straight ahead position.
2. Turn ignition switch to Off position and remove key.
3. Remove rear seat lower cushion.
4. Remove SIR fuse from rear fuse center.
5. Remove insulator panel from under lefthand side of instrument panel.
6. Remove Connector Position Assurance (CPA) cover from steering wheel module coil yellow connector. Connector is located near steering column.
7. Disconnect steering wheel module coil yellow connector.

Zone 5

1. Position steering wheel in straight ahead position.
2. Turn ignition switch to Off position and remove key.
3. Remove rear seat lower cushion.
4. Remove SIR fuse from rear fuse center.
5. Remove insulator panel from under righthand side of instrument panel.
6. Remove Connector Position Assurance (CPA) from instrument panel module to vehicle harness yellow connector. Connector is located under righthand side of instrument panel.
7. Disconnect instrument panel module yellow connector.

Zone 6

1. Position steering wheel in straight ahead position.
2. Turn ignition switch to Off position and remove key.
3. Remove rear seat lower cushion.
4. Remove SIR fuse from rear fuse center.
5. Remove trim panel from righthand center pillar.
6. Remove Connector Position Assurance (CPA) cover from Side Impact Sensor (SIS) connector.
7. Disconnect SIS connector.

Zone 7

1. Position steering wheel in straight ahead position.
2. Turn ignition switch to Off position and remove key.
3. Remove rear seat lower cushion.
4. Remove SIR fuse from rear fuse center.
5. Remove Connector Position Assurance (CPA) covers from lefthand side impact module and pretensioner connectors. Connectors are located under driver's seat.
6. Disconnect lefthand side impact and pretensioner connectors.

Zone 9

1. Position steering wheel in straight ahead position.
2. Turn ignition switch to Off position and remove key.
3. Remove rear seat lower cushion.
4. Remove SIR fuse from rear fuse center.
5. Remove Connector Position Assurance (CPA) covers from righthand side impact module and pretensioner connectors. Connectors are located under passenger front seat.
6. Disconnect righthand side impact and pretensioner connectors.
7. Remove insulator panel from under righthand side of instrument panel.
8. Remove CPA from instrument panel module to vehicle harness yellow connector. Connector is located under righthand side of instrument panel.
9. Disconnect instrument panel module yellow connector.
10. Remove insulator panel from under lefthand side of instrument panel.
11. Remove CPA cover from steering wheel module coil yellow connector. Connector is located near steering column.
12. Disconnect steering wheel module coil yellow connector.
13. Remove CPA covers from lefthand side impact module and pretensioner connectors. Connectors are located under driver's seat.
14. Disconnect lefthand side impact and pretensioner connectors.

STS

ZONE 1

1. Ensure steering wheel is in straight ahead position.
2. Ensure ignition is in OFF position.
3. Remove rear seat cushion.
4. Remove AIR BAG (IGN) fuse in righthand rear fuse center and AIR BAG (BATT) fuse from lefthand rear fuse center.
5. Remove radiator cover, both upper radiator support brackets and push radiator toward engine to access front sensors.
6. Remove both CPA's from front end sensor connectors.
7. Remove both connectors from sensors.

ZONE 2

1. Ensure steering wheel is in straight ahead position.
2. Ensure ignition is in OFF position.
3. Remove rear seat cushion.
4. Remove AIR BAG (IGN) fuse in righthand rear fuse center and AIR BAG (BATT) fuse from lefthand rear fuse center.
5. Remove lefthand side carpet trim retainer and pull carpet back to access driver's side roof panel air bag module connector.
6. Remove CPA form roof panel air bag module yellow connector.
7. Disconnect module yellow connector from driver's side roof panel air bag module.

8. Remove lefthand side center pillar trim panel.
9. Remove driver's side impact sensor CPA from driver's side impact sensor connector.
10. Remove driver's side impact sensor connector from driver's side impact sensor.

ZONE 3

1. Ensure steering wheel is in straight ahead position.
2. Ensure ignition is in OFF position.
3. Remove rear seat cushion.
4. Remove AIR BAG (IGN) fuse in righthand rear fuse center and AIR BAG (BATT) fuse from lefthand rear fuse center.
5. Remove driver's side sound insulator from instrument panel.
6. Remove CPA from driver's side steering wheel module coil yellow connector.
7. Disconnect steering wheel module coil yellow connector from vehicle harness yellow connector.

ZONE 5

1. Ensure steering wheel is in straight ahead position.
2. Ensure ignition is in OFF position.
3. Remove rear seat cushion.
4. Remove AIR BAG (IGN) fuse in righthand rear fuse center and AIR BAG (BATT) fuse from lefthand rear fuse center.
5. Remove passenger side insulator from instrument panel.
6. Remove CPA from instrument panel yellow connector.
7. Disconnect instrument panel yellow connector from vehicle harness yellow connector.

ZONE 6

1. Ensure steering wheel is in straight ahead position.
2. Ensure ignition is in OFF position.
3. Remove rear seat cushion.
4. Remove AIR BAG (IGN) fuse in righthand rear fuse center and AIR BAG (BATT) fuse from lefthand rear fuse center.
5. Remove righthand side carpet trim retainers, then push rear seat back from rear pillar to access passenger side roof panel air bag module connector.
6. Remove CPA from passenger side roof panel air bag module yellow connector.
7. Disconnect passenger side roof panel air bag module yellow connector from passenger side roof panel air bag module.
8. Remove passenger side center trim panel.
9. Remove passenger side impact sensor CPA from sensor connector.
10. Remove passenger side impact sensor connector from sensor.

ZONE 7

1. Ensure steering wheel is in straight ahead position.
2. Ensure ignition is in OFF position.

3. Remove rear seat cushion.
4. Remove AIR BAG (IGN) fuse in right-hand rear fuse center and AIR BAG (BATT) fuse from lefthand rear fuse center.
5. Remove both CPA's from driver's side impact air bag module and seat belt pretensioner yellow connector from under driver's seat bottom.
6. Disconnect driver's side impact air bag module and pretensioner yellow connector from vehicle harness yellow connector.

ZONE 8

1. Ensure steering wheel is in straight ahead position.
2. Ensure ignition is in OFF position.
3. Remove rear seat cushion.
4. Remove AIR BAG (IGN) fuse in right-hand rear fuse center and AIR BAG (BATT) fuse from lefthand rear fuse center.
5. Remove righthand side carpet trim retainer, then push rear seat back to access passenger side roof panel air bag module connector.
6. Remove CPA from passenger side roof panel air bag module yellow connector.
7. Disconnect passenger side roof panel air bag module yellow connector from module.
8. Remove passenger side sound insulator from instrument panel.
9. Remove CPA from instrument panel yellow connector.
10. Disconnect instrument panel yellow connector from vehicle harness yellow connector.
11. Remove both CPA locks form passenger side impact air bag module and seat belt pretensioner yellow connector located under passenger seat bottom.
12. Disconnect passenger side impact air bag module and pretensioner yellow connector from vehicle harness yellow connector.
13. Remove driver's side sound insulator from instrument panel.
14. Remove CPA from steering wheel module coil yellow connector.
15. Disconnect steering wheel module coil yellow connector from vehicle harness yellow connector.
16. Remove both CPA's locks form driver's side impact air bag module and seat belt pretensioner yellow connector from under driver's seat.
17. Disconnect driver's side impact air bag module and pretensioner yellow connector from vehicle harness yellow connector.
18. Remove driver's side carpet trim retainers, then push rear seat back away from pillar to access driver's side roof panel air bag module connector.
19. Remove CPA from module yellow connector.
20. Disconnect module yellow connector from module.

ZONE 9

1. Ensure steering wheel is in straight ahead position.

2. Ensure ignition is in OFF position.
3. Remove rear seat cushion.
4. Remove AIR BAG (IGN) fuse in right-hand rear fuse center and AIR BAG (BATT) fuse from lefthand rear fuse center.
5. Remove both CPA's from passenger side impact air bag module and seat belt pretensioner yellow connector from under passenger seat bottom.
6. Disconnect passenger side impact air bag module and pretensioner yellow connector from vehicle harness yellow connector.

VIBE

ZONE 1

1. Ensure front wheels are pointed straight-ahead.
2. Turn ignition switch to Off position and remove key.
3. Remove SIR Fuse from junction block, located near base of steering column.
4. Locate righthand front end discriminating sensor electrical connector.
5. Remove Connector Position Assurance (CPA) from righthand front end discriminating sensor connector.
6. Remove righthand front end discriminating sensor electrical connector from front end discriminating sensor.
7. Open hood and locate lefthand front end discriminating sensor electrical connector.
8. Remove Connector Position Assurance (CPA) from lefthand front end discriminating sensor connector.
9. Remove lefthand front end discriminating sensor electrical connector from front end discriminating sensor.

ZONE 2

1. Ensure front wheels are pointed straight-ahead.
2. Turn ignition switch to Off position and remove key.
3. Remove SIR Fuse from junction block, located near base of steering column.
4. Remove lefthand front seat belt lower anchor bolt trim cover and front seat belt lower anchor bolt.
5. Remove lefthand front door and rear door sill plates.
6. Remove lefthand center pillar lower trim panel.
7. Remove front seat shoulder belt guide adjuster trim cover and bolt and left-hand front seat shoulder belt guide adjuster.
8. Disconnect pretensioner electrical connector, then remove bolts and front seat belt retractor.
9. Remove side impact sensor electrical connector.

ZONE 3

1. Ensure front wheels are pointed straight-ahead.
2. Turn ignition switch to Off position and remove key.
3. Remove SIR Fuse from junction block, located near base of steering column.
4. Remove lower steering column trim cover.
5. Release inflatable restraint steering

wheel module coil connector locking mechanism.
6. Disconnect inflatable restraint steering wheel module coil connector.

ZONE 4

1. Ensure front wheels are pointed straight-ahead.
2. Turn ignition switch to Off position and remove key.
3. Remove SIR Fuse from junction block, located near base of steering column.
4. Release inflatable restraint steering wheel module coil connector locking mechanism.
5. Disconnect inflatable restraint steering wheel module coil connector.
6. Open instrument panel compartment door and remove screw .
7. Compress each side of compartment, until upper tabs release and remove compartment by pulling out to disconnect lower tabs.
8. Release and unlock instrument panel module connector, then disconnect module pigtail.
9. Release, then unlock driver's and passenger seat module connectors.
10. Disconnect driver's and passenger seat modules.

ZONE 5

1. Ensure front wheels are pointed straight-ahead.
2. Turn ignition switch to Off position and remove key.
3. Remove SIR Fuse from junction block, located near base of steering column.
4. Open instrument panel compartment door and remove screw .
5. Compress each side of compartment, until upper tabs release and remove compartment by pulling out to disconnect lower tabs.
6. Release and unlock instrument panel module connector, then disconnect module pigtail.

ZONE 6

1. Ensure front wheels are pointed straight-ahead.
2. Turn ignition switch to Off position and remove key.
3. Remove SIR Fuse from junction block, located near base of steering column.
4. Remove righthand front seat belt lower anchor bolt trim cover and front seat belt lower anchor bolt.
5. Remove righthand front door and rear door sill plates.
6. Remove righthand center pillar lower trim panel.
7. Remove front seat shoulder belt guide adjuster trim cover and bolt and right-hand front seat shoulder belt guide adjuster.
8. Disconnect pretensioner electrical connector, then remove bolts and front seat belt retractor.
9. Remove side impact sensor electrical connector.

ZONE 7

1. Ensure front wheels are pointed straight-ahead.

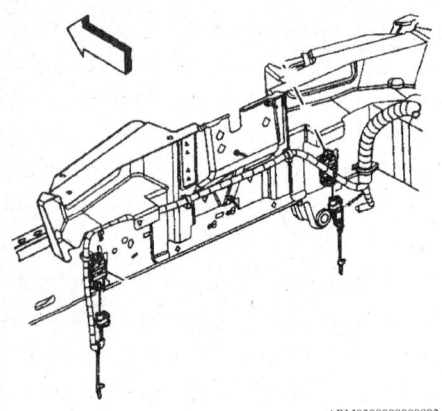

Fig. 2 Zone 1 component removal. XLR

ARM0300000000802

2. Turn ignition switch to Off position and remove key.
3. Remove SIR Fuse from junction block, located near base of steering column.
4. Release, then unlock driver's and passenger seat module connectors.
5. Disconnect driver's and passenger seat modules.

ZONE 9

1. Ensure front wheels are pointed straight-ahead.
2. Turn ignition switch to Off position and remove key.
3. Remove SIR Fuse from junction block, located near base of steering column.
4. Release, then unlock driver's and passenger seat module connectors.
5. Disconnect driver's and passenger seat modules.

ZONE 10

1. Ensure steering wheel is in straight ahead position.
2. Ensure ignition switch is in OFF position.
3. Remove AM2 fuse from function box at base of steering column.
4. Remove rear door sill plate.
5. Remove body side lower rear seat trim molding.
6. Disconnect side impact air bag sensor electrical connector.

ZONE 12

1. Ensure steering wheel is in straight ahead position.
2. Ensure ignition switch is in OFF position.
3. Remove AM2 fuse from function box at base of steering column.
4. Remove rear door sill plate.
5. Remove body side lower rear seat trim molding.
6. Disconnect side impact air bag sensor electrical connector.

XLR

ZONE 1

1. Ensure that steering wheel is pointed in straight ahead position.
2. Ensure ignition is in Off position.
3. Remove kick panel to access I/P fuse block.

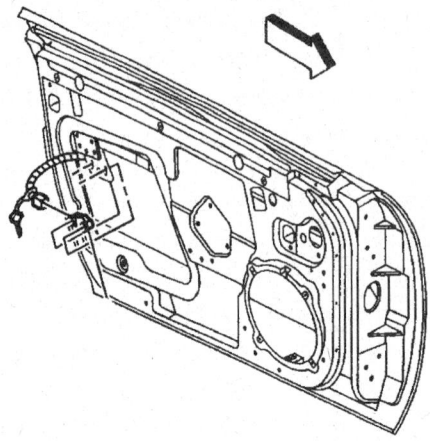

Fig. 3 Zone 2 component removal. XLR

ARM0300000000803

4. Remove SIR fuse (#16) from fuse block.
5. Open hood and remove air cleaner assembly.
6. Locate and remove lefthand and righthand electronic frontal sensors as indicated, **Fig. 2.**
7. Remove lefthand and righthand CPA's from connecting EFS as indicated, **Fig. 2.**
8. Remove lefthand and righthand EFS connector from EFS.

ZONE 2

1. Ensure that steering wheel is pointed in straight ahead position.
2. Ensure ignition is in Off position.
3. Remove kick panel to access I/P fuse block.
4. Remove SIR fuse (#16) from fuse block.
5. Open lefthand and righthand doors, then remove door trim panels.
6. Locate and remove CPA from SIS connector, then the SIS connector from SIS, **Fig. 3.**

ZONE 3

1. Ensure that steering wheel is pointed in straight ahead position.
2. Ensure ignition is in Off position.
3. Remove kick panel to access I/P fuse block.
4. Remove SIR fuse (#16) from fuse block.
5. Remove lefthand driver's side sound insulator from I/P.
6. Remove CPA from vehicle harness yellow connector.
7. Disconnect steering wheel module coil yellow connector from vehicle harness yellow connector, **Fig. 4.**

ZONE 4

1. Ensure that steering wheel is pointed in straight ahead position.
2. Ensure ignition is in Off position.
3. Remove kick panel to access I/P fuse block.
4. Remove SIR fuse (#16) from fuse block.
5. Remove righthand sound insulator from I/P.

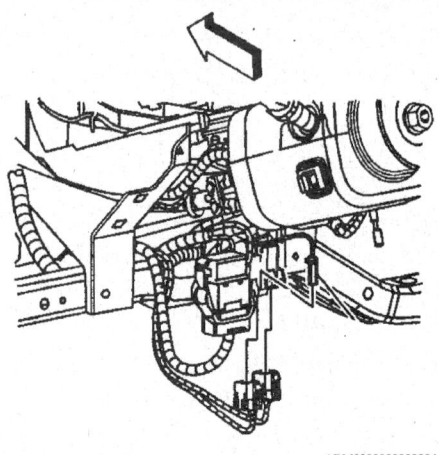

Fig. 4 Zone 3 component removal. XLR

ARM0300000000804

6. Remove CPA from vehicle harness yellow connector.
7. Disconnect I/P module yellow connector from vehicle harness yellow connector, **Fig. 5.**
8. Remove both CPA's from righthand front passenger side impact air bag module and seat belt pretensioner yellow connector under passenger seat, **Fig. 6.**
9. Remove lefthand driver's side sound insulator from I/P.
10. Remove CPA from vehicle yellow harness from under steering column.
11. Disconnect steering wheel module coil yellow connector from vehicle harness yellow connector.
12. Remove both CPA's from lefthand front driver's side impact air bag module and pretenstioner yellow connector under driver's seat, **Fig. 7.**
13. Disconnect vehicle harness yellow connector from lefthand front side impact air bag module and pretensioner yellow connector.

ZONE 5

1. Ensure that steering wheel is pointed in straight ahead position.
2. Ensure ignition is in Off position.
3. Remove kick panel to access I/P fuse block.
4. Remove SIR fuse (#16) from fuse block.
5. Remove righthand passenger side sound insulator panel.
6. Remove and disconnect CPA from vehicle harness yellow connector.

ZONE 6

1. Ensure that steering wheel is pointed in straight ahead position.
2. Ensure ignition is in Off position.
3. Remove kick panel to access I/P fuse block.
4. Remove SIR fuse (#16) from fuse block.
5. Open righthand side passenger door and remove door trim panel using suitable removal tool.
6. Remove CPA from SIS connector, then the SIS connector form SIS, **Fig. 3.**

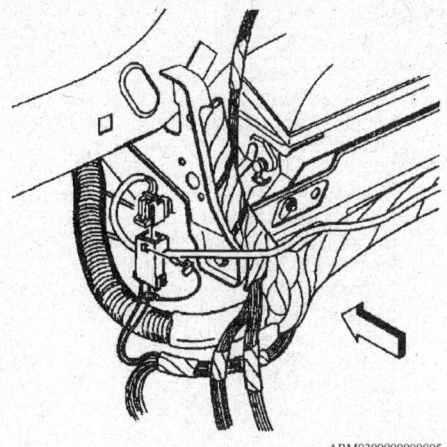

Fig. 5 Vehicle harness location. XLR

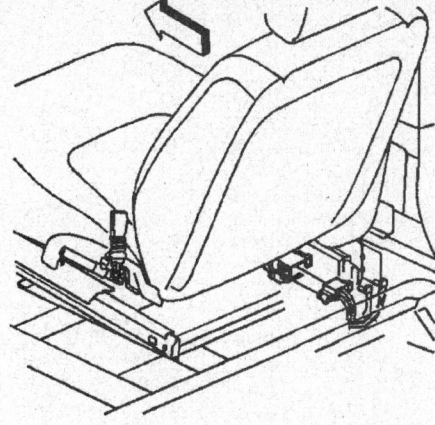

Fig. 6 Passenger's side impact air bag module connector. XLR

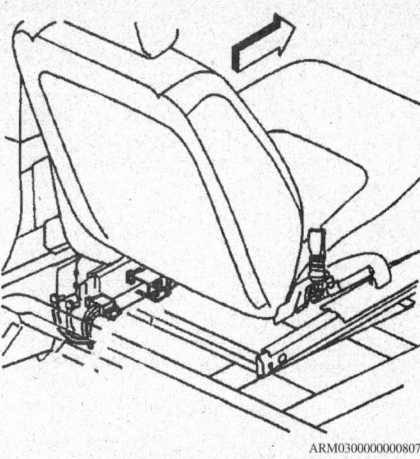

Fig. 7 Driver's seat electrical components. XLR

ZONE 7

1. Ensure that steering wheel is pointed in straight ahead position.
2. Ensure ignition is in Off position.
3. Remove kick panel to access I/P fuse block.
4. Remove SIR fuse (#16) from fuse block.
5. Remove both CPA's from lefthand from driver's side impact air bag module and pretensioner yellow connector from under driver's seat, **Fig. 7.**

ZONE 9

1. Ensure that steering wheel is pointed in straight ahead position.
2. Ensure ignition is in Off position.
3. Remove kick panel to access I/P fuse block.
4. Remove SIR fuse (#16) from fuse block.
5. Remove and disconnect both CPA's from righthand front passenger side impact air bag module and seat belt pretensioner yellow connector from under passenger seat, **Fig. 6.**

Arming

ALERO, GRAND AM, MALIBU & MALIBU MAXX

2001-02

1. Ensure front wheel are in straight ahead position.
2. Place ignition in Lock position and remove ignition key.
3. Connect yellow two-way connector to passenger air bag module pigtail and install CPA.
4. Connect yellow two-way SIR electrical connector and install CPA.
5. Install AIR BAG fuse into fuse block.
6. **From safe location at sides or below air bag modules,** turn ignition switch to On position.
7. Ensure SIR lamp flashes seven times and turns off.

2003-04

Zone 3

1. Connect steering wheel module coil connector.
2. Install Connector Position Assurance (CPA) cover onto steering wheel module coil connector. Connector is located under lefthand side of instrument panel.
3. Install AIR BAG fuse into junction block.
4. Install junction block access panel onto lefthand side of instrument panel.
5. **From safe location at sides or below air bag modules,** turn ignition switch to On position.
6. Ensure SIR lamp flashes seven times and turns off.

Zone 5

1. Connect instrument panel module electrical connector.
2. Install Connector Position Assurance (CPA) cover onto instrument panel module connector. Connector is located above righthand instrument panel wiring harness junction block.
3. Install junction block access panel onto righthand side of instrument panel.
4. Install AIR BAG fuse into lefthand junction block.
5. Install junction block access panel onto lefthand side of instrument panel.
6. **From safe location at sides or below air bag modules,** turn ignition switch to On position.
7. Ensure SIR lamp flashes seven times and turns off.

2005

Zone 1

1. Remove ignition key from switch.
2. Connect both front end sensor connectors to front end sensor.
3. Connect both CPA's to front end sensor connectors.
4. Install AIR BAG (IGN) and AIR BAG (BATT) fuses into BCM fuse center.
5. From a position away from air bag modules, turn ignition switch to ON position. AIR BAG indicator will flash the turn OFF.

Zone 2

1. Remove ignition key from switch.
2. Install driver's side impact sensor connector to side impact sensor.
3. Install CPA to driver's side impact sensor connector.
4. Install driver's side door trim panel.
5. Connect driver's side roof panel air bag module connector to vehicle harness connector.
6. Install CPA to roof panel air bag module connector.
7. Install garnish molding to upper lock pillar.
8. Connect driver's side seat belt pretensioner and install CPA.
9. Install lower center trim pillar.
10. Install AIR BAG (IGN) and AIR BAG (BATT) fuses into BCM fuse center, then the cover.
11. From a position away from air bag modules, turn ignition switch to ON position. AIR BAG indicator will flash the turn OFF.

Zone 3

1. Remove ignition key from switch.
2. Connect driver's side air bag module coil connector to vehicle harness connector.
3. Install CPA to steering wheel coil connector.
4. Install driver's side outer trim cover to instrument panel.
5. Install AIR BAG (IGN) and AIR BAG (BATT) fuses into BCM fuse center, then the cover.
6. From a position away from air bag modules, turn ignition switch to ON position. AIR BAG indicator will flash the turn OFF.

Zone 5

1. Remove ignition key from switch.
2. Connect passenger side air bag module connector to vehicle harness connector.
3. Install CPA to air bag module connector.
4. Install passenger side outer trim

cover to instrument panel.

5. Install AIR BAG (IGN) and AIR BAG (BATT) fuses into BCM fuse center, then the cover.
6. From a position away from air bag modules, turn ignition switch to ON position. AIR BAG indicator will flash the turn OFF.

Zone 6

1. Remove ignition key from switch.
2. Install passenger side impact air bag sensor connector to side impact sensor.
3. Install CPA to passenger side impact sensor.
4. Install passenger side door trim panel.
5. Connect roof panel air bag module connector to harness connector.
6. Install CPA to roof panel air bag module connector.
7. Install garnish trim panel molding.
8. Connect driver's side seat belt pretensioner and install CPA.
9. Install lower center pillar.
10. Install AIR BAG (IGN) and AIR BAG (BATT) fuses into BCM fuse center, then the cover.
11. From a position away from air bag modules, turn ignition switch to ON position. AIR BAG indicator will flash the turn OFF.

Zone 7

1. Remove ignition key from switch.
2. Connect vehicle harness yellow connector to driver's side impact module yellow connector.
3. Install CPA to driver's side impact yellow connector.
4. Install AIR BAG (IGN) and AIR BAG (BATT) fuses into BCM fuse center, then the cover.
5. From a position away from air bag modules, turn ignition switch to ON position. AIR BAG indicator will flash the turn OFF.

Zone 8

1. Remove ignition key from switch.
2. Connect driver's side roof panel air bag module connector to vehicle harness connector.
3. Install CPA to roof panel air bag module connector.
4. Install garnish trim panel molding.
5. Connect driver's side seat belt pretensioner connector.
6. Install CPA to seat belt pretensioner.
7. Install lower center trim panel.
8. Connect driver's side air bag module coil connector to vehicle harness connector.
9. Install CPA to steering wheel module coil connector.
10. Install driver's side outer trim cover panel.
11. Connect passenger side air bag module connector to vehicle harness connector.
12. Install CPA to passenger side air bag module connector.
13. Install righthand side outer trim panel.
14. Connect passenger side seat belt pre-

tensioner connector.

15. Install CPA to seat belt pretensioner connector.
16. Instal righthand side lower center trim panel.
17. Connect passenger side roof panel air bag module connector to vehicle harness connector.
18. Install CPA to module connector.
19. Install righthand side upper lock pillar garnish trim panel.
20. Install AIR BAG (IGN) and AIR BAG (BATT) fuses into BCM fuse center, then the cover.
21. From a position away from air bag modules, turn ignition switch to ON position. AIR BAG indicator will flash the turn OFF.

Zone 9

1. Remove ignition key from switch.
2. Connect vehicle harness yellow connector to passenger side impact module yellow connector.
3. Install CPA to passenger side impact module yellow connector.
4. Install AIR BAG (IGN) and AIR BAG (BATT) fuses into BCM fuse center, then the cover.
5. From a position away from air bag modules, turn ignition switch to ON position. AIR BAG indicator will flash the turn OFF.

AURORA

2001-02

1. Remove key from ignition switch.
2. Connect righthand side impact air bag module yellow connector to vehicle harness yellow connector located under righthand front seat.
3. Install connector position assurance (CPA) to righthand side impact air bag module yellow connector.
4. Connect lefthand side impact air bag module yellow connector to vehicle harness yellow connector located under driver's seat.
5. Install CPA to lefthand side impact air bag module yellow connector.
6. Connect passenger air bag module yellow connector to vehicle harness yellow connector located above righthand sound insulator.
7. Install CPA to passenger air bag module yellow connector.
8. Install instrument panel righthand side sound insulator.
9. Connect driver's air bag module yellow connector to vehicle harness yellow connector located next to steering column.
10. Install CPA to driver's air bag module yellow connector.
11. Install instrument panel lefthand side sound insulator.
12. Install SIR fuse to rear fuse block located under rear seat.
13. Staying well away from air bag modules and turn ignition switch to ON position.
14. AIR BAG warning lamp will flash seven times and turn OFF.

2003

Zone 1

1. Connect EFS connector. EFS is located on front lefthand side of engine compartment.
2. Install Connector Position Assurance (CPA) lock onto Electronic Frontal Sensor (EFS) connector.
3. Install SIR fuse into rear fuse center.
4. Install rear seat lower cushion.
5. **From safe location at sides or below air bag modules,** turn ignition switch to On position.
6. Ensure SIR lamp flashes seven times and turns off.

Zone 2

1. Connect lefthand Side Impact Sensor (SIS) connector.
2. Install Connector Position Assurance (CPA) lock onto SIS connector.
3. Install lefthand center pillar trim panel onto pillar.
4. Install front and rear carpet retainers onto lefthand center pillar trim panel.
5. Install SIR fuse into rear fuse center.
6. Install rear seat lower cushion.
7. **From safe location at sides or below air bag modules,** turn ignition switch to On position.
8. Ensure SIR lamp flashes seven times and turns off.

Zone 3

1. Connect steering wheel module yellow harness connector.
2. Install Connector Position Assurance (CPA) lock onto steering wheel module yellow connector.
3. Install lefthand closeout/insulator panel under lefthand side of instrument panel.
4. Install SIR fuse into rear fuse center.
5. Install rear seat lower cushion.
6. **From safe location at sides or below air bag modules,** turn ignition switch to On position.
7. Ensure SIR lamp flashes seven times and turns off.

Zone 5

1. Connect instrument panel module yellow harness connector.
2. Install Connector Position Assurance (CPA) lock onto instrument panel module yellow connector.
3. Install righthand closeout/insulator panel under righthand side of instrument panel.
4. Install SIR fuse into rear fuse center.
5. Install rear seat lower cushion.
6. **From safe location at sides or below air bag modules,** turn ignition switch to On position.
7. Ensure SIR lamp flashes seven times and turns off.

Zone 6

1. Connect righthand Side Impact Sensor (SIS) connector.
2. Install Connector Position Assurance (CPA) lock onto SIS connector.

3. Install righthand center pillar trim panel onto pillar.
4. Install front and rear carpet retainers onto righthand center pillar trim panel.
5. Install SIR fuse into rear fuse center.
6. Install rear seat lower cushion.
7. **From safe location at sides or below air bag modules,** turn ignition switch to On position.
8. Ensure SIR lamp flashes seven times and turns off.

Zone 7

1. Connect lefthand driver's side impact module and seat belt pretensioner yellow connector from harness connector. Connector is located under driver's seat.
2. Install Connector Position Assurance (CPA) lock onto lefthand driver's side impact module and seat belt pretensioner yellow connector.
3. Install fuse into rear fuse center.
4. Install rear seat lower cushion.
5. **From safe location at sides or below air bag modules,** turn ignition switch to On position.
6. Ensure SIR lamp flashes seven times and turns off.

Zone 8

1. Connect lefthand driver's side impact module and seat belt pretensioner yellow connector to vehicle harness connector. Connector is located under driver's seat.
2. Install Connector Position Assurance (CPA) lock onto lefthand driver's side impact module and seat belt pretensioner yellow connector.
3. Connect steering wheel module connector to yellow harness connector.
4. Install CPA lock onto steering wheel module yellow connector.
5. Install lefthand closeout/insulator panel under lefthand side of instrument panel.
6. Connect instrument panel module connector to yellow harness connector.
7. Install CPA lock onto instrument panel module yellow connector.
8. Install righthand closeout/insulator panel under righthand side of instrument panel.
9. Connect righthand side impact module and seat belt pretensioner yellow connector to vehicle harness connector. Connector is located under passenger front seat.
10. Install CPA lock onto righthand side impact module and seat belt pretensioner yellow connector.
11. Install SIR fuse into rear fuse center.
12. Install rear seat lower cushion.
13. **From safe location at sides or below air bag modules,** turn ignition switch to On position.
14. Ensure SIR lamp flashes seven times and turns off.

Zone 9

1. Connect righthand side impact module and seat belt pretensioner yellow connector to vehicle harness connector.

Connector is located under passenger seat.
2. Install Connector Position Assurance (CPA) lock onto righthand passenger side impact module and seat belt pretensioner yellow connector.
3. Install SIR fuse into rear fuse center.
4. Install rear seat lower cushion.
5. **From safe location at sides or below air bag modules,** turn ignition switch to On position.
6. Ensure SIR lamp flashes seven times and turns off.

BONNEVILLE & LESABRE

2001-02

1. Turn steering wheel to straight-ahead position.
2. Turn ignition to Lock position and remove key.
3. Connect yellow two-way connector and CPA at righthand side impact air bag module electrical connector under front seat.
4. Connect yellow two-way connector and CPA at lefthand side impact air bag module electrical connector under front seat.
5. Connect yellow two-way connector to passenger air bag module wiring and install CPA.
6. Install righthand sound insulator.
7. Connect yellow two-way SIR electrical connector at base of steering column and install CPA.
8. Install lefthand sound insulator.
9. Install SIR fuse into rear fuse block.
10. **From safe location at sides or below air bag modules,** turn ignition switch to On position.
11. Ensure SIR lamp flashes seven times and turns off.

2003-05

For arming procedures on these models, refer to "2003" in "Aurora."

CAMARO & FIREBIRD

1. Turn ignition key to Lock and remove key.
2. Connect yellow two-way connector to passenger air bag module and install CPA.
3. Install righthand instrument panel insulator.
4. Connect driver's air bag module yellow two-way SIR electrical connector.
5. Install CPA near base of steering column.
6. Install lefthand sound insulator.
7. Install AIR BAG fuse.
8. **From safe location at sides or below air bag modules,** turn ignition switch to On position.
9. Ensure SIR lamp flashes seven times and turns off.

CATERA

1. Turn steering wheel to straight-ahead position.
2. Turn ignition to Lock position.
3. Connect SDM electrical connectors if required.
4. Connect righthand side impact air bag

module electrical connector and install CPA.
5. Connect righthand front seat belt pretensioner electrical connector.
6. Install righthand front seat track trim cover.
7. Connect lefthand side impact air bag module electrical connector and install CPA.
8. Connect driver's seat belt pretensioner electrical connector.
9. Install driver's front seat track trim cover.
10. Connect passenger front air bag module electrical connector and install CPA.
11. Install passenger front air bag module cover.
12. Connect driver's air bag module electrical connector to SRS coil (clockspring).
13. Install steering column lower and upper covers.
14. **From safe location at sides or below air bag modules,** turn ignition switch to On position.
15. Ensure AIR BAG warning lamp flashes seven times and turns off.

CAVALIER & SUNFIRE

2001-02

1. Turn ignition to Lock position and remove key.
2. Connect both yellow SIR connectors at base of steering column.
3. Install CPAs and lefthand lower trim panel.
4. Install SIR AIR BAG fuse into fuse block.
5. Install instrument panel lefthand end cap.
6. **From safe location at sides or below air bag modules,** turn ignition switch to On position.
7. Ensure AIR BAG warning lamp flashes seven times and turns off.

2003-05

Zone 1

1. Connect Electronic Front Sensor (EFS) connector. Connector is located on front righthand side of engine compartment.
2. Install Connector Position Assurance (CPA) cover onto inflatable restraint EFS connector.
3. Install hood closeout filler panel onto front of engine compartment.
4. Install AIR BAG fuse into lefthand instrument panel junction block.
5. Install lefthand instrument panel outer trim cover.
6. **From safe location at sides or below air bag modules,** turn ignition switch to On position.
7. Ensure SIR lamp flashes seven times and turns off.

Zone 2, Coupe

1. Connect Side Impact Sensor (SIS) connector. Connector is located behind lefthand door panel.
2. Install Connector Position Assurance (CPA) cover onto SIS connector.

3. Install inflatable restraint Side Impact Sensor (SIS) onto door.
4. Install lefthand door trim panel and trim panel mounting screws.
5. Install window regulator handle.
6. **On models equipped with power door locks,** install power door lock switch.
7. **On all models,** install AIR BAG fuse into lefthand instrument panel junction block.
8. Install lefthand instrument panel outer trim cover.
9. **From safe location at sides or below air bag modules,** turn ignition switch to On position.
10. Ensure SIR lamp flashes seven times and turns off.

Zone 2, Sedan

1. Connect lefthand Side Impact Sensor (SIS) connector. Connector is located behind lefthand center pillar upper trim panel.
2. Install Connector Position Assurance (CPA) cover onto SIS connector.
3. Remove inflatable restraint Side Impact Sensor (SIS) from center pillar.
4. Install lefthand center pillar upper trim panel.
5. Install AIR BAG fuse into lefthand instrument panel junction block.
6. Install lefthand instrument panel outer trim cover.
7. **From safe location at sides or below air bag modules,** turn ignition switch to On position.
8. Ensure SIR lamp flashes seven times and turns off.

Zone 3

1. Connect steering wheel module coil connector. Connector is located under lefthand side of instrument panel, left of steering column.
2. Install Connector Position Assurance (CPA) cover onto inflatable restraint steering wheel module coil connector.
3. Install AIR BAG fuse into lefthand instrument panel junction block.
4. Install lefthand instrument panel outer trim cover.
5. **From safe location at sides or below air bag modules,** turn ignition switch to On position.
6. Ensure SIR lamp flashes seven times and turns off.

Zone 5

1. Connect inflatable restraint instrument panel module inline connector. Connector is located under lefthand side of instrument panel, left of steering column.
2. Install Connector Position Assurance (CPA) cover onto inflatable restraint instrument panel module inline connector.
3. Install AIR BAG fuse into lefthand instrument panel junction block.
4. Install lefthand instrument panel outer trim cover.
5. **From safe location at sides or below air bag modules,** turn ignition switch to On position.

6. Ensure SIR lamp flashes seven times and turns off.

Zone 6, Coupe

1. Connect righthand Side Impact Sensor (SIS) connector.
2. Install Connector Position Assurance (CPA) cover onto SIS connector.
3. Install SIS into righthand door.
4. Install righthand door trim panel and trim panel mounting screws.
5. **On models equipped with power door locks,** install power door lock switch.
6. **On all models,** install window regulator handle.
7. Install AIR BAG fuse into lefthand instrument panel junction block.
8. Install lefthand instrument panel outer trim cover.
9. **From safe location at sides or below air bag modules,** turn ignition switch to On position.
10. Ensure SIR lamp flashes seven times and turns off.

Zone 6, Sedan

1. Connect righthand Side Impact Sensor (SIS) connector.
2. Install Connector Position Assurance (CPA) cover onto SIS connector.
3. Install inflatable restraint SIS onto center pillar and pillar upper trim panel.
4. Install AIR BAG fuse into lefthand instrument panel junction block.
5. Install lefthand instrument panel outer trim cover.
6. **From safe location at sides or below air bag modules,** turn ignition switch to On position.
7. Ensure SIR lamp flashes seven times and turns off.

Zone 7

1. Connect inflatable restraint side impact module connector. Connector is located under driver's seat.
2. Install Connector Position Assurance (CPA) cover onto module connector.
3. Install AIR BAG fuse into lefthand instrument panel junction block.
4. Install lefthand instrument panel outer trim cover.
5. **From safe location at sides or below air bag modules,** turn ignition switch to On position.
6. Ensure SIR lamp flashes seven times and turns off.

Zone 9

1. Connect inflatable restraint side impact module connector. Connector is located under passenger front seat.
2. Install Connector Position Assurance (CPA) cover onto side impact module connector.
3. Install AIR BAG fuse into lefthand instrument panel junction block.
4. Install lefthand instrument panel outer trim cover.
5. **From safe location at sides or below air bag modules,** turn ignition switch to On position.
6. Ensure SIR lamp flashes seven times and turns off.

CENTURY & REGAL

2001–02

1. Ensure front wheels are in straight-ahead position and key is removed from ignition.
2. Connect side impact air bag module connector located under driver's seat.
3. Install Connector Position Assurance (CPA) to side impact module.
4. Connect passenger air bag module CPA and air bag module yellow connectors located to right of steering column.
5. Connect driver's air bag module CPA and yellow air bag module connectors at base of steering column.
6. Install AIR BAG or SIR fuse into fuse block.
7. **From safe location at sides or below air bag modules,** turn ignition switch to On position.
8. Ensure AIR BAG warning lamp flashes seven times and turns off.

2003–05

Zone 2

1. Connect lefthand Side Impact Sensor (SIS) connector.
2. Install Connector Position Assurance (CPA) cover onto SIS connector.
3. Install SIS on center pillar.
4. Install lefthand center pillar trim panel.
5. Install SIR fuse into fuse block.
6. Install instrument panel fuse block cover.
7. **From safe location at sides or below air bag modules,** turn ignition switch to On position.
8. Ensure SIR lamp flashes seven times and turns off.

Zone 3

1. Connect inflatable restraint steering wheel module coil connector. Connector is located at base of steering column.
2. Install Connector Position Assurance (CPA) cover onto steering wheel module coil connector.
3. Install lefthand insulator panel from under lefthand side of instrument panel.
4. Install SIR fuse into fuse block.
5. Install instrument panel fuse block cover.
6. **From safe location at sides or below air bag modules,** turn ignition switch to On position.
7. Ensure SIR lamp flashes seven times and turns off.

Zone 5

1. Connect instrument panel module connector. Connector is located on righthand side of steering column.
2. Install Connector Position Assurance (CPA) cover onto instrument panel module connector.
3. Install insulator panel under lefthand side of instrument panel.
4. Install SIR fuse into fuse block.
5. Install instrument panel fuse block cover.

6. **From safe location at sides or below air bag modules,** turn ignition switch to On position.
7. Ensure SIR lamp flashes seven times and turns off.

Zone 7

1. Connect side impact module connector. Connector is located under driver's seat.
2. Install Connector Position Assurance (CPA) cover onto side impact module connector.
3. Install SIR fuse into fuse block.
4. Install instrument panel fuse block cover.
5. **From safe location at sides or below air bag modules,** turn ignition switch to On position.
6. Ensure SIR lamp flashes seven times and turns off.

Zone 9

1. Connect Side Impact Sensor (SIS) connector.
2. Install Connector Position Assurance (CPA) cover onto SIS connector.
3. Install lefthand Side Impact Sensor (SIS) on center pillar.
4. Install lefthand center pillar trim panel.
5. Connect instrument panel module connector. Connector is located on righthand side of steering column.
6. Install CPA cover onto instrument panel module connector.
7. Connect steering wheel module coil connector. Connector is located at base of steering column.
8. Install CPA cover onto steering wheel module coil connector.
9. Install insulator panel under lefthand side of instrument panel.
10. Install SIR fuse into fuse block.
11. Install instrument panel fuse block cover.
12. **From safe location at sides or below air bag modules,** turn ignition switch to On position.
13. Ensure SIR lamp flashes seven times and turns off.

CORVETTE

2001-02

1. Turn ignition to Lock position and remove key.
2. Connect both yellow SIR connectors and install CPA.
3. Insert courtesy lamp through panel and install lefthand sound insulation panel.
4. Install push-on nut to steering column bracket stud and twist rivets clockwise to secure.
5. Align courtesy lamp and push into place.
6. Install SDM fuse into instrument panel fuse block.
7. Install front floor kick-up panel.
8. **From safe location at sides or below air bag modules,** turn ignition switch to On position.
9. Ensure AIR BAG warning lamp flashes seven times and turns off.

2003-04

Zone 3

1. Connect steering wheel module coil connector. Connector is located at base of steering column.
2. Install Connector Position Assurance (CPA) cover onto inflatable restraint steering wheel module coil connector.
3. Install sound insulator panel under lefthand side of instrument panel.
4. Install SDM fuse into fuse block.
5. Install kick-up panel.
6. **From safe location at sides or below air bag modules,** turn ignition switch to On position.
7. Ensure SIR lamp flashes seven times and turns off.

Zone 4

1. Connect steering wheel module coil connector. Connector is located at base of steering column.
2. Install Connector Position Assurance (CPA) cover onto inflatable restraint steering wheel module coil connector.
3. Connect inflatable restraint instrument panel module connector. Connector is located near base of steering column.
4. Install CPA cover onto inflatable restraint instrument panel module connector.
5. Install sound insulator panel under lefthand side of instrument panel.
6. Install SDM fuse into fuse block.
7. Install kick-up panel.
8. **From safe location at sides or below air bag modules,** turn ignition switch to On position.
9. Ensure SIR lamp flashes seven times and turns off.

Zone 5

1. Connect inflatable restraint instrument panel module connector. Connector is located near base of steering column.
2. Install Connector Position Assurance (CPA) cover onto inflatable restraint instrument panel module connector.
3. Install sound insulator panel under lefthand side of instrument panel.
4. Install SDM fuse into fuse block.
5. Install kick-up panel.
6. **From safe location at sides or below air bag modules,** turn ignition switch to On position.
7. Ensure SIR lamp flashes seven times and turns off.

2005

Zone 1

1. Remove ignition key from switch.
2. Connect lefthand and righthand side front end sensor connectors to sensors.
3. Connect lefthand and righthand side CPA's to front end sensor connectors.
4. Install air cleaner assembly.
5. Install SDM fuse, then the fuse block cover.
6. Install kick panel to fuse block.
7. From a position away from air bag modules, turn ignition switch to ON position. AIR BAG indicator will flash the

turn OFF.

Zone 2

1. Remove ignition key from switch.
2. Connect side impact sensor connector to side impact sensor.
3. Connect CPA to side impact sensor.
4. Install door trim panel.
5. Install SDM fuse to fuse block.
6. Install fuse block cover, then the kick panel to fuse block.
7. From a position away from air bag modules, turn ignition switch to ON position. AIR BAG indicator will flash the turn OFF.

Zone 3

1. Remove ignition key from switch.
2. Connect driver's side module coil yellow connector to vehicle harness yellow connector.
3. Install CPA to vehicle harness yellow connector.
4. Install lefthand side sound insulator panel to instrument panel.
5. Install SDM fuse to fuse block.
6. Install fuse block cover, then the kick panel to fuse block.
7. From a position away from air bag modules, turn ignition switch to ON position. AIR BAG indicator will flash the turn OFF.

Zone 4

1. Remove ignition key from switch.
2. Connect vehicle harness yellow connector to driver's side impact air bag module and pretensioner yellow connector.
3. Install both CPA's to driver's side impact air bag module and pretensioner yellow connectors.
4. Connect driver's side air bag module coil yellow connector to vehicle harness yellow connector.
5. Install CPA to vehicle harness yellow connector.
6. Install driver's side sound insulator panel to instrument panel.
7. Connect vehicle harness yellow connector to driver's side impact air bag module and pretensioner yellow connector.
8. Install both CPA's to driver's side impact air bag module pretensioner yellow connector.
9. Connect passenger side air bag module yellow connector to vehicle harness yellow connector.
10. Install CPA to vehicle harness yellow connector.
11. Install righthand side sound insulator panel.
12. Install SDM fuse to fuse block.
13. Install fuse block cover, then the kick panel to fuse block.
14. From a position away from air bag modules, turn ignition switch to ON position. AIR BAG indicator will flash the turn OFF.

Zone 5

1. Remove ignition key from switch.
2. Connect passenger side air bag module yellow connector to vehicle

harness yellow connector.

3. Install CPA to vehicle harness yellow connector.
4. Install righthand side sound insulator.
5. Install SDM fuse to fuse block.
6. Install fuse block cover, then the kick panel to fuse block.
7. From a position away from air bag modules, turn ignition switch to ON position. AIR BAG indicator will flash the turn OFF.

Zone 6

1. Remove ignition key from switch.
2. Connect side impact sensor connector to side impact sensor.
3. Connect CPA to side impact sensor connector.
4. Install door trim panel.
5. Install SDM fuse to fuse block.
6. Install fuse block cover, then the kick panel to fuse block.
7. From a position away from air bag modules, turn ignition switch to ON position. AIR BAG indicator will flash the turn OFF.

Zone 7

1. Remove ignition key from switch.
2. Connect vehicle harness yellow connector to driver's side impact air bag module and pretensioner yellow connector.
3. Install both CPA's to driver's side impact air bag module and pretensioner yellow connector.
4. Install SDM fuse to fuse block.
5. Install fuse block cover, then the kick panel to fuse block.
6. From a position away from air bag modules, turn ignition switch to ON position. AIR BAG indicator will flash the turn OFF.

Zone 9

1. Remove ignition key from switch.
2. Connect vehicle harness yellow connector to passenger side impact module and pretensioner yellow connector.
3. Install both CPA's to passenger side impact air bag module and pretensioner yellow connector.
4. Install SDM fuse to fuse block.
5. Install fuse block cover, then the kick panel to fuse block.
6. From a position away from air bag modules, turn ignition switch to ON position. AIR BAG indicator will flash the turn OFF.

CTS

ZONE 1

1. Ensure ignition is Off.
2. Connect Electronic Frontal Sensor (EFS) connector and install Connector Position Assurance (CPA) cover onto connector.
3. Install SIR fuse into righthand rear fuse center.
4. Install rear seat.
5. **From safe location at sides or below air bag modules,** turn ignition switch to On position.
6. Ensure AIR BAG warning lamp flashes seven times and turns off.

ZONE 2

1. Connect lefthand Side Impact Sensor (SIS) electrical connector.
2. Install Connector Position Assurance (CPA) cover onto lefthand Side Impact Sensor (SIS) connector.
3. Install lefthand center pillar trim panel onto pillar.
4. Instal front and rear carpet retainers onto lefthand center pillar trim panel.
5. Connect lefthand roof rail module connector.
6. Install Connector Position Assurance (CPA) cover onto lefthand roof rail module yellow electrical connector.
7. Install lefthand rear sail panel.
8. Install SIR fuse into righthand rear fuse center.
9. Install rear seat lower cushion.
10. **From safe location at sides or below air bag modules,** turn ignition switch to On position.
11. Ensure AIR BAG warning lamp flashes seven times and turns off.

ZONE 3

1. Connect steering wheel module connector to yellow harness connector.
2. Install Connector Position Assurance (CPA) cover onto steering wheel module yellow connector.
3. Install lefthand closeout/insulator panel on to lefthand side of instrument panel.
4. Install SIR fuse into righthand rear fuse center.
5. Install rear seat lower cushion.
6. **From safe location at sides or below air bag modules,** turn ignition switch to On position.
7. Ensure AIR BAG warning lamp flashes seven times and turns off.

ZONE 5

1. Connect instrument panel module connector to yellow harness connector.
2. Install Connector Position Assurance (CPA) cover onto instrument panel module yellow connector.
3. Install righthand closeout/insulator panel on to righthand side of instrument panel.
4. Install SIR fuse into righthand rear fuse center.
5. Install rear seat lower cushion.
6. **From safe location at sides or below air bag modules,** turn ignition switch to On position.
7. Ensure AIR BAG warning lamp flashes seven times and turns off.

ZONE 6

1. Connect righthand Side Impact Sensor (SIS) electrical connector.
2. Install Connector Position Assurance (CPA) cover onto righthand Side Impact Sensor (SIS) connector.
3. Install righthand center pillar trim panel onto pillar.
4. Instal front and rear carpet retainers onto righthand center pillar trim panel.
5. Connect righthand roof rail module connector.
6. Install Connector Position Assurance

(CPA) cover onto righthand roof rail module yellow electrical connector.
7. Install righthand rear sail panel.
8. Install SIR fuse into righthand rear fuse center.
9. Install rear seat lower cushion.
10. **From safe location at sides or below air bag modules,** turn ignition switch to On position.
11. Ensure AIR BAG warning lamp flashes seven times and turns off.

ZONE 7

1. Connect lefthand driver's side impact module and seat belt pretensioner yellow connector to vehicle harness connector. Connector is located under driver's seat.
2. Install Connector Position Assurance (CPA) cover on to lefthand driver's side impact module and seat belt pretensioner yellow connector.
3. Install SIR fuse into righthand rear fuse center.
4. Install rear seat lower cushion.
5. **From safe location at sides or below air bag modules,** turn ignition switch to On position.
6. Ensure AIR BAG warning lamp flashes seven times and turns off.

ZONE 8

1. Connect lefthand roof rail module connector.
2. Install Connector Position Assurance (CPA) lock onto lefthand roof rail module yellow electrical connector.
3. Install lefthand rear sail panel.
4. Install lefthand rear sail panel retaining clips.
5. Connect lefthand driver's side impact module and seat belt pretensioner yellow connector from harness connector. Connector is located under driver's seat.
6. Install CPA lock onto lefthand driver's side impact module and seat belt pretensioner yellow connector.
7. Connect steering wheel module connector to yellow harness connector.
8. Install CPA lock onto steering wheel module yellow connector.
9. Install lefthand closeout/insulator panel onto far lefthand side of instrument panel.
10. Connect righthand driver's side impact module and seat belt pretensioner yellow connector to vehicle harness connector. Connector is located under passenger front seat.
11. Install CPA lock onto righthand driver's side impact module and seat belt pretensioner yellow connector.
12. Connect instrument panel module connector to yellow harness connector.
13. Install CPA lock onto instrument panel module yellow connector.
14. Install righthand closeout/insulator panel onto far righthand side of instrument panel.
15. Connect righthand roof rail module connector.
16. Install CPA lock onto righthand roof rail module yellow electrical connector.

17. Install righthand rear sail panel.
18. Install righthand rear sail panel retaining clips.
19. Install SIR fuse into righthand rear fuse center.
20. Install rear seat lower cushion.
21. **From safe location at sides or below air bag modules,** turn ignition switch to On position.
22. Ensure AIR BAG warning lamp flashes seven times and turns off.

ZONE 9

1. Connect righthand passenger side impact module and seat belt pretensioner yellow connector to vehicle harness connector. Connector is located under passenger seat.
2. Install Connector Position Assurance (CPA) cover on to righthand side impact module and seat belt pretensioner yellow connector.
3. Install SIR fuse into righthand rear fuse center.
4. Install rear seat lower cushion.
5. **From safe location at sides or below air bag modules,** turn ignition switch to On position.
6. Ensure AIR BAG warning lamp flashes seven times and turns off.

DEVILLE

2001–02

1. Turn ignition to Lock and remove key.
2. **On models equipped with rear side impact air bag modules (AW9),** proceed as follows:
   a. Connect lefthand rear side impact air bag module yellow electrical connector.
   b. Install CPA for lefthand rear side impact air bag module yellow electrical connector.
   c. Connect righthand rear side impact air bag module yellow electrical connector.
   d. Install CPA for righthand rear side impact air bag module yellow electrical connector.
   e. Install rear seatback.
3. **On all models,** connect yellow two-way connector to passenger air bag module pigtail and install CPA.
4. Connect yellow two-way connector to driver's air bag module pigtail and install CPA.
5. Connect yellow two-way SIR electrical connector at base of steering column and install CPA.
6. Install lefthand sound insulator.
7. Install SIR fuse into fuse block.
8. **From safe location at sides or below air bag modules,** turn ignition switch to On position.
9. Ensure SIR lamp flashes seven times and turns off.

2003–05

Zone 1

1. Connect EFS connector. EFS is located on front lefthand side of engine compartment.
2. Install Connector Position Assurance (CPA) lock onto Electronic Frontal Sensor (EFS) connector.
3. Install SIR fuse into rear fuse center.
4. Install rear seat lower cushion.
5. **From safe location at sides or below air bag modules,** turn ignition switch to On position.
6. Ensure SIR lamp flashes seven times and turns off.

Zone 2

1. Connect lefthand Side Impact Sensor (SIS) connector.
2. Install Connector Position Assurance (CPA) lock onto SIS connector.
3. Install lefthand center pillar trim panel onto pillar.
4. Install front and rear carpet retainers onto lefthand center pillar trim panel.
5. Install SIR fuse into rear fuse center.
6. Install rear seat lower cushion.
7. **From safe location at sides or below air bag modules,** turn ignition switch to On position.
8. Ensure SIR lamp flashes seven times and turns off.

Zone 3

1. Connect steering wheel module yellow harness connector.
2. Install Connector Position Assurance (CPA) lock onto steering wheel module yellow connector.
3. Install lefthand closeout/insulator panel under lefthand side of instrument panel.
4. Install SIR fuse into rear fuse center.
5. Install rear seat lower cushion.
6. **From safe location at sides or below air bag modules,** turn ignition switch to On position.
7. Ensure SIR lamp flashes seven times and turns off.

Zone 5

1. Connect instrument panel module yellow harness connector.
2. Install Connector Position Assurance (CPA) lock onto instrument panel module yellow connector.
3. Install righthand closeout/insulator panel under righthand side of instrument panel.
4. Install SIR fuse into rear fuse center.
5. Install rear seat lower cushion.
6. **From safe location at sides or below air bag modules,** turn ignition switch to On position.
7. Ensure SIR lamp flashes seven times and turns off.

Zone 6

1. Connect righthand Side Impact Sensor (SIS) connector.
2. Install Connector Position Assurance (CPA) lock onto SIS connector.
3. Install righthand center pillar trim panel onto pillar.
4. Install front and rear carpet retainers onto righthand center pillar trim panel.
5. Install SIR fuse into rear fuse center.
6. Install rear seat lower cushion.
7. **From safe location at sides or below air bag modules,** turn ignition switch to On position.

8. Ensure SIR lamp flashes seven times and turns off.

Zone 7

1. Connect lefthand driver's side impact module and seat belt pretensioner yellow connector from harness connector. Connector is located under driver's seat.
2. Install Connector Position Assurance (CPA) lock onto lefthand driver's side impact module and seat belt pretensioner yellow connector.
3. Install fuse into rear fuse center.
4. Install rear seat lower cushion.
5. **From safe location at sides or below air bag modules,** turn ignition switch to On position.
6. Ensure SIR lamp flashes seven times and turns off.

Zone 8

1. Connect rear lefthand side impact module connector. Connector is located near lefthand rear door jamb.
2. Install Connector Position Assurance (CPA) lock onto rear lefthand side impact module and seat belt pretensioner yellow connector.
3. Install lefthand rear passenger seat back.
4. Connect lefthand driver's side impact module and seat belt pretensioner yellow connector to vehicle harness connector. Connector is located under driver's seat.
5. Install CPA lock onto lefthand driver's side impact module and seat belt pretensioner yellow connector.
6. Connect steering wheel module connector to yellow harness connector.
7. Install CPA lock onto steering wheel module yellow connector.
8. Install lefthand closeout/insulator panel under lefthand side of instrument panel.
9. Connect instrument panel module connector to yellow harness connector.
10. Install CPA lock onto instrument panel module yellow connector.
11. Install righthand closeout/insulator panel under righthand side of instrument panel.
12. Connect righthand side impact module and seat belt pretensioner yellow connector to vehicle harness connector. Connector is located under passenger front seat.
13. Remove CPA lock onto righthand front side impact module yellow connector.
14. Connect rear righthand side impact module connector. Connector is located near righthand rear door jamb.
15. Install Connector Position Assurance (CPA) lock onto rear righthand side impact module and seat belt pretensioner yellow connector.
16. Install righthand rear passenger seat back.
17. Install SIR fuse into rear fuse center.
18. Install rear seat lower cushion.
19. **From safe location at sides or below air bag modules,** turn ignition switch to On position.

20. Ensure SIR lamp flashes seven times and turns off.

Zone 9

1. Connect righthand side impact module and seat belt pretensioner yellow connector to vehicle harness connector. Connector is located under passenger seat.
2. Install Connector Position Assurance (CPA) lock onto righthand passenger side impact module and seat belt pretensioner yellow connector.
3. Install SIR fuse into rear fuse center.
4. Install rear seat lower cushion.
5. **From safe location at sides or below air bag modules,** turn ignition switch to On position.
6. Ensure SIR lamp flashes seven times and turns off.

Zone 10

1. Connect rear lefthand side impact module connector. Connector is located near lefthand rear door jamb.
2. Install Connector Position Assurance (CPA) lock onto rear lefthand side impact module and seat belt pretensioner yellow connector.
3. Install lefthand rear passenger seat back.
4. Install SIR fuse into rear fuse center.
5. Install rear seat lower cushion.
6. **From safe location at sides or below air bag modules,** turn ignition switch to On position.
7. Ensure SIR lamp flashes seven times and turns off.

Zone 12

1. Connect rear righthand side impact module connector. Connector is located near righthand rear door jamb.
2. Install Connector Position Assurance (CPA) lock onto rear righthand side impact module and seat belt pretensioner yellow connector.
3. Install righthand rear passenger seat back.
4. Install SIR fuse into rear fuse center.
5. Install rear seat lower cushion.
6. **From safe location at sides or below air bag modules,** turn ignition switch to On position.
7. Ensure SIR lamp flashes seven times and turns off.

ELDORADO

1. Turn ignition to Lock position and remove key.
2. Connect yellow two-way connector to passenger air bag module pigtail and install CPA.
3. Install glove compartment.
4. Connect yellow two-way SIR electrical connectors at base of steering column and install CPA.
5. Install lefthand sound insulator.
6. Install SIR fuse into fuse block.
7. **From safe location at sides or below air bag modules,** turn ignition switch to On position.
8. Ensure SIR lamp flashes seven times and turns off.

GRAND PRIX & INTRIGUE

2001-02

1. Ensure front wheels are in straight-ahead position and key is removed from ignition switch.
2. Connect passenger air bag module CPA and air bag module yellow connectors located to right of steering column.
3. Connect driver's air bag module CPA and yellow air bag module connectors at base of steering column.
4. Install AIR BAG or SIR fuse into fuse block.
5. Staying well away from both air bag modules, turn ignition On.
6. Ensure AIR BAG warning lamp flashes seven times and turns off.

2003-04

Zone 3

1. Connect steering wheel module coil connector. Connector is located at base of steering column.
2. Install Connector Position Assurance (CPA) cover onto inflatable restraint steering wheel module coil connector.
3. Install lefthand insulator panel under lefthand side of instrument panel.
4. Install SIR fuse into fuse block.
5. Install instrument panel fuse block cover.
6. **From safe location at sides or below air bag modules,** turn ignition switch to On position.
7. Ensure SIR lamp flashes seven times and turns off.

Zone 5

1. Connect inflatable restraint instrument panel module connector. Connector is located on righthand side of steering column.
2. Install Connector Position Assurance (CPA) cover onto inflatable restraint instrument panel module connector.
3. Install lefthand insulator panel under lefthand side of instrument panel.
4. Install SIR fuse into fuse block.
5. Install instrument panel fuse block cover.
6. **From safe location at sides or below air bag modules,** turn ignition switch to On position.
7. Ensure SIR lamp flashes seven times and turns off.

Zone 9

1. Connect SDM wiring harness connector. Connector is located under front righthand seat.
2. Install CPA cover onto Sensing and Diagnostic Module (SDM) connector.
3. Connect instrument panel module connector. Connector is located on righthand side of steering column.
4. Install CPA cover onto inflatable restraint instrument panel module connector.
5. Connect steering wheel module coil connector. Connector is located at base of steering column.
6. Install Connector Position Assurance

(CPA) cover onto inflatable restraint steering wheel module coil connector.
7. Install lefthand insulator panel under lefthand side of instrument panel.
8. Install SIR fuse into fuse block.
9. Install instrument panel fuse block cover.
10. **From safe location at sides or below air bag modules,** turn ignition switch to On position.
11. Ensure SIR lamp flashes seven times and turns off.

2005

Zone 1

1. Remove ignition key from switch.
2. Connect front end sensor connector to front end sensor.
3. Install CPA to front end sensor connector.
4. Install radiator upper shield and deflector.
5. Install SIR fuse.
6. Close underhood fuse cover.
7. From a position away from air bag modules, turn ignition switch to ON position. AIR BAG indicator will flash the turn OFF.

Zone 2

1. Remove ignition key from switch.
2. Install side impact sensor connector to side impact sensor.
3. Install side impact sensor CPA to side impact sensor connector.
4. Install water deflector shield over side impact sensor.
5. Install driver's door trim panel.
6. Connect driver's side roof panel air bag module wiring harness yellow connector to module.
7. Install CPA to driver's side roof panel air bag module connector.
8. Install lefthand side rear sail panel.
9. Install SIR fuse.
10. Close underhood fuse cover.
11. From a position away from air bag modules, turn ignition switch to ON position. AIR BAG indicator will flash the turn OFF.

Zone 3

1. Remove ignition key from switch.
2. Connect driver's side module coil yellow connector to vehicle harness yellow connector.
3. Install CPA to driver's side air bag module coil yellow connector.
4. Install lefthand side sound insulator to instrument panel.
5. Install SIR fuse.
6. Close underhood fuse cover.
7. From a position away from air bag modules, turn ignition switch to ON position. AIR BAG indicator will flash the turn OFF.

Zone 5

1. Remove ignition key from switch.
2. Connect passenger side air bag module yellow connector to vehicle harness yellow connector.
3. Install CPA to passenger side air bag module yellow connector.

4. Install righthand side sound insulator panel to instrument panel.
5. Install SIR fuse.
6. Close underhood fuse cover.
7. From a position away from air bag modules, turn ignition switch to ON position. AIR BAG indicator will flash the turn OFF.

Zone 6

1. Remove ignition key from switch.
2. Install passenger side impact sensor connector to side impact sensor.
3. Install passenger side impact sensor CPA to side impact sensor connector.
4. Replace water deflector shield covering side impact sensor.
5. Install passenger side door trim panel.
6. Connect passenger side roof panel air bag module wiring harness yellow connector to roof panel air bag module.
7. Install CPA to passenger side roof panel air bag module connector.
8. Install righthand side rear sail panel.
9. Install SIR fuse.
10. Close underhood fuse cover.
11. From a position away from air bag modules, turn ignition switch to ON position. AIR BAG indicator will flash the turn OFF.

Zone 7

1. Remove ignition key from switch.
2. Connect driver's side seat belt pretensioner connector to vehicle wiring harness connector.
3. Install CPA to seat belt pretensioner.
4. Install SIR fuse.
5. Close underhood fuse cover.
6. From a position away from air bag modules, turn ignition switch to ON position. AIR BAG indicator will flash the turn OFF.

Zone 9

1. Remove ignition key from switch.
2. Connect passenger side roof panel air bag module wiring harness yellow connector to roof panel air bag module.
3. Install CPA to passenger side roof panel air bag module connector.
4. Install righthand side rear sail panel.
5. Connect passenger side air bag module yellow connector to vehicle harness yellow connector.
6. Install CPA to passenger side air bag module connector.
7. Install righthand side insulator panel to instrument panel.
8. Connect driver's side air bag module coil yellow connector to vehicle harness yellow connector.
9. Install CPA to driver's side air bag module coil yellow connector.
10. Install lefthand side sound insulator to instrument panel.
11. Connect driver's side seat belt pretensioner connector to vehicle wiring harness connector.
12. Install CPA to seat belt pretensioner connector.

13. Connect driver's side roof panel air bag module wiring harness yellow connector to roof panel air bag module.
14. Install CPA to driver's side roof panel air bag module connector.
15. Install lefthand side rear sail panel.
16. Connect passenger side seat belt pretensioner connector to vehicle wiring harness connector.
17. Install CPA to seat belt pretensioner connector.
18. Install SIR fuse.
19. Close underhood fuse cover.
20. From a position away from air bag modules, turn ignition switch to ON position. AIR BAG indicator will flash the turn OFF.

GTO

ZONE 3

1. Remove ignition key from switch.
2. Install driver's side air bag module connector to coil.
3. Install upper steering column trim cover.
4. Connect battery ground cable.
5. Install SIR fuse to instrument panel fuse panel.
6. From a position away from air bag modules, turn ignition switch to ON position. AIR BAG indicator will flash the turn OFF.

ZONE 5

1. Remove ignition key from switch.
2. Install connector to passenger side air bag module.
3. Install glove compartment door.
4. Connect battery ground cable.
5. Install SIR fuse to fuse panel.
6. From a position away from air bag modules, turn ignition switch to ON position. AIR BAG indicator will flash the turn OFF.

ZONE 8

1. Remove ignition key from switch.
2. Install connector to passenger side air bag module.
3. Install glove compartment door.
4. Install connector to driver's side air bag module coil.
5. Install upper steering column cover.
6. Connect battery ground cable.
7. Install SIR fuse to fuse panel.
8. From a position away from air bag modules, turn ignition switch to ON position. AIR BAG indicator will flash the turn OFF.

G6

Refer to "2005" under "Alero, Grand Am, Malibu & Malibu Maxx" for disarming procedures.

IMPALA & MONTE CARLO

2001-02

1. Ensure front wheels are in straight-ahead position and key is removed from ignition.

2. **On models equipped with lefthand side impact air bag module,** connect yellow electrical connector under driver's seat and install CPA.
3. **On all models,** connect driver's air bag module CPA and yellow air bag module connector.
4. Install instrument panel righthand access hole cover.
5. Install SDM fuse into fuse block.
6. Install instrument panel fuse access cover.
7. **From safe location at sides or below air bag modules,** turn ignition switch to On position.
8. Ensure AIR BAG warning lamp flashes seven times and turns off.

2003-05

Zone 1

1. Connect front sensor to harness connector. Connector is located on front center of engine compartment.
2. Install orange Connector Position Assurance (CPA) cover onto yellow sensor harness connector.
3. Install upper air baffle and deflector onto radiator.
4. Install SIR fuse into fuse block.
5. Install instrument panel fuse block cover.
6. **From safe location at sides or below air bag modules,** turn ignition switch to On position.
7. Ensure SIR lamp flashes seven times and turns off.

Zone 2, Impala

1. Disconnect Side Impact Sensor (SIS) connector. Connector is located on lefthand center pillar.
2. Install Connector Position Assurance (CPA) cover onto SIS connector.
3. Install SIS onto center pillar.
4. Install lefthand center pillar trim panel.
5. Install SIR fuse into fuse block.
6. Install instrument panel fuse block cover.
7. **From safe location at sides or below air bag modules,** turn ignition switch to On position.
8. Ensure SIR lamp flashes seven times and turns off.

Zone 2, Monte Carlo

1. Connect Side Impact Sensor (SIS) connector. Sensor is located on lefthand front door impact beam.
2. Install Connector Position Assurance (CPA) cover onto SIS connector.
3. Install SIS onto door impact beam mounting bracket.

4. Install door trim panel, then connect power door lock and power window switch electrical connectors.
5. Install door trim panel to door mounting screws.
6. Install door handle trim bezel.
7. Install SIR fuse into fuse block.
8. Install instrument panel fuse block cover.
9. **From safe location at sides or below air bag modules,** turn ignition switch to On position.
10. Ensure SIR lamp flashes seven times and turns off.

Zone 3

1. Connect steering wheel module coil connector. Connector is located at base of steering column.
2. Install Connector Position Assurance (CPA) cover onto steering wheel module coil connector.
3. Install insulator panel under lefthand side of instrument panel.
4. Install SIR fuse into fuse block.
5. Install instrument panel fuse block cover.
6. **From safe location at sides or below air bag modules,** turn ignition switch to On position.
7. Ensure SIR lamp flashes seven times and turns off.

Zone 5

1. Connect instrument panel module connector. Connector is located behind access panel on far righthand side of instrument panel.
2. Install Connector Position Assurance (CPA) cover onto instrument panel module connector.
3. Install access panel on far righthand side of instrument panel.
4. Install SIR fuse into fuse block.
5. Install instrument panel fuse block cover.
6. **From safe location at sides or below air bag modules,** turn ignition switch to On position.
7. Ensure SIR lamp flashes seven times and turns off.

Zone 7

1. Connect lefthand side impact module connector. Connector is located under driver's seat.
2. Install Connector Position Assurance (CPA) cover onto lefthand side impact module connector.
3. Install SIR fuse into fuse block.
4. Install instrument panel fuse block cover.
5. **From safe location at sides or below air bag modules,** turn ignition switch to On position.
6. Ensure SIR lamp flashes seven times and turns off.

Zone 9

1. Connect lefthand side impact module connector. Connector is located under driver's seat.
2. Install Connector Position Assurance (CPA) cover onto lefthand side impact module connector.

3. Connect instrument panel module connector. Connector is located behind access panel on far righthand side of instrument panel.
4. Install CPA cover onto instrument panel module connector.
5. Install access panel onto far righthand side of instrument panel.
6. Connect steering wheel module coil connector. Connector is located at base of steering column.
7. Install CPA cover onto steering wheel module coil connector.
8. Install insulator panel under lefthand side of instrument panel.
9. Install SIR fuse into fuse block.
10. Install instrument panel fuse block cover.
11. **From safe location at sides or below air bag modules,** turn ignition switch to On position.
12. Ensure SIR lamp flashes seven times and turns off.

LACROSSE

ZONE 1

1. Remove key from ignition switch.
2. Connect both front end sensor connectors to each front end sensor.
3. Install both CPA's into each front end sensor connector.
4. Install radiator upper baffle and deflector.
5. Install SIR fuse to fuse panel.
6. Close underhood fuse cover.
7. From a position away from air bag modules, turn ignition switch to ON position. AIR BAG indicator will flash the turn OFF.

ZONE 2

1. Remove key from ignition switch.
2. Install driver's side impact sensor connector to side impact sensor.
3. Install side impact sensor CPA to connector.
4. Replace water deflector covering side impact sensor.
5. Install lefthand side door trim panel.
6. Connect driver's side roof panel air bag module wiring harness yellow connector to roof panel air bag module.
7. Install CPA to roof panel air bag module connector.
8. Install lefthand side rear panel.
9. Install SIR fuse to fuse panel.
10. Close underhood fuse cover.
11. From a position away from air bag modules, turn ignition switch to ON position. AIR BAG indicator will flash the turn OFF.

ZONE 3

1. Remove key from ignition switch.
2. Connect driver's side air bag module coil yellow connector to vehicle harness yellow connector.
3. Install CPA to driver's side air bag module coil yellow connector.
4. Install lefthand side sound insulator to instrument panel.
5. Install SIR fuse to fuse panel.
6. Close underhood fuse cover.
7. From a position away from air bag modules, turn ignition switch to ON po-

sition. AIR BAG indicator will flash the turn OFF.

ZONE 5

1. Remove key from ignition switch.
2. Connect passenger side air bag module yellow connector to vehicle harness yellow connector.
3. install CPA to passenger side air bag module yellow connector.
4. Install righthand side sound insulator to instrument panel.
5. Install SIR fuse to fuse panel.
6. Close underhood fuse cover.
7. From a position away from air bag modules, turn ignition switch to ON position. AIR BAG indicator will flash the turn OFF.

ZONE 6

1. Remove key from ignition switch.
2. Install passenger side impact sensor connector to side impact sensor.
3. Install passenger side impact sensor to side impact sensor connector.
4. Replace water deflector covering side impact sensor.
5. Install righthand side door trim panel.
6. Connect passenger side roof panel air bag module wiring harness yellow connector to roof panel air bag module.
7. Install CPA to passenger side roof panel air bag module connector.
8. Install righthand side rear panel.
9. Install SIR fuse to fuse panel.
10. Close underhood fuse cover.
11. From a position away from air bag modules, turn ignition switch to ON position. AIR BAG indicator will flash the turn OFF.

ZONE 7

1. Remove key from ignition switch.
2. Connect driver's side seat belt pretensioner connector to vehicle wiring harness connector.
3. Install CPA to driver's side seat belt pretensioner connector.
4. Install SIR fuse to fuse panel.
5. Close underhood fuse cover.
6. From a position away from air bag modules, turn ignition switch to ON position. AIR BAG indicator will flash the turn OFF.

ZONE 9

1. Remove key from ignition switch.
2. Connect passenger side seat belt pretensioner connector to vehicle wiring harness connector.
3. Install CPA to passenger side seat belt pretensioner connector.
4. Connect passenger side roof panel air bag module wiring harness yellow connector to roof panel air bag module.
5. Install CPA to passenger side air bag module connector.
6. Install righthand side rear panel.
7. Connect IPM yellow connector to vehicle harness yellow connector.
8. Install CPA to IPM yellow connector.
9. Install righthand side sound insulator to instrument panel.
10. Connect driver's side air bag module

coil yellow connector to vehicle harness yellow connector.

11. Install CPA to driver's side air bag module coil yellow connector.
12. Install lefthand side sound insulator to instrument panel.
13. Connect driver's side seat belt pretensioner connector to vehicle wiring harness connector.
14. Install CPA to driver's side seat belt pretensioner connector.
15. Connect driver's side roof panel air bag module wiring harness yellow connector to roof panel air bag module.
16. Install CPA to driver's side roo panel air bag module connector.
17. Install lefthand side rear trim panel.
18. Install SIR fuse to fuse panel.
19. Close underhood fuse cover.
20. From a position away from air bag modules, turn ignition switch to ON position. AIR BAG indicator will flash the turn OFF.

LUMINA

1. Ensure front wheels are in straight-ahead position and key is removed from ignition.
2. Connect passenger air bag module CPA and yellow air bag module connector, then close glove compartment door.
3. Install righthand sound insulator.
4. Connect CPA and yellow air bag module connectors at base of steering column.
5. Install lefthand sound insulator.
6. Install Fuse 21 into fuse block.
7. Install instrument panel fuse block door.
8. **From safe location at sides or below air bag modules,** turn ignition switch to On position.
9. Ensure AIR BAG warning lamp flashes seven times and turns off.

METRO

1. Turn ignition key to Lock position and remove key.
2. Connect passenger air bag module yellow electrical connector.
3. Install passenger air bag module CPA and close glove compartment.
4. Connect yellow two-way electrical connector inside steering wheel air bag module housing.
5. Install driver's air bag module CPA and steering wheel side cap.
6. Install AIR BAG fuse into Air Bag fuse block.
7. **From safe location at sides or below air bag modules,** turn ignition switch to On position.
8. Ensure AIR BAG lamp flashes seven times and turns off.

PARK AVENUE

2001-02

1. Turn steering wheel to straight-ahead position.
2. Turn ignition switch to Lock position and remove key.
3. Connect yellow two-way connector to passenger air bag module wiring and install CPA.

4. Install righthand sound insulator.
5. Connect yellow two-way SIR electrical connector at base of steering column and install CPA.
6. Install lefthand sound insulator.
7. Install SIR fuse into under hood bussed electrical center.
8. Staying well away from both air bag modules, turn ignition On.
9. Ensure SIR lamp flashes seven times and turns off.

2003-05

Zone 2

1. Connect lefthand Side Impact Sensor (SIS) connector.
2. Install Connector Position Assurance (CPA) cover onto SIS connector.
3. Install lefthand center pillar trim panel.
4. Install SIR fuse into underhood fuse center.
5. **From safe location at sides or below air bag modules,** turn ignition switch to On position.
6. Ensure SIR lamp flashes seven times and turns off.

Zone 3

1. Connect steering wheel module coil yellow connector. Connector is located near steering column.
2. Install Connector Position Assurance (CPA) cover onto steering wheel module coil yellow connector.
3. Install insulator panel under lefthand side of instrument panel.
4. Install SIR fuse into underhood fuse center.
5. **From safe location at sides or below air bag modules,** turn ignition switch to On position.
6. Ensure SIR lamp flashes seven times and turns off.

Zone 5

1. Connect instrument panel module connector. Connector is located under righthand side of instrument panel.
2. Install Connector Position Assurance (CPA) cover onto instrument panel module connector.
3. Install insulator panel under righthand side of instrument panel.
4. Install SIR fuse into underhood fuse center.
5. **From safe location at sides or below air bag modules,** turn ignition switch to On position.
6. Ensure SIR lamp flashes seven times and turns off.

Zone 6

1. Connect righthand Side Impact Sensor (SIS) connector.
2. Install Connector Position Assurance (CPA) cover onto SIS connector.
3. Install righthand center pillar trim panel.
4. Install SIR fuse into underhood fuse center.
5. **From safe location at sides or below air bag modules,** turn ignition switch to On position.

6. Ensure SIR lamp flashes seven times and turns off.

Zone 7

1. Connect driver's side impact module connector. Connector is located under driver's seat.
2. Install Connector Position Assurance (CPA) cover onto driver's side impact module connector.
3. Install SIR fuse into underhood fuse center.
4. **From safe location at sides or below air bag modules,** turn ignition switch to On position.
5. Ensure SIR lamp flashes seven times and turns off.

Zone 9

1. Connect driver's side impact module connector. Connector is located under driver's seat.
2. Remove Connector Position Assurance (CPA) cover onto driver's side impact module connector.
3. Connect steering wheel module coil yellow connector. Connector is located near steering column.
4. Install CPA cover onto steering wheel module coil yellow connector.
5. Install insulator panel under lefthand side of instrument panel.
6. Connect instrument panel module connector. Connector is located under righthand side of instrument panel.
7. Install CPA cover onto instrument panel module connector.
8. Install insulator panel under righthand side of instrument panel.
9. Connect passenger side impact module connector. Connector is located under passenger front seat.
10. Install CPA cover onto passenger side impact module connector.
11. Install SIR fuse into underhood fuse center.
12. **From safe location at sides or below air bag modules,** turn ignition switch to On position.
13. Ensure SIR lamp flashes seven times and turns off.

PRIZM

1. Turn ignition to Lock position and remove key.
2. Connect side impact air bag modules electrical connectors.
3. Connect passenger air bag module yellow two-way connector and secure with CPA.
4. Install glove compartment.
5. Connect yellow two-way connector on lower steering column and secure with CPA.
6. Install steering column lower trim cover.
7. Install CIG and IGN fuses in junction block.
8. **From safe location at sides or below air bag modules,** turn ignition switch to On position.
9. Ensure AIR BAG lamp lights for approximately six seconds and turns off.

SEVILLE

2001-02

1. Turn ignition to Lock and remove key.
2. **On models equipped with rear side impact air bag modules (AW9),** proceed as follows:
   a. Connect lefthand rear side impact air bag module yellow electrical connector.
   b. Install CPA for lefthand rear side impact air bag module yellow electrical connector.
   c. Connect righthand rear side impact air bag module yellow electrical connector.
   d. Install CPA for righthand rear side impact air bag module yellow electrical connector.
   e. Install rear seatback.
3. **On all models,** connect yellow two-way connector to passenger air bag module pigtail and install CPA.
4. Connect yellow two-way connector to driver's air bag module pigtail and install CPA.
5. Connect yellow two-way SIR electrical connector at base of steering column and install CPA.
6. Install lefthand sound insulator.
7. Install SIR fuse into fuse block.
8. **From safe location at sides or below air bag modules,** turn ignition switch to On position.
9. Ensure SIR lamp flashes seven times and turns off.

2003-04

Zone 2

1. Connect Side Impact Sensor (SIS connector.)
2. Install Connector Position Assurance (CPA) cover onto SIS connector.
3. Install lefthand center pillar trim panel.
4. Install SIR fuse into rear fuse center.
5. Install rear seat lower cushion.
6. **From safe location at sides or below air bag modules,** turn ignition switch to On position.
7. Ensure SIR lamp flashes seven times and turns off.

Zone 3

1. Connect steering wheel module coil yellow connector. Connector is located near steering column.
2. Install Connector Position Assurance (CPA) cover onto steering wheel module coil yellow connector.
3. Install insulator panel under lefthand side of instrument panel.
4. Install SIR fuse into rear fuse center.
5. Install rear seat lower cushion.
6. **From safe location at sides or below air bag modules,** turn ignition switch to On position.
7. Ensure SIR lamp flashes seven times and turns off.

Zone 5

1. Connect instrument panel module yellow connector. Connector is located under righthand side of instrument panel.

---

2. Install Connector Position Assurance (CPA) onto instrument panel module to vehicle harness yellow connector.
3. Install insulator panel under righthand side of instrument panel.
4. Install SIR fuse into rear fuse center.
5. Install rear seat lower cushion.
6. **From safe location at sides or below air bag modules,** turn ignition switch to On position.
7. Ensure SIR lamp flashes seven times and turns off.

Zone 6

1. Connect Side Impact Sensor (SIS) connector.
2. Install Connector Position Assurance (CPA) cover onto SIS connector.
3. Install righthand center pillar trim panel.
4. Install SIR fuse into rear fuse center.
5. Install rear seat lower cushion.
6. **From safe location at sides or below air bag modules,** turn ignition switch to On position.
7. Ensure SIR lamp flashes seven times and turns off.

Zone 7

1. Connect lefthand side impact and pretensioner connectors. Connectors are located under driver's seat.
2. Install Connector Position Assurance (CPA) covers onto lefthand side impact module and pretensioner connectors.
3. Install SIR fuse into rear fuse center.
4. Install rear seat lower cushion.
5. **From safe location at sides or below air bag modules,** turn ignition switch to On position.
6. Ensure SIR lamp flashes seven times and turns off.

Zone 9

1. Connect lefthand side impact and pretensioner connectors. Connectors are located under driver's seat.
2. Install Connector Position Assurance (CPA) covers onto lefthand side impact module and pretensioner connectors.
3. Connect steering wheel module coil yellow connector. Connector is located near steering column.
4. Install CPA cover on steering wheel module yellow connector.
5. Install insulator panel under lefthand side of instrument panel.
6. Connect instrument panel module yellow connector. Connector is located under righthand side of instrument panel.
7. Install CPA onto instrument panel module to vehicle harness yellow connector.
8. Install insulator panel under righthand side of instrument panel.
9. Connect righthand side impact and pretensioner connectors. Connectors are located under passenger front seat.
10. Install CPA covers onto righthand side impact module and pretensioner connectors.
11. Install SIR fuse into rear fuse center.
12. Install rear seat lower cushion.

---

13. **From safe location at sides or below air bag modules,** turn ignition switch to On position.
14. Ensure SIR lamp flashes seven times and turns off.

STS

ZONE 1

1. Remove key from ignition switch.
2. Connect both connectors to both front end sensors.
3. Connect both CPA's to both front end sensors.
4. Install upper radiator brackets, then the plastic cover.
5. Install AIR BAG (IGN) and AIR BAG (BATT) fuses in rear fuse centers.
6. Install covers and rear seat cushion.
7. From a position away from air bag modules, turn ignition switch to ON position. AIR BAG indicator will flash the turn OFF.

ZONE 2

1. Remove key from ignition switch.
2. Connect side impact sensor connector to side impact sensor.
3. Connect CPA to side impact sensor connector.
4. Install lefthand side center trim panel.
5. Connect driver's side roof panel air bag module yellow connector to module.
6. Install CPA to roof panel air bag module.
7. Release rear seat back.
8. Install lefthand side carpet trim.
9. Install AIR BAG (IGN) and AIR BAG (BATT) fuses in rear fuse centers.
10. Install covers and rear seat cushion.
11. From a position away from air bag modules, turn ignition switch to ON position. AIR BAG indicator will flash the turn OFF.

ZONE 3

1. Remove key from ignition switch.
2. Connect driver's side air bag module coil yellow connector to vehicle harness yellow connector.
3. Install CPA to driver's side air bag module coil connector.
4. Install lefthand side sound insulator to instrument panel.
5. Install AIR BAG (IGN) and AIR BAG (BATT) fuses in rear fuse centers.
6. Install covers and rear seat cushion.
7. From a position away from air bag modules, turn ignition switch to ON position. AIR BAG indicator will flash the turn OFF.

ZONE 5

1. Remove key from ignition switch.
2. Connect passenger side air bag module yellow connector to vehicle harness yellow connector.
3. Install CPA to passenger side air bag module yellow connector.
4. Install righthand side sound insulator to instrument panel.
5. Install AIR BAG (IGN) and AIR BAG (BATT) fuses in rear fuse centers.
6. Install covers and rear seat cushion.
7. From a position away from air bag

modules, turn ignition switch to ON position. AIR BAG indicator will flash the turn OFF.

ZONE 6

1. Remove key from ignition switch.
2. Connect side impact sensor connector to side impact sensor.
3. Connect CPA to side impact sensor.
4. Install righthand side center pillar trim panel.
5. Connect passenger side roof panel air bag module yellow connector to module.
6. Install CPA to module connector.
7. Release rear seat back.
8. Install righthand side carpet retainers and trim.
9. Install AIR BAG (IGN) and AIR BAG (BATT) fuses in rear fuse centers.
10. Install covers and rear seat cushion.
11. From a position away from air bag modules, turn ignition switch to ON position. AIR BAG indicator will flash the turn OFF.

ZONE 7

1. Remove key from ignition switch.
2. Connect driver's side impact air bag module and pretensioner yellow connector to vehicle harness yellow connector.
3. Install CPA locks to driver's side impact air bag module and pretensioner yellow connector.
4. Install AIR BAG (IGN) and AIR BAG (BATT) fuses in rear fuse centers.
5. Install covers and rear seat cushion.
6. From a position away from air bag modules, turn ignition switch to ON position. AIR BAG indicator will flash the turn OFF.

ZONE 8

1. Remove key from ignition switch.
2. Connect driver's side air bag module coil yellow connector to vehicle harness yellow connector.
3. Install CPA to driver's side air bag module coil yellow connector.
4. Install lefthand side sound insulator to instrument panel.
5. Connect driver's side impact air bag module and seat belt pretensioner yellow connector to vehicle harness yellow connector from under driver's seat.
6. Install CPA locks to driver's side impact air bag module and pretensioner yellow connector.
7. Connect driver's side roof panel air bag module yellow connector to roof panel air bag module.
8. Install CPA to driver's side roof panel air bag module connector.
9. Release rear seat back.
10. Install lefthand side carpet retainer and trim.
11. Connect passenger side air bag module yellow connector to vehicle harness yellow connector.
12. Install CPA to passenger side air bag module yellow connector.
13. Install passenger side sound insulator to instrument panel.
14. Connect passenger side impact air bag module and seat belt pretensioner

yellow connector to vehicle harness yellow connector located under front of passenger seat.
15. Install both CPA locks to side impact air bag module and pretensioner yellow connector.
16. Connect passenger side roof panel air bag module yellow connector to module.
17. Install CPA to module connector.
18. Release rear seat back.
19. Install righthand side carpet retainer and trim.
20. Install AIR BAG (IGN) and AIR BAG (BATT) fuses in rear fuse centers.
21. Install covers and rear seat cushion.
22. From a position away from air bag modules, turn ignition switch to ON position. AIR BAG indicator will flash the turn OFF.

ZONE 9

1. Remove key from ignition switch.
2. Connect passenger side impact air bag module and pretensioner yellow connector to vehicle harness yellow connector.
3. Install CPA locks to passenger side impact air bag module and pretensioner yellow connector.
4. Install AIR BAG (IGN) and AIR BAG (BATT) fuses in rear fuse centers.
5. Install covers and rear seat cushion.
6. From a position away from air bag modules, turn ignition switch to ON position. AIR BAG indicator will flash the turn OFF.

VIBE

ZONE 1

1. Connect lefthand front end discriminating sensor electrical connector from front end discriminating sensor.
2. Connect Connector Position Assurance (CPA) from lefthand front end discriminating sensor connector.
3. Connect righthand front end discriminating sensor electrical connector from front end discriminating sensor.
4. Connect Connector Position Assurance (CPA) from righthand front end discriminating sensor connector.
5. Install SIR Fuse into junction block.
6. **From safe location at sides or below air bag modules,** turn ignition switch to On position.
7. SIR indicator will flash then turn OFF.

ZONE 2

1. Install side impact sensor electrical connector.
2. Install lefthand front seat belt retractor to vehicle with mounting bolts.
3. Connect pretensioner electrical connector and install lefthand front seat shoulder belt guide adjuster bolt.
4. Install front seat shoulder belt guide trim cover.
5. Install center pillar lower trim panel, then lefthand front and rear side door sill trim plates.
6. Install lefthand front seat belt lower anchor bolt and trim cover to front lower anchor.
7. Install SIR Fuse into junction block.

8. **From safe location at sides or below air bag modules,** turn ignition switch to On position.
9. SIR indicator will flash then turn OFF.

ZONE 3

1. Install yellow two-way connector for inflatable restraint steering wheel module coil.
2. Connect connector and lock connector with connector lock lever.
3. Install lower steering column trim cover.
4. Install SIR Fuse into junction block.
5. **From safe location at sides or below air bag modules,** turn ignition switch to On position.
6. SIR indicator will flash then turn OFF.

ZONE 4

1. Remove key from ignition switch.
2. Install yellow two-way connectors to driver's and passenger seat modules.
3. Connect connectors and lock connectors with connector lock levers.
4. Install yellow two-way connector to inflatable restraint instrument panel module pigtail.
5. Connect connectors and lock connectors with connector lock levers.
6. Install instrument panel compartment and secure compartment until lower tabs engage.
7. Compress each side of compartment, until upper tabs engage, install screw and close door.
8. Install yellow two-way connector for inflatable restraint steering wheel module coil.
9. Install lower steering column trim cover.
10. Install SIR Fuse into junction block.
11. **From safe location at sides or below air bag modules,** turn ignition switch to On position.
12. SIR indicator will flash then turn OFF.

ZONE 5

1. Install yellow two-way connector to inflatable restraint instrument panel module pigtail.
2. Connect connector and lock connector with connector lock lever.
3. Install instrument panel compartment and secure compartment until lower tabs engage.
4. Compress each side of compartment, until upper tabs engage, install screw and close door.
5. Install SIR Fuse into junction block.
6. **From safe location at sides or below air bag modules,** turn ignition switch to On position.
7. SIR indicator will flash then turn OFF.

ZONE 6

1. Install side impact sensor electrical connector.
2. Install righthand front seat belt retractor to vehicle with mounting bolts.
3. Connect pretensioner electrical connector, then install righthand front seat shoulder belt guide adjuster bolt.
4. Install front seat shoulder belt guide trim cover.
5. Install center pillar lower trim panel,

then the righthand front and rear side door sill trim plates.

6. Install righthand front seat belt lower anchor bolt and trim cover to front lower anchor.
7. Install SIR Fuse into junction block.
8. **From safe location at sides or below air bag modules,** turn ignition switch to On position.
9. SIR indicator will flash then turn OFF.

ZONE 7

1. Install yellow two-way connectors to driver's and passenger seat modules.
2. Connect connectors and lock connectors with connector lock levers.
3. Install SIR Fuse into junction block.
4. **From safe location at sides or below air bag modules,** turn ignition switch to On position.
5. SIR indicator will flash then turn OFF.

ZONE 9

1. Install yellow two-way connectors to driver's and passenger seat modules.
2. Connect connectors and lock connectors with connector lock levers.
3. Install SIR Fuse into junction block.
4. **From safe location at sides or below air bag modules,** turn ignition switch to On position.
5. SIR indicator will flash then turn OFF.

ZONE 10

1. Connect side impact sensor electrical connector.
2. Install rear seat trim molding.
3. Install rear door sill plate.
4. Connect battery ground cable.
5. Install AM2 fuse into junction block.
6. **From safe location at sides or below air bag modules,** turn ignition switch to On position.
7. SIR indicator will flash then turn OFF.

ZONE 12

1. Connect side impact sensor electrical connector.
2. Install rear seat trim panel.
3. Install rear door sill plate.
4. Connect battery ground cable.
5. Install AM2 fuse into junction block.
6. **From safe location at sides or below air bag modules,** turn ignition switch to On position.
7. SIR indicator will flash then turn OFF.

XLR

ZONE 1

Refer to "Disarming" procedure for component locations.
1. Ensure ignition is in Off position.
2. Connect lefthand and righthand EFS connector to appropriate sensor.
3. Connect lefthand and righthand CPA to appropriate EFS connector.
4. Install SIR fuse into fuse block.
5. Install block cover.
6. Use caution while placing ignition to On position from below or side.
7. The AIR BAG indicator will flash, then turn Off. Refer to "Diagnosis & Testing" in **MOTOR's "Air Bag Manual" or "Air Bag Diagnostics CD"** for information.

ZONE 2

Refer to "Disarming" procedure for component locations.
1. Ensure ignition is in Off position.
2. Connect SIS connector to SIS, then the CPA to SIS connector.
3. Install door trim panel.
4. Install SIR fuse into fuse block.
5. Install fuse block cover and kick panel to I/P.
6. Use caution while placing ignition to On position from below or side.
7. The AIR BAG indicator will flash, then turn Off. Refer to "Diagnosis & Testing" in **MOTOR's "Air Bag Manual" or "Air Bag Diagnostics CD"** for information.

ZONE 3

Refer to "Disarming" procedure for component locations.
1. Ensure ignition is in Off position.
2. Connect wheel module coil yellow connector to vehicle harness yellow connector.
3. Install CPA to vehicle harness yellow connector.
4. Install lefthand sound insulator to I/P.
5. Install SIR fuse into fuse block.
6. Install kick panel and cover to I/P.
7. Use caution while placing ignition to On position from below or side.
8. The AIR BAG indicator will flash, then turn Off. Refer to "Diagnosis & Testing" in **MOTOR's "Air Bag Manual" or "Air Bag Diagnostics CD"** for information.

ZONE 4

Refer to "Disarming" procedure for component locations.
1. Ensure ignition is in Off position.
2. Connect vehicle harness yellow connector to lefthand side impact air bag module and pretensioner yellow connector.
3. Install CPA's to lefthand side impact air bag module and pretensioner yellow connector.
4. Connect steering wheel module coil yellow connector to vehicle harness yellow connector.
5. Install CPA to harness yellow connector.
6. Install lefthand sound insulator panel to I/P.
7. Connect vehicle harness yellow connector to lefthand side impact air bag module and pretensioner yellow connector.
8. Install both CPA's to lefthand side impact air bag module and pretensioner yellow connector.
9. Connect I/P module yellow connector to vehicle harness yellow connector.
10. Install CPA to vehicle harness yellow connector.
11. Install righthand sound insulator to I/P.
12. Install SIR fuse to fuse block.
13. Install kick panel to cover I/P.
14. Use caution while placing ignition to On position from below or side.
15. The AIR BAG indicator will flash, then turn Off. Refer to "Diagnosis & Testing" in **MOTOR's "Air Bag Manual" or**

"Air Bag Diagnostics CD" for information.

ZONE 5

Refer to "Disarming" procedure for component locations.
1. Ensure ignition is in Off position.
2. Connect I/P module yellow connector to vehicle harness yellow connector.
3. Install CPA to vehicle harness yellow connector.
4. Install righthand sound insulator to I/P.
5. Install SIR fuse to fuse block.
6. Install I/P fuse block cover, then the kick panel to cover I/P fuse block.
7. Use caution while placing ignition to On position from below or side.
8. The AIR BAG indicator will flash, then turn Off. Refer to "Diagnosis & Testing" in **MOTOR's "Air Bag Manual" or "Air Bag Diagnostics CD"** for information.

ZONE 6

Refer to "Disarming" procedure for component locations.
1. Ensure ignition is in Off position.
2. Connect SIS connector to SIS, then the CPA to SIS connector.
3. Install door trim panel(s).
4. Install SIR fuse to fuse block.
5. Install kick panel and cover to I/P fuse block.
6. Use caution while placing ignition to On position from below or side.
7. The AIR BAG indicator will flash, then turn Off. Refer to "Diagnosis & Testing" in **MOTOR's "Air Bag Manual" or "Air Bag Diagnostics CD"** for information.

ZONE 7

Refer to "Disarming" procedure for component locations.
1. Ensure ignition is in Off position.
2. Connect vehicle harness yellow connector to lefthand side impact air bag module and pretensioner yellow connector.
3. Install both CPA's to lefthand side impact air bag module and pretensioner yellow connector.
4. Install SIR fuse into fuse block.
5. Install I/P fuse block cover, then the kick panel to cover I/P.
6. Use caution while placing ignition to On position from below or side.
7. The AIR BAG indicator will flash, then turn Off. Refer to "Diagnosis & Testing" in **MOTOR's "Air Bag Manual" or "Air Bag Diagnostics CD"** for information.

ZONE 9

Refer to "Disarming" procedure for component locations.
1. Ensure ignition is in Off position.
2. Connect and install vehicle harness yellow connector to righthand side impact air bag module and pretensioner yellow connector.
3. Install SIR fuse to I/P fuse block.
4. Install I/P fuse block cover, then the kick panel to cover I/P fuse block.
5. Use caution while placing ignition to

On position from below or side.

6. The AIR BAG indicator will flash, then turn Off. Refer to "Diagnosis & Testing" in MOTOR's "Air Bag Manual" or "Air Bag Diagnostics CD" for information.

SATURN
Disarming

ION

ZONE 2

Coupe

1. Ensure front wheels are pointed straight-ahead.
2. Turn ignition key off and remove ignition key from switch.
3. Remove Air Bag fuse from Body Control Module (BCM) fuse center. Fuse center is located under center of instrument panel.
4. Remove coat hooks from headliner.
5. Pull trim panel from around high mount stop lamp.
6. Pull back headliner to access lefthand pretensioner connector.
7. Remove Connector Position Assurance (CPA) cover from lefthand pretensioner connector.
8. Disconnect lefthand pretensioner connector.
9. Remove garnish molding from lefthand upper lock pillar.
10. Remove CPA cover from lefthand roof rail module yellow connector.
11. Disconnect lefthand roof rail module yellow connector.

Sedan

1. Ensure front wheels are pointed straight-ahead.
2. Turn ignition key off and remove ignition key from switch.
3. Remove Air Bag fuse from Body Control Module (BCM) fuse center. Fuse center is located under center of instrument panel.
4. Remove trim panel from lefthand center pillar.
5. Remove Connector Position Assurance (CPA) cover from lefthand pretensioner yellow connector.
6. Disconnect lefthand pretensioner yellow connector.
7. Remove garnish molding from lefthand upper lock pillar.
8. Remove CPA cover from lefthand roof rail module yellow connector.
9. Disconnect lefthand roof rail module yellow connector.

ZONE 3

1. Ensure front wheels are pointed straight-ahead.
2. Turn ignition key off and remove ignition key from switch.
3. Remove Air Bag fuse from Body Control Module (BCM) fuse center. Fuse center is located under center of instrument panel.
4. Remove outer trim cover from lefthand side of instrument panel.

5. Remove Connector Position Assurance (CPA) cover from steering wheel module coil yellow connector.
6. Disconnect steering wheel module coil yellow connector.

ZONE 5

1. Ensure front wheels are pointed straight-ahead.
2. Turn ignition key off and remove ignition key from switch.
3. Remove Air Bag fuse from Body Control Module (BCM) fuse center. Fuse center is located under center of instrument panel.
4. Remove outer trim cover from righthand side of instrument panel.
5. Remove Connector Position Assurance (CPA) cover from instrument panel module yellow connector.
6. Disconnect instrument panel module yellow connector.

ZONE 6

Coupe

1. Ensure front wheels are pointed straight-ahead.
2. Turn ignition key off and remove ignition key from switch.
3. Remove Air Bag fuse from Body Control Module (BCM) fuse center. Fuse center is located under center of instrument panel.
4. Remove coat hooks from headliner.
5. Pull trim panel from around high mount stop lamp.
6. Pull back headliner to access righthand pretensioner connector.
7. Remove Connector Position Assurance (CPA) cover from righthand pretensioner connector.
8. Disconnect righthand pretensioner connector.
9. Remove garnish molding from righthand upper lock pillar.
10. Remove CPA cover from righthand roof rail module yellow connector.
11. Disconnect righthand roof rail module yellow connector.

Sedan

1. Ensure front wheels are pointed straight-ahead.
2. Turn ignition key off and remove ignition key from switch.
3. Remove Air Bag fuse from Body Control Module (BCM) fuse center. Fuse center is located under center of instrument panel.
4. Remove trim panel from righthand center pillar.
5. Remove Connector Position Assurance (CPA) cover from righthand pretensioner yellow connector.
6. Disconnect righthand pretensioner yellow connector.
7. Remove garnish molding from righthand upper lock pillar.
8. Remove CPA cover from righthand roof rail module yellow connector.
9. Disconnect righthand roof rail module yellow connector.

ZONE 8

Coupe

1. Ensure front wheels are pointed straight-ahead.
2. Turn ignition key off and remove ignition key from switch.
3. Remove Air Bag fuse from Body Control Module (BCM) fuse center. Fuse center is located under center of instrument panel.
4. Remove garnish molding from righthand upper lock pillar.
5. Remove Connector Position Assurance (CPA) cover from righthand roof rail module yellow connector.
6. Disconnect righthand roof rail module yellow connector.
7. Remove outer trim cover from righthand side of instrument panel.
8. Remove CPA cover from instrument panel module yellow connector.
9. Disconnect instrument panel module yellow connector.
10. Remove coat hooks from headliner.
11. Pull trim panel from around high mount stop lamp.
12. Pull back headliner to access righthand pretensioner connector.
13. Remove CPA cover from righthand pretensioner connector.
14. Disconnect righthand pretensioner connector.
15. Remove outer trim cover from lefthand side of instrument panel.
16. Remove CPA cover from steering wheel module coil yellow connector.
17. Disconnect steering wheel module coil yellow connector.
18. Pull back headliner to access lefthand pretensioner connector.
19. Remove CPA cover from lefthand pretensioner connector.
20. Disconnect lefthand pretensioner connector.
21. Remove garnish molding from lefthand upper lock pillar.
22. Remove CPA cover from lefthand roof rail module yellow connector.
23. Disconnect lefthand roof rail module yellow connector.

Sedan

1. Ensure front wheels are pointed straight-ahead.
2. Turn ignition key off and remove ignition key from switch.
3. Remove Air Bag fuse from Body Control Module (BCM) fuse center. Fuse center is located under center of instrument panel.
4. Remove garnish molding from righthand upper lock pillar.
5. Remove Connector Position Assurance (CPA) cover from righthand roof rail module yellow connector.
6. Disconnect righthand roof rail module yellow connector.
7. Remove outer trim cover from righthand side of instrument panel.
8. Remove CPA cover from instrument panel module yellow connector.
9. Disconnect instrument panel module yellow connector.

10. Remove trim panel from righthand center pillar.
11. Remove CPA cover from righthand pretensioner yellow connector.
12. Disconnect righthand pretensioner yellow connector.
13. Remove outer trim cover from lefthand side of instrument panel.
14. Remove CPA cover from steering wheel module coil yellow connector.
15. Disconnect steering wheel module coil yellow connector.
16. Remove trim panel from lefthand center pillar.
17. Remove CPA cover from lefthand pretensioner yellow connector.
18. Disconnect lefthand pretensioner yellow connector.
19. Remove garnish molding from lefthand upper lock pillar.
20. Remove CPA cover from lefthand roof rail module yellow connector.
21. Disconnect lefthand roof rail module yellow connector.

L-SERIES

1. Place front wheels in straight-ahead position.
2. Turn ignition to Lock position and remove key.
3. Remove IGN1 mini-fuse from underhood fuse block.
4. Remove instrument panel lefthand lower close-out panel.
5. Push out clips securing yellow two-way SIR connectors to instrument panel brace.
6. Disconnect SIR connectors.

S-SERIES

1. Place front wheels in straight-ahead position.
2. Turn ignition to Lock position and remove key.
3. Remove AIR BAG fuse from instrument panel fuse block.
4. Disconnect driver's air bag module two-way yellow electrical connector clipped to steering column brace.
5. Reach under instrument panel on righthand side and detach clip which retains yellow two-way SIR electrical connector to metal brace near HVAC fan.
6. Disconnect passenger air bag module connector.

Arming

ION

ZONE 2

Coupe

1. Connect lefthand roof rail module yellow connector.
2. Install Connector Position Assurance (CPA) cover onto lefthand roof rail module yellow connector.
3. Install lefthand upper lock pillar garnish molding.
4. Connect lefthand pretensioner connector.
5. Install CPA cover onto lefthand pretensioner connector.
6. Push headliner and high mount stop

lamp trim panel back into place.
7. Install coat hooks.
8. Install Air Bag fuse into Body Control Module (BCM) fuse panel.
9. **From safe location at sides or below air bag modules,** turn ignition switch to On position.
10. Ensure air bag lamp flashes seven times and turns off.

Sedan

1. Connect lefthand roof rail module yellow connector.
2. Install Connector Position Assurance (CPA) cover onto lefthand roof rail module yellow connector.
3. Install lefthand upper lock pillar garnish molding.
4. Connect lefthand pretensioner yellow connector.
5. Install CPA cover onto lefthand pretensioner yellow connector.
6. Install lefthand center pillar trim panel.
7. Install Air Bag fuse into Body Control Module (BCM) fuse panel.
8. **From safe location at sides or below air bag modules,** turn ignition switch to On position.
9. Ensure air bag lamp flashes seven times and turns off.

ZONE 3

1. Connect steering wheel module coil yellow connector.
2. Install Connector Position Assurance (CPA) cover onto steering wheel module coil yellow connector.
3. Install lefthand side of instrument panel outer trim cover.
4. Install Air Bag fuse into Body Control Module (BCM) fuse panel.
5. **From safe location at sides or below air bag modules,** turn ignition switch to On position.
6. Ensure air bag lamp flashes seven times and turns off.

ZONE 5

1. Connect instrument panel module yellow connector.
2. Install Connector Position Assurance (CPA) cover onto instrument panel module yellow connector.
3. Install righthand side of instrument panel outer trim cover.
4. Install Air Bag fuse into Body Control Module (BCM) fuse panel.
5. **From safe location at sides or below air bag modules,** turn ignition switch to On position.
6. Ensure air bag lamp flashes seven times and turns off.

ZONE 6

Coupe

1. Connect righthand roof rail module yellow connector.
2. Install Connector Position Assurance (CPA) cover onto righthand roof rail module yellow connector.
3. Install righthand upper lock pillar garnish molding.
4. Connect righthand pretensioner connector.
5. Install CPA cover onto righthand pre-

tensioner connector.
6. Push headliner and trim panel around high mount stop lamp back into place.
7. Install coat hooks into headliner.
8. Install Air Bag fuse into Body Control Module (BCM) fuse panel.
9. **From safe location at sides or below air bag modules,** turn ignition switch to On position.
10. Ensure air bag lamp flashes seven times and turns off.

Sedan

1. Connect righthand roof rail module yellow connector.
2. Install Connector Position Assurance (CPA) cover from righthand roof rail module yellow connector.
3. Install righthand upper lock pillar garnish molding.
4. Connect righthand pretensioner yellow connector.
5. Install CPA cover onto righthand pretensioner yellow connector.
6. Install righthand center pillar trim panel.
7. Install Air Bag fuse into Body Control Module (BCM) fuse panel.
8. **From safe location at sides or below air bag modules,** turn ignition switch to On position.
9. Ensure air bag lamp flashes seven times and turns off.

ZONE 8

Coupe

1. Connect lefthand roof rail module yellow connector.
2. Install Connector Position Assurance (CPA) cover onto lefthand roof rail module yellow connector.
3. Install lefthand upper lock pillar garnish molding.
4. Connect lefthand pretensioner connector.
5. Install CPA cover onto lefthand pretensioner connector.
6. Connect steering wheel module coil yellow connector.
7. Install CPA cover onto steering wheel module coil yellow connector.
8. Install lefthand side of instrument panel outer trim cover.
9. Connect righthand pretensioner connector.
10. Install CPA cover onto righthand pretensioner connector.
11. Push headliner and trim panel around high mount stop lamp back into place.
12. Install coat hooks.
13. Connect instrument panel module yellow connector.
14. Install CPA cover onto instrument panel module yellow connector.
15. Install righthand side of instrument panel outer trim cover.
16. Connect righthand roof rail module yellow connector.
17. Install CPA cover onto righthand roof rail module yellow connector.
18. Install righthand upper lock pillar garnish molding.
19. Install Air Bag fuse into Body Control Module (BCM) fuse panel.
20. **From safe location at sides or below**

air bag modules, turn ignition switch to On position.

21. Ensure air bag lamp flashes seven times and turns off.

Sedan

1. Connect lefthand roof rail module yellow connector.
2. Install Connector Position Assurance (CPA) cover onto lefthand roof rail module yellow connector.
3. Install lefthand upper lock pillar garnish molding.
4. Connect lefthand pretensioner yellow connector.
5. Install CPA cover onto lefthand pretensioner yellow connector.
6. Install lefthand center pillar trim panel.
7. Connect steering wheel module coil yellow connector.
8. Install CPA cover onto steering wheel module coil yellow connector.
9. Install instrument panel lefthand outer trim cover.
10. Connect righthand pretensioner yellow connector.
11. Install CPA cover onto righthand pretensioner yellow connector.
12. Install righthand center pillar trim panel.

13. Connect instrument panel module yellow connector.
14. Install CPA cover onto instrument panel module yellow connector.
15. Install instrument panel righthand outer trim cover.
16. Connect righthand roof rail module yellow connector.
17. Install CPA cover onto righthand roof rail module yellow connector.
18. Install righthand upper lock pillar garnish molding.
19. Install Air Bag fuse into Body Control Module (BCM) fuse panel.
20. **From safe location at sides or below air bag modules,** turn ignition switch to On position.
21. Ensure air bag lamp flashes seven times and turns off.

L-SERIES

1. Turn ignition to Lock position and remove key.
2. Connect SIR connectors.
3. Push in clips securing yellow two-way SIR connectors to instrument panel brace.
4. Install instrument panel lefthand lower close-out panel.

5. Install IGN1 mini-fuse in underhood fuse block.
6. **From safe location at sides or below air bag modules,** turn ignition switch to On position.
7. Ensure air bag lamp flashes seven times and turns off.

S-SERIES

1. Turn ignition to Lock position and remove key.
2. Connect passenger air bag module connector.
3. Reach under instrument panel on righthand side and install clip which retains yellow two-way SIR electrical connector to metal brace near HVAC fan.
4. Connect driver's air bag module two-way yellow electrical connector clipped to steering column brace.
5. Install AIR BAG fuse into instrument panel fuse block.
6. **From safe location at sides or below air bag modules,** turn ignition switch to On position.
7. Ensure air bag lamp flashes seven times and turns off.

COMPUTER RELEARN PROCEDURE

INDEX

DAIMLERCHRYSLER

Powertrain Control Module (PCM)

Anytime the PCM is replaced the VIN and vehicle mileage must be programmed into the new PCM. If the PCM is not programmed, Diagnostic Trouble Codes (DTCs) will set. To program the PCM, connect a DRB or suitably programmed scan tool to the Data Link Connector (DLC) and follow scan tool manufacturers' instructions. On models equipped with the Sentry Key Immobilizer System (SKIS), refer to "Sentry Key Immobilizer System (SKIS)" to program secret key into the PCM.

Sentry Key Immobilizer System (SKIS)

When replacing the PCM on these models, it will be required to program the SKIS I.D. code into the new PCM. The new PCM will not allow the engine to operate unless it receives the correct I.D. code from the Sentry Key Immobilizer Module (SKIM). Use the following procedure to program the secret key into the PCM.

1. Obtain vehicle's four-digit PIN number.
2. Ensure transmission or transaxle is in Park or Neutral and turn ignition to ON position.
3. Connect DRB or suitably programmed scan tool to Data Link Connector (DLC).
4. Select THEFT ALARM, SKIM, MISCELLANEOUS and PCM REPLACED from scan tool menu.
5. Enter secured access mode by entering vehicle's four-digit PIN number.
6. Press ENTER to transfer secret key code to PCM.
7. **If incorrect code is entered three times, secured access mode will be locked out for one hour. To exit lockout mode, turn ignition key to RUN position for one hour and enter correct PIN (ensure accessories are turned off and monitor state of battery charge, connect battery charger).**

FORD MOTOR CO.

Powertrain Control Module (PCM)

AUTOMATIC DATA TRANSFER

1. Prior to removing old PCM, connect suitably programmed scan tool to Data Link Connector (DLC).
2. Follow scan tool manufacturers' instructions to download data from old PCM.
3. Install new PCM and connect scan tool to DLC.
4. Follow scan tool manufacturers' instructions to download data from scan tool to replacement PCM.

MANUAL DATA ENTRY

1. Install new PCM.
2. Connect suitably programmed scan tool to Data Link Connector (DLC).
3. Follow scan tool manufacturers' instructions to manually program VID block data to PCM. If instructed by scan tool to contact "AS BUILT" data center, proceed as follows.
   a. Contact Fed World website at "fedworld.gov."
   b. Select auto service information and search for "Calibrations" or "Vehicle Calibrations."
   c. Specify vehicle manufacturer, model name and model year as required.

GENERAL MOTORS

Body Control Module (BCM)

ALERO & GRAND AM

This procedure must be performed if the BCM, Passlock sensor or PCM is replaced. If BCM is not properly programmed, it will not control the features properly.

1. Ensure battery is fully charged and ignition switch is in ON position.
2. Connect suitably programmed scan tool to Data Link Connector (DLC).
3. Access scan tool "Special Functions" menu and follow scan tool instructions to program BCM.
4. If BCM fails to accept program, inspect BCM connections and ensure scan tool is equipped with latest software.

AURORA

Refer to "Dash Integration Module (DIM)," "Instrument Panel Integration Module (IPM)" and "Rear Integration Module (RIM)" for programming procedures.

BONNEVILLE

Refer to "Dash Integration Module (DIM)," "Instrument Panel Integration Module (IPM)" and "Rear Integration Module (RIM)" for programming procedures.

CAMARO & FIREBIRD

This customer key learn procedure must be performed anytime the BCM is replaced.
1. Insert customer key into ignition cylinder and turn to ON position.
2. Start engine to ensure system operation.
3. Observe SECURITY indicator lamp, noting the following:
   a. If indicator lamp lights for approximately five seconds and then goes out, BCM is properly programmed.
   b. If indicator lamp flashes at rate of one flash per second, BCM is not properly programmed, inspect BCM wiring and connectors for fault.

CATERA

Anytime battery power is disconnected the following accessory programing procedure must be performed.

ELECTRONIC THROTTLE CONTROL (ETC)

1. Turn ignition switch to RUN position, but do not start engine.
2. Leave ignition switch in RUN position for approximately three minutes to allow ETC to cycle and relearn its home position.
3. Turn ignition switch off, start engine and allow to run for 30 seconds.

POWER SUNROOF

1. Turn ignition switch to RUN position.
2. Turn power sunroof switch to CLOSED position.
3. After sunroof fully closes and motor stops, press and hold switch in CLOSED position for three seconds.
4. Turn power sunroof switch to TILT position.
5. After sunroof reaches tilt position and motor stops, press and hold switch in TILT position for three seconds.
6. Turn power sunroof switch to FULL OPEN position.
7. After sunroof reaches full open position and motor stops, press and hold switch in FULL OPEN position for three seconds.

8. Turn power sunroof switch to CLOSED position.
9. After sunroof fully closes and motor stops, press and hold switch in CLOSED position for three seconds.

POWER WINDOWS

1. Turn ignition switch to RUN position.
2. Press power window switch to DOWN position.
3. After window reaches full down position, press and hold switch in DOWN position for three seconds.
4. Press power window switch to UP position.
5. After window reaches full up position, press and hold switch in UP position for three seconds.
6. Repeat procedure for each window.

HEAT & AIR CONDITIONING CONTROL HEAD

1. Turn ignition switch to RUN position.
2. Simultaneously press and hold AUTO and OFF buttons for at least five seconds.
3. Stepper motors should cycle from one stop to another while calibrating.
4. Ensure heater and air conditioning head operates correctly.

CAVALIER & SUNFIRE

This procedure must be performed if the BCM Is replaced. If BCM is not properly programmed with the proper RPO configurations, it will not control the features properly.
1. Ensure battery is fully charged.
2. Connect suitably programmed scan tool to Data Link Connector (DLC).
3. Turn ignition switch to ON position.
4. Access "SPECIAL FUNCTIONS" from scan tool menu, select "NEW BCM SETUP" and follow scan tool instructions to program new BCM.
5. If BCM fails to accept program, inspect BCM connections and ensure scan tool is equipped with latest software.
6. Anytime BCM is replaced, it will required for PCM to learn new fuel continue password, as follows:
   a. Turn ignition switch to ON position.
   b. Attempt to start engine and release key to ON (vehicle will not start).
   c. Observe "SECURITY" telltale lamp. After approximately 10 minutes lamp will turn off.
   d. Turn off ignition switch and wait five seconds.
   e. Repeat procedure two more times for total of three cycles/30 minutes.
   f. Turn ignition switch to OFF position.
   g. Start engine, vehicle has now learned Passlock sensor data password.

CENTURY

The following procedure must be performed anytime the BCM is replaced. After performing the BCM programming procedure, program the theft deterrent system as outlined in "Theft Deterrent Systems."
1. Connect suitably programmed scan tool to Data Link Connector (DLC).
2. Turn ignition switch to ON position.

3. Select "Diagnostics" from scan tool menu and enter vehicle data when prompted by scan tool.
4. Select "Body," then "Body Control Module" from scan tool menu.
5. Select "Special Functions" and "New VIN" from scan tool menu, then follow scan tool instructions to input required data.
6. Exit back to "Special Functions" menu and select "BCM Reprogramming."
7. Scan tool should inquire "Do you want to setup a Body Control Module?"
8. At prompt, select "Setup BCM" on scan tool.
9. Scan tool will display "Now setting up the new Body Control Module."
10. When successful programming is complete, scan tool will display "Body Control Module setup is complete."
11. Program theft deterrent system as outlined in "Theft Deterrent Systems."

CORVETTE

1. Ensure battery is fully charged.
2. Connect suitably programmed scan tool to Data Link Connector (DLC).
3. Select NEW BCM SETUP and program BCM with proper RPO configuration.
4. Turn ignition On and leave on for 11 minutes.
5. Turn ignition Off position for 30 seconds.
6. Turn ignition On for 11 minutes or until DTC P1630 sets.
7. Turn ignition Off for 30 seconds.
8. Turn ignition On for 30 seconds and start engine.
9. If engine starts, proceed as follows:
   a. Clear DTCs and turn ignition Off for 30 seconds.
   b. Ensure engine starts and runs.
10. If engine cranks but will not start, refer to **MOTOR's Domestic Engine Performance & Driveability Manual.**

CUTLASS & MALIBU

This procedure must be performed if the BCM, Passlock sensor or PCM is replaced. If BCM is not properly programmed, it will not control the features properly.
1. Ensure battery is fully charged and ignition switch is in ON position.
2. Connect suitably programmed scan tool to Data Link Connector (DLC).
3. Access scan tool "Special Functions" menu and follow scan tool instructions to program BCM.
4. If BCM fails to accept program, inspect BCM connections and ensure scan tool is equipped with latest software.

DEVILLE

Refer to "Dash Integration Module (DIM)," "Instrument Panel Integration Module (IPM)" and "Rear Integration Module (RIM)" for programming procedures.

GRAND PRIX & REGAL

2000

The following procedure must be performed anytime the BCM is replaced.
1. Connect suitably programmed scan tool to Data Link Connector (DLC).

2. Input required data when prompted by scan tool.
3. Turn ignition switch to RUN position.
4. Select "SPECIAL FUNCTIONS" from "MAIN MENU" screen.
5. Select "NEW VIN" and input required data.
6. Exit back to "SPECIAL FUNCTION" menu and select "BCM REPRO-GRAMMING."
7. Scan tool will display "DO YOU WANT TO SETUP A BODY CONTROL MOD-ULE?" Select "SETUP BCM" hotspot on scan tool.
8. Scan tool will display "NOW SETTING UP THE BODY CONTROL MODULE."
9. When BCM has been setup success-fully, scan tool will display "BODY CONTROL MODULE SETUP IS COMPLETE."
10. Program theft deterrent system as outlined in "Theft Deterrent Systems."

2001-04

The following procedure must be per-formed anytime the BCM is replaced. After performing the BCM programming proce-dure, program the theft deterrent system as outlined in "Theft Deterrent Systems."
1. Connect suitably programmed scan tool to Data Link Connector (DLC).
2. Turn ignition switch to ON position.
3. Select "Diagnostics" from scan tool menu and enter vehicle data when prompted by scan tool.
4. Select "Body," then "Body Control Module" from scan tool menu.
5. Select "Special Functions" and "New VIN" from scan tool menu, then follow scan tool instructions to input required data.
6. Exit back to "Special Functions" menu and select "BCM Reprogramming."
7. Scan tool should inquire "Do you want to setup a Body Control Module?"
8. At prompt, select "Setup BCM" on scan tool.
9. Scan tool will display "Now setting up the new Body Control Module."
10. When successful programming is complete, scan tool will display "Body Control Module setup is complete."
11. Program theft deterrent system as out-lined in "Theft Deterrent Systems."

IMPALA & MONTE CARLO

The following procedure must be per-formed anytime the BCM is replaced. After performing the BCM programming proce-dure, program the theft deterrent system as outlined in "Theft Deterrent Systems."
1. Connect suitably programmed scan tool to Data Link Connector (DLC).
2. Turn ignition switch to ON position.
3. Select "Diagnostics" from scan tool menu and enter vehicle data when prompted by scan tool.
4. Select "Body Control Module" from scan tool menu.
5. Select "Special Functions" and "New VIN" from scan tool menu, then follow scan tool instructions to input required data.
6. Exit back to "Special Functions" menu and select "BCM Reprogramming."
7. Scan tool should inquire "Do You Want To Setup A Body Control Module?"
8. At prompt, select "Setup BCM" on scan tool.
9. Scan tool will display "Now Setting Up The New Body Control Module."
10. When successful programming is complete, scan tool will display "Body Control Module Setup Is Complete."
11. Exit back to "Special Functions" menu and select "Set Options."
12. Select "Point Of Sale" and input re-quired data when prompted by scan tool.
13. Exit back to "Set Options" menu and select "Option Configuration."
14. Input required data when prompted by scan tool.
15. After BCM, VIN, Point Of Sale and Op-tion Configuration have been entered, program theft deterrent system as out-lined in "Theft Deterrent Systems."

INTRIGUE

The following procedure must be per-formed anytime the BCM is replaced. After performing the BCM programming proce-dure, program the theft deterrent system as outlined in "Theft Deterrent Systems."
1. Connect suitably programmed scan tool to Data Link Connector (DLC).
2. Turn ignition switch to ON position.
3. Select "Diagnostics" from scan tool menu and enter vehicle data when prompted by scan tool.
4. Select "Body," then "Body Control Module" from scan tool menu.
5. Select "Special Functions" and "New VIN" from scan tool menu, then follow scan tool instructions to input required data.
6. Exit back to "Special Functions" menu and select "BCM Reprogramming."
7. Scan tool should inquire "Do you want to setup a Body Control Module?"
8. At prompt, select "Setup BCM" on scan tool.
9. Scan tool will display "Now setting up new Body Control Module."
10. When successful programming is complete, scan tool will display "Body Control Module setup is complete."
11. Program theft deterrent system as out-lined in "Theft Deterrent Systems."

LESABRE

Refer to "Dash Integration Module (DIM)," "Instrument Panel Integration Mod-ule (IPM)" and "Rear Integration Module (RIM)" for programming procedures.

PARK AVENUE

The following procedure must be per-formed anytime the BCM is replaced.
1. Connect suitably programmed scan tool to Data Link Connector (DLC).
2. Turn ignition switch to ON position.
3. Select "Body Control Module" from scan tool menu.
4. Select "Special Functions," then "Setup SDM Serial Number In BCM," follow scan tool instructions to input re-quired data.
5. Exit back to "Special Functions" menu and select "Setup BCM."
6. Scan tool should inquire "Do you Want To Setup A Body Control Module?"
7. At prompt, select "Setup BCM" on scan tool.
8. Scan tool will display "Now Setting Up The New Body Control Module."
9. When successful programming is complete, scan tool will display "Body Control Module Setup Is Complete."
10. Exit back to "Special Functions" menu and select "Set Options."
11. Select "Point Of Sale" and input re-quired data when prompted by scan tool.
12. Exit back to "Set Options" menu and select "Load Management Option."
13. Input required data when prompted by scan tool.
14. Exit back to "Special Functions."

SEVILLE

Refer to "Dash Integration Module (DIM)," "Instrument Panel Integration Mod-ule (IPM)" and "Rear Integration Module (RIM)" for programming procedures.

Crankshaft Position System Variation Learn

2.2L & 2.4L ENGINES

The following procedure must be per-formed when any of the following proce-dures are performed; PCM is replaced, engine is replaced, crankshaft is replaced, crankshaft position sensor is replaced, or any engine repair that disturbs the crankshaft/harmonic balancer to the crank-shaft position sensor relationship.
1. Ensure battery is fully charged, park-ing brake is applied and vehicle wheels are blocked.
2. Place transaxle in Park or Neutral posi-tion.
3. Turn accessories off and connect suit-ably programmed scan tool to Data Link Connector (DLC).
4. Start and run engine until it reaches operating temperature of at least 185°F.
5. With engine running, enable "Crank-shaft Position System Variation Learn-ing" procedure with scan tool.
6. Press and hold brake pedal firmly and raise engine speed to 3,920 RPM, re-lease throttle as soon as engine cuts out.
7. With scan tool, ensure crankshaft vari-ation has been learned.
8. Perform this procedure up to 10 times. If PCM will not learn variation, DTC 1336 should set. Refer to **Motors' "Domestic Engine Performance & Driveability Manual"** for DTC P1336 diagnosis.

3.1L, 3.4L, 3800, 4.0L & 4.6L ENGINES

The crankshaft position system values are stored within PCM memory after a learn procedure is performed. If crankshaft posi-tion system variation is not within value stored in PCM memory, DTC P0300 may be set.

The crankshaft variation learn procedure must be performed under the following conditions: DTC P1336, PCM replacement, PCM reprogramming, engine replacement, crankshaft replacement, crankshaft damper replacement and crankshaft position sensor replacement.

When performing this procedure, ensure vehicle is at operating temperature, no DTCs other than P1336 are present and that no camshaft position sensor faults are present. Proceed as follows for CKP learn procedure:

1. Set parking brake and block drive wheels.
2. Start and run engine until it reaches operating temperature.
3. Turn engine off and turn ignition key to ON position.
4. Connect suitably programmed scan tool to Data Link Connector (DLC) and select "CKP Variation Learn Procedure" from scan tool function list.
5. Start engine and when instructed by scan tool, apply brake pedal firmly.
6. Ensure transaxle is in PARK and increase pedal position until CKP system variation learn fuel cut-off is reached at 5150 RPM.
7. Release accelerator pedal after second fuel cut-off is reached.
8. CKP system variation compensating values are learned when RPM decreases back to idle.
9. Monitor scan tool for DTC P1336. If scan tool indicates DTC P1336 ran and passed, learn procedure is complete. If scan tool indicates DTC P1336 failed or did not run, inspect for DTCs. If no DTCs other than P1336 exist, repeat learn procedure.

3.5L ENGINE

The crankshaft position system values are stored within PCM memory after a learn procedure is performed. If crankshaft position system variation is not within value stored in PCM memory, DTC P0300 may be set.

The crankshaft variation learn procedure must be performed under the following conditions: DTC P1336, PCM replacement, PCM reprogramming, engine replacement, crankshaft replacement, crankshaft damper replacement and crankshaft position sensor replacement.

When performing this procedure, ensure vehicle is at operating temperature, no DTCs other than P1336 are present and that no camshaft position sensor faults are present. Proceed as follows for CKP learn procedure:

1. Set parking brake and block drive wheels.
2. Start and run engine until it reaches operating temperature.
3. Turn engine off and turn ignition key to ON position.
4. Connect suitably programmed scan tool to Data Link Connector (DLC) and select "CKP Variation Learn Procedure" from scan tool function list.
5. Start engine and when instructed by scan tool, apply brake pedal firmly.
6. Ensure transaxle is in PARK.
7. **On 2000 models,** increase pedal position until CKP system variation learn fuel cut-off is reached at 4300 RPM.
8. **On 2001–04 models,** increase pedal position until CKP system variation learn fuel cut-off is reached at 4050 RPM.
9. **On all models,** release accelerator pedal after second fuel cut-off is reached.
10. CKP system variation compensating values are learned when RPM decreases back to idle.
11. Monitor scan tool for DTC P1336. If scan tool indicates DTC P1336 ran and passed, learn procedure is complete. If scan tool indicates DTC P1336 failed or did not run, inspect for DTCs. If no DTCs other than P1336 exist, repeat learn procedure.

5.7L ENGINE

CAMARO & FIREBIRD

1. Connect suitably programmed scan tool to Data Link Connector (DLC).
2. Apply parking brake, block drive wheels and close hood.
3. **On models equipped with automatic transmission,** place selector lever in PARK position.
4. **On models equipped with manual transmission,** place shift lever in NEUTRAL position.
5. **On all models,** start and run engine until coolant temperature is at least 150°F.
6. Turn off accessories and apply brakes.
7. Enable "Crankshaft Variation Learn Procedure" with scan tool.
8. Slowly raise engine speed to 4000 RPM and immediately release throttle when engine speed decreases.
9. Turn ignition off for 15 seconds after learn procedure is completed.

CORVETTE

Refer to "3.1L, 3.4L, 3800, 4.0L & 4.6L Engines" for CKP variation learn procedures on this engine.

Dash Integration Module (DIM)

AURORA, BONNEVILLE, DEVILLE, LESABRE & SEVILLE

1. Ensure battery is fully charged and modules on serial data line are connected.
2. Connect suitably programmed scan tool to Data Link Connector (DLC).
3. Turn ignition switch to ON position.
4. Access DIM menu on scan tool and select "Special Functions."
5. Select "New VIN" from special functions menu and follow scan tool instructions.
6. Select "Setup SDM Serial Number In DIM," scan tool should ask "Do you want to set up a Dash Integration Module?" Answer yes to set up module.
7. When scan tool displays "Module Initialized," DIM module is setup.
8. To program vehicle options, access "Special Functions" menu and select "Set Options."
9. Select "Automatic/Manual HVAC" and follow scan tool instructions to select RPO configuration.
10. Select "Options" and follow scan tool instructions to Select Headlamp Type option configuration.
11. Select "LH Drvr. Personalization" and follow scan tool instructions to select LH Drvr. Personalization option configuration.
12. Select "Magna Steer Option" and follow scan tool instructions to select RPO configuration.
13. Select "Miscellaneous Options No. 1" and follow scan tool instructions to select RPO configuration.
14. Select "Miscellaneous Options No. 2" and follow scan tool instructions to select RPO configuration.
15. Select "Universal Theft Deterrent" and follow scan tool instructions to select RPO configuration.
16. Exit back to "Special Functions" menu.

Engine Control Module (ECM)

CATERA

This procedure should only be performed when the ECM is replaced, when requested by the ECM or when informed by a service bulletin. In order to perform this programming procedure, access to a General Motors' Techline Information System 2000 PC Techline Terminal will be required.

1. Turn ignition switch off.
2. Select "Service Programming System" from Techline Terminal.
3. Select "Programming Process" and "Vehicle" for ECU location.
4. Turn ignition switch to ON position.
5. connect suitably programmed scan tool to Data Link Connector (DLC).
6. Connect cable tool No. RS-232, between Techline Terminal and scan tool.
7. Turn scan tool on and wait for start screen.
8. Ensure VIN displayed on Techline Terminal matches VIN.
9. Select type of module to be programmed and type of programming needed.
10. Select appropriate calibration file and ensure current calibration with selected calibration.
11. Select "Next" to initiate download of calibration files.
12. After download is complete, turn ignition switch off for at least 30 seconds and activate theft deterrent system immobilizer as follows:
    a. Select "Special Functions" from scan tool "Immobilizer" menu.
    b. Select "Program Immobilizer," then follow scan tool instructions to activate immobilizer.
13. After activating immobilizer, select "EXIT" service programming.

COMPUTER RELEARN PROCEDURE

Instrument Panel Integration Module (IPM)

AURORA, BONNEVILLE, DEVILLE, LESABRE & SEVILLE

1. Connect suitably programmed scan tool to Data Link Connector (DLC).
2. Turn ignition switch to ON position.
3. Select "Instrument Panel Module," then "Special Functions" from scan tool menu.
4. Select "Miscellaneous Test" and "IPM Recalibration."
5. After scan tool recalibrates IPM, ensure latest version has been installed by selecting "Data Display" and "Module Information", then view calibration ID number. ID number must match version loaded on scan tool.

Powertrain Control Module (PCM)

ALERO & GRAND AM

The following procedure must be performed anytime the PCM is replaced or Diagnostic Trouble Code (DTC) P0601 is set. Code P0601 indicates that EEPROM programming has faulted.
1. Ensure battery is fully charged.
2. Connect suitably programmed scan tool to Data Link Connector (DLC).
3. Follow scan tool instructions to program EEPROM.
4. If PCM will not program properly, replace PCM.
5. Perform CKP system variation learn procedure as outlined in "Crankshaft Position System Variation Learn."
6. Program theft deterrent system as outlined in "Theft Deterrent System Programming."

AURORA, BONNEVILLE, CAMARO, CENTURY, EIGHTY EIGHT, FIREBIRD, GRAND PRIX, IMPALA, INTRIGUE, LESABRE, LUMINA, MONTE CARLO, PARK AVENUE & REGAL

2000

The following procedure must be performed anytime the PCM is replaced or Diagnostic Trouble Code (DTC) P0602 is set. Code P0602 indicates that the EEPROM is not programmed or has faulted.
1. Ensure battery is fully charged.
2. Connect suitably programmed scan tool to Data Link Connector (DLC).
3. Follow scan tool instructions to program EEPROM.
4. If PCM will not program properly, replace PCM.

2001-04

This procedure should only be performed when the PCM is replaced, when requested by the PCM or when informed by a service bulletin. In order to perform this programming procedure, access to a General Motors' Techline Information System 2000 PC Techline Terminal will be required.
1. Turn ignition switch to OFF position.
2. Connect suitably programmed scan tool to Data Link Connector (DLC).
3. Turn ignition switch to ON position and turn accessories off.
4. Select "Service Programming" from scan tool menu.
5. Input vehicle information requested by scan tool.
6. Select type of module to be programmed and type of programming to be performed.
7. Compare VIN displayed on scan tool with VIN. If VIN does not match, write down actual VIN and correct at Techline terminal.
8. Exit "Service Programming" and turn off scan tool.
9. Disconnect scan tool from DLC connector and turn off ignition switch.
10. Connect scan tool to Techline Terminal and select "Service Programming."
11. Select type of scan tool and type of programming to be performed.
12. Ensure displayed VIN with VIN.
13. Select type of module to be programmed and identify type of programming to be performed as follows:
    a. Normal: This type of programming is for updating existing calibration or programming new controller.
    b. Vehicle Configuration Index (VCI): This selection is used if VIN is unavailable or is not recognized by Techline Terminal. Techline Customer Support center will have to be contacted to use this option.
    c. Reconfigure: This type of programming is used to reconfigure vehicle, such as tire size or axle ration changes.
14. Select appropriate calibration file and ensure connections are secure.
15. Select "Reprog" to initiate download of new calibration to scan tool.
16. After download is complete, turn off scan tool and disconnect from Techline Terminal.
17. Connect scan tool to DLC.
18. Turn scan tool and ignition switch to ON position.
19. Select "Service Programming" and "Select Program."
20. After download is complete, exit "Service Programming."
21. Turn ignition switch off for 30 seconds.
22. Turn scan tool off.
23. If control module was replaced, perform the following service procedures:
    a. CKP system variation learn.
    b. GM Oil Life System resetting.
    c. Program theft deterrent system.

CORVETTE

2000

The following procedure must be per-

formed anytime the PCM is replaced, when requested by the PCM or when informed by service bulletin.
1. Ensure battery is fully charged.
2. Connect suitably programmed scan tool to Data Link Connector (DLC).
3. Turn ignition switch off and remove passenger side floor access panel.
4. Remove splice pack/star connector shorting bars from both splice pack/star connectors, **Fig. 1.** It may be required to remove splice pack/star connectors from mounting positions.
5. Connect Star connector cable No. 1 of Serial Data Link Tester tool No. J-42236-A, or equivalent, to 12-pin splice pack connector No. 3 (8 or 9 wires).
6. Connect Star connector cable No. 2 of Serial Data Link Tester tool No. J-42236-A, or equivalent, to 12-pin splice pack connector No. 2 (4 wires).
7. Select Star connector No. 1 on Serial Data Link Tester tool toggle switch.
8. Select position "B" on Serial Data Link Tester.
9. Turn ignition switch to ON position.
10. Program PCM using latest software matching vehicle.
11. Enter "Service Programming System (SPS)" with scan tool.
12. Enter vehicle information requested.
13. Choose "Request Info" soft key on scan tool and select "Done."
14. Follow instructions on scan tool vehicle set-up screen.
15. Disconnect scan tool from DLC and connect scan tool to Techline Terminal.
16. Select "Service Programming System" at Techline Terminal.
17. Select terminal to Tech II programming method.
18. Select "Done," then follow remaining instructions from Techline Terminal.
19. Select "Vehicle Theft Re-Learn" option.
20. Select "Program" at summary screen, Techline Terminal will download information to Tech II.
21. Return scan tool to vehicle and connect to DLC.
22. Select "Service Programming" from scan tool main menu.
23. Answer prompts regarding model year and vehicle type.
24. Press "Theft Re-Learn" soft key on scan tool and follow instructions.
25. BCM and PCM will be prepared for relearn, security timer will be on for approximately 11 minutes or until DTC code P1630 sets. **It is important to keep scan tool connected to DLC during 11 minute wait.**
26. After 11 minute wait, turn ignition switch off for 30 seconds and start engine.
27. **On models equipped with automatic transmission,** perform idle learn procedure as follows:
    a. Turn off ignition switch and restore PCM battery feed.
    b. Turn off air conditioning controls, set parking brake and block drive wheels.
    c. Start and run engine until it reaches operating temperature of 176°F.

d. Shift transmission into Drive and allow engine to idle for approximately five minutes.

e. Shift transmission into Park and allow engine to idle for approximately five minutes.

f. Turn off engine for 30 seconds.

28. **On models equipped with manual transmissions,** perform idle learn procedure as follows:

a. Turn off ignition switch and restore PCM battery feed.

b. Turn off air conditioning controls, set parking brake and block drive wheels.

c. Place transmission in Neutral.

d. Start and run engine until it reaches operating temperature of 176°F.

e. Allow engine to idle for approximately five minutes.

f. Turn off engine for 30 seconds.

2001-04

Refer to "2001–04" in "Aurora" for PCM programming.

CUTLASS & MALIBU

DEVILLE, ELDORADO & SEVILLE

Refer to "Aurora" for PCM programming.

Rear Integration Module

AURORA, BONNEVILLE, DEVILLE, LESABRE & SEVILLE

1. Connect suitably programmed scan tool to Data Link Connector (DLC).
2. Turn ignition switch to ON position.
3. Access "Chassis Main" menu and select "Rear Integration Module."
4. Select "Recalibration" and follow scan tool instructions to calibrate automatic level control.

Theft Deterrent System Programming

ALERO, GRAND AM & MALIBU

The following procedure must be performed anytime the BCM, PCM or Passlock sensor is replaced.

1. Ensure battery is fully charged and there are no Diagnostic Trouble Codes (DTCs) present.
2. Turn ignition switch from OFF position to CRANK position attempting to start vehicle. Vehicle should start and then stall.
3. After vehicle stalls, leave ignition in ON position and observe security indicator on instrument cluster.
4. When security indicator turns off, turn ignition switch off and wait 10 seconds.
5. Repeat procedure two more times (three times total).
6. BCM and PCM will learn new code on next start attempt.

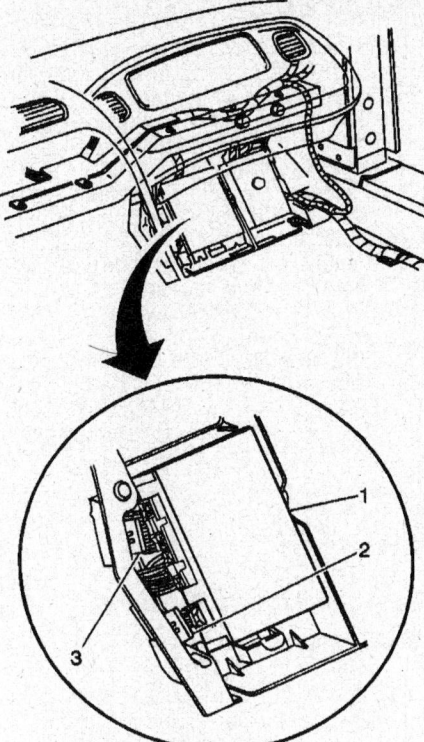

1- PCM
2- Star connector No. 2
3- Star connector No. 1

GC1029816660000X

Fig. 1 Splice pack/star connectors. 2000 Corvette

AURORA, BONNEVILLE, CTS, DEVILLE, GRAND PRIX, LESABRE, PARK AVENUE & SEVILLE

The following procedure must be performed when any of the following components are replaced; ignition keys, theft deterrent control module or PCM.

1. Connect suitably programmed scan tool to Data Link Connector (DLC).
2. Turn ignition switch to ON position.
3. Select "Setup New VTD Module" from scan tool special functions menu.
4. Follow scan tool instructions to setup theft deterrent control module.
5. Turn ignition switch to ON position, using master Passkey III key.
6. Observe instrument cluster security lamp, after approximately 10 minutes, lamp should turn off.
7. After lamp turns off, turn ignition switch to OFF position and wait five seconds.
8. Repeat procedure two more times (three times total).
9. With master Passkey III key, start vehicle.
10. Vehicle has now learned key transponder information and PCM has now learned fuel continue password.
11. Clear any Diagnostic Trouble Codes (DTCs) with scan tool.

CATERA

The following procedure must be performed anytime the theft deterrent control module is replaced.

Programming a new theft control module means the consecutive programming of the security code, engine type, key cylinder number, VIN number and ECM to learn the new frequency code. The engine type, VIN number and key cylinder number may also be programmed individually.

The security code and key cylinder number can be obtained by contacting GM TRACS 2000, phone number 1-800-433-6961.

1. Connect suitably programmed scan tool to Data Link Connector (DLC).
2. Access theft deterrent system on scan tool menu.
3. Use arrow keys on scan tool to enter security code obtained from General Motors. **Security code is four alpha numeric character combination and can only be programmed once. After it is entered, combination can not be altered or erased. However, security code is always entered twice for cross check. Scan tool will compare entered codes and evaluate results. If mismatch occurs, security code input must be repeated.**
4. If mistake is made when entering security code (more than two times), module will internally activate security wait time. After first and second attempts, waiting time of 10 seconds each will occur. After third attempt, waiting time of approximately 10 minutes occurs. Each attempt after that will double wait time. Any attempt to enter security code during wait time will fail.
5. Security wait time can be viewed through scan tool menu.
6. Access engine type on scan tool and follow scan tool instructions to program engine type.
7. Enter key cylinder number obtained from General Motors.
8. Program VIN number with scan tool.
9. New ECMs are delivered with immobilizer function deactivated, to activate immobilizer, proceed as follows:

a. Select "Special Functions" from scan tool "Immobilizer" menu.

b. Select "Program Immobilizer," then follow scan tool instructions to activate immobilizer.

CAVALIER & SUNFIRE

In order for a theft deterrent vehicle to run, a password is communicated between the PCM and Instrument Panel Cluster (IPC). If the PCM is replaced, the new PCM needs to learn the correct password for the vehicle. When the new PCM is installed, the EEPROM calibration is flashed into the PCM and the vehicle will learn its' new password upon initial ignition ON. If the IPC is replaced, the PCM needs to learn the new password from the IPC. Use the following procedure to learn the new password.

1. Attempt to start vehicle and leave ignition on.
2. Telltale "THEFT SYSTEM" lamp will flash for approximately 10 minutes.
3. When lamp stops flashing, start vehicle.
4. When vehicle is running, password is learned.

CENTURY, IMPALA, INTRIGUE, MONTE CARLO & REGAL

The following procedure must be performed anytime the BCM or PCM is replaced.

1. Ensure battery is fully charged and there are no Diagnostic Trouble Codes (DTCs) present.
2. Turn ignition switch from OFF position to CRANK position attempting to start vehicle. Vehicle should start and then stall.
3. After vehicle stalls, leave ignition in ON position and observe security indicator on instrument cluster.
4. When security indicator turns off, turn ignition switch off and wait five seconds.
5. Repeat procedure two more times (three times total).
6. Start engine, BCM and PCM have now learned new code.
7. Clear any Diagnostic Trouble Codes (DTCs) present.

CORVETTE

2000

The following procedure must be performed anytime the BCM or ignition key is replaced.

1. Connect suitably programmed scan tool to Data Link Connector (DLC).
2. Program BCM as outlined in "Body Control Module (BCM)."
3. Turn ignition switch to ON position for 11 minutes and turn ignition switch off for 30 seconds.
4. Turn ignition switch to ON position for 11 minutes and turn ignition switch off for 30 seconds.
5. Turn ignition switch to ON position for 11 minutes or until DTC P1630 sets and turn ignition switch off for 30 seconds.
6. Turn ignition switch to ON position for 30 seconds and attempt to start engine.
7. Engine should start, indicating password has been learned.
8. If engine still will not start, diagnose engine control system as outlined in **Motors' "Domestic Engine Performance & Driveability Manual."**
9. Clear Diagnostic Trouble Codes (DTCs).

2001-04

To program the theft deterrent system on these models, refer to "Century, Impala, Intrigue, Monte Carlo & Regal."

ELDORADO

The following procedure must be performed anytime the Instrument Panel Cluster (IPC) or PCM is replaced.

1. Turn ignition switch to ON position.
2. Attempt to start engine and release key to ON position.
3. Observe SECURITY telltale lamp, after approximately 10 minutes lamp should turn off.
4. After lamp turns off, turn ignition switch off and wait five seconds.
5. Repeat procedure two more times (total of three).
6. Start engine, vehicle has now learned password.
7. Clear any Diagnostic Trouble Codes (DTCs) with suitably programmed scan tool.

SATURN

Crankshaft Learn Procedure

The PCM uses crankshaft velocity calculations to determine engine misfire and to run misfire self-diagnostics. The PCM must know precisely the variability in crankshaft notches for this function. The PCM has a notch learn process that learns the variability between notches which must be reset if the crankshaft has been replaced. Using a suitably programmed scan tool, the "Crankshaft Learn Procedure" can be set to "Relearn."

Crankshaft Relearn Procedure

Any time a PCM or crankshaft position sensor is replaced the PCM must relearn the crankshaft notches. Using a suitably programmed scan tool, select Crankshaft Position Variation Learn under the SPECIAL FUNCTIONS menu and follow the on screen prompts. This procedure will not be initiated if a misfire has been detected. If misfire DTCs are present, diagnose and repair before proceeding with crankshaft relearn procedure.

Crankshaft Position System Variation Learn

ION

The following procedure must be performed when any of the following procedures are performed; ECM is replaced, engine is replaced, crankshaft is replaced, crankshaft position sensor is replaced, or any engine repair that disturbs the crankshaft/harmonic balancer to the crankshaft position sensor relationship.

1. Ensure battery is fully charged, parking brake is applied and vehicle wheels are blocked.
2. Place transaxle in Park or Neutral position.
3. Turn accessories off and connect suitably programmed scan tool to Data Link Connector (DLC).
4. Enable "Crankshaft Position System Variation Learning" procedure with scan tool.
5. Start and idle engine until it reaches operating temperature of at least 185°F.
6. Press and hold brake pedal firmly, then raise engine speed to 3,920 RPM, release throttle as soon as engine cuts out.
7. Ensure parking brake is set. **Do not apply brake pedal.**
8. Cycle ignition switch off to on, apply and hold brake pedal.
9. Start and run engine at idle speed.
10. Ensure air conditioning is off.
11. With scan tool, enable crankshaft variation system learn procedure.
12. Accelerate to Wide Open Throttle (WOT), release accelerator as soon as fuel cut-off occurs.
13. Scan tool will display learned procedure is complete by indicating DTC P0315 has been run and passed. If scan tool indicates DTC P0315 has failed or did not run. Refer to **Motors' "Domestic Engine Performance & Driveability Manual"** for DTC P0315 diagnosis.

L SERIES

2.2L ENGINE

Refer to "2.2L & 2.4L Engines" in "Crankshaft Position System Variation Learn" in "General Motors."

3.1L ENGINE

On these engines the Powertrain Control Module (PCM) will program crankshaft position variation automatically.

PCM/ECM Learning Procedure

If the battery is disconnected or if the PCM is replaced, the PCM must go through the learning process. To allow the PCM to relearn, proceed as follows:

1. Start vehicle and run until engine reaches normal operating temperature.
2. Drive vehicle at part throttle, with moderate acceleration and idle conditions until normal performance returns.
3. Park vehicle and engage parking brake with engine running.
4. **On models equipped with automatic transaxle,** place transaxle in Drive position.
5. **On models equipped with manual transaxle,** place transaxle in Neutral position.
6. **On all models,** allow vehicle to idle for

approximately two minutes until engine idle stabilizes. Ensure engine is at normal operating temperature.

Passlock Theft Deterrent Relearn Procedure

There are two methods used to reprogram the Passlock security system, the Seed and Key method and the Auto Learn method. If no components were replaced or the Passlock sensor was the only component replaced, the Auto Learn technique may be used to program the security system. If the BCM or PCM were replaced then the "Seed & Key" method must be used.

SEED & KEY METHOD

1. Turn ignition On.
2. Inspect for body control module (BCM) or powertrain control module (PCM) diagnostic trouble codes (DTCs) using suitably programmed scan tool.
3. Record and repair DTCs.
4. Turn ignition Off.
5. Select "Passlock Relearn" option using suitably programmed scan tool.
6. Wait for 10 minutes and observe security telltale changing from Flashing to On to Off.
7. If ignition is turned Off before telltale changes state, relearn procedure must be performed again.
8. Turn ignition Off.
9. Vehicle should start on next ignition switch cycle.

AUTO LEARN METHOD

1. Turn ignition On.
2. Momentarily turn ignition to Crank position, but do not start vehicle.
3. Wait for 10 minutes.
4. Observe SECURITY telltale changing from Flashing to On to Off.
5. If ignition is turned Off before telltale changes state, procedure will have to be performed again.
6. Turn Ignition Off.
7. Repeat procedure two more times.
8. If vehicle does not start on next ignition switch cycle, repeat procedure.

Remote Keyless Entry Synchronization

The remote keyless entry system does not send the same signal twice. The body control module (BCM) will not execute a signal if it has been sent previously. To synchronize a transmitter with the BCM, simultaneously press and hold the Lock and Unlock buttons on the transmitter for approximately ten seconds near the vehicle. The doors locks will cycle to confirm synchronization.

DaimlerChrysler Corp.

AIR BAG WARNING LAMP

If the Air Bag warning lamp lights and stays on, diagnosis and repair of the air bag system will be required to reset the lamp.

ANTI-LOCK BRAKE SYSTEM WARNING LAMP

This lamp should light when the ignition is turned On. The lamp may light for as long as 30 seconds as a bulb and system inspection. If the lamp remains lit or lights while operating the vehicle, a fault condition in the anti-lock brake system is indicated. When the lamp is lit, turn ignition Off and start the engine again. If the lamp still remains lit, the anti-lock brake system should be serviced. The brake system will remain functional, but without the anti-lock function. After servicing the anti-lock brake system, the lamp will automatically reset. On some models, it may be required to operate the vehicle at a speed over 18 mph and make several hard brake applications from 40 mph to reset the lamp.

CHECK ENGINE LAMP

The Check Engine lamp should light for approximately 3 seconds after the ignition has been turned On as a bulb inspection. If improper or no signals are received by the Single Board Engine Controller (SBEC) from various sensors or if the PCM enters its Limp-In mode, the SBEC will light the Check Engine lamp. After diagnosing and servicing the fuel injection system or emission related systems, the SBEC memory will be cleared after approximately 40–100 ignition key On-Off cycles.

The Check Engine lamp may light if the fuel filler cap has not been completely tightened. The lamp should turn off after the cap has been properly tightened and the vehicle has successfully completed a predetermined number of trip cycles.

On Monaco and Premier models, this lamp should light during engine starting as a bulb inspection. Once the engine has started, the lamp should go off. If the lamp remains lit, the fuel injection and emission control system diagnosis should be performed using tester DRB II. During the diagnosis and repair procedure with tester DRB II, the Check Engine lamp will be reset.

CHECK ENGINE OR MALFUNCTION INDICATOR LAMP

Except Colt & Summit

The powertrain control module monitors a variety of sensors in the fuel injection, ignition, emission and engines systems. Each time the ignition is turned On, the instrument panel MIL should light for approximately two seconds and then go out. If the PCM senses a fault condition with a monitored circuit often enough to indicate an actual fault condition or if it enters its Limp-In mode, it stores a Diagnostic Trouble Code (DTC) in the PCM's memory. If the code applies to a non-emissions related components or system and the fault condition is repaired or ceases to exist, the PCM cancels the code after 40 warm-up cycles. DTCs that affect vehicle emissions light the MIL. Use a suitably programmed scan tool to retrieve and erase DTC's and to reset the MIL.

On 1998 and newer models, the Check Engine lamp may light if the fuel filler cap has not been completely tightened. The

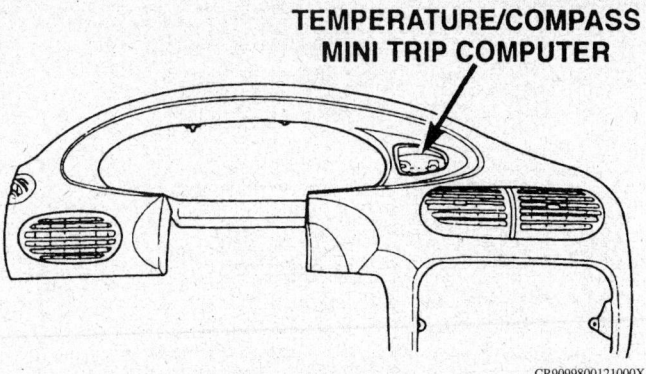

Fig. 1 Compass/temperature mini trip computer. Concorde, Intrepid, LHS, Vision, 300M & 1994–96 New Yorker

lamp should turn off after the cap has been properly tightened and the vehicle has successfully completed a predetermined number of trip cycles.

Colt & Summit

This lamp is used to monitor fuel injection and emission control system components for faults. When the ignition is turned On, the lamp will light for 2–3 seconds as a bulb inspection. If the lamp remains on, a fault in the fuel injection or emission control system is indicated. If fault is intermittent, the lamp will go off when the Electronic Control Unit (ECU) receives a normal signal from the faulting component. If the ECU receives an improper signal from a faulting component for a time longer than that programmed into the ECU, a code will be stored in the ECU memory and the Malfunction Indicator Lamp should light. After servicing the indicated component, the Malfunction Indicator Lamp can be reset by clearing the ECU memory. The ECU memory is cleared by using a suitable scan tool or disconnecting the battery ground cable for approximately 10 seconds.

COMPASS & TEMPERATURE MINI TRIP COMPUTER

Concorde, Intrepid, LHS, Vision, 300M & 1994–96 New Yorker

1. Set mini trip computer to Compass/Temperature mode, **Fig. 1.**
2. Press US/M and STEP buttons simultaneously until VAR and current variance zone number is displayed.
3. Press STEP until proper variance zone number is displayed, **Fig. 2.**
4. After 5 seconds of inactivity, displayed zone will be set automatically. Ensure accuracy of compass by pointing vehicle in N, S, E and W directions.

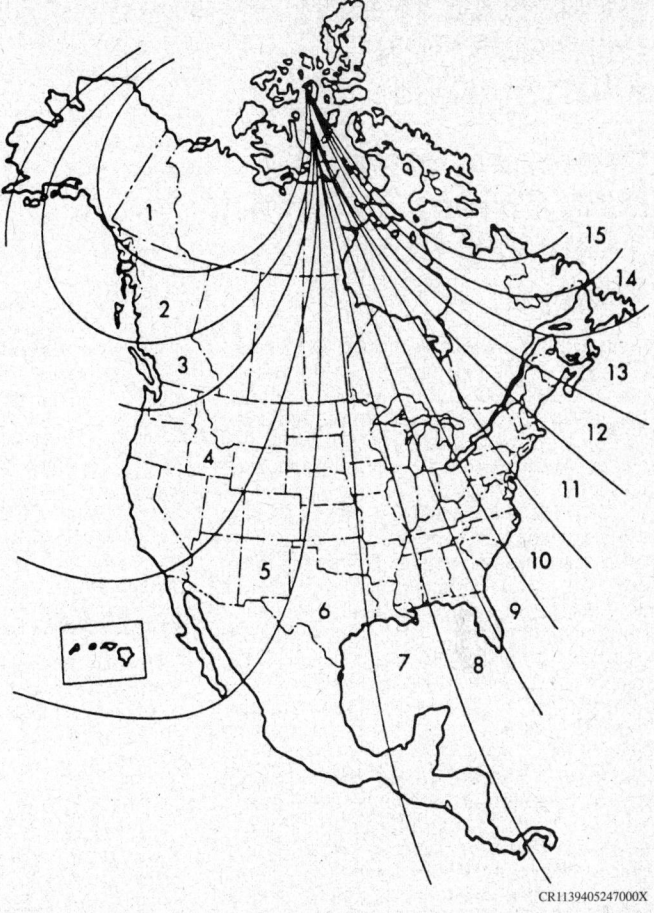

Fig. 2 Variance zone map. Concorde, Intrepid, LHS, Vision, 300M & 1994–96 New Yorker

Sebring Convertible

If the CAL indicator lights, the compass will need to be calibrated. This should be done on a level surface free of large metal objects such as other vehicles, bridges, buildings, railroads and underground cables. Proceed as follows:

1. Drive in complete circles, keeping steering wheel in fixed position, at speeds of 7–10 mph until CAL indicator turns Off. This may require two to six turns.
2. When CAL indicator turns Off, compass has been calibrated and should now display proper headings.
3. Inspect for proper calibrations by selecting North, South, East and West.
4. If compass does not appear to be reading accurately, calibration procedure should be repeated in another area.

ELECTRONIC VEHICLE INFORMATION CENTER

1992–93 Dynasty, Fifth Avenue, Imperial & New Yorker

The Electronic Vehicle Information Center is a computer controlled warning system which monitors various sensors used on the vehicle. The system supplements the warning indicators in the instrument cluster. When a warning message has been activated, a tone will sound to attract the driver's attention. The warning message will then be displayed on the overhead console until the condition has been corrected or a new display function is called up, **Fig. 3.** A tone will announce each new warning condition. The "Service Reminder" warning message will be indicated at 7,500 mile or 12 month intervals to indicate that required service is to be performed. After performing the required service, the Service Reminder message can be reset by using a DRB II diagnostic readout tool.

OVERHEAD TRAVEL INFORMATION SYSTEM (OTIS)

Concorde, Intrepid, LHS, Vision, 300M & 1994–96 New Yorker

Overhead Travel Information System (OTIS) is a module with six informational displays and four buttons. When the ignition is turned ON, OTIS blanks the display for one second and returns to the display active when the vehicle was last turned OFF.

LOW OIL PRESSURE—This message will be displayed when a low engine oil pressure condition exists. If message is encountered with vehicle operating at idle speed, increase engine RPM. If message remains or if message is encountered while operating vehicle, the engine lubricating system should be inspected and serviced immediately. After engine lubricating system has been serviced, the message will be automatically cancelled.

SERVICE REMINDER—This message will be indicated at 7,500 mile or 12 month intervals to indicate that required service is to be performed. After performing the required service, with the Service Reminder message displayed, depress the Vehicle Electronic Information Center Reset button.

TURN SIGNAL ON—This message will be indicated when the turn signal is on and the vehicle has traveled a distance over ½ mile at a speed more than 15 mph. The message will be reset when the turn signal lever has been returned to Off.

VOLTAGE IMPROPER—When this message is displayed, a fault condition in the charging or electrical system exists. After servicing, the message will be reset after the ignition has been cycled to the OFF position.

WASHER FLUID LOW—When this message is displayed, bring washer fluid to proper level. This message will be reset after the ignition has been cycled to the OFF position.

The six informational displays are:
1. Compass/temperature.
2. Average fuel economy.
3. Distance to empty.
4. Instantaneous fuel economy.
5. Trip odometer.
6. Elapsed time.

The four buttons on the OTIS are:
1. STEP—Depress this button to select display modes except Compass/temperature.
2. C/T—Depress this button to display compass (vehicle direction) and temperature.
3. U/SM—Switches display information between English and Metric readings.
4. RESET—Depress this button to reset current display (for displays that can be reset.)

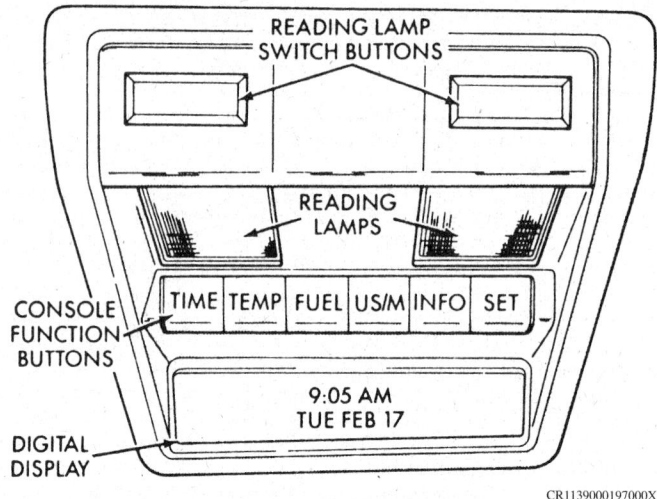

Fig. 3 Electronic Vehicle Information Center display console. 1992–93 Dynasty, Fifth Avenue, Imperial & New Yorker

COMPASS CALIBRATION

Do not attempt to set compass calibration near large metal objects, such as other vehicles, buildings or bridges.
1. Remove magnetic devices from roof panel.
2. Turn ignition On.
3. Press C/T button to select Compass/temperature display.
4. Depress and hold RESET button for approximately five seconds. VAR symbol will light during this time.
5. Continue to hold RESET button for approximately 10 seconds until CAL symbol lights.
6. Drive vehicle through three complete 360° turns in no less than 48 seconds. Compass will be calibrated when CAL symbol is extinguished.
7. Press and hold RESET button for approximately five seconds until VAR symbol is lit.
8. OTIS will display variance zone and VAR.
9. Press STEP button to display variance zone, **Fig. 2.**
10. Press RESET button to set new variance zone and resume normal operation.

LOW COOLANT WARNING LAMP

The Low Coolant warning lamp should light whenever coolant level in the coolant reservoir is below a predetermined level. Add coolant to bring reservoir to proper level to turn lamp off.

POWER LOSS/LIMIT LAMP

The Power Loss/Limit lamp should light for approximately 3 seconds after the ignition has been turned On as a bulb inspection. If improper or no signals are received by the logic module from various sensors, the logic module will light the Power Loss/Limit lamp. After diagnosing and servicing the fuel injection system or EGR system (California models with EGR sensor), the logic module memory can be cleared by disconnecting and connecting the battery quick-disconnect.

VEHICLE MAINTENANCE MONITOR (VMM) SYSTEM

This system, **Fig. 4,** monitors regular service and maintenance intervals, engine oil level, engine coolant level, windshield washer fluid level, brake and tail lamps, door ajar and oil, coolant and washer sensors.

When the vehicle is started and no faults are present, the display will indicate "MONITOR." If the monitor detects a fault, it will be noted on the display. If more than one fault is noted, the fault of the highest priority will be displayed first. The display will then note all existing faults and return to the fault of highest priority. The VMM fault messages are as follows:

DOOR—Door Ajar—Close door indicated on vehicle outline display to reset monitor.

LAMP—Brake or Tail Lamp Outage—The display should light when brake is applied or headlamp switch is in the On position and a burned out lamp bulb is present. To reset monitor, replace burned out bulb.

COOLANT—Low Engine Coolant Level—Bringing coolant to proper level will reset monitor.

OIL—Low Engine Oil Level—The system will inspect engine oil level approximately 12 minutes after the ignition has been turned Off. A low oil level condition must be indicated three consecutive times before the monitor will display "Oil." To reset monitor, add oil to bring to proper level. Then, while display is indicating the "Oil" message, depress RESET select switch

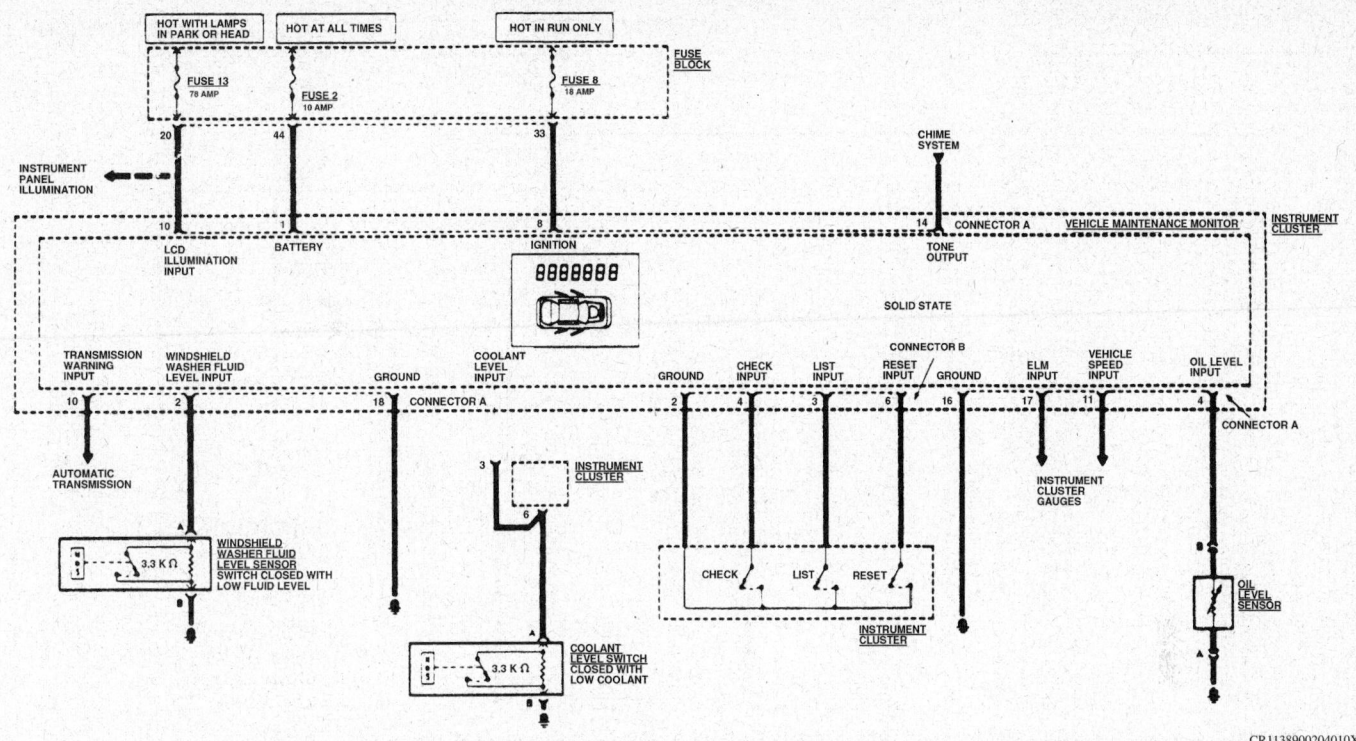

Fig. 4   Vehicle Maintenance Monitor (VMM) System wiring schematic (Part 1 of 2). Monaco & Premier

until a beep is noted. Even if RESET select switch is not depressed, the system will automatically reset monitor after three proper oil level readings have been obtained.

WASHER—Low Washer Fluid Level—Bringing washer fluid to proper level will reset monitor.

SERVICE—Perform Required Service and Maintenance—This message will be indicated at 7,500 mile intervals to indicate that required service is to be performed. After performing required service, depress the Reset select switch until a beep is noted.

SENSOR—This message will be indicated when a defect in the oil, coolant or washer sensor circuit is noted. Refer to "Self Diagnosis."

MILES (KMS)—Mile to next scheduled service interval.

Self Diagnosis

To diagnose, depress and hold the Check and List select switches, then turn ignition On. With the instrument cluster switch in the English mode, all diagnosis will be performed automatically in sequence. With the instrument cluster in the Metric mode, the Check select switch will have to be depressed to proceed to the next test. The display will indicate which

components are faulty or satisfactory. Refer to **Fig. 5.** After completing diagnosis, depress Check and List select switches to exit diagnosis mode.

Troubleshooting

1. If a condition of no display or improper information exists, start engine and inspect the following:
    a. **On models less passive restraint,** inspect fuses 8 and 19 in fuse panel. **On models equipped with passive restraint,** inspect fuses 2 and 8 in fuse panel. Replace any blown fuses.
    b. **On all models,** inspect terminal Nos. 1 and 5 of connector A using a suitable voltmeter, **Fig. 4.** Voltmeter should indicate battery voltage. If not, inspect for open circuit to fuse panel.
    c. Connect a suitable ohmmeter between terminal Nos. 15 and 18 of connector A, **Fig. 4.** Ohmmeter should indicate zero ohms. If a no display condition is present, replace monitor. If an improper information condition is present, refer to "Self Diagnosis." If reading is other than zero ohms, inspect for open circuit.
    d. With all doors closed, connect an

ohmmeter between terminal Nos. 6, 7, 8 and 9 of connector A, **Fig. 4.** Ohmmeter should indicate an infinite reading. If reading is other than infinite, inspect for short circuit to ground.

2. If monitor fails to change modes, disconnect electrical connector B, **Fig. 4,** and proceed as follows:
    a. With Check select switch depressed, connect ohmmeter between terminal Nos. 2 and 4 of connector B. If ohmmeter reading is zero ohms, proceed to step b. If ohmmeter reading is other than zero ohms, replace mode select switches.
    b. With List select switch depressed, connect ohmmeter between terminal Nos. 2 and 3 of connector B. If ohmmeter reading is zero ohms, proceed to step c. If ohmmeter reading is other than zero ohms, replace mode select switches.
    c. With Reset select switch depressed, connect ohmmeter between terminal Nos. 2 and 5 of connector B. Ohmmeter reading should be zero ohms. If ohmmeter reading is other than zero ohms, replace mode select switches.

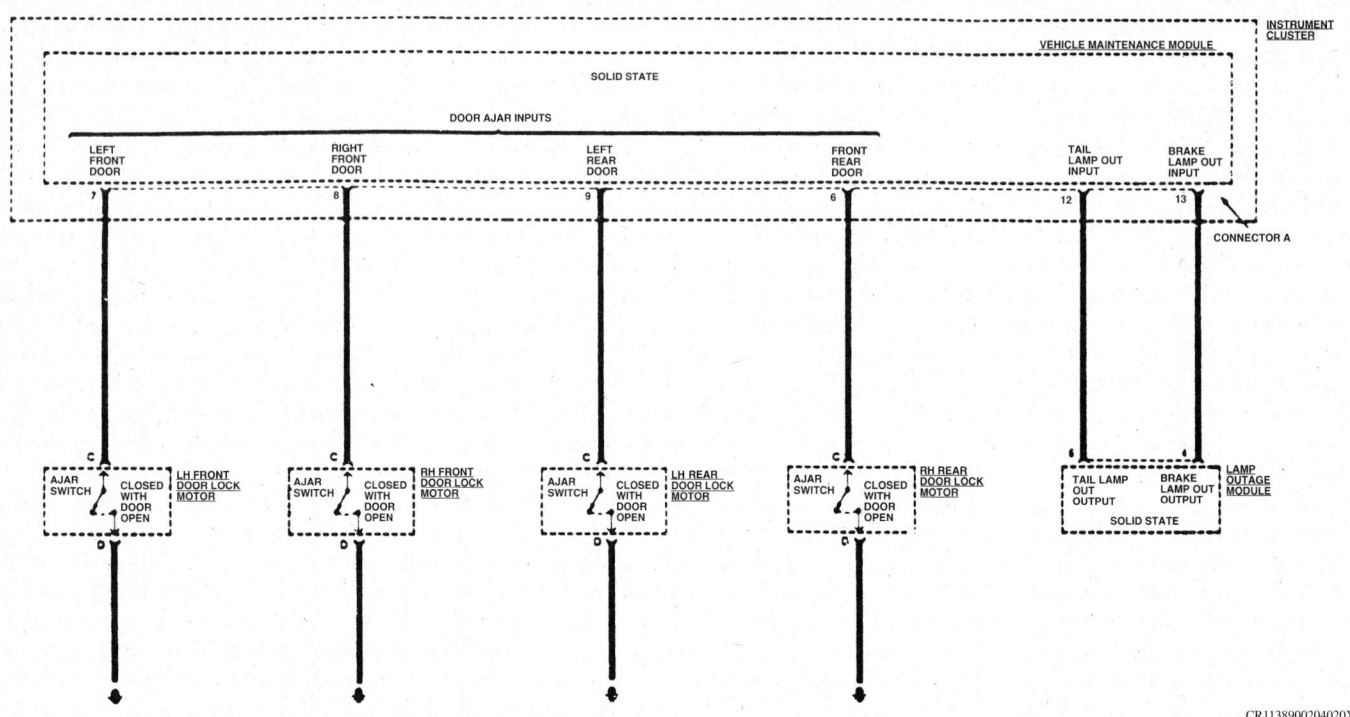

Fig. 4   Vehicle Maintenance Monitor (VMM) System wiring schematic (Part 2 of 2). Monaco & Premier

Ford Motor Co.

INDEX

AIR BAG WARNING LAMP

If the Air Bag warning lamp lights and stays on, diagnosis and repair of the air bag system will be required to reset the lamp.

ANTI-LOCK BRAKE WARNING LAMP

This lamp should light when the ignition is turned On. It may light for as long as 30 seconds as a bulb and system inspect. If the lamp remains lit or lights while operating the vehicle, a fault condition in the anti-lock brake system is indicated. When the lamp is lit, turn ignition Off and start engine again. If the lamp still remains lit, the anti-lock brake system should be serviced. The brake system will remain functional, but without the anti-lock function. After servicing the anti-lock brake system, the lamp will automatically reset when the vehicle is operated at a speed over 25 mph.

CHECK ENGINE LAMP

EEC-IV

1992-93

EXCEPT FESTIVA, PROBE w/2.2L ENGINE & ESCORT & TRACER w/1.8L ENGINE

This lamp should light when the ignition is turned On. After the engine is started, the lamp should go off, unless a fault condition is detected by the EEC-IV system. Following diagnosis and repair, the Check Engine/MIL lamp will automatically reset when the stored codes are cleared from the EEC-IV system memory. After diagnosis and repair, the EEC-IV memory may be cleared of stored codes as follows:

1. With ignition turned Off, connect a jumper wire between Self Test and Self Test Input (STI) connectors, **Fig. 1. On Crown Victoria, Grand Marquis and Town Car models,** the Self Test and STI connectors are gray in color and are located on the front of the lefthand fender apron, near the Electronic Engine Control (EEC) relay. **On Mustang models,** the Self Test and STI connectors are gray in color and are located on the lefthand fender apron. **On Tempo and Topaz models,** the Self Test connector is gray in color and the STI connector is black in color and they are both located on the righthand fender apron, near the front of the strut tower. **On Taurus and Sable models,** the Self Test and STI connectors are gray in color and are located on the righthand fender apron, near the front of the engine in the area of the AIR pump and alternator. **On 1992-93 Thunderbird and Cougar models,** the Self Test and STI connectors are gray in color and are located on the righthand fender apron, near the strut tower.
2. **On all models,** turn ignition On, then

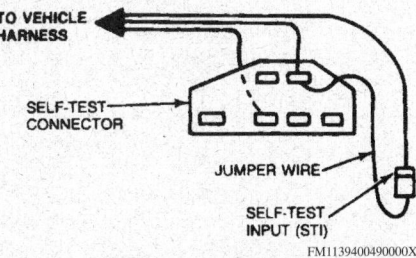

MESSAGE CENTER (CONTINENTAL ONLY)

Fig. 1 Jumper wire connections for resetting Check Engine lamp. EEC-IV Except Festiva, Probe w/2.2L Engine & Escort & Tracer w/1.8L Engine

disconnect jumper wire from test connector terminals. Disconnect jumper as soon as Check Engine lamp starts flashing.

FESTIVA

The Check Engine Indicator lamp should light when the ignition is in the RUN position with the engine not operating. When the engine is started, the Check Engine lamp should go off. If the lamp remains on, a service code has been stored in the EEC-IV self test system memory. After diagnosis and repair, the self test memory may be cleared of stored codes as follows:

1. With ignition turned Off, connect a jumper wire between Self Test Input (STI) connector terminal and ground. The STI connector is located in rear lefthand side of engine compartment, **Fig. 2.**
2. Turn ignition On, then disconnect and reconnect jumper wire connected between STI connector and ground.
3. Disconnect jumper from STI connector as soon as Check Engine lamp stops flashing.
4. Disconnect battery ground cable and depress brake pedal for approximately 5–10 seconds.
5. Connect battery ground cable.

PROBE w/2.2L ENGINE & ESCORT & TRACER w/1.8L ENGINE

This lamp should light when the ignition is turned On. After engine is started, the lamp should go off, unless a fault condition is detected by the system. After diagnosis and repair, the Check Engine lamp will automatically reset when stored codes are cleared from the system memory. After diagnosis and repair, memory may be cleared of stored codes as follows:

1. Disconnect battery ground cable, then depress brake pedal for approximately 5–10 seconds.
2. Connect battery ground cable again.

1995-97

This lamp should light when the ignition is turned On. After engine starts, the lamp should go off, unless a fault condition is de-

tected by the EEC-IV system. A diagnostic trouble code is stored in the PCM. Following diagnosis and repair, the Check Engine/MIL lamp will automatically reset when stored diagnostic trouble codes are cleared from PCM memory. The PCM reset procedure allows the scan tool to command the PCM to clear all diagnostic trouble codes.

PCM RESET USING STAR TESTER

1. Turn ignition Off.
2. Perform required vehicle preparation and visual inspection.
3. Connect Star tester, then select vehicle model and year.
4. Follow operating instructions on tester screen. Select Generic OBD II Functions.
5. Press CONT button if all OBD II monitors are not complete.
6. Turn ignition On.
7. Select Clear Diagnostic Codes and press Start key.

PCM RESET USING GENERIC SCAN TOOL

1. Turn ignition Off.
2. Connect scan tool to DLC.
3. Turn ignition On.
4. Perform scan tool reset, then turn ignition Off.

KEEP ALIVE MEMORY (KAM) RESET & PCM RESET LESS ELECTRONIC TESTER

To clear KAM, disconnect battery ground cable for at least 5 minutes. This will also result in PCM reset.

EEC-V

1. Turn ignition Off.
2. Connect scan tool to DLC.
3. Turn ignition On.
4. Perform scan tool reset and turn ignition Off.
5. **On 1998 and newer models,** Check Engine lamp may light if fuel filler cap has not been completely tightened. Lamp should turn off after cap has been properly tightened and vehicle has successfully completed predetermined number of trip cycles.

CHECK FUEL CAP LAMP

The Check Fuel Cap Lamp will illuminate momentarily when the ignition switch is placed in ON position as a bulb check. If the lamp remains On, inspect fuel cap for proper installation. After properly installing the fuel cap the lamp should go off after a normal period of driving.

ELECTRONIC COMPASS

Continental

1. Determine magnetic zone, **Fig. 3.**
2. Insert suitable rod into compass module, **Fig. 4,** and press internal switch until ZONE and current zone setting are displayed.
3. Turn ignition On and release switch.
4. Press internal switch until proper zone

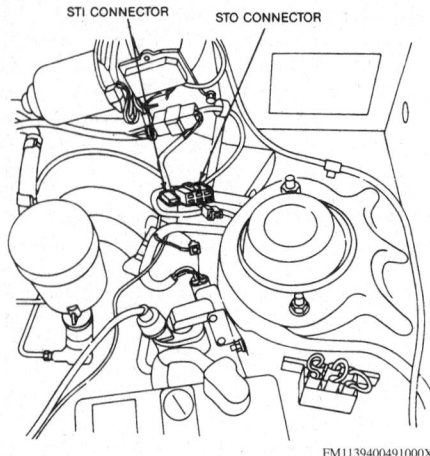

Fig. 2 STI connector location. Festiva

number is displayed, release to exit zone setting mode and lock in zone.

Mark VIII

1. Press and hold COMPASS button, then the RESET button until ECO-ZONE and RSETCAL is displayed.
2. Press FUEL ECONOMY button to enter the zone set mode.
3. Refer to **Fig. 3,** for proper compass zone selection.
4. Press RESET until correct zone is selected.
5. Press COMPASS button to end zone adjustment.

Town Car

The compass module is located at the back of the rearview mirror.
1. Select compass magnetic zone, **Fig. 3.**
2. Press and hold reset button on top of compass module until message center display reads current magnetic zone setting.
3. Press calibration button on compass module to select proper zone setting.
4. To exit zone setting mode, do not press any buttons for 10 seconds.

LOW COOLANT WARNING SYSTEM

The low coolant warning lamp should light whenever the coolant level in the coolant recovery bottle is ¼ to ¾ inch or more below the cold full mark. Raise coolant level in recovery bottle to the cold full mark to turn lamp off.

On models equipped with GEM module and low coolant level warning system, the low coolant level indicator lights for two seconds during engine startup or when ignition is turned to RUN. If coolant level falls below specification for more than 15 seconds, the GEM module generates a single one second tone. Raise coolant level in recovery bottle to specified level to turn lamp off.

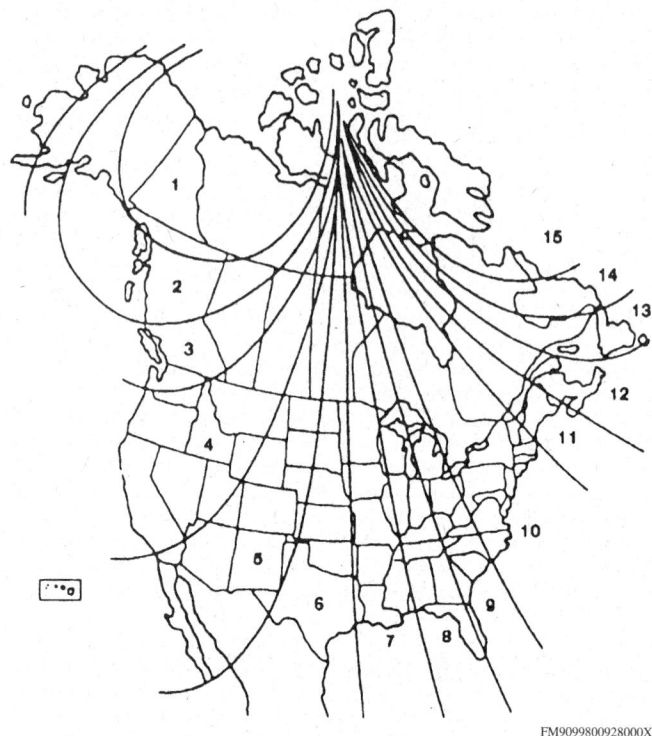

Fig. 3 Magnetic zone map. Continental & Town Car

LOW OIL LEVEL WARNING INDICATOR

This system is used to indicate when the engine oil level is 1½ quarts or more below the specified level. The lamp should light during engine starting. If the oil level is sufficient, the lamp will go off when the engine is operating. If the oil level is low, the lamp will remain on until engine oil is added and the ignition is turned Off. The module will take approximately 5 minutes to reset. If the engine is started during this period, the last recorded reading will be displayed.

MALFUNCTION INDICATOR LAMP (MIL)

Refer to "Check Engine Lamp" for lamp reset procedure.

MESSAGE CENTER

Crown Victoria, Grand Marquis & Town Car

The message center may be located to the right of the instrument cluster, or it may be a part of the cluster itself. It consists of three buttons: Select, E/M and Reset. The E/M button switches the display between English and Metric. The Reset button set data to zero of instantaneous information. The Select button cycles the message display through the following selections:
1. Average speed.

2. Fuel remaining.
3. Average fuel economy and instantaneous fuel economy.
4. Distance to empty.
5. Trip distance.

Mark VIII

AIR RIDE SWITCH OFF

This warning message is displayed when the air suspension service switch, located in the luggage compartment, is turned Off.

CHECK AIR RIDE SYSTEM

This warning message is displayed when an air suspension system diagnostic trouble code is detected by the air suspension/EVO control module.

CHECK CHARGING SYSTEM

This warning message is displayed when the electrical system is not maintaining a proper voltage at the message center.

CHECK ENGINE TEMP

This warning message is displayed when the coolant is overheating.

LOW ENGINE COOLANT

This warning message is displayed when the engine coolant level is below the cold line of the coolant recovery reservoir.

CHECK EXTERIOR LAMPS

This warning message is displayed when one of the following lamps is turned on and at least one is burned out: stop lamp, rear parking lamp or low beam headlamp.

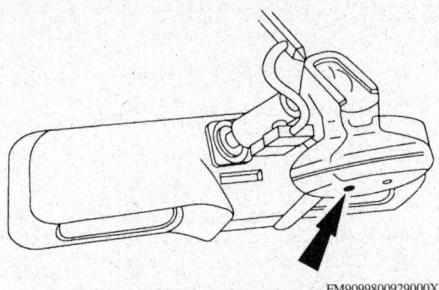

Fig. 4 Compass module location. Continental

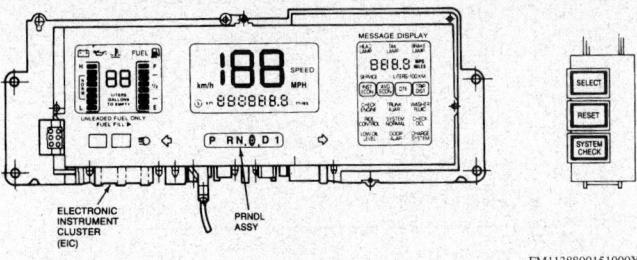

Fig. 5 Instrument cluster & message center. Continental

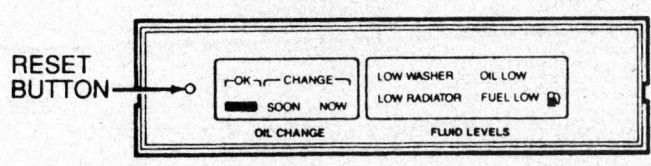

Fig. 6 Oil change interval indicator reset switch access hole location. 1992–93 Cougar & Thunderbird

CHANGE OIL SOON OR OIL CHANGE REQUIRED

The oil life functions include oil life, change oil soon and oil change required. The oil life is determined by three functions: Smart Tach pulses, miles driven and time elapsed.

When the oil life drops down to the range of 1–5%, the "Change Oil Soon" message will appear. When oil life is 0%, the "Oil Change Required" message will appear.

Depressing the oil change reset button will reset the oil life to 100%.

SERVICE INTERVAL REMINDER

Continental

After performing the required interval service, the service interval reminder mileage display on the instrument cluster can be reset as follows:
1. Depress System Check button on instrument panel. Service interval reminder mileage should be displayed on fuel computer display, **Fig. 5**.
2. Depress Reset button. Service interval reminder mileage should start flashing.
3. Depress Reset and System Check buttons at same time to reset mileage.

Cougar

1992-93

At approximately 7,500 miles, for models less super charged engine, the engine oil change indicator on the Vehicle Maintenance Monitor will indicate an oil change is needed. On models with super charged engine, the need for engine oil change will be indicated at 5,000 miles. After completing the required service, the oil change indicate can be reset by depressing the reset switch, **Fig. 6**.

1999

Some of these models are equipped with an optional overhead warning lamp system which includes a Service Interval reminder. This will light after approximately 358 days or 4800 miles to indicate that routine service is needed.

After service has been performed, the lamp can be reset by holding the trip computer SELECT and UNITS buttons for 5 seconds. The Service Interval lamp will light, then turn off after approximately four seconds.

2000-02

The maintenance interval warning indicator is controlled by the HEC. The HEC illuminates the indicator advising a scheduled maintenance (which is dependant on time of distance). The indicator is reset by placing the ignition switch in position II and depressing SELECT & UNITS buttons simultaneously for five seconds until maintenance light extinguishes.

LS

CHANGE OIL SOON OR OIL CHANGE REQUIRED

The oil life functions include "Oil Life OK, Change Oil Soon" and "Oil Change Required." The oil life is determined by the engine oil level and temperature sensors, ABS control module, odometer data and PCM RPM data.

When the oil life reaches the range of 1–5%, the "Change Oil Soon" message will appear. When oil life is 0%, the "Oil Change Required" message will appear.

Depressing the oil change RESET button will reset the oil life to 100%.

Mark VIII

CHANGE OIL SOON OR OIL CHANGE REQUIRED

The oil life functions include "Oil Life OK, Change Oil Soon" and "Oil Change Required." The oil life is determined by the engine oil level and temperature sensors, ABS control module, odometer data and PCM RPM data.

When the oil life reaches the range of 1–5%, the "Change Oil Soon" message will appear. When oil life is 0%, the "Oil Change Required" message will appear.

Depressing the oil change RESET button will reset the oil life to 100%.

Probe

ELECTRONIC INSTRUMENT CLUSTER

At 7,500 mile intervals, a Service Check message will be displayed under the System Scanner nomenclature on the instrument cluster for 3 minutes after engine starts, **Fig. 7**. After performing the required interval service, reset the service interval by depressing and holding the Service reset button, located on the speed alarm keyboard, until three tones have sounded, **Fig. 8**.

VEHICLE MAINTENANCE MONITOR

At 7,500 mile intervals a Service lamp, located on the overhead map lamp console, should light for 3 minutes after engine start, **Fig. 9**. After performing the required interval service, reset the service interval. **On models equipped with speed alarm keypad,** depress and hold the Service reset button, until three tones have sounded. **On models less speed alarm keypad,** locate reset hole in overhead console, then use a suitable tool to depress the reset button located behind the hole.

Thunderbird

1992-93

At approximately 7,500 miles, for models less super charged engine, the engine oil change indicator on the Vehicle Maintenance Monitor will indicate an oil change is needed. On models with super charged engine, the need for engine oil change will be indicated at 5,000 miles. After completing the required service, the oil change indicate can be reset by depressing the reset switch, **Fig. 6**.

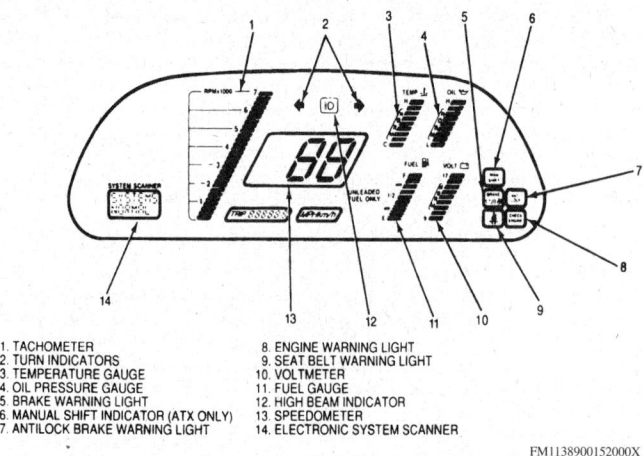

Fig. 7 Electronic instrument cluster. Probe

1. TACHOMETER
2. TURN INDICATORS
3. TEMPERATURE GAUGE
4. OIL PRESSURE GAUGE
5. BRAKE WARNING LIGHT
6. MANUAL SHIFT INDICATOR (ATX ONLY)
7. ANTILOCK BRAKE WARNING LIGHT
8. ENGINE WARNING LIGHT
9. SEAT BELT WARNING LIGHT
10. VOLTMETER
11. FUEL GAUGE
12. HIGH BEAM INDICATOR
13. SPEEDOMETER
14. ELECTRONIC SYSTEM SCANNER

FM1138900152000X

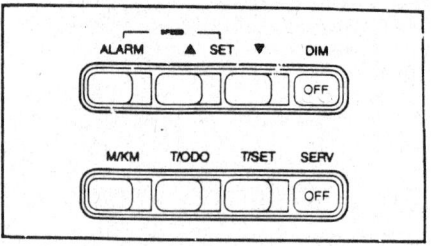

Fig. 8 Speed alarm keyboard. Probe

FM1138900153000X

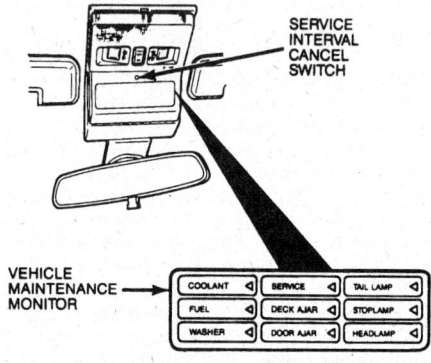

Fig. 9 Vehicle maintenance monitor. Probe

FM1138900154000X

General Motors Corp.

INDEX

AIR BAG WARNING LAMP

If the air bag warning lamp lights and stays on, diagnosis and repair of the air bag system will be required to reset the lamp.

ANTI-LOCK WARNING LAMP

This lamp should light when the ignition is turned On. The lamp may light for as long as 30 seconds as a bulb and system inspection. If lamp remains lit or lights while operating the vehicle, a fault condition in the anti-lock brake system is indicated. When lamp is lit, turn ignition Off and restart engine. If lamp still remains lit, the anti-lock brake system should be serviced. The brake system will remain functional, but without the anti-lock function. After servicing the anti-lock brake system the lamp will automatically reset. **On some models,** it may be required to operate vehicle at a speed over 18 mph to reset lamp.

CHANGE AUTOMATIC TRANSMISSION/ TRANSAXLE FLUID INDICATOR

DeVille & Seville

1. Turn ignition switch to ON position.
2. Press INFO button on Driver Information Center (DIC) button to display "Trans Fluid Life."
3. Press and hold Info RESET button on DIC until display reads "100% Trans Fluid Life."
4. Place ignition switch in Off position

Eldorado

2000

1. Turn ignition switch to ON position.
2. Press INFO button on Driver Information Center (DIC) button to display "Trans Fluid Life."
3. Press and hold Info RESET button on DIC until display reads "100% Trans Fluid Life."
4. Place ignition switch in Off position

2001-02

1. Turn ignition switch to ON position.
2. Press and hold OFF and REAR DEFOG buttons on climate control until "Trans Fluid Life Reset" appears on DIC
3. Place ignition switch in Off position

CHANGE ENGINE OIL MESSAGE

Buick

CENTURY & REGAL

1997

The Driver Information Center (DIC) en-gine oil life monitor indicates when to change oil. The "Change Oil" or "Change Oil Soon" messages might appear before 2,000 miles when operating under severe conditions.

To reset the oil change indicator after an oil change, proceed as follows:

1. Turn ignition On.
2. Fully depress and release accelerator pedal three times in 5 seconds.
3. If "Change Oil" or "Change Oil Soon" message flashes twice, indicator has properly reset.
4. If "Change Oil" or "Change Oil Soon" message stays on for 5 seconds, indicator has not properly reset and must be reset again.
5. **On models equipped with Oil Life Monitor,** press and hold RESET button for more than 5 seconds while oil monitor is being displayed or until oil life percentage reaches 100%.

1999

The Engine Oil Life monitor indicates when an oil and filter change are needed, usually from 3000–10,000 miles since the last change. The CHANGE OIL SOON indicator may light even before 3000 miles if the vehicle has been operated under severe service.

The monitor will not detect dust in the oil. If operating in dusty conditions be sure to change the oil and filter every 3000 miles or sooner if the CHANGE OIL SOON lamp lights.

To reset the Engine Oil Life monitor proceed as follows:

1. Turn ignition On, but do not start engine.
2. Fully depress and release accelerator pedal three times within 5 seconds.
3. If CHANGE OIL SOON lamp flashes twice, this means system is properly reset.
4. If CHANGE OIL SOON lamp lights and stays lit for 5 seconds, system did not reset. Repeat reset procedure.

2000-05

To reset the Engine Oil Life monitor proceed as follows:

1. Turn ignition On, but do not start engine.
2. Fully depress and release accelerator pedal three times within 5 seconds. The oil life indicator will begin to flash indicating the system is resetting.
3. Place ignition switch in Off position, then start engine.
4. The engine oil change light should illuminate as a bulb check and then go Off.
5. If oil change light remains On, repeat reset procedure.

LESABRE & PARK AVENUE

1992-95

After the engine oil has been changed, the "Change Oil Soon" lamp must be reset. With ignition On, use a pencil to depress the RESET button, located under the right-hand side of the instrument panel, for 5 sec-onds. The lamp should flash four times to indicate the Oil Life Monitor System has been reset.

1996-97

After the engine oil has been changed, display the oil life index on the DIC, then hold the RESET button for 5 seconds. When a DIC message of RESET is displayed and the oil life index equals 100%, the reset is complete.

1998

1. Turn ignition to Run.
2. Press TRIP button on driver's information center until OIL LIFE REMAINING is displayed.
3. Press and hold RESET for 6 seconds, then turn ignition off.

1999

1. Turn ignition On, then press TRIP button on driver's information center (DIC) switch to view various menu choices and stop on OIL LIFE REMAINING. A message will display percentage of oil life remaining.
2. Press and hold RESET button on DIC switch for at least two seconds. A message will display the percentage of oil life remaining as 99%. The engine oil life monitor is now reset.
3. Turn ignition Off.

2000-05

1. Turn ignition switch to On position.
2. Display Oil Life Index on Driver Information Center (DIC), then press and hold RESET button for more than 5 seconds until display reads 100%.
3. Turn ignition Off.

ROADMASTER

1994

After engine oil has been changed, the Change Oil lamp must be reset. Remove the instrument panel fuse box cover. With ignition On, depress the OIL RESET button for 5 seconds. The Change Oil lamp should go off.

1995-96

1. Turn ignition On, without starting engine.
2. Within 5 seconds, depress accelerator pedal to wide open position and release three times.
3. When lamp goes out, engine oil life monitor is reset. PCM will acknowledge if reset was successful by flashing Change Oil lamp twice, then will turn lamp off. If lamp does not reset, turn ignition Off and repeat procedure.

RIVIERA

1997-98

1. Turn ignition to Run.
2. Press TRIP button on driver's information center until OIL LIFE REMAINING is displayed.
3. Press and hold RESET for 6 seconds, then turn ignition off.

1999

1. Turn ignition to On, then press TRIP button on driver's information center (DIC) switch to view various menu choices and stop on OIL LIFE REMAINING. A message will display percentage of oil life remaining.
2. Press and hold RESET button on DIC switch for at least two seconds. A message will display percentage of oil life remaining as 99%. The engine oil life monitor is now reset.
3. Turn ignition Off.

Cadillac

ALLANTE

Press RANGE button until oil index appears, then simultaneously press and hold the AVG SPD and RANGE buttons for a minimum of 5 seconds.

CTS

LESS NAVIGATION SYSTEM

1. Access Driver Information Center (DIC) menu by pressing arrow key on INFO button located on righthand side of DIC.
2. When "100% ENGINE OIL LIFE" is highlighted, press and hold CLR button.
3. Percentage will return to 100 and oil life indicator will be reset.
4. If percentage will not return to 100, repeat procedure.

WITH NAVIGATION SYSTEM

1. Turn system on by pressing PWR/VOL knob once. PWR/VOL knob is located on lefthand side of Driver Information Center (DIC).
2. Access vehicle information menu by pressing INFO button on lefthand side DIC.
3. Turn TUNE/SEL knob on righthand side of DIC until "Engine Oil Life" is highlighted and press knob to select it.
4. When "100% Engine Oil Life" is displayed, press multi-function button next to "Reset" prompt in upper righthand corner of display.
5. Percentage will return to 100 and oil life indicator will reset.
6. If percentage does not return to 100, repeat procedure.

DEVILLE

1992

Press RANGE and FUEL USED buttons simultaneously to display oil life index, then press the RANGE and RESET buttons until "Change Oil Soon" light flashes (approximately 5 seconds). The oil life index will not remain displayed.

1993

Reset the Engine Oil Life Index (EOLI) after each oil change by pressing the RANGE and RESET keys on the Fuel Data Center for 5–50 seconds. The "Change Oil Soon" lamp will flash four times to indicate that the index has been reset.

1994-98

Press the INFORMATION button until Oil Life Index is displayed, then press and hold RESET button until Oil Life Index resets to 100 (approximately 5 seconds).

1999

1. Turn ignition On, then press TRIP button on driver's information center (DIC) switch to view various menu choices and stop on OIL LIFE REMAINING. A message will display percentage of oil life remaining.
2. Press and hold RESET button on DIC switch for at least two seconds. A message will display the percentage of oil life remaining as 99%. The engine oil life monitor is now reset.
3. Turn ignition Off.

2000-05

1. Turn ignition On, press Gauge Info button on Driver Information Center (DIC) switch to view various menu choices and stop on OIL LIFE REMAINING. Message will display percentage of oil life remaining.
2. Press and hold RESET button on DIC switch until display reads Oil Life Index 100% Normal.
3. Turn ignition Off.

FLEETWOOD (RWD)

REAR WHEEL DRIVE

1. Turn ignition On, without starting engine.
2. Press accelerator pedal to wide open throttle (WOT) position and release three times within 5 seconds.
3. If "Change Oil" warning indicator goes out, system has been reset.
4. If "Change Oil" warning indicator does not reset, turn ignition Off and repeat procedure.

1992 FRONT WHEEL DRIVE

Press RANGE and FUEL USED buttons simultaneously to display oil life index, then press the RANGE and RESET buttons until "Change Oil Soon" light flashes (approximately 5 seconds). The oil life index will not remain displayed.

ELDORADO & SEVILLE

1992

Press and hold the ENG DATA and RANGE buttons for a minimum of 5 seconds.

1993

Press the INFORMATION button until oil life index is displayed, then press STORE/RECALL until oil life index resets to 100 (approximately 5 seconds).

1994-98

Press the INFORMATION button until Oil Life Index is displayed, then press and hold RESET button until Oil Life Index resets to 100 (approximately 5 seconds).

1999

1. Turn ignition On, then press TRIP but-

ton on driver's information center (DIC) switch to view various menu choices and stop on OIL LIFE REMAINING. A message will display percentage of oil life remaining.
2. Press and hold RESET button on DIC switch for at least two seconds. A message will display the percentage of oil life remaining as 99%. The engine oil life monitor is now reset.
3. Turn ignition Off.

2000-04

1. Turn ignition On, press Gauge Info button on Driver Information Center (DIC) switch to view various menu choices and stop on OIL LIFE REMAINING. Message will display percentage of oil life remaining.
2. Press and hold RESET button on DIC switch until display reads Oil Life Index 100% Normal.
3. Turn ignition Off.

SIXTY SPECIAL

1993

Reset the Engine Oil Life Index (EOLI) after each oil change by pressing the RANGE and RESET keys on the Fuel Data Center for 5–50 seconds. The "Change Oil Soon" lamp will flash four times to indicate that the index has been reset.

Chevrolet

CAMARO

1. Turn ignition to Run, engine Off.
2. Press TRIP/OIL RESET button on instrument panel for 12 seconds. OIL CHANGE lamp will start to flash to confirm system is reset. When reset is complete lamp will go out.
3. Turn ignition Off.

CORVETTE

1992-96

1. Turn ignition key to On position, without starting engine.
2. Press ENG MET button on the trip monitor and release, then press and release again within 5 seconds.
3. Within 5 seconds of previous step, press and hold GAUGES button on trip monitor. "Change Oil" lamp will flash.
4. Hold GAUGES button until "Change Oil" lamp stops flashing and goes out.
5. When lamp goes out, engine oil life monitor is reset. If it does not reset, turn ignition Off and repeat procedure.

1997

1. Turn ignition to Run.
2. Press TRIP button on the Driver Information Center (DIC) switch to view menu. Stop at OIL LIFE REMAINING. A message will display percentage of oil life remaining.
3. Press and hold the DIC switch RESET button for at least two seconds. A message will display the percentage of oil life remaining as 100%. Oil life monitor has been reset.
4. Turn ignition Off.

1998-2000

The Driver Information Center (DIC) engine oil life monitor indicates when to change oil, usually 3000–7500 miles, although the "Change Oil" message might appear before 3000 miles when operating under severe conditions.

To reset the oil life monitor after an oil change, proceed as follows:
1. Turn ignition On.
2. Press TRIP button on DIC to view menu choices and stop on "Oil Life Remaining."
3. Press and hold RESET button for more than two seconds. When remaining oil life percentage changes to 99%, monitor has been properly reset.
4. Turn ignition Off.

2001-05

1. Turn ignition switch On with engine off.
2. Press TRIP button until "OIL LIFE" percentage is displayed.
3. Press RESET button and hold for two seconds, "OIL LIFE REMAIN" percent will appear.

IMPALA & MONTE CARLO

LESS DE SERIES RADIO

The Engine Oil Life monitor indicates when an oil and filter change are needed, usually 3000–10,000 miles since the last change. The CHANGE OIL SOON indicator may light even before 3000 miles if the vehicle has been operated under severe service.

The monitor will not detect dust in the oil. If operating in dusty conditions, change the oil and filter every 3000 miles, or less, if the CHANGE OIL SOON lamp lights.

To reset the Engine Oil Life monitor proceed as follows:
1. Turn ignition On, but do not start engine.
2. Fully depress and release accelerator pedal three times within five seconds.
3. If CHANGE OIL SOON lamp flashes twice, this means system is properly reset.
4. If CHANGE OIL SOON lamp lights and stays lit for five seconds, system did not reset. Repeat reset procedure.

WITH DE SERIES RADIO

1. Place ignition switch in On position with radio Off.
2. Press and hold Disp button on radio for at least five seconds until Settings is displayed.
3. Press Seek up or down arrow to scroll though main menu.
4. Scroll until Oil Life appears on display.
5. Press Rev or Next button to enter submenu. Reset will be displayed.
6. Press Disp button to reset. A chime will be heard to ensure new setting and Done will be displayed for one second.
7. Once message has been reset, scroll until Exit appears on display.
8. Press Disp button to exit programming. A chime will be heard to ensure exit.

CAPRICE & IMPALA SS

1994

After engine oil has been changed, the "Change Oil" lamp must be reset. Remove the instrument panel fuse box cover. With ignition On, depress the OIL RESET button for 5 seconds. The lamp should go off.

1995-96

1. Turn ignition On, without starting engine.
2. Within 5 seconds, depress accelerator pedal to wide open position and release three times.
3. When lamp goes out, engine oil life monitor is reset. PCM will acknowledge if reset was successful by flashing "Change Oil" lamp twice, then will turn lamp off. If lamp does not reset, turn ignition Off and repeat procedure.

LUMINA

1998-2001

The Engine Oil Life monitor indicates when an oil and filter change are needed, usually 3000–10,000 miles since the last change. The CHANGE OIL SOON indicator may light even before 3000 miles if the vehicle has been operated under severe service.

The monitor will not detect dust in the oil. If operating in dusty conditions, change the oil and filter every 3000 miles, or less, if CHANGE OIL SOON lamp lights.

To reset the Engine Oil Life monitor proceed as follows:
1. Turn ignition On, but do not start engine.
2. Fully depress and release accelerator pedal three times within five seconds.
3. If CHANGE OIL SOON lamp flashes twice, this means system is properly reset.
4. If CHANGE OIL SOON lamp lights and stays lit for five seconds, system did not reset. Repeat reset procedure.

Oldsmobile

ALERO

The Engine Oil Life monitor indicates when an oil and filter change are needed, usually 3000–7500 miles since the last change. The indicator may light even before 3000 miles if the vehicle has been operated under severe service.

The monitor will not detect dust in the oil. If operating in dusty conditions, change the oil and filter every 3000 miles, or less, if CHANGE OIL SOON lamp lights.

To reset the Engine Oil Life monitor proceed as follows:
1. Turn ignition On, but do not start engine.
2. Press and release RESET button. RESET button is located in driver's side instrument panel fuse block. CHANGE OIL indicator will begin flashing.
3. Press and release RESET button again.
4. Reset is complete when light goes out and chime sounds.

AURORA

1995

When the engine oil life index has reached 10 or less, the Driver Information System display will indicate distance to oil change and sound a beep when the ignition is placed in the RUN or ACC position for the first time each day. When the engine oil life index has reached zero, the Driver Information System display will indicate "Change Oil Now" and sound a beep, when ignition is turned to RUN or ACC for the first time each day. After engine oil change has been performed, the oil life index may be reset as follows:
1. Depress TEST button and release, then depress OIL button and release.
2. Depress and hold the RESET button for 5–7 seconds.

1996-99

After the engine oil has been changed, display the oil life index on the DIC, then hold the RESET button for 5 seconds. When a DIC message of RESET is displayed and the oil life index equals 100%, the reset is complete.

2001-03

1. Place ignition switch in On position.
2. Press the Select right arrow button on the driver's information center until the Oil Life % is displayed.
3. Press and hold the RESET button until the display indicates Oil Life 100%.
4. Engine oil life monitor is reset.

INTRIGUE

The "Change Oil" lamp will light when the engine oil's useful life is close to its expiration. This lighting may appear earlier than outlined in the owner's manual, depending on driving patterns.

To reset the oil life monitor after an oil change, proceed as follows:
1. Turn ignition On.
2. Fully depress and release accelerator pedal three times in five seconds.
3. If "Change Oil" message flashes, monitor has properly reset.
4. If "Change Oil" message stays on for five seconds, monitor has not properly reset and must be reset again.
5. **On models equipped with U20 option,** reset oil life low indicator as follows:
   a. Press and hold MODE button until light appears next to OIL LIFE.
   b. Press and hold trip RESET button until oil life percentage changes to 99%.

EIGHTY EIGHT, LSS, NINETY-EIGHT & REGENCY

1992-95

When the engine oil life index has reached 10 or less, the Driver Information System display will indicate distance to oil change and sound a beep when the ignition is placed in the RUN or ACC position for the first time each day. When the engine oil life index has reached zero, the Driver Information System display will indicate "Change

Oil Now" and sound a beep, when ignition is turned to RUN or ACC for the first time each day. After engine oil change has been performed, the oil life index may be reset as follows:

1. **On 1992–93 models,** depress TEST button and release, then depress OIL button and release.
2. **On 1994–95 models,** select OIL menu by depressing MODE button.
3. **On all models,** depress and hold the RESET button for 5–7 seconds.

1996-97

After the engine oil has been changed, display the oil life index on the DIC, then hold the RESET button for 5 seconds. When a DIC message of RESET is displayed and the oil life index equals 100%, the reset is complete.

1998-99

The Driver Information Center (DIC) engine oil life monitor indicates when to change oil, usually between 3000–7500 miles, although the "Change Oil" message might appear before 3000 miles when operating under severe conditions.

To reset the oil life monitor after an oil change, proceed as follows:

1. Turn ignition On.
2. Press TRIP button on DIC to view menu choices, then stop on "Oil Life Remaining."
3. Press and hold RESET button for more than 5 seconds. Monitor has been properly reset when remaining oil life percentage changes to 100%.
4. Turn ignition Off.

EXCEPT ALERO, AURORA, EIGHTY EIGHT, INTRIGUE, LSS, NINETY-EIGHT & TORONADO

When the engine oil life index has reached 10 or less, the Driver Information System display will indicate distance to oil change and sound a beep when ignition is turned to Run or Accessory for the first time each day. When the engine oil life index has reached 0, the Driver Information System display will indicate Change Oil Now and sound a beep when ignition is turned to Run or Accessory for the first time each day. After engine oil change has been performed, the oil life index may be reset by depressing and holding the Oil and Reset buttons for approximately 5 seconds, **Fig. 1.**

TORONADO

1992

Less CRT Driver Information Display

Oil life is displayed by pressing the ENG DATA button on the Driver Information System (DIS) keypad several times. To reset the oil life index, press and hold the RESET/ENTER key for 5 seconds while the oil life is displayed.

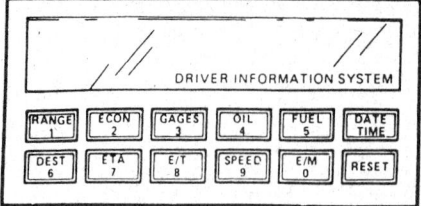
GC1138800168000X

Fig. 1   Driver Information Center. Oldsmobile except Alero, Aurora, Eighty Eight, Intrigue, LSS, Ninety-Eight & Toronado

With Driver Information Display

Oil life may be displayed by pressing the INFO button and then selecting the OIL LIFE option. Oil life is reset is reset by pressing RESET on the oil life display and then pressing YES on the confirmation screen. This will reset the oil life index and OIL LIFE INDEX 100. The Change Oil message will remain off until the next oil change is needed.

Pontiac

BONNEVILLE

1992-95

After changing engine oil and filter, if required, reset service interval indicator by depressing and releasing the service reminder button until the desired item is displayed. When the desired item is displayed, do not release service reminder button. After button has been depressed for approximately 10 seconds, the service interval mileage display will begin to count down in 500 mile intervals. When desired service interval mileage is reached, release button. The service interval reminder indicates miles to service, not miles from last service.

1996-97

After the engine oil has been changed, display the oil life index on the DIC, then hold the RESET button for 5 seconds. When a DIC message of RESET is displayed and the oil life index equals 99% or 100%, the reset is complete.

1998

1. Turn ignition switch to RUN position.
2. Press TRIP button on driver's information center (DIC) switch to view menu choices.
3. Select OIL LIFE REMAINING.
4. Press and hold RESET button on DIC for more than 5 seconds until oil life changes to 100%.
5. Turn ignition switch to OFF position.

1999

1. Turn ignition switch to RUN position.
2. Press and hold reset button in glove compartment for at least 5 seconds but not more than 60 seconds.
3. After 5 seconds, observe the CHANGE OIL SOON light flash four times before light turns OFF.

4. Engine oil life monitor has been reset.

2000-05

1. Turn ignition switch to On position.
2. Press MODE button on driver's information center (DIC) until VIEW DATA is visible.
3. Press SELECT button until OIL LIFE % is visible.
4. Press and hold RESET button on DIC until display reads OIL LIFE 100% NORMAL.
5. Engine oil life monitor is now reset.

FIREBIRD

1. Turn ignition to Run, engine Off.
2. Press TRIP/OIL RESET button on instrument panel for 12 seconds. OIL CHANGE lamp will start to flash to confirm system is reset. When reset is complete lamp will go out.
3. Turn ignition Off.

GRAND AM

The Engine Oil Life monitor indicates when an oil and filter change are needed. Usually 3000–7500 miles for 1999–2000 models, from 3000–12,500 miles for 2001 models, since the last change. The indicator may light even before 3000 miles if the vehicle has been operated under severe service.

The monitor will not detect dust in the oil. If operating in dusty conditions, change the oil and filter every 3000 miles, or less, if the CHANGE OIL SOON lamp lights.

To reset the Engine Oil Life monitor proceed as follows:

1. Turn ignition On, but do not start engine.
2. Press and release RESET button. CHANGE OIL indicator will begin flashing.
3. Press and release RESET button again.

GRAND PRIX

1992-96

Ensure oil life indicator is displayed by pressing Driver Information System SYSTEMS CHECK button. Press and hold the RESET button until oil life display is returned to 100%.

1997-99

Change Oil Soon Indicator

1. Turn ignition On, but do not start engine.
2. Fully depress and release accelerator three times within 5 seconds.
3. If "Change Oil Soon" lamp flashes this means system is resetting.
4. Turn ignition Off, then start engine.
5. If "Change Oil Soon" lamp lights, repeat procedure.

Oil Life Monitor

Press trip calculator MODE button until light appears next to "Oil Life," then press and hold RESET button until oil life percentage reaches 100%.

2000-05

To reset the Engine Oil Life monitor proceed as follows:

1. **On models equipped with DIC,** proceed as follows:
   a. Turn ignition On, but do not start engine.
   b. Fully depress and release accelerator pedal three times within five seconds. Oil life indicator will begin to flash indicating system is resetting.
   c. Place ignition switch in Off position and start engine.
   d. Engine oil change light should illuminate as bulb check and then go Off.
   e. If oil change light remains On, repeat reset procedure.
2. **On models equipped with trip computer,** proceed as follows:
   a. Depress Mode button until light appears next to Oil Life.
   b. Depress Trip Reset button until oil life percentage reads 99%.

Saturn

ION

1. Turn ignition key to RUN position.
2. Press trip odometer reset stem once or twice until "OIL LIFE" message is flashing on message center.
3. Press and hold instrument panel trip odometer button for few seconds until chime sounds five times.
4. When reset is complete "OIL LIFE" message will stay on without flashing.
5. Turn ignition switch off.
6. Turn ignition switch ON, if "OIL LIFE" lamp comes on and stays on for 30 seconds, lamp did not reset. Repeat procedure.

L SERIES

1. Turn ignition switch to RUN position.
2. Remove underhood fuse block cover, press red OIL RESET button and hold for five seconds.
3. Turn ignition switch off.
4. Turn ignition switch to RUN position and ensure "SERVICE OIL SOON" lamp turns off after 30 seconds.
5. If lamp does not turn off, repeat procedure.

S SERIES

The PCM has the ability to calculate when the engine oil needs to be changed based on vehicle mileage, engine revolutions and engine coolant temperature. The PCM bases the engine oil change interval within a window of 3000–6000 miles regardless of engine revolutions and engine coolant temperature. To reset the PCM oil life monitor, proceed as follows:

1. Remove cover from underhood fuse relay center.
2. Place ignition switch in On position.
3. Press red Oil Reset Button and hold for five seconds.
4. If "Change Engine Oil Soon" lamp is flashing, system is reset. Lamp will flash for 30 seconds or until ignition switch is placed in Off position.
5. If lamp comes On and remains On for 30 seconds at next ignition On cycle, lamp did not reset. Reset procedure must be performed again.

CHECK ENGINE OR SERVICE NOw/SOON ENGINE INDICATOR LAMPS

The Check Engine lamp may light if the fuel filler cap has not been completely tightened. This lamp should turn off after the cap has been properly tightened and the vehicle has successfully completed a predetermined number of trip cycles.

Except LeMans, Metro, Prizm & Storm

The Check Engine lamp should light when the ignition is turned On. When the engine is started, the lamp should go off. If the lamp remains On for 10 seconds or constantly after the engine is started, the self diagnosis system has detected a fault condition and has stored a code in the system Electronic Control Module (ECM) or Powertrain Control Module (PCM). After diagnosis and repair, the ECM memory can be cleared of codes as follows:

1. **On models except Cadillac with DEFI,** proceed as follows:
   a. Remove ECM/PCM fuse or disconnect battery ground cable for approximately 30 seconds, with ignition turned Off.
   b. If battery ground cable is disconnected to clear codes, components such as clocks, electronically tuned radios etc., will have to be reset.
2. **On Cadillac models equipped with DEFI,** the ECM/PCM power feed is connected by a pigtail, inline fuse holder, at the positive battery terminal. To clear codes within ECM/PCM system and protect components that need resetting, disconnect inline fuse.
3. **On Eldorado and Seville models,** stored codes are cleared during self-diagnostic procedure.

LeMans

The Check Engine lamp should light when the ignition is turned On. When the engine is started, them should go off. If the lamp remains On for 10 seconds or constantly after the engine is started, the self diagnosis system has detected a fault condition and has stored a code in the system Electronic Control Module (ECM). After diagnosis and repair, the ECM memory can be cleared of codes, by disconnecting battery ground cable for 10 seconds, with ignition turned Off.

Metro

The Check Engine lamp should light when the ignition is turned On with engine not operating. When engine is started, the Check Engine lamp should go off. If lamp remains on, a code has been stored by the Electronic Control Module (ECM) memory. After diagnosis and repair, turn ignition Off and clear codes stored in the ECM memory by disconnecting the battery ground cable, for approximately 20 seconds.

The Check Engine lamp may light if the fuel filler cap has not been completely tightened. This lamp should turn off after the cap has been properly tightened and the vehicle has successfully completed a predetermined number of trip cycles.

Prizm

The Check Engine lamp should light when the ignition is in ON position with engine not operating. When engine is started, the Check Engine lamp should go off. If lamp remains on, a code has been stored by the Electronic Control Unit (ECU) memory. After diagnosis and repair, turn ignition Off and clear codes stored in the ECU memory by removing the Stop Fuse. The Stop fuse is located in a fuse panel, in the passenger compartment, on driver's side, behind kick panel. The fuse must be removed for 10 seconds or longer, depending on ambient temperature. The lower the ambient temperature, the longer the fuse will have to be removed.

Storm

The Check Engine lamp should light when the ignition is in the On position with engine not operating. When engine is started, the Check Engine lamp should go off. If lamp remains on, a code has been stored by the Electronic Control Module (ECM) memory. After diagnosis and repair, turn ignition Off, then clear codes stored in the ECM memory by disconnecting the battery ground cable for approximately 30 seconds.

CHECK GAUGE WARNING LAMP

The Check Gauge warning lamp will light to warn the driver's to inspect the oil pressure gauge, engine coolant temperature gauge and the voltmeter. When lit, the "Check Gauge" lamp indicates that one of these gauges is operating in an abnormal range.

CHECK INFO CENTER WARNING LAMP

Eldorado & Seville

1992

This lamp will light for a few seconds when the ignition is turned On as a bulb inspection. If lamp remains lit, a message is stored in the Driver Information Center. Refer to "Driver Information Center."

DRIVER INFORMATION CENTER

Aurora

1995-99

The Driver Information Center Display is located on the instrument panel (Eighty-Eight and Ninety-Eight models with digital cluster or touring sedan gauge cluster). It provides traveling and performance information on the following:

1. Date and Time—This information is displayed for 5 seconds when the ignition is turned On. The DT/TM button may be depressed at any time to display current date and time.
2. Fuel Economy—The ECON button displays average fuel economy.
3. Remaining Fuel/Fuel Used—Depressing FUEL button displays amount of fuel used since reset button was last pressed. Depressing FUEL button a second time displays amount of fuel remaining.
4. Fuel Range—Depress RANGE to display distance that may be driven before refueling. To display amount of fuel used from a specific starting point, depress FUEL then RESET.
5. Average Speed—Depress SPEED to display average speed. To reset average speed, depress SPEED then RESET.
6. Remaining Oil Life and Oil Change Information—The OIL button displays information on oil life. Refer to "Change Oil Or Change Oil Now Message" for reset procedure.
7. Engine Coolant Temperature, Oil Pressure, Battery Voltage and Tachometer—Depressing GAGES once displays coolant temperature. Pressing GAGES a second time displays oil pressure. Pressing GAGES a third time displays battery voltage. Pressing GAGES a fourth time displays tachometer RPM.
8. Distance To Destination—Depress DEST then RESET and enter length of trip. Display will then count backwards to zero distance remaining. When the display reaches zero, "TRIP COMPLETE" is displayed. This message will clear when the TEST button is depressed or the ignition is turned Off.
9. Estimated Time of Arrival—After entering distance to destination, Press ETA button to display time remaining to destination (based on average speed).
10. Elapsed Time—Depressing the E/T button activates a stopwatch that records up to 100 hours.

Bonneville

The Driver Information Center Display is located on the instrument panel. When the ignition is turned On, the display will go through a bulb inspection in which the vehicle graph and message title will be displayed in sequence. After the sequence has been completed, all messages and ve- hicle graph will remain lit for approximately two seconds. After approximately two seconds, if all monitored systems are functioning properly, the message titles should go off and only the vehicle outline should be lit. If a fault condition in any of the monitored systems is present, the particular title for the monitored system should light and its approximate location on the vehicle graphic display should light. The following messages will be displayed:

1. **Function Monitor**—The coolant level, fuel level and windshield washer levels are monitored when ignition is turned On.
   a. Coolant Level—This message will be indicated when engine coolant level in the radiator drops below a predetermined level. To cancel message, inspect cooling system, then add coolant to bring system to proper level.
   b. Fuel Level—This message will be indicated when fuel level is 5 gallons or less. To cancel message add fuel to fuel tank.
   c. Washer Fluid—This message will be indicated when windshield washer fluid is at about 40% of capacity. To cancel message, add washer fluid to reservoir.
2. **Lamp Check**—The headlamps, tail lamps, brake lamps and turn signal lamps will be inspected whenever the lamp system is activated. To cancel this message, replace bulb or inspect and repair electrical system as required for lamp system indicated.
3. **Security**—Door, Hood Or Trunk Ajar are monitored. This message will appear when the indicated component is open or improperly closed. To cancel message, properly close indicated component.
4. **Service Reminder**—Oil change, oil filter change, engine tune-up and tire rotation intervals are monitored.
   a. After the bulb inspection sequence has been completed, the service interval can be inspected by depressing the service reminder button. Depressing the button once will display the Change Oil indication and mileage remaining to service interval. Depressing the button a second time, will display the Change Oil Filter indication and mileage remaining to service interval. Depressing the button a third time will display the Rotate Tires and mileage to service interval. Depressing the button a fourth time will display Tune-Up indication and mileage to service interval.
   b. After completing the required service, reset service interval indicator by depressing and releasing the service reminder button until the desired item is displayed. When the desired item is displayed, do not release service reminder button. After button has been depressed for approximately 10 seconds, the service interval mileage display will begin to count down in 500 mile intervals. When desired service inter- val mileage is reached, release button. The service interval reminder indicates miles to service, not miles from last service.

Eldorado & Seville

1992

This system incorporates a warning lamp, located on the instrument cluster, that is lit when the ignition is in the On position. After a few seconds the lamp should go off, unless a message in The Driver Information System is present. The driver's information center will display the following messages:

A/C Overheated—A/C Compressor Off—This message is displayed when excessive pressure in the refrigerant system is encountered. When this condition is encountered, the A/C Compressor clutch will be de-energized and cool air will not be delivered to the vehicle interior. The message will continue to appear and the A/C compressor clutch will continue to be de- energized until the system pressure returns to normal range. If this message frequently appears, the A/C system should be serviced.

A/C Sensor Fault—This message will be displayed when the sensor controlling A/C compressor clutch cycling has failed. When this sensor has failed, the A/C compressor will not operate and the A/C system will emit warmer air. After servicing system and replacing sensor, the display message will be cancelled.

Battery Volts High—This message will appear when the charging system is overcharging the battery. After completing charging system diagnosis and repair, the message will be cancelled when battery voltage returns to 11.5–15.5 volts with engine operating. Battery voltage can be displayed on the Drive Information Center Display by depressing the Eng-Data button three times.

Battery Volts Low—If this message is displayed while driving the vehicle or after vehicle has been started, a fault condition in the charging system is present or battery has been drained. After diagnosing charging system or electrical system for cause of battery drain, the message will be cancelled when engine is operating and battery voltage is between 11.5–15.5 volts. Battery voltage can be displayed on the Drive Information Center Display by depressing the Eng-Data button three times.

Change Engine Oil—When the engine oil life index has reached 0, the Change Engine Oil message will be indicated. After performing the engine oil change, the engine Oil Life Index may be reset by depressing and holding the Engine Data and Range buttons for at least 5 seconds

Cooling Fan Fault—This message will appear when the engine cooling fan system inoperative. After repairing cooling system the message will be automatically cancelled.

Engine Hot—A/C Compressor Off—This message will appear when A/C system is Auto or Defrost and engine coolant temperature is excessive. The A/C compressor

GENERAL MOTORS CORP.

Fig. 2 Driver information center. 1992–93 Eighty-Eight & Ninety-Eight

Fig. 3 Driver information center. LSS, 1994–96 Eighty Eight & Ninety Eight

clutch will be automatically de-energized when excessive engine coolant temperatures are encountered. When engine coolant temperature returns to normal, the A/C compressor clutch will be energized and the message on the display will be cancelled.

Front Or Rear Door Ajar—This message will appear when the transmission selector lever is moved out of the Park position and a door is not properly closed. The message can be cancelled by properly closing the indicated door.

Fuel Level Very Low—When low fuel level conditions are encountered this message will appear. To cancel message, add fuel.

Gear Select Problem—This message will appear if a fault condition in the transaxle gear select system is encountered while operating vehicle. After performing required service, the message will automatically be cancelled.

Headlamps Or Parking Lamps On—This message will be displayed when the headlamp switch is On, vehicle is moving and the sensed level of outside light indicates that headlamps should not be lit. This message may be cancelled by turning the headlamp switch Off.

Headlamps Suggested—This message will be displayed when the Twilight Sentinel is in the Off position, vehicle is moving and the sensed level of outside light indicates that headlamps should be lit. This message may be cancelled by activating the Twilight Sentinel System.

Low A/C Refrigerant—A/C Compressor Off—This message will be displayed when the A/C system detects a refrigerant charge low enough to cause compressor damage. When this condition is encountered, the A/C compressor clutch is de-energized and the A/C system is switched from AUTO to ECON. The system will remain in ECON until required repairs are made and system is recharged. After completing required repairs and recharging the system, A/C system operation will return to normal and the message on the display will be cancelled.

Low A/C Refrigerant—Service A/C Soon—This message will be displayed when the A/C system detects that refrigerant charge is low enough to cause a reduction in cooling capacity. This message will be displayed until system has been recharged.

Low Washer Fluid—This message will appear when windshield washer fluid level is low. To cancel message, refill windshield washer fluid reservoir.

Oil Life Index—The oil life index is a series of numerals ranging from 0–100. The 100 is indicated when engine oil has been drained and replacement engine oil has been installed. The 0 is an indication that the engine oil should be changed. The oil life index is accessed by depressing the Engine Data button four times.

Service Electrical System—This message will appear when a fault condition in the charging system is present. After repairing charging system, the message will be automatically cancelled.

Set Timing Mode—This message will appear if ignition timing is improperly set. After performing required service, the message will be automatically cancelled.

Starting Disabled/Due to Theft System/Remove Ignition Key—This message is an indication of a fault condition in the vehicle security system that may prohibit the vehicle from being restarted after the ignition has been turned Off. After servicing the vehicle security system the message will be automatically cancelled.

System Satisfactory—This message will be displayed for approximately 5 seconds after ignition has been turned On, unless a fault condition in the system has been detected. After approximately 5 seconds the display will return to the last display function selected.

System Problem—Service Car Soon—This message will be displayed when one or more of the vehicle computers supplying information to the Driver Information Center become faulty. After diagnosis and repair of the faulty computer, the message will be automatically cancelled.

Theft System Problem/Car May Not Start—This message will appear when the vehicle security system senses an improper ignition key has been placed in the ignition. After removing key from ignition, the Driver Information Center display will indicate "Wait 3 Minutes," "Wait 2 Minutes," Wait 1 Minute and then "Start Car." When the "Start Car" message appears, insert ignition key and attempt to start vehicle. If message appears again, inspect ignition key for damage and replace as required. If key appears to be satisfactory, clean pellet contacts with a soft cloth and attempt to restart vehicle.

Trunk Open—This message will appear when the ignition is the Run position and the trunk is not properly closed. The message can be cancelled by properly closing the trunk.

Eighty-Eight, LSS & Ninety-Eight

1992–93

The Driver Information Center Display, **Fig. 2**, is located on the instrument panel (Eighty-Eight and Ninety-Eight models with digital cluster or touring sedan gauge cluster). It provides traveling and performance information on the following:

1. Date and Time—This information is displayed for 5 seconds when the ignition is turned On. The DT/TM button may be depressed at any time to display current date and time.
2. Fuel Economy—The ECON button displays average fuel economy.
3. Remaining Fuel/Fuel Used—Depressing FUEL button displays amount of fuel used since reset button was last pressed. Depressing FUEL button a second time displays amount of fuel remaining.
4. Fuel Range—Depress RANGE to display distance that may be driven before refueling. To display amount of fuel used from a specific starting point, depress FUEL then RESET.
5. Average Speed—Depress SPEED to display average speed. To reset average speed, depress SPEED then RESET.
6. Remaining Oil Life and Oil Change Information—The OIL button displays information on oil life. Refer to "Change Oil Or Change Oil Now Message" for reset procedure.
7. Engine Coolant Temperature, Oil Pressure, Battery Voltage and Tachometer—Depressing GAGES once displays coolant temperature. Pressing GAGES a second time displays oil pressure. Pressing GAGES a third time displays battery voltage. Pressing GAGES a fourth time displays tachometer RPM.
8. Distance To Destination—Depress DEST then RESET and enter length of trip. Display will then count backwards to zero distance remaining. When the display reaches zero, "TRIP COMPLETE" is displayed. This message will clear when the TEST button is depressed or the ignition is turned Off.
9. Estimated Time of Arrival—After entering distance to destination, Press ETA button to display time remaining to destination (based on average speed).

10. Elapsed Time—Depressing the E/T button activates a stopwatch that records up to 100 hours.

1994-96

The Driver Information Center Display, **Fig. 3,** is located on the instrument panel. When the ignition is turned On, the display will go through a system inspection while the message "Monitored Systems OK" is displayed. If no fault conditions are detected, the screen returns to the mode displayed before the ignition was turned Off.

There are four buttons that control the functions of the driver's information center:
1. The MODE button, when pressed, cycles through a series of displays in the following order:
   a. ECON—Average fuel economy and instantaneous fuel economy.
   b. FUEL—Amount of fuel used since last fuel-used reset, and fuel remaining.
   c. RANGE—Fuel range and low fuel range.
   d. OIL—Oil life index and next required oil change.
   e. GAGES—Oil pressure, tachometer and battery voltage information.
   f. ET—Elapsed time since last reset.
   g. DT/TM—Date and time.
2. The ON/OFF button is used to input numbers and to blank out the display.
3. The RESET button is used with other buttons to reset the system. Depressing this button once enters the reset mode. Pressing this button again aborts the reset.
4. The SEL button is used to select different displays within a specific mode. For example, when the SEL button is depressed while in the GAGES mode, the display will cycle from oil pressure to battery voltage to tachometer.

ENGINE COOLANT TEMPERATURE TELLTALE LAMP

If the engine coolant temperature if more than 244°F, or if the transaxle fluid temperature if more than 284°F, the coolant temperature telltale lamp will light. The PCM will turn the cooling fan on if an ECT DTC is active.

LOW COOLANT LAMP

This lamp should light when engine coolant level in the radiator drops below a predetermined level. To turn lamp off, inspect cooling system and add coolant to bring system to proper level.

LOW OIL DIPSTICK

The Low Oil indicator ground is controlled by the PCM. To inspect for a low oil condition, the PCM inspects the low oil level sensor after the ignition has been turned to the Off or Lock position. The PCM inspects for a low oil condition 32 minutes after the ignition is turned Off if the previous ignition cycle was less than 12 minutes. The PCM inspects for a low oil condition 3 minutes after the ignition is turned off if the previous ignition cycle was less than 12 minutes.

LOW OIL PRESSURE TELLTALE LAMP

The engine oil pressure switch is normally closed and open when engine oil pressure is 1.4–5.8 psi. If the lamp is lit with engine running, inspect wiring for oil pressure switch circuit and the engine lubrication system for proper oil pump output pressure.

LOW WASHER FLUID INDICATOR

The windshield washer solvent tank has a switch that closes when the washer solvent level becomes low, illuminating the "Low Washer Fluid" indicator.

MALFUNCTION INDICATOR LAMP (MIL)

As a bulb and system check, the lamp will light with the ignition On and the engine not running. When the engine is started, the lamp will turn off. If the lamp remains On, the self diagnostic system has detected a fault. If the fault is intermittent or the system is repaired, the lamp will go Off after three trips but a diagnostic trouble code (DTC) will be stored in the PCM. Use a suitably programmed scan tool to retrieve and erase any DTCs using the "Clear DTC Information" option. If the lamp remains On while the engine is running or when a fault is suspected because of a driveability problem, perform an OBD system inspection. Scan the serial data stream using a suitably programmed scan tool.

PASSLOCK TELLTALE LAMP

The instrument panel cluster contains the security telltale lamp. The security telltale has three modes of operation: Off, Flashing & On. The security telltale will be off if ignition is in the Off position or if the ignition is in the Run, Start or ACC position and the security system diagnostics have all passed. The security telltale will be on if the body control module (BCM) is performing a bulb test at vehicle start up, the security system diagnostics have not yet completed at vehicle start up or if a security system diagnostic trouble code (DTC) is set in the BCM or PCM. The security telltale will be flashing if the tamper hall effect has been triggered, there was improper Passlock sensor data to the BCM for more than five seconds during vehicle start, there was no Passlock sensor data to the BCM for more than five seconds during vehicle start or there was improper password from the BCM to the PCM after five seconds during vehicle start. Repair or replace components. Retrieve and clear any associated DTCs to reset the telltale lamp.

SERVICE AIR COND LAMP

This lamp should light when the air conditioning system detects a low refrigerant charge. The lamp should light for approximately two seconds after ignition has been turned On as a bulb inspection.

If while operating vehicle, the lamp lights for approximately 60 seconds and then goes off, the refrigerant level is low enough to cause reduced cooling capacity. At this point the blower motor will increase speed to try to offset the loss in cooling capacity. The lamp will be automatically reset after system has been inspected and refrigerant charge has been brought to proper level.

If lamp is lit for approximately 60 seconds after engine start up, the refrigerant charge may be low enough to cause air conditioning compressor damage. When this condition is encountered, the air conditioning compressor clutch is de-energized and the air conditioning system is switched from Auto to Econ. The system will remain in ECON until required repairs are made and system is recharged. After completing required repairs and recharging the system, air conditioning system operation will return to normal and the lamp will be automatically reset.

SERVICE ELECTRICAL SYSTEM LAMP

This lamp should light when a fault condition in the charging system is present. The lamp should light during engine starting as a bulb inspection. If lamp is lit while engine is operating, the charging system should be inspected. After repairing charging system, the lamp will be automatically reset.

SERVICE TELLTALE LAMP

The service telltale lamp is used for non-emissions related failures which without being serviced could lead to component damage to other sub systems. As a bulb check, the lamp will light for 2–3 seconds and then turn off. If the lamp remains lit, the system has detected a fault condition. If the condition is intermittent or the system is repaired, the lamp will turn off 3 seconds after the PCM diagnostic test passes. Any DTCs will be stored in the freeze frame/failure records. Use a suitably programmed scan tool to retrieve and erase any DTCs using the "Clear DTC Information" option.

VEHICLE LIFT POINTS

TABLE OF CONTENTS

DaimlerChrysler

INDEX

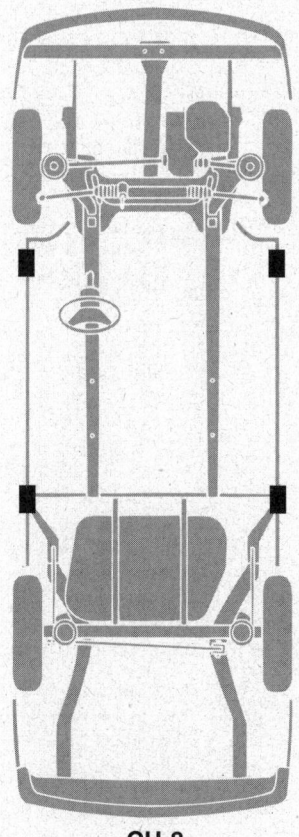

CH-8

ALCR00008

Fig. 1   Vehicle Lift Points. Sebring Coupe & Stratus Coupe

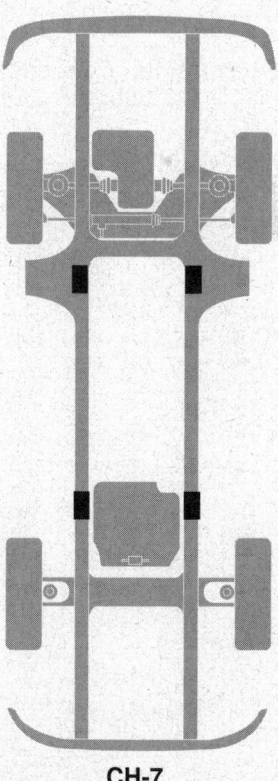

CH-7

ALCR00007

Fig. 2   Vehicle Lift Points. Sebring Sedan, Sebring Convertible & Stratus Sedan

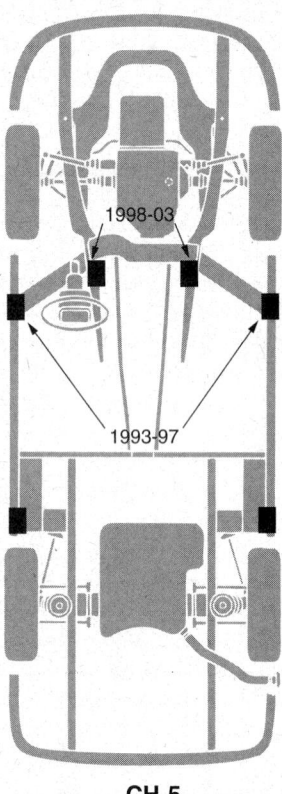

CH-5

ALCR00005

Fig. 3   Vehicle Lift Points. Concode, Intrepid, LHS, & 300M

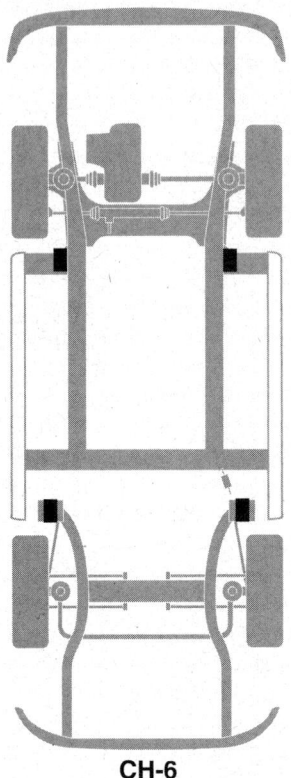

CH-6

ALCR00006

Fig. 4   Vehicle Lift Points. Neon

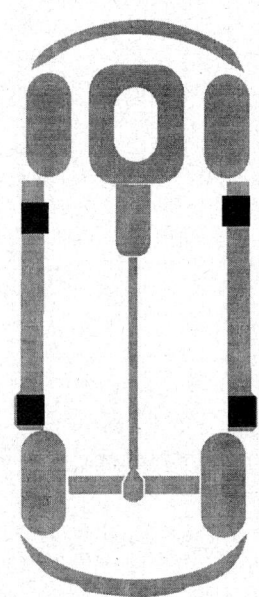

ALCR040006

Fig. 5   Vehicle Lift Points. Crossfire

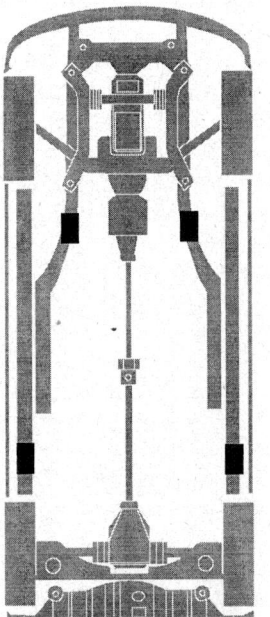

ALCR040009

Fig. 6   Vehicle Lift Points. Magnum & 300

Ford Motor Co.

INDEX

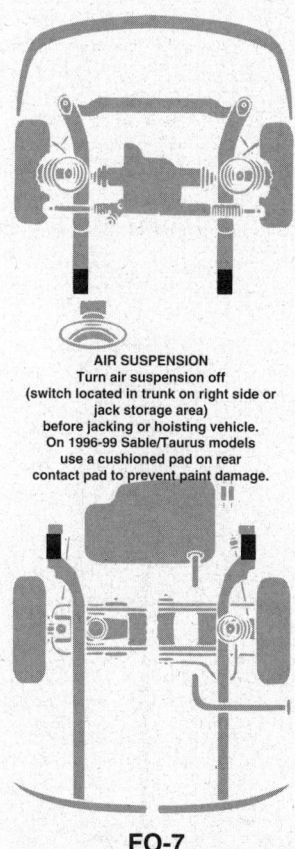

AIR SUSPENSION
Turn air suspension off
(switch located in trunk on right side or
jack storage area)
before jacking or hoisting vehicle.
On 1996-99 Sable/Taurus models
use a cushioned pad on rear
contact pad to prevent paint damage.

FO-7

ALFD00007

Fig. 1 Vehicle Lift Points. Continental,
Five-Hundred, Freestyle, Montego, Sable & Taurus

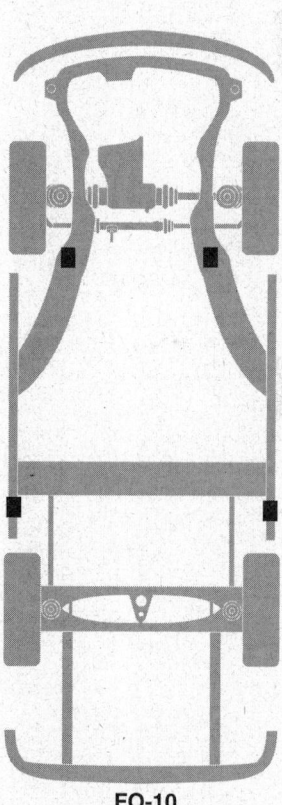

FO-10

ALFD00010

Fig. 2 Vehicle Lift Points. Cougar

VEHICLE LIFT POINTS

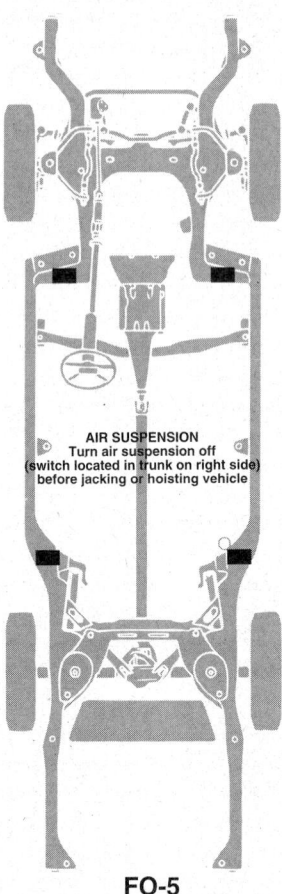

FO-5

Fig. 3 Vehicle Lift Points. Crown Victoria, Grand Marquis, Marauder & Town Car

ALFD00005

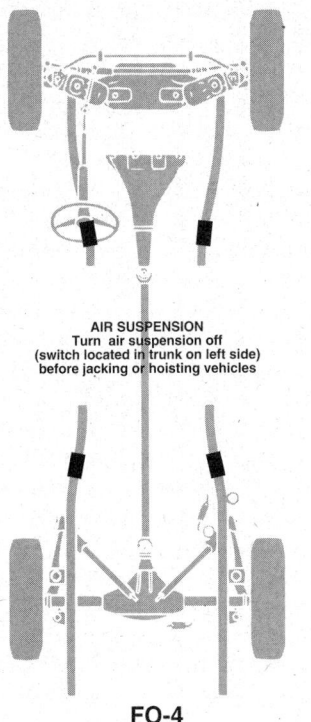

FO-4

Fig. 5 Vehicle Lift Points. Mustang

ALFD00004

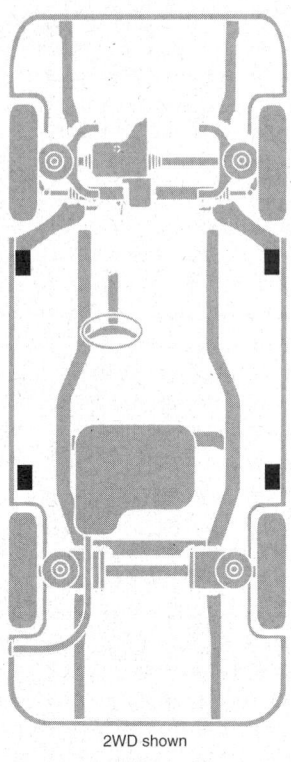

2WD shown

MA-2

ALMA00002

Fig. 4 Vehicle Lift Points. Escort, Focus & ZX2

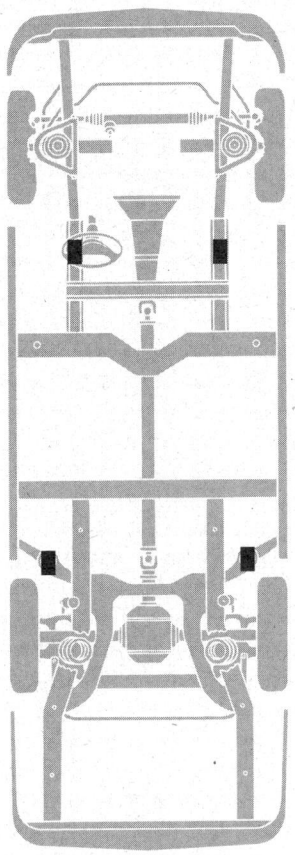

FO-12

ALFD00012

Fig. 6 Vehicle Lift Points. LS & Thunderbird

General Motors

INDEX

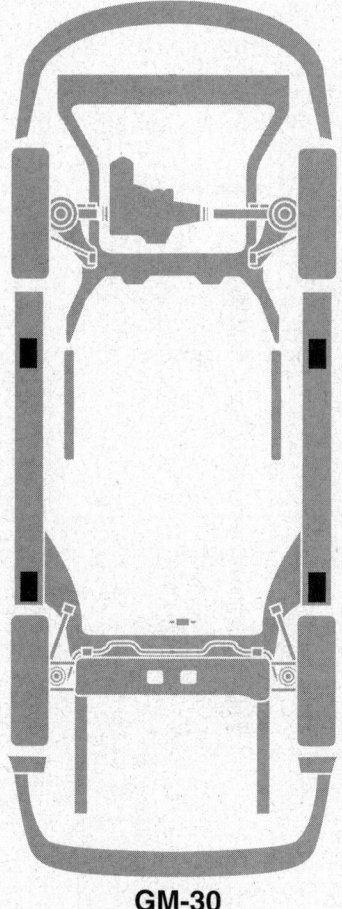

GM-30

ALGM00030

Fig. 1 Vehicle Lift Points. Alero, Grand Am & Malibu

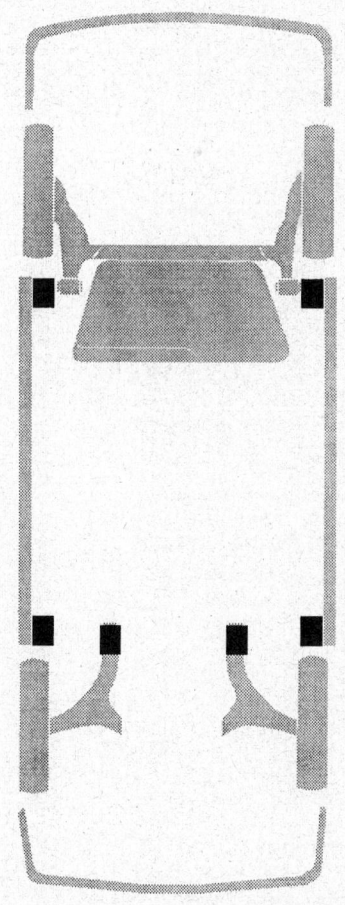

ALGM00037

Fig. 2 Vehicle Lift Points. Aveo

VEHICLE LIFT POINTS

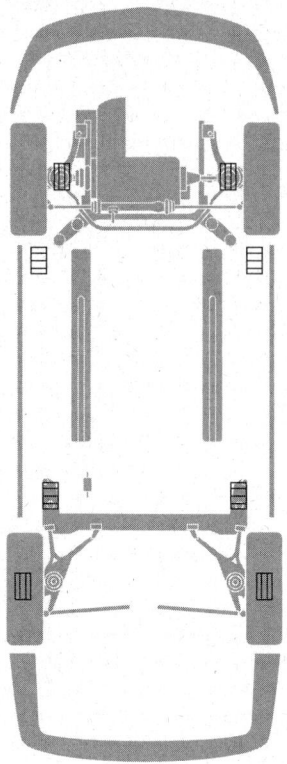

GM-29

ALGM00029

Fig. 3   Vehicle Lift Points. Aurora, Bonneville, DeVille & Seville

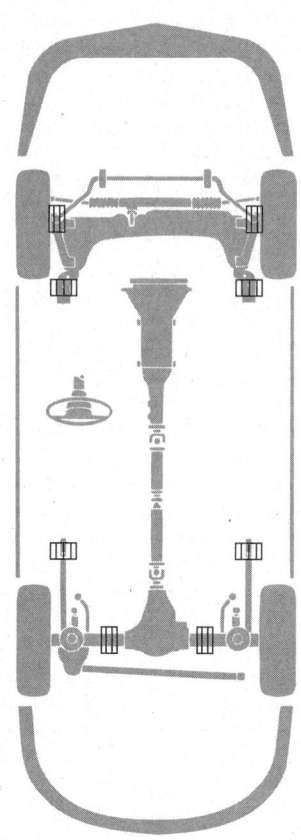

GM-28

ALGM00028

Fig. 4   Vehicle Lift Points. Camaro & Firebird

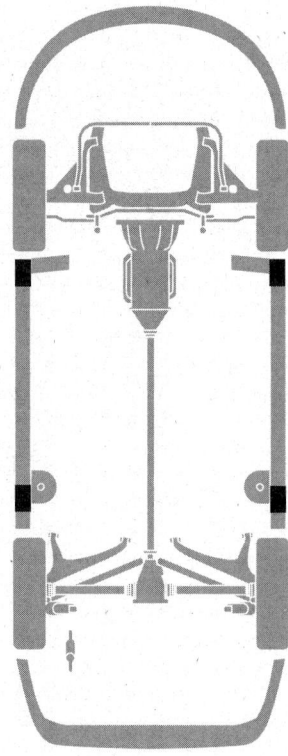

GM-32

ALGM00032

Fig. 5   Vehicle Lift Points. Catera

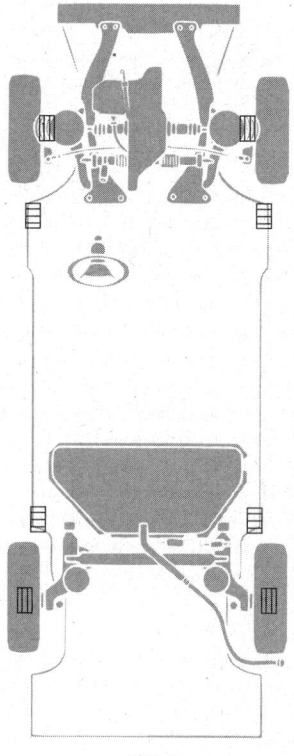

GM-2

ALGM00002

Fig. 6   Vehicle Lift Points. Cavalier & Sunfire

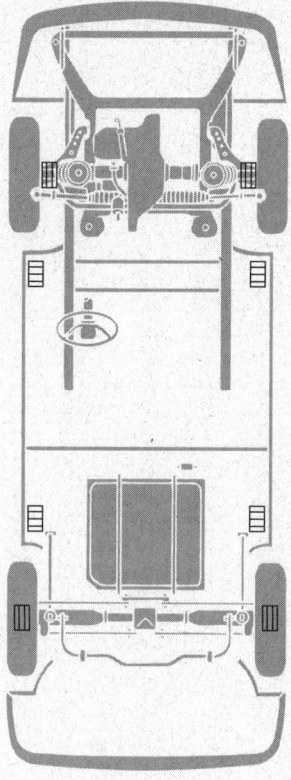

GM-18

ALGM00018

Fig. 7   Vehicle Lift Points. Century, Grand Prix, G6, Impala, Intrigue, Lumina, Monte Carlo & Regal

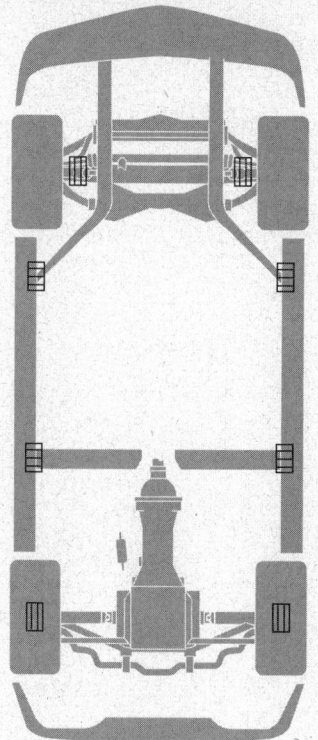

GM-33

Position lift pad as follows:
Front, immediately forward of the front frame rail shipping slot reinforcements.
Rear, install GM tool J 43625 into rear frame rail shipping slots, lock into place.
Then position rear hoist pad under J 43625.

ALGM00033

Fig. 8   Vehicle Lift Points. Corvette

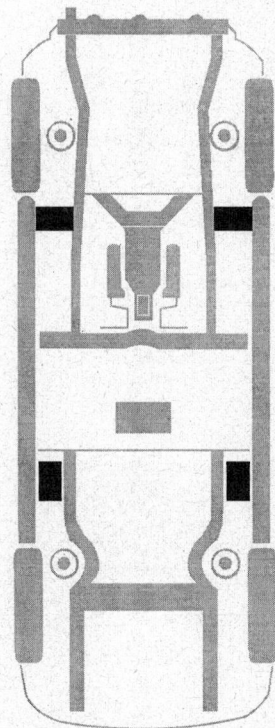

ALGM00035

Fig. 9   Vehicle Lift Points. CTS & STS

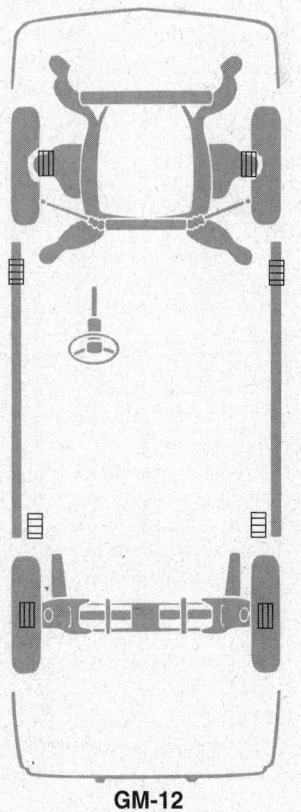

GM-12

ALGM00012

Fig. 10   Vehicle Lift Points. Eldorado

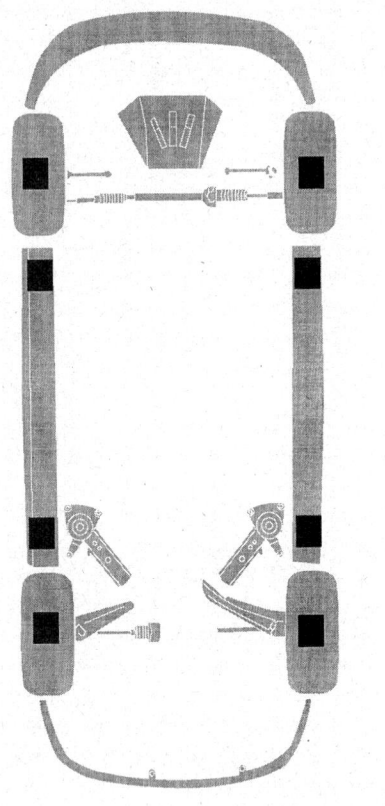

ALGM04038

Fig. 11   Vehicle Lift Points. GTO

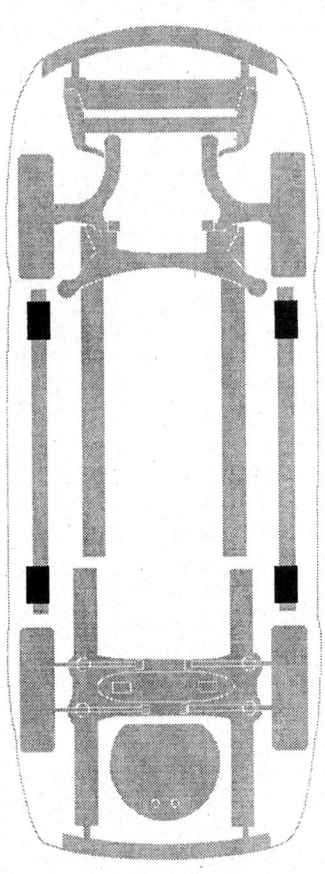

ALGM04039

Fig. 12   Vehicle Lift Points. LaCrosse

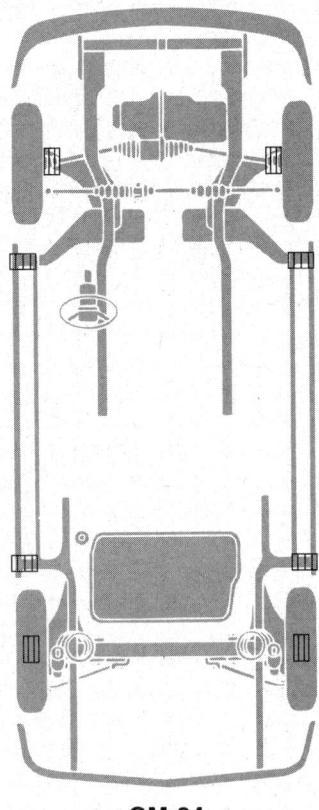

GM-34

ALGM00034

Fig. 13   Vehicle Lift Points. Metro

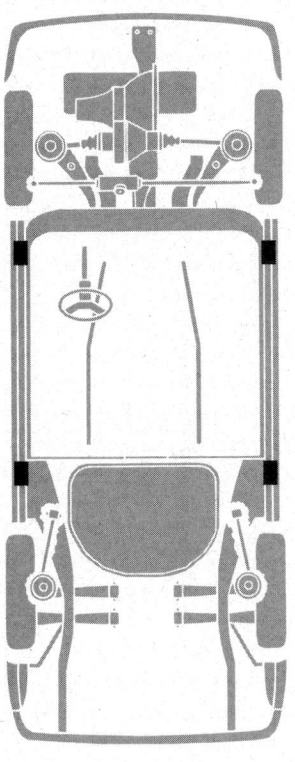

TO-3

ALTA00003

Fig. 14   Vehicle Lift Points. Prizm & Vibe

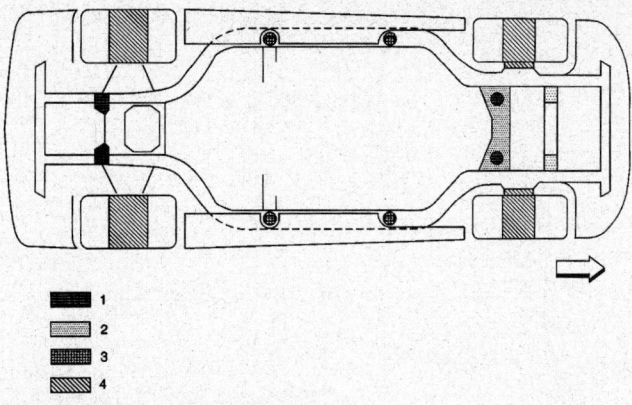

(1) Preferred Vehicle Jacking Locations
(2) Optional Vehicle Jacking Locations
(3) Frame Contact Hoist Locations, Optional Vehicle Jacking Locations
(4) Suspension Contact Hoist Locations

ARM0300000000689

Fig. 15 Vehicle Lift Points. XLR

Saturn

INDEX

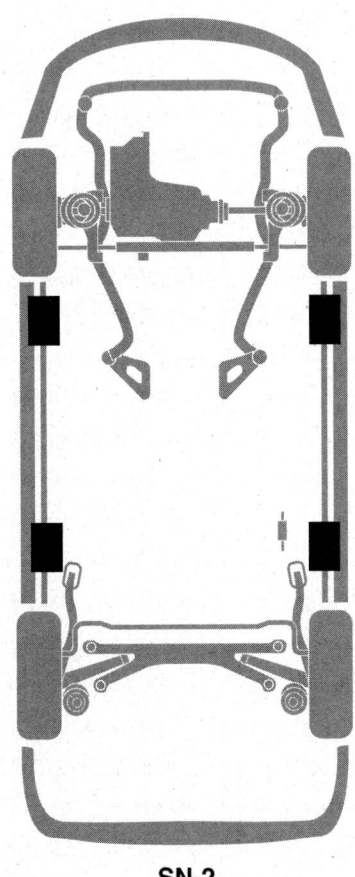

SN-2

ALSN00002

Fig. 1   Vehicle Lift Points. L-Series

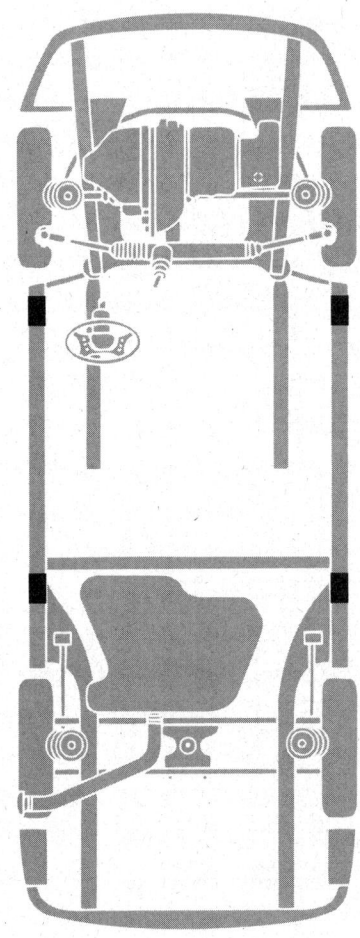

SN-1

ALSN00001

Fig. 2   Vehicle Lift Points. S-Series & ION

NON-STANDARD TIRE & WHEEL SIZE ADJUSTMENT TO RIDE HEIGHT SPECIFICATIONS & TIRE SIZE ADJUSTMENT CHARTS

INDEX

SECTION WIDTH ADJUSTMENT FOR METRIC RADIAL & BIAS PLY TIRES

These specifications are approximate and are only intended for use in making approximate ride height inspections and adjustments on models with non-standard tires. These specifications should not be used in place of those recommended by the vehicle manufacturer.

Standard Tire	Optional Tire, Tire Section Width Change Adjustment To Ride Height Specification, Inch													
	P145	P155	P165	P175	P185	P195	P205	P215	P225	P235	P245	P255	P265	P275
P145	0	+.25	+.50											
P155	−.25	0	+.25	+.50										
P165	−.50	−.25	0	+.25	+.50									
P175		−.50	−.25	0	+.25	+.50								
P185			−.50	−.25	0	+.25	+.50							
P195				−.50	−.25	0	+.25	+.50						
P205					−.50	−.25	0	+.25	+.50					
P215						−.50	−.25	0	+.25	+.50				
P225							−.50	−.25	0	+.25	+.50			
P235								−.50	−.25	0	+.25	+.50		
P245									−.50	−.25	0	+.25	+.50	
P255										−.50	−.25	0	+.25	+.50
P265											−.50	−.25	0	+.25
P275												−.50	−.25	0

ASPECT RATIO ADJUSTMENT FOR P145-215 METRIC RADIAL & BIAS PLY TIRES

These specifications are approximate and are only intended for use in making approximate ride height inspections and adjustments on models with non-standard tires. These specifications should not be used in place of those recommended by the vehicle manufacturer.

Standard Tire	Optional Tire, Tire Aspect Ratio Change to Ride Height Specification, Inch				
	60	65	70	75	80
60	0	+.38	+.75	—	—
65	−.38	0	+.38	+.75	—
70	−.75	−.38	0	+.38	+.75
75	—	−.75	−.38	0	+.38
80	—	—	−.75	−.38	0

ASPECT RATIO ADJUSTMENT FOR P225-275 METRIC RADIAL & BIAS PLY TIRES

These specifications are approximate and are only intended for use in making approximate ride height inspections and adjustments on models with non-standard tires. These specifications should not be used in place of those recommended by the vehicle manufacturer.

Standard Tire	Optional Tire, Tire Aspect Ratio Change to Ride Height Specification, Inch				
	60	65	70	75	80
60	0	+.50	+1.00	—	—
65	−.50	0	+.50	+1.00	—
70	−1.00	−.50	0	+.50	+1.00
75	—	−.75	−.50	0	+.50
80	—	—	−1.00	−.50	0

SECTION WIDTH ADJUSTMENT FOR ALPHA-NUMERIC RADIAL PLY TIRES

These specifications are approximate and are only intended for use in making approximate ride height inspections and adjustments on models with non-standard tires. These specifications should not be used in place of those recommended by the vehicle manufacturer.

Standard Tire	Optional Tire, Tire Section Width Change Adjustment To Ride Height Specification, Inch						
	DR	ER	FR	GR	HR	JR	LR
DR	0	+.19	+.44	—	—	—	—
ER	−.19	0	+.25	+.50	—	—	—
FR	−.44	−.25	0	+.25	+.63	—	—
GR	—	−.50	−.25	0	+.31	+.50	—
HR	—	—	−.63	−.31	0	+.19	+.44
JR	—	—	—	−.50	−.19	0	+.25
LR	—	—	—	—	−.44	−.25	0

ASPECT RATIO ADJUSTMENT FOR ALPHA-NUMERIC RADIAL PLY TIRES

These specifications are approximate and are only intended for use in making approximate ride height inspections and adjustments on models with non-standard tires. These specifications should not be used in place of those recommended by the vehicle manufacturer.

Standard Tire	Optional Tire, Change Adjustment to Ride Height Specification, Inch		
	60	70	78
60	0	+.50	+.62
70	−.50	0	+.13
78	−.62	−.13	0

SECTION WIDTH ADJUSTMENT FOR ALPHA-NUMERIC BIAS PLY TIRES

These specifications are approximate and are only intended for use in making approximate ride height inspections and adjustments on models with non-standard tires. These specifications should not be used in place of those recommended by the vehicle manufacturer.

Standard Tire	Optional Tire, Change Adjustment To Ride Height Specifications, Inch							
	A	B	C	D	E	F	G	H
A	0	+.25	+.50	—	—	—	—	—
B	−.25	0	+.25	+.38	—	—	—	—
C	−.50	−.25	0	+.13	+.37	—	—	—
D	—	−.37	−.13	0	+.25	+.50	—	—
E	—	—	−.38	−.25	0	+.25	+.50	—
F	—	—	—	−.50	−.25	0	+.25	+.56
G	—	—	—	—	−.50	−.25	0	+.31
H	—	—	—	—	—	−.56	−.31	0

ELECTRICAL SYMBOL & WIRE COLOR CODE IDENTIFICATION

TABLE OF CONTENTS

Electrical Symbol Identification

INDEX

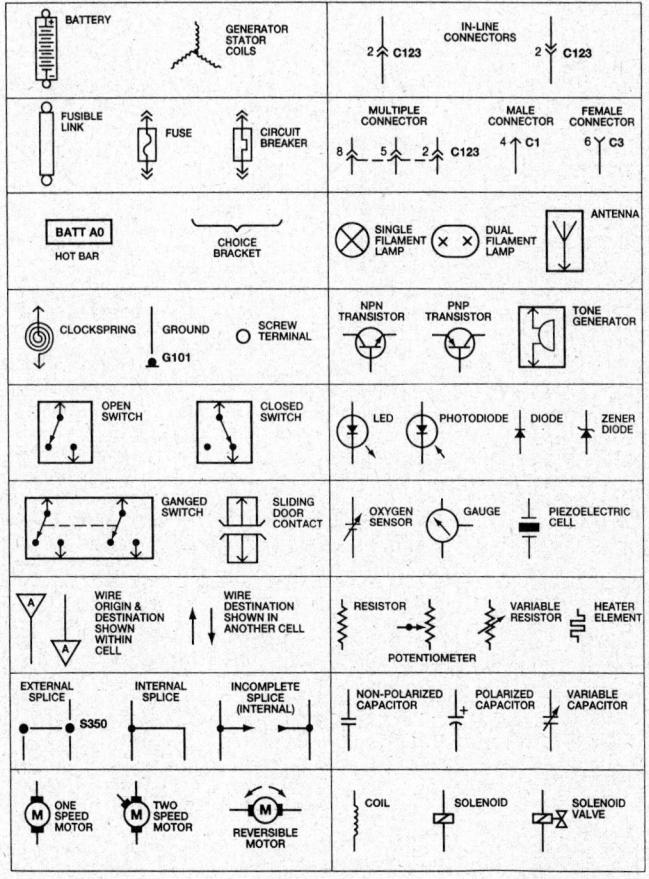

CR9049800087000X

Fig. 1 Symbol Identification. DaimlerChrysler

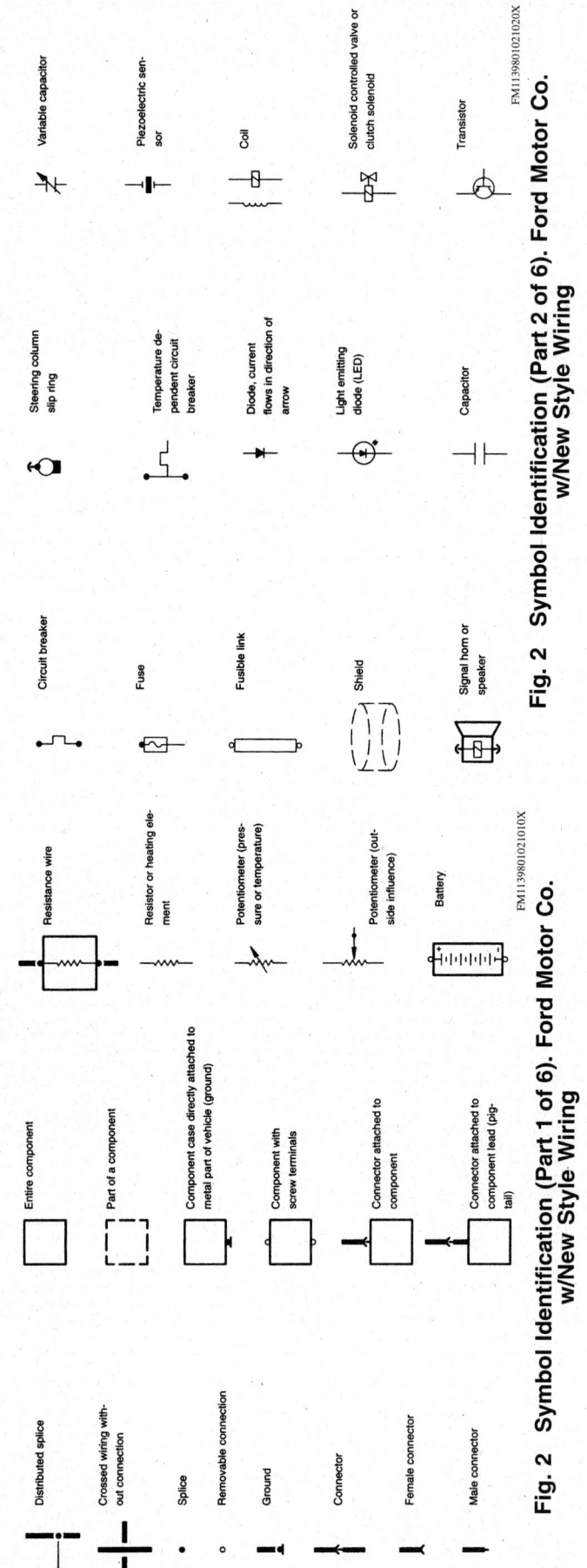

Fig. 2   Symbol Identification (Part 2 of 6). Ford Motor Co. w/New Style Wiring

Variable capacitor

Piezoelectric sensor

Coil

Solenoid controlled valve or clutch solenoid

Transistor

Steering column slip ring

Temperature dependent circuit breaker

Diode, current flows in direction of arrow

Light emitting diode (LED)

Capacitor

Circuit breaker

Fuse

Fusible link

Shield

Signal horn or speaker

Resistance wire

Resistor or heating element

Potentiometer (pressure or temperature)

Potentiometer (outside influence)

Battery

Fig. 2   Symbol Identification (Part 1 of 6). Ford Motor Co. w/New Style Wiring

Entire component

Part of a component

Component case directly attached to metal part of vehicle (ground)

Component with screw terminals

Connector attached to component

Connector attached to component lead (pigtail)

Distributed splice

Crossed wiring without connection

Splice

Removable connection

Ground

Connector

Female connector

Male connector

FM11398010210210X

FM11398010210110X

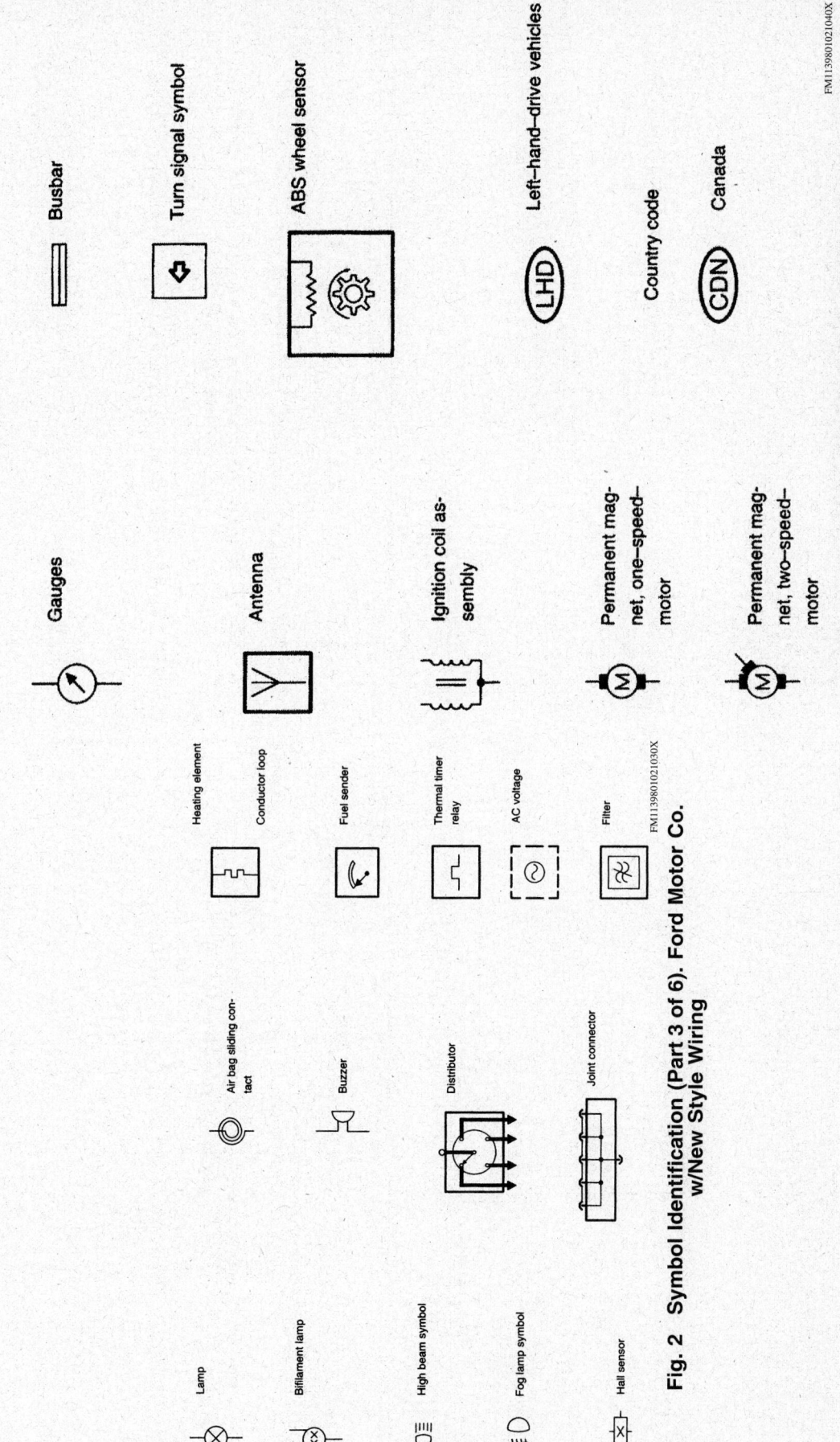

Busbar

Turn signal symbol

ABS wheel sensor

Left–hand–drive vehicles

LHD

Country code

CDN   Canada

Gauges

Antenna

Ignition coil as-sembly

Permanent mag-net, one–speed–motor

Permanent mag-net, two–speed–motor

Heating element

Conductor loop

Fuel sender

Thermal timer relay

AC voltage

Filter

Air bag sliding con-tact

Buzzer

Distributor

Joint connector

Lamp

Bifilament lamp

High beam symbol

Fog lamp symbol

Hall sensor

Fig. 2 Symbol Identification (Part 4 of 6). Ford Motor Co. w/New Style Wiring

Fig. 2 Symbol Identification (Part 3 of 6). Ford Motor Co. w/New Style Wiring

FM11398010210040X

FM11398010210030X

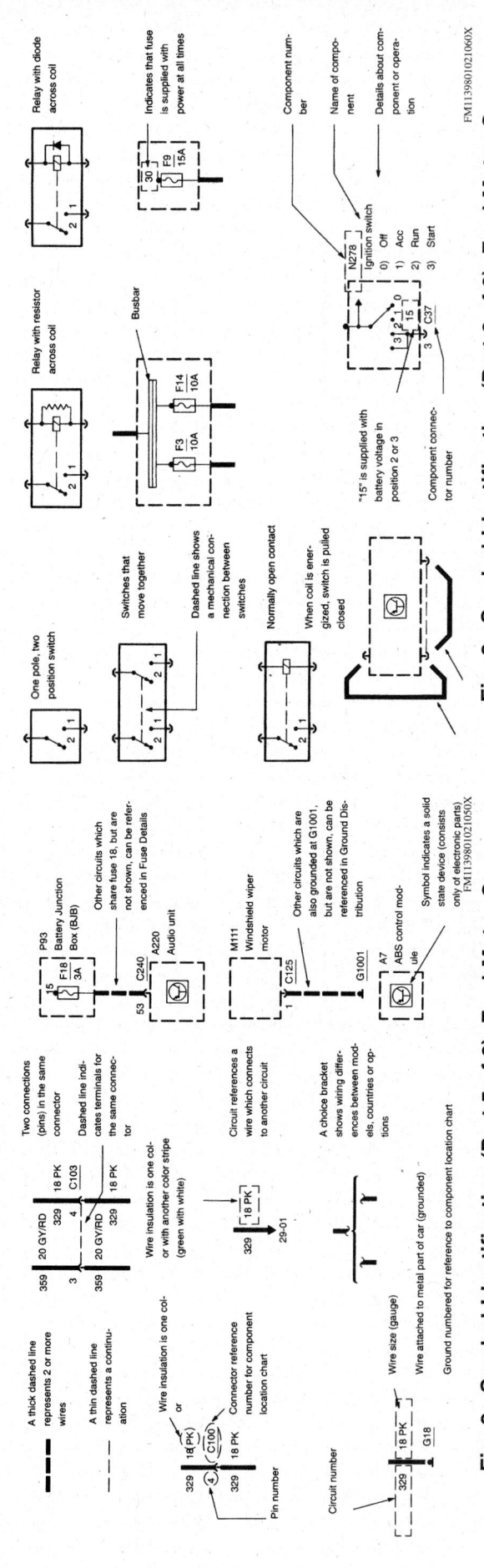

Fig. 2   Symbol Identification (Part 6 of 6). Ford Motor Co. w/New Style Wiring

Fig. 2   Symbol Identification (Part 5 of 6). Ford Motor Co. w/New Style Wiring

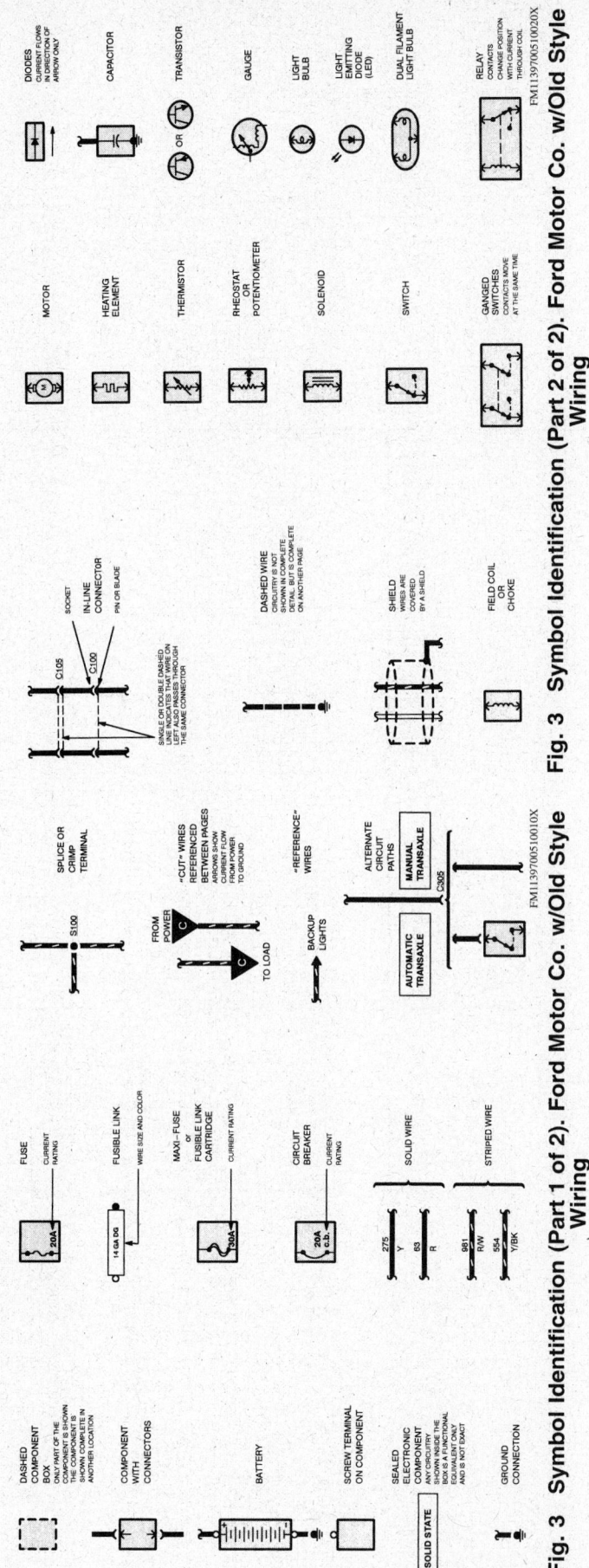

Fig. 3   Symbol Identification (Part 1 of 2). Ford Motor Co. w/Old Style Wiring

Fig. 3   Symbol Identification (Part 2 of 2). Ford Motor Co. w/Old Style Wiring

Symbol	Description
 ▲	Supplemental Inflatable Restraint (SIR) or Supplemental Restraint System (SRS) Icon This icon is used to alert the technician that the system contains SIR/SRS components that require certain precautions before servicing.
▲	On-Board Diagnostic (OBD II) Icon This icon is used to alert the technician that the circuit is essential for proper OBD II emission controls circuit operation. Any circuit which, if it fails, causes the malfunction indicator lamp (MIL) to turn on, is identified as an OBD II circuit.
▲	Important Icon This icon is used to alert the technician that there is additional information that will aid in servicing a system.
Hot At All Times Hot In Run Hot In Start Hot In Acc And Run Hot In Run And Start Hot In Run, Bulb Test And Start Hot With Headlamp Switch In Park Or Head Hot In Retained Accessory Power (RAP)	Voltage Indicator Boxes These boxes are used on schematics to indicate when voltage is present at a fuse.
⬚	Partial Component When a component is represented in a dashed box, the component or its wiring is not shown in its entirety.

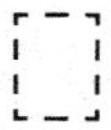

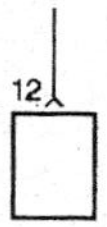

Symbol	Description
▢	Entire Component When a component is represented in a solid box the component or its wiring is shown in its entirety.
⌇	Fuse
⌒	Circuit Breaker
◆	Fusible Link
12 ▢	Connector Attached to Component

GC1139801141010X

Fig. 4 Symbol Identification (Part 1 of 4). General Motors

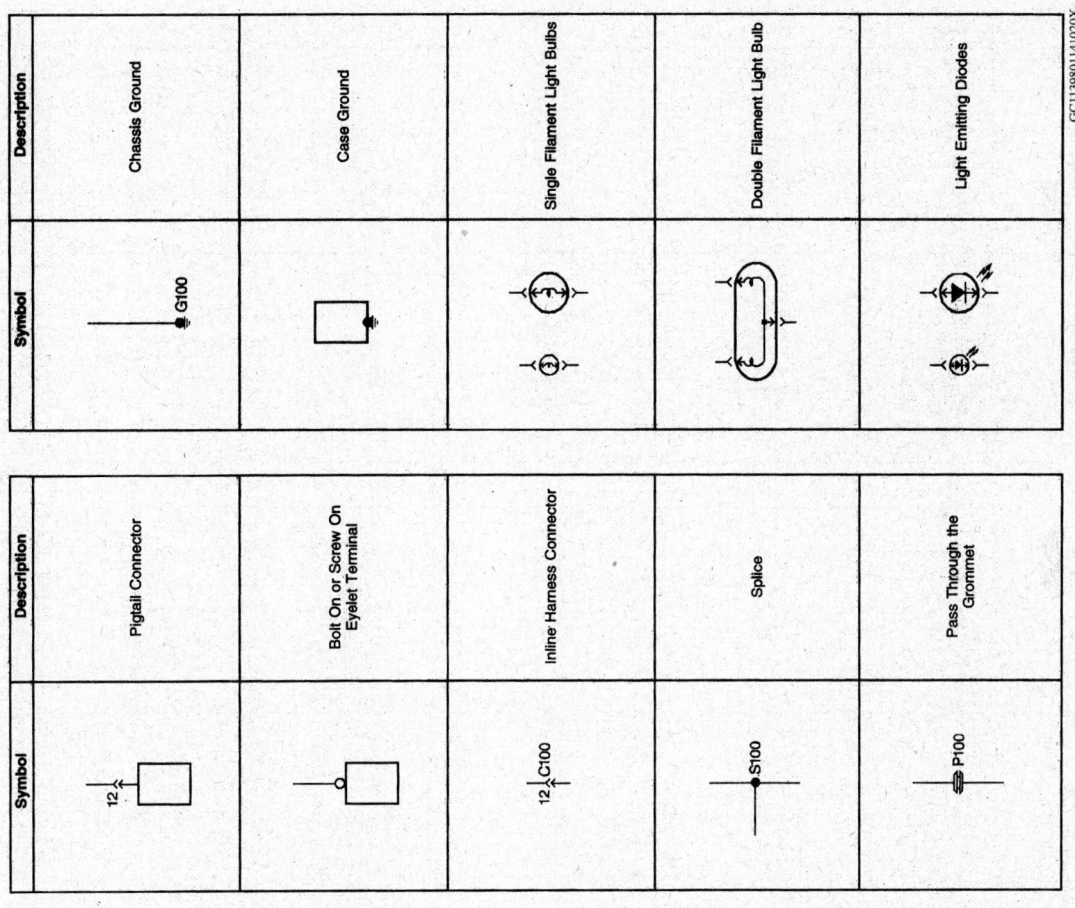

Symbol	Description
G100	Chassis Ground
	Case Ground
	Single Filament Light Bulbs
	Double Filament Light Bulb
	Light Emitting Diodes

Symbol	Description
12	Pigtail Connector
	Bolt On or Screw On Eyelet Terminal
12 C100	Inline Harness Connector
S100	Splice
P100	Pass Through the Grommet

GC113980114I020X

Fig. 4 Symbol Identification (Part 2 of 4). General Motors

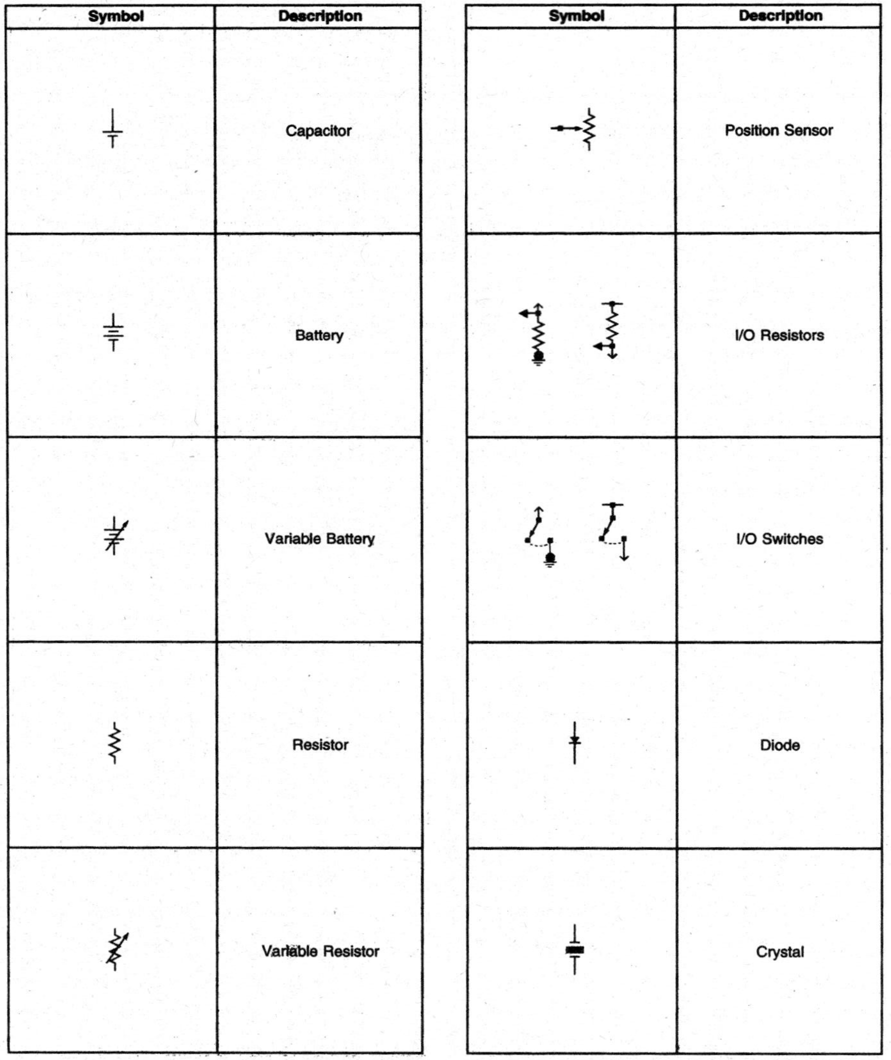

Symbol	Description
	Capacitor
	Battery
	Variable Battery
	Resistor
	Variable Resistor

Symbol	Description
	Position Sensor
	I/O Resistors
	I/O Switches
	Diode
	Crystal

Fig. 4 · Symbol Identification (Part 3 of 4). General Motors

GC113980114030X

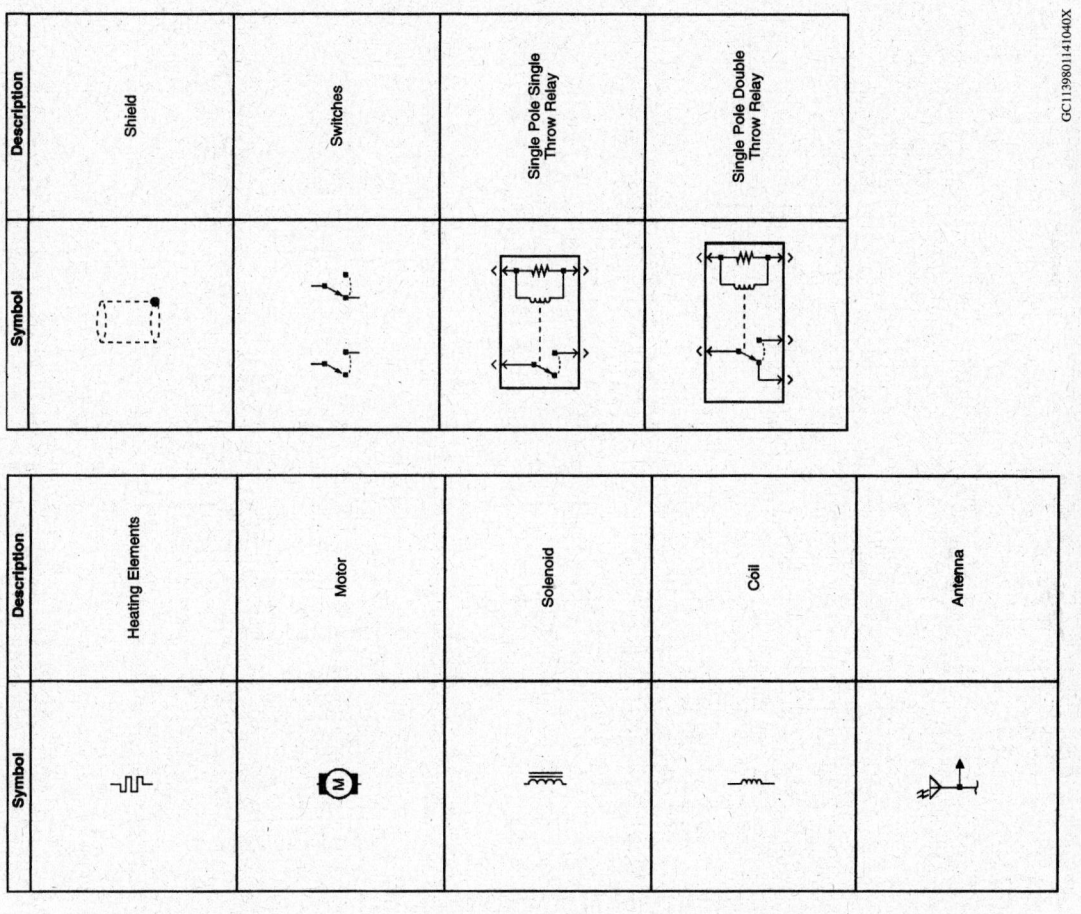

Fig. 4 Symbol Identification (Part 4 of 4). General Motors

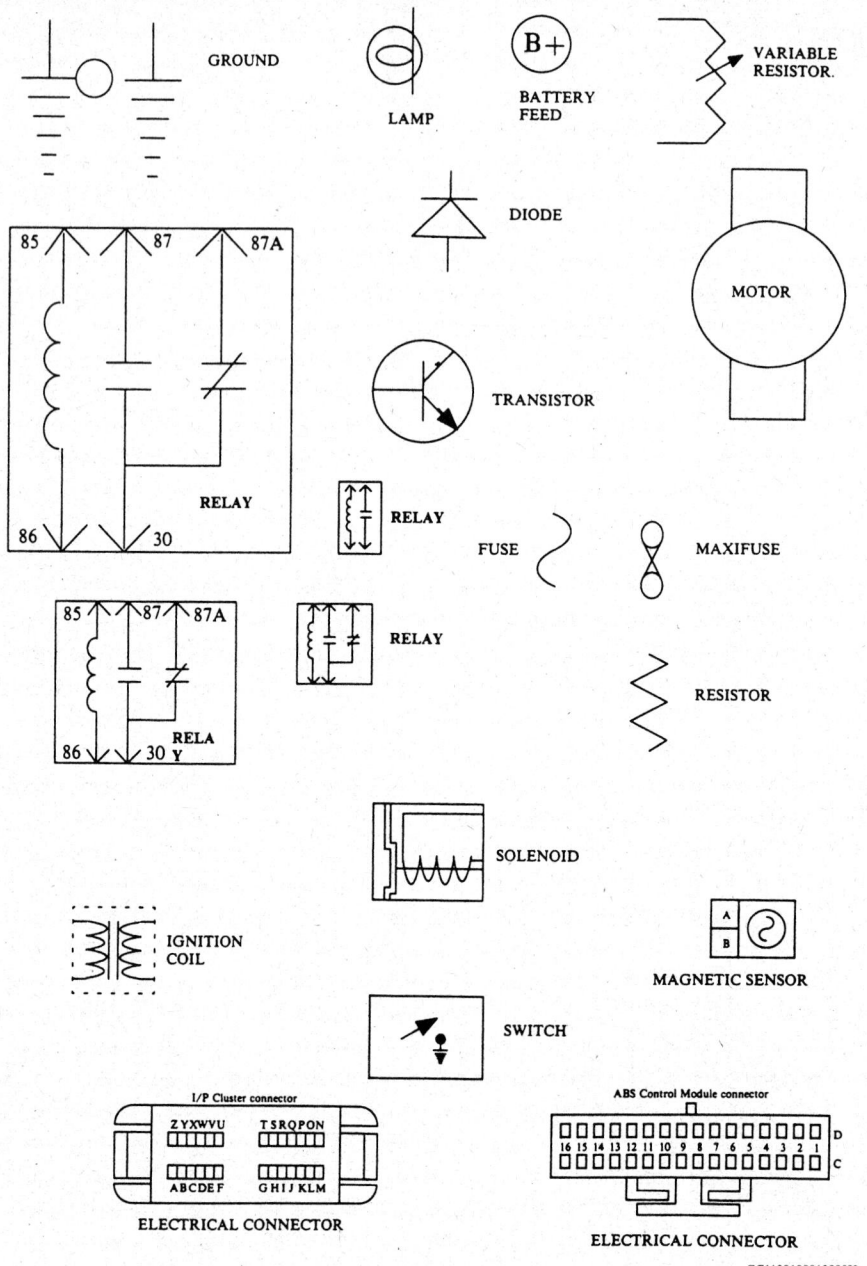

Fig. 5   Symbol Identification. Saturn

Wire Color Code Identification

Abbreviation	Wire Color
DAIMLERCHRYSLER DOMESTIC	
BL	Blue
BK	Black
BR	Brown
DB	Dark Blue
DG	Dark Green
GY	Gray
LB	Light Blue
LG	Light Green
OR	Orange
PK	Pink
RD	Red
TN	Tan
VT	Violet
WT	White
YL	Yellow
DAIMLERCHRYSLER IMPORTS	
B	Black
BR	Brown
G	Green
GR	Gray
L	Blue
LG	Light Green
O	Orange
P	Pink
R	Red
SB	Sky Blue
V	Violet
W	White
Y	Yellow
FORD MOTOR CO. w/NEW STYLE WIRING	
BK	Black
BN	Brown
BR	Brown
BU	Blue
GN	Green
GY	Gray
LG	Light Green
NA	Natural
OG	Orange
P	Purple
PK	Pink
RD	Red
SR	Silver
VT	Violet
WH	White
YE	Yellow

Continued

Abbreviation	Wire Color
FORD MOTOR CO. w/OLD STYLE WIRING	
BL	Blue
BK	Black
BN	Brown
BR	Brown
DB	Dark Blue
DG	Dark Green
GN	Green
GY	Gray
LB	Light Blue
LG	Light Green
N	Natural
O	Orange
P	Purple
PK	Pink
R	Red
T	Tan
W	White
Y	Yellow
GENERAL MOTORS & SATURN	
Black	BLK
Blue	BLU
Brown	BRN
DK BLU	Dark Blue
DK GRN	Dark Green
GRA/GRY	Gray
GRN	Green
LT BLU	Light Blue
LT GRAY	Light Gray
LT GRN	Light Green
ORN	Orange
PNK	Pink
PPL	Purple
RED	Red
TAN	Tan
WHT	White
YEL	Yellow

VEHICLE MAINTENANCE SCHEDULES

TABLE OF CONTENTS

Neon, Sebring Convertible, Sebring Sedan & Stratus Sedan

Recommended Service & Intervals (Months) — Service Interval In Miles①

Service	Interval / Notes
BODY	
Inspect Supplemental Restraint System	(X)
BRAKES	
Inspect Brake Connections, Hoses & Lines	Normal Service Every 6 Months Or 7500 Miles, Severe Service Every 3000 Miles
Inspect Brake Drums & Rotors (Normal Service Every 18 Mos.)	(S / N)
Inspect Brake Pads, Linings & Wheel Bearings, 2001–02	Normal Service Every 22,500 Miles; Severe Every 12,000 Miles
Inspect Brake Pads, Linings & Wheel Bearings, 2003	Normal Service Every 18,000 Miles; Severe Every 9000 Miles
Inspect Brake Pads, Linings & Wheel Bearings, 2004–05	Normal Service Every 18,000 Miles; Severe Service Every 12,000 Miles
CLUTCH & TRANSMISSION	
Change Automatic Transaxle Filter, Fluid & Adjust Bands. Stratus & 2001 Neon	Normal Service Every 30,000 Miles; Severe Service Every 15,000 Miles
Change Automatic Transaxle Filter, Fluid & Adjust Bands, Sebring Convertible & Stratus	Normal Service Every 100,000 Miles; Severe Service Every 48,000 Miles
Change Automatic Transaxle Filter, Fluid & Adjust Bands, 2001–03	Severe Service Every 48,000 Miles
Change Automatic Transaxle Filter, Fluid & Adjust Bands, 2004–05	Severe Service Every 60,000 Miles
DRIVESHAFT	
Inspect CV Joints	At 60 Months Or 100,000 Miles, Whichever Comes First (S / X)
ENGINE	
Change Engine Coolant	
Change Engine Oil (Normal Service Every 6 Mos.), 2001–02	(S / N)

Recommended Service & Intervals (Months)

Service Interval In Miles①

ENGINE

Recommended Service & Intervals	Notes
Change Engine Oil (Normal Service Every 6 Mos.), 2003–05	Normal Service Every 6000 Miles; Severe Service Every 3000 Miles
Change Engine Oil Filter, 2001–02	Normal Service Every 7500 Miles; Severe Service Every 3000 Miles
Change Engine Oil Filter, 2003–05	Normal Service Every 6000 Miles; Severe Service Every 3000 Miles
Inspect Air Filter, 2003②	S
Inspect Air Filter, 2004–05②	Normal Service Every 6000 Miles; Severe Service Every 3000 Miles
Inspect Coolant Level	At Every Engine Oil Change
Inspect EVAP & Fuel Systems Filler Pipe, Hoses, Lines, Tank & Cap	X
Inspect Exhaust System	S N S S S X S S S N S S S S S N S S S S N S
Inspect PCV Valve②	Normal Service Every 48 Months Or 60,000 Miles; Severe Service Every 30,000 Miles
Inspect & Adjust Drive Belts,	X
Replace Drive Belts. Except Sebring Convertible 2.7L	Every 60,000 Miles
Replace Drive Belts. Sebring Convertible 2.7L	Normal Service Inspect & Adjust At 60,000 Miles, Replace At 105,000 Miles; Severe Service Every 60,000 Miles
Replace Air Filter	Every 30,000 Miles
Replace Spark Plugs, 2.0L & 2.4L	X
Replace Spark Plugs, 2001 2.7L	Normal Service At 100,000 Miles; Severe Service Replace at 60,000 Miles Then Every 40,000 Miles Thereafter
Replace Spark Plugs, 2002–05 2.7L	Every 100,000 Miles
Replace Ignition Cables, 2002–05 2.4L	Every 60,000 Miles
Replace Timing Belt, 2001	At 105,000 Miles
Replace Timing Belt, 2002	Normal Service At 105,000 Miles; Severe Service At 90,000 Miles
Replace Timing Belt, 2003 2.0L	Normal Service At 105,000 Miles; Severe Service At 102,000 Miles
Replace Timing Belt, 2003–05 2.4L	Normal Service At 102,000 Miles; Severe Service At 90,000 Miles

STEERING, SUSPENSION & TIRES

Recommended Service & Intervals	Notes
Inspect Ball Joints	X
Lubricate Suspension & Steering Linkage	X
Rotate Tires & Adjust Pressure, 2001–02	Inspect And Rotate Tires Normal Service Every 7500 Miles; Severe Service Every 6000 Miles

Recommended Service & Intervals (Months)	Service Interval In Miles①																																
Months	3	6	9	12	15	18	21	24	27	30	33	36	39	42	45	48	51	54	57	60	63	66	69	72	75	78	81	84	87	90	93	96	99
Miles	3000	6000	9000	12000	15000	18000	21000	24000	27000	30000	33000	36000	39000	42000	45000	48000	51000	54000	57000	60000	63000	66000	69000	72000	75000	78000	81000	84000	87000	90000	93000	96000	99000

STEERING, SUSPENSION & TIRES

Rotate Tires & Adjust Pressure, 2003–05	Inspect And Rotate Tires Every 6000 Miles

Mos. — Months
N — Normal Service
S — Severe Service
X — Normal Or Severe Service
① — After vehicles passes 99,000 mile mark return to beginning of mileage table & start cycle over again.
② — This maintenance is recommended by DaimlerChrysler Corporation to the owner but is not required to maintain the emissions warranty.

Concorde, Intrepid, LHS & 300M

Recommended Service & Intervals (Months) — Service Interval In Miles[1]

The table below lists each service item together with its recommended interval. The maintenance grid to the right of each item marks the scheduled service points (S = Severe service, N = Normal service, X = perform service) across the mileage columns.

BODY

Service	Interval
Inspect Supplemental Restraint System	(X — at scheduled points)

BRAKES

Service	Interval
Inspect Brake Connections, Hoses & Lines, 2001–02	Normal Service Every 6 Mos. Or 7500 Miles; Severe Service Every 3000 Miles
Inspect Brake Connections, Hoses & Lines, 2003	Normal Service Every 6 Mos. Or 6000 Miles; Severe Service Every 3000 Miles
Inspect Brake Connections, Hoses & Lines, 2004	Normal Service Every 12,000 Miles; Severe Service Every 9000 Miles
Inspect Brake Drums & Rotors	(N / S — at scheduled points)
Inspect Brake Pads, Linings	(S — at scheduled points)

CLUTCH & TRANSMISSION

Service	Interval
Change Automatic Transaxle & Differential Fluid & Filter, 2001–03	Severe Service Every 48,000 Miles
Change Automatic Transaxle Fluid & Filter, 2004	Severe Service Every 60,000 Miles
Change Differential Fluid, 2004	Severe Service Every 48,000 Miles

DRIVESHAFT & CV JOINTS

Service	Interval
Inspect CV Joints	(S / N / X — at scheduled points)

ENGINE

Service	Interval
Change Engine Coolant	Every 60 Months Or 100,000 Miles
Change Engine Oil (Normal Service Every 6 Mos.), 2001–02	Normal Service Every 6000 Miles; Severe Service Every 3000 Miles
Change Engine Oil (Normal Service Every 6 Mos.), 2003–04	Normal Service Every 7500 Miles; Severe Service Every 3000 Miles
Change Engine Oil Filter (Normal Service Every 6 Mos.), 2001–02	Normal Service Every 6000 Miles; Severe Service Every 3000 Miles
Change Engine Oil Filter (Normal Service Every 6 Mos.), 2003–04	At Every Oil Change
Inspect Air Filter	

Service Interval In Miles①

Legend: **N** — Normal Service **S** — Severe Service **X** — Normal Or Severe Service

ENGINE

Recommended Service & Intervals (Months)	Service Interval / Marks
Inspect EVAP & Fuel Systems Filler Pipe, Hoses, Lines, Tank & Cap	X … X
Inspect Exhaust System	S S N S X S S X S S N S S S S N S S S S X S S S S N S
Inspect PCV Valve	S S N S X S S X S S N S S S S N S S S S X S S S S N S
Inspect & Adjust Drive Belts	Normal Service Replace at 60,000 Miles & Inspect Every 30,000 Miles Thereafter; Severe Service Replace Every 30,000 Miles
Replace Air Filter	X … X … X … X
Replace Drive Belts	S … S … S … S
Replace Spark Plugs, 2001–02	Every 100,000 Miles
Replace Spark Plugs, 2003–04	Normal Service Every 102,000 Miles; Severe Service Every 100,000 Miles
Replace Timing Belt, 3.2L & 3.5L, 2001–02②	At 100,000 Miles
Replace Timing Belt, 3.2L & 3.5L, 2003–04	Normal Service Every 102,000 Miles; Severe Service Federal Emissions Every 100,000 Miles; California Emissions Every 105,000 Miles
Replace Timing Belt, 3.2L & 3.5L, 2001–02③	At 105,000 Miles

STEERING, SUSPENSION & TIRES

Recommended Service & Intervals (Months)	Service Interval / Marks
Inspect Ball Joints	S N S N S N S S S S S S S
Lubricate Suspension & Steering Linkage	At Every Oil Change
Rotate Tires & Adjust Pressure, 2001–02	S N S N S N S N S N S N S N S N S N S N S N S N S N
Rotate Tires & Adjust Pressure, 2003–04	Every 6000 Miles

Mos. — Months
N — Normal Service
S — Severe Service
X — Normal Or Severe Service
① After vehicles passes 99,000 mile mark return to beginning of mileage table & start cycle over again.
② 2001–02 models w/Federal emissions.
③ 2001–02 models w/California emissions.

Sebring Coupe & Stratus Coupe

Service Interval In Miles ①

Recommended Service & Intervals (Months)	7500	15000	22500	30000	37500	45000	52500	60000	67500	75000	82500	90000	97500	105000	Notes
BODY															
Inspect Supplemental Restraint System Components															Every 10 Years From Vehicle Build Date
BRAKES															
Inspect Brake Connections, Hoses & Lines															Every 12 Months Or 15,000 Miles
Inspect Disc Brake Pads (Every 12 Mos.)															Normal Service Check for Wear Every 15,000 Miles; Severe Service Every 6000 Miles
Inspect Drum Brake Shoes (Every 24 Mos.)															Normal Service Check For Wear Every 30,000 Miles; Severe Service Every 15,000 Miles
CLUTCH & TRANSMISSION															
Change Or Inspect Automatic Transaxle Fluid & Filter															Normal Service, Inspect Every 15,000 Miles; Severe Service, Inspect Every 15,000 Miles, Change Fluid & Filter 30,000 Miles.
Change Manual Transaxle Lubricant				S							S				
DRIVESHAFT & CV JOINTS															
Inspect CV Joint Boots (Every 12 Mos.)		X		X		X		X		X		X		X	
ENGINE															
Change Engine Coolant															At 48 Months Or 60,000 Miles Then Every 24 Months Or 30,000 Miles
Change Engine Oil (Normal Service Every 6 Mos./Severe Service Every 3 Mos.)	S	S	S	S	S	S	S	S	S	S	S	S	S	S	
Change Engine Oil & Filter	S	N	S	X	S	N	S	X	S	N	S	X	S	N	
Inspect Air Filter		S		X		S		X		S		X		S	
Inspect Coolant Level															At Every Engine Oil Change
Inspect Distributor Cap & Rotor				X				X				X			
Inspect EVAP System				X				X				X			
Inspect Exhaust System & Heat Shields	S	S	S	S	S	S	S	S	S	S	S	S	S	S	
Inspect Fuel Filler Cap				X				X				X			
Inspect Fuel Hoses, Lines & Connections				X				X				X			
Inspect Fuel Tank				X				X				X			
Inspect & Adjust Drive Belts		X		X				X				X			
Replace Air Filter				X				X				X			Every 30,000 Miles
Replace Spark Plugs, DOHC				S				S				S			

Service Interval In Miles ①

Recommended Service & Intervals (Months)	3	6	9	12	15	18	21	24	27	30	33	36	39	42	45	48	51	54	57	60	63	66	69	72	75	78	81	84	87	90	93	96	99
Miles	3000	6000	9000	12000	15000	18000	21000	24000	27000	30000	33000	36000	39000	42000	45000	48000	51000	54000	57000	60000	63000	66000	69000	72000	75000	78000	81000	84000	87000	90000	93000	96000	99000
ENGINE																																	
Replace Spark Plugs, SOHC								Normal Service Every 100,000 Miles; Severe Service Every 15,000 Miles																									
Replace Timing Belt																				X													
STEERING, SUSPENSION & TIRES																																	
Inspect Ball Joints & Steering Linkage Grease Seals (Every 24 Mos.)								X								X								X								X	
Lubricate Suspension & Steering Linkage (Every 24 Mos.)								X								X								X								X	
Rotate Tires & Adjust Pressure (Every 6 Mos.)		X		X		X		X		X		X		X		X		X		X		X		X		X		X		X		X	

Mos. — Months
N — Normal Service
S — Severe Service
X — Normal Or Severe Service
① — After vehicles passes 99,000 mile mark return to beginning of mileage table & start cycle over again.

Crossfire

Service Interval In Miles①

Recommended Service & Intervals (Months)	3000	6000	9000	12000	15000	18000	21000	24000	27000	30000	33000	36000	39000	42000	45000	48000	51000	54000	57000	60000	63000	66000	69000	72000	75000	78000	81000	84000	87000	90000	93000	96000	99000
BODY																																	
Replace Cabin Air Filter	→ Every 18,500 Miles																																
BRAKES																																	
Inspect Brake Connections, Hoses & Lines	→ Normal Service Every 6 Months Or 7000 Miles; Severe Service Every 3 Months Or 3000 Miles																																
Inspect Brake Drums & Rotors					S	S	N			S		S		X		S		S		N		N		S		S		X		S		S	
Inspect Brake Drum	→ Normal Service Every 18,000 Miles; Severe Service Every 12,000 Miles				S					S				X		S		S		S		S				S				S			
Inspect Brake Pads & Linings					S	S	N			S		S		X		S		S		S		N		S		S		S		S		S	
Replace Brake Fluid																										S							
CLUTCH & TRANSMISSION																																	
Change Automatic Transmission Fluid & Filter	→ Replace Every 80,000 Miles																																
Check Transmission Lubricant & Level Condition	→ Severe Service At Every Oil Change																																
DRIVE AXLE & DRIVESHAFT																																	
Inspect CV & Driveshaft Joint Boots					X					X					X					X					X					X			X
ENGINE																																	
Change Engine Coolant	→ Every 60 Months Or 100,000 Miles																																
Change Engine Oil & Filter	→ Every 7000 Miles																																
Inspect Coolant Level, Hoses & Clamps	→ At Every Oil Change																																
Inspect Drive Belts					S					S					S					X					S					X			
Inspect Exhaust System	→ At Every Oil Change																																
Adjust Alternator Drive Belt Tension	→ Every 24 Months Or 30,000 Miles																																
Replace Air Filter	→ Normal Service 60,000 Miles																																
Replace Fuel Filter	→ Normal Service 60,000 Miles																																
Replace Spark Plugs	→ Every 60 Months Or 100,000 Miles																																

Service Interval In Miles①

Recommended Service & Intervals (Months)	3000	6000	9000	12000	15000	18000	21000	24000	27000	30000	33000	36000	39000	42000	45000	48000	51000	54000	57000	60000	63000	66000	69000	72000	75000	78000	81000	84000	87000	90000	93000	96000	99000
STEERING, SUSPENSION & TIRES																																	
Inspect Bushings, Arms, CV Joints, Seals, Springs & Jounce Bumpers	S	X	S	X	S	X	S	X	S	X	S	X	S	X	S	X	S	X	S	X	S	X	S	X	S	X	S	X	S	X	S	X	S
Inspect Tie Rod Ends & Boot Seals	Every 50,000 Miles																																
Lubricate Ball Joints (Every 18 Mos.)						X						X						X						X						X			
Lubricate Steering Linkage (Every 12 Mos.)				X				X				X				X				X				X				X				X	
Rotate Tires & Adjust Pressure	Every 7000 Miles																																

S — Severe Service
N — Normal Service
X — Normal Or Severe Service
① — After vehicles passes 99,000 mile mark return to beginning of mileage table & start cycle over again.

Magnum & 300

Service Interval In Miles[1]

Recommended Service & Intervals (Months)	3	6	9	12	15	18	21	24	27	30	33	36	39	42	45	48	51	54	57	60	63	66	69	72	75	78	81	84	87	90	93	96	99	102
Miles	3000	6000	9000	12000	15000	18000	21000	24000	27000	30000	33000	36000	39000	42000	45000	48000	51000	54000	57000	60000	63000	66000	69000	72000	75000	78000	81000	84000	87000	90000	93000	96000	99000	102000
BODY																																		
Replace Cabin Air Filter					X					X					X					X					X					X				
BRAKES																																		
Inspect Brake Linings & Rotors	Inspect Every 9000 Miles																																	
CLUTCH & TRANSMISSION																																		
Change Transfer Case Fluid (AWD)	Change Every 48,000 Miles																																	
Change Transmission Fluid & Filter	Change Every 60,000 Miles																																	
ENGINE																																		
Change Engine Oil & Filter	N	N	N	N	N	N	N	N	N	N	N	N	N	N	N	N	N	N	N	N	N	N	N	N	N	N	N	N	N	N	N	N	N	N
Change Engine Coolant	Normal Or Severe Service Every 102,000 Miles																																	
Replace Air Cleaner Filter										X										X										X				
Inspect Air Cleaner Filter		X		X		X		X				X		X		X		X				X		X		X		X				X		X
Replace Spark Plugs (2.7L & 3.5L Engines)	Change Every 100,000 Miles																																	
Replace Spark Plugs (5.7L Engine)										X										X										X				
Check/Replace PCV Valve (If Necessary)																																		X
Check/Inspect Drive Belt																																		X
Replace Engine Timing Belt	Change Every 105,000 Miles																																	
STEERING, SUSPENSION & TIRES																																		
Rotate Tires		X		X		X		X		X		X		X		X		X		X		X		X		X		X		X		X		X
Replace Rear Axle Fluid																X																		
Replace Power Steering Fluid	Change Every 60,000 Miles																																	

[1] — After vehicles passes 102,000 mile mark return to beginning of mileage table & start cycle over again.
N — Normal Service
S — Severe Service
X — Normal Or Severe Service

Crown Victoria, Grand Marquis & Marauder

Service Interval In Miles ① (values shown ×1,000 miles)

Recommended Service	3	6	9	12	15	18	21	24	27	30	33	36	39	42	45	48	51	54	57	60	Interval Notes
BODY																					
Inspect A/C Refrigerant Charge & System Operation																					Every 12 Months Or 15,000 Miles
Inspect Instrument Panel Warning Lamps & Gauges																					At Every Engine Oil Change
Lubricate Body Hardware & Hinges					X					X					X					X	
Lubricate Hood Latch Pivot Points & All Contact Areas					X					X					X					X	
Replace Cabin Air Filter																					Every 15,000 Miles If Equipped
BRAKES																					
Inspect Brake Drums, Linings, Pads, Rotors, Lubricate Caliper Slide Rails																					Normal Service Every 15,000 Miles; Severe Service Every 5000 Miles
Inspect Parking Brake System Operation					X					X					X					X	
CLUTCH & TRANSMISSION																					
Change Automatic Transmission Fluid & Filter																					Normal Service Inspect Every 15,000 Miles; Change Every 30,000 Miles
Lubricate Transmission Control Linkage					X					X					X					X	
DRIVE AXLE & DRIVESHAFT																					
Change Differential Lubricant																					②
Lubricate Driveshaft					X					X					X					X	
ENGINE																					
Change Engine Coolant, 2001-03																					Replace Green Coolant, Every 45,000 Miles, Then Every 30,000 Miles Thereafter, Orange Coolant, Every 150,000 Miles, Yellow Coolant Every 5 Years Or 100,000 Miles
Change Engine Coolant, 2004-05																					Replace Premium Gold Coolant, Every 5 Years Or 100,000 Miles Thereafter Replace Every 36 Months Or 50,000 Miles
Change Engine Oil & Filter, 2001-03	S	S	N	S	N	S	N	S	N	S	N	S	N	S	N	S	N	S	N	S	
Change Engine Oil & Filter, 2004-05																					Normal Service Every 5000 Miles; Severe Service Every 3000 Miles
Inspect Cooling System & Protection Level																					Annually Or Every 15,000 Miles
Inspect Drive Belts																					Every 100,000 Miles
Inspect Exhaust System										X										X	
Inspect Fluid & Lubricant Levels																					At Every Engine Oil Change
Inspect Fuel System Connections, Hoses & Lines					X					X					X					X	
Inspect & Replace Engine Air Filter					S					S					S					S	
Replace Engine Air Filter																					Every 30,000 Miles
Replace Fuel Filter Element & Housing O-Ring Seal, Drain Coalescent Filter Bowl, 2002–05 NGV																					Every 15 Years From Date On Tank From Manufacturer
Replace Fuel Filter Element & Housing O-Ring Seal, Drain Coalescent Filter Bowl, 2001 NGV																					Every 120,000 Miles
Replace Fuel Filter																					Normal Service Every 30,000 Miles; Severe Service Every 15,000 Miles
Replace PCV Valve																					Every 100,000 Miles

Service Interval In Miles①

Recommended Service	30000	50000	60000	75000	90000	105000	120000	150000	180000	210000	240000	270000	300000	330000	360000	390000	405000	420000	450000	480000	510000	525000	540000	570000	600000
ENGINE																									
Replace Spark Plugs, Except NGV	Normal Service Every 100,000 Miles; Severe Service Every 60,000 Miles																								
Replace Spark Plugs, NGV			X																						
STEERING, SUSPENSION & TIRES																									
Inspect & Repack Front Wheel Bearings							X				X				X					X					X
Lubricate Steering & Suspension Components						X					X				X					X					X
Rotate Tires	Normal Service Inspect for Wear & Rotate Every 5,000 Miles.																								

N — Normal Service
NGV — Natural Gas Vehicle
S — Severe Service
X — Normal Or Severe Service
① — After vehicle has passed 60,000 mile mark return to beginning of mileage table & start cycle over again.
② — Normal Vehicle Axle Maintenance: Rear axle units containing synthetic lubricant are lubricated for life. These lubricants are not to be checked or changed unless a leak is suspected, service is required or the axle assembly has been submerged in water. The axle lubricant should be changed anytime the axle has been submerged in water. Non-synthetic rear axle lubricants should be replaced every 100,000 miles under normal operating conditions. Non-synthetic rear axle lubricants should be replaced every 3000 miles or 3 months, whichever occurs first, during extended trailer tow operation above (70°F) ambient and wide open throttle for extended periods above 45 mph. The 3000 mile lube change interval may be waived if the axle was filled with 75W140 synthetic gear lubricant meeting Ford specification WSL-M2C192-A. Add four ounces of additive friction modifier C8AZ-19B546-A or equivalent for complete refill of Traction-Lok rear axles. The rear axle lubricant should be changed anytime the axle has been submerged in water. Police and Taxi Vehicle Axle Maintenance: Replace rear axle lubricant every 160,000 km (100,000 miles). Rear axle lubricant change may be waived if the axle was filled with 75W140 synthetic gear lubricant meeting Ford specification WSL-M2C192-A. Add four ounces of additive friction modifier C8AZ-19B546-A or equivalent for complete refill of Traction-Lok rear axles. The rear axle lubricant should be changed anytime the axle has been submerged in water.

Mustang

Service Interval In Miles ①

The service intervals are tabulated across columns from 35,000 miles through 360,000 miles. Each Recommended Service item and its interval note/marking is listed below.

Recommended Service	Service Interval / Notes
BODY	
Inspect A/C Refrigerant Charge & System Operation	Every 12 Months Or 15,000 Miles
Inspect Instrument Panel Warning Lamps & Gauges	At Every Engine Oil Change
Lubricate Body Hardware & Hinges	X
Lubricate Hood Latch Pivot Points & All Contact Areas	X
Replace Cabin Air Filter	Every 15,000 Miles, If Equipped
BRAKES	
Inspect Brake Drums, Linings, Pads, Rotors, Lubricate Caliper Slide Rails	Normal Service Every 15,000 Miles; Severe Service Every 5,000 Miles
Inspect Parking Brake System Operation	X
CLUTCH & TRANSMISSION	
Change Automatic Transmission Fluid & Filter	Inspect Every 15,000 Miles; Change Every 30,000 Miles.
Lubricate Transmission Control Linkage	X
DRIVE AXLE & DRIVESHAFT	
Change Differential Lubricant	③
Lubricate Driveshaft	X
ENGINE	
Change Engine Coolant, 2001–03	Green Coolant, Every 45,000 Miles, Then Every 30,000 Miles Thereafter. Replace Orange Coolant, Every 150,000 Miles, Replace Yellow Coolant Every 5 Years Or 100,000 Miles
Change Engine Coolant, 2004–05	Replace Premium Gold Coolant, Every 5 Years Or 100,000 Miles Thereafter Replace Every 36 Months Or 50,000 Miles
Change Engine Oil & Filter	S N S N S X S N S N S N S N S N S N S N S N S
Inspect Cooling System & Protection Level	Annually Or Every 15,000 Miles
Inspect Drive Belts	Every 100,000 Miles
Inspect Engine Air Filter	S
Inspect Exhaust System	X
Inspect Fluid & Lubricant Levels	At Every Engine Oil Change
Inspect Fuel System Connections, Hoses & Lines	X
Replace Engine Air Filter	Every 30,000 Miles
Replace Fuel Filter ②	Normal Service Every 30,000 Miles; Severe Service Every 15,000 Miles
Replace PCV Valve	Every 100,000 Miles
Replace Spark Plugs	Normal Service Every 100,000 Miles; Severe Service Every 60,000 Miles
STEERING, SUSPENSION & TIRES	
Inspect & Repack Front Wheel Bearings	X
Lubricate Steering & Suspension Components	X
Rotate Tires	Normal Service Inspect for Wear And Rotate Every 5,000 Miles.

N — Normal Service
S — Severe Service
X — Normal Or Severe Service

① — After vehicle has passed 60,000 mile mark return to beginning of mileage table & start cycle over again.

② — On All vehicles equipped with California emissions.

③ — Normal Vehicle Axle Maintenance: Rear axle units containing synthetic lubricant are lubricated for life. These lubricants are not to be checked or changed unless a leak is suspected, service is required or the axle assembly has been submerged in water. The axle lubricant should be changed anytime the axle has been submerged in water. Non-synthetic rear axle lubricants should be replaced every 3000 miles or 3 months, whichever occurs first, during extended trailer tow operation above (70°F) ambient and wide open throttle for extended periods above 45 mph. The 3000 mile lube change interval may be waived if the axle was filled with 75W140 synthetic gear lubricant meeting Ford specification WSL-M2C192-A. Add four ounces of additive friction modifier C8AZ-19B546-A or equivalent for complete refill of Traction-Lok rear axles. The rear axle lubricant should be changed anytime the axle has been submerged in water.

Escort & ZX2

Service Interval In Miles ①

Recommended Service	Service Interval / Frequency
BODY	
Inspect A/C Refrigerant Charge & System Operation	Every 12 Months Or 15,000 Miles
Inspect Instrument Panel Warning Lamps & Gauges	At Every Engine Oil Change
Lubricate Body Hardware & Hinges	X (marked at service intervals)
Lubricate Hood Latch Pivot Points & All Contact Areas	X (marked at service intervals)
Tighten Body Fasteners	S (marked at service intervals)
Replace Cabin Air Filter	Every 15,000 Miles If Equipped
BRAKES	
Inspect Brake Drums, Linings, Pads, Rotors, Lubricate Caliper Slide Rails	Normal Service Every 15,000 Miles; Severe Service Every 5000 Miles
Inspect Parking Brake System Operation	X (marked at service intervals)
CLUTCH & TRANSMISSION	
Change Automatic Transmission Fluid & Filter	Normal Service Inspect Every 15,000 Miles Change Every 150,000 Miles; Severe Service Change Every 30,000 Miles.
Inspect Clutch Pedal Operation	X (marked at service intervals)
Lubricate Transmission Control Linkage	X (marked at service intervals)
DRIVESHAFT	
Inspect CV Joint Boots	X (marked at service intervals)
ENGINE	
Change Engine Coolant	Replace Green Coolant, Every 45,000 Miles, Then Every 30,000 Miles Thereafter, Replace Orange Coolant, Every 150,000 Miles, Replace Yellow Coolant, Every 5 Years Or 100,000 Miles
Change Engine Oil & Filter	Normal Service Every 5000 Miles; Severe Service Every 3000 Miles
Inspect Cooling System & Protection Level	Annually Or Every 15,000 Miles
Inspect Drive Belts	Every 100,000 Miles
Inspect Engine Air Filter	X (marked at service intervals)
Inspect Exhaust System	X (marked at service intervals)
Inspect Fuel System Connections, Hoses & Lines	X (marked at service intervals)
Replace Fuel Filter	Normal Service Every 30,000 Miles; Severe Service Every 15,000 Miles
Replace PCV Valve, 2001	Every 60,000 Miles
Replace PCV Valve, 2002–03	Every 100,000 Miles
Replace Spark Plugs	Every 100,000 Miles
Replace Timing Belt	Every 120,000 Miles

STEERING, SUSPENSION & TIRES

Service Interval In Miles①

Recommended Service	15000	30000	45000	60000	75000	90000	105000	120000	135000	150000	165000	180000	195000	210000	225000	240000	255000	270000	285000	300000	315000	330000	345000	360000	375000	390000	405000	420000	435000	450000	465000	480000	495000	510000	525000	540000	555000	570000	585000	600000
Inspect & Repack Rear Wheel Bearings																						X																		X
Lubricate Steering & Suspension Components	X																					X								X										
Rotate Tires	Normal Service Inspect For Wear And Rotate Every 5000 Miles																																							
Tighten Chassis Fasteners	S																					S								S										X

N — Normal Service
S — Severe Service
X — Normal Or Severe Service
① — After vehicle has passed 60,000 mile mark return to beginning of mileage table & start cycle over again.

Focus

Service Interval In Miles ①

Recommended Service	15,000	30,000	45,000	60,000	Service Notes
BODY					
Inspect A/C Refrigerant Charge & System Operation					Every 12 Months Or 15,000 Miles
Inspect Instrument Panel Warning Lamps & Gauges					At Every Engine Oil Change
Lubricate Body Hardware & Hinges	X	X	X	X	
Lubricate Hood Latch Pivot Points & All Contact Areas	X	X	X	X	
Replace Cabin Air Filter					Every 15,000 Miles
Tighten Body Fasteners	S		S	X	
BRAKES					
Inspect Brake Drums, Linings, Pads, Rotors, Lubricate Caliper Slide Rails					Normal Service Every 15,000 Miles; Severe Service Every 5000 Miles
Inspect Parking Brake System Operation	X	X	X	X	
CLUTCH & TRANSMISSION					
Change Automatic Transmission Fluid & Filter					Inspect Every 15,000 Miles; Change Every 30,000 Miles
Inspect Clutch Pedal Operation	X	X		X	
Lubricate Transmission Control Linkage	X	X	X	X	
DRIVESHAFT					
Inspect CV Joint Boots	X	X	X	X	
ENGINE					
Change Engine Coolant, 2001–03					Replace Green Coolant, Every 45,000 Miles, Then Every 30,000 Miles Thereafter, Orange Coolant, Every 150,000 Miles, Yellow Coolant Every 5 Years Or 100,000 Miles
Change Engine Coolant, 2004–05					Replace Premium Gold Coolant, Every 5 Years Or 100,000 Miles Thereafter Replace Every 36 Months Or 50,000 Miles
Change Engine Oil & Filter					Normal Service Every 5000 Miles; Severe Service Every 3000 Miles
Inspect Cooling System & Protection Level					Annually Or Every 15,000 Miles
Inspect Drive Belts					Every 100,000 Miles
Inspect Exhaust System	X	X	X	X	
Inspect Fuel System Connections, Hoses & Lines	X	X	X	X	
Inspect Engine Air Filter	X	X	X	X	
Replace Fuel Filter					Normal Service Every 30,000 Miles; Severe Service Every 15,000 Miles
Replace PCV Valve, 2001					Every 60,000 Miles
Replace PCV Valve, 2002–05					Every 100,000 Miles
Replace Spark Plugs					Every 100,000 Miles
Replace Timing Belt					Every 120,000 Miles

Service Interval In Miles ①

Recommended Service

STEERING, SUSPENSION & TIRES

Recommended Service	3000	5000	6000	7500	9000	10500	12000	15000	18000	21000	22500	24000	25500	27000	30000	33000	36000	37500	39000	40500	42000	45000	48000	51000	52500	54000	55500	57000	60000
Inspect & Repack Rear Wheel Bearings															X														X
Lubricate Steering & Suspension Components								X							X							X							X
Rotate Tires																													
Tighten Chassis Fasteners								S							S							S							S

Rotate Tires: Normal Service — Inspect For Wear And Rotate Every 5000 Miles

N — Normal Service
S — Severe Service
X — Normal Or Severe Service
① — After vehicle has passed 60,000 mile mark return to beginning of mileage table & start cycle over again.

Taurus & Sable

Service Interval In Miles ①

Recommended Service

BODY

Recommended Service	Interval
Inspect A/C Refrigerant Charge & System Operation	Every 12 Months Or 15,000 Miles, Before Warm Season Arrives
Inspect Instrument Panel Warning Lamps & Gauges	At Every Engine Oil Change

Service Interval In Miles ①

The following schedule lists recommended service items against a grid of service intervals (in miles). Items marked with a descriptive note span the interval columns; items marked with N, S, or X apply at the indicated mileage columns of the grid.

Recommended Service	Interval / Notes
BODY	
Lubricate Body Hardware & Hinges	(marked X at grid intervals)
Lubricate Hood Latch Pivot Points & All Contact Areas	(marked X at grid intervals)
Replace Passenger Compartment Pollen Filter	(marked X at grid intervals)
BRAKES	
Inspect Brake Drums, Linings, Pads, Rotors, Lubricate Caliper Slide Rails	Normal Service Every 15,000 Miles; Severe Service Every 5000 Miles
Inspect Brake Lines & Hoses	(marked N / S at grid intervals)
Inspect Parking Brake System Operation	(marked X at grid intervals)
CLUTCH & TRANSMISSION	
Change Automatic Transmission Fluid & Filter	Inspect Every 15,000 Miles; Change Every 30,000 Miles
Lubricate Transmission Control Linkage	(marked X at grid intervals)
DRIVESHAFT	
Inspect CV Joint Boots	(marked X at grid intervals)
ENGINE	
Change Engine Coolant, 2001–03	Green Coolant, Every 45,000 Miles, Then Every 30,000 Miles Thereafter Replace Orange Coolant, Every 150,000 Miles, Replace Yellow Coolant, Every 5 Years Or 100,000 Miles
Change Engine Coolant, 2004–05	Replace Premium Gold Coolant, Every 5 Years Or 100,000 Miles Thereafter Replace Every 36 Months Or 50,000 Miles
Change Engine Oil & Filter	(marked S / N at grid intervals)
Inspect Cooling System & Protection Level	Annually Or Every 15,000 Miles
Inspect Drive Belts	Inspect Accessory Drive Belts Every 100,000 Miles.
Inspect Exhaust System	(marked X at grid intervals)
Inspect Fluid & Lubricant Levels	At Every Engine Oil Change
Inspect Fuel System Connections, Hoses & Lines	(marked X at grid intervals)
Inspect Engine Air Filter	(marked X at grid intervals)
Replace Fuel Filter	Normal Service Every 30,000 Miles; Severe Service Every 15,000 Miles
Replace PCV Valve	Every 100,000 Miles
Replace Spark Plugs	Normal Service Every 100,000 Miles; Severe Service Every 60,000 Miles
STEERING, SUSPENSION & TIRES	
Lubricate Steering & Suspension Components	(marked X at grid intervals)
Rotate Tires	Normal Service Inspect For Wear And Rotate Every 5000 Miles

N — Normal Service
S — Severe Service
X — Normal Or Severe Service
① — After vehicle has passed 60,000 mile mark return to beginning of mileage table & start cycle over again.

Thunderbird

Service Interval In Miles [1]

Columns (miles): 3,000 · 5,000 · 6,000 · 7,500 · 9,000 · 10,000 · 12,000 · 15,000 · 18,000 · 20,000 · 21,000 · 22,500 · 24,000 · 25,000 · 27,000 · 28,000 · 30,000 · 33,000 · 35,000 · 36,000 · 39,000 · 40,000 · 42,000 · 45,000 · 48,000 · 50,000 · 51,000 · 54,000 · 55,000 · 57,000 · 60,000

Recommended Service	Service Interval / Marks
BODY	
Inspect A/C Refrigerant Charge & System Operation	Every 12 Months Or 15,000 Miles
Inspect Instrument Panel Warning Lamps & Gauges	At Every Engine Oil Change
Lubricate Body Hardware & Hinges	X at 15,000 / 30,000 / 45,000 / 60,000
Lubricate Hood Latch Pivot Points & All Contact Areas	X at 6,000 / 15,000 / 30,000 / 45,000 / 60,000
BRAKES	
Inspect Brake Drums, Linings, Pads, Rotors, Lubricate Caliper Slide Rails	Normal Service Every 15,000 Miles; Severe Service Every 5000 Miles
Inspect Parking Brake System Operation	X at 15,000 / 30,000 / 45,000 / 60,000
CLUTCH & TRANSMISSION	
Change Automatic Transmission Fluid & Filter	Normal Service Inspect Every 15,000 Miles, Change Every 150,000 Miles; Severe Service Every 30,000 Miles (X at 30,000 / 60,000)
Lubricate Transmission Control Linkage	X at 15,000 / 30,000 / 45,000 / 60,000
DRIVE AXLE & DRIVESHAFT	
Lubricate Driveshaft	X at 15,000 / 30,000 / 45,000 / 60,000
ENGINE	
Change Engine Coolant	Green Coolant, Every 45,000 Miles, Then Every 30,000 Miles Thereafter. Replace Orange Coolant, Every 150,000 Miles, Replace Yellow Coolant Every 5 Years Or 100,000 Miles
Change Engine Oil & Filter	S / N marks at listed intervals (Severe / Normal service)
Inspect Cooling System & Protection Level	Annually Or Every 15,000 Miles
Inspect Drive Belts	Every 100,000 Miles
Inspect Exhaust System	X at 25,000 / 50,000
Inspect Fluid & Lubricant Levels	At Every Engine Oil Change
Inspect Fuel System Connections, Hoses & Lines	X at 30,000 / 60,000
Inspect & Replace Engine Air Filter	S at 30,000 / 60,000
Replace Engine Air Filter	Every 30,000 Miles
Replace Fuel Filter	Normal Service Every 30,000 Miles; Severe Service Every 15,000 Miles
Replace PCV Valve	4 Cylinder Every 60,000 Miles; V6 Every 100,000 Miles
Replace Spark Plugs	Normal Service Every 100,000 Miles; Severe Service Every 60,000 Miles
STEERING, SUSPENSION & TIRES	
Lubricate Steering & Suspension Components	X at 15,000 / 30,000 / 45,000 / 60,000
Rotate Tires	Normal Service Inspect For Wear And Rotate Every 5000 Miles

N — Normal Service
NGV — Natural Gas Vehicle
S — Severe Service
X — Normal Or Severe Service

Continental, LS & Town Car

① — After vehicle has passed 60,000 mile mark return to beginning of mileage table & start cycle over again.

Service Interval In Miles ①

Recommended Service	Interval / Notes
BODY	
Inspect A/C Refrigerant Charge & System Operation	Every 12 Months Or 15,000 Miles, Before Warm Season Arrives
Inspect Instrument Panel Warning Lamps & Gauges	At Every Engine Oil Change
Lubricate Body Hardware & Hinges	X
Lubricate Hood Latch Pivot Points & All Contact Areas	X
Replace Passenger Compartment Pollen Filter	Normal Service Every 15,000 Miles
BRAKES	
Inspect Brake Drums, Linings, Pads, Rotors, Lubricate Caliper Slide Rails	Normal Service Every 15,000 Miles; Severe Service Every 5000 Miles
Inspect Brake Lines & Hoses	Normal Service Every 30,000 Miles; Severe Service Every 12,000 Miles
Inspect Parking Brake System Operation	X
CLUTCH & TRANSMISSION	
Change Automatic Transmission Fluid & Filter, Continental & Town Car	
Change Automatic Transmission Fluid & Filter, LS	Normal Service Inspect Every 15,000 Miles, Change Every 150,000 Miles; Severe Service Change Every 30,000 Miles
Change Manual Transmission Fluid, Lincoln LS	Every 60,000 Miles.
Lubricate Transmission Control Linkage	X
DRIVE AXLE & DRIVESHAFT	
Change Differential Lubricant, Town Car, 2001–03	②
Inspect CV Joint Boots	X
Lubricate Driveshaft	X
ENGINE	
Change Engine Coolant, 2001–03	Green Coolant, Every 45,000 Miles, Then Every 30,000 Miles Thereafter. Replace Orange Coolant, Every 150,000 Miles, Replace Yellow Coolant, Every 5 Years Or 100,000 Miles
Change Engine Coolant, 2004–05	Replace Premium Gold Coolant, Every 5 Years Or 100,000 Miles Thereafter Replace Every 36 Months Or 50,000 Miles
Change Engine Oil & Filter	S N S N S X S N S X S N S X S N S X S N S
Inspect Cooling System & Protection Level	Annually Or Every 15,000 Miles
Inspect Drive Belts	Every 100,000 Miles
Inspect Exhaust System	X
Inspect Fuel System Connections, Hoses & Lines	X
Inspect Engine Air Filter	X
Replace PCV Valve	Every 100,000 Miles

Vehicle Maintenance Schedules

ENGINE

Recommended Service	Service Interval In Miles ①
Replace Fuel Filter	Normal Service Every 30,000 Miles; Severe Service Every 15,000 Miles
Replace Spark Plugs	Normal Service Every 100,000 Miles; Severe Service Every 60,000 Miles

STEERING, SUSPENSION & TIRES

Recommended Service	Service Interval In Miles ①
Inspect & Repack Front Wheel Bearings, Town Car	X (marked at 30,000 and 60,000 mile columns)
Lubricate Steering & Suspension Components	X (marked at 15,000 and 45,000 mile columns)
Rotate Tires	Normal Service Inspect for Wear And Rotate Every 5000 Miles

N — Normal Service
S — Severe Service
X — Normal Or Severe Service

① After vehicle has passed 60,000 mile mark return to beginning of mileage table & start cycle over again.

② Normal Vehicle Axle Maintenance: Rear axle units containing synthetic lubricant are lubricated for life. These lubricants are not to be checked or changed unless a leak is suspected, service is required or the axle assembly has been submerged in water. The axle lubricant should be changed anytime the axle has been submerged in water. Non-synthetic rear axle lubricants should be replaced every 100,000 miles under normal operating conditions. Non-synthetic rear axle lubricants should be replaced every 3000 miles or 3 months, whichever occurs first, during extended trailer tow operation above (70°F) ambient and wide open throttle for extended periods above 45 mph. The 3000 mile lube change interval may be waived if the axle was filled with 75W140 synthetic gear lubricant meeting Ford specification WSL-M2C192-A. Add four ounces of additive friction modifier C8AZ-19B546-A or equivalent for complete refill of Traction-Lok rear axles. The rear axle lubricant should be changed anytime the axle has been submerged in water.

Cougar

BODY

Recommended Service	Service Interval In Miles ①
Inspect A/C Refrigerant Charge & System Operation	Every 12 Months Or 15,000 Miles
Inspect Instrument Panel Warning Lamps & Gauges	At Every Engine Oil Change
Lubricate Body Hardware & Hinges	X (marked at repeated mileage columns)
Lubricate Hood Latch Pivot Points & All Contact Areas	X (marked at repeated mileage columns)
Replace Cabin Air Filter	Every 15,000 Miles

BRAKES

Recommended Service	Service Interval In Miles ①
Inspect Brake Drums, Linings, Pads, Rotors, Lubricate Caliper Slide Rails	Normal Service Every 15,000 Miles; Severe Service Every 5000 Miles
Inspect Parking Brake System Operation	X (marked at mileage columns)

Service Interval In Miles①

Recommended Service	Service Interval In Miles①
CLUTCH & TRANSMISSION	
Change Automatic Transmission Fluid & Filter	Normal Service Inspect Every 15,000 Miles, Change Every 150,000 Miles; Severe Service Every 30,000 Miles
Lubricate Transmission Control Linkage	X
ENGINE	
Change Engine Coolant	Green Coolant, Every 45,000 Miles, Then Every 30,000 Miles Thereafter. Replace Orange Coolant, Every 150,000 Miles, Replace Yellow Coolant Every 5 Years Or 100,000 Miles
Change Engine Oil & Filter	S N S N S X S N S N S X S N S N S X S N S N S X S N S N S X (per mileage table)
Inspect Cooling System & Protection Level	Annually Or Every 15,000 Miles
Inspect Drive Belts	Every 100,000 Miles
Inspect Exhaust System	X
Inspect Fluid & Lubricant Levels	At Every Engine Oil Change
Inspect Fuel System Connections, Hoses & Lines	X
Inspect & Replace Engine Air Filter	X / S
Replace Engine Air Filter	Every 30,000 Miles
Replace Fuel Filter	Normal Service Every 30,000 Miles; Severe Service Every 15,000 Miles
Replace PCV Valve	4 Cylinder Every 60,000 Miles; V6 Every 100,000 Miles
Replace Spark Plugs	Normal Service Every 100,000 Miles; Severe Service Every 60,000 Miles
Replace Timing Belt, 2.0L	Every 120,000 Miles
STEERING, SUSPENSION & TIRES	
Lubricate Steering & Suspension Components	X
Rotate Tires	Normal Service Inspect For Wear And Rotate Every 5000 Miles

N — Normal Service
NGV — Natural Gas Vehicle
S — Severe Service
X — Normal Or Severe Service
① — After vehicle has passed 60,000 mile mark return to beginning of mileage table & start cycle over again.

Five-Hundred, Freestyle & Montego

Recommended Service	Service Interval In Miles①
BODY	
Replace Seat Filters	Every 30,000 Miles
Replace Cabin Air Filter	Every 15,000 Miles
BRAKES	
Inspect Brake Pads, Shoes, Rotors, Drums, Brake Lines, Hoses & Parking Brake System	Normal Service Every 15,000 Miles; Severe Service Every 5000 Miles
CLUTCH & TRANSMISSION	
Replace Automatic Transmission Fluid & Filter	Inspect Every 15,000 Miles③
Replace Manual Transmission Fluid	N
ENGINE	
Change Engine Coolant	Replace Premium Gold Coolant Every 5 Years Or 100,000 Miles Thereafter Replace Every 3 Years Or 50,000 Miles
Change Engine Oil & Filter②	N N N N N N N N N N N N N N N N N N N N N N N N N N N N N N
Inspect Cooling System & Protection Level	Annually Or Every 15,000 Miles
Inspect Drive Belts	Every 100,000 Miles
Inspect Exhaust System	Every 90,000 Miles
Change Engine Air Filter	N
Replace Engine Fuel Filter	S
Replace PCV Valve	Every 100,000 Miles
Replace Spark Plugs	Normal Service Every 100,000 Miles; Severe Service Every 60,000 Miles
STEERING, SUSPENSION & TIRES	
Inspect Steering Linkage, Suspension, Ball Joints, Halfshafts, Driveshaft & U-Joints	X
Inspect Wheel Ends For End Play & Noise	X
Rotate Tires	Normal Service Every 5000 Miles

N — Normal Service
NGV — Natural Gas Vehicle
S — Severe Service
X — Normal Or Severe Service
① — After vehicle has passed 60,000 mile mark return to beginning of mileage table & start cycle over again.
② — Severe Service @ 3 mo/3000 miles or 200 hours of operation.
③ — Models equipped with 4F50N, 4R100, TorqShift and 4F27E, change fluid/filter every 30,000 miles. Models equipped with CVT transmission, change fluid and filter every 60,000 miles.

Aveo

Recommended Service

Service Interval In Miles①

Recommended Service	3000	6000	9000	12000	15000	18000	21000	24000	27000	30000	33000	36000	39000	42000	45000	48000	51000	54000	57000	60000	63000	66000	69000	72000	75000	78000	81000	84000	87000	90000	93000	96000	99000
BODY																																	
Replace Cabin Air Filter					X					X					X					X					X					X			
BRAKES																																	
Replace Brake Fluid	Every 24 Months/24,000 Miles																																
CLUTCH & TRANSAXLE																																	
Replace Clutch Fluid	Every 24 Months/24,000 Miles																																
ENGINE																																	
Replace Engine Coolant										X										X										X			
Replace Engine Oil & Filter	Normal Service Every 7500 Miles; Severe Service Every 3000 Miles																																
Inspect Engine Air Filter					X					X					X					X					X					X			
Inspect Drive Belts					N					N					N					N					N					N			
Replace Spark Plugs										X										X										X			
Inspect Timing Belt										X										X										X			
STEERING, SUSPENSION & TIRES																																	
Rotate Tires	Normal Service Every 7500 Miles; Severe Service Every 6000 Miles																																

N — Normal Service
S — Severe Service
X — Normal Or Severe Service
① — After vehicle passes 99,000 mile mark return to beginning of mileage table & start cycle over again.

Century, Regal, Impala, Lumina, Monte Carlo, Intrigue & Grand Prix

Service Interval In Miles①

Mileage columns (left → right): 3000, 6000, 7500, 9000, 12000, 15000, 18000, 21000, 24000, 27000, 30000, 33000, 36000, 39000, 45000, 48000, 51000, 54000, 57000, 60000, 63000, 66000, 67500, 69000, 72000, 75000, 78000, 81000, 84000, 87000, 90000, 93000, 96000, 99000, 100500

Recommended Service	Service Interval / Marks
BODY	
Inspect Lamps, Seat Belts & Warning Devices	At Least Once Every 6 Months
Lubricate Hinges, Latches, Lock Cylinders & Strikers	At Engine Oil Changes Or At Least Every 12 Months
Replace Passenger Compartment Air Filter	X at 15,000 / 45,000 / 75,000 miles
BRAKES	
Inspect Brake System,	Every 6 Months
Inspect Disc Brake Pads, Rotors, Shoes & Drums	At 7500 Miles, Then Every 15,000 Miles
Inspect Parking Brake Operation	At Least Once Every 12 Months
Lubricate Parking Brake Cable Guides	S / N marks at service intervals
CLUTCH & TRANSAXLE	
Change Automatic Transmission Fluid & Filter, Except Regal CNG	No Normal Service; Severe Service Every 50,000 Miles
Change Automatic Transmission Fluid & Filter, Regal CNG	Normal Service Every 100,000 Miles; Severe Service Every 50,000 Miles
Inspect Neutral Safety & BTSI & Lubricate Shift Linkage	S / N marks at service intervals
DRIVE AXLE & DRIVESHAFT	
Inspect CV Joint Boots	At Tire Rotations
ENGINE	
Change Engine Coolant	Every 60 Months Or 150,000 Miles
Change Engine Oil & Filter, Less Turbo②	S / N / X marks at service intervals
Change Engine Oil & Filter, w/Turbo②	X marks at service intervals
Inspect Drive Belts & EGR System	Inspect Every 60,000 Miles
Inspect Exhaust System	At Engine Oil Changes

Service Interval In Miles①

Recommended Service	3600	7500	9000	12000	15000	18000	21000	24000	27000	30000	33000	36000	39000	42000	45000	48000	51000	54000	57000	60000	63000	66000	69000	72000	75000	78000	81000	84000	87000	90000	93000	96000	99000
ENGINE																																	
Inspect Fuel Filter & PCV System										X										X										X			
Inspect Spark Plug Wires	At Spark Plug Changes →																																
Inspect Supercharger Oil Level, 3.8L Supercharged VIN 1	Every 30,000 Miles Or 36 Months →																																
Inspect TBI Unit Mounting Fastener Security	S	N																															
Inspect Throttle Linkage Operation	At Air Cleaner Element Changes →																																
Replace Air Filter & PCV Filter					S					X					S					X					S					X			
Replace Spark Plugs Except Regal CNG	Every 100,000 Miles →																																
STEERING, SUSPENSION & TIRES																																	
Inspect Steering & Suspension System	At Tire Rotations →																																
Lubricate Chassis & Suspension	S	N	S	N	S	N	S	N	S	N	S	N	S	N	S	N	S	N	S	N	S	N	S	N	S	N	S	N	S	N	S	N	S
Rotate Tires③	Inspect For Wear And Rotate Every 7500 Miles →																																

CNG — Compressed Natural Gas
N — Normal Service
S — Severe Service
X — Normal Or Severe Service
BTSI — Brake Transmission Shift Interlock
IAC — Idle Air Control
ISC — Idle Speed Control System

① — After vehicle passes 99,000 mile mark return to beginning of mileage table & start cycle over again.
② — If equipped, the engine oil life monitor will indicate when to change engine oil, usually 3000–10,000 miles. Under severe driving conditions, engine oil may need to be changed before 3000 miles. If vehicle is driven in a dusty area, change engine oil every 3000 miles.
③ — Tire Inflation Monitor System, if equipped, must be reset when tires are rotated.

LeSabre, Park Avenue & Bonneville

Service Interval In Miles①

Recommended Service	37500	67500	97500	75000	105000	125000	145000	180000	210000	240000	270000	300000	305000	335000	365000	395000	425000	450000	480000	515000	545000	575000	600000	630000	650000	675000	Notes
BODY																											
Clean Power Antenna Mast	S N	S N	S N	X	S N	S N	S N	S N	S N	X	S N	S N	S N	S N	S N	X	S N	S N	S N	S N	X	S N	S N	S N	X	S N	
Flush Vehicle Underside,																											At Least Every 12 Months
Inspect Drain Holes																											
Inspect Lamps & Seat Belts & Warning Devices																											At Least Once Every 6 Months
Lubricate Hinges, Latches, Lock Cylinders & Strikers																											At Engine Oil Changes Or At Least Every 12 Months
Replace Passenger Compartment Air Filter, 2001		X			X			X			X			X			X			X			X				
Replace Passenger Compartment Air Filter, 2002–05																											Normal Service Every 15,000 Miles; Severe Service Every 12,000 Miles
BRAKES																											
Inspect Brake Fluid Level																											Every 6 Months
Inspect Brake System																											Normal Service Every 7500 Miles; Severe Service Every 6000 Miles
Inspect Parking Brake Operation																											At Least Once Every 12 Months
Lubricate Parking Brake Cable Guides	S N	S N	S N	X	S N	S N	S N	X	S N	S N	S N	X	S N	S N	S N	X	S N	S N	S N	X	S N	S N	S N	X	S N	S N	
CLUTCH & TRANSAXLE																											
Change Automatic Transmission Fluid & Filter③																											Normal Service Every 100,000 Miles; Severe Service Every 50,000 Miles
Inspect Neutral Safety & BTSI & Lubricate Shift Linkage	S N	S N	S N	X	S N	S N	S N	X	S N	S N	S N	X	S N	S N	S N	X	S N	S N	S N	X	S N	S N	S N	X	S N	S N	
DRIVESHAFT																											
Inspect CV Joint Boots																											At Engine Oil Changes & Tire Rotations
ENGINE																											
Change Engine Coolant④																											Every 60 Months Or 150,000 Miles
Change Engine Oil & Filter②	S S	S S	S S	X S	S S	S S	S S	X S	S S	S S	S S	X S	S S	S S	S S	X S	S S	S S	S S	X S	S S	S S	S S	X S	S S	S S	
Inspect Drive Belts & EGR System																X											
Inspect Exhaust System																											At Engine Oil Changes
Inspect Fuel System & PCV Valve & Supercharger			X					X								X							X				
Lubricant Level④								X																			
Inspect Spark Plug Wires																											At Spark Plug Changes

Service Interval In Miles①

Service intervals (columns, left to right): 3000, 6000, 7500, 9000, 12000, 15000, 18000, 21000, 24000, 27000, 30000, 33000, 36000, 39000, 42000, 45000, 48000, 51000, 54000, 57000, 60000, 63000, 66000, 69000, 72000, 75000, 78000, 81000, 84000, 87000, 90000, 93000, 96000, 99000

Recommended Service	Service Interval / Marks
ENGINE	
Inspect TBI Unit Mounting Fastener Security	S, N
Inspect Thermostatically Controlled Air Cleaner Operation	X at 30,000 / 60,000 / 90,000
Inspect Throttle Linkage Operation	At Engine Oil Or Air Cleaner Element Changes
Replace Air Filter & PCV Filter④	Every 30,000 Miles
Replace Spark Plugs④	Every 100,000 Miles
STEERING, SUSPENSION & TIRES	
Inspect Power Steering Fluid Level & Suspension System	At Engine Oil Changes & Tire Rotations
Lubricate Chassis & Suspension	S N S N S X S N S N S X S N S X N
Rotate Tires	Normal Service Inspect For Wear & Rotate Every 7500 Miles; Severe Service Every 6000 Miles

N — Normal Service
S — Severe Service
X — Normal Or Severe Service
BTSI — Brake Transmission Shift Interlock
IAC — Idle Air Control
ISC — Idle Speed Control System

① — After vehicle passes 99,000 mile mark return to beginning of mileage table & start cycle over again.
② — If equipped, the engine oil life monitor will indicate when to change engine oil, usually 3,000–10,000 miles. Under severe driving conditions, engine oil may need to be changed before 3000 miles. If vehicle is driven in a dusty area, change engine oil every 3000 miles.
③ — If vehicle is used in hilly or mountainous terrain, heavy city traffic where outside temperature reaches 90°F or higher or uses such as high performance operation.
④ — The U.S. Environmental Protection Agency or the California Air Resources Board has determined the failure to perform this maintenance item will not nullify the emission warranty or limit recall liability prior to the completion of the vehicle's useful life. We, however, urge that all recommended maintenance services be performed at the indicated intervals and the maintenance be recorded.

Catera

Service Interval In Miles ①

Service Interval In Miles (in thousands): 3600, 7500, 9000, 12000, 15000, 18000, 21000, 24000, 27000, 30000, 33000, 36000, 39000, 42000, 45000, 48000, 51000, 54000, 57000, 60000, 63000, 66000, 69000, 72000, 75000, 78000, 81000, 84000, 87000, 90000, 93000, 96000, 99000

Recommended Service	Interval / Service Notes
BODY	
Flush Vehicle Underside, Inspect Drain Holes	At Least Every 12 Months, Especially In Winter & Springtime
Inspect Lamps, Seat Belts & Warning Devices	At Least Once Every 6 Months
Lubricate Hinges, Latches, Lock Cylinders & Strikers	At Engine Oil Changes Or At Least Every 12 Months
Replace Passenger Compartment Air Filter	X at 15000, 30000, 45000, 60000, 75000, 90000
BRAKES	
Inspect Brake System	Every 5000 Miles
Inspect Parking Brake Operation	S / N at each interval
Lubricate Parking Brake Cable Guides	At Least Once Every 12 Months
CLUTCH & TRANSAXLE	
Change Automatic Transmission Fluid & Filter	Normal Service Every 100,000 Miles; Severe Service Every 50,000 Miles (S / N marks)
Inspect Neutral Safety & BTSI Operation	S / N at each interval
Lubricate Transmission Shift Linkage	S / N at each interval
ENGINE	
Change Engine Coolant	Every 60 Months Or 150,000 Miles
Change Engine Oil & Filter	Normal Service Initially At 5000 Miles, Then Every 10,000 Miles Thereafter; Severe Service Every 5000 Miles
Inspect Air Cleaner Element	X at 15000, 45000, 75000
Inspect Drive Belts	Every 60,000 Miles (X at 60000)
Inspect EGR System	X at 30000, 60000, 90000
Inspect Exhaust System	At Engine Oil Changes (X at 30000, 60000, 90000)
Inspect Fuel Filler Cap	X at 30000, 60000, 90000
Inspect Fuel System Hoses, Lines & Connections	X at 30000, 60000, 90000
Inspect PCV Valve	X at 30000, 60000, 90000
Inspect Spark Plug Wires	At Spark Plug Changes
Replace Air Filter & PCV Filter	Every 30,000 Miles
Replace Fuel Filter	Every 100,000 Miles
Replace Spark Plugs	Every 100,000 Miles

Service Interval In Miles ①

Recommended Service	3000	6000	7500	9000	12000	15000	18000	21000	24000	27000	30000	33000	36000	39000	42000	45000	48000	51000	54000	57000	60000	63000	66000	69000	72000	75000	78000	81000	84000	87000	90000	93000	96000	99000
ENGINE																																		
Replace Timing Belt	Replace Every 100,000 Miles Under Normal Operating Conditions; Replace Every 60,000 Miles If Driven Without An Engine Coolant Heater At Ambient Temperatures Of –20°F Or Less, Then Inspect At 15,000 Mile Intervals.																																	
Replace Timing Belts, Reset Counter, ②	Every 60,000 Miles																																	
STEERING, SUSPENSION & TIRES																																		
Inspect Steering & Suspension System	At Tire Rotations																																	
Lubricate Chassis & Suspension	S	N	S	N	S	N	S	N	S	N	X	N	S	N	S	N	S	N	S	N	X	N	S	N	S	N	S	N	S	N	X	N	S	N
Rotate Tires	Initial Service At 5000 Miles, Then Every 10,000 Miles Thereafter																																	

N — Normal Service
S — Severe Service
X — Normal Or Severe Service
BTSI — Brake Transmission Shift Interlock
IAC — Idle Air Control
ISC — Idle Speed Control System
① — After vehicle passes 99,000 mile mark return to beginning of mileage table & start cycle over again.
② — If equipped.

CTS, STS & XLR

Service Interval In Miles[①]

Recommended Service	Interval (Miles)
BODY	
Replace Cabin Air Filter	Normal Service Every 12 Months/15,000 Miles
Underbody Flushing	At Least Once A Year
BRAKES	
Replace Brake Fluid	S (30,000 / 60,000 / 90,000 / 120,000 / 150,000 Miles)
CLUTCH & TRANSAXLE	
Replace Automatic Transmission Fluid & Filter	Normal Service Every 100,000 Miles; Severe Service Every 50,000 Miles
Replace Transfer Case Fluid	N (50,000 / 100,000 Miles)
Replace Manual Transaxle Fluid[②]	Severe Service Every 50,000 Miles
Replace Hydraulic Clutch Fluid	S (50,000 / 100,000 / 150,000 Miles)
ENGINE	
Change Engine Oil & Filer	[③]
Inspect Accessory Drive Belt	X (100,000 Miles)
Inspect Air Filter	Every Oil Change; Replace Every 50,000 Miles
Inspect Fuel System	As Required
Inspect Throttle Body System	X — 5 Years/150,000 Miles
Replace Coolant Fluid	Every 100,000 Miles
Replace Fuel Filter	Every 100,000 Miles
Replace Spark Plugs	Every 100,000 Miles
STEERING, SUSPENSION & TIRES	
Replace Rear Axle Fluid	S (50,000 / 100,000 / 150,000 Miles)

N — Normal Service
S — Severe Service
X — Normal Or Severe Service
BTSI — Brake Transmission Shift Interlock
IAC — Idle Air Control
ISC — Idle Speed Control System

① — After vehicle passes 150,000 mile mark return to beginning of mileage table & start cycle over again.

② — Change fluid whenever vehicle has been driven for 3,000 miles (5000 km) with transmission temperature at 290°F (143°C) or higher without using an auxiliary fluid cooler.

③ — Vehicle has a computer system that lets you know when to change the engine oil and filter. This is based on engine revolutions and engine temperature, and not on mileage. Based on driving conditions, the mileage at which an oil change will be indicated can vary considerably. For the oil life system to work properly, you must reset the system every time the oil is changed.

DeVille, Eldorado & Seville

Service Interval In Miles ① (values in thousands of miles)

Recommended Service	3	6	9	12	15	18	21	24	27	30	33	36	39	42	45	48	51	54	57	60	63	66	69	72	75	78	81	84	87	90	93	96	99
BODY																																	
Flush Vehicle Underside, Inspect Drain Holes	At Least Every 12 Months																																
Inspect Lamps, Seat Belts & Warning Devices	At Least Once Every 6 Months																																
Replace Passenger Compartment Air Filter					X					X					X					X					X					X			
BRAKES																																	
Inspect Brake System	Every 7500 Miles																																
Inspect Parking Brake Operation	At Least Once Every 12 Months																																
Lubricate Parking Brake Cable Guides	S	N	S	N	S	N	S	N	S	X	S	N	S	N	S	N	S	N	S	X	S	N	S	N	S	N	S	N	S	X	S	N	S
CLUTCH & TRANSAXLE																																	
Change Automatic Transmission Fluid & Filter, Eldorado	Normal Service Every 100,000 Miles; Severe Service Every 50,000 Miles																																
Change Automatic Transmission Fluid & Filter, Except Eldorado②	No Normal Service Required; Severe Service Every 50,000 Miles																																
Inspect Neutral Safety & BTSI Operation	S	N	S	N	S	N	S	N	S	X	S	N	S	N	S	N	S	N	S	X	S	N	S	N	S	N	S	N	S	X	S	N	S
Lubricate Transmission Shift Linkage	S	N	S	N	S	N	S	N	S	X	S	N	S	N	S	N	S	N	S	X	S	N	S	N	S	N	S	N	S	X	S	N	S
DRIVESHAFT																																	
Inspect CV Joint Boots	At Engine Oil Changes & Tire Rotations																																
ENGINE																																	
Change Engine Coolant	Every 60 Months Or 150,000 Miles																																
Change Engine Oil & Filter	S	S	N	S	S	N	S	S	N	S	S	N	S	S	N	S	S	N	S	S	N	S	S	N	S	S	N	S	S	N	S	S	N
Inspect Drive Belts & EGR System	Every 60,000 Miles																																
Inspect Exhaust System	At Engine Oil Changes																																
Inspect Fuel & PCV System										X										X										X			
Inspect Spark Plug Wires	At Spark Plug Changes																																
Inspect Thermostatically Controlled Air Cleaner Operation										X										X										X			

Service Interval In Miles ①

Service intervals (miles): 3000, 6000, 7500, 9000, 12000, 15000, 18000, 21000, 22500, 24000, 27000, 30000, 33000, 36000, 37500, 39000, 42000, 45000, 48000, 51000, 52500, 54000, 57000, 60000, 63000, 66000, 67500, 69000, 72000, 75000, 78000, 81000, 82500, 84000, 87000, 90000, 93000, 96000, 97500, 99000

Recommended Service	Interval / Service Note
ENGINE	
Inspect Throttle Linkage Operation	At Engine Oil Or Air Cleaner Element Changes
Replace Air Filter	Every 30,000 Miles
Replace PCV Valve	X (at 30,000 / 60,000 / 90,000 Miles)
Replace Spark Plugs	Every 100,000 Miles
STEERING, SUSPENSION & TIRES	
Inspect Steering & Suspension System	At Tire Rotations
Lubricate Chassis & Suspension	N at every 7,500-mile interval; S at intervening intervals
Rotate Tires	Inspect For Wear & Rotate Every 7500 Miles

N — Normal Service
S — Severe Service
X — Normal Or Severe Service
BTSI — Brake Transmission Shift Interlock
IAC — Idle Air Control
ISC — Idle Speed Control System
① — After vehicle passes 99,000 mile mark return to beginning of mileage table & start cycle over again.
② — No normal service required until message Change Trans Fluid appears on the drivers information center.

Camaro & Firebird

Service Interval In Miles①

Mileage interval column headers (left to right): 3,600 · 7,500 · 9,000 · 12,000 · 15,000 · 18,000 · 21,000 · 24,000 · 27,000 · 30,000 · 33,000 · 36,000 · 39,000 · 42,000 · 45,000 · 48,000 · 51,000 · 54,000 · 57,000 · 60,000 · 63,000 · 66,000 · 69,000 · 72,000 · 75,000 · 78,000 · 81,000 · 84,000 · 87,000 · 90,000 · 93,000 · 96,000 · 99,000

(S = Severe service, N = Normal service, X = service required at that interval)

Recommended Service

BODY

Recommended Service	Interval / Notes
Clean Power Antenna Mast	S, N at interval (X at 15,000 / 30,000 / 45,000 / 60,000 / 75,000 / 90,000)
Flush Vehicle Underside, Inspect Drain Holes	At Least Every 12 Months
Inspect Lamps, Seat Belts & Warning Devices	At Least Every 12 Months
Lubricate Hinges, Latches, Lock Cylinders & Strikers	At Least Once Every 6 Months
Replace Passenger Compartment Air Filter	At Engine Oil Changes Or At Least Every 12 Months — X at 15,000 / 30,000 / 45,000 / 60,000 / 75,000 / 90,000

BRAKES

Recommended Service	Interval / Notes
Inspect Brake System, 2001	Normal Service At 7500 Miles, Then Every 10,000 Miles Thereafter; Severe Service Every 7500 Miles
Inspect Parking Brake Operation	At Least Once Every 12 Months
Lubricate Parking Brake Cable Guides	S, N at interval

CLUTCH & TRANSAXLE

Recommended Service	Interval / Notes
Change Automatic Transmission Fluid & Filter	Normal Service Every 50,000 Miles; Severe Service Every 15,000 Miles
Inspect Neutral Safety & BTSI Operation	S, N at interval (X at 30,000 / 60,000 / 90,000)
Lubricate Transmission Shift Linkage	S, N at interval (X at 30,000 / 60,000 / 90,000)

ENGINE

Recommended Service	Interval / Notes
Change Engine Coolant	Every 60 Months Or 240,000 Miles
Change Engine Oil & Filter	S, N at interval
Inspect Drive Belts	Every 60,000 Miles
Inspect EGR System	X at 30,000 / 60,000 / 90,000
Inspect Exhaust System	At Engine Oil Changes
Inspect Fuel Filler Cap	At Engine Oil Changes — X at 30,000 / 60,000 / 90,000
Inspect Fuel System Hoses, Lines & Connections	X at 30,000 / 60,000 / 90,000
Inspect PCV Valve	X at 30,000 / 60,000 / 90,000
Inspect Spark Plug Wires	At Spark Plug Changes
Inspect TBI Unit Mounting Fastener Security	S, N at 3,600

Service Interval In Miles ①

Recommended Service	3000	6000	7500	9000	10500	12000	15000	18000	21000	22500	24000	27000	30000	33000	36000	37500	39000	42000	45000	48000	51000	52500	54000	57000	60000	63000	66000	67500	69000	72000	75000	78000	81000	82500	84000	87000	90000	93000	96000	97500	99000
ENGINE																																									
Inspect Thermostatically Controlled Air Cleaner Operation													X												X												X				
Inspect Throttle Linkage Operation																																									
Replace Air Filter															At Air Cleaner Element Changes																										
Replace Spark Plugs													Inspect & Replace If Necessary Every 15,000 Miles																				Every 100,000 Miles								
STEERING, SUSPENSION & TIRES																																									
Inspect Steering & Suspension System																							At Tire Rotations																	
Lubricate Chassis & Suspension	S	N		S		N	S	N	S		N	S	N	S	N		S	N	S	N	S		N	S	N	S	N		S	N	S	N	S		N	S	N	S	N		S
Rotate Tires	S	N		S		N	S	N	S		N	S	N	S	N		S	N	S	N	S		N	S	N	S	N		S	N	S	N	S		N	S	N	S	N		S

N — Normal Service
S — Severe Service
X — Normal Or Severe Service
BTSI — Brake Transmission Shift Interlock
IAC — Idle Air Control
ISC — Idle Speed Control System
① — After vehicle passes 99,000 mile mark return to beginning of mileage table & start cycle over again.

Cavalier & Sunfire

Recommended Service	Service Interval In Miles①												
	7500	15000	22500	30000	37500	45000	52500	60000	67500	75000	82500	90000	97500
BODY													
Inspect Lamps, Seat Belt & Warning Devices	At Least Once Every 6 Months →												
Lubricate Hinges, Latches, Lock Cylinders & Strikers	At Engine Oil Changes Or At Least Every 12 Months →												
Replace Passenger Compartment Air Filter			X			X			X			X	
BRAKES													
Inspect Brake System, 2001	Normal Service At 7500 Miles, Then Every 10,000 Miles Thereafter; Severe Service Every 6000 Miles →												
Inspect Brake System, 2002–05	Normal Service At 7500 Miles; Severe Service Every 6000 Miles →												
Inspect Parking Brake Operation	At Least Once Every 12 Months →												
Lubricate Parking Brake Cable Guides	S	S N	S	S N X	S	S N	S	S N X	S	S N	S	S N X	S
CLUTCH & TRANSAXLE													
Change Automatic Transmission Fluid & Filter	No Normal Service Required; Severe Service Every 50,000 Miles →												
Inspect Neutral Safety & BTSI Operation & Lubricate Shift Linkage	S	S N	S	S N X	S	S N	S	S N X	S	S N	S	S N X	S
DRIVESHAFT													
Inspect CV Joint Boots	At Tire Rotations →												
ENGINE													
Change Engine Coolant	Every 60 Months Or 150,000 Miles →												
Change Engine Oil & Filter, Less Turbo	S	S	S	S X	S	S	S	S X	S	S	S	S X	S
Change Engine Oil & Filter, w/Turbo	X	X	X	X	X	X	X	X	X	X	X	X	X
Inspect Drive Belt, 2004	Every 150,000 Miles →												
Inspect Drive Belts & EGR System & Fuel & PCV System												X	
Inspect Exhaust System	At Engine Oil Changes →												
Inspect Spark Plug Wires	At Spark Plug Changes →												
Inspect Thermostatically Controlled Air Cleaner Operation				X					X				

Service Interval In Miles ①

ENGINE

Recommended Service	Service Interval
Inspect Throttle Linkage Operation	At Engine Oil Or Air Cleaner Element Changes
Replace Air Filter & PCV Filter, 2001	15,000 – S; 30,000 – X; 45,000 – S; 60,000 – X; 75,000 – S; 90,000 – X
Replace Air Filter, 2002–05	30,000 – X; 60,000 – X; 90,000 – X
Replace Spark Plugs, Except CNG	Every 100,000 Miles

STEERING, SUSPENSION & TIRES

Recommended Service	Service Interval
Inspect Steering & Suspension System	At Tire Rotations
Lubricate Chassis & Suspension	S / N alternating across intervals (S N S N S N S N ...)
Rotate Tires	Normal Service Inspect For Wear & Rotate Every 7500 Miles; Severe Service Every 6000 Miles

CNG — Compressed Natural Gas
N — Normal Service
S — Severe Service
X — Normal Or Severe Service
BTSI — Brake Transmission Shift Interlock
IAC — Idle Air Control
ISC — Idle Speed Control System
① — After vehicle passes 99,000 mile mark return to beginning of mileage table & start cycle over again.

Corvette

Service Interval In Miles①

Recommended Service	Interval / Notes
BODY	
Clean Power Antenna Mast	S / N at intervals; X marks at every third interval
Inspect Lamps, Seat Belts & Warning Devices	At Least Once Every 6 Months
Lubricate Hinges, Latches, Lock Cylinders & Strikers	At Engine Oil Changes Or At Least Every 12 Months
Replace Passenger Compartment Air Filter	X (marked at regular intervals)
BRAKES	
Inspect Brake System	Normal Service At 7500 Miles, Then Every 10,000 Miles Thereafter; Severe Service Every 7500 Miles
Inspect Parking Brake Operation	At Least Once Every 12 Months
Lubricate Parking Brake Cable Guides	S / N at intervals
CLUTCH & TRANSAXLE	
Change Automatic Transmission Fluid & Filter	Normal Service Every 100,000 Miles; Severe Service Every 50,000 Miles
Inspect Neutral Safety & BTSI Operation & Lubricate Shift Linkage	S / N at intervals
ENGINE	
Change Engine Coolant	Every 60 Months Or 150,000 Miles
Change Engine Oil & Filter, ②	Normal Service Every 12 Months Or As Indicated By Oil Life Monitor; Severe Service Every 3000 Miles
Inspect Air Cleaner Element	Every 15,000 Miles — X
Inspect Drive Belts, EGR, Fuel & PCV System	X
Inspect Exhaust System	At Engine Oil Changes
Inspect Fuel System	Every 25,000 Miles
Inspect Spark Plug Wires	At Spark Plug Changes
Inspect TBI Unit Mounting Fastener Security	S / N
Inspect Thermostatically Controlled Air Cleaner Operation	X (marked at intervals)
Inspect Throttle Linkage Operation	At Air Cleaner Element Changes
Replace Air Filter	Every 30,000 Miles

Service Interval In Miles①

Recommended Service	3000	6000	9000	12000	15000	18000	21000	24000	27000	30000	33000	36000	39000	42000	45000	48000	51000	54000	57000	60000	63000	66000	69000	72000	75000	78000	81000	84000	87000	90000	93000	96000	99000
ENGINE																																	
Replace Spark Plugs																Every 100,000 Miles																	
STEERING, SUSPENSION & TIRES																																	
Inspect Steering & Suspension System																At Tire Rotations																	
Lubricate Chassis & Suspension	S	N	S	N	S	X	S	N	S	N	S	N	S	N	S	X	S	N	S	N	S	N	S	N	S	X	S	N	S	N	S	N	S	N

N — Normal Service
S — Severe Service
X — Normal Or Severe Service
BTSI — Brake Transmission Shift Interlock
IAC — Idle Air Control
ISC — Idle Speed Control System
① — After vehicle passes 99,000 mile mark return to beginning of mileage table & start cycle over again.
② — If equipped, the engine oil life monitor will indicate when to change engine oil, usually 3000–10,000 miles. Under severe driving conditions, engine oil may need to be changed before 3000 miles. If vehicle is driven in a dusty area, change engine oil every 3000 miles.

GTO & G6

Service Interval In Miles①

Recommended Service	Interval
BODY	
Underbody Flushing	At Least Once A Year
BRAKES	
Replace Brake Fluid	S
CLUTCH & TRANSAXLE	
Replace Automatic Transmission Fluid & Filter	Normal Service Every 100,000 Miles; Severe Service Every 50,000 Miles
ENGINE	
Replace Coolant Fluid	5 Years/150,000 Miles
Change Engine Oil & Filer	②
Inspect Throttle Body System	As Required
Inspect Fuel System	X
Inspect Accessory Drive Belt	X
Inspect Air Filter	Every Oil Change; Replace Every 50,000 Miles
Replace Fuel Filter	Every 100,000 Miles
Replace Spark Plugs	Every 100,000 Miles
STEERING, SUSPENSION & TIRES	
Replace Rear Axle Fluid	S

The mileage columns across the top run from 50,000 through 150,000 in 5,000-mile increments.

N — Normal Service
S — Severe Service
X — Normal Or Severe Service
BTSI — Brake Transmission Shift Interlock
IAC — Idle Air Control
ISC — Idle Speed Control System
① — After vehicle passes 150,000 mile mark return to beginning of mileage table & start cycle over again.
② — Vehicle has a computer system that lets you know when to change the engine oil and filter. This is based on engine revolutions and engine temperature, and not on mileage. Based on driving conditions, the mileage at which an oil change will be indicated can vary considerably. For the oil life system to work properly, you must reset the system every time the oil is changed.

LaCrosse

Service Interval In Miles①

(Mileage columns run in 5,000-mile increments from 50,000 to 150,000 miles.)

Recommended Service	Service Interval / Markers
BODY	
Replace Cabin Air Filter	Normal Service Every 12 Months/15,000 Miles
Underbody Flushing	At Least Once A Year
BRAKES	
Replace Brake Fluid	S
CLUTCH & TRANSAXLE	
Replace Automatic Transmission Fluid & Filter	Normal Service Every 100,000 Miles; Severe Service Every 50,000 Miles
Replace Hydraulic Clutch Fluid	S
Replace Manual Transaxle Fluid②	Severe Service Every 50,000 Miles
Replace Transfer Case Fluid	N
ENGINE	
Change Engine Oil & Filter	③
Inspect Throttle Body System	As Required
Inspect Fuel System	X
Inspect Accessory Drive Belt	X
Inspect Air Filter	Every Oil Change; Replace Every 50,000 Miles
Replace Coolant Fluid	5 Years/150,000 Miles
Replace Fuel Filter	Every 100,000 Miles
Replace Spark Plugs	Every 100,000 Miles
STEERING, SUSPENSION & TIRES	
Replace Rear Axle Fluid	S

N — Normal Service
S — Severe Service
X — Normal Or Severe Service
BTSI — Brake Transmission Shift Interlock
IAC — Idle Air Control
ISC — Idle Speed Control System

① — After vehicle passes 150,000 mile mark return to beginning of mileage table & start cycle over again.
② — Change fluid whenever vehicle has been driven for 3,000 miles (5000 km) with transmission temperature at 290°F (143°C) or higher without using an auxiliary fluid cooler.
③ — Vehicle has a computer system that lets you know when to change the engine oil and filter. This is based on engine revolutions and engine temperature, and not on mileage. Based on driving conditions, the mileage at which an oil change will be indicated can vary considerably. For the oil life system to work properly, you must reset the system every time the oil is changed.

Malibu, Alero & Grand Am

Recommended Service	Service Interval In Miles①																																							
	3000	6000	7500	9000	12000	15000	18000	21000	22500	24000	27000	30000	33000	36000	37500	39000	42000	45000	48000	51000	52500	54000	57000	60000	63000	66000	67500	69000	72000	75000	78000	81000	82500	84000	87000	90000	93000	96000	97500	99000
BODY																																								
Clean Power Antenna Mast		S	N		S	N	S		N	S		X		S	N		S	N	S		N	S		X		S	N		S	N	S		N	S		X		S	N	
Inspect Lamps, Seat Belts & Warning Devices	At Least Once Every 6 Months																																							
Lubricate Hinges, Latches, Lock Cylinders & Strikers	At Engine Oil Changes Or At Least Every 12 Months																																							
BRAKES																																								
Inspect Brake System	Every 7500 Miles																																							
Inspect Parking Brake Operation	At Least Once Every 12 Months																																							
Lubricate Parking Brake Cable Guides		S	N		S	N	S		N	S		X		S	N		S	N	S		N	S		X		S	N		S	N	S		N	S		X		S	N	
CLUTCH & TRANSAXLE																																								
Change Automatic Transmission Fluid & Filter	No Normal Service Required; Severe Service Every 50,000 Miles																																							
Inspect Neutral Safety & BTSI Operation & Lubricate Shift Linkage		S	N		S	N	S		N	S		X		S	N		S	N	S		N	S		X		S	N		S	N	S		N	S		X		S	N	
DRIVESHAFT																																								
Inspect CV Joint Boots	At Engine Oil Changes & Tire Rotations																																							
ENGINE																																								
Change Engine Coolant	Every 60 Months Or 150,000 Miles																																							
Change Engine Oil & Filter, Less Turbo②	S	S	N	S	S	X	S	S	N	S	S	X	S	S	N	S	S	X	S	S	N	S	S	X	S	S	N	S	S	X	S	S	N	S	S	X	S	S	N	S
Change Engine Oil & Filter, w/Turbo②	X	X		X	X	X	X	X		X	X	X	X	X		X	X	X	X	X		X	X	X	X	X		X	X	X	X	X		X	X	X	X	X		X
Inspect Accessory Drive Belts, 2004–05	Every 150,000 Miles																																							
Inspect Drive Belts & EGR System, 2001–03	Every 60,000 Miles																																							
Inspect Exhaust System, 2001–03	At Engine Oil Changes																																							
Inspect Exhaust System, 2004–05	Every 25,000 Miles																																							
Inspect Fuel System, 2001–03	At Each Oil Change																																							
Inspect Fuel System, 2004–05	Every 25,000 Miles																																							
Inspect Spark Plug Wires	At Spark Plug Changes																																							

Recommended Service — Service Interval In Miles[1]

Recommended Service	3000	6000	7500	9000	12000	15000	18000	21000	24000	27000	30000	33000	36000	39000	42000	45000	48000	51000	54000	57000	60000	63000	66000	69000	72000	75000	78000	81000	84000	87000	90000	93000	96000	99000
ENGINE																																		
Inspect Thermostatically Controlled Air Cleaner Operation & Fuel & PCV System											X										X										X			
Inspect Throttle Linkage Operation	At Air Cleaner Element Changes																																	
Replace Air Filter & PCV Filter, 2003[3]	Normal Service Every 30,000 Miles; Severe Service Inspect Every 15,000 Miles, Replace Every 30,000 Miles																																	
Replace Air Filter & PCV Filter, 2004–05[3]	Every 25,000 Miles																																	
Replace Spark Plugs[3]	Every 100,000 Miles																																	
Replace Timing Belt																					X													
STEERING, SUSPENSION & TIRES																																		
Inspect Steering & Suspension System	At Tire Rotations																																	
Lubricate Chassis & Suspension	S	N	S	N	S	N			X		S		X				S	N	S	N			X		S	N	S	X			S	N		
Rotate Tires	Inspect for Wear and Rotate Every 7500 Miles																																	

N — Normal Service
S — Severe Service
X — Normal Or Severe Service
BTSI — Brake Transmission Shift Interlock
IAC — Idle Air Control
ISC — Idle Speed Control System
[1] — After vehicle passes 99,000 mile mark return to beginning of mileage table & start cycle over again.
[2] — If equipped, the engine oil life monitor will indicate when to change engine oil, usually 3,000–10,000 miles. Under severe driving conditions, engine oil may need to be changed before 3000 miles. If vehicle is driven in a dusty area, change engine oil every 3000 miles.
[3] — The U.S. Environmental Protection Agency or the California air Resources Board has determined the failure to perform this maintenance item will not nullify the emission warranty or limit recall liability prior to the completion of the vehicle's useful life. The vehicle manufacturer, however, urge that all recommended maintenance services be performed at the indicated intervals & the maintenance be recorded.

Metro

Recommended Service

Service Interval In Miles ①

Recommended Service	7500	15000	22500	30000	37500	45000	52500	60000	67500	75000	82500	90000	97500
BODY													
Inspect Seat Belts & Related Components & Lubricate Lock Cylinders	At Least Once Every 12 Months												
Inspect Supplemental Restraint System	10 Years From Vehicle Build Date												
Inspect Warning Lamps & Devices	S	N	S	S	X	S	N	S	S	X	S	N	S
Lubricate Door Hinges	At Every Engine Oil Change												
BRAKES													
Change Brake Fluid				X				X				X	
Inspect Brake System	S	N	S	N	S	N	S	N	S	N	S	N	S
CLUTCH & TRANSAXLE													
Change Automatic Transaxle Fluid & Filter	No Normal Service Interval Recommended By Manufacturer; Severe Service Every 50,000 Miles												
Change Manual Transaxle Lubricant	S	N	S	X	S	N	S	X	S	N	S	X	S
Inspect Clutch Pedal Freeplay	S	N	S	X	S	N	S	X	S	N	S	X	S
Inspect Neutral Safety & Shift Interlock Switch Operation	S	N	S	X	S	N	S	X	S	N	S	X	S
Inspect Transaxle Fluid & Shift Control Operation	At Least Once Every 12 Months												
Replace Automatic Transaxle Fluid Cooler Hoses	At Every Engine Oil Change												
DRIVESHAFT													
Inspect CV Joint Boots	S	N	S	X	S	N	S	X	S	N	S	X	S
ENGINE													
Change Engine Coolant & Inspect Ignition Coils				X				X				X	
Change Engine Oil & Filter	S	S	S	S	S	S	S	S	S	S	S	S	S
Inspect Air Filter Element	S	S	S	X	S	S	S	X	S	S	S	X	S
Inspect Distributor Cap & Rotor & Drive Belts & PCV Valve				S				S				S	
Inspect Engine Valve Clearance				X				X				X	
Inspect Exhaust, Fuel & EVAP System & Coolant				X				X				X	

Recommended Service

Service Interval In Miles ①

Mileage interval columns (ascending): 3000, 6000, 7500, 9000, 12000, 15000, 18000, 21000, 24000, 27000, 30000, 33000, 36000, 39000, 42000, 45000, 48000, 51000, 54000, 57000, 60000, 63000, 66000, 69000, 72000, 75000, 78000, 81000, 84000, 87000, 90000, 93000, 96000, 99000

ENGINE

Recommended Service	Service Interval / Notes
Inspect Spark Plug Wires	S (Severe) / N (Normal) at listed service intervals
Inspect Warning Lamps	S / N / X at listed service intervals
Replace Engine Air Filter Element & PCV Filter	Normal Service Every 30,000 Miles; More Frequently In Severe Service Or Dusty Conditions
Replace EVAP Canister Filter	Every 10 Years Or 120,000 Miles
Replace Spark Plugs	X at 30,000 / 60,000 / 90,000
Replace Spark Plug Wires	X at 60,000
Replace Timing Belt	Every 100,000 Miles

STEERING, SUSPENSION & TIRES

Recommended Service	Service Interval / Notes
Inspect Power Steering, Steering & Suspension & Wheel Bearings	S / N / X at listed service intervals
Lubricate Chassis & Suspension	At Every Engine Oil Change
Rotate Tires	Normal Service Every 7500 Miles; Severe Service Every 6000 Miles

N — Normal Service
S — Severe Service
X — Normal Or Severe Service
① — After vehicle passes 99,000 mile mark return to beginning of mileage table & start cycle over again.

Prizm

Service Interval In Miles①

Mileage interval columns (left to right): 3000, 6000, 7500, 9000, 12000, 15000, 18000, 21000, 22500, 24000, 27000, 30000, 33000, 36000, 37500, 39000, 42000, 45000, 48000, 51000, 52500, 54000, 57000, 60000, 63000, 66000, 67500, 69000, 72000, 75000, 78000, 81000, 82500, 84000, 87000, 90000

Recommended Service	Service Interval / Marks
BODY	
Inspect Body Fastener Security	Severe Service Every 5000 Miles
Inspect Lamps & Warning Devices	S S N (pattern: S / N at intervals)
Inspect Seat Belts & Related Components	At Least Once Every 12 Months
Lubricate Lock Cylinders	
Supplemental Restraint System	10 Years From Vehicle Build Date, Then Every 24 Months Thereafter
BRAKES	
Inspect Brake System Hoses, Lines & Connections	Normal Service Every 15,000 Miles; Severe Service Every 5000 Miles
CLUTCH & TRANSAXLE	
Change Automatic Transmission Fluid & Filter	S (at intervals)
Change Differential & Manual Transaxle Lubricant	S (at intervals)
Inspect Neutral Safety & Shift Interlock Switch Operation	At Least Once Every 12 Months
Inspect Transaxle Lubricant Level	At Every Engine Oil Change
DRIVESHAFT	
Inspect CV Joint Boots & Tighten Driveshaft Flange	Normal Service Every 15,000 Miles; Severe Service Every 5000 Miles
ENGINE	
Change Engine Coolant	Every 24 Months Or 30,000 Miles
Change Engine Oil & Filter	Normal Service Every 7500 Miles; Severe Service Every 3000 Miles
Inspect Cooling System & Drive Belts	X (at 15,000; 30,000; 45,000; 60,000; 75,000; 90,000)
Inspect Engine Valve Clearance	X (at 15,000; 30,000; 45,000; 60,000; 75,000; 90,000)
Inspect EVAP Charcoal Canister	Every 72 Months Or 60,000 Miles
Inspect EVAP & Fuel System	X (at 30,000; 60,000; 90,000)
Inspect Exhaust System	X (at 15,000; 30,000; 45,000; 60,000; 75,000; 90,000)
Inspect Thermostatic Air Cleaner System Operation	X (at 15,000; 30,000; 45,000; 60,000; 75,000; 90,000)

Recommended Service — Service Interval In Miles①

Recommended Service	3000	6000	7500	9000	12000	15000	18000	21000	24000	27000	30000	33000	36000	39000	42000	45000	48000	51000	54000	57000	60000	63000	66000	69000	72000	75000	78000	81000	84000	87000	90000	93000	96000	99000
ENGINE																																		
Replace Air Filter Element & PCV Filter	Normal Service Every 30,000 Miles; More Frequently In Severe Service Or Dusty Conditions																																	
Replace Spark Plugs (Standard Type), 2001											X										X										X			
Replace Spark Plugs (Platinum Tip Type), 2001																					X													
Replace Spark Plugs, 2002	Every 120,000 Miles																																	
Replace Timing Belt																					X													
STEERING, SUSPENSION & TIRES																																		
Inspect Chassis Fastener Security	Severe Service Every 5000 Miles																																	
Inspect Steering & Suspension						S					S					S					S					S					S			
Lubricate Chassis & Suspension	At Every Engine Oil Change																																	
Rotate Tires	Normal Service Every 7500 Miles; Severe Service Every 6000 Miles																																	

N — Normal Service
S — Severe Service
X — Normal Or Severe Service
① — After vehicle passes 99,000 mile mark return to beginning of mileage table & start cycle over again.

Aurora

Service Interval In Miles ①

Recommended Service	3000	7500	9000	12000	15000	18000	21000	24000	27000	30000	33000	36000	39000	42000	45000	48000	51000	54000	57000	60000	63000	66000	69000	72000	75000	78000	81000	84000	87000	90000	93000	96000	99000
BODY																																	
Clean Power Antenna Mast	S	N	S	S	N	S	S	S	S	N	S	S	S	S	N	S	S	S	S	N	S	S	S	S	N	S	S	S	S	N	S	S	S
Inspect Lamps, Seat Belts & Warning Devices	S	N	S	S	N	S	S	S	S	N	S	S	S	S	N	S	S	S	S	N	S	S	S	S	N	S	S	S	S	N	S	S	S
Lubricate Hinges, Latches, Lock Cylinders & Strikers — At Least Every 6 Months																																	
Replace Passenger Compartment Air Filter — At Engine Oil Changes Or At Least Every 12 Months					X					X					X					X					X					X			
BRAKES																																	
Inspect Brake System — Every 7500 Miles																																	
Inspect Parking Brake Operation — At Least Once Every 12 Months																																	
Lubricate Parking Brake Cable Guides	S	N	S	S	N	S	S	S	S	N	S	S	S	S	N	S	S	S	S	N	S	S	S	S	N	S	S	S	S	N	S	S	S
CLUTCH & TRANSAXLE																																	
Change Automatic Transmission Fluid & Filter — Normal Service Every 100,000 Miles; Severe Service Every 50,000 Miles																																	
Inspect Neutral Safety & BTSI Operation	S	N	S	S	N	S	S	S	S	N	S	S	S	S	N	S	S	S	S	N	S	S	S	S	N	S	S	S	S	N	S	S	S
Lubricate Transmission Shift Linkage	S	N	S	S	N	S	S	S	S	N	S	S	S	S	N	S	S	S	S	N	S	S	S	S	N	S	S	S	S	N	S	S	S
DRIVESHAFT																																	
Inspect CV Joint Boots — At Tire Rotations																																	
ENGINE																																	
Change Engine Coolant — Every 60 Months Or 150,000 Miles																																	
Change Engine Oil & Filter, ②	S	N	S	S	N	S	S	S	S	N	S	S	S	S	N	S	S	S	S	N	S	S	S	S	N	S	S	S	S	N	S	S	S
Inspect Drive Belts										X										X										X			
Inspect EGR System										X										X										X			
Inspect Exhaust System — At Engine Oil Changes																																	
Inspect Fuel Filler Cap										X										X										X			
Inspect Fuel System Hoses, Lines & Connections										X										X										X			
Inspect PCV Valve										X										X										X			
Inspect Spark Plug Wires — At Spark Plug Changes																																	
Inspect Throttle Body Bores & Plates, Remove Any Deposits																									X								

Recommended Service

Service Interval In Miles ①

Recommended Service	3000	6000	7500	9000	12000	15000	18000	21000	24000	27000	30000	33000	36000	39000	42000	45000	48000	51000	54000	57000	60000	63000	66000	69000	72000	75000	78000	81000	84000	87000	90000	93000	96000	99000
ENGINE																																		
Inspect Throttle Linkage Operation	At Air Cleaner Element Changes																																	
Replace Air Filter & PCV Filter						S					X					S					X					S					X			
Replace Spark Plugs	Every 100,000 Miles																																	
STEERING, SUSPENSION & TIRES																																		
Inspect Steering & Suspension System	At Tire Rotations																																	
Lubricate Chassis & Suspension			S	N		S	N		X		S		N			S		N	X		S		N			S		N		S	N			
Rotate Tires	Inspect For Wear & Rotate Every 7500 Miles																																	

N — Normal Service
S — Severe Service
X — Normal Or Severe Service
BTSI — Brake Transmission Shift Interlock
IAC — Idle Air Control
ISC — Idle Speed Control System
① — After vehicle passes 99,000 mile mark return to beginning of mileage table & start cycle over again.
② — The Aurora is equipped with a GM Oil Life System which indicate when to change the engine oil & filter. Reset Oil Life System when oil & filter have been changed.

Vibe

Service Interval In Miles ①

Recommended Service	Interval / Service Notes
BODY	
Inspect Lamps, Seat Belts & Warning Devices	At Least Once Every 6 Months
Lubricate Hinges, Latches, Lock Cylinders & Strikers	At Engine Oil Changes Or At Least Every 12 Months
Replace Passenger Compartment Air Filter	Every 15,000 Miles
BRAKES	
Inspect Brake System, 2003	Every 7500 Miles
Inspect Brake System, 2004	Every 6000 Miles
Inspect Brake System, 2005	Every 5000 Miles
CLUTCH & TRANSMISSION	
Adjust Clutch Pedal Freeplay	At Least Once Every 6 Months
Change Automatic Transmission Fluid & Filter	Severe Service Every 60,000 Miles
Change Manual Transmission Fluid & Filter	Severe Service Every 30,000 Miles
Change Transfer Case Fluid	Severe Service Every 15,000 Miles
DRIVE AXLE	
Change Differential Lubricant	(service markers — see grid)
Lubricate Driveshaft	S S N S S X S S N S S X S S N S S X S S N S S X S S N S S X S S N S S S
ENGINE	
Change Engine Coolant	Every 30,000 Miles
Change Engine Oil & Filter ①	S S N S S X S S N S S X S S N S S X S S N S S X S S N S S X S S N S S S
Inspect Engine Air Filter	Severe Service Every 15,000 Miles
Inspect Exhaust System	At Engine Oil Changes
Inspect Fuel & Emission System	Every 30,000 Miles
Inspect Accessory Drive Belt	At 60,000 Miles
Inspect Spark Plug Wires	Every 100,000 Miles & At Spark Plug Replacements
Replace Engine Air Filter	X (replacement at specified intervals)
Replace Spark Plugs	Every 120,000 Miles
STEERING, SUSPENSION & TIRES	
Rotate Tires, 2003	Every 7500 Miles
Rotate Tires, 2004	Every 6000 Miles
Rotate Tires, 2005	Every 5000 Miles

N — Normal Service
S — Severe Service
X — Normal Or Severe Service
① — If equipped, the engine oil life monitor will indicate when to change engine oil, ususally 3000–10,000 miles. Under severe driving conditions, engine oil may need to be changed before 3000 miles. If vehicle is driven in a dusty area, change engine oil every 3000 miles.

Saturn

Service Interval In Miles[1]

Recommended Service	3000	6000	9000	12000	15000	18000	21000	24000	27000	30000	33000	36000	39000	42000	45000	48000	51000	54000	57000	60000	63000	66000	69000	72000	75000	78000	81000	84000	87000	90000	93000	96000	99000
BODY																																	
Inspect Seat Belts & Restraint Systems	At Least Once Every 6 Months																																
Inspect Wiper Blades & Inserts	At Least Once Every 6 Months																																
Lubricate Door Check Straps & Hinges					X					X					X					X					X					X			
Lubricate Hood Latch					X					X					X					X					X					X			
Lubricate Headlamp Doors					X					X					X					X					X					X			
Lubricate Sunroof					X					X					X					X					X					X			
Replace Cabin Air Filter, L-Series	Every 12 Months Or 12,000 Miles. In Dusty Areas Change More Often																																
Replace Cabin Air Filter, Ion	Every 18,000 Miles. In Dusty Areas Change More Often																																
BRAKES																																	
Add DEX-CVT Additive to VTi Variable Transmission, Ion	Every 50,000 Miles																																
Inspect Brake Drums & Shoes					X					X					X					X					X					X			
Inspect Disc Brake Calipers For Freedom Of Movement (Lubricate If Required)										X										X										X			
Inspect Disc Brake Pads & Rotors					X					X					X					X					X					X			
Inspect Brake Hoses, Lines & Connections					X					X					X					X					X					X			
CLUTCH & TRANSAXLE																																	
Change Automatic Transaxle Fluid & Filter, L-Series 2004–05	Normal Service Every 100,000 Miles; Severe Every 50,000 Miles																																
Change Automatic Transaxle Fluid & Filter, L-Series 2001–03	No Normal Service; Severe Every 50,000 Miles																																
Change Automatic Transaxle Fluid & Filter, S-Series 2001	No Normal Service; Severe Every 50,000 Miles																																
Change Automatic Transaxle Fluid & Filter, S-Series 2002	Normal Service Every 100,000 Miles; Severe Every 50,000 Miles																																
Change Automatic Or VTi Transaxle Fluid & Filter, Ion	No Normal Service; Severe Every 50,000 Miles																																
Change Automatic Or VTi Transaxle Fluid & Filter, Ion	Normal Service Every 100,000 Miles; Severe Every 50,000 Miles																																

Recommended Service	Service Interval In Miles①																																						
	3000	6000	7500	9000	12000	15000	18000	21000	22500	24000	27000	30000	33000	36000	37500	39000	42000	45000	48000	51000	52500	54000	57000	60000	63000	66000	67500	69000	72000	75000	78000	81000	82500	84000	87000	90000	93000	96000	97500	99000
DRIVESHAFT																																								
Inspect CV Joint Boots		X		X		X		X		X		X		X		X		X		X		X		X		X		X		X		X		X		X		X		X
ENGINE																																								
Change Engine Coolant & Inspect Pressure Cap, 2001–03	Every 60 Months Or 100,000 Miles																																							
Change Engine Coolant & Inspect Pressure Cap, 2004–05	Every 60 Months Or 150,000 Miles																																							
Change Engine Oil & Filter②	S	X	S	X	S	X	S	X	S	X	S	X	S	X	S	X	S	X	S	X	S	X	S	X	S	X	S	X	S	X	S	X	S	X	S	X	S	X	S	X
Inspect Air Filter	Severe Service Every 15,000 Miles																																							
Inspect Cooling System & Protection Level						X						X						X						X						X						X				
Inspect Drive Belts & Coolant Hoses, 2001–03	Every 18,000 Miles																																							
Inspect Drive Belts & Coolant Hoses, 2004–05	Every 25,000 Miles																																							
Inspect Emission Hoses, Lines & Connections, 2001–03	Every 30,000 Miles																																							
Inspect Exhaust System, 2001–03		X		X		X		X		X		X		X		X		X		X		X		X		X		X		X		X		X		X		X		X
Inspect Exhaust System, 2004–05	Every 25,000 Miles																																							
Inspect Fuel System, 2004–05	Every 25,000 Miles																																							
Inspect Fuel Hoses, Lines & Connections										X										X										X										X
Inspect Fuel Tank Filler Cap										X										X										X										X
Replace Air Filter, 2001–03	Normal Service Every 30,000 Miles; More Frequently In Severe Service Or Dusty Conditions																																							
Replace Air Filter, 2004–05	Every 25,000 Miles																																							
Replace Fuel Filter, 2002 S-Series																				X																				X
Replace Fuel Filter, Ion & 2001–03 L-Series	Every 100,000 Miles																																							
Replace Fuel Filter, 2004–05 L-Series	Every 25,000 Miles																																							
Replace Spark Plugs, S-Series 2001–02												X												X												X				
Replace Spark Plugs, L-Series & Ion	Every 100,000 Miles																																							
Replace Timing Belt, L-Series 3.0L V6	At 100,000 Miles																																							

STEERING, SUSPENSION & TIRES

Recommended Service	Service Interval In Miles ①																																
	3000	6000	9000	12000	15000	18000	21000	24000	27000	30000	33000	36000	39000	42000	45000	48000	51000	54000	57000	60000	63000	66000	69000	72000	75000	78000	81000	84000	87000	90000	93000	96000	99000
Inspect Ball Joint Seals					X					X					X					X					X					X			
Inspect Suspension					X					X					X					X					X					X			
Rotate Tires, S-Series					X					X					X					X					X					X			
Rotate Tires, L-Series	Every 12 Months Or 12,000 Miles																																
Rotate Tires, All Except L & S Series	Every 6000 Miles																																

N — Normal Service
S — Severe Service
X — Normal Or Severe Service
BTSI — Brake Transaxle Shift Interlock
① L-Series After vehicle passes 150,000 mile mark return to beginning of mileage table & start cycle over again. 2001–after vehicle passes 120,000 mile mark return to beginning of mileage table & start cycle over again.
② On models equipped with Engine Oil Life Monitor, change engine oil when message appears in message display center. Never drive vehicle more then 6000 miles or 6 months without changing oil and filter.

DAIMLERCHRYSLER CORP.

DAIMLERCHRYSLER CORP.

SEBRING COUPE & STRATUS COUPE

NOTE: Refer To The Rear Of This Manual For Vehicle Manufacturers Special Service Tool Suppliers.

INDEX OF SERVICE OPERATIONS

Specifications

GENERAL ENGINE SPECIFICATIONS

Year	Engine		Fuel System	Bore x Stroke, Inches	Comp. Ratio	Net HP @ RPM	Maximum Torque, Ft. Lbs. @ RPM	Normal Oil Pressure @ Idle, psi
	Liter	VIN Code①						
2001–05	2.4L	G	MFI	3.41 x 3.94	9.0	147 @ 5500	158 @ 4000	11.4
	3.0L	H	MFI	3.59 x 2.99	9.0	200 @ 5500	205 @ 4500	11.6

MFI — Multi-Port Fuel Injection

SMFI — Sequential Multi-Port Fuel Injection

① — Eighth digit of Vehicle Identification Number (VIN) denotes engine code.

TUNE UP SPECIFICATIONS

Engine Liter	Spark Plug Gap, Inch	Firing Order④	Ignition Timing °BTDC			Curb Idle Speed		Fuel Pump Pressure, psi.③	Valve Lash, Inch
			Man. Trans.	Auto. Trans.	Mark Fig.	Man. Trans.	Auto. Trans.		
2.4L	.039–.043	1-3-4-2	10	10	⑤	700②	700②	47–50	①
3.0L	.039–.043	1-2-3-4-5-6	15	15	⑤	700②	700②	47–50	①

BTDC — Before Top Dead Center
① — Equipped w/hydraulic lash adjusters.
② — Non-adjustable.
③ — Remove rear seat cushion, then the protector. Disconnect fuel pump connector. Start engine & let run until it stops naturally, then turn ignition to Off. Connect fuel pump connector, install protector & rear seat cushion. Remove cover from service valve on fuel rail. Connect suitable fuel pressure test gauge to service valve. Switch ignition in Run position, then use scan tool to activate fuel pump & pressurize system.
④ — Before disconnecting wires from coil unit, determine location of ignition wires in coil towers, as position may have been altered from that outlined.
⑤ — Equipped w/crankshaft position sensor.

FRONT WHEEL ALIGNMENT SPECIFICATIONS

Year	Camber Angle, Degrees ①		Toe, Inch③		Caster, Degrees		Ball Joint Wear
	Limits	Desired	Limits	Desired	Limits	Desired	
2001–05	-.5 to +.05	0	-.12 to +.12	0	+2.50 to +3.50	+3.00	②

① — Not adjustable.

② — Refer to "Ball Joint Inspection" in "Front Suspension & Steering."

③ — Toe in (+); toe out (-).

REAR WHEEL ALIGNMENT SPECIFICATIONS

Year	Camber, Degrees			Total Toe, Inch①	
	Limits	Desired	Max. LH/RH Deviation	Limits	Desired
2001–05	-1.83 to -.83	-1.33	.50	0 to +.24	+.12

① — Toe in (+); toe out (-).

VEHICLE RIDE HEIGHT SPECIFICATIONS

Model	Year	Body Style	Manufacturer's Original Tire Size	Front Dim.	Front Spec. Inches	Front Spec. mm	Rear Dim.	Rear Spec. Inches	Rear Spec. mm
Sebring Coupe	2001–02	All	①	G	5.90	150	H	5.90	150
	2003–05	2.4L	①	G	6.20	157	H	6.20	157
		3.0L	①	G	5.90	150	H	5.90	150
Stratus Coupe	2001–02	All	①	G	5.90	150	H	5.90	150
	2003–05	2.4L	①	G	6.20	157	H	6.20	157
		3.0L	①	G	5.90	150	H	5.90	150

G Dim — Ground to Front Rocker Panel

H Dim — Ground to Rear Rocker Panel

① — See door sticker or inside of glove box for manufacturer's original tire size specifications.

② — Measurement is w/fuel, radiator coolant & engine oil full, spare tire, jack, hand tools & mats in designated positions & tires properly inflated.

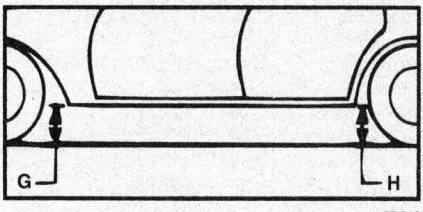

CRQ121

Fig. A   Dimensions G & H

FLUID CAPACITIES & COOLING SYSTEM DATA

Year	Engine	Coolant Capacity, Qts.	Coolant Type	Radiator Cap Relief Pressure, Lbs.	Thermo. Opening Temp. °F	Fuel Tank Capacity, Gals.	Engine Oil Refill, Qts.①	Transaxle Oil, Qts. Manual	Transaxle Oil, Qts. Auto.
2001–04	2.4L	7.4	Ethylene Glycol	11–15	190	16.4	4.2	2.3	8.1
	3.0L	8.5	Ethylene Glycol	11–15	190	16.4	4.2	3.0	8.5
2005	2.4L	8.4	Long Life	14–18	190		4.2	2.3	8.1
	3.0L	9.6	Long Life	14–18	190		4.2	3.0	8.9

① — Capacity without oil filter. Add additional 1/2 quart when changing filter.

LUBRICANT DATA

Year	Transaxle Manual	Transaxle Automatic	Power Steering	Brake System
2001–05	API GL-4	Diamond ATF SP-III or SP-IIM	ATF 59602	DOT 3 or 4

Electrical

NOTE: On Air Bag Equipped Models, Refer To "Air Bag System Precautions" Located In The Front Of This Manual For System Disarming & Arming Procedures.

NOTE: Refer To "Computer Relearn Procedures" Located In The Front Of This Manual When Battery Power To The Computer Has Been Interrupted.

INDEX

PRECAUTIONS

Air Bag Systems

Refer to "Air Bag System Precautions" in the front of this manual for system disarming and arming procedures.

Battery Ground Cable

Prior to service, disconnect battery ground cable and isolate as required.

FUSE PANEL & FLASHER LOCATION

The engine compartment fuse panel is located on the lefthand side of the engine compartment. The interior fuse panel is located behind the lefthand side of the instrument panel. The turn signal and hazard flashers are incorporated into the ETACS-ECU.

FUEL PUMP RELAY LOCATION

The fuel pump relay is located behind the lefthand side of the instrument panel, lefthand of the steering column, **Fig. 1.**

STARTER

REPLACE

1. Remove air cleaner assembly.
2. **On models equipped with 2.4L engines,** remove cover from starter.
3. **On all engines,** disconnect starter electrical connectors.

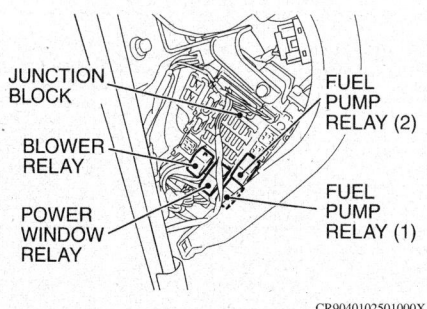

JUNCTION BLOCK
FUEL PUMP RELAY (2)
BLOWER RELAY
POWER WINDOW RELAY
FUEL PUMP RELAY (1)

CR9040102501000X

Fig. 1   Fuel pump relay location

4. Remove starter mounting bolts, then the starter.
5. Reverse procedure to install, noting the following:
   a. **Torque** starter mounting bolts to 21–25 ft. lbs.
   b. **Torque** battery cable to solenoid retaining bolt to 36–52 inch lbs.

ALTERNATOR

REPLACE

2.4L Engine

1. Remove oil pressure hose and tube assembly clamp bolts, **Fig. 2.**
2. Remove oil return tube assembly clamp bolt.
3. Remove drive belts, then the water pump pulley.
4. Remove oil level gauge unit.
5. Disconnect alternator electrical connector.
6. Remove alternator brace, then the alternator.

7. Reverse procedure to install. **Torque** alternator mounting bolts to 26–40 ft. lbs.

3.0L Engine

1. Remove drive belt, then the oil level gauge unit **Fig. 3.**
2. Disconnect alternator electrical connector.
3. Remove alternator.
4. Reverse procedure to install. **Torque** alternator mounting bolt to 26–40 ft. lbs.

DISTRIBUTOR

REPLACE

3.0L Engine

1. Disconnect distributor electrical connector, then the spark plug wires.
2. Remove intake manifold plenum as outlined in "Intake Manifold, Replace" in the "3.0L Engine" section.
3. Remove distributor assembly.
4. Reverse procedure to install, aligning mating marks on distributor housing and coupling.

COIL PACK

REPLACE

2.4L Engine

1. Remove spark plug wires.
2. Remove coil pack mounting bolts, then the coil pack.
3. Reverse procedure to install, noting the following:

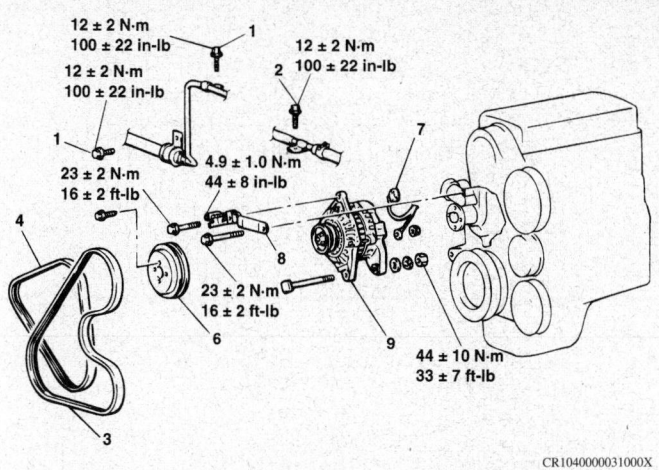

Fig. 2 Alternator replacement. 2.4L engine

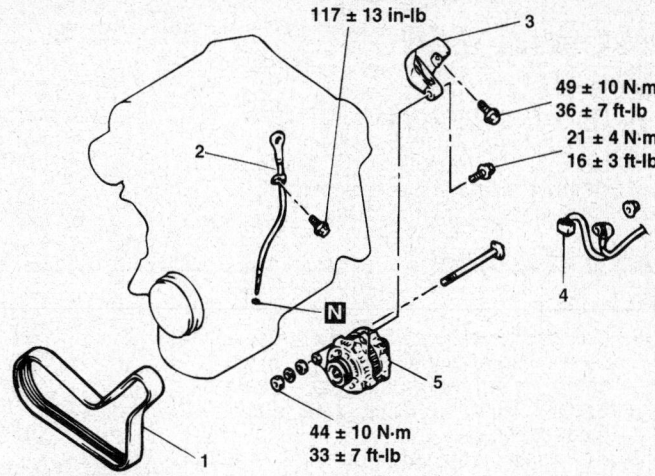

1- DRIVE BELT
2- OIL LEVEL GAUGE
3- ALTERNATOR BRACKET
4- ALTERNATOR HARNESS
5- ALTERNATOR

Fig. 3 Alternator replacement. 3.0L engine

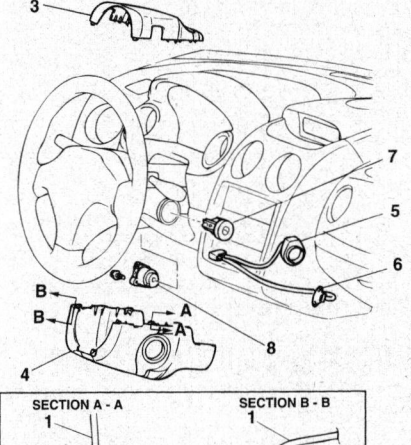

SECTION A - A   SECTION B - B

1. ETACS-ECU
2. IMMOBILIZER-ECU
3. COLUMN COVER UPPER
4. COLUMN COVER LOWER
5. KEY RING ANTENNA
6. KEY REMINDER SWITCH
7. STEERING LOCK CYLINDER
8. IGNITION SWITCH

Fig. 4 Ignition switch replacement

a. **Torque** mounting bolts to 70–104 inch lbs.

IGNITION LOCK
REPLACE

Refer to "Ignition Switch, Replace" for ignition lock replacement.

IGNITION SWITCH
REPLACE

1. Remove steering column upper and lower covers, **Fig. 4.**
2. Remove key ring antenna and key reminder switch.
3. Insert key into cylinder lock and turn to

ACC position, then the cylinder, using a suitable Phillips head screwdriver.
4. Remove ignition switch.
5. Reverse procedure to install, noting the following:
   a. If a new ignition key is used it must be registered using scan tool No. MB9911502, or equivalent.
   b. Follow scan tool manufactures instructions for key registration.

NEUTRAL SAFETY SWITCH
REPLACE

The neutral safety switch is located at the lower lefthand side of the transaxle housing, under the air cleaner assembly, **Fig. 5.**
1. Disconnect neutral safety switch electrical connector.
2. Remove switch from transaxle case.
3. Reverse procedure to install.

MULTI-FUNCTION SWITCH
REPLACE

1. Remove steering wheel as outlined in "Steering Wheel, Replace."
2. Remove instrument panel lower cover.
3. Remove upper and lower steering column cover.
4. Remove multi-function switch.
5. Reverse procedure to install.

STEERING WHEEL
REPLACE

1. Remove air bag module.
2. Remove steering wheel using suitable puller.
3. Reverse procedure to install. **Torque** steering wheel nut to 26–36 ft. lbs.

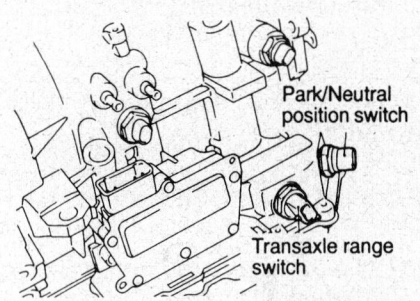

Park/Neutral position switch

Transaxle range switch

Fig. 5 Neutral safety switch

INSTRUMENT CLUSTER
REPLACE

1. Remove steering wheel as outlined in "Steering Wheel, Replace."
2. Remove meter hood from instrument panel.
3. Remove instrument cluster, disconnect electrical connectors and vehicle speed sensor.
4. Reverse procedure to install.

RADIO
REPLACE

1. Remove center panel assembly.
2. Remove radio, tape and/or CD player.
3. Remove radio bracket.
4. Reverse procedure to install.

WIPER MOTOR
REPLACE

1. Remove wiper arm and blade assembly.
2. Remove front deck garnish/cowl screen.
3. Remove wiper motor and link assembly, then disconnect motor electrical connector.

4. Reverse procedure to install.

BLOWER MOTOR
REPLACE

1. Remove glove compartment.
2. Remove air purifier assembly.
3. Remove joint duct, then the resistor.
4. Remove blower motor assembly.
5. Reverse procedure to install.

HEATER CORE
REPLACE

1. Remove driver's side front undercover panel, center panel assembly, glove compartment and passenger's side undercover panel using suitable flat-bladed tool.
2. Remove joint duct assembly.
3. **On models equipped with A/C,** proceed as follows:
   a. Remove automatic compressor controller.
   b. Recover refrigerant as outlined in "Air Conditioning."
   c. Remove A/C pipe, expansion valve, then the evaporator core.
   d. Remove drain hose.
4. **On all models,** drain coolant into suitable container.
5. Remove heater hoses.
6. Remove radio as outlined in "Radio, Replace."
7. Remove heater control assembly.
8. Remove steering wheel as outlined in "Steering Wheel, Replace."
9. Remove floor console in numbered sequence, **Fig. 6.**
10. Remove instrument panel as outlined in "Dash Panel Service."
11. Remove front deck crossmember, then the foot duct.
12. Remove heater/cooler unit, then the heater core.

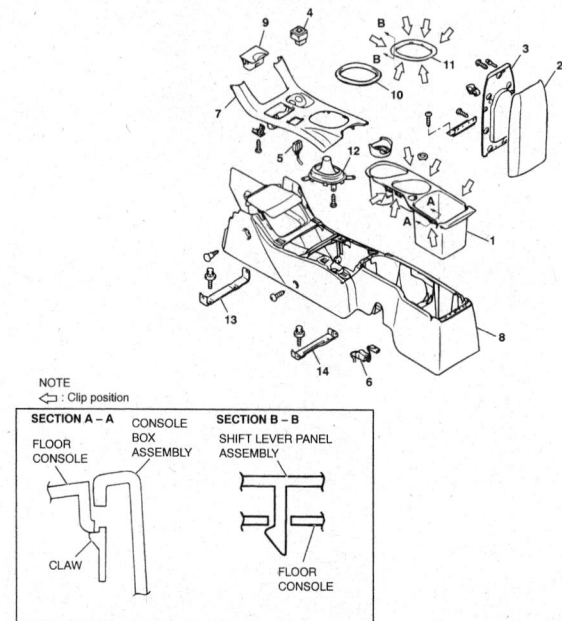

NOTE
⟵ : Clip position

1. CONSOLE BOX ASSEMBLY
2. CONSOLE LID
3. CONSOLE LID COVER
4. DOOR MIRROR CONTROL SWITCH
5. DOOR MIRROR CONTROL SWITCH HARNESS
6. ACCCESSARY SOCKET HARNESS
7. FLOOR CONSOLE INDICATOR PANEL
8. FLOOR CONSOLE
9. ASHTRAY
10. SHIFT LEVER PANEL ASSEMBLY <M/T>
11. GARNISH <A/T>
12. SHIFT LEVER BOOT <M/T>
13. FLOOR CONSOLE BRACKET A
14. FLOOR CONSOLE BRACKET B

CR9140000071000X

Fig. 6 Floor console removal

13. Reverse procedure to install.

EVAPORATOR CASE
REPLACE

Refer to "Heater Core, Replace" for evaporator case replacement.

EVAPORATOR CORE
REPLACE

Refer to "Heater Core, Replace" for evaporator core replacement.

2.4L Engine

NOTE: On Air Bag Equipped Models, Refer To "Air Bag System Precautions" Located In The Front Of This Manual For System Disarming & Arming Procedures.

NOTE: Refer To "Computer Relearn Procedures" Located In The Front Of This Manual When Battery Power To The Computer Has Been Interrupted.

INDEX

PRECAUTIONS

Air Bag Systems

Refer to "Air Bag System Precautions" in the front of this manual for system disarming and arming procedures.

Battery Ground Cable

Prior to service, disconnect battery ground cable and isolate as required.

Fuel System Pressure Relief

1. Remove fuel pump relay.
2. Start engine and let it run until it stops, then turn ignition switch off.
3. Reconnect fuel pump relay.

COMPRESSION PRESSURE

Perform compression test with engine at normal operating temperature, spark plugs removed, crankshaft position sensor disconnected and throttle wide open. Standard compression pressure at cranking speed is 185 psi. The minimum compression pressure is 139 psi with a maximum variation between cylinders of 14 psi.

ENGINE MOUNT

REPLACE

1. Hold engine with a chain block or similar tool.
2. Remove reserve tank.
3. Raise and support engine to remove weight from engine mount bracket using a suitable floor jack.
4. Remove engine mount insulator mounting bolt, mount bracket then the stopper.
5. Reverse procedure to install, tightening to specifications.

ENGINE

REPLACE

1. Release fuel pressure as outlined in "Precautions."
2. Mark and remove hood.
3. Remove strut tower bar.
4. Drain engine oil into suitable container.
5. Remove radiator as outlined in "Radiator, Replace."
6. Remove air cleaner, then the front exhaust pipe.
7. Disconnect accelerator cable, then the purge hose.
8. Disconnect necessary vacuum hose connections.
9. Disconnect the following electrical connections:
   a. Ignition coil.
   b. Fuel injectors.
   c. Ignition failure sensor.
   d. Manifold differential pressure sensor.
   e. Throttle position sensor.
   f. Heated oxygen sensor.
   g. Capacitor.
   h. Engine coolant temperature sensor.
   i. Camshaft position sensor.
   j. Knock sensor.
   k. Engine coolant temperature gauge unit.
   l. Idle air control motor.
   m. Evaporative emission purge solenoid valve.
   n. EGR solenoid valve.
   o. Alternator.
   p. Fuel high pressure hose.
   q. Fuel return hose.
   r. Oil pressure switch.
   s. Crankshaft position sensor.
   t. Power steering pressure switch.
10. Disconnect high pressure fuel hose, then the fuel return hose.
11. Remove oil dipstick and guide.
12. Remove pressure hose, then the heater hose.
13. Remove drive belts.
14. Remove power steering pump with hoses attached and position aside.
15. Remove A/C compressor with lines attached and position aside.
16. Remove transaxle as in **MOTOR's** "**Domestic Transmission, In-Vehicle Service**" manual.
17. Support engine with jack and hold engine with chain block or similar support tool.
18. Place jack under engine oil pan with piece of wood in between, then raise engine so that weight of engine is no longer on engine mount bracket.
19. Remove engine mount stopper, then the engine.
20. Reverse procedure to install. Tighten all fasteners to specifications.

INTAKE MANIFOLD

REPLACE

1. Release fuel pressure as outlined in "Precautions."
2. Drain engine coolant into suitable container, then remove air cleaner assembly.

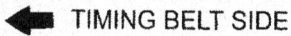

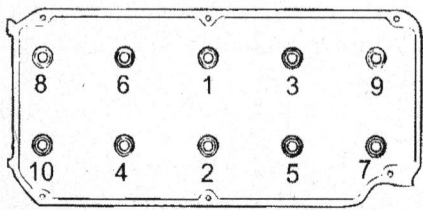

TIMING BELT SIDE

Fig. 1 Cylinder head bolt removal

ARM0400000000323

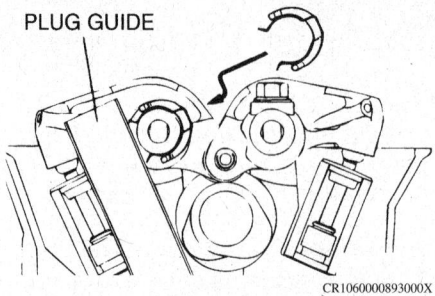

PLUG GUIDE

CR1060000893000X

Fig. 2 Rocker arm shaft spring installation

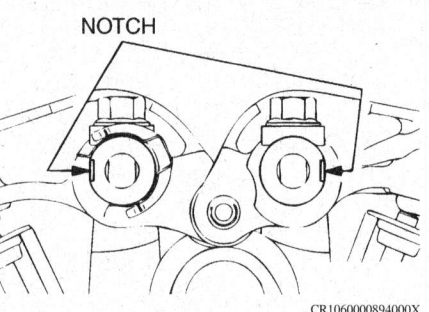

NOTCH

CR1060000894000X

Fig. 3 Rocker arm shaft notch direction

3. Disconnect accelerator cable.
4. Disconnect throttle position sensor and idle air control motor electrical connectors.
5. Remove throttle body assembly.
6. Disconnect purge hose, then the brake booster vacuum hose.
7. Disconnect ignition coil, fuel injectors, ignition failure sensor and manifold differential pressure sensor electrical connectors.
8. Disconnect evaporative emission purge solenoid valve and EGR solenoid valve connectors.
9. Disconnect high pressure and return fuel hoses.
10. Remove oil dipstick and guide.
11. Remove PCV hose and fuel hose.
12. Remove fuel rail, injector and fuel pressure regulator.
13. Remove insulator, then the vacuum pipe.
14. Remove EGR valve.
15. Remove intake manifold.
16. Reverse procedure to install.

EXHAUST MANIFOLD
REPLACE

1. Remove front heated oxygen sensor.
2. Remove heat protector, then the engine hanger.
3. Remove exhaust manifold and bracket.
4. Reverse procedure to install.

CYLINDER HEAD
REPLACE

1. Release fuel pressure as outlined in "Precautions," then drain cooling system.
2. Remove strut tower brace, then the air cleaner assembly.
3. Remove thermostat case assembly.
4. Remove front exhaust pipe.
5. Disconnect accelerator cable.
6. Disconnect purge hose, then the brake booster vacuum hose connections.
7. Disconnect the following electrical connectors:
   a. Ignition coil and injectors.
   b. Manifold differential pressure sensor.
   c. Throttle position sensor.
   d. Heated oxygen sensor.
   e. Capacitor.

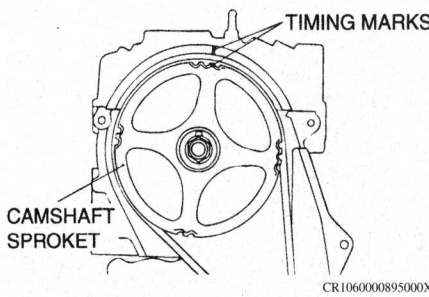

TIMING MARKS

CAMSHAFT SPROKET

CR1060000895000X

Fig. 4 Camshaft sprocket timing marks

   f. Engine coolant temperature sensor.
   g. Camshaft position sensor.
   h. Idle air control motor.
   i. Evaporative emission purge solenoid valve.
   j. EGR solenoid.
8. Disconnect fuel pressure and return hoses.
9. Remove oil dipstick and guide.
10. Remove spark plug wires, then the ignition coil.
11. Remove upper radiator hose.
12. Disconnect PCV hose.
13. Remove rocker cover, then the spark plug guide oil seal.
14. Remove timing belt as outlined in "Timing Belt, Replace."
15. Remove power steering pressure switch.
16. Remove power steering pump with hose attached and position aside.
17. Remove exhaust manifold bracket.
18. Loosen bolts in two or three steps using cylinder head bolt removal tool No. MB991654, or equivalent, in numbered sequence, **Fig. 1.**
19. Remove cylinder head, do not damage plug guides when removing bolts.
20. Reverse procedure to install, noting the following:
   a. Measure cylinder head bolts, if length below head of bolt is more than 3.91 inches, replace bolt.
   b. Tighten cylinder head bolts in five steps using reverse order of cylinder head bolt removal outlined in **Fig. 1.** First step, **torque** bolts to 55–61 ft. lbs. Second step; fully loosen bolts in sequence. Third step, **torque** bolts to 14–16 ft. lbs. Fourth step, tighten an additional

90.° Fifth step, tighten an additional 90.°

ROCKER ARMS
REPLACE

1. Remove breather hose, then the PCV hose and valve.
2. Remove valve cover.
3. Hold lash adjuster in place using lash adjuster holding tool No. MD998443, or equivalent, to remove rocker arm shafts.
4. Remove rocker arm shaft springs, then the rocker arms.
5. Remove lash adjusters.
6. Reverse procedure to install, noting the following:
   a. Install rocker arm shaft spring to intake side rocker arm shaft, **Fig. 2.**
   b. Ensure notch in end of rocker arm shaft is positioned as outlined, **Fig. 3.**

FRONT COVER
REPLACE

1. Remove drive belts.
2. Remove water pump pulley, then the crankshaft pulley.
3. Remove timing belt upper cover, then the lower cover.
4. Reverse procedure to install.

TIMING BELT
REPLACE

Front

REMOVAL

1. Remove front cover as outlined in "Front Cover, Replace."
2. Turn crankshaft clockwise to align camshaft sprocket timing marks, **Fig. 4.**
3. Loosen timing belt tensioner bolt.
4. If timing belt is to be re-used, mark flat side of belt with an arrow to indicate clockwise rotating direction.
5. Move tensioner pulley toward water pump side, then remove timing belt.

INSTALLATION

1. Align timing marks on camshaft

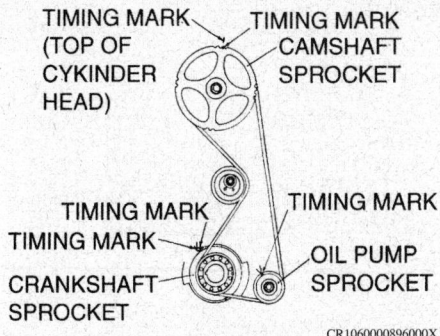

Fig. 5 Timing marks

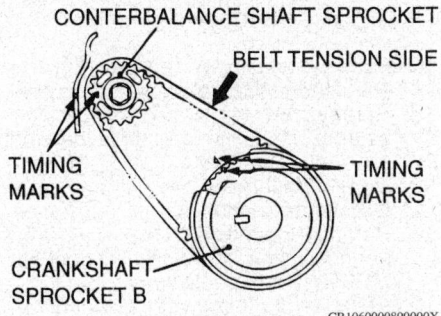

Fig. 8 Counterbalance shaft sprocket & crankshaft sprocket timing marks

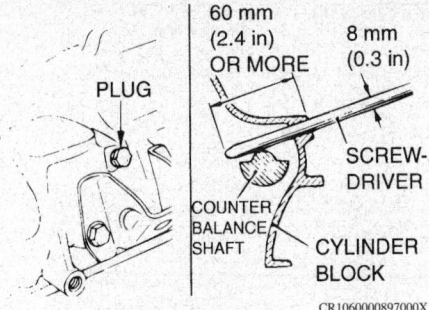

Fig. 6 Cylinder block plug location

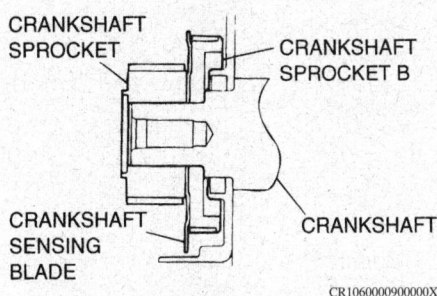

Fig. 9 Crankshaft sensing blade installation

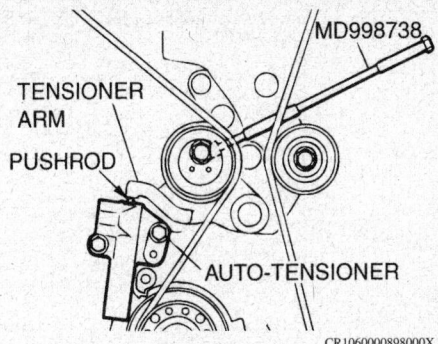

Fig. 7 Adjusting screw tool installation

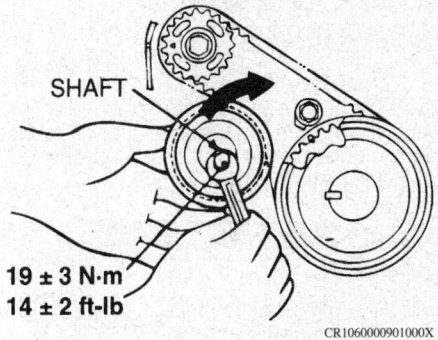

19 ± 3 N·m
14 ± 2 ft-lb

Fig. 10 Timing belt tensioner adjustment

sprocket, crankshaft sprocket and oil pump sprocket, **Fig. 5.**
2. Remove cylinder block plug and insert a suitable .3 inch Phillips head screw driver, **Fig. 6.**
3. Ensure screwdriver goes in 2.4 inches or more. If screwdriver will only go in 1.0 inch, turn sprocket one revolution and insert screw driver again. **Do not remove screw driver until timing belt is installed.**
4. To eliminate belt tension slack, install timing belt in the following order; over crankshaft sprocket, oil pump sprocket, then the camshaft sprocket.
5. Set tension pulley so pin holes are at bottom, then press lightly against timing belt. Temporarily tighten bolt.
6. Adjust timing belt tension as follows:
   a. Remove rubber plug from rear of timing belt cover, then tighten adjusting screw tool No. MD998738, or equivalent, by hand until tensioner arm is touching auto-tensioner pushrod, **Fig. 7.**
   b. Turn crankshaft ¼ turn counterclockwise, then turn clockwise until timing marks are aligned.
   c. Loosen tensioner pulley bolt, then use tensioner pulley socket tool No. MD998767, or equivalent, to **torque** bolt to 32–40 ft. lbs., while applying 31 inch lbs., of tension to belt.
   d. Turn crankshaft two revolutions clockwise to align timing marks.
   e. After 15 minutes, measure protrusion of auto tensioner pushrod. Protrusion should be .15–.18 inch. If protrusion is not as specified, repeat steps a through d.

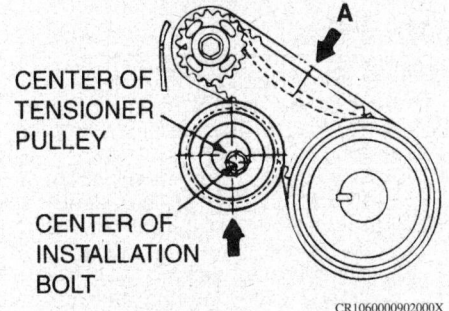

Fig. 11 Timing belt deflection

7. Ensure timing marks on each sprocket are aligned.
8. Install front cover.

Rear
REMOVAL
1. Remove front timing belt as outlined in "Timing Belt, Replace."
2. Remove crankshaft sprocket using crankshaft holding tool No. MB991367, or equivalent.
3. Remove crankshaft sensing blade.
4. Remove rear timing belt tensioner, then the rear timing belt.

INSTALLATION
1. Install rear timing belt crankshaft sprocket, ensure timing marks are aligned, **Fig. 8.**
2. Install rear timing belt, ensure there is no slack in belt.
3. Install crankshaft sensing as outlined, **Fig. 9.**
4. Adjust timing belt tension as follows:
   a. Temporarily fix timing belt tensioner so center of pulley is to lefthand and

above center of mounting bolt.
   b. Holding timing belt tensioner up in direction of arrow, **Fig. 10,** apply pressure on timing belt so belt is taut. **Torque** bolt to 12–16 ft. lbs.
   c. Ensure timing belt deflection at point (A) is .2–.3 inch, **Fig. 11.**

CAMSHAFT
REPLACE
1. Remove air cleaner assembly.
2. Remove rocker arms as outlined in "Rocker Arms, Replace."
3. Remove camshaft position sensor support.
4. Remove camshaft position sensing cylinder, then the camshaft sprocket.
5. Remove spark plug guide oil seal.
6. Remove camshaft sprocket using end yoke holder tool No. MB990767 and crankshaft pulley holding tool No. MD998719, or equivalents.
7. Remove camshaft oil seal, then the camshaft.
8. Reverse procedure to install, noting the following:
   a. Install camshaft oil seal using oil seal installer tool No. MD998713, or equivalent.

PISTON & ROD ASSEMBLY

The front mark on piston must face timing belt side of engine. Connecting rods and caps must be installed in original positions. **Torque** bolts to 13–15 ft. lbs., then an additional 90–94°.

CRANKSHAFT JOURNAL OUT-SIDE DIAMETER		CYLINDER BLOCK BEARING BORE	CRANKSHAFT BEARING	CRANKSHAFT BEARING FOR NO.3
IDENTIFICA-TION COLOR	SIZE mm (in)	IDENTIFICATION MARK	IDENTIFICATION MARK OR COLOR	IDENTIFICATION MARK OR COLOR
Yellow	56.994 - 57.000 (2.2439 - 2.2441)	0	1 or Green	0 or Black
		1	2 or Yellow	1 or Green
		2	3 or None	2 or Yellow
None	56.988 - 56.994 (2.2436 - 2.2439)	0	2 or Yellow	1 or Green
		1	3 or None	2 or Yellow
		2	4 or Blue	3 or None
White	56.982 - 56.988 (2.2438 - 2.2436)	0	3 or None	2 or Yellow
		1	4 or Blue	3 or None
		2	5 or Red	4 or Blue

CR1060000905000X

Fig. 12 Main bearing selection chart

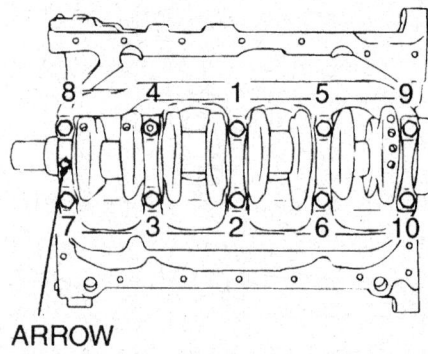

ARROW

CR1060000906000X

Fig. 13 Main bearing tightening sequence

MAIN & ROD BEARINGS

If bearing replacement is required, measure crankshaft journal diameter and select appropriate bearing from the chart, **Fig. 12.** **Torque** bolts to 17–19 ft. lbs., in sequence, **Fig. 13,** then an additional 90°.

CRANKSHAFT SEAL
REPLACE

1. Remove front timing belt as outlined in "Timing Belt, Replace."
2. Remove crankshaft position sensor.
3. Remove crankshaft sprocket using crankshaft spanner tool No. MB991367, or equivalent.
4. Remove crankshaft sensing blade.
5. Remove rear timing belt as outlined in "Timing Belt, Replace."
6. Remove rear timing belt crankshaft sprocket.
7. Remove key, then the crankshaft front oil seal.
8. Reverse procedure to install, noting the following:
   a. Apply engine oil to entire inside diameter of oil seal lip.
   b. Press in oil seal using crankshaft oil seal installer tool No. MD998375, or equivalent, until it is flush with front case.
   c. Install crankshaft sensing blade, **Fig. 9.**

CRANKSHAFT REAR OIL SEAL
REPLACE

1. Remove oil pan as outlined under "Oil Pan, Replace."
2. Remove transaxle as outlined in **MOTOR's "Domestic Transmission, In-Vehicle Service"** manual.
3. Remove flywheel, then the crankshaft bushing.
4. Remove crankshaft rear oil seal.
5. Reverse procedure to install, noting the following:
   a. Apply a small amount of engine oil to entire inside diameter of oil seal lip.
   b. Tap in oil seal using oil seal installer tool Nos. MB990938 and MD998776, or equivalents, **Fig. 14.**

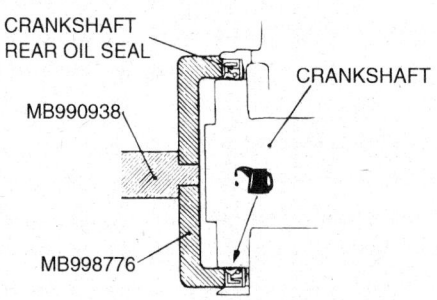

Fig. 14 Crankshaft rear oil seal installation

CR1060000903000X

CRANKSHAFT REAR OIL SEAL

MB990938

CRANKSHAFT

MB998776

OIL PAN
REPLACE

1. Drain engine oil, then remove dipstick.
2. Remove front exhaust pipe, then the bell housing cover.
3. Remove oil pan using oil pan removal tool No. MD998727, or equivalent.
4. Reverse procedure to install, noting the following:
   a. Apply sealant part No. MD970389, or equivalent, around gasket surface of oil pan.
   b. Install oil pan within 15 minutes of applying sealant.
   c. Allow sealant to dry at least one hour before starting engine.

OIL PUMP
REPLACE

1. Remove oil filter, then the oil pressure switch.
2. Remove oil pan as outlined in "Oil Pan, Replace."
3. Remove oil screen, then the oil screen gasket.
4. Remove plug on front case using plug wrench tool No. MD998162 and plug wrench retainer tool No. MD998783, or equivalents.
5. Remove plug on side of cylinder block.
6. Insert a suitable screw driver to lock counterbalance shaft, then remove flange bolt.
7. Remove relief plug, gasket, relief spring and the plunger.
8. Remove oil filter bracket, then the gasket.
9. Remove oil pump front case assembly.
10. Remove oil pump cover.

11. Remove oil pump driven gear, then the drive gear and crankshaft front oil seal.
12. Remove oil pump oil seal and counterbalance shaft oil seal, then the front case.
13. Remove righthand and lefthand counterbalance shafts.
14. Remove counterbalance shaft front bearing using bearing puller tool No. MD998371, or equivalent.
15. Remove righthand and lefthand rear counterbalance shaft bearings.
16. Reverse procedure to install, noting the following:
   a. Install righthand rear counterbalance shaft bearing ensuring oil holes are aligned, using bearing installer tool No. MD998705, or equivalent.
   b. Install lefthand rear counterbalance shaft bearing using bearing installer stopper tool No. MB991603, or equivalent installed on cylinder block.
   c. Install front counterbalance shaft bearing using bearing installer tool No. MD998705, or equivalent, ensuring oil holes are aligned.
   d. Install crankshaft front oil seal using oil seal installer tool No. MD998375, or equivalent.
   e. Ensure oil pump gear marks are aligned, **Fig. 15.**
   f. Install oil pump case assembly using crankshaft front oil seal guide tool No. MD998285, or equivalent set on front end of crankshaft.

OIL PUMP SERVICE

1. Ensure oil pump gears rotate smoothly with no looseness.
2. Inspect for ridge wear on contact surface between front case and gear surface of oil pump cover.
3. Inspect gear side clearance. Clearance should be .004–.006 inch for drive gear and .003–.004 inch for driven gear.

BELT TENSION DATA

Apply 22 lbs., of force to middle of belt between alternator pulley and water pump pulley. Deflection should be .26–.35 inch.

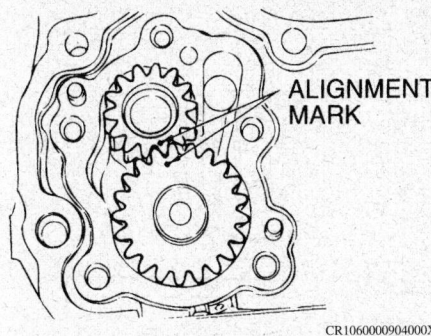

Fig. 15 Oil pump gear alignment marks

COOLING SYSTEM BLEED

Start and run engine until it reaches operating temperature. Accelerate engine repeatedly to 3000 RPM. After engine has cooled down remove radiator cap and fill to top.

THERMOSTAT
REPLACE

1. Drain coolant into suitable container.
2. Remove air cleaner assembly.
3. Disconnect lower radiator hose, then the water inlet fitting.
4. Remove thermostat.
5. Reverse procedure to install. Install thermostat with jiggle valve facing straight up.

WATER PUMP
REPLACE

1. Drain coolant into suitable container.
2. Remove timing belt tensioner as outlined in "Timing Belt, Replace."
3. Remove alternator brace as outlined in "Alternator, Replace" in the "Electrical" section.
4. Remove water pump assembly.
5. Reverse procedure to install.

RADIATOR
REPLACE

1. Drain coolant into suitable container, then disconnect radiator hoses.
2. Remove reserve tank assembly.
3. **On models equipped with automatic transaxles,** disconnect transaxle cooler lines.
4. **On all models,** remove radiator supports, then the radiator.
5. Remove radiator fan motor assembly.
6. Reverse procedure to install.

FUEL PUMP
REPLACE

1. Remove rear seat cushion, then the access plate.
2. Relieve fuel pressure as outlined in "Precautions."
3. Disconnect fuel hose and electrical connector.
4. Remove fuel pump module using tank cap wrench tool No. MB991480, or equivalent.

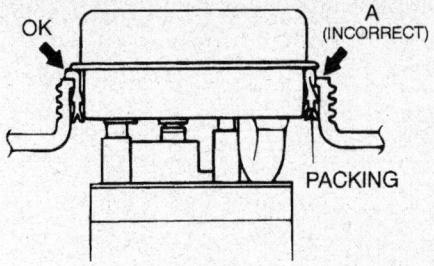

Fig. 16 Fuel pump packing installation

5. Reverse procedure to install, noting the following:
   a. Install packing to fuel tank **Fig. 16,** then install fuel pump module.
   b. Align mating mark on fuel pump module with mark on fuel tank.
   c. Tighten to specifications.

FUEL FILTER
REPLACE

1. Remove fuel pump as outlined in "Fuel Pump, Replace."
2. Remove thermistor case, then the fuel gage unit.
3. Remove packing, then the reservoir cup.
4. Remove pump support assembly.
5. Remove electrical harness, then the lock bracket.
6. Remove fuel pump, then the fuel filter.
7. Reverse procedure to install.

TIGHTENING SPECIFICATIONS

Year	Component	Torque Ft. Lbs.
2001–05	Auto-Tensioner Attaching Bolt	14–20
	Camshaft Position Sensor	10–11
	Camshaft Sprocket	58–72
	Connecting Rod Bearing Cap	③
	Crankshaft Pulley	14–22
	Crankshaft Sprocket	⑤
	Cylinder Head	②
	Drive Plate	94–102
	Engine Mount (M12x74)	56–74
	Engine Mount (M12x108)	51–69
	Engine Mount Bracket	56–72
	Exhaust Manifold	20–24
	Exhaust Manifold Bracket	22–30
	Flywheel (Manual Trans.)	95–101
	Front Case	15–19
	Ignition Coil Bolt	70–104①
	Intake Manifold Bolt	44–52①
	Intake Manifold Nut	12–16
	Intake Manifold Stay	21–23
	Main Bearing Cap	④
	Oil Filter Bracket	12–16
	Oil Pan	53–69①
	Oil Pan Drain Plug	25–33
	Oil Pump Cover	11–13
	Power Steering Pump	29–43
	Rocker Arm Shaft	21–25
	Rocker Cover	27–35
	Timing Belt Lower Cover	88–104①
	Timing Belt Tensioner	12–16
	Timing Belt Upper Cover	114–120①
	Water Pump Pulley	69–77

① — Inch lbs.
② — Refer to "Cylinder Head Replace" for tightening procedures & specifications.
③ — Refer to "Piston & Rod Assembly" for tightening procedure & specifications.
④ — Refer to "Main & Rod Bearings" for tightening procedure & specifications.
⑤ — 2001–2004 80–94 ft. lbs.; 2005 123 ft. lbs.

NOTE: On Air Bag Equipped Models, Refer To "Air Bag System Precautions" Located In The Front Of This Manual For System Disarming & Arming Procedures.

NOTE: Refer To "Computer Relearn Procedures" Located In The Front Of This Manual When Battery Power To The Computer Has Been Interrupted.

PRECAUTIONS

Air Bag Systems

Refer to "Air Bag System Precautions" in the front of this manual for system disarming and arming procedures.

Battery Ground Cable

Prior to service, disconnect battery ground cable and isolate as required.

Fuel System Pressure Relief

1. Remove fuel pump relay.
2. Start engine and let it run until it stops naturally, then turn ignition to off position.
3. Reconnect fuel pump relay.

COMPRESSION PRESSURE

Perform compression pressure inspection with throttle valve wide open and crankshaft position sensor disconnected. Standard compression pressure is 119 psi at cranking speed. The minimum pressure is 83 psi with a maximum variance between cylinders of 14 psi.

ENGINE MOUNT

REPLACE

1. Place a suitable jack under engine, then raise jack enough to remove weight from engine mount.
2. Remove coolant reserve tank, then the suction hose, **Fig. 1.**
3. Remove insulator mounting bolt, then the mount bracket, **Fig. 1.**
4. Remove engine mount stopper, then the dynamic damper, **Fig. 2.**
5. Reverse procedure to install.

ENGINE

REPLACE

1. Remove hood, then drain coolant into suitable container.
2. Release fuel pressure as outlined in "Precautions."
3. Remove strut tower brace, then the air cleaner assembly.
4. Remove radiator reserve tank, then the front exhaust pipe.
5. Disconnect accelerator cable.
6. Disconnect engine wiring harness electrical connections.
7. Disconnect high-pressure fuel hose, then the return hose.
8. Disconnect heater hoses.
9. Remove drive belts.
10. Remove A/C compressor with lines attached, then position aside.
11. Remove power steering pump with hose attached, then position aside.
12. Remove engine mount stay.
13. Remove transaxle as outlined in **MOTOR's "Domestic Transmission, In-Vehicle Service"** manual.
14. Remove engine mount bracket, then the stopper.
15. Remove engine assembly.
16. Reverse procedure to install.

INTAKE MANIFOLD

REPLACE

1. Release fuel pressure as outlined in "Precautions."
2. Drain engine coolant into suitable container.
3. Remove air cleaner assembly, then the throttle body.
4. Remove strut tower brace.
5. Disconnect engine wiring harness electrical connections.
6. Disconnect brake booster vacuum hose connection.
7. Remove EGR valve, then the pipe connection.
8. Remove power steering pump drive belt.
9. Remove power steering pump bracket stay.
10. Remove intake manifold plenum as outlined under "Intake Manifold Plenum, Replace."
11. Disconnect high-pressure fuel hose, then the return hose.
12. Remove fuel rail, then the fuel pressure regulator.
13. Remove timing belt lefthand and righthand and upper covers.
14. Remove intake manifold.
15. Reverse procedure to install, noting the following:
    a. Install intake gasket, **Fig. 3.**
    b. Tighten intake bolts to specification using sequence, **Fig. 4.**

INTAKE MANIFOLD PLENUM

REPLACE

1. Disconnect engine wiring harness

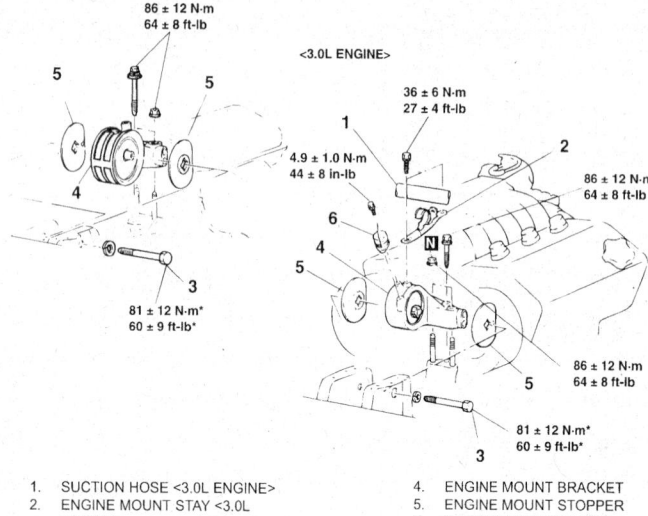

<3.0L ENGINE>

86 ± 12 N·m
64 ± 8 ft-lb

36 ± 6 N·m
27 ± 4 ft-lb

4.9 ± 1.0 N·m
44 ± 8 in-lb

86 ± 12 N·m
64 ± 8 ft-lb

81 ± 12 N·m*
60 ± 9 ft-lb*

86 ± 12 N·m
64 ± 8 ft-lb

81 ± 12 N·m*
60 ± 9 ft-lb*

1. SUCTION HOSE <3.0L ENGINE>
2. ENGINE MOUNT STAY <3.0L ENGINE>
3. ENGINE MOUNT INSULATOR MOUNTING BOLT
4. ENGINE MOUNT BRACKET
5. ENGINE MOUNT STOPPER
6. DYNAMIC DAMPER <3.0L ENGINE>

ARM0400000000322

Fig. 1   Engine mount replacement

ENGINE SIDE ➡

DYNAMIC DAMPER

ARROW

ENGINE MOUNT STOPPER

ENGINE MOUNT BRACKET

CR1060000907000X

Fig. 2   Engine mount stopper replacement

ORDER	MOUNTING NUTS	TIGHTENING TORQUE
1st	Right-bank nuts	6.4 ± 1.4 N·m (56 ± 13 in-lb)
2nd	Left-bank nuts	22 ± 1 N·m (16 ± 1 ft-lb)
3rd	Right-bank nuts	22 ± 1 N·m (16 ± 1 ft-lb)
4th	Left-bank nuts	22 ± 1 N·m (16 ± 1 ft-lb)
5th	Right-bank nuts	22 ± 1 N·m (16 ± 1 ft-lb)

CR1060000909000X

Fig. 4   Intake manifold bolt tightening sequence (Part 2 of 2)

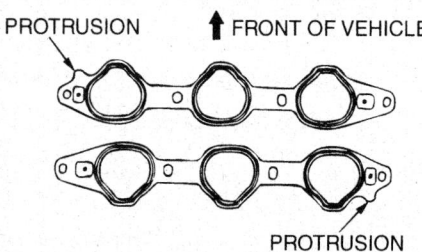

PROTRUSION   ⬆ FRONT OF VEHICLE

PROTRUSION

CR1060000908000X

Fig. 3   Intake manifold gasket installation

⬅ RIGHT BANK

⬅ LEFT BANK

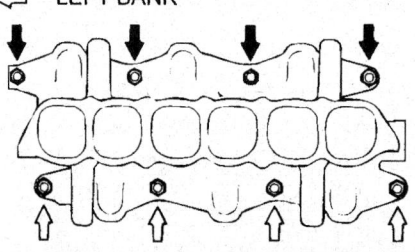

ARM0400000000324

Fig. 4   Intake manifold bolt tightening sequence (Part 1 of 2)

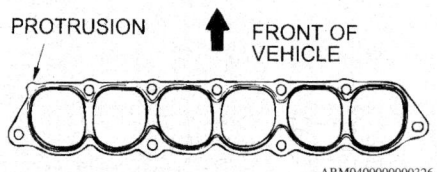

PROTRUSION   ⬆ FRONT OF VEHICLE

ARM0400000000326

Fig. 5   Intake manifold plenum gasket installation

electrical connectors.
2. Disconnect engine vacuum connectors.
3. Remove EGR Valve, then EGR pipe connection.
4. Remove drive belts, then the power steering bracket.
5. Remove front and rear intake manifold plenum stays.
6. Remove engine mount stay, then the intake manifold plenum.
7. Reverse procedure to install noting the following:
   a. Install Intake plenum gasket as shown, **Fig. 5.**
   b. Tighten all nuts and bolts to specifications.

EXHAUST MANIFOLD
REPLACE

1. Remove front exhaust pipe.
2. Remove air cleaner assembly, then the battery and battery tray.
3. Remove engine oil dipstick guide, then the strut tower brace.
4. Remove lefthand bank manifold upper and lower heat shields.
5. Remove lefthand exhaust manifold, then the EGR pipe.
6. Remove righthand bank manifold upper and lower heat shields.
7. Remove righthand exhaust manifold.

8. Reverse procedure to install.

CYLINDER HEAD
REPLACE

1. Drain engine coolant into suitable container.
2. Remove timing belt as outlined in "Timing Belt, Replace."
3. Remove alternator, then the intake manifold as outlined in "Intake Manifold, Replace."
4. Remove exhaust manifold as outlined in "Exhaust Manifold, Replace."
5. Remove water inlet pipe.
6. Remove valve cover blow by hose, then the breather hose.
7. Remove PCV hose, then the spark plug wires.
8. Remove valve covers, then the timing belt rear cover.
9. Loosen cylinder head bolts using cylinder head bolt wrench tool No. MD998051, or equivalent, in two or three steps in sequence, **Fig. 6.**
10. Reverse procedure to install, noting the following:
    a. Install cylinder head bolt washers with rounded shoulder facing up.
    b. **Torque** cylinder head bolts in two or

three steps to 77– 83 ft. lbs., using sequence, **Fig. 7.**
c. Loosen bolts in sequence, **Fig. 6.**
d. **Torque** cylinder head bolts in two or three steps to 77– 83 ft. lbs., using sequence, **Fig. 7.**

ROCKER ARMS
REPLACE

1. Remove intake manifold as outlined in "Intake Manifold, Replace."
2. Remove breather hose, then the PCV valve from valve cover.
3. Remove valve cover.
4. Remove rocker arm shaft cap.
5. Install lash adjuster holder tool No. MD998713, or equivalent, to prevent lash adjuster from coming free.
6. Remove rocker arms and shaft.
7. Reverse procedure to install, noting the following:
   a. Rotate camshaft until dowel pin on front end is located as outlined, **Fig. 8.**
   b. Ensure notch in end of rocker arm shaft is facing in direction outlined, **Fig. 9.**

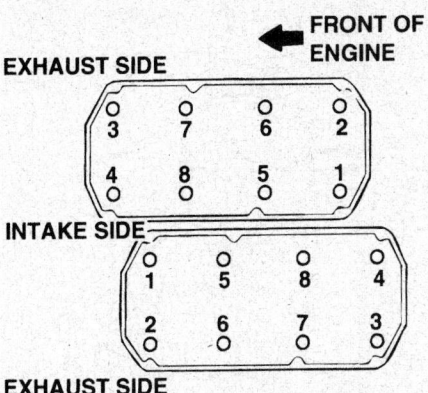

Fig. 6 Cylinder head bolt loosening sequence

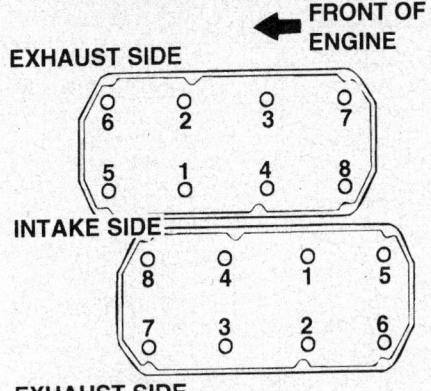

Fig. 7 Cylinder head bolt tightening sequence

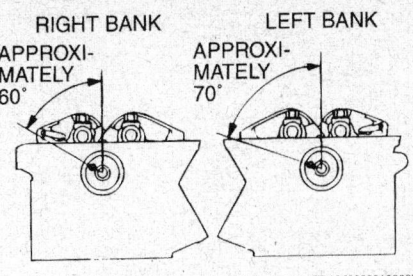

Fig. 8 Camshaft alignment

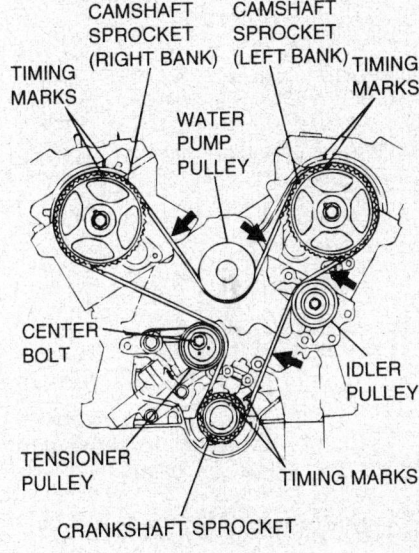

Fig. 10 Timing belt alignment marks

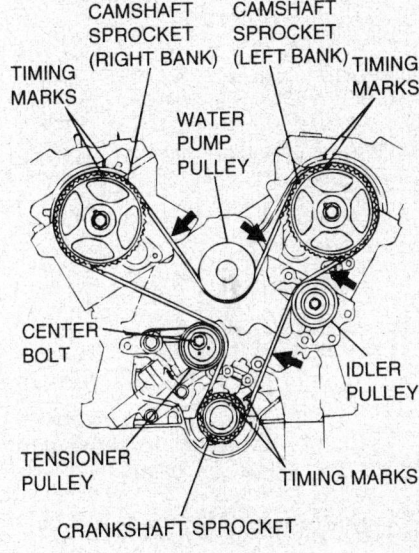

Fig. 9 Rocker arm shaft notch position

FRONT COVER

REPLACE

1. Remove power steering pump drive belt.
2. Remove crankshaft pulley using end yoke holder tool No. MB990767 and crankshaft pulley holder pin tool No. MD998715, or equivalents.
3. Remove power steering pump tensioner pulley.
4. Remove righthand and lefthand timing belt upper covers.
5. Remove timing belt lower cover.
6. Reverse procedure to install.

TIMING BELT

REPLACE

Removal

1. Remove alternator, then the engine mount as outlined in "Engine Mount, Replace."
2. Remove timing belt cover as outlined in "Front Cover, Replace."
3. Remove righthand side engine support bracket.
4. Turn crankshaft clockwise to align each timing mark, then set No. 1 cylinder at TDC on compression stroke, **Fig. 10.**
5. If reusing timing belt, chalk an arrow on flat side of belt to indicate clockwise direction.
6. Loosen center bolt of tensioner pulley, then remove timing belt.

7. Remove auto tensioner.

Installation

1. Align timing marks on camshaft sprockets with marks on rocker covers, then the timing mark on crankshaft with mark on engine block, **Fig. 10.**
2. Install timing belt in the following order:
   a. Crankshaft sprocket.
   b. Idler pulley.
   c. Lefthand bank camshaft sprocket.
   d. Water pump pulley.
   e. Righthand bank camshaft sprocket.
   f. Tensioner pulley.
3. Turn righthand bank camshaft sprocket counterclockwise until tension side of timing belt is firmly stretched, then inspect timing marks.
4. Push tensioner pulley into timing belt and temporarily tighten center bolt using tensioner wrench tool No. MD998767, or equivalent.
5. Turn crankshaft ¼ turn counterclockwise, then turn clockwise until timing marks are aligned using crankshaft pulley spacer tool No. MD998769, or equivalent.
6. Loosen center bolt of tensioner pulley.
7. Apply 39 inch lbs., of tension torque to timing belt using tensioner wrench tool No. MD998767, or equivalent and suitable torque wrench, **Fig. 11.** Tighten center bolt to specifications.
8. Place two wooden blocks in a suitable vise, then place auto-tensioner perpendicular between blocks. If there is a plug at base of tensioner, insert a washer to protect plug.
9. Slowly compress pushrod of auto-tensioner until pin hole (A) in pushrod is aligned with pin hole (B) in cylinder, then insert a suitable pin into holes, **Fig. 12.**
10. Install auto-tensioner on engine, then remove pin.
11. Turn crankshaft clockwise twice to align timing marks.
12. Wait at least five minutes, then inspect that auto-tensioner push rod extends .15–.20 inch. If not repeat steps 5 through 11.
13. Install engine support bracket, tighten

bolts in sequence, **Fig. 13,** to specifications.
14. Install timing belt cover as outlined in "Front Cover, Replace."

CAMSHAFT

REPLACE

Lefthand Bank

1. Remove timing belt as outlined in "Timing Belt, Replace."
2. Remove thermostat housing assembly.
3. Disconnect blow by hose, then the PCV hose from valve cover.
4. Remove spark plug wires, then the valve cover.
5. Remove rocker arm and shaft assembly as outlined in "Rocker Arms, Replace."
6. Remove camshaft sprocket using end yoke holder tool No. MB990767 and crankshaft pulley holder pin tool No. MD998715, or equivalents.
7. Remove thrust plate, then the camshaft.
8. Reverse procedure to install.

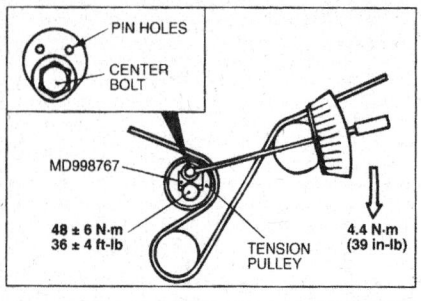

Fig. 11 Timing belt tension torque

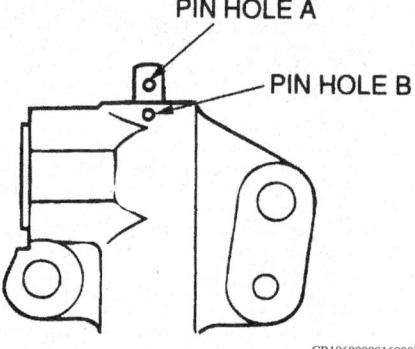

Fig. 12 Auto-tensioner pin hole alignment

CRANKSHAFT JOURNAL OUTSIDE DIAMETER		CYLINDER BLOCK BEARING BORE	CRANK-SHAFT BEARING
ID COLOR	SIZE mm (inch)	ID MARK	ID COLOR
Yellow	59.990 - 59.996 (2.3618 - 2.3620)	I	Pink
		II	Red
		III	Green
None	59.984 - 59.990 (2.3616 - 2.3618)	I	Red
		II	Green
		III	Black
White	59.978 - 59.984 (2.3613 - 2.3616)	I	Green
		II	Black
		III	Brown

Fig. 14 Crankshaft bearing selection chart

Righthand Bank

1. Remove timing belt as outlined in "Timing Belt, Replace."
2. Remove intake plenum as outlined in "Intake Manifold, Replace."
3. Disconnect breather hose, then the blow by hose from valve cover.
4. Remove spark plug wires, then the valve cover.
5. Remove rocker arms and shaft assembly as outlined in "Rocker Arms, Replace."
6. Remove distributor assembly.
7. Remove camshaft sprocket using end yoke holder tool No. MB990767 and crankshaft pulley holder pin tool No. MD998715, or equivalents.
8. Remove camshaft.
9. Reverse procedure to install, noting the following:
   a. Align timing mark on camshaft sprocket with mark on cylinder head.
   b. Align mating marks on distributor housing and coupling.

MAIN & ROD BEARINGS

If bearing replacement is required, measure crankshaft journal diameter and select correct bearing from chart, **Fig. 14.**

Cylinder block bearing bore diameter identification marks are stamped on block, **Fig. 15.**

Install bearing cap with arrow facing timing belt side, then **torque** bolts is sequence **Fig. 16,** to 65–73 ft. lbs.

CRANKSHAFT SEAL
REPLACE
Front

1. Remove timing belt as outlined in "Timing Belt, Replace."
2. Remove crankshaft position sensor, then the sensing blade.
3. Remove crankshaft spacer and key.
4. Remove crankshaft front oil seal.
5. Reverse procedure to install, noting the following:
   a. Apply a small amount of engine oil to seal lip before installing.
   b. Tap oil seal into front case using crankshaft front oil seal installer tool No. MD998717, or equivalent.

CRANKSHAFT REAR OIL SEAL
REPLACE

1. Remove transaxle as outlined in **MOTOR's "Domestic Transmission, In-Vehicle Service"** manual.
2. Remove flywheel or drive plate.
3. Remove rear oil seal.
4. Reverse procedure to install, noting the following:
   a. Apply a small amount of engine oil to seal lip before installing.
   b. Tap in rear oil seal using crankshaft rear seal installer tool No. MD998718, or equivalent.

OIL PAN
REPLACE

1. Drain engine oil into suitable container, then remove front exhaust pipe.
2. Remove lower oil pan bolts, then the lower oil pan.
3. Disconnect starter motor connector, then remove starter motor.
4. Remove oil dipstick, then the dipstick guide.
5. Remove upper oil pan bolts, then insert two M10 bolts into bolt holes and separate upper oil pan from cylinder block, **Fig. 17.**
6. Reverse procedure to install, noting the following:
   a. Tighten upper oil pan bolts to specifications using sequence, **Fig. 18.**

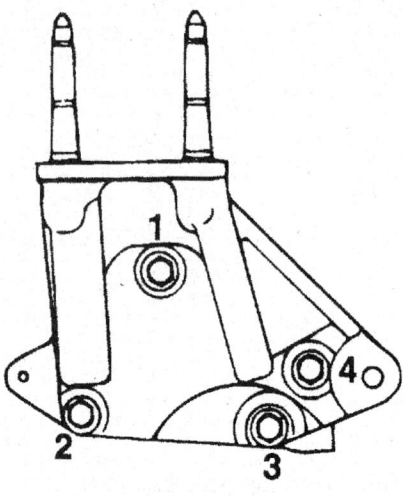

Fig. 13 Engine support bracket tightening sequence

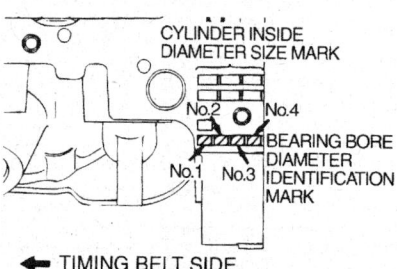

Fig. 15 Block bearing bore identification location

   b. Tighten upper oil pan bolts to specifications using sequence, **Fig. 19.**

OIL PUMP
REPLACE

1. Remove oil pressure switch.
2. Remove oil filter, then the oil filter bracket.
3. Remove oil pan as outlined in "Oil Pan, Replace."
4. Remove lower baffle plate, then the oil screen.
5. Remove upper baffle plate, then the plug.
6. Remove relief spring, then the relief plunger.
7. Remove crankshaft front oil seal as outlined in "Crankshaft Oil Seal, Replace."
8. Remove oil pump case assembly.
9. Reverse procedure to install.

OIL PUMP SERVICE
Disassemble

1. Remove oil pump cover.
2. Scribe alignment marks on outer and inner rotors for assembly reference.
3. Remove outer and inner rotors.

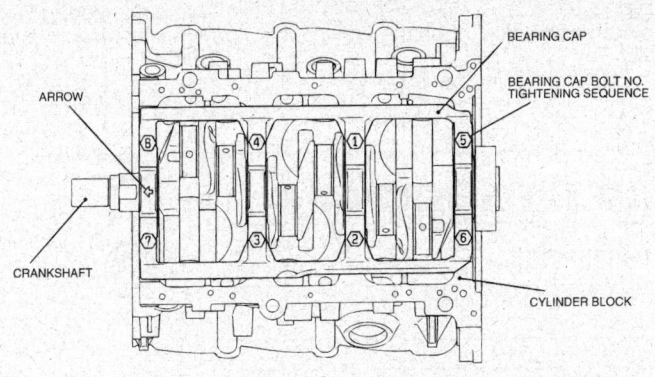

Fig. 16 Bearing cap bolt tightening sequence

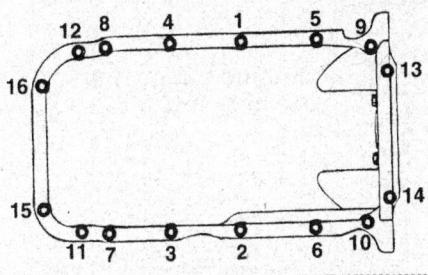

Fig. 18 Upper oil pan tightening sequence

ITEMS	WHEN CHECKED	DURING ADJUSTMENT	DURING REPLACEMENT
Vibration frequency Hz	125 - 154	133 - 148	160 - 183
Tension N (lb)	373 - 569 (84 - 128)	422 - 520 (95 - 117)	608 - 804 (137 - 181)
Deflection (Reference value) mm (in)	11.0 - 14.2 (0.43 - 0.56)	11.7 - 13.4 (0.46 - 0.53)	8.4 - 9.3 (0.33 - 0.37)

CR1060000922000X

Fig. 21 Power steering pump belt tension chart

Inspection

Refer to "Engine Rebuilding Specifications."

Assemble

1. Apply engine oil to rotors.
2. Align marks, then install rotors.

BELT TENSION DATA

Refer **Figs. 20 and 21,** to for belt tension data.

SERPENTINE DRIVE BELT

1. Loosen tensioner pulley fixing nut, then remove belt.
2. Install belt and **torque** fixing bolt temporarily to 11 ft. lbs., then adjust belt tension using adjusting bolt.

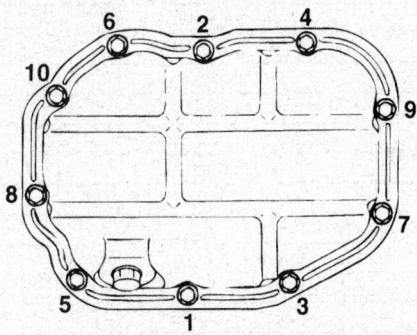

Fig. 19 Lower oil pan tightening sequence

COOLING SYSTEM BLEED

Start engine and bring to operating temperature. Rev engine repeatedly to 3000 RPM. After engine has cooled down remove radiator cap and fill to top of radiator.

THERMOSTAT
REPLACE

1. Drain engine coolant into suitable container.
2. Remove air cleaner assembly, then the lower radiator hose.
3. Remove thermostat housing, then the thermostat.
4. Reverse procedure to install. Ensure jiggle valve on thermostat is facing up.

WATER PUMP
REPLACE

1. Drain engine coolant into suitable container.
2. Remove timing belt as outlined in "Timing Belt, Replace."
3. Remove thermostat as outlined in "Thermostat, Replace."
4. Remove water pump assembly.
5. Reverse procedure to install.

RADIATOR
REPLACE

1. Drain engine coolant into suitable container.

Fig. 17 Upper oil pan removal

ITEMS	DURING ADJUSTMENT	DURING REPLACEMENT
Vibration frequency Hz	141 - 153	170 - 190
Tension N (lb)	539 - 637 (121 - 143)	785 - 981 (176 - 221)
Deflection (Reference value) mm (in)	9.0 - 10.1 (0.35 - 0.40)	6.2 - 7.6 (0.24 - 0.30)

CR1060000921000X

Fig. 20 Alternator & A/C compressor belt tension chart

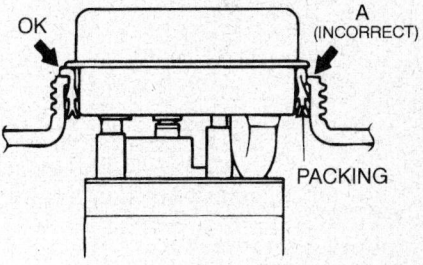

Fig. 22 Fuel pump packing installation

2. Disconnect reserve tank hose, then remove reserve tank.
3. Remove upper and lower radiator hoses.
4. **On models equipped with automatic transaxle,** disconnect oil cooler lines.
5. **On all models,** remove radiator supports.
6. Remove radiator, then the fan motor assembly.
7. Reverse procedure to install.

FUEL PUMP
REPLACE

1. Remove rear seat cushion, then the access plate.
2. Relieve fuel pressure as outlined in "Precautions."
3. Disconnect fuel hose and electrical connector.
4. Remove fuel pump module using tank cap wrench tool No. MB991480, or equivalent.
5. Reverse procedure to install, noting the following:
   a. Install packing to fuel tank and fuel pump module, **Fig. 22.**
   b. Align mating mark on fuel pump module with mark on fuel tank.

FUEL FILTER
REPLACE

1. Remove fuel pump as outlined in "Fuel Pump, Replace."
2. Remove thermistor case, then the fuel gage unit.
3. Remove packing, then the reservoir cup.
4. Remove pump support assembly.
5. Remove electrical harness, then the lock bracket.
6. Remove fuel pump, then the fuel filter.
7. Reverse procedure to install.

TIGHTENING SPECIFICATIONS

Year	Component	Torque Ft. Lbs.
2001–05	Alternator & A/C Compressor Belt Tensioner	29–43
	Camshaft Sprocket	58–73
	Connecting Rod Bearing Cap	37–39
	Crankshaft Bearing Cap	③
	Crankshaft Pulley	131–137
	Cylinder Head	②
	EGR Valve Bolt	12–14
	Engine Mount	51–69
	Engine Mount Bracket	58–72
	Engine Support Bracket	30–36
	Exhaust Manifold	30–36
	Intake Manifold Nuts	15–17
	Intake Manifold Plenum Nut & Bolts	12–14
	Intake Manifold Plenum Stay Bolts	④
	Oil Pan (Lower)	88–104①
	Oil Pan (Upper)	43–51①
	Oil Pump Case (M8 Bolt)	113–130①
	Oil Pump Case (M10 Bolt)	24–36
	Power Steering Pump Belt Tensioner	26–40
	Rocker Arm Shaft	21–25
	Thermostat Housing	100–130①
	Timing Belt Cover	88–104①
	Timing Belt Tensioner Pulley	32–40
	Valve Cover	27–35①
	Water Pump	14–20

① — Inch Lbs.
② — Refer to "Cylinder Head, Replace" for tightening procedures & specifications.
③ — Refer to "Main & Rod Bearings" for tightening procedures & specifications.
④ — M8 bolts, 12–14 ft. lbs.; M10 bolts, 22–30 ft. lbs.

Rear Suspension

NOTE: On Air Bag Equipped Models, Refer To "Air Bag System Precautions" Located In The Front Of This Manual For System Disarming & Arming Procedures.

NOTE: Refer To "Computer Relearn Procedures" Located In The Front Of This Manual When Battery Power To The Computer Has Been Interrupted.

NOTE: Prior To Performing Any Service Operations Listed In This Section, Consult The "Technical Service Bulletins" Section For Related Information.

INDEX

DESCRIPTION

The rear suspension is a modified double-wishbone design with coil springs and direct acting shock absorbers, **Fig. 1.** The rear axle consists of a knuckle, rear hub, unit bearing and axle shaft. The unit bearing is press-fitted to the rear axle shaft and bolted to the knuckle. On models equipped with Anti-Lock Brakes ABS, a rotor for detecting vehicle speed is located on the axle shaft and a speed sensor is located on the knuckle.

HUB & BEARING
REPLACE

1. Raise and support vehicle, then remove wheel and tire assembly.
2. **On models equipped with anti-lock brakes,** remove rear speed sensor.
3. **On models equipped with rear disc brakes,** remove brake caliper assembly and the disc, suspend brake caliper aside, **Fig. 2.**
4. **On models equipped with drum brakes,** remove brake drum and shoe.
5. **On all models,** remove rear hub and anti-lock brake rotor.
6. Reverse procedure to install.

SHOCK ABSORBER
REPLACE

1. Remove shock absorber cap.
2. Remove flange nuts under cap.
3. Remove shock absorber lower bolt and the shock absorber.
4. Reverse procedure to install.

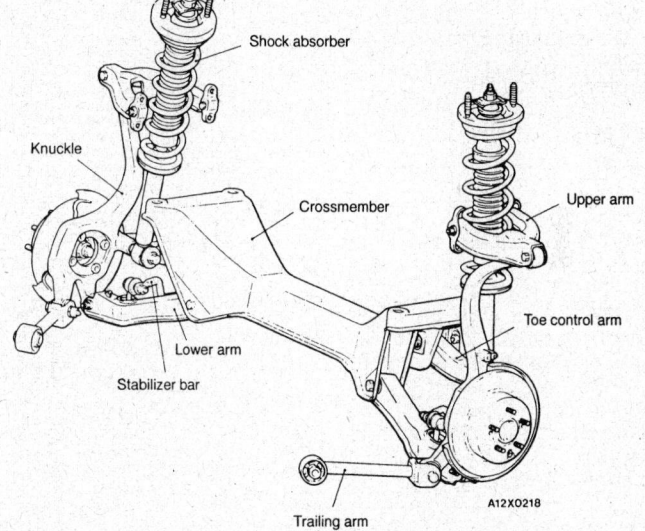

Fig. 1   Rear suspension

COIL SPRING
REPLACE

Disassemble as outlined, **Fig. 3.** Compress coil spring using compressor tool Nos. MB991237 and MB991239, or equivalents.

CONTROL ARM
REPLACE
Upper

1. Raise and support vehicle.
2. Remove upper arm to knuckle attaching bolt, **Fig. 4.**
3. Remove upper arm mounting bolt, then the upper arm assembly and bracket.
4. Reverse procedure to install.

Lower

1. Raise and support vehicle.
2. Remove stabilizer link, **Fig. 5.**
3. **On models equipped with anti-lock brakes,** remove wheel speed sensor clamp bolts.
4. **On all models,** remove lower arm assembly and knuckle connecting bolt.

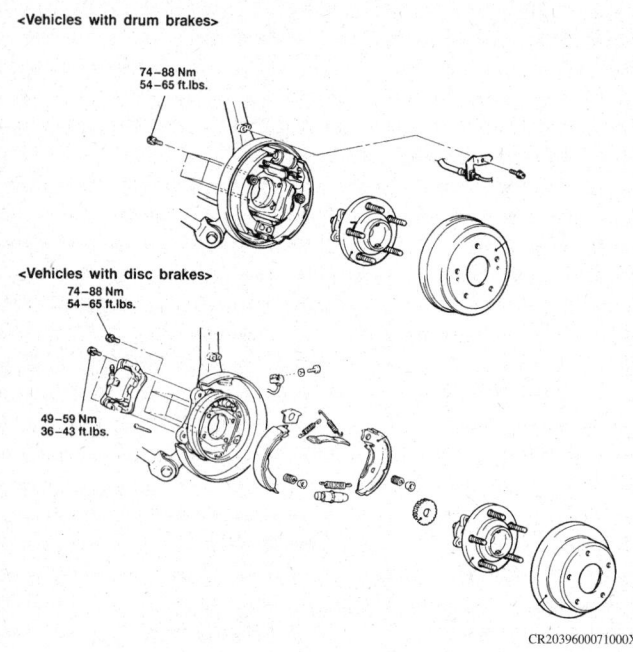

Fig. 2   Rear hub removal

5. Remove lower arm mounting bolt.
6. Disconnect toe control arm ball joint from knuckle.
7. Remove toe control arm mounting bolt.
8. Remove toe control arm assembly.
9. Reverse procedure to install.

KNUCKLE
REPLACE

1. Raise and support vehicle.
2. Remove rear hub as outlined in "Hub & Bearing, Replace."
3. Remove trailing arm, **Fig. 6.**
4. Remove lower arm and toe control arm. Loosen nut but do not remove.
5. Remove shock absorber and upper arm.
6. Remove knuckle.
7. **On models less anti-lock brakes,** remove hub cap.
8. **On all models,** reverse procedure to install.

TRAILING ARM
REPLACE

1. Raise and support vehicle.
2. Remove knuckle and trailing arm assembly attaching bolt.
3. Remove grommet.
4. Remove trailing arm assembly mounting bolt, then the stopper and trailing arm.
5. Reverse procedure to install.

STABILIZER BAR
REPLACE

1. Raise and support vehicle.
2. Remove stabilizer link mounting nuts.
3. Remove stabilizer link.
4. Remove stabilizer bar brackets and bushings.

5. Remove stabilizer bar.
6. Reverse procedure to install.

TECHNICAL SERVICE BULLETINS

Squeaking Or Hard Rubbing

2001

On these models there may be a squeaking or hard rubbing noise on bumps.
This condition may be caused by low lubricant in stopper bushings or the bushings

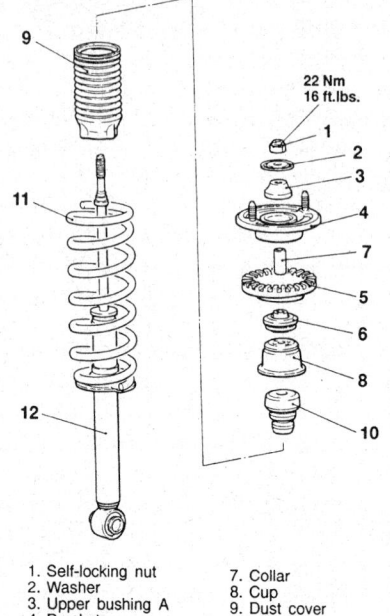

1. Self-locking nut
2. Washer
3. Upper bushing A
4. Bracket
5. Spring pad
6. Upper bushing B
7. Collar
8. Cup
9. Dust cover
10. Bump rubber
11. Coil spring
12. Shock absorber assembly

Fig. 3   Coil spring replacement

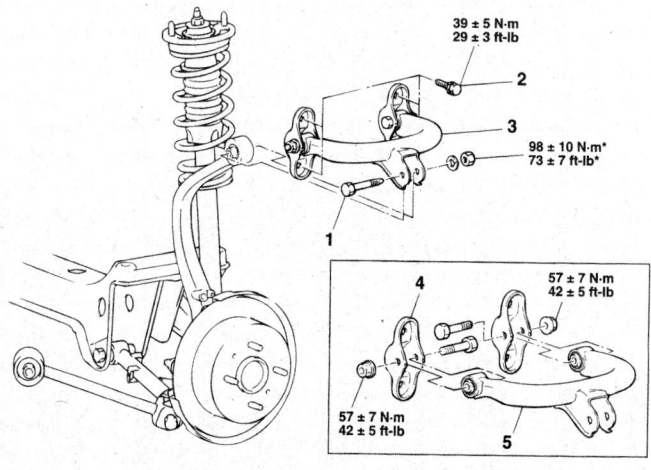

1. UPPER ARM AND KNUCKLE CONNECTING BOLT
2. UPPER ARM ASSEMBLY MOUNTING BOLTS
3. UPPER ARM ASSEMBLY
4. UPPER ARM BRACKET
5. UPPER ARM

Fig. 4   Upper control arm replacement

rubbing against the body bracket. To correct this condition proceed as follows:

1. Remove trailing arm as outlined in "Trailing Arm, Replace."
2. Place trailing arm on bench, mark original position of stoppers for reassembly.
3. Remove stopper and trim surface, **Fig. 7.**
4. Reverse procedure to install noting the following:
   a. Lubricate all surfaces of stoppers using Dielectric grease part No. J8126688, or equivalent.
   b. Tighten attaching bolts and nuts to specification.

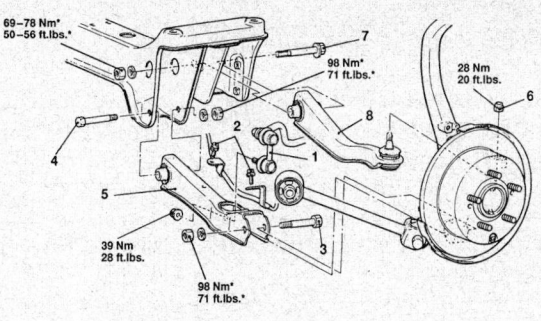

1. Stabilizer link
2. ABS wheel-speed sensor clamp bolts <Vehicles with ABS>
3. Lower arm assembly and knuckle connecting bolt
4. Lower arm assembly mounting bolt
5. Lower arm assembly

6. Toe control arm ball joint and knuckle connection
7. Toe control arm assembly mounting bolt
8. Toe control arm assembly

Caution
* : Indicates parts which should be temporarily tightened, and then fully tightened with the vehicles on the ground in the unladen condition.

CR2039600074000X

Fig. 5 Lower arm & toe control arm removal

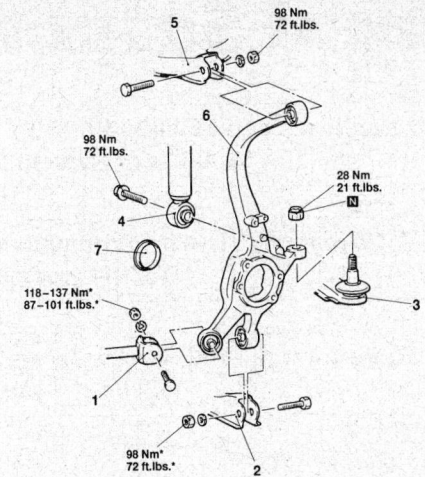

1. Trailing arm connection
2. Lower arm connection
3. Toe control arm connection
4. Shock absorber connection
5. Upper arm connection

6. Knuckle
7. Hub cap <Vehicles without ABS>

Caution
*: Indicates parts which should be temporarily tightened, and then fully tightened with the vehicle on the ground in the unladen condition.

CR2039600072000X

Fig. 6 Knuckle replacement

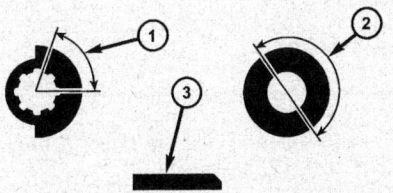

1 - Bevel Edge Of Outer Stopper - 1 to 3 O'clock Position

2 - Bevel Edge Of Inner Stopper - 11 to 5 O'clock Position

3 - Bevel Outer Edge (Away From Trailing Arm)

CR2030100109000X

Fig. 7 Trailing arm stopper trim angles. 2001

TIGHTENING SPECIFICATIONS

Year	Component	Torque/Ft. Lbs.
2001–05	Brake Hose Connection	11
	Caliper Mounting Bolts	36–43
	Crossmember Mounting Self-Locking Nuts	64
	Lower Arm & Knuckle Connecting Nut	71
	Lower Arm Mounting Nuts	71
	Shock Absorber Lower Bolt	72
	Shock Absorber Upper Flange Bolts	32
	Shock Tower Self-Locking Nut	16
	Stabilizer Bar Bracket Bolts	7–10
	Stabilizer Link Mounting Nuts	28
	Toe Control Arm Ball Joint & Knuckle Attaching Nut	20
	Trailing Arm Attaching Nut	87–101
	Trailing Arm Mounting Bolt	99–114
	Upper Arm Assembly Mounting Bolt	28
	Upper Arm Bracket Nuts	41
	Upper Arm & Knuckle Attaching Bolt	72
	Wheel Lug Nuts	87–101

NOTE: On Air Bag Equipped Models, Refer To "Air Bag System Precautions" Located In The Front Of This Manual For System Disarming & Arming Procedures.

NOTE: Refer To "Computer Relearn Procedures" Located In The Front Of This Manual When Battery Power To The Computer Has Been Interrupted.

NOTE: Prior To Performing Any Service Operations Listed In This Section, Consult The "Technical Service Bulletins" Section For Related Information.

INDEX

PRECAUTIONS

Air Bag Systems

Refer to "Air Bag System Precautions" in the front of this manual for system disarming and arming procedures.

Battery Ground Cable

Prior to service, disconnect battery ground cable and isolate as required.

HUB & BEARING

REPLACE

1. Raise and support vehicle, then remove tire.
2. **On models equipped with anti-lock brakes,** remove front speed sensor.
3. **On all models,** remove brake caliper assembly and suspend with wire.
4. Remove brake disc.
5. Remove driveshaft nut cotter pin.
6. Remove driveshaft end nut.
7. Remove tie rod and stabilizer link.
8. Disconnect lower arm from steering knuckle.
9. Remove hub assembly.
10. Reverse procedure to install.

DRIVESHAFT

REPLACE

1. **On models equipped with anti-lock brakes,** disconnect front speed sensor.
2. **On all models,** remove brake hose clip and cotter pin.
3. Remove drive shaft nut, **Fig. 1.**
4. Loosen but do not remove ball joint nut

using steering linkage puller tool No. MB991113, or equivalent.
5. Loosen but do not remove tie rod end using steering linkage puller tool No. MB991113, or equivalent.
6. Disconnect stabilizer link.
7. Push driveshaft out from hub using puller body tool No. MB991354, puller bar tool No. MB990242 and yoke holder tool No. MB990767, or equivalents.
8. Insert a suitable pry bar between transaxle case and driveshaft, then remove driveshaft.
9. Reverse procedure to install.

BALL JOINT INSPECTION

Use torque wrench tool No. MB990326, or equivalent, to measure ball joint breakaway torque. Breakaway torque should be as specified in **Fig. 2.**

COIL SPRING

REPLACE

Remove shock absorber as outlined in "Shock Absorber, Replace," then disassemble shock/coil spring unit, **Fig. 3.**

SHOCK ABSORBER

REPLACE

1. Remove stabilizer link mounting nut.
2. Remove shock absorber upper mounting nuts.
3. Raise and support vehicle.
4. Remove shock absorber lower mounting bolt.
5. Remove damper fork mounting bolt and damper fork.
6. Remove shock absorber from vehicle.

7. Reverse procedure to install.

CONTROL ARM

REPLACE

Upper

1. Raise and support vehicle.
2. Disconnect upper arm ball joint from knuckle, **Fig. 4.**
3. Remove self-locking nut, then the upper arm assembly.
4. Remove dust cover.
5. Reverse procedure to install. Install upper arm shaft at angle, **Fig. 5.**

Lower

1. Raise and support vehicle.
2. Disconnect lower ball joint from steering knuckle using ball joint remover/installer tool No. MB990799, or equivalent, **Fig. 6.**
3. Remove lower arm mounting bolt.
4. **On models equipped with 2.4L engine,** remove lower arm clamp, **Fig. 6.**
5. **On all models,** remove lower arm.
6. Reverse procedure to install.

STEERING KNUCKLE

REPLACE

1. Raise and support vehicle.
2. Remove front wheel and tire assembly.
3. **On models equipped with anti-lock brakes,** remove front wheel speed sensor.
4. **On all models,** remove hub assembly as outlined in "Hub & Bearing, Replace."
5. Refer to **Fig. 7,** for steering knuckle removal.

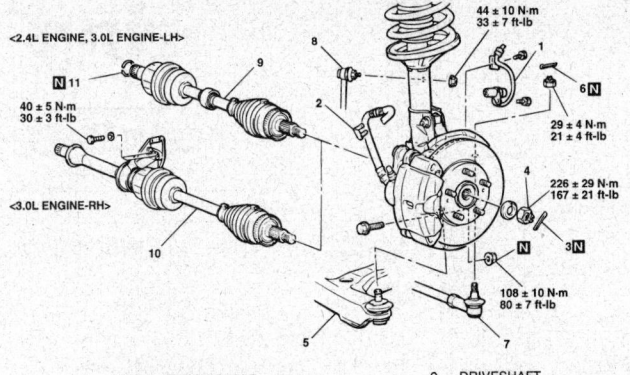

1. SPEED SENSOR CABLE CONNECTION <VEHICLES WITH ABS>
2. BRAKE HOSE CLIP
3. COTTER PIN
4. DRIVESHAFT NUT
5. LOWER ARM BALL JOINT CONNECTION
6. COTTER PIN
7. TIE ROD END CONNECTION
8. STABILIZER LINK CONNECTION
9. DRIVESHAFT
10. DRIVESHAFT AND INNER SHAFT
11. CIRCLIP

Fig. 1   Driveshaft replacement

Ball Joint	Breakaway Torque, Inch Lbs.
Lower Ball Joint	22–54
Stabilizer Link	30–80

Fig. 2   Ball joint specifications

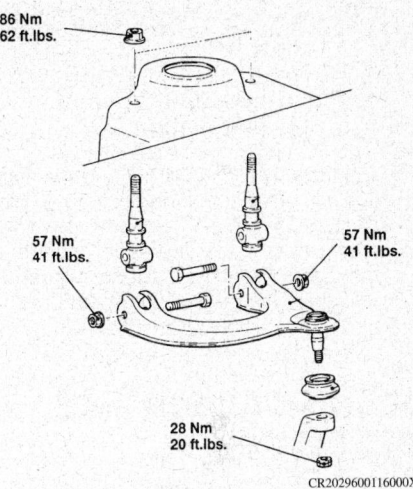

Fig. 4   Upper arm removal

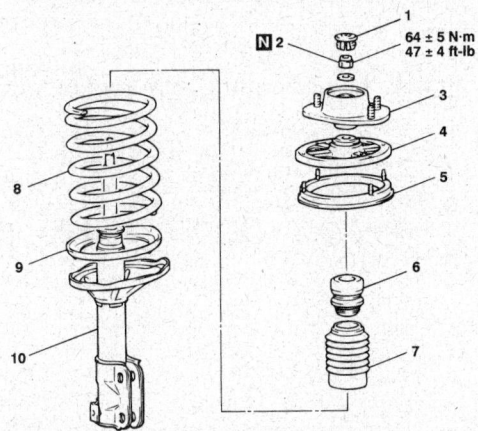

1. DUST COVER
2. JAM NUT
3. STRUT INSULATOR
4. SPRING SEAT, UPPER
5. SPRING PAD, UPPER
6. BUMP RUBBER
7. DUST COVER
8. COIL SPRING
9. SPRING PAD, LOWER
10. STRUT ASSEMBLY

Fig. 3   Coil spring replacement

6. Reverse procedure to install.

STABILIZER BAR
REPLACE
1. Raise and support vehicle.
2. Remove stabilizer link mounting nut.
3. Remove stabilizer link.
4. Remove stabilizer bar bracket and bushing.
5. Remove stabilizer bar.
6. Reverse procedure to install.

CROSSMEMBER
REPLACE
1. Drain power steering fluid, then remove center member.
2. Remove front exhaust pipe.
3. Remove stabilizer bar as outlined in "Stabilizer Bar, Replace."
4. Remove lower arm, then the clamp.
5. Remove crossmember mounting nuts, then the crossmember.
6. Reverse procedure to install.

POWER STEERING GEAR
REPLACE
1. Drain power steering fluid.
2. Remove transaxle and front roll stopper bolt, then the center member.
3. Remove front exhaust pipe.
4. Remove stabilizer bar as outlined in "Stabilizer Bar, Replace."
5. Remove steering shaft assembly connecting bolt.
6. Disconnect tie rod ends using steering linkage puller tool No. MB991113, or equivalent.

7. Disconnect return hose, then the pressure tube.
8. Remove cylinder clamp, then the steering gear.
9. Reverse procedure to install. Add power steering fluid and bleed as outlined in "Power Steering System Bleed."

POWER STEERING PUMP
REPLACE
1. Drain power steering fluid into a suitable container.
2. Remove power steering pump drive belt.
3. Disconnect suction hose.
4. Disconnect pressure hose from pump.
5. Remove gasket or O-ring.
6. Disconnect pressure switch electrical connector.
7. Remove oil pump and bracket.
8. Reverse procedure to install. Add power steering fluid and bleed system as outlined in "Power Steering System Bleed."

POWER STEERING SYSTEM BLEED
1. Raise and support front wheels.
2. Disconnect high tension ignition cable, then while operating starter motor intermittently, turn steering wheel full lefthand and full righthand five or six times.
3. Connect ignition cable, then start engine and run at idle.
4. Turn steering wheel to lefthand and righthand until there are no bubbles in the reservoir.

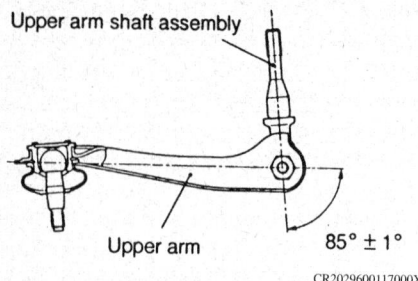

Upper arm shaft assembly

Upper arm

85° ± 1°

CR2029600117000X

Fig. 5   Upper arm shaft installation

5. Confirm fluid is not milky and that fluid level is up to specified position on dipstick.
6. Confirm there is very little change in fluid level when steering wheel is turned to lefthand or righthand.

TECHNICAL SERVICE BULLETINS

Front Stabilizer Bushing Noise

2001

On some of these models a creaking, popping or metallic clang sound may be heard from the front end. The sound may occur at low speed while braking hard or when accelerating briskly. This may be caused by the stabilizer bar moving in the mounting bushing.

To correct this condition replace stabilizer bushings using part No. MR589815 for models equipped with a 2.4L engine and part No. MR589817 for models equipped with a 3.0L engine.

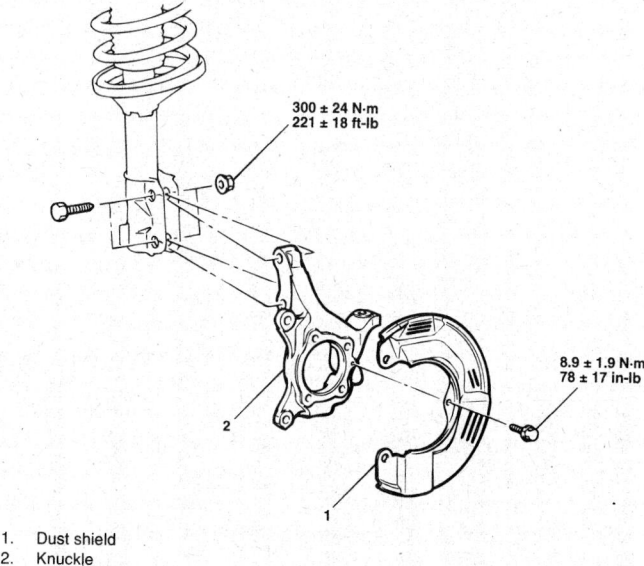

Grease: MOPAR® Multi-mileage Lubricant Part No. 2525035 or equivalent

<2.4L ENGINE>   <3.0L ENGINE>

108 ± 10 N·m
80 ± 7 ft-lb

108 ± 10 N·m*
80 ± 7 ft-lb*

99 ± 11 N·m
73 ± 8 ft-lb

81 ± 12 N·m
60 ± 9 ft-lb

1. LOWER ARM AND KNUCKLE CONNECTION
2. LOWER ARM MOUNTING BOLT
3. LOWER ARM CLAMP <2.4L ENGINE>
4. LOWER ARM

CR2020100178000X

Fig. 6   Lower control arm replacement

300 ± 24 N·m
221 ± 18 ft-lb

8.9 ± 1.9 N·m
78 ± 17 in-lb

1. Dust shield
2. Knuckle

CR2020000175000X

Fig. 7   Steering knuckle replacement

TIGHTENING SPECIFICATIONS

Year	Component	Torque/Ft. Lbs.
2001–05	Axle Nut	145–188
	Centermember Rear Assembly Bolts	64
	Centermember To Bracket Bolts	32
	Centermember To Crossmember Bolts	51–58
	Compression Lower Arm Ball Joint To Knuckle	43–51
	Compression Lower Arm Mounting Bolt	60
	Crossmember Lower Plate Bolts	71–85
	Crossmember To Rear Roll Bracket Bolts	32
	Damper Fork Mounting Bolt	75
	Damper Fork To Lateral Lower Arm Through Bolt	65
	Driveshaft Nut	145–188
	Driveshaft To Transaxle Bolt	30
	Hub Nut	145–188
	Joint Assembly & Steering Gear Connection	13
	Lateral Lower Arm Mounting Bolt & Nut	71–85
	Lateral Lower Arm To Knuckle Nuts	43–52
	Power Steering Gear Clamp Bolts	51
	Power Steering Pipe Connection	11
	Power Steering Pump Bracket Bolt (2.4L - M8)	18–24
	Power Steering Pump Bracket Bolt (2.4L - M10)	29–43
	Power Steering Pump Bracket Bolts (3.0L - M8)	14–20
	Power Steering Pump Bracket Bolts (3.0L - M10)	26–40
	Shock Absorber Lower Mounting Bolt	64
	Shock Absorber Upper Mounting Nut	32
	Stabilizer Bar Bracket	28
	Stabilizer Link Mounting Nut	28
	Tie Rod End To Steering Knuckle	18–25
	Upper Arm Self-Locking Nut	62
	Upper Arm Shaft To Control Arm	41

Wheel Alignment

INDEX

DESCRIPTION

Caster and camber are preset at the factory and cannot be adjusted. If camber is not within specifications, inspect and replace bent or damaged components.

PRELIMINARY INSPECTION

Wheel alignment should be measured with alignment equipment on a level surface. The suspension, steering system and wheels should be serviced to normal condition prior to measurement of wheel alignment. Inspect wheel runout as follows:
1. Raise and support vehicle.
2. While slowly turning wheel, measure runout with dial indicator.
3. Radial and lateral runout should be .05 inch or less for steel wheel, and .04 inch or less for aluminum wheel.
4. If wheel runout exceeds limit, replace wheel.

FRONT WHEEL ALIGNMENT

Caster

Caster is preset from the factory and cannot be adjusted.

Camber

1. Measure camber, use table, **Fig. 1,** to select proper camber adjusting bolt.
2. Replace upper and lower knuckle to strut attaching bolt with new bolts, **Fig. 2.**
3. Loosely tighten bolts, push or pull on front axle to adjust camber, **Fig. 3.**
4. **Torque** upper and lower knuckle to strut attaching bolt to 203–240 ft. lbs.

Toe-In

If toe measurement is not within specifications, adjust as follows:
1. Undo clips and turn lefthand and right-

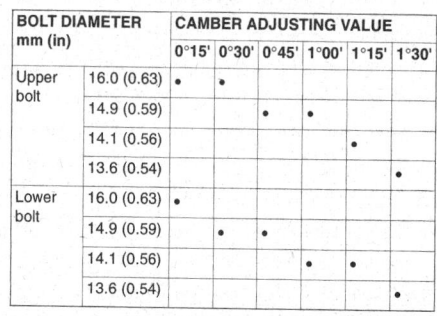

BOLT DIAMETER mm (in)		CAMBER ADJUSTING VALUE					
		0°15'	0°30'	0°45'	1°00'	1°15'	1°30'
Upper bolt	16.0 (0.63)	•	•				
	14.9 (0.59)			•	•		
	14.1 (0.56)					•	
	13.6 (0.54)						•
Lower bolt	16.0 (0.63)	•					
	14.9 (0.59)		•	•			
	14.1 (0.56)				•	•	
	13.6 (0.54)						•

CR2040100062000X

Fig. 1 Camber adjusting bolt selection table

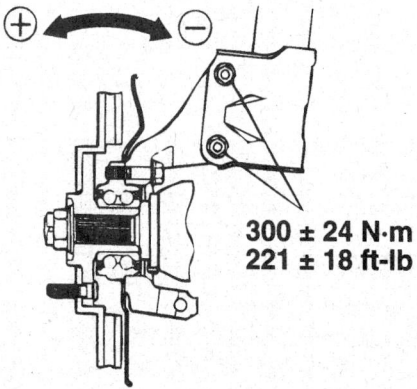

300 ± 24 N·m
221 ± 18 ft-lb

CR2040100064000X

Fig. 3 Camber adjustment

hand tie rod turnbuckles by the same amount in opposite directions, **Fig. 4.**
2. Toe will move out as lefthand turnbuckle is turned toward front of vehicle and righthand turnbuckle is turned toward rear of vehicle.

REAR WHEEL ALIGNMENT

Toe is adjusted by turning the toe control arm mounting bolt to the lefthand or righthand in equal amounts, **Fig. 5.** Turning the lefthand bolt clockwise adjusts in the toe-

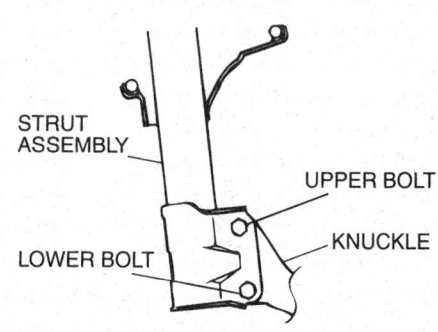

STRUT ASSEMBLY
UPPER BOLT
KNUCKLE
LOWER BOLT

CR2040100063000X

Fig. 2 Camber adjusting bolts

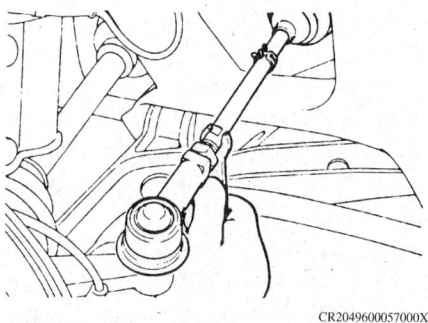

CR2049600057000X

Fig. 4 Front toe adjustment

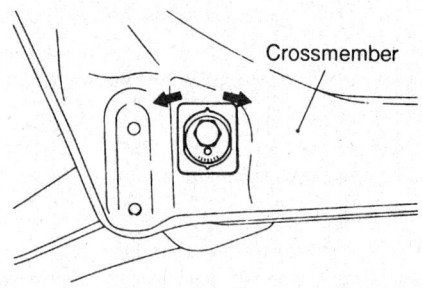

Crossmember

CR2049600058000X

Fig. 5 Rear toe adjustment

out direction. Turning the righthand bolt clockwise adjusts in the toe-in direction. Toe adjustments are made in graduations of .05 inch.

NOTE: Refer To The Rear Of This Manual For Manufacturer's Special Service Tool Supplies.

INDEX OF SERVICE OPERATIONS

Specifications

GENERAL ENGINE SPECIFICATIONS

| Year | Engine | | Fuel System | Bore & Stroke, Inches | Compression Ratio | Net HP @ RPM | Maximum Torque, Ft. Lbs. @ RPM | Normal Oil Pressure, psi @ 3000 RPM |
	Liter	VIN Code①						
2001	2.0L	C	SMPI	3.44 x 3.27	9.8	132 @ 6000	129 @ 5000	25–80
	2.4L	G/X	SMPI	3.44 x 3.98	②	150 @ 5200	167 @ 4000	25–80
	2.7L	U	SMPI	3.386 x 3.091	9.7	200 @ 5800	190 @ 4850	45–105
2002–05	2.4L	G/X	SMPI	3.44 x 3.98	②	150 @ 5200	167 @ 4000	25–80
	2.7L	U	SMPI	3.386 x 3.091	9.7	200 @ 5800	190 @ 4850	45–105

SMPI — Sequential Multi-Port Injection

① — Eighth digit of Vehicle Identification Number (VIN) denotes engine code.

② — 2001, 9.4:1; 2002–05 9.5:1.

TUNE UP SPECIFICATIONS

| Year & Engine | Spark Plug Gap, Inch | Ignition Timing | | | Minimum Air Flow Idle Speed, RPM② | Fuel Pump Pressure, psi | Valve Clearance |
		Firing Order	Firing Order Fig.	°BTDC			
2001							
2.0L	.035	1-3-4-2	A	②	600–1300	49	③
2.4L	.048	1-3-4-2	A	②	600–1300	58	①
2.7L	.048	1-2-3-4-5-6	B	②	350–700	58	①
2002–05							
2.4L	.048	1-3-4-2	A	②	600–1300	58	①
2.7L	.048	1-2-3-4-5-6	B	②	350–700	58	①

BTDC — Before Top Dead Center

① — Equipped w/hydraulic valve adjusters. No adjustment is required.

② — Controlled by PCM; not adjustable.

③ — Remove cap from fuel pressure test port on fuel rail. Connect suitable fuel pressure test gauge to fuel rail test port. Connect DRB scan tool, or equivalent. Place ignition switch in On position, then use scan tool to activate ADSD fuel system test.

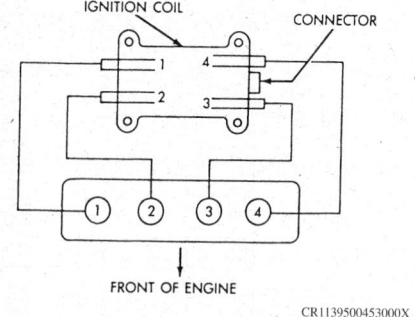

Fig. A

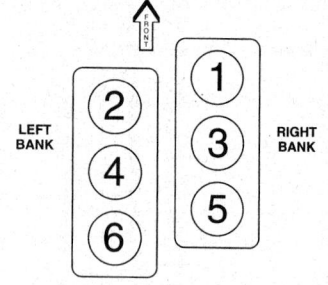

FIRING ORDER 1-2-3-4-5-6

Fig. B

FRONT WHEEL ALIGNMENT SPECIFICATIONS

| Year | Model | Camber Angle, Degrees | | Toe, Degrees③ | | Caster, Degrees① | Ball Joint Wear |
		Limits	Desired	Individual	Total		
2001	All	-.5 to +.7	+.1	+.05	+.10	+3.1	②
2002–05	All	-.9 to +.3	-.3	+.12	+.24	+3.3	②

① — Not adjustable.

② — Refer to "Ball Joint Inspection" in "Front Suspension & Steering" section.

③ — Toe in (+); toe out (-).

REAR WHEEL ALIGNMENT SPECIFICATIONS

Year	Model	Camber Angle, Degrees		Toe, Degrees①		Thrust Angle, Degrees	
		Limits	Desired	Individual	Total	Limits	Desired
2001	All	-.5 to +.3	-.1	+.05	+.1	-.15 to +.15	0
2002–05	All	-1.1 to +0.1	-.5	+.05	+.1	-.15 to +.15	0

① — Toe in (+); toe out (-).

VEHICLE RIDE HEIGHT SPECIFICATIONS

Year	Body Style	Manu-facturer's Original Tire Size	Measurement Points & Specifications②					
			Front			Rear		
			Dim.	Specification		Dim.	Specification	
				Inches	mm		Inches	mm
2001	All	①	A	28.00	710	B	28.00	710
2002–05	All	①	A	27.75	705	B	28.00	710

A Dim — Ground to lower edge of front wheelwell

B Dim — Ground to lower edge of rear wheelwell

① — See door sticker or inside of glove box for manufacturer's original tire size specifications. If tires on vehicle do not match manufactur-er's original tire size & measure-ment is not within limits, it will be required to refer to the "Non-

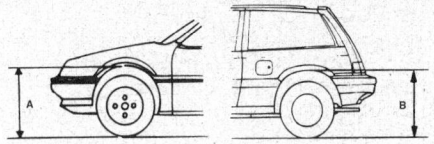

Fig. A   Dimensions A & B

CRQ124

Standard Tire & Wheel Size Adjust-ment To Ride Height Specification & Tire Size Adjustment Charts" in the front of this manual for approxi-mate changes in ride height specifi-cations.

② — Measurement is w/fuel, radiator coolant, engine oil full, jack, hand tools & mats in designated posi-tions and tires properly inflated.

FLUID CAPACITIES & COOLING SYSTEM DATA

Year	Engine	Coolant Capacity, Qts.	Coolant Type	Radiator Cap Relief Pressure, Lbs.	Thermo-stat Opening Tem-perature, °F	Fuel Tank Capacity, Gals.	Engine Oil Refill, Qts.①	Transaxle Oil, Qts.	
								Manual Trans.	Auto. Trans.
2001–02	2.0L	8.5	Ethylene Glycol	14–18	192–199	16	4.5	4.4	②
	2.4L	10.5	Ethylene Glycol	14–18	192–199	16	5.0	③	②
	2.7L	9.5	Ethylene Glycol	14–18	192–199	16	5.0	③	②
2003–05	2.4L	8.0	Ethylene Glycol	10–18	192–199	16	5.0	③	②
	2.7L	9.5	Ethylene Glycol	10–18	192–199	16	5.0	③	②

① — Includes filter change.

② — Service fill, 4.0 qts.; overhaul fill w/torque converter, 9.1 qts.

③ — T350 transaxle; 2.5 qts, T850 transaxle; 2.8 qts.

LUBRICANT DATA

Year	Lubricant Type			
	Transaxle		Power Steering	Brake System
	Manual	Automatic		
2001–05	Mopar ATF+4 Type 9602	Mopar ATF+4 Type 9602	Mopar ATF+4 Type 9602	DOT 3

Electrical

NOTE: On Air Bag Equipped Models, Refer To "Air Bag System Precautions" Located In The Front Of This Manual For System Disarming & Arming Procedures.

NOTE: Refer To "Computer Relearn Procedures" Located In The Front Of This Manual When Battery Power To The Computer Has Been Interrupted.

NOTE: Prior To Performing Any Service Operations Listed In This Section, Consult The "Technical Service Bulletins" Section For Related Information.

INDEX

PRECAUTIONS

Air Bag Systems

Refer to Air Bag System Precautions in the front of this manual for system disarming and arming procedures.

Battery Ground Cable

Prior to service, disconnect battery ground cable and isolate as required.

FUSE PANEL LOCATION

The interior accessory fuse panel is located between the instrument panel and the driver's side door. The door must be open to access the fuse panel. The fuse panel contains the headland relay, horn relay, rear window defogger relay, circuit breakers, and several fuses.

FUEL PUMP RELAY LOCATION

The fuel pump relay is located in the Power Distribution Center (PDC), which is near the battery on the lefthand side of the engine compartment.

RELAY CENTER LOCATION

The engine compartment relays are located in the Power Distribution Center (PDC) next to the battery. The PDC contains the starter relay, radiator fan relay, air conditioning compressor clutch relay, auto shutdown relay, wiper relay, back-up lamp relay, transaxle control relay, fuel pump relay and several fuses.

STARTER

REPLACE

2.0L Engine

AUTOMATIC TRANSAXLE

1. Remove air cleaner box.
2. Remove lower and upper bolt, then ground wire.
3. Remove starter and wires from starter.
4. Reverse procedure to install. **Torque** mounting bolts to 40 ft. lbs.

MANUAL TRANSAXLE

1. Remove air cleaner resonator.
2. Remove battery positive cable nut from starter, then remove battery positive cable and alternator output wire from starter.
3. Disconnect push on solenoid connector.
4. Remove two starter to transaxle housing mounting bolts and starter.
5. Reverse procedure to install.

2.4L Engine

1. Remove air cleaner box.
2. Remove lower and upper bolt, then ground wire.
3. Remove starter and wires from starter.
4. Reverse procedure to install. **Torque** mounting bolts to 40 ft. lbs.

2.7L Engine

1. Raise and support vehicle.
2. Disconnect electrical connector and remove O2 sensor.
3. Remove front mount bracket from engine block.
4. Disconnect battery cable from starter.
5. Remove lower mounting bolt and starter.
6. Reverse procedure to install noting the following:
   a. **Torque** upper and lower mounting

bolts to 40 ft. lbs.
b. **Torque** front mount through bolt to 45 ft. lbs.

ALTERNATOR
REPLACE

2.0L Engine

1. Unplug field circuit from alternator.
2. Remove B+ terminal cover by spreading cover with a small flat blade tool.
3. Remove B+ terminal nut and wire.
4. Loosen adjusting and pivot bolts. **Do not remove bolts.**
5. Loosen and remove adjusting bolt.
6. Remove pivot bolt. **Do not drop spacer.**
7. Release alternator from mounting bracket, move it toward passenger headlamp bucket and remove.
8. Reverse procedure to install.

2.4L Engine

1. Remove drive belt cover.
2. Unplug field circuit from alternator.
3. Remove B+ terminal cover by spreading cover using suitable small flat blade tool.
4. Remove B+ terminal nut and wire.
5. Raise and support vehicle.
6. Remove serpentine drive belt.
7. Lower vehicle and remove MAP sensor from intake manifold.
8. Remove mounting bolts and alternator.
9. Reverse procedure to install.

2.7L Engine

1. Raise and support vehicle.
2. Remove splash shield and loosen serpentine drive belt.
3. Remove lower mounting bolt, then lower vehicle.
4. Disconnect air conditioning pressure switch and clutch electrical connectors.
5. Remove engine oil dip stick.
6. Remove two upper mounting bolts and alternator.
7. Reverse procedure to install.

IGNITION COIL & COIL PACK
REPLACE

2.0L & 2.4L Engines

1. Disconnect coil pack electrical connector, **Fig. 1.**
2. Remove spark plug cables from coil pack by twisting cable and boot assembly, then pulling outward.
3. Remove mounting bolts and coil pack.
4. Reverse procedure to install.

2.7L Engine

1. Disconnect ignition coil electrical connector, **Fig. 2.**
2. Remove mounting bolts and coil.

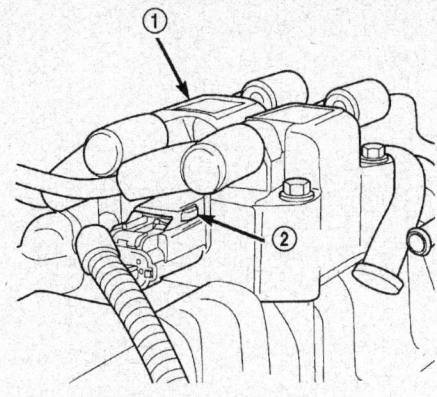

1 - COIL
2 - LOCKING TAB

CR1110200289000X

Fig. 1 Ignition coil pack replacement. 2.0L & 2.4L engines

3. Reverse procedure to install. **Torque** mounting bolts to 55 inch lbs.

IGNITION COIL CAPACITOR, REPLACE

1. Disconnect capacitor electrical connector, **Fig. 2.**
2. Remove mounting nut and capacitor.
3. Reverse procedure to install.

IGNITION LOCK
REPLACE

1. Remove upper steering column shroud.
2. Pull lower shroud down far enough to access lock cylinder retaining tab.
3. Place ignition key cylinder in RUN position.
4. Depress retaining tab and remove ignition lock.
5. Reverse procedure to install.

IGNITION SWITCH
REPLACE

1. Remove fuse panel cover from left-hand end of instrument panel.
2. Remove instrument panel top cover end mounting screw.
3. Pull center bezel off.
4. Remove top cover to center of instrument panel mounting screws.
5. Pull instrument panel top cover up enough to gain access to knee bolster screws.
6. Remove lower mounting screws and knee bolster.
7. Remove lower steering column shroud mounting screws.
8. Pull lower shroud to clear ignition cylinder and key release.
9. Hold tilt wheel lever down and remove lower shroud by sliding it forward.
10. Tilt wheel to full down position and remove upper steering column shroud.
11. Remove multiplication switch to lock housing mounting screws.
12. Place ignition key cylinder in RUN position.

13. Depress lock cylinder retaining tab and remove key cylinder.
14. Disconnect ignition switch electrical connectors.
15. Remove ignition switch mounting screw.
16. Depress retaining tabs and pull ignition switch from steering column.
17. Reverse procedure to install.

MULTI-FUNCTION SWITCH
REPLACE

1. Remove upper steering column cover.
2. Remove multiplication switch mounting screws.
3. Disconnect wire connectors. Lift switch straight up to remove.
4. Reverse procedure to install.

STEERING WHEEL
REPLACE

1. Place front wheels in straight ahead position.
2. Remove and disconnect speed control switches.
3. Disarm air bag system as outlined under "Precautions."
4. Remove speed control switch or covers from steering wheel, then disconnect electrical connectors.
5. Remove air bag module mounting bolts from steering wheel.
6. Lift module and disconnect wire connector by lifting secondary latch and using finger grips. **Do not use metallic tool to pry connector off.**
7. Disconnect horn wire.
8. Remove speed control wires from under brackets and from wire guides.
9. Remove driver's air bag module.
10. Disconnect horn wire from air bag mounting bracket and remove speed control wires from under bracket.
11. Loosen mounting bolt and steering wheel using suitable wheel puller tool.
12. Remove mounting bolt and steering wheel.
13. Reverse procedure to install, noting the following:
    a. **Torque** steering wheel bolt to 40 ft. lbs.
    b. **Torque** air bag module bolts to 75–95 inch lbs. Tighten lefthand side bolt first.

INSTRUMENT CLUSTER
REPLACE

1. Remove lefthand end cap.
2. Pry power mirror switch upward using trim stick tool No. C-4755, or equivalent.
3. Gently pry up on instrument panel center trim bezel.
4. Disconnect HVAC control connector.
5. Remove mounting screw and passenger side trim bezel by unsnapping retaining clips.
6. Remove lefthand lower instrument panel trim mounting screws.
7. Remove cluster bezel mounting screws.

8. **On models equipped with Mini-Trip Computer (CMTC/Traveler),** disconnect module.
9. **On all models,** pry cluster bezel from instrument panel.
10. Tilt steering column to its lowest position and depress hazard switch.
11. Remove cluster mounting screws.
12. Pull cluster rearward and disconnect 26-way electrical connector.
13. Remove cluster by tilting downward slightly and sliding sideways.
14. Reverse procedure to install.

RADIO

REPLACE

1. Remove center bezel and two radio mounting screws.
2. Pull radio straight out, then disconnect both electrical connectors, antenna cable and radio ground strap.
3. Remove radio.
4. Reverse procedure to install.

WIPER MOTOR

REPLACE

1. Remove wiper arms and blades.
2. Remove cowl screen.
3. Remove mounting screws and lift wiper motor to access harness clip.
4. Disconnect harness clip at forward mounting leg.
5. Disconnect motor electrical connector.
6. Disconnect drive linkage at motor output crank, then separate ball cap from ball using suitable ball joint separator tool.
7. Remove motor.
8. Reverse procedure to install. **Torque** mounting screws to 96–108 inch. lbs.

BLOWER MOTOR

REPLACE

1. Remove lower righthand silencer panel.
2. Remove righthand sill plate and kick panel.
3. Fold back righthand upper corner of carpet and disconnect blower motor electrical connector.
4. Remove three mounting screws and blower motor.
5. Reverse procedure to install.

HEATER CORE

REPLACE

1. Recover air conditioning system as outlined in "Air Conditioning" chapter.
2. Drain engine coolant into suitable container, then disconnect heater hoses from heater core.
3. Remove quick connect clips from air conditioning lines at expansion valve.
4. Remove air conditioning lines from expansion valve using quick connectors tool kit No. 7193, or equivalent. Cap air conditioning lines.
5. Remove expansion valve.
6. Remove shifter boot.
7. Remove console to shifter bracket front mounting screws.

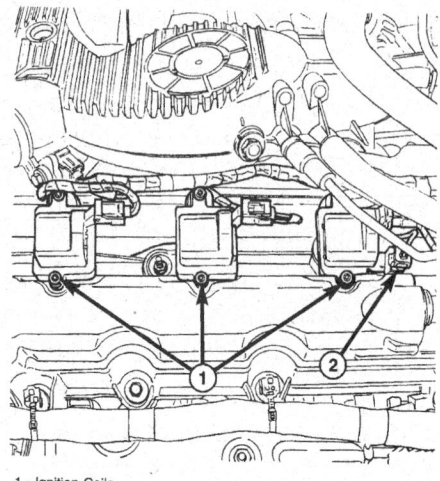

1 - Ignition Coils
2 - Ignition Capacitor

CR1110200290000X

Fig. 2   Ignition coils & ignition coil capacitor replacement. 2.7L engine

8. Remove console to floor bracket rear mounting screws.
9. Engage parking brake and pull console off of floor bracket.
10. Disconnect electrical connectors and remove floor console.
11. Remove rear heat ducts.
12. Remove HVAC housing to dash panel mounting nuts in engine compartment.
13. Remove instrument panel as outlined in "Dash Panel Service" chapter.
14. Disconnect electrical connector from lefthand side of HVAC housing.
15. Remove HVAC housing.
16. Disconnect recirculation motor electrical connector.
17. Remove wiring harness connector from top of housing.
18. Remove seal around evaporator core inlet/outlet.
19. Remove housing top mounting screw.
20. Separate upper from lower housing and remove heater core.
21. Reverse procedure to install.

EVAPORATOR CORE

REPLACE

1. Remove HVAC housing as outlined under "Heater Case, Replace."
2. Remove HVAC to instrument panel mounting bolts and separate HVAC housing from instrument panel.
3. Disconnect recirculation motor electrical connector.
4. Remove wiring harness connector from top of housing.
5. Remove seal around evaporator core inlet/outlet.
6. Remove housing to mounting screw.
7. Separate upper housing from lower.
8. Remove evaporator temperature sensor.
9. Remove evaporator and Styrofoam seal around evaporator.
10. Reverse procedure to install.

TECHNICAL SERVICE BULLETINS

Rear Window Defogger Inoperative

2001-02 SEBRING CONVERTIBLE

On some of these models built before May 1, 2001, the rear window defogger may be inoperative

This condition may be caused by the grid terminal(s) being separated or broken.

If the grid terminals are securely fastened to and the rear window defogger is inoperative, further diagnosis is required.

To correct this condition, proceed as follows:

1. **Failure to reorient terminal clips will result in additional failures.**
2. Remove screw from carpet and pull headliner from terminal clip area.
3. Remove terminal clip wire connector.
4. Remove broken or partial terminal clip in wire connector.
5. Place suitable protective mat below clip area to catch any dripping solder.
6. **Do not use flame-type soldering gun or gun rated at more than 500 watts.**
7. Apply heat with suitable solder gun to terminal clip until solder flows, then remove clip and smooth solder.
8. Wait five minutes for glass to cool.
9. Clean mating surfaces with 000 extra fine steel wool. **Avoid excessive abrasions.**
10. Solder new terminal clip in same area as original but with tip facing outboard.
11. Connect connector.
12. Repeat procedure on opposite side.

Flickering Panel, Overhead Or Dome Lamps

2001-02

On some of these models the trip computer and/or radio display, instrument panel, illumination, and/or overhead/dome lamps may flicker. This condition may be intermittent and noticed when operating the turn signals or beam change on the lefthand stalk switch. This condition may be temporarily corrected by adjusting the instrument panel illumination dimmer setting. **Do not change dimmer switch position prior to diagnosis.**

This condition may be caused by the multi-function switch.

To correct this condition, proceed as follows:

1. Ensure instrument panel cross-vehicle beam ground behind lefthand kick panel is satisfactory and not loose.
2. **Do not change dimmer switch position prior to monitoring voltage.**
3. Inspect dimmer switch output using suitably programmed scan tool.
4. While monitoring voltage, activate turn

Year	Radio Type	Part No.
2002	RBK	05091958AA
2003	RBB	05064335AF
		05064335AG
	RBK	05091958AA
		05054354AG

Fig. 3 Radio replacement chart

5. If measurement varies more than .2 volts, replace multi-function switch.
6. Ensure multi-function switch has build date of 2781, or higher.

Loud Burst Of Radio Static Or Distortion

2002-03

On some of these models the radio may have loud intermittent sound or burst of static within 30 seconds of radio being turned on.

This condition may be caused by software internal to the radio.

If the radio is listed, **Fig. 3,** it must be replaced.

Horn Self Actuates

2003 SEBRING SEDAN & STRATUS SEDAN

On some of these models, the horn may self actuate.

This condition may be caused by an electrostatic discharge causing the Body Control Module (BCM) to actuate the horn.

To correct this condition, flash program the BCM using a suitable programmed scan tool operating at CD 2123, or higher, with software level 55.3, or higher.

Center Lower Instrument Panel Rattle/Squeak

2003

On some of these models equipped with

six-disc CD changer (Code RDN) built July 15–Aug. 14, 2002, may have a road induced rattle/squeak from the lower center instrument panel stack area. Sound is more noticeable when interior temperatures are more than 110°F.

This condition may be caused by six-disc CD changer.

To correct this condition, proceed as follows:

1. Inspect fit between CD changer and trim bezel for witness mark of bezel contact on outer changer faceplate circumference.
2. Loosen mounting bolts and position changer to eliminate contact.
3. **Torque** mounting bolts to 20–28 inch lbs. Tighten lefthand first.
4. Install two ½ x 1 inch flocked tape strips over bottom two changer bezel clips.

2.0L & 2.4L Engines

NOTE: On Air Bag Equipped Models, Refer To "Air Bag System Precautions" Located In The Front Of This Manual For System Disarming & Arming Procedures.

NOTE: Refer To "Computer Relearn Procedures" Located In The Front Of This Manual When Battery Power To The Computer Has Been Interrupted.

NOTE: Prior To Performing Any Service Operations Listed In This Section, Consult The "Technical Service Bulletins" Section For Related Information.

INDEX

PRECAUTIONS

Air Bag Systems

Refer to "Air Bag System Precautions" in the front of this manual for system disarming and arming procedures.

Battery Ground Cable

Prior to service, disconnect battery ground cable and isolate as required.

Fuel System Pressure Relief

1. Remove fuel pump relay from power distribution center.
2. Start and run engine until it stalls.
3. Attempt to restart engine until it will no longer run, then turn ignition key to OFF position.
4. Install fuel pump relay, then erase any DTC's that may have been stored because of removing fuel pump relay.

COMPRESSION PRESSURE

Compression pressure should be 170–225 psi with no more than a 25% variation in pressure between cylinders.

ENGINE MOUNT

REPLACE

2.0L Engine

FRONT

1. Raise and support vehicle.
2. Remove front mount to bracket horizontal through bolt, **Fig. 1.**
3. Remove vertical bolts and front mount.
4. Reverse procedure to install.

LEFTHAND

1. Support transaxle with suitable jack.
2. Remove three engine mount to transaxle mounting bolts, **Fig. 2.**
3. Remove mounting bolts and lefthand mount.
4. Reverse procedure to install.

RIGHTHAND

1. Raise and support vehicle, then remove inner wheel splash guard.
2. Remove righthand engine support mounting bolts from frame rail, **Fig. 3.**
3. Lower vehicle and support engine with suitable floor jack.
4. Remove three engine support to engine bracket mounting bolts.
5. Reverse procedure to install.

REAR

1. Raise and support vehicle, then remove lefthand front tire and wheel assembly.
2. Support transaxle with suitable transaxle jack.
3. Remove mount and rear suspension crossover insulator mounting bolt, **Fig. 4.**
4. Remove four mounting bolts and transaxle mount.
5. Reverse procedure to install.

2.4L Engine

FRONT

1. Raise and support vehicle.
2. Remove front mount to bracket horizontal through bolt, **Fig. 1.**
3. Remove vertical bolts and front mount.
4. Reverse procedure to install.

LEFTHAND

1. Support transaxle with suitable jack.
2. Remove three engine mount to transaxle mounting bolts, **Fig. 5.**
3. Remove mounting bolts and lefthand mount.
4. Reverse procedure to install.

RIGHTHAND

1. Raise and support vehicle, then remove the inner wheel splash guard.
2. Remove righthand engine support assembly mounting bolts from frame rail, **Fig. 3.**
3. Lower vehicle and support engine with suitable floor jack.
4. Remove three engine support to engine bracket mounting bolts.
5. Reverse procedure to install.

REAR MOUNT

1. Raise and support vehicle, then remove lefthand front wheel.
2. Support transaxle with suitable transaxle jack.
3. Remove mount and rear suspension crossover insulator mounting bolt, **Fig. 6.**
4. Remove four mounting bolts and transaxle mount.
5. Reverse procedure to install.

ENGINE

REPLACE

1. Remove fuel pump relay from power distribution center.
2. Start and run engine until it stalls.
3. Attempt to restart engine until it will no longer run, then turn ignition key to OFF position.
4. Install fuel pump relay, then erase any DTC's that may have been stored because of removing fuel pump relay.
5. Drain coolant into suitable container.
6. Recover refrigerant as outlined in "Air Conditioning" chapter.
7. Remove throttle body air inlet hose and air cleaner assembly.
8. Remove upper radiator crossmember, then the upper and lower radiator hoses.
9. Disconnect transaxle oil cooler lines at transaxle. Plug lines and fittings.
10. Disconnect air conditioning lines from condenser and remove cooling module.
11. Disconnect electrical harness from transaxle and shift cable.
12. Disconnect engine electrical harness from PCM and bulkhead connector.
13. Raise and support vehicle, then remove front tire and wheel assemblies.
14. Remove both splash shields.
15. Remove both drive axles as outlined in "Front Wheel Drive Axles" chapter.
16. Drain engine oil into suitable container and remove accessory drive belts.
17. Remove power steering pump from bracket and position aside.
18. Disconnect heater return hose from pipe connection.
19. Disconnect air conditioning compressor electrical connector.
20. Disconnect oxygen sensor electrical connector.
21. Remove exhaust pipe to manifold mounting nuts and catalytic convertor pipe band clamp.
22. Remove catalytic convertor pipe from resonator pipe.

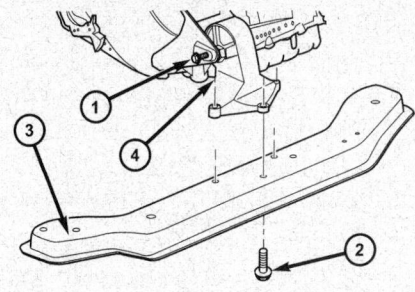

1 - HORIZONTAL THROUGH BOLT
2 - VERTICAL BOLT(S)
3 - LOWER RADIATOR CROSSMEMBER
4 - FRONT ENGINE MOUNT

CR1060100964000X

Fig. 1 Front engine mount replacement

23. Disconnect from hanger and remove catalytic convertor pipe.
24. Remove front and rear engine mount through bolts.
25. Remove rear mount bracket from transmission.
26. Remove structural collar and torque reaction bracket, **Fig. 7.**
27. Mark flex plate to torque converter position for installation alignment, then remove torque converter bolts.
28. Lower vehicle, then disconnect battery positive cable from Power Distribution Center (PDC).
29. Disconnect throttle and speed control cables, then the coolant recovery overflow hose.
30. Remove heater hose from thermostat housing and disconnect all engine ground straps.
31. Disconnect brake booster and vapor purge hoses, then the fuel line from fuel rail.
32. Remove intake manifold as outlined under "Intake Manifold, Replace."
33. Remove alternator.
34. Remove air conditioning suction line at compressor.
35. Remove compressor. Plug ports and lines.
36. Raise and support vehicle.
37. Support engine using dolly and cradle tool Nos. 6135 and 6710, or equivalents.
38. Install post tool No. 6848, or equivalent.
39. Loosen engine cradle mounts to position engine locating holes in bedplate.
40. Lower vehicle until engine rests on cradle mounts. Tighten mounts to cradle frame.
41. Lower vehicle so weight of engine and transaxle is only on cradle.
42. Remove left and righthand vertical mount mounting bolts.
43. Slowly raise and support vehicle.
44. Remove engine and transaxle on cradle around body flanges.
45. Reverse procedure to install, noting the following:
    a. Place structural collar into position between transaxle and oil pan, install transaxle bolt 1 hand tight, **Fig. 7.**

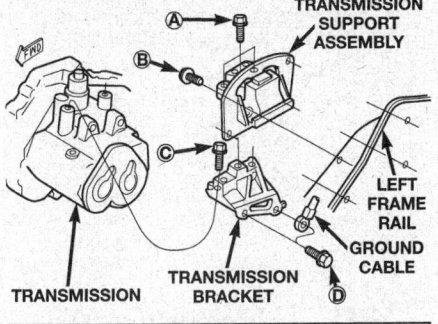

ITEM	DESCRIPTION	TORQUE
A	Bolt	61 N·m (45 ft. lbs.)
B	Bolt	33 N·m (24 ft. lbs.)
C	Bolt	61 N·m (45 ft. lbs.)
D	Bolt	61 N·m (45 ft. lbs.)

CR1069500597000X

Fig. 2 Lefthand engine mount replacement. 2.0L engine

b. Install collar to oil pan bolts 4 and 5 hand tight.
c. Position torque reaction bracket in place, then install bolts 2 and 3 hand tight.
d. **Torque** bolts 1–3 to 75 ft. lbs.
e. Install bolts 6 and 7 through torque reduction bracket into block hand tight.
f. **Torque** bolts 4 and 5 to 35 ft. lbs.
g. **Torque** bolts 6 and 7 to 45 ft. lbs.
h. **Torque** front engine mount through bolt to 45 ft. lbs.

INTAKE MANIFOLD
REPLACE

1. Remove fuel pump relay from power distribution center.
2. Start and run engine until it stalls.
3. Attempt to restart engine until it will no longer run, then turn ignition key to OFF position.
4. Install fuel pump relay, then erase any DTC's that may have been stored because of removing fuel pump relay.
5. Drain engine coolant into suitable container.
6. Remove throttle body air inlet hose and air cleaner housing assembly.
7. Remove throttle and speed control cables from throttle lever and bracket.
8. Remove EGR and oil dipstick tubes.
9. Disconnect vacuum hoses from intake manifold.
10. Disconnect fuel supply line at fuel rail.
11. Remove fastener holding fuel rail bracket to side of cylinder head.
12. Disconnect fuel injectors, then the knock and ECT sensors' electrical connectors.
13. Disconnect IAC, then the throttle position and MAP sensors' electrical connectors.
14. Disconnect air conditioning pressure switch and compressor clutch, then the alternator electrical connectors.

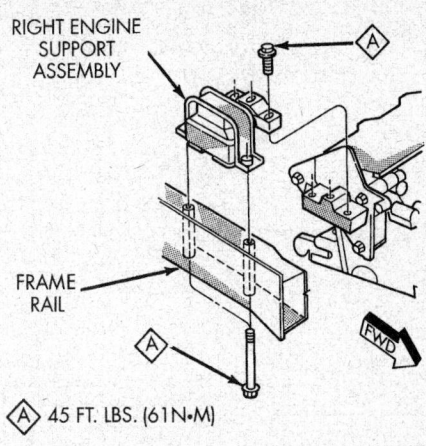

CR1069500593000X

Ⓐ 45 FT. LBS. (61N·M)

Fig. 3 Righthand engine mount replacement

15. Position wiring harness aside and remove fuel rail.
16. Remove coolant outlet connector.
17. Remove mounting bolts and intake manifold.
18. Reverse procedure to install, noting the following:
    a. Install new gasket.
    b. Tighten intake manifold bolts gradually in sequence, **Fig. 8.**

EXHAUST MANIFOLD
REPLACE

1. Raise and support vehicle.
2. Remove exhaust system, **Fig. 9.**
3. Raise and support vehicle, then remove lefthand front tire and wheel assembly.
4. Support transaxle with suitable transaxle jack.
5. Remove mount and rear suspension crossover insulator mounting bolt, **Figs. 4 and 6.**
6. Remove four mounting bolts and transaxle mount.
7. Remove exhaust manifold heat shield.
8. Disconnect oxygen sensor electrical connector.
9. Remove mounting bolts and exhaust manifold.
10. Reverse procedure to install noting the following:
    a. Install new gasket.
    b. Tighten bolts in sequence, **Fig. 10.**

CYLINDER HEAD
REPLACE

1. Remove fuel pump relay from power distribution center.
2. Start and run engine until it stalls.
3. Attempt to restart engine until it will no longer run, then turn ignition key to OFF position.
4. Install fuel pump relay, then erase any DTC's that may have been stored because of removing fuel pump relay.
5. Remove throttle body air inlet hose and air cleaner housing assembly.
6. Drain coolant into suitable container.
7. Remove intake manifold as outlined under "Intake Manifold, Replace."

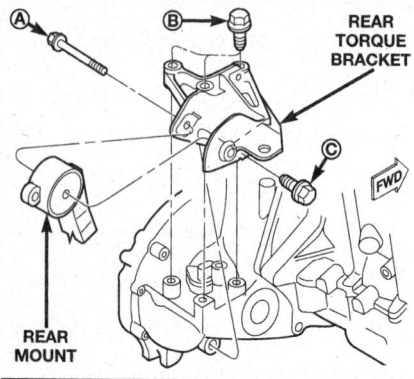

ITEM	DESCRIPTION	TORQUE
A	Bolt	61 N·m (45 ft. lbs.)
B & C	Bolt—w/Auto. Transaxle	110 N·m (80 ft. lbs.)
	Bolt—w/Manual Transaxle	61 N·m (45 ft. lbs.)

CR1069500599000X

Fig. 4   Rear engine mount replacement. 2.0L engine

8. Disconnect heater hose from thermostat housing.
9. Remove heater tube support bracket from cylinder head.
10. Disconnect Camshaft Position (CMP) sensor and EGR solenoid electrical connectors.
11. Raise and support vehicle, then disconnect exhaust pipe from exhaust manifold.
12. Remove accessory drive belts and crankshaft damper.
13. Remove timing belt as outlined under "Timing Belt, Replace."
14. Remove camshaft sprockets.
15. Remove timing belt idler pulley and rear timing belt cover.
16. Remove air cleaner inlet duct.
17. Disconnect coil pack electrical connector.
18. Remove spark plug cables from coil pack by twisting cable and boot assembly, then pulling outward.
19. Remove mounting bolts and coil pack.
20. Remove mounting bolts and valve cover.
21. Remove valve cover as outlined under "Valve Cover, Replace."
22. Remove camshafts and rocker arms.
23. Remove mounting bolts and cylinder head.
24. Reverse procedure to install, noting the following:
    a. Apply oil to cylinder head bolts
    b. **Torque** cylinder head bolts to 25 ft. lbs. in sequence, **Fig. 11.**
    c. **Torque** head bolts to 50 ft. lbs. in sequence.
    d. **Torque** bolts to 50 ft. lbs. in sequence.
    e. Tighten bolts an additional 90° in sequence.

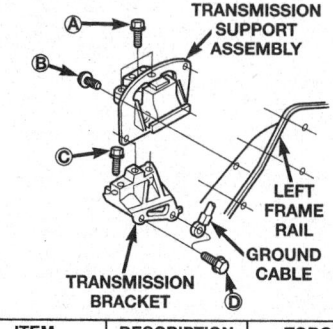

ITEM	DESCRIPTION	TORQUE
A	Bolt	61 N·m (45 ft. lbs.)
B	Bolt	33 N·m (24 ft. lbs.)
C	Bolt	61 N·m (45 ft. lbs.)
D	Bolt	61 N·m (45 ft. lbs.)

CR1069500598000X

Fig. 5   Lefthand engine mount replacement. 2.4L engine

VALVE COVER
REPLACE

2.0L Engine

1. Remove air cleaner inlet duct.
2. Disconnect coil pack electrical connector.
3. Remove spark plug cables from coil pack by twisting cable and boot assembly, then pulling outward.
4. Remove mounting bolts and coil pack.
5. Remove mounting bolts and valve cover.
6. Reverse procedure to install. Install new valve cover gasket.

2.4L Engine

1. Disconnect engine ground strap.
2. Disconnect coil pack electrical connector.
3. Remove spark plug cables from coil pack by twisting cable and boot assembly, then pulling outward.
4. Remove mounting bolts and coil pack.
5. Remove mounting bolts and valve cover.
6. Reverse procedure to install, noting the following:
    a. Install new valve cover gaskets and spark plug seals. **Do not allow oil or solvents to contact timing belt.**
    b. Apply silicone rubber adhesive sealant to camshaft cap corners and at top edge of half-round seal.
    c. **Torque** valve cover mounting bolts to 40 inch lbs.
    d. **Torque** mounting bolts to 80 inch lbs.
    e. **Torque** bolts to 105 inch lbs.

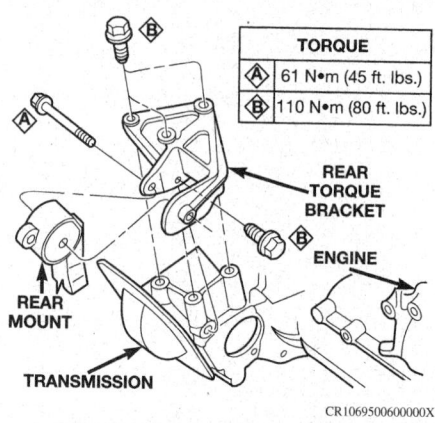

TORQUE	
Ⓐ	61 N·m (45 ft. lbs.)
Ⓑ	110 N·m (80 ft. lbs.)

CR1069500600000X

Fig. 6   Rear engine mount replacement. 2.4L engine

VALVE ARRANGEMENT

Intake valves are located on intake manifold side of engine and exhaust valves are located on exhaust manifold side of engine.

CAMSHAFT LOBE LIFT SPECIFICATIONS

Engine	Lift, Inch	
	Intake	Exhaust
2.0L	.340	.312
2.4L	.324	①

① — 2002–03, .256 inch; .2004–05, .259 inch

VALVE CLEARANCE SPECIFICATIONS

These engines are equipped with hydraulic lash adjusters designed to maintain zero lash at all times.

ROCKER ARMS
REPLACE

2.0L Engine

1. Remove air cleaner inlet duct.
2. Disconnect coil pack electrical connector.
3. Remove spark plug cables from coil pack by twisting cable and boot assembly, then pulling outward.
4. Remove mounting bolts and coil pack.
5. Remove mounting bolts and valve cover.
6. Identify rocker arm shaft assemblies for installation in original positions.
7. Remove mounting bolts and rocker arm shaft.
8. Reverse procedure to install, noting the following:
    a. Install rocker arm and shaft assemblies with notches on shafts facing

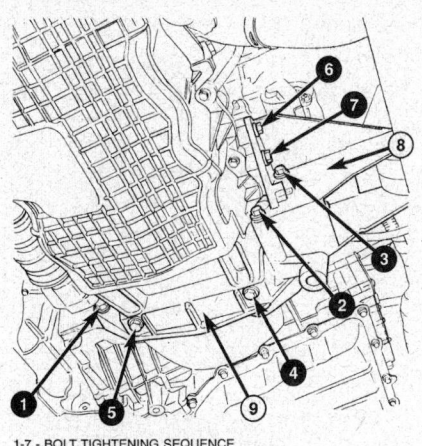

1-7 - BOLT TIGHTENING SEQUENCE
8 - TORQUE REACTION BRACKET
9 - STRUCTURAL COLLAR

CR1060100965000X

Fig. 7 Structural collar & torque reaction bracket replacement

up and toward timing belt side of engine, **Fig. 12.**
  b. Tighten bolts in sequence, **Fig. 13.**
9. Install new valve cover gasket.

2.4L Engine

1. Disconnect engine ground strap.
2. Disconnect coil pack electrical connector.
3. Remove spark plug cables from coil pack by twisting cable and boot assembly, then pulling outward.
4. Remove mounting bolts and coil pack.
5. Remove mounting bolts and valve cover.
6. Remove spark plugs.
7. Rotate engine until camshaft lobe on rocker being removed is positioned on its base circle. Piston should be a minimum of .25 inch below TDC.
8. Depress valve assembly until rocker arms can be removed using valve spring compressor tool Nos. 8215-A and 8436 or equivalents.
9. Reverse procedure to install, noting the following:
  a. Install new valve cover gaskets and spark plug seals. **Do not allow oil or solvents to contact timing belt.**
  b. Apply silicone rubber adhesive sealant to camshaft cap corners and at top edge of half-round seal.
  c. **Torque** valve cover mounting bolts to 40 inch lbs.
  d. **Torque** mounting bolts to 80 inch lbs.
  e. **Torque** bolts to 105 inch lbs.

FRONT COVER
REPLACE
2.0L Engine

1. Remove accessory drive belts.
2. Raise and support vehicle on suitable hoist and remove righthand inner splash shield.
3. Remove mounting bolt and crankshaft

using puller tool No. 1023 and insert tool No. C-4685-C2, or equivalents.
4. Lower vehicle and support engine using suitable jack.
5. Remove purge duty solenoid and wiring harness from righthand engine mount.
6. Remove righthand engine mount and bracket.
7. Remove mounting bolts and upper timing belt cover.
8. Remove mounting bolts and lower timing belt cover.
9. Reverse procedure to install.

2.4L Engine

1. Remove mounting bolts and upper cover, **Fig. 14.**
2. Raise and support vehicle, then remove righthand front tire and wheel assembly.
3. Remove belt splash shield and accessory drive belts.
4. Remove mounting bolt and crankshaft damper using puller tool No. 1026 and insert tool No. 6827, or equivalents.
5. Remove air conditioning alternator belt tensioner, then lower vehicle.
6. Remove drive belt cover.
7. Unplug field circuit from alternator.
8. Remove B+ terminal cover by spreading cover using suitable small flat blade tool.
9. Remove B+ terminal nut and wire.
10. Lower vehicle and remove MAP sensor from intake manifold.
11. Remove mounting bolts and alternator.
12. Remove alternator mounting bracket.
13. Raise and support vehicle.
14. Remove mounting bolts and lower cover, **Fig. 14.**
15. Reverse procedure to install.

TIMING BELT
REPLACE
2.0L Engine

The following procedure has been revised by a Technical Service Bulletin.

REMOVAL

1. Remove timing belt front cover as outlined under "Front Cover, Replace."
2. Align crankshaft and camshaft sprocket marks, **Fig. 15,** then loosen timing belt tensioner mounting bolts.
3. Remove timing belt. If belt is to be reused, mark running direction on belt for installation alignment.
4. Remove timing belt tensioner. **Fig. 16. Tensioner pivot bolt, should never be tightened, loosened or removed, as factory locking compound is not reusable. If pivot bolt is disturbed, entire pivot bracket assembly must be replaced.**
5. Inspect timing belt for cracks, missing teeth, rubber hardening and abnormal wear.

INSTALLATION

1. Position timing belt tensioner in suit-

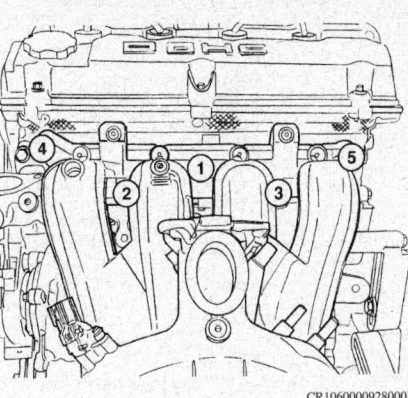

CR1060000928000X

Fig. 8 Intake manifold tightening sequence

able soft jawed vise, then slowly compress tensioner plunger into tensioner body.
2. With tensioner plunger compressed into body, insert $\frac{5}{64}$ inch hex wrench, or suitable locking pin, through holes in tensioner body, **Fig. 17.**
3. Align crankshaft sprocket mark with oil pump housing and back off to three sprocket teeth before Top Dead Center (TDC), **Fig. 18.**
4. Align camshaft sprocket mark with timing belt rear cover , **Fig. 15.**
5. Position crankshaft sprocket at ½ tooth before TDC, **Fig. 19.**
6. Position timing belt over crankshaft, around water pump and over camshaft sprockets, then around tensioner pulley.
7. Remove timing belt slack by placing crankshaft sprocket in TDC position.
8. Position timing belt tensioner on engine block and loosely install mounting bolts, **Fig. 16. Tensioner pivot bolt should never be tightened, loosened or removed, as factory locking compound is not reusable. If pivot bolt is disturbed, entire pivot bracket assembly must be replaced.**
9. Apply 20–21 ft. lbs. force to timing belt tensioner pulley using suitable torque wrench, **Fig. 15.**
10. While applying tension on tensioner pulley, move timing belt tensioner against tensioner pulley bracket and tighten mounting bolts.
11. Remove hex wrench or locking pin retaining tensioner plunger in body. Timing belt pretension is correct when wrench or pin can be freely removed and installed in tensioner body holes.
12. Rotate crankshaft two revolutions in normal rotation direction.
13. Inspect crankshaft and camshaft sprocket timing mark alignment, **Fig. 15.** If timing marks are not properly aligned, repeat belt installation procedure.
14. Install front cover as outlined under "Front Cover, Replace."
15. **After completing installation, perform camshaft and crankshaft alignment relearn procedure using suitably programmed scan tool and instructions.**
16. Remove park plug No. 1.

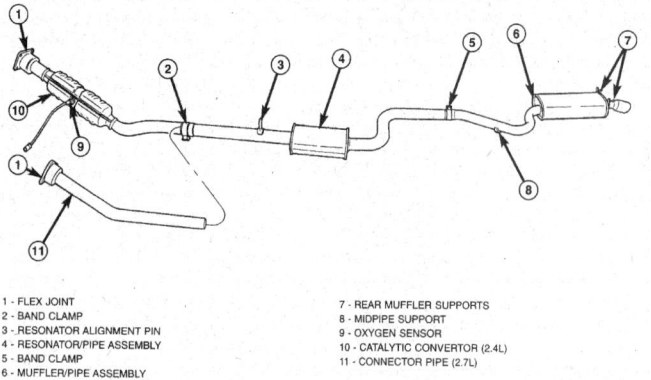

1 - FLEX JOINT
2 - BAND CLAMP
3 - RESONATOR ALIGNMENT PIN
4 - RESONATOR/PIPE ASSEMBLY
5 - BAND CLAMP
6 - MUFFLER/PIPE ASSEMBLY

7 - REAR MUFFLER SUPPORTS
8 - MIDPIPE SUPPORT
9 - OXYGEN SENSOR
10 - CATALYTIC CONVERTOR (2.4L)
11 - CONNECTOR PIPE (2.7L)

CR1070200020000X

Fig. 9 Exhaust system replacement. 2.0L & 2.4L engines

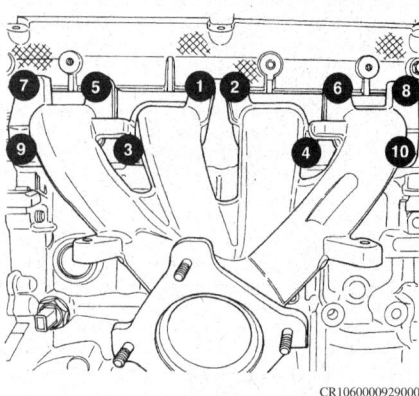

CR1060000929000X

Fig. 10 Exhaust manifold tightening sequence

17. Set cylinder No. 1 at TDC on compression stroke using suitable dial indicator.
18. Remove timing belt front cover access plug.
19. Camshaft sprocket timing mark should be aligned with timing belt rear cover arrow, **Fig. 15**.

2.4L Engine

REMOVAL

1. Remove timing belt front covers as outlined under "Front Cover, Replace."
2. Align crankshaft and camshaft sprocket timing marks, **Fig. 20**.
3. Position 6 mm hex head wrench to timing belt tensioner pulley and insert 3 mm hex head wrench into tensioner pulley pin hole, **Fig. 21**.
4. Rotate tensioner pulley counterclockwise until 3 mm hex head wrench can be inserted into cylinder block. locking hole.
5. Remove timing belt.

INSTALLATION

1. Ensure crankshaft sprocket timing mark is aligned.
2. Position camshaft sprockets so exhaust sprocket is ½ notch below intake sprocket, **Fig. 22**.
3. Install timing belt over crankshaft sprocket, then around water pump sprocket, idler pulley, camshaft sprockets and tensioner pulley.
4. Remove slack from belt by moving exhaust camshaft sprocket counterclockwise and align timing marks.
5. Remove 3 mm hex head wrench from cylinder block and tensioner.
6. Rotate crankshaft sprocket two revolutions in normal engine rotation direction.
7. Ensure all timing marks are aligned and install front covers as outlined under "Front Cover, Replace."

CAMSHAFT

REPLACE

2.0L Engine

1. Remove fuel pump relay from power

distribution center.
2. Start and run engine until it stalls.
3. Attempt to restart engine until it will no longer run, then turn ignition key to OFF position.
4. Install fuel pump relay, then erase any DTC's that may have been stored because of removing fuel pump relay.
5. Remove cylinder head as outlined under "Cylinder Head, Replace."
6. Remove camshaft sensor and camshaft target magnet, then the camshaft sprocket bolt.
7. Remove sprocket from camshaft with modified sprocket removal tool No. C-4687-1, or equivalent, **Fig. 23**. Hold camshaft sprocket with modified tool while removing bolt.
8. Remove camshaft seal using camshaft seal remover tool No. C-4679, or equivalent.
9. Remove camshaft from rear of cylinder head.
10. Reverse procedure to install, noting the following:
   a. Install new camshaft seal with seal insertion tool No. MD998306, or equivalent.
   b. Hold camshaft sprocket with tool No. C-4687 and adapter tool No. C-4687-1, or equivalents, and tighten.

2.4L Engine

1. Remove valve cover as outlined under "Valve Cover, Replace."
2. Remove timing belt, sprockets and covers as outlined under "Timing Belt, Replace."
3. Remove outside bearing caps L1, R1, L6 and R6.
4. Loosen camshaft bearing cap mounting bolts one camshaft at a time in sequence, **Fig. 24**.
5. Identify camshafts before removing from head. **Camshafts are not interchangeable.**
6. Reverse procedure to install, noting the following:
   a. Install left and righthand inside camshaft bearing caps, and R6 outside camshaft bearing cap.
   b. **Tighten** caps in sequence one camshaft at a time, **Fig. 25**.

c. **Outside camshaft bearing cap R6, is to be tightened as an inside bearing cap.**
d. Install outside camshaft bearing caps L1, R1 and L6, tighten.

BALANCE SHAFT

REPLACE

2.4L Engine

1. Remove timing belt front cover as outlined under "Front Cover, Replace."
2. Remove gear cover double ended retaining stud, chain covers and gears, **Fig. 26**.
3. Remove balance shaft gear and chain sprocket mounting bolts.
4. Remove crankshaft chain sprocket and chain using two pry bars to work sprocket back and forth.
5. Remove carrier rear cover and balance shafts.
6. Remove four carrier to crankcase mounting bolts.
7. Reverse procedure to install, noting the following:
   a. Align balance shaft gears dot marks and ensure keys face upward, **Fig. 27**.
   b. Align balance shaft timing chain and gear timing marks, **Fig. 28**.
   c. Position .039 inch thick and 2.75 inches long shim between tensioner and chain.
   d. Push tensioner and shim against timing chain with 5.5–6.6 lbs force, **Fig. 29**.
   e. Tighten top bottom tensioner bolts with force applied to timing chain.

PISTON & ROD ASSEMBLY

1. L or H stamping on front portion of piston must face toward front of engine.
2. Connecting rod and cap are stamped on side with cylinder number identification.
3. Numbered side of connecting rod cap must be installed on same side as numbered side of rod.
4. **Torque** cap bolts to 20 ft. lbs.
5. Tighten bolts an additional 90°.

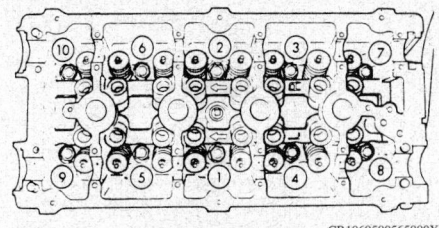

Fig. 11 Cylinder head tightening sequence

Fig. 12 Rocker arm shaft notch alignment. 2.0L engine

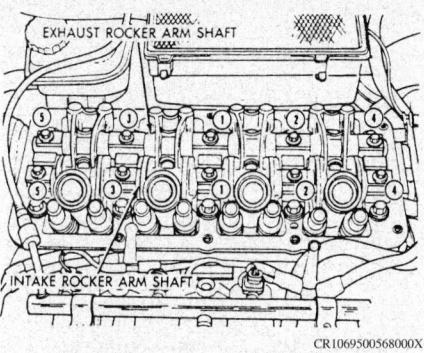

Fig. 13 Rocker arm shaft tightening sequence. 2.0L engine

MAIN & ROD BEARINGS

All upper and lower bearing shells in the crankcase have oil grooves.

Upper and lower bearing No. 3 halves are flanged to carry the crankshaft thrust loads and are not interchangeable with any other bearing halves.

All bearing cap bolts removed during service procedures are to be cleaned and oiled before installation.

Bearing shells are available in standard and .001 and .010 inch undersized: **Never install an undersize bearing that will reduce clearance below specifications.**

Torque main bearing M8 cap bolts to 20–21 ft. lbs., and M11 bolts to 30 ft. lbs., plus an additional ¼ turn, in sequence

1. Install main bearing shells with lubrication groove in cylinder block. Ensure oil holes in block line up with oil holes in bearings. Bearing tabs must seat in block tab slots.
2. Oil the bearings and journals, then install crankshaft. **Do not get oil on bedplate mating surface.**
3. Ensure both cylinder block and bedplate surfaces are clean.
4. Apply .059–.078 inch bead of anaerobic sealer Mopar Bed Plate Sealant, or equivalent, to cylinder block, **Fig. 30.**
5. Install lower main bearings into main bearing cap/bedplate. Ensure bearing tabs are seated into bedplate slots.
6. Position main bearing/bedplate onto engine block.
7. Lubricate bolt threads with suitable, clean engine oil. Wipe off any excess oil.
8. Install main bearing bedplate to engine block bolts 11, 17 and 20 hand tight, **Fig. 31.**
9. Tighten bolts down together until bedplate contacts cylinder block.
10. Rotate crankshaft until piston No. 4 is at TDC.
11. Move crankshaft rearward to limits of travel
12. Move crankshaft forward to limits of travel.
13. Hold crankshaft in it's furthest forward position by wedging an appropriate tool between rear of cylinder block (not bed plate) and rear crankshaft counterweight.
14. **Torque** mounting bolts 1–10 to 30 ft. lbs. in sequence, **Fig. 31.**
15. Remove wedge tool.

16. **Torque** bolts 1–10 to 30 ft. lbs. in sequence.
17. Tighten bolts and additional 90° in sequence.
18. Install main bearing bedplate engine block bolts 11–20.
19. **Torque** mounting bolts to 20 ft. lbs. in sequence.
20. After main bearing bedplate is installed, ensure crankshaft turning torque does not exceed 50 in. lbs.

CRANKSHAFT SEAL
REPLACE

1. Remove components to access crankshaft sprocket as outlined under "Timing Belt, Replace."
2. Remove crankshaft sprocket using sprocket remover tool No. 6793 and insert tool No. C-4685-C2, or equivalents, **Fig. 32.**
3. Remove front crankshaft seal using oil seal remover tool No. 6771, or equivalent, **Fig. 33.**
4. Reverse procedure to install, noting the following:
   a. Install new seal using seal installation tool No. 6780-1, or equivalent.
   b. Install crankshaft sprocket using installed tool No. 6792, or equivalent.

CRANKSHAFT REAR OIL SEAL
REPLACE

1. Remove transaxle as outlined in **MOTOR's "Domestic Transmission Manual, In-Vehicle Service."**
2. remove flex plate.
3. Insert suitable ³⁄₁₆ screwdriver between dust lip and metal case of seal seat. Pry out seal.
4. Reverse procedure to install, noting the following:
   a. Seal should be installed dry with THIS SIDE OUT mark facing away from block.
   b. Install seal flush with block surface using pilot tool No. 6926-1, seal installation tool No. 6926-2 and handle tool No. C-4171, or equivalents.

OIL PAN
REPLACE
2.0L Engine

1. Drain engine oil into suitable container.

2. Remove front engine mount bracket and bending strut.
3. Remove structural collar from oil pan to transaxle, then transaxle dust cover.
4. **On models equipped with air conditioning,** remove oil filter and adapter.
5. **On all models,** remove mounting bolts and oil pan.
6. Reverse procedure to install. Apply Molar silicone rubber adhesive sealant, or equivalent, at oil pump to engine block parting line, then to oil pan gasket to hold gasket in place.

2.4L Engine

1. Drain engine oil into suitable container.
2. Remove front engine torque bracket from bending strut and insulator mount.
3. Remove mounting bolts, then the collar and bending strut from engine, oil pan and transaxle.
4. Remove mounting bolts and oil pan.
5. Reverse procedure to install. Apply Molar silicone rubber adhesive sealant, or equivalent, at oil pump to engine block parting line and on oil pan gasket to hold gasket in place.

OIL PUMP
REPLACE

1. Remove components to access oil pump as outlined under "Timing Belt, Replace."
2. Remove oil pick-up tube.
3. Remove mounting bolts and oil pump.
4. Reverse procedure to install.

OIL PUMP SERVICE
Disassemble

1. Remove relief valve plug and gasket, then spring and relief valve.
2. Remove mounting bolts and cover.
3. Remove pump rotors.

Inspection

1. Clean all components thoroughly in suitable solvent. Mating surface of oil pump should be smooth. Replace pump cover if scratched or grooved.
2. Measure clearance between suitable

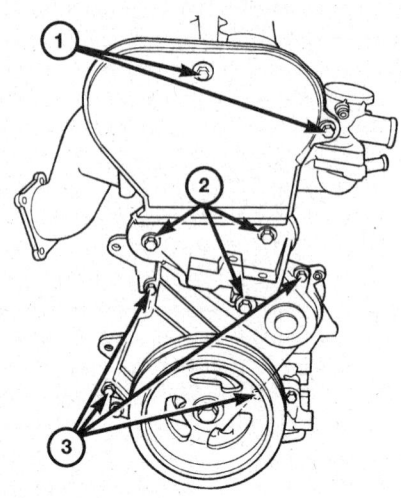

1 - UPPER TIMING BELT COVER FASTENERS
2 - ENGINE SUPPORT BRACKET FASTENERS
3 - LOWER TIMING BELT COVER FASTENERS

CR1060100966000X

Fig. 14 Front cover replacement. 2.4L engine

straightedge and pump cover. If measurement is more than . 001 inch, replace cover.

3. Measure thickness and diameter of outer rotor. If outer rotor thickness is .301 inch or less, or if diameter is 3.148 inches or less, replace outer rotor.
4. If inner rotor measures .301 inch or less, replace inner rotor.
5. Place outer rotor into pump housing and press to one side. Measure clearance between rotor and housing. If measurement is .015 inch or more, replace housing.
6. Install inner rotor into pump housing. If clearance between inner and outer rotors is .008 inch or more, replace rotors.
7. Measure clearance between straightedge and pump housing face between bolt holes. If measurement is .004 inch, or more, replace pump.
8. Inspect oil pressure relief valve plunger for scoring and for free operation within its bore. Small marks may be removed with 400 grit wet/dry sandpaper.
9. Oil pump relief valve spring should be approximately 2.39 inches long, Spring should have 18–19 lbs. of resistance when compressed to 1.6 inches. Replace spring if it is not within specifications.

Assemble

1. Install inner rotor with chamfer facing cast iron oil pump cover.
2. Apply Molar gasket maker lightly to cover mounting surface on pump body.
3. Install cover and tighten.
4. Install relief valve, spring, gasket and cap, then tighten.
5. Prime oil pump by filling rotor cavity with suitable, clean engine oil.

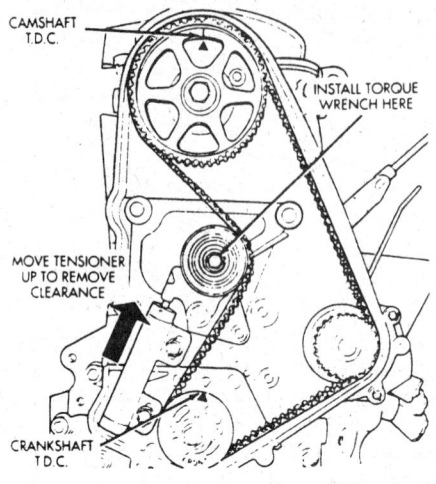

CR1069500620000X

Fig. 15 Crankshaft & camshaft timing mark alignment. 2.0L engine

6. Apply Molar gasket maker to oil pump.
7. Install oil-ring into counter bore on oil pump body discharge passage.
8. Install oil pump slowly onto crankshaft until seated to engine block.

BELT TENSION DATA

Refer to **Fig. 34** for belt tension data.

SERPENTINE DRIVE BELT

Air Conditioning Compressor & Alternator Belt

REMOVAL

1. Raise and support vehicle.
2. Remove righthand front tire and wheel assembly.
3. Remove drive belt splash shield.
4. Insert suitable ⅜ inch drive breaker bar into square opening of belt tensioner pivot plate.
5. Rotate belt tensioner clockwise until tensioner bottoms out, then remove belt from pulleys.

INSTALLATION

1. Insert suitable ⅜ inch drive breaker bar into square opening of belt tensioner pivot plate.
2. Install belt over all pulleys except air conditioning compressor drive pulley, **Fig. 35**.
3. Rotate belt tensioner clockwise until tensioner bottoms out and belt can be installed over air conditioning compressor pulley.
4. Gently release tensioner.
5. Install drive belt splash shield, then the tire and wheel assembly.

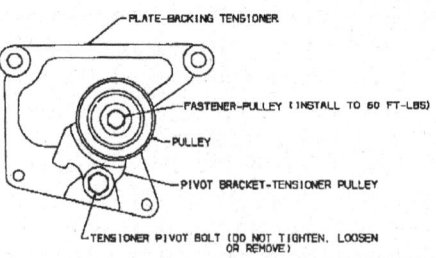

CR1069500679000X

Fig. 16 Tensioner pivot bracket. 2.0L engine

COOLING SYSTEM BLEED

This procedure has been revised by a Technical Service Bulletin.

1. Install cooling system filling aid tool No. 8195, or equivalent that looks like funnel that attaches to filler neck in place of pressure cap along with attached hose clip.
2. Pinch off overflow hose attach to fill neck.
3. Attach 5–6.5 foot length of clear ¼ inch I.D. clear hose to bleed valve. Pit other end of hose in suitable container.
4. Open cooling system bleed valve located on water outlet connector near front of engine.
5. Pour suitable coolant mixture into large side of filling aid tool.
6. Slowly fill cooling system, using large side of cooling aid.
7. When steady stream of coolant comes out of clear hose, close bleed valve. Continue filling to top of filling aid tool.
8. Remove overflow hose clip. Excess fluid will drain into coolant bottle overflow.
9. Remove filling aid.
10. Ensure pressure cap bottom seal and filler neck are clean and free of debris.
11. Install coolant bottle pressure cap.

THERMOSTAT
REPLACE

1. Drain coolant to below thermostat into suitable container.
2. Loosen clamp, then disconnect hoses at coolant outlet connector and thermostat housing.
3. Remove coolant outlet connector to thermostat housing mounting bolts.
4. Remove coolant outlet connector.
5. Remove thermostat and gasket.
6. Reverse procedure to install, noting the following:
   a. Install new gasket.
   b. Align air bleed with notch in coolant outlet connector.

WATER PUMP
REPLACE

1. Raise and support vehicle, then remove righthand inner splash shield.
2. Remove accessory drive belts
3. Drain coolant into suitable container.
4. Support engine from bottom and remove righthand engine mount.

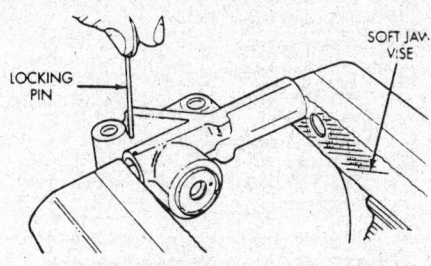

Fig. 17 Timing belt tensioner locking pin installation. 2.0L engine

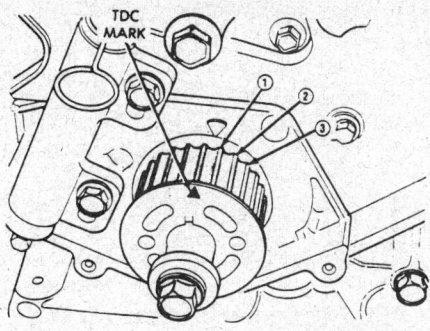

Fig. 18 Crankshaft sprocket & oil pump housing alignment . 2.0L engine

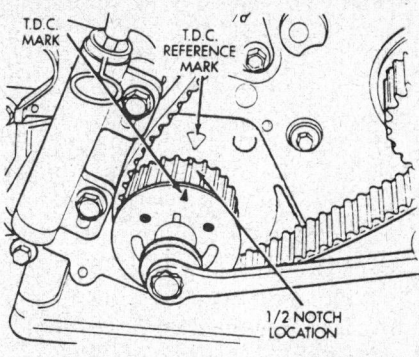

Fig. 19 Crankshaft sprocket ½ tooth rotation. 2.0L engine

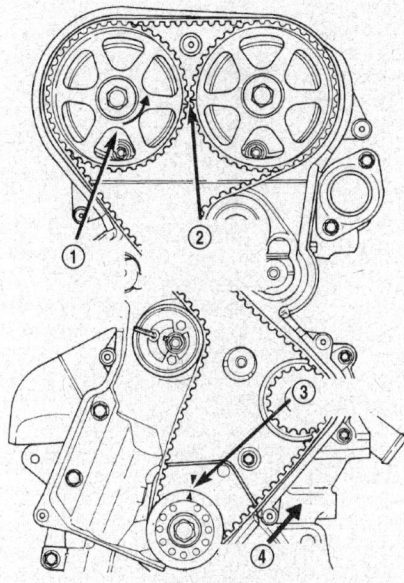

1 - ROTATE CAMSHAFT SPROCKET TO TAKE UP BELT SLACK
2 - CAMSHAFT TIMING MARKS 1/2 NOTCH LOCATION
3 - CRANKSHAFT AT TDC
4 - INSTALL BELT IN THIS DIRECTION

Fig. 20 Crankshaft & camshaft sprocket timing mark alignment. 2.4L engine

5. Remove mounting bolts, then position power steering pump and bracket aside. Power steering lines do not need to be disconnected.
6. Remove timing belt as outlined under "Timing Belt, Replace."
7. Remove mounting bolts water pump.
8. Reverse procedure to install. Install new O-ring gasket in water pump body O-ring groove.

RADIATOR
REPLACE

1. Drain coolant into suitable container, then remove upper radiator crossmember.
2. Disconnect electrical connector and remove radiator fan.
3. Disconnect hoses from radiator.
4. Remove screw holding support bracket for transmission cooler tubes to lefthand side of radiator.

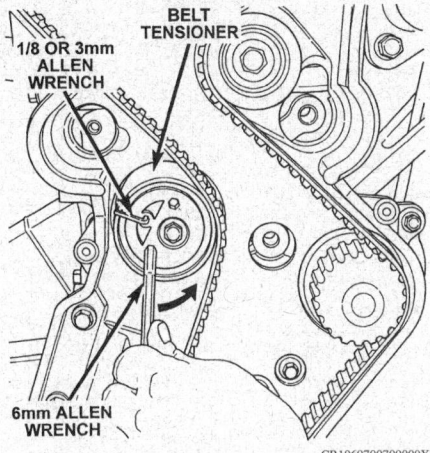

Fig. 21 Locking timing belt tensioner in release position. 2.4L engine

5. Remove air conditioning lines support bracket.
6. Carefully lift out radiator.
7. Reverse procedure to install.

FUEL PUMP
REPLACE

The electric fuel pump is not serviceable. If the fuel pump requires service, the entire fuel pump module must be replaced.
1. Remove fuel pump relay from power distribution center.
2. Start and run engine until it stalls.
3. Attempt to restart engine until it will no longer run, then turn ignition key to OFF position.
4. Install fuel pump relay, then erase any DTC's that may have been stored because of removing fuel pump relay.
5. Drain and remove fuel tank.
6. Disconnect fuel filter lines at fuel pump module.
7. Clean top of tank to remove dirt and debris.
8. Remove lockout securing pump module with fuel pump module ring spanner tool No. 6856, or equivalent, **Fig. 36.**
9. Remove fuel pump module and O-ring from tank. Discard O-ring.

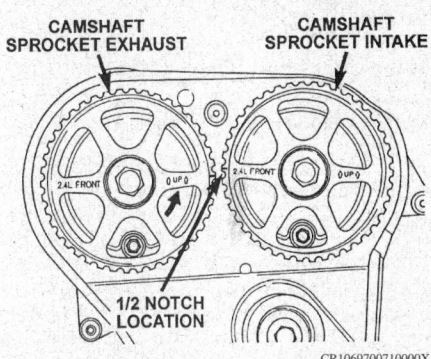

Fig. 22 Camshaft sprocket alignment. 2.4L engine

10. Reverse procedure to install. Install new pump module O-ring.

FUEL FILTER
REPLACE

The fuel filter is part of the fuel pressure regulator and is located on top of the fuel pump module.
1. Remove fuel pump relay from power distribution center.
2. Start and run engine until it stalls.
3. Attempt to restart engine until it will no longer run, then turn ignition key to OFF position.
4. Install fuel pump relay, then erase any DTC's that may have been stored because of removing fuel pump relay.
5. Drain fuel tank into suitable container.
6. Raise and support vehicle on hoist.
7. Support fuel tank with suitable transmission jack.
8. Remove strap bolts lower tank slightly.
9. Disconnect fuel filler vent tube, fuel line and vapor line.
10. Disconnect vacuum line from LDP.
11. Loosen clamp and remove fuel filler tube.
12. Unlock and disconnect fuel pump module electrical connector.
13. Lower fuel tank.
14. Disconnect fuel supply line at filter/regulator nipple.
15. Depress locking spring tab on side of fuel regulator, rotate 90° counterclockwise and remove.
16. Reverse procedure to install.

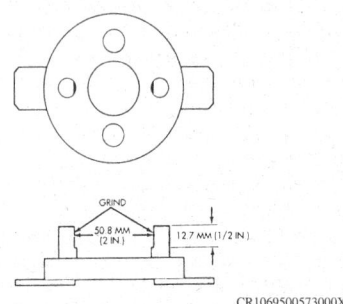

Fig. 23 Sprocket removal tool modification. 2.0L engine

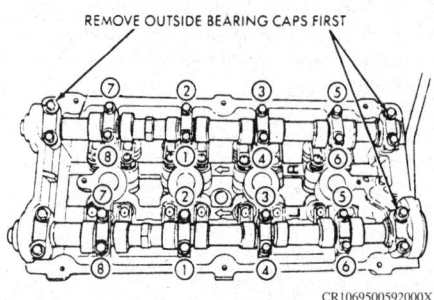

Fig. 24 Camshaft bearing cap removal sequence. 2.4L engine

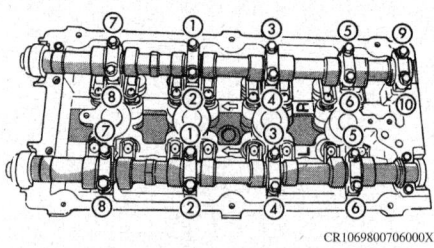

Fig. 25 Camshaft bearing cap tightening sequence. 2.4L engine

TECHNICAL SERVICE BULLETINS

Irregular Engine Snapping Sound

On some of these models there may be an irregular engine snapping sound. The sound is irregular, not periodic or harmonious. The sound is more higher pitch snapping, not low metallic knock. The sound may be noticed when the engine is idling in PARK between idle and 1400 RPM at normal operating temperature. The sound is on the upper end (cylinder head) toward the front (passenger side).

This condition may be caused the cam bearing caps L2–L5 and R2–R5.

To correct this condition, proceed as follows:

1. Remove valve cover as outlined under "Valve Cover, Replace."
2. Remove L2 cam bearing cap, **Fig. 37.**
3. **Do not remove L1/R1 or L6 cam bearing caps. Do not loosen L1/R1 or L6 cam bearing caps mounting bolts.**
4. **Remove one cam bearing cap at a time.**
5. Lightly chamfer two bores radius edges using suitable, small hand file, **Fig. 38.**
6. Create a 45° chamfer, .039–.059 inch wide along edge of each bore radios.
7. **Do not scratch bore surface.**
8. Clean part of aluminum filings.
9. Install L2 cam bearing cap and loosely install mounting bolts.
10. Twist cam bearing cap clockwise (as viewed from top of engine) by hand.
11. **Torque** bolts to 105 inch lbs while maintaining clockwise twisting force on cam bearing cap.
12. Repeat procedure on cam bearing caps L3, L4, L5, R2, R3, R4, R5 and R6.

Rattle Or Vibration Under Center Console

2001-02

On some of these models built before Dec. 17, 2001, there may be a rattle or vibration sound under the vehicle near the center console. The sound may be more pronounced during cold start up and the disappear when the engine reaches operating temperature.

This condition may be caused by the exhaust center isolator.

To correct this condition, proceed as follows:

1. Raise and support vehicle.
2. Spray water-based lubricate on exhaust center isolator and retaining pin, **Fig. 39.**
3. Pry center isolator off mounting pins.
4. Lubricate revised isolator (part No. 04879241AB) with suitable water-based lubricant and install.

Low Or No Cabin Heat

On some of these models there may be low or no cabin heat, engine overheating and/or coolant bottle damage after servicing the cooling system.

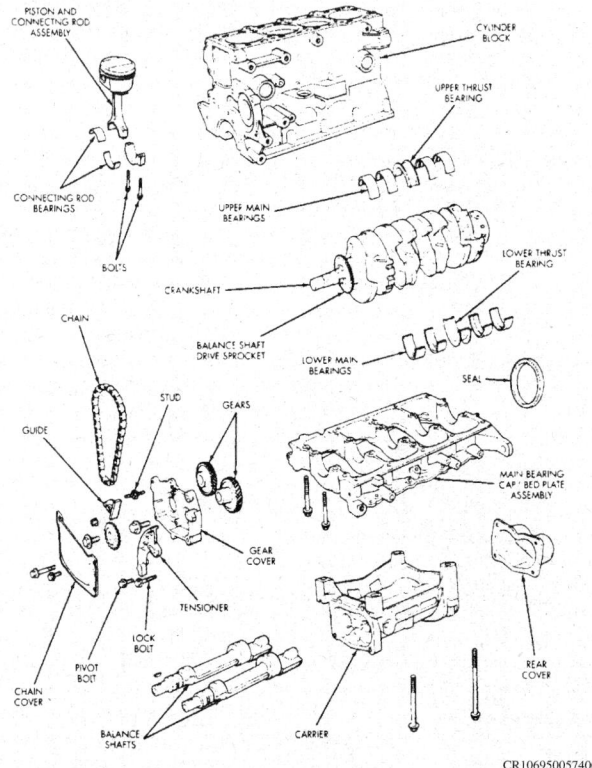

Fig. 26 Exploded view of cylinder block. 2.4L engine

This condition may be caused by not filling cooling system completely.

To correct this condition, proceed as follows:

1. Install cooling system filling aid tool No. 8195, or equivalent that looks like funnel that attaches to filler neck in place of pressure cap along with attached hose clip.
2. Pinch off overflow hose attach to fill neck.
3. Attach 5–6.5 foot length of clear ¼ inch I.D. clear hose to bleed valve. Pit other end of hose in suitable container.
4. Open cooling system bleed valve located on water outlet connector near front of engine.
5. Pour suitable coolant mixture into large side of filling aid tool.
6. Slowly fill cooling system, using large side of cooling aid.
7. When steady stream of coolant comes out of clear hose, close bleed valve.

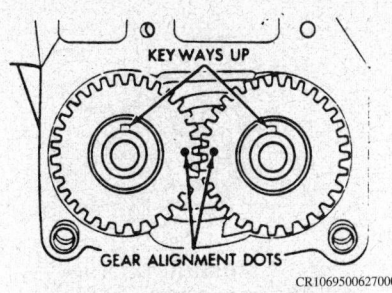

Fig. 27 Balance shaft gear alignment. 2.4L engine

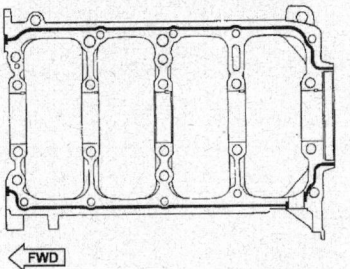

Fig. 30 Sealer application

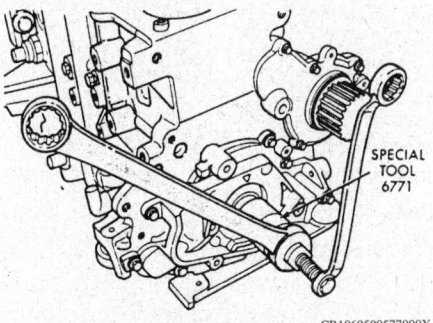

Fig. 33 Front crankshaft oil seal replacement

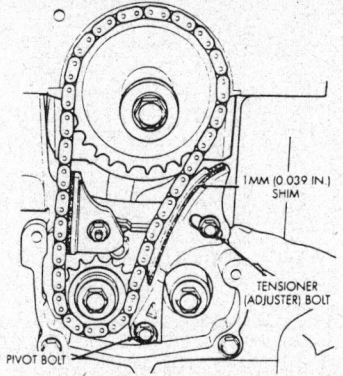

Fig. 28 Balance shaft timing chain & gears alignment. 2.4L engine

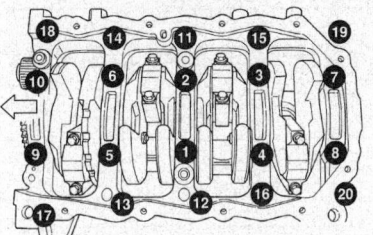

Fig. 31 Main bearing bolt tightening sequence

Accessory Drive Belt	Belt Tension		
Air Conditioning Compressor/ Generator	Dynamic Tensioned		
Power Steering Pump	New	120 - 180 lbs.	160 - 223 Hz
	Used*	70 - 115 lbs.	114 - 179 Hz

*A belt is considered used after 15 minutes of run-in time.

Fig. 34 Belt tension chart

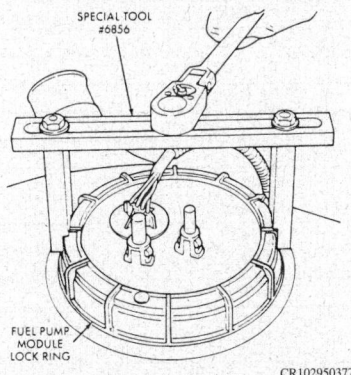

Fig. 36 Fuel pump module lockout

To correct this condition, install correct filter (part No. 04105409) on 2.4L DOHC engine.

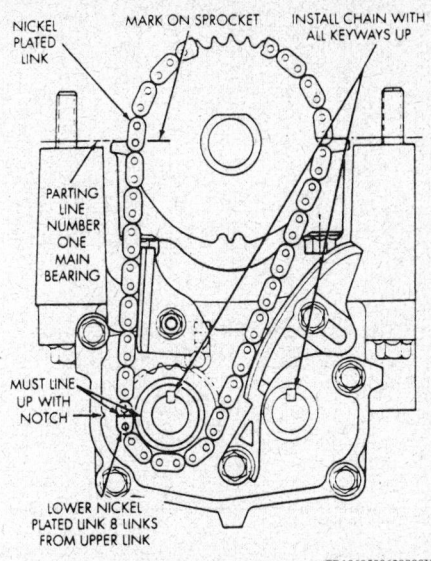

Fig. 29 Balance shaft timing chain tension adjustment. 2.4L engine

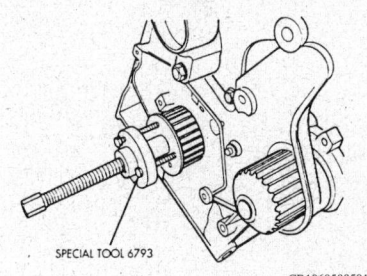

Fig. 32 Crankshaft sprocket replacement

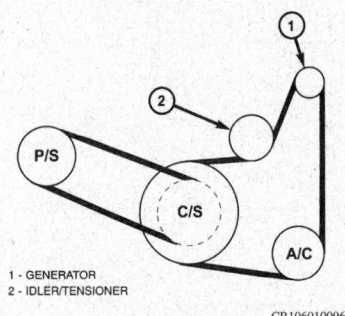

Fig. 35 Serpentine drive belt routing

Continue filling to top of filling aid tool.
8. Remove overflow hose clip. Excess fluid will drain into coolant bottle overflow.
9. Remove filling aid.
10. Ensure pressure cap bottom seal and filler neck are clean and free of debris.
11. Install coolant bottle pressure cap.

Incorrect Oil Filter

2.4L ENGINE

On some of these models there may be oil loss and engine damage.

This condition may be caused by installing oil filter (part No. MD360935) for 2.4L SOHC Mitsubidhi Motors Corp (MCC) used in Sebring Coupe and Stratus Coupe models on 2.4L DOHC DaimlerChrysler engine used in Sebring Convertible, Sebring Sedan and Stratus Sedan.

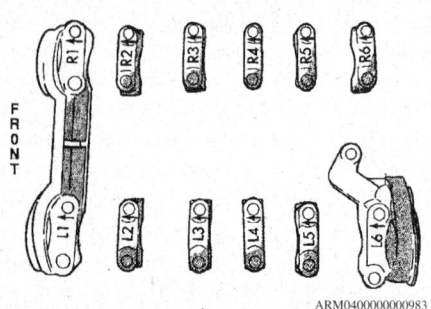

Fig. 37 Camshaft bearing cap identification

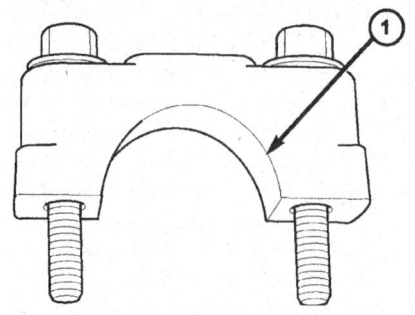

1- CAM BEARING CAP RADIUS

ARM0400000000984

Fig. 38 Camshaft bearing cap chamfer area

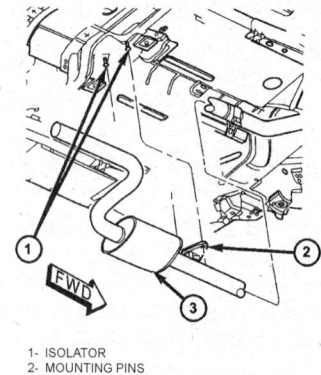

1- ISOLATOR
2- MOUNTING PINS
3- RESONATOR

ARM0400000000985

Fig. 39 Exhaust center isolator

TIGHTENING SPECIFICATIONS

Year	Component	Torque/Ft. Lbs.
2.0L DOHC ENGINE		
2001	Camshaft Sprocket	85
	Connecting Rod Cap	②
	Crankshaft Damper	105
	Crankshaft Main Bearing Bedplate (M8)	25
	Crankshaft Main Bearing Bedplate (M11)	60
	Cylinder Head	⑤
	Drive Plate	70
	Engine Mount	③
	Exhaust Manifold	17
	Exhaust Manifold Heat Shield	105①
	Fuel Pump Module Lock Ring	40
	Fuel Rail To Intake Manifold	16–17
	Fuel Tank Drain Plug	32①
	Hydraulic Timing Belt Tensioner	23
	Intake Manifold	105①
	Main Bearing Cap	④
	Oil Filter	15
	Oil Filter Adapter	40
	Oil Pan	105①
	Oil Pan Drain Plug	20
	Oil Pump	20
	Oil Pump Cover	105①
	Oil Pump Pickup Tube	20
	Oil Pump Relief Valve Retaining Cap	30
	PCV Valve	70①
	Spark Plugs	13
	Thermostat Housing	16–17
	Throttle Body Support Bracket	96–108①
	Throttle Body To Intake	16
	Timing Belt Cover	105①
	Timing Belt Tensioner	23
	Valve Cover	105①
	Water Pump	105①
2.4L DOHC ENGINE		
2001–05	Balance Shaft Carrier	40
	Balance Shaft Cover	105①
	Balance Shaft Sprocket	20
	Balance Shaft Timing Chain Tensioner	105①
	Camshaft Sprocket (2001)	75
	Camshaft Sprocket (2002–05)	85

Continued

TIGHTENING
SPECIFICATIONS—Continued

Year	Component	Torque/Ft. Lbs.
2.4L DOHC ENGINE		
2001–05	Connecting Rod Cap	②
	Crankshaft Damper	100
	Crankshaft Main Bearing Bedplate (M8) (2001)	25
	Crankshaft Main Bearing Bedplate (M11) (2001)	30⑦
	Crankshaft Main Bearing Bedplate (M8) (2002–05	20
	Crankshaft Main Bearing Bedplate (M11) (2001)	55
	Cylinder Head	⑤
	Engine Mount	③
	Exhaust Manifold	17
	Exhaust Manifold Heat Shield	105①
	Flex Plate	70
	Fuel Pump Module Lock Ring	40
	Fuel Rail To Intake Manifold	16–17
	Fuel Tank Drain Plug	32①
	Intake Manifold (2001)	105①
	Intake Manifold (2002–05)	20
	Oil Filter (2001)	15
	Oil Filter (2002)	10
	Oil Filter (2003–05)	97①
	Oil Pan	105①
	Oil Pan Drain Plug	20
	Oil Pump	20
	Oil Pump Cover	105①
	Oil Pump Pickup Tube (2001)	20
	Oil Pump Pickup Tube (2002–05)	17
	Oil Pump Relief Valve Retaining Cap	40
	Rocker Arm & Shaft	21
	Spark Plugs	13
	Thermostat Housing	16–17
	Throttle Body Support Bracket	96–108①
	Throttle Body To Intake	16
	Timing Belt Cover (M6) (2001)	40①
	Timing Belt Cover (M6) (2002–05)	105①
	Timing Belt Cover (M8)	20
	Timing Belt Cover, Screws (2001)	40①
	Timing Belt Cover, Screws (2002)	80①
	Timing Belt Cover, Screws (2003–05)	50①
	Timing Belt Tensioner	45
	Valve Cover	⑥
	Water Pump	105①

① — Inch Lbs.
② — Refer to "Piston & Rod Assembly" for tightening procedure & specifications.
③ — Refer to "Engine Mount, Replace" illustrations for tightening specifications.
④ — Refer to "Main & Rod Bearings" for tightening procedure & specifications.
⑤ — Refer to "Cylinder Head, Replace" for tightening procedure & specifications.
⑥ — Refer to "Valve Cover, Replace" for tightening procedure & specifications.
⑦ — Final tighten an additional 90°.

2.7L Engine

NOTE: Refer to "2.7L Engine" in "Concorde, Intrepid, LHS, Vision & 300M" Chapter For Procedures Not Covered In This Section.

NOTE: On Air Bag Equipped Models, Refer To "Air Bag System Precautions" Located In The Front Of This Manual For System Disarming & Arming Procedures.

NOTE: Refer To "Computer Relearn Procedures" Located In The Front Of This Manual When Battery Power To The Computer Has Been Interrupted.

NOTE: Prior To Performing Any Service Operations Listed In This Section, Consult The "Technical Service Bulletins" Section For Related Information.

INDEX

PRECAUTIONS

Air Bag Systems

Refer to "Air Bag System Precautions" in the front of this manual for system disarming and arming procedures.

Battery Ground Cable

Prior to service, disconnect battery ground cable and isolate as required.

Fuel System Pressure Relief

1. Remove fuel pump relay from power distribution center.
2. Start and run engine until it stalls.
3. Attempt to restart engine until it will no longer run, then turn ignition key to OFF position.
4. Install fuel pump relay, then erase any DTC's that may have been stored because of removing fuel pump relay.

COMPRESSION PRESSURE

The minimum compression pressure should be no less than 100 psi and the max-

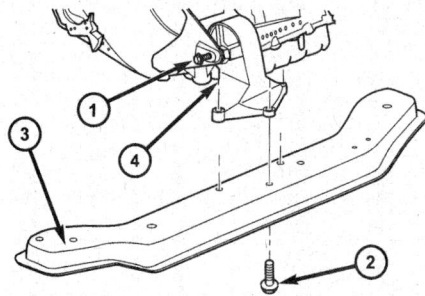

1 - HORIZONTAL THROUGH BOLT
2 - VERTICAL BOLT(S)
3 - LOWER RADIATOR CROSSMEMBER
4 - FRONT ENGINE MOUNT

CR1060000933000X

Fig. 1 Front engine mount replacement

imum variation between cylinders should be no more than 25%.

ENGINE MOUNT

REPLACE

Front

1. Raise and support vehicle, then re-

move front mount to bracket horizontal through bolt, **Fig. 1.**
2. Remove vertical bolts and front mount.
3. Reverse procedure to install.

Lefthand

1. Remove throttle body air inlet hose and air cleaner housing assembly.
2. Remove two mounting nuts and position speed control servo bracket aside.
3. Support transaxle with suitable floor jack and wooden block.
4. Remove three vertical bolts from mount to transaxle bracket, **Fig. 2.**
5. Slightly lower transaxle.
6. Remove frame rail bolts and mount.
7. Reverse procedure to install.

Rear

1. Remove throttle body air inlet hose and air cleaner housing assembly.
2. Remove three rear mount bracket to transaxle case vertical bolts, **Fig. 3.**
3. Raise and support vehicle, then remove rear mount bracket through bolt.
4. Remove rear mount bracket to transaxle case horizontal bolt.
5. Remove mount bracket.
6. Remove rear mount to suspension crossmember mounting bolts and rear mount.
7. Reverse procedure to install.

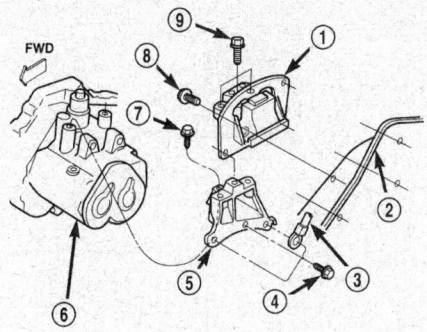

1 - TRANSMISSION SUPPORT ASSEMBLY
2 - LEFT FRAME RAIL
3 - GROUND CABLE
4 - BOLT (D)
5 - TRANSMISSION BRACKET
6 - TRANSMISSION
7 - BOLT (C)
8 - BOLT (B)
9 - BOLT (A)

CR1060000930000X

Fig. 2 Lefthand side engine mount replacement

Righthand

1. Remove engine coolant overflow container, then heater tube mounting screw.
2. Raise and support vehicle, then remove inner splash shield.
3. Remove heater tube rear mounting screw.
4. Remove righthand engine support assembly vertical bolts from frame rail, **Fig. 4.**
5. Lower vehicle, then support engine using suitable floor jack and block of wood placed under oil pan.
6. Remove mounting bolts and righthand engine mount.
7. Reverse procedure to install.

ENGINE
REPLACE

1. Remove fuel pump relay from power distribution center.
2. Start and run engine until it stalls.
3. Attempt to restart engine until it will no longer run, then turn ignition key to OFF position.
4. Install fuel pump relay, then erase any DTC's that may have been stored because of removing fuel pump relay.
5. Drain coolant into suitable container.
6. Recover air conditioning refrigerant as outlined in "Air Conditioning" chapter.
7. Remove throttle body air inlet hose and air cleaner housing assembly.
8. Raise and support vehicle, then remove both front tire and wheel assemblies.
9. Remove left and righthand splash shields.
10. Remove front fascia to and lower air shield to crossmember mounting bolts.
11. Remove front bumper fascia. Lower vehicle.
12. Remove upper radiator crossmember, then disconnect upper and lower radiator hoses at radiator.

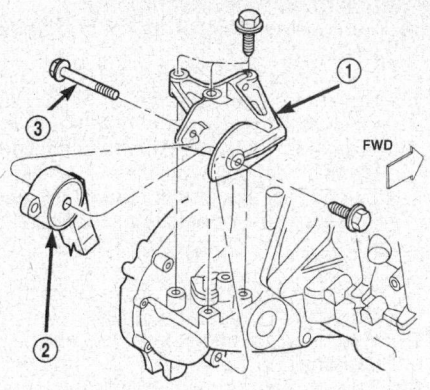

1 - REAR TORQUE BRACKET
2 - REAR MOUNT
3 - THROUGH BOLT

CR1060000931000X

Fig. 3 Rear engine mount replacement

13. Disconnect transaxle oil cooler lines at transaxle. Plug openings.
14. Disconnect air conditioning lines at condenser and remove cooling fan module.
15. Disconnect transaxle electrical connectors and shift cable.
16. Disconnect engine electrical harness from PCM and bulkhead connectors.
17. Remove ABS brake module and position aside.
18. Disconnect brake line from retaining clips, then raise and support vehicle.
19. Remove both axle shafts as outlined in "Front Drive Axle" chapter.
20. Remove through bolt and front engine mount from lower radiator crossmember.
21. Remove lower radiator crossmember and accessory drive belts.
22. Remove, then position power steering pump and bracket with lines attached aside.
23. Disconnect heater return from pipe connection at righthand front frame rail area.
24. Disconnect electrical connector, remove and position air conditioning compressor aside.
25. Remove structural collar and exhaust cross-under pipe.
26. Remove rear engine mount and transaxle bracket, then drain engine oil into suitable container.
27. Remove transaxle torque converter housing cover.
28. Mark flex plate to torque converter position for installation alignment, then remove torque converter bolts.
29. Lower vehicle, then disconnect positive cable from battery and PDC.
30. Disconnect ground cable from lefthand side transaxle mount bracket.
31. Disconnect throttle and speed control cables.
32. Disconnect coolant pressure bottle hose from engine outlet connector.
33. Disconnect heater hose from engine outlet connector.
34. Disconnect ground strap at righthand shock tower, then fuel line.

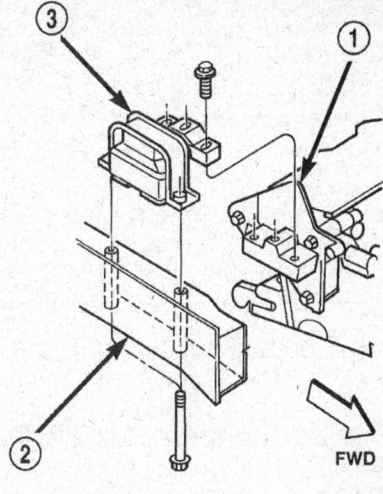

1 - ENGINE SUPPORT BRACKET
2 - FRAME RAIL
3 - RIGHT ENGINE MOUNT

CR1060000932000X

Fig. 4 Righthand side mount replacement

35. Disconnect brake booster and vapor purge vacuum hoses.
36. Disconnect all engine ground straps.
37. Lower vehicle enough to install engine dolly tool No. 6135 and cradle tool No. 6710 with posts tool No. 6848, or equivalents.
38. Loosen cradle engine mounts to allow movement for positioning onto engine locating holes on engine block, compressor mount bracket and oil pan rail.
39. Lower vehicle and position cradle until engine is resting on posts. Tighten post mounts to cradle frame.
40. Lower vehicle so only weight of engine is on cradle.
41. Remove left and righthand engine mount bolts.
42. Slowly raise vehicle and remove engine.
43. Reverse procedure to install.

BELT TENSION DATA

Refer to **Fig. 5** for belt tension data.

SERPENTINE DRIVE BELT

Air Conditioning Compressor/Alternator Belt

1. Raise and support vehicle, then remove righthand front tire and wheel assembly.
2. Remove splash shield.
3. Loosen tensioner locking bolt and pivot bolt.
4. Rotate tensioner clockwise and remove belt.
5. Reverse procedure to install.

Accessory Drive Belt		Belt Tension	
Air Conditioning Compressor/ Generator	New	185 - 235 lbs.	204 - 230 Hz
	Used*	110 - 160 lbs.	157 - 190 Hz
Power Steering Pump	New	120 - 180 lbs.	122 - 170 Hz
	Used*	70 - 115 lbs.	94 - 136 Hz
*A belt is considered used after 15 minutes of run-in time.			

CR1060200977000X

Fig. 5 Belt tension data. 2.7L engine

Power Steering Pump Belt

1. Raise and support vehicle, then remove righthand front tire and wheel assembly.
2. Remove splash shield.
3. Loosen tensioner locking bolt and pivot bolt.
4. Rotate tensioner clockwise and remove air conditioning compressor/ alternator belt.
5. Loosen adjusting bolt, then pivot power steering pump and remove belt.
6. Reverse procedure to install.

COOLING SYSTEM BLEED

This procedure has been revised by a Technical Service Bulletin.
1. Install cooling system filling aid tool No. 8195, or equivalent that looks like funnel that attaches to filler neck in place of pressure cap along with attached hose clip.
2. Pinch off overflow hose attach to fill neck.
3. Attach 5–6.5 foot length of clear ¼ inch I.D. clear hose to bleed valve. Pit other end of hose in suitable container.
4. Open cooling system bleed valve located on water outlet connector near front of engine.
5. Pour suitable coolant mixture into large side of filling aid tool.
6. Slowly fill cooling system, using large side of cooling aid.
7. When steady stream of coolant comes out of clear hose, close bleed valve. Continue filling to top of filling aid tool.
8. Remove overflow hose clip. Excess fluid will drain into coolant bottle overflow.
9. Remove filling aid.
10. Ensure pressure cap bottom seal and filler neck are clean and free of debris.
11. Install coolant bottle pressure cap.

THERMOSTAT
REPLACE

1. Drain cooling system into suitable container.

2. Raise and support vehicle.
3. Remove righthand front tire and wheel assembly.
4. Remove belt splash shield.
5. Remove accessory drive belts and lower alternator mounting bolt.
6. Lower vehicle and disconnect alternator electrical connectors.
7. Disconnect air conditioning clutch and pressure sensor electrical connectors.
8. Remove oil dipstick and tube, Plug hole.
9. Remove alternator and disconnect hoses at thermostat housing.
10. Remove mounting bolts and thermostat housing.
11. Reverse procedure to install. Install thermostat with bleed valve located at 12 o'clock position

WATER PUMP
REPLACE

1. Drain cooling system into suitable container.
2. Remove timing chain cover as outlined under "Front Cover, Replace."
3. Remove timing chain and guides as outlined under "Timing Chain, Replace."
4. Remove mounting bolts and water pump.
5. Reverse procedure to install.

RADIATOR
REPLACE

1. Drain cooling system into suitable container.
2. Remove upper radiator crossmember.
3. Disconnect electrical connector, and remove radiator fan.
4. Disconnect radiator hoses.
5. Remove screw holding support bracket for transaxle cooler tubes at lefthand side of radiator.
6. Remove air conditioning lines support bracket from righthand side of radiator.
7. Remove mounting screws and air conditioning condenser.
8. Remove radiator.
9. Reverse procedure to install.

FUEL PUMP
REPLACE

1. Remove fuel pump relay from power distribution center.
2. Start and run engine until it stalls.
3. Attempt to restart engine until it will no longer run, then turn ignition key to OFF position.
4. Install fuel pump relay, then erase any DTC's that may have been stored because of removing fuel pump relay.
5. Drain fuel tank into suitable container.
6. Raise vehicle and support on hoist.
7. Support fuel tank with suitable transmission jack.
8. Remove strap bolts and lower tank slightly.
9. Disconnect fuel filler vent tube, fuel line and vapor line.

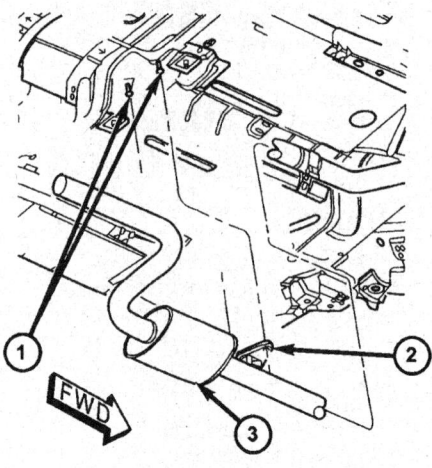

1- ISOLATOR
2- MOUNTING PINS
3- RESONATOR

ARM0400000000988

Fig. 6 Exhaust center isolator

10. Disconnect vacuum line from LDP.
11. Loosen clamp and remove fuel filler tube.
12. Unlock and disconnect fuel pump module electrical connector.
13. Lower fuel tank.
14. Disconnect fuel line from fuel pump module by depressing quick connect retainers.
15. Disconnect fuel pump electrical connector by pushing down on retainer and pulling connector off.
16. Remove fuel pump module lock nut using spanner wrench tool No. 6856, or equivalent.
17. Remove fuel pump and O-ring seal from tank. Discard old seal.
18. Reverse procedure to install.

FUEL FILTER
REPLACE

The fuel filter is part of the fuel pressure regulator and is located on top of the fuel pump module.
1. Remove fuel pump relay from power distribution center.
2. Start and run engine until it stalls.
3. Attempt to restart engine until it will no longer run, then turn ignition key to OFF position.
4. Install fuel pump relay, then erase any DTC's that may have been stored because of removing fuel pump relay.
5. Remove fuel tank as outlined under "Fuel Pump, Replace."
6. Disconnect fuel supply line at filter/ regulator nipple.
7. Depress locking spring tab on side of fuel regulator, rotate 90° counterclockwise and remove.
8. Slide tank forward allowing fill neck to clear suspension crossmember, then lower tank to remove.
9. Reverse procedure to install.

TECHNICAL SERVICE BULLETINS

Rattle Or Vibration Under Center Console

2001-02

On some of these models built before Dec. 17, 2001, there may be a rattle or vibration sound under the vehicle near the center console. The sound may be more pronounced during cold start up and the disappear when the engine reaches operating temperature.

This condition may be caused by the exhaust center isolator.

To correct this condition, proceed as follows:

1. Raise and support vehicle.
2. Spray water-based lubricate on exhaust center isolator and retaining pin, **Fig. 6.**
3. Pry center isolator off mounting pins.
4. Lubricate revised isolator (part No. 04879241AB) with suitable water-based lubricant and install.

Low Or No Cabin Heat

On some of these models there may be low or no cabin heat, engine overheating and/or coolant bottle damage after servicing the cooling system.

This condition may be caused by not filling cooling system completely.

To correct this condition, proceed as follows:

1. Install cooling system filling aid tool No. 8195, or equivalent that looks like funnel that attaches to filler neck in place of pressure cap along with attached hose clip.
2. Pinch off overflow hose attach to fill neck.

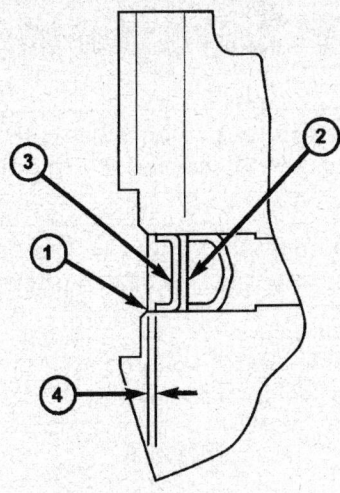

1- CUP PLUG BORE CHAMBER
2- ORIGINAL CUP PLUG
3- NEW CUP PLUG
4- 1-2 mm+

ARM0400000000986

Fig. 7   Cylinder head oil gallery cap plug installation

3. Attach 5–6.5 foot length of clear ¼ inch I.D. clear hose to bleed valve. Pit other end of hose in suitable container.
4. Open cooling system bleed valve located on water outlet connector near front of engine.
5. Pour suitable coolant mixture into large side of filling aid tool.
6. Slowly fill cooling system, using large side of cooling aid.
7. When steady stream of coolant comes out of clear hose, close bleed valve. Continue filling to top of filling aid tool.
8. Remove overflow hose clip. Excess fluid will drain into coolant bottle overflow.
9. Remove filling aid.

10. Ensure pressure cap bottom seal and filler neck are clean and free of debris.
11. Install coolant bottle pressure cap.

Cylinder Head Oil Gallery Cup Plug Leaking

2001-02

On some of these models, the cylinder head oil galley cup plug may be leaking.

This condition may be caused by a faulty oil gallery cup plug.

To correct this condition proceed as follows:

1. Determine which cup plug is leaking. Perform an engine oil leak dye test, as required.
2. Each head has six external oil gallery plugs. Cup plug bore is deep enough to allow for two plugs.
3. Some cup plugs may be serviced with head installed on engine, while other require cylinder head removal.
4. Remove components required to gain access to affected oil gallery cup plug.
5. Inspect cup plug bore in question and ensure that only one plug is present. If cup plug flange is just inside (.039–.079 inch) chamfered edge bore, two plugs are installed and cylinder head can not be repaired.
6. Clean plug bore with suitable brake cleaner and compressed air.
7. Lightly coat new plug (part No. 04792279) with gasket sealer No. 04318083, or equivalent.
8. Drive new plug into head using suitable installation drive tool until cup plug is .039–.079 inch inside chamfered edge of plug bore, **Fig. 7.**
9. Allow sealant to cure for at least 20 minutes.

TIGHTENING SPECIFICATIONS

Year	Component	Torque Ft. Lbs.
2001–05	Air Conditioning Compressor	21
	Alternator Bracket	30
	Front Engine Mount, Front	45
	Engine Mount To Bracket, Rear	45
	Engine Mount To Crossmember, Rear	45
	Engine Mount To Frame Rail, Lefthand	24
	Engine Mount To Frame Rail, Righthand	45
	Engine Mount To Support Bracket, Righthand	45
	Engine Mount To Transaxle Bracket, Lefthand	45
	Engine Mount Bracket To Transaxle, Rear	80
	Thermostat Housing	105①
	Water Pump	105①

① — Inch lbs.

Rear Suspension

NOTE: On Air Bag Equipped Models, Refer To "Air Bag System Precautions" Located In The Front Of This Manual For System Disarming & Arming Procedures.

NOTE: Refer To "Computer Relearn Procedures" Located In The Front Of This Manual When Battery Power To The Computer Has Been Interrupted.

NOTE: Prior To Performing Any Service Operations Listed In This Section, Consult The "Technical Service Bulletins" Section For Related Information.

INDEX

DESCRIPTION

The rear suspension is a fully independent short and long arm style suspension, **Fig. 1.** An upper control arm bolts to the top of each rear cast knuckle to the rear suspension crossmember. The movement of the rear knuckle is controlled laterally by two lower lateral links going from the front and rear of the knuckle to the rear crossmember and upper control arm. Fore and aft movement of the knuckle is controlled by a trailing arm.

HUB & BEARING
REPLACE

All models are equipped with permanently lubricated, sealed-for-life wheel bearings. There is no periodic lubrication or maintenance recommended for these units. If servicing is required, proceed as follows:
1. Raise and support vehicle, then remove rear tire and wheel assembly.
2. Remove brake drum.
3. Remove dust cap and from hub/bearing to spindle mounting nut.
4. Remove hub/bearing retainer from spindle by pulling straight on spindle by hand.
5. Reverse procedure to install.

SHOCK ABSORBER
REPLACE

1. Roll back carpeting and remove shock tower cover.
2. Remove two mounting nuts.
3. Raise and support vehicle, then remove tire and wheel assembly.
4. Remove shock clevis bracket to knuckle mounting bolt, **Fig. 2.**

5. Remove shock absorber clevis bracket from knuckle by pushing down on suspension.
6. Move shock absorber downward and tilt top of shock outward.
7. Remove shock through top of wheel-well opening.
8. Reverse procedure to install.

COIL SPRING
REPLACE

1. Position shock in suitable vise, **Fig. 3.**
2. Mark assembly right or lefthand.
3. Compress coil spring using coil spring compressor tool No. GP-2020-S2.5, or equivalent.
4. Keep shock shaft rod from turning using suitable tool and remove shock shaft nut.
5. Remove washer, shock mounting bracket, washer and dust shield.
6. Remove coil spring and spring compressor.
7. Reverse procedure to install.

CONTROL ARM
REPLACE

1. Raise and support vehicle, then remove both rear tire and wheel assemblies.
2. Roll back carpeting and remove shock tower cover.
3. Remove two mounting nuts.
4. Raise and support vehicle, then remove tire and wheel assembly.
5. Remove shock clevis bracket to knuckle mounting bolt, **Fig. 2.**
6. Remove shock absorber clevis bracket from knuckle by pushing down on suspension.
7. Move shock absorber downward and tilt top of shock outward.

8. Remove shock through top of wheel-well opening.
9. Remove muffler support bracket from rear frame, **Fig. 4.**
10. Remove hanger bracket from rear suspension crossmember and move exhaust down far as possible.
11. Remove cotter pin and castle nut from ball joint.
12. **On models equipped with ABS,** remove speed sensor heads from knuckle.
13. **On all models,** separate control arm ball joint from rear knuckle using puller tool No. CT-1106, or equivalent. **Install castle nut on ball joint stud to protect threads.**
14. Support crossmember by positioning suitable floor jack and block of wood under center of crossmember .
15. Remove routing clips for wheel speed sensor cable from brackets on both upper control arms.
16. Remove four rear suspension crossmember to rear frame rails mounting bolts.
17. Lower rear suspension crossmember far enough to access upper control arm pivot bar to crossmember mounting bolts.
18. Remove two mounting bolts and upper control arm, **Fig. 5.**
19. Reverse procedure to install, noting the following:
    a. Align upper control arm pivot bar with mounting holes in rear suspension crossmember.
    b. Position appropriate size drift into position hole in each side of rear suspension crossmember and crossmember locating holes in frame rails, then tighten frame rail mounting bolts.

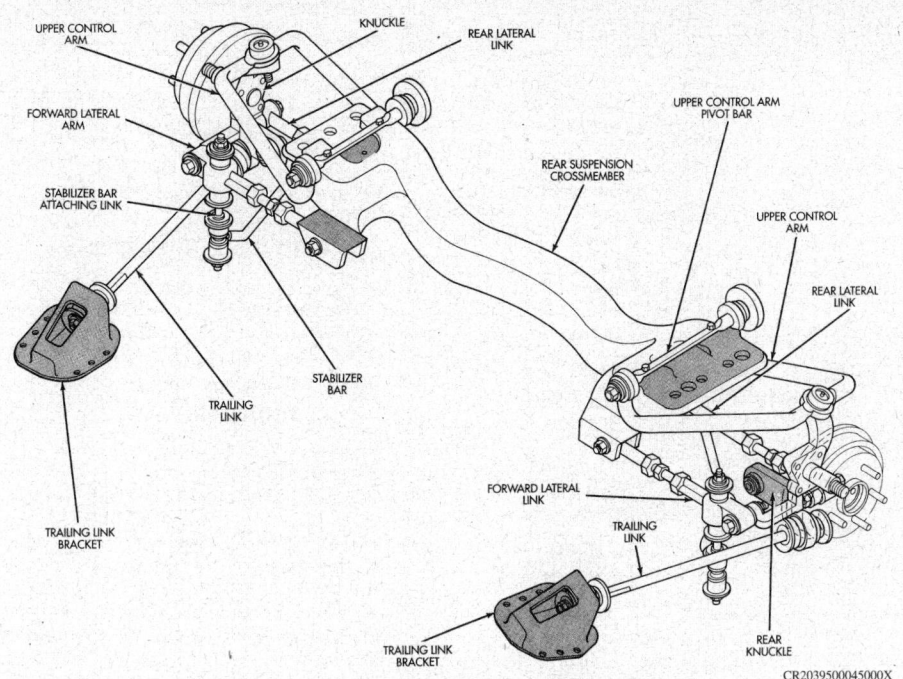

Fig. 1 Rear suspension components

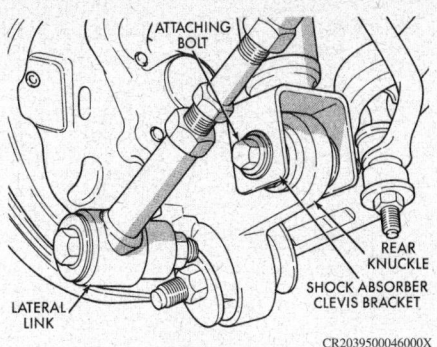

Fig. 2 Shock & knuckle replacement

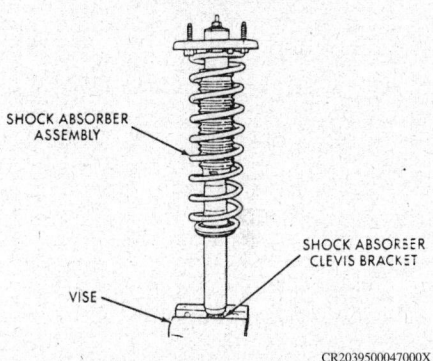

Fig. 3 Coil spring removal

KNUCKLE

REPLACE

1. Raise and support vehicle, then remove rear tire and wheel assembly.
2. Remove brake drum or disc brake.
3. Remove rear wheel speed sensor.
4. Remove parking brake cable from brake actuator lever.
5. Position a ½ inch box end wrench over parking brake cable retainer and collapse retaining tabs, **Fig. 6.**
6. Pull brake cable from brake support plate.
7. Remove mounting nut, washer, then the hub and bearing assembly from knuckle.
8. Remove four rear support plate to knuckle mounting bolts.
9. Remove brake support plate, brake shoes and wheel cylinder.
10. Remove forward and rear lateral links to knuckle mounting nuts and bolts.
11. Separate from rear knuckle using puller tool No. CT-1106, or equivalent. **Install castle nut on ball joint stud to protect threads.**
12. Remove knuckle.
13. Reverse procedure to install.

STABILIZER BAR

REPLACE

1. Raise and support vehicle, then remove both rear tire and wheel assemblies.

2. Remove nuts attaching stabilizer link isolator bushings to stabilizer links using suitable wrench to prevent stabilizer links from rotating.
3. Remove stabilizer bar bushing clamp to rear suspension crossmember mounting bolts, **Fig. 7.**
4. Remove rear stabilizer bar to crossmember bushing clamps and bushings from stabilizer bar.
5. Remove stabilizer bar.
6. Reverse procedure to install.

LATERAL LINK

REPLACE

Forward

1. Raise and support vehicle, then remove rear tire and wheel assembly.
2. Remove rear stabilizer bar attaching link from forward lateral link to knuckle, **Fig. 8.**
3. Remove lateral link to knuckle mounting nut and bolt.
4. Remove mounting bolt and lateral link.
5. Reverse procedure to install.

Rear

1. Raise and support vehicle, then remove rear tire and wheel assembly.
2. Remove lateral link to knuckle mounting nut and bolt, **Fig. 9.**
3. Remove mounting nut and bolt, then the lateral link.
4. Reverse procedure to install.

TECHNICAL SERVICE BULLETINS

Popping Or Squeaking From Rear Suspension

2001

On some of these models there may be a popping or squawking noise from the rear suspension. Noise may be mistaken for a strut or strut mount condition.

This condition may be caused play in the rear suspension upper control arm bushing because of improper installation.

To correct this condition, proceed as follows:

1. Inspect for improperly installed bushing.
2. Place suitable pry bar between control arm and bushing lip.
3. If there is movement between the two under light to moderate force, replace upper control arm.

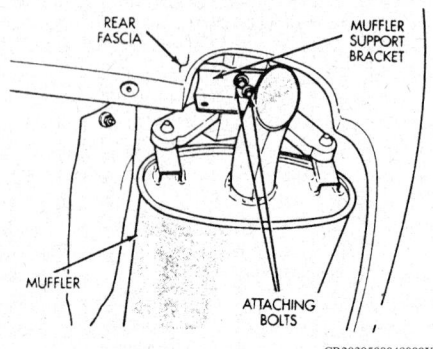

Fig. 4 Muffler support bracket replacement

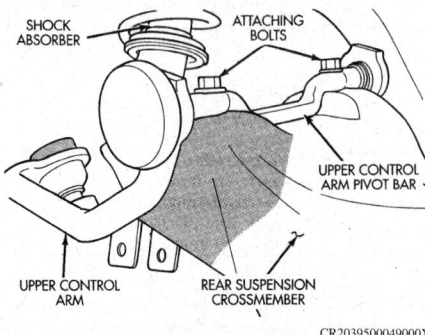

Fig. 5 Upper control arm & crossmember replacement

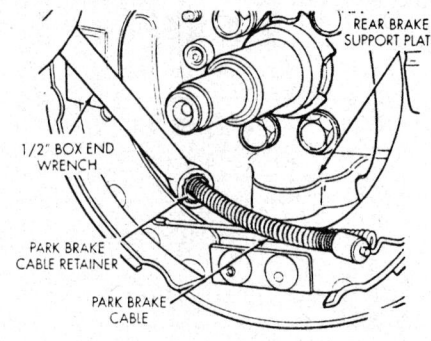

Fig. 6 Parking brake cable replacement

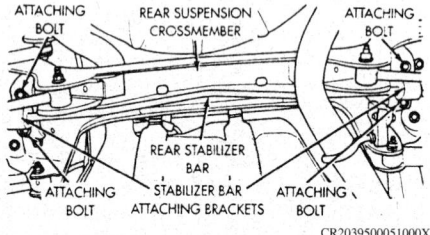

Fig. 7 Rear stabilizer bar replacement

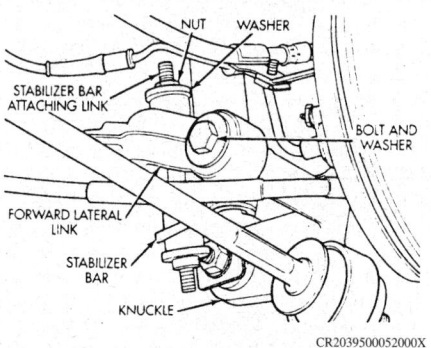

Fig. 8 Forward lateral link replacement

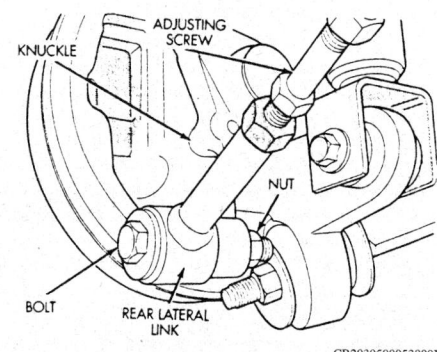

Fig. 9 Rear lateral link replacement

TIGHTENING SPECIFICATIONS

Year	Component	Torque/Ft. Lbs.
2001–05	Ball Joint	80
	Brake Support Plate To Knuckle	45
	Hub & Bearing	185
	Lateral Link	70
	Lateral Link To Knuckle	90
	Lateral Link To Suspension Crossmember	65
	Shock Assembly Clevis Bracket To Knuckle	70
	Shock Assembly Shaft	40
	Shock Assembly To Body	40
	Stabilizer Bar Bracket	24
	Stabilizer Bar Isolator Bushing	24
	Stabilizer Bar To Lateral Link	23
	Trailing Link Bracket	21
	Trailing Link Shaft	85
	Upper Ball Joint To Knuckle Castle Nut	63
	Upper Control Arm Pivot Bar To Crossmember	70
	Wheel Lug Nuts	100

Front Suspension & Steering

NOTE: On Air Bag Equipped Models, Refer To "Air Bag System Precautions" Located In The Front Of This Manual For System Disarming & Arming Procedures.

NOTE: Refer To "Computer Relearn Procedures" Located In The Front Of This Manual When Battery Power To The Computer Has Been Interrupted.

NOTE: Prior To Performing Any Service Operations Listed In This Section, Consult The "Technical Service Bulletins" Section For Related Information.

INDEX

WHEEL BEARING
ADJUST

These models are equipped with permanently-sealed front wheel bearings. There is no periodic lubrication or maintenance recommended.

HUB & BEARING
REPLACE

1. Raise and support vehicle.
2. Remove front stub axle cotter pin, lock nut and spring washer.
3. Lower vehicle, then loosen hub nut while vehicle is on ground and brakes are applied.
4. Raise and support vehicle, then remove from tire and wheel assembly.
5. Remove front disc brake caliper and brake disc assembly, then support aside from steering knuckle.
6. Remove outer tie rod end to steering knuckle.
7. Remove steering knuckle tie rod end using remover tool No. MB-991113, or equivalent.
8. Remove speed sensor cable routing bracket, **Fig. 1.**
9. Remove cotter pin and castle nut from stud of lower ball joint at steering knuckle.
10. Turn steering knuckle so front of steering knuckle is facing as far outboard in wheelwell as possible.
11. Separate steering knuckle from stud of lower ball joint by lightly tap boss. **Do not hit lower control arm or ball joint grease seal.**
12. Separate from ball joint stud by lifting up on steering knuckle. **Support driveshaft so it does not hang by inner Constant Velocity (CV) joint.**
13. Separate steering knuckle from outer CV joint by pulling away, **Fig. 2.**
14. Remove upper ball joint to steering knuckle cotter pin and nut.
15. Remove upper ball joint stud using puller tool No. C3894-A, or equivalent.
16. Remove steering knuckle.
17. Mount steering knuckle securely in suitable vise and remove three hub/bearing assembly to steering knuckle bolts.
18. Remove hub/bearing from steering knuckle. **If bearing does not come out, tap lightly using rubber mallet.**
19. Reverse remaining procedure to install.

DRIVESHAFT
REPLACE

1. Loosen, but do not remove, stub axle to hub/bearing mounting nut while vehicle is on ground and brakes applied.
2. Raise and support vehicle, then remove front tire and wheel assembly.
3. Remove brake caliper and support aside. Remove brake disc.
4. Remove tie rod end mounting nut and tie rod end stud from steering knuckle using remover tool No. MB-991113, or equivalent.
5. Remove vehicle speed sensor cable routing bracket.
6. Remove lower ball joint at steering knuckle. cotter pin and castle nut.
7. Turn steering knuckle so front of knuckle is facing as far outboard in wheelwell as possible.
8. Separate from stud of lower ball joint by lightly tap boss on steering knuckle.
9. Pull steering knuckle out and away from outer CV joint.
10. Support outer end of driveshaft, insert suitable pry bar between tripod joint and transaxle case side gear as far as possible by hand, **Fig. 3.**
11. Hold inner tripod joint and interconnecting shaft of driveshaft.
12. Remove inner tripod joint from transaxle by pulling it straight out of transaxle side gear.
13. Reverse procedure to install.

BALL JOINT INSPECTION

Lower

1. Raise and support vehicle.
2. Install dial indicator so it contacts top surface of steering knuckle near lower ball joint stud castle nut.
3. Grasp tire and wheel assembly, then push it up and down firmly.
4. Record amount of up and down movement of steering knuckle from dial indicator.
5. Replace lower control arm if movement exceeds .059 inch.

Upper

With the weight of the vehicle resting on its wheels, attempt to move the grease fitting with no mechanical assistance. If any movement of the grease fitting is detected, the ball joint is worn.

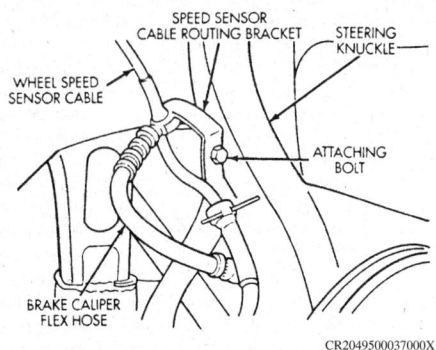

Fig. 1 Speed sensor cable routing bracket replacement

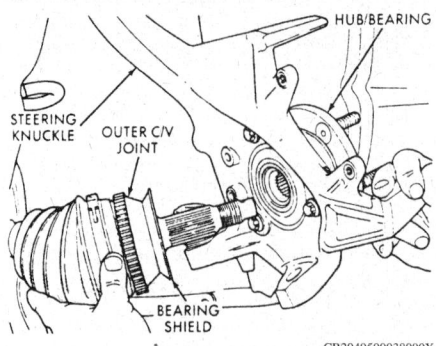

Fig. 2 Steering knuckle & outer CV joint replacement

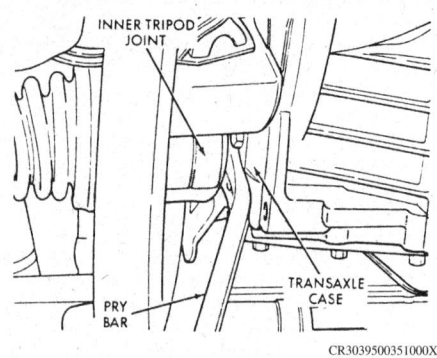

Fig. 3 Inner tripod joint replacement

BALL JOINT

REPLACE

The ball joints are not replaceable component of the control arms. If determined to be faulty, the entire control arm will have to be replaced.

SHOCK ABSORBER

REPLACE

1. Raise and support vehicle, then remove front tire and wheel assembly.
2. Remove vehicle speed sensor cable routing bracket.
3. Remove upper ball joint stud to steering knuckle cotter pin and castle nut.
4. Remove upper ball joint stud from steering knuckle using pull tool No. C-3894-A, or equivalent.
5. Position steering outward toward rear of wheelwell.
6. Remove shock clevis to shock pinch bolt.
7. Remove shock to lower control arm through bolt.
8. Remove clevis from shock by carefully tapping it off shock fluid reservoir with suitable soft brass drift,
9. Remove four shock/upper control arm mounting bracket to shock tower mounting bolts.
10. Remove shock and upper control arm mounting bracket through front area of wheelwell.
11. Reverse procedure to install.

CONTROL ARM

REPLACE

Lower

1. Raise and support vehicle, then remove front tire and wheel assembly.
2. Remove lower ball joint heat shield.
3. Remove disc brake caliper and support aside, then brake disc.
4. Disconnect ball joint from steering knuckle, then turn steering knuckle so front of knuckle is facing as far outboard as possible.
5. Separate steering knuckle from lower ball joint by lightly tapping with suitable rubber mallet.
6. Remove shock absorber clevis from lower control.

7. Remove nut attaching stabilizer bar link assembly to lower control arm using an Allen wrench to prevent stabilizer bar link from rotating.
8. Remove stabilizer bar bushing to front suspension crossmember and body mounting bolts.
9. Lower one side of stabilizer bar away from lower control arm.
10. Remove nut and bolt attaching rear isolator bushing of lower control arm, then nut and bolt attaching front isolator bushing of lower control arm, **Fig. 4.**
11. Remove front isolator bushing of lower control arm to front suspension crossmember.
12. Remove front of lower control arm from front suspension crossmember.
13. Remove rear of lower control arm from between top and bottom half of front suspension crossmember, keeping lower control arm as level as possible.
14. Reverse procedure to install.

Upper

1. Raise and support vehicle, then remove front tire and wheel assembly.
2. Remove vehicle speed sensor cable routing bracket.
3. Remove upper ball joint stud to steering knuckle cotter pin and castle nut.
4. Remove upper ball joint stud from steering knuckle using puller tool No. C-3894-A, or equivalent, then position steering outward toward rear of wheelwell.
5. Remove shock clevis to shock pinch bolt.
6. Remove shock to lower control arm through bolt.
7. Remove clevis from shock by carefully tapping clevis with suitable, soft brass drift off shock fluid reservoir.
8. Remove four upper control arm/shock absorber mounting bracket to shock tower mounting bolts.
9. Remove shock absorber and upper control arm mounting bracket.
10. Reverse procedure to install.

STEERING KNUCKLE

REPLACE

Refer to "Hub & Bearing, Replace" for knuckle replacement procedures.

STABILIZER BAR

REPLACE

1. Raise and support vehicle.
2. Remove stabilizer bar link to lower control arm nut using suitable hex wrench to prevent stabilizer bar link from rotating.
3. Remove stabilizer bar bushing to front suspension crossmember mounting bolts.
4. Remove bushings, bushing retainers, links and stabilizer bar.
5. Reverse procedure to install.

TIE ROD

REPLACE

1. Raise and support vehicle, then remove front tire and wheel assembly.
2. Remove tie rod end to steering knuckle mounting nuts.
3. Remove both tie rod end studs from steering knuckles using removal tool No. MB-991113, or equivalent.
4. Loosen inner to outer tie rod jam nut, then remove outer tie rod from inner tie rod, **Fig. 5.**
5. Remove jam nut.
6. Expand tie rod boot to inner tie rod clamp using suitable pliers, then remove inner tie rod from steering gear.
7. Reverse procedure to install.

POWER STEERING GEAR

REPLACE

1. Siphon power steering fluid from remote power steering reservoir.
2. Remove intermediate shaft coupler pinch bolt retaining pin from inside vehicle.
3. Remove pinch bolt from intermediate shaft coupler.
4. Separate intermediate shaft coupler from gear shaft.
5. Raise and support vehicle, then remove both front tire and wheel assemblies.
6. Remove both outer tie rod ends to steering knuckle mounting nuts.
7. Separate both tie rod end studs from steering knuckles using remover tool No. MB-991113, or equivalent.

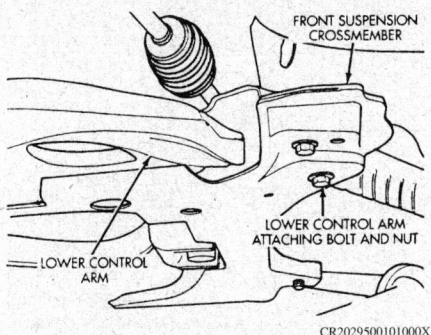

Fig. 4 Lower control arm replacement

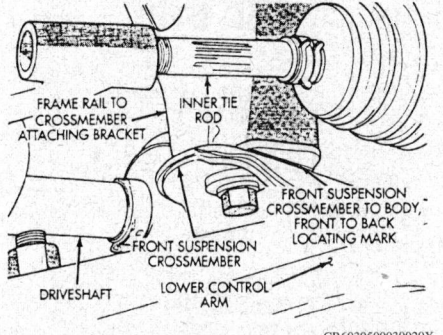

Fig. 6 Front suspension crossmember front to back locating mark (Part 2 of 2)

8. Mark front suspension crossmember on bod for installation alignment, **Fig. 6**.
9. Mark installed position (side to side) of front suspension crossmember, **Fig. 7**.
10. Remove stabilizer bar bushing clamp to body mounting bolts.
11. Remove three ABS control unit bolts, then secure unit to body for suspension crossmember removal. **Do not let unit hang by brake tubes.**
12. Remove shock absorber clevis to left and righthand lower control arms mounting bolts.
13. Remove two engine support bracket to front suspension crossmember mounting bolts.
14. Support front suspension crossmember using suitable jackstand.
15. Remove front suspension crossmember to frame rail mounting bolts from both sides of vehicle, then the rear mounting bolts.
16. Lower front suspension crossmember enough to allow steering gear to be removed from crossmember. **Ensure crossmember is supported by jackstand.**
17. Drain power steering gear fluid, pressure and return hoses into suitable container.
18. Disconnect power steering harness connector from fluid reservoir switch.
19. Remove steering gear mounting bolts, **Figs. 8 through 10**.
20. Remove steering gear.
21. Reverse procedure to install.

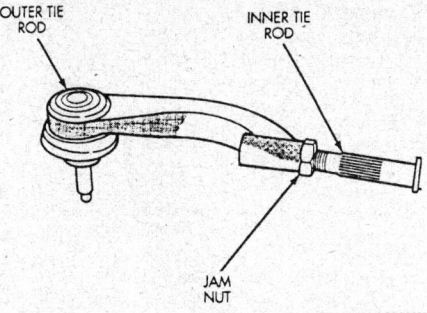

Fig. 5 Tie rod replacement

POWER STEERING PUMP
REPLACE
2.0L & 2.4L Engines

1. Siphon power steering fluid from remote power steering fluid reservoir.
2. Raise and support vehicle, then remove righthand tire and wheel assembly.
3. Remove splash shield from righthand front wheelwell.
4. Disconnect power steering fluid pressure hose from pressure fitting on power steering pump and drain remaining fluid into suitable container.
5. Remove hose clamp and power steering supply hose.
6. Remove power steering pump adjusting nut and pump to aluminum mounting bracket mounting bolt.
7. Remove ABS hydraulic control unit heat shield.
8. Remove speed sensor cable sealing grommet from inner fender, disconnect wheel speed sensor cable from wiring harness and secure aside.
9. Pull harness through hole in inner fender and unclip wiring harness through from frame rail.
10. Remove ABS sealing plug from hole in firewall.
11. Remove power steering pump front bracket to mounting bracket top mounting bolt, **Fig. 11**.
12. Remove power steering pump drive belt.
13. Remove power steering pump and bracket.
14. Reverse procedure to install.

2.7L Engine

1. Siphon power steering fluid out of remote power steering fluid reservoir.
2. Remove power steering pump supply fitting hose.
3. Raise and support vehicle, then remove drive belt splash shield.
4. Remove power steering fluid pressure hose from pump.
5. Remove oxygen sensor harness and clip from edge of pump heat shield.
6. Remove stamped pump adjuster bracket slot bolt and drive belt.
7. Pivot pump out past full-adjust position and remove three steering pump

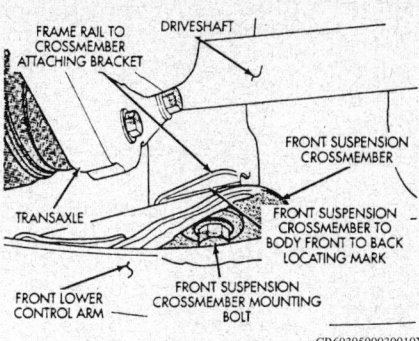

Fig. 6 Front suspension crossmember front to back locating mark (Part 1 of 2)

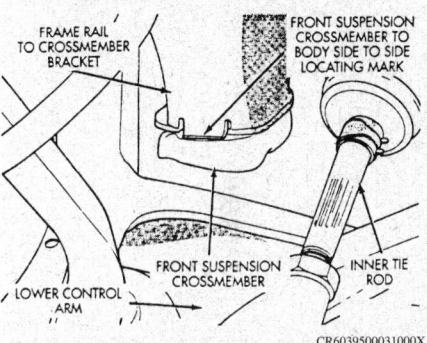

Fig. 7 Front suspension crossmember side to side locating mark

bracket mounting bolts.
8. Remove power steering pump through opening between frame rail and righthand driveshaft.
9. Reverse procedure to install.

TECHNICAL SERVICE BULLETINS
Pop Or Clunk From Front Of Vehicle

On some of these models there may be intermitten front end popping or clunk-type sound while driving over road that causes body to come under a twisting load. This sound may also be produced when parked and idling by turning steering wheel quickly 90° left, than right.

This condition may be caused by front shock tower/wheel well area.

To correct this condition, proceed as follows:

1. Raise and support vehicle, then remove both front tire and wheel assemblies.
2. Remove wheel splash shield.
3. Drill two $17/64$ inch diameter holes from inside shock tower/wheel wheel area into wet plenum, **Figs. 12 and 13**.
4. Apply suitable corrosion inhibitor to bare metal surfaces.
5. Install rivers (part No. 06033864) in holes using suitable riveter.
6. Install wheel well splash shield.
7. Repeat procedure on opposite side.

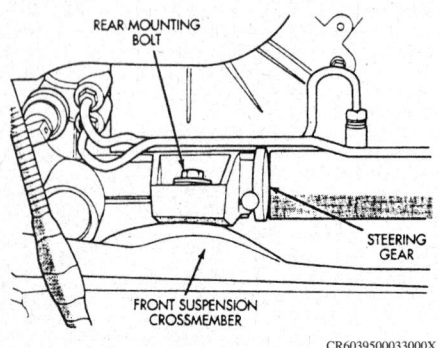

Fig. 8 Steering gear mounting isolator bolts. Rear

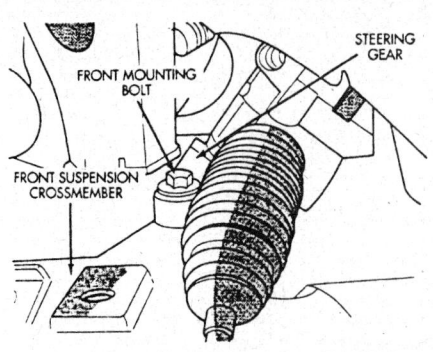

Fig. 9 Steering gear mounting isolator bolts. Front

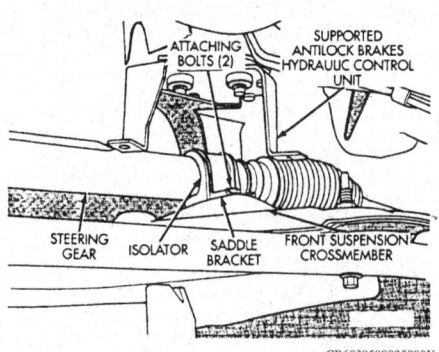

Fig. 10 Steering gear saddle bracket mounting bolts

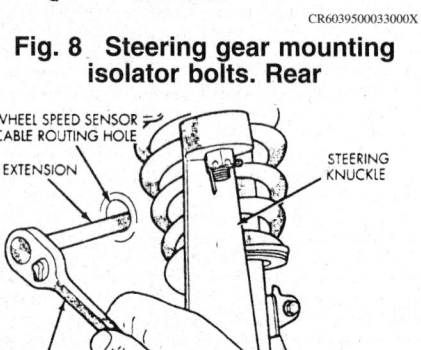

Fig. 11 Power steering pump mounting bracket replacement. 2.0L & 2.4L engines

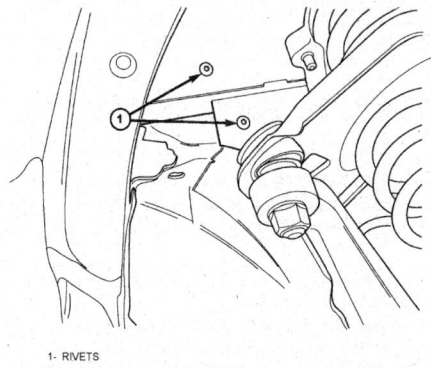

Fig. 12 Rivet location. Righthand

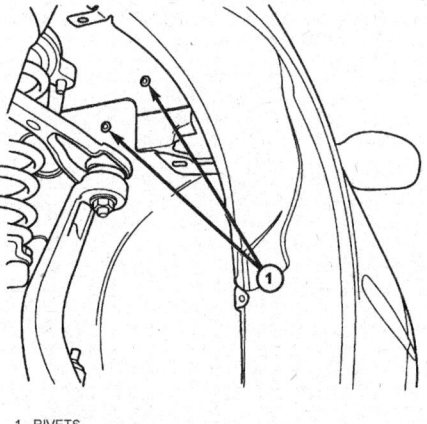

Fig. 13 Rivet location. Lefthand

TIGHTENING SPECIFICATIONS

Year	Component	Torque/Ft. Lbs.
2001–05	Ball Joint Stud To Shock Tower	23
	Ball Joint Stud To Steering Gear	70
	Disc Brake Caliper	16
	Front Cross-Member	120
	Front Stub Axle	180
	Lower Control Arm	120
	Outer Tie Rod To Inner Tie Rod Lock Nut	55
	Power Steering Bracket	40
	Power Steering Pump	40
	Power Steering & Return Hose	21–23
	Pressure Hose To Return Hose	84①
	Shock Absorber Shaft	40
	Shock Assembly Clevis Bracket	68
	Stabilizer Bar	75
	Stabilizer Bar Bushing	45
	Steering Gear	50
	Tie Rod End To Steering Knuckle	45
	Wheel Lug Nuts	100

① — Inch lbs.

Wheel Alignment

INDEX

PRECAUTIONS

When hoisting vehicle a frame contact type hoist must be used. Any equipment designed to lift vehicles by the rear axle cannot be used, as damage to rear suspension components will occur. Do not attempt to modify any suspension or steering components by heating or bending of the component.

DESCRIPTION

This vehicle is equipped with a non-adjustable front caster and camber suspension. Front caster and camber settings are determined at the time of design and require no adjustment during alignment. Though not adjustable, front caster and camber must be inspected and components replaced when outside of vehicle specification. Inspect all components for damage or signs of bending and replace as required.

PRELIMINARY INSPECTION

1. Ensure gas tank is full.
2. Inspect tire pressure and inflate specification. Ensure tires are of same size and tread.
3. Inspect front tire and wheel radial runout.
4. Ensure all suspension fasteners are tightened properly.
5. Inspect ball joints and steering linkage for wear, looseness or damage.
6. Inspect all suspension component rubber bushings for wear or deterioration.

FRONT WHEEL ALIGNMENT

Camber

Camber adjustment is not normally required. Inspect all front suspension components for damage or wear, then inspect rear alignment setting prior to adjusting camber setting.

1. Mark position of all shock assembly mounting bolts on shock tower of side to be adjusted.

2. Raise and support vehicle by frame until front tires and suspension are not supporting vehicle.
3. Loosen shock mounting bolts on side to be adjusted. Only loosen far enough to allow removal of plastic locating pins that align upper mounting bracket with shock tower.
4. Remove both plastic retaining pins using suitable punch or pliers.
5. Position shock assembly inboard or outboard as required to adjust camber. Ensure fore and aft position is same as marked and that rearward and forward bolts are moved an equal length.
6. **Do not enlarge any existing holes to increase adjustment range.**
7. **Torque** upper shock assembly mounting bolts to 68 ft. lbs.
8. Lower vehicle, then bounce front and rear of vehicle an equal amount of times.
9. Inspect camber setting and adjust as required.

Toe

1. Perform rear wheel alignment as outlined under "Rear Wheel Alignment."
2. Loosen front inner and outer tie rod jam nuts.
3. Rotate inner tie rod end at steering gear to set toe, **Fig. 1.**

REAR WHEEL ALIGNMENT

The following procedures have been revised by a Technical Service Bulletin.

2001–03

1. Center steering wheel and lock using suitable steering wheel clamp.
2. Loosen adjusting screw jam nuts on four of the lateral arms and adjusting screws. Each adjusting screw has one right-handed and one left-handed nut, **Fig. 2.**
3. When setting rear camber and toe, maximum lateral link lengths must not be exceeded, **Fig. 3.** If maximum length is exceeded, inadequate retention of adjustment link to inner and outer link may result.

4. Adjust rear lateral link adjusting screw to obtain approximate rear camber setting, **Fig. 2.**
5. Adjust forward lateral link adjusting screw in combination with rear lateral link to reach preferred specification.
6. Adjust forward lateral link adjusting screw to set preferred rear toe specification, **Fig. 2.**
7. **Toe adjustment will cause a slight change in camber setting. Should camber setting change during toe adjustment, continue to adjust camber and toe until both are at preferred specifications.**
8. **Torque** lateral link adjusting screw jam nuts to 48 ft. lbs., while holding adjustment screws from turning using crow foot and torque wrench.

2004–05

Rear Camber is adjustable on earlier production vehicles produced before Aug. 6, 2003. To verify whether rear camber is adjustable on a particular vehicle, look for the presence of an adjusting screw on the forward lateral links as well as the rearward lateral links of the rear suspension (Lateral link adjusting screws). Rear camber can be adjusted using the adjusting screws located in both the forward and rearward lateral links.

Vehicles without an adjusting screw on the rearward lateral link do not have camber adjustment capabilities, but still allow for toe adjustment using the adjusting screw in the forward lateral link.

If rear camber is outside of specifications on a vehicle without an adjustment screw on the rearward link, a service link with an adjustment screw (like early production vehicles) is available to provide that adjustment. Once installed, refer to "2001–03" for adjustment procedure.

THRUST ANGLE

The thrust angle is the average of the toe settings on each rear wheel. If measurement is not within specifications, adjust rear wheel toe to provide each wheel with ½ of the total toe measurement. When adjusting, do not exceed the total toe specification.

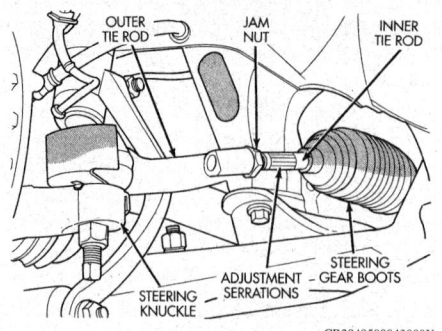

Fig. 1   Inner & outer tie rod adjustment

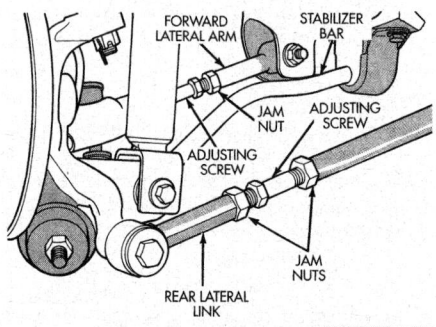

Fig. 2   Rear lateral arm adjustment

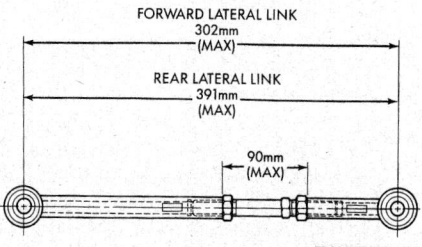

Fig. 3   Lateral link maximum length

CONCORDE, INTREPID, LHS & 300M

NOTE: Refer To Rear Of This Manual For Vehicle Manufacturer's Special Service Tool Suppliers.

INDEX OF SERVICE OPERATIONS

CONCORDE, INTREPID, LHS & 300M

Specifications

GENERAL ENGINE SPECIFICATIONS

Engine	Engine Code①	Fuel System	Bore & Stroke, Inch	Comp. Ratio	Brake HP @ RPM	Maximum Torque, Ft. Lbs. @ RPM	Normal Oil Pressure, psi	
							Idle	3000 RPM
2001								
2.7L	R/U	SMPI	3.386 x 3.091	9.7	200 @ 5800	190 @ 4850	5	45–105
3.2L	J	SMPI	3.622 x 3.189	9.5	222 @ 6400	222 @ 3950	5	45–105
3.5L	G/V	SMPI	3.780 x 3.189	9.9	250 @ 6400	250 @ 3900	5	45–105
2002–04								
2.7L	R	SMPI	3.386 x 3.091	9.7	200 @ 5800	190 @ 4850	5	45–105
3.5L	G/V	SMPI	3.780 x 3.189	9.9	250 @ 6400	250 @ 3900	5	45–105

SMPI — Sequential Multi-Port Fuel Injection

① — Eighth digit of VIN denotes engine code.

TUNE UP SPECIFICATIONS

Engine	Spark Plug Gap, Inch	Firing Order Fig.④	Ignition Timing		Idle Speed, RPM	Fuel Pump Pressure, psi⑥	Valve Clearance, Inch
			°BTDC	Mark			
2001							
2.7L	.048–.058	B	②	⑤	①	58	③
3.2L	.048–.053	B	②	⑤	①	58	③
3.5L	.048–.053	B	②	⑤	①	58	③
2002–04							
2.7L	.048–.058	B	②	⑤	①	58	③
3.5L	.048–.053	B	②	⑤	①	58	③

BTDC — Before Top Dead Center
N — Neutral
① — Controlled by PCM.
② — Direct (Distributorless) Ignition System (DIS). Not adjustable.
③ — Equipped w/hydraulic lash adjusters. No adjustment is required.

④ — Before disconnecting wires from coil unit, determine location of No. 1 wire, as position may have been altered from that in **Fig. A.**
⑤ — Equipped w/crankshaft position sensor.
⑥ — Remove cover from service valve

on fuel rail. Connect suitable fuel pressure test gauge to service valve. With ignition switch in Run position, use Diagnostic Read-Out Box to activate fuel pump & pressurize system.

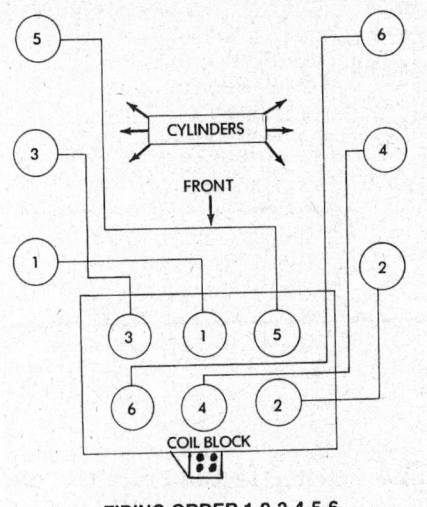

FIRING ORDER 1-2-3-4-5-6

CR1139800544000X

Fig. A

LEFT BANK

RIGHT BANK

FIRING ORDER 1-2-3-4-5-6

CR1139800545000X

Fig. B

FRONT WHEEL ALIGNMENT SPECIFICATIONS

Year	Camber Angle, Degrees①		Caster Angle, Degrees①		Toe In, Degrees		Ball Joint Wear
	Limits	Desired	Limits	Desired	Limits	Desired	
2001–04	–.6 to +.6②	0	+2 to +4③	+3	+.2 to –.2	0	④

① — Reference angle only. Not adjustable.

② — Side to side differential not to exceed .7°.

③ — Side to side differential not to exceed 1°.

④ — Refer to "Ball Joint Inspection" in "Front Suspension & Steering."

REAR WHEEL ALIGNMENT SPECIFICATIONS

Year	Camber Angle, Degrees①		Toe In, Degrees		Thrust Angle①
	Limits	Desired	Limits	Desired	
2001–04	–.70 to +.30	–.20	–.20 to +.40	+.10	–.15 to +.15

① — Reference angle only; not adjustable.

FLUID CAPACITIES & COOLING SYSTEM DATA

Engine	Coolant Capacity, Qts.	Recommended Engine Coolant Type	Radiator Cap Relief Pressure, Lbs.	Thermostat. Opening Temp., °F	Fuel Tank, Gals.	Engine Oil Refill, Qts.①	Transmission Oil, Qts.②	Differential Oil, Qts.
2001								
2.7L	9.4	Ethylene Glycol	14–18	203–220	18	5.0	9.3	.78
3.2L	9.4	Ethylene Glycol	14–18	203–220	18	5.0	9.3	.78
3.5L	9.4	Ethylene Glycol	14–18	203–220	18	5.0	9.3	.78
2002–04								
2.7L	9.4	Ethylene Glycol	16	203–220	17	5.0	9.3	.78
3.5L	9.4	Ethylene Glycol	16	203–220	17	5.0	9.3	.78

① — Includes oil filter.

② — Approximate; make final inspection w/dipstick. Includes torque converter sump.

LUBRICANT DATA

This chart has been revised by a Technical Service Bulletin.

Year	Lubricant Type			
	Transmission	Differential	Power Steering	Brake System
2001–04	Mopar ATF+ 4 Type 9602	Mopar 75W-90 Hypoid Gear Lubricant	ATF+4 (MS9602)①	DOT 3

① — 2001 model where factory filled with MS5931 (amber/yellow).

MS6902 (red) is recommended replace fluid.

Electrical

NOTE: On Air Bag Equipped Models, Refer To "Air Bag System Precautions" Located In The Front Of This Manual For System Disarming & Arming Procedures.

NOTE: Refer To "Computer Relearn Procedures" Located In The Front Of This Manual When Battery Power To The Computer Has Been Interrupted.

NOTE: Prior To Performing Any Service Operations Listed In This Section, Consult The "Technical Service Bulletins" Section For Related Information.

INDEX

PRECAUTIONS

Air Bag Systems

Refer to "Air Bag System Precautions" in the front of this manual for system disarming and arming procedures.

Battery Ground Cable

Prior to service, disconnect battery ground cable and isolate as required.

FUSE PANEL & FLASHER LOCATION

The fuse panel/junction block is located under the lefthand side of the instrument panel. The hazard flasher unit is located under the lefthand side of the instrument panel between the junction block and the brake pedal.

FUEL PUMP RELAY LOCATION

The fuel pump relay is located in the power distribution center. The power distribution center is located in the engine compartment in front coolant reservoir bottle.

STARTER

REPLACE

1. Raise and support vehicle using suitable lift.
2. Remove bolts mounting starter to transmission.
3. Remove battery feed wire from starter.
4. Remove starter solenoid assembly from transmission housing, then position starter to access Connector Positive Assurance (CPA) wiring connector.
5. Slightly lift engine to relieve lefthand engine mount pressure using suitable jack stand beneath engine.
6. Remove lefthand engine mount mounting bolts.
7. Raise engine slightly to allow for clearance for starter removal.
8. Slide starter motor out between catalyst and engine mount, disconnect posi-lock starter solenoid connector and remove starter.
9. Reverse procedure install. **Torque**

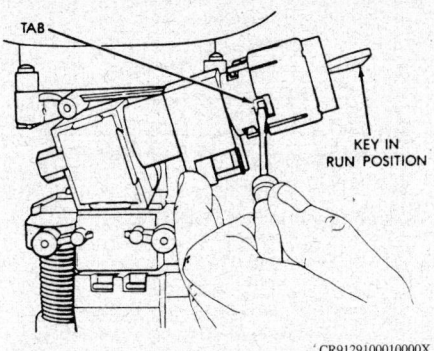

Fig. 1 Lock cylinder replacement

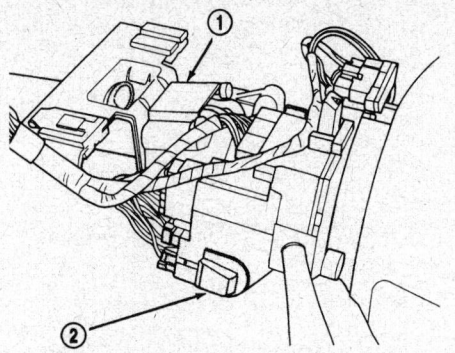

1 – STEERING COLUMN
2 – IGNITION SWITCH

CR1119900273000X

Fig. 2 Ignition switch replacement

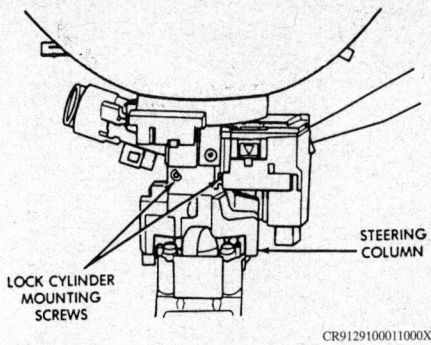

CR9129100011000X

Fig. 3 Lock cylinder housing replacement

starter mounting bolts to 40 ft. lbs., and solenoid battery nut to 90 inch lbs.

ALTERNATOR
REPLACE
2.7L Engine

1. Raise and support vehicle.
2. Remove lower plastic splash shield from under engine compartment.
3. Remove transmission cooler and position aside. **Do not disconnect cooler hydraulic lines.**
4. Remove lower radiator crossmember support, then support radiator with suitable jack stand.
5. Loosen alternator adjusting T-bolt, then the pivot bolt. Do not remove bolts.
6. Remove alternator drive belt.
7. Disconnect alternator field circuit plug.
8. Remove battery terminal retaining nut, then the battery terminal wire.
9. Remove pivot bolt, then the alternator. Do not lose spacer.
10. Reverse procedure to install, noting the following:
    a. **Torque** battery terminal nut to 90 inch lbs.
    b. **Torque** pivot bolt to 40 ft. lbs.

3.2L & 3.5L Engines

1. Remove upper radiator support and position aside.
2. Loosen lower alternator mounting bolt. Do not remove bolt.
3. Loosen pivot bolt and drive belt adjustment bolts, then remove drive belt.
4. Remove lower mounting bolt and disconnect alternator field circuit plug.
5. Remove battery terminal wire retaining nut and the terminal wire.
6. Remove pivot bolt, then the alternator.
7. Reverse procedure to install, noting the following:
    a. **Torque** battery terminal wire retaining nut to 85 inch lbs.
    b. **Torque** lower mounting bolt and pivot bolt to 40 ft. lbs.

COIL PACK
REPLACE

These engines are equipped with a coil on plug ignition system. Each cylinder has a dedicated coil sitting atop each plug. No secondary wires are required and connection from the coil to plug is made with a boot that is attached to the coil.

1. Clean area around coil and spark plug with compressed air spray.
2. Disconnect electrical connector from ignition coil.
3. **On models equipped with 3.2L and 3.5L engines,** alternately loosen coil retaining screws back and forth. **Do not lose spacers under coil.**
4. **On all models,** remove fasteners and ignition coil.
5. Reverse procedure to install, noting following:
    a. **On models equipped with 2.7L engines, torque** mounting screws to 55 inch lbs.
    b. **On models equipped with 3.2L and 3.5L engines, torque** mounting screws to 60 inch lbs.

IGNITION LOCK
REPLACE
Cylinder

1. Remove tilt lever.
2. Remove upper and lower column covers.
3. Turn ignition key to Run position, then depress lock cylinder mounting tab and slide cylinder out of housing, **Fig. 1.**
4. Reverse procedure to install.

Housing

1. Remove upper and lower column covers.
2. Remove tilt lever.
3. Remove tilt lever, then upper and lower column covers.
4. Remove Sentry Key Immobilizer Module (SKIM), if equipped.
5. Remove multi-function switch.
6. Disconnect electrical connector from ignition switch.
7. Remove ignition switch mounting screws and ignition switch, **Fig. 2.**
8. Center punch tamper proof screws, **Fig. 3.**
9. Drill out screw heads using a ¼ inch drill bit.
10. Remove lock cylinder housing from steering column.
11. Remove bolts from steering column.
12. Reverse procedure to install. Tighten new tamper proof screws until heads twist off.

IGNITION SWITCH
REPLACE

1. Remove tilt lever, then upper and lower column covers.
2. Remove Sentry Key Immobilizer Module (SKIM), if equipped.
3. Remove multi-function switch.
4. Disconnect electrical connector from ignition switch.
5. Remove ignition switch mounting screws and ignition switch, **Fig. 2.**
6. Reverse procedure to install. Align tab on ignition switch with slot on lock housing.

HEADLAMP SWITCH
REPLACE

1. Open front door and remove lefthand end cover.
2. Remove screw from lefthand end of instrument panel and pull headlight bezel rearward to disengage clips.
3. Remove headlight switch screws and pull switch out to disconnect electrical connectors.
4. Remove headlight switch.
5. Reverse procedure to install.

STOP LIGHT SWITCH
REPLACE
Removal

1. Press and hold brake pedal.
2. Rotate switch 30° counterclockwise, pull rearward and remove from bracket.
3. Disconnect wiring harness connector.

Installation

1. Hold stop lamp switch firmly in one hand, then using other hand, pull plunger outward until it ratchets to its fully extended position.

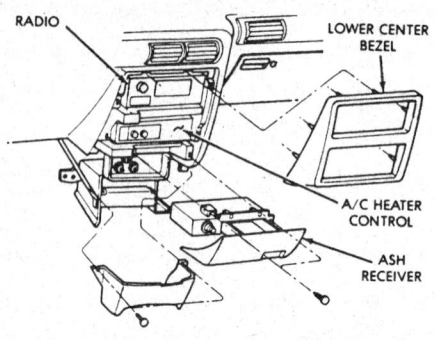

Fig. 4   Radio replacement

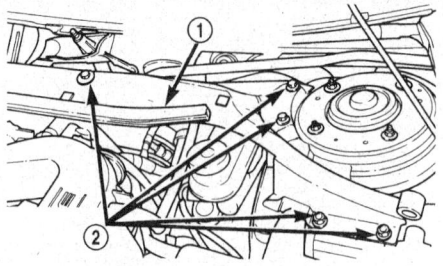

1 – TOWER TO TOWER SUPPORT
2 – RETAINING BOLTS

CR9020000443000X

Fig. 5   Tower to tower support removal

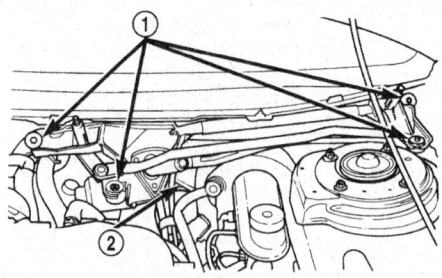

1 – RETAINING BOLTS
2 – WIPER MOTOR CONNECTOR

CR9020000444000X

Fig. 6   Wiper module retaining bolt removal

2. Connect wiring harness connector.
3. Press brake pedal as far down as possible, then install switch in bracket by aligning switch index key with mounting bracket square hole slot.
4. When fully installed, rotate switch 30° clockwise to lock.
5. Gently pull brake pedal back until pedal stops moving and switch plunger ratchets to correct position.

MULTI-FUNCTION SWITCH

REPLACE

1. Remove tilt lever, then the upper and lower steering column covers.
2. Remove multi-function switch to column mounting screws.
3. Disconnect multi-function switch electrical connections.
4. Reverse procedure to install. **Torque** multi-function switch to column screws to 17 inch lbs.

TURN SIGNAL SWITCH

REPLACE

1. Remove tilt lever, then the upper and lower steering column covers.
2. Remove multi-function switch to column mounting screws.
3. Disconnect multi-function switch electrical connections.
4. Reverse procedure to install. **Torque** multi-function switch to column screws to 17 inch lbs.

DIMMER SWITCH

REPLACE

1. Remove tilt lever, then the upper and lower steering column covers.
2. Remove multi-function switch to column mounting screws.
3. Disconnect multi-function switch electrical connections.
4. Reverse procedure to install. **Torque** multi-function switch to column screws to 17 inch lbs.

STEERING WHEEL

REPLACE

Removal

1. Lock steering column by turning steer-

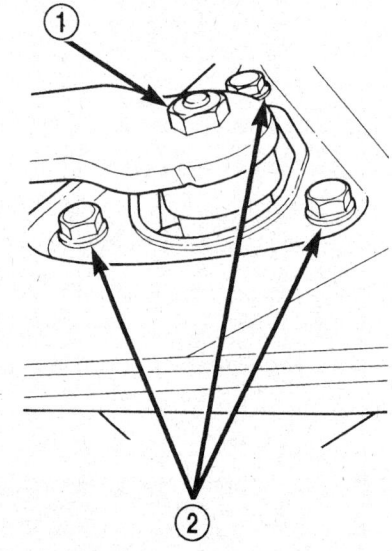

1 – CRANK ARM NUT
2 – WIPER MOTOR RETAINING BOLTS

CR9020000445000X

Fig. 7   Wiper motor crank arm removal

ing wheel ½ turn (180°) clockwise from straight ahead position.
2. Place ignition in Off/Lock position and remove ignition key. This will ensure no damage occurs to clockspring.
3. Remove driver's air bag module as outlined in "Passive Restraint Systems" chapter.
4. Remove steering wheel mounting nut from steering column shaft.
5. Remove steering wheel using steering wheel puller tool No. C-3428B, or equivalent.

Installation

1. Ensure steering wheel is positioned ½ turn (180°) to right.
2. Lock column into position with ignition cylinder lock.
3. Ensure turn signal stalk is in neutral, then pull all wires through larger opening of hub area on wheel.
4. Install steering wheel, ensure flats on hub align with clockspring.
5. Install steering wheel mounting nut and tighten nut to draw steering wheel onto column. **Torque** steering column shaft nut to 45 ft. lbs.

6. Connect wiring harness on air bag module.
7. Install drivers air bag module into steering wheel as outlined in "Passive Restraint Systems" chapter.

INSTRUMENT CLUSTER

REPLACE

1. Remove instrument panel lefthand end cap.
2. Remove steering column shroud cover, then tilt steering wheel down.
3. **On LHS and 300M models,** remove one screw from cluster bezel.
4. **On all models,** remove all items to expose bezel mounting screws.
5. Remove two screws over upper cluster bezel in instrument panel brow and all remaining screws.
6. Remove instrument panel cluster bezel using a trim stick tool No. C-4755, or equivalent.
7. Remove instrument cluster screws and disengage upper latch.
8. Remove instrument cluster from panel. **Instrument panel wiring harness connectors are mounted directly to rear panel. A force of approximately 20–30 lbs. will be required to disengage cluster from connectors.**
9. Reverse procedure to install.

RADIO

REPLACE

1. Remove lower center bezel, radio mounting screws, then remove radio, **Fig. 4.**
2. Pull radio straight out and disconnect electrical and antenna connections.
3. Remove radio ground strap, then the radio.
4. Reverse procedure to install.

WIPER MOTOR

REPLACE

1. Remove wiper arms.
2. Remove cowl screen panel.
3. Remove wiper module mounting bolt from top of tower to tower beam.
4. Remove tower to tower support bolts, **Fig. 5.**
5. Remove wiper module retaining bolts, **Fig. 6.**

6. Remove wiper module and disconnect electrical connector.
7. Disconnect wiper module master link from motor crank with ball and socket wedge. Do not damage ball, socket or seal when removing.
8. Remove nut to crank arm, **Fig. 7.**
9. Remove wiper motor from wiper module.
10. Reverse procedure to install.

WIPER SWITCH
REPLACE
1. Remove tilt lever, then the upper and lower steering column covers.
2. Remove multi-function switch to column mounting screws.
3. Disconnect multi-function switch electrical connections.
4. Reverse procedure to install. **Torque** multi-function switch to column screws to 17 inch lbs.

BLOWER MOTOR
REPLACE
1. Remove lower righthand under panel duct.
2. Disconnect blower motor connector from resistor block/power module.
3. Squeeze blower motor wiring grommet, push grommet through blower motor housing cover.
4. Remove blower motor housing cover.
5. Remove blower motor mounting screws, lower blower motor from housing.
6. Reverse procedure to install.

HEATER CORE
REPLACE
1. Remove heater and air conditioning housing as outlined under "Evaporator Core, Replace."
2. Remove heater core attaching screws, then the heater core.

3. Reverse procedure to install.

EVAPORATOR CORE
REPLACE
1. Recover refrigerant as outlined in "Air Conditioning" chapter.
2. Drain engine coolant into suitable container.
3. Remove instrument panel as outlined in "Dash Panel Service" chapter.
4. Remove air cleaner hose and distribution duct from engine.
5. Remove fasteners from heater hoses at dash panel and remove hoses from heater core.
6. Plug heater core inlet and outlet tubes to block coolant from entering interior.
7. Remove one nut at expansion valve retaining both air conditioning lines to expansion valve.
8. Cap expansion valve and air conditioning openings.
9. Remove three housing to dash panel retaining nuts from engine compartment side of dash panel.
10. Remove defrost duct retaining screws and the duct.
11. Remove housing to dash panel retaining nuts and screws.
12. Remove rear seat heat duct retaining screws and the duct.
13. Remove rear seat heat duct elbow push pin fastener.
14. Disconnect harness connector.
15. Gently pull housing rearward from dash panel.
16. Remove recirculation door actuator.
17. Remove recirculation door and housing.
18. Remove upper housing mounting screws, then the upper half of heater housing.
19. Lift evaporator out of lower housing.
20. Transfer expansion valve onto new evaporator using new gaskets.

21. Reverse procedure to install.

TECHNICAL SERVICE BULLETINS
Instrument Cluster Changes Brightness

On some of these models the instrument cluster illumination changes brightness. Models equipped with auto-lamp may also have headlamps or fog lamps come on at unexpected times.

This condition may be caused by the headlamp switch wiring connector.

To correct this condition, apply dielectric grease to headlamp switch wiring connector as follows:
1. Disconnect and isolate battery ground cable.
2. Remove instrument panel lefthand end cap.
3. Remove steering column shroud cover.
4. Tilt steering column down to lowest position.
5. **On Limited and 300M models,** remove cluster bezel mounting screw.
6. **On all models,** remove two mounting screws over upper cluster bezel in panel brow area.
7. **On Intrepid, Limited and 300M models,** remove four cluster mounting screws.
8. **On Concorde models,** remove five cluster mounting screws.
9. **On all models,** pry out instrument cluster pane; bezel using suit trim stick.
10. Clean contacts by disconnecting and connecting headlamp switch wire harness connector three times.
11. Disconnect connector and apply suitable dielectric grease to terminals.
12. Connect connector and assembly instrument panel.

2.7L Engine

NOTE: On Air Bag Equipped Models, Refer To "Air Bag System Precautions" Located In The Front Of This Manual For System Disarming & Arming Procedures.

NOTE: Refer To "Computer Relearn Procedures" Located In The Front Of This Manual When Battery Power To The Computer Has Been Interrupted.

INDEX

PRECAUTIONS

Air Bag Systems

Refer to "Air Bag System Precautions" in the front of this manual for system disarming and arming procedures.

Battery Ground Cable

Prior to service, disconnect battery ground cable and isolate as required.

Fuel System Pressure Relief

1. Remove fuel pump relay for power distribution center.
2. Start and run engine until it stalls.
3. Attempt to start engine until it no longer runs.
4. Turn ignition switch to Off position.
5. Place rag or towel under fuel line quick-connector fitting at fuel rail.
6. Install fuel pump relay.
7. One or more Diagnostic Trouble Codes (DTCs) may have been stored because of removing fuel pump relay. Clear these DTCs with suitably pro-grammed scan tool.

COMPRESSION PRESSURE

The minimum compression pressure should be no less than 100 psi and the maximum variation between cylinders should be no more than 25%.

ENGINE MOUNT
REPLACE

Lefthand & Righthand

1. Raise and support vehicle.
2. Remove isolator mounting nuts from top of mounting bracket.
3. Support engine with suitable jack, place suitable wood block between oil pan and jack.
4. Remove lower mounting nuts from frame.
5. Raise engine carefully, then remove isolator with heat shield.
6. Reverse procedure to install.

Rear

1. Raise and support vehicle.

2. Support transmission with suitable jack.
3. Remove mounting nuts, then the crossmember bolts and mount.
4. Reverse procedure to install.

STRUCTURAL COLLAR
REPLACE

1. Raise and support vehicle.
2. Remove mounting bolts, then the structural collar from oil pan and transmission housing.
3. Reverse procedure to install, noting the following:
   a. **Torque** vertical collar oil pan bolts to 10 inch lbs.
   b. **Torque** collar to transmission bolts to 40 ft. lbs.
   c. Start with center vertical bolt and work outward, **torque** mounting bolts to 40 ft. lbs.

ENGINE
REPLACE

1. Remove fuel pump relay for power distribution center.
2. Start and run engine until it stalls.
3. Attempt to start engine until it no longer runs.

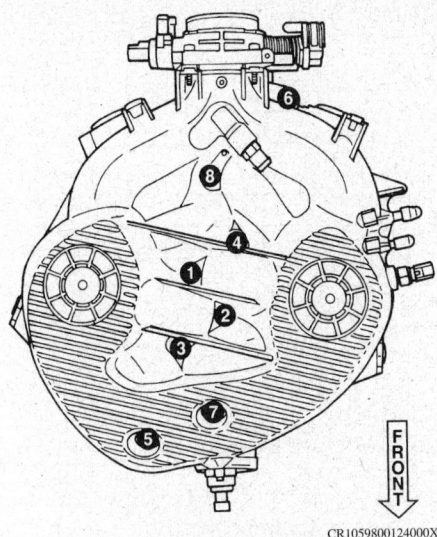

CR1059800124000X

Fig. 1 Upper intake manifold tightening sequence

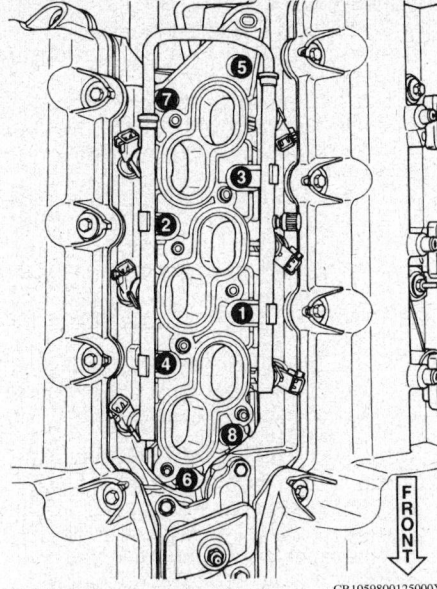

CR1059800125000X

Fig. 2 Lower intake manifold tightening sequence

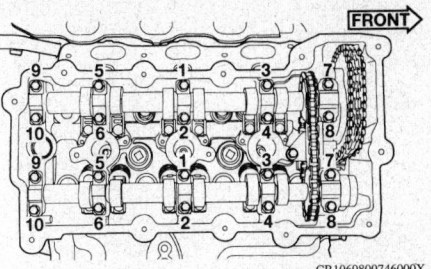

CR1069800746000X

Fig. 3 Camshaft bearing cap tightening sequence

4. Turn ignition switch to Off position.
5. Place rag or towel under fuel line quick-connector fitting at fuel rail.
6. Install fuel pump relay.
7. Mark hood position at hinges and remove, then drain cooling system into suitable container.
8. Remove wiper arms, left and righthand cowl screens (covers), then the cowl support.
9. Remove air cleaner assembly and air inlet hose, then the upper radiator crossmember.
10. Disconnect hood release cable from latch, then remove cooling fan module.
11. Disconnect upper radiator hose from engine and lower hose from radiator, then the transmission cooler lines from radiator.
12. Remove air conditioning condenser to radiator attaching bolts, then the transmission cooler line support bracket.
13. Remove mounting screw from lefthand side of radiator, then the radiator from engine compartment.
14. Remove accessory drive belts.
15. Remove power steering pump mounting bolts, then position pump aside.
16. Disconnect air conditioning compressor electrical connector, then remove compressor mounting bolts and position aside.
17. Remove exhaust manifold V-band clamps, then disconnect throttle and speed control cables.
18. Disconnect coolant pressure bottle and heater hoses.
19. Disconnect fuel line, vacuum lines, electrical connectors and engine ground straps.
20. Raise and support vehicle, then drain engine oil into suitable container.
21. Remove catalytic converter down pipe front and rear attaching bolts.
22. Remove structural collar mounting bolts and structural collar.
23. Mark flexplate to torque converter position for installation alignment, then remove converter mounting bolts.
24. Disconnect transmission cooler line

brackets from engine, then remove starter.
25. Remove crankshaft position sensor.
26. Remove lower transmission to cylinder block attaching bolts.
27. Lower vehicle and remove fuel line from throttle body.
28. Remove electrical harness bracket and to throttle body retaining screws.
29. Remove electrical harness and transmission shift cable retaining bracket.
30. Remove throttle body support bracket attaching bolts.
31. Remove transmission to cylinder block double-ended bolts.
32. Remove upper transmission to cylinder block bolts.
33. Remove left and righthand engine mount insulator to engine mount bracket mounting bolts.
34. Remove cam sensor from lefthand cylinder head.
35. Attach suitable lifting device to engine and support transmission with suitable floor jack, then remove engine.
36. Reverse procedure to install.

INTAKE MANIFOLD

REPLACE

Upper

1. Remove air inlet resonator and inlet tube.
2. Remove throttle and speed control cables from throttle arm and bracket, then the bracket.
3. Disconnect Manifold Absolute Pressure (MAP), Intake Air Temperature (IAT), Throttle Position (TPS) sensors, Manifold Tune Valve (MTV) and Idle Air Control (IAC) motor electrical connectors.
4. Disconnect vapor purge, brake booster, speed control servo and Positive Crankcase Ventilation (PCV) hoses.

5. Remove Exhaust Gas Recirculation (EGR) tube.
6. Loosen throttle body support bracket upper attaching bolt, then the left and righthand support bracket attaching bolts.
7. Release retaining clip and engine cover
8. Remove upper manifold mounting bolts and upper manifold.
9. Reverse procedure to install, noting the following:
   a. Ensure fuel injectors and wiring harnesses are positioned aside.
   b. Tighten manifold in sequence, **Fig. 1**.

Lower

1. Remove fuel pump relay for power distribution center.
2. Start and run engine until it stalls.
3. Attempt to start engine until it no longer runs.
4. Turn ignition switch to Off position.
5. Place rag or towel under fuel line quick-connector fitting at fuel rail.
6. Install fuel pump relay.
7. Remove air inlet resonator and inlet tube.
8. Remove throttle and speed control cables from throttle arm and bracket, then the bracket.
9. Disconnect Manifold Absolute Pressure (MAP), Intake Air Temperature (IAT), Throttle Position (TPS) sensors, Manifold Tune Valve (MTV) and Idle Air Control (IAC) motor electrical connectors.
10. Disconnect vapor purge, brake booster, speed control servo and Positive Crankcase Ventilation (PCV) hoses.
11. Remove Exhaust Gas Recirculation (EGR) tube.
12. Loosen throttle body support bracket upper attaching bolt, then the left and righthand support bracket attaching bolts.
13. Release retaining clip and engine cover
14. Remove upper manifold mounting bolts and upper manifold.
15. Remove fuel rail fuel supply hose, then the fuel rail support bracket to throttle body support bracket mounting screw.
16. Remove mounting bolts, then the fuel rail and injectors as an assembly.
17. Remove mounting bolts and the lower intake manifold.
18. Reverse procedure to install, noting the following:

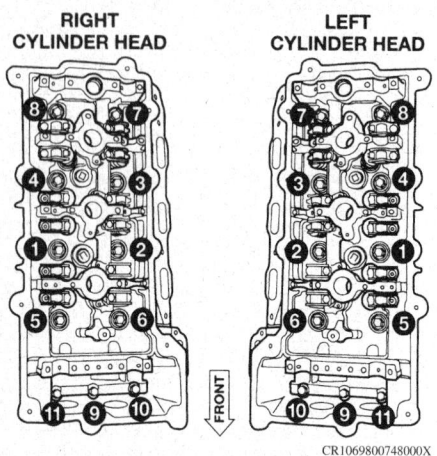

Fig. 4 Cylinder head bolt tightening sequence

a. To properly position manifold, install rearmost bolt and tighten 2–3 turns.
b. Tighten bolts in sequence, **Fig. 2.**

EXHAUST MANIFOLD

REPLACE

Lefthand

1. Raise and support vehicle.
2. Remove exhaust system and lefthand catalytic converter.
3. Remove transmission dipstick tube mounting bolt and rotate housing away from engine.
4. Lower vehicle.
5. Disconnect electrical connectors and remove harness mounting screws from support bracket, then the engine wiring harness support bracket from cylinder head.
6. Disconnect connector and remove exhaust manifold oxygen sensor.
7. Remove engine oil dipstick tube.
8. Remove mounting screws and heat shield.
9. Remove mounting bolts and exhaust manifold.
10. Reverse procedure to install.

Righthand

1. Remove air intake plenum and air filter housing.
2. Remove battery cable housing tube to transmission housing mounting bolt.
3. Remove EGR tube to exhaust manifold and EGR valve mounting bolts.
4. Disconnect electrical connector and exhaust manifold oxygen sensor.
5. Remove manifold to catalytic converter V-band clamp.
6. Remove mounting screws and heat shields.
7. Remove mounting bolts and exhaust manifold.
8. Reverse procedure to install.

CYLINDER HEAD

REPLACE

1. Remove fuel pump relay for power distribution center.
2. Start and run engine until it stalls.
3. Attempt to start engine until it no longer runs.
4. Turn ignition switch to Off position.
5. Place rag or towel under fuel line quick-connector fitting at fuel rail.
6. Install fuel pump relay.
7. Drain cooling system into suitable container and remove accessory drive belts.
8. Remove upper radiator crossmember and fan module.
9. Remove accessory and air conditioning belts.
10. Remove damper using crankshaft damper holder tool No. 8191, or equivalent, and three-jaw puller tool No. 1023, or equivalent.
11. Remove upper and lower intake manifolds as outlined under "Intake Manifold, Replace."
12. Remove cylinder head cover as outlined under "Valve Cover, Replace."
13. Remove upper radiator support crossmember, then the fan module and accessory drive belts.
14. Remove power steering pump from mounting bracket, then the accessory drive belt tensioner pulley and bracket.
15. Remove mounting bolts and timing chain cover.
16. Remove water outlet connector.
17. Rotate crankshaft until crankshaft sprocket timing mark aligns with oil pump housing timing mark, then remove timing chain.
18. Remove primary timing chain as outlined under "Timing Chain, Replace," then the secondary chain tensioner mounting bolts.
19. Loosen camshaft bearing cap bolts in reverse order of tightening sequence, **Fig. 3.**
20. Remove bearing caps, then the camshafts, secondary chain and tensioner as an assembly. **Mark bearing cap position for installation alignment.**
21. Remove catalytic converter pipe V-band clamps at exhaust manifold.
22. Remove cylinder head mounting bolts in reverse order of tightening sequence, **Fig. 4.**
23. Remove cylinder head.
24. Reverse procedure to install, noting the following:
    a. Cylinder head bolts are tightened using a torque plus angle procedure, bolts with stretched threads must be replaced.
    b. Lubricate bolt threads with suitable, clean engine oil.
    c. **Torque** cylinder head bolt Nos. 1–8 in sequence to 35 ft. lbs, **Fig. 4.**
    d. **Torque** head bolt bolts in sequence to 55 ft. lbs.
    e. Tighten bolts an additional 90° in sequence.
    f. **Torque** cylinder head bolt Nos. 9–11 in sequence to 21 ft. lbs.

VALVE COVER

REPLACE

1. Remove air inlet resonator and inlet tube.

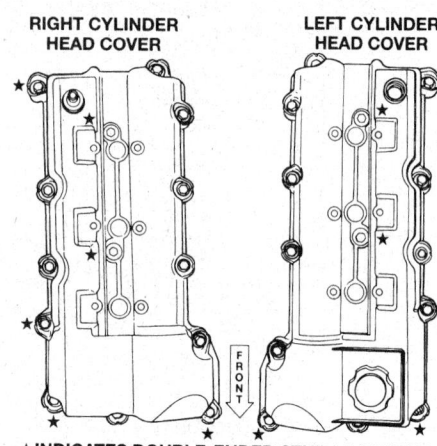

★INDICATES DOUBLE-ENDED STUD LOCATIONS

Fig. 5 Valve cover replacement

2. Remove throttle and speed control cables from throttle arm and bracket, then the bracket.
3. Disconnect Manifold Absolute Pressure (MAP), Intake Air Temperature (IAT), Throttle Position (TPS) sensors, Manifold Tune Valve (MTV) and Idle Air Control (IAC) motor electrical connectors.
4. Disconnect vapor purge, brake booster, speed control servo and Positive Crankcase Ventilation (PCV) hoses.
5. Remove Exhaust Gas Recirculation (EGR) tube.
6. Loosen throttle body support bracket upper attaching bolt, then the left and righthand support bracket attaching bolts.
7. Release retaining clip and engine cover
8. Remove upper manifold mounting bolts and upper manifold.
9. Disconnect ignition coil electrical connectors.
10. Remove ground strap from righthand cylinder head, then disconnect electrical and vacuum harness retaining clips from studs.
11. Remove ignition coil capacitor fasteners, then the left and righthand upper intake manifold support brackets.
12. Loosen mounting bolts and remove cylinder head covers. Mounting bolts will remain in cover.
13. Reverse procedure to install. Ensure double-ended studs are in correct locations, **Fig. 5.**

VALVE ADJUSTMENT

Equipped with hydraulic lash adjusters. No adjustment is required.

ROCKER ARMS

REPLACE

Removal

1. Remove valve covers as outlined under "Valve Cover, Replace."
2. Turn crankshaft to rotate engine until cam lobe is on base circle (heel) of rocker arm being removed.

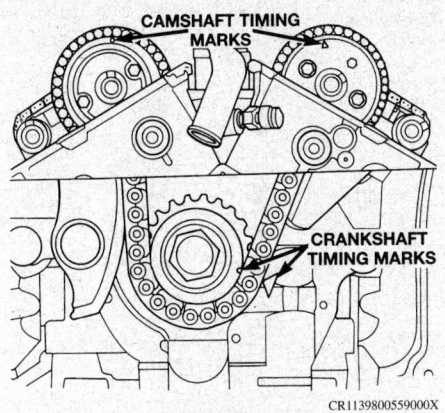

Fig. 6 Timing chain mark alignment

3. Depress valve spring enough to release tension and remove rocker arm using valve spring compressor tool No. 8215 and Adapter tool No. 8216, or equivalent.
4. Identify rocker arm position.

Installation

1. Lubricate rocker arm with suitable, clean engine oil.
2. Turn crankshaft until cam lobe is on base circle (heel) of rocker arm being removed.
3. Depress valve spring enough to release tension using valve spring compressor tool No. 8215 and adapter tool No. 8216, or equivalents.
4. Install rocker arm in original position and release valve spring tension.
5. Install valve cover as outlined under "Valve Cover, Replace."

VALVE SPRINGS
REPLACE

Ensure piston is at TDC on cylinder from which valve spring(s) is being removed.

1. Remove fuel pump relay for power distribution center.
2. Start and run engine until it stalls.
3. Attempt to start engine until it no longer runs.
4. Turn ignition switch to Off position.
5. Place rag or towel under fuel line quick-connector fitting at fuel rail.
6. Install fuel pump relay.
7. Remove air cleaner housing cover and inlet hose.
8. Remove air inlet resonator and inlet tube.
9. Remove throttle and speed control cables from throttle arm and bracket, then the bracket.
10. Disconnect Manifold Absolute Pressure (MAP), Intake Air Temperature (IAT), Throttle Position (TPS) sensors, Manifold Tune Valve (MTV) and Idle Air Control (IAC) motor electrical connectors.
11. Disconnect vapor purge, brake booster, speed control servo and Positive Crankcase Ventilation (PCV) hoses.

12. Remove Exhaust Gas Recirculation (EGR) tube.
13. Loosen throttle body support bracket upper attaching bolt, then the left and righthand support bracket attaching bolts.
14. Release retaining clip and engine cover
15. Remove upper manifold mounting bolts and upper manifold.
16. Remove valve covers as outlined under "Valve Cover, Replace."
17. Remove upper radiator crossmember and fan module.
18. Remove accessory and air conditioning belts.
19. Remove damper using crankshaft damper holder tool No. 8191, or equivalent, and three-jaw puller tool No. 1023, or equivalent.
20. Remove timing chain as outlined under "Timing Chain, Replace."
21. Remove primary timing chain as outlined under "Timing Chain, Replace," then the secondary chain tensioner mounting bolts.
22. Loosen camshaft bearing cap bolts in reverse order of tightening sequence, **Fig. 3.**
23. Remove bearing caps, then the camshafts, secondary chain and tensioner as an assembly. **Mark bearing cap position for installation alignment.**
24. Install suitable spark plug adapter into cylinder being serviced, then apply 90–100 psi air pressure to hold valves in place.
25. Compress valve spring using valve spring compressor tool No. MD-998772A with adapter tool No. 6779, or equivalent, then remove valve locks, retainer and spring.
26. Remove valve stem seals using suitable valve seal tool.
27. Reverse procedure to install, noting the following:
    a. Push valve steam seal/seat firmly and squarely over valve guide with stem as guide.
    b. Do not force seal against guide top.
    c. When install retainer locks, compress spring only enough to install locks.

HYDRAULIC LIFTERS
REPLACE

1. Remove rocker arm as outlined under "Rocker Arm, Replace."
2. Mark position of hydraulic lash adjuster installation alignment.
3. Remove hydraulic lash adjuster.
4. Reverse procedure to install. Ensure adjuster is partially full of oil.

CRANKSHAFT DAMPER
REPLACE

1. Remove upper radiator crossmember and fan module.
2. Remove accessory and air conditioning belts.
3. Remove damper using crankshaft damper holder tool No. 8191, or equiv-

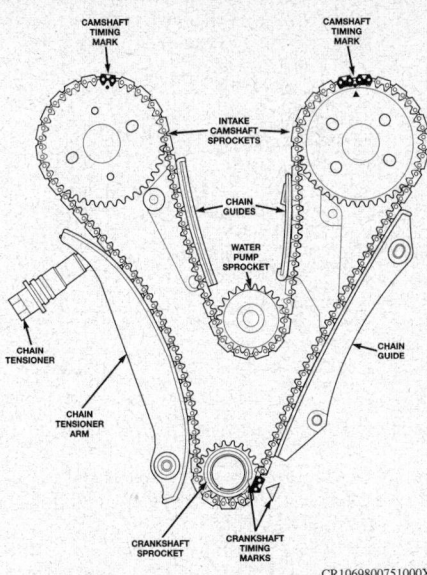

Fig. 7 Primary timing chain alignment marks

alent, and three-jaw puller tool No. 1023, or equivalent.
4. Reverse procedure to install.

FRONT COVER
REPLACE

1. Remove upper radiator support crossmember, then the fan module and accessory drive belts.
2. Remove upper radiator crossmember and fan module.
3. Remove accessory and air conditioning belts.
4. Remove damper using crankshaft damper holder tool No. 8191, or equivalent, and three-jaw puller tool No. 1023, or equivalent.
5. Remove power steering pump from mounting bracket, then the accessory drive belt tensioner pulley and bracket.
6. Remove mounting bolts and timing chain cover.
7. Reverse procedure to install, noting the following:
    a. Apply ⅛ inch bead of suitable silicone rubber adhesive sealant to parting lines between oil pan and cylinder block.
    b. Use crankshaft seal Installer and sleeve tool No. 6780-2, or equivalent, to install crankshaft seal.

TIMING CHAIN
REPLACE

With the timing chain removed, avoid turning the camshaft or crankshaft. If movement is required, exercise caution to avoid valve damage caused by piston contact.

Removal

1. Remove air inlet resonator and inlet tube.

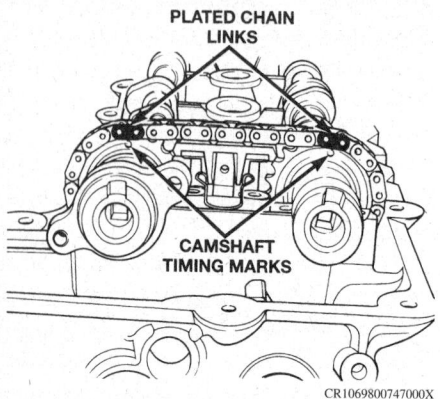

Fig. 8   Camshaft chain timing

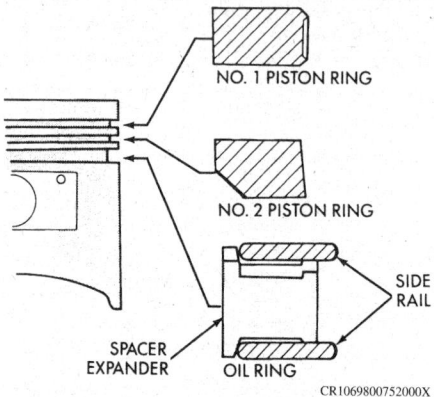

Fig. 9   Piston ring installation

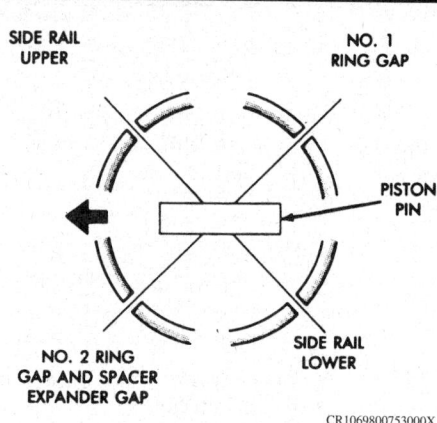

Fig. 10   Piston ring end gap positions

2. Remove throttle and speed control cables from throttle arm and bracket, then the bracket.
3. Disconnect Manifold Absolute Pressure (MAP), Intake Air Temperature (IAT), Throttle Position (TPS) sensors, Manifold Tune Valve (MTV) and Idle Air Control (IAC) motor electrical connectors.
4. Disconnect vapor purge, brake booster, speed control servo and Positive Crankcase Ventilation (PCV) hoses.
5. Remove Exhaust Gas Recirculation (EGR) tube.
6. Loosen throttle body support bracket upper attaching bolt, then the left and righthand support bracket attaching bolts.
7. Release retaining clip and engine cover
8. Remove upper manifold mounting bolts and upper manifold.
9. Remove valve covers as outlined under "Valve Cover, Replace."
10. Remove upper radiator crossmember and fan module.
11. Remove accessory and air conditioning belts.
12. Remove damper using crankshaft damper holder tool No. 8191, or equivalent, and three-jaw puller tool No. 1023, or equivalent.
13. Remove upper radiator crossmember and fan module.
14. Remove damper using crankshaft damper holder tool No. 8191, or equivalent, and three-jaw puller tool No. 1023, or equivalent.
15. Remove power steering pump from mounting bracket, then the accessory drive belt tensioner pulley and bracket.
16. Remove mounting bolts and timing chain cover.
17. Rotate crankshaft to align crankshaft sprocket timing marks and oil pump housing timing marks. Cylinder No. 1 should be at 60° ATDC.
18. Remove primary timing chain tensioner from righthand cylinder head.
19. Remove camshaft position sensor from lefthand cylinder head, then the chain guide access plug.
20. Remove righthand camshaft sprocket mounting bolts, then the damper and sprocket.
21. Remove mounting bolts and lefthand camshaft sprocket.

22. Remove lower chain guide, then the tensioner arm and primary timing chain.

Installation

1. Align crankshaft sprocket and oil pump housing timing marks, **Fig. 6.**
2. Place lefthand side primary chain sprocket on chain so timing mark is between two plated links.
3. Lower primary chain with lefthand side sprocket through lefthand cylinder head opening.
4. Loosely position lefthand side camshaft sprocket over camshaft hub.
5. Align plated link to crankshaft sprocket timing mark, **Fig. 7.**
6. Position primary chain onto water pump drive sprocket.
7. Align righthand camshaft sprocket timing mark to timing chain plated link and loosely position over camshaft hub.
8. Ensure all plated links are properly aligned to sprocket timing marks.
9. Install lefthand lower chain guide and tensioner arm.
10. Install chain guide access plug to lefthand cylinder head.
11. Remove tensioner from housing and place check ball end into shallow end of timing chain tensioner resetting gauge tool No. 8186, or equivalent.
12. Slowly depress tensioner until oil is purged from cylinder, then install into housing.
13. Position cylinder plunger into deeper end of timing chain tensioner resetting gauge tool No. 8186, or equivalent, then apply downward force until tensioner bottoms against top edge of tool.
14. Install chain tensioner into righthand cylinder head.
15. Insert suitable ⅜ inch square drive extension with breaker bar into righthand cylinder bank intake camshaft drive hub, then rotate until camshaft hub aligns with camshaft sprocket and damper bolt holes.
16. Install sprocket mounting bolts.
17. Insert suitable ⅜ inch square drive extension with breaker bar into lefthand cylinder bank intake camshaft drive hub, then rotate until camshaft hub aligns with camshaft sprocket and damper bolt holes.

18. Install sprocket mounting bolts.
19. Rotate engine slightly clockwise to remove timing chain slack.
20. Gently pry tensioner arm toward tensioner slightly, then release tensioner arm and ensure tensioner extends.
21. Install front cover, crankshaft damper, cylinder heads, camshaft position sensor and upper intake manifold.

TIMING CHAIN TENSIONER
REPLACE

Refer to "Timing Chain, Replace" for tensioner replacement.

TIMING CHAIN TENSIONER BLEED

Refer to "Timing Chain, Replace" for tensioner bleed.

CAMSHAFT
REPLACE

With the timing chain removed, avoid turning the camshaft or crankshaft. If movement is required, exercise caution to avoid valve damage caused by piston contact.

Removal

1. Remove primary timing chain as outlined under "Timing Chain, Replace," then the secondary chain tensioner mounting bolts.
2. Loosen camshaft bearing cap bolts in reverse order of tightening sequence, **Fig. 3.**
3. Remove bearing caps, then the camshafts, secondary chain and tensioner as an assembly. **Mark bearing cap position for installation alignment.**
4. Remove tensioner and chain from camshaft.

Installation

1. Assemble camshaft chain on cams

with plated links facing front and aligned with camshaft sprocket dots, **Fig. 8.**

2. **On models equipped with early build tensioners that separate into subcomponents,** proceed as follows:
   a. Separate cylinder from tensioner housing.
   b. Carefully drain housing oil without removing internal components.
   c. Assemble plunger to housing.
   d. Compress tensioner with hand pressure and lock with fabricated lock pin.

3. **On models equipped with late build tensioners that do not separate into subcomponents,** place tensioner into suitable soft jaw vise, slowly compress tensioner and install fabricated lock pin.

4. **On all models,** remove tensioner from vise and install between camshafts and chain.

5. Rotate cams so plated links and sprocket dots are at 12 o'clock position, then install to cylinder head. Ensure rocker arms are correctly seated and in proper positions.

6. Install bearing caps into their original positions.

7. **Torque** bearing cap retaining bolts gradually in sequence to 108 inch lbs., **Fig. 3.**

8. Install secondary chain tensioner mounting bolts.

9. Measure camshaft endplay.

10. Install primary timing chain as outlined under "Timing Chain, Replace."

PISTON & ROD ASSEMBLY

Removal

1. Remove cylinder bores top ridge with suitable ridge reamer before removing pistons.

2. Rotate crankshaft so connecting rod is centered in cylinder bore.

3. Mark connecting rod and bearing caps with permanent ink marker or suitable scribe tool for assembly. Do not use stamp or punch to mark connecting rods.

4. Remove connecting rod cap.

5. Remove piston and rod assembly from top of cylinder block. using connecting rod guide tools No. 8189, or equivalent.

6. Install bearing cap on mating rod.

Installation

1. Install oil ring expander.

2. Place one end of upper side rail between piston ring groove and expander, then hold end firmly and press down portion to be installed until side rail is in position. **Do not use piston ring expander.**

3. Place one end of lower side rail between piston ring groove and expander, then hold end firmly and press down

portion to be installed until side rail is in position. **Do not use piston ring expander.**

4. Install No. 2 intermediate piston ring. Ensure manufacturers I.D. dot mark faces up, towards top of piston, **Fig. 9.**

5. Install piston ring No. 1.

6. Position piston ring end gaps, **Fig. 10.**

7. Ensure compression ring gaps are staggered so neither is in line with oil ring rail gap.

8. Ensure oil ring expander ends are butted and rail gaps properly located before installing ring compressor.

9. Immerse piston head and rings in clean engine oil, slide ring compressor over piston and tighten. Ensure ring position does not change.

10. Position bearing onto connecting rod. Ensure bearing half hole aligns with connecting rod hole.

11. Lubricate bearing surface with engine oil.

12. Install connecting rod guide tools No. 8189, or equivalent.

13. Pistons are marked on top with arrow and F above pin boss. These marks must point toward front of engine in both cylinder banks.

14. Connecting rod oil squirt hole faces major thrust (righthand) side of block.

15. Rotate crankshaft so connecting rod journal is centered in cylinder bore, then insert rod and piston into bore and guide rod over crankshaft journal.

16. Tap piston down cylinder bore and guide connecting rod onto connecting rod journal using suitable hammer handle.

17. Lubricate rod bolts and bearing surfaces with engine oil.

18. Install connecting rod cap and bearing.

CRANKSHAFT

REPLACE

Removal

1. Remove engine as outlined under "Engine, Replace."

2. Drain engine oil into suitable container and remove oil filter.

3. Remove mounting bolts, then the structural collar from oil pan and transmission housing.

4. Remove mounting bolts, oil pan and gasket. Ensure timing cover to oil pan bolts are removed, before removing pan.

5. Remove accessory drive idler pulley bracket.

6. Remove air inlet resonator and inlet tube.

7. Remove throttle and speed control cables from throttle arm and bracket, then the bracket.

8. Disconnect Manifold Absolute Pressure (MAP), Intake Air Temperature (IAT), Throttle Position (TPS) sensors, Manifold Tune Valve (MTV) and Idle Air Control (IAC) motor electrical connectors.

9. Disconnect vapor purge, brake booster, speed control servo and Positive Crankcase Ventilation (PCV) hoses.

10. Remove Exhaust Gas Recirculation (EGR) tube.

11. Loosen throttle body support bracket upper attaching bolt, then the left and righthand support bracket attaching bolts.

12. Release retaining clip and engine cover

13. Remove upper manifold mounting bolts and upper manifold.

14. Remove valve covers as outlined under "Valve Cover, Replace."

15. Remove upper radiator support crossmember, then the fan module and accessory drive belts.

16. Remove upper radiator crossmember and fan module.

17. Remove accessory and air conditioning belts.

18. Remove damper using crankshaft damper holder tool No. 8191, or equivalent, and three-jaw puller tool No. 1023, or equivalent.

19. Remove power steering pump from mounting bracket, then the accessory drive belt tensioner pulley and bracket.

20. Remove mounting bolts and timing chain cover.

21. Remove timing chain as outlined under "Timing Chain, Replace."

22. Remove sprocket using crankshaft damper bolt and suitable puller.

23. Remove oil pump as outlined under "Oil Pump, Replace."

24. Remove transmission and drive plate.

25. Insert suitable 3/16 inch wide flat bladed screwdriver between lip and seal metal case.

26. Angle screwdriver through dust lip against metal case and pry out seal. **Do not allow screwdriver blade to contact seal surface.**

27. Remove structural windage tray.

28. Mark connecting rod cap position for assembly using permanent ink marker or suitable scribe tool. Do not use punch or stamp to mark connecting rods.

29. Remove connecting rod bearing caps.

30. Remove main bearing cap and tie bolts, then main bearing caps.

31. Remove crankshaft.

Installation

Upper and lower bearing halves are not interchangeable.

1. Lubricate upper main bearing halves with engine oil.

2. Push crankshaft forward.

3. Roll lubricate front thrust washer onto machined shelf between No. 3 upper main bulk head and crankshaft thrust surface. Ensure crankshaft thrust washer coated and oil groove side faces crankshaft thrust surface.

4. Move crankshaft rearward.

5. Roll lubricate rear thrust washer onto machined shelf between No. 3 upper main bulk head and crankshaft thrust surface. Ensure crankshaft thrust washer coated and oil groove side faces crankshaft thrust surface.

6. Lubricate lower main bearings with engine oil, then install main bearings and caps.

7. **Torque** inside main bearing cap bolts to 15 ft. lbs., then tighten an addition ¼ turn.
8. Measure crankshaft endplay.
9. Install connecting rods and measure side clearance.
10. Install windage tray.
11. Lubricate windage tray mounting bolts with engine oil, **torque** to 20 ft. lbs. then tighten an addition ¼ turn.
12. Install main cap tie bolts.
13. Install rear crankshaft oil seal retainer and oil seal.
14. Install oil pump, crankshaft sprocket, timing chain, front cover and valve covers.
15. Install accessory drive idler pulley bracket, then oil pickup tube and O-ring.
16. Install oil pan and filter, then oil dipstick tube.
17. Install engine and fill crankcase with suitable oil.

CRANKSHAFT SPROCKET

REPLACE

With the timing chain removed, avoid turning the camshaft or crankshaft. If movement is required, exercise caution to avoid valve damage caused by piston contact.

Removal

1. Remove timing chain as outlined under "Timing Chain, Replace."
2. Remove sprocket using crankshaft damper bolt and suitable puller.

Installation

1. Install sprocket until it bottoms against crankshaft step flange using crankshaft seal and sprocket installer tool No. 6780-1 and Crankshaft Damper Installer Screw tool No. 8179, or equivalent.
2. Measure from sprocket outer face to end of crankshaft. Ensure measurement is 1.5174–1.5574 inches.
3. Install primary timing chain.

MAIN & ROD BEARINGS

Refer to "Crankshaft, Replace" for main and rod bearings service.

CRANKSHAFT SEAL

REPLACE

1. Remove upper radiator crossmember and fan module.
2. Remove accessory and air conditioning belts.
3. Remove damper using crankshaft damper holder tool No. 8191, or equivalent, and three-jaw puller tool No. 1023, or equivalent.
4. Insert crankshaft damper remover insert tool No. 8194, or equivalent, into crankshaft nose.

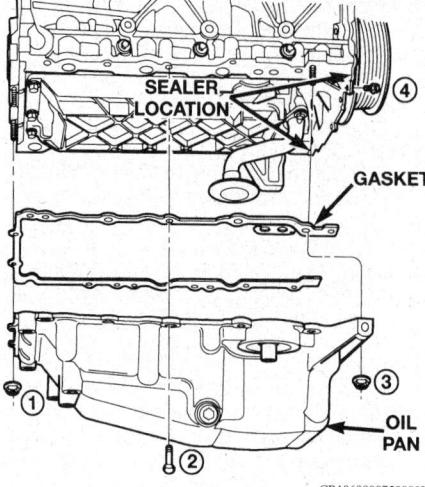

Fig. 11   Oil pan replacement

5. Remove seal using crankshaft seal remover tool No. 6771, or equivalent.
6. Reverse procedure to install. Using crankshaft seal protector tool No. 6780-2, crankshaft seal and sprocket installer tool 6780-1 and crankshaft damper installer screw tool No. 8179, or equivalents.

CRANKSHAFT REAR OIL SEAL

REPLACE

Removal

1. Remove transmission and drive plate.
2. Insert suitable ³⁄₁₆ inch wide flat bladed screwdriver between lip and seal metal case.
3. Angle screwdriver through dust lip against metal case and pry out seal. **Do not allow screwdriver blade to contact seal surface.**

Installation

1. Place magnetic base of crankshaft rear seal pilot guide tool No. 6926-1, or equivalent, on crankshaft.
2. Place seal over pilot tool, ensure seal lip faces towards crankshaft.
3. Drive seal into retainer housing until seal is flush with surface using crankshaft rear seal installer tool No. 6926-2 and handle tool No. C-4171, or equivalents.
4. Install drive plate and transmission.

OIL PAN

REPLACE

Removal

1. Remove dipstick and tube, then raise and support vehicle.
2. Drain engine oil into suitable container, then remove oil filter.
3. Disconnect suspension stabilizer bar and position aside.
4. Remove mounting bolts, then the

structural collar from oil pan and transmission housing.
5. Remove mounting bolts, oil pan and gasket. Ensure timing cover to oil pan bolts are removed, before removing pan.

Installation

1. Apply ⅛ inch bead of suitable silicone rubber adhesive sealant to front T-joints, **Fig. 11.**
2. Install gasket to block.
3. Install oil pan, then finger tighten bolts and nuts until gasket's rubber seal is compressed.
4. Install timing chain cover and **torque** mounting bolts (4) to 105 inch lbs.
5. **Torque** front mounting bolts to 21 ft. lbs.
6. **Torque** mounting nuts to 105 inch lbs.
7. **Torque** vertical collar oil pan bolts to 10 inch lbs.
8. **Torque** collar to transmission bolts to 40 ft. lbs.
9. Start with center vertical bolt and work outward, **torque** mounting bolts to 40 ft. lbs.
10. Install oil filter and drain plug, then lower vehicle and install dipstick and tube.
11. Connect stabilizer bar.
12. Fill crankcase with suitable oil.

OIL PUMP

REPLACE

1. Remove crankshaft damper as outlined under "Crankshaft, Replace."
2. Remove upper radiator support crossmember, then the fan module and accessory drive belts.
3. Remove upper radiator crossmember and fan module.
4. Remove accessory and air conditioning belts.
5. Remove damper using crankshaft damper holder tool No. 8191, or equivalent, and three-jaw puller tool No. 1023, or equivalent.
6. Remove power steering pump from mounting bracket, then the accessory drive belt tensioner pulley and bracket.
7. Remove mounting bolts and timing chain cover.
8. Remove timing chain as outlined under "Timing Chain, Replace."
9. Remove crankshaft sprocket as outlined under "Crankshaft, Replace."
10. Remove dipstick and tube, then raise and support vehicle.
11. Drain engine oil into suitable container, then remove oil filter.
12. Disconnect suspension stabilizer bar and position aside.
13. Remove mounting bolts, then the structural collar from oil pan and transmission housing.
14. Remove mounting bolts, oil pan and gasket. Ensure timing cover to oil pan bolts are removed, before removing pan.
15. Remove oil pickup tube and O-ring.
16. With cylinder No. 1 at 60° ATDC, ensure crankshaft sprocket timing marks and oil pump marks are aligned.

17. Remove mounting bolts, then the oil pump.
18. Reverse procedure to install, noting the following:
    a. Prime pump with suitable, clean engine oil before installation.
    b. Ensure crankshaft sprocket and oil pump marks align, with crankshaft positioned at cylinder No. 1 at 60° ATDC.

OIL PUMP SERVICE

1. Remove retaining cap, spring and pressure relief valve.
2. Remove mounting screws and lift cover plate off.
3. Remove pump rotors.
4. Wash components in suitable solvent, then inspect for damage or wear.
5. Lay straightedge across pump cover surface. If .001 inch feeler gauge can be inserted between cover and straight edge, replace cover.
6. Measure thickness and diameter of rotors.
7. If outer rotor thickness is less than .373 inch or rotor diameter is less than 3.5108 inches, replace rotor.
8. If inner rotor thickness is less than .373 inch, replace rotor.
9. Slide outer rotor into body, press to one side with fingers and measure clearance between rotor and body. If clearance is more than .015 inch, replace body.
10. Install inner rotor and measure clearance between rotors. If clearance is more than .003 inch, replace pump assembly.
11. Inspect oil pressure relief valve plunger for scoring and free operation in bore. Small marks may be removed with 400-grit wet or dry sandpaper.
12. Relief valve spring free length should be approximately 1.95 inches. Compress spring with 23–25 lbs. If length is not 1.34 inches, replace spring.
13. Reverse procedure to assemble.

BELT TENSION DATA

Belt	Belt Tension, Lbs.	
	New	Used
Accessory①	180–200	120
Air Conditioning②	150–170	120

① — Poly-V Belt.

② — V-Belt.

SERPENTINE DRIVE BELT

1. Loosen tensioner pulley locking nut.
2. Loosen belt adjusting bolt.
3. Remove accessory drive belt.
4. Reverse procedure to install.

SEPARATED ACCESSORY DRIVE SYSTEM

Air Conditioning

REMOVAL

1. Remove alternator/power steering serpentine drive belt.
2. Loosen tensioner locking and pivot bolts. Do not remove.
3. Insert suitable ½ inch drive breaker bar into belt tensioner square opening, rotate tensioner counterclockwise until belt can be removed from pulleys.
4. Slowly rotate tensioner clockwise to relieve spring load.

INSTALLATION

1. Insert suitable ½ inch drive breaker bar into tensioner square opening, then hold counterclockwise pressure on tensioner while removing locking bolt.
2. Carefully release tensioner torsion spring load.
3. Remove pivot bolt, tensioner and spring from front timing cover.
4. Insert spring arm into appropriate New or Used tensioner belt position.
5. Install torsion spring, tensioner and pivot bolt.
6. Apply counterclockwise pressure on tensioner until locking bolt can be installed using ½ inch drive breaker bar.
7. Rotate tensioner counterclockwise until belt can be installed on pulleys.
8. Release tensioner and remove socket wrench.
9. Install accessory drive belt.

COOLING SYSTEM BLEED

1. Close radiator drain hand tight.
2. Attach approximately 48 inches of ¼ inch I.D. clear hose to bleed valve.
3. Route hose away from accessory drive belt, drive pulleys and electrical cooling fan and into a clean container.
4. Open cooling system bleed valve, then attach filling aid funnel tool No. 8195, or equivalent, to pressure bottle filler neck.
5. Pinch overflow hose between coolant bottle chambers.
6. Pour 50/50 mix of suitable coolant and distilled water into large section of filling funnel.
7. Slowly fill until steady stream of coolant flows from bleed valve hose.
8. Close bleed valve and continue filling system to top of funnel.
9. Remove overflow hose clip and allow funnel to drain into overflow chamber.
10. Remove funnel and install coolant pressure bottle cap.
11. Remove bleed valve hose, then start and run engine until operating temperature is reached.
12. Shut off engine and allow to cool.

13. With engine cold, ensure pressure chamber level is between MIN and MAX marks.

THERMOSTAT

REPLACE

1. Drain cooling system into suitable container.
2. Remove oil dipstick tube, cover tube opening to prevent coolant from entering engine.
3. Raise and support vehicle.
4. Remove lefthand isolator mounting nuts from top of mounting bracket.
5. Support engine with suitable jack, place suitable wood block between oil pan and jack.
6. Remove lower mounting nuts from frame.
7. Raise engine carefully, then remove lefthand isolator with heat shield.
8. Remove alternator support strut, then disconnect electrical connector.
9. Remove transmission dipstick tube bracket mounting bolt.
10. Remove lower heater and radiator hoses from thermostat housing.
11. Remove thermostat housing mounting bolts, then the thermostat and housing.
12. Reverse procedure to install. Ensure thermostat is installed with bleed valve at 12 o'clock position.

WATER PUMP

REPLACE

1. Drain cooling system into suitable container.
2. Remove upper radiator crossmember.
3. Remove radiator fan assembly.
4. Remove accessory and air conditioning drive belts.
5. Remove timing chain and all chain guides as outlined under "Timing Chain, Replace."
6. Remove water pump mounting bolts, then the water pump and gasket.
7. Reverse procedure to install.

RADIATOR

REPLACE

1. Drain cooling system into suitable container.
2. Remove upper radiator crossmember, then the clamps and hoses from radiator.
3. Disconnect transmission hoses from cooler. Plug hose to prevent contamination.
4. Disconnect engine oil cooler lines.
5. Disconnect radiator fan electrical connector, then remove mounting bolts and fan module.
6. Remove air conditioning condenser mounting bolts and transmission cooler line bracket.
7. Lift condenser up enough to clear upper mounting clips, then rest condenser on lower radiator crossmember.
8. Remove radiator.
9. Reverse procedure to install.

FUEL PUMP
REPLACE

1. Remove fuel pump relay for power distribution center.
2. Start and run engine until it stalls.
3. Attempt to start engine until it no longer runs.
4. Turn ignition switch to Off position.
5. Place rag or towel under fuel line quick-connector fitting at fuel rail.
6. Install fuel pump relay.
7. Remove rear seat, then disconnect fuel pump electrical connector.
8. Raise and support vehicle, then drain fuel tank into suitable container.
9. Loosen brackets from body and swing rear stabilizer bar toward rear.
10. Remove fuel filler tube from tank, then disconnect fuel and EVAP lines.
11. Position suitable transmission jack under fuel tank, then remove fuel tank strap bolts, passenger side first.
12. Lower fuel tank, then remove purge and vent lines.
13. Depress quick connector retainers, then the fuel line from pump.
14. Slide fuel pump module electrical connector lock to unlock, then push connector retainer down and pull off module.
15. Remove fuel pump module locknut using fuel pump removal/installation tool No. 6856, or equivalent.
16. Remove fuel pump and O-ring seal.
17. Reverse procedure to install.

FUEL FILTER
REPLACE

A combination fuel filter/pressure regulator is located on top of fuel pump module. A separate frame mount filter is not used.

1. Remove fuel pump relay for power distribution center.
2. Start and run engine until it stalls.
3. Attempt to start engine until it no longer runs.
4. Turn ignition switch to Off position.
5. Place rag or towel under fuel line quick-connector fitting at fuel rail.
6. Install fuel pump relay.
7. Lower fuel tank as outlined under "Fuel Pump, Replace."
8. Remove fuel tank purge and vent lines.
9. Disconnect pressure regulator fuel line, then push locking tab in from locking slot and turn pressure regulator to unlock.
10. Pull regulator straight up and remove.
11. Reverse procedure to install.

TIGHTENING SPECIFICATIONS

Year	Component	Torque, Ft. Lbs.
2001–04	Fuel Pump Module	40
	Fuel Rail	16
	Fuel Tank Straps	44
	Intake Manifold	105①②
	Oil Pan	④
	Oil Pan Drain Plug	25
	Oil Pan Filter	15
	Oil Pump	21
	Oil Pump Cover	105①
	Oil Pump Pickup Tube	21
	Oil Pump Pressure Relief Valve Cap	105①
	PCV Valve	60①
	Rear Crankshaft Seal Retainer	108①
	Spark Plug	15
	Starter	30
	Structural Collar	③
	Thermostat Housing	105①
	Throttle Body	105①
	Throttle Body Support Bracket, Lower	50①
	Throttle Body Support Bracket, Upper	105①
	Timing Chain Cover, M6	105①
	Timing Chain Cover, M10	40
	Timing Chain Guide	21
	Timing Chain Guide Access Plug	15
	Timing Chain Tensioner	40
	Water Pump	105①
	Water Outlet Housing	105①
	Water Outlet Housing Bleed	105①

① — Inch lbs.
② — Refer to "Intake Manifold, Replace" for tightening specifications and sequence.
③ — Refer to "Structural Collar, Replace" for tightening specifications and sequence.
④ — Refer to "Oil Pan, Replace" for tightening specifications and sequence.

NOTE: On Air Bag Equipped Models, Refer To "Air Bag System Precautions" Located In The Front Of This Manual For System Disarming & Arming Procedures.

NOTE: Refer To "Computer Relearn Procedures" Located In The Front Of This Manual When Battery Power To The Computer Has Been Interrupted.

NOTE: Prior To Performing Any Service Operations Listed In This Section, Consult The "Technical Service Bulletins" Section For Related Information.

INDEX

PRECAUTIONS
Air Bag Systems

Refer to "Air Bag System Precautions" in the front of this manual for system disarming and arming procedures.

Battery Ground Cable

Prior to service, disconnect battery ground cable and isolate as required.

Fuel System Pressure Relief

1. Remove fuel pump relay for power distribution center.
2. Start and run engine until it stalls.
3. Attempt to start engine until it no longer runs.
4. Turn ignition switch to Off position.
5. Place rag or towel under fuel line quick-connector fitting at fuel rail.
6. Install fuel pump relay.
7. One or more Diagnostic Trouble Codes (DTCs) may have been stored because of removing fuel pump relay.

Clear these DTCs with suitably programmed scan tool.

COMPRESSION PRESSURE

The minimum compression pressure should be no less than 100 psi and the maximum variation between cylinders should be no more than 25%.

ENGINE MOUNT
REPLACE

Refer to "2.7L Engine" for engine mount replacement.

STRUCTURAL COLLAR
REPLACE

Refer to "2.7L Engine" for structural collar replacement.

ENGINE
REPLACE

1. Remove fuel pump relay for power distribution center.
2. Start and run engine until it stalls.
3. Attempt to start engine until it no longer runs.
4. Turn ignition switch to Off position.
5. Place rag or towel under fuel line quick-connector fitting at fuel rail.
6. Install fuel pump relay.
7. Mark hood position at hinges and remove, then drain cooling system into suitable container.
8. Remove wiper arms, left and righthand cowl covers, then cowl support.
9. remove wiper arms, left and righthand cowl screens, then the strut tower brace.
10. Remove air cleaner assembly and air inlet hose, then the upper radiator crossmember.
11. Disconnect hood release cable from latch, then remove radiator fan assembly and accessory drive belts.
12. Drain coolant into suitable container.
13. Disconnect upper radiator hose at engine and lower hose at radiator, then the engine oil and transmission cooler lines from radiator.
14. Remove power steering line bracket at lefthand side of radiator, then the air conditioning condenser to radiator attaching bolts.

15. Remove radiator, then the accessory drive belts.
16. Remove alternator, then the power steering pump mounting bolts. Position pump aside.
17. Remove air conditioning compressor mounting bolts. Position compressor aside.
18. Remove righthand exhaust manifold V-band clamps, then the righthand catalytic converter down pipe front and rear support bracket attaching bolts.
19. Remove fuel pump relay for power distribution center.
20. Start and run engine until it stalls.
21. Attempt to start engine until it no longer runs.
22. Turn ignition switch to Off position.
23. Place rag or towel under fuel line quick-connector fitting at fuel rail.
24. Install fuel pump relay.
25. Disconnect fuel line.
26. Disconnect throttle and speed control cables, then the coolant bottle hoses.
27. Disconnect vacuum lines and engine ground straps from both cylinder heads.
28. Remove air cleaner housing and inlet hose.
29. Remove throttle and speed control cables from throttle arm and bracket.
30. Disconnect Secondary Runner Valve (SRV), Manifold Tuning Valve (MTV), Throttle Position Sensor (TPS), Idle Air Control (IAC) and Intake Air Temperature/Manifold Absolute Pressure (TMAP) electrical connectors.
31. Disconnect SRV reservoir, speed control reservoir and Positive Crankcase Ventilation (PCV) vacuum hoses.
32. Remove left and righthand side intake manifold supports, then support brackets at intake manifold front corners and MTV.
33. Remove EGR tubes mounting clips.
34. Remove mounting bolts and upper manifold.
35. Disconnect heater hoses, then remove rear throttle body support bracket.
36. Remove water piper fastener at transmission to block bolt, then the four upper transmission to cylinder block bolts.
37. Disconnect all remaining electrical connections, then raise and support vehicle.
38. Drain engine oil into suitable container, then remove structural collar mounting bolts.
39. Mark flexplate to torque converter position, then remove converter attaching bolts.
40. Disconnect transmission cooler line brackets from engine.
41. Remove lefthand exhaust manifold V-band clamp, then the starter.
42. Remove left and righthand engine mount bolts.
43. Remove crankshaft position sensor and lower transmission to cylinder block bolts.
44. Lower vehicle, then attach suitable lifting device to engine.
45. Support transmission with suitable floor jack, place suitable block of wood between transmission and jack.

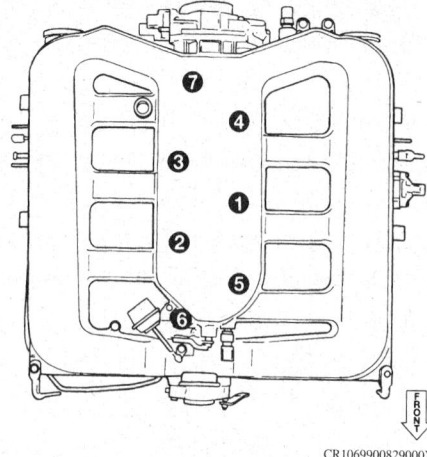

CR1069900829000X

Fig. 1 Upper intake manifold bolt tightening sequence

46. Remove engine from vehicle.
47. Reverse procedure to install.

INTAKE MANIFOLD
REPLACE
Upper

1. Remove air cleaner housing and inlet hose.
2. Remove throttle and speed control cables from throttle arm and bracket.
3. Disconnect Secondary Runner Valve (SRV), Manifold Tuning Valve (MTV), Throttle Position Sensor (TPS), Idle Air Control (IAC) and Intake Air Temperature/Manifold Absolute Pressure (TMAP) electrical connectors.
4. Disconnect SRV reservoir, speed control reservoir and Positive Crankcase Ventilation (PCV) vacuum hoses.
5. Remove left and righthand side intake manifold supports, then support brackets at intake manifold front corners and MTV.
6. Remove EGR tubes mounting clips.
7. Remove mounting bolts and upper manifold.
8. Reverse procedure to install, noting the following:
   a. Hand start all intake manifold mounting bolts.
   b. Tighten bolts in sequence, **Fig. 1**.

Lower

1. Remove fuel pump relay for power distribution center.
2. Start and run engine until it stalls.
3. Attempt to start engine until it no longer runs.
4. Turn ignition switch to Off position.
5. Place rag or towel under fuel line quick-connector fitting at fuel rail.
6. Install fuel pump relay.
7. Drain cooling system into suitable container.
8. Remove air cleaner housing and inlet hose.
9. Remove throttle and speed control cables from throttle arm and bracket.
10. Disconnect Secondary Runner Valve

(SRV), Manifold Tuning Valve (MTV), Throttle Position Sensor (TPS), Idle Air Control (IAC) and Intake Air Temperature/Manifold Absolute Pressure (TMAP) electrical connectors.
11. Disconnect SRV reservoir, speed control reservoir and Positive Crankcase Ventilation (PCV) vacuum hoses.
12. Remove left and righthand side intake manifold supports, then support brackets at intake manifold front corners and MTV.
13. Remove EGR tubes mounting clips.
14. Remove mounting bolts and upper manifold.
15. Disconnect fuel injectors and coolant temperature sensor electrical connectors, then the heater hose quick connect tee from heater tube.
16. Disconnect fuel rail fuel supply hose from fuel rail, then remove fuel rail support bracket to throttle body support bracket mounting screw.
17. Remove fuel rail and injector assembly mounting bolts, then the fuel rail and injectors.
18. Remove lower intake manifold mounting bolts and the manifold.
19. Reverse procedure to install. Gradually **torque** mounting bolts in sequence to 21 ft. lbs., **Fig. 2**.

EXHAUST MANIFOLD
REPLACE
Lefthand

1. Raise and support vehicle using suitable lift.
2. Remove exhaust system, then loosen converter pipe support mounting bolt at transmission.
3. Lower vehicle and remove exhaust manifold connector V-band clamp.
4. Disconnect connector and remove exhaust manifold oxygen sensor.
5. Remove mounting screws and heat shield.
6. Remove mounting bolts and exhaust manifold.
7. Reverse procedure to install.

Righthand

1. Raise and support vehicle, then remove exhaust system.
2. Loosen converter pipe support mounting bolt at transmission mount.
3. Loosen air conditioning drive belt, then lower vehicle.
4. Remove air cleaner housing and air inlet tube.
5. Remove manifold V-band clamp.
6. Remove air conditioning compressor mounting bolts, position compressor aside.
7. Remove engine oil dipstick tube, then the air conditioning compressor bracket.
8. Remove oxygen sensor and heat shields.
9. Remove exhaust manifold mounting bolts and the manifold.
10. Reverse procedure to install.

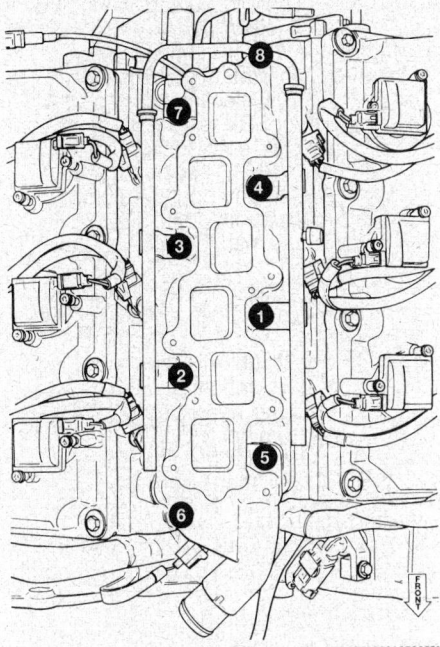

Fig. 2 Lower intake manifold bolt tightening sequence

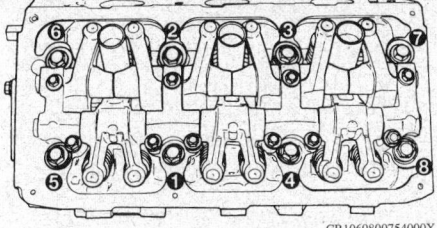

Fig. 3 Cylinder head bolt tightening sequence

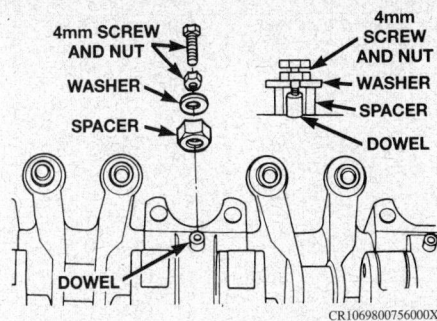

Fig. 4 Rocker arm dowel removal

CYLINDER HEAD
REPLACE

1. Remove upper radiator crossmember, then the fan module and accessory drive belts.
2. Remove upper radiator crossmember and fan module.
3. Remove damper using crankshaft damper holder tool No. 8191, or equivalent, and three-jaw puller tool No. 1023, or equivalent.
4. Remove damper using crankshaft damper holder tool No. 8191, or equivalent, and three-jaw puller tool No. 1023, or equivalent.
5. Remove lower belt cover, stamped steel cover and lefthand cast cover.
6. Remove camshaft sprockets as outlined under "Camshaft Sprocket, Replace."
7. Remove upper and lower intake manifolds as outlined under "Intake Manifold, Replace."
8. Remove exhaust manifold to catalytic converter pipe connection V-band clamps.
9. Remove rear timing belt cover to cylinder head attaching bolts, then the rear covers.
10. Remove mounting bolts and cylinder heads.
11. Reverse procedure to install, noting the following:
    a. **Cylinder head bolts with stretched threads must be replaced.**
    b. Lubricate bolt threads with suitable, clean engine oil.
    c. **Torque** cylinder head bolts in sequence to 45 ft. lbs. , **Fig. 3.**
    d. **Torque** head bolts in sequence to 65 ft. lbs.
    e. **Torque** bolts in sequence to 65 ft. lbs.
    f. Tighten bolts an additional 90° in sequence.
    g. If final cylinder head bolt **torque** is not 90 ft. lbs, replace bolts.
    h. Install new O-ring seal in righthand rear timing belt cover.

VALVE COVER
REPLACE

1. Remove air cleaner housing and inlet hose.
2. Remove throttle and speed control cables from throttle arm and bracket.
3. Disconnect Secondary Runner Valve (SRV), Manifold Tuning Valve (MTV), Throttle Position Sensor (TPS), Idle Air Control (IAC) and Intake Air Temperature/Manifold Absolute Pressure (TMAP) electrical connectors.
4. Disconnect SRV reservoir, speed control reservoir and Positive Crankcase Ventilation (PCV) vacuum hoses.
5. Remove left and righthand side intake manifold supports, then support brackets at intake manifold front corners and MTV.
6. Remove EGR tubes mounting clips.
7. Remove mounting bolts and upper manifold.
8. Cover lower intake manifold.
9. Disconnect electrical connectors and remove ignition coils.
10. Remove mounting bolts and cylinder head cover.
11. Reverse procedure to install, noting the following:
    a. Remove spark plug tube seals.
    b. Position new seal with part number facing cylinder head cover and install with Installer tool No. MB-998306, or equivalent.

SPARK PLUG TUBES
REPLACE

1. Remove cylinder head cover as outlined under "Valve Cover, Replace."
2. Remove tube from cylinder head using suitable locking pliers.
3. Apply suitable lubricant to new tube approximately .039 inch from tube end, in a .118 inch wide area.
4. Install seater end of tube into cylinder head, then carefully install tube using suitable hardwood block and mallet until seated into bore bottom.
5. Install cylinder head cover.

VALVE ADJUSTMENT

Rocker arms are equipped with hydraulic lash adjusters. No adjustment is required.

ROCKER ARMS
REPLACE
Removal

1. Remove cylinder head covers as outlined under "Valve Cover, Replace."
2. Identify rocker arm assembly and rocker arm for installation alignment.
3. Remove mounting bolts and rocker arm assembly. **To prevent air ingestion into lash adjusters, avoid turning rocker arm assembly upside down. Do not rest rocker arm assembly on lash adjusters.**
4. Install screw, nut, spacer and washer into pin, then tighten screw into pin, loosen nut and pull out shaft support dowel, **Fig. 4.**
5. Remove rocker arms and pedestals in order.

Installation

1. Install rocker arms and pedestals into shaft. Rocker shaft notches face up. Righthand cylinder bank notches face toward rear and lefthand notches face toward front.
2. Press new dowel pins until they bottom against shaft in pedestal. Pins pass through pedestal into exhaust rocker shafts.
3. Rotate camshafts until lobes are in neutral position, **Fig. 5.**
4. Install rocker arm and shaft assembly. Ensure identification marks face front of engine on lefthand head and toward rear of engine on righthand head.
5. Tighten mounting bolts in sequence, **Fig. 6.**

VALVE SPRINGS
REPLACE

Ensure piston is at TDC on cylinder from which valve spring(s) is being removed.

1. Remove fuel pump relay for power distribution center.
2. Start and run engine until it stalls.
3. Attempt to start engine until it no longer runs.

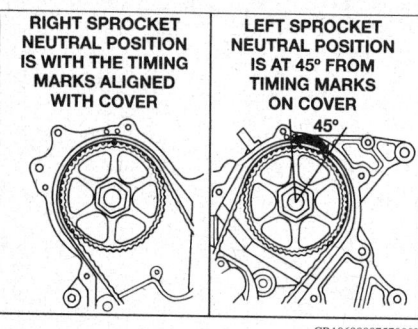

Fig. 5 Camshaft sprockets neutral position

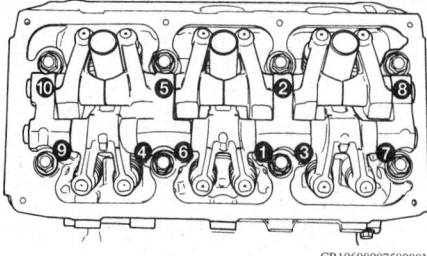

CR1069800758000X

Fig. 6 Rocker arm & shaft assembly bolt tightening sequence

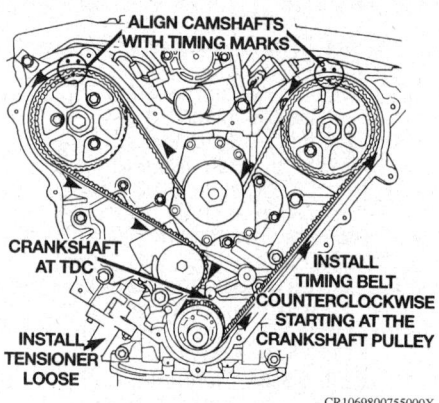

CR1069800755000X

Fig. 7 Camshaft sprocket timing mark alignment

4. Turn ignition switch to Off position.
5. Place rag or towel under fuel line quick-connector fitting at fuel rail.
6. Install fuel pump relay.
7. Remove air cleaner housing and hose.
8. Remove air cleaner housing and inlet hose.
9. Remove throttle and speed control cables from throttle arm and bracket.
10. Disconnect Secondary Runner Valve (SRV), Manifold Tuning Valve (MTV), Throttle Position Sensor (TPS), Idle Air Control (IAC) and Intake Air Temperature/Manifold Absolute Pressure (TMAP) electrical connectors.
11. Disconnect SRV reservoir, speed control reservoir and Positive Crankcase Ventilation (PCV) vacuum hoses.
12. Remove left and righthand side intake manifold supports, then support brackets at intake manifold front corners and MTV.
13. Remove EGR tubes mounting clips.
14. Remove mounting bolts and upper manifold.
15. Remove valve cover as outlined under "Valve Cover, Replace."
16. Turn crankshaft to rotate engine until cam lobe is on base circle (heel) of rocker arm being removed.
17. Depress valve spring enough to release tension and remove rocker arm using valve spring compressor tool No. 8215 and adapter tool No. 8216, or equivalent.
18. Rotate crankshaft clockwise until No. 1 piston is at TDC.
19. Install suitable spark plug adapter into cylinder being serviced, then apply 90–100 psi air pressure to hold valves in place.
20. Compress valve spring using valve spring compressor tool No. MD-998772-A with adapter tool No. 6527, or equivalent, then remove valve locks, retainer and spring.
21. Remove valve stem seals using suitable valve seal tool.
22. Repeat procedure in firing sequence 1-2-3-4-5-6. **Ensure piston is at TDC on cylinder from which valve spring(s) is being removed.**
23. Reverse procedure to install, noting the following:
    a. Push valve steam seal/seat firmly and squarely over valve guide with stem as guide.
    b. Do not force seal against guide top.
    c. When installer retainer locks, com-

press spring only enough to install locks.

CRANKSHAFT DAMPER
REPLACE

1. Remove upper radiator crossmember and fan module.
2. Remove accessory drive belts.
3. Hold crankshaft damper with holder tool No. 8191, or equivalent, then remove center bolt.
4. Remove damper using three-jaw puller tool No. 1023 and crankshaft damper remover insert tool No. C-4685-C2, or equivalents.
5. Reverse procedure to install.

FRONT COVER
REPLACE

1. Remove upper radiator support crossmember, then the fan module and accessory drive belts.
2. Remove upper radiator crossmember and fan module.
3. Remove accessory and air conditioning belts.
4. Remove damper using crankshaft damper holder tool No. 8191, or equivalent, and three-jaw puller tool No. 1023, or equivalent.
5. Remove lower belt cover, stamped steel cover and lefthand cast cover.
6. **Do not remove cover sealer.** If some sealer is missing, replace with suitable silicone rubber adhesive sealant.
7. Reverse procedure to install.

TIMING BELT
REPLACE

With the timing belt removed, avoid turning the camshaft or crankshaft. If movement is required, exercise caution to avoid valve damage caused by piston contact.

This procedure can only be used when camshaft sprockets have not been loosened or removed. If camshaft sprockets have been loosened or removed, refer to "Camshaft Timing, Adjust" for proper procedure.

Removal

1. Remove upper radiator crossmember and disconnect radiator fan electrical connector.

2. Remove fan module and accessory drive belts, then the fan module.
3. Remove damper using crankshaft damper holder tool No. 8191, or equivalent, and three-jaw puller tool No. 1023, or equivalent.
4. Remove lower belt cover, stamped steel cover and lefthand cast cover.
5. If reusing timing belt, mark rotational direction on belt.
6. Turn crankshaft clockwise until crankshaft mark aligns with oil pump housing TDC mark and camshaft sprocket timing marks are between rear cover marks, **Fig. 7.**
7. Mark camshaft sprocket timing mark position to two rear timing cover timing marks.
8. Remove timing belt tensioner and store with plunger facing up.
9. Remove timing belt.

Installation

1. Align crankshaft sprocket timing mark with oil pump housing TDC mark, **Fig. 7.**
2. Align camshaft sprocket marks between reference marks on rear cover.
3. Slowly preload tensioner with suitable vise, then install locking pin. Store pin with plunger facing up until ready to install.
4. Install timing belt in a counterclockwise direction starting at crankshaft sprocket.
5. Ensure camshaft sprocket marks are still between rear cover marks.
6. Hold tensioner pulley against belt, then install tensioner.
7. Pull retaining pin and allow tensioner to extend to pulley bracket.
8. Ensure camshaft sprocket marks are still aligned.
9. Rotate crankshaft sprocket two revolutions and ensure timing marks align.
10. Install front cover, crankshaft damper, accessory drive belts and cooling fan module.
11. Install upper radiator crossmember.

CAMSHAFT
REPLACE

With the timing belt removed, avoid turning the camshaft or crankshaft. If

movement is required, exercise caution to avoid valve damage caused by piston contact.

1. Remove timing belt as outlined under "Timing Belt, Replace."
2. Hold camshaft sprocket with suitable box wrench, then remove bolt and washer. If engine is in vehicle, it may be required to lift engine side.
3. Remove camshaft sprocket.
4. Camshaft sprockets are not interchangeable. Lefthand sprocket has DIS pickup slots, righthand sprocket does not.
5. Remove cylinder head as outlined under "Cylinder Head, Replace."
6. Remove rear camshaft cover and O-ring.
7. Carefully remove camshaft from rear of cylinder head.
8. Reverse procedure to install. Lubricate camshaft journals and cam with suitable, clean engine oil before installation.

CAMSHAFT OIL SEAL

REPLACE

1. Remove camshaft sprocket(s) as outlined under "Camshaft, Replace."
2. Remove oil seal using camshaft seal remover tool No. C-3981B, or equivalent.
3. Reverse procedure to install, noting the following:
   a. Lightly coat oil seal lip with suitable, clean engine oil.
   b. Install oil seal with seal protector sleeve tool No. 6788 and seal installer tool No. 6052, or equivalent.

CAMSHAFT TIMING

ADJUST

With the timing belt removed, avoid turning the camshaft or crankshaft. If movement is required, exercise caution to avoid valve damage caused by piston contact.

1. Align crankshaft sprocket timing mark with oil pump housing TDC mark, **Fig. 7**.
2. Install dial indicator into cylinder No. 1, then rotate crankshaft until piston is exactly at TDC.
3. Install camshaft alignment tools No. 6642, or equivalent, on rear of each cylinder head.
4. Slowly preload tensioner with suitable vise and install locking pin. Store pin with plunger facing up until ready to install.
5. Install camshaft sprockets, align timing marks between rear cover timing marks.
6. Install new mounting bolts. Lefthand mounting bolt is 10 inches long, righthand 8⅜ inches. Do not tighten at this time.
7. Install timing belt starting at crankshaft sprocket and going in counterclockwise direction. Maintain tension on belt when installing belt around tensioner pulley.

8. Ensure camshaft sprocket timing marks are still fall between rear cover marks.
9. Hold tensioner pulley against belt, install tensioner.
10. Pull retaining pin and allow tensioner to extend to pulley bracket.
11. Ensure No. 1 piston is at TDC, then hold camshaft sprocket hex with suitable wrench and tighten camshaft bolts.
12. Remove dial indicator and install spark plug.

TIMING BELT TENSIONER BLEED

Operate engine at 1600–2000 RPM for 10–15 minutes. This will purge air from tensioner and noise will dissipate.

PISTON & ROD ASSEMBLY

Refer to "2.7L Engine" for piston and rod assembly service.

CRANKSHAFT

REPLACE

Removal

1. Remove engine as outlined under "Engine, Replace."
2. Drain engine oil into suitable container.
3. Remove mounting bolts, then the structural collar from oil pan and transmission housing.
4. Remove engine oil cooler line, then the transmission oil cooler line clips.
5. Remove mounting bolts, oil pan and gasket.
6. Remove upper radiator crossmember and fan module.
7. Remove accessory and air conditioning belts.
8. Remove damper using crankshaft damper holder tool No. 8191, or equivalent, and three-jaw puller tool No. 1023, or equivalent.
9. Remove accessory drive belt idler pulley.
10. Remove lower belt cover, stamped steel cover and lefthand cast cover.
11. Remove timing belt and tensioner as outlined under "Timing Chain, Replace."
12. Remove damper using crankshaft damper holder tool No. 8191, or equivalent, and three-jaw puller tool No. 1023, or equivalent.
13. Insert crankshaft damper remover insert tool No. 8194, or equivalent, into crankshaft nose.
14. Remove seal using crankshaft seal remover tool No. 6771, or equivalent.
15. Tap crankshaft dowel pin out, then remove oil pump assembly.
16. Remove rear oil seal retainer.
17. Mark connecting rod bearing caps for assembly, then remove.
18. Mark main bearing caps for assembly, then remove.
19. Remove crankshaft.

Installation

Upper and lower bearing halves are not interchangeable.

1. Lubricate upper main bearing halves with engine oil.
2. Push crankshaft forward.
3. Roll lubricate front thrust washer onto machined shelf between No. 2 upper main bulk head and crankshaft thrust surface.
4. Move crankshaft rearward.
5. Roll lubricate rear thrust washer onto machined shelf between No. 2 upper main bulk head and crankshaft thrust surface.
6. Lubricate lower main bearings with engine oil, then install main bearings and caps.
7. **Torque** inside main bearing cap bolts to 15 ft. lbs., then tighten an additional ¼ turn.
8. Measure crankshaft end play.
9. Install connecting rods and measure side clearance.
10. Install windage tray.
11. Lubricate windage tray mounting bolts with engine oil, **torque** to 20 ft. lbs., then tighten an additional ¼ turn.
12. Install main cap tie bolts.
13. Install rear crankshaft oil seal retainer and oil seal.
14. Install oil pump, crankshaft dowel pin, crankshaft sprocket, timing belt, covers and crankshaft damper.
15. Install accessory drive idler pulley, then oil pickup tube and pan.
16. Install engine and fill crankcase with suitable oil.

MAIN & ROD BEARINGS

Removal

1. Remove dipstick and tube, then raise and support vehicle.
2. Drain engine oil into suitable container.
3. Remove mounting bolts, then the structural collar from oil pan and transmission housing.
4. Remove engine oil cooler line, then the transmission oil cooler line clips.
5. Remove mounting bolts, oil pan and gasket.
6. Mark bearing caps for assembly.
7. Remove bearing caps one at a time.
8. Insert main bearing tool No. C-3059, or equivalent, into crankshaft oil hole, rotate crankshaft clockwise and force bearing shell upper half out.

Installation

When installing new upper bearing shells, slightly chamfer sharp edges from plain side.

1. Lubricate main bearing with suitable, clean engine oil.
2. Start bearing in place and insert main bearing tool No. C-3059, or equivalent, into crankshaft oil hole.

3. Slowly rotate crankshaft counterclockwise, sliding bearing into place, then remove tool.
4. Lubricate and install lower bearing half.
5. Lubricate main bearing cap bolts and finger tighten.
6. Move crankshaft to forward travel limit.
7. Roll lubricate front thrust washer onto machined shelf between No. 2 upper main bulk head and crankshaft thrust surface.
8. Move crankshaft rearward.
9. Roll lubricate rear thrust washer onto machined shelf between No. 2 upper main bulk head and crankshaft thrust surface.
10. Install main bearing cap and tighten inner bolts finger tight.
11. **Torque** inside main bearing cap bolts to 15 ft. lbs., then tighten an additional ¼ turn.
12. Measure crankshaft end play.
13. Install windage tray.
14. Lubricate windage tray mounting bolts with engine oil, **torque** bolts to 20 ft. lbs., then tighten an additional ¼ turn.
15. Install main cap tie bolts.
16. Install oil pump, pickup tube and oil pan.
17. Install engine and fill crankcase with suitable oil.

CRANKSHAFT SEAL

REPLACE

Removal

1. Remove timing belt as outlined under "Timing Belt, Replace."
2. Remove crankshaft sprocket using crankshaft sprocket puller tool No. L-4407-A, or equivalent.
3. Tape dowel pin out of crankshaft.
4. Remove seal using crankshaft seal remover tool No. 6341A, or equivalent.

Installation

1. Install crankshaft seal using crankshaft seal installer tool No. 6342, or equivalent.
2. Install crankshaft dowel pin to .047 inch protrusion.
3. Install crankshaft sprocket using crankshaft sprocket installer tool No. 6641, or equivalent.
4. Install timing belt.

CRANKSHAFT REAR OIL SEAL

REPLACE

Refer to "2.7L Engine" for crankshaft rear oil seal replacement.

OIL PAN

REPLACE

1. Remove dipstick and tube, then raise and support vehicle.
2. Drain engine oil into suitable container.
3. Remove mounting bolts, then the structural collar from oil pan and transmission housing.
4. Remove engine oil cooler line, then the transmission oil cooler line clips.
5. Remove mounting bolts, oil pan and gasket.
6. Reverse procedure to install, noting the following:
   a. Apply ⅛ inch bead of suitable silicone rubber adhesive sealant to parting line of oil pump housing and rear seal retainer.

OIL PUMP

REPLACE

1. Drain cooling system into suitable container, then remove fan module and accessory drive belts.
2. Remove upper radiator crossmember and fan module.
3. Remove accessory and air conditioning belts.
4. Remove damper using crankshaft damper holder tool No. 8191, or equivalent, and three-jaw puller tool No. 1023, or equivalent.
5. Remove lower belt cover, stamped steel cover and lefthand cast cover.
6. Insert crankshaft damper remover insert tool No. 8194, or equivalent, into crankshaft nose.
7. Remove seal using crankshaft seal remover tool No. 6771, or equivalent.
8. Remove dipstick and tube, then raise and support vehicle.
9. Drain engine oil into suitable container.
10. Remove mounting bolts, then the structural collar from oil pan and transmission housing.
11. Remove engine oil cooler line, then the transmission oil cooler line clips.
12. Remove mounting bolts, oil pan and gasket.
13. Remove mounting bolts, then the oil pump and gasket.
14. Reverse procedure to install, noting the following:
   a. Prime oil pump before installing.
   b. Install new O-ring with oil pickup tube.

OIL PUMP SERVICE

1. Remove cotter pin and drill ⅛ inch hole into relief valve retainer cap, then insert self-threading sheet metal screw into cap.
2. Clamp screw into suitable vise, support oil pump body and remove cap by tapping on body with suitable soft hammer.
3. Discard cap, then remove spring and pressure relief valve.
4. Remove mounting screws and lift cover plate off.
5. Remove pump rotors.
6. Wash components in suitable solvent, then inspect for damage or wear.
7. Lay straightedge across pump cover surface. If .001 inch feeler gauge can be inserted between cover and straight edge, replace cover.
8. Measure thickness and diameter of rotors.
9. If outer rotor thickness is less than .563 inch, or rotor diameter is less than 3.141 inches, replace rotor.
10. If inner rotor thickness is less than .563 inch, replace rotor.
11. Slide outer rotor into body, press to one side with fingers and measure clearance between rotor and body. If clearance is more than .015 inch, replace body.
12. Install inner rotor and measure clearance between rotors. If clearance is more than .008 inch, replace pump assembly.
13. Place straightedge across body face between bolt holes. If clearance between rotors and straightedge is more than .003 inch replace pump assembly.
14. Inspect oil pressure relief valve plunger for scoring and free operation in bore. Small marks may be removed with 400-grit wet or dry sandpaper.
15. Relief valve spring free length should be approximately 1.95 inches. Compress spring with 23–25 lbs. If length is not 1.34 inches, replace spring.
16. Reverse procedure to assemble.

BELT TENSION DATA

Belt	Tension, Lbs.	
	New	Used
Accessory①	180–200	120
Air Conditioning②	150–170	120

① — Poly-V Belt.
② — V-Belt.

SERPENTINE DRIVE BELT

1. Remove tensioner pulley locking nut.
2. Raise and support vehicle.
3. Remove push clips attaching lower air shield to engine cradle, then the air shield from under vehicle.
4. Loosen tensioner adjusting bolt until belt can be removed.
5. Reverse procedure to install.

SEPARATED ACCESSORY DRIVE SYSTEM

Air Conditioning

1. Loosen tensioner pulley locking nut.
2. Loosen belt adjusting bolt.
3. Remove accessory drive belt.
4. Loosen tensioner pulley locknut, then the tensioner pulley adjusting bolt until belt can be removed.
5. Reverse procedure to install.

COOLING SYSTEM BLEED

1. Close radiator drain hand tight.
2. Attach approximately 48 inches of ¼ inch I.D. clear hose to bleed valve.
3. Route hose away from accessory drive

belt, drive pulleys and electrical cooling fan and into a clean container.

4. Open cooling system bleed valve, then attach filling aid funnel tool No. 8195, or equivalent, to pressure bottle filler neck.
5. Pinch overflow hose between coolant bottle chambers.
6. Pour 50/50 mix of suitable coolant and distilled water into large section of filling funnel.
7. Slowly fill until steady stream of coolant flows from bleed valve hose.
8. Close bleed valve and continue filling system to top of funnel.
9. Remove overflow hose clip and allow funnel to drain into overflow chamber.
10. Remove funnel and install coolant pressure bottle cap.
11. Remove bleed valve hose, then start and run engine until operating temperature is reached.
12. Shut off engine and allow to cool.
13. With engine cold, ensure pressure chamber level is between MIN and MAX marks.

THERMOSTAT
REPLACE

1. Drain cooling system into suitable container, then raise and support vehicle.
2. Disconnect engine oil pressure and power steering pressure switch electrical connectors.
3. Disconnect radiator and heater hoses from thermostat.
4. Remove mounting bolts, housing, thermostat and gasket.

5. Reverse procedure to install.

WATER PUMP
REPLACE

1. Drain cooling system into suitable container.
2. Remove accessory drive belts.
3. Remove timing belt components required to access water pump as outlined under "Timing Belt, Replace."
4. Remove mount bolt and water pump.
5. Reverse procedure to install. Apply suitable dielectric grease to O-ring.

RADIATOR
REPLACE

1. Drain cooling system into suitable container.
2. Remove upper radiator crossmember, then the clamps and hoses from radiator.
3. Disconnect transmission hoses from cooler. Plug hose to prevent contamination.
4. Disconnect engine oil cooler lines.
5. Disconnect radiator fan electrical connector, then remove mounting bolts and fan module.
6. Remove air conditioning condenser mounting bolts and transmission cooler line bracket.
7. Lift condenser up enough to clear upper mounting clips, then rest condenser on lower radiator crossmember.
8. Remove radiator.
9. Reverse procedure to install.

FUEL PUMP
REPLACE

Refer to "2.7L Engine" for fuel pump replacement.

FUEL FILTER
REPLACE

Refer to "2.7L Engine" for fuel filter replacement.

TECHNICAL SERVICE BULLETINS
Cold Engine Ticking
1998-2003

On some of these models built before March 31, 2003, there may be an engine ticking sound after cold engine start-up. The sound may last 2–3 seconds.

This condition may be caused by the exhaust rocker arms' swivel pads and retainer.

To correct this condition, replace the swivel pads and retainers as follows:

1. Remove valve covers as outlined under "Valve Cover, Replace."
2. Remove mounting bolts and rocker arm. **Do not turn rocker arms upside down.**
3. Remove retainers and swivel pads.
4. Install new swivel pads and retainers on exhaust rocker arms.
5. Install rocker arms and valve covers.

TIGHTENING SPECIFICATIONS

Year	Component	Torque, Ft. Lbs.
2001–04	Air Conditioning Belt Tensioner	40
	Air Conditioning Compressor To Bracket	21
	Air Conditioning Compressor To Engine Block	40
	Air Conditioning Condenser	45①
	Air Conditioning Condenser Inlet Tube Bracket	45①
	Alternator	40
	Camshaft Sprocket	②
	Camshaft Thrust Plate	21
	Cooling System Bleed	72①
	Connecting Rod Cap	③
	Crankshaft Damper	70
	Crankshaft Main Bearing Cap	③
	Crankshaft Main Bearing Cap, Tie Bolts	21
	Cylinder Head	⑥
	Cylinder Head Cover	105①
	Engine Mount Bracket	45
	Engine Mount Isolator	40
	Exhaust Manifold Heat Shield	105①
	Exhaust Manifold To Cylinder Head	17
	Exhaust Pipe Flange	25
	Fan Blade	45①
	Fan Module	45①
	Fan Motor	25①
	Fuel Pump Module	40
	Fuel Rail (3.2L)	16
	Fuel Rail (3.5L)	96①
	Fuel Tank Straps	40
	Intake Manifold, Lower	21④
	Intake Manifold, Upper	105④
	Oil Pan	105①
	Oil Pan Drain Plug	20
	Oil Pan Filter	15
	Oil Pump Cover	105①
	Oil Pump Pick-Up Tube	21
	PCV Valve	60①
	Rear Crankshaft Seal Retainer	105①
	Rocker Arm & Shaft	23
	Spark Plug	20
	Spark Plug Tube	45
	Structural Collar	⑤
	Thermostat Housing	105①
	Throttle Body	105①
	Timing Belt Cover, M6	105①
	Timing Belt Cover, M8	21
	Timing Belt Cover, M10	40
	Timing Belt Tensioner	21
	Timing Belt Tensioner Pulley	45
	Water Pump	105①
	Water Outlet Housing	72①

① — Inch Lbs.
② — Righthand side, 75 ft. lbs., then an additional ¼ turn; lefthand side, 85 ft. lbs., then an additional ¼.
③ — Refer to "Crankshaft, Replace" for tightening specifications and sequence.
④ — Refer to "Intake Manifold, Replace" for tightening procedure.
⑤ — Refer to "Structural Collar, Replace" for tightening specifications and sequence.
⑥ — Refer to "Cylinder Head, Replace" for tightening specifications and sequence.

Rear Axle & Suspension

NOTE: On Air Bag Equipped Models, Refer To "Air Bag System Precautions" Located In The Front Of This Manual For System Disarming & Arming Procedures.

NOTE: Refer To "Computer Relearn Procedures" Located In The Front Of This Manual When Battery Power To The Computer Has Been Interrupted.

NOTE: Prior To Performing Any Service Operations Listed In This Section, Consult The "Technical Service Bulletins" Section For Related Information.

INDEX

REAR WHEEL SPINDLE
REPLACE

1. Raise and support vehicle, then remove rear tire and wheel assemblies.
2. Remove rear caliper assembly and suspend from frame using suitable wire.
3. Remove rear disc brake rotor.
4. Remove rear hub and bearing assembly.
5. Remove speed sensor head from rear disc brake adapter, **Fig. 1.**
6. Remove speed sensor cable routing tube from trailing arm.
7. Remove disc brake adapter, disc shield, park brake shoes and park brake cable as an assembly, **Fig. 2.**
8. Disconnect trailing arm from trailing arm bracket, **Fig. 3.**
9. Disconnect lateral rod from spindle, **Fig. 4.**
10. Loosen and remove rear spindle to strut assembly pinch bolt.
11. Tap suitable center punch into hole on spindle until punch is jammed into hole, **Fig. 5. Do not punch hole in strut with center punch.**
12. Tap on top surface of spindle using suitable hammer, driving it down and off strut assembly, **Fig. 6.**
13. Remove spindle from vehicle.
14. Reverse procedure to install. Push or tap spindle assembly onto strut until notch in spindle is tightly seated against locating tab on strut assembly.

STRUT
REPLACE

1. Remove rear seat cushion and back assembly.

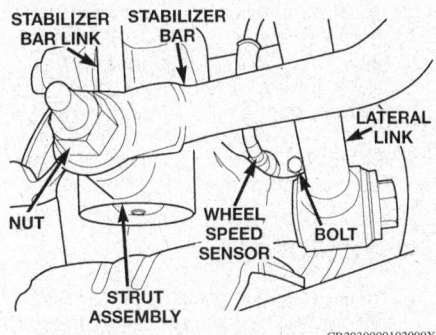

Fig. 1   Speed sensor head

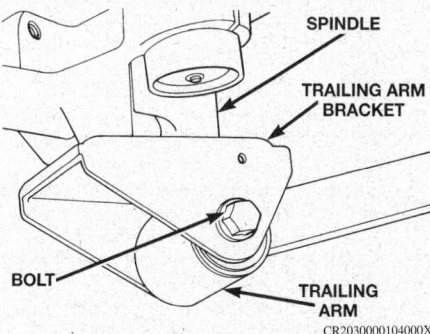

Fig. 3   Trailing arm to bracket bolt

2. Remove upper and lower quarter trim panels.
3. Remove rear parcel shelf trim panel.
4. Remove rear speakers and mounting plates, then disconnect speaker wiring.
5. Raise and support vehicle, then remove rear wheel and tire assembly.
6. Remove rear caliper assembly and suspend from frame using suitable wire.

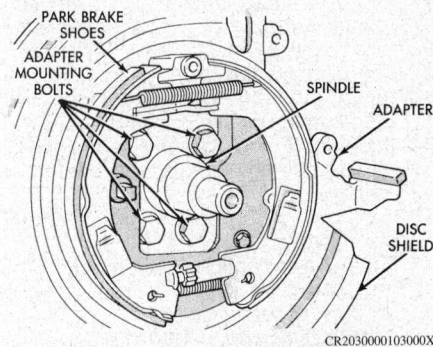

Fig. 2   Disc brake adapter mounting

7. Remove rear disc brake rotor.
8. Remove speed sensor cable routing tube on trailing arm bracket to spindle.
9. Remove bolt attaching lateral link to rear spindle assembly, **Fig. 7.**
10. Remove rear strut assembly to stabilizer bar attaching link at stabilizer bar.
11. Loosen and remove rear spindle to strut assembly pinch bolt.
12. Tap suitable center punch into hole on spindle until punch is jammed into hole, **Fig. 5. Do not punch hole in strut with center punch.**
13. Tap on top surface of spindle using suitable hammer, driving it down and off strut assembly, **Fig. 6.**
14. Let rear spindle and assembled components hang from trailing arm while strut is out of vehicle.
15. Lower vehicle.
16. Remove rear upper strut mount retaining nuts through luggage compartment.
17. Remove strut from vehicle.
18. Reverse procedure to install. Push or tap spindle assembly onto strut until

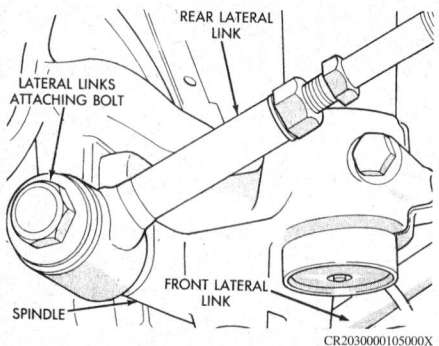

Fig. 4 Lateral links to spindle attaching bolts

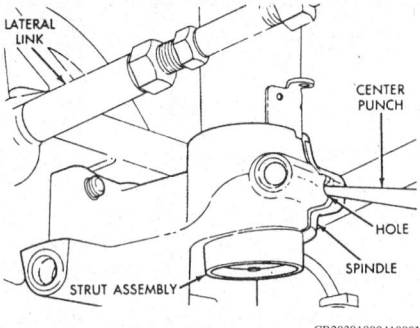

Fig. 5 Center punch installed in spindle

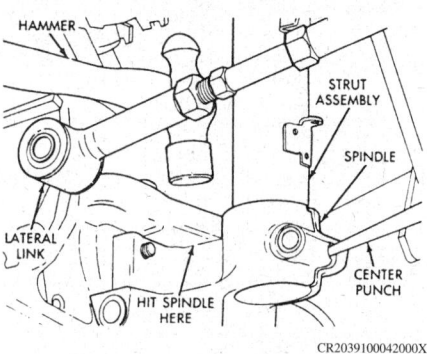

Fig. 6 Spindle removal

notch in spindle is tightly seated against locating tab on strut assembly.

STRUT SERVICE

1. Position strut assembly in suitable vise.
2. Mark strut assembly lower spring isolator, spring and upper strut mount for assembly reference.
3. Position spring compressor tool No. 7520, or equivalent, on strut assembly spring and compress coil spring until all load is removed from upper strut mount assembly.
4. Install strut rod ratchet socket tool No. 6864, or equivalent, on strut nut.
5. Insert an 8 mm Allen wrench into end of strut shaft and remove shaft nut from shaft.
6. Remove upper strut mount assembly from strut shaft.
7. Remove coil spring, plate, spring compressor, dust shield, jounce bumper and lower spring isolator.
8. Inspect all components for signs of abnormal wear or failure, replace as required.
9. Reverse procedure to install. Align marks made during disassembly.

REAR CROSSMEMBER
REPLACE
Removal

1. Open fuel filler door and remove filler neck mounting screws and cap.
2. Raise and support vehicle, then remove rear tire and wheel assemblies.
3. Remove lateral links mounting bolts and nuts. Lefthand front lateral link bolt cannot be removed until crossmember is lowered.
4. Remove brake tubes mounting screws from lefthand stabilizer bar isolator bushing retainer.
5. Remove stabilizer bar isolation bushing retaining frame rail mounting bolts and allow bar to hang down.
6. Remove tensioner from intermediate parking brake cable, then from lefthand rear parking brake cable.
7. Remove righthand rear parking brake cable from intermediate parking brake cable.

8. Remove retainer clips and rear parking brake cables from crossmember.
9. Remove brake proportioning valve mounting nuts.
10. Position suitable transmission jack under muffler.
11. Disconnect exhaust resonator hanger from rear frame rail, then muffler hangers on each side of muffler.
12. Lower jack and muffler enough to access crossmember.
13. Remove fuel filler neck lefthand frame rail mounting screw.
14. Remove crossmember rear corner mounting bolts, then lower crossmember as low as possible to access lateral link mounting bolt at lefthand front corner.
15. Remove mounting bolt and link, then the crossmember.

Installation

1. Install rear suspension crossmember above muffler. Ensure brake tubes are properly routed as crossmember is installed.
2. Install rear proportioning valve mounting brackets and nuts, then the intermediate parking brake cable routing clip.
3. Attach lefthand front lateral link to crossmember, then install mounting bolt through front of crossmember. Do not install nut at this time.
4. Raise crossmember against frame rails and install, but do not tighten two rear mounting bolts at this time.
5. Raise exhaust into place, then install hangers.
6. Install mounting screw and attach fuel filler neck to lefthand frame rail.
7. Position rear parking brake cables into crossmember alignment holes, then install retaining clips.
8. Connect righthand rear parking brake cable to intermediate parking brake cable, then install parking brake cable tensioner.
9. Install stabilizer bar isolator bushing retainer mounting bolts.
10. Tighten rear suspension crossmember rear mounting bolts.
11. Install brake tubes mounting screws.
12. Install remaining lateral links and mounting bolts. Forward mounting bolts must point towards rear and rear

mounting bolts should point towards front.
13. Install lateral link mounting nuts but do not tighten now. **Tighten mounting bolts when vehicle is at curb riding height.**
14. Install tire and wheel assemblies. Tighten wheel mounting stud nuts to half, then fill specifications.
15. Lower vehicle, then install filler neck mounting screws and fuel filler cap.
16. Tighten lateral arm to crossmember mounting bolts.
17. Inspect and set rear wheel toe.

STABILIZER BAR
REPLACE

1. Raise and support vehicle using suitable lift.
2. Remove stabilizer bar to strut attaching link stud nuts using suitable thin wrench to keep attaching link stud from turning.
3. Remove links from stabilizer bar.
4. Remove stabilizer bar isolator bushing retainers mounting bolts, then the stabilizer bar.
5. Mount bar in suitable soft jawed vise, then carefully pry back upper bushing retainer wider end tabs from lower half.
6. Tap bushing retainer upper half forward using suitable hammer and brass drift punch.
7. Remove lower half of bushing retainer, then the bushing.
8. Remove bar from vise, then repeat procedure to remove other bushing.
9. Reverse procedure to install. Bushing slit points toward front of vehicle.

LATERAL LINK
REPLACE
Lefthand
FRONT

1. Raise and support vehicle, then remove lefthand rear tire and wheel assembly.
2. Remove lateral link to spindle mounting nut and bolt.
3. Remove link to rear crossmember mounting nut. Bolt cannot be removed now.

4. Remove brake tubes to lefthand stabilizer bar isolator bushing retainer mounting screws.
5. Remove stabilizer bar isolator bushing retainers mounting bolts.
6. Remove fuel filler neck to frame rail mounting screw, then position suitable transmission jack under fuel tank.
7. Remove righthand, then lefthand fuel tank mounting strap mounting bolts, allow straps to hang.
8. Lower fuel tank enough to remove lateral link to crossmember mounting bolt, then the lefthand front lateral link.
9. Reverse procedure to install, noting the following:
   a. Do not tighten lateral link mounting bolt until vehicle is at curb riding height.
   b. Inspect and correct rear wheel toe.

REAR

1. Raise and support vehicle, then remove tire and wheel assemblies.
2. Remove lateral link to rear crossmember mounting nuts and bolts.
3. Remove lateral links.
4. Reverse procedure to install, noting the following:
   a. Do not tighten lateral link mounting bolt until vehicle is at curb riding height.
   b. Inspect and correct rear wheel toe.

Righthand

1. Raise and support vehicle, then remove tire and wheel assemblies.
2. Remove lateral link to rear crossmember mounting nuts and bolts.
3. Remove lateral links.
4. Reverse procedure to install, noting the following:
   a. Do not tighten lateral link mounting bolt until vehicle is at curb riding height.
   b. Inspect and correct rear wheel toe.

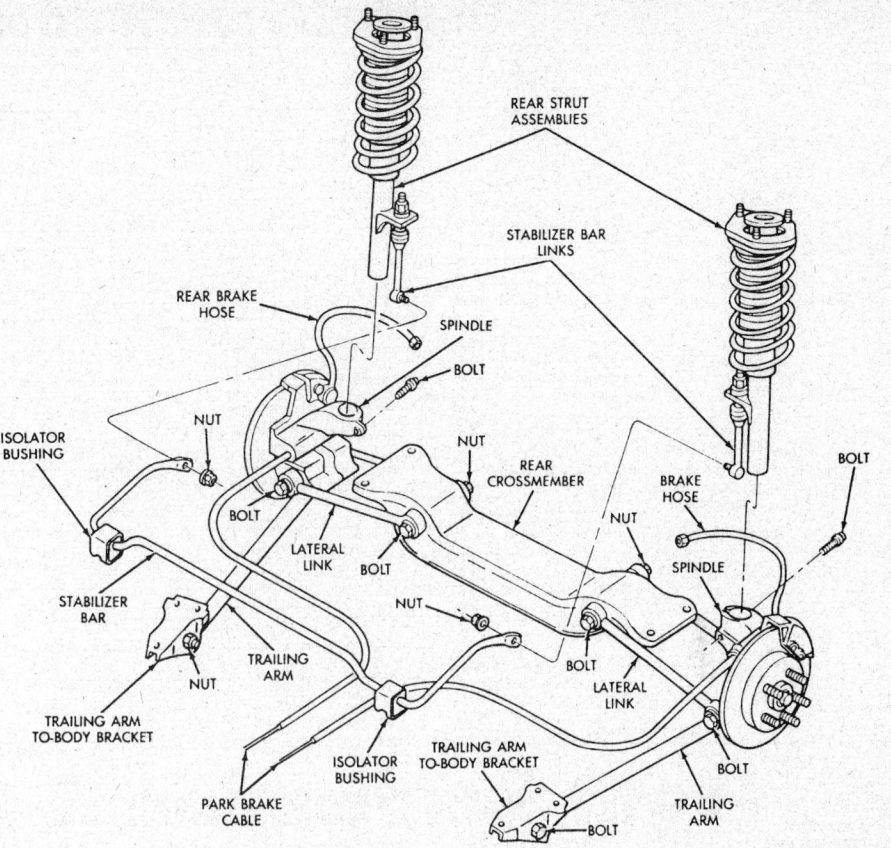

CR20391000400000X

Fig. 7 Exploded view of rear suspension

TECHNICAL SERVICE BULLETINS

Rear Strut Squeak

On some of these models there may be a rear strut squeaking during suspension jounce.

This condition may be caused by the rear strut striker cap.

To correct this condition, replace the rear strut striker as follows:
1. Remove and disassemble the rear struts as outlined in "Strut, Replace" and "Strut Service."
2. Remove strut striker cap.
3. Install revised strut striker cap (part No. 05194743AA).
4. Install strut.

TIGHTENING SPECIFICATIONS

Year	Component	Torque/Ft. Lbs.
2001–04	Brake Hose	35
	Brake Hose Bracket	17
	Brake Support Plate	80
	Caliper Adapter To Spindle	85
	Caliper To Adapter	16
	Crossmember To Body	75
	Hub & Bearing Assembly To Spindle	124
	Lateral Link Jam Nut	65
	Lateral Link To Spindle	100
	Lateral Link To Suspension Crossmember	70
	Spindle Mounting Bolts	80
	Stabilizer Bar Isolator Bushing Retainer	30
	Stabilizer Bar To Strut Link	70
	Strut Shaft To Upper Mount	55
	Strut To Body	19
	Strut To Spindle Pinch Bolt	40
	Strut To Stabilizer Bar Link	17
	Trailing Arm	75
	Trailing Arm Bracket	80
	Trailing Arm Bracket To Body	45
	Wheel Lug Nut	100

Front Suspension & Steering

NOTE: On Air Bag Equipped Models, Refer To "Air Bag System Precautions" Located In The Front Of This Manual For System Disarming & Arming Procedures.

NOTE: Refer To "Computer Relearn Procedures" Located In The Front Of This Manual When Battery Power To The Computer Has Been Interrupted.

NOTE: Prior To Performing Any Service Operations Listed In This Section, Consult The "Technical Service Bulletins" Section For Related Information.

INDEX

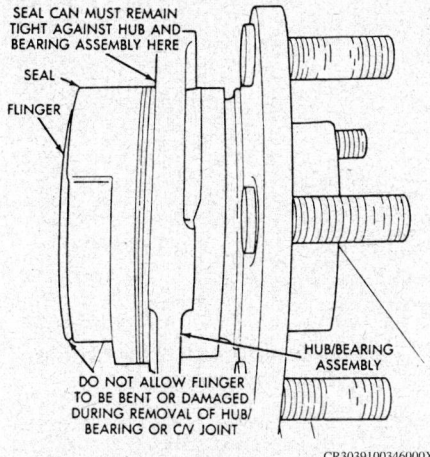

Fig. 1 Hub & bearing assembly

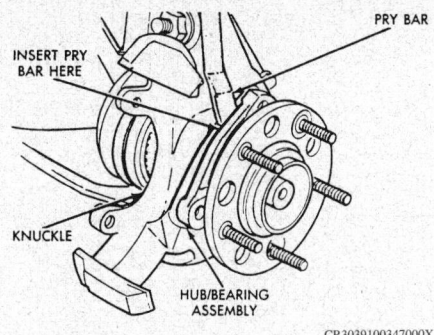

Fig. 2 Hub & bearing removal

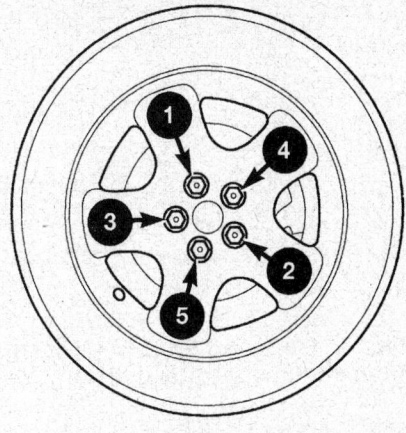

Fig. 3 Tire & wheel nut tightening sequence

PRECAUTIONS

Air Bag Systems

Refer to "Air Bag System Precautions" in the front of this manual for system disarming and arming procedures.

Battery Ground Cable

Prior to service, disconnect battery ground cable and isolate as required.

HUB & BEARING
REPLACE

1. Raise and support vehicle, then remove tire and wheel.
2. Remove front caliper assembly and rotor from steering knuckle as outlined in "Disc Brakes" chapter
3. Remove hub and bearing retaining nut.
4. Remove hub bolts, then the hub and bearing assembly from steering knuckle by sliding it straight off end of hub axle. **CAUTION: When removing hub and bearing assembly from steering knuckle, be careful not to damage flinger disc on hub and bearing assembly. If flinger disc is damaged, hub and bearing assembly must be replaced, Fig. 1.**
5. If hub and bearing will not slide out of knuckle, insert suitable pry bar between hub and steering knuckle, **Fig. 2.**
6. Reverse procedure to install, noting the following:
   a. Install new hub and bearing retaining nut.
   b. Install tire and wheel assembly tightening mounting nuts in sequence until all nuts are tightened to half specification, **Fig. 3.**
   c. Repeat tightening sequence to full specification.
   d. Lower vehicle, with brakes applied, tighten hub and braining retaining nut.

BALL JOINT INSPECTION

The lower ball joint is serviced with the lower control arm.
1. Raise and support front of vehicle.
2. Grasp tire at top and bottom, then apply in and out force on wheel and tire assembly.
3. While applying force to tire, look for movement between lower ball joint and lower control arm.
4. If there is any movement, replace lower control arm.

CONTROL ARM
REPLACE
LOWER

1. Raise and support vehicle, then remove tire and wheel assembly.
2. Remove ball joint stud to steering knuckle clamp nut and bolt, **Fig. 4.**
3. Insert suitable pry bar between lower control arm and steering knuckle to separate ball joint stud from steering knuckle, **Fig. 5. Do not pull steering knuckle away from vehicle after separating ball joint, this may allow the inner tripod joint to separate.**
4. Remove and discard tension strut to cradle nut and washer from end of tension strut, **Fig. 6. Never reuse tension strut nut.**
5. Loosen and remove lower control arm pivot bushing bolt.
6. Separate lower control arm and tension strut from cradle as an assembly by first removing pivot bushing from cradle and then sliding tension strut out of isolator bushing, **Fig. 7.**
7. Reverse procedure to install. Tighten lower control arm pivot bushing to cradle bracket attaching bolt with full weight of vehicle on suspension.

STEERING KNUCKLE
REPLACE

1. Raise and support vehicle, then remove tire and wheel assembly.
2. Remove brake caliper and rotor as outlined under "Caliper, Replace" in "Disc Brakes" chapter.
3. Remove ABS speed sensor screw.
4. Carefully remove speed sensor head from knuckle. If sensor has seized due to corrosion use a hammer and a punch to tap edge of sensor ear, rocking sensor until free, **Fig. 8. Do not use pliers on sensor head.**
5. Remove hub and bearing retaining nut.
6. Remove hub bolts, then the hub and bearing assembly from steering knuckle by sliding it straight off end of hub axle. **CAUTION: When removing hub and bearing assembly from steering knuckle, be careful not to damage flinger disc on hub and bearing assembly. If flinger disc is damaged, hub and bearing assembly must be replaced, Fig. 1.**
7. If hub and bearing will not slide out of knuckle, insert suitable pry bar between hub and steering knuckle, **Fig. 2.**
8. Remove ball joint stud to steering knuckle clamp nut and bolt, **Fig. 4.**
9. Insert suitable pry bar between lower control arm and steering knuckle to separate ball joint stud from steering knuckle, **Fig. 5. Do not pull steering knuckle away from vehicle after separating ball joint, this may allow the inner tripod joint to separate.**
10. Remove strut assembly to steering knuckle attaching bolts. **Strut bolts have a serrated shaft for a tight fit into steering knuckle. Turn nut on bolts only, do not turn bolts.**
11. Remove steering knuckle from vehicle.
12. Reverse procedure to install, noting the following:
    a. **Strut bolts have a serrated shaft so do not turn bolts in steering knuckle. Turn nut on bolts do not turn bolts.**
    b. Coat speed sensor head with high temperature multi-purpose EP grease before installing.
    c. Lower vehicle and with brake applied, tighten new hub and bearing retaining nut.

STABILIZER BAR
REPLACE

1. Remove righthand upper mount to strut tower mounting nut and washer.

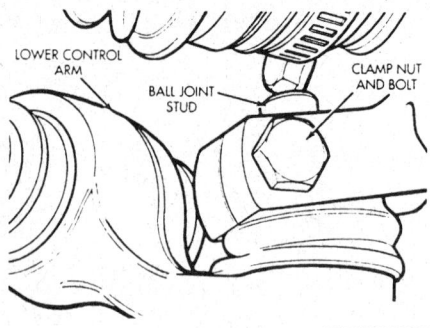

Fig. 4 Ball joint stud to steering knuckle clamp nut & bolt removal

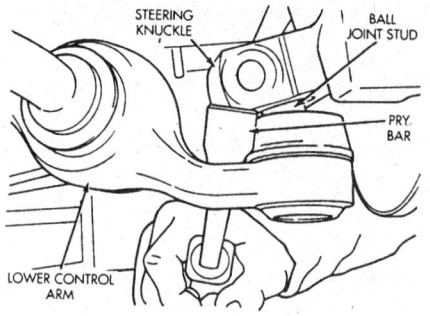

Fig. 5 Ball joint separation

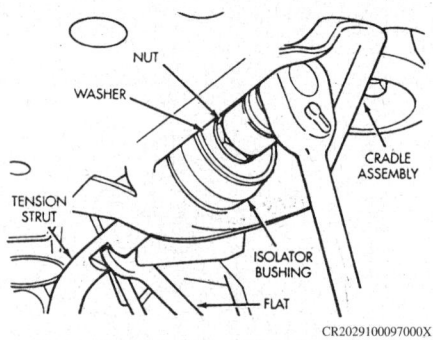

Fig. 6 Tension strut to cradle mounting

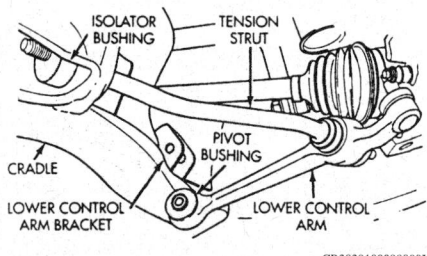

Fig. 7 Lower control arm removal

2. Raise and support vehicle, then remove righthand front tire and wheel assembly.
3. Remove mounting nut and righthand stabilizer bar attaching link at strut.
4. Remove mounting nut and lefthand stabilizer bar attaching link at strut.
5. Loosen but do not remove righthand outer tie rod end to strut arm mounting nut.
6. Release righthand outer tie rod end from strut steering arm using puller tool No. C-3894A, or equivalent, then remove nut and tire rod.
7. **On models equipped with anti-lock brakes,** remove speed sensor cable routing bracket.
8. **On all models,** remove strut to steering knuckle mounting bolts, then the righthand front strut.
9. Remove structural collar to engine oil pan mounting bolts, then stabilizer bushing retainers to cradle mounting bolts.
10. Remove stabilizer bar isolator bushing retainers and bushings.
11. Position suitable transmission jack under engine oil pan, place suitable wood block between jack and oil pan.
12. Carefully raise jack until motor mounts clear cradle.
13. Rotate stabilizer bar and remove through righthand wheel opening. **Be careful to not pull knuckle outward.**
14. Reverse procedure to install.

STRUT DAMPNER
REPLACE

1. Raise and support vehicle, then remove tire and wheel assembly.
2. Remove stabilizer bar link at strut assembly, **Fig. 9.**
3. Loosen, but do not remove, outer tie

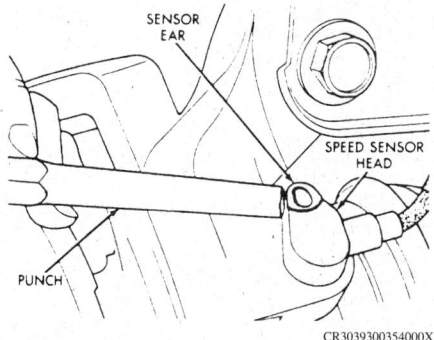

Fig. 8 Speed sensor removal

rod end nut, then remove outer tie rod end using suspension component puller tool No. C-3894A, or equivalent.
4. Remove speed sensor cable routing bracket from strut assembly.
5. Remove brake caliper and brake rotor as outlined in "Disc Brakes" chapter. Suspend caliper from frame using suitable wire.
6. Disconnect lower strut from steering knuckle. **Strut bolts have a serrated shaft for a tight fit into steering knuckle. Turn nut on bolts only, do not turn bolts.**
7. Disconnect upper strut from shock tower and remove strut assembly from vehicle.
8. To service damper, proceed as follows:
   a. Position strut assembly in suitable vise.
   b. Mark strut unit, lower spring isolator, spring and upper strut mount for assembly reference.
   c. Install spring compressor tool No. 7520, or equivalent, **Fig. 10,** on coil spring and compress coil spring to release load from upper strut mount assembly.
   d. Install strut rod socket tool No. 6864, or equivalent, on strut shaft nut; then remove strut shaft nut, **Fig. 11.**
   e. Remove upper strut mount, jounce bumper, seat/bearing, dust shield, coil spring and lower spring mount from strut, **Fig. 12.**
   f. Reverse procedure to assemble, align marks made during disassembly.
9. Reverse procedure to install. **Strut bolts have a serrated shaft; do not turn bolts in steering knuckle. Turn**

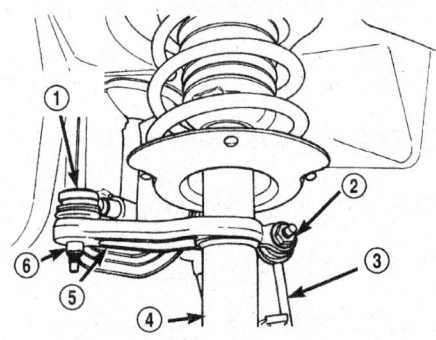

1 - OUTER TIE ROD
2 - NUT
3 - STABILIZER BAR ATTACHING LINK
4 - STRUT ASSEMBLY
5 - STEERING ARM
6 - NUT

Fig. 9 Stabilizer bar link at strut

nut on bolts instead of turning bolts.

TENSION STRUT
REPLACE

1. Raise and support vehicle, then remove tire and wheel assembly.
2. Remove ball joint stud to steering knuckle clamp nut and bolt, **Fig. 4.**
3. Insert suitable pry bar between lower control arm and steering knuckle to separate ball joint stud from steering knuckle, **Fig. 5. Do not pull steering knuckle away from vehicle after separating ball joint, this may allow the inner tripod joint to separate.**
4. Remove and discard tension strut to cradle nut and washer from end of tension strut, **Fig. 6. Never reuse tension strut nut.**
5. Loosen and remove lower control arm pivot bushing bolt.
6. Separate lower control arm and tension strut from cradle as an assembly by first removing pivot bushing from cradle and then sliding tension strut out of isolator bushing, **Fig. 7.**
7. Separate tension strut from lower control arm.
8. Install replacement tension strut into lower control arm. Position tension strut with word "Front" positioned away from control arm, **Fig. 13.**
9. Install lower control arm and tension strut into vehicle.

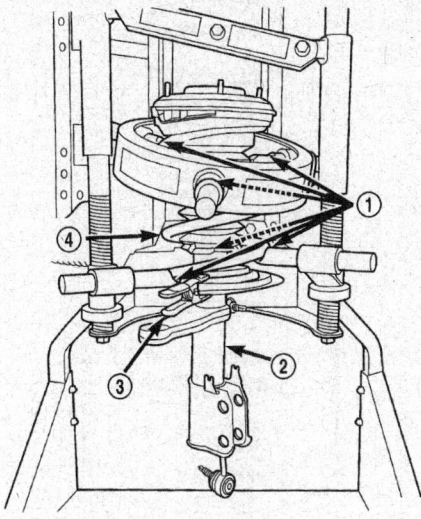

1 - HOOKS
2 - STRUT ASSEMBLY
3 - CLAMP
4 - COIL SPRING

CR2020100181000X

Fig. 10   Strut assembly in compressor

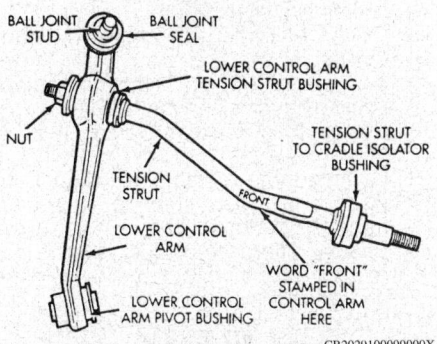

CR2029100099000X

Fig. 13   Tension strut removal from control arm

10. Install washer and new nut on tension strut.
11. Install tire and wheel assembly.
12. Tighten lower control arm pivot bushing to cradle bracket attaching bolt with full weight of vehicle on suspension.

TIE ROD END
REPLACE
Outer

1. Raise and support vehicle.
2. Remove tire and wheel assembly.
3. Loosen pinch bolt on tie rod sleeve, then remove tie rod to steering arm mounting nut.
4. Remove tie rod from steering arm using suspension component puller tool No. C-3894A, or equivalent.
5. Remove tie rod from sleeve.
6. Reverse procedure to install, noting the following:

Inner

1. Position wheels straight ahead.

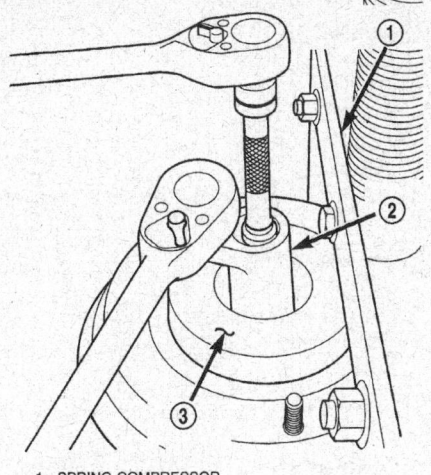

1 - SPRING COMPRESSOR
2 - SPECIAL TOOL 6864
3 - UPPER MOUNT

CR2020100182000X

Fig. 11   Strut shaft removal

2. Remove caps, mounting nuts and wiper arms, then the wiper module and cowl covers.
3. Remove mounting bolts, then the reinforcement.
4. Remove inline resonator and inlet hose from throttle body, then the air inlet hose from air cleaner housing.
5. Raise and support vehicle until wheels are just off the ground.
6. Remove wheel assembly.
7. Turn steering wheel to full righthand position.
8. Remove tie rod end to steering arm mounting nut, then remove tie rod using suspension component puller tool No. C-3894A, or equivalent.
9. Bend back tie rod to steering gear mounting bolt mounting plate retaining tabs.
10. Remove mounting bolts, mounting plate and washers.
11. Rotate loose end of mounting plate for clearance.
12. Remove tie rod assembly through wheel opening.
13. Loosen pinch bolt at inner to outer tie rod adjusting sleeve.
14. Remove tie rod from inner adjuster sleeve.
15. Reverse procedure to install.

POWER STEERING GEAR
REPLACE

1. Position wheels straight ahead.
2. Remove caps, mounting nuts and wiper arms, then the wiper module and cowl covers.
3. Remove mounting bolts, then the reinforcement.
4. Remove inline resonator and inlet hose from throttle body, then the air inlet hose from air cleaner housing.
5. Raise and support vehicle until wheels are just off the ground.
6. Lock steering wheel from rotating, **to avoid damaging clock spring.**

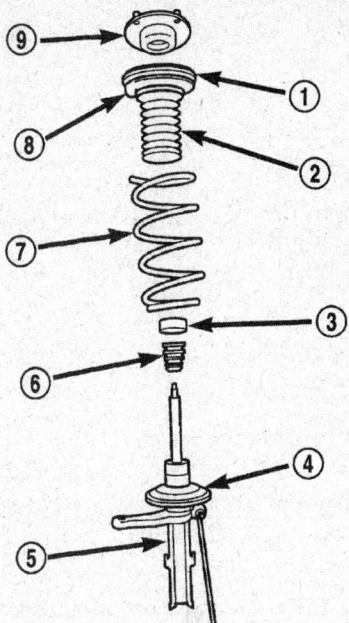

1 - SEAT AND BEARING
2 - DUST SHIELD
3 - CUP
4 - LOWER SPRING ISOLATOR
5 - STRUT
6 - JOUNCE BUMPER
7 - COIL SPRING
8 - UPPER SPRING ISOLATOR
9 - UPPER MOUNT

CR2020100180000X

Fig. 12   Exploded view of strut assembly

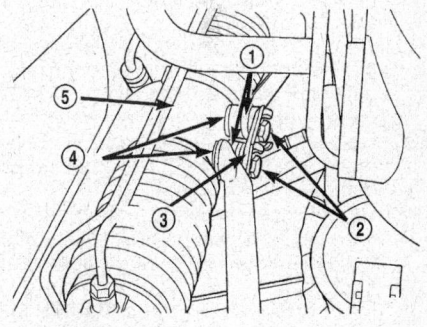

1 - TIE RODS
2 - BOLTS
3 - MOUNTING PLATE
4 - WASHERS
5 - STEERING GEAR

CR6030100231000X

Fig. 14   Tie rod to steering gear attaching bolts

7. Remove steering column coupler retaining pin and bolt, then separate intermediate steering shaft from column coupler.
8. Bend back tie rod to steering gear mounting bolt mounting plate retaining tabs.
9. Remove mounting bolts, mounting plate and washers, then lay tie rods on top of transmission bell housing, **Fig. 14.**
10. Drain as much power steering fluid as possible from reservoir.

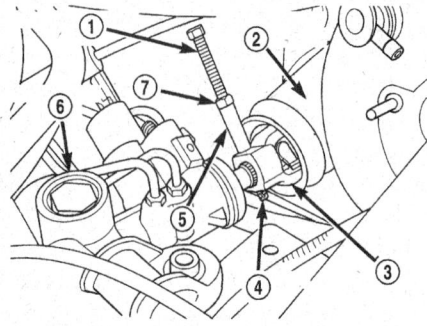

1 - SPECIAL TOOL 6831-A
2 - DASH PANEL SEAL & BOOT
3 - FLEX JOINT
4 - KNURLED NUT
5 - SLEEVE
6 - STEERING GEAR
7 - NUT

CR6030100232000X

Fig. 15　Steering gear roll pin removal

11. Remove power steering fluid pressure and return hoses from steering gear.
12. **On models equipped with speed proportional steering gear,** remove solenoid wiring harness connector.
13. **On all models,** remove mounting nuts, then the master cylinder with brake tubes connected from vacuum booster. Carefully position master cylinder upright on lefthand side valve cover.
14. Remove steering gear to crossmember lefthand, then the righthand side mounting bolts.
15. Slide steering gear and intermediate shaft into engine compartment to access intermediate shaft flex coupler roll pin, **Fig. 15.**
16. Remove roll pin and separate intermediate steering shaft from steering gear, using roll pin remover tool No. 6831-A, or equivalent.
17. Raise and support vehicle, then remove righthand front tire and wheel assembly.
18. Remove tie rod end to steering arm mounting nut, using suspension puller tool No. C-3894-A, or equivalent, then the tie rod.
19. **On models equipped with 2.7L engine,** turn front of lefthand front tire and wheel assembly as far outward as possible.
20. **On all models,** slide steering gear end through righthand side inner fender tie rod hole until approximately half gear is through hole.
21. Lift lefthand end of gear up between engine and cowl, then pull gear out.

POWER STEERING PUMP

REPLACE

1. Drain as much power steering fluid as possible from power steering reservoir.
2. Remove power steering fluid return hose from reservoir, then let fluid drain from reservoir and pump into suitable container.

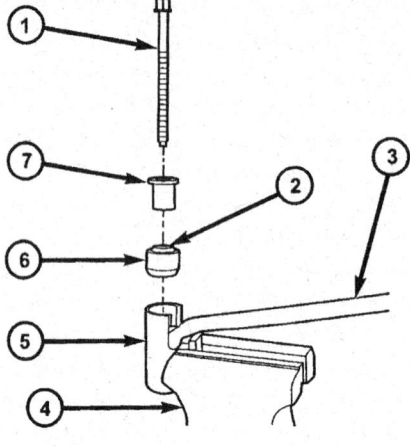

1 - 8438-3 SCREW
2 - BUSHING
3 - INNER TIE ROD END
4 - VISE
5 - 8438-1 (RECEIVER)
6 - 8438-2 (SIZER)
7 - 8438-4 (REMOVER/INSTALLER)

CR2020100185000X

Fig. 16　Receiver tool & tie rod end

3. Cap power steering fluid reservoir fitting.
4. Remove pressure hose from power steering pump and let remaining fluid drain from pump into container.
5. **On models equipped with 3.2 and 3.5L engines,** remove power steering pressure switch wiring harness connector.
6. **On all models,** loosen serpentine drive belt tensioner locknut, then remove power steering pump drive belt from power steering pump pulley.
7. Remove pump mounting bolts through pulley face holes.
8. Insert suitable screwdriver between pump and tensioner bracket sleeve, then push sleeve forward in tensioner bracket until it is flush with tensioner bracket back.
9. Remove pump and pulley as an assembly.
10. Reverse procedure to install, noting the following:
    a. Long mounting bolt is install in tensioner bracket sleeve.
    b. Ensure return hose clamp is installed past nipple upset bead.

POWER STEERING SYSTEM BLEED

During bleeding procedure, keep fluid in reservoir at correct level.
1. Raise and support front of vehicle.
2. Manually turn oil pump pulley a few times.
3. Turn steering wheel from stop to stop five or six times.
4. Disconnect high tension cable, then operate starter motor intermittently

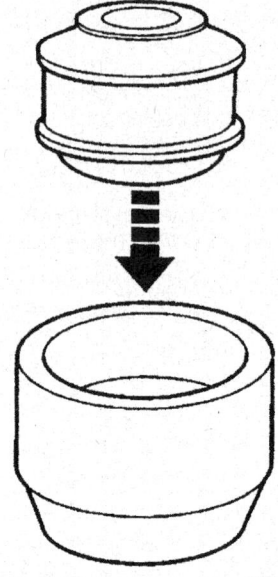

CR2020100186000X

Fig. 17　Bushing sizer tool & bushing

while turning steering wheel from stop to stop five or six times.
5. Connect high tension cable and start engine.
6. Turn steering wheel from stop to stop until no bubbles appear in reservoir.
7. Ensure fluid is not milky and that at proper level.
8. Confirm there is little or no change in fluid level when steering wheel is turned from stop to stop.
9. Ensure difference in fluid level is no more than .2 inch with engine running and when it is stopped.
10. If fluid level is not as specified, system is not completely bled. Repeat procedure.

TECHNICAL SERVICE BULLETINS

Loose Feel Or Clunk In Steering Wheel

1993-2001

On some these models there may be a loose feel or clunk in steering wheel as wheel is moved from side to side.

This condition may caused by inner tie rod bushings.

To correct this condition, install inner tie rod bushing kit part No. 05072586AA as follows:
1. Remove inner tie rods as outlined in "Tie Rod End, Replace."
2. Replace inner tie rod bushings using receiver tools Nos. 8438-1, 8438-3, 8438-4 and bushing sizer tool No. 8438-2, or equivalents, **Figs. 16 and 17.**
3. Mount receiver tool into suitable vise.
4. Place inner tie rod bushing end into receiver.

5. Place remover/installer tool No. 8438–4, or equivalent, small end down on top of bushing.
6. Insert screw tool No. 8438–3, or equivalent, through remover/installer tool and tie rod bushing until it threads into bottom of receiver.
7. To remove bushing hand tighten screw until it bottoms out.
8. Remove screw, receiver, tie rod end, then bushing from receiver.
9. Spray bushing, inner tie rod end, then inside bushing sizer with Mopar silicone spray part No. 04318070, or equivalent.
10. Place new bushing in bore of sizer tool, slide bushing to bottom of sizer bore. **Inner tie rod bushing is symmetrical. There is no designated top or bottom.**
11. Mount receiver into suitable vise, then place inner tie rod end into receiver.
12. Place sizer with bushing on top of tie rod bushing bore with tapered end facing downward.
13. Place installer tool No. 8438–4, or equivalent, small end down on top of bushing.
14. Insert screw tool No. 8438–3, or equivalent, through installer bushing with sizer, then tie rod end until threads bottom in receiver.
15. Slowly tighten screw, pushing bushing out of sizer into tie rod end bore until it bottoms out.
16. Disassemble receiver and sizer tools, then remove tie rod from receiver.
17. Bushing will appear slightly off center in tie rod.
18. Install tie rod end as outlined in "Tie Rod End, Replace."

TIGHTENING SPECIFICATIONS

Year	Component	Torque/Ft. Lbs.
2001–04	Ball Joint Stud To Steering Knuckle	40
	Disc Brake Caliper	16
	Front Cradle Assembly To Body	120
	Hub & Bearing Assembly To Steering Knuckle	80
	Hub & Bearing Axle Nut	105
	Inner Tie Rod To Steering Gear	74
	Lower Control Arm To Cradle Pivot	105
	Master Cylinder Mounting Nuts	21
	Outer Tie Rod Adjuster Pinch Bolt	28
	Outer Tie Rod To Steering Arm Nut	27
	Power Steering Fluid Pressure Hose To Discharge Fitting	62
	Power Steering Pressure Hose Tube	35
	Power Steering Pressure Switch	15
	Power Steering Pump To Bracket Bolts	21
	Power Steering Return Tube	23
	Reservoir Mounting Bolts, Pulley Side (2.7L)	10
	Reservoir Mounting Bolts, Rear (2.7L)	18
	Reservoir Mounting Bolts (3.2L & 3.5L)	①105
	Stabilizer Bar Attaching Link To Strut	17
	Stabilizer Bar Bushing Retainer To Cradle	45
	Stabilizer Bar Link Lower Nut	65
	Stabilizer Bar Link Upper Nut	70
	Steering Gear To Crossmember	43
	Strut Assembly Shaft	70
	Strut Assembly To Shock Tower	28
	Strut Assembly To Steering Knuckle	150②
	Sway Bar To Strut Link	70
	Tension Strut	95
	Wheel Lug Nut	100③

① — Inch lbs.
② — Strut bolts have a serrated shaft. Do not turn bolts in steering knuckle. Turn nuts on bolts. Do not turn bolts.
③ — Refer to "Hub & Bearing, Replace" for tightening sequence.

Wheel Alignment

INDEX

PRELIMINARY INSPECTION

Before any attempt is made to change or correct front wheel alignment, the following inspections and required corrections must be made.

1. Ensure tire pressure is at recommended pressure, all tires should be same size and in good condition and have approximately same wear.
2. Inspect front wheels and tire assembly for radial runout.
3. Inspect lower ball joint and steering linkage for looseness.
4. Inspect for broken or damaged front and rear springs.
5. **Just prior to each alignment reading, the vehicle should be jounced (rear first, then front) by grasping bumper at center and jouncing each end of vehicle an equal number of times. Always release bumpers at bottom of down cycle.**

FRONT WHEEL ALIGNMENT

Camber

If front camber is not within specifications, strut and steering knuckles are not bent or damaged there are special undersize camber adjustment bolts and nuts are available to allow adjustment. This involves replacing the original clevis to knuckle bolts using the following procedure.

1. Raise and support front of vehicle, then remove tire and wheel assemblies.
2. Remove strut assembly to steering knuckle attaching bolts. **Strut bolts have a serrated shaft for a tight fit into steering knuckle. Turn nut on bolts only, do not turn bolts.**

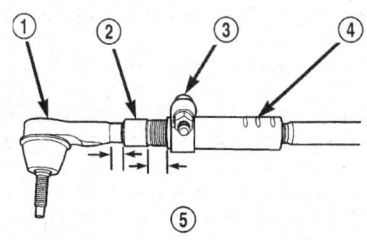

1 - OUTER TIE ROD
2 - ADJUSTER
3 - PINCH BOLT
4 - INNER TIE ROD
5 - ALLOWABLE THREADS EXPOSED ON OUTER TIE ROD AND ADJUSTER IS A MAXIMUM OF 20 MILLIMETERS. REFER TO AREA INDICATED ABOVE ON THE OUTER TIE ROD AND ADJUSTER.

CR2040100067000X

Fig. 1 Front tie rod adjustment dimensions

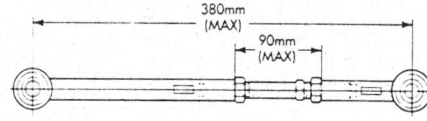

CR2049100035000X

Fig. 3 Rear tie rod adjustment dimensions

3. Loosely install special undersize camber bolts so nuts are toward front of vehicle.
4. Install wheels lower vehicle, then jounce front and rear of vehicle.
5. Adjust front camber to specifications by pulling in or pushing outward on top of wheel assembly.
6. Inspect and correct toe as required.

Toe

1. Center steering wheel and hold with steering wheel clamp.
2. Loosen tie rod adjustment sleeve jam nuts.
3. Rotate adjustment sleeve to align toe. **When setting toe, maximum threads exposed on inner and outer**

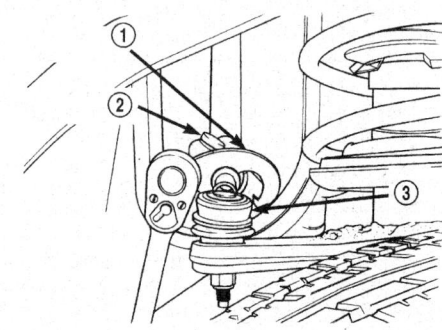

1 - ADJUSTMENT TOOL
2 - ADJUSTMENT PINCH BOLT
3 - TIE ROD END

CR2040100068000X

Fig. 2 Front wheel toe adjustment location

tie rod can not exceed 20 mm, Fig. 1.

4. Tighten adjustment pinch bolt as follows.
   a. Install a tie rod adjustment tool on neck area of outer tie rod to maintain correct perpendicular orientation of tie rod stud within tie rod end, **Fig. 2.**
   b. **Torque** tie rod adjustment pinch nut to 28 ft. lbs.
   c. Remove steering wheel clamp.

REAR WHEEL ALIGNMENT

Toe

1. Loosen lateral link adjustment link jam nuts.
2. Rotate adjustment link as required to set rear wheel toe.
3. **Do not exceed maximum length dimension of lateral links, Fig. 3. Both dimensions must be inspected.**
4. **Torque** lateral links locknuts to 65 ft. lbs.

CROSSFIRE

NOTE: Refer To Rear Of This Manual For Vehicle Manufacturer's Special Service Tool Suppliers.

INDEX OF SERVICE OPERATIONS

Specifications

GENERAL ENGINE SPECIFICATIONS

Engine	Engine VIN Code①	Fuel System	Bore & Stroke, Inches	Compression Ratio	Net HP @ RPM	Maximum Torque, Ft. Lbs. @ RPM	Normal Oil Pressure, psi	
							Curb Idle	3000 RPM
3.2L	L	MPFI	3.54 x 3.31	10.1:1	215 @ 5700	230 @ 3000	5	45–105
	N	MPFI	3.54 x 3.31	9.0:1	330 @ 6100	310 @ 3500	5	45–105

① — Eighth digit of VIN denotes engine code.

TUNE UP SPECIFICATIONS

Engine	Spark Plug Gap, Inch	Ignition Timing		Curb Idle Speed	Fuel Pump Pressure, psi	Valve Clearance, Inch
		Firing Order	°BTDC			
3.2L	.035	1-4-3-6-2-5	①	③	54–61	②

BTDC — Before Top Dead Center
① — Twin Ignition System not adjustable.

② — Equipped with hydraulic valve adjusters. No valve adjustment is required.

③ — Controlled by PCM.

FRONT WHEEL ALIGNMENT SPECIFICATIONS

Year	Camber, Degrees		Caster, Degrees		Toe In, Degrees ①		Ball Joint Wear
	Limits	Desired	Limits	Desired	Limits	Desired	
2004–05	—	-1.22	—	5.2	—	+2.5	②

① — The flexible mount of the control arms results in a correspondingly large toe value which reduces to

the correct dimension in the ready-to- drive condition.

② — Refer to "Ball Joint Inspection" in "Front Suspension & Steering."

REAR WHEEL ALIGNMENT SPECIFICATIONS

Year	Camber Angle, Degrees		Total Toe, Degrees		Thrust Angle, Degrees
	Limits	Desired	Limits	Desired	
2004–05	—	-1.13	—	1.2	—

FLUID CAPACITIES & COOLING SYSTEM DATA

Year	Coolant Capacity, Qts.	Coolant Type	Radiator Cap Relief Pressure, Lbs.	Thermostat. Opening Temp., °F	Fuel Tank, Gals.	Engine Oil Refill, Qts.①	Auto. Transaxle Oil, Qts.②	Man. Transaxle Oil, Pts.
2004–05	11.8③	Ethylene Glycol	14–18	192–195	15.8	6.1④	8.5	3.2

① — Includes oil filter.

② — Approximate, make final inspection w/dipstick.

③ — With supercharger 15.3 Qts.
④ — With supercharger 8.5 Qts.

LUBRICANT DATA

Year	Transaxle		Power Steering	Brake System
	Automatic	Manual		
2004–05	Mopar ATF+4 Type 9602	Mopar ATF+4 Type 9602	Mopar ATF+4 Type 9602	DOT 3–4

Electrical

NOTE: On Air Bag Equipped Models, Refer To "Air Bag System Precautions" Located In The Front Of This Manual For System Disarming & Arming Procedures.

NOTE: Refer To "Computer Relearn Procedures" Located In The Front Of This Manual When Battery Power To The Computer Has Been Interrupted.

INDEX

PRECAUTIONS

Air Bag Systems

Refer to "Air Bag System Precautions" in the front of this manual for system disarming and arming procedures.

Battery Ground Cable

Prior to service, disconnect battery ground cable and isolate as required.

FUSE PANEL & FLASHER LOCATION

This vehicle is equipped with two fuse panels. The engine compartment fuse panel is located on the lefthand side of the engine compartment, between the brake master cylinder and front fender. The second instrument panel fuse panel is located behind an access door on the lefthand side of the instrument panel.

The turn indicator signals are controlled by an Erasable Electronic Programmable Read Only Memory (EEPROM) chip that is integrated into the instrument cluster. If the turn indicators fail and the EEPROM is found at fault the instrument cluster must be replaced.

FUEL PUMP RELAY LOCATION

The fuel pump relay is housed within the relay control module located on the right-hand side of the engine compartment. The relay control module also contains the fuel pump relay fuse. If the fuel pump relay or circuitry fail the control module must be replaced as an assembly.

STARTER
REPLACE

1. Raise and support vehicle.
2. Remove lower engine panel.
3. Disconnect righthand O2 sensor electrical connector.
4. Remove righthand exhaust pipe from manifold and rear exhaust pipe.
5. Remove starter mounting bolts, then position starter to access posi-lock wiring connector.
6. Remove battery feed and solenoid wiring harness connectors.
7. Remove starter mounting bolts, then the starter.
8. Reverse procedure to install. **Torque** starter mounting bolts to 31 ft. lbs.

ALTERNATOR
REPLACE

1. Remove righthand air inlet tube.
2. Rotate accessory drive belt tensioner

in a counterclockwise direction, then lock belt tensioner with a locking pin.
3. Remove protective cap from alternator electrical cable, then disconnect the electrical cable.
4. Position wire harness aside and remove alternator mounting bolts, then the alternator.
5. Reverse procedure to install. **Torque** alternator mounting bolts to 31 ft. lbs.

COIL PACK
REPLACE

1. Remove air cleaner housing.
2. Disconnect ignition coil harness connector.
3. Disconnect spark plug cables from spark plugs.
4. Remove coil pack mounting bolts, then the coil pack.
5. Reverse procedure to install. **Torque** coil pack mounting bolts to 71 inch lbs.

IGNITION LOCK
REPLACE

1. Press out ignition lock cylinder escutcheon with suitable trim tool.
2. Remove transponder coil off key lock cylinder with suitable plastic wedge tool.
3. With ignition key in lock cylinder, push sleeve onto lock cylinder cap.
4. Turn lock cylinder to position No. 1, using ignition key.

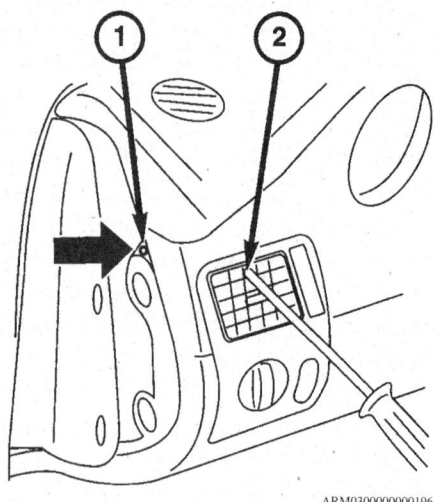

Fig. 1   Vent screw removal

5. Rotate lock cylinder cap 90° counter-clockwise to remove ignition lock cylinder.
6. Reverse procedure to install, noting the following:
   a. Lubricate outside of lock cylinder using suitable cylinder lock grease, then insert lock cylinder into cap.
   b. Push ignition key through lock cylinder cap until it stops.
   c. Rotate cap clockwise 90° until cylinder can be felt or heard lock into position.

IGNITION SWITCH
REPLACE

1. Remove lower lefthand instrument panel cover retaining clips, then the lower cover.
2. Remove two instrument cluster bezel retaining screws, then the bezel.
3. Remove four instrument cluster retaining screws, then move instrument cluster outwards.
4. Disconnect instrument cluster electrical connectors and harness retaining clips from back of instrument cluster.
5. Remove instrument cluster from vehicle.
6. Remove A-pillar trim panel.
7. Remove lefthand and righthand fuse covers.
8. Remove retaining screw located within the lefthand and righthand air vents, **Fig. 1.**
9. Remove retaining screw from inside of fuse panel covers.
10. Remove retaining screws from center console to top on instrument panel.
11. Remove retaining screws from inside glove compartment.
12. Remove defroster grille screws, then the defroster outwards.
13. Remove bolts from lefthand and righthand side under defroster grille, **Fig. 2.**
14. Remove sheet metal clips from both A-pillars.
15. Remove top panel of instrument panel.
16. Insert suitable plastic wedge directly between, ignition switch cover sleeve and transponder coil. Press transpon-

der coil off ignition switch cover sleeve using suitable plastic wedge, **Fig. 3.**
17. Disconnect 2–pin transponder coil electrical connector from control module.
18. **Steering lock and cylinder lock can only be installed in lock position. Never turn steering lock when ignition/starter switch is being installed.**
19. Remove ignition key cylinder.
20. Disconnect warning buzzer electrical contact and ignition/starter switch electrical contact.
21. Disconnect parking lock interlock cable.
22. Release locking pin clamp and pull steering lock from steering column.
23. Remove ignition switch.
24. Remove washer and parking lock valve.
25. Remove warning buzzer and contact switch.
26. Reverse procedure to install.

HEADLAMP SWITCH
REPLACE

1. Remove lower lefthand instrument panel cover retaining clips, then the lower cover.
2. Disconnect electrical connectors at back of headlamp switch.
3. Remove headlamp switches from interior trim panel using suitable trim stick.
4. Remove two headlamp switch to trim panel retaining screws, then the headlamp switch.
5. Reverse procedure to install.

STOP LIGHT SWITCH
REPLACE

1. Remove lower lefthand instrument panel cover retaining clips, then the lower cover.
2. Disconnect electrical connectors at back of stop light switch.
3. Press stop light switch locking tabs, then rotate stop light switch clockwise to release from brake pedal brace.
4. Remove stop lamp switch.
5. Reverse procedure to install.

MULTI-FUNCTION SWITCH
REPLACE

1. Remove steering wheel as outlined in "Steering Wheel, Replace."
2. Remove lower instrument panel retainers, then the lower instrument panel.
3. Remove cruise control to multi-function switch retaining screw.
4. Remove cruise control retaining screws from bracket below cruise control.
5. Remove multi-function switch to steering column retaining screws.
6. Disconnect multi-function switch electrical connectors and wire harness from steering column.
7. Remove multi-function switch.
8. Reverse procedure to install.

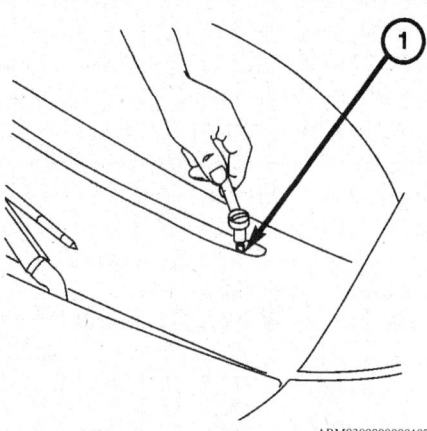

Fig. 2   Defroster grille bolt removal

TURN SIGNAL SWITCH
REPLACE

Refer to "Multi-Function Switch, Replace" for procedure.

DIMMER SWITCH
REPLACE

Refer to "Multi-Function Switch, Replace" for procedure.

STEERING WHEEL
REPLACE

Refer to **Fig. 4,** for exploded view of steering column to aid in replacement and installation. **Steering wheel does not require a wheel puller tool for removal.**
1. Place front wheels in straight ahead position.
2. Remove lefthand lower instrument panel fuse panel from below steering column.
3. Remove driver's air bag retaining screws, disconnect air bag electrical connector, then pass air bag connector wire through hole in steering column.
4. Remove driver's air bag module.
5. Remove steering wheel countersunk bolt, using a long Allen wrench, then the steering wheel.
6. Remove clockspring screws.
7. Reverse procedure to install, noting the following:
   a. **Torque** steering wheel mounting hex bolt to 60 ft. lbs.
   b. If steering wheel is offset by more than one tooth, turn signal indicator is no longer aligned properly.

INSTRUMENT CLUSTER
REPLACE

Remove instrument cluster as outlined in "Ignition Switch, Replace."

RADIO
REPLACE

1. Record customers defined presets.
2. Insert radio removal tools No. 3291, or

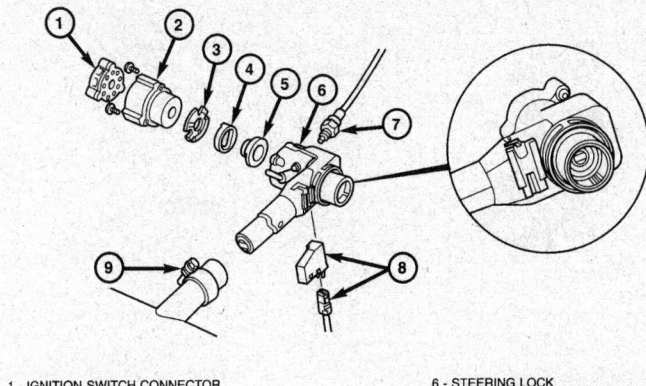

1 - IGNITION SWITCH CONNECTOR
2 - IGNITION SWITCH
3 - WASHER
4 - PARKING LOCK VALVE
5 - CAM
6 - STEERING LOCK
7 - PARK/BRAKE INTERLOCK CABLE
8 - BUZZER
9 - RELEASE CLAMP

ARM0300000000065

Fig. 3 Ignition switch replacement

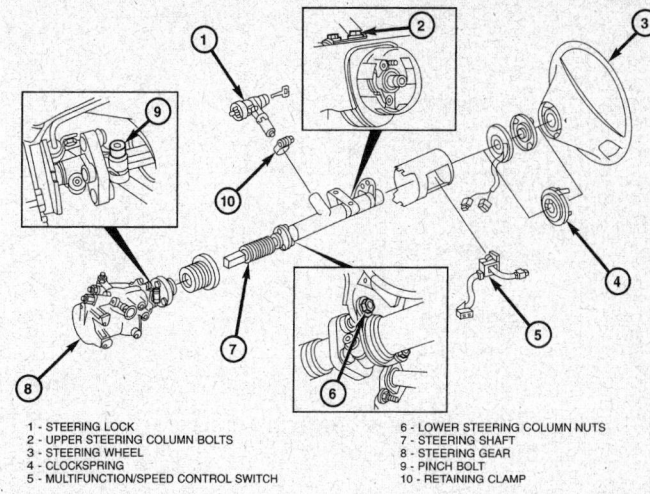

1 - STEERING LOCK
2 - UPPER STEERING COLUMN BOLTS
3 - STEERING WHEEL
4 - CLOCKSPRING
5 - MULTIFUNCTION/SPEED CONTROL SWITCH
6 - LOWER STEERING COLUMN NUTS
7 - STEERING SHAFT
8 - STEERING GEAR
9 - PINCH BOLT
10 - RETAINING CLAMP

ARM0300000000018

**Fig. 4 Exploded view of steering column
(Part 1 of 2)**

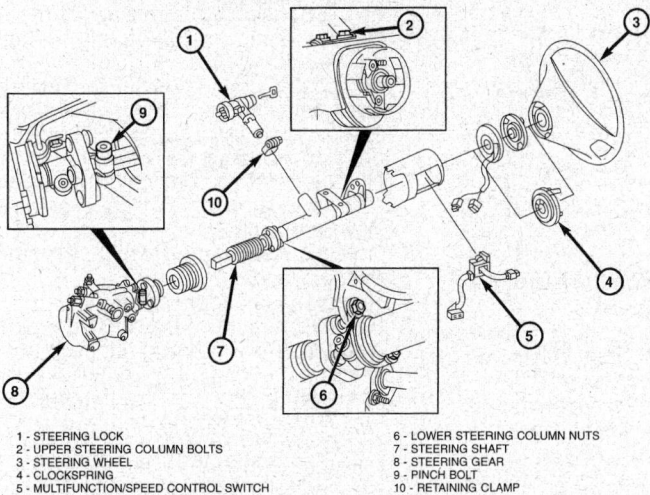

1 - STEERING LOCK
2 - UPPER STEERING COLUMN BOLTS
3 - STEERING WHEEL
4 - CLOCKSPRING
5 - MULTIFUNCTION/SPEED CONTROL SWITCH
6 - LOWER STEERING COLUMN NUTS
7 - STEERING SHAFT
8 - STEERING GEAR
9 - PINCH BOLT
10 - RETAINING CLAMP

ARM0300000000019

**Fig. 4 Exploded view of steering column
(Part 2 of 2)**

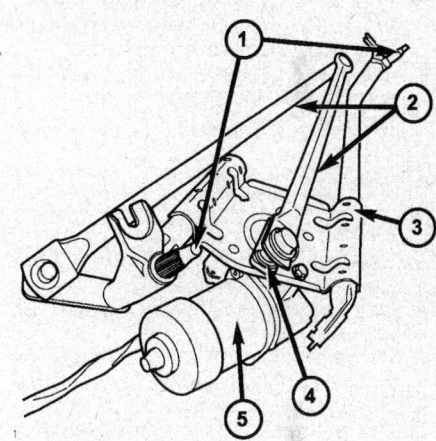

1 Wiper pivot shafts
2 Linkage
3 Module frame
4 Crank arm
5 Wiper motor

ARM0300000000582

Fig. 5 Wiper motor replacement

equivalents, into slots located on right-hand and lefthand sides of radio, with jagged edge of tools facing inward toward center of radio unit, push forward until a slight click is heard.
3. Gently pull tool rings along with radio rearward until radio is clear of dash panel.
4. Press flexible detentes in sides of radio after it has been remove, then release tools.
5. Disconnect radio electrical connectors and antenna.
6. Remove radio unit from vehicle.
7. Reverse procedure to install, then enter customer preset stations.

WIPER MOTOR
REPLACE

1. Open hood, then extend hood prop fully open to support hood.
2. Lift wiper arm to its over-center position.
3. Remove plastic nut cap at pivot arm end of wiper arm.
4. Remove wiper arm retaining nut from wiper pivot shaft.
5. Remove wiper arm from pivot shaft using suitable battery terminal puller to release wiper arm from pivot shaft.
6. Remove cowl grille retaining screws, then pull back on cowl grille to release retaining clips.
7. Disconnect hoses from under side of cowl grille.
8. Remove cowl grille from vehicle.
9. Remove control module box cover.
10. Disconnect wiper motor electrical connector from Body Control Module (BCM).
11. Remove wiper motor wire harness rubber grommet from BCM box and cowl ledge.
12. Remove cowl drain by rotating drain insert counterclockwise, then lift drain upward to remove.
13. Remove lower wiper module retaining bolts located under cowl ledge.
14. Remove two upper wiper module retaining bolts, then the wiper module and wiper motor assembly.
15. Remove wiper motor retaining bolts, then position wiper motor to access crank arm retaining nut, Fig. 5.
16. Remove crank arm retaining nut from wiper motor shaft.

17. Scribe a reference mark on both the wiper motor and wiper crank arm to ensure proper alignment during reassembly.
18. Remove crank arm from wiper motor shaft, then remove the wiper motor from wiper module.
19. Reverse procedure to install. **Torque** wiper motor retaining blots to 98 inch lbs.

WIPER SWITCH
REPLACE

Refer to "Multi-Function Switch, Replace" for procedure.

BLOWER MOTOR
REPLACE

1. Remove righthand lower instrument panel cover retainers, then the lower instrument panel cover.

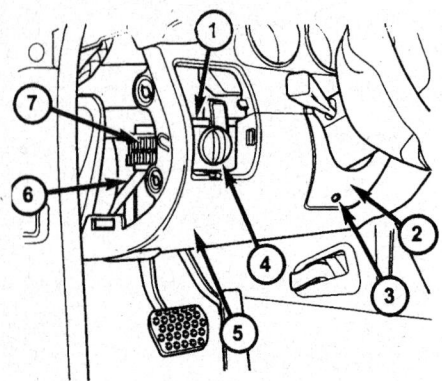

Fig. 6 Illumination control
module removal

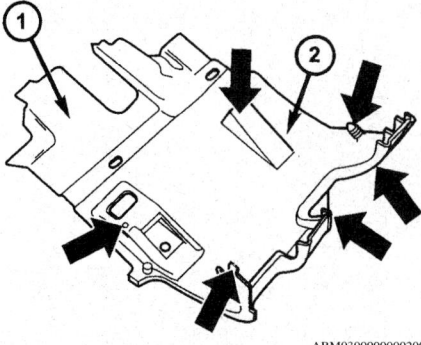

Fig. 7 Underside cover screw
removal

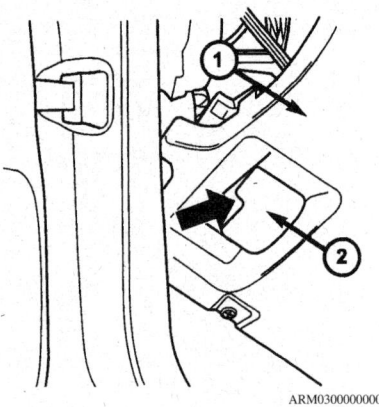

Fig. 8 Hood latch release
removal

2. Disconnect blower motor electrical connector from relief in blower motor door.
3. Position blower motor door release catches to one side, then swing blower motor cover door downward.
4. Remove blower motor retaining screws, then the blower motor.
5. Reverse procedure to install.

HEATER CORE
REPLACE

1. Recover refrigerant as outlined in "Air Conditioning" chapter.
2. Drain engine coolant into suitable container.
3. Remove top panel of dash panel as outlined in "Ignition Switch, Replace."
4. Remove air nozzles.
5. Remove steering column undercover attaching screw, then the cover.
6. Remove fuse panel cover.
7. Remove lower instrument cover retaining screws from illumination control module, side of instrument panel and support bar, **Fig. 6.**
8. Remove illumination control module.
9. Remove underside cover screws from cover, **Fig. 7.**
10. Remove lefthand lower instrument panel cover to upper instrument panel cover retaining screws, then the panel cover.
11. Remove hood latch release handle to lefthand lower instrument panel retaining screws, then guide handle through lower cover, **Fig. 8.**
12. Remove righthand lower instrument panel cover to upper instrument panel cover retaining screws, then the lower cover, **Fig. 9.**
13. Remove carpeting from righthand side passenger area.
14. Remove glove compartment to righthand lower instrument panel retaining screws, then the glove compartment, **Fig. 10.**
15. Remove instrument cluster as outlined in "Ignition Switch, Replace."
16. Ensure all wire harness to instrument panel nylon retaining straps are removed.
17. Remove lower instrument panel from vehicle.

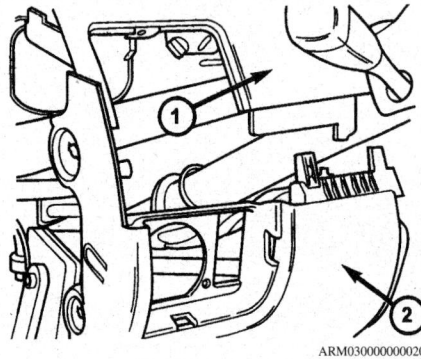

Fig. 9 Lefthand lower instrument
panel removal

18. Disconnect hot water hose located on firewall near brake booster.
19. Disconnect heater core supply hoses located on righthand side of firewall.
20. Remove green insulating mats.
21. Disconnect Sentry Key Entry Module (SKREM) electrical connectors by depressing retaining tabs.
22. Remove SKREM retaining screws, then the SKREM from mounting plate.
23. Ensure all wire harness to instrument panel support nylon retaining straps are removed.
24. Remove wire harness connectors and retainers from transmission tunnel.
25. Remove steering column to instrument panel support nuts, then position steering column aside.
26. Disconnect passenger's air bag module electrical connector.
27. Remove righthand and lefthand heater ducts to instrument panel support retaining screws, then the heater ducts.
28. Remove HVAC case to instrument panel support and transmission tunnel mounting bolts.
29. Remove instrument panel support to front vehicle bulkhead mounting bolts.
30. Remove instrument panel support to A-pillar support bolts.
31. Disconnect vacuum reservoir connectors.
32. Disconnect heater core and evaporator core temperature sensor electrical connectors located on lefthand side of HVAC housing.
33. Disconnect fresh air/recirculating flap switch-over valve electrical and vacuum reservoir connectors located on front of HVAC housing.
34. Remove remaining wire harness to heater housing nylon retaining ties.
35. Ensure to cap or plug off any coolant fluid lines.
36. Tip heater core housing and instrument panel support assembly forward and carefully remove through passenger's door opening.
37. Remove heater core cover retaining screws located on righthand side of HVAC housing.
38. Release heater core cover retaining spring clamps.
39. Remove heater core cover.
40. Remove heater core water flow pipe guide to HVAC housing retaining bolt.
41. Remove heating water return line to heater core retaining clip, then the return line from heater core.
42. Remove heater core to HVAC housing retaining screws, then the heater core and flow tube as an assembly.
43. Remove heater core water flow pipe retaining clip, then the flow pipe from heater core.
44. Reverse procedure to install.

EVAPORATOR CORE
REPLACE

1. Remove HVAC housing and heater core as outlined in "Heater Core, Replace."
2. Remove aluminum A/C lines from valve strip located on top of HVAC unit, **Fig. 11.**
3. Disconnect vacuum lines from reservoir element.
4. Separate blower housing from HVAC housing using suitable plastic trim stick to release sliding retaining clips, **Fig. 11.**
5. Remove blower motor housing to HVAC housing retaining spring clips, then separate blower motor housing from HVAC housing, **Fig. 12.**
6. Remove four expansion valve retaining screws and gasket located behind expansion valve.
7. Separate HVAC housing upper section by removing spring retainer clips.
8. Remove evaporator core from HVAC housing.
9. Reverse procedure to install.

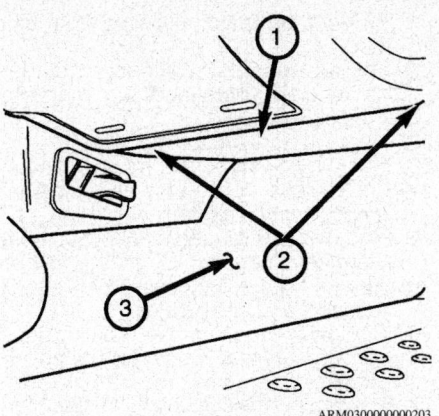

Fig. 10 Righthand lower instrument panel removal

ARM0300000000203

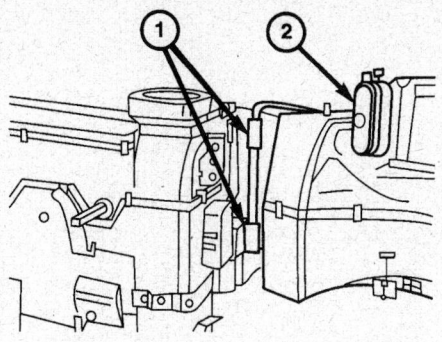

1 Sliding clips
2 Vacuum element

ARM0300000000583

Fig. 11 HVAC housing retaining clip & reservoir element locations

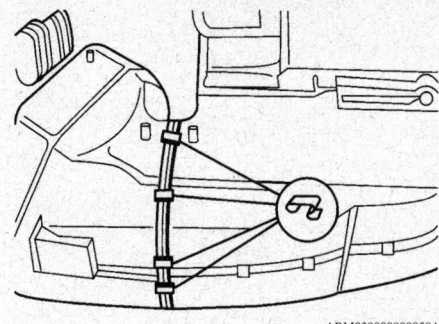

ARM0300000000584

Fig. 12 HVAC housing spring clip removal

3.2L Engine

NOTE: On Air Bag Equipped Models, Refer To "Air Bag System Precautions" Located In The Front Of This Manual For System Disarming & Arming Procedures.

NOTE: Refer To "Computer Relearn Procedures" Located In The Front Of This Manual When Battery Power To The Computer Has Been Interrupted.

INDEX

PRECAUTIONS
Air Bag Systems

Refer to "Air Bag System Precautions" in the front of this manual for system disarming and arming procedures.

Battery Ground Cable

Prior to service, disconnect battery ground cable and isolate as required.

Fuel System Pressure Relief

1. Remove fuel pump relay form power distribution center.
2. Start and run engine until it stalls.
3. Attempt to start engine until it no longer runs.
4. Turn ignition switch to Off position.
5. Place suitable rag or shop towel under fuel line quick-connector fitting at fuel rail.

6. Install fuel pump relay.
7. One or more Diagnostic Trouble Codes (DTCs) may have been stored because of removing fuel pump relay. Clear these DTCs with suitably programmed scan tool.

COMPRESSION PRESSURE

1. Drive vehicle until engine reaches normal operating temperature.

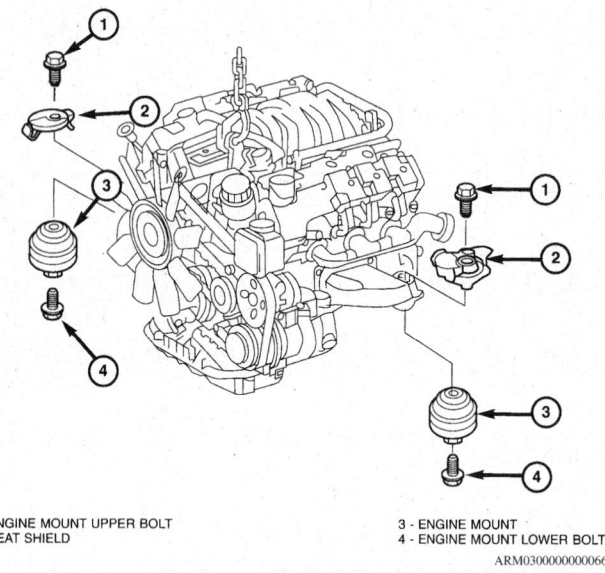

1 - ENGINE MOUNT UPPER BOLT
2 - HEAT SHIELD
3 - ENGINE MOUNT
4 - ENGINE MOUNT LOWER BOLT

ARM0300000000066

Fig. 1 Front engine mount replacement

2. Disconnect ignition coil cables from spark plugs.
3. Remove spark plugs from engine.
4. Inspect spark plugs for signs of abnormal firing or oil fouling.
5. Ensure throttle plate is fully open.
6. Install suitable compression gauge into number one spark plug hole.
7. Crank engine over with starter until maximum pressure is obtained. Repeat for remaining cylinders.
8. Compression pressure should be no less than 100 psi and maximum variation between cylinders should be no more than 25%.

ENGINE MOUNT
REPLACE
Front

1. Remove air cleaner housing.
2. Attach suitable engine support frame.
3. Remove upper engine mount bolt and heat shield, **Fig. 1.**
4. Slightly raise engine. Do not stretch hoses and lines while lifting engine.
5. Raise and support vehicle.
6. Remove lower splash shield mounting bolts, then the splash shield.
7. Remove engine mount.
8. Reverse procedure to install. Ensure arrows on engine mounts are aligned with engine bracket retaining slots.

Rear

1. Raise and support vehicle.
2. Support transmission with suitable transmission jack.
3. Remove lower engine mount retaining bolts.
4. Raise transmission slightly off crossmember support.
5. Remove upper engine mount bolts.
6. Remove rear engine mount.
7. Reverse procedure to install.

ENGINE
REPLACE

1. Relieve fuel pressure as outlined in "Precautions."
2. Remove air cleaner assembly housing.
3. Drain engine coolant into suitable container.
4. Remove cooling fan assembly as outlined in "Cooling Fans" chapter.
5. Remove radiator as outlined in "Radiator, Replace."
6. Remove serpentine drive belt as outlined in "Serpentine Drive Belt."
7. Disconnect mass air flow sensor connector and retaining screws, then remove the sensor.
8. Disconnect brake vacuum booster, intake manifold inspect valve and purge vacuum valve hoses.
9. Drain fluid from power steering pump reservoir using suitable fluid removal pump.
10. Disconnect ground lead at power steering pump.
11. Disconnect return and supply lines from power steering pump.
12. Disconnect fuel supply line at fuel rail.
13. Disconnect engine wire harness and connectors.
14. Raise and support vehicle.
15. Remove splash shield retaining bolts, then the splash shield.
16. Drain engine oil into suitable container.
17. Remove transmission to rear drive axle propeller shaft as outlined in "Rear Axle & Suspension" section.
18. Disconnect transmission wire connectors and wiring harness from retainers at transmission, then position aside.
19. **On models equipped with automatic transmission,** disconnect gear selector cable from transmission shift lever.
20. **On models equipped with manual transmission,** disconnect pressure line at clutch slave cylinder, reverse

lock-out cable and shift rod from ball stud.
21. **On all models,** disconnect starter motor connectors and wire harness from starter.
22. Remove front engine mount bolt.
23. Remove lower radiator hose and coolant bypass hose from water pump, then lower vehicle.
24. Remove upper radiator hose from thermostat housing.
25. Remove heater hoses from intake manifold and engine block.
26. Remove A/C compressor bolts, position compressor aside with lines attached.
27. Raise transmission slightly using suitable floor jack.
28. Remove transmission mount and crossmember mounting bolts, then the crossmember and transmission mount as an assembly.
29. Attach suitable engine lifting hoist to engine removal eyelets located on engine.
30. Lower rear of transmission with floor jack.
31. Lift engine and transmission as an assembly from vehicle.
32. Separate engine and transmission after mounting onto suitable stand.
33. Reverse procedure to install.

INTAKE MANIFOLD
REPLACE

1. Relieve fuel pressure as outlined in "Precautions."
2. Remove air cleaner housing.
3. Disconnect mass air flow sensor electrical connector and retaining bolts, then sensor.
4. Disconnect EGR, brake booster and ventilator purge valve vacuum hoses from intake manifold.
5. Disconnect engine wiring connectors and harnesses, then position aside.
6. Remove fuel supply line from fuel rail.
7. Remove fuel rail and injectors as an assembly.
8. Disconnect EGR pipe at EGR valve.
9. Remove air pump switch over valves and retainers.
10. Remove intake manifold mounting bolts and gaskets.
11. Reverse procedure to install, noting the following:
    a. Clean all gasket surfaces thoroughly.
    b. Install new gaskets.
    c. Tighten intake manifold bolts to specification.

EXHAUST MANIFOLD
REPLACE

1. Remove air cleaner housing.
2. Raise and support vehicle.
3. Remove splash shield retaining bolts, then the splash shield.
4. Disconnect catalytic converter sensor connector, then remove sensor and catalytic converter from vehicle.
5. Remove exhaust manifold nuts from cylinder head.

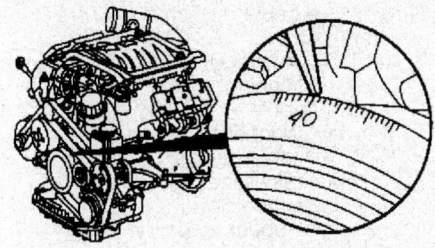

Fig. 2 Crankshaft positioned at 40° ATDC

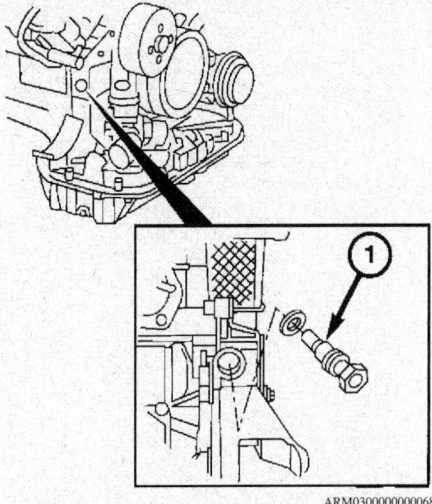

Fig. 3 Timing chain tensioner replacement

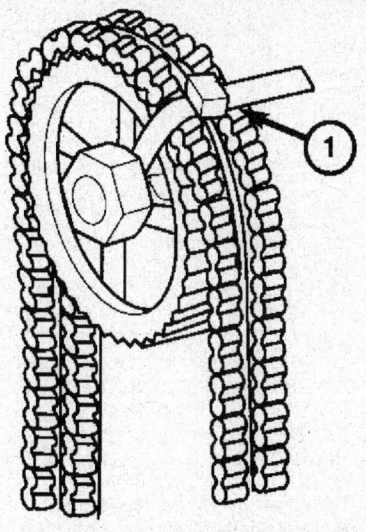

Fig. 4 Righthand timing chain & sprocket

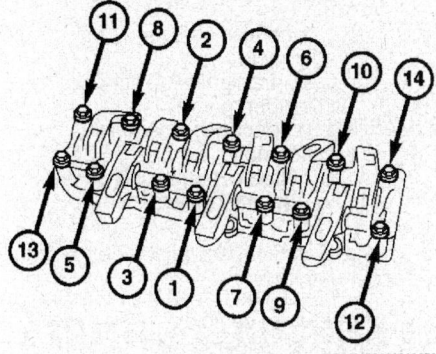

Fig. 5 Camshaft bearing bridge bolt tightening sequence (lefthand)

6. Lower vehicle.
7. Remove exhaust manifold and gasket from engine compartment.
8. Reverse procedure to install, noting the following:
   a. Clean all gasket surfaces thoroughly.
   b. Install new gaskets.
   c. Tighten exhaust manifold bolts to specification.

CYLINDER HEAD

REPLACE

Removal

1. Relive fuel pressure as outlined in "Precautions."
2. Remove air cleaner housing.
3. Disconnect mass air flow sensor electrical connector, then remove sensor.
4. Drain engine oil and coolant into suitable containers.
5. Remove radiator as outlined in "Radiator, Replace."
6. Remove righthand and lefthand camshaft position sensor connectors and retaining bolts, then the camshaft position sensors and wiring harnesses.
7. Remove drive belt as outlined in "Serpentine Drive Belt."
8. Remove intake manifold as outlined in "Intake Manifold, Replace."
9. Remove valve cover as outlined in "Valve Cover, Replace."
10. Disconnect righthand and lefthand exhaust system pipes at exhaust manifolds.
11. Position crankshaft at 40° ATDC, **Fig. 2.**

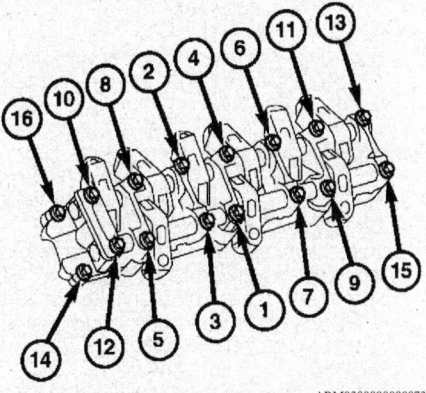

Fig. 6 Camshaft bearing bridge bolt tightening sequence (righthand)

12. Lock camshafts in position using camshaft locating plate tool No. 9104 and locking pin tool No. 9105, or equivalents, place locating plate tool flush on cylinder head and insert locking pin tool into groove located on camshaft.
13. Remove timing chain tensioner, **Fig. 3.**
14. Secure timing chain to righthand camshaft sprocket using plastic tie strap, **Fig. 4.**
15. Remove camshaft sprocket bolts, then the camshaft sprockets.
16. Remove camshaft locating plate tool No. 9104 and locking pin tool No. 9105, or equivalents.
17. Reverse sequence, **Figs. 5 and 6,** remove camshaft bearing bridge bolts in two steps.
18. Remove camshaft bearing bridges and camshafts.
19. Reverse sequence, **Fig. 7,** remove cylinder head bolts.
20. Remove cylinder head and gasket.

Installation

1. Clean cylinder head and block gasket surfaces of any foreign material.
2. Position new gasket and cylinder head

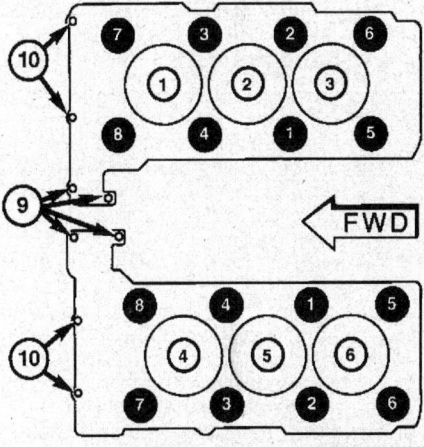

Fig. 7 Cylinder head bolt tightening sequence

on engine block dowels.
3. Measure and inspect cylinder head bolts prior to reuse. Do not reuse bolts that exceed, 5.66 of an inch (144 mm) in length, **Fig. 8.**
4. Tighten cylinder head bolts in four steps using sequence, **Fig. 7.**
   a. Step one, **torque** head bolts 1–8 to 15 ft. lbs.
   b. Step two, **torque** head bolts 1–8 to 37 ft. lbs.
   c. Step three, tighten head bolts 1–8 an additional 60–70°.
   d. Step four, tighten head bolts 1–8 an additional 60–70°.
   e. Tighten timing chain cover bolts 9–10 to 18 ft. lbs.
5. Ensure crankshaft is at 40° ATDC, **Fig. 2.**
6. Position camshaft bearing bridge on camshaft.
7. Lock camshafts in position by using camshaft locating plate tool No. 9104 and locking pin tool No. 9105, or equivalents, place locating plate tool flush on cylinder head and inserting locking

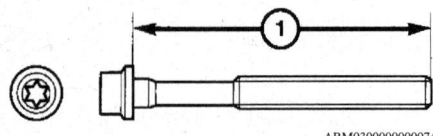

Fig. 8 Cylinder head bolt measurement

pin tool into grove located on camshaft.

8. **Torque** camshaft bridge bolts to 11 ft. lbs., then an additional 90° using sequence, **Figs. 5 and 6.**
9. Install camshaft sprockets and bolts, **torque** sprocket bolts to 37 ft. lbs., then tighten an additional 90°.
10. Install timing chain tensioner.
11. Remove plastic retaining tie from right-hand camshaft sprocket and chain.
12. Remove camshaft locating plate tool No. 9104 and locking pin tool No. 9105, or equivalents.
13. Install valve cover as outlined in "Valve Cover, Replace."
14. Install air cleaner housing.
15. Install mass air flow sensor.

VALVE COVER
REPLACE

1. Remove air cleaner housing.
2. Disconnect ignition coil electrical connectors and harness to valve cover retaining clips, then position harness assembly aside.
3. Disconnect spark plug wires at spark plugs.
4. Disconnect PCV, vacuum hoses and retainers from valve covers, then position them aside.
5. Remove valve cover retaining bolts, then the valve cover and gasket.
6. Reverse procedure to install, noting the following:
   a. Clean all gasket surfaces thoroughly.
   b. Install new gaskets.
   c. Tighten valve cover bolts to specification.

VALVE ADJUSTMENT

These engines are equipped with hydraulic lash adjusters. No adjustment required.

ROCKER ARMS
REPLACE
Removal

1. Remove camshaft bearing bridge as outlined in "Cylinder Head, Replace."
2. Remove rocker arm shaft from camshaft bearing bridge using a 16 mm drift to drive rocker arm shaft from camshaft bearing bridge, **Fig. 9.** If resistance is encountered while driving rocker arm shaft from bearing bridge, bearing must be heated. **Do not exceed 320°F.**
3. Remove rocker arms, inspect rocker arm bearing surfaces. If longitudal

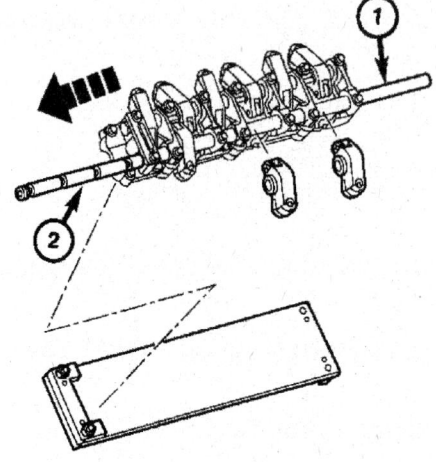

1 16mm Drift
2 Rocker arm shaft

ARM0300000000075

Fig. 9 Rocker arms & shaft removal

scoring is present on rocker arm bearing surface, replace effected rocker arms.

Installation

1. Allow rocker arm shaft and camshaft bearing bridge to cool.
2. Insert rocker arm shaft into camshaft bearing bridge and through rocker arms by gently tapping rocker arm shaft using suitable soft head mallet. Ensure rocker arms are aligned, **Fig. 10.**
3. Ensure oil supply holes in rocker arm shaft are facing downward, toward cylinder head.
4. Install camshaft bearing bridge as outlined in "Cylinder Head, Replace."

VALVE SPRINGS
REPLACE

1. Remove starter motor as outlined under "Starter, Replace" in "Electrical" section.
2. Remove camshafts as outlined in "Camshaft, Replace."
3. Remove spark plug from cylinder requiring valve spring replacement.
4. Position piston at TDC in cylinder requiring valve spring replacement.
5. Install flywheel locking tool No. 9102, or equivalent into starter motor opening.
6. Pressurize cylinder with compressed shop air using suitable adapter and air hose assembly.
7. Compress valve spring using suitable valve spring compression tool.
8. With valve spring compressed, remove collets, **Fig. 11.**
9. Slowly release valve spring compression tool.
10. Remove valve spring retainer, valve spring, valve stem seal and spring seat.
11. Reverse procedure to install. Always

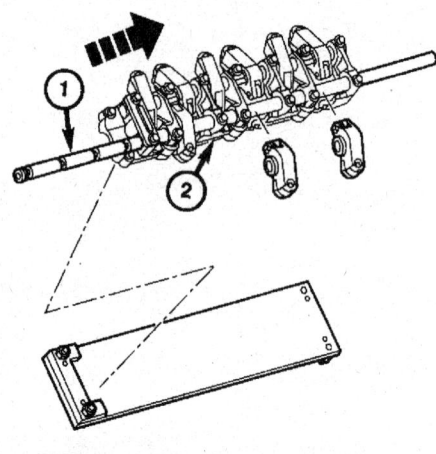

1 16mm Drift
2 Rocker arm shaft

ARM0300000000076

Fig. 10 Rocker arms & shaft installation

replace valve stem seal when replacing valve spring.

CRANKSHAFT DAMPER
REPLACE

1. Drain coolant into suitable container.
2. Remove radiator as outlined in "Radiator, Replace."
3. Remove drive belt as outlined in "Serpentine Drive Belt."
4. Remove starter motor as outlined under "Starter, Replace" in "Electrical" section.
5. Install flywheel locking tool No. 9102, or equivalent, into starter motor opening.
6. Remove crankshaft damper retaining bolt, then the crankshaft damper.
7. Reverse procedure to install. Replace damper retaining bolt if length exceeds 3.07 inch.

FRONT COVER
REPLACE

1. Remove engine as outlined in "Engine, Replace."
2. Separate transmission from engine, then mount engine on suitable engine stand.
3. **On models equipped with manual transmission,** remove clutch pressure plate, clutch disc and flywheel from engine crankshaft.
4. **On models equipped with automatic transmission,** remove drive flexplate from engine crankshaft.
5. **On all models,** remove upper and lower oil pan retaining bolts, then the upper and lower oil pans.
6. Remove drive belt as outlined in "Serpentine Drive Belt."
7. Remove power steering pump and idler pulley as outlined under "Power Steering Pump, Replace" in "Front Suspension & Steering" section.
8. Remove crankshaft damper as outlined in "Crankshaft Damper, Replace."

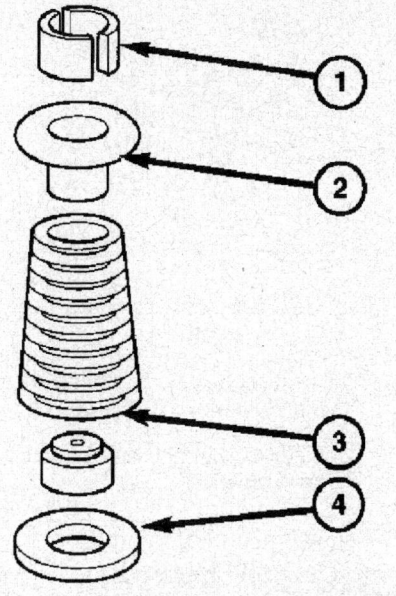

Fig. 11 Valve spring replacement

9. Remove alternator as outlined under "Alternator, Replace" in "Electrical" section.
10. Ensure crankshaft is at 40° ATDC, **Fig. 2.**
11. Remove starter motor as outlined under "Starter, Replace" in "Electrical" section.
12. Remove cylinder heads as outlined in "Cylinder Head, Replace."
13. Remove timing chain tensioner retaining bolt, then the tensioner.
14. Remove front timing cover retaining bolts, then the front timing chain cover.
15. Reverse procedure to install.

TIMING CHAIN
REPLACE
Removal

1. Remove timing chain cover as outlined in "Front Cover, Replace."
2. Remove oil pump drive chain and tensioner.
3. Remove lefthand and righthand camshaft sprocket retaining bolts.
4. Remove timing chain and camshaft sprockets.
5. Remove timing chain crankshaft sprocket.
6. Clean and inspect all gasket surfaces, chain guides and sprockets for wear or damage replace as required.

Installation

1. Invert engine on engine stand.
2. Install crankshaft sprocket, **Fig. 12.**
3. Ensure crankshaft is at 40° ATDC, **Fig. 2.**
4. Align balance shaft sprocket timing mark with copper teeth on timing chain.
5. Insert camshaft sprockets into timing

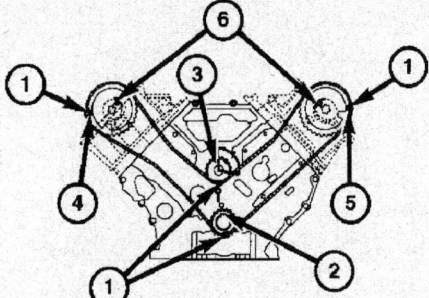

1 Copper teeth of timing chain
2 Crankshaft sprocket
3 Balance shaft sprocket timing mark
4 Camshaft sprocket timing mark
5 Camshaft sprocket timing mark
6 Camshaft sprockets

ARM0300000000080

Fig. 12 Timing chain replacement

chain and align camshaft sprocket timing marks with copper teeth on timing chain.
6. Install timing chain with sprockets and route within timing chain guides, **Fig. 13.**
7. Lock camshaft sprockets into position using camshaft locating plate tool No. 9104 and locking pin tool No. 9105, or equivalents, place locating plate tool flush on cylinder head and insert locking pin tool into groove located on camshaft.
8. Install oil pump, oil pump drive chain and oil pump drive chain tensioner.
9. Rotate engine to upright position on engine stand.
10. Install timing chain front cover as outlined in "Front Cover, Replace."
11. Remove camshaft locating plate tool No. 9104 and locking pin tool No. 9105, or equivalents.

TIMING CHAIN TENSIONER
REPLACE

1. Remove alternator as outlined under "Alternator, Replace" in "Electrical," section.
2. Remove timing chain tensioner retaining bolt, then the timing chain tensioner.
3. Reverse procedure to install.

CAMSHAFT
REPLACE

Refer to "Cylinder Head, Replace" for camshaft replacement procedure.

MAIN & ROD BEARINGS

1. Tighten main journal cap bolts as follows using sequence, **Fig. 14.**
   a. **Torque** M8 bolts to 15 ft. lbs., then tighten an additional 90°.
   b. **Torque** M10 bolts to 22 ft. lbs., then tighten an additional 90°.

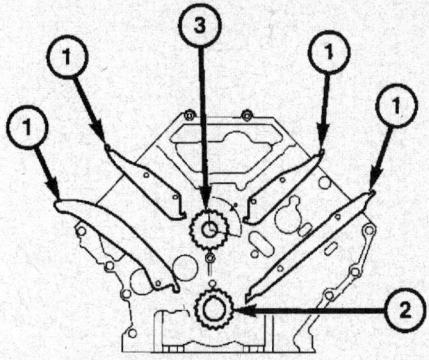

1 Timing chain guides
2 Crankshaft sprocket
3 Balance shaft sprocket timing mark

ARM0300000000081

Fig. 13 Timing chain guide locations

2. Tighten connecting rod bolts in three steps: First step, **torque** bolts to 44 inch lbs.; second step, **torque** bolts to 18 ft. lbs.; third step, tighten bolts an additional 90°.

CRANKSHAFT SEAL
REPLACE

1. Remove crankshaft damper as outlined in "Crankshaft Damper, Replace."
2. Remove crankshaft oil seal using suitable seal removal pry bar or screwdriver.
3. Reverse procedure to install. Lubricate crankshaft seal inner lips using suitable engine oil.

CRANKSHAFT REAR OIL SEAL
REPLACE

Crankshaft rear oil seal cannot be replaced separately. The end cover and seal are assembled at the factory and must be replaced as a set.
1. Remove engine as outlined in "Engine, Replace."
2. Separate transmission from engine, then mount engine on suitable engine stand.
3. **On models equipped with manual transmission,** remove clutch pressure plate, clutch disc and flywheel from engine crankshaft.
4. **On models equipped with automatic transmission,** remove drive flexplate from crankshaft.
5. **On all models,** remove crankshaft end cover retaining bolts, then the end cover seal assembly.
6. Reverse procedure to install, noting the following:
   a. Install new end cover and gaskets (without new crankshaft seal installed).
   b. Apply a 2 mm bead of Loctite sealer No. 5203, or equivalent, to areas

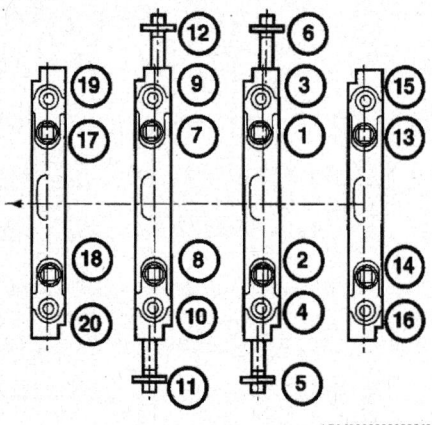

Fig. 14   Main bearing journal tightening sequence

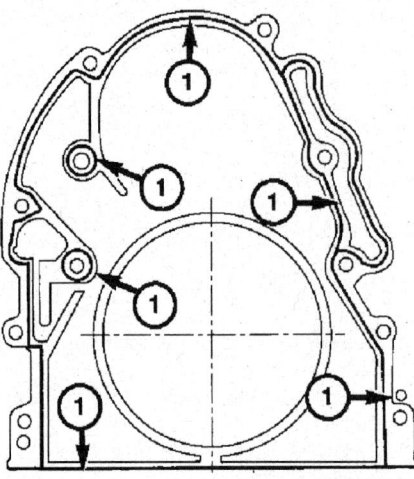

Fig. 15   End cover sealer locations

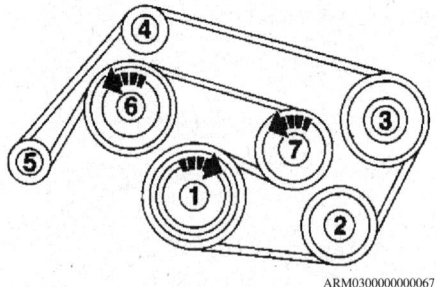

Fig. 16   Serpentine drive belt routing

outlined **Fig. 15.Components requiring sealer must be installed within 10 minutes after sealer is applied.**

c. Clean engine block and oil pan sealing surfaces of gasket material.
d. Ensure circumference of new crankshaft oil seal, sealing lips and crankshaft are oil and grease free.
e. Position crankshaft seal at right-hand angles to crankshaft to ensure proper seal.
f. Install new seal into crankshaft end cover using seal installation tool No. 9100, or equivalent.
g. Measure between edge of end cover and crankshaft oil seal, distance must be approximately .039 inch, around entire circumference.

OIL PAN
REPLACE

Lower

1. Raise and support vehicle.
2. Drain engine oil into suitable container.
3. Remove lower splash shield retaining screws, then the splash shield.
4. Remove transmission oil cooler line retaining bolts, then position oil cooler line aside.
5. Remove lower oil pan mounting bolts, then the oil pan.
6. Reverse procedure to install.

Upper

1. Remove engine as outlined in "Engine, Replace."
2. Separate transmission from engine, then mount engine on suitable engine stand.
3. **On models equipped with manual transmission,** remove clutch pressure plate, clutch disc and flywheel from engine crankshaft.
4. **On models equipped with automatic transmission,** remove drive flex-plate from engine crankshaft.
5. **On all models,** remove upper and lower oil pan retaining bolts, then the upper and lower oil pans.

6. Reverse procedure to install.

OIL PUMP
REPLACE

1. Raise and support vehicle.
2. Drain engine oil into suitable container.
3. Remove lower engine splash shield retaining bolts then the splash shield.
4. **On models equipped with automatic transmission,** remove transmission fluid cooler line retaining bolt, then position cooler lines aside.
5. **On all models,** remove lower oil pan retaining bolts, then the lower oil pan.
6. Remove oil pump retaining bolts.
7. Release oil pump drive chain tensioner.
8. Remove oil pump from drive chain and engine block.
9. Reverse procedure to install, noting the following:
   a. Inspect oil pump check valve operation by pressing and releasing plunger to ensure free movement of plunger.
   b. Fill oil pump (prime) with new suitable engine oil.
   c. Inspect oil pump drive chain for wear or damaged components.
   d. Position oil pump driven sprocket in drive chain, install oil pump, tighten retaining bolts to specification.

OIL PUMP SERVICE

The oil pump is not serviceable and will require replacement should failure occur.

BELT TENSION DATA

This engine is equipped with an automatic belt tensioner. Adjustment is not required.

SERPENTINE DRIVE BELT

For serpentine drive belt routing refer to, **Fig. 16.**

1. Pull accessory drive belt tensioner in a counterclockwise direction using suitable pry tool.
2. Lock belt tensioner with a locking pin.
3. Remove drive belt.

COOLING SYSTEM BLEED

1. Close radiator drain hand tight.
2. Attach approximately 48 inches of ¼ inch I.D. clear hose to bleed valve.
3. Route hose away from drive belt, drive pulleys and electrical cooling fan and into a clean container.
4. Open cooling system bleed valve, then attach filling aid funnel tool No. 8195, or equivalent, to pressure bottle filler neck.
5. Pinch overflow hose between coolant bottle chambers.
6. Pour 50/50 mix of suitable coolant and distilled water into large section of filling funnel.
7. Slowly fill until steady stream of coolant flows from bleed valve hose.
8. Close bleed valve and continue filling system to top of funnel.
9. Remove overflow hose clip and allow funnel to drain into overflow chamber.
10. Remove funnel and install coolant pressure bottle cap.
11. Remove bleed valve hose, then start and run engine until it reaches operating temperature.
12. Shut off engine and allow to cool.
13. With engine cold, ensure pressure chamber level is between MIN and MAX marks.

THERMOSTAT
REPLACE

Thermostat and housing are serviced as an assembly.
1. Remove air cleaner housing.
2. Partially drain cooling system into suitable container.
3. Disconnect upper radiator hose at thermostat housing.
4. Remove thermostat housing retaining bolts, then the thermostat and housing assembly.
5. Reverse procedure to install.

WATER PUMP
REPLACE

Less Supercharger

1. Remove air cleaner housing.
2. Drain engine coolant into suitable container.
3. Remove radiator as outlined in "Radiator, Replace."
4. Remove drive belt as outlined in "Serpentine Drive Belt."
5. Release belt tensioner locking pin.
6. Remove belt tensioner mounting bolts, then the belt tensioner.
7. Disconnect lower radiator hose and coolant bypass hose.
8. Remove water pump drive and idler pulleys.
9. Remove water pump retaining bolts, then the water pump and gasket, **Fig. 17.**
10. Reverse procedure to install, noting the following:
    a. Clean gasket surfaces.
    b. Position water pump with new gasket on locating pins.
    c. Ensure water pump retaining bolts are in correct locations, **Fig. 17.**

With Supercharger

1. Remove engine cover.
2. Drain coolant into suitable container.
3. Remove radiator as outlined in "Radiator, Replace."
4. Remove air pump mounting bolts, then the air pump assembly.
5. Remove drive belt as outlined in "Serpentine Drive Belt."
6. Remove supercharger idler pulley upper and lower mounting bolts, then the idler pulley.
7. Remove belt tensioner mounting bolts, then the tensioner.
8. Remove coolant bypass hose.
9. Remove alternator as outlined under "Alternator, Replace."
10. Remove water pump drive and idler pulleys.
11. Remove water pump retaining bolts, then the water pump and gasket, **Fig. 17.**
12. Reverse procedure to install.
    a. Clean gasket surfaces.
    b. Position water pump with new gasket on location pins.

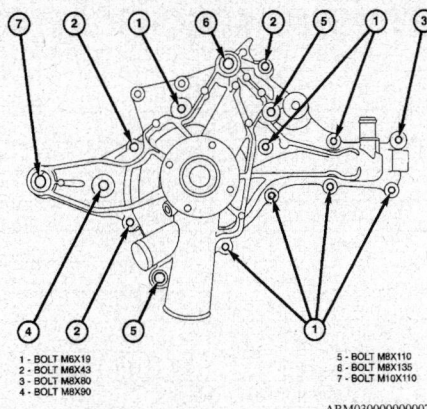

1 - BOLT M6X19
2 - BOLT M8X43
3 - BOLT M8X80
4 - BOLT M8X90
5 - BOLT M8X110
6 - BOLT M8X135
7 - BOLT M10X110

ARM0300000000078

Fig. 17 Water pump bolt identification & locations

RADIATOR
REPLACE

1. Remove radiator cooling fan as outlined under "Cooling Fans, Replace" in "Cooling Fans" chapter.
2. Drain coolant into suitable container.
3. Remove air cleaner inlet tubes.
4. Disconnect upper, lower and coolant recovery reservoir hoses.
5. **On models equipped with automatic transmission,** disconnect transmission fluid cooler lines, then plug openings to prevent leakage and contamination.
6. **On all models,** remove two radiator hold-down clamps.
7. Tilt radiator forward and remove A/C condenser to radiator retaining bolts.
8. Remove radiator from vehicle.
9. Reverse procedure to install.

FUEL PUMP
REPLACE

1. Relieve fuel pressure as outlined in "Precautions."
2. Raise and support vehicle.
3. Remove under vehicle splash shield retaining screws, then the splash shield.
4. Pinch off fuel suction hose and fuel supply hose, using suitable hose clamping pliers.
5. Disconnect fuel suction and supply hoses from fuel pump located on rear differential carrier.
6. Disconnect fuel pump electrical connector and harness at fuel pump.
7. Remove fuel pump to mounting bracket retaining clamp, then the fuel pump.
8. Reverse procedure to install.

FUEL FILTER
REPLACE

1. Relieve fuel pressure as outlined in "Precautions."
2. Raise and support vehicle.
3. Remove under vehicle splash shield retaining screws, then the splash shield.
4. Remove fuel filter/pressure regulator degassing line.
5. Remove fuel rail supply line at fuel filter/pressure regulator.
6. Remove fuel delivery hose at fuel filter/pressure regulator.
7. Remove fuel filter clamp retaining screw, then the fuel filter/pressure regulator assembly.
8. Reverse procedure to install.

SUPERCHARGER
REPLACE

1. Drain coolant into suitable container.
2. Remove engine cover and air cleaner.
3. Disconnect throttle body wire harness electrical connector.
4. Disconnect vacuum line at throttle body.
5. Remove righthand and lefthand intake plenums.
6. Remove throttle body mounting bolts, then the throttle body.
7. Remove supercharger outlet housing hose clamps, then the housing.
8. Disconnect fuel supply line at fuel rail.
9. Disconnect fuel injector harness electrical connector.
10. Remove fuel rail mounting bolts, then the fuel rail.
11. Disconnect charge air cooler coolant hoses from righthand front of engine.
12. Disconnect supercharger clutch electrical connector.
13. Remove secondary air injection valves.
14. Remove supercharger to cylinder head mounting bolts, then the supercharger. Do not reuse gasket.
15. Reverse procedure to install. Torque supercharger mounting bolts to 17 ft. lbs.

CROSSFIRE

TIGHTENING SPECIFICATIONS

Year	Component	Torque/Ft. Lbs.
2004–05	A/C Compressor Bolts	15
	Balance Shaft Bolts	15
	Camshaft Bearing Bridge Bolts	③
	Camshaft Sprocket Bolts	④
	Connecting Rod Cap Bolts	②
	Cooler Lines	84①
	Crankshaft Damper Bolt	148⑥
	Crankshaft Main Bearing Cap bolts	⑤
	Crossmember To Body Bolts	30
	Cylinder Head Bolts	③
	Cylinder Head Cover Bolts	84①
	Engine Lower Mount Bolt	26
	Engine Mount Bolts	22
	Engine Mount To Axle Carrier Bolts	41
	Engine Mount To Transmission Bolts	37
	Engine Support Bolts	15
	Engine Upper Mount Bolt	41
	Exhaust Flange Bolts	15
	Exhaust Manifold Heat Shield Bolts	12
	Exhaust Manifold To Cylinder Head Bolts	26
	Intake Manifold Bolts	15
	Lower Splash Shield Bolts	60①
	Oil Cooler Bolts	96①
	Oil Filter Adapter Center Bolt	52
	Oil Pan Lower Bolts	10
	Oil Pan Upper 6mm Bolts	89①
	Oil Pan Upper 8mm Bolts	15
	Oil Pump Retaining Bolts	21
	Oil Spray Nozzle Bolts	11
	Power Steering Pump Ground Bolt	18
	Power Steering Pump High Pressure Line	33
	Radiator To Body Screws	90①
	Thermostat Housing Bolts	17
	Timing Chain Cover Bolts	15
	Timing Chain Tensioner Bolt	59
	Transmission Mount Bolts	30

① — Inch lbs.
② — Refer to "Piston & Rod Assembly" for tightening procedure.
③ — Refer to "Cylinder Head, Replace" for tightening procedure.
④ — Refer to "Timing Chain, Replace" for tightening procedure.
⑤ — Refer to "Main & Rod Bearings" for tightening procedure.
⑥ — Plus 90°.

Rear Axle & Suspension

NOTE: On Air Bag Equipped Models, Refer To "Air Bag System Precautions" Located In The Front Of This Manual For System Disarming & Arming Procedures.

NOTE: Refer To "Computer Relearn Procedures" Located In The Front Of This Manual When Battery Power To The Computer Has Been Interrupted.

INDEX

REAR HALFSHAFT

REPLACE

1. Raise and support vehicle.
2. Remove rear tire and wheel assemblies.
3. Remove exhaust muffler.
4. Index mark across halfshaft flange and differential flange to ensure proper alignment during installation.
5. Remove halfshaft outer retaining nut, then push halfshaft through wheel hub.
6. Remove halfshaft flange to differential flange retaining bolts, then the halfshaft.
7. Reverse procedure to install. Ensure index markings are aligned properly.

DIFFERENTIAL HOUSING

REPLACE

1. Raise and support vehicle.
2. Remove propeller shaft as outlined in "Propeller Shaft, Replace."
3. Drain differential fluid into suitable container.
4. Support differential housing with suitable jack.
5. Separate halfshafts from rear differential as outlined in "Rear Halfshaft, Replace."
6. Remove front and rear differential housing to carrier mounting bolts.
7. Remove differential housing from vehicle.
8. Reverse procedure to install.

DIFFERENTIAL CARRIER

REPLACE

1. Remove righthand and lefthand brake caliper mounting bolts, then position calipers away from suspension components using suitable wire.
2. Remove rear portion of exhaust system including muffler.

3. Remove parking brake cable from brake cable equalizer.
4. Remove righthand and lefthand wheel speed sensor retaining bolts, then the sensors.
5. Remove righthand and lefthand halfshaft as outlined in "Rear Halfshaft, Replace."
6. Remove coil spring as outlined in "Coil Spring, Replace."
7. Remove shock absorbers as outlined in "Shock Absorber, Replace."
8. Remove propeller shaft as outlined in "Propeller Shaft, Replace."
9. Remove fuel pump retaining bolts, then position pump away from axle carrier using suitable wire. **Do not remove any fuel lines.**
10. Remove differential housing as outlined in "Differential Housing, Replace."
11. Support differential carrier with suitable transmission jack.
12. Remove differential carrier mounting bolts, then lower carrier assembly from frame.
13. Reverse procedure to install. Inspect rear wheel alignment.

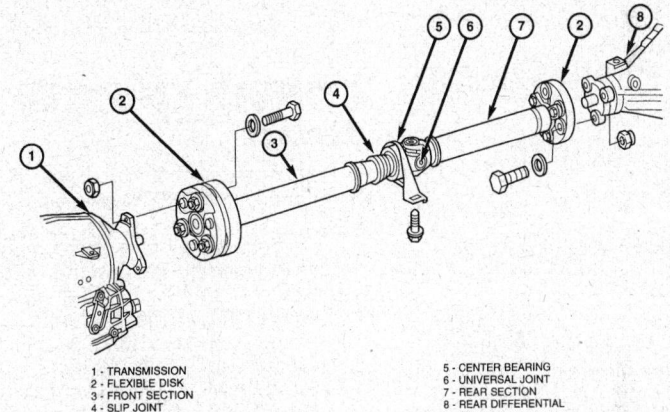

1 - TRANSMISSION
2 - FLEXIBLE DISK
3 - FRONT SECTION
4 - SLIP JOINT
5 - CENTER BEARING
6 - UNIVERSAL JOINT
7 - REAR SECTION
8 - REAR DIFFERENTIAL

ARM0300000000580

Fig. 1 Exploded view of propeller shaft

PROPELLER SHAFT

REPLACE

When removing or servicing the propeller shaft, never allow shaft to drop or hang from universal joints. Suspend shafts to the underside of the vehicle using suitable wire, **Fig. 1.**

1. Raise and support vehicle.
2. Remove exhaust system.
3. Remove center exhaust heat shield retaining nuts, then the heat shield.
4. Remove rear transmission tunnel support bracket bolts, then the support bracket.
5. Support transmission using suitable jack stand.
6. Remove transmission mount and transmission crossmember retaining bolts, then the crossmember.
7. Index mark across front driveshaft flange to transmission flange, and rear axle pinion to drive shaft flange to ensure proper alignment during installation.
8. Remove rear axle pinion to propeller shaft flange retaining bolts, then the

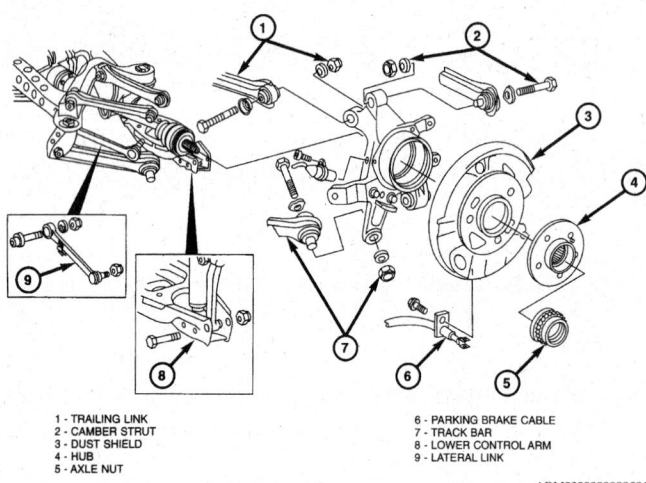

1 - TRAILING LINK
2 - CAMBER STRUT
3 - DUST SHIELD
4 - HUB
5 - AXLE NUT
6 - PARKING BRAKE CABLE
7 - TRACK BAR
8 - LOWER CONTROL ARM
9 - LATERAL LINK

ARM0300000000581

Fig. 2   Exploded view of rear wheel knuckle

propeller shaft from pinion flange.

9. Remove front propeller shaft flange to transmission flange retaining bolts, then the propeller shaft from transmission flange.
10. Remove center bearing retaining bolts, then the propeller shaft from vehicle, **Fig. 1.**
11. Reverse procedure to install. Ensure index markings are aligned properly.

HUB & BEARING
REPLACE

1. Remove disc brake caliper and rotor as outlined in "Disc Brakes" chapter.
2. Remove parking brake shoes as outlined in "Disc Brakes" chapter.
3. Remove rear halfshaft as outlined in "Rear Halfshaft, Replace."
4. Remove snap ring from rear hub assembly.
5. Remove bearing on hub using bearing tool No. 9181, or equivalent.
6. Clamp rear axle halfshaft flange into suitable soft jawed vise.
7. Remove inner bearing race from rear axle halfshaft flange by screwing suitable pair of clamping pliers onto bearing tool No. 9181, or equivalent, then tighten pliers.
8. Place thrust piece with large diameter on rear axle halfshaft flange, then position complete bearing tool No. 9181, or equivalent, over bearing race.
9. Clamp bearing race firmly at upper grooves of clamping pliers, above sleeve of bearing tool No. 9181, or equivalent.
10. Remove inner bearing race from halfshaft using bearing tool No. 9181, or equivalent.
11. Inspect halfshaft flange runout, allowable lateral and radial runout is .001–.018 inch.
12. Reverse procedure to install, noting the following:
    a. Install bearing onto wheel carrier until it touches shoulder of wheel carrier using bearing tool No. 9181, or equivalent.
    b. Install washer, ensure snap ring is

seated into wheel carrier retaining groove.
    c. Install halfshaft flange onto rear axle using soft faced mallet.

SPINDLE KNUCKLE
REPLACE

For component descriptions and locations when servicing wheel knuckle, refer to **Fig. 2.**

1. Remove disc brake caliper and rotor as outlined in "Disc Brakes" chapter.
2. Remove parking brake shoes as outlined in "Disc Brakes" chapter.
3. Remove parking brake cable retaining clip at caliper, then the cable.
4. Remove wheel speed sensor retaining bolt, then the wheel speed sensor.
5. Remove halfshaft as outlined in "Rear Halfshaft, Replace."
6. Remove disc brake dust shield retaining bolts, then the dust shield.
7. Remove camber strut, trailing link and lateral link bolts and nuts.
8. Remove track rod as outlined in "Track Rod, Replace."
9. Remove lower control arm as outlined in "Control Arm, Replace."
10. Remove wheel knuckle from vehicle.
11. Reverse procedure to install. Ensure rear axle halfshaft is horizontal before tightening bolts and nuts.

SHOCK ABSORBER
REPLACE

Vehicle must be standing with weight on all four wheels before removing shock absorber mounting hardware.

1. Remove upper shock absorber retaining nut and hardware.
2. Raise and support vehicle.
3. Remove lower control arm plastic protective cover retaining bolt, then the protective cover.
4. Remove lower shock absorber to control arm mounting bolt and nut.
5. Remove shock absorber from lower control arm.
6. Reverse procedure to install.

COIL SPRING
REPLACE

1. Raise and support vehicle.
2. Remove tire and wheel assembly.
3. Remove lower control arm plastic shield retaining bolts, then the plastic shield.
4. Remove shock absorber to control arm retaining bolts.
5. Raise control arm until axle shaft is in a horizontal position, using suitable floor jack.
6. Compress coil spring, using coil spring compressor tool No. 9152 and compressor plate tool No. 9150, or equivalents.
7. Remove control arm to frame retaining bolts.
8. Slowly lower control arm, then remove floor jack.
9. Swing control arm downward to release spring form mounting tabs.
10. Remove coil spring from vehicle.
11. Reverse procedure to install.

CONTROL ARM
REPLACE

1. Raise and support vehicle.
2. Remove tire and wheel assembly.
3. Remove coil spring as outlined in "Coil Spring, Replace."
4. Remove shock absorber as outlined in "Shock Absorber, Replace."
5. Remove stabilizer bar link to lower control arm retaining bolt, then the stabilizer bar link.
6. Remove lower control arm to wheel carrier bolts, then the lower control arm.
7. Reverse procedure to install.

CAMBER STRUT
REPLACE

1. Raise and support vehicle.
2. Remove tire and wheel assembly.
3. Remove camber strut to axle carrier retaining bolt.
4. Remove outer camber strut to wheel carrier retaining bolt.
5. Remove camber strut.
6. Reverse procedure to install. Vehicle must have full weight on four wheels before tightening retaining bolts.

TRAILING LINK
REPLACE

1. Raise and support vehicle.
2. Remove tire and wheel assembly.
3. Remove inner and outer trailing link to wheel carrier retaining bolts.
4. Remove trailing link from vehicle.
5. Reverse procedure to install. Vehicle must have full weight on four wheels before tightening retaining bolts.

TRACK ROD
REPLACE

1. Raise and support vehicle.
2. Remove tire and wheel assembly.

3. Remove inner track bar to axle carrier retaining bolt.
4. Remove outer track bar wheel carrier retaining bolt.
5. Remove track bar using suitable plastic headed hammer to loosen rubber mounts from guides.
6. Reverse procedure to install. Vehicle must have full weight on four wheels

before tightening retaining bolts.

LATERAL LINK
REPLACE

1. Raise and support vehicle.
2. Remove tire and wheel assembly.
3. Remove lateral link to axle carrier retaining bolt.

4. Remove lateral link ball joint stud to wheel carrier retaining nut.
5. Remove lateral link ball joint stud from carrier using ball joint removal tool No. 9168, or equivalent.
6. Remove lateral link from vehicle.
7. Reverse procedure to install. Axle shaft must be horizontal before tightening retaining bolts.

TIGHTENING SPECIFICATIONS

Year	Component	Torque/Ft. Lbs.
2004–05	Camber Strut Bolts	52
	Differential Housing To Carrier Bolt (Front)	82
	Differential Housing To Carrier Bolt (Rear)	33
	Differential Housing To Carrier Nut (Center)	66
	Halfshaft Connecting Flange Bolts	52
	Halfshaft Outer Nut	164
	Heat Shield Nuts	89①
	Lateral Link To Axle Carrier Bolt	52
	Lateral Link To Wheel Carrier Bolt	22
	Lower Control Arm To Axle Carrier Bolt	52
	Lower Control Arm To Wheel Carrier Bolt	88
	Pinion Shaft Nut	133
	Propeller Shaft Center Bearing Support Bolts	33
	Propeller Shaft To Axle Flange Bolts	44
	Propeller Shaft To Transmission Flange Bolts	44
	Track Bar Bolts	52
	Trailing Arm Bolts	52
	Transmission Crossmember Bolts	33
	Transmission Mount Bolts	33
	Transmission Tunnel Bolts	15
	Shock Absorber (Lower) Bolt	41
	Shock Absorber (Upper) Nut	13
	Stabilizer Bar Clamp Bolts	15
	Stabilizer Bar To Stabilizer Link Nut	15
	Stabilizer Link To Stabilizer Bar Bolt	22

① — Inch lbs.

Front Suspension & Steering

NOTE: On Air Bag Equipped Models, Refer To "Air Bag System Precautions" Located In The Front Of This Manual For System Disarming & Arming Procedures.

NOTE: Refer To "Computer Relearn Procedures" Located In The Front Of This Manual When Battery Power To The Computer Has Been Interrupted.

INDEX

PRECAUTIONS

Air Bag Systems

Refer to "Air Bag System Precautions" in the front of this manual for system disarming and arming procedures.

Battery Ground Cable

Prior to service, disconnect battery ground cable and isolate as required.

HUB & BEARING

REPLACE

1. Raise and support vehicle.
2. Remove tire and wheel assembly.
3. Remove brake caliper retaining bolts, then suspend caliper aside using suitable wire.
4. Remove bearing hub center dust cap, **Fig. 1.**
5. Remove brake rotor retaining bolt, then the brake rotor.
6. Remove bearing hub retaining nut, then the hub and tapered roller bearing from spindle.
7. Reverse procedure to install, then adjust wheel bearing end play as follows:
   a. Ensure brake pads are pushed back and not in contact with brake rotor.
   b. Loosen hub nut until a slight amount of endplay is achieved.
   c. Attach a dial indicator as outlined, **Fig. 2.**
   d. Adjust wheel bearing endplay by turning hub nut in stages while pushing and puling firmly on brake rotor.
   e. Dial indicator should show endplay of .004–.008 inch.

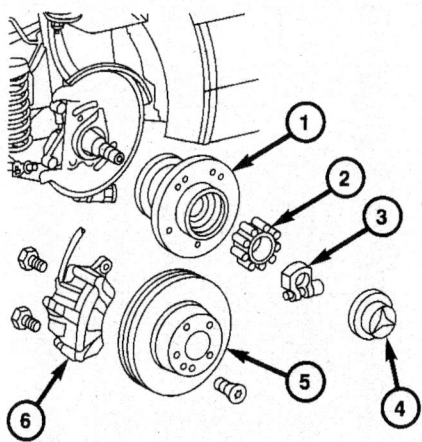

1 Front wheel hub
2 Tapered roller bearing
3 Hub nut and bolt
4 Dust cap
5 Brake rotor
6 Brake caliper

ARM0300000000575

Fig. 1 Hub & bearing replacement

BALL JOINT INSPECTION

The upper ball joint is serviced with the upper control arm.
1. Raise and support front of vehicle.
2. Grasp tire at top and bottom, then apply in and out force on wheel and tire assembly.
3. While applying force to tire, look for movement between upper or lower ball joint and control arm.
4. If there is any movement in upper or lower ball joints, replace ball joint as outlined in "Ball Joint, Replace."

BALL JOINT

REPLACE

Lower

1. Raise and support vehicle.
2. Remove tire and wheel assembly.
3. Remove front brake caliper retaining bolts, then position caliper aside using suitable wire to suspend caliper.
4. Remove one brake rotor to hub retaining bolt, then the brake rotor.
5. Remove three retaining bolts from front hub dust shield, then the dust shield.
6. Remove coil spring as outlined in "Coil Spring, Replace."
7. Remove ball joint retaining nuts, then using ball joint removal tool No. 9168, or equivalent, press ball joint from lower control arm and steering knuckle mountings.
8. Reverse procedure to install.

Upper

The upper ball joint is serviced with the upper control arm.

COIL SPRING

REPLACE

1. Remove tire and wheel assembly.
2. Remove shock absorber as outlined in "Shock Absorber, Replace."
3. Support lower control arm with suitable floor jack.
4. Raise lower control arm until arm is almost level.
5. Compress front spring carefully using spring compressor tools No. 9151 and 9152, or equivalent.
6. Remove sway bar retaining clamp nuts, then position sway bar aside.
7. Remove nuts from lower control arm

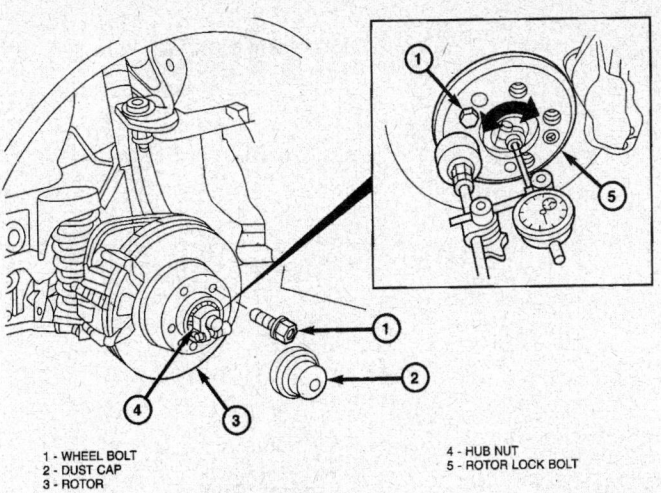

1 - WHEEL BOLT
2 - DUST CAP
3 - ROTOR

4 - HUB NUT
5 - ROTOR LOCK BOLT

ARM0300000000576

Fig. 2 Wheel bearing endplay adjustment

1 - UPPER CONTROL ARM
2 - TIE ROD END
3 - WHEEL SPEED SENSOR
4 - UPPER BALL JOINT NUT
5 - DUST SHIELD BOLT
6 - ROTOR LOCK BOLT
7 - ROTOR
8 - DUST CAP

9 - HUB NUT
10 - BEARING
11 - HUB
12 - DUST SHIELD
13 - TIE ROD END NUT
14 - LOWER BALL JOINT NUT
15 - CALIPER BOLT
16 - LOWER BALL JOINT

ARM0300000000574

Fig. 3 Steering knuckle replacement

retaining nuts, then the lower control arm while holding coil spring.
8. Slowly lower coil spring from vehicle.
9. Reverse procedure to install.

SHOCK ABSORBER
REPLACE

Vehicle must be standing with weight on all four wheels before removing shock absorber upper mounting hardware.
1. Remove upper shock absorber retaining nut, washer and rubber mount.
2. Raise and support vehicle.
3. Remove lower shock absorber to control arm mounting bolt and nut.
4. Remove shock absorber from lower control arm, then the shock absorber by pulling downward out form vehicle.
5. Remove mounting hardware from shock absorber.
6. Reverse procedure to install.

CONTROL ARM
REPLACE
Lower

Refer to "Coil Spring, Replace" for lower control arm replacement procedure.

Upper

The shock absorber must remain installed to remove the upper control arm.
1. Remove air cleaner housing to access upper control arm retaining bolt and nut located inside engine compartment.
2. Raise and support vehicle.
3. Remove tire and wheel assembly, then support lower control arm with suitable floor jack.
4. Raise floor jack to relieve any tension on brake lines or speed sensor electrical connection.
5. Secure steering knuckle to shock absorber using suitable wire.
6. Remove upper ball joint to steering knuckle retaining nut, then using ball joint removal tool No. 9168, or equivalent, press ball joint stud from steering knuckle.
7. Remove control arm upper retaining bolt and nut, then the upper control arm assembly.
8. Reverse procedure to install. **Tighten all bolts and nuts with vehicle at normal ride height.**

STEERING KNUCKLE
REPLACE

The shock absorber must remain installed when removing the steering knuckle.
1. Raise and support vehicle.
2. Remove hub and bearing assembly as outlined in "Hub & Bearing, Replace."
3. Remove three disc brake dust shield hex bolts, then the dust shield, **Fig. 3.**
4. Remove Wheel Speed Sensor (WSS) retaining bolt and pull sensor straight out of steering knuckle.
5. Remove tie rod end to steering knuckle retaining nut, then using tie rod end removal tool C-3894–A, or equivalent, press tie rod end stud from steering knuckle.
6. Remove lower ball joint to steering knuckle stud retaining nut, then using ball joint removal tool No. 9168, or equivalent, press ball joint stud from steering knuckle.
7. Remove upper ball joint to steering knuckle stud retaining nut, then using ball joint removal tool No. 9168, or equivalent, push upper ball joint stud from steering knuckle.
8. Remove steering knuckle.
9. Reverse procedure to install.

STABILIZER BAR
REPLACE

1. Remove righthand and lefthand stabilizer bar retaining nuts and clamps from lower control arms.
2. Remove righthand and lefthand stabilizer bar retaining nuts and clamps from front mounting brackets.
3. Remove stabilizer bar from vehicle.
4. Reverse procedure to install.

TIE ROD END
REPLACE

1. Raise and support vehicle, then remove tire and wheel assembly.
2. Loosen tie rod end locknut.
3. Remove outer tie rod to steering knuckle retaining nut.
4. Remove tie rod end from steering knuckle using tie rod end removal tool No. C-3894-A, or equivalent.
5. Remove tie rod end from drag link.
6. Reverse procedure to install. Inspect toe setting prior to tightening adjustment sleeve locknut.

PITMAN ARM
REPLACE

1. Raise and support vehicle.
2. Remove drag link to pitman arm retaining nut.
3. Remove drag link from pitman arm using ball joint removal tool No. 9168, or equivalent.
4. Measure and record distance between pitman arm and steering gear using suitable caliper gauge, **Fig. 4.**
5. Remove snap ring retainer from pitman arm shaft.
6. Remove pitman arm from gear box using suitable pitman arm removal tool.
7. Reverse procedure to install. Ensure distance between pitman arm and steering gear is same as recorded.

DRAG LINK
REPLACE

1. Raise and support vehicle.
2. Remove steering damper to drag link bolt and nut, then position damper aside.

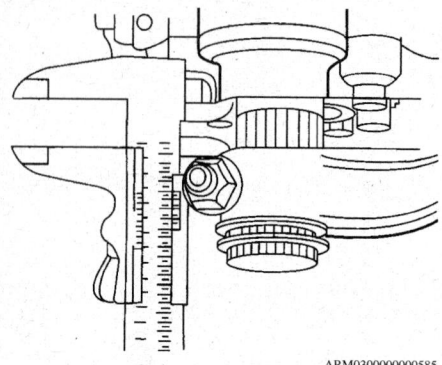

Fig. 4 Pitman arm measurement

3. Remove pitman arm and idler arm to drag link retaining nuts.
4. Remove pitman arm and idler arm from drag link using ball joint removal tool No. 9168, or equivalent.
5. Remove tie rod end as outlined in "Tie Rod End, Replace."
6. Remove drag link.
7. Reverse procedure to install.

POWER STEERING GEAR
REPLACE

Refer to **Fig. 5,** when replacing steering gear.

1. Lock steering wheel in straight ahead position. **Ensure steering wheel does not move when replacing steering gear or damage to clock spring will occur.**
2. Drain power steering fluid into suitable container.
3. Raise and support vehicle.
4. Remove drag link as outlined in "Drag Link, Replace."
5. Remove outer tie rod end as outlined in "Tie Rod End, Replace."
6. Remove pitman arm as outlined in "Pitman Arm, Replace."
7. Remove lefthand front cross brace, **Fig. 6.**
8. Remove steering fluid supply and return lines at steering gear.
9. Remove steering gear to steering shaft coupler pinch bolt.
10. Remove steering shaft from steering gear.
11. Remove engine ground strap from vehicle frame.
12. Remove lefthand and rigthand engine mount retaining bolts.
13. Raise engine approximately two inches using suitable transmission jack placed under lefthand side of engine.

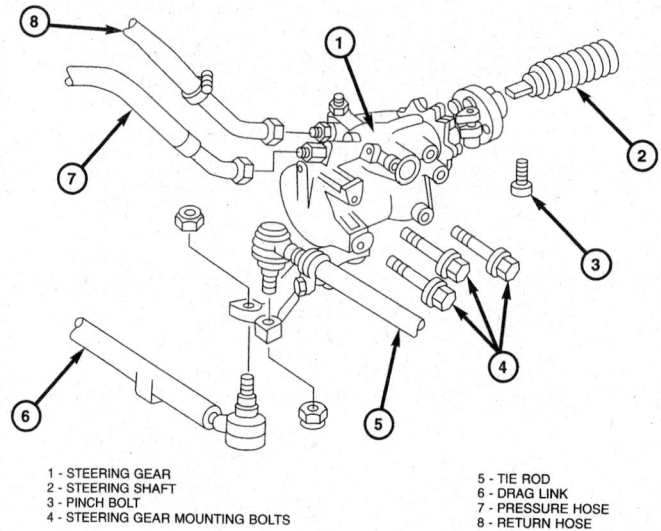

1 - STEERING GEAR
2 - STEERING SHAFT
3 - PINCH BOLT
4 - STEERING GEAR MOUNTING BOLTS
5 - TIE ROD
6 - DRAG LINK
7 - PRESSURE HOSE
8 - RETURN HOSE

Fig. 5 Exploded view of steering gear

14. Remove steering gear mounting bolts, carefully slide steering shaft from steering gear.
15. Remove steering gear from vehicle.
16. Reverse procedure to install, noting the following:
    a. Ensure steering gear is in center position, by aligning steering shaft and housing cover alignment marks.**Do not use force or damage will occur to lower steering shaft collapsible tubing.**
    b. Tighten mounting bolts and fluid lines.

POWER STEERING PUMP
REPLACE

1. Drain power steering fluid into suitable container.
2. Remove reservoir supply and return hoses.
3. Remove serpentine drive belt as outlined in "Engine" section.
4. Remove power steering pump to engine mounting bolts, then the steering pump.
5. Remove steering fluid reservoir C-type retaining clip.
6. Remove steering fluid reservoir.
7. Reverse procedure to install.

POWER STEERING SYSTEM BLEED

1. Fill fluid reservoir to correct level, allow fluid to settle for at least two minutes.

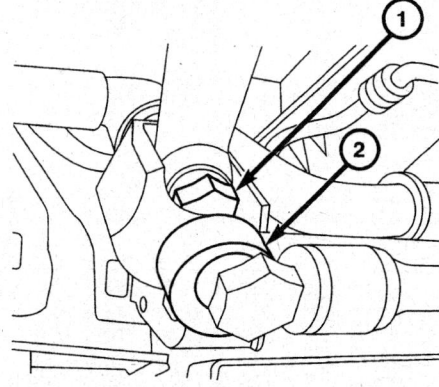

Fig. 6 Lefthand front cross brace replace

2. Start and allow engine to run for a few seconds, then turn engine off.
3. When fluid level remains constant after running engine, raise front wheels off ground.
4. Turn steering wheel righthand and left, lightly contacting wheel stops at least 20 times.
5. Add steering fluid if required.
6. Lower vehicle.
7. Start engine and turn steering wheel from lock to lock 2–3 times.
8. Inspect steering fluid and add if required.
9. If fluid is foamy or looks milky, allow vehicle to stand a few minutes, then repeat procedure.

TIGHTENING SPECIFICATIONS

Year	Component	Torque/Ft. Lbs.
2004–05	Drag Link To Idler Arm Nut	37
	Drag Link To Pitman Arm Nut	37
	Front Shock Absorber Lower Nut	41
	Front Shock Absorber Upper Nut	13
	Front Sway Bar Bushing Nut M8	15
	Front Sway Bar Bushing Nut M10	30
	Front Sway Bar To Lower Control Arm Nut	15
	Idler Arm Mounting Bolt	37
	Idler Arm Pinch Bolt	41
	Lower Ball Joint To Lower Control Arm	77
	Lower Ball Joint To Steering Knuckle	103
	Lower Control Arm To Frame Nut	88
	Outer Tie Rod To Steering Knuckle Nut	37
	Power Steering Fluid Pressure Hose	30
	Power Steering Pump Mounting	15
	Power Steering Return Tube	30
	Steering Column Pinch Bolt	22
	Steering Coupling Pinch Bolt	22
	Steering Gear Locknut	44
	Steering Gear Mounting Bolts	44
	Upper Control Arm To Body Nut	50
	Upper Control Arm To Steering Knuckle Bolt	33

Wheel Alignment

INDEX

PRELIMINARY INSPECTION

Before any attempt is made to change or correct wheel alignment, the following inspections and required corrections must be made.

1. Ensure tire pressure is at recommended pressure, all tires should be same size and in good condition and have approximately same wear.
2. Inspect both front tire and wheel assemblies for radial runout.
3. Inspect lower ball joint and steering linkage for looseness.
4. Inspect for broken or damaged front and rear springs.
5. Just prior to each alignment reading,

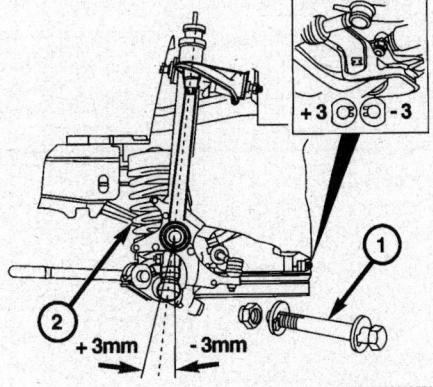

ARM0300000000578

Fig. 1 Caster repair bolt installation

the vehicle should be bounced (rear first, then front) by grasping bumper at center and bouncing each end of vehicle an equal number of times. Always release bumpers at bottom of down cycle.

FRONT WHEEL ALIGNMENT

Caster

1. Prepare vehicle as outlined in "Preliminary Inspection."
2. Compress front coil spring as outlined in "Front Suspension & Steering" section.

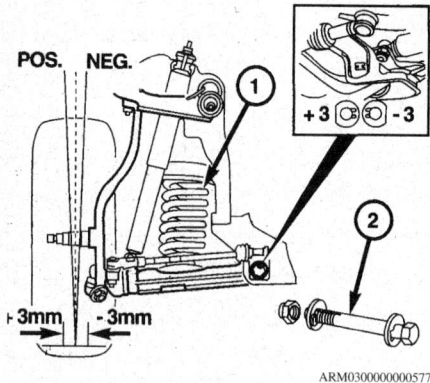

Fig. 2 Camber repair bolt installation

3. Install adjusting bolt, **Fig. 1,** then hand tighten nut.
4. Release coil spring as outlined in "Front Suspension & Steering" section.
5. Lower vehicle, then bounce vehicle several times to settle suspension.
6. Adjust caster to specifications by turning adjusting bolt using suitable wrench.
7. **Torque** adjusting bolt and nut to 88 ft. lbs., counter bolt movement using suitable hex wrench.

Camber

1. Prepare vehicle as outlined in "Preliminary Inspection."
2. Compress front coil spring as outlined in "Front Suspension & Steering" section.
3. Install adjusting bolt, **Fig. 2,** then hand tighten nut.
4. Release coil spring as outlined in "Front Suspension & Steering" section.
5. Lower vehicle, then bounced vehicle several times to settle suspension.
6. Adjust camber to specifications by turning adjusting bolt using suitable wrench.
7. **Torque** adjusting bolt and nut to 88 ft. lbs., counter bolt movement using suitable hex wrench.

Toe

The steering wheel is in the center position when the separating joint of the steering coupler and the notch on the steering gear are aligned above each other. If required offset the steering wheel by one tooth maximum.
1. Prepare vehicle as outlined in "Preliminary Inspection."
2. Ensure steering wheel is in center position, then hold with steering wheel clamp.
3. Loosen tie rod adjustment sleeve locknut.
4. Rotate adjustment sleeve to align toe to specifications. When setting toe, maximum threads exposed on tie rod can not exceed .78 inch (20mm).
5. **Torque** adjustment locknut to 37 ft. lbs.

REAR WHEEL ALIGNMENT
Caster

Rear axle caster is not adjustable. If

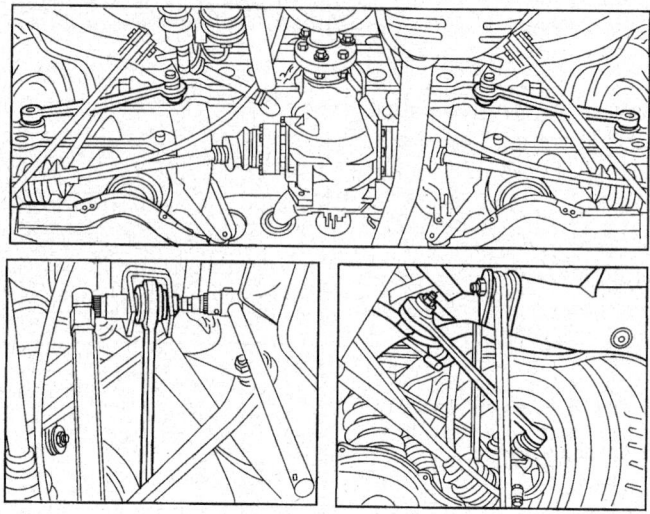

Fig. 3 Rear axle toe adjustment

caster is not within specifications, inspect rear suspension components for damage or wear as outlined in "Preliminary Inspection."

Camber

Rear axle camber is not adjustable. If caster is not within specifications, inspect rear suspension components for damage or wear as outlined in "Preliminary Inspection."

Toe

1. Prepare vehicle as outlined in "Preliminary Inspection."
2. Adjust toe to specification using left-hand and righthand tie rod to carrier mounting cam bolt, **Fig. 3.**

NOTE: Refer To The Rear Of This Manual For Manufacturer's Special Service Tool Supplies.

INDEX OF SERVICE OPERATIONS

Specifications

GENERAL ENGINE SPECIFICATIONS

Engine	Engine VIN Code①	Fuel System	Bore & Stroke, Inches	Compression Ratio	Net HP @ RPM	Maximum Torque, Ft. Lbs. @ RPM	Normal Oil Pressure, psi	
							Curb Idle	3000 RPM
2.0L SOHC	C	SMPI	3.45 X 3.27	9.8	132 @ 5600	130 @ 4600	4	25–80
2.0L SOHC	F	SMPI	3.45 X 3.27	9.8	150 @ 6500	135 @ 4400	4	25–80
2.4L DOHC	S	SMPI	3.45 X 3.98	8.1	220 @ 5100	245 @ 4400	4	25–80

DOHC — Dual Overhead Cam
SMPI — Sequential Multi-Port Fuel Injection

SOHC — Single Overhead Cam
① — Eighth digit of VIN denotes engine code.

TUNE UP SPECIFICATIONS

Engine	Spark Plug Gap, Inch	Ignition Timing		Curb Idle Speed	Fuel Pump Pressure, psi	Valve Clearance, Inch
		Firing Order ②	°BTDC			
2.0L	.035	1-3-4-2	①	550–1300	49–50	③
2.4L	.050	1-3-4-2	①	—	—	③

BTDC — Before Top Dead Center
① — Direct Ignition System (DIS); not adjustable.

② — Refer to **Fig. A,** for sparkplug wire connections.

③ — Equipped w/non-adjustable hydraulic lash adjusters.

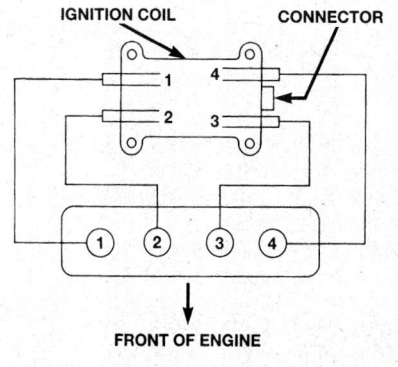

Fig. A

FRONT WHEEL ALIGNMENT SPECIFICATIONS

Year	Camber, Degrees①		Caster, Degrees①		Toe In, Degrees		Ball Joint Wear
	Limits	Desired	Limits	Desired	Limits	Desired	
2001–05	–.4 to +.4	0	+1.6 to +3.6②	+2.6	–.1 to +.3	+.1	③

① — Reference angle only; not adjustable.

② — Side to side differential not to exceed 0.1°.

③ — Refer to "Ball Joint Inspection" in "Front Suspension & Steering."

REAR WHEEL ALIGNMENT SPECIFICATIONS

Year	Camber Angle, Degrees①		Total Toe, Degrees①		Thrust Angle, Degrees①
	Limits	Desired	Limits	Desired	
2001–05	−.65 to +.15	−.25	−.10 to +.50	+.30	−.10 to +.10

① — Reference angle only. Non-adjustable.

VEHICLE RIDE HEIGHT SPECIFICATIONS

Year	Body Style	Manufacturer's Original Tire Size	Front Dim.	Front Specification Inches	Front Specification mm	Rear Dim.	Rear Specification Inches	Rear Specification mm
2001–05	Neon	①	A	26.14–26.78	664–680	B	26.41–27.05	671–687
2003–05	SRT-4	①	A	26.65–27.29	677–693	B	27.12–27.76	691–705

A Dim. — Ground to Lower Edge of Front Wheel Well

B Dim. — Ground to Lower Edge of Rear Wheel Well

① — See door sticker or inside of glove box for manufacturer's original tire size specifications. If tires on vehicle do not match manufacturer's original tire size & measurement is not within limits, it will be required to refer to the "Non-Standard Tire & Wheel Size Adjustment To Ride Height Specification & Tire Size Adjustment Charts" in the front of this manual for approximate changes in ride height specifications.

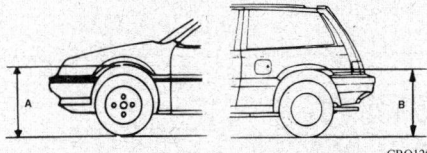

CRQ125

Fig. A   Dimensions A & B

FLUID CAPACITIES & COOLING SYSTEM DATA

Year	Engine	Coolant Capacity, Qts.	Coolant Type	Radiator Cap Relief Pressure, Lbs.	Thermo. Opening Temp., °F	Fuel Tank, Gals.	Engine Oil Refill, Qts.③	Auto. Transaxle Oil, Qts.②	Man. Transaxle Oil, Pts.
2001–05	2.0L	6.5	Ethylene Glycol	14–18	192–199	12.5	4.5	①	5.0–5.6
	2.4L	6.5	Ethylene Glycol	14–18	192–199	12.5	5.0	①	4.8–5.2

① — Fluid change only, 4.0 qts. After overhaul, 8.6 qts.

② — Approximate. Make final inspection w/dipstick.

③ — Includes oil filter.

LUBRICANT DATA

Year	Transaxle Automatic	Transaxle Manual	Power Steering	Brake System
2001	Mopar ATF+4 Type 9602	Mopar Type MS 9417	Mopar No. 5010304AA	DOT 3
2002–05	Mopar ATF+4 Type 9602	Mopar ATF+4 Type 9602	Mopar ATF+4 Type 9602	DOT 3

Electrical

NOTE: On Air Bag Equipped Models, Refer To "Air Bag System Precautions" Located In The Front Of This Manual For System Disarming & Arming Procedures.

NOTE: Refer To "Computer Relearn Procedures" Located In The Front Of This Manual When Battery Power To The Computer Has Been Interrupted.

INDEX

PRECAUTIONS

Air Bag Systems

Refer to "Air Bag System Precautions" in the front of this manual for system disarming and arming procedures.

Battery Ground Cable

Prior to service, disconnect battery ground cable and isolate as required.

FUSE PANEL LOCATION

The fuse block is positioned on a mounting bracket up and under the lefthand side of the instrument panel, secured by two screws. It can be accessed by removing the instrument panel end cap.

FUEL PUMP RELAY LOCATION

The fuel pump relay is located on the lefthand side of the engine compartment near the battery, in the Power Distribution Center (PDC).

RELAY CENTER LOCATION

The relay center is located on the lefthand side of the engine compartment, next to the battery.

STARTER

REPLACE

1. Raise and support vehicle using a suitable lift.
2. **On models equipped with 2.0L H/O engine and automatic transaxle,** disconnect inlet hose from intake manifold, then reposition air cleaner assembly.
3. **On models equipped with automatic transaxle,** remove two upper bracket bolts from intake support, then the oil pan and intake support brackets.
4. **On all models,** remove battery positive cable connector from starter assembly.
5. Disconnect latch and remove solenoid connector from starter assembly.
6. Remove starter attaching bolts, then the starter assembly.
7. Reverse procedure to install. **Torque** starter attaching bolts to 40 ft. lbs.

ALTERNATOR

REPLACE

2.0L Engine

1. Loosen alternator adjustment nut.
2. Raise and support vehicle.
3. Remove lower splash shield.
4. Disconnect alternator wiring.
5. Loosen alternator pivot bolt and remove alternator drive belt.
6. Remove pivot bracket mounting bolts.
7. Remove pivot nut from T-bolt while supporting alternator.
8. Lower alternator and remove through wheelwell.

9. Reverse procedure to install, noting the following:
   a. **Torque** alternator mounting bolts to 40 ft. lbs.
   b. **Torque** alternator feed terminal nut to 72 inch lbs.

2.4L Engine

1. Remove alternator heat shield attaching bolts.
2. Remove nut from upper T-bolt adjustment bracket.
3. Raise and support vehicle.
4. Remove right front wheel assembly.
5. Remove accessory drive splash shield from under righthand side of vehicle.
6. Remove drive axle retaining nut.
7. Remove lower control arm to steering knuckle retaining nut, then separate control arm from steering knuckle.
8. Remove axle shaft bearing support retaining bolts.
9. Remove axle shaft from transaxle. Place a suitable drain pan under transaxle to catch fluid.
10. Remove lower heat shield, then the alternator heat shield.
11. Disconnect alternator electrical connectors.
12. Loosen accessory drive belt T-bolt.
13. Remove pencil strut, **Fig. 1.**
14. Loosen lower alternator pivot bolt.
15. Remove alternator belt.
16. Remove alternator from lower mounting bracket and position aside.
17. Remove lower mounting bracket.
18. Remove alternator through axle shaft opening.
19. Reverse procedure to install, noting the following:

a. **Torque** lower bracket mounting bolts to 40 ft. lbs.
b. **Torque** axle shaft bearing support bolts to 40 ft. lbs.
c. **Torque** control arm to steering knuckle nut to 70 ft. lbs.
d. **Torque** axle shaft nut to 180 ft. lbs.
e. **Torque** accessory drive belt T-bolt to 40 ft. lbs.
f. **Torque** lower alternator pivot bolt to 40 ft. lbs.
g. **Torque** heat shield bolts to 40 ft. lbs.
h. **Torque** upper adjustment bracket nut sto 18 ft. lbs.

COIL PACK
REPLACE

1. Disconnect coil pack electrical connector and remove mounting bolts.
2. Remove coil pack from valve cover.
3. Reverse procedure to install. **Torque** coil pack to valve cover bolts to 106 inch lbs.

IGNITION LOCK
REPLACE

Refer to "Ignition Switch, Replace" for ignition lock replacement procedure.

IGNITION SWITCH
REPLACE

1. Turn ignition to Run position.
2. Depress lock cylinder retaining tab through hole in lower column shroud and remove lock cylinder using suitable tool.
3. Remove steering column upper and lower shrouds as required.
4. Disconnect ignition switch electrical connectors.
5. Remove ignition switch mounting screw.
6. Depress retaining tabs and pull ignition switch from steering column.
7. Reverse procedure to install, ensuring ignition switch and actuator rod in lock housing are both in Run position.

CLUTCH START SWITCH
REPLACE

1. Remove lefthand lower instrument panel bezel.
2. Disconnect clutch master cylinder rod from clutch pedal pin. **Inspect plastic retainer upon removal, it must be replaced if damaged.**
3. Remove brake booster push rod retaining clip from brake pedal, then disengage rod from pedal.
4. Remove pedal assembly bracket to instrument panel nuts, then brake booster/pedal bracket to cowl nuts.
5. From under hood, pull brake master cylinder/booster forward enough to obtain pedal to bracket stud clearance.
6. Remove pedal bracket assembly, then the pedal pivot shaft and brake/clutch pedals.
7. Remove interlock/upstop switch assembly from brake/clutch pedal brack-

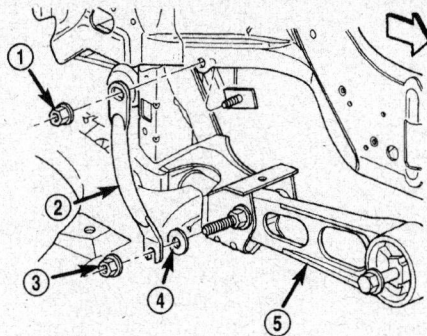

1 - NUT
2 - PENCIL STRUT
3 - NUT
4 - FLAT WASHER
5 - LOWER TORQUE STRUT

ARM0400000000242

Fig. 1 Pencil strut removal

et assembly by depressing four plastic wing tabs on each switch.
8. Reverse procedure to install, noting the following:
a. **Torque** pivot shaft nut, brake booster mounting nuts and pedal bracket to instrument panel nuts to 25 ft. lbs.
b. **Torque** adjustment screw to 70 inch lbs.

HEADLAMP SWITCH
REPLACE

Refer to "Multi-Function Switch, Replace" for procedures.

STOP LIGHT SWITCH
REPLACE

1. Depress brake pedal and rotate switch counterclockwise approximately 30°.
2. Pull switch rearward and remove from mounting bracket.
3. Disconnect electrical connector.
4. Pull switch plunger head out until ratchet sound stops.
5. Reverse procedure to install.

MULTI-FUNCTION SWITCH
REPLACE

1. Remove steering column upper and lower shrouds.
2. Disconnect all multi-function switch electrical connectors.
3. Remove mounting screws and multi-function switch.
4. Reverse procedure to install.

TURN SIGNAL SWITCH
REPLACE

Refer to "Multi-Function Switch, Replace" for procedure.

DIMMER SWITCH
REPLACE

Refer to "Multi-Function Switch, Replace" for procedure.

STEERING WHEEL
REPLACE

1. Place front wheels in straight ahead position.
2. Rotate steering wheel 180° clockwise.
3. Lock steering with column lock cylinder.
4. Remove speed control switch and connector.
5. Remove air bag as outlined in "Passive Restraint Systems" section.
6. Remove steering wheel mounting nut and vibration damper, if equipped.
7. Remove steering wheel while avoiding damage to clockspring wiring using appropriate puller tool.
8. Reverse procedure to install, noting the following:
a. Install steering wheel ensuring flats on hub align with clockspring.
b. **Torque** steering wheel mounting nut to 40 ft. lbs.

INSTRUMENT CLUSTER
REPLACE

1. Remove A-pillar moldings using trim stick tool No. C-4755, or equivalent.
2. Remove instrument panel top cover and cluster bezel.
3. Remove cluster housing to base panel mounting screws.
4. Pull cluster rearward to disconnect from base panel.
5. Remove cluster assembly.
6. Reverse procedure to install.

RADIO
REPLACE

1. Remove instrument panel center module bezel.
2. Remove radio mounting screws and pull radio out of instrument panel.
3. Disconnect radio electrical connectors, ground wire and antenna lead.
4. Reverse procedure to install.

WIPER MOTOR
REPLACE

1. Remove wiper arms and blades.
2. Remove cowl cover to cowl screws at base of windshield opening.
3. Remove hood to cowl seal at leading edge of cowl cover. Pull seal toward front of vehicle.
4. Remove cowl cover.
5. Disconnect electrical connectors at wiper motor.
6. Remove windshield wiper module.
7. Remove motor crank linkage by inserting suitable screwdriver between crank and linkage, then twisting and lifting straight up.
8. Remove mounting screws and separate windshield wiper motor from linkage.
9. Reverse procedure to install, noting the following:
a. Add suitable unilube grease to socket.
b. **Torque** motor mounting screws to 45–55 inch lbs.

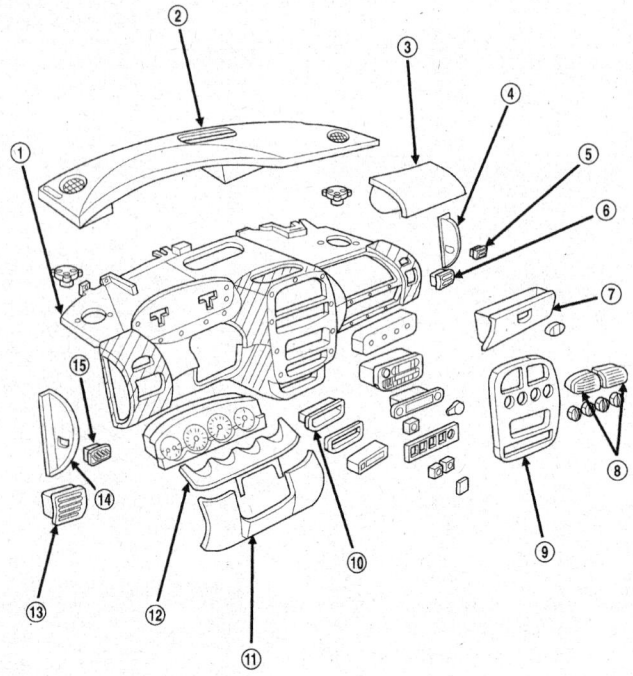

1 - INSTRUMENT PANEL ASSEMBLY
2 - UPPER COVER INSTRUMENT PANEL
3 - MODULE, PASSENGER SIDE AIRBAG
4 - END CAP, RIGHT
5 - DEMISTER GRILLE, RIGHT
6 - LOUVER, AIR OUTLET, RIGHT
7 - DOOR, GLOVE BOX
8 - LOUVER, AIR OUTLET, CENTER

9 - BEZEL INSTRUMENT PANEL, CENTER
10 - BIN, LOWER STORAGE
11 - COVER, LOWER INSTRUMENT PANEL
12 - CLUSTER BEZEL
13 - LOUVER, AIR OUTLET, LEFT
14 - END CAP, LEFT
15 - DEMISTER GRILLE, LEFT

CR9140100078000X

Fig. 2 Exploded view of instrument panel. Neon

c. **Torque** drive link nut to 98–106 inch lbs.

WIPER SWITCH

REPLACE

Refer to "Multi-Function Switch, Replace" for procedures.

BLOWER MOTOR

REPLACE

Less A/C

1. Disconnect blower motor electrical connector.
2. Turn blower motor approximately ⅛ turn counterclockwise while pulling down on locking tab.
3. Remove blower motor from housing,
4. Reverse procedure to install.

With A/C

1. Remove righthand side scuff plate and pull back carpet.
2. Disconnect blower motor wiring connector.
3. Remove mounting screws and lower blower motor from housing.
4. Reverse procedure to install, taping silencer in position.

HEATER CORE

REPLACE

1. Drain coolant into suitable container.

2. Move front seats as far rearward as possible.
3. Ensure front wheels are locked in straight-ahead position, to prevent clockspring damage.
4. Remove A-pillar trim using trim stick tool No. C-4755, or equivalent.
5. Remove instrument panel top cover, **Fig. 2.**
6. Remove instrument cluster bezel.
7. Remove lefthand lower instrument panel cover by gently pulling rearward.
8. Remove steering column lower cover.
9. **On models equipped with speed control,** remove speed control switches from steering wheel.
10. **On all models,** remove driver's side air bag module to steering wheel mounting screws.
11. Disconnect air bag module electrical connectors, then remove module from steering wheel.
12. Hold steering wheel firmly in place, then remove steering wheel retaining nut.
13. **On models equipped with steering wheel damper weight,** remove weight from steering wheel.
14. **On all models,** remove steering wheel from steering column using a suitable steering wheel puller tool. **Do not pound on shaft.**
15. Remove key from ignition.
16. Remove steering column lower and upper shrouds.
17. Remove steering column coupler retaining pin.
18. Loosen pinch bolt nut, then remove

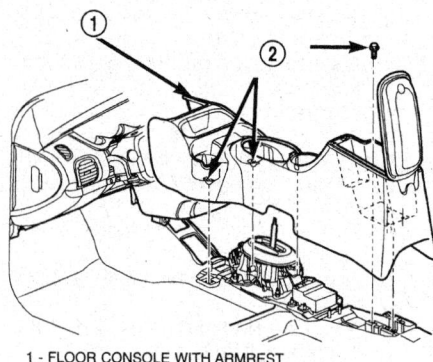

1 - FLOOR CONSOLE WITH ARMREST
2 - ATTACHING SCREWS

CR9140100079000X

Fig. 3 Floor center console. Neon

coupling pinch bolt.
19. Separate upper and lower steering column couplings.
20. **On models equipped with automatic transaxle,** disconnect transaxle ignition interlock cable from column. Depress tab on top of cable connector and remove cable from rear side of ignition cylinder housing.
21. **On all models,** remove two column to instrument panel lower mounting nuts.
22. Remove two column to instrument panel upper mounting nuts.
23. Lower steering column away from instrument panel.
24. Disconnect air bag clockspring electrical connector.
25. Disconnect electrical connectors at multi-function, windshield wiper, ignition and Sentry Key Immobilizer Module (SKIM) switches.
26. Carefully remove steering column from vehicle.
27. Remove instrument panel lefthand and righthand end covers.
28. Remove lefthand and righthand cowl side panels.
29. Apply parking brake, then remove floor center console, **Fig. 3.**
30. Remove Data Link Connector (DLC) from instrument panel by depressing side tabs.
31. Remove four instrument panel to firewall retaining bolts.
32. Remove two bolts on top of brake pedal support bracket.
33. Remove two center support bolts.
34. Remove lefthand and righthand A-pillar mounting bolts.
35. Disconnect vanity and rearview mirror electrical connector at top lefthand side of instrument panel.
36. Disconnect two harness connectors to heater HVAC at top righthand of instrument panel.
37. Remove both A/C outlet barrels.
38. Remove heater and A/C control knobs.
39. Gently pry outward on center bezel and remove from instrument panel.
40. Remove two heater and A/C control head retaining screws.
41. Disconnect electrical and vacuum connectors at heater and A/C control head.
42. Pull heater and A/C control head out of instrument panel, twist 90° and push back through opening. **Leave control**

cables in place.

43. Disconnect electrical connectors at Air Bag Control Module (ACM), parking brake warning lamp switch and PRNDL lamp.
44. Remove two bolts at top of brake pedal bracket, then carefully remove instrument panel from vehicle.
45. Disconnect heater hoses at dash panel.
46. Plug heater core outlets to prevent coolant spillage during housing removal.
47. **On models equipped with A/C,** evacuate and recover A/C refrigerant.
48. **On all models,** remove coolant reservoir fasteners and position reservoir aside.
49. Remove suction line at expansion valve. Plug refrigerant lines to prevent contamination of system.
50. Remove expansion valve. Plug all fittings.
51. Remove rubber drain tube extension from evaporator drain.
52. Disconnect vacuum harness at brake booster.
53. Unsnap and remove defroster duct.

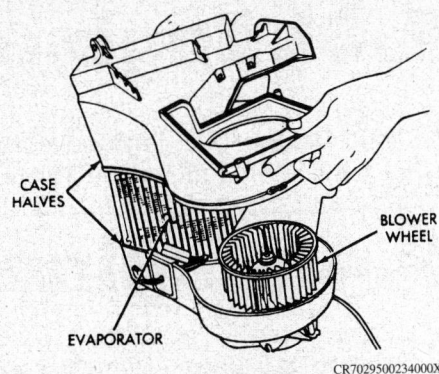

CR7029500234000X

Fig. 4 Evaporator case separation

54. Remove engine side of firewall housing mounting nuts.
55. Remove righthand side mounting screw.
56. Remove one remaining nut located on dash panel stud.
57. Disconnect electrical connectors as required.
58. Remove unit housing.

59. Separate air distribution outlet foam seals at case halves.
60. Remove foam seals at evaporator and heater core tubes.
61. Remove retaining clips and screws holding halves together.
62. Separate housing halves.
63. Lift heater core out of housing.
64. Reverse procedure to install.

EVAPORATOR CORE
REPLACE

1. Remove unit housing as outlined in "Heater Core, Replace."
2. Remove clips and screws to separate evaporator/blower case.
3. Remove evaporator case foam seal.
4. Remove mounting screws and air duct with recirculation door assembly.
5. Disconnect fin sensing switch.
6. Remove upper and lower clips and screws, then separate case halves, **Fig. 4**.
7. Remove evaporator.
8. Reverse procedure to install.

2.0L Engine

NOTE: Refer To "2.0L & 2.4L Engine" Section In The "Sebring Convertible, Sebring Sedan & Stratus Sedan" Chapter For Service Procedures On This Engine.

2.4L Engine

NOTE: On Air Bag Equipped Models, Refer To "Air Bag System Precautions" Located In The Front Of This Manual For System Disarming & Arming Procedures.

NOTE: Refer To "Computer Relearn Procedures" Located In The Front Of This Manual When Battery Power To The Computer Has Been Interrupted.

INDEX

PRECAUTIONS

Air Bag Systems

Refer to "Air Bag System Precautions" in the front of this manual for system disarming and arming procedures.

Battery Ground Cable

Prior to service, disconnect battery ground cable and isolate as required.

Fuel System Pressure Relief

1. Remove fuel pump relay from Power Distribution Center (PDC).
2. Start and run engine until it stalls.
3. Attempt restarting engine until it will no longer run.
4. Turn ignition key to Off position.
5. Place a rag or shop towel below fuel line quick connect fitting at fuel rail.

6. Return fuel pump relay to (PDC).
7. One or more diagnostic trouble codes may have been stored in PCM memory due to fuel pump relay removal. Use suitable scan tool to erase codes.

COMPRESSION PRESSURE

Recommended compression pressures are 170–225 psi. Recommended pressures are used only as a guide to diagnosing engine problem. An engine should not be disassembled to determine the cause of low compression unless a fault is present.
1. Ensure battery is fully charged and starter is in good operating condition.
2. Inspect engine oil level and top up if required.
3. Drive vehicle until engine is at normal operating temperature.
4. Remove spark plugs from engine and inspect for abnormal firing indicators.
5. Disconnect coil wire from distributor

and secure to good ground. For direct ignition system, disconnect coil connector.
6. Ensure throttle blade is fully open during compression test.
7. Insert compression gauge adapter tool No. 8116, or equivalent, into No. 1 cylinder spark plug hole.
8. Connect 0–500 psi (Blue) transducer with cable adapters to DRBIII.
9. Crank engine until maximum pressure is reached on gauge, repeat for all cylinders.
10. Compression should not be less than 100 psi or vary by more than 25 percent from cylinder to cylinder.

ENGINE MOUNT
REPLACE
Left

1. Remove air cleaner assembly.
2. Remove bolts attaching PDC bracket to left mount and battery tray.

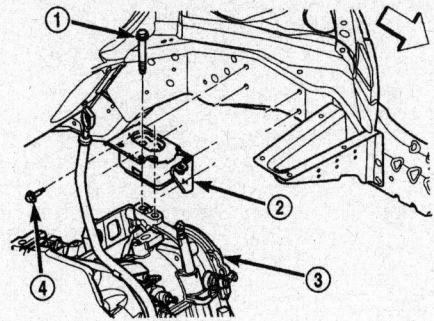

1 - BOLT
2 - LEFT MOUNT
3 - TRANSAXLE
4 - BOLT

ARM0400000000243

Fig. 1 Left engine mount

3. Support transaxle with suitable jack.
4. Remove mount to transaxle bolts, **Fig. 1.**
5. Remove left mount bracket to body frame rail fasteners, then the motor mount.
6. Reverse procedure to install.

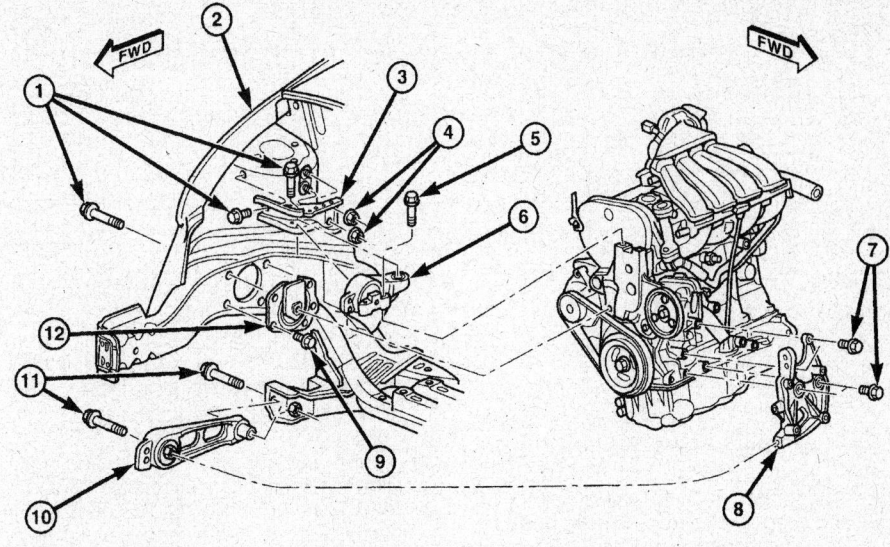

1 - BOLT
2 - RIGHT FENDER
3 - UPPER TORQUE STRUT BRACKET
4 - NUTS
5 - BOLT
6 - UPPER TORQUE STRUT

7 - BOLT
8 - LOWER TORQUE STRUT BRACKET
9 - BOLT
10 - LOWER TORQUE STRUT
11 - BOLT
12 - RIGHT ENGINE MOUNT

ARM0400000000244

Fig. 2 Right engine mount & torque struts

Right

Engine removal is required for required clearance to access the right motor mount. The right engine mount attaching holes are slightly oversize to compensate for manufacturing tolerances. The mount has been set at the factory for proper powertrain alignment. If mount is to be removed, it will be required to mark the position of the mount before removing the attaching bolts.
1. Remove engine assembly as outlined under "Engine, Replace."
2. Mark position of engine mount to body frame rail using a suitable permanent marker.
3. Remove bolts attaching mount to body, **Fig. 2,** then the mount.
4. Reverse procedure to install.

Torque Struts

UPPER

1. Remove bolts attaching strut to shock tower bracket and engine mount bracket, **Fig. 2.**
2. **On models equipped with A/C,** remove timing belt front upper cover.
3. **On all models,** remove upper torque strut.
4. Reverse procedure to install, adjust torque strut according to adjustment procedure.

LOWER

1. Raise and support vehicle.
2. Remove accessory belt splash shield.
3. Remove pencil strut, **Fig. 1.**
4. Remove bolts attaching lower strut to crossmember and strut bracket, then the lower torque strut.
5. Reverse procedure to install, adjust torque strut according to adjustment procedure.

ADJUSTMENT PROCEDURE

The upper and lower torque struts need to be adjusted together to assure proper engine mount load balance and engine positioning. Whenever a torque strut bolt is loosened, the following adjustment procedure must be performed.
1. Remove pencil strut.
2. Loosen upper and lower torque strut attaching bolt at suspension crossmember and shock tower bracket.
3. Position a suitable floor jack on forward edge of transmission bell housing, **Fig. 3.**
4. Floor jack must be positioned to prevent minimal upward lifting of engine.
5. Apply upward force, allowing upper engine to rotate rearward until distance between center or rearmost attaching bolt on engine mount bracket (point "A") and center of hole on shock tower bracket (point "B") is 4.70 inches, **Fig. 4.**
6. With engine held at proper position, **torque** upper and lower torque strut bolts to 85 ft. lbs.
7. Remove floor jack.
8. Install pencil strut and **torque** nuts to 43 ft. lbs.

STRUCTURAL COLLAR
REPLACE
Removal

1. Raise and support vehicle.
2. Remove bolts attaching bending strut to engine and transaxle, **Fig. 5,** then the strut.
3. Remove bolts attaching collar and clutch slave cylinder to oil pan and transaxle, then the collar.

Installation

Torque procedure for structural collar and bending strut must be followed or damage could occur to oil pan, collar and/or bending strut. Refer to **Fig. 5,** for bolt position when performing this procedure.
1. Place collar into position between transaxle and oil pan. Install collar to transaxle bolt (1), hand tighten only.
2. Position power steering hose support bracket and install collar to oil pan bolt (2), hand tighten only.
3. Position clutch slave cylinder into mounting position and install bolts (3) and (4), hand tighten only.
4. Position power steering hose support bracket and install remaining collar to oil pan bolt (5), hand tighten only.
5. Tighten all bolts in sequence as follows:
   a. **Torque** bolt (1) to 75 ft. lbs.
   b. **Torque** bolts (2) and (5) to 45 ft. lbs.
   c. **Torque** bolts (3) and (4) to 20 ft. lbs.

ENGINE
REPLACE

1. Relieve fuel system pressure as outlined under "Precautions."
2. Remove air cleaner housing assembly and clean air hose.
3. Disconnect both battery cables.
4. Remove battery and battery tray.
5. Drain cooling system into suitable container.
6. **On models equipped with A/C,** recover refrigerant as outlined in "Air Conditioning" section.
7. **On all models,** disconnect throttle and speed control cables.
8. Disconnect engine wiring harness at PCM connector.

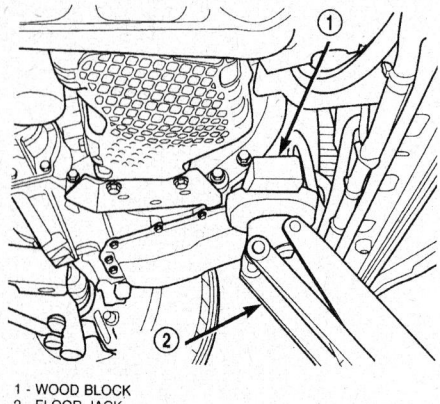

1 - WOOD BLOCK
2 - FLOOR JACK

ARM0400000000245

Fig. 3 Floor jack positioning

9. Disconnect positive cable from PDC and ground wire from vehicle body.
10. Remove power distribution center attaching bolts and set PDC aside.
11. Disconnect wiring connectors at lower battery tray support.
12. Disconnect ground wire from vehicle body to engine at right side strut tower.
13. Disconnect brake booster vacuum hose from intake manifold.
14. Disconnect proportional purge hoses from intake manifold.
15. Disconnect coolant reserve/recovery hose from coolant outlet connector.
16. Disconnect heater hoses.
17. Remove upper radiator support cross-member.
18. Remove upper and lower radiator hoses.
19. Disconnect upper A/C line from condenser.
20. Disconnect A/C lines at junction near upper torque strut.
21. Disconnect electrical fan connector and remove cooling module assembly fan.
22. Disconnect shift linkage and transaxle electrical connectors.
23. Disconnect clutch hydraulic line at quick disconnect fitting using removal tool No. 6638, or equivalent.
24. Raise and support vehicle.
25. Remove front wheels, right inner splash shield and axle shafts.
26. Remove accessory drive belts, alternator and support brackets.
27. Remove charge air cooler hoses.
28. Drain engine oil into suitable container.
29. Disconnect downstream oxygen sensor connector.
30. Disconnect exhaust system from manifold.
31. Disconnect power steering pressure hose from steering gear.
32. Remove upper and lower heat shields, elbow support bracket, turbocharger support bracket and elbow.
33. Remove lower engine torque strut and structural collar.
34. Remove torque converter bolts.
35. Lower vehicle and remove A/C compressor.
36. Disconnect power steering fluid return line from reservoir.
37. Remove power steering pump.

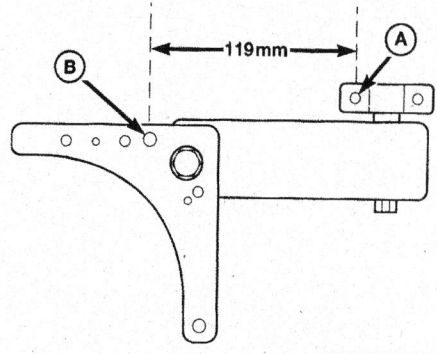

ARM0400000000246

Fig. 4 Engine position measurement

38. Raise and support vehicle, and position engine dolly and cradle tool No. 6135 and tool No. 6710, or equivalents, **Fig. 6,** below engine and transaxle assembly.
39. Loosen engine support posts to allow movement for positioning onto engine locating holes and flange on engine bedplate.
40. Lower vehicle and position cradle until engine is resting on support posts.
41. Tighten mounts to cradle frame.
42. Install suitable safety straps around engine to cradle. Tighten straps and lock into position.
43. Raise vehicle enough to determine if straps are secure enough to hold cradle assembly to engine.
44. Lower vehicle so weight of engine and transmission is on cradle assembly.
45. Remove upper engine torque strut.
46. Remove right mount through bolt and left mount attaching bolt.
47. Raise vehicle slowly until engine/transaxle assembly clears engine compartment. It may be required to move engine/transmission assembly with cradle to allow for removal around body flanges.
48. Reverse procedure to install.

INTAKE MANIFOLD
REPLACE

1. Relieve fuel system pressure as outlined under "Precautions."
2. Remove fuel rail trim cover.
3. Disconnect charge air cooler to throttle body hose.
4. Disconnect vacuum hoses from throttle body and intake manifold.
5. Disconnect throttle cable from throttle body.
6. Disconnect Throttle Position (TP) sensor and Idle Air Control (IAC) valve electrical connectors.
7. Remove intake manifold support bracket.
8. Disconnect fuel injector electrical connectors, then unclip wiring harness from fuel rail.
9. Disconnect Manifold Absolute Pressure (MAP) sensor electrical connector.
10. Disconnect fuel supply line quick connect at fuel rail assembly.

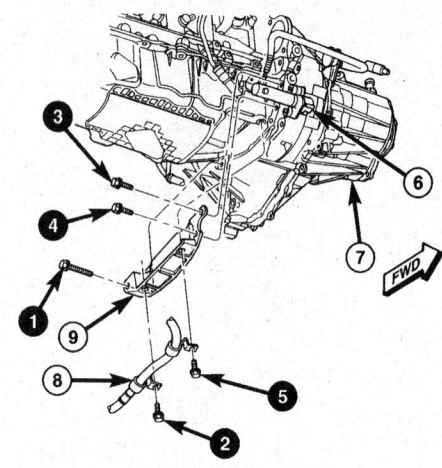

1–5 – BOLT TIGHTENING SEQUENCE
6 – HYDRAULIC CLUTCH SLAVE CYLINDER
7 – TRANSAXLE
8 – POWER STEERING HOSE
9 – COLLAR

ARM0400000000247

Fig. 5 Structural collar & bending strut. With manual transaxle

11. Remove intake manifold attaching bolts, then the intake manifold.
12. Reverse procedure to install.

EXHAUST MANIFOLD
REPLACE

The exhaust manifold must be serviced as an assembly with the turbocharger. Refer to "Turbocharger, Replace" for replacement procedure.

CYLINDER HEAD
REPLACE

1. Perform fuel system pressure relief procedure as outlined under "Precautions."
2. Remove clean air hose and air cleaner housing.
3. Drain cooling system into suitable container.
4. Disconnect fuel supply line quick connect at fuel rail assembly.
5. Remove heater tube support bracket from cylinder head.
6. Disconnect upper radiator and heater supply hoses from coolant outlet connections.
7. Disconnect Engine Coolant Temperature (ECT) sensor electrical connector.
8. Remove accessory drive belts.
9. Raise and support vehicle.
10. Disconnect exhaust pipe from manifold.
11. Remove turbocharger heat shields.
12. Remove elbow and turbocharger support brackets.
13. Remove oil supply and return lines.
14. Remove coolant supply and return lines.
15. Lower vehicle and disconnect ignition coil wiring connector.
16. Remove ignition coil and plug wires.
17. Disconnect Camshaft Position (CMP) sensor electrical connector.

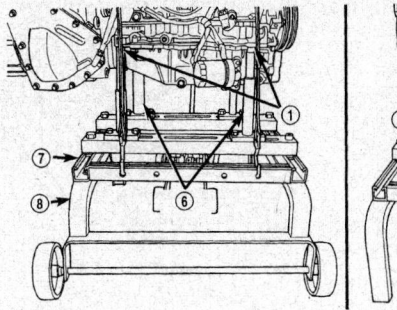
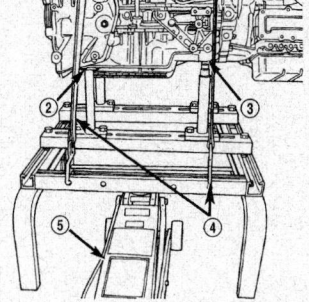

1 - POST LOCATING HOLES IN BLOCK
2 - POST POSITIONED UNDER BRACKET
3 - POST LOCATING HOLE IN STRUT
4 - SAFETY STRAPS

5 - FLOOR JACK
6 - SPECIAL TOOL 6848
7 - SPECIAL TOOL 6135
8 - SPECIAL TOOL 6710

ARM0400000000248

Fig. 6 Engine cradle support

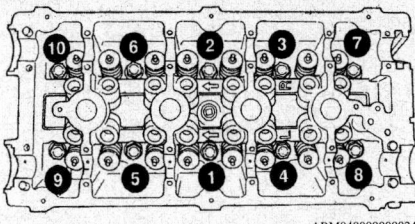

ARM0400000000249

Fig. 7 Cylinder head tightening sequence

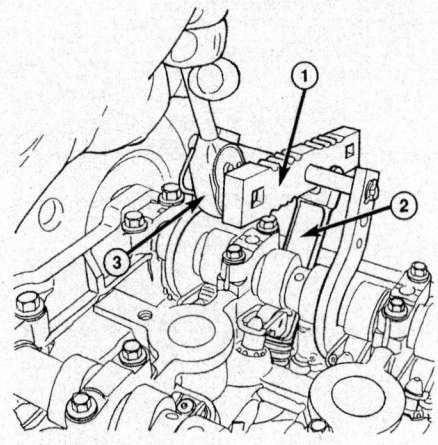

1 - SPECIAL TOOL 8215A
2 - SPECIAL TOOL 8436
3 - 3/8" DRIVE RACHET

ARM0400000000250

Fig. 8 Rocker arm (camshaft follower) replacement

18. Remove valve cover as outlined under "Valve Cover, Replace."
19. Remove timing belt and camshafts as outlined under "Timing Belt, Replace" and "Camshaft, Replace."
20. Remove rocker arms.
21. Remove cylinder head bolts in reverse order of tightening sequence, **Fig. 7.**
22. Remove cylinder head from engine block.
23. Reverse procedure to install, noting the following:
   a. Install new cylinder head gasket on cylinder block with part number facing up.
   b. Before installing bolts, lightly coat threads with engine oil.
   c. Using sequence, **Fig. 7,** tighten cylinder head bolts in four steps: First step, **torque** all bolts to 25 ft. lbs.; second step, **torque** all bolts to 50 ft. lbs.; third step, **torque** all bolts to 50 ft. lbs. again; fourth step, tighten all bolts an additional 90.°

CYLINDER HEAD COVER
REPLACE

1. Disconnect ignition coil connector.

2. Disconnect spark plug wires and remove ignition coil.
3. Disconnect PCV and make-up air hoses from cover.
4. Remove wire harness from cover studs.
5. Remove coolant return line bracket to cover stud retaining nut.
6. Remove remaining cover attaching bolts and nuts, then the cover.
7. Reverse procedure to install.

VALVE ADJUSTMENT

These engines use hydraulic lifters. No adjustment is required.

ROCKER ARMS
REPLACE

This procedure is for in-vehicle service with camshafts installed.
1. Remove valve cover as outlined under "Valve Cover, Replace."
2. Remove spark plugs.
3. Rotate engine until camshaft lobe, on follower being removed, is positioned on it's base circle (heel). Piston should be a minimum of .025 inch below TDC position.
4. If cam follower assemblies are to be reused, mark followers for installation reference.
5. Slowly depress valve assembly until cam follower can be removed using valve spring compressor tool No. 8215 and adapter tool No. 8436, or equivalent, **Fig. 8.**
6. It may be required to remove additional brackets to allow clearance for tool handle movement.
7. Reverse procedure to install.

CRANKSHAFT DAMPER
REPLACE

1. Raise and support vehicle.
2. Remove right front wheel.
3. Remove right splash shield.
4. Remove accessory drive belts.
5. Remove crankshaft damper retaining bolt.
6. Remove crankshaft damper using puller tool No. 1026, or equivalent.
7. Reverse procedure to install.

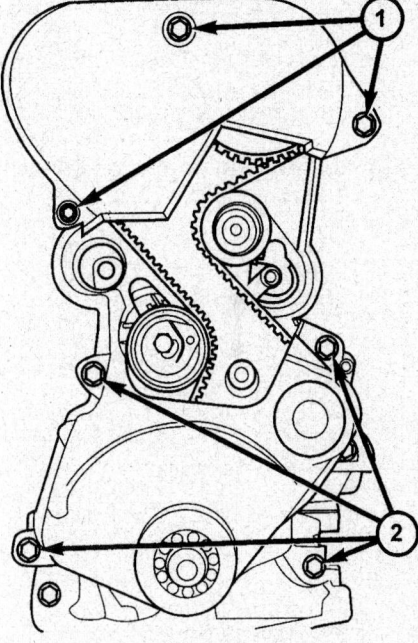

1 - UPPER COVER FASTENERS
2 - LOWER COVER FASTENERS

ARM0400000000251

Fig. 9 Upper & lower timing belt covers

HYDRAULIC LASH ADJUSTERS
REPLACE

1. Remove rocker arm as outlined under "Rocker Arms, Replace."
2. Remove hydraulic lash adjusters from cylinder head. If reusing lash adjusters, mark each adjuster for installation reference.
3. Reverse procedure to install. Before installing, ensure lash adjuster is at least partially full of engine oil.

FRONT COVER
REPLACE

Upper

1. Remove upper torque strut as outlined under "Engine Mounts, Replace."
2. Remove upper timing belt cover attaching bolts, then the cover, **Fig. 9.**
3. Reverse procedure to install.

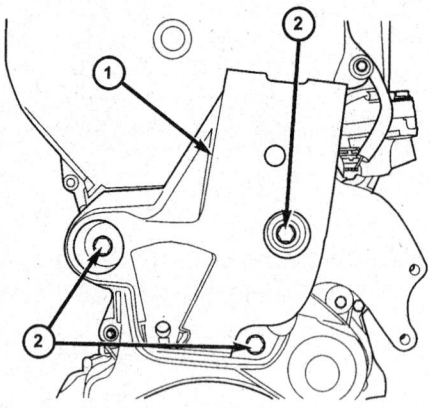

1 - ENGINE SUPPORT BRACKET
2 - BOLTS - 61 N·m (45 ft. lbs.)

ARM0400000000252

Fig. 10   Engine support bracket

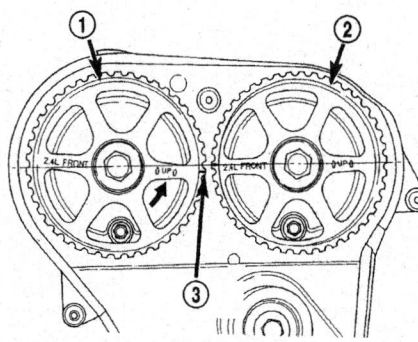

1 - CAMSHAFT SPROCKET-EXHAUST
2 - CAMSHAFT SPROCKET-INTAKE
3 - 1/2 NOTCH LOCATION

ARM0400000000255

Fig. 13   Camshaft sprocket alignment

Lower

1. Remove crankshaft damper as outlined under "Crankshaft Damper, Replace."
2. Remove lower torque strut as outlined under "Engine Mounts, Replace."
3. Disconnect exhaust system from manifold.
4. Disconnect A/C pressure switch at rear of compressor housing.
5. Lower vehicle and support engine with suitable jack.
6. Remove upper torque strut.
7. Remove power steering pump and bracket. Set pump aside. Do not disconnect lines from pump.
8. Remove right engine mount through bolt.
9. Raise engine with suitable jack until engine support bracket bolts are accessible, **Fig. 10.**
10. Remove engine support bracket, then the lower timing belt cover.

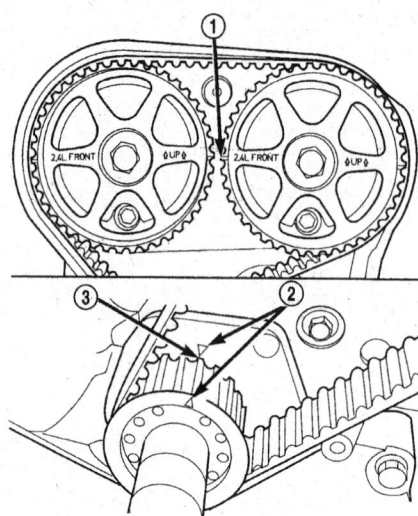

1 - CAMSHAFT TIMING MARKS
2 - CRANKSHAFT TDC MARKS
3 - TRAILING EDGE OF SPROCKET TOOTH

ARM0400000000253

Fig. 11   Crankshaft & camshaft timing marks

11. Reverse procedure to install.

TIMING BELT
REPLACE
Removal

1. Raise and support vehicle.
2. Remove timing belt covers as outlined under "Front Cover, Replace."
3. Before removing timing belt, rotate crankshaft until TDC mark on oil pump housing aligns with TDC mark on crankshaft sprocket, **Fig. 11.**
4. When aligning crankshaft and camshaft timing marks, always rotate engine from crankshaft. **Do not rotate camshaft after timing belt has been removed.**
5. Install a 6mm Allen wrench into top plate of belt tensioner opening, **Fig. 12.**
6. Rotate top plate of belt tensioner clockwise, then remove timing belt.

Installation

1. Set crankshaft sprocket to TDC by aligning sprocket with arrow on oil pump housing, **Fig. 11.**
2. Set camshaft sprocket timing marks so exhaust camshaft timing mark is ½ notch below intake camshaft sprocket, **Fig. 13.**
3. Ensure arrows on both camshaft sprockets are facing up.
4. Install timing belt. Starting at crankshaft, go around water pump sprocket, idler pulleys, camshaft sprockets and tensioner.

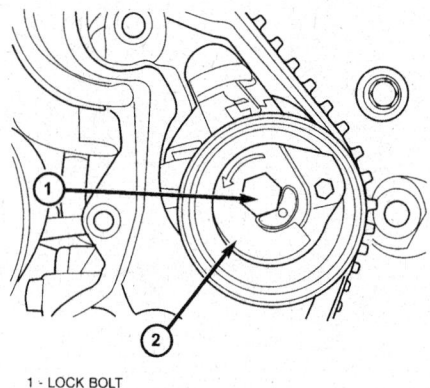

1 - LOCK BOLT
2 - TOP PLATE

ARM0400000000254

Fig. 12   Locking timing belt tensioner

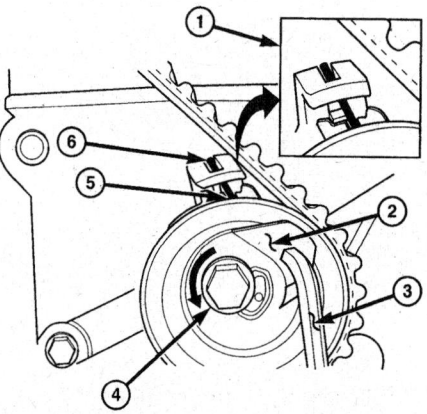

1 - ALIGN SETTING NOTCH WITH SPRING TANG
2 - TOP PLATE
3 - 6mm ALLEN WRENCH
4 - LOCK BOLT
5 - SETTING NOTCH
6 - SPRING TANG

ARM0400000000256

Fig. 14   Timing belt tension adjustment

5. Move exhaust camshaft sprocket counterclockwise to take up belt slack and align marks.
6. Install a 6mm Allen wrench into top plate of belt tensioner opening, **Fig. 12.**
7. Rotate top plate of belt tensioner counterclockwise. Tensioner pulley will move against belt and setting notch will start to move clockwise, **Fig. 14.**
8. Watching movement of setting notch, continue rotating top plate until setting notch is aligned with spring tang.
9. Use allen wrench to prevent top plate from moving, then **torque** tensioner bolt to 18 ft. lbs.
10. Remove allen wrench.
11. Rotate crankshaft two complete revolutions and verify camshaft and crankshaft timing marks are aligned, **Fig. 11.**
12. Ensure spring tang is within tolerance window, **Fig. 14.**

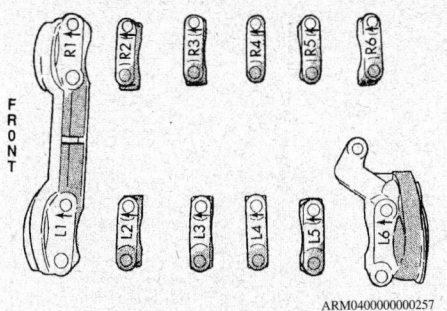

Fig. 15 Camshaft bearing cap identification

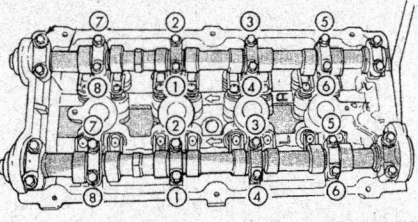

Fig. 16 Camshaft bearing cap removal sequence

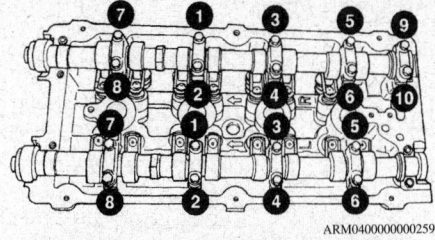

Fig. 17 Camshaft bearing cap tightening sequence

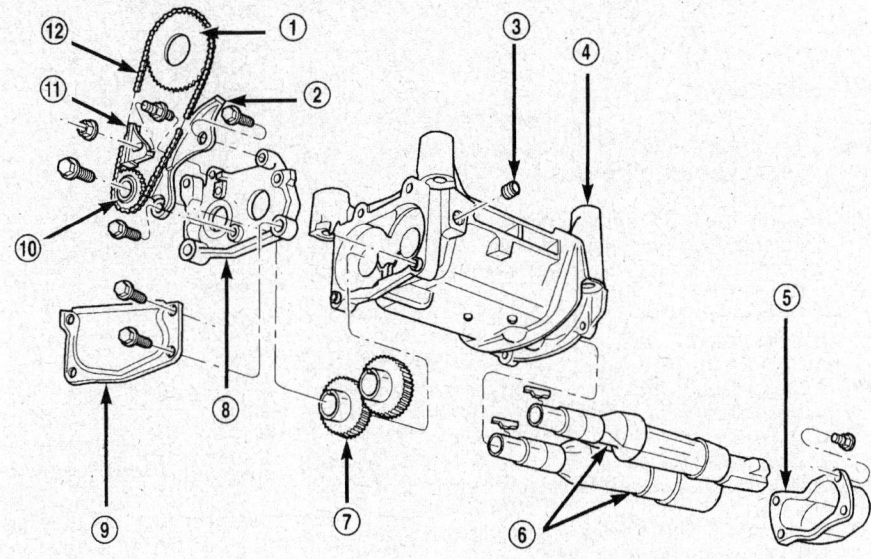

1 - SPROCKET
2 - TENSIONER
3 - PLUG
4 - CARRIER
5 - REAR COVER
6 - BALANCE SHAFTS
7 - GEARS
8 - GEAR COVER
9 - CHAIN COVER
10 - SPROCKET
11 - GUIDE
12 - CHAIN

ARM0400000000260

Fig. 18 Exploded view of balance shaft & carrier assembly

1 - NICKEL PLATED LINK AND MARK
2 - GEAR/SPROCKET SCREWS
3 - NICKEL PLATED LINK AND DOT

ARM0400000000261

Fig. 19 Drive chain & sprockets

13. Install lower and upper timing belt covers as outlined under "Front Cover, Replace.".

TIMING BELT REAR COVER

REPLACE

1. Remove timing belt as outlined under "Timing Belt, Replace."
2. Remove timing belt idler pulley retaining bolt, then the idler pulley.
3. Hold camshaft sprocket in place with holding tool No. 6847, or equivalent, then remove camshaft sprocket retaining bolt and sprocket.
4. Remove rear timing belt cover attaching bolts, then the rear cover.
5. Reverse procedure to install.

CAMSHAFT

REPLACE

Removal

Camshafts are not interchangeable. The left (intake) camshaft thrust bearing face (No. 6) spacing is wider.

1. Remove cylinder head cover as outlined under "Cylinder Head Cover, Replace."
2. Remove camshaft position sensor and camshaft target magnet.
3. Remove timing belt as outlined under "Timing Belt, Replace."
4. Remove rear timing belt cover as outlined under "Timing Belt Rear Cover, Replace."
5. Bearing caps are identified for location, remove outside bearing caps first, Fig. 15.
6. Loosen camshaft bearing cap attaching bolts in sequence, Fig. 16.
7. Identify camshafts, then remove from cylinder head.

Installation

Ensure no piston is at TDC when installing camshafts.

1. Lubricate all camshaft bearing journals, cam followers and camshafts.
2. Install cam followers and camshafts.

3. Install right and left camshaft bearing caps No. 2–5 and right No. 6. Torque M6 fasteners to 105 inch lbs. in sequence, Fig. 17.
4. Apply Mopar Gasket Maker, or equivalent, to No. 1 and left No. 6 bearing caps. Install caps and tighten M8 fasteners to specification.
5. Camshaft end caps must be installed before camshaft seals are installed.
6. Install camshaft seals, rear timing belt cover, camshaft sprockets and timing belt as outlined under "Timing Belt, Replace.".
7. Install camshaft target magnet and camshaft position sensor.
8. Install cylinder head cover.

BALANCE SHAFT

REPLACE

Balance Shafts

1. Drain engine oil into suitable container.
2. Remove oil pan and oil pickup tube.
3. Remove chain cover, guide and tensioner, Fig. 18.
4. Remove balance shaft drive spocket retaining bolt, Fig. 19.
5. Remove chain and sprocket assembly. Using two wide pry bars, work sprocket back and forth until it is off of crankshaft.
6. Remove gear cover retaining stud

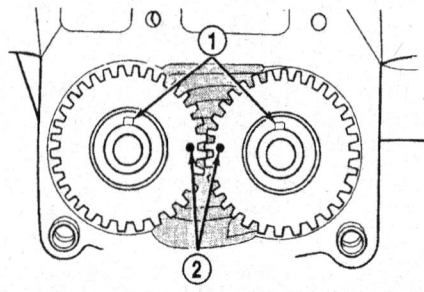

1 - KEY WAYS UP
2 - GEAR ALIGNMENT DOTS

ARM0400000000262

Fig. 20   Gear timing

(double ended to also retain chain guide), gear cover and balance shaft gears.

7. Remove gear cover and balance shafts.
8. Remove four carrier to crankcase attaching bolts to separate carrier from engine bedplate.

INSTALLATION

1. With balance shafts installed in carrier, **Fig. 18,** position carrier on crankcase and install four attaching bolts.
2. Turn balance shafts until both shaft keyways are up, parallel to vertical centerline of engine.
3. Install short hub drive gear on sprocket driven shaft and long hub gear on gear driven shaft.
4. Gear and balance shaft keyways must be up with gear timing marks meshed, **Fig. 20.**
5. Install gear cover and tighten double ended stud/washer to specification.
6. Align flat on balance shaft sprocket to flat on crankshaft, **Fig. 21.**
7. Install balance shaft drive sprocket on crankshaft using sprocket installer tool No. 6052, or equivalent.
8. Turn crankshaft until No. 1 cylinder is at TDC, timing marks on chain sprocket should align with parting line on left side of No. 1 main bearing cap, **Fig. 22.**
9. Place chain over crankshaft sprocket so that plated link of chain is over No. 1 cylinder timing mark on balance shaft crankshaft sprocket, **Fig. 22.**
10. Place balance shaft sprocket into timing chain and align timing mark on sprocket with lower plated link on chain, **Fig. 22.**
11. Lower plated link is eight links from upper link.
12. With balance shaft keyways pointing up, slide balance shaft sprocket onto nose of balance shaft. Balance shaft may have to be pushed in slightly to allow for clearance.
13. Timing mark on sprocket, lower nickel plated link and arrow on side of gear cover should align when balance shafts are timed correctly.
14. Install balance shaft bolts. Place a wood block between crankcase and crankshaft counterbalance to prevent crankshaft and gear rotation.
15. Install chain tensioner loosely.

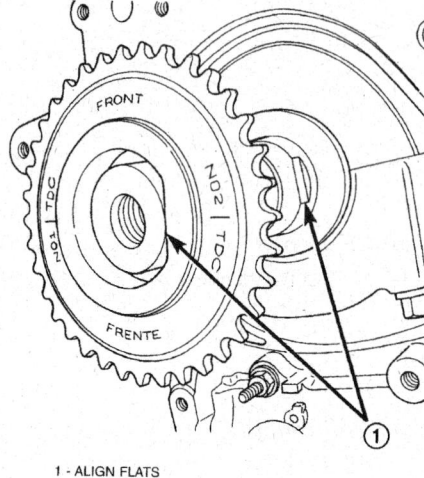

1 - ALIGN FLATS

ARM0400000000263

Fig. 21   Balance shaft sprocket to crankshaft alignment

16. Position guide on double ended stud. Ensure tab on guide fits into slot on gear cover, then install nut and **torque** to 105 inch lbs.
17. Place a shim .039 inch thick and 2.75 inches long between tensioner and chain, **Fig. 23.**
18. Push tensioner and shim up against chain. Apply firm pressure (5.5–6.6 lbs.) directly behind adjustment slot to take up all slack.
19. Chain must have shoe radius contact, **Fig. 23.**
20. With load applied, tighten top bolt first, then the bottom pivot bolt. Tighten bolts to specification, then remove shim.
21. Install carrier covers, pickup tube and oil pan.

BALANCE SHAFT CARRIER

REPLACE

1. Remove oil pan and pickup tube as outlined under "Oil Pan, Replace."
2. Remove chain cover, guide and tensioner, **Fig. 18.**
3. Remove balance shaft drive sprocket retaining bolt, **Fig. 19.**
4. Move driven balance shaft inboard through driven chain sprocket. Sprocket will hang in lower chain loop.
5. Remove carrier to crankcase attaching bolts, then the carrier.
6. Reverse procedure to install.

PISTON & ROD ASSEMBLY

The directional stamp on the piston should face toward the front of the engine.

MAIN & ROD BEARINGS

The crankshaft and main bearings are supported by a bedplate. When installing bedplate, refer to **Fig. 24,** for bolt tightening

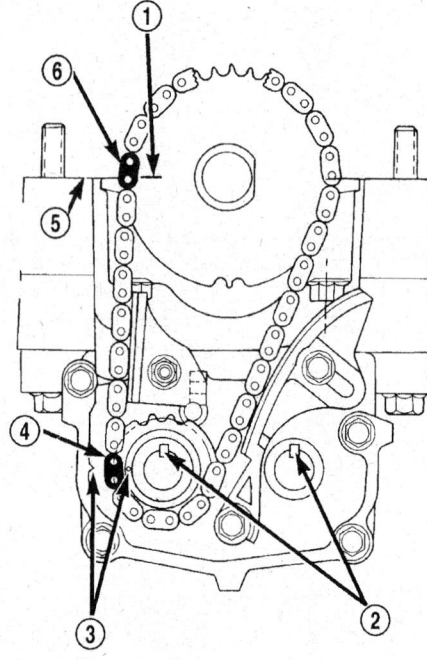

1 - MARK ON SPROCKET
2 - KEYWAYS UP
3 - ALIGN MARKS
4 - PLATED LINK
5 - PARTING LINE (BEDPLATE TO BLOCK)
6 - PLATED LINK

ARM0400000000264

Fig. 22   Balance shaft timing

sequence and identification. Tighten bedplate retaining bolts in five steps. First step, **torque** bolts numbered 1–10 to 30 ft.lbs.; second step, **torque** bolts numbered 1–10 to 30 ft. lbs.; Third step, **torque** bolts numbered 11–20 fo 21 ft. lbs.; Fourth step, **torque** bolts numbered 1–10 to 55 ft. lbs.; Fifth step, **torque** bolts numbered 11–20 to 21 ft. lbs.

CRANKSHAFT REAR OIL SEAL

REPLACE

Removal

1. Remove transaxle and flexplate as outlined in **MOTOR'S "Domestic Transmission, In-Vehicle Service"** manual.
2. Insert a 3/16 inch flat bladed screwdriver between dust lip and metal case of crankshaft seal.
3. Pry out seal.
4. Do not allow screwdriver blade to contact crankshaft seal surface.
5. If burrs or scratches are present on crankshaft edge, polish with 400 grit sand paper to prevent seal damage during installation of new seal.

Installation

When installing new seal, no lube on seal is needed.
1. Place seal guide tool No. 6926–1, or equivalent, on crankshaft.

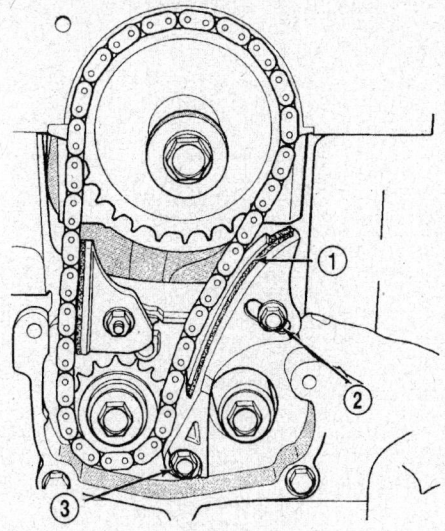

1 - 1MM (0.039 IN.) SHIM
2 - TENSIONER (ADJUSTER) BOLT
3 - PIVOT BOLT

ARM0400000000265

Fig. 23 Chain tension adjustment

2. Position seal over guide tool, guide tool should remain on crankshaft during installation of seal.
3. Ensure lip of seal is facing toward crankcase during installation.
4. Drive seal into block using seal driver tool No. 6926–2 and handle tool No. C-4171, or equivalents, until tool bottoms out against block.
5. Install flexplate.
6. Apply Mopar Lock and Seal adhesive to bolt threads and tighten to specification.
7. Install transaxle as outlined in **MOTOR'S "Domestic Transmission, In-Vehicle Service"** manual.

OIL PAN
REPLACE

1. Raise and support vehicle.
2. Drain engine oil into suitable container.
3. Remove oil filter.
4. Remove right inner splash shield.
5. Remove turbocharger to charge air cooler hose assembly.
6. Remove oil cooler connector bolt. **Do not disconnect coolant lines from oil cooler.**
7. Remove structural collar as outlined under "Structural Collar, Replace."
8. Remove lower torque strut.
9. Remove oil filter adapter and gasket.
10. Remove oil pan and gasket.
11. Reverse procedure to install, noting the following:
    a. Clean oil pan and all gasket surfaces.
    b. Apply Mopar Engine RTV GEN II, or equivalent, at oil pump to engine block parting lines.
    c. Install oil pan and gasket, tighten to specification.
    d. Install oil filter adapter and gasket, tighten to specification.

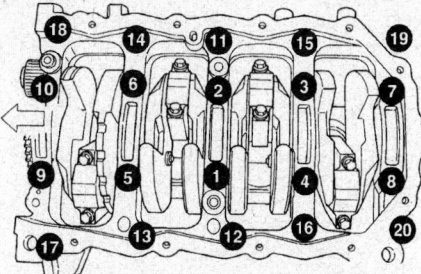

ARM0400000000266

Fig. 24 Bedplate bolt identification & tightening sequence

OIL PUMP
REPLACE

1. Remove timing belt and timing belt rear cover as outlined under "Timing Belt, Replace" and "Timing Belt Rear Cover, Replace.".
2. Remove oil pan as outlined under "Oil Pan, Replace."
3. Remove crankshaft sprocket using puller tool Nos. 6793 and C-4685–C2, or equivalents.
4. Remove crankshaft key.
5. Remove oil pickup tube.
6. Remove oil pump and front crankshaft seal, **Fig. 25.**
7. Reverse procedure to install, noting the following:
    a. Ensure all surfaces are clean and free of oil and dirt.
    b. Apply Mopar Gasket Maker, or equivalent, to oil pump, **Fig. 26.**
    c. Install O-ring into oil pump body discharge passage.
    d. Prime oil pump with engine oil before installation.

ACCESSORY DRIVE BELTS
REPLACE

A/C & Power Steering

1. Raise and support vehicle.
2. Remove splash shield.
3. Rotate belt tensioner clockwise and remove belt from power steering and compressor pulleys.
4. Reverse procedure to install.

Alternator

1. Remove A/C and power steering pump belt.
2. Loosen alternator pivot bolt.
3. Loosen locking nut and adjusting bolt, then remove belt.
4. Reverse procedure to install.

COOLING SYSTEM BLEED

1. Open cooling system bleed valve, **Fig. 27.**

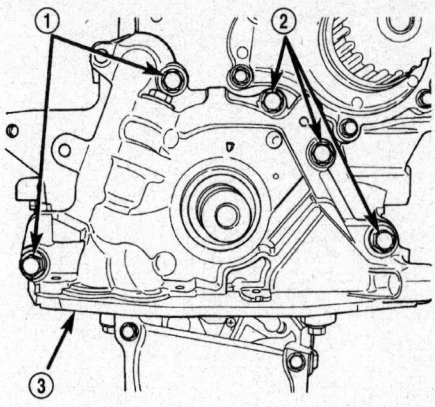

1 – BOLTS
2 – BOLTS
3 – OIL PUMP

CR1060000866000X

Fig. 25 Oil pump

2. Attach a four foot length of clear hose to bleed valve, route hose away from accessory drive and radiator fan.
3. Place other end of hose into suitable container.
4. Fill cooling system with proper amount of recommended coolant.
5. Slowly continue filling system until a steady stream of coolant flows from attached hose on bleed valve.
6. Close bleed valve and remove hose.
7. Fill coolant level to top of pressure cap neck, then install pressure cap.
8. Fill coolant recovery bottle to at least Full Hot mark.
9. Perform 3–4 warm up and cool down cycles, top up coolant as required.

THERMOSTAT
REPLACE

1. Remove upper intake manifold as outlined under "Intake Manifold, Replace."
2. Drain cooling system into suitable container to level below thermostat.
3. Remove upper radiator hose from outlet connector.
4. Remove coolant recovery system hose from outlet connector.
5. Remove thermostat/outlet connector.
6. Remove thermostat assembly.
7. Reverse procedure to install, noting the following:
    a. Clean sealing surfaces.
    b. Place new thermostat into coolant outlet connector aligning air bleed with location notch on outlet connector, **Fig. 28.**

WATER PUMP
REPLACE

1. Drain cooling system into suitable container.
2. Remove timing belt as outlined under "Timing Belt, Replace."
3. Remove camshaft sprockets and rear timing belt cover as outlined under "Rear Timing Belt Cover, Replace."
4. Remove water pump attaching bolts, then the water pump.

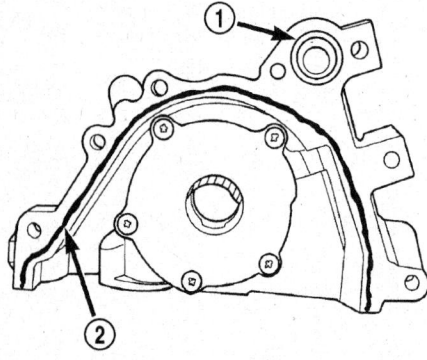

1 – O-RING
2 – SEALER LOCATION

Fig. 26 Oil pump sealing

5. Reverse procedure to install, noting the following:
   a. Apply Mopar Dielectric Grease, or equivalent, to new O-ring.
   b. Ensure O-ring seal is properly seated in water pump groove.

RADIATOR
REPLACE

1. Remove battery and battery tray.
2. Drain cooling system into suitable container.
3. Recover refrigerant as outlined under "Air Conditioning."
4. Remove grille and upper radiator support crossmember.
5. Remove upper radiator hose from radiator.
6. Raise and support vehicle.
7. Disconnect and cap automatic transmission cooler hoses.
8. Disconnect radiator fan motor electrical connector.
9. Remove lower radiator hose.
10. Lower vehicle, then remove A/C lines from condenser.
11. Remove cooling module assembly (radiator, fan and A/C condenser).
12. Place cooling module on workbench and remove radiator fan to radiator attaching bolts.
13. Remove A/C condenser and transmission oil cooler to radiator attaching bolts.
14. Remove lower air shield from radiator.
15. Reverse procedure to install.

FUEL PUMP
REPLACE

The fuel pump is part of the fuel pump module assembly which includes the fuel pump, fuel pump reservoir, inlet strainer, fuel pressure regulator, fuel gauge sending unit, fuel supply line connection and the fuel filter. The fuel pump module is located on the top of the fuel tank. The fuel level sensor is the only serviceable component on the fuel pump module. If any other components are faulty, the entire fuel pump module must be replaced.

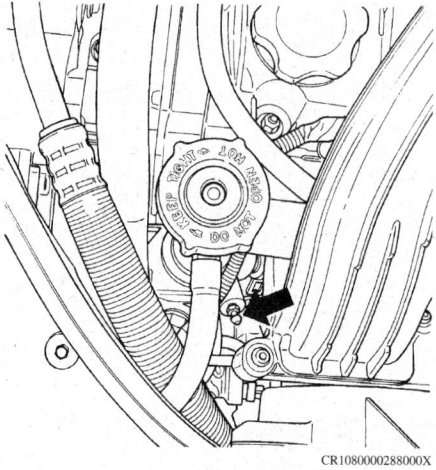

Fig. 27 Cooling system bleed valve

1. Remove fuel filler cap and relieve fuel system pressure as outlined under "Precautions."
2. Remove air cleaner lid.
3. Disconnect inlet air temperature sensor and makeup air hose.
4. Raise and support vehicle.
5. Drain fuel into a suitable container.
6. Support fuel tank with a suitable jack.
7. Disconnect fuel tank rubber fill hose.
8. Remove bolts from fuel tank straps.
9. Lower fuel tank, then remove EVAP line and recirculation line.
10. Remove vacuum line from LDP.
11. Disconnect quick connect fuel line fitting in front of fuel tank.
12. Unlock electrical connector, then disconnect connector.
13. Remove hoses from EVAP canister.
14. Remove fuel tank from vehicle.
15. Clean top of fuel tank to remove loose dirt and debris.
16. Disconnect fuel lines from fuel pump module.
17. Remove fuel pump module locknut using spanner wrench tool No. 6856, or equivalent.
18. Remove fuel pump module and seal from tank. Fuel reservoir of fuel pump module does not empty out when fuel tank is drained. Ensure residual fuel does not spill onto vehicle surfaces.
19. Reverse procedure to install.

TURBOCHARGER
REPLACE

If turbocharger is being replaced due to a bearing failure, replacement of oil pressure feed line is required. Oil return tube should be cleaned also.

1. Drain engine cooling system.
2. Remove air cleaner housing and lid.
3. Disconnect clean air hose from turbocharger.
4. Disconnect throttle and speed control cables from throttle body.
5. Disconnect IAT, MAP, IAC motor, TP, ignition coil capacitor and upstream HO2 sensor electrical connectors.

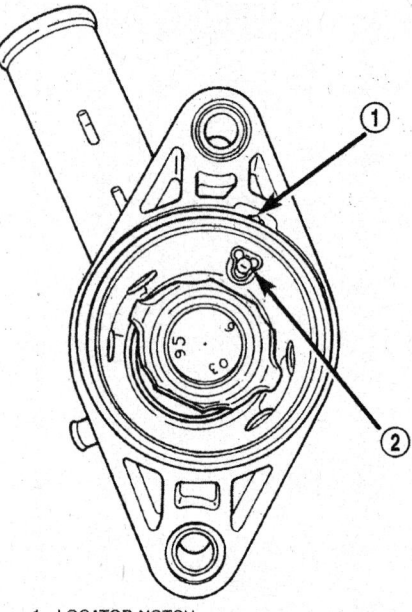

1 - LOCATOR NOTCH
2 - AIR BLEED

Fig. 28 Thermostat installation

6. Disconnect air inlet hose from throttle body.
7. Disconnect vacuum hoses from throttle body and upper intake manifold.
8. Remove upper intake manifold support bracket.
9. Remove upper intake manifold as outlined under "Intake Manifold, Replace." Cover lower intake manifold to prevent foreign objects from entering engine.
10. Remove turbocharger upper heat shield.
11. Disconnect oil supply line, coolant return line and vacuum hoses from turbocharger.
12. Raise and support vehicle.
13. Remove muffler ground strap, then disconnect downstream oxygen sensor.
14. Remove bolts securing catalytic converter to exhaust manifold.
15. Remove catalytic converter and intermediate pipe as an assembly.
16. Remove turbocharger to charge air cooler hose assembly.
17. Remove turbocharger and elbow support brackets.
18. Remove oil return tube, then the turbocharger coolant supply line.
19. Remove turbocharger lower heat shield, then the elbow.
20. Remove lower exhaust manifold bolts, then lower vehicle.
21. Remove upper exhaust manifold bolts.
22. Remove turbocharger/exhaust manifold assembly from engine and cowl panel.
23. Reverse procedure to install. Install a new exhaust manifold gasket, position steel layer of gasket against cylinder head.

TIGHTENING SPECIFICATIONS

Year	Component	Torque Ft. Lbs.
2003–05	Balance Shaft Carrier	40
	Balance Shaft Chain Tensioner	105①
	Balance Shaft Gear Cover	105①
	Balance Shaft Sprockets	21
	Camshaft Bearing Caps (M-6)	105①
	Camshaft Bearing Caps (M-8)	18
	Catalytic Converter To Exhaust Manifold	21
	Coolant Line Banjo Bolt	22
	Coolant/Oil Line Brass Bolt	30
	Coolant/Oil Line Flared Fitting	23
	Connecting Rod Cap	20②
	Crankshaft Damper	100
	Crankshaft Main Bearing Cap (Bedplate)	④
	Cylinder Head	③
	EGR Retainer Plate (Small Bolt)	95①
	EGR Retainer Plate (Large Bolt)	20
	Exhaust Manifold	17
	Exhaust Manifold/Turbocharger Assembly	21
	Exhaust Manifold Heat Shields	105①
	Exhaust Pipe To Manifold	21
	Flex Plate	70
	Fuel Pump Module Locknut	55
	Fuel Rail Assembly To Intake Manifold	18
	Intake Manifold	17
	Motor Mount (L) Bracket To Body Rail	21
	Motor Mount (L) To Transaxle	87
	Motor Mount (R)	21
	Oil Filter Adapter	105①
	Oil Pan	105①
	Thermostat Outlet	110①
	Turbocharger Support Bracket	40
	Water Pump	105①

① — Inch Lbs.
② — Plus ¼ turn.
③ — Refer to "Cylinder Head, Replace" for bolt tightening sequence and procedure.
④ — Refer to "Main & Rod Bearings" for bolt tightening sequence and procedure.

Rear Suspension

NOTE: On Air Bag Equipped Models, Refer To "Air Bag System Precautions" Located In The Front Of This Manual For System Disarming & Arming Procedures.

NOTE: Refer To "Computer Relearn Procedures" Located In The Front Of This Manual When Battery Power To The Computer Has Been Interrupted.

INDEX

DESCRIPTION

Because the construction of this type of suspension, only frame contact or wheel lift type hoisting equipment should be used to raise vehicle.

Rear suspension components which become damaged must be replaced. No attempt should be made to repair these components.

The rear suspension is a fully independent strut type, **Fig. 1.** A forged spindle knuckle is bolted to the strut assembly. Lateral links and tension struts are used to control position and movement of the rear suspension.

HUB & BEARING
REPLACE

The rear hub and bearing are serviced as an assembly.
1. Raise and support vehicle, then remove wheel and tire.
2. **On models equipped with rear disc brakes,** remove caliper and disc as outlined in "Disc Brakes" chapter.
3. **On models equipped with rear drum brakes,** remove brake drum as outlined in "Drum Brakes" chapter of this manual.
4. **On all models,** remove mounting nut, hub and bearing assembly.
5. Reverse procedure to install.

SPINDLE KNUCKLE
REPLACE

Removal

1. Remove rear hub and bearing as outlined in "Hub & Bearing, Replace."
2. **On models equipped with ABS,** remove sensor bracket to strut screw.
3. **On models equipped with rear drum brakes,** proceed as follows:
   a. Remove four brake support plate to knuckle bolts.
   b. Remove brake support plate, brake

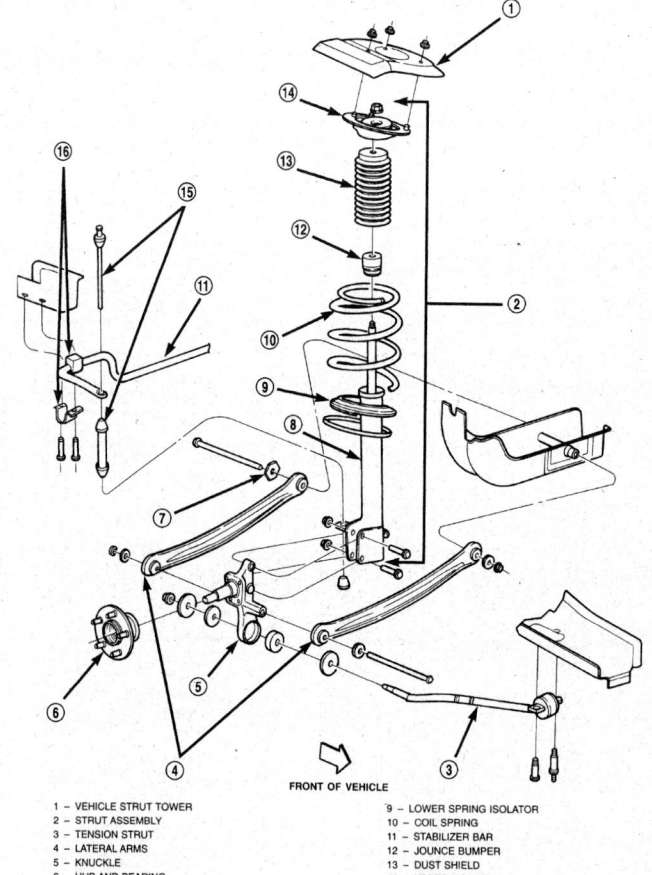

1 – VEHICLE STRUT TOWER		9 – LOWER SPRING ISOLATOR	
2 – STRUT ASSEMBLY		10 – COIL SPRING	
3 – TENSION STRUT		11 – STABILIZER BAR	
4 – LATERAL ARMS		12 – JOUNCE BUMPER	
5 – KNUCKLE		13 – DUST SHIELD	
6 – HUB AND BEARING		14 – UPPER MOUNT	
7 – WHEEL ALIGNMENT ADJUSTMENT CAM		15 – STABILIZER BAR LINK	
8 – STRUT		16 – STABILIZER BAR CUSHION AND RETAINER	

CR2039900089000X

Fig. 1 Exploded view of rear suspension

shoes and wheel cylinder as an assembly from knuckle. Leave brake hose intact.
   c. Tie assembly aside with suitable cord or string. **Avoid overextending brake hose.**
4. **On models equipped with rear disc brakes,** proceed as follows:

   a. Remove four brake adapter to knuckle bolts.
   b. Remove adapter, rotor shield, parking brake shoes and cable as an assembly.
   c. Tie assembly aside with suitable cord or string.
5. **On all models,** loosen, but do not

completely remove, two knuckle to strut nuts and bolts. **These bolts are serrated and must not be turned during removal. Hold bolts in place in knuckle while removing nuts and tap bolts out using suitable pin punch.**

6. Remove rear knuckle to lateral arm nuts and bolt.
7. Remove tension strut rear nut using suitable wrench on strut's flat to prevent tension strut from turning.
8. Remove tension strut retainer.
9. Remove rear tension strut bayonet bushing from strut.
10. Remove rear knuckle to strut mounting nuts and bolts. Tap out bolts using suitable pin punch.
11. Remove knuckle.

Installation

1. Align hole in lower end of rear knuckle with forward bayonet bushing on tension strut. Ensure bushing's stepped area seats squarely into knuckle's hole.
2. Rotate knuckle until its upper mounting holes align with holes in strut's clevis bracket.
3. Install strut to rear knuckle mounting bolts from front side. Install nuts on bolts.
4. Align lateral arms with hole in center of knuckle. Install arm to knuckle bolts. Start bolt from front side. Install nut, but do not tighten completely.
5. Install rear bayonet bushing onto tension strut. Ensure stepped area seats squarely into hole in knuckle.
6. Install rear tension strut retainer and nut. Tighten nut to specifications while holding strut in place with suitable wrench on flat area.
7. Install brake support plate or adapter onto knuckle.
8. **On models equipped with Anti-Lock Brakes,** install sensor bracket to strut screw.
9. **On all models,** install tire and wheel. Tighten lugnuts in proper sequence to half specification. Repeat sequence again to full specification.
10. Lower vehicle to ground and rock to bring to curb height.
11. Tighten lateral arm to knuckle mounting bolt to specifications.
12. Inspect and adjust rear toe. Refer to "Rear Wheel Alignment Specifications" in "Specifications" section.

STRUT
REPLACE

1. Raise and support vehicle.
2. Remove wheel and tire.
3. **On models equipped with rear drum brakes,** remove brake hose bracket to strut screw.
4. **On models equipped with anti-lock brakes,** remove wheel speed sensor bracket to strut screw.
5. **On all models,** remove nut from end of rear stabilizer bar link bolt. Pull bolt out through top and remove link.

6. **On models equipped with rear disc brakes,** proceed as follows:
   a. Remove four brake adapter to knuckle bolts.
   b. Remove adapter, rotor shield, parking brake shoes and cable as an assembly.
   c. Tie assembly aside with suitable cord or string.
7. **On all models,** remove two knuckle to strut nuts and bolts. **These bolts are serrated and must not be turned during removal. Hold bolts in place in knuckle while removing nuts and tap bolts out using suitable pin punch.**
8. Lower vehicle only enough to climb into luggage compartment without tires reaching ground.
9. Remove carpeting from top of strut tower inside luggage compartment.
10. Loosen, but do not completely remove, three strut to tower nuts.
11. Hold strut firmly in place and remove mounting nuts.
12. Remove strut from knuckle by sliding it away from knuckle and lowering it between lateral arms, then angle top outward and out through wheelwell opening.
13. Reverse procedure to install, noting the following:
   a. Align holes in strut clevis bracket on strut's lower end with knuckle's mounting holes.
   b. Lower vehicle to ground and rock to bring to curb height.
   c. Inspect and adjust rear toe. Refer to "Rear Wheel Alignment Specifications" in "Specifications" section.

STRUT SERVICE

Coil springs on these models are available in different load rates. Spring rates may be different on each side of the vehicle depending on how the vehicle is equipped. Ensure proper spring rates are chosen during assembly.

The gas-charged strut damper cannot be rebuilt and is serviced as a unit.

1. Remove strut as outlined in "Strut, Replace."
2. Record orientation of all markings, letters and assembly tips before proceeding.
3. Place match marks on components to aid alignment.
4. Position strut in compressor tool No. PSE W-7200, or equivalent, following tool manufacturer's instructions.
5. Compress coil spring until all spring tension is off upper mount.
6. Install strut nut socket tool No. 6864, or equivalent, on strut shaft mounting nut.
7. Install socket on shaft's end hex.
8. Remove shaft nut while preventing strut shaft from turning.
9. Remove upper mount from strut shaft.
10. Remove clamp from bottom of spring.
11. Pull strut through bottom of spring.
12. Remove dust shield and jounce bumper by pulling them straight up.
13. Remove lower spring isolator from strut's lower spring seat.

14. If coil spring is being replaced, proceed as follows:
   a. Record spring's position in compressor tool for easier assembly.
   b. Back off compressor drive completely to release spring tension.
   c. Push hooks back and remove spring.
15. Reverse procedure to install, noting the following:
   a. Mount coil spring into original position.
   b. Inspect upper mount before installation. Ensure proper mount is being installed. Righthand mounts are marked R, while lefthand has L marking.

TENSION STRUT
REPLACE

1. Remove wheel and tire as required.
2. Remove nuts from both ends of tension strut using suitable wrench on flat to prevent tension strut from turning.
3. Record orientation of tension strut bushings and washers.
4. Remove bushings, washers and tension strut.
5. Reverse procedure to install noting. Inspect and adjust rear wheel alignment as outlined in "Wheel Alignment."

ROLL BAR
REPLACE

1. Raise and support vehicle, then remove both rear wheels.
2. Disconnect roll bar from mounting links at each side and swing bar down to clear links.
3. Remove mounting bracket and roll bar. **Record bushing orientation.**
4. Reverse procedure to install. Ensure bushings are installed in original positions.

LATERAL LINK
REPLACE

Removal

1. Raise and support vehicle.
2. Remove tire and wheel.
3. Remove lateral link to knuckle nut, bolt and washers.
4. Remove nut, washer, bolt and wheel alignment cam mounting lateral arms to rear crossmember.
5. Remove lateral arms.

Installation

The lateral arms have a specific installation orientation. The arm with identical size bushing sleeves on both ends must be mounted on the forward side of the crossmember and knuckle with the trimmed outer edge facing rearward. This front arm also displays the word FORWARD facing forward.

The arm with differing size bushing sleeves mounts on the rearward side of the crossmember and knuckle. Position the smaller sleeve end at the knuckle and the larger end at the rear crossmember. **If the rear arm will be mounted on the right-hand side,** the trimmed outer edge must face rearward. **If the rear arm will be mounted on the lefthand side,** the trimmed outer edge must face forward.

1. Place forward lateral arm against leading edge of knuckle.
2. Install short lateral arm mounting bolt with washer through lateral arm and knuckle and out trailing end of knuckle.
3. Install small sleeved end of rear lateral arm onto end of bolt previously installed.
4. Install washer and nut onto end of mounting bolt, but do not tighten completely.
5. Install alignment cam on long arm mounting bolt.
6. Hold rear lateral arm up against crossmember and install long mounting bolt with adjustment cam through lateral arm bushing and rear crossmember. Ensure bolt is installed with alignment cam's notch pointing straight up.
7. Position forward lateral arm against rear crossmember hole.
8. Route long mounting bolt through lateral arm bushing sleeve.
9. Install washer and nut onto end of mounting bolt at rear crossmember, but do not tighten completely. Note the following:
   a. When properly installed, each lateral arm will have bow in its length facing downward.
   b. Both righthand side arms will have trimmed outer edges facing rear of vehicle.
   c. Lefthand side arms will have trimmed outer edges facing each other.
   d. Mounting bolt at knuckle will have nut at rear, while mounting bolt at crossmember will have nut at front.
10. Install tire and wheel. Tighten lugnuts in proper sequence to half specification. Repeat sequence again to full specification.
11. Lower vehicle to ground and rock to bring to curb height.
12. Tighten lateral arm mounting bolt nut at knuckle to specifications.
13. Tighten lateral arm mounting bolt nut at crossmember to specifications.
14. Inspect and adjust rear toe. Refer to "Rear Wheel Alignment Specifications" in "Specifications" section.

TIGHTENING SPECIFICATIONS

Year	Component	Torque/Ft. lbs.
2001–05	Brake Hose Bracket	23
	Brake Support Plate	55
	Disc Brake Adapter	55
	Hub & Bearing To Knuckle	160
	Knuckle	65
	Lateral Arm Nut At Crossmember	65
	Lateral Arm Nut At Knuckle	70
	Parking Brake Cable	21
	Roll Bar Cushion Retainer	25
	Roll Bar Link	17
	Strut Assembly Shaft	55
	Tension Strut Frame Rail	70
	Tension Strut Rear	70
	Tower	25
	Wheel Lugnuts	100①

① — Tighten lugnuts in proper sequence to half specification. Repeat sequence again to full specification.

Front Suspension & Steering

NOTE: On Air Bag Equipped Models, Refer To "Air Bag System Precautions" Located In The Front Of This Manual For System Disarming & Arming Procedures.

NOTE: Refer To "Computer Relearn Procedures" Located In The Front Of This Manual When Battery Power To The Computer Has Been Interrupted.

NOTE: Prior To Performing Any Service Operations Listed In This Section, Consult The "Technical Service Bulletins" For Related Information.

INDEX

DESCRIPTION

This suspension is a gas pressurized strut system used in place of front suspension upper ball joint and upper control arm. The bottom of the strut is attached directly to the steering knuckle using two mounting bolts and nuts going through the clevis bracket and steering knuckle, **Fig. 1,**

A cast lower arm assembly is attached to the front suspension crossmember using two rubber isolator bushings and to the steering knuckle by means of a ball joint.

A sealed for life front hub and bearing assembly is attached to the front steering knuckle. The outer CV joint assembly is splined to the front hub and bearing assembly.

HUB & BEARING
REPLACE

The cartridge type front wheel bearing on these models is not transferable to a new knuckle. If a new knuckle does not arrive with a new bearing, a new bearing must be installed. This must be done before the knuckle is installed on the vehicle.
1. Raise and support vehicle.
2. Remove tire and wheel.
3. Remove cotter pin, locknut and spring washer from hub nut.
4. Apply brakes, then remove hub nut on end of driveshaft.
5. Remove caliper to knuckle guide pin bolts.
6. Remove caliper from knuckle and position aside with suitable cord or wire. **Do not let caliper hang by brake hose.**

7. Remove any clips from wheel studs.
8. Remove rotor from hub.
9. Remove outer tie rod to knuckle nut.
10. Remove tie rod end from knuckle using tie rod remover tool No. MB991113, or equivalent.
11. Remove tie rod heat shield.
12. Remove ball joint stud to knuckle nut and pinch bolt.
13. Remove two strut to knuckle bolts. **These bolts are serrated and must not be turned during removal. Hold bolts in place in knuckle while removing nuts and tap bolts out using suitable pin punch.**
14. Separate ball joint from knuckle by prying down on lower control arm and up against ball joint knuckle boss. **Do not cutting or tearing seal.**
15. Pull knuckle off driveshaft outer CV joint splines and remove knuckle. **Do not let driveshaft hang by inner CV joint. Support it with suitable cord.**
16. Refer to "Hub & Bearing Service" for continuation of bearing replacement procedure.

HUB & BEARING SERVICE
Disassemble

The cartridge type front wheel bearing on these models is not transferable to a new knuckle. If a new knuckle does not arrive with a new bearing, a new bearing must also be installed. This must be done before the knuckle is installed on the vehicle.

1. Press one wheel stud out of hub flange using stud remover tool No. 4150A, or equivalent.
2. Rotate hub until removed stud aligns with bearing retainer plate notch.
3. Remove stud from hub.
4. Rotate hub until open stud hole faces away from caliper lower rail on knuckle.
5. Install one half of bearing splitter tool No. 1130, or equivalent between hub and bearing plate.
6. Align threaded hole in first half of bearing splitter with caliper rail on knuckle.
7. Install remaining portions of splitter. Hand tighten nuts to hold splitter in place on knuckle.
8. Ensure retainer plate to knuckle bolts are contacting splitter. **Retainer plate should not support knuckle or contact splitter.**
9. Mount knuckle in suitable arbor press supported by bearing splitter.
10. Position driver tool No. 6644-2, or equivalent on hub's small end.
11. Remove hub from wheel bearing using arbor press. Outer race normally comes out of bearing when hub is pressed.
12. Remove bearing splitter tool from knuckle.
13. Remove mounting bolts and bearing retainer plate.
14. Mount knuckle in arbor press again, supported by press blocks. Ensure press blocks do not obstruct knuckle bore or bearing will not slide out.
15. Place bearing driver tool No. MB990799, or equivalent on bearing's outer race.
16. Press bearing out of knuckle.

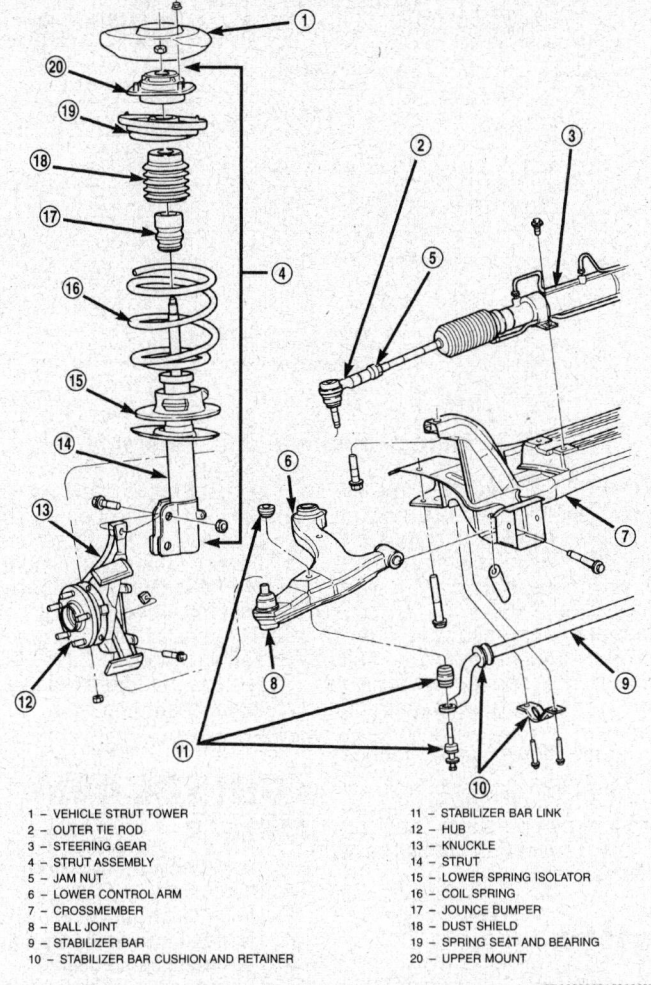

1 – VEHICLE STRUT TOWER
2 – OUTER TIE ROD
3 – STEERING GEAR
4 – STRUT ASSEMBLY
5 – JAM NUT
6 – LOWER CONTROL ARM
7 – CROSSMEMBER
8 – BALL JOINT
9 – STABILIZER BAR
10 – STABILIZER BAR CUSHION AND RETAINER
11 – STABILIZER BAR LINK
12 – HUB
13 – KNUCKLE
14 – STRUT
15 – LOWER SPRING ISOLATOR
16 – COIL SPRING
17 – JOUNCE BUMPER
18 – DUST SHIELD
19 – SPRING SEAT AND BEARING
20 – UPPER MOUNT

CR2029900153000X

Fig. 1 Exploded view of front suspension

17. Install bearing splitter tool on hub between hub flange and outer bearing race.
18. Place hub, race and splitter in arbor press.
19. Place driver tool on end of hub.
20. Press hub out of bearing race.

Assemble

The cartridge type front wheel bearing on these models is not transferable to a new knuckle. If a new knuckle does not arrive with a new bearing, a new bearing must also be installed. This must be done before the knuckle is installed on the vehicle.

1. Wipe knuckle bore clean with clean, dry lint free towel. Ensure no dirt or grease remains.
2. Place new bearing into knuckle bore, perfectly square.
3. Place knuckle in arbor press with receiver tool No. C-4698-2, or equivalent supporting knuckle.
4. Place driver tool 5052, or equivalent, on bearing outer race.
5. Press bearing into knuckle until it has fully bottomed. Remove knuckle from press.
6. Install bearing retainer plate onto knuckle with three original or exact re-

placement bolts. **Do not use substitutions.**
7. Place previously removed wheel stud back into hub flange.
8. Place hub in arbor press supported by tool No. C-4698-1, or equivalent.
9. Press stud into hub flange until it seats fully against flange's rear side. Remove hub from press.
10. Place knuckle with its newly installed bearing back into arbor press with receiver tool No. MB990799, or equivalent, supporting bearing inner race.
11. Place hub in bearing, ensuring it is square with inner race.
12. Press hub into bearing until it fully bottoms in bearing.
13. Remove knuckle from press.

BALL JOINT INSPECTION

With weight of vehicle resting on wheels, grasp grease fitting and, with no mechanical assistance or added force, attempt to move grease fitting, **Fig. 2.**

If the ball joint is worn the grease fitting will move easily. If there is movement replace ball joint as required.

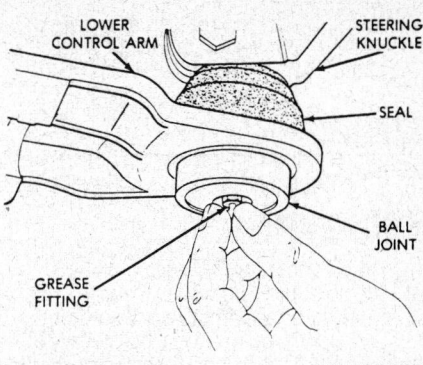

CR2029500103000X

Fig. 2 Ball joint wear inspection

BALL JOINT

REPLACE

Removal

1. Remove lower control arm following procedure outlined in "Control Arm, Replace."
2. Pry ball joint seal boot off ball joint using suitable screwdriver.
3. Position receiver tool No. 6908-2, or equivalent, on hydraulic press to support lower control arm while receiving ball joint.
4. Place control arm on top of receiver tool so bottom of ball joint sits in receiver cup.
5. Place larger end of adapter tool No. 6804, or equivalent, on top of ball joint.
6. Press ball joint completely out of control arm use hydraulic press.
7. Remove arm and all tools from press.

Installation

1. Position new ball joint by hand into its control arm bore, with notch in stud facing control arm front isolator bushing, to ease assembly. Ensure it moves in straight and square.
2. Position installer tool No. 6758, or equivalent on hydraulic press to support control arm. Place control arm on top of installer in upside-down position, aligning ball joint stud squarely with installer cup.
3. Place larger end of adapter tool No. 6804, or equivalent on top of ball joint.
4. Use hydraulic press to press ball joint into control arm until joint's shoulder bottoms in its bore. **Do not apply excessive pressure after joint has bottomed.**
5. Remove all tools and control arm from press.
6. Install new ball joint seal over stud. Position upward lip on outside perimeter of seal boot outward away from control arm once installed. Start installation by hand.
7. Position installer tool No. 6758, or equivalent over boot's outer diameter. Use hand pressure on top of tool until boot is pressed squarely down against top surface of control arm.

8. Install lower control arm following procedure outlined in "Control Arm, Replace."

STRUT

REPLACE

Removal

1. Raise and support vehicle on hoist.
2. Remove tire and wheel.
3. Mark strut assemblies if both lefthand and righthand units will be replaced.
4. Remove ground wire screw at rear of strut.
5. **On models equipped with ABS,** remove ABS sensor bracket screw at rear of strut.
6. **On all models,** remove two strut to knuckle bolts. Hold bolts in place in knuckle while removing nuts and tap bolts out using suitable pin punch. **These bolts are serrated and must not be turned during removal.**
7. Lower vehicle enough to open hood, but do not let tires reach ground.
8. Remove three strut to tower mounting nuts.
9. Remove strut.

Installation

1. Install new strut into tower. Ensure three studs align with tower holes.
2. Close hood.
3. Position lower end of strut in line with upper end of knuckle and align mounting holes.
4. Install strut to knuckle bolts with nuts facing front of vehicle.
5. Tighten mounting nuts to specifications, then an additional 90.° **These bolts are serrated and must not be turned during removal. Hold bolts in place in knuckle while installing nuts.**
6. **On models equipped with ABS,** mount wheel speed sensor to rear ear of strut.
7. **On all models,** attach ground wire to rear of strut.
8. Install tire and wheel. Tighten lugnuts in proper sequence to half specification. Repeat sequence again to full specification.

STRUT SERVICE

Removal

1. Remove strut as outlined in "Strut, Replace."
2. Position strut into coil spring compressor tool No. PSE W-7200, or equivalent, following manufacturer's instructions. Set lower and upper hooks.
3. Place clamp on lower end of spring to hold strut in place when shaft nut is removed. **Do not remove strut shaft nut until after spring has been compressed.**
4. Compress spring until all tension is gone from upper mount.

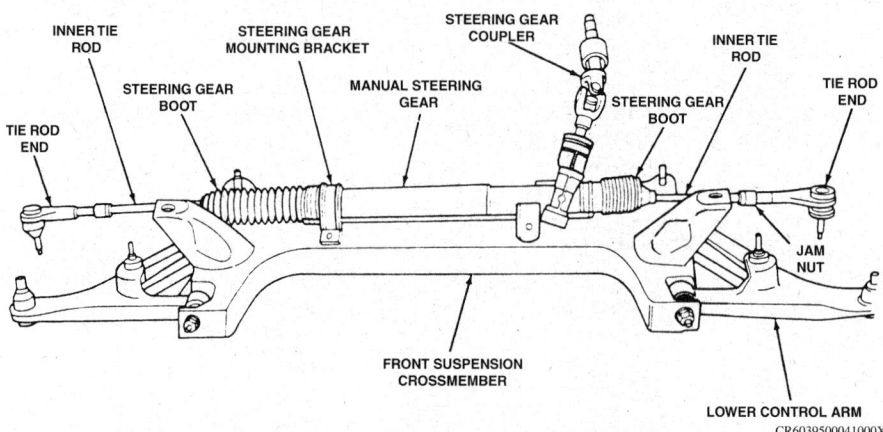

Fig. 3   Manual steering gear assembly

5. When spring has been sufficiently compressed, install strut nut socket tool No. 6864, or equivalent on nut.
6. Install suitable socket on strut shaft hex end, then hold shaft in place and remove nut.
7. Remove upper spring seat and bearing with upper spring isolator as a unit from top of coil spring by pulling straight up. Isolator can be separated after removal.
8. Remove dust shield and jounce bumper by pulling straight up.
9. If coil spring is being replaced, release spring tension by completely backing off compressor drive. Push hooks back and remove spring.

Installation

1. Place coil spring into compressor tool following manufacturer's instructions.
2. Rotate spring so end of top coil is directly in rear.
3. Slowly compress spring until strut can be assembled.
4. Install lower spring isolator on strut's lower spring seat.
5. Install strut through bottom of spring until clevis bracket is positioned straight outward away from compressor.
6. Install clamp on lower end of spring and strut so strut stays in place.
7. Install jounce bumper on strut shaft, with smaller end pointing downward toward lower seat.
8. Install dust shield on strut shaft. Shield's bottom will snap past retainer on top of strut housing.
9. Install upper spring isolator on upper spring seat and bearing.
10. Install upper spring seat and bearing on top of spring. Position notch in upper edge of seat straight out away from compressor.
11. Install strut upper mount over strut shaft, onto top of upper spring seat and bearing.
12. Loosely install strut shaft mounting nut.
13. Install strut nut socket tool No. 6864, or equivalent, on strut shaft mounting nut.
14. Install suitable socket on hex end of strut shaft, hold shaft in place and tight-

en nut to specifications.
15. Slowly release coil spring tension by completely backing off tensioner drive. Ensure upper mount, seat and bearing properly align, and upper mount does not bind.
16. Remove clamp from lower end of spring and strut. Push hooks back and remove strut from compressor.
17. Install strut.

CONTROL ARM

REPLACE

This procedure has been revised by a Technical Service Bulletin.

1. Raise and support vehicle.
2. Remove tires and wheels.
3. Remove stabilizer links.
4. Rotate forward ends of stabilizer bar downward. Loosen bar cushion retainers if required.
5. Remove ball joint stud nut and pinch bolt at knuckle. **Do not pull outward on knuckle. This might separate inner CV joint on driveshaft.**
6. Separate ball joint stud from knuckle, avoiding seal cuts and tears. Pry downward on control arm and up against knuckle's ball joint boss.
7. On righthand control arm, remove mounting bolts and engine torque strut.
8. Remove control arm front pivot bolt at crossmember.
9. Remove control arm rear pivot bolt at crossmember and frame rail.
10. Remove control arm from crossmember.
11. Reverse procedure to install, noting the following:
    a. Position control arm into crossmember.
    b. Install rear pivot bolt at crossmember and frame rail, but do not fully tighten at this time.
    c. Install control arm front pivot bolt at crossmember.
    d. If righthand control arm was replaced, install engine torque strut and adjust as outlined in "Adjustment" in "Engine Mount, Replace" section.
    e. Install new ball joint pinch bolt.

f. Lower vehicle to ground and rock to bring to curb height.

g. If original stabilizer link bolts are being installed, clean all grease, oil and loose material, then apply two drops of Mopar Lock And Seal part No. 4318031, or equivalent, to last ½ inch of each bolt's threads.

STEERING KNUCKLE
REPLACE

Refer to "Hub & Bearing, Replace" for procedure.

POWER STEERING GEAR
REPLACE

1. Ensure front wheels are in straight ahead position and lock it using steering wheel holder tool.
2. Remove steering column coupler retainer pin inside passenger compartment.
3. Back nut off and remove coupling pinch bolt.
4. Separate steering column upper and lower couplings.
5. Raise and support vehicle.
6. Remove both front tires and wheels.
7. Remove both outer tie rod to knuckle nuts. Hold tie rods stationary while removing nuts.
8. Remove outer tie rods from knuckles using tie rod remover tool No. MB991113, or equivalent.
9. Remove tie rod heat shield.
10. Release locking tab and disconnect power steering fluid pressure switch wiring electrical connector.
11. Back out tube nut securing power steering fluid pressure hose to gear.
12. **On models less power steering fluid cooler,** disconnect fluid return hose from gear and remove hose from C-clamps on outside of two routing clips on gear's front side.
13. **On models equipped with power steering fluid cooler,** disconnect cooler hose from steering gear, then remove mounting screws and allow cooler to hang aside.
14. **On all models,** remove pressure hose from front of steering gear.
15. Remove engine torque strut to right-hand forward corner of crossmember.
16. Scribe alignment marks on crossmember and body for installation reference.
17. Support crossmember with suitable transmission jack under center.

18. Loosen and completely remove two front crossmember to frame rail bolts.
19. Loosen, but do not remove, two rear crossmember to frame rail bolts.
20. Lower front crossmember with jack enough to allow steering gear removal from rear of crossmember.
21. Remove roll pin where steering column lower coupling meets pinion shaft using suitable punch. Push lower coupling up and off pinion shaft.
22. Release pinion shaft firewall cover seal from tabs cast into steering gear housing and remove seal from gear.
23. Loosen and remove four steering gear to crossmember bolts.
24. Remove steering gear from front crossmember.
25. Reverse procedure to install, noting the following:
    a. Install front crossmember to frame rail mounting bolts.
    b. Temporarily tighten mounting bolts to 20 inch lbs.
    c. Tap crossmember back into place and align with marks made during removal using suitable soft-faced hammer.
    d. Ensure grease is present on dash to coupling seal lip where it meets plastic collar.
    e. Fill and bleed power steering fluid system.
    f. Inspect and adjust front toe setting as outlined in "Wheel Alignment."

POWER STEERING PUMP
REPLACE

1. Siphon all possible power steering fluid from pump reservoir.
2. Remove steering pump drive belt.
3. Disconnect fluid return hose from reservoir.
4. Disconnect fluid pressure hose from steering pump.
5. Remove steering pump to rear support bracket bolt.
6. Loosen two support bracket to engine block bolts.
7. Working through pump pulley holes, remove three pump to cast bracket bolts.
8. Remove power steering pump with reservoir.
9. Reverse procedure to install, noting the following:
    a. Fill and bleed power steering fluid system.
    b. Inspect for and correct any leaks.

MANUAL STEERING GEAR
REPLACE

Refer to "Power Steering Gear, Replace" and **Fig. 3,** for service procedures.

TECHNICAL SERVICE BULLETINS

Snapping Noise

2001

On some of these models there may be a snapping noise from front suspension.

This condition may be caused by front crossmember tightening.

To correct this condition, proceed as follows:
1. Raise and support vehicle.
2. **Torque** front crossmember rear mounting bolts to 175 ft. lbs.

Power Steering Moan

2001

On some of these models there may be a power steering moan at low engine speeds during slow turns and parking.

This condition may be caused by low, aerated fluid level.

To correct this condition, proceed as follows:
1. Remove power steering fluid cap.
2. Raise and support front wheels enough to allow wheels to be turned side to side.
3. Cycle steering wheel lock to lock three times.
4. Inspect fluid level and adjust as required.
5. Apply 15–20 in Hg vacuum to power steering system at reservoir neck for five minutes.
6. Remove vacuum.
7. Start engine and slow turn steering wheel lock to lock 10 times while maintaining approximately 1850–2150 RPM. **Do not hold steering against lock.**
8. Allow engine to idle three minutes.
9. Turn ignition switch to Off position and lower vehicle.
10. Inspect fluid level and adjust as required.

TIGHTENING SPECIFICATIONS

Year	Component	Torque/Ft. Lbs.
2001–05	ABS Wheel Speed Sensor	10
	Ball Joint Pinch Bolt	70
	Brake Caliper Guide Bolts	16
	Control Arm Front Pivot Bolt	120
	Control Arm Rear Pivot Bolt	150
	Driveshaft Hub	180
	Front Crossmember, Front	105
	Front Crossmember, Rear	150
	Ground Wire To Strut	10
	Hub Bearing Retainer Plate	21
	Power Steering Cooler	90①
	Power Steering Fluid Pressure Switch	70①
	Power Steering Hose Tube	25
	Power Steering Pump	21
	Power Steering Pump Pressure Fitting	65
	Power Steering Pump Pressure Hose Tube	25
	Power Steering Pump Rear Support Bracket To Engine	40
	Stabilizer Bar Cushion	21
	Stabilizer Link	22
	Steering Column Lower Coupling Pinch Bolt	21
	Strut Shaft	55
	Strut To Knuckle	40②
	Strut To Tower	25
	Wheel Lugnuts	100③

① — Inch lbs.

② — Tighten an additional 90°.

③ — Tighten lugnuts in proper sequence to half specification. Repeat sequence again to full specification.

Wheel Alignment

INDEX

PRELIMINARY INSPECTION

Ensure vehicle has a full tank of gas when wheel alignment specifications are inspected or adjusted. If tank is not full, this change in weight will affect curb height of vehicle and alignment specifications. Inspect and adjust tire pressure. Ensure all tires are the same size. Inspect all suspension components for looseness or damage. Components showing signs of wear or damage should be replaced before alignment.

FRONT WHEEL ALIGNMENT

Caster and camber settings are determined by the location of vehicle's suspension components, **Fig. 1.** No adjustment of caster and camber is possible after vehicle is built or when servicing suspension components. Caster and camber are not normally considered an adjustable specification when performing an alignment on these models.

Caster

If caster is not within specifications, inspect for damaged suspension components or body damage causing component locations to change. No adjustment is possible for caster.

Camber

1. Properly position vehicle on alignment rack and install all required equipment per alignment equipment specifications.
2. Center steering wheel and lock in place using steering wheel clamp.
3. Jounce vehicle, read front alignment settings and compare to specifications.
4. If camber readings obtained are not within specifications, Mopar Service Kit will be required. Different kits are designed for front and rear suspension.
5. Raise and support vehicle, then remove original front strut clevis bracket to steering knuckle upper mounting bolt. **These bolts are serrated and must not be turned during removal. Hold bolts in place in knuckle while**

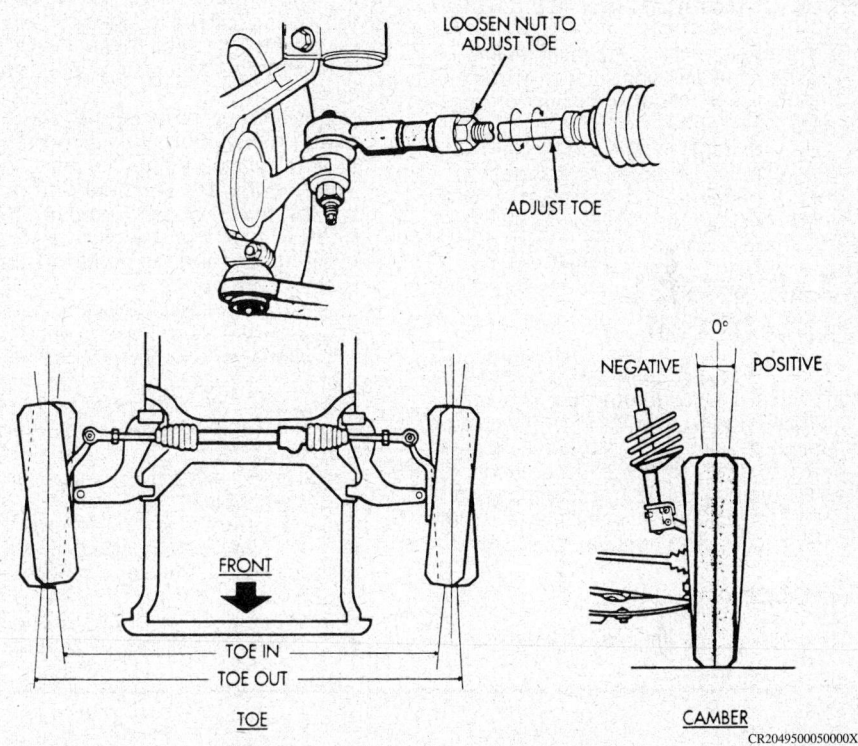

Fig. 1 Camber & toe alignment

CR2049500050000X

removing nuts and tap bolts out using suitable pin punch.
6. Loosen strut clevis bracket to steering knuckle mounting lower bolt enough to allow knuckle to move in clevis bracket.
7. Install bolt from service kit into upper strut clevis bracket to steering knuckle mounting hole.
8. Install nut provided by service kit on replacement bolt.
9. Tighten upper bolt and nut from service kit until snug, but still allowing movement between strut clevis bracket and knuckle.
10. Remove original lower bolt and install bolt from service kit into lower strut clevis bracket hole. Install nut and tighten until snug.
11. Lower vehicle until full weight is supported by suspension.
12. Jounce front and rear of vehicle equal number of times.
13. Adjust camber to preferred setting by pushing or pulling top of tire.
14. Tighten upper and lower strut clevis bracket bolts.
15. Jounce vehicle equal number of times and ensure rear camber setting. When vehicle is at proper setting, **torque** both front strut clevis brackets to 40 ft. lbs., plus additional ¼ turn.

Toe

Rear wheel toe must be set prior to setting front wheel toe. Proceed as follows:

1. Center steering wheel and lock in place using steering wheel clamp.
2. Loosen lefthand and righthand lateral links to rear crossmember mounting bolts' nuts, **Fig. 2.**
3. Rotate lateral link adjustment cams until preferred rear toe specification is obtained, **Fig. 3.**
4. Tighten righthand and lefthand lateral links to rear crossmember mounting bolt nuts while holding toe adjustment cams from turning. This will securely hold adjustment cams in position.

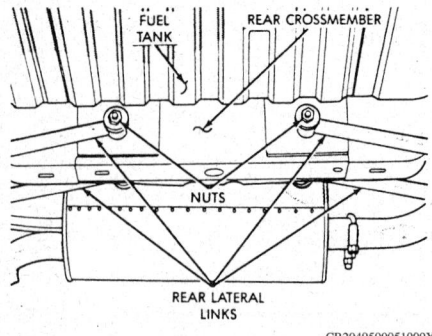

Fig. 2 Rear lateral link toe setting

5. **Torque** lateral link mounting bolt to 70 ft. lbs., while prevent lateral link mounting bolt and adjustment cam from turning.
6. Loosen front inner tie rod end jam nuts and grasp inner tie rods at serration.
7. Rotate inner tie rods of steering gear and set front toe specifications.
8. **Torque** tie rod locknuts to 55 ft. lbs.

REAR WHEEL ALIGNMENT

Caster and camber settings are determined by the location of vehicle's suspension components, **Fig. 1.** No adjustment of caster is possible after vehicle is built or when servicing suspension components. Caster and camber are not normally considered an adjustable specification when performing an alignment on this vehicle.

Caster

If caster is not within specifications, inspect for damaged suspension components or body damage causing component locations to change. No adjustment is possible for caster.

Camber

1. Properly position vehicle on alignment rack and install all required equipment, per alignment equipment specifications.
2. Jounce vehicle and read rear alignment settings and compare to specifications.
3. If camber readings obtained are not within specifications, Mopar Service Kit will be required. Different kits are designed for front and rear suspension.
4. Raise and support vehicle, then remove original rear strut clevis bracket to rear knuckle upper mounting bolt. **These bolts are serrated and must not be turned during removal. Hold bolts in place in knuckle while removing nuts and tap bolts out using suitable pin punch.**
5. Loosen strut clevis bracket to rear knuckle lower mounting bolt enough to allow knuckle to move in clevis bracket.
6. Install bolt from service kit into upper strut clevis bracket to rear knuckle mounting hole.
7. Install nut provided by service kit on replacement bolt.
8. Tighten upper bolt and nut from service kit until snug, but still allowing movement between strut clevis bracket and knuckle.
9. Remove original lower bolt and install bolt from service kit into lower strut cle-

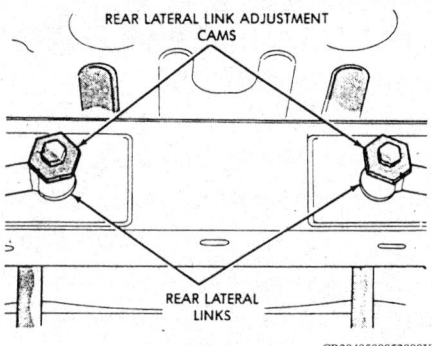

Fig. 3 Rear wheel toe adjustment cams

vis bracket hole. Install nut and tighten until snug.
10. Lower vehicle until full weight is supported by suspension.
11. Jounce front and rear of vehicle equal number of times.
12. Adjust camber to preferred setting by pushing or pulling top of tire.
13. Tighten upper and lower strut clevis bracket bolts.
14. Jounce vehicle equal number of times and ensure rear camber setting. When vehicle is at proper setting, **torque** rear strut clevis brackets to 70 ft. lbs.

Toe

Rear wheel toe must be set prior to setting front wheel toe. Refer to "Front Wheel Alignment" in this section for front and rear wheel toe setting procedures.

MAGNUM, 300 & 300C

NOTE: Refer To Rear Of This Manual For Vehicle Manufacturer's Special Service Tool Suppliers.

INDEX OF SERVICE OPERATIONS

Specifications

GENERAL ENGINE SPECIFICATIONS

Engine	Engine Code①	Fuel System	Bore & Stroke, Inch	Comp. Ratio	Brake HP @ RPM	Maximum Torque, Ft. Lbs. @ RPM	Normal Oil Pressure, psi	
							Idle	3000 RPM
2005								
2.7L	R	MPI	3.386 x 3.091	9.67	190 @ 6400	190 @ 4000	5	45–105
3.5L	G	MPI	3.780 x 3.189	10.0	250 @ 6400	250 @ 3800	5	45–105
5.7L	H	MPI	3.910 x 3.580	9.6	340 @ 5000	390 @ 4000	4	25–110

MPI — Multi-Port Electronic Fuel Injection

① — Eighth digit of VIN denotes engine code.

TUNE UP SPECIFICATIONS

Engine	Spark Plug Gap, Inch	Firing Order Fig.④	Ignition Timing		Idle Speed, RPM	Fuel Pump Pressure, psi⑥	Valve Clearance, Inch
			°BTDC	Mark			
2005							
2.7L	.048–.058	⑨	②	⑤	①	53–63	③
3.5L	.048–.053	⑨	②	⑤	①	53–63	③
5.7L	.045	A	⑦	Damper	⑧	53–63	③

BTDC — Before Top Dead Center

N — Neutral

① — Controlled by PCM.

② — Direct (Distributorless) Ignition System (DIS). Not adjustable.

③ — Equipped w/hydraulic lash adjusters. No adjustment is required.

④ — Before disconnecting wires from coil unit, determine location of No. 1 wire, as position may have been altered.

⑤ — Equipped w/crankshaft position sensor.

⑥ — Remove cover from service valve on fuel rail. Connect suitable fuel pressure test gauge to service valve. With ignition switch in Run position, use Diagnostic Read-Out Box to activate fuel pump & pressurize system.

⑦ — Non-adjustable.

⑧ — Controlled by an idle speed control motor.

⑨ — Firing order, 1-2-3-4-5-6.

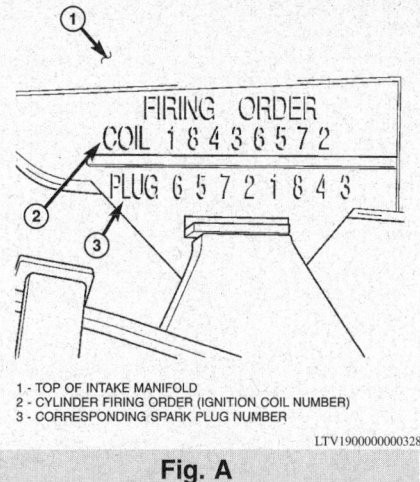

1 - TOP OF INTAKE MANIFOLD
2 - CYLINDER FIRING ORDER (IGNITION COIL NUMBER)
3 - CORRESPONDING SPARK PLUG NUMBER

LTV1900000000328

Fig. A

FRONT WHEEL ALIGNMENT SPECIFICATIONS

Year	Camber Angle, Degrees⑤		Caster Angle, Degrees⑥		Toe In, Degrees④		Ball Joint Wear
	Limits	Desired	Limits	Desired	Limits	Desired	
2005	-.60 to +.40	-.10	+9.00 to +12.10	①	-.05 to +.15③	+.10②	

This chart has been revised by a Technical Service Bulletin.
① — Lefthand, +10.30°; righthand, +11.10°.
② — Total toe, +.20°.
③ — Total toe, 0° to +.40°.

④ — Maximum side-to-side difference: desired, 0°; limits, +.06°.
⑤ — Maximum side-to-side difference: desired, +.20°; limits, -.30° to +.60°.

⑥ — Maximum side-to-side difference: desired, -.80°; limits, -1.30° to -.50°.

REAR WHEEL ALIGNMENT SPECIFICATIONS

This chart has been revised by a Technical Service Bulletin.

Year	Camber Angle, Degrees①②		Toe In, Degrees		Thrust Angle, Degrees	
	Limits	Desired	Limits	Desired	Limits	Desired
2005	-1.25 to -.25	-.75	-.05 to +.25	+.10	-.50 to +.50	0

① — Reference angle only; not adjustable.

② — Maximum side-to-side difference: desired, 0°; limits, -.50° to +.50°.

VEHICLE RIDE HEIGHT SPECIFICATIONS

This chart has been revised by a Technical Service Bulletin.

Model	Year	Drive	Manufacturer's Original Tire Size①	Measurement Points & Specifications②					
				Front③			Rear③		
				Dim.	Specification④		Dim.	Specification⑦	
					Inches	mm		Inches	mm
Magnum, 300 & 300C	2005	AWD	—	6-4	13.9000⑧	353⑨	3	12.099⑩	307⑪
		RWD	—	6-4	12.9375②	328③	3	11.625⑤	296⑥

① — See door sticker or inside of glove compartment for manufacturer's original tire size specifications. If tires on vehicle do not match manufacturer's original tire size & measurement is not within limits, it will be required to refer to the "Non-Standard Tire & Wheel Size Adjustment To Ride Height Specification & Tire Size Adjustment Charts" in the front of this manual for approximate changes in ride height specifications.
② — Limits, 12.500–13.375 inches.
③ — Limits, 318–338 mm.
④ — Cross ride height, .5 inch or -12 to +12 mm.
⑤ — Limits, 11.25–12.00 inches.

⑥ — Limits, 286–306 mm.
⑦ — Cross ride height, 0 inch or -12 to +12 mm.
⑧ — Limits, 13.51–14.29 inches.
⑨ — Limits, 243–363 mm.
⑩ — Limits, 11.70–12.48 inches.
⑪ — Limits, 297–317 mm.

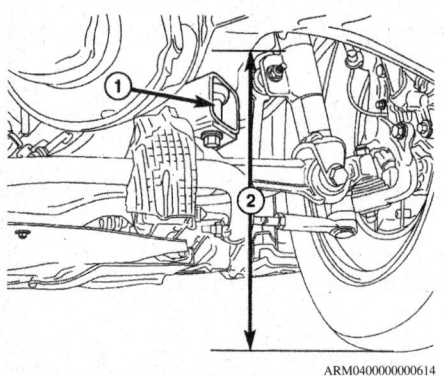

Fig. 1 Front ride height (1) Engine cradle rear mount (2) Dimension

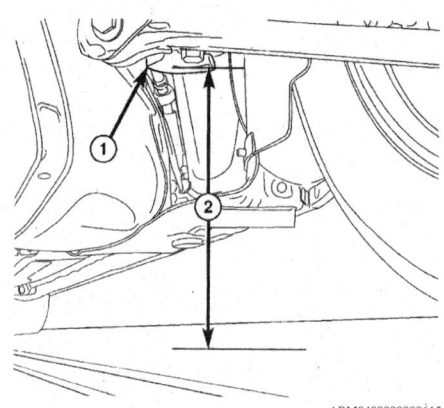

Fig. 2 Rear ride height (1) Travel limiter (2) Dimension

FLUID CAPACITIES & COOLING SYSTEM DATA

Engine	Coolant Capacity, Qts.	Recommended Engine Coolant Type	Radiator Cap Relief Pressure, Lbs.	Thermostat. Opening Temp., °F	Fuel Tank, Gals.	Engine Oil Refill, Qts.①	Transmission Oil, Qts.②	Transfer Case, Pts	Differential Oil, Qts. Front	Differential Oil, Qts. Rear
2005										
2.7L	9.7	Ethylene Glycol	16	203–220	18	6.0	③⑤	1.3	—	⑦
3.5L	10.6	Ethylene Glycol	16	203–220	19	6.0	③⑥	1.3	.78	⑦
5.7L	14.6	Ethylene Glycol	16	195	19	7/0	③⑥	1.3	④	⑦

① — Includes oil filter.
② — Approximate; make final inspection w/dipstick. Includes torque converter sump.
③ — 42RLE, overhaul fill, 16,0 pts,; Service fill, 17.6 pts.
④ — 10 ½ inch, 4.75 pts.; 11 ½ inch, 7.65 pts.
⑤ — NAG1, overhaul fill, 10.6 pts., service fill, 16.3 pts.;
⑥ — Dry fill capacity depends on type and size of internal cooler, length and inside diameter of cooler lines, or use of an auxiliary cooler, these figures may vary.
⑦ — 198 mm RII Axle, 1.5 Qts.; 210 MM RII Axle, 1.7 Qts.

LUBRICANT DATA

Year	Lubricant Type					
	Transmission	Transfer Case	Differential Front	Differential Rear	Power Steering	Brake System
2005	ATF+4 (MS9602)	Mopar Transfer Case Lubricant	Mopar Synthetic Gear & Axle Lubricant 75W-90	Mopar Synthetic Gear & Axle Lubricant 75W-140	ATF+4 (MS9602)	DOT 3

Electrical

NOTE: On Air Bag Equipped Models, Refer To "Air Bag System Precautions" Located In The Front Of This Manual For System Disarming & Arming Procedures.

NOTE: Refer To "Computer Relearn Procedures" Located In The Front Of This Manual When Battery Power To The Computer Has Been Interrupted.

NOTE: Prior To Performing Any Service Operations Listed In This Section, Consult The "Technical Service Bulletins" Section For Related Information.

NOTE: Refer To The Rear Of This Manual For Vehicle Manufacturer's Special Tool Suppliers.

INDEX

PRECAUTIONS

Air Bag Systems

Refer to "Air Bag System Precautions" in the front of this manual for system disarming and arming procedures.

Battery Ground Cable

Prior to service, disconnect battery ground cable and isolate as required.

RECALIBRATION

Anytime the battery has been disconnect or has lost its charge, the following must be recalibrated:

EXPRESS WINDOW

1. Turn ignition switch to RUN position.
2. Move driver's window upward until it stalls in full up position. Allow window motor to stall for at least two seconds before releasing switch.
3. Move driver's window downward until it stalls in full down position. Allow window motor to stall for at least two seconds before releasing switch.
4. Move driver's window upward until it stalls in full up position. Allow window motor to stall for at least two seconds before releasing switch.
5. Move passenger's window upward until it stalls in full up position. Allow window motor to stall for at least two seconds before releasing switch.
6. Move passenger's window downward until it stalls in full down position. Allow window motor to stall for at least two seconds before releasing switch.
7. Move passenger's window upward until it stalls in full up position. Allow window motor to stall for at least two seconds before releasing switch.

ELECTRONIC STABILITY PROGRAM (ESP) STEERING ANGLE SENSOR

1. Start engine.
2. Turn steering wheel right until wheel locks full right.
3. Turn steering wheel left until wheel locks full left.
4. Turn steering wheel right until wheels are centered.
5. Cycle ignition switch OFF and ON. Do not start engine.

FUSE PANEL & FLASHER LOCATION

The majority of electrical system fuses and relays are housed in the two Power Distribution Centers (PDC). The engine compartment PDC and the Front Control Module (FCM) are combined to form the Integrated Power Module (IPM). The other PDC is located next to the battery, at the rear of the vehicle.

The FCM is a micro controller based module located in the righthand front corner of the engine compartment. The IPM connects directly to the battery and provides the primary means of circuit protection and power distribution for all vehicle electrical systems. The FCM controls power to some of these vehicle systems electrical and electromechanical loads based on inputs received from hard wired switch inputs and data received on the CAN bus circuit.

FUEL PUMP RELAY LOCATION

The fuel pump relay is located in the Power Distribution Center (PDC) in the righthand front corner of the engine compartment.

STARTER
REPLACE

2.7L & 3.5L Engines

1. Lock steering wheel in straight-ahead position using suitable wheel holder.
2. Raise vehicle and support.
3. Remove underbody splash shield.
4. Remove center pinch bolt, then separate intermediate steering shaft upper from lower shaft.
5. Disconnect starter electrical connector.
6. Remove three starter mounting bolts and wiring clip.
7. Pull starter forward and down, then around exhaust.
8. Move starter past intermediate steering shaft and remove.
9. Reverse procedure to install, noting the following:
   a. **Torque** starter mounting bolts 40 ft. lbs.
   b. **Torque** intermediate shaft pinch bolt to 32 ft. lbs.

5.7L Engine

1. Raise and support vehicle.
2. **On AWD models,** proceed as follows:
   a. Remove steering gear to steering column pinch bolt.
   b. Remove three mounting bolts and slightly lower steering gear.
   c. Temporarily support steering gear. **Do not disconnect any hydraulic hoses or remove steering linkage.**
   d. Remove steering gear heat-shield.
3. **On all models,** remove mounting bolts and move starter motor towards front of vehicle for nose to clear. **Support starter motor during process.**
4. Remove nut and solenoid wire from solenoid stud. **Do not let starter motor hang from wire harness.**
5. Remove starter motor.
6. Reverse procedure to install.

ALTERNATOR
REPLACE

2.7L Engine

1. Rotate belt tensioner counterclockwise until it contacts it's stop.
2. Remove belt and slowly rotate tensioner into freearm position. **Do not let tensioner arm snap back to freearm position.**
3. Disconnect field circuit plug.
4. Remove B+ terminal nut and wire.
5. Remove two lower mounting bolts, upper bolt and alternator.
6. Reverse procedure to install, noting the following:
   a. **Torque** alternator mounting bolts to 48 ft. lbs.
   b. **Torque** B+ terminal nut to 115 inch lbs.
   c. Route belt around all pulleys except idler pulley.
   d. Rotate tensioner arm until it contacts it's stop position.
   e. Route belt around idler and slowly let tensioner rotate into belt.
   f. Ensure belt is seated onto all pulleys.

3.5L Engine

1. Rotate belt tensioner counterclockwise until it contacts it's stop.
2. Remove belt and slowly rotate tensioner into freearm position. **Do not let tensioner arm snap back to freearm position.**
3. Remove bracket mounting bolts.
4. Remove alternator upper mounting bolt.
5. Raise and support vehicle.
6. Remove middle splash pan.
7. Disconnect field circuit plug.
8. Remove B+ terminal nut and wire.
9. Remove lower mounting bolts and alternator.
10. Reverse procedure to install, noting the following:
    a. **Torque** alternator mounting bolts to 48 ft. lbs.
    b. **Torque** B+ terminal nut to 115 in. lbs.
    c. **Torque** bracket mounting bolts to 40 ft. lbs.
    d. Route belt around all pulleys except idler pulley.
    e. Rotate tensioner arm until it contacts it's stop position.
    f. Route belt around idler and slowly let tensioner rotate into belt.
    g. Ensure belt is seated onto all pulleys.

5.7L Engine

1. Rotate belt tensioner counterclockwise until it contacts it's stop.
2. Remove belt and slowly rotate tensioner into freearm position. **Do not let tensioner arm snap back to freearm position.**
3. Raise and support vehicle.
4. Unsnap plastic insulator cap from B+ output terminal.
5. Remove B+ terminal mounting nut, then disconnect terminal and field wire connector.
6. Remove mounting nut, bolt and support bracket.
7. Remove two mounting bolts and alternator.
8. Reverse procedure to install, noting the following
   a. **Torque** alternator mounting bolts to 48 ft. lbs.
   b. **Torque** B+ terminal nut to 115 in. lbs.
   c. **Torque** bracket mounting bolts to 30 ft. lbs.
   d. Route belt around all pulleys except idler pulley.
   e. Rotate tensioner arm until it contacts it's stop position.
   f. Route belt around idler and slowly let tensioner rotate into belt.
   g. Ensure belt is seated onto all pulleys.

COIL PACK
REPLACE

2.7L Engine

1. Remove intake manifold as outlined under "Intake Manifold, Replace" in "2.7L Engine" section.
2. Clean around coil area and spark plug using suitable compressed air.
3. Remove electrical connector.
4. Remove two mounting screws and ignition coil.
5. Reverse procedure to install. **Torque** mounting screws to 57 inch lbs.

3.5L Engine

1. Remove intake manifold as outlined under "Intake Manifold, Replace" in "3.5L Engine" section.
2. Clean around coil area and spark plug using suitable compressed air.
3. Remove electrical connector.
4. Remove two mounting screws, loosen screws by alternating back and forth. **Do not lose spacers under coil**
5. Remove ignition coil.
6. Reverse procedure to install. **Torque** mounting screws to 60 inch lbs. alternating back and forth.

5.7L Engine

Before removing or disconnecting any spark plug cables, mark their original position for installation reference. Remove cables one-at-a-time. To prevent ignition crossfire, spark plug cables must be placed in cable tray (routing loom) into their original position.
1. Depending on which coil is being removed, the throttle body air intake tube or intake box may need to be removed to gain access.
2. Disconnect electrical connector by moving slide lock first
3. Press release lock while pulling electrical connector from coil.
4. Disconnect secondary high-voltage cable from coil with twisting action.
5. Clean area at base of coil with suitable compressed air.
6. Remove two mounting bolts (mounting bolts are retained to coil).
7. Pull up and remove coil from cylinder head opening with slight twisting action.
8. Reverse procedure to install, noting the following

a. Apply dielectric grease to inside of boots.
b. **Torque** mounting bolts to 105 inch lbs.

IGNITION LOCK
REPLACE

1. Remove bezel ignition switch ring.
2. Pull center console bezel loose from instrument panel.
3. Insert ignition key and turn to switch ON position.
4. Depress ignition switch housing locking tab.
5. Remove key cylinder from ignition switch housing.
6. Reverse procedure to install.

IGNITION SWITCH
REPLACE

1. Disconnect snap retainers using trim stick tool No. C-4755, or equivalent, between ignition switch bezel and instrument cluster.
2. Remove ignition switch bezel.
3. Disconnect wire harness connector from headlamp switch and remove cluster bezel.
4. Remove side trim panel to steering column cover.
5. Remove steering column cover to instrument panel and relocate panel mounting screws.
6. Disconnect snap retainers by pulling steering column cover rearward at top and righthand side.
7. Remove instrument panel steering column cover reinforcement to bracket mounting screws.
8. Remove reinforcement.
9. Remove two front mounting nuts and lower mounting nut, then slide switch rearward.
10. Disconnect ignition switch and SKREEM module electrical connector.
11. Remove interlock cable by depressing locking tab and pulling straight out.
12. Remove mounting screw, squeeze two locking tabs and remove ignition switch.
13. Reverse procedure to install.

NEUTRAL SAFETY SWITCH
REPLACE

1. Place ignition key in ACC position.
2. Remove lower instrument panel trim and disconnect park lock cable from ignition cylinder.
3. Apply parking brake and turn ignition switch to ON position.
4. Apply brakes and place gear selector lever into Neutral position.
5. Turn ignition switch to OFF position and release brakes.
6. Remove floor console front cubby bin mat.
7. Open lid of console rear bin and remove mat.
8. Remove two front of console shifter bezel to console mountings screws.

9. Disconnect console bezel from console using suitable trim stick.
10. Remove shifter bezel from around gear selector lever.
11. Remove three console to floor panel transmission tunnel mounting bolts from rear bin.
12. Remove two front of console to instrument panel mounting screws.
13. Slide console rearward and disconnect accessory power outlet jumper wire connector.
14. Remove floor console.
15. Remove mounting bolts, then the shield covering gearshift and park lock cables.
16. Disconnect park lock cable from shift mechanism.
17. Reverse procedure to install.

HEADLAMP SWITCH
REPLACE

1. Remove steering column cover to instrument panel mounting screws.
2. Disconnect snap retainers from instrument panel by pulling steering column cover rearward at top and righthand side.
3. Disconnect trunk release switch wire harness connector.
4. Disconnect emergency bracket release handle release cable.
5. Remove steering column cover.
6. From underneath and behind instrument panel, push up on lower clip on headlamp switch, then wiggle it down and out of instrument panel.
7. Disconnect headlamp switch electrical connector.
8. Reverse procedure to install.

STOP LIGHT SWITCH
REPLACE

1. Depress and hold brake pedal.
2. Rotate stop lamp switch counterclockwise approximately 30° from its mounting position.
3. Pull switch rearward and remove it from mounting bracket.
4. Disconnect wiring harness connector.
5. Reverse procedure to install.

MULTI-FUNCTION SWITCH
REPLACE

The multi-function switch is located on the steering column, just below the steering wheel, within the Steering Column Control Module (SCCM). The only visible components of the multi-function switch are the control stalk and control knob that extend through the SCCM on the lefthand side of the column. The multi-function switch cannot be adjusted or repaired. If any function of the switch is faulty, or if the switch is damaged, the entire switch must be replaced.

1. Position front wheels straight-ahead.
2. Fully extend or pull out adjustable steering column.
3. Remove two driver's air bag module

covers and mounting screws from behind steering wheel.
4. Pull air bag module rearward, then disconnect two air bag squib connectors and horn connector. **Do not pull on horn switch feed pigtail wire.**
5. Separate driver's air bag module from steering column.
6. Remove mounting bolt and slide steering wheel off shaft.
7. Back out set screw through access hole in bottom of SCCM.
8. Pull SCCM off steering column shaft.
9. Remove three clockspring screws.
10. Remove clockspring by pulling it straight up.
11. **If equipped with ESP,** remove mounting screw at six o'clock position and remove steering angle sensor.
12. **If not equipped with ESP,** lift out a plastic strengthening insert.
13. **If equipped with manual telescoping column,** remove mounting screw at six o'clock position and strut.
14. **If equipped with electronic telescoping column,** remove mounting screw at six o'clock position, then the stalk and switch.
15. **On all models,** remove speed control switch.
16. Remove steering column tilt/telescoping lever mounting screw at six o'clock position.
17. Remove three mounting screws from bottom and separate multi-function switch from SCCM circuit board.
18. Reverse procedure to install, noting the following:
    a. **Torque** steering wheel mounting bolt to 52 ft. lbs.
    b. **Torque** driver' air bag module mounting screws to 89 inch lbs.

TURN SIGNAL SWITCH
REPLACE

Refer to "Multi-Function Switch, Replace" for the turn signal switch replacement procedure

DIMMER SWITCH
REPLACE

Refer to "Multi-Function Switch, Replace" for the dimmer switch replacement procedure

STEERING WHEEL
REPLACE

1. Position front wheels straight-ahead.
2. Fully extend or pull out adjustable steering column.
3. Remove two driver's air bag module mounting covers and mounting screws from behind steering wheel.
4. Pull air bag module rearward, then disconnect two air bag squib connectors and horn connector. **Do not pull on horn switch feed pigtail wire.**
5. Separate driver's air bag module from steering column.
6. Reverse procedure to install, noting the following:

a. **Torque** steering wheel mounting bolt to 52 ft. lbs.
b. **Torque** driver' air bag module mounting screws to 89 inch lbs.

INSTRUMENT CLUSTER
REPLACE

1. Disconnect snap retainers using trim stick tool No. C-4755, or equivalent, between ignition switch bezel and instrument cluster.
2. Remove ignition switch bezel.
3. Disconnect wire harness connector from headlamp switch and remove cluster bezel.
4. Remove four mounting screws and disconnect cluster electrical connectors.
5. Remove instrument cluster.
6. Reverse procedure to install

RADIO
REPLACE

1. Remove center bezel from instrument panel by releasing snap retainers using trim stick tool No. C-4755, or equivalent.
2. Disconnect air conditioning/heater control and switch pod electrical connectors.
3. Remove center bezel.
4. Remove mounting bolts.
5. Disconnect antenna cable by pulling locking antenna connector away from radio.
6. Disconnect electrical harness connector and remove radio.
7. Reverse procedure to install.

WIPER MOTOR
REPLACE
Front

1. Remove caps and mounting nuts, then separate wiper arm from pivot using suitable two-jaw puller.
2. Remove wiper arms.
3. Remove cowl top panel to each front fender push-pin.
4. Disconnect two ¼ turn fasteners securing cowl top panel to dash panel.
5. Remove six cowl top panel to strut tower support push-pins.
6. Disconnect integral cowl top panel to dash panel retaining clips.
7. Remove cowl panel.
8. Disconnect wiper motor electrical connector.
9. Remove two mounting bolts and wiper module.
10. Remove bellcrank to motor shaft mounting nut.
11. Pry bellcrank from wiper motor shaft using suitable, flat bladed tool.
12. Remove two motor mounting bolts.
13. Separate wiper motor from module/linkage. **Do not loose two pocket nuts.**
14. Reverse procedure to install, noting the following:
    a. **Torque** wiper module mounting bolts to 70 inch lbs.

b. **Torque** wiper arm nuts to 13 ft. lbs.

Rear

1. Remove rear wiper arm caps and mounting nuts.
2. Remove wiper arm by rocking it from side to side.
3. Remove lamp from lower liftgate trim panel.
4. Remove two lower trim panel to inside of liftgate mounting screws in pull cup formation to right of latch.
5. Disconnect seven push-in plastic fasteners securing panel to liftgate by prying trim panel away from inside of liftgate using suitable trim stick.
6. Remove liftgate lower trim panel.
7. Remove two upper trim panel lower corner screws.
8. Disconnect eight panel to liftgate push-in plastic fasteners using suitable trim stick.
9. Remove liftgate upper trim panel.
10. Remove three mounting nuts and disconnect electrical harness connector.
11. Remove wiper motor.
12. Reverse procedure to install. **Torque** mounting nuts to 70 inch lbs.

WIPER SWITCH
REPLACE

Refer to "Multi-Function Switch, Replace" for the wiper switch replacement procedure

WIPER TRANSMISSION
REPLACE

1. Remove caps and mounting nuts, then separate wiper arm from pivot using suitable two-jaw puller.
2. Remove wiper arms.
3. Remove cowl top panel to each front fender push-pin.
4. Disconnect two ¼ turn fasteners securing cowl top panel to dash panel.
5. Remove six cowl top panel to strut tower support push-pins.
6. Disconnect integral cowl top panel to dash panel retaining clips.
7. Remove cowl panel.
8. Disconnect wiper motor electrical connector.
9. Remove two mounting bolts and wiper module.
10. Reverse procedure to install, noting the following:
    a. **Torque** wiper module mounting bolts to 70 inch lbs.
    b. **Torque** wiper arm nuts to 13 ft. lbs.

CABIN AIR FILTER
REPLACE

1. Remove air inlet grille from wiper module screen near dash panel in engine compartment.
2. Open filter door on top of particulate air filter housing inside of dash panel plenum.
3. Remove air filter.
4. Reverse procedure to install with air flow indicated by arrow on filter.

BLOWER MOTOR
REPLACE

1. Remove two righthand side instrument panel silencer to instrument pane push-pins.
2. Disconnect brackets near dash panel by pulling instrument panel silencer rearward.
3. Remove instrument panel silencer.
4. Disconnect locking tab, wire harness connector and retainers.
5. Remove four blower motor mounting screws.
6. Reverse procedure to install. **Torque** mounting screws to 20 inch lbs.

HEATER CORE
REPLACE

1. Drain engine cooling system into suitable container.
2. Disconnect heater hoses from core tubes.
3. Remove two lefthand side instrument panel silencer to bracket push-pins.
4. Disconnect brackets by pulling instrument panel silencer rearward.
5. Remove lefthand side instrument panel silencer.
6. Remove three mounting screws and lefthand blend door actuator from air distribution housing.
7. Disconnect HVAC wire harness connector and remove blend door actuator.
8. Remove two mounting screw and flange from front of HVAC housing.
9. Remove clamps and disconnect tubes from heater core. Discard O-ring seals.
10. Pull heater core tubes through dash panel. Plug or tape over opened heater core ports.
11. Remove mounting screw and heater core bracket.
12. Pull heater core out of air distribution housing.
13. Reverse procedure to install, noting the following:
    a. **Torque** heater core bracket mounting screws to 20 inch lbs.
    b. Install new rubber O-ring seals lubricated with suitable, clean engine coolant.
    c. **Torque** flange mounting screws to 20 inch lbs.
    d. **Torque** blend door mounting screws to 17 inch lbs.

EVAPORATOR CORE
REPLACE

1. Recover refrigerant as outlined in "Air Conditioning" chapter.
2. Drain engine cooling system into suitable container.
3. Remove caps and mounting nuts, then separate wiper arm from pivot using suitable two-jaw puller.
4. Remove wiper arms.
5. Remove cowl top panel to each front fender push-pin.
6. Disconnect two ¼ turn fasteners securing cowl top panel to dash panel.

7. Remove six cowl top panel to strut tower support push-pins.
8. Disconnect integral cowl top panel to dash panel retaining clips.
9. Remove cowl panel.
10. Disconnect wiper motor electrical connector.
11. Remove two mounting bolts and wiper module.
12. Raise and support vehicle.
13. Remove front splash shields.
14. Remove mounting nut and disconnect air conditioning liquid line from condenser. Discard dual plane seal.
15. Install plugs, or tape over opened liquid line fitting and condenser outlet port.
16. Lower vehicle.
17. Remove mounting nut and disconnect front section of air conditioning liquid line from rear section. Discard dual plane seal.
18. Install plugs in, or tape over opened liquid line fittings.
19. **On models equipped with 2.7L engine,** proceed as follows:
    a. Remove front section of air conditioning liquid line.
    b. Disconnect Mass Air Flow (MAF) sensor electrical connector
    c. Remove clean air duct between throttle body and air filter housing.
    d. Remove vent tube.
    e. Remove mounting bolt and air filter housing.
    f. Raise and support vehicle.
    g. Partially remove front fascia to gain access to air filter resonator.
    h. Remove mounting bolt and air cleaner resonator.
20. **On models equipped with 3.5L engine,** proceed as follows:
    a. Separate air inlet duct at element housing.
    b. Disconnect PCV hose at element housing.
    c. Remove housing mounting bolt.
    d. Pull housing up and off of locating pin.
    e. Remove element housing.
21. **On models equipped with 5.7L engine,** proceed as follows:
    a. Loosen clamp and disconnect air duct at air cleaner cover.
    b. Lift entire housing assembly from four locating pins.
22. **On all models,** disconnect air conditioning pressure transducer wire harness.
23. Remove refrigerant line mounting bracket to lefthand front shock tower mounting bolt.
24. Remove liquid and suction line tapping block to expansion valve mounting nut.
25. Disconnect rear section of air conditioning liquid and suction lines from expansion valve. Discard liquid line fittings and dual plane seal.
26. Install plugs in, or tape over opened suction and liquid line fittings, and expansion valve ports.
27. Remove rear section of air conditioning liquid and suction lines.
28. Disconnect hoses from heater core tubes.
29. Remove two mounting nuts and air

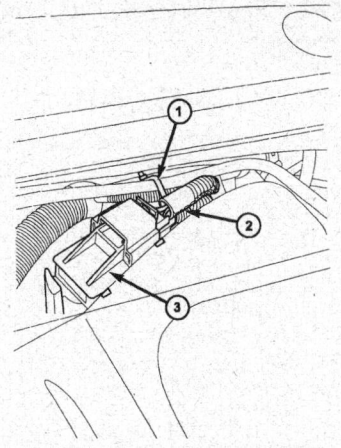

1 - TIE STRAP WIRING TO THE PURGE SOLENOID VACUUM LINE
2 - DO NOT PULL ON WIRING
3 - MAP SENSOR

ARM0400000000613

Fig. 1 MAP sensor wiring position

inlet water separator, or cabin air filter and housing.
30. Remove HVAC housing mounting nut inside fresh air inlet housing.
31. Remove two HVAC housing engine compartment mounting nuts.
32. Remove instrument panel as outlined in "Dash Panel Service" chapter.
33. Remove floor console front cubby bin mat.
34. Open lid of console rear bin and remove rear bin mat.
35. Remove two front of console shifter bezel to console mountings screws.
36. Disconnect console bezel from console using suitable trim stick.
37. Remove shifter bezel from around gear selector lever.
38. Remove three console to floor panel transmission tunnel mounting bolts from rear bin.
39. Remove two front of console to instrument panel mounting screws.
40. Slide console rearward and disconnect accessory power outlet jumper wire connector.
41. Remove floor console.
42. Remove mounting bolts, then the shield covering gearshift and park lock cables.
43. Remove two duct to center floor panel mounting screws.
44. Disconnect and remove floor console ducts.
45. Remove six mounting screws and floor distribution duct.
46. Remove four mounting screws and defroster duct.
47. Remove two HVAC housing passenger compartment mounting nuts.
48. Pull HVAC housing rearward to clear mounting studs.
49. Lift housing so condensate drain tube clears floor panel grommet.
50. Remove HVAC housing.
51. Remove air distribution and inlet housings.
52. Remove two mounting screws, then the flange and heater core tubes.

53. Disconnect evaporator temperature sensor, blower motor resistor or power module, and blower motor wiring harnesses.
54. Disconnect two wire harness retainers and remove blower motor.
55. Remove blower motor resistor or power module.
56. Remove evaporator temperature sensor.
57. Remove two mounting bolts and expansion valve.
58. Discard evaporator tube fittings O-ring seals.
59. Install plugs in, or tape over opened evaporator tube fittings and all expansion valve ports.
60. Remove HVAC wiring harness.
61. Remove 10 mounting screws, then separate upper half from lower half of HVAC housing.
62. Lift evaporator and foam seal out of lower half of housing.
63. Reverse procedure to install, noting the following:
    a. **Torque** wiper module mounting bolts to 70 inch lbs.
    b. **Torque** wiper arm nuts to 13 ft. lbs.

TECHNICAL SERVICE BULLETINS

Radio DTC221E

On some of these models equipped with navigation radios, Diagnostic Trouble Code (DTC) B221E may be set when the ignition is turned ON.

This is an erroneous code. Do not replace the radio based solely on internal radio DTC B221.E

Rain Sensor Switch Setting Not Sensitive Enough

On some of these models the rain sensor switch settings do not differ or are not sensitive enough.

These conditions may be caused by the Light Rain Sensor Module (LRSM) programming.

To correct this situation, program LRSM with latest software version.

Wiper Linkage Contacts MAP Sensor Wiring

On some of these models built before April 14, 2004, with 5.7L engine, the wiper linkage may contact and move the MAP sensor wiring. Overtime, this may break the wires and/or the MAP sensor.

This condition may be caused by MAP sensor wiring.

To correct this condition, secure MAP sensor wiring to the purge solenoid vacuum line and away from wiper linkage using suitable tie strap, **Fig. 1.**

Audio System Intermittent Output

On some of these models built before May 10, 2004, and equipped with premium audio system. may occasionally not produce audio for an entire ignition cycle. The radio display and control may work normally, but no sound is produced.

These condition may be caused by Audio Amplifier (AMP) programming.

To correct this situation, program AMP with latest software version.

Loss of Communications w/Multiple Module DTCs Set

On some of these models there may be loss of communications and multitple module Diagnostic Trouble Codes (DTCs) set.

This condition may be caused by dislodged diodes in cavity 31, 32 and/or 33 in the Rear Power Distribution Center (RPDC), located in the truck next to the battery.

CAVITY 31 DISLODGED

If cavity 31 diode becomes dislodged, DTCs will be set for these modules, the air bag lamp will illuminate and the Front Control Module (FCM) will set DTC B2124, ignition run control circuit open.

If cavity 31 diode becomes dislodged, ignition run feed will be lost to the following modules/components:

1. Occupant Restraint Control (ORC) module.
2. Automatic Temperature Control (ATC) control head.
3. Manual Temperature Control (MTC) and ATC blower motor.
4. High Intensity Discharge (HID) module and associated sensors/headlamps, and
5. Parktronics module.

CAVITY 32 DISLODGED

If cavity 32 diode becomes dislodged, the following will occur:

1. All modules capable will set loss of communication DTCs with the Transmission Control Module.
2. Transmission will go into second gear limp-in mode.
3. Anti-Lock Brake System (ABS) lamp will illuminate.

CAVITY 33 DISLODGED

If cavity 33 diode becomes dislodged, no DTC or any noticeable functions are affected. Cavity 33 diode provides charging system over voltage protection.

To correct this condition, ensure all diodes and fuses are securely seated by pressing down on them. If diodes becomes complete separated from RPDC cavity, note the following:

1. Diodes are keyed and can only be install in one direction.
2. Diode arrow symbol on top of diodes in slots 31 and 32 point toward spare tire.
3. Diode arrow symbol on top of diode 33 points toward vehicle rear.
4. Ensure diode 33 is properly orientated as reverse terminal contact will cause fuse No. 5 to fail.

2.7L Engine

NOTE: On Air Bag Equipped Models, Refer To "Air Bag System Precautions" Located In The Front Of This Manual For System Disarming & Arming Procedures.

NOTE: Refer To "Computer Relearn Procedures" Located In The Front Of This Manual When Battery Power To The Computer Has Been Interrupted.

NOTE: Refer To The Rear Of This Manual For Vehicle Manufacturer's Special Tool Suppliers.

INDEX

PRECAUTIONS

Air Bag Systems

Refer to "Air Bag System Precautions" in the front of this manual for system disarming and arming procedures.

Battery Ground Cable

Prior to service, disconnect battery ground cable and isolate as required.

RECALIBRATION

Anytime the battery has been disconnect or has lost its charge, the following must be recalibrated:

EXPRESS WINDOW

1. Turn ignition switch to RUN position.
2. Move driver's window upward until it stalls in full up position. Allow window motor to stall for at least two seconds before releasing switch.
3. Move driver's window downward until it stalls in full down position. Allow window motor to stall for at least two seconds before releasing switch.
4. Move driver's window upward until it stalls in full up position. Allow window motor to stall for at least two seconds before releasing switch.
5. Move passenger's window upward until it stalls in full up position. Allow window motor to stall for at least two seconds before releasing switch.
6. Move passenger's window downward until it stalls in full down position. Allow window motor to stall for at least two seconds before releasing switch.
7. Move passenger's window upward until it stalls in full up position. Allow window motor to stall for at least two seconds before releasing switch.

ELECTRONIC STABILITY PROGRAM (ESP) STEERING ANGLE SENSOR

1. Start engine.
2. Turn steering wheel right until wheel locks full right.
3. Turn steering wheel left until wheel locks full left.
4. Turn steering wheel right until wheels are centered.
5. Cycle ignition switch OFF and ON. Do not start engine.

Fuel System Pressure Relief

1. Remove fuel pump relay for Power Distribution Center (PDC).
2. Start and run engine until it stalls.
3. Attempt to start engine until it no longer runs.
4. Turn ignition switch to OFF position.
5. Install fuel pump relay.

COMPRESSION PRESSURE

1. Ensure battery is completely charged and engine starter motor is in good operating condition
2. Ensure engine oil level is correct.
3. Drive vehicle until engine reaches normal operating temperature.
4. Remove all spark plugs. Check electrodes for abnormal firing indicators fouled, hot, oily, etc.
5. Record cylinder number of spark plug for future reference.
6. Remove Auto Shutdown (ASD) relay from PDC.
7. Ensure throttle blade is fully open during compression check.
8. Insert compression gauge adaptor tool No. 8116, or equivalent, into spark plug hole No. 1.
9. Connect suitable 0–500 psi pressure gauge.
10. Crank engine until maximum pressure is reached on gauge. Record this pressure.
11. Repeat previous step for all remaining cylinders.
12. Compression should not be less than 100 psi and not vary more than 25% from cylinder to cylinder.
13. If one or more cylinders have abnormally low compression pressures, repeat compression test.
14. If same cylinder, or cylinders, repeat an abnormally low reading on second compression test, it could indicate existence of problem in cylinder.

ENGINE MOUNT
REPLACE
Left & Righthand

1. Disconnect Mass Air Flow (MAF) sensor electrical connector.
2. Remove clean air duct between throttle body and air filter housing.
3. Remove vent tube.
4. Remove mounting bolt and air filter housing.
5. Raise and support vehicle.
6. Remove three per side wheel house splash shield rivets.
7. Remove nine belly pan mounting screws.
8. Remove two fascia to fender mounting screw, one per side.
9. Open hood and remove upper push pin fasteners (four per sedan and six per wagon).
10. Partially remove front fascia to gain access to air filter resonator.
11. Remove air cleaner resonator.
12. Remove mounting bolts and lower splash shield.
13. Remove lefthand engine mount nuts and studs.
14. Place suitable wooden block under oil pan and raise engine with suitable jackstand.

15. Remove mounting bolts and engine mount isolator.
16. Reverse procedure to install. Do not do not let mount contact frame when lowering engine.

Rear

1. Raise and support vehicle on hoist.
2. Remove crossmember to mount bolts.
3. Raise transmission using suitable jack under transmission pan.
4. Remove mounting bolts and crossmember.
5. Remove mounting bolts and rear mount
6. Reverse procedure to install.

STRUCTURAL COLLAR
REPLACE

1. Raise and support vehicle on hoist.
2. Remove mounting bolts and lower splash shield.
3. Remove transmission mount bolts.
4. Place suitable transmission jack under transmission pan, then raise engine and transmission.
5. Remove mounting bolts and structural collar to right, then rear.
6. Reverse procedure to install, noting the following:
   a. Hand tighten mounting bolts.
   b. Ensure structural collar is flush with oil pan and transmission bell housing.
   c. **Torque** vertical collar bolts to oil pan to 10 inch lbs.
   d. **Torque** horizontal collar bolts to transmission to 40 ft. lbs.
   e. **Torque** mounting bolts, starting with center vertical bolts and working outward to 40 ft. lbs.

ENGINE
REPLACE

1. Remove hood.
2. Remove fuel pump relay for Power Distribution Center (PDC).
3. Start and run engine until it stalls.
4. Attempt to start engine until it no longer runs.
5. Turn ignition switch to OFF position.
6. Install fuel pump relay.
7. Disconnect Intake Air Temperature (IAT) sensor electrical connector.
8. Disconnect Manifold Absolute Pressure (MAP) sensor electrical connector.
9. Remove clean air duct between throttle body and air filter housing.
10. Remove vent tube.
11. Remove mounting bolt and air filter housing.
12. Rotate belt tensioner counterclockwise until it contacts it's stop.
13. Remove belt and slowly rotate tensioner into freearm position. **Do not let tensioner arm snap back to freearm position.**
14. Disconnect power steering pump lines.

15. Remove mounting bolts and position power steering pump aside.
16. Recover refrigerant as outlined in "Air Conditioning" chapter.
17. Disconnect compressor electrical connectors.
18. Disconnect wire harness connector from air conditioning compressor clutch coil connector.
19. Remove mounting nuts, then disconnect suction and discharge lines from compressor. Discard dual plane seals. Install plugs in, or tape over all of opened refrigerant line fittings and compressor ports.
20. Raise and support vehicle.
21. Remove mounting bolts and splash shield.
22. Remove automatic transmission cooler line bracket and air conditioning compressor mounting bolts.
23. Position cooler lines aside and remove compressor.
24. Drain cooling system into suitable container.
25. Drain engine oil into suitable container and remove oil filter.
26. Disconnect downstream oxygen sensor connectors.
27. Disconnect exhaust pipes at manifolds.
28. Disconnect electrical connectors, then remove mounting bolts and position starter aside.
29. Disconnect coolant pipe near starter from hose.
30. Disconnect electrical connector, then remove mounting bolt and Crankshaft Position (CKP) sensor.
31. Disconnect ground strap.
32. Disconnect oil pressure sensor electrical connector.
33. Remove four engine mount nuts and studs.
34. Remove mounting bolts and lower steering gear for clearance.
35. Raise engine using suitable wooden block and lifting device under oil pan.
36. Remove mounting bolts and structural collar.
37. Remove lower bell housing bolts.
38. Lower engine and remove jack stand.
39. Mark flexplate to torque converter for installation alignment.
40. Remove torque converter mounting bolts.
41. Lower vehicle.
42. Remove caps and mounting bolts, then separate wiper arm from pivot using suitable two-jaw puller.
43. Remove wiper arms.
44. Remove two push pins securing front cowl top panel to righthand rear corner of engine compartment.
45. Remove front cowl top panel.
46. Remove push-pin securing each end of cowl top panel to each front fender.
47. Disconnect two 1/4 turn fasteners securing cowl top panel to dash panel.
48. Remove six push-pins securing cowl top panel to strut tower support.
49. Disengage integral retaining clips securing cowl top panel to dash panel.
50. Remove cowl panel.
51. Remove strut tower support and posi-

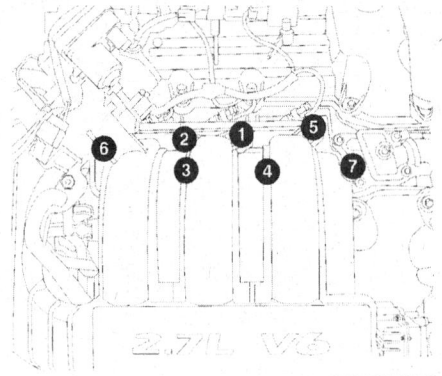

Fig. 1 Upper intake manifold tightening sequence

tion purge solenoid aside.
52. Remove intake manifold as outlined under "Intake Manifold, Replace."
53. Disconnect vacuum lines and electrical connectors.
54. Disconnect ground straps.
55. Disconnect fuel line at fuel rail.
56. Disconnect coil, injector, capacitor and knock sensor connectors.
57. Remove from bracket and position purge solenoid aside.
58. Unlock and disconnect EGR valve electrical connector.
59. Disconnect electrical connector, then remove two mounting bolts and wiper module.
60. Remove and position shock tower brace aside.
61. Remove upper intake manifold as outlined under "Intake Manifold, Replace."
62. Remove mounting bolts and EGR valve tube. **Do not drop silicone rubber seals into intake manifold.**
63. Remove mounting bolts and EGR valve.
64. Remove upper bellhousing bolts and position electrical harness aside.
65. Attach suitable lifting fixture to front of lefthand cylinder head and rear of right hand cylinder head.
66. Support transmission with suitable wooden block and floor jack.
67. Remove engine.
68. Reverse procedure to install.

INTAKE MANIFOLD
REPLACE
Upper

1. Disconnect Manifold Absolute Pressure (MAP) sensor electrical connector.
2. Remove clean air duct between throttle body and air filter housing.
3. Remove vent tube.
4. Remove mounting bolt and air filter housing.
5. Disconnect electronic throttle control and manifold tuning valve electrical connectors.
6. Disconnect vapor purge, brake boost-

er and Positive Crankcase Ventilation (PCV) hoses.
7. Remove manifold support brackets.
8. Remove mounting bolts, upper manifold and foam insulator.
9. Reverse procedure to install, noting the following:
   a. Ensure fuel injectors and wiring harnesses are in correct position to not interfere with upper manifold installation.
   b. Tighten mounting bolts in sequence, **Fig. 1.**

Lower

1. Remove fuel pump relay for Power Distribution Center (PDC).
2. Start and run engine until it stalls.
3. Attempt to start engine until it no longer runs.
4. Turn ignition switch to OFF position.
5. Install fuel pump relay.
6. Disconnect Manifold Absolute Pressure (MAP) sensor electrical connector.
7. Remove clean air duct between throttle body and air filter housing.
8. Remove vent tube.
9. Remove mounting bolt and air filter housing.
10. Disconnect electronic throttle control and manifold tuning valve electrical connectors.
11. Disconnect vapor purge, brake booster hose and Positive Crankcase Ventilation (PCV) hoses.
12. Remove manifold support brackets.
13. Remove mounting bolts, upper manifold and foam insulator.
14. Disconnect injector electrical connectors.
15. Disconnect fuel supply hose from fuel rail
16. Remove mounting bolts, then the fuel rail and injectors.
17. Remove mounting bolts and lower manifold.
18. Remove fuel rail fuel supply hose, then the fuel rail support bracket to throttle body support bracket mounting screw.
19. Reverse procedure to install, noting the following:
   a. Position manifold on cylinder head surfaces by installing upper intake manifold bolt 2-3 turns in rearmost hole.
   b. Install fuel rail with injectors and start bolts 1-4, **Fig. 2.**
   c. **Torque** mounting bolts in sequence, **Fig. 2.**

EXHAUST MANIFOLD
REPLACE
Lefthand

1. Disconnect Intake Air Temperature (IAT) sensor connector.
2. Disconnect Manifold Absolute Pressure (MAP) sensor electrical connector.
3. Remove clean air duct between throttle body and air filter housing.

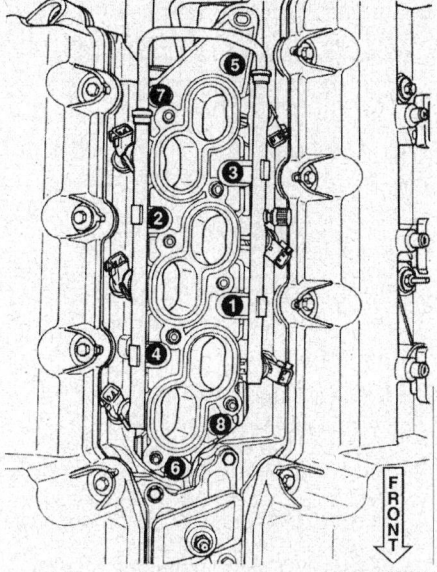

Fig. 2 Lower intake manifold tightening sequence

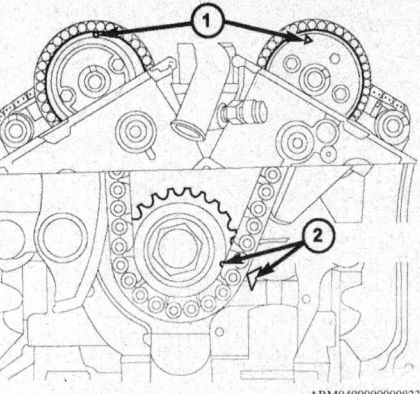

ARM0400000000823

Fig. 3 Timing mark alignment

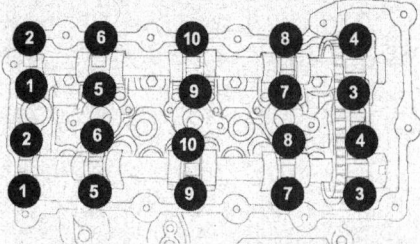

ARM0400000000824

Fig. 4 Camshaft loosening sequence

4. Remove vent tube.
5. Remove mounting bolt and air filter housing.
6. Remove oil dipstick tube.
7. Disconnect and remove oxygen sensor.
8. Remove upper and lower heat shields.
9. Raise and support vehicle on hoist.
10. Disconnect downstream oxygen sensor connector.
11. Remove catalytic converter to muffler and resonator clamps.
12. Remove isolators, then the muffler and tailpipe by twisting/turning while pulling assembly out of catalytic converters.
13. Remove ball flange nuts, then the ball flange nut and catalytic converter.
14. Remove mounting bolts and exhaust manifold
15. Reverse procedure to install, noting the following:
    a. Tighten exhaust manifold mounting bolts starting at center working outward.
    b. **Torque** manifold ball flange nut to 106 inch lbs.
    c. Measure exhaust module and fuel tank clearance. Clearance should be .62 inch.
    d. Measure clearance at rear tunnel reinforcement. Clearance .59–.78 inch.
    e. **Torque** ball flange nuts to 25 ft. lbs.

Righthand

1. Disconnect and remove upstream oxygen sensor.
2. Raise and support vehicle.
3. Remove tube at EGR valve and manifold.
4. Disconnect downstream oxygen sensor electrical connector.
5. Remove catalytic converter to muffler

and resonator clamps.
6. Remove isolators, then the muffler and tailpipe by twisting/turning while pulling assembly out of catalytic converters.
7. Remove mounting nuts and cross-brace.
8. Remove ball flange nuts and catalytic converter.
9. Remove upper and lower heat shields.
10. Remove mounting bolts and exhaust manifold.
11. Reverse procedure to install, noting the following:
    a. Tighten exhaust manifold mounting bolts starting at center working outward.
    b. **Torque** manifold ball flange nut to 106 inch lbs.
    c. Measure exhaust module and fuel tank clearance. Clearance should be .62 inch.
    d. Measure clearance at rear tunnel reinforcement. Clearance .59–.78 in.
    e. **Torque** ball flange nuts to 25 ft. lbs.

CYLINDER HEAD
REPLACE

1. Remove fuel pump relay for Power Distribution Center (PDC).
2. Start and run engine until it stalls.
3. Attempt to start engine until it no longer runs.
4. Turn ignition switch to OFF position.
5. Install fuel pump relay.
6. Raise and support vehicle on hoist.
7. Drain cooling system into suitable container.
8. Rotate belt tensioner counterclockwise until it contacts it's stop.
9. Remove belt and slowly rotate tensioner into freearm position. **Do not let tensioner arm snap back to freearm position.**
10. Hold damper using damper holder tool No. 9365, or equivalent, then remove damper mounting bolts.
11. Remove damper using suitable three-jaw puller.

12. Disconnect Camshaft Position (CMP) and coolant temperature sensors' connectors.
13. Remove upper and lower intake manifolds as outlined under "Intake Manifold, Replace."
14. Remove cylinder head covers as outlined under "Valve Cover, Replace."
15. Remove radiator as outlined under "Radiator, Replace."
16. Remove radiator upper hose at tube.
17. Remove heater hose from heater tube at rear of engine.
18. Disconnect heater tube from retaining clip at rear of engine.
19. Remove mounting screws, then disconnect and remove heater tube from outlet connector.
20. Rotate crankshaft until crankshaft sprocket timing mark aligns with timing mark on oil pump housing, **Fig. 3.** Mark on oil pump housing is 60° ATDC of cylinder No. 1.
21. Remove primary timing chain as outlined under "Timing Chain, Replace."
22. Remove upper primary timing chain guides.
23. Remove camshaft bearing caps gradually in sequence, **Fig. 4.**
24. Mark position for install alignment, then remove camshafts and valve train components from cylinder head.
25. **For lefthand cylinder head,** proceed as follows:
    a. Remove oil dipstick tube to cylinder head mounting bolt.
    b. Remove engine oil dipstick tube.
    c. Remove alternator.
26. **For righthand cylinder head,** proceed as follows:
    a. Remove cylinder head ground strap.
    b. Disconnect electrical connector and remove EGR valve from head.
27. **On all models,** ensure cylinder head bolts No. 1–3 are removed before attempting removal of cylinder head.
28. Remove cylinder head bolts in sequence, **Fig. 5.**
29. Reverse procedure to install, noting the following:
    a. Cylinder head bolts are tightened using torque plus angle procedure. Bolts with stretched threads must be replaced.
    b. Install new head gasket over locating dowels.

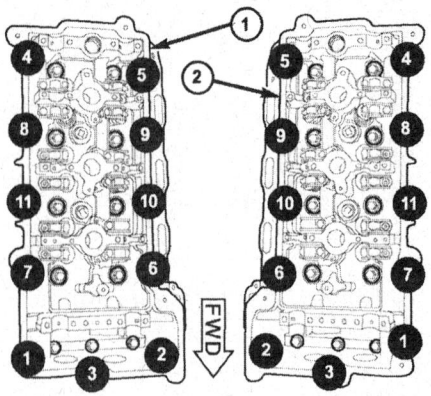

Fig. 5 Cylinder head removal sequence

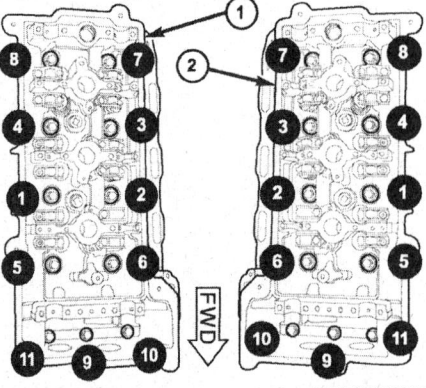

Fig. 6 Cylinder head tightening sequence

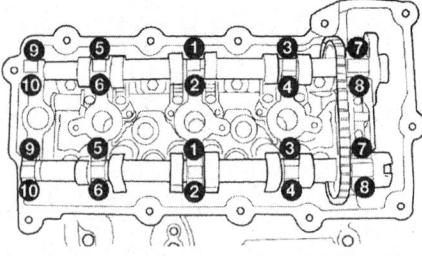

Fig. 7 Camshaft bearing cap tightening sequence

c. Ensure head is properly positioned over locating dowels.
d. Lubricate bolt threads with suitable, clean engine oil.
e. **Torque** cylinder head bolts Nos. 1–8 in sequence to 35 ft. lbs., **Fig. 6.**
f. **Torque** head bolts Nos. 1–8 in sequence to 55 ft. lbs.
g. **Torque** bolts Nos. 1–8 in sequence to 55 ft. lbs.
h. Tighten bolts Nos. 1–8 an additional 90° in sequence.
i. **Torque** cylinder head bolts Nos. 9–11 in sequence to 21 ft. lbs.
j. **Torque** cylinder head bolts 9–11 to 21 ft. lbs.
k. Tighten camshaft bearing caps in sequence, **Fig. 7.**

VALVE COVER

REPLACE

Lefthand

1. Disconnect Manifold Absolute Pressure (MAP) sensor electrical connector.
2. Remove clean air duct between throttle body and air filter housing.
3. Remove vent tube.
4. Remove mounting bolt and air filter housing.
5. Disconnect electronic throttle control and manifold tuning valve electrical connectors.
6. Disconnect vapor purge, brake booster hose and Positive Crankcase Ventilation (PCV) hoses.
7. Remove manifold support brackets.
8. Remove mounting bolts, upper manifold and foam insulator.
9. Disconnect ignition coils electrical connectors.
10. Remove ground strap from cylinder head cover stud and disconnect capacitor connector.
11. Position electrical harness aside.
12. Disconnect retaining clips from cylinder head cover studs and position electrical harness aside.
13. Remove make up air hose.

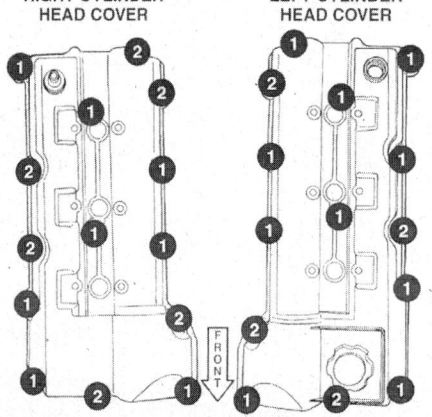

RIGHT CYLINDER HEAD COVER   LEFT CYLINDER HEAD COVER

Fig. 8 Valve cover loosening & tightening sequence

14. Remove capacitor mounting bolts and ignition coils.
15. Loosen valve cover mounting bolts, **Fig. 8. Cylinder head cover mounting bolts are captured in cover. Ensure double ended studs in center of cover are loose before attempting to remove cover.**
16. Remove valve cover.
17. Reverse procedure to install. Ensure double-ended studs are in correct locations.

Righthand

1. Disconnect Manifold Absolute Pressure (MAP) sensor electrical connector.
2. Remove clean air duct between throttle body and air filter housing.
3. Remove vent tube.
4. Remove mounting bolt and air filter housing.
5. Disconnect electronic throttle control and manifold tuning valve electrical connectors.
6. Disconnect vapor purge, brake booster hose and Positive Crankcase Ventilation (PCV) hoses.
7. Remove manifold support brackets.
8. Remove mounting bolts, upper mani-

fold and foam insulator.
9. Disconnect ignition coils electrical connectors.
10. Disconnect capacitor electrical connector
11. Remove PCV hose from cylinder head cover grommet.
12. Remove ground strap from cylinder head cover stud.
13. Disconnect retaining clips from cylinder head cover studs and position electrical harness aside.
14. Remove ignition coil capacitor mounting bolts and ignition coils.
15. Remove foam insulator.
16. Loosen valve cover mounting bolts, **Fig. 8. Cylinder head cover mounting bolts are captured in cover.**
17. Remove valve cover.
18. Reverse procedure to install. Ensure double-ended studs are in correct locations.

CAMSHAFT LOBE LIFT SPECIFICATIONS

Intake ....3543 inch
Exhaust ....3150 inch

VALVE CLEARANCE SPECIFICATIONS

This engine is equipped with hydraulic lifters and valves are lashed with zero clearance.

VALVE ADJUSTMENT

This engine is equipped with hydraulic lash adjusters. No adjustment is required.

ROCKER ARMS

REPLACE

1. Remove cylinder head cover(s) as outlined under "Valve Cover, Replace."
2. Rotate engine until cam lobe is on its base circle (heel), on rocker arm being removed.
3. Mark rocker arms for installation in original positions.
4. Depress valve spring using spring removal tools Nos. 8215 and 8216, suitable adaptor and ratchet
5. Repeat procedure for each rocker arm removed.
6. Reverse procedure to install using spring installation tools Nos. 8215-A

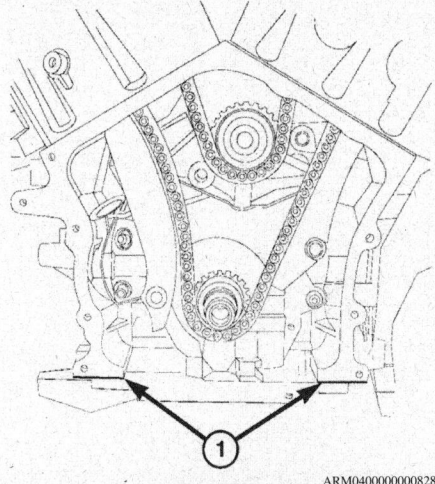

Fig. 9   Front cover RTV application

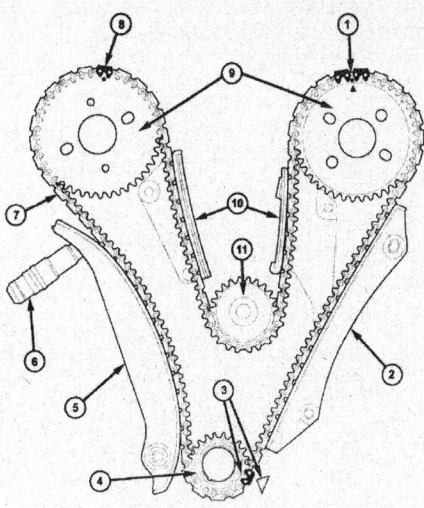

1- TWO (PLATED) TIMING LINKS
2- CHAIN GUIDE
3- OIL PUMP HOUSING
4- CRANKSHAFT SPROCKET
5- CHAIN GUIDE
6- CHAIN TENSIONER
7- TIMING CHAIN
8- TIMING (PLATED) LINK
9- CAMSHAFT SPROCKETS
10- CHAIN GUIDE
11- WATER PUMP DRIVE SPROCKET

ARM0400000000829

Fig. 10   Timing chain alignment

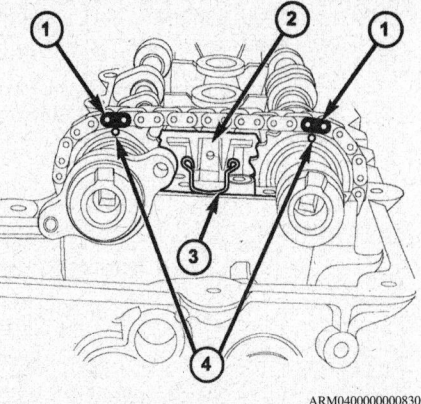

ARM0400000000830

Fig. 11   Camshaft cam alignment

and 8216-A, suitable adaptor and ratchet

HYDRAULIC LIFTERS
REPLACE

1. Remove rocker arm as outlined under "Rocker Arm, Replace."
2. Mark hydraulic lash adjuster for installation in original position
3. Remove hydraulic lash adjuster.
4. Reverse procedure to install. Ensure adjuster is partially full of oil (little or no plunger travel when lash adjuster is depressed).

CRANKSHAFT DAMPER
REPLACE

1. Rotate belt tensioner counterclockwise until it contacts it's stop.
2. Remove belt and slowly rotate tensioner into freearm position. **Do not let tensioner arm snap back to freearm position.**
3. Hold damper using damper holder tool No. 9365, or equivalent, then remove damper mounting bolts.
4. Remove damper using suitable three-jaw puller.
5. Reverse procedure to install, using installer tool No. 6792-1, screw tool No. 8179, and nut and thrust bearing tool No. 6792, or equivalents.

FRONT COVER
REPLACE

1. Drain cooling system into suitable container.
2. Remove coolant pressure container
3. Raise and support vehicle on hoist.
4. Remove mounting bolts and lower splash shield.
5. Rotate belt tensioner counterclockwise until it contacts it's stop.
6. Remove belt and slowly rotate tensioner into freearm position. **Do not let tensioner arm snap back to freearm position.**

7. Hold damper using damper holder tool No. 9365, or equivalent, then remove damper mounting bolts.
8. Remove damper using suitable three-jaw puller.
9. Lower vehicle.
10. Remove mounting bolts and timing chain cover. Discard timing chain cover gasket
11. Remove front crankshaft oil seal from cover.
12. Reverse procedure to install. Apply ⅛ inch bead of Mopar Engine RTV GEN II, or equivalent, to the parting lines between oil pan and cylinder block, **Fig. 9.**

TIMING CHAIN
REPLACE

With the timing chain removed, avoid turning the camshaft or crankshaft. If movement is required, exercise extreme caution to avoid valve damage caused by piston contact.

Removal

1. Drain cooling system into suitable container.
2. Remove cylinder heads as outlined under "Cylinder Head, Replace."
3. Remove timing chain cover as outlined under "Front Cover, Replace."
4. Rotate crankshaft until crankshaft sprocket timing mark aligns with timing mark on oil pump housing, **Fig. 3.** Mark on oil pump housing is 60° ATDC of cylinder No. 1.
5. Remove cap and primary timing chain

tensioner retainer cap from righthand cylinder head.
6. Disconnect and remove Camshaft Position (CMP) sensor from lefthand cylinder head.
7. Remove timing chain guide access plugs from cylinder heads.
8. Remove mounting bolts, righthand camshaft damper and sprocket. **When camshaft sprocket bolts are removed, camshafts rotate in clockwise direction.**
9. Remove mounting bolts and lefthand camshaft sprocket.

Installation

1. Install left and righthand side short chain guides.
2. Align crankshaft sprocket timing to oil pump housing marks, **Fig. 10.**
3. Lubricate timing chain and guides with suitable engine oil.
4. Place lefthand side primary chain sprocket onto chain so timing mark is located between two (plated) timing links.
5. Lower primary chain with lefthand side sprocket through lefthand cylinder head opening.
6. **Camshaft sprockets can be allowed to float on camshaft hub during installation.**
7. Loosely position lefthand side camshaft sprocket over camshaft hub.
8. Align timing (plated) link to crankshaft sprocket timing mark.
9. Position primary chain onto water pump drive sprocket.
10. Align righthand camshaft sprocket timing mark to timing (plated) link on timing chain and loosely position over camshaft hub.
11. Ensure all chain timing (plated) links are properly aligned to timing marks on all sprockets.
12. Install lefthand side lower chain guide and tensioner arm.
13. Install chain guide access plugs to cylinder heads.
14. Place check ball end of tensioner into shallow end of timing chain tensioner reset gauge tool No. 8186, or equivalent.
15. Slowly depress tensioner using hand

Crankshaft Main Journal Grade Mark	Main Bearing Bore Grade Mark		
	1	2	3
1	(3) Standard	(2) +.0001 inch	(1) +.0002 inch
2	(4) -.0001 inch	(3) Standard	(2) +.0001 inch
3	(5) -.0002 inch	(4) -0.0001 inch	(3) Standard

Fig. 12 Main bearing selection chart

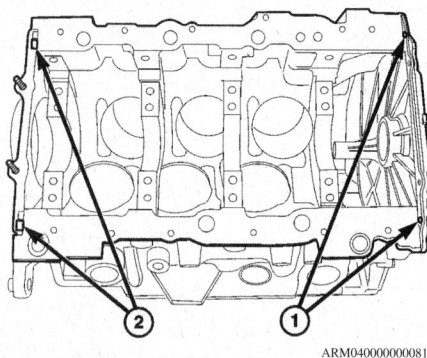

ARM0400000000819

Fig. 13 Oil pan RTV application

pressure until oil is purged from tensioner.

16. Position tensioner cylinder plunger into deeper end of tensioner reset gauge tool.

17. Apply downward force until tensioner is reset.

18. Install reset chain tensioner into right-hand cylinder head, position tensioner retaining and tighten mounting bolts.

19. Starting at righthand cylinder bank, position camshaft damper on camshaft hub, then insert ⅜ inch square drive extension with breaker bar into intake camshaft drive hub.

20. Rotate camshaft until camshaft hub aligns to camshaft sprocket and damper attaching holes.

21. Install and tighten sprocket mounting bolts.

22. Turn lefthand side camshaft by inserting ⅜ inch square drive extension with breaker bar into intake camshaft drive hub until sprocket mounting bolts can be installed and tightened.

23. Remove timing chain slack by rotating engine slightly clockwise.

24. Activate timing chain tensioner by gently pry tensioner arm towards tensioner slightly using suitable flat bladed pry tool. Release tensioner arm.

25. Ensure tensioner is activated (extends).

26. Install CMP sensor and connect electrical connector.

27. Install cylinder heads as outlined under "Cylinder Head, Replace."

28. Install timing chain cover as outlined under "Front Cover, Replace."

29. After installation of reset tensioner, engine noise will occur after initial start-up. Noise will normally disappear within 5–10 seconds.

30. Fill cooling system

TIMING CHAIN TENSIONER

REPLACE

1. Remove timing chain cover as outlined under "Front Cover, Replace."
2. Align timing marks, **Fig. 10.**
3. Remove cover and timing chain tensioner.
4. Reverse procedure to install, noting the following:
   a. Ensure proper timing alignment prior to tensioner installation.
   b. Position tensioner cylinder plunger

into deeper end of tensioner reset gauge tool No. 8186, or equivalent.

c. Apply downward force until tensioner is reset.

d. Tensioner retaining plate dowel pin must aligned with hole in cylinder head.

TIMING CHAIN TENSIONER BLEED

1. Place check ball end of tensioner into shallow end of timing chain tensioner reset gauge tool No. 8186, or equivalent.
2. Slowly depress tensioner using hand pressure until oil is purged from tensioner.

CAMSHAFT

REPLACE

With the timing chain removed, avoid turning the camshaft or crankshaft. If movement is required, exercise caution to avoid valve damage caused by piston contact.

Removal

1. Remove primary timing chain as outlined under "Timing Chain, Replace."
2. Remove secondary chain tensioner mounting bolts.
3. Slowly loosen and remove camshaft bearing caps gradually in sequence, **Fig. 4.**
4. Camshaft bearing caps have been marked during engine manufacturing. For example, No. 1 exhaust camshaft bearing is marked 1E.
5. Remove intake camshaft, exhaust camshaft), secondary timing chain and secondary timing chain tensioner as an assembly.
6. Remove secondary timing chain tensioner and secondary timing chain from camshafts.

Installation

When the timing chain is removed and the cylinder heads are installed, do not rotate the camshafts or crankshaft without first locating the proper crankshaft position.

1. Assemble camshaft chain on cams.
2. Ensure plated links are facing toward front, **Fig. 11.**

3. Align plated links to camshaft sprockets' dots.

4. If camshaft chain tensioner is already in compressed and locked position, proceed to next step. When camshaft chain tensioner has been removed, proceed as follows:
   a. Place tensioner into suitable soft jaw vise.
   b. Slowly compress tensioner until fabricated lock pin can be inserted into locking holes.

5. Install compressed and locked camshaft chain tensioner between camshafts and chain

6. Rotate cams so plated links and dots are facing 12 O'clock position.

7. Install cams to cylinder head. Ensure rocker arms are correctly seated and in proper positions.

8. Install camshaft bearing caps. Ensure bearing caps are installed in original positions.

9. Tighten camshaft bearing cap bolts gradually in sequence, **Fig. 7.**

10. Install and tighten secondary chain tensioner mounting bolts.

11. Remove locking pin from secondary tensioners.

12. Measure camshafts end play. Endplay should be .0051–.0110 inch.

13. Install primary timing chain as outlined under "Timing Chain, Replace."

PISTON & ROD ASSEMBLY

1. Position bearing onto connecting rod. Ensure bearing half and connecting rod holes align.

2. Lubricate bearing surface with suitable, clean engine oil.

3. Install connecting rod guides tools No. 8189, or equivalent, into connecting rod.

4. Ensure pistons top mark arrow and F (front) above pin boss. pointing towards front of engine in both cylinder banks.

5. Connecting rod oil squirt hole faces major thrust (righthand) side of block.

6. Rotate crankshaft so connecting rod journal is on center of cylinder bore.

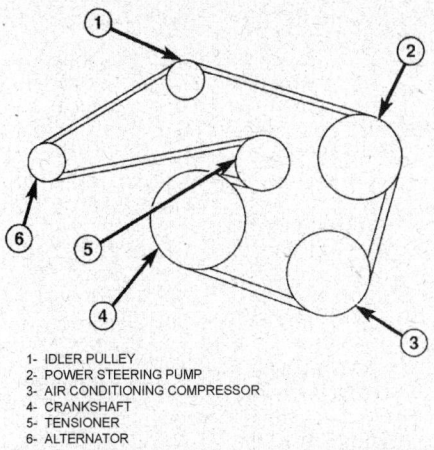

1- IDLER PULLEY
2- POWER STEERING PUMP
3- AIR CONDITIONING COMPRESSOR
4- CRANKSHAFT
5- TENSIONER
6- ALTERNATOR

ARM0400000000616

Fig. 14 Serpentine drive belt routing

7. Insert rod and piston into cylinder bore, then guide rod over crankshaft journal.
8. **Do not interchange piston assemblies bank to bank.**
9. Tap piston down in cylinder bore, using suitable hammer handle while guide connecting rod into position on connecting rod journal.
10. Lubricate rod bolts and bearing surface with suitable engine oil.
11. Install and connecting rod cap and bearing, then tighten bolts.

MAIN & ROD BEARINGS

Upper and lower bearing halves are not interchangeable.
1. Refer to **Fig. 12** to select main bearings.
2. Install main bearing in block and main caps ensuring tangs engage slots in block and main caps.
3. Lubricate upper main bearing halves with suitable engine oil.
4. Install crankshaft. **Do not damage bearing surfaces on crankshaft.**
5. Ensure coated and oil groove side of crankshaft thrust washer faces crankshaft thrust surface.
6. Push crankshaft forward.
7. Lubricate and install front thrust washer by rolling thrust washer onto machined shelf between upper main bulk head No. 3 and crankshaft thrust surface.
8. Move crankshaft rearward.
9. Lubricate and install rear thrust washer by rolling thrust washer onto machined shelf between upper main bulk head No. 3 and crankshaft thrust surface.
10. Lubricate lower main bearings with suitable engine oil.
11. Install main bearings caps.
12. Lubricate main bearing cap bolts with suitable engine oil.
13. **Torque** inner main cap bolts to 15 ft. lbs., then tighten additional 90°.
14. Measure crankshaft end play. End play should be .0019–.0108 inch.
15. Install connecting rods and measure

side clearance. using plastigage. Side clearance should be .0052–.015 inch.
16. Install windage tray with slots to right-hand side of engine.
17. Lubricate mounting bolts with suitable engine oil and **Torque** to 20 ft. lbs., then tighten additional 90°.
18. Install main cap tie (horizontal) bolts and **torque** to 20 ft. lbs.

CRANKSHAFT SEAL
REPLACE

1. Rotate belt tensioner counterclockwise until it contacts it's stop.
2. Remove belt and slowly rotate tensioner into freearm position. **Do not let tensioner arm snap back to freearm position.**
3. Hold damper using damper holder tool No. 9365, or equivalent, then remove damper mounting bolts.
4. Remove damper using suitable three-jaw puller.
5. Remove seal using remover tool Nos. 6771 and 8194, or equivalents.
6. Reverse procedure to install using crankshaft seal protector tool No. 6780-2, crankshaft seal and sprocket installer tool 6780-1 and crankshaft damper installer screw tool No. 8179, or equivalents.

CRANKSHAFT REAR OIL SEAL
REPLACE

The crankshaft rear oil seal is incorporated in the seal adapter and can not be removed from the adapter. The crankshaft rear oil seal/seal adapter are serviced as an assembly.

The integrated stamped steel rear crankshaft seal is not interchangeable with the cast aluminum rear seal adapter and seal assembly.
1. Raise and support vehicle.
2. Remove mounting bolts and splash shield.
3. Raise and support vehicle on hoist.
4. Remove mounting bolts and lower splash shield.
5. Remove transmission mount bolts.
6. Place suitable transmission jack under transmission pan, then raise engine and transmission.
7. Remove mounting bolts and structural collar to right, then rear.
8. Remove transmission as outlined in **MOTOR's "Domestic Transmission Manual, In-Vehicle Service."**
9. Remove mounting bolts, then the backing and flex plates.
10. Remove oil pan as outlined under "Oil Pan, Replace."
11. Remove mounting screws and crankshaft rear oil seal/adapter.
12. Reverse procedure to install, noting the following:
   a. Install seal assembly using seal installer tool No. 6926-1, or equivalent.
   b. Install seal mounting bolts hand tight.

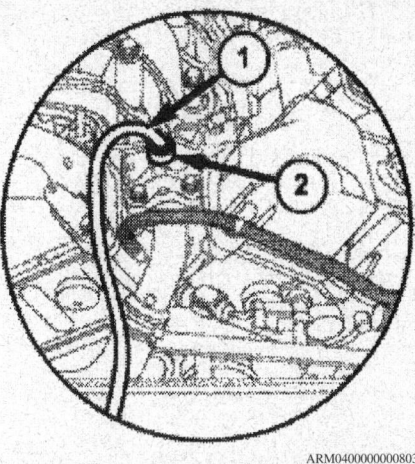

ARM0400000000803

Fig. 15 Cooling system bleed

   c. Attach alignment tools No. 8225, or equivalent to pan rail.
   d. Ensure 2.7L stamped on special tool is facing cylinder block (flat side of tools against pan rail).
   e. Apply firm pressure to seal assembly against special tools and **torque** seal screws 105 inch lbs.

OIL PAN
REPLACE

1. Remove engine oil indicator.
2. Raise and support vehicle on hoist.
3. Remove mounting bolts and lower splash shield.
4. Drain engine oil into suitable container and remove oil filter.
5. Remove bolt and steering separate coupler from rack.
6. Disconnect power steering pressure switch electrical connector.
7. Remove steering rack mounting bolts and power steering line support from frame.
8. Position rack aside.
9. Raise and support vehicle on hoist.
10. Remove mounting bolts and lower splash shield.
11. Remove transmission mount bolts.
12. Place suitable transmission jack under transmission pan, then raise engine and transmission.
13. Remove mounting bolts and structural collar to right, then rear.
14. Remove alternator mounting bracket to oil pan lower bolt.
15. Remove air conditioning compressor bracket to oil pan lower bolt.
16. Remove lower timing chain cover to oil pan bolts.
17. Remove mounting bolts, oil pan and gasket. **Ensure four lower timing cover bolts are removed.**
18. Reverse procedure to install, noting the following:
   a. Apply ⅛ inch bead of Mopar Engine RTV GEN II, or equivalent, to front T-joints (oil pan gasket to timing cover gasket interface) and rear T-joints (oil pan gasket to crankshaft rear oil seal retainer gasket interface), **Fig. 13.**

b. Install oil pan bolts and nuts, then hand tighten just tight enough to compress gasket's rubber seal

c. Line up front of oil pan to be flush with front face of block.

d. Install lower timing chain cover bolts and **torque** to 105 inch lbs.

e. **Torque** oil pan bolts to 20 ft. lbs.

f. **Torque** oil pan nuts to 105 inch lbs.

g. Hand tighten structural collar mounting bolts.

h. Ensure structural collar is flush with oil pan and transmission bell housing.

i. **Torque** vertical collar bolts to oil pan to 10 inch lbs.

j. **Torque** horizontal collar bolts to transmission to 40 ft. lbs.

k. **Torque** mounting bolts, starting with center vertical bolts and working outward to 40 ft. lbs.

OIL PUMP

REPLACE

1. Remove timing chain and sprockets as outlined under "Timing Chain, Replace."

2. Remove oil pan as outlined under "Oil Pan, Replace."

3. Remove oil pick-up tube and O-ring.

4. Ensure crankshaft position is at 60° ATDC of cylinder No. 1 or crankshaft sprocket and oil pimp marks align.

5. Remove mounting bolts and oil pump.

6. Reverse procedure to install, noting the following:

a. Prime oil pump before installation by filling rotor cavity with suitable engine oil.

b. Ensure crankshaft position is at 60° ATDC of cylinder No. 1 or crankshaft sprocket.

c. Install new oil pick-up tube O-ring lubricated with suitable, clean engine oil.

OIL PUMP SERVICE

Do not remove oil pressure relief valve. If the oil pressure relief valve is suspect, replace the oil pump assembly.

Disassemble

1. Remove mounting screws and oil pump cover.

2. Remove inner and outer pump rotors.

Inspection

1. Wash all parts in suitable solvent.

2. Inspect mating surface of oil pump housing and cover. Replace oil pump if deeply scratched or grooved.

3. Lay straightedge across pump cover surface. Replace cover is gap is .001 inch or more.

4. Measure thickness and diameter of outer rotor. If outer rotor thickness is .373 inch, or less, or if diameter is 3.5108 inches, or less, replace outer rotor.

5. Measure inner rotor. If inner rotor is .373 inch, or less, replace inner rotor.

6. Slide outer rotor into body, press to one side with fingers, then measure clearance between rotor and body. If measurement is 015 inch, or more, replace body only if outer rotor is within specifications.

7. Install inner rotor into body. If clearance between inner and outer rotors is .008 inch, or more, replace both rotors.

8. Place straightedge across face of body, between bolt holes. If clearance between rotors and straightedge is .003 inch, or more, replace pump assembly if rotors are within specification.

Assemble

1. Install rotor.

2. Tighten cover mounting screws.

3. Prime oil pump before installation by filling rotor cavity with suitable engine oil.

BELT TENSION DATA

Belt adjustment is maintained by an automatic (spring load) belt tensioner.

SERPENTINE DRIVE BELT

Routing

Refer to **Fig. 14** for serpentine drive belt routing.

Replacement

REMOVAL

1. Rotate belt tensioner counterclockwise until it contacts it's stop.

2. Remove belt and slowly rotate tensioner into freearm position. **Do not let tensioner arm snap back to freearm position.**

INSTALLATION

1. Route belt around all pulleys except idler pulley.

2. Rotate tensioner arm until it contacts it's stop position.

3. Route belt around idler and slowly let tensioner rotate into belt.

4. Ensure belt is seated onto all pulleys.

5. Tensioner is equipped with indexing tang on back and indexing stop on housing.

6. If new belt (used 15 minutes or less) is being installed, tang must be within approximately .24–.32 inch of indexing stop.

COOLING SYSTEM BLEED

1. Attach 4–6 feet long ¼ inch ID clear hose to bleeder fitting located on lower intake manifold, left of center and below upper intake plenum, **Fig. 15. When installing drain hose to air bleed valve, route hose away from accessory drive belts, accessory drive pulleys, and electric cooling fan motors.**

2. Route hose away from accessory drive belt, drive pulleys and electric cooling fan

3. Place other end of hose into clean container.

4. **Ensure cooling system air bleed valve is opened before any coolant is added to cooling system.**

5. Attach filling aid funnel tool No. 8195, or equivalent, to pressure bottle filler neck.

6. Pinch overflow hose that connects between two chambers of coolant bottle using suitable hose pinch-off pliers.

7. Open bleed fitting.

8. Pour suitable antifreeze mixture into larger section of filling aid funnel (smaller section of funnel is to allow air to escape).

9. Slowly fill cooling system until steady stream of coolant flows from hose attached to bleed valve.

10. Close bleed valve and continue filling system to top of filling aid funnel tool.

11. Remove pinch-off pliers from overflow hose.

12. Allow coolant in filling funnel to drain into overflow chamber of pressure bottle.

13. Remove funnel and install coolant pressure bottle cap.

14. Remove hose from bleed valve.

15. Start engine and run at 1500–2000 RPM for 30 minutes, noting the following:

a. Engine cooling system will push any remaining air into coolant bottle within about an hour of normal driving. As a result, a drop in coolant level in pressure bottle may occur.

b. If engine cooling system overheats and pushes coolant into overflow side of coolant bottle, this coolant will be sucked back into cooling system, **only if pressure cap is left on bottle.**

c. Removing pressure cap breaks vacuum path between two bottle sections and coolant will not return to cooling system.

16. Shut off engine allow it to cool down for 30 minutes. This permits coolant to be drawn into pressure chamber.

17. With engine cold, ensure coolant level should be within MIN and MAX marks. Coolant will normally only be in inboard of coolant bottle two chambers. Outboard chamber is only to recover coolant in event of an overheat or after recent service fill.

THERMOSTAT

REPLACE

1. Drain cooling system into suitable container.

2. Remove radiator lower hose from thermostat housing

3. Remove nuts from heater tube flange studs.

4. Loosen starter bolt at heater tube bracket.

5. Remove and position heater tube aside.

6. Remove mounting bolt, two studs, thermostat housing, O-ring and thermostat.
7. Remove thermostat housing bolts.
8. Reverse procedure to install, noting the following:
   a. Install thermostat with bleed valve located at 12 o'clock position, between tabs on seal.
   b. Lubricate new heater return tube O-ring with suitable

WATER PUMP
REPLACE

1. Drain cooling system into suitable container.
2. Remove upper radiator hose.
3. Disconnect cooling fan electrical connector.
4. Remove mounting bolts and radiator cooling fan.
5. Rotate belt tensioner counterclockwise until it contacts it's stop.
6. Remove belt and slowly rotate tensioner into freearm position. **Do not let tensioner arm snap back to freearm position.**
7. Remove timing chain and guides as outlined under "Timing Chain, Replace."
8. Remove mounting bolts, water pump and gasket.
9. Reverse procedure to install.

RADIATOR
REPLACE

1. Drain cooling system into suitable container.
2. Remove upper radiator hose.
3. Remove upper radiator closure panels.
4. Disconnect cooling fan electrical connector, then remove mounting bolts and cooling fan.
5. Raise and support vehicle.
6. Remove lower splash shield.
7. Remove lower radiator hose.
8. Remove lower condenser mount bolts.
9. Lower vehicle.
10. Remove mounting bolts and upper radiator mounting brackets.
11. Remove upper condenser mounting bolts.
12. Separate condenser from radiator.
13. Tilt radiator toward engine and remove it.
14. Reverse procedure to install.

FUEL PUMP
REPLACE

1. Remove fuel pump relay for Power Distribution Center (PDC).
2. Start and run engine until it stalls.
3. Attempt to start engine until it no longer runs.
4. Turn ignition switch to OFF position.
5. Install fuel pump relay.
6. Drain partial fuel from fuel tank through filler tube using hard nylon tube, with 30° cut on end, to push check valve open to drain fuel from tank. **Fuel level of vehicle must be below ⅝ of tank before removing module lock-rings.**
7. Remove rear lower seat cushion by pushing seat back and up.
8. Fold back foam pad covering access cover for modules.
9. Disconnect electrical connector from lefthand side module.
10. Mark module orientation for installation alignment.
11. Remove lefthand side module lock ring use lock ring tool No. 9340, or equivalent.
12. Drain fuel from lefthand side of fuel tank. Lift module up enough to push hose into tank and drain. **Do not spill fuel in interior of vehicle.**
13. Disconnect electrical connectors from module top.
14. Remove module top half.
15. Remove module fuel level sending card, fuel return lines and supply line.
16. Press in fuel line release tab and remove fuel line by pulling it up.
17. Unsnap and remove fuel return line from lower module.
18. Tip module on its side and drain remaining fuel from reservoir.
19. Remove module.
20. Reverse procedure to install.

FUEL FILTER
REPLACE

The fuel filter is replaceable only as part of the fuel pump module.

TIGHTENING SPECIFICATIONS

Year	Component	Torque Ft. Lbs.
2005	Air Conditioning Compressor	21
	Alternator/Compressor Mounting Bracket, No. 1 & 2	40
	Alternator/Compressor Mounting Bracket, No. 3	30
	Automatic Belt Tensioner	40
	Camshaft Bearing Cap	105①
	Camshaft Chain Tensioner	105①
	Camshaft Sprocket	20
	Connecting Rod Cap	20②
	Cooling Fan	50①
	Cooling System Bleed Screw	110①
	Crankshaft Damper	125
	Crankshaft Rear Seal Retainer	105①
	Cross-Brace	40
	Crossmember	50
	Cylinder Head	③
	Cylinder Head Cover	105①
	EGR Tube	95①
	Engine Mount	45
	Engine Mount Adapter	55
	Engine Mount Isolator	106
	Engine Mount, Rear	35
	Exhaust Manifold	17
	Exhaust Manifold Heat Shield	20
	Fan Blade	17
	Fan Shroud	50①
	Fuel Line Clamps	31①
	Hose Clamp	31①
	Heater Supply Tube	30①
	Idler Pulley	20
	Intake Manifold	105①
	Main Bearing Cap	⑤
	Oil Pan	④
	Oil Pan Drain Plug	20
	Oil Pump	20
	Oil Pump Cover	105①
	Oil Pump Pick Up Tube	20
	Radiator to Support Bracket	105①
	Starter	30
	Steering Coupling	22
	Steering Gear	95
	Structural Collar	⑥
	Thermostat Housing	105①
	Thermostat Housing/Water Inlet Connector	105①
	Throttle Body	105①
	Timing Chain Cover, M6	105①
	Timing Chain Cover, M10	40
	Timing Chain Guide Access Plug	15
	Timing Chain Tensioner	105①
	Torque Converter	55
	Transmission Mount	35
	Upper Radiator Closure Panel	90①
	Water Pump	105①

① — Inch lbs.
② — Plus an additional 90°.
③ — Refer to "Cylinder Head, Replace" for tightening specifications and sequence.
④ — Refer to "Oil Pan, Replace" for tightening specifications and sequence.
⑤ — Refer to "Main & Rod Bearings" for tightening specifications and sequence.
⑥ — Refer to "Structure Collar, Replace" for tightening specifications and sequence.

3.5L Engine

NOTE: On Air Bag Equipped Models, Refer To "Air Bag System Precautions" Located In The Front Of This Manual For System Disarming & Arming Procedures.

NOTE: Refer To "Computer Relearn Procedures" Located In The Front Of This Manual When Battery Power To The Computer Has Been Interrupted.

NOTE: Refer To The Rear Of This Manual For Vehicle Manufacturer's Special Tool Suppliers.

INDEX

PRECAUTIONS

Air Bag Systems

Refer to "Air Bag System Precautions" in the front of this manual for system disarming and arming procedures.

Battery Ground Cable

Prior to service, disconnect battery ground cable and isolate as required.

RECALIBRATION

Anytime the battery has been disconnect or has lost its charge, the following must be recalibrated:

EXPRESS WINDOW

1. Turn ignition switch to RUN position.
2. Move driver's window upward until it stalls in full up position. Allow window motor to stall for at least two seconds before releasing switch.
3. Move driver's window downward until it stalls in full down position. Allow window motor to stall for at least two seconds before releasing switch.
4. Move driver's window upward until it stalls in full up position. Allow window motor to stall for at least two seconds before releasing switch.
5. Move passenger's window upward until it stalls in full up position. Allow window motor to stall for at least two seconds before releasing switch.
6. Move passenger's window downward until it stalls in full down position. Allow window motor to stall for at least two seconds before releasing switch.
7. Move passenger's window upward until it stalls in full up position. Allow window motor to stall for at least two seconds before releasing switch.

ELECTRONIC STABILITY PROGRAM (ESP) STEERING ANGLE SENSOR

1. Start engine.
2. Turn steering wheel right until wheel locks full right.
3. Turn steering wheel left until wheel locks full left.
4. Turn steering wheel right until wheels are centered.
5. Cycle ignition switch OFF and ON. Do not start engine.

Fuel System Pressure Relief

1. Remove fuel pump relay for Power Distribution Center (PDC).
2. Start and run engine until it stalls.
3. Attempt to start engine until it no longer runs.
4. Turn ignition switch to OFF position.
5. Install fuel pump relay.

COMPRESSION PRESSURE

Refer to "2.7L Engine" section for compression pressure procedures.

ENGINE MOUNT

REPLACE

AWD

LEFTHAND

1. Raise and support vehicle, then remove lefthand front tire and wheel assembly.

2. Remove lefthand engine mount to cradle mounting bolt.
3. Support engine using suitable jack stand.
4. Remove mounting bolts and nuts, then the engine mount.
5. Reverse procedure to install.

REAR

1. Raise and support vehicle on hoist.
2. Remove crossmember to mount bolts.
3. Raise transmission using suitable transmission jack.
4. Remove mounting bolts and crossmember.
5. Remove mounting bolts and rear mount.
6. Reverse procedure to install.

RIGHTHAND

1. Raise and support vehicle, then remove righthand front tire and wheel assembly.
2. Support engine using suitable jack stand.
3. Remove engine mount to cradle mounting bolt.
4. Raise and support engine with jack stand.
5. Remove mounting bolts and righthand engine mount.
6. Reverse procedure to install.

RWD

LEFTHAND

1. Raise and support vehicle, then remove both engine mount to cradle nuts and lefthand engine mount studs.
2. Raise engine approximately .20 inch using suitable jack and wooden block under oil pan.
3. Remove lefthand engine mount heat shield.
4. Remove mounting bolts and lefthand engine mount.
5. Reverse procedure to install.

REAR

1. Raise and support vehicle on hoist.
2. Remove crossmember to mount bolts.
3. Raise transmission using suitable transmission jack.
4. Remove mounting bolts and crossmember.
5. Remove mounting bolts and rear mount.
6. Reverse procedure to install.

RIGHTHAND

1. Raise and support vehicle, then remove both of engine mount to cradle nuts.
2. Remove both the engine mount through studs.
3. Raise engine approximately .20 inch using suitable jack stand and wooden block under oil pan.
4. Remove righthand mount heat shield mounting bolts.
5. Remove righthand engine mount.
6. Reverse procedure to install.

ENGINE

REPLACE

1. Remove fuel pump relay for Power Distribution Center (PDC).
2. Start and run engine until it stalls.
3. Attempt to start engine until it no longer runs.
4. Turn ignition switch to OFF position.
5. Install fuel pump relay.
6. Center and secure steering wheel.
7. Recover refrigerant as outlined in "Air Conditioning" chapter.
8. Remove hood.
9. Remove windshield cowl.
10. Raise and support vehicle.
11. Remove lower engine close out panel.
12. Drain cooling system into suitable container.
13. Disconnect lower radiator hose.
14. **On AWD models,** remove front drive axles and housing.
15. **On all models,** disconnect alternator electrical connectors
16. Separate column coupling from steering gear.
17. Remove underbody splash shield.
18. Remove center bolt, then separate intermediate steering shaft upper and lower shaft.
19. Disconnect starter electrical connector.
20. Remove three starter mounting bolts and wiring clip.
21. Pull starter forward and down, then work it up and around exhaust.
22. Work starter past intermediate steering shaft and remove it.
23. Disconnect hose at oil cooler and remove cooler hose retainer at transmission.
24. Disconnect transmission line bracket at air conditioning compressor and allow bolt to rest on cradle.
25. Disconnect ground strap at righthand transmission housing.
26. Disconnect and position engine block heater wiring connector aside.
27. Disconnect connector, then remove mounting bolt and Crankshaft Position (CKP) sensor.
28. Disconnect lefthand No. 2 oxygen senor electrical connector and separate exhaust manifold from lefthand exhaust pipe.
29. Disconnect righthand No. oxygen senor electrical connector and separate exhaust manifold from righthand exhaust pipe.
30. Remove flex plate inspection cover and torque converter bolts.
31. Remove transmission housing to engine mounting bolts.
32. Remove engine mounting to cradle mounting bolts and nuts.
33. Lower vehicle.
34. Remove upper intake manifold as outlined under "Intake Manifold, Replace."
35. Disconnect heater and coolant reservoir hoses from rear coolant pipe.
36. Disconnect oxygen sensor connector and ground wire on lefthand cylinder head cover.

37. Disconnect coolant temperature, cam position, oil pressure sensors' electrical connectors.
38. Disconnect lefthand ignition coil and fuel injector harness connectors, then position wiring harness aside.
39. Remove righthand intake manifold support braces.
40. Disconnect capacitor and ground strap from righthand cylinder head cover.
41. Disconnect oxygen sensor, knock, EGR, injector and ignition coil harness connectors, then position wiring harness aside.
42. Disconnect engine wiring harness from transmission housing and remove remaining transmission housing bolts.
43. Connect driveline support fixture tool No. 8534B, or equivalent, engine lifting bracket to righthand rear of cylinder head outer most bolt access hole.
44. Install bolt into inner most bolt access hole next to engine lift bracket to assure lifting bracket positioning.
45. Connect suitable engine hoisting chain to lefthand timing chain cover engine lifting point and engine lift bracket.
46. Remove engine constantly checking to ensure proper positioning and no damage to other components or wiring harnesses. As engine is hoisted from engine bay area, remove loosened air conditioning compressor bolt retaining transmission cooler lines and direct lines aside.
47. Reverse procedure to install. **Do not pinch power steering rack sensor with lefthand engine mount.**

INTAKE MANIFOLD

REPLACE

Upper

1. Disconnect Intake Air temperature (IAT) sensor electrical connector.
2. Remove air inlet hose from throttle body.
3. Disconnect Manifold Absolute Pressure (MAP) sensor electrical connector.
4. Disconnect engine electrical harness connectors from intake manifold.
5. Disconnect EGR tube, PCV, Purge and power brake booster vacuum hoses from upper intake manifold.
6. Disconnect throttle control electrical electronic connector.
7. Remove throttle bracket mounting bolts from throttle body and cylinder head.
8. Disconnect Manifold Tuning Valve (MTV) and Short Runner Valve (SRV) electrical connectors.
9. Remove righthand intake manifold support brackets.
10. Remove mounting bolts, insulation foam pad and upper intake manifold.
11. Reverse procedure to install, noting the following:
    a. Install new gasket.
    b. Tighten mounting bolts starting in

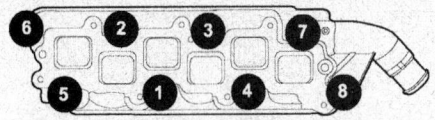

Fig. 1 Lower intake manifold tightening sequence

ARM0400000000834

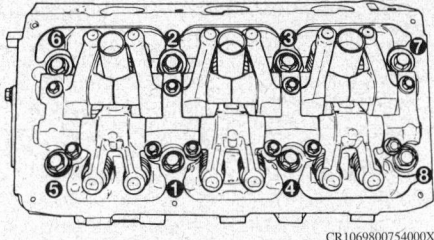

CR1069800754000X

Fig. 2 Cylinder head bolt tightening sequence

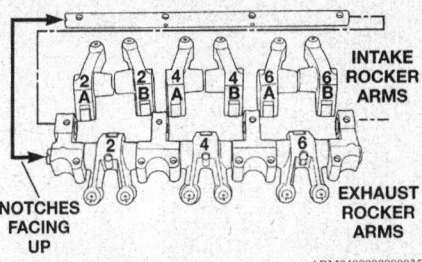

ARM0400000000835

Fig. 3 Rock arm identification

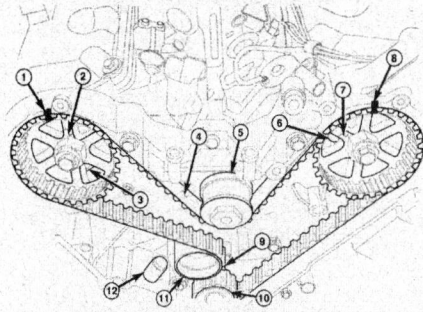

1- RIGHTHAND CAMSHAFT GEAR ALIGNMENT MARK
2- RIGHTHAND CAMSHAFT GEAR
3- CYLINDER HEAD TO INNER TIMING BELT COVERS BOLTS- RIGHTHAND
4- TIMING BELT
5- WATER PUMP PULLEY
6- CYLINDDER HEAD TO INNER TIMING BELT COVER BOLTS- LEFTHAND
7- LEFTHAND CAMSHAFT GEAR
8- LEFTHAND CAMSHAFT GEAR ALIGNMENT MARK
9- CRANKSHAFT GEAR ALIGNMENT MARK
10- CRANKSHAFT GEAR
11- TIMING BELT TENSIONER PULLEY
12- TIMING BELT TENSIONER

ARM0400000000836

Fig. 4 Camshaft timing position

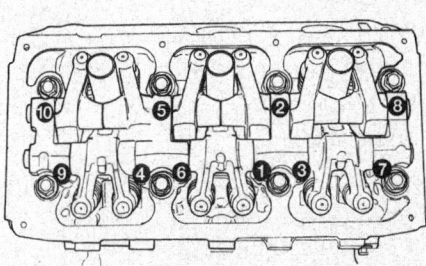

ARM0400000000837

Fig. 5 Rocker arm tightening sequence

EXHAUST MANIFOLD
REPLACE
Lefthand

1. Raise and support vehicle.
2. Separate front exhaust pipe to manifold union.
3. Lower vehicle.
4. Disconnect and remove oxygen sensor from exhaust manifold.
5. Remove shield mounting bolts and exhaust manifold. Discard gasket
6. Reverse procedure to install. Tighten mounting bolts starting at center working outward.

Righthand

1. Disconnect upstream oxygen sensor electrical connector.
2. Raise and support vehicle
3. Remove exhaust manifold to exhaust pipe flange mounting bolts.
4. Lower vehicle.
5. Remove heat shield and exhaust manifold manifold.
6. Remove oxygen sensor from exhaust manifold.
7. Reverse procedure to install. Tighten mounting bolts starting at center working outward.

CYLINDER HEAD
REPLACE

1. Remove upper radiator crossmember, then the fan module and accessory drive belts.
2. Remove upper radiator crossmember and fan module.
3. Remove damper using crankshaft damper holder tool No. 8191, or equivalent, and three-jaw puller tool No. 1023, or equivalent.
4. Remove damper using crankshaft damper holder tool No. 8191, or equivalent, and three-jaw puller tool No. 1023, or equivalent.
5. Remove lower belt cover, stamped steel cover and lefthand cast cover.
6. Remove camshaft sprockets as outlined under "Camshaft Sprocket, Replace."
7. Remove upper and lower intake manifolds as outlined under "Intake Manifold, Replace."

8. Remove exhaust manifold to catalytic converter pipe connection V-band clamps.
9. Remove rear timing belt cover to cylinder head mounting bolts and rear covers.
10. Remove mounting bolts and cylinder heads.
11. Reverse procedure to install, noting the following:
    a. **Cylinder head bolts with stretched threads must be replaced.**
    b. Lubricate bolt threads with suitable, clean engine oil.
    c. **Torque** cylinder head bolts in sequence to 45 ft. lbs., **Fig. 2.**
    d. **Torque** head bolts in sequence to 65 ft. lbs.
    e. **Torque** bolts in sequence to 65 ft. lbs.
    f. Tighten bolts an additional 90° in sequence.
    g. If final cylinder head bolt **torque** is not 90 ft. lbs, replace bolts.
    h. Install new O-ring seal in righthand rear timing belt cover.

VALVE COVER
REPLACE

1. Remove upper intake manifold as outlined under "Intake Manifold, Replace."
2. Cover lower intake manifold.
3. Disconnect and remove three ignition coils.
4. Remove ground strap/resistor mounting bolt from cylinder head cover.
5. Lift wire harness track retaining tabs.
6. Loosen mounting bolts and remove cylinder head cover.
7. Reverse procedure to install. Install

center working outward in cross sequence pattern.

Lower

1. Remove fuel pump relay for Power Distribution Center (PDC).
2. Start and run engine until it stalls.
3. Attempt to start engine until it no longer runs.
4. Turn ignition switch to OFF position.
5. Install fuel pump relay.
6. Drain cooling system into suitable container.
7. Disconnect upper radiator hose from thermostat housing.
8. Remove upper intake manifold as outlined under "Upper."
9. Position power steering fluid reservoir and bracket aside.
10. Disconnect fuel injectors and coolant temperature sensor electrical connectors.
11. Disconnect heater hose from rear intake manifold.
12. Disconnect coolant container hose at rear intake manifold.
13. Disconnect fuel supply hose from rail.
14. Remove mounting bolts, then the fuel rail and injectors as an assembly.
15. Remove mounting bolts and lower intake manifold.
16. Reverse procedure to install, noting the following:
    a. Install new gaskets.
    b. Gradually tighten intake manifold mounting bolts in sequence. **Fig. 1.**

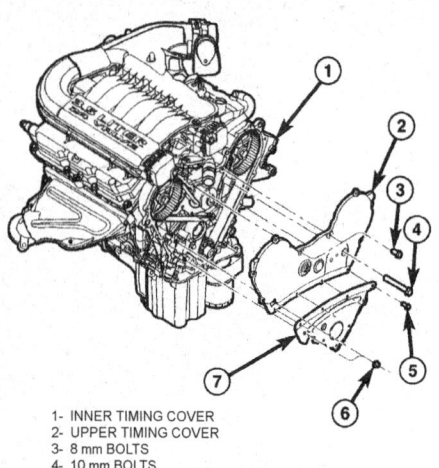

1- INNER TIMING COVER
2- UPPER TIMING COVER
3- 8 mm BOLTS
4- 10 mm BOLTS
5- 6 mm BOLTS
6- NUTS
7- LOWER TIMING COVER

ARM0400000000838

Fig. 6   Timing belt cover replacement

new spark plug tube seals using spark plug tube seal installation tool No. MD-998306, or equivalent

CAMSHAFT LOBE LIFT SPECIFICATIONS

Intake ....3367 inch
Exhaust ....3367 inch

VALVE CLEARANCE SPECIFICATIONS

This engine is equipped with hydraulic lifters and valves are lashed with zero clearance.

VALVE ADJUSTMENT

Rocker arms are equipped with hydraulic lash adjusters. No adjustment is required.

ROCKER ARMS
REPLACE

The rocker arm and shaft assembly on the righthand side of the engine has an oil passage hole from the cylinder head to the third rocker shaft support. The rocker arm shaft assembly on the lefthand side of the engine has an oil passage hole from the cylinder head to the second rocker shaft support.

1. Remove upper intake manifold as outlined under "Intake Manifold, Replace."
2. Cover lower intake manifold.
3. Disconnect and remove three ignition coils.
4. Remove ground strap/resistor retaining bolt from cylinder head cover.
5. Lift up wire harness track retaining tabs.
6. Loosen mounting bolts and remove cylinder head cover.
7. Identify rocker arm assembly and rocker arms for installation alignment, **Fig. 3**.
8. Remove mounting bolts and rocker arm assembly. **Avoid turning rocker arm assembly upside down. Do not allow rocker arm assembly to rest on lash adjusters.**
9. Reverse procedure to install, noting the following:
   a. Rotate camshaft gears to timing position were lobes are in a neutral position (no load to the valve), **Fig. 4**.
   b. Install rocker arm and shaft assembly ensuring identification marks face toward front of engine for lefthand head and toward rear of engine for righthand head.
   c. Tighten rocker arm/shaft assembly bolts in sequence, **Fig. 5**.

CRANKSHAFT DAMPER
REPLACE

1. Rotate belt tensioner counterclockwise until it contacts it's stop.
2. Remove belt and slowly rotate tensioner into the freearm position. **Do not let tensioner arm snap back to freearm position.**
3. Raise and support vehicle on hoist.
4. Remove crankshaft damper bolt.
5. Remove crankshaft damper using suitable three-jaw puller.
6. Reverse procedure to install, using damper install bolt tool No. C-4685-C1, with nut and thrust bearing from tools Nos. 6792 and 6792-1, or equivalents.

FRONT COVER
REPLACE

1. Remove fuel pump relay for Power Distribution Center (PDC).
2. Start and run engine until it stalls.
3. Attempt to start engine until it no longer runs.
4. Turn ignition switch to OFF position.
5. Install fuel pump relay.
6. Rotate belt tensioner counterclockwise until it contacts it's stop.
7. Remove belt and slowly rotate tensioner into the freearm position. **Do not let tensioner arm snap back to freearm position.**
8. Remove mounting bolts and position power steering pump aside.
9. Raise and support vehicle on hoist.
10. Remove crankshaft damper bolt.
11. Remove crankshaft damper using suitable three-jaw puller.
12. Remove lower front timing belt cover mounting bolts and nuts, **Fig. 6**.
13. Lower vehicle.
14. Remove upper mounting bolts and front timing belt cover.
15. Reverse procedure to install.

REAR TIMING BELT COVER
REPLACE

With the timing belt removed, avoid turning the camshaft or crankshaft. If

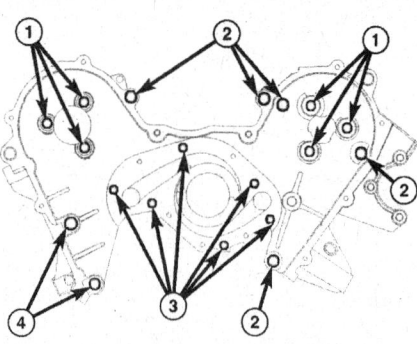

1- M8 FASTENERS (APPLY THREAD SEAALANT)
2- M10 FASTENERS
3- M6 FASTENERS
4- M10 FASTENERS (STUD/NUT)

ARM0400000000840

Fig. 7   Rear timing belt cover replacement

movement is required, exercise extreme caution to avoid valve damage caused by piston contact.

1. Remove fuel pump relay for Power Distribution Center (PDC).
2. Start and run engine until it stalls.
3. Attempt to start engine until it no longer runs.
4. Turn ignition switch to OFF position.
5. Install fuel pump relay.
6. Remove timing belt as outlined under "Timing Belt, Replace."
7. Camshaft timing gears are keyed to camshaft.
8. Hold lefthand camshaft sprocket with box end wrench.
9. Loosen and remove mounting bolt (bolt is 10 inches long) and washer, then the camshaft sprocket.
10. Righthand camshaft must be pushed rearward approximately 3 ½ inches to remove camshaft gear retaining bolt and gear. **Do not scratch or nick camshaft or cylinder head journals when moving camshaft.**
11. Hold righthand camshaft sprocket with box end wrench.
12. Loosen and remove mounting bolt (righthand bolt is 8 ⅜ inches long) and washer, then the righthand camshaft sprocket.
13. Remove mounting bolts and rear timing belt cover, **Fig. 7**.
14. Reverse procedure to install. Install new O-rings lubricates with Mopar Dielectric Grease, or equivalent.

TIMING BELT
REPLACE

With the timing belt removed, avoid turning the camshaft or crankshaft. If movement is required, exercise extreme caution to avoid valve damage caused by piston contact.

Removal

The 3.5L is not a freewheeling engine. Loosen the valve train rocker assemblies before servicing the timing drive.

Crankshaft Main Journal Grade Mark	Main Bearing Bore Grade Mark		
	1	2	3
A	(3) Standard	(2) +.0001 inch	(1) +.0002 inch
B	(4) -.0001 inch	(3) Standard	(2) +.0001 inch
C	(5) -.0002 inch	(4) -0.0001 inch	(3) Standard

Fig. 8 Main bearing selection chart

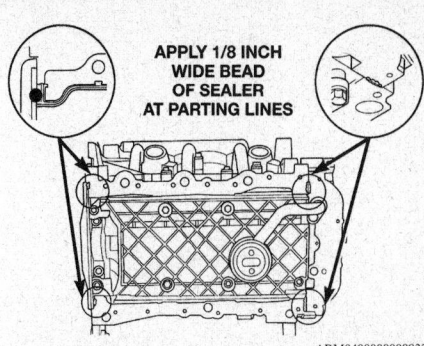

APPLY 1/8 INCH WIDE BEAD OF SEALER AT PARTING LINES

ARM040000000832

Fig. 9 Oil pan RTV application

1. Remove fuel pump relay for Power Distribution Center (PDC).
2. Start and run engine until it stalls.
3. Attempt to start engine until it no longer runs.
4. Turn ignition switch to OFF position.
5. Install fuel pump relay.
6. Remove both cylinder head covers as outlined under "Valve Cover, Replace" and loosen rocker arm assemblies as outlined under "Rocker Arm, Replace."
7. Remove front timing belt cover as outlined under "Front Cover, Replace."
8. Mark belt running direction if timing belt is to be reused.
9. Rotate engine clockwise by turning crankshaft until crankshaft mark aligns with TDC mark on oil pump housing and camshaft sprocket timing marks are aligned with marks on rear cover, **Fig. 4.**
10. Remove timing belt tensioner and timing belt.
11. Place tensioner into suitable vise. Index tensioner in vise same way it is installed on engine.
12. Compress plunger. Total bleed down of tensioner should take approximately five minutes.
13. When plunger is compressed into tensioner body install suitable pin through body and plunger to retain plunger in place for installation.

Installation

If camshafts have moved from the timing marks, always rotate camshaft towards the direction nearest to the timing marks, **Do not turn camshafts a full revolution or damage to valves and/or pistons could result.**

1. Align crankshaft sprocket with TDC mark on oil pump cover, **Fig. 4.**
2. Align camshaft sprockets timing reference marks with marks on rear cover.
3. Install timing belt starting at crankshaft sprocket going in counterclockwise direction.
4. Install belt around last sprocket. Maintain tension on belt as it is positioned around tensioner pulley.
5. If camshaft gears have been removed it is only necessary to have camshaft gear mounting bolts installed to snug torque at this time.
6. Holding tensioner pulley against belt, install tensioner into housing and tighten.
7. Each camshaft sprocket mark should remain aligned with cover marks.
8. When tensioner is in place pull retaining pin to allow tensioner to extend to pulley bracket.
9. Rotate crankshaft sprocket two revolutions and check timing marks on camshafts and crankshaft. If marks do not line up within their respective locations, repeat procedure.
10. If camshaft gears have been removed and timing is correct, counterhold and tighten camshaft gears to final specification.
11. Install front timing belt cover as outlined under "Front Cover, Replace."
12. Tighten the rocker arm assemblies as outlined under "Rocker Arm, Replace."
13. Install cylinder head covers as outlined under "Valve Cover, Replace."

CAMSHAFT
REPLACE

1. Remove cylinder head as outlined under "Cylinder Head, Replace."
2. Carefully remove camshaft from rear of cylinder head. **Do not to nick or scratch journals when removing camshaft.**
3. Reverse procedure to install. Lubricate camshaft bearing journals, lobes and seal with suitable, clean engine oil.

CAMSHAFT OIL SEAL
REPLACE

Lefthand

1. Drain cooling system into suitable container.
2. Remove front timing cover as outlined under "Front Cover, Replace."
3. Align camshaft gear and crankshaft gear timing marks to TDC, **Fig. 4.**
4. Remove rear timing cover as outlined under "Rear Timing Belt Cover, Replace."
5. Remove rocker arm assembly as outlined under "Rocker Arm, Replace."
6. Remove camshaft thrust plate from rear of cylinder head.
7. Maneuver camshaft rearward and out of cylinder head approximately 3.5 inches.
8. Remove camshaft oil seal using suitable driver. **Do no damage cylinder head to seal or camshaft journal surfaces.**
9. Reverse procedure to install, noting the following:
   a. Tap seal into place using camshaft seal installer tool No. MD-998306, or equivalent.
   b. Light coat camshaft oil seal lip and seal protector sleeve tool 6788, or equivalent, with suitable, clean engine oil.
   c. Install oil tool onto camshaft
   d. Slide camshaft forward, inserting seal protector through camshaft seal until camshaft seats. Remove special tool.
   e. Install camshaft thrust plate and new seal.

Righthand

1. Remove timing belt as outlined under "Timing Belt, Replace."
2. Righthand camshaft must be pushed rearward approximately 3 1/2 inches to remove camshaft gear retaining bolt and gear. **Do not scratch or nick camshaft or cylinder head journals when moving camshaft.**
3. Hold righthand camshaft sprocket with box end wrench.
4. Loosen and remove mounting bolt (righthand bolt is 8 3/8 inches long) and washer, then the righthand camshaft sprocket.
5. Remove EGR valve and camshaft thrust plate from rear of cylinder head.
6. Remove rocker arm assembly as outlined under "Rocker Arm, Replace."
7. Maneuver camshaft rearward and out of cylinder head approximately 3.5 inches.
8. Remove camshaft oil seal using suitable driver tool. **Do not damage cylinder head to seal or camshaft journal surfaces.**
9. Reverse procedure to install, noting the following:
   a. Tap seal into place using camshaft seal installer tool No. MD-998306, or equivalent.
   b. Light coat camshaft oil seal lip and seal protector sleeve tool 6788, or equivalent, with suitable, clean engine oil.
   c. Install oil tool onto camshaft
   d. Slide camshaft forward, inserting seal protector through camshaft seal until camshaft seats. Remove special tool.
   e. Install camshaft thrust plate and new seal.

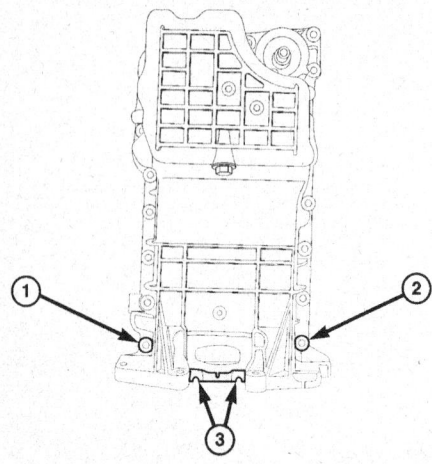

Fig. 10 Oil pan alignment tightening sequence

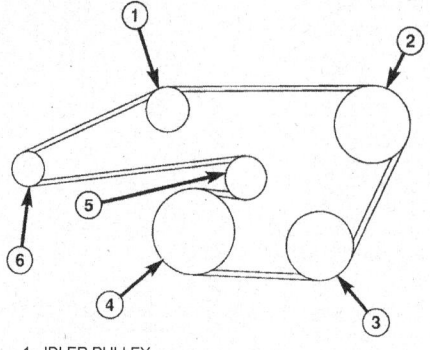

1- IDLER PULLEY
2- POWER STEERING PUMP
3- AIR CONDITIONING COMPRESSOR
4- CRANKSHAFT
5- TENSIONER
6- ALTERNATOR

Fig. 11 Serpentine drive belt routing

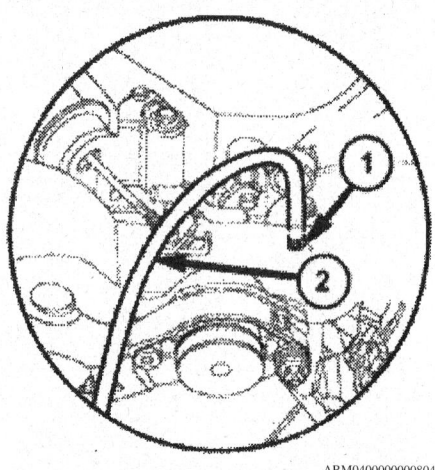

Fig. 12 Cooling system bleed

PISTON & ROD ASSEMBLY

Refer to "2.7L Engine" section for piston and rod assembly service.

MAIN & ROD BEARINGS

Bearing caps are not interchangeable and are marked to insure correct installation. Upper and lower bearing halves are not interchangeable.

1. Remove upper half of bearing by inserting main bearing tool No. C-3059, or equivalent, into crankshaft oil hole. Slowly rotate crankshaft clockwise, forcing out upper half of bearing shell.
2. Refer to **Fig. 8** to select main bearings.
3. Lubricate main bearing with suitable, clean engine oil.
4. Start bearing in place and insert main bearing tool C-3059, or equivalent, into crankshaft oil hole.
5. Slowly rotate crankshaft counterclockwise sliding bearing into position.
6. Move crankshaft forward to limit of travel.
7. Lubricate and install front thrust washer by rolling washer onto machined shelf between upper main bulk head No. 2 and crankshaft thrust surface.
8. Move crankshaft rearward to limit of travel.
9. Lubricate and install rear thrust washer by rolling washer onto machined shelf between upper main bulk head No. 2 and crankshaft thrust surface.
10. Install lower main bearings into main bearing caps.
11. Lubricate lower main bearings with suitable, clean engine oil.
12. Lubricate main bearing cap bolts with suitable engine oil.
13. Install each main cap and tighten bolts hand tight.
14. Install inside main bearing cap bolts and **torque** to 15 ft. lbs., then tighten an additional 90°.

15. Measure crankshaft end play. Endplay should be 004–.012 inch.
16. Install connecting rods and measure side clearance. Maximum clearance is .153 inch.
17. Install windage tray.
18. Lubricate bolts with suitable engine oil and **torque** to 20 ft. lbs., then tighten an additional 90°.
19. Install main cap tie (horizontal) bolts and **torque** to 20 ft. lbs.

CRANKSHAFT SEAL
REPLACE

1. Drain cooling system into suitable container.
2. Remove timing belt as outlined under "Timing Belt, Replace."
3. Remove crankshaft sprocket using crankshaft sprocket removal tool No. L-4407-A, or equivalent.
4. Tap dowel pin out of crankshaft.
5. Remove crankshaft seal using crankshaft oil seal removal tool No. 6341A, or equivalent. **Do not nick shaft seal surface or seal bore.**
6. Reverse procedure to install noting the following:
   a. Install crankshaft seal using crankshaft oil seal installer tool No. 6342, or equivalent.
   b. Install dowel pin into crankshaft to .047 inch protrusion.

CRANKSHAFT REAR OIL SEAL
REPLACE

1. Remove engine oil pan as outlined under "Oil Pan, Replace."
2. Lower weight of engine back onto engine mounts.
3. Remove transmission as outlined in **MOTOR's "Domestic Transmission Manual, In-Vehicle Service."**
4. Remove flexplate.
5. Remove mounting bolts and rear crankshaft oil seal.

6. Reverse procedure to install, noting the following:
   a. **Do not separate seal protector from rear crankshaft oil seal before installation.**
   b. Position oil seal, retainer and seal protector on crankshaft, then push firmly into place on engine block (seal protector will be removed from rear oil seal assembly as a result of installing rear oil seal).
   c. Hand tighten rear oil seal mounting bolts.
   d. Attach alignment tools No. 8225, or equivalent to pan rail. Tool notch should be located away seal retainer.
   e. While applying firm pressure to seal retainer against special tools, tighten seal retainer screws

OIL PAN
REPLACE

AWD

1. Drain cooling system into suitable container.
2. Remove oil level indicator tube mounting bolt at righthand exhaust manifold.
3. Raise and support vehicle.
4. Drain engine oil into suitable container and remove oil filter.
5. Remove lefthand axle shaft.
6. Disconnect power steering power steering rack.
7. Remove lefthand front axle intermediate shaft support bracket and housing.
8. Remove front drive shaft heat shield.
9. Mark for installation alignment and remove righthand front drive shaft.
10. Remove righthand catalytic converter.
11. Separate from cradle hold down and position power steering hose aside.
12. Remove lower engine mount to cradle mounting bolts and nuts.
13. Remove front sway bar.
14. Raise and support engine with suitable jack stand.
15. Remove front axle housing support bracket.

16. Remove mounting bolts, then rotate and remove front axle housing.
17. Lower engine and remove jack stand.
18. Remove hoses from and oil cooler.
19. Separate oil level indicator tube from oil pan.
20. Remove torque converter access cover.
21. Remove mounting bolts and oil pan.
22. Reverse procedure to install, noting the following:
    a. Install new oil level indicator tube seal.
    b. Apply ⅛ inch bead of Mopar Engine RTV GEN II, or equivalent, at parting line of oil pump housing and rear seal retainer, **Fig. 9.**
    c. Install oil pan mounting bolts hand tight.
    d. Ensure rear face of oil pan is flush to transmission bell housing.
    e. **Torque** horizontal rear oil pan to transmission bolts to 12 inch lbs.
    f. **Torque** lefthand M8 oil pan alignment bolt to 21 ft. lbs, **Fig. 10.**
    g. **Torque** righthand M8 oil pan alignment bolt to 21 ft. lbs.
    h. **Torque** remaining M8 bolts and nuts to 21 ft. lbs.
    i. **Torque** M6 bolts to 1 105 inch lbs.
    j. **Torque** four M10 oil pan to transmission bolts to 40 ft. lbs.

RWD

1. Lock steering wheel in center position.
2. Remove engine oil indicator.
3. Raise and support vehicle, then remove splash shield.
4. Drain engine oil into suitable container and remove the oil filter.
5. Remove oil filter/oil cooler mounting stud and position oil cooler aside
6. Separate steering column coupler from steering gear.
7. Remove steering gear to cradle mounting bolts and suspend steering gear aside.
8. Remove flexplate access cover.
9. Remove rear oil pan to transmission mounting bolts.
10. Remove two rear oil pan bolts.
11. Remove remaining oil pan bolts.
12. Loosen engine mount bolts at cradle.
13. Raise and support engine using suitable floor jack with wooden block at transmission housing.
14. Remove oil pan.
15. Reverse procedure to install, noting the following:
    a. Apply ⅛ inch bead of Mopar Engine RTV GEN II, or equivalent, at parting line of oil pump housing and rear seal retainer, **Fig. 9.**
    b. Install oil pan mounting bolts hand tight.
    c. Ensure rear face of oil pan is flush to transmission bell housing.
    d. **Torque** horizontal rear oil pan to transmission bolts to 12 inch lbs.
    e. **Torque** lefthand M8 oil pan alignment bolt to 21 ft. lbs, **Fig. 10.**
    f. **Torque** righthand M8 oil pan alignment bolt to 21 ft. lbs.
    g. **Torque** remaining M8 bolts and nuts to 21 ft. lbs.

h. **Torque** M6 bolts to 1 105 inch lbs.
i. **Torque** four M10 oil pan to transmission bolts to 40 ft. lbs.

OIL PUMP
REPLACE

1. Drain cooling system into suitable container.
2. Remove timing belt as outlined under "Timing Belt, Replace."
3. Remove crankshaft sprocket using crankshaft sprocket removal tool No. L-4407-A, or equivalent.
4. Remove oil pan as outlined under "Oil Pan, Replace."
5. Remove oil pickup tube.
6. Remove mounting bolts, oil pump and gasket.
7. Reverse procedure to install, noting the following:
    a. Prime oil pump before installation by filling rotor cavity with suitable, clean engine oil.
    b. Install new oil pickup tube O-ring.

OIL PUMP SERVICE
Disassemble

1. Remove mounting screws and oil pump cover.
2. Remove pump rotors.

Inspect

Do not inspect the oil relief valve assembly. If the oil relief valve is suspect, replace the oil pump.
1. Clean all parts thoroughly.
2. Ensure mating surface of oil pump housing is smooth. Replace pump cover if scratched or grooved.
3. Lay straightedge across pump cover surface. If clearance is .001 inch or more between cover and straight edge, cover should be replaced.
4. Measure thickness and diameter of outer rotor. If outer rotor thickness is .563 inch, or less, or if diameter is 3.141 inches. or less, replace outer rotor.
5. If inner rotor measures .563 inch, or less, replace inner rotor.
6. Slide outer rotor into body, press to one side with fingers and measure clearance between rotor and body. If clearance is .015 inch, or more, replace body only if outer rotor is within specifications.
7. Install inner rotor into body. If clearance between inner and outer rotors is .008 inch, or more, replace both rotors.
8. Place straightedge across face of body, between bolt holes. If clearance is .003 inch, or more, between rotors and straightedge, replace pump assembly only if rotors are within specifications.

Assemble

Prime oil pump before installation by filling rotor cavity with engine oil.

OIL COOLER
REPLACE

1. Drain cooling system into suitable container.
2. Raise and support vehicle on hoist.
3. Disconnect coolant hoses from oil cooler.
4. Remove oil filter.
5. Remove mounting bolts and oil cooler.
6. Reverse procedure to install, noting the following:
    a. Oil cooler seal retainer flange cut out section (top), must be aligned with tab on oil pan.
    b. Oil cooler must be prevented from turning during tightening.

BELT TENSION DATA

Belt adjustment is maintained by an automatic (spring load) belt tensioner.

SERPENTINE DRIVE BELT
Routing

Refer to **Fig. 11** for serpentine drive belt routing.

Replacement
REMOVAL

1. Rotate belt tensioner counterclockwise until it contacts it's stop.
2. Remove belt and slowly rotate tensioner into the freearm position. **Do not let tensioner arm snap back to freearm position.**

INSTALLATION

1. Route belt around all pulleys except idler pulley.
2. Rotate tensioner arm until it contacts it's stop position.
3. Route belt around idler and slowly let tensioner rotate into belt.
4. Ensure belt is seated onto all pulleys.
5. Tensioner is equipped with indexing tang on back and indexing stop on tensioner housing.
6. If new belt (used 15 minutes or less) is being installed, tang must be within approximately .24–.32 inch of indexing stop.

COOLING SYSTEM BLEED

1. Attach 4–6 feet long ¼ inch ID clear hose to bleeder fitting located on lower intake manifold, left of center and below upper intake plenum, **Fig. 12. When installing drain hose to air bleed valve, route hose away from accessory drive belts, accessory drive pulleys, and electric cooling fan motors.**
2. Route hose away from accessory drive belt, drive pulleys and electric cooling fan

3. Place other end of hose into clean container.
4. **Ensure cooling system air bleed valve is opened before any coolant is added to cooling system.**
5. Attach filling aid funnel tool No. 8195, or equivalent, to pressure bottle filler neck.
6. Pinch overflow hose that connects between two chambers of coolant bottle using suitable hose pinch-off pliers.
7. Open bleed fitting.
8. Pour suitable antifreeze mixture into larger section of filling aid funnel (smaller section of funnel is to allow air to escape).
9. Slowly fill cooling system until steady stream of coolant flows from hose attached to bleed valve.
10. Close bleed valve and continue filling system to top of filling aid funnel tool.
11. Remove pinch-off pliers from overflow hose.
12. Allow coolant in filling funnel to drain into overflow chamber of pressure bottle.
13. Remove funnel and install coolant pressure bottle cap.
14. Remove hose from bleed valve.
15. Start engine and run at 1500–2000 RPM for 30 minutes, noting the following:
    a. Engine cooling system will push any remaining air into coolant bottle within about an hour of normal driving. As a result, a drop in coolant level in pressure bottle may occur.
    b. If engine cooling system overheats and pushes coolant into overflow side of coolant bottle, this coolant will be sucked back into cooling system, **only if pressure cap is left on bottle.**
    c. Removing pressure cap breaks vacuum path between two bottle sections and coolant will not return to cooling system.
16. Shut off engine allow it to cool down for 30 minutes. This permits coolant to be drawn into pressure chamber.
17. With engine cold, ensure coolant level should be within MIN and MAX marks. Coolant will normally only be in inboard of coolant bottle two chambers. Outboard chamber is only to recover coolant in event of an overheat or after recent service fill.

THERMOSTAT
REPLACE

1. Drain cooling system into suitable container.
2. Remove radiator lower hose from thermostat housing.
3. Remove bypass hose.
4. Remove mounting bolts, housing and thermostat.
5. Reverse procedure to install.

WATER PUMP
REPLACE

1. Drain cooling system into suitable container.
2. Rotate belt tensioner counterclockwise until it contacts it's stop.
3. Remove belt and slowly rotate tensioner into the freearm position. **Do not let tensioner arm snap back to freearm position.**
4. Remove engine timing belt as outlined under "Timing Belt, Replace."
5. Remove mounting bolts and water pump. Record position of longer bolts for installation alignment.
6. Reverse procedure to install.

RADIATOR
REPLACE

Refer to "Radiator, Replace" in the "2.7L Engine" section for radiator replacement procedure.

FUEL PUMP
REPLACE

Refer to "Fuel Pump, Replace" in "2.7L Engine" section for fuel pump replacement procedure

FUEL FILTER
REPLACE

The fuel filter is replaceable only as part of the fuel pump module.

TIGHTENING SPECIFICATIONS

Year	Component	Torque, Ft. Lbs.
2005	Alternator/Compressor Mounting Bracket, Nos. 1 & 2	40
	Alternator/Compressor Mounting Bracket, No. 3	30
	Automatic Belt Tensioner	40
	Camshaft Sprocket	75②
	Camshaft Thrust Plate	20
	Connecting Rod Cap	20②
	Crankshaft Damper	70
	Crankshaft Main Bearing Cap	④
	Crankshaft Rear Seal Retainer	105①
	Cylinder Head	③
	Engine Mount Heat Shield	97①
	Engine Mount to Cradle	55
	Engine Mount to Mounting Bracket	55
	Engine Mount Through Studs	106
	Exhaust Manifold	17
	Exhaust Manifold Heat Shield	105①
	Fan Blade	17
	Fan Shroud	50①
	Flexplate Inspection Cover	97①
	Flexplate to Crankshaft	70
	Flexplate to Torque Converter	55
	Front Drive Axle Housing	48
	Front Drive Axle Intermediate Shaft Housing & Support Bracket, Lefthand	19
	Fuel Line Clamps	31①
	Heater Supply Tube	30①
	Idler Pulley	20
	Intake Manifold, Lower	20
	Intake Manifold, Upper	105①
	Main Bearings	④
	Oil Cooler Connector	55
	Oil Pan, M6	105①
	Oil Pan, M8	20
	Oil Pan Drain Plug	20
	Oil Pan to Transmission Bell Housing	40
	Oil Pump	20
	Oil Pump Cover	105①
	Oil Pump Pick Up Tube	20
	Radiator to Support Bracket	106①
	Rocker Shaft Pedestal Retaining	23
	Thermostat Housing	105①
	Timing Belt Cover, M6	105①
	Timing Belt Cover, M8	20
	Timing Belt Cover, M10	40
	Timing Belt Tensioner	20
	Timing Belt Tensioner Pulley	45
	Upper Radiator Closure Panel	90①
	Valve Cover	105①
	Water Pump	105①
	Windage Tray	④

① — Inch Lbs.
② — Plus an additional 90°.
③ — Refer to "Cylinder Head, Replace" for tightening specifications and sequence.
④ — Refer to "Main & Rod Bearings" for tightening specifications and sequence.

5.7L Engine

NOTE: On Air Bag Equipped Models, Refer To "Air Bag System Precautions" Located In The Front Of This Manual For System Disarming & Arming Procedures.

NOTE: Refer To "Computer Relearn Procedures" Located In The Front Of This Manual When Battery Power To The Computer Has Been Interrupted.

NOTE: Refer To The Rear Of This Manual For Vehicle Manufacturer's Special Tool Suppliers.

INDEX

PRECAUTIONS

Air Bag Systems

Refer to "Air Bag System Precautions" in the front of this manual for system disarming and arming procedures.

Battery Ground Cable

Prior to service, disconnect battery ground cable and isolate as required.

RECALIBRATION

Anytime the battery has been disconnect or has lost its charge, the following must be recalibrated:

EXPRESS WINDOW

1. Turn ignition switch to RUN position.
2. Move driver's window upward until it stalls in full up position. Allow window motor to stall for at least two seconds before releasing switch.
3. Move driver's window downward until it stalls in full down position. Allow window motor to stall for at least two seconds before releasing switch.
4. Move driver's window upward until it stalls in full up position. Allow window motor to stall for at least two seconds before releasing switch.
5. Move passenger's window upward until it stalls in full up position. Allow window motor to stall for at least two seconds before releasing switch.
6. Move passenger's window downward until it stalls in full down position. Allow window motor to stall for at least two seconds before releasing switch.
7. Move passenger's window upward until it stalls in full up position. Allow window motor to stall for at least two seconds before releasing switch.

ELECTRONIC STABILITY PROGRAM (ESP) STEERING ANGLE SENSOR

1. Start engine.
2. Turn steering wheel right until wheel locks full right.
3. Turn steering wheel left until wheel locks full left.
4. Turn steering wheel right until wheels are centered.
5. Cycle ignition switch OFF and ON. Do not start engine.

Fuel System Pressure Relief

1. Remove fuel pump relay for Power Distribution Center (PDC).
2. Start and run engine until it stalls.
3. Attempt to start engine until it no longer runs.
4. Turn ignition switch to OFF position.
5. Install fuel pump relay.

COMPRESSION PRESSURE

The minimum compression pressure should be no less than 100 psi and the maximum variation between cylinders should be no more than 25%.

1. Ensure battery is completely charged and engine starter motor is in good operating condition.
2. Clean spark plug recesses with compressed air
3. Remove fuel pump relay for Power Distribution Center (PDC).
4. Start and run engine until it stalls.
5. Attempt to start engine until it no longer runs.
6. Turn ignition switch to OFF position.
7. Install fuel pump relay.
8. Remove Auto Shutdown (ASD) relay.
9. Insert suitable compression pressure gauge and rotate engine with engine starter motor for three revolutions.
10. Record compression pressure on third revolution.
11. Continue test for remaining cylinders.

Fig. 1 Exhaust manifold loosening & tightening sequence (Part 1 of 2)

ARM0400000000810

INTAKE SIDE

EXHAUST SIDE

ARM0400000000813

Fig. 3 Rocker shaft loosening & tightening sequence

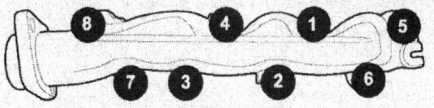

ARM0400000000811

Fig. 1 Exhaust manifold loosening & tightening sequence (Part 2 of 2)

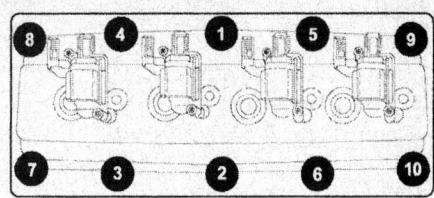

ARM0400000000812

Fig. 2 Valve cover loosening & tightening sequence

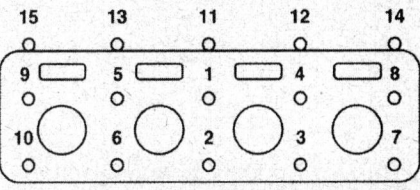

ARM0400000000814

Fig. 4 Cylinder head loosening & tightening sequence

ENGINE MOUNT

REPLACE

Front

1. Raise and support vehicle.
2. Remove mounting bolt, nut and alternator support bracket.
3. Remove hydromount to frame studs and nuts.
4. Raise engine using suitable jack.
5. Remove bracket mounting bolts and hydromount.
6. Mounting bolts and engine mount brackets.
7. Reverse procedure to install.

Rear

1. Raise and support vehicle on hoist, then support transmission using suitable jack.
2. Remove mounting bolts and crossmember.
3. Remove mounting bolts and transmission mount.
4. Remove mounting bolts and transmission mount bracket.
5. Reverse procedure to install.

ENGINE

REPLACE

1. Remove engine cover.
2. Remove fuel pump relay for Power Distribution Center (PDC).
3. Start and run engine until it stalls.
4. Attempt to start engine until it no longer runs.
5. Turn ignition switch to OFF position.
6. Install fuel pump relay.

7. Remove air cleaner resonator and duct work.
8. Remove caps and mounting nuts, then separate wiper arm from pivot using suitable two-jaw puller.
9. Remove wiper arms.
10. Remove cowl top panel to each front fender push-pin.
11. Disconnect two ¼ turn fasteners securing cowl top panel to dash panel.
12. Remove six cowl top panel to strut tower support push-pins.
13. Disconnect integral cowl top panel to dash panel retaining clips.
14. Remove cowl panel.
15. Drain cooling system into suitable container.
16. Rotate belt tensioner counterclockwise until it contacts it's stop.
17. Remove belt and slowly rotate tensioner into the freearm position. **Do not let tensioner arm snap back to freearm position.**
18. Remove upper radiator hose.
19. Remove upper radiator closure panels.
20. Disconnect cooling fan electrical connector, then remove mounting bolts and cooling fan.
21. Remove air conditioning compressor with lines attached and position aside.
22. Raise and support vehicle.
23. Unsnap plastic insulator cap from B+ output terminal.
24. Remove B+ terminal mounting nut, then disconnect terminal and field wire connector.
25. Remove mounting nut, bolt and support bracket.
26. Remove two mounting bolts and alternator.
27. Remove intake manifold and IAFM as outlined under "Intake Manifold, Replace."
28. Remove ground wires from rear of each cylinder head.
29. Disconnect heater hoses.
30. Remove power steering pump and set aside. It is not necessary to disconnect hoses.
31. Disconnect fuel supply line.
32. Raise and support vehicle on hoist.
33. Drain engine oil into suitable container.
34. Remove mounting screws and front belly pan.
35. Remove engine front mount to frame nuts.
36. **On AWD models,** proceed as follows:
    a. Mark front driveshaft to flange at both ends for installation alignment.
    b. Remove front drive shaft mounting bolts from differential and transfer

case.
    c. Remove driveshaft.
    d. Remove left and righthand front drive axles.
    e. Remove support bracket from differential to engine block.
    f. Unbolt differential from oil pan.
    g. Rotate differential so drive flange is facing forward and oil pan side is facing up.
    h. Remove differential through opening at rear of cradle.
    i. Remove intermediate shaft from oil pan.
37. **On all models,** disconnect transmission oil cooler lines from oil pan bolts retainers.
38. Disconnect exhaust pipe at manifolds.
39. Disconnect wires and remove starter motor.
40. Remove torque converter access cover.
41. Remove drive plate to converter bolts.
42. Remove transmission bell housing to engine block bolts
43. Lower vehicle
44. Install engine lift fixture tool Nos. 8984 and 8984-UPD, or equivalents.
45. Separate engine from transmission, then remove engine and install it on suitable repair stand.
46. Reverse procedure to install.

INTAKE MANIFOLD

REPLACE

1. Remove engine cover.
2. Remove fuel pump relay for Power Distribution Center (PDC).
3. Start and run engine until it stalls.
4. Attempt to start engine until it no longer runs.
5. Turn ignition switch to OFF position.
6. Install fuel pump relay.
7. Remove air inlet hose.
8. Remove ignition wires from on top of intake manifold.

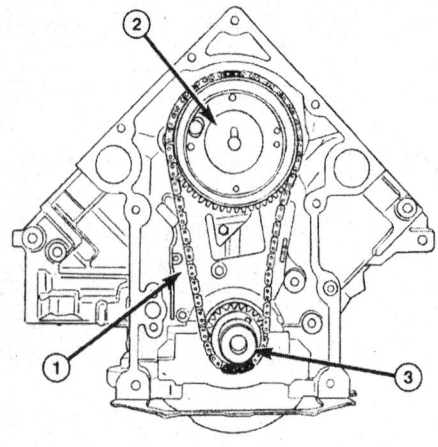

Fig. 5   Timing chain alignment

GRADE	SIZE mm (in.)	FOR USE WITH
MARKING		JOURNAL SIZE
A	0.008 mm U/S	64.988–64.995 mm
	(0.0004 in.) U/S	(2.5585– 2.5588in.)
B	NOMINAL	64.996–65.004 mm
		(2.5588–2.5592 in.)
C	0.008 mm O/S	65.005–65.012 mm
	(0.0004 in.) O/S	(2.5592–2.5595 in.)

ARM0400000000816

Fig. 6   Main bearing selection chart

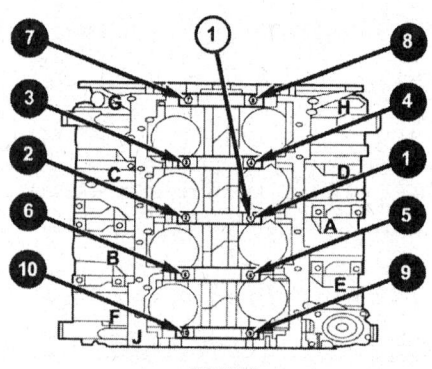

FRONT

ARM0400000000817

Fig. 7   Main bearing tightening sequence

9. Disconnect Manifold Absolute Pressure (MAP) sensor, fuel injectors and Electric Throttle Control (ETC) electrical connectors.
10. Remove wire harness from intake manifold.
11. Disconnect brake booster, purge and Make Up Air (MUA) hoses.
12. Remove EGR tube from intake manifold.
13. Remove intake manifold mounting bolts in crisscross pattern starting from outside bolts and ending at middle bolts.
14. Remove intake manifold.
15. Reverse procedure to install.

EXHAUST MANIFOLD
REPLACE

1. Raise and support vehicle.
2. Remove exhaust pipe to manifold bolts.
3. Remove engine mount to frame mounting bolts.
4. Raise engine enough to remove exhaust manifolds using suitable jack. **Do not damage engine harness.**
5. Remove bracket mounting bolts and hydromount.
6. Mounting bolts and engine mount brackets.
7. Remove heat shield
8. Remove exhaust manifold bolts in sequence, then the exhaust manifold, **Fig. 1.**
9. Reverse procedure to install, noting the following:
   a. **Torque** manifold ball flange nut to 106 inch lbs.
   b. Measure exhaust module and fuel tank clearance. Clearance should be .55 inch.
   c. Measure clearance at rear tunnel reinforcement. Clearance .59–.78 in.
   d. **Torque** ball flange nuts to 25 ft. lbs.

CYLINDER HEAD
REPLACE

The head gaskets are not interchangeable between left and righthand sides.

They are marked L and R to indicate left and righthand sides.
1. Remove fuel pump relay for Power Distribution Center (PDC).
2. Start and run engine until it stalls.
3. Attempt to start engine until it no longer runs.
4. Turn ignition switch to OFF position.
5. Install fuel pump relay.
6. Disconnect fuel supply line.
7. Drain cooling system into suitable container.
8. Loosen clamp and disconnect air duct at air cleaner cover.
9. Remove air cleaner resonator and duct work from four locating pins.
10. Remove closed crankcase ventilation system.
11. Disconnect exhaust at exhaust manifolds
12. Disconnect evaporation control system.
13. Disconnect heater hoses.
14. Remove power steering pump.
15. Disconnect coil on plug electrical connectors.
16. Remove valve cover mounting bolts and ground straps, **Fig. 2. Ground straps must be installed in original locations**
17. Remove valve cover.
18. Remove intake manifold and throttle body as outlined under "Intake Manifold, Replace."
19. Install pushrod retaining plate tool No. 9070, or equivalent.
20. Loosen rocker shafts in sequence, **Fig. 3.**
21. Mark locations for installation alignment and remove rocker shafts.
22. Mark locations for installation alignment and remove push rods.
23. **Do not remove retainers from rocker shaft.**
24. Remove head bolts in sequence and cylinder heads, **Fig. 4.**
25. Discard cylinder head gasket.
26. Reverse procedure to install, noting the following:
   a. Head gaskets are marked TOP to indicate which side goes up.
   b. **Torque** M12 cylinder head bolts in sequence to 25 ft. lbs. and M8 bolts to 15 ft. lbs., **Fig. 4.**
   c. **Torque** M12 cylinder head bolts in sequence to 40 ft. lbs. and ensure M8 bolts as at 15 ft. lbs.
   d. Tighten M12 cylinder head bolts and additional 90° in sequence.
   e. **Torque** M8 bolts to 25 ft. lbs.

VALVE COVER
REPLACE

1. Disconnect coil on plug electrical connectors.
2. Remove valve cover mounting bolts and ground straps, **Fig. 2. Ground straps must be installed in original locations.**
3. Remove valve cover.
4. Reverse procedure to install, noting the following:
   a. Hand start all valve cover mounting bolts.
   b. Ensure all double ended studs are in correct location
   c. Righthand ground strap is located on front inboard stud and lefthand is on rear inboard stud.
   d. Tighten valve cover bolts is sequence, **Fig. 2.**

CAMSHAFT LOBE LIFT SPECIFICATIONS
Intake ....472 inch
Exhaust ....460 inch

VALVE CLEARANCE SPECIFICATIONS

This engine is equipped with hydraulic lifters and valves are lashed with zero clearance.

VALVE ADJUSTMENT

This engine is equipped with hydraulic lash adjusters. No adjustment is required.

ROCKER ARMS
REPLACE

The rocker arms are not interchangeable between intake and exhaust. The intake rocker arms are marked with an I.
1. Disconnect coil on plug electrical connectors.
2. Remove valve cover mounting bolts and ground straps, **Fig. 2. Ground straps must be installed in original positions.**
3. Remove valve cover.

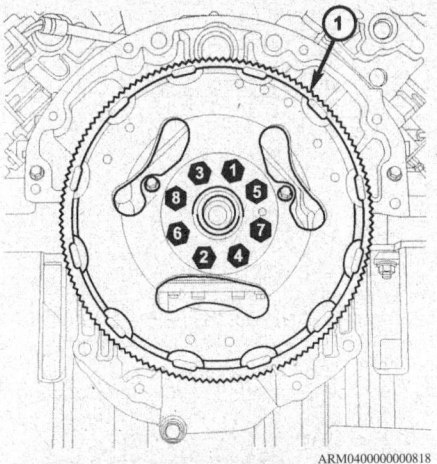

Fig. 8 Flexplate tightening sequence

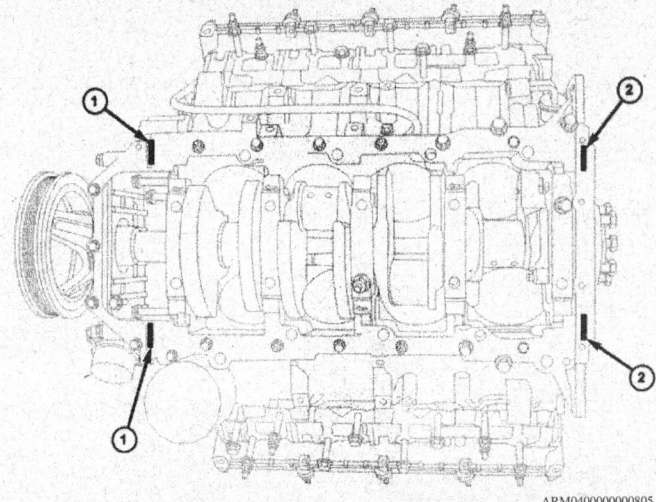

Fig. 9 Oil pan RTV sealing

4. Install pushrod retaining plate tool No. 9070, or equivalent.
5. Loosen rocker shafts in sequence, **Fig. 3.**
6. Mark locations for installation alignment and remove rocker shafts.
7. Mark locations for installation alignment and remove push rods.
8. **Do not remove retainers from rocker shaft.**
9. Reverse procedure to install, noting the following:
   a. Longer push rods are for exhaust side and shorter ones intake.
   b. Ensure retainers and rocker arms are not overlapped when tightening bolts.
   c. Ensure pushrod is installed into rocker arm and tappet correctly.
   d. Tighten rocker shaft bolts in sequence, **Fig. 3.**
   e. Do not rotate or crank engine during or immediately after rocker arm installation. Allow hydraulic tappets five minutes to bleed down.

HYDRAULIC LIFTERS
REPLACE

1. Remove cylinder head as outlined under "Cylinder Head, Replace."
2. Remove mounting bolt and tappet guide holder
3. If all tappets are to be removed and reused, identify tappets to ensure installation in original location.
4. Pull tappet out of bore with twisting motion.
5. Reverse procedure to install.

CRANKSHAFT DAMPER
REPLACE

1. Rotate belt tensioner counterclockwise until it contacts it's stop.
2. Remove belt and slowly rotate tensioner into the freearm position. **Do not let tensioner arm snap back to freearm position.**
3. Drain cooling system into suitable container.

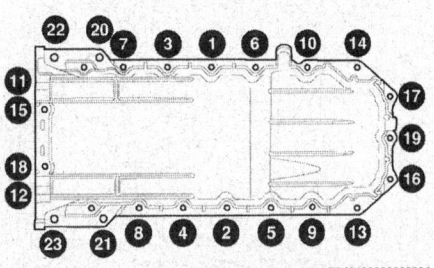

Fig. 10 Oil pan tightening sequence

4. Remove radiator upper hose.
5. Remove upper radiator hose and disconnect cooling fan electrical connector.
6. Remove mounting bolts and cooling fan.
7. Remove crankshaft damper bolt.
8. Remove damper using suitable three-jaw puller tool.
9. Reverse procedure to install, using crankshaft, damper tool No. 8512-A, as follows:
   a. Thread nut onto shaft first.
   b. Place roller bearing onto threaded rod.
   c. Ensure hardened bearing surface of bearing faces nut.
   d. Slide hardened washer onto threaded rod,
   e. Coat threaded rod's threads with Mopar Nickel Anti-Seize, or Loctite No. 771, or equivalent.
   f. Press damper onto crankshaft.

FRONT COVER
REPLACE

1. Remove engine cover.
2. Loosen clamp and disconnect air duct at air cleaner cover.
3. Remove air cleaner resonator and duct work from four locating pins.
4. Drain cooling system into suitable container.

5. Rotate belt tensioner counterclockwise until it contacts it's stop.
6. Remove belt and slowly rotate tensioner into the freearm position. **Do not let tensioner arm snap back to freearm position.**
7. Remove upper radiator hose and disconnect cooling fan electrical connector.
8. Remove mounting bolts and cooling fan.
9. Remove thermostat housing radiator hose.
10. Remove coolant and washer bottles.
11. Remove fan shroud.
12. Remove air conditioning compressor and position it aside. **It is not necessary to disconnect lines or recover refrigerant.**
13. Remove alternator and upper radiator hose.
14. Disconnect both heater hoses at timing cover.
15. Disconnect lower radiator hose at engine.
16. Remove accessory drive belt tensioner and both idler pulleys.
17. Remove crankshaft damper bolt.
18. Remove damper using suitable three-jaw puller tool.
19. Remove power steering pump and position it aside. **Do not remove power steering pump hoses.**
20. Remove dipstick support bolt.
21. Remove oil pan and pick up tube as outlined under "Oil Pan, Replace."
22. Remove mounting bolts and timing cover. **It is not necessary to remove water pump for timing cover removal.**
23. Reverse procedure to install, noting the following:
   a. Ensure slide bushings are located in timing cover.
   b. Install new gasket.

TIMING CHAIN
REPLACE

1. Remove timing chain cover as outlined under "Front Cover, Replace."

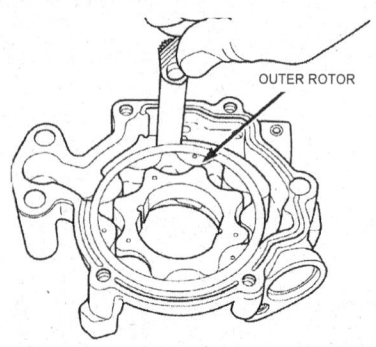

Fig. 11   Outer rotor to body clearance

ARM0400000000807

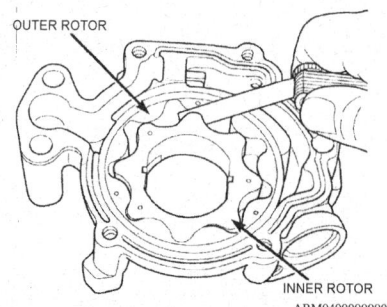

Fig. 12   Clearance between rotors

ARM0400000000808

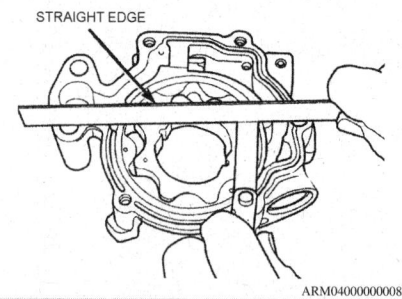

Fig. 13   Clearance over rotors

ARM0400000000809

2. Install vibration damper bolt hand tight.
3. Align timing chain sprockets and keyways using suitable socket and breaker bar to rotate crankshaft, **Fig. 5**, noting the following:
   a. Camshaft pin and slot in cam sprocket must be at 12 o'clock position.
   b. Crankshaft keyway must be at 2 o'clock position.
   c. Crankshaft sprocket must be installed so dots and or paint marking is at 6 o'clock position.
4. Remove four mounting bolts and oil pump.
5. Retract tensioner shoe until hole in shoe lines up with hole in bracket.
6. Slide suitable pin into holes.
7. Remove camshaft sprocket mounting bolt, then the timing chain with crankshaft and camshaft sprockets.
8. Reverse procedure to install, noting the following:
   a. Install timing chain with single plated link aligned with dot and or paint marking on camshaft sprocket.
   b. Crankshaft sprocket is aligned with dot and or paint marking on sprocket between two plated timing chain links.

TIMING CHAIN TENSIONER

REPLACE

1. Remove timing chain as outlined under "Timing Chain, Replace."
2. Remove mounting bolts and tensioner.
3. Reverse procedure to install.

CAMSHAFT

REPLACE

The 5.7L engine uses a unique camshaft for use with the multi displacement system. When installing a new camshaft, the replacement camshaft must be compatible with the multi displacement system.
1. Remove cylinder heads as outlined under "Cylinder Head, Replace."
2. Remove oil pan as outlined under "Oil Pan, Replace."
3. Remove timing chain as outlined under "Timing Chain, Replace."

4. Remove camshaft tensioner/thrust plate.
5. Identify lifters for installation in original location.
6. Remove tappets and retainer.
7. Install long bolt into front of camshaft.
8. Remove camshaft. **Do not damage cam bearings with cam lobes**
9. Reverse procedure to install, noting the following:
   a. Lubricate camshaft lobes and camshaft bearing journals.
   b. Measure camshaft end play. If measurement is not .0031–.0114 inch, install new thrust plate.
   c. This engine uses both standard roller tappets and deactivating roller tappets with the multi displacement system. Deactivating roller tappets must be used in cylinders Nos. 1, 4, 6 and 7.
   d. Deactivating tappets can be identified by two holes in side of tappet body, for latching pins.

PISTON & ROD ASSEMBLY

Install pistons with raised mark or arrow facing toward front of engine.

Install connecting rod with oil slinger slot facing toward front of engine.

Connecting rod bolts are torque to yield. **Install new bolts when they are loosened or removed.**

MAIN & ROD BEARINGS

1. Identify rod bearing caps for installation in original positions before removal.
2. Identify main bearing caps for installation in original positions before removal.
3. Select proper main bearings, **Fig. 6**
4. Install main bearings in block and caps, then lubricate bearings.
5. Position crankshaft into cylinder block.
6. Install thrust washers.
7. Install new washer/seal on crossbolts.
8. Clean and oil all cap bolts.
9. Install all main bearing caps.
10. **Torque** cap bolts in sequence to 20 ft. lbs., **Fig. 7.**
11. Tighten main cap bolts an additional 90°.

12. Install crossbolts with new washer/gasket.
13. **Torque** crossbolts to 21 ft. lbs.
14. Repeat crossbolt tightening.
15. Measure crankshaft end play. End play should be 0031–.0114 inch.

CRANKSHAFT SEAL

REPLACE

1. Rotate belt tensioner counterclockwise until it contacts it's stop.
2. Remove belt and slowly rotate tensioner into the freearm position. **Do not let tensioner arm snap back to freearm position.**
3. Drain cooling system into suitable container.
4. Remove radiator upper hose.
5. Remove upper radiator hose and disconnect cooling fan electrical connector.
6. Remove mounting bolts and cooling fan.
7. Remove crankshaft damper bolt.
8. Remove damper using suitable three-jaw puller tool.
9. Remove crankshaft front seal using seal tool No. 9071, or equivalent.
10. Reverse procedure to install, :
    a. Front crankshaft seal must be installed dry. **Do not apply lubricant to sealing lip or to outer edge.**
    b. Install crankshaft front seal using driver tools Nos. 8348 and 8512A, or equivalents.

CRANKSHAFT REAR OIL SEAL

REPLACE

Removal

1. Remove transmission as outlined in **MOTOR's "Domestic Transmission Manual, In-Vehicle Service."**
2. Remove mounting bolts and flexplate.
3. Remove crankshaft rear oil seal using remover Tool No. 8506, or equivalent.

Installation

Rear seal must be installed dry. **Do not lubricate the seal lip or outer edge.**
1. Position plastic seal guide onto crankshaft rear face.
2. Position crankshaft rear oil seal onto guide.

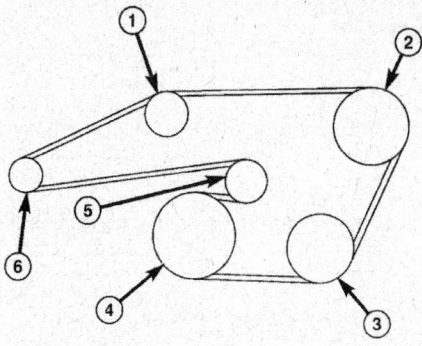

1- IDLER PULLEY
2- POWER STEERING PUMP
3- AIR CONDITIONING COMPRESSOR
4- CRANKSHAFT
5- TENSIONER
6- ALTERNATOR

ARM0400000000618

Fig. 14 Serpentine drive belt routing

3. Tap seal into place using crankshaft rear oil seal installer tool No. 8349 and driver handle tool No, C-4171, or equivalents.
4. Continue to tap on driver handle until seal installer seats against cylinder block crankshaft bore.
5. Tighten flexplate mounting bolts in sequence, **Fig. 8.**

OIL PAN
REPLACE

Gasket is integral to engine windage tray and does not come out with oil pan. When the oil pan is removed, a new oil pan gasket/windage tray assembly must be installed. The old gasket cannot be reused.

AWD

1. Remove engine cover.
2. Remove intake manifold as outlined under "Intake Manifold, Replace."
3. Install engine lift fixture tool No. 8984 and adapter No. 8984-UPD, or equivalent. **Do not use air tools when installing mounting bolts and nuts.**
4. Raise and support vehicle.
5. Remove mounting screws and front belly pan.
6. Remove left and righthand side engine mount to frame mounting bolts.
7. Drain engine oil into suitable container and remove oil filter.
8. Remove mounting bolts and lower steering rack. **Do not remove power steering hoses, tie rod ends or disconnect steering column.**
9. Remove engine oil dipstick and tube from oil pan.
10. Disconnect downstream oxygen sensor connectors.
11. Remove catalytic converter to muffler and resonator clamps.
12. Remove mounting nuts and tunnel reinforcement
13. Remove two mounting nuts and isolators, then the lefthand resonator and tailpipe.

14. Remove isolators, then the muffler and tailpipe by twisting/turning while pulling assembly out of catalytic converters.
15. Remove ball flange nuts and catalytic converter.
16. Mark front driveshaft to flange at both ends for installation alignment.
17. Remove front drive shaft mounting bolts from differential and transfer case.
18. Remove driveshaft.
19. Remove left and righthand front drive axles.
20. Remove differential support bracket.
21. Remove mounting bolts and differential support bracket.
22. Turn differential so drive flange is facing forward and oil pan side is facing up.
23. Remove differential through opening at rear of cradle.
24. Remove intermediate shaft from oil pan.
25. Lower vehicle.
26. Install engine support fixture tool No. 8534, or equivalent. **Do not fasten fixture to vehicle body, or attach third support leg to radiator support.**
27. Raise engine to provide oil pan removal clearance.
28. Raise and support vehicle.
29. Mark oil pan mounting bolts for installation alignment. **Horizontal M10 fasteners are .20 inch longer and must be installed in original locations.**
30. Remove oil pan to transmission, then the engine rear vertical and horizontal mounting bolts.
31. Remove mounting bolts and oil pan. **Do not pry on oil pan or gasket.**
32. Discard integral windage tray and gasket.
33. Reverse procedure to install, noting the following:
   a. Apply .177 x .985 inch Mopar Engine RTV, or equivalent, bead to four T-joints, (area where front cover, rear retainer, block, and oil pan gasket meet). Bead should cover bottom of gasket, **Fig. 9.**
   b. Install new oil pan gasket/windage tray assembly.
   c. Horizontal M10 fasteners are .20 inch longer and must be installed in original locations.
   d. Align oil pan rear with engine block rear face.
   e. Install M10 and M6 oil pan fasteners hand tight.
   f. **Torque** M6 mounting bolts in sequence to 44 inch lbs., **Fig. 10.**
   g. **Torque** M10 oil pan mounting bolts in sequence to 39 ft. lbs
   h. **Torque** M6 oil pan mounting bolts to 106 inch lbs.

RWD

1. Remove intake manifold as outlined under "Intake Manifold, Replace."
2. Install engine lift fixture tool No. 8984 and adapter No. 8984-UPD, or equivalent. **Do not use air tools when installing mounting bolts and nuts.**
3. Raise and support vehicle.

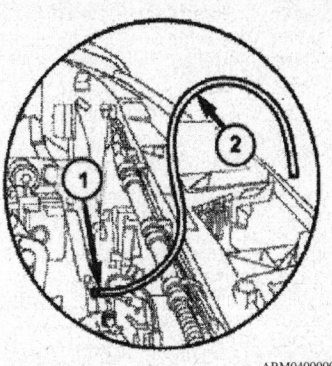

ARM0400000000802

Fig. 15 Cooling system bleed

4. Remove mounting screws and front belly pan.
5. Drain engine oil into suitable container and remove oil filter.
6. Remove mounting bolts and lower steering rack. **Do not remove power steering hoses, tie rod ends or disconnect steering column.**
7. Remove left and righthand side engine hydromount to frame nuts and studs.
8. Remove engine oil dipstick and tube from oil pan.
9. Lower vehicle.
10. Raise engine to provide oil pan removal clearance.
11. Raise and support vehicle.
12. Mark oil pan mounting bolts for installation alignment. **Horizontal M10 fasteners are .20 inch longer length and must be installed in original locations.**
13. Remove oil pan to transmission, then the engine rear vertical and horizontal mounting bolts.
14. Remove mounting bolts and oil pan. **Do not pry on oil pan or gasket.**
15. Discard integral windage tray and gasket.
16. Reverse procedure to install, noting the following:
   a. Apply .177 x .985 inch Mopar Engine RTV, or equivalent, bead to four T-joints, (area where front cover, rear retainer, block, and oil pan gasket meet). Bead should cover bottom of gasket, **Fig. 9.**
   b. Install new oil pan gasket/windage tray assembly.
   c. Horizontal M10 fasteners are .20 inch longer, and must be installed in original locations.
   d. Align oil pan rear with engine block rear face.
   e. Install M10 and M6 oil pan fasteners hand tight.
   f. **Torque** M6 mounting bolts in sequence to 44 inch lbs. **Fig. 10.**
   g. **Torque** M10 oil pan mounting bolts in sequence to 39 ft. lbs
   h. **Torque** M6 oil pan mounting bolts to 106 inch lbs.

OIL PUMP
REPLACE

1. Remove oil pan as outlined under "Oil Pan, Replace."

2. Remove mounting bolt and pick-up tube
3. Remove timing chain cover as outlined under "Front Cover, Replace."
4. Remove four mounting bolts and oil pump.
5. Reverse procedure to install.

OIL PUMP SERVICE

The oil pump pressure relief valve and spring should not be removed from the oil pump. If these components are disassembled and/or removed from the pump. The entire oil pump assembly must be replaced.

1. Remove pump cover.
2. Clean all parts thoroughly.
3. Mating surface of oil pump housing should be smooth. If pump cover is scratched or grooved oil pump assembly should be replaced.
4. Slide outer rotor into body of oil pump.
5. Press outer rotor to one side of oil pump body and measure clearance between outer rotor and body, **Fig. 11.**
6. If clearance is .009 inch, or more, oil pump assembly must be replaced.
7. Install inner rotor in into oil pump body.
8. Measure clearance between inner and outer rotors, **Fig. 12.**
9. If clearance between rotors is .006 inch, or more, oil pump assembly must be replaced.
10. Place suitable straight edge across body of oil pump between bolt holes and measure clearance, **Fig. 13.**
11. If clearance is .0038 inch, or more, pump must be replaced.
12. Install pump cover.

BELT TENSION DATA

Belt adjustment is maintained by an automatic (spring load) belt tensioner.

SERPENTINE DRIVE BELT

Routing

Refer to **Fig. 14** for serpentine drive belt routing

Replacement

REMOVAL

1. Rotate belt tensioner counterclockwise until it contacts it's stop.
2. Remove belt and slowly rotate tensioner into the freearm position. **Do not let tensioner arm snap back to freearm position.**

INSTALLATION

1. Route belt around all pulleys except idler pulley.
2. Rotate tensioner arm until it contacts it's stop position.
3. Route belt around idler and slowly let tensioner rotate into belt.
4. Ensure belt is seated onto all pulleys.

5. Tensioner is equipped with indexing tang on back and indexing stop on tensioner housing.
6. If new belt (used 15 minutes or less) is being installed, tang must be within approximately .24–.32 inch of indexing stop.

COOLING SYSTEM BLEED

1. Attach 4–6 feet long ¼ inch ID clear hose to bleeder fitting located on front of water outlet housing at front of engine, **Fig. 15.** It may be necessary to install bleed fitting. **When installing drain hose to air bleed valve, route hose away from accessory drive belts, accessory drive pulleys, and electric cooling fan motors.**
2. Route hose away from accessory drive belt, drive pulleys and electric cooling fan
3. Place other end of hose into clean container.
4. **Ensure cooling system air bleed valve is opened before any coolant is added to cooling system.**
5. Install threaded and barbed fitting (¼ - 18 npt) into water pump housing.
6. Attach filling aid funnel tool No. 8195, or equivalent, to pressure bottle filler neck.
7. Pinch overflow hose that connects between two chambers of coolant bottle using suitable hose pinch-off pliers.
8. Open bleed fitting.
9. Pour suitable antifreeze mixture into larger section of filling aid funnel (smaller section of funnel is to allow air to escape).
10. Slowly fill cooling system until steady stream of coolant flows from hose attached to bleed valve.
11. Close bleed valve and continue filling system to top of filling aid funnel tool.
12. Remove pinch-off pliers from overflow hose.
13. Allow coolant in filling funnel to drain into overflow chamber of pressure bottle.
14. Remove funnel and install coolant pressure bottle cap.
15. Remove hose from bleed valve.
16. Install fitting into thermostat housing. Coat threads with Mopar Thread Sealant with Teflon, or equivalent.
17. Start engine and run at 1500–2000 RPM for 30 minutes, noting the following:
    a. Engine cooling system will push any remaining air into coolant bottle within about an hour of normal driving. As a result, a drop in coolant level in pressure bottle may occur.
    b. If engine cooling system overheats and pushes coolant into overflow side of coolant bottle, this coolant will be sucked back into cooling system, **only if pressure cap is left on bottle.**
    c. Removing pressure cap breaks vacuum path between two bottle

sections and coolant will not return to cooling system.
18. Shut off engine allow it to cool down for 30 minutes. This permits coolant to be drawn into pressure chamber.
19. With engine cold, ensure coolant level should be within MIN and MAX marks. Coolant will normally only be in inboard of coolant bottle two chambers. Outboard chamber is only to recover coolant in event of an overheat or after recent service fill.

THERMOSTAT
REPLACE

1. Drain coolant into suitable container.
2. Remove thermostat housing radiator hose.
3. Remove mounting bolts, housing and thermostat.
4. Reverse procedure to install. Install thermostat (spring side down) into recessed machined groove on timing chain cover with bleed valve located at 12 o'clock position.

WATER PUMP
REPLACE

1. Drain coolant into suitable container.
2. Remove upper radiator hose and disconnect cooling fan electrical connector.
3. Remove mounting bolts and cooling fan.
4. Rotate belt tensioner counterclockwise until it contacts it's stop.
5. Remove belt and slowly rotate tensioner into the freearm position. **Do not let tensioner arm snap back to freearm position.**
6. Remove thermostat housing radiator hose.
7. Remove mounting bolts, housing and thermostat.
8. Mark location of different length water pump mounting bolts.
9. Remove mounting bolts and water pump.
10. Reverse procedure to install.

RADIATOR
REPLACE

Refer to "Radiator, Replace" in the "2.7L Engine" section for radiator replacement procedure.

FUEL PUMP
REPLACE

Refer to "Fuel Pump, Replace" in "2.7L Engine" section for fuel pump replacement procedure.

FUEL FILTER
REPLACE

The fuel filter is replaceable only as part of the fuel pump module.

TIGHTENING SPECIFICATIONS

Year	Component	Torque Ft. Lbs.
2005	Air Cleaner	30①
	Alternator	40
	Automatic Belt Tensioner to Block	40
	Camshaft Sprocket	20
	Camshaft Tensioner Plate	20
	Connecting Rod Cap	15②
	Cooling Fan	50
	Crossbolts	20
	Cylinder Head	③
	Cylinder Head Cover	70①
	Exhaust Manifold	18
	Exhaust Manifold Ball Flange	⑥
	Exhaust Manifold Heat Shield	70①
	Fan Blade to Fan Motor	17
	Fan Shroud	50①
	Flexplate To Crankshaft	55
	Front Insulator	70
	Heater Supply Tube	30①
	Housing, Coolant Outlet	105①
	Idler Pulley	40
	Intake Manifold	105①
	Lifter Guide Holder	106
	Lifting Stud	40
	Main Bearing Cap	④
	Oil Pan	⑤
	Oil Dipstick Tube	105
	Oil Pan Drain Plug	20
	Oil Pump	20
	Oil Pump Pickup Tube	20
	Radiator to Support Bracket	106①
	Rear Seal Retainer	11
	Rear Insulator to Bracket	50
	Rear Insulator to Crossmember	30
	Rear Insulator to Transmission	50
	Rear Insulator Bracket	50
	Rocker Arm	16
	Tappet Guide Yoke	106①
	Thermostat Housing	112
	Throttle Body	105①
	Timing Chain Case Cover	112①
	Upper Radiator Closure Panel	90①
	Vibration Damper	129
	Water Pump	20
	Water Pump to Timing Chain	20

① — Inch lbs.
② — Plus an additional 90°.
③ — Refer to "Cylinder Head, Replace" for tightening specifications and sequence.
④ — Refer to "Main & Rod Bearings" for tightening specifications and sequence.
⑤ — Refer to "Oil Pan, Replace" for tightening specifications and sequence.
⑥ — Refer to "Exhaust Manifold, Replace" for tightening specifications and sequence.

Rear Axle & Suspension

NOTE: On Air Bag Equipped Models, Refer To "Air Bag System Precautions" Located In The Front Of This Manual For System Disarming & Arming Procedures.

NOTE: Refer To "Computer Relearn Procedures" Located In The Front Of This Manual When Battery Power To The Computer Has Been Interrupted.

NOTE: Refer To The Rear Of This Manual For Vehicle Manufacturer's Special Tool Suppliers.

INDEX

PRECAUTIONS

Air Bag Systems

Refer to "Air Bag System Precautions" in the front of this manual for system disarming and arming procedures.

Battery Ground Cable

Prior to service, disconnect battery ground cable and isolate as required.

RECALIBRATION

Anytime the battery has been disconnect or has lost its charge, the following must be recalibrated.

EXPRESS WINDOW

1. Turn ignition switch to RUN position.
2. Move driver's window upward until it stalls in full up position. Allow window motor to stall for at least two seconds before releasing switch.
3. Move driver's window downward until it stalls in full down position. Allow window motor to stall for at least two seconds before releasing switch.
4. Move driver's window upward until it stalls in full up position. Allow window motor to stall for at least two seconds before releasing switch.
5. Move passenger's window upward until it stalls in full up position. Allow window motor to stall for at least two seconds before releasing switch.
6. Move passenger's window downward until it stalls in full down position. Allow

window motor to stall for at least two seconds before releasing switch.
7. Move passenger's window upward until it stalls in full up position. Allow window motor to stall for at least two seconds before releasing switch.

ELECTRONIC STABILITY PROGRAM (ESP) STEERING ANGLE SENSOR

1. Start engine.
2. Turn steering wheel right until wheel locks full right.
3. Turn steering wheel left until wheel locks full left.
4. Turn steering wheel right until wheels are centered.
5. Cycle ignition switch OFF and ON. Do not start engine.

DESCRIPTION

This vehicle utilizes a five-link rear suspension including the following major components: camber link, compression link, spring link, tension link, toe link, coil spring crossmember, hub and bearing, knuckle, shock absorber and stabilizer bar.

The knuckle, camber link, compression link and tension link are aluminum castings.

Both AWD and RWD models utilize a two-piece rear propeller shaft design to transmit torque to the rear axle assembly. **Fig. 1.** This two-piece design consists of: front and rear shaft segments, center support bearing/bracket assembly, single-cardan U-joint at rear segment/bearing interface, rubber couplers at transmission

and rear axle flanges, and, on 2.7L and 3.5L models, fore-mounted vibration damper.

The front shaft segment is designed with a collapsing feature, consisting of two concentric tubes secured by shear pins. This feature allows the tubes to telescope up to eight inches during certain impacts. The flexible rubber couplers at the transmission and axle flanges absorb vibration. The low-travel single-cardan universal joint permits the minimal axial and angular variations that occur with independent rear suspension. Additionally, models equipped with 2.7L and 3.5L engines utilize a vibration damper which is designed to absorb and isolate driveline vibrations and harmonics. This damper is mounted to the front segment, sandwiched between the coupler and propeller shaft.

AWD models utilize a two-piece front propeller shaft design to transmit torque to the front axle assembly, **Fig. 2.** This two-piece design consists of: front and rear shaft segments, single-cardan U-joints at end flanges and rubber boot at front/rear segment interface.

REAR HALFSHAFT
REPLACE

This procedure requires the compression of the rear suspension to ride height. A drive-on hoist should be used. If a drive-on hoist is not used, screw-style under-hoist jack stands are required to compress the rear suspension, facilitating rear halfshaft removal.

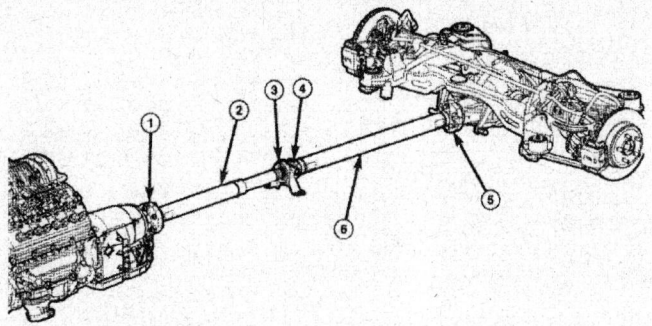

1- FRONT COUPLER
2- FRONT SEGMENT
3- BEARING/BRACKET ASSEMBLY
4- SINGLE-CARDAN U-JOINT
5- REAR COUPLER
6- REAR SEGMENT

ARM0400000000640

Fig. 1   Propeller shaft. Rear

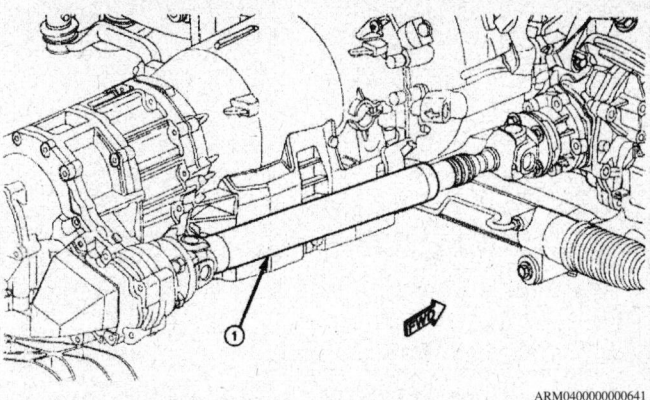

ARM0400000000641

Fig. 2   Propeller shaft. Front

Halfshaft inner and outer boots are not serviceable separately. Boot replacement requires entire shaft assembly replacement.

Removal

1. Raise and support vehicle on hoist.
2. Drain rear axle fluid into suitable container suitable. Install drain plug.
3. **On models equipped with 5.7L engine,** remove rear exhaust system.
4. **On all models,** remove tire an wheel assembly.
5. Remove wheel hub nut and discard.
6. Mark propeller shaft rubber coupler and axle flange for installation alignment.
7. Remove three propeller shaft coupler-to-axle flange bolt/nuts.
8. Partially disengage halfshaft from axle using suitable screwdriver.
9. **If drive-on hoist is not used,** compress rear suspension using screw-style under-hoist jack stands.
10. **On all models,** position transmission jack to rear axle.
11. Remove rear axle forward mount isolator bolt/nut.
12. Remove rear axle-to-crossmember bolts using short socket and flexible-head ratchet.
13. Lower rear axle. While lowering axle, separate propeller shaft from axle and support with suitable rope or wire.
14. Lower axle just enough to remove halfshafts one at a time.
15. Shift axle assembly in one direction, compressing one halfshaft while removing other. **Protect axle seal and journal.**
16. Unequal-length halfshafts are used. **Lefthand halfshaft is shorter. Identify and tag halfshafts upon removal to ensure proper installation.**
17. **Never grasp halfshaft assembly by inner or outer boots.**

18. Remove halfshaft from hub.
19. Remove and inspect rubber isolation washer.
20. Remove axle seals using suitable screwdriver.

Installation

1. Install new axle seal using driver tool No. 9223, or equivalent.
2. Install halfshaft isolation washer. Washer is bi-directional and can be installed in either direction.
3. Install halfshaft to wheel hub/knuckle assembly.
4. Install new hub nut by hand.
5. Lubricate halfshaft inner joint bearing journal with Mopar Gear and Axle Lubricant 75W-140, or equivalent.
6. Install halfshaft to rear axle using new circlip. **Do not damage axle seals.**
7. Ensure proper installation by pulling outward on joint by hand.
8. Raise rear axle into position.
9. Align propeller shaft and start propeller shaft coupler-to-axle bolt/nuts by hand.
10. Install two rear axle-to-crossmember bolts and tighten.
11. Install rear axle front mount isolator and tighten.
12. Ensure halfshaft inner joints are fully engaged to axle.
13. Remove transmission jack and/or screw-type under-hoist jack stands.
14. Tighten propeller shaft coupler-to-axle flange bolt/nuts.
15. Remove rear axle fill plug and fill axle with Mopar 75W-140 Synthetic Gear & Axle Lubricant, or equivalent.
16. Install and tighten fill plug.
17. **On models equipped with 5.7L engine,** install exhaust system. Tighten band clamps
18. **On all models,** lower vehicle and tighten halfshaft hub nut.
19. Install wheel center cap.

20. Install tie and wheel assembly and tighten lug nuts.

DIFFERENTIAL CARRIER
REPLACE

This procedure requires the compression of the rear suspension to ride height. A drive-on hoist should be used. If a drive-on hoist is not used, screw-style under-hoist jack stands are required to compress the rear suspension, facilitating rear halfshaft removal.

Never grasp halfshaft assembly by inner or outer boots.

1. Raise and support vehicle on hoist.
2. Drain rear axle fluid in suitable container. Install drain plug
3. **On models equipped with dual outlet exhaust,** remove rear exhaust system.
4. **On models not equipped with dual outlet exhaust,** lower exhaust system at rear hanger(s) to provide adequate clearance.
5. **On all models,** mark propeller shaft rubber coupler and axle flange for installation alignment.
6. Remove three propeller shaft coupler to axle flange bolt/nuts.
7. Partially disengage halfshaft from axle using suitable screwdriver.
8. **If a drive-on hoist is not used,** compress rear suspension using screw-style jack stands.
9. **On all models,** support rear axle with suitable transmission jack.
10. Remove rear axle forward mount isolator bolt/nut.
11. Remove two rear axle to crossmember bolts.
12. Lower rear axle. While lowering axle, separate propeller shaft from axle and support with suitable rope or wire.
13. Lower axle just enough to remove both halfshafts one at a time.
14. Shift axle assembly in one direction, compressing one halfshaft while removing the other. **Protect axle seal and journal.**
15. Remove axle assembly and transfer to bench.

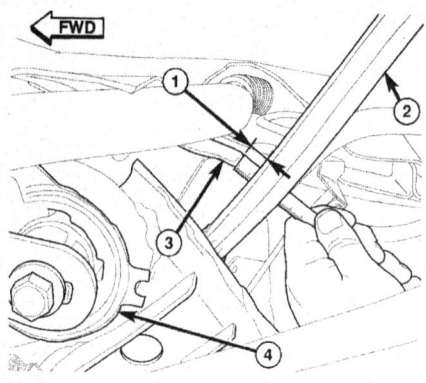

1- CLEARANCE
2- TENSION LINK
3- WELD FLANGE
4- FRONT MOUNT BUSHING

ARM0400000000638

Fig. 3 Suspension movement clearance

16. Remove and discard axle seals using suitable screwdriver.
17. Reverse procedure to install, noting the following:
    a. Install new axle sea using driver tool No. 9223, or equivalent.
    b. Halfshaft installation angle should be minimized to avoid damage to seal.
    c. Use new circlip(s).

PROPELLER SHAFT
REPLACE

1. Raise and support vehicle on hoist.
2. Mark transmission and axle flanges and rubber couplers for installation alignment.
3. Remove crossmember, rear exhaust system and heat shield.
4. Remove propeller shaft front and rear coupler-to-flange bolts.
5. Remove center bearing mounting bolts.
6. Remove propeller shaft with aid of helper.**Never allow propeller shaft to hang from center bearing, or while only connected to transmission or rear axle flanges.**
7. Remove three coupler-to-propeller shaft bolt/nuts.
8. Record orientation and direction of components for install alignment.
9. Separate coupler and damper from propeller shaft.
10. Reverse procedure to install.

HUB & BEARING
REPLACE

1. Raise and support vehicle, then remove tire and wheel assembly.
2. While helper applies brakes to keep hub from rotating, remove half shaft hub nut.
3. Remove two mounting bolts, disc brake caliper and adapter.
4. Hang assembly aside using suitable wire. **Do not overextend brake hose.**

5. Remove clips, then slide brake rotor off hub and bearing.
6. Loosen each hub and bearing mounting bolt a turn or two at a time while pulling outward on hub and bearing to avoid bolt contact with half shaft outer joint.
7. Once removed from threads in hub and bearing (but not knuckle), allow bolts to stay in and protrude through knuckle and brake support plate.
8. Slide hub and bearing off knuckle and half shaft.
9. Reverse procedure to install. Ensure isolation washer is present on end of half shaft. Washer can be installed in either direction on shaft.

HUB & BEARING SERVICE

The rear wheel bearing and wheel hub are a one piece sealed unit or hub and bearing unit type assembly. The wheel mounting studs used to mount the tire and wheel to the vehicle are the only replaceable components of the hub and bearing. Otherwise, the hub and bearing is serviced only as a complete assembly.

SHOCK ABSORBER
REPLACE
Load-Leveling
REMOVAL

1. Raise and support vehicle, then remove both rear tire and wheel assemblies.
2. **If servicing lefthand side,** proceed as follows:
   a. Drain fuel from tank into suitable container.
   b. Open filler tube door and remove retaining wire from inside filler tube rubber.
   c. Start removing rubber from body sheet metal, squeeze rubber and push in.
   d. Remove lefthand inner splash shield.
   e. Disconnect filler tube vent line.
   f. Remove filler tube mounting bolt.
   g. Remove under body splash shield.
   h. Loosen filler tube hose clamp. Leave clamp tight on hose and fuel tank location.
   i. Move clamp toward fuel tank and remove filler tube.
3. **On all models,** position an extra pair of suitable jack stands under and support forward end of engine cradle.
4. **If servicing righthand side or on models with dual-exhaust,** proceed as follows:
   a. Position under-hoist utility jack or stand several inches below exhaust at muffler.
   b. Disconnect exhaust isolators at muffler and resonators hangers.
   c. Lower exhaust down to rest upon top of jack or stand.
5. **On all models,** position suitable

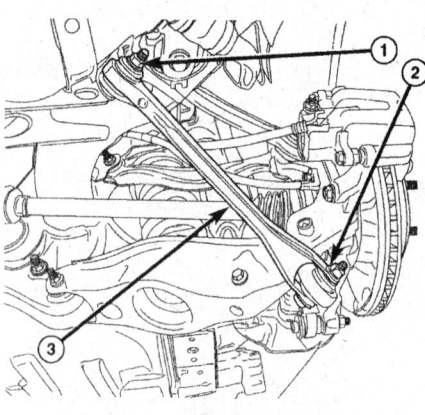

1- CROSSMEMBER BOLT & NUT
2- KNUCKLE BOLT & NUT
3- COMPRESSION LINK

ARM0400000000639

Fig. 4 Compression link replacement

under-hoist utility jack or transmission jack under center of rear axle differential.
6. Raise jack head to contact differential and secure in place. **Do not secure stabilizer bar.**
7. Remove shock absorber upper mounting screws, lower mounting bolt and nut.
8. Remove both front and rear crossmember mounting bolts on repair-side of vehicle. **Do not loosen or remove crossmember mounting bolts on opposite side of vehicle. On models equipped with AWD, do not misplace spacers between crossmember mounts and body.**
9. Slowly lower jack allowing repair-side of crossmember to drop. Lower jack just enough to allow top of shock absorber to clear body flange. **Do not lower crossmember any further than required to remove shock absorber.**
10. Remove shock absorber by tipping top outward and lifting lower end out of pocket in spring link.

INSTALLATION

1. Install shock absorber by setting lower end into pocket in spring link, then tipping top inward until aligned with upper mounting holes.
2. Install lower shock mounting bolt and nut. **Do not tighten now.**
3. **On models equipped with AWD,** ensure spacers on top of crossmember mount bushings.
4. **On all models,** raise jack, guiding coil spring and upper end of shock absorber into mounted positions.
5. Install and tighten shock absorber upper mounting screws.
6. Install crossmember mounting bolts. Snug, but do not fully tighten bolts now. **Rear crossmember mounting bolts are longer than front mounting bolts. Do not interchange mounting bolts.**
7. Measure distance between tension link and weld flange on body directly in

front of it, just outboard of front mount bushing, **Fig. 3.**

8. This distance must be at least .47 inch to allow proper clearance for suspension movement, noting the following:
   a. If distance is less than specified on either side of vehicle, shift that side of rear crossmember directly rearward until distance is .47 inch, or more.
   b. To do so, loosen three mounting bolts slightly, leaving one on opposite side of shift snugged to pivot off of.
   c. Shift crossmember rearward and snug loosened bolts.
   d. Measure opposite side to ensure it still maintains minimum .47 inch distance.
9. Tighten all crossmember mounting bolts.
10. Remove jack from under rear axle differential.
11. If previously lowered, raise rear exhaust back to mounted position and connect exhaust isolators at muffler and resonators hangers. Remove jack or stand below exhaust muffler.
12. Insert filler tube into fuel tank rubber hose.
13. Slide hose clamp into place and tighten.
14. Hose clamp in place and tighten.
15. Install filler tube mounting bolt and vent line.
16. Install underbody splash shield.
17. Install lefthand inner splash shield.
18. Pull rubber through opening and install to body. Ensure sheet metal is in rubber groove.
19. Start metal wire retaining wire in groove on inside of filler tube rubber.
20. Work wire retaining wire around rubber and install wire retainer.
21. Install tire and wheel assemblies, then tighten wheel mounting nuts.
22. Lower and position vehicle on alignment rack/drive-on lift.
23. Raise lift as required to access lower mounting bolt.
24. Tighten shock absorber lower mounting bolt nut.

Standard

1. Raise and support vehicle, then remove tire and wheel assembly.
2. Position suitable under-hoist utility jack or jack stand under outer spring link adding just enough support to keep suspension from going into full-rebound when shock absorber mounting bolts.
3. Remove lower mounting bolt, nut, upper mounting bolts and shock absorber.
4. Reverse procedure to install, noting the following:
   a. Tighten upper mounting bolt when installed.
   b. **Do not tighten lower mounting bolt nut when installed.**
   c. Lower and position vehicle on alignment rack/drive-on lift.
   d. Raise lift as required to access lower mounting bolt.

e. Tighten shock absorber lower mounting bolt nut.

COIL SPRING
REPLACE

Rear coil springs are interchangeable.
1. Remove shock absorber as outlined under "Shock Absorber, Replace," "Load-Leveling."
2. Disconnect brake hose at bracket mounted to body.
3. Slowly lower jack until crossmember is low enough to remove coil spring. **Do not lower jack any further than required to remove spring.**
4. Remove coil spring and isolators.
5. Reverse procedure to install, noting the following:
   a. Install upper and lower isolators on coil spring.
   b. Ensure isolators are completely installed on ends of spring.
   c. Install coil spring with isolators into spring pocket of spring link fitting lower isolator to shape of pocket, then align top of spring with body mount.

CAMBER LINK
REPLACE

1. Remove shock absorber as outlined under "Shock Absorber, Replace," "Load-Leveling."
2. Remove mounting link to knuckle nut and bolt, then the mounting link to crossmember nut bolt.
3. Remove link.
4. Reverse procedure to install, noting the following:
   a. Heavier, thicker end goes toward crossmember.
   b. Fore-or-aft bow faces forward (curves around coil spring).
   c. Up-or-down bow faces downward.

COMPRESSION LINK
REPLACE

1. Raise and support vehicle, then remove rear tire and wheel assembly.
2. Remove mounting link bolt and nut at knuckle, **Fig. 4.**
3. Remove mounting link bolt and nut at crossmember.
4. Remove link.
5. Reverse procedure to install, noting the following:
   a. Although compression link is different end-to-end, there is no top and bottom.
   b. **Do not tighten mounting bolts and nuts when installed.**
   c. Lower and position vehicle on alignment rack/drive-on lift.
   d. Raise vehicle as required to access link fasteners
   e. Tighten crossmember bolt, then the knuckle bolt.

TOE LINK
REPLACE

Lefthand

REMOVAL

1. Raise and support vehicle, then remove both rear tire and wheel assemblies.
2. Drain fuel from tank into suitable container.
3. Open filler tube door and remove retaining wire from inside filler tube rubber.
4. Start removing rubber from body sheet metal, squeeze rubber and push in.
5. Remove lefthand inner splash shield.
6. Disconnect filler tube vent line.
7. Remove filler tube mounting bolt.
8. Remove under body splash shield.
9. Loosen filler tube hose clamp. Leave clamp tight on hose and fuel tank location.
10. Move clamp toward fuel tank and remove filler tube.
11. Position suitable extra pair of jack stands under and support forward end of engine cradle.
12. **On models with dual-exhaust,** proceed as follows:
    a. Position under-hoist utility jack or stand several inches below exhaust at muffler.
    b. Disconnect exhaust isolators at muffler and resonators hangers.
    c. Lower exhaust down to rest upon top of jack or stand.
13. **On all models,** support rear axle differential by positioning suitable under-hoist utility jack or transmission jack under center.
14. Remove shock absorber lower mounting bolt and nut.
15. Remove both front and rear crossmember mounting bolts on repair-side of vehicle. **Do not loosen or remove crossmember mounting bolts on opposite side of vehicle. On models equipped with AWD, do not misplace spacers between crossmember mounts and body.**
16. Slowly lower jack allowing repair-side of crossmember to drop just enough to access toe link mounting bolt at crossmember.
17. Remove wheel speed sensor cable from toe link.
18. While holding toe adjustment cam bolt from rotating, remove nut securing toe link at crossmember.
19. Slide cam bolt rearward out of crossmember and link,
20. Remove mounting bolt and nut at knuckle, then the toe link.

INSTALLATION

1. Slide crossmember end of toe link into box bracket on crossmember.
2. Slide cam bolt through bracket and link from rear.
3. Install bolt and nut to knuckle. **Do not tighten bolt now.**
4. While holding toe adjustment cam bolt

from rotating (cam facing upward), install cam washer and nut at crossmember. **Do not tighten nut now.**

5. Attach wheel speed sensor cable to toe link.
6. Carefully raise jack, guiding coil spring and lower end of shock absorber into mounted positions.
7. When lower shock mounting bolt holes line up, install bolt and nut. **Do not tighten now.**
8. Install crossmember mounting bolts. Snug, but do not fully tighten bolts now. **Rear crossmember mounting bolts are longer than front mounting bolts. Do not interchange mounting bolts.**
9. Measure distance between tension link and weld flange on body directly in front of it, just outboard of front mount bushing, **Fig. 3.**
10. This distance must be at least .47 inch to allow proper clearance for suspension movement, noting the following:
    a. If distance is less than specified on either side of vehicle, shift that side of rear crossmember directly rearward until distance is .47 inch, or more.
    b. To do so, loosen three mounting bolts slightly, leaving one on opposite side of shift snugged to pivot off of.
    c. Shift crossmember rearward and snug loosened bolts.
    d. Measure opposite side to ensure it still maintains minimum .47 inch distance.
11. Tighten all crossmember mounting bolts.
12. Remove jack from under rear axle differential.
13. If previously lowered, raise rear exhaust back to mounted position and connect exhaust isolators at muffler and resonators hangers.
14. Remove jack or stand below exhaust muffler.
15. Insert filler tube into fuel tank rubber hose.
16. Slide hose clamp into place and tighten.
17. Hose clamp in place and tighten.
18. Install filler tube mounting bolt and vent line.
19. Install underbody splash shield.
20. Install lefthand inner splash shield.
21. Pull rubber through opening and install to body. Ensure sheet metal is in rubber groove.
22. Start metal wire retaining wire in groove on inside of filler tube rubber.
23. Work wire retaining wire around rubber and install wire retainer.
24. Install tire and wheel assemblies, then tighten wheel mounting nuts.
25. Lower and position vehicle on alignment rack/drive-on lift.
26. Raise vehicle as required to access mounting bolts.
27. Tighten shock absorber lower mounting bolt nut.
28. Tighten toe link nut at crossmember. This nut may be tightened after rear wheel alignment toe is set. **Do not tighten from bolt head end.**
29. Tighten tow link bolt at knuckle.

Righthand

REMOVAL

1. Raise and support vehicle, then remove rear tire and wheel assembly
2. Remove wheel speed sensor cable from toe link.
3. While holding toe adjustment cam bolt from rotating, remove nut securing toe link at crossmember.
4. Slide cam bolt rearward out of crossmember and link.
5. Remove mounting bolt and nut at knuckle, then the link,

INSTALLATION

1. Slide crossmember end of toe link into box bracket on crossmember.
2. Slide cam bolt through bracket and link from rear of vehicle.
3. Install bolt and nut securing link to knuckle. Do not tighten bolt now.
4. While holding toe adjustment cam bolt from rotating (cam facing upward), install cam washer and nut securing toe link at crossmember. **Do not tighten nut now.**
5. Attach wheel speed sensor cable to toe link.
6. Raise rear exhaust back to mounted position and connect exhaust isolators at muffler and resonators hangers.
7. Remove jack or stand below exhaust muffler.
8. Install tire and wheel assembly, then tighten wheel mounting nuts.
9. Lower and position vehicle on alignment rack/drive-on lift.
10. Raise vehicle as required to access mounting bolts.
11. Tighten toe link nut at crossmember. This nut may be tightened after rear wheel alignment toe is set. **Do not tighten from bolt head end.**
12. Tighten bolt at knuckle,

SPRING LINK

REPLACE

Removal

1. Raise and support vehicle.
2. Remove spring link-to-knuckle nut and bolt
3. Place guide tool No. 9361-2, or equivalent, against sleeve in knuckle to keep tap tool No, 9361-1, or equivalent, straight.
4. Cut threads approximately halfway through bushing (or about six complete threads) using tap with suitable handle.
5. Thread remover tool No. 9361, noting the following:
    a. **On AWD models lefthand side,** use bolt No. 9361-3, nut, spherical

washer, thrust bearing and sleeve tool No. 9361-5, or equivalents.
    b. **On AWD models righthand side,** use bolt No. 9361-3, nut, spherical washer, thrust bearing and sleeve tool No. 9361-6, or equivalents.
    c. **On RWD models,** use bolt No. 9361-3, nut, spherical washer, thrust bearing and sleeve tool No. 9361-4, or equivalents.
    d. **On all models,** ensure to place hardened side against nut.
6. Rotate nut down, matching sleeve angled end with angled face of knuckle. Continue to rotate nut until knuckle sleeve is removed from knuckle. Discard knuckle sleeve.
7. Remove crossmember mounting bolt and nut, then the spring link.

Installation

1. Guide ball joint end of spring link into mounting pocket of knuckle, then swing opposite end up to bushing in crossmember and install bolt and nut. **Do not tighten bolt now**
2. Place new knuckle sleeve onto installer bolt tool No. 9361-7, or equivalent, slide it up to bolt's head.
3. Slide bolt tool with sleeve through knuckle and spring link ball joint, starting from knuckle forward end.
4. Install thrust bearing and nut on end of bolt tool.
5. While holding bolt head stationary, rotate nut (using hand tools) installing sleeve in knuckle. Install sleeve until nut stops turning. **Do not overtighten nut.**
6. Remove special tool.
7. Install spring link-to-knuckle bolt front-to-rear through knuckle and link, then install nut.
8. While holding bolt head stationary, tighten nut.
9. Lower and position vehicle on alignment rack/drive-on lift.
10. Raise vehicle as required to access mounting bolt.
11. Tighten spring link bolt at crossmember.

TENSION LINK

REPLACE

1. Remove shock absorber as outlined under "Shock Absorber, Replace," "Load-Leveling."
2. Remove mounting link to knuckle nut and bolt, then the mounting link to crossmember nut bolt.
3. Remove link.
4. Reverse procedure to install, noting the following:
    a. Although link is same end-to-end, ensure that center bow is facing downward.
    b. **Do not tighten mounting bolts and nuts when installed.**
    c. Lower and position vehicle on alignment rack/drive-on lift.

d. Raise vehicle as required to access link fasteners
e. Tighten crossmember bolt, then the knuckle bolt.

KNUCKLE
REPLACE

Removal

1. Raise and support vehicle.
2. Unclip wheel speed sensor cable at rear brake rotor shield.
3. Remove mounting screw and wheel speed sensor head from knuckle.
4. Remove tire and wheel assembly.
5. While helper applies brakes to keep hub from rotating, remove half shaft hub nut.
6. Remove two mounting bolts, disc brake caliper and adapter.
7. Hang assembly aside using suitable wire. **Do not overextend brake hose.**
8. Remove clips, then slide brake rotor off hub and bearing.
9. Loosen each hub and bearing mounting bolt a turn or two at a time while pulling outward on hub and bearing to avoid bolt contact with half shaft outer joint.
10. Once removed from threads in hub and bearing (but not knuckle), allow bolts to stay in and protrude through knuckle and brake support plate.
11. Slide hub and bearing off knuckle and half shaft.
12. Completely back off parking brake shoe adjustment.
13. Remove spring and parking brake shoe adjuster.
14. Remove hold-down clip and pin, then the upper brake shoe from return spring and shoe actuator lever.
15. Remove return spring from lower shoe.
16. Remove shoe actuator lever from end of cable.
17. Remove hold-down clip and pin, then the lower shoe.
18. If not removed, remove parking brake shoe actuator lever from end of cable and shoe support from knuckle.
19. Remove parking brake cable screw at knuckle and pull cable out.
20. Support contact spring link at shock mount using suitable under-hoist utility jack or jack stand under spring link.
21. Remove spring link-to-knuckle nut and bolt.
22. Place guide tool No. 9361-2, or equivalent, against sleeve in knuckle to keep tap tool No. 9361-1, or equivalent, straight.
23. Cut threads approximately halfway through bushing (or about six complete threads) using tap with suitable handle.
24. Thread remover tool No. 9361, noting the following:
    a. **On AWD models lefthand side,** use bolt No. 9361-3, nut, spherical washer, thrust bearing and sleeve tool No. 9361-5, or equivalents.
    b. **On AWD models righthand side,** use bolt No. 9361-3, nut, spherical

washer, thrust bearing and sleeve tool No. 9361-6, or equivalents.
    c. **On RWD models,** use bolt No. 9361-3, nut, spherical washer, thrust bearing and sleeve tool No. 9361-4, or equivalents.
    d. **On all models,** ensure to place hardened side against nut.
25. Rotate nut down, matching sleeve angled end with angled face of knuckle. Continue to rotate nut until knuckle sleeve is removed from knuckle. Discard knuckle sleeve.
26. Remove compression link to knuckle mounting bolt and nut.
27. Remove toe link to knuckle mounting bolt.
28. Remove stabilizer link to knuckle mounting nut and bolt.
29. Remove tension link to knuckle mounting nut and bolt.
30. Remove camber link to knuckle mounting nut and bolt.
31. Remove knuckle and hub mounting bolts.

INSTALLATION

1. Install four hub mounting bolts through knuckle from inboard side allowing ends to protrude from opposite side.
2. Position knuckle, then install camber link to knuckle mounting bolt and nut. **Do not tighten bolt now.**
3. Install tension link to knuckle mounting bolt and nut. **Do not tighten bolt now.**
4. Install stabilizer link to knuckle mounting bolt and nut. **Do not tighten bolt now.**
5. Install toe link to knuckle mounting **Do not tighten bolt now.**
6. Install compression link to knuckle mounting bolt and nut. **Do not tighten bolt now.**
7. Place new knuckle sleeve onto installer bolt tool No. 9361-7, or equivalent, slide it up to bolt's head.
8. Slide bolt tool with sleeve through knuckle and spring link ball joint, starting from knuckle forward end.
9. Install thrust bearing and nut on end of bolt tool.
10. While holding bolt head stationary, rotate nut (using hand tools) installing sleeve in knuckle. Install sleeve until nut stops turning. **Do not overtighten nut.**
11. Remove special tool.
12. Install spring link-to-knuckle bolt front-to-rear through knuckle and link, then install nut.
13. While holding bolt head stationary, tighten nut.
14. Remove under-hoist utility jack or jack stand from under spring link.
15. Insert end of cable through rear knuckle and install mounting screw.
16. Install parking brake shoe support over hub and bearing mounting screws and onto face of knuckle.
17. Install shoe actuator lever on end of parking brake cable. Ensure actuator lever is positioned with word UP facing outward.
18. Install parking brake shoes as well as all components necessary to access them

19. Ensure isolation washer is present on end of half shaft. Washer can be installed in either direction on shaft.
20. Install hub and bearing as well as all components necessary to access it.
21. Insert wheel speed sensor head into mounting hole in rear of knuckle and install mounting screw.
22. Install sensor cable at rear brake rotor shield.
23. Lower vehicle and adjust parking brake shoes as required.
24. Position vehicle on alignment rack/drive-on hoist and raise vehicle as required to access mounting bolts.
25. Tighten mounting bolts and nuts at knuckle with vehicle at curb height in following order:
    a. Camber link;
    b. Compression link;
    c. Stabilizer link,
    d. Tension Link, and
    e. Toe link.

STABILIZER BAR
REPLACE

Removal

1. Raise and support vehicle, then remove both tire and wheel assemblies.
2. Remove rear exhaust system.
3. Mark to propeller shaft rubber coupler and axle flange for installation alignment.
4. Remove three propeller shaft coupler-to-axle flange bolts and nuts.
5. Support propeller shaft using suitable bungee cord attached to fuel tank straps.
6. Disconnect righthand rear front parking brake cable at connector.
7. Remove front parking brake cable from equalizer.
8. On each rear disc brake, while holding guide pins from turning, remove disc brake caliper guide pin bolts.
9. Remove brake caliper from brake adapter and pads.
10. Guide brake caliper up through suspension, following brake hose path.
11. Support caliper above rear suspension to keep caliper from overextending brake hose when crossmember is lowered.
12. Remove retaining clip, wheel speed sensor connector from body wiring harness connector and pull sensor connector outward.
13. Remove wheel speed sensor connectors from body wiring harness connector located in luggage compartment floor pan
14. Unclip lefthand wheel speed sensor cable from routing clip near body connector.
15. Remove shock absorber lower mounting bolt and nut.
16. Mark location of rear crossmember on body at all four mount (bushing) locations for installation alignment.
17. Support forward end of engine cradle by positioning an extra pair of suitable jack stands under.

18. Support rear axle differential with suitable under-hoist utility jack or transmission jack. **Do not secure stabilizer bar.**
19. Drain fuel from tank into suitable container.
20. Open filler tube door and remove retaining wire from inside filler tube rubber.
21. Start removing rubber from body sheet metal, squeeze rubber and push in.
22. Remove lefthand inner splash shield.
23. Disconnect filler tube vent line.
24. Remove filler tube mounting bolt.
25. Remove under body splash shield.
26. Loosen filler tube hose clamp. Leave clamp tight on hose and fuel tank location.
27. Move clamp toward fuel tank and remove filler tube.
28. Remove both front and rear crossmember mounting bolts. **On models equipped with AWD, do not misplace spacers between crossmember mounts and body.**
29. Slowly lower crossmember just enough to allow propeller shaft removal from rear axle differential.
30. Slide propeller shaft out of rear axle differential and support it with bungee cord.
31. Slowly lower crossmember several inches.
32. Remove front parking brake cable routing bracket to rear crossmember mounting screw.
33. Continue to lower jack until crossmember is at comfortable working level to access stabilizer bar.
34. On each end, remove stabilizer bar to stabilizer link mounting bolt and nut.
35. Remove each stabilizer bar isolator retainer to crossmember mounting bolt.
36. Remove stabilizer bar with isolators and retainers.
37. Remove retainers from isolators, then the isolators from stabilizer bar utilizing slits in bushings.

Installation

1. Install isolators on stabilizer bar utilizing slits in bushings.
2. Install each isolator so its slit faces forward and flat side is positioned toward crossmember.
3. Install retainers on isolators.
4. Install stabilizer bar with isolators and retainers on crossmember.
5. Install isolator retainer mounting bolts. **Do not tighten now.**
6. Install stabilizer bar ends to each stabilizer links mounting bolt and nut. **Do not tighten now.**
7. Tighten isolator retainer mounting bolts.
8. Remove coil springs with isolators from spring links.
9. Raise crossmember until there is approximately 10 inches clearance to body mounting points.
10. Install front parking brake cable routing bracket to rear crossmember screw.
11. Raise crossmember to body mounting points.

12. As crossmember is raised, slide propeller shaft onto rear axle differential flange and align shocks with pockets in spring links.
13. Continue to raise crossmember until crossmember mounting bolts can be installed.
14. Install lefthand side crossmember mounting bolts, but not righthand side bolts. Rear mounting bolts are longer than front mounting bolts. **Do not interchange mounting bolts. Do not tighten bolts now.**
15. Slowly lower jack allowing righthand side of crossmember to drop. Lower jack just enough to allow spring installation. **Do not lower jack any further than required.**
16. Ensure isolators are completely installed on ends of spring.
17. Install coil spring with isolators into spring pocket of spring link fitting lower isolator to shape of pocket, then align top of spring with body mount.
18. Carefully raise jack, guiding coil spring and lower end of shock absorber into mounted positions.
19. Once shock absorber lower mounting hole lines up with hole in spring link, stop jacking.
20. Install lower shock mounting bolt and nut. **Do not tighten now.**
21. **On models equipped with AWD,** insert spacers on top of righthand crossmember mount bushings before crossmember is raised into place.
22. **On all models,** raise righthand side of crossmember into mounted position.
23. Install righthand side crossmember mounting bolts. Rear mounting bolts are longer than front mounting bolts. **Do not interchange mounting bolts.**
24. Snug, but do not fully tighten bolts now.
25. Remove both lefthand side front and rear crossmember mounting bolts.
26. Slowly lower jack allowing lefthand side of crossmember to drop. Lower jack just enough to allow spring Installation. **Do not lower jack any further than required.**
27. Ensure isolators are completely installed on ends of spring.
28. Install coil spring with isolators into spring pocket of spring link fitting lower isolator to shape of pocket, then align top of spring with body mount.
29. Carefully raise jack, guiding coil spring and lower end of shock absorber into mounted positions.
30. Once shock absorber lower mounting hole lines up with hole in spring link, stop jacking.
31. Install lower shock mounting bolt and nut. **Do not tighten now.**
32. **On models equipped with AWD,** insert spacers on top of lefthand crossmember mount bushings before crossmember is raised into place.
33. **On all models,** raise lefthand side of crossmember into mounted position
34. Install lefthand side crossmember mounting bolts. Rear mounting bolts are longer than front mounting bolts. **Do not interchange mounting bolts.**
35. Snug, but do not fully tighten bolts now.
36. Shift crossmember to line up mounts

with location marks.
37. Once mounts are lined up with location marks, on both sides of vehicle, measure distance between tension link and weld flange on body directly in front of it, just outboard of front mount bushing, **Fig. 3.**
38. This distance must be at least .47 inch to allow proper clearance for suspension movement, noting the following:
   a. If distance is less than specified on either side of vehicle, shift that side of rear crossmember directly rearward until distance is .47 inch, or more.
   b. To do so, loosen three mounting bolts slightly, leaving one on opposite side of shift snugged to pivot off of.
   c. Shift crossmember rearward and snug loosened bolts.
   d. Measure opposite side to ensure it still maintains minimum .47 inch distance.
39. Tighten four crossmember mounting bolts.
40. Remove jack from under rear axle differential.
41. Align propeller shaft index marks.
42. Install propeller shaft rear coupler to axle flange bolts and nuts by hand.
43. Tighten propeller shaft rear coupler to axle flange bolts.
44. Insert filler tube into fuel tank rubber hose.
45. Slide hose clamp into place and tighten.
46. Hose clamp in place and tighten.
47. Install filler tube mounting bolt and vent line.
48. Install underbody splash shield.
49. Install lefthand inner splash shield.
50. Pull rubber through opening and install to body. Ensure sheet metal is in rubber groove.
51. Start metal wire retaining wire in groove on inside of filler tube rubber.
52. Work wire retaining wire around rubber and install wire retainer.
53. Clip lefthand rear wheel speed sensor cable to routing clip near body connector.
54. Match lefthand rear wheel speed sensor connector to righthand sensor connector to make one connector.
55. Insert speed sensor connectors into body wiring harness connector in luggage compartment floor pan.
56. Ensure retaining clip on body connector is properly in place and sensor connector cannot be pulled out.
57. On each rear disc brake, push caliper guide pins into caliper adapter to clear caliper mounting bosses.
58. Guide caliper and brake hose down through rear suspension, then slide caliper over brake pads and onto caliper adapter.
59. Align caliper mounting holes with guide pins and install guide pin bolts. **Do not to cross-thread caliper guide pin bolts.**
60. While holding guide pins from turning, tighten bolts.
61. Ensure brake hose is properly routed

and will not come in contact with suspension components.

62. Route parking brake cable above rear crossmember and slide cable through equalizer above rear differential.

63. Because of short travel and low spring tension, it is not required to lock-out parking brake lever to service parking brake components.

64. Connect front parking brake cable at connector to righthand rear parking brake cable.

65. Install rear exhaust system.
66. Install tire and wheel assemblies, then tighten wheel mounting nuts.
67. Lower vehicle until rear wheels are just above floor level.
68. Apply parking brake lever. Release lever and apply.
69. Ensure rear wheels will not rotate with lever applied.
70. Lower vehicle.
71. Connect battery negative cable to battery post.

72. Pump brake pedal several times to ensure vehicle has firm brake pedal before moving vehicle.
73. Position vehicle on alignment rack/drive-on hoist.
74. Raise vehicle as required to access mounting bolts.
75. Tighten shock absorber lower mounting bolt nuts and stabilizer link fasteners.

TIGHTENING SPECIFICATIONS

Year	Component	Torque/Ft. Lbs.
2005	Axle Front Mount Isolator	48
	Axle Housing-to-Crossmember	162
	Axle Hub	157
	Brake Caliper Adapter Knuckle	88
	Camber Link Crossmember	63
	Camber Link Knuckle	72
	Center Bearing-To-Body (Rear)	20
	Compression Link Crossmember	63
	Compression Link Knuckle	60
	Coupler/Damper-To-Propeller Shaft (Rear)	43
	Crossmember	133
	Differential Cover (198 mm)	22①
	Differential Cover (210 mm)	37
	Exhaust System Band Clamp	45
	Front Propeller Shaft To Axle/Transfer Case Flange	22
	Hub	157
	Hub & Bearing	50
	Parking Brake Cable Knuckle	71
	Rear Axle Drain/Fill Plug (198 mm)	44
	Rear Axle Drain/Fill Plug (210 mm)	37
	Ring Gear-to-Differential Case	63
	Shaft Coupler-To-Rear Axle	43
	Shaft Coupler-To-Transmission	43
	Shock Absorber, Lower	53
	Shock Absorber, Upper	38
	Spring Link Crossmember	80
	Spring Link Knuckle	102
	Stabilizer Bar Isolator Retainer	45
	Stabilizer Link	45
	Tension Link Crossmember	63
	Tension Link Knuckle	72
	Toe Link Crossmember	80
	Toe Link Knuckle	60
	Wheel Lug Nut	110

① — Plus an additional 45°.

Front Suspension & Steering

NOTE: On Air Bag Equipped Models, Refer To "Air Bag System Precautions" Located In The Front Of This Manual For System Disarming & Arming Procedures.

NOTE: Refer To "Computer Relearn Procedures" Located In The Front Of This Manual When Battery Power To The Computer Has Been Interrupted.

NOTE: Refer To The Rear Of This Manual For Vehicle Manufacturer's Special Tool Suppliers.

INDEX

PRECAUTIONS

Air Bag Systems

Refer to "Air Bag System Precautions" in the front of this manual for system disarming and arming procedures.

Battery Ground Cable

Prior to service, disconnect battery ground cable and isolate as required.

RECALIBRATION

Anytime the battery has been disconnect or has lost its charge, the following must be recalibrated:

EXPRESS WINDOW

1. Turn ignition switch to RUN position.
2. Move driver's window upward until it stalls in full up position. Allow window motor to stall for at least two seconds before releasing switch.
3. Move driver's window downward until it stalls in full down position. Allow window motor to stall for at least two seconds before releasing switch.
4. Move driver's window upward until it stalls in full up position. Allow window motor to stall for at least two seconds before releasing switch.
5. Move passenger's window upward until it stalls in full up position. Allow window motor to stall for at least two seconds before releasing switch.
6. Move passenger's window downward until it stalls in full down position. Allow window motor to stall for at least two seconds before releasing switch.
7. Move passenger's window upward until it stalls in full up position. Allow window motor to stall for at least two seconds before releasing switch.

ELECTRONIC STABILITY PROGRAM (ESP) STEERING ANGLE SENSOR

1. Start engine.
2. Turn steering wheel right until wheel locks full right.
3. Turn steering wheel left until wheel locks full left.
4. Turn steering wheel right until wheels are centered.
5. Cycle ignition switch OFF and ON. Do not start engine.

DESCRIPTION

The front suspension for both All-Wheel-Drive (AWD) and Rear-Wheel-Drive (RWD) vehicles is a long and short arm design.

On AWD models, the front suspension includes: hub and bearing knuckle, lower control arm, shock assembly, stabilizer bar and link, and upper control arm, **Fig. 1.**

On RWD models the front suspension includes: hub and bearing knuckle, lower control arm, shock assembly, stabilizer bar and link, tension strut, and upper control arm, **Fig. 2.**

The power steering systems consist of: steering column rack and pinion steering gear, belt driven hydraulic steering pump, pump pressure, return and supply hoses, oil cooler, remote reservoir, and inner and outer tie rod ends, **Figs. 3 and 4.**

HUB & BEARING

REPLACE

AWD

1. Raise and support vehicle, then remove tire and wheel assembly.
2. While a helper applies brakes to keep hub from rotating, remove hub nut from axle half shaft.
3. Remove two mounting bolts, then remove disc brake caliper and adapter from knuckle.
4. Hang assembly aside using suitable wire. **Do not overextend brake hose.**
5. Remove wheel studs' clips, then slide brake rotor off hub and bearing.
6. Remove four mounting bolts, then slide hub and bearing off axle half shaft and knuckle.
7. Reverse procedure to install. Ensure isolation washer is present on end of half shaft.

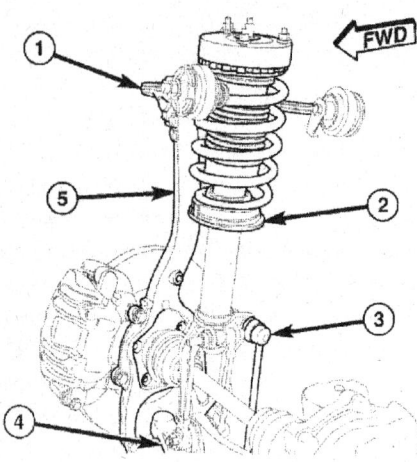

1- UPPER CONTROL ARM
2- STRUT
3- STABILIZER BAR AND LINK
4- LOWER CONTROL ARM
5- KNUCKLE

ARM0400000000630

Fig. 1   Front suspension. AWD

RWD

1. Raise and support vehicle, then remove tire and wheel assembly.
2. While a helper applies brakes to keep hub from rotating, remove hub nut from axle half shaft.
3. Remove two mounting bolts, then remove disc brake caliper and adapter from knuckle.
4. Hang assembly aside using suitable wire. **Do not overextend brake hose.**
5. Remove dust cap. **Do not damaging internal bore of hub.**
6. Remove hub nut, then slide hub and bearing off knuckle spindle.
7. Reverse procedure to install. Install new dust cap.

DRIVESHAFT

REPLACE

Halfshaft inner and outer boots are not serviceable separately. Boot replacement requires entire shaft assembly replacement.

Lefthand halfshaft is shorter than right. Identify and tag halfshafts upon removal to ensure proper installation.

1. Raise and support vehicle, then remove tire and wheel assembly.
2. While holding link ball joint stem from rotating, remove stabilizer link to shock clevis bracket nut.
3. Slide link ball joint stem from clevis bracket.

4. Remove clevis bracket to bottom of shock nut and pinch bolt.
5. Remove shock clevis bracket to lower control arm nut and bolt.
6. Pull lower end of clevis bracket outward away from lower control arm bushing, then slide it off shock.
7. While helper applies brakes to keep hub from rotating, remove hub nut from axle half shaft.
8. Remove two mounting bolts, then the disc brake caliper and adapter from knuckle.
9. Hang assembly aside using suitable wire. **Do not overextend brake hose.**
10. Remove wheel studs' clips, then slide brake rotor off hub and bearing.
11. Separate upper ball joint stud from knuckle using puller tool No. 9360, or equivalent, **Do not damage ball joint seal boot.**
12. Remove upper ball joint stud nut.
13. Remove wheel speed sensor to knuckle clip.
14. Disconnect righthand halfshaft from axle and remove.
15. Remove lefthand halfshaft.
16. Remove four assembly-to-oil pan mounting bolts and intermediate shaft.
17. Reverse procedure to install, noting the following:
    a. Install new axle seal using driver tool No. C-4193-A, or equivalent.
    b. Ensure isolation washer is present on end of half shaft. Washer is bi-directional and can be installed in either direction on shaft.
    c. Lubricate halfshaft inner joint bearing journal with Mopar Gear and Axle Lubricant 75W-140, or equivalent.
    d. Install new circlip(s).

BALL JOINT

REPLACE

Lower

1. Remove knuckle as outlined under "Steering Knuckle, Replace."
2. Remove bottom ball joint snap ring using suitable snap-ring pliers.
3. Support knuckle and ball joint using support clamp tool No. 9320-1, or equivalent.
4. Remove ball joint using press tool No. C-4212F, or equivalent, and suitable vice.
5. Reverse procedure to install.

Upper

The upper ball joint is pressed into the upper control arm. The ball joint is a sealed for life component and cannot be maintenance lubricated. Neither the upper ball joint, nor the seal boot can be serviced as a

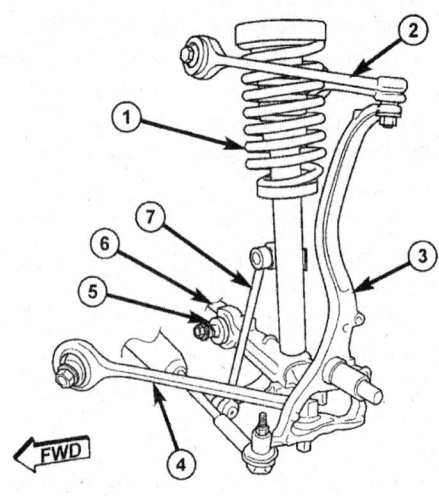

1- STRUT
2- UPPER CONTROL ARM
3- KNUCKLE
4- TENSION STRUT
5- LOWER CONTROL ARM
6- STABILIZER BAR
7- STABILIZER LINK (7)

ARM0400000000629

Fig. 2   Front suspension. RWD

separate component. The entire upper control arm must be replaced if either are damaged.

COIL SPRING

REPLACE

Refer to "Coil Spring & Strut Service" for coil spring replacement procedure.

STRUT

REPLACE

AWD

1. Raise and support vehicle, then remove tire and wheel assembly.
2. While holding link ball joint stem from rotating, remove stabilizer link to shock clevis bracket nut.
3. Slide link ball joint stem from clevis bracket.
4. Remove clevis bracket to bottom of strut shock mounting nut and pinch bolt.
5. Remove strut clevis bracket to lower control arm mounting nut and bolt.
6. Pull lower end of clevis bracket outward away from lower control arm bushing, then slide it off strut.
7. Lower vehicle just enough to access upper strut mounting nuts.
8. Remove strut tower cap, three nuts and strut.
9. Reverse procedure to install.

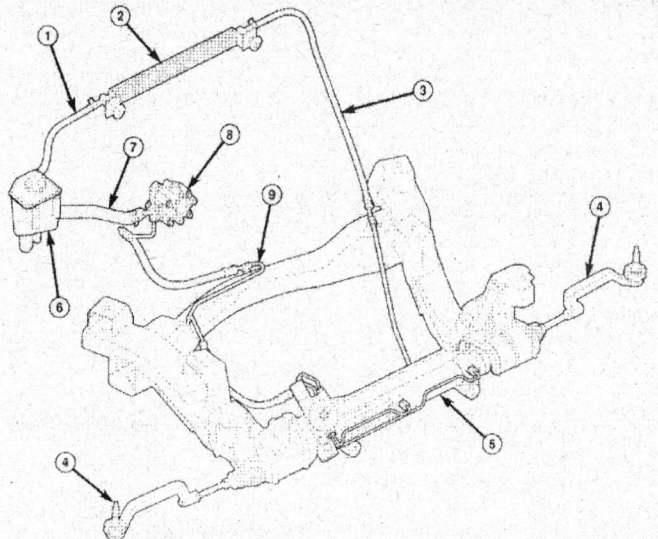

1- RETURN HOSES
2- OIL COOLER
3- RETURN HOSES
4- OUTER TIE ROD ENDS
5- RACK & PINION STEERING GEAR
6- REMOTE RESERVOIR
7- SUPPLY HOSES
8- BELT DRIVEN HYDRAULIC STEERING PUMP
9- PUMP PRESSURE HOSES

ARM0400000000631

Fig. 3   Power steering system. AWD

1- RETURN HOSES
2- OIL COOLER
3- RETURN HOSES
4- INNER & OUTER TIE ROD ENDS
5- REMOTE RESERVOIR
6- SUPPLY HOSES
7- BELT DRIVEN HYDRAULIC STEERING PUMP
8- PUMP PRESSURE HOSES
9- RACK & PINION STEERING GEAR

ARM0400000000632

Fig. 4   Power steering system. RWD

RWD

1. Remove front strut tower cap and upper three mounting nuts.
2. Raise and support vehicle, then remove tire and wheel assembly.
3. Remove stabilizer link to strut mounting nut.
4. Slide link ball joint stem from strut.
5. Remove strut to lower control arm mounting bolt.
6. Disconnect wheel speed sensor cable routing clip at brake tube bracket.
7. Loosen upper ball joint stud to knuckle nut. Back nut off until nut is even with end of stud.
8. Separate upper ball joint stud from knuckle using puller tool No. 9360, or equivalent. **Do not damage ball joint seal boot.**
9. Remove end of upper ball joint stud nut and tip knuckle top outward. **Do not overextend brake flex hose.**
10. Remove strut.
11. Reverse procedure to install.

COIL SPRING & STRUT SERVICE

Left and righthand springs must not be interchanged.
1. Remove strut as outlined under "Strut, Replace."

2. Position strut coil spring on spring compressor tool No. W-7200, or equivalent, hooks.
3. Install clamp securing shock to lower spring coil.
4. Position compressor tool upper hooks on upper coil spring.
5. Rotate strut as required positioning shock in compressor so that upper spring coil ends (step in upper mount) at straight outward position from tool.
6. Compress coil spring until all spring tension is removed from upper mount.
7. Holding shaft from turning using position wrench tool No. 9362, or equivalent, remove shaft nut.
8. Remove clamp from bottom of coil spring, then the strut and lower isolator out through bottom of coil spring.
9. Remove upper mount from shaft and coil spring.
10. Mark lower spring coil end relationship to compressor for assembly alignment.
11. Back off compressor drive and releasing tension from coil spring.
12. Push back compressor upper hooks and remove coil spring from tool.
13. Remove jounce bumper from shaft by pulling straight up and off.
14. Remove lower isolator from body by pulling straight up and off shaft.
15. Reverse procedure to assemble, noting the following:
   a. Place coil spring with part number

tag end upward in compressor lower hooks.
   b. Rotate coil spring around until upper coil ends at straight outward position from compressor, **Fig. 5.**
   c. Install jounce bumper on shock shaft, small end first.

CONTROL ARM
REPLACE

Lower

AWD

1. Raise and support vehicle, then remove tire and wheel assembly.
2. While helper applies brakes to keep hub from rotating, remove hub nut from the axle half shaft.
3. Remove mounting screws and belly pan.
4. Loosen lower control arm ball joint stud to knuckle nut. Back nut off until nut is even with end of stud.
5. Separate ball joint stud from knuckle using puller tool No. 9360, or equivalent. **Do not damage ball joint seal boot.**
6. Remove nut from end of ball joint stud.
7. Back off shock clevis bracket to lower control arm nut until it is flush with end of bolt.
8. Tap bolt out of clevis bracket until bolt

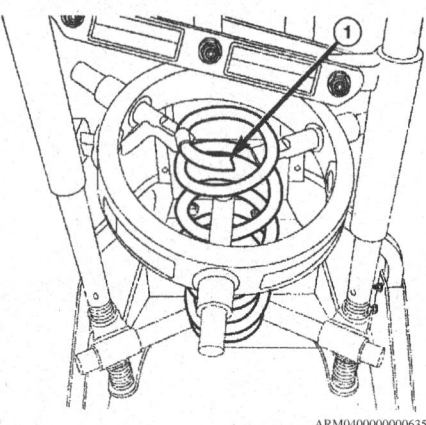

Fig. 5 Coil spring alignment

ARM0400000000635

serrations clear bracket using suitable brass drift punch.

9. Remove clevis bracket and control arm mounting nut and bolt.

10. Remove mounting screws and heat shields above both inner tie rod bellows

11. On lefthand side arm, remove bolts (3) and (4), **Fig. 6.**. Loosen, but do not remove bolt. **Do not drop gear too far.**

12. One righthand side arm, remove bolts (2) and (3). Loosen, but do not remove bolt (4).

13. Remove bolt and nut securing rearward end of lower control arm to engine cradle. If lower control arm bolt at engine cradle has lengthwise grooved shaft, note the following:
   a. Bolt is special wheel alignment adjustment bolt.
   b. Bolt head must not be rotated in vehicle or damage to bolt and engine cradle will result.
   c. While holding bolt in place with suitable wrench, remove nut.
   d. Slide bolt out of bushing and cradle recording of bolt positioning in engine cradle for installation alignment.
   e. Bolt needs to be installed in same position as removed to ensure wheel camber and caster return to adjusted position.

14. Slide lower control arm from engine cradle and knuckle.

15. Reverse procedure to install. Install new ball joint stud nuts.

RWD

1. Raise and support vehicle, then remove tire and wheel assembly.

2. Remove mounting screws and belly pan.

3. Remove stabilizer bar heat shield mounting screws on side of control arm repair.

4. Remove stabilizer bar bushing retainer mounting bolts on side of control arm repair.

5. Remove retainer halves from around stabilizer bar bushing.

6. Utilizing slit, remove bushing from stabilizer bar.

7. Remove bolt and nut securing lower control arm to engine cradle. If lower control arm bolt at engine cradle has lengthwise grooved shaft, note the following:
   a. Bolt is special wheel alignment adjustment bolt.
   b. Bolt head must not be rotated in vehicle or damage to bolt and engine cradle will result.
   c. While holding bolt in place with suitable wrench, remove nut.
   d. Slide bolt out of bushing and cradle recording of bolt positioning in engine cradle for installation alignment.
   e. Bolt needs to be installed in same position as removed to ensure wheel camber and caster return to adjusted position.

8. Remove strut to lower control mounting bolt.

9. Remove wheel speed sensor to knuckle mounting screw. Remove sensor head.

10. Remove wheel speed sensor cable routing clip from brake flex hose routing bracket.

11. Loosen ball joint stud to lower control arm nut. Back nut off until nut is even with end of stud.

12. Separate ball joint stud from lower control arm using puller, tool No. 9360, or equivalent.

13. Remove nut from end of ball joint stud attaching lower control arm to knuckle.

14. Pry knuckle downward and slide ball joint stud out of lower control arm.

15. Position knuckle outward, away from lower control arm. Slide lower control arm out of engine cradle.

16. Reverse procedure to install.
   a. Measure height of ball joint seal boot mounted on knuckle, **Fig. 7.**
   b. If seal boot height is above 1.00 inch, any air inside seal boot must be expelled.
   c. Tip ball joint stud completely to one side. Using thumb and index finger, gently squeeze seal boot together at center expelling any air. **Do not allow grease to be release.**
   d. Push down very top of seal boot.
   e. Return ball joint stud to original centered position.
   f. Install new ball joint stud nuts.

Upper

Although AWD and RWD upper control arms are similar, they are not interchangeable.

1. **If removing lefthand upper control**

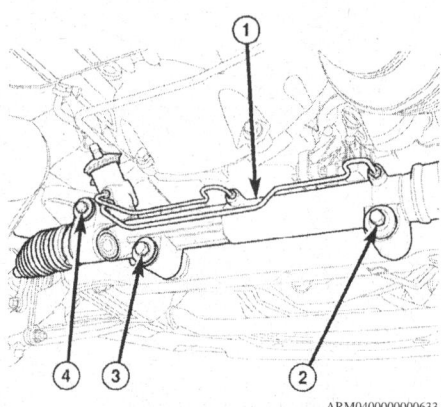

Fig. 6 Steering gear replacement. AWD

ARM0400000000633

arm, proceed as follows:
   a. Remove coolant recovery container pressure cap
   b. Remove and plug coolant recovery tube.
   c. Remove mounting nuts and position coolant recovery container aside.

2. **If removing rightright upper control arm,** proceed as follows:
   a. Open battery cable nut cover.
   b. Remove battery cable nut and cable from the Integrated Power Module (IPM).
   c. Disconnect outboard retaining clip and rotate IPM to access wire harness connectors.
   d. Disconnect wire harness connectors.
   e. Disconnect inboard retaining clips and remove IPM.

3. **On all models,** remove front shock tower cap and three upper strut mounting nuts.

4. Remove nuts from upper control arm mounting bolts.

5. Raise and support vehicle, then remove tire and wheel assembly.

6. Disconnect wheel speed sensor cable routing clip at brake tube bracket.

7. Loosen upper ball joint stud to knuckle mounting nut. Back nut off until nut is even with end of stud.

8. Separate upper ball joint stud from knuckle using puller tool No. 9360, or equivalent. **Do not damage ball joint seal boot.**

9. Remove nut from end of upper ball joint stud.

10. Pull strut downward until its clear shock tower, then pull it outward allowing access to upper control arm mounting bolts.

11. Remove mounting bolts and upper control arm.

12. Reverse procedure to install.

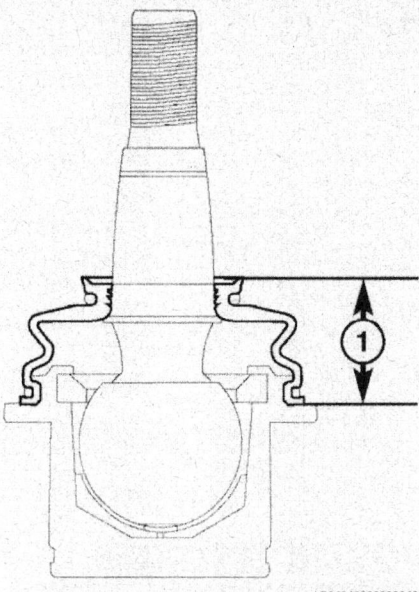

Fig. 7 Ball joint seal boot measurement

STEERING KNUCKLE
REPLACE
AWD

1. Raise and support vehicle, then remove tire and wheel assembly.
2. While helper applies brakes to keep hub from rotating, remove hub nut from axle half shaft.
3. Remove clip fastening wheel speed sensor to knuckle.
4. Remove screw fastening wheel speed sensor) to knuckle.
5. Pull sensor head out of knuckle.
6. Remove two mounting bolts, then the caliper and adapter. Hang assembly aside using suitable wire. **Do not overextend brake hose.**
7. Remove nut from outer tie rod end) stud.
8. Separate tie rod stud from knuckle using puller tool No. 9360, or equivalent.
9. Loosen lower control arm ball joint stud to knuckle nut. Back nut off until nut is even with end of stud.
10. Separate ball joint stud from knuckle using puller tool No. 9360, or equivalent. **Do not damage ball joint seal boot.**
11. Remove ball joint stud nut.
12. Loosen nut attaching upper ball joint stud to knuckle. Back nut off until nut is even with end of stud.
13. Separate ball joint stud from knuckle

using puller tool No. 9360, or equivalent. **Do not damage ball joint seal boot.**
14. Remove nut from end of upper ball joint stud.
15. Slide knuckle off half shaft and remove.
16. If hub and bearing, and dust shield are to be removed, remove four mounting bolts, then slide hub and bearing out of knuckle along with shield.
17. Reverse procedure to install, noting the following:
    a. Ensure isolation washer is present on end of half shaft. Washer can be installed in either direction on shaft.
    b. Install new ball joint stud nuts.

RWD

1. Raise and support vehicle, then remove tire and wheel assembly.
2. Remove fastening wheel speed sensor to knuckle mounting screw. Pull sensor head out of knuckle
3. Remove wheel speed sensor cable routing clip from brake flex hose routing bracket.
4. Remove brake flex hose routing bracket to knuckle mounting screw.
5. Remove two mounting bolts, then the brake caliper and adapter. Hang assembly aside using suitable wire.
6. Remove nut from outer tie rod end stud.
7. Separate tie rod stud from knuckle using puller tool No. 9360, or equivalent.
8. Loosen nut attaching upper ball joint stud to knuckle. Back nut off until nut is even with end of stud.
9. Separate upper ball joint stud from knuckle using puller tool No. 9360, or equivalent. **Do not damage ball joint seal boot.**
10. Remove nut from end of upper ball joint stud.
11. Loosen nut attaching tension strut ball joint stud to knuckle. Back nut off until nut is even with end of stud.
12. Separate strut ball joint stud from knuckle using puller tool No. 9360, or equivalent. **Do not damage ball joint seal boot.**
13. Remove nut from end of tension strut ball joint stud.
14. Loosen nut attaching ball joint stud to lower control arm. Back nut off until nut is even with end of stud.
15. Separate ball joint stud from lower control arm using puller tool No. 9360, or equivalent. **Do not damage ball joint seal boot.**
16. Remove nut from end of ball joint stud attaching lower control arm to knuckle. Remove knuckle.
17. If hub and bearing, and dust shield are

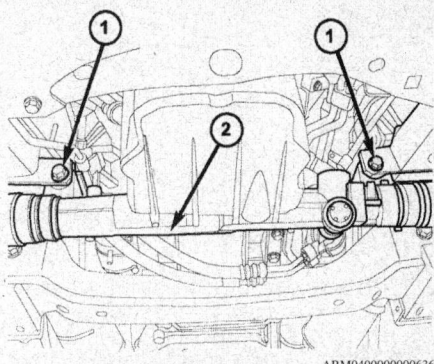

Fig. 8 Steering gear replacement. RWD

to be removed, remove four mounting bolts, then slide hub and bearing out of knuckle along with shield.
18. Reverse procedure to install.
    a. Install new dust cap.
    b. Measure height of ball joint seal boot mounted on knuckle, **Fig. 7.**
    c. If seal boot height is above 1.00 inch, any air inside seal boot must be expelled.
    d. Tip ball joint stud completely to one side. Using thumb and index finger, gently squeeze seal boot together at center expelling any air. **Do not allow grease to be release.**
    e. Push down very top of seal boot.
    f. Return ball joint stud to original centered position.
    g. Install new ball joint stud nuts.

STABILIZER BAR
REPLACE
AWD

1. Raise and support vehicle.
2. Remove mounting screws and belly pan.
3. On each side of vehicle, remove stabilizer link to stabilizer bar mounting nut.
4. Slide link ball joint stem from bar.
5. On each side of vehicle, remove stabilizer bar isolator retainer mounting bolts.
6. Remove stabilizer bar with isolators and retainers.
7. On each side of bar, remove stabilizer bar isolators retainers.
8. Utilizing slit and remove each isolator.
9. Reverse procedure to install, noting the following:
    a. Ensure isolator slit is positioned toward rear of vehicle.
    b. Ensure link ball joint stem is pointed inboard toward engine cradle.

RWD

1. Raise and support vehicle.
2. Remove mounting screws and belly pan.
3. On each side of vehicle, remove mounting screws and stabilizer bar heat shield.
4. On each side of vehicle, remove stabilizer bar isolator retainer mounting bolts.
5. On each side of vehicle, remove stabilizer bar isolator retainer halves.
6. Remove each isolator utilizing slit.
7. On each side of vehicle, remove stabilizer link to stabilizer bar mounting nut.
8. Slide link ball joint stem from bar and remove bar.
9. Reverse procedure to install, noting the following:
   a. Ensure link ball joint stem is pointed inboard toward engine cradle.
   b. Ensure sure slit in isolator is positioned toward rear of vehicle.

TENSION STRUT

REPLACE

1. Raise and support vehicle, then remove tire and wheel assembly.
2. Remove mounting screws and belly pan.
3. Loosen tension strut ball joint stud to knuckle mounting nut. Back nut off until nut is even with end of stud.
4. Separate tension strut ball joint stud from knuckle using puller special tool No. 9360, or equivalent. **Do not damage ball joint seal boot.**
5. Remove nut from end of tension strut ball joint stud.
6. Rotate knuckle outward and push ball joint upward, out of knuckle.
7. Remove bolt and nut securing tension strut to engine cradle. If lower tension strut bolt at engine cradle has lengthwise grooved shaft, note the following:
   a. Bolt is special wheel alignment adjustment bolt.
   b. Bolt head must not be rotated in vehicle or damage to bolt and engine cradle will result.
   c. While holding bolt in place with suitable wrench, remove nut.
   d. Slide bolt out of bushing and cradle recording of bolt positioning in engine cradle for installation alignment.
   e. Bolt needs to be installed in same position as removed to ensure wheel camber and caster return to adjusted position.

8. Slide tension strut out of cradle bracket.
9. Reverse procedure to install. Install new ball joint stud nuts.

TIE ROD

REPLACE

Outer

1. Raise and support vehicle, then remove tire and wheel assembly.
2. Remove clamp at inner tie rod and ensuring bellows moves freely before rotating inner tie rod. **Do not twist bellows at inner tie rod.**
3. Loosen tie rod jam nut at outer tie rod.
4. Remove outer tie rod end nut at knuckle.
5. Separate outer tie rod end from knuckle using remover tool No. 9630, or equivalent.
6. Unthread outer tie rod from inner tie rod. Count number of turns when removing outer tie rod for good starting point when installing and setting toe.
7. Reverse procedure to install.

POWER STEERING GEAR

REPLACE

1. Center steering wheel and lock it with suitable steering wheel holder.
2. Siphon power steering fluid from pump reservoir.
3. Raise and support vehicle, then remove both front tire and wheel assemblies.
4. Remove clamp at inner tie rod and ensure bellows moves freely before rotating inner tie rod. **Do not twist bellows at inner tie rod.**
5. Loosen tie rod jam nut at each outer tie rod.
6. Remove outer tie rod end nut at each knuckle.
7. Separate outer tie rod from each knuckle using remover tool No. 9630, or equivalent.
8. Fully extend or pull out adjustable steering column.
9. Remove pinch bolt connecting steering shaft to lower steering coupling shaft.
10. Separate lower coupling from steering shaft.
11. Remove pinch bolt from steering coupling at steering gear.
12. Slide coupling from steering gear.

13. Unthread tube nut from steering gear and remove return hose from steering gear.
14. Unthread tube nut and remove pressure hose from steering gear.
15. Remove mounting screws and heat shield above each inner tie rod bellows.
16. **On AWD models,** proceed as follows:
    a. Remove steering gear upper mounting bolt and nut, **Fig. 6.**
    b. Remove lower mounting bolts and steering gear.
17. **On RWD models,** remove mounting bolts and steering gear, **Fig. 8.**
18. **On all models,** reverse procedure to install.
    a. Install new O-ring lubricated with suitable, clean power steering fluid on steering hoses' ends.
    b. Install new pinch bolts to steering couplings.

POWER STEERING PUMP

REPLACE

1. Siphon power steering fluid from pump reservoir.
2. Disconnect Mass Air Flow (MAF) sensor electrical connector.
3. Remove clean air duct between throttle body and air filter housing.
4. Remove vent tube.
5. Remove mounting bolt and air filter housing.
6. Raise and support vehicle.
7. Remove wheel house splash shield rivets three per side.
8. Remove nine belly pan mounting screws.
9. Remove two fascia to fender screw (one per side).
10. Open hood and remove upper push pin fasteners (four per sedan and six per wagon), then partially remove front fascia.
11. Remove mounting bolt and air cleaner resonator.
12. Rotate belt tensioner counterclockwise until it contacts it's stop.
13. Remove belt and slowly rotate tensioner into **Do not let tensioner arm snap back to the freearm position.**
14. Remove hose clamp and supply hose from pump.
15. Unthread tube nut and remove pressure hose from pump.
16. Remove three mounting bolts through pulley access holes and pump from engine bracket.
17. Reverse procedure to install. Install new O-rings lubricated with suitable, clean power steering fluid

POWER STEERING SYSTEM BLEED

1. Wipe filler cap clean and check fluid level.
2. Turn steering wheel all way to left.
3. Fill pump fluid reservoir to proper level and let fluid settle for least two minutes.
4. Raise and support front wheels off ground.
5. Slowly turn steering wheel lock-to-lock 20 times with engine off while checking fluid level. Vehicles with long return lines or oil coolers turn wheel 40 times.
6. Start engine.
7. With engine idling maintain fluid level.
8. Lower front wheels and let engine idle for two minutes.
9. Turn steering wheel in both direction, and verify power assist and quiet operation of pump.
10. If fluid is extremely foamy or milky looking, allow vehicle to stand few minutes and repeat procedure. **Do not run vehicle with foamy fluid for an extended period.**

TIGHTENING SPECIFICATIONS

Year	Component	Torque/Ft. Lbs.
2005	Air Cleaner Resonator (2.7L & 3.5L)	89①
	Air Filter	89①
	Ball Stud Joint	35②
	Caliper Adapter To Knuckle	125
	Engine Cradle	136
	Hub Bearing	50
	Hub Nut, AWD	157
	Hub Nut, RWD	184
	Intermediate Shaft-To-Oil Pan	18
	Knuckle Dust Shield	89①
	Lower Control Arm, Cradle	130
	Lower Control Arm, Ball Joint IAWD)	90
	Lower Control Arm, Ball Joint (RWD)	50②
	Outer Tie Rod Ball Joint	63
	Power Steering Gear (AWD)	75
	Power Steering Gear (RWD)	70
	Power Steering Hose Tube	35
	Power Steering Pump	21
	Stabilizer Bar, Heat Shield	62①
	Stabilizer Bar, Isolator Retainer	44
	Stabilizer Bar, Link (Lower)	95
	Stabilizer Bar, Link (Upper)	95
	Steering Coupling Lower Shaft Pinch Bolt	23
	Steering Coupling To Steering Gear Pinch Bolt	40
	Steering Gear	90
	Strut, Clevis Bracket (Lower)	128
	Strut, Clevis Bracket (Pinch)	45
	Strut, Lower (RWD)	128
	Strut, Shaft	70
	Strut, Upper	20
	Tension Strut, Cradle	130
	Tension Strut, Ball Joint	50②
	Tie Rod Jam Nut	55
	Upper Control Arm, Ball Joint	35②
	Wheel Lug Nut	110

① — Inch lbs.
② — Tighten an additional 90°.

Wheel Alignment

NOTE: On Air Bag Equipped Models, Refer To "Air Bag System Precautions" Located In The Front Of This Manual For System Disarming & Arming Procedures.

NOTE: Refer To "Computer Relearn Procedures" Located In The Front Of This Manual When Battery Power To The Computer Has Been Interrupted.

NOTE: Prior To Performing Any Service Operations Listed In This Section, Consult The "Technical Service Bulletins" Section For Related Information.

NOTE: Refer To The Rear Of This Manual For Vehicle Manufacturer's Special Tool Suppliers.

INDEX

PRELIMINARY INSPECTION

Before any attempt is made to change or correct the wheel alignment, the following inspection and necessary corrections must be made to ensure proper alignment.
1. Ensure fuel tank is full of fuel.
2. Ensure passenger and luggage compartments are free of any load that is not factory equipment.
3. Ensure all tires are same size and in good condition with approximately same amount of tread wear.
4. Inflate all tires to recommended air pressure.
5. Check wheel and tire assemblies for excessive radial runout.
6. Inspect lower ball joints and all steering linkage for looseness, binding, wear or damage.
7. Check suspension fasteners for proper torque.
8. Inspect all suspension component rubber bushings for signs of wear or deterioration.
9. Check vehicle's curb height to ensure it is within specifications.

FRONT WHEEL ALIGNMENT

On this vehicle, four-wheel alignment is recommended.
1. Position vehicle on alignment rack.
2. Install all required alignment equipment on vehicle per alignment equipment manufacturer's instructions.
3. Prior to reading vehicle's alignment readouts, front and rear of vehicle should be jounced (suspension compressed/released).
4. Induce jounce (rear first, then front) by grasping center of bumper and jouncing each end of vehicle an equal number of times.
5. Bumper should always be released when vehicle is at bottom of jounce cycle.
6. Record vehicle's current front and rear alignment settings. Compare settings to vehicle specifications for camber, caster and toe-in.
7. If caster and camber are within specifications, proceed to roe.
8. Rear camber and caster are not adjustable. If found not to be within specifications, inspect for damaged suspension or body components.
9. If rear toe is not within specifications, adjust rear toe before proceeding to adjust front toe.

Camber & Caster

Camber and caster settings on this vehicle are determined at the time the vehicle is designed, by the location of the vehicle's suspension components. This is referred to as net build. The result is no required adjustment of camber and caster after the vehicle is built or when servicing the suspension components. Thus, when performing a wheel alignment, caster and camber are not normally considered adjustable angles.

Camber and caster should be checked to ensure they meet vehicle specifications.

If individual front camber or caster is found not to meet alignment specifications, each can be adjusted by shifting the engine cradle if cross-camber and cross-caster are within specifications, or by using an available service adjustment bolt package. Always try to shift the cradle first (if camber and caster are off slightly) to correct the misalignment before installing an adjustment bolt package. If an adjustment bolt package installation is required, inspect the suspension components for any signs of damage or bending first.

Do not attempt to adjust the vehicles wheel alignment by heating, bending or by performing any other modification to the vehicle's front suspension components or body.

ADJUSTMENT BY SHIFTING CRADLE

1. Loosen four engine cradle mounting bolts enough to allow movement of cradle, **Fig. 1.**
2. Shift cradle to bring camber or caster into specifications. **When shifting cradle, use care not to move other angles (camber or caster) that are within specifications, out of specifications.**
3. Tighten four mounting bolts
4. Jounce rear, then front of vehicle an equal amount of times.
5. Measure camber and caster.
6. If camber and caster are within specifications, proceed to roe.
7. If camber or caster cannot be brought into specifications, perform the "Adjustment Bolt Package Installation."

ADJUSTMENT BOLT PACKAGE INSTALLATION

Adjustment bolts for AWD and RWD are not interchangeable.
1. Adjustment bolt package contains two

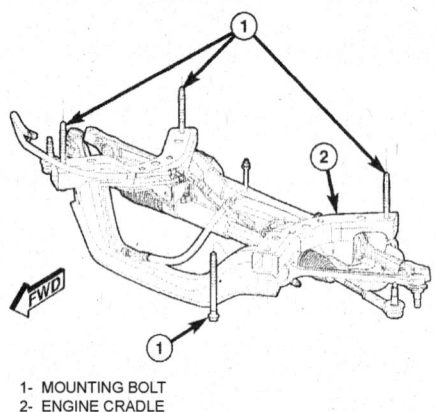

1- MOUNTING BOLT
2- ENGINE CRADLE

ARM0400000000619

Fig. 1   Engine cradle adjustment

special bolts, **Fig. 2.**
2. These bolts can be identified by offset grooves cut into thread section.
3. These bolts are designed to replace inboard mounting bolts of lower control arm at engine cradle.
4. Each bolt allows approximately .3° movement.
5. **To adjust camber only,** use both bolts, one at each leg of control arm.
6. **To adjust caster only,** use one bolt at front leg only
7. **On all models,** raise and support vehicle by frame until tires are not supporting vehicle weight.
8. Remove mounting screws and front belly pan.
9. **On AWD models,** proceed as follows:
   a. Remove mounting screws and heat shields covering steering gear inner tie rod boots.
   b. Loosen (do not remove) steering gear mounting bolt furthest from side of adjustment bolt installation.
   c. Remove two remaining mounting bolts and allow steering gear to relax on side of adjustment bolt installation, proving access to lower control arm rear mounting bolt.
10. **On RWD models,** proceed as follows:
    a. Remove mounting screws and heat shields covering stabilizer bar bushing retainers to cradle.
    b. Remove four stabilizer bar bushing retainers mounting bolts, then position stabilizer bar rearward and down out of way of control arm mounting bolts.
11. **On all models,** hold head of control arm or tension strut mounting bolt stationary and remove nut. **Do not rotate bolt.**
12. Slide bolt straight out of bushing and discard. **Do not damage bat wings in bushing inner metal or cradle.**
13. **When installing an adjustment bolt, ensure it is install in correct direction. Lower control arm rear mounting bolts must be installed from rear-forward and lower control arm front mounting bolts must be installed from front-rearward.**

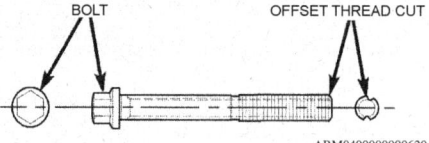

BOLT   OFFSET THREAD CUT

ARM0400000000620

Fig. 2   Adjustment bolt

14. Grooves on adjustment bolts are off-center forcing bolt to be installed in one of two ways depending on whether more positive or negative camber or caster is required. Bolts must be rotated 180° to achieve either more positive or negative camber or caster.
15. **Do not force adjustment bolt.**
16. **To achieve more positive camber,** proceed as follows:
    a. Move control arm in desired direction.
    b. Insert adjustment bolt with washer installed through bat wing hole in engine cradle and round hole in bushing inner metal, **Fig. 3.**
17. **To achieve more negative camber,** proceed as follows:
    a. Move control arm in desired direction.
    b. Insert adjustment bolt with washer installed through bat wing hole in engine cradle and round hole in bushing inner metal, **Fig. 4.**
18. **To achieve more positive caster,** proceed as follows:
    a. Move lower control arm in desired direction.
    b. Insert adjustment bolt with washer installed through bat wing hole in engine cradle and round hole in bushing inner metal, **Fig. 3.**
19. **To achieve more negative caster,** proceed as follows:
    a. Move lower control arm in desired direction.
    b. Insert adjustment bolt with washer installed through bat wing hole engine cradle and round hole in bushing inner metal, **Fig. 4.**
20. **On all adjustments,** start new nut and washer (on RWD vehicles) on end of mounting bolt by hand, then while holding head of bolt stationary, install nut. **Do not tighten nut now.**
21. Install steering gear and heat shields.
22. Lower vehicle to curb position.
23. Jounce rear, then front of vehicle an equal amount of times.
24. **Torque** adjustment bolt nut using suitable crowfoot wrench to 130 ft. lbs. while holding bolt stationary. Socket on end of breaker bar works well for holding rear bolt stationary with steering gear is installed.
25. Measure camber and caster.
26. If camber and caster are not within specifications, inspect suspension components for any signs of damage or bending.
27. If camber and caster (and cross-camber and cross-caster) are within specifications, proceed with toe to check and adjust toe.

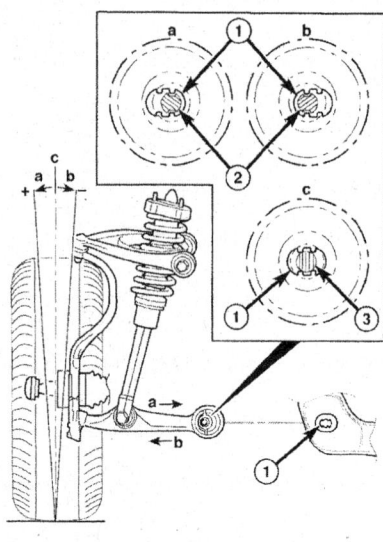

1- ENGINE CRADLE
2- ADJUSTMENT BOLT
3- ORIGINAL (NON-GROOVED) MOUNTING BOLT

ARM0400000000621

Fig. 3   Positive camber adjustment

28. Install the belly pan.

Toe

When performing the toe adjustment procedure, set rear toe to specifications before setting front toe.

Do not twist the inner tie rod-to-steering gear boots during front wheel toe adjustment.

Perform the following procedure to each side of the vehicle as required.
1. Center steering wheel and lock in place using suitable steering wheel clamp.
2. Remove boot clamps at inner tie rods and ensure boots move freely on inner tie rods.
3. Loosen jam nut at inner-to-outer tie rod connection, **Figs. 5 and 6.**
4. Grasp inner tie rod at hex and rotate as required to adjust front toe.
5. **Torque** tie rod jam nut to 55 ft. lbs.
6. Ensure inner tie rod-to-steering gear boot is not twisted, then install boot clamp at inner tie rod.
7. Adjust front toe on opposite side as outlined in previous steps.

REAR WHEEL ALIGNMENT

Rear camber and caster are not adjustable. If found not to be within specifications, inspect for damaged suspension or body components If rear toe is not within specifications, adjust rear toe before proceeding to adjust front toe.

Toe

When performing the toe adjustment

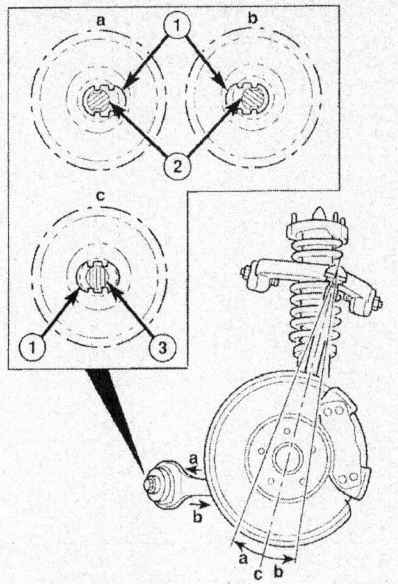

1- ENGINE CRADLE
2- ADJUSTMENT BOLT
3- ORIGINAL (NON-GROOVED) MOUNTING BOLT

ARM0400000000622

Fig. 4   Negative camber adjustment

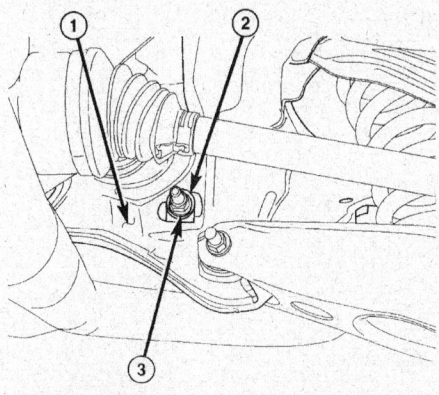

1- REAR CROSSMEMBER
2- ECCENTRIC LOBE
3- CAM BOLT

ARM0400000000623

Fig. 7   Rear toe adjustment (Part 1 of 2)

procedure, set rear toe to specifications before setting front toe.
1. Center steering wheel and lock in place using suitable steering wheel clamp.
2. Loosen toe link to rear crossmember cam bolt nut (front of rear crossmember) just enough to rotate cam bolt, **Fig. 7.**
3. Rotate cam bolt head on opposite side (rear) of crossmember in either direction until preferred specification is obtained.**When adjusting rear toe, eccentric lobes on toe adjustment cam bolts and washers are not to be facing downward. Lobes should only be facing upward or up to 90° to one side or other from 12 O'clock position.**

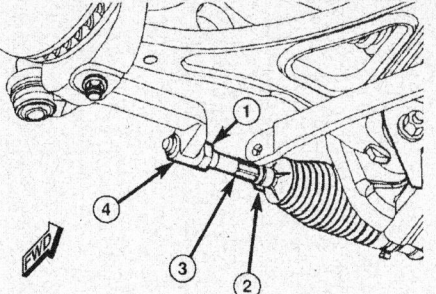

1- JAM NUT
2- CLAMP
3- INNER TIE ROD CONNECTION
4- OUTER TIE ROD CONNECTION

ARM0400000000626

Fig. 5   Jam nut. AWD

4. While holding cam bolt from turning, tighten cam bolt nut.
5. Adjust rear toe on opposite side of vehicle as outlined in previous test.
6. Once rear toe is set, proceed to front toe to set vehicle's front toe.

VEHICLE RIDE HEIGHT

1. Vehicle height is checked with vehicle on flat, level surface, preferably vehicle alignment rack.
2. Ensure tires inflated to recommended pressure.
3. Ensure all tires are same size as standard equipment.
4. Vehicle height is checked with fuel tank full of fuel, and no passenger or luggage compartment load.
5. Vehicle height is not adjustable.
6. If measurement is not within specifications, inspect vehicle for bent or weak suspension components.
7. Compare parts tag on suspect coil spring(s) to parts book and vehicle sales code, checking for match.
8. Once removed from vehicle, compare coil spring height to correct new or known good coil spring.
9. Heights should vary if suspect spring is weak.
10. **To measure front ride height,** on each side of vehicle, measure distance from frame rail just behind engine cradle rear mount to floor or alignment rack/lift runway surface, **Fig. 8.**
11. **To measure rear ride height,** on each side of vehicle, measure distance from travel limiter attached to front rear crossmember mount bushing to floor or alignment rack/lift runway surface
12. **On all height measurements,** it may be necessary to measure to bottom of straight edge, placed from lift runway to runway, to get an accurate measurement.

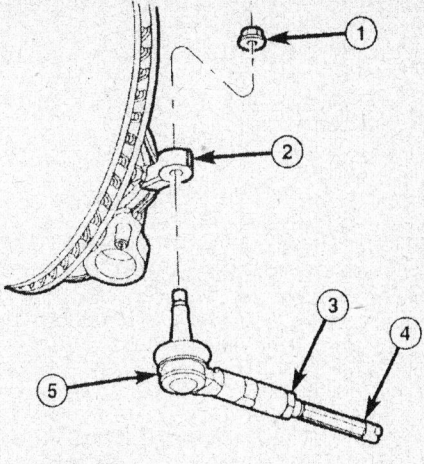

1- NUT
2- STEERING KNUCKLE
3- JAM NUT
4- INNER TIR ROD CONNECTION
5- OUTER TIE ROD CONNECTION

ARM0400000000627

Fig. 6   Jam nut. RWD

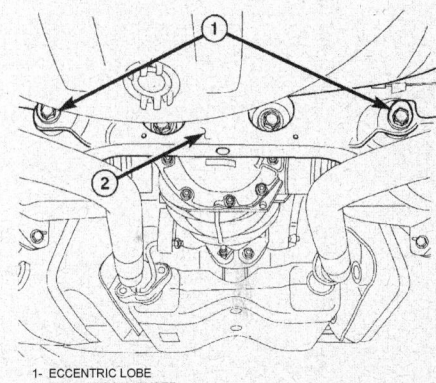

1- ECCENTRIC LOBE
2- REAR CROSSMEMBER

ARM0400000000624

Fig. 7   Rear tow adjustment (Part 2 of 2)

TECHNICAL SERVICE BULLETINS

Lead To Right

Some of these vehicles built before April 25, 2004, may lead to right.

This condition may be caused by alignment bias.

To correct this condition, proceed as follows:
1. Ensure vehicle is not being affected by crown sensitivity (vehicle drives straight on flat road).

2. Adjust all four tire pressures to door placard standards.
3. Ensure all four tires are same size and type.
4. Set alignment to specifications, noting the following:
   a. Set more caster on righthand side than on left.
   b. There will be more camber on left-hand side than right.
   c. Utilize cradle shift before using caster/camber adjustment bolt kit (part No. 05134117AA). adjustment bolts only provide approximately .2–.3° change.
   d. Shift cradle will move passenger's side forward and driver's side rear-ward.
   e. If installing adjustment bolt, do not allow bolt head to turn as cradle tension link joint or lower control

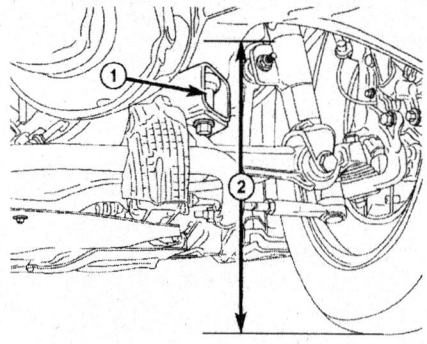

1- ENGINE CRADLE REAR MOUNT
2- FRONT RIDE HEIGHT

ARM0400000000628

Fig. 8   Front ride height measurement

arm bushing inner metal sleeve will be destroyed.
   f. Nut must be untorqued and re-moved before bolt.
   g. Once nut is removed, bolt can be slid out.

AIR CONDITIONING

NOTE: Prior To Performing Any Service Operations Listed In This Section, Consult The "Technical Service Bulletins" Section For Related Information.

TABLE OF CONTENTS

System Testing

NOTE: On Air Bag Equipped Models, Refer To "Air Bag System Precautions" Located In The Front Of This Manual For System Disarming & Arming Procedures.

NOTE: Refer To "Computer Relearn Procedures" Located In The Front Of This Manual When Battery Power To The Computer Has Been Interrupted.

INDEX

PRECAUTIONS

Battery Ground Cable

Prior to service, disconnect battery ground cable and isolate as required.

R-134a Systems

R-134a refrigerant is a non-toxic, non-flammable, clear, colorless, odorless liquefied gas.

R-134a refrigerant is not compatible with R-12 refrigerant. Even small amounts of R-12 in an R-134a system will cause lubricant contamination, compressor failure, or improper air conditioning performance. Never add R-12 to an R-134a system.

New service ports have been added to the compressor to prevent charging the system with R-12 refrigerant. R-134a systems require a special compressor lubricant. Use PAG compressor oil when servicing system.

Avoid breathing air conditioning R-134a refrigerant and lubricant vapor or mist. Exposure may irritate eyes, nose and throat. Use only approved service equipment to discharge R-134a systems.

Always wear eye protection when servicing the air conditioning system. Serious injury may result from eye contact with refrigerant. If this happens, seek prompt medical attention.

EXERCISE SYSTEM

Air conditioning units must be used periodically. Manufacturers caution that when the air conditioner is not used regularly, particularly during cold months, it should be turned on for a few minutes once every two or three weeks while the engine is running. This keeps the system in good operating condition.

Inspecting the system for effects of infrequent usage before the onset of summer is one of the most important aspects of air conditioning servicing.

First, clean out the condenser core, in all cases in front of the radiator. All obstructions such as leaves, bugs and dirt must be removed, as they will reduce heat transfer and impair the efficiency of the system. Ensure the space between the condenser and the radiator is also free of foreign matter.

Ensure evaporator water drain is open. The evaporator cools and dehumidifies the air before it enters the passenger compartment. At that point, the refrigerant is changed from a liquid to a vapor. As the core cools the air, moisture condenses on it but is prevented from collecting in the evaporator by the water drain.

PERFORMANCE TEST

Vehicle should not be in sunlight when performing this test.

Concorde, Intrepid, LHS & 300M

1. Ensure ambient air temperature of vehicle and location are at least 70° F.
2. Ensure evaporator temperature sensor probe (between evaporator fins) is at least 65° F.
3. Connect suitable tachometer and manifold gauge set to vehicle.
4. **On models equipped with Manual Temperature Control (MTC),** set air conditioning controls as follows:
   a. Blower motor control to highest speed position.
   b. Temperature control to full cool position.
   c. Mode control to recirculation (MAX-A/C) position.
   d. Air conditioning switch to MAX A/C.
   e. A/C control to ON position.
5. **On models equipped with Automatic Temperature Control (ATC),** set air conditioning controls as follows:
   a. Blower motor control to the highest speed position.
   b. Temperature control to the LO position.
   c. Recirculation control ON (A/C and RECIRC symbols should be lit).
   d. Mode control to PANEL position.
   e. MANUAL should appear in ATC display, confirming system is set manually.
6. **On all models,** adjust idle to 1000 RPM with air conditioning clutch engaged. Engine should be at normal operating temperature. Doors and windows should be closed.
7. Insert thermometer in left center air conditioning outlet and operate the engine for 20 minutes.
8. Evaporator inlet line temperature should be no more than 10°F cooler than discharged air temperature.
9. If discharge air temperature fails to meet specifications, further diagnosis of air conditioning system should be performed.
10. Start engine and hold idle at 1000 RPM with compressor clutch engaged. If compressor does not engage, inspect pressure.
11. Engine should be warmed to operating temperature with doors closed and windows open.
12. Insert suitable thermometer in driver side center panel outlet and operate system until it stabilizes.
13. With compressor clutch engaged, compare air temperature at center panel outlet and compressor discharge pressure (high side) to chart, **Fig. 1.**
14. Compressor clutch may cycle, depending upon ambient temperature and humidity. If clutch cycles, use readings obtained before clutch disengaged.
15. If air outlet temperature fails to meet specifications, or if compressor discharge pressure is high, inspect pressure.

Ambient Temperature, Deg. F	70	80	90	100	110
Maximum Allowable Air Temperature At Center Left Panel Outlet, Deg. F	42	45	50	54	59
Compressor Discharge Pressure, psi	200–230	210–250	240–280	280–320	320–365
Compressor Suction Pressure, psi	15–25	20–30	25–35	30–40	35–45

Fig. 1 Performance temperature & pressure test. Concorde, Intrepid, LHS, 300M, 2004–05 Sebring Convertible, Sebring Sedan & Stratus Sedan

Crossfire

Air temperature in the test room must be at least 70° F.

1. Connect suitable manifold gauge set.
2. Set air conditioning heater mode control switch knob in Panel position.
3. Set temperature control knob to cool position, and A/C button to On position.
4. Rotate blower motor control knob to highest speed position.
5. Start engine and hold at 1300 RPM with compressor clutch engaged.
6. Ensure all vehicle windows and doors, then allow engine to reach operating temperature.
7. Insert suitable thermometer in lefthand center vent and allow engine to run for five minutes. Air conditioning clutch may cycle depending on ambient conditions.
8. With compressor clutch engaged, record discharge air temperature and compressor discharge pressure.
9. Compare discharge air temperature to chart, **Fig. 2.** Reading should be taken with compressor clutch engaged.

Magnum, 300 & 300C

1. Connect suitable tachometer and manifold gauge set.
2. Set system control to recirculation mode (MAX-A/C) position, the temperature control to full cool position and blower motor control to highest speed position.
3. Start engine and hold idle at 1000 RPM with compressor clutch engaged.
4. If compressor does not engage, diagnosis system.
5. Engine should be at operating temperature, doors closed and windows opened.
6. Insert suitable thermometer in driver side center panel outlet.
7. Operate system until it stabilizes.
8. With compressor clutch engaged, compare air temperature at center panel outlet and compressor discharge pressure (high side) to chart, **Fig. 3.**
9. Compressor clutch may cycle, depending upon ambient temperature and humidity. If clutch cycles, use readings obtained before clutch disengaged.

Neon

1. Connect suitable tachometer and manifold gauge set.
2. Attach suitable thermocouple to evaporator inlet line.
3. Set controls to A/C, RECIRC and PANEL Set temperature lever to full cool and blower on high.
4. Start and hold engine at 1000 RPM with compressor clutch engaged.
5. Engine should be warmed with doors close and windows open.
6. Insert suitable thermometer in lefthand center vent and operate engine for five minutes. If compressor clutch cycles, disconnect low pressure cycling clutch switch connector.
7. With clutch engaged, compare center panel outlet air temperature and compressor discharge pressure to chart, **Figs. 4 and 5.**
8. If clutch cycles, obtained reading before clutch disengaged.

Sebring Convertible, Sebring Sedan & Stratus Sedan

2001-03

1. Connect suitable tachometer and manifold gauge set.
2. Attach suitable thermocouple to evaporator outlet line.
3. Set control to A/C, RECIRC, and PANEL, temperature lever on full cool and blower on high.
4. Start engine and hold at 1000 RPM with air conditioning clutch engaged.
5. Engine should be warmed up with doors and windows closed.
6. Insert suitable thermometer in lefthand center air conditioning outlet and operate engine for five minutes.
7. Clutch may cycle depending on ambient conditions.
8. With compressor clutch engaged, compare discharge air temperature to evaporator inlet line temperature.
9. Evaporator outlet line temperature should be at least 10°F cooler than discharge air temperature.
10. If discharge air temperature fails to meet the specifications, inspect for leaks.

2004-05

Refer to "Concorde, Intrepid, LHS & 300M" for performance testing.

Sebring Coupe & Stratus Coupe

1. Ensure vehicle is not in direct sunlight.
2. Connect suitable gauge manifold to high and low-pressure valves.
3. Start engine.
4. Set system controls as follows:
   a. A/C switch to ON position.
   b. Model selection to FACE position.
   c. Temperature control to MAXIMUM COOLING position.
   d. Air selection to RECIRCULATION position.
   e. Blower switch to F (Fast) position.
5. Adjust engine sped to 1500 RPM with compressor clutch engaged.
6. Engine should be warmed with doors and windows closed.
7. Insert suitable thermometer in center air outlets and operate engine for 20 minutes.
8. Record discharge temperature.
9. If clutch cycles, take reading before clutch disengages.
10. Compare readings to chart, **Fig. 6**.

LEAK TEST

Do not pressure test R-134a systems with compressed air. Some mixtures of air and R-134a have been indicated to be combustible at higher pressures.

A leak detector designed for R-12 will not detect leaks in an R-134a system.

Park vehicle in a wind-free work area, then proceed as follows:

1. Inspect charge level as outlined under "Performance Test" in this section.
2. When performing this test with original discharge pressure less than 30 psi, reclaim remaining refrigerant, then connect suitable vacuum pump and evacuate system to lowest vacuum possible.
3. Ensure system holds vacuum reading for at least 15 minutes. If system holds vacuum for 15 minutes a leak is probably not present. If vacuum did not hold for 15 minutes proceed as follows:
   a. Ensure transaxle is in Park.
   b. Run engine for five minutes, then ensure engine is idling at 700 RPM.
   c. Charge system with 10 ounces of R-134a refrigerant.
   d. Set air conditioning control to 100% outside air.
   e. Set panel mode to full cool.
   f. Set blower to high speed.
   g. Place air conditioning button in ON position.
   h. Open vehicle windows.
4. Turn engine Off, wait approximately five minutes, then use suitable electronic leak detector designed for R-134a refrigerant systems and inspect system for leakage. If a leak is found repair as required. If no leak was found fill system as outlined under "Performance Test."

Ambient Air Temperature, Deg F, & Humidity	70 @ 80	80 @ 80	90 @ 80	100 @ 50	110 @ 20
Air Temperature at Center Panel Outlet, Deg. F①	50–55	58–63	60–65	63–68	58–63
Evaporator Inlet Pressure at Charge Port, psi	35–40	38–42	39–43	40–44	38–42
Compressor Discharge Pressure, psi	18–260	200–280	200–280	240–320	220–300

① — The discharge air temperatures will be lower if the humidity is less than the percentages shown.

Fig. 2   Performance temperature & pressure chart. Crossfire

DISCHARGING SYSTEM

The use of refrigerant recovery and recycling stations allows the recovery and reuse of refrigerant after contaminants and moisture have been removed.

Follow the recovery or recycling station manufacturer's operating instructions.

SYSTEM EVACUATION

Using Vacuum Pump

Vacuum pumps suitable for removing air and moisture from air conditioning systems are commercially available. A specification for system pump-down used here is 26–29 ½ inches of vacuum. This reading can be attained at or near sea level only. For each 1000 feet of altitude this operation is being performed, the vacuum reading will be 1 inch lower. As an example, at 5000 feet elevation, only 21–24 ½ inches of vacuum can be obtained.

The system must be completely discharged before it can be evacuated. Damage to vacuum pump may result if pressurized refrigerant is allowed to enter.

1. With gauges connected into system, remove cap from vacuum hose connector. Install center hose from gauge manifold to vacuum pump connector. Mid-position the high and low side compressor service valves (if used). Open high and low side gauge manifold hand valves.
2. Operate vacuum pump a minimum of 45 minutes for air and moisture removal. Watch compound gauge that system pumps down into a vacuum. System will reach 26–29 ½ inches vacuum in 5 minutes or less. If system does not pump down, inspect all connections and leak-test if required.
3. Close gauge manifold hand valves and shutoff vacuum pump.
4. Inspect ability of system to hold vacuum. Watch compound gauge to ensure gauge does not rise at a faster rate than 1 inch of vacuum every 4 or 5 minutes. If compound gauge rises at too rapid a rate, install partial charge and leak-test, then evacuate system as outlined above.
5. If system holds vacuum, charge system with refrigerant.

Using Charging Station

On systems using R-134a refrigerant use a charging station designed for R-134a refrigerant systems.

A vacuum pump is built into the charging station and is constructed to withstand repeated and prolonged use without damage. Complete moisture removal from the system is possible only with a vacuum pump constructed for the purpose.

The system must be completely discharged before it can be evacuated. Damage to the vacuum pump may result if pressurized refrigerant is allowed to enter.

1. Connect hose to vacuum pump if system was discharged through charging station.
2. Open high and low side gauge valves of charging station.
3. Connect station to proper electrical outlet.
4. Engage Off-On switch to vacuum pump according to directions of specific station being used.
5. System should pump down into a 28–29 ½ inches vacuum in 5 minutes or less. If system fails to meet this specification, repair as required.
6. Operate pump a minimum of 45 minutes to remove all air and moisture.
7. Close high and low side gauge valves. Open switch to turn off pump.
8. Inspect ability of system to hold vacuum by watching compound gauge to ensure it does not rise at a rate higher than 1 inch of vacuum every 4 or 5 minutes. If rise rate is not within specifications, repair system as required. If rise rate is within specifications, charge system with refrigerant.

CHARGING SYSTEM

Concorde, Intrepid, LHS & 300M

Use a suitable refrigerant recovery station to discharge and charge the system. Follow the station manufacturer's instructions.

Crossfire

1. Connect suitable pressure gauge to discharge side of compressor, then attach two thermocouple probes on evaporator coil inlet and outlet tubes just before refrigerant line connector fitting.
2. With transaxle in Park and engine idling at 1000 RPM, set air conditioning controls as follows:
   a. Air conditioning control set to outside air.
   b. Set panel mode to full cool.
   c. Blower to high speed.
   d. Air conditioning button in On position.
   e. Turn Recirc button Off.
3. Open all vehicle windows, operate system and allow to stabilize, then set system pressure to 260 psi by placing piece of cardboard over part of condenser to obtain specified gauge reading.
4. Observe discharge pressure and evaporator coil inlet and outlet tube temperature, then determine system charge, **Fig. 7**.
5. If charge is not within specification, add or reclaim two ounces of refrigerant at a time.
6. Read gauge pressure and liquid line temperature. Continue procedure until proper charge is obtained.

Magnum, 300 & 300C

1. Connect suitable manifold gauge set and R-134a refrigerant recovery/recycling/charging station.
2. Measure proper amount of refrigerant and heat it to 125° F with charging station.
3. Open both suction and discharge valves, then open charge valve to allow heated refrigerant to flow into system.
4. When transfer of refrigerant has stopped, close both suction and discharge valves.

Ambient Temperature, Deg. F	70	80	90	100	110
Maximum Allowable Air Temperature At Center Left Panel Outlet, Deg. F	48	48	54	59	65
Compressor Suction Pressure, psi	20–30	20–30	30–40	30–40	35–45
Discharge Pressure at Service Port, psi	150–200	200–300	225–325	250–350	300–400

Fig. 3 Performance Temperature & Pressure. Magnum, 300 & 300C

5. If all of refrigerant charge did not transfer from dispensing device, open all of windows in vehicle and set system controls so that the compressor is engaged and blower motor is operating at its lowest speed setting.
6. Run the engine at steady high idle (more than 1400 RPM).
7. If compressor does not engage, test and repair compressor clutch control circuit.
8. Open low-side valve to allow remaining refrigerant to transfer to system.
9. **Do not open discharge (high pressure) valve now.**
10. Disconnect charging station and manifold gauge set from refrigerant system service ports.
11. Install caps onto refrigerant system service ports.

Neon

1. Connect suitable manifold gauge set to service ports.
2. Measure refrigerant.
3. Ensure engine is shut off.
4. Open suction and discharge valves.
5. Open charge valve to allow refrigerant to flow into system.
6. When transfer of refrigerant has stopped, close suction and discharge valve.
7. If all of charge did not transfer from dispensing device, put vehicle controls into the following mode:
   a. Automatic transaxle in park or manual transaxle in neutral position.
   b. Engine idling at 700 RPM.
   c. Control set in 100 percent outside air, panel mode and Blower motor ON high speed with vehicle windows closed
8. If compressor does not engage, test compressor clutch control circuit.
9. Open suction valve to allow remaining refrigerant to transfer to system.
10. Close all valves and test performance.
11. Disconnect charging station or manifold gauge set.
12. Install service port caps.

Sebring Convertible, Sebring Sedan & Stratus Sedan

1. Disconnect charging station or manifold gauge, install service port caps.
2. Measure proper amount of refrigerant and heat it to 125° F with charging station.
3. Open both suction and discharge valves, then open charge valve to allow heated refrigerant to flow into system.
4. When transfer of refrigerant has stopped, close both suction and discharge valves.
5. **If all refrigerant charge did not transfer from dispensing device,** proceed as follows:
   a. Open all windows.
   b. Set system controls so that compressor is engaged and blower motor is operating at its lowest speed setting.
   c. Run engine at steady high idle about 1400 RPM.
   d. If compressor does not engage, test and repair compressor clutch control circuit.
   e. Open low-side valve to allow remaining refrigerant to transfer to system.
6. **Do not to open discharge (high pressure) valve now.**
7. Disconnect charging station and manifold gauge set from refrigerant system service ports.
8. Install caps onto service ports.

Sebring Coupe & Stratus Coupe

Use a suitable refrigerant recovery station to discharge and charge the system. Follow the station manufacturer's instructions.

Ambient Temperature	21°C (70°F)	26.5°C (80°F)	32°C (90°F)	37°C (100°F)	43°C (110°F)
Air Temperature at Left Center Panel Outlet	1-8°C (34-46°F)	3-9°C (37-49°F)	4-10°C (39-50°F)	6-11°C (43-52°F)	7-18°C (45-65°F)
Compressor Discharge Pressure After the Filter Drier	1034-1724 kPa (150-250 PSI)	1517-2275 kPa (220-330 PSI)	1999-2620 kPa (290-380 PSI)	2068-2965 kPa (300-430 PSI)	2275-3421 kPa (330-496 PSI)
Evaporator Suction Pressure	103-207 kPa (15-30 PSI)	117-221 kPa (17-32 PSI)	138-241 kpa (20-35 PSI)	172-269 kpa (25-39 PSI)	207-345 kPa (30-50 PSI)

CR702000584000X

Fig. 4   Performance temperature chart. 2001 Neon & 2004–05 Neon w/2.4L Turbo engine

Ambient Temperature, Deg. F	70	80	90	100	110
Air Temperature At Lefthand Center Panel Outlet, Deg. F	42	48	53	57	69
Compressor Discharge Pressure, psi	125	150	215	275	350
Evaporator Suction Pressure, psi	26	35	38	45	57

Fig. 5   Performance temperature chart. 2002–05 Neon w/2.0L engine

Ambient Temperature, Deg. F	68	77	95	104
Discharge Air Temperature. Deg F	42–50	43–51	46–54	46–55
Compressor High Pressure, psi	224–281	235–290	301–320	311–380
Compressor Low Pressure, psi	18–23	18–23	22–26	21–38

Fig. 6   Performance temperature & pressure test. Sebring Coupe & Stratus Coupe

Compressor Discharge Pressure Chart					
Ambient Temperature	16°C (60°F)	21°C (70°F)	27°C (80°F)	32°C (90°F)	38°C (100°F)	43°C (110°F)
Compressor Discharge Pressure	1378 kPa (200 psi)	1516 kPa (220 psi)	1723 kPa (250psi)	1930 kPa (280 psi)	2206 kPa (320 psi)	2413 kPa (350 psi)

ARM030000000005

Fig. 7   Charge determination chart. Crossfire

System Service

INDEX

OIL CHARGE

To obtain proper oil fill capacities when replacing air conditioning compressors, measure the amount of oil removed from the failed compressor using a suitable measurement container, then add the same amount of manufactures recommended oil to the new compressor unit.

Model	Year	Compressor	Compressor Oil Viscosity	Component	Oil, Ounces
Concorde, Intrepid, LHS & 300M②	2001–04	Nippondenso 10PA17	ND-8 PAG	Compressor	①
				Condenser	1.00
				Evaporator	2.00
				Lines	1.50
				Receiver-Dryer	1.00
Crossfire	2004–05	Nippondenso 10S17	ND-8 PAG	Compressor	①
				Condenser	.34
				Evaporator	1.69
				Lines	1.5
				Receiver-Dryer	2.37
Magnum, 300 & 300C	2005	Denso 10S17	ND-8 PAG	Compressor	①
				Condenser	1.0
				Evaporator	2.0
				Lines	1.5
				Receiver-Dryer	1.0
Neon	2001	Nippondenso 10S17	ND-8 PAG	Compressor	①
				Condenser	1.0
				Evaporator	2.0
				Lines	1.5
				Receiver-Dryer	1.0
	2002 w/Auto Trans.	Nippondenso 10S17	ND-8 PAG	Compressor	①
				Condenser	1.0
				Evaporator	2.0
				Lines	1.5
				Receiver-Dryer	1.0
	2002 w/Manual Trans.	Nippondenso 10S17	ND-8 PAG	Compressor	①
				Condenser	1.0
				Evaporator	2.0
				Lines	1.5
				Receiver-Dryer	1.0

Continued

Model	Year	Compressor	Compressor Oil Viscosity	Component	Oil, Ounces
Neon	2003	Nippondenso 10S15	ND-8 PAG	Compressor	①
				Condenser	1.0
				Evaporator	2.0
				Lines	1.5
				Receiver-Dryer	1.0
	2004–05 w/2.0L	Nippondenso 10S15	ND-8 PAG	Compressor	①
				Condenser	1.0
				Evaporator	2.0
				Lines	1.5
				Receiver-Dryer	1.0
	2004–05 W/2.4L	Nippondenso 10S17	ND-8 PAG	Compressor	①
				Condenser	1.0
				Evaporator	2.0
				Lines	1.5
				Receiver-Dryer	1.0
Sebring Convertible, Sebring Sedan & Stratus Sedan	2001–03	Sanden TRS-090 Scroll Type	ND-15 PAG	Compressor	①
				Condenser	1.0
				Evaporator	2.0
				Filter/Drier	1.0
				Lines	1.5
	2004–05 (2.0L & 2.4L Turbo)	Sanden TRS - 090	ND-15 PAG	Compressor	①
				Condenser	1.0
				Evaporator	2.0
				Filter/Drier	1.0
				Lines	1.5
	2004–05 (2.4L Non-Turbo & 2.7L)	Visteon HS-15	VC-46 PAG	Compressor	①
				Condenser	1.0
				Evaporator	2.0
				Filter/Drier	1.0
				Lines	1.5
Sebring Coupe & Stratus Coupe	2001–05	MSC90C Scroll Type	SUN PAG 56	Compressor	4.1
				Condenser	.5
				Evaporator	2.0
				Lines	.3
				Receiver	.3

① — Drained refrigerant oil from old compressor and measure. Drain all refrigerant oil from new compressor, then fill new compressor with same amount of refrigerant oil that was drained out of old compressor.

OIL LEVEL CHECK

The oil level of these compressors should be inspected whenever refrigerant has been lost due to leakage or through normal system servicing.

Specifications

INDEX

A/C SPECIFICATIONS

Model	Year	Refrigerant		Compressor Oil Viscosity	Total System Capacity, Ounces	Compressor Clutch Air Gap, Inch
		Capacity, Lbs.	Type			
Concorde, Intrepid, LHS & 300M	2001–04	①	R-134a	ND8 PAG	5.0	.014–.026
Crossfire	2004–05	1.97	R-134a	ND8 PAG	4.4	.025–.035
Magnum, 300 & 300C	2005	①	R-134a	ND8 PAG	6.1	014–.024
Neon	2001–02	1.875	R-134a	ND8 PAG	6.1	.014–.026
	2003 w/2.0L	1.875	R-134a	ND8 PAG	6.1	.014–.026
	2003 w/2.4L Turbo	①	R-134a	ND8 PAG	5.4	.014–.026
	2004–05	①	R-134a	ND8 PAG	6.1	.014–.026
Sebring Convertible, Sebring Sedan & Stratus Sedan	2001–03	1.69	R-134a	SP-15 PAG	5.0	.016–.031
	2004–05 w/2.0L & 2.4L Turbo	①	R-134a	SP-15 PAG	5.0	013–.025
	2004–05 w/2.4L Non-Turbo & 2.7L	①	R-134a	VC-46 PAG	5.0	014–.030
Sebring Coupe & Stratus Coupe	2001–05	.88–.97	R-134a	SUN PAG 56	5.1	②

① — Refer to underhood label for refrigerant capacity.

② — 2.4L engine, .012–.020 inch; 3.0L engine, .016–.024.

CHARGING VALVE LOCATION

Concorde, Intrepid, LHS & 300M

On models equipped with 2.7L engines, the high pressure gauge port is located on the liquid line and the low pressure gauge port is located on the suction line.

On models equipped with 3.2L and 3.5L engines, the high and low side pressure connectors are located on the air conditioning compressor.

Crossfire

The high pressure service port is located on the liquid line near the front of the engine compartment behind the grille, **Fig. 1.**

The suction line is located on the left-hand side of the engine compartment near the strut mounting, **Fig. 2.**

Magnum, 300 & 300C

The high side service port is located on the liquid line near lefthand shock tower.

The low side service port is located on the suction line near the lefthand shock tower.

Neon

On 2001 models, the high side valve is located on the liquid line or on the liquid tube of the accumulator assembly, depending on engine application. The low side valve is located on the suction line or on the suction tube of the accumulator assembly, depending on engine application.

On 2002 models, the high side valve is located on the filter-drier. The low side valve is situated on the suction line, near the washer fluid reservoir filler.

On 2003 models with 2.0L engine, the high side valve is located on the liquid line or on the liquid tube of the accumulator assembly, depending on engine application. The low side valve is located on the suction

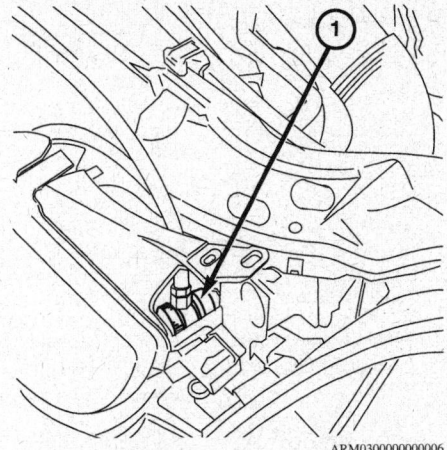

Fig. 1 High pressure service port location. Crossfire

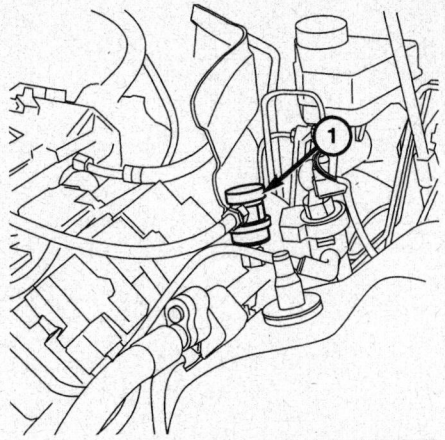

Fig. 2 Suction line service port location. Crossfire

line or on the suction tube of the accumulator assembly, depending on engine application.

On 2004–05 models with 2.0L engine, the low side valve is located on the liquid line between the condenser and the evaporator. The high side valve is located on the discharge line fitting at condenser.

On 2003–05 models with 2.4L engine, the low side valve is located on the suction line near the receiver/drier. The high side valve is located on the liquid line fitting at the receiver/drier outlet port.

Sebring Convertible, Sebring Sedan & Stratus Sedan

The high side service port is located on the receiver/drier. The low side service port is located on the suction line, near the right-hand strut tower.

Sebring Coupe & Stratus Coupe

The low side valve is located on the suction line. The high side valve is located on the high pressure lines.

BELT TENSION

Concorde, Intrepid, LHS & 300M

1. Loosen tensioner pulley locking nut, **Figs. 3 and 4.**
2. Measure tension using belt tensioning tool No. C-7198, or equivalent, **Fig. 5.**
3. **Torque** locking nut to 40 ft. lbs.

Crossfire

Belt adjustment is maintained by an automatic (spring load) belt tensioner.

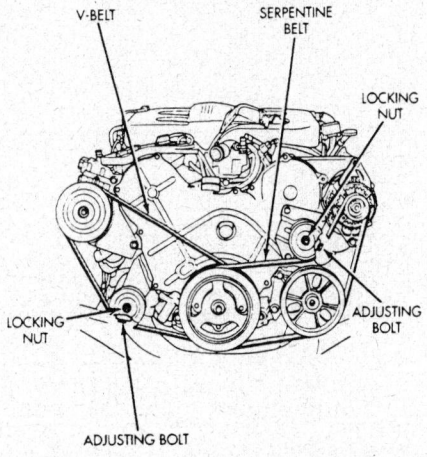

Fig. 4 Belt tension inspection. Concorde, Intrepid, LHS & 300M w/3.2L & 3.5L engines

Magnum, 300 & 300C

Belt adjustment is maintained by an automatic (spring load) belt tensioner.

Neon

1. Install drive belt over all pulleys except for power steering pump pulley.
2. Rotate belt tensioner clockwise using 17 mm wrench until belt can be installed on power steering pulley.
3. Release spring tension onto belt.
4. Inspect belt length indicator marks. Indicator mark should be within minimum belt length and maximum belt length marks, **Fig. 6.** On new belt, indicator mark should align approximately with nominal belt length mark.

Sebring Coupe & Stratus Coupe

1. Loosen tension pulley fixing nut A behind tension pulley, **Figs. 7 and 8.**

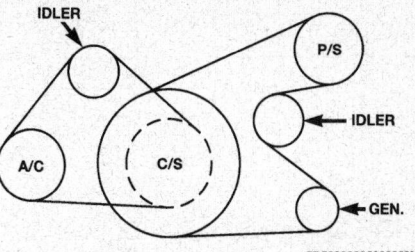

Fig. 3 Belt tension inspection. Concorde, Intrepid, LHS & 300M w/2.7L engine

2. Adjust belt tension amount using adjusting bolt B.
3. **Torque** fixing nut to 26–40 ft. lbs.
4. **If using scan tool,** proceed as follows:
   a. Connect belt tension meter set tool No. MB991668 to scan tool MUT-II No. MB991502, or equivalents.
   b. Connect scan tool to data Link Connector.
   c. Turn ignition switch to ON position and select belt tension measurement from menu screen,
   d. Hold microphone from tension meter drive belt center between pulleys approximately .4–.8 inch away from and perpendicular to rear surface of belt.
   e. Gently tap middle of belt with finger and measure vibration frequency, **Fig. 9.**
5. **If using tension gauge,** refer to **Figs. 10 and 11.**
6. **If measuring deflection,** apply 22 lbs. force in middle of drive belt between pulleys and measure, **Figs. 12 and 13.**

Sebring Convertible, Sebring Sedan & Stratus Sedan

2.0L & 2.4L ENGINES

Belt adjustment is maintained by an automatic (spring load) belt tensioner.

2.7L ENGINE

1. Engage suitable torque wrench, with maximum two-inch extension in ½ inch square opening of tensioner bracket.
2. Apply 104 ft. lbs. of torque, counterclockwise to tensioner bracket while tightening upper fastener.
3. **Torque** fastener to 20 ft. lbs.
4. Remove torque wrench from tensioner bracket and **torque** lower tensioner bracket fastener to 20 ft. lbs.
5. Connect belt tension gauge adapter tool No. 8371 to DRBIII following tool instructions.
6. Place end of microphone probe approximately 1 inch from belt at one of belt center span locations, **Fig. 14.**
7. Pluck belt at least three times using finger, or other suitable tool.
8. Adjust belt to obtain proper tension frequency hertz (Hz), **Fig. 15.**

AIR CONDITIONING

Engine	Condition	Tension, Lbs.
2.7L	New	180–200
	Used	120
3.2L & 3.5L	New	150–170
	Used	120

Fig. 5 Belt tension. Concorde, Intrepid, LHS & 300M

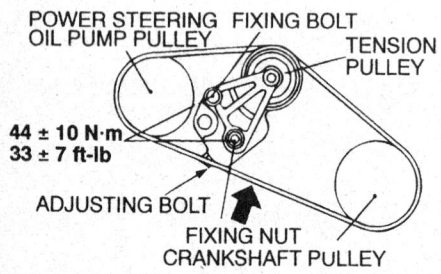

POWER STEERING FIXING BOLT
OIL PUMP PULLEY
TENSION PULLEY
44 ± 10 N·m
33 ± 7 ft-lb
ADJUSTING BOLT
FIXING NUT
CRANKSHAFT PULLEY

CR7020000624000X

Fig. 8 Belt tension inspection. Sebring Coupe & Stratus Coupe w/3.0L engine

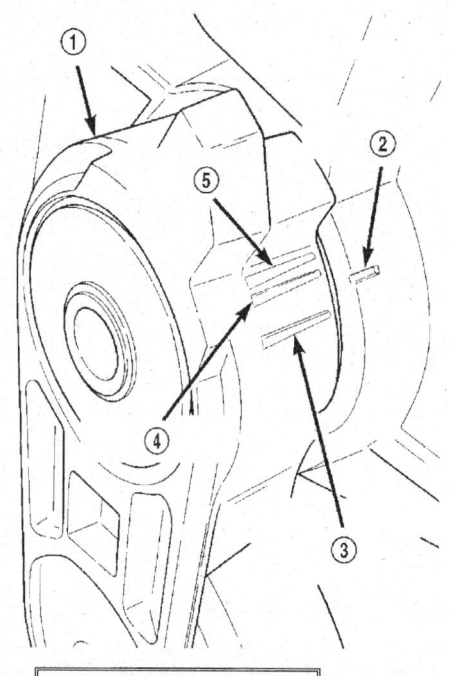

| 1 - AUTOMATIC BELT TENSIONER |
| 2 - BELT LENGTH INDICATOR |
| 3 - MAXIMUM BELT LENGTH |
| 4 - NOMINAL BELT LENGTH |
| 5 - MINIMUM BELT LENGTH |

ARM0400000000851

Fig. 6 Belt tensioning. Neon

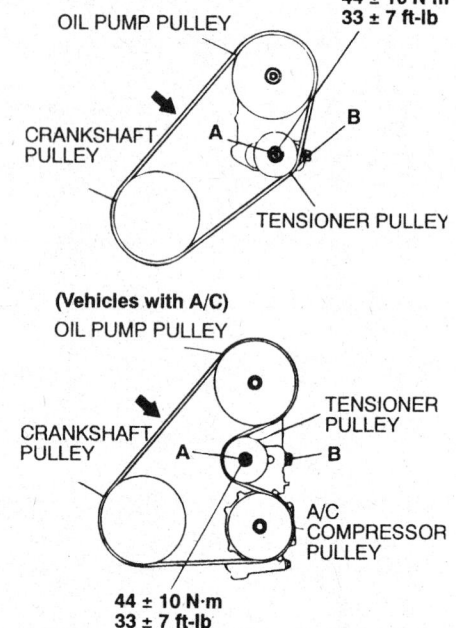

(Vehicles without A/C)
OIL PUMP PULLEY
44 ± 10 N·m
33 ± 7 ft-lb
CRANKSHAFT PULLEY
A
B
TENSIONER PULLEY

(Vehicles with A/C)
OIL PUMP PULLEY
CRANKSHAFT PULLEY
A
B
TENSIONER PULLEY
A/C COMPRESSOR PULLEY
44 ± 10 N·m
33 ± 7 ft-lb

CR7020000623000X

Fig. 7 Belt tension inspection. Sebring Coupe & Stratus Coupe w/2.4L engine

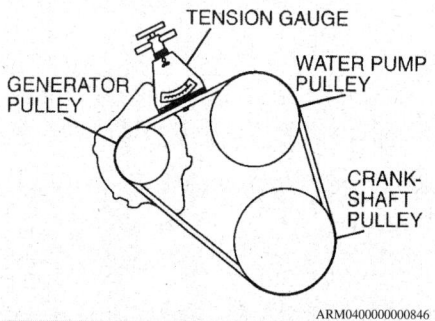

TENSION GAUGE
GENERATOR PULLEY
WATER PUMP PULLEY
CRANK-SHAFT PULLEY

ARM0400000000846

Fig. 10 Tension gauge measurement. Sebring Coupe & Stratus Coupe w/2.4L engine

Engine	Method	When Checked	During Adjustment	During Replacement
2.4L	Vibration Frequency, Hz	114–140	121–134	145–166
	Tension, Lbs.	88–132	99–121	143–187
	Deflection, Inch	.46–.61	.50–.57	.35–.44
3.0L	Vibration Frequency, Hz	134–165	142–158	171–196
	Tension, Lbs.	84–128	95–117	137–181
	Deflection, Inch	.43–.56	.46–.52	.33–.41

Fig. 9 Belt tension table. Sebring Coupe & Stratus Coupe

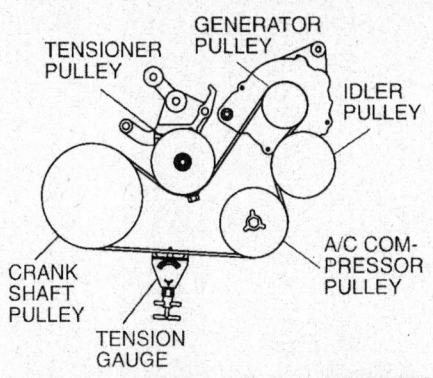

ARM0400000000847

Fig. 11 Tension gauge measurement. Sebring Coupe & Stratus Coupe w/3.0L engine

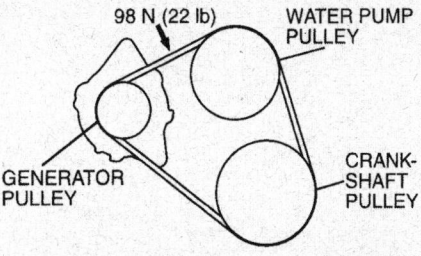

ARM0400000000848

Fig. 12 Deflection measurement. Sebring Coupe & Stratus Coupe w/2.4L engine

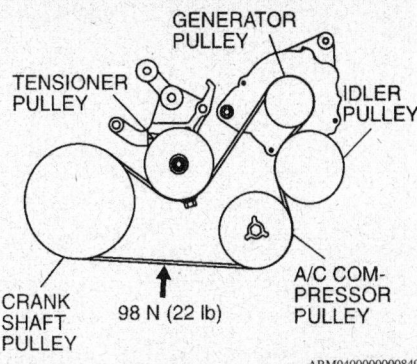

ARM0400000000849

Fig. 13 Deflection measurement. Sebring Coupe & Stratus Coupe w/3.0L engine

TECHNICAL SERVICE BULLETINS

Erratic Air Conditioning Operation

CONCORDE, INTREPID, LHS, SEBRING CONVERTIBLE, SEBRING SEDAN, STRATUS SEDAN & 300M

On some of these models the air conditioning and heater systems may operate erratically to include: lack of cold air, lack of hot air, unrequested mode change on Automatic Temperature Control (ATC), no control of mode or temperature control or dithering/tapping blend door noise. These symptoms may be accompanied by the following Diagnostic Trouble Codes (DTCs) blend door feedback, blend door stall, air conditioning control mode door input shorted to battery, in-vehicle temperature sensor failure, ATC messages not received, or mode door stall.

This condition may be caused by the HVAC control assembly.

To correct this condition, proceed as follows

1. Verify symptoms and inspect for DTCs using suitably programmed scan tool.
2. With vehicle at room temperature (50–80°F), remove fuse 19 from junction block M-1 circuit for 10 minutes to erase DTC's.
3. Replace fuse and start vehicle to calibrate HVAC system. Allow approximately five minutes for recalibration to complete.
4. Operate vehicle and air conditioning heater system to ensure symptoms and/or DTCs are gone.
5. If dithering/tapping noise is still present, additional diagnosis is required.

Honk Or Fog Horn Sound

2001–02 SEBRING CONVERTIBLE, SEBRING SEDAN & STRATUS SEDAN

On some of these models there may be a honk or fog horn sound coming from the air conditioning expansion valve within a few seconds of air conditioning clutch engagement, or immediately after air conditioning clutch engagement. This sound may last 1–3 seconds and can be confused with the sound that a vehicle braking system makes when the vehicle is allowed to creep forward at curb idle. Vibration from this condition may be felt in the passenger compartment especially in the steering wheel and seats.

This condition may be caused by the expansion valve.

To correct this condition replace the expansion valve with a revised unit (part No. 04596318AA). Replacing the expansion valve will not improve any vehicle noise conditions that last longer than three seconds.

Window Fogging In Certain Climate Conditions

2001–04 SEBRING CONVERTIBLE/SEBRING SEDAN & STRATUS SEDAN

On some of these models the windows may fog with the HVAC system In Floor Mode.

This condition may be caused by the Body Control Computer (BCM) programing.

To correct this condition, program BCM with latest software.

Clunk Sound At Initial Engine Startup

2001 NEON

On some of these models if the vehicle is shut off with the air conditioning compressor engaged and allowed to sit overnight, an audible clunk may be heard from the engine compartment at the initial engine startup. This condition is most noticeable in moderate to warm ambient temperatures and is not detrimental to the operation and performance of the compressor.

This condition may be caused by the when the compressor ingests the first liquid refrigerant after sitting overnight or for extended periods of time.

To correct this condition, install an updated expansion valve.

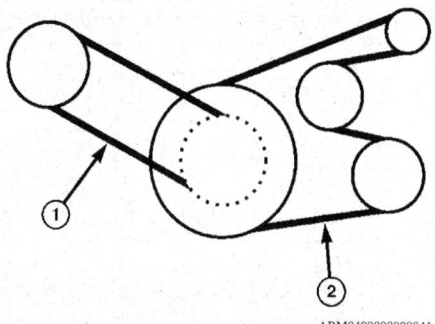

ARM040000000841

Fig. 14 Belt center span locations. 2.7L engine

Condition①	Lbs	Hz.
New	185–235	204–230
Used	110–160	157–190

① — A belt is considered used after 15 minutes of run-in time.

Fig. 15 Belt tension specifications. 2.7L engine

COOLING FANS

NOTE: On Air Bag Equipped Models, Refer To "Air Bag System Precautions" Located In The Front Of This Manual For System Disarming & Arming Procedures.

NOTE: Refer To "Computer Relearn Procedures" Located In The Front Of This Manual When Battery Power To The Computer Has Been Interrupted.

NOTE: "Electrical Symbol And Wire Color Code Identification" Located In Front Of This Manual Can Be Used As An Aid When Using Wiring Circuits Found In This Section.

INDEX

PRECAUTIONS

Air Bag Systems

Refer to "Air Bag System Precautions" in the front of this manual for system disarming and arming procedures.

Battery Ground Cable

Prior to service, disconnect battery ground cable and isolate as required.

DESCRIPTION

Concorde, Intrepid, LHS & 300M

Radiator fan control is accomplished in two ways. A pressure transducer on the compressor discharge line sends a signal to the Powertrain Control Module (PCM) which activates the fans. The fans are also activated when the coolant temperature sensor sends a signal to the PCM. The engine controller then sends a signal to the fan relay which turns the coolant fans on.

Radiator fan control can be accomplished five ways.
1. Pressure transducer on air conditioning compressor discharge line sends signal to Powertrain Control Module (PCM) which will activate both fans.
2. In addition to this control, fans are turned on based output to the PCM from:
   a. Coolant temperature sensor;
   b. Intake air temperature sensor;
   c. Output speed sensor, and;
   d. Transmission oil temperature sensor
3. Regardless of coolant temperature fan will not run during cranking until engine starts.
4. Fans will run in accordance with specifications, **Figs. 1 and 2.**

Crossfire

The Radiator Cooling Fan System is comprised of the radiator fan control module, Powertrain Control Module (PCM) and the radiator fan motor. The Radiator fan control module acts as the relay for the cooling fan circuit. The module is mounted to the inner fender. The PCM acts as the input to the module to command the fan operation. The radiator cooling fan is made up of a multiple bladed fan. The cooling fan motor is a high speed DC type.

Neon

The radiator fan is a single speed electric motor driven fan.

Depending on engine/transmission combination, the vehicle may be equipped with a single fan or a dual fan. Vehicles

Fan Speed	ENGINE COOLANT TEMPERATURE						INTAKE (CHARGE) TEMPERATURE	
	A/C Off		A/C On		Engine @ Idle < 13 Km/h (8 MPH) Vehicle Speed		Vehicle Speed < 45 Km/h (28 MPH)**	
	Low	High	Low	High	Low	High	Low	High
Fan On:	106°C (223°F)	110°C (230°F)	105°C (221°F)	110°C (230°F)	104°C (219°F) - After 1st Fan Cycle	110°C (230°F)	65°C (149°F) if coolant <93°C (199°F) 61°C (142°F) if coolant >105°C (221°F)	After Low Fan On for 8 minutes.
Fan Off:	102°C (216°F)	107°C (225°F)	102°C (216°F)	106°C (223°F)	Fan on time = 4 minutes*	105°C (221°F)	64°C (147°F) if coolant <92°C (197°F) 60°C (140°F) if coolant >104°C (219°F	Fan on time = 4 minutes*

*Minimum fan on time = 90 seconds
**Note: If low fan is on for 8 minutes, fan turns on high speed for 4 minutes, then goes back to low speed.

Fan Speed	A/C PRESSURE		TRANSMISSION OIL TEMPERATURE	
	Low	High	Low	High
Fan On:	1,448 Kpa (210 psi)	1,717 Kpa (249 psi)	109°C (228°F)	111°C (232°F)
Fan Off:	1,207 Kpa (175 psi)	1,503 Kpa (218 psi)	104°C (220°F)	109°C (228°F)

CR1080200345000X

Fig. 1 Fan operating mode conditions. Concorde & Intrepid w/2.7L engine

Fan Speed	ENGINE COOLANT TEMPERATURE				INTAKE (CHARGE) AIR TEMPERATURE	
	A/C Off/On		Engine @ Idle < 13 Km/h (8 MPH) Vehicle Speed		Vehicle Speed < 45 Km/h (28 MPH)	
	Low	High	Low	High	Low	High
Fan On:	102°C (216°F)	110°C (230°F)	99°C (210°F) - After 2nd Fan Cycle	110°C (230°F)	71°C (159°F) if coolant <93°C (199°F) 66°C (150°F) if coolant >99°C (210°F)	72°C (162°F)
Fan Off:	99°C (210°F)	105°C (221°F)	Fan on time = 4 minutes*	105°C (221°F)	Fan on time = 8 minutes*	Fan on time = 4 minutes*

*Minimum fan on time = 90 seconds

Fan Speed	A/C PRESSURE		TRANSMISSION OIL TEMPERATURE	
	Low	High	Low	High
Fan On:	1,448 Kpa (210 psi)	1,717 Kpa (249 psi)	102°C (216°F)	109°C (228°F)
Fan Off:	1,207 Kpa (219 psi)	1,510 Kpa (219 psi)	98°C (208°F)	107°C (224°F)

CR1080200346000X

Fig. 2 Fan operating mode conditions. LHS, Concorde, Intrepid & 300M w/3.2L & 3.5L engines

Radiator Fan Control			A/C Pressure	
A/C Off	Low	High		
Fan On:	104°C (220°F)	110°C (230°F)		
Fan Off:	98°C (208°F)	105°C (221°F)		
A/C On	Low	High	Low	High
Fan On:	99°C (210°F)	110°C (230°F)	1,448 Kpa (210 psi)	1,718 Kpa (249 psi)
Fan Off:	93°C (199°F)	105°C (221°F)	1,207 Kpa (175 psi)	1,585 kpa (229 psi)
EATX Fluid Temperature	Low Speed	High Speed		
Fan On:	109°C (228°F)	111°C (232°F)		
Fan Off:	104°C (220°F)	109°C (228°F)		

CR1080100329000X

Fig. 5 Fan operating mode conditions. Sebring Convertible, Sebring Sedan & Stratus Sedan w/2.7L engine

Radiator Fan Control			A/C Pressure	
A/C Off	Low	High		
Fan On:	104°C (220°F)	110°C (230°F)		
Fan Off:	99°C (210°F)	104°C (220°F)		
A/C On	Low	High	Low	High
Fan On:	99°C (210°F)	110°C (230°F)	1,466 Kpa (209 psi)	1,717 Kpa (249 psi)
Fan Off:	93°C (200°F)	104°C (220°F)	1,172 Kpa (170 psi)	1,579 Kpa (229 psi)
EATX Fluid Temperature	Low Speed	High Speed		
Fan On:	116°C (240°F)	120°C (248°F)		
Fan Off:	109°C (228°F)	116°C (240°F)		

CR1080100327000X

Fig. 3 Fan operating mode conditions. Sebring Sedan & Stratus Sedan w/2.0L engine

Radiator Fan Control			A/C Pressure	
A/C Off	Low	High		
Fan On:	104°C (219°F)	110°C (230°F)		
Fan Off:	99°C (210°F)	105°C (221°F)		
A/C On	Low	High	Low	High
Fan On:	99°C (210°F)	110°C (230°F)	1,448 Kpa (210 psi)	1,718 Kpa (249 psi)
Fan Off:	93°C (199°F)	105°C (221°F)	1,207 Kpa (175 Psi)	1,585 Kpa (229 Psi)
EATX Fluid Temperature	Low Speed	High Speed		
Fan On:	109°C (228°F)	111°C (232°F)		
Fan Off:	104°C (220°F)	109°C (228°F)		

CR1080100325000X

Fig. 4 Fan operating mode conditions. Sebring Convertible, Sebring Sedan & Stratus Sedan w/2.4L engine

equipped with dual fans, each fan blade is different from the other.

Sebring Convertible, Sebring Sedan & Stratus Sedan

Fan control is accomplished three ways.
1. Fan runs when air conditioning pressure reaches set psi.
2. In addition to this control, fan is turned on by temperature of coolant which is sensed by coolant temperature sensor which sends message to Powertrain Control Module (PCM). The PCM turns on fan through fan relay.
3. On models equipped with automatic transmission, transmission fluid thermistor may have some influences on fan operation.
4. The PCM provides fan control for the following conditions:
   1. Fan will not run during cranking until engine starts no matter what coolant temperature is.
   2. Fan will run when air conditioning clutch is engaged, low pressure cutout switch is closed and once set compressor head pressure is reached.
   3. Fan will run according to, **Figs. 3 through 5.**

Sebring Coupe & Stratus Coupe

On models equipped with manual transaxle, the Engine Control Module (ECM) and on models equipped with automatic transaxle the Powertrain Control Module (PCM) judge radiator and condenser fan motors' required speed using input signals from the air conditioning switch, automatic compressor controller, vehicle or output shaft speed sensor and engine coolant temperature sensor. The ECM or PCM activates the fan control module to drive the radiator and condenser fan motors.

SYSTEM DIAGNOSIS & TESTING

Accessing Diagnostic Trouble Codes

Connect a suitably programmed scan tool to Data Link Connector (DLC), and follow manufacturer's instructions.

Test	Description
P0110	Intake Air Temperature Sensor Stuck
P0111	Intake Air Temperature Sensor Performance
P0112	Intake Air Temperature Sensor Voltage Low
P0113	Intake Air Temperature Sensor Voltage High
P0116	Engine Coolant Temperature Performance
P0117	Engine Coolant Temperature Sensor Too Low
P0118	Engine Coolant Temperature Sensor Too High
P0480	Low Speed Fan Control Relay Circuit
P0481	High Speed Fan Control Relay Circuit
P0532	Air Conditioning Pressure Sensor Low
P0533	Air Conditioning Pressure Sensor High
P0711	Transmission Temperature Sensor Performance
P0712	Transmission Temperature Sensor Low
P0713	Transmission Temperature Sensor High
P0714	Transmission Temperature Sensor Intermittent
P0720	Output Speed Sensor Error
P1489	High Speed Fan Control Relay Circuit Test
P1490	Low Speed Fan Control Relay Circuit Test
P1491	Fan Control Relay Circuit Test
P1738	High Temperature Operation Activated

Fig. 6 DTC interpretation

Diagnostic Trouble Code Interpretation

Refer to **Fig. 6** for Diagnostic Trouble Code (DTC) interpretation.

Wiring Diagrams

CONCORDE, INTREPID, LHS & 300M

Refer to **Figs. 7 through 10** for cooling fan wiring diagrams.

CROSSFIRE

Refer to **Fig. 11** for cooling fan wiring diagrams.

MAGNUM, 300 & 300C

Refer to **Fig. 12** for engine cooling fan wiring diagram.

NEON

Refer to **Figs. 13 through 16** for cooling fan wiring diagrams.

SEBRING CONVERTIBLE, SEBRING SEDAN & STRATUS SEDAN

Refer to **Fig. 17 and 18** for cooling fan wiring diagrams.

SEBRING COUPE & STRATUS COUPE

Refer to **Fig. 19 and 20** for cooling fan wiring diagrams.

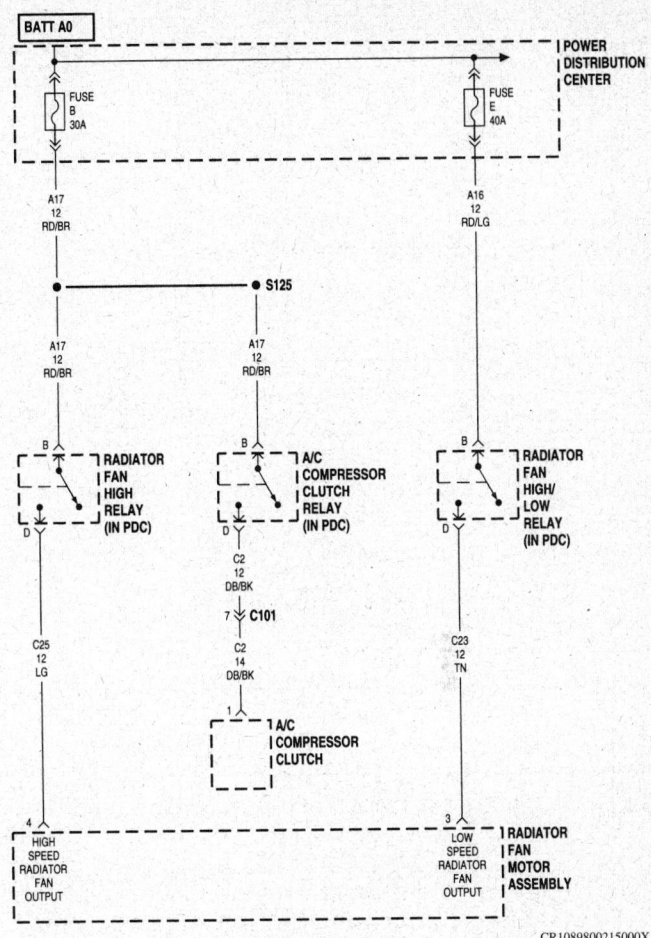

CR1089800215000X

Fig. 7 Engine cooling fan wiring diagram. Intrepid, LHS & 300M

Symptom Based Test

CROSSFIRE

RADIATOR COOLING FAN ALWAYS ON

1. Turn ignition Switch to ON position.
2. Inspect air conditioning switch using DRB III, or suitably programmed scan tool. If tool displays air conditioning off, proceed to next step. If tool displays air conditioning on, repair switch circuit.
3. Turn ignition switch to OFF position.
4. Disconnect radiator fan control module harness connector.
5. Disconnect radiator fan motor harness connector.
6. Turn ignition Switch to ON position.
7. Measure voltage on radiator fan control module output circuit. If measurement is less than 1 volt, proceed to next step. If voltage is not as specified, inspect for short to voltage in radiator fan control module output circuit.
8. Turn ignition switch to OFF position.
9. Disconnect Powertrain Control Module (PCM) harness connector.
10. Measure resistance between ground and radiator fan control circuit. Is resistance more than 100 kohms, proceed to next step. If resistance is not as specified, inspect for short to ground in radiator fan control circuit.
11. Turn ignition switch to OFF position.
12. Connect PCM harness connector.
13. Measure resistance between ground and radiator fan control circuit at radiator fan control module harness connector. If resistance is more than 100 kohms, replace radiator fan control module. If resistance is not as specified, replace PCM.

RADIATOR COOLING FAN INOPERATIVE

1. Turn ignition Switch to ON position.
2. Actuate radiator cooling fan using DRB III, or suitably programmed scan tool. If fan is not operating, proceed to next step. If fan is operating, replace Powertrain Control Module (PCM).
3. Turn ignition Switch to OFF position.
4. Disconnect PCM harness connector.
5. Turn ignition Switch to ON position.
6. Connect suitable jumper wire between ground and radiator fan control circuit at PCM harness connector cavity 39. If

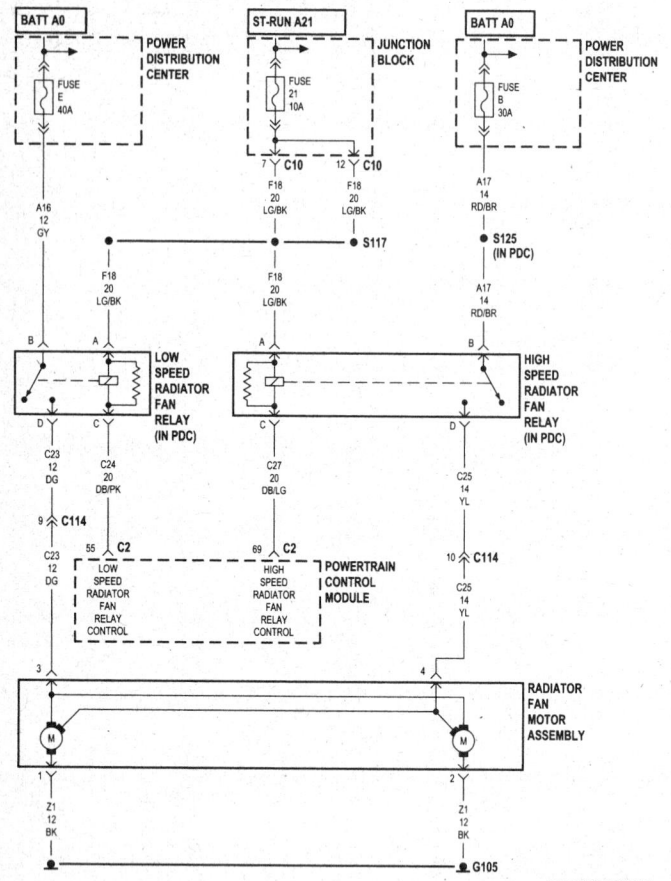

Fig. 8   Engine cooling fan wiring diagram. LHS, 2001–02 Concorde, Intrepid & 300M

CR1080000272000X

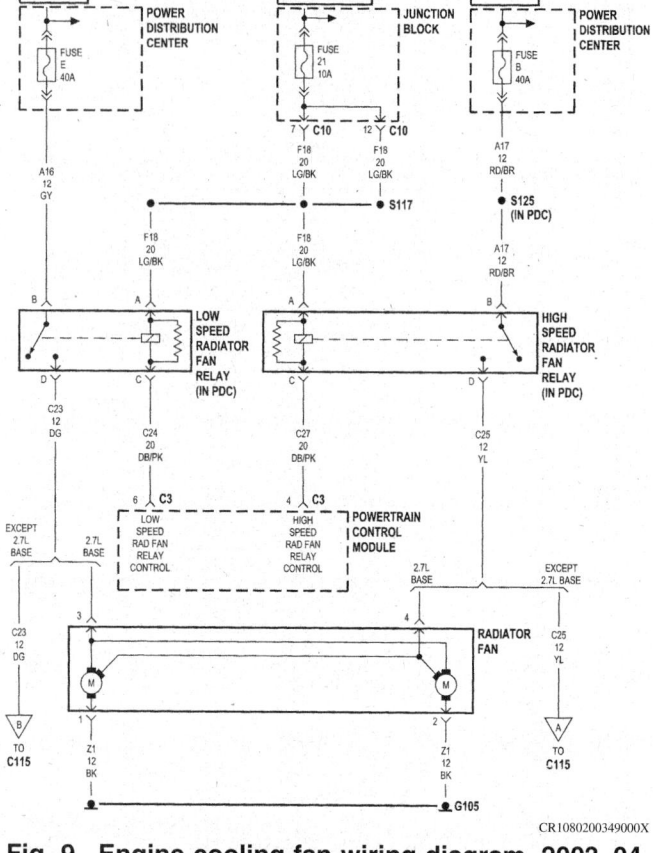

Fig. 9   Engine cooling fan wiring diagram. 2003–04 Concorde & Intrepid w/2.7L engine

CR1080200349000X

cooling fan is running, replace PCM. If fan is not running, proceed to next step.

7. Turn ignition Switch to OFF position.
8. Disconnect radiator fan control module harness connector.
9. Turn ignition Switch to ON position.
10. Measure voltage of fused B + circuit at the radiator fan control module harness connector. If measurement is more than 11 volts, proceed to next step. If measurement is not as specified, inspect for open in fused B + circuit.
11. Turn ignition switch to OFF position.
12. Measure resistance between ground and the module ground circuit. If the resistance is less than 5. ohms, proceed to next step. If resistance is not as specified, inspect for open in module ground circuit.
13. Ensure ignition switch is in OFF position.
14. Disconnect PCM harness connector.
15. Measure resistance of radiator fan control circuit from radiator fan control module harness connector to the PCM harness connector. If resistance is less than 5.0 ohms, go to next step, If resistance is not as specified, inspect for an open in radiator fan control circuit.
16. Ensure ignition switch is in OFF position.
17. Disconnect radiator fan motor harness connector.

18. Measure resistance of radiator fan control module output circuit from radiator fan control module harness connector to radiator fan motor harness connector. If resistance is less than 5 ohms, proceed to next step. If resistance is not as specified, inspect for open in radiator fan control module output circuit.
19. Ensure ignition switch is in OFF position.
20. Measure resistance of radiator fan control module ground circuit from radiator fan control module harness connector to radiator fan motor harness connector. If resistance is less than 5 ohms, proceed to next step. If resistance is not as specified, inspect for open in radiator fan control module ground circuit.
21. Ensure ignition switch is in OFF position.
22. Measure resistance of radiator fan motor. If resistance is less than 5 ohms, replace radiator fan control module. If resistance is not as specified, replace radiator fan motor.

SEBRING COUPE & STRATUS COUPE

Refer to **Figs. 21 through 30** for radiator and condenser fan motor troubleshooting.

Diagnostic Tests

CONCORDE, INTREPID, LHS & 300M

Refer to **Figs. 31 through 53** for diagnostic tests.

NEON

Refer to **Fig. 54 through 63** for diagnostic tests.

SEBRING CONVERTIBLE, SEBRING SEDAN & STRATUS SEDAN

Refer to **Figs. 64 through 73** for diagnostic test.

Clearing Diagnostic Trouble Codes

Connect a suitably programmed scan tool to Data Link Connector (DLC), and follow manufacturer's instructions.

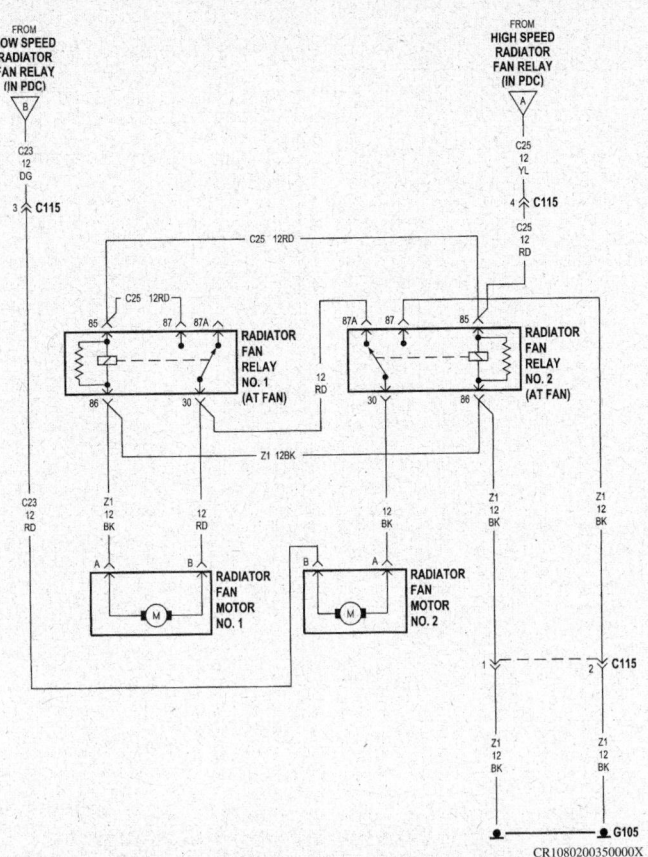

Fig. 10   Engine cooling fan wiring diagram. 2003–04 Concorde, Intrepid & 300M except 2.7L engine

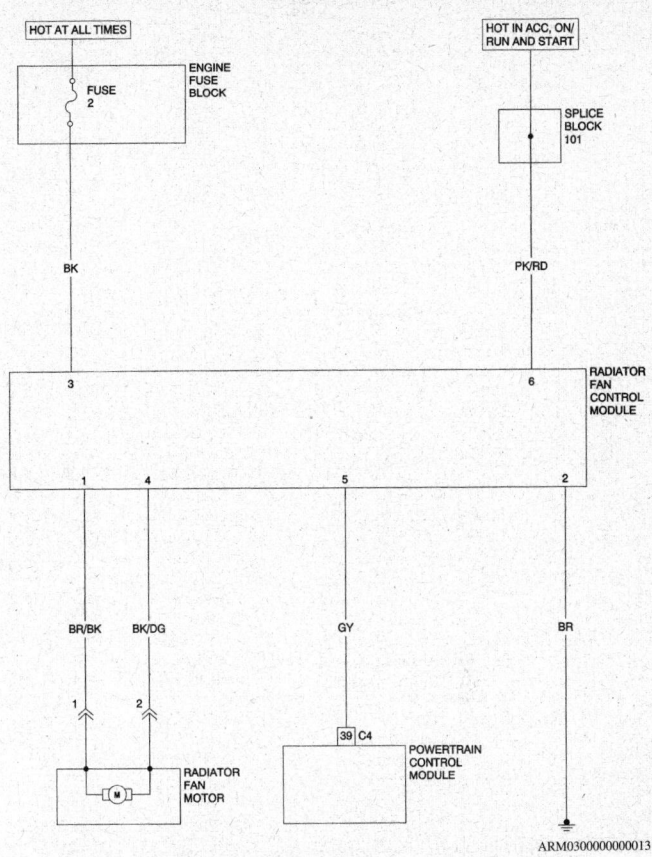

Fig. 11   Engine cooling fan wiring diagram. Crossfire

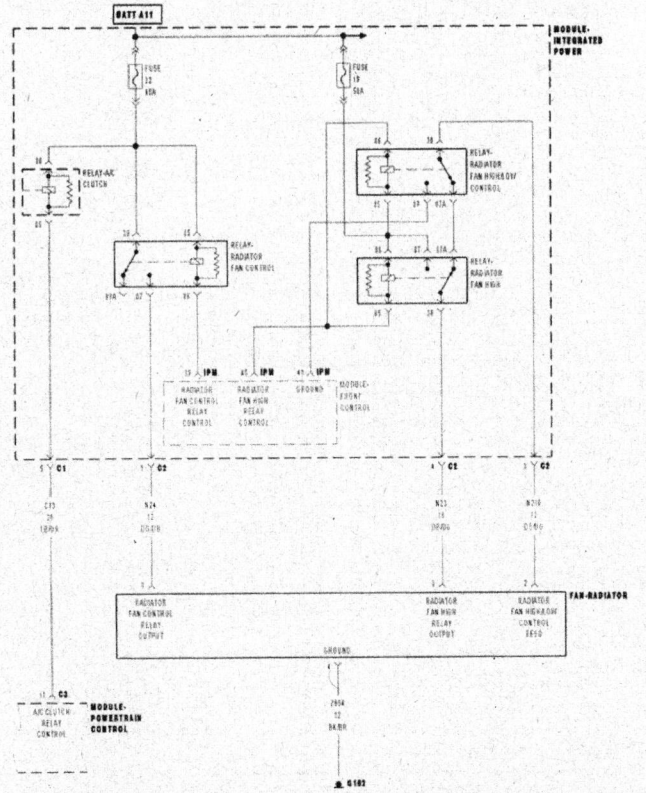

Fig. 12   Engine cooling fan wiring diagram (Part 1 of 4). Magnum, 300 & 300C

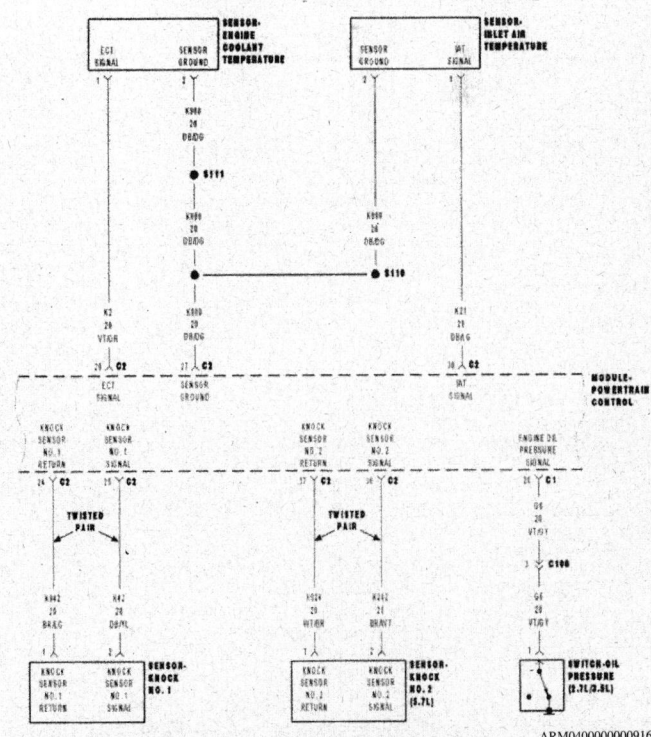

Fig. 12   Engine cooling fan wiring diagram (Part 2 of 4). Magnum, 300 & 300C

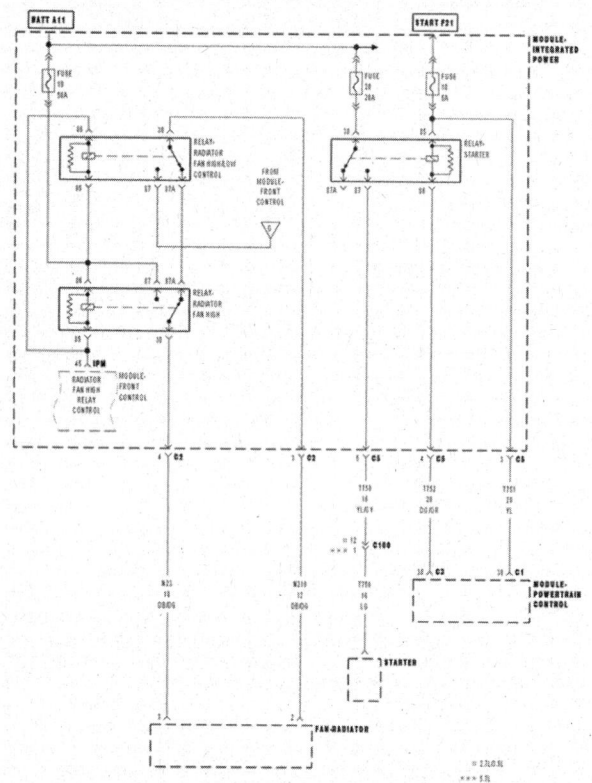

Fig. 12 Engine cooling fan wiring diagram (Part 3 of 4). Magnum, 300 & 300C

ARM0400000000917

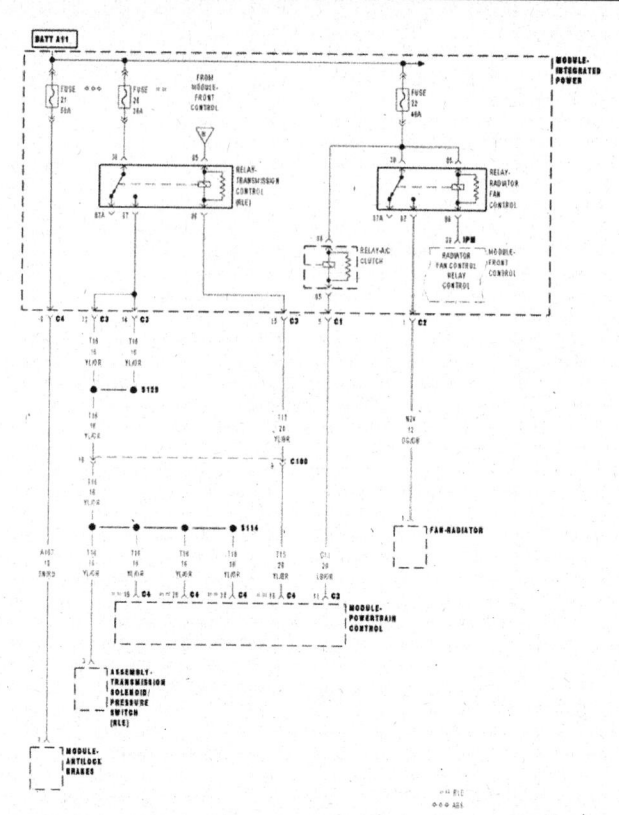

Fig. 12 Engine cooling fan wiring diagram (Part 4 of 4). Magnum, 300 & 300C

ARM0400000000918

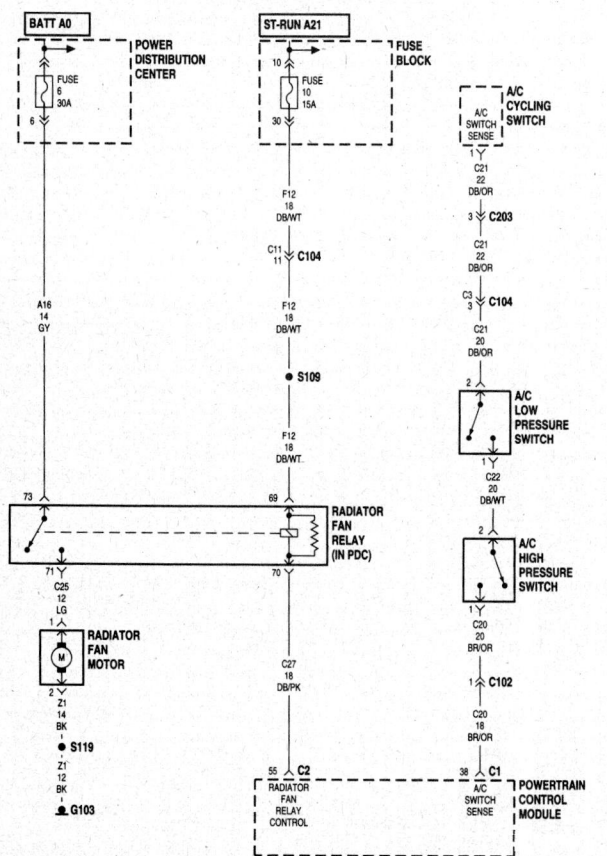

Fig. 13 Engine cooling fan wiring diagram (Part 1 of 2). 2001 Neon

CR1080000275000X

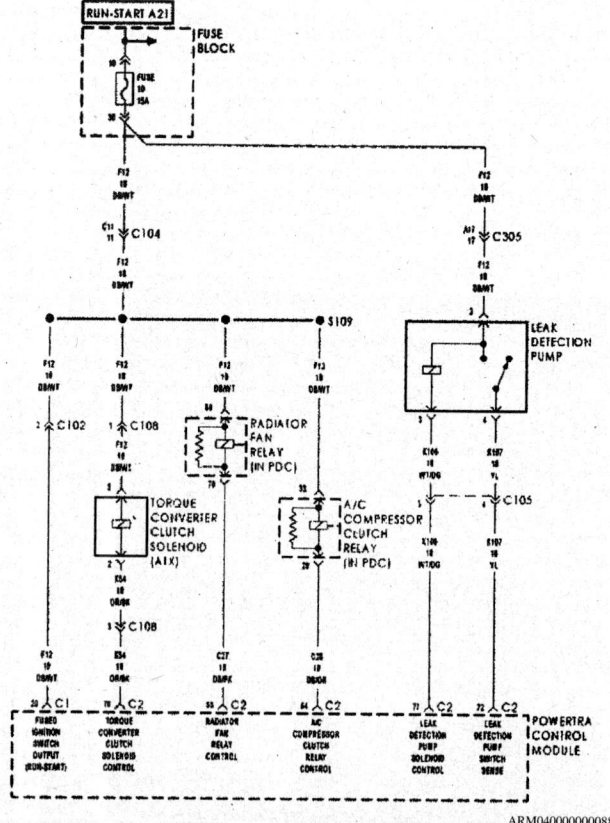

Fig. 13 Engine cooling fan wiring diagram (Part 2 of 2). 2001 Neon

ARM0400000000880

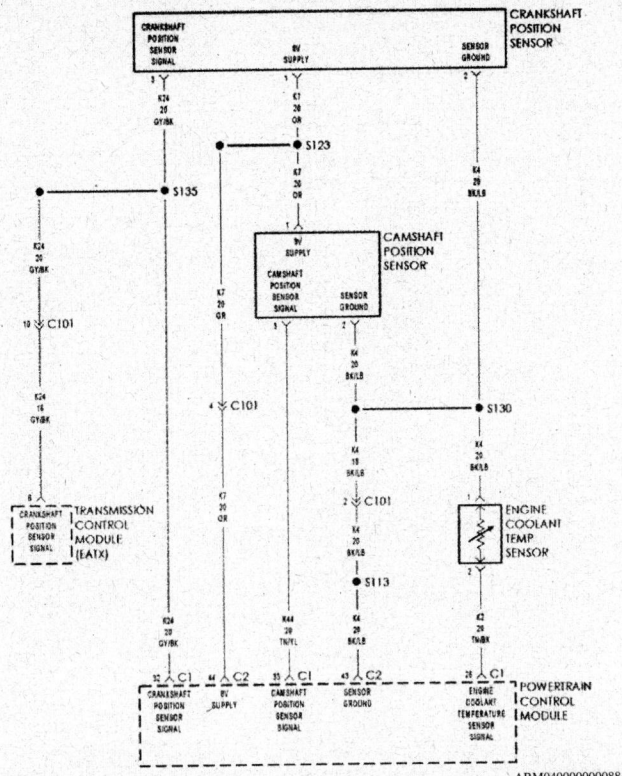

Fig. 14   Engine cooling fan wiring diagram. 2002 Neon

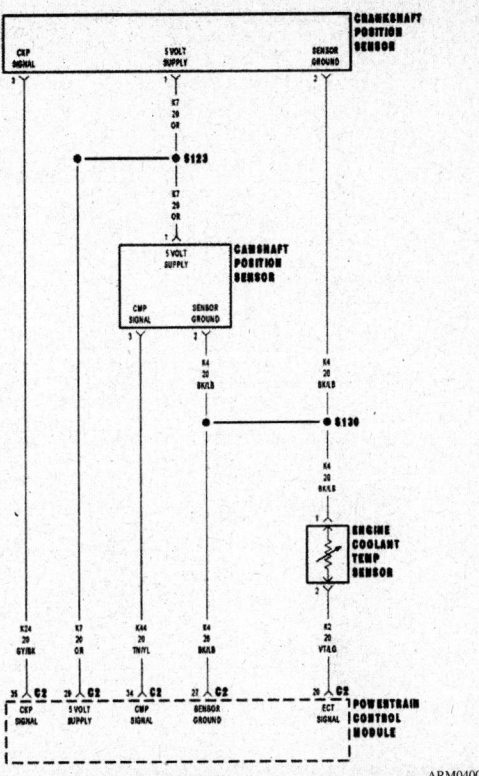

Fig. 15   Engine cooling fan wiring diagram (Part 1 of 3). 2003–05 Neon w/2.0L engine

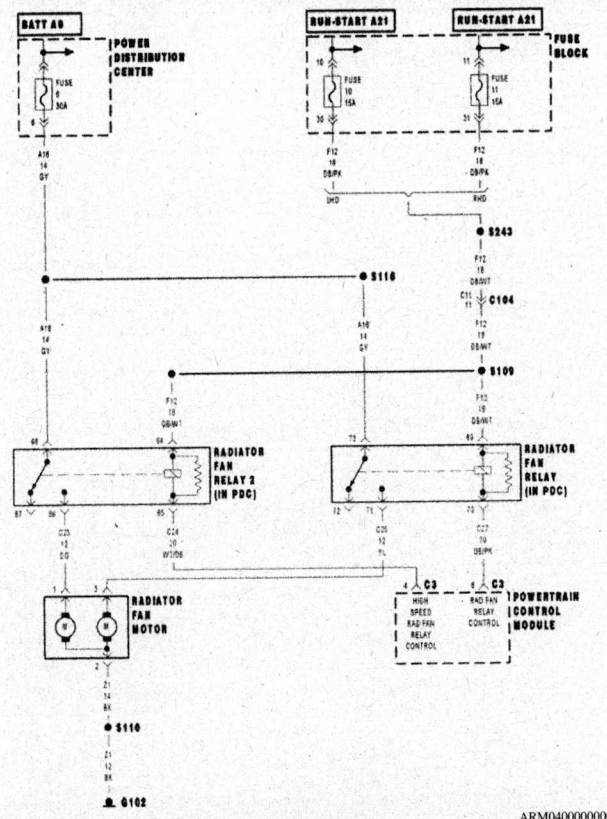

Fig. 15   Engine cooling fan wiring diagram (Part 2 of 3). 2003–05 Neon w/2.0L engine & automatic transaxle

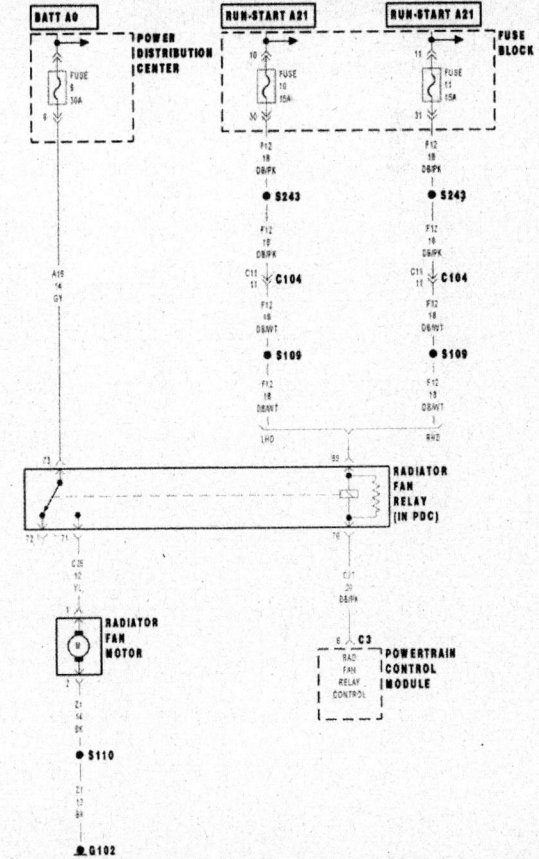

Fig. 15   Engine cooling fan wiring diagram (Part 2 of 3). 2003–05 Neon w/2.0L engine & manual transaxle

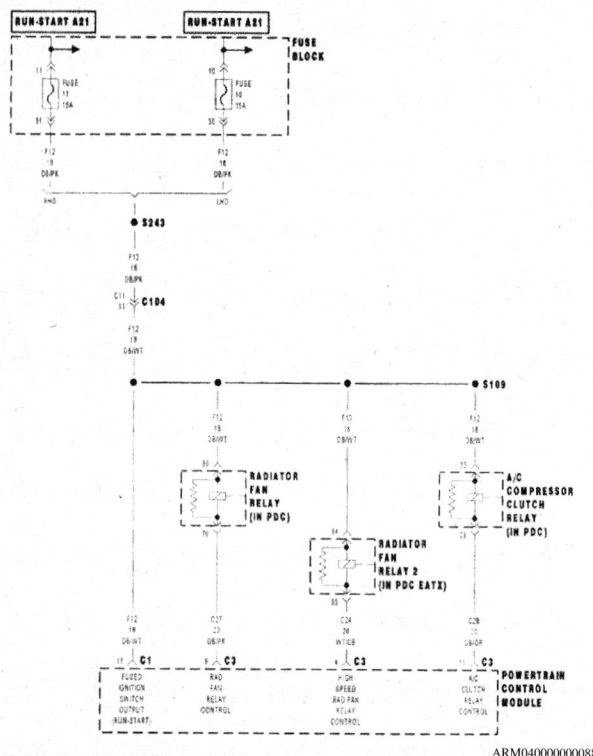

Fig. 15   Engine cooling fan wiring diagram (Part 3 of 3). 2003–05 Neon w/2.0L engine

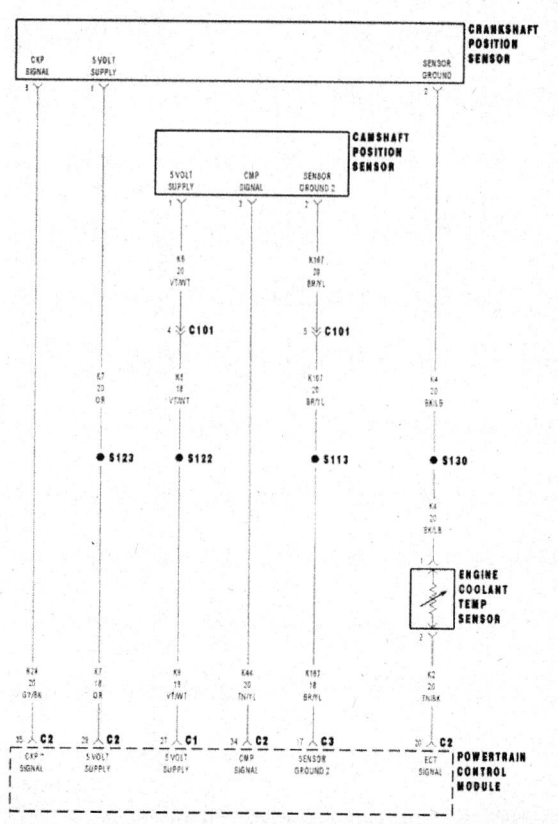

Fig. 16   Engine cooling fan wiring diagram (Part 1 of 4). 2003–05 Neon w/2.4L engine

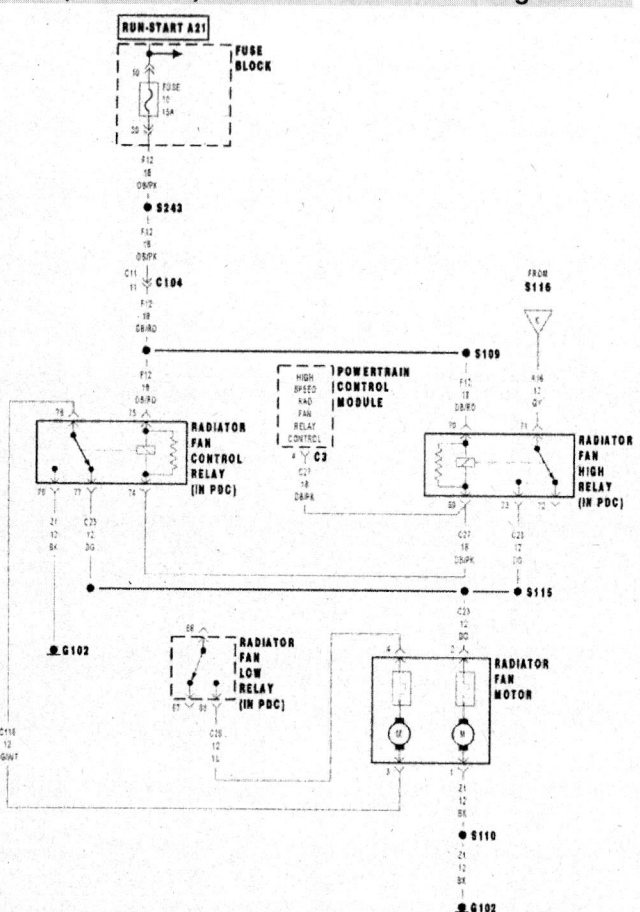

Fig. 16   Engine cooling fan wiring diagram (Part 2 of 4). 2003–05 Neon w/2.4L engine

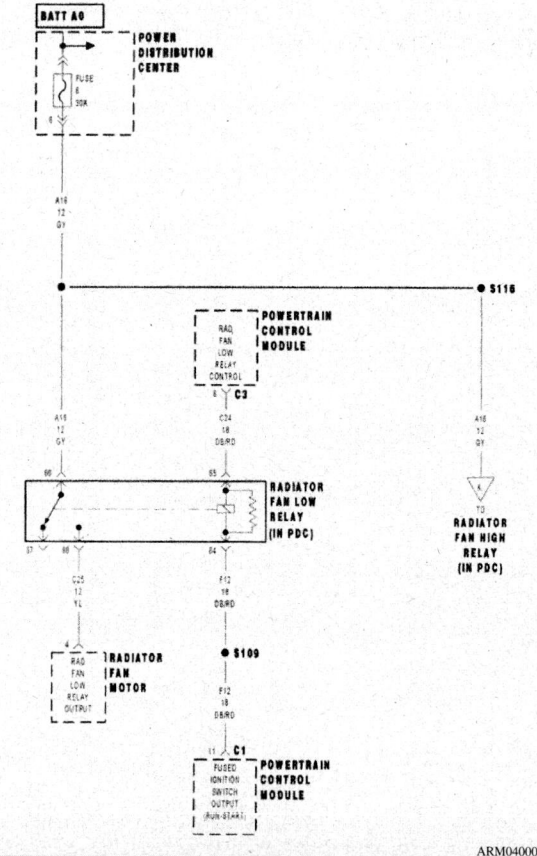

Fig. 16   Engine cooling fan wiring diagram (Part 3 of 4). 2003–05 Neon w/2.4L engine

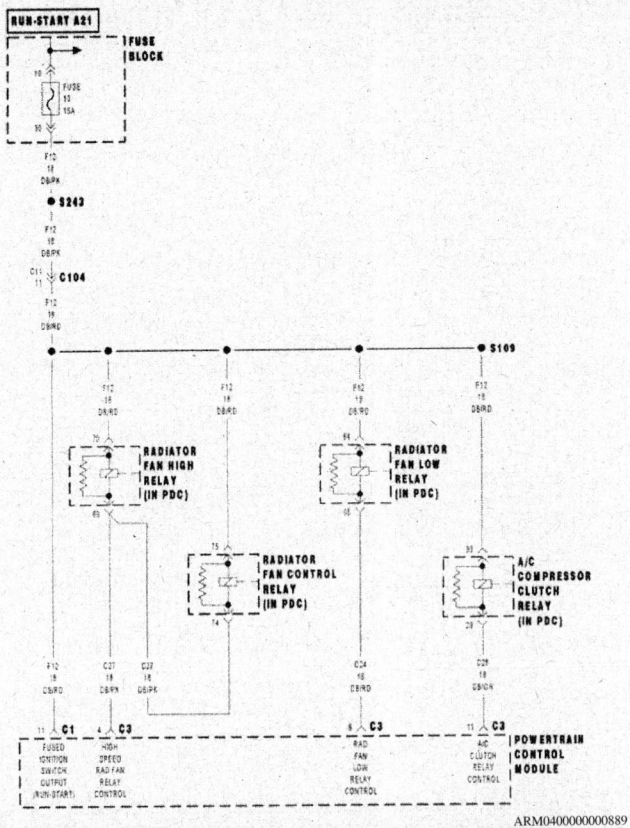

Fig. 16 Engine cooling fan wiring diagram (Part 4 of 4). 2003–05 Neon w/2.4L engine

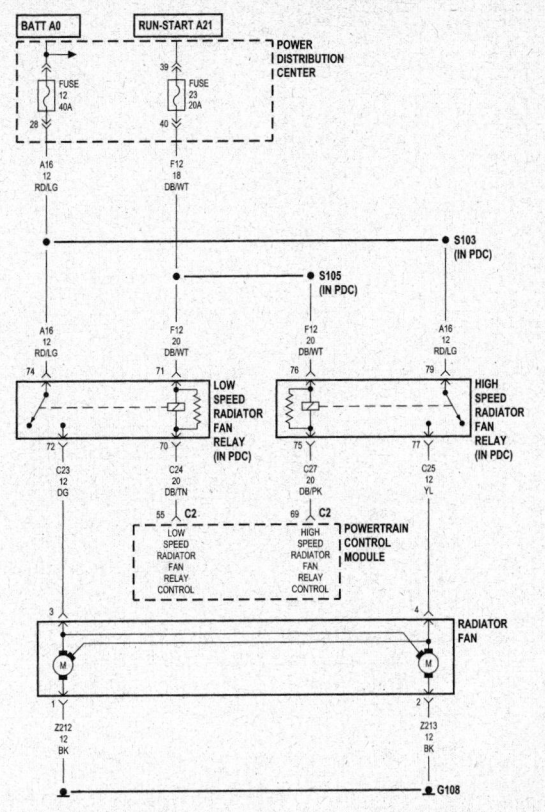

Fig. 17 Engine cooling fan wiring diagram (Part 1 of 3). 2001 Sebring Convertible, Sebring Sedan & Stratus Sedan

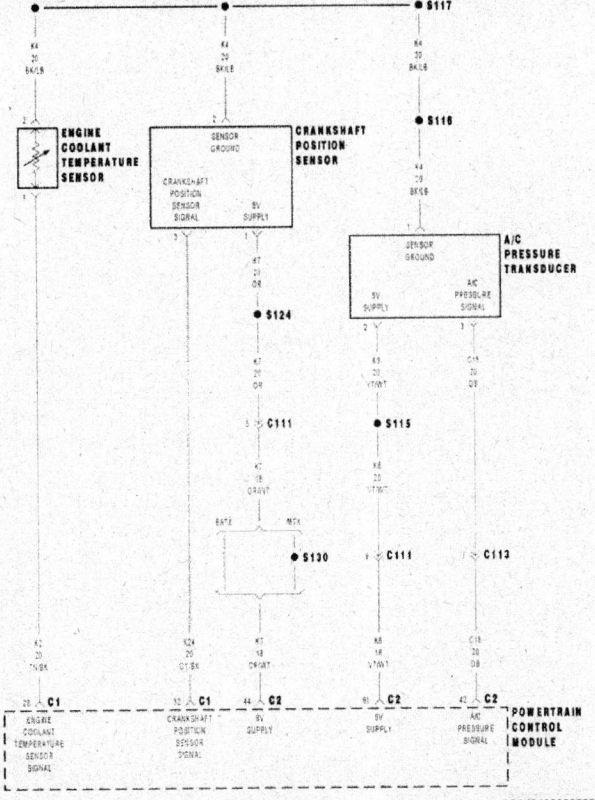

Fig. 17 Engine cooling fan wiring diagram (Part 2 of 3). 2001 Sebring Convertible, Sebring Sedan & Stratus Sedan

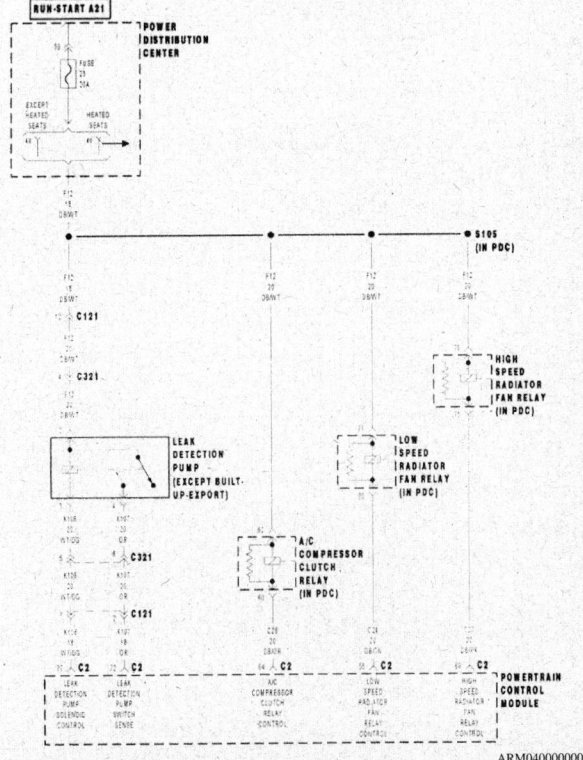

Fig. 17 Engine cooling fan wiring diagram (Part 3 of 3). 2001 Sebring Convertible, Sebring Sedan & Stratus Sedan

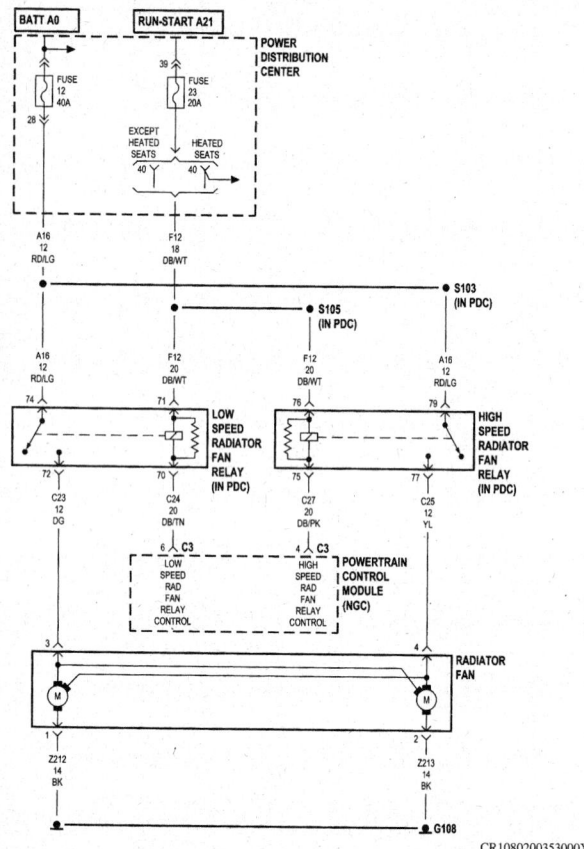

Fig. 18 Engine cooling fan wiring diagram (Part 1 of 3). 2003–05 Sebring Convertible, Sebring Sedan & Stratus Sedan

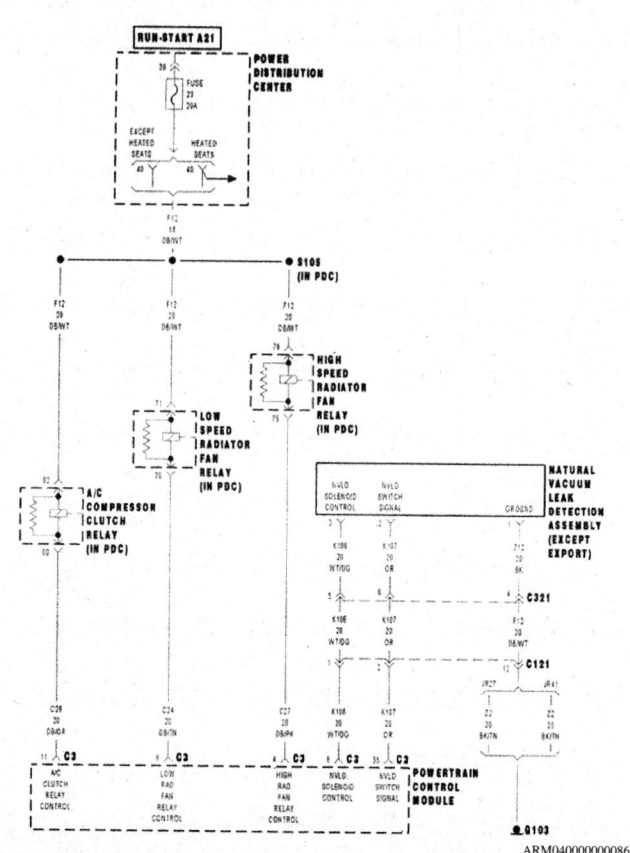

Fig. 18 Engine cooling fan wiring diagram (Part 2 of 3). 2003–05 Sebring Convertible, Sebring Sedan & Stratus Sedan

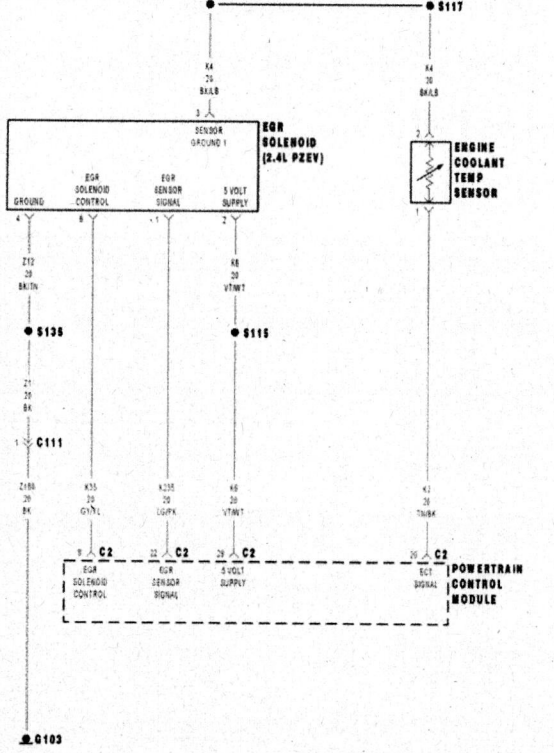

Fig. 18 Engine cooling fan wiring diagram (Part 3 of 3). 2003–05 Sebring Convertible, Sebring Sedan & Stratus Sedan w/2.0L & 2.4L engines

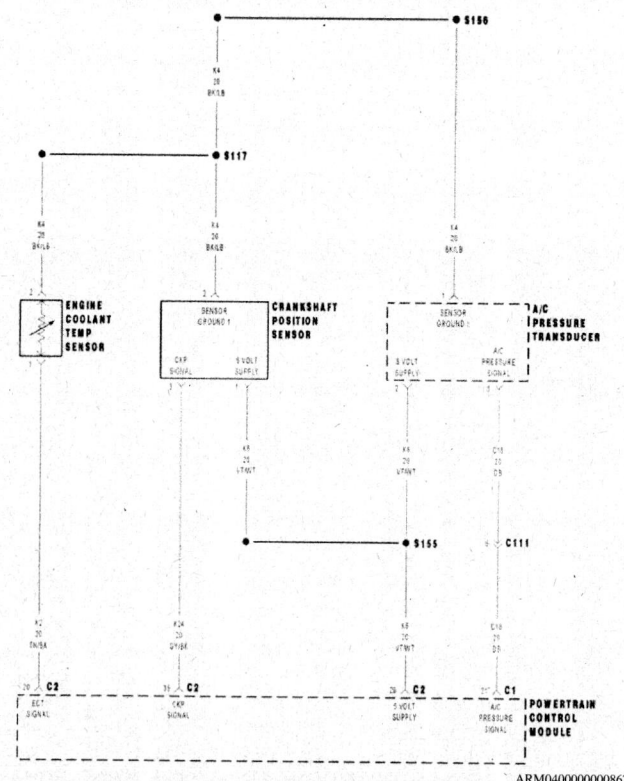

Fig. 18 Engine cooling fan wiring diagram (Part 3 of 3). 2003–05 Sebring Convertible, Sebring Sedan & Stratus Sedan w/2.7L engine

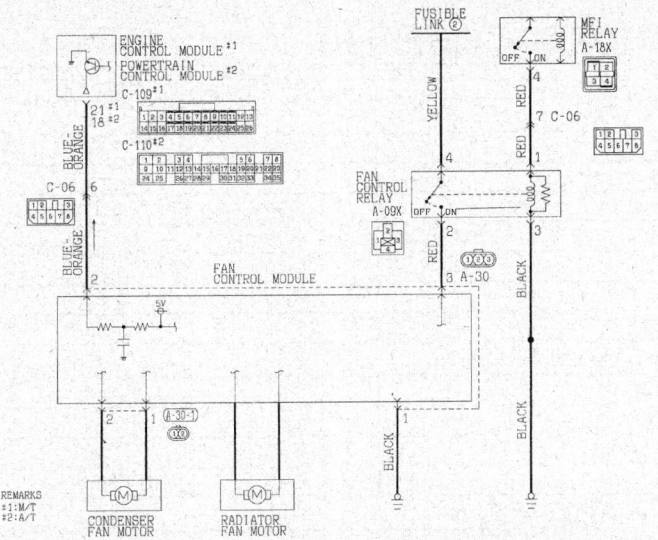

Fig. 19 Radiator & condenser fan wiring diagram. Sebring Coupe & Stratus Coupe w/2.4L engine

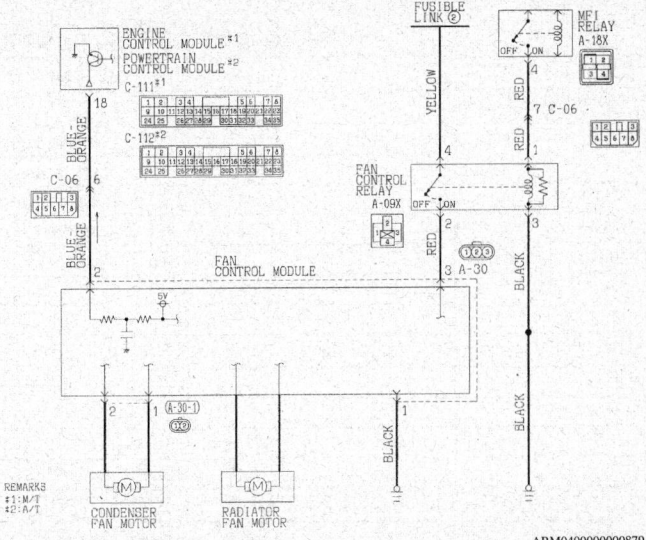

Fig. 20 Radiator & condenser fan wiring diagram. Sebring Coupe & Stratus Coupe w/3.0L engine

DIAGNOSTIC CHART INDEX

Test	Description	Page No.	Fig. No.
2002–04 CONCORDE, INTREPID & 300M			
P0110	IAT Sensor Stuck	8-25	39
P0111	IAT Sensor Performance	8-25	39
P0112	IAT Sensor Low	8-26	40
P0113	IAT Sensor High	8-26	41
P0116	ECT Performance	8-27	42
P0117	ECT Sensor Low	8-28	43
P0118	ECT Sensor High	8-28	44
P0480	Low Speed Fan Control Relay Circuit	8-29	45
P0481	High Speed Fan Control Relay Circuit	8-29	46
P0532	Air Conditioning Pressure Sensor Low	8-30	47
P0533	Air Conditioning Pressure Sensor High	8-30	48
P0711	Transmission Temperature Sensor Performance	8-31	49
P0712	Transmission Temperature Sensor Low	8-32	50
P0713	Transmission Temperature Sensor High	8-33	51
P0714	Transmission Temperature Sensor Intermittent	8-34	52
P0720	Output Speed Sensor Error	8-34	53
CROSSFIRE			
—	Refer to "Symptom Based Testing"	—	—
LHS, 2001 CONCORDE, INTREPID & 300M			
P0112	IAT Sensor Voltage Low	8-20	31
P0113	IAT Sensor Voltage High	8-21	32
P0117	ECT Sensor Voltage Low	8-21	33
P0118	ECT Sensor Voltage High	8-22	34
P0720	Output Speed Sensor Error	8-22	35
P1489	High Speed Fan Control Relay Circuit	8-23	36
P1490	Low Speed Fan Control Relay Circuit	8-24	37
P1738	High Temperature Operation Activated	8-25	38
2001–02 NEON			
P0117	ECT Sensor Voltage Too Low	8-35	54
P0118	ECT Sensor Voltage Too High	8-36	55
P1490	Low Speed Fan Control Relay Circuit	8-36	56

Continued

DIAGNOSTIC CHART INDEX—Continued

Test	Description	Page No.	Fig. No.
2003–05 NEON			
P0116	ECT Performance (2003)	8-37	57
	ECT Performance (2004–05)	8-38	58
P0117	ECT Temperature Sensor Low	8-39	59
P0118	ECT Temperature Sensor High	8-39	60
P0480	Cooling Fan No 1 Control Circuit	8-40	61
P0481	Cooling Fan No 2 Control Circuit Open (w/2.0L Engine)	8-40	62
	Cooling Fan No 2 Control Circuit Open (w/2.4L Engine)	8-41	63
2001–02 SEBRING CONVERTIBLE, SEBRING SEDAN & STRATUS SEDAN			
P0117	ECT Sensor Voltage Too Low	8-41	64
P0118	ECT Sensor Voltage Too High	8-42	65
P1489	High Speed Fan Control Relay Circuit	8-43	66
P1490	Low Speed Fan Control Relay Circuit	8-43	67
2003–05 SEBRING CONVERTIBLE, SEBRING SEDAN & STRATUS SEDAN			
P0116	ECT Performance	8-44	68
P0117	ECT Sensor Low	8-45	69
P0118	ECT Sensor High	8-45	70
P0480	Low Speed Fan Control Relay Circuit	8-46	71
P1489	High Speed Fan Control Relay Circuit	8-46	72
P1490	Low Speed Fan Control Relay Circuit	8-47	73
2001 SEBRING COUPE & STRATUS COUPE			
—	Condenser Fan Inoperative	8-14	23
—	Radiator & Condenser Fans Do Not Change Speed Or Stop	8-14	22
—	Radiator & Condenser Fans Inoperative	8-13	21
—	Radiator Fan Inoperative	8-15	24
2002 SEBRING COUPE & STRATUS COUPE			
—	Radiator & Condenser Fans Do Not Change Speed Or Stop	8-16	26
—	Radiator & Condenser Fans Do Not Operate	8-15	25
2003–05 SEBRING COUPE & STRATUS COUPE			
—	Condenser Fan Does Not Operate	8-20	30
—	Radiator & Condenser Fans Do Not Change Speed Or Stop	8-19	28
—	Radiator & Condenser Fans Do Not Operate.	8-17	27
—	Radiator Fan Does Not Operate	8-19	29

CIRCUIT OPERATION
- The fan control module is powered from fusible link number 5.
- The ECM <M/T> or PCM <A/T> judges the required revolution speed of radiator fan motor and condenser fan motor using the input signals transmitted from A/C switch, automatic compressor controller, vehicle speed sensor and engine coolant temperature sensor. The ECM <M/T> or PCM <A/T> activates the fan control module to drive the radiator fan motor and condenser fan motor.

TECHNICAL DESCRIPTION
- The cause could be a malfunction of the fan control module power supply or ground circuit.
- The cause could also be a malfunction of the fan control module or the ECM <M/T> or PCM <A/T>.

TROUBLESHOOTING HINTS
- Malfunction of fusible link
- Malfunction of fan control relay
- Malfunction of fan control module
- Malfunction of ECM <M/T> or PCM <A/T>
- Damaged wiring harness or connector

DIAGNOSIS

Required Special Tool:
MB991223: Harness Set

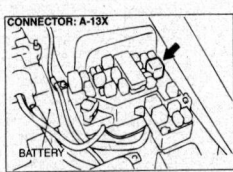

STEP 1. Check the circuit at fan control module connector A-30.
(1) Disconnect fan control module connector A-30, and measure at the harness side connector.
(2) Measure the voltage between terminal number 3 and ground.
  - When the ignition switch is turned to "ON" position, voltage should be battery positive voltage.
Q: Is the voltage battery positive voltage when the ignition switch is turned to "ON" position?
YES : Go to Step 7.
NO : Go to Step 2.

STEP 2. Check the fan control relay.
Q: Is the fan control relay in good condition?
YES : Go to Step 3.
NO : Replace it, then go to Step 10.

CR1080000297010X

Fig. 21 Radiator & Condenser Fans Inoperative (Part 1 of 6). 2001 Sebring Coupe & Stratus Coupe

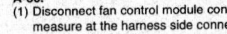

STEP 6. Check for continuity between fan control relay connector A-13X and ground.
Q: Are the harness wires between fan control relay connector A-13X and ground damaged?
YES : Repair or replace them, then go to Step 12.
NO : There is no action to be taken.

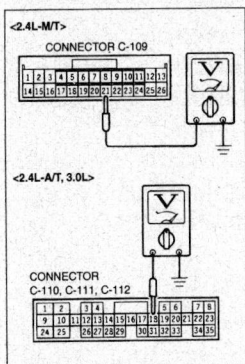

STEP 7. Check the circuit at fan control module connector A-30.
(1) Disconnect fan control module connector A-30, and measure at the harness side connector.
(2) Measure the resistance between terminal number 1 and ground.
Q: Is the resistance less than 2 ohm?
YES : Go to Step 9.
NO : Go to Step 8.

STEP 8. Check the harness wire between fan control module connector A-30 and ground.
Q: Are the harness wires between fan control connector A-30 and ground damaged?
YES : Repair or replace them, then go to Step 12.
NO : There is no action to be taken.

CR1080000297030X

Fig. 21 Radiator & Condenser Fans Inoperative (Part 3 of 6). 2001 Sebring Coupe & Stratus Coupe

STEP 9. Check the circuit at ECM connector C-109 <2.4L-M/T>, C-111 <3.0L-M/T>or PCM connector C-110 <2.4L-A/T>, C-112 <3.0L-A/T>.
(1) Connect ECM connector C-109 <2.4L-M/T>, C-111 <3.0L-M/T> or PCM connector C-110 <2.4L-A/T>, C-112 <3.0L-A/T>.
(2) Start the engine and allow it to idle.
(3) Measure the voltage between terminal number 21 <2.4L-M/T> or 18 <2.4L-A/T, 3.0L> and ground.
Q: Is the voltage 0.7 volt or more when the radiator fan is operating?
YES : Go to Step 11.
NO : Go to Step 10.

CR1080000297040X

Fig. 21 Radiator & Condenser Fans Inoperative (Part 4 of 6). 2001 Sebring Coupe & Stratus Coupe

STEP 3. Check for continuity between fusible link number 5 and fan control relay connector A-13X.
Q: Are the harness wires between fusible link number 5 and fan control relay connector A-13X damaged?
YES : Repair or replace them, then go to Step 12.
NO : Go to Step 4.

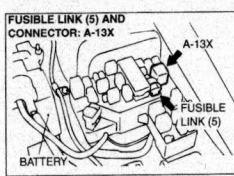

STEP 4. Check for continuity between fan control relay connector A-13X and fan control module connector A-30.
Q: Are the harness wires between fan control relay connector A-13X and fan control module connector A-30 damaged?
YES : Repair or replace them, then go to Step 12
NO : Go to Step 5.

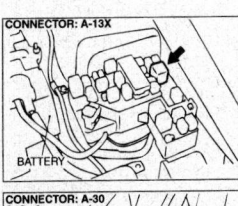

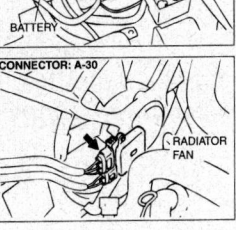

STEP 5. Check for continuity between MFI relay connector A-21X and fan control relay connector A-13X .
Q: Are the harness wires between MFI relay connector A-21X and fan control relay connector A-13X damaged?
YES : Repair or replace them, then go to Step 12.
NO : Go to Step 6.

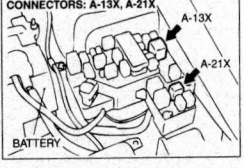

CR1080000297020X

Fig. 21 Radiator & Condenser Fans Inoperative (Part 2 of 6). 2001 Sebring Coupe & Stratus Coupe

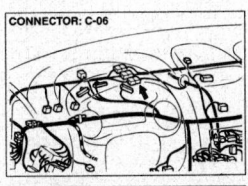

STEP 10. Check the harness wire between ECM connector C-109 <2.4L-M/T>, C-111 <3.0L-M/T>or PCM connector C-110 <2.4L-A/T>, C-112 <3.0L-A/T> and fan control module connector A-30.
NOTE: If intermediate connector C-06 is damaged, repair or replace it.

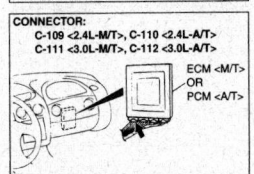

Q: Are the harness wires between ECM connector C-109 <2.4L-M/T>or, C-111 <3.0L-M/T>or PCM connector C-110 <2.4L-A/T> , C-112 <3.0L-A/T> and fan control module connector A-30 damaged?
YES : Repair or replace them, then go to Step 12.
NO : Go to Step 11.

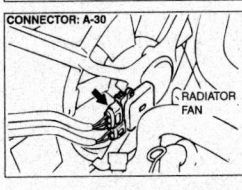

CR1080000297050X

Fig. 21 Radiator & Condenser Fans Inoperative (Part 5 of 6). 2001 Sebring Coupe & Stratus Coupe

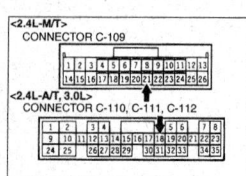

STEP 11. Check the fan control module at ECM connector C-109 <2.4L-M/T>, C-111 <3.0L-M/T>or PCM connector C-110 <2.4L-A/T> , C-112 <3.0L-A/T>.

(1) Disconnect ECM connector C-109 <2.4L-M/T>, C-111 <3.0L-M/T> or PCM connector C-110 <2.4L-A/T>, C-112 <3.0L-A/T>.
(2) Pull out pin 21 <2.4L-M/T> or 18 <2.4L-A/T, 3.0L> to disconnect it.
(3) Reconnect ECM connector C-109 <2.4L-M/T>, C-111 <3.0L-M/T> or PCM connector C-110 <2.4L-A/T>, C-112 <3.0L-A/T> with pin 21 <2.4L-M/T> or 18 <2.4L-A/T, 3.0L> still removed.
(4) Turn the ignition switch to "ON" position.

Q: Do the radiator fan motor and condenser fan motor operate?
   YES : Replace the ECM <M/T> or PCM <A/T>. Then go to Step 12.
   NO : Replace the radiator fan motor and fan control module assembly.Then go to Step 12 .

STEP 12. Check the symptoms.
Q: Do the radiator fan and condenser fan operate correctly?
   YES : This diagnosis is complete.
   NO : Return to Step 1.

CR1080000297060X

Fig. 21 Radiator & Condenser Fans Inoperative (Part 6 of 6). 2001 Sebring Coupe & Stratus Coupe

STEP 1. Check the fan control relay.
Refer to P.7-18.

Q: Is the fan control relay in good condition?
   YES : Go to Step 2.
   NO : Replace the part, then go to Step 6.

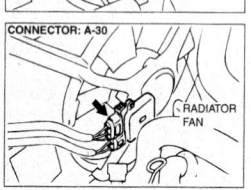

STEP 2. Check the harness wire between fan control relay connector A-13X and fan control module connector A-30.
Q: Are the harness wire between fan control relay connector A-13X and fan control module connector A-30 damaged?
   YES : Repair or replace the part, then go to Step 6.
   NO : Go to Step 3.

STEP 3. Check the circuit at ECM connector C-109 <2.4L-M/T>, C-111 <3.0L-M/T>or PCM connector C-110 <2.4L-A/T> , C-112 <3.0L-A/T>.
(1) Connect ECM connector C-109 <2.4L-M/T>, C-111 <3.0L-M/T> or PCM connector C-110 <2.4L-A/T>, C-112 <3.0L-A/T>.
(2) Start the engine and run it at idle. [Engine coolant temperature: 80°C (176°Φ) ορ λεσσ]
(3) Measure the voltage between terminal number 21 <2.4L-M/T> or 18 <2.4L-A/T, 3.0L> and ground.

Q: Is the voltage 0 - 0.3 volt when radiator fan is not operating?
   YES : Go to Step 6.
   NO : Go to Step 4.

CR1080000298020X

Fig. 22 Radiator & Condenser Fans Do Not Change Speed Or Stop (Part 2 of 3). 2001 Sebring Coupe & Stratus Coupe

TECHNICAL DESCRIPTION
The cause could be a malfunction of the radiator fan motor or an open circuit between the fan control module and the radiator fan motor.

TROUBLESHOOTING HINTS
- Malfunction of radiator fan motor
- Malfunction of fan control module

CR1080000299010X

Fig. 23 Condenser Fan Inoperative (Part 1 of 2). 2001 Sebring Coupe & Stratus Coupe

---

Radiator Fan and Condenser Fan Drive Circuit

CIRCUIT OPERATION
- The fan control module is powered from fusible link number 5.
- The ECM <M/T> or PCM <A/T> judges the required revolution speed of radiator fan motor and condenser fan motor using the input signals transmitted from A/C switch, automatic compressor controller, vehicle speed sensor and engine coolant temperature sensor. The ECM <M/T> or PCM <A/T> activates the fan control module to drive the radiator fan motor and condenser fan motor.

TECHNICAL DESCRIPTION
The fan control module has variable control of the radiator fan motor and the condenser fan motor speeds using signals transmitted from the ECM <M/T> or PCM <A/T>.

TROUBLESHOOTING HINTS
- Malfunction of fan control relay
- Malfunction of fan control module
- Malfunction of ECM <M/T> or PCM <A/T>
- Malfunction of ECM <M/T> or PCM <A/T>

DIAGNOSIS

Required Special Tool:
MB991223: Harness Set

CR1080000298010X

Fig. 22 Radiator & Condenser Fans Do Not Change Speed Or Stop (Part 1 of 3). 2001 Sebring Coupe & Stratus Coupe

STEP 4. Check the harness wire between ECM connector C-109 <2.4L-M/T>, C-111 <3.0L-M/T> or PCM connector C-110 <2.4L-A/T> , C-112 <3.0L-A/T> and fan control module connector A-30.
NOTE: If intermediate connector C-06 is damaged, repair or replace it.

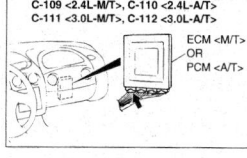

Q: Are the harness wires between ECM connector C-109 <2.4L-M/T>, C-111 <3.0L-M/T>or PCM connector C-110 <2.4L-A/T> , C-112 <3.0L-A/T> and fan control module connector A-30 damaged?
   YES : Repair or replace them, then go to Step 6.
   NO : Go to Step 5.

STEP 5. Check the fan control module at ECM connector C-109 <2.4L-M/T>, C-111 <3.0L-M/T>or PCM connector C-110 <2.4L-A/T> , C-112 <3.0L-A/T>.
(1) Connect ECM connector C-109 <2.4L-M/T>, C-111 <3.0L-M/T> or PCM connector C-110 <2.4L-A/T>, C-112 <3.0L-A/T>.
(2) Turn the ignition switch to " ON" position.
(3) Pull out the terminal number 21 <2.4L-M/T> or 18 <2.4L-A/T, 3.0L> and connect it to the body ground.

Q: Do the radiator fan motor and condenser fan motor stop?
   YES : Replace the ECM <M/T> or PCM <A/T>. Then go to Step 6.
   NO : Replace the radiator fan motor and fan control module assembly. Then go to Step 6 .

STEP 6. Check the symptoms.
Q: Do the radiator fan and condenser fan operate correctly?
   YES : This diagnosis is complete.
   NO : Return to Step 1.

CR1080000298030X

Fig. 22 Radiator & Condenser Fans Do Not Change Speed Or Stop (Part 3 of 3). 2001 Sebring Coupe & Stratus Coupe

DIAGNOSIS

Replace the radiator fan motor and fan control module assembly.

Q: Does the radiator fan operate correctly?
   YES : There is no action to be taken?
   NO : Repair the wiring harness between the fan control module and the radiator fan motor.

CR1080000299020X

Fig. 23 Condenser Fan Inoperative (Part 2 of 2). 2001 Sebring Coupe & Stratus Coupe

Radiator Fan and Condenser Fan Drive Circuit

CIRCUIT OPERATION

- The fan control module is powered from fusible link number 5.
- The ECM <M/T> or PCM <A/T> judges the required revolution speed of radiator fan motor and condenser fan motor using the input signals transmitted from A/C switch, automatic compressor controller, vehicle speed sensor and engine coolant temperature sensor. The ECM <M/T> or PCM <A/T> activates the fan control module to drive the radiator fan motor and condenser fan motor.

TECHNICAL DESCRIPTION
The cause could be a malfunction of the condenser fan motor or of the fan control module.

TROUBLESHOOTING HINTS
- Malfunction of condenser fan motor
- Malfunction of fan control module

DIAGNOSIS

STEP 1. Check the condenser fan motor.
Q: Is the condenser fan in good condition?
YES : Replace the radiator fan motor and fan control module assembly. Then go to Step 3.
NO : Go to Step 2.

STEP 2. Check the fan control module.
Refer to P.7-18.
Q: Is the fan control module in good condition?
YES : Go to Step 3.
NO : Replace the fan control module, then go to Step 3.

STEP 3. Check the symptoms.
Q: Does the condenser fan operate correctly?
YES : This diagnosis is complete.
NO : Return to Step1.

CR1080000300000X

Fig. 24 Radiator Fan Inoperative. 2001 Sebring Coupe & Stratus Coupe

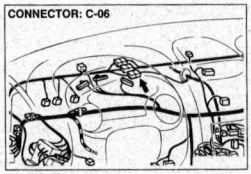

CONNECTOR: C-06

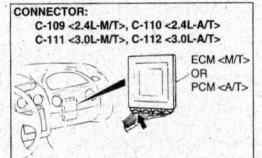

CONNECTOR:
C-109 <2.4L-M/T>, C-110 <2.4L-A/T>
C-111 <3.0L-M/T>, C-112 <3.0L-A/T>
ECM <M/T> OR PCM <A/T>

CIRCUIT OPERATION

- The fan control module is powered from fusible link number 2.
- The ECM <M/T> or PCM <A/T> judges the required revolution speed of radiator fan motor and condenser fan motor using the input signals transmitted from A/C switch, automatic compressor controller, vehicle speed sensor <M/T>, output shaft speed sensor <A/T> and engine coolant temperature sensor. The ECM <M/T> or PCM <A/T> activates the fan control module to drive the radiator fan motor and condenser fan motor.

TECHNICAL DESCRIPTION

- The cause could be a malfunction of the fan control module power supply or ground circuit.
- The cause could also be a malfunction of the fan control module or the ECM <M/T> or PCM <A/T>.

TROUBLESHOOTING HINTS
- Malfunction of fusible link
- Malfunction of fan control relay
- Malfunction of fan control module
- Malfunction of ECM <M/T> or PCM <A/T>
- Damaged wiring harness or connector

DIAGNOSIS

Required Special Tool:
MB991223: Harness Set

STEP 1. Check the fusible link number 2.
Q: Is the fusible link number 2 good condition?
YES : Go to Step 2.
NO : Replace it, then go to Step 13.

STEP 2. Check the circuit at fan control module connector A-30.
(1) Disconnect fan control module connector A-30, and measure at the harness side connector.
(2) Measure the voltage between terminal number 3 and ground.
- When the ignition switch is turned to "ON" position, voltage should be battery positive voltage.
Q: Is the voltage battery positive voltage when the ignition switch is turned to "ON" position?
YES : Go to Step 8.
NO : Go to Step 3.

CR1080200331020X

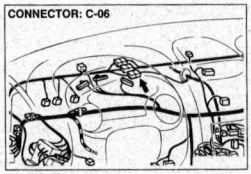

CONNECTOR A-30

Fig. 25 Radiator & Condenser Fans Do Not Operate (Part 2 of 7). 2002 Sebring Coupe & Stratus Coupe

---

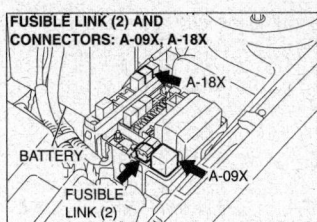

FUSIBLE LINK (2) AND CONNECTORS: A-09X, A-18X
A-18X
BATTERY
A-09X
FUSIBLE LINK (2)

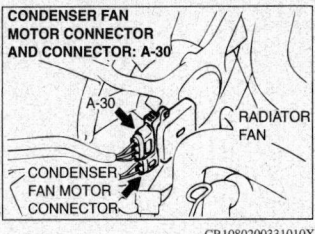

CONDENSER FAN MOTOR CONNECTOR AND CONNECTOR: A-30
A-30
RADIATOR FAN
CONDENSER FAN MOTOR CONNECTOR

CR1080200331010X

Fig. 25 Radiator & Condenser Fans Do Not Operate (Part 1 of 7). 2002 Sebring Coupe & Stratus Coupe

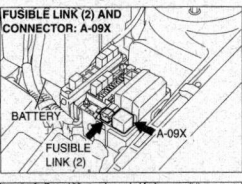

FUSIBLE LINK (2) AND CONNECTOR: A-09X
BATTERY
FUSIBLE LINK (2)
A-09X

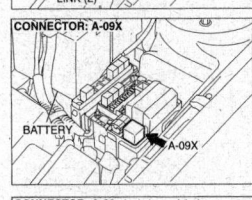

CONNECTOR: A-09X
BATTERY
A-09X

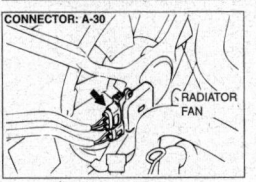

CONNECTOR: A-30
RADIATOR FAN

STEP 3. Check the fan control relay.
Refer to P.7-18.
Q: Is the fan control relay in good condition?
YES : Go to Step 4.
NO : Replace it, then go to Step 11.

STEP 4. Check for continuity between fusible link number 2 and fan control relay connector A-09X.
Q: Are the harness wires between fusible link number 2 and fan control relay connector A-09X damaged?
YES : Repair or replace them, then go to Step 13.
NO : Go to Step 5.

STEP 5. Check for continuity between fan control relay connector A-09X and fan control module connector A-30.
Q: Are the harness wires between fan control relay connector A-09X and fan control module connector A-30 damaged?
YES : Repair or replace them, then go to Step 13.
NO : Go to Step 6.

CR1080200331030X

Fig. 25 Radiator & Condenser Fans Do Not Operate (Part 3 of 7). 2002 Sebring Coupe & Stratus Coupe

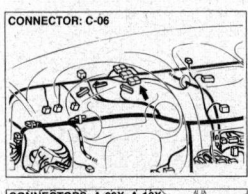

CONNECTOR: C-06

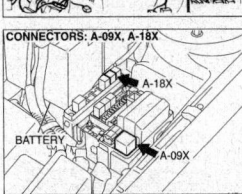

CONNECTORS: A-09X, A-18X
A-18X
BATTERY
A-09X

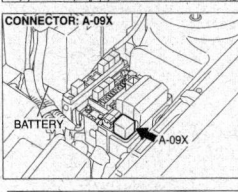

CONNECTOR: A-09X
BATTERY
A-09X

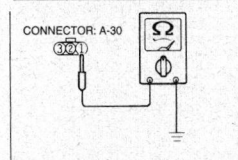

CONNECTOR: A-30

STEP 6. Check for continuity between MFI relay connector A-18X and fan control relay connector A-09X.
NOTE: If intermediate connector C-06 is damaged, repair or replace it.

Q: Are the harness wires between MFI relay connector A-18X and fan control relay connector A-09X damaged?
YES : Repair or replace them, then go to Step 13.
NO : Go to Step 7.

STEP 7. Check for continuity between fan control relay connector A-09X and ground.
Q: Are the harness wires between fan control relay connector A-09X and ground damaged?
YES : Repair or replace them, then go to Step 13.
NO : There is no action to be taken.

STEP 8. Check the circuit at fan control module connector A-30.
(1) Disconnect fan control module connector A-30, and measure at the harness side connector.
(2) Measure the resistance between terminal number 1 and ground.
Q: Is the resistance less than 2 ohm?
YES : Go to Step 10.
NO : Go to Step 9.

CR1080200331040X

Fig. 25 Radiator & Condenser Fans Do Not Operate (Part 4 of 7). 2002 Sebring Coupe & Stratus Coupe

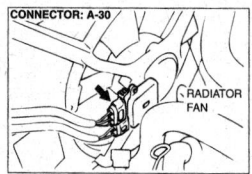

CONNECTOR: A-30

RADIATOR FAN

STEP 9. Check the harness wire between fan control module connector A-30 and ground.

Q: Are the harness wires between fan control module connector A-30 and ground damaged?

   YES : Repair or replace them, then go to Step 13.
   NO : There is no action to be taken.

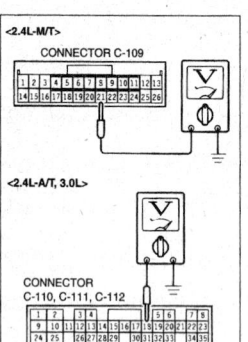

<2.4L-M/T>
CONNECTOR C-109

<2.4L-A/T, 3.0L>

CONNECTOR
C-110, C-111, C-112

STEP 10. Check the circuit at ECM connector C-109 <2.4L-M/T>, C-111 <3.0L-M/T> or PCM connector C-110 <2.4L-A/T>, C-112 <3.0L-A/T>.

(1) Connect ECM connector C-109 <2.4L-M/T>, C-111 <3.0L-M/T> or PCM connector C-110 <2.4L-A/T>, C-112 <3.0L-A/T>.

(2) Start the engine and allow it to idle.

(3) Measure the voltage between terminal number 21 <2.4L-M/T> or 18 <2.4L-A/T, 3.0L> and ground.

Q: Is the voltage 0.7 volt or more when the radiator fan is operating?

   YES : Go to Step 12.
   NO : Go to Step 11.

CR1080200331050X

Fig. 25 Radiator & Condenser Fans Do Not Operate (Part 5 of 7). 2002 Sebring Coupe & Stratus Coupe

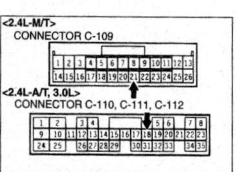

<2.4L-M/T>
CONNECTOR C-109

<2.4L-A/T, 3.0L>
CONNECTOR C-110, C-111, C-112

STEP 12. Check the fan control module at ECM connector C-109 <2.4L-M/T>, C-111 <3.0L-M/T> or PCM connector C-110 <2.4L-A/T>, C-112 <3.0L-A/T>.

(1) Disconnect ECM connector C-109 <2.4L-M/T>, C-111 <3.0L-M/T> or PCM connector C-110 <2.4L-A/T>, C-112 <3.0L-A/T>.

(2) Pull out pin 21 <2.4L-M/T> or 18 <2.4L-A/T, 3.0L> to disconnect it.

(3) Reconnect ECM connector C-109 <2.4L-M/T>, C-111 <3.0L-M/T> or PCM connector C-110 <2.4L-A/T>, C-112 <3.0L-A/T> with pin 21 <2.4L-M/T> or 18 <2.4L-A/T, 3.0L> still removed.

(4) Turn the ignition switch to "ON" position.

Q: Do the radiator fan motor and condenser fan motor operate?

   YES : Replace the ECM <M/T> or PCM <A/T>. Then go to Step 13.
   NO : Replace the radiator fan motor and fan control module assembly. Then go to Step 13.

STEP 13. Check the symptoms.

Q: Do the radiator fan and condenser fan operate correctly?

   YES : This diagnosis is complete.
   NO : Return to Step 1.

CR1080200331070X

Fig. 25 Radiator & Condenser Fans Do Not Operate (Part 7 of 7). 2002 Sebring Coupe & Stratus Coupe

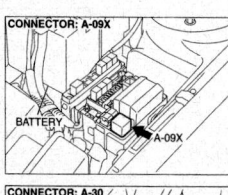

CONNECTOR: A-09X

BATTERY

A-09X

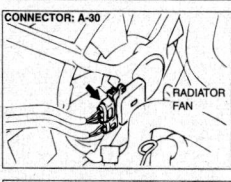

CONNECTOR: A-30

RADIATOR FAN

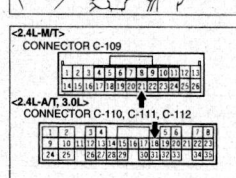

<2.4L-M/T>
CONNECTOR C-109

<2.4L-A/T, 3.0L>
CONNECTOR C-110, C-111, C-112

STEP 1. Check the fan control relay.

Q: Is the fan control relay in good condition?

   YES : Go to Step 2.
   NO : Replace the part, then go to Step 6.

STEP 2. Check the harness wire between fan control relay connector A-09X and fan control module connector A-30.

Q: Are the harness wire between fan control relay connector A-09X and fan control module connector A-30 damaged?

   YES : Repair or replace the part, then go to Step 6.
   NO : Go to Step 3.

STEP 3. Check the circuit at ECM connector C-109 <2.4L-M/T>, C-111 <3.0L-M/T> or PCM connector C-110 <2.4L-A/T>, C-112 <3.0L-A/T>.

(1) Connect ECM connector C-109 <2.4L-M/T>, C-111 <3.0L-M/T> or PCM connector C-110 <2.4L-A/T>, C-112 <3.0L-A/T>.

(2) Start the engine and run it at idle. [Engine coolant temperature: 80°C (176°F) or less]

(3) Measure the voltage between terminal number 21 <2.4L-M/T> or 18 <2.4L-A/T, 3.0L> and ground.

Q: Is the voltage 0 – 0.3 volt when radiator fan is not operating?

   YES : Go to Step 6.
   NO : Go to Step 4.

CR1080200332020X

Fig. 26 Radiator & Condenser Fans Do Not Change Speed Or Stop (Part 2 of 3). 2002 Sebring Coupe & Stratus Coupe

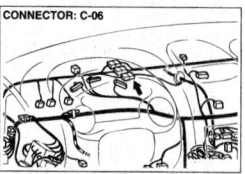

CONNECTOR: C-06

STEP 11. Check the harness wire between ECM connector C-109 <2.4L-M/T>, C-111 <3.0L-M/T> or PCM connector C-110 <2.4L-A/T>, C-112 <3.0L-A/T> and fan control module connector A-30.

NOTE: If intermediate connector C-06 is damaged, repair or replace it.

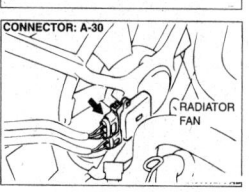

CONNECTOR:
C-109 <2.4L-M/T>, C-110 <2.4L-A/T>
C-111 <3.0L-M/T>, C-112 <3.0L-A/T>

ECM <M/T>
OR
PCM <A/T>

CONNECTOR: A-30

RADIATOR FAN

Q: Are the harness wires between ECM connector C-109 <2.4L-M/T>, C-111 <3.0L-M/T> or PCM connector C-110 <2.4L-A/T>, C-112 <3.0L-A/T> and fan control module connector A-30 damaged?

   YES : Repair or replace them, then go to Step 13.
   NO : Go to Step 12.

CR1080200331060X

Fig. 25 Radiator & Condenser Fans Do Not Operate (Part 6 of 7). 2002 Sebring Coupe & Stratus Coupe

CIRCUIT OPERATION

- The fan control module is powered from fusible link number 2.
- The ECM <M/T> or PCM <A/T> judges the required revolution speed of radiator fan motor and condenser fan motor using the input signals transmitted from A/C switch, automatic compressor controller, vehicle speed sensor <M/T>, output shaft speed sensor <A/T> and engine coolant temperature sensor. The ECM <M/T> or PCM <A/T> activates the fan control module to drive the radiator fan motor and condenser fan motor.

TECHNICAL DESCRIPTION

The fan control module has variable control of the radiator fan motor and the condenser fan motor speeds using signals transmitted from the ECM <M/T> or PCM <A/T>.

TROUBLESHOOTING HINTS

- Malfunction of fan control relay
- Malfunction of fan control module
- Malfunction of ECM <M/T> or PCM <A/T>
- Damaged wiring harness or connector

CR1080200332010X

Fig. 26 Radiator & Condenser Fans Do Not Change Speed Or Stop (Part 1 of 3). 2002 Sebring Coupe & Stratus Coupe

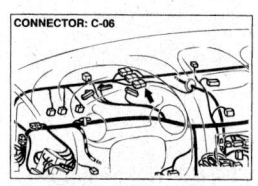

CONNECTOR: C-06

CONNECTOR:
C-109 <2.4L-M/T>, C-110 <2.4L-A/T>
C-111 <3.0L-M/T>, C-112 <3.0L-A/T>

ECM <M/T>
OR
PCM <A/T>

<2.4L-M/T>
CONNECTOR C-109

<2.4L-A/T, 3.0L>
CONNECTOR C-110, C-111, C-112

STEP 4. Check the harness wire between ECM connector C-109 <2.4L-M/T>, C-111 <3.0L-M/T> or PCM connector C-110 <2.4L-A/T>, C-112 <3.0L-A/T> and fan control module connector A-30.

NOTE: If intermediate connector C-06 is damaged, repair or replace it.

Q: Are the harness wires between ECM connector C-109 <2.4L-M/T>, C-111 <3.0L-M/T> or PCM connector C-110 <2.4L-A/T>, C-112 <3.0L-A/T> and fan control module connector A-30 damaged?

   YES : Repair or replace them, then go to Step 6.
   NO : Go to Step 5.

STEP 5. Check the fan control module at ECM connector C-109 <2.4L-M/T>, C-111 <3.0L-M/T> or PCM connector C-110 <2.4L-A/T>, C-112 <3.0L-A/T>.

(1) Connect ECM connector C-109 <2.4L-M/T>, C-111 <3.0L-M/T> or PCM connector C-110 <2.4L-A/T>, C-112 <3.0L-A/T>.

(2) Turn the ignition switch to "ON" position.

(3) Pull out the terminal number 21 <2.4L-M/T> or 18 <2.4L-A/T, 3.0L> and connect it to the body ground.

Q: Do the radiator fan motor and condenser fan motor stop?

   YES : Replace the ECM <M/T> or PCM <A/T>. Then go to Step 6.
   NO : Replace the radiator fan motor and fan control module assembly. Then go to Step 6.

STEP 6. Check the symptoms.

Q: Do the radiator fan and condenser fan operate correctly?

   YES : This diagnosis is complete.
   NO : Return to Step 1.

CR1080200332030X

Fig. 26 Radiator & Condenser Fans Do Not Change Speed Or Stop (Part 3 of 3). 2002 Sebring Coupe & Stratus Coupe

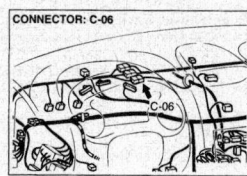

CONNECTOR: C-06

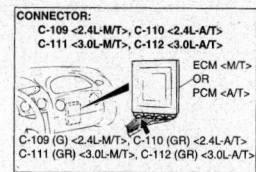

CONNECTOR:
C-109 <2.4L-M/T>, C-110 <2.4L-A/T>
C-111 <3.0L-M/T>, C-112 <3.0L-A/T>

ECM <M/T>
OR
PCM <A/T>

C-109 (G) <2.4L-M/T>, C-110 (GR) <2.4L-A/T>
C-111 (GR) <3.0L-M/T>, C-112 (GR) <3.0L-A/T>

CIRCUIT OPERATION

- The fan control module is powered from fusible link number 2.
- The ECM <M/T> or PCM <A/T> judges the required revolution speed of radiator fan motor and condenser fan motor using the input signals transmitted from A/C switch, automatic compressor controller, vehicle speed sensor <M/T>, output shaft speed sensor <A/T> and engine coolant temperature sensor. The ECM <M/T> or PCM <A/T> activates the fan control module to drive the radiator fan motor and condenser fan motor.

TECHNICAL DESCRIPTION

- The cause could be a malfunction of the fan control module power supply or ground circuit.
- The cause could also be a malfunction of the fan control module.

TROUBLESHOOTING HINTS

- Malfunction of fusible link
- Malfunction of fan control relay
- Malfunction of fan control module
- Malfunction of ECM <M/T> or PCM <A/T>
- Damaged wiring harness or connector

DIAGNOSIS

Required Special Tool:
MB991223: Harness Set

STEP 1. Check the fusible link number 2.
Q: Is the fusible link number 2 in good condition?
  YES : Go to Step 2.
  NO : Replace it. go to Step 13.

CR1080200343010X

Fig. 27   Radiator & Condenser Fans Do Not Operate (Part 1 of 8). 2003–05 Sebring Coupe & Stratus Coupe

STEP 4. Check fan control relay connector A-09X and fan control module connector A-30 for loose, corroded or damaged terminals, or terminals pushed back in the connector.
Q: Are the connectors and terminals in good condition?
  YES : Go to Step 5.
  NO : Repair or replace the faulty components.

    Go to Step 13.

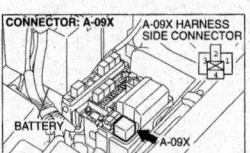

CONNECTOR: A-09X

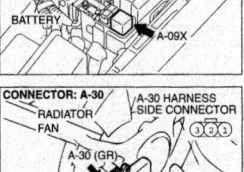

CONNECTOR: A-30

STEP 5. Check the harness wires between fusible link (2) and fan control module connector A-30 terminal 3 for damage.
Q: Are the harness wires between in good condition?
  YES : It can be assumed that this malfunction is intermittent.
    Go to Step 6.
  NO : Repair the damaged harness wires. Go to Step 13.

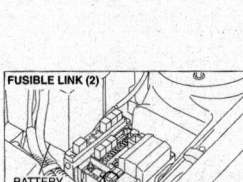

FUSIBLE LINK (2)

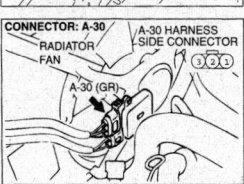

CONNECTOR: A-30

CR1080200343030X

Fig. 27   Radiator & Condenser Fans Do Not Operate (Part 3 of 8). 2003–05 Sebring Coupe & Stratus Coupe

STEP 2. Measure the power supply voltage signal at fan control module connector A-30.
(1) Disconnect fan control module connector A-30.

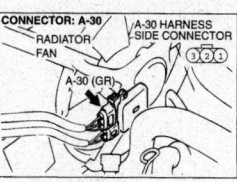

CONNECTOR: A-30

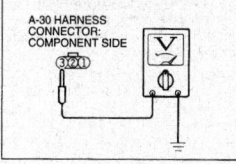

A-30 HARNESS CONNECTOR: COMPONENT SIDE

(2) Measure the voltage between fan control module connector A-30 terminal number 3 and ground.
  - The measured voltage should measure battery positive voltage. (When the ignition switch is turned to "ON" position).
(3) Connect fan control module connector A-30.
Q: Is the measured voltage battery positive voltage?
  YES : Go to Step 8.
  NO : Go to Step 3.

STEP 3. Check the fan control relay.
Refer to P.7-22.
Q: Is the fan control relay in good condition?
  YES : Go to Step 4.
  NO : Replace it. Go to Step 13.

CR1080200343020X

Fig. 27   Radiator & Condenser Fans Do Not Operate (Part 2 of 8). 2003–05 Sebring Coupe & Stratus Coupe

STEP 6. Check fan control relay connector A-09X and intermediate connector C-06 for loose, corroded or damaged terminals, or terminals pushed back in the connector.
Q: Are the connectors and terminals in good condition?
  YES : Go to Step 7.
  NO : Repair or replace the faulty components.

    Go to Step 13.

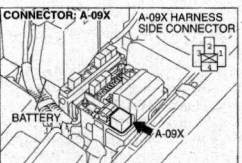

CONNECTOR: A-09X

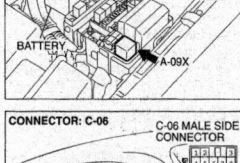

CONNECTOR: C-06

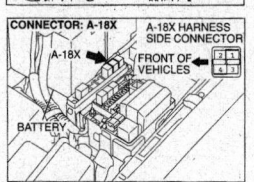

CONNECTOR: A-18X

STEP 7. Check the harness wires between MFI relay connector A-18X terminal 4 and grounding point (2) for damage.
Q: Are the harness wires between in good condition?
  YES : It can be assumed that this malfunction is intermittent.
    Go to Step 13.
  NO : Repair the damaged harness wires. Go to Step 13.

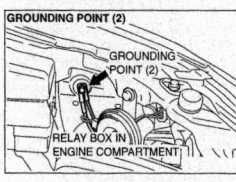

GROUNDING POINT (2)

CR1080200343040X

Fig. 27   Radiator & Condenser Fans Do Not Operate (Part 4 of 8). 2003–05 Sebring Coupe & Stratus Coupe

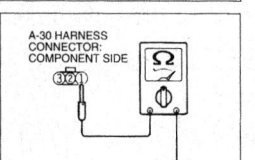

STEP 8. Measure the continuity between fan control module connector A-30 and ground.

(1) Disconnect fan control module connector A-30.

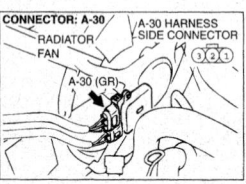

(2) Measure the resistance between fan control module connector A-30 terminal number 1 and ground.
  • The measured resistance should be less than 2 ohms.
(3) Connect fan control module connector A-30.

Q: Is the measured resistance less than 2 ohms?
  YES : Go to Step 11.
  NO : Go to Step 9.

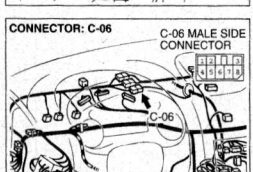

STEP 9. Check fan control module connector A-30 for loose, corroded or damaged terminals, or terminals pushed back in the connector.

Q: Is the connector and terminals in good condition?
  YES : Go to Step 10.
  NO : Repair or replace the faulty components.

2). Go to Step 13.

Fig. 27   Radiator & Condenser Fans Do Not Operate (Part 5 of 8). 2003–05 Sebring Coupe & Stratus Coupe

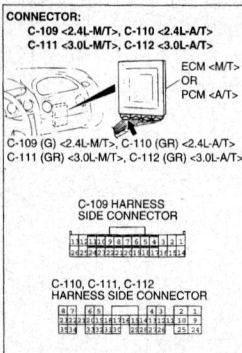

STEP 11. Check fan control module connector A-30, intermediate connector C-06 and ECM connector C-109 <2.4L-M/T> or C-111 <3.0L-M/T>, or PCM connector C-110 <2.4L-A/T> or C-112 <3.0L-A/T> for loose, corroded or damaged terminals, or terminals pushed back in the connector.

Q: Are the connectors and terminals in good condition?
  YES : Go to Step 12.
  NO : Repair or replace the faulty components.

Go to Step 13.

Fig. 27   Radiator & Condenser Fans Do Not Operate (Part 7 of 8). 2003–05 Sebring Coupe & Stratus Coupe

STEP 10. Check the harness wires between fan control module connector A-30 terminal 1 and grounding point (2) for damage.

Q: Are the harness wires between in good condition?
  YES : It can be assumed that this malfunction is intermittent.

Go to Step 13.
  NO : Repair the damaged harness wires. Go to Step 13.

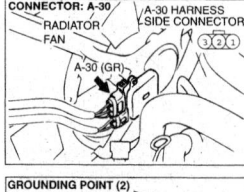

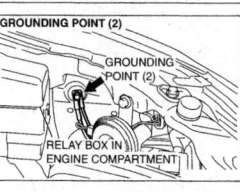

CR1080200343060X

Fig. 27   Radiator & Condenser Fans Do Not Operate (Part 6 of 8). 2003–05 Sebring Coupe & Stratus Coupe

STEP 12. Check the harness wires between fan control module connector A-30 terminal 2 and ECM connector C-109 terminal 21 <2.4L-M/T> or C-111 terminal 18 <2.4L-M/T>, or PCM connector C-110 terminal 18 <2.4L-A/T> or C-112 terminal 18 <3.0L-A/T> for damage.

Q: Are the harness wires between in good condition?
  YES : Check that the malfunction is eliminated. If the malfunction is eliminated, it can be assumed that this malfunction is intermittent. (Refer to INTRODUCTION, How to Use Troubl Inspection Service Points P.-6). If the malfunction is not eliminated, replace the fun control module.(Refer to P.7-23), then go to Step 13.
  NO : Repair the damaged harness wires. Go to Step 13.

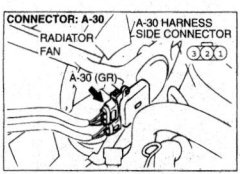

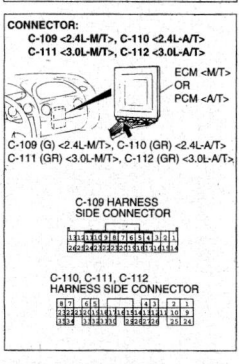

STEP 13. Retest the system.

Q: Do the radiator fan and condenser fan operate correctly?
  YES : The procedure is complete.
  NO : Replace the ECM <M/T> or PCM <A/T>.

CR1080200343080X

Fig. 27   Radiator & Condenser Fans Do Not Operate (Part 8 of 8). 2003–05 Sebring Coupe & Stratus Coupe

CR1080200343070X

Fig. 27   Radiator & Condenser Fans Do Not Operate (Part 7 of 8). 2003–05 Sebring Coupe & Stratus Coupe

NOTE: If the engine coolant temperature reaches 110°C (230°F) or higher, the radiator fan control rotates the radiator fan for up to 5 minutes even after the ignition switch is turned to the "LOCK" (OFF) position [the fan stops its rotation when the engine coolant temperature decreases to 110°C (230°F) or lower.]

Radiator Fan and Condenser Fan Drive Circuit

CIRCUIT OPERATION
- The fan control module is powered from fusible link number 2.
- The ECM <M/T> or PCM <A/T> judges the required revolution speed of radiator fan motor and condenser fan motor using the input signals transmitted from A/C switch, automatic compressor controller, vehicle speed sensor <M/T>, output shaft speed sensor <A/T> and engine coolant temperature sensor. The ECM <M/T> or PCM <A/T> activates the fan control module to drive the radiator fan motor and condenser fan motor.

TECHNICAL DESCRIPTION
The fan control module has variable control of the radiator fan motor and the condenser fan motor speeds using signals transmitted from the ECM <M/T> or PCM <A/T>.

TROUBLESHOOTING HINTS
- Malfunction of fan control relay
- Malfunction of fan control module
- Malfunction of ECM <M/T> or PCM <A/T>
- Damaged wiring harness or connector

DIAGNOSIS
Required Special Tool:
MB991223: Harness Set

STEP 1. Check the fan control relay.

Q: Is the fan control relay in good condition?
YES : Go to Step 2.
NO : Replace it. Go to Step 5.

CR1080200344010X

Fig. 28 Radiator & Condenser Fans Do Not Change Speed Or Stop (Part 1 of 4). 2003–05 Sebring Coupe & Stratus Coupe

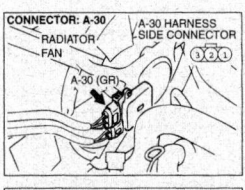

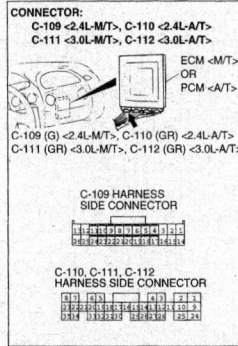

STEP 3. Check fan control module connector A-30, intermediate connector C-06 and ECM connector C-109 <2.4L-M/T> or C-111 <3.0L-M/T>, or PCM connector C-110 <2.4L-A/T> or C-112 <3.0L-A/T> for loose, corroded or damaged terminals, or terminals pushed back in the connector.
Q: Are the connectors and terminals in good condition?
YES : Go to Step 4.
NO : Repair or replace the faulty components.

Go to Step 5.

CR1080200344030X

Fig. 28 Radiator & Condenser Fans Do Not Change Speed Or Stop (Part 3 of 4). 2003–05 Sebring Coupe & Stratus Coupe

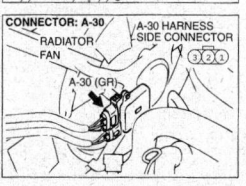

STEP 2. Check the harness wire between fan control relay connector A-09X terminal 2 and fan control module connector A-30 terminal 3 for damage.
Q: Is the harness wire in good condition?
YES : Go to Step 3.
NO : Repair the damaged harness wire. Go to Step 5.

CR1080200344020X

Fig. 28 Radiator & Condenser Fans Do Not Change Speed Or Stop (Part 2 of 4). 2003–05 Sebring Coupe & Stratus Coupe

STEP 4. Check the harness wires between fan control module connector A-30 terminal 2 and ECM connector C-109 terminal 21 <2.4L-M/T> or C-111 terminal 18 <2.4L-M/T>, or PCM connector C-110 terminal 18 <2.4L-A/T> or C-112 terminal 18 <3.0L-A/T> for damage.
Q: Are the harness wires between in good condition?
YES : Check that the malfunction is eliminated. If the malfunction is eliminated, it can be assumed that this malfunction is intermittent.

If the malfunction is not eliminated, replace the fun control module then go to Step 5.
NO : Repair the damaged harness wires. Go to Step 5.

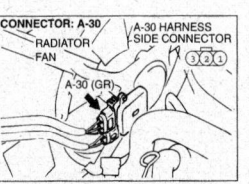

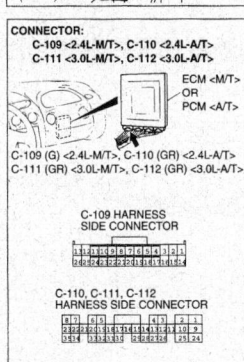

STEP 5. Retest the system.
Q: Do the radiator fan and condenser fan operate correctly?
YES : The procedure is complete.
NO : Replace the ECM <M/T> or PCM <A/T>.

CR1080200344040X

Fig. 28 Radiator & Condenser Fans Do Not Change Speed Or Stop (Part 4 of 4). 2003–05 Sebring Coupe & Stratus Coupe

TECHNICAL DESCRIPTION
The cause could be a malfunction of the radiator fan motor or an open circuit between the fan control module and the radiator fan motor.

TROUBLESHOOTING HINTS
- Malfunction of radiator fan motor
- Malfunction of fan control module

DIAGNOSIS
Replace the radiator fan motor and fan control module assembly.

Q: Does the radiator fan operate correctly?
YES : There is no action to be taken?
NO : Repair the wiring harness between the fan control module and the radiator fan motor.

CR1080200333000X

Fig. 29 Radiator Fan Does Not Operate. 2003–05 Sebring Coupe & Stratus Coupe

COOLING FANS

Radiator Fan and Condenser Fan Drive Circuit

CIRCUIT OPERATION

- The fan control module is powered from fusible link number 2.
- The ECM <M/T> or PCM <A/T> judges the required revolution speed of radiator fan motor and condenser fan motor using the input signals transmitted from A/C switch, automatic compressor controller, vehicle speed sensor <M/ T>, output shaft speed sensor <A/T> and engine coolant temperature sensor. The ECM <M/T> or PCM <A/T> activates the fan control module to drive the radiator fan motor and condenser fan motor.

TECHNICAL DESCRIPTION

The cause could be a malfunction of the condenser fan motor or of the fan control module.

TROUBLESHOOTING HINTS

- Malfunction of condenser fan motor
- Malfunction of fan control module

DIAGNOSIS

STEP 1. Check the condenser fan motor.

Q: Is the condenser fan in good condition?
   YES : Go to Step 2.
   NO : Replace the condenser fan motor. Then go to Step 3.

STEP 2. Check the fan control module.

Q: Is the fan control module in good condition?
   YES : Go to Step 3.
   NO : Replace the fan control module, then go to Step 3.

CR1080200334010X

Fig. 30 Condenser Fan Does Not Operate (Part 1 of 2). 2003–05 Sebring Coupe & Stratus Coupe

When Monitored and Set Condition:

P0112-INTAKE AIR TEMP SENSOR VOLTAGE LOW

When Monitored: With the ignition on. Battery voltage greater than 10 volts.

Set Condition: The Intake Air Temperature (IAT) sensor circuit voltage at the PCM goes below 0.5 volt.

POSSIBLE CAUSES
INTERMITTENT CONDITION
IAT SENSOR INTERNAL FAILURE
IAT SENSOR SIGNAL SHORTED TO GROUND
IAT SENSOR SIGNAL SHORTED TO SENSOR GROUND CIRCUIT
PCM

TEST	ACTION

1	Turn the ignition on.
	With the DRBIII®, read the IAT voltage.
	Is the voltage below 1.0 volt?
	
	    Yes → Go To 2
	
	    No → Go To 6

2	Turn the ignition off.
	Disconnect the IAT harness connector.
	Turn the ignition on.
	With the DRBIII®, read IAT voltage.
	Is the voltage above 1.0 volt?
	
	    Yes → Replace the IAT Sensor.
	
	    No → Go To 3

3	Turn the ignition off.
	Disconnect the IAT Sensor harness connector.
	Disconnect the PCM harness connector.
	Measure the resistance of the IAT Sensor Signal circuit in the IAT Sensor harness connector and ground.
	Is the resistance below 100 ohms?
	
	    Yes → Repair the IAT Sensor Signal circuit for a short to ground.
	
	    No → Go To 4

ARM0400000000919

Fig. 31 Code P0112: IAT Sensor Voltage Low (Part 1 of 2). LHS, 2001 Concorde, Intrepid & 300M

STEP 3. Check the symptoms.

Q: Does the condenser fan operate correctly?
   YES : This diagnosis is complete.
   NO : Return to Step1.

CR1080200334020X

Fig. 30 Condenser Fan Does Not Operate (Part 2 of 2). 2003–05 Sebring Coupe & Stratus Coupe

TEST	ACTION

4	Turn the ignition off.
	Disconnect the IAT Sensor harness connector.
	Disconnect the PCM harness connector.
	Measure the resistance between the IAT Sensor Signal circuit and the Sensor ground circuit in the IAT Sensor harness connector.
	Is the resistance below 100 ohms?
	
	    Yes → Repair the IAT Sensor Signal circuit for a short to the Sensor ground circuit.
	
	    No → Go To 5

5	If there are no possible causes remaining, view repair.
	
	    Repair
	        Replace and program the Powertrain Control Module Module

6	WARNING: WHEN THE ENGINE IS OPERATING, DO NOT STAND IN A DIRECT LINE WITH THE FAN. DO NOT PUT YOUR HANDS NEAR THE PULLEYS, BELTS OR FAN. DO NOT WEAR LOOSE CLOTHING.
	NOTE: The conditions that set the DTC are not present at this time. The following list may help in identifying the intermittent condition.
	With the engine running at normal operating temperature, monitor the DRB parameters related to the DTC while wiggling the wiring harness. Look for parameter values to change and/or a DTC to set.
	Review the DRB Freeze Frame information. If possible, try to duplicate the conditions under which the DTC was set.
	Refer to any Technical Service Bulletins (TSB) that may apply.
	Visually inspect the related wiring harness. Look for any chafed, pierced, pinched, or partially broken wires.
	Visually inspect the related wiring harness connectors. Look for broken, bent, pushed out, or corroded terminals.
	Were any of the above conditions present?
	
	    Yes → Repair as necessary
	
	    No → Test Complete.

ARM0400000000920

Fig. 31 Code P0112: IAT Sensor Voltage Low (Part 2 of 2). LHS, 2001 Concorde, Intrepid & 300M

When Monitored and Set Condition:

P0113-INTAKE AIR TEMP SENSOR VOLTAGE HIGH

When Monitored: With the ignition on. Battery voltage greater than 10 volts.

Set Condition: The Intake Air Temperature (IAT) sensor circuit voltage at the PCM goes above 4.9 volts.

POSSIBLE CAUSES
INTERMITTENT CONDITION
IAT SENSOR SIGNAL CIRCUIT SHORTED TO BATTERY VOLTAGE
IAT SENSOR INTERNAL FAILURE
IAT SENSOR SIGNAL CIRCUIT OPEN
SENSOR GROUND CIRCUIT OPEN
PCM

TEST	ACTION
1	Turn the ignition on. With the DRBIII®, read the IAT voltage. Is the voltage above 4.6 volts? Yes → Go To 2 No → Go To 7
2	Turn the ignition off. Disconnect the IAT Sensor harness connector. Turn the ignition on. Measure the voltage of the IAT Sensor Signal circuit in the IAT Sensor harness connector. Is the voltage above 5.2 volts? Yes → Repair the IAT Sensor Signal circuit for a short to battery voltage. No → Go To 3
3	Turn the ignition off. Disconnect the IAT harness connector. Connect a jumper wire between the IAT Sensor Signal circuit and the Sensor ground circuit in the IAT harness connector. Turn the ignition on. With the DRBIII®, read IAT voltage? Is the voltage below 1.0 volt? Yes → Replace the IAT Sensor. No → Go To 4

ARM0400000000921

Fig. 32 Code P0113: IAT Sensor Voltage High (Part 1 of 2). LHS, 2001 Concorde, Intrepid & 300M

When Monitored and Set Condition:

P0117-ECT SENSOR VOLTAGE TOO LOW

When Monitored: With the ignition on. Battery voltage greater than 10 volts.

Set Condition: The Engine Coolant Temperature (ECT) sensor circuit voltage at the PCM is less than 0.8 volt for more than 2.6 seconds.

POSSIBLE CAUSES
INTERMITTENT CONDITION
ECT SENSOR INTERNAL FAILURE
ECT SENSOR SIGNAL SHORTED TO GROUND
ECT SENSOR SIGNAL SHORTED TO SENSOR GROUND CIRCUIT
PCM

TEST	ACTION
1	Turn the ignition on. With the DRBIII®, read the ECT voltage. Is the voltage below 1.0 volt? Yes → Go To 2 No → Go To 6
2	Turn the ignition off. Disconnect the ECT harness connector. Turn the ignition on. With the DRBIII®, read ECT voltage. Is the voltage above 1.0 volt? Yes → Replace the ECT Sensor. No → Go To 3
3	Turn the ignition off. Disconnect the ECT Sensor harness connector. Disconnect the PCM harness connector. Measure the resistance of the ECT Sensor Signal circuit in the ECT Sensor harness connector to ground. Is the resistance below 100 ohms? Yes → Repair the ECT Sensor Signal circuit for a short to ground. No → Go To 4

ARM0400000000923

Fig. 33 Code P0117: ECT Sensor Voltage Low (Part 1 of 2). LHS, 2001 Concorde, Intrepid & 300M

TEST	ACTION
4	Turn the ignition off. Disconnect the IAT Sensor harness connector. Disconnect the PCM harness connector. Measure the resistance of the IAT Sensor Signal circuit between the IAT Sensor harness connector and the PCM harness connector. Is the resistance below 5 ohms? Yes → Go To 5 No → Repair the IAT Sensor Signal circuit for an open.
5	Turn the ignition off. Disconnect the IAT Sensor harness connector. Disconnect the PCM harness connector. Measure the resistance of the Sensor ground circuit between the IAT Sensor harness connector and the PCM harness connector. Is the resistance below 5.0 ohms? Yes → Go To 6 No → Repair the Sensor ground circuit for an open.
6	If there are no possible causes remaining, view repair. Repair 　Replace and program the Powertrain Control Module Module
7	**WARNING: WHEN THE ENGINE IS OPERATING, DO NOT STAND IN A DIRECT LINE WITH THE FAN. DO NOT PUT YOUR HANDS NEAR THE PULLEYS, BELTS OR FAN. DO NOT WEAR LOOSE CLOTHING.** **NOTE: The conditions that set the DTC are not present at this time. The following list may help in identifying the intermittent condition.** With the engine running at normal operating temperature, monitor the DRB parameters related to the DTC while wiggling the wiring harness. Look for parameter values to change and/or a DTC to set. Review the DRB Freeze Frame information. If possible, try to duplicate the conditions under which the DTC was set. Refer to any Technical Service Bulletins (TSB) that may apply. Visually inspect the related wiring harness. Look for any chafed, pierced, pinched, or partially broken wires. Visually inspect the related wiring harness connectors. Look for broken, bent, pushed out, or corroded terminals. Were any of the above conditions present? Yes → Repair as necessary No → Test Complete.

ARM0400000000922

Fig. 32 Code P0113: IAT Sensor Voltage High (Part 2 of 2). LHS, 2001 Concorde, Intrepid & 300M

TEST	ACTION
4	Turn the ignition off. Disconnect the ECT Sensor harness connector. Disconnect the PCM harness connector. Measure the resistance between the ECT Sensor Signal circuit and the Sensor ground circuit in the ECT Sensor harness connector. Is the resistance below 100 ohms? Yes → Repair the ECT Sensor Signal circuit for a short to the Sensor ground circuit. No → Go To 5
5	If there are no possible causes remaining, view repair. Repair 　Replace and program the Powertrain Control Module Module
6	**WARNING: WHEN THE ENGINE IS OPERATING, DO NOT STAND IN A DIRECT LINE WITH THE FAN. DO NOT PUT YOUR HANDS NEAR THE PULLEYS, BELTS OR FAN. DO NOT WEAR LOOSE CLOTHING.** **NOTE: The conditions that set the DTC are not present at this time. The following list may help in identifying the intermittent condition.** With the engine running at normal operating temperature, monitor the DRB parameters related to the DTC while wiggling the wiring harness. Look for parameter values to change and/or a DTC to set. Review the DRB Freeze Frame information. If possible, try to duplicate the conditions under which the DTC was set. Refer to any Technical Service Bulletins (TSB) that may apply. Visually inspect the related wiring harness. Look for any chafed, pierced, pinched, or partially broken wires. Visually inspect the related wiring harness connectors. Look for broken, bent, pushed out, or corroded terminals. Were any of the above conditions present? Yes → Repair as necessary No → Test Complete.

ARM0400000000924

Fig. 33 Code P0117: ECT Sensor Voltage Low (Part 2 of 2). LHS, 2001 Concorde, Intrepid & 300M

When Monitored and Set Condition:

P0118-ECT SENSOR VOLTAGE TOO HIGH

When Monitored: With the ignition on. Battery voltage greater than 10 volts.

Set Condition: The Engine Coolant Temperature (ECT) sensor circuit voltage at the PCM is greater than 4.96 volts for more than 2.6 seconds.

POSSIBLE CAUSES
INTERMITTENT CONDITION
ECT SENSOR SIGNAL CIRCUIT SHORTED TO BATTERY VOLTAGE
ECT SENSOR INTERNAL FAILURE
ECT SENSOR SIGNAL CIRCUIT OPEN
SENSOR GROUND CIRCUIT OPEN
PCM

TEST	ACTION
1	Turn the ignition on. With the DRBIII®, read the ECT voltage. Is the voltage above 4.6 volts? Yes → Go To 2 No → Go To 7
2	Turn the ignition off. Disconnect the ECT Sensor harness connector. Turn the ignition on. Measure the voltage of the ECT Sensor Signal circuit in the ECT Sensor harness connector. Is the voltage above 5.2 volts? Yes → Repair the ECT Sensor Signal circuit for a short to battery voltage. No → Go To 3

ARM0400000000925

Fig. 34 Code P0118: ECT Sensor Voltage High (Part 1 of 3). LHS, 2001 Concorde, Intrepid & 300M

TEST	ACTION
7	WARNING: WHEN THE ENGINE IS OPERATING, DO NOT STAND IN A DIRECT LINE WITH THE FAN. DO NOT PUT YOUR HANDS NEAR THE PULLEYS, BELTS OR FAN. DO NOT WEAR LOOSE CLOTHING. NOTE: The conditions that set the DTC are not present at this time. The following list may help in identifying the intermittent condition. With the engine running at normal operating temperature, monitor the DRB parameters related to the DTC while wiggling the wiring harness. Look for parameter values to change and/or a DTC to set. Review the DRB Freeze Frame information. If possible, try to duplicate the conditions under which the DTC was set. Refer to any Technical Service Bulletins (TSB) that may apply. Visually inspect the related wiring harness. Look for any chafed, pierced, pinched, or partially broken wires. Visually inspect the related wiring harness connectors. Look for broken, bent, pushed out, or corroded terminals. Were any of the above conditions present? Yes → Repair as necessary No → Test Complete.

ARM0400000000927

Fig. 34 Code P0118: ECT Sensor Voltage High (Part 3 of 3). LHS, 2001 Concorde, Intrepid & 300M

TEST	ACTION
3	Turn the ignition off. Disconnect the ECT harness connector. Connect a jumper wire between the ECT Sensor Signal circuit and the Sensor ground circuit in the ECT harness connector. Turn the ignition on. With the DRBIII®, read ECT voltage. Is the voltage below 1.0 volt? Yes → Replace the ECT Sensor. No → Go To 4
4	Turn the ignition off. Disconnect the ECT Sensor harness connector. Disconnect the PCM harness connector. Measure the resistance of the ECT Sensor Signal circuit between the ECT Sensor harness connector and the PCM harness connector. Is the resistance below 5 ohms? Yes → Go To 5 No → Repair the ECT Sensor Signal circuit for an open.
5	Turn the ignition off. Disconnect the ECT Sensor harness connector. Disconnect the PCM harness connector. Measure the resistance of the Sensor ground circuit between the ECT Sensor harness connector and the PCM harness connector. Is the resistance below 5.0 ohms? Yes → Go To 6 No → Repair the Sensor ground circuit for an open.
6	If there are no possible causes remaining, view repair. Repair Replace and program the Powertrain Control Module Module

ARM0400000000926

Fig. 34 Code P0118: ECT Sensor Voltage High (Part 2 of 3). LHS, 2001 Concorde, Intrepid & 300M

When Monitored and Set Condition:

P0720-OUTPUT SPEED SENSOR ERROR

When Monitored: The transmission gear ratio is monitored continuously while the transmission is in gear.

Set Condition: If there is an excessive change in output RPM in any gear.

POSSIBLE CAUSES
INTERMITTENT WIRING AND CONNECTORS
OUTPUT SPEED SENSOR SIGNAL CIRCUIT OPEN
SPEED SENSOR GROUND CIRCUIT OPEN
OUTPUT SPEED SENSOR SIGNAL CIRCUIT SHORT TO GROUND
OUTPUT SPEED SENSOR SIGNAL CIRCUIT SHORT TO VOLTAGE
SPEED SENSOR GROUND CIRCUIT SHORT TO VOLTAGE
OUTPUT SPEED SENSOR
TCM - OUTPUT SPEED SENSOR

TEST	ACTION
1	NOTE: Low fluid level can be the cause of many transmission problems. If the fluid level is low locate and repair the leak then check and adjust the fluid level per the service information. NOTE: Always perform diagnostics with a fully charged battery to avoid false symptoms. With the DRBIII®, read the engine DTC's. Check and repair all engine DTC's prior to performing transmission symptom diagnostics. With the DRBIII®, read Transmission DTC's. Record all DTC's and 1 Trip Failures. NOTE: Diagnose 1 Trip Failures as a fully matured DTC. Using the wiring diagram/schematic as a guide, inspect the wiring and connectors. Repair as necessary. Perform the Shift Lever Position Test. If the test does not pass, refer to Symptom test for P0705 Check Shifter Signal. For Gear Ratio DTC's, check and record all CVI's. Most DTC's set on start up but some must be set by driving the vehicle such that all diagnostic monitors have run. Note: Verify flash level of transmission controller. Some problems are corrected by software upgrades to the transmission controller. NOTE: Check for applicable TSB's related to the problem. Perform this procedure prior to Symptom diagnosis. Continue Go To 2

ARM0400000000968

Fig. 35 Code P0720: Output Speed Sensor Error (Part 1 of 4). LHS, 2001 Concorde, Intrepid & 300M

TEST	ACTION
2	Start the engine in park. Raise the drive wheels off of the ground. **WARNING: PROPERLY SUPPORT THE VEHICLE.** Place transmission in drive, release foot from brake. **WARNING: BE SURE TO KEEP HANDS AND FEET CLEAR OF ROTATING WHEELS.** Note: The drive wheels must be turning at this point. With the DRBIII®, read the Output RPM Is the Output RPM below 100? Yes → Go To 3 No → Go To 11
3	Turn ignition off to the lock position. **CAUTION: Remove the Starter Relay from the PDC. This will prevent the vehicle from being started in gear.** **NOTE: Failure to remove the Starter Relay can cause a TCM - No Response condition.** Install Transmission Simulator, Miller tool #8333 and the FWD adapter cable kit, Miller tool #8333-1. Ignition on, engine not running. Using the Transmission Simulator, set the rotary knob to the 1000/3000 position. Turn the Input/Output switch ON. **NOTE: After competition of this procedure, make sure to disconnect Transmission Simulator, Miller tool #8333 and FWD adaptor cable kit, Miller tool #8333-1 and reconnect all connectors.** With the DRBIII®, read the Input RPM and Output RPM. Does the Input RPM read 3000 and the Output RPM read 1250 (within 50 RPM)? Yes → Go To 4 No → Go To 5
4	If there are no possible causes remaining, view repair. Repair Replace the Output Speed Sensor in accordance with the Service Information.
5	Turn ignition off to the lock position. Disconnect the TCM harness connector. Disconnect the Output Speed Sensor harness connector. **Note: Check connectors - Clean/repair as necessary.** Measure the resistance of the Output Speed Sensor Signal circuit from the TCM harness connector to the Output Speed Sensor harness connector. Is the resistance above 5.0 ohms? Yes → Repair the Output Speed Sensor Signal circuit for an open. No → Go To 6

ARM0400000000969

Fig. 35 Code P0720: Output Speed Sensor Error (Part 2 of 4). LHS, 2001 Concorde, Intrepid & 300M

TEST	ACTION
6	Turn the ignition off to the lock position. Disconnect the TCM harness connector. Disconnect the Output Speed Sensor harness connector. **Note: Check connectors - Clean/repair as necessary.** Measure the resistance of the Speed Sensor Ground circuit from the TCM harness connector to the Output Speed Sensor harness connector. Is the resistance above 5.0 ohms? Yes → Repair the Speed Sensor Ground circuit for an open. No → Go To 7
7	Turn ignition off to the lock position. Disconnect the TCM harness connector. Disconnect the Output Speed Sensor harness connector. **Note: Check connectors - Clean/repair as necessary.** Measure the resistance between ground and the Output Speed Sensor Signal circuit. Is the resistance Below 5.0 ohms? Yes → Repair the Output Speed Sensor Signal circuit for a short to ground. No → Go To 8
8	Turn the ignition off to the lock position. Disconnect the TCM harness connector. Disconnect the Output Speed Sensor harness connector. Remove the Transmission Control Relay. **Note: Check connectors - Clean/repair as necessary.** Connect a jumper wire between the Fused B+ circuit and Transmission Control Relay Output circuit in the Transmission Control Relay connector. Ignition on, engine not running. Measure the voltage of the Output Speed Sensor Signal circuit in the TCM harness connector. Is the voltage above 0.5 volt? Yes → Repair the Output Speed Sensor Signal circuit for a short to voltage. No → Go To 9
9	Turn the ignition off to the lock position. Disconnect the TCM harness connector. Disconnect the TRS harness connector. Remove the Transmission Control Relay. **Note: Check connectors - Clean/repair as necessary.** Connect a jumper wire between the Fused B+ and Transmission Control Relay Output circuits in the Transmission Control Relay connector. Ignition on, engine not running. Measure the voltage of the Speed Sensor Ground circuit in the TCM harness connector. Is the voltage above 0.5 volts? Yes → Repair the Speed Sensor Ground circuit for a short to voltage. No → Go To 10

ARM0400000000970

Fig. 35 Code P0720: Output Speed Sensor Error (Part 3 of 4). LHS, 2001 Concorde, Intrepid & 300M

TEST	ACTION
10	If there are no possible causes remaining, view repair. Repair Replace the Transmission Control Module
11	The conditions necessary to set the DTC are not present at this time. Using the schematics as a guide, inspect the wiring and connectors specific to this circuit. Wiggle the wiring and connectors while checking for shorts and open circuits. Were any problems found? Yes → Repair as necessary. No → Test Complete.

ARM0400000000971

Fig. 35 Code P0720: Output Speed Sensor Error (Part 4 of 4). LHS, 2001 Concorde, Intrepid & 300M

When Monitored and Set Condition:

P1489-HIGH SPEED FAN CONTROL RELAY CIRCUIT

When Monitored: With the ignition on. Battery voltage greater than 10.0 volts.

Set Condition: An open or shorted circuit is detected in the radiator fan relay control circuit.

POSSIBLE CAUSES
HIGH SPEED RADIATOR FAN RELAY INTERMITTENT OPERATION
INTERMITTENT CONDITION
FUSED IGNITION SWITCH OUTPUT CIRCUIT
HIGH SPEED RADIATOR FAN RELAY RESISTANCE
HIGH SPEED RADIATOR FAN RELAY CONTROL CIRCUIT OPEN
HIGH SPEED RADIATOR FAN RELAY CONTROL CIRCUIT SHORT TO GROUND
PCM

TEST	ACTION
1	Turn the ignition on. With the DRBIII®, actuate the High Speed Radiator Fan Relay. Is the High Speed Radiator Fan Relay operating? Yes → Go To 2 No → Go To 4
2	Turn the ignition on. With the DRBIII®, actuate the High Speed Radiator Fan Relay. Wiggle the wiring harness from the High Speed Radiator Fan Relay to the PCM while the relay is actuating. Did the High Speed Radiator Fan Relay stop when wiggling the wiring harness? Yes → Repair as necessary. No → Go To 3

ARM0400000000972

Fig. 36 Code P1489: High Speed Fan Control Relay Circuit (Part 1 of 3). LHS, 2001 Concorde, Intrepid & 300M

TEST	ACTION
3	WARNING: WHEN THE ENGINE IS OPERATING, DO NOT STAND IN A DIRECT LINE WITH THE FAN. DO NOT PUT YOUR HANDS NEAR THE PULLEYS, BELTS OR FAN. DO NOT WEAR LOOSE CLOTHING. NOTE: The conditions that set the DTC are not present at this time. The following list may help in identifying the intermittent condition. With the engine running at normal operating temperature, monitor the DRB parameters related to the DTC while wiggling the wiring harness. Look for parameter values to change and/or a DTC to set. Review the DRB Freeze Frame information. If possible, try to duplicate the conditions under which the DTC was set. Refer to any Technical Service Bulletins (TSB) that may apply. Visually inspect the related wiring harness. Look for any chafed, pierced, pinched, or partially broken wires. Visually inspect the related wiring harness connectors. Look for broken, bent, pushed out, or corroded terminals. Were any of the above conditions present? Yes → Repair as necessary No → Test Complete.
4	Turn the ignition off. Remove the High Speed Radiator Fan Relay from the PDC. Turn the ignition on. Measure the voltage of the Fused Ignition Switch Output circuit in the PDC. Is the voltage above 11.0 volts? Yes → Go To 5 No → Repair the Fused Ignition Switch Output circuit. Check and replace any open fuses.
5	Turn the ignition off. Remove the High Speed Radiator Fan Relay from the PDC. Measure the resistance of the High Speed Radiator Fan Relay between the Fused Ignition Switch Output terminal and the High Speed Radiator Fan Relay Control terminal. Is the resistance between 60 to 80 ohms? Yes → Go To 6 No → Replace the High Speed Radiator Fan Relay.
6	Turn the ignition off. Remove the High Speed Radiator Fan Relay from the PDC. Disconnect the PCM harness connector. Measure the resistance of the High Speed Radiator Fan Relay Control circuit between the PDC and the PCM harness connector. Is the resistance below 5.0 ohms. Yes → Go To 7 No → Repair the High Speed Radiator Fan Relay Control circuit for an open.

ARM0400000000973

Fig. 36   Code P1489: High Speed Fan Control Relay Circuit (Part 2 of 3). LHS, 2001 Concorde, Intrepid & 300M

When Monitored and Set Condition:

P1490-LOW SPEED FAN CONTROL RELAY CIRCUIT

When Monitored: With the ignition on. Battery voltage greater than 10 volts.

Set Condition: An open or shorted circuit is detected in the radiator fan relay control circuit.

POSSIBLE CAUSES
LOW SPEED RADIATOR FAN RELAY INTERMITTENT OPERATION
INTERMITTENT CONDITION
FUSED IGNITION SWITCH OUTPUT CIRCUIT
LOW SPEED RADIATOR FAN RELAY RESISTANCE
LOW SPEED RADIATOR FAN RELAY CONTROL CIRCUIT OPEN
LOW SPEED RADIATOR FAN RELAY CONTROL CIRCUIT SHORT TO GROUND
PCM

TEST	ACTION
1	Turn the ignition on. With the DRBIII®, actuate the Low Speed Radiator Fan Relay. Is the Low Speed Radiator Fan Relay operating? Yes → Go To 2 No → Go To 4
2	Turn the ignition on. With the DRBIII®, actuate the Low Speed Radiator Fan Relay. Wiggle the wiring harness from the Low Speed Radiator Fan Relay to the PCM while the relay is actuating. Did the Low Speed Radiator Fan Relay stop when wiggling the wiring harness? Yes → Repair as necessary. No → Go To 3

ARM0400000000975

Fig. 37   Code P1490: Low Speed Fan Control Relay Circuit (Part 1 of 3). LHS, 2001 Concorde, Intrepid & 300M

TEST	ACTION
7	Turn the ignition off. Remove the High Speed Radiator Fan Relay from the PDC. Disconnect the PCM harness connector. Measure the resistance of the High Speed Radiator Fan Relay Control circuit in the PDC to ground. Is the resistance below 5.0 ohms. Yes → Repair the High Speed Radiator Fan Relay Control circuit for a short to ground. No → Go To 8
8	If there are no possible causes remaining, view repair. Repair Replace and program the Powertrain Control Module Module

ARM0400000000974

Fig. 36   Code P1489: High Speed Fan Control Relay Circuit (Part 3 of 3). LHS, 2001 Concorde, Intrepid & 300M

TEST	ACTION
3	WARNING: WHEN THE ENGINE IS OPERATING, DO NOT STAND IN A DIRECT LINE WITH THE FAN. DO NOT PUT YOUR HANDS NEAR THE PULLEYS, BELTS OR FAN. DO NOT WEAR LOOSE CLOTHING. NOTE: The conditions that set the DTC are not present at this time. The following list may help in identifying the intermittent condition. With the engine running at normal operating temperature, monitor the DRB parameters related to the DTC while wiggling the wiring harness. Look for parameter values to change and/or a DTC to set. Review the DRB Freeze Frame information. If possible, try to duplicate the conditions under which the DTC was set. Refer to any Technical Service Bulletins (TSB) that may apply. Visually inspect the related wiring harness. Look for any chafed, pierced, pinched, or partially broken wires. Visually inspect the related wiring harness connectors. Look for broken, bent, pushed out, or corroded terminals. Were any of the above conditions present? Yes → Repair as necessary No → Test Complete.
4	Turn the ignition off. Remove the Low Speed Radiator Fan Relay from the PDC. Turn the ignition on. Measure the voltage of the Fused Ignition Switch Output circuit in the PDC. Is the voltage above 11.0 volts? Yes → Go To 5 No → Repair the Fused Ignition Switch Output circuit. Check and replace any open fuses.
5	Turn the ignition off. Remove the Low Speed Radiator Fan Relay from the PDC. Measure the resistance of the Low Speed Radiator Fan Relay between the Fused Ignition Switch Output terminal and the Low Speed Radiator Fan Relay Control terminal. Using a jumper wire, momentarily jumper the Radiator Fan Relay Control circuit to ground. Is the resistance between 60 to 80 ohms? Yes → Go To 6 No → Replace the Low Speed Radiator Fan Relay.
6	Turn the ignition off. Remove the Low Speed Radiator Fan Relay from the PDC. Disconnect the PCM harness connector. Measure the resistance of the Low Speed Radiator Fan Relay Control circuit between the PDC and the PCM harness connector. Is the resistance below 5.0 ohms. Yes → Go To 7 No → Repair the Low Speed Radiator Fan Relay Control circuit for an open.

ARM0400000000976

Fig. 37   Code P1490: Low Speed Fan Control Relay Circuit (Part 2 of 3). LHS, 2001 Concorde, Intrepid & 300M

TEST	ACTION
7	Turn the ignition off. Remove the Low Speed Radiator Fan Relay from the PDC. Disconnect the PCM harness connector. Measure the resistance of the Low Speed Radiator Fan Relay Control circuit in the PDC to ground. Is the resistance below 5.0 ohms. Yes → Repair the Low Speed Radiator Fan Relay Control circuit for a short to ground. No → Go To 8
8	If there are no possible causes remaining, view repair. Repair Replace and program the Powertrain Control Module Module

ARM0400000000977

Fig. 37   Code P1490: Low Speed Fan Control Relay Circuit (Part 3 of 3). LHS, 2001 Concorde, Intrepid & 300M

TEST	ACTION
4	This DTC is an informational DTC designed to aid the Technician in diagnosing shift quality complaints. This DTC indicates that the transmission has been operating in the "Overheat" shift schedule which may generate a customer complaint. The customer driving patterns may indicate the need for an additional transmission oil cooler. View repair options.. Repair Repair cause of transmission overheating

ARM0400000000979

Fig. 38   Code P1738: High Temperature Operation Activated (Part 2 of 2). LHS, 2001 Concorde, Intrepid & 300M

When Monitored and Set Condition:

P0110-INTAKE AIR TEMPERATURE SENSOR STUCK

When Monitored: Engine Running.

Set Condition: After 4 warm-up cycles, the PCM did not see a 2°C (6°F) change in the IAT Sensor voltage within 200 miles . Two Trip Fault

P0111-INTAKE AIR TEMPERATURE SENSOR PERFORMANCE

When Monitored: Engine off time is greater than 480 minutes. Ambient temperature is greater than -23°C (-10°F).

Set Condition: After a calibrated amount of cool down time, the PCM compares the ECT Sensor, IAT Sensor and the Ambient Air Temperature Sensor values. If the IAT Sensor value is not within calibrated temperature amount of the other two temperature sensors an error is detected. Two Trip Fault.

POSSIBLE CAUSES
GOOD TRIP EQUAL TO ZERO
(K21) IAT SIGNAL CIRCUIT SHORTED TO BATTERY VOLTAGE
IAT SENSOR VOLTAGE BELOW 1.0 VOLTS
(K21) IAT SIGNAL CIRCUIT OPEN
(K4) SENSOR GROUND CIRCUIT OPEN
(K21) IAT SIGNAL SHORTED TO GROUND
(K21) IAT SIGNAL CIRCUIT SHORTED TO (K4) SENSOR GROUND
PCM HIGH
PCM LOW

ARM0400000000938

Fig. 39   Code P0110 & P0111: IAT Sensor Stuck Or Performance (Part 1 of 3). 2002–04 Concorde, Intrepid & 300M

When Monitored and Set Condition:

P1738-HIGH TEMPERATURE OPERATION ACTIVATED

When Monitored: Whenever the engine is running.

Set Condition: Immediately when the Overheat shift schedule is activated (240 degrees Transmission oil temp).

POSSIBLE CAUSES
ENGINE COOLING SYSTEM MALFUNCTION
INCORRECT FLUID LEVEL
TRANSMISSION OIL COOLER PLUGGED
HIGH TEMPERATURE OPERATIONS ACTIVATED

TEST	ACTION
1	Perform engine cooling system diagnostics in accordance to Service Information. Is the engine cooling system functioning properly? Yes → Go To 2 No → Repair cause of engine overheating.
2	Check the Transmission Fluid Level in accordance with the Service Information. **NOTE: Make sure to use proper fluid level instructions in accordance with the Service Information. Failure to do so can lead to a over or under filled Transmission fluid level.** Is the fluid level OK? Yes → Go To 3 No → Adjust the Fluid Level
3	Perform Transmission Cooler Flow Check in accordance with the Service Information. Did the Transmission Cooler Flow Check test pass? Yes → Go To 4 No → Repair the cause of the plugged Transmission Oil Cooler as necessary. Repair or replace the plugged Transmission Oil Cooler

ARM0400000000978

Fig. 38   Code P1738: High Temperature Operation Activated (Part 1 of 2). LHS, 2001 Concorde, Intrepid & 300M

TEST	ACTION
1	Ignition on, engine not running. With the DRBIII®, read DTCs and record the related Freeze Frame data. Is the Good Trip Counter displayed and equal to zero? Yes → Go To 2 No → Diagnose intermittent condition.
2	Turn the ignition off. Disconnect the IAT Sensor harness connector. **NOTE: Visually inspect both the component and the PCM connectors. Look for damaged, partially broken wires, and backed out or corroded terminals.** Ignition on, engine not running. Measure the voltage on the (K21) IAT Signal circuit in the IAT Sensor harness connector. Is the voltage above 5.2 volts? Yes → Repair the short to battery voltage in the (K21) IAT Signal circuit. No → Go To 3
3	Turn the ignition off. Disconnect the IAT Sensor harness connector. Ignition on, engine not running. With the DRBIII®, read the IAT Sensor voltage. Is the voltage above 4.9 volts? Yes → Go To 4 No → Go To 7
4	Turn the ignition off. Disconnect the IAT Sensor harness connector. Using a jumper wire, jumper across the IAT Sensor harness connector. Ignition on, engine not running. With the DRBIII®, read the IAT Sensor voltage. Is the voltage below 1.0 volt? Yes → Replace the IAT Sensor. No → Go To 5
5	Turn the ignition off. Disconnect the IAT Sensor harness connector. Disconnect the PCM harness connector. **CAUTION: DO NOT PROBE THE PCM HARNESS CONNECTORS. PROBING THE PCM HARNESS CONNECTORS WILL DAMAGE THE PCM TERMINALS RESULTING IN POOR TERMINAL TO PIN CONNECTION. INSTALL MILLER SPECIAL TOOL #8815 TO PERFORM DIAGNOSIS.** Measure the resistance of the (K21) IAT Signal circuit from the IAT Sensor harness connector to the appropriate terminal of special tool #8815. Is the resistance below 5.0 ohms? Yes → Go To 6 No → Repair the open in the (K21) IAT Signal circuit.

ARM0400000000939

Fig. 39   Code P0110 & P0111: IAT Sensor Stuck Or Performance (Part 2 of 3). 2002–04 Concorde, Intrepid & 300M

TEST	ACTION
6	Turn the ignition off. Disconnect the IAT Sensor harness connector. Disconnect the PCM harness connector. **CAUTION: DO NOT PROBE THE PCM HARNESS CONNECTORS. PROBING THE PCM HARNESS CONNECTORS WILL DAMAGE THE PCM TERMINALS RESULTING IN POOR TERMINAL TO PIN CONNECTION. INSTALL MILLER SPECIAL TOOL #8815 TO PERFORM DIAGNOSIS.** Measure the resistance of the (K4) Sensor ground circuit from the IAT Sensor harness connector to the appropriate terminal of special tool #8815. Is the resistance below 5.0 ohms? Yes → NOTE: Before continuing, check the PCM harness connector terminals for corrosion, damage, or terminal push out. Repair as necessary. Replace and program the Powertrain Control Module in accordance with the Service Information. No → Repair the open in the (K4) Sensor ground circuit.
7	Turn the ignition off. Disconnect the IAT Sensor harness connector. Disconnect the PCM harness connector. Measure the resistance between ground and the (K21) IAT Signal circuit in the IAT Sensor harness connector. Is the resistance below 100 ohms? Yes → Repair the short to ground in the (K21) IAT Signal circuit. No → Go To 8
8	Turn the ignition off. Disconnect the IAT Sensor harness connector. Disconnect the PCM harness connector. Measure the resistance between the (K4) Sensor ground circuit and the (K21) IAT Sensor Signal circuit at the IAT Sensor harness connector. Is the resistance below 5.0 ohms? Yes → Repair the (K4) Sensor ground circuit shorted to the (K21) IAT Signal circuit. No → NOTE: Before continuing, check the PCM harness connector terminals for corrosion, damage, or terminal push out. Repair as necessary. Replace and program the Powertrain Control Module

ARM0400000000940

Fig. 39   Code P0110 & P0111: IAT Sensor Stuck Or Performance (Part 3 of 3). 2002–04 Concorde, Intrepid & 300M

TEST	ACTION
4	Turn the ignition off. Disconnect the IAT Sensor harness connector. Disconnect the PCM harness connector. Measure the resistance between the (K21) IAT Sensor Signal circuit and the (K4) Sensor ground circuit in the IAT Sensor harness connector. Is the resistance below 100 ohms? Yes → Repair the (K4) Sensor ground shorted to the (K21) IAT Signal circuit. No → Go To 5
5	**NOTE: Before continuing, check the PCM harness connector terminals for corrosion, damage, or terminal push out. Repair as necessary.** If there are no possible causes remaining, view repair. Repair Replace and program the Powertrain Control Module

ARM0400000000942

Fig. 40   Code P0112: IAT Sensor Low (Part 2 of 2). 2002–04 Concorde, Intrepid & 300M

When Monitored and Set Condition:

P0112-INTAKE AIR TEMPERATURE SENSOR LOW

When Monitored: With the ignition on. Battery voltage greater than 10 volts.

Set Condition: The Intake Air Temperature (IAT) sensor voltage is less than 0.0784 of a volt. One trip Fault.

POSSIBLE CAUSES
IAT SENSOR VOLTAGE BELOW 1.0 VOLT
IAT SENSOR INTERNAL FAILURE
(K21) IAT SIGNAL SHORTED TO GROUND
(K21) IAT SIGNAL SHORTED TO (K4) SENSOR GROUND CIRCUIT
PCM

TEST	ACTION
1	Ignition on, engine not running. With the DRBIII®, read the IAT Sensor voltage. Is the voltage below 1.0 volt? Yes → Go To 2 No → Diagnose intermittent condition.
2	Turn the ignition off. Disconnect the IAT harness connector. Ignition on, engine not running. With the DRBIII®, read IAT Sensor voltage. Is the voltage above 1.0 volt? Yes → Replace the IAT Sensor. No → Go To 3
3	Turn the ignition off. Disconnect the IAT Sensor harness connector. Disconnect the PCM harness connector. Measure the resistance between ground and the (K21) IAT Signal circuit at the IAT Sensor harness connector. Is the resistance below 100 ohms? Yes → Repair the short to ground in the (K21) IAT Signal circuit. No → Go To 4

ARM0400000000941

Fig. 40   Code P0112: IAT Sensor Low (Part 1 of 2). 2002–04 Concorde, Intrepid & 300M

When Monitored and Set Condition:

P0113-INTAKE AIR TEMPERATURE SENSOR HIGH

When Monitored: With the ignition on. Battery voltage greater than 10 volts.

Set Condition: The Intake Air Temperature (IAT) sensor voltage at the PCM is greater than 4.98 volts. One trip Fault.

POSSIBLE CAUSES
IAT SENSOR VOLTAGE ABOVE 4.6 VOLTS
(K21) IAT SIGNAL CIRCUIT SHORTED TO BATTERY VOLTAGE
IAT SENSOR INTERNAL FAILURE
(K21) IAT SIGNAL CIRCUIT OPEN
(K4) SENSOR GROUND CIRCUIT OPEN
PCM

TEST	ACTION
1	Ignition on, engine not running. With the DRBIII®, read the IAT Sensor voltage. Is the voltage above 4.6 volts? Yes → Go To 2 No → Diagnose intermittent condition.
2	Turn the ignition off. Disconnect the IAT Sensor harness connector. Ignition on, engine not running. Measure the voltage of the (K21) IAT Signal circuit in the IAT Sensor harness connector. Is the voltage above 5.2 volts? Yes → Repair the short to battery voltage in the (K21) IAT Signal circuit. No → Go To 3

ARM0400000000943

Fig. 41   Code P0113: IAT Sensor High (Part 1 of 2). 2002–04 Concorde, Intrepid & 300M

TEST	ACTION

3	Turn the ignition off.
	Disconnect the IAT harness connector.
	Connect a jumper wire between the (K21) IAT Signal circuit and the (K4) Sensor ground circuit in the IAT harness connector.
	Ignition on, engine not running.
	With the DRBIII®, read IAT voltage.
	Is the voltage below 1.0 volt?
	
	    Yes → Replace the IAT Sensor.
	
	    No → Go To 4

4	Turn the ignition off.
	Disconnect the IAT Sensor harness connector.
	Disconnect the PCM harness connector.
	CAUTION: DO NOT PROBE THE PCM HARNESS CONNECTORS. PROBING THE PCM HARNESS CONNECTORS WILL DAMAGE THE PCM TERMINALS RESULTING IN POOR TERMINAL TO PIN CONNECTION. INSTALL MILLER SPECIAL TOOL #8815 TO PERFORM DIAGNOSIS.
	Measure the resistance of the (K21) IAT Signal circuit from the IAT Sensor harness connector to the appropriate terminal of special tool #8815.
	Is the resistance below 5.0 ohms?
	
	    Yes → Go To 5
	
	    No → Repair the open in the (K21) IAT Signal circuit.

5	Turn the ignition off.
	Disconnect the IAT Sensor harness connector.
	Disconnect the PCM harness connector.
	CAUTION: DO NOT PROBE THE PCM HARNESS CONNECTORS. PROBING THE PCM HARNESS CONNECTORS WILL DAMAGE THE PCM TERMINALS RESULTING IN POOR TERMINAL TO PIN CONNECTION. INSTALL MILLER SPECIAL TOOL #8815 TO PERFORM DIAGNOSIS.
	Measure the resistance of the (K4) Sensor ground circuit from the IAT Sensor harness connector to the appropriate terminal of special tool #8815.
	Is the resistance below 5.0 ohms?
	
	    Yes → Go To 6
	
	    No → Repair the open in the (K4) Sensor ground circuit.

6	NOTE: Before continuing, check the PCM harness connector terminals for corrosion, damage, or terminal push out. Repair as necessary.
	If there are no possible causes remaining, view repair.
	
	    Repair
	
	    Replace and program the Powertrain Control Module

ARM0400000000944

Fig. 41   Code P0113: IAT Sensor High (Part 2 of 2). 2002–04 Concorde, Intrepid & 300M

TEST	ACTION

2	Turn the ignition off.
	Disconnect the ECT Sensor harness connector.
	NOTE: Visually inspect both the component and the PCM connectors. Look for damaged, partially broken wires, and backed out or corroded terminals.
	Ignition on, engine not running.
	Measure the voltage on the (K2) ECT Signal circuit in the ECT Sensor harness connector.
	Is the voltage above 5.2 volts?
	
	    Yes → Repair the short to battery voltage in the (K2) ECT Signal circuit.
	
	    No → Go To 3

3	Turn the ignition off.
	Disconnect the ECT Sensor harness connector.
	Ignition on, engine not running.
	With the DRBIII®, read the ECT Sensor voltage.
	Is the voltage above 4.6 volts?
	
	    Yes → Go To 4
	
	    No → Go To 7

4	Turn the ignition off.
	Disconnect the ECT Sensor harness connector.
	Using a jumper wire, jumper across the ECT Sensor harness connector.
	Ignition on, engine not running.
	With the DRBIII®, read the ECT Sensor voltage.
	Is the voltage below 1.0 volt?
	
	    Yes → Replace the ECT Sensor.
	
	    No → Go To 5

5	Turn the ignition off.
	Disconnect the ECT Sensor harness connector.
	Disconnect the PCM harness connector.
	CAUTION: DO NOT PROBE THE PCM HARNESS CONNECTORS. PROBING THE PCM HARNESS CONNECTORS WILL DAMAGE THE PCM TERMINALS RESULTING IN POOR TERMINAL TO PIN CONNECTION. INSTALL MILLER SPECIAL TOOL #8815 TO PERFORM DIAGNOSIS.
	Measure the resistance of the (K2) ECT Signal circuit from the ECT Sensor harness connector to the appropriate terminal of special tool #8815.
	Is the resistance below 5.0 ohms?
	
	    Yes → Go To 6
	
	    No → Repair the open in the (K2) ECT Signal circuit.

ARM0400000000946

Fig. 42   Code P0116: ECT Performance (Part 2 of 3). 2002–04 Concorde, Intrepid & 300M

When Monitored and Set Condition:

P0116-ENGINE COOLANT TEMPERATURE PERFORMANCE

When Monitored: Engine off time is greater than 480 minutes. Ambient temperature is greater than 4°C (39°F) 02 MY or -23°C (-10°F) 03 MY.

Set Condition: After a calibrated amount of cool down time, the PCM compares the ECT Sensor, IAT Sensor and the Ambient Air Temperature Sensor values. If the ECT Sensor value is not within calibrated temperature amount of the other two temperature sensors an error is detected. Two Trip Fault.

POSSIBLE CAUSES
GOOD TRIP EQUAL TO ZERO
(K2) ECT SIGNAL CIRCUIT SHORTED TO BATTERY VOLTAGE
ECT SENSOR VOLTAGE BELOW 1.0 VOLT
(K2) ECT SIGNAL CIRCUIT OPEN
(K4) SENSOR GROUND CIRCUIT OPEN
(K2) ECT SIGNAL CIRCUIT SHORTED TO GROUND
(K2) ECT SIGNAL SHORTED TO (K4) SENSOR GROUND
PCM HIGH
PCM LOW

TEST	ACTION

1	NOTE: Due to the fact that the PCM compares the IAT, AAT and ECT sensor to see if they are within a calibrated temp of one another, the use of a block heater can cause false readings for the PCM. Check with the customer to see if they use a block heater.
	Ignition on, engine not running.
	With the DRBIII®, read DTCs and record the related Freeze Frame data.
	Is the Good Trip Counter displayed and equal to zero?
	
	    Yes → Go To 2
	
	    No → Diagnose intermittent condition.

ARM0400000000945

Fig. 42   Code P0116: ECT Performance (Part 1 of 3). 2002–04 Concorde, Intrepid & 300M

TEST	ACTION

6	Turn the ignition off.
	Disconnect the ECT harness connector.
	Disconnect the PCM harness connector.
	CAUTION: DO NOT PROBE THE PCM HARNESS CONNECTORS. PROBING THE PCM HARNESS CONNECTORS WILL DAMAGE THE PCM TERMINALS RESULTING IN POOR TERMINAL TO PIN CONNECTION. INSTALL MILLER SPECIAL TOOL #8815 TO PERFORM DIAGNOSIS.
	Measure the resistance of the (K4) Sensor ground circuit from the ECT Sensor harness connector to the appropriate terminal of special tool # 8815.
	Is the resistance below 5.0 ohms?
	
	    Yes → NOTE: Before continuing, check the PCM harness connector terminals for corrosion, damage, or terminal push out. Repair as necessary. Replace and program the Powertrain Control Module
	
	    No → Repair the open in the (K4) Sensor ground circuit.

7	Disconnect the ECT Sensor harness connector.
	Turn the ignition off.
	Disconnect the PCM harness connector.
	Measure the resistance between ground and the (K2) ECT Signal circuit in the ECT Sensor harness connector.
	Is the resistance below 100 ohms?
	
	    Yes → Repair the short to ground in the (K2) ECT Signal circuit.
	
	    No → Go To 8

8	Turn the ignition off.
	Disconnect the ECT Sensor harness connector.
	Disconnect the PCM harness connector.
	Measure the resistance between the (K2) ECT Sensor Signal circuit and the (K4) Sensor ground circuit at the ECT Sensor harness connector.
	Is the resistance below 5.0 ohms?
	
	    Yes → Repair the (K4) Sensor ground shorted to the (K2) ECT Sensor Signal circuit.
	
	    No → NOTE: Before continuing, check the PCM harness connector terminals for corrosion, damage, or terminal push out. Repair as necessary. Replace and program the Powertrain Control Module

ARM0400000000947

Fig. 42   Code P0116: ECT Performance (Part 3 of 3). 2002–04 Concorde, Intrepid & 300M

When Monitored and Set Condition:

P0117-ENGINE COOLANT TEMPERATURE SENSOR LOW

When Monitored: With the ignition on. Battery voltage greater than 10 volts.

Set Condition: The Engine Coolant Temperature (ECT) sensor circuit voltage at the PCM is less than 0.0782 of a volt. One Trip Fault.

POSSIBLE CAUSES
ECT SENSOR VOLTAGE BELOW 1.0 VOLTS
ECT SENSOR INTERNAL FAILURE
(K2) ECT SIGNAL SHORTED TO GROUND
(K2) ECT SIGNAL SHORTED TO (K4) SENSOR GROUND CIRCUIT
PCM

TEST	ACTION
1	Ignition on, engine not running. With the DRBIII®, read the ECT Sensor voltage. Is the voltage below 1.0 volt? Yes → Go To 2 No → Diagnose intermittent condition.
2	Turn the ignition off. Disconnect the ECT harness connector. Ignition on, engine not running. With the DRBIII®, read ECT Sensor voltage. Is the voltage between 4.8 and 5.2 volts? Yes → Replace the ECT Sensor. No → Go To 3
3	Turn the ignition off. Disconnect the ECT Sensor harness connector. Disconnect the PCM harness connector. Measure the resistance between ground and the (K2) ECT Signal circuit in the ECT Sensor harness connector. Is the resistance below 100 ohms? Yes → Repair the ground shorted to the (K2) ECT Signal circuit. No → Go To 4

ARM0400000000948

Fig. 43   Code P0117: ECT Sensor Low (Part 1 of 2). 2002–04 Concorde, Intrepid & 300M

When Monitored and Set Condition:

P0118-ENGINE COOLANT TEMPERATURE SENSOR HIGH

When Monitored: With the ignition on. Battery voltage greater than 10 volts.

Set Condition: The Engine Coolant Temperature (ECT) sensor voltage at the PCM is greater than 4.9 volts. One trip Fault.

POSSIBLE CAUSES
ECT SENSOR VOLTAGE ABOVE 4.9 VOLTS
(K2) ECT SIGNAL CIRCUIT SHORTED TO BATTERY VOLTAGE
ECT SENSOR INTERNAL FAILURE
(K2) ECT SIGNAL CIRCUIT OPEN
(K4) SENSOR GROUND CIRCUIT OPEN
PCM

TEST	ACTION
1	Ignition on, engine not running. With the DRBIII®, read the ECT Sensor voltage. Is the voltage above 4.9 volts? Yes → Go To 2 No → Diagnose intermittent condition.
2	Turn the ignition off. Disconnect the ECT Sensor harness connector. Ignition on, engine not running. Measure the voltage of the (K2) ECT Signal circuit in the ECT Sensor harness connector. Is the voltage above 5.2 volts? Yes → Repair the short to battery voltage in the (K2) ECT Signal circuit. No → Go To 3

ARM0400000000950

Fig. 44   Code P0118: ECT Sensor High (Part 1 of 2). 2002–04 Concorde, Intrepid & 300M

TEST	ACTION
4	Turn the ignition off. Disconnect the ECT Sensor harness connector. Disconnect the PCM harness connector. Measure the resistance between the (K2) ECT Sensor Signal circuit and the (K4) Sensor ground circuit in the ECT Sensor harness connector. Is the resistance below 100 ohms? Yes → Repair the (K4) Sensor ground shorted to the (K2) ECT Sensor Signal circuit. No → Go To 5
5	NOTE: Before continuing, check the PCM harness connector terminals for corrosion, damage, or terminal push out. Repair as necessary. If there are no possible causes remaining, view repair. Repair Replace and program the Powertrain Control Module

ARM0400000000949

Fig. 43   Code P0117: ECT Sensor Low (Part 2 of 2). 2002–04 Concorde, Intrepid & 300M

TEST	ACTION
3	Turn the ignition off. Disconnect the ECT harness connector. Connect a jumper wire between the (K2) ECT Signal circuit and the (K4) Sensor ground circuit in the ECT harness connector. Ignition on, engine not running. With the DRBIII®, read ECT Sensor voltage. Is the voltage below 1.0 volt? Yes → Replace the ECT Sensor. No → Go To 4
4	Turn the ignition off. Disconnect the ECT Sensor harness connector. Disconnect the PCM harness connector. CAUTION: DO NOT PROBE THE PCM HARNESS CONNECTORS. PROBING THE PCM HARNESS CONNECTORS WILL DAMAGE THE PCM TERMINALS RESULTING IN POOR TERMINAL TO PIN CONNECTION. INSTALL MILLER SPECIAL TOOL #8815 TO PERFORM DIAGNOSIS. Measure the resistance of the (K2) ECT Signal circuit from the ECT Sensor harness connector to the appropriate terminal of special tool #8815. Is the resistance below 5.0 ohms? Yes → Go To 5 No → Repair the open in the (K2) ECT Signal circuit.
5	Turn the ignition off. Disconnect the ECT Sensor harness connector. Disconnect the PCM harness connector. CAUTION: DO NOT PROBE THE PCM HARNESS CONNECTORS. PROBING THE PCM HARNESS CONNECTORS WILL DAMAGE THE PCM TERMINALS RESULTING IN POOR TERMINAL TO PIN CONNECTION. INSTALL MILLER SPECIAL TOOL #8815 TO PERFORM DIAGNOSIS. Measure the resistance from the (K4) Sensor ground circuit from the ECT Sensor harness connector to the appropriate terminal of special tool #8815. Is the resistance below 5.0 ohms? Yes → Go To 6 No → Repair the open in the (K4) Sensor ground circuit.
6	NOTE: Before continuing, check the PCM harness connector terminals for corrosion, damage, or terminal push out. Repair as necessary. If there are no possible causes remaining, view repair. Repair Replace and program the Powertrain Control Module

ARM0400000000951

Fig. 44   Code P0118: ECT Sensor High (Part 2 of 2). 2002–04 Concorde, Intrepid & 300M

When Monitored and Set Condition:

P0480-LOW SPEED FAN CONTROL RELAY CIRCUIT

When Monitored: With the ignition on. Battery voltage greater than 10 volts.

Set Condition: An open or shorted circuit is detected in the radiator fan relay control circuit. One Trip Fault.

POSSIBLE CAUSES
LOW SPEED RADIATOR FAN RELAY OPERATION
(A16) FUSED B+ FEED CIRCUITS
LOW SPEED RADIATOR FAN RELAY RESISTANCE
(C24) LOW SPEED RAD FAN RELAY CONTROL CIRCUIT OPEN
(C24) LOW SPEED RAD FAN RELAY CONTROL CIRCUIT SHORT TO GROUND
PCM

TEST	ACTION
1	Ignition on, engine not running. With the DRBIII®, actuate the Radiator Fan Relay. Is the Low Speed Radiator Fan Relay operating? Yes → Diagnose intermittent condition. No → Go To 2
2	Turn the ignition off. Remove the Low Speed Radiator Fan Relay from the PDC. Ignition on, engine not running. Measure the voltage of the (A16) Fused B+ Feed circuit in the PDC. Is the voltage above 11.0 volts? Yes → Go To 3 No → Repair the (A16) Fused B+ Output circuit. Inspect the related fuse and repair as necessary.

ARM0400000000928

Fig. 45   Code P0480: Low Speed Fan Control Relay Circuit (Part 1 of 2). 2002–04 Concorde, Intrepid & 300M

When Monitored and Set Condition:

P0481-HIGH SPEED FAN CONTROL RELAY CIRCUIT

When Monitored: With the ignition on. Battery voltage greater than 10 volts.

Set Condition: An open or shorted circuit is detected in the radiator fan relay control circuit. One trip Fault.

POSSIBLE CAUSES
HIGH SPEED RADIATOR FAN RELAY OPERATION
(A16) FUSED IGNITION SWITCH OUTPUT CIRCUIT
HIGH SPEED RADIATOR FAN RELAY RESISTANCE
(C27) HIGH SPEED RAD FAN RELAY CONTROL CIRCUIT OPEN
(C27) HIGH SPEED RAD FAN RELAY CONTROL CIRCUIT SHORT TO GROUND
PCM

TEST	ACTION
1	Turn the ignition on. With the DRBIII®, actuate the High Speed Radiator Fan Relay. Is the High Speed Radiator Fan Relay operating? Yes → Diagnose intermittent condition. No → Go To 2
2	Turn the ignition off. Remove the High Speed Radiator Fan Relay from the PDC. Turn the ignition on. Measure the voltage of the (A16) Fused Ignition Switch Output circuit in the PDC. Is the voltage above 11.0 volts? Yes → Go To 3 No → Repair the (A16) Fused Ignition Switch Output circuit. Check and replace any open fuses.

ARM0400000000930

Fig. 46   Code P0481: High Speed Fan Control Relay Circuit (Part 1 of 2). 2002–04 Concorde, Intrepid & 300M

TEST	ACTION
3	Turn the ignition off. Remove the Low Speed Radiator Fan Relay from the PDC. Measure the resistance of the Low Speed Radiator Fan Relay between the Fused Ignition Switch Output terminal and the Low Speed Rad Fan Relay Control terminal. Is the resistance between 60 to 85 ohms? Yes → Go To 4 No → Replace the Low Speed Radiator Fan Relay.
4	Turn the ignition off. Remove the Low Speed Radiator Fan Relay from the PDC. Disconnect the PCM harness connector. **CAUTION: DO NOT PROBE THE PCM HARNESS CONNECTORS. PROBING THE PCM HARNESS CONNECTORS WILL DAMAGE THE PCM TERMINALS RESULTING IN POOR TERMINAL TO PIN CONNECTION. INSTALL MILLER SPECIAL TOOL #8815 TO PERFORM DIAGNOSIS.** Measure the resistance of the (C24) Low Speed Rad Fan Relay Control circuit from the PDC to the appropriate terminal of special tool #8815. Is the resistance below 5.0 ohms? Yes → Go To 5 No → Repair the open in the (C24) Low Speed Rad Fan Relay Control circuit.
5	Turn the ignition off. Remove the Low Speed Radiator Fan Relay from the PDC. Disconnect the PCM harness connector. Measure the resistance between ground and the (C24) Low Speed Rad Fan Control circuit at the PDC. Is the resistance below 100 ohms? Yes → Repair the short to ground in the (C24) Low Speed Rad Fan Relay Control circuit. No → Go To 6
6	**NOTE: Before continuing, check the PCM harness connector terminals for corrosion, damage, or terminal push out. Repair as necessary.** If there are no possible causes remaining, view repair. Repair Replace and program the Powertrain Control Module

ARM0400000000929

Fig. 45   Code P0480: Low Speed Fan Control Relay Circuit (Part 2 of 2).2002–04 Concorde, Intrepid & 300M

TEST	ACTION
3	Turn the ignition off. Remove the High Speed Radiator Fan Relay from the PDC. Measure the resistance of the High Speed Radiator Fan Relay between the Fused Ignition Switch Output terminal and the High Speed Rad Fan Relay Control terminal. Is the resistance between 60 to 85 ohms? Yes → Go To 4 No → Replace the High Speed Radiator Fan Relay.
4	Turn the ignition off. Remove the High Speed Radiator Fan Relay from the PDC. Disconnect the PCM harness connector. **CAUTION: DO NOT PROBE THE PCM HARNESS CONNECTORS. PROBING THE PCM HARNESS CONNECTORS WILL DAMAGE THE PCM TERMINALS RESULTING IN POOR TERMINAL TO PIN CONNECTION. INSTALL MILLER SPECIAL TOOL #8815 TO PERFORM DIAGNOSIS.** Measure the resistance of the (C27) High Speed Rad Fan Relay Control circuit from the PDC to the appropriate terminal of special tool #8815. Is the resistance below 5.0 ohms? Yes → Go To 5 No → Repair the open in the (C27) High Speed Rad Fan Relay Control circuit.
5	Turn the ignition off. Remove the High Speed Radiator Fan Relay from the PDC. Disconnect the PCM harness connector. Measure the resistance between ground and the (C27) High Speed Rad Fan Relay Control circuit in the PDC. Is the resistance below 5.0 ohms? Yes → Repair the short to ground in the (C27) High Speed Rad Fan Relay Control circuit. No → Go To 6
6	**NOTE: Before continuing, check the PCM harness connector terminals for corrosion, damage, or terminal push out. Repair as necessary.** If there are no possible causes remaining, view repair. Repair NOTE: Before continuing, check the PCM harness connector terminals for corrosion, damage or terminal push out. Repair as necessary. Replace and program the Powertrain Control Module

ARM0400000000931

Fig. 46   Code P0481: High Speed Fan Control Relay Circuit (Part 2 of 2). 2002–04 Concorde, Intrepid & 300M

When Monitored and Set Condition:

P0532-A/C PRESSURE SENSOR LOW

When Monitored: The engine running. The A/C relay energized.

Set Condition: The A/C pressure sensor signal voltage at the PCM goes below 0.58 volts for 2.6 seconds. One Trip Fault.

POSSIBLE CAUSES
A/C PRESSURE SENSOR VOLTAGE BELOW 0.6 VOLTS
(K7) 5 VOLT SUPPLY CIRCUIT SHORTED TO GROUND
(K7) 5 VOLT SUPPLY CIRCUIT OPEN
A/C PRESSURE SENSOR INTERNAL FAILURE
(C18) A/C PRESSURE SIGNAL CIRCUIT SHORTED TO GROUND
(C18) A/C PRESSURE SIGNAL CIRCUIT SHORTED TO (K4) SENSOR GROUND CIRCUIT
PCM (K7) 5 VOLT SUPPLY CIRCUIT
PCM A/C PRESSURE SENSOR SIGNAL

TEST	ACTION
1	NOTE: Ensure the A/C refrigerant System is properly charged per the Service Information. Start the engine. With the DRBIII®, read the A/C Pressure Sensor voltage. Is the voltage below 0.6 of a volt? Yes → Go To 2 No → Diagnose intermittent condition.
2	Turn the ignition off. Disconnect the A/C Pressure Sensor harness connector. Turn the ignition on. Measure the voltage of the (K7) 5 Volt Supply circuit in the A/C Pressure Sensor harness connector. Is the voltage between 4.5 to 5.2 volts? Yes → Go To 3 No → Go To 7

ARM0400000000932

Fig. 47 Code P0532: Air Conditioning Pressure Sensor Low (Part 1 of 3). 2002–04 Concorde, Intrepid & 300M

TEST	ACTION
8	Turn the ignition off. Disconnect the A/C Pressure Sensor harness connector. Disconnect the PCM harness connector. **CAUTION: DO NOT PROBE THE PCM HARNESS CONNECTORS. PROBING THE PCM HARNESS CONNECTORS WILL DAMAGE THE PCM TERMINALS RESULTING IN POOR TERMINAL TO PIN CONNECTION. INSTALL MILLER SPECIAL TOOL #8815 TO PERFORM DIAGNOSIS.** Measure the resistance of the (K7) 5 Volt Supply circuit from the A/C Pressure Sensor harness connector to the appropriate terminal of special tool #8815. Is the resistance below 5.0 ohms? Yes → Go To 9 No → Repair the open in the (K7) 5 Volt Supply circuit.
9	NOTE: Before continuing, check the PCM harness connector terminals for corrosion, damage, or terminal push out. Repair as necessary. If there are no possible causes remaining, view repair. Repair Replace and program the Powertrain Control Module

ARM0400000000934

Fig. 47 Code P0532: Air Conditioning Pressure Sensor Low (Part 3 of 3). 2002–04 Concorde, Intrepid & 300M

TEST	ACTION
3	Turn the ignition off. Disconnect the A/C Pressure Sensor harness connector. With the DRBIII®, monitor the A/C Pressure Sensor voltage. Turn the ignition on. Is the voltage above 0.6 of a volt? Yes → Replace the A/C Pressure Sensor. No → Go To 4
4	Turn the ignition off. Disconnect the A/C Pressure Sensor harness connector. Disconnect the PCM harness connector. Measure the resistance between ground and the (C18) A/C Pressure Signal circuit in the A/C Pressure Sensor harness connector. Is the resistance below 100 ohms? Yes → Repair the short to ground in the (C18) A/C Pressure Signal circuit. No → Go To 5
5	Turn the ignition off. Disconnect the A/C Pressure Sensor harness connector. Disconnect the PCM harness connector. Measure the resistance between the (C18) A/C Pressure Sensor Signal circuit and the (K4) Sensor ground circuit in the A/C Pressure Sensor harness connector. Is the resistance below 100 ohms? Yes → Repair the short to the (K4) Sensor ground circuit in the (C18) A/C Pressure Signal circuit. No → Go To 6
6	NOTE: Before continuing, check the PCM harness connector terminals for corrosion, damage, or terminal push out. Repair as necessary. If there are no possible causes remaining, view repair. Repair Replace and program the Powertrain Control Module
7	Turn the ignition off. Disconnect the A/C Pressure Sensor harness connector. Disconnect the PCM harness connector. Measure the resistance between ground and the (K7) 5 Volt Supply circuit in the A/C Pressure Sensor harness connector. Is the resistance below 100 ohms? Yes → Repair the short to ground in the (K7) 5 Volt Supply circuit. No → Go To 8

ARM0400000000933

Fig. 47 Code P0532: Air Conditioning Pressure Sensor Low (Part 2 of 3). 2002–04 Concorde, Intrepid & 300M

When Monitored and Set Condition:

P0533-A/C PRESSURE SENSOR HIGH

When Monitored: The engine running. The A/C relay energized.

Set Condition: The A/C pressure sensor signal at the PCM goes above 4.92 volts. One trip Fault.

POSSIBLE CAUSES
A/C PRESSURE SENSOR VOLTAGE ABOVE 4.6 VOLTS
(C18) A/C PRESSURE SIGNAL CIRCUIT SHORTED TO (K7) 5 VOLT SUPPLY CIRCUIT
(C18) A/C PRESSURE SIGNAL CIRCUIT SHORTED TO BATTERY VOLTAGE
A/C PRESSURE SENSOR INTERNAL FAILURE
(C18) A/C PRESSURE SIGNAL CIRCUIT OPEN
(K4) SENSOR GROUND CIRCUIT OPEN
PCM

TEST	ACTION
1	NOTE: Ensure the A/C refrigerant System is properly charged per the Service Information. Start the engine. With the DRBIII®, read the A/C Pressure Sensor voltage. Is the voltage above 4.6 volts? Yes → Go To 2 No → Diagnose intermittent condition.
2	Turn the ignition off. Disconnect the A/C Pressure Sensor harness connector. Disconnect the PCM harness connector. Measure the resistance between the (C18) A/C Pressure Signal circuit and the (K7) 5 Volt Supply circuit in the A/C Pressure Sensor harness connector. Is the resistance below 5.0 ohms? Yes → Repair the (C18) A/C Pressure Signal circuit for a short to the (K7) 5 Volt Supply circuit. No → Go To 3

ARM0400000000935

Fig. 48 Code P0533: Air Conditioning Pressure Sensor High (Part 1 of 3). 2002–04 Concorde, Intrepid & 300M

TEST	ACTION
3	Turn the ignition off. Disconnect the A/C Pressure Sensor harness connector. Turn the ignition on. Measure the voltage on the (C18) A/C Pressure Sensor Signal circuit at the A/C Pressure Sensor harness connector. Is the voltage above 5.2 volts? Yes → Repair the (C18) A/C Pressure Signal circuit for a short to battery voltage. No → Go To 4
4	Turn the ignition off. Disconnect the A/C Pressure Sensor harness connector. Connect a jumper wire between the (C18) A/C Pressure Signal circuit and the (K4) Sensor ground circuit. With the DRBIII®, monitor the A/C Pressure Sensor voltage. Turn the ignition on. Is the voltage below 1.0 volt? Yes → Replace the A/C Pressure Sensor. No → Go To 5
5	Turn the ignition off. Disconnect the A/C Pressure Sensor harness connector. Disconnect the PCM harness connector. **CAUTION: DO NOT PROBE THE PCM HARNESS CONNECTORS. PROBING THE PCM HARNESS CONNECTORS WILL DAMAGE THE PCM TERMINALS RESULTING IN POOR TERMINAL TO PIN CONNECTION. INSTALL MILLER SPECIAL TOOL #8815 TO PERFORM DIAGNOSIS.** Measure the resistance of the (C18) A/C Pressure Sensor Signal circuit from the A/C Pressure Sensor harness connector to the appropriate terminal of special tool #8815. Is the resistance below 5.0 ohms? Yes → Go To 6 No → Repair the (C18) A/C Pressure Signal circuit for an open.
6	Turn the ignition off. Disconnect the A/C Pressure Sensor harness connector. Disconnect the PCM harness connector. **CAUTION: DO NOT PROBE THE PCM HARNESS CONNECTORS. PROBING THE PCM HARNESS CONNECTORS WILL DAMAGE THE PCM TERMINALS RESULTING IN POOR TERMINAL TO PIN CONNECTION. INSTALL MILLER SPECIAL TOOL #8815 TO PERFORM DIAGNOSIS.** Measure the resistance of the (K4) Sensor ground circuit from the A/C Pressure Sensor harness connector to the appropriate terminal of special tool #8815. Is the resistance below 5.0 ohms? Yes → Go To 7 No → Repair the (K4) Sensor ground circuit for an open.

ARM0400000000936

Fig. 48 Code P0533: Air Conditioning Pressure Sensor High (Part 2 of 3). 2002–04 Concorde, Intrepid & 300M

When Monitored and Set Condition:

P0711-TRANSMISSION TEMPERATURE SENSOR PERFORMANCE

When Monitored: Continuously with the ignition on and engine running.

Set Condition: This DTC will set when the desired transmission temperature does not reach a normal operating temperature within a given time frame. Time is variable due to ambient temperature. Approximate times are starting temperature to warm up time: (-40° F / -40° C - 35 min) (-20° F / -28° C - 25 min) (20° F / -6.6° C - 20 min) (60° F / 15.5 °C - 10 min)

POSSIBLE CAUSES
RELATED DTC'S PRESENT
TRANSMISSION TEMPERATURE SENSOR
POWERTRAIN CONTROL MODULE
INTERMITTENT WIRING AND CONNECTORS

TEST	ACTION
1	**NOTE: Low fluid level can be the cause of many transmission problems. If the fluid level is low locate and repair the leak then check and adjust the fluid level per the Service Information.** **NOTE: Always perform diagnostics with a fully charged battery to avoid false symptoms.** With the DRBIII®, read Engine DTC's. Check and repair all Engine DTC's prior to performing any transmission symptom diagnostics. With the DRBIII®, read Transmission DTC's. Record all DTC's and 1 Trip Failures. **NOTE: Diagnose 1 Trip Failures as a fully matured DTC.** Using the wiring diagram/schematic as a guide, inspect the wiring and connectors. Repair as necessary. Perform the Shift Lever Position Test. If the test does not pass, refer to Symptom test for P0706 Check Shifter Signal. For Gear Ratio DTC's, check and record all CVI's. Most DTC's set on start up but some must be set by driving the vehicle such that all diagnostic monitors have run. **NOTE: Verify flash level of Powertrain Control Module. Some problems are corrected by software upgrades to the Transmission and Engine software.** **NOTE: Check for applicable TSB's related to the problem.** Perform this procedure prior to Symptom diagnosis. Continue Go To 2

ARM0400000000952

Fig. 49 Code P0711: Transmission Temperature Sensor Performance (Part 1 of 3). 2002–04 Concorde, Intrepid & 300M

TEST	ACTION
7	**NOTE: Before continuing, check the PCM harness connector terminals for corrosion, damage, or terminal push out. Repair as necessary.** If there are no possible causes remaining, view repair. Repair Replace and program the Powertrain Control Module

ARM0400000000937

Fig. 48 Code P0533: Air Conditioning Pressure Sensor High (Part 3 of 3). 2002–04 Concorde, Intrepid & 300M

TEST	ACTION
2	With the DRBIII®, check Transmission DTC's. Are there any other Transmission Temperature Sensor related DTCs present? Yes → Refer to the Transmission category and perform the appropriate symptom. No → Go To 3
3	With the DRBIII®, Check the STARTS SINCE SET counter for P0711. **NOTE: This counter only applies to the last DTC set.** Is the STARTS SINCE SET counter 2 or less? Yes → Go To 4 No → Go To 7
4	Turn the ignition off to the lock position. Remove the Starter Relay. **CAUTION: Removal of the Starter Relay is to prevent a Transmission, NO RESPONSE, condition and disable the starter.** Install the Transmission Simulator, Miller tool #8333 and the Electronic Transmission Adapter kit 8333-1A. **Note: Check connectors - Clean/repair as necessary.** Ignition on, engine not running. With the Transmission Simulator, turn the Input/Output switch to OFF. With the DRBIII®, monitor the TRANS TEMP VOLTS while turning the Thermistor Voltage switch to all three positions on the Transmission Simulator. Compare the DRBIII® readings with the numbers listed on the Transmission Simulator. Do the readings on the Transmission Simulator match the DRBIII® readings ± 0.2 volts? Yes → Go To 5 No → Go To 6
5	If there are no possible causes remaining, view repair. Repair Replace Transmission Solenoid/TRS assembly
6	Using the schematics as a guide, inspect the wiring and connectors. Repair as necessary. Pay particular attention to all power and ground circuits. If there are no possible causes remaining, view repair. Repair Replace the Powertrain Control Module

ARM0400000000953

Fig. 49 Code P0711: Transmission Temperature Sensor Performance (Part 2 of 3). 2002–04 Concorde, Intrepid & 300M

TEST	ACTION

7	The conditions necessary to set this DTC are not present at this time.
	Using the schematics as a guide, inspect the wiring and connectors specific to this circuit.
	Wiggle the wires while checking for shorted and open circuits.
	With the DRBIII®, check the EATX EVENT DATA to help identify the conditions in which the DTC was set.
	Were there any problems found?
	
	    Yes → Repair as necessary.
	
	    No → Test Complete.

ARM0400000000954

Fig. 49 Code P0711: Transmission Temperature Sensor Performance (Part 3 of 3). 2002–04 Concorde, Intrepid & 300M

TEST	ACTION

3	With the DRBIII®, Check the STARTS SINCE SET counter for P0712.
	NOTE: This counter only applies to the last DTC set.
	Is the STARTS SINCE SET counter 2 or less?
	
	    Yes → Go To 4
	
	    No → Go To 8

4	Turn the ignition off to the lock position.
	Remove the Starter Relay.
	CAUTION: Removal of the Starter Relay is to prevent a Transmission, NO RESPONSE, condition and disable the starter.
	Install the Transmission Simulator, Miller tool #8333 and the Electronic Transmission Adapter kit 8333-1A.
	Note: Check connectors - Clean/repair as necessary.
	Ignition on, engine not running.
	With the Transmission Simulator, turn the Input/Output switch to OFF.
	With the DRBIII®, monitor the TRANS TEMP VOLTS while turning the Thermistor Voltage switch to all three positions on the Transmission Simulator.
	Compare the DRBIII® readings with the numbers listed on the Transmission Simulator.
	Do the readings on the Transmission Simulator match the DRBIII® readings ± 0.2 volts?
	
	    Yes → Go To 5
	
	    No → Go To 6

5	If there are no possible causes remaining, view repair.
	
	    Repair
	        Replace Transmission Solenoid/TRS assembly

6	Turn the ignition off to the lock position.
	Disconnect the PCM C4 harness connector.
	Disconnect the Transmission Solenoid/TRS Assembly harness connector.
	Note: Check connectors - Clean/repair as necessary.
	CAUTION: DO NOT PROBE THE PCM HARNESS CONNECTORS. PROBING THE PCM HARNESS CONNECTORS WILL DAMAGE THE PCM TERMINALS RESULTING IN POOR TERMINAL TO PIN CONNECTION. INSTALL MILLER SPECIAL TOOL #8815 TO PERFORM DIAGNOSIS.
	Measure the resistance between ground and the Transmission Temperature Sensor Signal circuit.
	Is the resistance below 5.0 ohms?
	
	    Yes → Repair the Transmission Temperature Sensor Signal circuit for a short to ground.
	
	    No → Go To 7

ARM0400000000956

Fig. 50 Code P0712: Transmission Temperature Sensor Low (Part 2 of 3). 2002–04 Concorde, Intrepid & 300M

When Monitored and Set Condition:

P0712-TRANSMISSION TEMPERATURE SENSOR LOW

When Monitored: Continuously with the ignition on and engine running.

Set Condition: The DTC will set when the monitored Temperature Sensor voltage drops below 0.078 volts for the period of 0.45 seconds.

POSSIBLE CAUSES
RELATED DTC'S PRESENT
TRANSMISSION TEMPERATURE SENSOR SIGNAL CIRCUIT SHORT TO GROUND
TRANSMISSION TEMPERATURE SENSOR
POWERTRAIN CONTROL MODULE
INTERMITTENT WIRING AND CONNECTORS

TEST	ACTION

1	**NOTE: Low fluid level can be the cause of many transmission problems. If the fluid level is low locate and repair the leak then check and adjust the fluid level per the Service Information.**
	NOTE: Always perform diagnostics with a fully charged battery to avoid false symptoms.
	With the DRBIII®, read Engine DTC's. Check and repair all Engine DTC's prior to performing any transmission symptom diagnostics.
	With the DRBIII®, read Transmission DTC's. Record all DTC's and 1 Trip Failures.
	NOTE: Diagnose 1 Trip Failures as a fully matured DTC.
	Using the wiring diagram/schematic as a guide, inspect the wiring and connectors. Repair as necessary.
	Perform the Shift Lever Position Test. If the test does not pass, refer to Symptom test for P0706 Check Shifter Signal.
	For Gear Ratio DTC's, check and record all CVI's.
	Most DTC's set on start up but some must be set by driving the vehicle such that all diagnostic monitors have run.
	NOTE: Verify flash level of Powertrain Control Module. Some problems are corrected by software upgrades to the Transmission and Engine software.
	NOTE: Check for applicable TSB's related to the problem.
	Perform this procedure prior to Symptom diagnosis.
	
	    Continue
	        Go To 2

2	With the DRBIII®, check Transmission DTC's.
	Are there any Speed Sensor DTCs present?
	
	    Yes → Refer to the Transmission category and perform the appropriate symptom.
	
	    No → Go To 3

ARM0400000000955

Fig. 50 Code P0712: Transmission Temperature Sensor Low (Part 1 of 3). 2002–04 Concorde, Intrepid & 300M

TEST	ACTION

7	Using the schematics as a guide, inspect the wiring and connectors. Repair as necessary. Pay particular attention to all power and ground circuits.
	If there are no possible causes remaining, view repair.
	
	    Repair
	        Replace the Powertrain Control Module

8	The conditions necessary to set this DTC are not present at this time.
	Using the schematics as a guide, inspect the wiring and connectors specific to this circuit.
	Wiggle the wires while checking for shorted and open circuits.
	With the DRBIII®, check the EATX EVENT DATA to help identify the conditions in which the DTC was set.
	Were there any problems found?
	
	    Yes → Repair as necessary.
	
	    No → Test Complete.

ARM0400000000957

Fig. 50 Code P0712: Transmission Temperature Sensor Low (Part 3 of 3). 2002–04 Concorde, Intrepid & 300M

When Monitored and Set Condition:

P0713-TRANSMISSION TEMPERATURE SENSOR HIGH

When Monitored: Continuously with the ignition on and engine running.

Set Condition: The DTC will set when the monitored Temperature Sensor voltage rises above 4.94 volts for the period of 0.45 seconds.

POSSIBLE CAUSES
RELATED DTC'S PRESENT
TRANSMISSION TEMPERATURE SENSOR SIGNAL CIRCUIT OPEN
TRANSMISSION TEMPERATURE SENSOR SIGNAL CIRCUIT SHORT TO VOLTAGE
TRANSMISSION TEMPERATURE SENSOR
POWERTRAIN CONTROL MODULE
INTERMITTENT WIRING AND CONNECTORS

TEST	ACTION
1	NOTE: Low fluid level can be the cause of many transmission problems. If the fluid level is low locate and repair the leak then check and adjust the fluid level per the Service Information. NOTE: Always perform diagnostics with a fully charged battery to avoid false symptoms. With the DRBIII®, read Engine DTC's. Check and repair all Engine DTC's prior to performing any transmission symptom diagnostics. With the DRBIII®, read Transmission DTC's. Record all DTC's and 1 Trip Failures. NOTE: Diagnose 1 Trip Failures as a fully matured DTC. Using the wiring diagram/schematic as a guide, inspect the wiring and connectors. Repair as necessary. Perform the Shift Lever Position Test. If the test does not pass, refer to Symptom test for P0706 Check Shifter Signal. For Gear Ratio DTC's, check and record all CVI's. Most DTC's set on start up but some must be set by driving the vehicle such that all all diagnostic monitors have run. NOTE: Verify flash level of Powertrain Control Module. Some problems are corrected by software upgrades to the Transmission and Engine software. NOTE: Check for applicable TSB's related to the problem. Perform this procedure prior to Symptom diagnosis. Continue Go To 2

ARM0400000000958

Fig. 51   Code P0713: Transmission Temperature Sensor High (Part 1 of 4). 2002–04 Concorde, Intrepid & 300M

TEST	ACTION
6	Turn the ignition off to the lock position. Disconnect the PCM C4 harness connector.. Disconnect the Transmission Solenoid /TRS Assembly harness connector Note: Check connectors - Clean/repair as necessary. CAUTION: DO NOT PROBE THE PCM HARNESS CONNECTORS. PROBING THE PCM HARNESS CONNECTORS WILL DAMAGE THE PCM TERMINALS RESULTING IN POOR TERMINAL TO PIN CONNECTION. INSTALL MILLER SPECIAL TOOL #8815 TO PERFORM DIAGNOSIS. Measure the resistance of the Transmission Temperature Sensor Signal circuit from the appropriate terminal of special tool #8815 to the Transmission Solenoid/TRS Assembly harness connector. Is the resistance above 5.0 ohms? Yes → Repair the Transmission Temperature Sensor Signal circuit for an open. No → Go To 7
7	Turn the ignition off to the lock position. Disconnect the PCM C4 harness connector. Remove the Transmission Control Relay. Note: Check connectors - Clean/repair as necessary. CAUTION: DO NOT PROBE THE PCM HARNESS CONNECTORS. PROBING THE PCM HARNESS CONNECTORS WILL DAMAGE THE PCM TERMINALS RESULTING IN POOR TERMINAL TO PIN CONNECTION. INSTALL MILLER SPECIAL TOOL #8815 TO PERFORM DIAGNOSIS. Connect a jumper wire between the Fused B+ circuit and the Transmission Control Relay Output circuit in the Transmission Control Relay connector. Ignition on, engine not running. Measure the voltage of the Transmission Temperature Sensor Signal circuit in the appropriate terminal of special tool #8815. Is the voltage above 0.5 volts? Yes → Repair the Transmission Temperature Sensor Signal circuit for a short to voltage. No → Go To 8
8	Using the schematics as a guide, inspect the wiring and connectors. Repair as necessary. Pay particular attention to all power and ground circuits. If there are no possible causes remaining, view repair. Repair Replace the Powertrain Control Module

ARM0400000000960

Fig. 51   Code P0713: Transmission Temperature Sensor High (Part 3 of 4). 2002–04 Concorde, Intrepid & 300M

TEST	ACTION
2	With the DRBIII®, check Transmission DTC's. Are there any Speed Sensor DTCs present? Yes → Refer to the Transmission category and perform the appropriate symptom. No → Go To 3
3	With the DRBIII®, Check the STARTS SINCE SET counter for P0713. NOTE: This counter only applies to the last DTC set. Is the STARTS SINCE SET counter 2 or less? Yes → Go To 4 No → Go To 9
4	Turn the ignition off to the lock position. Remove the Starter Relay. CAUTION: Removal of the Starter Relay is to prevent a Transmission, NO RESPONSE, condition and disable the starter. Install the Transmission Simulator, Miller tool #8333 and the Electronic Transmission Adapter kit 8333-1A. Note: Check connectors - Clean/repair as necessary. Ignition on, engine not running. With the Transmission Simulator, turn the Input/Output switch to OFF. With the DRBIII®, monitor the TRANS TEMP VOLTS while turning the Thermistor Voltage switch to all three positions on the Transmission Simulator. Compare the DRBIII® readings with the numbers listed on the Transmission Simulator. Do the readings on the Transmission Simulator match the DRBIII® readings ± 0.2 volts? Yes → Go To 5 No → Go To 6
5	If there are no possible causes remaining, view repair. Repair Replace Transmission Solenoid/TRS assembly

ARM0400000000959

Fig. 51   Code P0713: Transmission Temperature Sensor High (Part 2 of 4). 2002–04 Concorde, Intrepid & 300M

TEST	ACTION
9	The conditions necessary to set this DTC are not present at this time. Using the schematics as a guide, inspect the wiring and connectors specific to this circuit. Wiggle the wires while checking for shorted and open circuits. With the DRBIII®, check the EATX EVENT DATA to help identify the conditions in which the DTC was set. Were there any problems found? Yes → Repair as necessary. No → Test Complete.

ARM0400000000961

Fig. 51   Code P0713: Transmission Temperature Sensor High (Part 4 of 4). 2002–04 Concorde, Intrepid & 300M

When Monitored and Set Condition:

P0714-TRANSMISSION TEMPERATURE SENSOR INTERMITTENT

When Monitored: Continuously with the ignition on and engine running.

Set Condition: The DTC will set when the monitored Temperature Sensor voltage fluctuates or changes abruptly within a predetermined period of time.

POSSIBLE CAUSES
RELATED DTC'S PRESENT
TRANSMISSION TEMPERATURE SENSOR
POWERTRAIN CONTROL MODULE
INTERMITTENT WIRING AND CONNECTORS

TEST	ACTION
1	NOTE: Low fluid level can be the cause of many transmission problems. If the fluid level is low locate and repair the leak then check and adjust the fluid level per the Service Information. NOTE: Always perform diagnostics with a fully charged battery to avoid false symptoms. With the DRBIII®, read Engine DTC's. Check and repair all Engine DTC's prior to performing any transmission symptom diagnostics. With the DRBIII®, read Transmission DTC's. Record all DTC's and 1 Trip Failures. NOTE: Diagnose 1 Trip Failures as a fully matured DTC. Using the wiring diagram/schematic as a guide, inspect the wiring and connectors. Repair as necessary. Perform the Shift Lever Position Test. If the test does not pass, refer to Symptom test for P0706 Check Shifter Signal. For Gear Ratio DTC's, check and record all CVI's. Most DTC's set on start up but some must be set by driving the vehicle such that all diagnostic monitors have run. NOTE: Verify flash level of Powertrain Control Module. Some problems are corrected by software upgrades to the Transmission and Engine software. NOTE: Check for applicable TSB's related to the problem. Perform this procedure prior to Symptom diagnosis. Continue Go To 2
2	With the DRBIII®, check Transmission DTC's. Are there any Speed Sensor and/or other Temperature Sensor DTCs present? Yes → Refer to the Transmission category and perform the appropriate symptom. No → Go To 3

ARM0400000000962

Fig. 52   Code P0714: Transmission Temperature Sensor Intermittent (Part 1 of 2). 2002–04 Concorde, Intrepid & 300M

When Monitored and Set Condition:

P0720-OUTPUT SPEED SENSOR ERROR

When Monitored: The transmission gear ratio is monitored continuously while the transmission is in gear.

Set Condition: If there is an excessive change in the Output RPM in any gear.

POSSIBLE CAUSES
OUTPUT SPEED SENSOR SIGNAL CIRCUIT OPEN
SPEED SENSOR GROUND CIRCUIT OPEN
OUTPUT SPEED SENSOR SIGNAL CIRCUIT SHORT TO GROUND
OUTPUT SPEED SENSOR SIGNAL CIRCUIT SHORT TO VOLTAGE
SPEED SENSOR GROUND CIRCUIT SHORT TO VOLTAGE
OUTPUT SPEED SENSOR
POWERTRAIN CONTROL MODULE
INTERMITTENT WIRING AND CONNECTORS

TEST	ACTION
1	NOTE: Low fluid level can be the cause of many transmission problems. If the fluid level is low locate and repair the leak then check and adjust the fluid level per the Service Information. NOTE: Always perform diagnostics with a fully charged battery to avoid false symptoms. With the DRBIII®, read Engine DTC's. Check and repair all Engine DTC's prior to performing any transmission symptom diagnostics. With the DRBIII®, read Transmission DTC's. Record all DTC's and 1 Trip Failures. NOTE: Diagnose 1 Trip Failures as a fully matured DTC. Using the wiring diagram/schematic as a guide, inspect the wiring and connectors. Repair as necessary. Perform the Shift Lever Position Test. If the test does not pass, refer to Symptom test for P0706 Check Shifter Signal. For Gear Ratio DTC's, check and record all CVI's. Most DTC's set on start up but some must be set by driving the vehicle such that all diagnostic monitors have run. NOTE: Verify flash level of Powertrain Control Module. Some problems are corrected by software upgrades to the Transmission and Engine software. NOTE: Check for applicable TSB's related to the problem. Perform this procedure prior to Symptom diagnosis. Continue Go To 2

ARM0400000000964

Fig. 53   Code P0720: Output Speed Sensor Error (Part 1 of 4). 2002–04 Concorde, Intrepid & 300M

TEST	ACTION
3	With the DRBIII®, Check the STARTS SINCE SET counter for P0714. NOTE: This counter only applies to the last DTC set. Is the STARTS SINCE SET counter 2 or less? Yes → Go To 4 No → Go To 7
4	Turn the ignition off to the lock position. Remove the Starter Relay. CAUTION: Removal of the Starter Relay is to prevent a Transmission, NO RESPONSE, condition and disable the starter. Install the Transmission Simulator, Miller tool #8333 and the Electronic Transmission Adapter kit 8333-1A. Note: Check connectors - Clean/repair as necessary. Ignition on, engine not running. With the Transmission Simulator, turn the Input/Output switch to OFF. With the DRBIII®, monitor the TRANS TEMP VOLTS while turning the Thermistor Voltage switch to all three positions on the Transmission Simulator. Compare the DRBIII® readings with the numbers listed on the Transmission Simulator. Do the readings on the Transmission Simulator match a non-fluctuating DRBIII® reading ± 0.2 volts? Yes → Go To 5 No → Go To 6
5	If there are no possible causes remaining, view repair. Repair Replace Transmission Solenoid/TRS assembly
6	Using the schematics as a guide, inspect the wiring and connectors. Repair as necessary. Pay particular attention to all power and ground circuits. If there are no possible causes remaining, view repair. Repair Replace the Powertrain Control Module
7	The conditions necessary to set this DTC are not present at this time. Using the schematics as a guide, inspect the wiring and connectors specific to this circuit. Wiggle the wires while checking for shorted and open circuits. With the DRBIII®, check the EATX EVENT DATA to help identify the conditions in which the DTC was set. Were there any problems found? Yes → Repair as necessary. No → Test Complete.

ARM0400000000963

Fig. 52   Code P0714: Transmission Temperature Sensor Intermittent (Part 2 of 2). 2002–04 Concorde, Intrepid & 300M

TEST	ACTION
2	Start the engine in park. Raise the drive wheels off of the ground. WARNING: PROPERLY SUPPORT THE VEHICLE. Firmly apply the brakes and place the transmission selector in drive. WARNING: BE SURE TO KEEP HANDS AND FEET CLEAR OF ROTATING WHEELS. Release the brakes and allow the drive wheels to spin freely. Note: The drive wheels must be turning at this point. With the DRBIII®, read the Output RPM Is the Output RPM below 100? Yes → Go To 3 No → Go To 11
3	Turn the ignition off to the lock position. Remove the Starter Relay. CAUTION: Removal of the Starter Relay is to prevent a Transmission, NO RESPONSE, condition and disable the starter. Install the Transmission Simulator, Miller tool #8333 and the Electronic Transmission Adapter kit 8333-1A. Ignition on, engine not running. With the Transmission Simulator, set the "Input/Output Speed" switch to "ON" and the rotary switch to the "3000/1250" position. With the DRBIII®, read the Input and Output RPM. Does the Input RPM read 3000 and the Output RPM read 1250 (within 50 RPM)? Yes → Go To 4 No → Go To 5
4	If there are no possible causes remaining, view repair. Repair Replace the Output Speed Sensor
5	Turn the ignition off to the lock position. Disconnect the PCM harness connector. Disconnect the Output Speed Sensor harness connector. Note: Check connectors - Clean/repair as necessary. CAUTION: DO NOT PROBE THE PCM HARNESS CONNECTORS. PROBING THE PCM HARNESS CONNECTORS WILL DAMAGE THE PCM TERMINALS RESULTING IN POOR TERMINAL TO PIN CONNECTION. INSTALL MILLER SPECIAL TOOL #8815 TO PERFORM DIAGNOSIS. Measure the resistance of the Output Speed Sensor Signal circuit from appropriate terminal of special tool #8815 to the Output Speed Sensor harness connector. Is the resistance above 5.0 ohms? Yes → Repair the Output Speed Sensor Signal circuit for an open. No → Go To 6

ARM0400000000967

Fig. 53   Code P0720: Output Speed Sensor Error (Part 2 of 4). 2002–04 Concorde, Intrepid & 300M

TEST	ACTION
6	Turn the ignition off to the lock position. Disconnect the PCM harness connector. Disconnect the Output Speed Sensor harness connector. **Note: Check connectors - Clean/repair as necessary.** **CAUTION: DO NOT PROBE THE PCM HARNESS CONNECTORS. PROBING THE PCM HARNESS CONNECTORS WILL DAMAGE THE PCM TERMINALS RESULTING IN POOR TERMINAL TO PIN CONNECTION. INSTALL MILLER SPECIAL TOOL #8815 TO PERFORM DIAGNOSIS.** Measure the resistance of the Speed Sensor Ground circuit from the appropriate terminal of special tool #8815 to the Output Speed Sensor harness connector. Is the resistance above 5.0 ohms? Yes → Repair the Speed Sensor Ground circuit for an open. No → Go To 7
7	Turn the ignition off to the lock position. Disconnect the PCM harness connector. Disconnect the Output Speed Sensor harness connector. **Note: Check connectors - Clean/repair as necessary.** **CAUTION: DO NOT PROBE THE PCM HARNESS CONNECTORS. PROBING THE PCM HARNESS CONNECTORS WILL DAMAGE THE PCM TERMINALS RESULTING IN POOR TERMINAL TO PIN CONNECTION. INSTALL MILLER SPECIAL TOOL #8815 TO PERFORM DIAGNOSIS.** Measure the resistance between ground and the Output Speed Sensor Signal circuit. Is the resistance below 5.0 ohms? Yes → Repair the Output Speed Sensor Signal circuit for a short to ground. No → Go To 8
8	Turn the ignition off to the lock position. Disconnect the PCM harness connector. Disconnect the Output Speed Sensor harness connector. Remove the Transmission Control Relay. **Note: Check connectors - Clean/repair as necessary.** Connect a jumper wire between the Fused B+ circuit and Transmission Control Relay Output circuit in the Transmission Control Relay connector. Ignition on, engine not running. **CAUTION: DO NOT PROBE THE PCM HARNESS CONNECTORS. PROBING THE PCM HARNESS CONNECTORS WILL DAMAGE THE PCM TERMINALS RESULTING IN POOR TERMINAL TO PIN CONNECTION. INSTALL MILLER SPECIAL TOOL #8815 TO PERFORM DIAGNOSIS.** Measure the voltage of the Output Speed Sensor Signal circuit. Is the voltage above 0.5 volt? Yes → Repair the Output Speed Sensor Signal circuit for a short to voltage. No → Go To 9

ARM0400000000965

Fig. 53 Code P0720: Output Speed Sensor Error (Part 3 of 4). 2002–04 Concorde, Intrepid & 300M

TEST	ACTION
9	Turn the ignition off to the lock position. Disconnect the PCM harness connector. Disconnect the TRS harness connector. Remove the Transmission Control Relay. **Note: Check connectors - Clean/repair as necessary.** Connect a jumper wire between the Fused B+ and Transmission Control Relay Output circuits in the Transmission Control Relay connector. Ignition on, engine not running. **CAUTION: DO NOT PROBE THE PCM HARNESS CONNECTORS. PROBING THE PCM HARNESS CONNECTORS WILL DAMAGE THE PCM TERMINALS RESULTING IN POOR TERMINAL TO PIN CONNECTION. INSTALL MILLER SPECIAL TOOL #8815 TO PERFORM DIAGNOSIS.** Measure the voltage of the Speed Sensor Ground circuit. Is the voltage above 0.5 volts? Yes → Repair the Speed Sensor Ground circuit for a short to voltage. No → Go To 10
10	Using the schematics as a guide, inspect the wiring and connectors. Repair as necessary. Pay particular attention to all power and ground circuits. If there are no possible causes remaining, view repair. Repair Replace the Powertrain Control Module
11	The conditions necessary to set the DTC are not present at this time. Using the schematics as a guide, inspect the wiring and connectors specific to this circuit. Wiggle the wiring and connectors while checking for shorted and open circuits. With the DRBIII®, check the EATX EVENT DATA to help identify the conditions in which the DTC was set. Were there any problems found? Yes → Repair as necessary. No → Test Complete.

ARM0400000000966

Fig. 53 Code P0720: Output Speed Sensor Error (Part 4 of 4). 2002–04 Concorde, Intrepid & 300M

When Monitored and Set Condition:

P0117-ECT SENSOR VOLTAGE TOO LOW

When Monitored: With the ignition on. Battery voltage greater than 10 volts.

Set Condition: The Engine Coolant Temperature (ECT) sensor circuit voltage at the PCM is less than 0.8 volt for more than 2.6 seconds.

POSSIBLE CAUSES
INTERMITTENT CONDITION
ECT SENSOR INTERNAL FAILURE
ECT SENSOR SIGNAL SHORTED TO GROUND
ECT SENSOR SIGNAL SHORTED TO SENSOR GROUND CIRCUIT
PCM

TEST	ACTION
1	Turn the ignition on. With the DRBIII®, read the ECT voltage. Is the voltage below 1.0 volt? Yes → Go To 2 No → Go To 6
2	Turn the ignition off. Disconnect the ECT harness connector. Turn the ignition on. With the DRBIII®, read ECT voltage. Is the voltage above 1.0 volt? Yes → Replace the ECT Sensor. No → Go To 3
3	Turn the ignition off. Disconnect the ECT Sensor harness connector. Disconnect the PCM harness connector. Measure the resistance of the ECT Sensor Signal circuit in the ECT Sensor harness connector to ground. Is the resistance below 100 ohms? Yes → Repair the ECT Sensor Signal circuit for a short to ground. No → Go To 4

ARM0400000000890

Fig. 54 Code P0117: ECT Sensor Voltage Too Low (Part 1 of 2). 2001–02 Neon

TEST	ACTION
4	Turn the ignition off. Disconnect the ECT Sensor harness connector. Disconnect the PCM harness connector. Measure the resistance between the ECT Sensor Signal circuit and the Sensor ground circuit in the ECT Sensor harness connector. Is the resistance below 100 ohms? Yes → Repair the ECT Sensor Signal circuit for a short to the Sensor ground circuit. No → Go To 5
5	If there are no possible causes remaining, view repair. Repair Replace and program the Powertrain Control Module in accordance with the Service Information.
6	**WARNING: WHEN THE ENGINE IS OPERATING, DO NOT STAND IN A DIRECT LINE WITH THE FAN. DO NOT PUT YOUR HANDS NEAR THE PULLEYS, BELTS OR FAN. DO NOT WEAR LOOSE CLOTHING.** **NOTE: The conditions that set the DTC are not present at this time. The following list may help in identifying the intermittent condition.** With the engine running at normal operating temperature, monitor the DRB parameters related to the DTC while wiggling the wiring harness. Look for parameter values to change and/or a DTC to set. Review the DRB Freeze Frame information. If possible, try to duplicate the conditions under which the DTC was set. Refer to any Technical Service Bulletins (TSB) that may apply. Visually inspect the related wiring harness. Look for any chafed, pierced, pinched, or partially broken wires. Visually inspect the related wiring harness connectors. Look for broken, bent, pushed out, or corroded terminals. Were any of the above conditions present? Yes → Repair as necessary. No → Test Complete.

ARM0400000000891

Fig. 54 Code P0117: ECT Sensor Voltage Too Low (Part 2 of 2). 2001–02 Neon

When Monitored and Set Condition:

P0118-ECT SENSOR VOLTAGE TOO HIGH

When Monitored: With the ignition on. Battery voltage greater than 10 volts.

Set Condition: The Engine Coolant Temperature (ECT) sensor circuit voltage at the PCM goes above 4.96 volts for more than 2.6 seconds.

POSSIBLE CAUSES
INTERMITTENT CONDITION
ECT SENSOR SIGNAL CIRCUIT SHORTED TO BATTERY VOLTAGE
ECT SENSOR INTERNAL FAILURE
ECT SENSOR SIGNAL CIRCUIT OPEN
SENSOR GROUND CIRCUIT OPEN
PCM

TEST	ACTION
1	Turn the ignition on. With the DRBIII®, read the ECT voltage. Is the voltage above 4.6 volts? Yes → Go To 2 No → Go To 7
2	Turn the ignition off. Disconnect the ECT Sensor harness connector. Turn the ignition on. Measure the voltage of the ECT Sensor Signal circuit in the ECT Sensor harness connector. Is the voltage above 5.2 volts? Yes → Repair the ECT Sensor Signal circuit for a short to battery voltage. No → Go To 3

ARM0400000000892

Fig. 55   Code P0118: ECT Sensor Voltage Too High (Part 1 of 3). 2001–02 Neon

TEST	ACTION
7	**WARNING: WHEN THE ENGINE IS OPERATING, DO NOT STAND IN A DIRECT LINE WITH THE FAN. DO NOT PUT YOUR HANDS NEAR THE PULLEYS, BELTS OR FAN. DO NOT WEAR LOOSE CLOTHING.** **NOTE: The conditions that set the DTC are not present at this time. The following list may help in identifying the intermittent condition.** With the engine running at normal operating temperature, monitor the DRB parameters related to the DTC while wiggling the wiring harness. Look for parameter values to change and/or a DTC to set. Review the DRB Freeze Frame information. If possible, try to duplicate the conditions under which the DTC was set. Refer to any Technical Service Bulletins (TSB) that may apply. Visually inspect the related wiring harness. Look for any chafed, pierced, pinched, or partially broken wires. Visually inspect the related wiring harness connectors. Look for broken, bent, pushed out, or corroded terminals. Were any of the above conditions present? Yes → Repair as necessary No → Test Complete.

ARM0400000000894

Fig. 55   Code P0118: ECT Sensor Voltage Too High (Part 3 of 3). 2001–02 Neon

TEST	ACTION
3	Turn the ignition off. Disconnect the ECT harness connector. Connect a jumper wire between the ECT Sensor Signal circuit and the Sensor ground circuit in the ECT harness connector. Turn the ignition on. With the DRBIII®, read ECT voltage. Is the voltage below 1.0 volt? Yes → Replace the ECT Sensor. No → Go To 4
4	Turn the ignition off. Disconnect the ECT Sensor harness connector. Disconnect the PCM harness connector. Measure the resistance of the ECT Sensor Signal circuit between the ECT Sensor harness connector and the PCM harness connector. Is the resistance below 5 ohms? Yes → Go To 5 No → Repair the ECT Sensor Signal circuit for an open.
5	Turn the ignition off. Disconnect the ECT Sensor harness connector. Disconnect the PCM harness connector. Measure the resistance of the Sensor ground circuit between the ECT Sensor harness connector and the PCM harness connector. Is the resistance below 5.0 ohms? Yes → Go To 6 No → Repair the Sensor ground circuit for an open.
6	If there are no possible causes remaining, view repair. Repair Replace and program the Powertrain Control Module

ARM0400000000893

Fig. 55   Code P0118: ECT Sensor Voltage Too High (Part 2 of 3). 2001–02 Neon

When Monitored and Set Condition:

P1490-LOW SPEED FAN CONTROL RELAY CIRCUIT

When Monitored: With the ignition on. Battery voltage greater than 10 volts.

Set Condition: An open or shorted circuit is detected in the radiator fan relay control circuit.

POSSIBLE CAUSES
LOW SPEED RADIATOR FAN RELAY INTERMITTENT OPERATION
INTERMITTENT CONDITION
FUSED IGNITION SWITCH OUTPUT CIRCUIT
LOW SPEED RADIATOR FAN RELAY RESISTANCE
LOW SPEED RADIATOR FAN RELAY CONTROL CIRCUIT OPEN
LOW SPEED RADIATOR FAN RELAY CONTROL CIRCUIT SHORT TO GROUND
PCM

TEST	ACTION
1	Turn the ignition on. With the DRBIII®, actuate the Low Speed Radiator Fan Relay. Is the Low Speed Radiator Fan Relay operating? Yes → Go To 2 No → Go To 4
2	Turn the ignition on. With the DRBIII®, actuate the Low Speed Radiator Fan Relay. Wiggle the wiring harness from the Low Speed Radiator Fan Relay to the PCM while the relay is actuating. Did the Low Speed Radiator Fan Relay stop when wiggling the wiring harness? Yes → Repair as necessary. No → Go To 3

ARM0400000000895

Fig. 56   Code P1490: Low Speed Fan Control Relay Circuit (Part 1 of 3). 2001–02 Neon

TEST	ACTION
3	**WARNING: WHEN THE ENGINE IS OPERATING, DO NOT STAND IN A DIRECT LINE WITH THE FAN. DO NOT PUT YOUR HANDS NEAR THE PULLEYS, BELTS OR FAN. DO NOT WEAR LOOSE CLOTHING.** **NOTE: The conditions that set the DTC are not present at this time. The following list may help in identifying the intermittent condition.** With the engine running at normal operating temperature, monitor the DRB parameters related to the DTC while wiggling the wiring harness. Look for parameter values to change and/or a DTC to set. Review the DRB Freeze Frame information. If possible, try to duplicate the conditions under which the DTC was set. Refer to any Technical Service Bulletins (TSB) that may apply. Visually inspect the related wiring harness. Look for any chafed, pierced, pinched, or partially broken wires. Visually inspect the related wiring harness connectors. Look for broken, bent, pushed out, or corroded terminals. Were any of the above conditions present? Yes → Repair as necessary No → Test Complete.
4	Turn the ignition off. Remove the Low Speed Radiator Fan Relay from the PDC. Turn the ignition on. Measure the voltage of the Fused Ignition Switch Output circuit in the PDC. Is the voltage above 11.0 volts? Yes → Go To 5 No → Repair the Fused Ignition Switch Output circuit. Check and replace any open fuses.
5	Turn the ignition off. Remove the Low Speed Radiator Fan Relay from the PDC. Measure the resistance of the Low Speed Radiator Fan Relay between the Fused Ignition Switch Output terminal and the Low Speed Radiator Fan Relay Control terminal. Using a jumper wire, momentarily jumper the Radiator Fan Relay Control circuit to ground. Is the resistance between 60 to 80 ohms? Yes → Go To 6 No → Replace the Low Speed Radiator Fan Relay.
6	Turn the ignition off. Remove the Low Speed Radiator Fan Relay from the PDC. Disconnect the PCM harness connector. Measure the resistance of the Low Speed Radiator Fan Relay Control circuit between the PDC and the PCM harness connector. Is the resistance below 5.0 ohms? Yes → Go To 7 No → Repair the Low Speed Radiator Fan Relay Control circuit for an open.

ARM0400000000896

Fig. 56   Code P1490: Low Speed Fan Control Relay Circuit (Part 2 of 3). 2001–02 Neon

When Monitored and Set Condition:

P0116-ENGINE COOLANT TEMPERATURE PERFORMANCE

When Monitored: Engine off time is greater than 480 minutes. Ambient temperature is greater than 0°C (32°F).

Set Condition: After a calibrated amount of cool down time, the PCM compares the ECT Sensor, IAT Sensor and the Ambient Air Temperature Sensor values. If the ECT Sensor value is not within calibrated temperature amount of the other two temperature sensors an error is detected. Two Trip Fault.

POSSIBLE CAUSES
GOOD TRIP EQUAL TO ZERO
(K2) ECT SIGNAL CIRCUIT SHORTED TO BATTERY VOLTAGE
ECT SENSOR VOLTAGE BELOW 0.1 VOLT
(K2) ECT SIGNAL CIRCUIT OPEN
(K167) SENSOR GROUND CIRCUIT OPEN
(K2) ECT SIGNAL CIRCUIT SHORTED TO GROUND
(K2) ECT SIGNAL SHORTED TO (K167) SENSOR GROUND
PCM HIGH
PCM LOW

TEST	ACTION
1	**NOTE: Due to the fact that the PCM compares the IAT, AAT and ECT sensor to see if they are within a calibrated temp of one another, the use of a block heater can cause false readings for the PCM. Check with the customer to see if they use a block heater.** Ignition on, engine not running. With the DRBIII®, read DTCs and record the related Freeze Frame data. Is the Good Trip Counter displayed and equal to zero? Yes → Go To 2 No → Diagnose intermittent condition.

ARM0400000000898

Fig. 57   Code P0116: ECT Performance (Part 1 of 3). 2003 Neon

TEST	ACTION
7	Turn the ignition off. Remove the Low Speed Radiator Fan Relay from the PDC. Disconnect the PCM harness connector. Measure the resistance of the Low Speed Radiator Fan Relay Control circuit in the PDC to ground. Is the resistance below 5.0 ohms. Yes → Repair the Low Speed Radiator Fan Relay Control circuit for a short to ground. No → Go To 8
8	If there are no possible causes remaining, view repair. Repair Replace and program the Powertrain Control Module

ARM0400000000897

Fig. 56   Code P1490: Low Speed Fan Control Relay Circuit (Part 3 of 3). 2001–02 Neon

TEST	ACTION
2	Turn the ignition off. Disconnect the ECT Sensor harness connector. **NOTE: Visually inspect both the component and the PCM connectors. Look for damaged, partially broken wires, and backed out or corroded terminals.** Ignition on, engine not running. Measure the voltage on the (K2) ECT Signal circuit in the ECT Sensor harness connector. Is the voltage above 5.2 volts? Yes → Repair the short to battery voltage in the (K2) ECT Signal circuit. No → Go To 3
3	Turn the ignition off. Disconnect the ECT Sensor harness connector. Ignition on, engine not running. With the DRBIII®, read the ECT Sensor voltage. Is the voltage above 4.6 volts? Yes → Go To 4 No → Go To 7
4	Turn the ignition off. Disconnect the ECT Sensor harness connector. Using a jumper wire, jumper across the ECT Sensor harness connector. Ignition on, engine not running. With the DRBIII®, read the ECT Sensor voltage. Is the voltage below 0.1 volt? Yes → Replace the ECT Sensor. No → Go To 5
5	Turn the ignition off. Disconnect the ECT Sensor harness connector. Disconnect the PCM harness connector. **CAUTION: DO NOT PROBE THE PCM HARNESS CONNECTORS. PROBING THE PCM HARNESS CONNECTORS WILL DAMAGE THE PCM TERMINALS RESULTING IN POOR TERMINAL TO PIN CONNECTION. INSTALL MILLER SPECIAL TOOL #8815 TO PERFORM DIAGNOSIS.** Measure the resistance of the (K2) ECT Signal circuit from the ECT Sensor harness connector to the appropriate terminal of special tool #8815. Is the resistance below 5.0 ohms? Yes → Go To 6 No → Repair the open in the (K2) ECT Signal circuit.

ARM0400000000899

Fig. 57   Code P0116: ECT Performance (Part 2 of 3). 2003 Neon

TEST	ACTION
6	Turn the ignition off. Disconnect the ECT harness connector. Disconnect the PCM harness connector. **CAUTION: DO NOT PROBE THE PCM HARNESS CONNECTORS. PROBING THE PCM HARNESS CONNECTORS WILL DAMAGE THE PCM TERMINALS RESULTING IN POOR TERMINAL TO PIN CONNECTION. INSTALL MILLER SPECIAL TOOL #8815 TO PERFORM DIAGNOSIS.** Measure the resistance of the (K167) Sensor ground circuit from the ECT Sensor harness connector to the appropriate terminal of special tool # 8815. Is the resistance below 5.0 ohms? Yes → NOTE: Before continuing, check the PCM harness connector terminals for corrosion, damage, or terminal push out. Repair as necessary. Replace and program the Powertrain Control Module No → Repair the open in the (K167) Sensor ground circuit.
7	Disconnect the ECT Sensor harness connector. Turn the ignition off. Disconnect the PCM harness connector. Measure the resistance between ground and the (K2) ECT Signal circuit in the ECT Sensor harness connector. Is the resistance below 100 ohms? Yes → Repair the short to ground in the (K2) ECT Signal circuit. No → Go To 8
8	Turn the ignition off. Disconnect the ECT Sensor harness connector. Disconnect the PCM harness connector. Measure the resistance between the (K2) ECT Sensor Signal circuit and the (K167) Sensor ground circuit at the ECT Sensor harness connector. Is the resistance below 5.0 ohms? Yes → Repair the (K167) Sensor ground shorted to the (K2) ECT Sensor Signal circuit. No → NOTE: Before continuing, check the PCM harness connector terminals for corrosion, damage, or terminal push out. Repair as necessary. Replace and program the Powertrain Control Module

ARM0400000000900

Fig. 57   Code P0116: ECT Performance (Part 3 of 3). 2003 Neon

TEST	ACTION
2	Turn the ignition off. Disconnect the ECT Sensor harness connector. NOTE: Visually inspect both the component and the PCM connectors. Look for damaged, partially broken wires, and backed out or corroded terminals. Ignition on, engine not running. Measure the voltage on the (K2) ECT Signal circuit in the ECT Sensor harness connector. Is the voltage above 5.2 volts? Yes → Repair the short to battery voltage in the (K2) ECT Signal circuit. No → Go To 3
3	Turn the ignition off. Disconnect the ECT Sensor harness connector. Ignition on, engine not running. With the DRBIII®, read the ECT Sensor voltage. Is the voltage above 4.9 volts? Yes → Go To 4 No → Go To 7
4	Turn the ignition off. Disconnect the ECT Sensor harness connector. Using a jumper wire, jumper across the ECT Sensor harness connector. Ignition on, engine not running. With the DRBIII®, read the ECT Sensor voltage. Is the voltage below 0.1 volt? Yes → Replace the ECT Sensor. No → Go To 5
5	Turn the ignition off. Disconnect the ECT Sensor harness connector. Disconnect the PCM harness connector. **CAUTION: DO NOT PROBE THE PCM HARNESS CONNECTORS. PROBING THE PCM HARNESS CONNECTORS WILL DAMAGE THE PCM TERMINALS RESULTING IN POOR TERMINAL TO PIN CONNECTION. INSTALL MILLER SPECIAL TOOL #8815 TO PERFORM DIAGNOSIS.** Measure the resistance of the (K2) ECT Signal circuit from the ECT Sensor harness connector to the appropriate terminal of special tool #8815. Is the resistance below 5.0 ohms? Yes → Go To 6 No → Repair the open in the (K2) ECT Signal circuit.

ARM0400000000906

Fig. 58   Code P0116: ECT Performance (Part 2 of 3). 2004–05 Neon

When Monitored and Set Condition:

P0116-ENGINE COOLANT TEMPERATURE PERFORMANCE

When Monitored: Engine off time is greater than 480 minutes. Ambient temperature is greater than -23°C (-9°F).

Set Condition: After a calibrated amount of cool down time, the PCM compares the ECT Sensor, IAT Sensor and the Ambient Air Temperature Sensor values. If the ECT Sensor value is not within calibrated temperature amount of the other two temperature sensors an error is detected. Two Trip Fault.

POSSIBLE CAUSES
GOOD TRIP EQUAL TO ZERO
(K2) ECT SIGNAL CIRCUIT SHORTED TO BATTERY VOLTAGE
ECT SENSOR VOLTAGE BELOW 0.1 VOLT
(K2) ECT SIGNAL CIRCUIT OPEN
(K167) SENSOR GROUND CIRCUIT OPEN
(K2) ECT SIGNAL CIRCUIT SHORTED TO GROUND
(K2) ECT SIGNAL SHORTED TO (K167) SENSOR GROUND
PCM HIGH
PCM LOW

TEST	ACTION
1	NOTE: The PCM compares IAT, AAT and ECT to determine if they are within a calibrated temp of one another. Using a block heater that does not meet OEM specifications or that is not installed at the proper location can defeat the algorithm in the PCM. Ignition on, engine not running. NOTE: Check with the customer to determine if such a block heater is installed on the vehicle. With the DRBIII®, read DTCs and record the related Freeze Frame data. Is the Good Trip Counter displayed and equal to zero? Yes → Go To 2 No → Diagnose intermittent condition.

ARM0400000000905

Fig. 58   Code P0116: ECT Performance (Part 1 of 3). 2004–05 Neon

TEST	ACTION
6	Turn the ignition off. Disconnect the ECT harness connector. Disconnect the PCM harness connector. **CAUTION: DO NOT PROBE THE PCM HARNESS CONNECTORS. PROBING THE PCM HARNESS CONNECTORS WILL DAMAGE THE PCM TERMINALS RESULTING IN POOR TERMINAL TO PIN CONNECTION. INSTALL MILLER SPECIAL TOOL #8815 TO PERFORM DIAGNOSIS.** Measure the resistance of the (K167) Sensor ground circuit from the ECT Sensor harness connector to the appropriate terminal of special tool # 8815. Is the resistance below 5.0 ohms? Yes → NOTE: Before continuing, check the PCM harness connector terminals for corrosion, damage, or terminal push out. Repair as necessary. Replace and program the Powertrain Control Module No → Repair the open in the (K167) Sensor ground circuit.
7	Disconnect the ECT Sensor harness connector. Turn the ignition off. Disconnect the PCM harness connector. Measure the resistance between ground and the (K2) ECT Signal circuit in the ECT Sensor harness connector. Is the resistance below 100 ohms? Yes → Repair the short to ground in the (K2) ECT Signal circuit. No → Go To 8
8	Turn the ignition off. Disconnect the ECT Sensor harness connector. Disconnect the PCM harness connector. Measure the resistance between the (K2) ECT Sensor Signal circuit and the (K167) Sensor ground circuit at the ECT Sensor harness connector. Is the resistance below 5.0 ohms? Yes → Repair the (K167) Sensor ground shorted to the (K2) ECT Sensor Signal circuit. No → NOTE: Before continuing, check the PCM harness connector terminals for corrosion, damage, or terminal push out. Repair as necessary. Replace and program the Powertrain Control Module

ARM0400000000907

Fig. 58   Code P0116: ECT Performance (Part 3 of 3). 2004–05 Neon

When Monitored and Set Condition:

P0117-ENGINE COOLANT TEMPERATURE SENSOR LOW

When Monitored: With the ignition on. Battery voltage greater than 10 volts.

Set Condition: The Engine Coolant Temperature (ECT) sensor circuit voltage at the PCM is less than 0.0782 of a volt. One Trip Fault.

POSSIBLE CAUSES
ECT SENSOR VOLTAGE BELOW 0.1 VOLTS
ECT SENSOR INTERNAL FAILURE
(K2) ECT SIGNAL SHORTED TO GROUND
(K2) ECT SIGNAL SHORTED TO (K167) SENSOR GROUND CIRCUIT
PCM

TEST	ACTION
1	Ignition on, engine not running. With the DRBIII®, read the ECT Sensor voltage. Is the voltage below 0.1 volt? Yes → Go To 2 No → Diagnose intermitten condition.
2	Turn the ignition off. Disconnect the ECT harness connector. Ignition on, engine not running. With the DRBIII®, read ECT Sensor voltage. Is the voltage between 4.8 and 5.2 volts? Yes → Replace the ECT Sensor. No → Go To 3
3	Turn the ignition off. Disconnect the ECT Sensor harness connector. Disconnect the PCM harness connector. Measure the resistance between ground and the (K2) ECT Signal circuit in the ECT Sensor harness connector. Is the resistance below 100 ohms? Yes → Repair the ground shorted to the (K2) ECT Signal circuit. No → Go To 4

ARM0400000000901

Fig. 59 Code P0117: ECT Temperature Sensor Low (Part 1 of 2). 2003–05 Neon

When Monitored and Set Condition:

P0118-ENGINE COOLANT TEMPERATURE SENSOR HIGH

When Monitored: With the ignition on. Battery voltage greater than 10 volts.

Set Condition: The Engine Coolant Temperature (ECT) sensor voltage at the PCM is greater than 4.9 volts. One trip Fault.

POSSIBLE CAUSES
ECT SENSOR VOLTAGE ABOVE 4.9 VOLTS
(K2) ECT SIGNAL CIRCUIT SHORTED TO BATTERY VOLTAGE
ECT SENSOR INTERNAL FAILURE
(K2) ECT SIGNAL CIRCUIT OPEN
(K167) SENSOR GROUND CIRCUIT OPEN
PCM

TEST	ACTION
1	Ignition on, engine not running. With the DRBIII®, read the ECT Sensor voltage. Is the voltage above 4.9 volts? Yes → Go To 2 No → Diagnsoe intermittent condition.
2	Turn the ignition off. Disconnect the ECT Sensor harness connector. Ignition on, engine not running. Measure the voltage of the (K2) ECT Signal circuit in the ECT Sensor harness connector. Is the voltage above 5.2 volts? Yes → Repair the short to battery voltage in the (K2) ECT Signal circuit. No → Go To 3

ARM0400000000903

Fig. 60 Code P0118: ECT Temperature Sensor High (Part 1 of 2). 2003–05 Neon

TEST	ACTION
4	Turn the ignition off. Disconnect the ECT Sensor harness connector. Disconnect the PCM harness connector. Measure the resistance between the (K2) ECT Sensor Signal circuit and the (K167) Sensor ground circuit in the ECT Sensor harness connector. Is the resistance below 100 ohms? Yes → Repair the (K167) Sensor ground shorted to the (K2) ECT Sensor Signal circuit. No → Go To 5
5	**NOTE: Before continuing, check the PCM harness connector terminals for corrosion, damage, or terminal push out. Repair as necessary.** If there are no possible causes remaining, view repair. Repair Replace and program the Powertrain Control Module

ARM0400000000902

Fig. 59 Code P0117: ECT Temperature Sensor Low (Part 2 of 2). 2003–05 Neon

TEST	ACTION
3	Turn the ignition off. Disconnect the ECT harness connector. Connect a jumper wire between the (K2) ECT Signal circuit and the (K4) Sensor ground circuit in the ECT harness connector. Ignition on, engine not running. With the DRBIII®, read ECT Sensor voltage. Is the voltage below 1.0 volt? Yes → Replace the ECT Sensor. No → Go To 4
4	Turn the ignition off. Disconnect the ECT Sensor harness connector. Disconnect the PCM harness connector. **CAUTION: DO NOT PROBE THE PCM HARNESS CONNECTORS. PROBING THE PCM HARNESS CONNECTORS WILL DAMAGE THE PCM TERMINALS RESULTING IN POOR TERMINAL TO PIN CONNECTION. INSTALL MILLER SPECIAL TOOL #8815 TO PERFORM DIAGNOSIS.** Measure the resistance of the (K2) ECT Signal circuit from the ECT Sensor harness connector to the appropriate terminal of special tool #8815. Is the resistance below 5.0 ohms? Yes → Go To 5 No → Repair the open in the (K2) ECT Signal circuit.
5	Turn the ignition off. Disconnect the ECT Sensor harness connector. Disconnect the PCM harness connector. **CAUTION: DO NOT PROBE THE PCM HARNESS CONNECTORS. PROBING THE PCM HARNESS CONNECTORS WILL DAMAGE THE PCM TERMINALS RESULTING IN POOR TERMINAL TO PIN CONNECTION. INSTALL MILLER SPECIAL TOOL #8815 TO PERFORM DIAGNOSIS.** Measure the resistance of the (K167) Sensor ground circuit from the ECT Sensor harness connector to the appropriate terminal of special tool #8815. Is the resistance below 5.0 ohms? Yes → Go To 6 No → Repair the open in the (K167) Sensor ground circuit.
6	**NOTE: Before continuing, check the PCM harness connector terminals for corrosion, damage, or terminal push out. Repair as necessary.** If there are no possible causes remaining, view repair. Repair Replace and program the Powertrain Control Module

ARM0400000000904

Fig. 60 Code P0118: ECT Temperature Sensor High (Part 2 of 2). 2003–05 Neon

When Monitored and Set Condition:

P0480-COOLING FAN 1 CONTROL CIRCUIT

When Monitored: With the ignition on. Battery voltage greater than 10 volts.

Set Condition: An open or shorted circuit is detected in the radiator fan relay control circuit. One Trip Fault.

POSSIBLE CAUSES
LOW SPEED RADIATOR FAN RELAY OPERATION
(A16) FUSED B+ FEED CIRCUITS
LOW SPEED RADIATOR FAN RELAY RESISTANCE
(C24) LOW SPEED RAD FAN RELAY CONTROL CIRCUIT OPEN
(C24) LOW SPEED RAD FAN RELAY CONTROL CIRCUIT SHORT TO GROUND
PCM

TEST	ACTION

1	Ignition on, engine not running.
	With the DRBIII®, actuate the Radiator Fan Relay.
	Is the Low Speed Radiator Fan Relay operating?
	
	    Yes → Diagnose intermittent condition.
	
	    No → Go To 2

2	Turn the ignition off.
	Remove the Low Speed Radiator Fan Relay from the PDC.
	Ignition on, engine not running.
	Measure the voltage of the (A16) Fused B+ Feed circuit in the PDC.
	Is the voltage above 11.0 volts?
	
	    Yes → Go To 3
	
	    No → Repair the (A16) Fused B+ Output circuit. Inspect the related fuse and repair as necessary.
	Perform POWERTRAIN VERIFICATION TEST VER - 5.

ARM0400000000908

Fig. 61   Code P0480: Cooling Fan No 1 Control Circuit (Part 1 of 2). 2004–05 Neon

When Monitored and Set Condition:

P0481-COOLING FAN 2 CONTROL CIRCUIT (NON-TURBO)

When Monitored: With the ignition on. Battery voltage greater than 10 volts.

Set Condition: An open or shorted circuit is detected in the radiator fan relay control circuit. One trip Fault.

POSSIBLE CAUSES
HIGH SPEED RADIATOR FAN RELAY OPERATION
(A110) FUSED IGNITION SWITCH OUTPUT CIRCUIT
HIGH SPEED RADIATOR FAN RELAY RESISTANCE
(C27) HIGH SPEED RAD FAN RELAY CONTROL CIRCUIT OPEN
(C27) HIGH SPEED RAD FAN RELAY CONTROL CIRCUIT SHORT TO GROUND
PCM

TEST	ACTION

1	Turn the ignition on.
	With the DRBIII®, actuate the High Speed Radiator Fan Relay.
	Is the High Speed Radiator Fan Relay operating?
	
	    Yes → Diagnose intermittent condition.
	
	    No → Go To 2

2	Turn the ignition off.
	Remove the High Speed Radiator Fan Relay from the PDC.
	Turn the ignition on.
	Measure the voltage of the (A110) Fused Ignition Switch Output circuit in the PDC.
	Is the voltage above 11.0 volts?
	
	    Yes → Go To 3
	
	    No → Repair the (A110) Fused Ignition Switch Output circuit. Check and replace any open fuses.

ARM0400000000910

Fig. 62   Code P0481: Cooling Fan No 2 Control Circuit Open (Part 1 of 2). 2004–05 Neon w/2.0L Engine

TEST	ACTION

3	Turn the ignition off.
	Remove the Low Speed Radiator Fan Relay from the PDC.
	Measure the resistance of the Low Speed Radiator Fan Relay between the Fused Ignition Switch Output terminal and the Low Speed Rad Fan Relay Control terminal.
	Is the resistance between 60 to 85 ohms?
	
	    Yes → Go To 4
	
	    No → Replace the Low Speed Radiator Fan Relay.

4	Turn the ignition off.
	Remove the Low Speed Radiator Fan Relay from the PDC.
	Disconnect the PCM harness connector.
	CAUTION: DO NOT PROBE THE PCM HARNESS CONNECTORS. PROBING THE PCM HARNESS CONNECTORS WILL DAMAGE THE PCM TERMINALS RESULTING IN POOR TERMINAL TO PIN CONNECTION. INSTALL MILLER SPECIAL TOOL #8815 TO PERFORM DIAGNOSIS.
	Measure the resistance of the (C24) Low Speed Rad Fan Relay Control circuit from the PDC to the appropriate terminal of special tool #8815.
	Is the resistance below 5.0 ohms?
	
	    Yes → Go To 5
	
	    No → Repair the open in the (C24) Low Speed Rad Fan Relay Control circuit.

5	Turn the ignition off.
	Remove the Low Speed Radiator Fan Relay from the PDC.
	Disconnect the PCM harness connector.
	Measure the resistance between ground and the (C24) Low Speed Rad Fan Control circuit at the PDC.
	Is the resistance below 100 ohms?
	
	    Yes → Repair the short to ground in the (C24) Low Speed Rad Fan Relay Control circuit.
	
	    No → Go To 6

6	**NOTE: Before continuing, check the PCM harness connector terminals for corrosion, damage, or terminal push out. Repair as necessary.**
	If there are no possible causes remaining, view repair.
	
	    Repair
	        Replace and program the Powertrain Control Module

ARM0400000000909

Fig. 61   Code P0480: Cooling Fan No 1 Control Circuit (Part 2 of 2). 2004–05 Neon

TEST	ACTION

3	Turn the ignition off.
	Remove the High Speed Radiator Fan Relay from the PDC.
	Measure the resistance of the High Speed Radiator Fan Relay between the Fused Ignition Switch Output terminal and the High Speed Rad Fan Relay Control terminal.
	Is the resistance between 60 to 85 ohms?
	
	    Yes → Go To 4
	
	    No → Replace the High Speed Radiator Fan Relay.

4	Turn the ignition off.
	Remove the High Speed Radiator Fan Relay from the PDC.
	Disconnect the PCM harness connector.
	CAUTION: DO NOT PROBE THE PCM HARNESS CONNECTORS. PROBING THE PCM HARNESS CONNECTORS WILL DAMAGE THE PCM TERMINALS RESULTING IN POOR TERMINAL TO PIN CONNECTION. INSTALL MILLER SPECIAL TOOL #8815 TO PERFORM DIAGNOSIS.
	Measure the resistance of the (C27) High Speed Rad Fan Relay Control circuit from the PDC to the appropriate terminal of special tool #8815.
	Is the resistance below 5.0 ohms?
	
	    Yes → Go To 5
	
	    No → Repair the open in the (C27) High Speed Rad Fan Relay Control circuit.

5	Turn the ignition off.
	Remove the High Speed Radiator Fan Relay from the PDC.
	Disconnect the PCM harness connector.
	Measure the resistance between ground and the (C27) High Speed Rad Fan Relay Control circuit in the PDC.
	Is the resistance below 5.0 ohms?
	
	    Yes → Repair the short to ground in the (C27) High Speed Rad Fan Relay Control circuit.
	
	    No → Go To 6

6	**NOTE: Before continuing, check the PCM harness connector terminals for corrosion, damage, or terminal push out. Repair as necessary.**
	If there are no possible causes remaining, view repair.
	
	    Repair
	        NOTE: Before continuing, check the PCM harness connector terminals for corrosion, damage or terminal push out. Repair as necessary. Replace and program the Powertrain Control Module

ARM0400000000911

Fig. 62   Code P0481: Cooling Fan No 2 Control Circuit Open (Part 2 of 2). 2004–05 Neon w/2.0L Engine

When Monitored and Set Condition:

P0481-COOLING FAN 2 CONTROL CIRCUIT (TURBO)

When Monitored: With the ignition on. Battery voltage greater than 10 volts.

Set Condition: An open or shorted circuit is detected in the radiator fan relay control circuits. One Trip Fault.

POSSIBLE CAUSES
RADIATOR FAN RELAYS 2 AND 3 OPERATION
FUSED IGNITION SWITCH OUTPUT CIRCUIT
RADIATOR FAN RELAY #2 CONTROL CIRCUIT OPEN BEFORE THE SPLICE
RADIATOR FAN RELAY #3 CONTROL CIRCUIT OPEN BEFORE SPLICE
RADIATOR FAN RELAY CONTROL CIRCUITS SHORT TO GROUND
RADIATOR FAN RELAY CONTROL CIRCUIT OPEN AFTER THE SPLICE
RADIATOR FAN RELAY #2 OR #3
PCM

TEST	ACTION
1	Turn the ignition on. With the DRBIII®, actuate the High Speed Radiator Fan Relay. Are both Radiator Fan operating at high speed? Yes → Refer to the INTERMITTENT CONDITION symptom in the Driveability category. No → Go To 2
2	Turn the ignition off. Remove both of the Radiator Fan Relays (#2 and #3) from the PDC. Turn the ignition on. NOTE: A voltage measurement must be taken at both Radiator Fan Relay Fused Ignition Switch Output circuits in the PDC. Measure the voltage of the Fused Ignition Switch Output circuit at the radiator Fan Relay connector in the PDC. Is the voltage above 11.0 volts at both relay connectors? Yes → Go To 3 No → Repair the Fused Ignition Switch Output circuit. Check and replace any open fuses.

ARM0400000000912

Fig. 63 Code P0481: Cooling Fan No 2 Control Circuit Open (Part 1 of 3). 2004–05 Neon w/2.4L Engine

TEST	ACTION
5	NOTE: Both Radiator Fan Relays must be removed from the PDC during the following steps. Turn the ignition off. Disconnect the PCM harness connector. CAUTION: DO NOT PROBE THE PCM HARNESS CONNECTORS. PROBING THE PCM HARNESS CONNECTORS WILL DAMAGE THE PCM TERMINALS RESULTING IN POOR TERMINAL TO PIN CONNECTION. INSTALL MILLER SPECIAL TOOL #8815 TO PERFORM DIAGNOSIS. Measure the resistance of the Radiator Fan Relay #3 Control circuit from the PDC to the appropriate terminal of special tool #8815. Is the resistance below 5.0 ohms? Yes → NOTE: Before continuing, check the PCM harness connector terminals for corrosion, damage or terminal push out. Repair as necessary. Replace and program the Powertrain Control Module No → Repair the open in the Radiator Fan Relay Control circuit.

ARM0400000000914

Fig. 63 Code P0481: Cooling Fan No 2 Control Circuit Open (Part 3 of 3). 2004–05 Neon w/2.4L Engine

TEST	ACTION
3	NOTE: Both Radiator Fan Relays must be removed from the PDC during the following steps. Turn the ignition on. Using the DRBIII®, actuate the High Speed Radiator Fan Relay. Using a test light connected to battery voltage, probe both of the Radiator Fan Relay Control circuits (relays #2 and #3). NOTE: The test light should flash at both control circuits. Choose a conclusion that best matches the result of the above test. Does NOT flash for Relay #2 (ONLY). Repair the open in the Radiator Fan Relay #2 Control circuit between the PDC and the splice. Does NOT flash for Relay #3 (ONLY). Repair the open in the Radiator Fan Relay #3 Control circuit between the PDC and the splice. Does NOT flash for both #2 and #3 Relays Go To 4 Flashes at both Relays. Install a substitute relay in place of the Radiator Fan Relays #2 and #3 to determine the faulty relay. Replace the appropriate Radiator Fan Relay.
4	NOTE: Both Radiator Fan Relays must be removed from the PDC during the following steps. Turn the ignition off. Disconnect the PCM harness connector. Measure the resistance between ground and the Radiator Fan Relay #2 Control circuit in the PDC. Is the resistance below 100 ohms? Yes → Repair the short to ground in the Radiator Fan Relay Control circuits. No → Go To 5

ARM0400000000913

Fig. 63 Code P0481: Cooling Fan No 2 Control Circuit Open (Part 2 of 3). 2004–05 Neon w/2.4L Engine

When Monitored and Set Condition:

P0117-ECT SENSOR VOLTAGE TOO LOW

When Monitored: With the ignition on. Battery voltage greater than 10 volts.

Set Condition: The Engine Coolant Temperature (ECT) sensor circuit voltage at the PCM is less than 0.5 volt for more than 2.6 seconds.

POSSIBLE CAUSES
INTERMITTENT CONDITION
ECT SENSOR INTERNAL FAILURE
ECT SENSOR SIGNAL SHORTED TO GROUND
ECT SENSOR SIGNAL SHORTED TO SENSOR GROUND CIRCUIT
PCM TERMINAL CONDITION
PCM

TEST	ACTION
1	Turn the ignition on. With the DRBIII®, read the ECT voltage. Is the voltage below 1.0 volt? Yes → Go To 2 No → Go To 6
2	Turn the ignition off. Disconnect the ECT harness connector. Turn the ignition on. With the DRBIII®, read ECT voltage. Is the voltage above 1.0 volt? Yes → Replace the ECT Sensor. No → Go To 3
3	Turn the ignition off. Disconnect the ECT Sensor harness connector. Disconnect the PCM harness connector. Measure the resistance of the ECT Sensor Signal circuit in the ECT Sensor harness connector to ground. Is the resistance below 100 ohms? Yes → Repair the ECT Sensor Signal circuit for a short to ground. No → Go To 4

ARM0400000000870

Fig. 64 Code P0117: ECT Sensor Voltage Too Low (Part 1 of 2). 2001–02 Sebring Convertible, Sebring Sedan & Stratus Sedan

TEST	ACTION
4	Turn the ignition off. Disconnect the ECT Sensor harness connector. Disconnect the PCM harness connector. Measure the resistance between the ECT Sensor Signal circuit and the Sensor ground circuit in the ECT Sensor harness connector. Is the resistance below 100 ohms? Yes → Repair the ECT Sensor Signal circuit for a short to the Sensor ground circuit. No → Go To 5
5	Turn the ignition off. Disconnect the PCM harness connector. Inspect the ECT Signal and Sensor Ground terminals. Check for corrosion, damage or terminal push out. If there are no possible causes remaining, view repair. Yes → Repair as necessary. Perform POWERTRAIN VERIFICATION TEST VER - 5. No → Replace and program the Powertrain Control Module
6	WARNING: WHEN THE ENGINE IS OPERATING, DO NOT STAND IN A DIRECT LINE WITH THE FAN. DO NOT PUT YOUR HANDS NEAR THE PULLEYS, BELTS OR FAN. DO NOT WEAR LOOSE CLOTHING. NOTE: The conditions that set the DTC are not present at this time. The following list may help in identifying the intermittent condition. With the engine running at normal operating temperature, monitor the DRBIII® parameters related to the DTC while wiggling the wiring harness. Look for parameter values to change and/or a DTC to set. Review the DRBIII® Freeze Frame information. If possible, try to duplicate the conditions under which the DTC was set. Refer to any Technical Service Bulletins (TSB) that may apply. Visually inspect the related wiring harness. Look for any chafed, pierced, pinched, or partially broken wires. Visually inspect the related wiring harness connectors. Look for broken, bent, pushed out, or corroded terminals. Were any of the above conditions present? Yes → Repair as necessary No → Test Complete.

ARM0400000000871

Fig. 64 Code P0117: ECT Sensor Voltage Too Low (Part 2 of 2). 2001–02 Sebring Convertible, Sebring Sedan & Stratus Sedan

TEST	ACTION
3	Turn the ignition off. Disconnect the ECT harness connector. Connect a jumper wire between the ECT Sensor Signal circuit and the Sensor ground circuit in the ECT harness connector. Turn the ignition on. With the DRBIII®, read ECT voltage. Is the voltage below 1.0 volt? Yes → Replace the ECT Sensor. No → Go To 4
4	Turn the ignition off. Disconnect the ECT Sensor harness connector. Disconnect the PCM harness connector. Measure the resistance of the ECT Sensor Signal circuit between the ECT Sensor harness connector and the PCM harness connector. Is the resistance below 5.0 ohms? Yes → Go To 5 No → Repair the ECT Sensor Signal circuit for an open.
5	Turn the ignition off. Disconnect the ECT Sensor harness connector. Disconnect the PCM harness connector. Measure the resistance of the Sensor ground circuit between the ECT Sensor harness connector and the PCM harness connector. Is the resistance below 5.0 ohms? Yes → Go To 6 No → Repair the Sensor ground circuit for an open.
6	Turn the ignition off. Disconnect the PCM harness connector. Inspect the ECT Signal and Sensor Ground terminals. Check for corrosion, damage or terminal push out. Were any of the above condition present? Yes → Repair as necessary. Perform POWERTRAIN VERIFICATION TEST VER - 5. No → Replace and program the Powertrain Control Module

ARM0400000000873

Fig. 65 Code P0118: ECT Sensor Voltage Too High (Part 2 of 3). 2001–02 Sebring Convertible, Sebring Sedan & Stratus Sedan

When Monitored and Set Condition:

P0118-ECT SENSOR VOLTAGE TOO HIGH

When Monitored: With the ignition on. Battery voltage greater than 10 volts.

Set Condition: The Engine Coolant Temperature (ECT) sensor circuit voltage at the PCM is greater than 4.96 volts for more than 2.6 seconds.

POSSIBLE CAUSES
INTERMITTENT CONDITION
ECT SENSOR SIGNAL CIRCUIT SHORTED TO BATTERY VOLTAGE
ECT SENSOR INTERNAL FAILURE
ECT SENSOR SIGNAL CIRCUIT OPEN
SENSOR GROUND CIRCUIT OPEN
PCM TERMINAL CONDITION
PCM

TEST	ACTION
1	Turn the ignition on. With the DRBIII®, read the ECT voltage. Is the voltage above 4.6 volts? Yes → Go To 2 No → Go To 7
2	Turn the ignition off. Disconnect the ECT Sensor harness connector. Turn the ignition on. Measure the voltage of the ECT Sensor Signal circuit in the ECT Sensor harness connector. Is the voltage above 5.2 volts? Yes → Repair the ECT Sensor Signal circuit for a short to battery voltage. No → Go To 3

ARM0400000000872

Fig. 65 Code P0118: ECT Sensor Voltage Too High (Part 1 of 3). 2001–02 Sebring Convertible, Sebring Sedan & Stratus Sedan

TEST	ACTION
7	WARNING: WHEN THE ENGINE IS OPERATING, DO NOT STAND IN A DIRECT LINE WITH THE FAN. DO NOT PUT YOUR HANDS NEAR THE PULLEYS, BELTS OR FAN. DO NOT WEAR LOOSE CLOTHING. NOTE: The conditions that set the DTC are not present at this time. The following list may help in identifying the intermittent condition. With the engine running at normal operating temperature, monitor the DRBIII® parameters related to the DTC while wiggling the wiring harness. Look for parameter values to change and/or a DTC to set. Review the DRBIII® Freeze Frame information. If possible, try to duplicate the conditions under which the DTC was set. Refer to any Technical Service Bulletins (TSB) that may apply. Visually inspect the related wiring harness. Look for any chafed, pierced, pinched, or partially broken wires. Visually inspect the related wiring harness connectors. Look for broken, bent, pushed out, or corroded terminals. Were any of the above conditions present? Yes → Repair as necessary No → Test Complete.

ARM0400000000874

Fig. 65 Code P0118: ECT Sensor Voltage Too High (Part 3 of 3). 2001–02 Sebring Convertible, Sebring Sedan & Stratus Sedan

P1489-HIGH SPEED FAN CONTROL RELAY CIRCUIT

When Monitored: With the ignition on. Battery voltage greater than 10.0 volts.

Set Condition: An open or shorted circuit is detected in the radiator fan relay control circuit.

POSSIBLE CAUSES
HIGH SPEED RADIATOR FAN RELAY INTERMITTENT OPERATION
INTERMITTENT CONDITION
FUSED IGNITION SWITCH OUTPUT CIRCUIT
HIGH SPEED RADIATOR FAN RELAY RESISTANCE
HIGH SPEED RADIATOR FAN RELAY CONTROL CIRCUIT OPEN
HIGH SPEED RADIATOR FAN RELAY CONTROL CIRCUIT SHORT TO GROUND
PCM

TEST	ACTION
1	Turn the ignition on. With the DRBIII®, actuate the High Speed Radiator Fan Relay. Is the High Speed Radiator Fan Relay operating? Yes → Go To 2 No → Go To 4
2	Turn the ignition on. With the DRBIII®, actuate the High Speed Radiator Fan Relay. Wiggle the wiring harness from the High Speed Radiator Fan Relay to the PCM while the relay is actuating. Did the High Speed Radiator Fan Relay stop when wiggling the wiring harness? Yes → Repair as necessary. No → Go To 3

CR1080000303010X

Fig. 66   Code P1489: High Speed Fan Control Relay Circuit (Part 1 of 3). 2001–02 Sebring Convertible, Sebring Sedan & Stratus Sedan

TEST	ACTION
7	Turn the ignition off. Remove the High Speed Radiator Fan Relay from the PDC. Disconnect the PCM harness connector. Measure the resistance of the High Speed Radiator Fan Relay Control circuit in the PDC to ground. Is the resistance below 5.0 ohms. Yes → Repair the High Speed Radiator Fan Relay Control circuit for a short to ground. No → Go To 8
8	If there are no possible causes remaining, view repair. Repair Replace and program the Powertrain Control Module in accordance with the Service Information.

CR1080000303030X

Fig. 66   Code P1489: High Speed Fan Control Relay Circuit (Part 3 of 3). 2001–02 Sebring Convertible, Sebring Sedan & Stratus Sedan

P1490-LOW SPEED FAN CONTROL RELAY CIRCUIT

When Monitored: With the ignition on. Battery voltage greater than 10 volts.

Set Condition: An open or shorted circuit is detected in the radiator fan relay control circuit.

POSSIBLE CAUSES
LOW SPEED RADIATOR FAN RELAY INTERMITTENT OPERATION
INTERMITTENT CONDITION
FUSED IGNITION SWITCH OUTPUT CIRCUIT
LOW SPEED RADIATOR FAN RELAY RESISTANCE
LOW SPEED RADIATOR FAN RELAY CONTROL CIRCUIT OPEN
LOW SPEED RADIATOR FAN RELAY CONTROL CIRCUIT SHORT TO GROUND
PCM

TEST	ACTION
1	Turn the ignition on. With the DRBIII®, actuate the Low Speed Radiator Fan Relay. Is the Low Speed Radiator Fan Relay operating? Yes → Go To 2 No → Go To 4
2	Turn the ignition on. With the DRBIII®, actuate the Low Speed Radiator Fan Relay. Wiggle the wiring harness from the Low Speed Radiator Fan Relay to the PCM while the relay is actuating. Did the Low Speed Radiator Fan Relay stop when wiggling the wiring harness? Yes → Repair as necessary. No → Go To 3

CR1080000302010X

Fig. 67   Code P1490: Low Speed Fan Control Relay Circuit (Part 1 of 3). 2001–02 Sebring Convertible, Sebring Sedan & Stratus Sedan

TEST	ACTION
3	WARNING: WHEN THE ENGINE IS OPERATING, DO NOT STAND IN A DIRECT LINE WITH THE FAN. DO NOT PUT YOUR HANDS NEAR THE PULLEYS, BELTS OR FAN. DO NOT WEAR LOOSE CLOTHING. NOTE: The conditions that set the DTC are not present at this time. The following list may help in identifying the intermittent condition. With the engine running at normal operating temperature, monitor the DRB parameters related to the DTC while wiggling the wiring harness. Look for parameter values to change and/or a DTC to set. Review the DRB Freeze Frame information. If possible, try to duplicate the conditions under which the DTC was set. Refer to any Technical Service Bulletins (TSB) that may apply. Visually inspect the related wiring harness. Look for any chafed, pierced, pinched, or partially broken wires. Visually inspect the related wiring harness connectors. Look for broken, bent, pushed out, or corroded terminals. Were any of the above conditions present? Yes → Repair as necessary No → Test Complete.
4	Turn the ignition off. Remove the High Speed Radiator Fan Relay from the PDC. Turn the ignition on. Measure the voltage of the Fused Ignition Switch Output circuit in the PDC. Is the voltage above 11.0 volts? Yes → Go To 5 No → Repair the Fused Ignition Switch Output circuit. Check and replace any open fuses.
5	Turn the ignition off. Remove the High Speed Radiator Fan Relay from the PDC. Measure the resistance of the High Speed Radiator Fan Relay between the Fused Ignition Switch Output terminal and the High Speed Radiator Fan Relay Control terminal. Is the resistance between 60 to 80 ohms? Yes → Go To 6 No → Replace the High Speed Radiator Fan Relay.
6	Turn the ignition off. Remove the High Speed Radiator Fan Relay from the PDC. Disconnect the PCM harness connector. Measure the resistance of the High Speed Radiator Fan Relay Control circuit between the PDC and the PCM harness connector. Is the resistance below 5.0 ohms? Yes → Go To 7 No → Repair the High Speed Radiator Fan Relay Control circuit for an open.

CR1080000303020X

Fig. 66   Code P1489: High Speed Fan Control Relay Circuit (Part 2 of 3). 2001–02 Sebring Convertible, Sebring Sedan & Stratus Sedan

TEST	ACTION
3	WARNING: WHEN THE ENGINE IS OPERATING, DO NOT STAND IN A DIRECT LINE WITH THE FAN. DO NOT PUT YOUR HANDS NEAR THE PULLEYS, BELTS OR FAN. DO NOT WEAR LOOSE CLOTHING. NOTE: The conditions that set the DTC are not present at this time. The following list may help in identifying the intermittent condition. With the engine running at normal operating temperature, monitor the DRB parameters related to the DTC while wiggling the wiring harness. Look for parameter values to change and/or a DTC to set. Review the DRB Freeze Frame information. If possible, try to duplicate the conditions under which the DTC was set. Refer to any Technical Service Bulletins (TSB) that may apply. Visually inspect the related wiring harness. Look for any chafed, pierced, pinched, or partially broken wires. Visually inspect the related wiring harness connectors. Look for broken, bent, pushed out, or corroded terminals. Were any of the above conditions present? Yes → Repair as necessary No → Test Complete.
4	Turn the ignition off. Remove the Low Speed Radiator Fan Relay from the PDC. Turn the ignition on. Measure the voltage of the Fused Ignition Switch Output circuit in the PDC. Is the voltage above 11.0 volts? Yes → Go To 5 No → Repair the Fused Ignition Switch Output circuit. Check and replace any open fuses.
5	Turn the ignition off. Remove the Low Speed Radiator Fan Relay from the PDC. Measure the resistance of the Low Speed Radiator Fan Relay between the Fused Ignition Switch Output terminal and the Low Speed Radiator Fan Relay Control terminal. Is the resistance between 60 to 80 ohms? Yes → Go To 6 No → Replace the Low Speed Radiator Fan Relay.
6	Turn the ignition off. Remove the Low Speed Radiator Fan Relay from the PDC. Disconnect the PCM harness connector. Measure the resistance of the Low Speed Radiator Fan Relay Control circuit between the PDC and the PCM harness connector. Is the resistance below 5.0 ohms? Yes → Go To 7 No → Repair the Low Speed Radiator Fan Relay Control circuit for an open.

CR1080000302020X

Fig. 67   Code P1490: Low Speed Fan Control Relay Circuit (Part 2 of 3). 2001–02 Sebring Convertible, Sebring Sedan & Stratus Sedan

TEST	ACTION

7	Turn the ignition off.
	Remove the Low Speed Radiator Fan Relay from the PDC.
	Disconnect the PCM harness connector.
	Measure the resistance of the Low Speed Radiator Fan Relay Control circuit in the PDC to ground.
	Is the resistance below 5.0 ohms?
	
	      Yes → Repair the Low Speed Radiator Fan Relay Control circuit for a short to ground.
	
	      No → Go To 8

8	If there are no possible causes remaining, view repair.
	
	      Repair
	            Replace and program the Powertrain Control Module

CR1080000302030X

Fig. 67   Code P1490: Low Speed Fan Control Relay Circuit (Part 3 of 3). 2001–02 Sebring Convertible, Sebring Sedan & Stratus Sedan

TEST	ACTION

2	Turn the ignition off.
	Disconnect the ECT Sensor harness connector.
	NOTE: Visually inspect both the component and the PCM connectors. Look for damaged, partially broken wires, and backed out or corroded terminals.
	Ignition on, engine not running.
	Measure the voltage on the (K2) ECT Signal circuit in the ECT Sensor harness connector.
	Is the voltage above 5.2 volts?
	
	      Yes → Repair the short to battery voltage in the (K2) ECT Signal circuit.
	
	      No → Go To 3

3	Turn the ignition off.
	Disconnect the ECT Sensor harness connector.
	Ignition on, engine not running.
	With the DRBIII®, read the ECT Sensor voltage.
	Is the voltage above 4.6 volts?
	
	      Yes → Go To 4
	
	      No → Go To 7

4	Turn the ignition off.
	Disconnect the ECT Sensor harness connector.
	Using a jumper wire, jumper across the ECT Sensor harness connector.
	Ignition on, engine not running.
	With the DRBIII®, read the ECT Sensor voltage.
	Is the voltage below 1.0 volt?
	
	      Yes → Replace the ECT Sensor.
	
	      No → Go To 5

5	Turn the ignition off.
	Disconnect the ECT Sensor harness connector.
	Disconnect the PCM harness connector.
	CAUTION: DO NOT PROBE THE PCM HARNESS CONNECTORS. PROBING THE PCM HARNESS CONNECTORS WILL DAMAGE THE PCM TERMINALS RESULTING IN POOR TERMINAL TO PIN CONNECTION. INSTALL MILLER SPECIAL TOOL #8815 TO PERFORM DIAGNOSIS.
	Measure the resistance of the (K2) ECT Signal circuit from the ECT Sensor harness connector to the appropriate terminal of special tool #8815.
	Is the resistance below 5.0 ohms?
	
	      Yes → Go To 6
	
	      No → Repair the open in the (K2) ECT Signal circuit.

ARM0400000000855

Fig. 68   Code P0116: ECT Performance. (Part 2 of 3). 2003–05 Sebring Convertible, Sebring Sedan & Stratus Sedan

When Monitored and Set Condition:

P0116-ENGINE COOLANT TEMPERATURE PERFORMANCE

When Monitored: Engine off time is greater than 480 minutes. Ambient temperature is greater than 4°C (39°F).

Set Condition: After a calibrated amount of cool down time, the PCM compares the ECT Sensor, IAT Sensor and the Ambient Air Temperature Sensor values. If the ECT Sensor value is not within calibrated temperature amount of the other two temperature sensors an error is detected. Two Trip Fault.

POSSIBLE CAUSES
GOOD TRIP EQUAL TO ZERO
(K2) ECT SIGNAL CIRCUIT SHORTED TO BATTERY VOLTAGE
ECT SENSOR VOLTAGE BELOW 1.0 VOLT
(K2) ECT SIGNAL CIRCUIT OPEN
(K4) SENSOR GROUND CIRCUIT OPEN
(K2) ECT SIGNAL CIRCUIT SHORTED TO GROUND
(K2) ECT SIGNAL SHORTED TO (K4) SENSOR GROUND
PCM HIGH
PCM LOW

TEST	ACTION

1	**NOTE: Due to the fact that the PCM compares the IAT, AAT and ECT sensor to see if they are within a calibrated temp of one another, the use of a block heater can cause false readings for the PCM. Check with the customer to see if they use a block heater.**
	Ignition on, engine not running.
	With the DRBIII®, read DTCs and record the related Freeze Frame data.
	Is the Good Trip Counter displayed and equal to zero?
	
	      Yes → Go To 2
	
	      No → Diagnose intermittent condition.

ARM0400000000854

Fig. 68   Code P0116: ECT Performance. (Part 1 of 3). 2003–05 Sebring Convertible, Sebring Sedan & Stratus Sedan

TEST	ACTION

6	Turn the ignition off.
	Disconnect the ECT harness connector.
	Disconnect the PCM harness connector.
	CAUTION: DO NOT PROBE THE PCM HARNESS CONNECTORS. PROBING THE PCM HARNESS CONNECTORS WILL DAMAGE THE PCM TERMINALS RESULTING IN POOR TERMINAL TO PIN CONNECTION. INSTALL MILLER SPECIAL TOOL #8815 TO PERFORM DIAGNOSIS.
	Measure the resistance of the (K4) Sensor ground circuit from the ECT Sensor harness connector to the appropriate terminal of special tool # 8815.
	Is the resistance below 5.0 ohms?
	
	      Yes → NOTE: Before continuing, check the PCM harness connector terminals for corrosion, damage, or terminal push out. Repair as necessary. Replace and program the Powertrain Control Module
	
	      No → Repair the open in the (K4) Sensor ground circuit.

7	Disconnect the ECT Sensor harness connector.
	Turn the ignition off.
	Disconnect the PCM harness connector.
	Measure the resistance between ground and the (K2) ECT Signal circuit in the ECT Sensor harness connector.
	Is the resistance below 100 ohms?
	
	      Yes → Repair the short to ground in the (K2) ECT Signal circuit.
	
	      No → Go To 8

8	Turn the ignition off.
	Disconnect the ECT Sensor harness connector.
	Disconnect the PCM harness connector.
	Measure the resistance between the (K2) ECT Sensor Signal circuit and the (K4) Sensor ground circuit at the ECT Sensor harness connector.
	Is the resistance below 5.0 ohms?
	
	      Yes → Repair the (K4) Sensor ground shorted to the (K2) ECT Sensor Signal circuit.
	
	      No → NOTE: Before continuing, check the PCM harness connector terminals for corrosion, damage, or terminal push out. Repair as necessary. Replace and program the Powertrain Control Module

ARM0400000000856

Fig. 68   Code P0116: ECT Performance. (Part 3 of 3). 2003–05 Sebring Convertible, Sebring Sedan & Stratus Sedan

When Monitored and Set Condition:

P0117-ENGINE COOLANT TEMPERATURE SENSOR LOW

When Monitored: With the ignition on. Battery voltage greater than 10 volts.

Set Condition: The Engine Coolant Temperature (ECT) sensor circuit voltage at the PCM is less than 0.0782 of a volt. One Trip Fault.

POSSIBLE CAUSES
ECT SENSOR VOLTAGE BELOW 1.0 VOLTS
ECT SENSOR INTERNAL FAILURE
(K2) ECT SIGNAL SHORTED TO GROUND
(K2) ECT SIGNAL SHORTED TO (K4) SENSOR GROUND CIRCUIT
PCM

TEST	ACTION
1	Ignition on, engine not running. With the DRBIII®, read the ECT Sensor voltage. Is the voltage below 1.0 volt? Yes → Go To 2 No → Diagnose INTERMITTENT CONDITION
2	Turn the ignition off. Disconnect the ECT harness connector. Ignition on, engine not running. With the DRBIII®, read ECT Sensor voltage. Is the voltage between 4.8 and 5.2 volts? Yes → Replace the ECT Sensor. No → Go To 3
3	Turn the ignition off. Disconnect the ECT Sensor harness connector. Disconnect the PCM harness connector. Measure the resistance between ground and the (K2) ECT Signal circuit in the ECT Sensor harness connector. Is the resistance below 100 ohms? Yes → Repair the ground shorted to the (K2) ECT Signal circuit. No → Go To 4

ARM0400000000857

Fig. 69   Code P0117: ECT Sensor Low (Part 1 of 2). 2003–05 Sebring Convertible, Sebring Sedan & Stratus Sedan

When Monitored and Set Condition:

P0118-ENGINE COOLANT TEMPERATURE SENSOR HIGH

When Monitored: With the ignition on. Battery voltage greater than 10 volts.

Set Condition: The Engine Coolant Temperature (ECT) sensor voltage at the PCM is greater than 4.98 volts. One trip Fault.

POSSIBLE CAUSES
ECT SENSOR VOLTAGE ABOVE 4.9 VOLTS
(K2) ECT SIGNAL CIRCUIT SHORTED TO BATTERY VOLTAGE
ECT SENSOR INTERNAL FAILURE
(K2) ECT SIGNAL CIRCUIT OPEN
(K4) SENSOR GROUND CIRCUIT OPEN
PCM

TEST	ACTION
1	Ignition on, engine not running. With the DRBIII®, read the ECT Sensor voltage. Is the voltage above 4.9 volts? Yes → Go To 2 No → Diagnose INTERMITTENT CONDITION
2	Turn the ignition off. Disconnect the ECT Sensor harness connector. Ignition on, engine not running. Measure the voltage of the (K2) ECT Signal circuit in the ECT Sensor harness connector. Is the voltage above 5.2 volts? Yes → Repair the short to battery voltage in the (K2) ECT Signal circuit. No → Go To 3

ARM0400000000859

Fig. 70   Code P0118: ECT Sensor High (Part 1 of 2). 2003–05 Sebring Convertible, Sebring Sedan & Stratus Sedan

TEST	ACTION
4	Turn the ignition off. Disconnect the ECT Sensor harness connector. Disconnect the PCM harness connector. Measure the resistance between the (K2) ECT Sensor Signal circuit and the (K4) Sensor ground circuit in the ECT Sensor harness connector. Is the resistance below 100 ohms? Yes → Repair the (K4) Sensor ground shorted to the (K2) ECT Sensor Signal circuit. No → Go To 5
5	NOTE: Before continuing, check the PCM harness connector terminals for corrosion, damage, or terminal push out. Repair as necessary. If there are no possible causes remaining, view repair. Repair Replace and program the Powertrain Control Module

ARM0400000000858

Fig. 69   Code P0117: ECT Sensor Low (Part 2 of 2). 2003–05 Sebring Convertible, Sebring Sedan & Stratus Sedan

TEST	ACTION
3	Turn the ignition off. Disconnect the ECT harness connector. Connect a jumper wire between the (K2) ECT Signal circuit and the (K4) Sensor ground circuit in the ECT Sensor harness connector. Ignition on, engine not running. With the DRBIII®, read ECT Sensor voltage. Is the voltage below 1.0 volt? Yes → Replace the ECT Sensor. No → Go To 4
4	Turn the ignition off. Disconnect the ECT Sensor harness connector. Disconnect the PCM harness connector. CAUTION: DO NOT PROBE THE PCM HARNESS CONNECTORS. PROBING THE PCM HARNESS CONNECTORS WILL DAMAGE THE PCM TERMINALS RESULTING IN POOR TERMINAL TO PIN CONNECTION. INSTALL MILLER SPECIAL TOOL #8815 TO PERFORM DIAGNOSIS. Measure the resistance of the (K2) ECT Signal circuit from the ECT Sensor harness connector to the appropriate terminal of special tool #8815. Is the resistance below 5.0 ohms? Yes → Go To 5 No → Repair the open in the (K2) ECT Signal circuit.
5	Turn the ignition off. Disconnect the ECT Sensor harness connector. Disconnect the PCM harness connector. CAUTION: DO NOT PROBE THE PCM HARNESS CONNECTORS. PROBING THE PCM HARNESS CONNECTORS WILL DAMAGE THE PCM TERMINALS RESULTING IN POOR TERMINAL TO PIN CONNECTION. INSTALL MILLER SPECIAL TOOL #8815 TO PERFORM DIAGNOSIS. Measure the resistance of the (K4) Sensor ground circuit from the ECT Sensor harness connector to the appropriate terminal of special tool #8815. Is the resistance below 5.0 ohms? Yes → Go To 6 No → Repair the open in the (K4) Sensor ground circuit.
6	NOTE: Before continuing, check the PCM harness connector terminals for corrosion, damage, or terminal push out. Repair as necessary. If there are no possible causes remaining, view repair. Repair Replace and program the Powertrain Control Module

ARM0400000000860

Fig. 70   Code P0118: ECT Sensor High (Part 2 of 2). 2003–05 Sebring Convertible, Sebring Sedan & Stratus Sedan

COOLING FANS

When Monitored and Set Condition:

P0480-LOW SPEED FAN CONTROL RELAY CIRCUIT

When Monitored: With the ignition on. Battery voltage greater than 10 volts.

Set Condition: An open or shorted circuit is detected in the radiator fan relay control circuit. One Trip Fault.

POSSIBLE CAUSES
LOW SPEED RADIATOR FAN RELAY OPERATION
(A16) FUSED B+ FEED CIRCUITS
LOW SPEED RADIATOR FAN RELAY RESISTANCE
(C24) LOW SPEED RAD FAN RELAY CONTROL CIRCUIT OPEN
(C24) LOW SPEED RAD FAN RELAY CONTROL CIRCUIT SHORT TO GROUND
PCM

TEST	ACTION
1	Ignition on, engine not running. With the DRBIII®, actuate the Radiator Fan Relay. Is the Low Speed Radiator Fan Relay operating? Yes → Diagnose intermittent condition. No → Go To 2
2	Turn the ignition off. Remove the Low Speed Radiator Fan Relay from the PDC. Ignition on, engine not running. Measure the voltage of the (A16) Fused B+ Feed circuit in the PDC. Is the voltage above 11.0 volts? Yes → Go To 3 No → Repair the (A16) Fused B+ Output circuit. Inspect the related fuse and repair as necessary.

ARM0400000000861

Fig. 71 Code P0480: Low Speed Fan Control Relay Circuit (Part 1 of 2). 2003–05 Sebring Convertible, Sebring Sedan & Stratus Sedan

P1489-HIGH SPEED FAN CONTROL RELAY CIRCUIT

When Monitored: With the ignition on. Battery voltage greater than 10.0 volts.

Set Condition: An open or shorted circuit is detected in the radiator fan relay control circuit.

POSSIBLE CAUSES
HIGH SPEED RADIATOR FAN RELAY OPERATION
FUSED IGNITION SWITCH OUTPUT CIRCUIT
HIGH SPEED RADIATOR FAN RELAY RESISTANCE
(C27) HIGH SPEED RADIATOR FAN RELAY CONTROL CIRCUIT OPEN
(C27) HIGH SPEED RADIATOR FAN RELAY CONTROL CIRCUIT SHORT TO GROUND
PCM

TEST	ACTION
1	Turn the ignition on. With the DRBIII®, actuate the High Speed Radiator Fan Relay. Is the High Speed Radiator Fan Relay operating? Yes → Refer to the INTERMITTENT CONDITION symptom in the Driveability category. Perform POWERTRAIN VERIFICATION TEST VER - 5. No → Go To 2
2	Turn the ignition off. Remove the High Speed Radiator Fan Relay from the PDC. Turn the ignition on. Using a 12-volt test light connected to ground, probe the (F12) Fused Ignition Switch Output circuit in the PDC. Did the test light illuminate brightly? Yes → Go To 3 No → Repair the Fused Ignition Switch Output circuit. Check and replace any open fuses. Perform POWERTRAIN VERIFICATION TEST VER - 5.

CR1080200351010X

Fig. 72 Code P1489: High Speed Fan Control Relay Circuit (Part 1 of 2). 2003–05 Sebring Convertible, Sebring Sedan & Stratus Sedan

TEST	ACTION
3	Turn the ignition off. Remove the Low Speed Radiator Fan Relay from the PDC. Measure the resistance of the Low Speed Radiator Fan Relay between the Fused Ignition Switch Output terminal and the Low Speed Rad Fan Relay Control terminal. Is the resistance between 60 to 85 ohms? Yes → Go To 4 No → Replace the Low Speed Radiator Fan Relay.
4	Turn the ignition off. Remove the Low Speed Radiator Fan Relay from the PDC. Disconnect the PCM harness connector. **CAUTION: DO NOT PROBE THE PCM HARNESS CONNECTORS. PROBING THE PCM HARNESS CONNECTORS WILL DAMAGE THE PCM TERMINALS RESULTING IN POOR TERMINAL TO PIN CONNECTION. INSTALL MILLER SPECIAL TOOL #8815 TO PERFORM DIAGNOSIS.** Measure the resistance of the (C24) Low Speed Rad Fan Relay Control circuit from the PDC to the appropriate terminal of special tool #8815. Is the resistance below 5.0 ohms? Yes → Go To 5 No → Repair the open in the (C24) Low Speed Rad Fan Relay Control circuit.
5	Turn the ignition off. Remove the Low Speed Radiator Fan Relay from the PDC. Disconnect the PCM harness connector. Measure the resistance between ground and the (C24) Low Speed Rad Fan Control circuit at the PDC. Is the resistance below 100 ohms? Yes → Repair the short to ground in the (C24) Low Speed Rad Fan Relay Control circuit. No → Go To 6
6	NOTE: Before continuing, check the PCM harness connector terminals for corrosion, damage, or terminal push out. Repair as necessary. If there are no possible causes remaining, view repair. Repair Replace and program the Powertrain Control Module

ARM0400000000862

Fig. 71 Code P0480: Low Speed Fan Control Relay Circuit (Part 2 of 2). 2003–05 Sebring Convertible, Sebring Sedan & Stratus Sedan

TEST	ACTION
3	Turn the ignition off. Remove the High Speed Radiator Fan Relay from the PDC. Measure the resistance of the High Speed Radiator Fan Relay between the Fused Ignition Switch Output terminal and the High Speed Radiator Fan Relay Control terminal. Is the resistance between 60 to 80 ohms? Yes → Go To 4 No → Replace the High Speed Radiator Fan Relay.
4	Turn the ignition off. Remove the High Speed Radiator Fan Relay from the PDC. Disconnect the PCM harness connector. Measure the resistance of the (C27) High Speed Radiator Fan Relay Control circuit between the PDC and the PCM harness connector. Is the resistance below 5.0 ohms? Yes → Go To 5 No → Repair the open in the (C27) High Speed Radiator Fan Relay Control circuit.
5	Turn the ignition off. Remove the High Speed Radiator Fan Relay from the PDC. Disconnect the PCM harness connector. Measure the resistance between ground and the (C27) High Speed Radiator Fan Relay Control circuit in the PDC. Is the resistance below 5.0 ohms? Yes → Repair the short to ground in the (C27) High Speed Radiator Fan Relay Control circuit. No → Go To 6
6	NOTE: Before Continuing: Disconnect the PCM harness connector and check the related wiring terminals for corrosion, damage or terminal push out. Repair as necessary. Using the schematics as a guide, inspect the wire harness and connectors. Pay particular attention to all Power and Ground circuits. If there are no possible causes remaining, view repair. Repair Replace and program the Powertrain Control Module in accordance with the Service Information.

CR1080200351020X

Fig. 72 Code P1489: High Speed Fan Control Relay Circuit (Part 2 of 2). 2003–05 Sebring Convertible, Sebring Sedan & Stratus Sedan

P1490-LOW SPEED FAN CONTROL RELAY CIRCUIT

When Monitored: With the ignition on. Battery voltage greater than 10 volts.

Set Condition: An open or shorted circuit is detected in the radiator fan relay control circuit.

POSSIBLE CAUSES
LOW SPEED RADIATOR FAN RELAY OPERATION
(F12) FUSED IGNITION SWITCH OUTPUT CIRCUIT
LOW SPEED RADIATOR FAN RELAY RESISTANCE
(C24) LOW SPEED RADIATOR FAN RELAY CONTROL CIRCUIT OPEN
(C24) LOW SPEED RADIATOR FAN RELAY CONTROL CIRCUIT SHORT TO GROUND
PCM

TEST	ACTION
1	Turn the ignition on. With the DRBIII®, actuate the Low Speed Radiator Fan Relay. Is the Low Speed Radiator Fan Relay operating? Yes → Perform POWERTRAIN VERIFICATION TEST No → Go To 2
2	Turn the ignition off. Remove the Low Speed Radiator Fan Relay from the PDC. Turn the ignition on. using a 12-volt test light connected to ground, probe the (F12) Fused Ignition Switch Output circuit in the PDC. Did the test light illuminate brightly? Yes → Go To 3 No → Repair the (F12) Fused Ignition Switch Output circuit. Check and replace any open fuses.

CR1080200352010X

Fig. 73 Code P1490: Low Speed Fan Control Relay Circuit (Part 1 of 2). 2003–05 Sebring Convertible, Sebring Sedan & Stratus Sedan

TEST	ACTION
3	Turn the ignition off. Remove the Low Speed Radiator Fan Relay from the PDC. Measure the resistance of the Low Speed Radiator Fan Relay between the Fused Ignition Switch Output terminal and the Low Speed Radiator Fan Relay Control terminal. Is the resistance between 60 to 80 ohms? Yes → Go To 4 No → Replace the Low Speed Radiator Fan Relay.
4	Turn the ignition off. Remove the Low Speed Radiator Fan Relay from the PDC. Disconnect the PCM harness connector. Measure the resistance of the (C24) Low Speed Radiator Fan Relay Control circuit between the PDC and the PCM harness connector. Is the resistance below 5.0 ohms? Yes → Go To 5 No → Repair the open in the (C24) Low Speed Radiator Fan Relay Control circuit.
5	Turn the ignition off. Remove the Low Speed Radiator Fan Relay from the PDC. Disconnect the PCM harness connector. Measure the resistance of the (C24) Low Speed Radiator Fan Relay Control circuit in the PDC to ground. Is the resistance below 100 ohms? Yes → Repair the short to ground in the (C24) Low Speed Radiator Fan Relay Control circuit. No → Go To 6
6	NOTE: Before continuing, check the PCM harness connector terminals for corrosion, damage, or terminal push out. Repair as necessary. Using the schematics as a guide, inspect the wire harness and connectors. Pay particular attention to all Power and Ground circuits. If there are no possible causes remaining, view repair. Repair Replace and program the Powertrain Control Module in accordance with the Service Information.

CR1080200352020X

Fig. 73 Code P1490: Low Speed Fan Control Relay Circuit (Part 2 of 2). 2003–05 Sebring Convertible, Sebring Sedan & Stratus Sedan

POSSIBLE CAUSES
ECT SENSOR OPERATION
ECT SENSOR

TEST	ACTION
1	NOTE: The engine coolant temperature must be below 62°C (150°F). Turn the ignition on. With the DRBIII®, monitor the ECT value. Start the engine. Does the ECT reach 82°C (180°F) and was it a smooth transition? Yes → Engine Coolant Temperature sensor is operating normally. No → Replace the Engine Coolant Temperature Sensor.

ARM0400000000875

Fig. 74 Engine Coolant Temperature (ECT) sensor testing. 2001–02 Sebring Convertible, Sebring Sedan & Stratus Sedan

COMPONENT DIAGNOSIS & TESTING

Coolant Temperature Sensor

CONCORDE, INTREPID, LHS & 300M

1. Turn ignition switch to OFF position.
2. Disconnect coolant temperature sensor connector.
3. Measure resistance between sensor terminals when engine is at 200°F.
4. If resistance is not 700–1000 ohms, replace sensor.

NEON

1. Ensure ignition is in OFF position and disconnect coolant temperature sensor electrical connector.
2. Measure resistance between sensor terminals. Resistance should be 7–13 kohms.
3. Run engine until coolant temperature reaches approximately 200°F, then measure resistance. Resistance should be 700–1000 ohms.
4. Measure wiring harness resistance between Powertrain Control Module (PCM) terminal No. 28 and coolant sensor harness connector. Resistance should not exceed 1 ohm.
5. Measure wiring harness resistance between PCM terminal No. 51 and coolant sensor harness connector. Resistance should not exceed 1 ohm.
6. If resistance is not as specified, replace coolant sensor or repair wiring harness.

SEBRING CONVERTIBLE, SEBRING SEDAN & STRATUS SEDAN

2001-02

Refer to **Fig. 74** for Engine Coolant Temperature (ECT) sensor testing.

2003-05

Refer to appropriate Diagnostic Trouble Code (DTC) in "System Diagnosis & Testing" section for coolant temperature sensor testing.

Fan Control Module

SEBRING COUPE & STRATUS COUPE

1. Disconnect condenser fan motor electrical connector.
2. Start engine and allow it to idle.

3. Turn air conditioning switch on and maintain engine coolant temperature of 176°F, or less.
4. Measure voltage between fan control module side connector terminal, **Fig. 75.**
5. Ensure voltage changes repeatedly as follows:
   a. Zero volts.
   b. 5.6–10.8 volts.
   c. Battery positive voltage ± 2.6 volts.
6. If voltage does not repeatedly change as specified, replace radiator fan motor and control module.

Fan Control Relay

CONCORDE, INTREPID, LHS & 300M

Refer to appropriate Diagnostic Trouble Code (DTC) in "System Diagnosis & Testing" section for fan control relay testing.

COOLING FANS

CROSSFIRE

1. Disconnect radiator fan electrical harness connector at fan motor.
2. Remove radiator cooling fan module retaining bolts.
3. Remove cooling fan module.
4. Reverse procedures to install. **Torque** module retaining bolts to 89 inch lbs.

NEON

NON-TURBO ENGINES

1. Turn ignition switch to ON position.
2. Actuate radiator fan relay using DRBIII, or suitably programmed scan tool.
3. If relay does not actuate, turn ignition switch to OFF position.
4. Disconnect radiator fan harness connector.
5. Measure resistance between ground circuit and fan harness connector to ground. If resistance is less than 5 ohms, proceed to next step. If resistance is not as specified, inspect ground circuit for open.
6. Turn ignition switch to ON position.
7. Actuate radiator fan relay using DRBIII, or suitably programmed scan tool.
8. Measure voltage of relay output circuit in harness connector. If measurement is note more than 11 volts, , proceed to next step. If measurement is more than 11 volts, replace fan motor.
9. Turn ignition switch to OFF position.
10. Remove radiator fan relay from PDC.
11. Probe fused B+ circuit in PDC using suitable 12-volt test light connected to ground. If test light illuminates brightly, proceed to next step. If light does not illuminate, repair fused B+ circuit, then inspect fuses.
12. Measure resistance of relay output circuit between PDC and fan harness connector. If resistance is less than 5 ohms, replace relay. If resistance is not less than 5 ohms, inspect circuit for open.

TURBO ENGINE

Low Speed

1. Turn ignition switch to ON position.
2. Actuate low speed radiator relay using DRBIII, or suitably programmed scan tool.
3. If only fan No. 2 is operating, proceed to next step. If fans are not operating, proceed as follows:
   a. Remove low speed relay No. 1 from PDC.
   b. Probe fused B+ circuit in PDC using suitable 12-volt test light connected to ground. If test light illuminates brightly, proceed to next step. If light does not illuminate, repair fused B+ circuit, then inspect fuses.
   c. Turn ignition switch to OFF position.
   d. Install substitute relay.
   e. Turn ignition switch to ON position.
   f. Actuate low speed radiator relay using DRBIII, or suitably programmed scan tool.

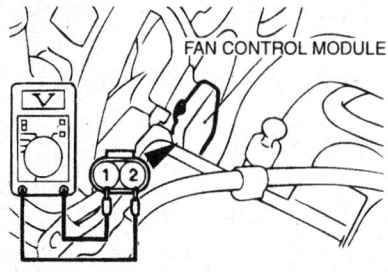

CR1080000296000X

Fig. 75 Fan control module terminal identification. Sebring Coupe & Stratus Coupe

   g. If fan did not operate, proceed to next step. If fan did operate, replace relay.
   h. Turn ignition switch to OFF position.
   i. Disconnect radiator fan No. 1 harness connector.
   j. Measure resistance between fan No. 1 harness connector ground circuit and ground. If resistance is less than 5 ohms, proceed to next step. If resistance in not as specified, inspect for open in ground circuit.
   k. Remove radiator fan replay No. 3 from PDC.
   l. Turn ignition switch to ON position.
   m. Actuate low speed radiator relay No. 1 using DRBIII, or suitably programmed scan tool.
   n. Connect probe to low speed radiator relay output in control relay No. 3 using fused jumper wire.
   o. If radiator fan No. 2 operates, inspect for open between relay No. 3 and fan No. 1 in relay output circuit. If circuit is satisfactory, replace fan assembly.
   p. If radiator fan No. 2 does not operates, inspect for open between relay No. 2 and fan No. 3 in relay output circuit. If circuit is satisfactory, replace fan assembly.
4. Actuate low speed radiator relay No. 1 using DRBIII, or suitably programmed scan tool.
5. Turn ignition switch to ON position.
6. Remove relay control No. 3 from PDC. If fan No. 2 continued to operate, proceed to next step. If fan No. 2 stopped operating, replace relay control No. 3.
7. Turn ignition switch to OFF position.
8. Remove low speed radiator fan relay No. 1 from PDC.
9. Measure resistance between ground and low speed radiator fan out circuit at relay No. 1 connect in PDC. If resistance is not less than 5 ohms, proceed to next step. If resistance is 5 ohms, repair short to ground in low speed radiator fan output circuit.
10. Connect all relays and connectors.
11. Turn ignition switch to ON position.
12. Actuate low speed radiator relay using DRBIII, or suitably programmed scan tool.
13. Disconnect radiator fan No. 1 connector. If fan No. 2 still operates, inspect low speed radiator fan output circuit for

short to ground. If fan does not operate, replace radiator fan assembly.

High Speed

The low speed fan operation must be checked first.
1. Turn ignition switch to ON position.
2. Actuate high speed radiator fan relay using DRBIII, or suitably programmed scan tool.
3. If fan No. 1 does not operate, proceed to next step. If fan does operator, proceed as follows:
   a. Acutate low speed radiator fan relay No. 1 using DRBIII, or suitably programmed scan tool.
   b. Fan No. 2 should operate at high speed.
   c. If fan No. 2 does not operate on high speed, inspect radiator fan control relay No. 3 connector in PDC for open ground circuit.
   d. If circuit is satisfactory, replace radiator fan control relay No. 3
4. Turn ignition switch to OFF position.
5. Disconnect radiator fan No. 1 harness connector.
6. Measure resistance between harness connector ground circuit and ground. If resistance is less than 5 ohms, proceed to next step. If resistance is not as specified, inspect ground circuit for open.
7. Turn ignition switch to ON position.
8. Actuate high speed radiator fan relay No. 2 using DRBIII, or suitably programmed scan tool.
9. Measure voltage of relay output circuit in harness connector. If measurement is not more than 11 volts, proceed to next step. If measurement is more than 11 volts, replace radiator fan assembly.
10. Turn ignition switch to OFF position.
11. Remove high speed radiator fan relay No. 2 from PDC.
12. Probe fused B+ circuit in PDC using suitable 12-volt test light connected to ground. If test light illuminates brightly, proceed to next step. If light does not illuminate, repair fused B+ circuit, then inspect fuses.
13. Remove high speed radiator fan relay from PDC.
14. Disconnect radiator fan No. 1 harness connector.
15. Measure resistance of high speed radiator fan relay output circuit between PDC and fan harness connector. If resistance is less than 5 ohms, replace relay. If resistance is not less than 5 ohms, inspect circuit for open.

SEBRING CONVERTIBLE, SEBRING SEDAN & STRATUS SEDAN

2001-02

Refer to **Fig. 76** for fan control relay testing.

2003-05

Refer to appropriate Diagnostic Trouble Code (DTC) in "System Diagnosis & Testing" section for fan control relay testing.

POSSIBLE CAUSES
RADIATOR FAN RELAY OPERATION
GROUND CIRCUIT OPEN
RADIATOR FAN MOTOR
FUSED B+ CIRCUIT
RADIATOR FAN RELAY OUTPUT CIRCUIT
RADIATOR FAN RELAY

TEST	ACTION
1	NOTE: This test can be used for either Low or High Speed Relay Output circuits. Turn the ignition on. With the DRBIII®, actuate the Radiator Fan Relay. Is the Radiator Fan actuating? Yes → The Radiator Fan System operating properly at this time. No → Go To 2
2	Turn the ignition off. Disconnect the Radiator Fan harness connector. Measure the Ground circuit in the Radiator Fan harness connector to ground. Is the resistance below 5.0 ohms? Yes → Go To 3 No → Repair the Ground circuit for an open.
3	Disconnect the Radiator Fan harness connector. Turn the ignition on. With the DRBIII®, actuate the Radiator Fan Relay. Measure the voltage of the Radiator Fan Relay Output circuit in the Radiator Fan harness connector. Is the voltage above 11.0 volts? Yes → Replace the Radiator Fan Motor. No → Go To 4
4	Turn the ignition off. Remove the Radiator Fan Relay from the PDC. Using a 12-volt test light connected to ground, probe the Fused B+ circuit in the PDC. Does the test light illuminate brightly? Yes → Go To 5 No → Repair the Fused B+ circuit. Inspect fuses and replace as necessary.

ARM0400000000876

Fig. 76 Radiator fan relay output testing (Part 1 of 2). 2001–02 Sebring Convertible, Sebring Sedan & Stratus Sedan

TEST	ACTION
5	Turn the ignition off. Remove the Radiator Fan Relay from the PDC. Disconnect the Radiator Fan harness connector. Measure the resistance of the Radiator Fan Relay Output circuit between the PDC and the Radiator Fan harness connector. Is the resistance below 5.0 ohms? Yes → Replace the Radiator Fan Relay. No → Repair the Radiator Fan Relay Output circuit for an open.

ARM0400000000877

Fig. 76 Radiator fan relay output testing (Part 2 of 2). 2001–02 Sebring Convertible, Sebring Sedan & Stratus Sedan

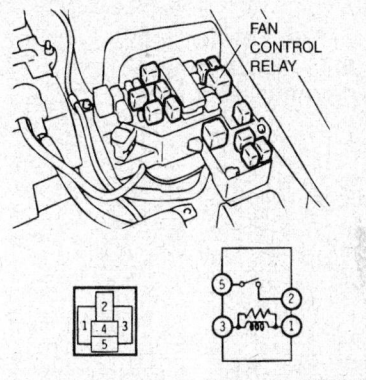

CR1080000294000X

Fig. 77 Fan control relay location. 2001–02 Sebring Coupe & Stratus Coupe

SEBRING COUPE & STRATUS COUPE

Refer to **Figs. 77 and 78** for fan control relay location and **Fig. 79 and 80** for continuity inspection.

Radiator Fan Motor

CONCORDE, INTREPID, LHS & 300M

Refer to appropriate Diagnostic Trouble Code (DTC) in "System Diagnosis & Testing" section for radiator fan motor testing.

NEON

1. Disconnect fan motor electrical connector.
2. Connect suitable 14 gauge jumper wire between battery positive terminal and fan motor terminal No. 1.
3. If fan motor does not operate normally, inspect circuit between fan motor electrical connector terminal No. 2 and ground.
4. If ground circuit is satisfactory, replace fan motor.

SEBRING CONVERTIBLE, SEBRING SEDAN & STRATUS SEDAN

Refer to appropriate Diagnostic Trouble Code (DTC) in "System Diagnosis & Testing" section for radiator fan motor testing.

COMPONENT REPLACEMENT

Fan Motor

CONCORDE, INTREPID, LHS & 300M

1. Disconnect electrical connector, **Fig. 81.**
2. Remove fan module to radiator clips and bolts, **Fig. 81.**
3. Remove fan module from radiator.
4. Bench support motor and motor shaft.
5. Remove fan retaining clip or nut. Remove burrs before removing fans from shaft. **Do not let fan blades touch bench when removing.**
6. Remove mounting bolts and motor from support.
7. Reverse procedure to install, noting the following:
   a. **Torque** lefthand fan motor mounting bolts to 45 inch lbs., and righthand bolts to 25 inch lbs.
   b. **Torque** shroud to radiator mounting bolts to 45 inch lbs.

CROSSFIRE

1. Drain engine coolant into suitable container.
2. Loosen upper coolant hose clamp then, remove hose and position aside.
3. Disconnect radiator fan harness connector at fan motor.

4. Remove radiator fan hold-down clamps.
5. Lift radiator cooling fan assembly upward to remove from vehicle.
6. Reverse procedure to install noting the following:
   a. Lightly lubricate two lower retaining studs with suitable grease.
   b. Lower radiator cooling fan rubber mounts onto retaining studs.
   c. Install radiator fan hold-down clamps.
   d. Connect upper coolant hose and tighten clamp.
   e. Refill engine coolant, then inspect for leaks.

MAGNUM, 300 & 300C

1. Partially drain cooling system into suitable container.
2. Remove upper radiator hose and disconnect cooling fan electrical connector,
3. Remove mounting bolts and radiator cooling fan assembly.
4. Reverse procedure to install.

NEON

2001

1. Drain cooling system to below upper radiator hose level into suitable container.
2. Remove upper hose from radiator.
3. Disconnect electrical connector from motor.
4. Remove fan mounting screws.
5. Lift fan shroud up and out of lower clips.

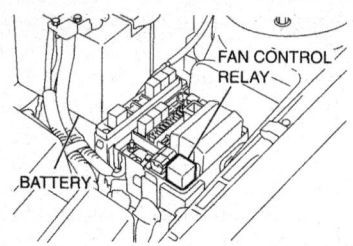

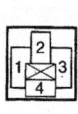 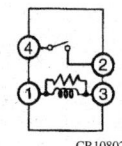

CR1080200348000X

Fig. 78 Fan control relay location. 2003–05 Sebring Coupe & Stratus Coupe

TESTER CONNECTION	BATTERY VOLTAGE	SPECIFIED CONDITION
1 – 3	Not applied	Approximately 2Ω
2 – 5	Not applied	Open circuit
	Applied (Connect "+" to the terminal 3 and "–" to the terminal 1.)	Less than 2Ω

CR1080000295000X

Fig. 79 Fan control relay continuity inspection. 2001–02 Sebring Coupe & Stratus Coupe

TESTER CONNECTION	BATTERY VOLTAGE	SPECIFIED CONDITION
1 – 3	Not applied	Approximately 2 ohms
2 – 4	Not applied	Open circuit
	Applied (Connect "+" to the terminal 1 and "–" to the terminal 3.)	Less than 2 ohms

CR1080200347000X

Fig. 80 Fan control relay continuity inspection. 2003–05 Sebring Coupe & Stratus Coupe

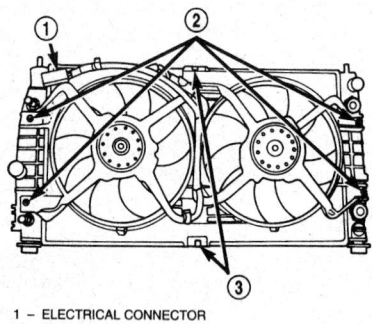

1 – ELECTRICAL CONNECTOR
2 – FASTENERS
3 – CLIPS

CR1080000273000X

Fig. 81 Fan module removal. Concorde, Intrepid, LHS & 300M

6. Remove in-rush current suppressor mounting screw.
7. Remove mounting screws and fan motor.
8. Remove hub mounting nut and fan from motor shaft.
9. Reverse procedure to install.

2002–05

1. Drain cooling system to below upper radiator hose level into suitable container.
2. Remove upper hose from radiator.
3. Remove mounting bolts and nuts, then position air cleaner housing aside.
4. Raise and support vehicle.
5. Disconnect Powertrain Control Module (PCM) electrical connectors and remove wiring harness clip from bracket.
6. Remove mounting bolts and PCM with bracket.
7. Disconnect electrical connector from motor.
8. Lower vehicle.
9. Remove radiator upper support mounts.
10. Remove air conditioning line support bracket screw.
11. Remove radiator fan mounting screws.
12. Lift radiator fan assembly up and out of lower shroud clips.
13. Remove in-rush current suppressor mounting screw.

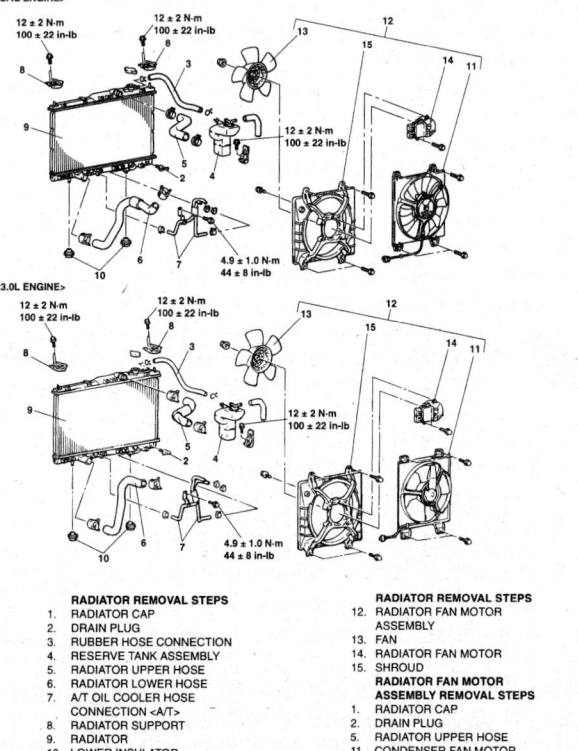

RADIATOR REMOVAL STEPS
1. RADIATOR CAP
2. DRAIN PLUG
3. RUBBER HOSE CONNECTION
4. RESERVE TANK ASSEMBLY
5. RADIATOR UPPER HOSE
6. RADIATOR LOWER HOSE
7. A/T OIL COOLER HOSE CONNECTION <A/T>
8. RADIATOR SUPPORT
9. RADIATOR
10. LOWER INSULATOR
11. CONDENSER FAN MOTOR ASSEMBLY

RADIATOR REMOVAL STEPS
12. RADIATOR FAN MOTOR ASSEMBLY
13. FAN
14. RADIATOR FAN MOTOR
15. SHROUD
RADIATOR FAN MOTOR ASSEMBLY REMOVAL STEPS
1. RADIATOR CAP
2. DRAIN PLUG
5. RADIATOR UPPER HOSE
11. CONDENSER FAN MOTOR ASSEMBLY
12. RADIATOR FAN MOTOR ASSEMBLY

CR1080000301000X

Fig. 82 Radiator fan replacement. Sebring Coupe & Stratus Coupe

14. Remove mounting screws and fan motor.
15. Remove hub mounting nut and fan from motor shaft.
16. Reverse procedure to install.

SEBRING CONVERTIBLE, SEBRING SEDAN & STRATUS SEDAN

1. Remove upper radiator crossmember.
2. Disconnect fan motor electrical connector.
3. Remove fan module to radiator mounting bolts.
4. Remove fan from motor shaft.
5. Remove mounting bolts and motor.
6. Reverse procedure to install. **Torque** mounting bolts to 45 inch lbs.

SEBRING COUPE & STRATUS COUPE

1. Drain cooling system into suitable container.

2. Remove upper radiator hose, **Fig. 82.**
3. Remove mounting bolts and condenser fan motor assembly.
4. Remove mounting bolts and radiator fan motor assembly.
5. Remove mounting nut and fan, then mounting bolts and motor.
6. Reverse procedure to install.

Fan Control Module

CROSSFIRE

1. Disconnect radiator fan control module harness connector.
2. Remove mounting and cooling fan module.
3. Reverse procedure to install.

STARTER MOTORS

TABLE OF CONTENTS

Application Chart

Model	Year	Engine	Starter		
			Manufacturer	No.	Type
Concorde, Intrepid, LHS & 300M	2001–04	2.7L	Melco	—	Direct Drive
		3.2L	Nippondenso	—	Gear Reduction
		3.5L	Nippondenso	—	Gear Reduction
Crossfire	2004–05	3.2L	Nippondenso	—	Gear Reduction
Magnum, 300 & 300C	2005	2.7L	Melco	—	Direct Drive
		3.5L	Nippondenso	—	Gear Reduction
		5.7L	Nippondenso	—	Gear Reduction
Neon	2001–05	2.0L & 2.4L	Bosch	—	Gear Reduction
Sebring Convertible, Sebring Sedan & Stratus Sedan	2001–05	2.4L	Nippondenso	—	Gear Reduction
		2.7L	Melco	—	Direct Drive
Sebring Coupe & Stratus Coupe	2001	2.4L	Mitsubishi	M1T84883	Gear Reduction
		3.0L	Mitsubishi	M000T80783	Gear Reduction
Sebring Coupe & Stratus Coupe	2002–05	2.4L	Mitsubishi	M1T84883	Gear Reduction
		3.0L	Mitsubishi	M0T80784	Gear Reduction

Bosch Starter Motors

NOTE: On Air Bag Equipped Models, Refer To "Air Bag System Precautions" Located In The Front Of This Manual For System Disarming & Arming Procedures.

NOTE: Refer To "Computer Relearn Procedures" Located In The Front Of This Manual When Battery Power To The Computer Has Been Interrupted.

INDEX

STARTER MOTORS

DESCRIPTION

Bosch starter motor is a permanent magnet starter motor. The fields have six permanent magnets. A planetary gear train transmits power between starter motor and pinion shaft. The starter provides mechanical torque to rotate the crankshaft at an RPM (crank speed) necessary for self-sustained spark/ignition

TROUBLESHOOTING

Refer to **Fig. 1** when troubleshooting the starting system.

DIAGNOSIS & TESTING

In-Vehicle Tests

Before starting any tests, ensure the battery is fully charged and all connections are secure.

The following tests will require a suitable volt-ohmmeter tester accurate to .10 volt.

On models equipped with manual transaxle, apply parking brake and depress clutch pedal whenever a test step calls for turning the ignition switch to START position.

STARTER FEED CIRCUIT TEST

1. Connect suitable tester to battery remote terminals following manufacturer's instructions.
2. Disable ignition and fuel systems by disconnecting Automatic Shutdown (ASD) relay in Power Distribution Center (PDC).
3. Ensure all electrical accessories are off, transmission is in Park or Neutral position and parking brake is set.
4. Turn ignition switch to START position.
5. If measurement is 9.6–12.4 volts and amperage draw more than 280 amps, perform test outlined under "Starter Feed Circuit Resistance Test."
6. If measurement is 12.4 volts. or more. and amperage 0–10 amps, perform "Starter Control Circuit Test."
7. After starting system conditions have been corrected, ensure battery is fully charged.
8. If voltage is less than 9.6 volts and amperage draw more than 300 amps, replace starter motor.

STARTER FEED CIRCUIT RESISTANCE (VOLTAGE DROP) TEST

1. Disable ignition and fuel system by disconnecting Automatic Shutdown (ASD) relay in power distribution center.
2. Connect suitable voltmeter negative lead to battery ground post and positive lead to battery ground clamp.
3. Turn ignition switch to START position.
4. If voltage is detected, correct poor contact between cable clamp and post.
5. Connect voltmeter positive lead to positive battery terminal and negative lead to battery positive cable clamp.
6. Turn ignition switch to START position.

7. If voltage is detected, correct poor contact between cable clamp and post.
8. Connect voltmeter negative lead to battery ground terminal and positive lead to engine block near battery cable attaching point.
9. Turn ignition switch to START position.
10. If measurement is more than .2 volt, correct poor contact at ground cable attaching point.
11. If measurement is still more than .2 volt, replace ground cable.
12. Remove starter heat shield.
13. Connect positive voltmeter lead to starter motor housing and negative lead to battery ground terminal.
14. Turn ignition switch to START position.
15. If measurement is more than .2 volt, correct poor starter to engine ground.
16. Connect positive voltmeter lead to battery positive terminal and negative lead to battery cable terminal on starter solenoid.
17. Turn ignition switch to START position.
18. If measurement is more than .2 volt correct poor contact at battery cable to solenoid connection.
19. If measurement is still more than .2 volt, replace battery positive cable.
20. If resistance tests do not detect feed circuit failures, replace starter motor.

STARTER CONTROL CIRCUIT TEST

Perform the starter solenoid test before performing the starter relay test.

STARTER SOLENOID TEST

1. Raise and support vehicle.
2. Inspect starter and starter solenoid for corrosion or loose wiring.
3. Lower vehicle and remove starter relay from connector.
4. Connect suitable remote starter switch or jumper wire between battery remote positive post and terminal 87 on starter relay connector.
5. If engine cranks, starter and starter solenoid are operating properly. Perform

starter relay test as outlined under "Starter Relay Test."
6. If engine does not crank or solenoid chatters, inspect wiring and connectors from relay to starter for loose or corroded connections.
7. Repeat test and, if engine still does not crank properly, repair or replace starter or starter solenoid.

STARTER RELAY TEST

1. Remove starter relay from power distribution center.
2. With relay in de-energized position, continuity should exist between terminals 87A and 30, but not between terminals 87 and 30.
3. Measure resistance between terminals 85 and 86. Resistance should be 70–80 ohms.
4. Connect battery positive lead to terminal 86 and ground lead to terminal 85. Relay should click.
5. With relay in energized position, continuity should exist between terminals 30 and 87, but not between terminals 87A and 30.
6. If any one inspection failed, replace relay.

IGNITION SWITCH TEST

After testing starter solenoid and relay, test ignition switch and wiring. Inspect all wiring for opens and shorts and all connectors for looseness or corrosion.

Bench Tests

STARTER SOLENOID

1. Disconnect field coil wire from field coil terminal.
2. Inspect for continuity between solenoid terminal and field coil terminal. Continuity should exist.
3. Inspect for continuity between solenoid terminal and solenoid housing. Continuity should exist.
4. If continuity does not exist in either test, replace solenoid.

CONDITION	POSSIBLE CAUSE	CORRECTION
STARTER FAILS TO ENGAGE.	1. BATTERY DISCHARGED OR FAULTY.	1. REFER TO THE BATTERY SECTION FOR MORE INFORMATION. CHARGE OR REPLACE BATTERY, IF REQUIRED.
	2. STARTING CIRCUIT WIRING FAULTY.	2. REFER TO FEED CIRCUIT RESISTANCE TEST AND FEED CIRCUIT TEST IN THIS SECTION.
	3. STARTER RELAY FAULTY.	3. REFER TO RELAY TEST, IN THIS SECTION. REPLACE RELAY, IF NECESSARY.
	4. IGNITION SWITCH FAULTY.	4. REFER TO IGNITION SWITCH TEST, IN THE STEERING SECTION OR 8 WIRING DIAGRAMS. REPLACE SWITCH, IF NECESSARY.
	5. PARK/NEUTRAL POSITION SWITCH (AUTO TRANS) FAULTY OR MIS-ADJUSTED.	5. REFER PARK/NEUTRAL POSITION SWITCH TEST, IN THE TRANSAXLE. SECTION FOR MORE INFORMATION. REPLACE SWITCH, IF NECESSARY.
	6. CLUTCH INTERLOCK SWITCH (MAN TRANS) FAULTY.	6. REFER TO CLUTCH PEDAL POSITION SWITCH TEST, IN THE CLUTCH. SECTION. REPLACE SWITCH, IF NECESSARY.
	7. STARTER SOLENOID FAULTY.	7. REFER TO SOLENOID TEST, IN THIS SECTION. REPLACE STARTER ASSEMBLY, IF NECESSARY.
	8. STARTER ASSEMBLY FAULTY.	8. IF ALL OTHER STARTING SYSTEM COMPONENTS AND CIRCUITS CHECK OK, REPLACE STARTER ASSEMBLY.
	9. FAULTY TEETH ON RING GEAR.	9. ROTATE FLYWHEEL 360°, AND INSPECT TEETH AND RING GEAR REPLACED IF DAMAGED.
	10. PCM DOUBLE START OVERRIDE OUTPUT FAILURE.	10. REFER TO PCM DIAGNOSTIC. CHECK FOR CONTINUITY BETWEEN PCM AND TERMINAL 85. REPAIR OPEN CIRCUIT AS REQUIRED. IF OK, PCM MAY BE DEFECTIVE.
STARTER ENGAGES, FAILS TO TURN ENGINE.	1. BATTERY DISCHARGED OR FAULTY.	1. REFER TO THE BATTERY SECTION FOR MORE INFORMATION. CHARGE OR REPLACE BATTERY AS NECESSARY.

CR1120200465010X

Fig. 1 Starting system troubleshooting (Part 1 of 2)

CONDITION	POSSIBLE CAUSE	CORRECTION
	2. STARTING CIRCUIT WIRING FAULTY.	2. REFER TO THE FEED CIRCUIT RESISTANCE TEST AND THE FEED CIRCUIT TEST IN THIS SECTION. REPAIR AS NECESSARY.
	3. STARTER ASSEMBLY FAULTY.	3. IF ALL OTHER STARTING SYSTEM COMPONENTS AND CIRCUITS CHECK OK, REPLACE STARTER ASSEMBLY.
	4. ENGINE SEIZED.	4. REFER TO THE ENGINE SECTION, FOR DIAGNOSTIC AND SERVICE PROCEDURES.
	5. LOOSE CONNECTION AT BATTERY, PDC, STARTER, OR ENGINE GROUND.	5. INSPECT FOR LOOSE CONNECTIONS.
	6. FAULTY TEETH ON RING GEAR.	6. ROTATE FLYWHEEL 360°, AND INSPECT TEETH AND RING GEAR REPLACED IF DAMAGED.
STARTER ENGAGES, SPINS OUT BEFORE ENGINE STARTS.	1. BROKEN TEETH ON STARTER RING GEAR.	1. REMOVE STARTER. INSPECT RING GEAR AND REPLACE IF NECESSARY.
	2. STARTER ASSEMBLY FAULTY.	2. IF ALL OTHER STARTING SYSTEM COMPONENTS AND CIRCUITS CHECK OK, REPLACE STARTER ASSEMBLY.
STARTER DOES NOT DISENGAGE.	1. STARTER IMPROPERLY INSTALLED.	1. INSTALL STARTER. TIGHTEN STARTER MOUNTING HARDWARE TO CORRECT TORQUE SPECIFICATIONS.
	2. STARTER RELAY FAULTY.	2. REFER TO RELAY TEST, IN THIS SECTION. REPLACE RELAY, IF NECESSARY.
	3. IGNITION SWITCH FAULTY.	3. REFER TO IGNITION SWITCH TEST, IN THE STEERING SECTION. REPLACE SWITCH, IF NECESSARY.
	4. STARTER ASSEMBLY FAULTY.	4. IF ALL OTHER STARTING SYSTEM COMPONENTS AND CIRCUITS CHECK OK, REPLACE STARTER ASSEMBLY.
	5. FAULTY TEETH ON RING GEAR.	5. ROTATE FLYWHEEL 360°, AND INSPECT TEETH AND RING GEAR REPLACED IF DAMAGED.

CR1120200465020X

Fig. 1 Starting system troubleshooting (Part 2 of 2)

STARTER SPECIFICATIONS

Year	Free Speed Test			Minimum RPM	Cranking Amp Draw Test
	Power Rating, KW	Max. Amps	Volts		
2001–05	1.1	—	12	—	150–280

Melco Starters

NOTE: On Air Bag Equipped Models, Refer To "Air Bag System Precautions" Located In The Front Of This Manual For System Disarming & Arming Procedures.

NOTE: Refer To "Computer Relearn Procedures" Located In The Front Of This Manual When Battery Power To The Computer Has Been Interrupted.

INDEX

DESCRIPTION

Melco starter is direct drive, **Fig. 1.** They have an overrunning clutch starter drive and a solenoid switch mounted on the starter motor.

DIAGNOSIS & TESTING

Refer to the "Nippondenso Starter Motors" section for Melco starter diagnosis and testing procedures.

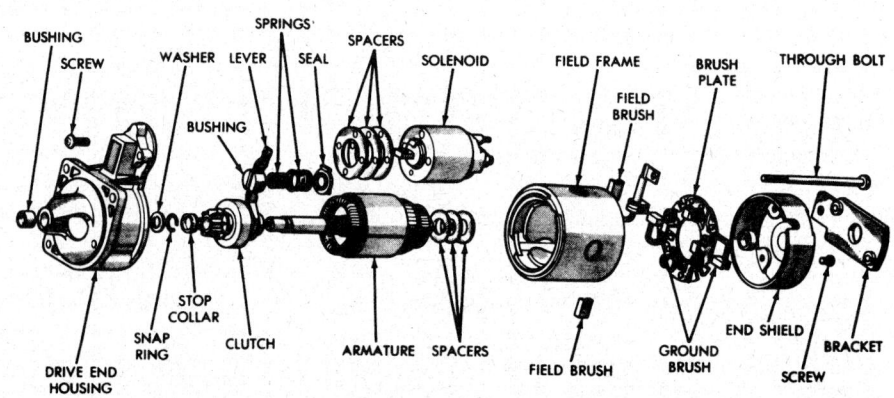

CR1129100075000X

Fig. 1   Exploded view of direct drive starter

STARTER SPECIFICATIONS

Engine	Free Speed Test		Cranking Amp Draw Test
	Power Rating, KW	Volts	
2.7L	1.4	12	150–280

Mitsubishi Starter Motors

NOTE: On Air Bag Equipped Models, Refer To "Air Bag System Precautions" Located In The Front Of This Manual For System Disarming & Arming Procedures.

NOTE: Refer To "Computer Relearn Procedures" Located In The Front Of This Manual When Battery Power To The Computer Has Been Interrupted.

INDEX

DESCRIPTION

Mitsubishi starter is a gear reduction type utilizing a planetary gear assembly to obtain higher rotational speeds with the same torque output, **Fig. 1.**

TROUBLESHOOTING

Starter Motor Does Not Operate

1. Inspect starter coil.
2. Inspect for poor contact at battery terminals and starter.
3. **On 2001–03 models equipped with automatic transaxle,** inspect park/neutral position switch.
4. **On 2004–05 models equipped with automatic transaxle,** inspect transmission range switch.
5. **On models equipped with manual transaxle,** inspect starter relay.
6. **On 2001–03 models equipped with manual transaxle,** inspect clutch pedal position switch
7. **On 2004–05 models equipped with manual transaxle,** inspect interlock switch.
8. **On 2001–03 models,** inspect theft-alarm starter relay.

Starter Does Not Stop

Inspect the starter magnetic switch.

DIAGNOSIS & TESTING

System Diagnosis

1. Inspect battery. If battery is in good condition, proceed to next step. If battery is not as specified, charge or replace it.

2. Disconnect starter motor solenoid terminal connector.
3. Apply battery positive voltage to starter motor solenoid terminal using suitable jumper wire.
4. If starter motor does not operate normally, proceed to next step. If starter operates normally, proceed as follows:
   a. Inspect ignition switch.
   b. Inspect starter relay.
   c. **On 2001–03 models equipped with automatic transaxle,** inspect park/neutral position switch.
   d. **On 2004–05 models equipped with automatic transaxle,** inspect transmission range switch.
   e. **On models equipped with manual transaxle,** inspect starter relay.
   f. **On 2001–03 models equipped with manual transaxle,** inspect clutch pedal position switch
   g. **On 2004–05 models equipped with manual transaxle,** inspect interlock switch.
   h. **On all models,** inspect line between battery and starter motor solenoid terminal.
5. Inspect cable connection and continuity between starter motor battery terminal and battery positive terminal.
6. Inspect starter motor. If motor is in satisfactory condition, inspect engine rotational resistance.

Starter Relay Test

Refer to **Figs. 2 through 7** for starter relay continuity tests.

Magnetic Switch Pull-In Test

1. Disconnect field coil wire from M terminal, **Figs. 8 and 9.**
2. Connect 12-volt battery between terminals S and M. **This test must be performed in less than 10 seconds to prevent coil from burning.**
3. If pinion moves out, pull-in coil is satisfactory.
4. If pinion does not move out, replace magnetic switch.

Magnetic Switch Hold-In Test

1. Disconnect field coil wire from terminal M of switch, **Figs. 10 and 11.**
2. Connect 12-volt battery between terminal S and starter body. **This test must be performed in less than 10 seconds to prevent coil from burning.**
3. Pull out pinion by hand until it hits stopper.
4. If pinion remains out, switch is operating properly.
5. If pinion moves in, hold-in circuit is open. Replace magnetic switch.

Free Running Test

1. Place starter motor assembly in suitable soft-jawed vise.
2. Connect suitable 100-amp scale test voltmeter and carbon pile rheostat in series with positive post of fully charged battery and starter motor terminal, **Figs. 12 and 13.**
3. Connect suitable 15-volt scale voltmeter across starter motor.
4. Rotate carbon pile to full resistance position.
5. Connect battery ground cable to starter body.
6. Adjust rheostat until battery voltage outlined by voltmeter matches voltage listed under "Starter Specifications."
7. Confirm amperage is as specified and starter motor turns smoothly and freely.

STARTER MOTORS

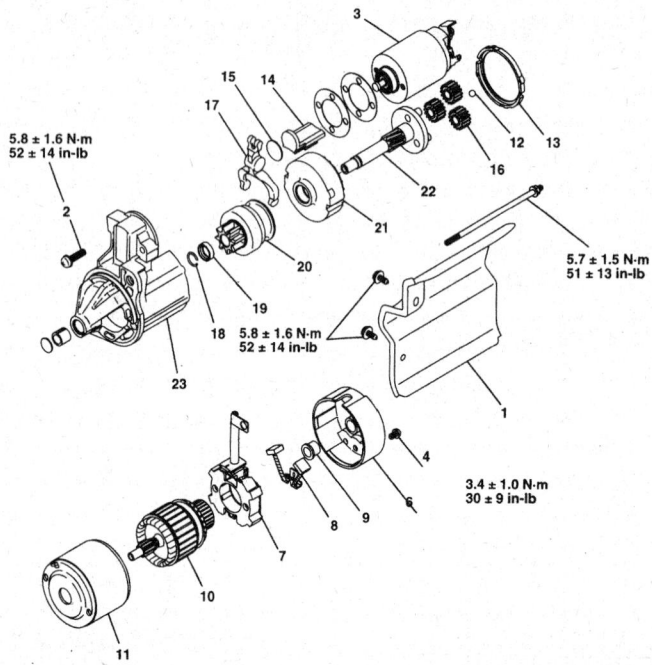

1. COVER
2. SCREW
3. MAGNETIC SWITCH
4. SCREW
5. SCREW
6. REAR BRACKET
7. BRUSH HOLDER
8. BRUSH
9. REAR BEARING
10. ARMATURE
11. YOKE ASSEMBLY
12. BALL
13. PACKING A
14. PACKING B
15. PLATE
16. PLANETARY GEAR
17. LEVER
18. SNAP RING
19. STOP RING

Fig. 1   Exploded view of Mitsubishi gear reduction starter

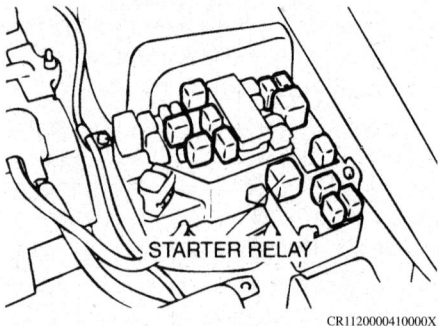

Fig. 2   Starter relay location. 2001 Sebring Coupe & Stratus Coupe

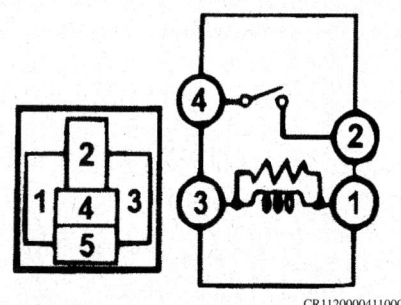

Fig. 3   Starter relay terminal identification. 2001 Sebring Coupe & Stratus Coupe

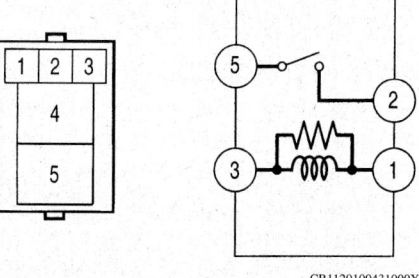

Fig. 6   Starter relay terminal identification. 2002–05 Sebring Coupe & Stratus Coupe

TESTER CONNECTION	BATTERY VOLTAGE	SPECIFIED CONDITION
1 – 3	Not applied	Approximately 2Ω
2 – 4	Not applied	Open circuit
	Applied (Connect "+" to the terminal 3 and "–" to the terminal 1.)	Less than 2Ω

Fig. 4   Starter relay test. 2001 Sebring Coupe & Stratus Coupe

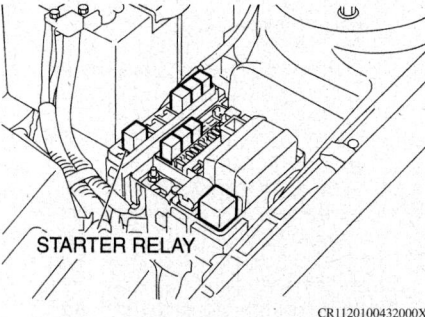

Fig. 5   Starter relay location. 2002–05 Sebring Coupe & Stratus Coupe

BATTERY VOLTAGE	TERMINAL NO. TO BE CONNECTED TO BATTERY	TERMINAL NO. TO PERFORM CONTINUITY TEST
Not applied	2 – 5	Open circuit
1 – Battery (–) terminal 3 – Battery (+) terminal	2 – 5	Less than 2 ohm

Fig. 7   Starter relay test. 2002–05 Sebring Coupe & Stratus Coupe

Magnetic Switch Return Test

1. Disconnect field coil wire from terminal M from magnetic switch, **Figs. 14 and 15.**
2. Connect 12-volt battery between terminals M and starter body. **This test** must be performed in less than 10 seconds to prevent coil from burning.
3. Pull pinion out and release.
4. If pinion quickly returns to original position, switch is operating properly.
5. If pinion does not quickly return to original position, replace magnetic switch.

Theft Alarm Starter Relay Test

Refer to **Figs. 16 through 19** for theft alarm starter relay continuity tests.

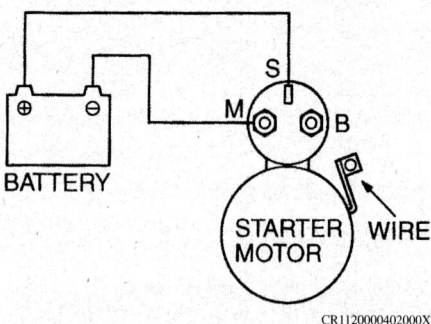

Fig. 8   Magnetic switch pull-in test. Sebring Coupe & Stratus Coupe w/2.4L engine

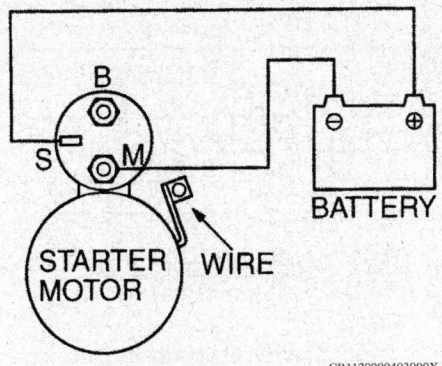

Fig. 9   Magnetic switch pull-in test. Sebring Coupe & Stratus Coupe w/3.0L engine

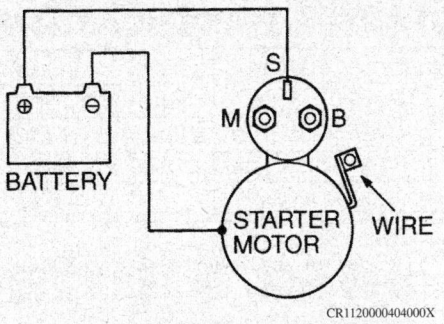

Fig. 10   Magnetic switch hold-in test. Sebring Coupe & Stratus Coupe w/2.4L engine

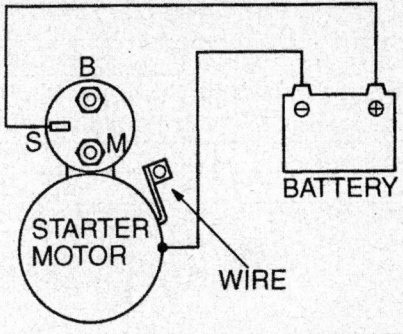

Fig. 11   Magnetic switch hold-in test. Sebring Coupe & Stratus Coupe w/3.0L engine

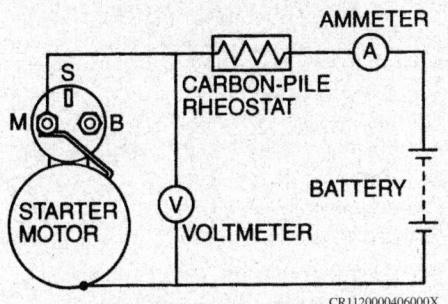

Fig. 12   Free running test. Sebring Coupe & Stratus Coupe w/2.4L engine

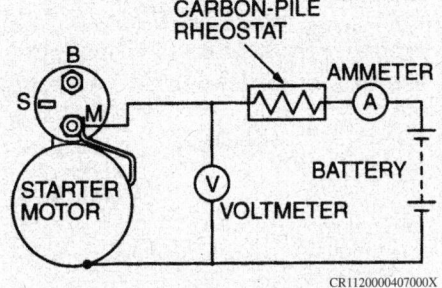

Fig. 13   Free running test. Sebring Coupe & Stratus Coupe w/3.0L engine

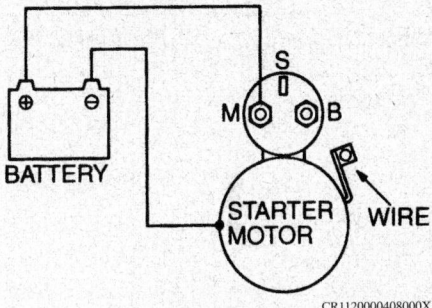

Fig. 14   Magnetic switch return test. Sebring Coupe & Stratus Coupe w/2.4L engine

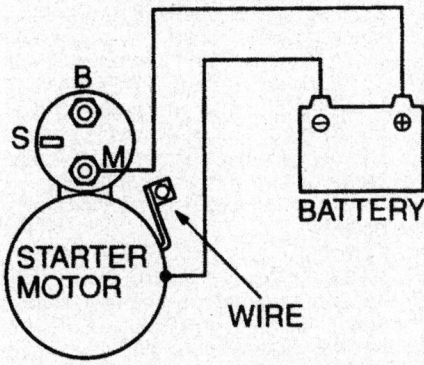

Fig. 15   Magnetic switch return test. Sebring Coupe & Stratus Coupe w/3.0L engine

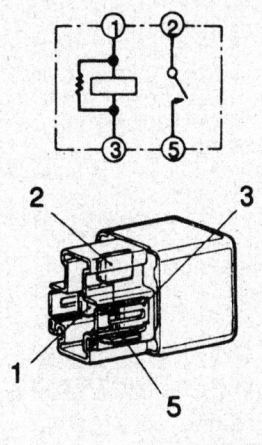

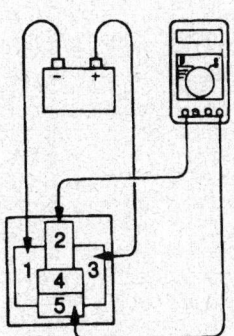

Fig. 16   Theft alarm starter relay terminal identification. Manual transaxle

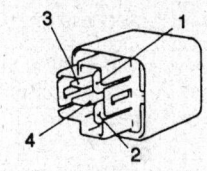

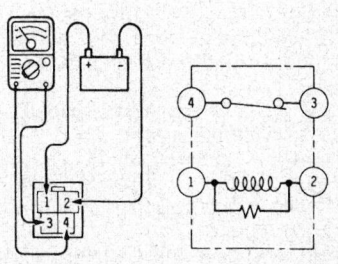

Fig. 18   Theft alarm starter relay terminal identification. Automatic transaxle

Battery voltage	Terminal			
	1	2	3	5
Not applied	◯――――――◯			
Applied	⊖--------⊕			
		◯――――――◯		

NOTE
◯――◯ indicates that there is continuity between the terminals.
⊕--⊖ indicates terminals to which battery voltage is applied.

Fig. 17   Theft alarm starter relay test. Manual transaxle

Battery voltage	Terminal			
	1	2	3	4
Not applied	◯――◯		◯――◯	
Applied	⊕--⊖			

NOTE
◯――◯ indicates that there is continuity between the terminals.
⊕--⊖ indicates terminals to which battery voltage is applied.

Fig. 19   Theft alarm starter relay test. Automatic transaxle

STARTER SPECIFICATIONS

Engine	Rated Output, kW/V	Free Speed Test			Pinion Gap, Inch	Commutator				Undercut Depth, Inch	
		Terminal Voltage	Currant, Amps	Speed, RPM		Run-Out, Inch		Diameter, Inch			
						Standard	Limit	Standard	Limit	Standard	Limit
2.4L	1.33	11	90	2400	.02–.07	.002	.004	1.16	1.13	.02	.008
3.0L	1.17	11	90	2800	.02–.07	.002	.004	1.16	1.13	.02	.008

Nippondenso Starter Motors

NOTE: On Air Bag Equipped Models, Refer To "Air Bag System Precautions" Located In The Front Of This Manual For System Disarming & Arming Procedures.

NOTE: Refer To "Computer Relearn Procedures" Located In The Front Of This Manual When Battery Power To The Computer Has Been Interrupted.

INDEX

DESCRIPTION

Nippondenso starters are gear reduction types, **Fig. 1.** The structure of the gear reduction type starter differs from that of the direct drive type, but the electrical wiring is the same for both types.

DIAGNOSIS & TESTING

The following tests will require a voltmeter accurate to .10 volt.

Before starting any tests, ensure the battery is fully charged and that all connections are good, then disable ignition system as follows:
1. **On models equipped with distributor ignition system,** disconnect ignition coil cable from distributor cap, then connect suitable jumper wire between coil cable end terminal and good body ground.
2. **On models equipped with direct ignition system,** proceed as follows:
   a. Disconnect ignition coils electrical connector.
   b. Disconnect Automatic Shutdown (ASD) relay in Power Distribution Center (PDC).

On models equipped with manual transaxle, apply parking brake and depress clutch pedal whenever test step calls for turning the ignition switch to START position.

In-Vehicle Tests

STARTER FEED CIRCUIT TEST

1. Connect tester to battery terminals following manufacturer's instructions.
2. Ensure all electrical accessories are off, transmission is in Park or Neutral and parking brake is set.
3. Turn ignition switch to START position.
4. If measurement is more than 9.6 volts and amperage draw more than 280 amps, inspect for engine seizure or faulty starter.
5. If measurement is 12.4 volts, or more, and amperage is 0–10 amps, inspect and correct corroded cables and poor connections.
6. If measurement is less than 9.6 volts and amperage more than 300 amps, replace starter motor.

STARTER FEED CIRCUIT RESISTANCE (VOLTAGE DROP) TEST

1. Connect voltmeter negative lead to battery ground post and positive lead to battery ground clamp.
2. Turn ignition switch to START position.
3. If voltage is detected, correct poor contact between cable clamp and post.
4. Connect voltmeter positive lead to positive battery terminal and negative lead to battery positive cable clamp.
5. Turn ignition switch to START position and observe voltmeter.
6. If voltage is detected, correct poor contact between cable clamp and post.
7. Connect voltmeter negative lead to battery ground terminal, and positive lead to engine block near battery cable attaching point.
8. Turn ignition switch to START position.
9. If measurement is more than .2 volt, correct poor contact at ground cable attaching point.
10. If voltage reading is still more than .2

volt after correcting poor contacts, replace ground cable.
11. Remove starter heat shield if required.
12. Connect positive voltmeter lead to starter motor housing and negative lead to battery ground terminal.
13. Turn ignition switch to START position.
14. If measurement is more than .2 volt, correct poor starter to engine ground.
15. Connect positive voltmeter lead to battery positive terminal, and negative lead to battery cable terminal on starter solenoid.
16. Turn ignition switch to START position.
17. If measurement is more than .2 volt correct poor contact at battery cable to solenoid connection.
18. If reading is still more than .2 volt after correcting poor contacts, replace battery positive cable.
19. If resistance tests do not detect feed circuit failures, replace starter motor as outlined under "Starter Motor, Replace."

STARTER CONTROL CIRCUIT TEST

The starter control circuit consists of the starter solenoid, starter relay, ignition switch, neutral safety switch and all related wiring and connections.

On models equipped with manual transaxle, apply parking brake and depress clutch pedal whenever a test step calls for turning the ignition switch to START position.

STARTER RELAY TEST

1. Disconnect Automatic Shutdown (ASD) relay in Power Distribution Center (PDC).

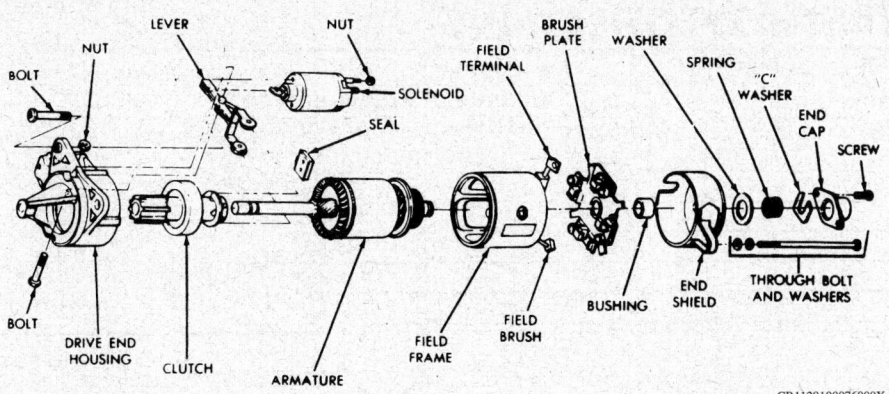

Fig. 1 Exploded view of Nippondenso gear reduction starter

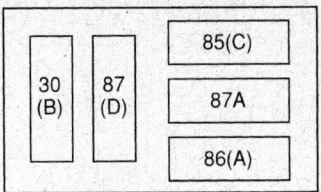

CAV	COLOR	FUNCTION
30 (B)	RD	B (+)
85 (C)	TN	P/N POSITION SW.SENSE (AUTO)
86 (A)	YL	IGNITION SWITCH OUTPUT
87 (D)	LG	STARTER RELAY OUTPUT

CR1129100065000X

Starter Relay Pinout

Fig. 2 Starter relay terminal identification. Concorde, Crossfire, Intrepid, LHS, 300M & 2001–04 Sebring Sedan & Convertible & Stratus Sedan

2. Remove starter relay from power distribution center.
3. With relay in de-energized position, continuity should exist between terminals 87A and 30, but not between terminals 87 and 30.
4. Measure resistance between terminals 85 and 86, which should be 70–80 ohms.
5. Connect battery positive lead to terminal 86 and ground lead to terminal 85. Relay should click.
6. With relay in energized position, continuity should exist between terminals 30 and 87, but not between terminals 87A and 30.
7. If any one inspection failed, replace relay.

STARTER SOLENOID TEST

1. Disconnect Automatic Shutdown (ASD) relay in Power Distribution Center (PDC).

2. Ensure battery is fully charged and in good condition.
3. Raise and support vehicle.
4. Inspect starter and starter solenoid for corrosion or loose wiring.
5. Lower vehicle.
6. Remove starter relay from connector.
7. Connect suitable remote starter switch or jumper wire between battery positive post and terminal 87, **Fig. 2.**
8. If engine cranks, starter and starter solenoid are operating properly.
9. Perform starter relay test as outlined under "Starter Control Circuit Test."
10. If engine does not crank or solenoid chatters, inspect wiring and connectors from relay to starter for loose or corroded connections.
11. Repeat test and, if engine still does not crank properly, repair or replace starter or starter solenoid as required.

IGNITION SWITCH TEST

After testing starter solenoid and relay, test ignition switch and wiring. Inspect all wiring for opens or shorts and all connectors for looseness or corrosion.

Bench Testing

STARTER SOLENOID

Refer to "Bench Tests" in the "Bosch Starter Motors" section.

STARTER MOTORS

STARTER SPECIFICATIONS

Engine	Free Speed Test			Minimum RPM	Cranking Amp Draw Test
	Power Rating, KW	Max. Amps	Volts		
2.4L	1.4	—	12	—	150–280
2.7L	1.4	—	12	—	150–280
3.2L	1.4	—	12	—	150–280
3.5L	1.4	—	12	—	150–280
5.7L	2.4	73	11	3601	125–250

ALTERNATORS

NOTE: On Air Bag Equipped Models, Refer To "Air Bag System Precautions" Located In The Front of This Manual For System Disarming & Arming Procedures.

NOTE: Refer To "Computer Relearn Procedure" Located In The Front of This Manual When Battery Power To The Computer Has Been Interrupted.

NOTE: "Electrical Symbol & Wire Color Code Identification" Located In The Front of This Manual May Be Used As An Aid When Using Wiring Circuits Found In This Section.

TABLE OF CONTENTS

Application Chart

Model	Year	Engine	Part No.
Concorde, Intrepid, LHS & 300M	2001–04	2.7L, 3.2L & 3.5L	Nippondenso
Crossfire	2004–05	3.2L	Bosch
Magnum, 300 & 300C	2005	2.7L, 3.5L & 5.7L	Nippondenso
Neon	2001–05	2.0L & 2.4L	Mitsubishi
Sebring Convertible & Sedan & Stratus Sedan	2001–05	2.0L, 2.4L & 2.7L	Nippondenso
Sebring Coupe & Stratus Coupe	2001–05	2.4L & 3.0L	Mitsubishi

ALTERNATORS

Bosch

INDEX

PRECAUTIONS

Battery Ground Cable

Prior to service, disconnect battery ground cable and isolate as required.

DESCRIPTION

The generator is belt-driven by the engine using a serpentine type accessory drive belt). It is serviced only as a complete assembly. If the generator fails for any reason, the entire assembly must be replaced. The only component that is replaceable is the voltage regulator.

DIAGNOSIS & TESTING

Wiring Diagrams

Refer to **Fig. 1** for wiring diagrams.

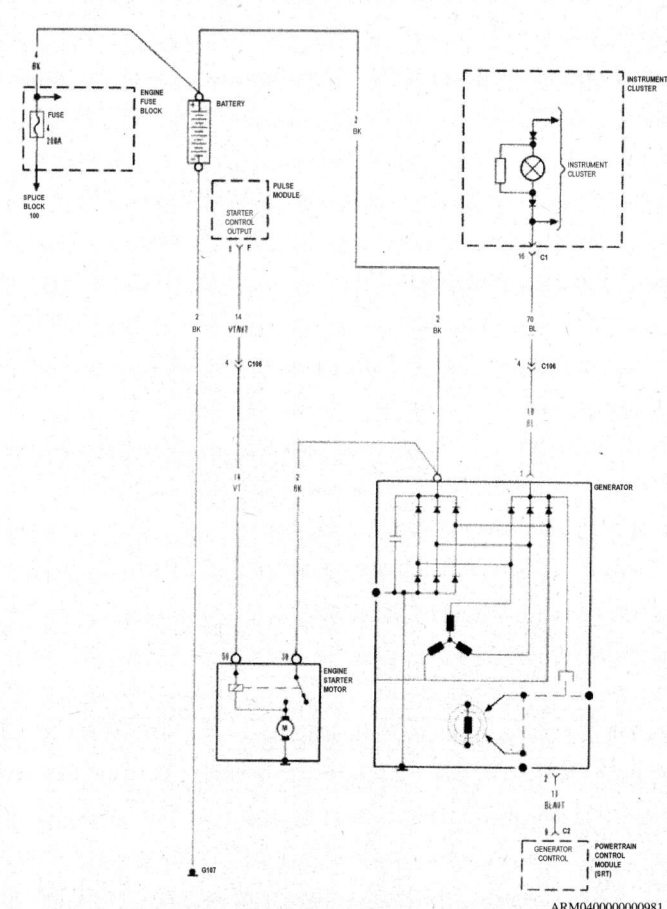

Fig. 1   Wiring Diagram. Crossfire

ALTERNATOR SPECIFICATIONS

Model & Year	Engine	No.	Rated Output Amps
Crossfire	3.2L	05097756AA	120

Nippondenso

INDEX

APPLICATION CHART

Model	Engine	Type
Concorde, Intrepid, LHS & 300M	2.7L	Nippondenso
	3.2L & 3.5L	Nippondenso
Magnum, 300 & 300C	2.7L, 3.5L & 5.7L	Nippondenso
Sebring Convertible & Sedan & Stratus Sedan	2.0L, 2.4L & 2.7L	Nippondenso

PRECAUTIONS

Battery Ground Cable

Prior to service, disconnect battery ground cable and isolate as required.

GENERAL INFORMATION

The power source of the charging system is the alternator. Current is transmitted from the field terminal of the regulator through a slip ring to the field coil and back to ground through another slip ring. The strength of the field regulates the output of the alternating current. This alternating current is then transmitted from the alternator to the rectifier where it is converted to direct current.

These alternators employ a three-phase stator winding in which the phase windings are electrically 120° apart. The rotor consists of a field coil encased between interleaved sections producing a magnetic field with alternate north and south poles. By rotating the rotor inside the stator, the alternating current is induced in the stator windings. This alternating current is rectified (changed to DC) by silicon diodes and sent to the output terminal of the alternator.

Diode Rectifiers

Six or more silicon diode rectifiers are used and act as electrical one-way valves. One half of the diodes have ground polarity and are pressed or screwed into a heat sink which is grounded. The other diodes (ungrounded) are pressed or screwed into and insulated from the end head. These diodes are connected to the alternator output terminal.

Since the diodes have a high resistance to the flow of current in one direction and a low resistance in the opposite direction, they may be connected in a manner which allows current to flow from the alternator to the battery in the low resistance direction. The high resistance in the opposite direction prevents the flow of current from the battery to the alternator. Because of this feature no circuit breaker is required between the alternator and battery.

DESCRIPTION

The main components of the alternator are the rotor, stator, rectifier, end shields and drive pulley. Direct current is available at the output B terminal.

Alternator output is controlled by voltage regulator circuitry contained within the power and logic modules of the engine controller.

DIAGNOSIS & TESTING

Wiring Diagrams

CONCORDE, INTREPID, LHS & 300M

Refer to **Figs. 1 through 4** for wiring diagrams.

MAGNUM, 300 & 300C

Refer to **Fig. 5** for wiring diagrams.

SEBRING CONVERTIBLE, SEBRING SEDAN & STRATUS SEDAN

Refer to **Figs. 6 and 7** for wiring diagrams.

Diagnostic Tests

CONCORDE, INTREPID, LHS & 300M

2001

Refer to **Figs. 8 through 16** for diagnostic tests.

2002-04

Refer to **Figs. 17 through 21** for diagnostic tests.

SEBRING CONVERTIBLE, SEBRING SEDAN & STRATUS SEDAN

Refer to **Figs. 22 through 28** for diagnostic tests.

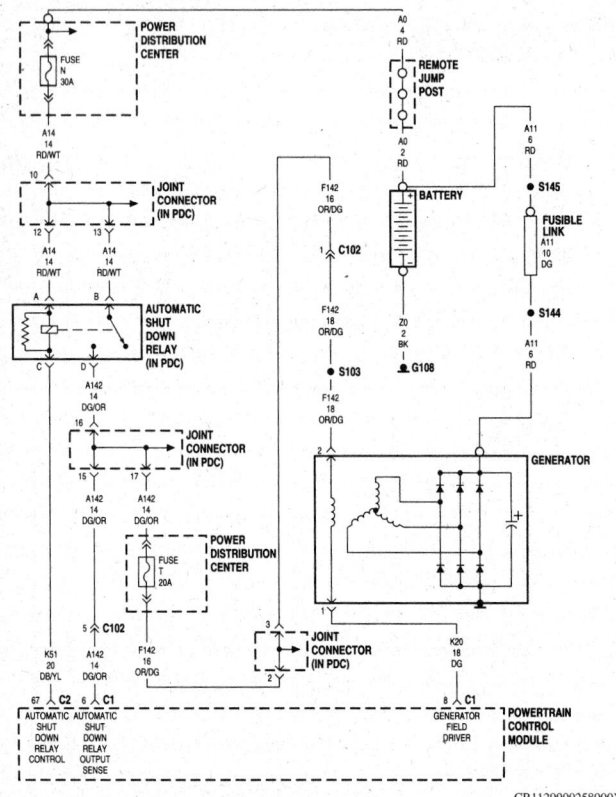

Fig. 1 Wiring diagram. LHS & 2001 Concorde, Intrepid & 300M

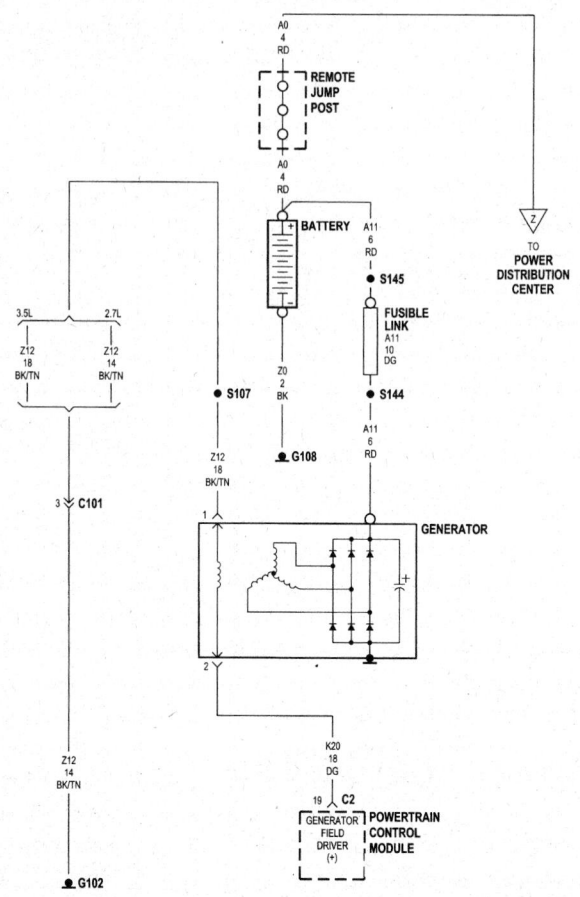

Fig. 2 Wiring diagram (Part 1 of 2). 2002 Concorde, Intrepid, LHS & 300M

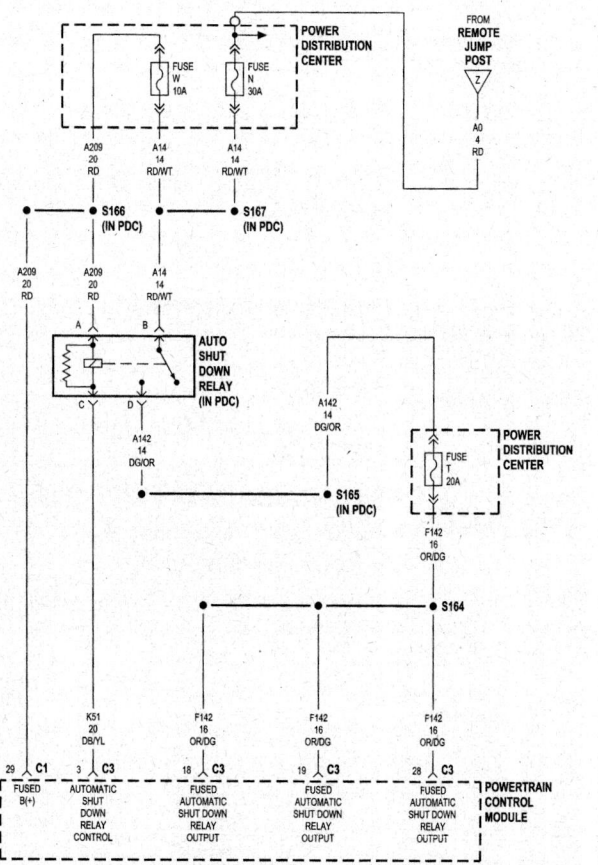

Fig. 2 Wiring diagram (Part 2 of 2). 2002 Concorde, Intrepid, LHS & 300M

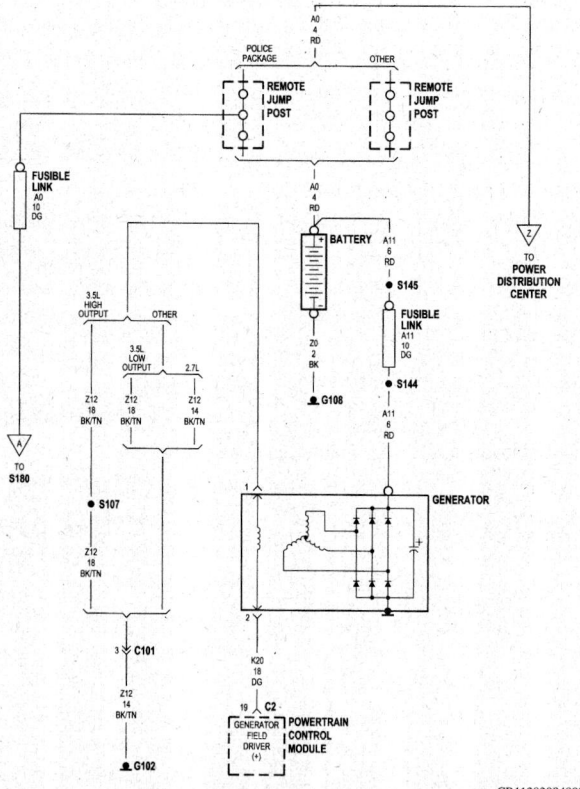

Fig. 3 Wiring diagram (Part 1 of 3). 2003–04 Concorde, Intrepid, LHS & 300M

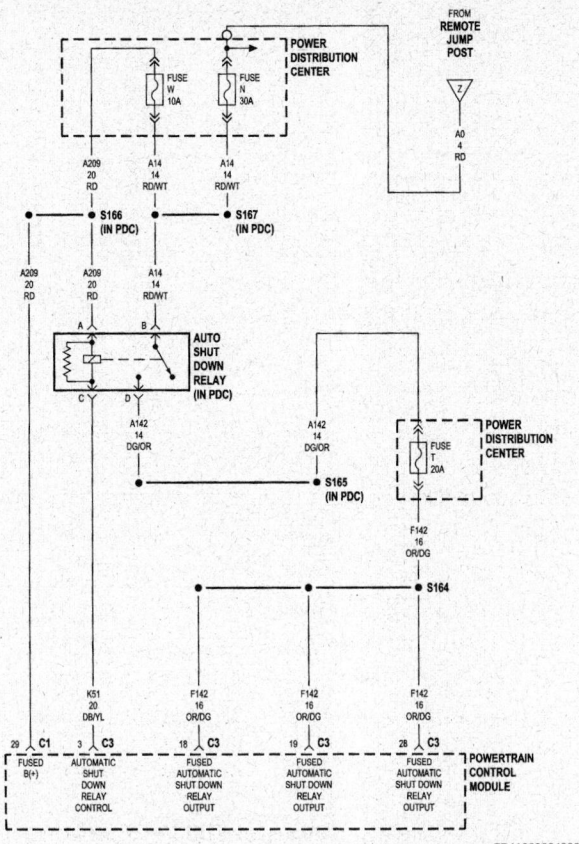

Fig. 3   Wiring diagram (Part 2 of 3). 2003–04 Concorde, Intrepid, LHS & 300M

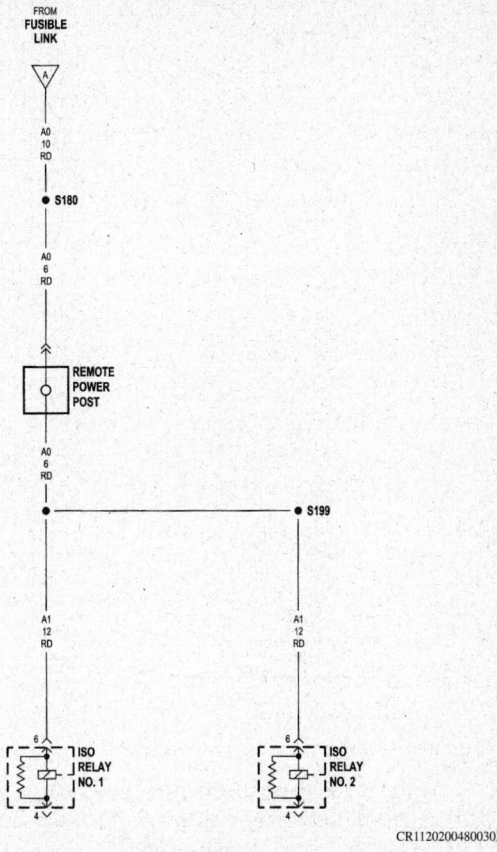

Fig. 3   Wiring diagram (Part 3 of 3). 2003–04 Concorde, Intrepid, LHS & 300M w/police package

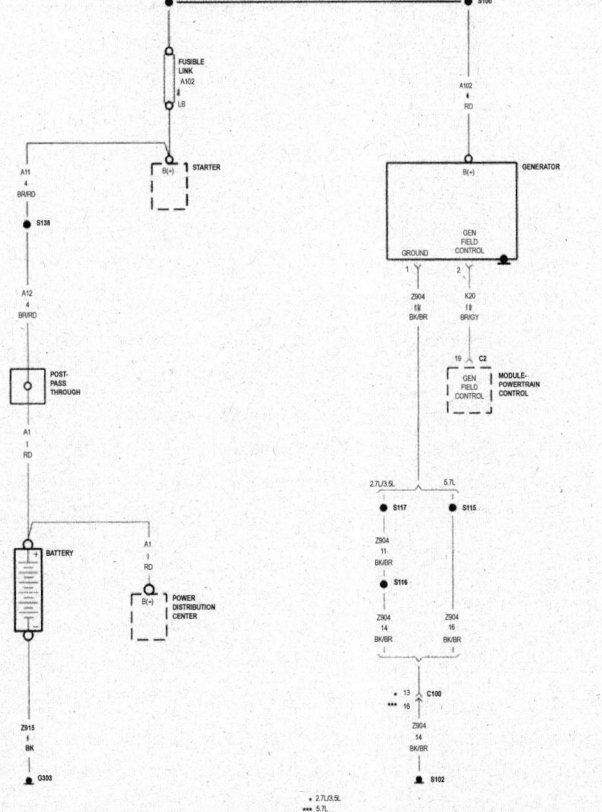

Fig. 4   Wiring diagram. Magnum, 300 & 300C

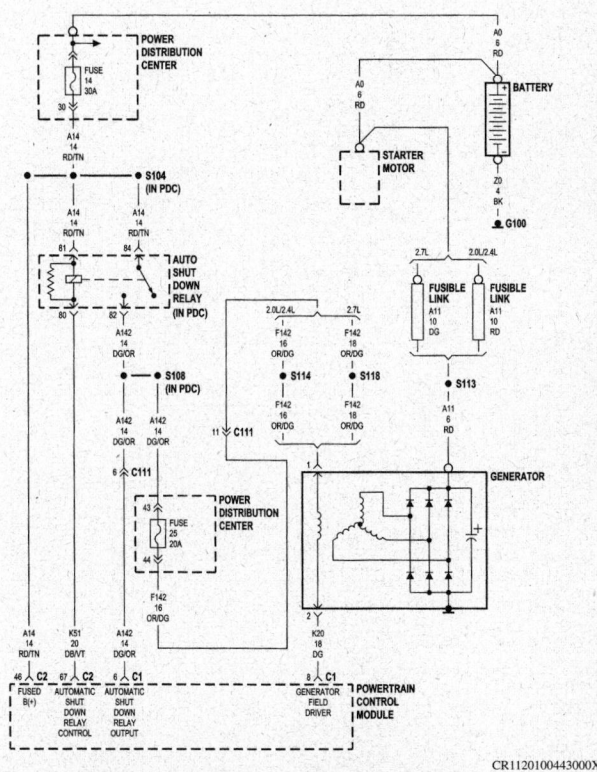

Fig. 5   Wiring diagram. 2002 Sebring Convertible, Sebring Sedan & Stratus Sedan

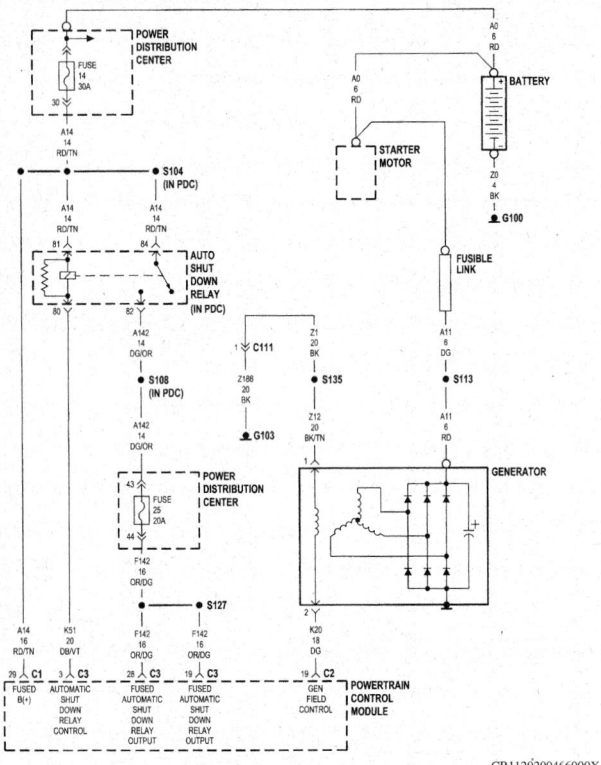

Fig. 6 Wiring diagram. 2003–05 Sebring Convertible, Sebring Sedan & Stratus Sedan w/2.4L engine

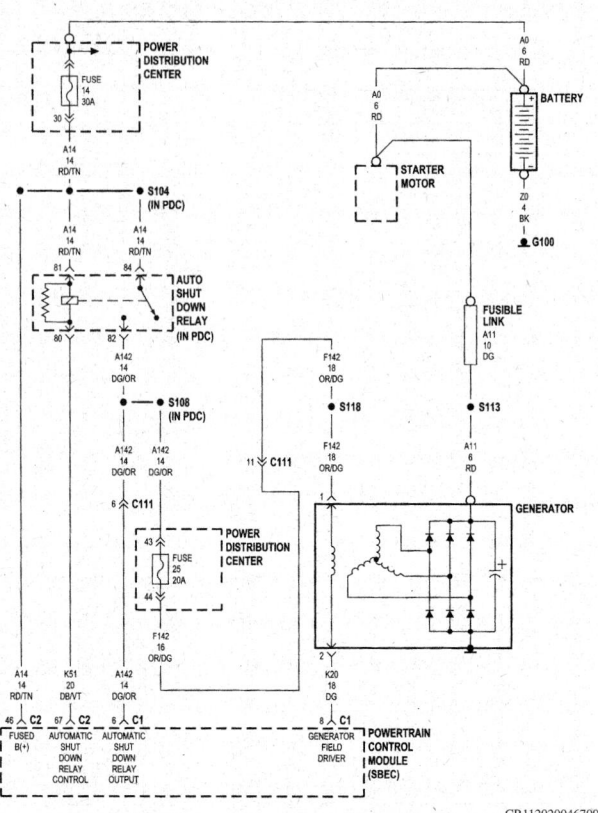

Fig. 7 Wiring diagram. 2003–05 Sebring Convertible, Sebring Sedan & Stratus Sedan w/2.7L engine

DIAGNOSTIC CHART INDEX

Code/Test	Description	Page No.	Fig. No.
2002–04 CONCORDE, INTREPID, LHS & 300M			
—	Verification Test VER-3.	10-14	21
P0562	Battery Voltage Low	10-11	17
P0563	Battery Voltage High	10-12	18
P0622	Alternator Field Control Circuit	10-13	19
P2503	Charging System Voltage Low	10-13	20
LHS & 2001 CONCORDE, INTREPID & 300M			
—	Ambient/Battery Temperature Sensor Diagnosis	10-10	13
—	Charging System Diagnosis w/No Code	10-10	14
—	Verification Test VER-3	10-11	15
—	Verification Test VER-5	10-11	16
P0622	Alternator Field Not Switching Properly	10-8	8
P1478	Battery Temperature Sensor Voltage Out of Limit	10-8	9
P1492	Ambient/Battery Temperature Sensor Voltage Out of Range	10-8	10
P1493	Ambient/Battery Temperature Sensor Voltage Out of Range	10-8	10
P1594	Charging System Voltage Too High	10-9	11
P1682	Charging System Voltage Too Low.	10-9	12
SEBRING CONVERTIBLE, SEBRING SEDAN & STRATUS SEDAN			
—	Verification Test VER-3.	10-17	27
—	Verification Test VER-5	10-17	28
P0622	Alternator Field Not Switching Properly	10-15	22
P1492	Ambient/Battery Temperature Sensor Voltage Too High	10-15	23
P1493	Ambient/Battery Temperature Sensor Voltage Too Low	10-15	24
P1594	Charging System Voltage Too High	10-16	25
P1682	Charging System Voltage Too Low	10-16	26

TEST	ACTION
1	Ignition On, Engine Not Running With the DRB actuate the Generator Field Driver Circuit. Using a 12-volt test light, backprobe the Generator Field Driver Circuit at the back of the Generator. Did the light blink? Yes → Go To 2 No → Go To 4
2	Ignition On, Engine Not Running With the DRB actuate the Generator Field Driver Circuit. **Note: Actuator Test should still be running.** Wiggle Wiring Harness from the Generator to PCM. With the DRB, read Codes. Does the Generator Field Driver (-) Circuit code return? Yes → Repair as necessary where wiggling caused problem to appear. Perform the Powertrain Verification Test - Ver 3 No → Go To 3
3	Turn ignition off. Using the schematic as a guide, inspect the Wiring and Connectors. Were any problems found? Yes → Repair as necessary. Perform the Powertrain Verification Test - Ver 3 No → Test Complete.

CR1129900321010X

Fig. 8   Code P0622: Alternator Field Not Switching Properly (Part 1 of 2). LHS & 2001 Concorde, Intrepid & 300M

TEST	ACTION
1	The Powertrain Control Module is reporting an internal trouble code and must be replaced. View repair options. Repair Replace the Powertrain Control Module.

CR1129900322000X

Fig. 9   Code P1478: Battery Temperature Sensor Voltage Out of Limit. LHS & 2001 Concorde, Intrepid & 300M

TEST	ACTION
1	Turn ignition on. With the DRBIII®, read DTC's. Is the DTC Global Good Trip Counter displayed and equal to zero? Yes → Go To 2 No → Go To 11

CR1129900323010X

Fig. 10   Codes P1492 & P1493: Ambient/Battery Temperature Sensor Voltage Out of Range (Part 1 of 3). LHS & 2001 Concorde, Intrepid & 300M

TEST	ACTION
4	Ignition On, Engine Not Running Record all DTC's and freeze frame data, now erase Codes. Carefully inspect all Connectors for corrosion or spread Terminals before continuing. With the DRB actuate the Generator Field Driver Circuit. Backprobe the ASD Relay Output Circuit at back of Generator. Is the voltage above 10.0 volts? Yes → Go To 5 No → Repair the open ASD Relay Output Circuit. Perform the Powertrain Verification Test - Ver 3
5	Turn ignition off. Disconnect the PCM Connectors. Disconnect the Generator Field harness connector. Using an Ohmmeter, measure the Generator Field Driver Circuit from PCM Connector to ground. Is the resistance below 5.0 ohms? Yes → Repair the Generator Field Driver Circuit shorted to ground. Perform the Powertrain Verification Test - Ver 3 No → Go To 6
6	Turn ignition off. Disconnect the PCM harness connectors. Disconnect the Generator Field harness connector. **Note: Check Connectors - Clean/repair as necessary.** Using an Ohmmeter, measure the Generator Field Driver Circuit from PCM to Generator. Is the resistance below 5.0 ohms? Yes → Go To 7 No → Repair the open Generator Field Driver Circuit. Perform the Powertrain Verification Test - Ver 3
7	Turn ignition off. Disconnect the Generator Field harness connector at back of the Generator. **Note: Check connectors - Clean/repair as necessary.** Use an Ohmmeter in the following steps. Measure resistance across the Generator Field Terminals at the Generator. Is the resistance below 5.0 ohms? Yes → Repair the Generator as necessary. Perform the Powertrain Verification Test - Ver 3 No → Go To 8
8	If there are no possible causes remaining, replace the Powertrain Control Module. View repair options. Repair Replace the Powertrain Control Module. Perform the Powertrain Verification Test - Ver 3

CR1129900321020X

Fig. 8   Code P0622: Alternator Field Not Switching Properly (Part 2 of 2). LHS & 2001 Concorde, Intrepid & 300M

TEST	ACTION
2	Disconnect the Ambient Temperature Sensor. Remove the Ambient Temperature Sensor. Using an ohmmeter, measure the resistance of the Ambient Temperature Sensor across the Sensor. Compare the readings with the Ambient Temp Sensor Specifications Do the readings compare with the values listed? Yes → Go To 3 No → Replace the Ambient Temperature Sensor. Perform the Powertrain Verification Test - Ver 5
3	Turn the ignition off. Disconnect the Ambient Temperature Sensor connector. Close all doors , insure all lights are off, then wait one minute. Measure the resistance of the sensor ground circuit to ground. Is the resistance below 30 ohms? No → Go To 4 Yes → Go To 6
4	Turn ignition off. Disconnect the Ambient Temperature Sensor connector. Disconnect the BCM connector. Measure the resistance of the Sensor Ground circuit between the Ambient Temperature Sensor connector and the BCM. Is the resistance below 5.0 ohms? No → Repair the open Sensor Ground circuit. Perform the Powertrain Verification Test - Ver 5 Yes → Go To 5
5	If there are no possible causes remaining, replace the BCM. View repair options. Repair Replace the BCM. Perform the Powertrain Verification Test - Ver 5
6	Turn ignition off. Disconnect the Ambient Temperature Sensor connectors. Disconnect the BCM connectors. Using an Ohmmeter, measure the resistance of the Ambient Temperature Sensor Signal circuit from the Sensor connector to the BCM connector. Is the resistance below 5.0 ohms? No → Repair the open circuit. Perform the Powertrain Verification Test - Ver 5 Yes → Go To 7

CR1129900323020X

Fig. 10   Codes P1492 & P1493: Ambient/Battery Temperature Sensor Voltage Out of Range (Part 2 of 3). LHS & 2001 Concorde, Intrepid & 300M

TEST	ACTION
7	Turn ignition off. Disconnect the Ambient Temperature Sensor connector. Disconnect the BCM connector. Using an Ohmmeter, measure the resistance between the Sensor Ground circuit and ground at the BCM. Is the resistance below 500K (500,000) ohms? No → Go To 8. Yes → Repair the Sensor Ground circuit for a partial short to ground. Perform the Powertrain Verification Test - Ver 5
8	Turn ignition off. Disconnect the Ambient Temperature Sensor connector. Disconnect the BCM connector. Using an Ohmmeter, measure the Ambient Temperature Sensor Signal circuit to ground. Is the resistance below 50K (50,000) ohms? Yes → Repair the Ambient Temperature Sensor signal circuit for a partial short to ground. Perform the Powertrain Verification Test - Ver 5. No → Go To 9.
9	Turn ignition off. Disconnect the Ambient Temperature Sensor connector. Disconnect the BCM connector. Using an Ohmmeter, measure the resistance between the Ambient Temperature Sensor Signal circuit and the Sensor Ground circuit. Is the resistance below 50K (50,000) ohms? Yes → Repair the Ambient Temperature Sensor Signal Circuit for a short to the Sensor Ground Circuit. Perform the Powertrain Verification Test - Ver 5. No → Go To 10.
10	If there are no possible causes remaining, replace the BCM. View repair options. Repair: Replace the BCM. Perform the Powertrain Verification Test - Ver 5.
11	Turn ignition off. Note: Visually inspect the related wiring harness. Look for any chafed, pierced, pinched, or partially broken wires. Note: Visually inspect the related wire harness connectors. Look for broken, bent, pushed out, or corroded terminals. Note: Refer to any Technical Service Bulletins (TSB) that may apply. Were any problems found? Yes → Repair wiring harness/connectors as necessary. Perform the Powertrain Verification Test - Ver 5. No → Test Complete.

CR1129900323030X

Fig. 10 Codes P1492 & P1493: Ambient/Battery Temperature Sensor Voltage Out of Range (Part 3 of 3). LHS & 2001 Concorde, Intrepid & 300M

TEST	ACTION
4	Turn ignition off. Note: Battery must be fully charged. Note: Generator Belt tension and condition must be checked before continuing. Start engine and allow it to reach operating temperature. With the DRB, read the BTS temperature. Using a Thermometer, measure under hood temperature. Is the temperature within 10 F degrees of Battery temperature? Yes → Test Complete. No → Replace Powertrain Control Module. Perform the Powertrain Verification Test - Ver 3.
5	Turn ignition off. Disconnect the PCM Connectors. Disconnect the Generator Field harness connector. Using an Ohmmeter, measure the Generator Field Driver Circuit from PCM Connector to ground. Is the resistance below 5.0 ohms? Yes → Repair the Generator Field Driver Circuit shorted to ground. Perform the Powertrain Verification Test - Ver 3. No → Go To 6.
6	Turn ignition off. Disconnect the Field Harness Connector at back of the Generator. Note: Check connectors - Clean/repair as necessary. Measure resistance of the Generator Field Driver Circuit at the Generator to Ground. Is the resistance below 5.0 ohms? Yes → Repair or replace the shorted Generator as necessary. Perform the Powertrain Verification Test - Ver 3. No → Go To 7.
7	If there are no possible causes remaining, replace the Powertrain Control Module. View repair options. Repair: Replace the Powertrain Control Module. Perform the Powertrain Verification Test - Ver 3.

CR1129900324020X

Fig. 11 Code P1594: Charging System Voltage Too High (Part 2 of 2). LHS & 2001 Concorde, Intrepid & 300M

TEST	ACTION
1	Ignition On, Engine Not Running. With DRB, actuate the Generator Field Driver. With a 12-volt test light, backprobe the Generator Field Driver Circuit in back of Generator. Did the light blink? Yes → Go To 2. No → Go To 5.
2	Ignition On, Engine Not Running. With the DRB, actuate the Generator Field Driver. With DRB, stop the Generator Field Driver actuation. With DRB, read the Target Charging voltage. Is the Target Charging voltage above 13 volts? Yes → Go To 3. No → Go To 4.
3	Start the engine. Manually set the engine speed to 1600 RPM. With DRB, read both the Battery voltage and the Target Charging voltage. Compare the "Target Voltage" to the "Battery Voltage" reading. Monitor voltage for 5 minutes, if necessary. Look for a 1.0 volt difference or more. Was there more than a 1.0 volt difference? Yes → Replace the Powertrain Control Module. Perform the Powertrain Verification Test - Ver 3. No → Test Complete.

CR1129900324010X

Fig. 11 Code P1594: Charging System Voltage Too High (Part 1 of 2). LHS & 2001 Concorde, Intrepid & 300M

TEST	ACTION
1	Turn Ignition Off. Note: Battery must be fully charged. Note: Generator Belt tension and condition must be checked before continuing. Start Engine. With the DRB, read the target charging voltage. Is the target charging voltage above 15.1 volts? Yes → Go To 2. No → Go To 3.
2	Turn ignition off. Note: Battery must be fully charged. Note: Generator Belt tension and condition must be checked before continuing. Start engine and allow it to reach operating temperature. With the DRB, read the BTS temperature. Using a Thermometer, measure under hood temperature. Is the temperature within 10 F degrees of Battery temperature? Yes → Go To 3. No → Replace the PCM. Perform the Powertrain Verification Test - Ver 3.

CR1129900325010X

Fig. 12 Code P1682: Charging System Voltage Too Low (Part 1 of 3). LHS & 2001 Concorde, Intrepid & 300M

TEST	ACTION

3	Turn ignition on, engine not running.
	Using a Voltmeter, measure voltage between the Generator B(+) Terminal and the Battery (+) Post.
	Caution: Ensure all wires are clear of the engine's moving parts.
	Start engine.
	Is the voltage above 0.4 volt?
	
	    Yes → Repair the B(+) Circuit for high resistance between the Generator and Battery.
	            Perform the Powertrain Verification Test - Ver 3
	
	    No → Go To 4

4	Start engine.
	Warm the engine to operating temperature.
	Caution: Ensure all wires are clear of the engine's moving parts.
	Using a Voltmeter, measure voltage between the Generator case and Battery (-) Post.
	Is the voltage above 0.1 volt?
	
	    Yes → Repair Generator Ground for high resistance, Generator Case to Battery (-) side.
	            Perform the Powertrain Verification Test - Ver 3
	
	    No → Go To 5

5	Start engine.
	Turn on all accessories, manually set engine speed to 1600 RPM.
	With DRB, read Target Charging and Charging voltage.
	Compare the two readings.
	Is there more than a 1.0 volt difference?
	
	    Yes → Go To 6
	
	    No → Test Complete.

6	Ignition On, Engine Not Running
	With the DRB, actuate the Generator Field.
	Using a Voltmeter, measure the voltage at both Generator Field Terminals.
	Is the voltage below 3.0 volts at either Terminal?
	
	    Yes → Go To 7
	
	    No → Test Complete.

7	Ignition On, Engine Not Running
	Record all DTC's and freeze frame data, now erase Codes.
	Carefully inspect all Connectors for corrosion or spread Terminals before continuing.
	With the DRB actuate the Generator Field Driver Circuit.
	Backprobe the ASD Relay Output Circuit at back of Generator.
	Is the voltage above 10.0 volts?
	
	    Yes → Go To 8
	
	    No → Repair the open ASD Relay Output Circuit.
	           Perform the Powertrain Verification Test - Ver 3

CR1129900325020X

Fig. 12 Code P1682: Charging System Voltage Too Low (Part 2 of 3). LHS & 2001 Concorde, Intrepid & 300M

TEST	ACTION

8	Turn ignition off.
	Disconnect the PCM Connectors.
	Disconnect the Generator Field harness connector.
	Using an Ohmmeter, measure the Generator Field Driver Circuit from PCM Connector to ground.
	Is the resistance below 5.0 ohms?
	
	    Yes → Repair the Generator Field Driver Circuit shorted to ground.
	           Perform the Powertrain Verification Test - Ver 3
	
	    No → Go To 9

9	Turn ignition off.
	Disconnect ASD Relay Connector.
	Note: Check connectors - Clean/repair as necessary.
	Disconnect the generator field connector.
	Note: Check Connectors - Clean/repair as necessary.
	Using an Ohmmeter, measure the ASD Relay Output Circuit from ASD Relay Connector to ground.
	Is the resistance below 5.0 ohms?
	
	    Yes → Repair the ASD Relay Output Circuit shorted to ground.
	           Perform the Powertrain Verification Test - Ver 3
	
	    No → Go To 10

10	Turn ignition off.
	Disconnect the PCM harness connectors.
	Disconnect the Generator Field harness connector.
	Note: Check Connectors - Clean/repair as necessary.
	Using an Ohmmeter, measure the Generator Field Driver Circuit from PCM to Generator.
	Is the resistance below 5.0 ohms?
	
	    Yes → Go To 11
	
	    No → Repair the open Generator Field Driver Circuit.
	           Perform the Powertrain Verification Test - Ver 3

11	If there are no possible causes remaining, replace the Powertrain Control Module.
	View repair options.
	
	    Repair
	           Replace the Powertrain Control Module.
	           Perform the Powertrain Verification Test - Ver 3

CR1129900325030X

Fig. 12 Code P1682: Charging System Voltage Too Low (Part 3 of 3). LHS & 2001 Concorde, Intrepid & 300M

TEST	ACTION

1	Turn ignition off.
	Note: Visually inspect the related wiring harness. Look for any chafed, pierced, pinched, or partially broken wires.
	Note: Visually inspect the related wire harness connectors. Look for broken, bent, pushed out, or corroded terminals.
	Note: Refer to any Technical Service Bulletins (TSB) that may apply.
	Were any problems found?
	
	    Yes → Repair wiring harness/connectors as necessary.
	           Perform the Powertrain Verification Test - Ver 5
	
	    No → Go To 2

2	Turn ignition on.
	With the DRB in sensors, read the "Ambient/Bat Tmp Deg" value and record the reading.
	Using a temp probe, measure the air temperature near the BTS.
	Is the recorded BTS temperature value within 10° of the temperature probe reading?
	
	    Yes → Test Complete.
	
	    No → Replace the BTS.
	           Perform the Powertrain Verification Test - Ver 5

CR1129900327000X

Fig. 13 Ambient/Battery Temperature Sensor Diagnosis. LHS & 2001 Concorde, Intrepid & 300M

TEST	ACTION

1	Turn ignition off.
	Note: Battery condition must be verified prior to this test.
	Inspect the Generator Belt tension and condition.
	Is the Generator Belt OK?
	
	    Yes → Go To 2
	
	    No → Repair as necessary.
	           Perform the Powertrain Verification Test - Ver 3

2	Start the Engine.
	Turn on all accessories.
	Raise engine speed to 2000 RPM for 30 seconds then return to idle.
	With the DRB III read DTC's.
	Are there any "Charging System" Trouble Codes?
	
	    Yes → Refer to Symptom list for problems related to Charging.
	           Perform the Powertrain Verification Test - Ver 3
	
	    No → Go To 3

3	Ignition On, Engine Not Running
	With the DRB, actuate the Generator Field.
	Using a 12-volt test light, backprobe the Generator Field Driver Terminal at the back of the Generator.
	Note: The test light should blink On and Off every 1.4 seconds.
	While monitoring the 12-volt test light, wiggle the Field Terminals back to the PCM and ASD Relay.
	Was there any interruption in the normal cycle of the test light?
	
	    Yes → Repair the wire where wiggling interrupted the voltage cycle.
	           Perform the Powertrain Verification Test - Ver 3
	
	    No → Go To 4

CR1129900326010X

Fig. 14 Charging System Diagnosis w/No Code (Part 1 of 3). LHS & 2001 Concorde, Intrepid & 300M

TEST	ACTION
4	Ignition On, Engine Not Running With the DRB, read trouble codes. Are there any "Charging System" trouble codes? Yes → Refer to Symptom list for problems related to Charging. Perform the Powertrain Verification Test - Ver 3 No → Go To 5
5	Turn ignition on, engine not running. Using a Voltmeter, measure voltage between the Generator B(+) Terminal and the Battery (+) Post. **Caution: Ensure all wires are clear of the engine's moving parts.** Start engine. Is the voltage above 0.4 volt? Yes → Repair the B(+) Circuit for high resistance between the Generator and Battery. Perform the Powertrain Verification Test - Ver 3 No → Go To 6
6	Start engine. Warm the engine to operating temperature. **Caution: Ensure all wires are clear of the engine's moving parts.** Using a Voltmeter, measure voltage between the Generator case and Battery (-) Post. Is the voltage above 0.1 volt? Yes → Repair Generator Ground for high resistance, Generator Case to Battery (-) side. Perform the Powertrain Verification Test - Ver 3 No → Go To 7
7	Ignition On, Engine Not Running. With the DRB, read the Battery voltage and record the results. Using a Voltmeter, measure Battery voltage B(+) to B(-) Terminal and record the results. Compare the two voltage readings. Is the voltage difference less than one volt? Yes → Test Complete. No → Go To 8
8	Ignition On, Engine Not Running. With the DRB, read the Battery voltage and record the results. Turn Ignition off. Disconnect the PCM. **Note: Check connectors - Clean/repair as necessary.** Turn Ignition off. Turn Ignition on, with the engine off. Using a Voltmeter, measure the Fused B(+) at PCM Connector. Is the voltage within one volt of the DRB recorded reading? Yes → Go To 9 No → Repair the B(+) Circuit for high resistance between the PCM and the Battery. Perform the Powertrain Verification Test - Ver 3

CR1129900326020X

Fig. 14 Charging System Diagnosis w/No Code (Part 2 of 3). LHS & 2001 Concorde, Intrepid & 300M

POWERTRAIN VERIFICATION TEST VER - 3

1. Inspect the vehicle to ensure that all engine components are properly installed and connected. Reassemble and reconnect components as necessary.
2. Connect the DRB to the Data Link Connector and erase the codes.
3. If the PCM has been replaced perform steps 4 through 6 then continue the verification.
4. If PCM has been changed and correct VIN and mileage have not been programmed, a DTC will be set in ABS and Air bag modules. In addition, if vehicle is equipped with a Sentry Key Immobilizer Module (SKIM), Secret Key data must be updated to enable start.
5. For ABS and Air Bag systems: Enter correct VIN and Mileage in PCM. Erase codes in ABS and Air Bag modules.
6. For SKIM theft alarm: Connect DRB to data link conn. Go to Theft Alarm, SKIM, Misc. and place SKIM in secured access mode, by using the appropriate PIN code for this vehicle. Select Update the Secret Key data. Data will be transferred from SKIM to PCM.
7. Ensure no other charging system problems remain by doing the following: Start the engine. Perform generator output per service manual.
8. Raise the engine speed to 2000 rpm for at least 30 seconds.
9. Allow the engine to idle.
10. Turn the engine off.
11. Turn the ignition key on.
12. With the DRB, read trouble code messages.
13. If repaired code has reset, or any other one has set, check all pertinent Technical Service Bulletins and return to Symptom List if necessary.
14. If there are no codes, the repair is now complete.

Repair is not complete, refer to appropriate symptom.

CR1129900328000X

Fig. 15 Verification Test VER-3. LHS & 2001 Concorde, Intrepid & 300M

TEST	ACTION
9	If there are no possible causes remaining, replace the Powertrain Control Module. View repair options. Repair Replace the PCM. Perform the Powertrain Verification Test - Ver 3

CR1129900326030X

Fig. 14 Charging System Diagnosis w/No Code (Part 3 of 3). LHS & 2001 Concorde, Intrepid & 300M

POWERTRAIN VERIFICATION TEST VER - 5

1. Inspect the vehicle to ensure that all engine components are properly installed and connected. Reassemble and reconnect components as necessary.
2. If any existing diagnostic trouble codes have not been repaired, go to Symptom List and follow path specified.
3. Connect the DRBIII® to the data link connector.
4. Ensure the fuel tank has at least a quarter tank of fuel. Turn off all accessories.
5. Perform steps 6 through 8 if the PCM has been replaced. Then proceed with the verification. If the PCM has not been replaced skip those steps and continue verification.
6. If PCM has been changed and correct VIN and mileage have not been programmed, a DTC will be set in ABS and Air bag modules. In addition, if vehicle is equipped with a Sentry Key Immobilizer Module (SKIM), Secret Key data must be updated to enable start.
7. For ABS and Air Bag systems: Enter correct VIN and Mileage in PCM. Erase codes in ABS and Air Bag modules.
8. For SKIM theft alarm: Connect DRB to data link conn. Go to Theft Alarm, SKIM, Misc. and place SKIM in secured access mode, by using the appropriate PIN code for this vehicle. Select Update the Secret Key data. Data will be transferred from SKIM to PCM.
9. If a Comprehensive Component DTC was repaired, perform steps 10-13. If a Major OBDII Monitor DTC was repaired skip those steps and continue verification.
10. After the ignition has been off for at least 10 seconds, restart the vehicle and run 2 minutes.
11. If the Good Trip counter changed to one or more and there are no new DTC's, the repair was successful and is now complete. Erase DTC's and disconnect the DRBIII®.
12. If the repaired DTC has reset, the repair is not complete. Check for any related TSB's or flash updates and return to the Symptom list.
13. If another DTC has set, return to the Symptom List and follow the path specified for that DTC.
14. With the DRBIII®, monitor the appropriate pre-test enabling conditions until all conditions have been met. Once the conditions have been met, switch screen to the appropriate OBDII monitor, (Audible beeps when the monitor is running).
15. If the monitor ran, and the Good Trip counter changed to one or more, the repair was successful and is now complete. Erase DTC's and disconnect the DRBIII®.
16. If the repaired OBDII trouble code has reset or was seen in the monitor while on the road test, the repair is not complete. Check for any related technical service bulletins or flash updates and return to Symptom List.
17. If another DTC has set, return to the Symptom List and follow the path specified for that DTC.

Repair is not complete, refer to appropriate symptom.

CR1129900329000X

Fig. 16 Verification Test VER-5. LHS & 2001 Concorde, Intrepid & 300M

Set Condition: The battery sensed voltage is 1 volt below the charging goal for 13.47 seconds. The PCM senses the battery voltage turns off the field driver and senses the battery voltage again. If the voltages are the same, the code is set. One trip Fault.

POSSIBLE CAUSES

POSSIBLE CAUSES
INTERMITTENT CONDITION
B+ CIRCUIT HIGH RESISTANCE
GENERATOR GROUND HIGH RESISTANCE
GENERATOR OPERATION
GENERATOR FIELD GROUND CIRCUIT OPEN
GENERATOR FIELD CONTROL CIRCUIT SHORTED TO GROUND
GENERATOR FIELD CONTROL CIRCUIT OPEN
PCM

TEST	ACTION
1	**NOTE: Ensure the Battery is in good condition. Using the Midtronics Battery Tester, test the Battery before continuing.** **NOTE: Inspect the vehicle for aftermarket accessories that may exceed the Generator System output.** Turn the ignition off. **NOTE: Ensure the generator drive belt is in good operating condition.** **NOTE: Inspect the fuses in the PDC. If a fuse is found to be open use the wiring diagram/schematic as a guide, inspect the wiring and connectors for damage.** Ignition on, engine not running. With the DRBIII®, read DTCs and record the related Freeze Frame data. Is the Good Trip Counter displayed and equal to zero? Yes → Go To 2 No → Go To 9

CR1120100445010X

Fig. 17 Code P0562: Battery Voltage Low (Part 1 of 3). 2002–04 Concorde, Intrepid, LHS & 300M

TEST	ACTION
2	**WARNING: WHEN THE ENGINE IS OPERATING, DO NOT STAND IN A DIRECT LINE WITH THE FAN. DO NOT PUT YOUR HANDS NEAR THE PULLEYS, BELTS OR FAN. DO NOT WEAR LOOSE CLOTHING.** Ignition on, engine not running. **NOTE: Ensure all wires are clear of the engine's moving parts.** Measure the voltage between the Generator B+ Terminal and the Battery+ Post. Start the engine. Is the voltage above 0.4 of a volt? Yes → Repair the B+ circuit for high resistance between the Generator and Battery. Perform POWERTRAIN VERIFICATION TEST VER - 3. No → Go To 3
3	**WARNING: WHEN THE ENGINE IS OPERATING, DO NOT STAND IN A DIRECT LINE WITH THE FAN. DO NOT PUT YOUR HANDS NEAR THE PULLEYS, BELTS OR FAN. DO NOT WEAR LOOSE CLOTHING.** Start the engine. Allow the engine to reach normal operating temperature. **NOTE: Ensure all wires are clear of the engine's moving parts.** Measure the voltage between the Generator case and Battery ground post. Is the voltage above 0.1 of a volt? Yes → Repair Generator Ground for high resistance, Generator Case to Battery ground side. Perform POWERTRAIN VERIFICATION TEST VER - 3. No → Go To 4
4	Turn the ignition off. Disconnect the Generator Field harness connector. Using a 12-volt test light, jumper it across the Generator Field harness connector. Ignition on, engine not running. With the DRBIII®, actuate the Generator Field Driver circuit. Does the test light illuminate brightly and flash on and off? Yes → Replace the Generator. Perform POWERTRAIN VERIFICATION TEST VER - 3. No → Go To 5
5	Turn the ignition off. Disconnect the Generator Field harness connector. Using a 12-volt test connected to battery voltage, probe the Generator Ground circuit in the Generator Field harness connector. Does the test light illuminate brightly? Yes → Go To 6 No → Repair the open in the Generator Field Ground circuit. Perform POWERTRAIN VERIFICATION TEST VER - 3.

CR1120100445020X

Fig. 17   Code P0562: Battery Voltage Low (Part 2 of 3). 2002–04 Concorde, Intrepid, LHS & 300M

When Monitored: The engine running. The engine speed greater than 380 RPM.

Set Condition: Battery voltage is 1 volt greater than desired system voltage. One Trip Fault

POSSIBLE CAUSES
GENERATOR FIELD CONTROL CIRCUIT SHORTED TO GROUND
GENERATOR FIELD CONTROL CIRCUIT OPEN
GENERATOR FIELD GROUND CIRCUIT OPEN
INTERMITTENT CONDITION
GENERATOR OPERATION
GENERATOR FIELD CONTROL CIRCUIT SHORTED TO BATTERY VOLTAGE
PCM

TEST	ACTION
1	**NOTE: Ensure the Battery is in good condition. Using the Midtronics Battery Tester, test the Battery before continuing.** **NOTE: Inspect the vehicle for aftermarket accessories that may exceed the Generator System output.** Turn the ignition off. **NOTE: Ensure the generator drive belt is in good operating condition.** **NOTE: Inspect the fuses in the PDC. If a fuse is found to be open use the wiring diagram/schematic as a guide, inspect the wiring and connectors for damage.** Ignition on, engine not running. With the DRBIII®, read DTCs and record the related Freeze Frame data. Is the Good Trip Counter displayed and equal to zero? Yes → Go To 2 No → Go To 8
2	Turn the ignition off. Disconnect the Generator Field harness connector. Using a 12-volt test light, jumper it across the Generator Field harness connector. Ignition on, engine not running. With the DRBIII®, actuate the Generator Field Driver circuit. Does the test light illuminate brightly and flash on and off? Yes → Go To 4 No → Go To 3

CR1120100446010X

Fig. 18   Code P0563: Battery Voltage High (Part 1 of 3). 2002–04 Concord, Intrepid, LHS & 300M

TEST	ACTION
6	Ignition on, engine not running. Disconnect the Generator Field harness connector. Disconnect the PCM harness connector. Measure the resistance between ground and the Generator Field Control circuit in the Generator Field harness connector. Is the resistance below 100 ohms? Yes → Repair the Generator Field Control circuit for a short to ground. Perform POWERTRAIN VERIFICATION TEST VER - 3. No → Go To 7
7	Turn the ignition off. Disconnect the Generator Field harness connector. Disconnect the PCM harness connector. **CAUTION: DO NOT PROBE THE PCM HARNESS CONNECTORS. PROBING THE PCM HARNESS CONNECTORS WILL DAMAGE THE PCM TERMINALS RESULTING IN POOR TERMINAL TO PIN CONNECTION. INSTALL MILLER SPECIAL TOOL #8815 TO PERFORM DIAGNOSIS.** Measure the resistance of the Generator Field Control circuit from the Generator Field harness connector to the appropriate terminal of the special tool #8815. Is the resistance below 5.0 ohms? Yes → Go To 8 No → Repair the open in the Generator Field Control circuit. Perform POWERTRAIN VERIFICATION TEST VER - 3.
8	**NOTE: Before continuing, check the PCM harness connector terminals for corrosion, damage or terminal push out. Repair as necessary.** If there are no possible causes remaining, view repair. Repair Replace and program the Powertrain Control Module in accordance with the Service Information. Perform POWERTRAIN VERIFICATION TEST VER - 3.
9	**NOTE: Ensure the Battery is in good condition. Using the Midtronics Battery Tester, test the Battery before continuing.** **NOTE: The conditions that set the DTC are not present at this time. The following list may help in identifying the intermittent condition.** **WARNING: WHEN THE ENGINE IS OPERATING, DO NOT STAND IN A DIRECT LINE WITH THE FAN. DO NOT PUT YOUR HANDS NEAR THE PULLEYS, BELTS OR FAN. DO NOT WEAR LOOSE CLOTHING.** With the engine running at normal operating temperature, monitor the DRBIII® parameters related to the DTC while wiggling the wire harness. Look for parameter values to change and/or a DTC to set. Review the DRBIII® Freeze Frame information. If possible, try to duplicate the conditions under which the DTC was set. Refer to any Technical Service Bulletins (TSB) that may apply. Visually inspect the related wire harness. Look for any chafed, pierced, pinched, or partially broken wires. Visually inspect the related wire harness connectors. Look for broken, bent, pushed out, or corroded terminals. Were any of the above conditions present? Yes → Repair as necessary Perform POWERTRAIN VERIFICATION TEST VER - 3. No → Test Complete.

CR1120100445030X

Fig. 17   Code P0562: Battery Voltage Low (Part 3 of 3). 2002–04 Concorde, Intrepid, LHS & 300M

TEST	ACTION
3	Turn the ignition off. Disconnect the Generator Field harness connector. Disconnect the PCM harness connector. Measure the voltage on the Generator Field Control circuit at the Generator Field harness connector. Is the voltage above 1.0 volt? Yes → Repair the short to voltage in the Generator Field Control circuit. Perform POWERTRAIN VERIFICATION TEST VER - 3. No → Go To 4
4	Turn the ignition off. Disconnect the Generator Field harness connector. Using a 12-volt test connected to battery voltage, probe the Generator Ground circuit in the Generator Field harness connector. Does the test light illuminate brightly? Yes → Go To 5 No → Repair the open in the Generator Field Ground circuit. Perform POWERTRAIN VERIFICATION TEST VER - 3.
5	Ignition on, engine not running. Disconnect the Generator Field harness connector. Measure the resistance between ground and the Generator Field Control circuit in the Generator Field harness connector. Is the resistance below 100 ohms? Yes → Repair the Generator Field Control circuit for a short to ground. Perform POWERTRAIN VERIFICATION TEST VER - 3. No → Go To 6
6	Turn the ignition off. Disconnect the Generator Field harness connector. Disconnect the PCM harness connector. **CAUTION: DO NOT PROBE THE PCM HARNESS CONNECTORS. PROBING THE PCM HARNESS CONNECTORS WILL DAMAGE THE PCM TERMINALS RESULTING IN POOR TERMINAL TO PIN CONNECTION. INSTALL MILLER SPECIAL TOOL #8815 TO PERFORM DIAGNOSIS.** Measure the resistance of the Generator Field Control circuit from the Generator Field harness connector to the appropriate terminal of the special tool #8815. Is the resistance below 5.0 ohms? Yes → Go To 7 No → Repair the open in the Generator Field Control circuit. Perform POWERTRAIN VERIFICATION TEST VER - 3.
7	**NOTE: Before continuing, check the PCM harness connector terminals for corrosion, damage or terminal push out. Repair as necessary.** If there are no possible causes remaining, view repair. Repair Replace and program the Powertrain Control Module in accordance with the Service Information. Perform POWERTRAIN VERIFICATION TEST VER - 3.

CR1120100446020X

Fig. 18   Code P0563: Battery Voltage High (Part 2 of 3). 2002–04 Concord, Intrepid, LHS & 300M

TEST	ACTION
8	NOTE: The conditions that set the DTC are not present at this time. The following list may help in identifying the intermittent condition. NOTE: Ensure the Battery is in good condition. Using the Midtronics Battery Tester, test the Battery before continuing. WARNING: WHEN THE ENGINE IS OPERATING, DO NOT STAND IN A DIRECT LINE WITH THE FAN. DO NOT PUT YOUR HANDS NEAR THE PULLEYS, BELTS OR FAN. DO NOT WEAR LOOSE CLOTHING. With the engine running at normal operating temperature, monitor the DRBIII® parameters related to the DTC while wiggling the wire harness. Look for parameter values to change and/or a DTC to set. Review the DRBIII® Freeze Frame information. If possible, try to duplicate the conditions under which the DTC was set. Refer to any Technical Service Bulletins (TSB) that may apply. Visually inspect the related wire harness. Look for any chafed, pierced, pinched, or partially broken wires. Visually inspect the related wire harness connectors. Look for broken, bent, pushed out, or corroded terminals. Were any of the above conditions present? Yes → Repair as necessary Perform POWERTRAIN VERIFICATION TEST VER - 3. No → Test Complete.

CR1120100446030X

Fig. 18   Code P0563: Battery Voltage High (Part 3 of 3). 2002–04 Concord, Intrepid, LHS & 300M

TEST	ACTION
3	Turn the ignition off. Disconnect the Generator Field harness connector. Using a 12-volt test light, jumper it across the Generator Field harness connector. Ignition on, engine not running. With the DRBIII®, actuate the Generator Field Driver circuit. Does the test light illuminate brightly and flash on and off? Yes → Replace the Generator. Perform POWERTRAIN VERIFICATION TEST VER - 3. No → Go To 4
4	Turn the ignition off. Disconnect the Generator Field harness connector. Using a 12-volt test connected to battery voltage, probe the Generator Ground circuit in the Generator Field harness connector. Does the test light illuminate brightly? Yes → Go To 5 No → Repair the open in the Generator Field Ground circuit. Perform POWERTRAIN VERIFICATION TEST VER - 3.
5	Turn the ignition off. Disconnect the Generator Field harness connector. Disconnect the PCM harness connector. Measure the voltage on the Generator Field Control circuit in the Generator Field harness connector. Is the voltage above 1.0 volts? Yes → Repair the short to voltage in the Generator Field Control circuit. Perform POWERTRAIN VERIFICATION TEST VER - 3. No → Go To 6
6	Turn the ignition on. Disconnect the Generator Field harness connector. Disconnect the PCM harness connector. Measure the resistance between ground and the Generator Field Control circuit in the Generator Field harness connector. Is the resistance below 100 ohms? Yes → Repair the Generator Field Control circuit for a short to ground. Perform POWERTRAIN VERIFICATION TEST VER - 3. No → Go To 7
7	Turn the ignition off. Disconnect the Generator Field harness connector. Disconnect the PCM harness connector. CAUTION: DO NOT PROBE THE PCM HARNESS CONNECTORS. PROBING THE PCM HARNESS CONNECTORS WILL DAMAGE THE PCM TERMINALS RESULTING IN POOR TERMINAL TO PIN CONNECTION. INSTALL MILLER SPECIAL TOOL #8815 TO PERFORM DIAGNOSIS. Measure the resistance of the Generator Field Control circuit from the Generator Field harness connector to the appropriate terminal of the special tool #8815. Is the resistance below 5.0 ohms? Yes → Go To 8 No → Repair the open in the Generator Field Control circuit. Perform POWERTRAIN VERIFICATION TEST VER - 3.

CR1120100447020X

Fig. 19   Code P0622: Low (Part 2 of 3). 2002–04 Concorde, Intrepid, LHS & 300M

When Monitored: With the ignition on. Engine running.

Set Condition: When the PCM tries to regulate the generator field with no result during monitoring. One Trip Fault.

POSSIBLE CAUSES
WIRING HARNESS INTERMITTENT
GENERATOR OPERATION
GENERATOR FIELD GROUND CIRCUIT OPEN
GENERATOR FIELD CONTROL CIRCUIT SHORTED TO BATTERY VOLTAGE
GENERATOR FIELD CONTROL CIRCUIT SHORTED TO GROUND
GENERATOR FIELD CONTROL CIRCUIT OPEN
PCM

TEST	ACTION
1	Ignition on, engine not running. With the DRBIII®, read DTCs and record the related Freeze Frame data. Does the test light illuminate brightly and flash? Yes → Go To 2 No → Go To 3
2	With the DRBIII®, erase DTCs. WARNING: WHEN THE ENGINE IS OPERATING, DO NOT STAND IN A DIRECT LINE WITH THE FAN. DO NOT PUT YOUR HANDS NEAR THE PULLEYS, BELTS OR FAN. DO NOT WEAR LOOSE CLOTHING. Start the engine and allow it to idle. Wiggle the wire harness from the Generator to PCM. With the DRBIII®, read DTCs. Did the DTC reset? Yes → Repair as necessary . Perform POWERTRAIN VERIFICATION TEST VER - 3. No → Test Complete.

CR1120100447010X

Fig. 19   Code P0622: Alternator Field Control Circuit (Part 1 of 3). 2002–04 Concorde, Intrepid, LHS & 300M

TEST	ACTION

8	NOTE: Before continuing, check the PCM connector terminals for corrosion, damage, or terminal push out. Repair as necessary.
	If there are no possible causes remaining, view repair.
	
	Repair
	     Replace and program the Powertrain Control Module in accordance with the Service Information.
	     Perform POWERTRAIN VERIFICATION TEST VER - 3.

CR1120100447030X

Fig. 19   Code P0622: Battery Voltage Low (Part 3 of 3). 2002–04 Concorde, Intrepid, LHS & 300M

When Monitored: The engine running. The engine speed greater than 1157 RPM.

Set Condition: The battery sensed voltage is 1 volt below the charging goal for 13.47 seconds. The PCM senses the battery voltage turns off the field driver and senses the battery voltage again. If the voltages are the same, the code is set.

POSSIBLE CAUSES
B+ CIRCUIT HIGH RESISTANCE
GENERATOR GROUND HIGH RESISTANCE
GENERATOR OPERATION
INTERMITTENT CONDITION
GENERATOR FIELD GROUND CIRCUIT OPEN
GENERATOR FIELD CONTROL CIRCUIT SHORTED TO BATTERY VOLTAGE
GENERATOR FIELD CONTROL CIRCUIT SHORTED TO GROUND
GENERATOR FIELD CONTROL CIRCUIT OPEN
PCM

TEST	ACTION
1	NOTE: Inspect the vehicle for aftermarket accessories that may exceed the Generator System output. Turn the ignition off. NOTE: The battery must be fully charged. NOTE: The Generator belt tension and condition must be checked before continuing. Start the engine. Allow the idle to stabilize. With the DRBIII®, read the Target Charging Voltage. Is the Target Charging Voltage above 15.1 volts? Yes → Go To 2 No → Go To 3

CR1120100448010X

Fig. 20   Code P2503: Charging System Voltage Low (Part 1 of 4). 2002–04 Concorde, Intrepid, LHS & 300M

TEST	ACTION
2	**NOTE: The conditions that set the DTC are not present at this time. The following list may help in identifying the intermittent condition.** **WARNING: WHEN THE ENGINE IS OPERATING, DO NOT STAND IN A DIRECT LINE WITH THE FAN. DO NOT PUT YOUR HANDS NEAR THE PULLEYS, BELTS OR FAN. DO NOT WEAR LOOSE CLOTHING.** With the engine running at normal operating temperature, monitor the DRBIII® parameters related to the DTC while wiggling the wire harness. Look for parameter values to change and/or a DTC to set. Review the DRBIII® Freeze Frame information. If possible, try to duplicate the conditions under which the DTC was set. Refer to any Technical Service Bulletins (TSB) that may apply. Visually inspect the related wire harness. Look for any chafed, pierced, pinched, or partially broken wires. Visually inspect the related wire harness connectors. Look for broken, bent, pushed out, or corroded terminals. Were any of the above conditions present? Yes → Repair as necessary Perform POWERTRAIN VERIFICATION TEST VER - 3. No → Test Complete.
3	**WARNING: WHEN THE ENGINE IS OPERATING, DO NOT STAND IN A DIRECT LINE WITH THE FAN. DO NOT PUT YOUR HANDS NEAR THE PULLEYS, BELTS OR FAN. DO NOT WEAR LOOSE CLOTHING.** Ignition on, engine not running. **NOTE: Ensure all wires are clear of the engine's moving parts.** Measure the voltage between the Generator B+ Terminal and the Battery+ Post. Start the engine. Is the voltage above 0.4 of a volt? Yes → Repair the B+ circuit for high resistance between the Generator and Battery. Perform POWERTRAIN VERIFICATION TEST VER - 3. No → Go To 4
4	**WARNING: WHEN THE ENGINE IS OPERATING, DO NOT STAND IN A DIRECT LINE WITH THE FAN. DO NOT PUT YOUR HANDS NEAR THE PULLEYS, BELTS OR FAN. DO NOT WEAR LOOSE CLOTHING.** Start the engine. Warm the engine to operating temperature. **NOTE: Ensure all wires are clear of the engine's moving parts.** Measure the voltage between the Generator case and Battery ground post. Is the voltage above 0.1 of a volt? Yes → Repair Generator Ground for high resistance, Generator Case to Battery ground side. Perform POWERTRAIN VERIFICATION TEST VER - 3. No → Go To 5

CR1120100448020X

Fig. 20 Code P2503: Charging System Voltage Low (Part 2 of 4). 2002–04 Concorde, Intrepid, LHS & 300M

TEST	ACTION
10	If there are no possible causes remaining, view repair. **Repair** Replace and program the Powertrain Control Module in accordance with the Service Information. Perform POWERTRAIN VERIFICATION TEST VER - 3.

CR1120100448040X

Fig. 20 Code P2503: Charging System Voltage Low (Part 4 of 4). 2002–04 Concorde, Intrepid, LHS & 300M

TEST	ACTION
5	Turn the ignition off. Disconnect the Generator Field harness connector. Using a 12-volt test light, jumper it across the Generator Field harness connector. Ignition on, engine not running. With the DRBIII®, actuate the Generator Field Driver circuit. Does the test light illuminate brightly and flash on and off? Yes → Replace the Generator. Perform POWERTRAIN VERIFICATION TEST VER - 3. No → Go To 6
6	Turn the ignition off. Disconnect the Generator Field harness connector. Using a 12-volt test connected to battery voltage, probe the Generator Ground circuit in the Generator Field harness connector. Does the test light illuminate brightly? Yes → Go To 7 No → Repair the open in the Generator Field Ground circuit. Perform POWERTRAIN VERIFICATION TEST VER - 3.
7	Turn the ignition off. Disconnect the Generator Field harness connector. Disconnect the PCM harness connector. Measure the voltage on the Generator Field Control circuit at the Generator Field harness connector. Is the voltage above 1.0 volt? Yes → Repair the short to voltage in the Generator Field Control circuit. Perform POWERTRAIN VERIFICATION TEST VER - 3. No → Go To 8
8	Turn the ignition on. Disconnect the Generator Field harness connector. Disconnect the PCM harness connector. Measure the resistance between ground and the Generator Field Control circuit in the Generator Field harness connector. Is the resistance below 100 ohms? Yes → Repair the Generator Field Control circuit for a short to ground. Perform POWERTRAIN VERIFICATION TEST VER - 3. No → Go To 9
9	Turn the ignition off. Disconnect the Generator Field harness connector. Disconnect the PCM harness connector. **CAUTION: DO NOT PROBE THE PCM HARNESS CONNECTORS. PROBING THE PCM HARNESS CONNECTORS WILL DAMAGE THE PCM TERMINALS RESULTING IN POOR TERMINAL TO PIN CONNECTION. INSTALL MILLER SPECIAL TOOL #8815 TO PERFORM DIAGNOSIS.** Measure the resistance of the Generator Field Control circuit from the Generator Field harness connector to the appropriate terminal of the special tool #8815. Is the resistance below 5.0 ohms? Yes → Go To 10 No → Repair the open in the Generator Field Control circuit. Perform POWERTRAIN VERIFICATION TEST VER - 3.

CR1120100448030X

Fig. 20 Code P2503: Charging System Voltage Low (Part 3 of 4). 2002–04 Concorde, Intrepid, LHS & 300M

POWERTRAIN VERIFICATION TEST VER - 3
1. NOTE: After completing the Powertrain Verification Test the Transmission Verification Test must be performed. 2. NOTE: If the PCM has been replaced and the correct VIN and mileage have not been programmed, a DTC will be set in the ABS Module, Airbag Module and the SKIM. 3. NOTE: If the vehicle is equipped with a Sentry Key Immobilizer System, Secret Key data must be updated. Refer to the Service Information for the PCM, SKIM and the Transponder (ignition key) for programming information. 4. Inspect the vehicle to ensure that all components related to the repair are connected properly. 5. With the DRBIII®, clear DTCs. 6. Perform generator output test. Refer to the appropriate service information as necessary. 7. Start the engine and set engine speed to 2000 RPM for at least thirty seconds. 8. Cycle the ignition key off and on. 9. With the DRBIII®, read the DTCs. If the DTC returns, or any other symptom or DTC is present, refer to the appropriate category and perform the corresponding symptom. 10. If there are no DTCs present and all components are functioning properly, the repair is complete. Are any DTCs present? Yes → Repair is not complete, refer to appropriate symptom. No → Repair is complete.

CR1120100449000X

Fig. 21 Verification Test VER-3. 2002–04 Concorde, Intrepid, LHS & 300M

TEST	ACTION	APPLICABILITY
1	Turn the ignition on. With the DRBIII®, actuate the Generator Field Driver circuit. Using a 12-volt test light connected to ground, backprobe the Generator Field Driver circuit in the back of the Generator. Does the test light illuminate brightly and flash? Yes → Go To 2 No → Go To 4	All
2	Turn the ignition on. With the DRBIII® actuate the Generator Field Driver circuit. Wiggle the wiring harness from the Generator to PCM. With the DRBIII®, read DTC's. Did the DTC reset? Yes → Repair as necessary. Perform POWERTRAIN VERIFICATION TEST VER - 3. No → Go To 3	All
3	Turn the ignition off. Using the schematic as a guide, inspect the Wiring and Connectors. Were any problems found? Yes → Repair as necessary. Perform POWERTRAIN VERIFICATION TEST VER - 3. No → Test Complete.	All

CR1120100394010X

Fig. 22   Code P0622: Alternator Field Not Switching Properly (Part 1 of 2). Sebring Convertible, Sebring Sedan & Stratus Sedan

TEST	ACTION
1	Turn the ignition on. With the DRBIII®, read the Ambient Temperature Sensor voltage. Is the voltage above 4.8 volts? Yes → Go To 2 No → Go To 7
2	Turn the ignition off. Disconnect the Ambient Temperature Sensor harness connector. Turn the ignition on. Measure the voltage of the Ambient Temperature Sensor Signal circuit in the Ambient Temperature Sensor harness connector. Is the voltage above 5.2 volts? Yes → Repair the Ambient Temperature Sensor Signal circuit for a short to battery voltage. Perform POWERTRAIN VERIFICATION TEST VER - 5. No → Go To 3

CR1120100395010X

Fig. 23   Code P1492: Ambient/Battery Temperature Sensor Voltage Too High (Part 1 of 2). Sebring Convertible, Sebring Sedan & Stratus Sedan

TEST	ACTION
3	Turn the ignition off. Disconnect the Ambient Temperature Sensor harness connector. Connect a jumper wire between the Ambient Temperature Sensor Signal circuit and the Sensor ground circuit in the Ambient Temperature Sensor harness connector. Turn the ignition on. With the DRBIII®, read Ambient Temperature Sensor voltage. Is the voltage below 1.0 volt? Yes → Replace the Ambient Temperature Sensor. Perform POWERTRAIN VERIFICATION TEST VER - 5. No → Go To 4
4	Turn the ignition off. Disconnect the Ambient Temperature Sensor harness connector. Disconnect the PCM harness connector. Measure the resistance of the Ambient Temperature Sensor Signal circuit between the Ambient Temperature Sensor harness connector and the PCM harness connector. Is the resistance below 5.0 ohms? Yes → Go To 5 No → Repair the Ambient Temperature Sensor Signal circuit for an open. Perform POWERTRAIN VERIFICATION TEST VER - 5.
5	Turn the ignition off. Disconnect the Ambient Temperature Sensor harness connector. Disconnect the PCM harness connector. Measure the resistance of the Sensor ground circuit between the Ambient Temperature Sensor harness connector and the PCM harness connector. Is the resistance below 5.0 ohms? Yes → Go To 6 No → Repair the Sensor ground circuit for an open. Perform POWERTRAIN VERIFICATION TEST VER - 5.
6	If there are no possible causes remaining, view repair. Repair Replace and program the Powertrain Control Module Perform POWERTRAIN VERIFICATION TEST VER - 5.

CR1120100395020X

Fig. 23   Code P1492: Ambient/Battery Temperature Sensor Voltage Too High (Part 2 of 2). Sebring Convertible, Sebring Sedan & Stratus Sedan

TEST	ACTION
4	**NOTE: Carefully inspect all Connectors for corrosion or spread Terminals before continuing.** Disconnect the Generator Field harness connector. Turn the ignition on. With the DRBIII® actuate the Generator Field Driver circuit. Using a 12-volt test light connected to ground, probe the ASD Relay Output circuit. Does the test light illuminate brightly? Yes → Go To 5 No → Repair the ASD Relay Output circuit. Perform POWERTRAIN VERIFICATION TEST VER - 3.
5	Turn the ignition off. Disconnect the PCM harness connector. Disconnect the Generator Field harness connector. Measure the resistance of the Generator Field Driver circuit from PCM harness connector to ground. Is the resistance below 5.0 ohms? Yes → Repair the Generator Field Driver circuit for a shorted to ground. Perform POWERTRAIN VERIFICATION TEST VER - 3. No → Go To 6
6	Turn the ignition off. Disconnect the PCM harness connector. Disconnect the Generator Field harness connector. Measure the resistance of the Generator Field Driver circuit from the PCM harness connector to the Generator Field harness connector. Is the resistance below 5.0 ohms? Yes → Go To 7 No → Repair the Generator Field Driver circuit for an open. Perform POWERTRAIN VERIFICATION TEST VER - 3.
7	Turn the ignition off. Disconnect the Generator Field harness connector. Measure the resistance across the Generator Field Terminals at the Generator. Is the resistance above 15.0 ohms? Yes → Replace the Generator. Perform POWERTRAIN VERIFICATION TEST VER - 3. No → Go To 8
8	Turn the ignition off. Disconnect the Generator Field harness connector. Measure the resistance across the Generator Field Terminals at the Generator. Is the resistance below 0.5 ohms? Yes → Replace the Generator. Perform POWERTRAIN VERIFICATION TEST VER - 3. No → Go To 9
9	If there is no more possible causes remaining, view repair. Repair Replace and program the Powertrain Control Module in accordance with the Service Information. Perform POWERTRAIN VERIFICATION TEST VER - 3.

CR1120100394020X

Fig. 22   Code P0622: Alternator Field Not Switching Properly (Part 2 of 2). Sebring Convertible, Sebring Sedan & Stratus Sedan

TEST	ACTION
1	Turn the ignition on. With the DRBIII®, read the Ambient Temperature Sensor voltage. Is the voltage below 0.3 volt? Yes → Go To 2 No → Go To 6
2	Turn the ignition off. Disconnect the Ambient Temperature Sensor harness connector. Turn the ignition on. With the DRBIII®, read Ambient Temperature Sensor voltage. Is the voltage above 1.0 volt? Yes → Replace the Ambient Temperature Sensor. Perform POWERTRAIN VERIFICATION TEST VER - 5. No → Go To 3
3	Turn the ignition off. Disconnect the Ambient Temperature Sensor harness connector. Disconnect the PCM harness connector. Measure the resistance of the Ambient Temperature Sensor Signal circuit in the Ambient Temperature Sensor harness connector to chassis ground. Is the resistance below 100 ohms? Yes → Repair the Ambient Temperature Sensor Signal circuit for a short to ground. Perform POWERTRAIN VERIFICATION TEST VER - 5. No → Go To 4

CR1120100396010X

Fig. 24   Code P1493: Ambient/Battery Temperature Sensor Voltage Too Low (Part 1 of 2). Sebring Convertible, Sebring Sedan & Stratus Sedan

ALTERNATORS

TEST	ACTION
4	Turn the ignition off. Disconnect the Ambient Temperature Sensor harness connector. Disconnect the PCM harness connector. Measure the resistance between the Ambient Temperature Sensor Signal circuit and the Sensor ground circuit in the Ambient Temperature Sensor harness connector. Is the resistance below 100 ohms? Yes → Repair the Ambient Temperature Sensor Signal circuit for a short to the Sensor ground circuit. Perform POWERTRAIN VERIFICATION TEST VER - 5. No → Go To 5
5	If there are no possible causes remaining, view repair. Repair Replace and program the Powertrain Control Module in accordance with the Service Information. Perform POWERTRAIN VERIFICATION TEST VER - 5.
6	WARNING: WHEN THE ENGINE IS OPERATING, DO NOT STAND IN A DIRECT LINE WITH THE FAN. DO NOT PUT YOUR HANDS NEAR THE PULLEYS, BELTS OR FAN. DO NOT WEAR LOOSE CLOTHING. NOTE: The conditions that set the DTC are not present at this time. The following list may help in identifying the intermittent condition. With the engine running at normal operating temperature, monitor the DRB parameters related to the DTC while wiggling the wiring harness. Look for parameter values to change and/or a DTC to set. Review the DRB Freeze Frame information. If possible, try to duplicate the conditions under which the DTC was set. Refer to any Technical Service Bulletins (TSB) that may apply. Visually inspect the related wiring harness. Look for any chafed, pierced, pinched, or partially broken wires. Visually inspect the related wiring harness connectors. Look for broken, bent, pushed out, or corroded terminals. Were any of the above conditions present? Yes → Repair as necessary Perform POWERTRAIN VERIFICATION TEST VER - 5. No → Test Complete.

CR1120100396020X

Fig. 24   Code P1493: Ambient/Battery Temperature Sensor Voltage Too Low (Part 2 of 2). Sebring Convertible, Sebring Sedan & Stratus Sedan

TEST	ACTION
4	WARNING: WHEN THE ENGINE IS OPERATING, DO NOT STAND IN A DIRECT LINE WITH THE FAN. DO NOT PUT YOUR HANDS NEAR THE PULLEYS, BELTS OR FAN. DO NOT WEAR LOOSE CLOTHING. NOTE: The conditions that set the DTC are not present at this time. The following list may help in identifying the intermittent condition. With the engine running at normal operating temperature, monitor the DRB parameters related to the DTC while wiggling the wiring harness. Look for parameter values to change and/or a DTC to set. Review the DRB Freeze Frame information. If possible, try to duplicate the conditions under which the DTC was set. Refer to any Technical Service Bulletins (TSB) that may apply. Visually inspect the related wiring harness. Look for any chafed, pierced, pinched, or partially broken wires. Visually inspect the related wiring harness connectors. Look for broken, bent, pushed out, or corroded terminals. Were any of the above conditions present? Yes → Repair as necessary Perform POWERTRAIN VERIFICATION TEST VER - 3. No → Test Complete.
5	Turn the ignition off. Disconnect the PCM harness connector. Disconnect the Generator Field harness connector. Measure the resistance of the Generator Field Driver circuit from the PCM harness connector to ground. Is the resistance below 5.0 ohms? Yes → Repair the Generator Field Driver circuit shorted to ground. Perform POWERTRAIN VERIFICATION TEST VER - 3. No → Go To 6
6	Turn the ignition off. Disconnect the Generator Field harness connector. Measure resistance of the Generator Field Driver terminal on the Generator to ground. Is the resistance below 5.0 ohms? Yes → Repair or replace the shorted Generator as necessary. Perform POWERTRAIN VERIFICATION TEST VER - 3. No → Go To 7
7	If there are no possible causes remaining, view repair. Repair Replace and program the Powertrain Control Module Perform POWERTRAIN VERIFICATION TEST VER - 3.

CR1120100397020X

Fig. 25   Code P1594: Charging System Voltage Too High (Part 2 of 2). Sebring Convertible, Sebring Sedan & Stratus Sedan

TEST	ACTION
1	Note: Battery must be fully charged. Note: Generator Belt tension and condition must be checked before continuing. Turn the ignition on. With DRBIII®, actuate the Generator Field Driver. With a 12-volt test light connected to ground, backprobe the Generator Field Driver circuit in the back of Generator Field harness connector. Does the test light illuminate brightly and flash? Yes → Go To 2 No → Go To 5
2	With DRBIII®, stop all actuation. Turn the ignition on. With DRBIII®, read the Target Charging voltage. Is the Target Charging voltage above 13 volts? Yes → Go To 3 No → Go To 4
3	Start the engine. With the DRBIII®, manually set the engine speed to 1600 RPM. With DRBIII®, read both the Battery voltage and the Target Charging voltage. Compare the Target Charging Voltage to the Battery Voltage reading. Monitor voltage for 5 minutes, if necessary. Look for a 1.0 volt difference or more. Was there more than a 1.0 volt difference? Yes → Replace the Powertrain Control Module in accordance with the Service Information. Perform POWERTRAIN VERIFICATION TEST VER - 3. No → Go To 4

CR1120100397010X

Fig. 25   Code P1594: Charging System Voltage Too High (Part 1 of 2). Sebring Convertible, Sebring Sedan & Stratus Sedan

TEST	ACTION
1	NOTE: Inspect the vehicle for aftermarket accessories that may exceed the Generator System output. Turn the ignition off. NOTE: The battery must be fully charged. NOTE: The Generator belt tension and condition must be checked before continuing. Start the engine. Allow the idle to stabilize. With the DRBIII®, read the Target Charging Voltage. Is the Target Charging Voltage above 15.1 volts? Yes → Go To 8 No → Go To 2
2	WARNING: WHEN THE ENGINE IS OPERATING, DO NOT STAND IN A DIRECT LINE WITH THE FAN. DO NOT PUT YOUR HANDS NEAR THE PULLEYS, BELTS OR FAN. DO NOT WEAR LOOSE CLOTHING. Turn the ignition on. NOTE: Ensure all wires are clear of the engine's moving parts. Measure the voltage between the Generator B+ Terminal and the Battery+ Post. Start the engine. Is the voltage above 0.4 volt? Yes → Repair the B+ circuit for high resistance between the Generator and Battery. Perform POWERTRAIN VERIFICATION TEST VER - 3. No → Go To 3

CR1120100398010X

Fig. 26   Code P1682: Charging System Voltage Too Low (Part 1 of 3). Sebring Convertible, Sebring Sedan & Stratus Sedan

TEST	ACTION
3	**WARNING: WHEN THE ENGINE IS OPERATING, DO NOT STAND IN A DIRECT LINE WITH THE FAN. DO NOT PUT YOUR HANDS NEAR THE PULLEYS, BELTS OR FAN. DO NOT WEAR LOOSE CLOTHING.** Start the engine. Warm the engine to operating temperature. **NOTE: Ensure all wires are clear of the engine's moving parts.** Measure the voltage between the Generator case and Battery ground post. Is the voltage above 0.1 volt? Yes → Repair Generator Ground for high resistance, Generator Case to Battery ground side. Perform POWERTRAIN VERIFICATION TEST VER - 3. No → Go To 4
4	Start the engine. **WARNING: WHEN THE ENGINE IS OPERATING, DO NOT STAND IN A DIRECT LINE WITH THE FAN. DO NOT PUT YOUR HANDS NEAR THE PULLEYS, BELTS OR FAN. DO NOT WEAR LOOSE CLOTHING.** Turn on all accessories, manually set engine speed to 1600 RPM. With DRBIII®, read Target Charging and Charging voltage. Compare the two readings. Is there more than a 1.0 volt difference? Yes → Go To 5 No → Go To 8
5	Turn the ignition off. Disconnect the PCM harness connector. Disconnect the Generator Field harness connector. Measure the resistance of the Generator Field Driver circuit from the PCM harness connector to Generator harness connector. Is the resistance below 5.0 ohms? Yes → Go To 6 No → Repair the Generator Field Driver circuit for an open. Perform POWERTRAIN VERIFICATION TEST VER - 3.
6	Disconnect the Generator Field harness connector. Turn the ignition on. With the DRBIII® actuate the Generator Field Driver. Using a 12-volt test light connected to ground, probe the ASD Relay Output circuit in the Generator harness connector. Does the test light illuminate brightly? Yes → Go To 7 No → Repair the ASD Relay Output circuit. Perform POWERTRAIN VERIFICATION TEST VER - 3.
7	If there is no possible causes remaining, view repair. Yes → Repair or replace the Generator as necessary.. Perform POWERTRAIN VERIFICATION TEST VER - 3.

CR1120100398020X

Fig. 26 Code P1682: Charging System Voltage Too Low (Part 2 of 3). Sebring Convertible, Sebring Sedan & Stratus Sedan

POWERTRAIN VERIFICATION TEST VER - 3
1. NOTE: If the PCM has been replaced and the correct VIN and mileage have not been programmed, a DTC will be set in the ABS Module, Airbag Module and the SKIM.
2. NOTE: If the vehicle is equipped with a Sentry Key Immobilizer System, Secret Key data must be updated. Refer to the Service Information for the PCM, SKIM and the Transponder (ignition key) for programming information.
3. Inspect the vehicle to ensure that all components related to the repair are connected properly.
4. With the DRBIII®, clear DTCs.
5. Perform generator output test. Refer to the appropriate service information as necessary.
6. Start the engine and set engine speed to 2000 RPM for at least thirty seconds.
7. Cycle the ignition key off and on.
8. With the DRBIII®, read the DTCs. If the DTC returns, or any other symptom or DTC is present, refer to the appropriate category and perform the corresponding symptom.
9. If there are no DTCs present and all components are functioning properly, the repair is complete.
Are any DTCs present?
Yes → Repair is not complete, refer to appropriate symptom.
No → Repair is complete.

CR1120100399000X

Fig. 27 Verification Test VER-3. Sebring Convertible, Sebring Sedan & Stratus Sedan

TEST	ACTION
8	**WARNING: WHEN THE ENGINE IS OPERATING, DO NOT STAND IN A DIRECT LINE WITH THE FAN. DO NOT PUT YOUR HANDS NEAR THE PULLEYS, BELTS OR FAN. DO NOT WEAR LOOSE CLOTHING.** **NOTE: The conditions that set the DTC are not present at this time. The following list may help in identifying the intermittent condition.** With the engine running at normal operating temperature, monitor the DRB parameters related to the DTC while wiggling the wiring harness. Look for parameter values to change and/or a DTC to set. Review the DRB Freeze Frame information. If possible, try to duplicate the conditions under which the DTC was set. Refer to any Technical Service Bulletins (TSB) that may apply. Visually inspect the related wiring harness. Look for any chafed, pierced, pinched, or partially broken wires. Visually inspect the related wiring harness connectors. Look for broken, bent, pushed out, or corroded terminals. Were any of the above conditions present? Yes → Repair as necessary Perform POWERTRAIN VERIFICATION TEST VER - 3. No → Test Complete.

CR1120100398030X

Fig. 26 Code P1682: Charging System Voltage Too Low (Part 3 of 3). Sebring Convertible, Sebring Sedan & Stratus Sedan

POWERTRAIN VERIFICATION TEST VER - 5
1. NOTE: If the PCM has been replaced and the correct VIN and mileage have not been programmed, a DTC will be set in the ABS Module, Airbag Module and the SKIM.
2. NOTE: If the vehicle is equipped with a Sentry Key Immobilizer System, Secret Key data must be updated. Refer to the Service Information for the PCM, SKIM and the Transponder (ignition key) for programming information.
3. Inspect the vehicle to ensure that all engine components are properly installed and connected. Reassemble and reconnect components as necessary.
4. Connect the DRBIII® to the data link connector.
5. Ensure the fuel tank has at least a quarter tank of fuel. Turn off all accessories.
6. If a Comprehensive Component DTC was repaired, perform steps 5 - 8. If a Major OBDII Monitor DTC was repaired skip those steps and continue verification.
7. After the ignition has been off for at least 10 seconds, restart the vehicle and run 2 minutes.
8. If the Good Trip counter changed to one or more and there are no new DTC's, the repair was successful and is now complete. Erase DTC's and disconnect the DRBIII®.
9. If the repaired DTC has reset, the repair is not complete. Check for any related TSB's or flash updates and return to the Symptom list.
10. If another DTC has set, return to the Symptom List and follow the path specified for that DTC.
11. With the DRBIII®, monitor the appropriate pre-test enabling conditions until all conditions have been met. Once the conditions have been met, switch screen to the appropriate OBDII monitor, (Audible beeps when the monitor is running).
12. If the monitor ran, and the Good Trip counter changed to one or more, the repair was successful and is now complete. Erase DTC's and disconnect the DRBIII®.
13. If the repaired OBDII trouble code has reset or was seen in the monitor while on the road test, the repair is not complete. Check for any related technical service bulletins or flash updates and return to Symptom List.
14. If another DTC has set, return to the Symptom List and follow the path specified for that DTC.
Are any DTCs present?
Yes → Repair is not complete, refer to appropriate symptom.
No → Repair is complete.

CR1120100400000X

Fig. 28 Verification Test VER-5. Sebring Convertible, Sebring Sedan & Stratus Sedan

ALTERNATOR SPECIFICATIONS

Model & Year	Engine	Type	Rated Output Amps
Concorde, Intrepid, LHS & 300M	2.7L	Nippondenso	105
	3.2L & 3.5L	Nippondenso	125
Magnum, 300 & 300C	2.7L, 3.5L & 5.7L	Nippondenso	—
Sebring Convertible, Sebring Sedan & Stratus Sedan	2.0L	Nippondenso	135
	2.4L	Nippondenso	135
	2.7L	Nippondenso	135

Mitsubishi

INDEX

APPLICATION CHART

Model	Year	Engine	Part No.
Neon	2001	2.0L	4794222AA
	2002–05	2.0L	4794222AC
	2004–05	2.4L	—
Sebring & Stratus Coupe	2001	2.4L	MD362870
		3.0L	MD362301
	2002–05	2.4L	MD362870
		3.0L	MD373093

PRECAUTIONS

Battery Ground Cable

Prior to service, disconnect battery ground cable and isolate as required.

Service

1. Ensure battery polarity is proper when servicing units. Reversed battery polarity will damage rectifiers and regulators.
2. If booster battery is used for starting, use proper polarity in hookup.
3. When a fast charger is used to charge a vehicle battery, vehicle battery cables should be disconnected unless fast charger is equipped with a special alternator protector, in which case vehicle battery cables need not be disconnected. Also, fast chargers should never be used to start a vehicle, as damage to rectifiers will result.
4. Lead connections to grounded rectifiers (negative) should never be soldered, as excessive heat may damage rectifiers.
5. Unless system includes a load relay or field relay, grounding alternator output terminal will damage alternator and/or circuits. This is true even when system is not in operation, since no circuit breaker is used and battery voltage is applied to alternator output terminal at all times. Field or load relay acts as a circuit breaker in that it is controlled by ignition switch.
6. Before making any in-vehicle tests of alternator or regulator, battery should be inspected and circuit inspected for faulty wiring or insulation, loose or corroded connections and poor ground circuits.
7. Inspect alternator belt tension to ensure belt is tight enough to prevent slipping under load.
8. To prevent system damage, turn ignition off before making any test connections.
9. Vehicle battery must be fully charged or a fully charged battery may be installed for test purposes.

GENERAL INFORMATION

The power source of the charging system is the alternator. Current is transmitted from the field terminal of the regulator through a slip ring to the field coil and back to ground through another slip ring. The strength of the field regulates the output of the alternating current. This alternating current is then transmitted from the alternator to the rectifier where it is converted to direct current.

These alternators employ a three-phase stator winding in which the phase windings are electrically 120° apart. The rotor consists of a field coil encased between interleaved sections producing a magnetic field with alternate north and south poles. By rotating the rotor inside the stator the alternating current is induced in the stator windings. This alternating current is rectified (changed to D.C.) by silicon diodes and brought out to the output terminal of the alternator.

Diode Rectifiers

Six or more silicon diode rectifiers are used and act as electrical one-way valves. One half of the diodes have ground polarity and are pressed or screwed into a heat sink which is grounded. The other diodes (ungrounded) are pressed or screwed into and

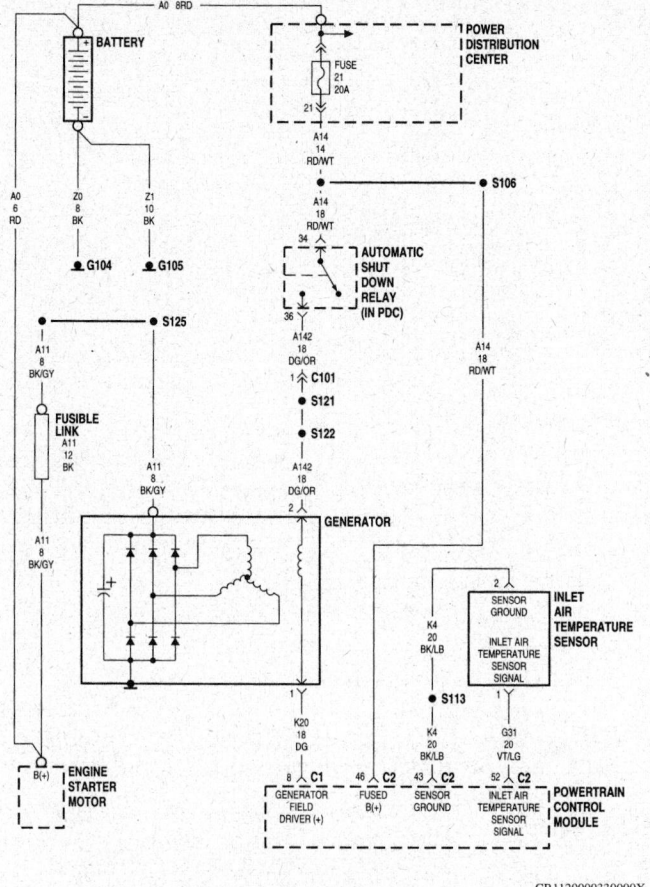

Fig. 1 Wiring diagram. 2001–02 Neon

CR1120000330000X

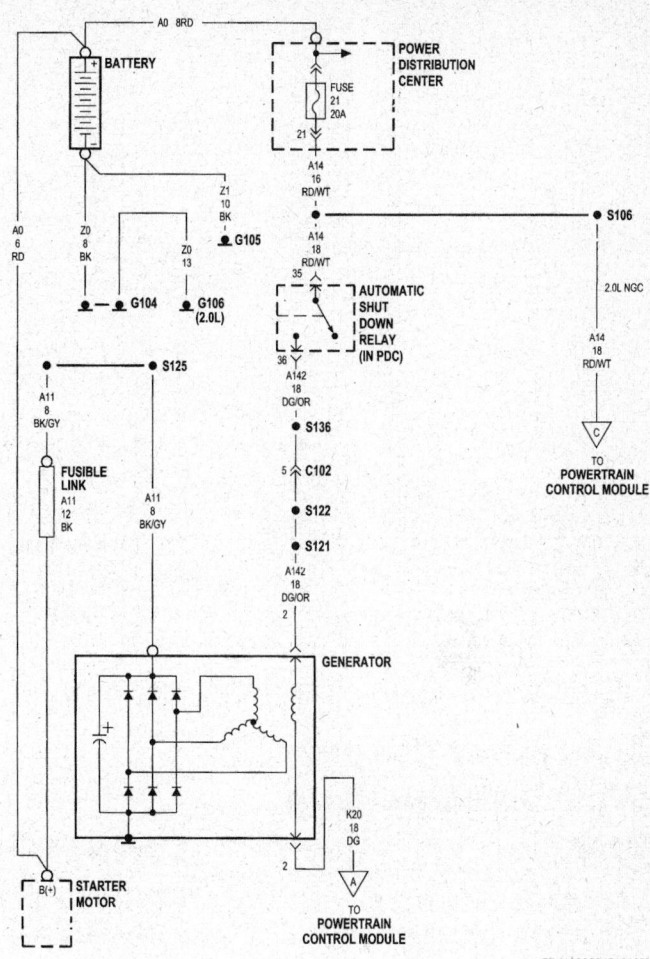

Fig. 2 Wiring diagram (Part 1 of 2). 2003–05 Neon

CR1120200471010X

insulated from the end head. These diodes are connected to the alternator output terminal.

Since the diodes have a high resistance to the flow of current in one direction and a low resistance in the opposite direction, they may be connected in a manner which allows current to flow from the alternator to the battery in the low resistance direction. The high resistance in the opposite direction prevents the flow of current from the battery to the alternator. Because of this feature, no circuit breaker is required between the alternator and battery.

Service Precautions

1. Ensure battery polarity is proper when servicing units. Reversed battery polarity will damage rectifiers and regulators.
2. If booster battery is used for starting, use proper polarity in hookup.
3. When a fast charger is used to charge a vehicle battery, vehicle battery cables should be disconnected unless fast charger is equipped with a special alternator protector, in which case vehicle battery cables need not be disconnected. Also, fast chargers should never be used to start a vehicle, as damage to rectifiers will result.

4. Lead connections to grounded rectifiers (negative) should never be soldered, as excessive heat may damage rectifiers.
5. Unless system includes a load relay or field relay, grounding alternator output terminal will damage alternator and/or circuits. This is true even when system is not in operation, since no circuit breaker is used and battery is applied to alternator output terminal at all times. Field or load relay acts as a circuit breaker in that it is controlled by ignition switch.
6. Before making any in-vehicle tests of alternator or regulator, battery should be inspected and circuit inspected for faulty wiring or insulation, loose or corroded connections and poor ground circuits.
7. Inspect alternator belt tension to ensure belt is tight enough to prevent slipping under load.
8. To prevent system damage, turn ignition off before making any test connections.
9. The vehicle battery must be fully charged or a fully charged battery may be installed for test purposes.

DESCRIPTION

On these units, the regulator is incorporated into the alternator rear housing. The electronic voltage regulator has the ability to vary regulated system voltage upward or downward as temperature changes. No voltage regulator adjustments are required on these units.

DIAGNOSIS & TESTING

Wiring Diagrams

Refer to **Figs. 1 through 7** for wiring diagrams when diagnosing the charging system.

Diagnostic Tests

NEON

2001

Refer to **Figs. 8 through 12** for diagnostic tests.

2002–05

Refer to **Figs. 13 through 20** for diagnostic tests.

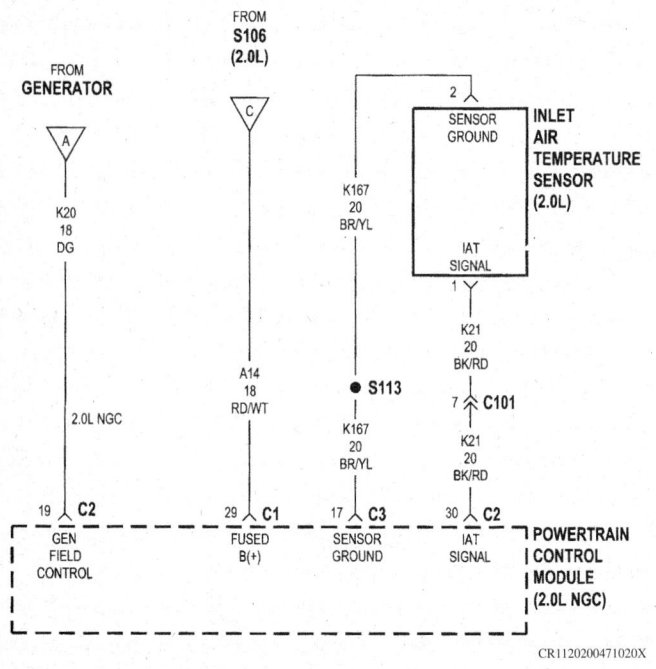

Fig. 2 Wiring diagram (Part 2 of 2). 2003–05 Neon

CR1120200471020X

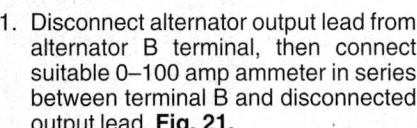

CR1120100387010X

Fig. 3 Wiring diagram (Part 1 of 2). 2001 Sebring Coupe & Stratus Coupe w/manual transmission

Alternator Output Wire Voltage Drop Test

SEBRING COUPE & STRATUS COUPE

1. Disconnect alternator output lead from alternator B terminal, then connect suitable 0–100 amp ammeter in series between terminal B and disconnected output lead, **Fig. 21**.
2. Connect suitable digital voltmeter between alternator B terminal and battery positive terminal.
3. Connect battery ground cable and leave hood open.
4. With engine running at approximately 2500 RPM, turn headlamps and other lamps on and off to adjust alternator load on ammeter to slightly more than 30 amps.
5. Decrease engine speed gradually until value displayed on ammeter is 30 amps and read voltmeter. Limit value should be .3 volts maximum.
6. If alternator output is high and value does not decrease to 30 amps, set value to 40 amps. Limit value should be .4 volts maximum.
7. If value is still more than limit value, a fault in alternator output wire may exist.
8. Inspect wiring between alternator B terminal and battery positive terminal, including fusible link.
9. If terminal is not sufficiently tight or if harness has become discolored because of overheating, repair and test again.

Current Output Test

SEBRING COUPE & STRATUS COUPE

1. Disconnect wire from alternator terminal B then connect suitable 0–100 amp ammeter in series between B terminal and disconnected output wire, **Fig. 22**.
2. Connect suitable 0–20 volt voltmeter between alternator and ground, noting the following:
3. Connect battery ground cable. Leave hood open.
4. Ensure voltmeter reading is equal to battery voltage. If voltage is 0 volts, cause is probably an open circuit in wire or fusible link between alternator B terminal and battery positive terminal.
5. Turn headlamps on at low beam, then start engine.
6. Turn headlamps to high beam, HVAC blower switch to High, increase engine speed to approximately 2500 RPM and record maximum current output. Limit should be 70% of nominal current output.
7. Reading should be more than limit value. If reading is below limit value and alternator output wire is in good condition, replace alternator.

Voltage Regulator Test

SEBRING COUPE & STRATUS COUPE

1. Connect suitable, digital voltmeter be-

tween alternator S terminal and ground using harness tool No. MB991519, or equivalent, **Fig. 23**.
2. Disconnect alternator output wire from alternator B terminal, then connect suitable 0–100 amp ammeter in series between B terminal and output wire.
3. Connect battery ground cable, then ensure all lamps and accessories are off.
4. Connect suitable tachometer and turn ignition On.
5. Ensure voltmeter reading is equal to battery positive voltage. If voltage is 0 volts, cause is probably an open circuit in wire or fusible link between alternator S terminal and battery positive terminal.
6. Ensure all lights and accessories are turned off.
7. Start engine and increase speed to approximately 2500 RPM.
8. Read voltmeter when current output by alternator becomes 10 amps or less.
9. If voltage reading is as specified voltage regulator is operating properly, **Fig. 24**.
10. If voltage is not within specification, voltage regulator or alternator fault exists.

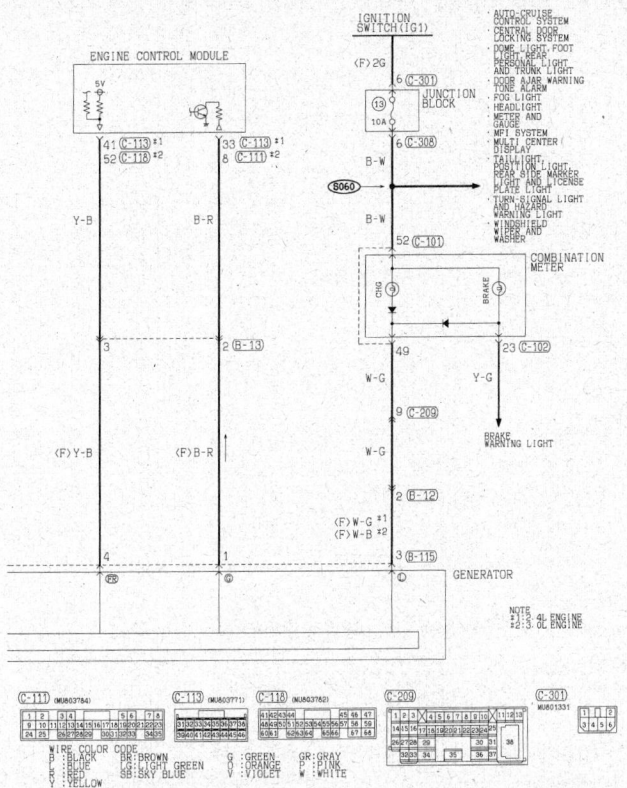

Fig. 3   Wiring diagram (Part 2 of 2). 2001 Sebring Coupe & Stratus Coupe w/manual transmission

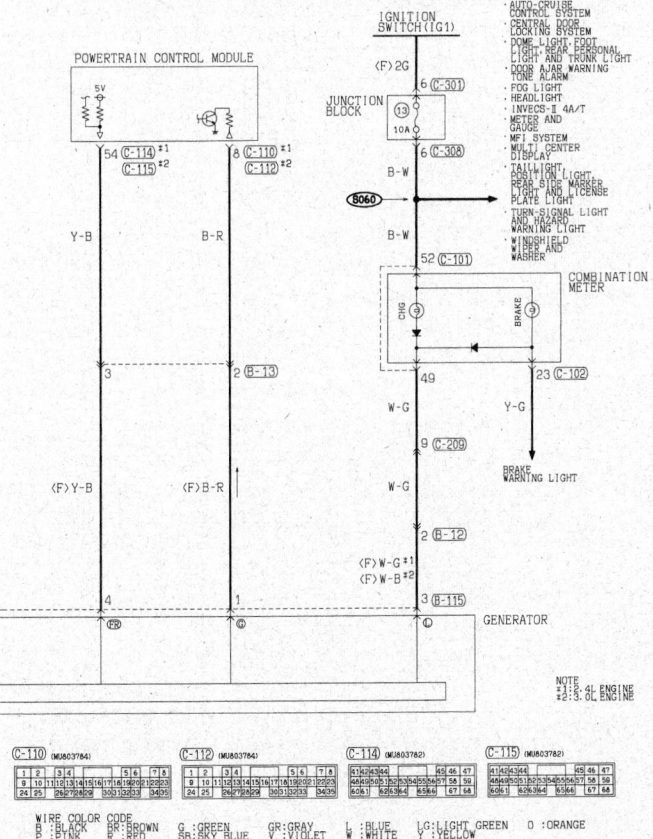

Fig. 4   Wiring diagram (Part 2 of 2). 2001 Sebring Coupe & Stratus Coupe w/automatic transmission

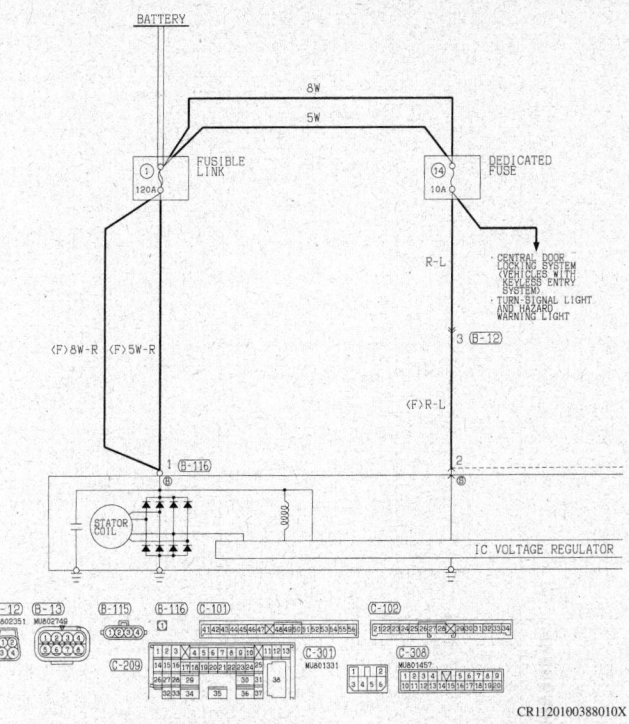

Fig. 4   Wiring diagram (Part 1 of 2). 2001 Sebring Coupe & Stratus Coupe w/automatic transmission

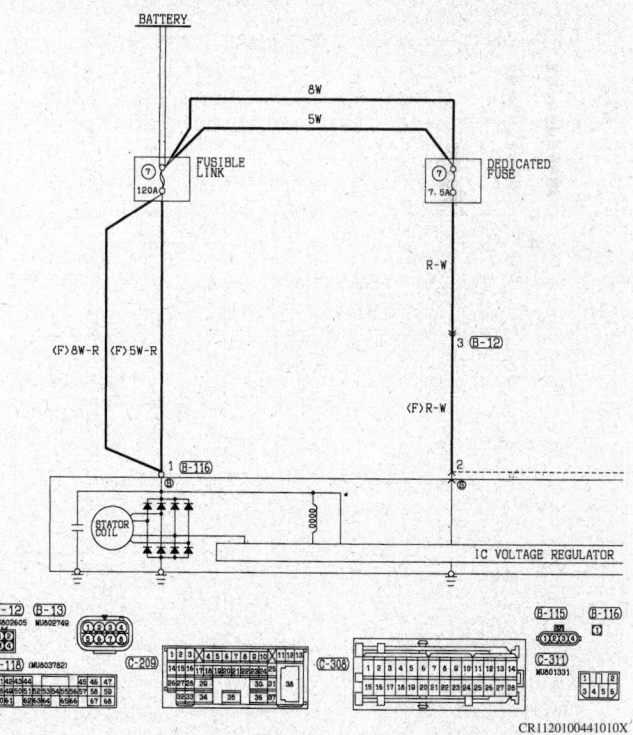

Fig. 5   Wiring diagram (Part 1 of 4). 2002 Sebring Coupe & Stratus Coupe w/manual transmission

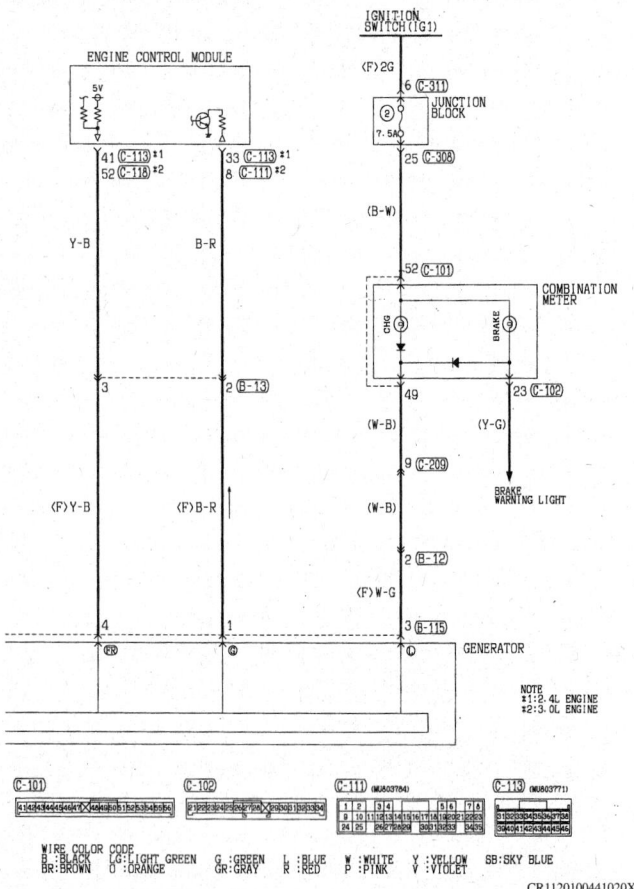

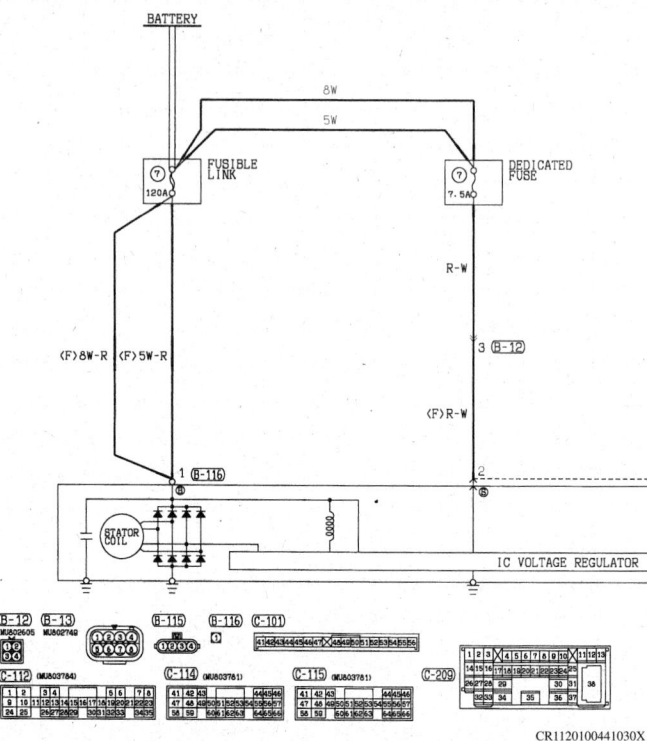

Fig. 5   Wiring diagram (Part 3 of 4). 2002 Sebring Coupe & Stratus Coupe w/automatic transmission

Fig. 5   Wiring diagram (Part 2 of 4). 2002 Sebring Coupe & Stratus Coupe w/manual transmission

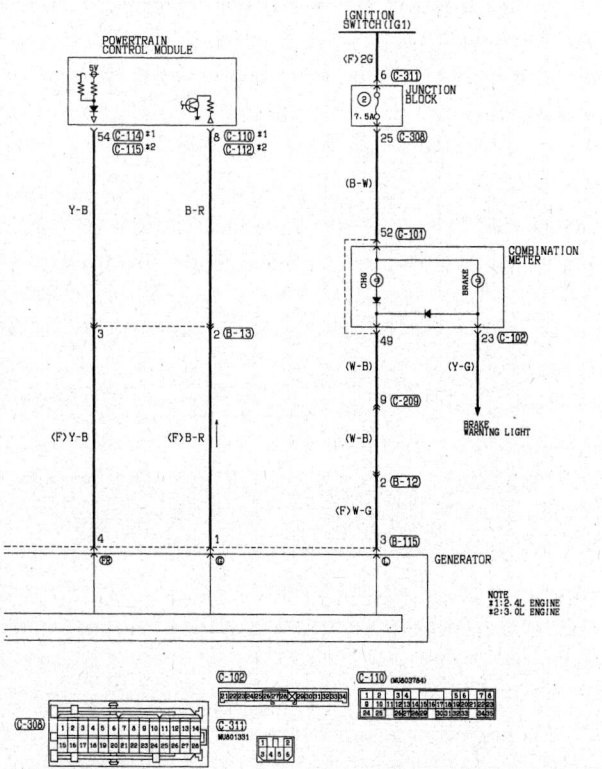

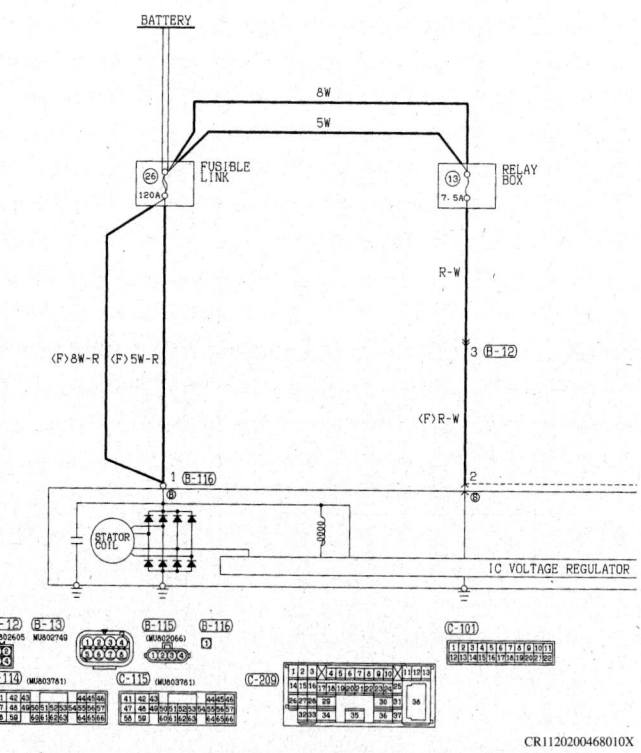

Fig. 6   Wiring diagram (Part 1 of 2). 2003–05 Sebring Coupe & Stratus Coupe w/automatic transmission

Fig. 5   Wiring diagram (Part 4 of 4). 2002 Sebring Coupe & Stratus Coupe w/automatic transmission

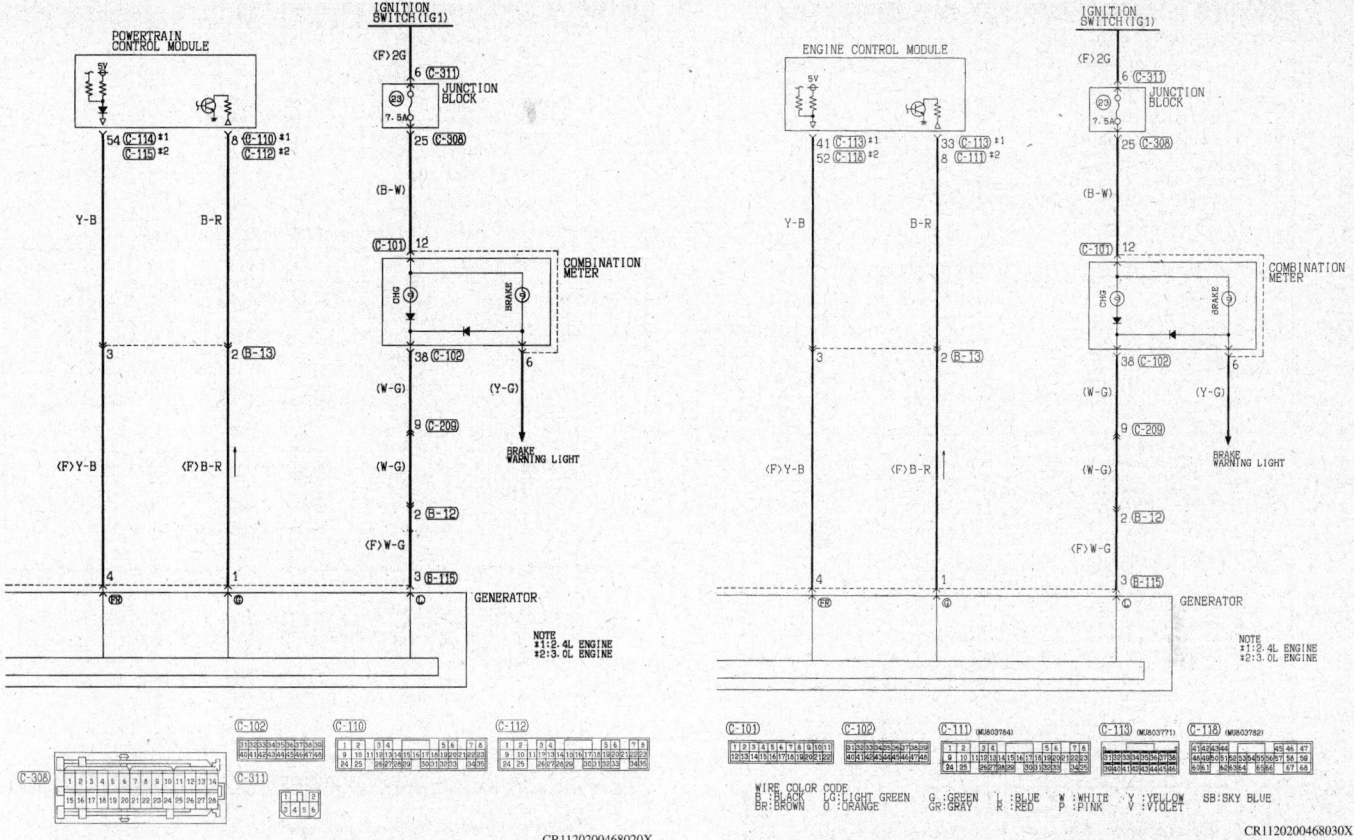

Fig. 6   Wiring diagram (Part 2 of 2). 2003–05 Sebring Coupe & Stratus Coupe w/automatic transmission

Fig. 7   Wiring diagram. 2003–05 Sebring Coupe & Stratus Coupe w/manual transmission

DIAGNOSTIC CHART INDEX

Code/Test	Description	Page No.	Fig No.
2001 NEON			
—	Charging System Diagnosis w/No Code	10-25	11
—	Verification Test VER-3A	10-26	12
P0622	Alternator Field Not Switching Properly	10-24	8
P1594	Charging System Voltage Too High	10-24	9
P1682	Charging System Voltage Too Low	10-25	10
2002–05 NEON			
—	Verification Test VER-3	10-30	20
P0562	Charging System Voltage Too Low	10-26	13
P0563	Charging System Voltage Too High	10-27	14
P0622	Alternator Field Not Switching Properly	10-27	15
P0625	Alternator Field Control Circuit Low	10-28	16
P0626	Alternator Field Control High. 2002–05	10-28	17
P1594	Charging System Voltage Too High	10-29	18
P1682	Charging System Voltage Too Low	10-29	19

TEST	ACTION
1	Ignition On, Engine Not Running With the DRB actuate the Generator Field Driver Circuit. Using a 12-volt test light, backprobe the Gen Field Driver Circuit at the back of the Generator. Did the light blink? Yes → Go To 2 No → Go To 4
2	Ignition On, Engine Not Running With the DRB actuate the Generator Field Driver Circuit. **Note: Actuator Test should still be running.** Wiggle Wiring Harness from the Generator to PCM. With the DRB, read Codes. Does the Generator Field Driver (-) Circuit code return? Yes → Repair as necessary where wiggling caused problem to appear. Perform Powertrain Verification Test VER-3A. No → Go To 3
3	Turn ignition off. Using the schematic as a guide, inspect the Wiring and Connectors. Were any problems found? Yes → Repair as necessary. Perform Powertrain Verification Test VER-3A. No → Test Complete.
4	Ignition On, Engine Not Running Record all DTC's and freeze frame data, now erase Codes. Carefully inspect all Connectors for corrosion or spread Terminals before continuing. With the DRB actuate the Generator Field Driver Circuit. Backprobe the ASD Relay Output Circuit at back of Generator. Is the voltage above 10.0 volts? Yes → Go To 5 No → Repair the open ASD Relay Output Circuit. Perform Powertrain Verification Test VER-3A.
5	Turn ignition off. Disconnect the PCM Connectors. **Note: Check connectors - Clean/repair as necessary.** Disconnect the generator field connector. **Note: Check Connectors - Clean/repair as necessary.** Using an Ohmmeter, measure the Generator Field Driver Circuit from PCM Connector to ground. Is the resistance below 5.0 ohms? Yes → Repair the Generator Field Driver Circuit shorted to ground. Perform Powertrain Verification Test VER-3A. No → Go To 6

CR1120000331010X

Fig. 8 Code P0622: Alternator Field Not Switching Properly (Part 1 of 2). 2001 Neon

TEST	ACTION
9	Ignition On, Engine Not Running With DRB, actuate the Generator Field Driver. With a 12-volt test light, backprobe the Generator Field Driver Circuit in back of Generator. Did the light blink? Yes → Go To 10 No → Go To 13
10	Ignition On, Engine Not Running With the DRB, actuate the Generator Field Driver. With DRB, stop the Generator Field Driver actuation. With DRB, read the Target Charging voltage. Is the Target Charging voltage above 13 volts? Yes → Go To 11 No → Go To 12
11	Start the engine. Manually set the engine speed to 1600 RPM. With DRB, read both the Battery voltage and the Target Charging voltage. Compare the "Target Voltage" to the "Battery Voltage" reading. Monitor voltage for 5 minutes, if necessary. Look for a 1.0 volt difference or more. Was there more than a 1.0 volt difference? Yes → Replace the Powertrain Control Module. Perform Powertrain Verification Test VER-3A. No → Test Complete.
12	Turn ignition off. **Note: Battery must be fully charged.** **Note: Generator Belt tension and condition must be checked before continuing.** Start engine and allow it to reach operating temperature. With the DRB, read the BTS temperature. Using a Thermometer, measure under hood temperature. Is the temperature within 10 F degrees of Battery temperature? Yes → Test Complete. No → Replace Powertrain Control Module. Perform Powertrain Verification Test VER-3A.
13	Turn ignition off. Disconnect the PCM Connectors. **Note: Check connectors - Clean/repair as necessary.** Disconnect the generator field connector. **Note: Check Connectors - Clean/repair as necessary.** Using an Ohmmeter, measure the Generator Field Driver Circuit from PCM Connector to ground. Is the resistance below 5.0 ohms? Yes → Repair the Generator Field Driver Circuit shorted to ground. Perform Powertrain Verification Test VER-3A. No → Go To 14

CR1120000332010X

Fig. 9 Code P1594: Charging System Voltage Too High (Part 1 of 2). 2001 Neon

TEST	ACTION
6	Turn ignition off. Disconnect the PCM Connectors. Disconnect the generator field connector. **Note: Check Connectors - Clean/repair as necessary.** Using an Ohmmeter, measure the Generator Field Driver Circuit from PCM to Generator. Is the resistance below 5.0 ohms? Yes → Go To 7 No → Repair the open Generator Field Driver Circuit. Perform Powertrain Verification Test VER-3A.
7	Turn ignition off. Disconnect the Gen Field Harness Connector at back of the Generator. **Note: Check connectors - Clean/repair as necessary.** Use an Ohmmeter in the following steps. Measure resistance across the Generator Field Terminals at the Generator. Is the resistance below 5.0 ohms? Yes → Repair the Generator as necessary. Perform Powertrain Verification Test VER-3A. No → Go To 8
8	If there are no potential causes remaining, the PCM is assumed to be defective. View repair options. Repair Replace the Powertrain Control Module. Perform Powertrain Verification Test VER-3A.

CR1120000331020X

Fig. 8 Code P0622: Alternator Field Not Switching Properly (Part 2 of 2). 2001 Neon

TEST	ACTION
14	Turn ignition off. Disconnect the Field Harness Connector at back of the Generator. **Note: Check connectors - Clean/repair as necessary.** Measure resistance of the Generator Field Driver Circuit at the Generator to Ground. Is the resistance below 5.0 ohms? Yes → Repair or replace the shorted Generator as necessary. Perform Powertrain Verification Test VER-3A. No → Go To 15
15	If there are no potential causes remaining, the Powertrain Control Module is assumed to be defective. View repair options. Repair Replace the Powertrain Control Module. Perform Powertrain Verification Test VER-3A.

CR1120000332020X

Fig. 9 Code P1594: Charging System Voltage Too High (Part 2 of 2). 2001 Neon

TEST	ACTION

16	Turn Ignition Off.
	Note: Battery must be fully charged.
	Note: Generator Belt tension and condition must be checked before continuing.
	Start Engine.
	With the DRB, read the target charging voltage.
	Is the target charging voltage above 15.1 volts?
	
	    Yes → Go To 17
	
	    No → Go To 18

17	Turn ignition off.
	Note: Battery must be fully charged.
	Note: Generator Belt tension and condition must be checked before continuing.
	Start engine and allow it to reach operating temperature.
	With the DRB, read the BTS temperature.
	Using a Thermometer, measure under hood temperature.
	Is the temperature within 10 F degrees of Battery temperature?
	
	    Yes → Go To 18
	
	    No → Replace the PCM.
	        Perform Powertrain Verification Test VER-3A.

18	Turn ignition on, engine not running.
	Using a Voltmeter, measure voltage between the Generator B(+) Terminal and the Battery (+) Post.
	Caution: Ensure all wires are clear of the engine's moving parts.
	Start engine.
	Is the voltage above 0.4 volt?
	
	    Yes → Repair the B(+) Circuit for high resistance between the Generator and Battery.
	        Perform Powertrain Verification Test VER-3A.
	
	    No → Go To 19

19	Start engine.
	Warm the engine to operating temperature.
	Caution: Ensure all wires are clear of the engine's moving parts.
	Using a Voltmeter, measure voltage between the Generator case and Battery (-) Post.
	Is the voltage above 0.1 volt?
	
	    Yes → Repair Generator Ground for high resistance, Generator Case to Battery (-) side.
	        Perform Powertrain Verification Test VER-3A.
	
	    No → Go To 20

20	Start engine.
	Turn on all accessories, manually set engine speed to 1600 RPM.
	With DRB, read Target Charging and Charging voltage.
	Compare the two readings.
	Is there more than a 1.0 volt difference?
	
	    Yes → Go To 21
	
	    No → Test Complete.

CR1120000333010X

Fig. 10 Code P1682: Charging System Voltage Too Low (Part 1 of 3). 2001 Neon

TEST	ACTION

26	If there are no potential causes remaining, the PCM is assumed to be defective.
	View repair options.
	
	    Repair
	        Replace the Powertrain Control Module.
	        Perform Powertrain Verification Test VER-3A.

CR1120000333030X

Fig. 10 Code P1682: Charging System Voltage Too Low (Part 3 of 3). 2001 Neon

TEST	ACTION

21	Ignition On, Engine Not Running
	With the DRB, actuate the Generator Field.
	Using a Voltmeter, measure the voltage at both Generator Field Terminals.
	Is the voltage below 3.0 volts at either Terminal?
	
	    Yes → Go To 22
	
	    No → Test Complete.

22	Ignition On, Engine Not Running
	Record all DTC's and freeze frame data, now erase Codes.
	Carefully inspect all Connectors for corrosion or spread Terminals before continuing.
	With the DRB actuate the Generator Field Driver Circuit.
	Backprobe the ASD Relay Output Circuit at back of Generator.
	Is the voltage above 10.0 volts?
	
	    Yes → Go To 23
	
	    No → Repair the open ASD Relay Output Circuit.
	        Perform Powertrain Verification Test VER-3A.

23	Turn ignition off.
	Disconnect the PCM Connectors.
	Note: Check connectors - Clean/repair as necessary.
	Disconnect the generator field connector.
	Note: Check Connectors - Clean/repair as necessary.
	Using an Ohmmeter, measure the Generator Field Driver Circuit from PCM Connector to ground.
	Is the resistance below 5.0 ohms?
	
	    Yes → Repair the Generator Field Driver Circuit shorted to ground.
	        Perform Powertrain Verification Test VER-3A.
	
	    No → Go To 24

24	Turn ignition off.
	Disconnect ASD Relay Connector.
	Note: Check connectors - Clean/repair as necessary.
	Disconnect the generator field connector.
	Note: Check Connectors - Clean/repair as necessary.
	Using an Ohmmeter, measure the ASD Relay Output Circuit from ASD Relay Connector to ground.
	Is the resistance below 5.0 ohms?
	
	    Yes → Repair the ASD Relay Output Circuit shorted to ground.
	        Perform Powertrain Verification Test VER-3A.
	
	    No → Go To 25

25	Turn ignition off.
	Disconnect the PCM Connectors.
	Disconnect the generator field connector.
	Note: Check Connectors - Clean/repair as necessary.
	Using an Ohmmeter, measure the Generator Field Driver Circuit from PCM to Generator.
	Is the resistance below 5.0 ohms?
	
	    Yes → Go To 26
	
	    No → Repair the open Generator Field Driver Circuit.
	        Perform Powertrain Verification Test VER-3A.

CR1120000333020X

Fig. 10 Code P1682: Charging System Voltage Too Low (Part 2 of 3). 2001 Neon

TEST	ACTION

27	Turn ignition off.
	Note: Battery condition must be verified prior to this test.
	Inspect the Generator Belt tension and condition.
	Is the Generator Belt OK?
	
	    Yes → Go To 28
	
	    No → Repair as necessary.
	        Perform Powertrain Verification Test VER-3A.

28	Start the Engine.
	Turn on all accessories.
	Raise engine speed to 2000 RPM for 30 seconds then return to idle.
	With the DRB III read DTC's.
	Are there any "Charging System" Trouble Codes?
	
	    Yes → Refer to Symptom list for problems related to Charging.
	        Perform Powertrain Verification Test VER-3A.
	
	    No → Go To 29

29	Ignition On, Engine Not Running
	With the DRB, actuate the Generator Field.
	Using a 12-volt test light, backprobe the Generator Field Driver Terminal at the back of the Generator.
	Note: The test light should blink On and Off every 1.4 seconds.
	While monitoring the 12-volt test light, wiggle the Field Terminals back to the PCM and ASD Relay.
	Was there any interruption in the normal cycle of the test light?
	
	    Yes → Repair the wire where wiggling interrupted the voltage cycle.
	        Perform Powertrain Verification Test VER-3A.
	
	    No → Go To 30

30	Ignition On, Engine Not Running
	With the DRB, read trouble codes.
	Are there any "Charging System" trouble codes?
	
	    Yes → Refer to Symptom list for problems related to Charging.
	        Perform Powertrain Verification Test VER-3A.
	
	    No → Go To 31

31	Turn ignition on, engine not running.
	Using a Voltmeter, measure voltage between the Generator B(+) Terminal and the Battery (+) Post.
	Caution: Ensure all wires are clear of the engine's moving parts.
	Start engine.
	Is the voltage above 0.4 volt?
	
	    Yes → Repair the B(+) Circuit for high resistance between the Generator and Battery.
	        Perform Powertrain Verification Test VER-3A.
	
	    No → Go To 32

CR1120000334010X

Fig. 11 Charging System Diagnosis w/No Code (Part 1 of 2). 2001 Neon

TEST	ACTION
32	Start engine. Warm the engine to operating temperature. **Caution: Ensure all wires are clear of the engine's moving parts.** Using a Voltmeter, measure voltage between the Generator case and Battery (-) Post. Is the voltage above 0.1 volt? Yes → Repair Generator Ground for high resistance, Generator Case to Battery (-) side. Perform Powertrain Verification Test VER-3A. No → Go To 33
33	Ignition On, Engine Not Running. With the DRB, read the Battery voltage and record the results. Using a Voltmeter, measure Battery voltage B(+) to B(-) Terminal and record the results. Compare the two voltage readings. Is the voltage difference less than one volt? Yes → Test Complete. No → Go To 34
34	Ignition On, Engine Not Running With the DRB, read the Battery voltage and record the results. Turn Ignition off. Disconnect the PCM. **Note: Check connectors - Clean/repair as necessary.** Turn Ignition on, with the engine off. Using a Voltmeter, measure the Fused B(+) at PCM Connector. Is the voltage within one volt of the DRB recorded reading? Yes → Go To 35 No → Repair the B(+) Circuit for high resistance between the PCM and the Battery. Perform Powertrain Verification Test VER-3A.
35	If there are no potential causes remaining, the PCM is assumed to be defective. View repair options. Repair Replace the PCM. Perform Powertrain Verification Test VER-3A.

CR1120000334020X

Fig. 11   Charging System Diagnosis w/No Code (Part 2 of 2). 2001 Neon

VERIFICATION TEST VER-3A
1. Inspect the vehicle to ensure that all engine components are properly installed and connected. Reassemble and reconnect components as necessary. 2. Connect the DRB to the Data Link Connector and erase the codes. 3. If the PCM has been replaced perform steps 4 through 6 then continue the verification. 4. If PCM has been changed and correct VIN and mileage have not been programmed, a DTC will be set in ABS and Air bag modules. In addition, if vehicle is equipped with a Sentry Key Immobilizer Module (SKIM), Secret Key data must be updated to enable start. 5. For ABS and Air Bag systems: Enter correct VIN and Mileage in PCM. Erase codes in ABS and Air Bag modules. 6. For SKIM theft alarm: Connect DRB to data link conn. Go to Theft Alarm, SKIM, Misc. and place SKIM in secured access mode, by using the appropriate PIN code for this vehicle. Select Update the Secret Key data. Data will be transferred from SKIM to PCM. 7. Ensure no other charging system problems remain by doing the following: Start the engine. Perform generator output per service manual. 8. Raise the engine speed to 2000 rpm for at least 30 seconds. 9. Allow the engine to idle. 10. Turn the engine off. 11. Turn the ignition key on. 12. With the DRB, read trouble code messages. 13. If repaired code has reset, or any other one has set, check all pertinent Technical Service Bulletins and return to Symptom List if necessary. 14. If there are no codes, the repair is now complete.

CR1120000335000X

Fig. 12   Verification Test VER-3A. 2001 Neon

When Monitored: With the engine running for more than 30 seconds.

Set Condition: When battery voltage is less than 11.5 volts for more than 5 seconds.

POSSIBLE CAUSES
B+ CIRCUIT HIGH RESISTANCE
GENERATOR GROUND HIGH RESISTANCE
INTERMITTENT CONDITION
GENERATOR FIELD DRIVER CIRCUIT OPEN
ASD RELAY OUTPUT CIRCUIT OPEN
GENERATOR

TEST	ACTION
1	**NOTE: Inspect the vehicle for aftermarket accessories that may exceed the Generator System output.** Turn the ignition off. **NOTE: Verify that the battery is fully charged and capable of passing a load test before continuing.** **NOTE: The Generator belt tension and condition must be checked before continuing.** Start the engine. Allow the idle to stabilize. With the DRBIII®, read the Target Charging Voltage. Is the Target Charging Voltage above .15.1 volts? Yes → Go To 7 No → Go To 2
2	**WARNING: WHEN THE ENGINE IS OPERATING, DO NOT STAND IN A DIRECT LINE WITH THE FAN. DO NOT PUT YOUR HANDS NEAR THE PULLEYS, BELTS OR FAN. DO NOT WEAR LOOSE CLOTHING.** Turn the ignition on. **NOTE: Ensure all wires are clear of the engine's moving parts.** Measure the voltage between the Generator B+ Terminal and the Battery+ Post. Start the engine. Is the voltage above 0.4 volt? Yes → Repair the B+ circuit for high resistance between the Generator and Battery. Perform POWERTRAIN VERIFICATION TEST VER - 3. No → Go To 3

CR1120100434010X

Fig. 13   Code P0562: Charging System Voltage Too Low (Part 1 of 3). 2002–05 Neon

TEST	ACTION
3	**WARNING: WHEN THE ENGINE IS OPERATING, DO NOT STAND IN A DIRECT LINE WITH THE FAN. DO NOT PUT YOUR HANDS NEAR THE PULLEYS, BELTS OR FAN. DO NOT WEAR LOOSE CLOTHING.** Start the engine. Warm the engine to operating temperature. **NOTE: Ensure all wires are clear of the engine's moving parts.** Measure the voltage between the Generator case and Battery ground post. Is the voltage above 0.1 volt? Yes → Repair Generator Ground for high resistance, Generator Case to Battery ground side. Perform POWERTRAIN VERIFICATION TEST VER - 3. No → Go To 4
4	Start the engine. **WARNING: WHEN THE ENGINE IS OPERATING, DO NOT STAND IN A DIRECT LINE WITH THE FAN. DO NOT PUT YOUR HANDS NEAR THE PULLEYS, BELTS OR FAN. DO NOT WEAR LOOSE CLOTHING.** Turn on all accessories, manually set engine speed to 1600 RPM. With DRBIII®, read Target Charging and Charging voltage. Compare the two readings. Is there more than a 1.0 volt difference? Yes → Go To 5 No → Go To 7
5	Turn the ignition off. Disconnect the PCM harness connector. Disconnect the Generator Field harness connector. Measure the resistance of the Generator Field Driver circuit from the PCM harness connector to Generator harness connector. Is the resistance below 5.0 ohms? Yes → Go To 6 No → Repair the Generator Field Driver circuit for an open. Perform POWERTRAIN VERIFICATION TEST VER - 3.
6	Disconnect the Generator Field harness connector. Turn the ignition on. With the DRBIII® actuate the Generator Field Driver. Using a 12-volt test light connected to ground, probe the ASD Relay Output circuit in the Generator harness connector. Does the test light illuminate brightly? Yes → Repair or replace the Generator as necessary. Perform POWERTRAIN VERIFICATION TEST VER - 3. No → Repair the ASD Relay Output circuit. Perform POWERTRAIN VERIFICATION TEST VER - 3.

CR1120100434020X

Fig. 13   Code P0562: Charging System Voltage Too Low (Part 2 of 3). 2002–05 Neon

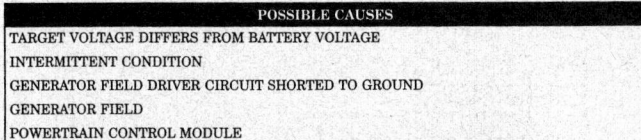

TEST	ACTION
7	**WARNING: WHEN THE ENGINE IS OPERATING, DO NOT STAND IN A DIRECT LINE WITH THE FAN. DO NOT PUT YOUR HANDS NEAR THE PULLEYS, BELTS OR FAN. DO NOT WEAR LOOSE CLOTHING.** **NOTE: The conditions that set the DTC are not present at this time. The following list may help in identifying the intermittent condition.** With the engine running at normal operating temperature, monitor the DRBIII® parameters related to the DTC while wiggling the wiring harness. Look for parameter values to change and/or a DTC to set. Review the DRBIII® Freeze Frame information. If possible, try to duplicate the conditions under which the DTC was set. Refer to any Technical Service Bulletins (TSB) that may apply. Visually inspect the related wiring harness. Look for any chafed, pierced, pinched, or partially broken wires. Visually inspect the related wiring harness connectors. Look for broken, bent, pushed out, or corroded terminals. Were any of the above conditions present? Yes → Repair as necessary. Perform POWERTRAIN VERIFICATION TEST VER - 3. No → Test Complete.

CR1120100434030X

Fig. 13 Code P0562: Charging System Voltage Too Low (Part 3 of 3). 2002–05 Neon

TEST	ACTION
3	Start the engine. With the DRBIII®, manually set the engine speed to 1600 RPM. With DRBIII®, read both the Battery voltage and the Target Charging voltage. Compare the Target Charging Voltage to the Battery Voltage reading. Monitor voltage for 5 minutes, if necessary. Look for a 1.0 volt difference or more. Was there more than a 1.0 volt difference? Yes → Replace the Powertrain Control Module in accordance with the Service Information. Perform POWERTRAIN VERIFICATION TEST VER - 3. No → Go To 4
4	**WARNING: WHEN THE ENGINE IS OPERATING, DO NOT STAND IN A DIRECT LINE WITH THE FAN. DO NOT PUT YOUR HANDS NEAR THE PULLEYS, BELTS OR FAN. DO NOT WEAR LOOSE CLOTHING.** **NOTE: The conditions that set the DTC are not present at this time. The following list may help in identifying the intermittent condition.** With the engine running at normal operating temperature, monitor the DRBIII® parameters related to the DTC while wiggling the wiring harness. Look for parameter values to change and/or a DTC to set. Review the DRBIII® Freeze Frame information. If possible, try to duplicate the conditions under which the DTC was set. Refer to any Technical Service Bulletins (TSB) that may apply. Visually inspect the related wiring harness. Look for any chafed, pierced, pinched, or partially broken wires. Visually inspect the related wiring harness connectors. Look for broken, bent, pushed out, or corroded terminals. Were any of the above conditions present? Yes → Repair as necessary. Perform POWERTRAIN VERIFICATION TEST VER - 3. No → Test Complete.
5	Turn the ignition off. Disconnect the PCM harness connector. Disconnect the Generator Field harness connector. Measure the resistance of the Generator Field Driver circuit from the PCM harness connector to ground. Is the resistance below 5.0 ohms? Yes → Repair the Generator Field Driver circuit shorted to ground. Perform POWERTRAIN VERIFICATION TEST VER - 3. No → Go To 6
6	Turn the ignition off. Disconnect the Generator Field harness connector. Measure resistance of the Generator Field Driver terminal pin to ground. Is the resistance below 5.0 ohms? Yes → Repair or replace the shorted Generator as necessary. Perform POWERTRAIN VERIFICATION TEST VER - 3. No → Replace and program the Powertrain Control Module in accordance with the Service Information. Perform POWERTRAIN VERIFICATION TEST VER - 3.

CR1120100435020X

Fig. 14 Code P0563: Charging System Voltage Too High (Part 2 of 2). 2002–05 Neon

When Monitored: With the engine running for more than 30 seconds.

Set Condition: When battery voltage is greater than 1 volt over target voltage for more than 5 seconds.

POSSIBLE CAUSES
TARGET VOLTAGE DIFFERS FROM BATTERY VOLTAGE
INTERMITTENT CONDITION
GENERATOR FIELD DRIVER CIRCUIT SHORTED TO GROUND
GENERATOR FIELD
POWERTRAIN CONTROL MODULE

TEST	ACTION
1	**NOTE: Verify that the battery is fully charged and capable of pass a load test before continuing.** **Note: Generator Belt tension and condition must be checked before continuing.** Turn the ignition on. With DRBIII®, actuate the Generator Field Driver. With a 12-volt test light connected to ground, backprobe the Generator Field Driver circuit in the back of Generator Field harness connector. Does the test light illuminate brightly and flash? Yes → Go To 2 No → Go To 5
2	With DRBIII®, stop all actuation. Turn the ignition on. With DRBIII®, read the Target Charging voltage. Is the Target Charging voltage above 13.0 volts? Yes → Go To 3 No → Go To 4

CR1120100435010X

Fig. 14 Code P0563: Charging System Voltage Too High (Part 1 of 2). 2002–05 Neon

When Monitored: With the ignition on. Engine running.

Set Condition: When the PCM tries to regulate the generator field with no result during monitoring.

POSSIBLE CAUSES
WIRING HARNESS INTERMITTENT
INSPECT WIRING HARNESS
ASD RELAY OUTPUT CIRCUIT OPEN
GENERATOR FIELD DRIVER CIRCUIT SHORTED TO GROUND
GENERATOR FIELD DRIVER CIRCUIT OPEN
GENERATOR FIELD COIL OPEN
GENERATOR FIELD COIL SHORTED
POWERTRAIN CONTROL MODULE

TEST	ACTION
1	Turn the ignition on. With the DRBIII®, actuate the Generator Field Driver circuit. Using a 12-volt test light connected to ground, backprobe the Generator Field Driver circuit in the back of the Generator. Does the test light illuminate brightly and flash? Yes → Go To 2 No → Go To 4
2	Turn the ignition on. With the DRBIII® actuate the Generator Field Driver circuit. Wiggle the wiring harness from the Generator to PCM. With the DRBIII®, read DTC's. Did the DTC reset? Yes → Repair as necessary. Perform POWERTRAIN VERIFICATION TEST VER - 3. No → Go To 3
3	Turn the ignition off. Using the schematic as a guide, inspect the Wiring and Connectors. Were any problems found? Yes → Repair as necessary. Perform POWERTRAIN VERIFICATION TEST VER - 3. No → Test Complete.

CR1120100436010X

Fig. 15 Code P0622: Alternator Field Not Switching Properly (Part 1 of 2). 2002–05 Neon

TEST	ACTION
4	**NOTE: Carefully inspect all Connectors for corrosion or spread Terminals before continuing.** Disconnect the Generator Field harness connector. Turn the ignition on. With the DRBIII® actuate the Generator Field Driver circuit. Using a 12-volt test light connected to ground, probe the ASD Relay Output circuit. Does the test light illuminate brightly? Yes → Go To 5 No → Repair the ASD Relay Output circuit. Perform POWERTRAIN VERIFICATION TEST VER - 3.
5	Turn the ignition off. Disconnect the PCM harness connector. Disconnect the Generator Field harness connector. Measure the resistance of the Generator Field Driver circuit from PCM harness connector to ground. Is the resistance below 100 ohms? Yes → Repair the Generator Field Driver circuit for a shorted to ground. Perform POWERTRAIN VERIFICATION TEST VER - 3. No → Go To 6
6	Turn the ignition off. Disconnect the PCM harness connector. Disconnect the Generator Field harness connector. Measure the resistance of the Generator Field Driver circuit from the PCM harness connector to the Generator Field harness connector. Is the resistance below 5.0 ohms? Yes → Go To 7 No → Repair the Generator Field Driver circuit for an open. Perform POWERTRAIN VERIFICATION TEST VER - 3.
7	Turn the ignition off. Disconnect the Generator Field harness connector. Measure the resistance across the Generator Field Terminals at the Generator. Is the resistance above 15.0 ohms? Yes → Replace the Generator. Perform POWERTRAIN VERIFICATION TEST VER - 3. No → Go To 8
8	Turn the ignition off. Disconnect the Generator Field harness connector. Measure the resistance across the Generator Field Terminals at the Generator. Is the resistance below 0.5 ohms? Yes → Replace the Generator. Perform POWERTRAIN VERIFICATION TEST VER - 3. No → Go To 9
9	If there is no more possible causes remaining, view repair. Repair Replace and program the Powertrain Control Module in accordance with the Service Information. Perform POWERTRAIN VERIFICATION TEST VER - 3.

CR1120100436020X

Fig. 15 Code P0622: Alternator Field Not Switching Properly (Part 2 of 2). 2002–05 Neon

TEST	ACTION
3	Turn the ignition off. Disconnect the PCM harness connector. Disconnect the Generator Field harness connector. Measure the resistance of the Generator Field Driver circuit from PCM harness connector to ground. Is the resistance below 5.0 ohms? Yes → Repair the Generator Field Driver circuit for a shorted to ground. Perform POWERTRAIN VERIFICATION TEST VER - 3. No → Go To 4
4	Turn the ignition off. Disconnect the Generator Field harness connector. Measure resistance of the Generator Field Driver terminal on the Generator to ground. Is the resistance below 5.0 ohms? Yes → Repair or replace the shorted Generator as necessary. Perform POWERTRAIN VERIFICATION TEST VER - 3. No → Go To 5
5	Turn the ignition off. Disconnect the PCM harness connector. Disconnect the Generator Field harness connector. Measure the resistance of the Generator Field Driver circuit from the PCM harness connector to the Generator Field harness connector. Is the resistance below 5.0 ohms? Yes → Go To 6 No → Repair the Generator Field Driver circuit for an open. Perform POWERTRAIN VERIFICATION TEST VER - 3.
6	Turn the ignition off. Disconnect the Generator Field harness connector. Measure the resistance across the Generator Field Terminals at the Generator. Is the resistance above 15.0 ohms? Yes → Replace the Generator. Perform POWERTRAIN VERIFICATION TEST VER - 3. No → Go To 7
7	If there is no more possible causes remaining, view repair. Repair Replace and program the Powertrain Control Module in accordance with the Service Information. Perform POWERTRAIN VERIFICATION TEST VER - 3.

CR1120100437020X

Fig. 16 Code P0625: Alternator Field Control Circuit Low (Part 2 of 2). 2002–05 Neon

When Monitored: With the engine running for more than 25 seconds.

Set Condition: When the Generator Field Circuit is open or shorted to ground.

POSSIBLE CAUSES
WIRING HARNESS INTERMITTENT
GENERATOR FIELD DRIVER CIRCUIT SHORTED TO GROUND
GENERATOR FIELD
GENERATOR FIELD DRIVER CIRCUIT OPEN
GENERATOR FIELD COIL OPEN
POWERTRAIN CONTROL MODULE

TEST	ACTION
1	**NOTE: Verify that the battery is capable of passing a load test and is fully charged before continuing.** Turn the ignition on. With the DRBIII®, actuate the Generator Field Driver circuit. Using a 12-volt test light connected to ground, backprobe the Generator Field Driver circuit in the back of the Generator. Does the test light illuminate brightly and flash? Yes → Go To 2 No → Go To 3
2	Turn the ignition off. Using a schematic as a guide, inspect the related Wiring and Connectors. Turn the ignition on, engine not running. With the DRBIII® actuate the Generator Field Driver circuit. Wiggle the wiring harness from the Generator to PCM. With the DRBIII®, read DTC's. Did the DTC reset? Yes → Repair as necessary. Perform POWERTRAIN VERIFICATION TEST VER - 3. No → Test Complete.

CR1120100437010X

Fig. 16 Code P0625: Alternator Field Control Circuit Low (Part 1 of 2). 2002–05 Neon

When Monitored: With the engine running for more than 25 seconds.

Set Condition: When the Generator Field circuit is shorted to B+.

POSSIBLE CAUSES
WIRING HARNESS INTERMITTENT
GENERATOR FIELD CKT SHORT TO VOLTAGE
POWERTRAIN CONTROL MODULE

TEST	ACTION
1	**NOTE: Verify that the battery is capable of passing a load test and is fully charged before continuing.** Turn the ignition on. With the DRBIII®, actuate the Generator Field Driver circuit. Using a 12-volt test light connected to ground, backprobe the Generator Field Driver circuit in the back of the Generator. Does the test light illuminate brightly and flash? Yes → Go To 2 No → Go To 3
2	Turn the ignition off. Using a schematic as a guide, inspect the related Wiring and Connectors. Turn the ignition on, engine not running. With the DRBIII® actuate the Generator Field Driver circuit. Wiggle the wiring harness from the Generator to PCM. With the DRBIII®, read DTC's. Did the DTC reset? Yes → Repair as necessary. Perform POWERTRAIN VERIFICATION TEST VER - 3. No → Test Complete.
3	Turn the ignition off. Disconnect PCM harness connector. Using a 12-volt test light connect to Ground (B-), backprobe the Generator Field circuit at the PCM harness connector. Does the test light illuminate brightly? Yes → Repair the Generator Field Driver circuit short to B+. Perform POWERTRAIN VERIFICATION TEST VER - 3. No → Replace and program the Powertrain Control Module in accordance with the Service Manual. Perform POWERTRAIN VERIFICATION TEST VER - 3.

CR1120100438000X

Fig. 17 Code P0626: Alternator Field Control High. 2002–05 Neon

When Monitored: The engine running. The engine speed greater than 380 RPM.

Set Condition: Battery voltage is 1 volt greater than desired system voltage.

POSSIBLE CAUSES
TARGET VOLTAGE DIFFERS FROM BATTERY VOLTAGE
INTERMITTENT CONDITION
GENERATOR FIELD DRIVER CIRCUIT SHORTED TO GROUND
GENERATOR FIELD
POWERTRAIN CONTROL MODULE

TEST	ACTION
1	**Note: Battery must be fully charged.** **Note: Generator Belt tension and condition must be checked before continuing.** Turn the ignition on. With DRBIII®, actuate the Generator Field Driver. With a 12-volt test light connected to ground, backprobe the Generator Field Driver circuit in the back of Generator Field harness connector. Does the test light illuminate brightly and flash? Yes → Go To 2 No → Go To 5
2	With DRBIII®, stop all actuation. Turn the ignition on. With DRBIII®, read the Target Charging voltage. Is the Target Charging voltage above 13.0 volts? Yes → Go To 3 No → Go To 4
3	Start the engine. With the DRBIII®, manually set the engine speed to 1600 RPM. With DRBIII®, read both the Battery voltage and the Target Charging voltage. Compare the Target Charging Voltage to the Battery Voltage reading. Monitor voltage for 5 minutes, if necessary. Look for a 1.0 volt difference or more. Was there more than a 1.0 volt difference? Yes → Replace the Powertrain Control Module in accordance with the Service Information. Perform POWERTRAIN VERIFICATION TEST VER - 3. No → Go To 4

CR1120100439010X

Fig. 18 Code P1594: Charging System Voltage Too High. (Part 1 of 2). 2002–05 Neon

When Monitored: With the ignition on. Engine RPM greater than 1152 RPM. With no other charging system codes set.

Set Condition: The battery sensed voltage is 1 volt below the charging goal for 13.47 seconds. The PCM senses the battery voltage, then turns off the field driver, and then senses the battery voltage again. If the voltages are the same, the code is set.

POSSIBLE CAUSES
B+ CIRCUIT HIGH RESISTANCE
GENERATOR GROUND HIGH RESISTANCE
INTERMITTENT CONDITION
GENERATOR FIELD DRIVER CIRCUIT OPEN
ASD RELAY OUTPUT CIRCUIT OPEN
GENERATOR

TEST	ACTION
1	NOTE: Inspect the vehicle for aftermarket accessories that may exceed the Generator System output. Turn the ignition off. NOTE: The battery must be fully charged. NOTE: The Generator belt tension and condition must be checked before continuing. Start the engine. Allow the idle to stabilize. With the DRBIII®, read the Target Charging Voltage. Is the Target Charging Voltage above 15.1 volts? Yes → Go To 7 No → Go To 2
2	WARNING: WHEN THE ENGINE IS OPERATING, DO NOT STAND IN A DIRECT LINE WITH THE FAN. DO NOT PUT YOUR HANDS NEAR THE PULLEYS, BELTS OR FAN. DO NOT WEAR LOOSE CLOTHING. Turn the ignition on. NOTE: Ensure all wires are clear of the engine's moving parts. Measure the voltage between the Generator B+ Terminal and the Battery+ Post. Start the engine. Is the voltage above 0.4 volt? Yes → Repair the B+ circuit for high resistance between the Generator and Battery. Perform POWERTRAIN VERIFICATION TEST VER - 3. No → Go To 3

CR1120100440010X

Fig. 19 Code P1682: Charging System Voltage Too Low (Part 1 of 3). 2002–05 Neon

TEST	ACTION
4	WARNING: WHEN THE ENGINE IS OPERATING, DO NOT STAND IN A DIRECT LINE WITH THE FAN. DO NOT PUT YOUR HANDS NEAR THE PULLEYS, BELTS AND FAN. DO NOT WEAR LOOSE CLOTHING. NOTE: The conditions that set the DTC are not present at this time. The following list may help in identifying the intermittent condition. With the engine running at normal operating temperature, monitor the DRBIII® parameters related to the DTC while wiggling the wiring harness. Look for parameter values to change and/or a DTC to set. Review the DRBIII® Freeze Frame information. If possible, try to duplicate the conditions under which the DTC was set. Refer to any Technical Service Bulletins (TSB) that may apply. Visually inspect the related wiring harness. Look for any chafed, pierced, pinched, or partially broken wires. Visually inspect the related wiring harness connectors. Look for broken, bent, pushed out, or corroded terminals. Were any of the above conditions present? Yes → Repair as necessary. Perform POWERTRAIN VERIFICATION TEST VER - 3. No → Test Complete.
5	Turn the ignition off. Disconnect the PCM harness connector. Disconnect the Generator Field harness connector. Measure the resistance of the Generator Field Driver circuit from the PCM harness connector to ground. Is the resistance below 5.0 ohms? Yes → Repair the Generator Field Driver circuit shorted to ground. Perform POWERTRAIN VERIFICATION TEST VER - 3. No → Go To 6
6	Turn the ignition off. Disconnect the Generator Field harness connector. Measure resistance of the Generator Field Driver terminal pin to ground. Is the resistance below 5.0 ohms? Yes → Repair or replace the shorted Generator as necessary. Perform POWERTRAIN VERIFICATION TEST VER - 3. No → Replace and program the Powertrain Control Module in accordance with the Service Information. Perform POWERTRAIN VERIFICATION TEST VER - 3.

CR1120100439020X

Fig. 18 Code P1594: Charging System Voltage Too High. (Part 2 of 2). 2002–05 Neon

TEST	ACTION
3	WARNING: WHEN THE ENGINE IS OPERATING, DO NOT STAND IN A DIRECT LINE WITH THE FAN. DO NOT PUT YOUR HANDS NEAR THE PULLEYS, BELTS OR FAN. DO NOT WEAR LOOSE CLOTHING. Start the engine. Warm the engine to operating temperature. NOTE: Ensure all wires are clear of the engine's moving parts. Measure the voltage between the Generator case and Battery ground post. Is the voltage above 0.1 volt? Yes → Repair Generator Ground for high resistance, Generator Case to Battery ground side. Perform POWERTRAIN VERIFICATION TEST VER - 3. No → Go To 4
4	Start the engine. WARNING: WHEN THE ENGINE IS OPERATING, DO NOT STAND IN A DIRECT LINE WITH THE FAN. DO NOT PUT YOUR HANDS NEAR THE PULLEYS, BELTS OR FAN. DO NOT WEAR LOOSE CLOTHING. Turn on all accessories, manually set engine speed to 1600 RPM. With DRBIII®, read Target Charging and Charging voltage. Compare the two readings. Is there more than a 1.0 volt difference? Yes → Go To 5 No → Go To 7
5	Turn the ignition off. Disconnect the PCM harness connector. Disconnect the Generator Field harness connector. Measure the resistance of the Generator Field Driver circuit from the PCM harness connector to Generator harness connector. Is the resistance below 5.0 ohms? Yes → Go To 6 No → Repair the Generator Field Driver circuit for an open. Perform POWERTRAIN VERIFICATION TEST VER - 3.
6	Disconnect the Generator Field harness connector. Turn the ignition on. With the DRBIII® actuate the Generator Field Driver. Using a 12-volt test light connected to ground, probe the ASD Relay Output circuit in the Generator harness connector. Does the test light illuminate brightly? Yes → Repair or replace the Generator as necessary. Perform POWERTRAIN VERIFICATION TEST VER - 3. No → Repair the ASD Relay Output circuit. Perform POWERTRAIN VERIFICATION TEST VER - 3.

CR1120100440020X

Fig. 19 Code P1682: Charging System Voltage Too Low (Part 2 of 3). 2002–05 Neon

TEST	ACTION
7	**WARNING: WHEN THE ENGINE IS OPERATING, DO NOT STAND IN A DIRECT LINE WITH THE FAN. DO NOT PUT YOUR HANDS NEAR THE PULLEYS, BELTS OR FAN. DO NOT WEAR LOOSE CLOTHING.** **NOTE: The conditions that set the DTC are not present at this time. The following list may help in identifying the intermittent condition.** With the engine running at normal operating temperature, monitor the DRBIII® parameters related to the DTC while wiggling the wiring harness. Look for parameter values to change and/or a DTC to set. Review the DRBIII® Freeze Frame information. If possible, try to duplicate the conditions under which the DTC was set. Refer to any Technical Service Bulletins (TSB) that may apply. Visually inspect the related wiring harness. Look for any chafed, pierced, pinched, or partially broken wires. Visually inspect the related wiring harness connectors. Look for broken, bent, pushed out, or corroded terminals. Were any of the above conditions present? Yes → Repair as necessary Perform **POWERTRAIN VERIFICATION TEST VER - 3.** No → Test Complete.

CR1120100440030X

Fig. 19 Code P1682: Charging System Voltage Too Low (Part 3 of 3). 2002–05 Neon

POWERTRAIN VERIFICATION TEST VER - 3

1. NOTE: If the PCM has been replaced and the correct VIN and mileage have not been programmed, a DTC will be set in the ABS Module, Airbag Module and the SKIM.
2. NOTE: If the vehicle is equipped with a Sentry Key Immobilizer System, Secret Key data must be updated. Refer to the Service Information for the PCM, SKIM and the Transponder (ignition key) for programming information.
3. Inspect the vehicle to ensure that all components related to the repair are connected properly.
4. With the DRBIII®, clear DTCs.
5. Perform generator output test. Refer to the appropriate service information as necessary.
6. Start the engine and set engine speed to 2000 RPM for at least thirty seconds.
7. Cycle the ignition key off and on.
8. With the DRBIII®, read the DTCs. If the DTC returns, or any other symptom or DTC is present, refer to the appropriate category and perform the corresponding symptom.
9. If there are no DTCs present and all components are functioning properly, the repair is complete.
Are any DTCs present?

Yes → Repair is not complete, refer to appropriate symptom.

No → Repair is complete.

CR1120100442000X

Fig. 20 Verification Test VER-3. 2002–05 Neon

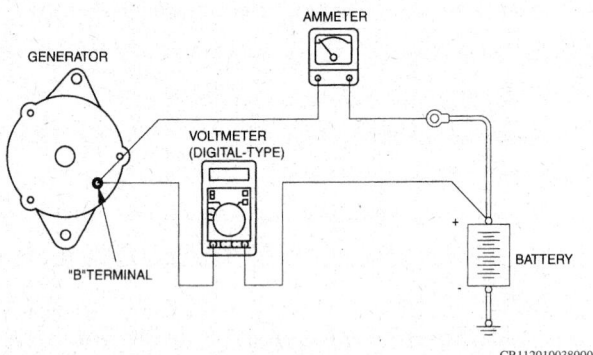

Fig. 21 Alternator output wire voltage drop test connection. Sebring Coupe & Stratus Coupe

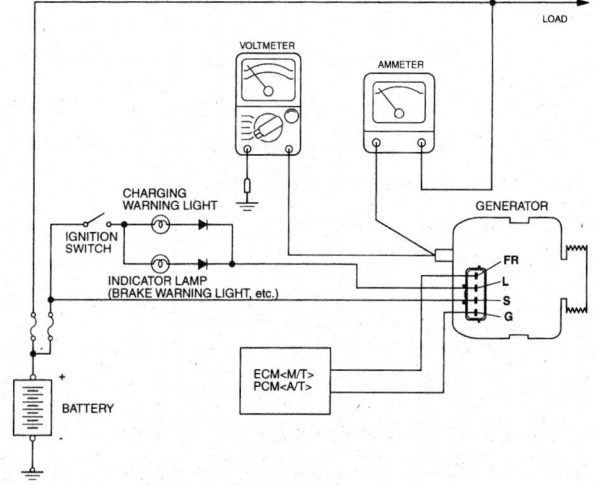

Fig. 22 Alternator output test connection. Sebring Coupe & Stratus Coupe

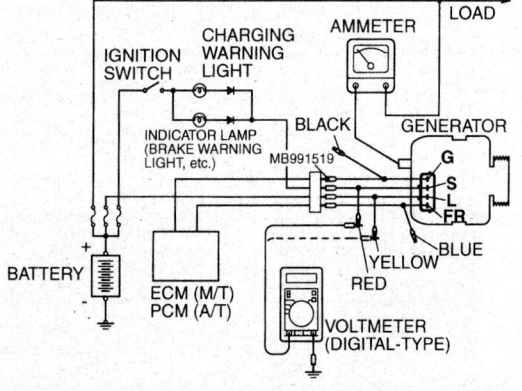

Fig. 23 Voltage regulator test connections. Sebring Coupe & Stratus Coupe

INSPECTION TERMINAL	VOLTAGE REGULATOR AMBIENT TEMPERATURE [°C(°F)]	STANDARD VALUE (V)
Terminal "S"	-20 (-4)	14.2 - 15.4
	20 (68)	13.9 - 14.9
	60 (140)	13.4 - 14.5
	80 (176)	13.1 - 14.5

CR1120100392000X

Fig. 24 Regulated voltage specifications

ALTERNATOR SPECIFICATIONS

Model	Engine	Type	Rated Output Amps
Neon	2.0L	Mitsubishi	85
Sebring Coupe & Stratus Coupe	2.4L	Mitsubishi	95
	3.0L	Mitsubishi	85

STEERING COLUMNS

NOTE: On Air Bag Equipped Models, Refer To "Air Bag System Precautions" Located In The Front Of This Manual For System Disarming & Arming Procedures.

NOTE: Refer To "Computer Relearn Procedures" Located In The Front Of This Manual When Battery Power To The Computer Has Been Interrupted.

NOTE: Prior To Performing Any Service Operations Listed In This Section, Consult The "Technical Service Bulletins" Section For Related Information.

INDEX

PRECAUTIONS

Air Bag Systems

Refer to "Air Bag System Precautions" in the front of this manual for system disarming and arming procedures.

Battery Ground Cable

Prior to service, disconnect battery ground cable and isolate as required.

Column Service

When servicing collapsible steering columns, care should be exercised since they are extremely susceptible to damage. Dropping of or leaning on column or striking sharp blows on end of steering shaft or shift levers could loosen or shear plastic fasteners which maintain column rigidity.

It is important only the specified screws, bolts and nuts be used during the assembly sequence and tightened to specifications to ensure proper breakaway action of column under impact. Avoid using excessively long bolts, as they may prevent a portion of the steering column from collapsing under impact.

If there is evidence of a sheared plastic shift tube injection, a new shift tube must be installed. If plastic injections are sheared but steering shaft is not bent, repairs may be possible using a service steering shaft repair kit containing instructions and dimensions for all steering columns. On some models, the mounting brackets will shear under impact and must also be replaced.

DIAGNOSIS & TESTING

Diagnostic Trouble Code Interpretation

Refer to **Fig. 1** for Diagnostic Trouble Code (DTC) interpretation.

Wiring Diagrams

STEERING COLUMN
REPLACE

Concorde, Intrepid, LHS & 300M

1. Remove instrument panel lefthand end fuse panel cover.
2. Remove lower instrument panel cover to instrument panel mounting bracket mounting screws from behind fuse panel cover.
3. Remove lower instrument panel cover.
4. Remove trunk release switch wiring harness connector.
5. Remove park release handle cable.
6. Remove mounting bolts and instrument panel reinforcement.
7. Remove diagnostic connector.
8. Ensure front wheels are in straight ahead position. If steering column is to be removed as one assembly, or without removing steering wheel, steering wheel must be turned to righthand 180° from straight ahead position and locked in place.
9. If removing steering wheel as outlined under "Electrical" section of "Concorde, Intrepid, LHS & 300M" chapter.
10. Push in righthand seam between upper and lower shrouds.
11. When upper shroud unsnaps, pull upper shroud away from lower.
12. Remove steering column upper shroud by repeating previous steps on lefthand side.
13. Remove tilt lever.
14. Remove mounting screws and lower steering column shroud.
15. Remove clockspring wiring harness connectors.
16. Remove mounting screws and clockspring.
17. Disconnect module wire harness connector.
18. Remove mounting screw and unclip module from key cylinder halo bezel.
19. Disconnect multi-function switch wiring harness from routing clip.
20. Remove mounting screws and multi-function switch.
21. Remove mounting screws and ignition switch.
22. **On models equipped with floor mounted shifter,** depress lock tab and remove shifter/ignition interlock cable from key lock housing.
23. **On models equipped with steering column mounted shifter,** proceed as follows:

Test	Description
B1489	Steering Wheel Control Audio Switch Circuit
B148A	Steering Wheel Control Menu Switch Circuit
B148B	Steering Wheel Control Up Switch Circuit
B148C	Steering Wheel Control Down Switch Circuit
B148D	Steering Wheel Control Side Switch Circuit
B148E	Steering Wheel Control + Switch Circuit
B148F	Steering Wheel Control - Switch Circuit
B1490	Steering Wheel Control C/T Switch Circuit
B1D8D	Steering Column Control Telescope Position Sensor Circuit Low
B1D8E	Steering Column Control Telescope Position Sensor Circuit High
B1D91	Steering Column Control Tilt Position Sensor Circuit Low
B1D92	Steering Column Control Tilt Position Sensor Circuit High
B1D93	Steering Column Control Telescope Motor Control Circuit Performance
B1D97	Steering Column Control Tilt Motor Control Circuit Performance
B1DA0	Steering Column Control Tilt Switch Circuit Stuck
B1DA5	Steering Column Control Telescope Switch Circuit Stuck
B2225	Steering Column Control Module Internal
B2332	Horn Switch Input Circuit/Performance
C1219	Steering Angle Sensor Erratic Performance
P0562	Battery Voltage Low
P0563	Battery Voltage High
P0585	Speed Control Multiplex Switch 1/2 Correlation
P1593	Speed Control Switch 1/2 Stuck
U0002	CAN-C BUS Off Performance
U0019	CAN-B BUS Circuit
U0121	Lost Communication w/Anti-Lock Brake System Control Module
U0141	Lost Communication w/Front Control Module
U0155	Lost Communication w/Cluster/CCN
U0212	Lost Communication w/Steering Column Control Module
U1109	Lost Communication w/Lin/Steering Wheels Controls

Fig. 1 DTC interpretation

a. Remove cable from shifter mechanism.
b. Unlock cable lock, then remove shift cable by inserting suitable screwdriver between shift cable and shifter mechanism, and prying cable off pin.
24. **On all models,** remove mounting screws and cable mounting bracket.
25. Remove air ducts under steering column.
26. Remove retaining pin and steering column coupler pinch bolt.
27. Remove mounting bracket to support bracket mounting nuts and loosen steering column lower mounting bracket to support bracket mounting bolts.
28. Remove steering column support bracket by pulling rearward and out.
29. Reverse procedure to install, noting the following:
   a. **Torque** bracket to support bracket fasteners to 96 inch lbs.
   b. **Torque** coupler pinch bolt to 20 ft. lbs.
   c. **Torque** steering wheel mounting nut to 45 ft. lbs.
   d. **Torque** air bag module bolts to 96 inch lbs.

Crossfire

1. Place front wheels in straight ahead position.
2. Remove lefthand lower instrument panel fuse panel from below steering column.
3. Remove driver's air bag screws, disconnect air bag electrical connector, then pass air bag connector wire through whole in steering column.
4. Remove air bag module.
5. Remove steering wheel countersunk bolt, **Fig. 2.**
6. Remove clockspring screws.
7. Remove mounting screws and instrument cluster.
8. Remove ashtray from center console, then press locking tabs together and push ignition lock cable from ignition starter switch.
9. Remove mounting screws and position center console bezel aside.

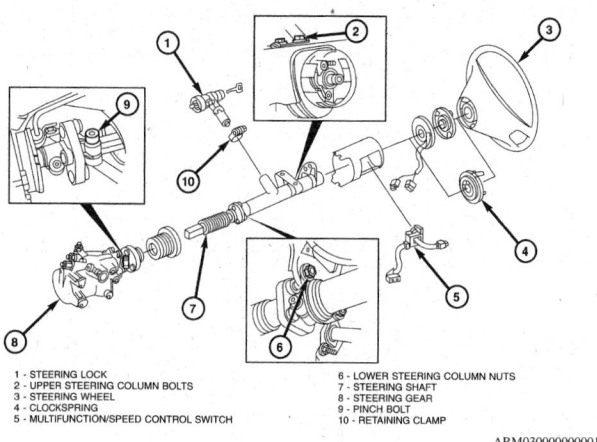

1 - STEERING LOCK
2 - UPPER STEERING COLUMN BOLTS
3 - STEERING WHEEL
4 - CLOCKSPRING
5 - MULTIFUNCTION/SPEED CONTROL SWITCH
6 - LOWER STEERING COLUMN NUTS
7 - STEERING SHAFT
8 - STEERING GEAR
9 - PINCH BOLT
10 - RETAINING CLAMP

ARM0300000000018

Fig. 2 Exploded view of steering column (Part 1 of 2). Crossfire

10. Turn ignition lock cable 90° to lefthand and pull cable straight out.
11. Remove mounting screws, electrical connector and speed control switch.
12. Remove mounting screws, electrical connector and multi-function switch.
13. Remove steering column trim ring.
14. Remove pinch bolt from steering column to steering gear coupling.
15. Remove lower steering column mounting nuts.
16. Remove upper steering column to instrument panel support bolts.
17. Slowly lower steering column, then pull column outward away from instrument panel.
18. Reverse procedure to install, noting the following:
   a. **Torque** lower steering column mounting nuts to 71 inch lbs.
   b. **Torque** upper steering column bolts to 15 ft. lbs.
   c. **Torque** steering column to steering gear pinch bolt to 22 ft. lbs.
   d. **Torque** steering wheel mounting hex bolt to 60 ft. lbs.
   e. If steering wheel is offset by more than one tooth, turn signal indicator is no longer aligned properly.

Magnum, 300 & 300C

1. **On models equipped with electric telescoping column,** place column mid-tilt position.
2. **On all models,** removing steering wheel as outlined under "Electrical" section of "Magnum, 300 & 300C" chapter.
3. Remove mounting screw, then disconnect steering column cover snap retainers by pulling it rearward at top and righthand side.
4. Disconnect wire harness connector from the trunk release switch.
5. Disconnect emergency bracket release handle release cable and remove steering column cover.
6. Remove steering column opening reinforcement.
7. Remove at least one clockspring

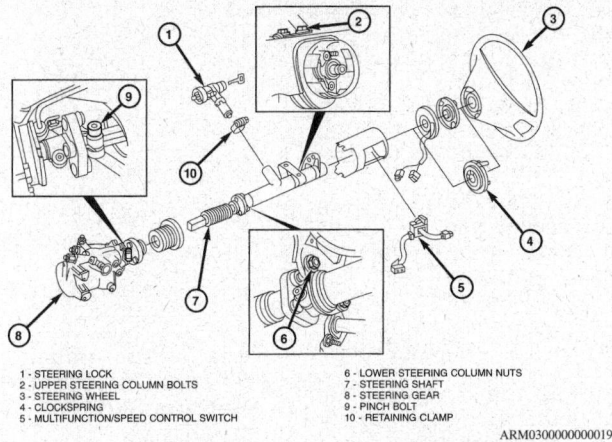

1 - STEERING LOCK
2 - UPPER STEERING COLUMN BOLTS
3 - STEERING WHEEL
4 - CLOCKSPRING
5 - MULTIFUNCTION/SPEED CONTROL SWITCH
6 - LOWER STEERING COLUMN NUTS
7 - STEERING SHAFT
8 - STEERING GEAR
9 - PINCH BOLT
10 - RETAINING CLAMP

ARM0300000000019

Fig. 2 Exploded view of steering column (Part 2 of 2). Crossfire

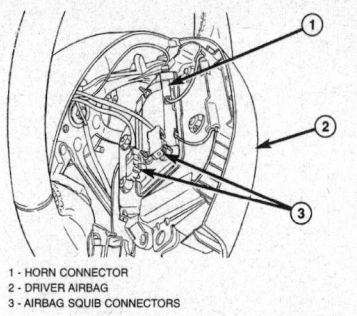

1 - HORN CONNECTOR
2 - DRIVER AIRBAG
3 - AIRBAG SQUIB CONNECTORS

CR6040100156000X

Fig. 3 Air bag electrical connector. 2001–04 Sebring Convertible, Sebring Sedan & Stratus Sedan

mounting screw.

8. **On models equipped with manual tilt and telescoping columns,** disconnect unlatch lever from column.
9. **On all models,** remove four mounting screws and roll top shroud.
10. Back set screw out through access hole and remove Steering Column Control Module (SCCM).
11. Remove two steering column mounting nuts at bulkhead.
12. Remove instrument cluster as outlined under "Electrical" section of "Magnum, 300 & 300C" chapter.
13. Raise and support vehicle.
14. Remove lower coupling shaft pinch bolt.
15. Slide steering shaft out of lower coupling shaft.
16. Lower vehicle.
17. **On models equipped with electronic telescoping column,** remove mounting screws, brace and support beam bracket.
18. **On all models,** remove lower steering column mounting pivot bolt and nut.
19. Remove two upper mounting bolts and steering column.
20. Reverse procedure to install, noting the following:
    a. **Torque** steering column upper mounting screws to 22 ft. lbs.
    b. **Torque** pivot bolt to 22 ft. lbs.
    c. **Torque** support beam bracket mounting screw at column to 21 ft. lbs.
    d. **Torque** support beam bracket mounting screw at support beam to 106 in. lbs.
    e. **Torque** steering column to bulkhead to 62 inch lbs.
    f. **Torque** new pinch bolt to 23 ft. lbs.
    g. **Torque** new steering wheel nut to 52 ft. lbs.

Neon

1. Ensure front wheels in straight-ahead position.
2. Remove instrument panel top cover lefthand end mounting just above left instrument panel end cap.

3. Starting at lefthand end, push upward on instrument panel top cover, disconnecting its retainer clips along face. Disconnect just enough clips to allow access to upper ends of instrument cluster bezel.
4. Disconnect clips along outer edge and remove instrument cluster bezel.
5. Remove two mounting screws along bottom of steering column cover below instrument panel.
6. Disconnect upper end clips and remove steering column cover.
7. If removing steering wheel as outlined under "Electrical" section of "Neon" chapter.
8. Remove key from ignition cylinder.
9. Remove two lower shroud to the steering column and upper shroud mounting screws.
10. Disconnect clips from each other, then remove lower shroud from upper shroud and column.
11. Remove upper shroud.
12. Remove steering column coupling retainer pin at base of column, back off pinch bolt nut and remove steering column coupling pinch bolt. Pinch bolt nut is caged to coupling and is not removable.
13. Separate upper and lower steering column couplings.
14. **On models equipped with automatic transaxle,** depress cable connector top tab and remove ignition interlock cable from back side of the steering column ignition cylinder housing.
15. **On all models,** remove two lower and two upper steering column to instrument panel mounting nuts.
16. Lower steering column away from instrument panel.
17. Disconnect clockspring wiring harness electrical connector.
18. Disconnect multi-function, windshield wiper and ignition switches' wiring harness electrical connectors.
19. **On models equipped with Sentry Key Immobilizer Module (SKIM),** disconnect SKIM electrical connector.
20. **On all models,** remove the steering column.
21. If steering column is being replaced,

proceed as follows:
    a. Insert key and turn ignition key cylinder to ON position.
    b. Depress retaining tab and remove Ignition key cylinder by pulling key and cylinder straight out of column.
    c. Disconnect latch hooks on back of clockspring by lifting clockspring slightly to clear column housing with top latch hook.
    d. Lower clockspring slightly and disconnect lower latch hook.
    e. Remove clockspring.
    f. Remove two mounting screws and multi-function/windshield wiper switch.
    g. **On models equipped (SKIM,** remove two mounting screws and slide SKI off non-halo trim ring, then remove non-halo trim ring.
22. **On all models,** reverse procedure to install, noting the following:
    a. **Torque** SKIM mounting screws to 25 inch lbs.
    b. **Torque** steering column mounting nuts to 12 ft. lbs.
    c. **Do not tighten coupling pinch bolt anytime vehicle is not at curb riding height.**
    d. **Torque** coupling pinch bolt to 12 ft. lbs.

Sebring Convertible, Sebring Sedan & Stratus Sedan

1. Place wheels in straight ahead position.
2. Remove fuse panel cover and instrument panel top cover mounting screws.
3. Remove radio bezel and climate control panel from top cover of instrument panel.
4. Remove instrument panel mounting screws from rear of climate control panel.
5. Remove knee bolster and cruise control switches from steering wheel.
6. Remove driver's air bag module and disconnect electrical connector from module, **Fig. 3.**
7. Remove steering wheel using suitable

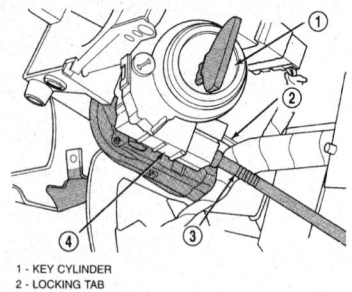

1 - KEY CYLINDER
2 - LOCKING TAB
3 - SHIFTER IGNITION INTERLOCK CABLE
4 - KEY LOCK HOUSING

CR6040100157000X

Fig. 4 Shifter/ignition interlock cable removal. Sebring Convertible, Sebring Sedan & Stratus Sedan

steering wheel puller.
8. Remove upper shroud by pressing inward on upper shroud while pulling apart upper and lower shrouds.
9. Place column tilt in highest position and remove lower shroud.
10. Remove electrical connectors from clockspring, ignition switch and multifunction switch.
11. **On models equipped with automatic transmissions,** proceed as follows:
    a. Place key cylinder in OFF position.
    b. Depress locking tab on shifter/ignition interlock cable, **Fig. 4.**
    c. Remove cable from key lock housing.
12. **On all models,** remove and position steering column wiring harness aside.
13. Remove pinch bolt from intermediate shaft and slide shaft up and off steering gear, **Fig. 5.**
14. Remove mounting bolts, nuts and steering column.
15. Reverse procedure to install, noting the following:
    a. **Torque** steering column mounting brackets nuts and bolts to 150 inch lbs.
    b. **Torque** intermediate shaft coupler pinch bolt to 32 ft. lbs.
    c. Depress plastic locking pin to disengage clockspring mechanism. Rotate clockspring clockwise to end of travel.
    d. Slowly rotate counterclockwise until yellow appears in centering window of clockspring and the drive pin on rotor is in front of arrow on clockspring label. Engage clockspring.
    e. **Torque** upper and lower shroud bolts to 17 inch lbs.
    f. **Torque** steering wheel bolt to 40 ft. lbs.
    g. **Torque** driver's air bag module mounting screws to 17 inch lbs.
    h. **Torque** cruise control switch mounting screws to 12 inch lbs.

Sebring Coupe & Stratus Coupe

1. Remove mounting screws and driver's air bag module, **Fig. 6. Do not remove screws from holder.**

2. Disconnect driver's air bag module clockspring connect by pressing lock toward outer side using suitable flat-tipped screwdriver.
3. Remove mounting nut and steering wheel using puller tool No. MB-990803, or equivalent. **Do not hammer.**
4. Remove mounting screws and instrument panel under cover.
5. Remove mounting bolts, then the lower and upper column covers.
6. Remove mounting screws and clockspring.
7. Remove mounting bolts and column switch.
8. **On models equipped with automatic transaxle,** remove cover and disconnect key interlock cable.
9. **On all models,** remove mounting and pinch bolts, then the steering column.
10. Remove mounting bolt and steering cover.
11. Reverse procedure to install, noting the following:
    a. **Torque** steering cover mounting bolts to 36–52 inch lbs.
    b. **Torque** pinch bolt to 12–14 ft. lbs. and mounting bolts to 78–122 inch lbs.
    c. **Torque** install column switch mounting bolts to 14–22 ft. lbs.
    d. **Torque** steering wheel mounting nut to 26–36 ft. lbs.
    e. **Torque** air bag module mounting bolts to 61–95 inch lbs.

STEERING COLUMN SERVICE

Concorde, Intrepid, LHS & 300M

The steering column has been designed to be serviced as an assembly less wiring, switches, clockspring, gear shift lever, shift ignition interlock, brake lock solenoid, shrouds and steering wheel. **Fig. 7.**

The steering column intermediate shaft must be replaced as an entire assembly.

Crossfire

The steering column has been designed to be serviced as an assembly less wiring, switches, clockspring, gear shift lever, shift ignition interlock, brake lock solenoid, shrouds and steering wheel.

DISASSEMBLY

1. Remove pinch bolt from intermediate shaft, then intermediate shaft, **Fig. 8.**
2. Remove retaining ring, disk spring and thrust ring.
3. Push intermediate shaft outward slightly.
4. Remove locking ring and thrust ring.
5. Press ball bearing from steering column using intermediate shaft.

ASSEMBLE

1. Press new bearing up to stop in steering column using suitable press tool.

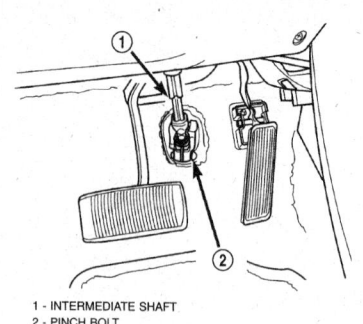

1 - INTERMEDIATE SHAFT
2 - PINCH BOLT

CR6040100158000X

Fig. 5 Intermediate shaft pinch bolt removal. Sebring Convertible, Sebring Sedan & Stratus Sedan

2. Slide intermediate shaft into inner column tube, then press second bearing in using suitable press tool.
3. Ensure locking rings, position correctly in upper steering shaft lock grooves.
4. Push thrust and locking ring together onto intermediate shaft.
5. Slide thrust ring and disk spring into intermediate shaft.
6. Ensure disk spring is fully preloaded using lower steering shaft, if required.
7. If disk spring preload is to high, upper steering shaft will turn unevenly and bind.
8. If disk spring preload is to low, detectable movement will result when steering wheel jacket tube is installed.
9. Mount retaining ring on intermediate shaft, using suitable tool, push disk spring on until it is fully loaded.
10. Attach lower tube to upper tube by screwing countersunk screw to protect splines.
11. Slide lower intermediate shaft onto upper intermediate shaft, then install the mounting nut and bolt.
12. Cover to protect lower intermediate shaft.
13. Install lower intermediate shaft onto upper shaft until disc spring is fully preloaded. Use a suitable press to fully preload intermediate shaft disc spring.
14. Inspect steering column for ease of movement, by turning steering wheel at same time, tighten nut and bolt in this position.

Magnum, 300 & 300C

Do not attempt to remove or modify any part of the column.

Neon

The steering column on these models has been designed to be serviced as a complete assembly, only. The shaft, bearings and upper coupling are all serviced with the column.

The replaceable components on the steering column are the key cylinder, ignition switch, multi-function switch, trim shrouds, steering wheel, air bag module and the clockspring.

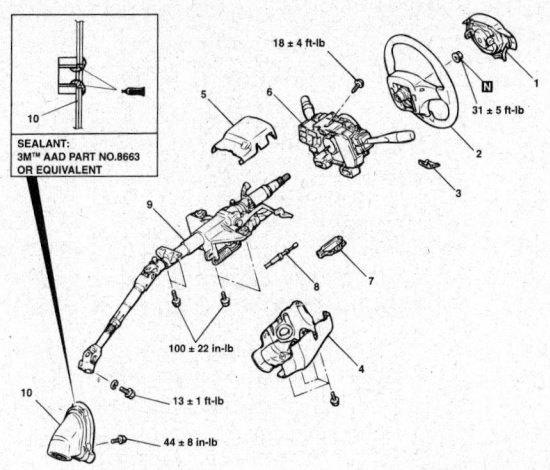

1. AIR BAG MODULE
2. STEERING WHEEL
3. COVER
   • INSTRUMENT PANEL UNDER COVER
4. LOWER COLUMN COVER
5. UPPER COLUMN COVER
6. CLOCK SPRING AND COLUMN SWITCH ASSEMBLY
7. COVER <A/T>
8. KEY INTERLOCK CABLE <A/T>
9. STEERING SHAFT ASSEMBLY
10. STEERING COVER ASSEMBLY

CR6040000152000X

Fig. 6 Steering column replacement. Sebring Coupe & Stratus Coupe

Sebring Convertible, Sebring Sedan & Stratus Sedan

The steering column has been designed to be serviced as an assembly except for wiring, switches, key cylinder, shrouds and the steering wheel.

The only other serviceable component is the intermediate shaft. If the shaft requires replacement, proceed as follows:

1. Remove steering column as outlined under "Steering Column, Replace."
2. Remove roll pin from flex joint using remover/installer tool No. 6831-A, or equivalent, **Fig. 9.**
3. Pry intermediate shaft off steering column using a suitable screwdriver.
4. Reverse procedure to install.

Sebring Coupe & Stratus Coupe

The steering column has been designed to be serviced as an assembly except for wiring, switches, shrouds and the steering wheel.

The only serviceable component is the steering lock cylinder, **Fig. 10.** To remove cylinder lock proceed as follows:

1. Cut bolts at steering column lock bracket, **Fig. 11.** Discard old bolts.
2. Remove bracket and cylinder lock.
3. Install new steering lock cylinder in alignment with column boss. Do not completely tighten new twist off bolts.
4. Ensure lock is working properly. Tighten new bolts until head twists off.

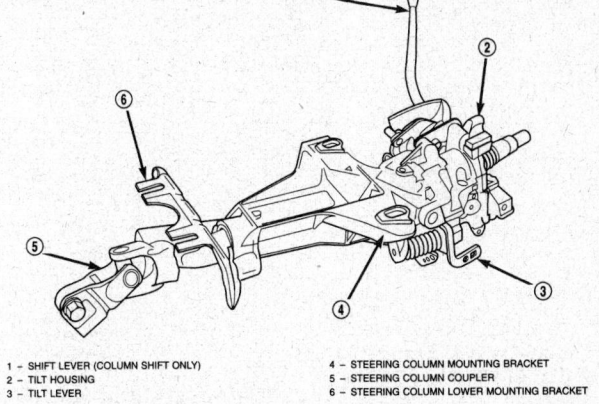

1 – SHIFT LEVER (COLUMN SHIFT ONLY)
2 – TILT HOUSING
3 – TILT LEVER
4 – STEERING COLUMN MOUNTING BRACKET
5 – STEERING COLUMN COUPLER
6 – STEERING COLUMN LOWER MOUNTING BRACKET

CR6009900147000X

Fig. 7 Steering column components. Concorde, Intrepid, LHS & 300M

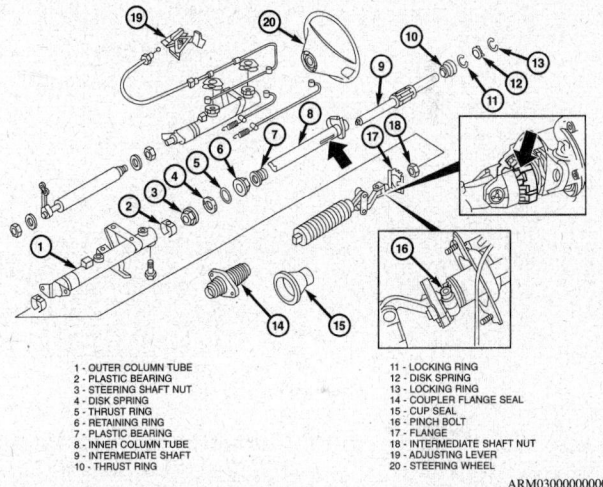

1 – OUTER COLUMN TUBE
2 – PLASTIC BEARING
3 – STEERING SHAFT NUT
4 – DISK SPRING
5 – THRUST RING
6 – RETAINING RING
7 – PLASTIC BEARING
8 – INNER COLUMN TUBE
9 – INTERMEDIATE SHAFT
10 – THRUST RING
11 – LOCKING RING
12 – DISK SPRING
13 – LOCKING RING
14 – COUPLER FLANGE SEAL
15 – CUP SEAL
16 – PINCH BOLT
17 – FLANGE
18 – INTERMEDIATE SHAFT NUT
19 – ADJUSTING LEVER
20 – STEERING WHEEL

ARM0300000000020

Fig. 8 Exploded view of steering column. Crossfire

TECHNICAL SERVICE BULLETINS

Steering Column Clicking

2001–04 SEBRING CONVERTIBLE, SEBRING SEDAN, STRATUS SEDAN & 2002–03 NEON

Some of these models there maybe a clicking sound when the steering wheel is turned.

This condition may be caused by steering column alignment.

To correct this condition proceed as follows:

1. Remove steering column shrouds. If click sound remains, proceed to next step. If click sound is eliminated, inspect for steering column shroud interference.
2. Remove steering wheel as outlined under "Electrical" section of "Sebring Convertible, Sebring Sedan & Stratus Sedan" or "Neon" chapters.
3. Disconnect intermediate shaft to steering gear lower coupling.
4. Install steering wheel.
5. Ensure clockspring is centered.
6. **Torque** coupling pinch bolt to 21 ft. lbs.
7. **Torque** steering wheel bolt to 40 ft. lbs.
8. If click sound returns, loosen lower coupling pinch bolt and four steering column mounting bracket nuts.
9. Jiggle steering column and **torque** coupling pinch bolt to 21 ft. lbs.
10. Hold steering column in place by tightening two lower mounting nuts.
11. Ensure both break-away capsules are fully seated in upper steering column mounting bracket slots.
12. Ensure mounting studs are centered fore-and-aft in plastic capsules.
13. Equally tighten both steering column mounting nuts, until upper steering column back is seated against support bracket.
14. **Torque** four steering column bracket to support bracket nuts to 12 ft. lbs.
15. If click sound remains, proceed to next

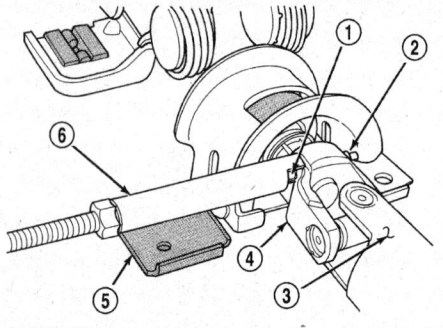

1 - ROLL PIN
2 - KNURLED NUT
3 - INTERMEDIATE SHAFT
4 - UNIVERSAL JOINT
5 - STEERING COLUMN LOWER MOUNTING BRACKET
6 - SPECIAL TOOL 6831-A

CR6040100162000X

Fig. 9   Roll pin removal. Sebring Convertible, Sebring Sedan & Stratus Sedan

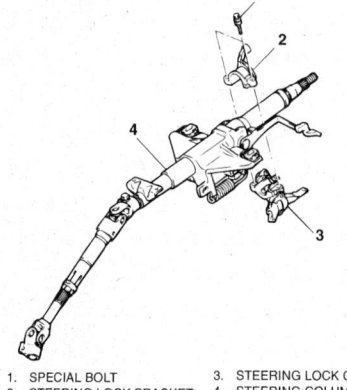
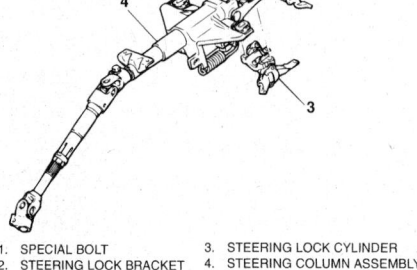

1. SPECIAL BOLT   3. STEERING LOCK CYLINDER
2. STEERING LOCK BRACKET   4. STEERING COLUMN ASSEMBLY

CR6040100154000X

Fig. 10   Steering lock cylinder & bracket. Sebring & Stratus Coupe

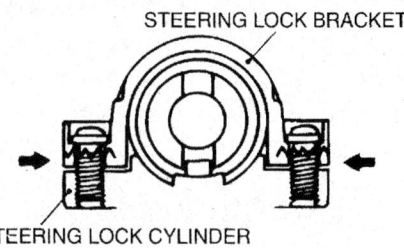

CR6040100155000X

Fig. 11   Steering lock bracket bolts removal. Sebring & Stratus Coupe

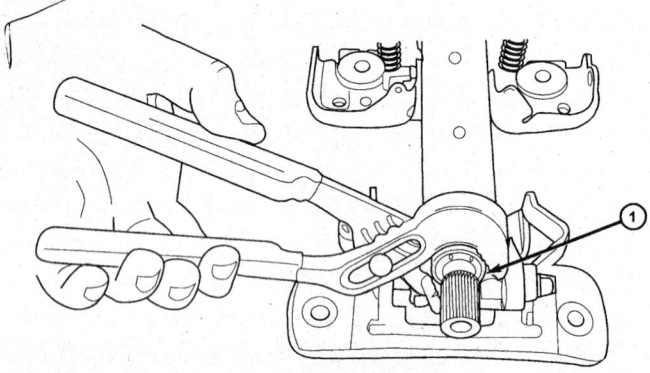

1 - DEFORM OUTSIDE DIAMETER OF RETAINER TO REMOVE

CR6040100159000X

Fig. 12   Spring retainer replacement. 2001–04 Sebring Convertible, Sebring Sedan, Stratus Sedan & 2002–03 Neon

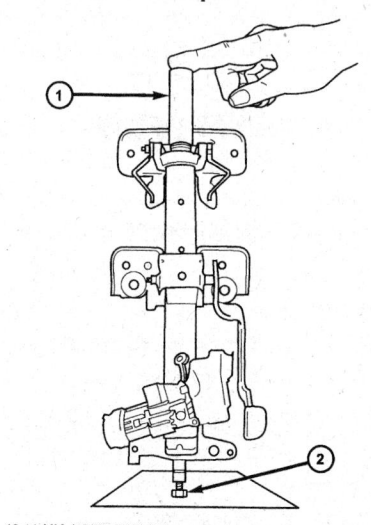

1 - 12-14 MM (15/32-17/32 IN.)

2 - INSURE SURFACE IS FLAT AND DOES NOT DAMAGE THE SHAFT

CR6040100160000X

Fig. 13   Retainer installation. 2001–04 Sebring Convertible, Sebring Sedan, Stratus Sedan & 2002–03 Neon

step. If click sound is eliminated, replace lower coupling pinch bolt (part No. 06506382AA) and **torque** it to 21 ft. lbs.
16. Remove clockspring and disconnect lower coupling.
17. If click sound remains, proceed to next step. If click sound is eliminated, inspect for clockspring interference.
18. Remove steering column as outlined under "Steering Column, Replace."
19. Remove two mounting screws and separate multi-function switch from column.
20. Remove intermediate shaft universal joint roll pin using remover/installer tool No. 6831-A, or equivalent.
21. Pry column intermediate shaft from steering column shaft using suitable screwdriver between universal joint and lower mounting bracket.
22. Remove spring retainer by pinching outside of retainer using suitable pliers and sliding it off steering column shaft, **Fig. 12.**
23. Remove spring, wedge and steering column shaft.
24. Inspect and replace bearings (upper part No. 04690507AB, lower part No.

04690344AB), as required.
25. Stand steering column on end with upper bearing outer race supported on 1¹⁄₁₆ inches socket.
26. Tap bearing downward several times until bearing is fully seated using ⅞ inch deep well socket, or suitable tool, against lower bearing outer race and brass hammer.
27. Ensure there is no clearance between lower casting and lower bearing outer race using .005 inch feeler gauge.
28. **On models built after Sept. 30, 2001,** install original steering column shaft.
29. **On models built before Oct. 1, 2001,** install revised steering column shaft (part No. 04690852AA), revised edge (part No. 04690570) and revised spring (part No. 05057088AA).
30. **On all models,** thread steering wheel bolt into shaft.
31. Stand column on bolt head.
32. Install new retainer (part No. 04664130), onto shaft using ⅞ inch deep well socket and suitable small hammer to tap retainer into place, **Fig. 13,**
33. Ensure distance between lower housing and outside face of retainer is ¹⁵⁄₃₂–

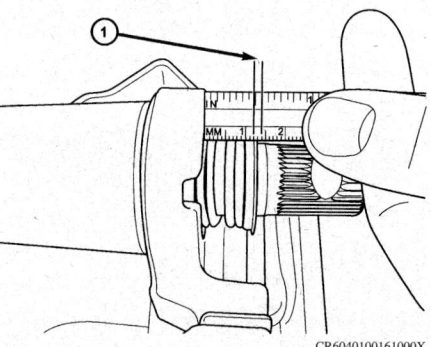

CR6040100161000X

Fig. 14   Spring retainer measurement. 2001–04 Sebring Convertible, Sebring Sedan, Stratus Sedan & 2002–03 Neon

¹⁷⁄₃₂ inch, **Fig. 14.**
34. If distance is less than ¹⁵⁄₃₂–¹⁷⁄₃₂ inch, remove retainer and install new one until specified distance is obtained.
35. Ensure click sound is corrected. If should is still present, further diagnosis is required.

POWER STEERING

TABLE OF CONTENTS

Concorde, Intrepid, LHS & 300M

NOTE: On Air Bag Equipped Models, Refer To "Air Bag System Precautions" Located In The Front Of This Manual For System Disarming & Arming Procedures.

NOTE: Refer To "Computer Relearn Procedures" Located In The Front Of This Manual When Battery Power To The Computer Has Been Interrupted.

NOTE: Prior To Performing Any Service Operations Listed In This Section, Consult The "Technical Service Bulletins" Section For Related Information.

INDEX

POWER STEERING PRESSURE SPECIFICATIONS

Model	Year	Power Steering Pump Pressure, psi		Max Relief Pressure	Output Flow, Gallons Per Minute①
		Test Valve			
		Open	Closed		
Concorde, Intrepid, LHS & 300M	2001–04	50–125	1250–1350	1250–1350	2.1–2.5

① — At 1500 RPM & minimum pressure.

PRECAUTIONS

Air Bag Systems

Refer to "Air Bag System Precautions" in the front of this manual for system disarming and arming procedures.

Battery Ground Cable

Prior to service, disconnect battery ground cable and isolate as required.

DESCRIPTION

Power assist is provided by an open center, rotary type control valve. It is used to direct oil from the power steering pump to either side of the integral steering rack piston. These vehicles may be equipped with

CONDITION	POSSIBLE CAUSES	CORRECTION
OBJECTIONABLE HISS OR WHISTLE*	1. Damaged or mispositioned steering column shaft/coupling dash panel seal. 2. Noisy valve in power steering gear.	1. Reposition or replace steering column shaft/coupling dash panel seal. 2. Replace power steering gear.
RATTLE OR CLUNK	1. Power steering gear loose on front suspension crossmember. 2. Front suspension crossmember mounting fasteners loose at frame. 3. Loose tie rod (outer or inner). 4. Loose lower control arm mounting bolts at front suspension crossmember. 5. Loose shock assembly mounting fasteners at shock tower. 6. Power steering fluid pressure hose touching the body of the vehicle. 7. Internal power steering gear noise. 8. Damaged front suspension crossmember.	1. Inspect power steering gear mounting bolts. Replace as necessary. Tighten to the specified torque. 2. Tighten the front suspension crossmember mounting fasteners to the specified torque. 3. Check tie rod pivot points for wear. Replace worn/loose parts as required. 4. Tighten control arm mounting bolts to the specified torque. 5. Tighten shock assembly fasteners to the specified torques. 6. Adjust hose to proper position by loosening, repositioning, and tightening fitting to specified torque. Do not bend tubing. 7. Replace power steering gear. 8. Replace front suspension crossmember.

CR6029700192010X

Fig. 1 Troubleshooting (Part 1 of 6)

three different types of power steering. They are base, firm feel and speed proportional power steering.

TROUBLESHOOTING

Refer to **Fig. 1** when troubleshooting the power steering system.

DIAGNOSIS & TESTING

Accessing Diagnostic Trouble Codes

Connect the DRB III, or suitably programmed scan tool, to the Data Link Connector (DLC), **Fig. 2**. The diagnostic cycle begins when the ignition is turned On.

Connector Terminal Identification

Refer to **Fig. 3** for connector terminal identification.

Diagnostic Tests

Refer to **Figs. 4 through 7** for diagnostic tests.

Clearing Diagnostic Trouble Codes

Follow tool manufacturer's instructions to clean DTCs.

SYSTEM SERVICE

Power Steering System Bleed

1. Ensure power steering fluid remote reservoir is full, then start engine and turn steering wheel from stop to stop several times.
2. Stop engine and inspect fluid level again. If required, add fluid until proper fluid level is reached.

3. Repeat procedure until fluid level is consistent. Inspect system for leaks.

Component Service

FLUID COOLER, REPLACE

1. Remove as much power steering fluid as possible from reservoir using suitable siphon pump.
2. Raise and support vehicle on suitable frame contact hoist or with suitable jack stands.
3. **On 300M models,** remove front fascia.
4. **On all models,** remove clamp and lower hose, then drain fluid into suitable container.
5. Remove clamp and upper hose.
6. Remove mounting clips and air dam from lower radiator support.
7. Remove mounting nuts and cooler.
8. Reverse procedure to install, noting following:
   a. Install air dam with new retaining clips.
   b. Ensure clamps are installed on hoses past cooler retention beads.

RESERVOIR, REPLACE

2.7L ENGINE

1. Remove power steering pump as outlined under "Power Steering Pump, Replace" in "Front Suspension & Steering" of "Concorde, Intrepid, LHS & 300M" chapter.
2. Remove mounting bolts and reservoir.
3. Reverse procedure to install, noting following:
   a. Lubricate reservoir O-ring seal with suitable, fresh, clean power steering fluid.
   b. Press reservoir nipple straight into pump without rotating or twisting.

CONDITION	POSSIBLE CAUSES	CORRECTION
POPPING NOISE	1. Worn outer tie rod.	1. Replace outer tie rod.
CHIRP OR SQUEAL (POWER STEERING PUMP)	1. Loose power steering pump drive belt.	1. Check and adjust power steering pump drive belt to specifications. Replace belt if worn or glazed.
WHINE OR GROWL (POWER STEERING PUMP)**	1. Low fluid level. 2. Power steering hose touching vehicle body or frame. 3. Extreme wear of power steering pump internal components.	1. Fill power steering fluid reservoir to proper level and check for leaks (make sure all air is bled from the system fluid). 2. Adjust hose to proper position by loosening, repositioning, and tightening fitting to specified torque. Do not bend tubing. Replace hose if damaged. 3. Replace power steering pump and flush system as necessary.
SUCKING AIR SOUND	1. Loose clamp on power steering fluid return hose. 2. Missing O-Ring on power steering hose connection. 3. Low power steering fluid level. 4. Air leak between power steering fluid reservoir and power steering pump.	1. Tighten or replace hose clamp. 2. Inspect connection and replace O-Ring as required. 3. Fill power steering fluid reservoir to proper level and check for leaks. 4. Replace power steering pump (with reservoir).
SQUEAK OR RUBBING SOUND	1. Steering column shroud rubbing. 2. Steering column shaft rubbing. 3. Clockspring noisy. 4. Steering gear internally noisy.	1. Realign shrouds as necessary. 2. Move or realign item rubbing shaft. 3. Remove clockspring. Reinstall wheel. If noise is gone, replace clockspring. 4. Replace steering gear.
SCRUBBING OR KNOCKING NOISE.	1. Incorrect tire or wheel size. 2. Interference between steering gear and other vehicle components. 3. Steering gear internal stops worn excessively allowing tires to be steered excessively far.	1. Replace incorrect size tire or wheel with size used as original equipment. 2. Check for bent or misaligned components and correct as necessary. 3. Replace steering gear.

CR6029700192020X

Fig. 1 Troubleshooting (Part 2 of 6)

3.2 & 3.5L ENGINES

1. Raise and support vehicle on suitable frame contact hoist or with suitable jack stands.
2. Remove reservoir hoses and drain fluid into suitable container.
3. Lower vehicle, then rotate and remove reservoir's rear side toward engine, out of its bracket.
4. Reverse procedure to install, noting following:
   a. Ensure reservoir bottom tab is inserted into frame rail hole.
   b. Ensure clamps are installed on hoses past retention beads.

DRIVE PULLEY, REPLACE

REMOVAL

1. Remove power steering pump as outlined under "Power Steering Pump, Replace" in "Front Suspension & Steering Section" of "Concorde, Intrepid, LHS & 300M." chapter.
2. Mount pump by mounting boss in suitable vise. **Do not clamp pump body.**
3. Remove pulley using puller tool No. C-4333, or equivalent. **Do not use press or hammer on pump shaft.**

INSTALLATION

1. Place pulley squarely on shaft end and install spacer provided with pump or pulley into pulley hub.
2. Remove spacer tool No. 6936, or equivalent, into pulley hub, **Fig. 8.**
3. Thread installer tool No. C-4063, or equivalent, into pump shaft.
4. Holding installer tool with one wrench, turn installer hex down threaded rod pushing pulley onto shaft. Ensure tool and pulley remain aligned.
5. Ensure spacer is fully seated against

CONDITION	POSSIBLE CAUSES	CORRECTION
STEERING WHEEL/ COLUMN CLICKING, CLUNKING OR RATTLING.	1. Steering column preload is not set properly.	1. Loosen steering column coupling pinch bolt. Replace pinch bolt and torque to specifications.
	2. Loose steering coupling pinch bolt.	2. Replace pinch bolt and torque to specifications.
	3. Steering column bearings.	3. Replace steering column.
STEERING WHEEL HAS FORE AND AFT LOOSENESS.	1. Steering wheel retaining nut not properly tightened and torqued.	1. Tighten the steering wheel retaining nut to its specified torque.
	2. Steering column preload is not set properly.	2. Loosen steering column coupling pinch bolt to reset steering column preload. Replace pinch bolt and torque to specifications.
	3. Steering column lower bearing spring retainer slipped on steering column shaft.	3. Replace steering column.
STEERING WHEEL OR DASH VIBRATES DURING LOW SPEED OR STANDSTILL STEERING MANEUVERS.	1. Air in the fluid of the power steering system.	1. Bleed air from system following the power steering pump initial operation service procedure.*
	2. Tires not properly inflated.	2. Inflate tires to the specified pressure.
	3. Excessive engine vibration.	3. Ensure that the engine is running properly.
	4. Loose tie rod end jam nut.	4. Tighten the inner to outer tie rod jam nut to the specified torque.
	5. Overcharged air conditioning system.	5. Check air conditioning pump head pressure and correct as necessary.
STEERING CATCHES, STICKS IN CERTAIN POSITIONS OR IS DIFFICULT TO TURN.	1. Low power steering fluid level.	1. Fill power steering fluid reservoir to specified level and check for leaks.
	2. Tires not inflated to specified pressure.	2. Inflate tires to the specified pressure.
	3. Lack of lubrication in front suspension control arm ball joints.	3. Lubricate ball joints if ball joints are not a lubricated-for-life type ball joint. If ball joint is a lubricated-for-life ball joint, replace ball joint or control arm.
	4. Worn upper or lower control arm ball joint.	4. Replace ball joint or control arm.
	5. Lack of lubrication in steering gear outer tie rod ends.	5. Lubricate tie rod ends if they are not a lubricated-for-life type. If tie rod end is a lubricated-for-life type, replace tie rod end.

CR6029700192030X

Fig. 1 Troubleshooting (Part 3 of 6)

CONDITION	POSSIBLE CAUSES	CORRECTION
	6. Loose power steering pump drive belt.	6. Tighten the power steering pump drive belt to specifications. If drive belt is worn or glazed, replace belt.
	7. Faulty power steering pump flow control (Perform Power Steering System Flow and Pressure Test).	7. Replace power steering pump.
	8. Excessive friction in steering column or intermediate shaft.	8. Isolate and correct condition.
	9. Binding upper or lower control arm ball joint.	9. Replace the upper or lower ball joint.
	10. Excessive friction in power steering gear.	10. Replace power steering gear.
STIFF, HARD TO TURN, SURGE, MOMENTARY INCREASE IN EFFORT WHEN TURNING.	1. Tires not properly inflated.	1. Inflate tires to specified pressure.
	2. Low power steering fluid level.	2. Add power steering fluid as required to power steering fluid reservoir to obtain proper level. Check for leaks.
	3. Loose power steering pump drive belt.	3. Tighten the power steering pump drive belt to specifications. If drive belt is worn or glazed, replace belt.
	4. Lack of lubrication in control arm ball joints.	4. Lubricate ball joints if ball joints are not a lubricated-for-life type ball joint. If ball joint is a lubricated-for-life ball joint, replace ball joint or control arm.
	5. Low power steering pump pressure (Perform Power Steering System Flow and Pressure Test).	5. Replace the power steering pump as necessary.
	6. High internal leak in power steering gear (Perform Power Steering System Flow and Pressure Test).	6. Replace power steering gear.
STEERING WHEEL DOES NOT RETURN TO CENTER POSITION.	1. Tires not inflated properly.	1. Inflate tires to specified pressure.
	2. Improper front wheel alignment.	2. Check and adjust wheel alignment as necessary.
	3. Lack of lubrication in front suspension control arm ball joints.	3. Lubricate ball joints if ball joints are not a lubricated for life type of ball joint. If ball joint is a lubricated for life ball joint, replace ball joint or control arm.
	4. Steering column coupling joints misaligned.	4. Realign steering column coupling joints.
	5. Steering wheel rubbing.	5. Adjust steering column shrouds to eliminate rubbing condition.

CR6029700192040X

Fig. 1 Troubleshooting (Part 4 of 6)

shaft front, then remove tool and spacer.

PRESSURE SWITCH, REPLACE

1. **On models equipped with 3.2 and 3.5L engines,** raise and support vehicle.
2. **On all models,** disconnect electrical connector and remove power steering pressure switch.
3. Reverse procedure to install.

SOLENOID CONTROL VALVE CONTROL MODULE, REPLACE

1. Remove electrical connector from control module.
2. Depress two locking tabs on bottom of control module and disconnect control module from steering gear end cap.
3. Rotate control module upward, until retaining tabs can be removed from steering gear end cap.
4. Remove control module from steering gear.
5. Reverse procedure to install.

SOLENOID CONTROL VALVE, REPLACE

1. Remove solenoid control valve electrical connector.
2. Remove power steering pressure and return hoses from steering gear. Allowing fluid to drain into suitable container.
3. Loosen and remove solenoid control valve from steering gear using a suitable crowfoot wrench.
4. Reverse procedure to install.

TECHNICAL SERVICE BULLETINS

Loose Feel Or Clunk In Steering Wheel

LHS, 2001 CONCORDE, INTREPID & 300M

On some of these models, there may be a loose feel or clunk in steering wheel as it is moved side to side.

This condition may be caused by the inner tie rod bushings.

To correct this condition, proceed as follows:

1. Remove inner tie rods as outlined under "Tie Rod End, Replace" in "Front Suspension & Steering" section of "Concorde, Intrepid, LHS & 300M" chapter.
2. Replace inner tie rod bushings using receiver tool No. 8438-1, 8438-3, 8438-4 and bushing sizer tool No. 8438-2, or equivalents.
3. Spray bushing using Mopar silicone spray part No. 04318070, or equivalent, to inner tie rod end and inside bushing sizer.
4. **Inner tie rod bushing is symmetrical. There is no designated top or bottom.**

CONDITION	POSSIBLE CAUSES	CORRECTION
	6. Damaged, mis-positioned or un-lubricated steering column coupler to dash seal.**	6. Replace, reposition, or lubricate dash seal.
	7. Binding upper or lower control arm ball joint.	7. Replace the upper or lower control arm ball joint.
	8. Tight shaft bearing in steering column.	8. Replace the steering column.
	9. Excessive friction in steering column coupling.	9. Replace steering column coupling.
	10. Excessive friction in power steering gear.	10. Replace power steering gear.
EXCESSIVE STEERING WHEEL KICKBACK OR TOO MUCH STEERING WHEEL FREE PLAY.	1. Air in the fluid of the power steering system.	1. Bleed air from system following the the power steering pump initial operation service procedure. *
	2. Power steering gear loose on front suspension crossmember.	2. Inspect power steering gear mounting bolts. Replace as necessary. Tighten to the specified torque.
	3. Steering column coupling worn, broken or loose.	3. Replace steering column coupling.
	4. Free play in steering column.	4. Check all components of the steering system and repair or replace as required.
	5. Worn control arm ball joints.	5. Replace ball joint or control arm as required.
	6. Loose steering knuckle to ball joint stud pinch bolt.	6. Inspect pinch bolts, replace as necessary, and tighten to specified torque.
	7. Front wheel bearings loose or worn.	7. Replace wheel bearing or knuckle as necessary.
	8. Loose outer tie rod ends.	8. Replace outer tie rod ends that have excessive free play.
	9. Loose inner tie rod ends.	9. Replace power steering gear.
	10 Defective steering gear rotary valve.	10. Replace power steering gear.

NOTE: * Steering shudder can be expected in new vehicles and vehicles with recent steering system repairs. Shudder should dissipate after the vehicle has been driven several weeks.

CR6029700192050X

Fig. 1 Troubleshooting (Part 5 of 6)

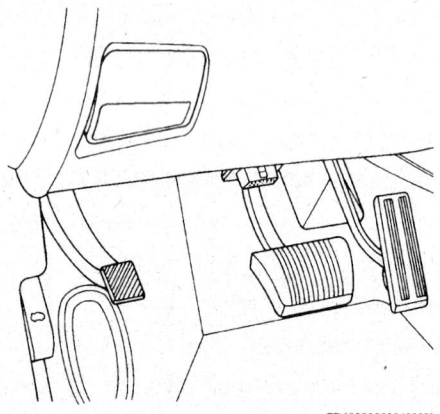

CR6029800204000X

Fig. 2 Data link connector location

CAV	CIRCUIT	FUNCTION
1	L60 18TN	RIGHT TURN SIGNAL
2	L61 18LG	LEFT TURN SIGNAL
3	G9 20GY/BK	RED BRAKE WARNING INDICATOR DRIVER
4	L34 20GY/OR	FUSED RIGHT HIGH BEAM OUTPUT
5	-	-
6	L1 20VT/BK	BACK-UP LAMP FEED
7	F18 20LG/BK	FUSED IGNITION SWITCH OUTPUT (RUN-START)
8	S77 18VT/OR (EXCEPT BUILT-UP EXPORT)	SPEED PROPORTIONAL STEERING SOLENOID (+)
9	-	-
10	S76 18LG/PK (EXCEPT BUILT-UP EXPORT)	SPEED PROPORTIONAL STEERING SOLENOID (-)

JUNCTION BLOCK - C10

CR6020000215000X

Fig. 3 Connector terminal identification (Part 2 of 3)

CONDITION	POSSIBLE CAUSES	CORRECTION
LOW FLUID LEVEL WITH VISIBLE LEAK.	1. Loose power steering hose fittings.	1. Tighten the fitting to its specified torque.
	2. Damaged or missing fitting seal, gasket, or O-ring.	2. Replace as necessary.
	3. Power steering pump or power steering gear leaking.	3. Repair or replace the leaking component as required.
AERATED FLUID.	1. Low fluid level.*	1. Fill power steering fluid reservoir to proper level.
	2. Air leak between power steering fluid reservoir and pump.	2. Inspect for proper sealing. Replace the power steering pump (with reservoir).
	3. Cracked power steering pump housing.	3. Replace the power steering pump.
RESERVOIR FLUID OVERFLOW AND FLUID THAT IS MILKY IN COLOR	1. Water contamination.	1. Drain the power steering fluid from the system. Flush the system with fresh clean power steering fluid, drain, then refill to the proper level.

CR6029700192060X

Fig. 1 Troubleshooting (Part 6 of 6)

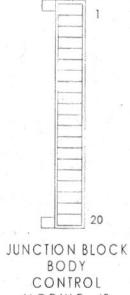

JUNCTION BLOCK BODY CONTROL MODULE - JB

CAV	CIRCUIT	FUNCTION
1	Z20	GROUND
2	M2	COURTESY LAMP DRIVER
3	S76	SPEED PROPORTIONAL STEERING SOLENOID (-)
4	S77	SPEED PROPORTIONAL STEERING SOLENOID (+)
5	G5	FUSED IGNITION SWITCH OUTPUT (RUN-START)
6	L7	PARK LAMP RELAY OUTPUT
7	M1	FUSED B(+)
8	P2	DECKLID RELEASE CONTROL
9	-	
10	D25	PCI BUS (OTIS)
11	-	
12	-	-
13	P109	DRIVER DOOR UNLOCK RELAY CONTROL
14	L307	LOW BEAM RELAY CONTROL
15	P38	DOOR LOCK RELAY CONTROL
16	L308	PARK LAMP RELAY CONTROL
17	L26	FOG LAMP RELAY CONTROL
18	X3	HORN RELAY CONTROL
19	P36	DOOR UNLOCK RELAY CONTROL
20	Z2	GROUND

CR6020000214000X

Fig. 3 Connector terminal identification (Part 1 of 3)

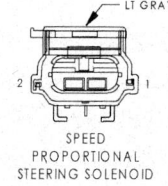
← LT GRAY

SPEED PROPORTIONAL STEERING SOLENOID

CAV	CIRCUIT	FUNCTION
1	S76 18LG/PK	SPEED PROPORTIONAL STEERING SOLENOID (-)
2	S77 18VT/OR	SPEED PROPORTIONAL STEERING SOLENOID (+)

CR6020000216000X

Fig. 3 Connector terminal identification (Part 3 of 3)

TEST	ACTION
1	Start the engine. While turning the Steering Wheel, monitor the amount of force it takes to turn the Steering Wheel. With the DRBIII®, de-activate the Speed Pro Steering Solenoid for 15 seconds. Again turn the Steering Wheel and monitor the amount of force it takes to turn the Steering Wheel. Was the Steering Wheel harder to turn with the Speed Pro Steering Solenoid de-activated? Yes → System is operating properly at this time. Erase DTC, inspect the wiring and connectors and repair as necessary. Perform SPEED PRO STEERING VERIFICATION TEST - VER 1. No → Go To 2
2	Turn the ignition off. Disconnect the Speed Pro Steering Solenoid harness connector. Measure the resistance of the Speed Pro Steering Solenoid. Is the resistance between 5.7 and 6.3 ohms at 20 C (68° F)? Yes → Go To 3 No → Replace the Speed Pro Steering Solenoid. Perform SPEED PRO STEERING VERIFICATION TEST - VER 1.

CR6020000217010X

Fig. 4 Speed Pro Steering Circuit Short to Voltage (Part 1 of 2)

TEST	ACTION
3	Turn the ignition off. Disconnect the Speed Pro Steering Solenoid harness connector. Start the engine. Measure the voltage of the Speed Pro Steering Solenoid (+) circuit in the Speed Pro Steering Solenoid harness connector. Is there any voltage present? Yes → Repair the Seed Pro Steering Solenoid (+) circuit for a short to voltage. Perform SPEED PRO STEERING VERIFICATION TEST - VER 1. No → Go To 4
4	Turn the ignition off. Disconnect the Speed Pro Steering Solenoid harness connector. Start the engine. Measure the voltage of the Speed Pro Steering Solenoid (-) circuit in the Speed Pro Steering Solenoid harness connector. Is there any voltage present? Yes → Repair the Speed Pro Steering Solenoid (-) circuit for a short to voltage and replace the Body Control Module (BCM will be damaged). Perform BODY VERIFICATION TEST - VER 1. No → Go To 5
5	Turn the ignition off. Disconnect the Speed Pro Steering Solenoid harness connector. Remove the Body Control Module from the Junction Block. Measure the resistance of the Speed Pro Steering Solenoid (+) circuit to the Speed Pro Steering Solenoid (-) circuit in the Junction Block BCM Internal connector. Is the resistance below 100.0 ohms Yes → Repair the Speed Pro Steering Solenoid (+) circuit for a short to the Speed Pro Steering Solenoid (-) circuit. Perform SPEED PRO STEERING VERIFICATION TEST - VER 1. No → Go To 6
6	If there are no possible causes remaining, view repair. Repair Replace the Body Control Module. Perform BODY VERIFICATION TEST - VER 1.

CR6020000217020X

Fig. 4   Speed Pro Steering Circuit Short to Voltage (Part 2 of 2)

TEST	ACTION
3	Turn the ignition off. Disconnect the Speed Pro Steering Solenoid harness connector. Measure the resistance between ground and the Speed Pro Steering Solenoid (+) circuit in the Speed Pro Steering Solenoid harness connector. Is the resistance below 100 ohms? Yes → Repair the Speed Pro Steering (+) circuit for a short to ground. Perform SPEED PRO STEERING VERIFICATION TEST - VER 1. No → Go To 4
4	Turn the ignition off. Disconnect the Speed Pro Steering Solenoid harness connector. Measure the resistance between ground and the Speed Pro Steering Solenoid (-) circuit in the Speed Pro Steering Solenoid harness connector. Is the resistance below 100 ohms? Yes → Repair the Speed Pro Steering (-) circuit for a short to ground. Perform SPEED PRO STEERING VERIFICATION TEST - VER 1. No → Go To 5
5	Turn the ignition off. Disconnect the Speed Pro Steering Solenoid harness connector. Remove the Body Control Module from the Junction Block. Measure the resistance of the Speed Pro Steering Solenoid (-) circuit between the Junction Block BCM connector and the Speed Pro Steering Solenoid harness connector. Is the resistance below 5.0 ohms? Yes → Go To 6 No → Repair the open Speed Pro Steering Solenoid (-) circuit. Perform SPEED PRO STEERING VERIFICATION TEST - VER 1.
6	Turn the ignition off. Disconnect the Speed Pro Steering Solenoid harness connector. Remove the Body Control Module from the Junction Block. Measure the resistance of the Speed Pro Steering Solenoid (-) circuit to the Speed Pro Steering Solenoid (+) circuit in the Junction Block BCM Internal connector. Is the resistance below 100.0 ohms Yes → Repair the Speed Pro Steering Solenoid (+) circuit for a short to the Speed Pro Steering Solenoid (-) circuit. Perform SPEED PRO STEERING VERIFICATION TEST - VER 1. No → Go To 7
7	Turn the ignition off. Disconnect the Speed Pro Steering Solenoid harness connector. Remove the Body Control Module from the Junction Block. Measure the resistance of the Speed Pro Steering Solenoid (+) circuit between the Junction Block BCM connector and the Speed Pro Steering Solenoid connector. Is the resistance below 5.0 ohms? Yes → Go To 8 No → Repair the open Speed Pro Steering Solenoid (+) circuit. Perform SPEED PRO STEERING VERIFICATION TEST - VER 1.
8	If there are no possible causes remaining, view repair. Repair Replace the Body Control Module. Perform BODY VERIFICATION TEST - VER 1.

CR6020000218020X

Fig. 5   Speed Pro Steering Solenoid Circuit Open/ Shorted to Ground (Part 2 of 2)

TEST	ACTION
1	Start the engine. While turning the Steering Wheel, monitor the amount of force it takes to turn the Steering Wheel With the DRBIII®, de-activate the Speed Pro Steering Solenoid for 15 seconds. Again turn the steering wheel and monitor the amount of force it takes to turn the Steering Wheel. Was the Steering Wheel harder to turn while the Speed Pro Steering Solenoid was de-activated? Yes → System is operating properly at this time. Erase the DTC, inspect the wiring and connectors and repair as necessary. Perform SPEED PRO STEERING VERIFICATION TEST - VER 1. No → Go To 2
2	Turn the ignition off. Disconnect the Speed Pro Steering Solenoid harness connector. Measure the resistance of the Speed Pro Steering Solenoid. Is the resistance between 5.7 and 6.3 ohms at 20 C (68° F)? Yes → Go To 3 No → Replace the Speed Pro Steering Solenoid. Perform SPEED PRO STEERING VERIFICATION TEST - VER 1.

CR6020000218010X

Fig. 5   Speed Pro Steering Solenoid Circuit Open/ Shorted to Ground (Part 1 of 2)

TEST	ACTION
1	Start the engine. While turning the Steering Wheel, monitor the amount of force it takes to turn the Steering Wheel. With the DRBIII®, de-activate the Speed Pro Steering Solenoid for 15 seconds. Again turn the steering wheel and monitor the amount of force it takes to turn the Steering Wheel. Was the Steering Wheel harder to turn while the Speed Pro Steering Solenoid was de-activated? Yes → System is operating properly at this time. Erase the DTC, inspect the wiring and connectors and repair as necessary. Perform SPEED PRO STEERING VERIFICATION TEST - VER 1. No → Go To 2
2	Turn the ignition off. Disconnect the Speed Pro Steering Solenoid harness connector. Measure the resistance of the Speed Pro Steering Solenoid. Is the resistance between 5.7 and 6.3 ohms at 20 C (68° F)? Yes → Go To 3 No → Replace the Speed Pro Steering Solenoid. Perform SPEED PRO STEERING VERIFICATION TEST - VER 1.

CR6020000219010X

Fig. 6   Speed Pro Steering Solenoid Over Temperature (Part 1 of 2)

TEST	ACTION
3	Using the wiring diagram/schematic as a guide, inspect the wiring and connectors from the BCM to the Speed Pro Steering Solenoid. Check for chafed, pinched, open or shorted wiring. Were there any problems found? Yes → Repair the Speed Pro Steering Solenoid wiring and/or connectors as necessary. Perform SPEED PRO STEERING VERIFICATION TEST - VER 1. No → Go To 4
4	If there are no possible causes remaining, view repair. Repair Replace the Body Control Module. Perform BODY VERIFICATION TEST - VER 1.

CR6020000219020X

Fig. 6   Speed Pro Steering Solenoid Over Temperature (Part 2 of 2)

BODY VERIFICATION TEST - VER 1

1. Disconnect all jumper wires and reconnect all previously disconnected components and connectors.
2. If the Sentry Key Immobilizer Module (SKIM) or the Powertrain Control Module (PCM) was replaced, proceed to number 6. If the SKIM or PCM was not replaced, continue to the next number.
3. If the Body Control Module was replaced, turn the ignition on for 15 seconds (to allow the new BCM to learn VIN) or engine may not start (if VTSS equipped). If the vehicle is equipped with VTSS, use the DRBIII® and enable VTSS.
4. Program all other options as needed.
5. If any repairs were made to the HVAC System, disconnect the battery or, using the DRBIII®, recalibrate the HVAC doors. Proceed to number 13.
6. Obtain the Vehicle's unique PIN assigned to it's original SKIM from either the vehicle's invoice or from Chrysler's Customer Assistance Center (1-800-992-1997).
7. NOTE: Once Secured Access Mode is active, the SKIM will remain in that mode for 60 seconds.
8. With the DRBIII®, select THEFT ALARM, SKIM, MISCELLANEOUS and select SKIM REPLACED. Enter the 4 digit PIN to put the SKIM in Secured Access Mode.
9. The DRBIII® will prompt for the following steps. (1) Program the country code into the SKIM's memory. (2) Program the vehicle's VIN into the SKIM memory. (3) Transfer the vehicle's Secret Key data from the PCM.
10. Using the DRBIII®, program all customer keys into the SKIM memory. This requires that the SKIM be in Secured Access Mode, using the 4 digit PIN.
11. Note: If the PCM is replaced, the VIN and the unique Secret Key data must be transferred from the SKIM to the PCM. This procedure requires the SKIM to be placed in Secured Access Mode using the 4-digit PIN.
12. Note: If 3 attempts are made to enter Secured Access Mode using an incorrect PIN, Secured Access Mode will be locked out for 1 hour which causes the DRBIII® to display "Bus +\- Signals Open". To exit this mode, turn ignition to Run for 1 hour.
13. Ensure that all accessories are turned off and the battery is fully charged.
14. Ensure that the Ignition is on.
15. With the DRBIII®, record and erase all DTCs from ALL modules. Start and run the engine for 2 minutes. Operate all functions of the system that caused the original concern.
16. Turn the ignition off and wait 5 seconds. Turn the ignition on and using the DRBIII®, read DTCs from ALL modules.
Are any DTC's present or is the original condition still present?

Yes → Repair is not complete, refer to appropriate symptom.

No → Repair is complete.

CR6020000220000X

Fig. 7   Verification Test VER-1

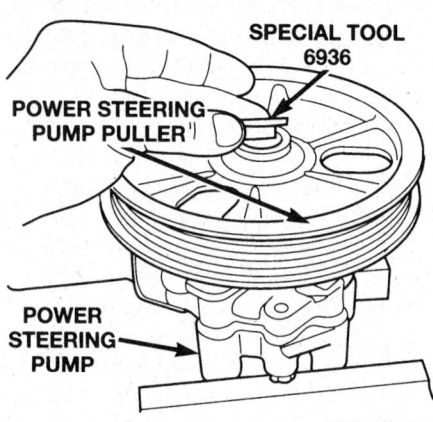

CR6029800208000X

Fig. 8   Spacer tool installation into pulley

TIGHTENING SPECIFICATIONS

Year	Component	Torque Ft. Lbs.
2001–04	Air Bag Module	75①
	Hose Tube Nuts	35
	Power Steering Gear Mounting	43
	Power Steering Pump	21
	Power Steering Pump Discharge Fitting	62
	Reservoir, Pulley Side	10
	Reservoir, Rear (2.7L)	18
	Speed Control Switch	13①
	Steering Column Coupler	20
	Steering Column	105①
	Steering Wheel	45
	Tie Rod Adjuster Pinch Bolt	28
	Tie Rod Steering Arm	27
	Tie Rod Steering Gear	74

① — Inch lbs.

Crossfire

NOTE: On Air Bag Equipped Models, Refer To "Air Bag System Precautions" Located In The Front Of This Manual For System Disarming & Arming Procedures.

NOTE: Refer To "Computer Relearn Procedures" Located In The Front Of This Manual When Battery Power To The Computer Has Been Interrupted.

POWER STEERING PRESSURE SPECIFICATIONS

Model	Year	Power Steering Pump Pressure, psi		Output Flow, Gallons Per Minute③
		Test Valve	Max Relief Pressure	
		Open①	Closed②		
Crossfire	2004–05	50–80	1250–1350	1250–1350	2.4–2.8

① — Initial pressure.

② — Do not leave valve closed for more than five seconds.

③ — At 1500 RPM & minimum pressure.

PRECAUTIONS

Air Bag Systems

Refer to "Air Bag System Precautions" in the front of this manual for system disarming and arming procedures.

Battery Ground Cable

Prior to service, disconnect battery ground cable and isolate as required.

DESCRIPTION

The power steering pump on this model, uses a constant flow rate displacement vane type pump with the fluid reservoir attached to the pump body, **Fig. 1.** The steering gear used is a recirculating ball type gear, input is provided by the steering column input, **Fig. 2.**

TROUBLESHOOTING

Refer to **Figs. 3 through 5** for steering system troubleshooting.

DIAGNOSIS & TESTING

Accessing Diagnostic Trouble Codes

Connect the DRB III, or suitably programmed scan tool, to the Data Link Connector (DLC) located near hood release, **Fig. 6.** The diagnostic cycle begins when the ignition is turned On.

Connector Terminal Identification

Refer to **Fig. 7** for connector terminal identification.

Diagnostic Tests

Refer to **MOTOR's "Domestic Engine Performance & Driveability Manual"** for DTC diagnostic test procedures.

Clearing Diagnostic Trouble Codes

Follow tool manufacturer's instructions to clean DTCs.

Component Testing

POWER STEERING PUMP & GEAR

1. Connect pressure gauge hose from power steering analyzer to tube No. 6865. or equivalent, **Fig. 8.**
2. Connect adapter tool No. 6826, or equivalent. to steering analyzer test valve.
3. Disconnect high pressure hose from steering pump.

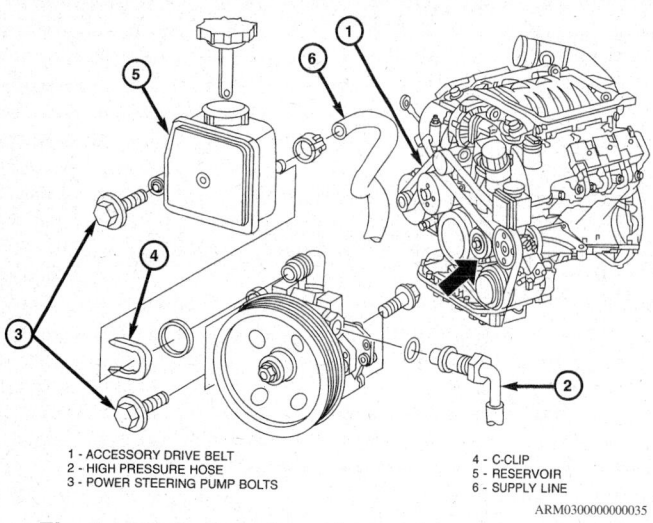

1 - ACCESSORY DRIVE BELT
2 - HIGH PRESSURE HOSE
3 - POWER STEERING PUMP BOLTS
4 - C-CLIP
5 - RESERVOIR
6 - SUPPLY LINE

ARM0300000000035

Fig. 1   Exploded view of power steering pump

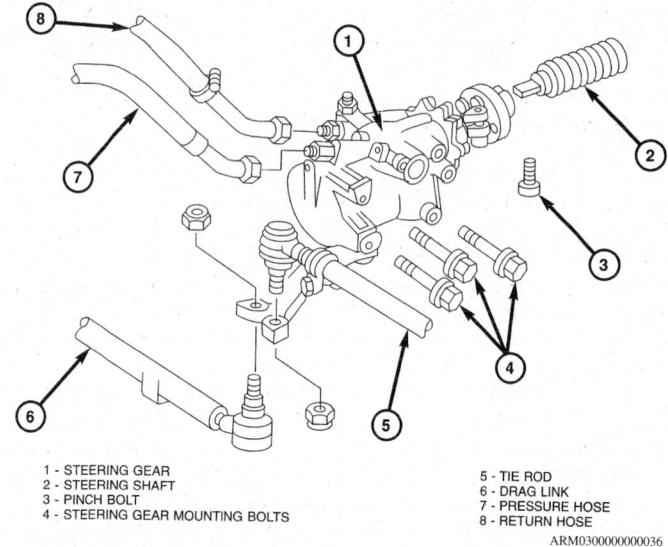

1 - STEERING GEAR
2 - STEERING SHAFT
3 - PINCH BOLT
4 - STEERING GEAR MOUNTING BOLTS
5 - TIE ROD
6 - DRAG LINK
7 - PRESSURE HOSE
8 - RETURN HOSE

ARM0300000000036

Fig. 2   Exploded view of power steering gear

STEERING NOISE

CONDITION	POSSIBLE CAUSES	CORRECTION
HISS OR WHISTLE	1. Steering intermediate shaft to dash panel seal.	1. Check and repair seal at dash panel.
	2. Noisy valve in power steering gear.	2. Replace steering gear.
RATTLE OR CLUNK	1. Gear mounting bolts loose.	1. Tighten bolts to specification.
	2. Loose or damaged suspension components.	2. Inspect and repair suspension.
	3. Loose or damaged steering linkage.	3. Inspect and repair steering linkage.
	4. Internal gear noise.	4. Replace gear.
	5. Pressure hose in contact with other components.	5. Reposition hose.
CHIRP OR SQUEAL	1. Loose belt.	1. Adjust or replace.
	2. Belt routing.	2. Verify belt routing is correct.
WHINE OR GROWL	1. Low fluid level.	1. Fill to proper level.
	2. Pressure hose in contact with other components.	2. Reposition hose.
	3. Internal pump noise.	3. Replace pump.
	4. Air in the system.	4. Perform pump initial operation.
SUCKING AIR SOUND	1. Loose return line clamp.	1. Replace clamp.
	2. O-ring missing or damaged on hose fitting.	2. Replace o-ring.
	3. Low fluid level.	3. Fill to proper level.
	4. Air leak between pump and reservoir.	4. Repair as necessary.
SCRUBBING OR KNOCKING	1. Wrong tire size.	1. Verify tire size.
	2. Wrong gear.	2. Verify gear.

ARM0300000000037

Fig. 3   Steering noise

4. Connect tube 6865 onto pump hose fitting.
5. Connect power steering hose from steering gear to adapter tool No. 6826, or equivalent.
6. Fully open test valve.
7. Start engine and let idle long enough to circulate fluid pressure test gauge.
8. Turn engine off, then inspect and adjust fluid level.
9. Start engine and allow to idle.
10. If pressure is higher than specified, inspect hoses for restrictions.
11. Close valve fully three times, for no more the three seconds or pump damage could occur.
12. Record highest pressure indicated. All reading must be within 50 psi of each other.
13. Is pressure are not within 50 psi, replace power steering pump.
14. Open test valve and turn steering wheel to extreme left and righthand positions against stops. **Do not force**

BINDING AND STICKING

CONDITION	POSSIBLE CAUSE	CORRECTION
DIFFICULT TO TURN WHEEL STICKS OR BINDS	1. Low fluid level.	1. Fill to proper level.
	2. Tire pressure.	2. Adjust tire pressure.
	3. Steering component.	3. Inspect and lube.
	4. Loose belt.	4. Adjust or replace.
	5. Low pump pressure.	5. Pressure test and replace if necessary.
	6. Column shaft coupler binding.	6. Replace coupler.
	7. Steering gear worn or out of adjustment.	7. Repair or replace gear.
	8. Ball joints binding.	8. Inspect and repair as necessary.
	9. Belt routing.	9. Verify belt routing is correct.

INSUFFICIENT ASSISTANCE. OR POOR RETURN TO CENTER

CONDITION	POSSIBLE CAUSE	CORRECTION
HARD TURNING OR MOMENTARY INCREASE IN TURNING EFFORT	1. Tire pressure.	1. Adjust tire pressure.
	2. Low fluid level.	2. Fill to proper level.
	3. Loose belt.	3. Adjust or replace.
	4. Lack of lubrication.	4. Inspect and lubricate steering and suspension components.
	5. Low pump pressure or flow.	5. Pressure and flow test and repair as necessary.
	6. Internal gear leak.	6. Pressure and flow test, and repair as necessary.
	7. Belt routing.	7. Verify belt routing is correct.
STEERING WHEEL DOES NOT WANT TO RETURN TO CENTER POSITION	1. Tire pressure.	1. Adjust tire pressure.
	2. Wheel alignment.	2. Align front end.
	3. Lack of lubrication.	3. Inspect and lubricate steering and suspension components.
	4. High friction in steering gear.	4. Test and adjust as necessary.
	5. Ball joints binding.	5. Inspect and repair as necessary.

Note:
Some roads will cause a vehicle to drift, due to the crown in the road.

ARM0300000000038

Fig. 4   Binding & sticking

pump to operate against stops for more than 2–4 seconds at a time.
15. Record highest pressure indicated at each steering stop position. All readings must be within 50 psi of each other. If pressure readings are not as specified, steering gear is leaking internally and must be repaired or replaced.

SYSTEM SERVICE

Power Steering System Bleed

1. Ensure power steering fluid reservoir

is full, then start engine and turn steering wheel from stop to stop approximately 20 times times.
2. Stop engine and inspect fluid level again. Add fluid until proper fluid level is reached.
3. Repeat procedure until fluid level is consistent. Inspect system for leaks.

Component Service

DRIVE PULLEY, REPLACE

REMOVAL

1. Remove power steering pump as outlined under "Power Steering Pump, Replace" in "Front Suspension &

CONDITION	POSSIBLE CAUSE	CORRECTION
EXCESSIVE PLAY IN STEERING WHEEL	1. Worn or loose suspension or steering components.	1. Repair as necessary.
	2. Worn or loose wheel bearings.	2. Repair as necessary.
	3. Steering gear mounting.	3. Tighten gear mounting bolts to specification.
	4. Gear out of adjustment.	4. Adjust gear to specification.
	5. Worn or loose steering coupler.	5. Repair as necessary.
VEHICLE PULLS TO ONE SIDE DURING BRAKING	1. Tire Pressure.	1. Adjust tire pressure.
	2. Air in brake hydraulics system.	2. Bleed brake system.
	3. Worn brake components.	3. Repair as necessary.
VEHICLE LEADS OR DRIFTS FROM STRAIGHT AHEAD DIRECTION ON UNCROWNED ROAD.	1. Tire pressure.	1. Adjust tire pressure.
	2. Radial tire lead.	2. Cross front tires.
	3. Brakes dragging.	3. Repair as necessary.
	4. Wheel alignment.	4. Align vehicle.
	5. Weak or broken spring.	5. Replace spring.
	6. Loose or worn steering/suspension components.	6. Repair as necessary.

ARM0300000000039

Fig. 5   Loose steering & vehicle leads or drifts

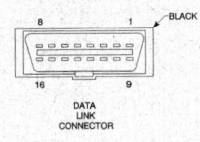

CAVITY	COLOR	GAUGE	FUNCTION
1	BK/WT	20	SCI TRANSMIT
2	—	—	—
3	DG/YL	20	SCI RECEIVE
4	BR	18	GROUND
5	BR/WT	20	SENSOR GROUND
6	—	—	—
7	BL	20	SCI TRANSMIT
8	RD/WT	20	SCI TRANSMIT
9	RD/YL	20	SCI TRANSMIT
10	—	—	—
11	DG	20	SCI TRANSMIT
12	YL/DG	20	SCI TRANSMIT
13	YL	20	SCI TRANSMIT
14	—	—	—
15	BK/BL	20	SCI TRANSMIT
16	RD/DG	18	FUSED B(+)

DATA LINK CONNECTOR — BLACK 16 WAY

ARM0300000000042

Fig. 7   Connector terminal identification

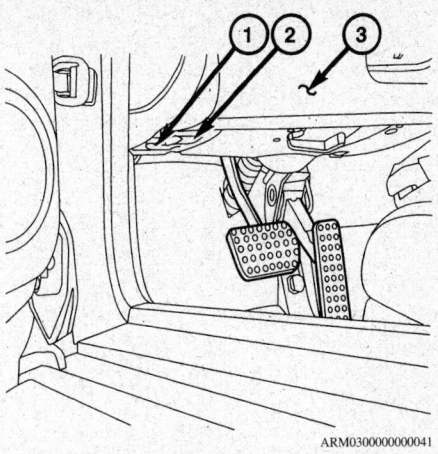

ARM0300000000041

Fig. 6   Data link connector location

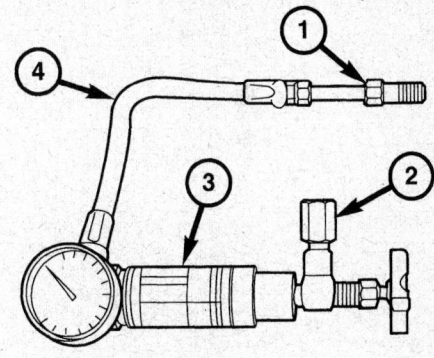

1 Gauge adapter
2 Test valve
3 Gauge assembly
4 Analyzer gauge tubr #6865

ARM0300000000040

Fig. 8   Power steering pump analyzer

Steering" section of "Crossfire" chapter.

2. Mount pump by mounting pump flange boss in suitable vise. **Do not clamp pump body or reservoir in vise.**
3. Remove mounting nut and drive pulley using drive pulley removal tool No. C-4333, or equivalent. **Do not use press or hammer on pump shaft.**

INSTALLATION

1. Place pulley squarely on shaft end and install spacer provided with pump or pulley.
2. Install spacer tool No. 6936, or equivalent, into pulley hub.
3. Thread spacer installation tool No. C-4063, or equivalent, into pump shaft.
4. Holding installer tool with one wrench, turn installer hex down threaded rod pushing pulley onto shaft. Ensure tool and pulley remain aligned.
5. Ensure spacer is fully seated against shaft front, then remove tool and spacer.

PITMAN SHAFT & SEAL, REPLACE

1. Measure distance of point (A) between pitman arm point (2) and steering gear point (1), using caliper gauge, **Fig. 9.**
2. Remove lower snap ring and pitman arm from shaft, **Fig. 10.**
3. Remove pitman shaft seal upper locking ring.
4. Remove pitman shaft seal from steering gear housing using suitable pry tool.
5. Install new seal using seal installer tool No. 9159, or equivalent, **Fig. 11.**
6. Reverse procedures to install.

IDLER ARM, REPLACE

1. Raise and support vehicle.
2. Remove mounting bolt and idler arm drag link, **Fig. 12.**
3. Remove steering linkage heat shield.
4. Remove mounting bolts and idler arm.
5. Remove pinch bolt, and idler arm bushing.

6. Reverse procedure to install.

STEERING DAMPER, REPLACE

1. Remove nut and bolt from steering damper mounting bracket, **Fig. 13.**
2. Remove drag link mounting nut and bolt.
3. Remove steering damper.
4. Reverse procedure to install.

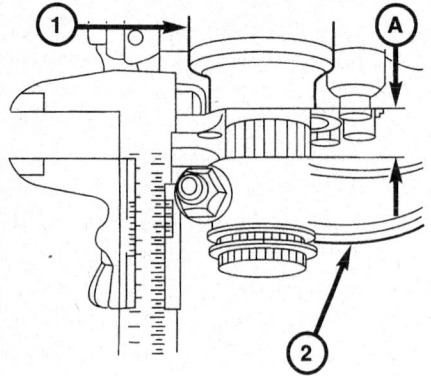

1. Caliper gauge
2. Steering gear
A. Distance pitman arm

ARM0300000000046

Fig. 9   Pitman arm measurement points

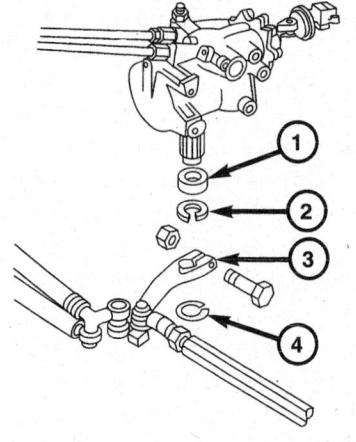

1. Pitman shaft seal
2. Upper locking ring
3. Pitman arm
4. lower snap ring

ARM0300000000047

Fig. 10   Pitman arm shaft & seal replacement

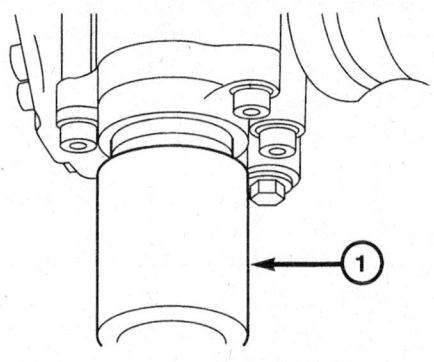

1. Pitman seal installer tool No. 9159

ARM0300000000048

Fig. 11   Pitman shaft & seal installation

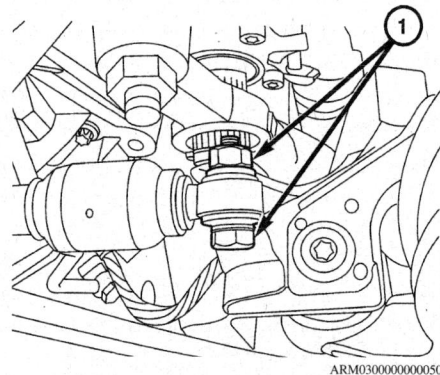

ARM0300000000050

Fig. 13   Steering damper replacement. Crossfire

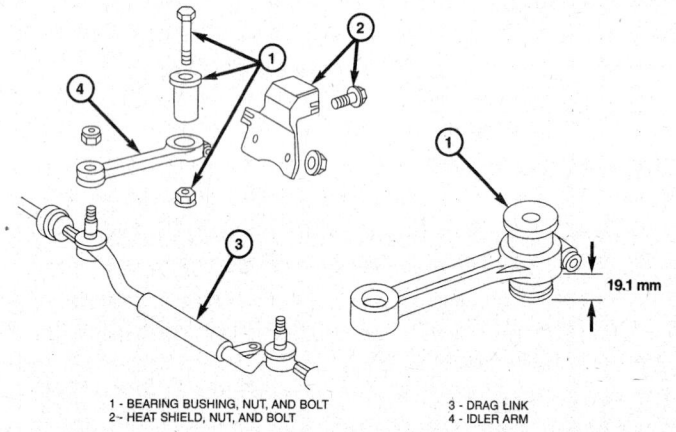

1 - BEARING BUSHING, NUT, AND BOLT
2 - HEAT SHIELD, NUT, AND BOLT

3 - DRAG LINK
4 - IDLER ARM

ARM0300000000049

Fig. 12   Idler arm replacement

TIGHTENING SPECIFICATIONS

Year	Component	Torque Ft. Lbs.
2004	Air Bag Module	71①
	Draglink To Idler Arm	37
	Draglink To Pitman Arm	37
	Engine Mount	18
	Hose Tube Nuts	22
	Idler Arm	37
	Idler Arm Pinch Bolt	22
	Pitman Arm Pinch Bolt	41
	Power Steering Gear	44
	Power Steering Pump	15
	Power Steering High Pressure Hose	22
	Power Steering Pump Discharge Fitting	30
	Steering Damper	29
	Tie Rod Steering Arm	37

① — Inch lbs.

Magnum, 300 & 300C

NOTE: On Air Bag Equipped Models, Refer To "Air Bag System Precautions" Located In The Front Of This Manual For System Disarming & Arming Procedures.

NOTE: Refer To "Computer Relearn Procedures" Located In The Front Of This Manual When Battery Power To The Computer Has Been Interrupted.

INDEX

POWER STEERING PRESSURE SPECIFICATIONS

Model	Year	Power Steering Pump Pressure, psi			Output Flow, Gallons Per Minute①
		Test Valve		Max Relief Pressure	
		Open	Closed		
Magnum, 300 & 300C	2005	50–125	1640–1740	1640–1740	2.2

① — At 1100 RPM & minimum pressure.

PRECAUTIONS

Air Bag Systems

Refer to "Air Bag System Precautions" in the front of this manual for system disarming and arming procedures.

Battery Ground Cable

Prior to service, disconnect battery ground cable and isolate as required.

DESCRIPTION

Hydraulic pressure for operation of the power steering gear is provided by a belt-driven all-aluminum power steering pump. It is a droop flow rate and constant displacement type pump. A common power steering pump, mounted in a common location (left front of engine), is standard on all models.

TROUBLESHOOTING

Refer to "Concorde, Intrepid, LHS & 300M" when troubleshooting the power steering system.

SYSTEM SERVICE

Power Steering System Bleed

1. Wipe filler cap clean and adjust fluid level. Dipstick should indicate COLD when fluid is at normal temperature.
2. Turn steering wheel all way to left.
3. Adjust pump fluid reservoir to proper level and let fluid settle for at least two minutes.
4. Raise and support front wheels off ground.
5. Slowly turn steering wheel lock-to-lock 20 times with engine off while checking fluid level. On vehicles with long return lines or oil coolers turn wheel 40 times.
6. Start engine and idling maintain fluid level.
7. Lower front wheels and let engine idle for two minutes.
8. Turn steering wheel in both direction, then ensure power assist and quiet operation.
9. If fluid is extremely foamy or milky looking, allow vehicle to stand few minutes and repeat procedure.
10. Do not run vehicle with foamy fluid for extended period.

Component Service

PUMP PULLEY, REPLACE

1. Siphon power steering fluid from pump reservoir.
2. Remove air cleaner housing and inlet tube to throttle body.
3. Remove clamps, then the reservoir supply and return hoses.
4. Remove reservoir from coolant bottle by sliding it out of guide.
5. Reverse procedure to install.

OIL COOLER, REPLACE

1. Siphon power steering fluid from pump reservoir.
2. Raise and support vehicle.
3. Remove mounting screws and belly pan.
4. Remove clamps, then return hose from steering gear at cooler and to reservoir at cooler.
5. Push in on clip tabs and remove cooler from clips mounted to cooling module.
6. Reverse procedure to install.

TIGHTENING SPECIFICATIONS

Year	Component	Torque Ft. Lbs.
2005	Hose Tube	35
	Outer Tie Rod Ball Joint	63
	Power Steering Gear, AWD	75
	Power Steering Gear, RWD	70
	Power Steering Pump	21
	Tie Rod Jam Nut	55

Neon, Sebring Convertible, Sebring Sedan & Stratus Sedan

NOTE: On Air Bag Equipped Models, Refer To "Air Bag System Precautions" Located In The Front Of This Manual For System Disarming & Arming Procedures.

NOTE: Refer To "Computer Relearn Procedures" Located In The Front Of This Manual When Battery Power To The Computer Has Been Interrupted.

INDEX

POWER STEERING PRESSURE SPECIFICATIONS

Model	Year	Power Steering Pump Pressure, psi			Output Flow, Gallons Per Minute③
		Test Valve		Max Relief Pressure	
		Open①	Closed		
Neon	2001–05	50–80	1350–1450②	1350–1450	1.5–1.7
Sebring Sedan, Stratus Sedan & Sebring Convertible	2001–05	50–80	1195–1293	1195–1293	1.3–1.6

① — Initial pressure.

② — Do not leave valve closed for more than five seconds.

③ — At 1500 RPM & minimum pressure.

PRECAUTIONS

Air Bag Systems

Refer to "Air Bag System Precautions" in the front of this manual for system disarming and arming procedures.

Battery Ground Cable

Prior to service, disconnect battery ground cable and isolate as required.

DESCRIPTION

The steering gear is a rack and pinion type using power assist. These models have two versions depending upon production date. Early production models have two parallel flats on end where steering column intermediate shaft would bolt up. Later production models have two flats that are at 60° angles to one another where steering column intermediate shaft would bolt up.

The hydraulic pressure for operation of the power steering gear is provided by a belt driven power steering pump. Early production models are equipped with variable

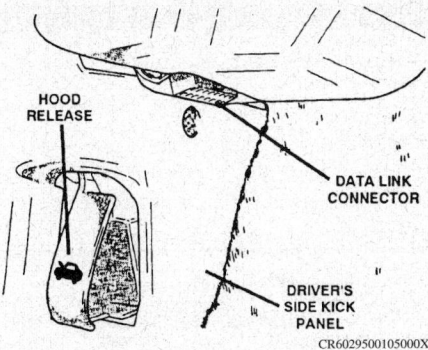

Fig. 1 DLC location

assist power steering pumps. Later production models are equipped with standard power steering pumps only.

TROUBLESHOOTING

Refer to "Concorde, Intrepid, LHS & 300M" when troubleshooting the power steering system.

DIAGNOSIS & TESTING

Accessing Diagnostic Trouble Codes

Connect DRB, or suitable programmed scan tool, to the Data Link Connector (DLC), **Fig. 1**. The diagnostic cycle begins when the ignition is turned On.

Connector Terminal Identification

Refer to **Fig. 2** for connector terminal identification.

Diagnostic Tests

Refer to **Figs. 3 and 4** for diagnostic and testing procedures.

Clearing Diagnostic Trouble Codes

Follow tool manufacturer's instructions to clean DTCs.

SYSTEM SERVICE

Power Steering System Bleed

To avoid personal injury, power steering fluid level should be inspected with engine Off. Use only approved fluid. Do not use automatic transmission fluid. Do not overfill fluid system.
1. Wipe filler cap clean and inspect fluid level.
2. Dipstick should indicate Full Cold when fluid is at normal temperature, approximately 70–80° F.
3. Fill power steering pump fluid reservoir

to proper level with approved power steering fluid.
4. Start and run engine for few seconds, then turn engine Off.
5. Adjust fluid level.
6. Repeat previous procedure until fluid level remains constant after running engine.
7. Raise front wheels off ground and start engine.
8. Slowly turn steering wheel left and right, lightly contacting wheel stops.
9. Turn engine off and adjust fluid level.
10. Lower vehicle and start engine.
11. Turn steering wheel slowly from lock to lock.
12. Stop engine and adjust fluid level.
13. If fluid is extremely foamy, wait few minutes, then repeat entire bleeding procedure.

Pump Pressure Inspection

NON-VARIABLE & ELECTRONICALLY CONTROLLED VARIABLE ASSIST

1. Disconnect power steering fluid pressure hose at power steering pump.
2. Connect inlet hose on pressure gauge tool No. 6815, or equivalent, using suitable adapter to pressure fitting on power steering pump.
3. Connect pressure hose power steering pump to outlet port of pressure gauge using suitable adapter fitting. **Pressure gauge is to be installed in series with power steering pressure hose, between pump and steering gear. It must also be installed so it is in proper direction of fluid flow.**
4. Completely open valve on gauge.
5. Start engine and let idle long enough to circulate fluid through flow/pressure test and get air out of fluid.
6. Turn off engine and adjust inspect fluid level.
7. Start engine. Pressure gauge should read less than 125 psi. If reading is more than specified, inspect hoses for restrictions.
8. Initial pressure reading should be 50–80 psi and flow meter should read 1.3–1.6 GPM.
9. Close pressure gauge valve fully three times and record highest pressure each time. Readings must be more than specified and within 50 psi of each other. **Do not leave valve closed for more than five seconds as pump could be damaged.**
10. Open test valve, then turn steering wheel to left and right until against stops, recording highest pressure at each position. **Do not force pump to operate against stops for more than 2–4 seconds as pump damage will result.**
11. Compare pressure gauge readings to specifications.
12. If highest output pressures are not same against either stop, steering

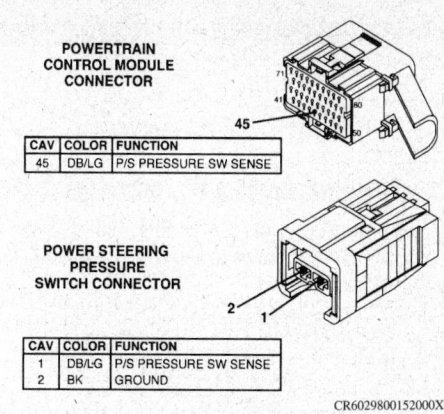

Fig. 2 Connector terminal identification

gear is leaking internally and must be replaced.

DROOP FLOW VARIABLE ASSIST

1. Connect together pressure hose tool No. 6713 and 6905, or equivalents, **Fig. 5**.
2. Install adapter tool No. 6866, or equivalent, on end of pressure hose, then the quick disconnect.
3. Install pressure hose in inlet and outlet fitting of pressure/flow tester.
4. Disconnect power steering fluid pressure hose at pump.
5. Install adapter tool No 6972-1, or equivalent, in pressure fitting on pump, then adapter tool No 6972-2, or equivalent, in banjo fitting on power steering fluid pressure hose and nut tool No. 6972-3, or equivalent, on adapter tool 6972-2 in banjo fitting, **Fig. 6**.
6. Connect inlet hose of pressure/flow tester tool No. 6815, or equivalent, to pressure fitting on pump using adapter tool No. 6866 in pressure hose tool No. 6713, or equivalent, **Fig. 7**.
7. Connect outlet hose on pressure/flow tester to adapter tool No. 6972-2, or equivalent, installed in pressure hose using quick disconnect.
8. Completely open valve on pressure/flow tester.
9. Start engine and idle long enough to circulate fluid through tester and extract air from fluid, then turn off engine.
10. Inspect and adjust fluid level.
11. Start and idle engine.
12. Pressure gauge should read less than 125 psi. If reading is above specification, inspect hoses for restrictions.
13. Initial pressure reading should be 50–80 psi and flow meter should read 1.3–1.6 GPM.
14. Close pressure gauge valve fully three times and record highest pressure each time. Readings must be above specification and within 50 psi of each other. **Do not leave valve closed for more than 2–4 seconds as pump will be damaged.**
15. Open test valve, then turn steering wheel to left and righthand positions until against stops, recording highest

	POSSIBLE CAUSES
POWER STEERING PRESSURE SWITCH OPERATION	
GROUND CIRCUIT	
POWER STEERING PRESSURE SWITCH SENSE CIRCUIT SHORTED TO GROUND	
POWER STEERING PRESSURE SENSE CIRCUIT OPEN	
PCM	

TEST	ACTION
1	Turn the ignition off. Disconnect the Power Steering Pressure Switch harness connector. Turn the ignition on. With the DRBIII®, monitor the Power Steering Pressure Switch. Using a jumper wire, connect one end to the Power Steering Pressure Switch Sense circuit. With the other end of the jumper tap the ground circuit in the Power Steering Pressure Switch harness connector. Does the Power Steering Pressure Switch display change from HI to LOW? Yes → Replace the Power Steering Pressure Switch Perform POWERTRAIN VERIFICATION TEST VER - 5. No → Go To 2
2	Turn the ignition off. Disconnect Power Steering Pressure Switch harness connector. Using a 12-volt test light connected to 12-volts, probe the ground circuit in the Power Steering Pressure Switch harness connector. Does the test light illuminate? Yes → Go To 3 No → Repair the ground circuit for an open. Perform POWERTRAIN VERIFICATION TEST VER - 5.

CR6020100222010X

Fig. 3 DTC P0551: Power Steering Switch Failure (Part 1 of 2)

TEST	ACTION
3	Turn the ignition off. Disconnect the Power Steering Pressure Switch harness connector. Disconnect the PCM harness connector. Measure the resistance of the Power Steering Pressure Switch Sense circuit in the PSP Switch harness connector to ground. Is the resistance below 100 ohms? Yes → Repair the Power Steering Pressure Sense circuit for a short to ground. Perform POWERTRAIN VERIFICATION TEST VER - 5. No → Go To 4
4	Turn the ignition off. Disconnect the Power Steering Pressure Switch harness connector. Disconnect the PCM harness connector. Measure the resistance of the Power Steering Pressure Switch Sense circuit between the PSP Switch harness connector and the PCM harness connector. Is the resistance below 5.0 ohms? Yes → Go To 5 No → Repair the Power Steering Pressure Sense circuit for an open. Perform POWERTRAIN VERIFICATION TEST VER - 5.
5	If there are no possible causes remaining, view repair. Repair Replace and program the Powertrain Control Module in accordance with the Service Information. Perform POWERTRAIN VERIFICATION TEST VER - 5.

CR6020100222020X

Fig. 3 DTC P0551: Power Steering Switch Failure (Part 2 of 2)

POWERTRAIN VERIFICATION TEST VER - 5
1. NOTE: If the PCM has been replaced and the correct VIN and mileage have not been programmed, a DTC will be set in the ABS Module, Airbag Module and the SKIM. 2. NOTE: If the vehicle is equipped with a Sentry Key Immobilizer System, Secret Key data must be updated. Refer to the Service Information for the PCM, SKIM and the Transponder (ignition key) for programming information. 3. Inspect the vehicle to ensure that all engine components are properly installed and connected. Reassemble and reconnect components as necessary. 4. Connect the DRBIII® to the data link connector. 5. Ensure the fuel tank has at least a quarter tank of fuel. Turn off all accessories. 6. If a Comprehensive Component DTC was repaired, perform steps 5 - 8. If a Major OBDII Monitor DTC was repaired skip those steps and continue verification. 7. After the ignition has been off for at least 10 seconds, restart the vehicle and run 2 minutes. 8. If the Good Trip counter changed to one or more and there are no new DTC's, the repair was successful and is now complete. Erase DTC's and disconnect the DRBIII®. 9. If the repaired DTC has reset, the repair is not complete. Check for any related TSB's or flash updates and return to the Symptom list. 10. If another DTC has set, return to the Symptom List and follow the path specified for that DTC. 11. With the DRBIII®, monitor the appropriate pre-test enabling conditions until all conditions have been met. Once the conditions have been met, switch screen to the appropriate OBDII monitor, (Audible beeps when the monitor is running). 12. If the monitor ran, and the Good Trip counter changed to one or more, the repair was successful and is now complete. Erase DTC's and disconnect the DRBIII®. 13. If the repaired OBDII trouble code has reset or was seen in the monitor while on the road test, the repair is not complete. Check for any related technical service bulletins or flash updates and return to Symptom List. 14. If another DTC has set, return to the Symptom List and follow the path specified for that DTC. Are any DTCs present? Yes → Repair is not complete, refer to appropriate symptom. No → Repair is complete.

CR6020100223000X

Fig. 4 Verification Test VER-5

pressure at each position. **Do not force pump to operate against stops for more than 2–4 seconds as pump damage will result.**

16. Compare pressure gauge readings to pump specifications. If highest output pressures are not same against either stop, steering gear is leaking internally and must be replaced.

Component Service

POWER STEERING PRESSURE SWITCH, REPLACE

1. Raise and support vehicle.
2. Disconnect its electrical connector.

3. Remove pressure switch from steering gear using crowfoot and long extension, **Fig. 8.**
4. Reverse procedure to install, noting the following:
   a. Install and hand tighten switch into gear until fully seated.
   b. Tighten switch using crowfoot and extension. **Do not overtighten.**
   c. Connect pressure switch electrical connector, ensuring latch is securely engaged with locking tab.

SOLENOID CONTROL MODULE, REPLACE

1. Disconnect solenoid control module electrical connectors, **Fig. 9.**
2. Unclip locking tab, holding module to

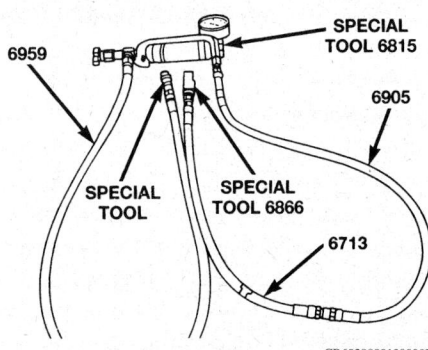

CR6029800139000X

Fig. 5 Power steering flow/pressure tester & fittings. Droop flow variable assist

fluid lines, on bottom side of control module.
3. Rotate module upward and remove two upper attaching clips from steering gear, **Fig. 10.**
4. Reverse procedure to install.

SOLENOID CONTROL VALVE, REPLACE

1. Remove steering gear as outlined under "Power Steering Gear, Replace" in "Front Suspension & Steering" section of appropriate chassis chapter.
2. Disconnect solenoid control valve electrical connector at solenoid control module, **Fig. 10.**
3. Remove solenoid from steering gear using suitable crowfoot, **Fig. 11.**
4. Reverse procedure to install, noting the following:
   a. Coat O-ring seals with suitable, fresh, clean power steering fluid prior
   b. Install solenoid control valve by hand until fully seated, then using crowfoot tool to tighten.

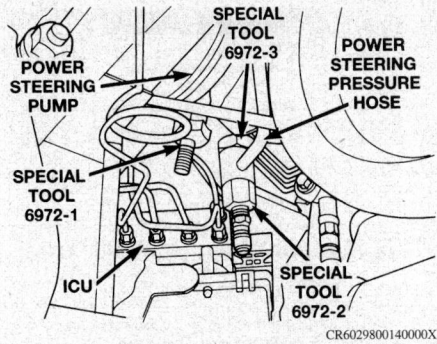

Fig. 6 Adapter fitting installation. Droop flow variable assist

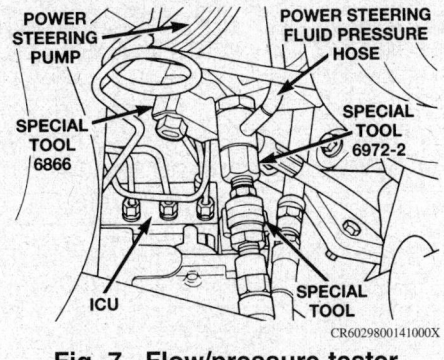

Fig. 7 Flow/pressure tester connections. Droop flow variable assist

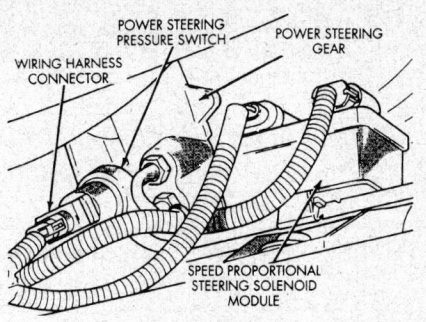

Fig. 8 Pressure switch replacement.

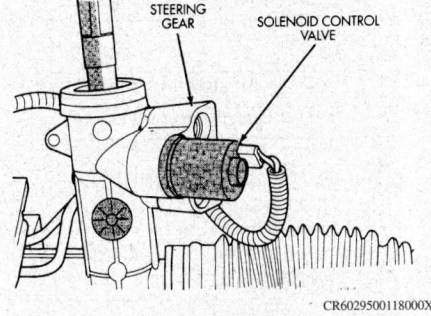

Fig. 9 Solenoid module electrical connectors

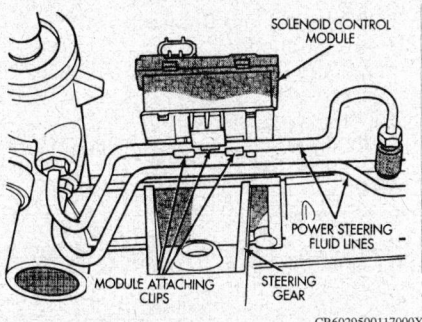

Fig. 10 Solenoid control module replacement

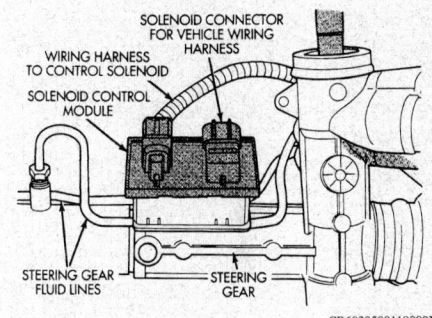

Fig. 11 Solenoid control valve replacement

TIGHTENING SPECIFICATIONS

Year	Component	Torque Ft. Lbs.
2001–05	Air Bag Module	90①
	Flex Coupler	12
	Outer To Inner Tie Rod Jam Nut	55
	Power Steering Fluid Hose Banjo Fitting	33
	Power Steering Fluid Hose Pressure Hose To Return Hose Bracket	75①
	Power Steering Fluid Hose Return Hose Bracket To Head	21
	Power Steering Fluid Hose Tube Nuts	23
	Power Steering Fluid Reservoir	21
	Power Steering Pump Bracket To Engine	40
	Power Steering Pump Discharge Fitting	55
	Steering Column Mounting Bracket	105①
	Steering Gear To Crossmember	50
	Steering Wheel	45
	Tie Rod To Steering Knuckle	45

① — Inch lbs.

Sebring Coupe & Stratus Coupe

NOTE: On Air Bag Equipped Models, Refer To "Air Bag System Precautions" Located In The Front Of This Manual For System Disarming & Arming Procedures.

NOTE: Refer To "Computer Relearn Procedures" Located In The Front Of This Manual When Battery Power To The Computer Has Been Interrupted.

INDEX

POWER STEERING PRESSURE SPECIFICATIONS

Model	Year	Power Steering Pump Pressure, psi		Max Relief Pressure	Output Flow, Gallons Per Minute①
		Test Valve			
		Open	Closed②		
Sebring Coupe & Stratus Coupe	2001–05	116–145	1209–1280	1209–1280	—

① — At 1500 RPM & minimum pressure.

② — At 1000 RPM & minimum pressure.

PRECAUTIONS
Air Bag Systems

Refer to "Air Bag System Precautions" in the front of this manual for system disarming and arming procedures.

Battery Ground Cable

Prior to service, disconnect battery ground cable and isolate as required.

DESCRIPTION

The type of power steering which is responsive to engine speed has been added to all models. The steering column has a shock absorber mechanism and a tilt steering mechanism.

A vane type oil pump with fluid flow control system has been added to all models. The steering gear and linkage is an integral rack and pinion type.

DIAGNOSIS & TESTING
Accessing Diagnostic Trouble Codes

Connect DRB, or suitable programmed

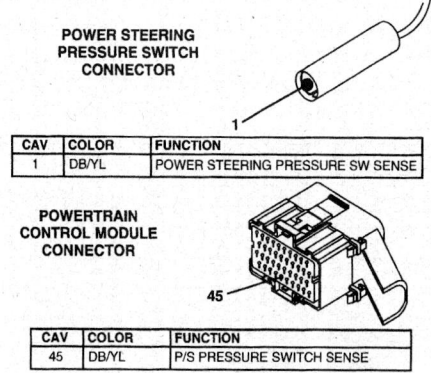

Fig. 1   Connector terminal identification

scan tool, to the Data Link Connector (DLC) under the lefthand side of the instrument panel near the hood release. The diagnostic cycle begins when the ignition is turned On.

Connector Terminal Identification

Refer to **Fig. 1** for connector terminal identifications.

Diagnostic Tests

Refer to "Neon, Sebring Convertible, Sebring Sedan & Stratus Sedan" for power steering system diagnostic tests.

Clearing Diagnostic Trouble Codes

Follow tool manufacturer's instructions to clean DTCs.

Component Testing
OIL PUMP RELIEF PRESSURE TEST

1. Disconnect pressure hose and connect oil pump pressure test tools, **Fig. 2.**
2. Bleed air, then turn steering wheel several times while vehicle is not moving.
3. Start engine and idle at 900–1100 RPM.
4. Fully close shutoff valve on pressure gauge, and measure oil pump relief pressure. **Pressure gauge shutoff valve must not remain closed for more than 10 seconds.**
5. If pressure is not as specified, replace oil pump.
6. Remove pressure test tools

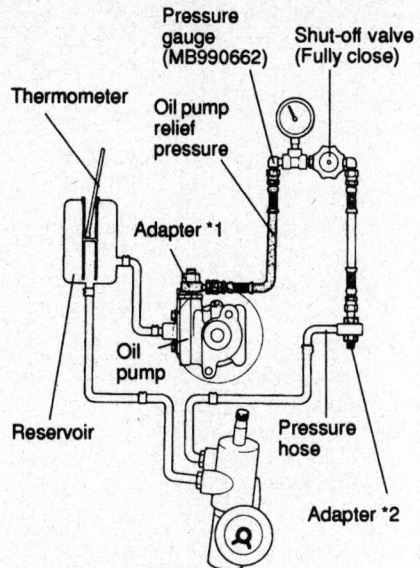

NOTE
*1: MB990993 or MB991217 <SOHC>
MB991548 <DOHC>

*2: MB990994 <SOHC>
MB991549 <DOHC>

CR6029500087000X

Fig. 2   Oil pump relief pressure test tool installation

NO-LOAD CONDITION PRESSURE TEST

1. Disconnect pressure hose from oil pump and connect no-load condition pressure test tool, **Fig. 3.**
2. Bleed air, then turn steering wheel several times while vehicle is not moving so fluid temperature rises.
3. Start engine and idle at 900–1100 RPM.
4. Inspect and ensure hydraulic pressure is at standard value of 116–145 psi when no-load conditions are created by fully opening pressure gauge shut-off valve.
5. If pressure is not as specified, condition's probable cause is oil line or steering gearbox. Inspect and repair as required.

STEERING GEAR RETENTION HYDRAULIC PRESSURE TEST

1. Disconnect pressure hose from oil pump and connect retention hydraulic pressure test tools, **Fig. 4.**
2. Bleed air, then turn steering wheel several times while vehicle is not moving so fluid temperature rises.
3. Start engine, then idle at 900–1100 RPM.
4. Fully close, then fully open shutoff valve on pressure gauge.
5. Turn steering wheel all way to left or right and record retention hydraulic pressure.
6. If pressure is not within standard value, overhaul steering gearbox.

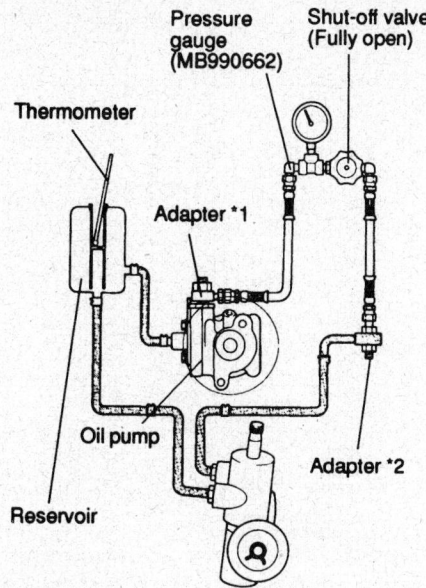

NOTE
*1: MB990993 or MB991217 <SOHC>
MB991548 <DOHC>

*2: MB990994 <SOHC>
MB991549 <DOHC>

CR6029500088000X

Fig. 3   No-load pressure test tool installation

POWER STEERING PRESSURE SWITCH INSPECTION

1. Disconnect pressure hose from oil pump and connect power steering pressure switch test tools, **Fig. 5.**
2. Bleed air, then turn steering wheel several times while vehicle is not moving so fluid temperature rises.
3. Idle engine.
4. Disconnect pressure switch connector and connect suitable ohmmeter.
5. Gradually close shutoff valve at pressure gauge and increase hydraulic pressure.
6. Turn steering wheel all way to left or right and record retention hydraulic pressure.
7. Ensure pressures are within specifications.
8. Gradually open shutoff valve and reduce hydraulic pressure.
9. Ensure hydraulic pressure deactivates switch at standard value of 116–348 psi.
10. Remove tools and tighten pressure hose.

SYSTEM SERVICE
Power Steering System Bleed

1. Raise and support front wheels.
2. Manually turn oil pump pulley several times.

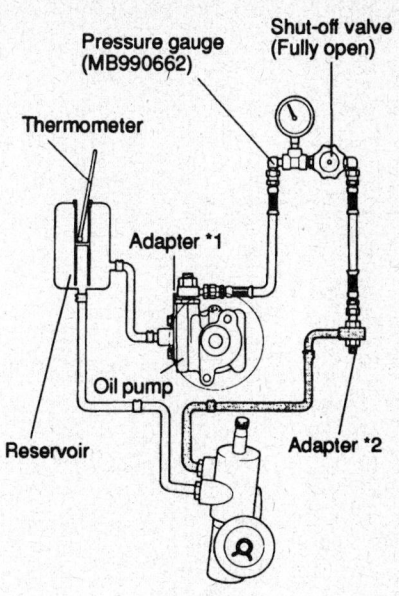

NOTE
*1: MB990993 or MB991217 <SOHC>
MB991548 <DOHC>

*2: MB990994 <SOHC>
MB991549 <DOHC>

CR6029500089000X

Fig. 4   Retention pressure test tool installation

3. Turn steering wheel all way left and right 5–6 times.
4. Disconnect high-tension cable and crank starter motor intermittently, while turning steering wheel fully to left and right , 5–6 times for 15–20 seconds.
5. Refill fluid supply during air bleeding so level never falls below lower position of filter.
6. If air bleeding is done while engine is running, air will be broken up and absorbed into fluid. Ensure bleeding is done only while cranking.
7. Connect high-tension cable and start engine.
8. Turn steering wheel to left and right until there are no air bubbles in reservoir.
9. Ensure fluid is not milky and adjust inspect fluid level.
10. Ensure level does not change when steering wheel is turned left or right.
11. Ensure level is within .2 inch when engine is stopped compared to when it is running.
12. If fluid level variation is more than .2 inch, air still exists in system, requiring additional bleeding.

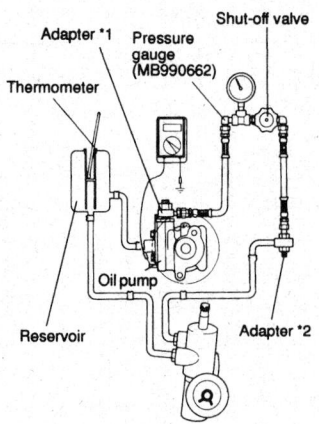

NOTE
*1: MB990993 or MB991217 <SOHC>
MB991548 <DOHC>

*2: MB990994 <SOHC>
MB991549 <DOHC>

CR6029500090000X.

Fig. 5 Pressure switch test tool installation

TIGHTENING SPECIFICATIONS

Year	Component	Torque Ft. Lbs.
2001–05	Clockspring & Column Switch	18
	Gear Box Cylinder Clamp	51
	Gear Box End Plug	44
	Gear Box Feed Tube Flare	10
	Gear Box Pinion & Valve	18
	Gear Box Rack Support Cover	109①
	Gear Box Rack Support Cover, Jam Nut	44
	Gear Box Return & Pressure Hose Flare Nut	11
	Gear Box Stay (2.4L Engine)	55
	Gear Box Steering Shaft & Gear Box	13
	Gear Box Tie Rod	65
	Gear Box Tie Rod End	38
	Gear Box Tie Rod End To Knuckle	21
	Gear Box Valve Housing	14
	Hose Oil Pump Eye	42
	Hose Oil Reservoir & Pressure Hose	100①
	Hose Pressure Tube Flare, Gear Box Side	107①
	Hose Return Tube & Cooler Tube	100①
	Hose Pressure Tube Flare, Pressure Hose Side	11
	Oil Pump Front/Rear Bracket (3.0L Engine)	12
	Oil Pump Oil Pump Bracket Bolt M8 (2.4L)	21
	Oil Pump (3.0L Engine)	31
	Oil Pump Bracket (2.4L Engine)	36
	Oil Pump Bracket (3.0L Engine)	17
	Oil Pump Eye Bolt	42
	Oil Pump Pressure Hose (2.4L Engine)	100①
	Oil Pump Pressure Switch	15
	Steering Shaft & Gear Box	13
	Steering Column	100①
	Steering Cover	44①
	Steering Wheel	31

① — Inch lbs.

DISC BRAKES

TABLE OF CONTENTS

Concorde, Intrepid, LHS & 300M

NOTE: On Air Bag Equipped Models, Refer To "Air Bag System Precautions" Located In The Front Of This Manual For System Disarming & Arming Procedures.

NOTE: Refer To "Computer Relearn Procedures" Located In The Front Of This Manual When Battery Power To The Computer Has Been Interrupted.

INDEX

DESCRIPTION

The front single piston, floating caliper disc brake consists of rotor, caliper, pads and driving hub, **Fig. 1.** The caliper is mounted to steering knuckle using bushings, sleeves and two thru bolts which thread directly into steering knuckle.

This assembly has an anti-rattle clip attached to outer pad and an inner pad-piston retainer clip.

All of braking force is taken directly by adapter. The caliper is a one piece casting with inboard side containing a single piston cylinder bore.

A square cut rubber piston seal is located in a machined groove in caliper bore and provides a seal between piston and caliper bore.

A molded rubber dust boot installed in a groove in cylinder bore and piston keeps contamination from caliper bore and piston. The boot mounts in caliper bore and in a groove in piston.

The rear single piston, floating caliper rear disc brake includes a hub assembly, adapter, rotor, caliper, shoes and pads, **Fig. 2.** The parking brake system consists of a small duo-servo brake mounted to an

adapter which expands out against the hat section on inside of rotor. The caliper has either a 1.338 or 1.420 inch piston located on inboard side.

The caliper floats on rubber bushings with metal sleeves on two bolts that are threaded into adapter. Two machined abutments on adapter position and align caliper and brake pads for movement fore and aft.

TROUBLESHOOTING

Refer to **Fig. 3** for system troubleshooting.

Lateral Runout Inspection

1. Raise and support vehicle, then remove wheel and tire assemblies.
2. Ensure wheel bearings are properly adjusted.
3. Install lug nuts or bolts.
4. Mount suitable dial indicator and position plunger so it contacts rotor at point one inch from outer edge.
5. Rotate rotor and note dial indicator

readings. Perform this inspection on both inboard and outboard rotor faces.
6. If runout exceeds specifications, proceed as follows:
  a. Position rotor on hub and inspect runout.
  b. If runout still exceeds specifications, replace or machine rotor.

Parallelism Inspection

Measure the rotor at 12 equally spaced points at a radius approximately one inch from edge of disc using suitable micrometer.

BRAKE SYSTEM BLEED

Refer to "Hydraulic Brake Systems" chapter for brake system bleeding procedures.

BRAKE PAD SERVICE

1. Raise and support vehicle, then remove wheel and tire assembly.

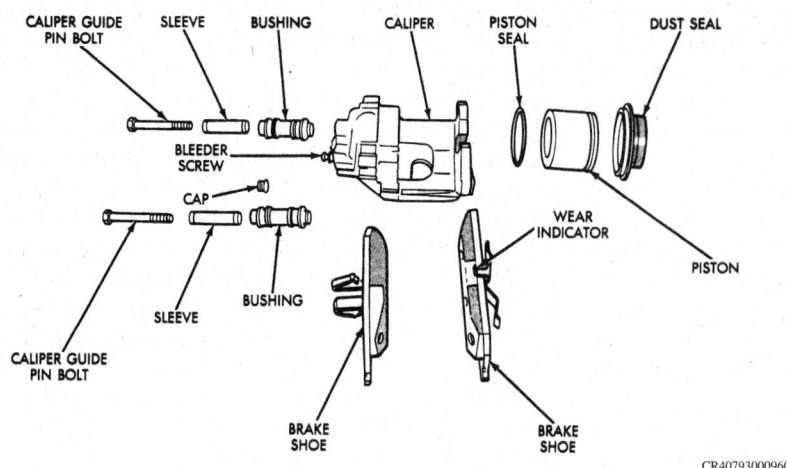

Fig. 1 Dual pin floating caliper disc brake. Front

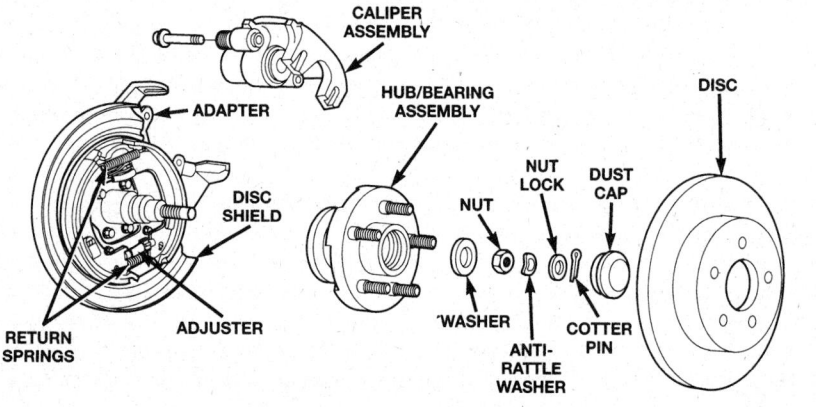

Fig. 2 Dual pin floating caliper disc brake. Rear

2. Remove caliper assembly to steering knuckle guide pin bolts.
3. Rotate top of caliper away from steering knuckle.
4. Lift caliper off bottom machined abutment on steering knuckle.
5. Support caliper to prevent damage of flexible brake hose.
6. Remove outboard brake shoe by prying shoe retaining clip over raised area of caliper.
7. Pull inboard brake shoe away from piston until retaining clip is free from cavity in piston.
8. Reverse procedure to install, noting the following:
   a. Press caliper piston back into piston bore of caliper using suitable tool.
   b. Apply brake pedal several times, then inspect master cylinder brake fluid level and adjust fluid.

CALIPER SERVICE

Replacement

1. Remove caliper from brake rotor and brake pads from caliper as outlined under "Brake Pad Service."
2. Disconnect brake hose at brake caliper. Cap brake line.
3. Reverse procedure to install.

Overhaul

FRONT

DISASSEMBLE

1. Place suitable wood block between caliper piston and caliper fingers.
2. With brake hose attached to caliper, carefully depress brake pedal to push piston out of caliper bore.
3. Prop brake pedal to any position below first inch of brake pedal travel to prevent brake fluid loss.
4. If pistons are to be removed from both calipers, disconnect brake hose at frame bracket after removing piston, then cap brake line and repeat procedure to remove piston from other caliper.
5. Disconnect brake hose from caliper.
6. Mount caliper in suitable soft jawed vice.
7. Support caliper, then remove and discard dust boot.
8. Remove seal from groove in piston bore and discard using a small wooden or plastic stick. **Do not use screwdriver or other metal tool.**
9. Remove caliper bushings.

ASSEMBLE

1. Mount caliper in suitable soft jawed vice.

2. Lubricate piston seal with clean brake fluid and install seal in caliper bore groove. Ensure seal is properly seated.
3. Lubricate piston boot with clean brake fluid and position over piston.
4. Install piston and boot assembly, pushing it past piston seal until it bottoms in caliper bore.
5. Drive dust boot into counterbore until properly seated using suitable hammer and dust boot installer No. C-4689 with handle No. C-4171 or equivalents.
6. Compress flanges of bushings and install on caliper housing. Ensure bushing flanges extend evenly over caliper housing on both sides.
7. Remove Teflon sleeves from guide pin bushings prior to installing bushings into caliper. After bushings are installed into caliper, install Teflon sleeves into bushings.
8. Connect brake hose to brake line at frame bracket.

REAR

1. Remove caliper from rotor as outlined under "Brake Pad Service."
2. Place a small piece of wood approximately 1 inch thick between piston and caliper fingers, then carefully depress brake pedal to hydraulically push piston out of bore. Prop brake pedal to any position below first inch of brake pedal travel to prevent brake fluid loss.
3. If pistons are to be removed from both calipers, disconnect brake hose at frame bracket after removing piston, then cap brake line and repeat procedure to remove piston from other caliper.
4. Disconnect brake hose from caliper.
5. Mount caliper in suitable soft jawed vice.
6. Support caliper, then remove and discard dust boot.
7. Remove seal from groove in piston bore and discard using a small wooden or plastic stick. **Do not use screwdriver or other metal tool.**
8. If required, remove bushing and sleeve assembly, as follows:
   a. Push inner sleeve until it pops out of bushing, then pull inner sleeve completely out of bushing.
   b. Collapse one side of bushing. Pull opposite side of bushing to remove from caliper.
9. Thoroughly clean piston and caliper grooves, caliper housing and bushing mounting surfaces.
10. Dip new piston seal in clean brake fluid and install in groove in bore.
11. Coat new piston boot with clean brake fluid leaving a generous amount inside boot.
12. Coat piston with clean brake fluid, then position dust boot over piston.
13. Install piston into bore pushing it past piston seal until it bottoms in bore.
14. Position dust boot in counterbore, then using suitable hammer and installer No. C-4383-7 or equivalent, drive boot into counterbore of caliper.
15. If removed, install guide pin sleeve bushings as follows:

RED BRAKE WARNING LAMP

CONDITION	POSSIBLE CAUSES	CORRECTION
RED BRAKE WARNING LAMP ON	1. Parking brake lever not fully released.	1. Release parking brake lever.
	2. Parking brake warning lamp switch on parking brake lever.	2. Inspect and replace switch as necessary.
	3. Brake fluid level low in reservoir.	3. Fill reservoir. Check entire system for leaks. Repair or replace as required.
	4. Brake fluid level switch.	4. Disconnect switch wiring connector. If lamp goes out, replace switch.
	5. Mechanical instrument cluster (MIC) problem.	5. Refer to Chassis Diagnostic Procedures manual.

BRAKE NOISE

CONDITION	POSSIBLE CAUSES	CORRECTION
DISC BRAKE CHIRP	1. Excessive brake rotor runout.	1. Follow brake rotor diagnosis and testing. Correct as necessary.
	2. Lack of lubricant on brake caliper slides.	2. Lubricate brake caliper slides.
DISC BRAKE RATTLE OR CLUNK	1. Broken or missing anti-rattle spring clips on shoes.	1. Replace brake shoes.
	2. Caliper guide pins loose.	2. Tighten guide pins.
DISC BRAKE SQUEAK AT LOW SPEED (WHILE APPLYING LIGHT BRAKE PEDAL EFFORT)	1. Brake shoe linings.	1. Replace brake shoes.
SCRAPING (METAL-TO-METAL).	1. Foreign object interference with brakes.	1. Inspect brakes and remove foreign object.
	2. Brake shoes worn out.	2. Replace brake shoes. Inspect rotors. Reface or replace as necessary.

CR4079900136010X

Fig. 3   Brake system troubleshooting (Part 1 of 3)

a. Fold bushing in half lengthwise at solid middle section.
b. Insert folded bushing into caliper. Do not use sharp object to perform this step.
c. Unfold bushing until it is fully seated in caliper. Flanges should be seated evenly on both sides of bushing hole.

16. If removed, install guide pin sleeve as follows:
a. Hold end of bushing, then push sleeve through bushing until end of bushing is fully seated into seal groove of sleeve.
b. Holding sleeve in place, install other end of bushing into seal groove.
c. Ensure bushing is in seal groove on both sides.

17. Install brake fluid line, then install caliper as outlined under "Brake Pad Service."

ROTOR

REPLACE

1. Remove caliper from brake rotor as outlined under "Brake Pad Service."
2. Remove parking brake adjustment hole plug from brake disc hub.
3. Remove rotor. Use suitable soft face hammer to tap rotor free of hub as required.
4. Reverse procedure to install.

ADJUSTMENTS
Parking Brake

1. Release parking brake.

OTHER BRAKE CONDITIONS

CONDITION	POSSIBLE CAUSES	CORRECTION
BRAKES CHATTER	1. Disc brake rotor has excessive thickness variation.	1. Isolate condition as rear or front. Reface or replace brake rotors as necessary.
BRAKES DRAG (FRONT OR ALL)	1. Contaminated brake fluid.	1. Check for swollen seals. Replace all system components containing rubber.
	2. Binding caliper pins or bushings.	2. Replace pins and bushings.
	3. Binding master cylinder.	3. Replace master cylinder.
	4. Binding brake pedal.	4. Replace brake pedal.
BRAKES DRAG (REAR ONLY)	1. Parking brake cables binding or froze up.	1. Check cable routing. Replace cables as necessary.
	2. Parking brake cable return spring not returning shoes.	2. Replace cables as necessary.
	3. Obstruction inside the center console preventing full return of the parking brake cables.	3. Remove console and remove obstruction.
BRAKES GRAB	1. Contaminated brake shoe linings.	1. Inspect and clean, or replace shoes. Repair source of contamination.
	2. Improper power brake booster assist.	2. Refer to Power Brake Booster in the diagnosis and testing section.
EXCESSIVE PEDAL EFFORT	1. Obstruction of brake pedal.	1. Inspect, remove or move obstruction.
	2. Low power brake booster assist.	2. Refer to power brake booster in the diagnosis and testing section.
	3. Glazed brake linings.	3. Reface or replace brake rotors as necessary. Replace brake shoes.
	4. Brake shoe lining transfer to brake rotor.	4. Reface or replace brake rotors as necessary. Replace brake shoes.
EXCESSIVE PEDAL TRAVEL (VEHICLE STOPS OK)	1. Air in brake lines.	1. Bleed brakes.
EXCESSIVE PEDAL TRAVEL (PEDAL GOES TO FLOOR - CAN'T SKID WHEELS)	1. Power brake booster runout (vacuum assist).	1. Check booster vacuum hose and engine tune for adequate vacuum supply. Refer to power brake booster in the diagnosis and testing section.
EXCESSIVE PEDAL TRAVEL (ONE FRONT WHEEL LOCKS UP DURING HARD BRAKING)	1. One of the two hydraulic circuits to the front brakes is malfunctioning.	1. Inspect system for leaks. Check master cylinder for internal malfunction.
PEDAL PULSATES/ SURGES DURING BRAKING	1. Disc brake rotor has excessive thickness variation.	1. Isolate condition as rear or front. Reface or replace brake rotors as necessary.

CR4079900136020X

Fig. 3   Brake system troubleshooting (Part 2 of 3)

CONDITION	POSSIBLE CAUSES	CORRECTION
PEDAL IS SPONGY	1. Air in brake lines.	1. Bleed brakes.
	2. Power brake booster runout (vacuum assist).	2. Check booster vacuum hose and engine tune for adequate vacuum supply. Refer to power brake booster in the diagnosis and testing section.
PREMATURE REAR WHEEL LOCKUP	1. Contaminated brake shoe linings.	1. Inspect and clean, or replace shoes. Repair source of contamination.
	2. Inoperative proportioning valve.	2. Test proportioning valves folowing procedure listed in diagnosis and testing section. Replace valves as necessary.
	3. Improper power brake booster assist.	3. Refer to power brake booster in the diagnosis and testing section.
STOP LAMPS STAY ON	1. Brake lamp switch out of adjustment.	1. Adjust brake lamp switch.
	2. Brake pedal binding.	2. Inspect and replace as necessary.
	3. Obstruction in pedal linkage.	3. Remove obstruction.
	4. Power Brake Booster not allowing pedal to return completely.	4. Replace power brake booster.
VEHICLE PULLS TO RIGHT OR LEFT ON BRAKING	1. Frozen brake caliper piston.	1. Replace frozen piston or caliper. Bleed brakes.
	2. Contaminated brake shoe lining.	2. Inspect and clean, or replace shoes. Repair source of contamination.
	3. Pinched brake lines.	3. Replace pinched line.
	4. Leaking piston seal.	4. Replace piston seal or brake caliper.
	5. Suspension problem.	5. Refer to the Suspension group.
PARKING BRAKE - EXCESSIVE LEVER TRAVEL	1. Rear parking brake shoes out of adjustment.	1. Adjust rear parking brake shoes.

CR4079900136030X

Fig. 3   Brake system troubleshooting (Part 3 of 3)

2. Raise and support vehicle.
3. Adjust parking brake cable until there is slack in cable.
4. Tighten adjusting nut until slight drag is felt when rotating rear wheels.
5. Back off adjusting nut two full turns past point when both rear wheels rotate freely.
6. Inspect parking brake operation.

DISC BRAKE SPECIFICATIONS
Rotor Specifications

Year	Brake Lining Wear Limit, Inch③	Front Disc Brake					Brake Lining Wear Limit, Inch③	Rear Disc Brake				
		Rotor			Thickness Variation Parallelism Inch	Lateral Run Out (T.I.R.) Inch		Rotor			Thickness Variation Parallelism Inch	Lateral Run Out (T.I.R.) Inch
		Thickness, Inch						Thickness, Inch				
		Nominal	Min. Refinish	Discard Limit②				Nominal	Min. Refinish	Discard Limit②		
2001–04	.312①	1.019–1.029	—	.960	.0005	.003	.281①	.458–.478	—	.409	.0005	.003

① — Includes backing plate.
② — Discard thickness is stamped on rotor.

⑫ — Above rivet head or backing plate. Original equipment type brake lining.

Caliper Specifications

Location, Type	Caliper Piston O.D., Inch
Front	2.36
Rear, Solid	1.34
Rear, Vented	1.42

TIGHTENING SPECIFICATIONS

Year	Component	Torque/Ft. Lbs.
2001–04	Bearing Retainer	21
	Bleed Screws	10
	Brake Hose To Caliper Banjo Bolt	35
	Brake Line Fitting	12
	Caliper	16
	Caliper Guide Pins	30
	Front Brake Hose Intermediate Bracket	108①
	Support Plate To Rear Axle	80
	Wheel Lug Nuts	85–110

① — Inch lbs.

Crossfire

NOTE: On Air Bag Equipped Models, Refer To "Air Bag System Precautions" Located In The Front Of This Manual For System Disarming & Arming Procedures.

NOTE: Refer To "Computer Relearn Procedures" Located In The Front Of This Manual When Battery Power To The Computer Has Been Interrupted.

INDEX

DESCRIPTION

On models equipped less supercharger, the front calipers are a single piston type. The calipers are free to slide laterally on the anchor.

On models equipped with supercharger, the front calipers are a two piston type. The calipers are fixed.

On 2004 models, the rear disc brakes consist of fixed single piston style calipers with solid rotors.

On 2005 models, the rear disc brakes consist of fixed two piston style calipers with solid rotors on models equipped less supercharger and ventilated rotors on models with supercharger.

On all models the rear caliper is mounted to the rear wheel hub. The calipers are directly bolted to the wheel hub with mounting bolts. The disc brake rotor dust shield is mounting to the hub.

The disc brake rotor has a built in drum used for the parking brakes. The parking brake shoes are mounted to the wheel hub.

TROUBLESHOOTING

Refer to "Concorde, Intrepid, LHS & 300M" for troubleshooting procedures.

BRAKE SYSTEM BLEED

Refer to "Hydraulic Brake Systems" chapter for brake system bleeding procedures.

BRAKE PAD SERVICE

Front

1. Raise and support vehicle, then remove front wheel and tire assemblies.
2. Drain small amount of brake fluid from master cylinder reservoir using suitable, clean suction gun.
3. Bottom caliper piston into bore by prying caliper body against rotor.

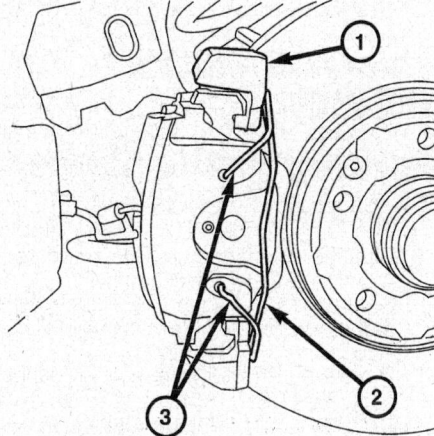

1 CALIPER
2 SUPPORT SPRING
3 SUPPORT SPRING RETAINING HOLE LOCATIONS

ARM0300000000052

Fig. 1 Front brake caliper retaining spring removal

4. Remove caliper support spring by prying support spring from retaining holes located in caliper body, **Fig. 1**.
5. Disconnect brake pad wear indicator wiring harness connector.
6. Remove protective caps, caliper slide pins and caliper.
7. Support caliper using suitable wire.
8. Remove inboard and outboard pads.
9. Reverse procedure to install, noting the following:
   a. Bottom piston is caliper using suitable C-clamp.
   b. Lubricate slide pins with suitable silicone grease.
   c.

Rear

1. Raise and support vehicle, then remove rear wheel and tire assemblies.

2. Drain small amount of brake fluid from master cylinder reservoir using suitable, clean suction gun.
3. Remove mounting bolts and caliper from knuckle.
4. Remove brake hose by rotating caliper while holding brake hose with suitable line wrench.
5. Knock retaining pin out using suitable punch.
6. Remove anti-rattle clip and brake pads.
7. Reverse procedure to install. Bottom piston is caliper using suitable C-clamp.

CALIPER SERVICE

Replacement

FRONT

1. Raise and support vehicle, then remove front wheel and tire assemblies.
2. Drain small amount of fluid from master cylinder reservoir using suitable, clean suction gun.
3. Disconnect harness connector, then remove mounting bolt and brake pad wear indicator.
4. Bottom piston into caliper by prying caliper over.
5. Remove support spring by prying it out of caliper.
6. Remove caps, slide pins and caliper from mounting bracket.
7. Remove caliper brake hose.
8. Remove brake pads.
9. Reverse procedure to install. Lubricate slide pins with suitable silicone grease.

REAR

1. Raise and support vehicle, then remove rear wheel and tire assemblies.
2. Drain small amount of fluid from master cylinder reservoir using suitable, clean suction gun.
3. Remove mounting bolts and caliper.

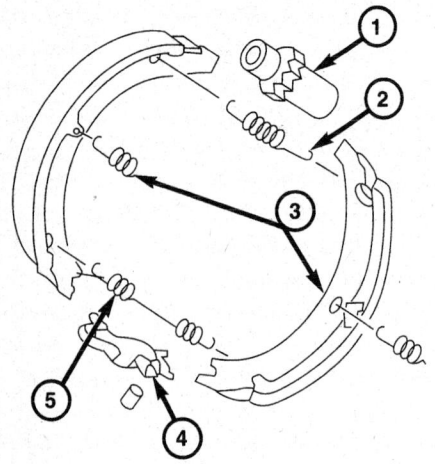

(1) Adjuster.
(2) Upper return spring.
(3) Hold down spring.
(4) Expanding lock.
(5) Lower return spring.

ARM0300000000055

Fig. 2   Exploded view of parking brake

4. Remove brake hose by rotating caliper while holding hose with suitable line wrench.
5. Knock pad retaining pin out using suitable punch.
6. Remove anti-rattle clip and brake pads.
7. Reverse procedure to install.

Overhaul

1. Place suitable small piece of wood pad with one-inch thickness of shop towels outboard of caliper in front of piston.
2. Remove caliper piston by apply short burst of low pressure air with suitable blow gun through brake hose port. **Do not attempt to catch piston. Do not use sustained air pressure.**
3. Remove piston dust boot with suitable pry tool.
4. Remove piston seal with suitable tool.
5. Remove bleed screw.
6. Clean caliper.
7. Lubricate piston, seals and bore with suitable, clean brake fluid.
8. Install new seal into groove. **Ensure seal is fully seated and not twisted.**
9. Install new dust boot and seat it into piston.
10. Stretch dust boot rearward to straighten folds, then move it forward until fold snaps into place.
11. Install piston into bore and press down to bottom of caliper by hand or with

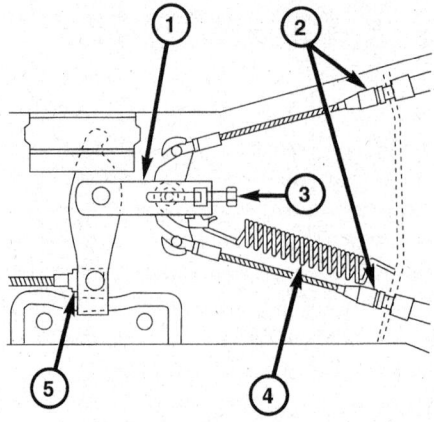

1 CABLE EQUALIZER MECHANISIM
2 PARKING BRAKE CABLES
3 EQUALIZER TENSIONER BOLT
4 RETURN RING
5 FRONT CABLE BOLTED TO EQUALIZER

ARM0300000000056

Fig. 3   Parking brake cable

handle of suitable hammer.
12. Seat dust boot.
13. Install new bleed screw.

PARKING BRAKE SERVICE

Parking Brake Shoes, Replace

1. Raise and support vehicle, then remove tire and wheel assembly.
2. Remove rear disc brake caliper assembly as outlined under "Caliper Service."
3. Remove rear rotor from hub and dust cap.
4. Remove cotter pin, nut retainer, wave washer, rear hub/bearing retaining nut and washer from rear spindle.
5. Remove rear hub and bearing from rear spindle.
6. Release parking brake equalizer tensioning bolts.
7. Remove parking brake shoe lower return spring using suitable hooked pick spring release tool, **Fig. 2.**
8. Remove parking brake shoe hold-down spring using suitable needle-nose pliers.
9. Remove parking brake shoe lower return spring using suitable hooked pick spring release tool.
10. Remove parking brake expanding lock from lower parking brake shoes.
11. Remove parking brake shoes by lifting them over rear axle shaft flange.
12. Reverse procedure to install.

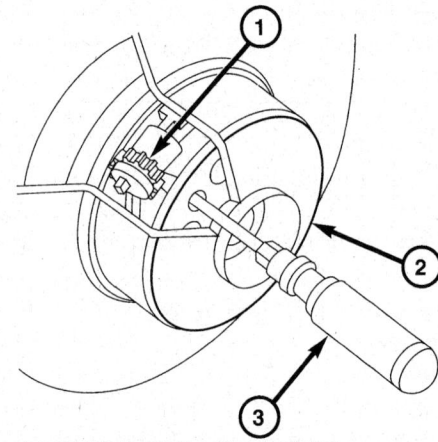

1 PARKING BRAKE ADJUSTER WHEEL
2 REAR WHEEL
3 SUITABLE SCREWDRIVER

ARM0300000000057

Fig. 4   Parking brake adjuster wheel

ADJUSTMENTS
Parking Brake

1. Raise and support vehicle.
2. Loosen parking brake cable tensioning bolt, **Fig. 3.**
3. Remove one wheel lug bolt on each rear wheel.
4. Rotate wheel until parking brake adjuster wheel can be seen through removed wheel bolt hole **Fig. 4.**
5. **On righthand side,** turn adjusting wheel from bottom to top.
6. **On lefthand side,** turn adjusting wheel from top to bottom.
7. **On all sides,** turn adjusting wheel until parking brake shoes are applied and rear wheels no longer turn freely.
8. Tighten parking brake cable tensioning bolt until cables no longer sag and firmly apply parking brake several time.
9. To fine adjust parking brake, tighten parking brake cable tensioning bolt until parking brake lever can be moved one tooth with moderate effort of approximately, 66–88 ft. lbs.

ROTOR
REPLACE

1. Remove caliper from brake rotor as outlined under "Brake Pad Service."
2. Remove parking brake adjustment hole plug from brake disc hub.
3. Remove rotor. Use suitable soft face hammer to tap rotor free of hub as required.
4. Reverse procedure to install.

DISC BRAKE SPECIFICATIONS
Rotor Specifications

Year/ Engine	Front Disc Brake						Rear Disc Brake					
	Brake Lining Wear Limit, Inch③	Rotor					Brake Lining Wear Limit, Inch③	Rotor				
		Thickness, Inch			Thickness Variation Parallelism Inch	Lateral Run Out (T.I.R.) Inch		Thickness, Inch			Thickness Variation Parallelism Inch	Lateral Run-Out (T.I.R.) Inch
		Nominal	Min. Refinish	Discard Limit②				Nominal	Min. Refinish	Discard Limit②		
2004–05												
3.2L ④	.55	1.10	1.02	.99	.0005	.002	.43	.35	.30	.29	.0005	.003
3.2L ①	.55	1.25	1.18	1.16	.0005	.002	.43	.87	.79	.76	.0005	.003

① — With supercharged engine.
② — Discard thickness is stamped on rotor.
③ — Above rivet head or backing plate. Original equipment type brake lining.
④ — Less supercharged engine.

Caliper Specifications

Rotor Type	Caliper Piston O.D., Inch
Solid	1.34
Vented	1.42

TIGHTENING SPECIFICATIONS

Year	Component	Torque/Ft. Lbs.
2004–05	Bearing Retainer	21
	Bleed Screw	62①
	Brake Hose To Caliper Banjo Bolt	35
	Brake Line Fitting	12
	Caliper Guide Pins	18
	Caliper Anchor, Front	85
	Caliper Anchor, Rear	41
	Support Plate To Rear Axle	80
	Wheel Lug Nuts	85–100

① — Inch lbs.

Magnum, 300 & 300C

NOTE: On Air Bag Equipped Models, Refer To "Air Bag System Precautions" Located In The Front Of This Manual For System Disarming & Arming Procedures.

NOTE: Refer To "Computer Relearn Procedures" Located In The Front Of This Manual When Battery Power To The Computer Has Been Interrupted.

INDEX

DESCRIPTION

Four-wheel disc brakes are standard on these vehicle. There are two four-wheel disc brake systems available, a standard and a premium. The standard disc brake system is referred to as 17-inch. The premium disc brake system is referred to as 18-Inch.

Seventeen-inch four-wheel disc brakes (so called because they are designed to fit inside 17-inch wheels) are standard on rear-wheel drive models with V6 engines. They feature single-piston aluminum calipers and vented rotors in the front and single-piston aluminum calipers with solid rotors in the rear.

Eighteen-inch four-wheel disc brakes (so called because they are designed to fit inside 18-inch wheels) are standard on Chrysler 300 Hemi C and all international models, and optional on other models. They feature twin-piston aluminum calipers and vented rotors in the front and single-piston aluminum calipers with vented rotors in the rear.

Although the rear calipers appear the same as the 17-inch system, the rear calipers used with this system feature a wider jaw to compensate for the wider, vented brake rotors used.

Although the twin-piston caliper used is the same, Rear-Wheel-Drive (RWD) models mount the caliper to the rear (trailing end) of the knuckle while All-Wheel-Drive (AWD) models mount the caliper to the front (leading end) of the knuckle.

All calipers are aluminum construction and are the low-drag type, which allows minimal drag of the pads on the discs with low clearance to the rotors to maintain maximum pedal feel and responsiveness.

All calipers are anodized, giving them an off-black appearance. This coating offers corrosion protection and a long-term neat appearance. Phenolic pistons are used in all calipers. The premium twin caliper pistons have stainless steel caps for protection against damage because of contact with the brake pads. All brake rotors are fully coated with Geomet, a water-soluble, environmental friendly corrosion preventive. Both the friction surfaces and the vents are coated. During initial brake applications of a new rotor, the brake pads scrub the coating off the friction surfaces, ensuring that the remainder will be rust free. Coating the vents also ensures that there will not be a loss of heat capacity over time.

BRAKE SYSTEM BLEED

Refer to "Hydraulic Brake Systems" chapter for brake system bleeding procedures.

BRAKE PAD SERVICE

1. Raise and support vehicle, then remove wheel and tire assembly.
2. Retract caliper piston in bore by grasping rear of caliper and pulling outward working with guide pins. **Never push on piston directly.**
3. Remove caliper guide pin bolt by holding it while turning bolt.
4. Rotate caliper upward. **Do not overextend brake hose.**
5. Remove brake pads from caliper, then the anti-rattle clips.
6. Remove caliper to steering knuckle guide pin bolts.
7. Reverse procedure to install, noting the following:
   a. Use hand pressure or suitable C-clamp to retract piston, first placing wood block over piston.
   b. Inboard and outboard pads are interchangeable.

CALIPER SERVICE

Replacement

1. Depress brake pedal past its first inch of travel and hold it in position using brake pedal holding tool.
2. Raise and support vehicle, then remove tire and wheel assembly.
3. Remove banjo bolt connecting flexible brake hose to caliper.
4. While holding guide pins from turning, remove caliper guide pin bolts.
5. Remove brake caliper from brake adapter and pads.
6. Reverse procedure to install, noting the following:
   a. Completely retract caliper piston back into bore of caliper using hand pressure or suitable C-clamp by first placing suitable wood block over piston.
   b. **Do not crossthread caliper guide pin bolts.**
   c. Install new washers on each side of hose fitting as banjo bolt is placed through fitting.

Overhaul

DISASSEMBLE

1. Drain brake fluid from caliper into suitable container.
2. Mount caliper in suitable vise equipped with protective jaws.
3. Place suitable wooden block (padded with approximately one-inch thickness of shop towels) in front of caliper piston.
4. Padded block should be sized to allow piston to push out of bore far enough to be removed by hand after being loosened by air pressure, yet large enough to keep piston from coming completely out.
5. Apply low pressure compressed air to caliper fluid inlet in short spurts to ease piston out of bore. **Do not use high pressure.**
6. Remove piston from caliper.
7. Remove and discard dust boot using suitable tool.
8. Work piston seal out of groove caliper

piston bore using suitable, soft tool such as plastic trim stick. **Do not use screw driver or other metal tool for seal removal.**

9. Remove caliper bleeder screw.
10. Clean piston bore and drilled passage ways with alcohol, or suitable solvent.
11. Wipe it dry using only a lint-free cloth.
12. Inspect both piston and bore for scoring or pitting. **Do not hone caliper bore.**

ASSEMBLE

1. Lubricate caliper piston, piston seal and piston bore with suitable, clean, fresh brake fluid.
2. Install new piston sea in groove. Seal should be started at one area of groove and gently worked around and into groove using only clean fingers to seat it.
3. Install new dust boot on piston and work boot lip into groove at top of piston.
4. Stretch boot downward, straightening boot folds, then move boot back upward until folds snap uniformly into place.
5. Install piston into bore, pressing piston down to bottom of bore using hand-pressure. Dust boot will not seat now.
6. Seat dust boot in caliper counterbore using installer tool No. 9315, with handle tool No. C-4171, or equivalents.
7. Install dust boot until it bottoms.**Do not over-seat dust boot.**
8. Install bleeder screw in threaded hole that will be uppermost once caliper is installed.

ROTOR
REPLACE

1. Raise and support vehicle, then remove tire and wheel assembly.
2. Grasp rear of caliper and pull outward working with guide pins to retract piston. **Never push on piston directly.**
3. Remove disc brake caliper and adapter from knuckle, then support it using suitable wire or bungee cord. **Do not to overextend brake hose.**
4. Remove clips, then slide brake rotor off hub and bearing.
5. Reverse procedure to install.

PARKING BRAKE SERVICE
Shoe

1. Raise and support vehicle, then remove tire and wheel assembly.
2. While helper applies brakes, remove hub nut from half shaft.
3. Remove two mounting bolts, disc brake caliper and adapter. Suspend assembly aside using suitable wire or bungee cord. **Do not overextend brake hose.**
4. Remove clips and brake rotor.
5. Loosen each hub and bearing mounting bolt 1–2 turns at a time while pulling outward on hub and bearing.
6. Once removed from threads in hub and bearing, but not knuckle allow bolts to stay in and protrude through knuckle and brake support plate.
7. Slide hub and bearing off knuckle and half shaft.

8. Completely back off parking brake shoe adjustment.
9. Remove spring and parking brake shoe adjuster.
10. Remove shoe adjuster.
11. Remove upper brake shoe hold-down clip and pin.
12. Remove upper shoe from return spring and shoe actuator lever.
13. Remove return spring from lower shoe.
14. Remove lower brake shoe hold-down clip and pin.
15. Remove lower shoe.
16. Reverse procedure to install.

ADJUSTMENTS
Parking Brake

1. Place parking brake lever in full released position.
2. Raise and support vehicle.
3. Remove plug in parking brake shoe support to access adjuster star-wheel.
4. Through access hole, rotate adjuster star wheel to expand shoes outward against drum.
5. Turn adjuster star wheel until wheel will not rotate using suitable tool.
6. Back off adjuster six detents.
7. Rotate wheel to ensure light drag. If drag is too heavy, continue to back off adjuster one detent at a time until light drag is present. **Do not back off star-wheel more than 17 detents from wheel lock.**
8. Install access plug. Adjust opposite wheel parking brake shoes using same method.

DISC BRAKE SPECIFICATIONS
Rotor Specifications

	Front Disc Brake						Rear Disc Brake					
	Brake Lining Wear Limit, Inch①	Rotor					Brake Lining Wear Limit, Inch①	Rotor				
		Thickness, Inch			Thickness Variation Parallelism Inch	Lateral Run Out (T.I.R.) Inch		Thickness, Inch			Thickness Variation Parallelism Inch	Lateral Run-Out (T.I.R.) Inch
Year/ Brake Size		Nominal	Min. Refinish	Discard Limit②				Nominal	Min. Refinish	Discard Limit②		
2005												
17-inch Brakes	—	1.097–1.107	—	1.040	.0004	.0014	—	.389–.399	—	.335	.0004	.0014
18-inch Brakes	—	1.097–1.107	—	1.040	.0004	.0014	—	.861–.871	—	807	.0004	.0014

① — Above rivet head or backing plate. Original equipment type brake lining.

② — Discard thickness is stamped on rotor.

TIGHTENING SPECIFICATIONS

Year	Component	Torque/Ft. Lbs.
2005	Bleeder Screw	97①
	Brake Tube Nut	10
	Brake Hose-to-Front knuckle Bracket	97①
	Brake Hose Caliper Banjo Bolt	32
	Caliper Adapter, Front	70
	Caliper Adapter, Rear	85
	Caliper Guide Pin, Front	44
	Caliper Guide Pin	44
	Parking Brake Cable Knuckle	71①
	Wheel Lug Nuts	110

① — Inch lbs.

Neon

NOTE: On Air Bag Equipped Models, Refer To "Air Bag System Precautions" Located In The Front Of This Manual For System Disarming & Arming Procedures.

NOTE: Refer To "Computer Relearn Procedures" Located In The Front Of This Manual When Battery Power To The Computer Has Been Interrupted.

INDEX

DESCRIPTION

The front single piston, floating caliper disc brake consists of rotor, caliper, pads and driving hub. The caliper is mounted to steering knuckle using bushings, sleeves and two thru bolts which thread directly into steering knuckle.

This assembly has an anti-rattle clip attached to outer pad and an inner pad-piston retainer clip.

All of braking force is taken directly by adapter. The caliper is a one piece casting with inboard side containing a single piston cylinder bore.

A square cut rubber piston seal is located in a machined groove in caliper bore and provides a seal between piston and caliper bore.

A molded rubber dust boot installed in a groove in cylinder bore and piston keeps contamination from caliper bore and piston. The boot mounts in caliper bore and in a groove in piston.

The rear single piston, floating caliper rear disc brake includes a hub assembly, adapter, rotor, caliper, shoes and pads. The parking brake system consists of a small duo-servo brake mounted to an adapter which expands out against the hat section on inside of rotor. The caliper has either a 1.338 or 1.420 inch piston located on inboard side.

The caliper floats on rubber bushings with metal sleeves on two bolts that are threaded into adapter. Two machined abutments on adapter position and align caliper and brake pads for movement fore and aft.

TROUBLESHOOTING

Refer to "Concorde, Intrepid, LHS & 300M" for troubleshooting procedures.

BRAKE SYSTEM BLEED

Refer to "Hydraulic Brake Systems" chapter for brake system bleeding procedures.

BRAKE PAD SERVICE

Front

1. Raise and support vehicle, then remove front wheel and tire assemblies
2. Remove caliper to steering knuckle guide pin bolts.
3. Rotate top of caliper away from steering knuckle.
4. Lift caliper off bottom machined abutment on steering knuckle.
5. Support caliper to prevent damage of flexible brake hose.
6. Remove outboard brake shoe by prying shoe retaining clip over raised area of caliper.
7. Pull inboard brake shoe away from piston until retaining clip is free from cavity in piston.
8. Reverse procedure to install, noting the following:
   a. Press caliper piston back into piston bore of caliper using suitable tool.
   b. Apply brake pedal several times, then inspect master cylinder brake fluid level and adjust fluid.

Rear

1. Raise and support vehicle, then remove rear wheels and tires.
2. Remove caliper guide pin bolts.
3. Rotate top of caliper away from adapter, then lift caliper off lower machined abutment on adapter.
4. Support caliper from rear strut using suitable wire.
5. Remove outboard brake pad from caliper by prying brake pad retaining clip over raised area on caliper.
6. Pull inboard pad away from caliper piston until retaining clip is free from piston cavity.
7. Press piston completely into caliper bore.
8. Lubricate adapter abutments with Mopar multi-purpose grease, or equivalent.
9. Install inboard and outboard pads.
10. Place bottom of caliper over abutment, then rotate top of caliper into place.
11. Install caliper guide pin bolts.
12. Install tire and wheel assemblies, then lower vehicle and inspect brake fluid level.
13. Road test vehicle to remove any foreign material from brakes and seat brake pads.

CALIPER SERVICE

Replace

1. Remove caliper from brake rotor and brake pads from caliper as outlined under "Brake Pad Service."
2. Disconnect brake hose at brake caliper, then cap brake line.
3. Reverse procedure to install.

Overhaul

DISASSEMBLE

1. Place suitable wood block between caliper piston and caliper fingers.
2. With brake hose attached to caliper, depress brake pedal to push piston out of caliper bore.
3. Prop brake pedal to any position below first inch of brake pedal travel to prevent brake fluid loss.
4. If pistons are to be removed from both calipers, disconnect brake hose at frame bracket after removing piston. Cap brake line and repeat procedure to remove piston from other caliper.
5. Disconnect brake hose from caliper.
6. Mount caliper in suitable soft jawed vice.
7. Support caliper, then remove and discard dust boot.
8. Remove seal from groove in piston bore using suitable small wooden or

plastic stick. **Do not use screwdriver or other metal tool.**

9. Remove caliper bushings.

ASSEMBLE

1. Mount caliper in suitable soft jawed vice.
2. Lubricate piston seal with suitable, clean brake fluid.
3. Install seal in caliper bore groove. Ensure seal is properly seated.
4. Lubricate piston boot with suitable, clean brake fluid and position over piston.
5. Install piston and boot, pushing it past seal until it bottoms in caliper bore.
6. Drive dust boot into counterbore until properly seated using suitable hammer and dust boot installer No. C-4689 with handle No. C-4171, or equivalents.
7. Compress flanges of bushings and install on caliper housing.
8. Ensure bushing flanges extend evenly over caliper housing on both sides.
9. Remove Teflon sleeves from guide pin bushings prior to installing bushings into caliper.
10. After bushings are installed into caliper, install Teflon sleeves into bushings.

11. Connect brake hose to brake line at frame bracket.

ROTOR
REPLACE

1. Remove caliper from brake rotor as outlined under "Brake Pad Service."
2. Remove parking brake adjustment hole plug from brake disc hub.
3. Remove rotor using suitable soft face hammer to tap rotor free of hub as required.
4. Reverse procedure to install.

PARKING BRAKE SERVICE
Parking Brake Shoes, Replace

1. Remove rear disc brake caliper assembly as outlined under "Caliper Service."
2. Remove rear rotor and dust cap hub.
3. Remove cotter pin, nut retainer, wave washer and rear hub/bearing retaining nut and washer from rear spindle.
4. Remove rear hub and bearing.

5. Remove rear brake shoe hold-down clip.
6. Turn brake shoe adjuster wheel until adjuster is at shortest length.
7. Remove adjuster from parking brake.
8. Remove lower shoe to shoe spring.
9. Pull front parking brake shoe away from anchor pin, then remove front parking brake shoe and lower spring.
10. Pull rear brake shoe away from anchor.
11. Remove rear brake shoe and upper spring.
12. Remove hold-down clip and front brake shoe.
13. Reverse procedure to install.

ADJUSTMENTS
Parking Brake

1. Release parking brake.
2. Raise and support vehicle.
3. Adjust parking brake cable until there is slack in cable.
4. Tighten adjusting nut until slight drag is felt when rotating rear wheels.
5. Back off adjusting nut two full turns past point when both rear wheels rotate freely.
6. Inspect parking brake operation.

DISC BRAKE SPECIFICATIONS
Rotor Specifications

Year/ Engine	Front Disc Brake						Rear Disc Brake					
	Brake Lining Wear Limit, Inch①	Rotor			Thickness Variation Parallelism Inch	Lateral Run Out (T.I.R.) Inch	Brake Lining Wear Limit, Inch①	Rotor			Thickness Variation Parallelism Inch	Lateral Run-Out (T.I.R.) Inch
		Thickness, Inch						Thickness, Inch				
		Nominal	Min. Refinish	Discard Limit②				Nominal	Min. Refinish	Discard Limit②		
2001–03												
2.0L	—	.861–.871	—	.803	.0005	.005	—	.344–.364	—	.285	.0005	.005
2004–05												
2.0L	—	.861–.871	—	.803	.0005	.005	—	.344–.364	—	.285	.0005	.005
2.4L	—	1.1099–1.106	—	1.039	.0004	.005	—	.463–.482	—	.404	.0005	.005

① — Above rivet head or backing plate. Original equipment type brake lining.

② — Discard thickness is stamped on rotor.

Caliper Specifications

Location, Type	Caliper Piston O.D., Inch
Front	2.125
Rear, Solid	1.340
Rear, Vented	1.420

TIGHTENING SPECIFICATIONS

Year	Component	Torque/Ft. Lbs.
2001–05	Bearing Retainer	21
	Bleed Screws	10
	Brake Hose To Caliper Banjo Bolt	18
	Brake Line Fitting	12
	Caliper	16
	Caliper Guide Pins	30
	Caliper Adapter (To Knuckle), Rear	55
	Front Brake Hose Intermediate Bracket	108①
	Support Plate To Rear Axle	80
	Wheel Lug Nuts	85–110

① — Inch lbs.

DISC BRAKES

Sebring Convertible, Sebring Sedan & Stratus Sedan

NOTE: On Air Bag Equipped Models, Refer To "Air Bag System Precautions" Located In The Front Of This Manual For System Disarming & Arming Procedures.

NOTE: Refer To "Computer Relearn Procedures" Located In The Front Of This Manual When Battery Power To The Computer Has Been Interrupted.

INDEX

TROUBLESHOOTING

Lateral Runout Inspection

1. Remove caliper as outlined under "Brake Pad Service."
2. Inspect disc surface for grooves, cracks and rust.
3. Tighten rotor to hub.
4. Place suitable dial indicator approximately 1 inch from outer circumference of brake rotor, **Fig. 1.**
5. Measure brake rotor runout.
6. If runout of rotor is equal to or exceeds specifications, proceed as follows:
   a. Before removing brake rotor, chalk both sides of wheel stud on side at which runout is greatest.
   b. Remove brake rotor and place dial gauge, **Fig. 2.**
   c. Move hub in axial direction and measure play. If play exceeds .002 inch, disassemble hub knuckle and inspect each part.
   d. If play does not exceed specifications, install brake rotor 180° away from chalk marks.
   e. Inspect runout of brake rotor again.
   f. If runout cannot be corrected by changing phase of rotor, replace or machine rotor.

Parallelism Inspection

Measure the rotor thickness at 12 posi-

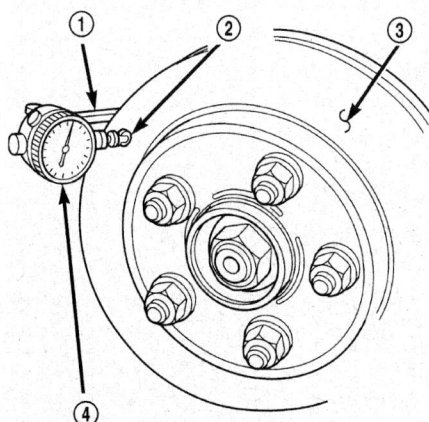

1 - SPECIAL TOOL SP-1910
2 - 25 mm FROM EDGE
3 - DISC SURFACE
4 - SPECIAL TOOL C-3339

CR4070100146000X

Fig. 1 Dial indicator mounting for rotor lateral runout

tions with suitable micrometer 1 inch in from outer edge of disc.

BRAKE SYSTEM BLEED

Refer to "Hydraulic Brake Systems" chapter for brake system bleeding procedures.

BRAKE PAD SERVICE

Front

1. Raise and support vehicle, then remove tire and wheel assemblies.

2. Remove anti-rattle spring from outboard side of caliper and adapter.
3. Remove caps, guide pin bolts and caliper.
4. Remove pads.
5. Reverse procedure to install, noting the following:
   a. Press caliper piston back into piston bore of caliper.
   b. Apply brake pedal several times, then inspect master cylinder brake fluid level and adjust fluid.

Rear

1. Raise and support vehicle, then rear wheel and tire assemblies.
2. Remove caliper guide pin bolts.
3. Rotate top of caliper away from adapter, then lift caliper off lower machined abutment on adapter.
4. Support caliper from rear strut assembly using suitable wire.
5. Remove outboard brake pad from caliper by prying brake pad retaining clip over raised area on caliper.
6. Pull inboard pad away from caliper piston until retaining clip is free from piston cavity.
7. Press piston completely into caliper bore.
8. Lubricate adapter abutments with Mopar multi-purpose grease, or equivalent.
9. Install inboard and outboard pads.
10. Place bottom of caliper over abutment, then rotate top of caliper into place.
11. Install caliper guide pin bolts.
12. Install tire and wheel assemblies, then lower vehicle and inspect brake fluid level.

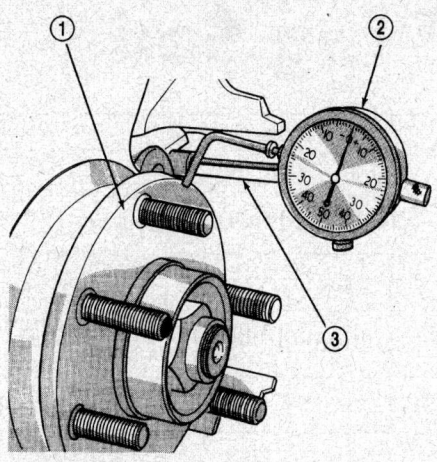

1 - HUB SURFACE
2 - SPECIAL TOOL C-3339
3 - SPECIAL TOOL SP-1910

CR4070100147000X

Fig. 2   Dial gauge mounting for hub lateral runout

13. Road test vehicle to remove any foreign material from brakes and seat brake pads.

CALIPER SERVICE
Replacement

1. Remove caliper from brake rotor and brake pads from caliper as outlined under "Brake Pad Service."
2. Disconnect brake hose at brake caliper. Cap brake line.
3. Reverse procedure to install.

Overhaul

1. Remove brake pads as outlined under "Brake Pad Service."
2. Hang caliper on suitable wire away from rotor.
3. Place suitable, small piece of wood between piston and caliper fingers.
4. Depress brake pedal to hydraulically push piston out of bore.
5. Apply and hold-down brake pedal to any position beyond first inch of brake travel to prevent master cylinder brake fluid loss.
6. Disconnect brake line from caliper. Plug brake line to avoid any additional brake fluid loss.
7. Mount brake caliper in suitable, soft jawed vise. **Excessive vise pressure will cause bore distortion and binding of piston.**

8. Remove guide pin bushings.
9. Remove and discard piston dust boot .
10. Work piston seal out of its groove using suitable plastic trim stick. **Do not use screw driver or other metal tool.**
11. Clean all components using alcohol, or suitable solvent, and wipe dry using a lint free cloth. **No lint residue can be left in caliper bore.**
12. Inspect piston bore for scoring or pitting. Light scratches or corrosion can usually be cleared from bores using crocus cloth. Bores that show deep scratches or scoring should be honed. **Bore diameter should not be honed more than .001 inch. If bore does not clean up within specification, replace caliper housing.**
13. When honing brake caliper housing, coat stones and bore with brake fluid.
14. After honing bore, clean seal and boot grooves with suitable, stiff non-metallic rotary brush.
15. Remove all dirt and grit by flushing caliper with brake fluid, wipe dry with lint free cloth.
16. Replace caliper piston if there is any pitting, scratches or physical damage.
17. Dip new piston seal in clean brake fluid and install in caliper bore groove. Seal should be positioned at one area in groove and gently worked around groove using only fingers until properly seated. **Never install old piston seal.**
18. Coat new piston boot with clean brake fluid leaving generous amount inside boot.
19. Coat dust boot with clean brake fluid and position over piston.
20. Install piston into caliper bore pushing it past piston seal until it bottoms in caliper bore.
21. Position dust boot in counterbore of caliper piston bore.
22. Drive boot into counterbore of caliper using suitable hammer and piston caliper boot installer No. C-4689 and handle No. C-4171, or equivalents, **Fig. 3.**
23. Install guide pin bushings and dust boots.
24. Attach hydraulic brake line to caliper. Use new seal washers when installing brake line to caliper.

ROTOR
REPLACE

1. Remove caliper from brake rotor as outlined under "Brake Pad Service."
2. Remove retaining clips and rotor. Use suitable soft face hammer to tap rotor free of hub as required.
3. Reverse procedure to install.

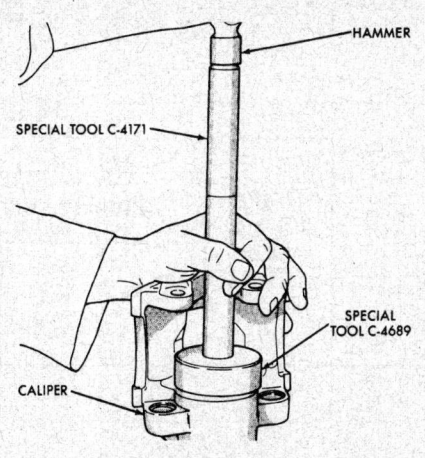

CR4079500099000X

Fig. 3   Caliper piston boot installation

ADJUSTMENTS
Parking Brake Lever

1. Remove center floor console and lower parking brake handle.
2. Position lever to its fully released position.
3. Tighten adjusting nut on parking brake lever output cable until approximately 1.02 inch of thread is past edge of adjusting nut.
4. Actuate parking brake lever to its fully applied position (22 clicks) one time, then position lever to its fully released position.
5. Raise and support rear of vehicle.
6. Turn rear wheel with parking brake in released position to confirm rear brakes are not dragging.

Parking Brake Shoe

1. Raise and support vehicle, then remove rear wheels.
2. Remove adjusting hole plug from hub of brake disc.
3. Turn adjusting nut until brake disc cannot be turned by hand using suitable tool.
4. Back off adjusting nut five notches.
5. Firmly apply, then release parking brake lever several times to seat and center parking brake shoes.
6. Adjust parking brake lever as outlined under "Parking Brake Lever, Adjust"
7. Install rear wheels, then lower vehicle.

DISC BRAKES

DISC BRAKE SPECIFICATIONS
Rotor Specifications

Year	Front Disc Brake						Rear Disc Brake					
	Brake Lining Wear Limit, Inch①	Rotor					Brake Lining Wear Limit, Inch①	Rotor				
		Thickness, Inch			Thickness Variation Parallelism Inch	Lateral Run Out (T.I.R.) Inch		Thickness, Inch			Thickness Variation Parallelism Inch	Lateral Run-Out (T.I.R.) Inch
		Nominal	Min. Refinish	Discard Limit②				Nominal	Min. Refinish	Discard Limit②		
2001–05	—	.900–.911	—	.843	.0005	.004	—	.350–.360	—	.285	.0005	.005

① — Above rivet head or backing plate. Original equipment type brake lining.

② — Discard thickness is stamped on rotor.

TIGHTENING SPECIFICATIONS

Year	Component	Torque/Ft. Lbs.
2001–05	Bleed Screws	10
	Brake Hose Intermediate Bracket	105①
	Brake Hose To Caliper (Banjo Bolt)	26
	Brake Tube	12
	Caliper Adapter	60
	Caliper Guide & Lockpins	26
	Wheel Lug Nuts	100

① — Inch lbs.

Sebring Coupe & Stratus Coupe

NOTE: On Air Bag Equipped Models, Refer To "Air Bag System Precautions" Located In The Front Of This Manual For System Disarming & Arming Procedures.

NOTE: Refer To "Computer Relearn Procedures" Located In The Front Of This Manual When Battery Power To The Computer Has Been Interrupted.

INDEX

TROUBLESHOOTING

Refer to **Fig. 1** for brake system troubleshooting.

Lateral Runout Inspection

1. Remove mounting bolts and caliper.
2. Inspect disc surface for grooves, cracks and rust.
3. Place suitable dial gauge approximately .2 inch from outer circumference of brake rotor.
4. Measure runout of rotor.
5. If runout of rotor is equal to or exceeds specifications, proceed as follows:
   a. Before removing brake rotor, chalk both sides of wheel stud on side at which runout is greatest.
   b. Remove brake rotor and place dial gauge as outlined, **Fig. 2.**
   c. Move hub in axial direction and measure play. If play exceeds .002 inch disassemble hub knuckle and inspect each part.
   d. If play does not exceed limit specification, install brake rotor 180° away from chalk marks.
   e. Inspect runout of brake rotor again.
   f. If runout cannot be corrected by changing phase of rotor, replace or machine rotor.

Parallelism Inspection

Measure the rotor thickness at eight positions approximately 45° apart and .39 inch in from outer edge of disc, using suitable micrometer.

BRAKE SYSTEM BLEED

Refer to "Hydraulic Brake Systems" chapter for brake system bleeding procedures.

BRAKE PAD SERVICE

Front

1. Raise and support vehicle, then remove tire and wheel assemblies.
2. Remove guide pin, lift caliper body upward and secure with suitable wire, **Fig. 3.**
3. Remove inner shims, anti-squeak shims, brake pad and clips from support mounting.
4. Reverse procedure to install, noting the following:
   a. Press caliper piston back into piston bore of caliper using suitable tool.
   b. Apply brake pedal several times, then inspect master cylinder brake fluid level and adjust fluid.

Rear

1. Raise and support vehicle, then remove rear wheel and tire assemblies.
2. Remove pin bolts and lift caliper from support.
3. Support caliper from rear strut using suitable wire.
4. Remove outboard brake pad and wear indicator.
5. Remove inner shims and inboard pad.
6. Remove outer shim and clip.
7. Reverse procedure to install.

CALIPER SERVICE

Replacement

1. Remove caliper from brake rotor and brake pads from caliper as outlined under "Brake Pad Service."
2. Disconnect brake hose at brake caliper. Cap brake line.
3. Reverse procedure to install.

Overhaul

FRONT

1. Remove caliper assembly as outlined under "Replacement."
2. Remove lockpin, bushing, caliper support, guide pin and lockpin boots, **Fig. 3.**
3. Remove boot ring using suitable flat blade screwdriver.
4. Position shop towel in caliper body, then apply compressed air through brake hose fitting hole to remove piston and dust boot. **Apply air gently.**
5. Remove piston seal using finger tips. **Do not use screwdriver or other tool.**
6. Reverse procedure to assemble, noting following:
   a. Inspect cylinder and piston for wear or damage and/or corrosion. Inspect caliper body and sleeve for wear.
   b. Apply suitable brake fluid to inner cylinder, then install piston seal into cylinder groove. **Do not wipe special grease from piston seal.**
   c. Apply suitable brake fluid to piston and insert into cylinder without twisting.
   d. Fill piston edge with grease from seal and boot repair kit, or equivalent, then install piston boot.
   e. Lubricate sliding surface of lockpin and guide pin boots, caliper support and bushing with grease from seal and boot repair kit.
   f. Install guide and lockpins with their head marks matched with identification marks on caliper body.

REAR

1. Remove caliper assembly as outlined under "Replacement."
2. Remove caliper support, **Fig. 4.**
3. Remove pin boots and boot ring.
4. Position suitable wood block in caliper body, then apply compressed air

through brake hose fitting hole to remove piston and dust boot. **Apply air gently.**

5. Remove piston seal using finger tip.
6. Reverse procedure to assemble, noting following:
   a. Inspect cylinder and piston for wear, damage and/or corrosion. Inspect caliper body and sleeve for wear.
   b. Apply brake fluid to inner cylinder, then install piston seal into cylinder groove. **Do not wipe grease from piston seal.**
   c. Apply brake fluid to pistons and insert into cylinders by pushing downward into caliper. **Do not twist pistons into caliper.**
   d. Fill piston edge with grease from seal and boot repair kit, then install piston boot.
   e. Lubricate bushing, pin boot and slide pins with grease from seal and boot repair kit.
   f. Install guide and lockpins. Ensure head marks match with identification marks on caliper body.

ROTOR

REPLACE

1. Remove caliper from brake rotor as outlined under "Brake Pad Service."
2. Remove rotor. Use suitable soft face hammer to tap rotor free of hub as required.
3. Reverse procedure to install.

ADJUSTMENTS

Parking Brake Lever

1. Pull parking brake lever with approximately 45 ft. lbs. force and count number of notches.
2. Standard value is 5–7 notches with drum brakes and 3–5 notches with disc brakes. If parking brake lever stroke is not as specified, proceed to next step.
3. Remove inner compartment mat of floor console.
4. Loosen adjusting nut to end of cable rod to free cable.
5. Remove adjustment hole plug and to turn adjuster using suitable flat tipped screwdriver.
6. Turn adjuster in direction which expands shoes so disc will not rotate.
7. Return adjuster five notches in opposite direction.
8. Turn adjusting nut to adjust parking brake lever stroke within standard

Symptom	Probable cause	Remedy
Vehicle pulls to one side when brakes are applied	Grease or oil on pad or lining surface	Replace
	Inadequate contact of pad or lining	Correct
	Auto adjuster malfunction	Adjust
	Drum out of round or uneven wear	Repair or replace as necessary
Insufficient braking power	Low or deteriorated brake fluid	Refill or change
	Air in brake system	Bleed air from system
	Overheated brake rotor due to dragging of pad or lining	Correct
	Inadequate contact of pad or lining	
	Brake booster malfunction	
	Clogged brake line	
	Grease or oil on pad or lining surface	Replace
	Proportioning valve malfunction	
	Auto adjuster malfunction	Adjust
Increased pedal stroke (Reduced pedal to floorboard clearance)	Air in brake system	Bleed air from system
	Worn lining or pad	Replace
	Broken vacuum hose	
	Faulty master cylinder	
	Brake fluid leaks	Correct
	Auto adjuster malfunction	Adjust
	Excessive push rod to master cylinder clearance	
Brake drag	Incomplete release of parking brake	Correct
	Clogged master cylinder return port	
	Incorrect parking brake adjustment	Adjust
	Incorrect push rod to master cylinder clearance	
	Faulty master cylinder piston return spring	Replace
	Worn brake pedal return spring	
	Broken rear drum brake shoe return spring	
	Lack of lubrication in sliding parts	Lubricate

CR4079100038010X

Fig. 1   Brake system troubleshooting (Part 1 of 3)

value. **If number of brake lever notches engaged is less than standard value, cable has been excessively pulled.**

9. Inspect to ensure there is no play between adjusting nut and pin.
10. Raise and support rear of vehicle.
11. Turn rear wheel with parking brake in released position to confirm rear brakes are not dragging.

Parking Brake Shoe

1. Raise and support vehicle, then remove rear wheels.
2. Firmly apply, then release parking brake lever several times to seat and center parking brake shoes.
3. Remove adjusting hole plug from hub of brake disc.
4. Turn adjusting nut until brake disc cannot be turned by hand using suitable tool.
5. Back off adjusting nut five notches.
6. Repeat above steps on opposite side.
7. Firmly apply, then release parking brake lever several times to seat and center parking brake shoes.

Symptom	Probable cause	Remedy
Insufficient parking brake function	Worn brake lining	Replace
	Grease or oil on lining surface	
	Parking brake cable sticking	
	Stuck wheel cylinder or caliper piston	
	Excessive parking brake lever stroke	Adjust the parking brake lever stroke or check the parking brake cable routing
	Auto adjuster malfunction	Adjust
Scraping or grinding noise when brakes are applied	Worn brake lining or pad	Replace
	Caliper to wheel interference	Correct or replace
	Dust cover to disc interference	
	Bent brake backing plate	
	Cracked drums or brake disc	
Squealing, groaning or chattering noise when brakes are applied	Missing or damaged brake pad anti-squeak shim	Replace
	Brake drums and linings, discs and pads worn or scored	Correct or replace
	Incorrect parts	
	Burred or rusted calipers	Clean or deburr
	Dirty, greased, contaminated or glazed linings	Clean or replace
	Drum brakes-weak, damaged or incorrect shoe hold-down springs, loose or damaged shoe hold-down pins and springs	Correct or replace
	Incorrect brake pedal or booster push rod setting	Adjust
Squealing noise when brakes are not applied	Bent or warped backing plate causing interference with drum	Replace
	Drum brakes-weak, damaged or incorrect shoe-to-shoe spring	
	Poor return of brake booster, master cylinder or wheel cylinder	
	Loose or extra brake parts	Retighten

CR4079100038020X

Fig. 1   Brake system troubleshooting (Part 2 of 3)

Symptom	Probable cause	Remedy
Squealing noise when brakes are not applied	Improper positioning of pads in caliper	Correct
	Improper installation of support mounting to caliper body	
	Improper machining of drum causing interference with backing plate or shoe	Replace drum
	Disc brakes-rusted, stuck	Lubricate or replace
	Worn, damaged or insufficiently lubricated wheel bearings	
	Incorrect brake pedal or booster push rod setting	Adjust
Groaning clicking or rattling noise when brakes are not applied	Stones or foreign material trapped inside wheel covers	Remove stones, etc.
	Loose wheel nuts	Retighten
	Disc brakes-loose installation bolt	
	Worn, damaged or dry wheel bearings	Lubricate or replace
	Disc brakes-failure of anti-rattle shim	Replace
	Disc brakes-wear on sleeve	
	Incorrect brake pedal or booster push rod setting	Adjust

CR4079100038030X

Fig. 1   Brake system troubleshooting (Part 3 of 3)

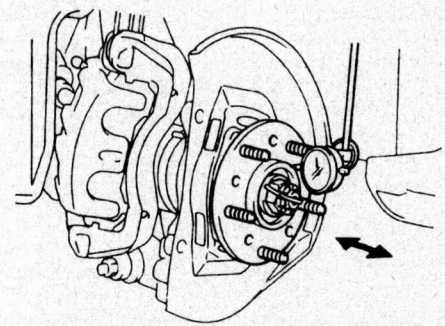

CR4079700112000X

Fig. 2   Dial gauge mounting

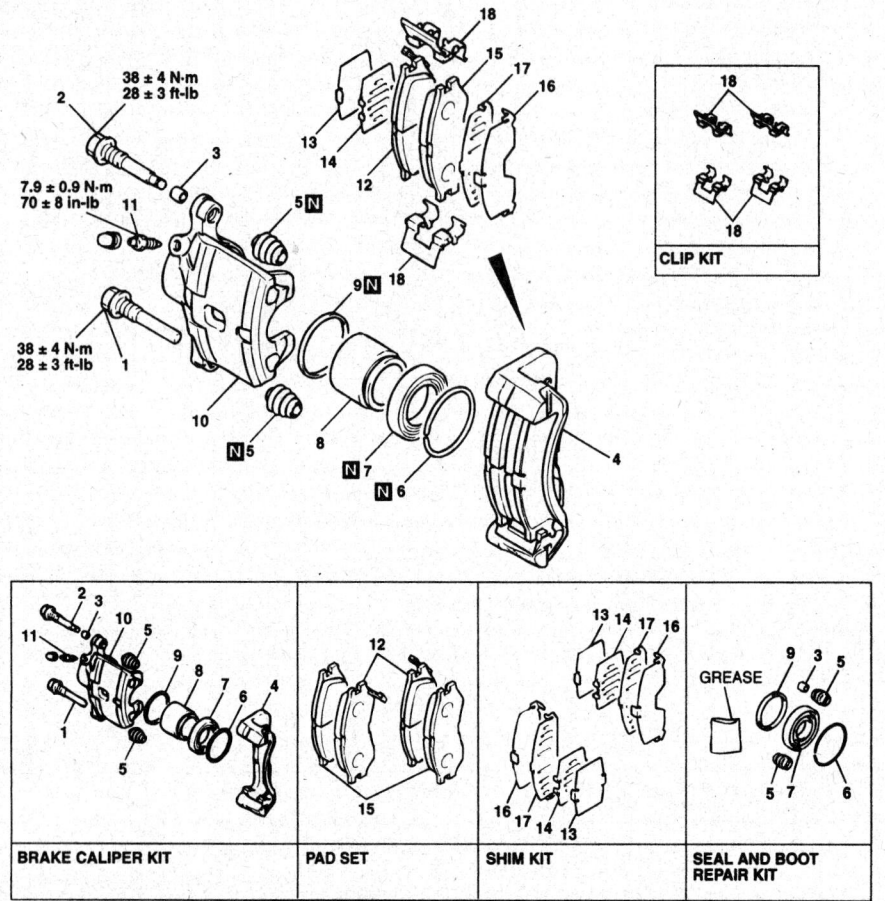

Fig. 3   Disc brake

CR4070000144000X

**CALIPER ASSEMBLY DISASSEM-
BLY STEPS**
1. GUIDE PIN
2. LOCK PIN
3. BUSHING
4. CALIPER SUPPORT, PAD, CLIP
    AND SHIM ASSEMBLY
5. PIN BOOT
6. BOOT RING
7. PISTON BOOT
8. PISTON
9. PISTON SEAL
10. CALIPER BODY
11. BLEEDER SCREW

**PAD ASSEMBLY DISASSEMBLY
STEPS**
1. GUIDE PIN
2. LOCK PIN
3. BUSHING
4. CALIPER SUPPORT, PAD, CLIP
    AND SHIM ASSEMBLY
12. PAD AND WEAR INDICATOR AS-
    SEMBLY
13. INNER SHIM B
14. INNER SHIM A
15. PAD ASSEMBLY
16. OUTER SHIM B
17. OUTER SHIM A
18. CLIP

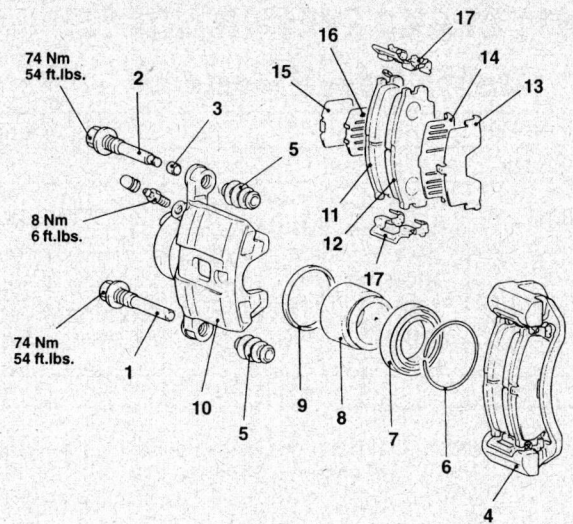

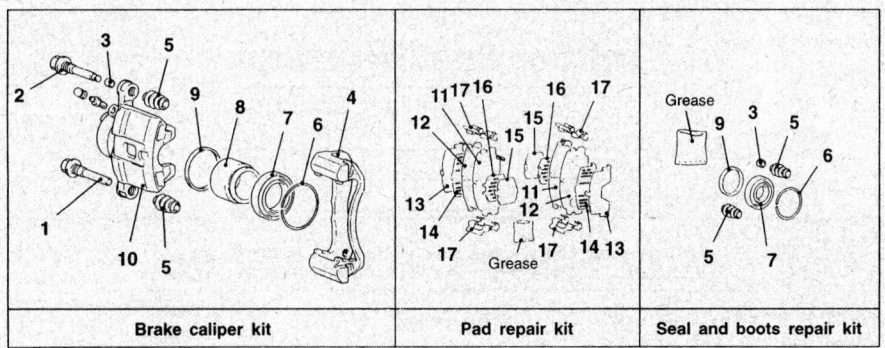

| Brake caliper kit | Pad repair kit | Seal and boots repair kit |

Caliper assembly

1. Guide pin
2. Lock pin
3. Bushing
4. Caliper support (pad, clip, shim)
5. Boot
6. Boot ring
7. Piston boot
8. Piston
9. Piston seal
10. Caliper body

Pad assembly

1. Guide pin
2. Lock pin
3. Bushing
4. Caliper support (pad, clip, shim)
11. Pad and wear indicator assembly
12. Pad assembly
13. Outer shim (stainless)
14. Outer shim (coated with rubber)
15. Inner shim (stainless)
16. Inner shim (coated with rubber)
17. Clip

CR4079100045000X

Fig. 4   Dual pin floating caliper disc brake. Rear

DISC BRAKE SPECIFICATIONS
Rotor Specifications

Year	Front Disc Brake						Rear Disc Brake					
	Brake Lining Wear Limit, Inch③	Rotor			Thickness Variation Parallelism Inch	Lateral Run Out (T.I.R.) Inch	Brake Lining Wear Limit, Inch③	Rotor			Thickness Variation Parallelism Inch	Lateral Run-Out (T.I.R.) Inch
		Thickness, Inch						Thickness, Inch				
		Nominal	Min. Re-finish	Discard Limit②				Nominal	Min. Re-finish	Discard Limit②		
2001–05	.08	①	—	④	—	.002	.08	.40	—	.33	—	.003

① — 2.4L engine, .90 inch; 3.0L engine, 1.02 inches.
② — Discard thickness is stamped on rotor.
③ — Above rivet head or backing plate. Original equipment type brake lining.
④ — 2.4L engine, .88 inch; 3.0L engine, .96 inch.

Caliper Specifications

Location	Caliper Bore Dia. Inch
Front	2.375
Rear	1.375

TIGHTENING SPECIFICATIONS

Year	Component	Torque/Ft. Lbs.
2001–05	Backing Plate	36–43
	Bleed Screws	50–84①
	Brake Hose To Rear Caliper Banjo Bolt (2001–02)	18–25
	Brake Hose To Rear Caliper Banjo Bolt (2003–05)	11–12
	Caliper Guide & Lockpins, Front (2001–02)	54
	Caliper Guide & Lockpins, Front (2003–05)	28–31
	Caliper Guide & Lockpins, Rear	32
	Caliper Support To Front Axle	65
	Caliper Support To Rear Axle	36–43
	Wheel Lug Nuts	87–101

① — Inch lbs.

DRUM BRAKES

TABLE OF CONTENTS

Neon

NOTE: On Air Bag Equipped Models, Refer To "Air Bag System Precautions" Located In The Front Of This Manual For System Disarming & Arming Procedures.

NOTE: Refer To "Computer Relearn Procedures" Located In The Front Of This Manual When Battery Power To The Computer Has Been Interrupted.

INDEX

PRECAUTIONS

When working on or around brake assemblies, care must be taken to prevent breathing asbestos dust. During routine service operations, the amount of asbestos dust from brake lining wear is at a low level because of a chemical breakdown during use. A few precautions will minimize exposure.

Do not sand or grind brake linings unless suitable exhaust ventilation equipment is used to prevent excessive asbestos exposure.

1. Wear suitable respirator approved for asbestos dust use during repair procedures.
2. When cleaning brake dust from brake components, use vacuum cleaner with highly efficient filter system. If suitable vacuum cleaner is not available, use water soaked rag. **Do not use compressed air or dry brush to clean brake components.**
3. Keep work area clean.
4. Properly dispose of rags and vacuum cleaner bags by placing them in plastic bags.
5. Do not smoke or eat while working on brake systems.
6. Never use any fluid containing mineral oil to clean brake system components.

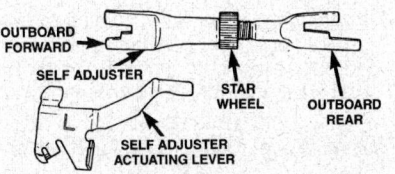

CR4089800040020X

Fig. 1 Automatic self-adjuster mechanism

INSPECTION

Brake Drums

Any time the brake drums are removed for brake service, the braking surface diameter should be inspected with a suitable brake drum micrometer at several points to determine if they are within the safe oversize limit stamped on the brake drum outer surface. If the braking surface diameter exceeds specifications, the drum must be replaced. If the braking surface diameter is within specifications, drums should be cleaned and inspected for cracks, scores, deep grooves, taper, out of round and heat spotting. If drums are cracked or heat spotted, they must be replaced. Scoring and

grooves in the braking surface can only be removed by machining with special equipment, as long as the braking surface is within specifications. Any brake drum showing taper or sufficient out of round to cause vehicle vibration or noise while braking should also be machined, removing only enough stock to true up the drum.

After a brake drum is machined, wipe the braking surface diameter with a denatured alcohol soaked cloth. If one brake drum is machined, the other should also be machined to the same diameter to maintain equal braking forces.

Brake Linings & Springs

Inspect brake linings for excessive wear, damage, oil, grease or brake fluid contamination. If any of the these conditions exist, brake linings should be replaced as an axle set to maintain equal braking forces. Examine brake shoe webbing, hold-down and return springs for signs of overheating indicated by a slight blue color. Any component which exhibits overheating signs should be replaced. Overheated springs lose their pull and could cause brake linings to wear out prematurely. Inspect springs for

DRUM BRAKES

RED BRAKE WARNING LAMP

CONDITION	POSSIBLE CAUSES	CORRECTION
RED BRAKE WARNING LAMP ON	1. Parking brake lever not fully released.	1. Release parking brake lever.
	2. Parking brake warning lamp switch on parking brake lever.	2. Inspect and replace switch as necessary.
	3. Brake fluid level low in reservoir.	3. Fill reservoir. Check entire system for leaks. Repair or replace as required.
	4. Brake fluid level switch.	4. Disconnect switch wiring connector. If lamp goes out, replace switch.
	5. Mechanical instrument cluster (MIC) problem.	5. Diagnose Instrument Cluster Fault Condition.
	6. ABS EBD malfunction. .	6. Refer to ABS section

BRAKE NOISE

CONDITION	POSSIBLE CAUSES	CORRECTION
DISC BRAKE CHIRP	1. Excessive brake rotor runout.	1. Follow brake rotor diagnosis and testing. Correct as necessary.
	2. Lack of lubricant on brake caliper slides.	2. Lubricate brake caliper slides.
DISC BRAKE RATTLE OR CLUNK	1. Broken or missing anti-rattle spring clips on shoes.	1. Replace brake shoes.
	2. Caliper guide pins loose.	2. Tighten guide pins.
DISC BRAKE SQUEAK AT LOW SPEED (WHILE APPLYING LIGHT BRAKE PEDAL EFFORT)	1. Brake shoe linings.	1. Replace brake shoes.
DRUM BRAKE CHIRP	1. Lack of lubricant on brake shoe support plate where shoes ride.	1. Lubricate shoe contact areas on brake shoe support plates.
	2. Wheel cylinder out of alignment.	2. Loosen wheel cylinder mounting bolts, realign wheel cylinder with brake shoes and tighten mounting bolts.
DRUM BRAKE CLUNK	1. Drum(s) have threaded machined braking surface.	1. Reface or replace drake drums as necessary.
DRUM BRAKE HOWL OR MOAN	1. Lack of lubricant on brake shoe support plate where shoes ride and at the anchor.	1. Lubricate shoe contact areas on brake shoe support plates and at the anchor.
	2. Rear brake shoes.	2. Replace rear brake shoes.
DRUM BRAKE SCRAPING OR WHIRRING	1. ABS wheel speed sensor or tone wheel.	1. Inspect, correct or replace faulty component(s).
SCRAPING (METAL-TO-METAL).	1. Foreign object interference with brakes.	1. Inspect brakes and remove foreign object.
	2. Brake shoes worn out.	2. Replace brake shoes. Inspect rotors and drums. Reface or replace as necessary.

CR4089900044010X

Fig. 2   Brake system troubleshooting (Part 1 of 3)

CONDITION	POSSIBLE CAUSES	CORRECTION
BRAKES CHATTER	1. Rear brake drum out of round or disc brake rotor has excessive thickness variation.	1. Isolate condition as rear or front. Reface or replace brake drums or rotors as necessary.
BRAKES DRAG (FRONT OR ALL)	1. Contaminated brake fluid.	1. Check for swollen seals. Replace all system components containing rubber.
	2. Binding caliper pins or bushings.	2. Replace pins and bushings.
	3. Binding master cylinder.	3. Replace master cylinder.
	4. Binding brake pedal.	4. Replace brake pedal.
BRAKES DRAG (REAR ONLY)	1. Parking brake cables binding or froze up.	1. Check cable routing. Replace cables as necessary.
	2. Parking brake cable return spring not returning shoes.	2. Replace cables as necessary.
	3. Service brakes not adjusted properly (rear drum brakes only).	3. Follow the procedure listed in the adjustment section.
	4. Obstruction inside the center console preventing full return of the parking brake cables.	4. Remove console and remove obstruction.
BRAKES GRAB	1. Contaminated brake shoe linings.	1. Inspect and clean, or replace shoes. Repair source of contamination.
	2. Improper power brake booster assist.	2. Refer to power brake booster in the diagnosis and testing section.
EXCESSIVE PEDAL EFFORT	1. Obstruction of brake pedal.	1. Inspect, remove or move obstruction.
	2. Low power brake booster assist.	2. Refer to power brake booster in the diagnosis and testing section.
	3. Glazed brake linings.	3. Reface or replace brake rotors as necessary. Replace brake shoes.
	4. Brake shoe lining transfer to brake rotor.	4. Reface or replace brake rotors as necessary. Replace brake shoes.
EXCESSIVE PEDAL TRAVEL (VEHICLE STOPS OK)	1. Air in brake lines.	1. Bleed brakes.
	2. Rear drum brake auto-adjuster malfunctioning.	2. Inspect and replace drum brake components as necessary. Adjust rear brakes.
EXCESSIVE PEDAL TRAVEL (PEDAL GOES TO FLOOR - CAN'T SKID WHEELS)	1. Power brake booster runout (vacuum assist).	1. Check booster vacuum hose and engine tune for adequate vacuum supply. Refer to power brake booster in the diagnosis and testing section.
EXCESSIVE PEDAL TRAVEL (ONE FRONT WHEEL LOCKS UP DURING HARD BRAKING)	1. One of the two hydraulic circuits to the front brakes is malfunctioning.	1. Inspect system for leaks. Check master cylinder for internal malfunction.

CR4089900044020X

Fig. 2   Brake system troubleshooting (Part 2 of 3)

sags, bends and external damage and replace as required.

Inspect hold-down retainers and pins for bends, rust and corrosion. Replace faulty components as required.

Wheel Cylinder

With brake drum removed, inspect the wheel cylinder for fluid leaks. Inspect wheel cylinder boots for cuts, tears, or heat cracks. Replace faulty components as required.

Backing Plate

Inspect backing plate shoe contact surface for grooves that may restrict shoe movement and cannot be removed by lightly sanding with emery cloth or other suitable abrasive. If backing plate exhibits these condition, it should be replaced. Also inspect for signs of cracks, warpage and excessive rust, indicating need for replacement.

Adjuster Mechanism

1. Ensure quadrant rotates freely throughout its tooth contact range, **Fig. 1**.
2. Ensure quadrant slides freely entire length of its mounting slot.
3. Inspect quadrant spring for any signs of damage.
4. Ensure knurled pin is securely attached to adjuster mechanism and teeth are not damaged.

5. Examine adjuster mechanism for excessive wear or damage. Replace as required.
6. If adjuster mechanism will be used again, apply light coat of suitable multi-purpose lubricant between quadrant and strut of adjuster mechanism.

Parking Brake Cable

Inspect parking brake cable end for kinks, fraying and elongation and replace as required. Use a small hose clamp to compress clamp where it enters backing plate during removal.

TROUBLESHOOTING

Refer to **Fig. 2** for brake system troubleshooting.

BRAKE SERVICE

Because of the automatic adjustment feature of the parking brake, only remove brake shoes from one side of the vehicle at a time.

Removal

1. Raise and support vehicle, then remove rear wheel and tire assembly.
2. Remove retaining clips, then the drum from hub and bearing.

3. Remove self-adjuster lever to brake shoe spring.
4. Remove self-adjustment lever from shoe.
5. Remove brake shoe to support plate hold-down clips and pins.
6. Remove lower brake shoe to anchor plate return spring.
7. Remove park brake lever pin to shoe retaining clip.
8. Remove leading and trailing brake shoes, upper return spring and self-adjuster screw from support plate.

Installation

1. Lubricate brake shoe contact areas on brake support plate and anchor, with suitable multi-purpose lubricant, **Fig. 3**.
2. Assemble front and rear shoes, self-adjuster screw and upper return spring.
3. Install brake shoe components.
4. Install wave washer on park brake lever pin.
5. Install both shoe to support plate hold-down pins and clips.
6. Install lower shoe to anchor plate return spring.
7. Install self-adjustment lever on leading brake shoe.
8. Install self-adjustment lever to shoe spring.

CONDITION	POSSIBLE CAUSES	CORRECTION
PEDAL PULSATES/SURGES DURING BRAKING	1. Rear brake drum out of round or disc brake rotor has excessive thickness variation.	1. Isolate condition as rear or front. Reface or replace brake drums or rotors as necessary.
PEDAL IS SPONGY	1. Air in brake lines. 2. Power brake booster runout (vacuum assist).	1. Bleed brakes. 2. Check booster vacuum hose and engine tune for adequate vacuum supply. Refer to power brake booster in the diagnosis and testing section.
PREMATURE REAR WHEEL LOCKUP	1. Contaminated brake shoe linings. 2. Inoperative proportioning valve (non-ABS vehicles only). 3. ABS EBD not functioning. 4. Improper power brake booster assist.	1. Inspect and clean, or replace shoes. Repair source of contamination. 2. Test proportioning valves following procedure listed in diagnosis and testing section. Replace valves as necessary. 3. Refer to the ABS section 4. Refer to power brake booster in the diagnosis and testing section.
STOP LAMPS STAY ON	1. Brake lamp switch out of adjustment. 2. Brake pedal binding. 3. Obstruction in pedal linkage. 4. Power Brake Booster not allowing pedal to return completely.	1. Adjust brake lamp switch. 2. Inspect and replace as necessary. 3. Remove obstruction. 4. Replace power brake booster.
VEHICLE PULLS TO RIGHT OR LEFT ON BRAKING	1. Frozen brake caliper piston. 2. Contaminated brake shoe lining. 3. Pinched brake lines. 4. Leaking piston seal. 5. Suspension problem.	1. Replace frozen piston or caliper. Bleed brakes. 2. Inspect and clean, or replace shoes. Repair source of contamination. 3. Replace pinched line. 4. Replace piston seal or brake caliper. 5. Refer to the Suspension section.
PARKING BRAKE - EXCESSIVE HANDLE TRAVEL	1. Rear brakes out of adjustment.	1. Adjust rear drum brake shoes, or rear parking brake shoes on vehicles with rear disc brakes.

CR4089900044030X

Fig. 2 Brake system troubleshooting (Part 3 of 3)

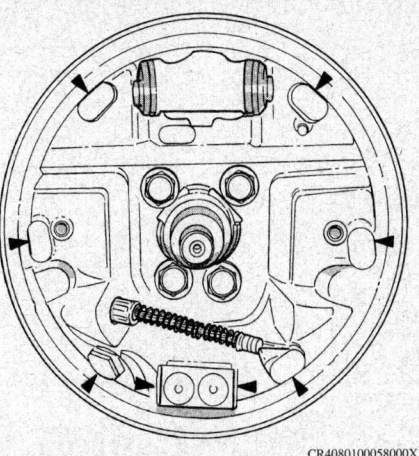

CR4080100058000X

Fig. 3 Brake shoe contact areas

9. Adjust shoes out until drum drags lightly when installed. **Do not over-adjust.**
10. Install brake drum.

ADJUSTMENTS
Service Brake

1. Ensure parking brake is in its fully released position.

2. Raise and support vehicle.
3. Remove brake adjusting hole plug from rear brake shoe support plate.
4. Insert brake adjustment tool, or suitable thin screwdriver, through support plate adjusting hole and against star wheel of adjustment screw.
5. Rotate adjuster downward until slight drag is felt when wheel is rotated.
6. Push adjustment lever out of engagement with star wheel using suitable

thin screwdriver or welding rod through adjustment hole. **Do not bend adjusting lever or distort lever spring.**
7. If brakes are over-adjusted, insert second screwdriver and engage it with star wheel while holding adjuster actuator lever away from star wheel.
8. Back off star wheel until there is no brake shoe drag. Repeat adjustment procedure.
9. Install brake adjusting hole plug.
10. Repeat procedure at other rear wheel.

Parking Brake

Because of the self-adjusting feature of the parking brake lever, adjustment of the parking brake system relies on proper brake shoe adjustment. Refer to "Service Brake."

DRUM BRAKE SPECIFICATIONS

Year	Brake Lining Wear Limit, Inch①	Brake Drum Inside Diameter, Inches			Drum Runout Limit, Inch	Drum Maximum Out Of Roundness, Inch③
		Nominal	Maximum Refinish④	Maximum Inside Diameter (Discard Limit)②		
2001–05	.030	7.875	7.904	7.921	.006	.0035

① — Above rivet head or shoe. Original equipment type brake linings.

② — Maximum brake drum inside diameter (discard limit) is stamped on drum.

③ — In 360°.

④ — Maximum refinishing diameter is stamped on outer face of drum.

TIGHTENING SPECIFICATIONS

Year	Component	Torque/Ft. Lbs.
2001–05	Bearing Retainer	160
	Brake Line Fitting	12
	Support Plate To Rear Axle	55
	Wheel Cylinder Bleed Screw	80②
	Wheel Cylinder To Backing Plate	115②
	Wheel Lugnuts	100①

① — Tighten to half specification in star pattern, then to full specification in star pattern.
② — Inch lbs.

Sebring Coupe & Stratus Coupe

NOTE: On Air Bag Equipped Models, Refer To "Air Bag System Precautions" Located In The Front Of This Manual For System Disarming & Arming Procedures.

NOTE: Refer To "Computer Relearn Procedures" Located In The Front Of This Manual When Battery Power To The Computer Has Been Interrupted.

INDEX

PRECAUTIONS

When working on or around brake assemblies, care must be taken to prevent breathing asbestos dust. During routine service operations, the amount of asbestos dust from brake lining wear is at a low level because of a chemical breakdown during use. A few precautions will minimize exposure.

Do not sand or grind brake linings unless suitable local exhaust ventilation equipment is used to prevent excessive asbestos exposure.

1. Wear suitable respirator approved for asbestos dust use during repair procedures.
2. When cleaning brake dust from brake components, use vacuum cleaner with highly efficient filter system. If suitable vacuum cleaner is not available, use water soaked rag. **Do not use compressed air or dry brush to clean brake components.**
3. Keep work area clean.
4. Properly dispose of rags and vacuum cleaner bags by placing them in plastic bags.
5. Do not smoke or eat while working on brake systems.

DIAGNOSIS

STEP 1. Check for oil, water, etc., on the pad or lining contact surface of all brakes.
Q: Is oil, water, etc., on the pad or lining contact surface?
   YES : Replace the part and determine and repair source/cause of foreign material. Then go to Step 8.
   NO : Go to Step 2.

STEP 2. Check the lining and brake drum contact (Vehicles equipped with rear drum brake).
(1) If equipped with rear disc brake, go to Step 5.
(2) Put chalk on the inner surface of the brake drum. Rub the lining against the drum inner surface.
   NOTE: Clean off chalk after check.

Q: Does the lining wipe off or smudge the chalk across the full width of the lining?
   YES : Go to Step 3.
   NO : Replace the shoe and lining assemblies on both sides. Then go to Step 4.

CR4080100049010X

Fig. 1 Vehicle pulls to one side when brakes are applied (Part 1 of 2)

6. Never use any fluid containing mineral oil to clean brake system components.

INSPECTION

Brake Drums

Any time the brake drums are removed for brake service, the braking surface diameter should be inspected with a suitable brake drum micrometer at several points to determine if they are within the safe oversize limit stamped on the brake drum outer surface. If the braking surface diameter exceeds specifications, the drum must be replaced. If the braking surface diameter is within specifications, drums should be cleaned and inspected for cracks, scores, deep grooves, taper, out of round and heat spotting. If drums are cracked or heat spotted, they must be replaced. Scoring and grooves in the braking surface can only be removed by machining with special equipment, as long as the braking surface is within specifications. Any brake drum showing taper or sufficiently out of round to cause vehicle vibration or noise while braking should also be machined, removing only enough stock to true up the drum.

After a brake drum is machined, wipe the braking surface diameter with a denatured alcohol soaked cloth. If one brake drum is machined, the other should also be machined to the same diameter to maintain equal braking forces.

STEP 3. Check the auto adjuster function

Q: Is there fault?
YES : Repair it. Then go to step 8.
NO : Go to Step 4.

STEP 4. Check the brake drum inside diameter

Q: Is the brake drum inside diameter outside of specifications?
YES : Replace the part. Then go to Step 8.
NO : Go to Step 5.

STEP 5. Check disc brake pistons for smooth operation.
(1) With engine not running, depress the brake pedal rapidly several times to deplete booster vacuum reserves.
(2) Test each disc brake assembly one at a time.
  a. 1) Remove the lower caliper bolt, then remove caliper from mount.
  b. 2) Have an assistant slowly depress the brake pedal. Confirm piston(s) extend slowly and smoothly with no jumpiness. Repeat for each disc brake assembly.
Q: Do (does) the piston(s) move correctly?
YES : Go to Step 6.
NO : Disassemble and inspect brake assembly Then go to Step 8.

STEP 6. Check brake disc(s) for run out

Q: Is runout outside of specifications?
YES : Repair and replace as necessary. Then go to Step 8.
NO : Go to Step 7.

STEP 7. Check brake discs for correct thickness

Q: Is the thickness outside of specifications?
YES : Repair or replace as necessary. Then go to Step 8.
NO : Go to Step 8.

STEP 8. Check symptoms.
Q: Is the symptom eliminated?
YES : Repair complete.
NO : Start over at Step 1. If a new symptom appears, refer to the symptom chart.

CR4080100049020X

Fig. 1   Vehicle pulls to one side when brakes are applied (Part 2 of 2)

Brake Linings & Springs

Inspect brake linings for excessive wear, damage, oil, grease or brake fluid contamination. If any of the these conditions exist, brake linings should be replaced as an axle set to maintain equal braking forces. Examine brake shoe webbing, hold-down and return springs for signs of overheating indicated by a slight blue color. Any component which exhibits overheating signs should be replaced. Overheated springs lose their pull and could cause brake linings to wear out prematurely. Inspect springs for sags, bends and external damage and replace as required.

Inspect hold-down retainers and pins for bends, rust and corrosion. If any of these are found, replace as required.

Backing Plate

Inspect backing plate shoe contact surface for grooves that may restrict shoe movement and cannot be removed by lightly sanding with emery cloth or other suit-

DIAGNOSIS

STEP 1. Check whether the brake fluid is low, is the correct fluid (A/T fluid, engine oil, etc.) or is contaminated (debris, sand, etc.).

Q: Is there fault?
YES : Refill or replace with the specified brake fluid DOT 3 or DOT 4. Bleed the brakes if necessary Then go to Step 9.
NO : Go to Step 2.

STEP 2. Check for spongy (not firm brakes).
(1) With engine not running, depress the brake pedal rapidly several times to deplete booster vacuum reserve.
(2) With the brake pedal fully released, depress the brake pedal slowly until it stops.
(3) With a measuring stick (ruler, etc.) next to the brake pedal, depress the pedal firmly and measure the distance the pedal traveled.
Q: Is the distance greater than 20 mm (0.8 inch)?
YES : Bleed the brakes to remove air in the fluid. Then go to Step 9.
NO : Go to Step 3.

STEP 3. Check the lining and brake drum contact (Vehicles equipped with rear drum brake).
(1) If equipped with rear disc brake, go to Step 4.
(2) Put chalk on the inner surface of the brake drum. Rub the lining against the drum inner surface.
  NOTE: Clean off chalk after check.
Q: Does the lining wipe off or smudge the chalk across the full width of the lining?
YES : Go to Step 5.
NO : Replace the shoe and lining assemblies on both sides. Go to Step 9.

STEP 4. Check the auto adjuster function.
Q: Is there fault?
YES : Repair it. Then go to Step 9.
NO : Go to Step 6.

STEP 5. Check the brake booster function.
Q: Is there fault?
YES : Replace the part. Then go to Step 9.
NO : Go to Step 5.

CR4080100050010X

Fig. 2   Insufficient braking power (Part 1 of 2)

able abrasive. If backing plate exhibits these condition, it should be replaced. Also inspect for signs of cracks, warpage and excessive rust, indicating need for replacement.

Adjuster Mechanism

Inspect components for rust, corrosion, bends and fatigue. Replace as required. On adjuster mechanism equipped with adjuster cable, inspect cable for kinks, fraying or elongation of eyelet and replace as required.

Parking Brake Cable

Inspect parking brake cable end for kinks, fraying and elongation and replace as required. Use a small hose clamp to compress clamp where it enters backing plate to remove.

TROUBLESHOOTING

Refer to **Figs. 1 through 8** for brake system troubleshooting.

STEP 6. Check for pinched or restricted brake tube or hose.

Q: Is there pinched or restricted brake tube or hose?
YES : Replace that complete section of brake tube or brake hose. Then go to Step 9.
NO : Go to Step 7.

STEP 7. Check for oil, water, etc., on the pad or lining contact surfaces of all brakes.
Q: Is oil, water, etc., on the pad or lining contact surface?
YES : replace the part and determine and repair source/cause of foreign material. Recheck symptom. Then go to Step 9.
NO : Diagnosis is complete. If condition persists, go to Step 8.

STEP 8. Check the proportioning valve operation.

Q: Is there fault?
YES : Replace the part. Then go to Step 9.
NO : Go to Step 9.

STEP 9. Recheck symptom.
Q: Is the symptom eliminated?
YES : Diagnosis is complete.
NO : Start over at step 1. If a new symptom surfaces, refer to the symptom chart.

CR4080100050020X

Fig. 2   Insufficient braking power (Part 2 of 2)

BRAKE SERVICE

Shoe, Replace

1. Raise and support vehicle, then remove tire and wheel assembly.
2. Loosen park brake cable adjusting nut.
3. Drain brake fluid into suitable container.
4. Remove brake drum, **Fig. 9.**
5. Remove shoe-to-lever spring, adjuster lever and auto adjuster assembly.
6. Remove retainer spring, then the hold-down cup, spring and cup.
7. Remove shoe-to-shoe spring, then the shoe and lining assemblies.
8. Remove retainer, wave washer and parking lever.
9. Remove hold-down pin, brake tube connection, snap ring and rear hub.
10. Reverse procedure to install.

Wheel Cylinder, Replace

1. Raise and support vehicle, then remove tire and wheel assembly.
2. Drain brake fluid into suitable container.
3. Remove brake drum, **Fig. 10.**
4. Remove shoe-to-lever and shoe-to-shoe springs.
5. Remove auto adjuster.
6. Remove connection pipe and wheel cylinder.
7. Reverse procedure to install.

DRUM BRAKES

DIAGNOSIS

STEP 1. Check for spongy (not firm brakes).
(1) With engine not running, depress the brake pedal rapidly several times to deplete booster vacuum reserve.
(2) With the brake pedal fully released, depress the brake pedal slowly until it stops.
(3) With a measuring stick (ruler, etc.) next to the brake pedal, depress the pedal firmly and measure the distance the pedal traveled.

Q: Is the distance greater than 20 mm (0.8 inch)?
    YES : Bleed the brakes to remove air in the fluid. Then go to Step 8 .
    NO : Go to Step 2.

STEP 2. Check the pad or lining for wear.
Q: Is the pad or lining thickness outside of specifications?
    YES : Replace the part. Then go to Step 8.
    NO : Go to Step 3.

STEP 3. Check the vacuum hose and check valve for damage.
Q: Is there damage?
    YES : Replace the part. Then go to Step 8.
    NO : Go to Step 4.

CR4080100051010X

Fig. 3 Increased pedal stroke (Part 1 of 2)

DIAGNOSIS

STEP 1. Check the parking brake lever return.
Q: Is there fault?
    YES : Repair it. Then go to Step 10.
    NO : Go to Step 2.

CR4080100052010X

Fig. 4 Brake drag (Part 1 of 3)

DIAGNOSIS

STEP 1. Check the front brakes, then rear brakes, for metal-to-metal condition.

Q: Is the metal-to-metal contact evicent?
    YES : Repair or replace components. Then go to Step 6.
    NO : Go to Step 2.

STEP 2. Check for interference between the caliper and wheel.

Q: Is there interference?
    YES : Repair or replace the part. Then go to Step 6.
    NO : Go to Step 3.

CR4080100053010X

Fig. 5 Scraping or grinding noise when brakes are applied (Part 1 of 2)

ADJUSTMENTS

Parking Brake

These brakes are equipped with self adjusting mechanisms. Periodic adjustments are not required. If stopping power is insufficient, or if brake pedal travel is excessive, brakes and self adjusting mechanism should be cleaned and inspected.

After performing brake service, adjust parking brake as follows:
1. Apply parking brake lever with force of approximately 45 lbs. while counting clicks. Lever should click 5–7 times.
2. If not within specifications, release parking brake lever and remove center console.

STEP 2. Check the parking brake pull amount.
Q: Is there fault?
    YES : Adjust it. Then go to Step 10.
    NO : Go to Step 3.

STEP 3. Check the brake pedal return spring for deterioration.
Q: Is there deterioration?
    YES : Replace the spring. Then go to Step 10.
    NO : Go to Step 4.

STEP 4. Check the brake shoe springs for breakage.
Q: Are the brake shoe springs broken?
    YES : Replace the spring. Then go to Step 10.
    NO : Go to Step 5.

STEP 5. Check the amount of grease at each sliding section.
Q: Is the grease amount low?
    YES : Apply grease. Then go to Step 10.
    NO : Go to Step 6.

CR4080100052020X

Fig. 4 Brake drag (Part 2 of 3)

3. Free parking brake cables by loosen parking brake lever adjusting nut.
4. Depress brake pedal several times to ensure shoe to drum clearance is properly maintained by self-adjusters.
5. Tighten adjusting nut until brake lever can be raised 5–7 notches with force of approximately 45 lbs. **If adjusting nut is tightened excessively, self-adjuster mechanism will be inoperative.**
6. Raise and support rear of vehicle, then ensure brakes do not drag with parking brake lever released.

STEP 4. Check the master cylinder function.
Q: Is there fault?
    YES : Repair it. Then go to Step 8.
    NO : Go to Step 5.

STEP 5. Check for brake fluid leaks.
Q: Is there leaks?
    YES : Check the connection for looseness, corrosion, etc. Clean and repair as necessary. If leaking in any tube or hose section, replace the complete tube or hose. Then go to Step 8.
    NO : Go to Step 6.

STEP 6. Check the auto adjuster function.
Q: Is there fault?
    YES : Repair the part. Then go to Step 8.
    NO : Go to Step 7.

STEP 7. Check the clearance (too much) between the pushrod and primary piston.
Q: Is the clearance outside of specifications?
    YES : Adjust the clearance. Then go to Step 8.
    NO : Go to Step 8.

STEP 8. Recheck symptom.
Q: Is the symptom eliminated?
    YES : Diagnosis is complete.
    NO : Start over at step 1. If a new symptom surfaces, refer to the symptom chart.

CR4080100051020X

Fig. 3 Increased pedal stroke (Part 2 of 2)

STEP 6. Check the clearance (too low) between the pushrod and primary piston.

Q: Is there fault?
    YES : Adjust the clearance. Then go to Step 10.
    NO : Go to Step 7.

STEP 7. Check the master cylinder piston return spring for damage and return port for clogging.
Q: Is there damage?
    YES : Replace the part. Then go to Step 10.
    NO : Go to Step 8.

STEP 8. Check port for clogging.
Q: Is the port clogged?
    YES : Repair it. Then go to Step 10.
    NO : Go to Step 9.

STEP 9. Check disc brake pistons for sticking.
Depress the brake pedal, then release. Confirm each wheel spins freely.

Q: Are all wheels stuck?
    YES : Inspect that brake assembly. Then go to Step 10.
    NO : Go to Step 10.

STEP 10. Recheck symptom.
Q: Is the symptom eliminated?
    YES : Diagnosis is complete.
    NO : Start over at step 1. If a new symptom surfaces, refer to the symptom chart.

CR4080100052030X

Fig. 4 Brake drag (Part 3 of 3)

STEP 3. Check for interference between the dust cover and brake disc.
Q: Is there interference?
    YES : Repair or replace the part. Then go to Step 6.
    NO : Go to Step 4.

STEP 4. Check the brake drums or discs for cracks.
Q: Are there cracks?
    YES : Repair or replace the part. Then go to Step 6.
    NO : Go to Step 5.

STEP 5. Check for bent backing plate(s).
Q: Is(Are) the backing plate(s) bent?
    YES : Repair or replace the part. Then go to Step 6.
    NO : Go to Step 6.

STEP 6. Recheck symptom.
Q: Is the symptom eliminated?
    YES : Diagnosis is complete.
    NO : Start over at step 1. If a new symptom surfaces, refer to the symptom chart.

CR4080100053020X

Fig. 5 Scraping or grinding noise when brakes are applied (Part 2 of 2)

DIAGNOSIS

STEP 1. Check the brake drums and lining or brake disc and pads for wear or cutting.

Q: Is there wear or cutting?
- YES : Repair or replace the part. Then go to Step 7.
- NO : Go to Step 2.

STEP 2. Check the calipers for rust.

Q: Is there rust?
- YES : Remove the rust. Then go to Step 7.
- NO : Go to Step 3.

STEP 3. Check the lining parts for damage.
If equipped with rear disc brakes, go to Step 6.

Q: Is there damage?
- YES : Repair or replace the part. Then go to Step 7.
- NO : Go to Step 4.

STEP 4. Check whether the lining is dirty or greasy.

Q: Is the lining dirty or greasy?
- YES : Clean or replace the part. Then go to Step 7.
- NO : Go to Step 5.

STEP 5. Check whether the shoe hold-down springs are weak or the shoe-hold-down pins and springs are loose or damaged.

Q: Is there fault?
- YES : Repair or replace the part. Then go to Step 7.
- NO : Go to Step 6.

STEP 6. Adjust the brake pedal or brake booster pushrod.

Q: Is the adjustment value come?
- YES : Adjust. Then go to Step 7.
- NO : Go to Step 7.

STEP 7. Recheck symptom.

Q: Is the symptom eliminated?
- YES : Diagnosis is complete.
- NO : Start over at step 1. If a new symptom surfaces, refer to the symptom chart.

CR4080100054000X

Fig. 6 Squealing, groaning or chattering noise when brakes are applied.

DIAGNOSIS

STEP 1. Check whether foreign material has entered the wheel covers.

Q: Is there foreign material?
- YES : Remove it. Then go to Step 5.
- NO : Go to Step 2.

STEP 2. Check for looseness of the wheel nuts.

Q: Are the wheel nuts loose?
- YES : Tighten to 98 ± 10 N·m (73 ± 7 ft-lb). Then go to Step 5.
- NO : Go to Step 3.

STEP 3. Check for looseness of the caliper installation bolt.

Q: Is the caliper installation bolt loose?
- YES : Tighten to 100 ± 10 N·m (74 ± 7 ft-lb) for the front caliper, or 60 ± 5 N·m (45 ± 3 ft-lb) for the rear caliper. Then go to Step 5.
- NO : Go to Step 4.

CR4080100056010X

Fig. 8 Groaning, clicking or rattling noise when brakes are not applied (Part 1 of 2)

DIAGNOSIS

STEP 1. Check whether the backing plate is bent or loose and interfering with the drum

If equipped with rear disc brakes, go to Step 4.

Q: Is there fault?
- YES : Replace the part. Then go to Step 10.
- NO : Go to Step 2.

STEP 2. Check whether the drum is damaged due to interference with the backing plate or shoe.

Q: Is there damage?
- YES : Replace the part. Then go to Step 10.
- NO : Go to Step 3.

STEP 3. Check the brake drum for wear and the shoe-to-shoe spring for damage.

Q: Is there wear or damage?
- YES : Replace the part. Then go to Step 10.
- NO : Go to Step 4.

STEP 4. Check the brake discs for rust.

Q: Are the brake discs rusted?
- YES : Remove the rust by using sand paper. If still rusted, turn the rotors with an on-the-car brake lathe. Then go to Step 10.
- NO : Go to Step 5.

STEP 5. Check the brake pads for correct installation.

Q: Are the pads installed incorrectly?
- YES : Repair it. Then go to Step 10.
- NO : Go to Step 6.

STEP 6. Check the calipers for correct installation.

Q: Are the calipers installed incorrectly?
- YES : Repair it. Then go to Step 10.
- NO : Go to Step 7.

CR4080100055010X

Fig. 7 Squealing noise when brakes are not applied (Part 1 of 2)

STEP 7. Check the wheel bearings for deterioration or damage, and the quality and quantity.

Q: Are the wheel bearings damaged or out of grease?
- YES : Apply grease or replace the part. Then go to Step 10.
- NO : Go to Step 8.

STEP 8. Check whether the brake booster, master cylinder or wheel cylinder return is insufficient.

Q: Is the brake booster, master cylinder or wheel cylinder return insufficient?
- YES : Replace the part. Then go to Step 10.
- NO : Go to Step 9.

STEP 9. Adjust the brake pedal or brake booster pushrod.

Q: Is the adjustment value come?
- YES : Adjust. Then go to Step 10.
- NO : Go to Step 10.

STEP 10. Recheck symptom.

Q: Is the symptom eliminated?
- YES : Diagnosis is complete.
- NO : Start over at step 1. If a new symptom surfaces, refer to the symptom chart.

CR4080100055020X

Fig. 7 Squealing noise when brakes are not applied (Part 2 of 2)

STEP 4. Check the wheel bearings for wear, damage or dryness.

Q: Is there fault?
- YES : Apply grease or replace the part. Then go to Step 5.
- NO : Go to Step 5.

STEP 5. Recheck symptom.

Q: Is the symptom eliminated?
- YES : Diagnosis is complete.
- NO : Start over at step 1. If a new symptom surfaces, refer to the symptom chart.

CR4080100056020X

Fig. 8 Groaning, clicking or rattling noise when brakes are not applied (Part 2 of 2)

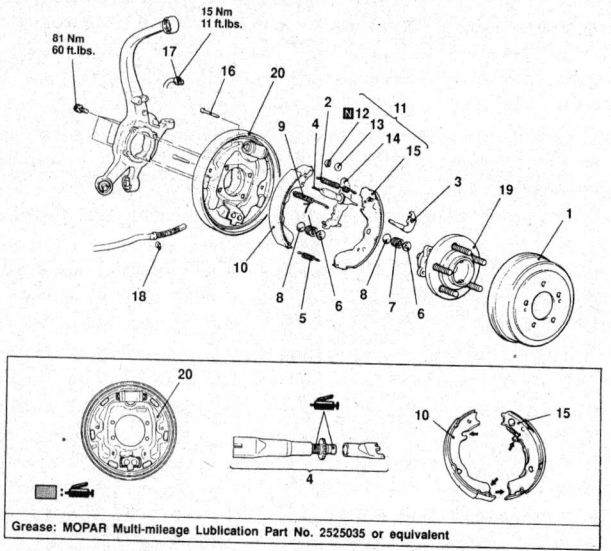

1. Brake drum
2. Shoe-to-lever spring
3. Adjuster lever
4. Auto adjuster assembly
5. Retainer spring
6. Shoe hold-down cup
7. Shoe hold-down spring
8. Shoe hold-down cup
9. Shoe-to-shoe spring
10. Shoe and lining assembly
11. Shoe and lever assembly
12. Retainer
13. Wave washer
14. Parking lever
15. Shoe and lining assembly
16. Shoe hold-down pin
17. Brake pipe connection
18. Snap ring
19. Rear hub assembly
20. Backing plate

Grease: MOPAR Multi-mileage Lubrication Part No. 2525035 or equivalent

CR4089500024000X

Fig. 9   Exploded view of drum brake

1. Brake drum
2. Retainer
3. Shoe-to-shoe spring
4. Auto adjuster assembly
5. Connection for the brake tube
6. Wheel cylinder
7. Bleeder screw

CR4089500023000X

Fig. 10   Rear drum brake wheel cylinder replacement

DRUM BRAKE SPECIFICATIONS
DRUM BRAKE

Year	Brake Lining Wear Limit, Inch①	Brake Drum Inside Diameter, Inches			Drum Runout Limit, Inch	Drum Maximum Out Of Roundness, Inch③
		Nominal	Maximum Refinish	Maximum Inside Diameter (Discard Limit)②		
2001–05	.040	9.00	—	9.08	—	—

① — Above rivet head or shoe. Original equipment type brake linings.

② — Maximum brake drum inside diameter (discard limit) is stamped on drum.

③ — In 360°.

TIGHTENING SPECIFICATIONS

Year	Component	Torque/Ft. Lbs.
2001–05	Backing Plate To Rear Axle	60
	Brake Line Fittings	11
	Wheel Cylinder Bleed Screw	96①
	Wheel Cylinder To Backing Plate	84①
	Wheel Lugnuts	65–80

① — Inch lbs.

HYDRAULIC BRAKE SYSTEMS

NOTE: On Air Bag Equipped Models, Refer To "Air Bag System Precautions" Located In The Front Of This Manual For System Disarming & Arming Procedures.

NOTE: Refer To "Computer Relearn Procedures" Located In The Front Of This Manual When Battery Power To The Computer Has Been Interrupted.

NOTE: Refer To "Anti-Lock Brakes" Chapter When Servicing ABS System.

INDEX

DESCRIPTION

Master Cylinder

The master cylinder is a center valve master cylinder used for all applications. The brake fluid reservoir mounted on top and brake fluid level switch is mounted on the side of the reservoir.

The reservoir is indexed to prevent installation in the wrong direction. The cap diaphragm is slit to allow atmospheric pressure to equalize on both sides of diaphragm.

The primary and secondary outlet tubes of the master cylinder are connected to a junction block on non-ABS equipped vehicles. The master cylinder primary outlet port connects to the inboard port of the junction block and the secondary outlet port connects to the outboard port of the junction block. The inboard port of the junction block supplies the righthand front and lefthand rear brakes. The outboard port of the junction block supplies the lefthand front and righthand rear brakes.

On vehicles equipped with ABS the master cylinder primary outlet port outlet tubes connect to the inboard port of the ICU and the secondary outlet port outlet tubes connect to the outboard port of the ICU.

TROUBLESHOOTING

Refer to "Troubleshooting" in "Disc Brakes" chapter for troubleshooting of the hydraulic brake system.

DIAGNOSIS & TESTING

Proportioning Valve

CONCORDE, INTREPID, LHS & 300M

ABS

2001

Not all components use the same type tubing flare. The tube leading into the proportioning valve has an ISO flare, while the flex hose coming out of the proportioning valve has a standard double-inverted flare. Use the correct adapters when installing gauges to test proportioning valves.

1. Raise and support vehicle.
2. Clean any debris away from suspect proportioning valve, connections and area.
3. Remove chassis brake tube from suspect proportioning valve, **Fig. 1.**
4. Remove proportioning valve from rear flex hose which is held stationary by bracket mounted on back side of crossmember.
5. Remove retainer clip securing rear flex hose from its bracket.
6. Ensure pressure test fittings being installed into proportioning valve have correct thread sizes for installation into proportioning valve and installation of chassis brake tubes.
7. Install pressure test fittings tool No. 6892-2, or equivalent, into inlet port and No. 8187-2, or equivalent, into outlet port of proportioning valve, **Fig. 2.**
8. Install portioning valve and pressure test fittings into chassis brake tube.
9. Connect tool No. 6892-2 to chassis brake tube and No. 8187-2 to brake flex hose.
10. Install pressure gauge tool No. C-4007-A, or equivalent, into each pressure test fitting, **Fig. 3.**
11. Bleed air out of system including air from hose between pressure test fitting and pressure gauge at pressure gauge.
12. Have helper apply pressure to brake pedal until reading on proportioning valve inlet gauge is at specified pressure.
13. Check pressure reading on proportioning valve outlet gauge.
14. If proportioning valve outlet pressure is not within specifications once inlet pressure is obtained, , replace proportioning valve.
15. If pressure is within specifications, do not replace proportioning valve.
16. Remove pressure gauges from fittings.
17. Remove proportioning valve and the pressure test fittings tools from chassis brake tube and rear flex hose.
18. Remove pressure test fittings from proportioning valve.
19. Install rear brake flex hose to its mounting bracket using new retainer clip.
20. Install proportioning valve to rear brake flex hose.
21. Install chassis brake tube to proportioning valve.
22. Bleed affected brake line.

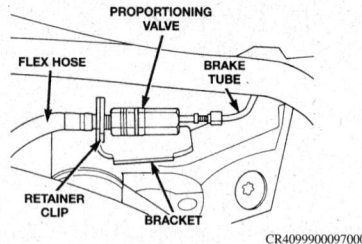

Fig. 1 Proportioning valve replacement. Concorde, Intrepid, LHS & 300M w/ABS

23. Repeat procedure on other proportioning valve.

2002–04

These models with ABS do not have proportioning valves to test, they use Electronic Variable Brake Proportioning which is built into the Integrated Control Unit (ICU).

NON-ABS

On early production non-ABS applications, refer to "ABS" for testing procedure.

On later production non-ABS applications, proceed as follows;

1. **If lefthand rear proportioning valve is suspect,** disconnect tube nut fitting at master cylinder primary port (port closest to power brake booster) and install adapter tool No. 8494-2, or equivalent, in its place on master cylinder.
2. **If the right rear proportioning valve is suspect,** disconnect tube nut fitting at master cylinder secondary port (port furthest from power brake booster) and install adapter tool No. 8494-1, or equivalent, in its place on master cylinder.
3. **On all conditions,** connect primary brake tube to adapter.
4. Install pressure gauge tool No. C-4007-A, or equivalent, to adapter.
5. Remove speed control servo to upper radiator closure panel mounting screw.
6. Remove washer filler tube to the upper radiator closure panel mounting screw.
7. Remove Transmission Control Module (TCM) mounting nut and screw. Position TCM with speed control servo attached aside ensure not to strain wires and speed control servo cable.
8. Clean any debris away from fittings on top of junction block.
9. Remove chassis brake tube leading to either left or righthand rear brake at junction block.
10. **If lefthand rear proportioning valve is suspect,** install adapter tool No. 8494-3, or equivalent, in its place on junction block.
11. **If righthand rear proportioning valve is suspect,** install adapter tool No. 8494-4, or equivalent, in its place on junction block.
12. **On all conditions,** install pressure gauge tool No. C-4007-A, or equivalent, to adapter.
13. Bleed air out of system including air from hose between pressure test fitting

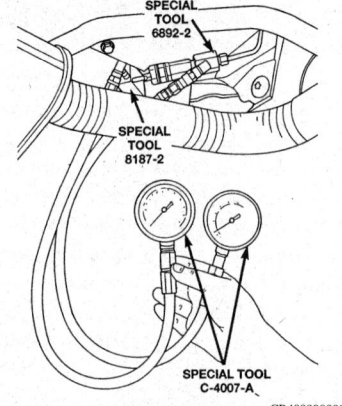

Fig. 2 Pressure test fittings. Concorde, Intrepid, LHS & 300M w/ABS

and pressure gauge at pressure gauge.

14. With the aid of a helper, apply pressure to brake pedal until reading on proportioning valve inlet gauge at master cylinder is at specifications.
15. Then check pressure reading on proportioning valve outlet gauge at junction block outlet to rear brake.
16. If proportioning valve outlet pressure is not within specifications once inlet pressure is obtained, replace junction block with internal proportioning valves.
17. Remove pressure gauge and adapter tools from junction block.
18. Install chassis brake tube to junction block port.
19. Install TCM with speed control servo attached.
20. Install washer filler tube to upper radiator closure panel mounting screw.
21. Install speed control servo to upper radiator closure panel mounting screw.
22. Remove the pressure gauge and adapter tools from master cylinder.
23. the brake tube to master cylinder primary or secondary port.
24. Bleed affected brake line.

CROSSFIRE

These models are not equipped with a proportioning valve, junction block or splitter. The Hydraulic Control Unit (HCU) monitors and controls these functions.

NEON

LESS ANTI-LOCK BRAKE SYSTEM

1. Remove hydraulic brake line from proportioning valve to be tested, **Fig. 4.**
2. Remove master cylinder outlet port valve.
3. Install pressure test fitting tool No. 6805-1, 6805-2, or equivalent, into outlet port of master cylinder.
4. Install pressure test fitting tool No. 6805-1, 6805-2, or equivalent, into rear brake tube.
5. Install proportioning valve into pressure test fitting.
6. Install pressure test fitting tool Nos.

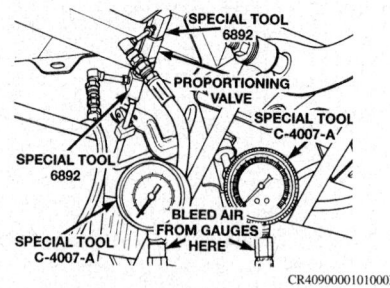

Fig. 3 Pressure gauge installation. Concorde, Intrepid, LHS & 300M w/ABS

6805-3 and 6805-4, or equivalents, into outlet port or proportioning valve.

7. Connect brake hydraulic line onto pressure test fitting on proportioning valve.
8. Install pressure gauge set tool No. C-4007-A, or equivalent, into test fitting and bleed air from pressure gauge hose.
9. Apply pressure to brake pedal until proportioning valve inlet test fitting pressure is appropriate, then record outlet test fitting pressure.
10. If proportioning valve is not within specifications when inlet pressure is obtained, replace valve.
11. Install proportioning valve into master cylinder body until O-ring is seated.
12. Install brake tube onto proportioning valve.
13. Bleed brake line.

WITH ANTI-LOCK BRAKE SYSTEM

1. Remove hydraulic brake line from proportioning valve to be tested, **Fig. 5.**
2. Remove master cylinder outlet port valve.
3. Install pressure test fitting tool No. 6805-1 or 6805-2, or equivalent, into outlet port of master cylinder.
4. Install proportioning valve into pressure test fitting in master cylinder outlet port.
5. Install pressure test fitting tool No. 6805-3 or 6805-4, or equivalent, into outlet port of proportioning valve.
6. Connect brake hydraulic line onto pressure test fitting on proportioning valve.
7. Install pressure gauge set tool No. C-4007-A, or equivalent, into test fitting and bleed air from pressure gauge hose.
8. Apply pressure to brake pedal until proportioning valve inlet test fitting pressure is appropriate, then record outlet test fitting pressure.
9. If outlet test fitting pressure is not within specifications, replace proportioning valve.
10. Install proportioning valve into master cylinder body until O-ring is seated.
11. Install brake tube onto proportioning valve.
12. Bleed brake line.

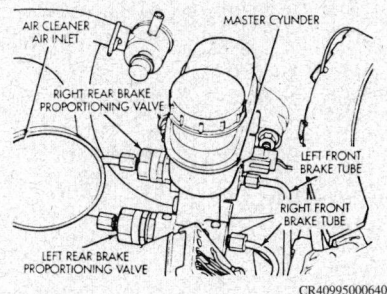

Fig. 4 Proportioning valve. Neon less ABS

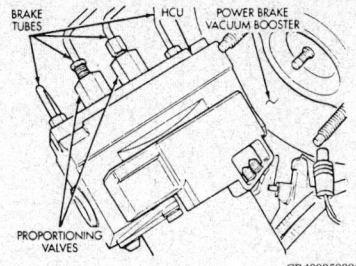

CR4099500068000X

Fig. 5 Proportioning valve. Neon w/ABS

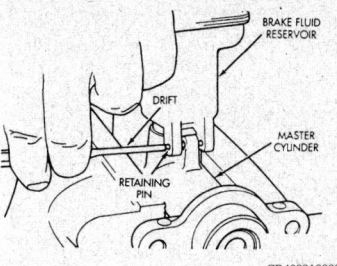

CR4099100031000X

Fig. 6 Retaining pin removal

SEBRING COUPE & STRATUS COUPE

1. Install suitable pressure gauges, one each on input and output side of proportioning valve.
2. Bleed brake line and pressure gauge, then gradually depress brake pedal and observe gauge.
3. Observe left and righthand output pressures.
4. Pressure difference between left and righthand sides should not be more than 57 psi.
5. If pressure is not within specifications, replace proportioning valve.

COMPONENT REPLACEMENT

Fluid Reservoir

These models use ISO style flares that are of metric dimension. Use ISO style tubing flares and metric tubing when performing any repairs.
1. Remove reservoir caps.
2. Remove reservoir brake fluid.
3. Remove master cylinder as outlined in "Master Cylinder, Replace."
4. Secure master cylinder in suitable vise.
5. Remove two reservoir to master cylinder retaining pins, **Fig. 6.**
6. Rock reservoir side to side and remove from master cylinder. **Do not use any tools when removing reservoir.**
7. Remove sealing grommets.
8. Reverse procedure to install, noting the following:
   a. Lubricate new sealing grommets with suitable brake fluid.
   b. Ensure reservoir is seated properly against sealing grommets.
   c. Bench bleed master cylinder as outlined in "Brake System Bleed."

Junction Block

1. Depress pedal one inch down and hold in position using suitable tool, **Fig. 7.**
2. **On Sebring Sedan and Stratus Sedan,** remove air cleaner housing.
3. **On all models,** raise and support vehicle.
4. Remove lefthand inner fender shield.
5. **On 2001–04 Concorde, Intrepid, LHS and 300M models,** proceed as follows:

CROSSFIRE

a. Remove speed control servo to upper radiator closure panel mounting screw, **Fig. 8.**
b. Remove washer filler tube to upper radiator closure panel. mounting screw.
c. Remove Transmission Control Module (TCM) mounting nut and screw.
d. Remove TCM with servo attached from mount and set aside with wiring harness connected.
e. Remove primary and secondary master cylinder ports tubes at junction block.
6. **On all models,** remove four chassis brake tubes mounted across front top of junction block.
7. Remove two brake tubes from primary and secondary ports, and top of junction block.
8. Remove three mounting bolts and junction block.
9. Reverse procedure to install.

Master Cylinder

CONCORDE, INTREPID, LHS & 300M

1. Disconnect brake fluid level sensor wire connector from reservoir side.
2. Disconnect master cylinder, primary and secondary brake lines. Plug or cap lines and openings.
3. Remove mounting nuts and slide master cylinder away from brake booster, **Fig. 9.**
4. Reverse procedure to install.

CROSSFIRE

1. Disconnect brake fluid level sensor harness at brake fluid reservoir, **Fig. 10.**
2. Disconnect master cylinder brake fluid sensor harness connectors.
3. Disconnect master cylinder primary and secondary brake lines. Plug or cap lines and openings.
4. Remove mounting nuts and master cylinder. **Do not tilt master cylinder when removing from brake booster.**
5. Reverse procedure to install. Bend bleed master cylinder, **Fig. 11.**

MAGNUM, 300 & 300C

1. Pump brake pedal with vehicle's engine not running until firm feeling brake pedal is achieved, 4–5 strokes.
2. Remove cowl area access panel.
3. Thoroughly clean all surfaces of brake fluid reservoir and master cylinder. using suitable brake parts cleaner.
4. Disconnect brake fluid level sensor wiring harness.
5. Disconnect Electronic Stability Program wiring harness connector.
6. Disconnect primary and secondary brake tubes from master cylinder. Plug or cap lines and openings.
7. Remove two mounting nuts and slide master cylinder straight out of power brake booster, then remove vacuum seal.
8. Reverse procedure to install using new vacuum seal.

NEON

LESS ANTI-LOCK BRAKE SYSTEM

1. Remove brake fluid level sensor wiring harness connector.
2. Disconnect master cylinder housing primary and secondary brake tubes. Plug or cap lines and openings.
3. Remove master cylinder to power brake vacuum booster mounting nuts.
4. Slide master cylinder forward out of power brake vacuum booster.
5. Reverse procedure to install.

WITH ANTI-LOCK BRAKE SYSTEM

1. Ensure ignition switch is in OFF position.
2. Pumped down power booster vacuum by pumping brake pedal until it is firm.
3. Remove brake fluid level sensor wiring harness connector.
4. Disconnect master cylinder housing primary and secondary brake tubes. Plug or cap lines and openings.
5. Clean area where master cylinder attaches to power brake vacuum booster using suitable brake cleaner.
6. Remove master cylinder to power brake vacuum booster mounting nuts.
7. Slide master cylinder forward out of power brake vacuum booster.
8. Remove vacuum seal by carefully inserting suitable, small screwdriver between master cylinder push rod and vacuum seal.
9. Prying seal out of booster, **Fig. 12.**
10. **Do not attempt to pry seal out by inserting screwdriver between seal and booster.**
11. Reverse procedure to install, noting the following:
    a. Lubricate master cylinder push rod using suitable silicone lubricant.

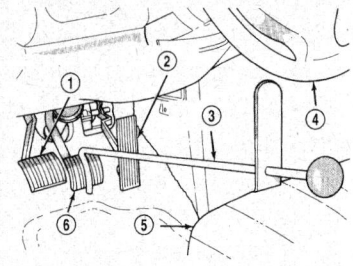

1 – CLUTCH PEDAL (IF EQUIPPED WITH MANUAL TRANSAXLE)
2 – THROTTLE PEDAL
3 – BRAKE PEDAL HOLDING TOOL
4 – STEERING WHEEL
5 – DRIVER'S SEAT
6 – BRAKE PEDAL

CR4090000104000X

Fig. 7 Brake pedal holding tool

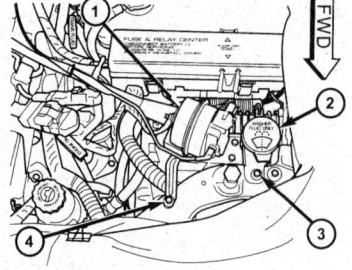

1 - SPEED CONTROL SERVO
2 - WINDSHIED WASHER FILLER TUBE
3 - SCREW
4 - SCREW

CR4090000105000X

Fig. 8 Speed control servo & filler tube replacement. 2001–04 Concorde, Intrepid, LHS & 300M

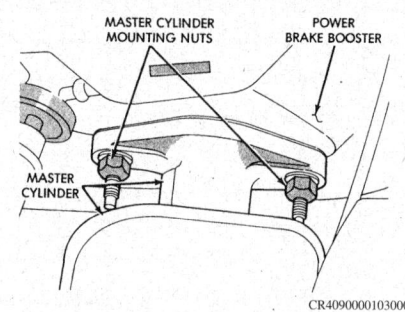

CR4090000103000X

Fig. 9 Master cylinder replacement. Concorde, Intrepid, LHS, Sebring Convertible, Sebring Sedan & Stratus Sedan & 300M

b. Slide vacuum seal onto master cylinder push rod with notches on seal pointing toward and seated against master cylinder housing.
c. Slide master cylinder into power brake vacuum booster and position on mounting studs.

SEBRING CONVERTIBLE, SEBRING SEDAN & STRATUS SEDAN

Refer to "Concorde, Intrepid, LHS & 300M" for master cylinder replacement procedure.

SEBRING COUPE & STRATUS COUPE

1. Drain brake fluid into suitable container.
2. Disconnect brake tube connection, **Fig. 13.**
3. Remove mounting nuts and master cylinder.
4. Reverse procedure to install.

Proportioning Valve

CONCORDE, INTREPID, LHS & 300M

2001

This procedure applies to ABS and early production non-ABS applications. Later production Non-ABS proportioning valves are located in the junction block and cannot be serviced separately.
1. Raise and support vehicle.
2. Clean debris away from proportioning valve and connections.
3. Remove proportioning valve chassis brake tube.
4. Remove rear flex hose proportioning valve.
5. Reverse procedure to install.

2002-04

Less Anti-Lock Brake System

These models use a proportioning valve that is integrated with the junction block. The proportioning valve cannot be serviced separately.

Anti-Lock Brake System

These models use electronic variable

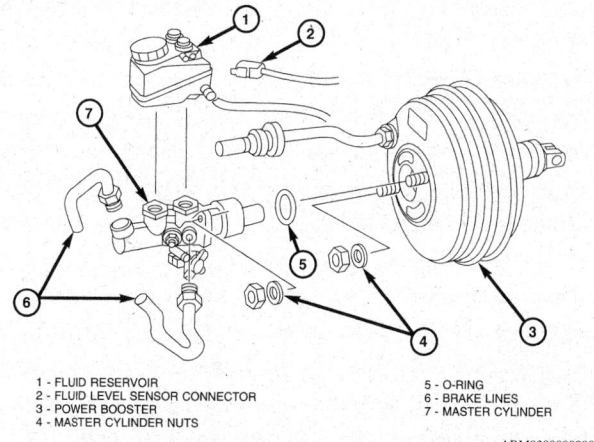

1 – FLUID RESERVOIR
2 – FLUID LEVEL SENSOR CONNECTOR
3 – POWER BOOSTER
4 – MASTER CYLINDER NUTS
5 – O-RING
6 – BRAKE LINES
7 – MASTER CYLINDER

ARM0300000000059

Fig. 10 Master cylinder components & locations. Crossfire

brake proportioning built into the Integral Control Unit (ICU).

NEON

1. Depress brake pedal past its first one inch of travel and hold it in position using suitable brake pedal holder too.
2. Disconnect brake tube from proportioning valve requiring removal.
3. Remove proportioning valve from master cylinder.
4. Reverse procedure to install. Lubricate new O-ring with suitable brake fluid.

COMPONENT SERVICE

The only serviceable component on master cylinder(s) are the reservoir and sealing grommets. The master cylinder(s) are not to be serviced, they must be replaced as an assembly.

BRAKE SYSTEM BLEED

Pressure Bleed

Use bleeder tank tool No. C-3496-B, or equivalent, and adapter tool No. BB400-9A, or equivalent, to pressurize hydraulic system.

Normal pressure bleeder pressure should not be more than 35 psi. **On models equipped with plastic reservoirs, do not exceed 25 psi bleeding pressure.**
1. Attach suitable clear plastic hose to bleeder screw and submerge other end into clear container with clean brake fluid.
2. Open bleeder screw at least one full turn.
3. Bleed 4–8 ounces of fluid through system until air free flow is maintained.
4. Repeat procedure at all screws.
5. If pedal travel is excessive or has not improved, repeat procedure.

Manual Bleed

On models with power brakes, if bleeding the hydraulic system without the engine running, first reduce vacuum in the power unit to zero by pumping the brake pedal several times with the engine off.
1. Remove four bleeder screws' rubber dust caps.
2. Attach suitable clear plastic tubing to bleeder screw and submerge other end of tube into clear container of clean brake fluid.
3. Pump brake pedal three or four times and hold it down.
4. Open bleeder screw at least one full turn.
5. Release brake pedal only after bleeder

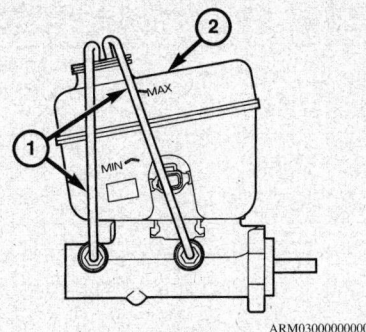

Fig. 11   Bench bleeding master cylinder. Crossfire

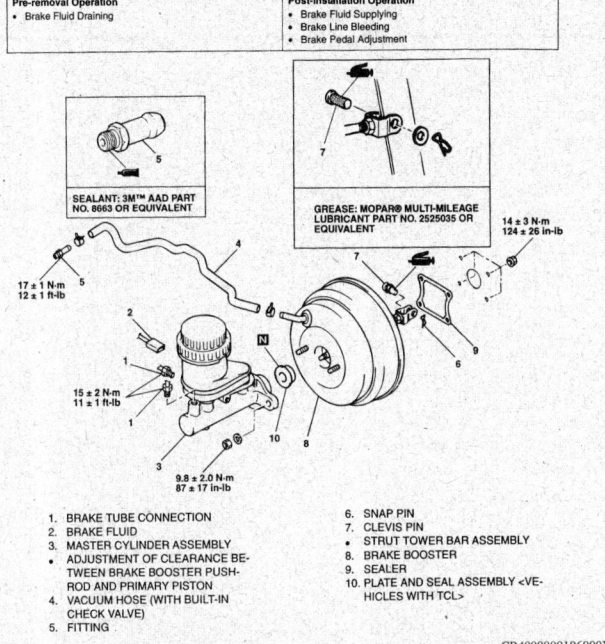

Pre-removal Operation	Post-installation Operation
• Brake Fluid Draining	• Brake Fluid Supplying • Brake Line Bleeding • Brake Pedal Adjustment

SEALANT: 3M™ AAD PART NO. 8663 OR EQUIVALENT

GREASE: MOPAR® MULTI-MILEAGE LUBRICANT PART NO. 2525035 OR EQUIVALENT

14 ± 3 N·m
124 ± 26 in-lb

17 ± 1 N·m
12 ± 1 ft-lb

15 ± 2 N·m
11 ± 1 ft-lb

9.8 ± 2.0 N·m
87 ± 17 in-lb

1. BRAKE TUBE CONNECTION
2. BRAKE FLUID
3. MASTER CYLINDER ASSEMBLY
• ADJUSTMENT OF CLEARANCE BETWEEN BRAKE BOOSTER PUSHROD AND PRIMARY PISTON
4. VACUUM HOSE (WITH BUILT-IN CHECK VALVE)
5. FITTING

6. SNAP PIN
7. CLEVIS PIN
• STRUT TOWER BAR ASSEMBLY
8. BRAKE BOOSTER
9. SEALER
10. PLATE AND SEAL ASSEMBLY <VEHICLES WITH TCL>

Fig. 13   Master cylinder replacement. Sebring Coupe & Stratus Coupe

screw is closed.
6. Repeat procedure four or five times at all bleeder screw locations. Ensure fluid level in master cylinder stays at proper level.

Master Cylinder Bleed
BENCH BLEEDING

When clamping master cylinder in

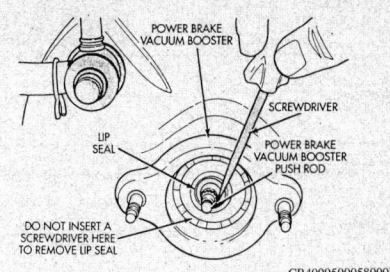

Fig. 12   Vacuum seal removal. Neon w/ABS

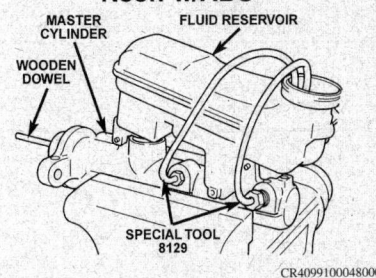

Fig. 14   Master cylinder bench bleeding

vise for bleeding, carefully tighten vise just enough to hold master cylinder from moving. Excessive pressure can damage master cylinder.

1. Support master cylinder and attach bleeding tubes, **Fig. 14.**
2. Fill reservoir with approved brake fluid.
3. Depress pushrod slowly using suitable wooden stick or dowel, then allow pistons to return under pressure of springs. Do this several times until all air bubbles are expelled.
4. Remove cylinder bleeding tubes and install reservoir cover.
5. Install master cylinder onto vehicle as outlined in "Component Replacement."
6. Bleed hydraulic system as outlined in "Brake System Bleed."

ON-VEHICLE BLEEDING

Master cylinders may be bled manually or by pressure bleeding. It is recommended that the master cylinder be bled before bleeding the wheel cylinders and calipers.

HYDRAULIC BRAKE SYSTEMS

HYDRAULIC BRAKE SYSTEM SPECIFICATIONS

Model	Year	Master Cylinder Bore Dia., Inch	Booster to Primary Piston Clearance, Inch	Wheel Bleed Sequence
Concorde, Intrepid, LHS & 300M	2001–04	.937	—	LR, RF, RR, LF
Crossfire	2004	.937	—	LR, RF, RR, LF
Magnum, 300 & 300C	2005	—	—	—
Neon	2001–05①	.875	—	LR, RF, RR, LF
	2001–05②	.937	—	LR, RF, RR, LF
Sebring Convertible, Sebring Sedan & Stratus Sedan	2001–05	—	—	LR, RF, RR, LF
Sebring Coupe & Stratus Coupe	2001–05	1.06	.404–.415	RR, LF, LR, RF

① — Less ABS.   ② — With ABS.

HYDRAULIC BRAKE CONTROL SPECIFICATIONS

Model	Year	Valve Identification	Valve Tag Color①	Split Point		Master Cylinder Inlet Pressure, psi	Rear Brake Outlet Pressure, psi
				Pressure, psi	Slope		
LESS ABS							
Concorde, Intrepid & LHS & 300M	2001–04	③	Bar Coded Label	400	.34	1000	525–625
Magnum, 300 & 300C	2005	⑥	—	—	—	—	—
Neon	2001–05②	③	Purple	350	.34	1000	525–625
	2001–05④	③	Red	300	.34	1000	480–580
Sebring Convertible, Sebring Sedan & Stratus Sedan	2001–04	⑥	—	—	—	—	—
Sebring Coupe & Stratus Coupe	2001–05	⑥	—	391–462	—	—	—
WITH ABS							
Concorde, Intrepid & LHS & 300M	2001–04	③	Bar Code Label	400	.34	1000	525–625
Crossfire	2004–05	③	Bar Coded Label	400	.34	1000	525–625
Magnum, 300 & 300C	2005	⑤	—	—	—	—	—
Neon	2001–05	③	Black Band	300	.34	1000	550–650
Sebring Convertible, Sebring Sedan & Stratus Sedan	2001–04	⑤	—	—	—	—	—
Sebring Coupe & Stratus Coupe	2001–05	⑤	—	391–462	—	—	—

① — Color tag located under boot of valve stem.
② — 14-inch disc/disc.
③ — Proportioning valve.
④ — 14-inch disc/drum.
⑤ — Electronic variable brake proportioning.
⑥ — Proportioning valves are included in junction block, they are not serviceable.

TIGHTENING SPECIFICATIONS

Year	Component	Torque/Ft. Lbs.
CONCORDE, INTREPID, LHS & 300M		
2001–04	Bleeder Screw	125①
	Brake Booster	21
	Brake Line	105①
	Junction Block	19
	Master Cylinder	21
	Tube	12
CROSSFIRE		
2004–05	Bleeder Screw	62①
	Brake Booster	15
	Brake Line	10
	Master Cylinder	15
MAGNUM, 300 & 300C		
2005	Booster	18
	Master Cylinder	19
	Tube	10
NEON		
2001–05	Bleeder Screw	11
	Brake Booster	25
	Brake Line	13
	Master Cylinder	13
	Tube	12
SEBRING CONVERTIBLE, SEBRING SEDAN & STRATUS SEDAN		
2001–05	Bleeder Screw	11
	Brake Line	13
	Junction Block	21
	Master Cylinder	19
	Tube	12
SEBRING COUPE & STRATUS COUPE		
2001–05	Bleeder Screw	62–78①
	Brake Booster	11–17
	Brake Line	10–12
	Master Cylinder	70–104①

① — Inch Lbs.

POWER BRAKE UNITS

NOTE: On Air Bag Equipped Models, Refer To "Air Bag System Precautions" Located In The Front Of This Manual For System Disarming & Arming Procedures.

NOTE: Refer To "Computer Relearn Procedures" Located In The Front Of This Manual When Battery Power To The Computer Has Been Interrupted.

INDEX

DESCRIPTION

System

These units are of the vacuum suspended type. Some units are of the single diaphragm type, while others are of the tandem diaphragm type, both single piston and double piston or split system type master cylinders are used, **Figs. 1 and 2.**

The vacuum suspended diaphragm type units utilize engine manifold vacuum and atmospheric pressure for its power. It consists of three basic elements combined into a single power unit. The three basic elements of the single diaphragm type are:

1. A vacuum power section which includes a front and rear shell, a power diaphragm, a return spring and a pushrod.
2. A control valve, built integral with power diaphragm and connected through a valve rod to brake pedal, controls degree of brake application or release in accordance with pressure applied to brake pedal.
3. A hydraulic master cylinder, attached to vacuum power section which contains all elements of conventional brake master cylinder except for pushrod, supplies fluid under pressure to wheel brakes in proportion to pressure applied to brake pedal.

Operation

Upon application of the brakes, the valve rod and plunger move to the left in the power diaphragm to close the vacuum port and open the atmospheric port to admit air

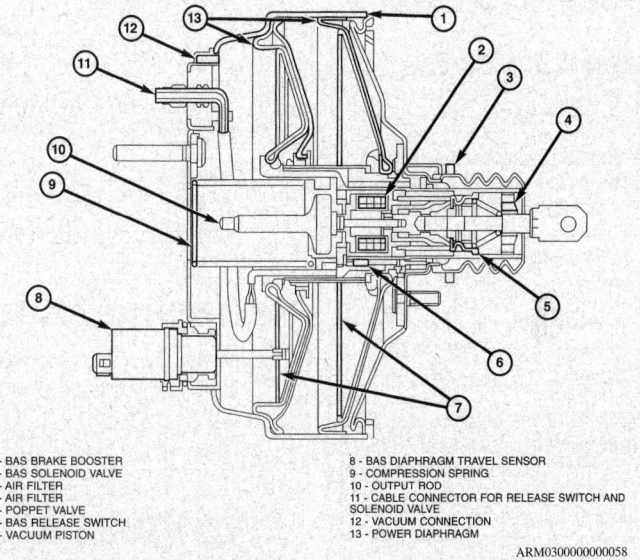

1 - BAS BRAKE BOOSTER
2 - BAS SOLENOID VALVE
3 - AIR FILTER
4 - AIR FILTER
5 - POPPET VALVE
6 - BAS RELEASE SWITCH
7 - VACUUM PISTON
8 - BAS DIAPHRAGM TRAVEL SENSOR
9 - COMPRESSION SPRING
10 - OUTPUT ROD
11 - CABLE CONNECTOR FOR RELEASE SWITCH AND SOLENOID VALVE
12 - VACUUM CONNECTION
13 - POWER DIAPHRAGM

ARM0300000000058

Fig. 1 Dual diaphragm vacuum power booster

through the air cleaner and valve at the rear diaphragm chamber. With vacuum present in the rear chamber, a force is developed to move the power diaphragm, hydraulic pushrod and hydraulic piston or pistons to close the compensating port or ports and force fluid under pressure through the residual check valve or valves and lines into the front and rear wheel cylinders to actuate the brakes.

As pressure is developed within the master cylinder a counter force acting through the hydraulic pushrod and reaction disc against the vacuum power diaphragm and valve plunger sets up a reaction force opposing the force applied to the valve rod and plunger. This reaction force tends to close the atmospheric port and reopen the vacuum port. Since this force is in opposition to the force applied to the brake pedal by the driver it gives the driver a feel of the amount of brake applied. The proportion of reactive force applied to the valve plunger through reaction disc is designed into the Master-Vac to ensure maximum power consistent with maintaining pedal feel. The reaction force is in direct proportion to the hydraulic pressure developed within the brake system.

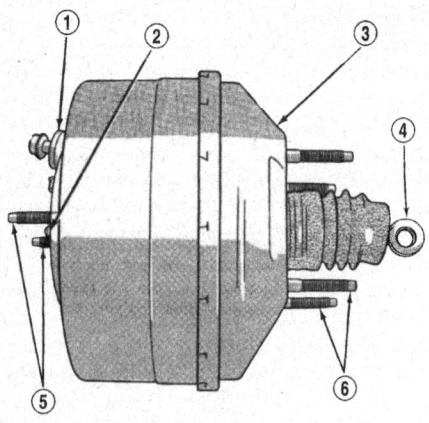

1 - VACUUM CHECK VALVE
2 - OUTPUT ROD
3 - POWER BRAKE BOOSTER ASSEMBLY
4 - INPUT ROD
5 - MASTER CYLINDER MOUNTING STUDS (2)
6 - POWER BOOSTER ASSEMBLY TO DASH PANEL MOUNTING STUDS (4)

ARM0300000000061

Fig. 2 Single diaphragm vacuum power booster

TROUBLESHOOTING

Decreasing Brake Pedal Travel

If a decreasing brake pedal is encountered, the power brake unit may be binding internally. To test the power brake unit for this condition proceed as follows:

1. Place transmission shift lever into Neutral and start engine.
2. Increase engine speed to approximately 1500 RPM, close throttle and completely depress brake pedal.
3. Slowly release brake pedal and stop engine.
4. Remove vacuum check valve and hose from power brake unit. Observe for backward movement of brake pedal.
5. If brake pedal moves backward, power brake unit has internal binding. Replace power brake unit.

Hard Brake Pedal

An internal bind or a failed vacuum check valve would cause this condition. Refer to Previous to test power brake unit for an internal bind. To inspect for a failed vacuum check valve proceed as follows:

1. Start engine and increase engine speed to approximately 1500 RPM, then close throttle and stop engine.
2. Wait 90 seconds, then try brake action.
3. If brakes are not vacuum assisted for two or more applications, replace check valve.

Dragging Brakes

If slow or incomplete release of brakes (dragging brakes) is encountered the power brake unit has an internal bind condition. Test for an internal bind condition as outlined in "Decreasing Brake Pedal Travel."

DIAGNOSIS & TESTING

Refer to **Fig. 3** for power brake system diagnosis and testing.

GENERAL SERVICE

The BAS diaphragm travel sensor and the BAS control module are the only components that can be serviced. If any other repairs are required it will be required to replace the entire booster assembly, Fig. 1.

In order to properly service and repair available brake systems, a thorough understanding of the power assist systems is required. The vacuum assist diaphragm assembly multiplies the force exerted on the master cylinder piston in order to increase the hydraulic pressure delivered to the wheel cylinders or calipers while decreasing the effort required to obtain acceptable stopping performance.

Vacuum assist units get their energy by opposing engine vacuum to atmospheric pressure. A piston, cylinder and flexible diaphragm utilize this energy to provide brake assistance. The diaphragm is balanced with engine vacuum until the brake pedal is depressed, allowing atmospheric pressure to unbalance the unit and apply force to the brake system.

Brakes will operate even if the power unit fails. This means the conventional brake system and the power assist system are completely separate. Troubleshooting conventional and power assist systems are exactly the same until the power unit is reached. As with conventional hydraulic brakes, a spongy pedal still means air is trapped in the hydraulic system. Power brakes give higher line pressure, making leaks more critical.

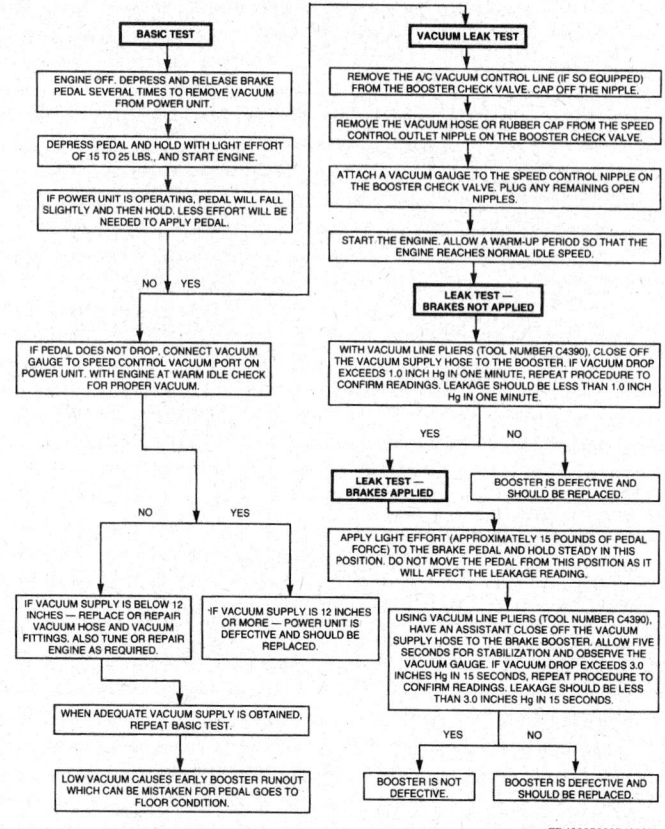

CR4099700074000X

Fig. 3 Power brake system diagnosis

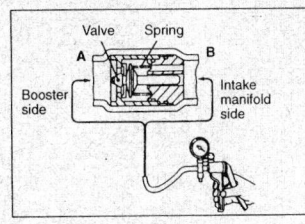

Vacuum pump connection	Accept/reject criteria
Connection at the brake booster side (A)	A negative pressure (vacuum) is created and held.
Connection at the intake manifold side (B)	A negative pressure (vacuum) is not created.

CR4099700073000X

Fig. 4 Vacuum pump connection locations

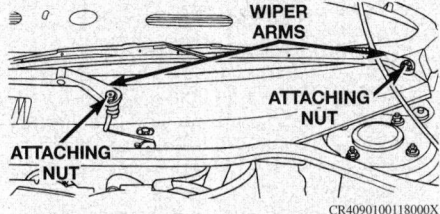

CR4090100118000X

Fig. 7 Wiper arm replacement. Concorde, Intrepid, LHS & 300M

Brake Booster Operation Test

1. Start and run engine for one to two minutes, then shut engine off and inspect pedal operation as follows.
   a. If brake pedal depresses fully first time but gradually becomes higher when depressed succeeding times, booster is operating properly.
   b. If pedal height remains unchanged, booster is faulty.
2. With engine off, step on brake pedal several times, then step on brake pedal, start engine and inspect pedal operation as follows.
   a. If pedal moves downward slightly, booster is satisfactory.
   b. If pedal does not change position, booster is faulty.
3. Step on brake pedal and stop engine, continue to depress pedal for 30 seconds, then inspect brake operation as follows:
   a. If pedal height does not change, booster is satisfactory.
   b. If pedal height rises, booster is faulty.
4. If brake booster does not pass all three tests, inspect check valve and vacuum hose as outlined in "Check Valve Operation Test." If check valve and vacuum hose are satisfactory, replace booster.

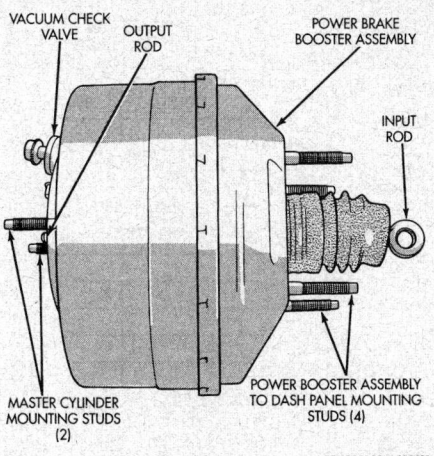

CR4090100116000X

Fig. 5 Teves Power brake booster assembly. Concorde, Intrepid, LHS & 300M

Check Valve Operation Test

1. Remove vacuum hose. **Check valve is press fitted inside vacuum hose.**
2. Inspect operation of check valve by using a vacuum pump. Refer to **Fig. 4** for vacuum pump connection locations.
3. Connect vacuum pump at brake booster side (A). A negative pressure (vacuum) should be created and held.
4. Connect vacuum pump at intake manifold side (B). A negative pressure (vacuum) is not created.
5. If check valve is faulty, replace it as an assembly unit together with vacuum hose.

POWER BRAKE UNIT SERVICE

Power Booster, Replace

CONCORDE, INTREPID, LHS & 300M

Two different power brake vacuum booster designs are used, although externally they appear the same. On some models, use a Teves booster while others use a Bosch power brake booster, **Figs. 5 and 6.**

Do not attempt to disassemble or service power brake unit. Brake unit is serviced only as a complete unit.
1. Remove caps, mounting nuts and wiper arms, **Fig. 7.**
2. Remove wiper module and cowl cover, **Fig. 8.**
3. Remove eight reinforcement to strut towers mounting bolts and one wiper module to reinforcement mounting bolt, then the reinforcement, **Fig. 9.**

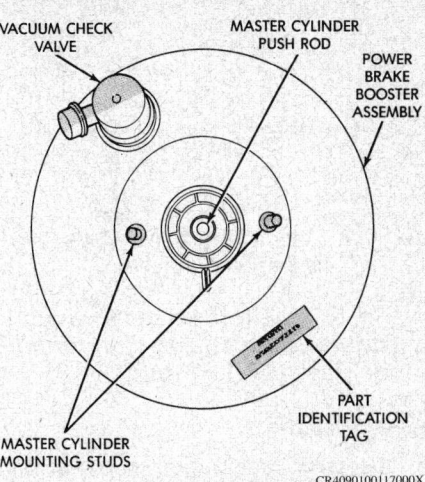

CR4090100117000X

Fig. 6 Bosch Power brake booster identification. Concorde, Intrepid, LHS & 300M

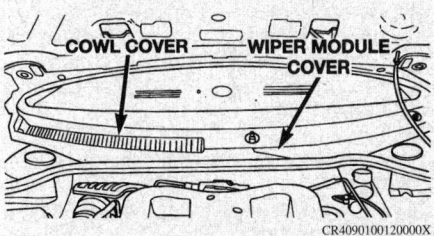

CR4090100120000X

Fig. 8 Wiper module & cowl cover replacement. Concorde, Intrepid, LHS & 300M

4. Disconnect brake fluid level sensor wire connector on righthand side of master cylinder reservoir.
5. Remove two mounting nuts and slide master cylinder off mounting studs with brake lines attached.
6. Position master cylinder backwards on lefthand engine valve cover.
7. Disconnect booster check valve vacuum hose. **Do not remove check valve from booster.**
8. Rotate windshield wiper motor crank lever until lever is at 12 o'clock position, **Fig. 10.**
9. From under instrument panel, position suitable, small screwdriver between center tang of booster input rod to brake pedal pin retaining clip, then rotate screwdriver so retainer clip center tang passes over end of brake pedal pin and pull retainer clip off. Discard old retainer clip.
10. From under instrument panel remove four mounting nuts, slide booster up and to right on dash panel, then tilt outward and up to remove.
11. Reverse procedure to install noting following:
    a. **Torque** booster to dash panel and master cylinder to booster mounting nuts to 21 ft. lbs.
    b. Install new connecting booster input rod to brake pedal pin retainer clip.

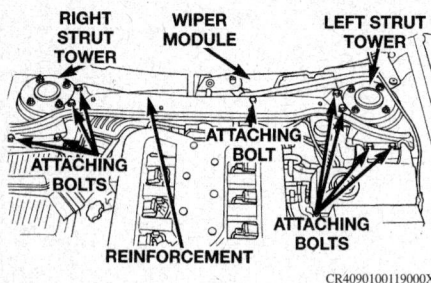

Fig. 9 Reinforcement & wiper module replacement. Concorde, Intrepid, LHS & 300M

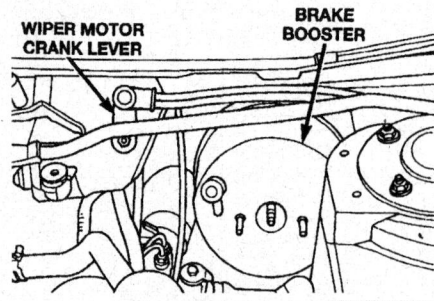

Fig. 10 Wiper crank lever position. Concorde, Intrepid, LHS & 300M

CROSSFIRE

The BAS diaphragm travel sensor and the BAS control module are the only components that can be serviced. If any other repairs are required, replace the entire power booster assembly.

1. Remove master cylinder as outlined under "Master Cylinder, Replace" in "Hydraulic Brake Systems" chapter.
2. Disconnect power booster check valve vacuum hose, **Fig. 11**.
3. Remove retaining clip and slide booster push rod off brake pedal lever, **Fig. 12**.
4. Reverse procedure to install, noting the following:
   a. Install new gasket.
   b. Lubricate pushrod to brake pedal retaining pin with suitable multi-purpose grease.
   c. Install new pushrod to brake pedal pin retainer clip.
   d. **Torque** power booster mounting nuts to 29 ft. lbs.

MAGNUM, 300 & 300C

1. Move driver's seat to full rearward position.
2. Remove master cylinder as outlined under "Master Cylinder, Replace" in "Hydraulic Brake Systems" chapter.
3. **On models equipped with Electronic Stability Program (ESP),** disconnect wiring harness connectors at pedal travel sensor on power brake booster and at active brake booster solenoid.
4. **On all models,** disconnect check valve vacuum hose on face of booster. **Do not remove booster check valve.**
5. Remove brake lamp switch.
6. Remove booster push rod from pin on brake pedal by positioning suitable, small screwdriver between center tang on power brake booster brake pedal pin retaining clip. Rotate screwdriver enough to allow retaining clip center tang to pass over end of brake pedal pin, then slide retaining clip off brake pedal pin. Discard retaining clip.

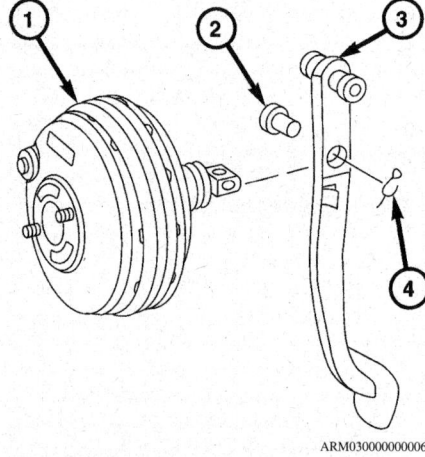

Fig. 12 Power booster brake lever replacement. Crossfire

7. Slide booster push rod off brake pedal pin.
8. Remove four power brake booster mounting nuts and remove windshield wiper module.
9. Slide power brake booster forward out of dash panel and remove through opening between cross-brace and windshield.
10. Reverse procedure to install, noting the following:
    a. Install new booster seal.
    b. **Torque** power brake booster mounting nuts to 19 ft. lbs.

NEON
LESS ABS

1. Remove battery .
2. Remove air cleaner box mounting bolt and disconnect air inlet sensor electrical connector.
3. Lift air cleaner box upward to clear alignment post, then move air cleaner box forward to access battery tray mounting bolts and remove battery tray.
4. Disconnect brake fluid level sensor

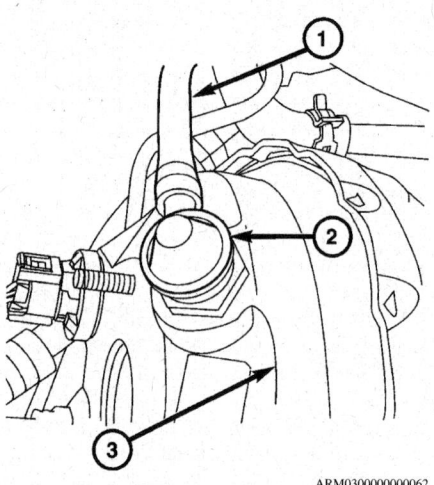

Fig. 11 Power booster replacement. Crossfire

wiring harness on fluid reservoir.
5. Disconnect primary and secondary brake tubes from master cylinder housing. Plug or cap master cylinder outlets.
6. Remove mounting nuts and slide master cylinder forward out of booster.
7. Disconnect power booster check valve vacuum hoses. **Do not remove check valve from power booster.**
8. Position suitable small screwdriver between center tang on input rod to brake pedal pin retaining clip.
9. Rotate screwdriver to allow retaining clip center tang to pass over end of brake pedal pin. Discard retaining clip.
10. Remove mounting nuts and slide power booster forward until mounting studs clear dash, then tilt unit upward to remove.
11. Reverse procedure to install, noting the following:
    a. **Torque** power booster mounting nuts to 21 ft. lbs.
    b. **Torque** master cylinder mounting bolts to 13 ft. lbs.
    c. Install new brake booster input rod to brake pedal retaining clip.
    d. **Torque** master cylinder primary and secondary brake tube nuts to 12 ft. lbs.

WITH ABS

1. Pump brake with ignition off until firm pedal is achieved.
2. Ensure ignition switch is in Off position.
3. Remove battery.
4. Remove air cleaner box mounting bolt and disconnect air inlet sensor electrical connector.
5. Lift air cleaner box upward to clear alignment post, then move air cleaner box forward to access battery tray mounting bolts and remove battery tray.

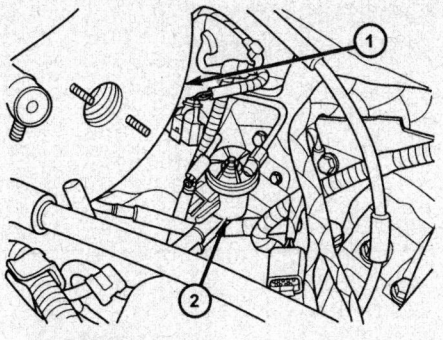

1 - POWER BRAKE BOOSTER
2 - PURGE SOLENOID

CR4090000108000X

Fig. 13 Purge solenoid replacement. Sebring Convertible, Sebring Sedan & Stratus Sedan

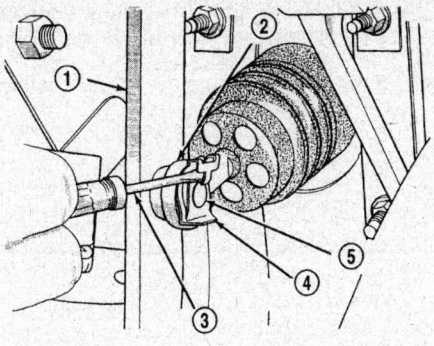

1 - BRAKE PEDAL
2 - INPUT ROD
3 - SCREWDRIVER
4 - RETAINING CLIP
5 - BRAKE PEDAL PIN

CR4090000109000X

Fig. 14 Input rod retaining pin replacement. Sebring Convertible, Sebring Sedan & Stratus Sedan

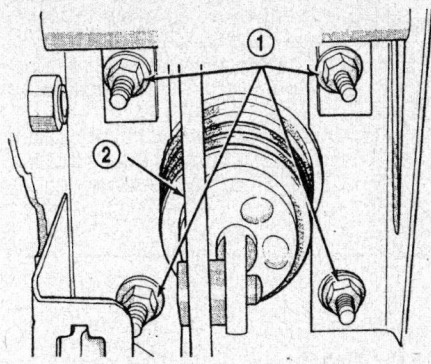

1 - POWER BRAKE BOOSTER MOUNTING NUTS
2 - BRAKE PEDAL

CR4090000110000X

Fig. 15 Power brake booster mounting nuts. Sebring Convertible, Sebring Sedan & Stratus Sedan

6. Disconnect brake fluid level sensor wiring harness mounted on fluid reservoir.
7. Disconnect primary and secondary brake tubes from master cylinder housing. Plug master cylinder outlets.
8. Clean area where master cylinder attaches to power booster using suitable cleaner.
9. Remove mounting nuts and slide master cylinder forward out of booster.
10. Remove vacuum seal in front of power brake vacuum booster by carefully inserting suitable, small screwdriver between master cylinder push rod and vacuum seal and prying seal out of booster. **Do not attempt to pry seal out by inserting screwdriver between seal and booster.**
11. Disconnect power booster check valve vacuum hoses. **Do not remove check valve from power booster.**
12. Remove Integrated Hydraulic Control Unit (ICU) and mounting bracket.
13. Position suitable, small screwdriver between center tang on input rod to brake pedal pin retaining clip.
14. Rotate screwdriver to allow retaining clip center tang to pass over end of brake pedal pin. Discard retaining clip.
15. Remove mounting nuts and slide power booster forward until mounting studs clear dash, then tilt unit upward to remove.
16. Reverse procedure to install, noting the following:
    a. Lubricate master cylinder push rod with suitable silicone lubricant.
    b. Install new vacuum seal onto push rod with notches on seal pointing toward master cylinder housing.
    c. **Torque** power booster mounting nuts to 21 ft. lbs.
    d. **Torque** master cylinder mounting bolts to 13 ft. lbs.
    e. **Torque** master cylinder primary and secondary brake tube nuts to 12 ft. lbs.

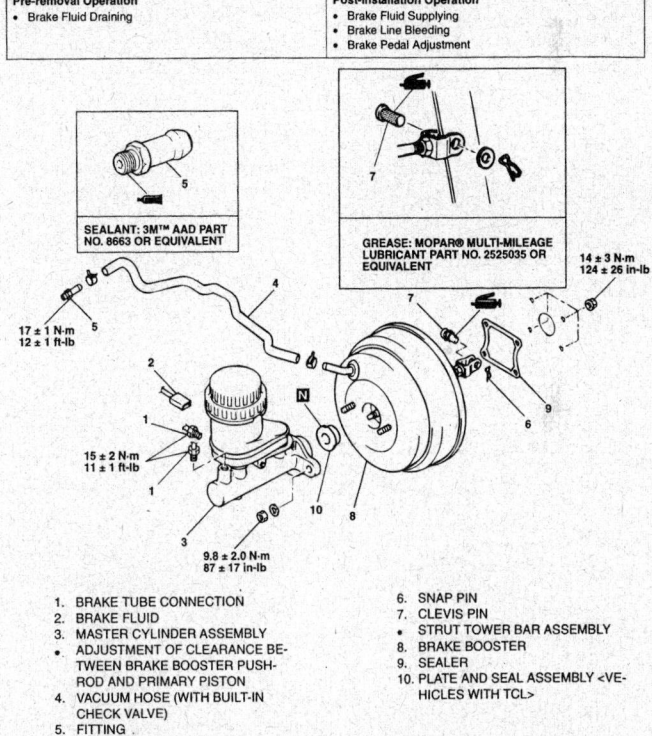

Pre-removal Operation	Post-installation Operation
• Brake Fluid Draining	• Brake Fluid Supplying • Brake Line Bleeding • Brake Pedal Adjustment

SEALANT: 3M™ AAD PART NO. 8663 OR EQUIVALENT

GREASE: MOPAR® MULTI-MILEAGE LUBRICANT PART NO. 2525035 OR EQUIVALENT

14 ± 3 N·m
124 ± 26 in-lb

17 ± 1 N·m
12 ± 1 ft-lb

15 ± 2 N·m
11 ± 1 ft-lb

9.8 ± 2.0 N·m
87 ± 17 in-lb

1. BRAKE TUBE CONNECTION
2. BRAKE FLUID
3. MASTER CYLINDER ASSEMBLY
   • ADJUSTMENT OF CLEARANCE BETWEEN BRAKE BOOSTER PUSH-ROD AND PRIMARY PISTON
4. VACUUM HOSE (WITH BUILT-IN CHECK VALVE)
5. FITTING
6. SNAP PIN
7. CLEVIS PIN
   • STRUT TOWER BAR ASSEMBLY
8. BRAKE BOOSTER
9. SEALER
10. PLATE AND SEAL ASSEMBLY <VEHICLES WITH TCL>

CR4090000106000X

Fig. 16 Brake booster & master cylinder replacement. Sebring & Stratus Coupe

SEBRING CONVERTIBLE, SEBRING SEDAN & STRATUS SEDAN

1. Disconnect speed control servo wiring harness connector and vacuum hose.
2. Remove speed control servo mounting nuts. Leave cable attached and position servo aside.
3. Remove master cylinder from booster as outlined under, "Hydraulic Brake Systems."
4. Remove vacuum booster check valve vacuum hoses.
5. Disconnect electrical connector, mounting screw and solenoid from frame rail, **Fig. 13**.
6. Insert small screwdriver between center tang on power brake booster input rod and brake pedal retaining clip, **Fig. 14**.

7. Rotate screwdriver to allow retaining clip center tang to pass over end of brake pedal pin, then pull retaining clip off brake pedal pin. **Discard retaining clip.**

8. Remove power brake vacuum booster to dash panel mounting nuts. Nuts are accessible from under dash panel, **Fig. 15.**

9. Slide power brake vacuum booster straight forward until mounting studs clear dash panel.

10. Reverse procedure to install, noting the following:
   a. **Torque** power booster mounting nuts to 21 ft. lbs.
   b. **Torque** speed control servo mounting nuts to 55 inch lbs.

SEBRING COUPE & STRATUS COUPE

Refer to **Fig. 16** for power booster removal procedures.

FRONT WHEEL DRIVE AXLES

TABLE OF CONTENTS

Application Chart

Model	Year	Type No.
Concorde, Intrepid, LHS & 300M	2001–04	2
Magnum, 300 & 300C	2005	3
Neon	2001–05	2
Sebring Convertible, Sebring Sedan & Stratus Sedan	2001–05	2
Sebring Coupe & Stratus Coupe	2001–05	1

Type 1

NOTE: On Air Bag Equipped Models, Refer To "Air Bag System Precautions" Located In The Front Of This Manual For System Disarming & Arming Procedures.

NOTE: Refer To "Computer Relearn Procedures" Located In The Front Of This Manual When Battery Power To The Computer Has Been Interrupted.

INDEX

DRIVESHAFT

REPLACE

1. Raise and support vehicle, then remove tire and wheel assembly.
2. **On models equipped with ABS,** disconnect speed sensor cable connector, **Fig. 1.**
3. **On all models,** disconnect brake hose clip.
4. Ensure vehicle weight is not applied to wheel bearing.
5. Remove cotter pin and driveshaft nut.
6. Loosen lower arm ball joint nut. **Do not remove nut.**
7. Disconnect lower arm ball joint using steering linkage puller tool No. MB99113, or equivalent, **Fig. 2.**
8. Remove cotter pin and loosen tie rod end nut. **Do not remove nut.**
9. Disconnect tie rod end using steering linkage puller.
10. Remove mounting nut and disconnect stabilizer link connector.
11. Push drive shaft from hub using axle puller tool No. MB990242, adapter MB991354 and end yoke holder tool No. MB990767, or equivalents, **Fig. 3,** noting the following:
    a. **On models equipped with ABS,** do not damage ABS rotor.
    b. **On all models,** do not pull driveshaft, use pry bar.
    c. Do inset pry bar deep enough to damage oil seal.
    d. Do not damage transaxle oil seal with driveshaft splines.
12. Remove driveshaft by inserting a suitable pry bar between transaxle case and driveshaft, **Fig. 4. Do damage transaxle oil seal with inner driveshaft spline.**
13. **On models equipped with 3.0L engine,** if righthand side inner shaft and transaxle are tightly joined, tap center bearing bracket lightly with suitable plastic hammer.
14. **On all models,** cover transaxle case with suitable shop towel.
15. Reverse procedure to install, noting the following:
    a. Washer convex side must face drive shaft nut.
    b. Use end yoke holder tool No. MB990767, or equivalent, when tightening driveshaft nut.

DRIVESHAFT SERVICE

When servicing the drive axle, never disassemble the Birfield joint except when replacing the boot.

2.4L Engine

DISASSEMBLE

1. Remove tripod joint bands, **Fig. 5.**
2. Remove circlip, snap ring and spider.

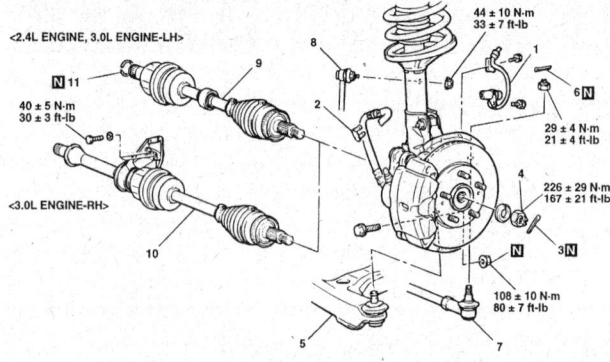

1. SPEED SENSOR CABLE CONNECTION <VEHICLES WITH ABS>
2. BRAKE HOSE CLIP
3. COTTER PIN
4. DRIVESHAFT NUT
5. LOWER ARM BALL JOINT CONNECTION
6. COTTER PIN
7. TIE ROD END CONNECTION
8. STABILIZER LINK CONNECTION
9. DRIVESHAFT
10. DRIVESHAFT AND INNER SHAFT
11. CIRCLIP

Required Special Tools:
- MB990242: Puller Bar
- MB990767: End Yoke Holder
- MB990998: Front Hub Remover and Installer
- MB991345: Puller Body

CR3030000478000X

Fig. 1   Exploded view of driveshaft

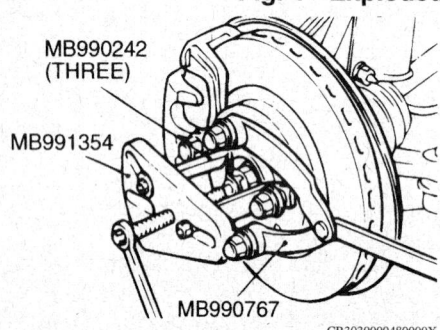

CR3030000480000X

Fig. 3   Driveshaft replacement

3. Wrap Birfield joint with suitable plastic tape.
4. Ensure plastic tape is around spline part on Birfield joint so tripod joint boot is not damaged when they are removed.
5. Remove bands and tripod boot.
6. Remove bands and dynamic damper.

ASSEMBLE

1. Install dynamic damper, **Fig. 6,** noting the following:
   a. **Ensure no grease adheres to rubber part of dynamic damper.**
   b. **Damper band and tripod joint boot band are different in shape, ensure proper band is installed.**
2. Wrap suitable plastic tape around shaft spline, then install tripod joint boot and band.
3. Apply drive axle repair kit grease to spider axles and rollers.

4. Install spider spline chamfered portion toward driveshaft and spider to driveshaft, **Fig. 7.**
5. Fill tripod joint with 3.1–3.9 ounces of repair kit grease, then install snap ring, case and circlip.

3.0L Engine

LEFTHAND

Refer to "2.4L Engine" for lefthand shaft replacement procedure

RIGHTHAND

DISASSEMBLE

1. Disassemble outer shaft as outlined under "2.4L Engine."
2. Remove tripod joint bands, **Fig. 5.**
3. Press and deform seal plate, then remove it with suitable press.
4. Remove inner shaft from tripod case using inner shaft remove tool No. MB991248, or MD998801, or equivalents, **Fig. 8.**
5. Remove dust covers.
6. Remove inner shaft and dust shields from center bearing bracket using inner shaft remove tool, **Fig. 9.**
7. Remove center bearing from bracket using adapter tool No. MB990930 and rear suspension bush base tool No. MB990938, or equivalents, **Fig. 10.**

ASSEMBLE

1. Assemble outer shaft as outlined under "2.4L Engine."

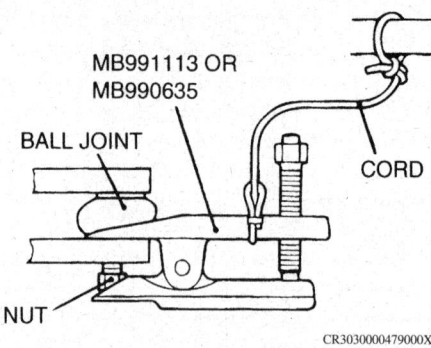

CR3030000479000X

Fig. 2   Ball joint/tie rod end disconnection

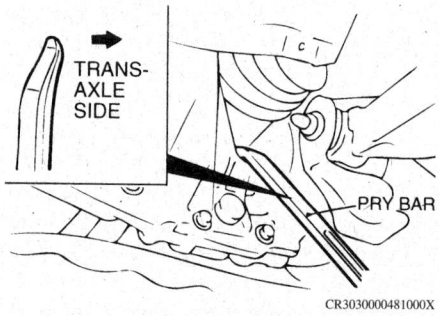

CR3030000481000X

Fig. 4   Pry bar installation

2. Install center bearing into center bearing bracket using adapter tool No. MB990930 and rear suspension bush base tool No. MB990938, or equivalents, **Fig. 10.**
3. Pack .5–.7 ounces suitable multimileage grease into inner dust seal and .3–.4 ounces into outer, **Fig. 11.**
4. Install oil seal into center bearing bracket adapter and rear suspension bush base tools.
5. Apply suitable grease to dust seal lip of dust seal. **Do not damage outer dust seal surface rubber portion. Do not apply grease to outside of lip.**
6. Hold center bearing inner race using adapter tool No. MB991172, or equivalent, and press-in inner shaft, **Fig. 12.**
7. Install suitable grease to inner shaft serration and press inner shaft into tripod joint case.
8. Fill tripod joint with 3.3–4.1 ounces of repair kit grease, then install seal plate, case and circlip.
9. Position tripod joint outer race so distance between boot bands is 3.3 inches, **Fig. 13.**
10. Remove part of tripod joint outer race to release air pressure inside boot.

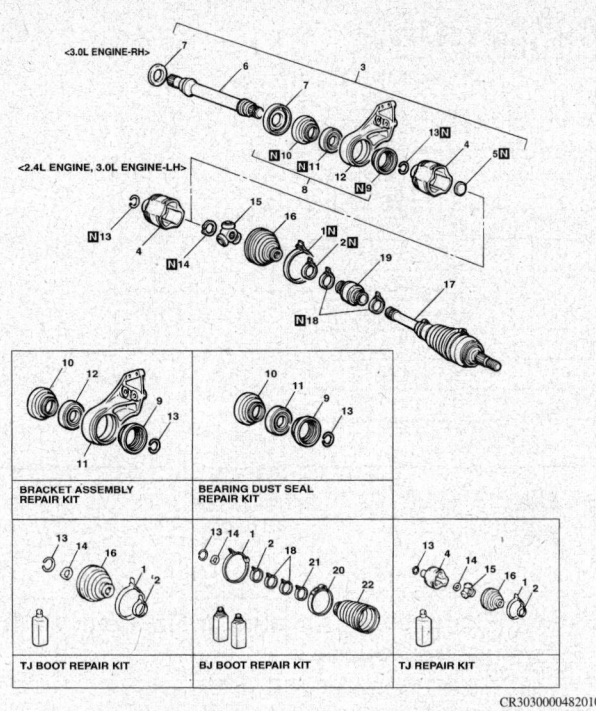

1. TJ BOOT BAND (LARGE)
2. TJ BOOT BAND (SMALL)
3. TJ CASE INNER SHAFT ASSEMBLY
4. TJ CASE
5. SEAL PLATE
6. INNER SHAFT
7. DUST COVER
8. BRACKET ASSEMBLY
9. DUST SEAL OUTER
10. DUST SEAL INNER
11. CENTER BEARING
12. CENTER BEARING BRACKET
13. CIRCLIP
14. SNAP RING
15. SPIDER ASSEMBLY
16. TJ BOOT
17. BJ ASSEMBLY
18. DAMPER BAND <2.4L ENGINE, 3.0L ENGINE-LH>
19. DYNAMIC DAMPER <2.4L ENGINE, 3.0L ENGINE-LH>
20. BJ BOOT BAND (LARGE)
21. BJ BOOT BAND (SMALL)
22. BJ BOOT

NOTE: BJ: Birfield Joint
TJ: Tripod Joint

Required Special Tool:
- MB990890: Rear Suspension Bush Base
- MB990930: Installation Adapter
- MB990932: Installation Adapter
- MB990934: Installation Adapter
- MB990938: Installation Adapter
- MB991172: Adapter
- MB991248 or MD998801: Inner Shaft Remover
- MB991561: Boot Band Crimping Tool

CR3030000482020X

Fig. 5   Exploded view of driveshaft assembly (Part 2 of 2). w/2.4L engine

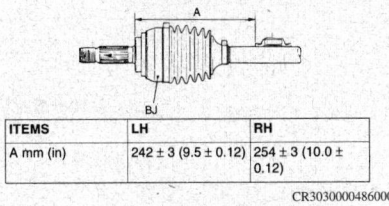

CR3030000482010X

Fig. 5   Exploded view of driveshaft assembly (Part 1 of 2) w/2.4L engine

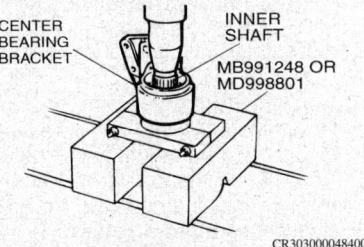

ITEMS	LH	RH
A mm (in)	242 ± 3 (9.5 ± 0.12)	254 ± 3 (10.0 ± 0.12)

CR3030000486000X

Fig. 6   Dynamic damper installation. w/2.4L engine

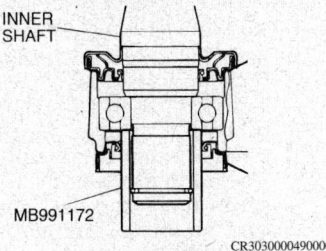

CR3030000484000X

Fig. 9   Inner shaft from center bearing bracket removal. Sebring Coupe & Stratus Coupe w/3.0L engine

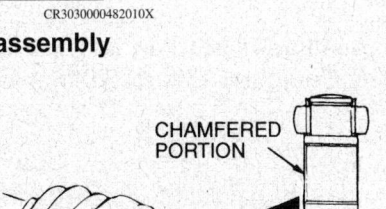

Fig. 7   Spider installation. Sebring Coupe & Stratus Coupe w/2.4L engine

CR3030000487000X

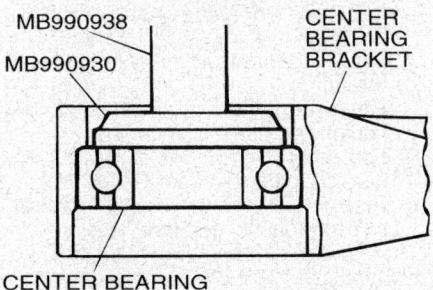

CR3030000485000X

Fig. 10   Center bearing replacement. w/3.0L engine

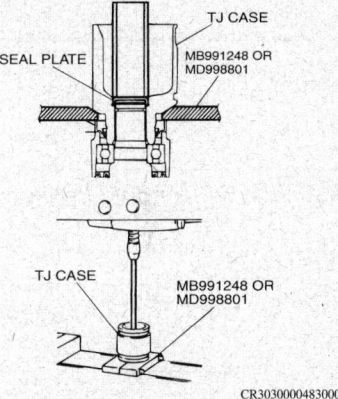

CR3030000483000X

Fig. 8   Inner shaft from case removal. w/3.0L engine

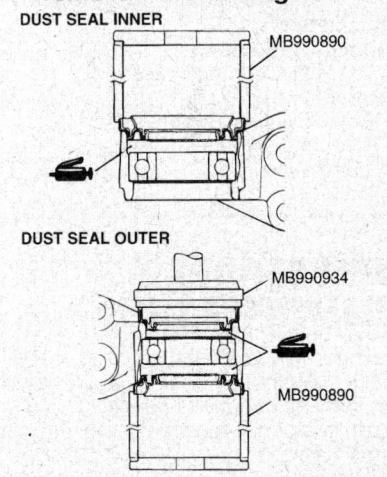

CR3030000489000X

Fig. 11   Dust seal installation. w/3.0L engine

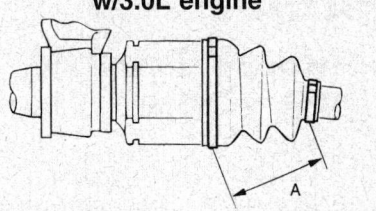

CR3030000490000X

Fig. 12   Inner shaft installation. w/3.0L engine

CR3030000491000X

Fig. 13   Boot band installation. w/3.0L engine

TIGHTENING SPECIFICATIONS

Year	Component	Torque Ft. Lbs.
2001–05	Caliper	67–81
	Center Bearing	27–33
	Driveshaft Nut	146–188
	Driveshaft & Inner Shaft Bracket	27–33
	Dust Shield	61–95①
	Front Strut	203–239
	Knuckle To Front Hub	58–72
	Lower Arm Ball Joint	73–87
	Stabilizer Link	26–40
	Tie Rod End & Ball Joint	17–25

① — Inch Lbs.

Type 2

NOTE: On Air Bag Equipped Models, Refer To "Air Bag System Precautions" Located In The Front Of This Manual For System Disarming & Arming Procedures.

NOTE: Refer To "Computer Relearn Procedures" Located In The Front Of This Manual When Battery Power To The Computer Has Been Interrupted.

INDEX

DRIVESHAFT IDENTIFICATION

The unequal length system used on these models has a short solid interconnecting shaft on one side with a longer tubular interconnecting shaft on the other, **Figs. 1 and 2.**

DRIVESHAFT

REPLACE

Concorde, Intrepid, LHS & 300M

1. Raise and support vehicle, then remove wheel and tire assemblies.
2. Remove brake caliper as outlined in "Disc Brakes" chapter.
3. Remove brake rotor by pulling it straight off mounting studs.
4. Remove speed sensor cable routing bracket from strut.
5. Remove stub axle and hub mounting nut.
6. Install puller tool No. 6790, or equivalent, on hub and bearing assembly using wheel lugnuts.
7. Install lugnut on wheel stud to protect threads.
8. Prevent hub from turning. by inserting suitable flat-bladed pry tool.
9. Force outer stub axle from hub and bearing assembly using puller tool.
10. Disconnect inner tripod joint from transaxle stub shaft retaining ring.
11. Pry driveshaft from transmission by inserting suitable pry bar between transmission case and driveshaft, **Fig. 3,** noting the following:
    a. **Do not pull on driveshaft.**
    b. **Do not insert pry bar deep enough to damage oil seal.**
    c. **Only pry inner joint from retaining snap ring.**
    d. **Do not attempt to remove inner tripod joint from transaxle stub shaft.**
12. Support steering knuckle, then disconnect and remove strut from steering knuckle.
13. Support outer CV joint assembly with one hand and grasp steering knuckle with other hand.
14. Rotate outer CV out and to rear, until it clears hub and bearing assembly.
15. Remove driveshaft inner tripod joint from transaxle stub shaft. **Do not pull on interconnecting shaft.**
16. Reverse procedure to install, noting the following:
    a. Install new O-ring seal and tripod joint retaining circlip.
    b. Apply thin, even bead suitable of multi-purpose lubricant grease around inner tripod joint splines where O-rings seats against joint.
    c. When installing outer CV joint into hub and bearing assembly, do not damage flinger disc, **Fig. 4.**
    d. **Ensure snap rings are securely seated in grooves because strut bolts have serrated shaft. Turn nut on bolts, but do not turn bolts.**
    e. Install new hub and bearing stub shaft mounting nut. Tighten, but do not torque nut now.
    f. Apply vehicle brakes, then tighten new hub and bearing stub shaft nut.

Neon, Sebring Convertible, Sebring Sedan & Stratus Sedan

If the vehicle will be moved on its wheels when a driveshaft has been removed, install a properly sized bolt and nut through the front hub. **Torque to 180 ft. lbs. to ensure the hub bearing will not loosen.**

1. Place transaxle in Park position.
2. Raise and support vehicle, then remove wheel and tire assembly.
3. **On models equipped with ABS,** disconnect front wheel speed sensor and position harness aside.
4. **On all models,** remove ball joint to knuckle mounting nut and bolt.
5. Separate ball joint stud from knuckle by prying down on lower control arm. **Avoid damaging joint seal.**
6. Remove driveshaft from knuckle by pulling outward on knuckle while pressing in on driveshaft. Support outer end of driveshaft. If separation is difficult, proceed as follows:
   a. Install puller tool No. 6790, or equivalent, on hub and bearing using lugnuts.
   b. Install axle nut to protect threads.
   c. Prevent hub from turning by inserting suitable flat-bladed pry tool.
   d. Force driveshaft outer stub axle from hub and bearing assembly using puller tool.
   e. Remove axle nut, then pull knuckle out and away from outer CV joint.
7. Support driveshaft outer end.
8. Remove inner tripod joints from transaxle side gears using suitable punch to disconnect inner joint retaining ring from side gear, noting the following:
   a. On righthand side joint, position punch against inner joint.
   b. On lefthand side joint, position punch in joint groove.
9. Position suitable oil resistant container under driveshaft where it enters transaxle.
10. Support inner tripod joint and driveshaft interconnecting shaft.
11. Remove inner joint from transaxle by pulling it straight out of side gear and oil seal. **Do not let spline or snap ring drag across oil sealing lip.**
12. Reverse procedure to install, noting the following:
    a. Thoroughly clean spline and oil sealing surface on tripod joint.
    b. Lubricate oil seal sealing surface with transaxle fluid.
    c. Ensure snap ring is fully seated in its groove. Tripod joint will not be removable by hand when snap ring is properly installed.
    d. Install new knuckle to ball joint stud bolt and nut.
    e. Clean dirt and debris from driveshaft outer stub shaft threads.
    f. Inspect transaxle fluid level.

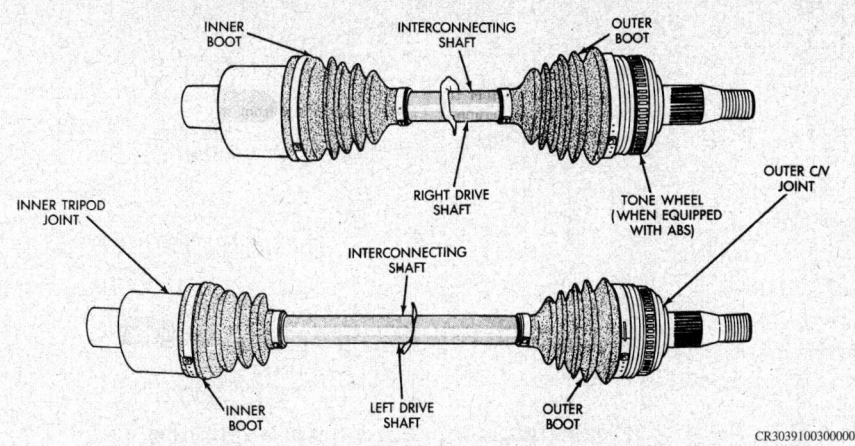

Fig. 1 Driveshaft identification. Concorde, Intrepid, LHS & 300M

DRIVESHAFT SERVICE

The driveshaft is a non-serviceable item, except for the inner and outer driveshaft boots, **Fig. 4.** If any failure of internal components is diagnosed, the driveshaft must be replaced as an assembly.

Inner Driveshaft Boot, Replace

REMOVAL

1. Remove driveshaft as outlined under "Driveshaft, Replace."
2. Remove inner joint boot clamps and slide boot down interconnecting shaft.
3. Remove joint housing interconnecting shaft and spider. **Do not pull on interconnecting shaft.**
4. Remove snap ring and spider from interconnecting shaft using suitable brass drift. **Hold bearings in place on spider trunnions to prevent them from falling away. Do not hit outer tripod bearings when removing spider.**
5. Remove interconnecting shaft joint boot.
6. Clean and inspect spider, tripod joint housing and interconnecting shaft for signs of excessive wear. **If excessive wear is present, replace entire driveshaft.**

INSTALLATION

Two different types of boots are used on these models. One is a high temperature, soft and pliable type, the other is a normal temperature, soft and rigid type. The replacement boot must be of the same type that was removed.

1. **On Concorde, Intrepid, LHS and 300M models,** install new boot clamps and boot onto interconnecting shaft. **Boot must be positioned on interconnecting shaft so only thinnest shaft groove is visible.**
2. **On Neon, Sebring Convertible, Sebring Sedan and Stratus Sedan models,** install new boot clamps and boot onto interconnecting shaft. **Boot must be positioned so raised bead on inside of boot is in groove on in-**
   terconnecting shaft.
3. **On all models,** install spider onto interconnecting shaft and retaining snap ring. **Ensure retaining snap ring is fully installed and seated into shaft groove.**
4. Distribute ½ of grease provided in boot service package into tripod housing and remaining grease into boot. **Do not use any other type of grease.**
5. Install spider into tripod housing.
6. Position boot over boot retaining groove on interconnecting shaft and install boot retaining clamp using crimper tool No. C-4975-A, or equivalent.
7. Position boot into tripod housing retaining groove.
8. **On Neon, Sebring Convertible, Sebring Sedan and Stratus Sedan models,** proceed as follows:
   a. Insert suitable trim stick between joint and boot to vent inner joint, **Fig. 5.** If inner joint has hard plastic boot, trim stick must be inserted between soft rubber insert and joint housing.
   b. With trim stick inserted between sealing boot and tripod joint housing, position interconnecting shaft in center of travel in tripod joint housing.
   c. **On models equipped with Hytrel, hard plastic sealing boot,** insert trim stick between soft rubber and tripod housing not hard plastic sealing boot and soft rubber insert.
   d. **On all models,** position inner tripod joint on halfshaft until correct sealing boot edge to edge length is obtained, **Fig. 6.**
   e. **On models with hard plastic sealing boot,** edge to edge length is 4.213 inches.
   f. **On models with soft sealing boot,** edge to edge length is 4.134 inches.
   g. **On all models,** position boot to interface with tripod housing. Boot lobes must be properly aligned with tripod housing recesses.
9. **On models equipped with crimp type boot clamp,** proceed as follows:
   a. Clamp sealing boot onto tripod housing using crimper tool No.

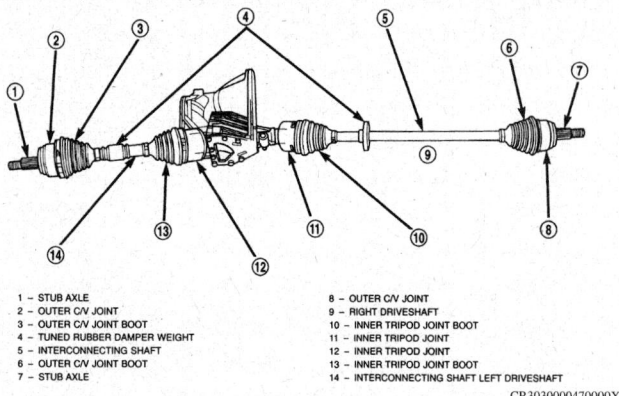

1 – STUB AXLE
2 – OUTER C/V JOINT
3 – OUTER C/V JOINT BOOT
4 – TUNED RUBBER DAMPER WEIGHT
5 – INTERCONNECTING SHAFT
6 – OUTER C/V JOINT BOOT
7 – STUB AXLE

8 – OUTER C/V JOINT
9 – RIGHT DRIVESHAFT
10 – INNER TRIPOD JOINT BOOT
11 – INNER TRIPOD JOINT
12 – INNER TRIPOD JOINT
13 – INNER TRIPOD JOINT BOOT
14 – INTERCONNECTING SHAFT LEFT DRIVESHAFT

CR3030000470000X

Fig. 2 Driveshaft identification. Neon, Sebring Convertible, Sebring Sedan & Stratus Sedan

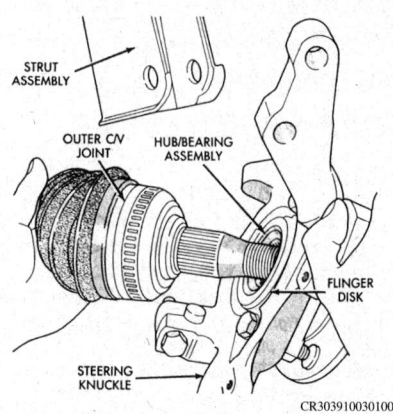

CR3039100301000X

Fig. 3 Outer CV joint separation from hub. Concorde, Intrepid, LHS & 300M

C-4975-A, or equivalent.

b. Place crimping tool over clamp bridge.

c. Tighten nut on crimper tool until tool's jaws are completely closed together, face to face.

10. **On models equipped with latching type boot clamp,** proceed as follows:

a. Clamp sealing boot onto tripod housing using clamp locking tool No. YA3050, or equivalent.

b. Place tool's prongs in clamp hole.

c. Squeeze tool together until clamp's top band is latched behind two tabs on lower clamp band.

11. **On all models,** install driveshaft as outlined under "Driveshaft, Replace."

Outer Driveshaft Boot, Replace

CONCORDE, INTREPID, LHS & 300M

REMOVAL

1. Remove driveshaft as outlined under "Driveshaft, Replace."

2. Remove outer joint boot clamps and slide boot down interconnecting shaft.

3. Remove grease to expose outer CV joint retaining ring, **Fig. 7.**

4. Spread retaining ring and slide CV joint off interconnecting shaft.

5. Remove and discard failed boot and clamps.

6. Clean and inspect spider, CV joint and interconnecting shaft for signs of excessive wear. **If excessive wear is present, entire driveshaft must be replacement.**

INSTALLATION

1. Install new boot clamps and boot onto interconnecting shaft.

2. Install CV joint onto interconnecting shaft by pushing shaft into CV joint

until retaining snap ring is seated in shaft groove, **Fig. 7.**

3. Distribute ½ of grease provided in boot service package into CV joint and remaining grease into boot.

4. Position boot over boot retaining grove on interconnecting shaft with thinnest shaft groove is visible.

5. Install boot retaining clamp using crimper tool No. C-4975-A, or equivalent.

6. Position boot over boot retaining grove on CV joint housing and install boot retaining clamp using crimper tool. Ensure seal is not dimpled, stretched or distorted.

7. Install driveshaft as outlined under "Driveshaft, Replace."

NEON, SEBRING CONVERTIBLE, SEBRING SEDAN & STRATUS SEDAN

REMOVAL

1. Remove driveshaft as outlined under "Driveshaft, Replace."

2. Remove and discard large boot clamp retaining CV joint sealing boot to CV joint housing.

3. Remove and discard small clamp retaining outer CV joint sealing boot to interconnecting shaft.

4. Slide outer CV joint housing sealing boot down interconnecting shaft.

5. Wipe away grease to expose outer CV joint and interconnecting shaft.

6. Support interconnecting shaft in suitable soft jawed vice with protective jaw caps.

7. Disconnect CV joint housing from interconnecting shaft internal circlip by strike end using suitable soft faced hammer.

8. CV joint may have to be tapped off interconnecting shaft using suitable soft faced hammer.

9. Remove interconnecting shaft large circlip.

10. Slide boot off interconnecting shaft.

11. Thoroughly clean and inspect outer CV and interconnecting joints for signs of excessive wear. **If components show signs of excessive wear, replace driveshaft.**

INSTALLATION

1. Slide new sealing boot to interconnecting shaft retaining clamp and onto interconnecting shaft, **Fig. 8. Ensure seal boot is positioned on interconnecting shaft so raised bead on inside of seal boot is in groove on interconnecting shaft.**

2. Align interconnecting shaft and outer CV joint cross splines, then start outer CV joint onto interconnecting shaft.

3. Install outer CV joint assembly onto interconnecting shaft using suitable soft faced hammer, **Fig. 9.**

4. Distribute ½ of grease provided in seal boot service package into outer CV joint housing. **Do not use any other type of grease.**

5. Put remaining grease into sealing boot.

6. Install outer CV joint boot to interconnecting shaft clamp evenly on sealing boot.

7. Clamp sealing boot onto interconnecting shaft using clamp crimper tool No. C-4975-A, or equivalent, **Fig. 10.**

8. Position outer CV joint sealing boot into outer CV joint housing retaining groove.

9. Install sealing boot to outer CV joint retaining clamp evenly on sealing boot.

10. Clamp sealing boot onto CV joint housing using clamp crimper tool No. C-4975-A, or equivalent. **Ensure jaws of crimper tool are closed completely together.**

11. Install driveshaft as outlined under "Driveshaft, Replace."

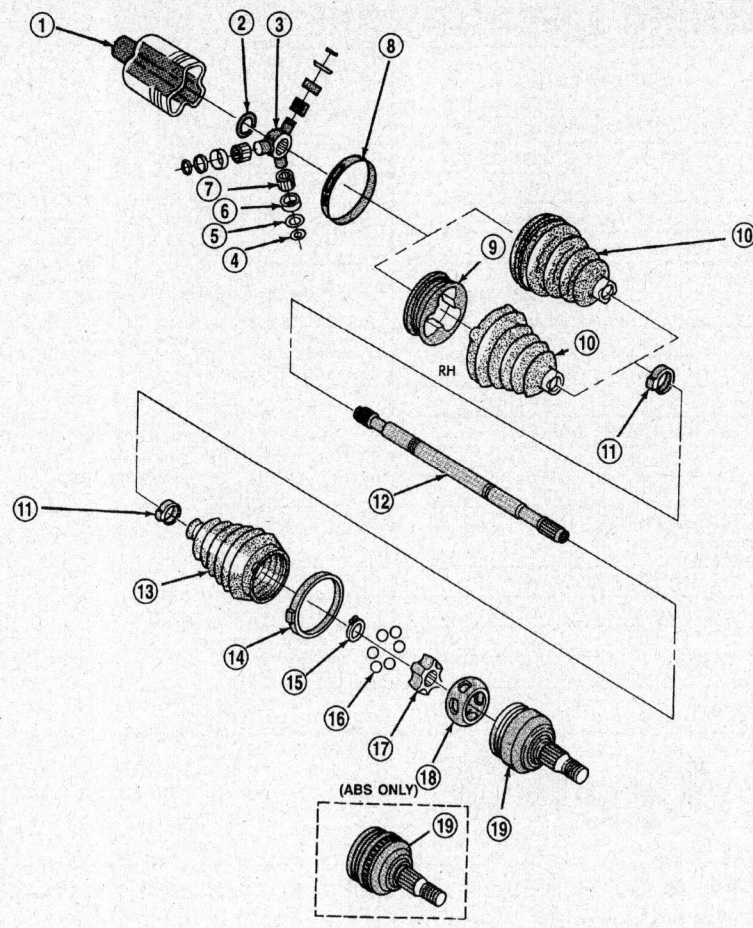

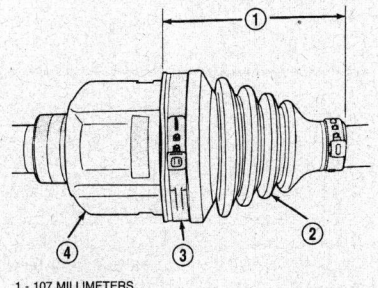

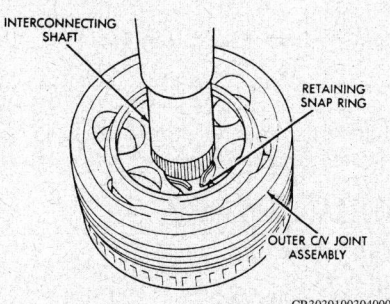

1 - HOUSING ASM, RETAINER
2 - RING, SPACER
3 - SPIDER, TRIPOD JOINT
4 - RING, RETAINING
5 - RETAINER, BALL & ROLLER
6 - BALL, TRIPOD JOINT
7 - ROLLER, NEEDLE
8 - CLAMP, SEAL RETAINING
9 - BUSHING, TRILOBAL TRIPOD
10 - SEAL, DRIVE AXLE INBOARD

11 - CLAMP, SEAL RETAINING
12 - SHAFT, AXLE (RH SHOWN, LH SIMILAR)
13 - SEAL, DRIVE AXLE OUTBOARD
14 - CLAMP, SEAL RETAINING
15 - RING, RACE RETAINING
16 - BALL, CHROME ALLOY
17 - RACE, C/V JOINT INNER
18 - CAGE, C/V JOINT
19 - RACE, C/V JOINT OUTER

CR3030000477000X

Fig. 4   Exploded view of driveshaft

1 - 107 MILLIMETERS
2 - HYTREL SEALING BOOT
3 - SEALING BOOT CLAMP
4 - INNER TRIPOD JOINT

CR3030100504000X

Fig. 6   Sealing boot edge to edge length

INTERCONNECTING SHAFT

RETAINING SNAP RING

OUTER C/V JOINT ASSEMBLY

CR3039100304000X

Fig. 7   Outer CV joint retaining snap ring location. Concorde, Intrepid, LHS & 300M

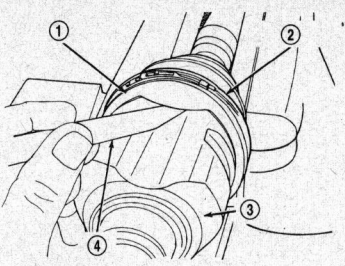

1 - INNER TRIPOD JOINT SEALING BOOT
2 - SEALING BOOT CLAMP
3 - INNER TRIPOD JOINT HOUSING
4 - TRIM STICK

CR3030100503000X

Fig. 5   Venting tripod joint assembly

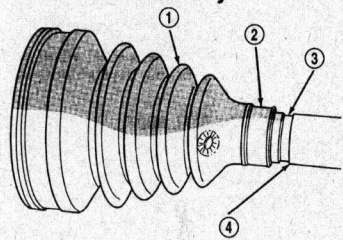

1 - SEALING BOOT
2 - RAISED BEAD IN THIS AREA OF SEALING BOOT
3 - GROOVE
4 - INTERCONNECTING SHAFT

CR3039800401000A

Fig. 8   Outer sealing boot installation. Sebring Convertible, Sebring Sedan & Stratus Sedan

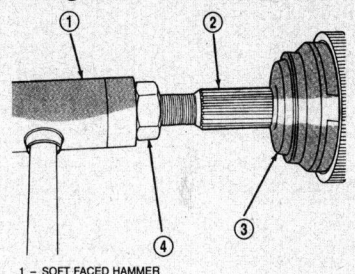

1 - SOFT FACED HAMMER
2 - STUB AXLE
3 - OUTER C/V JOINT
4 - NUT

CR3039800402000A

Fig. 9   Outer CV joint installation. Neon, Sebring Convertible, Sebring Sedan & Stratus Sedan

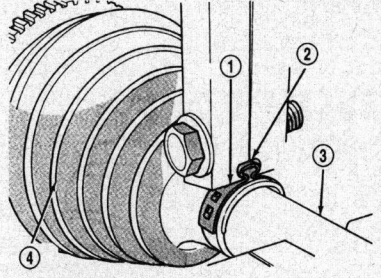

1 - CLAMP
2 - JAWS OF SPECIAL TOOL C-4975A MUST BE CLOSED COMPLETELY TOGETHER HERE
3 - INTERCONNECTING SHAFT
4 - SEALING BOOT

CR3039800403000A

Fig. 10   CV boot clamp installation. Neon, Sebring Convertible, Sebring Sedan & Stratus Sedan

TIGHTENING SPECIFICATIONS

Year	Component	Torque Ft. Lbs.
CONCORDE, INTREPID, LHS & 300M		
2001–04	Halfshaft To Hub Bearing	105
	Knuckle To Ball Stud	70
	Knuckle To Strut Bolt	155
	Tie Rod End To Knuckle	27
	Wheel Lugnuts	100
NEON		
2001–05	Caliper To Knuckle	16
	Halfshaft To Hub Bearing	180
	Knuckle To Ball Joint Stud	70
	Knuckle To Strut Bolt	40①
	Tie Rod End To Knuckle	45
	Wheel Lugnuts	95
SEBRING CONVERTIBLE, SEBRING SEDAN & STRATUS SEDAN		
2001–05	Ball Joint To Knuckle	70
	Halfshaft To Hub Bearing	110
	Tie Rod To Knuckle	41
	Wheel Lugnuts	100

① — Final tighten an additional 90°.

Type 3

NOTE: On Air Bag Equipped Models, Refer To "Air Bag System Precautions" Located In The Front Of This Manual For System Disarming & Arming Procedures.

NOTE: Refer To "Computer Relearn Procedures" Located In The Front Of This Manual When Battery Power To The Computer Has Been Interrupted.

INDEX

DESCRIPTION

The inner joints of both half shaft assemblies are cross-groove joints. The outer joints of both assemblies are Rzeppa Joints. The cross-groove joints are true Constant Velocity (CV) joints, which allow for the changes in half shaft length through the jounce and rebound travel of the rear suspension.

The inner cross-groove joint of the left-hand halfshaft assembly is splined to the intermediate shaft and retained with a snap ring. The right halfshaft is splined to the front axle assembly and retained with a snap ring. The outer CV joint has a stub shaft that is splined into the wheel hub and retained by a steel hub nut.

DRIVESHAFT
REPLACE
Removal

1. Raise and support vehicle, then remove tire and wheel assembly.
2. While holding link ball joint stem from rotating, remove stabilizer link (1) to shock clevis bracket nut.
3. Slide link ball joint stem from clevis bracket.
4. Remove clevis bracket to bottom of shock mounting nut and pinch bolt.
5. Remove shock clevis bracket to lower control arm mounting nut and bolt.
6. Pull lower end of clevis bracket outward away from lower control arm bushing, then slide it off shock. **If required, to use an appropriate prying tool to spread clamp area of clevis bracket.**
7. While helper applies brakes to keep hub from rotating, remove hub nut from axle half shaft.
8. Grasp rear of caliper and pull outward working with guide pins to retract caliper piston. **Never push on piston directly.**

9. Remove two disc brake caliper and adapter to knuckle mounting bolts.
10. Remove disc brake caliper and adapter from knuckle, then hang aside using suitable wire or bungee cord. **Do care not to overextend brake hose.**
11. Remove clips, then slide brake rotor off hub and bearing.
12. Separate upper ball joint stud from knuckle. using puller tool No. 9360, or equivalent. **Do not damage ball joint seal boot while sliding tool into place past seal boot.**
13. Remove tool and nut from end of upper ball joint stud.
14. Remove wheel speed sensor to knuckle clip.
15. Disconnect and remove righthand halfshaft from axle.
16. Remove lefthand halfshaft.

Installation

1. If previously removed, install and tighten intermediate shaft .
2. Install lefthand halfshaft.
3. Install new axle seal using seal installer tool No. C-4193-A, or equivalent.
4. Install righthand halfshaft.
5. Install halfshaft isolation washer. Washer is bi-directional and can be installed in either direction on shaft.
6. Install halfshaft into hub/bearing .
7. Loosely install halfshaft hub nut. **Do not tighten now.**
8. Place upper ball joint stud through hole in top of knuckle and install nut.
9. Tighten nut by holding ball joint stud with suitable hex wrench while turning nut with wrench. Tighten nut using crow foot wrench on torque wrench.
10. Clean hub face to remove dirt or corrosion where rotor mounts.
11. Install brake rotor over studs on hub and bearing.
12. Install disc brake caliper and adapter over brake rotor.
13. Install and tighten caliper adapter to knuckle mounting bolts.
14. Pull lower end of shock outward, then slide clevis bracket onto lower end.
15. Slide clevis bracket onto shock until bracket contacts collar on shock housing.
16. Install clevis bracket to bottom of shock pinch bolt and nut. Install pinch bolt from rear. **Do not tighten now.**
17. Slide clevis bracket over bushing mounted in lower control arm.
18. Install shock clevis bracket to lower control arm bolt and nut. **Do not tighten now.**
19. Slide stabilizer link ball joint stem into clevis bracket.
20. Install link to clevis bracket nut.
21. Tighten ball joint stud turning nut using crow foot wrench on torque wrench.
22. Attach wheel speed sensor cable routing clip at knuckle.
23. Install hub nut on end of axle half shaft.
24. While helper applies brakes to keep hub from turning tighten hub nut.
25. Install tire and wheel assembly.
26. Lower vehicle.
27. Tighten lower shock clevis bracket bolt nut. **When tightening lower shock**

clevis mounting bolt, do not attempt rotating bolt. Bolt shaft is serrated. Turn nut only.

DRIVESHAFT SERVICE
CV Boot
INNER
REMOVAL

1. Remove large boot clamp which retains inner tripod joint sealing boot to tripod joint housing and discard.
2. Remove small clamp which retains inner tripod joint sealing boot to interconnecting shaft and discard.
3. Remove the sealing boot from the tripod housing and slide it down interconnecting shaft.
4. Slide tripod joint housing off spider assembly and interconnecting shaft. Hold bearings in place on spider trunions.
5. Remove snap ring which retains spider assembly to interconnecting shaft.
6. Remove spider from interconnecting shaft. If spider will not come off interconnecting shaft by hand, remove it by tapping spider with suitable brass drift. **Do not hit outer tripod bearings.**
7. Slide sealing boot off interconnecting shaft.

INSTALLATION

1. Slide inner tripod joint seal boot retaining clamp, onto interconnecting shaft.
2. Slide replacement inner tripod joint sealing boot onto interconnecting shaft. Inner tripod joint seal boot must be positioned on interconnecting shaft, so raised bead on inside of seal boot is in groove on interconnecting shaft.
3. Install spider assembly onto interconnecting shaft. Spider must be installed on interconnecting shaft far enough to fully install spider retaining snap ring.
4. If spider will not fully install on interconnecting shaft by hand, it can be installed by tapping spider body with suitable brass drift. **Do not hit the outer tripod bearings.**
5. Install spider assembly to interconnecting shaft retaining snap ring into groove on end of interconnecting shaft. Ensure snap ring is fully seated into groove on interconnecting shaft.
6. Distribute half grease provided in seal boot service package into tripod housing. **Do not use any other type of grease.**
7. Put remaining amount into sealing boot.
8. Align tripod housing with spider, then slide tripod housing over spider and interconnecting shaft.
9. Install inner tripod joint seal boot to interconnecting shaft clamp evenly on sealing boot.
10. Place crimping tool C-4975-A, or equivalent, over bridge of clamp and tighten nut until tool jaws are closed, face to face.
11. **Seal must not be dimpled, stretched or out of shape.** If seal is not shaped

correctly, equalize pressure in seal and shape it by hand.
12. Position sealing boot into tripod housing retaining groove.
13. Install seal boot retaining clamp evenly on sealing boot.
14. **Do not puncture or damage sealing boot.**
15. Insert suitable trim stick between tripod joint and sealing boot to vent inner tripod joint. Ensure trim stick is held flat and firmly against tripod housing. If inner tripod joint has Hytrel (hard plastic) sealing boot, ensure trim stick is inserted between soft rubber insert and tripod housing not hard plastic sealing boot and soft rubber insert.
16. Position interconnecting shaft so it is at center of its travel in tripod joint housing
17. Remove trim stick from between sealing boot and tripod joint housing to equalize air pressure in tripod joint.
18. Position trilobal boot to interface with tripod housing. Boot lobes must be properly aligned with recess's of tripod housing.
19. **On models equipped with crimp type boot clamp,** place crimping tool C-4975-A, or equivalent, over bridge of clamp and tighten nut until tool jaws are closed, face to face.
20. **On models equipped with latching type boot clamp,** proceed as follows:
    a. Place prongs of Snap-On clamp locking tool No. YA3050, or equivalent, in clamp holes.
    b. Squeeze tool together until top band of clamp is latched behind two tabs on lower band.

OUTER
REMOVAL

1. Remove large boot clamp retaining C/V joint sealing boot to C/V joint housing and discard.
2. Remove small clamp that retains outer C/V joint sealing boot to interconnecting shaft and discard.
3. Remove sealing boot from outer C/V joint housing and slide it down interconnecting shaft.
4. Wipe away grease to expose outer C/V joint and interconnecting shaft.
5. Support interconnecting shaft in suitable vise equipped with protective caps on jaws.
6. Sharply hit end of C/V joint housing to dislodge housing from internal circlip on interconnecting shaft using suitable, soft-faced hammer.
7. Slide outer C/V joint off end of interconnecting shaft. Joint may have to be tapped off shaft using suitable, soft-faced hammer.
8. Remove large circlip from interconnecting shaft.
9. Slide sealing boot off interconnecting shaft.

INSTALLATION

1. Slide new sealing boot to interconnecting shaft retaining clamp onto interconnecting shaft.
2. Slide outer C/V joint sealing boot onto

interconnecting shaft.

3. Seal boot be positioned on interconnecting shaft so raised bead on inside of seal boot is in groove on interconnecting shaft.

4. Align splines on interconnecting shaft with splines on cross of outer C/V joint assembly and start outer C/V joint onto interconnecting shaft.

5. Install outer C/V joint onto interconnecting shaft by using suitable, soft-faced hammer and tapping end of stub axle with nut installed until outer C/V joint is fully seated on interconnecting shaft.

6. Outer C/V joint must be installed on interconnecting shaft until cross of outer C/V joint is seated against circlip on interconnecting shaft.

7. Distribute half of grease provided in seal boot service package into outer C/V joint assembly housing. **Do not use any other type of grease**

8. Put remaining grease into sealing boot.

9. Install outer C/V joint sealing boot to interconnecting shaft clamp evenly on sealing boot.

10. Place crimping tool C-4975-A, or equivalent, over bridge of clamp and tighten nut until tool jaws are closed, face to face.

11. **Seal must not be dimpled, stretched, or out-of-shape.** If seal is not shaped correctly, equalize pressure in seal and shape it by hand.

12. Position outer C/V joint sealing boot into its retaining groove on outer C/V joint housing.

13. Install sealing boot to outer C/V joint retaining clamp evenly on sealing boot.

14. Clamp sealing boot onto outer C/V joint housing using crimper tool.

15. Place tool over bridge of clamp and tighten nut until jaws are closed completely.

INTERMEDIATE SHAFT

REPLACE

1. Remove lefthand halfshaft as outlined under "Driveshaft, Replace."

2. Remove four intermediate shaft assembly-to-oil pan mounting bolts.

3. Remove intermediate shaft.

4. Reverse procedure to install. **Torque** intermediate shaft-to-oil pan bolts to 18 ft. lbs.

INTERMEDIATE SHAFT SERVICE

The intermediate shaft assembly is serviced only as an assembly.

TIGHTENING SPECIFICATIONS

Year	Component	Torque Ft. Lbs.
2005	Caliper Adapter To Knuckle	125
	Clevis Bracket To Shock	45
	Hub Nut	157
	Intermediate Shaft-To-Oil Pan	18
	Lower Shock Clevis Bracket	128
	Stabilizer Link Ball Joint	108
	Upper Ball Joint Stud	35①
	Wheel Lug Nut	110

① — Final tighten an additional 90°.

ENGINE REBUILDING SPECIFICATIONS

NOTE: For Engine Tightening Specifications, Refer To The Engine Section In The Appropriate Chassis Chapter Of This Manual.

INDEX

CYLINDER HEAD, VALVE GUIDE & VALVE SEATS

All measurements given in inches, unless otherwise specified.

Engine Liter	Year	Cylinder Head Warpage Limit①	Cylinder Head Overall Thickness②	Valve Guides (Standard) Inside Diameter	Stem To Guide Clearance Intake	Exhaust	Valve Seats Angle, Degrees	Width Intake	Exhaust	Runout
2.0L DOHC	2001	.004	—	.235–.236	.0018–.0030	.0736–.0040	44.5–45.0	.035–.079	.035–.098	.002
2.0L SOHC	2001–05	.004		.2350–.2360	.0018–.0030	.0029–.0040	44.5–45.0	.035–.079	.035–.098	.002
2.4L DOHC	2001–05	.004		.2350–.2360	.0018–.0030	.0029–.0040	44.5–45.0	.035–.079	.035–.098	.002
2.4L SOHC	2001–05	.007	4.70	.2400	.0008–.0030	.0012–.0050	45.0–45.5	.040–.050	.040–.050	—
2.7L DOHC	2001–04	.008	—	.2353–.2363	.0009–.0114	.0020–.0146	45.0–45.5	.0394–.0591	.0492–.0689	.002
3.0L SOHC	2001–05	.007	4.70	.3200	.0008–.0030	.0016–.0050	45.0–45.5	.040–.050	.049–.069	—
3.2L SOHC 18-Valve	2004–05	.008	—	—	—	—	45.0	1.220–1.221	1.378–1.379	—
3.2L SOHC 24-Valve	2001	.008		.2746–.2756	.0009–.0026	.0020–.0037	45.0–45.5	.0295–.0492	.0492–.0689	.002
3.5L SOHC	2001–05	.008		.2746–.2756	.0009–.0114	.0020–.0146	45.0–45.5	.0295–.0492	.0492–.0689	.002
5.7L	2005	.002	—	.313–.314	.008–.0025	.0019–.0037	44.5–45.0	.0464–.0637	.0582–.0755	.0019

DOHC — Dual Overhead Cam
SOHC — Single Overhead Cam
① — Measurement is a combined total dimension of stock removal limit from cylinder head and block surface (deck) together.
② — Overall thickness, less warpage limit.

VALVE SPRINGS

All measurements given in inches, unless otherwise specified.

Engine	Year	Free Length Intake	Exhaust	Installed Height	Spring Pressure, Lbs. @ Inches Intake	Exhaust	Maximum Straightness Deviation
2.0L DOHC	2001	1.940	1.940	1.453–1.532	66.0–74.0 @ 1.496	66.0–74.0 @ 1.496	—
2.0L SOHC	2001–05	①	①	1.580	②	②	—
2.4L DOHC	2001–05	1.943	1.943	1.496	70 @ 1.496	70 @ 1.496	—
2.4L SOHC	2001–05	1.960–2.000	1.960–2.000	1.740	60 @ 1.74	60 @ 1.74	4°
2.7L DOHC	2001–04	1.7965	1.7965	1.4961	56–64 @ 1.4961	56–64 @ 1.4961	—
3.0L SOHC	2001–05	1.970–2.010	1.970–2.010	1.740	60 @ 1.74	60 @ 1.74	4°
3.2L SOHC 18-Valve	2004–05	—	—	—	—	—	—

Continued

VALVE SPRINGS—Continued
All measurements given in inches, unless otherwise specified.

Engine	Year	Free Length		Installed Height	Spring Pressure, Lbs. @ Inches		Maximum Straightness Deviation
		Intake	Exhaust		Intake	Exhaust	
3.2L SOHC 24-Valve	2001	1.7195	1.7448	1.4961	69.5–80.5 @ 1.4961	71.0–79.0 @ 1.4961	—
3.5L SOHC	2001–05	1.7195	1.7448	1.4961	19.5–80.5 @ 1.4961	71.0–79.0 @ 1.4961	—
5.7L	2005	2.256	2.256	1.81	86–100 @ 1.811	86–100 @ 1.811	—

DOHC — Dual Overhead Cam

SOHC — Single Overhead Cam

① — Standard engine, 1.84 inches; High Output R/T engine, 2.13 inches.

② — Standard engine, 70 lbs. @ 1.57 inches; High Output R/T engine, 72 lbs. @ 1.57 inches

VALVES
All measurements given in inches, unless otherwise specified.

Engine	Year	Stem Diameter		Clearance		Stem Tip Height		Maximum Tip Refinish	Face Angle, Degrees	Margin (Minimum)	
		Intake	Exhaust	Intake	Exhaust	Intake	Exhaust			Intake	Exhaust
2.0L DOHC	2001	.2337–.2344	.2326–.2333	—	—	1.891	1.889	—	44.5–45.0	.047–.066	.038–051
2.0L SOHC	2001–05	.2337–.2344	.2326–.2333	.046	.050	1.76–1.80	1.71–1.75	—	45.0	.038–.058	.042–.071
2.4L DOHC	2001–05	.2337–.2344	.2326–.2333	—	—	1.891	1.889	—	44.5–45.0	.047–.066	.038–.051
2.4L SOHC	2001–05	.2400	.2300	—	—	1.941–1.960	1.941–1.960	—	45.0–45.5	.040–.050	.040–.050
2.7L DOHC	2001–04	.2337–.2344	.2326–.2333	—	—	1.8326–1.85694	1.91436–1.91804	—	44.5–45.0	—	—
3.0L SOHC	2001–05	.2400	.2400	.0008–.0030	.0016–.0050	1.941–1.960	1.941–1.960	—	45.0–45.5	.020–.040	.030–.050
3.2L SOHC 18-Valve	2004–05	.2740	.2740	.0009–.0025	.0020–.0037	—	—	—	45.0	.047	.062
3.2L SOHC 24-Valve	2001	.2730–.2737	.2719–.2726	—	—	1.6680–1.7187	1.7600–1.8105	—	44.5–45.0	—	—
3.5L SOHC	2001–05	.2730–.2737	.2719–.2726	—	—	1.6680–1.7187	1.7600–1.8105	—	44.5–45.0	.0329–.0459	0.567–.0697
5.7L	2005	.312–.313	.311–.312	—	—	—	—	—	45.0–45.5	—	—

DOHC — Dual Overhead Cam.

SOHC — Single Overhead Cam.

CAMSHAFT
All measurements given in inches, unless otherwise specified.

Engine	Year	Camshaft Journal Diameter	Camshaft Bearing Clearance	Camshaft Endplay	Lifter Bore Diameter	Lifter Diameter	Lifter To Bore Clearance
2.0L DOHC	2001	1.021–1.022	.0027–.006	.002–.006	—	.6206–.6264	—
2.0L SOHC	2001–05	①	.0021–.0047	.0020–.0150	—	—	—
2.4L DOHC	2001–05	1.0220–1.0230	.0009–.0025	.0019–.0066	—	—	—
2.4L SOHC	2001–05	1.8000	—	—	—	—	—
2.7L DOHC	2001–04	.9449–.9441	.0020–.0051	.0051–.0110	—	—	—
3.0L SOHC	2001–05	1.8000	—	—	—	—	—
3.2L SOHC 18-Valve	2004–05	—	—	—	—	—	—
3.2L SOHC 24-Valve	2001	1.6905–1.6913	.0030–.0059	.0040–.0140	—	—	—
3.5L SOHC	2001–05	1.6905–1.6913	.0030–.0059	.0040–.0140	—	—	—
5.7L	2005	②	③	.0031–.0114	—	.8420–.8427	.0007–.0024

DOHC — Dual Overhead Cam

SOHC — Single Overhead Cam

① — Journal No. 1, 1.6190–1.6199 inches; No. 2, 1.634–1.635 inches; No. 3, 1.650–1.651 inches; No. 4,

1.666–1.668 inches; No. 5, 1.6820–1.6829 inches.

② — Journal No. 1, 2.29 inches; No. 2 2.27 inches; No. 3, 2.26 inches; No. 4, 2.24 inches; No. 5 1.72 inches.

③ — Journals Nos. 1, 3 & 5, .0015–.0030 inches; Journals Nos. 2 and 4, .0019–.0035 inch.

CRANKSHAFT, BEARINGS & RODS

All measurements given in inches, unless otherwise specified.

| Engine | Year | Crankshaft | | | | Bearing Clearance | | Connecting Rods | | Crank-shaft Endplay |
		Main Bearing Journal Diameter	Connecting Rod Journal Diameter	Max. Out Of Round	Max. Taper	Main Bearings	Con-necting Rod Bearings	Pin Bore Diameter	Side Clear-ance	
2.0L DOHC	2001	2.0469–2.0475	1.8894–1.8900	.0001	.0001	.0008–.0024	.0010–.0023	.8252–.8260	.005–.015	.0035–.0150
2.0L SOHC	2001–05	2.0469–2.0475	1.8894–1.8900	.0001	.0001	.0008–.0024	.0010–.0023	.8252–.8260	.0050–.0150	.0035–.0150
2.4L DOHC	2001–05	2.3620–2.3625	1.9680–1.9685	.0003	.0001	.0007–.0024	.0009–.0027	.8264–.8267	.0051–.0160	.0035–.0150
2.4L SOHC	2001–05	2.2400	1.7700	—	—	.0008–.0030	.0004–.0150	—	.0040–.0150	.0020–.0150
2.7L DOHC	2001–04	2.4997–2.5004	2.1067–2.1060	.0006	.0006	.0014–.0034	.0010–.0026	.8665–.8668	.0052–.0170	.0019–.0170
3.0L SOHC	2001–05	2.4000	2.000	—	—	.0008–.0030	.0008–.0030	—	—	.002–.0100
3.2L SOHC 18-Valve	2004–05	—	—	.0006	.0006	.0030–.0100	.0030–.0100	—	—	—
3.2L SOHC 24-Valve	2001	2.519–2.520	2.283–2.284	.0006	.0006	.0007–.0034	.00075–.00340	.9452–.9455	—	.004–.017
3.5L SOHC	2001–05	2.519–2.520	2.283–2.284	.0006	.0006	.0007–.0034	.00075–.00340	.9452–.9455	.0153	.0040–.0170
5.7L	2005	2.5585–2.5595	2.125–2.126	.0002	.0001	.0009–.0020	.0007–.0023	.9431–.9438	.0030–.0137	.011

DOHC — Dual Overhead Cam.   SOHC — Single Overhead Cam.

PISTONS, PINS & RINGS

All measurements given in inches, unless otherwise specified.

| Engine | Year | Piston Diame-ter (Std.) | Piston Clear-ance | Piston Pin Di-ameter | Piston Pin To Piston Clearance | Piston Ring End Gap (Minimum) | | | Piston Ring Side Clearance | | |
| | | | | | | Compression | | Oil | Compression | | Oil |
						Top	2nd		Top	2nd	
2.0L DOHC	2001	3.4434–3.441	.0007–.0020④	.8267–.8269	.0003–.0008	.0090–.0310	.0190–.0310	.0090–.0390	.0010–.0040	.0010–.0040	.0002–.0070
2.0L SOHC	2001–05	3.4432–3.4439	.0008–.0020②	.8268–.8269	.0003–.0006	.0900–.0310	.0190–.0390	.0090–.0390	.0010–.0040	.0010–.0040	.0002–.0070
2.4L DOHC	2001–05	3.4424–3.4431	.0009–.0022①	.8660–.8661	.0002–.0007	.0078–.0310	.007–.0310	.005–.0390	.001–.004	.001–.004	.001–.006
2.4L SOHC	2001–05	3.4000	.0008–.0015	.8700	.0008–.0030	.0100–.0300	.0160–.0300	.0040–.0300	.0008–.0030	.0012–.0030	—
2.7L DOHC	2001–04	3.3345–3.3868	.0003–.0016	.8661–.8662	.0002–.0005	.0080–.0140	.0146–.0240	.0100–.0300	.0013–.0032	.0016–.0031	.0022–.0080
3.0L SOHC	2001–05	3.5800	.0008–.0015	.8700	—	.0120–.0030	.0180–.0300	.0080–.0300	.0012–.0030	.0080–.0030	—
3.2L SOHC 18-Valve	2004–05	3.538–3.539	.0003–.0018	—	—	.0070–.0130	.0070–.0150	—	.0016–.0031	.0016–.0031	.0015–.0073
3.2L SOHC 24-Valve	2001	3.6205–3.6221	.0003–.0018	.9448–.9449	.0002–.0006	.0080–.0140	.0087–.0193	.0100–.0300	.0016–.0031	.0016–.0031	.0015–.0073
3.5L SOHC	2001–05	3.7780–3.7796	.0000–.0018	.9448–.9449	.0002–.0006	.0080–.0140	.0091–.0197	.0100–.0300	.0016–.0031	.0016–.0031	.0015–.0073

Continued

PISTONS, PINS & RINGS—Continued

All measurements given in inches, unless otherwise specified.

Engine	Year	Piston Diameter (Std.)	Piston Clearance	Piston Pin Diameter	Piston Pin To Piston Clearance	Piston Ring End Gap (Minimum)			Piston Ring Side Clearance		
						Compression		Oil	Compression		Oil
						Top	2nd		Top	2nd	
5.7L	2005	—	.0008–.0019③	.9448–.9449	.00035–.00070	.0090.0149	.0137–.0236	.0059–.0259	.0007–.0026	.0007–.0026	.0007–.0091

DOHC — Dual Overhead Cam
SOHC — Single Overhead Cam
① — Measured at .866 inch from bottom of skirt.

② — Measured at .42 inch from bottom of skirt.
③ — Measure 1.5 inches below deck.

④ — Measure .6875 inch from bottom of skirt

CYLINDER BLOCK

All measurements given in inches, unless otherwise specified.

Engine	Year	Cylinder Bore Diameter (Std.)	Cylinder Bore Taper (Max.)	Cylinder Bore Out Of Round (Max.)
2.0L DOHC	2001	3.4446–3.4452	.002	.002
2.0L SOHC	2001–05	3.4446–3.4452	.002	.002
2.4L DOHC	2001–05	3.4446–3.4452	.002	.002
2.4L SOHC	2001–05	3.4100–3.4110	.0003	.00003
2.7L DOHC	2001–04	3.3856–3.3862	.002	.003
3.0L SOHC	2001–05	3.5900–3.5910	.0003	.0003
3.2L SOHC 18-Valve	2004–05	3.5390–3.5400	.011	.005
3.2L SOHC 24-Valve	2001	3.6217–3.6223	.002	.003
3.5L SOHC	2001–05	3.7797–3.7803	.002	.003
5.7L	2005	3.917	.0005	.0003

DOHC — Dual Overhead Cam   SOHC — Single Overhead Cam

OIL PUMP

All measurements given in inches, unless otherwise specified.

Engine	Year	Rotor Backlash	Rotor To Body Clearance②	Rotor Endplay①	Rotor Thickness (Minimum)		Outer Rotor Diameter (Minimum)	Maximum Cover Flatness Variation	Relief Spring Free Length	Relief Spring Pressure, Lbs. @ Inches
					Inner	Outer				
2.0L DOHC	2001	.008	.004	.0040	.301	.301	3.148	.003	—	—
2.0L SOHC	2001–05	.008	.004	.0040	.301†	.301	3.148	.003	2.390	18.0–19.0 @ 1.600
2.4L DOHC	2001–05	.0080	.004	.0040	.421	.421	3.383	.001	—	—
2.4L SOHC	2001–05	—	③	—	—	—	—	—	—	—
2.7L DOHC	2001–04	.0080	.0030	—	.3731–.3741	.3731–.3741	3.5109	.001	—	—
3.0L SOHC	2001–05	.0030–.0070	.0040–.0130	.0020–.0030	—	—	—	—	—	—
3.2L SOHC 18-Valve	2004–05	—	—	—	—	—	—	—	—	—
3.2L SOHC 24-Valve	2001	.0080	.0150	.0030	.563	.563	3.149	.001	—	—
3.5L SOHC	2001–05	.003	.0150	.0030	.563	.563	3.149	.001	—	—
5.7L	2005	.006	.0038	.009	—	—	—	—	—	—

DOHC — Dual Overhead Cam
SOHC — Single Overhead Cam
① — Measured between pump cover

mounting surface & end of gear using straightedge & feeler gauge.
② — Maximum inner & outer rotor tip clearance.

③ — Drive gear, .004–.006 inch. Driven gear, .003–.004 inch.

FORD MOTOR COMPANY

FORD MOTOR COMPANY

COUGAR

INDEX OF SERVICE OPERATIONS

COUGAR

Specifications

GENERAL ENGINE SPECIFICATIONS

Year	Engine Liter (Code) ①	Fuel System	Bore & Stroke, Inches	Compression Ratio	Net HP @ RPM	Maximum Torque, Ft. Lbs. @ RPM	Normal Oil Pressure, psi
2001–02	2.0L (3)	SEFI	3.34 X 3.46	9.6	125 @ 5500	130 @ 4000	35–65
	2.5L (L)	SEFI	3.24 X 3.13	9.7	170 @ 6250	165 @ 4250	20–45

SEFI — Sequential Electronic Fuel Injection

① — Eighth digit of Vehicle Identifications Number (VIN) denotes engine code.

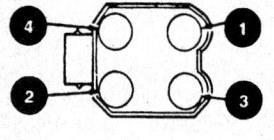

FIRING ORDER:
1- 3- 4- 2

FM1139500409000X

Fig. A

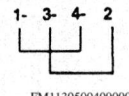

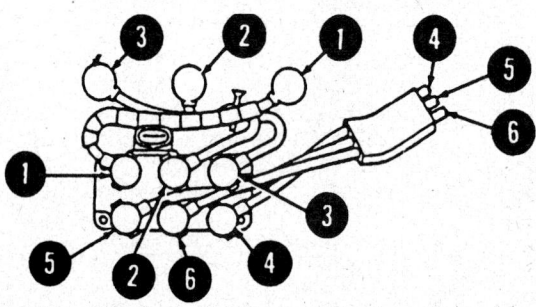

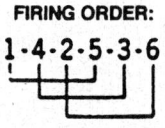

FIRING ORDER:
1-4-2-5-3-6

FM1139500410000X

Fig. B

TUNE UP SPECIFICATIONS

Engine (Code)③	Spark Plug Gap, Inch	Ignition Timing; °BTDC			Curb Idle Speed⑦		Fast Idle Speed⑦		Fuel Pump Pressure, psi ②	Valve Clearance, Inch
		Firing Order Fig.①	Man. Trans.	Auto Trans.	Mark Fig.	Man. Trans.	Auto Trans.	Man. Trans.	Auto Trans.		

Engine (Code)③	Spark Plug Gap, Inch	Firing Order Fig.①	Man. Trans.	Auto Trans.	Mark Fig.	Man. Trans.	Auto Trans.	Man. Trans.	Auto Trans.	Fuel Pump Pressure, psi ②	Valve Clearance, Inch
2001–02											
2.0L (3)	.052	A	⑧	⑧	④	⑤	⑤	⑤	⑤	35–60	⑨
2.5L (L, G)	.052	B	⑧	⑧	④	⑤	⑤	⑤	⑤	35–60	⑥

BTDC — Before Top Dead Center

① — Before disconnecting wires from distributor coil unit, determine location of ignition wires, as position may have been altered from that outlined at end of this chart.

② — Wrap shop towel around diagnostic valve to prevent fuel spillage. Connect suitable fuel pressure gauge to fuel diagnostic valve. Place ignition switch in On position to energize fuel pump & inspect pressure gauge reading.

③ — Eighth digit of Vehicle Identification Number (VIN) denotes engine code.

④ — Equipped w/crankshaft position sensor.

⑤ — Controlled by Idle air control valve.

⑥ — Valve clearance is hydraulically controlled, no adjustment is required.

⑦ — When adjusting idle speed, set parking brake & chock drive wheels.

⑧ — Non-adjustable.

⑨ — Intake, .0043–.0071 inch; exhaust, .0106–.0134 inch.

FRONT WHEEL ALIGNMENT SPECIFICATIONS

Model	Caster Angle, Degrees		Camber Angle, Degrees		Total Toe, Inch①		Toe-Out On Turns, Degrees		Ball Joint Wear, Inch
	Limits	Desired	Limits	Desired	Limits	Desired	Outer Wheel	Inner Wheel	
2001–02									
Cougar	+1.52 to +3.52	+2.52	-2.11 to +.890	-.61	-.09 to +..09	0	—	—	②

① — Toe-in (+), toe-out (-).

② — Refer to "Ball Joint Inspection," in "Front Suspension & Steering" section, for inspection procedure.

REAR WHEEL ALIGNMENT SPECIFICATIONS

Model	Camber Angle, Degrees		Total Toe, Inches①	
	Limits	Desired	Limits	Desired
2001–02				
Cougar	-2.20 to +.80	-.70	+.06 to +.26	+.16

① — Toe-in (+), toe-out (-).

VEHICLE RIDE HEIGHT

Model	Body Style	Manufacturer's Original Tire Size	Measurement Points & Specifications②					
			Front			Rear		
			Dim.	Specification		Dim.	Specification	
				Inches	mm		Inches	mm
Cougar	All	①	A	7.21	183	B	7.18	156

A Dim. — Distance from Front Rocker Panel to Ground

B Dim. — Distance from Rear Rocker Panel to Ground

Dim. — Dimension

① — See door sticker or inside of glove box for manufacturers original tire size specifications. If tires on vehicle do not match manufacturers original tire size & measurement is not within limits, it will be required to refer to the "Non-Standard Tire & Wheel Size Adjustment To Ride Height Specification & Tire Size Adjustment Charts" in the front of this manual for approximate changes in ride height specifications.

② — Measurement is w/fuel, radiator coolant & engine oil full, spare tire, jack, hand tools & mats in designated positions & tires properly inflated.

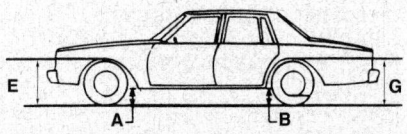

CRQ166

Fig. A   Dimensions A, B, E & G

FLUID CAPACITIES & COOLING SYSTEM DATA

Year	Engine	Coolant Capacity, Qts.		Coolant Type	Radiator Cap Relief Pressure, Lbs.	Thermo Opening Temp., Deg. F	Fuel Tank, Gals.	Engine Oil Refill, Qts.②	Transaxle Oil	
		Automatic Trans.	Manual Trans.						Manual Trans., Pts.	Automatic Trans., Qts.①
2001–02	2.0L	7	7	EG	13–18	187–194	15.5	4.5	5.4	4.0
	2.5L	10.2	10	EG	13–18	183–190	15.5	5.8	5.4	4.0

EG — Ethylene Glycol ① — Approximate. Make final inspect w/dipstick. ② — Includes filter.

LUBRICANT DATA

Year	Model	Lubricant Type				
		Transaxle		Hydraulic Clutch Fluid	Power Steering	Brake System
		Manual	Automatic			
2001–02	All	Mercon XT-M5-QS	Mercon	DOT 3	Mercon	DOT 3

Electrical

NOTE: On Air Bag Equipped Models, Refer To "Air Bag System Precautions" Located In The Front Of This Manual For System Disarming & Arming Procedures.

NOTE: Refer To "Computer Relearn Procedures" Located In The Front Of This Manual When Battery Power To The Computer Has Been Interrupted.

INDEX

PRECAUTIONS

Battery Ground Cable

Prior to service, disconnect battery ground cable and isolate as required.

Air Bag Systems

Refer to "Air Bag System Precautions" in front of this manual for system disarming and arming procedures.

Fuel Pressure Relief

1. Remove air cleaner outlet tube.
2. Remove Schrader valve cap.
3. Connect fuel pressure gauge tool No. T80L-9974-B, or equivalent, to Schrader valve.
4. When relieving fuel pressure, catch any displaced fuel in suitable container. Turn tap on fuel pressure gauge fully counterclockwise to relieve fuel pressure.

FUSE PANEL & FLASHER LOCATION

Fuse junction panel is located to left of steering column and is attached to instrument panel

Indicator flasher is located at turn and emergency warning indicator switch at steering column tube.

FUEL PUMP RELAY LOCATION

Fuel pump relay is located in front lefthand corner of engine compartment, in engine compartment fuse box.

RELAY CENTER LOCATION

Relays are contained in power distribution box, located in engine compartment on lefthand fender apron.

STARTER
REPLACE

2.0L Engine

1. Remove air cleaner.
2. Remove starter motor upper mounting bolts.
3. Cut cable ties, then raise and support vehicle.
4. Disconnect starter motor electrical connectors.
5. Remove starter motor.
6. Reverse procedure to install. **Torque** starter motor bolts to 15–20 ft. lbs.

2.5L Engine

1. Drain cooling system into suitable container.
2. Remove lower intake manifold as out-

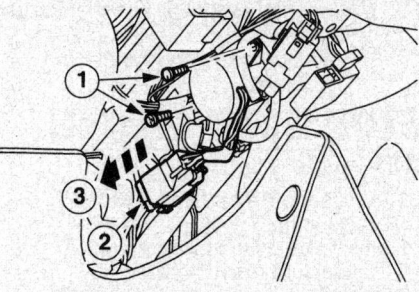

Fig. 1   Ignition switch replacement

FM9049800063000X

lined under "Intake Manifold, Replace" in "2.5L Engine" section
3. Remove air cleaner and air cleaner bracket.
4. Disconnect starter motor electrical connectors.
5. Remove bracket bolts and disconnect shift cable.
6. Remove starter motor support bracket and Schrader valve cap.
7. Relieve fuel pressure as outlined under "Precautions."
8. Disconnect fuel return and supply lines using fuel line tool No. 310-D005 or 310-D004, or equivalent.
9. Disconnect cooling system hoses from crossover pipe and coolant temperature sensor electrical connector.
10. Remove accelerator cable guide and PCV pipe nut and hose.
11. Remove water crossover pipe, then the mounting bolts and starter motor
12. Reverse procedure to install.

ALTERNATOR
REPLACE

2.0L Engine

1. Disconnect air cleaner outlet pipe.
2. Remove bolts and nuts, then the intake air resonator.
3. Disconnect coolant hose from retaining clip.
4. Remove radiator splash shield.
5. Disconnect cable and wiring from alternator.
6. Disconnect ground cable on eye hook, then raise and support vehicle.
7. Remove radiator splash shield.
8. Remove righthand front wheel, then the mounting bolts and splash shield.
9. Remove accessory drive belt and alternator lower mounting bolts.
10. Lower vehicle and remove alternator upper mounting bolt.
11. Lift alternator clear of engine. **Do not overstress or damage hoses or cables.**
12. Reverse procedure to install. **Torque** alternator bolt to 33 ft. lbs.

2.5L Engine

1. Remove alternator drive belt form alternator pulley.
2. Separate tie rod from wheel knuckle using tie rod separator tool No. 211-001 or equivalent.

3. Remove wheelwell liner.
4. Disconnect alternator electrical connector.
5. Remove rear support bracket bolt, then the alternator upper and lower bolts.
6. Remove alternator through wheel opening.
7. Reverse procedure to install, noting the following:
   a. **Torque** alternator bracket bolts to 18 ft. lbs.
   b. **Torque** alternator bolts to 33 ft. lbs.
   c. **Torque** tie rod end nut to 35 ft. lbs.

COIL PACK
REPLACE

1. Disconnect ignition coil electrical connector and spark plug wires from coil.
2. Remove ignition coil mounting screws.
3. Reverse procedure to install. **Torque** coil mounting screws to 48 inch lbs.

IGNITION LOCK
REPLACE

Non-Functional Lock Cylinder
REMOVAL

Following procedure is for vehicles in which ignition switch lock cylinder is inoperative and ignition switch lock cylinder cannot be rotated because of a lost or broken lock cylinder key, unknown key number or with an ignition switch lock cylinder cap damaged and/or broken to extent key cannot be rotated.

1. Remove mounting screws, then the upper and lower steering column shrouds.
2. Drill out ignition switch lock cylinder pin using ⅛ inch drill.
3. Pull lock cylinder from steering column housing.
4. Inspect housing for damage. If damaged, replace steering column as outlined in "Steering Columns" chapter.

INSTALLATION

1. Thoroughly clean all drill shavings and other foreign materials from steering column housing.
2. Install new lock cylinder by turning it to accessory position and pressing in pin.
3. Insert ignition switch lock cylinder into lock cylinder housing, then turn lock cylinder to OFF position to extend pin into lock cylinder housing hole.
4. Turn lock cylinder, using key, to inspect for proper operation.
5. Install steering column shrouds and mounting screws.
6. Connect battery ground cable.

Functional Lock Cylinder

1. Remove steering column lower shroud.

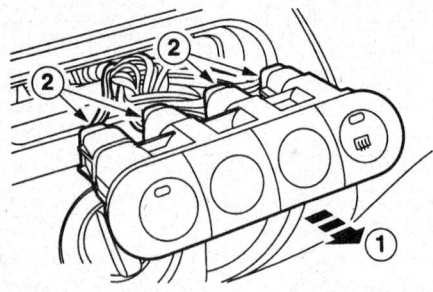

Fig. 2   Center switch replacement

2. Remove anti-theft system transceiver screw and transceiver.
3. Insert and turn key to accessory.
4. Depress retainer and remove ignition switch lock cylinder.
5. Reverse procedure to install.

IGNITION SWITCH
REPLACE

1. Remove mounting screws and steering column shroud.
2. Disconnect ignition switch electrical connector.
3. Remove two mounting screws and ignition switch, **Fig. 1.**
4. Reverse procedure to install.

CLUTCH START SWITCH
REPLACE

1. Disconnect harness connector from clutch pedal position switch.
2. Turn switch approximately 45° and pull switch from bracket.
3. Reverse procedure to install.

TRANSAXLE RANGE (TR) SENSOR
REPLACE

1. Place manual control lever in NEUTRAL position.
2. Remove battery tray and disconnect electrical harness from sensor.
3. Remove two mounting bolts and sensor.
4. Reverse procedure to install, noting following:
   a. Ensure manual control lever is in NEUTRAL position.
   b. Align TR sensor slots using TR sensor tool No. T94P-70010-AH, or equivalent.
   c. **Torque** TR sensor bolts to 84–108 inch lbs.
   d. **Torque** MAF sensor bolts to 25 inch lbs.
   e. **Torque** engine air cleaner tube clamps to 24–48 inch lbs.

HEADLAMP SWITCH
REPLACE

1. Remove instrument panel lower panel.
2. Remove lamp switch panel screws and disconnect instrument panel from clips.

3. Disconnect electrical connectors and remove switch.
4. Reverse procedure to install.

STOP LIGHT SWITCH
REPLACE

1. Disconnect stop lamp switch electrical connector.
2. Remove switch by rotating 90° counterclockwise and pulling toward rear of vehicle.
3. Reverse procedure to install.

MULTI-FUNCTION SWITCH
REPLACE

1. Remove mounting screws and steering column upper shroud.
2. Press locking tab, then slide multi-function switch up and off of steering column.
3. Press locking tabs on multi-function switch electrical connector and remove connector from switch.
4. Reverse procedure to install.

STEERING WHEEL
REPLACE

1. Remove air bag module screws and air bag module.
2. Disconnect air bag wire harness from driver side air bag module and remove module from steering wheel.
3. Center front wheels to straight ahead position and disconnect speed control wire harness from steering wheel.
4. Remove steering wheel bolt.
5. Route air bag sliding contact wire harness through steering wheel opening while lifting steering wheel off shaft.
6. Reverse procedure to install, noting following:
   a. Ensure front wheels are in straight-ahead position.
   b. Ensure steering wheel and steering shaft alignment marks are aligned and air bag contact wire is not pinched.
   c. **Torque** new steering wheel bolt to 37 ft. lbs.
   d. **Torque** air bag module screws to 96–120 inch lbs.

INSTRUMENT CLUSTER
REPLACE

1. Remove ashtray and cigar lighter bezel, then the radio.
2. Remove center switch and disconnect electrical connectors, **Fig. 2.**
3. Remove heater control panel and radio unit bezel.
4. Remove heater control radio unit bezel, then disconnect electrical connectors and vacuum line.
5. Remove instrument panel lower trim panel.
6. Remove lamp switch panel and disconnect electrical connectors.

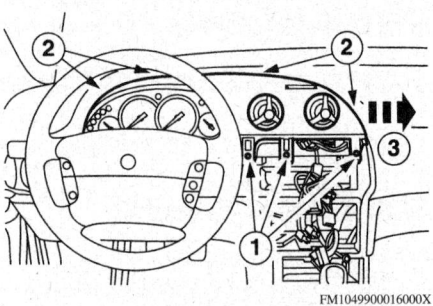

Fig. 3   Instrument cluster bezel replacement

7. Remove instrument cluster bezel screws, release clips and bezel, **Fig. 3.**
8. Pull instrument cluster forward, release locking tangs and disconnect electrical connectors.
9. Remove cluster.
10. Reverse procedure to install.

RADIO
REPLACE

1. Record preset stations.
2. Install radio removing tool No. T87P-19061-A, or equivalent, into radio chassis and push tools in approximately 1 inch to release retaining clips, **Fig. 4. Do not use excessive force when installing radio removing tool.**
3. Apply light spreading force on tools and pull radio chassis out of instrument panel.
4. Disconnect wiring connectors and antenna cable.
5. Reverse procedure to install. Inspect radio chassis operation and set preset radio stations.

WIPER MOTOR
REPLACE

Front

1. Ensure wiper motor is in Park position and remove wiper arms.
2. Remove cowl grille, then the wiper motor and linkage.
3. Mark position of wiper pivot arm in relation to wiper motor mounting bracket, **Fig. 5.**
4. Remove windshield wiper linkage to upper cowl panel bolts, **Fig. 6.**
5. Remove wiper motor nut and bolt from mounting plate and linkage.
6. Disconnect harness from wiper motor.
7. Reverse procedure to install, noting the following:
   a. **Torque** wiper motor mounting plate bolts to 106 inch lbs.
   b. **Torque** wiper motor output arm bolt to 19 ft. lbs.
   c. **Torque** wiper linkage bolts to 72 inch lbs.
   d. **Torque** wiper pivot arm nuts to 18 ft. lbs.
   e. **Torque** wiper motor bolts to 106 inch lbs.

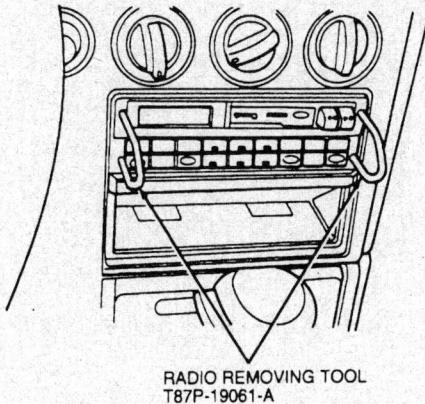

RADIO REMOVING TOOL
T87P-19061-A

FM9039500009000X

Fig. 4 Radio chassis replacement

Rear

1. Open wiper cover and loosen mounting nut.
2. Open liftgate and remove liftgate trim panel.
3. Loosen ground connection and bolts, then disconnect rear wiper motor electrical connector.
4. Remove rear window wiper motor.
5. Reverse procedure to install.

WIPER SWITCH

REPLACE

1. Remove mounting screws and steering column upper shroud.
2. Press locking tab, slide multi-function switch up and off of steering column.
3. Press locking tabs on multi-function switch electrical connector and remove connector from switch.
4. Reverse procedure to install.

BLOWER MOTOR

REPLACE

1. Working from inside vehicle, remove push pins and upper foothill trim panel from passenger side.
2. Disconnect blower motor wire harness electrical connector.
3. Lift retaining lug on air conditioning blower motor flange, **Fig. 7.**
4. Turn blower motor counterclockwise approximately 30° to disconnect it from air conditioning evaporator housing.
5. Pull blower motor out of air conditioning evaporator housing.
6. Reverse procedure to install. Install blower motor into air conditioning evaporator housing and turn clockwise until retaining lug engages.

CABIN AIR FILTER

REPLACE

Under normal operating conditions the cabin air filter should be replaced 15,000 miles. In dusty areas change the cabin air filter more often.

1. Position windshield wipers in Park position.
2. Lift plastic wiper arm mounting nut covers.
3. Remove wiper arm mounting nuts.
4. Lift up wiper arms.
5. Remove wiper arms by moving them from side to side.
6. Open hood.
7. Remove plastic screw covers from cowl grille mounting screws.
8. Remove cowl grille mounting screws, **Fig. 8.**
9. Remove hood rear weather seal.
10. Disconnect cowl grille at rear and remove grille.
11. Remove cabin air filter element from housing, **Fig. 9.**
12. Position new cabin air filter element into filter housing. Ensure filter is firmly seated in housing.
13. Install cowl grille and close hood.
14. Install windshield wiper arms. **Torque** mounting nuts to 18 ft. lbs.

HEATER CORE

REPLACE

1. Drain coolant into suitable container.
2. Raise and support vehicle, then disconnect heater hoses from heater core.
3. Disconnect vacuum line.
4. Lower vehicle.
5. **On models equipped with manual transaxle,** remove gearshift knob, spring, damping sleeve and gearshift lever boot.
6. **On models equipped with armrest,** raise armrest to gain access.
7. **On models equipped less armrest,** remove rear cup holder to gain access.
8. **On all models,** remove ashtray and cigar lighter bezel.
9. Remove stowage tray by pushing down on power socket aperture and pulling out stowage tray.
10. Remove floor console front screws.
11. Fully raise parking brake control lever, then remove console and disconnect cigar lighter/power socket electrical connector.
12. Remove air bag diagnostic monitor and position aside.
13. Disconnect vacuum supply line from vacuum reservoir tank.
14. Remove screws from heater outlet floor duct.
15. Remove heater/evaporator core housing screws, slide air duct upwards, release retaining tabs on each side and remove heater outlet floor duct.
16. Disconnect electrical connector from De-Ice sensor.
17. Remove four retaining clips, cover and heater core.
18. Remove de-ice sensor by pulling out cable and unclipping sensor from heater core.
19. Reverse procedure to install.

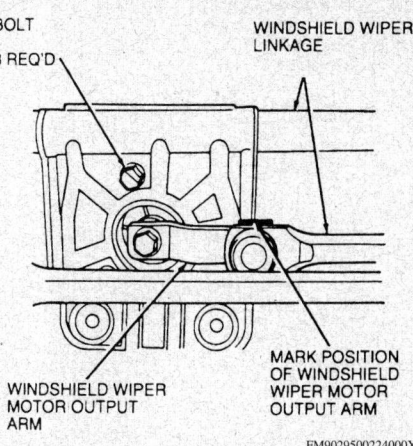

BOLT
3 REQ'D

WINDSHIELD WIPER
LINKAGE

WINDSHIELD WIPER
MOTOR OUTPUT
ARM

MARK POSITION
OF WINDSHIELD
WIPER MOTOR
OUTPUT ARM

FM9029500224000X

Fig. 5 Wiper pivot arm position marking

EVAPORATOR CORE

REPLACE

1. Recover refrigerant from air conditioning system as outlined in "Air Conditioning" chapter.
2. Drain coolant into suitable container.
3. Remove instrument panel as outlined in "Dash Panel Service" chapter.
4. Raise and support vehicle, then disconnect heater hoses from heater core and vacuum line.
5. Lower vehicle and disconnect blower motor and resistor electrical connector.
6. **On models equipped with 2.5L engine,** remove ignition.
7. **On all models,** pull clips off air conditioning lines.
8. Disconnect line to accumulator/drier at evaporator using disconnect tool No. T84L-19623-B, or equivalent. Seal line and evaporator with plugs.
9. Disconnect line from condenser at evaporator using disconnect tool.
10. Remove nut on heater/evaporator core housing.
11. Remove lower defroster air duct screw from heater/evaporator core housing and release retaining tabs.
12. Disconnect left and righthand air hose from heater/evaporator core housing.
13. Disconnect air distributor from heater/air conditioning.
14. Remove heater/evaporator core housing.
15. Separate heater/air conditioning housing.
16. Remove screws at front of heater/air conditioning housing and rubber seal.
17. Remove evaporator nut, unclip vacuum hose and disconnect housing components.
18. Remove evaporator.
19. Reverse procedure to install, noting the following:
    a. Install new rings and coat them with refrigerant oil.
    b. When installing new evaporator, install gaskets as they were on old evaporator.

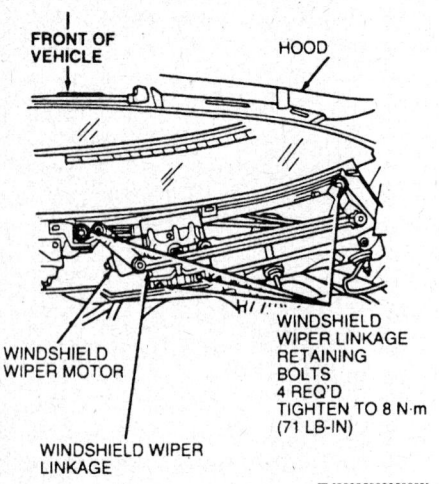

Fig. 6   Wiper linkage replacement

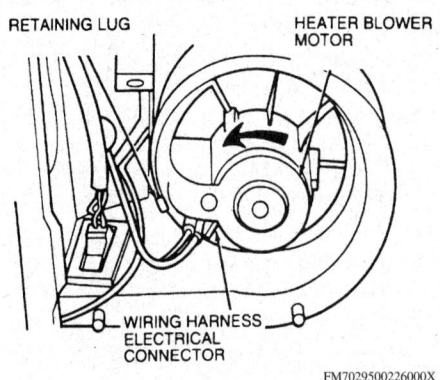

Fig. 7   Blower motor replacement

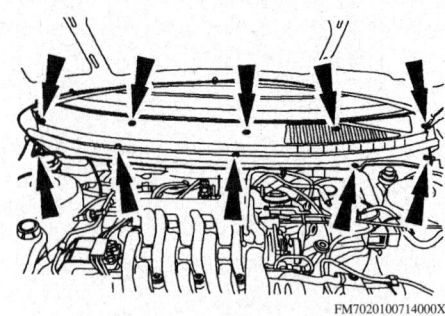

Fig. 8   Cowl grille replacement

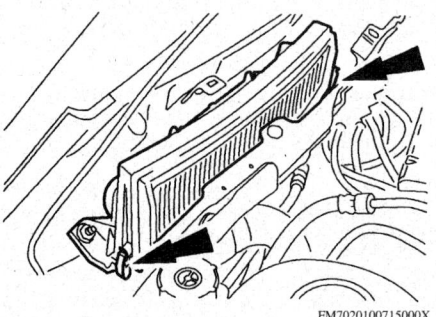

Fig. 9   Cabin air filter replacement

2.0L Engine

NOTE: On Air Bag Equipped Models, Refer To "Air Bag System Precautions" Located In The Front Of This Manual For System Disarming & Arming Procedures.

NOTE: Refer To "Computer Relearn Procedures" Located In The Front Of This Manual When Battery Power To The Computer Has Been Interrupted.

INDEX

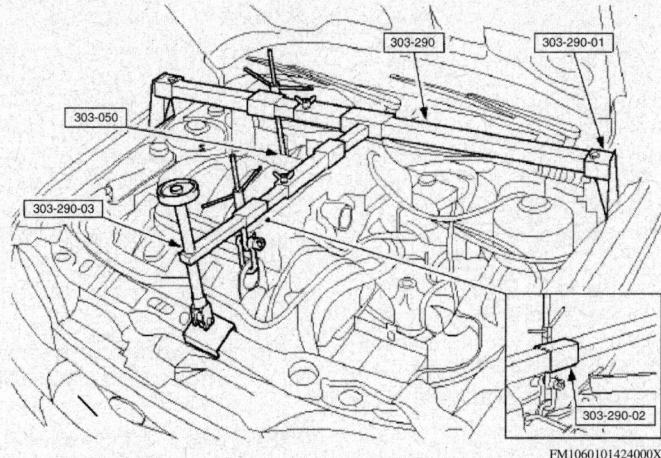

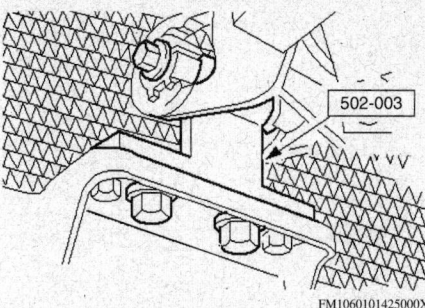

Fig. 2 Powertrain alignment gauge

Fig. 1 Engine mount replacement

PRECAUTIONS

Battery Ground Cable

Prior to service, disconnect battery ground cable and isolate as required.

Air Bag Systems

Refer to "Air Bag System Precautions" in front of this manual for system disarming and arming procedures.

Cooling System

This engine has an aluminum cylinder head and requires a special corrosion inhibiting coolant to avoid cooling system damage. Use only specified coolant in this engine.

Fuel System Pressure Relief

1. Remove engine air intake resonators from air cleaner.
2. Connect Multiport Fuel Injection (MFI) fuel pressure gauge tool No. T80L-9974-B, or equivalent, to fuel pressure relief valve cap on fuel injection supply manifold.
3. Open manual valve on gauge tool to relieve fuel system pressure.

COMPRESSION PRESSURE

Compression pressure should be inspected with engine at normal operating temperature, spark plugs removed and throttle plate wide open. Cylinder compression pressure is considered within specification if lowest reading cylinder is within 75 percent of highest reading and no reading is less than 101 psi.

ENGINE MOUNT
REPLACE
Removal

1. Remove coolant expansion tank hose from clip, bolts and water pump pulley shield.
2. Install engine support bar tool No. 303-290, adapters, tool Nos. 303-290-01, 303-290-02 and 303-290-03 and engine lifting bracket tool no. 303-050, or equivalents, **Fig. 1.**
3. Remove ignition wires and retainer from upper front engine support bracket.
4. Remove power steering pressure line bracket bolt and ground strap.
5. Disconnect power steering pressure line and position it aside.
6. Remove mounting nuts and upper front engine support bracket nuts. **Mark nuts' position on engine support bracket for installation alignment.**
7. Remove bolts and position radiator coolant expansion tank aside.
8. Remove three bolts and upper front engine support insulator.

Installation

1. Raise and support vehicle.
2. Remove through bolt and lefthand front engine support insulator.
3. Replace lefthand engine support insulator with powertrain alignment gauge tool No. 502-003, or equivalent, **Fig. 2.** Tighten through bolt hand tight.
4. Remove righthand engine support insulator through bolt and loosen mounting bolts.
5. Lower vehicle.
6. Install front engine support insulator and radiator coolant expansion tank.
7. Install upper front engine support bracket. **Use new nuts and ensure nuts align with marks on engine support bracket.**
8. Remove three bar engine support and universal lifting eye.
9. Raise and support vehicle.
10. Install righthand engine support insu-

lator bolt. **Ensure righthand engine support insulator is center in transaxle bracket and in front to rear alignment before tightening through bolt.**
11. Remove powertrain alignment gauge, then install lefthand support insulator and through bolt. **Ensure lefthand engine support insulator is centered in transaxle bracket and in front to rear alignment before tightening through bolt.**
12. Lower vehicle, install power steering pressure line to power steering pump.
13. Install ignition wires and retainer to upper front engine support bracket stud.
14. Install water pump pulley shield.

ENGINE
REPLACE
Automatic Transaxle

1. Move selector lever to D position.
2. Raise and support vehicle and remove front wheels.
3. Remove radiator splash shield and brace on both sides.
4. Drain engine coolant into suitable container.
5. Lower vehicle and remove battery.
6. Remove air intake tube, then disconnect mass air flow and intake air temperature sensor connectors.
7. Remove air cleaner and crankcase ventilation hose.
8. Attach condenser core on hood lock panel.
9. Loosen suspension strut locknuts five turns on both sides using suitable Allen key to stop piston rod from turning, Support suspension strut steady.
10. Disconnect engine wiring harness and automatic transaxle ground cable, then remove cable tie.
11. Unclip wiring harness and disconnect transaxle range switch electrical connector.
12. Disconnect crankshaft position sensor and engine coolant temperature sensor electrical connectors.
13. Remove selector cable abutment bracket, unclip selector cable from selector lever and disconnect selector cable.
14. Disconnect throttle cable by pulling out clip and unhooking cable.

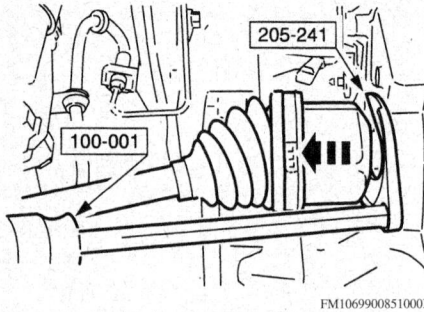

Fig. 3 Halfshaft removal

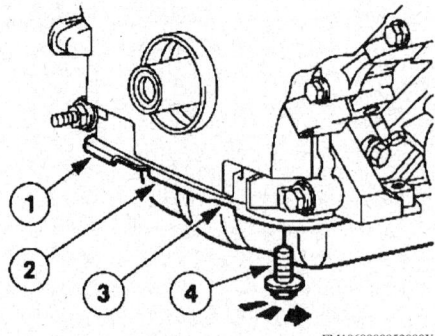

Fig. 4 Manual gear lever alignment tool installation

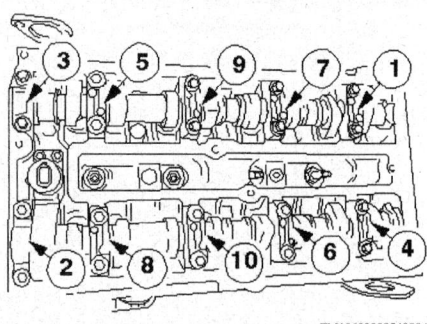

Fig. 5 Camshaft bearing caps loosening sequence

15. Remove upper accessory drive belt cover, then raise and support vehicle.
16. Remove righthand splash shield, then loosen and remove accessory drive belt.
17. Disconnect lower suspension arm ball joints and stabilizer link rods, then the ABS wiring harness bracket from suspension strut. **Do not damage boot and ABS sensor ring.**
18. Disconnect radiator at bottom and both heated oxygen sensor electrical connectors. Cut cable ties.
19. Remove power steering hoses from subframe.
20. Remove mounting bolt and vehicle speed sensor.
21. Disconnect brake booster vacuum line from of intake manifold.
22. Remove righthand engine support insulator bolts and engine support insulator.
23. Remove steering gear heat shield, then the power steering line bracket and coolant line bracket.
24. Remove front exhaust tube and discard gasket.
25. Remove steering gear two bolts using steering gear wrench tool No. T97P-3504-A, or equivalent, and position aside.
26. Raise automatic transaxle slightly with suitable transmission jack to remove lefthand engine support insulator nuts, center bolt and insulator.
27. Remove suction accumulator bolts.
28. Remove subframe. Take out rubber guides from lower radiator supports. Support subframe using suitable powertrain lift.
29. Drain automatic transmission fluid into suitable container and install drain plug.
30. Remove lefthand halfshaft using slide hammer tool No. T50T-100-A and halfshaft remover tool No. T86P-3514-A, or equivalents, **Fig. 3. To avoid damage to halfshaft joints and boots, do not bend inner halfshaft joint more than 18° and outer one no more than 45°.**
31. Disconnect fluid tube and close off openings with suitable plugs.
32. Disconnect turbine shaft speed sensor electrical connector.
33. Remove fluid cooler tube from transaxle.
34. Remove righthand drive halfshaft and intermediate shaft. Position righthand drive halfshaft aside with suitable mechanic's wire.
35. Disconnect coolant hose from heater coolant tube and remove bracket.
36. Disconnect lower coolant hose and lower vehicle.
37. Disconnect two ground cables and hoses from oil cooler.
38. Disconnect fan motor and power steering pressure switch electrical connectors, then remove upper coolant hose.
39. Remove air conditioning tube/hose bracket and power steering line.
40. Remove upper bolts from power steering pump, wiring clamp from fender apron panel and coolant hoses.
41. Raise and support vehicle and disconnect air conditioning compressor electrical connector.
42. Separate radiator from condenser core.
43. Remove air conditioning compressor bolts and position compressor aside with suitable mechanic's wire.
44. Remove power steering pump and position it aside.
45. Disconnect heater coolant hose and lower vehicle.
46. Remove power steering reservoir (push fit) and position it aside.
47. Disconnect main wiring harness from powertrain control module.
48. Disconnect vacuum hoses from intake manifold.
49. Relieve fuel pressure as outlined under "Precautions."
50. Disconnect fuel lines using quick disconnect connect tool Nos. D87L-9280-A or D87L-9280-B, or equivalents.
51. Raise and support vehicle.
52. Lower vehicle and place engine/transaxle on powertrain lift, Secure engine/transaxle with retaining straps.
53. Remove coolant expansion tank and position it aside. Disconnect speed control cable from coolant expansion tank.
54. Remove front engine mounting bracket nuts and loosen bolts two turns.
55. Remove rear engine mounting bracket.
56. Raise vehicle and pull out powertrain lift with engine/automatic transaxle from underneath.
57. Reverse procedure to install.

Manual Transaxle

1. Put gearshift lever into neutral and lock shifter into neutral, using gear lever alignment tool No. T97P-7025-A, or equivalent, **Fig. 4.**
2. Disconnect hose and remove hood bolts and hood.
3. Loosen suspension strut locknut five turns on both sides using suitable Allen key to stop piston rod from turning.
4. Raise and support vehicle, then remove front wheels.
5. Remove radiator splash shield and brackets on both sides.
6. Drain engine coolant into suitable container.
7. Disconnect mass air flow and intake air temperature sensor electrical connectors, then remove air intake tube.
8. Remove crankcase ventilation hose and air hose.
9. Unhook rubber ring and remove air cleaner.
10. Remove battery, loosen central junction box and position it aside.
11. Remove four battery bracket bolts and two ground cables.
12. Remove power steering reservoir (push fit) and position it aside. Disconnect main wiring harness from PCM.
13. Remove ground cable from engine lifting eye and disconnect power steering pressure switch.
14. Disconnect speed control cable from throttle valve, then gently move cable up and down and pull it out of retaining bush. Press retaining bush out of bracket.
15. Disconnect throttle cable by unhooking cable and pulling off plastic clip. Position throttle cable aside.
16. Disconnect vacuum hoses from intake manifold.
17. Remove heat shield and coolant hose brackets, then pull out engine oil dipstick tube.
18. Remove coolant hose from coolant pipe and coolant hose from water pump.
19. Remove three-way catalytic converter from exhaust manifold.
20. Disconnect air conditioning compressor electrical connector.
21. Disconnect engine coolant temperature sensor electrical connector.

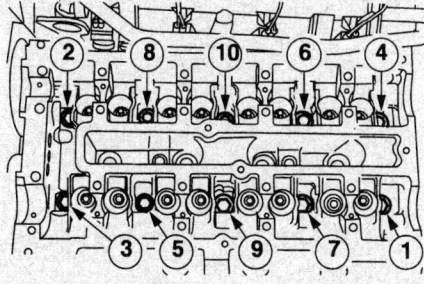

Fig. 6 Cylinder head bolt removal sequence

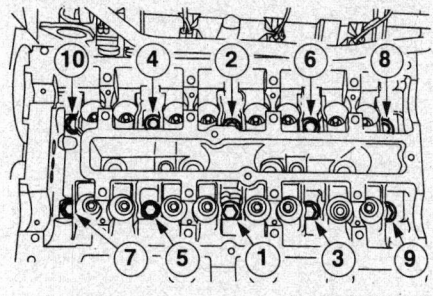

Fig. 7 Cylinder head bolt tightening sequence

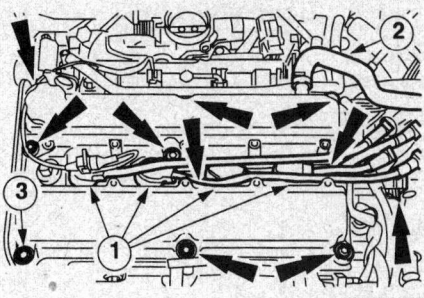

Fig. 8 Valve cover bolt loosening sequence

22. Disconnect fan motor electrical connector and remove upper coolant hoses.
23. Remove clamp from fender apron panel and coolant hoses.
24. Remove upper accessory drive belt cover.
25. Pull out clip and disconnect from slave cylinder.
26. Remove slave cylinder from transaxle and tie it aside.
27. Disconnect ground cable from transaxle.
28. Raise and support vehicle.
29. Remove righthand fender splash shields.
30. Loosen and remove accessory drive belt, then disconnect brake booster vacuum line from intake manifold.
31. Remove radiator brackets and disconnect both Heated Oxygen Sensor (HO2S) electrical connectors. Cut cable ties.
32. Disconnect front exhaust tube and discard gasket.
33. Disconnect lower suspension arm ball joints from wheel knuckles and ABS wiring harness bracket from suspension strut. **Do not damage boot and ABS sensor ring.**
34. **To avoid to damage halfshaft joints and boots, do not bend inner halfshaft joint more than 18° or outer halfshaft no more than 45°.**
35. Remove left and righthand halfshafts using slide hammer tool No. T50T-100-A and halfshaft remover tool No. T86-P3514-A, or equivalents, **Fig. 3.** Secure halfshafts with suitable wire.
36. Remove righthand engine support insulator center bolt and engine support insulator.
37. Remove bracket for righthand engine support insulator from transaxle.
38. Raise transaxle slightly with suitable transmission jack, then remove lefthand engine support insulator and Three-Way Catalytic Converter (TWC).
39. Remove suction accumulator bracket bolts and lower coolant hoses.
40. Disconnect heater coolant hoses, remove compressor bolts and position compressor aside with suitable mechanic's wire aside.
41. Disconnect shift cable from gear selector lever, release abutment bracket by turning it counterclockwise and removing cable from bracket. Release ad-

justment mechanism by pressing it in.
42. Lower vehicle and relieve fuel pressure as outlined under "Precautions."
43. Disconnect fuel lines using fuel line quick disconnect tool No. D87L-9280-A/B, or equivalent.
44. Disconnect coolant expansion tank and position it aside.
45. Disconnect speed control cable from coolant expansion tank.
46. Remove TWC bracket.
47. Raise engine/transaxle slightly to remove pressure from support insulator using lifting bracket tool No. T70P-6000 and spreader bar tool No. D93P-6001-A3, or equivalents, and suitable floor crane.
48. Remove front engine support insulator nuts and loosen bolts two turns.
49. Mark up position, then remove rear transaxle support insulator nuts and bolts.
50. Raise engine/transaxle, until power steering pump is accessible, then remove mounting bolts and position power steering pump aside with suitable mechanic's wire.
51. Remove engine/transaxle.
52. Separate transaxle from engine.
53. Reverse procedure to install.

INTAKE MANIFOLD
REPLACE

1. Remove air cleaner outlet tube.
2. Disconnect throttle position sensor, idle air control and engine control sensor wiring.
3. Relieve fuel system pressure as outlined under "Precautions."
4. Remove fuel supply manifold.
5. Remove engine wiring harness screws and position aside.
6. Disconnect vacuum supply hoses from intake manifold by squeezing tabs, twisting hoses and pulling away from intake manifold.
7. Disconnect brake booster vacuum line from intake manifold.
8. Remove fuel charging wiring and accessory drive belt.
9. Remove alternator bolts and position aside.
10. Remove seven mounting bolts, two nuts and intake manifold.
11. Remove manifold gasket and discard.
12. Reverse procedure to install.

EXHAUST MANIFOLD
REPLACE

1. Remove heat shield, coolant hose bracket and engine lifting eye and pull out engine oil dipstick tube.
2. **When repairing exhaust system or removing exhaust components, disconnect Heated Oxygen Sensor (HO2S) at the wiring harness to prevent damage to sensors and the harness.** Disconnect HO2S wiring connector.
3. Remove catalytic converter from exhaust manifold.
4. Raise and support vehicle.
5. Loosen catalytic converter bracket bolt and drop converter down so studs clear exhaust manifold.
6. Lower vehicle.
7. Remove exhaust manifold bolts, manifold and gasket.
8. Reverse procedure to install.

CYLINDER HEAD
REPLACE

The maximum amount by which the engine management system will adjust the camshaft timing (VCT control unit) is limited to 2°. As a result of this an extremely high degree of accuracy is required for any work which affects the valve timing.
1. Release coolant expansion tank cap.
2. Loosen righthand front wheel.
3. Raise and support vehicle.
4. Remove righthand front tire and wheel.
5. Remove radiator splash shield and drain coolant into suitable container.
6. Remove power steering lower bolts.
7. Disconnect brake booster line and crankcase ventilation hose from intake manifold.
8. Disconnect oil pressure switch and knock sensor electrical connectors.
9. Lower vehicle.
10. Remove intake pipe by disconnecting Mass Air Flow (MAF) and Inlet Air Temperature (IAT) sensors, then remove one bolt and two screws.
11. Remove air cleaner by disconnecting intake hose and crankcase ventilation hose.
12. Disconnect speed control cable from throttle valve.
13. Move cable up and down and pull it out of retaining bushing. Remove retaining bushing from bracket.
14. Disconnect throttle cable.

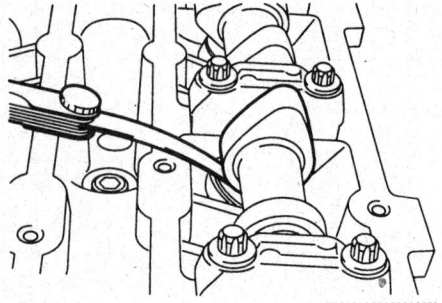

Fig. 9 Valve clearance measurement

FM1009800008000X

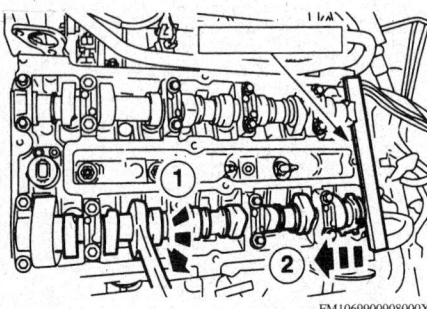

Fig. 12 Camshaft locking tool installation

FM1069900908000X

15. Remove plastic clip from bracket and position cable aside.
16. Disconnect wiring harness rail and vacuum hoses connected to intake manifold.
17. Remove undershield and disconnect starter positive lead. **Do not bend fusible element when removing nut as there is risk of it breaking.**
18. Remove electrical connector from radio interference suppressor, ignition coil, Engine Coolant Temperature (ECT) switch, Power Steering Pressure (PSP) switch and place harness aside.
19. Disconnect Camshaft Position (CMP) sensor electrical connector.
20. Disconnect coolant hoses and remove thermostat housing.
21. Remove upper bolts, coolant hose bracket and engine lifting eye, pull out engine oil dipstick tube, bracket for air conditioning tube/hose, lower bolts and heat shield.
22. Disconnect catalytic converter from exhaust manifold and Heated Oxygen Sensor (HO2S) electrical connector.
23. Remove belt pulley cover.
24. Remove power steering pump bracket from cylinder head and upper power steering pump bolts.
25. Remove electrical connectors and remove alternator.
26. Remove alternator mounting bracket.
27. Raise and support vehicle.
28. Loosen water pump belt pulley bolts, then working clockwise, loosen and remove drive belt.
29. Remove water pump belt pulley and drive belt idler pulley.
30. Remove crankshaft vibration damper and lower timing belt cover.
31. **On models equipped with manual**

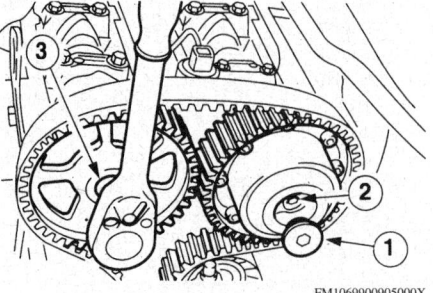

Fig. 10 Loosening camshaft sprockets

FM1069900905000X

transaxle, loosen center bolt of right-hand engine support insulator two turns.
32. **On models equipped with automatic transaxle,** loosen center bolt of righthand engine support insulator two turns.
33. Loosen center bolt of lefthand engine support insulator two turns.
34. Lower vehicle and support engine with suitable jack.
35. Disconnect coolant expansion tank and position aside.
36. Remove front engine mounting and upper timing belt cover.
37. Disconnect solenoid valve connector and remove cylinder head cover plate.
38. Disconnect spark plug wires from spark plugs, then the crankcase ventilation hose.
39. Loosen bolt and release timing belt tensioner by turning it clockwise. Loosen bolt four turns and unhook timing belt tensioner.
40. Remove timing belt, unscrew blanking plug from exhaust camshaft timing belt pulley. **Support camshaft by hexagon with open ended wrench to stop it from turning.** Remove exhaust camshaft pulley.
41. Remove intake camshaft pulley.
42. Remove bolts from Variable Camshaft Timing (VCT) oil feed flange and upper part of engine front cover.
43. Loosen camshaft bearing caps in sequence, **Fig. 5.** Working evenly in several stages, loosen each bolt two turns at a time.
44. Remove intake camshaft and exhaust camshaft with VCT control unit.
45. Remove valve tappets.
46. Cool cylinder head to ambient temperature and remove cylinder head bolts in sequence, **Fig. 6.**
47. Remove cylinder head from block.
48. Reverse procedure to install, noting the following:
    a. **Cylinder head bolts must be replaced with new bolts.**
    b. **Torque** cylinder head bolts to 18 ft. lbs., in sequence, **Fig. 7.**
    c. **Torque** head bolts to 33 ft. lbs., in sequence.
    d. Final tighten bolts an additional 105° in sequence.

VALVE COVER
REPLACE

1. Disconnect oil feed sensor connector

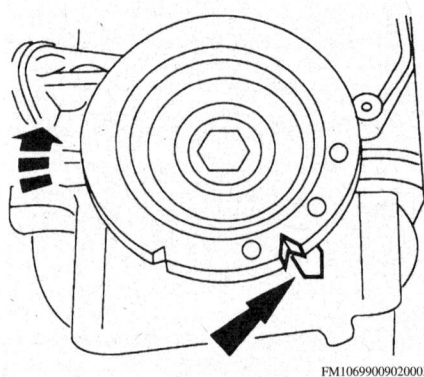

FM1069900902000X

Fig. 11 Crankshaft timing marks

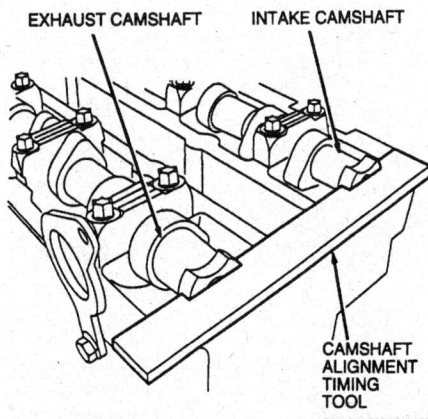

FM1069500554000X

Fig. 13 Camshaft alignment.

and remove crankcase ventilation tube.
2. Position throttle and speed control cables aside, then remove eight bolts and appearance cover.
3. Remove spark plug wires.
4. Remove four bolts and position front cover aside.
5. Position throttle cable and speed control cable aside, remove bolts and valve cover, **Fig. 8.**
6. Reverse procedure to install. Inspect valve cover gasket and O-rings for damage or signs of leakage.

CAMSHAFT LOBE LIFT SPECIFICATIONS

Camshaft lobe lift for intake and exhaust is .245 inch.

VALVE CLEARANCE SPECIFICATIONS

Intake valve clearance is .004–.007 inch, exhaust valve clearance is .010–.013.

VALVE ADJUSTMENT

1. Disconnect oil feed sensor connector and remove crankcase ventilation tube.
2. Position throttle and speed control cables aside, then remove eight bolts and appearance cover.
3. Remove spark plug wires.

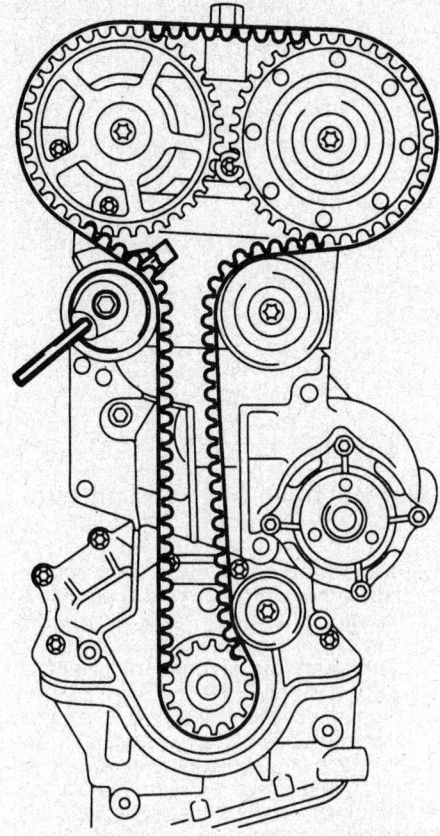

Fig. 14 Timing belt installation

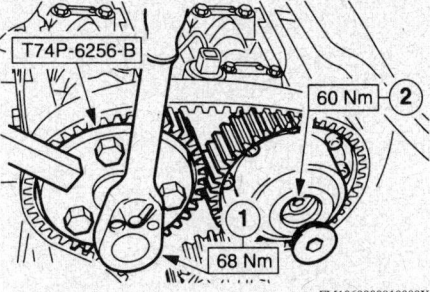

Fig. 15 Tightening camshaft sprockets

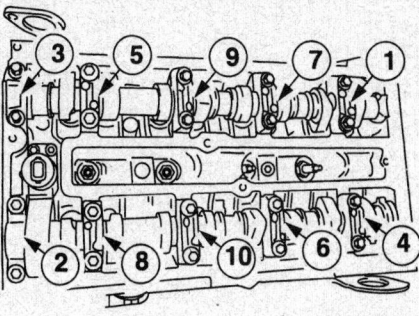

Fig. 16 Camshaft journal cap removal sequence

4. Remove four bolts and position front cover aside.
5. Position throttle cable and speed control cable aside , remove bolts and valve cover, **Fig. 8.**
6. Turn crankshaft until camshaft reaches base circle and measure valve clearance with suitable feeler gauge, **Fig. 9.**
7. Repeat for all valves and record measurement.
8. If valve clearance is not within specifications, remove camshafts as outlined under "Camshaft, Replace."

HYDRAULIC VALVE TAPPETS

REPLACE

1. Remove camshafts as outlined under "Camshaft, Replace."
2. If camshafts and valve tappets are to be reused, mark tappet locations for assembly.
3. Remove valve tappets.
4. If valve tappet is pitted, scored, excessively worn or if plunger is not free in body, replace tappet.
5. Reverse procedure to install.

FRONT COVER

REPLACE

1. Remove bolts and position power steering line aside.
2. Remove front engine support insulator.

3. Remove upper engine front cover studs, bolts and cover.
4. Remove splash shields bolts and splash shields.
5. Loosen but do not remove water pump pulley bolts.
6. Turn belt tensioner clockwise and remove accessory drive belt.
7. Remove idler pulley and water pump pulley.
8. Remove center engine front cover bolts and center engine front cover.
9. Remove bolt and crankshaft pulley.
10. Remove bolts and lower engine front cover.
11. Reverse procedure to install.

TIMING BELT

REPLACE

Removal

With timing belt removed, avoid turning camshaft or crankshaft. If movement is required, exercise extreme caution to avoid valve damage caused by piston contact.

1. Loosen righthand front wheel lug nuts.
2. Raise and safely support vehicle.
3. Remove righthand front wheel and tire.
4. Remove righthand front splash shield.
5. Remove engine undercover, then the serpentine belt.
6. Loosen water pump pulley bolts.
7. Loosen belt tensioner in clockwise direction and remove tensioner.
8. Remove water pump and belt idler pulleys.
9. Insert suitable tool into access hole in bottom of transaxle case to prevent engine rotation.
10. Remove crankshaft pulley using suitable puller tool.
11. Remove lower portion of engine front cover.
12. Loosen righthand engine support insulator center bolt two turns.
13. Loosen lefthand engine support insulator center bolt two turns.
14. Lower vehicle.
15. Remove mounting bolts and position coolant expansion tank aside.
16. Disconnect speed control cable from coolant expansion tank.
17. Position suitable floor jack and suitable block of wood under engine oil pan.
18. Mark engine front support insulator mounting position.
19. Remove pressure from engine front

support insulator by raising jack, then remove insulator.
20. Disconnect power steering pipe bracket from engine lifting eye.
21. Remove upper and center portions of engine front cover.
22. Unhook throttle and speed control cables from engine appearance cover.
23. Disconnect solenoid valve electrical connector.
24. Remove engine appearance cover.
25. Tag spark plug wires and disconnect at spark plugs.
26. Disconnect crankcase ventilation hose.
27. Remove mounting bolts working diagonally from outside to inside and valve cover.
28. Remove spark plugs.
29. Turn crankshaft until cylinder No. 1 is approximately at TDC position.
30. Record timing belt tensioner alignment marks and loosen tensioner bolt.
31. Turn belt tensioner clockwise to release tension.
32. Loosen belt tensioner bolt four turns and unhook tensioner.
33. Hold camshafts by hexagons suitable wrench.
34. Remove blanking plug from exhaust camshaft sprocket, **Fig. 10.**
35. Loosen exhaust and intake camshaft sprockets.
36. Remove timing belt.

Installation

1. Remove tool from access hole in bottom of transaxle case.
2. Turn crankshaft until cylinder No. 1 reaches TDC, **Fig. 11.**
3. Support camshafts by hexagons and turn in direction of engine rotation using suitable wrench , **Fig. 12.**
4. Install camshaft alignment tool No. T94P-6256-CH, or equivalent, **Fig. 13.**
5. Ensure crankshaft is still resting against timing peg. **Do not turn crankshaft.**
6. Ensure timing belt tensioner lug is not hooked in sheet metal cover during belt installation.
7. Install new timing belt. Start at crankshaft sprocket, work in counterclockwise direction and keep belt under tension, **Fig. 14.**
8. Hook belt tensioner into sheet metal cover and loosely turn bolt in.

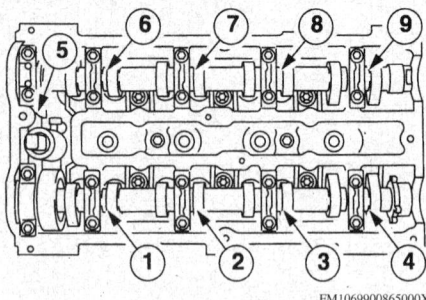

Fig. 17 Camshaft journal cap tightening sequence

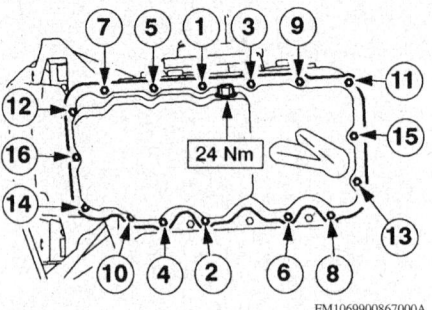

Fig. 18 Oil pan tightening sequence

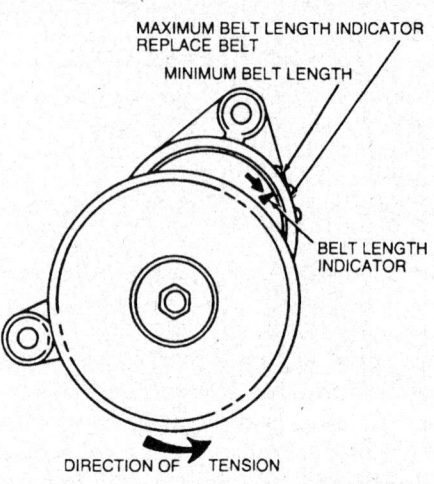

Fig. 19 Drive belt wear indicator mark

9. Turn belt tensioner counterclockwise until pointer and mark are properly aligned. **Torque** tensioner bolt to 18 ft. lbs.
10. Prevent intake camshaft sprocket from turning using holding tool No. T74P-6256-B, or equivalent, **Fig. 15.**
11. **Torque** intake camshaft sprocket to 50 ft. lbs.
12. Support exhaust camshaft by its hexagon using suitable wrench. **Torque** exhaust camshaft sprocket to 44 ft. lbs.
13. Remove timing peg and install blanking plug. **Torque** to 18 ft. lbs.
14. Remove camshaft locking tool.
15. Support exhaust camshaft by its hexagon. **Torque** exhaust camshaft sprocket again to 89 ft. lbs.
16. Ensure camshaft timing is properly set by installing aligning tool No. T94P-6256-CH, or equivalent, onto camshafts. If aligning tool refuses to fit into both slots, loosen tensioner and both camshaft sprocket bolts, then tension timing belt.
17. Install new blanking plug onto exhaust camshaft sprocket. **Torque** to 27 ft. lbs.
18. Install valve cover. **Torque** mounting bolts to 62 inch lbs.
19. Install spark plugs. **Torque** to 11 ft. lbs.
20. Connect crankcase ventilation hose.
21. Connect spark plug wires.
22. Install engine appearance cover.
23. Connect solenoid valve electrical connector.
24. Hook throttle and speed control cables at engine appearance cover.
25. Install center and upper portions of engine front cover.
26. Connect power steering pipe bracket at engine lifting eye.
27. Raise up slightly on floor jack and install engine support insulator. **Torque** mounting bolts to 60 ft. lbs.
28. Install coolant expansion tank.
29. Connect speed control cable at coolant expansion tank.
30. Raise and safely support vehicle.
31. **On models equipped with automatic transaxle,** ensure center bolt is properly centered in righthand engine support insulator. **Torque** bolt to 86 ft. lbs.
32. **On models equipped with manual transaxle,** ensure center bolt is properly centered in righthand engine support insulator. **Torque** bolt to 34 ft. lbs.
33. **On all models,** ensure center bolt is properly centered in lefthand engine

support insulator. **Torque** bolt to 86 ft. lbs.
34. Install lower portion of engine front cover.
35. Insert suitable tool into access hole in bottom of transaxle case to prevent engine rotation.
36. Install crankshaft pulley. **Torque** mounting bolt to 85 ft. lbs.
37. Install serpentine belt idler and water pump pulleys.
38. Turn serpentine belt tensioner clockwise and install belt.
39. **Torque** water pump pulley bolts to 13 ft. lbs.
40. Install engine undercover, then the righthand splash shield.
41. Install righthand front wheel and tire.
42. Lower vehicle to ground.
43. Tighten righthand front wheel lug nuts.
44. Connect battery ground cable.
45. Start engine and inspect for proper operation. **Some abnormal drive symptoms may appear for approximately 10 miles while vehicle relearns its adaptive strategy.**

CAMSHAFT
REPLACE
Removal

1. Disconnect oil feed sensor connector and remove crankcase ventilation tube.
2. Position throttle and speed control cables, then remove eight bolts and appearance cover.
3. Remove spark plug wires.
4. Remove four bolts and position front cover aside.
5. Position throttle cable and speed control cable aside, remove bolts and valve cover, **Fig. 8.**
6. Turn crankshaft until camshaft reaches base circle and measure valve clearance with suitable feeler gauge, **Fig. 9.**
7. Repeat for all valves and record measurement.
8. Remove timing belt as outlined under "Timing Belt, Replace."
9. Remove camshaft sprockets.
10. Mark cylinder head camshaft journal cap number on outside edge of camshaft journal caps and cylinder head. **Cylinder head camshaft journal caps and cylinder head should be**

numbered to ensure they are installed in original positions. Keep camshaft journal caps from cylinder head together. Do not mix with camshaft journal caps from another cylinder head.
11. Remove cylinder head camshaft journal cap bolts in pairs, loosening one turn at a time, beginning at rear of cylinder head, **Fig. 16.** Remove cylinder head camshaft journal thrust caps last to ensure proper camshaft position in cylinder head.
12. Remove intake and exhaust camshaft and camshafts.
13. Inspect camshafts and cylinder head for wear or damage. Replace components as required.

Installation

1. Ensure crankshaft is at Top Dead Center (TDC) of cylinder No. 1.
2. Lubricate camshafts with engine assembly lubricant part No. D9AZ-19579-D, or equivalent.
3. Install camshafts into cylinder head. Camshafts are marked for identification. Intake camshaft also has additional cam lobe for camshaft position sensor.
4. Apply 1/8 inch bead of silicone gasket and sealant part No. F1AZ-19562-A, or equivalent, to sealing surfaces of camshaft journal thrust caps and cylinder head.
5. Loosely install cylinder head camshaft journal caps and camshafts. **Install camshaft journal thrust caps last.**
6. **Torque** camshaft journal cap bolts in several steps to 11 ft. lbs., in sequence, **Fig. 17.**
7. Install valve cover and mounting bolts.
8. Install front cover and mount bolts, then the spark plug wires.
9. Install throttle and speed control cables, then the appearance cover.
10. Install crankcase ventilation tube and connect oil feed sensor connector.
11. Thinly coat camshaft bearing cap Nos. 0 and 5 with sealer.
12. Bring oil feed ring hole to top.

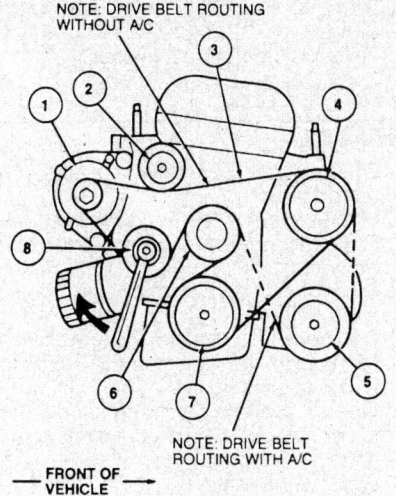

NOTE: DRIVE BELT ROUTING WITHOUT A/C

NOTE: DRIVE BELT ROUTING WITH A/C

FRONT OF VEHICLE →

Item	Description
1	Generator
2	Drivebelt Idler Pulley
3	Accessory Drive Belt
4	Power Steering Pump Pulley
5	A/C Compressor
6	Water Pump Pulley
7	Crankshaft Pulley
8	Drive Belt Tensioner

FM1069500410000X

Fig. 20   Drive belt routing

13. If lug is not centered between oil bores and mark, install new exhaust camshaft timing belt pulley.
14. Install camshaft sprockets, camshaft bearing cap No. 5 and camshaft oil seals,
15. Install timing belt as outlined under "Timing Belt, Replace."

CAMSHAFT FRONT SEALS
REPLACE

1. Remove timing belt as outlined under "Timing Belt, Replace."
2. Remove camshaft sprockets, camshaft bearing cap No. 5 and camshaft oil seals,
3. Reverse procedure to install, noting the following:
   a. Thinly coat camshaft bearing cap Nos. 0 and 5 with sealer.
   b. Bring oil feed ring hole to top.
   c. If lug is not centered between oil bores and mark, install new exhaust camshaft timing belt pulley.

CRANKSHAFT SEAL
REPLACE

1. Remove timing belt as outlined under "Timing Belt, Replace," then the crankshaft sprocket and washer.
2. Remove crankshaft front seal from oil pump using seal remover tool No. T92C-6700-CH, or equivalent.
3. Clean and inspect crankshaft front seal bore.
4. Lubricate crankshaft front oil seal bore

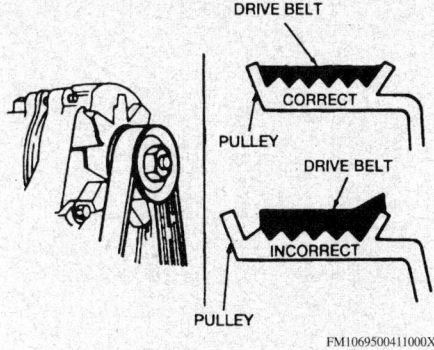

DRIVE BELT

CORRECT

PULLEY

DRIVE BELT

INCORRECT

PULLEY

FM1069500411000X

Fig. 21   Drive belt installation

and crankshaft front seal with engine assembly lubricant D9AZ-19579-D, or equivalent.
5. Install crankshaft front seal using seal replacer tool No. T81P-6700-A, or equivalent.
6. Install crankshaft timing sprocket and timing belt as outlined under "Timing Belt, Replace."

CRANKSHAFT REAR OIL SEAL
REPLACE

1. Remove transaxle as outlined in **MOTOR's "Domestic Transmission Manual, In-Vehicle Service."**
2. Record position of flywheel on crankshaft flange, then remove flywheel bolts, flywheel and reinforcement plate.
3. Remove rear oil seal using seal remover tool No. T92C-6700-CH, or equivalent.
4. Reverse procedure to install. Install oil seal using crankshaft rear seal replacer tool No. T88P-6701-B1, or equivalent, and three flywheel bolts.

OIL PAN
REPLACE

1. Remove heat shield and coolant hose bracket.
2. Remove engine lifting eye and pull out engine oil dipstick tube.
3. Remove catalytic converter from exhaust manifold.
4. Raise vehicle.
5. Remove mounting bolt, retaining and catalytic converter from exhaust system.
6. Disconnect heated oxygen sensor connector and remove catalytic converter from bracket.
7. Drain engine oil into suitable container.
8. Remove mounting bolts and oil pan.
9. Reverse procedure to install, noting the following:
   a. **Do not damage mating faces.** Remove any traces of sealer or gasket residue from mating faces using suitable spatula or scraper.
   b. Mating faces must be free of oil and gasket residue. Clean oil pan to remove any oil residue or sludge.
   c. Apply .118-inch bead of sealer to

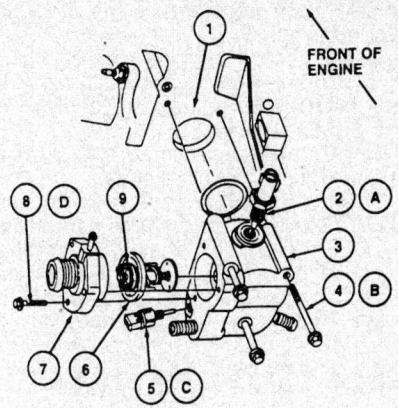

FRONT OF ENGINE

Item	Description
1	Cylinder Block
2	Engine Coolant Temperature Sensor
3	Water Thermostat Housing
4	Bolt (3 Req'd)
5	Water Temperature Indicator Sender Unit
6	O-Ring
7	Water Hose Connection
8	Bolt (3 Req'd)
9	Water Thermostat
A	Tighten to 10-14 N·m (89-124 Lb-In)
B	Tighten to 18-22 N·m (13-16 Lb-Ft)
C	Tighten to 7-10 N·m (62-89 Lb-In)
D	Tighten to 8-11 N·m (71-97 Lb-In)

FM1089500091000X

Fig. 22   Thermostat replacement

mating face of oil pan and install oil pan within 10 minutes of applying sealer.
   d. **Torque** oil pan bolts to 53 inch lbs in sequence, **Fig. 18.**
   e. **Final torque** bolts to 88 inch lbs.

OIL PUMP
REPLACE

1. Remove timing belt as outlined under "Timing Belt, Replace," then the crankshaft sprocket.
2. Remove heat shield and coolant hose bracket.
3. Remove engine lifting eye and pull out engine oil dipstick tube.
4. Remove catalytic converter from exhaust manifold.
5. Raise vehicle.
6. Remove mounting bolt, retaining clip and catalytic converter from exhaust system.
7. Disconnect heated oxygen sensor connector and remove catalytic converter from bracket.
8. Drain engine oil into suitable container.
9. Remove mounting bolts and oil pan.
10. Remove oil pump screen cover and tube.
11. Remove lower air conditioning bracket bolts and lower crankcase to transmission bolts.
12. Remove lower crankcase to upper crankcase bolts and lower crankcase.
13. Remove mounting bolts and oil pump.

14. Reverse procedure to install, noting following:
    a. Clean oil pump to cylinder block gasket sealing surfaces with wire brush. Do not damage sealing surfaces.
    b. Turn oil pump inner rotor to align with flats on crankshaft.
    c. Install pump with new gasket flush to cylinder block at oil pan sealing surface, using straight edge. Clearance between oil pan and oil pump sealing surfaces should not be more than .012–.031 inch.

BELT TENSION DATA

Drive belts have an automatic drive belt tensioner and do not require adjustment.

Automatic belt tensioner has a drive belt wear indicator mark, **Fig. 19.** If indicator mark is not between tabs on front cover, belt is worn or an incorrect belt is installed.

SERPENTINE DRIVE BELT

Routing

Refer to **Fig. 20,** for belt routing.

Belt Replacement

Minor cracks in V-grooved portion of drive belt are considered normal and acceptable. Drive belt should be replaced if it has chunks missing from ribs, severe glazing or frayed cords.
1. Raise and support vehicle.
2. Loosen drive belt tensioner pulley mounting bolt and turn drive belt tensioner away from accessory drive belt using 13 mm wrench.
3. Lift belt over pulley flanges and remove.
4. Reverse procedure to install. Ensure drive belt is properly installed on each pulley, with all V-grooves making proper contact with each pulley, **Fig. 21.**

Tensioner Replacement

1. Raise and support vehicle.
2. Loosen drive belt tensioner pulley mounting bolt and turn drive belt tensioner away from accessory drive belt using 13 mm wrench.
3. Lift belt over pulley flanges and remove.
4. Loosen belt tensioner bolts and remove tensioner from front of engine.
5. Install tensioner and bolts to front of engine and tighten bolts.
6. Ensure drive belt is properly installed

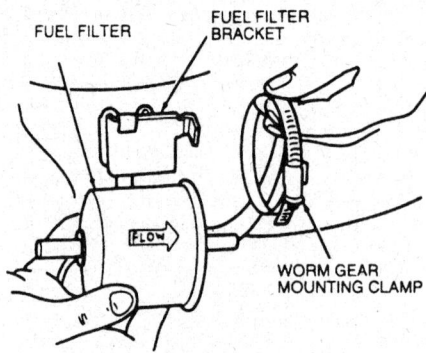

FM1029500156000X

Fig. 23 Inline fuel filter replacement

on each pulley, with all V-grooves making proper contact with each pulley, **Fig. 21.**

COOLING SYSTEM BLEED

These engines do not require a specific bleed procedure. To ensure coolant level is satisfactory, start the engine, turn heater control to its maximum heat and vent positions. After engine reaches normal operating temperature, hot air should be blowing from the air conditioning vents. If cool air is blowing from the vents, coolant level is low, turn engine off and add coolant as required.

THERMOSTAT
REPLACE

1. Remove engine air intake resonators from air cleaner assembly.
2. Drain engine cooling system so engine coolant level is below thermostat, then disconnect upper radiator hose and overflow hose from water hose connection.
3. Remove bolts and water outlet connection from thermostat housing, **Fig. 22.**
4. Remove thermostat and seal from housing.
5. Reverse procedure to install.

WATER PUMP
REPLACE

1. Drain engine coolant into suitable container.
2. Remove righthand front wheel and lower splash shield.
3. Lower vehicle.
4. Disconnect hoses and remove coolant expansion tank.
5. Loosen water pump pulley bolts and remove accessory drive belt.
6. Remove water pump pulley bolts and pulley.

7. Remove mounting bolts and water pump.
8. Reverse procedure to install.

RADIATOR
REPLACE

1. Drain engine coolant into suitable container.
2. Remove motor, fan and shroud.
3. Remove upper shield and support condenser.
4. Disconnect radiator upper cooling hose.
5. **On models equipped with automatic transaxle,** disconnect radiator upper cooling hose.
6. **On all models,** disconnect radiator lower cooling hose and disconnect air conditioning condenser.
7. Remove radiator.
8. Reverse procedure to install.

FUEL PUMP
REPLACE

1. Remove fuel tank.
2. Fuel supply line connectors are white or are identified by white band. Fuel return line connectors are red or are identified by red band. Disconnect fuel feed pipe.
3. Remove fuel pump locking ring using fuel sender ring wrench tool No. D84P-9275-A, or equivalent.
4. Remove fuel pump.
5. Reverse procedure to install. Install new O-ring.

FUEL FILTER
REPLACE

In-Tank

1. Remove fuel pump as outlined under "Fuel Pump, Replace."
2. Remove filter mounted on fuel pump inlet.
3. Reverse procedure to install.

Inline

1. Relieve fuel system pressure as outlined under "Precautions."
2. Remove push connect fittings at both ends of fuel filter and install retainer clips in each connect fitting.
3. Remove fuel filter from bracket by loosening worm gear mounting clamp enough to allow filter to pass through, **Fig. 23.**
4. Reverse procedure to install, noting the following:
    a. Locate fuel filter against tab at lower end of bracket. Ensure proper direction of fuel flow, **Fig. 23.**
    b. Tighten worm gear mounting clamp.

TIGHTENING SPECIFICATIONS

Year	Component	Torque/Ft. Lbs.
2001–02	Accelerator Cable Bracket	72–108①
	Air Cleaner Bracket	15–22
	Battery Ground Cable To Engine At Transaxle	15–22
	Camshaft Journal Cap	④
	Camshaft Sprocket	47–53
	Catalytic Converter Bracket	72–108①
	Catalytic Converter Clamp	15–22
	Catalytic Converter To Exhaust Manifold	26–33
	Center & Lower Timing Belt Cover	60–72①
	Crankshaft Pulley	81–89
	Cylinder Head	②
	Drive Belt Idler Pulley	30
	Drive Belt Tensioner	15–22
	EGR Valve To Exhaust Manifold Tube	44
	Engine Air Cleaner Tube Clamps	24–48①
	Engine & Transaxle Support Insulator	62
	Engine & Transaxle Support Insulator To Front Fender Apron	52–70
	Engine Lifting Eye	⑥
	Engine Rear Plate	79–86③
	Exhaust Manifold Heat Shield	72–108①
	Exhaust Manifold	13–16
	Exhaust Manifold Shield Retainers	72–108①
	Flywheel, Bolt	81
	Flywheel, Nut	54–64③
	Front Engine Support Bracket To Front Sub-Frame Bolts	20
	Front Engine Support Bracket To Transaxle	⑤
	Front Engine Support Insulator	20
	Front Engine Support Insulator Through Bolt	20
	Front Stabilizer Bar Link To Stabilizer Bar	35
	Heated Oxygen Sensor	44
	Heater Water Tube	72–108①
	Intake Manifold	13
	Lefthand Engine Support Insulator Through Bolt	62
	Lower Engine Rear Plate	72–108①
	Main Bearing	63
	Oil Dipstick Tube	72–108①
	Oil Pan Drain Plug	20
	Oil Pan	⑨
	Oil Pump Screen Cover & Tube	72–96①
	Power Steering Pump Mounting Bracket Support Bracket	29–41
	Radiator Coolant Recovery Reservoir	72–108①
	Radiator Supports To Front Sub-Frame	72–96①
	Righthand Front Engine Support Insulator Through Bolt	62
	Self-Locking Oil Pump Screen Cover & Tube Support	13–15
	Shift Cable Bracket	15–19

Continued

TIGHTENING
SPECIFICATIONS—Continued

Year	Component	Torque/Ft. Lbs.
2001–02	Shift Rod	17
	Stabilizer	41
	Steering Shaft To Joint	18
	Thermostat Housing	15
	Throttle Body	72–108①
	Tie Rod End	⑧
	Timing Belt Pulley	26–30
	Timing Belt Tensioner Pulley	72–96①
	Transaxle Oil Cooler Lines	17
	Transaxle To Engine	25–34
	Upper Front Engine Support	52–70
	Upper Front Engine Support Bracket	52–70
	Upper Timing Belt Cover	27–44①
	Valve Cover	⑦
	VCT Oil Feed Flange To Cylinder Head	84①
	Water Hose Connection	71–97
	Water Pump Pulley	89–124
	Wheel Knuckle To Lower Arm	37–43
	Wheel Lug Nuts	94
	Worm Gear Mounting Clamp	15–25①

① — Inch lbs.
② — Refer to "Cylinder Head, Replace."
③ — Tighten in alternating sequence.
④ — Refer to "Camshaft, Replace" for tighten specifications and sequence.
⑤ — Lefthand side, 30–40 ft. lbs.; righthand side, 40–55 ft. lbs.
⑥ — Lefthand side, 10–13 ft. lbs.; righthand side, 30–40 ft. lbs.
⑦ — Refer to "Valve Cover, Replace" for tighten specifications and sequence.
⑧ — Refer to "Engine, Replace" for tighten specifications and sequence.
⑨ — Refer to "Oil Pan, Replace" for tighten specifications and sequence.

2.5L Engine

NOTE: On Air Bag Equipped Models, Refer To "Air Bag System Precautions" Located In The Front Of This Manual For System Disarming & Arming Procedures.

NOTE: Refer To "Computer Relearn Procedures" Located In The Front Of This Manual When Battery Power To The Computer Has Been Interrupted.

INDEX

PRECAUTIONS

Battery Ground Cable

Prior to service, disconnect battery ground cable and isolate as required.

Air Bag Systems

Refer to "Air Bag System Precautions" in front of this manual for system disarming and arming procedures.

Cooling System

This engine has an aluminum cylinder head and requires a special corrosion inhibiting coolant to avoid cooling system damage. Use only specified coolant in this engine.

Fuel System Pressure Relief

Fuel supply lines will remain pressurized for long periods of time after engine shutdown. Pressure must be relieved before servicing fuel system.

1. Remove engine air intake resonators.
2. Disconnect engine control sensor wiring connectors from Mass Air Flow (MAF) sensor and Intake Air Temperature (IAT) sensor.
3. Remove engine air cleaner to body O-ring retainer.
4. Remove engine air cleaner body and intake tube from bracket and intake tube and duct.
5. Connect Multi-Port Fuel Injection (MFI) fuel pressure gauge tool No. T80L-9974-B, or equivalent, to fuel pressure relief valve cap on fuel injection supply manifold.
6. Open manual valve on gauge tool to relieve fuel system pressure.

COMPRESSION PRESSURE

Compression pressure should be inspected at normal operating temperature with spark plugs removed and throttle plate wide open. Cylinder compression pressure is considered within specification if lowest reading cylinder is within 75 percent of highest reading.

ENGINE MOUNT

REPLACE

Refer to "Engine Mount, Replace" in the "2.0L Engine" section for replacement procedure.

ENGINE

REPLACE

Automatic Transaxle

1. Remove front wheels, battery and hood.
2. Remove coolant hose from clip, then the mounting bolts and water pump pulley.
3. Remove air cleaner and drain engine coolant into suitable container.
4. Disconnect accelerator and speed control cables from bracket.
5. Remove transaxle selector cable bolts and cable.
6. Remove bolt from bulkhead connector and disconnect electrical connector.
7. Loosen central junction box and position it aside.
8. Disconnect ground cable and fan motor connector.
9. Remove four battery bracket bolts, battery bracket and two ground cables.
10. Relieve fuel pressure as outlined under "Precautions."
11. Disconnect fuel lines using fuel line disconnect tool Nos. D87L-9280-A (3/8 inch) or D87L-9280-B (1/2 inch), or equivalent.
12. Disconnect all heater hoses.

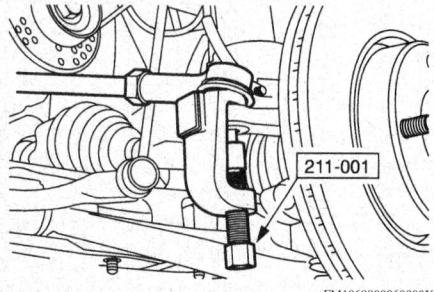

Fig. 1 Tie rod end replacement

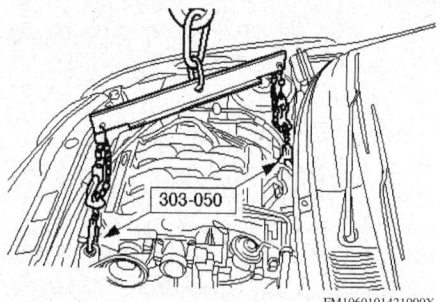

Fig. 2 Engine lifting tool. Manual transaxle

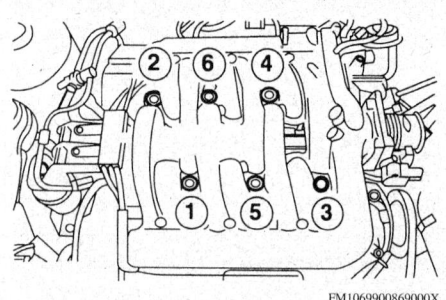

Fig. 3 Upper intake removal sequence

13. Disconnect suction accumulator electrical connector and evaporative emission hose.
14. Loosen both suspension strut nuts five turns.
15. Disconnect upper intake vacuum supply line and heater control vacuum hoses.
16. Drain power steering fluid reservoir into suitable container, pull reservoir out (push fit) and position it aside.
17. Disconnect power steering lines and position aside.
18. Disconnect PCM and ground cable.
19. Disconnect coolant expansion tank hoses and remove tank.
20. Remove upper transaxle cooling tube. Close off openings with plugs for transaxle opening
21. Remove fan, then raise and support vehicle.
22. Drain engine oil into suitable container.
23. Disconnect heated oxygen sensor electrical connector.
24. Remove dual converter Y-pipe and righthand fender splash shields.
25. Remove righthand control arm and intermediate shaft bearing with righthand front drive halfshaft from transaxle. Support halfshaft aside using suitable cable ties.
26. Disconnect stabilizer link rod and remove tie rod end using stabilizer link rod tool No. 211-001, or equivalent, **Fig. 1.**
27. Disconnect ABS wiring harness bracket from suspension strut. **Do not damage boot and ABS sensor ring.**
28. Remove lefthand front drive halfshaft from transaxle and hang it up.
29. Disconnect and remove HO2S electrical connector.
30. Remove transaxle cooling lines.
31. Remove coolant hose from radiator.
32. Disconnect air conditioning compressor electrical connector.
33. Remove condenser core and tie it up.
34. Remove radiator and disconnect HO2S sensor.
35. Remove coolant pipe.
36. Remove accessory drive belt and compressor heat shield.
37. Remove compressor bracket bolts and position compressor aside with suitable mechanic's wire.
38. Remove lefthand support insulator nuts, center bolt and insulator.
39. Remove center bolt from righthand support insulator.
40. Lower vehicle.
41. Raise engine slightly to remove pressure from support insulator using lifting bracket tool No. T70P-6000, or equivalent, and suitable floor crane.
42. Remove upper front support insulator from side member and rear support insulator from side member.
43. Remove engine and transaxle as assembly.
44. Separate transaxle from engine.
45. Reverse procedure to install.

Manual Transaxle

1. Remove battery and hood.
2. Remove water pump pulley cover.
3. Remove air cleaner and drain brake fluid into suitable container.
4. **On models equipped with speed control,** disconnect accelerator and speed control cables.
5. **On models equipped less speed control,** disconnect accelerator.
6. **On all models,** disconnect bulkhead connector, then loosen central junction box and place aside.
7. Remove fan motor electrical connectors from battery tray.
8. Remove three battery ground straps and battery tray.
9. Disconnect fuel lines and coolant hoses. Position aside.
10. Remove ground strap from transaxle bolt.
11. Disconnect suction accumulator and two fan motor electrical connectors.
12. Disconnect engine coolant temperature sensor and reverse lamp connector.
13. Disconnect evaporative emission hose, upper intake vacuum supply lines and heater control vacuum hoses.
14. Loosen suspension strut lock nuts five turns on both sides.
15. Drain power steering reservoir into suitable container, then pull it out and position it aside.
16. Disconnect power steering lines.
17. Remove Powertrain Control Module (PCM) cover plate.
18. Disconnect PCM electrical connector and coolant expansion tank hoses.
19. Remove coolant level sensor electrical connector and expansion tank.
20. Remove oil dipstick and oxygen sensor electrical connector bracket.
21. Loosen fan from radiator, then raise and support vehicle.
22. Remove radiator splash shield and drain cooling system into suitable container.
23. Drain transmission fluid into suitable container.
24. Remove coolant hose from radiator and drain engine oil.
25. Disconnect air conditioning compressor electrical connector and remove condenser core from radiator.
26. Remove radiator and fans.
27. Disconnect oxygen sensor connector and remove coolant pipe.
28. Remove Y-pipe and three-way catalytic converter.
29. Remove righthand front fender splash shield and accessory drive belt.
30. Remove compressor heat shield and bracket bolts. Position compressor aside.
31. Disconnect shifter cables and brackets.
32. Remove both control arms and righthand front driveshaft from intermediate shaft bearing using suitable copper drift. Support aside.
33. Remove lefthand front drive halfshaft from transaxle using suitable tire level. and position it aside.
34. Remove lefthand support insulator through bolt and bracket.
35. Remove righthand support insulator through bolt, support insulator and bracket.
36. Lower vehicle. Install engine lifting bracket tool No. 303-050 or equivalent, **Fig. 2.**
37. Remove starter motor bracket and ground cable from transaxle flange.
38. Remove ACL bracket and rear upper support insulator.
39. Raise engine slightly, then remove front upper support through bolt and insulator.
40. Remove engine/transaxle assembly.
41. Reverse procedure to install.

INTAKE MANIFOLD
REPLACE

Upper

1. Remove air cleaner and water pump pulley shield.
2. Disconnect exhaust gas recirculation valve, accelerator and speed control cables, then remove accelerator cable bracket.
3. Disconnect black retainer, two vacuum

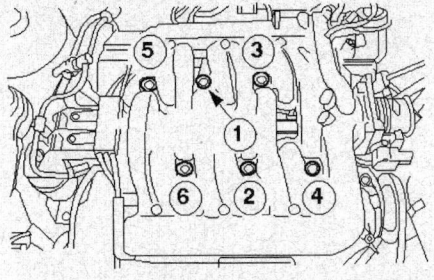

Fig. 4 Upper intake manifold bolt tightening sequence

supply lines from upper intake and vacuum regulator solenoid vacuum hose.
4. Disconnect positive crankcase ventilation hose, throttle position sensor and Idle air control valve electrical connector.
5. Disconnect EGR vacuum regulator solenoid electrical connector.
6. Remove intake bolts in sequence, **Fig. 3.**
7. Reverse procedure, noting the following:
   a. Position new gasket on lower intake manifold.
   b. **Torque** bolts to 84 inch lbs., in sequence, **Fig. 4.**

Lower

1. Relieve fuel system pressure as outlined under "Precautions."
2. Remove air cleaner and water pump pulley shield.
3. Disconnect exhaust gas recirculation valve, accelerator and speed control cables, then remove accelerator cable bracket.
4. Disconnect black retainer, two vacuum supply lines from upper intake and vacuum regulator solenoid vacuum hose.
5. Disconnect positive crankcase ventilation hose, throttle position sensor and Idle air control valve electrical connector.
6. Disconnect EGR vacuum regulator solenoid electrical connector.
7. Remove intake bolts in sequence, **Fig. 3.**
8. Disconnect fuel supply and return lines from fuel injection supply manifold.
9. Disconnect engine control sensor wiring from fuel injectors and valve cover studs. Position wiring aside.
10. Disconnect vacuum supply line from fuel pressure regulator and Intake Manifold Runner Control (IMRC) vacuum solenoid. Position line aside.
11. Remove fuel injection supply manifold and fuel injectors from lower intake manifold.
12. Remove IMRC vacuum solenoid from lower intake manifold.
13. Remove lower intake manifold to cylinder head bolts in sequence, **Fig. 5.**
14. Remove lower intake manifold from cylinder heads and intake manifold gaskets from cylinder heads, **Fig. 6.** Discard gaskets.

15. Reverse procedure to install, noting following:
   a. Verify IMRC vacuum solenoid and plate operation using hand vacuum pump. Install new intake manifold gaskets.
   b. **Torque** lower intake manifold bolts to 72–108 inch lbs., in sequence, **Fig. 7.**

EXHAUST MANIFOLD
REPLACE
Righthand

1. Disconnect engine control sensor extension wire from righthand heated oxygen sensor.
2. Raise and support vehicle, then remove alternator and bracket as outlined in "Electrical" section.
3. Remove converter outlet flange nuts, then the muffler and converter outlet gasket from converter.
4. Remove converter nuts and exhaust pipe flange hold-down springs.
5. Remove converter and inlet gasket from Y-pipe, then discard gasket.
6. Remove front and rear Y-pipe flange fasteners from exhaust manifolds.
7. Remove stud bolt and nut retainer from oil pan, then the Y-pipe.
8. Remove righthand halfshaft support bearing bracket from support bearing and cylinder block as outlined in "Front Wheel Drive Axles" chapter.
9. Remove heated oxygen sensor from righthand exhaust manifold using oxygen sensor wrench tool No. T94P-9472-A, or equivalent. If excessive force is required to remove sensor, lubricate sensor with penetrating oil before removal.
10. Loosen EGR valve to exhaust manifold tube from exhaust manifold.
11. Remove exhaust manifold nuts from cylinder head studs, then the manifold and gasket,
12. Reverse procedure to install, noting following:
   a. **Torque** exhaust manifold nuts to 15 ft. lbs., in sequence, **Fig. 8.**
   b. Tighten EGR valve to exhaust manifold tube nuts and heated oxygen sensor.

Lefthand

1. Disconnect lefthand heated oxygen sensor from engine control sensor wiring.
2. Raise and support vehicle.
3. Remove front and rear flange pipe fasteners from exhaust manifolds, then the stud bolt and nut retainer from oil pan.
4. Remove two remaining nuts and bolts from Y-pipe outlet connection.
5. Discard exhaust converter inlet gasket, then remove Y-pipe.
6. Remove lower radiator hose tube bracket nuts from stud bolts and exhaust manifold nuts from lefthand cylinder head studs.
7. Position lower radiator hose tube aside

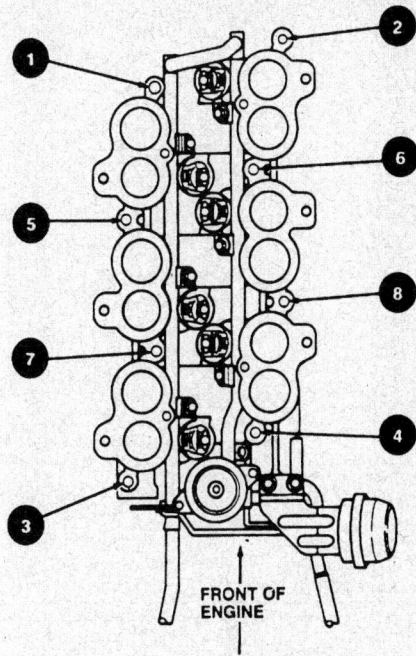

REMOVE BOLTS IN SEQUENCE SHOWN

LOWER INTAKE MANIFOLD

Fig. 5 Lower intake manifold bolt removal sequence

, then remove lefthand exhaust manifold and gasket.
8. Remove heated oxygen sensor from lefthand exhaust manifold using oxygen sensor wrench tool No. T94P-9472-A, or equivalent. If excessive force is required to remove sensor, lubricate sensor with penetrating oil before removal.
9. Reverse procedure to install. **Torque** lefthand exhaust manifold nuts to 15 ft. lbs., in sequence, **Fig. 8.**

CYLINDER HEAD
REPLACE

1. Drain engine coolant from radiator and cylinder block drain plugs into suitable containers.
2. Remove upper and lower intake manifolds as outlined under "Intake Manifold, Replace."
3. Remove alternator and alternator bracket as outlined in "Electrical" section.
4. Remove heated oxygen sensor from righthand exhaust manifold using oxygen sensor wrench tool No. T94P-9472-A, or equivalent. If excessive force is required to remove sensor, lubricate sensor with penetrating oil before removal.
5. **On lefthand cylinder head,** proceed as follows:
   a. Disconnect lefthand heated oxygen sensor from engine control sensor wiring.
   b. Raise and support vehicle.
   c. Remove front and rear flange pipe fasteners from exhaust manifolds,

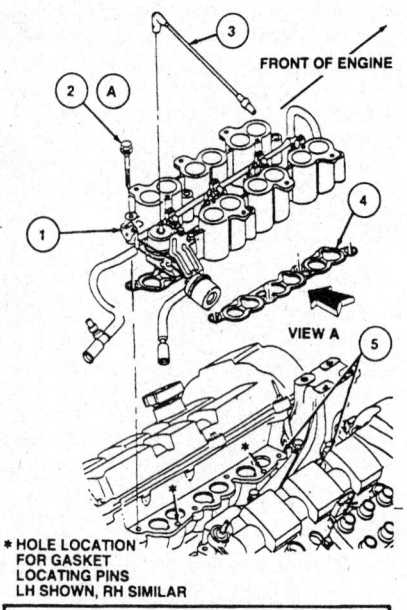

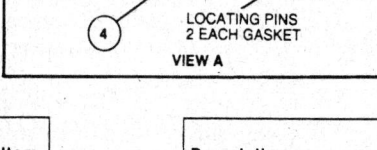

* HOLE LOCATION
FOR GASKET
LOCATING PINS
LH SHOWN, RH SIMILAR

LOCATING PINS
2 EACH GASKET
VIEW A

Item	Description
1	Lower Intake Manifold
2	Bolt (8 Req'd)
3	Main Emission Vacuum Control Connector
4	Intake Manifold Gasket (2 Req'd)
5	Cylinder Head (2 Req'd)
A	Tighten to 8-12 N·m (71-106 Lb-In)

FM1059500073000X

Fig. 6   Lower intake manifold replacement

then the stud bolt and nut retainer from oil pan.

d. Remove two remaining nuts and bolts from Y-pipe outlet connection.

e. Discard exhaust converter inlet gasket, then remove Y-pipe.

f. Remove lower radiator hose tube bracket nuts from stud bolts and exhaust manifold nuts from lefthand cylinder head studs.

g. Position lower radiator hose tube aside , then remove lefthand exhaust manifold and gasket.

h. Remove heated oxygen sensor from lefthand exhaust manifold using oxygen sensor wrench tool No. T94P-9472-A, or equivalent. If excessive force is required to remove sensor, lubricate sensor with penetrating oil before removal.

i. Remove water pump as outlined under "Water Pump, Replace."

6. **On both cylinder heads,** remove lefthand and righthand valve covers as outlined under "Valve Cover, Replace."

7. Remove exhaust Y-pipe, exhaust support bracket nuts and support bracket.

8. Remove air conditioning compressor heat shield nuts and heat shield.

9. Drain engine oil into suitable container.

10. Remove flywheel access cover and oil pan bolts from transaxle housing.

11. Remove oil pan bolts and studs in sequence, **Fig. 9.** Discard gasket

12. Remove alternator and power steering pump.

13. Disconnect camshaft and crankshaft position sensor electrical connectors and remove.

14. Remove mounting bolts, studs and front cover, **Fig. 10.**

15. Remove camshafts as outlined under "Camshaft, Replace."

16. **Piston must be at bottom of its stroke with both valves closed. Any loss of air pressure will allow to fall into cylinder.** Remove spark plug.

17. Install adapter into spark plug bore and connect compressed air supply at 102–144 psi.

18. Compress valve spring using valve spring compressor tool No. T94P-6565-BH or equivalent, and remove roller follower.

19. Remove hydraulic lash adjusters.

20. Install upper front engine support insulator and front engine support bracket to front of engine and righthand front fender apron.

21. Remove three bar engine support tool No. D88L-6000-A, or equivalent.

22. **On righthand cylinder head,** proceed as follows:

    a. Disconnect hoses from EGR pressure sensor to exhaust manifold tube and pressure sensor electrical connector.

    b. Disconnect interior vacuum source hose from main emission vacuum harness and fuel vapor hose from PCV valve.

    c. Disconnect EGR transducer electrical connector.

    d. Remove EGR exhaust manifold tube and fuel charging wiring bracket from EGR transducer bracket.

23. **On both cylinder heads,** loosen engine air cleaner tube clamps on outlet tube, then disconnect crankcase ventilation hoses and IAC valve tube from air cleaner outlet tube fitting.

24. Remove air cleaner outlet tube from MAF sensor and throttle body.

25. Disconnect engine control sensor wiring connector form MAF and IAT sensor.

26. Remove engine air cleaner to body O-ring retainer, air cleaner and intake tube from bracket.

27. Remove engine air cleaner intake tube and duct.

28. Remove crankcase ventilation tube from water crossover and oil separator, **Fig. 11.**

29. Remove water crossover bolt and stud bolt from righthand cylinder head. Position crossover aside.

30. **On lefthand cylinder head,** remove oil level dipstick.

31. **On both cylinder heads,** remove cylinder head bolts in sequence, **Fig. 12.**

32. Remove cylinder heads. Remove righthand cylinder head with exhaust manifold and EGR transducer bracket attached.

33. Remove exhaust manifold and EGR

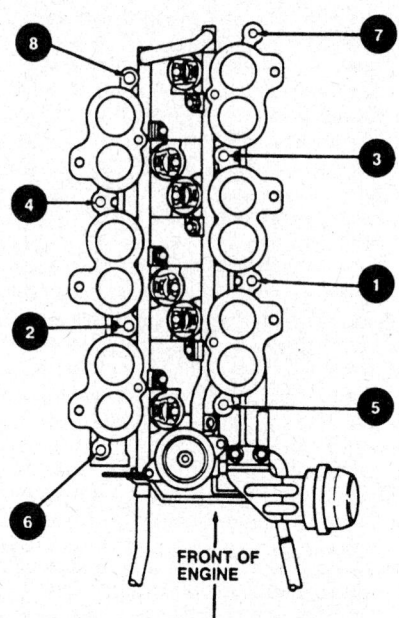

● INSTALL BOLTS IN SEQUENCE SHOWN

LOWER INTAKE MANIFOLD

FM1059500074000X

Fig. 7   Intake manifold bolt tightening sequence

transducer bracket from righthand cylinder head.

34. Reverse procedure to install, noting following:

    a. Clean cylinder heads, lower intake manifold valve cover and cylinder gasket surfaces. If cylinder heads were removed to replace cylinder gasket, inspect flatness of cylinder heads and cylinder block gasket surfaces.

    b. Install new head gaskets on cylinder block.

    c. **Cylinder head bolts are torque-to-yield designed and must be replaced with new bolts. If reused, damage to engine may occur.**

    d. **Torque** cylinder head bolts to 29 ft. lbs., in sequence, **Fig. 13.**

    e. Tighten head bolts an additional 90° in sequence.

    f. Loosen bolts one full turn.

    g. **Torque** bolts to 29 ft. lbs., in sequence.

    h. Tighten bolts an additional 90°.

    i. Final tighten bolts an additional 90.°

    j. Inspect water crossover O-rings for wear or damage.

    k. Lubricate water crossover O-rings with specified engine coolant.

VALVE COVER

REPLACE

Righthand

1. Remove upper intake manifold as outlined under "Intake Manifold, Replace."

2. Remove ignition wires from ignition coils and spark plugs.

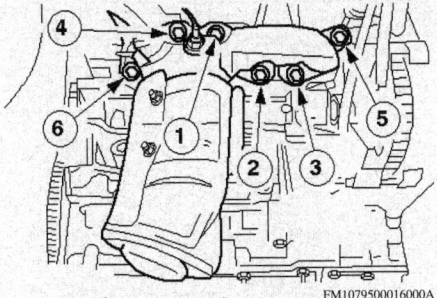

Fig. 8 Exhaust manifold tightening sequence

3. Disconnect engine control sensor wiring from ignition coil and radio ignition interference capacitor.
4. Remove EGR vacuum regulator control from upper intake manifold.
5. Disconnect ignition wires by squeezing locking tabs and twisting while pulling upward.
6. Remove mounting bolts and ignition coil.
7. Remove radio ignition interference capacitor and disconnect coil ground wire.
8. Remove crankcase ventilation tube from righthand valve cover.
9. Remove fuel charging wiring retainer and inline connector wiring bracket nuts and bracket from righthand valve cover stud bolts. Position bracket and fuel charging wiring aside.
10. Remove engine control sensor wiring nuts and wiring from righthand valve cover stud bolts. Position engine control sensor wiring aside.
11. Loosen valve cover bolts and stud bolts in sequence, **Fig. 14.**
12. Remove valve cover from cylinder head and gaskets from cover.
13. Reverse procedure to install, noting following:
    a. Clean valve cover sealing surfaces using shop towel and suitable metal cleaner.
    b. Apply .31 inch diameter bead of black silicone rubber sealant, part No. F4AZ-19562-B, or equivalent, at two places on valve cover sealing surfaces where front cover and cylinder heads contact.
    c. Install new valve cover gaskets onto valve cover.
    d. Within six minutes of applying sealer, **torque** valve cover bolts and studs to 89 inch lbs., in sequence, **Fig. 15.**

Lefthand

1. Remove upper intake manifold as outlined under "Intake Manifold, Replace."
2. Remove crankcase ventilation tube from lefthand valve cover and fuel charging wiring brackets from lefthand valve cover stud bolts. Position fuel charging wiring aside.
3. Remove ignition wires from spark plugs and valve cover, then loosen valve cover bolts and stud bolts in se-

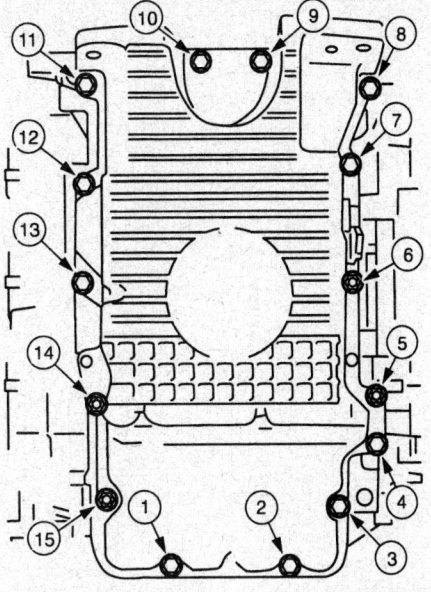

Fig. 9 Oil pan removal sequence

quence, **Fig. 14.**
4. Remove valve cover from lefthand cylinder head and gaskets from cover.
5. Reverse procedure to install, noting following:
    a. Clean valve cover sealing surfaces using shop towel and suitable metal cleaner.
    b. Apply .31 inch diameter bead of black silicone rubber sealant, part No. F4AZ-19562-B, or equivalent, at two places on valve cover sealing surfaces where front cover and cylinder heads contact and two places on rear of cylinder head where camshaft seal retainer contacts cylinder head.
    c. Install new valve cover gaskets onto valve cover.
    d. Within six minutes of applying sealer, **torque** valve cover bolts and studs to 89 inch lbs., in sequence, **Fig. 15.**

VALVE ARRANGEMENT

Front To Rear

Lefthand Intake: .....Secondary-Primary-Secondary-Primary-Secondary-Primary.
Righthand Intake: ..Primary-Secondary-Primary-Secondary-Primary-Secondary.

CAMSHAFT LOBE LIFT SPECIFICATIONS

Camshaft lobe lift for primary and secondary intake and exhaust is .188 inch with zero allowable lobe lift loss.

VALVE CLEARANCE SPECIFICATIONS

Valve clearance is hydraulically controlled and not adjustable.

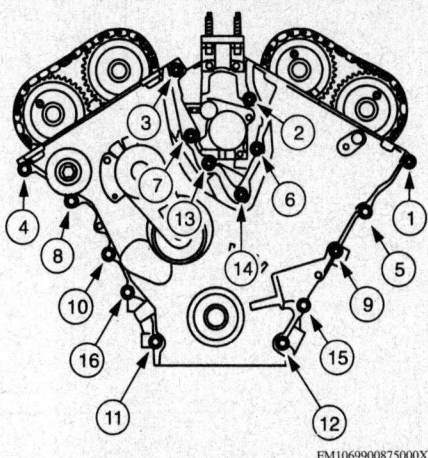

Fig. 10 Front engine cover bolt removal sequence

VALVE ADJUSTMENT

Valve clearance is hydraulically controlled and not adjustable.

CAMSHAFT FOLLOWERS
REPLACE

1. Remove valve covers and gaskets as outlined under "Valve Cover, Replace."
2. **Piston must be at bottom of its stroke with both valves closed. Any loss of air pressure will allow to fall into cylinder.** Remove spark plug.
3. Install adapter into spark plug bore and connect compressed air supply at 102–144 psi.
4. Compress valve spring using valve spring compressor tool No. T94P-6565-BH or equivalent, and remove roller follower.
5. Reverse procedure to install.

HYDRAULIC LASH ADJUSTER
REPLACE

Mark the position of camshaft follower and hydraulic lash adjuster to ensure they are assembled in original position if they are to be reused.
1. Remove valve covers and gaskets as outlined under "Valve Cover, Replace."
2. **Piston must be at bottom of its stroke with both valves closed. Any loss of air pressure will allow to fall into cylinder.** Remove spark plug.
3. Install adapter into spark plug bore and connect compressed air supply at 102–144 psi.
4. Compress valve spring using valve spring compressor tool No. T94P-6565-BH or equivalent, and remove roller follower.
5. Remove hydraulic lash adjusters.
6. Lubricate adjusters with engine assembly lubricant and install. Ensure lash adjusters are installed in original positions.

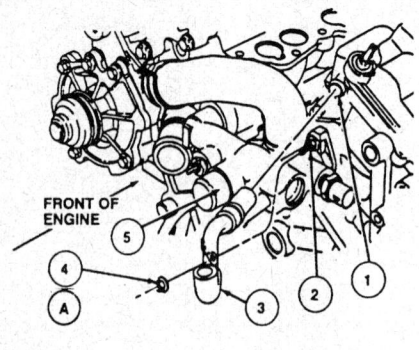

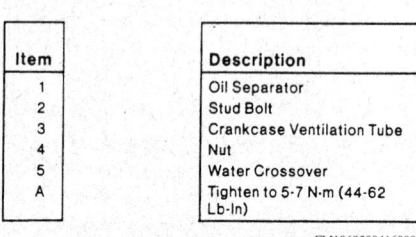

Item	Description
1	Oil Separator
2	Stud Bolt
3	Crankcase Ventilation Tube
4	Nut
5	Water Crossover
A	Tighten to 5-7 N·m (44-62 Lb-In)

FM1069500416000X

Fig. 11 Cylinder head replacement

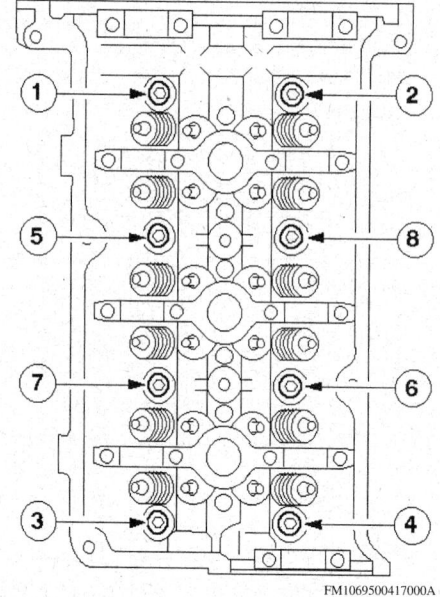

FM1069500417000A

Fig. 12 Cylinder head bolt removal sequence

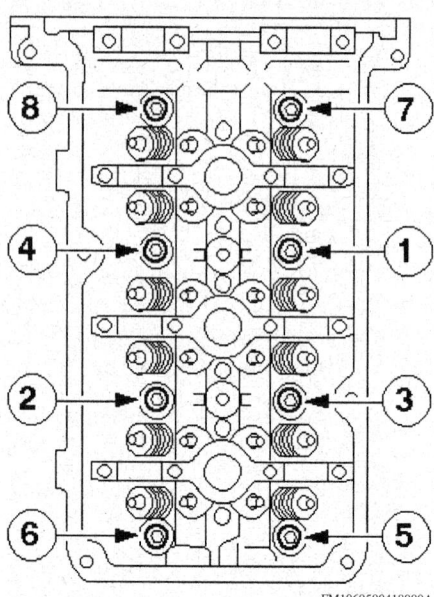

FM1069500418000A

Fig. 13 Cylinder head bolt tightening sequence

FRONT COVER
REPLACE

1. Remove lefthand and righthand valve covers as outlined under "Valve Cover, Replace."
2. Remove exhaust Y-pipe, exhaust support bracket nuts and support bracket.
3. Remove air conditioning compressor heat shield nuts and heat shield.
4. Drain engine oil into suitable container.
5. Remove flywheel access cover and oil pan bolts from transaxle housing.
6. Remove oil pan bolts and studs in sequence, **Fig. 9.** Discard gasket
7. Remove alternator and power steering pump.
8. Disconnect camshaft and crankshaft position sensor electrical connectors and remove.
9. Remove mounting bolts, studs and front cover, **Fig. 10.**
10. Reverse procedure to install, noting the following:
    a. Prior to applying sealer clean front cover to cylinder block and cylinder head sealing surfaces with metal surface cleaner F4AZ-19A536-RA.
    b. Install bolts and studs in indicated sequence, **Fig. 16.**
    c. Tighten seven bolts and studs one quarter turn (90°) after engine front cover contacts cylinder block and cylinder heads.
    d. Install remaining engine front cover bolts and studs, then **torque** to 18 ft. lbs., in sequence, **Fig. 17.**
    e. Lubricate new O-rings with engine oil before installation.
    f. Install position sensors and bolts.

TIMING CHAIN
REPLACE
Removal

1. Remove lefthand and righthand valve covers as outlined under "Valve Cover, Replace."
2. Remove exhaust Y-pipe, exhaust support bracket nuts and support bracket.
3. Remove air conditioning compressor heat shield nuts and heat shield.
4. Drain engine oil into suitable container.
5. Remove flywheel access cover and oil pan bolts from transaxle housing.
6. Remove oil pan bolts and studs in sequence, **Fig. 9.** Discard gasket
7. Remove alternator and power steering pump.
8. Disconnect camshaft and crankshaft position sensor electrical connectors and remove.
9. Remove mounting bolts, studs and front cover, **Fig. 10.**
10. Remove camshaft oil seal retainer, **Fig. 18.**
11. Remove crankshaft position sensor pulse wheel.
12. Install crankshaft pulley bolt and washer and turn crankshaft keyway clockwise to 11 o'clock position and engine at TDC of cylinder No. 1. Roller finger follower marks on back of camshaft sprockets must line up with one another, **Fig. 19.**
13. Turn crankshaft clockwise to position crankshaft keyway in 3 o'clock position.
14. Mark position of all chain drive components to ensure installation in original positions.
15. Remove righthand chain tensioner and tensioner arm bolts, chain tensioner and tensioner adapter plate.
16. Remove righthand timing chain guide and timing chain.
17. Remove righthand camshaft as follows:
    a. Remove camshaft thrust caps Nos. 1R and 5R. **Fig. 20.**
    b. Loosen camshaft bearing caps in several passes in sequence, **Fig. 20.**
    c. Remove bearing caps.
18. **Piston must be at bottom of its stroke with both valves closed. Any loss of air pressure will allow to fall into cylinder.** Remove spark plug.
19. Install adapter into spark plug bore and connect compressed air supply at 102–144 psi.
20. Compress valve spring using valve spring compressor tool No. T94P-6565-BH or equivalent, and remove roller follower.
21. Turn crankshaft clockwise two revolutions until keyway is in 11 o'clock position.
22. Remove crankshaft pulley bolt and washer.
23. Remove lefthand chain tensioner and tensioner arm.
24. Remove lefthand timing chain fixed chain guide and timing chain.
25. Remove lefthand camshaft as follows:
    a. Remove camshaft thrust caps Nos. 1L and 5L. **Fig. 21.**
    b. Loosen camshaft bearing caps in several passes in sequence, **Fig. 21.**
    c. Remove bearing caps.
26. **Piston must be at bottom of its stroke with both valves closed. Any loss of air pressure will allow to fall into cylinder.** Remove spark plug.
27. Install adapter into spark plug bore and connect compressed air supply at 102–144 psi.
28. Compress valve spring using valve spring compressor tool No. T94P-6565-BH or equivalent, and remove roller follower.
29. Remove righthand and lefthand timing chain sprockets.

Installation

1. Install crankshaft pulley washer and bolt.
2. Install righthand and lefthand timing

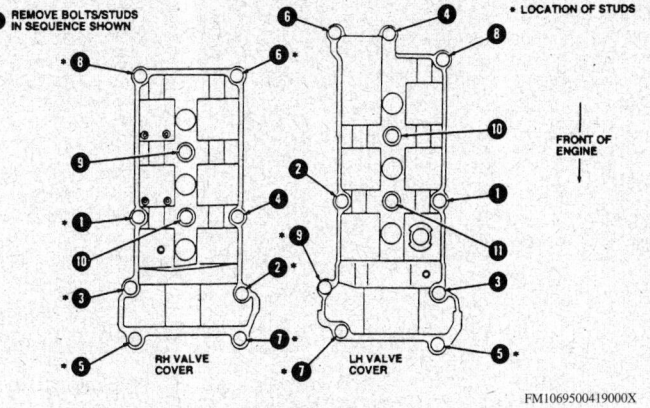

Fig. 14 Valve cover bolt removal sequence

Fig. 15 Valve cover bolt tightening sequence

chain sprocket, washer and bolt.
3. Turn crankshaft clockwise to position key to 11 o'clock position.
4. Remove crankshaft pulley bolt and washer.
5. Lubricate camshafts with engine assembly lubricator.
6. Install lefthand chain guide and bolts (black material), then timing chain. **Timing chain colored links and marks on timing sprockets must line up.**
7. Position timing chain tensioner in suitable vise with jaw protectors.
8. During tensioner compression, do not release ratchet stem until tensioner piston is fully bottomed in its bore or damage to ratchet stem will result.
9. Support timing chain tensioner ratchet lock mechanism away from ratchet stem with small pick.
10. Slowly compress timing chain tensioner. **Piston should retract with minimal force. If binding occurs, reposition tensioner to eliminate side loading.**
11. Retain piston with suitable paper clip. **Wire must remain in timing chain tensioner until tensioner is installed onto engine with piston bottomed in bore.**
12. Install lefthand tensioner arm (black material), tensioner adapter plate and timing chain tensioner.
13. Install righthand chain guide and bolts (tan material), then timing chain. **Timing chain colored links and marks on timing sprockets must line up.**
14. Set tensioner as outlined in previous steps.
15. Install righthand tensioner arm (tan material), tensioner adapter plate and timing chain tensioner.
16. Install lefthand roller finger followers.
17. Install lefthand camshaft bearing caps and tighten to sequence, **Fig. 22.** Do not install thrust caps until camshaft journal caps are installed.
18. Install crankshaft pulley bolt and washer.
19. Rotating crankshaft counterclockwise may cause timing chains to bind and may cause engine damage. Turn engine clockwise to locate crankshaft keyway to 3 o'clock position.
20. Install righthand roller finger followers.

21. Install righthand camshaft bearing caps and tighten to sequence, **Fig. 22.** Do not install thrust caps until camshaft journal caps are installed.
22. Remove righthand and lefthand chain tensioner retaining wires.
23. Remove crankshaft pulley bolt and washer.
24. Install camshaft oil seal retainer.
25. Install pulse wheel with keyway in slot stamped 25, color code blue.
26. Install new camshaft oil seal.
27. Install engine front cover.

TIMING CHAIN TENSIONER

REPLACE

Refer to "Timing Chain, Replace" for timing chain tensioner replacement procedure.

CAMSHAFT

REPLACE

Refer to "Timing Chain, Replace" for camshaft replacement procedures.

CRANKSHAFT SEAL

REPLACE

1. Raise and support vehicle, then remove righthand front wheel and tire assembly.
2. Remove righthand splash shield from fender apron for access to crankshaft pulley.
3. Turn accessory drive belt using suitable breaker bar installed in ⅜ inch square hole in drive belt tensioner.
4. Lift accessory drive belt over pulley flanges and remove.
5. Remove crankshaft pulley bolt and washer from crankshaft, then, using crankshaft damper remover tool No. T58P-6316-D, or equivalent, remove crankshaft pulley from crankshaft.
6. Remove crankshaft front seal from front cover using seal remover tool No. T92C-6700-CH, or equivalent.
7. Reverse procedure to install, noting following:
   a. Lubricate seal sealing surfaces with suitable engine assembly lubricant, then, using crankshaft seal

replacer tool No. T88T-6701-A and crankshaft damper replacer tool No. T74P-7316-B, or equivalents, install crankshaft front seal into front cover.
   b. Clean crankshaft pulley sealing surfaces with suitable metal cleaner to remove all residues which could interfere with sealer's ability to adhere.
   c. Apply black silicone rubber part No. F4AZ-19562-B, or equivalent, to front of crankshaft on inside diameter surface of pulley at keyway.
   d. Install crankshaft pulley using crankshaft damper replacer tool No. T74P-6316-B, or equivalent, and washer from bolt.
   e. **Torque** crankshaft pulley bolt to 89 ft. lbs., and loosen bolt one full turn.
   f. **torque** bolt to 35–39 ft. lbs., and tighten bolt an additional 85–95°.

CRANKSHAFT REAR OIL SEAL

REPLACE

1. Remove transaxle as outlined in **MOTOR's "Domestic Transmission Manual, In-Vehicle Service."**
2. Record position of flywheel on crankshaft flange and remove flywheel bolts.
3. Install rear crankshaft seal remover tool No. T95P-6701-EH, or equivalent, **Fig. 23.** Install slide hammer and remove rear crankshaft seal. **Avoid scratching or damaging oil seal sealing surfaces on crankshaft and cylinder block.**
4. Reverse procedure to install, noting the following:
   a. Clean and inspect crankshaft rear oil seal sealing surfaces.
   b. Lubricate crankshaft flange, crankshaft rear oil seal bore and oil seal lip with Engine Assembly Lubricant D9AZ-19579-D, or equivalent.
   c. Alternately tighten bolt until crankshaft rear oil seal is flush with cylinder block, using rear main seal replacer tool No. T82L-6701-A, or equivalent, **Fig. 24.**

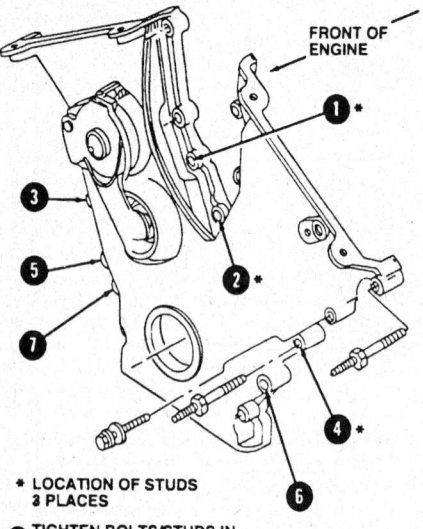

* LOCATION OF STUDS
  3 PLACES
● TIGHTEN BOLTS/STUDS IN
  SEQUENCE SHOWN

FM1069500428000X

Fig. 16 Front cover bolt & stud bolt installation sequence

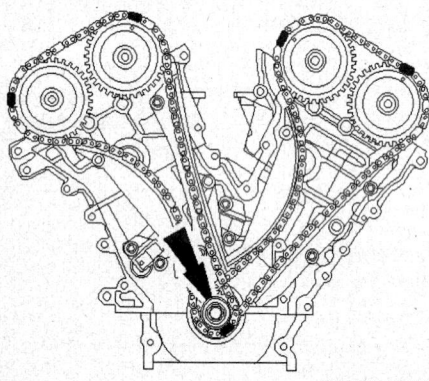

FM1060101422000X

Fig. 19 Crankshaft & camshaft alignment

OIL PAN
REPLACE

1. Remove exhaust Y-pipe, exhaust support bracket nuts and support bracket.
2. Remove air conditioning compressor heat shield nuts and heat shield.
3. Drain engine oil into suitable container.
4. Remove flywheel access cover and oil pan bolts from transaxle housing.
5. Remove oil pan bolts and studs in sequence, **Fig. 9**. Discard gasket.
6. Reverse procedure to install, noting the following:
   a. Position oil pan and loosely install bolts and studs.
   b. Install oil pan to transaxle housing bolts.
   c. Tighten bolts in sequence, **Fig. 25**.

OIL PUMP
REPLACE

1. Remove lefthand and righthand valve covers as outlined under "Valve Cover, Replace."
2. Remove exhaust Y-pipe, exhaust support bracket nuts and support bracket.

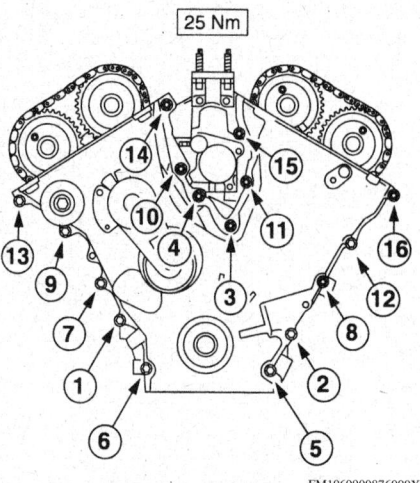

FM1069900876000X

Fig. 17 Front engine cover tightening sequence

3. Remove air conditioning compressor heat shield nuts and heat shield.
4. Drain engine oil into suitable container.
5. Remove flywheel access cover and oil pan bolts from transaxle housing.
6. Remove oil pan bolts and studs in sequence, **Fig. 9**. Discard gasket
7. Remove alternator and power steering pump.
8. Disconnect camshaft and crankshaft position sensor electrical connectors and remove.
9. Remove mounting bolts, studs and front cover, **Fig. 10**.
10. Remove timing chains as outlined under "Timing Chain, Replace."
11. Remove crankshaft sprocket and oil pump bolts in sequence, **Fig. 26**.
12. Remove pump from cylinder block.
13. Reverse procedure to install. **Torque** oil pump bolts to 72–108 inch lbs., in sequence, **Fig. 27**.

BELT TENSION DATA

Drive belts have an automatic drive belt tensioner and do not require adjustment.

The automatic belt tensioner is a spring loaded device which sets and maintains drive belt tension. Drive belts should not require tension adjustment for the life of the drive belt.

SERPENTINE DRIVE BELT
Routing

Refer to **Figs. 28 and 29**, for belt routing.

Belt Replacement
WATER PUMP

1. Remove engine cover and turn drive belt tensioner clockwise by hand.
2. Lift drive belt over pulley flanges and remove.
3. Reverse procedure to install.

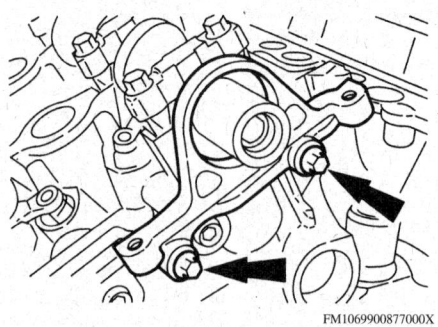

FM1069900877000X

Fig. 18 Camshaft oil seal removal

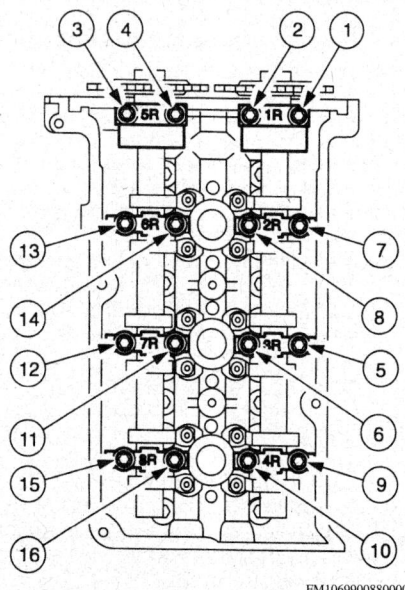

FM1069900880000X

Fig. 20 Righthand camshaft cap bolts loosening sequence

ACCESSORY DRIVE

1. Raise and support vehicle.
2. Turn drive belt using suitable breaker bar installed in ⅜ inch square hole in drive belt tensioner.
3. Lift accessory drive belt over pulley flanges and remove.
4. Reverse procedure to install.

TENSIONER REPLACEMENT
ACCESSORY DRIVE

1. Raise and support vehicle.
2. Turn drive belt using suitable breaker bar installed in ⅜ inch square hole in drive belt tensioner.
3. Lift accessory drive belt over pulley flanges and remove.
4. Loosen belt tensioner bolts and remove tensioner from front of engine.
5. Align drive belt tensioner spring to slot in front cover and install tensioner onto front cover.

WATER PUMP

1. Remove tensioner bolt and tensioner from water pump.
2. Align tab on tensioner with hole in mounting area on water pump and install tensioner onto pump.

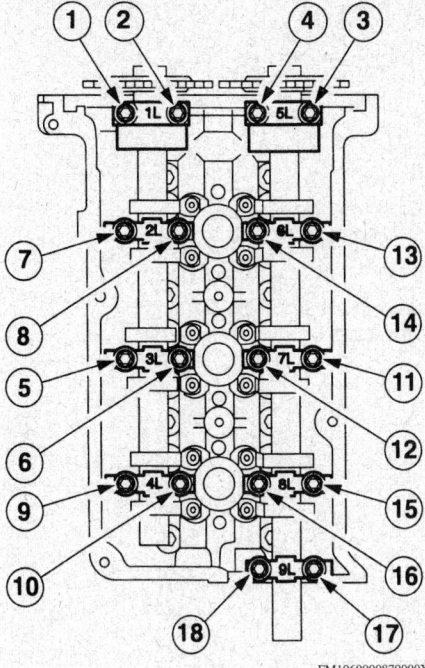

Fig. 21 Lefthand camshaft cap bolt loosening sequence

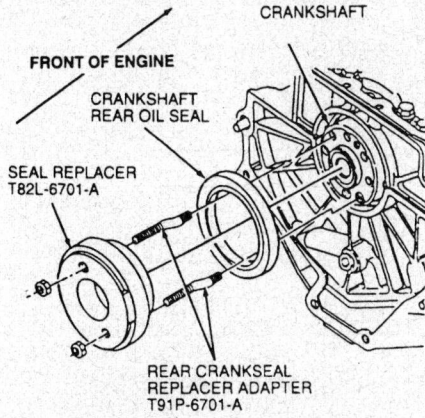

NOTE: LUBRICATE CRANKSHAFT FLANGE AND REAR OIL SEAL BORE WITH ENGINE ASSY LUBRICANT D9AZ-19579-D OR EQUIVALENT MEETING FORD SPECIFICATION ESR-M99C80-A PRIOR TO INSTALLATION OF SEAL

Fig. 24 Crankshaft rear oil seal installation

COOLING SYSTEM BLEED

These engines do not require a specific bleed procedure. To ensure coolant level is satisfactory, start the engine, turn heater control to its maximum heat and vent positions. After engine reaches normal operat-

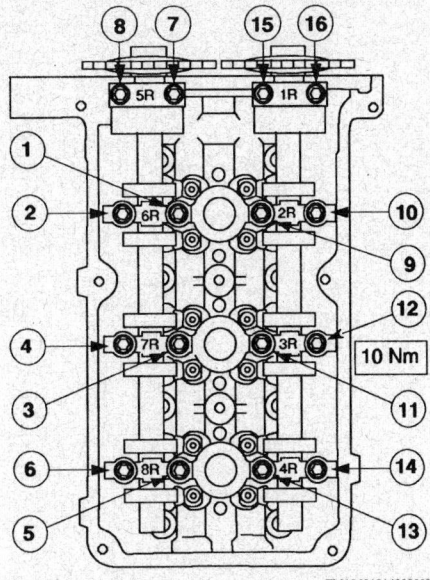

Fig. 22 Camshaft cap bolt tightening sequence

ing temperature, hot air should be blowing from the air conditioning vents. If cool air is blowing from the vents, coolant level is low, turn engine off and add coolant as required.

THERMOSTAT
REPLACE

1. Drain engine cooling system into suitable container so engine coolant level is below water thermostat.
2. Remove engine cover, if equipped
3. Disconnect radiator hoses from thermostat housing and remove housing.
4. Remove housing bolts and separate thermostat housings.
5. Remove O-ring seal and thermostat from housing.
6. Reverse procedure to install.

WATER PUMP
REPLACE

1. Remove battery and air cleaner.
2. Remove thermostat housing and engine cover.
3. Turn belt tensioner clockwise by hand and remove belt.
4. **On models equipped with automatic transmission,** disconnect transmission range selector electrical connector.
5. **On all models,** remove water pump bolts, coolant hoses and water pump.
6. Remove water pump from housing.
7. Reverse procedure to install. Replace gasket and O-ring.

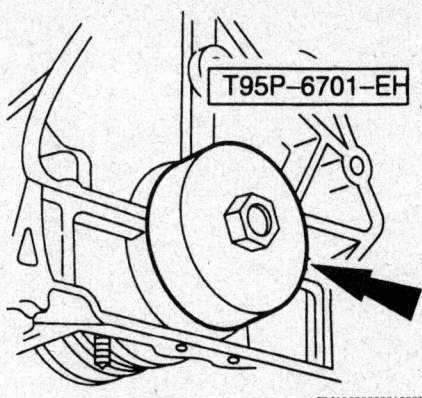

Fig. 23 Rear crankshaft seal remover tool installation

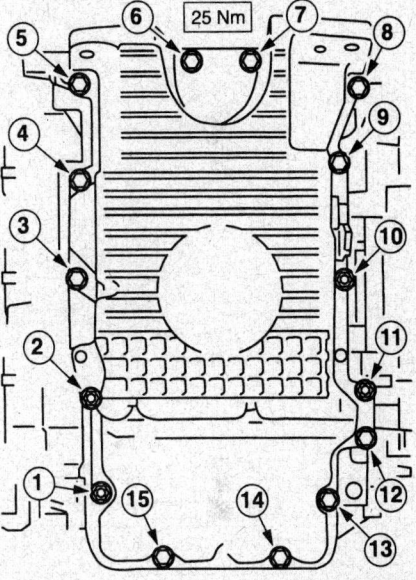

Fig. 25 Oil pan tightening sequence

RADIATOR
REPLACE

Refer to "2.0L Engine" for radiator replacement procedure.

FUEL PUMP
REPLACE

Refer to "2.0L Engine" for fuel pump replacement procedure.

FUEL FILTER
REPLACE

Refer to "2.0L Engine" for fuel filter replacement procedure.

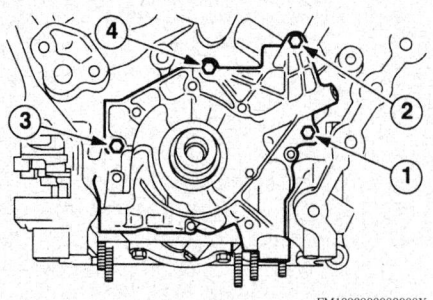

FM1099900080000X

Fig. 26 Oil pump bolt removal sequence

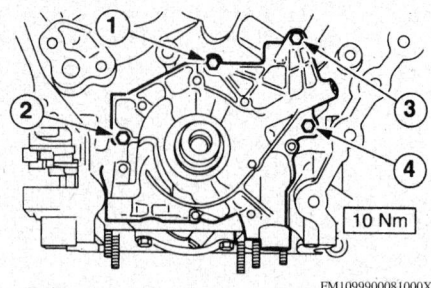

FM1099900081000X

Fig. 27 Oil pump bolt tightening sequence

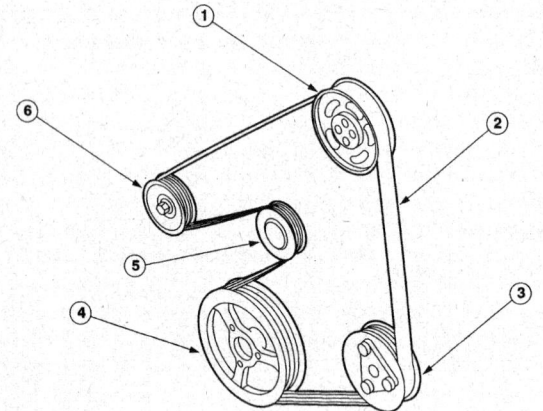

Item	Description
1	Power steering pump pulley
2	Accesory drive belt
3	Air conditioning pump pulley

Item	Description
4	Crankshaft pulley
5	Belt tensioner
6	Generator pulley

FM1069500439000A

Fig. 28 Accessory drive belt routing. With air conditioning

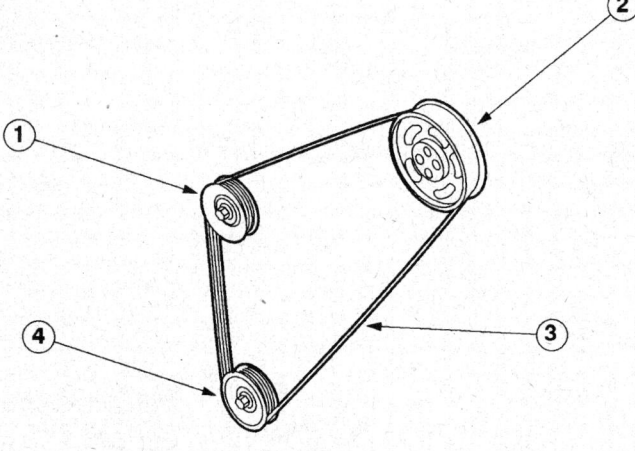

Item	Description
1	Belt tensioner
2	Water pump pulley
3	Water pump belt
4	Water pump drive pulley

FM1069500440000A

Fig. 29 Water pump drive belt routing

TIGHTENING SPECIFICATIONS

Year	Component	Torque/Ft. Lbs.
2001–02	Air Conditioning Compressor	15–22
	Air Conditioning Condenser Core To Radiator	60①
	Air Conditioning Hose Bracket To Front Cover	72–108①
	Accelerator Cable Bracket To Throttle Body	72–108①
	Accessory Drive Belt Tensioner	15–22
	Battery Ground Cable To Engine/ Transaxle Stud	15–22
	Camshaft Journal Cap	72–108①
	Camshaft Journal Thrust Cap	72–108①
	Camshaft Rear Oil Seal Retainer	72–108①
	Crankcase Ventilation Tube	44–62①
	Crankshaft Pulley	⑦
	Cylinder Head	②
	Drive Belt Idler Pulley	15–22
	EGR Valve To Exhaust Manifold Tube	26–33
	Engine Air Cleaner Tube Clamps	24–48①
	Engine Rear Plate	54–64③
	Engine & Transaxle Support Insulator	④
	Exhaust Manifold	15
	Fan Shroud	24–48①
	Flywheel	59③
	Front Engine Support Bracket	61
	Front Engine Support Bracket To Sub-Frame	20
	Front Stabilizer Link To Front Stabilizer Bar	35
	Front Tie Rod End	⑥
	Front Wheel Knuckle To Front Suspension Lower Arm	40
	Heated Oxygen Sensor	30
	Inline Fuel Filter Worm Gear Mounting Clamp	15–25①
	Intake Manifold	⑤
	Lower Radiator Hose Tube	72–108①
	Lower Radiator Support	72–96①
	Muffler Inlet Flange	26–33
	Oil Pan Drain Plug	19
	Oil Pan To Transaxle	25–34
	Oil Pan To Transaxle Housing	25–34
	Oil Pump	72–108①
	Oil Pump Screen Cover & Tube	72–108①
	Oil Pump Screen Cover & Tube Support	15–22
	Power Steering Pressure Hose Bracket	72–108①
	Power Steering Pump	18
	Power Steering Pump Pulley	18
	Power Steering Pump Support	72–108①
	Radiator To Front Sub-Frame	72–96①
	Shift Cable Bracket	17
	Shift Rod	17
	Stabilizer Bar	41
	Steering Shaft Pinch Bolt	18
	Thermostat Housing	18
	Three-Way Catalytic Converter	27
	Transaxle Oil Cooler Line Bracket	20

Continued

TIGHTENING SPECIFICATIONS—Continued

Year	Component	Torque/Ft. Lbs.
2001–02	Transaxle Oil Cooler Tube To Fitting	21
	Transaxle Stabilizer Bar	41
	Transaxle To Engine	30
	Torque Converter To Flywheel	59
	Upper Intake Manifold	84①
	Valve Cover	72–108①
	Water Crossover Pipe (Bypass Tube) To Cylinder Head	72–108①
	Water Pump	13
	Water Pump Drive Belt Tensioner	72–108①
	Wheel Lug Nuts	94

① — Inch lbs.
② — Refer to "Cylinder Head, Replace" for tighten specifications and sequence.
③ — Tighten in an alternating pattern.
④ — Automatic transaxle, 30–41 ft. lbs.; manual transaxle, 52–70 ft. lbs.
⑤ — Refer to "Intake Manifold, Replace" for tighten specifications and sequence.
⑥ — Refer to "Engine, Replace" for tighten specifications and sequence.
⑦ — Refer to "Crankshaft Seal, Replace" for tighten specifications and sequence.

Rear Suspension

NOTE: On Air Bag Equipped Models, Refer To "Air Bag System Precautions" Located In The Front Of This Manual For System Disarming & Arming Procedures.

NOTE: Refer To "Computer Relearn Procedures" Located In The Front Of This Manual When Battery Power To The Computer Has Been Interrupted.

INDEX

DESCRIPTION

Rear suspension has a quadralink design, **Fig. 1.** This is basically two horizontal, pressed steel, lateral arms each side of the vehicle, attached to a pressed steel crossmember at the inner pivots and cast iron spindle assemblies at the outer pivots. The lateral arms control the toe change of the rear wheels. The third link of the quadralink system is a tie bar which connects the wheel spindle to a forward body mounted bracket. The fourth link is a McPherson strut mounted on top of the wheel spindle. The strut controls the camber and reacts to braking torque. The tie bar and lateral arms connect through rubber bushes, the strut is mounted to the spindle assembly. The rear lateral arm joint to the crossmember allows toe adjustment by rotation of a cam bolt. The system has additional roll control by use of a stabilizer bar, connected between the crossmember and the front lateral arms. A hub and bearing assembly runs on the wheel spindle and locates on the brake drum or disc, and the wheel.

HUB & BEARING
REPLACE

1. Raise and support vehicle, then remove wheel.

2. **On models equipped with rear disc brakes,** remove caliper and brake rotor. **It is not required to disconnect hydraulic line from caliper; support caliper aside to prevent hydraulic line damage.**
3. **On models equipped with rear drum brakes,** remove retainer and brake drum.
4. **On all models,** remove rear axle wheel hub retainer and remove wheel hub. **Do not use impact wrench to loosen retainer; spindle damage may result.**
5. Reverse procedure to install. Tighten new retainer and wheel lug nuts.

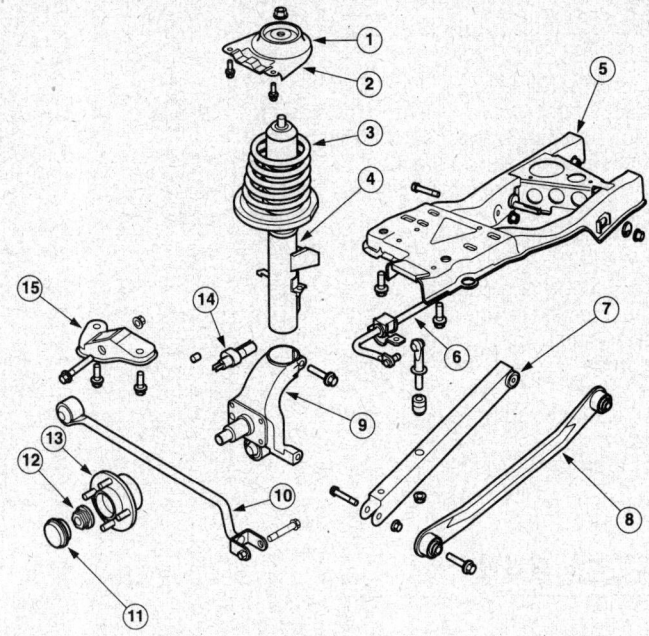

**Fig. 1 Exploded view of rear suspension
(Part 1 of 2)**

Item	Description
1	Body mounting cup
2	Spring seat
3	Spring
4	Strut
5	Crossmember
6	Stabilizer bar
7	Front lower arm
8	Rear lower arm
9	Wheel spindle
10	Tie-bar
11	Dust cap
12	Hub retaining nut
13	Hub and bearing assembly
14	Wheel speed sensor
15	Tie-bar mounting bracket

FM2039700060020X

**Fig. 1 Exploded view of rear
suspension (Part 2 of 2)**

WHEEL BEARING

ADJUST

Wheel bearings are pre-greased and sealed. Bearing require no periodic maintenance. Cartridge design prohibits adjustment.

REAR WHEEL SPINDLE

REPLACE

1. Raise and support vehicle, then remove wheel and rear anti-lock brake sensor.
2. **On models equipped with rear disc brakes,** remove caliper and brake rotor. **It is not required to disconnect hydraulic line from caliper; support caliper aside to prevent hydraulic line damage.**
3. **On models equipped with rear drum brakes,** remove retainer and brake drum.
4. **On all models,** remove rear axle wheel hub retainer and remove wheel hub. **Do not use impact wrench to loosen retainer; spindle damage may result.**
5. **On models equipped with rear disc brakes,** remove disc brake shield.
6. **On models equipped with rear drum brakes,** proceed as follows:
    a. Remove brake backing plate and position aside.
    b. Disconnect stabilizer bar link from lateral arm.
7. **On all models,** disconnect rear suspension tie rod and bushing at spindle, **Fig. 2.**
8. Disconnect rearward and forward suspension arms with bushings from spindle, then remove strut to spindle pinch bolt.
9. Remove spindle from strut assembly.
10. Reverse procedure to install, noting the following:
    a. When installing rear suspension arms, tie rods and respective bushings on spindle.
    b. Tighten bolts snugly, but do not final tighten until other components have been installed and vehicle weight is on wheels.
    c. **Do not use impact wrench to tighten new wheel hub retainer.**

STRUT

REPLACE

1. Raise and support vehicle, then remove wheel.
2. Disconnect anti-lock brake sensor wiring from strut assembly and remove sensor.
3. **On models equipped with drum brakes,** clamp and disconnect rear brake hose from brake tube, then remove hose and retainer from strut.
4. **On models equipped with disc brakes,** remove brake hose.
5. **On all models,** remove wheel spindle to suspension unit pinch bolt.
6. Remove wheel spindle from suspension unit.
7. Raise suspension unit of suitable jack and remove suspension unit from crossmember.
8. Remove suspension unit.

STRUT SERVICE

1. Position strut assembly in Rotunda strut spring compressor tool No. 014-00781, or equivalent, and compress spring.
2. Remove top nut, bracket, bushing and spring seat, then slowly release spring compressor tool, **Fig. 3.**
3. Remove spring, dust shield and jounce bumper.
4. Reverse procedure to assemble. Tighten top nut.

CONTROL ARM

REPLACE

LOWER

FRONT ARM

1. Raise and support vehicle, then remove wheel.
2. Remove stabilizer bar link and bushing from front lateral arm, then the front lateral arm from spindle.
3. Remove tie bar from spindle carrier, release three exhaust mounting and support exhaust system.
4. Support crossmember and remove crossmember bolts and lower.
5. Reverse procedure to install, noting following:
    a. When installing forward arm and bushing to crossmember bolt and nut, ensure bolt head faces fuel tank.
    b. Tighten bolt and nut snugly, but do not final tighten until vehicle weight is resting upon rear wheels.

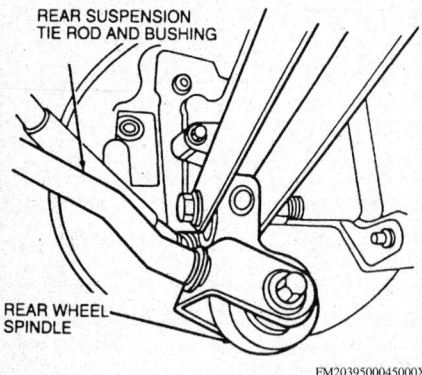

REAR SUSPENSION
TIE ROD AND BUSHING

REAR WHEEL
SPINDLE

FM2039500045000X

Fig. 2 Rear spindle assembly

REAR ARM

1. Raise and support vehicle, then remove wheel and disconnect rear arm from spindle.
2. Remove rear lateral arm from crossmember.
3. Reverse procedure to install, noting following:
   a. When installing rearward arm, connect to spindle and tighten bolts and nuts snugly, but do not final tighten until vehicle weight is resting upon rear wheels. **Tighten wheel lug nuts before lowering vehicle.**
   b. After vehicle weight is resting on rear wheels, tighten rearward arm bolts and nuts.

TIE ROD
REPLACE

1. Raise and support vehicle, then remove wheel.
2. Disconnect parking brake cable and conduit from forward tie rod bracket.
3. Remove exhaust rubber from tie bar bracket.
4. Remove tie strap securing parking brake rear cable and conduit to rear suspension tie rod and bushing.
5. Disconnect tie rod and bushing assembly at spindle.
6. Remove bolts, tie rod, bushing and front bracket.
7. Remove bolt, tie rod and front bracket assembly.
8. Reverse procedure to install.

STABILIZER BAR
REPLACE

1. Raise and support vehicle.
2. Remove stabilizer bar links and bushings from front lateral arms.
3. Remove stabilizer bar bushings.
4. Remove righthand tie bar from wheel spindle and stabilizer bar.
5. Reverse procedure to install.

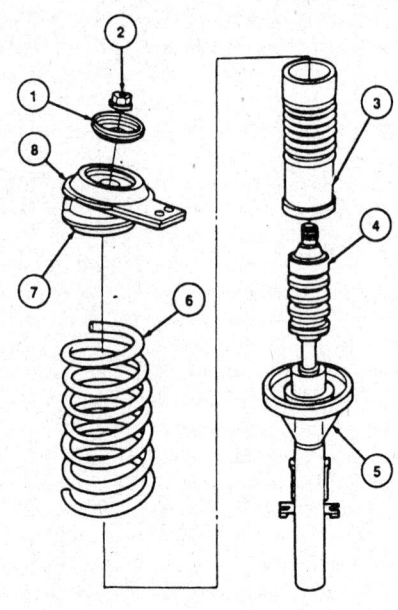

Item	Description
1	Rear Shock Absorber Bracket
2	Shock Absorber Mounting Nut
3	Rear Shock Absorber Dust Boot
4	Rear Suspension Jounce Bumper
5	Shock Absorber
6	Rear Spring
7	Spring Seat
8	Shock Absorber Bushing

FM2039500047000X

Fig. 3 Exploded view of strut assembly

TIGHTENING SPECIFICATIONS

Year	Component	Torque/Ft. Lbs.
2001–02	Anti-Lock Sensor	90①
	Drum Brake Backing Plate	33–40
	Rearward Rear Suspension Arm To Crossmember	52–79
	Spindle To Forward Rear Suspension Arm	52–79
	Spindle To Rearward Rear Suspension Arm	75–102
	Stabilizer Bar Bracket	14–19
	Stabilizer Bar Link To Rear Suspension Arm	22–30
	Strut Mount	17–22
	Strut, Top	30–43
	Strut To Spindle Pinch Bolt	52–72
	Tie Rod Forward Bracket To Body	75–102
	Tie Rod To Spindle	75–102
	Wheel Hub Retainer	214
	Wheel Lug Nuts	94

① — Inch lbs.

Front Suspension & Steering

NOTE: On Air Bag Equipped Models, Refer To "Air Bag System Precautions" Located In The Front Of This Manual For System Disarming & Arming Procedures.

NOTE: Refer To "Computer Relearn Procedures" Located In The Front Of This Manual When Battery Power To The Computer Has Been Interrupted.

INDEX

PRECAUTIONS

Battery Ground Cable

Prior to service, disconnect battery ground cable and isolate as required.

Air Bag Systems

Refer to "Air Bag System Precautions" in front of this manual for system disarming and arming procedures.

DESCRIPTION

Front suspension utilizes McPherson struts, a stabilizer bar, lower control arms and a tubular perimeter frame. Steering control is maintained by an integral power rack and pinion steering gear coupled with a belt driven, vane type power steering pump. Power steering fluid is contained in a remote reservoir.

WHEEL BEARING

ADJUST

Wheel bearings are pre-greased and sealed. Bearing require no periodic maintenance. Cartridge design prohibits adjustment.

HUB & BEARING

REPLACE

1. Raise and support vehicle, then remove wheel, caliper and rotor. **It is not required to disconnect brake hydraulic line to caliper. However, support caliper chassis.**
2. Remove front brake anti-lock sensor and tie rod end cotter pin and loosen tie rod end to knuckle nut.
3. Separate tie rod end from knuckle

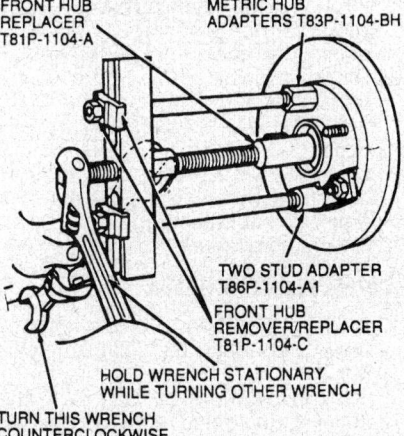

MAKE SURE THE HUB REMOVER ADAPTER IS FULLY THREADED ONTO THE HUB STUD AND IS POSITIONED OPPOSITE THE TWO STUD ADAPTER

FRONT HUB REPLACER T81P-1104-A

METRIC HUB ADAPTERS T83P-1104-BH

TWO STUD ADAPTER T86P-1104-A1

FRONT HUB REMOVER/REPLACER T81P-1104-C

HOLD WRENCH STATIONARY WHILE TURNING OTHER WRENCH

TURN THIS WRENCH COUNTERCLOCKWISE

FM2029500093000X

Fig. 1 Hub assembly replacement

using rod end remover tool No. 3290-D, or equivalent.
4. Insert steel rod into front disc brake rotor to prevent turning and remove front axle wheel hub mounting nut.
5. Separate halfshaft from wheel hub using special tools, **Fig. 1. Support halfshaft during separation from wheel hub.**
6. Reverse procedure to install.

BALL JOINT INSPECTION

1. Raise and support vehicle.
2. Grasp lower control arm, then attempt to move it up and down while listening and watching for any free movement.

3. An audible click noise usually appears if free movement is present, which must be corrected by replacing lower control arm.

BALL JOINT

REPLACE

Removal

1. Raise and support vehicle, then remove wheel and lower arm as outlined under "Control Arm, Replace."
2. Drill .118 inch pilot hole through each rivet and drill .354 inch hole in rivets to depth of .472 inch, **Fig. 2.**
3. Drive rivets out using suitable .275–.314 inch diameter punch and remove ball joint.

Installation

1. Allow protective cover to remain on ball joint to protect seal and position ball joint in lower arm.
2. Install three bolts and nuts in lower arm to replace rivets **Fig. 3.**
3. Install lower arm as outlined under "Control Arm, Replace," then install wheel and lower vehicle.

STRUT

REPLACE

1. Raise and support vehicle.
2. Remove wheel and while supporting piston rod with suitable hex wrench, **Fig. 4.**
3. Remove strut top nut.
4. Disconnect stabilizer bar link from strut assembly, then disconnect brake hose and anti-lock brake sensor wiring from strut brackets.

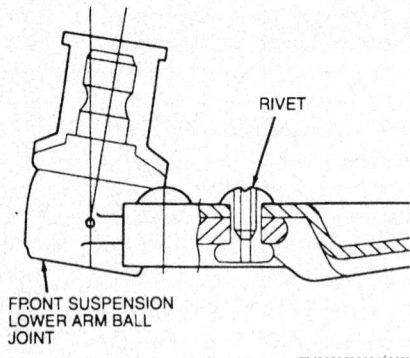

Fig. 2   Ball joint rivets

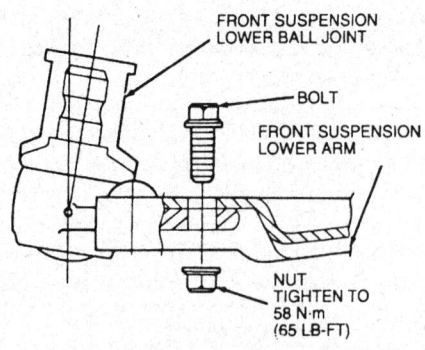

Fig. 3   Ball joint bolt installation

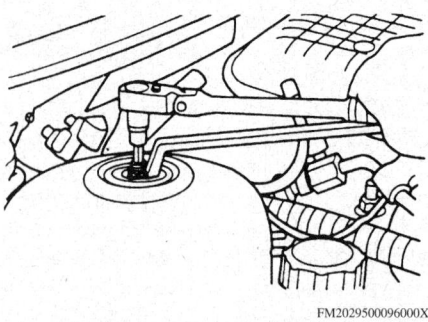

Fig. 4   Strut top nut replacement

5. Remove strut to knuckle pinch bolt and strut assembly.
6. Reverse procedure to install, noting following:
   a. Install strut top nut before tightening strut to knuckle pinch bolt, **Fig. 4.**
   b. During stabilizer bar link installation, avoid damaging ball joint seal.

COIL SPRING & STRUT SERVICE

1. Raise and support vehicle.
2. Remove wheel and while supporting piston rod with suitable hex wrench, **Fig. 4.**
3. Remove strut top nut.
4. Disconnect stabilizer bar link from strut assembly, then disconnect brake hose and anti-lock brake sensor wiring from strut brackets.
5. Remove strut to knuckle pinch bolt and strut assembly.
6. Position assembly in Rotunda spring compressor tool No. 086-00029, or equivalent.
7. Compress coil spring and remove thrust bearing retainer nut, thrust bearing, spring seat and dust shield, **Fig. 5.**
8. Release spring compressor tension, then remove coil spring from strut assembly and jounce bumper, **Fig. 5.**
9. Reverse procedure to assemble, noting following:
   a. Compress coil spring for installation using Rotunda spring compressor tool No. 086-0029B, or equivalent.
   b. Ensure coil spring seats properly in spring seat notch.

CONTROL ARM
REPLACE
Lower
LEFTHAND SIDE

1. Support radiator assembly.
2. **On models equipped with 2.0L engine,** remove heat shield and catalytic converter mounting nuts from exhaust manifold.

3. **On all models,** raise and support vehicle, then remove three-way catalytic converter.
4. Disconnect steering column lower yoke.
5. **On models equipped with manual transaxle,** disconnect gearshift rod and clevis.
6. **On all models,** remove lower front radiator cover, radiator supports and ball joint to knuckle pinch bolts.
7. Remove lower arm ball joints from knuckle, then disconnect power steering cooler lines at righthand front subframe and stabilizer bar link at front stabilizer bar.
8. Remove front and rear engine mount through bolts, then position Rotunda powertrain lift tool No. 014-00765, or equivalent, under front subframe.
9. Remove lower arm bushing to subframe nuts and lower subframe to gain access to lower suspension mounting bolts.
10. Remove four lower arm to subframe bolts and nuts, then separate lower arm from subframe, **Fig. 6.**
11. Reverse procedure to install.

RIGHTHAND SIDE

1. Raise and support vehicle, then remove wheel and ball joint to knuckle pinch bolt.
2. Separate lower arm ball joint from knuckle and remove four lower arm bushing to subframe bolts, **Fig. 6.**
3. Reverse procedure to instal.

STEERING KNUCKLE
REPLACE

1. Raise and support vehicle, then remove wheel, caliper and rotor. **It is not required to disconnect brake hydraulic line to caliper. However, support caliper chassis.**
2. Remove front brake anti-lock sensor and tie rod end cotter pin and loosen tie rod end to knuckle nut.
3. Separate tie rod end from knuckle using rod end remover tool No. 3290-D, or equivalent.
4. Insert steel rod into front disc brake rotor to prevent turning and remove front axle wheel hub mounting nut.
5. Separate halfshaft from wheel hub

using special tools, **Fig. 1. Support halfshaft during separation from wheel hub.**
6. Remove pinch bolt securing knuckle to lower arm ball joint.
7. Remove strut to knuckle pinch bolt and knuckle, **Fig. 7.**
8. Reverse procedure to install. Install new pinch bolts and nuts on knuckle mounts.

STABILIZER BAR
REPLACE

1. Raise and support vehicle, then remove both front wheels.
2. Remove stabilizer bar link from strut assembly, **Fig. 8,** then use ball joint remover tool No. D88L-3006-A, or equivalent, to remove link from stabilizer bar. **Do not damage stabilizer bar link ball joint seal during removal. Link assembly must be replaced if seal is damaged.**
3. Remove four stabilizer bar insulator bracket to subframe bolts and stabilizer bar.
4. Reverse procedure to install. **Do not damage stabilizer bar link ball joint seal during installation. Link assembly must be replaced if seal is damaged.**

TIE ROD END
REPLACE

1. Remove and discard cotter pin and nut from tie rod end.
2. Separate tie rod end from steering knuckle using tie rod end remover tool No. 3290-D, or equivalent.
3. While supporting tie rod end with suitable wrench, loosen jam nut slightly. **Allow jam nut to remain as close to its original position as possible for tie rod end installation depth reference.**
4. Remove tie rod end from tie rod using suitable pliers.
5. Reverse procedure to install, noting following:
   a. Thread new tie rod end onto tie rod only until it reaches jam nut.
   b. Support with jam nut until wheel alignment can be inspected and set.
   c. Install new tie rod end stud nut and cotter pin.
   d. Tighten tie rod end to knuckle nut and tie rod end jam nut.

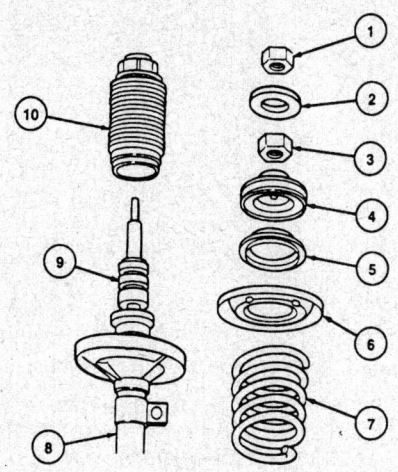

Fig. 5 Exploded view of strut assembly

Item	Description
1	Nut
2	Retainer
3	Upper Mount Retainer Nut
4	Upper Mount
5	Bearing
6	Spring Seat
7	Front Coil Spring
8	Front Shock Absorber
9	Jounce Bumper
10	Dust Shield

FM2029500097000X

e. Set front wheel toe as outlined in "Wheel Alignment" section.

POWER STEERING GEAR

REPLACE

1. Center steering wheel and lock in position.
2. Working from inside passenger compartment, remove clamp plate bolt securing steering column shaft to flexible coupling.
3. Turn clamp plate to disconnect from steering gear pinion shaft. Carefully remove floor seal.
4. Remove pinch bolt from flexible coupling and slide coupling from steering gear pinion shaft.
5. Remove as much power steering fluid from pump auxiliary reservoir as possible using suction gun, or equivalent, fluid suction tool.
6. Disconnect power steering return hose from pump auxiliary reservoir, then raise and support vehicle.
7. Remove front subframe assembly and remove steering gear cover plate from subframe, **Fig. 9.**
8. Disconnect pressure and return hose unions from power steering gear, then remove two bolts securing gear to subframe.

9. Separate steering gear from subframe. **Do not attempt to disassemble any part of steering gear. Entire unit must be replaced.**
10. Remove spindle connecting rods and boots from steering gear assembly.
11. Reverse procedure to install, noting following:
    a. Install new plastic seals on hydraulic lines.
    b. Fill power steering fluid reservoir and bleed system as outlined under "Power Steering System Bleed."
    c. If tie rod ends were loosened during procedure, inspect and adjust wheel alignment as outlined in "Wheel Alignment" section.

POWER STEERING PUMP

REPLACE

2.0L Engine

1. Raise and support vehicle, then remove lower splash shield.
2. Turn drive belt tensioner clockwise and remove drive belt.
3. Disconnect power steering pump high pressure line union and drain fluid into suitable container.
4. Disconnect power steering low pressure hose.
5. Remove four mounting bolts and power steering pump.
6. Reverse procedures to install.

2.5L Engine

1. Turn drive belt tensioner clockwise and remove drive belt.
2. Disconnect power steering line and hose from pump.
3. Support engine using engine support tool No. D88L-6000-A, or equivalent, and remove engine mount bracket, **Fig. 10.**
4. Drain cooling system into suitable container and remove coolant expansion tank.
5. Remove mounting bolts and engine mount.
6. Support center of power steering pump pulley with suitable hex head wrench and remove four power steering pump mounting bolts.
7. Remove pump bracket mounting bolt, then the retaining plate nuts and bolts, **Fig. 11.**
8. Remove mounting bolts and power steering pump.
9. Reverse procedures to install.

POWER STEERING SYSTEM BLEED

LESS AIR EVACUATOR TOOL

1. Raise and support front of vehicle,

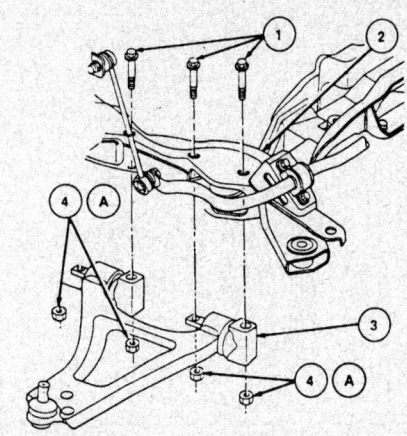

Item	Description
1	Bolts (4 Req'd)
2	Sub-frame
3	Front Suspension Lower Arm
4	Nuts (4 Req'd)
A	Tighten to 130 N·m (96 Lb-Ft)

FM2029500098000X

Fig. 6 Lower arm replacement

then fill power steering pump reservoir until fluid level is between MIN and MAX marks.

2. Disconnect Ignition Control Module (ICM) lead to prevent engine from starting, then crank engine for 30 seconds.
3. Inspect fluid level and add as required; then, while cranking engine again for 30 seconds, turn steering wheel from lock to lock repeatedly. **Do not hold wheel at either lock more than five seconds, power steering pump damage may result.**
4. Inspect and adjust fluid.
5. Connect ICM and lower vehicle.

WITH AIR EVACUATOR TOOL

1. Fill pump reservoir to MAX mark.
2. Start engine and slowly turn steering wheel from lock to lock
3. Switch engine off and inspect fluid level, add fluid as required.
4. Connect suitable stopper to hand vacuum pump tube and insert into reservoir filler neck.
5. Start engine and slowly turn steering wheel to right, just off stop.
6. Turn engine off and apply 5 inches Hg of vacuum pressure until air is purged from system, minimum of five minutes. If pressure drops by more than 2 inches Hg in five minutes, system should be inspected for leaks.
7. Depressurize system at vacuum pump and repeat bleed operation turning steering wheel to left, just off stop.
8. If noise level is still unacceptable, leave vehicle standing overnight then repeat bleed procedure.

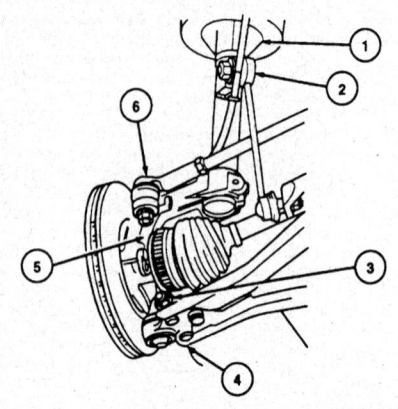

Item	Description
1	Front Shock Absorber
2	Stabilizer Bar Link
3	Lower Ball Joint-To-Knuckle Pinch Bolt
4	Front Suspension Lower Arm
5	Front Wheel Knuckle
6	Front Wheel Spindle Connecting Rod

FM2029500099000X

Fig. 7   Knuckle assembly

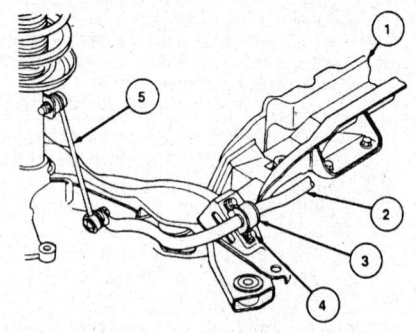

Item	Description
1	Front Sub-Frame
2	Stabilizer Bar
3	Stabilizer Bar Bracket
4	Stabilizer Bar Bracket Bolt (4 Req'd)
5	Stabilizer Bar Link

FM2029500100000X

Fig. 8   Stabilizer bar assembly

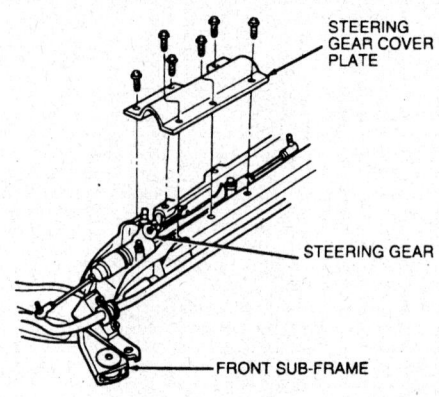

FM6029500193000X

Fig. 9   Steering gear cover plate replacement

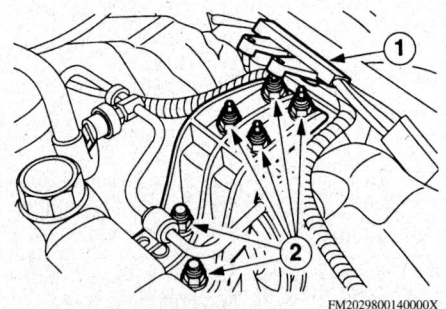

FM2029800140000X

Fig. 10   Engine mount bracket. 2.5L engine

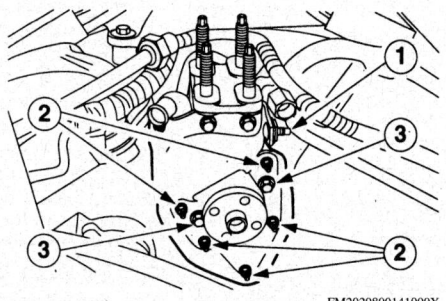

FM2029800141000X

Fig. 11   Retaining plate & bracket. 2.5L engine

TIGHTENING SPECIFICATIONS

Year	Component	Torque/Ft. Lbs.
2001–02	Engine Mount Through Bolts	40–55
	Exhaust Manifold Heat Shield	53①
	Lower Arm To Subframe	96
	Lower Ball Joint Pinch Bolt	65
	Power Steering Hose To Bracket	53①
	Power Steering Hose To Power Steering Pump Fittings	48
	Power Steering Hose Union To Steering Gear	23
	Power Steering Pump	18
	Power Steering Pump Pulley (2.5L)	96①
	Stabilizer Bar Insulator Mounting Bracket To Subframe	37
	Stabilizer Bar Link Nut	37
	Steering Gear Cover Plate To Subframe	37
	Steering Gear To Subframe	101
	Steering Shaft Clamp Plate	18
	Steering Shaft Flex Coupling Pinch Bolt	21
	Strut Thrust Bearing	44
	Strut To Front Wheel Knuckle Pinch Bolt	62
	Strut Top	37
	Tie Rod End Jam Nut	35–50
	Tie Rod End To Knuckle	18–22
	Traction Assist Module	53①
	Wheel Hub Retainer	210
	Wheel Lug Nuts	94

① — Inch lbs.

Wheel Alignment

INDEX

PRELIMINARY INSPECTION

1. Ensure tires are inflated to proper pressure.
2. Inspect tire for wear patterns may indicate improper wheel alignment, tire imbalance or damage because of bulges or separation.
3. Inspect suspension for modifications such as trailer towing equipment or heavy duty handling components.
4. Inspect vehicle for signs of overloading or sagging; ensure luggage compartment does not contain heavy objects.
5. Road test vehicle to isolate area of concern.

FRONT WHEEL ALIGNMENT

All wheel alignment inspections must be performed on an alignment rack leveled to within 1/16 inch side to side and front to rear. Alignment equipment must be capable of compensating for wheel runout and of measuring left and righthand front wheel toe independently.

Caster & Camber

Front wheel caster and camber are preset by manufacturer and are not adjustable. If caster and camber are not as indicated under "Front Wheel Alignment Specifications" in "Specifications" section, inspect suspension components for damage, modification or excessive wear.

Toe

1. Start engine and turn steering wheel back and forth several times, then place it in its centered position (wheels straight ahead).
2. Stop engine and lock steering wheel in position, then loosen steering ball stud dust seal outer clamp and slide off end of seal to prevent seal from twisting during adjustment.
3. Loosen tie rod end jam nuts, then adjust left and righthand tie rod ends until each wheel's toe measurement is 1/2 of total toe as specified under "Front Wheel Alignment Specifications" in "Specifications" section.
4. **Torque** tie rod end jam nuts to 35–46 ft. lbs., then position steering ball stud dust seal outer clamp over seal and tighten. **Ensure seal is not twisted.**

REAR WHEEL ALIGNMENT

1. Loosen bolt attaching rear suspension arm and bushing to subframe.
2. Turn alignment cam to obtain specified toe.
3. **Torque** rear suspension arm and bushing mounting nut to 62 ft. lbs.

CROWN VICTORIA, GRAND MARQUIS, MARAUDER & TOWN CAR

NOTE: Refer To Rear Of This Manual For Vehicle Manufacturer's Special Service Tool Suppliers.

INDEX OF SERVICE OPERATIONS

Specifications

GENERAL ENGINE SPECIFICATIONS

Engine Liter (VIN)①	Fuel System	Bore & Stroke	Compression Ratio	Net H.P. @ RPM	Maximum Torque Ft. Lbs. @ RPM	Normal Oil Pressure, psi
2001–02						
4.6L (W)	SEFI	3.55 x 3.54	9.40	⑦	⑥	40–70③
4.6L (9)⑤	SEFI	3.55 x 3.54	10.00	175 @ 4500	235 @ 3500	40–70③
2003–05						
4.6L (V)	SEFI	3.60 x 3.60	9.85	302 @ 5700	318 @ 4300	20–45③
4.6L (W)	SEFI	3.55 x 3.54	9.40	224 @ 4800	②	40–70③
4.6L (W)④	SEFI	3.55 x 3.54	9.40	239 @ 4900	287 @ 4100	40–70③
4.6L (9)⑤	SEFI	3.55 x 3.54	10.00	175 @ 4500	235 @ 3500	40–70③

SEFI — Sequential Multi-Port Electronic Fuel Injection

① — The eighth digit of VIN denotes engine code.

② — 272 @ 4100 RPM w/single exhaust; 287 @ 4100 RPM w/dual exhaust.

③ — At 200°F.

④ — Sport.

⑤ — Natural Gas Vehicle (NGV).

⑥ — 265 hp @ 4000 RPM w/single exhaust; 275 hp @ 4000 RPM w/dual exhaust.

⑦ — 220 hp @ 4750 RPM w/single exhaust; 235 hp @ 4750 RPM w/dual exhaust.

TUNE UP SPECIFICATIONS

Engine Liter (VIN)①	Spark Plug Gap	Ignition Timing, BTDC			Curb Idle Speed, RPM③		Fast Idle Speed, RPM③		Fuel Pump Pressure, psi	Valve Clearance, Inch
		Firing Order Fig.	Man. Trans.	Auto. Trans.	Mark Fig.	Man. Trans.	Auto. Trans.	Man. Trans.	Auto. Trans.	
2001										
4.6L (W)	.054	A⑩	—	10⑤ ②	—	⑥	—	⑥	30–45⑦	⑧
4.6L (9)⑨	.044	A⑩	—	10⑤ ②	—	⑥	—	⑥	80–120④	⑧
2002										
4.6L (W)	.052–.056	A⑩	—	⑤ ②	—	⑥	—	⑥	⑪	⑧
4.6L (9)⑨	.052–.056	A⑩	—	⑤ ②	—	⑥	—	⑥	⑪	⑧
2003–05										
4.6L (V,W)	.052–.056	A⑩	—	8–12⑤ ②	—	⑥	—	⑥	⑪	⑧
4.6L (9)⑨	.052–.056	A⑩	—	⑤ ②	—	⑥	—	⑥	⑪	⑧

BTDC — Before Top Dead Center

① — The eighth digit of Vehicle Identification Number (VIN) denotes engine code.

② — Equipped w/crankshaft sensor.

③ — When inspecting idle speed, set parking brake & block drive wheels.

④ — Locate vehicle in a well ventilated area away from heat, spark & flame producing equipment. Using extreme caution, connect a suitable natural gas approved fuel pressure gauge to the fuel pressure Schraeder valve. Release fuel pressure in fuel injection supply manifold back to fuel tanks. Place ignition switch in On position, then start engine if possible. Place igni-

tion switch in Off position. After two minutes, inspect fuel pressure reading on gauge.

⑤ — Non-adjustable.

⑥ — Idle speed is controlled by an automatic idle speed control. No adjustment is required.

⑦ — Wrap shop towel around fuel diag-

nostic valve to prevent fuel spillage. Connect suitable fuel pressure gauge to fuel diagnostic valve. Place ignition switch in On position to energize fuel pump & inspect pressure gauge reading.

⑧ — Equipped w/hydraulic lifters.

⑨ — Natural Gas Vehicle.

⑩ — Equipped w/coil on spark plug ignition. Cylinder numbering front to rear, righthand bank, 1-2-3-4; lefthand bank 5-6-7-8. Firing order, 1-3-7-2-6-5-4-8.

⑪ — Key On, Engine Off, 35–45 psi. Key On, Engine Running, 30–45 psi.

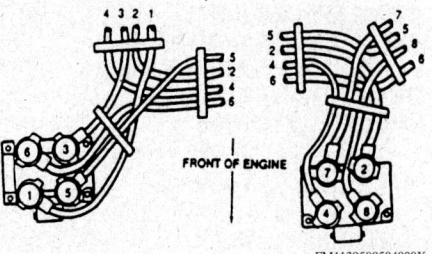

FM11139500504000X

Fig. A

FRONT WHEEL ALIGNMENT SPECIFICATIONS

Model	Caster Angle, Degrees		Camber Angle, Degrees		Total Toe, Inch①		Toe-Out On Turns, Degrees		Ball Joint Wear, Inch
	Limits	Desired	Limits	Desired	Limits	Desired	Outer Wheel	Inner Wheel	
2001–02									
Crown Victoria & Grand Marquis	+4.75 to +6.25	+5.5	-1.25 to +.25	-.5	-.20 to +.06	-.07	18.51	20	①②
Town Car	+5.25 to +6.75	+6.0	-1.25 to +.25	-.5	-.20 to +.06	-.07	—	—	①
2003–05									
Crown Victoria & Grand Marquis	+5.35 to +6.85	+6.1	-.75 to +.55	-.1	-.07 to +1.90	+.06	—	—	①
Marauder	+4.75 to +6.25	+5.5	-1.45 to +.05	-.7	-.18 to +.06	-.06	—	—	①
Town Car	+5.45 to +6.95	+6.2	-1.35 to +.15	-.6	④	③	—	—	①

① — Refer to "Ball Joint Inspection" in "Front Suspension & Steering" section.

② — Lower ball joint backlash, .03937 inch maximum; Upper ball joint backlash, .015 inch maximum; Ball joint endplay, .02 inch maximum.

③ — +.12°.

④ — +.13 to +37°.

VEHICLE RIDE HEIGHT SPECIFICATIONS

Model	Year	Body Style	Manufacturer's Original Tire Size	Measurement Points & Specifications②					
				Front③			Rear③		
				Dim.	Specification⑤		Dim.	Specification④	
					Inches	mm		Inches	mm
Crown Victoria	2001–02	Base	①	1	1.2	29.6	2	5.4	138.0
		Air Suspension	①	1	1.1	27.4	2	5.2	132.4
		Handling Package	①	1	1.0	26.0	2	5.2	132.4
		Police/NGV	①	1	1.0	26.4	2	5.2	132.3
	2003–05	All	①	2	2.4	60.0	2	4.74	118.0
Grand Marquis	2001–02	Base	①	1	1.2	29.6	2	5.4	138.0
		Air Suspension	①	1	1.1	27.4	2	5.2	132.4
		Handling Package	①	1	1.0	26.0	2	5.2	132.4
	2003–05	All	①	2	2.4	60.0	2	4.7	118.0
Marauder	2003–05	All	①	2	2.4	60.0	2	4.7	118.0
Town Car	2001–02	All	①	1	+.6 to +1.6③	+15.3 to +40.7③	2	+4.8 to +5.4③	+121.0 to +136.2③
	2003–04	All	P225/60R17	1	+2.0 to +2.8③	+50.0 to +70.0③	2	+4.4 to +5.0	+110.4 to +125.6

1 Dim. — Distance from lower control arm bolt head center to ground minus distance from ball stud center to ground

2 Dim. — 2001–02 distance between top of rear axle and inner frame reinforcement; 2003–05 distance from ground to center of lower control arm mounting bolt minus distance from ground to center of shock absorber mounting bolt

Dim. — Dimension

① — See door sticker or inside of glove box for manufacturer's original tire size specifications. If tires on vehicle do not match manufacturer's original tire size & measurement is not within limits, it will be required to refer to the "Non-Standard Tire & Wheel Size Adjustment To Ride Height Specification & Tire Size Adjustment Charts" in the front of this manual for approximate changes in ride height specifications.

② — Measurement is with fuel, radiator coolant and engine oil full, spare tire, jack, hand tools and mats in designated positions and tires properly inflated.

③ — Ride height lean (side to side) should be within .50 inch (12.7 mm).

④ — ± .3 inch (7.6 mm).

⑤ — ± .5 inch (12.7 mm)

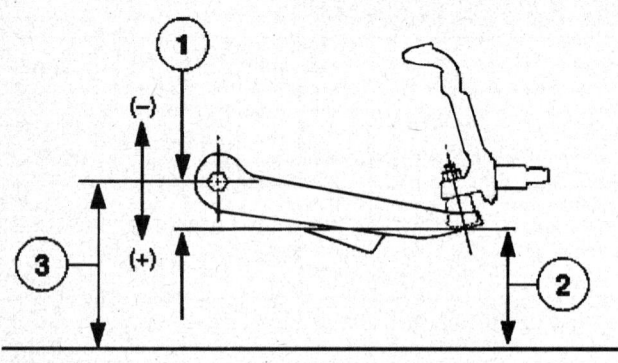

Item	Description
1	Ride height
2	Measurement (center of ball stud to ground)
3	Measurement (center of bolt head to ground)

FM2020100206000X

Fig. A   Front ride height measurement. 2001–02

Item	Description
1	Distance between the ground and the center of the shock absorber mounting bolt
2	Ride height = 3-1
3	Distance between the ground and the center of the lower arm mounting bolt

ARM66FM000000041

Fig. B   Front ride height measurement. 2003–05

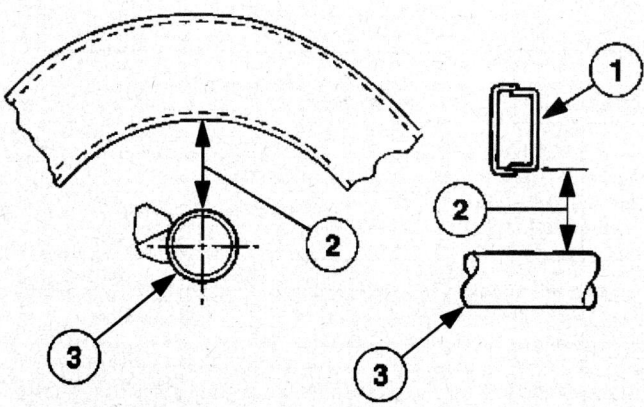

Item	Description
1	Inner frame reinforcement
2	Ride height
3	Rear axle

FM2030100153000X

Fig. C   Rear ride height measurement

FLUID CAPACITIES & COOLING SYSTEM DATA

Year & Engine	Coolant Capacity, Qts.	Coolant Type	Radiator Cap Relief Pressure, psi	Thermo. Opening Temp.	Fuel Tank Gals.	Engine Refill Qts.	Transmission Oil		Rear Axle Oil Pts.
							Man. Trans. Pts.	Auto. Trans. Qts.①	
2001–02									
4.6 SOHC	15.8	EG	13–18	188–193	19	5.0②	—	11.9③	3.75④
2003–05									
4.6 DOHC	14.5	⑤	13–18	183–190	19	6.0②	—	11.9③	3.75
4.6 SOHC	15.8	⑤	13–18	188–193	19	5.0②	—	11.9③	3.75

EG — Ethylene Glycol
① — Approximate, make final inspection w/dipstick.
② — Includes filter. Final inspection is made w/dipstick.
③ — Police model, 12.8 qts.
④ — Traction-Lok axles, add 4 oz. of Ford Motor Co. Friction Modifier No. C8AZ-19B546-A, or equivalent.
⑤ — Always fill cooling system with same coolant that is present in the system. Do not mix coolant types. For models w/green coolant use ethylene glycol, Motorcraft Premium Engine Coolant VC-4 (in Oregon VC-5), or equivalent meeting Ford specification ESE-M97B44-A. For models w/orange coolant use coolant Motorcraft Premium Gold Engine Coolant VC-7-A meeting Ford specifications WSS-M97B51-A1.

LUBRICANT DATA

Year	Model	Lubricant Type				
		Transmission		Rear Axle	Power Steering	Brake System
		Manual	Automatic			
2001–05	All	—	Mercon V	80-90W GL-5①②	Mercon ATF	DOT 3

① — Premium thermally stable rear axle lubricant P/N XY-80–90W-QL, or equivalent, meeting Ford specification WSP-M2C197-A.
② — Traction-Lok axles, add 4 oz. of Ford Motor Co. Friction Modifier No. C8AZ-19B546-A, or equivalent.

Electrical

NOTE: On Air Bag Equipped Models, Refer To "Air Bag System Precautions" Located In The Front Of This Manual For System Disarming & Arming Procedures.

NOTE: Refer To "Computer Relearn Procedures" Located In The Front Of This Manual When Battery Power To The Computer Has Been Interrupted.

NOTE: Prior To Performing Any Service Operations Listed In This Section, Consult The "Technical Service Bulletins" Section For Related Information.

INDEX

PRECAUTIONS

Air Bag Systems

Refer to "Air Bag System Precautions" in the front of this manual for system disarming and arming procedures.

Battery Ground Cable

Prior to service, disconnect battery ground cable and isolate as required.

FUSE PANEL & FLASHER LOCATION

Crown Victoria, Grand Marquis & Marauder

The fuse panel is located behind the lefthand side of the instrument panel.

The emergency flashers are located on the lefthand rear of the trunk, front flasher is located in righthand rear of engine compartment and the rear flasher is located center rear of trunk.

Town Car

2001–02

The instrument panel fuse panel is located behind the lefthand side of the instrument panel to the lefthand side of the steering column.

The turn signal and hazard flashers are a component of the Lighting Control Module (LCM), located behind the instrument panel.

2003-05

The instrument panel fuse panel is located behind the lefthand side of the instrument panel to the lefthand side of the steering column.

The engine compartment power distribution box is located next to the battery on the righthand front of the engine compartment.

The turn signal and hazard flashers are a component of the Lighting Control Module (LCM), located behind the lefthand side of instrument panel.

FUEL PUMP RELAY LOCATION

Crown Victoria, Grand Marquis & Marauder

2001-02

The fuel pump relay is located on the lefthand side of engine compartment, in the relay center.

2003-05

The fuel pump relay is located on the righthand side of the engine compartment, in the relay center.

Town Car

2001-02

The fuel pump relay is located in the power distribution box located on the rear lefthand side of the engine compartment.

2003-05

The fuel pump relay is located on the righthand side of the engine compartment, in the relay center.

RELAY CENTER LOCATION

2001-02

The relay center is located on the lefthand side of the engine compartment.

2003-05

The relay center is located on the righthand side of the engine compartment.

STARTER
REPLACE

1. Raise and support front of vehicle.
2. Remove starter motor solenoid terminal cover and disconnect cables.
3. Remove bolt, then position transmission cooler lines and bracket aside.

---

4. Remove two upper mounting bolts, lower bolt and starter motor.
5. Reverse procedure to install, noting the following:
   a. **Torque** starter bolts to 15–20 ft. lbs.
   b. **Torque** S-terminal cable eyelet with washer nut to 40–57 inch lbs.
   c. **Torque** starter cable B-terminal nut to 72–120 inch ft. lbs.
   d. **Torque** transmission cooler line bracket bolt to 84 inch lbs.

COIL PACK
REPLACE

Crown Victoria, Grand Marquis & Marauder

1. Disconnect engine control sensor wiring from ignition coil and radio ignition interference capacitor.
2. Disconnect ignition wires by squeezing locking tabs and twisting while pulling upward.
3. Remove ignition coil mounting screws and ignition coil with radio ignition interference capacitor.
4. Reverse procedure to install, noting the following:
   a. **Torque** coil pack mounting bolts to 40–61 inch lbs.
   b. Apply dielectric compound No. D7AZ-19A331-A, or equivalent, to ignition wire boots.

Town Car

2001-02

1. Remove air cleaner outlet tube.
2. Remove lefthand and righthand spark plug/ignition coil covers.
3. Disconnect spark plug ignition coil wire.
4. Disconnect ignition coil connector.
5. Remove spark plug ignition coil.
6. Inspect coil for cracks, dirt and carbon fouling.
7. Reverse procedure to install. **Torque** spark plug/ignition coil covers to 89 inch lbs.

2003-05

1. Remove air cleaner outlet tube.
2. Disconnect coil electrical connector.
3. Remove bolt and coil.
4. Reverse procedure to install. **Torque** mounting bolts to 89 inch lbs.

COIL UNITS
REPLACE

2001-02

1. Remove air cleaner outlet tube.
2. Remove fuel rail and disconnect engine control sensor wiring connector from coil per plug units.
3. Remove mounting bolts and coil per plug units.

---

4. Reverse procedure to install. **Torque** mounting bolts to 72–108 inch lbs.

2003-05

1. Remove air cleaner outlet tube.
2. **On models equipped with DOHC engine,** remove coil cover bolts.
3. **On all models,** disconnect coil electrical connector.
4. Remove mounting bolt and coil.
5. Reverse procedure to install. **Torque** mounting bolts to 89 inch lbs.

IGNITION LOCK
REPLACE

Functional Lock

The following procedures are for vehicles that have a functioning ignition switch lock, ignition key is available, or the lock cylinder key numbers are known and key can be made.

1. Turn lock cylinder to Run position.
2. Insert 1/8 inch diameter wire pin or small drift punch in hole in trim shroud under lock cylinder.
3. Depress retaining pin while pulling out on lock cylinder to remove from column housing.
4. Install lock cylinder by turning to Run position and depressing retaining pin.
5. Insert lock cylinder into housing.
6. Ensure cylinder is fully seated and aligned in interlocking washer before turning key to OFF position. This will permit cylinder retaining pin to extend into cylinder housing hole.
7. Lock cylinder using key.
8. Ensure correct mechanical operation in all positions.

Non-Functional Lock

The following procedure is for vehicles that have a inoperative ignition lock cylinder and the ignition switch cannot be rotated because of a lost or broken lock cylinder key, unknown key number, or an ignition switch cap that has been damaged to the extent that the key cannot be rotated.

1. Center front wheels to straight ahead position.
2. Remove driver's air bag module as outlined in "Passive Restraint Systems" chapter.
3. Disconnect speed control wire harness from steering wheel.
4. Remove and discard steering wheel mounting bolt.
5. Remove steering wheel using suitable steering wheel puller.
6. Route contact wire harness through steering wheel as wheel is lifted off of shaft.
7. Twist ignition cap or bezel using suitable channel lock or vise-grip type pliers until it separates from ignition switch.
8. Drill down middle of key slot approximately 1¾ inches using suitable ⅜ inch diameter drill until ignition switch

lock cylinder breaks loose from break-away base of ignition switch lock cylinder.

9. Remove lock cylinder and drill shavings from steering column tube flange.

10. Remove steering column upper bearing retainer, steering column lock housing bearing, ignition switch lock cylinder and steering column lock gear. Thoroughly clean drill shavings and other foreign material from casting.

11. Install new ignition lock cylinder as outlined under "Lock Cylinder, Functioning."

IGNITION SWITCH
REPLACE

1. Remove pin-type retainers and position lefthand instrument panel insulator aside.
2. Disconnect courtesy lamp and remove lefthand instrument panel insulator.
3. Remove lower instrument panel steering column opening cover.
4. Remove five bolts and instrument panel steering column opening cover reinforcement.
5. Disconnect ignition switch electrical connector.
6. Ensure ignition key is in Off position.
7. Remove ignition switch bolts and switch.
8. Reverse procedure to install.

HEADLAMP SWITCH
REPLACE

1. Remove instrument panel cluster finish panel.
2. Unclip switch and remove headlamp switch.
3. Reverse procedure to install.

STOP LIGHT SWITCH
REPLACE
2001–02
REMOVAL

The switch side plate nearest brake pedal is slotted, it is not required to remove brake master cylinder push rod and one spacer washer from brake pedal pin.

1. Lift locking tab and disconnect connector.
2. Remove hairpin retainer and slide switch, pushrod, nylon washers and bushings away from brake pedal.

INSTALLATION

1. Position switch so U-shaped side is nearest brake pedal and directly over or under pin.
2. Slide switch down or up trapping master cylinder pushrod and black bushing between switch and side plates.
3. Push switch and pushrod firmly toward brake pedal arm.
4. Assemble outside white plastic washer to pin and install hairpin retainer to trap whole assembly.

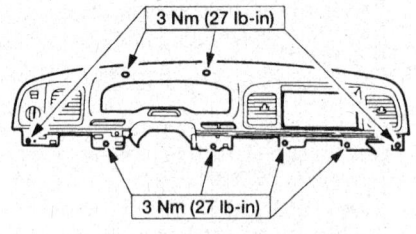

FM9099901237000X

Fig. 1 Instrument panel cluster finish trim panel replacement. 2001–02

5. Ensure switch wire harness has sufficient length to travel with switch during full stroke of brake pedal.
6. Inspect switch for proper operation.

2003–05

1. Remove pin-type retainers and lefthand instrument panel insulator.
2. Disconnect stop light switch electrical connector.
3. Remove stop light switch self locking pin and brake master cylinder push rod spacer.
4. Remove stop light switch from brake master cylinder push rod.
5. Reverse procedure to install.

MULTI-FUNCTION SWITCH
REPLACE

1. Tilt column to lowest position and remove tilt lever, as required.
2. Remove ignition lock cylinder.
3. Remove mounting screws, then the upper and lower shrouds.
4. Remove two multi-function switch to steering column casting mounting screws.
5. Disconnect switch.
6. Disconnect two electrical connectors.
7. Reverse procedure to install. **Torque** mounting screws to 18–26 inch lbs.

TURN SIGNAL SWITCH
REPLACE

1. Tilt column to lowest position and remove tilt lever, as required.
2. Remove ignition lock cylinder.
3. Remove mounting screws, then the upper and lower shrouds.
4. Remove two multi-function switch to steering column casting mounting screws.
5. Disconnect switch.
6. Disconnect two electrical connectors.
7. Reverse procedure to install. **Torque** mounting screws to 18–26 inch lbs.

STEERING WHEEL
REPLACE

1. Center front wheels to straight ahead position.
2. Remove driver's air bag module as

outlined in "Passive Restraint Systems" chapter.

3. Disconnect speed control wire harness from steering wheel.
4. Remove and discard steering wheel mounting bolt.
5. Remove steering wheel using suitable steering wheel puller.
6. Route contact wire harness through steering wheel as wheel is lifted off of shaft.
7. Reverse procedure to install, noting the following:
   a. Align steering wheel and shaft marks.
   b. Route contact wire harness through steering wheel opening at three o'clock position.
   c. Ensure air bag contact wire is not pinched and speed control wiring does not get trapped between steering wheel and contact.
   d. **Torque** steering wheel mounting bolt to 25–34 ft. lbs.
   e. **Torque** air bag module mounting nuts to 108 inch lbs.

INSTRUMENT CLUSTER
REPLACE
2001–02

1. Pull radio out from instrument cluster finish panel with radio removal tool No. T87P-19061-A, or equivalent.
2. Disconnect radio electrical connectors and antenna cable, then remove radio.
3. Remove lefthand and righthand instrument panel finish panels, then disconnect electrical connectors.
4. Place gearshift lever in 1 position.
5. Place steering column in full tilt position.
6. Remove screws and disconnect electrical connectors, **Fig. 1.**
7. Remove instrument panel cluster finish panel.
8. Remove lower steering column cover.
9. Remove instrument panel steering column opening cover reinforcement.
10. Disconnect transmission range indicator cable and position aside.
11. Remove four mounting screws and instrument cluster.
12. Reverse procedure to install.

2003–05

1. Remove instrument cluster finish panel.
2. **On Crown Victoria and Grand Marquis models,** proceed as follows:
   a. Remove lower steering column cover.
   b. Remove lower steering column reinforcement.
   c. Disconnect transmission range indicator cable and position aside.
3. **On models equipped with electronic cluster,** loosen steering column assembly.
4. **On all models,** remove instrument cluster, pull cluster out from instrument panel and disconnect electrical connectors.

5. Reverse procedure to install. **Torque** steering column to 11 ft. lbs.

RADIO
REPLACE

1. Release retaining clips by pushing radio removal tools No. T87P-19061-A, or equivalents, into face plate.
2. Slightly spread tools and pull radio from dash.
3. Disconnect power, antenna and speaker leads.
4. Reverse procedure to install. Ensure rear bracket is engaged on lower support rail.

WIPER MOTOR
REPLACE

1. Remove cowl top vent panel.
2. **On 2001–02 models,** remove evaporative emission canister purge valve and set aside.
3. **On all models,** remove mounting bolts, then position mounting arm and pivot shaft aside.
4. Remove wiper motor cover.
5. Remove clip and disconnect linkage from wiper motor.
6. Remove mounting bolts and wiper motor.
7. Reverse procedure to install.

WIPER SWITCH
REPLACE

1. Tilt column to lowest position and remove tilt lever, as required.
2. Remove ignition lock cylinder.
3. Remove mounting screws, then the upper and lower shrouds.
4. Remove two multi-function switch to steering column casting mounting screws.
5. Disconnect switch.
6. Disconnect two electrical connectors.
7. Reverse procedure to install. **Torque** mounting screws to 18–26 inch lbs.

BLOWER MOTOR
REPLACE

1. Remove mounting nut and position windshield washer fluid reservoir aside.
2. Remove righthand fender apron mounting screws and position apron aside.
3. Disconnect wire harness connector from retainer and blower motor electrical connector.
4. Disconnect blower motor rubber hose.
5. Remove mounting screws and blower motor.
6. Reverse procedure to install.

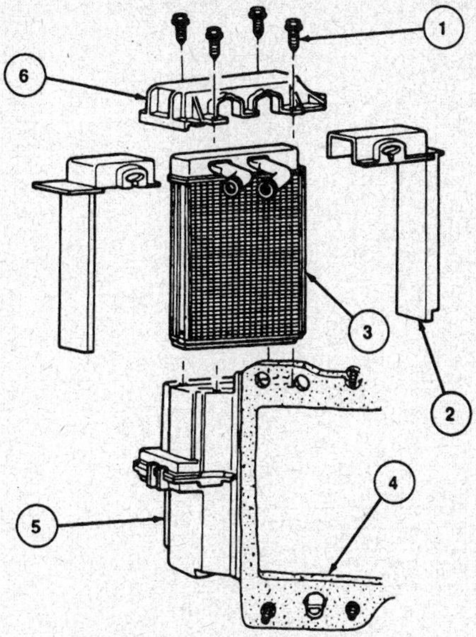

Item	Description
1	Screw (4 Req'd)
2	Heater Core Case Seal
3	Heater Core
4	Heater Dash Gasket
5	Heater Air Plenum Chamber
6	Heater Core Cover

FM7029800510000X

Fig. 2 Heater core replacement

HEATER CORE
REPLACE

Crown Victoria, Grand Marquis & Marauder
2001-02

1. Remove heater outlet floor duct.
2. Remove instrument panel as outlined in "Dash Panel Service" chapter.
3. Disconnect heater water hoses from heater core tubes.
4. Plug heater water hose ends and core tubes.
5. Remove evaporator core housing upper lefthand corner mounting nut.
6. Disconnect two vacuum supply hoses from vacuum source. Push grommet and vacuum supply hose into passenger compartment.
7. Disconnect wiring harness from air conditioning electronic blend door actuator.
8. Disconnect white vacuum hose from heater and air conditioning air inlet duct door vacuum control motor.
9. Remove nuts from studs along lower flange of heater air plenum chamber.
10. Disconnect connectors to air conditioning electronic blend door actuator and module on side of heater air plenum chamber.
11. Remove heater air plenum chamber by pulling rearward.

12. Remove four mounting screws and heater core cover, **Fig. 2.**
13. Pull heater core from heater air plenum chamber.
14. Reverse procedure to install. Ensure heater core case seal is properly positioned.

2003-05

1. Remove instrument panel as outlined in "Dash Panel Service" chapter.
2. Clamp off and disconnect heater hoses.
3. Remove plenum chamber nuts from inside vehicle and disconnect electrical connectors.
4. **On five-passenger models,** loosen center console rear footwell duct nuts.
5. **On six-passenger models,** position back carpet from plenum chamber. Cut each side of rear footwell duct and bend back. **Only cut footwell duct enough to allow heater flow duct to be removed with plenum chamber as an assembly.**
6. **On all models,** remove in-vehicle temperature sensor hose.
7. Remove plenum chamber, then the heater core mounting screws.
8. Carefully cut seal above heater core inlet and outlet tubes, then remove heater core.
9. Reverse procedure to install.

Town Car
2001-02

1. Remove instrument panel as outlined in "Dash Panel Service" chapter.
2. Drain coolant into suitable container until level is below heater core.
3. Remove windshield wiper arms.
4. Remove cowl top cover.
5. Remove fresh air inlet duct.
6. Remove windshield wiper mounting arm and pivot shaft with cowl extension as an assembly.
7. Disconnect heater hoses at heater core.
8. Remove nut at cowl side stud.
9. Remove mounting screw and nut from evaporator core housing.
10. Disconnect vacuum hoses and electrical connectors.
11. Position carpet back from plenum chamber.
12. Cut each side of rear footwell duct and bend duct back. **Do not cut too much of duct. Cut only to point of allowing heater floor duct to be removed with plenum chamber as an assembly.**
13. Remove plenum chamber lower flange mounting nuts.
14. Remove upper flange mounting nut and plenum chamber.
15. Remove mounting screws, heater core cover and seal.
16. Remove heater core.
17. Reverse procedure to install, noting the following:
    a. Ensure to sufficiently seal rear footwell duct to heater outlet floor duct.
    b. Close rear footwell duct around heater outlet floor duct.
    c. Install suitable tie strap.

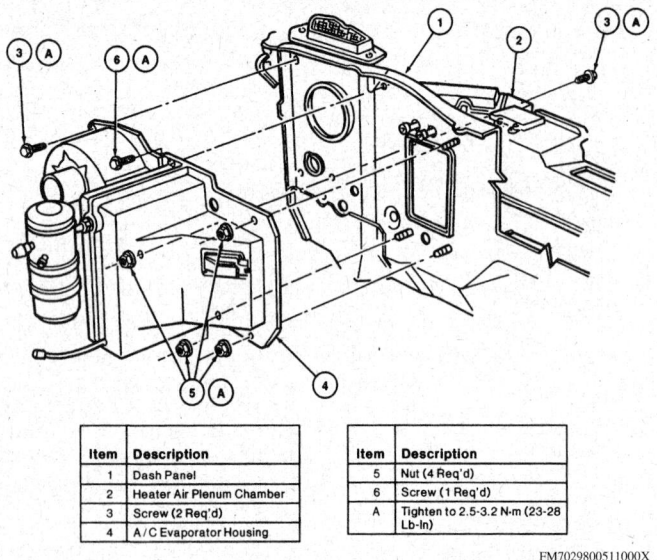

Item	Description
1	Dash Panel
2	Heater Air Plenum Chamber
3	Screw (2 Req'd)
4	A/C Evaporator Housing

Item	Description
5	Nut (4 Req'd)
6	Screw (1 Req'd)
A	Tighten to 2.5-3.2 N-m (23-28 Lb-In)

FM7029800511000X

Fig. 3 Evaporator core housing removal

2003-05

1. Remove instrument panel as outlined in "Dash Panel Service" chapter.
2. Remove evaporator core housing as outlined under "Evaporator Core, Replace."
3. Disconnect electrical connectors.
4. Position seal aside, the remove mounting screws and rear seat duct.
5. Remove air cleaner outlet pipe.
6. Disconnect wiring clip and remove dash panel nut.
7. Remove mounting nuts and heater core housing.
8. Remove mounting screws and heater core tube cover.
9. Remove mounting screws and floor duct.
10. Remove mounting screws, cover and heater core.
11. Reverse procedure to install.

EVAPORATOR CORE
REPLACE

Crown Victoria, Grand Marquis & Marauder

2001-02

Whenever an evaporator core is replaced, replace the suction accumulator/drier.

1. Recover air conditioning refrigerant system as outlined in "Air Conditioning" chapter.
2. Remove heater blower motor switch resistor.
3. Disconnect evaporator to compressor suction line from suction accumulator/drier using suitable spring lock coupling disconnect tools.
4. Plug openings. Position hose away from suction accumulator/drier.
5. Disconnect condenser to evaporator tube from evaporator core inlet tube using suitable spring lock coupling disconnect tools.
6. Position condenser to evaporator tube away from evaporator core housing.
7. Drain radiator coolant into suitable container.
8. Loosen clamps and disconnect heater water hoses from heater core tubes.
9. Remove two purge valve mounting bracket to cowl top extension mounting nuts. Position purge valve and bracket away from evaporator core housing.
10. Remove radiator coolant recovery reservoir. Position forward, away from evaporator core housing.
11. Disconnect air conditioning blower motor lead from main wiring harness, then remove hard shell connector from air conditioning blower motor speed control and air conditioning cycling switch.
12. Disconnect main wire harness (which crosses evaporator core housing) at hard shell connecting point and position it away from evaporator core housing.
13. Remove instrument panel lower insulator from bottom of instrument panel on passenger side by disengaging four push pins and disconnecting power point electrical connector.
14. Fold carpeting back on righthand side of floor. Remove air conditioning recirculating air duct bottom lefthand screw.
15. Raise and support vehicle, then remove righthand front tire and wheel assembly.
16. Remove mounting bolts from rear of righthand fender apron. Position apron down in rear to improve access to evaporator core housing.
17. From engine side of instrument panel, remove three nuts from evaporator mounting studs and two screws from top of evaporator core housing, **Fig. 3.**
18. Pull bottom of evaporator core housing away from instrument panel to disconnect two bottom studs.

19. Move top of evaporator core housing away from instrument panel, disconnect it from top stud, then maneuver case up and over fender apron.
20. Remove six evaporator core housing halves mounting screws, **Fig. 4.**
21. Separate evaporator core housing halves and carefully cutting evaporator case instrument panel seal at seams using suitable razor blade.
22. Disconnect suction accumulator/drier inlet from evaporator core outlet tube.
23. Remove suction accumulator/drier and evaporator core mounting bracket screw, then the suction accumulator/drier from evaporator core.
24. Remove mounting screw from inlet tube bracket and evaporator core.
25. Reverse procedure to install.

2003-05

1. Recover air conditioning refrigerant system as outlined in "Air Conditioning" chapter.
2. Raise and support vehicle, then remove righthand front wheel and tire.
3. Remove mounting screws and righthand fender apron.
4. Remove evaporator core mounting nuts, **Fig. 5.**
5. Lower vehicle.
6. **On models equipped with manual air conditioning,** disconnect blower motor resister electrical connector.
7. **On models equipped with automatic temperature control,** disconnect blower motor speed control electrical connector.
8. **On all models,** disconnect evaporator air discharge temperature sensor electrical connector.
9. Disconnect evaporator inlet and outlet spring lock couplings. Discard O-ring seals.
10. Remove mounting nuts, then position purge valve and bracket away from evaporator core housing.
11. Clamp off and disconnect heater hoses at heater core.
12. Disconnect electrical connectors from bracket, **Fig. 6.**
13. Disconnect blower motor electrical connector.
14. Remove mounting nut and position wire harness away from evaporator housing.
15. Disconnect wire harness from bracket.
16. Remove retainers and instrument panel lower insulator.
17. Fold back carpet and remove mounting screw.
18. From inside vehicle remove mounting screw, **Fig. 7.**
19. Remove evaporator core housing mounting bolts.
20. **On models equipped with automatic temperature control,** remove in-vehicle temperature sensor hose and elbow from evaporator housing.
21. **On all models,** remove evaporator core housing.
22. Reverse procedure to install using new O-rings lubricated with clean PAG oil.

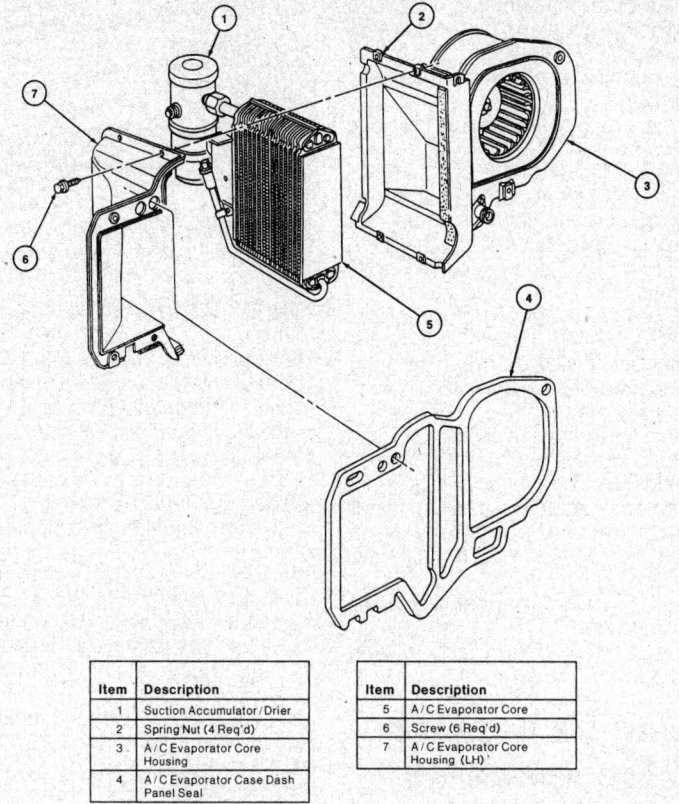

Item	Description
1	Suction Accumulator / Drier
2	Spring Nut (4 Req'd)
3	A/C Evaporator Core Housing
4	A/C Evaporator Case Dash Panel Seal

Item	Description
5	A/C Evaporator Core
6	Screw (6 Req'd)
7	A/C Evaporator Core Housing (LH)

FM7029800512000X

Fig. 4   Evaporator core replacement

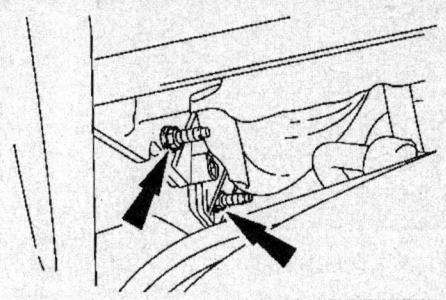

ARM66FM000000002

Fig. 5   Nut removal. 2003–05

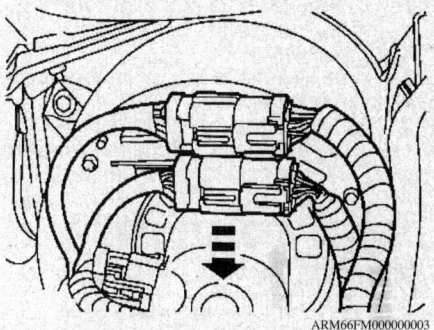

ARM66FM000000003

Fig. 6   Electrical connectors. 2003–05

Town Car

2001-02

On **2001–02 models,** the evaporator core is not available separately. It is serviced only with the evaporator core housing assembly. The old evaporator core housing components will have to be transfer to the new one.

1. Recover air conditioning refrigerant system as outlined in "Air Conditioning" chapter.
2. Drain coolant into suitable container.
3. Remove screws and righthand cowl vent screen.
4. Disconnect EVAP canister purge valve vacuum hoses and electrical connector.
5. Remove EVAP canister purge valve.
6. Remove heater core hoses.
7. Remove mounting screw and position windshield washer fluid reservoir aside.
8. Disengage four wire harness retainers from top of righthand fender apron.
9. Remove righthand front wheel and tire.
10. Remove righthand front fender apron.
11. Disconnect A/C cycling switch and blower motor electrical connectors.
12. Disconnect suction accumulator/dryer evaporator to compressor suction line.
13. Disconnect suction accumulator/dryer from evaporator core.
14. Remove accumulator mounting bracket to evaporator core housing screw, then the suction accumulator/dryer.
15. Disconnect condenser to evaporator tube from evaporator core.
16. Remove righthand instrument panel insulator.
17. Remove in-vehicle temperature sensor hose and elbow from evaporator housing.
18. Remove nuts at top and bottom of evaporator housing.
19. Remove screws and nut near blower motor.
20. Separate housing portions, then remove blower motor and evaporator core.
21. Disconnect electrical connector.
22. Remove evaporator core cover.
23. Reverse procedure to install, noting the following:
    a. Lubricate A/C O-ring seals with suitable PAG refrigerant compressor oil.
    b. Evacuate and charge refrigerant system.
    c. Fill cooling system with proper coolant.

2003-05

The evaporator core is not available separately. It is serviced only with the evaporator core housing assembly. The old evaporator core housing components will have to be transfer to the new one.

1. Recover air conditioning refrigerant system as outlined in "Air Conditioning" chapter.
2. Drain engine coolant into suitable container.
3. Disconnect spring lock couplings and discard O-ring seals.
4. Remove mounting screws and righthand cowl vent screen.
5. Remove cowl mounting bolts.
6. Disconnect EVAP canister purge valve vacuum hoses and wire harness connector.
7. Remove evaporator core engine compartment mounting nuts.
8. Disconnect evaporator core electrical connectors.
9. Disconnect clamps and heater core hoses.
10. Disconnect clamp and engine heater hose.
11. Remove nuts, then position purge valve and bracket away from evaporator core housing.
12. Remove mounting nuts, stud and position windshield washer fluid reservoir aside.
13. Loosen mounting bolts and position junction box aside.
14. Remove evaporator core mounting bolts.
15. Raise and support vehicle, then remove righthand tire and wheel assembly.
16. Remove mounting screws and fender apron, then disconnect wiring harness retainers.

Fig. 7 Screw removal. 2003–05

17. Remove lower evaporator core housing mounting nuts.
18. Lower vehicle.
19. Remove upper evaporator core housing mounting nuts.
20. Remove evaporator core housing.
21. Reverse procedure to install using new O-rings lubricated with clean PAG oil.

CABIN AIR FILTER

REPLACE

Under normal operating conditions, cabin air filter should be replaced every 15,000 miles. Under severe operating conditions replace, cabin air filter should be replaced every 12,000 miles.
1. Open hood.
2. Pull hood pad away from righthand cowl vent screen.
3. Remove righthand cowl vent screen.
4. Remove water shield.
5. Remove cabin air filter element from filter housing, **Fig. 8.**
6. Reverse procedure to install.

TECHNICAL SERVICE BULLETINS

Repeated Heater Core Failure

On some of these models there may be repeated heater core leaks.

This condition may be caused by a chemical reaction (electrolysis).

To correct this condition, proceed as follows:
1. Place positive probe of suitable digital volt/ohm meter in engine coolant and negative probe on battery ground terminal.
2. Adjust engine to 2000 RPM.
3. If more than .4 volt is recorded, flush coolant and measure voltage, again.
4. If voltage is still excessive, inspect body/battery grounds.
5. If condition still exists, add extra grounds to heater core and engine, as follows:
   a. Secure 16 gauge stranded copper wire to heater core inlet tube using suitable hose clamp.
   b. Secure other end of wire to existing body sheet metal fastener.
   c. Secure another extra ground between existing engine and body sheet metal fasteners.

   d. Ensure there is continuity between added grounds and battery ground terminal.
6. If condition still exists, install restrictor as follows:
   a. Cut line as close to engine block as possible.
   b. Install restrictor (P/N F1UZ-18D406-A) on inlet hose with arrow facing coolant flow direction (toward heater core).
   c. Secure with two suitable hose clamps.
7. Bleed cooling system trapped air as follows:
   a. Disconnect heater hose at righthand front or rear of engine.
   b. Remove thermostat and housing.
   c. Fill engine with suitable coolant until mixture is seen at engine side heater hose connection.
   d. Connect heater hose, then install thermostat and housing.
   e. Fill degas bottle to coolant fill level mark.
   f. Fun engine to normal operating temperature.
   g. Select MAX heat and blower speeds

Whining Or Buzzing On Radio Speakers

2001–02 TOWN CAR

On some of these models there may be a whining or buzzing noise in the radio speakers.

This condition may be caused by the in-tank electric fuel pump.

To correct this condition, proceed as follows:
1. Remove fuel pump sender as outlined under "Fuel Pump, Replace" in "4.6L Engine" section.
2. Remove negative and positive connectors.
3. Cut and discard wires 3 inches from fuel pump flange.
4. Connect Radio Frequency Interference (RFI) filter No. F1PZ-18B925-A, connectors to fuel pump spade terminal.
5. Cut and solder filter wires to flange wires. Cover solder connections with heat shrink tubing.
6. Secure RFI filter to fuel pump and sending unit with suitable bundling strap.
7. Install fuel pump as outlined under "Fuel Pump, Replace" in "4.6L Engine" section.

Sticking Or Binding Ignition Switch: DTCs P0500, P1502 & U1039

On some of these models there may roughness and/or excessive effort required to turn key from RUN to START position, or key may not fully return from START to

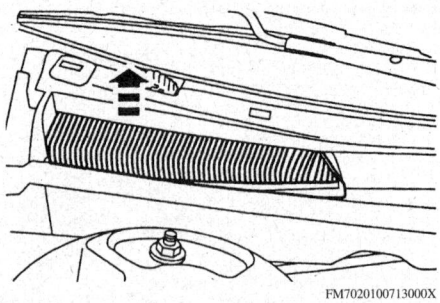

Fig. 8 Cabin air filter replacement

RUN position after starting vehicle. On some of these Continental models, the Malfunction Indicator Lamp (MIL) may illuminate with Diagnostic Trouble Codes P0500, P1502 and U1039 stored.

This condition may be caused the key-in-ignition warning chime switch.

To correct this condition, proceed as follows:
1. Remove ignition switch as outlined under "Ignition Switch, Replace."
2. Remove plastic key chime warning switch by prying rear tine up while sliding switch away from key insertion end, **Fig. 9.**
3. Install new key-in-ignition warning chime switch, P/N XL2Z-11A127-AB.
4. Install lock as outlined under "Ignition Switch, Replace."

Erratic Blower Motor Operation

2003 TOWN CAR

On some of these models there may be intermittent, erratic climate control blower motor operation. The blower may operate at high speed uncommanded, and/or unable to control blower motor sped when using the Dual electronic Automatic Temperature Control (DEATC) system. This condition may be present under aggressive braking, turning and acceleration.

This condition may be caused by chafing of the blower motor speed control wire harness behind the righthand valve cover at the starter cable bracket, near the evaporator case.

To correct this condition, install revised blower motor speed control wire harness (P/N 19C603) as follows:
1. Ensure harness is chaffed behind righthand engine cam cover at starter cable bracket near evaporate case.
2. Raise and support vehicle, then disconnect four oxygen sensor wire connectors.
3. Remove lefthand and righthand catalytic converter to exhaust manifold nuts. Allow exhaust to hang.
4. Remove wiring harness to evaporator case mounting screw between bulkhead and righthand rear of engine.
5. Disconnect blower motor speed control connector.
6. Lower vehicle.
7. Disconnect engine compartment temperature sensor connector near engine on evaporator case.

8. Disconnect blower motor connector.
9. Remove two wiring harness to evaporator case mounting screws.
10. Disconnect retainer and inline connector.
11. Remove wiring harness.
12. Position new wiring harness between two heater hoses at righthand rear of engine near heater core inlet tubes.
13. Direct harness down back of engine on driver's side of blower motor speed control. Allow enough length to connect to blower motor speed control.
14. Connect engine compartment temperature sensor.
15. Route harness across engine compartment toward blower motor.
16. Connect blower motor.
17. Slip retainer on harness over evaporator case.
18. Route harness between two mounting bosses on evaporator case.
19. Secure wiring harness to top mounting boss with mounting screw.
20. Connect inline connector.
21. Install blower motor insulator, righthand fender apron and windshield washer reservoir.
22. Raise and support vehicle.
23. Inspect wire harness routed down driver's side of blower motor speed control.

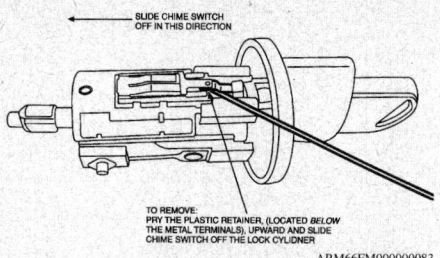

Fig. 9 Chime warning switch replacement. Continental & 2001–02 Town Car

24. Connect harness to blower motor speed control.
25. Install new exhaust mounting bolts and nuts. **Torque** bolts and nuts to 30 ft. lbs.
26. Connect oxygen sensors.

Poor AM Reception

2003 TOWN CAR

On some of these models built before Dec. 4, 2002, may have poor AM radio reception.

This condition may be caused by the antenna wiring harness.

To correct this condition, install AM reception service kit (P/N 3W1Z-18K891-AA) according to included instructions.

Climate Control Whistle

2003 TOWN CAR

On some of these models built before Sept. 25, 2002, there may be a whistle from the heating ventilation air condition system, This condition occurs when the blower fan is operating at MAX speed with temperature set to MAX heat.

This condition may be caused by air escaping from between heater core case and the temperature blend door actuators.

To correct this condition, install a foam seal between the heater core case and blend door actuators as follows:
1. Remove righthand temperature blend door actuator for heater case.
2. Install foam seal (P/N F57Z-19A672-CA) on actuator so it will seal interface between case it and case.
3. Install actuator.
4. Repeat procedure on lefthand temperature blend door actuator.

4.6L Engine

NOTE: On Air Bag Equipped Models, Refer To "Air Bag System Precautions" Located In The Front Of This Manual For System Disarming & Arming Procedures.

NOTE: Refer To "Computer Relearn Procedures" Located In The Front Of This Manual When Battery Power To The Computer Has Been Interrupted.

NOTE: Prior To Performing Any Service Operations Listed In This Section, Consult The "Technical Service Bulletins" Section For Related Information.

INDEX

PRECAUTIONS

Air Bag Systems

Refer to "Air Bag System Precautions" in the front of this manual for system disarming and arming procedures.

Battery Ground Cable

Prior to service, disconnect battery ground cable and isolate as required.

Fuel System Pressure Relief

GASOLINE ENGINE

The fuel system remains under high pressure even when the engine is not running. To avoid injury or fire, release pressure from the fuel system before disconnecting any fuel line. Proceed as follows:
1. Ensure ignition switch is in Off position.
2. Remove fuel tank cap to release residual fuel pressure.
3. Connect fuel pressure gauge tool No. T80L-9974-B, or equivalent, to fuel rail valve located on fuel rail.
4. Gradually open testing kit valve to relieve fuel pressure in system.
5. Drain fuel into suitable container or return to fuel tank.
6. When repair is completed, turn ignition On and Off several times to pressurize fuel system. **Do not start engine.**
7. Inspect for fuel leaks at pressure regulator, fuel injectors and fuel fittings. Repair as required.

NATURAL GAS ENGINE

SYSTEM

When servicing any component of the fuel charging system, fuel pressure should be released using the following procedures.

When venting fuel system, venting into a vent stack is recommended, **Fig. 1.** If using a vent stack, ensure local regulations are followed. Before venting occurs, battery should be disconnected and isolated, as required.

Natural gas O-rings are identified with a yellow stripe. Do not use unapproved O-rings.

Before performing pressure relief procedures, refer to "Fuel Tank Solenoid Valve Test" to determine status of fuel tank solenoid valves.

If a manual override tool has been used to open fuel tank solenoid valve, solenoid valve must be replaced, Fig. 2.

Do not vent fuel tank unless tank or fuel tank solenoid valve is being replaced. Unnecessary venting of good tanks will damage fuel tank solenoid valve.

FUEL TANK SOLENOID VALVE TEST

Prior to relieving fuel pressure on NGV vehicles, the following diagnosis should be performed to determine whether or not the fuel tank solenoid valve is stuck open or closed.
1. Inspect fuel system and determine if any of the following apply:
   a. Damaged fuel tanks.
   b. Damaged fuel tank solenoid valve.
   c. Damaged lines or hoses.
   d. Damaged fuse or relay.
   e. Damaged power distribution box.
   f. Damaged, loose or corroded electrical connections.
2. If any of preceding conditions were found during visual inspection, repair as require.
3. If none of preceding conditions were found during visual inspection, refer to symptom chart, **Fig. 3.**
4. Refer to **Fig. 4,** for pinpoint tests A.

5. If fuel tank solenoid valve requires replacement, refer to **MOTOR's "Domestic Engine Performance & Driveability Manual"** for procedure.

LINE PRESSURE

1. Connect grounding cable tool No. 134-00121, or equivalent, to fuel supply manifold and ground.
2. Ensure bleed valve on fuel rail pressure test kit is closed before installing.
3. Install fuel rail pressure test kit tool No. 134-00116, or equivalent, to fuel supply manifold Schraeder valve.
4. Connect vent hose to pressure test kit and vent stack.
5. Slowly open bleed valve of fuel rail pressure tester and allow fuel lines to vent to atmosphere for one minute. If pressure gauge still registers 95–125 psi, refer to **MOTOR's "Domestic Engine Performance & Driveability Manual."**

TANK PRESSURE

Solenoid Normally Operating

1. Remove vapor vent box from fuel tank, as required.
2. Disconnect fuel tank electrical connectors and **torque** manual lockdown jackscrews to 80 inch lbs., on fuel tanks not to be vented. If neither of rear or upper tanks need to be vented, rear upper fuel tank rack harness connector may be disconnected without removing rear or upper fuel tank rack vent box.
3. Connect grounding cable 134-00121, or equivalent, to back side of fuel fill valve at fuel line connection and ground.
4. Ensure manual bleed valve on fuel vent kit is closed before connecting to fuel filler valve.
5. Connect fuel filler neck venting kit tool No. 134-00117, or equivalent, to fuel filler valve.

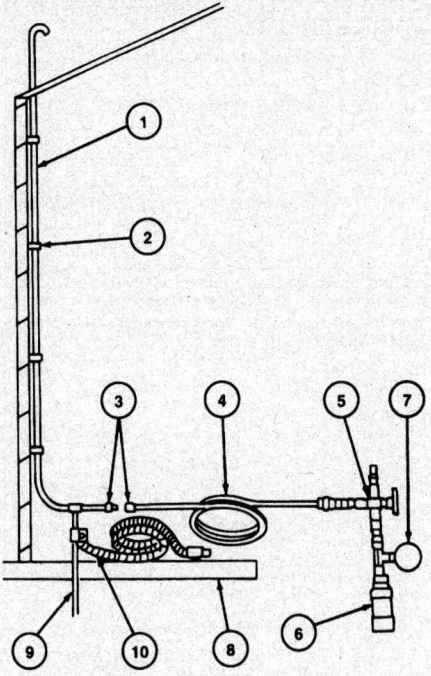

Item	Description
1	1/2 Inch Pipe
2	Vent Stack Support
3	Vent Stack Connectors
4	Rotunda Venting Hose
5	Rotunda Fuel Filter Neck Venting Kit
6	Fill Valve Connector
7	Gauge
8	Building Floor
9	Support / Grounding Rod
10	Grounding Cable

FM1029900308000X

Fig. 1 Typical vent stack installation

6. Connect vent hose tool No. 134-00118, or equivalent, to filler neck vent kit and vent stack.
7. Remove fuel valve relay from power distribution box.
8. Connect wire sockets Nos. 87 and 30 in fuel pump relay socket of power distribution box using suitable jumper wire constructed of six inches of 18 gauge wire and two spade terminals.
9. Slowly open manual backflow valve on fuel filler valve using suitable 3/16 inch Allen wrench.
10. Ensure gauge on fuel filler neck vent kit indicates tank pressure.
11. Slowly open bleed valve on fuel filler neck vent kit and allow fuel tank to vent to atmosphere. Venting process may take one hour or more.
12. Close bleed valve on fuel filler neck vent kit. Ensure gauge pressure is zero psi.
13. Remove fuel tank solenoid manual lockdown valve.
14. **Ensure jackscrew in manual override tool is retracted fully (counterclockwise) prior to installation into fuel tank solenoid valve. If tool is in-**

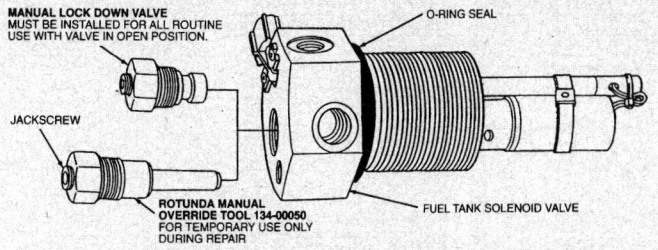

Fig. 2 Fuel tank solenoid valve replacement

Condition	Possible Source	Action
• Unable to Vent Fuel Tanks or Fuel Lines	• Damaged fuel tank solenoids. • Damaged lines or hoses. • Circuitry.	• GO to Pinpoint Test A.

FM1029900301000X

Fig. 3 NGV fuel tank solenoid valve symptom chart

stalled in vent position, fuel will be immediately released.
15. Install Rotunda manual override tool No. 134-00050, or equivalent, to tank solenoid and **torque** to 30 ft. lbs.
16. Turn override tool jackscrew clockwise until fuel flows.
17. Vent system until fuel flow stops.
18. Close manual backflow valve on fuel filler valve after tank has been vented.
19. Vent fuel lines.
20. Remove manual override tool from fuel tank solenoid valve.
21. Install fuel tank solenoid manual lockdown valve and **torque** to 30 ft. lbs.
22. **Torque** manual lockdown valve jackscrew on fuel tank solenoid valve to 80 inch lbs.
23. Repeat procedure until affected tanks are vented.

Solenoid Stuck Open

1. Disconnect fuel tank electrical connectors and **torque** manual lockdown jackscrews to 80 inch lbs., on fuel tanks not to be vented. If neither of rear or upper tanks need to be vented, rear upper fuel tank rack harness connector may be disconnected without removing rear or upper fuel tank rack vent box.
2. Remove vent box from upper fuel tank rack, as required.
3. Connect grounding cable tool No. 134-00121, or equivalent, to back side of fuel fill valve and ground.
4. Ensure manual bleed valve on fuel filler neck vent kit is closed before connecting to fuel filler valve.
5. Connect fuel filler vent kit tool No. 134-00117, or equivalent, to fuel filler valve.
6. Connect vent hose tool No. 134-00118, or equivalent, to filler neck vent kit and vent stack.
7. Slowly open manual backflow valve on fuel filler valve.
8. Ensure filler neck vent kit pressure gauge indicates tank pressure.
9. Slowly open bleed valve on filler neck vent kit and allow contents of fuel tank to vent to atmosphere. Vent process may take one hour or more.
10. Close bleed valve on fuel filler neck vent kit. Ensure pressure is zero psi.
11. Remove fuel tank solenoid manual

lockdown valve.
12. **Ensure jackscrew in manual override tool is retracted fully (counterclockwise) prior to installation into fuel tank solenoid valve. If tool is installed in vent position, fuel will be immediately released.**
13. Install Rotunda manual override tool No. 134-00050, or equivalent, to tank solenoid and **torque** to 30 ft. lbs.
14. Turn override tool jackscrew clockwise until fuel flows.
15. Open manual bleed valve on fuel filler neck vent kit and vent system until fuel flow stops.
16. Close manual backflow valve on fuel filler valve after tank has been vented.
17. Vent fuel lines.
18. Remove manual override tool from fuel tank solenoid valve.
19. Install fuel tank solenoid manual lockdown valve and **torque** to 30 ft. lbs.
20. **Torque** manual lockdown valve jackscrew on fuel tank solenoid valve to 80 inch lbs.
21. Repeat procedure until affected tanks are vented.

Solenoid Stuck Closed

1. Disconnect fuel tank electrical connectors and **torque** manual lockdown jackscrews to 80 inch lbs., on fuel tanks not to be vented. If neither of rear or upper tanks need to be vented, rear upper fuel tank rack harness connector may be disconnected without removing rear or upper fuel tank rack vent box.
2. Remove vent box from upper fuel tank rack, as required.
3. Connect grounding cable tool No. 134-00121, or equivalent, to back side of fuel fill valve and ground.
4. Ensure manual bleed valve on fuel filler neck vent kit is closed before connecting to fuel filler valve.
5. Connect fuel filler vent kit tool No. 134-00117, or equivalent, to fuel filler valve.
6. Connect vent hose tool No. 134-00118, or equivalent, to filler neck vent kit and vent stack.
7. Open manual bleed valve on fuel filler neck vent kit for one minute to bleed residual fuel system pressure. Close manual bleed valve.

TEST CONDITIONS	TEST DETAILS/RESULTS/ACTIONS
A1 CHECK FUEL SYSTEM SOLENOID OPERATION	

Note: The battery must be fully charged to carry out solenoid diagnostics.

Note: Whenever connecting the vent tool make sure the bleed valve on the tool is closed.

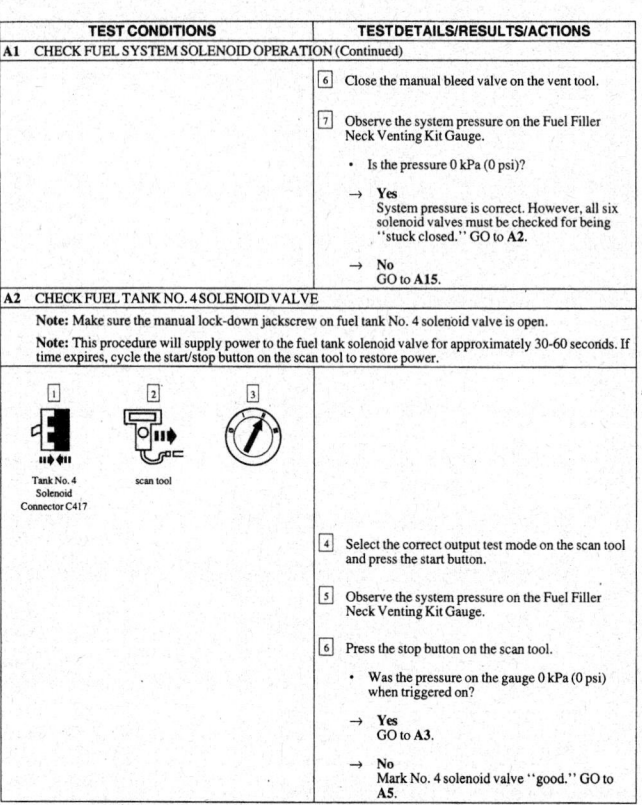

	2 Connect the grounding cable, the venting hose assembly and the Fuel Filler Neck Venting Kit to the vent stack and the fuel fill valve.
	Tank No. 3 Solenoid Connector C416. Tank No. 4 Solenoid Connector C417. 8-Pin Upper Tank Rack Harness Connector C421.
	4 Open the manual back flow valve on the fuel filler valve.
	5 Open the bleed valve on the vent tool for 60 seconds.

FM1029900362010X

Fig. 4   Pinpoint Test A: Fuel tank solenoid valve diagnosis (Part 1 of 26)

TEST CONDITIONS	TEST DETAILS/RESULTS/ACTIONS
A3 CHECK POWER SUPPLY TO FUEL TANK NO. 4 SOLENOID VALVE	

Note: This procedure will supply power to the fuel tank solenoid valves for approximately 30-60 seconds. If time expires, cycle the start/stop button on the scan tool.

Tank No. 4 Solenoid Connector C417

Output Test Mode

	3 Connect a multimeter to C417 between circuits 787 (PK/BK) and ground.
	6 Press the start button on the scan tool.
	7 Observe the voltage reading on the multimeter.
	8 Press the stop button on the scan tool.
	• Was the voltage equal to battery voltage when triggered on?
	→ **Yes** GO to **A4**.
	→ **No** REPAIR circuit 787 (PK/BK) for an open. REPEAT Test **A2**.

FM1029900362030X

Fig. 4   Pinpoint Test A: Fuel tank solenoid valve diagnosis (Part 3 of 26)

TEST CONDITIONS	TEST DETAILS/RESULTS/ACTIONS
A1 CHECK FUEL SYSTEM SOLENOID OPERATION (Continued)	

	6 Close the manual bleed valve on the vent tool.
	7 Observe the system pressure on the Fuel Filler Neck Venting Kit Gauge.
	• Is the pressure 0 kPa (0 psi)?
	→ **Yes** System pressure is correct. However, all six solenoid valves must be checked for being "stuck closed." GO to **A2**.
	→ **No** GO to **A15**.

TEST CONDITIONS	TEST DETAILS/RESULTS/ACTIONS
A2 CHECK FUEL TANK NO. 4 SOLENOID VALVE	

Note: Make sure the manual lock-down jackscrew on fuel tank No. 4 solenoid valve is open.

Note: This procedure will supply power to the fuel tank solenoid valve for approximately 30-60 seconds. If time expires, cycle the start/stop button on the scan tool to restore power.

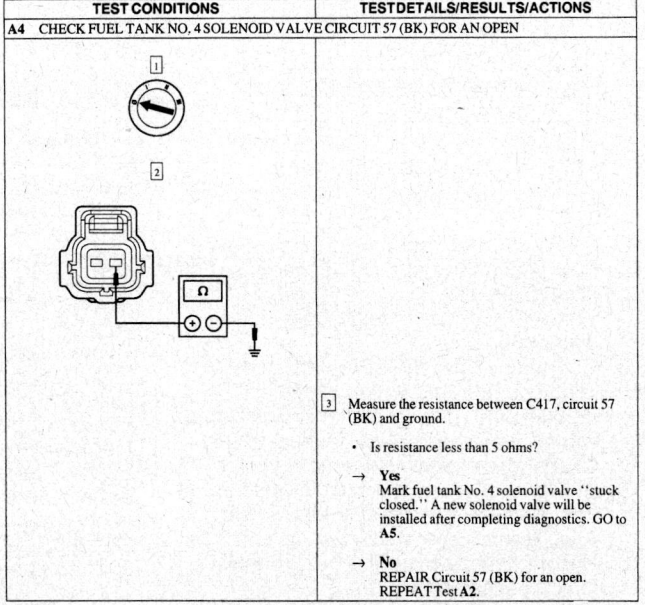

Tank No. 4 Solenoid Connector C417   scan tool

	4 Select the correct output test mode on the scan tool and press the start button.
	5 Observe the system pressure on the Fuel Filler Neck Venting Kit Gauge.
	6 Press the stop button on the scan tool.
	• Was the pressure on the gauge 0 kPa (0 psi) when triggered on?
	→ **Yes** GO to **A3**.
	→ **No** Mark No. 4 solenoid valve "good." GO to **A5**.

FM1029900362020X

Fig. 4   Pinpoint Test A: Fuel tank solenoid valve diagnosis (Part 2 of 26)

TEST CONDITIONS	TEST DETAILS/RESULTS/ACTIONS
A4 CHECK FUEL TANK NO. 4 SOLENOID VALVE CIRCUIT 57 (BK) FOR AN OPEN	

	3 Measure the resistance between C417, circuit 57 (BK) and ground.
	• Is resistance less than 5 ohms?
	→ **Yes** Mark fuel tank No. 4 solenoid valve "stuck closed." A new solenoid valve will be installed after completing diagnostics. GO to **A5**.
	→ **No** REPAIR Circuit 57 (BK) for an open. REPEAT Test **A2**.

FM1029900362040X

Fig. 4   Pinpoint Test A: Fuel tank solenoid valve diagnosis (Part 4 of 26)

8. Remove manual lockdown valve from fuel tank solenoid valve of fuel tank to be vented.

9. **Ensure jackscrew in manual override tool is retracted fully (counterclockwise) prior to installation into fuel tank solenoid valve. If tool is installed in vent position, fuel will be immediately released.**

10. Install Rotunda manual override tool No. 134-00050, or equivalent, to tank solenoid and **torque** to 30 ft. lbs.

11. Turn override tool jackscrew clockwise until fuel flows.

12. Slowly open manual backflow valve on fuel filler valve and ensure pressure gauge on vent kit reads tank pressure.

13. Slowly open bleed valve on fuel filler neck vent kit and allow tank to vent to atmosphere. Vent process may take one hour or more.

14. Vent tank until fuel flow stops.

15. Close manual backflow valve on fuel filler valve when tank venting is complete.

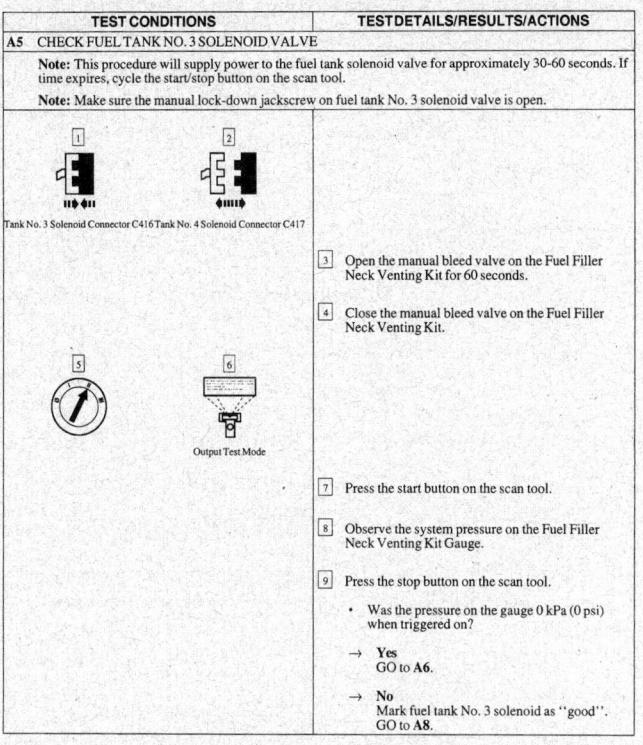

TEST CONDITIONS	TEST DETAILS/RESULTS/ACTIONS
A5 CHECK FUEL TANK NO. 3 SOLENOID VALVE	

Note: This procedure will supply power to the fuel tank solenoid valve for approximately 30-60 seconds. If time expires, cycle the start/stop button on the scan tool.

Note: Make sure the manual lock-down jackscrew on fuel tank No. 3 solenoid valve is open.

3. Open the manual bleed valve on the Fuel Filler Neck Venting Kit for 60 seconds.

4. Close the manual bleed valve on the Fuel Filler Neck Venting Kit.

7. Press the start button on the scan tool.

8. Observe the system pressure on the Fuel Filler Neck Venting Kit Gauge.

9. Press the stop button on the scan tool.

- Was the pressure on the gauge 0 kPa (0 psi) when triggered on?

→ **Yes** GO to **A6**.

→ **No** Mark fuel tank No. 3 solenoid as "good". GO to **A8**.

FM1029900362050X

Fig. 4 Pinpoint Test A: Fuel tank solenoid valve diagnosis (Part 5 of 26)

16. Vent fuel lines.
17. Remove manual override tool from fuel tank solenoid valve.
18. Install fuel tank solenoid manual lock-down valve and **torque** to 30 ft. lbs.
19. **Torque** manual lockdown valve jackscrew on fuel tank solenoid valve to 80 inch lbs.
20. Repeat procedure until affected tanks are vented.

COMPRESSION PRESSURE

Cylinder compression pressure should be 134–250 psi at an engine cranking speed of 180 RPM minimum. The compression in each cylinder should fall within the specified compression pressure range with no more than a 75% variance in compression.

ENGINE MOUNT

REPLACE

Crown Victoria, Grand Marquis & Marauder

1. **On 2001–02 models,** for righthand engine mount, remove starter.
2. **On 2001–02 models,** for lefthand engine mount, remove oil dipstick tube.
3. **On all models,** support vehicle engine with suitable engine support device.
4. Remove mounting bolts and mount(s).
5. Reverse procedure to install.

Town Car

2001–02

LEFTHAND

1. Remove oil dipstick tube.
2. Support engine using suitable lifting device.
3. Remove three lefthand engine mount bolts.
4. Remove lefthand engine mount.
5. Reverse procedure to install.

RIGHTHAND

1. Remove starter motor as outlined in "Electrical" chapter.
2. Support engine using suitable lifting device.
3. Remove three righthand engine mount bolts.
4. Remove righthand engine mount.
5. Reverse procedure to install.

2003–05

LEFTHAND

1. Support with engine lift bracket tool No. 303-F047 and support bar tool No. 3030-D063, or equivalents.
2. Raise and support vehicle.
3. Remove oil filter.
4. Remove mounting nut, bolts and lefthand engine mount.
5. Reverse procedure to install.

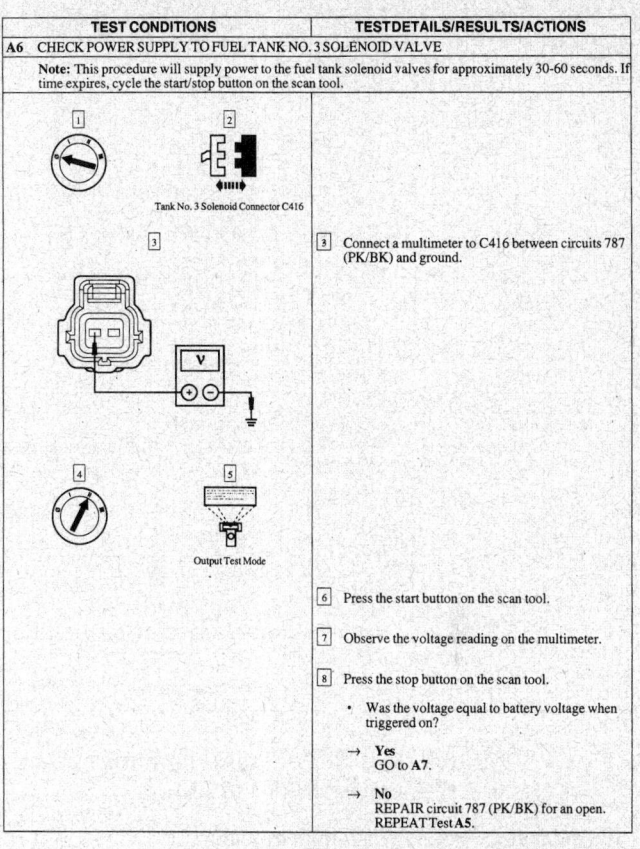

TEST CONDITIONS	TEST DETAILS/RESULTS/ACTIONS
A6 CHECK POWER SUPPLY TO FUEL TANK NO. 3 SOLENOID VALVE	

Note: This procedure will supply power to the fuel tank solenoid valves for approximately 30-60 seconds. If time expires, cycle the start/stop button on the scan tool.

3. Connect a multimeter to C416 between circuits 787 (PK/BK) and ground.

6. Press the start button on the scan tool.

7. Observe the voltage reading on the multimeter.

8. Press the stop button on the scan tool.

- Was the voltage equal to battery voltage when triggered on?

→ **Yes** GO to **A7**.

→ **No** REPAIR circuit 787 (PK/BK) for an open. REPEAT Test **A5**.

FM1029900362060X

Fig. 4 Pinpoint Test A: Fuel tank solenoid valve diagnosis (Part 6 of 26)

RIGHTHAND

1. Support with engine lift bracket tool No. 303-F047 and support bar tool No. 3030-D063, or equivalents.
2. Raise and support vehicle.
3. Remove mounting nut, bolts and righthand engine mount.
4. Reverse procedure to install.

ENGINE

REPLACE

2001–02

1. Remove hood.
2. Evacuate air conditioning system as outlined in "Air Conditioning" chapter.
3. Remove air cleaner outlet tube.
4. Relieve fuel pressure as outlined under "Precautions."
5. Disconnect fuel lines.
6. Remove wiper arm and pivot shaft.
7. Raise and support vehicle.
8. Drain engine coolant and oil into suitable containers.
9. Disconnect lower radiator hose from oil filter adapter.
10. **On models equipped with oil cooler,** disconnect two coolant hoses, remove oil cooler and secure to front of engine.
11. **On all models,** remove battery.

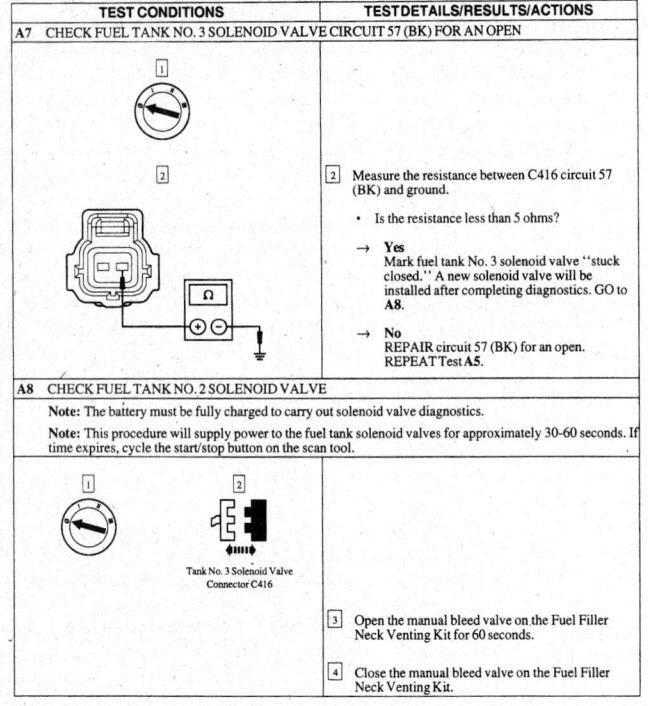

TEST CONDITIONS	TEST DETAILS/RESULTS/ACTIONS
A7 CHECK FUEL TANK NO. 3 SOLENOID VALVE CIRCUIT 57 (BK) FOR AN OPEN	

[2] Measure the resistance between C416 circuit 57 (BK) and ground.

• Is the resistance less than 5 ohms?

→ **Yes**
Mark fuel tank No. 3 solenoid valve "stuck closed." A new solenoid valve will be installed after completing diagnostics. GO to **A8**.

→ **No**
REPAIR circuit 57 (BK) for an open. REPEAT Test **A5**.

| **A8** CHECK FUEL TANK NO. 2 SOLENOID VALVE | |

Note: The battery must be fully charged to carry out solenoid valve diagnostics.

Note: This procedure will supply power to the fuel tank solenoid valves for approximately 30-60 seconds. If time expires, cycle the start/stop button on the scan tool.

Tank No. 3 Solenoid Valve
Connector C416

[3] Open the manual bleed valve on the Fuel Filler Neck Venting Kit for 60 seconds.

[4] Close the manual bleed valve on the Fuel Filler Neck Venting Kit.

FM1029900362070X

Fig. 4   Pinpoint Test A: Fuel tank solenoid valve diagnosis (Part 7 of 26)

TEST CONDITIONS	TEST DETAILS/RESULTS/ACTIONS
A8 CHECK FUEL TANK NO. 2 SOLENOID VALVE (Continued)	

[5] Install Rotunda Electrical Harness for Venting Tanks between male and female halves of upper tank assembly harness connector C421.

Output Test Mode

[8] Hold the Rotunda Electrical Harness for Venting Tanks to the tank No. 2 position.

[9] Press the start button on the scan tool.

[10] Observe the system pressure on the Fuel Filler Neck Venting Kit Gauge.

[11] Press the stop button on the scan tool.

• Was the pressure on the gauge 0 kPa (0 psi) when triggered on?

→ **Yes**
Mark fuel tank No. 2 solenoid valve "may be stuck closed." GO to **A9**.

→ **No**
Mark fuel tank No. 2 solenoid valve as "good." GO to **A9**.

FM1029900362080X

Fig. 4   Pinpoint Test A: Fuel tank solenoid valve diagnosis (Part 8 of 26)

1. Disconnect hoses from transmission fluid cooler and power steering cooler.
2. Remove radiator upper sight shield.
3. Position clamp and disconnect upper radiator hose from water hose connection. Secure hose to radiator.
4. Disconnect fan motor electrical connector and position aside.
5. Remove nuts and separate lines from air conditioning condenser core.
6. Remove mounting bolts, support brackets and radiator.
7. Disconnect engine bulkhead connectors, **Fig. 5.**
8. Disconnect accelerator and speed control actuator cables.
9. **On models equipped with gasoline engine,** remove accelerator and speed control actuator cables from clips and position aside.
10. **On all models,** disconnect main vacuum supply hose.
11. Remove ground wire bolt, **Fig. 6.**
12. Raise and support vehicle, then remove starter motor.
13. Support exhaust system and remove mounting nuts.
14. Remove torque converter inspection cover.
15. Remove torque converter nut access plug, **Fig. 7.**
16. Remove transmission cooler line bracket bolt, **Fig. 8.**
17. Remove nut and ground wire, **Fig. 9.**
18. Remove five starter bolts and one stud, **Fig. 10.**
19. **On models equipped with gasoline engine,** proceed as follows:
    a. Remove evaporative emission canister purge valve, **Fig. 11.**
    b. Position clamps aside and remove heater hoses.
    c. Remove nut and disconnect electrical connectors on righthand inner fender, **Fig. 12.**
20. **On models equipped with natural gas engine,** proceed as follows:
    a. Disconnect electrical connectors, **Fig. 13.**
    b. Remove cover, nut and wiring, **Fig. 14.**
21. **On all models,** remove bolt and body ground, **Fig. 15.**
22. Disconnect air conditioning cycling switch electrical connector and remove nut, **Fig. 16.**
23. Disconnect air conditioning lines.
24. Disconnect and unplug righthand heated oxygen sensor connector.
25. Disconnect lefthand heated oxygen sensor and separate transmission harness from rear of lefthand cylinder head.
26. Disconnect power steering pressure hose.
27. Remove bolt from bracket, **Fig. 17.**
28. Raise and support vehicle.
29. Remove lefthand engine mount through bolts, **Fig. 18.**
30. Remove righthand engine mount through bolt, **Fig. 19.**
31. Lower vehicle.
32. Install suitable engine lifting equipment.
33. Support transmission.
34. Remove engine.
35. Reverse procedure to install.

2003-05

DOHC

1. Remove hood.
2. Remove air cleaner outlet tube.
3. Drain coolant into suitable container.
4. Remove fan shroud assembly.
5. Remove pin retainers, nuts and bolts, then the righthand cowl extension.
6. Disconnect electrical connector, then remove bolts and lefthand extension cover.
7. Disconnect power distribution power supply electrical connector.
8. Disconnect ground wire and air conditioning electrical connector.
9. Disconnect fuel hose spring lock coupling.
10. Remove accelerator controls splash shield.
11. Disconnect accelerator cable, speed control cable and return spring.
12. Remove accelerator and speed control cables from bracket.
13. Disconnect vacuum hoses and EAR system module electrical connector.
14. Remove mounting bolt and position accelerator cables aside.
15. Disconnect coolant hoses.
16. Disconnect engine bulkhead electrical connectors.
17. Disconnect lower radiator hose from oil filter adapter.
18. Raise and support vehicle, then drain

TEST CONDITIONS	TEST DETAILS/RESULTS/ACTIONS
A9 CHECK FUEL TANK NO. 1 SOLENOID VALVE	

Note: This procedure will supply power to the fuel tank solenoid valves for approximately 30-60 seconds. If time expires, cycle the start/stop button on the scan tool.

Note: Leave the Rotunda Electrical Harness for Venting Tanks tool used in Step **A8** connected to the upper fuel tank rack harness connector C420F.

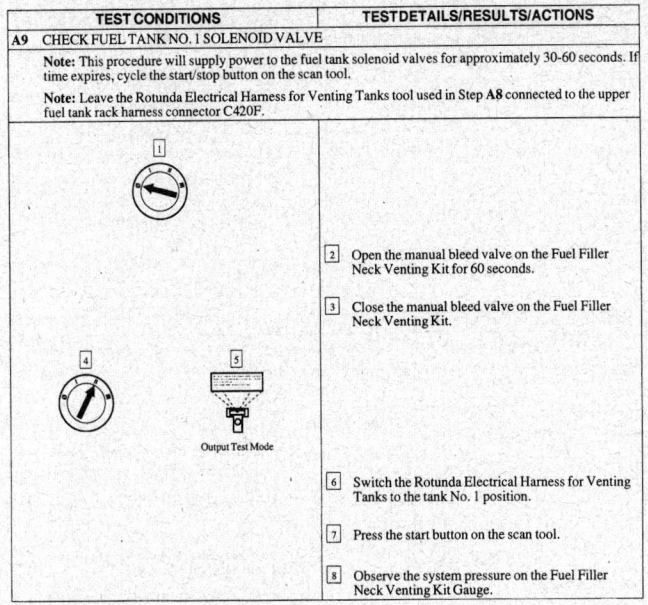

Output Test Mode

2 Open the manual bleed valve on the Fuel Filler Neck Venting Kit for 60 seconds.

3 Close the manual bleed valve on the Fuel Filler Neck Venting Kit.

6 Switch the Rotunda Electrical Harness for Venting Tanks to the tank No. 1 position.

7 Press the start button on the scan tool.

8 Observe the system pressure on the Fuel Filler Neck Venting Kit Gauge.

FM1029900362090X

Fig. 4 Pinpoint Test A: Fuel tank solenoid valve diagnosis (Part 9 of 26)

TEST CONDITIONS	TEST DETAILS/RESULTS/ACTIONS
A9 CHECK FUEL TANK NO. 1 SOLENOID VALVE (Continued)	

9 Press the stop button on the scan tool.

- Was the pressure on the gauge 0 kPa (0 psi) when triggered on?

→ **Yes**
Fuel tank No. 1 solenoid valve "may be stuck closed." GO to **A10**.

→ **No**
Mark fuel tank No. 1 solenoid valve "good." To complete diagnostics, install a new solenoid valve if the solenoid valve is marked "stuck closed." If fuel tank No. 2 solenoid valve was marked "may be stuck closed," GO to **A10**. If all solenoid valves were marked "good," diagnostics are complete. RESTORE the vehicle and test the system for normal operation.

| **A10 CHECK UPPER AND REAR TANK RACK CIRCUIT 57 (BK)** | |

Note: At this point in the diagnostics it is necessary to access the upper and rear fuel tank rack harness connections. Due to packaging considerations, it will be necessary to remove the upper and rear tank rack assemblies to remove the upper and rear tank rack vent boxes.

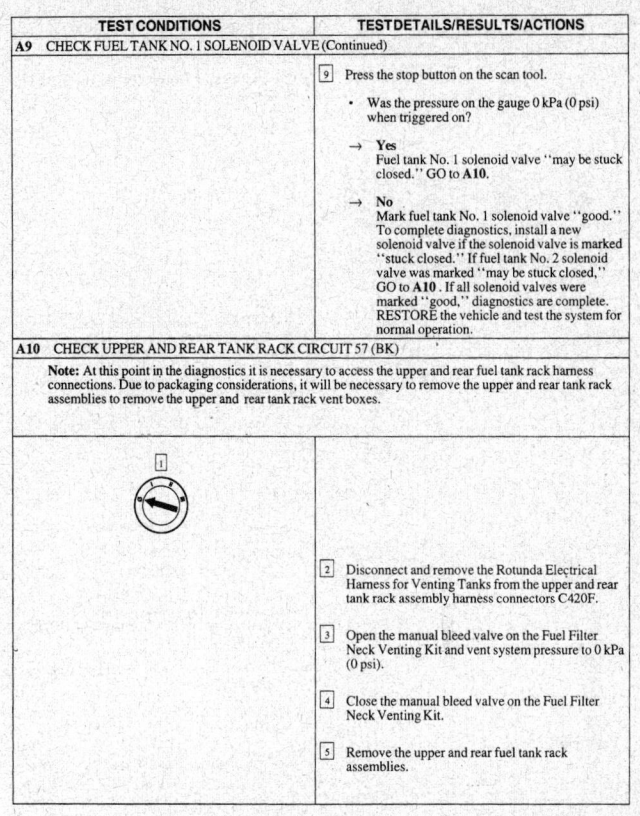

2 Disconnect and remove the Rotunda Electrical Harness for Venting Tanks from the upper and rear tank rack assembly harness connectors C420F.

3 Open the manual bleed valve on the Fuel Filler Neck Venting Kit and vent system pressure to 0 kPa (0 psi).

4 Close the manual bleed valve on the Fuel Filler Neck Venting Kit.

5 Remove the upper and rear fuel tank rack assemblies.

FM1029900362100X

Fig. 4 Pinpoint Test A: Fuel tank solenoid valve diagnosis (Part 10 of 26)

engine oil into suitable container.

19. Disconnect power steering and power steering pressure switch electrical connectors.
20. Remove mounting nut and transmission cooler tube support bracket.
21. Disconnect CKP electrical connector.
22. Disconnect engine wiring harness retainers from air conditioning compressor.
23. Disconnect air conditioning compressor electrical connector.
24. Remove bolts, then position air conditioning compressor and power steering pump aside.
25. Remove starter motor and engine oil cooler tubes bracket.
26. Disconnect transmission and heated oxygen sensors electrical connectors.
27. Remove four exhaust pipe to manifold mounting nuts.
28. Remove inspection cover and torque converter nut access plug.
29. Remove engine support insulator nuts and lower vehicle.
30. Support transmission using suitable transmission jack.
31. Remove mounting bolts and separate transmission from engine.
32. Install engine lift bracket set tool No. D93P-6001-A, or equivalent.
33. Lift and remove engine.
34. Reverse procedure to install.

SOHC

1. Remove hood.
2. Evacuate air conditioning system as outlined in "Air Conditioning" chapter.
3. Remove air cleaner outlet tube.
4. Relieve fuel pressure as outlined under "Precautions."
5. Remove wiper arm and pivot shaft.
6. Rotate tensioner clockwise and remove accessory drive belt.

7. Remove lefthand and righthand cowl extensions.
8. Drain engine coolant into suitable container.
9. Remove accelerator splash shield and disconnect vacuum hose.
10. Disconnect EVAP canister purge valve hoses and electrical connector, then remove EVAP canister purge valve.
11. Disconnect accelerator cable and speed control actuator cable.
12. Remove accelerator and speed control actuator cables from clips, then position them aside.
13. Disconnect fuel spring lock connector.
14. Disconnect power distribution power supply electrical connector.
15. Disconnect ground wire, **Fig. 20**.
16. Disconnect air conditioning electrical connector and heater water hoses.
17. Remove ground strap, **Fig. 21**.
18. Disconnect engine bulkhead electrical connectors.
19. Remove mounting bolt and position power steering pump reservoir aside.
20. Disconnect upper radiator hose and secure it to radiator assembly.
21. Disconnect lower radiator hose from oil filter adapter.
22. Remove cooling fan, then raise and support vehicle.
23. Drain engine oil into suitable container.
24. Disconnect power steering and power steering pressure switch electrical connectors.
25. Remove mounting nut and the transmission cooler tube support bracket.

26. Disconnect CKP electrical connector.
27. Disconnect engine wiring harness retainers from air conditioning compressor, then the air conditioning compressor electrical connector.
28. Remove mounting bolts and position air conditioning compressor aside.
29. Remove mounting bolts and position power steering pump aside.
30. Remove starter motor and lower vehicle.
31. Remove and discard pinch bolt, then disconnect lower intermediate steering shaft from upper intermediate shaft.
32. Remove and discard pinch bolt, then disconnect upper intermediate steering shaft from isolator.
33. Remove mounting nuts, bearing and seal, then the upper intermediate steering shaft.
34. Remove and discard pinch bolt, then remove lower intermediate steering shaft. **Do not allow steering wheel to rotate while steering shaft is removed.**
35. Disconnect transmission and heated oxygen sensors electrical connectors.
36. Remove four mounting nuts from front exhaust pipes.
37. Remove mounting bolts inspection cover.
38. Remove torque converter nut access plug.
39. Remove lower engine to transmission mounting bolts.
40. Remove engine support insulator

TEST CONDITIONS	TEST DETAILS/RESULTS/ACTIONS
A10 CHECK UPPER AND REAR TANK RACK CIRCUIT 57 (BK) (Continued)	

	[6] Remove the upper and rear fuel tank rack assembly vent boxes.
	[11] With the upper and rear fuel tank rack assemblies removed, measure the resistance between fuel tank No. 1 solenoid valve connector C416 circuit 57 (BK), fuel tank No. 2 solenoid connector C417 circuit 57 (BK), fuel tank No. 5 solenoid connector C418 circuit 57 (BK), fuel tank No. 6 solenoid connector C419 circuit 57 (BK), and ground. • Is the resistance less than 5 ohms on both circuits? → **Yes** GO to **A11**. → **No** REPAIR circuit 57 (BK) for an open. GO to **A11**.
A11 CHECK UPPER AND REAR TANK RACK CIRCUIT 787 (PK/BK)	
	[1] Measure the resistance between connector C466 at the inertial fuel shut-off switch, and solenoid valve connectors C418, C419, C416 and C417, (PK/BK) circuit 787. • Is the resistance less than 5 ohms on both circuits? → **Yes** GO to **A12**. → **No** REPAIR circuit 787 (PK/BK) for an open. INSTALL complete upper and rear tank rack assemblies (including the vent boxes) in the vehicle. REPEAT Test **A8**.

FM1029900362110X

Fig. 4 Pinpoint Test A: Fuel tank solenoid valve diagnosis (Part 11 of 26)

TEST CONDITIONS	TEST DETAILS/RESULTS/ACTIONS
A12 CHECK UPPER FUEL TANK RACK ASSEMBLY MANUAL LOCK-DOWNS	
	[1] With the upper and rear fuel tank rack assemblies still removed, check the fuel tank No. 1 and No. 2 solenoid valves manual lock-downs. • Are the manual lock-downs open? → **Yes** INSTALL new upper fuel tank rack assembly solenoids if marked "may be stuck closed." INSTALL the complete upper tank rack assembly (including vent box) in the vehicle. REPEAT Test **A8**. → **No** INSTALL the upper and rear tank rack assemblies without the vent boxes. Make all fuel line connections. GO to **A13**.
A13 CHECK FUEL TANK NO. 2 SOLENOID VALVE MANUAL LOCK-DOWN	
Note: Make sure the bleed valve on the Fuel Filler Neck Venting Kit is closed before proceeding with this test.	
	[1] Open fuel tank No. 2 solenoid valve manual lock-down jackscrew.
	[2] Open the bleed valve on the Fuel Filler Neck Venting Kit for 60 seconds.
	[3] Close the bleed valve on the Fuel Filler Neck Venting Kit.
	[4] Observe the system pressure on the Fuel Filler Neck Venting Kit Gauge. • Is the pressure on the gauge 0 kPa (0 psi)? → **Yes** Mark fuel tank No. 2 solenoid valve "good." GO to **A14**. → **No** Mark fuel tank No. 2 solenoid valve "stuck open." GO to **A14**.
A14 CHECK FUEL TANK NO. 1 SOLENOID VALVE MANUAL LOCK-DOWN	
	[1] Tighten the manual lock-down jackscrew on fuel tank No. 2 solenoid valve to 9 Nm (79 lb/in).
	[2] Open fuel tank No. 1 solenoid valve manual lock-down jackscrew.

FM1029900362120X

Fig. 4 Pinpoint Test A: Fuel tank solenoid valve diagnosis (Part 12 of 26)

mounting nuts.
41. Install engine lifting bracket set tool No. 303-DS086, or equivalent.
42. Remove remaining engine to transmission bolts and engine.
43. Reverse procedure to install.

INTAKE MANIFOLD
REPLACE
Gasoline Engine
DOHC
LOWER

1. Drain engine coolant into suitable container.
2. Remove upper intake manifold as outlined under "Upper."
3. Disconnect engine coolant temperature sensor electrical connector and coolant hoses.
4. Remove serpentine drive belt and crossover tube.
5. Remove mounting bolts and alternator support bracket.
6. Remove mounting bolts and alternator.
7. Disconnect electrical connector and vacuum hose from fuel pressure sensor.
8. Separate wiring harness from fuel injection supply manifold studs in four places.
9. Disconnect eight fuel injector electrical connectors.
10. Remove lower intake manifold bolts in sequence, then raise slightly, **Fig. 22.**
11. Disconnect fuel charging wiring harness from rear of lower intake manifold.
12. Remove lower intake manifold.
13. Reverse procedure to install. **Torque** lower intake manifold bolts to 89 inch lbs., in sequence, **Fig. 23.**

UPPER

1. Remove air cleaner outlet tube and accelerator control splash shield.
2. Disconnect accelerator cable, speed control cable and return spring.
3. Disconnect fuel vapor hose.
4. Remove accelerator and speed control cables from bracket.
5. Disconnect vacuum hoses.
6. Remove mounting bolt and position accelerator control cables aside.
7. Disconnect EAR system module tube from EAR system module.
8. Disconnect throttle position sensor and IAC sensor electrical connectors.
9. Disconnect PCV ventilation tube.
10. Disconnect EAR system module electrical connector.
11. Disconnect vacuum hoses and PCV coolant hoses.
12. Remove mounting bolts in sequence and upper intake manifold, **Fig. 24.**
13. Reverse procedure to install, noting the following:

a. Inspect and clean sealing surfaces, then install new upper intake manifold gasket.
b. **Torque** upper intake manifold bolts to 89 inch lbs., in sequence, **Fig. 25.**

SOHC

1. Drain engine coolant into suitable container.
2. Remove air cleaner outlet tube.
3. Relieve fuel pressure as outlined under "Precautions."
4. Remove wiper arm and pivot shaft.
5. Remove drive belt.
6. Raise and support vehicle.
7. Disconnect electrical connectors at crankshaft position sensor and air conditioning compressor.
8. Remove oil filter.
9. Disconnect oil pressure sensor electrical connector and power steering switch electrical connector.
10. Disconnect EAR valve from manifold.
11. Disconnect two differential pressure feedback hoses.
12. Disconnect righthand heated oxygen sensor electrical connector.
13. Disconnect fuel charging wiring electrical connectors from ignition coils and fuel injectors.
14. Disconnect accelerator cable and speed control actuator cable.
15. Remove cables from EAR tube heat shield and position aside.

TEST CONDITIONS	TESTDETAILS/RESULTS/ACTIONS
A14 CHECK FUEL TANK NO. 1 SOLENOID VALVE MANUAL LOCK-DOWN (Continued)	

3. Open the bleed valve on the Fuel Filler Neck Venting Kit for 60 seconds.

4. Close the bleed valve on the Fuel Filler Neck Venting Kit.

5. Observe the system pressure on the Fuel Filler Neck Venting Kit Gauge.

- Is the system pressure on the Fuel Filler Neck Venting Kit Gauge 0 kPa (0 psi)?

→ **Yes**
Mark fuel tank No. 1 solenoid valve "good." GO to **A8** to retest the upper tank rack.

→ **No**
MARK fuel tank No. 1 solenoid valve "stuck open." INSTALL new upper fuel tank rack assembly solenoid valves if marked "stuck open." GO to **A8**.

TEST CONDITIONS	TESTDETAILS/RESULTS/ACTIONS
A15 CHECK ALL SOLENOID CIRCUITS 787 (PK/BK) FOR A SHORT TO B+	

2. Measure the voltage between fuel tank No. 3 (C414) and No. 4 (C415) solenoid connectors circuit 787 (PK/BK) and ground. Measure the voltage between the upper fuel tank rack assembly harness connectors C416 and C417 Circuit 787 (PK/BK) and ground. Measure the voltage between the rear fuel tank rack assembly harness connectors C418 and C419 Circuit 787 (PK/BK) and ground

- Is battery voltage present on any connector 787 (PK/BK) circuit?

→ **Yes**
REPAIR circuit 787 (PK/BK) for a short to B+. REPEAT Test **A1**.

→ **No**
GO to **A16**.

FM1029900362130X

Fig. 4 Pinpoint Test A: Fuel tank solenoid valve diagnosis (Part 13 of 26)

TEST CONDITIONS	TESTDETAILS/RESULTS/ACTIONS
A16 ISOLATE UPPER AND LOWER TANK RACK ASSEMBLIES	
Note: At this point in the diagnostics it is necessary to remove the rear rack assembly.	

1. Tighten the manual lock-down jackscrew on fuel tank No. 3 and No. 4 solenoid valves to 9 Nm (79 lb/in).

2. Open the manual bleed valve on the Fuel Filler Neck Venting Kit for 60 seconds.

3. Close the manual bleed valve on the Fuel Filler Neck Venting Kit.

4. Observe the system pressure on the Fuel Filler Neck Venting Kit Gauge.

- Is the pressure on the gauge 0 kPa (0 psi)?

→ **Yes**
GO to **A21**.

→ **No**
GO to **A17**.

TEST CONDITIONS	TESTDETAILS/RESULTS/ACTIONS
A17 CHECK FUEL TANK NO. 1 CIRCUIT 787 (PK/BK)	
Note: At this point in the diagnostics it is necessary to access the upper fuel tank rack harness connectors. Due to packaging considerations, it will be necessary to remove the upper tank rack assembly to remove the upper tank rack vent box.	

2. Make sure the manual lock-downs on fuel tank No. 3 and No. 4 are still closed from Step **A16**.

3. Open the manual bleed valve on the Fuel Filler Neck Venting Kit and vent the system pressure to 0 kPa (0 psi).

4. Close the manual bleed valve on the Fuel Filler Neck Venting Kit.

5. Remove the upper tank rack assembly.

FM1029900362140X

Fig. 4 Pinpoint Test A: Fuel tank solenoid valve diagnosis (Part 14 of 26)

16. Remove EAR tube heat shield.
17. Disconnect evaporative emissions return tube, main chassis vacuum supply line and EAR valve vacuum supply.
18. Disconnect PCV tube at two locations and remove.
19. Disconnect electrical connector from EAR vacuum regulator.
20. Disconnect vacuum line from evaporative emission canister purge valve.
21. Disconnect alternator cable and position aside.
22. Remove upper mounting bracket and electrical connector from alternator.
23. Remove upper radiator and heater hose.
24. Disconnect electrical connector from idle air control valve and throttle position sensor.
25. Disconnect EAR tube from EAR valve.
26. Remove lefthand oxygen sensor and transmission electrical connectors from wiring bracket, then the bracket.
27. Remove throttle body.
28. Separate fuel charging wiring pushpin connector from crash bracket, then remove bolt, stud and crash bracket.
29. Disconnect vacuum lines and remove vacuum harness.
30. Remove fuel injection supply manifold and fuel injectors as an assembly.
31. Remove eight ignition coils.
32. Remove water outlet adapter, thermostat and gasket.
33. Remove intake manifold and gaskets, clean gasket sealing surfaces.

34. Reverse procedure to install, noting the following:
    a. Install new gaskets.
    b. Install intake manifold and hand tighten bolts, **Fig. 26.**
    c. Install ignition coils and tighten bolts.
    d. Install fuel injection supply manifold and tighten studs.
    e. Install crash bracket loosely.
    f. Install thermostat and water outlet adapter loosely with bolts.
    g. **Torque** intake manifold bolts to 15–22 ft. lbs., in sequence, **Figs. 27 and 28.**

Natural Gas Engine

1. Remove wiper arm & pivot shaft.
2. Remove air cleaner outlet tube.
3. Relieve fuel pressure as outlined under "Precautions."
4. Disconnect fuel charging wiring electrical connectors from ignition coils and fuel injectors.
5. Disconnect fuel charging electrical connectors from fuel pressure, fuel pump temperature and engine coolant temperature sensors.
6. Remove isolation valve wiring lead from upper alternator support bracket and disconnect connector.
7. Disconnect alternator battery cable.
8. Remove power distribution box access cover, nut and wiring.
9. Disconnect fuel charging wiring electrical connectors from the following components:
    a. Inner fender splash shield connectors.
    b. Air conditioning pressure transducer.
    c. Cylinder head temperature sensor jumper.
    d. Camshaft position sensor.
    e. Alternator.
    f. Throttle position sensor.
    g. Radio ignition interference capacitor.
    h. EAR vacuum regulator solenoid.
    i. Differential pressure feedback EAR.
    j. Idle air control valve.
10. Disconnect throttle cable and speed control actuator cable from throttle body.
11. Remove mounting bolt, then position cables and bracket aside.
12. Remove fuel charging wiring mounting bolts and position harness aside.
13. Disconnect fuel lines and hoses from differential pressure feedback EAR and vacuum line from EAR valve.
14. Disconnect main chassis vacuum line.
15. Disconnect crankcase vent tube at two locations and remove.
16. Disconnect vacuum lines from throttle body adapter and EAR vacuum regulator solenoid.
17. Disconnect EAR tube from EAR valve.
18. Remove isolation valve bolts.
19. Remove fuel injection supply manifold

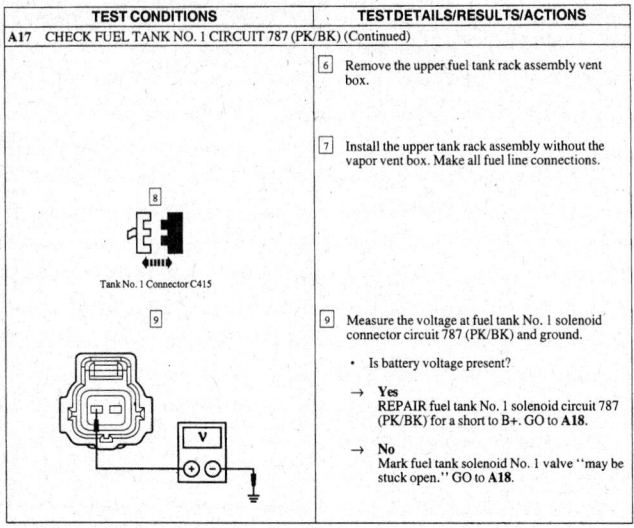

TEST CONDITIONS	TEST DETAILS/RESULTS/ACTIONS
A17 CHECK FUEL TANK NO. 1 CIRCUIT 787 (PK/BK) (Continued)	

6 Remove the upper fuel tank rack assembly vent box.

7 Install the upper tank rack assembly without the vapor vent box. Make all fuel line connections.

8 Tank No. 1 Connector C415

9 Measure the voltage at fuel tank No. 1 solenoid connector circuit 787 (PK/BK) and ground.

• Is battery voltage present?

→ **Yes**
REPAIR fuel tank No. 1 solenoid circuit 787 (PK/BK) for a short to B+. GO to **A18**.

→ **No**
Mark fuel tank solenoid No. 1 valve "may be stuck open." GO to **A18**.

FM1029900362150X

Fig. 4   Pinpoint Test A: Fuel tank solenoid valve diagnosis (Part 15 of 26)

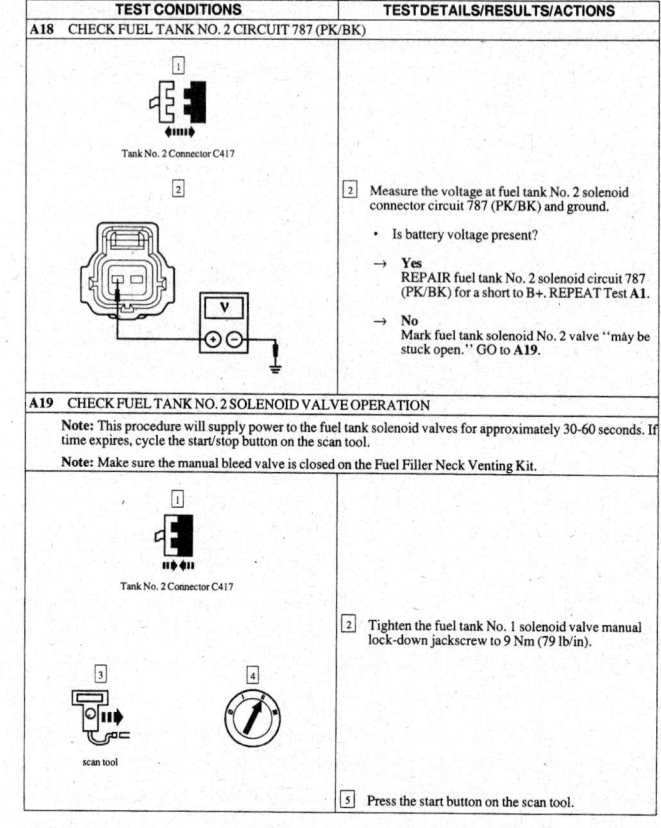

TEST CONDITIONS	TEST DETAILS/RESULTS/ACTIONS
A18 CHECK FUEL TANK NO. 2 CIRCUIT 787 (PK/BK)	

1 Tank No. 2 Connector C417

2 Measure the voltage at fuel tank No. 2 solenoid connector circuit 787 (PK/BK) and ground.

• Is battery voltage present?

→ **Yes**
REPAIR fuel tank No. 2 solenoid circuit 787 (PK/BK) for a short to B+. REPEAT Test **A1**.

→ **No**
Mark fuel tank solenoid No. 2 valve "may be stuck open." GO to **A19**.

A19 CHECK FUEL TANK NO. 2 SOLENOID VALVE OPERATION	

Note: This procedure will supply power to the fuel tank solenoid valves for approximately 30-60 seconds. If time expires, cycle the start/stop button on the scan tool.

Note: Make sure the manual bleed valve is closed on the Fuel Filler Neck Venting Kit.

1 Tank No. 2 Connector C417

2 Tighten the fuel tank No. 1 solenoid valve manual lock-down jackscrew to 9 Nm (79 lb/in).

3 scan tool

4

5 Press the start button on the scan tool.

FM1029900362160X

Fig. 4   Pinpoint Test A: Fuel tank solenoid valve diagnosis (Part 16 of 26)

and fuel injectors as an assembly.

20. Disconnect heater hose from intake manifold.
21. Disconnect upper radiator hose from water outlet adapter.
22. Remove eight ignition coils.
23. Remove upper alternator support bracket.
24. Remove water outlet adapter, thermostat and O-ring.
25. Remove mounting bolts and intake manifold.
26. Remove intake manifold gaskets and clean all surfaces.
27. Reverse procedure to install, noting the following:
    a. Install new intake manifold gaskets.
    b. **Torque** bolts to 15–22 ft. lbs., in sequence, **Fig. 29.**

EXHAUST MANIFOLD
REPLACE
DOHC

1. Remove front tire and wheel assembly.
2. Disconnect exhaust pipe from exhaust manifold.
3. Disconnect EAR system module tube from exhaust manifold.
4. Remove exhaust manifold heat shield.
5. Remove eight mounting nuts and exhaust manifold.
6. Reverse procedure to install. **Torque** bolts to 108 inch lbs., in sequence, **Figs. 30 and 31.**

SOHC

1. Raise and support vehicle.
2. Disconnect oxygen sensor connectors.
3. Remove exhaust manifold to catalytic converter nuts and disconnect converters at exhaust inlet pipes.
4. Remove catalytic converters.
5. Disconnect EAR tube at exhaust manifold connector.

6. Remove nuts, exhaust manifolds and gaskets.
7. Reverse procedure to install. **Torque** manifold nuts to 14–16 ft. lbs., in sequence, **Figs. 32 and 33.**

CYLINDER HEAD
REPLACE
DOHC

1. Remove engine as outlined under "Engine, Replace."
2. Remove flexplate and engine/transmission spacer plate.
3. Mount engine on suitable work stand.
4. Remove engine lift bracket tools.
5. Remove mounting bolts and righthand engine mount.
6. Remove engine block drain plug and drain coolant into suitable container. Install drain plugs.
7. Disconnect PCV tube, then the vacuum and PCV valve coolant hoses.
8. Remove mounting bolt and EAR system module bracket, then disconnect module tube.
9. Disconnect EAR system module tube.
10. Disconnect Throttle Position (TP) and Idle Air Control (IAC) sensor electrical connectors.
11. Remove mounting bolts in sequence and upper intake manifold, **Fig. 24.**
12. Disconnect electrical connector, alternator cable and harness retainer.

13. Remove mounting bolts and alternator bracket.
14. Disconnect Engine Coolant Temperature (ECT) sensors.
15. Remove crossover tube.
16. Remove mounting bolts and alternator.
17. Disconnect fuel pressure sensor electrical connector and vacuum hose.
18. Disconnect fuel charging wiring from fuel injection supply manifold studs.
19. Disconnect fuel injector electrical connectors.
20. Remove mounting bolts and studs in sequence, then slightly raise lower intake manifold, **Fig. 22.**
21. Disconnect fuel charging wiring harness from lower intake manifold rear, the remove manifold and gaskets.
22. Remove covers and disconnect ignition coil electrical connectors.
23. Remove ignition coils.
24. Disconnect Knock Sensor (KC) jumper harness from fuel charging harness.
25. Remove mounting bolts and water pump pulley.
26. Remove mounting bolt and crankshaft pulley using crankshaft vibration damper tool No. 303-009, or equivalent.
27. Remove crankshaft front seal using crankshaft front oil seal remover tool No. 303-107, or equivalent.
28. Remove belt idler pulleys.
29. Disconnect Camshaft Position (CMP)

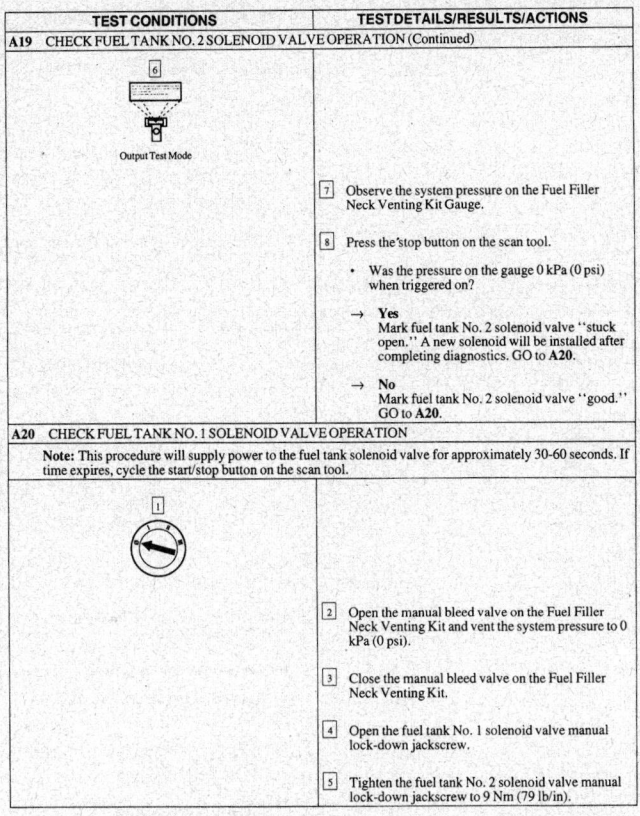

TEST CONDITIONS	TEST DETAILS/RESULTS/ACTIONS
A19 CHECK FUEL TANK NO. 2 SOLENOID VALVE OPERATION (Continued)	
Output Test Mode	**7** Observe the system pressure on the Fuel Filler Neck Venting Kit Gauge. **8** Press the stop button on the scan tool. • Was the pressure on the gauge 0 kPa (0 psi) when triggered on? → **Yes** Mark fuel tank No. 2 solenoid valve "stuck open." A new solenoid will be installed after completing diagnostics. GO to **A20**. → **No** Mark fuel tank No. 2 solenoid valve "good." GO to **A20**.
A20 CHECK FUEL TANK NO. 1 SOLENOID VALVE OPERATION	
Note: This procedure will supply power to the fuel tank solenoid valve for approximately 30-60 seconds. If time expires, cycle the start/stop button on the scan tool.	
	2 Open the manual bleed valve on the Fuel Filler Neck Venting Kit and vent the system pressure to 0 kPa (0 psi). **3** Close the manual bleed valve on the Fuel Filler Neck Venting Kit. **4** Open the fuel tank No. 1 solenoid valve manual lock-down jackscrew. **5** Tighten the fuel tank No. 2 solenoid valve manual lock-down jackscrew to 9 Nm (79 lb/in).

FM1029900362170X

Fig. 4   Pinpoint Test A: Fuel tank solenoid valve diagnosis (Part 17 of 26)

TEST CONDITIONS	TEST DETAILS/RESULTS/ACTIONS
A20 CHECK FUEL TANK NO. 1 SOLENOID VALVE OPERATION (Continued)	
Tank No. 2 Connector C417 Tank No. 1 Connector C416 Output Test Mode	**10** Press the start button on the scan tool. **11** Observe the system pressure on the Fuel Filler Neck Venting Kit Gauge. **12** Press the stop button on the scan tool. • Was the pressure on the gauge 0 kPa (0 psi) when triggered on? → **Yes** Mark fuel tank No. 1 solenoid valve "stuck open." INSTALL new upper tank rack assembly valves if marked "stuck open." GO to **A21**. → **No** Mark fuel tank No. 1 solenoid valve "good." GO to **A21**.
A21 CHECK FUEL TANK NO. 3 SOLENOID VALVE FOR STUCK OPEN CONDITION	
	2 Open the manual lock-down jackscrew on fuel tank No. 3 solenoid valve. **3** Make sure the manual lock-down jackscrew on fuel tank No. 4 solenoid valve is still closed from Step **A16**. **4** Open the manual bleed valve on the Fuel Filler Neck Venting Kit for 60 seconds. **5** Close the manual bleed valve on the Fuel Filler Neck Venting Kit.

FM1029900362180X

Fig. 4   Pinpoint Test A: Fuel tank solenoid valve diagnosis (Part 18 of 26)

sensor and engine wiring harness retainers.

30. Disconnect oil pressure sensor electrical connector.
31. Disconnect electrical connectors, then remove mounting nuts and radio capacitors.
32. Disconnect retainers and remove fuel charging wiring harness.
33. Remove spark plugs.
34. Remove mounting bolts, valve covers and gaskets.
35. Remove mounting nuts, lefthand exhaust manifold and gaskets.
36. Remove oil dipstick tube.
37. Remove mounting nuts, righthand exhaust manifold and gaskets.
38. Remove mounting nut, ground strap and coolant bypass tube.
39. Remove mounting nut and position wiring harness bracket aside.
40. Remove front cover lower mounting bolts.
41. Remove mounting bolts and front cover.
42. Position piston at bottom of stroke and camshaft lobe at base circle.
43. Compress intake valve spring using intake valve spring compressor tool No. 303-452, or equivalent, and remove roller follower.
44. Compress exhaust valve spring using exhaust valve spring compressor tool No. 303-4567, or equivalent, and remove roller follower.
45. Repeat previous steps on all cylinders.
46. Remove mounting bolts, timing chain tensioners and tensioner arms.
47. Remove lefthand and righthand timing chains, then the crankshaft sprocket.
48. Remove lefthand and righthand timing chain guides.
49. Mark for installation alignment, then remove hydraulic lash adjusters.
50. Remove mounting bolts, cylinder head and gasket. Discard cylinder head bolts.
51. Reverse procedure to install, noting the following:
    a. **Torque** new cylinder head bolt to 30 ft. lbs., in sequence, **Fig. 34**.
    b. Tighten an additional 90° in sequence.
    c. Loosen bolts minimum of one full turn.
    d. **Torque** to 30 ft. lbs., in sequence.
    e. Tighten an additional 90° in sequence.
    f. Tighten an additional 90° in sequence.
    g. Align timing chain and sprockets as outlined under "Timing Chain, Replace."

SOHC

2001-02

RIGHTHAND

1. Remove intake manifold as outlined under "Intake Manifold, Replace."
2. Remove valve covers as outlined under "Valve Cover, Replace."
3. Remove engine front cover as outlined under "Front Cover, Replace."
4. Remove spark plugs.
5. Remove evaporator housing.
6. Position clamp aside and remove coolant hose.
7. Remove nut and cylinder head ground strap.
8. Disconnect EAR transducer.
9. Remove ground strap stud.
10. Remove water bypass tube. Replace O-rings, as required.
11. Remove timing chains as outlined under "Timing Chain, Replace."
12. Remove lefthand and righthand timing chain guides.
13. Remove any remaining hardware or wiring from cylinder head.
14. Raise and support vehicle.
15. Disconnect lefthand and righthand exhaust manifolds.
16. Lower vehicle.
17. Loosen righthand side cylinder head bolts in three one turn passes in sequence, **Fig. 35**.
18. Remove cylinder head and gasket.
19. Clean gasket sealing surfaces and bolt holes.
20. Reverse procedure to install, noting the following:
    a. Install new gasket.
    b. **Torque** bolts to 28–31 ft. lbs., in sequence, **Fig. 35**.
    c. Tighten bolts an additional 85–95°.

TEST CONDITIONS	TEST DETAILS/RESULTS/ACTIONS
A21 CHECK FUEL TANK NO. 3 SOLENOID VALVE FOR STUCK OPEN CONDITION (Continued)	
	6 Observe the system pressure on the Fuel Filler Neck Venting Kit Gauge. • Is the pressure on the gauge 0 kPa (0 psi)? → **Yes** Mark fuel tank No. 3 solenoid valve "good." GO to **A22**. → **No** Mark fuel tank No. 3 solenoid valve "stuck open." A new solenoid valve will be installed when diagnostics are complete. GO to **A22**.
A22 CHECK FUEL TANK NO. 4 SOLENOID FOR STUCK OPEN CONDITION	
1	
	2 Close the manual lock-down jackscrew fuel tank No. 3 solenoid valve to 9 Nm (79 lb/in).
	3 Open the manual bleed valve on the Fuel Filler Neck Venting Kit and vent the system pressure to 0 kPa (0 psi).
	4 Close the manual bleed valve on the Fuel Filler Neck Venting Kit.
	5 Open the manual lock-down jackscrew on fuel tank No. 4 solenoid valve.
	6 Open the manual bleed valve on the Fuel Filler Neck Venting Kit for 60 seconds.
	7 Close the manual bleed valve on the Fuel Filler Neck Venting Kit.

FM1029900362190X

Fig. 4   Pinpoint Test A: Fuel tank solenoid valve diagnosis (Part 19 of 26)

d. Loosen bolts at least one full turn (360°).
e. **Torque** bolts to 28–31 ft. lbs., in sequence.
f. Tighten bolts an additional 85–95°.
g. Tighten bolts additional 85–95°.

LEFTHAND

1. Remove intake manifold as outlined under "Intake Manifold, Replace."
2. Remove timing chains as outlined under "Timing Chain, Replace."
3. Remove lefthand side exhaust manifold.
4. Disconnect radio ignition interference capacitor and remove engine control sensor wiring.
5. Remove oil dipstick tube. Replace O-rings, as required.
6. Remove lefthand and righthand timing chain guide.
7. Cylinder No. 8 head bolt cannot be completely removed, it will be required to support cylinder No. 8 head bolt with rubber band or tape to keep bolt from interfering with removal, **Fig. 36.**
8. Loosen cylinder head bolts in three one turn passes in sequence, **Fig. 37.**
9. Remove cylinder head and gasket.
10. Reverse procedure to install, noting the following:
    a. Install new gasket.
    b. **Torque** bolts to 28–31 ft. lbs., in sequence, **Fig. 37.**
    c. Tighten bolts an additional 85–95°.
    d. Loosen bolts at least one full turn (360°).
    e. **Torque** bolts to 28–31 ft. lbs., in sequence.
    f. Tighten bolts an additional 85–95°.
    g. Tighten bolts additional 85–95°.

2003-05

1. Remove engine as outlined under "Engine, Replace."
2. Remove mounting bolts and flexplate.
3. Remove eight mounting bolts and crankcase rear oil seal retainer.
4. Install engine on suitable engine stand.
5. Disconnect EAR system module tube from exhaust manifold connector.
6. Remove intake manifold as outlined under "Intake Manifold, Replace."
7. Remove valve cover as outlined under "Valve Cover, Replace."
8. Remove mounting bolts, water pump pulley and water pump.
9. Remove crankshaft pulley using removal tool No. 303-009, or equivalent.
10. Remove crankshaft front seal using removal tool No. 303-107, or equivalent.
11. Remove front cover as outlined under "Front Cover, Replace."
12. Remove timing chain as outlined under "Timing Chain, Replace."
13. Remove mounting nuts and exhaust manifold and gasket.
14. Remove cylinder head bolts in three one turn loosening passes in sequence, **Fig. 38.**
15. Remove cylinder head and gasket.
16. Reverse procedure to install noting the following:
    a. **Torque** cylinder head bolts to 30 ft. lbs., in sequence, **Figs. 35 through 37.**

TEST CONDITIONS	TEST DETAILS/RESULTS/ACTIONS
A22 CHECK FUEL TANK NO. 4 SOLENOID FOR STUCK OPEN CONDITION (Continued)	
	8 Observe the system pressure on the Fuel Filler Neck Venting Kit Gauge. • Is the pressure on the gauge 0 kPa (0 psi)? → **Yes** Mark fuel tank No. 4 solenoid valve "good." If No. 3 solenoid valve was marked "stuck open," INSTALL a new solenoid valve at this time. GO to **A23**. → **No** Fuel tank No. 4 solenoid valve is stuck open. INSTALL a new fuel tank No. 4 solenoid valve. GO to **A23**.
A23 CHECK FUEL TANK NO. 6 SOLENOID VALVE	
Note: Install the rear rack assembly fuel without the vent boxes. Make sure the manual lock-down jackscrew on fuel tank No. 6 solenoid valve is open. **Note:** This procedure will supply power to the fuel tank solenoid valve for approximately 30-60 seconds. If time expires, cycle the start/stop button on the scan tool to restore power.	
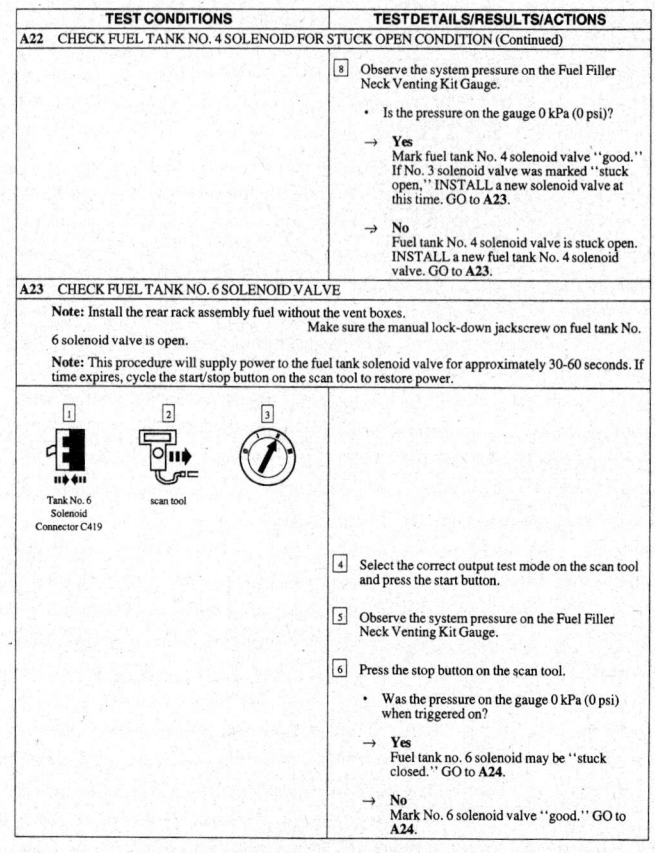 1 Tank No. 6 Solenoid Connector C419 2 scan tool 3	
	4 Select the correct output test mode on the scan tool and press the start button.
	5 Observe the system pressure on the Fuel Filler Neck Venting Kit Gauge.
	6 Press the stop button on the scan tool. • Was the pressure on the gauge 0 kPa (0 psi) when triggered on? → **Yes** Fuel tank no. 6 solenoid may be "stuck closed." GO to **A24**. → **No** Mark No. 6 solenoid valve "good." GO to **A24**.

FM1029900362200X

Fig. 4   Pinpoint Test A: Fuel tank solenoid valve diagnosis (Part 20 of 26)

b. Tighten cylinder head bolts an additional 85–95° in sequence.
c. Loosen cylinder head bolts a minimum of one full turn.
d. Tighten cylinder head bolts an additional 85–95° in sequence.
e. Tighten cylinder head bolts an additional 85–95° in sequence.
f. **Torque** crankshaft pulley bolt to 66 ft. lbs.
g. Loosen crankshaft pulley bolt 360°.
h. **Torque** crankshaft pulley bolt to 37 ft. lbs, then rotate and additional 85–90°
i. Tighten flexplate bolts in sequence, **Fig. 39.**

VALVE COVER
REPLACE
DOHC

LEFTHAND

1. Remove throttle body and ignition coils.
2. Disconnect camshaft position sensors and engine wiring harness retainers.
3. Remove mounting nut and position oil lever indicator aside.
4. Remove mounting bolts and lefthand valve cover.
5. Reverse procedure to install noting the following:

TEST CONDITIONS	TEST DETAILS/RESULTS/ACTIONS
A24 CHECK FUEL TANK NO. 5 SOLENOID VALVE	

Note: This procedure will supply power to the fuel tank solenoid valves for approximately 30-60 seconds. If time expires, cycle the start/stop button on the scan tool.

Note: Install the Rotunda Electrical Harness for Venting Tanks 134-00120 or equivalent to the rear fuel tank rack harness connector C420F.

	2 Open the manual bleed valve on the Fuel Filler Neck Venting Kit for 60 seconds.
	3 Close the manual bleed valve on the Fuel Filler Neck Venting Kit.
	6 Switch the Rotunda Electrical Harness for Venting Tanks to the tank No. 1 position.
	7 Press the start button on the scan tool.
	8 Observe the system pressure on the Fuel Filler Neck Venting Kit Gauge.
	9 Press the stop button on the scan tool.
	• Was the pressure on the gauge 0 kPa (0 psi) when triggered on?
	→ **Yes** Fuel tank No. 5 solenoid valve "may be stuck closed." GO to **A25**.
	→ **No** Mark fuel tank No. 5 solenoid valve "good." GO to **A25**.

FM1029900362210X

Fig. 4 Pinpoint Test A: Fuel tank solenoid valve diagnosis (Part 21 of 26)

TEST CONDITIONS	TEST DETAILS/RESULTS/ACTIONS
A25 CHECK REAR FUEL TANK RACK ASSEMBLY MANUAL LOCK-DOWNS	

	1 With the rear fuel tank rack assembly installed without the vent box, check the fuel tank No. 5 and No. 6 solenoid valves manual lock-downs.
	• Are the manual lock-downs open?
	→ **Yes** INSTALL new solenoids for those marked "stuck closed." If no. 5 or 6 solenoid valve was marked may be "stuck closed," INSTALL a new solenoid at this time. RESTORE the vehicle. RETEST the system for normal operation.
	→ **No** GO to **A26**.

TEST CONDITIONS	TEST DETAILS/RESULTS/ACTIONS
A26 CHECK FUEL TANK NO. 6 SOLENOID VALVE MANUAL LOCK-DOWN	

Note: Make sure the bleed valve on the Fuel Filler Neck Venting Kit is closed before proceeding with this test.

	1 Open fuel tank No. 6 solenoid valve manual lock-down jackscrew.
	2 Open the bleed valve on the Fuel Filler Neck Venting Kit for 60 seconds.
	3 Close the bleed valve on the Fuel Filler Neck Venting Kit.
	4 Observe the system pressure on the Fuel Filler Neck Venting Kit Gauge.
	• Is the pressure on the gauge 0 kPa (0 psi)?
	→ **Yes** If fuel tank no. 5 solenoid valve manual lock down is open GO to **A23**. If closed GO to **A27**.
	→ **No** Mark fuel tank No. 6 solenoid valve "stuck open." GO to **A15**.

TEST CONDITIONS	TEST DETAILS/RESULTS/ACTIONS
A27 CHECK FUEL TANK NO. 5 SOLENOID VALVE MANUAL LOCK-DOWN	

	1 Tighten the manual lock-down jackscrew on fuel tank No.6 solenoid valve to 9 Nm (79 lb/in).
	2 Open fuel tank No. 5 solenoid valve manual lock-down jackscrew.

FM1029900362220X

Fig. 4 Pinpoint Test A: Fuel tank solenoid valve diagnosis (Part 22 of 26)

a. Apply silicone gasket and sealant No. F7AZ-19554-EA, or equivalent, **Fig. 40**.
b. **Torque** bolts to 89 inch lbs., in sequence, **Fig. 41**.

RIGHTHAND

1. Drain engine cooling system into suitable container.
2. Disconnect fuel hose spring lock coupling.
3. Disconnect coolant hose and EVAP tube, then position aside.
4. Disconnect engine wiring harness retainer.
5. Remove righthand ignition coils.
6. Remove mounting bolts and righthand valve cover.
7. Reverse procedure to install noting the following:
   a. Apply silicone gasket and sealant No. F7AZ-19554-EA, or equivalent, **Fig. 40**.
   b. **Torque** bolts to 89 inch lbs., in sequence, **Fig. 41**.

SOHC

LEFTHAND

1. Raise and support vehicle.
2. Remove oil bypass filter.
3. Disconnect Power Steering Pressure (PSP) switch and oil pressure sensor connectors.
4. Lower vehicle.
5. Disconnect cylinder head temperature sensor jumper wire connector.

6. Remove bolt and two studs and position bracket aside.
7. Disconnect Camshaft Position (CMP) sensor connector.
8. Disconnect alternator connector and fuel charging wiring connectors from coils and fuel injectors.
9. Disconnect Idle Air Control (IAC) valve and Throttle Position (TP) sensor connector.
10. Disconnect 42-pin connector, 16-pin connector and transmission connector.
11. Remove six bolts, five studs and cam cover.
12. Reverse procedure to install, noting the following:
    a. Apply silicone gasket and sealant No. F7AZ-19554-EA, or equivalent, **Fig. 42**.
    b. Adjust engine oil level.
13. **Torque** bolts to 89 inch lbs., in sequence, **Fig. 43**.

RIGHTHAND

1. Raise and support vehicle.
2. Disconnect Crankshaft Position (CKP) sensor and air conditioning compressor electrical connectors.
3. Lower vehicle and disconnect air conditioning cycling switch connector.
4. Relieve fuel pressure as outlined under "Precautions."
5. Disconnect fuel lines.
6. Disconnect ignition coils and fuel injec-

tor connectors.
7. Disconnect fuel injector electrical connectors.
8. Remove Positive Crankcase Ventilation (PCV) tube and position aside.
9. Remove Evaporative Emission (EVAP) canister purge valve.
10. Position hold-down clamp and remove hose from bypass tube.
11. Disconnect harness retainers from valve cover and position harness aside.
12. Remove studs, bolts and cam cover.
13. Reverse procedure to install, noting the following:
    a. Apply silicone gasket and sealant No. F7AZ-19554-EA, or equivalent, **Fig. 42**.
    b. **Torque** bolts 89 inch lbs., in sequence, **Fig. 44**.

VALVE ARRANGEMENT

DOHC

FRONT TO REAR

Righthand ..S-P-E-E-S-P-E-E-S-P-E-E-S-P-E-E①

Lefthand .E-E-P-S-E-E-P-S-E-E-P-S-E-E-P-S

① —S-Secondary Intake; P-Primary Intake; E-Exhaust.

TEST CONDITIONS	TEST DETAILS/RESULTS/ACTIONS
A27 CHECK FUEL TANK NO. 5 SOLENOID VALVE MANUAL LOCK-DOWN (Continued)	

3 Open the bleed valve on the Fuel Filler Neck Venting Kit for 60 seconds.

4 Close the bleed valve on the Fuel Filler Neck Venting Kit.

5 Observe the system pressure on the Fuel Filler Neck Venting Kit Gauge.

- Is the system pressure on the Fuel Filler Neck Venting Kit Gauge 0 kPa (0 psi)?
→ **Yes** GO to **A23**.
→ **No** MARK fuel tank No. 5 solenoid valve "stuck open." GO to **A15**.

TEST CONDITIONS	TEST DETAILS/RESULTS/ACTIONS
A28 CHECK FUEL TANK NO. 6 SOLENOID VALVE OPERATION	

Note: The battery must be fully charged to carry out solenoid valve diagnostics.

Note: This procedure will supply power to the fuel tank solenoid valves for approximately 30-60 seconds. If time expires, cycle the start/stop button on the scan tool.

Upper and Lower Rack Solenoid Valve Connectors C420F, C421M

3 Open the manual bleed valve on the Fuel Filler Neck Venting Kit for 60 seconds.

4 Close the manual bleed valve on the Fuel Filler Neck Venting Kit.

FM1029900362230X

Fig. 4 Pinpoint Test A: Fuel tank solenoid valve diagnosis (Part 23 of 26)

TEST CONDITIONS	TEST DETAILS/RESULTS/ACTIONS
A28 CHECK FUEL TANK NO. 6 SOLENOID VALVE OPERATION (Continued)	

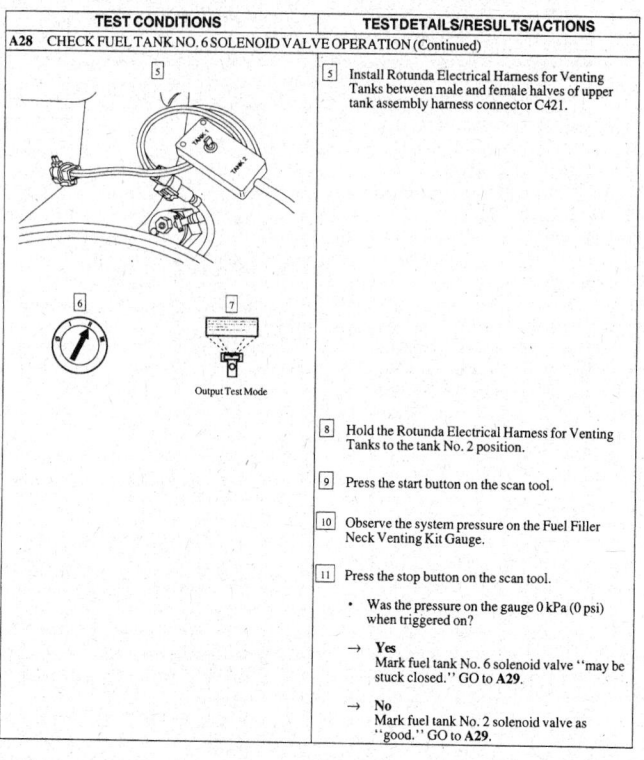

5 Install Rotunda Electrical Harness for Venting Tanks between male and female halves of upper tank assembly harness connector C421.

8 Hold the Rotunda Electrical Harness for Venting Tanks to the tank No. 2 position.

9 Press the start button on the scan tool.

10 Observe the system pressure on the Fuel Filler Neck Venting Kit Gauge.

11 Press the stop button on the scan tool.

- Was the pressure on the gauge 0 kPa (0 psi) when triggered on?
→ **Yes** Mark fuel tank No. 6 solenoid valve "may be stuck closed." GO to **A29**.
→ **No** Mark fuel tank No. 2 solenoid valve as "good." GO to **A29**.

FM1029900362240X

Fig. 4 Pinpoint Test A: Fuel tank solenoid valve diagnosis (Part 24 of 26)

SOHC

FRONT TO REAR
Righthand Bank ....I-E-I-E-I-E-I-E
Lefthand Bank ....E-I-E-I-E-I-E-I

CAMSHAFT LOBE LIFT SPECIFICATIONS

Engine	Intake, Inch	Exhaust, Inch
DOHC	.2200	.2186
SOHC	.2591	.2597

VALVE ADJUSTMENT

These engines are equipped with hydraulic valve lash adjusters. The intake and exhaust valves cannot be adjusted.

ROCKER ARMS
REPLACE
DOHC

1. Remove valve covers as outlined under "Valve Cover, Replace."
2. Position piston of cylinder being repaired at bottom of stroke and camshaft lobe at base circle.
3. Compress valve spring and remove roller follower using valve spring compressor tool No. T93P-6565-AR, or equivalent.
4. Repeat previous steps for remaining cylinders.
5. Reverse procedure to install.

SOHC

1. Remove camshaft covers as outlined under "Valve Cover, Replace."
2. Position piston of cylinder at bottom of stroke and camshaft lobe at base circle.
3. Install valve spring spacer tool No. T91P-6565-AH, or equivalent, between spring coils.
4. Compress valve spring using valve spring compressor tool No. T91P-6565-AH, or equivalent, and remove rocker arm, **Fig. 45**.
5. Remove valve spring compressor and spacer.
6. Repeat previous steps for remaining cylinders.
7. Reverse procedure to install. Apply clean engine oil to valve stem and tip, rocker arm roller contact surfaces and valve tappet.

HYDRAULIC LIFTERS
REPLACE

1. Remove rocker arms as outlined under "Rocker Arms, Replace."
2. Remove valve tappets from cylinder heads.
3. Clean and inspect valve tappets.
4. Reverse procedure to install, noting the following:
   a. Apply clean engine oil to valve stem and tip, rocker arm roller contact surfaces and valve tappets and cylinder head valve tappet bore.
   b. Valve tappets must have no more

than .039 inches of plunger travel prior to installation.

VALVE SPRING & VALVE STEM OIL SEAL
REPLACE
Removal

If, during this procedure, air pressure has forced the piston to the bottom of the cylinder, any loss of air pressure will allow the valve to fall into the cylinder. A rubber band, tape or string wrapped around the end of the valve stem will prevent this and still allow enough travel to inspect the valve for binding and excess guide to valve stem clearance.

1. Remove camshaft covers as outlined under "Valve Cover, Replace."
2. Remove rocker arms/roller followers as outlined under "Rocker Arms, Replace."
3. Remove spark plug and position piston at top of stroke with both valves closed.
4. Install suitable air line with adapter in spark plug opening and apply air pressure.
5. Install valve spring spacer tool No. T91P-6565-AH, or equivalent, between valve spring coils.
6. Compress valve spring using valve spring compressor tool No. T91P-6565-A, or equivalent.
7. Remove keys, retainer and valve spring.
8. Remove valve stem seal using suitable locking pliers.

TEST CONDITIONS	TEST DETAILS/RESULTS/ACTIONS
A29 CHECK FUEL TANK NO. 5 SOLENOID VALVE OPERATION	

Note: This procedure will supply power to the fuel tank solenoid valves for approximately 30-60 seconds. If time expires, cycle the start/stop button on the scan tool.

Note: Leave the Rotunda Electrical Harness for Venting Tanks tool used in Step **A28** connected to the upper fuel tank rack harness connector C420F.

	2 Open the manual bleed valve on the Fuel Filler Neck Venting Kit for 60 seconds.
	3 Close the manual bleed valve on the Fuel Filler Neck Venting Kit.
	6 Switch the Rotunda Electrical Harness for Venting Tanks to the tank No. 1 position.
	7 Press the start button on the scan tool.
	8 Observe the system pressure on the Fuel Filler Neck Venting Kit Gauge.

FM1029900362250X

Fig. 4 Pinpoint Test A: Fuel tank solenoid valve diagnosis (Part 25 of 26)

TEST CONDITIONS	TEST DETAILS/RESULTS/ACTIONS
A29 CHECK FUEL TANK NO. 5 SOLENOID VALVE OPERATION (Continued)	

	9 Press the stop button on the scan tool.
	• Was the pressure on the gauge 0 kPa (0 psi) when triggered on?
	→ **Yes** MARK fuel tank no. 5 solenoid valve "Does not Operate." INSTALL new solenoids for those marked "Stuck Closed" at this time. RESTORE the vehicle. TEST the system for normal operation.
	→ **No** Mark fuel tank No. 5 solenoid valve "good." To complete diagnostics, install a new solenoid valve if the solenoid valve is marked "stuck closed." If fuel tank No. 6 solenoid valve was marked "may be stuck closed," INSTALL a new solenoid at this time. If all solenoid valves were marked "good," diagnostics are complete. RESTORE the vehicle. TEST the system for normal operation.

FM1029900362260X

Fig. 4 Pinpoint Test A: Fuel tank solenoid valve diagnosis (Part 26 of 26)

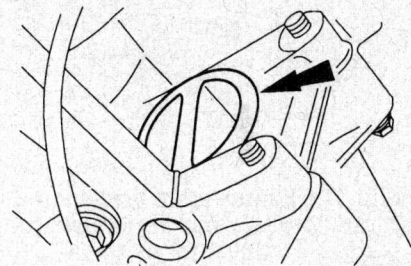

FM1069901022000X

Fig. 7 Torque converter nut access plug replacement. 2001–02

8. Remove mounting bolts and position air conditioning compressor aside.
9. Drain engine oil into suitable container.
10. Remove four front oil pan mounting bolts.
11. Remove serpentine belt idler pulleys.
12. Remove mounting bolts, studs and front cover.
13. Reverse procedure to install, noting the following:
   a. Clean and inspect sealing surfaces. **Do not use metal scrapers, wire brushes or other abrasive means to clean sealing surfaces.**
   b. Apply silicone and gasket sealant No. F7AZ-19554-EA, or equivalent, **Fig. 46.**
   c. **Torque** front cover mounting bolts Nos. 1–7 to 15–22 ft. lbs., in sequence, **Fig. 47.**
   d. **Torque** bolts Nos. 6–15 to 29–40 ft. lbs., in sequence.
   e. **Torque** oil pan front mounting bolts to 18 inch lbs., in sequence, **Fig. 48.**
   f. **Torque** mounting bolts to 15 ft. lbs., in sequence.
   g. Final tighten an additional 60°.

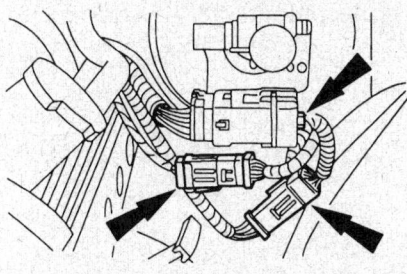

FM1069901020000X

Fig. 5 Engine bulkhead connectors replacement. 2001–02

9. Repeat previously steps as required until all seals are removed.

Installation

Piston must be at Top Dead Center (TDC) of cylinder being serviced.
1. Remove air pressure and inspect valve stem for damage. Rotate valve and inspect valve stem tip eccentric movement during rotation.
2. Position valve up and down through normal travel and inspect stem for binding. **If valve has been damaged. It will be required to remove cylinder head for service.**
3. If valve condition is good, apply engine oil to valve stem and hold valve closed.
4. Apply air pressure in cylinder.
5. Install valve stem seal using valve stem seal replacer tool No. T91P-6571-A, or equivalent.
6. Position valve spring and retainer over valve stem.
7. Compress valve spring using valve spring spacer tool No. T91P-6565-AH, or equivalent, between coils.
8. Install valve spring retainer key using valve spring compressor tool No.

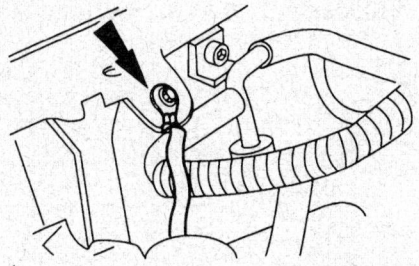

FM1069901021000X

Fig. 6 Ground wire mounting bolt replacement. 2001–02

T91P-6565-A, or equivalent.
9. Turn off air supply and remove adapter from spark plug opening.
10. Install spark plug, roller follower and camshaft cover.
11. Start engine and inspect for leaks.

FRONT COVER
REPLACE
DOHC

1. Remove valve covers as outlined under "Valve Cover, Replace."
2. Remove cooling fan.
3. Remove mounting bolts and water pump pulley.
4. Remove crankshaft front seal as outlined under "Front Cover Seal, Replace."
5. Remove mounting bolts and position power steering pump aside.
6. Disconnect air conditioning compressor and crankshaft position sensor electrical connectors.
7. Disconnect engine wiring harness retainers from air conditioning compressor.

SOHC

1. Remove both cam covers and water pump.
2. Raise and support vehicle.
3. Remove power steering bolts and position pump aside.
4. Drain engine oil into suitable container.
5. Remove oil pan to front cover bolts.
6. Remove crankshaft front seal.

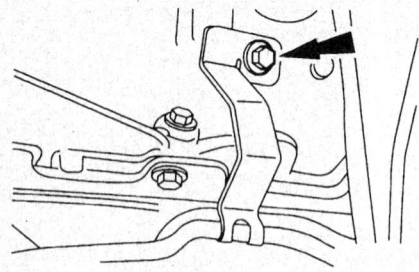

Fig. 8 Transmission cooler line bracket. 2001–02

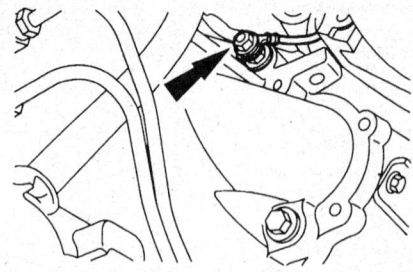

Fig. 9 Starter nut & ground wire replacement. 2001–02

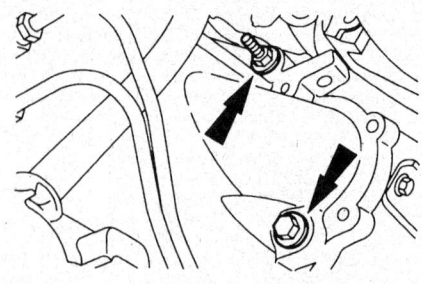

Fig. 10 Starter bolts & stud replacement. 2001–02

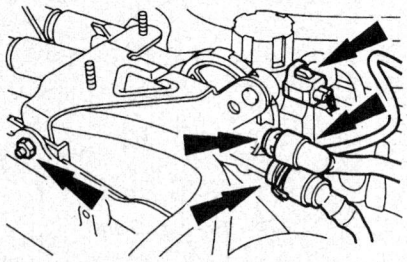

Fig. 11 Evaporative emission canister purge valve replacement. 2001–02

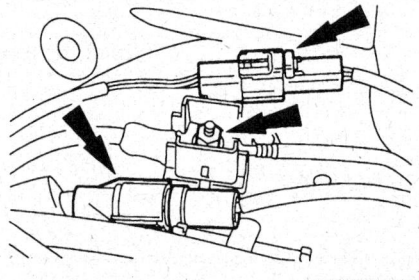

Fig. 12 Electrical connectors replacement. 2001–02 righthand inner fender

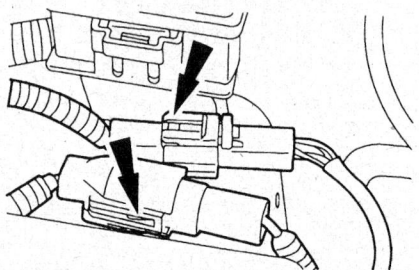

Fig. 13 Electrical connectors replacement. 2001–02 w/natural gas engine

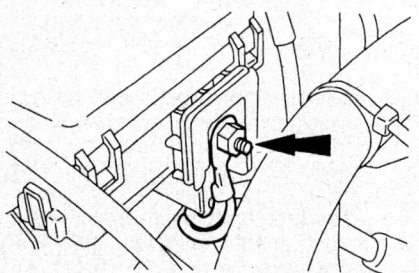

Fig. 14 Cover, nut & wiring replacement. 2001–02 w/natural gas engine

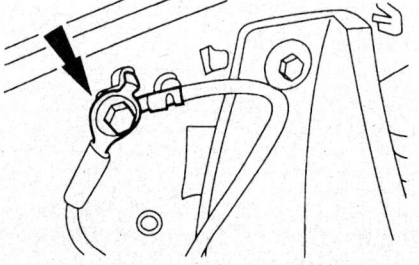

Fig. 15 Body ground wires replacement. 2001–02

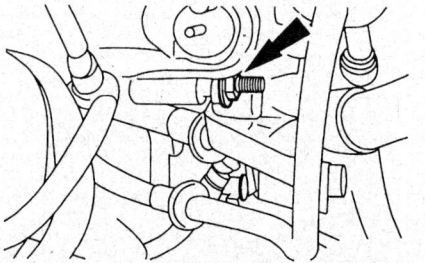

Fig. 16 Air conditioning line bracket replacement. 2001–02

7. Remove belt idler pulley.
8. Remove front cover bolts and stud bolts.
9. Remove engine front cover from front cover to cylinder block dowel.
10. Reverse procedure to install, noting the following:
   a. If engine front cover is not secured within four minutes, sealant must be removed and sealing area cleaned with metal surface cleaner No. F4AZ-19A536-RA , or equivalent. Allow to dry until there is no sign of wetness, or for four minutes, whichever is longer.
   b. Apply silicone along cylinder head-to-block surface and oil pan-to-cylinder block surface.
   c. Use silicone gasket and sealant No. F7AZ-19554-EA, or equivalent.
   d. Ensure crankshaft key and keyway are aligned, using crankshaft damper replacer tool No. T74P-6316-B, or equivalent.
   e. Install crankshaft pulley.

f. **Torque** bolts Nos. 1–7 to 15–22 ft. lbs., in sequence, **Fig. 49**.
g. **Torque** bolts Nos. 6–15 to 29–40 ft. lbs., in sequence.
h. **Torque** four oil pan to engine front cover bolts to 15 ft. lbs., in sequence, **Fig. 50**.
i. Final tighten bolts an additional 60° in sequence.

FRONT COVER SEAL
REPLACE

1. Release belt tensioner and remove serpentine drive belt.
2. Raise and support vehicle, then remove crankshaft damper mounting bolt and washer.
3. Remove crankshaft damper using crankshaft damper removal tool No. T58P-6316-D, or equivalent.
4. Remove front cover seal using front cover seal removal tool No. T74P-6700-A, or equivalent.
5. Reverse procedure to install, noting the following:

   a. Install front cover seal using replacement tool No. T88T-6701-A, or equivalent.
   b. Apply silicone gasket and sealant P/N F6AZ-19562-AA, or equivalent, in damper keyway.
   c. Ensure crankshaft key and keyway are aligned.
   d. Install crankshaft damper using crankshaft damper replacer tool No. T74P-6316-B, or equivalent.
   e. **Torque** bolt to 66 ft. lbs.
   f. Loosen one complete turn.
   g. **Torque** bolts to 35–39 ft. lbs.
   h. Final tighten bolts an additional 85–95°.

TIMING CHAIN
REPLACE
2001–02
REMOVAL

Do not rotate the crankshaft and/or

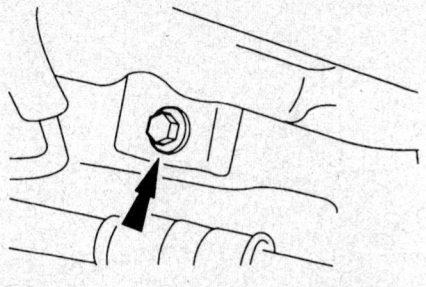

FM1069901032000X

Fig. 17 Bracket bolt replacement 2001–02

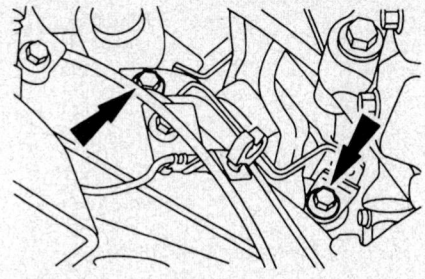

FM1069901033000X

Fig. 18 Lefthand engine mount through bolts replacement. 2001–02

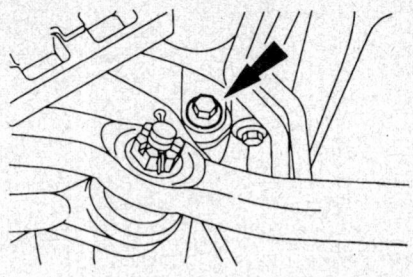

FM1069901034000X

Fig. 19 Righthand engine mount through bolt replacement. 2001–02

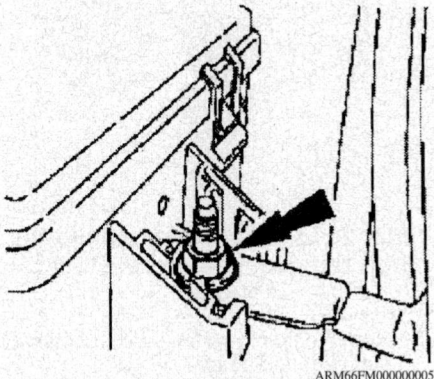

ARM66FM000000005

Fig. 20 Ground wire removal. 2003–05 SOHC engine

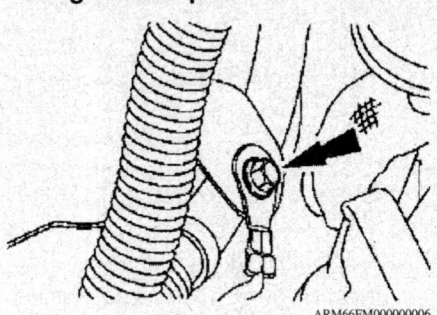

ARM66FM000000006

Fig. 21 Ground strap removal. 2003–05 SOHC engine

camshaft with the timing chains removed and the cylinder heads installed. Rotation of camshaft or crankshaft may result in valve and/or piston damage.

If engine has jumped time, cylinder heads must be removed to repair damage to valves and/or pistons.

1. Remove components to access timing chains, as required.
2. Remove crankshaft position sensor tooth wheel and rotate engine to cylinder No. 1 TDC.
3. Prevent accidental rotation of camshafts by installing cam positioning tools No. T92P-6256-A, or equivalents, to flats on camshafts, **Fig. 51**.
4. Remove two bolts and righthand tensioner.
5. Remove righthand tensioner arm, two mounting bolts and righthand chain guide.
6. Remove righthand camshaft sprocket mounting bolt, washer, gear and spacer, as required.
7. Remove two mounting bolts and lefthand tensioner.
8. Remove tensioner arm, mounting bolts and lefthand chain guide.
9. Remove lefthand chain and camshaft gears.
10. Remove lefthand camshaft sprocket mounting bolt, washer, gear and spacer, as required.

INSTALLATION

If engine has jumped time, ensure all repairs to engine components and/or valve train are completed. Then rotate engine

counterclockwise 45° to position pistons below top of deck face. Install cylinder heads.

1. Prevent camshafts from rotating using cam positioning tools No. T92P-6256-A, or equivalent.
2. Install timing chain guides (both sides) and tighten bolts.
3. Position lefthand and righthand camshaft spacers and gears on camshaft, if removed.
4. Install washer and camshaft gear mounting bolt. **Do not tighten now.**
5. Install lefthand crankshaft gear. Ensure tapered portion of gear faces away from engine block.
6. If copper links of timing chain are not visible, split chain in half and mark two opposing links, **Fig. 52**.
7. Install lefthand timing chain on camshaft gear. Ensure copper link is aligned with timing mark of camshaft gear, **Fig. 53**.
8. Install lefthand timing chain on crankshaft gear. Ensure copper link is aligned with timing mark on crankshaft gear.
9. Install righthand crankshaft gear. Ensure tapered portion of gear faces toward engine block.
10. Install righthand timing chain on camshaft gear. Ensure copper link is aligned with timing mark of camshaft gear.
11. Install righthand timing chain on crankshaft gear. Ensure copper link is aligned with crankshaft gear.
12. Lubricate tensioner arm contact surfaces with engine oil, then install lefthand and righthand tensioner arms on dowels, **Fig. 54**.
13. Install lefthand and righthand timing chain tensioners and tighten. **Do not remove lockpins until timing chain guides are installed.**
14. Install chain guides and tighten.
15. Remove lockpins from timing chain tensioners and ensure timing marks are aligned.
16. Remove cam positioning tools and install components removed during removal procedure.

2003–05

REMOVAL

Do not rotate the crankshaft and/or

camshaft with the timing chains removed and the cylinder heads installed. Rotation of camshaft or crankshaft may result in valve and/or piston damage.

If engine has jumped time, cylinder heads must be removed to repair damage to valves and/or pistons.

1. Remove front cover as outlined under "Front Cover, Replace."
2. Remove rocker arms as outlined under "Rocker Arms, Replace."
3. Remove crankshaft sensor ring from crankshaft.
4. Install camshaft aligner tool No. T91P-6256-A, or equivalent, **Fig. 51**.
5. Rotate crankshaft until timing mark on righthand camshaft sprocket is approximately at 11 o'clock position and timing mark on lefthand camshaft sprocket is approximately at 12 o'clock position, **Fig. 55**.
6. Inspect correct positioning of camshaft sprockets by install crankshaft holding tool No. T93P-6303-A, or equivalent, **Fig. 56**.
7. Remove crankshaft holding tool, then the timing chain tensioners and arms.
8. Remove righthand timing chain from camshaft and crankshaft sprockets.
9. Remove lefthand timing chain from camshaft and crankshaft sprockets.
10. Remove mounting bolts, then the lefthand and righthand timing chain guides.

INSTALLATION

1. Compress tensioner plunger using suitable vise and hold plunger in place by installing retaining clip.
2. If copper links on timing chain are not visible, mark one link on one end and one link on opposite end to use as timing marks, **Fig. 57**.
3. Rotate crankshaft until timing mark on

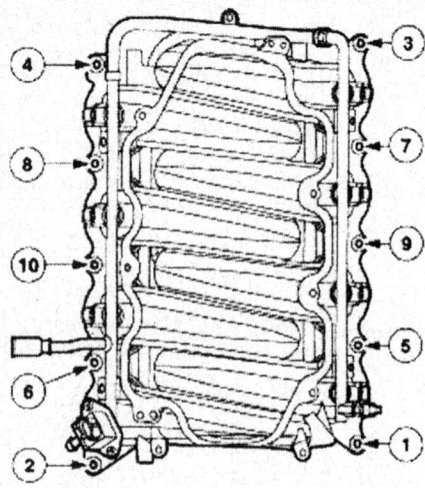

Fig. 22 Lower intake manifold bolt removal sequence. DOHC engine

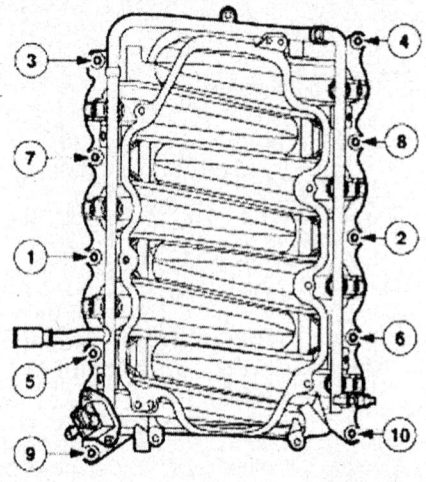

Fig. 23 Lower intake manifold tightening sequence. DOHC engine

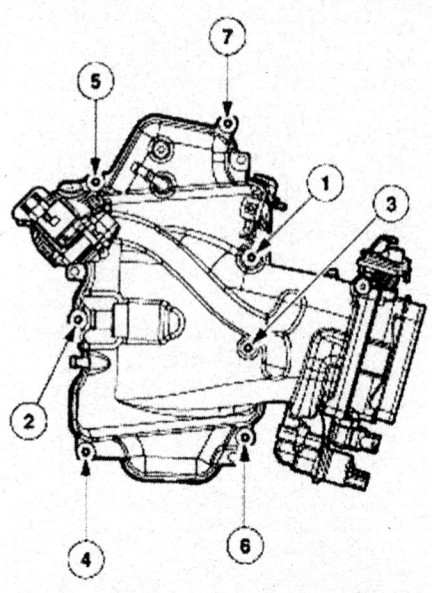

Fig. 24 Upper intake manifold bolt removal sequence. DOHC engine

righthand camshaft sprocket is approximately at 11 o'clock position and timing mark on lefthand camshaft sprocket is approximately at 12 o'clock position, **Fig. 55.**

4. Remove camshaft alignment tools.
5. Install crankshaft sprocket ensuring flange faces forward, **Fig. 58.**
6. Install timing chain guides.
7. Position crankshaft so cylinder No. 1 is at TDC using crankshaft holding tool No. T93P-6303-A, or equivalent, **Fig. 59.** Cylinder No. 1 is at TDC when stud on engine block fits into slot on holding tool.
8. Remove crankshaft holding tool.
9. Position lefthand timing chain on crankshaft sprocket aligning copper (marked) link with timing mark on sprocket, **Fig. 60.**
10. Install lefthand timing chain on camshaft sprocket aligning copper (marked) link with timing marks on sprocket, **Fig. 61.**
11. Position lefthand timing chain tensioner arm on dowel pin and install timing chain tensioner. Remove retaining clip from tensioner.
12. Position righthand timing chain on crankshaft sprocket aligning copper (marked) link with timing mark on sprocket, **Fig. 62.**
13. Install righthand timing chain on camshaft sprocket, aligning copper (marked) link with timing marks on sprocket, **Fig. 63.**
14. Position righthand timing chain tensioner arm on dowel pin and install timing chain tensioner. Remove retaining clip from tensioner.
15. Install crankshaft sensor ring on crankshaft.
16. Install rocker arms as outlined under "Rocker Arms, Replace."
17. Install front cover as outlined under "Front Cover, Replace."

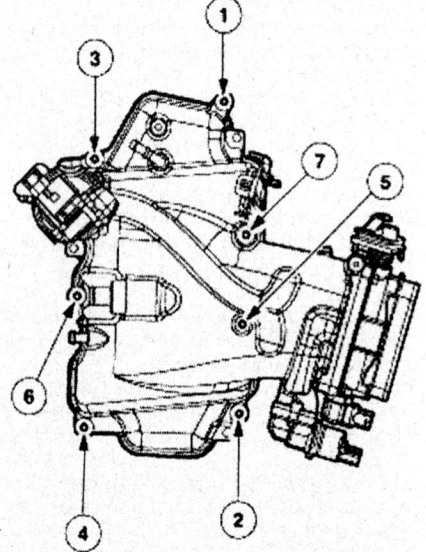

Fig. 25 Upper intake manifold tightening sequence. DOHC engine

CAMSHAFT
REPLACE
DOHC

1. Remove rocker arms as outlined under "Rocker Arms, Replace."
2. Remove timing chains as outlined under "Timing Chain, Replace."
3. Install camshaft holding tool No. T93P-6256-AHR, or equivalent, onto camshafts.
4. Remove exhaust camshaft sprocket, then the intake camshaft bolt, washer and spacer.
5. Remove camshaft holding tool.
6. Compress chain tensioner and install lock pin.

7. Remove timing chain, intake camshaft sprocket and spacer.
8. Remove timing chain tensioner bolts.
9. Mark camshaft bearing caps for installation alignment. Caps are not interchangeable.
10. Remove mounting bolts and camshaft bearing cap. **Outer bolts on outer cam bearing cap (exhaust) are longer and must be installed in same location.**
11. Remove camshafts.
12. Reverse procedure to install, noting the following:
    a. Lubricate camshafts with clean engine oil.
    b. Tighten camshaft bearing cap bolts to 14 ft. lbs., in sequence, **Fig. 64.**
    c. Align camshaft sprockets timing marks to 12 o'clock position, **Fig. 65,** then install camshaft sprockets and chain as assembly.

SOHC
2001-02

1. Remove cooling fan and shroud.
2. Relieve fuel system pressure as outlined under "Precautions."
3. Remove camshaft covers as outlined under "Valve Cover, Replace."
4. Remove front cover as outlined under "Front Cover, Replace."
5. Remove timing chains as outlined under "Timing Chain, Replace."
6. Rotate crankshaft counterclockwise 45°. Ensure pistons are below top of engine deck face. **Crankshaft must be in position prior to rotating camshafts or piston and/or valve damage may result.**
7. Install valve spring compressor tool

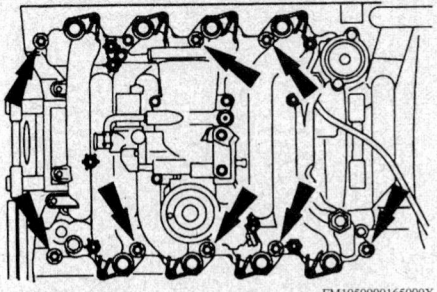

Fig. 26 Intake manifold initial tightening sequence. SOHC gasoline engine

No. T91P-6565-A, or equivalent, under camshaft and on valve spring retainer.

8. Install valve spring spacer tool No. T91P-6565-AH, or equivalent, between spring coils and camshaft to prevent damage.
9. With camshaft at base circle, compressing valve spring and remove followers by rotating camshaft, as required.
10. Repeat previous steps until all roller followers are removed.
11. Remove camshaft cap cluster mounting bolt, **Fig. 66.**
12. Tap upward, then remove cap and camshaft, **Fig. 67.**
13. Reverse procedure to install. Tighten camshaft cap cluster to 71–107 inch lbs., in sequence, **Fig. 66.**

2003–05

1. Remove rocker arms as outlined under "Rocker Arms, Replace."
2. Remove timing chain as outlined under "Timing Chain, Replace."
3. Remove mounting bolt, camshaft sprocket and spacer.
4. Remove 13 camshaft bearing cap bolts.
5. Remove bearing cap ladders and camshaft.
6. Reverse procedure to install noting the following:
   a. Lubricate camshaft journals and bearing cap ladders with clean engine oil.
   b. Tighten bearing cap bolts to 89 inch lbs., in sequence, **Fig. 66.**

PISTON & ROD ASSEMBLY

DOHC

1. Rod bearing cap bolts are torque-to-yield bolts, **Do not reuse bolts.**
2. Install connecting rod to piston with marks facing toward front of engine.
3. Install piston with arrow facing toward front of engine.

SOHC

If old pistons are serviceable, ensure they are installed on original rods. Inspect

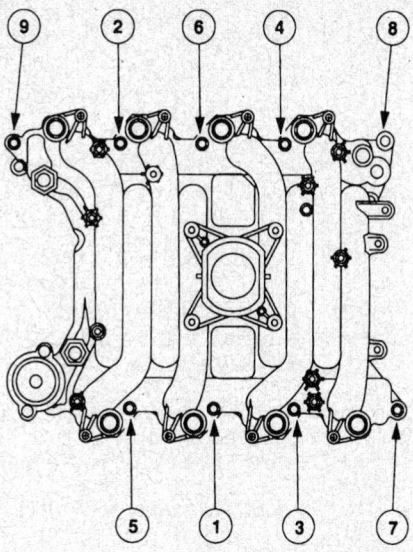

Fig. 27 Intake manifold bolt tightening sequence. 2001–02 w/SOHC gasoline engine

Installation Sequence — Gasoline Engine

FRONT OF ENGINE →

Installation Sequence — Natural Gas Engine

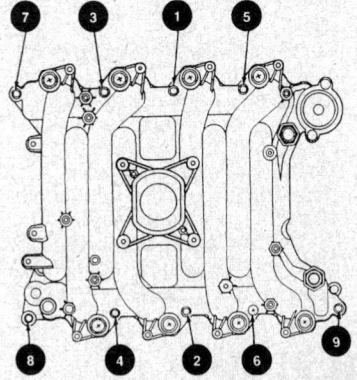

Fig. 29 Intake manifold tightening sequence. SOHC natural gas engine

side clearance between connecting rods and crankshaft journal. Correct clearance is .00059–.01772 inch.

1. Assemble pistons, pins, bearings, caps, nuts and bolts in original positions.

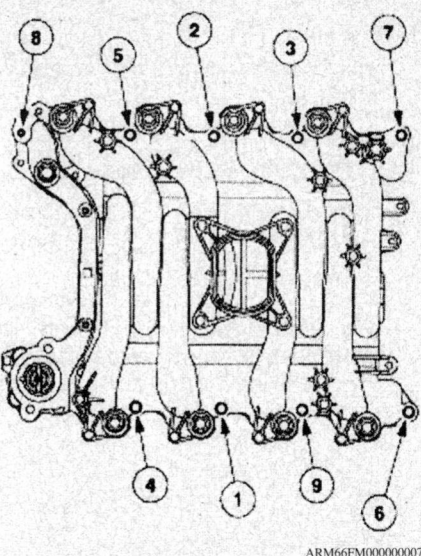

Fig. 28 Intake manifold bolt tightening sequence. 2003–05 w/SOHC gasoline engine

2. Install pistons with notch to front of engine.
3. Alternatively tighten connecting rod caps.
4. Rotate crankshaft to ensure smooth operation.

MAIN & ROD BEARINGS

DOHC

MAIN

1. **Torque** vertical main bearing bolts to 89 inch lbs., in sequence, **Fig. 68.**
2. **Torque** vertical bolts to 18 ft. lbs., in sequence.
3. **Torque** vertical bolts to 30 ft. lbs., in sequence.
4. Tighten vertical bolts an additional 90° in sequence.
5. **Torque** cross mounted bolts to 30 ft. lbs., then an additional 90°.

SOHC

MAIN

1. **Torque** cross mounted bolts to 89 inch lbs., in sequence, **Fig. 69.**
2. **Torque** cross mounted bolts to 15 ft. lbs., in sequence.
3. **Torque** vertical bolts to 30 ft. lbs., in sequence, **Fig. 70.**
4. Then tighten an additional 90°.

CRANKSHAFT REAR OIL SEAL

REPLACE

1. Lower transmission and support using suitable jack.
2. Remove flywheel.
3. Remove crankshaft oil slinger using

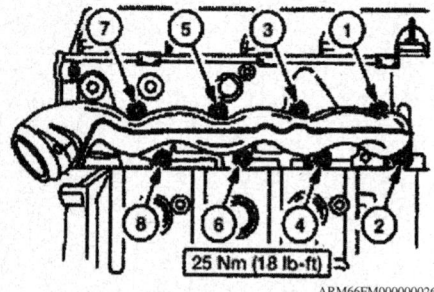

Fig. 30 Righthand exhaust manifold tightening sequence. DOHC engine

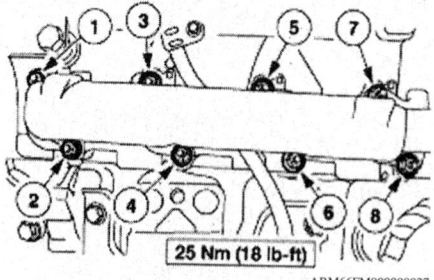

Fig. 31 Lefthand exhaust manifold tightening sequence. DOHC engine

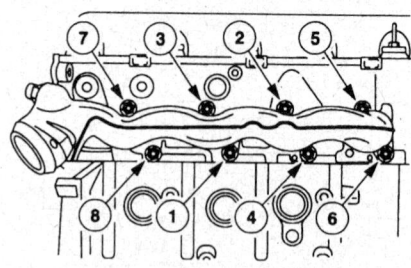

Fig. 32 Righthand exhaust manifold tightening sequence. SOHC engine

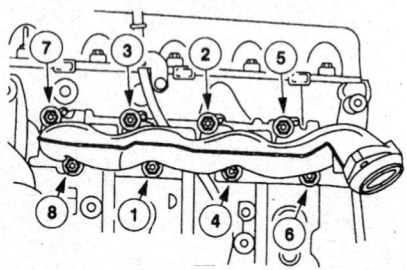

Fig. 33 Lefthand exhaust manifold tightening sequence. SOHC engine

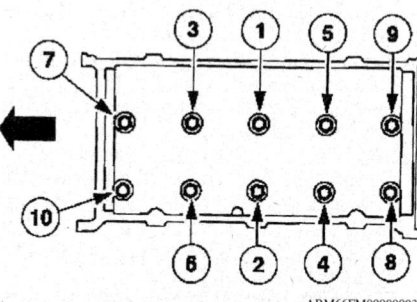

Fig. 34 Cylinder head tightening sequence. DOHC engine

rear crankshaft slinger remover tool No. T95P-6701-AH and slide hammer tool No. T50T-100-A, or equivalents.

4. Remove crankshaft rear oil seal using rear crankshaft seal remover tool No. T95P-6701-EH and slide hammer tool No. T50T-100-A, or equivalents.
5. Remove crankshaft rear oil seal retainer, as required.
6. Reverse procedure to install, noting the following:
   a. Use suitable plastic scraping tool to remove all traces of old sealant. **Do not use metal scrapers, wire brushes, power abrasive discs or other abrasive means to clean sealing surfaces.**
   b. Clean sealing surfaces with metal surface cleaner No. F4AZ-19A536-RA, or equivalent. Allow to dry until there is no sign of wetness, or four minutes, whichever is longer.
   c. Use silicone gasket and sealant No. F7AZ-19554-EA, or equivalent.

OIL PAN
REPLACE
2001-02

1. Remove air cleaner outlet tube.
2. Remove wiper arm and pivot shaft.
3. Remove drive belt, fan motor and shroud.
4. Relieve fuel system pressure as outlined under "Precautions."
5. Disconnect fuel lines.
6. Remove Exhaust Gas Recirculation (EAR) tube.
7. Remove alternator and blower motor speed control.

8. Remove righthand engine mount bolt.
9. Raise and support vehicle.
10. Remove two lefthand engine mount bolts.
11. Remove four nuts and support exhaust.
12. Remove bolt for transmission line support bracket.
13. Loosen nuts for transmission mount.
14. Lower vehicle.
15. Remove second righthand motor mount bolt from top.
16. Raise engine with suitable floor crane and support engine.
17. Raise and support vehicle.
18. Remove mounting bolts and position oil pan aside. Remove oil pickup tube bolts.
19. Remove oil pickup tube bracket bolt.
20. Remove O-ring and inspect.
21. Remove oil pan and gasket through front.
22. Reverse procedure to install. **Torque** oil pan mounting bolts to 15–20 ft. lbs., in sequence, **Fig. 71.**

2003-05

1. Remove engine as outlined under "Engine, Replace."
2. Remove mounting bolts and flywheel.
3. Mount engine on suitable engine stand.
4. Remove oil pan mounting bolts in sequence, **Fig. 71.**
5. Remove oil pan and gasket.
6. Reverse procedure to install, noting the following:
7. **On models equipped with DOHC engine, torque** oil pan mounting bolts to 15 ft. lbs., in sequence, **Fig. 71.**
8. **On models equipped with SOHC engine, torque** oil pan mounting bolts to 108 inch lbs., in sequence, **Fig. 71.**

OIL PUMP
REPLACE

1. Remove camshaft covers as outlined under "Valve Cover, Replace."
2. Remove front cover as outlined under "Front Cover, Replace."
3. Remove oil pan as outlined under "Oil Pan, Replace."
4. Remove timing chains as outlined under "Timing Chain, Replace."
5. Remove mounting bolts and oil pump, **Fig. 72.**

6. Reverse procedure to install. Align oil pump inner rotor with flat of crankshaft.

BELT TENSION DATA

Automatic belt tensioners are spring loaded devices which set and maintain drive belt tension. The drive belt should not require tension adjustment. Automatic tensioners have belt wear indicator marks. If indicator mark is not between indicator lines, belt is worn or an incorrect belt is installed.

SERPENTINE DRIVE BELT
Belt Routing

Refer to **Fig. 73,** for drive belt routing.

Replacement

1. Rotate tensioner away from belt using suitable breaker bar installed in ½ inch square hole in tensioner arm.
2. Lift old belt over alternator pulley flange and remove.
3. When installing, position new belt over pulleys. Ensure all V-grooves make proper contact with pulley.
4. Ensure belt is properly installed on each pulley.

COOLING SYSTEM BLEED
DOHC

1. Remove coolant bleed plug from coolant bypass tube, **Fig. 74.**

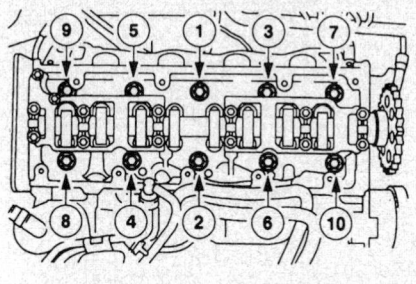

Fig. 35 Righthand cylinder head bolt tightening sequence. SOHC engine

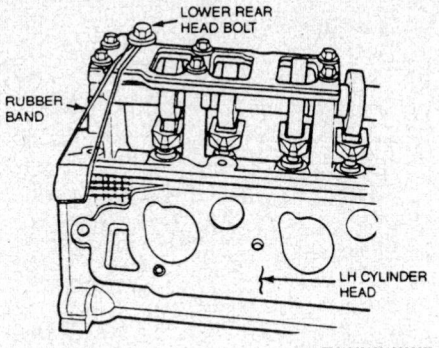

Fig. 36 Lefthand lower rear head bolt removal. 2001–02 SOHC engine

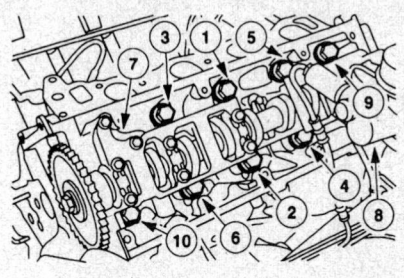

Fig. 37 Lefthand cylinder head bolt tightening sequence. SOHC engine

2. Disconnect heater core coolant supply hose.
3. Add coolant through water bypass tube opening until coolant appears at heater core coolant supply hose.
4. Install heater hose and bypass bleed plug.
5. Fill coolant over flow bottle to COOLANT FILL LEVEL marks and install pressure cap.
6. Select maximum heater temperature and blower speed settings, then position control to discharge air at air conditioning vents.
7. Run engine until it reaches operating temperature.
8. Fill coolant over flow bottle to COOLANT FILL LEVEL marks.
9. Repeat two previous steps until coolant level is between COOLANT FILL LEVEL on over flow bottle.

SOHC

1. Place heater temperature switch in maximum heat position.
2. Start engine and allow to idle. While engine is idling, feel for hot air at air conditioning vents.
3. If air discharge remains cool and engine coolant temperature gauge does not move, engine coolant level is low in engine and must be filled.
4. Stop engine, allow to cool and fill cooling system.
5. Start engine and allow to idle until normal operating temperature is reached, noting the following:
   a. Hot air should discharge from air conditioning vents.
   b. Engine coolant temperature gauge should maintain stabilized reading in middle of NORMAL range.
   c. Upper radiator hose should feel hot to touch.
6. Shut engine off and allow to cool.
7. Inspect engine for coolant leaks.
8. Adjust engine coolant level in overflow bottle, as required.

THERMOSTAT

REPLACE

DOHC

1. Drain cooling system into suitable container, then raise and support vehicle.

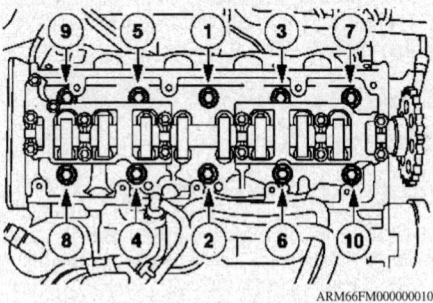

Fig. 38 Cylinder head bolt loosening sequence. 2003–05 SOHC engine

2. Disconnect coolant hose.
3. Remove mounting bolts and coolant outlet.
4. Remove thermostat and O-ring seal.
5. Reverse procedure to install using new hose clamps.

SOHC

1. Drain coolant into suitable container until level is below upper radiator hose and thermostat housing.
2. Remove engine appearance cover.
3. Disconnect upper radiator hose at thermostat housing.
4. Remove two thermostat housing mounting bolts.
5. Remove O-ring seal and thermostat from intake manifold. Replace O-ring, as required.
6. Reverse procedure to install.

WATER PUMP

REPLACE

1. Drain coolant into suitable container.
2. Loosen water pump mounting bolts, release belt tensioner and remove accessory drive belt.
3. Remove mounting bolts and water pump pulley.
4. Loosen mounting bolts and remove water pump.
5. Reverse procedure to install. Replace O-ring.

RADIATOR

REPLACE

1. Raise and support vehicle.
2. Drain engine coolant into suitable container.
3. Remove fan blade, motor and shroud.
4. Release three hold downs and remove radiator sight shield.
5. Remove upper and lower radiator hoses from radiator.
6. Remove radiator support bolts and supports.
7. Remove bolts and position air conditioning condenser core and transmission oil cooler away from radiator.
8. Reverse procedure to install.

FUEL PUMP

REPLACE

1. Relieve fuel system pressure as outlined under "Precautions."
2. Drain fuel tank into suitable container, then raise and support vehicle.
3. Remove fuel tank and disconnect pressure transducer connector on top rear corner of fuel tank.
4. Remove six mounting bolts and fuel pump module.
5. Reverse procedure to install, noting the following:
   a. Turn ignition from Off to On position for three seconds using fuel pressure gauge tool No. T80L-9974-B, or equivalent, on fuel charging Schraeder valve.
   b. Repeat off to on switching 5–10 times until pressure gauge shows at least 35 psi.

FUEL FILTER

REPLACE

1. Turn engine off and relieve fuel system pressure as outlined under "Precautions."
2. Raise and support vehicle.
3. Remove push connect fittings at both ends of filter. Install new retainer clips in each push connect fitting.
4. Remove two mounting bolts and fuel filter from metal bracket.
5. Remove filter from retainer. Record direction of flow. Arrow points to open end of retainer.
6. Remove rubber insulator rings from filter.

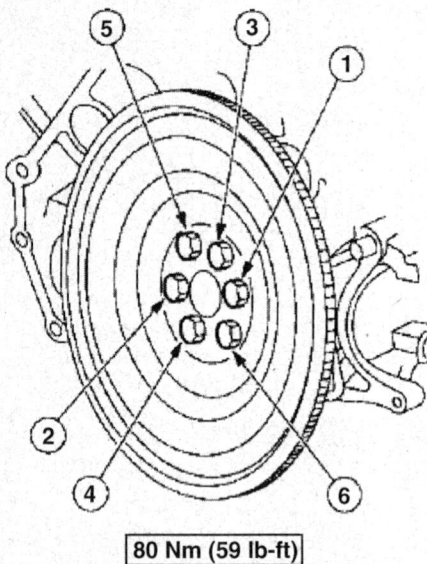

Fig. 39 Flexplate bolt tightening sequence. 2003–05 SOHC engine

80 Nm (59 lb-ft)

ARM66FM000000011

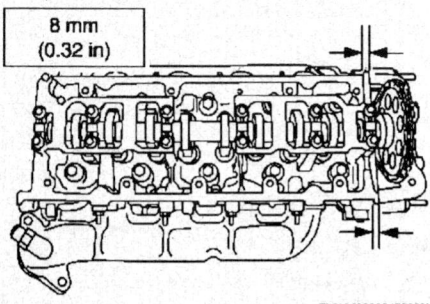

Fig. 42 Sealant application locations. SOHC engine

8 mm (0.32 in)

FM1069900847000X

7. Reverse procedure to install, noting the following:
   a. Replace insulator if filter moves freely.
   b. Start engine and inspect for fuel leaks.

TECHNICAL SERVICE BULLETINS

Intake Manifold Crossover Coolant Leak

2001 TOWN CAR

On some of these models, there may coolant seeps at the intake manifold crossover first runner.

This condition may be caused by a intake manifold coolant crossover leak.

To correct this condition, install service kits, **Fig. 75,** which include intake manifold, alternator brace, water outlet connection bolts, intake manifold gasket, thermostat O-ring, upper radiator hose, water outlet connector, engine cover, nut, stud and instruction sheet for 2000 models, and intake

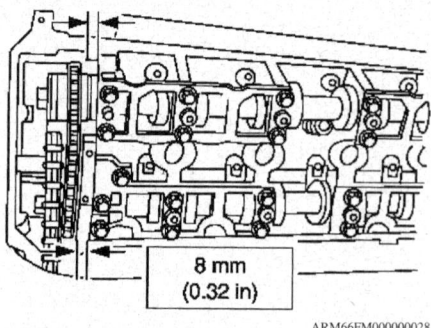

Fig. 40 Sealant location. DOHC engine

8 mm (0.32 in)

ARM66FM000000028

manifold, alternator brace, water outlet connection bolts, intake manifold gasket, thermostat O-ring and instruction sheet for 2001 models.

Engine Mounts Lack Durability

2001–02 TOWN CAR

On some of these models the engine mounts may lack satisfactory durability under severe operating conditions encountered by limo/livery service where there is extended idling at high ambient temperature.

This condition may be caused by extreme heat generated by engine.

To correct this condition install revised engine mounts with built-in heat shields (P/N F8VZ-6028-AA and righthand P/N F8VZ-6028-BA).

Engine Tick

2001–04 TOWN CAR

On some of these models with engines built before Aug. 29, 2003, there may be an engine tick noise at all temperatures during idle. The noise may be prevalent in the front wheel well area, but may be heard with the hood open.

This condition may be caused by the cylinder head valve guide area.

To correct this condition, proceed as follows:

1. Ensure noise is coming from back of cylinder head near exhaust ports by listening with suitable stethoscope.
2. Ensure noise is heard in wheel well or catalytic converter and from under vehicle.
3. Ensure there are no exhaust manifold leaks.
4. Ensure noise is present when canceling each cylinder by unplugging injectors one at a time.
5. Ensure camshaft spacers are in place.
6. Ensure cam sprocket is tightened to specifications.
7. Inspect hydraulic lash adjusters for spongy condition.
8. Ensure timing chain tensioner pin has been removed.
9. Replace cylinder head and cam (P/N 1L2Z-6049-LA).

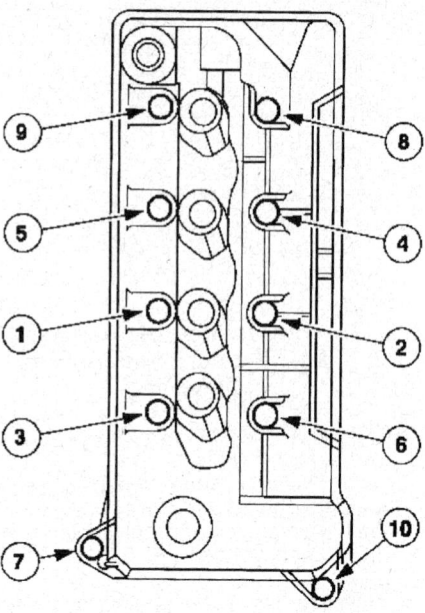

Fig. 41 Valve cover tightening sequence. DOHC engine

ARM66FM000000029

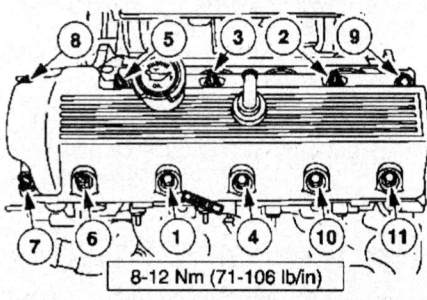

Fig. 43 Lefthand cam cover bolt tightening sequence. SOHC engine

8-12 Nm (71-106 lb/in)

FM1069900849000X

Idle Or Low Speed Engine Vibration

2003 TOWN CAR

On some of these models there may be an engine vibration at idle and/or low engine speeds. This condition may be more pronounced when the engine is cold. The vibration may be felt through the steering wheel, brake pedal or floor.

To correct this condition, proceed as follows:

This condition may be caused by the engine mounts, idle speed strategy and exhaust damper turning.

1. Remove and replace engine mounts (P/N 3W1Z-6038-EA, P/N 3W1Z-6038-DB).
2. **On models built before Dec. 2, 2002,** remove and discard two exhaust system H-pipe original rubber dampers.
3. **On all models,** remove and discard one original rubber damper from each muffler.
4. **On models built before Dec. 2, 2002,** proceed as follows:

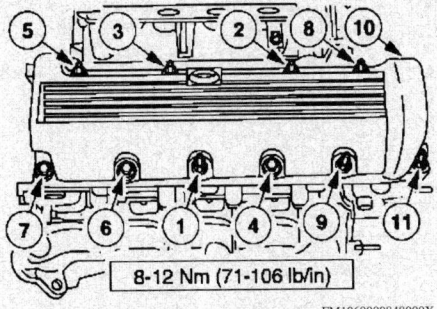

Fig. 44 Righthand cam cover tightening sequence. SOHC engine

8-12 Nm (71-106 lb/in)

FM1069900848000X

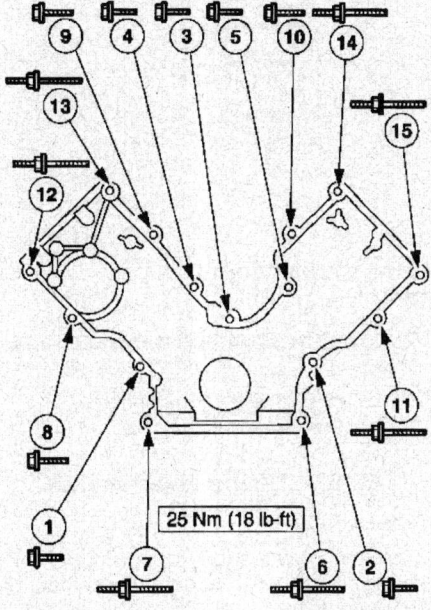

25 Nm (18 lb-ft)

ARM66FM000000031

Fig. 47 Front cover tightening sequence (Part 1 of 2). DOHC engine

a. Remove exhaust H-pipe righthand flange mounting bolts and nuts.
b. Install righthand exhaust H-pipe flange damper (P/N 3W1Z-5F240-AA). **Torque** to 30 ft. lbs.
5. **On all models,** remove and discard lefthand front muffler to exhaust pipe clamps.
6. Install muffler damper (P/N 4W1Z-5F240-AA) using U-bolt (P/N W710145-S306). **Torque** to 33 ft. lbs.
7. **On models built before June 10, 2002,** program Powertrain Control Module (PCM) with latest calibration.

Cylinder Head Oil Leak

2001-02 TOWN CAR

On some of these models there may be an oil leak or weepage from cylinder head gasket at lefthand front or righthand rear of engine.

This condition may be caused by metal chip debris lodged between the head gas-

---

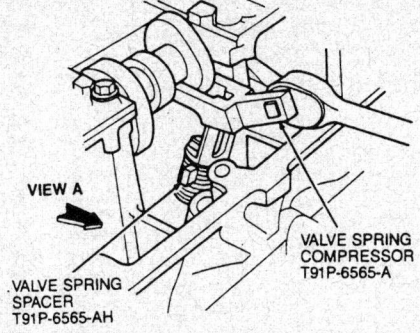

VIEW A

VALVE SPRING COMPRESSOR T91P-6565-A

VALVE SPRING SPACER T91P-6565-AH

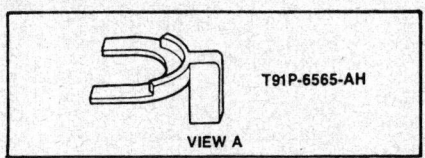

T91P-6565-AH

VIEW A

FM1069100137000X

Fig. 45 Valve spring compression. SOHC engine

ket and block, chip debris between the head gasket and block, chip debris between the cylinder head and gasket, or sealing surface damage during manufacturing.

To correct this condition, replace head gasket (P/N 3U7Z-6051-BA; P/N 3U7Z-6051-AA) on side with leak only. If head was damaged by chip contamination, replace cylinder head.

Fuel Pump Whining/ Buzzing Through Radio Speaker

2001

On some of these models there may be a whining or buzzing in speakers.

This condition may be caused by fuel pump electrical noise.

To correct this condition install an electronic noise Radio Frequency Interference (RFI) filter (P/N F1PZ-18B925-A) on fuel pump inside the fuel tank, as follows:
1. Remove fuel pump sender from fuel tank as outlined under "Fuel Pump, Replace."
2. Cut fuel pump wires three inches from flange. Discard wires.
3. Connect RFI filter connectors to fuel pump spade terminal.
4. Cut and solder both RFI filter red and black wires to flange red and black wires.
5. Install suitable heat shrink tubing over solder connectors.
6. Secure RFI filter to fuel pump using suitable bundling strap.
7. Install fuel pump sender.

Engine Mounts Lack Durability

2001

On some of these models the engine mounts may lack satisfactory durability

---

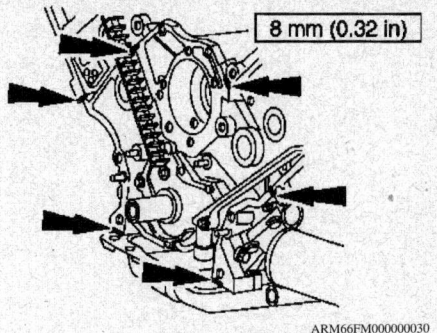

8 mm (0.32 in)

ARM66FM000000030

Fig. 46 Front cover sealant application. DOHC engine

Item	Part Number	Description
1	N806177	Bolt, Hex Flange Head Pilot, M8 x 1.25 x 53
2	N806177	Bolt, Hex Flange Head Pilot, M8 x 1.25 x 53
3	N806177	Bolt, Hex Flange Head Pilot, M8 x 1.25 x 53
4	N806177	Bolt, Hex Flange Head Pilot, M8 x 1.25 x 53
5	N806177	Bolt, Hex Flange Head Pilot, M8 x 1.25 x 53
6	W706508	Stud, Hex Shldr Pilot, M8 x 1.25 x 50 — M6 x 1 x 10
7	N808586	Stud and Washer, Hex Head Pilot, M8 x 1.25 x 60 — M6 x 1 x 26
8	N806177	Bolt, Hex Flange Head Pilot, M8 x 1.25 x 53
9	N806177	Bolt, Hex Flange Head Pilot, M8 x 1.25 x 53
10	N806177	Bolt, Hex Flange Head Pilot, M8 x 1.25 x 53
11	N806300	Stud, Hex Shldr Pilot, M8 x 1.25 x 65 — M8 x 1.25 x 26
12	W706560	Stud, Hex Head Pilot, M8 x 1.25 x 65 — M8 x 1.25 x 16
13	W706560	Stud, Hex Shldr Pilot, M8 x 1.25 x 65 — M8 x 1.25 x 26
14	W706560	Stud, Hex Shldr Pilot, M8 x 1.25 x 65 — M8 x 1.25 x 26
15	N806300	Stud, Hex Shldr Pilot, M8 x 1.25 x 65 — M8 x 1.25 x 26

ARM66FM000000032

Fig. 47 Front cover tightening sequence (Part 2 of 2). DOHC engine

under severe operating conditions encountered by police, taxi or limo/livery service where there is extended idling at high ambient temperature.

This condition may be caused by extreme heat generated by engine.

To correct this condition install revised engine mounts with built-in heat shields (P/N F8VZ-6028-AA and P/N F8VZ-6028-BA).

Engine Tick

2001-05 SOHC ENGINE

On some of these models with engines built before Aug. 29, 2003, there may be an engine tick noise at all temperatures during idle. The noise may be prevalent in the front wheel well area, but may be heard with the hood open.

This condition may be caused by the cylinder head valve guide area.

To correct this condition, proceed as follows:
1. Ensure noise is coming from back of cylinder head near exhaust ports by listening with suitable stethoscope.
2. Ensure noise is heard in wheel well or catalytic converter and from under vehicle.
3. Ensure there are no exhaust manifold leaks.

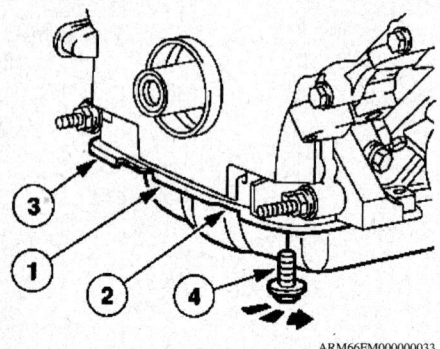

Fig. 48 Oil pan front bolts tightening sequence. DOHC engine

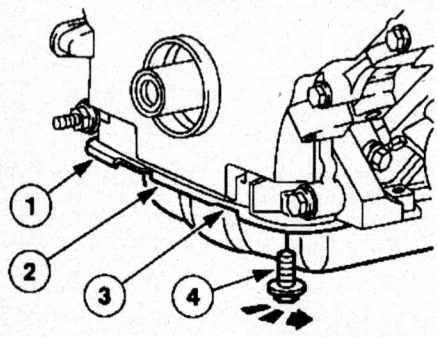

Fig. 50 Oil pan to front cover bolt tightening sequence

4. Ensure noise is present when canceling each cylinder by unplugging injectors one at a time.
5. Ensure camshaft spacers are in place.
6. Ensure cam sprocket is tightened to specifications.
7. Inspect hydraulic lash adjusters for spongy condition.
8. Ensure timing chain tensioner pin been removed.
9. Replace cylinder head and cam (P/N 1L2Z-6049-LA).

Timing Chain Area Grinding

2001–03

On some of these models there may be a grinding noise from the timing chain area.

This condition may be caused by excessive wear of the timing chain tensioner arm.

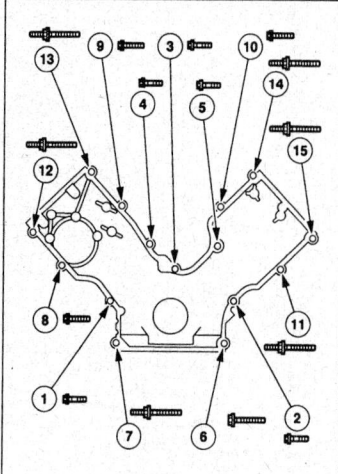

Item	Description
1	Bolt, Hex Flange Head Pilot, M8 x 1.25 x 53
2	Bolt, Hex Flange Head Pilot, M8 x 1.25 x 53
3	Bolt, Hex Flange Head Pilot, M8 x 1.25 x 53

Item	Description
4	Bolt, Hex Flange Head Pilot, M8 x 1.25 x 53
5	Bolts, Hex Flange Head Pilot, M8 x 1.25 x 53
6	Bolt, Hex-Head Pilot, M10 x 1.5 x 1.5 x 103.1
7	Stud, Hex-Head Pilot, M10 x 1.5 x 1.5 x 103.1
8	Screw and Washer, Hex Pilot, M10 x 1.5 x 57.5
9	Screw and Washer, Hex Pilot, M10 x 1.5 x 57.5
10	Screw and Washer, Hex Pilot, M10 x 1.5 x 57.5
11	Stud and Washer, Hex Head Pilot, M10 x 1.5 x M8 x 1.25 x 109.6
12	Stud and Washer, Hex Head Pilot, M10 x 1.5 x M8 x 1.25 x 109.6
13	Stud and Washer, Hex Head Pilot, M10 x 1.5 x M8 x 1.25 x 109.6
14	Stud and Washer, Hex Head Pilot, M10 x 1.5 x M8 x 1.25 x 109.6
15	Stud and Washer, Hex Head Pilot, M10 x 1.5 x M8 x 1.25 x 109.6

Fig. 49 Front cover tightening sequence. SOHC engine

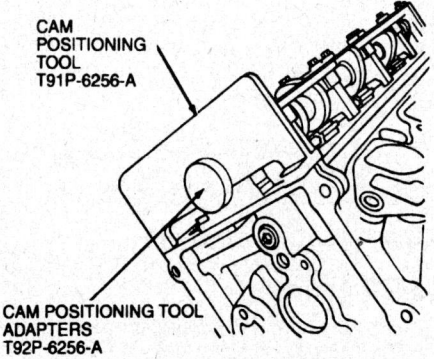

Fig. 51 Camshaft positioning tool installation

To correct this condition, replace timing chains, tensioners and tensioner arm.

Cylinder Head Oil Leak

2001–02

On some of these models there may be

NOTE: WITH EITHER CHAIN POSITIONED AS SHOWN, MARK EACH END AND USE MARKS AS TIMING MARKS

Fig. 52 Timing chain marks. 2001–02

an oil leak or weepage from cylinder head gasket at lefthand front or righthand rear of engine.

This condition may be caused by metal chip debris lodged between the head gasket and block, chip debris between the head gasket and block, chip debris between the cylinder head and gasket, or sealing surface damage during manufacturing.

To correct this condition, replace head gasket (P/N 3U7Z-6051-BA; P/N 3U7Z-6051-AA) on side with leak only. If head was damaged by chip contamination, replace cylinder head.

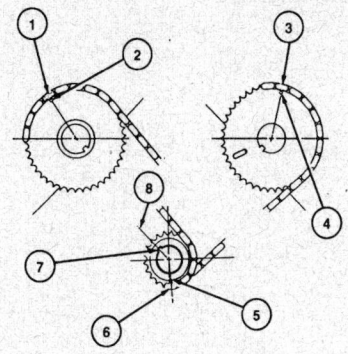

Item	Part Number	Description
1	—	RH Camshaft Timing Chain Mark
2	—	RH Camshaft Sprocket Mark
3	—	LH Camshaft Timing Chain Mark
4	—	RH Camshaft Sprocket Mark
5	—	Crankshaft Sprocket Mark
6	—	Crankshaft Timing Chain Mark
7	6306	Crankshaft Sprocket
8	—	Crankshaft Keyway Center Line

FM1069100143000X

Fig. 53 Lefthand timing chain installation. 2001–02

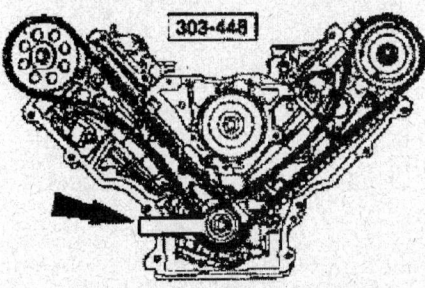

ARM66FM000000009

Fig. 56 Crankshaft holding tool. 2003–05

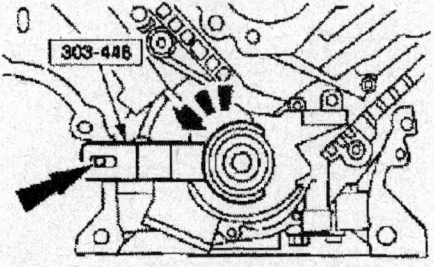

ARM66FM000000015

Fig. 59 Crankshaft holding tool installation. 2003–05

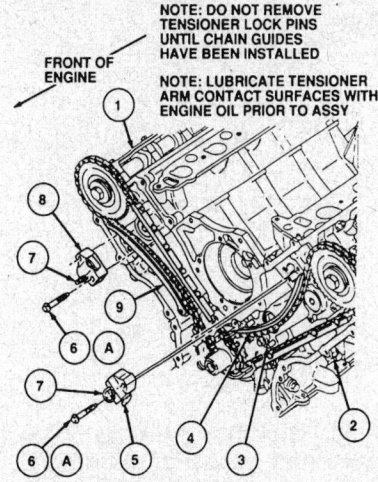

NOTE: DO NOT REMOVE TENSIONER LOCK PINS UNTIL CHAIN GUIDES HAVE BEEN INSTALLED

NOTE: LUBRICATE TENSIONER ARM CONTACT SURFACES WITH ENGINE OIL PRIOR TO ASSY

FRONT OF ENGINE

Item	Part Number	Description
1	6049	Cylinder Head (RH)
2	6049	Cylinder Head (LH)
3	N806007	Dowel
4	6L253	Timing Chain Tensioner Arm (LH)
5	6L266	Timing Chain Tensioner (LH)
6	N606543-S2	Bolt (2 Req'd)
7	—	Lock Pin (Part of 6L266)
8	6L266	Timing Chain Tensioner (RH)
9	6L253	Timing Chain Tensioner Arm (RH)
A	—	Tighten to 20-30 N·m (15-22 Lb-Ft)

FM1069100144000X

Fig. 54 Tensioner arm installation. 2001–02

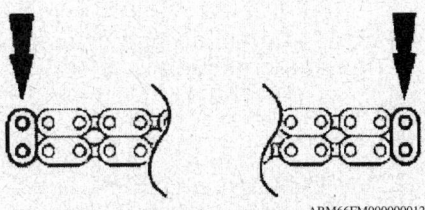

ARM66FM000000012

Fig. 57 Timing chain marks. 2003–05

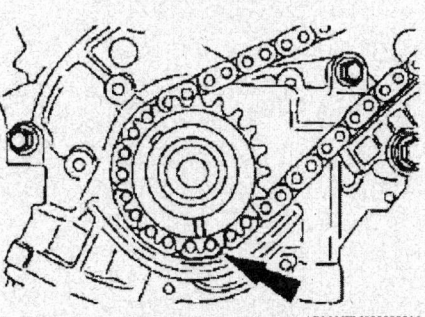

ARM66FM000000016

Fig. 60 Lefthand timing chain to crankshaft sprocket alignment. 2003–05

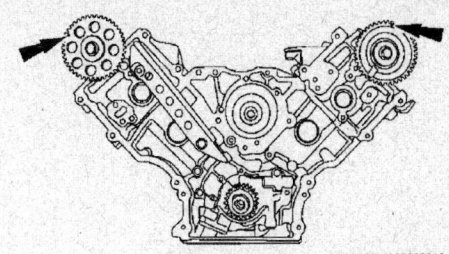

ARM66FM000000013

Fig. 55 Camshaft timing marks. 2003–05

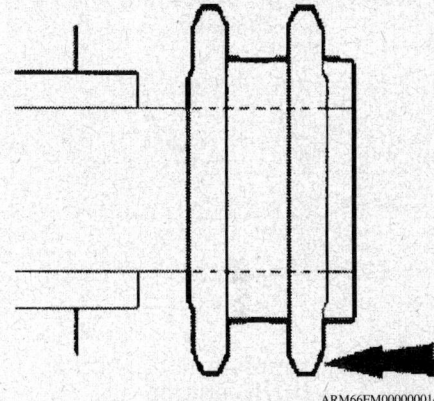

ARM66FM000000014

Fig. 58 Crankshaft sprocket installation. 2003–05

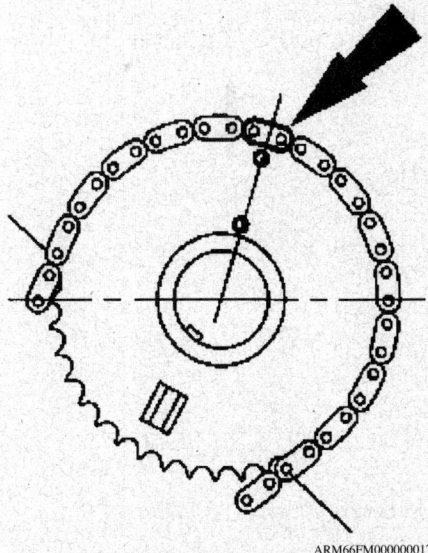

ARM66FM000000017

Fig. 61 Lefthand timing chain to camshaft sprocket alignment. 2003–05

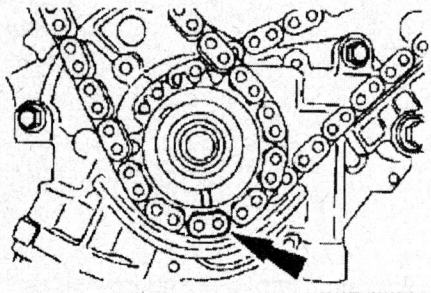

Fig. 62 Righthand timing chain to crankshaft sprocket alignment. 2003–05

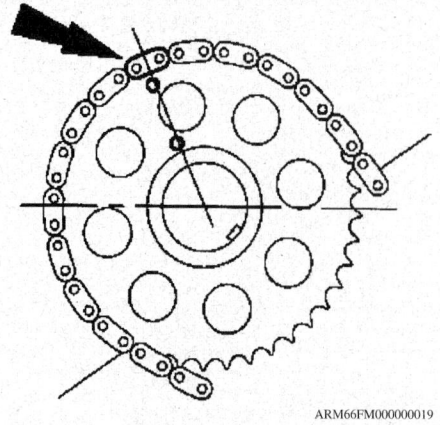

Fig. 63 Righthand timing chain to camshaft sprocket alignment. 2003–05

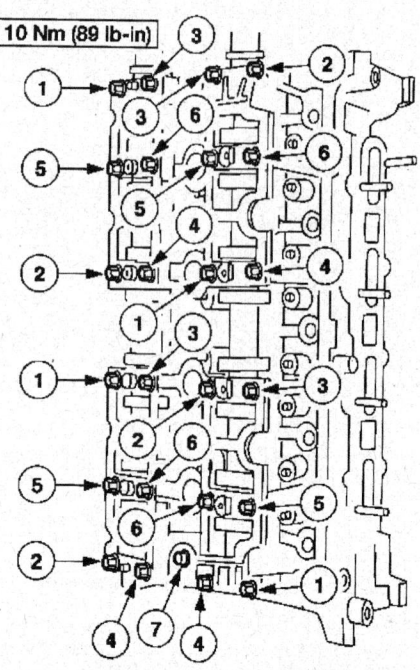

Fig. 64 Camshaft bearing tightening sequence. DOHC engine

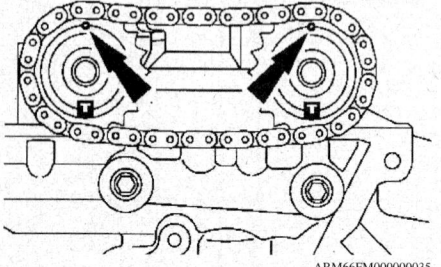

Fig. 65 Camshaft timing marks. DOHC engine

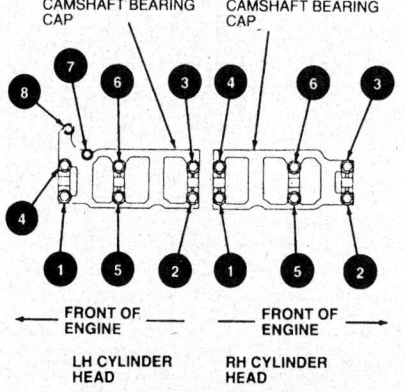

Fig. 66 Camshaft cap cluster tightening sequence. SOHC engine

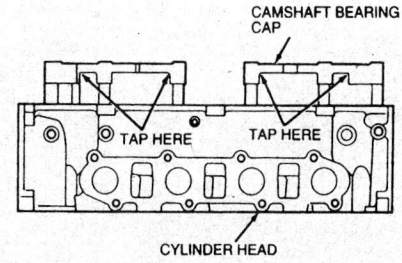

Fig. 67 Camshaft replacement. 2001–02 SOHC engine

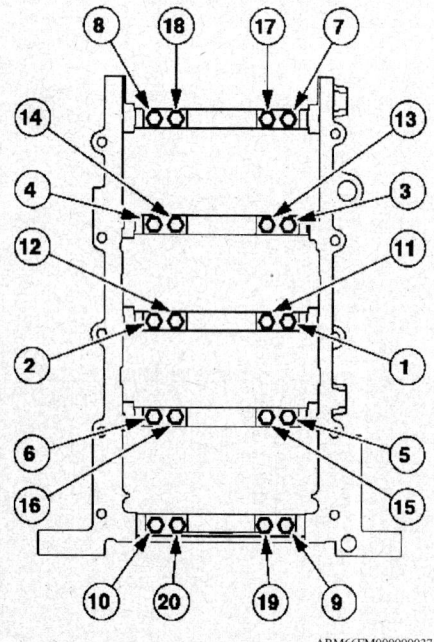

Fig. 68 Main bearing vertical bolts tightening sequence. DOHC engine

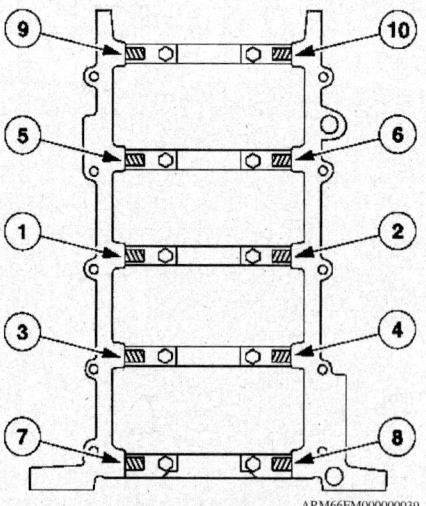

Fig. 69 Main bearing cross mounted bolts tightening sequence. SOHC engine

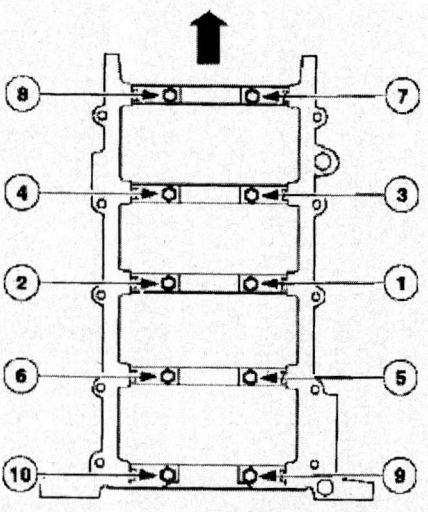

Fig. 70 Main bearing vertical mounted bolts tightening sequence. SOHC engine

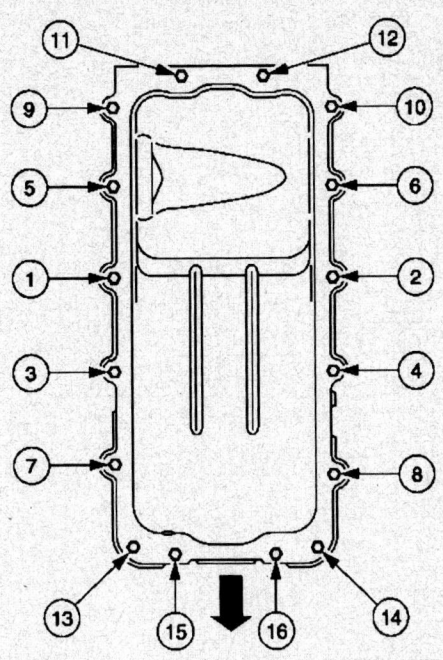

Fig. 71 Oil pan tighten sequence

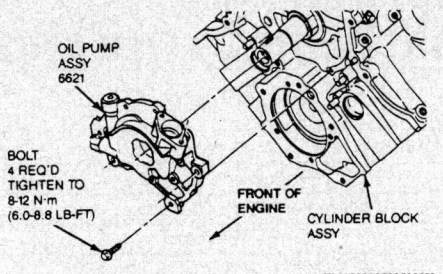

Fig. 72 Oil pump assembly

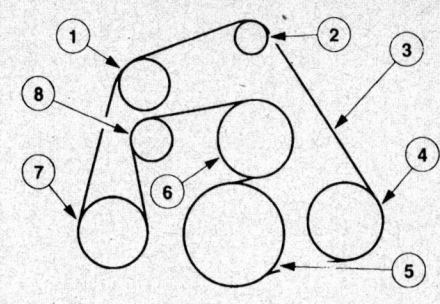

Item	Description
1	Belt idler pulley
2	Generator pulley
3	Drive belt
4	Power steering pump pulley
5	Crankshaft pulley
6	Water pump pulley
7	A/C clutch pulley
8	Drive belt tensioner pulley

FM1069901042000X

Fig. 73 Serpentine drive belt routing

Year	Model	Service Kit No.
2001	All	1W7Z-9424-AAA

Fig. 75 Intake manifold replacement kits. 2001 Town Car

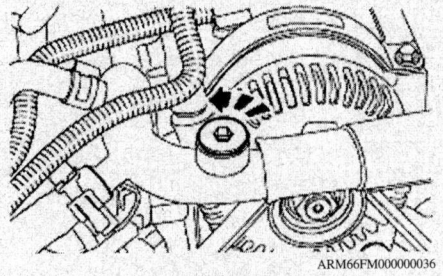

Fig. 74 Coolant bleed plug. DOHC engine

TIGHTENING SPECIFICATIONS

Year	Component	Torque/Ft. Lbs.
DOHC ENGINE		
2003–05	Air Conditioning Compressor	18
	Alternator Mounting Bracket	89①
	Camshaft Cap	⑫
	Camshaft Sprocket	85
	Connecting Rod	⑦
	Cylinder Head	⑤
	EAR Valve To Exhaust Manifold Tube	30
	Engine Mount	52
	Exhaust Manifold	⑩
	Flex Plate	59
	Front Cover	⑥
	Heater Coolant Outlet To Cylinder Head	89①
	Lower Intake Manifold	⑨
	Main Rod Bearing Cap	⑦
	Oil Filter Adapter	18
	Oil Pan	⑧
	Oil Pump Screen Cover & Tube To Oil Pump	89①
	Oil Pump Screen & Pickup Tube To Main Bearing Cap Stud Spacer	18
	Oil Pump To Cylinder Block	89①
	Outlet Heater Water Hose To Engine Front Cover	18
	Power Steering Pump	18
	Serpentine Belt Idler Pulley	18
	Serpentine Belt Tensioner	18
	Thermostat	18
	Timing Chain Guide	89
	Timing Chain Tensioner (Primary)	18
	Timing Chain Tensioner (Secondary)	89①
	Upper Intake Manifold	⑨
	Valve Cover	⑪
	Water Pump	18
	Water Pump Pulley	18
SOHC ENGINE		
2001–02	Air Conditioning Compressor	15–22
	Alternator	15–22
	Camshaft Bearing Caps	⑫
	Camshaft Gear	82–95
	Connecting Rod	③
	Cylinder Head	⑤
	Damper	④
	EAR Tube Connector	33–48
	EAR Valve	15–22
	EAR Valve Line	26–33
	ECT Sensor	12–17
	Engine Mount	45–59
	Engine Mount Through Bolt	15–22
	Engine To Transmission	30–44
	Engine To Transmission Brace	18–31
	Exhaust Manifold	⑩
	Exhaust Pipe To Exhaust Manifold	20–30
	Flywheel	54–64
	Front Cover	⑥
	Fuel Rail	71–106

TIGHTENING
SPECIFICATIONS—Continued

Year	Component	Torque/Ft. Lbs.
2001–02	Fuel Tank Strap	22–30
	HEGO Sensors	27–33
	Intake Manifold	⑨
	Main Bearing Cap	22–25
	Oil Filter Adapter	15–22
	Oil Inlet Tube To Main Bearing Cap	15–22
	Oil Inlet Tube To Oil Pump	72–106①
	Oil Pan	⑧
	Oil Pan Drain Plug	98–143①
	Oil Pump To Cylinder Block	72–107①
	Power Steering Pump To Engine	15–22
	Rear Engine Mount	35–47
	Rear Engine Mount To Crossmember	51–67
	Rear Oil Seal Retainer	71–106①
	Spark Plug	15
	Thermostat	15–22
	Throttle Body & Adapter	71–106①
	Timing Chain Guides	71–106①
	Timing Chain Tensioner	15–22
	Torque Converter	22–25
	Water Pump	15–22
	Water Pump Pulley	15–22
2003–05	Camshaft Bearing Cap	⑫
	Camshaft Sprocket	89
	Connecting Rod Bearing Cap	③
	Crankshaft Main Bearings	②
	Cylinder Head	⑤
	EAR Tube	30
	Engine Mount	52
	Exhaust Manifold	25
	Exhaust Manifold To Converter	25
	Flywheel	59
	Front Cover	⑥
	Fuel Injection Supply Manifold Studs	89①
	Idler Pulley	18
	Intake Manifold	18
	Motor Mount To Crossmember	44
	Oil Filter Adapter	18
	Oil Pan	⑧
	Oil Pan Drain Plug	10①
	Oil Pump	89①
	Oil Pump Screen Cover & Tube To Oil Pump Screen Cover & Tube Spacer	18

Continued

TIGHTENING
SPECIFICATIONS—Continued

Year	Component	Torque/Ft. Lbs.
2003–05	Oil Pump Screen Cover & Tube Bolts	89①
	Oil Pump Screen Cover & Tube Spacer	18
	Power Steering High Pressure Line	18
	Power Steering Pump	18
	Rear Main Seal Retainer Plate	89①
	Starter Motor	18
	Thermostat	18
	Throttle Body	89①
	Timing Chain Guide	89①
	Timing Chain Tensioner	18
	Torque Converter	27
	Transmission Mount	76
	Valve Cover	⑪
	Water Bypass Tube Stud	18
	Water Outlet Adapter	18
	Water Pump	18
	Water Pump Pulley	18

① — Inch lbs.
② — Torque to 30 ft. lbs., and final tighten an additional 90°.
③ — Torque to 30–33 ft. lbs., and final tighten an additional 90–120°.
④ — Refer to "Front Cover Seal, Replace" for tightening specifications and sequence
⑤ — Refer to "Cylinder Head, Replace" for tightening specifications and sequence.
⑥ — Refer to "Front Cover, Replace" for tightening specifications and sequence.
⑦ — Refer to "Main & Rod Bearings" for tightening specifications and sequence.
⑧ — Refer to "Oil Pan, Replace" for tightening specifications and sequence.
⑨ — Refer to "Intake Manifold, Replace" for tightening specifications and sequence.
⑩ — Refer to "Exhaust Manifold, Replace" for tightening specifications and sequence.
⑪ — Refer to "Valve Cover, Replace" for tightening specifications and sequence.
⑫ — Refer to "Camshaft, Replace" for tightening specifications and sequence.

Rear Axle & Suspension

NOTE: On Air Bag Equipped Models, Refer To "Air Bag System Precautions" Located In The Front Of This Manual For System Disarming & Arming Procedures.

NOTE: Refer To "Computer Relearn Procedure" Located In The Front Of This Manual When Battery Power To The Computer Has Been Interrupted.

INDEX

PRECAUTIONS

Air Bag Systems

Refer to "Air Bag System Precautions" in the front of this manual for system disarming and arming procedures.

Air Suspension Pressure Relief

Before servicing any air suspension components, disconnect power to system by turning air suspension switch OFF or by disconnecting battery ground cable.

Do not remove an air spring under any circumstances when there is pressure in the air spring. Do not remove any component supporting an air spring without either exhausting the air or providing support for air spring. Refer to the "Active Suspension Systems" chapter to vent air from spring.

Battery Ground Cable

Prior to service, disconnect battery ground cable and isolate as required.

DESCRIPTION

Crown Victoria, Grand Marquis & Marauder

The rear suspension is composed of the upper and lower suspension arms, lateral arm, Watts link pivot, rear stabilizer bar and air or coil springs, **Fig. 1.**

Town Car

The rear suspension is composed of the upper and lower suspension arms, lateral arm, Watts link pivot, rear stabilizer bar and air or coil springs, **Fig. 2.**

REAR AXLE
REPLACE

1. **On models equipped with air suspension,** turn air suspension switch to Off position, then vent air from system as outlined in "Active Suspension Systems" chapter.
2. **On all models,** raise and support vehicle and position safety stands below rear frame crossmember.
3. Mark driveshaft flange and pinion flange for correct alignment during installation.
4. Remove four mounting bolts and disconnect driveshaft.
5. Remove rear wheels, calipers and brake discs. Support caliper with suitable wire.
6. Remove rear disc rotor, parking brake rear cable and conduit from parking brake cable equalizer. Reroute parking brake rear cable and conduit aside.
7. Remove anti-lock brake sensors. Reroute anti-lock brake sensor wiring.
8. Remove rear stabilizer bar from rear stabilizer bar link and bushing.
9. Remove rear stabilizer bar bracket bolts, rear stabilizer bar brackets and rear stabilizer bar.
10. Remove rear air springs height sensor, as required.
11. Separate Watts linkage from rear axle housing.
12. Remove bellcrank stud nut. **Do not damage bellcrank stud threads.**
13. Secure rear axle to jack using additional support straps.

14. Support rear axle housing with suitable jack.
15. Remove lower mounting nuts and shock absorbers from brackets.
16. Remove lower control arm retainer, then the upper control arm mounting nuts and bolts.
17. Unseat air springs and lower rear axle.
18. Reverse procedure to install.

REAR AXLE SHAFT
REPLACE

Removal

1. **On models equipped with air suspension,** turn air suspension switch to Off position, then vent air from system as outlined in "Active Suspension Systems" chapter.
2. **On all models,** raise and support vehicle, then remove rear wheel and tire assembly.
3. Remove disc brake calipers and rotors, then the rear anti-lock brake sensor.
4. Drain rear axle fluid into suitable container by removing cover.
5. Remove differential pinion shaft lock bolt and differential pinion shaft, **Fig. 3.**
6. Push flanged end of axle shafts toward center of vehicle and remove C-lock from button end of axle shaft, **Fig. 4.**
7. Remove axle shaft from housing. **Do not damage oil seal and ABS sensor ring.**

Installation

1. Ensure O-ring is present on spline end of axle shaft.
2. Slide axle shaft into axle housing. **Do not damage bearing seal or ABS sensor ring.**
3. Start splines into side gear and push

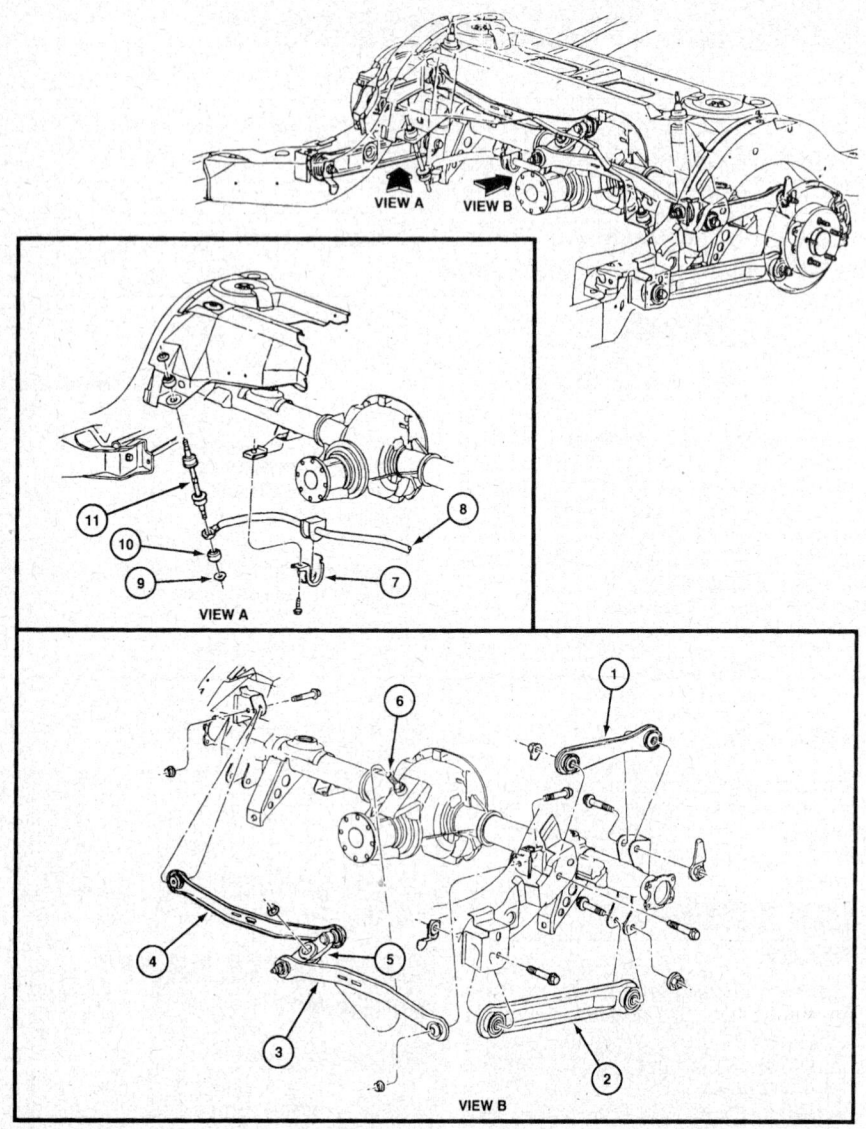

Item	Description
1	Rear Suspension Upper Arm
2	Rear Suspension Lower Arm
3	Lateral Arm, LH (Part of 4264)
4	Lateral Arm, RH (Part of 4264)
5	Watts Link Pivot (Part of 4264)

Item	Description
6	Watts Link Pivot Stud
7	Stabilizer Bar Bracket
8	Stabilizer Bar and Isolator Assy
9	Stabilizer Bar Link Retaining Nut
10	Stabilizer Bar Bushing
11	Stabilizer Bar Link

FM2039800059020X

Fig. 1 Exploded view of rear suspension (Part 2 of 2). Crown Victoria, Grand Marquis & Marauder

FM2039800059010X

Fig. 1 Exploded view of rear suspension (Part 1 of 2). Crown Victoria, Grand Marquis & Marauder

firmly until button end of axle shaft can be seen in differential case.

4. Install C-lock on button end of axle shaft splines. Push shaft outboard until splines engage and C-lock seats in counterbore of differential side gear.
5. Position differential pinion shaft through case and pinion gears, aligning hole in shaft with lock bolt hose.
6. Apply rear axle lubricant No. E0AZ-19554-BA, or equivalent, to pinion shaft lock bolt and tighten.
7. Install cover and tighten.
8. Install ABS speed sensor, rotors and calipers.

PROPELLER SHAFT
REPLACE

To maintain proper drive line balance, mark the driveshaft, universal joints, slip yoke and companion flange before removing the shaft so it can be installed in its original position.

1. Remove companion flange to drive pinion flange mounting bolts.
2. Pull driveshaft rearward until slip yoke clears transmission extension housing.
3. Reverse procedure to install.

SHOCK ABSORBER
REPLACE

1. **On models equipped with air suspension,** turn air suspension switch to Off position, then vent air from system as outlined in "Active Suspension Systems" chapter.
2. **On all models,** raise and support vehicle.
3. **On models equipped with plastic dust tube,** place suitable open end wrench on hex stamped into dust tube's metal cap.
4. **On models equipped with steel dust**

tube, grasp tube to prevent stud rotation when loosening mounting nut.
5. **On all models,** remove shock absorber mounting nut, washer and insulator from stud on upper side of frame.
6. Compress shock absorber to clear hole in frame, then remove inner insulator and washer from upper stud.
7. Remove self-locking nut and disconnect shock absorber lower stud from mounting bracket on rear axle tube.
8. Reverse procedure to install.

COIL SPRING
REPLACE

1. Mark rear shock absorber relative to protective sleeve with vehicle in static, level ground position (curb height).
2. Raise and support vehicle on suitable hoist.
3. Remove both wheel and tire assemblies.
4. Remove nuts and bushings, then rotate stabilizer bar off links.
5. Support rear axle.
6. All vehicles are equipped with gas pressurized shock absorbers which will extend unassisted. **Do not apply heat or flame to shock absorbers during removal or component servicing.**
7. Remove nuts and disconnect shock absorbers. Discard nuts.
8. Lower axle, then remove springs and spring insulators.
9. Reverse procedure to install.

AIR SPRING
REPLACE

2001-02

1. Turn air suspension switch to Off position, then vent air from system as outlined in "Active Suspension Systems" chapter.
2. Remove rear air spring retainer.
3. Lift bottom of air spring off rear axle.
4. Disconnect electrical connector.
5. Push on red retaining ring and disconnect air line.
6. Remove air spring.
7. Reverse procedure to install.

2003-05

Do not remove an air spring when there is pressure in the air spring.

Do not attempt to install any air spring that has become unfolded.

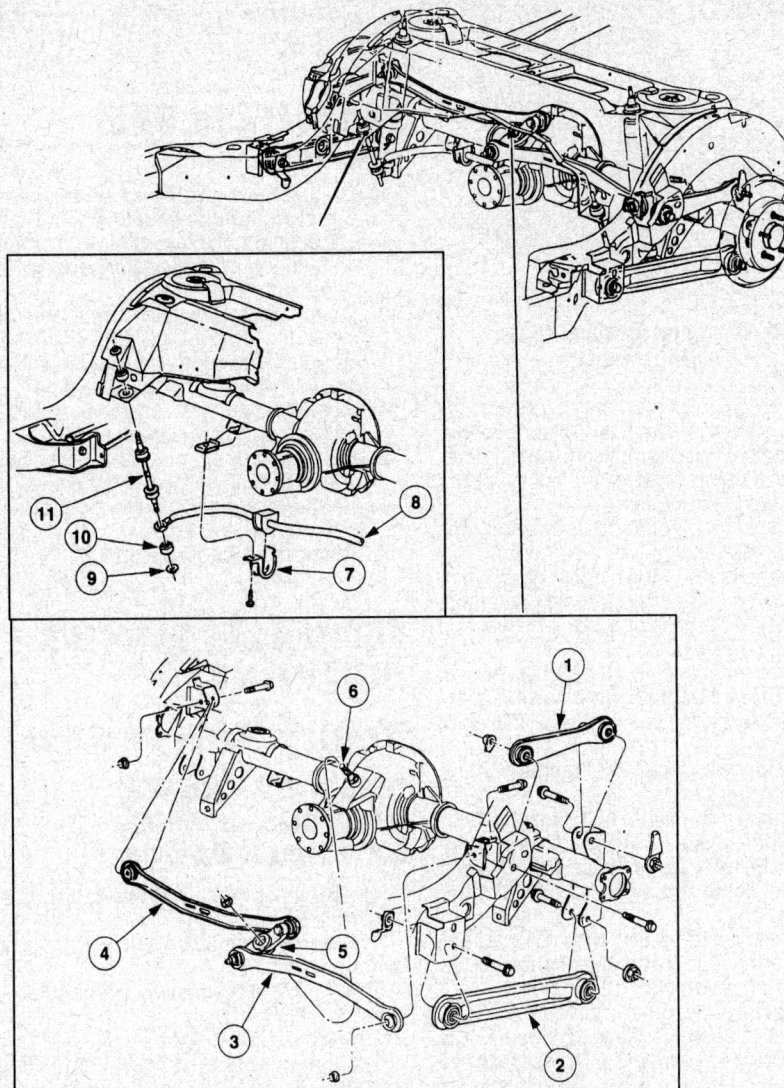

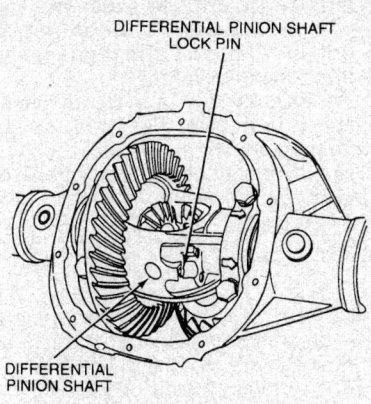

DIFFERENTIAL PINION SHAFT
LOCK PIN

DIFFERENTIAL
PINION SHAFT

FM3039200211000X

Fig. 3 Differential pinion shaft replacement

Item	Description
1	Rear Suspension Upper Arm
2	Rear Suspension Lower Arm
3	Lateral Arm, LH
4	Lateral Arm, RH
5	Watts Link Pivot

Item	Description
6	Watts Link Pivot Stud
7	Stabilizer Bar Bracket
8	Stabilizer Bar and Isolator Assy
9	Stabilizer Bar Link Retaining Nut
10	Stabilizer Bar Bushing
11	Stabilizer Bar Link

FM2039800062000X

Fig. 2 Exploded view of rear suspension. Town Car

1. Raise and support vehicle until tires are slightly above ground.
2. Vent air springs as outlined in "Active Suspensions" chapter.
3. Remove air spring retainer, then detach air spring from rear axle.
4. Disconnect air spring electrical connector, then quick connect locking ring and pull out air line.
5. Remove air spring.
6. Reverse procedure to install.

CONTROL ARM
REPLACE

Lower

1. **On models equipped with air suspension,** turn air suspension switch to Off position, then vent air from system as outlined in "Active Suspension Sys-

tems" chapter.
2. **On all models,** mark rear suspension shock tube relative to protective sleeve with vehicle on level ground.
3. Raise and support vehicle, then remove wheel and tire assembly.
4. Support rear axle.
5. Remove and discard rear suspension lower arm pivot bolt and nut from axle bracket.
6. Remove and discard rear suspension lower arm pivot bolt and nut from frame bracket.
7. Remove rear suspension lower arm.
8. Reverse procedure to install, noting the following:
   a. Rear suspension lower arm bolts must be tightened with vehicle at curb height.
   b. Rear suspension lower arms are interchangeable from side to side with "OUTBOARD" stamped on side of arm for positioning during installation.
   c. Position rear suspension lower arm to frame bracket and install new pivot bolt and nut. Insert bolt so nut faces inboard. **Do not tighten now.**
   d. Raise axle to compresses shock absorber to previously established alignment mark (curb height).
   e. Tighten rear suspension lower arm to frame bracket pivot bolt.

Upper

1. **On models equipped with air suspension,** turn air suspension switch to Off position, then vent air from system as outlined in "Active Suspension Systems" chapter.
2. **On all models,** mark rear suspension shock absorber relative to protective sleeve with vehicle in static, level ground position (curb height).
3. Raise and support vehicle.
4. Support rear axle.
5. Remove and discard rear suspension upper arm pivot bolt and nut from axle

bracket. **Do not use excessive force when removing pivot bolt and flag nut on righthand upper suspension arm to axle bracket.**

6. Remove and discard rear suspension upper arm pivot bolt and nut from frame bracket.
7. Remove rear suspension upper arm.
8. Reverse procedure to install, noting the following:
   a. Rear suspension upper arm bolts must be tightened with vehicle at curb height.
   b. Rear suspension upper arms are interchangeable from side to side with "FRONT" and "OUTBOARD" stamped on side of arms for positioning during installation.
   c. Position rear suspension upper arm to frame bracket and install new pivot bolt and nut. Insert bolt so nut faces inboard. **Do not tighten now.**
   d. Raise axle to compresses shock absorber to previously established alignment mark (curb height).
   e. Tighten bolts.

LATERAL CONTROL ARM

REPLACE

1. **On models equipped with air suspension,** turn air suspension switch to Off position, then vent air from system as outlined in "Active Suspension Systems" chapter.
2. **On all models,** mark rear suspension shock absorber relative to protective sleeve with vehicle in static, level ground position (curb height).
3. Raise and support vehicle.
4. Support rear axle.
5. Disconnect height sensor from mounting bracket.
6. Remove and discard both lateral arm pivot bolts and nuts.

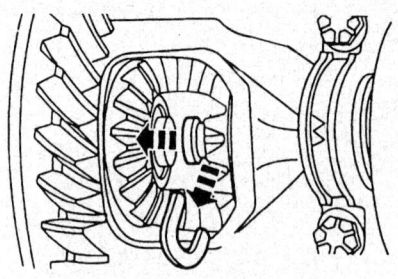

FM3039100209000X

Fig. 4 Axle shaft C-lock replacement

7. Watts link pivot stud is coated with dry adhesive and must be replaced whenever pivot nut or stud is loosened or removed using new Watts link pivot nut and stud service kit.
8. If Watts link pivot stud on axle loosens while removing pivot nut, continue to loosen pivot stud until open end wrench can inserted to hold pivot stud. While holding pivot stud, remove and discard pivot nut.
9. Lower axle until Watts link is free of pivot stud. Remove lateral arm.
10. Remove and discard Watts link pivot stud.
11. Reverse procedure to install, noting the following:
    a. Install new Watts link pivot stud.
    b. Rear suspension lateral arm pivot bolts and Watts link pivot nut must be tightened with vehicle at curb height.
    c. Install lateral arm on pivot stud ensuring righthand arm flange faces front of vehicle.
    d. Raise axle until lateral arm aligns with frame brackets and install new pivot bolts and nuts. **Do not tighten now.**
    e. Raise axle to compresses shock absorber to previously established

alignment mark (curb height). Tighten bolts.

STABILIZER BAR

REPLACE

1. **On models equipped with air suspension,** turn air suspension switch to Off position, then vent air from system as outlined in "Active Suspension Systems" chapter.
2. **On all models,** raise and support vehicle.
3. Support rear axle using hi-lift jack tool No. 014-00942, or equivalent.
4. Remove both stabilizer bar link lower mounting nuts and bushings.
5. Remove upper mounting nuts, bushings and both stabilizer bar links.
6. Remove mounting bolts, both stabilizer bars and brackets.
7. Reverse procedure to install.

TECHNICAL SERVICE BULLETINS

Vehicle Low In Rear

2001-02 CROWN VICTORIA w/CNG EXTENDED RANGE

On some of these models the rear end may sit low.

This condition may be caused by the rear springs.

To correct this condition, proceed as follows:

1. Measure ride height.
2. If measurement is less than 4.9–5.5 inches (137–153 mm), replace rear spring with revised unit (P/N D9AZ-5560-AE).

TIGHTENING SPECIFICATIONS

Year	Component	Torque/Ft. Lbs.
2001–02	Caliper Locating Pin	21–26
	Driveshaft Flange Bolt	70–95
	Height Sensor Mounting Bracket To Lateral Arm	9–12
	Lateral Arm To Frame Bracket	65–88
	Lateral Arm To Watts Link Pivot	60–77
	Lower Arm To Axle & Frame	95–127
	Lower Arm To Frame	120–150
	Pinion Shaft Lock Bolt	15–29
	Rear Cover	25–34
	Shock Absorber To Axle Bracket	57–75
	Shock Absorber Upper	26–34
	Stabilizer Bar Bracket Bolt To Axle	16–21
	Stabilizer Link Nut To Stabilizer Bar	13–16
	Upper Arm To Axle	65–88
	Upper Arm To Frame	95–127
	Watts Link Pivot, Nut	158–212
	Watts Link Pivot, Stud	189–211
	Wheel Lug Nut	80–106

Front Suspension & Steering

NOTE: On Air Bag Equipped Models, Refer To "Air Bag System Precautions" Located In The Front Of This Manual For System Disarming & Arming Procedures.

NOTE: Refer To "Computer Relearn Procedure" Located In The Front Of This Manual When Battery Power To The Computer Has Been Interrupted.

INDEX

PRECAUTIONS

Air Bag Systems

Refer to "Air Bag System Precautions" in the front of this manual for system disarming and arming procedures.

Air Suspension Pressure Relief

Before servicing any air suspension components, disconnect power to system by turning air suspension switch OFF or by disconnecting battery ground cable.

Do not remove an air spring under any circumstances when there is pressure in the air spring. Do not remove any component supporting an air spring without either exhausting the air or providing support for air spring. Refer to the "Active Suspension Systems" chapter to vent air from spring.

Battery Ground Cable

Prior to service, disconnect battery ground cable and isolate as required.

WHEEL BEARING

ADJUST

These models are equipped with sealed bearing units which do not require adjustment or maintenance. If the bearing is found to be faulty, then the hub and bearing must be replaced as an assembly.

KNUCKLE ASSY   HUB AND BEARING ASSY
BRAKE DUST SHIELD

FM2049200025000X

Fig. 1 Hub & wheel bearing assembly

WHEEL BEARING

REPLACE

2001–02

1. Raise and support front of vehicle, then remove wheel and tire assembly.
2. Remove grease cap from hub.
3. Remove disc brake caliper with brake hose attached. Suspend caliper from suspension with suitable wire. **Do not allow caliper to hang from brake hose.**
4. Remove brake rotor.
5. Remove nut, then the hub and bearing, **Fig. 1.** If hub is difficult to remove, use hub removal tool No. T81P-1104-C, or equivalent.
6. Reverse procedure to install. Install new hub nut.

2003–05

1. Remove tire and wheel assembly.
2. Remove bolts, then position brake caliper, pads and anchor plate aside.
3. Remove brake rotor.
4. Disconnect electrical connector and unclip retainers.
5. Remove bolts, then the wheel bearing and hub assembly.
6. Reverse procedure to install.

BALL JOINT INSPECTION

On models equipped with air suspension, turn switch to Off position prior to raising and supporting vehicle.

Refer to "Specifications" section maximum backlash and endplay measurements.

1. Raise and support vehicle.
2. Inspect ball joint boos for tears. Replace ball joint as required.
3. Inspect wheel bearings.
4. Support lower control arm with suitable safety stand.
5. While assistant pushes and pulls equally on top and bottom of tire, observe any relative lateral backlash between upper control arm and front wheel spindle. Replace ball joint if lateral backlash is at or exceeds specifications.
6. While assistant moves tire up and down, observe any relative endplay between upper arm and front wheel spindle. Replace ball joint if endplay is at or exceeds specifications.

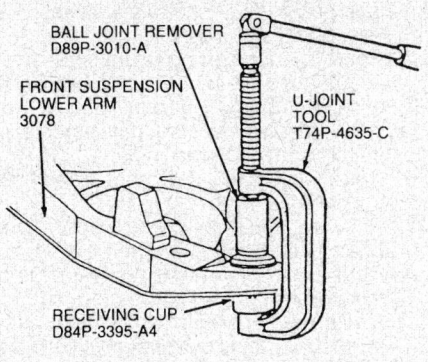

Fig. 2 Lower ball joint removal. 2001–02

7. Remove tire and wheel assembly.
8. Separate lower arm from front wheel spindle. Disconnect mounting bolts and nuts.
9. Measure lateral backlash using suitable dial indicator while moving ball joint side to side. Replace ball joint if lateral backlash is at or exceeds specifications.
10. Measure endplay using suitable dial indicator while moving ball joint up and down. Replace ball joint if endplay is at or exceeds specifications.

BALL JOINT
REPLACE
2001-02
LOWER

1. Raise and support vehicle.
2. Remove front wheel spindle.
3. Remove and discard ball joint boot seal.
4. Press out arm bushing joint using U-joint tool No. T74P-4635-C, ball joint remover tool No. D89P-3010-A, and receiving cup tool No. D84P-3395-A4, or equivalents, **Fig. 2.**
5. Reverse procedure to install, noting the following:
   a. When installing new front suspension arm bushing joint, protective cover must remain in place. It may be required to cut off end of cover to allow it to pass through receiving cup.
   b. Install ball joint with ball joint replacer tool No. D89P-3010-B, receiving cup tool No. D84P-3395-A4 and U-joint tool No. T74P-4635-C, or equivalents, **Fig. 3.**
   c. Inspect wheel alignment.

UPPER

1. Raise and support vehicle, then remove wheel and tire assembly.
2. Position suitable jack under lower control arm at ball joint.
3. Remove mounting nut and punch bolt from upper ball joint stud.
4. Mark position of alignment cams.
5. Remove ball joint mounting nuts.
6. Remove ball joint and separate ball

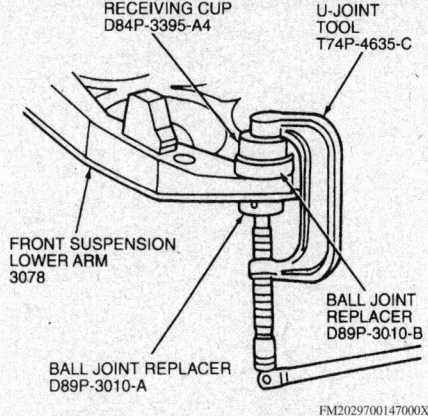

Fig. 3 Lower ball joint installation. 2001–02

joint stud from spindle by spreading slot with suitable pry bar.
7. Reverse procedure to install.

2003-05

The ball joint is not serviced separately. If the ball joint requires service, the lower or upper control arm will need to be replaced.

COIL SPRING
REPLACE
2001-02

1. Raise and support vehicle, then remove wheel and tire assembly.
2. Remove two front shock absorber to suspension lower arm mounting bolts.
3. Remove upper nut, retainer, grommet and front shock absorber.
4. Install one plate with pivot ball seat facing downward into coils of front coil spring, using coil spring compressor tool D78P-5310-A, or equivalent.
5. Rotate plate so it is flush with upper surface of front suspension lower arm.
6. Install other plate with pivot ball seat facing upward into coils of front coil spring.
7. Insert upper ball joint nut through coils of front coil spring so nut rests in upper plate. This pin can only be inserted one way into upper ball nut because of stepped-hole design.
8. Insert compression rod into opening in front suspension lower arm, through upper and lower plate and upper ball nut.
9. Insert securing pin through upper ball nut and compression rod, **Fig. 4.**
10. With upper ball nut secured, turn upper plate so it walks up coil until it contacts upper front spring insulator. Back nut off one-half turn.
11. Install lower ball nut and thrust washer on compression rod and screw on forcing nut, **Fig. 5.**
12. Tighten forcing nut until front coil spring is compressed enough so it is free in its front spring insulator.
13. Remove two front lower arm pivot

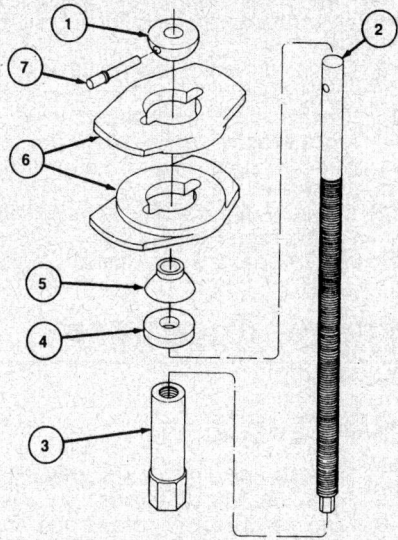

Item	Description
1	Upper Ball (Part of 204-D001 (D78P-5310-A))
2	Compression Rod (Part of 204-D001 (D78P-5310-A))
3	Forcing Nut (Part of 204-D001 (D78P-5310-A))
4	Thrust Washer (Part of 204-D001 (D78P-5310-A))
5	Lower Ball Nut (Part of 204-D001 (D78P-5310-A))
6	Plate (Part of 204-D001 (D78P-5310-A))
7	Pin (Part of 204-D001 (D78P-5310-A))

Fig. 4 Compression rod assembly. 2001–02

bolts, disconnect lower arm from crossmember and remove coil spring.
14. If new front coil spring is to be installed proceed as follows:
   a. Mark position of upper and lower plates on front coil spring.
   b. Compress new front coil spring for installation with an assistant.
   c. Measure compressed length and amount of curvature of old front coil spring.
15. Loosen forcing nut to relieve spring tension and remove tools from front coil spring.
16. Reverse procedure to install.

2003-05

1. Remove and discard three upper shock absorber nuts.
2. Remove tire and wheel assembly.
3. Remove bolts, then position brake caliper, pads and anchor plate aside.
4. Remove brake rotor.
5. Remove nuts, then the stabilizer link. Discard nuts.
6. Remove and discard remaining shock absorber nuts.
7. Remove shock absorber and spring assembly.
8. Mount shock absorber and spring assembly in suitable holding device, then

mark upper mount, spring and shock absorber for reference during assembly.
9. Compress spring using suitable spring compressor.
10. While holding shock absorber rod, remove and discard nut.
11. Remove upper mount and dust boot assembly.
12. Carefully remove spring and spring compressor.
13. Reverse procedure to install.

SHOCK ABSORBER
REPLACE
2001-02

1. Remove upper shock absorber nut.
2. Raise and support vehicle.
3. Remove two lower screws and shock absorber.
4. Reverse procedure to install.

2003-05

1. Remove and discard three upper shock absorber nuts.
2. Remove tire and wheel assembly.
3. Remove bolts, then position brake caliper, pads and anchor plate aside.
4. Remove brake rotor.
5. Remove nuts, then the stabilizer link. Discard nuts.
6. Remove and discard remaining shock absorber nuts.
7. Remove shock absorber and spring assembly.
8. Reverse procedure to install.

CONTROL ARM
REPLACE
2001-02
LOWER

1. Raise and support vehicle, then remove wheel and tire assembly.
2. Remove cotter pin and nut from tie rod end.
3. Remove tie rod end from front wheel spindle using tie rod end removal tool No. 211-001, or equivalent.
4. Remove coil spring as outlined under "Coil Spring, Replace"
5. Remove and discard lower ball joint nut.
6. Remove ball joint from steering knuckle using pitman arm puller tool No. 211-003, or equivalent.
7. Remove lower control arm.
8. Reverse procedure to install.

UPPER

1. Raise and support vehicle, then remove wheel and tire assembly.
2. Place suitable jack under front suspension lower arm and lower vehicle until lower arm begins to move.
3. Secure front wheel spindle to frame using suitable piece of safety wire.

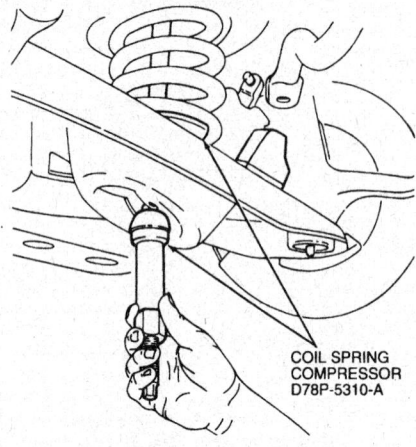
Spring Compressor Installation

COIL SPRING COMPRESSOR D78P-5310-A

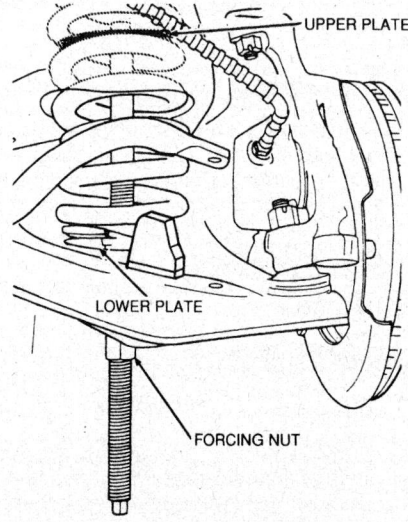
Spring Compressor Location

UPPER PLATE

LOWER PLATE

FORCING NUT

FM2029700149000X

Fig. 5 Spring compressor installation. 2001-02

4. Remove upper steering knuckle bolt and nut to release upper ball joint from knuckle.
5. Remove mounting bolts, nuts and control arm.
6. Reverse procedure to install. Inspect wheel alignment.

2003-05
LOWER

1. Remove tire and wheel assembly.
2. Remove and discard lower nut.
3. Remove nut and flag bolt. Discard nut.
4. Remove and discard nuts and bolts.
5. Remove studs, then position steering gear upward to access cam bolt.
6. Remove cam bolt, then the lower control arm.
7. Reverse procedure to install. Do not tighten nuts and bolts until weight of vehicle is resting on control arm.

UPPER

1. Remove tire and wheel assembly.
2. Remove bolts, then position brake cal-

iper, pads and anchor plate aside.
3. Remove brake rotor.
4. Raise suspension arms until pressure is released from stabilizer bar links using suitable jack stand.
5. Remove stabilizer bar nuts, then the stabilizer bar. Discard nuts.
6. Detach electrical retainers from arm and wheel knuckle.
7. Remove nuts, bolts and upper arm. Discard nuts.
8. Reverse procedure to install, noting the following:
    a. Do not tighten upper arm to crossmember nuts until weight of vehicle is resting on tire and wheel assemblies.
    b. Inspect wheel alignment.

STABILIZER BAR
REPLACE
2001-02

1. Raise and support vehicle.
2. Remove stabilizer bar link nuts.
3. Remove four stabilizer bar brackets mounting nuts and lower arm stabilizer bar insulator from stabilizer bar.
4. Remove stabilizer bar.
5. Reverse procedure to install.

2003-05

1. Remove tire and wheel assemblies.
2. Remove bolts, then position brake caliper, pads and anchor plate aside.
3. Remove brake rotor.
4. Raise suspension arms until pressure is released from stabilizer bar links using suitable jack stand.
5. Remove nuts, then the stabilizer bar links. Discard nuts.
6. Remove nuts, brackets and stabilizer bar. Discard nuts.
7. Reverse procedure to install.

POWER STEERING GEAR
REPLACE
2001-02

1. Remove stone shield, as required.
2. Disconnect steering gear pressure and return lines . Plug lines and ports.
3. Remove flex coupling to steering gear and column clamp bolt.
4. Raise and support vehicle.
5. Remove sector shaft nut.
6. Remove pitman arm using pitman arm puller tool No. T64P-3590-F, or equivalent.
7. Support steering gear and remove mounting bolts.
8. Remove steering gear by working if free of flex coupling.
9. Reverse procedure to install.

2003-05

1. Hold steering wheel in straight ahead position using suitable holding device.

2. Remove tire and wheel assemblies.
3. Remove nuts, then detach tie rods from wheel knuckles.
4. Remove bolt, then detach intermediate shaft from steering gear. **Do not allow intermediate shaft to rotate while it is disconnected from steering gear.**
5. Disconnect power steering lines and drain fluid into suitable container.
6. Disconnect electrical connector.
7. Remove nuts, studs and power steering gear.
8. Reverse procedure to install.

POWER STEERING PUMP
REPLACE

1. Disconnect power steering pump return line and allow power steering pump fluid to drain into suitable container.

2. Disconnect power steering pump pressure hose from pump fitting.
3. Disconnect drive belt, then remove pulley and power steering pump.
4. Reverse procedure to install, noting the following:
   a. **Do not overtighten pressure hose fitting.**
   b. Swivel and/or endplay of fitting is normal and does not indicate loose fitting.

TECHNICAL SERVICE BULLETINS
Harsh Ride
2003

On some of these models the front end ride may be harsh.

This condition may be caused by front springs.

To correct this condition, proceed as follows:
1. Measure front ride height.
2. If measurement is less than 63 mm but more than 57 mm, replace front spring (P/N 3W1Z-5310-EA).
3. If measurement is less than 57 mm, replace front spring (P/N 3W1Z05310-HA).

TIGHTENING SPECIFICATIONS

Year	Component	Torque/Ft. Lbs
2001–02	Axle Nut	189–254
	Ball Joint To Lower Spindle	107–129
	Ball Joint To Upper Spindle	56–76
	Brake Caliper	24
	Flex Coupling to Gear Input Shaft	20–30
	Lower Arm To Crossmember	110–148
	Lower Arm To Frame	110–148
	Pinch Bolt & Nut	56–76
	Pitman Arm	35–46
	Pressure Hose To Gear	16–25
	Quick Connect Tube	35–45
	Return Hose To Gear	26–34
	Shock Absorber, Top Stud	25–33
	Shock Absorber, Lower Bolt	10–12
	Stabilizer Bar Link To Spindle	20–25
	Stabilizer Link To Bar	34–46
	Steering Gear To Side Rail	50–65
	Steering Pump To Engine	15–22
	Tie Rod End To Spindle	35–46
	Upper Ball Joint To Upper Arm	107–129
	Wheel Lug Nut	85–104
2003–05	Brake Caliper Anchor Plate To Wheel Knuckle	118
	Hub To Wheel Knuckle	74
	Lower Arm To Crossmember To Cam Bolt	166
	Lower Arm To Frame	85
	Lower Ball Joint To Wheel Knuckle Nut	111
	Power Steering Pump	18
	Shock Absorber To Crossmember Upper Nuts	22
	Shock Absorber To Lower Arm Nut & Flag Bolt	166
	Shock Absorber Top Stud Nut	37
	Stabilizer Bar Bracket To Frame	46
	Stabilizer Bar Links	46
	Steering Gear To Crossmember Stud Nuts	76
	Steering Gear To Crossmember Studs	13
	Tie Rod End To Wheel Knuckle	59
	Upper Arm To Crossmember	111
	Upper Ball Joint To Wheel Knuckle	111
	Wheel Bearing	74

Wheel Alignment

INDEX

PRELIMINARY INSPECTION

Prior to performing the front wheel alignment, a preliminary inspection should be made to determine the condition of the vehicle's suspension components. The following inspections and procedures should be made prior to performing front wheel alignment:

1. Vehicle must be leveled by performing air suspension system test. as outlined in "Active Suspensions" chapter.
2. Inflate tires to specified pressure (cold).
3. Measure vehicle ride height.
4. Inspect suspension and steering components for looseness.
5. Inspect existing caster, camber and toe settings prior to alignment.
6. Inspect suspension mounting bolts for proper tightness.
7. Alignment equipment must be capable of four wheel alignment.
8. Alignment rack must be leveled to 1/16 inch, side to side and front to rear, and be equipped with wheel runout compensation.

FRONT WHEEL ALIGNMENT

Caster & Camber

2001–02

Adjusting cams are provided for caster and camber adjustment, **Fig. 1**.

1. Inspect caster and camber and record readings.
2. Vehicle within minimum to maximum tolerances may require alignment adjustment to nominal setting because side to side setting is out of specification.
3. If adjustment is required, loosen two nuts on top of adjusting cams.
4. Turn hex cams as required to obtain desired valve.

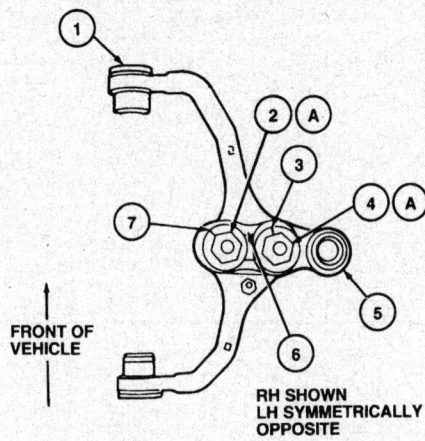

FRONT OF VEHICLE

RH SHOWN
LH SYMMETRICALLY OPPOSITE

Item	Description
1	Front Suspension Lower Arm
2	Camber Adjust
3	Reference Mark
4	Caster Adjust
5	Front Suspension Upper Ball Joint
6	RH Identification on Forging

FM2049700059010X

Fig. 1 Caster & camber adjustment (Part 1 of 2). 2001–02

5. Hold each cam and **torque** nuts to 109–148 ft. lbs.
6. Inspect toe-in and steering wheel spoke position. Adjust both at same time, as required.

2003–05

1. Remove and discard cam bolt retainer flag or lefthand caster bushing centering washer.
2. Inspect caster and chamber and record readings.
3. Loosen cam bolt nut, then rotate cam bolt to adjust camber, **Fig. 2**.
4. While holding cam bolt, **torque** nut to 166 ft. lbs.

Item	Description
7	Reference Mark
A	Turn Adjusting Cams Clockwise to Increase and Counterclockwise to Decrease

FM2049700059020X

Fig. 1 Caster & camber adjustment (Part 2 of 2). 2001–02

5. Loosen nut and move arm inward to decrease caster and outward to increase caster, **Fig. 3**.
6. While holding arm **torque** nut to 111 ft. lbs.

Toe-In & Steering Wheel Spoke Position

After adjusting caster and camber, inspect steering wheel spoke position with front wheels in straight ahead position. If spokes are not in normal position, adjusted while toe is being adjusted.

1. Loosen two clamp bolts on each front wheel spindle tie rod adjusting sleeve, **Fig. 4**.
2. Adjust toe-in. If steering wheel spokes are in normal position, lengthen or shorten both rods equally to obtain correct toe.
3. If steering wheel spokes are not correct, make required rod adjustments to obtain correct toe-in and steering wheel alignment.
4. When toe-in and steering wheel position are both correct, lubricate clamp, bolts and nuts.
5. **Torque** clamp bolts on both connecting rod sleeves to 20–22 ft. lbs.
6. Sleeve position should not be changed when clamp bolts are tightened for proper clamp bolt orientation.

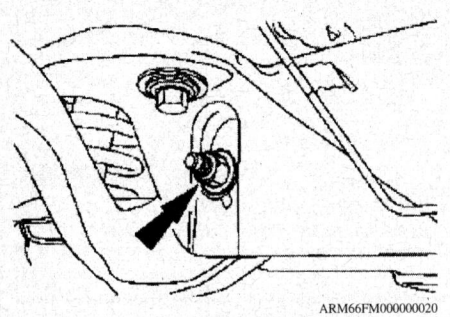

Fig. 2 Camber adjustment. 2003–05

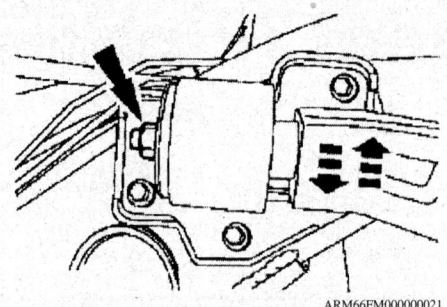

Fig. 3 Caster adjustment. 2003–05

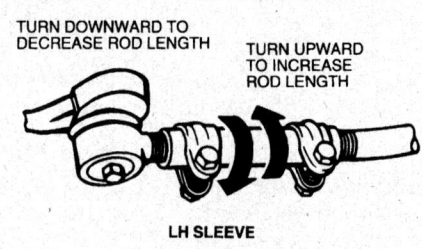

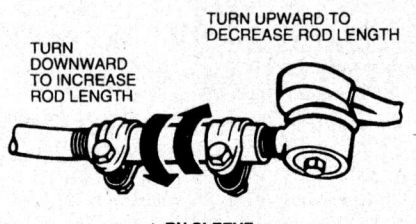

Fig. 4 Toe adjustment

ESCORT & ZX2

NOTE: Refer To Rear Of This Manual For Vehicle Manufacturer's Special Service Tool Suppliers.

INDEX OF SERVICE OPERATIONS

Specifications

GENERAL ENGINE SPECIFICATIONS

Year & Engine (Code)①	Fuel System	Bore & Stroke, Inches	Compression Ratio	Net H.P. @ RPM	Maximum Torque Ft. Lbs. @ RPM	Normal Oil Pressure, psi
2001–03						
2.0L DOHC (3)	SEFI	3.34 x 3.46	9.6	130 @ 5750	127 @ 4250	54–80
2.0L SOHC (P)	SEFI	3.34 x 3.46	9.2	114 @ 5000	126 @ 3750	35–65

SEFI — Sequential Electronic Fuel Injection

① — The eighth digit of VIN denotes engine code.

TUNE UP SPECIFICATIONS

Engine	Spark Plug Gap, Inch	Ignition Timing, °BTDC — Firing Order Fig.	Ignition Timing, °BTDC — Man. Trans.	Ignition Timing, °BTDC — Auto. Trans.	Ignition Timing, °BTDC — Timing Mark Fig.	Curb Idle Speed① — Man. Trans.	Curb Idle Speed① — Auto. Trans.	Fast Idle Speed① — Man. Trans.	Fast Idle Speed① — Auto. Trans.	Fuel Pump Pressure, psi	Valve Clearance, Inch
2001–03											
2.0L DOHC	.052–.056	③	8–12②	8–12②	⑦	⑥	⑥	⑥	⑥	50–85	⑤
2.0L SOHC	.044	③	8–12②	8–12②	⑦	⑥	⑥	⑥	⑥	50–85	④

BTDC — Before Top Dead Center
N — Neutral
① — When adjusting idle speed, set parking brake & chock drive wheels.
② — Computer controlled, non-adjustable.

③ — Firing order, 1-3-4-2. Refer to **Fig. A,** for spark plug wire connections at ignition coil pack.
④ — Equipped with hydraulic lash adjusters.

⑤ — Intake, .0043–.0071 inch; exhaust, .0106–.0134 inch.
⑥ — Idle speed controlled by an automatic idle speed control.
⑦ — Equipped with a crankshaft position sensor. Timing is not adjustable.

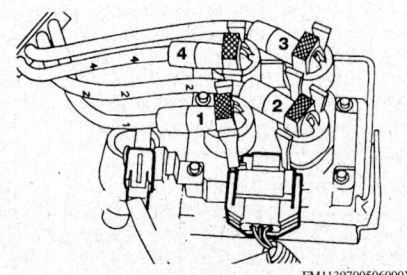

FM1139700506000X

Fig. A

FRONT WHEEL ALIGNMENT SPECIFICATIONS

Model	Caster Angle, Degrees — Limits	Caster Angle, Degrees — Desired	Camber Angle, Degrees — Limits	Camber Angle, Degrees — Desired	Total Toe, Inch① — Limits	Total Toe, Inch① — Desired	Toe-Out On Turns, Degrees — Outer Wheel	Toe-Out On Turns, Degrees — Inner Wheel	Ball Joint Wear, Inch
2001–02									
Escort	+1.20 to +3.20	+2.20	-1.40 to +.60	-.40	-.07 to +.23	+.10	—	—	②
ZX2	+1.30 to +3.30	+2.30	-1.40 to +.60	-.40	-.07 to +.23	+.10	—	—	②
2003									
ZX2	+1.00 to +3.00	+2.00	-1.00 to +1.00	0	-.02 to +1.80	+.08	—	—	②

① — Toe-in (+), toe-out (-).
② — Refer to "Ball Joint Inspection," in

"Front Suspension & Steering" section, for inspection procedure.

REAR WHEEL ALIGNMENT SPECIFICATIONS

Model	Camber Angle, Degrees		Total Toe, Inches①	
	Limits	Desired	Limits	Desired
2001–02				
Escort	-1.70 to +.30	-.70	-.05 to +.25	+.10
ZX2	-2.20 to -.20	-1.20	-.05 to +.25	+.10
2003				
ZX2	-2.00 to 0	-1.00	-.04 to +.20	+.08

① — Toe-in (+), toe-out (-).

VEHICLE RIDE HEIGHT SPECIFICATIONS

Model	Year	Body Style	Manufacturer's Original Tire Size	Measurement Points & Specifications②					
				Front			Rear		
				Dim.	Specification		Dim.	Specification	
					Inches	mm		Inches	mm
Escort	2001–02	All	①	A	5.9	151	B	5.9	151

A Dim. — Distance from Front Rocker Panel to Ground
B Dim. — Distance from Rear Rocker Panel to Ground
E Dim. — Ground to Front Wheel Opening Through Centerline of Wheel
G Dim. — Ground to Rear Wheel Opening Through Centerline of Wheel
L Dim. — Ground to Bottom of Front Bumper

M Dim. — Ground to Bottom of Rear Bumper
Dim. — Dimension
N/A — Not Available
① — See door sticker or inside of glove box for manufacturers original tire size specifications. If tires on vehicle do not match manufacturers original tire size & measurement is not within limits, it will be required to refer to the "Non-Standard Tire & Wheel Size

Adjustment To Ride Height Specification & Tire Size Adjustment Charts" in the front of this manual for approximate changes in ride height specifications.

② — Measurement is with fuel, radiator coolant and engine oil full, spare tire, jack, hand tools and mats in designated positions and tires properly inflated.

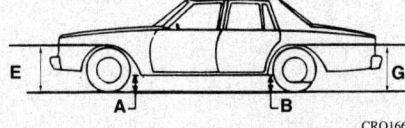

Fig. A   Dimensions A, B, E & G

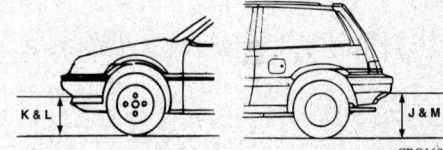

Fig. B   Dimensions J, K, L & M

FLUID CAPACITIES & COOLING SYSTEM DATA

Year/ Engine (Code)③	Coolant Capacity, Qts.		Coolant Type	Radiator Cap Relief Pressure, Lbs.	Thermo. Opening Temp.	Fuel Tank Gals.	Engine Oil Refill Qts.①	Transaxle Oil	
	Manual Transaxle	Automatic Transaxle						Manual Transaxle Pints	Auto. Transaxle Qts.②
2.0L (P)	5.3	6.3	EG	14.4–17.6	188–195	12.8	4.0	—	4.1
2.0L(3)	5.3	6.3	EG	14.4–17.6	194–201	12.8	4.5	7.1	4.1

EG — Ethylene Glycol
① — Includes filter.

② — Approximate. Make final inspection w/dipstick.

③ — The eighth digit of VIN denotes engine code.

LUBRICANT DATA

Year	Lubricant Type			
	Transaxle		Power Steering	Brake System
	Manual	Automatic		
2001–03	Mercon	Mercon	Mercon	DOT 3

Electrical

NOTE: On Air Bag Equipped Models, Refer To "Air Bag System Precautions" Located In The Front Of This Manual For System Disarming & Arming Procedures.

NOTE: Refer To "Computer Relearn Procedures" Located In The Front Of This Manual When Battery Power To The Computer Has Been Interrupted.

INDEX

PRECAUTIONS

Battery Ground Cable

Prior to service, disconnect battery ground cable and isolate as required.

Air Bag Systems

Refer to "Air Bag System Precautions" in the front of this manual for system disarming and arming procedures.

FUSE PANEL & FLASHER LOCATION

These vehicles use two fuse panels. The passenger compartment fuse panel is located below the instrument panel, to the left of the steering wheel. The engine compartment fuse panel is located on the lefthand side of the engine compartment.

The flasher unit is located at the relay panel behind the lefthand side of the instrument panel.

FUEL PUMP RELAY LOCATION

Fuel pump output is controlled by the Constant Control Relay Module (CCRM), located in the front lefthand corner of the engine compartment.

RELAY CENTER LOCATION

The relay panel is located behind the lefthand side of the instrument panel, above the instrument panel fuse panel.

STARTER
REPLACE
DOHC Engine

1. Remove air cleaner outlet tube, then raise and support vehicle.
2. Remove lower starter bolt and lower vehicle.
3. Remove remaining two starter bolts, then raise and support vehicle.
4. Remove starter motor from block mounting surface, then the connector mounting nut.
5. Remove starter.
6. Reverse procedure to install. **Torque** connector nut to 60 inch lbs., and mounting bolts to 15–20 ft. lbs.

SOHC Engine

1. Remove air duct from throttle body to resonance chamber.
2. Remove starter motor upper mount bolts, then raise and support vehicle.
3. Disconnect S terminal connector from starter solenoid. When disconnecting connector from S terminal, grasp connector and depress plastic tab to remove.
4. Remove B terminal mounting nut and disconnect cable from terminal.
5. Remove lower mounting bolt and starter motor.
6. Reverse procedure to install. **Torque** upper and lower mounting bolts to 18–20 ft. lbs., and B terminal mounting nut to 84–144 inch lbs.

COIL PACK
REPLACE

1. Disconnect ignition coil electrical connector.
2. Disconnect spark plug wires from ignition coil by squeezing locking tabs to release coil boot retainers.
3. Remove four ignition coil mounting bolts and noise filter condenser.
4. Save noise filter condenser for installation with new ignition coil.
5. Reverse procedure to install. **Torque** bolts to 40–60 inch lbs.

IGNITION LOCK
REPLACE

1. Remove driver's air bag sliding contact as outlined in "Passive Restraint Systems" chapter
2. Remove upper and lower steering column shrouds.
3. Remove turn signal switch, windshield

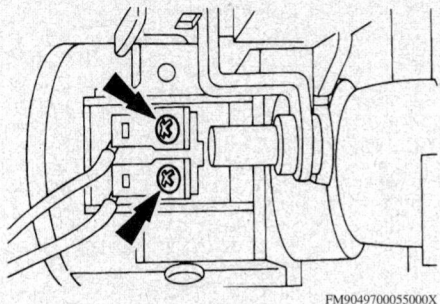

Fig. 1   Ignition key reminder switch screws

wiper switch and hazard/flasher switch from multi-function switch.
4. Disconnect electrical connectors.
5. Remove mounting screws and multi-function switch housing.
6. Disconnect ignition switch electrical connectors.
7. Remove ignition/shifter interlock cable mounting bracket bolt and position bracket and cable aside.
8. Groove head of ignition switch lock cylinder bracket bolts with hammer and chisel.
9. Remove ignition switch lock cylinder bracket bolts, ignition switch lock cylinder and bracket. Discard bolts.
10. Reverse procedure to install. Tighten lock cylinder bracket bolts until bolt heads break off.

IGNITION SWITCH
REPLACE

1. Remove upper and lower steering column shrouds.
2. Disconnect ignition switch electrical connector.
3. Remove ignition switch electrical connector cover screws.
4. Remove ignition key reminder switch screws, **Fig. 1.**
5. Remove ignition switch, **Fig. 2.**
6. Reverse procedure to install.

HEADLAMP SWITCH
REPLACE

1. Remove driver's air bag sliding contact as outlined in "Passive Restraint Systems" chapter
2. Remove upper and lower steering column shrouds.
3. Remove turn signal switch, windshield wiper switch and hazard/flasher switch from multi-function switch.
4. Disconnect electrical connectors.
5. Remove mounting screws and multi-function switch housing.
6. Reverse procedure to install.

FOG LAMP SWITCH
REPLACE

1. Remove driver's air bag sliding contact as outlined in "Passive Restraint Systems" chapter.
2. Remove upper and lower steering column shrouds.
3. Remove turn signal switch, windshield

wiper switch and hazard/flasher switch from multi-function switch.
4. Disconnect electrical connectors.
5. Remove mounting screws and multi-function switch housing.
6. Reverse procedure to install.

STOP LIGHT SWITCH
REPLACE

1. Disconnect stop lamp switch electrical connector.
2. Remove locknut and stop lamp switch.
3. Reverse procedure to install. Adjust stop lamp switch by turning switch until it contacts brake pedal, then tighten an additional half turn.

MULTI-FUNCTION SWITCH
REPLACE

1. Remove driver's air bag sliding contact as outlined in "Passive Restraint Systems" chapter.
2. Remove upper and lower steering column shrouds.
3. Remove turn signal switch, windshield wiper switch and hazard/flasher switch from multi-function switch.
4. Disconnect electrical connectors.
5. Remove mounting screws and multi-function switch housing.
6. Reverse procedure to install.

TURN SIGNAL SWITCH
REPLACE

1. Remove driver's air bag sliding contact as outlined in "Passive Restraint Systems" chapter.
2. Remove upper and lower steering column shrouds.
3. Remove turn signal switch, windshield wiper switch and hazard/flasher switch from multi-function switch.
4. Disconnect electrical connectors.
5. Remove mounting screws and multi-function switch housing.
6. Reverse procedure to install.

DIMMER SWITCH
REPLACE

Escort

1. Disconnect hood release cable, then remove four mounting screws and left-hand lower dash trim panel.
2. Disconnect electrical connector, squeeze two lock tabs and remove dimmer switch through front of trim panel.
3. Reverse procedure to install.

ZX2

1. Remove instrument panel upper finish panel insert and hood latch release handle mounting nut.
2. Remove mounting screw and instrument panel steering column cover.
3. Disconnect light switch rheostat resistor electrical connector.

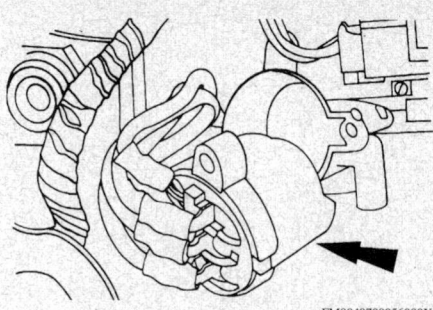

Fig. 2   Ignition switch replacement

4. Depress locking tabs and remove light switch from instrument panel steering column cover.
5. Reverse procedure to install.

STEERING WHEEL
REPLACE

1. Ensure front wheels are in straight-ahead position.
2. Remove two driver's air bag module mounting bolts, then disconnect air bag sliding contact and horn electrical connectors.
3. Carefully lift driver's air bag module away from steering wheel.
4. Remove steering wheel bolt.
5. Remove steering wheel using suitable steering wheel puller tool.
6. Reverse procedure to install, noting the following:
   a. **Torque** steering wheel mounting bolt to 34–46 ft. lbs.
   b. **Torque** driver's air bag module mounting bolts to 72–103 inch lbs.

INSTRUMENT CLUSTER
REPLACE

Escort

1. If equipped with tilt steering wheel, tilt steering wheel downward.
2. Remove hood latch release handle bolt.
3. Remove five mounting screws and instrument panel finish panel, **Fig. 3.**
4. Remove four mounting screws and pull cluster from instrument panel, then disconnect electrical connectors at back of instrument cluster.
5. Reverse procedure to install.

ZX2

1. Remove instrument panel upper finish panel insert, then the hood latch release handle mounting nut.
2. Remove mounting screw and instrument panel steering column cover.
3. Disconnect light switch rheostat resistor electrical connector.
4. Remove mounting screw and instrument panel upper finish panel.
5. Disconnect power mirrors switch electrical connector.
6. Remove four instrument cluster

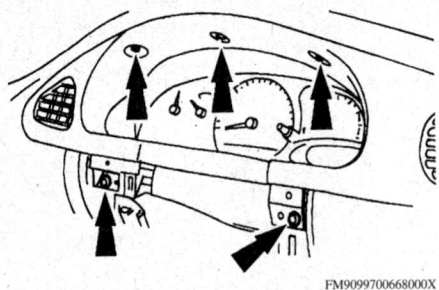

Fig. 3 Instrument panel finish panel replacement. Escort

FM9099700668000X

mounting screws, then disconnect three electrical connectors.
7. Remove instrument cluster.
8. Reverse procedure to install.

RADIO
REPLACE

1. Set temperature control switch to Cold position.
2. Disconnect heater temperature cable.
3. Pull out integrated control panel using radio removal tool No. T87P-19061-A, or equivalent, **Fig. 4.**
4. Disconnect radio antenna lead and electrical connectors.
5. Remove radio from instrument panel.
6. Reverse procedure to install.

WIPER MOTOR
REPLACE

Front

1. Ensure windshield wiper motor is in Off position and wiper pivot arms are parked in highest position on windshield.
2. Remove windshield wiper pivot arms.
3. Raise and support hood, then remove five center cowl top vent grille retainers and screws.
4. Remove two outer cowl top vent grille retainers and screws.
5. Lift clip up and off windshield wiper mounting arm and pivot shaft.
6. Slide windshield wiper mounting arm and pivot shaft off windshield wiper motor.
7. Disconnect windshield wiper motor electrical connector, then remove wiper motor bolts and wiper motor.
8. Reverse procedure to install. **Torque** wiper motor mounting bolts to 60–84 inch lbs.

Rear

1. Lift wiper arm mounting nut cover and remove nut, then pull wiper arm from pivot shaft.
2. Remove shaft seal from outer bushing mounting nut, then remove outer bushing mounting nut and outer bushing.
3. Remove liftgate trim panel as follows:
   a. Remove three push-in retainers and hi-mount stop lamp cover.
   b. Remove liftgate seaming welt from

along trim panel, then disconnect 10 retaining clips and remove trim panel.
   c. Remove cargo area lamp.
4. Disconnect wiper motor electrical connector, then remove three wiper motor mounting bolts and wiper motor.
5. Reverse procedure to install noting the following:
   a. **Torque** wiper motor mounting bolts to 60–84 inch lbs., and outer bushing mounting nut to 35–52 inch lbs.
   b. Turn wiper switch to ON position and allow pivot shaft to move through 3–4 cycles, then turn wiper switch off.
   c. Position wiper arm on pivot shaft so tip of blade is .79–.98 inch from rear window molding.
   d. **Torque** wiper arm mounting nut to 60–84 inch lbs.

WIPER SWITCH
REPLACE

1. Remove driver's air bag sliding contact as outlined in "Passive Restraint Systems" chapter.
2. Remove upper and lower steering column shrouds.
3. Remove turn signal switch, windshield wiper switch and hazard/flasher switch from multi-function switch.
4. Disconnect electrical connectors.
5. Remove mounting screws and multi-function switch housing.
6. Reverse procedure to install.

WIPER TRANSMISSION
REPLACE

Escort

1. With hood closed, remove seven screw covers from cowl grille screws.
2. Remove seven mounting screws and cowl grille.
3. Pry up four baffle retaining clips, then remove baffle trim piece.
4. Remove mounting screws, pivot shafts and wiper linkage.
5. Reverse procedure to install. **Torque** pivot shaft mounting screws to 60–84 inch lbs.

ZX2

1. Remove windshield wiper pivot arms, then raise and support hood.
2. Remove five center cowl top vent grille retainers and screws, then the two outer cowl top vent grille retainers, screws and washers.
3. Remove pushpins from left and right-hand air distribution flange baffles.
4. Remove windshield wiper mounting arm and pivot shaft retaining clip, then slide arm and shaft off windshield wiper motor.
5. Remove windshield wiper mounting arm and pivot shaft mounting screws, then pull arm and pivot shaft out through righthand air distribution flange baffle opening.

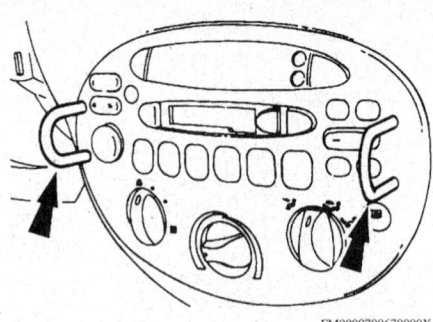

FM90997700670000X

Fig. 4 Radio replacement

6. Reverse procedure to install. **Torque** pivot shaft mounting screws to 60–84 inch lbs.

BLOWER MOTOR
REPLACE

Escort

1. Remove trim panel below glove compartment.
2. Remove wiring bracket and bolt, then disconnect blower motor electrical connector.
3. Remove three blower motor mounting bolts, then blower motor.
4. Remove retaining clip and blower wheel from motor.
5. Reverse procedure to install.

ZX2

1. Remove three mounting screw and blower motor.
2. Disconnect blower motor electrical connector.
3. Remove retainer and blower wheel.
4. Reverse procedure to install. **Torque** blower motor mounting screws to 21–23 inch lbs.

HEATER CORE
REPLACE

Escort

1. Disconnect heater hoses at bulkhead.
2. Disconnect mode selector and temperature control cables from cams and retaining clips.
3. Loosen heater to blower clamp, then remove three heater unit mounting nuts, **Fig. 5.**
4. Remove instrument panel as outlined in "Dash Panel Service" chapter.
5. Disconnect antenna lead from retaining clip and remove heater unit.
6. Remove insulator, then four brace capscrews and brace.
7. Disconnect vacuum control motor vacuum connector.
8. Remove windshield defroster nozzle connectors.
9. Loosen air conditioning evaporator outlet duct clamp screw.
10. Remove lower heater core housing mounting nut.

11. Remove mounting nuts and upper heater core housing.
12. Remove heater dash panel seal.
13. Remove screws and heater core cover.
14. Remove heater core.
15. Reverse procedure to install.

ZX2

1. Drain coolant into suitable container.
2. Remove air cleaner outlet tube and disconnect heater hoses from heater core.
3. Remove instrument panel as outlined in "Dash Panel Service" chapter.
4. Disconnect antenna lead from heater core housing, then the vacuum control motor vacuum connector.
5. Disconnect vacuum lines from air conditioning evaporator housing retainer.
6. Remove windshield defroster nozzle pushpins and mounting screws.
7. Loosen air conditioning evaporator outlet duct clamp screw, then remove lower heater core housing mounting nut.
8. Remove upper heater core housing mounting nuts and heater core housing.
9. Remove heater dash panel seal, mounting screws and heater core cover.
10. Remove heater core.
11. Reverse procedure to install.

EVAPORATOR CORE
REPLACE

Escort

Do not disassemble air conditioning evaporator housing. If the evaporator core must be replaced, replace the entire air conditioning evaporator as a unit.

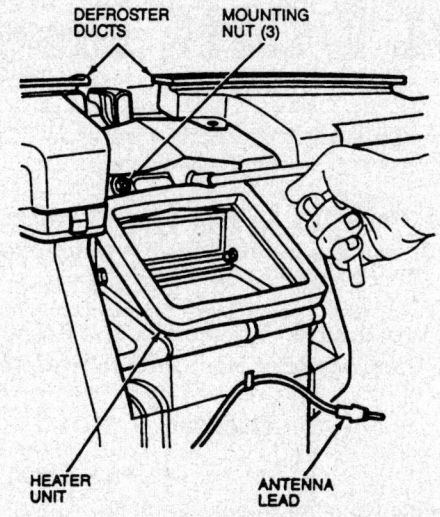

Fig. 5   Heater unit replacement. Escort

1. Recover refrigerant as outlined in "Air Conditioning" chapter.
2. Disconnect air conditioning vacuum line from evaporator housing.
3. Disconnect rear condenser to evaporator tube spring lock coupling.
4. Disconnect accumulator/drier spring lock coupling.
5. Remove instrument panel as outlined in "Dash Panel Service" chapter.
6. Loosen air conditioning evaporator outlet duct clamp bolt.
7. Disconnect air conditioning blower motor electrical connector.
8. Disconnect vacuum control motor vacuum connector.
9. Disconnect vacuum lines from air conditioning evaporator housing retainer.
10. Remove four mounting nuts and air conditioning evaporator housing.
11. Reverse procedure to install.

ZX2

1. Recover refrigerant as outlined in "Air Conditioning" chapter.
2. Disconnect air conditioning vacuum line, then remove spring lock coupling from rear condenser to evaporator line.
3. Remove suction line support clip mounting nuts.
4. Disconnect suction line spring lock coupling.
5. Remove instrument panel as outlined in "Dash Panel Service" chapter.
6. Remove pushpins, mounting screws and righthand windshield defroster nozzle.
7. Loosen air conditioning evaporator outlet duct clamp bolt, then disconnect air conditioning blower motor electrical connector.
8. Disconnect vacuum control motor vacuum connector and air conditioning evaporator housing retainer vacuum lines.
9. Remove nuts and air conditioning evaporator housing, then disconnect vacuum line.
10. Remove screws and air conditioning vacuum reservoir tank and bracket.
11. Remove two inlet duct door vacuum control motor mounting nuts.
12. Remove push nut and vacuum control motor, then the air inlet duct mounting screws.
13. Remove blower motor and heater blower motor switch resistor.
14. Remove evaporator tube and drain tube dash panel seals.
15. Remove evaporator core.
16. Reverse procedure to install.

2.0L DOHC Engine

NOTE: For procedures not outlined in this section, refer to "Contour, Cougar & Mystique"

NOTE: On Air Bag Equipped Models, Refer To "Air Bag System Precautions" Located In The Front Of This Manual For System Disarming & Arming Procedures.

NOTE: Refer To "Computer Relearn Procedures" Located In The Front Of This Manual When Battery Power To The Computer Has Been Interrupted.

INDEX

PRECAUTIONS

Air Bag Systems

Refer to "Air Bag System Precautions" in the front of this manual for system disarming and arming procedures.

Battery Ground Cable

Prior to service, disconnect battery ground cable and isolate as required.

Fuel System Pressure Relief

2001

1. Remove Schrader valve cap from end of fuel injection supply manifold, **Fig. 1.**
2. Attach fuel pressure gauge No. T80L-9974-B, or equivalent, to Schrader valve cap opening.
3. Open pressure gauge manual valve to relieve fuel system pressure.

2002-03

1. Remove fuel pump fuse.
2. Start engine and let it run until it stalls.
3. Crank engine two more times to remove fuel pressure.
4. Turn ignition switch to Off position and install fuel pump fuse.

COMPRESSION PRESSURE

1. Relieve fuel system pressure as outlined under "Precautions."
2. Remove spark plugs.
3. Install compression tester.
4. Install auxiliary starter switch in starting circuit.
5. With ignition switch Off, crank engine using auxiliary starter at least five times and record highest reading.
6. Repeat test on each cylinder, cranking engine same number of strokes per cylinder.
7. Install components as required, installing spark plugs into indicated cylinder.
8. Reset PCM fault memory as outlined under "Computer Relearn Procedures."

ENGINE

REPLACE

1. Remove hood.
2. Remove battery and battery tray.
3. Remove air cleaner.
4. Remove throttle return spring and constant control relay module bracket as an assembly.
5. Disconnect heated oxygen sensor.
6. Drain coolant into suitable container.
7. Recover refrigerant as outlined in "Air Conditioning" chapter.
8. Remove catalytic converter and splash shield.
9. Disconnect starter motor wiring and remove accessory drive belt.
10. Remove air conditioning compressor, then disconnect lower radiator hose and heater hose.
11. Disconnect power steering pressure line.
12. **On models equipped with automatic transaxle,** remove torque converter inspection cover and converter nuts.
13. **On all models,** remove front roll restrictor nuts and restrictor.
14. Remove axle shafts as outlined in "Front Wheel Drive Axles" chapter.
15. Disconnect transaxle cooler lines.
16. **On models equipped with automatic transaxle,** remove mounting bolts and transaxle cooler lines, then disconnect transaxle shift cable.
17. **On models equipped with manual transaxle,** disconnect transaxle control rod and support.
18. **On all models,** disconnect fuel charging wiring from transaxle internal wiring harness connector, turbine shaft speed sensor, transaxle range sensor and heated oxygen sensor connectors.
19. Remove radiator, fan shroud and fan motor as an assembly.
20. Disconnect accelerator cable and speed control actuator cable.
21. Disconnect power steering return hose and remove radiator coolant recovery reservoir.
22. Disconnect alternator wiring and vacuum lines.
23. Disconnect fuel charging wiring harness connectors, heater water hoses, vehicle speed sensor and ground strap.

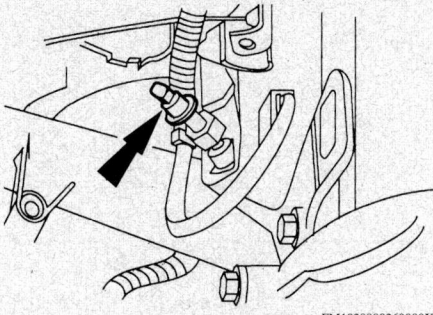

Fig. 1 Schrader valve cap location. 2001

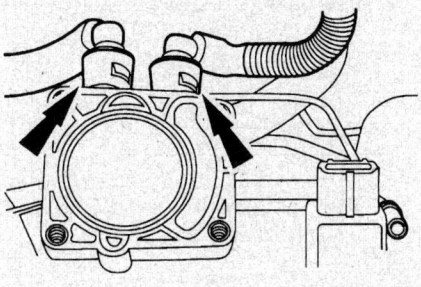

Fig. 2 Heater line bolt replacement

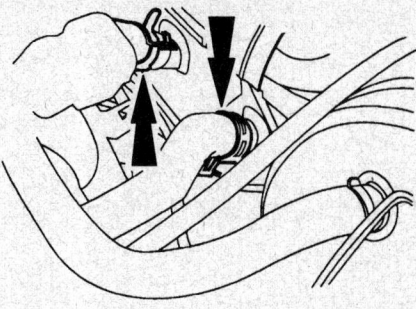

Fig. 3 Heater hose replacement

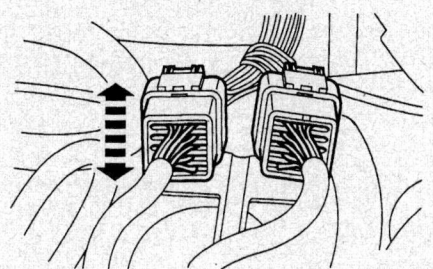

Fig. 4 Main engine control connector replacement

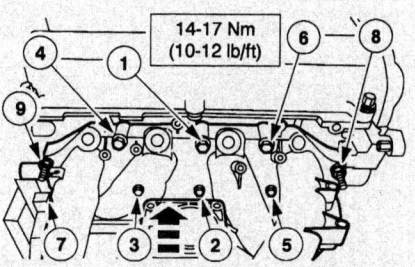

Fig. 5 Vacuum hose replacement

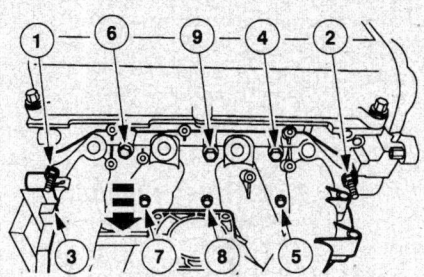

Fig. 6 Intake manifold replacement

24. Disconnect fuel line and support engine with suitable lifting device.
25. Remove remaining engine mount nuts and bolts.
26. Remove engine and transaxle as an assembly with engine lifting brackets tool No. T70P-6000, or equivalent, and engine lift.
27. Reverse procedure to install.

INTAKE MANIFOLD
REPLACE

1. Remove air cleaner outlet tube and disconnect throttle position sensor wiring.
2. Remove throttle body from intake manifold.
3. Raise and support vehicle.
4. Drain coolant into suitable container.
5. Remove heater line bolt, **Fig. 2.**
6. Lower vehicle.
7. Disconnect heater hoses from heater core, **Fig. 3.**
8. Disconnect main engine control sensor wiring and remove connectors from mounting bracket, **Fig. 4.**
9. Disconnect vacuum supply hoses from intake manifold, **Fig. 5.**
10. Disconnect crankcase ventilation hose from valve cover, then remove fuel charging wiring and drive belt.
11. Remove alternator mounting bolt and position alternator aside.
12. Disconnect fuel line, then remove intake manifold mounting bolts and nuts in sequence, **Fig. 6.**
13. Reverse procedure to install. **Torque** intake manifold bolts to 12–15 ft. lbs., in sequence, **Fig. 7.**

Fig. 7 Intake manifold tightening sequence

14-17 Nm (10-12 lb/ft)

EXHAUST MANIFOLD
REPLACE

1. Disconnect fan motor wiring and remove fan shroud.
2. Raise and support vehicle.
3. Disconnect HO2S wiring connector.
4. Remove catalytic converter from exhaust manifold and lower vehicle.
5. Remove oil dipstick tube bracket bolt.
6. Remove exhaust manifold heat shield.
7. Remove exhaust manifold mounting bolts and studs in sequence, **Fig. 8.**
8. Reverse procedure to install. **Torque** exhaust manifold to 10–12 ft. lbs., in sequence, **Fig. 9.**

FUEL INJECTION SUPPLY MANIFOLD
REPLACE

1. Disconnect spring lock coupling with tool Nos. D87L-9280-A or D87L-9280-B, or equivalent.
2. Remove air cleaner outlet tube and throttle body.
3. Disconnect fuel injector electrical connectors.

4. Disconnect fuel pressure sensor vacuum line and electrical connector.
5. Disconnect fuel temperature sensor wiring connector, then remove fuel charging wiring and position aside, **Fig. 10.**
6. Disconnect vacuum line and wiring from fuel pressure sensor.
7. Disconnect fuel temperature sensor wiring connector.
8. Remove fuel charging wiring.
9. Remove mounting bolts and fuel injection supply manifold.
10. Reverse procedure to install.

CYLINDER HEAD
REPLACE

1. Remove air cleaner outlet tube.
2. Remove timing belt as outlined under "Timing Belt, Replace."
3. Remove valve cover and camshaft sprockets.
4. Remove oil control solenoid flange bolts and flange, **Fig. 11.**
5. Remove camshaft journal caps in sequence, **Fig. 12.**
6. Remove camshafts, oil control sensor and bushing.
7. Remove thermostat housing.
8. Remove coolant recovery reservoir.
9. Relieve fuel system pressure as outlined under "Precautions."
10. Disconnect fuel line.
11. Remove power steering pump and bracket.
12. Remove alternator.
13. Remove oil dipstick and tube.
14. Disconnect speed control cables, accelerator cables, main engine electrical connectors and crankshaft position sensor electrical connector.
15. Raise and support vehicle.

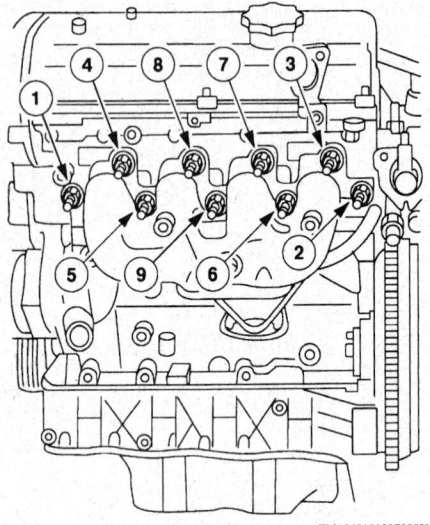

Fig. 8 Exhaust manifold replacement

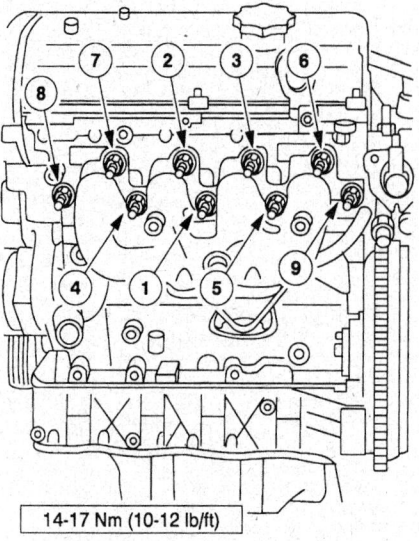

14-17 Nm (10-12 lb/ft)

Fig. 9 Exhaust manifold tightening sequence

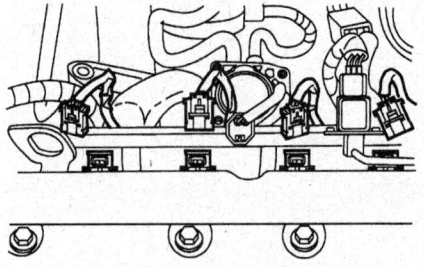

Fig. 10 Fuel charging wiring replacement

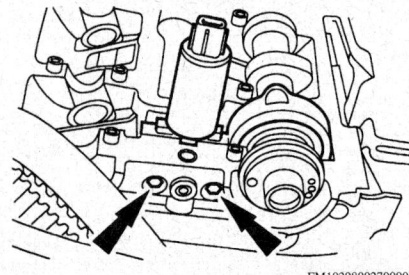

Fig. 11 Oil control solenoid flange replacement

16. Remove mounting bolts and splash shield.
17. Lower vehicle.
18. Remove bolts, cylinder head and gasket.
19. Reverse procedure to install, noting the following:
    a. Do not use abrasive grinding discs to remove gasket material, use only plastic scrapers. Do not gouge or scratch aluminum sealing surface.
    b. Install new gasket and bolts. **Head bolts are torque to yield design and cannot be reused.**
    c. **Torque** cylinder heads bolts to 15 ft. lbs., in sequence, **Fig. 13.**
    d. **Torque** head bolts to 30 ft. lbs., in sequence.
    e. Tighten bolts an additional 105°.
    f. Ensure valve clearance as outlined under "Valve Clearance Specifications."
    g. Install oil control solenoid bushing and flange on exhaust camshaft, **Fig. 14.**
    h. **Torque** camshaft journal caps bolts to 10–12 ft. lbs., in sequence, **Fig. 15.**

VALVE COVER

REPLACE

1. Disconnect crankcase ventilation hose from fitting on valve cover.

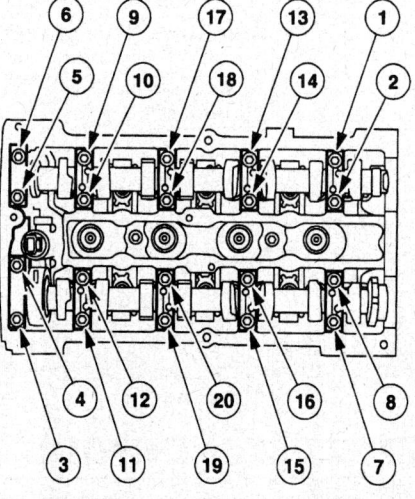

Fig. 12 Camshaft loosening sequence

2. Disconnect oil control solenoid electrical connector and remove appearance cover.
3. Position accelerator cable and speed control cable aside.
4. Remove spark plug wires and upper timing belt cover, **Fig. 16.**
5. Remove mounting bolts and valve cover, **Fig. 17.**
6. Reverse procedure to install.

TIMING BELT COVER

REPLACE

1. Remove mounting bolts and upper timing belt cover, **Fig. 16.**
2. Loosen water pump pulley bolts.
3. Remove drive belt.
4. Remove idler pulley.
5. Remove pulley mounting bolts and water pump, **Fig. 18.**
6. Raise and support vehicle.

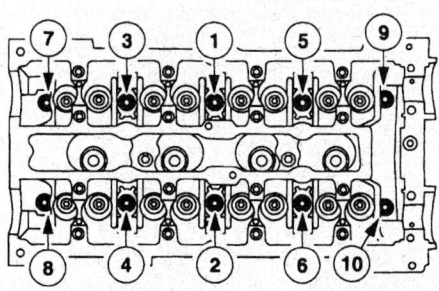

Fig. 13 Cylinder head bolt tightening sequence

7. Remove mounting bolts and middle timing belt cover, **Fig. 19.**
8. Remove crankshaft pulley.
9. Remove mounting bolts and lower timing cover, **Fig. 20.**
10. Reverse procedure to install.

TIMING BELT

REPLACE

1. Remove catalytic converter.
2. Remove spark plugs.
3. Turn crankshaft clockwise until cylinder No. 1 reaches TDC, **Fig. 21.**
4. Remove bolt and instal crankshaft TDC timing peg tool No. T97P-6000-A, or equivalent, **Fig. 22.**
5. Remove mounting bolts and timing belt upper cover.
6. Raise and support front of vehicle with suitable jack stands.
7. Remove splash shield.
8. Loosen water pump pulley bolts.
9. Remove accessory drive belt.
10. Remove accessory drive belt idler pulley.
11. Remove water pump pulley.
12. Remove center timing belt cover.
13. Remove crankshaft pulley.
14. Remove timing belt lower cover.
15. Lower vehicle.
16. Disconnect PCV hose from valve cover fitting.
17. Disconnect oil control solenoid electrical connector.
18. Remove appearance cover.
19. Position accelerator control and speed control cables aside.
20. Remove ignition wires and brackets.
21. Remove valve cover and discard gasket.
22. Align camshafts using camshaft alignment tool No. T94P-6256-CH, or

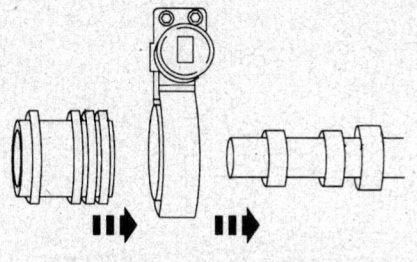

Fig. 14 Oil control solenoid bushing & flange installation

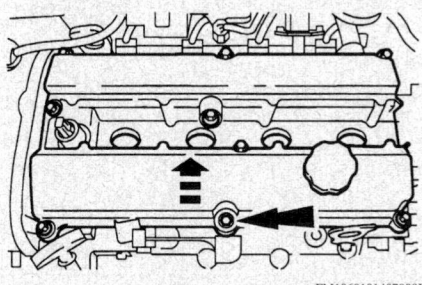

Fig. 17 Valve cover replacement

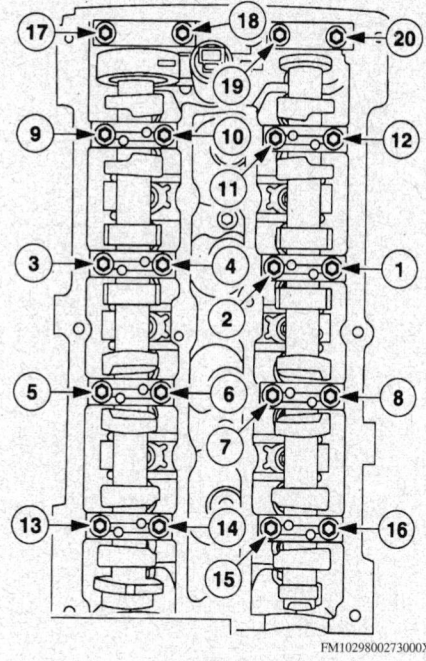

Fig. 15 Camshaft tightening sequence

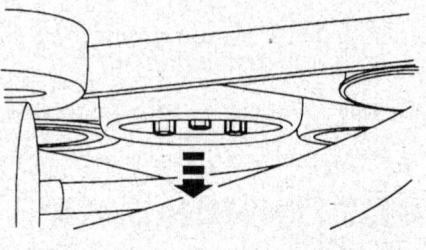

Fig. 18 Water pump pulley bolt replacement

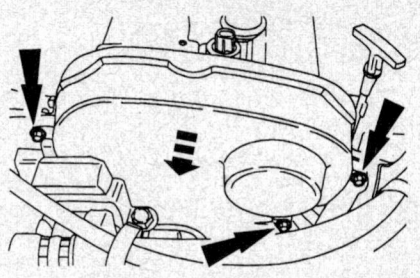

Fig. 16 Upper timing belt cover replacement

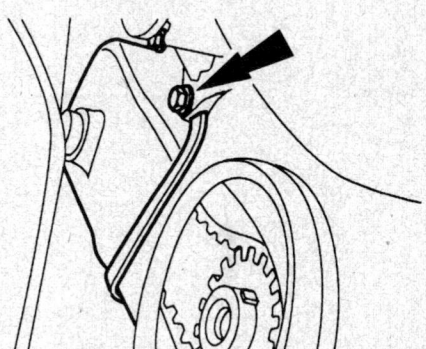

Fig. 19 Middle timing belt cover replacement

equivalent. It may be required to turn exhaust camshaft clockwise to install alignment tool, **Fig. 23.**
23. Loosen timing belt tensioner pulley bolt.
24. Release belt tension by disconnecting tensioner tab from timing cover backplate.
25. Carefully slide timing belt off camshaft and crankshaft sprockets.
26. Ensure camshafts are properly aligned using camshaft alignment tool.
27. Turn crankshaft clockwise against TDC timing peg.
28. Engage timing belt tensioner tab into upper timing cover backplate.
29. With timing belt tensioner bolt backed out four full turns, position tensioner so location tab is at approximately four o'clock position, **Fig. 24.**
30. Line up hex key slot in tensioner adjusting washer with pointer which is located behind pulley.
31. Starting at crankshaft and working counterclockwise, install new timing belt.
32. Turn timing belt tensioner locating tab counterclockwise and insert locating tab into slot in rear timing cover, **Fig. 25.**
33. Position hex key slot in tensioner adjusting washer to 4 o'clock position.
34. Tighten tensioner enough to seat tensioner firmly against rear timing belt cover, but still loose enough to allow tensioner adjusting washer to be turned with hex wrench.
35. Turn adjusting washer counterclockwise using suitable hex wrench until notch in pointer is centered over index line on locating tab, **Fig. 26.** During adjustment pointer will move in clockwise direction.
36. While holding adjusting washer in position, **torque** tensioner mounting bolt to 16–20 ft. lbs, **Fig. 27.**

37. After tightening tensioner bolt, ensure tensioner pointer is still aligned with index line. If not, repeat previous three steps.
38. Remove TDC peg and install bolt.
39. Remove camshaft alignment tool.
40. Reverse procedure to install, noting the following:
   a. Install accessory drive belts.
   b. Install new valve cover gasket and apply .1 inch bead of suitable silicone rubber sealer in two places where front camshaft bearing cap meets cylinder head.

CAMSHAFT
REPLACE
1. Remove timing belt as outlined under "Timing Belt, Replace."
2. Remove valve cover and camshaft sprockets.
3. Remove oil control solenoid flange bolts and flange, **Fig. 11.**
4. Remove camshaft journal caps in sequence, **Fig. 12.**
5. Remove camshafts, oil control sensor and bushing.
6. Reverse procedure to install, noting the following:

a. Ensure valve clearance as outlined under "Valve Clearance Specifications."
b. Install oil control solenoid bushing and flange on exhaust camshaft, **Fig. 14.**
c. **Torque** camshaft journal caps bolts to 10–12 ft. lbs., in sequence, **Fig. 15.**

CRANKSHAFT SEAL
REPLACE
1. Remove timing belt as outlined under "Timing Belt, Replace."
2. Remove crankshaft sprocket and timing belt guide washer.
3. Remove front seal from oil pump using seal remover tool No. T92C-6700-CH, or equivalent. **Do not damage crankshaft surface.**
4. Reverse procedure to install using oil pump replacer toll No. T81P-6700-A, or equivalent.

CRANKSHAFT REAR OIL SEAL
REPLACE
1. Remove transaxle as outlined in **MOTOR's** "Domestic Transmission Manual, In-Vehicle Service."
2. Remove seal using seal remover tool No. T92C-6700-CH, or equivalent. **Do not damage cranking sealing surface.**
3. Inspect crankshaft rear oil seal area, then coat seal and seal area with suitable engine oil.

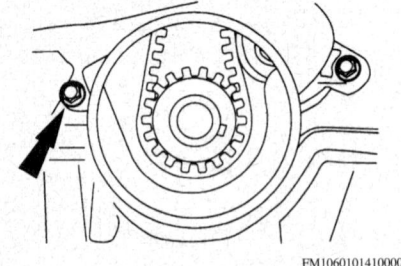

Fig. 20   Lower timing chain cover replacement

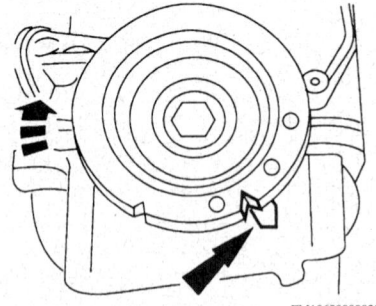

Fig. 21   Crankshaft timing marks

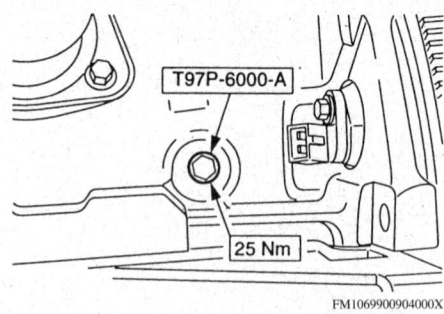

Fig. 22   Timing peg installation

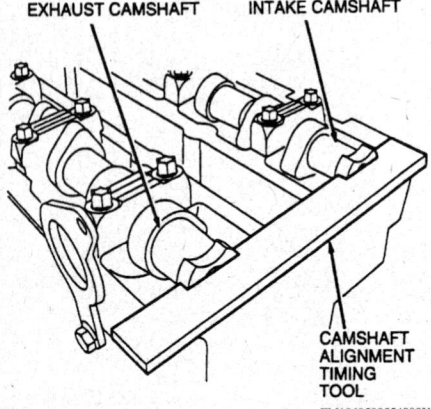

Fig. 23   Camshaft alignment

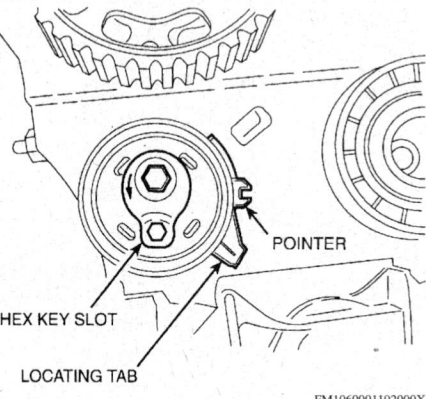

Fig. 24   Position timing belt tensioner

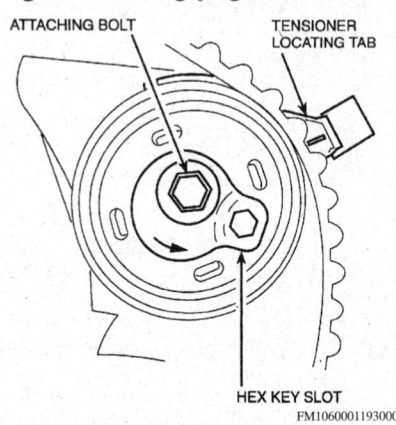

Fig. 25   Position timing belt tensioner adjusting washer

4. Ensure edges of crankshaft rear oil seal are not rolled over.
5. Install rear oil seal using crankshaft rear seal pilot tool No. T88P-6701-B2 and crankshaft rear seal replacer tool No. T88P-6701-B1, or equivalents.

OIL PAN
REPLACE

1. Raise and support vehicle, then drain engine oil into suitable container.
2. Remove catalytic convertor.
3. Remove seventeen mounting bolts evenly and oil pan.
4. Reverse procedure to install, noting the following:
   a. Clean and inspect mounting faces of oil pan and cylinder block.
   b. Apply .1 inch continuous bead of silicone gasket and sealant F6AZ-19562-AA, or equivalent, to oil pan. **Install oil pan within four minutes after sealer has been applied.**
   c. **Torque** oil pan bolts in sequence to 15–22 ft. lbs., **Fig. 28.**

OIL PUMP SERVICE

Oil Pump Screen Cover & Tube

1. Raise and support vehicle, then drain engine oil into suitable container.
2. Remove catalytic convertor.
3. Remove seventeen mounting bolts evenly and oil pan.

4. Remove oil pump screen bolts and discard oil pump inlet tube.
5. Reverse procedure to install.

BELT TENSION DATA

Automatic drive belt tensioners are spring loaded devices which set and maintain drive belt tension. The drive belt should not require tension adjustment for the life to the belt. Automatic drive belt tensioners have drive belt wear indicator marks. If the indicator mark is not approximately in the middle between MIN and MAX tabs on the engine front cover, the drive belt is worn or an incorrect drive belt is installed.

SERPENTINE DRIVE BELT

Refer to **Fig. 29,** for serpentine drive belt routing.

COOLING SYSTEM BLEED

1. Select maximum heater temperature and blower motor speed settings. Position control to discharge air through vents.
2. Start engine and allow to idle. While engine is idling, feel for hot air at vents.
3. If air discharge remains cool and engine coolant temperature gauge does not move, coolant level is low and must be filled. Stop engine, allow to cool and fill coolant.
4. Start engine and allow to idle until normal operating temperature is reached.

Hot air should blow from vents and engine temperature gauge should maintain stabilized reading in NORMAL range and upper radiator hose should feel hot to touch.

THERMOSTAT
REPLACE

1. Drain coolant into suitable container.
2. Disconnect camshaft position sensor electrical connector, **Fig. 30.**
3. Remove mounting bolts and position water hose connection aside, **Fig. 31.**
4. Remove water thermostat and seal from housing, **Fig. 32.**
5. Reverse procedure to install.

RADIATOR
REPLACE

1. Raise and support vehicle.
2. Drain radiator coolant into suitable container.
3. Remove mounting bolts and righthand splash shield, **Fig. 33.**
4. Disconnect lower radiator hose and lower oil cooler outlet tube, **Fig. 34.**
5. Remove two oil cooler tube bracket bolts.
6. Lower vehicle.
7. Disconnect connector at fan motor, **Fig. 35.**
8. Remove radiator cap and disconnect overflow hose.
9. Remove four support bracket mounting bolts and radiator, **Fig. 36.**
10. Remove radiator and shroud.
11. Remove fan motor, blade and shroud, **Fig. 37.**

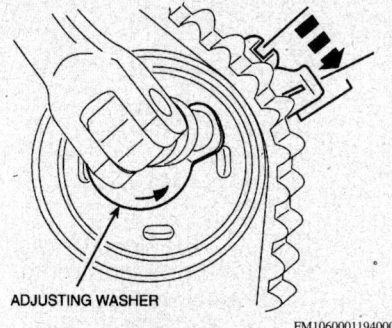

Fig. 26 Aligning timing belt tensioner

FM1060001194000X

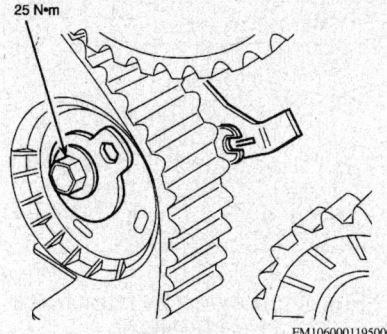

Fig. 27 Tightening timing belt tensioner bolt

FM1060001195000X

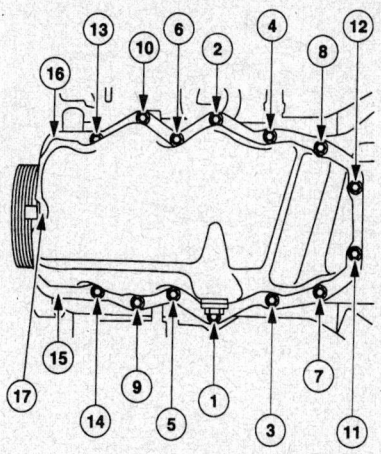

FM1029800274000X

Fig. 28 Oil pan tightening sequence

Item	Description
1	Generator
2	Drive Belt Idler Pulley
3	Power Steering Pump Pulley
4	Water Pump Pulley
5	Drive Belt Tensioner
6	A/C Compressor
7	Crankshaft
8	Drive Belt Idler Pulley
9	Accessory Drive Belt

FM1139800548000X

Fig. 29 Serpentine drive belt routing

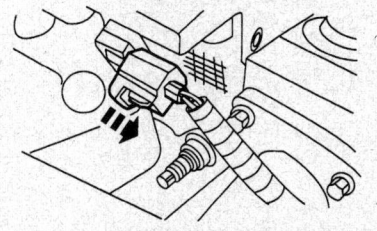

Fig. 30 Camshaft position sensor connector replacement

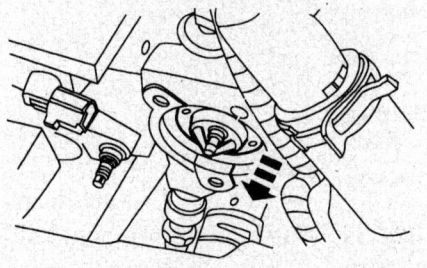

FM1060101413000X

Fig. 32 Water thermostat replacement

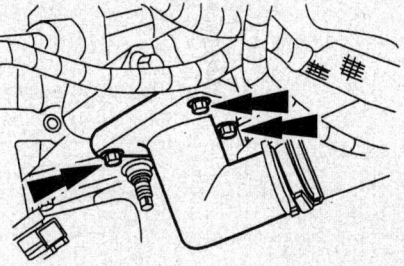

FM1060101412000X

Fig. 31 Water hose replacement

12. Reverse procedure to install. Fill cooling system and bleed as outlined under "Cooling System Bleed."

WATER PUMP

REPLACE

1. Raise and support vehicle.
2. Drain radiator into suitable container.
3. Remove mounting bolts and splash shield.
4. Loosen water pump pulley mounting bolts and drive belt.
5. Remove mounting bolts and position air conditioning compressor aside, **Fig. 38**.
6. Remove water pump from middle timing belt cover, **Fig. 39**.
7. Reverse procedure to install.

FUEL PUMP

REPLACE

1. Remove rear seat cushion and disconnect fuel pump electrical connector.
2. Remove four mounting screws and fuel pump access cover.
3. Remove fuel line clips and disconnect top fuel pump lines.

4. Remove locking retainer ring and fuel pump.
5. Reverse procedure to install.

FUEL FILTER

REPLACE

1. Place suitable container under fuel filter.
2. Loosen fuel filter bracket clamp.
3. Remove fuel line clips.
4. Disconnect fuel tubes and remove fuel filter, **Fig. 40**.
5. Reverse procedure to install.

TECHNICAL SERVICE BULLETINS

Idle Vibration

2001-02

1. Shift transaxle to Neutral position and apply parking brake.
2. Remove battery and tray.
3. Support engine with three-bar engine

support tool No. 303-D063 and lifting brackets tools No. 303-050, or equivalents.
4. Raise and support vehicle.
5. Remove mounting bolts and rear lower crossmember.
6. Remove two front mounting bolts, two rear mounting bolts, then two front and four rear engine mounts Nos. 1 and 2 nuts.
7. Remove engine support crossmember running on engine's front to rear.
8. **On models built before Dec. 3, 2001,** discard two engine mount No. 1 flat washers.
9. **On models built before July 15, 2002,** slot engine mount No. 1 holes approximately .25 inch in front of rear direction.
10. **On all models,** loosen rear lower engine mount (No. 1) center bolt.
11. Loosen front lower engine mount (No. 2) center bolt.
12. Install front mounting point of belly band with original bolts. Apply 2–3 drops of suitable threadlocker to bolts.
13. Install rear mounting point with original nuts.
14. **Torque** mounting bolts and nuts to 47–65 ft. lbs.
15. Install engine mounts Nos. 1 and 2 nuts. **Do not tighten now.**
16. Lower vehicle.
17. Remove engine mount No. 3 and damper.
18. **On models built before June 15, 2002,** proceed as follows:
    a. Raise and support vehicle.

Fig. 33 Splash shield replacement

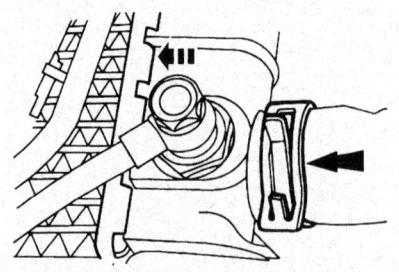

Fig. 34 Lower radiator hose replacement

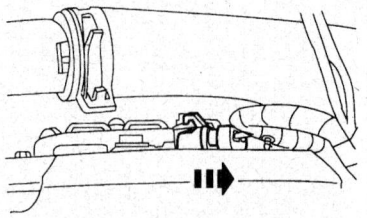

Fig. 35 Fan motor connector replacement

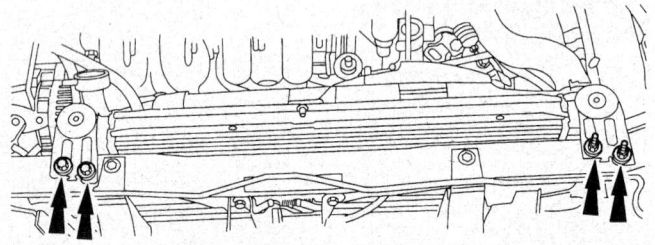

Fig. 36 Radiator support bracket bolt replacement

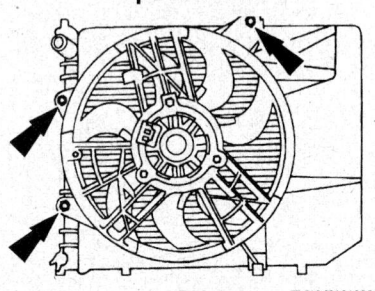

Fig. 37 Fan motor, blade & shroud replacement

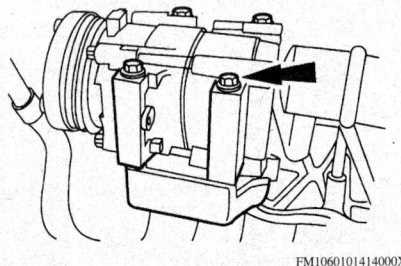

Fig. 38 Air conditioning compressor replacement

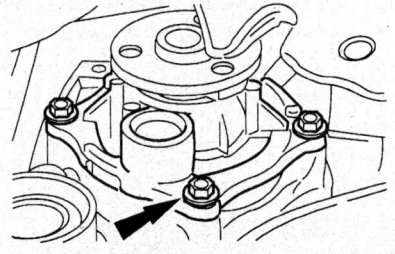

Fig. 39 Water pump replacement

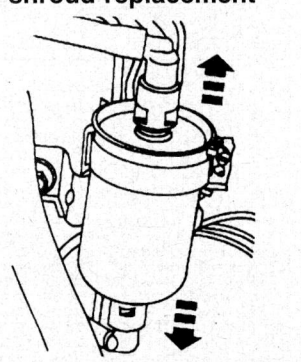

Fig. 40 Fuel filter replacement

b. Remove power steering bracket to frame bolt.
c. Lower vehicle.
d. Remove power steering/air conditioning bracket nut and power steering bracket bolt, then position bracket aside.
e. Raise engine using three-bar support.
f. Remove mounting bolt and engine mount bracket.
g. Install new bracket (part No. 2S4Z-6028-AA) and **torque** bolt to 12–17 ft. lbs.
h. Lower engine.
i. Position lines, then **torque** power steering/air condition bracket nuts and power steering bracket to 71–89 inch lbs.
j. Raise vehicle.
k. **Torque** power steering to frame bolt to 71–89 inch lbs.
19. Install original No. 3 engine mount, Leave center through-bolt loose.
20. **On all models,** remove three-bar engine support tool and lifting brackets.
21. Install battery and tray.
22. **On models equipped with manual transaxle,** proceed as follows:
a. Start engine.
b. Rev engine.

c. Allow vehicle to move slightly forward and reverse in normal manner.
d. Allow engine to assume neutral position on mounts.
e. Turn engine off.
f. Allow engine to establish neutral position.
23. **On models equipped with automatic transaxle,** proceed as follows:
a. Start engine.
b. Engage transaxle from Neutral to Reverse, Reverse to Neutral, Neutral to Drive and Drive to Neutral positions.
c. Allow vehicle to move slightly forward and reverse in normal manner.
d. Turn engine off.
e. Allow engine to establish neutral position.
24. **On all models, torque** engine mount No. 3 center through-bolt to 50–68 ft. lbs.
25. Raise and support vehicle.
26. **Torque** engine mount Nos. 1 and 2 nuts to 26–38 ft. lbs.
27. **Torque** front engine mount (No. 2) center bolt to 50–68 ft. lbs.
28. **On models equipped with automatic transaxle,** ensure rear engine mount (No. 1) center bolt is at bottom

of slot using suitable pry bar.
29. **On all models, torque** rear engine mount (No. 1) center bolt to 50–68 ft. lbs.
30. **On models built before June 25, 2001,** install two new spacers (part No. 2S4Z-5L0200-AA) between lower crossmember and frame.
31. **On all models,** install rear lower crossmember and **torque** mounting bolts to 70–95 ft. lbs.

2003

On some of these models there may be an idle vibration.

This condition may be caused by engine mounting system.

To correct this condition, proceed as follows:
1. Raise and support vehicle.
2. Loosen but do not remove engine/transaxle mount bolts and nuts.
3. Lower vehicle.
4. Move vehicle back and forward 2–4 feet.
5. Raise and support vehicle.
6. Tighten mount bolts and nuts.
7. Lower vehicle.

TIGHTENING SPECIFICATIONS

Year	Component	Torque/Ft. Lbs.
2001–03	Accelerator & Speed Control Bracket	72–84①
	Air Conditioning Compressor	15–22
	Air Conditioning Line Bracket	15–18
	Alternator	34
	Appearance Cover	48–84①
	Camshaft	⑥
	Camshaft Position Sensor	48–84①
	Catalytic Converter Bracket	15–20
	Catalytic Converter To Exhaust Mounting	30–40
	Catalytic Converter To Oil Pan Bracket	30–40
	Constant Control Relay Module	72–96①
	Crankshaft Pulley	81–89
	Cylinder Head	②
	Exhaust Camshaft Sprocket, Bolt	88
	Exhaust Camshaft Sprocket, Plug	26–30
	Exhaust Manifold Heat Shield	72–96①
	Exhaust Manifold	⑤
	Flywheel	54–67
	Front Roll Restrictor, Nut	48–65
	Front Roll Restrictor, Bolt	50–69
	Front Engine Support Isolator	50–69
	Ignition Coil	40–61①
	Ignition Coil Bracket	14–16
	Intake Camshaft Sprocket	48–53
	Intake Manifold	④
	Engine Mount	50–69
	Oil Control Solenoid Flange	72–96①
	Oil Dipstick Tube	72–96①
	Oil Pan	③
	Oil Pan Drain Plug	29–41
	Oil Pump	84–108①
	Oil Pump Screen Cover & Tube	72–96①
	Oil Pressure Sensor Switch	19
	Power Steering Pump	30–41
	Rear Engine Support Isolator	50–69
	Rear Roll Restrictor	28–38
	Splash Shield	72–96①
	Timing Belt Tensioner	18
	Valve Cover	60–72①
	Water Pump	16

① — Inch Lbs.
② — Refer to "Cylinder Head, Replace" for tightening specifications and sequence.
③ — Refer to "Oil Pan, Replace" for tightening specifications and sequence.
④ — Refer to "Intake Manifold, Replace" for tightening specifications and sequence.
⑤ — Refer to "Exhaust Manifold, Replace" for tightening specifications and sequence.
⑥ — Refer to "Camshaft, Replace" for tightening specifications and sequence.

2.0L SOHC Engine

NOTE: On Air Bag Equipped Models, Refer To "Air Bag System Precautions" Located In The Front Of This Manual For System Disarming & Arming Procedures.

NOTE: Refer To "Computer Relearn Procedures" Located In The Front Of This Manual When Battery Power To The Computer Has Been Interrupted.

INDEX

PRECAUTIONS

Air Bag Systems

Refer to "Air Bag System Precautions" in the front of this manual for system disarming and arming procedures.

Battery Ground Cable

Prior to service, disconnect battery ground cable and isolate as required.

Fuel System Pressure Relief

1. Remove Schrader valve cap at end of fuel injection supply manifold, **Fig. 1.**
2. Attach fuel pressure gauge No. T80L-9974-B, or equivalent.
3. Open pressure gauge manual valve to relieve fuel system pressure.

COMPRESSION PRESSURE

1. Relieve fuel system pressure as outlined under "Precautions."
2. Remove spark plugs.
3. Install compression tester.
4. Install auxiliary starter switch in starting circuit.
5. With ignition switch Off, crank engine using auxiliary starter at least five times and record highest reading.
6. Repeat test on each cylinder, cranking engine same number of strokes per cylinder.
7. Install components as required, installing spark plugs into indicated cylinder.
8. Reset PCM fault memory as outlined under "Computer Relearn Procedures."

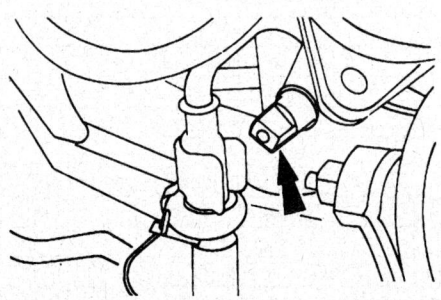

FM1029700252000X

Fig. 1 Schrader valve cap location

ENGINE

REPLACE

1. Remove hood.
2. Recover refrigerant as outlined in "Air Conditioning" chapter.
3. Remove battery and battery tray.
4. Remove air cleaner outlet tube.
5. Disconnect vacuum hoses from Exhaust Gas Recirculation (EGR) valve, brake booster, throttle body, fuel pressure regulator and intake manifold, **Fig. 2.**
6. Disconnect two vacuum lines, remove two mounting bolts and position vacuum tree aside, **Fig. 3.**
7. Disconnect speed control, accelerator and throttle valve control actuating cables from throttle control lever.
8. Disconnect shift cable from bracket and set aside.
9. Disconnect two main engine/fuel charging wiring connectors.
10. Disconnect electrical connector, then remove Constant Control Relay Module (CCRM) and bracket.
11. Disconnect EGR back pressure transducer electrical connector and two vacuum hoses, then remove transducer.

12. Disconnect transaxle range sensor electrical and transaxle solenoid connectors, then remove two mounting bolts, CCRM and bracket.
13. Disconnect transaxle range sensor, transaxle solenoid and turbine speed connectors.
14. Disconnect vehicle speed sensor electrical connector.
15. Disconnect upstream Heated Oxygen Sensor (HO2S) electrical connector mounted on cooling fan shroud.
16. Disconnect downstream HO2S electrical connector.
17. Remove mounting screw and position ground strap aside.
18. Disconnect engine cooling fan electrical connector.
19. Remove three mounting bolts and position power steering pressure hose aside.
20. Disconnect fuel return line from fuel injection supply manifold using disconnect tool No. D87L-9280-B (½ inch), or equivalent.
21. Remove exhaust manifold heat shield.
22. Remove four exhaust manifold to catalytic converter nuts.
23. Remove upper starter bolt and position bracket aside.
24. Disconnect transaxle fluid cooler lines from transaxle.
25. Remove air conditioning line bracket bolt.
26. Disconnect air conditioning manifold and tube spring lock coupling at accumulator/drier.
27. Disconnect air conditioning manifold and tube spring lock coupling at condenser.
28. Remove accessory drive belt and automatic tensioner.
29. Drain power steering reservoir fluid into suitable container.
30. Position drain pan under power steering reservoir and disconnect power

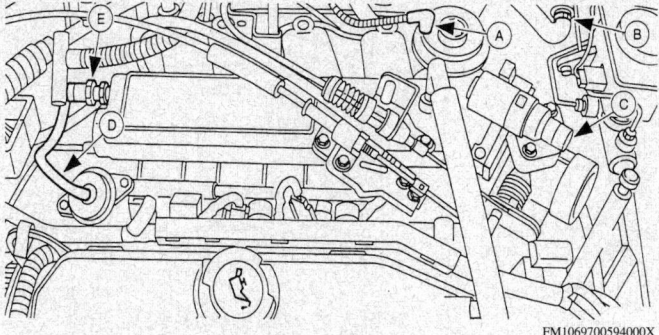

Fig. 2 Vacuum hose locations (Part 1 of 2)

FM1069700594000X

A- EGR VALVE
B- BRAKE BOOSTER
C- THROTTLE BODY
D- FUEL PRESSURE REGULATOR
E- INTAKE MANIFOLD

ARM66FM000000174

Fig. 2 Vacuum hose locations (Part 2 of 2)

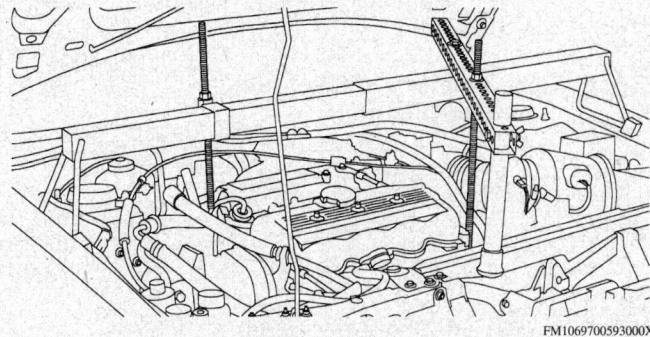

FM1069700593000X

Fig. 4 Engine support tool installation

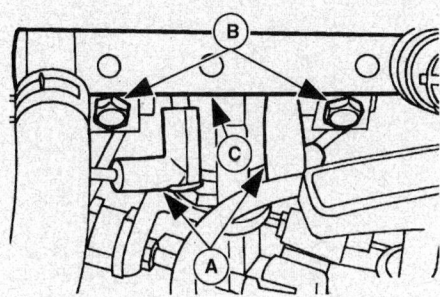

A- VACUUM LINES
B- BOLTS
C- VACUUM TREE

ARM66FM000000175

Fig. 3 Vacuum tree

steering lines.
31. Raise and support vehicle.
32. Remove lug nuts and front wheel and tire assemblies.
33. Remove lefthand splash shield.
34. Remove righthand splash shield.
35. Drain coolant and engine oil into suitable containers.
36. Remove four bolts and crossmember.
37. Remove mounting bolts and catalytic converter.
38. Remove front wheel driveshafts and joints.
39. Disconnect S-terminal wire, then the B-terminal nut and cable from starter solenoid.
40. Disconnect oil pressure switch electrical connector.
41. Disconnect air conditioning compressor electrical connector.
42. Remove four mounting bolts, air conditioning compressor and manifold lines.
43. Remove hose clamp and disconnect lower radiator hose from radiator.
44. Remove mounting bolt and camshaft pulley.
45. Lower vehicle.
46. Loosen heater hose clamp at water outlet connection and disconnect heater hose.
47. Loosen heater hose clamp at bulkhead and remove heater hose.
48. Disconnect upper radiator hose and remove radiator.
49. Disconnect alternator electrical connectors.

50. Disconnect battery positive cable from alternator.
51. Attach engine lifting bracket tool No. T70P-6000, or equivalent, on lefthand rear side of cylinder head.
52. Install three-bar engine support tool No. D88L-6000-A, or equivalent, **Fig. 4.**
53. Raise and support vehicle.
54. Remove transaxle support crossmember.
55. Lower vehicle.
56. Remove four nuts and transaxle mount.
57. Remove righthand engine support insulator through bolt.
58. Attach suitable lifting eye on transaxle and use for balance, if required.
59. Attach suitable lifting device, then remove engine and transaxle.
60. Separate transaxle from engine.
61. Mount engine on stand and remove lifting device.
62. Reverse procedure to install.

INTAKE MANIFOLD
REPLACE

1. Drain coolant system into suitable container.
2. Remove air cleaner outlet tube.
3. Disconnect vacuum hoses, **Fig. 2.**
4. Disconnect speed control and accelerator cables, then the throttle control lever, **Fig. 5.**
5. Remove speed control cable bracket bolt, **Fig. 6.**
6. Disconnect idle air control valve and throttle position sensor connectors, **Fig. 7.**
7. Remove oil dipstick tube bracket bolt from manifold.
8. Disconnect EGR manifold tube, **Fig. 8.**
9. Raise and support vehicle.
10. Remove oil dipstick tube.

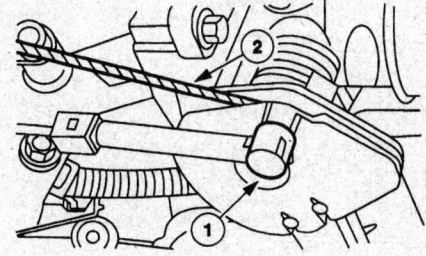

FM1060101363000X

Fig. 5 Accelerator cable &
throttle control cable replacement

11. Remove four manifold nuts, **Fig. 9.**
12. Lower vehicle.
13. Remove mounting nuts and intake manifold, **Fig. 10.** Discarding gasket.
14. Reverse procedure to install.

EXHAUST MANIFOLD
REPLACE

1. Remove engine drive belt.
2. Disconnect forward HO2S electrical connector mounted to cooling fan shroud, **Fig. 11.**
3. Remove five mounting nuts and exhaust shield.
4. Remove two EGR tubes to exhaust manifold mounting nuts and studs, **Fig. 12.**
5. Remove mounting bolts and position power steering hose aside, **Fig. 13.**
6. Loosen lower alternator bolt, remove upper bolt and pivot alternator forward, **Fig. 14.**
7. Remove exhaust manifold to TWC nuts, **Fig. 15.**
8. Remove mounting nuts, exhaust manifold and gasket, **Fig. 16.**
9. Reverse procedure to install.

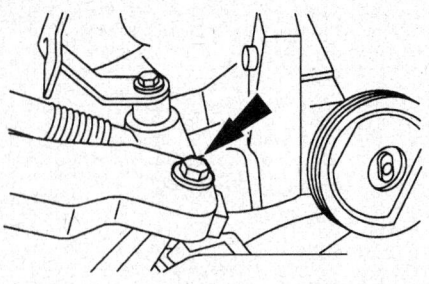

Fig. 6 Speed control bracket bolt replacement

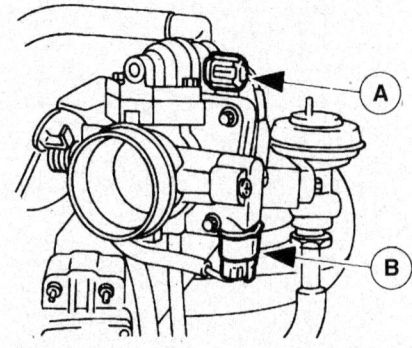

A- IDLE AIR CONTROL (IAC) VALVE
B- THROTTLE POSITION (TP) SENSOR

ARM66FM000000176

Fig. 7 Idle air control valve & throttle position sensor connectors

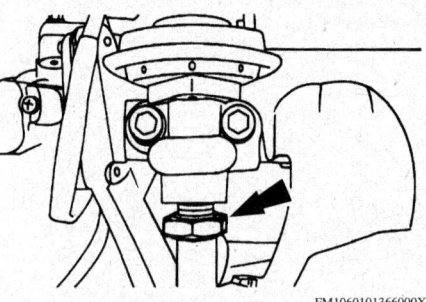

Fig. 8 EGR manifold bolt replacement

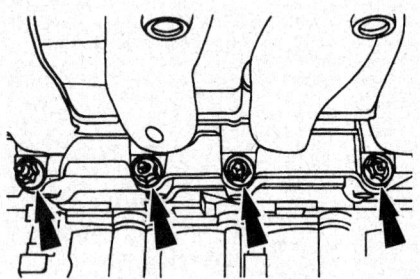

Fig. 9 Intake manifold nut replacement

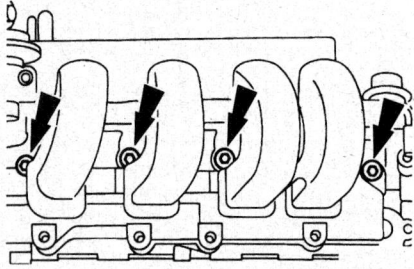

Fig. 10 Intake manifold & nut replacement

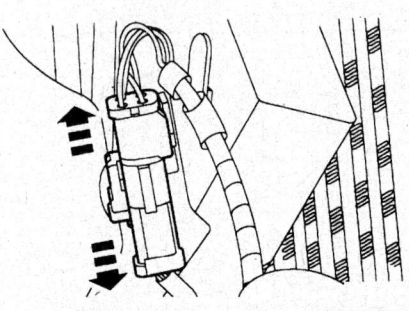

Fig. 11 HO2S connector replacement

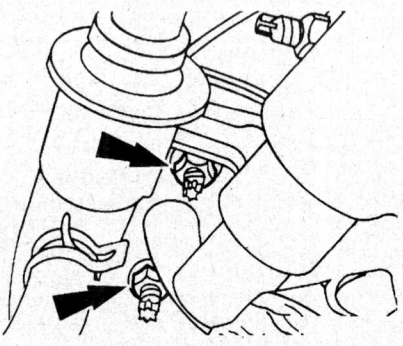

Fig. 12 EGR nut & stud replacement

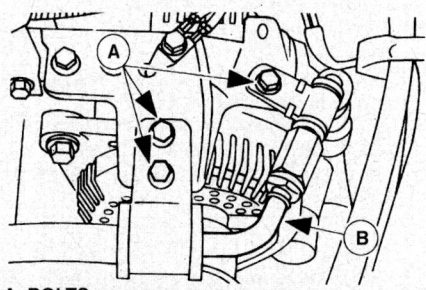

A- BOLTS
B- POWER STEERING PRESSURE HOSE

ARM66FM000000177

Fig. 13 Power steering hose removal

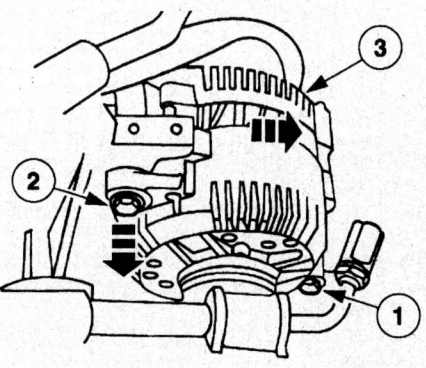

Fig. 14 Alternator forward pivot

FUEL INJECTION SUPPLY MANIFOLD
REPLACE

1. Disconnect crankshaft position sensor electrical connector, **Fig. 17.**
2. Disconnect two main engine harness electrical connectors above righthand front wheel well, **Fig. 18.**
3. Disconnect four fuel injector electrical connectors, **Fig. 19.**
4. Disconnect fuel pressure sensor electrical connector, **Fig. 20.**
5. Disconnect camshaft position sensor electrical connector, **Fig. 21.**
6. Remove wiring harness routing rail pulling upward from fuel injection supply manifold.
7. Disconnect fuel inlet line from fuel injection supply manifold using suitable disconnect tool.
8. Disconnect fuel supply line from fuel injection supply manifold using suitable disconnect tool.

9. Remove two fuel injection supply manifold bolts, **Fig. 22.**
10. Disconnect fuel injection supply manifold from fuel injectors and remove manifold.
11. Reverse procedure to install.

CYLINDER HEAD
REPLACE

1. Remove timing belt as outlined under "Timing Belt, Replace."
2. Remove air cleaner intake tube and outlet half of engine air cleaner.
3. Disconnect vacuum hoses from Exhaust Gas Recirculation (EGR) valve, brake booster, throttle body, fuel pressure regulator and intake manifold, **Fig. 2.**
4. Disconnect speed control cable, accel-

erator cable and throttle valve control actuating cable from throttle control lever.
5. Remove two speed control cable bracket bolts and position bracket and cables aside.
6. Disconnect two fuel charging wiring electrical connectors.
7. Disconnect crankshaft position sensor electrical connector.
8. Disconnect upstream heated oxygen sensor electrical connector mounted on cooling fan shroud.
9. Disconnect fuel supply line and fuel return line from fuel injection supply manifold using disconnect tool No. D87L-9280-A, or equivalent.
10. Remove power steering pressure hose bracket and position hose aside.
11. Loosen alternator lower bolt, remove alternator upper bolt and tilt alternator forward.
12. Remove oil dipstick tube bracket bolt from intake manifold.
13. Disconnect EGR tube from EGR valve.

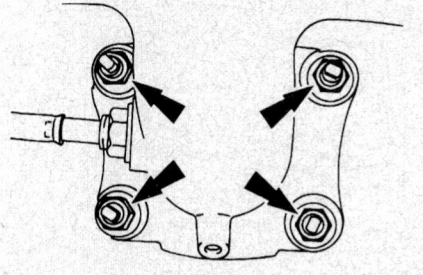

Fig. 15 Exhaust manifold to TWC nut replacement

FM1060101373000X

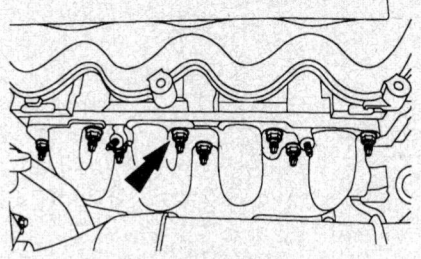

Fig. 16 Exhaust manifold replacement

FM1060101374000X

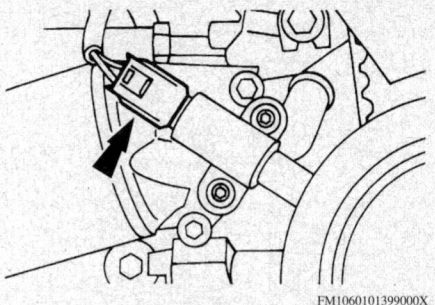

Fig. 17 Crankshaft sensor electrical connector replacement

FM1060101399000X

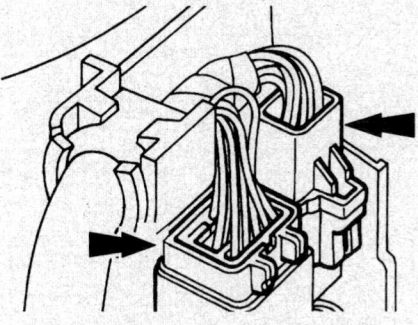

Fig. 18 Main engine harness replacement

FM1060101400000X

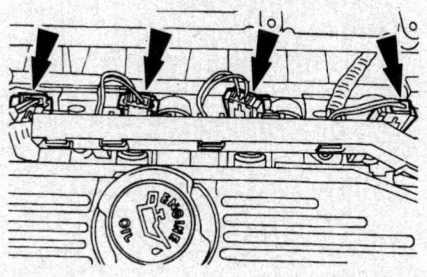

Fig. 19 Fuel injector connector replacement

FM1060101401000X

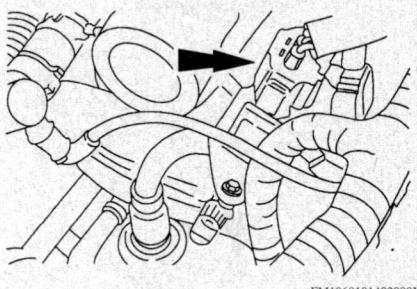

Fig. 20 Fuel pressure connector replacement

FM1060101402000X

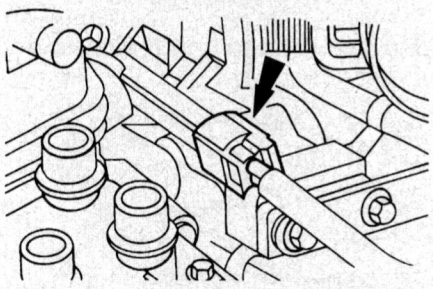

Fig. 21 Camshaft sensor connector replacement

FM1060101403000X

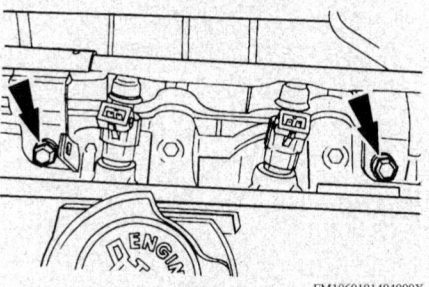

Fig. 22 Fuel injection supply manifold replacement

FM1060101404000X

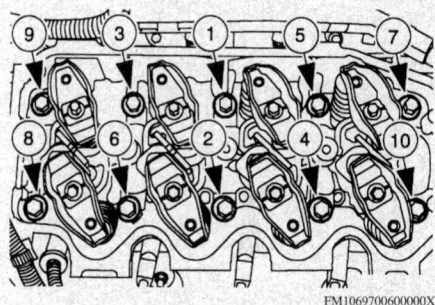

Fig. 23 Cylinder head bolt tightening sequence

FM1069700600000X

14. Disconnect EGR tube from exhaust manifold.
15. Remove exhaust manifold shield.
16. Remove exhaust manifold to catalytic converter nuts.
17. Raise and support vehicle.
18. Drain coolant into suitable container.
19. Remove righthand splash shield.
20. Remove oil dipstick tube from cylinder block.
21. Disconnect air conditioning compressor electrical connector.
22. Remove air conditioning compressor mounting bolts and suspend compressor with wire.
23. Loosen front engine accessory drive bracket lower four bolts and one mounting out four turns. **Do not remove.**
24. Lower vehicle.
25. Remove uppermost front engine accessory drive bracket to cylinder head bolt.
26. Remove air conditioning line bracket to front engine accessory drive bracket bolt.
27. Remove valve cover.
28. Disconnect upper radiator hose from thermostat housing water hose connection.
29. Disconnect heater hose from thermostat housing.
30. Remove cylinder head bolts, cylinder head and gasket.
31. Reverse procedure to install, noting the following:
    a. **Torque** cylinder head bolts to 30–44 ft. lbs., in sequence, **Fig. 23.**
    b. Back off bolts ½ turn.
    c. **Torque** head bolts to 30–44 ft. lbs., in sequence.
    d. Tighten bolts an additional 90° in sequence.
    e. Tighten bolts an additional 90° in sequence.

VALVE ADJUSTMENT

This engine uses hydraulic valve lash adjusters. Valve clearance is adjusted automatically.

TIMING BELT
REPLACE

Removal

1. Remove drive belt and tensioner.
2. Remove front cover, **Fig. 24.**
3. Raise and support vehicle, then remove righthand wheel and tire assembly.
4. Remove righthand splash shield.
5. Remove mounting bolt and crankshaft pulley.
6. Align timing marks, **Fig. 25.**
7. Loosen timing belt tensioner bolt.
8. Turn timing belt counterclockwise ¼ turn using suitable Allen wrench.
9. Insert ⅛ inch drill bit to lock timing belt tensioner in place.
10. Remove timing belt.

Installation

1. Install timing belt in counterclockwise direction, over crankshaft pulley and camshaft pulley.

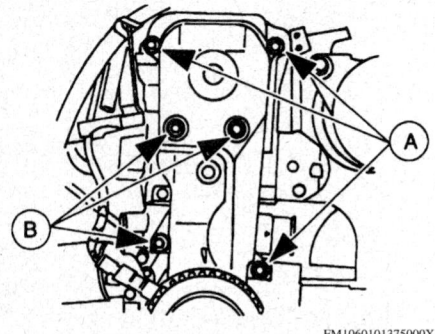

Fig. 24 Engine front cover replacement

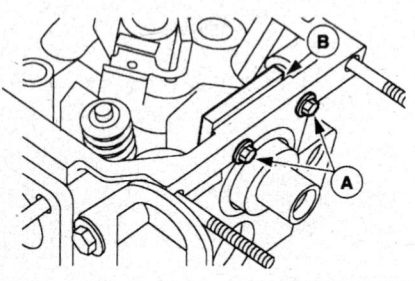

Fig. 27 Camshaft thrust plate replacement

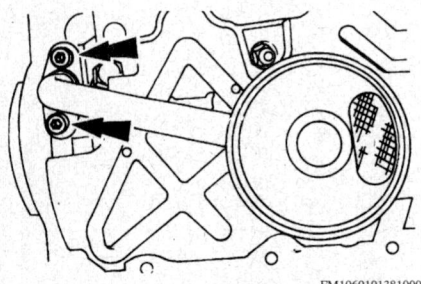

Fig. 30 Oil pump screen cover replacement

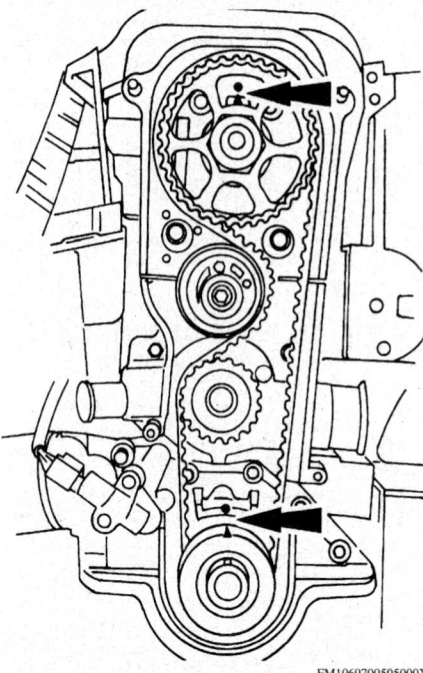

Fig. 25 Timing mark alignment

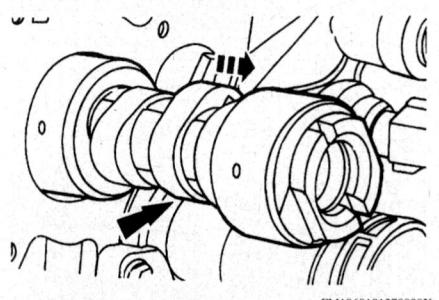

Fig. 28 Camshaft replacement

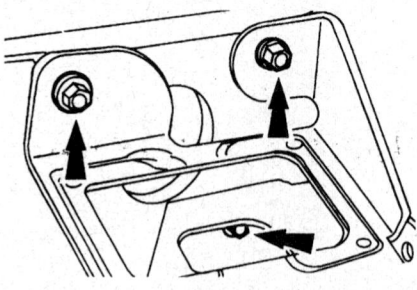

Fig. 26 Ignition coil bracket replacement

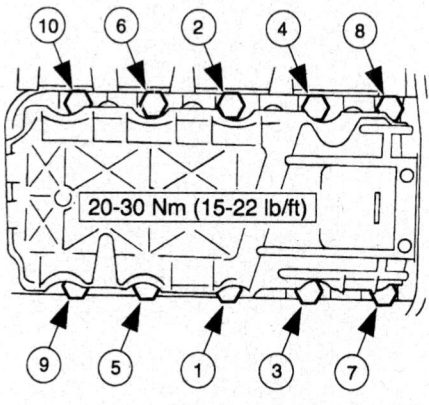

20-30 Nm (15-22 lb/ft)

Fig. 29 Oil pan bolt replacement

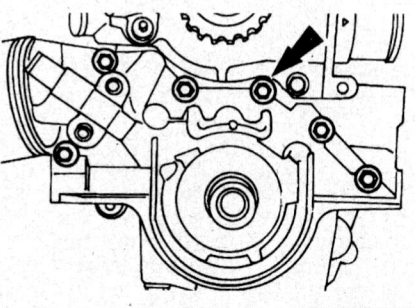

Fig. 31 Oil pump replacement

2. Install belt under timing belt tensioner and over water pump sprocket. **During installation, maintain belt span between crankshaft and camshaft sprockets.**
3. Remove ⅛ inch drill bit holding timing belt tensioner in position.
4. Allow tensioner to tension timing belt, then tighten tensioner bolt.
5. Turn crankshaft two turns in normal direction of rotation.
6. Ensure crankshaft and camshaft timing marks are aligned, **Fig. 25.** If timing mark are not aligned, timing belt must be removed and installed.
7. Install engine front cover and crankshaft pulley.
8. Install splash shield, then the wheel and tire assembly.
9. Lower vehicle, then install accessory drive belt tensioner and drive belt.

CAMSHAFT
REPLACE

1. Remove engine air cleaner.
2. Remove three bolts, valve cover and gasket.
3. Remove camshaft front seal.
4. Remove ignition coil as outlined under "Ignition Coil, Replace" in "Electrical" section.
5. Remove ignition coil bracket, **Fig. 26.**
6. Remove valve tappet guide plate retainer, plate and eight valve tappets.
7. Remove two mounting bolts and camshaft thrust plate, **Fig. 27.**
8. Remove and discard cylinder head rear cup plug.
9. Remove camshaft from rear of cylinder head, **Fig. 28.**
10. Reverse procedure to install.

OIL PAN
REPLACE

1. Remove TWC converter.
2. Drain engine oil into suitable container.

3. Remove mounting bolts and TWC to oil pan bracket.
4. Remove oil pan bolts in sequence, **Fig. 29.**
5. Remove oil pan.
6. Reverse procedure to install.

OIL PUMP
REPLACE

1. Remove timing belt as outlined under "Timing Belt, Replace."
2. Raise and support vehicle.
3. Remove TWC converter.
4. Drain engine oil into suitable container.
5. Remove mounting bolts and TWC to oil pan bracket.
6. Remove oil pan mounting bolts in sequence, **Fig. 29.**
7. Remove oil pan.

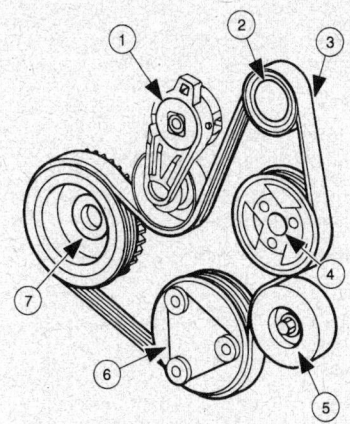

Item	Part Number	Description
1	6B209	Drive Belt Tensioner
2	10346	Generator
3	8620	Drive Belt
4	3A733	Power Steering Pump Pulley
5	6C348	Accessory Drive Belt Routing Pulley
6	19703	A/C Compressor
7	6A312	Crankshaft Pulley

FM1069700596000X

Fig. 32 Drive belt routing. With A/C

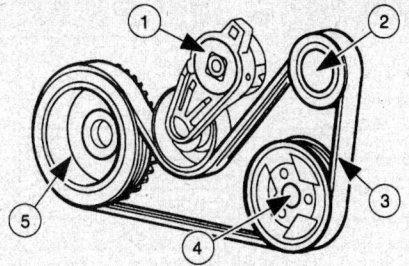

Item	Part Number	Description
1	6B209	Drive Belt Tensioner
2	10346	Generator
3	8620	Drive Belt
4	3A733	Power Steering Pump Pulley
5	6A312	Crankshaft Pulley

FM1069700597000X

Fig. 33 Drive belt routing. Less A/C

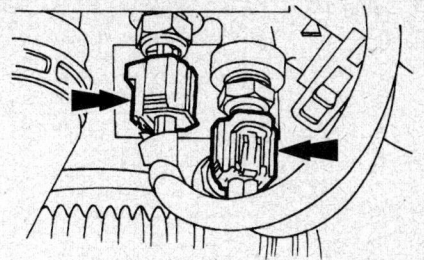

FM1060101383000X

Fig. 34 Sender unit & sensor replacement

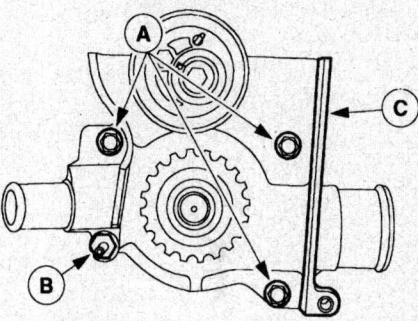

A- BOLTS
B- STUD
C- WATER PUMP

ARM66FM000000178

Fig. 37 Water pump replacement

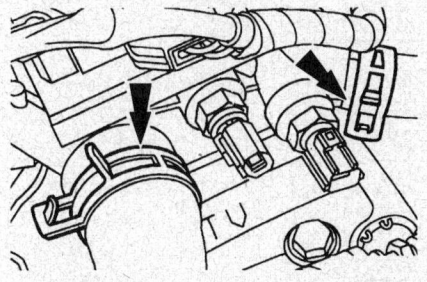

FM1060101384000X

Fig. 35 Upper radiator & heater coolant hoses replacement

8. Disconnect crankshaft position sensor electrical connector.
9. Remove two mounting bolts, oil pump screen cover and tube, **Fig. 30.**
10. Remove oil pump and gasket, **Fig. 31.**
11. Reverse procedure to install.

BELT TENSION DATA

No manual drive belt tension adjustments are required. The drive belt tensioner automatically adjusts belt tension.

SERPENTINE DRIVE BELT

Refer to **Figs. 32 and 33,** for serpentine drive belt routing.

COOLING SYSTEM BLEED

After filling cooling system, run engine for approximately 12 minutes with radiator

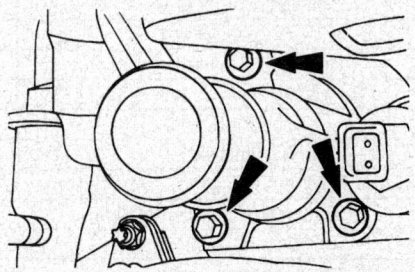

FM1060101385000X

Fig. 36 Thermostat replacement

pressure cap off, then top off radiator. Secure cap and with engine running, fill coolant reservoir to FULL HOT mark with coolant.

THERMOSTAT
REPLACE

1. Remove air cleaner outlet tube.
2. Drain coolant into suitable container.
3. Disconnect water temperature indicator sender unit and engine coolant temperature sensor electrical connectors, **Fig. 34.**
4. Disconnect upper radiator and thermostat housing heater coolant hoses, **Fig. 35.**
5. Remove mounting bolts, housing and thermostat, **Fig. 36.**
6. Reverse procedure to install.

RADIATOR
REPLACE

Refer to "2.0L DOHC Engine" for radiator replacement procedure.

WATER PUMP
REPLACE

1. Drain coolant into suitable container.
2. Remove timing belt as outlined under

"Timing Belt, Replace."
3. Remove timing belt tensioner bolt and timing belt tensioner.
4. Remove lower radiator hose from water pump.
5. Lower vehicle.
6. Disconnect heater hose from water pump.
7. Remove three bolts, one stud and water pump, **Fig. 37.**
8. Reverse procedure to install.

FUEL PUMP
REPLACE

1. Remove rear seat cushion and disconnect fuel pump electrical connector.
2. Remove four mounting screws and fuel pump access cover.
3. Remove fuel line clips and disconnect top fuel pump lines.
4. Remove locking retainer ring and fuel pump.
5. Reverse procedure to install.

FUEL FILTER
REPLACE

1. Place suitable container under fuel filter.
2. Loosen fuel filter bracket clamp.
3. Remove fuel line clips.
4. Disconnect fuel tubes and remove fuel filter.
5. Reverse procedure to install.

TIGHTENING SPECIFICATIONS

Year	Component	Torque/Ft. Lbs.
2001–02	Air Conditioning Compressor	15–22
	Air Conditioning Line Bracket	15–18
	Alternator, Lower	15–22
	Alternator, Upper	30–40
	Camshaft Position Sensor	15–22
	Camshaft Sprocket	70–85
	Camshaft Thrust Plate	6–10
	Catalytic Converter Bracket	15–20
	Catalytic Converter To Exhaust	26–34
	Catalytic Converter To Oil Pan Bracket	30–40
	Connecting Rod Cap	26–30
	Constant Control Relay Module	72–96①
	Crankshaft Main Bearing Cap	66–79
	Crankshaft Pulley	81–96
	Cylinder Head	②
	EGR Manifold Tube	15–20
	Engine Front Cover	72–96①
	Engine Mount	50–69
	Engine Mounting Bracket	31–42
	Exhaust Manifold Heat Shield	45–61①
	Exhaust Manifold	15–17
	Flywheel	54–67
	Front Engine Accessory Drive Bracket	30–40
	Fuel Injection Supply Manifold	15–22
	Ignition Coil Bracket	72–96①
	Ignition Coil	40–61①
	Intake Manifold	15–22
	Intake Manifold Runner Control Actuator	72–96①
	Lefthand Splash Shield	69–98①
	Oil Dipstick Tube	72–96①
	Oil Pan	15–22
	Oil Pan Baffle	15–22
	Oil Pan Drain Plug	15–22
	Oil Pump	8–12
	Oil Pump Screen Cover & Tube	72–96①
	Oil Pressure Sensor Switch	8–12
	Power Steering Pressure Hose Bracket	64–87①
	Power Steering Pump	30–41
	Power Steering Pump Pulley	15–22
	Righthand Engine Support Insulator Through Bolt	50–69
	Righthand Splash Shield	72–96①
	Rocker Arm	17–22
	Speed Control Cable Bracket	64–87①
	Starter	18–20
	Thermostat Housing	8–12
	Timing Belt Tensioner	15–22
	Valve Cover	72–96①
	Water Outlet Connection	8–11
	Water Pump	15–22

① — Inch Lbs.
② — Refer to "Cylinder Head, Replace" for tightening sequence.

Rear Suspension

NOTE: On Air Bag Equipped Models, Refer To "Air Bag System Precautions" Located In The Front Of This Manual For System Disarming & Arming Procedures.

NOTE: Refer To "Computer Relearn Procedures" Located In The Front Of This Manual When Battery Power To The Computer Has Been Interrupted.

INDEX

DESCRIPTION

The rear strut and spring assemblies can be disassembled to replace any of the individual components, **Figs. 1 and 2.** The rear strut and spring assemblies can be replaced independently. The rear wheel hubs cannot be disassembled. The rear wheel hubs contain the rear wheel bearings and must be replaced as an assembly. The left-hand and righthand rear wheel spindles can be replaced individually. The rear suspension arm bushings can be replaced individually, only the toe can be adjusted on the rear suspension.

HUB & BEARING
REPLACE

1. Raise and support vehicle.
2. **On models equipped with disc brakes,** remove brake caliper and rotor as outlined in "Disc Brakes" chapter.
3. **On models equipped with drum brakes,** remove drum brake as outlined in "Drum Brakes" chapter.
4. **On all models,** unstake rear axle wheel hub retainer.
5. Remove rear axle wheel hub retainer and discard.
6. Remove wheel hub.
7. Reverse procedure to install. Install new anti-lock brake sensor indicator to wheel hub using suitable press with steel plate, **Fig. 3.**

REAR WHEEL SPINDLE
REPLACE

1. Raise and support vehicle.
2. Remove rear wheel hub as outlined under "Hub & Bearing, Replace."
3. **On models equipped with disc brakes,** remove rear disc plate shield as outlined under "Disc Brakes."
4. **On models equipped with drum brakes,** remove brake backing plate as outlined under "Drum Brakes."
5. **On models equipped with anti-lock brakes,** remove anti-lock brake system sensor bracket bolt and sensor, **Figs. 4 and 5.**
6. **On all models,** remove lower strut and spring mounting nuts, **Fig. 6.**
7. Remove rear suspension trailing link bolt, **Fig. 7.**
8. Remove rear suspension arm and bushing nut, then the rear wheel spindle, **Fig. 8.**
9. Reverse procedure to install.

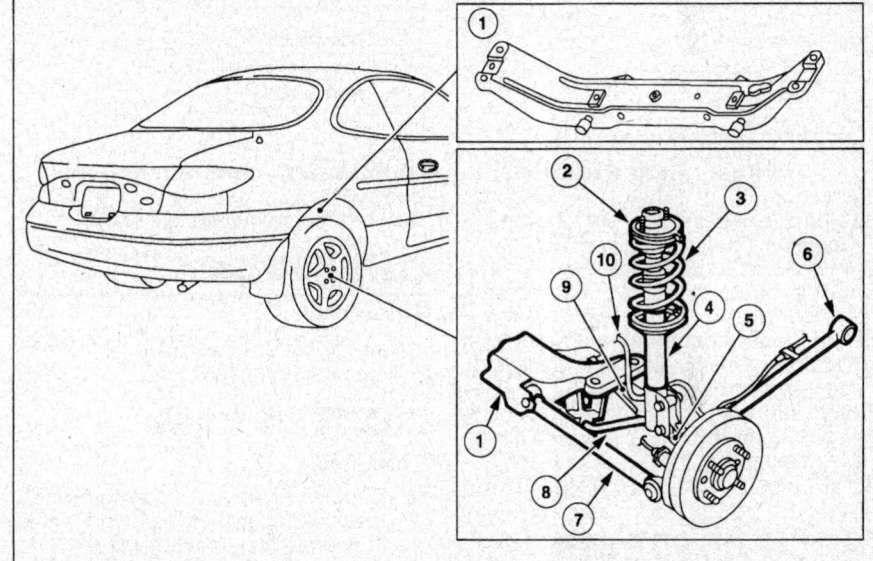

Item	Description
1	Rear Floor Cross Member
2	Rear Shock Absorber Insulator
3	Rear Spring
4	Rear Shock Absorber
5	Rear Wheel Spindle
6	Rear Suspension Tie Rod and Bushing

Item	Description
7	Rear Suspension Arm and Bushing (Rear)
8	Rear Stabilizer Bar
9	Rear Suspension Arm and Bushing (Front)
10	Rear Wheel Brake Hose

FM1060101416000X

Fig. 1 Rear suspension components

STRUT
REPLACE

1. Remove high mount stop lamp cover and lamp.
2. Remove pushpins and package tray trim panel.

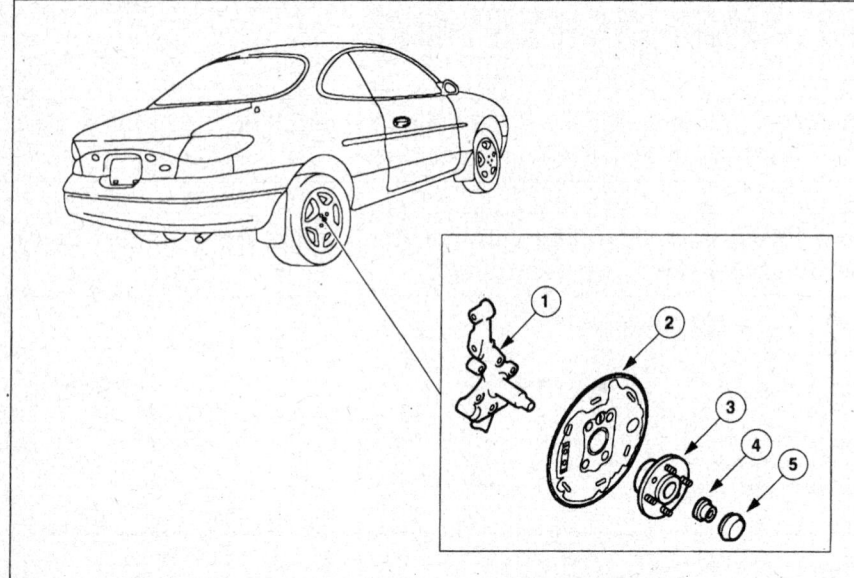

Item	Description
1	Rear Wheel Spindle
2	Brake Backing Plate
3	Wheel Hub

Item	Description
4	Rear Axle Wheel Hub Retainer
5	Hub Grease Cap

FM1060101417000X

Fig. 2   Rear wheel bearing & hub system components

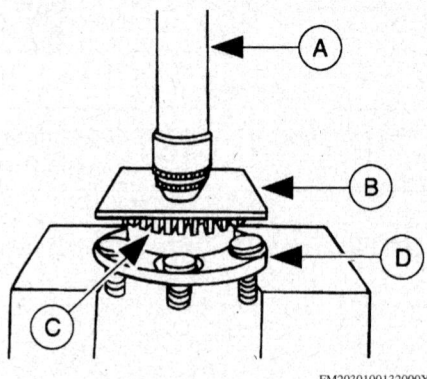

FM2030100132000X

Fig. 3   Anti-lock brake sensor installation

3. Remove upper strut and spring mounting nuts, **Fig. 9**.
4. Raise and support vehicle.
5. Slide brake hose clip off, position aside, **Fig. 10**.
6. **On models equipped with anti-lock brakes,** remove anti-lock brake system sensor bracket bolt.
7. **On all models,** remove mounting bolts, then the lower strut and spring assembly, **Fig. 11**.
8. Reverse procedure to install.

SHOCK ABSORBER
REPLACE

1. Remove high mount stop lamp cover and lamp.
2. Remove pushpins and package tray trim panel.
3. Remove upper strut and spring mounting nuts, **Fig. 9**.
4. Raise and support vehicle.
5. Slide brake hose clip off, position aside, **Fig. 10**.
6. **On models equipped with anti-lock brakes,** remove anti-lock brake system sensor bracket bolt.
7. **On all models,** remove mounting bolts, then the lower strut and spring assembly, **Fig. 11**.
8. Compress rear spring using tool No. 014-00781, or equivalent, to compress rear spring, **Fig. 12**.
9. Remove shock absorber top mounting cover, **Fig. 13**.
10. Remove piston rod nut, retainers and shock absorber insulator.
11. Remove spring compressor.
12. Remove rear shock, **Fig. 14**.

13. Reverse procedure to install.

COIL SPRING
REPLACE

Refer to "Shock Absorber, Replace" for replacement procedure.

CONTROL ARM
REPLACE

1. Remove wheel and tire assemblies.
2. Install floor jack to support vehicle under rear floor crossmember.
3. Remove rear stabilizer bar end bolt and nut, **Fig. 15**.
4. Remove retainer and upper rear stabilizer bar end bushings, then the retainer spacer and lower rear stabilizer bar end bushings.
5. Remove retainer.
6. Remove rear crossmember bolts, **Fig. 16**.
7. Remove rear suspension arm and bushing nut, **Fig. 17**.
8. Remove mounting bolt, rear suspension arm and bushing, **Fig. 18**.
9. Reverse procedure to install.

REAR CROSSMEMBER
REPLACE

1. Raise and support vehicle.
2. Remove wheel and tire assemblies.
3. Install floor jack to support vehicle under rear floor crossmember.
4. Remove rear stabilizer bar end bolt and nut, **Fig. 15**.
5. Remove retainer and upper rear stabilizer bar end bushings, then the retain-

er spacer and lower rear stabilizer bar end bushings.
6. Remove retainer.
7. Remove rear crossmember bolts, **Fig. 16**.
8. Remove rear suspension arm and bushing nut, **Fig. 17**.
9. Remove mounting bolt, rear suspension arm and bushing, **Fig. 18**.
10. Remove two bracket bolts and stabilizer bar, **Fig. 19**.
11. Remove two brake hose support brackets and disconnect hose.
12. Remove three-way connector bolt, **Fig. 20**.
13. **Locate alignment of both alignment shims prior to removal.**
14. Remove rear suspension alignment shims and bolts, **Fig. 21**.
15. Install suitable jack under rear floor crossmember.
16. Remove rear floor crossmember bolts, **Fig. 16**.
17. Remove rear suspension arm and bushing nut.
18. Remove mounting bolt, rear suspension arm and bushing, **Fig. 18**.
19. Lower and remove rear floor crossmember.
20. Reverse procedure to install.

STABILIZER BAR
REPLACE

1. Raise and support vehicle.
2. Remove wheel and tire assemblies.
3. Install floor jack to support vehicle under rear floor crossmember.
4. Remove rear stabilizer bar end bolt and nut, **Fig. 15**.
5. Remove retainer and upper rear stabilizer bar end bushings, then the retainer spacer and lower rear stabilizer bar end bushings.
6. Remove retainer.
7. Remove rear crossmember bolts, **Fig. 16**.
8. Remove rear suspension arm and bushing nut, **Fig. 17**.
9. Remove mounting bolt, rear suspension arm and bushing, **Fig. 18**.
10. Remove two bracket bolts and stabilizer bar, **Fig. 19**.
11. Reverse procedure to install.

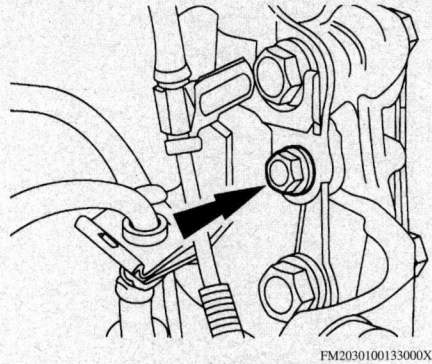

FM2030100133000X

Fig. 4   Anti-lock brake bracket bolt replacement

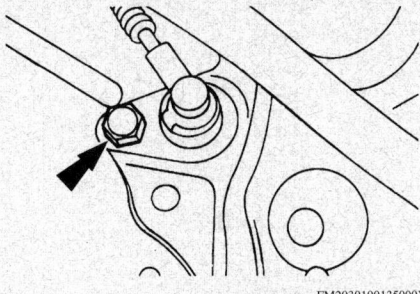

FM2030100135000X

Fig. 5   Anti-lock brake sensor bolt replacement

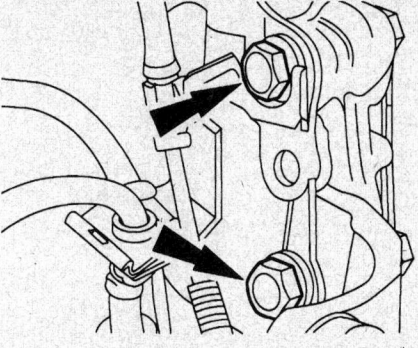

FM2030100134000X

Fig. 6   Lower strut & spring replacement

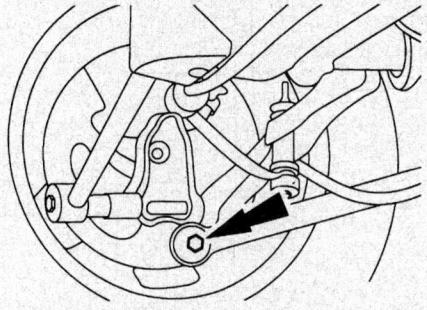

FM2030100136000X

Fig. 7   Trailing link bolt replacement

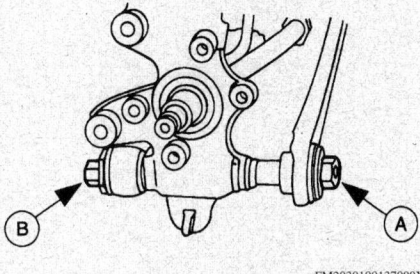

FM2030100137000X

Fig. 8   Rear wheel spindle replacement

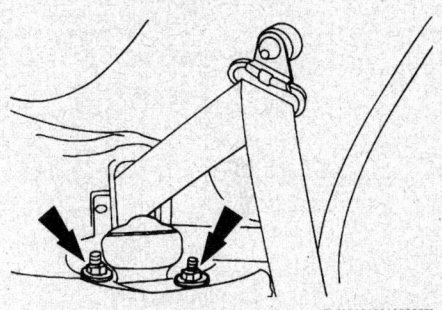

FM2030100138000X

Fig. 9   Upper strut & spring nut replacement

FM2030100139000X

Fig. 10   Brake hose clip replacement

FM2030100140000X

Fig. 11   Lower strut & spring bolt replacement

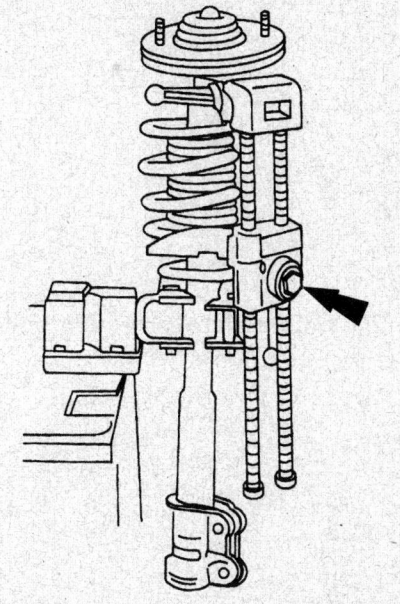

FM2030100141000X

Fig. 12   Rear spring compression

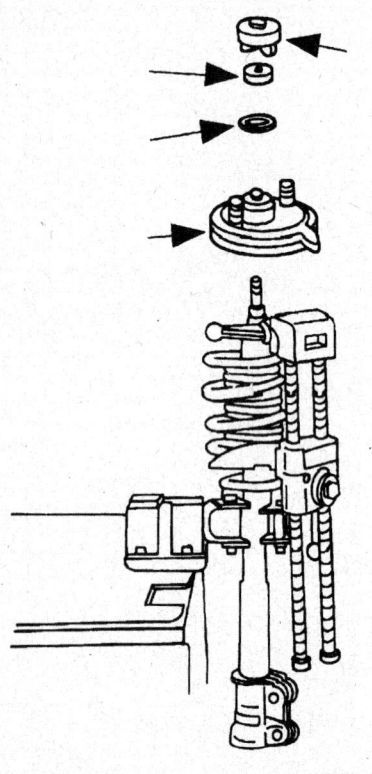

Fig. 13 Top mounting cover & component replacement

FM2030100142000X

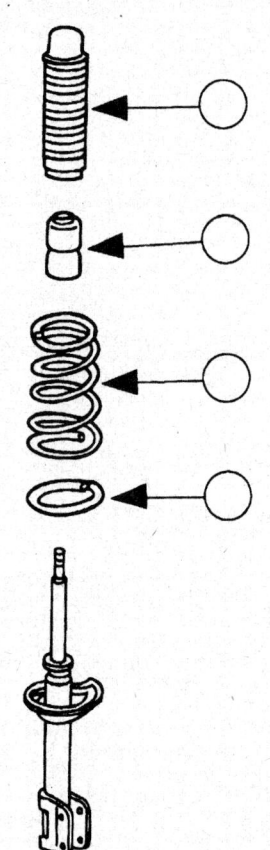

FM2030100143000X

Fig. 14 Rear shock replacement

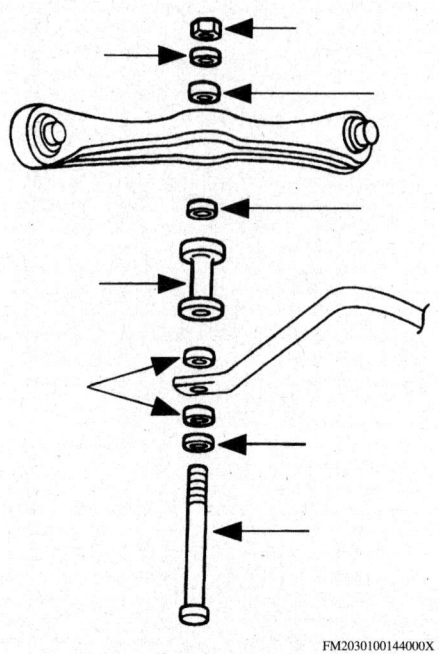

FM2030100144000X

Fig. 15 Rear stabilizer bar link replacement

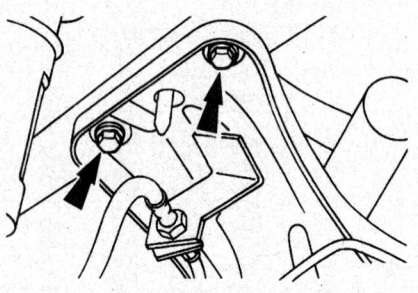

FM2030100145000X

Fig. 16 Rear crossmember bolt replacement

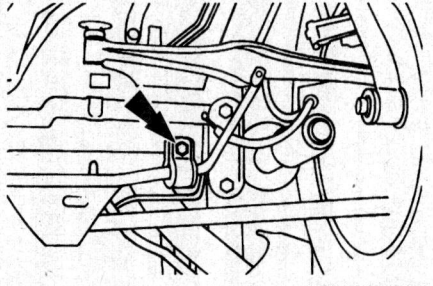

FM2030100148000X

Fig. 19 Stabilizer bar replacement

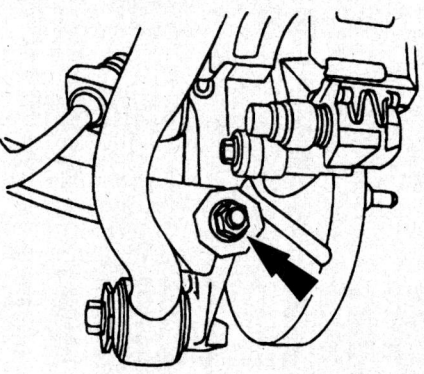

FM2030100146000X

Fig. 17 Rear suspension arm & bushing nut replacement

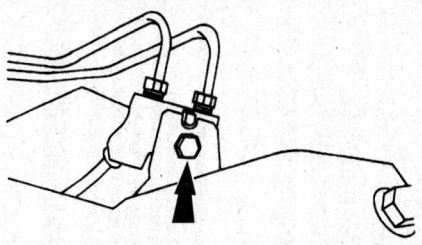

FM2030100149000X

Fig. 20 Three-way bolt replacement

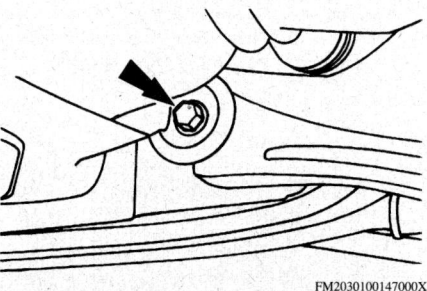

FM2030100147000X

Fig. 18 Rear suspension arm & bushing bolt replacement

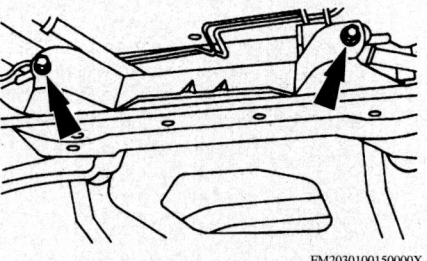

FM2030100150000X

Fig. 21 Rear suspension alignment shims & bolt replacement

TIGHTENING SPECIFICATIONS

Year	Component	Torque/Ft. Lbs.
2001–03	Anti-Lock Brake System Sensor	14–18
	Lower Strut & Spring	76–100
	Piston Rod	41–49
	Rear Anti-Lock Brake System Sensor Bracket	14–18
	Rear Axle Wheel Hub Retainer	130–174
	Rear Floor Crossmember	34–46
	Rear Suspension Arm & Bushing	64–86
	Rear Suspension Trailing Link	69–94
	Rear Wheel Disc Brake Shield	34–44
	Stabilizer Bar Bracket	32–43
	Upper Strut & Spring	34–46
	Wheel Lug Nuts	74–100

Front Suspension & Steering

NOTE: On Air Bag Equipped Models, Refer To "Air Bag System Precautions" Located In The Front Of This Manual For System Disarming & Arming Procedures.

NOTE: Refer To "Computer Relearn Procedures" Located In The Front Of This Manual When Battery Power To The Computer Has Been Interrupted.

INDEX

DESCRIPTION

The front suspension is a McPherson strut design with cast steering knuckles. The shock absorber strut assembly includes a mounting block, a thrust bearing, an upper spring seat, a rubber spring seat, a bound stopper and coil spring mounted to the shock strut, **Fig. 1.**

The front wheels and brake rotors are supported by a sealed roller bearing mounted in the steering knuckle. A snap ring holds the bearing in the knuckle. The halfshaft is secured to the front hub assembly with a staked nut. The staked nut cannot be reused, **Fig. 2.**

WHEEL BEARING

REPLACE

1. Remove front wheel knuckle as outlined under "Steering Knuckle, Replace."
2. Remove and discard inner wheel bearing oil seal.
3. Press wheel hub from front wheel knuckle using bearing puller attachment tool No. 205-D064, or equivalent, **Fig. 3.**
4. Remove retainer ring from front wheel knuckle, **Fig. 4.**
5. Press front wheel bearing from front wheel knuckle using bearing pulling attachment tool, **Fig. 5.**
6. Reverse procedure to install.

STEERING KNUCKLE

REPLACE

1. Raise and support vehicle.
2. Remove wheel and tire assembly.
3. Remove brake caliper bolts and rotor, then secure caliper with wire as outlined in "Disc Brakes" chapter.
4. Carefully raise staked portion of front axle wheel hub retainer and remove retainer, **Fig. 6.**
5. Remove cotter pin and tie rod end nut from tie rod end, **Fig. 7.**
6. Separate tie rod end nut from front wheel knuckle using tie rod end separator tool No. T85M-3395-A, or equivalent, **Fig. 8.**
7. **On models equipped with anti-lock brakes,** remove anti-lock brake sensor, **Fig. 9.**
8. **On all models,** remove ball joint nut and through bolt.
9. Separate front suspension lower arm ball joint from front wheel knuckle, **Fig. 10.**
10. Remove two strut mounting bolts from front wheel knuckle.
11. Separate and remove strut from front wheel knuckle.
12. Reverse procedure to install.

BALL JOINT INSPECTION

1. Raise and support vehicle.
2. Grasp lower edge of tire, then move wheel in and out from pivot center line.
3. Ball joint should be replaced if excessive movement is felt (more than 1/32 inch).

BALL JOINT

REPLACE

1. Raise and support vehicle.

2. Remove wheel and tire assembly.
3. Remove ball joint nut and through bolt.
4. Separate front suspension lower arm ball joint from front wheel knuckle.
5. Remove two ball joint nuts and front suspension lower arm ball joint.
6. Reverse procedure to install.

COIL SPRING
REPLACE

1. Raise and support vehicle, then remove front tire and wheel assembly.
2. Remove flexible brake hose to shock/strut assembly clip.
3. Remove two shock/strut assembly to steering knuckle mounting nuts and bolts.
4. Remove upper mounting block nuts on strut tower and shock/strut assembly, **Fig. 11.**
5. Remove cap from top of shock/strut assembly.
6. Secure shock/strut assembly mounting block in suitable vise and turn piston rod nut one full revolution to loosen.
7. Compress spring using suitable spring compressor tool.
8. Remove nut, mounting block, thrust bearing, upper spring seat, rubber spring seat, coil spring and bound stopper.
9. Reverse procedure to install. Ensure shock/strut assembly mounting block direction indicator faces inboard.

STRUT
REPLACE

1. Raise and support vehicle, then remove front tire and wheel assembly.
2. Remove flexible brake hose to shock/strut assembly clip.
3. Remove two shock/strut assembly to steering knuckle mounting nuts and bolts.
4. Remove upper mounting block nuts on strut tower and shock/strut assembly, **Fig. 11.**
5. Reverse procedure to install. Ensure shock/strut assembly mounting block direction indicator faces inboard.

CONTROL ARM
REPLACE

1. Raise and support vehicle.
2. Remove stabilizer bar nuts, washers, bushings, sleeves and bolts, **Fig. 12.**
3. Remove lower control arm front bushing bolt and washer.
4. Remove lower control arm rear bushing retaining strap mounting bolt.
5. Remove lower ball joint to steering knuckle mounting nut and bolt.
6. Separate steering knuckle from lower ball joint.
7. Remove mounting bolts and lower control arm, **Fig. 13.**
8. Reverse procedure to install. Tighten stabilizer bar bolts, sleeves, bushings,

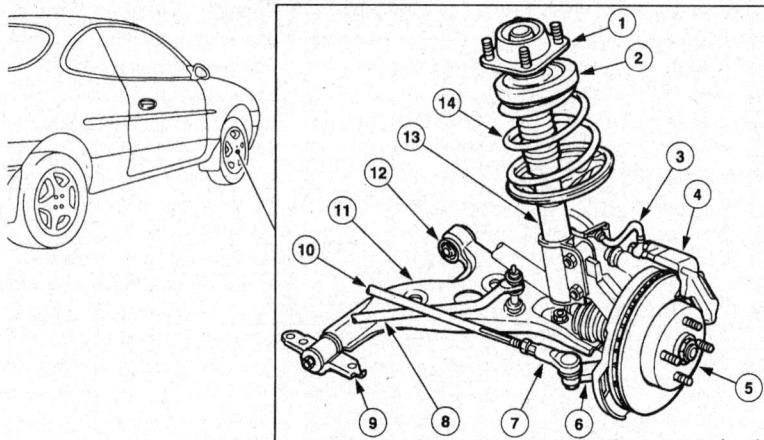

Item	Description
1	Front Shock Absorber Mounting Bracket
2	Upper Spring Seat (Part of 18198)
3	Front Brake Hose
4	Disc Brake Caliper
5	Front Disc Brake Rotor
6	Front Wheel Knuckle
7	Tie Rod End

Item	Description
8	Front Stabilizer Bar
9	Front Suspension Lower Arm Mounting Bolt Bushing (Rear)
10	Front Wheel Spindle Tie Rod
11	Front Suspension Lower Arm
12	Front Suspension Lower Arm Mounting Bolt Bushing (Front)
13	Front Shock Absorber
14	Front Coil Spring

FM2020100184000X

Fig. 1   Front suspension components

washers and nuts so .67–.75 inch of thread is showing.

STABILIZER BAR
REPLACE

1. Support engine with three bar engine support tool No. D88L-6000-A, or equivalent.
2. Raise and support vehicle.
3. Remove front wheel and tire assembly.
4. Remove mounting bolts and crossmember, **Fig. 14.**
5. Remove steering gear mounting bracket nuts, **Fig. 15.**
6. Position steering gear slightly forward, then remove stabilizer bar nuts, washers, bushings, sleeves and bolts from lower control arm.
7. Remove front stabilizer bar link, **Fig. 12.**
8. Remove transaxle insulator nuts and rear engine support to vehicle frame nuts, **Fig. 16.**
9. Lower end of transaxle support crossmember, **Fig. 17.**
10. Install position high lift trans jack to support subframe, **Fig. 18.**
11. Remove two subframe to frame nuts.
12. Remove front subframe to vehicle mounting nuts, **Fig. 19.**
13. Lower subframe.
14. Remove four mounting bolts and stabilizer bar, **Fig. 20.**
15. Reverse procedure to install. Tighten front stabilizer bar link nuts so .67–.75 inch thread is exposed.

POWER STEERING GEAR
REPLACE

1. Turn ignition switch to ACC position.
2. Remove five mounting nuts and steering column tube boot.
3. Remove steering column input shaft coupling to steering gear input shaft and control bolt.
4. Raise and support vehicle.
5. Remove front tire and wheel assemblies.
6. Remove and discard cotter pin from tie rod end nut.
7. Remove tie rod end nut and separate tie rod from wheel knuckle using tie rod end separator tool No. T85M-3395-A, or equivalent, **Fig. 21.**
8. Remove righthand splash shield.
9. Remove crossmember.
10. Disconnect power steering return hose and plug line.
11. Remove strap attaching hoses to steering gear housing.
12. **On models equipped with manual transaxle, proceed as follows:**
    a. Disconnect transmission gearshift rod and clevis from transaxle.
    b. Remove extension bar nut, then disconnect gearshift lever stabilizer bar and support from transaxle.
13. **On all models,** remove steering gear mounting brackets.
14. Remove two nuts from each bracket.
15. Remove two steering gear mounting brackets.

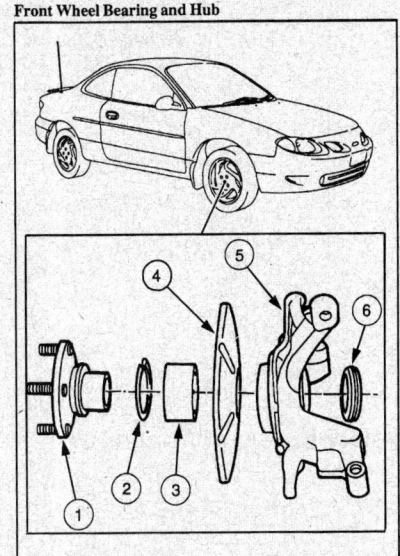

Fig. 2   Front wheel bearing & hub

Item	Description	Item	Description
1	Wheel Hub	3	Front Wheel Bearing
2	Retainer Ring	4	Front Disc Brake Rotor Shield
		5	Front Wheel Knuckle
		6	Inner Wheel Bearing Oil Seal

FM2020100185000X

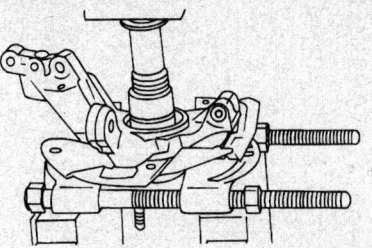

Fig. 3   Wheel hub from wheel knuckle replacement

FM2020100186000X

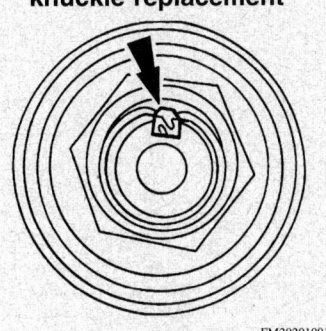

Fig. 6   Wheel hub retainer replacement

FM2020100189000X

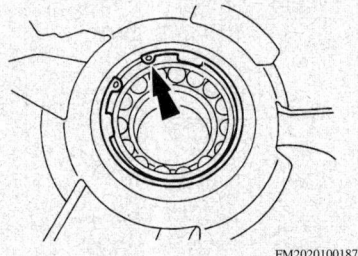

FM2020100187000X

Fig. 4   Retaining ring replacement

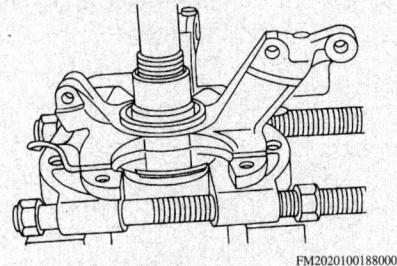

FM2020100188000X

Fig. 5   Bearing replacement

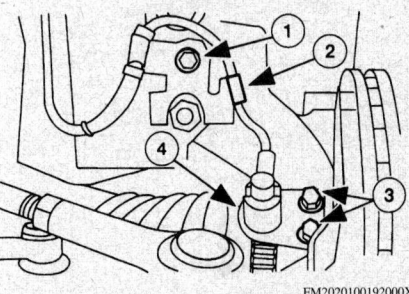

FM2020100192000X

Fig. 9   Anti-lock brake sensor replacement

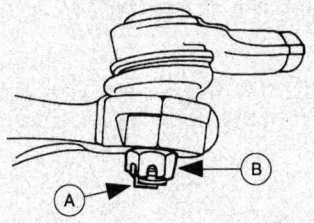

FM2020100190000X

Fig. 7   Cotter pin & nut replacement

16. Remove pushpin and position right-hand boot shield aside.
17. Remove steering gear from righthand side of vehicle.
18. Reverse procedure to install.

POWER STEERING PUMP

REPLACE

DOHC Engine

1. Disconnect radiator overflow tube and position aside.
2. Remove air conditioning hose clamp

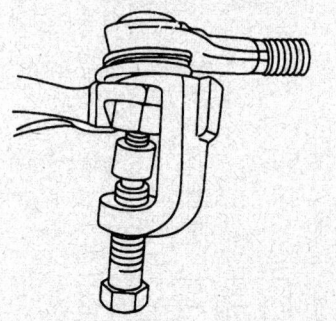

FM2020100191000X

Fig. 8   Tie rod separator tool installation

bolt and disconnect speed control cable from air conditioning hose bracket.
3. Remove air conditioning hose bracket, then raise and support vehicle.
4. Remove mounting bolts and lower righthand splash shield.
5. Turn belt tensioner bolt clockwise and remove accessory drive belt.
6. Disconnect power steering pressure hose from power steering pump and lower vehicle.

7. Remove power steering hose brackets and disconnect heated oxygen sensor connector.
8. Remove engine block ground bracket and disconnect power steering return hose from power steering pump.
9. Raise and support vehicle, then remove power steering pressure hose.
10. Lower vehicle, then remove four mounting bolts and pump.
11. Reverse procedure to install. Install new power steering pump heat shield.

SOHC Engine

1. Remove power steering pump reservoir.
2. Remove power steering pump pulley.
3. Raise and support vehicle.
4. Remove six bolts and righthand splash shield.
5. Disconnect power steering pressure hose.
6. Lower vehicle.
7. Loosen clamp and disconnect power steering reservoir to pump hose.
8. Remove mounting bolts and power steering pump.
9. Reverse procedure to install.

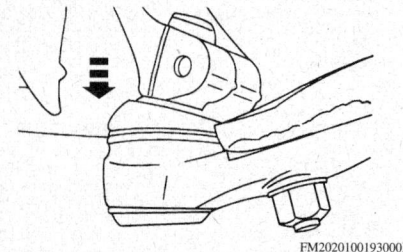

Fig. 10 Front suspension lower arm ball joint replacement

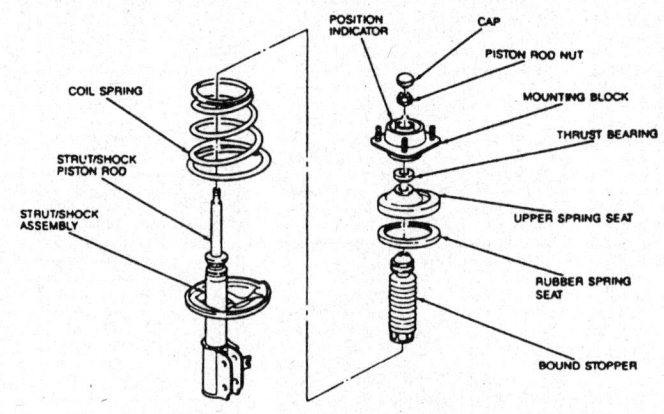

Fig. 11 Exploded view of front strut

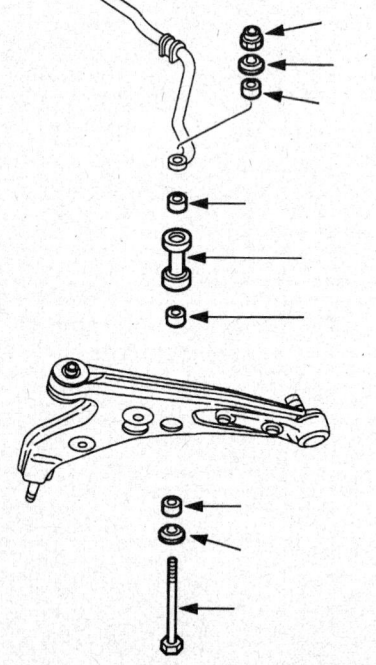

Fig. 12 Stabilizer bar link replacement

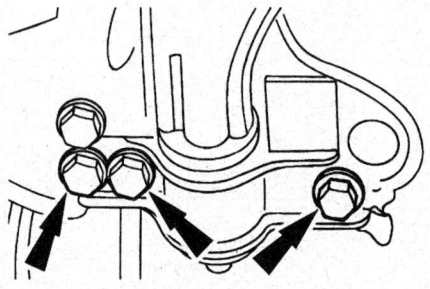

Fig. 13 Lower control arm replacement

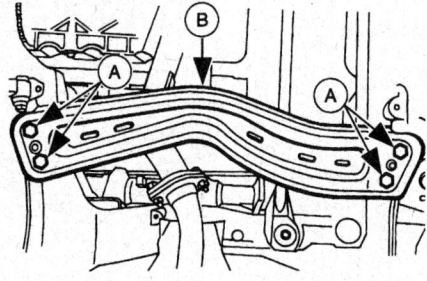

Fig. 14 Crossmember replacement

Fig. 16 Transaxle insulator nut replacement

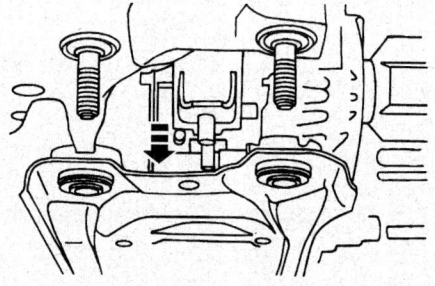

Fig. 17 Transaxle support crossmember replacement

Fig. 15 Steering gear mounting bracket nut replacement

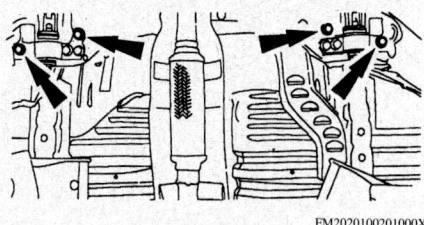

Fig. 19 Front subframe nut replacement

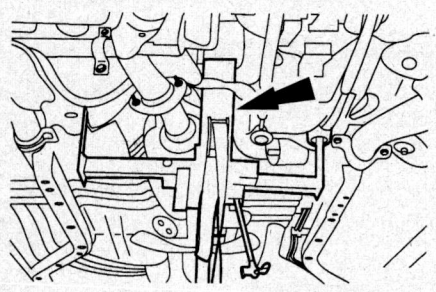

Fig. 18 Subframe replacement

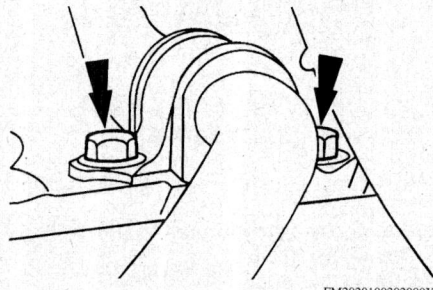

Fig. 20 Stabilizer bar replacement

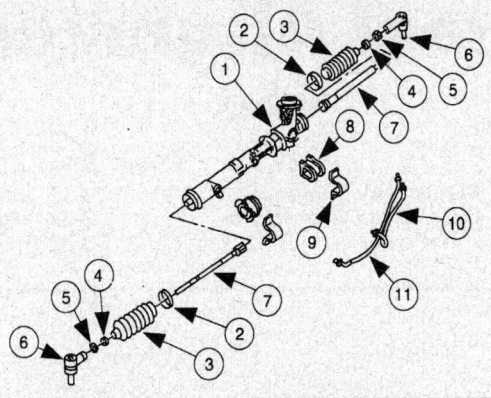

Item	Description	Item	Description
1	Steering Gear	6	Tie Rod End
2	Inner Front Suspension Steering Ball Stud Dust Seal (Part of 3332)	7	Front Wheel Spindle Tie Rod
		8	Steering Gear Insulator
3	Front Suspension Steering Ball Stud Dust Seal	9	Steering Gear Mounting Bracket
4	Outer Front Suspension Steering Ball Stud Dust Seal (Part of 3332)	10	Power Steering Left Turn Pressure Hose
5	Tie Rod End Jam Nut (Part of 3A130)	11	Power Steering Right Turn Pressure Hose

FM6029700218000X

Fig. 21 Power steering gear components

TIGHTENING SPECIFICATIONS

Year	Component	Torque/Ft. Lbs.
2001–03	Lower Alternator, Lower	15–22
	Upper Alternator, Upper	30–40
	Crossmember	69–97
	Engine Block Ground Bracket	71–89①
	Front Wheel Spindle Tie Rod	40–50
	Lower Power Steering Hose Retaining Bracket	70–96①
	Power Steering Fluid Cooler Bracket	70–96①
	Power Steering Pressure Hose Bracket	71–89①
	Power Steering Pressure Hose Fitting	20–25
	Power Steering Pressure Hose To Pump Fitting	40–54
	Power Steering Pressure Hose To Steering Gear Fitting	21–25
	Power Steering Pressure Hose Bracket	70–96①
	Power Steering Pulley	15–22
	Power Steering Pump, SOHC Engine	30–41
	Power Steering Pump, DOHC Engine	15–22
	Power Steering Pump Reservoir	70–96①
	Power Steering Return Hose Retainer Bracket	70–96①
	Power Steering Return Hose To Steering Gear Fitting	20–25
	Righthand Splash Shield	69–98①
	Steering Column Input Shaft Coupling To Steering Gear Input Shaft Pinch Bolt	30–36
	Steering Column Tube Boot	18–52①
	Steering Gear Mounting Bracket	28–38
	Tie Rod End	25–33
	Tie Rod End Jam Nut	25–37
	Upper Power Steering Hose Bracket	30–40
	Wheel Lug Nuts	74–100

① — Inch lbs.

Wheel Alignment

INDEX

PRELIMINARY INSPECTION

1. Inspect tires for proper inflation and similar tread wear.
2. Inspect hub and bearing for excessive wear, repair as required.
3. Inspect ball joints.
4. Inspect tie rod ends for excessive looseness.
5. Inspect wheel and tire runout.
6. Inspect vehicle ride height.
7. Inspect rack and pinion for looseness at frame.
8. Ensure proper strut operation.
9. Inspect suspension and steering components for damage, replace as required.

FRONT WHEEL ALIGNMENT

Camber

1. Raise and support vehicle.
2. Remove front shock absorber upper mounting bracket nuts.
3. Push front shock absorber upper mounting bracket downward and turn to desired position to set camber/caster, **Fig. 1.**
4. **Torque** front shock absorber upper mounting bracket nuts to 35–47 ft. lbs.

Toe

The lefthand and righthand front wheel spindle rods are both righthand threaded. To increase the toe-in, turn the righthand front wheel spindle tie rod toward the front of the vehicle and turn the lefthand front wheel spindle tie rod the same amount toward the rear of the vehicle. One turn of the front wheel spindle tie rod (both sides) makes a toe-in change of .24 inch.

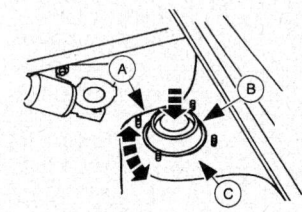

Direction Indicator	Difference From Standard Position	
	Camber Angle	Caster Angle
A	+ 14 Minutes	+ 14 Minutes
B	+ 29 Minutes	0 Degrees
C	+ 14 Minutes	- 14 Minutes

FM2020100203000X

Fig. 1 Camber adjustment specifications

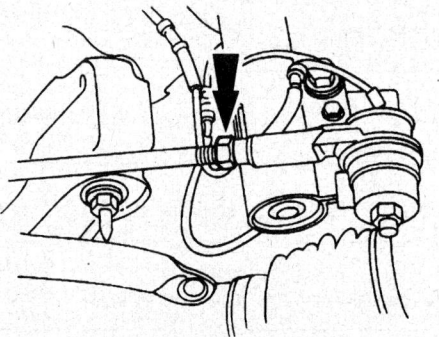

FM2020100204000X

Fig. 2 Tie rod end jam nut

1. Loosen left and righthand tie rod end jam nuts, **Fig. 2.**
2. Turn front wheel spindle tie rods equally until toe-in setting is within specifications.
3. **Torque** tie rod end jam nuts to 25–29 ft. lbs.

REAR WHEEL ALIGNMENT

Toe

1. Loosen lefthand and righthand rear suspension arm and bushing bolt.

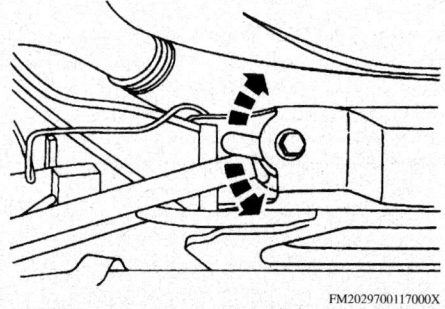

FM2029700117000X

Fig. 3 Rear toe adjustment

2. Turn lefthand and righthand adjusting cams together until toe is within specifications, **Fig. 3.**
3. **Torque** lefthand and righthand rear suspension arm and bushing bolt to 63–86 ft. lbs.

CONTINENTAL

INDEX OF SERVICE OPERATIONS

Specifications

GENERAL ENGINE SPECIFICATIONS

Year	Engine, Liter (Code)①	Fuel System	Bore & Stroke	Compression Ratio	Net HP @ RPM	Maximum Torque, Ft. Lbs. @ RPM	Normal Oil Pressure, psi
2001–02	4.6L DOHC (V)	SFI	3.55 × 3.54	9.85	275 @ 5750	275 @ 4750	20–45

SFI — Sequential Fuel Injection
DOHC — Dual Overhead Cam

① — The eighth digit of VIN denotes engine code.

TUNE UP SPECIFICATIONS

Year & Engine/ Liter (Code)①	Spark Plug Gap, Inch	Ignition Timing, °BTDC Firing Order, Fig.④	Ignition Timing, °BTDC Degrees	Ignition Timing, °BTDC Timing Mark, Fig.	Curb Idle Speed, RPM⑨	Fast Idle Speed, RPM⑨	Fuel Pump Pressure, psi③	Valve Clearance⑧
2001								
4.6L DOHC (V)	.054	⑦	②	⑤	⑥	⑥	35–45	.0018–.0033
2002								
4.6L DOHC (V)	.052–.056	⑦	②	⑤	⑥	⑥	35–55	.0018–.0033

BTDC — Before Top Dead Center
DOHC — Dual Overhead Cam
① — The eighth digit of VIN denotes engine code.
② — Not adjustable.
③ — Key on engine off. Wrap shop towel around fuel diagnostic valve to prevent fuel spillage. Connect suitable fuel pressure gauge to fuel diagnostic valve. Energize fuel pump and record fuel pressure gauge reading.

④ — Before disconnecting wires from distributor cap, determine location of No. 1 wire in cap, as distributor position may have been altered from that illustrated at the end of this chart.
⑤ — Equipped w/crankshaft sensor.
⑥ — Idle speed is controlled by an automatic idle speed control. No adjustment is required.
⑦ — Equipped w/coil on spark plug ignition. Cylinder numbering front to

rear, righthand bank, 1-2-3-4; lefthand bank 5-6-7-8. Firing order, 1-3-7-2-6-5-4-8.
⑧ — Equipped w/hydraulic lifters.
⑨ — When inspecting idle speed, set parking brake & block drive wheels.

FRONT WHEEL ALIGNMENT SPECIFICATIONS

Year	Caster Angle, Degrees Limits	Caster Angle, Degrees Desired	Camber Angle, Degrees Limits	Camber Angle, Degrees Desired	Total Toe, Inch① Limits	Total Toe, Inch① Desired	Toe-Out On Turns, Degrees Outer Wheel	Toe-Out On Turns, Degrees Inner Wheel	Ball Joint Wear, Inch
2001–02	+3.40 to + 5.40	+4.40	-1.20 to 0	-.60	-.23 to +.07	-.10	—	—	①

① — Refer to "Ball Joint Inspection" in "Front Suspension & Steering" section.

REAR WHEEL ALIGNMENT SPECIFICATIONS

Year	Camber Angle, Degrees Limits	Camber Angle, Degrees Desired	Total Toe, Inch Limits	Total Toe, Inch Desired
2001–02	-1.2 to +.2	-.7	-.03 to +.23	+.10

VEHICLE RIDE HEIGHT SPECIFICATIONS

Year	Manu-facturer's Original Tire Size	Measurement Points & Specifications②					
		Front			Rear		
		Dim.	Specification		Dim.	Specification	
			Inches	mm		Inches	mm
2001–02	P225/60HR16	1	+3.3 to +3.9①③	+90.7 to +92.1①③	2	-1.1 to -.9①③	-28.06 to -24.76①③

Dim. — Dimension
N/A — Not Available
① — After Accurate Trim Test.
② — Measurement is with fuel, radiator coolant and engine oil full, spare

tire, jack, hand tools and mats in designated positions and tires properly inflated.
③ — Ride height side to side at wheel opening should be within .01 inch

(.25 mm). Ride height front to rear (average front to average rear) should be with in .03 inch (.75 mm).

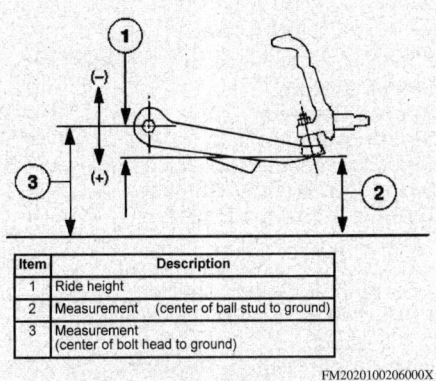

Item	Description
1	Ride height
2	Measurement (center of ball stud to ground)
3	Measurement (center of bolt head to ground)

FM2020100206000X

Fig. A Front ride height measurement

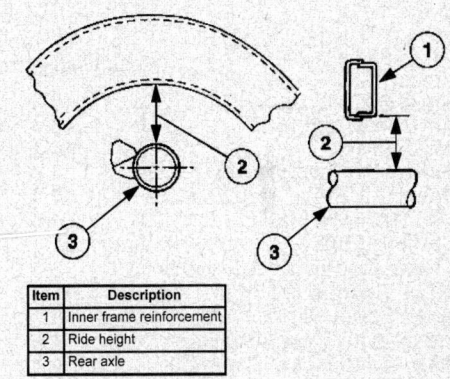

Item	Description
1	Inner frame reinforcement
2	Ride height
3	Rear axle

FM2030100153000X

Fig. B Rear ride height measurement

FLUID CAPACITIES & COOLING SYSTEM DATA

Year	Engine	Coolant Capacity, Qts.	Coolant Type	Radiator Cap Relief Pressure, psi	Thermo. Opening Temp., Deg. F	Fuel Tank, Gal.	Engine Oil Refill, Qts.①②	Automatic Trans., Qts.②	Rear Axle Oil, Pints③
2001	4.6L DOHC	15.8	EG	13–18	183–190	20	6	13.7	—
2002	4.6L DOHC	15.8	④	13–18	183–190	20	6	13.7	—

EG — Ethylene Glycol
① — With filter change.
② — Approximate. Make final inspection w/dipstick.
③ — Differential w/tractional, add 4 oz. friction modifier.

④ — Yellow-colored, Motorcraft Premium Gold Engine Coolant extended-life engine coolant meeting Ford Specification WSS-M97B51-A1 (P/N VC-7-A and VC-7-C for U.S. except California

and Oregon, and VC-7-B for California and Oregon only). Use only the type of engine coolant with which the vehicle was originally equipped. Do not mix coolant types.

LUBRICANT DATA

Year	Lubricant Type			
	Automatic Transmission/ Transaxle	Rear Axle	Power Steering	Brake System
2001–02	Mercon V	①	Mercon	DOT 3

① — Use premium axle lubricant P/N XY-80W90-QL, or an equivalent meeting Ford specification WSP-

M2C197-A. On models equipped with traction lock axles, add four ounces of friction modifier P/N

C8AZ-19B546-A, or equivalent meeting Ford specification EST-M2C118-A.

CONTINENTAL

Electrical

NOTE: On Air Bag Equipped Models, Refer To "Air Bag System Precautions" Located In The Front Of This Manual For System Disarming & Arming Procedures.

NOTE: Refer To "Computer Relearn Procedures" Located In The Front Of This Manual When Battery Power To The Computer Has Been Interrupted.

NOTE: Prior To Performing Any Service Operations Listed In This Section, Consult The "Technical Service Bulletins" Section For Related Information.

INDEX

PRECAUTIONS

Air Bag Systems

Refer to "Air Bag System Precautions" in the front of this manual for system disarming and arming procedures.

Battery Ground Cable

Prior to service, disconnect battery ground cable and isolate as required.

FUSE PANEL & FLASHER LOCATION

The fuse panel is located under the instrument panel to the lefthand side of the steering column.

The turn signal and hazard flashers are a component of the Lighting Control Module (LCM) located under the righthand side of the instrument panel.

RELAY CENTER LOCATION

The relay center, known as the Constant Control Relay Module (CCRM), is located on the radiator support in the lower front center of the engine compartment. The relay center contains the following relays: fuel pump, air conditioning fan, PCM power and air conditioning control.

FUEL PUMP RELAY LOCATION

The fuel pump relay is a component of the CCRM. The fuel pump control module is located at the front righthand side of the luggage compartment.

STARTER

REPLACE

The starter solenoid heavy gauge input lead is hot at all times. Ensure protective cap is installed over terminal and is replaced after service. When battery has been disconnected and connected, some abnormal drive symptoms may occur while the EEC processor relearns its adaptive strategy. The vehicle may need to be driven 10 miles or more to relearn strategy.
1. Raise and support vehicle.
2. Remove lower air deflector.
3. Disconnect starter cable and push-on connector at starter solenoid. **When disconnecting hard shell connector at S terminal, pull plastic shell straight out. Do not pull on wire.**
4. Remove mounting bolts and starter.

5. Reverse procedure to install. **Torque starter mounting bolts to 20–27 ft. lbs.**

COIL PACK

REPLACE

The PCM controls the eight separate ignition coils. Each coil is mounted directly above its respective spark plug.
1. Remove air cleaner outlet tube.
2. Remove left and righthand spark plug/ignition coil covers.
3. Disconnect spark plug ignition coil wire.
4. Disconnect ignition coil connector.
5. Remove spark plug ignition coil.
6. Inspect coil for cracks, dirt and carbon fouling.
7. Reverse procedure to install. **Torque spark plug/ignition coil covers to 89 inch lbs.**

IGNITION LOCK

REPLACE

Functional Lock

1. Turn ignition lock cylinder to Run position.
2. Press ignition switch lock cylinder release pin while pulling on lock cylinder.
3. Reverse procedure to install.

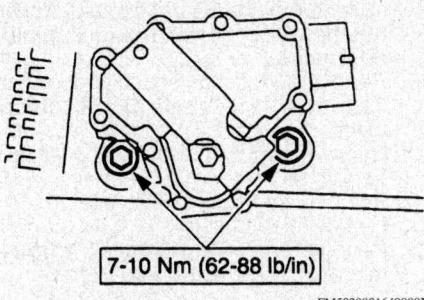

7-10 Nm (62-88 lb/in)

FM5029801649000X

Fig. 1 TR sensor alignment

Non-Functional Lock

REMOVAL

1. Ensure front wheels are in straight-ahead position.
2. Disconnect back-up power supply and remove air bag module as outlined in "Passive Restraint Systems"
3. chapter.
4. Disconnect steering wheel speed control wiring harness.
5. Remove and discard steering wheel mounting bolt.
6. Remove steering wheel using steering wheel puller tool No. T67L-3600-A, or equivalent.
7. Disconnect key warning switch electrical connector.
8. **On models equipped with ignition switch cap,** use channel-lock or vise-grip type pliers to twist cap from lock cylinder.
9. **On all models,** drill out retaining pin using suitable ⅛ inch drill bit. **Do not drill deeper than ½ inch.**
10. Break cap away from cylinder by striking sharp blows to suitable chisel at base of ignition lock cylinder cap.
11. Drill down middle of ignition lock key slot 1¾ inches using suitable ⅜ inch drill bit until lock cylinder breaks loose from lock cylinder breakaway base.
12. Remove lock cylinder and drill shavings from lock cylinder housing.
13. Remove retainer, washer, ignition switch and actuator. Clean drill shavings from casting.
14. Inspect lock cylinder housing.

INSTALLATION

1. Install actuator and ignition switch.
2. Install trim and electrical components.
3. Install new ignition lock cylinder.
4. Install steering wheel.
5. Ensure lock operates properly.
6. Ensure electrical connectors and wiring are properly routed to avoid pinching.
7. **Torque** new steering wheel bolt to 30 ft. lbs.
8. **Torque** steering wheel mounting bolt to 25–34 ft. lbs.

IGNITION SWITCH

REPLACE

1. Remove lefthand instrument panel steering column opening cover.

2. Remove mounting bolts and position hood latch release handle aside.
3. Remove mounting bolts and position parking brake handle aside.
4. Remove instrument panel steering column opening cover reinforcement.
5. Loosen mounting bolt and disconnect ignition switch electrical connector.
6. Remove mounting screws and ignition switch.
7. Reverse procedure to install, noting the following:
   a. **Torque** ignition switch mounting screws to 47–64 inch lbs.
   b. **Torque** ignition switch electrical connector mounting bolt to 7–10 inch lbs.
   c. **Torque** parking brake handle and hood release handle mounting bolts to 24–33 inch lbs.

NEUTRAL SAFETY SWITCH

REPLACE

The Transmission Range (TR) sensor is located on the outside of the transmission. It completes the start circuit in Park or Neutral and the backup lamp circuit in Reverse. The sensor also opens and closes a set of four switches that are monitored by the Powertrain Control Module (PCM) to determine the position of the manual PRND21 lever.

1. Apply parking brake.
2. Place gearshift lever in Neutral and remove engine air cleaner.
3. Disconnect TR sensor electrical connector.
4. Remove mounting nut and manual control lever to manual shaft.
5. Remove mounting bolts and TR sensor.
6. Reverse procedure to install, adjusting sensor as follows:
   a. Loosely install TR sensor mounting bolts.
   b. Ensure manual shift lever is in Neutral position.
   c. Align TR sensor using TR sensor alignment tool No. T97L-70010-A, or equivalent, **Fig. 1.**
   d. **Torque** mounting bolts to 62–88 inch lbs.

HEADLAMP SWITCH

REPLACE

1. Uploading Lighting Control Module (LCM) configuration using Worldwide Diagnostic System (WDS) 418-F224 New Generation STAR (NGS) tester tool No. 418-F052, or equivalent, suitably programmed scan tool.
2. Remove instrument panel steering column opening cover.
3. Remove LCM to instrument panel mounting screws.
4. Pull LCM from instrument panel and disconnect electrical connectors.
5. Reverse procedure to install. Download module configuration information to new LCM using STAR (NGS) tester, or equivalent, suitably programmed scan tool.

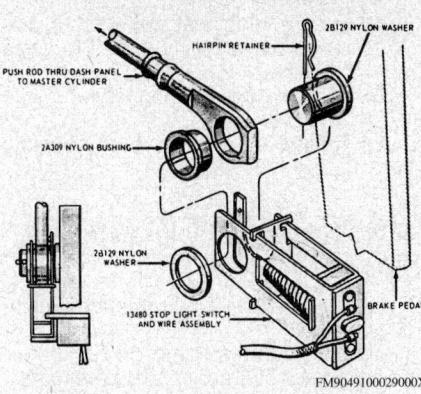

FM9049100029000X

Fig. 2 Stop lamp switch

STOP LIGHT SWITCH

REPLACE

1. Disconnect wires at switch connector.
2. Remove hair pin retainer.
3. Slide switch, pushrod and nylon washers and bushing away from brake pedal, then remove switch, **Fig. 2.**
4. Reverse procedure to install.

MULTI-FUNCTION SWITCH

REPLACE

1. Remove ignition lock cylinder.
2. Place tilt column in lowest position and remove tilt lever.
3. Remove mounting screws, then the upper and lower column shrouds.
4. Remove wiring harness retainer and disconnect electrical connectors.
5. Remove mounting screws and multi-function switch.
6. Reverse procedure to install.

TURN SIGNAL SWITCH

REPLACE

1. Remove ignition lock cylinder.
2. Place tilt column in lowest position and remove tilt lever.
3. Remove mounting screws, then the upper and lower column shrouds.
4. Remove wiring harness retainer and disconnect electrical connectors.
5. Remove mounting screws and multi-function switch.
6. Reverse procedure to install.

STEERING WHEEL

REPLACE

1. Ensure front wheels are in straight-ahead position.
2. Disconnect back-up power supply and remove air bag module as outlined in "Passive Restraint Systems" chapter
3. Disconnect steering wheel speed control wiring harness.
4. Remove and discard steering wheel mounting bolt.
5. Remove steering wheel using puller tool No. T67L-3600-A, or equivalent.
6. Reverse procedure to install, noting the following:

a. Ensure electrical connectors and wiring are properly routed to avoid pinching.
b. **Torque** new steering wheel bolt to 30 ft. lbs.
c. **Torque** air bag module mounting nuts to 108 inch lbs.

INSTRUMENT CLUSTER
REPLACE

1. Remove lefthand instrument panel insulator.
2. Remove courtesy lamp.
3. Remove instrument panel lower cover.
4. Remove mounting screws and position hood release handle aside.
5. Remove mounting screws and position parking brake handle aside.
6. Remove steering column opening cover reinforcement.
7. Remove mounting screws and steering column shroud.
8. Disconnect electrical connectors and wiring.
9. Remove mounting nuts and lower steering column to floor.
10. Remove instrument panel finish panel.
11. Remove instrument cluster finish panel.
12. Disconnect electrical connectors at clock and message center.
13. Pull instrument cluster out and disconnect transaxle range indicator.
14. Reverse procedure to install, noting the following:
    a. Ensure electrical connectors and wiring are properly routed to avoid pinching.
    b. **Torque** steering column mounting nuts to 10–12 ft. lbs.
    c. **Torque** steering column impact absorber nuts to 10–14 ft. lbs.
    d. Cycle ignition to Run using two encoded ignition keys. Clear DTCs and test system for normal operation.
    e. Passive Anti-Theft System (PATS) must be configured after instrument cluster has been replaced, refer to NGS Tester configuration card HELP screen.

RADIO
REPLACE

1. Remove instrument panel trim and insulation panels to access radio mounting and electrical connectors.
2. Disconnect wiring connectors and antenna cable.
3. Reverse procedure to install.

WIPER MOTOR
REPLACE

1. Remove cap, nut and wiper pivot arm
2. Remove cowl top vent panels.
3. Disconnect wiper motor electrical connector.
4. Remove mounting bolts, arm and pivot shaft.
5. Remove mounting bolt and disconnect wiper motor crank.

6. Remove mounting bolts and wiper motor.
7. Reverse procedure to install, noting the following:
    a. **Torque** motor mounting bolts to 10–13 ft. lbs.
    b. **Torque** motor crank mounting bolt to 12–16 ft. lbs.
    c. **Torque** mounting arm and pivot shaft mounting bolts to 79–106 inch lbs.

WIPER SWITCH
REPLACE

1. Remove ignition lock cylinder.
2. Place tilt column in lowest position and remove tilt lever.
3. Remove mounting screws, then the upper and lower column shrouds.
4. Remove wiring harness retainer and disconnect electrical connectors.
5. Remove mounting screws and multifunction switch.
6. Reverse procedure to install.

BLOWER MOTOR
REPLACE

1. Remove instrument panel insulator fasteners.
2. Disconnect courtesy lamp and remove insulator.
3. Remove righthand scuff plate.
4. Remove instrument panel upper finish panel and disconnect air conditioning sunload sensor wire harness connector.
5. Remove righthand and center instrument panel to dash panel mounting screws.
6. Remove righthand instrument panel to cowl mounting nut.
7. Disconnect blower motor electrical connector.
8. Remove mounting screws and blower motor.
9. Reverse procedure to install, noting the following:
    a. **Torque** righthand instrument panel to cowl mounting nut to 89–123 inch lbs.
    b. **Torque** blower motor mounting screws to 18–26 ft. lbs.

HEATER CORE
REPLACE

1. Remove instrument panel as outlined in "Dash Panel Service" chapter.
2. Drain coolant into suitable container until level is below heater core.
3. Disconnect Powertrain Control Module (PCM) electrical connector.
4. Disconnect hoses at heater core.
5. Remove mounting screws and metal cover.
6. Remove air conditioning electronic blend door actuator.
7. Remove air conditioning air intake flue damper assist spring.
8. Depress locking ramp and remove air conditioning damper door shaft from

air temperature control door shaft. **Do not bend air conditioning damper door shaft .**
9. Remove air conditioning evaporator case outlet door shaft. **Do not bend lever.**
10. Remove mounting screws and heater core cover.
11. Remove heater core cover seal.
12. Remove heater core.
13. Reverse procedure to install, **torque** mounting screws to 18–26 inch lbs.

EVAPORATOR CORE
REPLACE

The evaporator core is serviced as a core and housing assembly. The core, internal doors, seals and door linkage are with the housing. The blower motor and wheel assembly, heater core and cover, dash panel seals and vacuum actuators will be required fore new housing.
1. Remove seats.
2. Remove rear seat airflow duct.
3. Remove instrument panel as outlined in "Dash Panel Service" chapter.
4. Drain coolant into suitable container until level is below heater core.
5. Recover air conditioning refrigerant system as outlined in "Air Conditioning" chapter.
6. Disconnect PCM electrical connector.
7. Disconnect heater hoses at heater core.
8. Disconnect vacuum supply hose.
9. Disconnect condenser to evaporator tube and evaporator to accumulator tube spring lock couplings from evaporator core.
10. Disconnect evaporator housing electrical connectors.
11. Remove nuts and washers at cowl panel.
12. Remove evaporator housing mounting screws.
13. Remove mounting screws and metal cover.
14. Remove screws and air conditioning electronic blend door actuator.
15. Remove air conditioning air intake flue damper assist spring.
16. Depress locking ramp and remove air conditioning damper door shaft from air temperature control door shaft. **Do not bend air conditioning damper door shaft.**
17. Remove air conditioning evaporator case outlet door shaft. **Do not bend lever.**
18. Remove air conditioning tube dash panel seal and evaporator drain tube seal.
19. Remove 15 screws and evaporator housing cover.
20. Remove evaporator core.
21. Reverse procedure to install, noting the following:
    a. Lubricate replacement evaporator core with proper amount of suitable PAG refrigerant oil.
    b. Fill cooling system with proper coolant.
    c. Charge air conditioning refrigerant system.

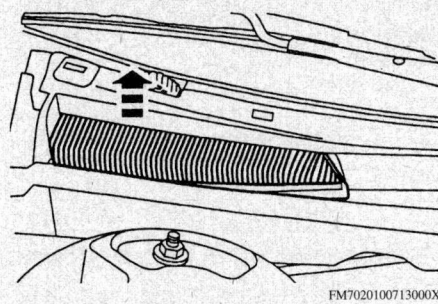

Fig. 3 Cabin air filter replacement

CABIN AIR FILTER
REPLACE

1. Open hood.
2. Pull hood pad away from righthand cowl vent screen.
3. Remove righthand cowl vent screen.
4. Remove water shield.
5. Remove cabin air filter element from filter housing, **Fig. 3**.
6. Reverse procedure to install.

TECHNICAL SERVICE BULLETINS

Sticking Or Binding Ignition Switch: DTCs P0500, P1502 & U1039

On some of these models there may roughness and/or excessive effort required to turn key from RUN to START position, or key may not fully return from START to RUN position after starting vehicle. On some of these models, the Malfunction Indicator Lamp (MIL) may illuminate with Diagnostic Trouble Codes P0500, P1502 and U1039 stored.

This condition may be caused the key-in-ignition warning chime switch.

To correct this condition, proceed as follows:

1. Remove ignition switch as outlined under "Ignition Switch, Replace."

2. Remove plastic key chime warning switch by prying rear tine up while sliding switch away from key insertion end, **Fig. 4**.
3. Install new key-in-ignition warning chime switch, P/N XL2Z-11A127-AB.
4. Install lock as outlined under "Ignition Switch, Replace."

Repeated Heater Core Failure

On some of these models there may be repeated heater core leaks.

This condition may be caused by a chemical reaction (electrolysis).

To correct this condition, proceed as follows:

1. Place positive probe of suitable digital volt/ohm meter in engine coolant and negative probe on battery ground terminal.
2. Adjust engine to 2000 RPM.
3. If more than .4 volt is recorded, flush coolant and inspect voltage, again.
4. If voltage is still excessive, inspect body/battery grounds.
5. If condition still exists, add extra grounds to heater core and engine, as follows:
   a. Secure 16 gauge stranded copper wire to heater core inlet tube using suitable hose clamp.
   b. Secure other end of wire to existing body sheet metal fastener.
   c. Secure another extra ground between existing engine and body sheet metal fasteners.
   d. Ensure there is continuity between added grounds and battery ground terminal.
6. If condition still exists, install restrictor as follows:
   a. Cut line as close to engine block as possible.
   b. Install restrictor (P/N F1UZ-18D406-A) on inlet hose with arrow facing coolant flow direction (toward heater core).
   c. Secure with two suitable hose clamps.
7. Bleed cooling system trapped air as follows:
   a. Disconnect heater hose at right-

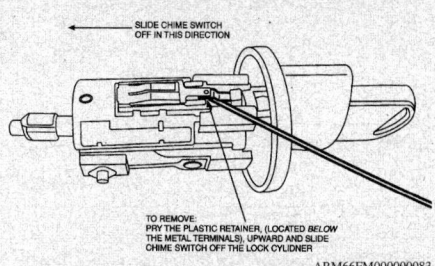

Fig. 4 Chime warning switch replacement

hand front or rear of engine.
b. Remove thermostat and housing.
c. Fill engine with suitable coolant until mixture is seen at engine side heater hose connection.
d. Connect heater hose, then install thermostat and housing.
e. Fill degas bottle to coolant fill level mark.
f. Fun engine to normal operating temperature.
g. Select MAX heat and blower speeds.

Erratic Cool/Warm Function

On some of these models warm air may constantly discharge from climate control system.

This condition may be caused by distorted and binding climate control stratification door.

To correct this condition, install revised door (P/N 3F1Z-19D842-AA) as follows:

1. Remove instrument panel as outlined in "Dash Panel Service" chapter.
2. Remove temperature blend door actuator.
3. Disconnect nylon link from stratification door (inside plenum).
4. Remove door (it will be easier to cut it near pivots).
5. Place new door inside and slide large pivot point first, then the door into position until small door pivot on front of case clicks into place.
6. Connect nylon link, install actuator and instrument panel.

4.6L DOHC Engine

NOTE: On Air Bag Equipped Models, Refer To "Air Bag System Precautions" Located In The Front Of This Manual For System Disarming & Arming Procedures.

NOTE: Refer To "Computer Relearn Procedures" Located In The Front Of This Manual When Battery Power To The Computer Has Been Interrupted.

INDEX

PRECAUTIONS

Air Bag Systems

Refer to "Air Bag System Precautions" in the front of this manual for system disarming and arming procedures.

Battery Ground Cable

Prior to service, disconnect battery ground cable and isolate as required.

Fuel System Pressure Relief

Fuel supply lines will remain pressurized after the engine is shutoff. Pressure must be relieved prior to any fuel system servicing. Relieve fuel system pressure as follows:
1. Remove fuel tank cap.
2. Attach fuel pressure gauge tool No. T80L-9974-B, or equivalent, to fuel rail pressure relief Schrader valve.
3. Place tool outlet hose in suitable container.
4. Slowly open tool valve to relieve pressure.

COMPRESSION PRESSURE

Cylinder compression pressure should be 134–250 psi at an engine cranking speed of 180 RPM minimum. The compression in the cylinder with the lowest reading should be within 75% of highest reading cylinder.

ENGINE MOUNT

REPLACE

Engine Mount

1. Turn off air suspension system.
2. Raise and safely support vehicle.
3. Drain coolant into suitable container.
4. Disconnect lower radiator hose at coolant inlet.
5. Lower vehicle.
6. Disconnect upper radiator hose at coolant outlet.
7. Remove PCV valve from valve cover.
8. Disconnect main vacuum supply tube.
9. Remove radiator upper sight shield.
10. Remove windshield wiper mounting arm and pivot shaft.
11. Remove nut and position engine control sensor wiring aside.
12. Disconnect heater hose at tube.
13. Disconnect PCM electrical connector.
14. Disconnect ground wires as required.
15. Install lefthand engine lifting bracket from three-bar engine support set tool No. 303-290-A, or equivalent, on righthand , rear of engine.
16. Install righthand engine lifting bracket on lefthand (front) side of engine.
17. Raise and safely support vehicle.
18. **If replacing righthand engine mount,** remove righthand front wheel and tire.
19. Remove radiator air deflector.
20. **If replacing lefthand engine mount,** remove oil filter.
21. **On all models,** remove mounting bolts, nut and engine support insulator.
22. Remove mounting bolts and engine support insulator bracket.
23. Reverse procedure to instal. Apply suitable threadlock to mounting bolts and nuts.

Transaxle Mount

1. Turn off air suspension system.
2. Remove lefthand front wheel and tire.
3. Remove lefthand front fender splash shield and position aside.
4. Support transaxle with suitable jack.
5. Remove transaxle upper support insulator nut.
6. Remove transaxle upper support bracket bolts and bracket.
7. Remove transaxle upper support insulator bolts and insulator.
8. Reverse procedure to install.

ENGINE

REPLACE

The engine will separate from the transaxle during removal.
1. Drain coolant into suitable container.
2. Turn air suspension system off.

3. Remove lefthand dash closeout panel and disconnect courtesy lamp.
4. Remove steering column boot.
5. Mark steering column and coupler for installation alignment.
6. Remove steering column coupler pinch bolt and disconnect column from steering gear.
7. Remove air cleaner outlet tube.
8. Remove bolt and position roll restrictor aside.
9. Raise and safely support vehicle.
10. Lower vehicle and recover air conditioning refrigerant system as outlined in "Air Conditioning" chapter.
11. Remove fuel tank cap.
12. Attach fuel pressure gauge tool No. T80L-9974-B, or equivalent, to fuel rail pressure relief Schraeder valve.
13. Place tool outlet hose in suitable container.
14. Slowly open tool valve to fuel system pressure.
15. Disconnect fuel line.
16. Disconnect main chassis vacuum supply hose.
17. Disconnect PCM ground straps.
18. Disconnect PCM engine control sensor wiring.
19. Remove engine control sensor wiring to righthand valve cover mounting nut.
20. Disconnect engine control sensor wiring from main engine wiring harness, MAF sensor and TP sensor.
21. Remove accelerator cable snow shield.
22. Disconnect accelerator and speed control actuator cables from throttle body.
23. Remove bolts and accelerator cable bracket and position it aside.
24. Disconnect manual control cable from transaxle shift selector.
25. Disconnect engine control sensor wiring from three main engine compartment wiring harness connectors.
26. Remove bracket mounting bolt and position main engine compartment harness aside.
27. Disconnect EVAP return line.
28. Disconnect transaxle cooler inlet and outlet tubes.
29. Remove engine oil dipstick.
30. Disconnect heater hoses from water bypass tube and engine connections.
31. Disconnect power steering return hose and allow fluid to drain into suitable container.
32. Remove nut and bolt and position alternator battery lead aside.
33. Raise and support vehicle, then remove front tire and wheel assemblies.
34. Disconnect connectors, then remove left and righthand sensor links.
35. Separate left and righthand tie rod ends from front wheel knuckles.
36. Separate left and righthand halfshafts from front wheel knuckles.
37. Remove radiator air deflector.
38. Remove dual converter Y-pipe.
39. Disconnect power steering cooler line and allow fluid to drain into suitable container.
40. Disconnect air conditioning compressor refrigerant lines.

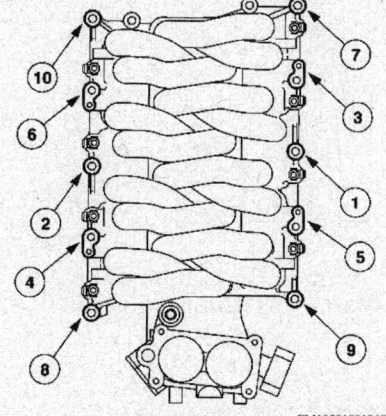

Fig. 1 Intake manifold loosening & tightening sequence

41. Disconnect lower radiator hose and bypass hose.
42. Disconnect starter motor wiring and electrical connectors.
43. Remove inspection cover.
44. Mark torque converter and flexplate for proper installation alignment, then remove four mounting nuts.
45. Support front subframe with suitable powertrain jack and universal powertrain removal bracket.
46. Remove four mounting bolts and lower subframe.
47. Support engine and transaxle using spreader bar set tool No. D93P-6001-A3 , or equivalent, and suitable floor crane.
48. Disconnect EVO sensor electrical connector.
49. Disconnect power steering gear return hose and allow fluid to drain into suitable container.
50. Disconnect turbine shaft speed sensor, transaxle range (TR) sensor and internal transmission wiring harness electrical connectors.
51. Disconnect engine righthand support insulator.
52. Remove bellhousing to engine block bolts.
53. Remove engine righthand support insulator bracket.
54. Separate engine from transaxle.
55. Remove engine.
56. Reverse procedure to install, noting the following:
   a. Ensure torque converter to flexplate marks are properly aligned.
   b. Apply suitable threadlock to engine mount, support and insulator mounting bolts and nuts.
   c. Install new castle nuts at tie rod ends.
   d. Ensure match marks at steering column to steering gear are properly aligned.

INTAKE MANIFOLD
REPLACE

1. Drain coolant into suitable container.
2. Remove air cleaner outlet tube.
3. Relive fuel system pressure as outlined in "Precautions."

4. Disconnect fuel line.
5. Remove two engine sensor control wiring to valve covers mounting nuts.
6. Remove mounting nut and bolt, then position alternator battery lead aside.
7. Disconnect alternator electrical connector.
8. Remove alternator mounting bracket.
9. Disconnect coolant hoses from water bypass tube.
10. Disconnect ECT sensor electrical connector.
11. Remove studs bypass tube. Discard O-rings.
12. Separate MAF sensor connector from accelerator snow shield.
13. Remove bolt, pushpin and snow shield.
14. Disconnect accelerator and speed control actuator cables from throttle body.
15. Remove mounting bolts and bracket, then position accelerator cable aside.
16. Disconnect chassis vacuum supply tube, PCV tube and engine vacuum supply line.
17. Disconnect fuel pressure sensor vacuum line and electrical connector.
18. Disconnect EVAP return line.
19. Disconnect heater hose.
20. Disconnect vacuum lines from EGR vacuum regulator solenoid and EGR valve.
21. Remove engine wiring harness covers.
22. Disconnect electrical connectors at fuel injectors.
23. Disconnect engine control sensor wiring electrical connectors from IAC valve, TP sensor and MAF sensor.
24. Disconnect EGR tube at EGR valve.
25. Disconnect ignition coils as required.
26. Disconnect starter motor electrical connectors.
27. Remove intake manifold studs holders and position engine wiring harness aside.
28. Remove mounting bolts and studs in sequence in three stages, **Fig. 1.**
29. Remove intake manifold and discard gaskets.
30. Reverse procedure to install. **Torque** intake manifold bolts in sequence to 89 inch lbs, **Fig. 1.**

EXHAUST MANIFOLD
REPLACE

Lefthand

1. Recover air conditioning refrigerant system as outlined in "Air Conditioning" chapter.
2. Raise and support vehicle.
3. Remove radiator air deflector.
4. Remove dual converter Y-pipe.
5. Disconnect air conditioning suction discharge manifold from compressor.
6. Remove manifold.
7. Reverse procedure to install. Tighten exhaust manifold nuts in sequence, **Fig. 2.**

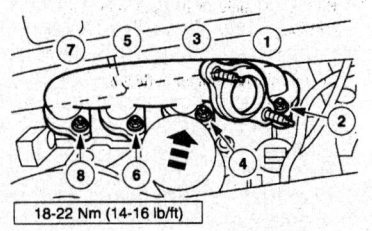

Fig. 2 Lefthand exhaust manifold tightening sequence

18-22 Nm (14-16 lb/ft)

FM1059800145000X

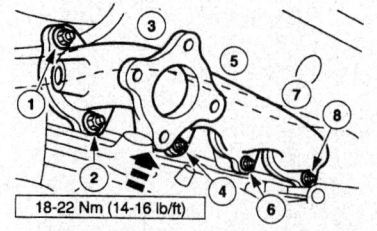

Fig. 3 Righthand exhaust manifold tightening sequence

18-22 Nm (14-16 lb/ft)

FM1059800143000X

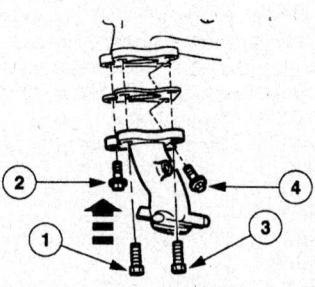

FM1059800144000X

Fig. 4 Righthand exhaust manifold connector tightening sequence

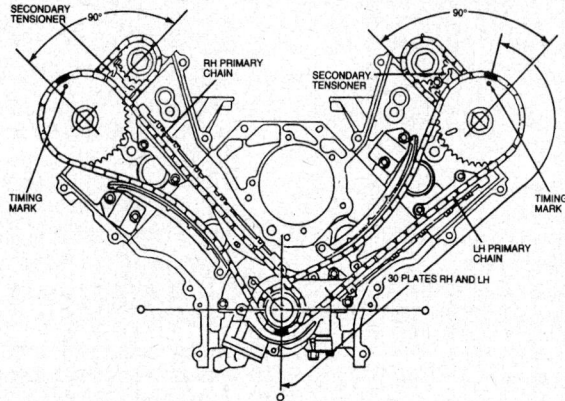

SECONDARY TENSIONER 90°

RH PRIMARY CHAIN

SECONDARY TENSIONER

90°

TIMING MARK

TIMING MARK

LH PRIMARY CHAIN

30 PLATES RH AND LH

FM1069300462000X

Fig. 5 Setting cylinder No. 1 to TDC

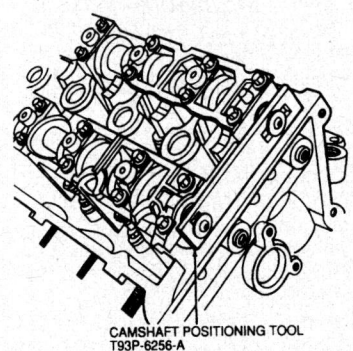

CAMSHAFT POSITIONING TOOL T93P-6256-A

FM1069300463000X

Fig. 6 Camshaft positioning tool installation

Righthand

1. Raise and support vehicle.
2. Remove righthand front wheel and tire assembly.
3. Remove radiator air deflector.
4. Remove dual converter Y-pipe.
5. Remove four bolts to exhaust manifold connector and gasket.
6. Disconnect EGR valve tube from exhaust manifold.
7. Remove engine support insulator strut.
8. Remove exhaust manifold.
9. Reverse procedure to install, noting the following:
   a. Tighten exhaust manifold nuts in sequence, **Fig. 3.**
   b. **Torque** exhaust manifold connector bolts in sequence to 13–17 ft. lbs., **Fig. 4.**
   c. Final **torque** connector bolts to in sequence 31–39 ft. lbs.

CYLINDER HEAD
REPLACE

This procedure has been revised by a Technical Service Bulletin.

1. Remove engine from vehicle as outlined under "Engine, Replace."
2. Remove valve covers as outlined under "Valve Cover, Replace."
3. Remove engine front cover as outlined under "Front Cover, Replace."
4. Remove intake manifold as outlined under "Intake Manifold, Replace."
5. Remove crankshaft position sensor pulse wheel.
6. Position piston of cylinder being re-

paired at bottom of stroke and camshaft lobe at base circle.

7. Compress valve spring using spring compressor tool No. T93P-6565-AR, or equivalent, and remove roller follower.
8. Repeat previous steps for remaining cylinders.
9. Remove exhaust manifolds as outlined under "Exhaust Manifold, Replace."
10. Rotate engine to No. 1 cylinder TDC, **Fig. 5.**
11. Install camshaft positioning tool No. T93P-6256-A, or equivalent, to camshafts, **Fig. 6.**
12. Remove primary timing chain as outlined under "Timing Chain, Replace." **Do not remove camshaft sprocket and secondary timing chain now.**
13. Remove heater hose tube from righthand cylinder head.
14. Loosen cylinder head bolts in sequence, **Fig. 7.**
15. Remove and discard cylinder head bolts.
16. Remove cylinder head and gaskets, discard gaskets.
17. If head casting is to be replaced, proceed as follows:
   a. Remove secondary timing chain and sprockets as outlined under "Timing Chain, Replace."
   b. Rotate crankshaft key counterclockwise 45° from vertical. Ensure pistons are below top of engine deck face. **Crankshaft must be in position prior to rotating camshafts or piston and/or valve damage may result if rocker**

arms have not been removed.
   c. Remove camshaft cap cluster mounting bolts, **Fig. 8.**
   d. Remove first exhaust.
   e. Remove intake camshaft cap cluster.
   f. Tap camshaft cap upward.
   g. Remove cap and camshaft.
18. Reverse procedure to install, noting the following:
   a. Aluminum cylinder heads must be cleaned of residue left behind by multi-layered steel (MLS) head gaskets. **Do not use power sanding, grinding or buffing equipment. Do not use manual grinding and scraping aids such as sandpaper, razor blades or metal scrapers.**
   b. Soften RTV using Motorcraft Silcone Gasket Remover (P/N ZC-30), or equivalent.
   c. Remove as much old material as possible using suitable plastic or wooden scraper. **Do not damage aluminum with score marks or depressions.**
   d. Clean surface with coat of Motorcraft Metal Surface Prep (P/N ZC-31), or equivalent. Wipe clean with suitable lint-free rag.
   e. **Use new cylinder head bolts and gaskets.**
   f. Lightly oil new cylinder head bolts with clean motor oil.
   g. **Torque** cylinder head bolts in sequence to 27–32 ft. lbs., **Fig. 9.**
   h. Tighten head bolts an additional 85–95° in sequence.

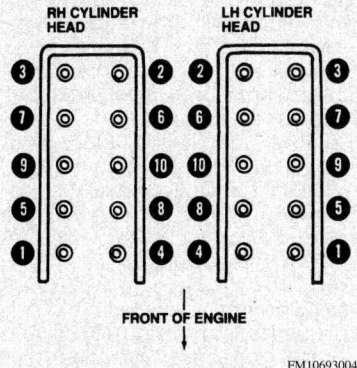

Fig. 7 Cylinder head bolt loosening sequence

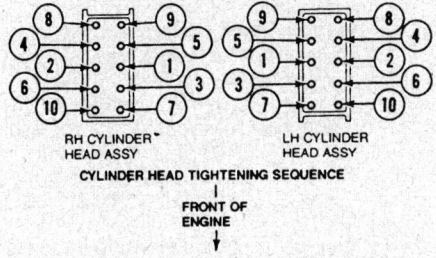

Fig. 9 Cylinder head tightening sequence

i. Tighten bolts an additional 85–95° in sequence.

VALVE COVER
REPLACE
Lefthand

1. Remove water bypass tube.
2. Remove crankcase ventilation tube from valve cover.
3. Remove two engine control sensor wiring harness to valve cover mounting nuts.
4. Disconnect camshaft position sensor.
5. Remove ignition coil cover and disconnect coil wiring harness connectors.
6. Remove ignition coils.
7. Disconnect air suspension relay electrical connector remove mounting bolt.
8. Position air suspension relay and bracket aside.
9. Remove mounting bolts, studs and valve cover.
10. Reverse procedure to install, noting the following:
    a. Install new spark plug bore O-rings and valve cover gaskets.
    b. Apply suitable silicone gasket and sealant to two places where engine front cover meets valve cover.
    c. Tighten mounting bolts in sequence, Fig. 10.

Righthand

1. Remove cross vehicle support.
2. Remove water bypass tube.
3. Remove fuel tank cap.
4. Attach fuel pressure gauge tool No.

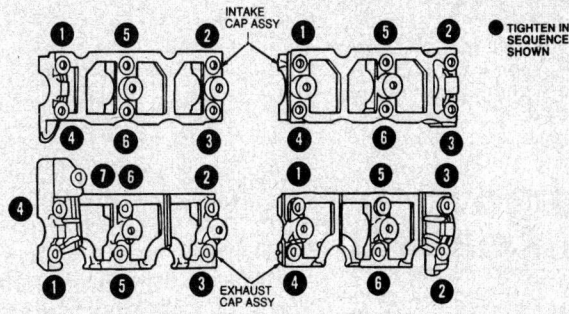

Fig. 8 Camshaft cap cluster loosening & tightening sequence

T80L-9974-B, or equivalent, to fuel rail pressure relief Schrader valve.
5. Place tool outlet hose in suitable container.
6. Slowly open tool valve to fuel system pressure.
7. Disconnect fuel line.
8. Disconnect main vacuum supply tube and PCV valve and tube.
9. Remove wiring harness mounting nut from valve cover.
10. Disconnect heater hose from heater water outlet tube.
11. Disconnect powertrain control module grounds.
12. Disconnect engine control sensor wiring from PCM.
13. Remove ignition coil cover, ignition coil electrical connectors and ignition coils.
14. Remove engine control sensor wiring mounting nut from valve cover front.
15. Disconnect fuel injection pressure sensor.
16. Remove engine control sensor wiring cover.
17. Disconnect four fuel injectors and position wiring harness out of way.
18. Remove mounting bolts, studs and valve cover.
19. Reverse procedure to install, noting the following:
    a. Install new spark plug bore O-rings and valve cover gaskets.
    b. Apply suitable silicone gasket and sealant to two places where engine front cover meets valve cover.
    c. Position valve cover and tighten bolts in sequence, Fig. 11.

VALVE ARRANGEMENT
Front To Rear

Righthand Side .S-P-E-E-S-P-E-E-S-P-E-E-S-P-E-E①
Lefthand Side ....E-E-P-S-E-E-P-S-E-E-P-S-E-E-P-S

①—S-Secondary Intake; P-Primary Intake; E-Exhaust.

CAMSHAFT LOBE LIFT SPECIFICATIONS

Engine	Intake, Inch	Exhaust, Inch
4.6L DOHC	.2200	.2186

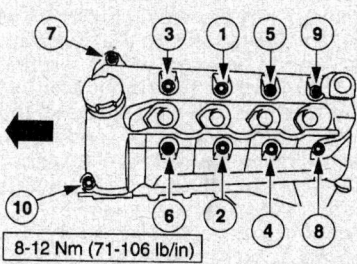

Fig. 10 Lefthand valve cover tightening sequence

VALVE ADJUSTMENT

These engines are equipped with hydraulic valve lash adjusters. No valve adjustment is required.

ROCKER ARMS
REPLACE

1. Remove valve covers as outlined under "Valve Cover, Replace."
2. Position piston of cylinder being repaired at bottom of stroke and camshaft lobe at base circle.
3. Compress valve spring using spring compressor tool No. T93P-6565-AR, or equivalent, and remove roller follower.
4. Repeat previous steps for remaining cylinders.
5. Reverse procedure to install.

HYDRAULIC LIFTERS
REPLACE

1. Remove valve covers as outlined under "Valve Cover, Replace."
2. Position piston of cylinder being repaired at bottom of stroke and camshaft lobe at base circle.
3. Compress valve spring using spring compressor tool No. T93P-6565-AR, or equivalent, and remove roller follower.
4. Repeat previous steps for remaining cylinders.
5. Remove valve tappets from cylinder heads.
6. Clean and inspect valve tappets.
7. Reverse procedure to install, noting the following:

a. Apply clean engine oil to valve stem and tip, rocker arm roller contact surfaces and valve tappets and cylinder head valve tappet bore.

b. Valve tappets must have no more than .039 inches of plunger travel prior to installation.

VALVE SPRING & VALVE STEM OIL SEAL
REPLACE
Removal

If, during this procedure, air pressure has forced the piston to the bottom of the cylinder, any loss of air pressure will allow the valve to fall into the cylinder. A rubber band, tape or string wrapped around the end of the valve stem will prevent this and still allow enough travel to inspect the valve for binding and excess guide to valve stem clearance.

1. Remove valve covers as outlined under "Valve Cover, Replace."
2. Position piston of cylinder being repaired at bottom of stroke and camshaft lobe at base circle.
3. Compress valve spring using spring compressor tool No. T93P-6565-AR, or equivalent, and remove roller follower.
4. Remove spark plug and position piston at top of stroke with both valves closed.
5. Install suitable air line with adapter in spark plug opening and apply air pressure. Failure of air pressure to hold valves closed is indication of valve or valve seat damage that may require cylinder head removal.
6. Install .40 inch shim between spring coils.
7. Compress valve spring using valve spring compressor tool No. T91P-6565-A, or equivalent.
8. Remove keepers, retainer and valve spring.
9. Remove valve stem seal using suitable locking pliers.

Installation

1. **Piston must be at Top Dead Center (TDC) of cylinder being serviced.**
2. Remove air pressure and inspect valve stem for damage.
3. Rotate valve and inspect valve stem tip eccentric movement during rotation.
4. Position valve up and down through normal travel and inspect stem for binding. **If valve has been damaged, remove cylinder head for service.**
5. If valve condition is good, apply engine oil to valve stem and hold valve closed.
6. Apply air pressure in cylinder.
7. Install valve stem seal using valve stem seal replacer tool No. T88T-6571-A, or equivalent.
8. Position valve spring and retainer over valve stem.
9. Install .40 inch shim between spring coils.
10. Compress valve spring and install keepers.

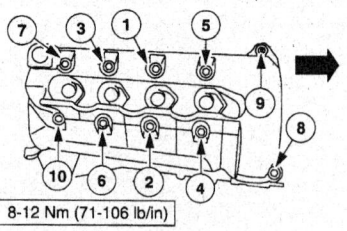

8-12 Nm (71-106 lb/in)

FM1059800149000X

Fig. 11 Righthand valve cover tightening sequence

11. Turn off air supply and remove spark plug opening adapter.
12. Install spark plug, roller follower and valve cover.

FRONT COVER
REPLACE

1. Remove valve covers as outlined under "Valve Cover, Replace."
2. Remove cooling fan.
3. Remove mounting bolts and water pump pulley.
4. Remove crankshaft front seal as outlined under "Front Cover Seal, Replace."
5. Remove mounting bolts and position power steering pump aside.
6. Disconnect air conditioning compressor and crankshaft position sensor electrical connectors.
7. Disconnect engine wiring harness retainers from air conditioning compressor.
8. Remove mounting bolts and position air conditioning compressor aside.
9. Drain engine oil into suitable container.
10. Remove four front oil pan mounting bolts.
11. Remove serpentine belt idler pulleys.
12. Remove mounting bolts, studs and front cover.
13. Reverse procedure to install, noting the following:
    a. Clean and inspect sealing surfaces. **Do not use metal scrapers, wire brushes or other abrasive means to clean sealing surfaces.**
    b. Apply suitable silicone and gasket sealant, **Fig. 12.**
    c. Tighten front cover mounting bolts in sequence, **Fig. 13.**
    d. **Torque** oil pan front mounting bolts in sequence to 18 inch lbs., **Fig. 14.**
    e. **Torque** mounting bolts in sequence to 15 ft. lbs.
    f. Final tighten bolts an additional 60° in sequence.

FRONT COVER SEAL
REPLACE

1. Remove drive belt.
2. Disconnect upper motor mount.
3. Raise and support vehicle.
4. Remove righthand front wheel and tire assembly.
5. Remove righthand inner fender.
6. Support engine, transaxle and front

sub frame with suitable powertrain lift and universal powertrain removal bracket.
7. Remove front subframe brackets.
8. Lower engine transaxle and front subframe as an assembly.
9. Remove crankshaft pulley using crankshaft damper remover tool No. TP58P-6316-D, or equivalent.
10. Remove front cover seal using front cover seal remover tool No. T74P-6700-A, or equivalent.
11. Reverse procedure to install, noting the following:
    a. Lubricate engine front cover seal and front cover with clean engine oil.
    b. Install oil seal using crankshaft seal replacer tool No. T88T-6701-A, or equivalent.
    c. Apply suitable silicone gasket and sealant to woodruff key slot on crankshaft pulley.
    d. Install crankshaft pulley using crankshaft damper replacer tool No. T74P-6316-D, or equivalent.
    e. **Torque** crankshaft bolt to 66 ft. lbs.
    f. Loosen crankshaft bolt at least 360°.
    g. **Torque** crankshaft mounting bolt to 35–39 ft. lbs.
    h. Tighten mounting bolt an additional 85–90°.

TIMING CHAIN
REPLACE

These engines have an interference fit design. If engine has jumped time cylinder heads must be removed to repair damage to valves and/or pistons.

At no time, when the timing chains are removed and the cylinder heads are installed, may the crankshaft and/or camshaft be rotated unless all rocker arms have been removed. Rotation may result in valve and/or piston damage.

These engines have a primary timing chain and use a secondary timing chain between intake and exhaust camshafts.

Before loosening or tightening camshaft sprocket nuts and bolts, ensure camshaft positioning and locking devices are in place.

Primary
REMOVAL

1. Remove engine as outlined under "Engine, Replace."
2. Remove valve covers as outlined under "Valve Cover, Replace."
3. Position piston of cylinder being repaired at bottom of stroke and camshaft lobe at base circle.
4. Compress valve spring using spring compressor tool No. T93P-6565-AR, or equivalent, and remove roller follower.
5. Repeat previous steps for remaining cylinders.
6. Remove front engine cover as outlined under "Front Engine Cover, Replace."
7. Remove crankshaft position pulse

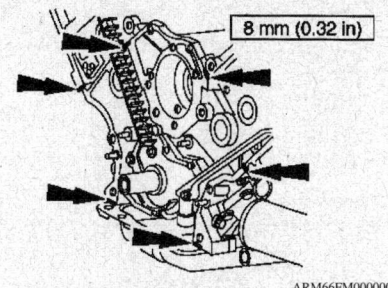

Fig. 12 Front cover sealant application

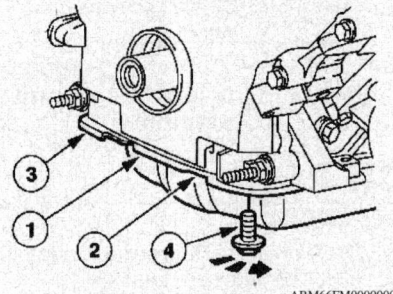

Fig. 14 Oil pan front bolts tightening sequence

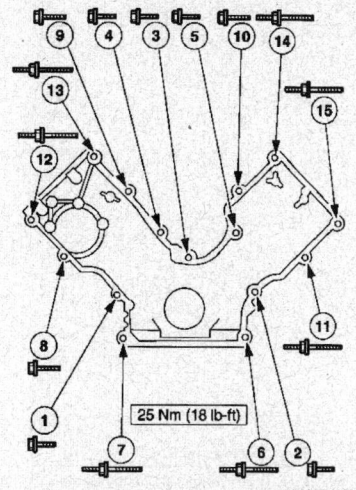

Fig. 13 Front cover tightening sequence (Part 1 of 2)

Item	Part Number	Description
1	N806177	Bolt, Hex Flange Head Pilot, M8 x 1.25 x 53
2	N806177	Bolt, Hex Flange Head Pilot, M8 x 1.25 x 53
3	N806177	Bolt, Hex Flange Head Pilot, M8 x 1.25 x 53
4	N806177	Bolt, Hex Flange Head Pilot, M8 x 1.25 x 53
5	N806177	Bolt, Hex Flange Head Pilot, M8 x 1.25 x 53
6	W706508	Stud, Hex Shldr Pilot, M8 x 1.25 x 50 — M6 x 1 x 10
7	N808586	Stud and Washer, Hex Head Pilot, M8 x 1.25 x 60 — M6 x 1 x 26
8	N806177	Bolt, Hex Flange Head Pilot, M8 x 1.25 x 53
9	N806177	Bolt, Hex Flange Head Pilot, M8 x 1.25 x 53
10	N806177	Bolt, Hex Flange Head Pilot, M8 x 1.25 x 53
11	N806300	Stud, Hex Shldr Pilot, M8 x 1.25 x 65 — M8 x 1.25 x 26
12	W706560	Stud, Hex Head Pilot, M8 x 1.25 x 65 — M8 x 1.25 x 16
13	W706560	Stud, Hex Shldr Pilot, M8 x 1.25 x 65 — M8 x 1.25 x 26
14	W706560	Stud, Hex Shldr Pilot, M8 x 1.25 x 65 — M8 x 1.25 x 26
15	N806300	Stud, Hex Shldr Pilot, M8 x 1.25 x 65 — M8 x 1.25 x 26

Fig. 13 Front cover tightening sequence (Part 2 of 2)

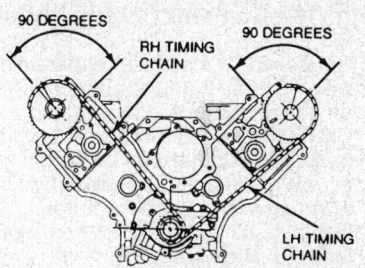

Fig. 15 Engine rotation to TDC

wheel and rotate engine to cylinder No. 1 TDC, **Figs. 5 and 15.**
8. Install camshaft positioning tool No. T93P-6256-A, **Fig. 6,** and camshaft holding tool No. T93P-6256-AH, **Fig. 16,** or equivalents, to camshafts.
9. Remove mounting bolts, righthand tensioner and arm.
10. Remove mounting bolts and righthand chain guide. **Record bolt lengths for installation alignment.**
11. Remove righthand timing chain and crankshaft sprocket. **Record sprocket position for installation alignment.**
12. Remove righthand camshaft gear mounting bolt, washer, gear and spacer.
13. Remove mounting bolts, lefthand tensioner and arm.
14. Remove mounting bolts and lefthand chain guide. **Record bolt lengths for installation alignment.**
15. Remove lefthand timing chain and crankshaft sprocket. **Record gear position for installation alignment.**
16. Remove lefthand camshaft gear mounting bolt, washer and sprocket.

INSTALLATION

If engine has jumped time, ensure all repairs to engine components and/or valve train are completed. During timing chain installation ensure all rocker arm have been remove, if cam or crank should turn with rockers installed engine damage will result.
1. Rotate engine until keyway is 45° counterclockwise from vertical.
2. Ensure secondary timing chain and tensioner are properly installed.
3. Install camshaft positioning tool No. T93P-6256-A, **Fig. 6,** and camshaft holding tool No. T93P-6256-AH, or equivalents, **Fig. 16,** to camshafts.

4. If removed, install primary timing chain cam sprockets onto camshaft, and hand tighten nuts.
5. Install lefthand timing chain onto camshaft sprocket and ensure one timing chain colored link is aligned with camshaft sprocket timing marks, **Fig. 17.**
6. Install lefthand timing chain onto crankshaft sprocket and ensure one timing chain colored link is aligned with camshaft sprocket timing marks. Ensure tapered boss of crankshaft sprocket is facing away from engine block, **Fig. 18.**
7. Bleed timing chain tensioner as outlined under "Timing Chain Tensioner Bleed."
8. Install lefthand chain rail, tensioner and arm.
9. Remove timing chain slack using suitable C-clamp across both timing chain rails and release timing chain tensioner.
10. Repeat procedures for righthand timing chain. Ensure crankshaft sprocket tapered boss faces toward engine block, **Fig. 18.**
11. Tighten camshaft sprocket nuts.
12. Install crankshaft position pulse wheel.
13. Install front engine cover as outlined under "Front Engine Cover, Replace."
14. Position piston of cylinder being repaired at bottom of stroke and camshaft lobe at base circle.
15. Compress valve spring using spring compressor tool No. T93P-6565-AR, or equivalent, and install roller follower.
16. Install valve covers as outlined under "Valve Cover, Replace."
17. Install engine as outlined under "Engine, Replace."

Secondary

Ensure camshaft locking tools are in place before loosening or tightening cam sprocket bolts. Engine damage will result if tools are not properly installed.
1. Remove primary timing chain as outlined under "Primary."
2. Compress and lock spring loaded sec-

ondary timing chain tensioner.
3. Remove intake camshafts mounting bolt . Record spacers sprockets and washers positions for installation alignment.
4. Remove secondary timing chain and sprockets.
5. Remove mounting bolts and secondary timing chain tensioner.
6. Reverse procedure to install.

TIMING CHAIN TENSIONER BLEED

1. Position timing chain tensioner in suitable soft-jawed vise.
2. Lock ratchet stem mechanism position using suitable tool and slowly compress tensioner plunger by rotating vise handle. **Tensioner must be compressed slowly.**
3. When tensioner plunger bottoms in bore, continue holding ratchet lock mechanism and push ratchet mechanism down until flush with tensioner face.
4. While holding ratchet stem flush to tensioner face, release ratchet lock mechanism and install paper clip or suitable tool to lock tensioner in collapsed position, **Fig. 19.**
5. **Do not remove paper clip or suitable tool until timing chain, tensioner arm, tensioner and timing chain guide are installed on engine.**

CAMSHAFT
REPLACE

1. Remove timing chains as outlined under "Timing Chain, Replace."

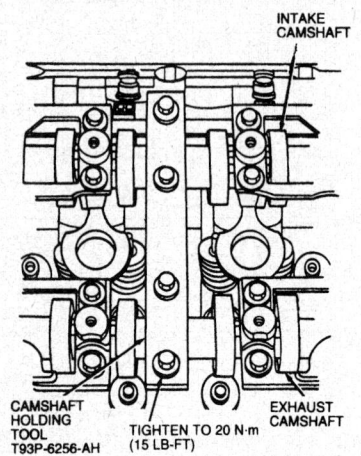

Fig. 16 Camshaft holding tool

2. Rotate crankshaft key counterclockwise 45° from vertical. Ensure pistons are below top of engine deck face. **Crankshaft must be in position prior to rotating camshafts or piston and/or valve damage may result if rocker arms have not been removed.**
3. Remove camshaft cap cluster mounting bolts, **Fig. 8.**
4. Remove first exhaust.
5. Remove intake camshaft cap cluster.
6. Tap camshaft cap upward.
7. Remove cap and camshaft.
8. Reverse procedure to install.

PISTON & ROD ASSEMBLY

1. Rod bearing cap bolts are torque-to-yield bolts, do not reuse bolts.
2. Install connecting rod to piston with marks facing toward front of engine.
3. Install piston with arrow facing toward front of engine.
4. **Torque** connecting rod bearing cap bolts to 18 ft. lbs.
5. **Torque** cap bolts to 33 ft. lbs.
6. Final tighten bolts an additional 90°.

MAIN & ROD BEARINGS

Main bearing vertical bolts and rod bolts used in these engines are of the "Torque To Yield" type and can not be reused. Ensure replacement bolts are available before servicing main or rod bearings.

1. Loosen bolts in sequence, **Fig. 20.**
2. Seat bearing caps using suitable brass hammer.
3. **Torque** vertical main bearing bolts 1–20 in sequence to 72–108 inch lbs., **Fig. 21.**
4. **Torque** vertical main bearing bolts 1–10 in sequence to 16–21 ft. lbs.
5. **Torque** main bearing bolts 11–20 in sequence to 28–32 ft. lbs.
6. Tighten vertical main bearing bolts 1–20 an additional 85–90° in sequence.

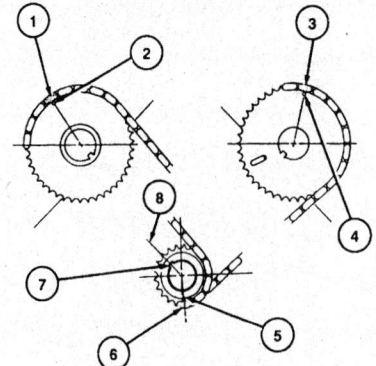

Item	Description
1	RH Camshaft Timing Chain Mark
2	RH Camshaft Sprocket Mark
3	LH Camshaft Timing Chain Mark
4	RH Camshaft Sprocket Mark
5	Crankshaft Sprocket Mark
6	Crankshaft Timing Chain Mark
7	Crankshaft Sprocket
8	Crankshaft Keyway Center Line

FM1069300467000X

Fig. 17 Crankshaft to camshaft timing mark alignment

7. **Torque** main bearing cap adjusting screws 21–30 in sequence to 80–97 inch lbs.
8. **Torque** main bearing cap adjusting screws in sequence to 14–17 ft. lbs.
9. **Torque** main bearing cap side bolts 31–40 in sequence to 84 inch lbs.
10. **Torque** main bearing cap side bolts in sequence to 14–17 ft. lbs.

CRANKSHAFT REAR OIL SEAL

REPLACE

1. Remove transaxle/transmission as outlined in **MOTOR's "Domestic Transmission, In-Vehicle Service"** manual.
2. Remove flywheel.
3. Remove crankshaft oil slinger using rear crankshaft slinger remover tool No. T-95P-6701-AH, or equivalent, and suitable slide hammer.
4. Remove crankshaft rear oil seal using rear crankshaft seal remover tool No. T95P-6701-BH, or equivalent, and suitable slide hammer.
5. Reverse procedure to install, noting the following:
   a. Install rear oil seal using crankshaft seal replacer tool No. T-95P-6701-AH and rear crankshaft seal adapter tool No. T-95P-6701-DH, or equivalents.
   b. With rear crankshaft seal adapter still installed, use rear crankshaft slinger replacer and rear crankshaft seal replacer to install crankshaft oil slinger.

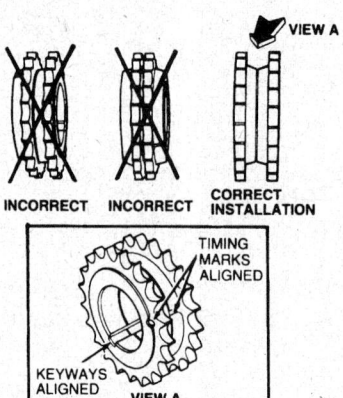

Fig. 18 Crankshaft sprocket position

OIL PAN

REPLACE

1. Drain engine oil into suitable container.
2. Remove dual converter Y-pipe.
3. Disconnect sensor wiring from low oil level sensor and oil pan rail.
4. Remove 16 mounting bolts and oil pan.
5. Reverse procedure to install, noting the following:
   a. **Torque** oil pan mounting bolts in sequence to 14 ft. lbs., **Fig. 22.**
   b. Final tighten mounting bolts an additional 60° in sequence.

OIL PUMP

REPLACE

This procedure has been revised by a Technical Service Bulletin.
1. Remove valve covers as outlined under "Valve Cover, Replace."
2. Remove front cover as outlined under "Front Engine Cover, Replace."
3. Drain engine oil into suitable container.
4. Remove dual converter Y-pipe.
5. Disconnect sensor wiring from low oil level sensor and oil pan rail.
6. Remove 16 mounting bolts and oil pan.
7. Remove timing chains as outlined under "Timing Chain, Replace."
8. Remove mounting bolts and oil pump, **Fig. 23.**
9. Reverse procedure to install, noting the following:
   a. Align oil pump inner rotor with flat of crankshaft.
   b. Prime oil pump and system prior to starting engine.

BELT TENSION DATA

Automatic belt tensioners are spring loaded devices which set and maintain the drive belt tension. The belt should not require tension adjustments during its lifetime. Automatic tensioners have belt wear indicator marks. If the indicator mark is not between the indicator lines, the belt is worn or an improper belt is installed.

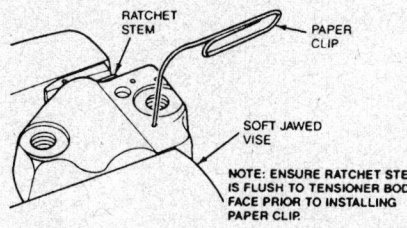

Fig. 19 Timing chain tensioner bleed

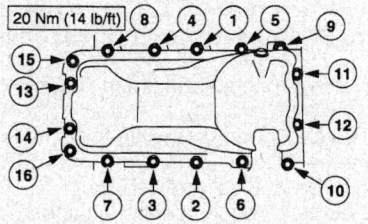

Fig. 22 Oil pan tightening sequence

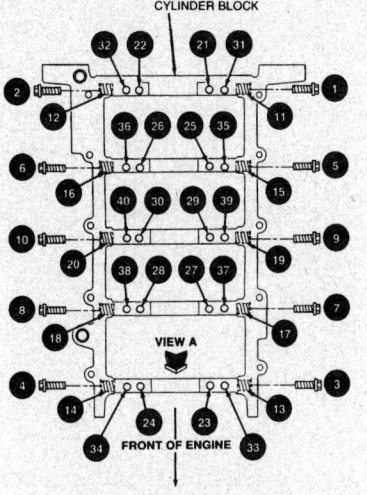

Fig. 20 Main bearing cap loosening sequence

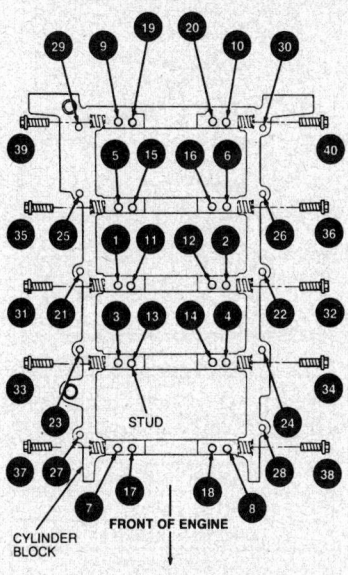

Fig. 21 Main bearing cap tightening sequence

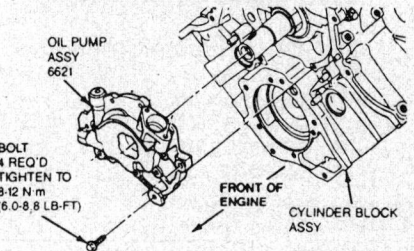

Fig. 23 Exploded view of oil pump

SERPENTINE DRIVE BELT

Belt Routing

Refer to **Fig. 24,** for drive belt routing.

Belt Replacement

1. Rotate tensioner away from belt using suitable breaker bar installed in ½ inch square hole in tensioner arm.
2. Lift old belt over alternator pulley flange and remove.
3. When installing new belt over pulleys. Ensure V grooves make proper contact with pulley.
4. Ensure belt is properly installed on each pulley.

COOLING SYSTEM BLEED

A pressurized reservoir system is used which constantly separates the air from the cooling system. When the thermostat is open, coolant flows through a small hose from the top of the radiator outlet tank to the reservoir. The reservoir separates any entrapped air from the coolant and replenishes the system through the lower hose. The reservoir serves as the location for service fill, coolant expansion during warm up, system pressurization from the pressure cap and air separation during operation. The reservoir is designed to have approximately ½–1 quart of air when cold to allow for coolant expansion.

Add coolant to the minimum level on the reservoir.

THERMOSTAT

REPLACE

1. Drain coolant level below upper radia-

tor hose and thermostat housing.
2. Disconnect lower radiator, coolant recovery and engine return hoses at thermostat housing, **Fig. 25.**
3. Remove two thermostat housing mounting bolts.
4. Remove O-ring seal and thermostat from housing.
5. Reverse procedure to install.

WATER PUMP

REPLACE

1. Drain cooling system into suitable container, then remove engine cooling fan and shroud.
2. Release belt tensioner and remove accessory drive belt, **Fig. 26.**
3. Remove mounting bolts and water pump pulley.
4. Remove mounting bolts and water pump.
5. Reverse procedure to install.

RADIATOR

REPLACE

1. Drain engine coolant into suitable container, then disconnect deceleration and radiator hoses.
2. Disconnect automatic transmission fluid inlet and outlet lines using suitable back-up wrench to hold fitting.
3. **On models equipped with fan shroud,** proceed as follows:
   a. Remove upper shroud mounting bolts at radiator support.
   b. Remove air conditioning condenser core to radiator upper mounting bolts.
   c. Lift fan shroud enough to disengage lower retaining clips and lay shroud over fan.
4. **On all models,** remove mounting bolts and radiator upper supports.
5. Reverse procedure to install.

FUEL PUMP

REPLACE

1. Remove fuel tank cap.
2. Attach fuel pressure gauge tool No. T80L-9974-B, or equivalent, to fuel rail pressure relief Schrader valve.
3. Place tool outlet hose in suitable container.
4. Slowly open tool valve to fuel system pressure.
5. Drain fuel tank at fuel filler neck.
6. Raise and support vehicle.
7. Disconnect fuel supply and return line fittings and vent line.
8. Disconnect fuel pump and sender electrical connectors.
9. Remove mounting support straps and lower fuel tank . Ensure dirt does not enter tank or fuel system.
10. Remove fuel pump locking ring by turning it counterclockwise using fuel tank sender wrench No. D74P-9275-A, or equivalent.
11. Remove fuel pump and discard seal ring.
12. Reverse procedure to install, noting the following:
    a. Install fuel pressure gauge tool No. T80L-9974-B, or equivalent, on fuel charging Schrader valve.
    b. Turn ignition from Off to On position

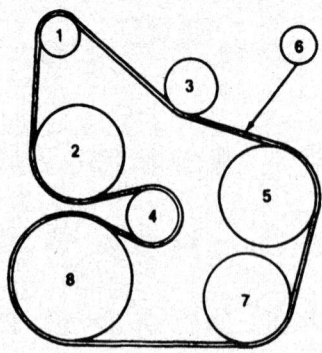

Item	Description
1	Generator
2	Water Pump Pulley
3	Belt Idler Pulley
4	Drive Belt Tensioner
5	Power Steering Pump
6	Drive Belt
7	A/C Compressor
8	Crankshaft Pulley

FM1069300469000X

Fig. 24   Drive belt routing

for three seconds.

c. Repeat Off to On switching 5–10 times until pressure gauge shows at least 35 psi.

FUEL FILTER
REPLACE

1. Turn engine off.

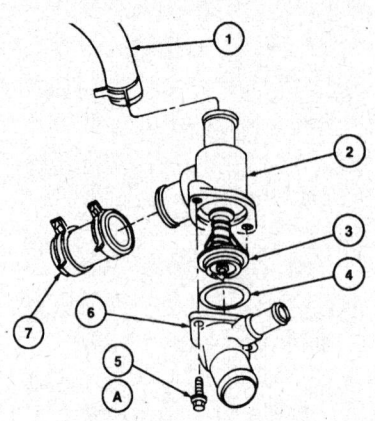

Item	Description
1	Water Bypass Hose
2	Lower Water Thermostat Housing
3	Water Thermostat
4	O-Ring Seal
5	Bolt (2 Req'd)
6	Upper Water Thermostat Housing
7	Engine Return Hose
A	Tighten to 20-30 N·m (15-22 Lb-Ft)

FM1069300471000X

Fig. 25   Exploded view of thermostat housing

2. Remove fuel tank cap.
3. Attach fuel pressure gauge tool No. T80L-9974-B, or equivalent, to fuel rail pressure relief Schrader valve.

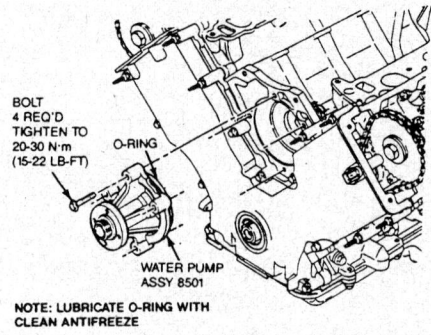

BOLT 4 REQ'D TIGHTEN TO 20-30 N·m (15-22 LB-FT)

O-RING

WATER PUMP ASSY 8501

NOTE: LUBRICATE O-RING WITH CLEAN ANTIFREEZE

FM1089100059000X

Fig. 26   Water pump replacement

4. Place tool outlet hose in suitable container.
5. Slowly open tool valve to fuel system pressure.
6. Raise and support vehicle.
7. Remove push connect fittings at both ends of fuel filter. Install new retainer clips in each push connect fitting.
8. Remove fuel filter and retainer from metal bracket by removing two mounting bolts.
9. Remove filter from retainer. Record flow arrow direction.
10. Remove rubber insulator rings from filter.
11. Reverse procedure to install. Replace insulator(s) if filter moves freely after retainer installation.

TIGHTENING SPECIFICATIONS

Year	Component	Torque/Ft. Lbs.
2001–02	Alternator Bracket	15–22
	Belt Idler Pulley	15–22
	Belt Tensioner	15–22
	Camshaft	81–95
	Camshaft Cover	72–108①
	Camshaft Sprocket	81–95
	Crankshaft Damper	114–121
	Crankshaft Pulley	②
	Connecting Rod	18–24④
	Cylinder Front Cover	15–22
	Cylinder Head	③
	Drive Belt Tensioner	15–22
	EGR Tube Connector	30–33
	EGR Valve To Intake Manifold	15–22
	EGR Valve To Exhaust Manifold Tube	26–33
	Engine Insulators	15–22
	Engine To Transmission	30–44
	Exhaust Manifold	15–22
	Exhaust Manifold Studs	96–108①
	Exhaust Pipe	20–30
	Flywheel	54–64
	Front Engine Cover	15–22

Continued

TIGHTENING
SPECIFICATIONS—Continued

Year	Component	Torque/Ft. Lbs.
2001–02	Front Engine Mount	45–59
	Front Engine Mount Through Bolts	15–22
	Fuel Filer	27–44①
	Heater Outlet Hose	15–22
	Idle Air Control	14
	IMRC	⑦
	Intake Manifold	53–64
	Low Oil Level Sensor	15–22
	Lower Control Arm To Strut	118–162
	Main Bearing	⑤
	Oil Filter Adapter	15–22
	Oil Inlet Tube To Main Bearing Cap	15–22
	Oil Inlet Tube To Oil Pump	72–108①
	Oil Pan	⑥
	Oil Pan Drain Plug	8–12
	Oil Pump	72–108①
	Oxygen Sensor	27–33
	Power Steering Pump Reservoir	72–96①
	Power Steering Pump	15–22
	Powertrain Frame	73–100
	Rear Axle To Rear Subframe	72–89
	Rear Engine Mount, Bolt	50–70
	Rear Engine Mount, Nut	35–50
	Rear Engine Support	15–22
	Spark Plug	84–96①
	Thermostat Housing	15–22
	Throttle Body	72–108①
	Torque Converter	22–25
	Upper Control Arm To Steering Knuckle	50–68
	Upper Manifold	15–22
	Valve Cover	72–108①
	Water Bypass Tube	72–96①
	Water Pump	15–22
	Water Pump Pulley	15–22

① — Inch lbs.
② — Refer to "Front Cover Seal, Replace." for tightening specifications and sequence.
③ — Refer to "Cylinder Head, Replace" for tightening specifications and sequence.
④ — Tighten an additional 85–90°.
⑤ — Refer to "Main & Rod Bearings" for tightening specifications and sequence.
⑥ — Refer to "Oil Pan, Replace" for tightening specifications and sequence.
⑦ — Refer to "Intake Manifold, Replace" for tightening specifications and sequence.

Rear Axle & Suspension

NOTE: On Air Bag Equipped Models, Refer To "Air Bag System Precautions" Located In The Front Of This Manual For System Disarming & Arming Procedures.

NOTE: Refer To "Computer Relearn Procedures" Located In The Front Of This Manual When Battery Power To The Computer Has Been Interrupted.

INDEX

PRECAUTIONS

Air Bag Systems

Refer to "Air Bag System Precautions" in the front of this manual for system disarming and arming procedures.

Air Suspension Pressure Relief

Before servicing any air suspension components, disconnect power to system by turning air suspension switch OFF or by disconnecting battery ground cable.

Do not remove an air spring under any circumstances when there is pressure in the air spring. Do not remove any component supporting an air spring without either exhausting the air or providing support for air spring. Refer to "Functional Test" in the "Active Suspension Systems" chapter to vent air from spring.

Battery Ground Cable

Prior to service, disconnect battery ground cable and isolate as required.

DESCRIPTION

The rear suspension utilizes a fully independent rear suspension which includes lower suspension arms, suspension upper arm and bushings, spring, tension strut and bushing, wheel spindle, shock absorbers and stabilizer bar, **Figs. 1 through 3.**

The air suspension system incorporates a rear load leveling system that maintains the vehicle at the proper ride height under varying conditions of vehicle load, and an optional road calibrated suspension ride control system that varies the damping of the shock absorbers between soft and firm, **Fig. 4.**

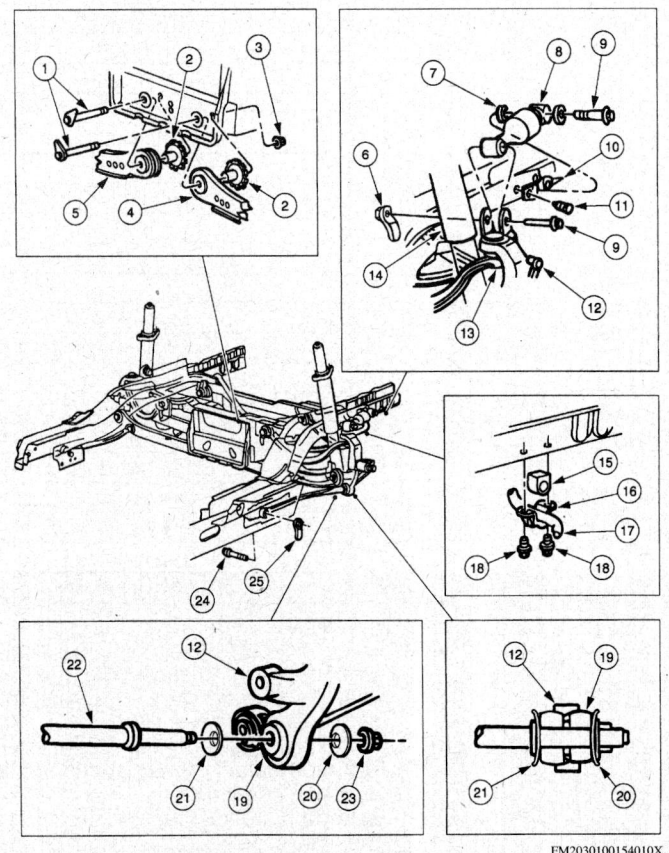

FM2030100154010X

Fig. 1 Exploded view of rear suspension (Part 1 of 2)

SHOCK ABSORBER
REPLACE

1. Turn air suspension switch off.
2. Raise and support vehicle.
3. Support rear axle with suitable jack.
4. Release air pressure from air springs.
5. Remove shock absorber upper mounting nut, washer and insulator.
6. Remove self-locking mounting nut from lower shock absorber stud, discard nut.
7. Remove shock absorber.
8. Reverse procedure to install.

AIR SPRING
REPLACE

1. Turn air suspension switch to Off position.
2. Turn ignition switch to Run position, then connect suitably programmed scan tool to DLC.
3. Select air suspension control module

Item	Description
1	Bolt (4 Req'd)
2	Rear Suspension Arm Adjusting Cam (4 Req'd)
3	Nut (4 Req'd)
4	Rear Lower Suspension Arm (Front LH and Rear RH)
5	Front Lower Suspension Arm (Front RH and Rear LH)
6	Nut (2 Req'd)
7	Washer (4 Req'd)
8	Rear Suspension Damper
9	Bolt (4 Req'd)
10	Damper Bracket
11	Bolt (4 Req'd)
12	Rear Wheel Spindle
13	Rear Suspension Arm and Bushing

Item	Description
14	Shock Absorber
15	Lower Suspension Arm Stabilizer Bar Insulator (2 Req'd)
16	Stabilizer Bar Bracket
17	Rear Stabilizer Bar
18	Bolt (4 Req'd)
19	Rear Suspension Tie Rod Bushing (4 Req'd)
20	Washer (2 Req'd)
21	Washer (2 Req'd)
22	Rear Suspension Tension Strut and Bushing
23	Nut (2 Req'd)
24	Bolt (2 Req'd)
25	Nut Assy (2 Req'd)

FM2030100154020X

Fig. 1 Exploded view of rear suspension (Part 2 of 2)

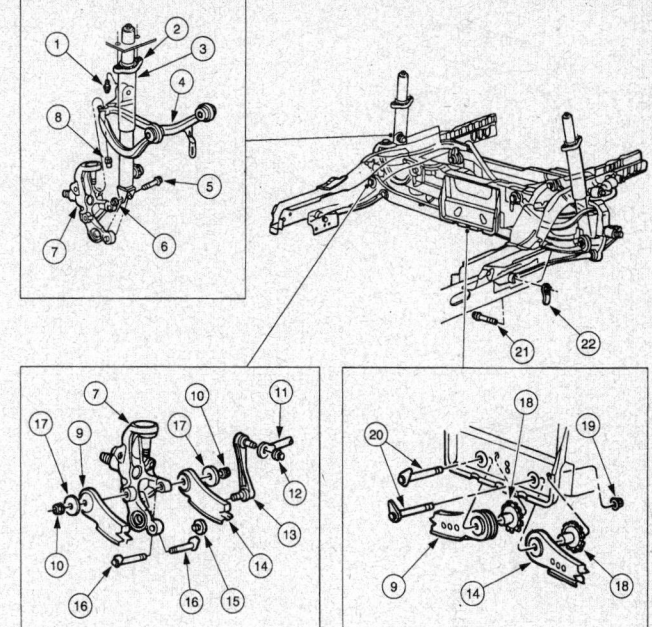

FM2030100155010X

Fig. 2 Exploded view of rear shock absorber & components (Part 1 of 2)

Item	Description
1	Bolt (4 Req'd)
2	Rear Shock Absorber Bracket
3	Shock Absorber
4	Rear Suspension Arm and Bushing
5	Bolt (2 Req'd)
6	Nut

Item	Description
7	Rear Wheel Spindle
8	Nut (2 Req'd)
9	Front Lower Suspension Arm (RH)
10	Nut (4 Req'd)
11	Rear Stabilizer Bar

Item	Description
12	Nut (2 Req'd)
13	Rear Stabilizer Bar Link
14	Rear Lower Suspension Arm (Rear RH and Front LH)
15	Nut (2 Req'd)
16	Bolt (4 Req'd)

Item	Description
17	Bolt (4 Req'd)
18	Rear Suspension Arm Adjusting Cam (4 Req'd)
19	Nut (4 Req'd)
20	Washer (4 Req'd)
21	Bolt (2 Req'd)
22	Nut Assy (2 Req'd)

FM2030100155020X

Fig. 2 Exploded view of rear shock absorber & components (Part 2 of 2)

active command LR_SOL or RR_SOL from off to on.
4. Select air suspension control module active command AS_VENT to deflate air springs or AS_COMP to inflate air springs. **When using AS_COMP command, do not run air compressor for more than three minutes to prevent overheating.**
5. Remove rear air spring retainer.
6. Lift bottom of air spring off rear axle.
7. Disconnect electrical connector.
8. Push on red retaining ring and disconnect air line.
9. Remove air spring.
10. Reverse procedure to install.

CONTROL ARM
REPLACE

Upper

1. Turn air suspension switch Off.
2. Raise and support vehicle.
3. Remove wheel and tire assembly.
4. Deflate air spring.
5. Disconnect air suspension height sensor from ball stud pin on rear suspension arm and bushing.
6. Remove lower shock absorber mounting nut and bolt.
7. Loosen but do not remove upper ball joint to upper rear suspension arm nut.
8. Separate ball joint from rear suspension arm and bushing and remove nut.
9. Remove rear upper suspension arm to body nuts and bolts.
10. Remove rear suspension arm and bushing.
11. Reverse procedure to install.

Lower

1. Turn air suspension to Off position.
2. Raise and support vehicle.
3. Remove tire and wheel assembly.
4. Deflate air spring.
5. Remove air spring seat and air spring.
6. Remove brake anti-lock sensor wiring, rear parking brake cable conduit and routing clips from front lower suspension arm.
7. Remove front lower suspension arm to rear wheel spindle nut, washer and bolt.
8. Remove front lower suspension arm to body nut and bolt and front lower suspension arm.
9. Remove rear suspension arm adjusting cam from front lower suspension arm, if damaged.
10. Reverse procedure to install.

STABILIZER BAR
REPLACE

1. Disconnect air suspension electrical wiring and related components that interfere with stabilizer bar removal.
2. Raise and support vehicle.
3. Remove stabilizer bar to link mounting nuts, washers and insulators.
4. Remove U-bracket mounting bolts and stabilizer bar.
5. Reverse procedure to install, using new mounting bolts and nuts.

CONTINENTAL

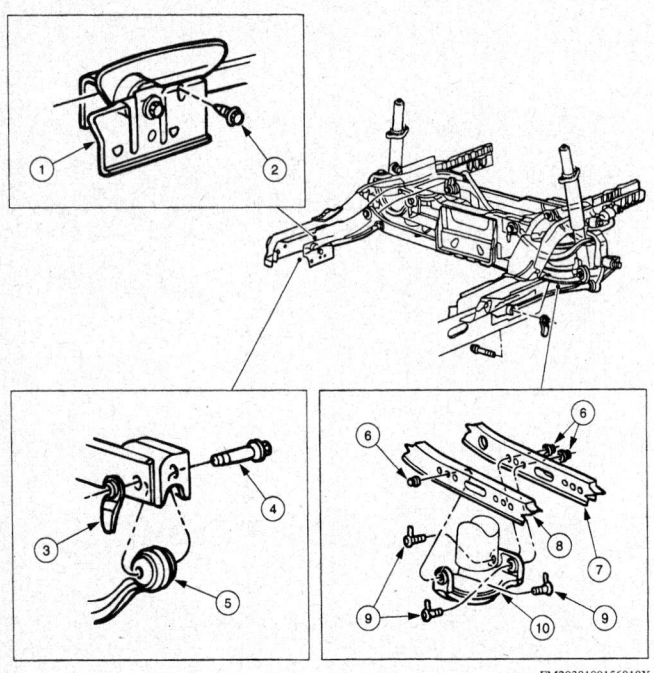

Item	Description
1	Bracket (2 Req'd)
2	Bolt (2 Req'd)
3	Nut (4 Req'd)
4	Bolt (4 Req'd)
5	Rear Suspension Arm and Bushing

Item	Description
6	Nut (6 Req'd)
7	Rear Lower Suspension Arm (Rear RH and Front LH)
8	Front Lower Suspension Arm (Front RH and Rear LH)
9	Bolt (6 Req'd)
10	Spring Seat (2 Req'd)

FM2030100156020X

Fig. 3 Exploded view of rear subframe & components (Part 2 of 2)

FM2030100156010X

Fig. 3 Exploded view of rear subframe & components (Part 1 of 2)

Item	Description
7	Air Spring Solenoid
8	Shock Absorber
9	Shock Actuator
10	Lamp Switch

Item	Description
11	Air Suspension Height Sensor
12	Vent Solenoid
13	Air Compressor

FM2019800374020X

Fig. 4 Air suspension component locations (Part 2 of 2)

Item	Description
1	Front Spring and Shock Absorber Assembly
2	Shock Actuator (Part of 3C098)
3	Message Center Indicator

Item	Description
4	Vehicle Dynamic Module (VDM)
5	Rear Suspension Leveler Compressor Switch
6	Rear Air Spring

FM2019800374010X

Fig. 4 Air suspension component locations (Part 1 of 2)

TIGHTENING SPECIFICATIONS

Year	Component	Torque/Ft. Lbs.
2001–02	Anti-Lock Brake Sensor	53①
	Disc Brake Adapter To Caliper	64–88
	Disc Brake Shield	89①
	Lower Suspension Arm	59
	Rear Spring Seat	50–68
	Shock Absorber, Lower	59
	Shock Absorber, Upper	30
	Shock Absorber Mass Damper	21
	Stabilizer Bar Bracket	22
	Stabilizer Bar Link	30
	Tension Strut To Body	77
	Tension Strut To Rear Wheel Spindle	41
	Upper Ball Joint	59
	Upper Suspension Arm	85
	Wheel Hub Retainer	188–254
	Wheel Lug	85–104

① — Inch lbs.

Front Suspension & Steering

NOTE: On Air Bag Equipped Models, Refer To "Air Bag System Precautions" Located In The Front Of This Manual For System Disarming & Arming Procedures.

NOTE: Refer To "Computer Relearn Procedures" Located In The Front Of This Manual When Battery Power To The Computer Has Been Interrupted.

INDEX

PRECAUTIONS

Air Bag Systems

Refer to "Air Bag System Precautions" in the front of this manual for system disarming and arming procedures.

Air Suspension System

Always place the air suspension switch in the Off position before performing any work, or whenever raising the front suspension.

WHEEL BEARING

ADJUST

On these models the wheel bearings are preset and cannot be adjusted.

WHEEL BEARING

REPLACE

Wheel hub is not pressed into front wheel knuckle. Do not use a slide hammer or strike back of inner bearing race to remove a stuck wheel hub. Apply rust penetrant and inhibitor to the inboard and outboard wheel hub/knuckle mating surface, then remove wheel hub from front wheel knuckle.

1. Turn air suspension switch to Off position.
2. Raise and support vehicle.
3. Remove wheel and tire assembly.
4. Remove brake disc.
5. Remove and discard front axle wheel hub retainer.
6. Ensure steering column is in unlocked position.
7. Remove and discard front suspension lower ball joint nut.
8. Separate ball joint from lower suspension arm. using suitable joint removal tool.
9. Press front driveshaft joint out of wheel hub using hub remover/replacer tool No. T81P-1104-C, or equivalent.

10. Remove and discard three wheel hub mounting bolts.
11. Remove wheel hub and bearing assembly.

BALL JOINT INSPECTION

1. Raise and support vehicle.
2. Connect dial indicator gauge and holding fixture tool No. 100-D00 (D78P-4201-B), or equivalent, to vehicle.
3. Alternate pulling downward and pushing upward on lower arm by hand.
4. Measure and record any vertical movement between knuckle and lower arm.
5. If movement is or exceeds .03 inch, install new front wheel knuckle.

BALL JOINT
REPLACE

The ball joint is not serviceable. If the ball joint requires replacement, the front wheel knuckle must be replaced.

COIL SPRING
REPLACE

Refer to "Strut, Replace" for coil spring replacement procedure.

STRUT
REPLACE

1. Remove hub nut and loosen upper strut mounting nuts, **Fig. 1.**
2. Raise and support vehicle. **Do not lift vehicle from lower control arm.**
3. Disconnect air suspension electrical wiring and related components that interfere with strut removal.
4. Remove wheel and tire assembly.
5. Remove brake caliper and suspend with suitable wire.
6. Disconnect tie rod end.
7. Remove mounting nut and remove stabilizer bar link from strut.
8. Remove lower control arm to steering knuckle pinch nut and bolt.
9. Spread joint and disconnect control arm from knuckle.
10. Press axle from hub/rotor using suitable hub installation/removal tool. Wire axle shaft to maintain level position. **Do not permit axle shaft to move outward during disengagement from hub.**
11. Remove strut to steering knuckle pinch bolt.
12. Spread joint and remove steering knuckle and hub assembly.
13. Remove mounting nuts and strut upper.
14. Reverse procedure to install.

SHOCK ABSORBER
REPLACE

Refer to "Strut, Replace" for coil spring replacement procedure.

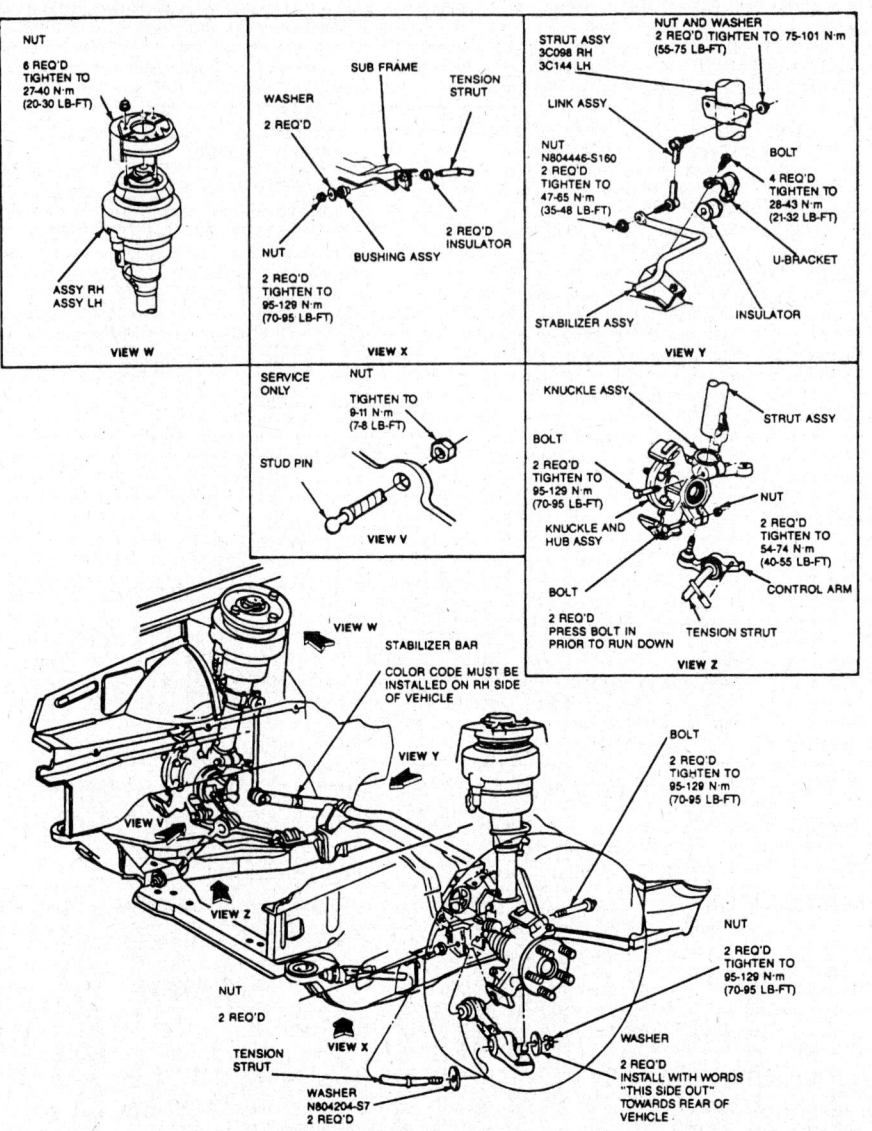

Fig. 1 Front suspension components

CONTROL ARM
REPLACE

Lower

1. Raise and support vehicle.
2. Disconnect air suspension electrical wiring and related components that interfere with control arm removal.
3. Remove wheel and tire assembly, then the tension strut nut and washer.
4. Separate ball joint from lower arm using suitable joint removal tool.
5. Remove inner pivot bolt, nut and lower control arm.
6. Reverse procedure to install.

STABILIZER BAR
REPLACE

1. Turn air suspension switch to off position.
2. Raise and support vehicle.
3. Position safety stands behind front subframe.
4. Remove and discard stabilizer bar link mounting nut.
5. Position another set of safety stands under front subframe.
6. Remove bolts and brackets as required to lower rear of subframe enough to gain access to stabilizer bar brackets.
7. Remove brackets and stabilizer bar.
8. Reverse procedure to install.

POWER STEERING GEAR
REPLACE

1. Remove instrument panel lower trim panel.
2. Remove steering column lower trim panel and reinforcement panel.
3. Remove universal joint pinch and intermediate shaft to steering gear coupling bolts.
4. Slide shaft upward to remove from

steering gear and downward to remove from steering column.

5. Loosen mounting screw and disconnect engine compartment wiring harness.
6. Remove bolt and position upper motor mount out of way.
7. Remove ground strap mounting bolt.
8. Raise and support vehicle.
9. Separate tie rod ends from steering knuckle.
10. Disconnect height sensors.
11. Disconnect heated oxygen sensors.
12. Remove catalytic converter and brackets.
13. Remove subframe insulator braces.

14. Remove steering gear nuts.
15. Support subframe with suitable lifting device, then remove rear and loosen front mounting bolts.
16. Lower lifting device.
17. Remove push pins, heat shield and bracket.
18. Disconnect wiring at steering gear.
19. Rotate steering gear to clear subframe bolt and pull it to left to access power steering lines.
20. Disconnect pressure and return lines at steering gear.
21. Remove steering gear through left-hand wheelwell.
22. Reverse procedure to install.

POWER STEERING PUMP
REPLACE

1. Remove radiator upper sight shield.
2. Disconnect power steering reservoir pump hose.
3. Evacuate air conditioning system as outlined in "Air Conditioning" chapter.
4. Remove air conditioning compressor.
5. Remove routing bracket and disconnect power steering pressure hose.
6. Remove power steering pump.
7. Reverse procedure to install.

TIGHTENING SPECIFICATIONS

Year	Component	Torque/Ft. Lbs.
2001–02	Combination Power Steering & Transmission Fluid Cooler	62–88①
	Front Wheel Spindle Tie Rod	67–81
	Intermediate Hose Connection	42–53
	Intermediate Shaft To Steering Column	16–24
	Intermediate Shaft To Steering Gear	31–37
	Power Steering Oil Pressure Switch	62–123①
	Power Steering Pump	15–22
	Power Steering Return Hose Bracket	80–106①
	Power Steering Secondary VAPS Actuator	25–30
	Pressure Line Fitting At Pump	31–39
	Pressure Line Fitting Into Banjo Bolt	25–30
	Reservoir	54–61①
	Return Line Fitting	25–30
	Steering Gear	84–112
	Subframe	100–144
	Tie Rod End	35–46
	Vehicle Dynamics Module Connector Screw	45–61①
	Wheel Lug	85–104

① — Inch lbs.

Wheel Alignment

INDEX

PRELIMINARY INSPECTION

Prior to performing the front wheel alignment, a preliminary inspection should be made to determine the condition of the vehicle's suspension components. The following inspections and procedures should be made prior to performing front wheel alignment:

Do not attempt to adjust alignment by heating or bending.

1. Vehicle must be leveled by performing air suspension system test. as outlined in "Active Suspensions" chapter.
2. Inflate tires to specified pressure (cold).
3. Measure vehicle ride height.
4. Inspect suspension and steering components for looseness.
5. Inspect existing caster, camber and toe settings prior to alignment.
6. Inspect suspension mounting bolts for proper tightness.
7. Alignment equipment must be capable of four wheel alignment.
8. Alignment rack must be leveled to 1/16 inch, side to side and front to rear, and be equipped with wheel runout compensation.

FRONT WHEEL ALIGNMENT

Caster & Camber

1. Measure camber and caster using suitable alignment rack.
2. Inspect subframe alignment. If subframe alignment does not correct camber and caster, proceed to next step.
3. Loosen nuts on top of strut tower.
4. Remove two mounting nuts and Noise/Vibration/Harness (NVH) brace.
5. Remove six spot welds, the mounting nuts and alignment plate. **Do not cut deeper than required to remove plate.**
6. Remove burrs, then clean and paint exposed metal of shock tower and alignment plate surfaces.
7. Install alignment plate and loosely install mounting nuts.
8. Adjust camber and caster, noting the following:
   a. Adjust caster by turning left or righthand wheel through prescribed angle.
   b. **Do not sweep past prescribed angle.**
9. **Torque** adjusting plate nuts to 20–29 ft. lbs.
10. Ensure camber and caster are within specifications.
11. Drill three holes into shock tower not more than 3/8 inch deep. Clean and

paint exposed metal.
12. Install three 1/8 X 1/4 inch grip range steel pop rivets.
13. Install brace and **torque** mounting nuts to 22–30 ft. lbs.

Toe-In

1. Lock steering wheel in straight ahead position using suitable steering wheel holder.
2. Loosen, then slide off small outer clamps from steering boot to prevent boot from twisting during adjustment procedure.
3. Loosen tie rod adjusting and jam nuts.
4. Adjust length of left and righthand tie rods until each wheel has 1/2 desired total toe specification.
5. After adjustment is completed, tighten jam nuts, install outer clamps and remove steering wheel holder.

REAR WHEEL ALIGNMENT

Camber

Camber is factory set and cannot be adjusted.

Toe-In

Toe-in is adjusted by rotating the cams located inside the rear inner lower control arm bushings.

NOTE: Refer To Rear Of This Manual For Vehicle Manufacturer's Special Service Tool Suppliers.

INDEX OF SERVICE OPERATIONS

Specifications

GENERAL ENGINE SPECIFICATIONS

Year	Engine (Code)①	Fuel System	Bore x Stroke, Inches	Comp. Ratio	Net HP @ RPM	Maximum Torque, Ft. Lbs. @ RPM	Normal Oil Pressure, psi
2001	3.0L (S)	SFI	3.50 x 3.13	10.5	210 @ 6500	205 @ 4750	20–45②
	3.9L (A)	SFI	3.38 x 3.35	10.5	252 @ 6100	267 @ 4300	61–73③
2002	3.0L (S)	SFI	3.50 x 3.13	10.5	220 @ 6400	215 @ 4800	20–45②
	3.9L (A)	SFI	3.38 x 3.35	10.6	252 @ 6100	261 @ 4300	61–73③
2003–05	3.0L (S)	SFI	3.50 x 3.13	10.5	232 @ 6750	220 @ 4500	20–45②
	3.9L (A)	SFI	3.38 x 3.35	10.8	280 @ 6000	286 @ 4000	61–73③

① — The eighth digit of the VIN denotes engine code.

② — At operating temperature & 1500 RPM.

③ — At operating temperature & 400 RPM.

TUNE UP SPECIFICATIONS

Year & Engine (Code)①	Spark Plug Gap, Inch	Ignition Timing BTDC			Idle Speed⑩		Fuel Pump Pressure	Valve Lash, Inch
		Firing Order Fig.⑨	Degrees BTDC	Mark Fig.	Curb	Fast		
3.0L	.051–.057	④	⑤	⑥	②	②	30–65	⑦
3.9L	.039–.043	⑧	⑤	⑥	②	②	30–65	③

BTDC — Before Top Dead Center

D — Drive

① — Eighth digit of Vehicle Identification Number (VIN) denotes engine code.

② — Idle speed is electronically controlled and is non-adjustable.

③ — Intake, .007–.009 inch. Exhaust, .009–.011 inch.

④ — Cylinder numbering from front to rear of engine, righthand bank, 1-2-3; lefthand bank, 4-5-6. Firing order, 1-4-2-5-3-6.

⑤ — Non-adjustable.

⑥ — Equipped w/crankshaft sensor.

⑦ — Intake, .007–.009 inch. Exhaust, .012–.015 inch.

⑧ — Equipped with coil on plug ignition system. Firing order, 1-5-4-2-6-3-7-8.

⑨ — Before disconnecting wires from coil unit, determine location of ignition wires, as position may have been altered from that outlined at end of this chart.

⑩ — When adjusting idle speed, set parking brake & chock drive wheels.

FRONT WHEEL ALIGNMENT SPECIFICATIONS

Year	Caster Angle, Degrees				Camber Angle, Degrees				Toe-In, Degrees	Ball Joint Wear, Inch[1]
	Limits	Desired	Split		Limits	Desired	Split			
			Limits	Desired			Limits	Desired		
2001–05	+7.6 to +8.6	+8.1	-.7 to +.7	0	-.65 to +.35	-.15	-.7 to +.7	0	-.09 to +.41	1/32

[1] — Radial play.

REAR WHEEL ALIGNMENT SPECIFICATIONS

Year	Camber, Degrees		Toe-In, Degrees				Ball Joint Wear, Inch[1]
	Limits	Desired	Limits	Desired	Split		
					Limits	Desired	
2001–05	-1.75 to -.25	-1	-.13 to +.37	+.12	-.01 to +.49	+.24	1/32

[1] — Radial play.

VEHICLE RIDE HEIGHT SPECIFICATIONS

Year	Front, Inches[1]	Rear, Inches[1]	Ride Height Difference, Inches	
			Side To Side	Front To Rear
2001–05	2.1–2.7[2]	.7–1.3[3]	.5	.6

[1] — See door sticker or inside of glove box for manufacturers original tire size specifications. If tires on vehicle do not match manufacturers original tire size & measurement is not within limits, it will be required to refer to the "Non-Standard Tire & Wheel Size Adjustment To Ride Height Specification & Tire Size Adjustment Charts" in the front of this manual for approximate changes in ride height specifications.

[2] — Measure front vehicle ride height, **Fig. A.**

[3] — Measure rear vehicle ride height, **Fig. B.**

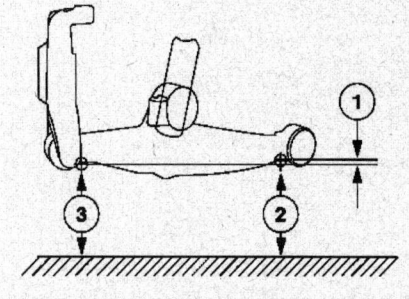

Item	Description
1	Ride height = A-B
2	Measurement A
3	Measurement B

FM2049900064000X

Fig. B   Rear ride height measurement

Item	Description
1	Ride height = B-A
2	Measurement A
3	Measurement B

FM2049900063000X

Fig. A   Front ride height measurement

FLUID CAPACITIES & COOLING SYSTEM DATA

Year	Engine	Coolant Capacity, Qts.		Coolant Type	Radiator Cap Relief Pressure, Lbs.	Thermo. Opening Temp.	Fuel Tank, Gals.	Engine Oil Refill, Qts.④	Rear Axle, Pts.③	Transmission Oil	
		Less A/C	With A/C							Man. Trans., Pts.	Auto. Trans., Qts.
2001–05	3.0L	10.6	10.6	Ethylene Glycol	16	①	18	6.9	3	②	11.9
	3.9L	11.3	11.3	Ethylene Glycol	16	①	18	6.0	3	—	11.9

① — Thermostat begins to open at 192–199°F and is fully open at 219°F.

② — Fill transmission to .02 inch below lower edge of fill plug bore.

③ — Fill ⅛–³⁄₁₆ inch from bottom of filler hole.

④ — Includes engine oil filter.

LUBRICANT DATA

Year	Lubricant Type					
	Transmission		Rear Axle	Power Steering	Brake System	Hydraulic Clutch Fluid
	Manual	Automatic				
2001–05	Mercon ATF	Mercon V XT-5-Q-M	①	②	DOT 3	DOT 3

① — Use 75W-140 synthetic rear axle lubricant F1TZ-19580-B, or equivalent, meeting Ford specification WSL-M2C192-A.

② — Use Motorcraft Mercon multi-purpose ATF transmission fluid XT-2-QDX, or equivalent, meeting Ford specification Mercon.

Electrical

NOTE: On Air Bag Equipped Models, Refer To "Air Bag System Precautions" Located In The Front Of This Manual For System Disarming & Arming Procedures.

NOTE: Refer To "Computer Relearn Procedures" Located In The Front Of This Manual When Battery Power To The Computer Has Been Interrupted.

INDEX

PRECAUTIONS

Air Bag Systems

Refer to "Air Bag System Precautions" in the front of this manual for system disarming and arming procedures.

Battery Ground Cable

Prior to service, disconnect battery ground cable and isolate as required.

Electrostatic Discharge

Electronic modules are sensitive to electrical charges. Ensure modules are not exposed to these charges or damage may result.

MODULE CONFIGURATION

Newly released modules will require configuration after being installed on the vehicle. All configurable modules will be packaged in a kit which contains a warning label and multi-language sheet which lists requirements to configure the modules.

There are two types of configuration data. The first type is used by the module so that it can interact with the vehicle correctly. The second type is customer preference driven. These are items that the customer may or may not want to have enabled. To program customer driven preferences, a Ford Service Function (FSF) card and the New Generation Star Tester (NGS), tool No. 007-00500, or equivalents, must be used to toggle preferences on or off.

The New Generation Star Tester (NGS), tool No. 007-00500, or equivalent, must be used to retrieve configuration data from the old module before it is removed from the vehicle. This information will be transferred into the new module so that the new module will contain the same settings as the old module.

The following modules require configuration when being replaced: Anti-Lock Brake System (ABS) module, ABS module with traction control, Interactive Vehicle Dynamic (IVD) module, Instrument Cluster Module (ICM), ICM with message center, Message Center Module (MCM), Rear Electronic Module (REM), Front Electronic Module (FEM), Driver Door Module (DDM), Dual Automatic Temperature Control (DATC) module, Remote Emergency Satellite Cellular Unit (RESCU) module, Audio Control Module (ACM), Steering Column Lock Module (SCLM) and the Powertrain

Control Module (PCM) when it is replaced on models equipped with a manual transmission. If configuring the PCM, a NGS tester flash cable tool No. 007-00531, or equivalent, must be used.

To perform the configuration process, proceed as follows:

1. Connect New Generation Star Tester tool No. 007-00500 with Ford Service Function (FSF) card, or equivalents, to vehicle DLC.
2. Follow scan tool instructions to upload configuration data.
3. Install new module. **NGS will not retain configuration data for more than 24 hours.**
4. Download stored configuration information to new module using FSF card and NGS tester.
5. If unable to carry out configuration process, proceed as follows:
   a. Inspect for signs of electrical damage.
   b. If NGS does not communicate with vehicle, ensure program card is correctly installed, vehicle connections are secure and ignition switch is in run position.
   c. If NGS still does not communicate

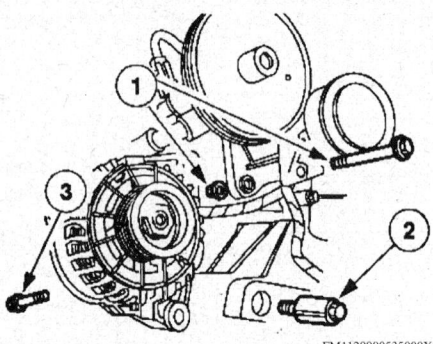

Fig. 1 Alternator bolt tightening sequence. 3.9L engine

with vehicle, diagnose module communications network concern.

FUSE PANEL & FLASHER LOCATION

Battery Junction Box

The battery junction box is located under the rear righthand side of the luggage compartment floor lining.

Central Junction Box

The central junction box is located under the righthand side of the instrument panel.

Interior Auxiliary Junction Box

The interior auxiliary junction box is located under the lefthand side of the instrument panel. This junction box contains a power junction stud and the DLC.

Underhood Auxiliary Junction Box

The underhood auxiliary junction box is located on the rear righthand side of the engine compartment.

Trailer Tow Auxiliary Junction Box

The trailer tow auxiliary junction box is located in the rear center of the luggage compartment.

Flasher

The flashing function is controlled by the front electronic module. The module is located at the lefthand A pillar.

FUEL PUMP RELAY LOCATION

The fuel pump relay is located under the luggage compartment floor lining in the battery junction box.

STARTER
REPLACE

1. Raise and support vehicle.
2. Remove ground strap from starter mounting stud.
3. Remove start cover and cables.
4. Remove mounting bolts and starter.
5. Reverse procedure to install. **Torque** starter mounting bolts to 18 ft. lbs.

ALTERNATOR
REPLACE

3.0L Engine

1. Remove accessory drive belt.
2. Raise and support vehicle.
3. Remove lower splash shield.
4. Support alternator, then remove mounting bolts.
5. Disconnect alternator electrical connections and remove alternator.
6. Reverse procedure to install, noting the following:
   a. **Torque** alternator electrical connectors to 71 inch lbs.
   b. **Torque** alternator mounting bolts to 33 ft. lbs.

3.9L Engine

1. Remove engine appearance cover.
2. Disconnect IAT sensor, breather hose and idle air control valve inlet tube.
3. Remove air intake tube support nut and washer.
4. Loosen tube clamps and remove tube.
5. Remove accessory drive belt.
6. Raise and support vehicle, then remove front lower splash shield.
7. Support alternator, then remove mounting bolts.
8. Turn alternator and remove positive cable.
9. Lower alternator and disconnect electrical connector.
10. Turn and remove alternator.
11. Reverse procedure to install, noting the following:
    a. **Torque** alternator electrical connector to 71 inch lbs.
    b. **Torque** alternator mounting bolts to 15 ft. lbs., then tighten an additional 90°, in sequence, **Fig. 1**.

IGNITION COIL
REPLACE

These engines use a coil on plug ignition system with an individual coil mounted on top of each spark plug.

3.0L Engine

1. Remove engine appearance cover.
2. If replacing righthand ignition coils, remove upper intake manifold as outlined under "Intake Manifold, Replace" in "3.0L Engine" section.
3. Disconnect coil electrical connector.
4. Remove mounting bolts and ignition coil.

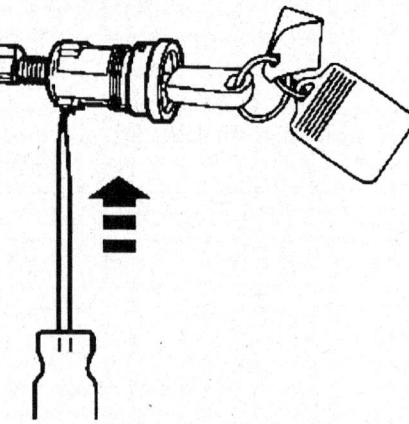

Fig. 2 Ignition lock cylinder replacement

5. Reverse procedure to install, noting the following:
   a. Ensure coils are seated and boot is not damaged. If boot is damaged, coil must be replaced.
   b. **Torque** coil mounting bolts to 53 inch lbs.

3.9L Engine

1. Remove engine appearance cover.
2. Disconnect IAT sensor, breather hose and idle air control valve inlet tube.
3. Remove air intake tube support nut and washer.
4. Loosen tube clamps and remove tube.
5. Remove ignition coil cover.
6. Disconnect coil electrical connectors.
7. Remove mounting bolts and ignition coils.
8. Reverse procedure to install. **Torque** mounting bolts to 44 inch lbs.

IGNITION LOCK
REPLACE

1. Remove steering column lower cover.
2. Remove mounting bolts and hood release handle.
3. Remove lower dash heater duct from below steering column.
4. Remove steering column opening cover reinforcement.
5. Place ignition switch in run position.
6. Depress ignition switch lock cylinder tab using suitable screwdriver, **Fig. 2**.
7. Remove ignition switch lock cylinder.
8. Reverse procedure to install.

IGNITION SWITCH
REPLACE

1. Adjust steering column to full tilt down and full extended position.
2. Remove mounting bolts and hood release handle.
3. Disconnect electrical connectors, then remove lower steering column cover.
4. Disconnect electrical connectors and remove outer instrument panel finish panel, **Fig. 3**.
5. Remove inner instrument panel finish

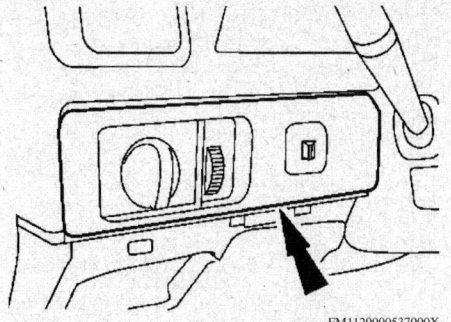

FM1129900537000X

Fig. 3 Outer instrument panel finish panel replacement

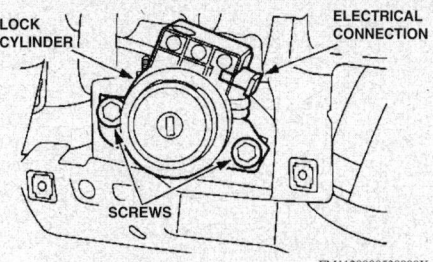

FM1129900538000X

Fig. 4 Ignition switch lock cylinder replacement

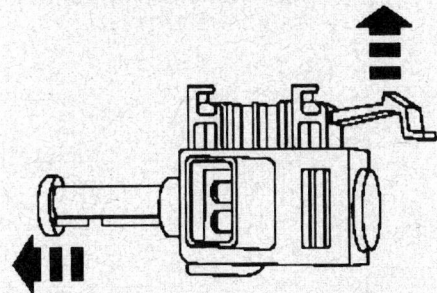

FM1069900968000X

Fig. 6 Clutch pedal position switch

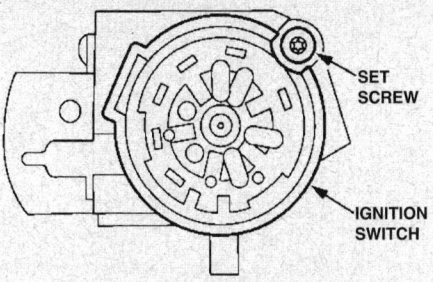

FM1129900539000X

Fig. 5 Ignition switch replacement

panel and instrument cluster finish panel mounting screws.
6. Disconnect in-vehicle air temperature sensor electrical connector and remove instrument cluster finish panel.
7. Remove mounting bolts and steering column reinforcement.
8. Disconnect ignition switch electrical connector and remove ignition switch lock cylinder mounting screws.
9. Remove ignition switch lock cylinder, **Fig. 4.**
10. With ignition switch in OFF position, remove set screw and ignition switch, **Fig. 5.**
11. Reverse procedure to install.

CLUTCH START SWITCH
REPLACE
1. Disconnect clutch pedal position switch electrical connector.
2. Lift retaining tag and remove switch, **Fig. 6.**
3. Reverse procedure to install.

NEUTRAL SAFETY SWITCH
REPLACE
Refer to "Digital Transmission Range (TR) Sensor, Replace" for neutral safety switch replacement procedure.

DIGITAL TRANSMISSION RANGE (TR) SENSOR
REPLACE
Removal
1. Raise and support vehicle.
2. Disconnect oxygen sensor and catalyst monitor electrical connectors.
3. Remove mounting nuts and three-way catalytic converter.
4. Remove mounting nuts and heat shield.
5. Make index marks on bolts, washers and nuts, to indicate installation position of driveshaft flex coupling to transmission flange and pinion flanges.
6. Make index marks on front driveshaft companion flange and transmission flange, then remove companion flange

to transmission flange mounting bolts. **Do not remove driveshaft flex coupling mounting bolts.**
7. Slide front driveshaft rearward and support transmission with suitable transmission jack. Secure transmission to jack using suitable safety chain.
8. Remove transmission mount, then lower transmission to gain access to digital TR sensor.
9. Disconnect shift cable.
10. Disconnect TR sensor electrical connector, then remove sensor.

Installation
1. Place TR sensor flush against boss on transmission case, then loosely install sensor mounting bolts.
2. Place manual lever in neutral position.
3. Align TR sensor using sensor alignment tool No. T97L-70010-A, or equivalent.
4. **Torque** sensor screws evenly to 89 inch lbs., then connect TR sensor electrical connector.
5. Connect shift cable and install rear transmission support.
6. Adjust shift cable as outlined in MOTOR's "Domestic Transmission Manual, In-Vehicle Service."
7. Align index marks and **torque** companion flange to transmission flange bolts to 60 ft. lbs.
8. Install heat shield and catalytic converter, lower vehicle.

HEADLAMP SWITCH
REPLACE
1. Remove lower instrument panel steering column cover.
2. Remove outer instrument panel finish panel located on lefthand side of steering column.

3. Release four retaining clips, then remove headlamp switch from outer instrument panel finish panel.
4. Reverse procedure to install.

STOP LIGHT SWITCH
REPLACE
1. Remove instrument panel insulator.
2. Disconnect and remove brake pedal position switch.
3. Reverse procedure to install.

MULTI-FUNCTION SWITCH
REPLACE
1. Ensure front wheels are in straight ahead position.
2. Remove driver's air bag module as outlined in "Passive Restraints Systems" chapter.
3. Remove horn switch.
4. Loosen steering wheel mounting bolt.
5. Loosen steering wheel using differential bearing cone removal tool No. T77F-4220-B1, or equivalent, **Fig. 7.**
6. Remove steering wheel puller, steering wheel mounting bolt and steering wheel. Discard steering wheel mounting bolt.
7. Remove mounting bolts and hood release handle.
8. Disconnect electrical connectors, then remove lower steering column cover.
9. Disconnect electrical connectors and remove outer instrument panel finish panel, **Fig. 3.**
10. Remove inner instrument panel finish panel and instrument cluster finish panel mounting screws.
11. Disconnect in-vehicle air temperature sensor electrical connector and remove instrument cluster finish panel.
12. Apply two strips of masking tape across air bag sliding contact to prevent rotation.
13. Depress three clips and position air bag sliding contact aside.
14. Disconnect multi-function switch electrical connector, then remove switch.
15. Reverse procedure to install. **Torque** steering wheel bolt to 30 ft. lbs.

STEERING WHEEL
REPLACE
1. Ensure front wheels are in straight ahead position.

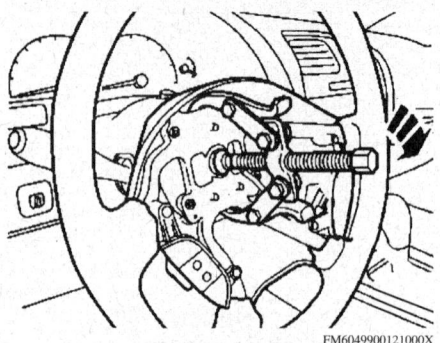

Fig. 7 Steering wheel replacement

2. Remove driver's air bag module as outlined in "Passive Restraints Systems" chapter.
3. Remove horn switch.
4. Loosen steering wheel mounting bolt.
5. Loosen steering wheel using differential bearing cone removal tool No. T77F-4220-B1, or equivalent, **Fig. 7**.
6. Remove steering wheel puller, steering wheel mounting bolt and steering wheel. Discard steering wheel mounting bolt.
7. Reverse procedure to install. **Torque** new steering wheel mounting bolt to 30 ft. lbs.

INSTRUMENT CLUSTER
REPLACE

Prior to instrument cluster removal, module configuration must be retrieved. Refer to "Module Configuration" for procedure.
1. Remove mounting bolts and hood release handle.
2. Disconnect electrical connectors, then remove lower steering column cover.
3. Disconnect electrical connectors and remove outer instrument panel finish panel, **Fig. 3**.
4. Remove inner instrument panel finish panel and instrument cluster finish panel mounting screws.
5. Disconnect in-vehicle air temperature sensor electrical connector and remove instrument cluster finish panel.
6. Remove floor heat duct.
7. Remove steering column reinforcement.
8. Loosen steering column mounting bolts and lower steering column.
9. Place suitable cloth over upper steering column cover to prevent damage to instrument cluster lens.
10. Remove mounting bolts and instrument cluster.
11. Reverse procedure to install. Download module configuration from NGS tester into new module.

RADIO
REPLACE

Prior to radio removal, module configuration must be retrieved. Refer to "Module Configuration" for procedure.
1. Remove air conditioning register finish panel.

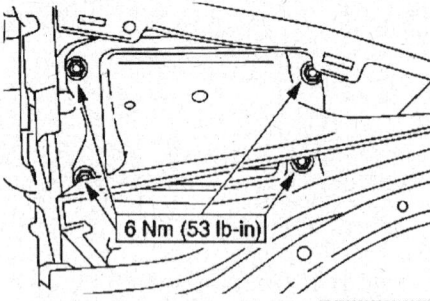

Fig. 8 Cabin air filter housing bolt locations

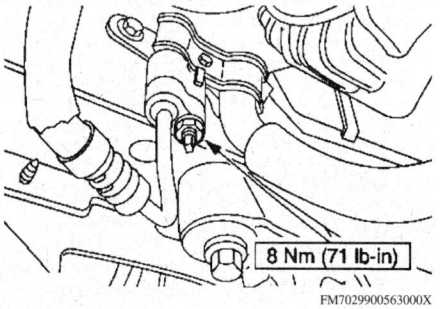

Fig. 10 Peanut fitting location

2. Remove ash tray finish panel.
3. Remove audio/climate control mounting bolts.
4. Disconnect electrical connectors and antenna cable.
5. Remove audio/climate control unit.
6. Separate audio unit from audio/climate control assembly.
7. Reverse procedure to install. Download module configuration from NGS tester into new module.

WIPER MOTOR
REPLACE
LS

1. Remove mounting nuts and wiper pivot arms.
2. Remove two part pin retainers and separate Velcro attachment of rubber hinge cover to rear outboard corner of cowl vent screen.
3. Lift cowl vent screen to release clips.
4. Remove cowl vent screen.
5. Remove strut tower support brace.
6. Remove coolant overflow bottle and position aside.
7. Remove wiper mounting arm and pivot shaft bolts.
8. Disconnect drain boot from windshield wiper mounting arm and pivot shaft.
9. Position windshield wiper mounting arm and pivot shaft aside, then loosen upper windshield wiper motor bolt.
10. Turn wiper output arm to 6 o'clock position.
11. Remove lower wiper motor bolts.
12. Turn bottom of wiper mounting arm and pivot shaft upward.
13. Remove windshield wiper mounting arm and pivot shaft.
14. Remove remaining mounting bolts and wiper motor.

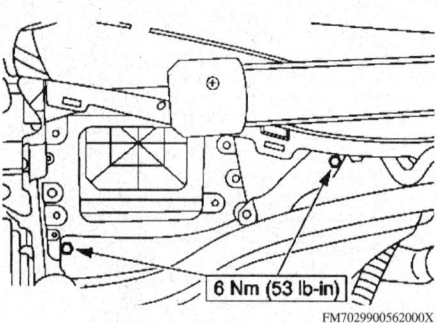

Fig. 9 Plenum panel replacement

15. Reverse procedure to install, noting the following:
   a. **Torque** wiper pivot arm nuts to 18 ft. lbs.
   b. **Torque** strut support brace bolts to 15 ft. lbs.
   c. **Torque** mounting arm and pivot shaft bolts to 108 inch lbs.
   d. **Torque** wiper motor crank bolt and mounting bolts to 108 inch lbs.

Thunderbird

1. Remove mounting nuts and wiper arm pivot arms.
2. Remove lefthand and righthand cowl vent screen extension panels.
3. Disconnect windshield washer nozzle hoses from engine main wiring harness at lower righthand side of engine compartment.
4. Remove pin-type retainers and cowl vent screen.
5. Remove strut tower support brace.
6. Remove degas bottle and position aside. Route degas bottle lower hose in front of brake booster.
7. Remove wiper mounting arm and pivot shaft mounting bolts.
8. Disconnect drain boot from wiper mounting arm and pivot shaft,
9. Position wiper arm and pivot shaft aside, then loosen wiper motor mounting bolt.
10. Turn wiper output arm to 6 o'clock position, then remove lower wiper motor bolts.
11. Remove wiper mounting arm and pivot shaft by rotating upward.
12. Remove upper mounting and crank bolts, then the wiper motor.
13. Reverse procedure to install, noting the following:
   a. **Torque** wiper motor mounting bolts to 11 ft. lbs.
   b. **Torque** wiper motor crank bolt and to 13 ft. lbs.
   c. **Torque** strut support brace bolts to 15 ft. lbs.
   d. **Torque** mounting arm and pivot shaft bolts to 108 inch lbs.

WIPER SWITCH
REPLACE

Refer to "Multi-Function Switch, Replace" for wiper switch replacement procedure.

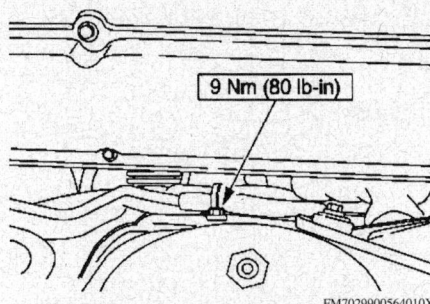

FM7029900564010X

Fig. 11 Air conditioning line bracket location (Part 1 of 2)

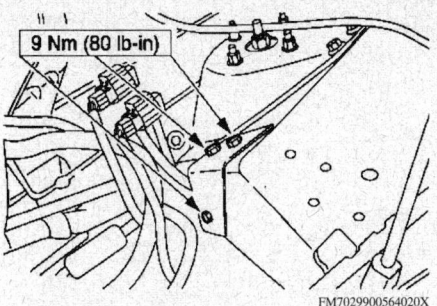

FM7029900564020X

Fig. 11 Air conditioning line bracket location (Part 2 of 2)

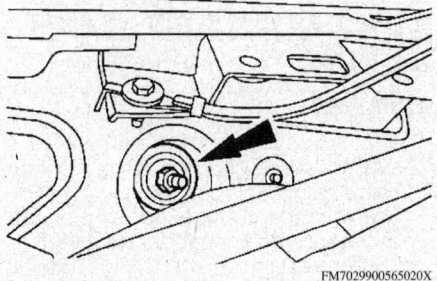

FM7029900565020X

Fig. 12 Engine compartment evaporator housing bolt location (Part 2 of 3)

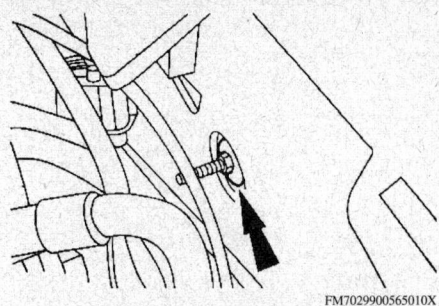

FM7029900565010X

Fig. 12 Engine compartment evaporator housing bolt location (Part 1 of 3)

WIPER TRANSMISSION

REPLACE

Refer to "Wiper Motor, Replace" for wiper transmission replacement procedure.

BLOWER MOTOR

REPLACE

1. Remove passenger side floor duct.
2. Remove blower motor cover.
3. Disconnect blower motor electrical connector.
4. Remove blower motor.
5. Reverse procedure to install.

CABIN AIR FILTER

REPLACE

LS

1. Remove mounting nuts and wiper pivot arms.
2. Remove two part pin retainers and separate Velcro attachment of rubber hinge cover to rear outboard corner of cowl vent screen.
3. Lift cowl vent screen to release clips.
4. Remove righthand cowl cover.
5. Push on righthand corner of filter to release clip.
6. Release lefthand clip and remove cabin air filter.
7. Reverse procedure to install.

Thunderbird

1. Remove left and righthand cowl side trim pieces.
2. Remove mounting nuts and wiper arms.
3. Remove pin-type retainers and cowl vent screen.
4. Push on righthand corner of cabin air filter and release righthand clip.
5. Release lefthand clip and cabin air filter.
6. Reverse procedure to install.

HEATER CORE

REPLACE

LS

1. Recover air conditioning refrigerant as outlined in "Air Conditioning" chapter.

2. Disconnect heater hose from heater core.
3. Remove mounting nuts and wiper pivot arms.
4. Remove two part pin retainers and separate Velcro attachment of rubber hinge cover to rear outboard corner of cowl vent screen.
5. Lift cowl vent screen to release clips.
6. Remove righthand cowl cover.
7. Push on righthand corner of filter to release clip.
8. Release lefthand clip and remove cabin air filter.
9. Remove strut tower support brace.
10. Remove cabin air filter housing mounting bolts, **Fig. 8.**
11. Remove mounting bolts and plenum panel, **Fig. 9.**
12. Disconnect coolant recovery line.
13. Remove forward heater hose mounting bolt at righthand shock tower.
14. Raise and support vehicle.
15. Remove rear heater hose mounting bolt from body side and position heater hose aside.
16. Disconnect spring lock coupling using spring lock coupling tool T84L-19623-B, or equivalent.
17. Remove nut and disconnect peanut fitting, **Fig. 10.**
18. Remove peanut fitting bracket bolt.
19. Remove air conditioning line bracket bolts, **Fig. 11.**
20. Remove thermostatic expansion valve manifold and tube.
21. Remove instrument panel as outlined in "Dash Panel Service" chapter.
22. Disconnect electrical connector at top of evaporator core housing.
23. Remove cowl top mounting bolt.
24. Remove evaporator housing attachment bolt.

25. Remove engine compartment nuts, **Fig. 12.**
26. Remove evaporator core housing.
27. Remove evaporator core housing to air inlet housing screws, **Fig. 13.**
28. Disconnect clip and separate evaporator core housing from air inlet housing.
29. Remove housing gasket.
30. Remove nine screws, then disconnect clip and separate evaporator core housing halves.
31. Disconnect bypass door connector and position harness aside.
32. Remove mounting screws, **Fig. 14.**
33. Remove heater core.
34. Reverse procedure to install noting the following:
   a. Lubricate air conditioning O-ring seal using PAG refrigerant oil YN-12-C, F7AZ-19589-DA, or equivalent.
   b. **Torque** air conditioning peanut fitting to 71 inch lbs.
   c. **Torque** expansion valve fitting to 15 ft. lbs.
   d. **Torque** evaporator housing to engine compartment nuts and cowl top attachment bolt to 62 inch lbs.
   e. **Torque** evaporator housing bolt to 44 inch lbs.
   f. Ensure heater hoses are correctly connected to heater core.

Thunderbird

1. Recover refrigerant as outlined in "Air Conditioning" chapter.
2. Partially drain cooling system into suitable container, then disconnect heater hose from heater core.
3. Remove manifold and tube to expansion valve mounting bolt, then disconnect assembly from expansion valve. Discard O-rings.
4. Remove instrument panel as outlined in "Dash Panel Service" chapter.
5. Disconnect electrical connector located on top of evaporator core housing.
6. Remove cowl top and evaporator housing mounting bolts.
7. Remove evaporator housing to bulkhead mounting nuts and washers from engine compartment side of bulkhead.
8. Remove evaporator housing to bulkhead mounting nut and washer from passenger compartment side of bulkhead.
9. Remove evaporator core housing.
10. Remove evaporator core housing to

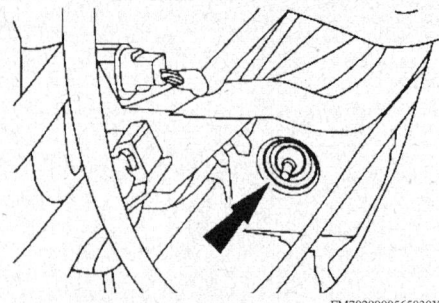

Fig. 12 Engine compartment evaporator housing bolt location (Part 3 of 3)

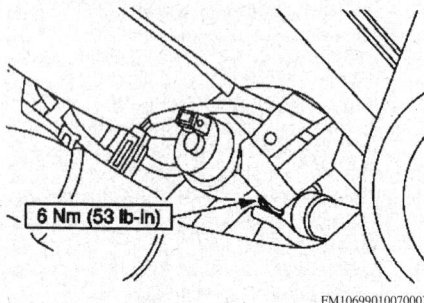

Fig. 15 Auxiliary coolant pump replacement

air inlet housing mounting screws.
11. Release clip and separate evaporator core housing from air inlet housing.
12. Remove evaporator core housing screws, then separate housing halves.
13. Remove mounting screws and heater core.
14. Remove heater core tube gasket.
15. Reverse procedure to install.

EVAPORATOR CORE
REPLACE

1. Remove evaporator housing and separate housing halves as outlined under "Heater Core, Replace."
2. Remove evaporator core from housing.
3. Remove evaporator core to thermostatic expansion valve fittings and expansion valve from evaporator core.
4. Reverse procedure to install.

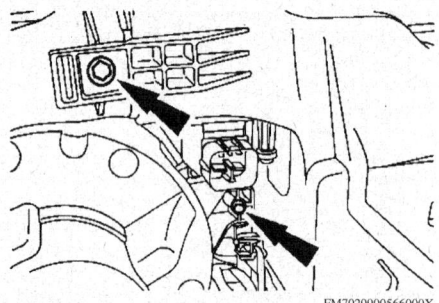

Fig. 13 Evaporator housing to air inlet housing screw location

DUAL COOLANT FLOW VALVE
REPLACE

1. Ensure engine is cold.
2. Wrap suitable shop towel around pressure relief cap, then remove cap. **Ensure coolant does not come into contact with accessory drive belt.**
3. Drain radiator coolant into suitable container.
4. **On models equipped with oil cooler,** disconnect coolant return hose at oil cooler.
5. **On models equipped with 3.9L engine,** remove auxiliary coolant pump as follows:
   a. Ensure engine is cold.
   b. Wrap suitable shop towel around pressure relief cap, then remove cap.
   c. **Ensure coolant does not come into contact with accessory drive belt.**
   d. **On models equipped with oil cooler,** disconnect coolant return hose at oil cooler.
   e. **On all models,** disconnect auxiliary coolant pump electrical connector.
   f. Remove coolant pump to fan shroud mounting bolts, **Fig. 15.**
   g. Disconnect coolant pump hoses, then remove pump.
6. **On all models,** disconnect coolant valve electrical connector.
7. Place identification marks on dual coolant flow valve for installation alignment, **Fig. 16.**
8. Raise and support vehicle.
9. Remove coolant valve mounting nut and bolt.

Fig. 14 Heater core cover screw location

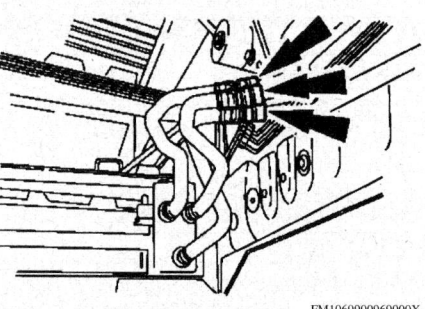

Fig. 16 Dual coolant flow valve

10. Raise valve and disconnect coolant supply and return lines.
11. Remove coolant flow valve.
12. Reverse procedure to install.

AUXILIARY COOLANT FLOW PUMP
REPLACE

1. Ensure engine is cold.
2. Wrap suitable shop towel around pressure relief cap, then remove cap.
3. **Ensure coolant does not come into contact with accessory drive belt.**
4. Drain radiator coolant into suitable container.
5. **On models equipped with oil cooler,** disconnect coolant return hose at oil cooler.
6. **On all models,** disconnect auxiliary coolant pump electrical connector.
7. Remove coolant pump to fan shroud mounting bolts, **Fig. 15.**
8. Disconnect coolant pump hoses, then remove pump.
9. Reverse procedure to install. **Torque** auxiliary coolant pump mounting bolts to 53 inch lbs.

3.0L Engine

NOTE: On Air Bag Equipped Models, Refer To "Air Bag System Precautions" Located In The Front Of This Manual For System Disarming & Arming Procedures.

NOTE: Refer To "Computer Relearn Procedures" Located In The Front Of This Manual When Battery Power To The Computer Has Been Interrupted.

INDEX

PRECAUTIONS

Air Bag Systems

Refer to "Air Bag System Precautions" in the front of this manual for system disarming and arming procedures.

Battery Ground Cable

Prior to service, disconnect battery ground cable and isolate as required.

Fuel System Pressure Relief

1. Remove Schrader valve cap and install fuel pressure gauge tool No. T80L-9974-B, or equivalent, to Schrader valve.
2. Slowly open manual valve on pressure gauge and drain fuel into suitable container.

QUICK DISCONNECT HOSES

R-Clip

When working with R-clip type connections do not use tools to disconnect, **Fig. 1.** Use of tools may deform clip components and could cause leaks.

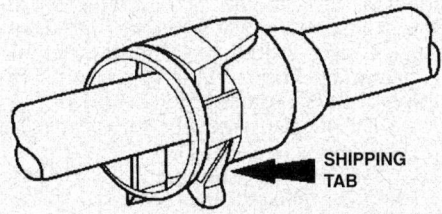

SHIPPING TAB

FM1069900923000X

Fig. 1   R-clip connection

To disconnect, bend shipping tab downward, **Fig. 1.** Spread R-clip and push clip into fitting. Separate fitting from tube.

To install, first inspect fitting and tube for damage and ensure connections are clean. Apply a light coat of clean 5W-30 motor oil to male end of tube. Insert R-clip into fitting. Align tube and fitting, then insert tube into fitting and push together until a click is heard. Pull on connection to ensure it is fully engaged.

Spring Lock

When working with spring lock type connections spring lock tool set No. T84L-19623-B, or equivalent, must be used to disconnect fittings, **Fig. 2.** When connecting spring lock type fittings, inspect and clean both coupling ends. Lubricate fuel line O-ring seals with clean 5W-30 motor oil. When connection is made, pull on line to ensure it is fully engaged.

Vapor Tube

To disconnect vapor tube connections, squeeze fitting and disconnect vapor tube from fitting, **Fig. 3.** To connect, ensure fittings are clean and free from damage. Push tube onto fitting until it snaps into place. Pull on connection to ensure fitting is secure.

COMPRESSION PRESSURE

Before performing compression test, ensure the crankcase oil is of correct viscosity and at correct level. Ensure battery is fully charged and engine is at normal operating temperature.

1. Turn ignition switch to OFF position.
2. Remove spark plugs.
3. Set throttle plates to wide open position.
4. Install suitable compression gauge in cylinder No. 1.
5. Install auxiliary starter switch in starting circuit.
6. With ignition switch in OFF position, use auxiliary starter switch to crank engine at least five compression strokes.
7. Count number of compression strokes required to reach highest reading and record highest reading.
8. Repeat test on each cylinder, cranking engine same number of compression strokes.

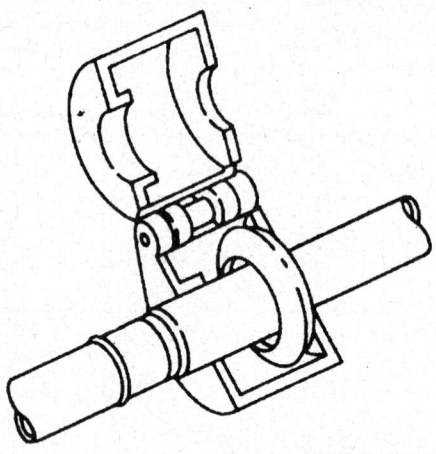

Fig. 2 Spring lock connection

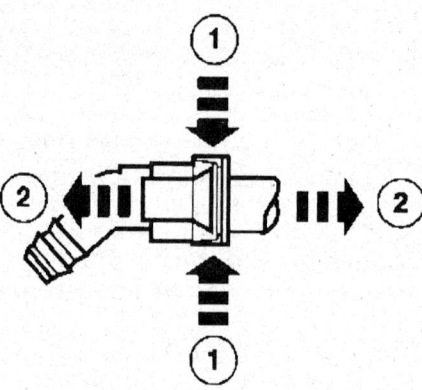

Fig. 3 Vapor tube connection

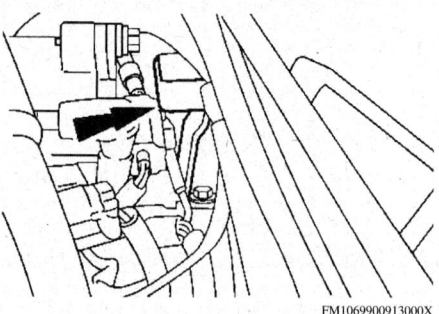

Fig. 4 Wire harness bracket replacement

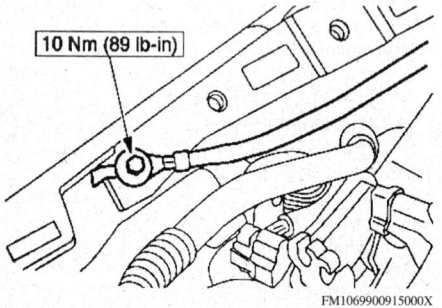

Fig. 5 Ground strap location

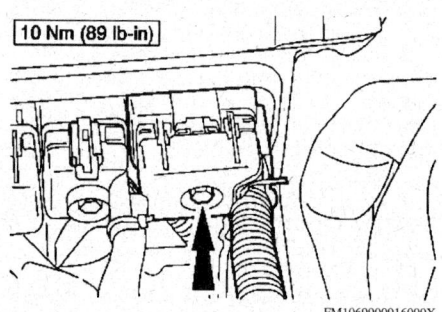

Fig. 6 Main engine harness connector

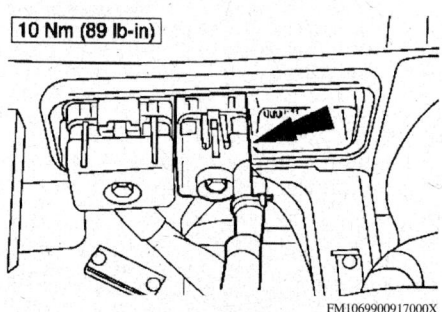

Fig. 7 Main transmission harness connector

9. Indicated compression pressures are considered within specifications if lowest reading cylinder is within 75 percent of highest reading.

ENGINE MOUNT

REPLACE

1. Remove cowl vent screen as outlined under "Wiper Motor, Replace" in "Electrical" section.
2. Remove strut brace.
3. Remove wire harness bracket, **Fig. 4.**
4. Disconnect intake manifold tuning valve electrical connector.
5. Remove mounting bolts and intake manifold tuning valve.
6. Remove cabin air filter plenum as outlined under "Heater Core, Replace" in "Electrical" section.
7. Remove engine mount upper nut.
8. Raise and support vehicle.
9. Remove engine mount lower nut.
10. Raise engine and remove mount.
11. Reverse procedure to install, noting the following:
    a. **Ensure intake manifold tuning valve is fully seated into intake before installing bolts.**
    b. **Torque** intake manifold tuning valve to 89 inch lbs.
    c. **Torque** upper mount nut to 30 ft. lbs.
    d. **Torque** lower mount nut to 46 ft. lbs.

ENGINE

REPLACE

When carrying out operations which involve the removal and installation of the driveshaft, always inspect the joint angles and adjust as outlined under "Driveline Angle Measurement" in "Rear Axle & Suspension" section.

1. Disconnect IAT sensor electrical connector.
2. Disconnect aspirator and PCV hose from air cleaner outlet tube.
3. Remove air cleaner outlet tube.
4. Remove engine appearance cover.
5. Ensure engine is cold.
6. Wrap suitable shop towel around pressure relief cap, then remove cap.
7. **Ensure coolant does not come into contact with accessory drive belt.**
8. Open radiator draincock and drain coolant into suitable container.
9. **On models equipped with oil cooler,** disconnect coolant return hose at oil cooler.
10. **On all models,** recover air conditioning refrigerant as outlined in "Air Conditioning" chapter.
11. Remove upper radiator sight shield and upper radiator support brackets.
12. Disconnect air conditioning pressure switch connector.
13. Remove power steering reservoir bolts and position reservoir aside.
14. Disconnect fuel lines.
15. Disconnect brake aspirator vacuum hose, then remove left and righthand cowl trim panels.
16. Unclip chassis vacuum lines from support bracket, then disconnect lines.

17. Remove strut brace support.
18. Remove cabin air filter plenum as outlined under "Heater Core, Replace" in "Electrical" section.
19. Disconnect main vacuum hose from rear of intake manifold.
20. Disconnect throttle and speed control cables and unclip from bracket.
21. Remove ground strap bolt, **Fig. 5.**
22. Disconnect main engine wiring harness and transmission harness connectors, **Figs. 6 and 7.**
23. Disconnect fuel charging wiring, **Fig. 8.**
24. Disconnect wiring harness retainer from bracket.
25. Remove air conditioning line mounting bracket.
26. Remove hydraulic cooling fan reservoir and position aside.
27. Unclip line from frame, **Fig. 9.**
28. Raise and support vehicle.
29. Drain engine oil into suitable container.
30. Remove left and righthand splash shields.
31. Remove air conditioning manifold bolt, then position manifold aside.
32. Place reference marks on dual coolant flow valve coolant lines for installation alignment.
33. Disconnect coolant hoses from dual coolant flow valve using quick disconnect tool No. T85T-18539-AH, or equivalent, **Fig. 10.**
34. Remove exhaust system and heat shields.
35. Remove driveshaft as outlined in "Rear Axle & Suspension" section
36. Disconnect shift cable at transmission.
37. Remove shift cable bracket bolt.
38. Remove front tires.
39. Disconnect left and righthand front ABS sensors.

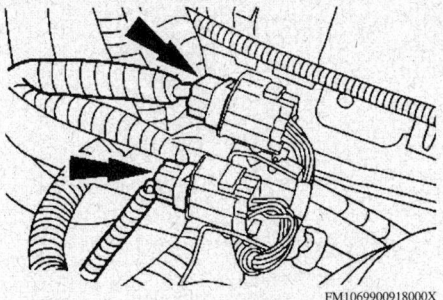

Fig. 8 Fuel charging wiring connectors

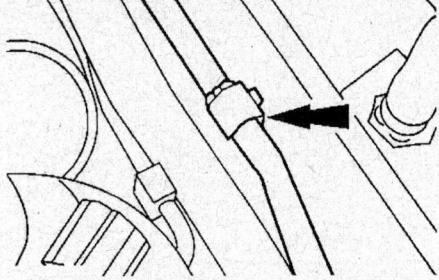

Fig. 9 Frame line location

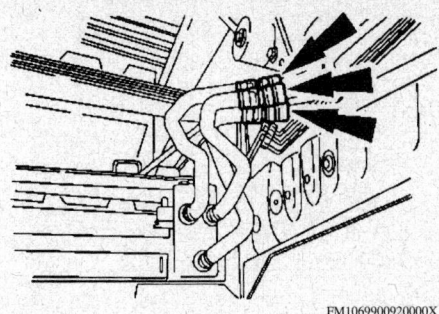

Fig. 10 Dual coolant flow valve

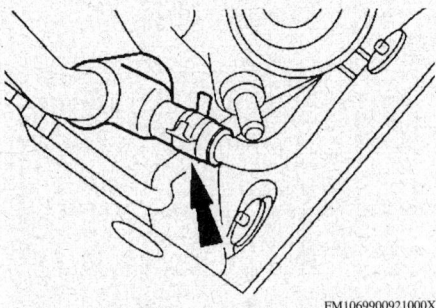

Fig. 11 Hose disconnect location

40. Remove bolts, then position from brake calipers aside.
41. Disconnect stabilizer link lower mounts and upper ball joints.
42. Remove lower strut mount bolts.
43. Disconnect starter wiring harness at starter.
44. Disconnect power steering pressure electrical connectors.
45. Remove steering shaft clamp bolt.
46. Remove torque converter nuts.
47. Disconnect hose, **Fig. 11.**
48. Support rear of vehicle using suitable safety stands.
49. Support engine, transmission, front and center crossmembers and cooling system with suitable powertrain lift and transmission support bracket.
50. Remove four transmission crossmember bolts.
51. Remove four front and four center crossmember bolts.
52. Lower engine and transmission.
53. Install two engine lifting brackets tool No. 303-050, or equivalent, to engine.
54. Support engine and transmission in front subframe using suitable engine lift and spreader bar.
55. Disconnect two wire harness retainers and position harness aside.
56. Remove starter and oxygen sensor bracket.
57. Remove upper then lower transmission to engine mounting bolts.
58. Remove left and righthand engine mount upper mounting nuts.
59. Remove accessory drive belt.
60. Disconnect power steering pump electrical connector.
61. Remove power steering pump and position aside.
62. Disconnect hydraulic cooling fan pump electrical connector.
63. Remove hydraulic cooling fan pump

and position aside.
64. Disconnect upper radiator hose.
65. **On models equipped with automatic transmission,** disconnect cooler line bracket from oil pan, then remove transmission cooler lines from transmission and plug fittings.
66. **On models equipped with oil cooler,** disconnect oil cooler hoses.
67. **On all models,** remove remaining transmission to engine mounting bolts and separate transmission from engine.
68. **On models equipped with manual transmission,** remove clutch.
69. **On all models,** remove flywheel.
70. Unclip left and righthand wire harness retainers.
71. Remove rear separator plate.
72. Mount engine to suitable workstand, then remove lifting equipment.
73. Reverse procedure to install.

INTAKE MANIFOLD
REPLACE
Upper

1. Ensure engine is cold.
2. Wrap suitable shop towel around pressure relief cap, then remove cap.
3. **Ensure coolant does not come into contact with accessory drive belt.**
4. Open radiator draincock and drain coolant into suitable container.
5. **On models equipped with oil cooler,** disconnect coolant return hose at oil cooler.
6. **On all models,** remove air cleaner outlet tube.
7. Disconnect TP sensor and IAC electrical connectors.
8. Disconnect speed control and accelerator cables and position aside.
9. Disconnect coolant hoses, PCV hose and vapor purge hose from throttle body.
10. Disconnect EGR vacuum hose and EGR tube.
11. Remove cowl vent screen.
12. Remove vacuum hoses and cruise control cables from mounting brackets.
13. Disconnect differential pressure feedback EGR electrical connector.
14. Remove differential pressure feedback EGR transducer and position aside.
15. Remove fuel pressure sensor shield.

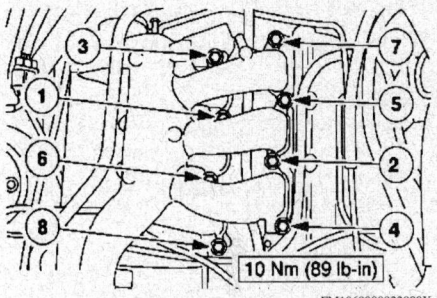

Fig. 12 Upper intake manifold bolt tightening sequence

16. Disconnect vacuum hose from rear of intake manifold.
17. Disconnect intake manifold tuning valve electrical connector.
18. Disconnect exhaust vacuum regulator electrical connector and vacuum line.
19. Remove upper intake support bolt.
20. Remove mounting bolts and upper intake manifold.
21. Reverse procedure to install. **Torque** manifold bolts to 89 inch lbs., in sequence, **Fig. 12.**

Lower

1. Remove upper intake manifold as outlined under "Upper."
2. Disconnect fuel lines.
3. Remove fuel line bracket bolt.
4. Disconnect fuel pressure sensor vacuum line and fuel charging wiring harness connector.
5. Disconnect crankcase ventilation tube and position aside.
6. Remove mounting bolts and lower intake manifold. **Fuel injection supply manifold and lower intake manifold must be removed as an assembly.**
7. Reverse procedure to install, noting the following:
   a. Inspect fuel injector O-rings.
   b. Inspect lower intake manifold gaskets.
   c. **Torque** mounting bolts to 89 inch lbs., in sequence, **Fig. 13.**

EXHAUST MANIFOLD
REPLACE
Lefthand

1. Remove heat shield.
2. Remove three upper nuts on manifold.

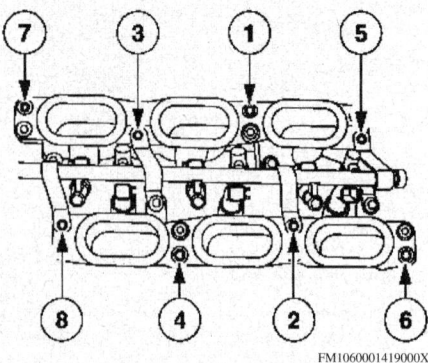

Fig. 13 Lower intake manifold tightening sequence

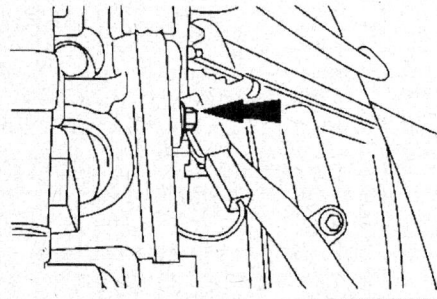

Fig. 16 Lefthand noise suppressor bolt location

3. Remove secondary air tube from exhaust manifold.
4. Remove dual converter Y-pipe.
5. Remove three lower nuts and exhaust manifold.
6. Reverse procedure to install. Install new gasket and **torque** mounting nuts to 15 ft. lbs., in sequence, **Fig. 14.**

Righthand

1. Remove heat shield.
2. Remove secondary air tube from exhaust manifold.
3. Remove dual Y-pipe.
4. Disconnect EGR valve to exhaust manifold tube.
5. Remove mounting nuts and manifold.
6. Reverse procedure to install. Install new gasket and **torque** mounting nuts to 15 ft. lbs in sequence, **Fig. 14.**

CYLINDER HEAD
REPLACE

When cleaning cylinder head surfaces, do not use metal scrapers, wires brushes, power abrasive discs or other abrasive methods to clean sealing surfaces. Use only a plastic scraping tool to remove all traces of gasket material.

Cylinder head bolts are of torque-to-yield style and must be replaced when removed.

Lefthand and righthand cylinder head gaskets are not interchangeable.

Lefthand

1. Remove camshafts as outlined under "Camshaft, Replace."

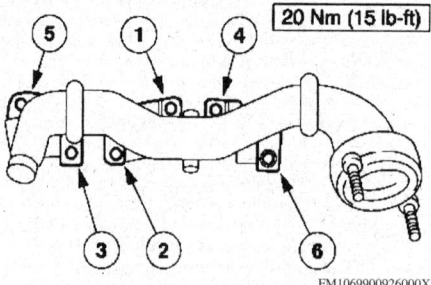

Fig. 14 Exhaust manifold tightening sequence

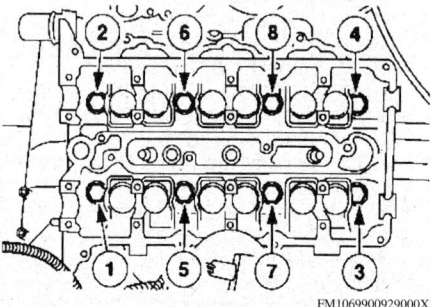

Fig. 17 Cylinder head bolt loosening sequence

2. Remove exhaust manifold as outlined under "Exhaust Manifold, Replace."
3. Remove lower intake manifold as outlined under "Intake Manifold, Replace."
4. Remove cylinder head ground strap, stud and bolt, **Fig. 15.**
5. Remove noise suppressor bolt, **Fig. 16.**
6. Disconnect coolant outlet hose from thermostat housing.
7. Remove thermostat housing.
8. Remove oil dipstick tube stud bolt.
9. Remove cylinder head bolts in sequence, **Fig. 17.**
10. Reverse procedure to install, noting the following:
    a. **Torque** cylinder head bolts to 22 ft. lbs., in sequence, **Fig. 18.**
    b. Tighten head bolts an additional 90° in sequence.
    c. Loosen bolts 360° in sequence.
    d. **Torque** to 22 ft. lbs., in sequence.
    e. Tighten an additional 90° in sequence.
    f. Tighten an additional 90° in sequence.

Righthand

1. Remove camshafts as outlined under "Camshaft, Replace."
2. Remove exhaust manifold as outlined under "Exhaust Manifold, Replace."
3. Remove lower intake manifold as outlined under "Intake Manifold, Replace."
4. Remove noise suppressor bolt, **Fig. 19.**
5. Disconnect outlet hose from thermostat housing.
6. Remove thermostat housing.
7. Remove cylinder head bolts in sequence, **Fig. 17.**

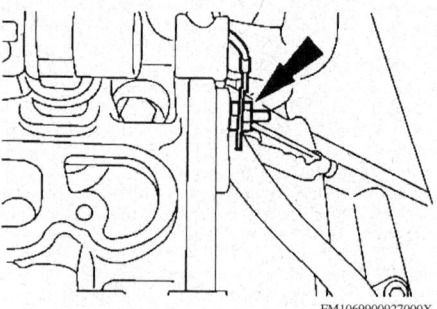

Fig. 15 Lefthand cylinder head ground strap location

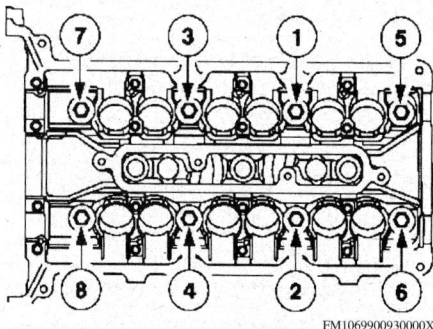

Fig. 18 Cylinder head bolt tightening sequence

8. Reverse procedure to install, noting the following:
    a. **Torque** cylinder head bolts to 22 ft. lbs., in sequence, **Fig. 18.**
    b. Tighten head bolts an additional 90° in sequence.
    c. Loosen bolts 360° in sequence.
    d. **Torque** to 22 ft. lbs., in sequence.
    e. Tighten an additional 90° in sequence.
    f. Tighten an additional 90° in sequence.

VALVE COVER
REPLACE

Lefthand

1. Remove engine appearance cover.
2. Disconnect coil electrical connector.
3. Remove mounting bolts and ignition coil.
4. Remove cylinder head temperature sensor.
5. Remove vacuum hoses from appearance cover support bracket.
6. Remove appearance cover support bracket.
7. Disconnect PCV tube and position aside.
8. Remove ignition coil harness from retainers.
9. Remove studs, bolts and valve cover.
10. Reverse procedure to install, noting the following:
    a. Apply .2 inch bead of silicone gasket sealant part No. F7AZ-19554-EA, or equivalent, to front cover joints.
    b. **Torque** mounting bolts to 89 inch lbs., in sequence, **Fig. 20.**

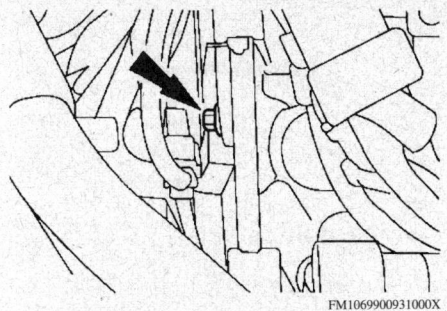

Fig. 19 Righthand noise suppressor bolt location

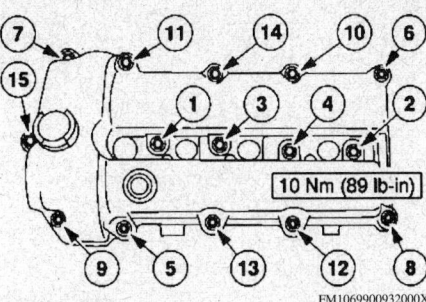

Fig. 20 Valve cover tightening sequence

10 Nm (89 lb-in)

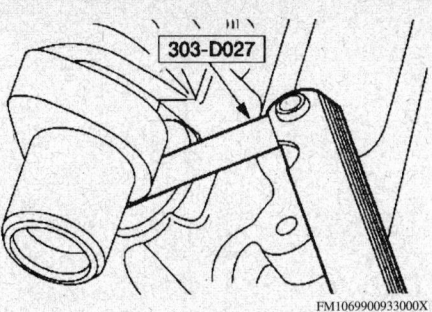

303-D027

Fig. 21 Valve lash measurement

Righthand

1. Remove upper intake manifold as outlined under "Intake Manifold, Replace."
2. Disconnect PCV tube and position aside.
3. Disconnect coil electrical connector.
4. Remove mounting bolts and ignition coil.
5. Remove wiring harness retainer from stud.
6. Remove upper intake manifold support bracket and position aside.
7. Remove wiring harness bracket nuts and position aside.
8. Remove mounting bolts, studs and valve cover.
9. Reverse procedure to install, noting the following:
   a. Apply .2 inch bead of silicone gasket sealant part No. F7AZ-19554-EA, or equivalent, to front cover joints.
   b. **Torque** mounting bolts to 89 inch lbs., in sequence, **Fig. 20.**

VALVE ARRANGEMENT

Inner .... I-I-I-I-I-I
Outer .... E-E-E-E-E-E

VALVE ADJUSTMENT

Rotating the engine in a counterclockwise direction will cause engine damage.

Mark shims with permanent marker. Scratches or paint on shim will cause incorrect lash adjustment and severe engine damage.

When measuring valve lash, ensure camshaft lobes are 180° away from each valve tappet.

1. Remove left and righthand valve covers as outlined under "Valve Cover, Replace."
2. Turn engine clockwise to position camshaft lobe away from shim surface.
3. Measure clearance between camshaft and shim surface using feeler gauge set tool No. D81L-4201-A, or equivalent, **Fig. 21.** Refer to "Specifications" section for correct valve clearance.
4. Mark position of timing chain in relation to camshaft sprockets to ensure timing remains correct.
5. Place alignment marks on camshaft

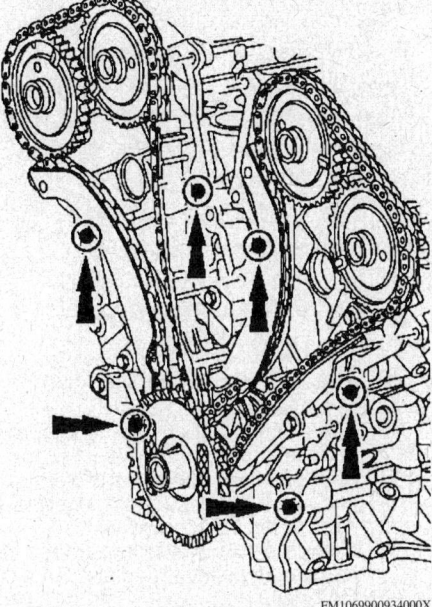

Fig. 22 Front cover sealant application points

caps for installation alignment. Caps should be marked for location and orientation.

6. Remove camshaft thrust cap and rear camshaft cap from camshaft that requires adjustment.
7. Install camshaft lift tools, tool No. 303-659, or equivalents, and hand tighten. Taller tool should be installed in place of rear camshaft cap to allow camshaft to be lifted for shim removal.
8. Remove center camshaft caps.
9. Mark location of each shim.
10. Remove shims that require adjustment using rubber tipped air gun and compressed air.
11. Measure and record thickness of each shim to correspond with valve clearance.
12. Calculate required shim thickness by adding original shim thickness to measured clearance and subtracting desired clearance.
13. Reverse procedure to install, noting the following:
    a. Apply coat of clean 5W-30 motor oil to replacement shims and install shims.
    b. Apply coat of clean 5W-30 motor oil to camshaft journals and bearing caps.

c. Turn crankshaft in clockwise direction to turn camshafts two full revolutions. Inspect valve clearance and timing.

CRANKSHAFT DAMPER
REPLACE

1. Remove accessory drive belt.
2. Remove secondary air valve, bracket and tube.
3. Raise and support vehicle.
4. Remove front center splash panel.
5. Remove crankshaft pulley bolt and washer.
6. Remove crankshaft damper using damper removal tool No. 303-D121, or equivalent. **Ensure removal tool grabs inside of damper or damage will occur.**
7. Reverse procedure to install, noting the following:
   a. Ensure damper and crankshaft surfaces are clean.
   b. Apply silicone gasket and sealant part No. F7AZ-19554-EA, or equivalent, to end of keyway slot.
   c. Lubricate outside sealing surface of crankshaft pulley with clean 5W-30 motor oil.
   d. Install damper using damper installer tool No. T74P-6316-B, or equivalent.
   e. **Torque** crankshaft pulley bolt to 89 ft. lbs.
   f. Loosen pulley bolt 360°.
   g. **Torque** bolt to 37 ft. lbs.
   h. Tighten bolt an additional 90°.

FRONT COVER
REPLACE

1. Remove left and righthand valve covers as outlined under "Valve Cover, Replace."
2. Support engine with three bar engine support kit tool No. 303-F072, or equivalent.
3. Raise and support vehicle.
4. Remove splash shields.
5. Ensure engine is cold, then wrap suitable shop towel around pressure relief cap and remove cap. **Ensure coolant does not come into contact with accessory drive belt.**
6. Drain radiator coolant into suitable container.
7. **On models equipped with oil cooler,** disconnect coolant return hose at oil cooler.

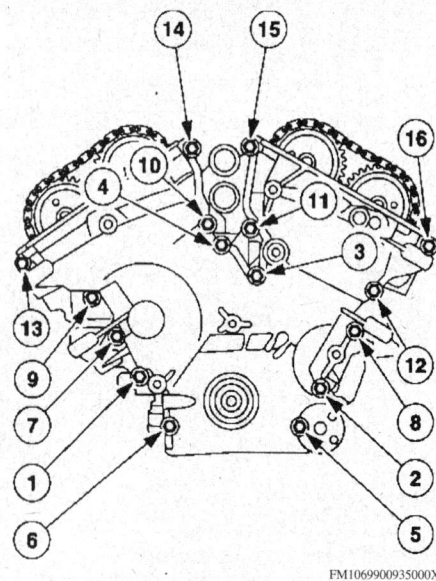

Fig. 23 Front cover tightening sequence

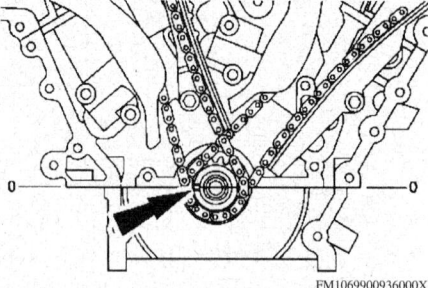

Fig. 24 Crankshaft keyway alignment

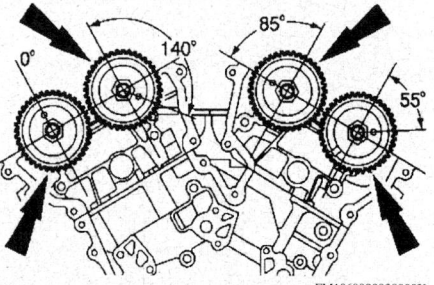

Fig. 26 Camshaft neutral positions

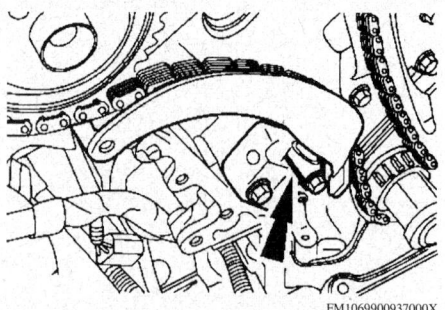

Fig. 25 Timing chain tensioner retention

8. **On all models,** disconnect upper water pump hose, then the upper and lower radiator hoses.
9. Disconnect and remove radiator hose.
10. Disconnect lower water pump hose.
11. Remove accessory drive belt.
12. Remove water pump as outlined under "Water Pump, Replace."
13. Remove oil pan as outlined under "Oil Pan, Replace."
14. Remove power steering pump as outlined under "Power Steering Pump, Replace" in "Front Suspension & Steering" section.
15. Remove lower cooling fan pump bolt, then disconnect hose.
16. Disconnect cooling fan pump electrical connector.
17. Remove high pressure line bracket.
18. Disconnect high pressure line.
19. Remove two upper mounting bolts and cooling fan pump.
20. Remove idler pulley and belt tensioner.
21. Remove secondary air valve, bracket and tube.
22. Remove crankshaft pulley bolt and washer.
23. Remove crankshaft damper using damper removal tool No. 303-D121, or equivalent. **Ensure removal tool grabs inside of damper or damage will occur.**
24. Remove crankshaft front oil seal using seal removal tool No. T92C-6700-CH, or equivalent.
25. Remove mounting bolts and front cover.
26. Reverse procedure to install, noting the following:
    a. Apply .24 inch diameter dot of silicone gasket and sealant part No. F7AZ-19554-EA, or equivalent, **Fig. 22.** Ensure front cover is installed within 6 minutes of sealer application.
    b. **Torque** front cover mounting bolts to 18 ft. lbs., in sequence, **Fig. 23.**
    c. Install front crankshaft seal using

seal installer tool No. T88T-6701-1, or equivalent.
d. Ensure all damper and crankshaft surfaces are clean.
e. Apply silicone gasket and sealant part No. F7AZ-19554-EA, or equivalent, to end of keyway slot.
f. Lubricate outside sealing surface of crankshaft pulley with clean 5W-30 motor oil.
g. Install damper using damper installer tool No. T74P-6316-B, or equivalent.
h. **Torque** crankshaft pulley bolt to 89 ft. lbs.
i. Loosen pulley bolt 360°.
j. **Torque** bolt to 37 ft. lbs.
k. Tighten bolt an additional 90°.

FRONT COVER SEAL

REPLACE

1. Remove accessory drive belt.
2. Remove secondary air valve, bracket and tube.
3. Raise and support vehicle.
4. Remove front center splash panel.
5. Remove crankshaft pulley bolt and washer.
6. Remove crankshaft damper using damper removal tool No. 303-D121, or equivalent. **Ensure removal tool grabs inside of damper or damage will occur.**
7. Remove front cover seal using seal remover tool No. T92C-6700-CH, or equivalent.
8. Reverse procedure to install, noting the following:
    a. Lubricate inside diameter of seal using clean 5W-30 motor oil.
    b. Install front cover seal using seal installer tool No. T88T-6701-A, or equivalent.

c. Ensure all damper and crankshaft surfaces are clean.
d. Apply silicone gasket and sealant part No. F7AZ-19554-EA, or equivalent, to end of keyway slot.
e. Lubricate outside sealing surface of crankshaft pulley with clean 5W-30 motor oil.
f. Install damper using damper installer tool No. T74P-6316-B, or equivalent.
g. **Torque** crankshaft pulley bolt to 89 ft. lbs.
h. Loosen pulley bolt 360°.
i. **Torque** bolt to 37 ft. lbs.
j. Tighten bolt an additional 90°.

TIMING CHAIN

REPLACE

Rotating the engine in a counter-clockwise direction will cause engine damage.

Removal

1. Remove front cover as outlined under "Front Cover, Replace."
2. Remove ignition pulse ring.
3. Install crankshaft damper bolt and washer.
4. Turn crankshaft clockwise until keyway is positioned in 9 o'clock position, **Fig. 24.**
5. If timing chain tensioner and chain are to be reused, place identification marks on them for installation alignment. **Do not interchange left and righthand timing components.**
6. Place suitable paper clip into righthand timing chain tensioner before removing bolts, **Fig. 25.**
7. Remove righthand timing chain tensioner and arm.
8. Remove righthand timing chain and chain guide.
9. Install suitable paper clip into lefthand timing chain tensioner.
10. Remove lefthand timing chain tensioner and arm, then the timing chain and guide.

Installation

Ensure crankshaft keyway remains in 9 o'clock position until cams are properly positioned or valve damage will occur.

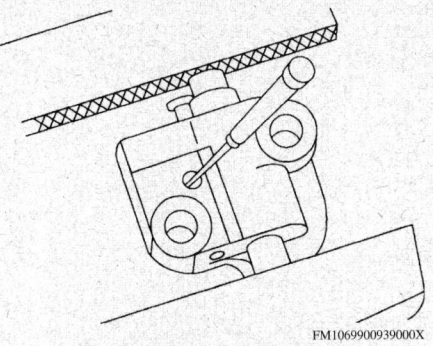

Fig. 27 Timing chain tensioner ratchet lock access hole

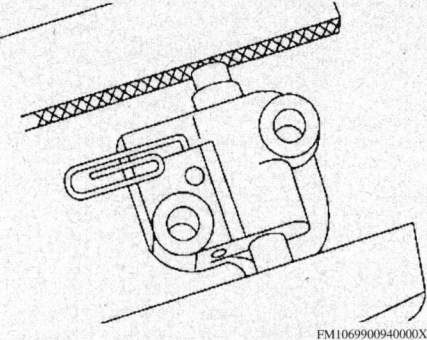

Fig. 28 Timing chain tensioner piston retention

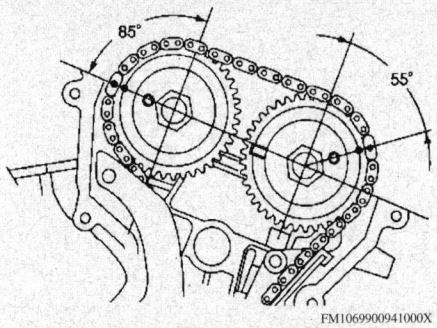

Fig. 29 Primary lefthand timing chain alignment mark inspection

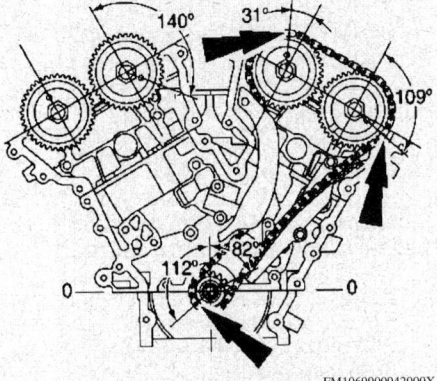

Fig. 30 Secondary lefthand timing chain alignment mark inspection

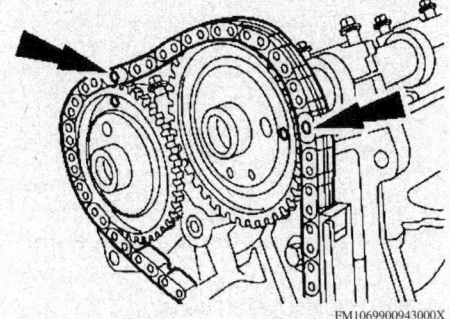

Fig. 31 Primary righthand timing chain alignment mark inspection

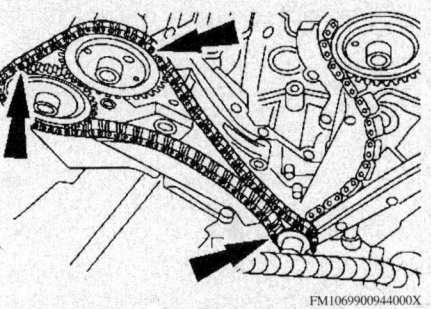

Fig. 32 Secondary righthand timing chain alignment mark inspection

1. Ensure crankshaft keyway is in 9 o'clock position, **Fig. 24.**
2. Turn left and righthand camshafts to locate them to neutral positions, **Fig. 26.**
3. Place lefthand chain tensioner into suitable soft-jawed vise.
4. Hold tensioner ratchet lock mechanism away from ratchet stem using suitable pick, **Fig. 27.**
5. **During tensioner compression, do not release ratchet stem until tensioner piston is fully bottomed in bore or stem will become damaged.** Slowly compress chain tensioner.
6. Retain lefthand tensioner piston using suitable paper clip, **Fig. 28.**
7. Turn crankshaft clockwise to 11 o'clock position.
8. Remove crankshaft damper bolt and washer.
9. Install lefthand timing chain guide and tighten. Ensure short bolt is installed into upper hole and long bolt into lower hole.
10. Install lefthand timing chain. Align gold timing chain index link with marks on camshaft and crankshaft sprockets, **Fig. 29.**
11. Install lefthand timing chain tensioner and tighten. Ensure tensioner piston is fully engaged in tensioner arm.
12. Remove paper clip from lefthand tensioner and install crankshaft damper bolt and washer.
13. Turn crankshaft clockwise until keyway is positioned between 2 and 3 o'clock position.

14. Ensure gold timing chain index links on lefthand timing chain are still aligned with timing index marks on crankshaft and camshaft sprockets, **Fig. 30.**
15. Place righthand chain tensioner into suitable soft-jawed vise.
16. Hold tensioner ratchet lock mechanism away from ratchet stem using suitable pick, **Fig. 27.**
17. **During tensioner compression, do not release ratchet stem until tensioner piston is fully bottomed in bore or stem will become damaged.** Slowly compress chain tensioner.
18. Retain righthand tensioner piston using suitable paper clip, **Fig. 28.**
19. Install righthand timing chain guide and tighten.
20. Install righthand timing chain. Align gold chain index marks with camshaft and crankshaft alignment marks, **Fig. 31.**
21. Install righthand timing chain tensioner and tighten.
22. Remove paper clip from righthand tensioner.
23. Ensure gold timing index links on righthand timing chain are still aligned with timing index marks on camshaft and crankshaft sprockets, **Fig. 32.**
24. Remove crankshaft damper bolt and washer.
25. Install ignition pulse ring.
26. Install front cover as outlined under "Front Cover, Replace."

CAMSHAFT
REPLACE

When removing camshafts, camshaft journal thrust caps must be removed prior to loosening other camshaft journal cap bolts.

When installing camshafts, camshaft bearing caps must be installed prior to installing thrust caps.

Camshaft journal caps and cylinder heads are numbered to ensure they are installed in original positions.

Removal

1. Remove upper intake manifold as outlined under "Intake Manifold, Replace."
2. Remove front cover as outlined under "Front Cover, Replace."
3. Remove timing chains as outlined under "Timing Chain, Replace."
4. Remove camshaft journal thrust caps, **Fig. 33.**
5. Remove remaining journal caps and camshafts.

Installation

1. Ensure bearing caps are installed to original positions.
2. Lubricate camshafts and bearing surfaces with clean 5W-30 motor oil.
3. Install camshaft bearing caps. **Do not tighten bolts now.**
4. Install camshaft thrust caps. **Do not tighten bolts now.**
5. **Torque** camshaft bearing caps to 89 inch lbs., in sequence, **Figs. 34 and 35.**
6. If new camshafts were installed, adjust valve lash as outlined under "Valve Adjustment."
7. **Ensure crankshaft keyway is in 9 o'clock position before rotating**

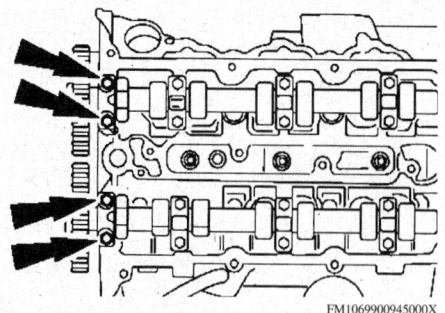

Fig. 33 Camshaft journal thrust cap location

camshafts or engine damage will result.

8. Turn camshafts to ensure they are not binding. If binding occurs, ensure bearing caps are in original positions. Loosen bearing caps in reverse order and tighten.
9. Install timing chains as outlined under "Timing Chain, Replace."
10. Install front cover as outlined under "Front Cover, Replace."
11. Install upper intake manifold as outlined under "Intake Manifold, Replace."

PISTON & ROD ASSEMBLY

When removing pistons and connecting rods, place reference marks on components involved for installation alignment.

When installing pistons, ensure arrow on piston is facing toward front of engine.

MAIN & ROD BEARINGS

Connecting Rod Bearings

Connecting rod bearing caps are cracked and split from connecting rods during the manufacturing process. When assembling components, ensure mating surfaces are clean and ensure identification marks on cap and rod are aligned.

Connecting rod bolts are of torque-to-yield design and must be replaced when removed.

1. **Torque** new bolts to 17 ft. lbs.
2. **Torque** bolts to 32 ft. lbs.
3. Final tighten bolts additional 90°.

Main Bearings

When cleaning gasket surfaces, do not use metal scrapers, wires brushes, power abrasive discs or other abrasive methods to clean sealing surfaces. Use only a plastic scraping tool to remove all traces of gasket material.

Lower cylinder block bolts and studs are of torque-to-yield design and must be replaced when removed.

To select and install main bearings, proceed as follows:

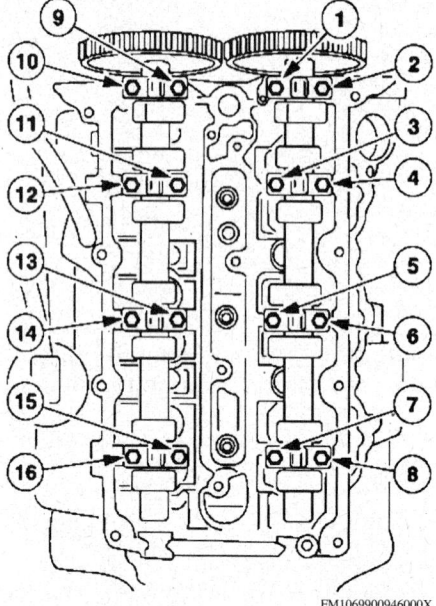

Fig. 34 Lefthand camshaft bearing cap tightening sequence

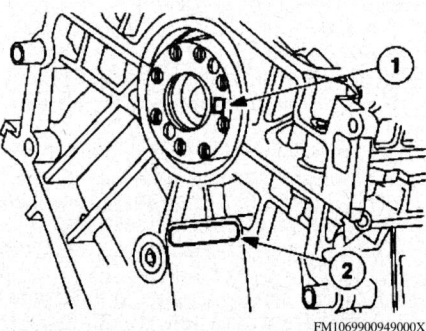

Fig. 36 Cylinder block and crankshaft bearing reference marks

1. Read crankshaft flange and engine block rear face codes, **Fig. 36.**
2. First two numbers after asterisk are code for main No. 1 and next two numbers for main No. 2.
3. First two numbers after second asterisk are code for main No. 3 and last two numbers for main No. 4.
4. Refer to **Fig. 37,** for bearing grade selection chart.
5. For example, if block code is *0609*0711* and crankshaft code is *8480*8082*, main No. 1 will use grade 1 bearings as determined by intersection of 06 block column and 84 crankshaft row, **Fig. 37.** Using these codes as, main Nos. 2, 3 and 4 will use grade 2.
6. Install upper main bearing and upper thrust bearing to cylinder block in proper locations.
7. Lubricate bearings using clean 5W-30 motor oil, then install crankshaft to cylinder block.
8. Install lower main bearings and lower thrust bearing into lower cylinder block in proper locations.
9. Ensure all gasket surfaces are clean

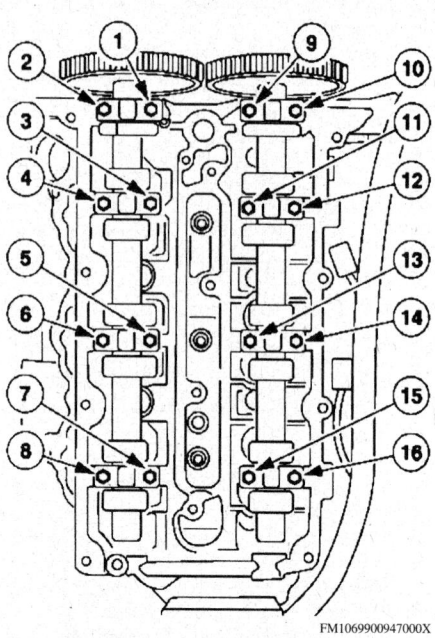

Fig. 35 Righthand camshaft bearing cap tightening sequence

using Ford Metal Surface Cleaner part No. F4AZ-19A536-RA, or equivalent. Allow to dry until there is no sign of wetness present.
10. Apply .12 inch bead of silicone gasket sealant part No. F7AZ-19554-EA, or equivalent, to lower cylinder block. End bead of gasket material .24 inch from rear crankshaft seal bore on both sides, **Fig. 38.** Bolts and studs must be tightened within four minutes of applying sealant.
11. Install lower cylinder block studs and bolts, **Fig. 39.**
12. Install new bolts and studs.
13. **Torque** bolts 1–8 to 18 ft. lbs., in sequence, **Fig. 40.**
14. **Torque** bolts 9–16 to 30 ft. lbs., in sequence.
15. Tighten bolts 1–16 an additional 90° in sequence.
16. **Torque** bolts 17–22 to 18 ft. lbs., in sequence.
17. Remove excess sealer from front cover and rear seal bore inner diameter areas.
18. Turn crankshaft in clockwise direction to ensure free rotation.

CRANKSHAFT REAR OIL SEAL
REPLACE

1. Remove transaxle as outlined in **MOTOR's** "Domestic Transmission Manual, In-Vehicle Service."
2. Remove flywheel.
3. Remove rear crankshaft seal using seal removal tool No. T95P-6701-EH and slide hammer tool No. 307-005, or equivalents.
4. Lubricate outer lips and inner seal of new crankshaft rear seal with clean 5W-30 motor oil.
5. Install rear oil seal using seal installer

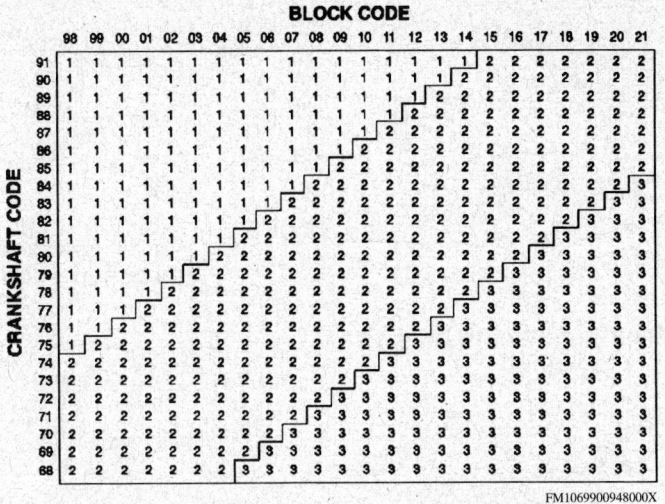

BLOCK CODE

Fig. 37 Bearing grade selection chart

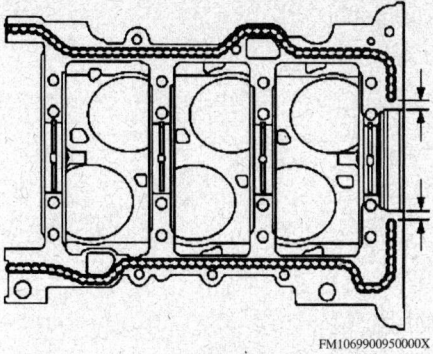

Fig. 38 Lower cylinder block sealant application

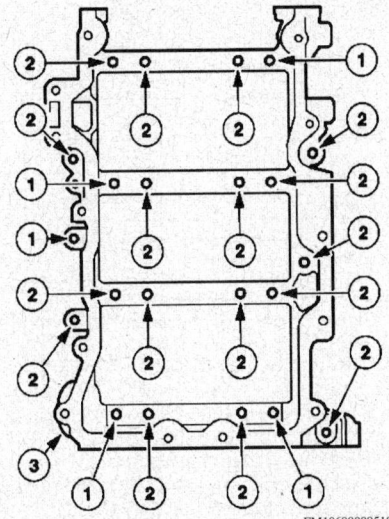

Fig. 39 Lower cylinder block bolt identification

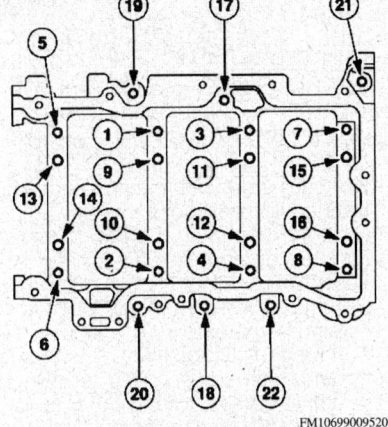

Fig. 40 Lower cylinder block tightening sequence

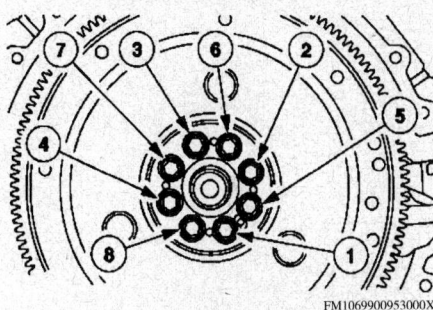

Fig. 41 Flywheel tightening sequence

tool No. T82L-6701-A and rear adapter bolts tool No. T91P-6701-A, or equivalents.

6. Install flywheel with elongated hole over crankshaft dowel.
7. **Torque** flywheel bolts to 59 ft. lbs., in sequence, **Fig. 41.**
8. **On models equipped with automatic transmissions,** install transmission as outlined in **MOTOR's "Domestic Transmission, In-Vehicle Service."**
9. **On models equipped with manual transmissions,** install transmission as outlined in **MOTOR's "Domestic Transmission, In-Vehicle Service."**

OIL PAN
REPLACE

1. Support engine using three bar engine support tool No. 303-F072, or equivalent.
2. Remove accessory drive belt.
3. Raise and support vehicle.
4. Drain engine oil into suitable container.
5. Remove lower splash shield.

6. Support alternator, then remove mounting bolts.
7. Disconnect alternator electrical connections and remove alternator.
8. Remove air conditioning compressor mounting bolts, then support compressor aside using suitable mechanics wire.
9. Remove electronic thermactor air bracket bolts.
10. Remove power steering line from oil pan stud.
11. Remove steering gear mounting nuts and support steering gear.
12. Remove left and righthand control arm through bolts, then the left and righthand motor mount nuts.
13. Remove left and righthand subframe bolts, **Figs. 42 and 43.**
14. Remove transmission cooler line bracket nut.
15. Remove transmission to oil pan bolts.
16. Remove oil pan mounting bolts.
17. Pry subframe downward and remove oil pan.
18. Reverse procedure to install, noting the following:
   a. Install new gasket to oil pan.
   b. Apply .4 inch dot of silicone gasket sealant part No. F7AZ-19554-EA,

or equivalent, to oil pan, **Fig. 44.**
   c. Oil pan must be installed and bolts tightened within six minutes of sealant application.
   d. **Torque** oil pan mounting bolts to 18 ft. lbs., in sequence, **Fig. 45.**
   e. Ensure vehicle suspension alignment is within specifications. Refer to "Specifications" section.

OIL PUMP
REPLACE

1. Remove timing chains as outlined under "Timing Chain, Replace."
2. Remove oil pan as outlined under "Oil Pan, Replace."
3. Remove oil pump screen tube.
4. Remove mounting bolts and oil pump, **Fig. 46.**
5. Reverse procedure to install.

OIL COOLER
REPLACE

1. Ensure engine is cold.
2. Wrap suitable shop towel around pressure relief cap, then remove cap. **Ensure coolant does not come into contact with accessory drive belt.**
3. Drain radiator coolant into suitable container.
4. Disconnect coolant hoses at oil cooler.
5. Remove mounting bolt and oil cooler.
6. Reverse procedure to install, noting the following:
   a. Position oil cooler and gasket.
   b. Install mounting bolt, then turn cooler clockwise until locating pin hits stop.

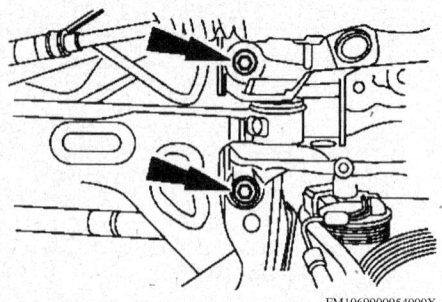

Fig. 42 Lefthand subframe bolt location

FM1069900954000X

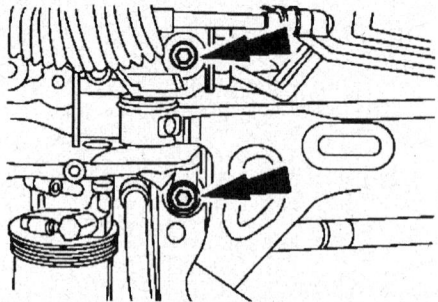

Fig. 43 Righthand subframe bolt location

FM1069900955000X

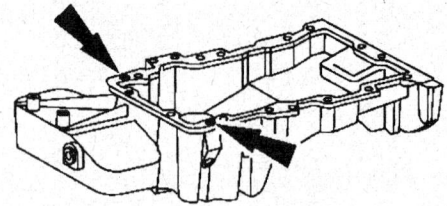

FM1069900956000X

Fig. 44 Oil pan sealant application points

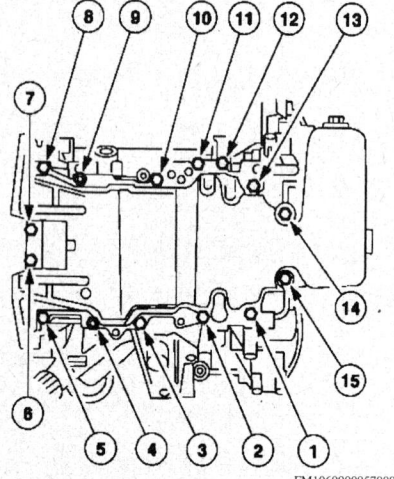

FM1069900957000X

Fig. 45 Oil pan tightening sequence

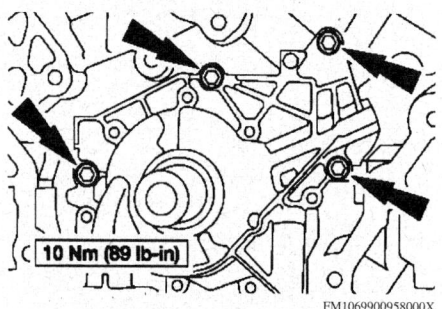

10 Nm (89 lb-in)

FM1069900958000X

Fig. 46 Oil pump replacement

9. Reopen heater air bleed to release any trapped air, then close.
10. Operate engine at 1500 RPM for 3–5 minutes or until hot air comes from heater.
11. Return to idle and ensure hot air is still coming from heater.
12. Turn engine off and allow to cool. After engine has cooled, add coolant to overflow bottle to bring level to MAX cold fill mark.

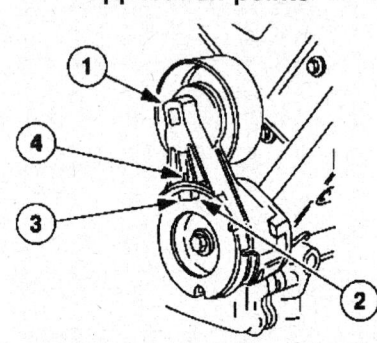

Item	Description
1	Belt tension relief point
2	Unacceptable belt wear range
3	Acceptable belt installation and wear range
4	Belt length indicator

FM1069900959000X

Fig. 47 Belt tensioner inspection

SERPENTINE DRIVE BELT

Tension

Vehicle is equipped with an automatic belt tensioner and tension is not adjustable. Refer to **Fig. 47,** to inspect tensioner.

Routing

Refer to **Fig. 48,** for serpentine drive belt routing.

COOLING SYSTEM BLEED

1. Open engine air bleed fitting, **Fig. 49.**
2. Open heater air bleed fitting, **Fig. 50.**
3. Add coolant to overflow bottle. Allow system to equalize until no more coolant can be added.
4. Close engine air bleed when coolant begins to escape.
5. Install cap to overflow bottle.
6. Start and run engine at idle speed with heater air bleed open. Turn heater to MAX position.
7. Close heater air bleed when steady stream of coolant starts to flow.
8. Allow engine to idle for 5 minutes, then add coolant to overflow bottle until it reaches MAX mark.

THERMOSTAT
REPLACE

1. Ensure engine is cold.
2. Wrap suitable shop towel around pressure relief cap, then remove cap. **Ensure coolant does not come into contact with accessory drive belt.**
3. Drain radiator coolant into suitable container.
4. Disconnect coolant hoses at oil cooler.
5. Remove air cleaner outlet tube.
6. Disconnect hoses from thermostat housing, **Fig. 51.**
7. Remove housing, thermostat and seal.
8. Reverse procedure to install.

WATER PUMP
REPLACE

1. Ensure engine is cold.
2. Wrap suitable shop towel around pressure relief cap, then remove cap. **Ensure coolant does not come into contact with accessory drive belt.**
3. Drain radiator coolant into suitable container.
4. Disconnect coolant hoses at oil cooler.
5. Remove air cleaner outlet tube.
6. Disconnect engine vent hose, **Fig. 49.**
7. Disconnect upper and lower radiator hoses, then the heater supply and water pump hoses.
8. Remove water crossover.
9. Disconnect water inlet hose from coolant outlet tube.
10. Disconnect and remove water inlet hose from pump.
11. Remove serpentine drive belt.
12. Remove water pump mounting bolts, studs and water pump. Record location of water pump studs for installation alignment.
13. Reverse procedure to install.

RADIATOR
REPLACE

1. Ensure engine is cold.
2. Wrap suitable shop towel around pressure relief cap, then remove cap. **Ensure coolant does not come into contact with accessory drive belt.**
3. Drain radiator coolant into suitable container.
4. Disconnect coolant hoses at oil cooler.
5. Remove upper radiator sight shield.
6. Remove air cleaner outlet tube.
7. Remove radiator support brackets and upper radiator hose.
8. Remove receiver drier mounting bolt and position receiver drier aside.
9. Disconnect high pressure cooling fan line and return hose.
10. Separate return hose from fan shroud and position aside.

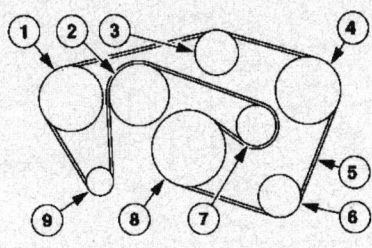

Item	Description
1	Hydraulic fan pump pulley
2	Water pump pulley
3	Belt idler pulley
4	Power steering pump pulley
5	Drive belt
6	A/C clutch pulley
7	Drive belt tensioner
8	Crankshaft vibration damper
9	Generator pulley

FM1069900960000X

Fig. 48   Serpentine drive belt routing

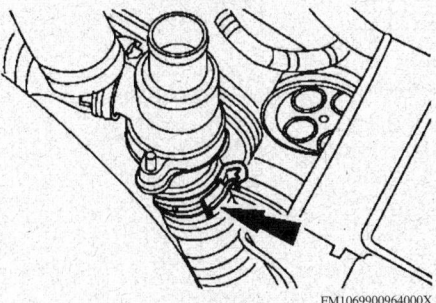

FM1069900964000X

Fig. 51   Thermostat housing location

11. Remove fan shroud.
12. Support air conditioning condenser using suitable mechanics wire.
13. Raise and support vehicle.
14. Remove left and righthand splash shields, then the radiator air deflector.
15. Disconnect lower radiator hose.
16. Remove condenser to radiator mounting bolts.
17. Remove condenser support brackets and radiator through bottom of vehicle.
18. Reverse procedure to install.

HYDRAULIC FAN MOTOR
REPLACE

Refer to "Radiator, Replace" for hydraulic fan motor replacement procedure.

HYDRAULIC COOLING FAN PUMP
REPLACE

1. Remove accessory drive belt.
2. Remove lower cooling fan pump bolt.
3. Disconnect hose and allow to drain into suitable container, **Fig. 52.**

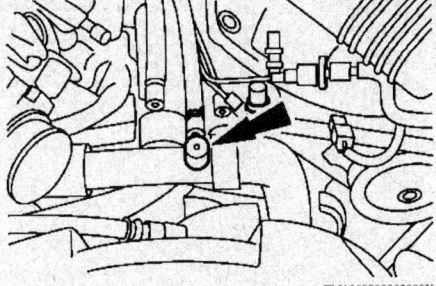

FM1069900962000X

Fig. 49   Engine air bleed location

4. Disconnect cooling fan pump electrical connector.
5. Remove high pressure line bracket.
6. Disconnect high pressure line.
7. Remove two upper mounting bolts and cooling fan pump.
8. Reverse procedure to install.

FUEL PUMP
REPLACE

The fuel system contains two pumps. One is the "fuel delivery module" which provides fuel pressure to the engine. The second pump is a jet pump or transfer pump which maintains fuel levels in both sides of the fuel tank.

The jet pump is located on the lefthand side of the fuel tank and contains a fuel level sensor and a check valve which maintains system pressure after the pump is shut off.

The fuel delivery module is located on the righthand side of the fuel tank and contains a fuel level sensor and an inlet screen on the bottom of the pump.

To disconnect fuel lines from pumps, press down on fuel line connector while pressing release tabs. Pull straight up to remove.

Whenever fuel pumps are removed, new fuel pump gaskets must be installed.

Fuel Delivery Module

1. Relieve fuel pressure as outlined under "Precautions."
2. Release rear seat mini-buckle.
3. Depress two seat cushion latches, then remove rear seat cushion and insulation.
4. Remove fuel pump access covers. Ensure fuel pump connectors are fully seated.
5. Remove black connector elbow on transfer pump, **Fig. 53.**
6. Attach fuel line draining connector to suitable fuel storage tanker hose and outlet fitting on transfer pump.
7. Siphon fuel until tank side is empty.
8. Attach fuel draining connector to fuel delivery module and repeat previous three steps, **Fig. 54.**
9. Disconnect remaining fuel line from fuel delivery module.
10. Disconnect fuel delivery module electrical connector.
11. Loosen fuel pump lockring using fuel sender wrench tool No. 310-069, or equivalent.

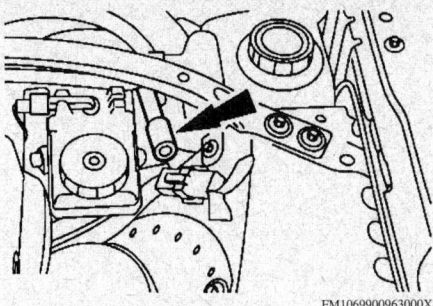

FM1069900963000X

Fig. 50   Heater air bleed location

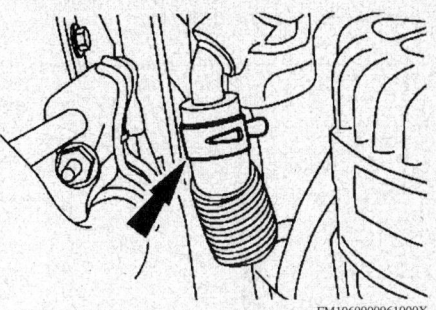

FM1069900961000X

Fig. 52   Hose location

12. Remove fuel delivery module lockring.
13. Position pump flange clear of pump opening, then press lock tabs and release pump from tank mounting flange.
14. Lift pump straight up and out of retainer cup, then tilt while in tank to drain fuel from reservoir.
15. Straighten and lift straight up and out of tank. Drain excess fuel into suitable container.
16. Reverse procedure to install.

Jet (Transfer) Pump

1. Relieve fuel pressure as outlined under "Precautions."
2. Drain fuel tank as outlined under "Fuel Delivery Module."
3. Ensure fuel line connectors are fully seated prior to pressing release tabs.
4. Disconnect fuel lines from transfer pump.
5. Disconnect electrical connector from transfer pump.
6. Loosen transfer pump lockring using fuel sender wrench tool No. 310-069, or equivalent.
7. Remove lockring and transfer pump.
8. Reverse procedure to install.

FUEL FILTER
REPLACE

1. Relieve fuel pressure as outlined under "Precautions."
2. Raise and support vehicle.
3. Remove lefthand front tire and wheel assembly.
4. Remove splash shield fasteners.
5. Disconnect fuel line R-clip fittings, **Fig. 55.**
6. Remove mounting bolt and filter.
7. Reverse procedure to install.

Fig. 53 Transfer pump fuel line connections

FM1069900965000X

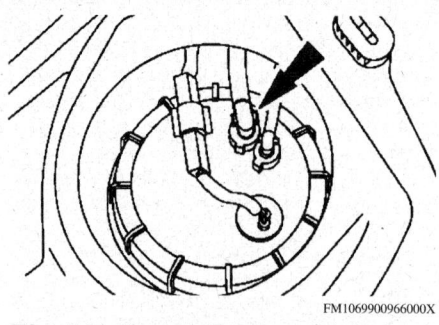

Fig. 54 Fuel delivery module fuel line connections

FM1069900966000X

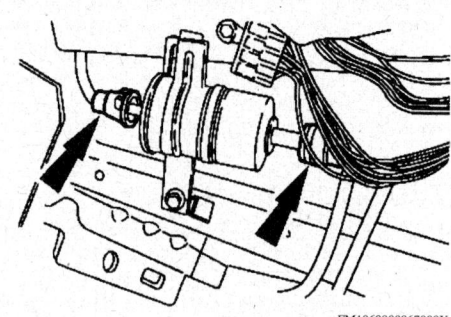

Fig. 55 Fuel filter

FM1069900967000X

TIGHTENING SPECIFICATIONS

Year	Component	Torque, Ft. Lbs.
2001–05	Air Conditioning Compressor	18
	Alternator	35
	Belt Tensioner	35
	Camshaft Bearing Caps	⑨
	CKP Sensor	89①
	CMP Sensor	89①
	Connecting Rod	②
	Coolant Inlet Tube	18
	Coolant Outlet Tube	18
	Crankshaft Damper	③
	Cylinder Head	④
	Dipstick Tube	89①
	EGR Tube To EGR Valve	30
	Engine Appearance Cover Bracket	53
	Engine Mount	46
	Exhaust Manifold Heat Shield	89①
	Exhaust Manifold To Cylinder Head	⑥
	Exhaust Pipe To Exhaust Manifold	30
	Flywheel	⑩
	Front Brake Caliper	76
	Front Cover	⑦
	Front & Center Crossmember, Bolts	76
	Front Intake Manifold Support, Nut	89①
	Hydraulic Cooling Fan Pump	18
	Hydraulic Cooling Fan Reservoir	108①
	Idler Pulley	18
	Lower Control Arm, Through Bolt	129
	Lower Cylinder Block	②
	Lower Intake Manifold To Cylinder Head	⑤
	Lower Stabilizer Link	41
	Lower Strut Mount Bolts	129
	Main Bearing Cap	②
	Oil Cooler	42
	Oil Pan	⑧
	Oil Pan To Transmission	35
	Oil Pump	89①
	Oil Pump Screen	89①
	Power Steering Pump	18
	Power Steering Reservoir	108①
	Radiator Support Brackets	89①

Continued

TIGHTENING
SPECIFICATIONS—Continued

Year	Component	Torque, Ft. Lbs.
2001–05	Starter Motor	18
	Steering Gear	76
	Steering Shaft Clamp Bolt	18
	Subframe	77
	Thermostat Housing	96①
	Timing Chain Guide	18
	Timing Chain Tensioner	18
	Torque Converter	23–28
	Transmission Crossmember	41
	Transmission Cooler Lines	15
	Transmission To Engine	35
	Transmission To Oil Pan	35
	Upper Ball Joint	66
	Upper Intake Manifold Support Bracket, Bolt	89①
	Upper Intake Manifold Support Bracket, Nut	53①
	Upper Intake Manifold To Lower Intake Manifold	⑤
	Valve Cover	⑦
	Water Pump	18
	Wheel Lug Nuts	100

① — Inch lbs.
② — Refer to "Main & Rod Bearings" for tightening specifications & sequence.
③ — Refer to "Crankshaft Damper, Replace" for tightening specifications & sequence.
④ — Refer to "Cylinder Head, Replace" for tightening specifications & sequence.
⑤ — Refer to "Intake Manifold, Replace" for tightening specifications & sequence.
⑥ — Refer to "Exhaust Manifold, Replace" for tightening specifications & sequence.
⑦ — Refer to "Valve Cover, Replace" for tightening specifications & sequence.
⑧ — Refer to "Oil Pan, Replace" for tightening specifications & sequence.
⑨ — Refer to "Camshaft, Replace" for tightening specifications & sequence.
⑩ — Refer to "Crankshaft Rear Oil Seal, Replace" for tightening specifications & sequence.

3.9L Engine

NOTE: On Air Bag Equipped Models, Refer To "Air Bag System Precautions" Located In The Front Of This Manual For System Disarming & Arming Procedures.

NOTE: Refer To "Computer Relearn Procedures" Located In The Front Of This Manual When Battery Power To The Computer Has Been Interrupted.

INDEX

PRECAUTIONS

Air Bag Systems

Refer to "Air Bag System Precautions" in the front of this manual for system disarming and arming procedures.

Battery Ground Cable

Prior to service, disconnect battery ground cable and isolate as required.

Fuel System Pressure Relief

1. Remove Schrader valve cap and install fuel pressure gauge tool No. T80L-9974-B, or equivalent, to Schrader valve.
2. Slowly open manual valve on pressure gauge and drain fuel into suitable container.

QUICK DISCONNECT HOSES

R-Clip

When working with R-clip type connections, do not use tools to disconnect, **Fig. 1.** Use of tools may deform clip components and could cause leaks.

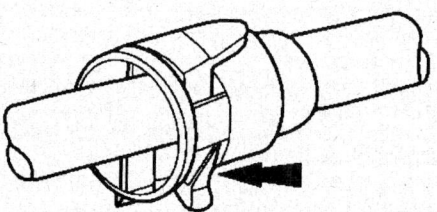

FM1069900970000X
Fig. 1 R-clip connection

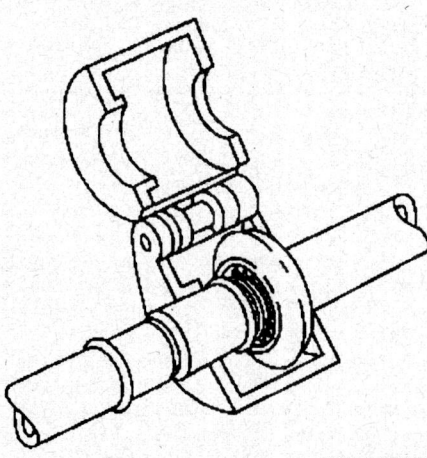

FM1069900971000X
Fig. 2 Spring lock connection

To disconnect, bend shipping tab downward, **Fig. 1.** Spread R-clip and push clip into fitting. Separate fitting from tube.

To install, first inspect fitting and tube for damage and ensure connections are clean. Apply a light coat of clean 5W-30 motor oil to male end of tube. Insert R-clip into fitting. Align tube and fitting, then insert tube into fitting and push together until a click is heard. Pull on connection to ensure it is fully engaged.

Spring Lock

When working with spring lock type connections, spring lock tool set No. T84L-19623-B, or equivalent, must be used to disconnect fittings, **Fig. 2.** When connecting spring lock type fittings, inspect and clean both coupling ends. Lubricate fuel line O-ring seals with clean 5W-30 motor oil. When connection is made, pull on line to ensure it is fully engaged.

Vapor Tube

To disconnect vapor tube connections, squeeze fitting and disconnect vapor tube from fitting, **Fig. 3.** To connect, ensure fittings are clean and free from damage. Push tube onto fitting until it snaps into place. Pull on connection to ensure fitting is secure.

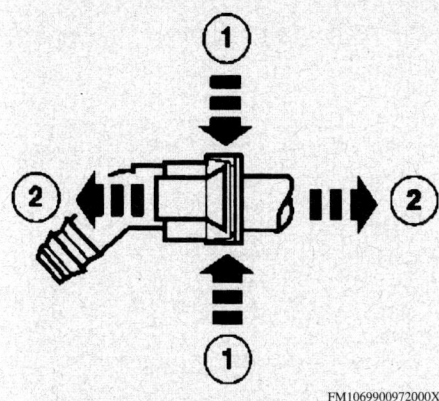

Fig. 3 Vapor tube connection

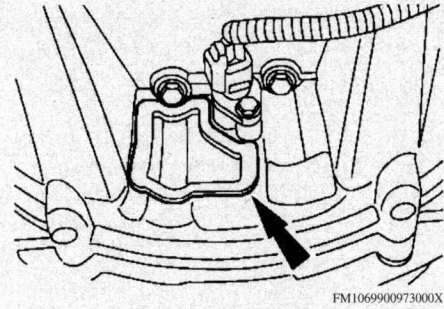

Fig. 4 Flywheel inspection cover

Fig. 5 Front & center support bolt location

COMPRESSION PRESSURE

Before performing compression test, ensure crankcase oil is of correct viscosity and at correct level. Ensure battery is fully charged and engine is at normal operating temperature.

1. Turn ignition switch to OFF position.
2. Remove spark plugs.
3. Set throttle plates to wide open position.
4. Install suitable compression gauge in cylinder No. 1.
5. Install auxiliary starter switch in starting circuit.
6. With ignition switch in OFF position, use auxiliary starter switch to crank engine at least five compression strokes.
7. Count number of compression strokes required to reach highest reading and record highest reading.
8. Repeat test on each cylinder, cranking engine same number of compression strokes.
9. Indicated compression pressures are considered within specifications if lowest reading cylinder is within 75 percent of highest reading.

ENGINE MOUNT
REPLACE

1. Support engine using engine lifting eye kit tool No. D81L-6001-D and three bar engine support kit tool No. D88L-6000-A, or equivalents.
2. Raise and support vehicle.
3. Remove upper and lower engine mount nuts.
4. Remove engine mount and bracket.
5. Reverse procedure to install.

ENGINE
REPLACE

When carrying out operations which involve the removal and installation of the driveshaft, always inspect the joint angles and adjust as outlined under "Driveline Angle Measurement" in "Rear Axle & Suspension" section.

1. Remove air cleaner and outlet tube.
2. Remove engine appearance cover.
3. Ensure engine is cold.
4. Wrap suitable shop towel around pressure relief cap, then remove cap.
5. **Ensure coolant does not come into contact with accessory drive belt.**
6. Open radiator draincock and drain coolant into suitable container.
7. **On models equipped with oil cooler,** disconnect coolant return hose at oil cooler.
8. **On all models,** remove upper radiator sight shield.
9. Remove upper radiator support brackets.
10. Recover refrigerant as outlined in "Air Conditioning" chapter.
11. Disconnect air conditioning pressure switch.
12. Release power steering line from frame rail.
13. Remove power steering reservoir and position aside.
14. Disconnect fuel lines.
15. Disconnect evaporative canister purge hose and main vacuum supply hose.
16. Remove cowl panels.
17. Remove cowl panel support bracket.
18. Disconnect throttle and speed control cables, then the engine ground strap.
19. Remove cabin air filter and plenum as outlined under "Heater Core, Replace" in "Electrical" section.
20. Disconnect powertrain bulkhead connectors located on rear side of righthand strut tower and position aside.
21. Remove cowl to engine insulation panel.
22. Disconnect remaining bulkhead connectors.
23. Place reference marks on heater hoses for installation alignment.
24. Disconnect four heater hoses at water control valve.
25. Remove hydraulic cooling fan reservoir and position aside.
26. Disconnect water valve electrical connector from radiator support and position harness aside.
27. Raise and support vehicle.
28. Remove front wheels.
29. Remove front anti-lock brake sensors.
30. Remove front calipers as outlined in "Disc Brakes" chapter and position aside.
31. Remove two sway bar link lower bolts.
32. Hold ball joint external hex, then remove upper ball joint nuts.
33. Separate upper ball joints from spindles.
34. Remove lower strut mount bolts.
35. Remove left, righthand and center splash shields.
36. Remove mounting nut, then disconnect air conditioning high pressure line.
37. Disconnect low pressure air conditioning quick disconnect coupler.
38. Remove exhaust system.
39. Remove driveshaft as outlined under "Propeller Shaft, Replace" in "Rear Axle & Suspension" section.
40. Disconnect shift cable and shift cable bracket bolt.
41. Disconnect hydraulic cooling fan lines from righthand frame rail.
42. Disconnect power steering lines from lefthand frame rail.
43. Disconnect steering gear electrical connectors.
44. Disconnect steering coupling.
45. Disconnect starter motor and alternator electrical connectors.
46. Remove flywheel inspection cover, **Fig. 4.**
47. Place reference marks on torque converter stud, nut and adapter plate for installation alignment.
48. Remove eight torque converter nuts from flywheel spacer.
49. **On models equipped with engine block heater,** disconnect engine block heater plug at grille opening.
50. **On all models,** support rear of vehicle using suitable safety stands.
51. Support engine transmission, front suspension, front and center crossmemebers and cooling system using suitable powertrain lift and transmission support bracket. Disconnect transmission support system.
52. Remove four front and four center support bolts, **Fig. 5.**
53. Lower powertrain assembly.
54. Disconnect engine block heater.
55. Disconnect air conditioning manifold hose from compressor.
56. Disconnect power steering pump and hydraulic cooling fan return hoses. Drain fluid into suitable container.
57. Remove lower radiator hose bolts.
58. Disconnect radiator and heater hoses.
59. Remove transmission cooler line bracket nut.
60. Disconnect transmission cooler and power steering pressure lines.
61. Remove power steering line bracket.
62. Install engine lifting eye kit tool No. D81L-6001-D, or equivalent, to engine.
63. Remove six lower transmission bolts.

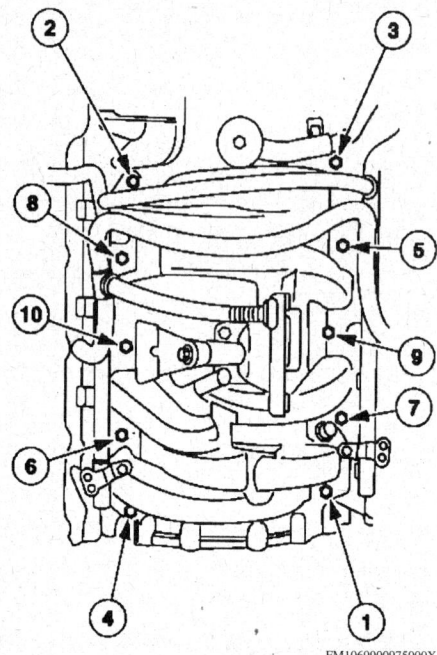

Fig. 6   Intake manifold loosening & tightening sequence

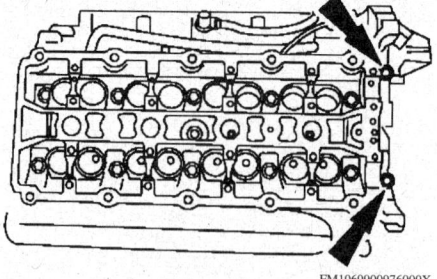

Fig. 7   Front cylinder head bolt location

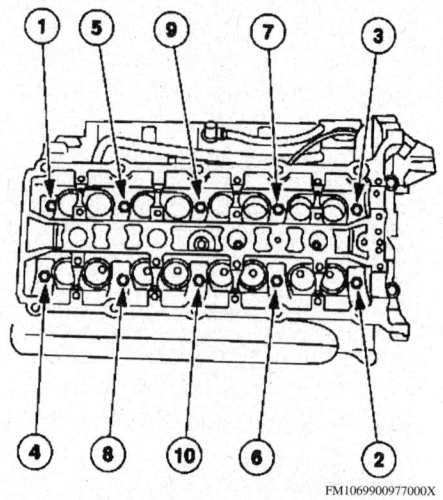

Fig. 8   Righthand cylinder head loosening sequence

64. Install spreader bar tool No. D93P-6001-A3, or equivalent, to engine lifting eyes.
65. Attach suitable engine crane to spreader bar and support engine and transmission.
66. Remove engine mount upper nuts.
67. Remove engine and transmission from subframe and place on floor.
68. Remove wiring harness mounting nuts and remaining transmission to engine mounting bolts.
69. Separate engine from transmission, then mount engine to suitable stand.
70. Reverse procedure to install.

INTAKE MANIFOLD
REPLACE

When cleaning cylinder head surfaces, do not use metal scrapers, wires brushes, power abrasive discs or other abrasive methods to clean sealing surfaces. Use only a plastic scraping tool to remove all traces of gasket material.

1. Remove air cleaner outlet tube.
2. Ensure engine is cold.
3. Wrap suitable shop towel around pressure relief cap, then remove cap. **Ensure coolant does not come into contact with accessory drive belt.**
4. Drain radiator coolant into suitable container.
5. Disconnect coolant return hose at oil cooler.
6. Remove wiper motor and arm as outlined under "Wiper Motor, Replace" in "Electrical" section.
7. Remove engine compartment brace.
8. Disconnect accelerator and speed control cables.
9. Disconnect main vacuum hose and vacuum harness.

10. Disconnect EGR vacuum line and EGR valve to exhaust manifold tube.
11. Disconnect camshaft position sensor and evaporative emission canister purge valve line.
12. Remove fuel pressure sensor connector.
13. Disconnect inline vacuum connector to fuel pressure sensor.
14. Relieve fuel pressure as outlined under "Precautions."
15. Disconnect fuel line, then the knock sensor and cylinder head temperature sensor connectors from bracket.
16. Raise wiring harness, then disconnect lefthand fuel injector connectors.
17. Disconnect idle air control, TP sensor and crankcase ventilation tube.
18. Disconnect coolant hoses from throttle body.
19. Raise wiring harness and disconnect righthand fuel injectors.
20. Remove manifold mounting bolts in sequence, **Fig. 6.**
21. Reverse procedure to install. **Torque** intake manifold bolts to 15 ft. lbs., in sequence, **Fig. 6.**

EXHAUST MANIFOLD
REPLACE
Lefthand

1. Remove dipstick tube.
2. Raise and support vehicle.
3. Remove exhaust catalyst pipe.
4. Remove eight mounting bolts and exhaust manifold.
5. Reverse procedure to install.

Righthand

1. Raise and support vehicle.
2. Disconnect exhaust catalyst from manifold.
3. Disconnect starter motor electrical connectors.
4. Disconnect EGR tube from exhaust manifold.
5. Remove eight mounting bolts and exhaust manifold.
6. Reverse procedure to install.

CYLINDER HEAD
REPLACE

When cleaning cylinder head surfaces, do not use metal scrapers, wires brushes, power abrasive discs or other abrasive methods to clean sealing surfaces. Use only a plastic scraping tool to remove all traces of gasket material.

Cylinder head bolts should be replaced when removed.

Marking shims with permanent marker. Scratches or paint on shim will cause incorrect lash adjustment and severe engine damage.

1. Remove intake manifold as outlined under "Intake Manifold, Replace."
2. Remove engine sound insulator.
3. Remove camshafts as outlined under "Camshaft, Replace."
4. Place reference marks on bucket and shim tappets for installation alignment, then remove.
5. Remove water crossover tube.
6. Disconnect cylinder head temperature and camshaft position sensors.
7. Raise and support vehicle.
8. Disconnect exhaust system from exhaust manifolds.
9. Disconnect EGR tube from exhaust manifold, then lower vehicle.
10. Remove left and righthand front cylinder head bolts, **Fig. 7.**
11. Remove righthand cylinder head bolts in sequence, **Fig. 8.**
12. Remove righthand cylinder head and gasket.
13. Remove lefthand cylinder head bolts in sequence, **Fig. 9.** If bolt 2 cannot be fully removed, hold bolt above decking surface using suitable rubber band when removing cylinder head.
14. Remove lefthand cylinder head and gasket.
15. Reverse procedure to install, noting the following:
    a. Hand tighten cylinder head bolts.
    b. **Torque** cylinder head bolts to 15 ft. lbs., in sequence, **Figs. 10 and 11.**
    c. **Torque** head bolts to 26 ft. lbs., in sequence.
    d. **Torque** bolts to 33 ft. lbs., in sequence.
    e. Tighten an additional 90° in sequence
    f. Tighten an additional 90° in sequence.

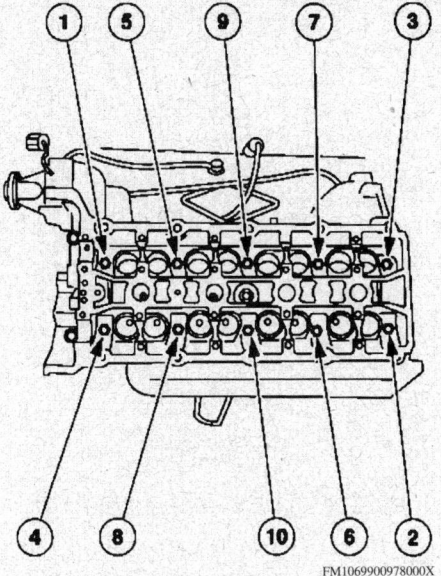

Fig. 9   Lefthand cylinder head loosening sequence

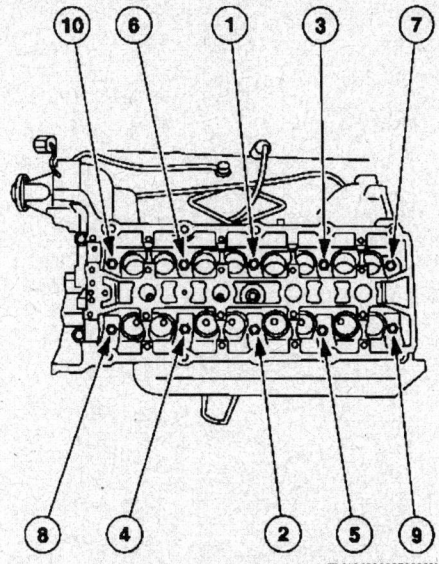

Fig. 10   Lefthand cylinder head tightening sequence

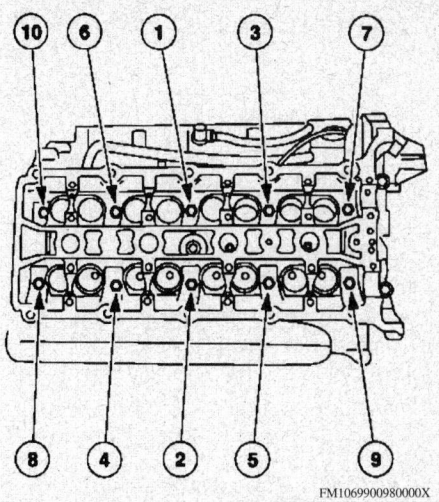

Fig. 11   Righthand cylinder head tightening sequence

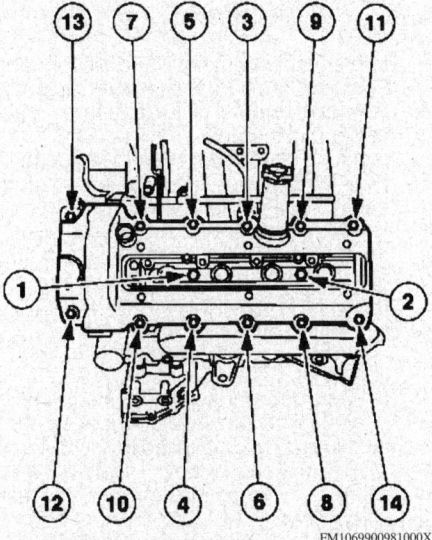

Fig. 12   Lefthand valve cover loosening & tightening sequence

g. **Torque** front cylinder head bolts to 15 ft. lbs., then tighten an additional 90°.

VALVE COVER

REPLACE

Lefthand

1. Remove engine appearance cover.
2. Remove air cleaner housing.
3. Disconnect crankcase ventilation tube.
4. Relieve fuel system pressure as outlined under "Precautions."
5. Disconnect fuel line.
6. Disconnect evaporative emission canister purge valve hose, then the air assist tube.
7. Remove vapor management valve appearance cover and disconnect hose.

8. Position evaporative emission canister purge valve, engine vacuum regulator and bracket aside.
9. Position engine wiring harness upward, then remove ignition coil cover and ignition coils.
10. Disconnect three front and one rear wiring harness retainers.
11. Remove fuel line bracket bolt.
12. Remove reservoir mounting bolts and position aside.
13. Remove oil dipstick tube.
14. Remove brake line bracket, then the lefthand valve cover mounting bolts in sequence, **Fig. 12**.
15. Reverse procedure to install, noting the following:
    a. Apply .12 inch bead of silicone gasket and sealant part No. F7AZ-19554-EA, or equivalent, to cover joints, **Fig. 13**.
    b. **Torque** mounting bolts to 89 inch lbs., in sequence, **Fig. 12**.

Righthand

1. Remove air cleaner outlet tube.
2. Remove hydraulic cooling fan reservoir and position aside.
3. Disconnect crankcase ventilation hose.
4. Disconnect wiring harness brackets and position aside.
5. Remove ignition coil cover, then disconnect ignition coils.
6. Raise engine wiring harness and disconnect fuel injectors.
7. Disconnect three front and one rear wiring harness retainer, then remove ignition coils.
8. Remove righthand valve cover mounting bolts in sequence, then the valve cover, **Fig. 14**.
9. Reverse procedure to install, noting the following:
    a. Apply silicone gasket and sealant part No. F7AZ-19554-EA, or equivalent, to cover joints, **Fig. 13**.

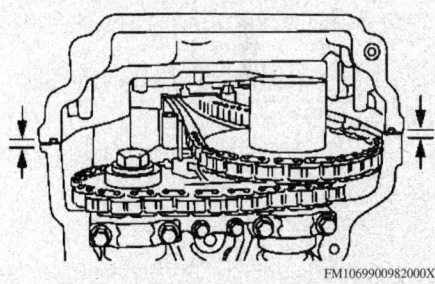

Fig. 13   Valve cover sealant application points

b. **Torque** valve cover mounting bolts to 89 inch lbs., in sequence, **Fig. 14**.

VALVE ARRANGEMENT
Inner...I-I-I-I-I-I-I-I-I
Outer............................E-E-E-E-E-E-E-E

VALVE ADJUSTMENT

1. Remove valve covers as outlined under "Valve Cover, Replace."
2. Remove spark plugs.
3. When measuring valve clearance, ensure camshaft is on base circle, **Fig. 15**.
4. Measure and record valve clearances using suitable feeler gauge. Refer to "Specifications" section for valve clearance.
5. If adjustment is required, remove camshafts as outlined under "Camshaft, Replace."
6. Remove shims from bucket tappet. Shims are marked for thickness (for example, 222 equals 2.22 mm shim).
7. Select shims by adding base shim thickness to measured clearance, then subtract desirable clearance (intake, .006 inch; exhaust, .012 inch).
8. Reverse procedure to install. Ensure new valve clearance is within specifications.

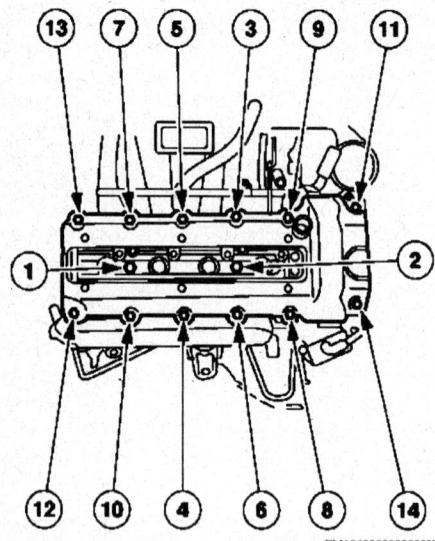

Fig. 14 Righthand valve cover loosening & tightening sequence

FM1069900983000X

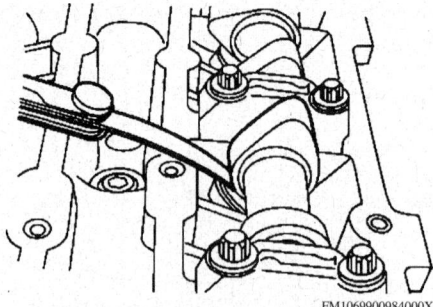

Fig. 15 Valve clearance measurement

FM1069900984000X

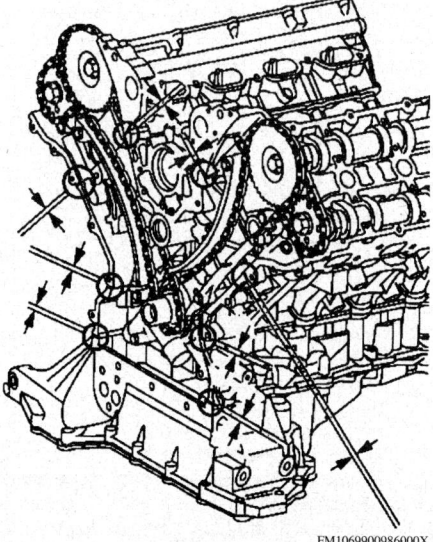

Fig. 17 Front cover sealant application points

FM1069900986000X

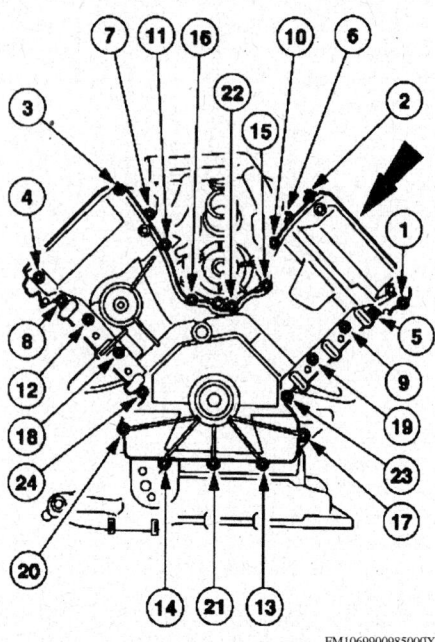

Fig. 16 Front cover removal sequence

FM1069900985000X

CRANKSHAFT DAMPER

REPLACE

1. Remove hydraulic cooling fan as outlined under "Radiator, Replace."
2. Remove accessory drive belt.
3. Remove crankshaft pulley mounting bolt.
4. Remove crankshaft damper using damper remover tool No. T58P-6316-D, or equivalent.
5. Reverse procedure to install, noting the following:
   a. Apply silicone gasket and sealant part No. F7AZ-19554-EA, or equivalent, to damper keyway.
   b. Install damper using damper installation tool No. T74P-6316-B, or equivalent.
   c. **Torque** crankshaft damper bolt to 59 ft. lbs.
   d. Loosen damper bolt two full turns.
   e. **Torque** bolt to 37 ft. lbs.
   f. Tighten an additional 90°.

FRONT COVER

REPLACE

1. Ensure engine is cold.
2. Wrap suitable shop towel around pressure relief cap, then remove cap. **Ensure coolant does not come into contact with accessory drive belt.**
3. Drain radiator coolant into suitable container.
4. **On models equipped with oil cooler,** disconnect coolant return hose at oil cooler.
5. **On all models,** remove valve covers as outlined under "Valve Cover, Replace."
6. Remove cooling fan as outlined under "Radiator, Replace."
7. Loosen water pump bolts.
8. Remove accessory drive belts.
9. Remove water pump pulley, then cover alternator.
10. Remove lower radiator hose bolts.

11. Disconnect upper radiator hose from water crossover.
12. Disconnect heater hose.
13. Remove idler pulleys.
14. Remove crankshaft pulley mounting bolt.
15. Remove crankshaft damper using damper remover tool No. T58P-6316-D, or equivalent.
16. Recover refrigerant as outlined in "Air Conditioning." chapter.
17. Raise and support vehicle.
18. Remove splash shields.
19. Remove power steering hose bracket and position aside.
20. Remove air conditioning compressor manifold from compressor.
21. Disconnect compressor electrical connector.
22. Remove mounting bolts and air conditioning compressor.
23. Drain power steering reservoir into suitable container, then disconnect reservoir hose.
24. Remove power steering pump and position aside.
25. Remove power steering pump bracket.
26. Remove alternator as outlined under "Alternator, Replace" in "Electrical" section.
27. Drain hydraulic cooling fan reservoir

into suitable container and disconnect hydraulic fan pump reservoir hose.
28. Remove hydraulic cooling fan pump and pump bracket.
29. Remove front cover bolts in sequence, **Fig. 16.** Clean gasket surfaces using suitable plastic scraper.
30. Reverse procedure to install, noting the following:
   a. Inspect front cover gaskets.
   b. Apply .12 inch wide bead of silicone gasket and sealant part No. F7AZ-19554-EA, or equivalent, to eight points, **Fig. 17.**
   c. **Torque** front cover mounting bolts to 44 inch lbs., in sequence **Fig. 18.**
   d. **Torque** mounting bolts to 89 inch lbs., in sequence
   e. Apply silicone gasket and sealant part No. F7AZ-19554-EA, or equivalent, to damper keyway.
   f. Install damper using damper installation tool No. T74P-6316-B, or equivalent.
   g. **Torque** crankshaft damper bolt to 59 ft. lbs.
   h. Loosen damper bolt two full turns.
   i. **Torque** bolt to 37 ft. lbs.
   j. Tighten an additional 90°.

FRONT COVER SEAL

REPLACE

1. Remove hydraulic cooling fan as outlined under "Radiator, Replace."
2. Remove accessory drive belt.
3. Remove crankshaft pulley mounting bolt.
4. Remove crankshaft damper using damper remover tool No. T58P-6316-D, or equivalent.
5. Remove front seal using seal removal tool No. 303-409, or equivalent.
6. Reverse procedure to install, noting the following:

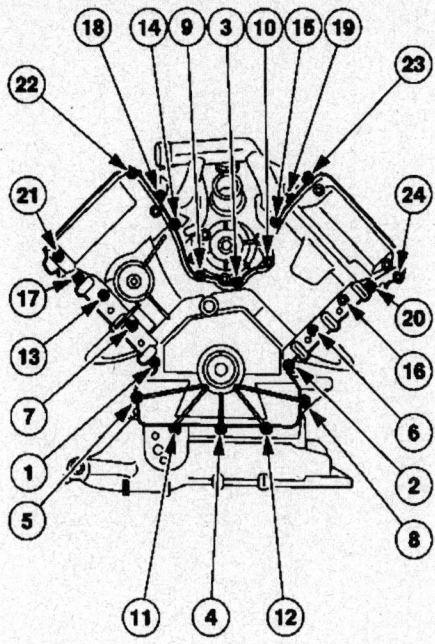

Fig. 18   Front cover tightening sequence

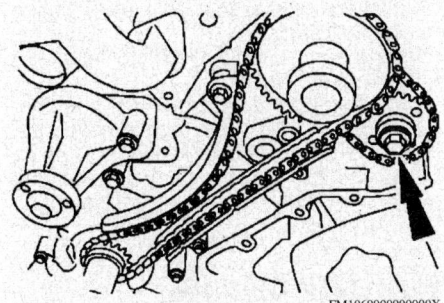

Fig. 21   Lefthand outer camshaft bolt

a. Install new seal using seal installer tool No. 303-646, or equivalent.
b. Apply silicone gasket and sealant part No. F7AZ-19554-EA, or equivalent, to damper keyway.
c. Install damper using damper installation tool No. T74P-6316-B, or equivalent.
d. **Torque** crankshaft damper bolt to 59 ft. lbs.
e. Loosen damper bolt two full turns.
f. **Torque** bolt to 37 ft. lbs.
g. Tighten an additional 90°.

TIMING CHAIN
REPLACE
Primary
REMOVAL

There are no timing alignment marks for this engine. The proper alignment is achieved using suitable crankshaft locking tool and camshaft positioning/locking tools.
1. Remove front cover as outlined under "Front Cover, Replace."
2. Raise and support vehicle.

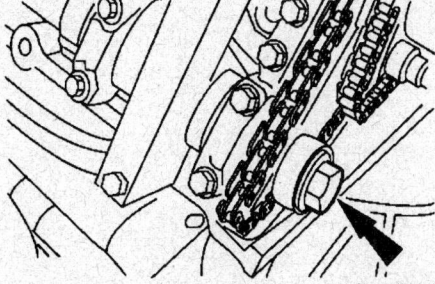

Fig. 19   Righthand outer camshaft bolt

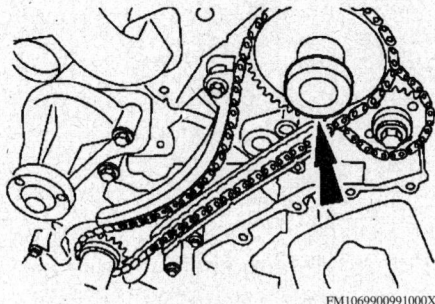

Fig. 22   Lefthand camshaft damper bolt

3. Remove crankshaft position sensor and torque converter access cover.
4. Turn crankshaft to 45° ATDC and ensure crankshaft keyway is at 6 o'clock position.
5. Install crankshaft positioning tool No. 303-645, or equivalent, to ignition pulse wheel.
6. Lower vehicle, then install camshaft locking tool No. 303-530, or equivalent, to righthand cylinder head.
7. Loosen outer camshaft bolt, **Fig. 19**.
8. Loosen camshaft damper bolt and slide camshaft sprockets forward on bolts, **Fig. 20**.
9. Remove righthand timing chain tensioner and blanking plate.
10. Remove tensioner arm and timing chain guide.
11. Remove righthand primary timing chain and crankshaft sprocket as an assembly.
12. Remove camshaft locking tool from righthand cylinder head.
13. Install camshaft locking tool to lefthand cylinder head.
14. Loosen outer camshaft bolt, **Fig. 21**.
15. Loosen lefthand camshaft damper bolt and slide camshaft sprockets forward on bolts, **Fig. 22**.
16. Remove lefthand timing chain tensioner and blanking plate, then the tensioner arm.
17. Remove lefthand timing chain guide.
18. Remove lefthand timing chain and crankshaft gear as an assembly.

INSTALLATION

There are no timing alignment marks for this engine. The proper alignment is achieved using suitable crankshaft locking tool and camshaft positioning/locking tools.
1. Insert suitable wire into timing chain

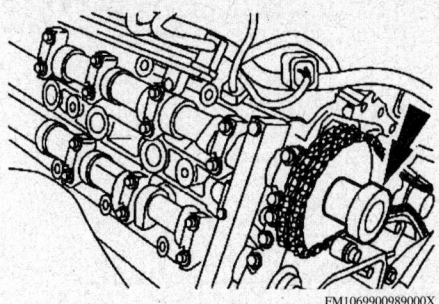

Fig. 20   Righthand camshaft damper bolt

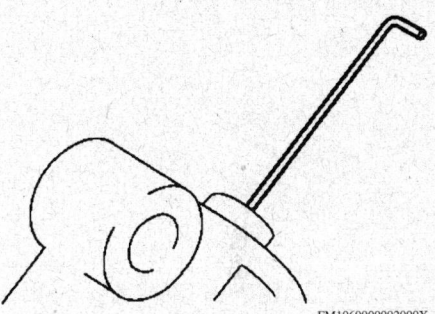

Fig. 23   Timing chain tensioner reset

tensioner and dislodge check ball, **Fig. 23**.
2. Compress tensioner using hand pressure and remove wire.
3. If timing mark on lefthand timing chain crankshaft gear is facing toward rear of engine, install righthand timing chain crankshaft gear with mark facing forward. If timing mark on lefthand timing chain crankshaft gear is facing toward front of engine, install righthand timing chain crankshaft gear with mark facing toward rear of engine.
4. Ensure camshaft holding tool is installed on lefthand cylinder head.
5. Position timing chain over lefthand intake camshaft sprocket.
6. Position crankshaft gear into timing chain.
7. Position timing chain and crankshaft gear over crankshaft as an assembly.
8. Install lefthand timing chain guide and tensioner arm.
9. Position lefthand blanking plate, **Fig. 24. If blanking plate is not positioned properly, oil galley will not seal resulting in low oil pressure and engine damage.**
10. Install lefthand timing chain tensioner and blanking plate.
11. Install suitable tie strap to take up timing chain slack, **Fig. 25**.
12. Apply tension to lefthand exhaust camshaft sprocket using timing chain tensioning tool No. 303-532, or equivalent.
13. **Torque** camshaft sprocket bolts to 15 ft. lbs., then tighten an additional 90°.
14. Install camshaft holding tool to righthand cylinder head. It may be required to adjust camshafts to install holding tool.
15. If timing mark on lefthand timing chain

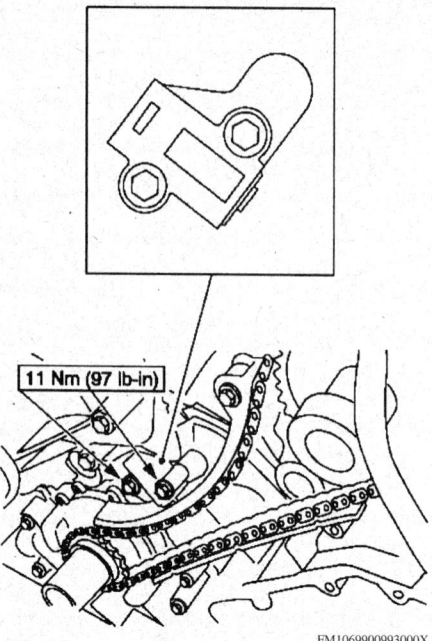

Fig. 24 Lefthand blanking plate installation

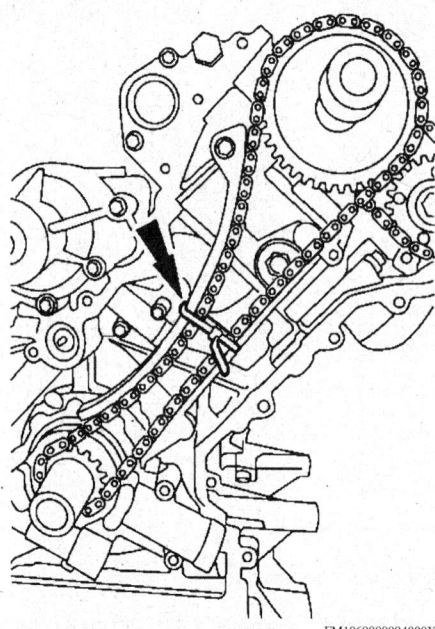

Fig. 25 Timing chain installation

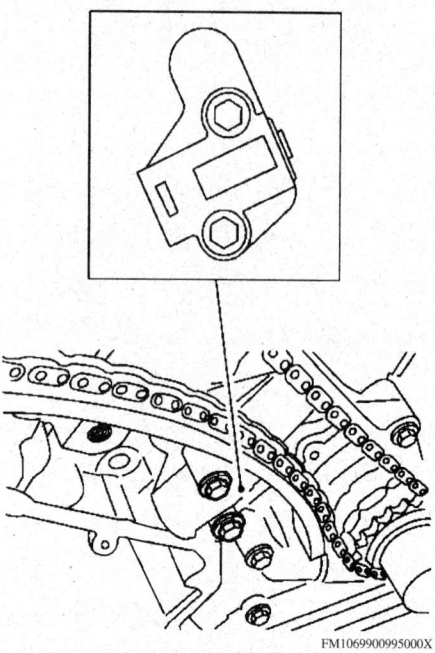

Fig. 26 Righthand blanking plate installation

crankshaft gear is facing toward rear of engine, install righthand timing chain crankshaft gear with mark facing forward. If timing mark on lefthand timing chain crankshaft gear is facing toward front of engine, install righthand timing chain crankshaft gear with mark facing toward rear of engine.

16. Position timing chain over righthand intake camshaft sprocket.
17. Place crankshaft gear into timing chain.
18. Install timing chain and crankshaft gear over crankshaft as an assembly.
19. Install righthand chain guide and tensioner arm.
20. Position righthand blanking plate, **Fig. 26. If blanking plate is not positioned properly, oil galley will not seal resulting in low oil pressure and engine damage.**
21. Install righthand timing chain tensioner and blanking plate.
22. Install suitable tie strap to take up timing chain slack, **Fig. 25.**
23. Exhaust camshaft sprocket bolt must be fully tightened before tightening intake camshaft sprocket bolt.
24. Apply tension to righthand exhaust camshaft sprocket using timing chain tensioning tool No. 303-532, or equivalent.
25. **Torque** sprocket bolts to 15 ft. lbs., then tighten an additional 90°.
26. Remove camshaft locking tool and tie straps.
27. Raise and support vehicle.
28. Remove crankshaft locking tool.
29. Install crankshaft position sensor and torque converter cover.
30. Lower vehicle.
31. Install front cover as outlined under "Front Cover, Replace."

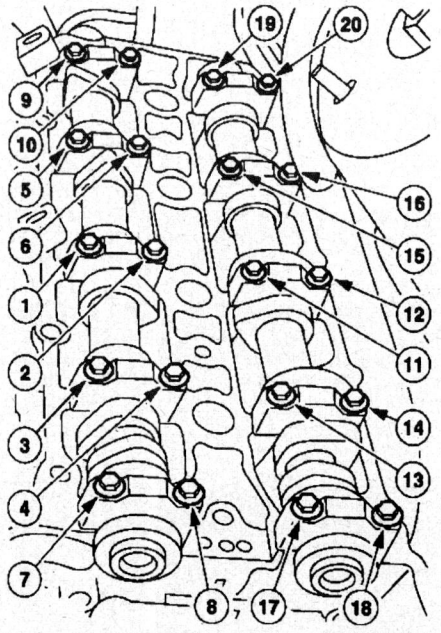

Fig. 27 Lefthand cylinder head camshaft tightening sequence

Secondary

There are no timing alignment marks for this engine. The proper alignment is achieved using suitable crankshaft locking tool and camshaft positioning/locking tools.

1. Remove primary timing chains as outlined under "Primary."
2. Remove exhaust camshaft sprocket and intake camshaft sprocket bolts.
3. Remove sprockets, damper and chain as an assembly.
4. Remove secondary timing chain tensioner.

5. Reverse procedure to install, noting the following:
   a. Insert suitable wire into tensioner check valve.
   b. Apply hand pressure until tensioner is fully collapsed, then remove wire.
   c. When installing secondary timing chains, ensure camshaft holding tool No. 303-530, or equivalent, is in place.

TIMING CHAIN TENSIONER
REPLACE

Refer to "Timing Chain, Replace" for timing chain tensioner replacement procedure.

CAMSHAFT
REPLACE
Removal

1. Remove primary and secondary timing chains as outlined under "Timing Chain, Replace."
2. Remove camshaft locking tool.
3. Place reference marks on camshaft bearing caps and record locations for installation alignment.
4. Remove left and righthand camshaft bearing caps, then the camshafts.
5. Place reference marks on shims and bucket tappets, then record for installation alignment. **Mark shims and bucket tapperts with permanent marker. Scratches or paint on shims will result in incorrect lash adjustments and engine damage.**

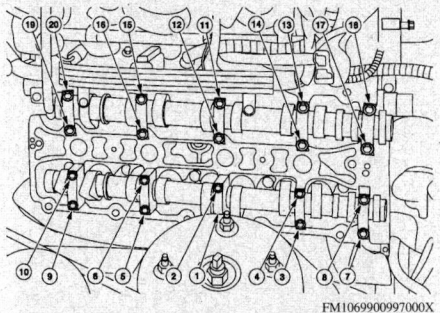

Fig. 28 Righthand cylinder head camshaft tightening sequence

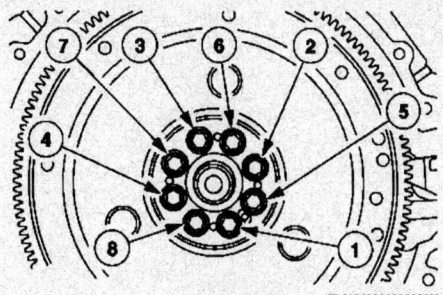

Fig. 29 Flywheel tightening sequence

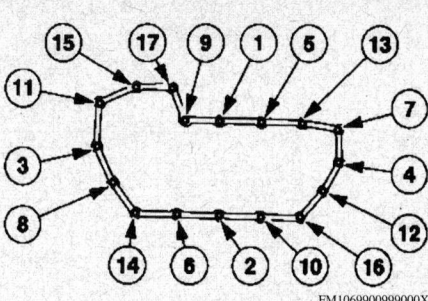

Fig. 30 Oil pan tightening sequence

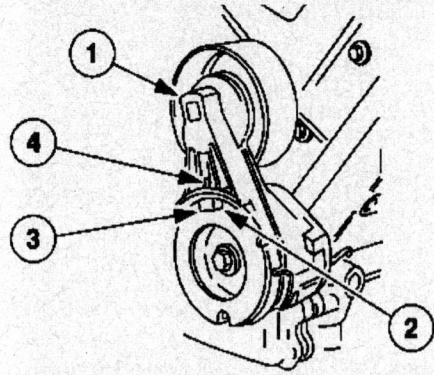

Item	Description
1	Belt tension relief point
2	Unacceptable belt wear range
3	Acceptable belt installation and wear range
4	Belt length indicator

Fig. 31 Belt tensioner inspection

Installation

1. Apply clean 5W-30 motor oil to camshaft journals, camshaft caps and camshaft lobes.
2. Install left and righthand cylinder head camshafts.
3. Hand tighten mounting bolts in sequence, **Figs. 27 and 28.**
4. **Torque** bolts to 53 inch lbs.
5. Final tighten bolts an additional 90°.
6. If any valve train components were replaced, perform valve lash adjustment as outlined under "Valve Adjustment."
7. Install camshaft locking tool No. 303-530, or equivalent, to lefthand cylinder head.
8. Install primary and secondary timing chains as outlined under "Timing Chain, Replace."

CRANKSHAFT REAR OIL SEAL

REPLACE

1. Raise and support vehicle.
2. Remove transaxle as outlined in **MO-**

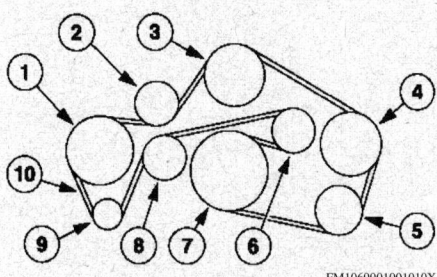

Fig. 32 Serpentine drive belt routing (Part 1 of 2)

TOR's "Domestic Transmission Manual, In-Vehicle Service."
3. Remove flywheel.
4. Remove rear crankshaft oil seal using screw tool No. T95T-5310-AR2 and seal remover/installer tool No. 303-647, or equivalents.
5. Reverse procedure to install, noting the following:
   a. Lubricate outer lips and inner seal of new oil seal before installation.
   b. Install new seal using seal remover/installer tool No. 303-647, or equivalent.
   c. **Torque** flywheel mounting bolts to 11 ft. lbs., in sequence, **Fig. 29.**
   d. **Torque** mounting bolts to 81 ft. lbs., in sequence.

OIL PAN

REPLACE

1. Raise and support vehicle.
2. Drain engine oil into suitable container.
3. Remove mounting bolts and oil pan.
4. Reverse procedure to install, noting the following:
   a. Inspect oil pan gasket.
   b. **Torque** mounting bolts to 44 inch lbs., in sequence, **Fig. 30.**
   c. **Torque** mounting bolts to 108 inch lbs., in sequence.

OIL PUMP

REPLACE

1. Remove primary timing chains as outlined under "Timing Chain, Replace."
2. Remove mounting bolts and oil pump.
3. Reverse procedure to install.

OIL COOLER

REPLACE

1. Ensure engine is cold.

Item	Description
1	Hydraulic fan pump pulley
2	Belt idler pulley—unflanged
3	Water pump pulley
4	Power steering pump pulley
5	A/C clutch pulley
6	Drive belt tensioner
7	Crankshaft vibration damper
8	Belt idler pulley—flanged
9	Generator pulley
10	Drive belt

Fig. 32 Serpentine drive belt routing (Part 2 of 2)

2. Wrap suitable shop towel around pressure relief cap, then remove cap. **Ensure coolant does not come into contact with accessory drive belt.**
3. Drain radiator coolant into suitable container.
4. Disconnect coolant return hose at oil cooler.
5. Remove center air deflector and oil filter.
6. Disconnect oil cooler coolant hoses.
7. Remove mounting bolts and oil cooler.
8. Reverse procedure to install.

SERPENTINE DRIVE BELT

Tension Data

Vehicle is equipped with an automatic belt tensioner. Belt tension is not adjustable. Refer to **Fig. 31,** to inspect tensioner.

Routing

Refer to **Fig. 32,** for serpentine drive belt routing.

COOLING SYSTEM BLEED

1. Remove engine fill cap, **Fig. 33.**

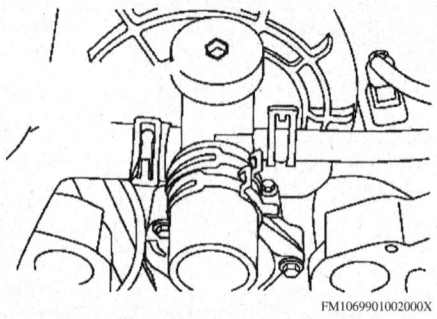

Fig. 33 Engine fill cap location

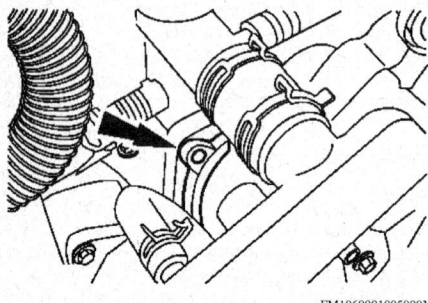

Fig. 36 Thermostat housing cover replacement

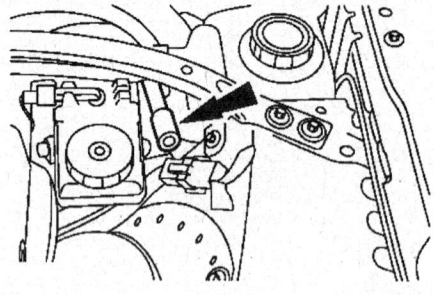

Fig. 34 Heater air bleed location

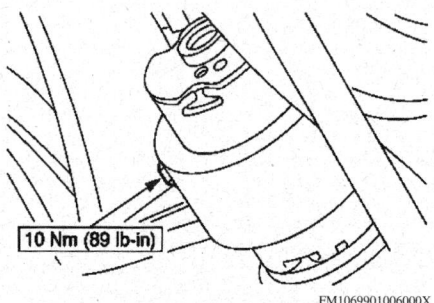

Fig. 37 Electric water pump location

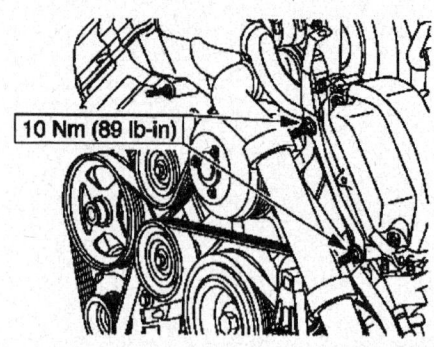

Fig. 35 Coolant tube replacement

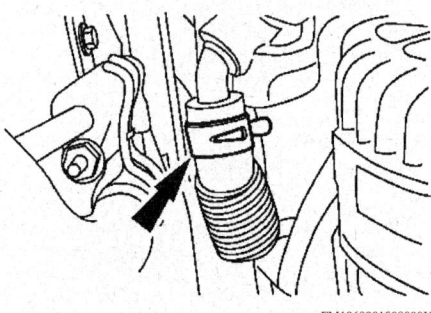

Fig. 38 Fan pump hose location

2. Open heater air bleed, **Fig. 34.**
3. Add coolant to overflow bottle allowing system to equalize until no more coolant can be added.
4. Install overflow bottle cap.
5. Add as much coolant as possible to engine fill cap opening. Ensure coolant does not come in contact with accessory drive belt.
6. Install engine fill cap.
7. Start engine and turn heater to Max position.
8. Close heater bleed when steady stream of coolant is present.
9. Allow engine to idle for five minutes adding coolant to overflow bottle to maintain cold fill Max mark.
10. Open heater air bleed to release any trapped air and close again.
11. Operate engine at 2000 RPM for 3–5 minutes or until hot air comes from heater.
12. Return engine to idle and ensure hot air is still coming from heater.
13. Turn engine off and allow to cool.
14. Add coolant to overflow bottle to bring level to cold fill Max level.

THERMOSTAT
REPLACE

1. Ensure engine is cold.
2. Wrap suitable shop towel around pressure relief cap, then remove cap. **Ensure coolant does not come into contact with accessory drive belt.**
3. Drain radiator coolant into suitable container.
4. **On models equipped with oil cooler,** disconnect coolant return hose at oil cooler.
5. **On all models,** remove air cleaner outlet tube.

6. Remove coolant tube from front of engine, **Fig. 35.**
7. Remove coolant tube bracket studs.
8. Disconnect lower radiator hose from thermostat housing.
9. Remove housing cover and thermostat, **Fig. 36.**
10. Reverse procedure to install.

WATER PUMP
REPLACE

1. Ensure engine is cold.
2. Wrap suitable shop towel around pressure relief cap, then remove cap. **Ensure coolant does not come into contact with accessory drive belt.**
3. Drain radiator coolant into suitable container.
4. **On models equipped with oil cooler,** disconnect coolant return hose at oil cooler.
5. **On all models,** loosen water pump pulley bolts.
6. Remove accessory drive belt.
7. Remove mounting bolts and water pump pulley.
8. Remove mounting bolts and water pump. Inspect water pump O-ring seal.
9. Reverse procedure to install, noting the following:
   a. Lubricate water pump O-ring using premium engine coolant part No. E2FZ-19549-AA, or equivalent.
   b. Bleed cooling system as outlined under "Cooling System Bleed."

RADIATOR
REPLACE

1. Ensure engine is cold.
2. Wrap suitable shop towel around pressure relief cap, then remove cap. **En-**

sure coolant does not come into contact with accessory drive belt.
3. Drain radiator coolant into suitable container.
4. **On models equipped with oil cooler,** disconnect coolant hoses at oil cooler.
5. **On all models,** remove upper radiator sight shield.
6. Remove air cleaner outlet tube.
7. Remove radiator support brackets and upper radiator hose.
8. Remove receiver drier mounting bolt and position receiver drier aside.
9. Remove electric water pump bolt and position aside, **Fig. 37.**
10. Disconnect high pressure cooling fan line and return hose.
11. Separate return hose from fan shroud and position aside.
12. Remove fan shroud.
13. Support air conditioning condenser using suitable mechanics wire.
14. Raise and support vehicle.
15. Remove left and righthand splash shields, then the radiator air deflector.
16. Disconnect lower radiator hose.
17. Remove condenser to radiator mounting bolts.
18. Remove condenser support brackets and radiator through bottom of vehicle.
19. Reverse procedure to install.

HYDRAULIC FAN MOTOR
REPLACE

Refer to "Radiator, Replace" for hydraulic fan motor replacement procedure.

HYDRAULIC COOLING FAN PUMP
REPLACE

1. Remove engine appearance cover.
2. Disconnect IAT sensor, breather hose and idle air control valve inlet tube.
3. Remove air intake tube support nut and washer.
4. Loosen tube clamps and remove tube.
5. Remove accessory drive belt.
6. Raise and support vehicle, then remove mounting bolts.
7. Turn alternator and remove positive cable from alternator.
8. Lower alternator and disconnect elec-
trical connector.
9. Turn alternator and remove.
10. Disconnect hose and drain fluid into suitable container, **Fig. 38.**
11. Disconnect fan pump electrical connector.
12. Remove high pressure line bracket and disconnect high pressure line.
13. Remove pump mounting bolts and cooling fan.
14. Reverse procedure to install.

FUEL PUMP
REPLACE

Refer to "Fuel Pump, Replace" in the
"3.0L Engine" section for fuel pump replacement procedures.

FUEL FILTER
REPLACE

1. Relieve fuel pressure as outlined under "Precautions."
2. Raise and support vehicle.
3. Remove lefthand front tire and wheel assembly.
4. Remove splash shield fasteners.
5. Disconnect fuel line R-clip fittings.
6. Remove mounting bolt and filter.
7. Reverse procedure to install.

TIGHTENING SPECIFICATIONS

Year	Component	Torque, Ft. Lbs.
2001–05	Air Conditioning Compressor	18
	Air Conditioning Manifold To Compressor	15
	Alternator	⑤
	Belt Tensioner	37
	Camshaft Bearing Caps	⑩
	Camshaft Sprockets	15⑦
	Condenser To Radiator	89①
	Cowl Panel Support Bracket	80①
	Crankshaft Damper	③
	Crankshaft Position Sensor	89①
	Cylinder Head	②
	EGR Tube To EGR Valve	30
	EGR Tube To Exhaust Manifold	30
	Electric Water Pump	89①
	Engine Mount Bracket To Cylinder Block	34
	Engine Mount	30
	Exhaust Catalyst To Exhaust Manifold	30
	Exhaust Manifold To Cylinder Head	18
	Flywheel	⑧
	Front Cover	④
	Front & Center Support Bolts	76
	Hydraulic Cooling Fan Pump	18
	Hydraulic Cooling Fan Pump Bracket	18
	Hydraulic Cooling Fan Reservoir, Lower	106①
	Hydraulic Cooling Fan Reservoir, Upper	53①
	Idler Pulley	18
	Intake Manifold	⑫
	Lower Strut	129
	Lower Sway Bar Link	41
	Oil Cooler	43
	Oil Pan	⑨
	Oil Pump	53①⑦
	Power Steering Pressure Line	89①
	Power Steering Pump Bracket	18
	Power Steering Pump To Bracket	18
	Power Steering Reservoir, Lower	106①
	Power Steering Reservoir, Upper	53①

Continued

TIGHTENING
SPECIFICATIONS—Continued

Year	Component	Torque, Ft. Lbs.
2001–05	Primary Timing Chain Guide	97①
	Primary Timing Chain Tensioner	97①
	Receiver/Drier Bracket	8
	Secondary Timing Chain Tensioner	97①
	Steering Coupling	26
	Thermostat Housing	80①
	Torque Converter To Flywheel	28
	Transmission Cooler Lines	89①
	Transmission To Engine	35
	Upper Ball Joint	66
	Upper Radiator Support Brackets	89①
	Valve Cover	⑪
	Water Pump	71①⑦
	Water Pump Pulley	89①⑥
	Wheel Lug Nuts	100

① — Inch lbs.
② — Refer to "Cylinder Head, Replace."
③ — Refer to "Crankshaft Damper, Replace."
④ — Refer to "Front Cover, Replace."
⑤ — Refer to "Alternator, Replace" in "Electrical" section.
⑥ — Tighten an additional 45°.
⑦ — Tighten an additional 90°.
⑧ — Refer to "Crankshaft Rear Oil Seal, Replace" for tightening procedure.
⑨ — Refer to "Oil Pan, Replace" for tightening procedure.
⑩ — Refer to "Camshaft, Replace."
⑪ — Refer to "Valve Cover, Replace," for tightening specifications and sequence.
⑫ — Refer to "Intake Manifold, Replace," for tightening specifications and sequence.

Rear Axle & Suspension

NOTE: On Air Bag Equipped Models, Refer To "Air Bag System Precautions" Located In The Front Of This Manual For System Disarming & Arming Procedures.

NOTE: Refer To "Computer Relearn Procedures" Located In The Front Of This Manual When Battery Power To The Computer Has Been Interrupted.

NOTE: Prior To Performing Any Service Operations Listed In This Section, Consult The "Technical Service Bulletins" Section For Related Information.

INDEX

PRECAUTIONS
Air Bag Systems

Refer to "Air Bag System Precautions" in the front of this manual for system disarming and arming procedures.

Battery Ground Cable

Prior to service, disconnect battery ground cable and isolate as required.

DESCRIPTION

The rear axle is an integral-type housing hypoid gear design, **Fig. 1.** The ring and pinion consists of an eight inch ring gear and an overhung drive pinion which is supported by two opposed tapered roller bearings. Pinion preload is maintained by a drive pinion collapsible spacer on the pinion shaft and is adjusted by the pinion nut. Differential bearing preload and ring gear backlash are adjusted by differential bearing shims located between differential bearing cup and rear axle housing.

Halfshafts are held in the differential case by a driveshaft bearing retainer circlip which engages a step in the differential side gear.

The suspension is an independent design featuring upper and lower control arms, shock absorber and spring, adjustable toe links, stabilizer bar and wheel knuckles, **Fig. 2.**

When servicing suspension components, always use new nuts and bolts when removed.

When carrying out operations which involve the removal and installation of the driveshaft, always inspect the joint angles and adjust as outlined under "Driveline Angle Measurement."

REAR AXLE
REPLACE

1. Remove halfshafts as outlined under "Rear Halfshaft, Replace."
2. Remove exhaust system and heat shield.
3. Place reference marks on pinion flange, flex coupling and driveshaft to pinion flange bolts, nuts, washers and weighted washers for installation alignment.
4. Support driveshaft, then remove driveshaft to pinion flange bolts and nuts. **Do not remove flex coupling on driveshaft flange.**
5. Loosen driveshaft yoke adjuster nut using driveshaft coupler wrenches, tool No. 205-474, or equivalents.
6. Remove center bearing mounting bolts and shims. Mark position of shims for installation alignment.
7. Slide rear driveshaft to full forward position and tighten adjuster nut.

8. Position suitable jack under axle housing and secure axle to jack.
9. Remove three axle mounting nuts, **Fig. 3.**
10. Lower axle housing.
11. Reverse procedure to install.

STUB SHAFT BEARING & SEAL
REPLACE

1. Remove halfshaft as outlined under "Rear Halfshaft, Replace."
2. Remove stub shaft bearing housing seal and bearing using bearing cup remover tool No. T77F-1102-A and slide hammer tool No. T50T-100-A, or equivalents.
3. Lubricate new bearing with SAE 75W-140 synthetic rear axle lubricant F1TZ-19580-B, or equivalent.
4. Install bearing into rear axle housing bore using bearing replacer tool No. T89P-1244-A and handle tool No. T80T-4000-W, or equivalents.
5. Lubricate lip of seal with premium long life grease XG-1-C, or equivalent.
6. Install seal using seal replacer tool No. T89P-4850-A and handle tool No. T80T-4000-W, or equivalents.
7. Install halfshaft as outlined under "Rear Halfshaft, Replace."

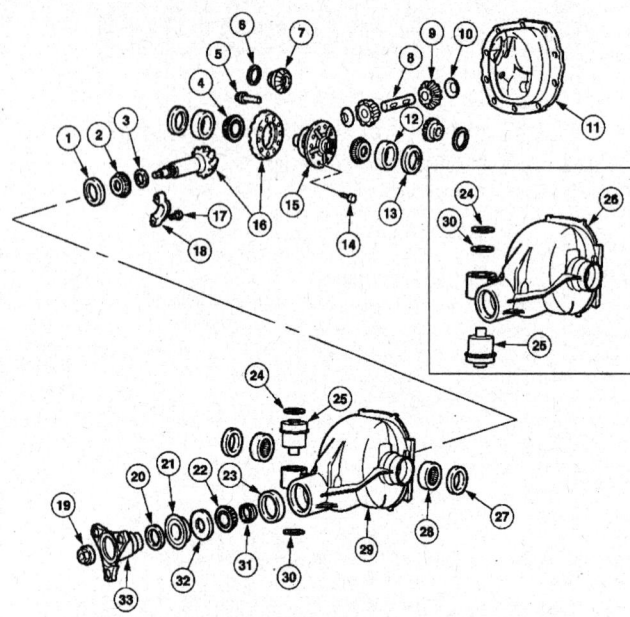

Item	Description
1	Rear axle pinion bearing cup
2	Pinion bearing
3	Drive pinion bearing adjustment shim
4	Differential bearing
5	Differential pinion shaft lock bolt
6	Differential side gear thrust washer
7	Differential side gear
8	Differential pinion shaft
9	Differential pinion gear
10	Differential pinion thrust washer
11	Differential housing cover
12	Differential bearing cup
13	Differential bearing shim
14	Rear axle ring gear case bolt
15	Differential case

FM2039900064010X

Fig. 1 Exploded view of rear axle (Part 1 of 2)

16	Ring gear and pinion
17	Bolt
18	Differential bearing cap (part of 4010)
19	Pinion nut
20	Drive pinion oil seal deflector
21	Rear axle drive pinion seal
22	Pinion bearing
23	Differential drive pinion bearing cup
24	Front mount shim
25	Rear axle differential front lower insulator
26	Rear axle housing (aluminum)
27	Inboard CV joint stub shaft pilot bearing housing seal
28	Inboard CV joint stub shaft pilot bearing housing
29	Rear axle housing (nodular iron)
30	Rear axle differential front lower insulator cap
31	Differential drive pinion collapsible spacer
32	Rear axle drive pinion shaft oil slinger
33	Rear axle pinion flange

FM2039900064020X

Fig. 1 Exploded view of rear axle (Part 2 of 2)

PINION FLANGE & SEAL

REPLACE

Removal

1. Raise and support vehicle, then remove rear wheels.
2. Remove mounting bolts and rear brake calipers. Position calipers aside.
3. Disconnect propeller shaft as outlined under "Propeller Shaft, Replace."
4. Record torque required to maintain rotation of pinion gear using suitable inch lb. torque wrench.
5. Install flange holding tool No. 205-478, or equivalent, and cotter pin, **Fig. 4.**
6. Remove and discard pinion nut using suitable breaker bar.
7. Place reference mark on pinion flange in relation to drive pinion stem for installation alignment, **Fig. 5.**
8. Remove flange from axle using flange removal tool No. 307-408, or equivalent.
9. Remove pinion seal.

Installation

1. Lubricate new seal using premium long life grease XG-1-C, or equivalent.
2. Install seal using seal installer tool No. T79P-4676-A, or equivalent.
3. Lubricate pinion flange spines using SAE 75W-140 synthetic rear axle lubricant F1TZ-19580-B, or equivalent.
4. Polish pinion flange seal journal using suitable crocus cloth.
5. Align pinion flange with drive pinion shaft.
6. Install flange using holding tool No. 205-478 and pinion flange installer tool No. 205-479, or equivalents.
7. Install cotter pin, **Fig. 4.**
8. Install new pinion nut.
9. Hold pinion flange using suitable flange holding tool, tighten new pinion nut until proper preload (used bearings, 8–10 inch lbs.; new bearings, 16–28 inch lbs.) is reached. **New collapsible spacer and pinion nut must be installed to reduce preload.**

REAR HALFSHAFT

REPLACE

Halfshafts are not serviceable. If wear or damage is present, replace entire halfshaft. When servicing halfshafts, ensure excessive angle is not applied to CV joints and that joints are not pulled apart or separated.

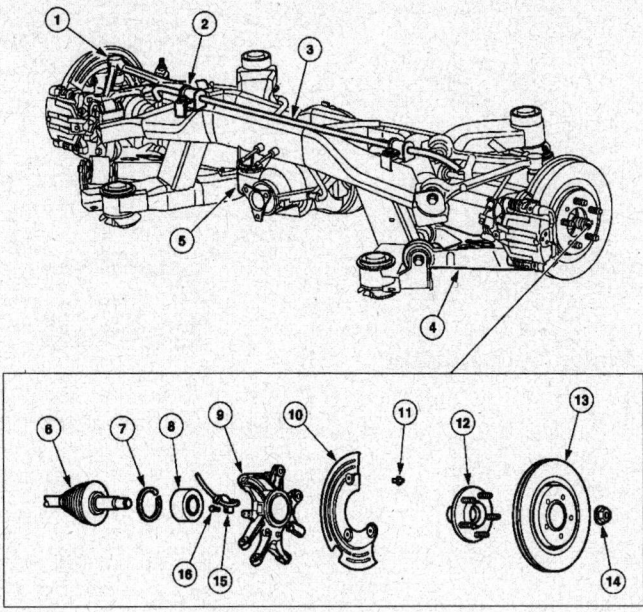

Item	Description
12	Hub
13	Rear brake disc
14	Hub retainer
15	ABS sensor
16	Screw

FM2039900065020X

Fig. 2 Rear suspension components (Part 2 of 2)

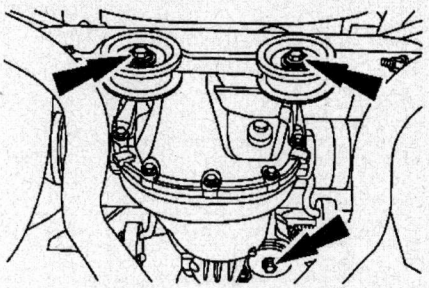

FM2039900066000X

Fig. 3 Axle mounting nuts

Item	Description
1	Upper arm
2	Stabilizer bar link
3	Stabilizer bar retaining bracket
4	Stabilizer bar
5	Lower arm
6	Axle shaft
7	Snap ring
8	Wheel hub bearing
9	Knuckle
10	Rear brake disc shield
11	Rivet

FM2039900065010X

Fig. 2 Rear suspension components (Part 1 of 2)

The halfshafts on models equipped with 3.9L engine are larger in diameter and are not interchangeable with halfshafts on models equipped with a 3.0L engine.

1. Raise and support vehicle.
2. Remove rear tires.
3. Remove and discard axle wheel hub nut.
4. Remove rear brake rotors as outlined in "Disc Brakes" chapter.
5. Remove ABS sensors as outlined in "Anti-Lock Brakes" chapter.
6. Remove lower knuckle mounting bolt.
7. Press CV joint from hub using hub remover/replacer tool No. T81P-1104-C, hub remover adapter tool No. T86P-1104-A1 and hub remover adapter tool No. T83P-1104-BH, or equivalents.
8. Raise and support knuckle, then remove CV joint from hub.
9. Separate CV joint from differential side gear using halfshaft removal tool No. 205-472, or equivalent. Ensure crown of tool forks face away from axle housing.

10. Remove halfshaft from axle housing.
11. Install differential plug tool No. T89P-4850-B, or equivalent, to differential.
12. Reverse procedure to install, noting the following:
    a. Install new axleshaft circlip.
    b. Before installing halfshaft into differential housing, install seal protector tool No. 205-461, or equivalent.
    c. Slide CV joint into housing until splines are past seal, then remove seal protector tool.
    d. Ensure halfshaft is fully seated into differential.
    e. Install new wheel hub nut.

DRIVELINE ANGLE MEASUREMENT

1. Park vehicle on level surface.
2. Remove mounting bolts and slide exhaust heat shield as far forward as possible to expose driveshaft to axle coupling.

3. Turn driveshaft several times by hand to neutralize center support bearing and flex couplings.
4. Place pinion angle level gauge tool No. T86P-4602-A, or equivalent, on left-hand frame rail with tool facing passenger side, **Fig. 6.**
5. Zero angle gauge tool using thumbscrew.
6. Mark location where tool was zeroed. **Do not remove flange bolts when measuring driveline angle.**
7. Remove one nut from flex coupling to transmission flange.
8. Install driveline adapter tool No. 205-449, or equivalent, to front of flex coupling and tighten nut. Ensure adapter contacts flex coupling bolt sleeve to obtain accurate reading.
9. Place pinion angle gauge in angle adapter with angle gauge facing passenger side and record transmission angle A, **Fig. 7.**
10. Remove one nut from flex coupling to front driveshaft connection.
11. Install driveline adapter tool No. 205-449, or equivalent, to front of flex coupling and tighten nut. Ensure adapter contacts flex coupling bolt sleeve to obtain accurate reading.
12. Place pinion angle gauge in angle adapter with angle gauge facing passenger side and record front driveshaft angle B.
13. Remove one nut from flex coupling to rear driveshaft connection.
14. Install driveline adapter tool No. 205-449, or equivalent, to front of flex coupling and tighten nut. Ensure adapter contacts flex coupling bolt sleeve to obtain accurate reading.
15. Place pinion angle gauge in angle adapter with angle gauge facing passenger side and record rear driveshaft angle C.

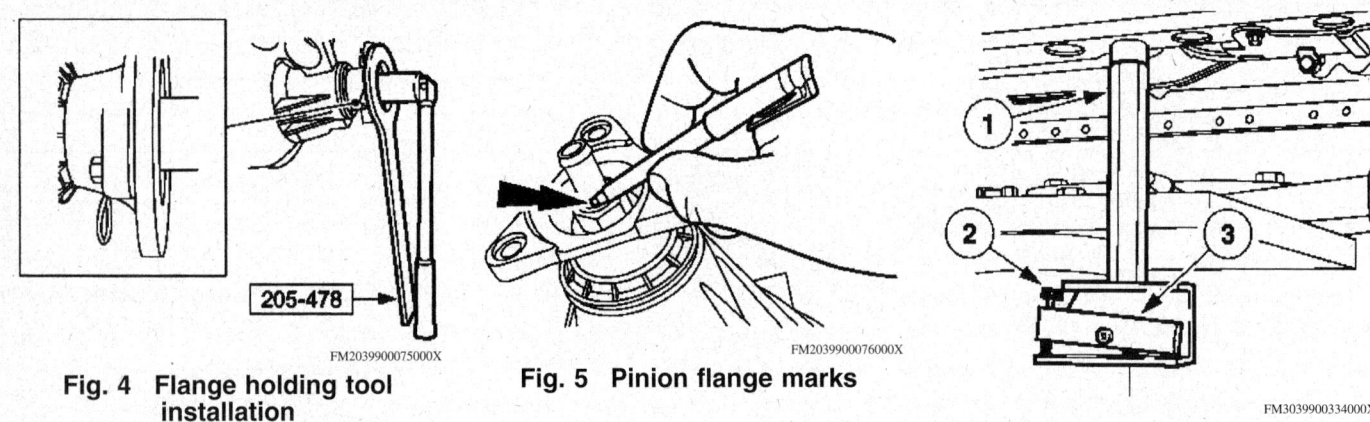

Fig. 4 Flange holding tool installation

Fig. 5 Pinion flange marks

Fig. 6 Pinion angle gauge setup

Fig. 7 Driveline angle inspection points

16. Remove one nut from flex coupling to pinion flange connection.
17. Install driveline adapter tool No. 205-449, or equivalent, to front of flex coupling and tighten nut. Ensure adapter contacts flex coupling bolt sleeve to obtain accurate reading.
18. Place pinion angle gauge in angle adapter with angle gauge facing passenger side and record differential pinion angle D.
19. Calculate joint 1 angle by subtracting front driveshaft angle B from transmission angle A.
20. Calculate joint 2 angle by subtracting rear driveshaft angle C from front driveshaft angle B.
21. Calculate joint 3 angle by subtracting differential pinion angle D from rear driveshaft angle C
22. If adjustment is required, install suitable center support bearing adjusting washers. Ensure left and righthand washers are of equal thickness.

PROPELLER SHAFT
REPLACE

1. Raise and support vehicle.
2. Remove muffler, extension pipe and body brace.
3. Remove heat shield.
4. Inspect and record driveline angles as outlined under "Driveline Angle Measurement."
5. Place reference marks on bolts, washers, nuts and flex coupling to transmission flange and pinion flange for installation alignment.
6. Remove driveshaft to axle flange mounting nuts. **Do not remove flex coupling to driveshaft mounting bolts, Fig. 8.**
7. Loosen driveshaft length adjustment nut using driveshaft coupler wrenches, tool No. 205-474, or equivalents.
8. Remove transmission flange to driveshaft mounting nuts. **Do not remove flex coupling to driveshaft mounting bolts.**
9. Slide front shaft rearward, then hand tighten adjustment nut to prevent separation of front and rear shafts.
10. Remove center bearing support brace nuts and driveshaft.
11. Reverse procedure to install, noting the following:
   a. Add one gram of premium long life grease XG-1-C, or equivalent, to both alignment bushing cavities.

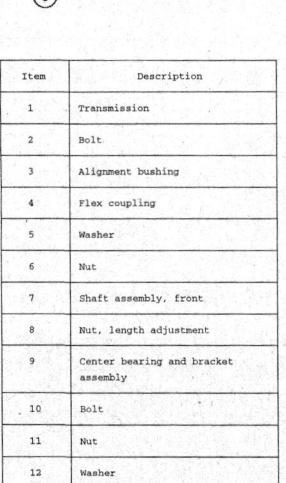

Item	Description
1	Transmission
2	Bolt
3	Alignment bushing
4	Flex coupling
5	Washer
6	Nut
7	Shaft assembly, front
8	Nut, length adjustment
9	Center bearing and bracket assembly
10	Bolt
11	Nut
12	Washer
13	Shaft assembly, rear
14	Flex coupling
15	Bolt

Fig. 8 Driveshaft components

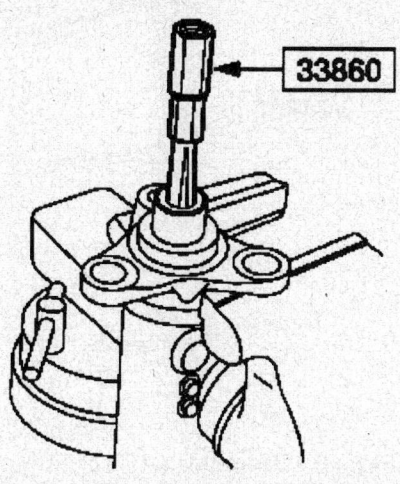

FM2039900067010X

Fig. 9 Propeller shaft bushing inner core removal (Part 1 of 4)

b. Apply Threadlock 262 E2FZ-19554-B, or equivalent, to driveshaft to flange nuts and bolts.

U-JOINT
REPLACE

The single center U-joint is of a lubed for life design that requires no periodic lubrication. This U-joint is staked to the yoke and is not removable.

PROPELLER SHAFT CENTER BEARING
REPLACE

1. Remove propeller shaft as outlined under "Propeller Shaft, Replace."
2. Place alignment marks on driveshaft for installation alignment.
3. Loosen adjustment nut, then separate front and rear shaft.
4. Place propeller shaft in suitable vise and clamp at driveshaft weld yoke.
5. Remove retaining ring, center bearing and bracket using two-jaw puller tool No. D80L-1002-L and bearing puller tool No. D84L-1123-A, or equivalents.
6. Reverse procedure to install. Install center bearing and retaining ring to driveshaft using driveshaft alignment bushing remover tube tool No. 205-D073, or equivalent, and suitable hammer.

PROPELLER SHAFT ALIGNMENT BUSHING
Removal

1. Remove propeller shaft as outlined under "Propeller Shaft, Replace."
2. Place alignment marks on front and rear driveshafts for installation alignment.
3. Loosen length adjustment nut, then separate front and rear shaft.
4. Remove mounting nuts, bolts and flex coupling.

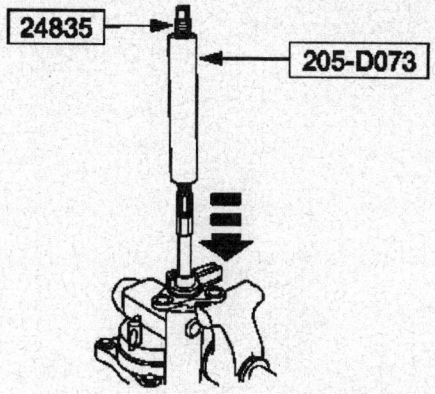

FM2039900067020X

Fig. 9 Propeller shaft bushing inner core removal (Part 2 of 4)

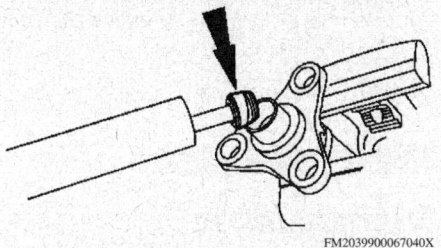

FM2039900067040X

Fig. 9 Propeller shaft bushing inner core removal (Part 4 of 4)

5. Place driveshaft end yoke into suitable vise.
6. Remove alignment bushing inner core using blind hole puller set tool No. D80L-100A, driveshaft alignment bushing remover tube tool No. 205-D073 and handle tool No. T80T-4000-W, or equivalents, **Fig. 9.**
7. Remove bushing shell using removal tools, **Fig. 10.**

Installation

There are six bushings in each flex coupling. Three bushings protrude from each side of coupling. Arrows on the side of coupling point toward protruding end of bushing. When installing flex coupling, protruding end of bushing must seat in driveshaft flange counterbore or damage will occur to coupling during operation.

1. Align bushing with propeller shaft, then install using handle tool No. T80T-4000-W and alignment bearing installer tool No. 205-D074, or equivalents.
2. Install flex coupling as follows:
   a. Position protruding end of bushing against driveshaft flange, **Fig. 11.**
   b. Apply Threadlock 262 E2FZ-19554-B, or equivalent, to flex coupling bolts and nuts, then install. Ensure bolt heads seat against driveshaft flange and nuts against flex coupling. Bolt heads are serrated and must be held in place while nut is tightened.
3. Align front and rear propeller shaft reference marks, then assemble both shafts. Hand tighten nut to prevent separation of shaft.

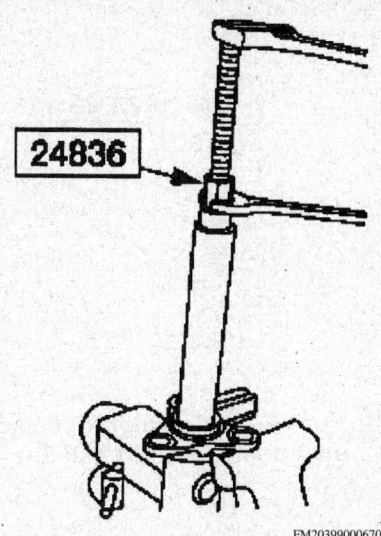

FM2039900067030X

Fig. 9 Propeller shaft bushing inner core removal (Part 3 of 4)

4. Add one gram of premium long life grease XG-1-C, or equivalent, to both alignment bushing cavities before installing propeller shaft.
5. Install propeller shaft as outlined under "Propeller Shaft, Replace."

HUB & BEARING
REPLACE

1. Remove knuckle as outlined under "Knuckle, Replace."
2. Drill out dust shield rivets using .22 inch drill bit. **Do not use drill bit larger than .24 inch.**
3. Remove dust shield.
4. Place knuckle in suitable press. Ensure knuckle is level and is supported as close to bearing bore as possible. Knuckle extremities should not be used for support.
5. Remove hub from knuckle using step plate adapter set tool No. D80L-630-A and bearing puller tool No. T71P-4621-B, or equivalents. When hub is pressed from bearing, bearing inner race will also be removed. **Do not install race back into bearing.**
6. Remove bearing retaining snap ring.
7. Support knuckle in press as close to bearing bore as possible.
8. Remove bearing from knuckle using suitable step plate adapter.
9. If hub is reused, remove inner bearing race from hub using suitable press and bearing puller tool No. T71P-4621-B, or equivalent.
10. Reverse procedure to install, noting the following:
    a. Attach dust shield using aluminum rivets.
    b. When installing hub to bearing, ensure bearing inner race is properly supported.

BALL JOINT INSPECTION

1. Raise and support vehicle.

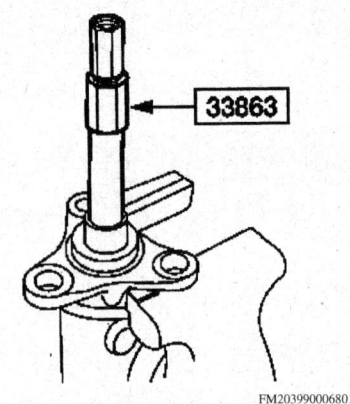

Fig. 10 Propeller shaft bushing shell removal (Part 1 of 4)

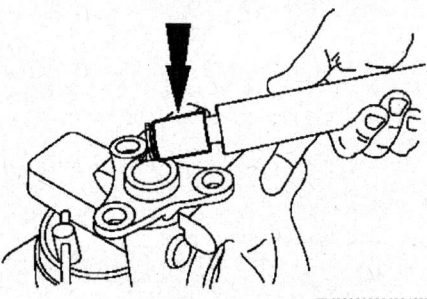

Fig. 10 Propeller shaft bushing shell removal (Part 4 of 4)

2. Ensure brake pads are retracted enough to allow free movement of tire.
3. Grasp tire at top and bottom and move wheel inward and outward while lifting weight of tire off bearing.
4. If tire is loose on spindle or does not turn freely, install new hub and bearing.
5. Position suitable safety stand under lower suspension arm.
6. Grasp tire at top and bottom and attempt to move inward and outward.
7. If movement is more than 1/32 inch replace control arm.

WHEEL BEARING INSPECTION

1. Raise and support vehicle.
2. Ensure brake pads are retracted enough to allow free movement of tire.
3. Grasp tire at top and bottom and move wheel inward and outward while lifting weight of tire off bearing.
4. If tire is loose on spindle or does not turn freely, install new hub and bearing.

STRUT
REPLACE

When working with strut, do not apply heat during removal or service.
1. Open luggage compartment.
2. Remove carpet and spare tire.
3. Remove trim covers to access strut upper mounting bolts.
4. Remove four strut upper mounting nuts and discard, **Fig. 12.**

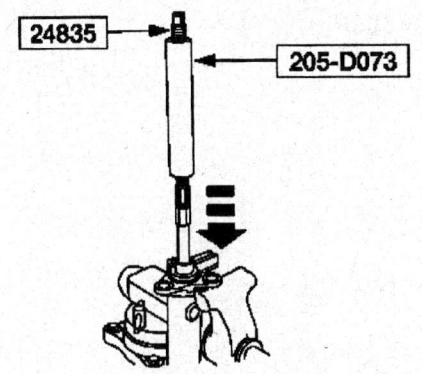

Fig. 10 Propeller shaft bushing shell removal (Part 2 of 4)

5. Raise and support vehicle.
6. Remove strut lower mounting bolt and nut and discard.
7. Remove strut.
8. Reverse procedure to install.

STRUT SERVICE
Disassemble

When working with strut, do not apply heat during removal or service.
If reusing components, place alignment marks for installation alignment.
1. Place strut into suitable vise, **Fig. 13.**
2. Compress spring using suitable spring compressor.
3. Remove center nut while holding shock absorber rod, **Fig. 14.**
4. Remove upper mount and dust boot.
5. Release spring and remove from strut.

Assemble

1. Inspect strut components for damage or wear. If spring paint is damaged, new spring should be installed.
2. Compress spring using suitable spring compressor.
3. Position upper mount and dust boot on spring. Ensure components are properly aligned.
4. Install new upper strut mount nut.
5. Remove strut from spring compressor and vise.

BALL JOINT
REPLACE

Refer to "Control Arm, Replace" for ball joint replacement procedure.

CONTROL ARM
REPLACE
Lower
REMOVAL

If lower arm bushings require service, entire lower control arm must be replaced.
1. With vehicle at static level position, re-

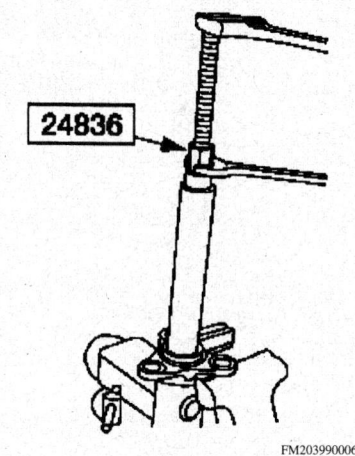

Fig. 10 Propeller shaft bushing shell removal (Part 3 of 4)

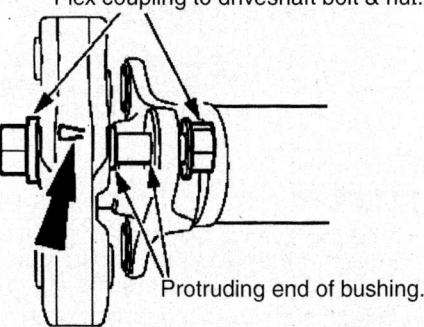

Fig. 11 Flex coupling installation

move hub cap and measure distance from center of hub to lip of fender, **Fig. 15.**
2. Raise and support vehicle, then remove rear wheels.
3. Remove rear brake rotor as outlined in "Disc Brakes" chapter.
4. Remove lower strut to control arm mounting bolt and nut, discard nut and bolt.
5. Remove lower stabilizer link to control arm mounting nut, discard nut.
6. Remove lower knuckle to control arm mounting nut and bolt, discard nut and bolt.
7. Remove lower arm to subframe mounting bolts and nuts, discard nuts and bolts.
8. Remove lower control arm.

INSTALLATION

Do not tighten lower arm to subframe or knuckle bolts and nuts until curb height is at correct level.
1. Connect lower arm to subframe.
2. Install knuckle to lower arm.
3. Connect stabilizer bar link to lower suspension arm.
4. Install strut to lower control arm.
5. Position suitable jackstand under lower arm and raise suspension until distance between center of hub and lip of fender is as recorded during removal procedure.
6. Tighten lower arm mounting nuts and

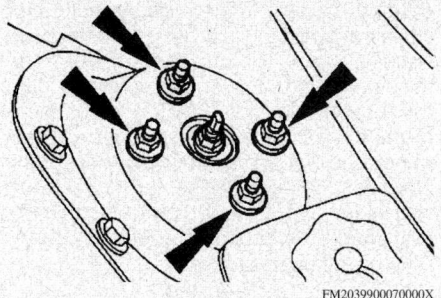

Fig. 12 Strut upper mounting nuts

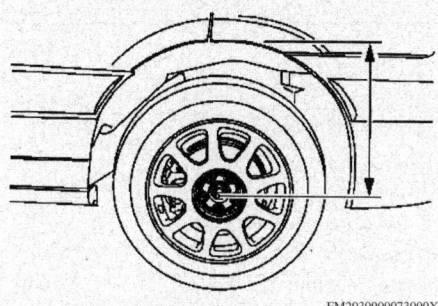

Fig. 15 Curb height measurement

remove jackstand.
7. Install rear rotors as outlined in "Disc Brakes" chapter.
8. Install wheels, then lower vehicle.

Upper
REMOVAL

If upper arm bushings and ball joints require service, entire upper control arm must be replaced.

1. With vehicle at static level position, remove hub cap and measure distance from center of hub to lip of fender, **Fig. 15.**
2. Raise and support vehicle.
3. Remove rear wheels.
4. Unclip ABS sensor wire retainer from suspension arm.
5. Disconnect and remove ABS sensor and position aside.
6. Remove and discard upper ball joint to knuckle nut, then separate knuckle from ball joint.
7. Remove upper arm to subframe nuts and bolts, discard nuts and bolts.
8. Remove upper suspension arm.

INSTALLATION

Do not tighten upper arm to subframe or knuckle nuts and bolts until suspension is at proper curb height.

1. Install upper arm to subframe and knuckle.
2. Clip ABS sensor wire to upper suspension arm.
3. Position suitable jack under suspension lower arm.
4. Raise suspension until distance between center of hub and lip of fender is as recorded during removal procedure.
5. Tighten upper arm to subframe and knuckle mounting nuts.

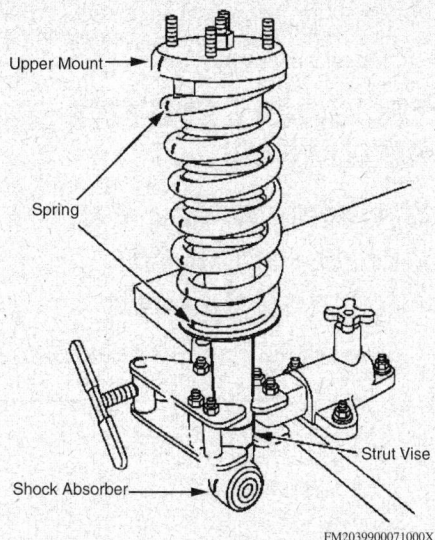

Fig. 13 Rear strut components

6. Lower suspension and remove jack.
7. Install wheels and lower vehicle.

TOE LINK
REPLACE

1. Raise and support vehicle.
2. Remove rear wheels.
3. Disconnect toe link from knuckle, **Fig. 16.**
4. Remove toe link.
5. Reverse procedure to install. Use new toe link mounting nuts and ensure wheel alignment is within specifications. Refer to "Specifications" section.

KNUCKLE
REPLACE

1. With vehicle at static level position, remove hub cap, then measure and record distance from center of hub to lip of fender, **Fig. 15.**
2. Raise and support vehicle, then remove rear wheels.
3. Remove and discard hub nut.
4. Remove rear rotors as outlined in "Disc Brakes" section.
5. Disconnect toe link from knuckle.
6. Remove ABS sensor and position aside.
7. Disconnect lower suspension arm from knuckle.
8. Support axleshaft.
9. Remove axleshaft from hub using hub remover/replacer tool No. T81P-1104-C, hub remover adapter tool No. T86P-1104-A and hub remover adapters tool No. T83P-1104-BH, or equivalents.
10. Remove upper ball joint and knuckle.
11. Reverse procedure to install, noting the following:
    a. Before tightening knuckle mounting bolts, raise suspension and ensure distance between center of hub and lip of fender is as recorded.
    b. When servicing suspension components, always use new nuts and bolts.

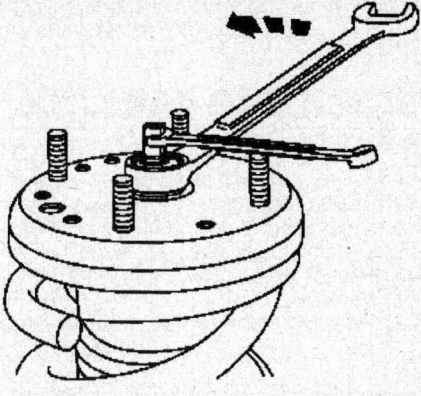

Fig. 14 Rear strut center nut replacement

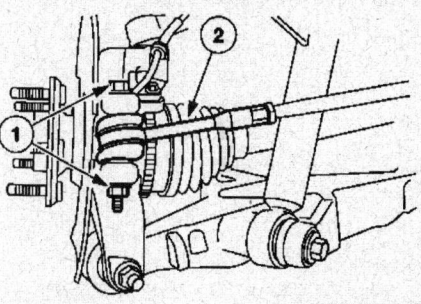

Fig. 16 Toe link replacement

STABILIZER BAR
REPLACE

1. With vehicle at static level position, remove hub cap, then measure and record distance from center of hub to lip of fender, **Fig. 15.**
2. Raise and support vehicle, then remove wheels.
3. Disconnect propeller shaft from axle as outlined under "Propeller Shaft, Replace."
4. Place Rotunda powertrain lift tool No. 014-00765, or equivalent, under rear subframe.
5. Place reference marks on subframe mounting bolts for installation alignment.
6. Remove subframe mounting bolts and lower subframe eight inches.
7. Remove stabilizer link caps from left and righthand stabilizer links.
8. Disconnect left and righthand stabilizer links from stabilizer bar.
9. Remove stabilizer bar brackets and bushings.
10. Secure left and righthand knuckles to subframe using suitable mechanics wire.
11. Disconnect left and righthand upper control arms from subframe.
12. Remove stabilizer bar.
13. Reverse procedure to install, noting the following:
    a. Before tightening knuckle mounting bolts, raise suspension and ensure distance between center of hub and lip of fender is as recorded.

b. When servicing suspension components, always use new nuts and bolts.

STABILIZER BAR LINK
REPLACE

1. Raise and support vehicle, then remove rear wheels.
2. Disconnect stabilizer bar link from suspension lower arm.
3. Remove protective cap from stabilizer bar link.
4. Remove stabilizer link from stabilizer bar.

5. Reverse procedure to install. When servicing suspension components, always use new nuts and bolts.

TECHNICAL SERVICE BULLETINS

Droning Noise On Acceleration At Highway Speeds

Some vehicles may exhibit a moaning or droning noise during light acceleration while transmission is in 5th gear at highway speeds. Noise will disappear if the transmission is shifted to 4th gear or when lifting the throttle. The noise may be because of the body reacting to a resonant frequency generated by the powertrain. To correct this condition, install revised larger diameter rear halfshafts. Larger diameter halfshafts will reduce the resonant frequencies generated by the powertrain.

TIGHTENING SPECIFICATIONS

Year	Component	Torque, Ft. Lbs.
2001–05	Anti-Lock Brake Sensor	89①
	Axle Fill Plug	25
	Center Bearing	32
	Driveshaft Length Adjustment	58
	Flex Coupling To Driveshaft	60
	Front Differential	52
	Hub Nut	221
	Lower Arm & Bushing To Knuckle Pivot	111
	Lower Arm & Bushing To Subframe Pivot	111
	Pinion Nut	②
	Rear Differential	76
	Shock & Spring To Lower Arm	98
	Stabilizer Bar Bracket	41
	Stabilizer Bar Link	35
	Subframe To Body	76
	Toe Link	41
	Upper Arm & Bushing To Subframe Pivot	66
	Upper Ball Joint	66
	Upper Shock Absorber Mount To Body	21
	Upper Shock Absorber Rod To Upper Shock Mount	37
	Wheel Lug Nuts	100
	Yoke Adjuster	66

① — Inch lbs.
② — Refer to "Pinion Flange & Seal, Replace" for proper preload.

NOTE: On Air Bag Equipped Models, Refer To "Air Bag System Precautions" Located In The Front Of This Manual For System Disarming & Arming Procedures.

NOTE: Refer To "Computer Relearn Procedures" Located In The Front Of This Manual When Battery Power To The Computer Has Been Interrupted.

INDEX

PRECAUTIONS

Air Bag Systems

Refer to "Air Bag System Precautions" in the front of this manual for system disarming and arming procedures.

Battery Ground Cable

Prior to service, disconnect battery ground cable and isolate as required.

DESCRIPTION

The front suspension is an aluminum short-arm-long-arm that features struts, stabilizer bar and stabilizer bar links, **Fig. 1.**
When servicing suspension components, always use new nuts and bolts.

HUB & BEARING

REPLACE

1. Raise and support vehicle.
2. Remove front wheels.
3. Remove brake rotor as outlined in "Disc Brakes" chapter.
4. Remove inner fender splash shield and position aside.
5. Disconnect ABS wheel speed sensor and separate from wire retainers. **Do not remove ABS sensor from hub unless new sensor and wire are being installed.**
6. Remove wheel hub and bearing mounting bolts and discard, **Fig. 2.**
7. Remove wheel hub and bearing from knuckle. **Do not use suitable slide hammer or strike back of wheel hub and bearing to remove. Hub and bearing should slide out from knuckle.**

8. Reverse procedure to install, noting the following:
   a. Ensure knuckle bore is clean enough to allow hub and bearing to be seated by hand.
   b. Apply Motorcraft high temperature nickel anti-seize lubricant F6AZ-9L494-AA, or equivalent, to bearing carrier and wheel knuckle
   c. Install new suspension mounting bolts and nuts.

BALL JOINT INSPECTION

1. Raise and support vehicle.
2. Ensure brake pads are retracted enough to allow free movement of tire.
3. Grasp tire at top and bottom and move wheel inward and outward while lifting weight of tire off vehicle.
4. If tire is loose on spindle or does not turn freely, install new hub and bearing.
5. Position suitable safety stand under lower suspension arm.
6. Grasp tire at top and bottom and attempt to move inward and outward.
7. If movement is more than 1/32 inch on upper or lower ball joint, replace control arm.

WHEEL BEARING INSPECTION

1. Raise and support vehicle.
2. Ensure brake pads are retracted enough to allow free movement of tire.
3. Grasp tire at top and bottom and move wheel inward and outward while lifting weight of tire off bearing.

4. If tire is loose on spindle or does not turn freely, install new hub and bearing.

STRUT

REPLACE

Do not use heat to remove strut mounting bolts.
1. Raise and support vehicle, then remove front wheels.
2. Disconnect stabilizer bar link from control arm and discard nut.
3. Remove and discard strut to lower control arm mounting bolt.
4. Remove strut to body mounting bolts, **Fig. 3. Do not remove strut center nut.**
5. Reverse procedure to install. Install new suspension mounting bolts and nuts.

COIL SPRING & STRUT SERVICE

Do not use heat to remove strut mounting bolts.
1. Raise and support vehicle, then remove front wheels.
2. Disconnect stabilizer bar link from control arm and discard nut.
3. Remove and discard strut to lower control arm mounting bolt.
4. Remove strut to body mounting bolts, **Fig. 3. Do not remove strut center nut.**
5. Mount strut in suitable vise, **Fig. 4.**
6. Place reference marks on strut components for assembly alignment.
7. Compress spring using suitable spring compressor.
8. Hold shock absorber center rod and remove center nut from strut.
9. Remove upper mount and dust boot.

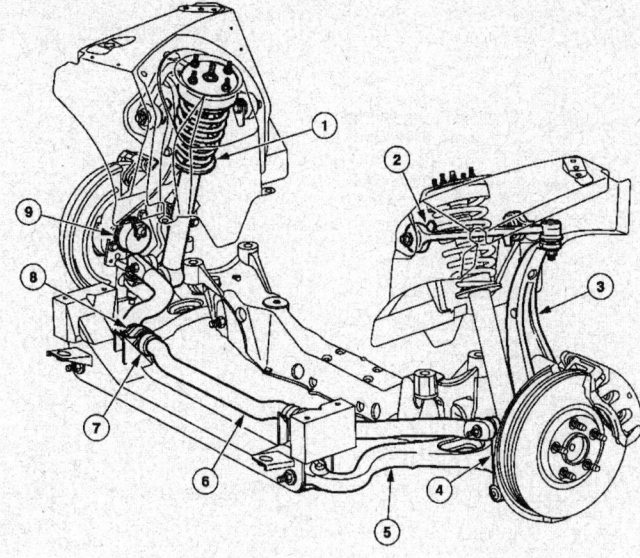

Item	Description
1	Shock absorber and spring assy
2	Upper arm and bushing
3	Wheel knuckle
4	Stabilizer bar link
5	Lower arm and bushing
6	Stabilizer bar
7	Stabilizer bar bushing
8	Stabilizer bar bracket
9	Wheel hub and bearing

FM2029900148000X

Fig. 1 Front suspension components

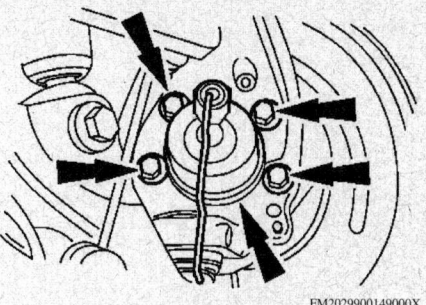

FM2029900149000X

Fig. 2 Wheel hub & bearing replacement

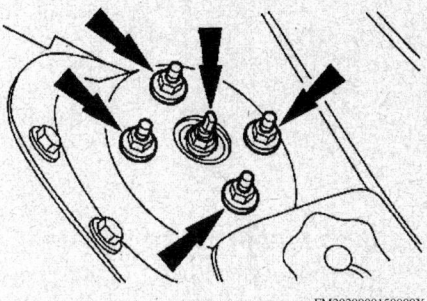

FM2029900150000X

Fig. 3 Strut mounting bolts

9. Install wheels, then lower vehicle and ensure wheel alignment is within specifications.

Upper
LEFTHAND

1. Remove hub cap.
2. Measure and record distance from lip of fender to center of wheel hub, **Fig. 8.**
3. Remove air cleaner.
4. Remove upper control arm nut and discard, **Fig. 9.**
5. Raise and support vehicle, then remove front wheel.
6. Disconnect stabilizer bar link from control arm and discard nut.
7. Remove and discard strut to lower control arm mounting bolt.
8. Remove strut to body mounting bolts, **Fig. 3. Do not remove strut center nut.**
9. Secure knuckle to body using suitable mechanics wire.
10. Disconnect upper control arm from steering knuckle and discard nut.
11. Remove control arm from body and discard nuts and bolts.
12. Reverse procedure to install, noting the following:
    a. Ensure suspension is at recorded distance, before tightening control arm mounting bolts.
    b. When servicing suspension components, always use new nuts and bolts.

RIGHTHAND

1. Remove hub cap.
2. Measure and record distance from lip of fender to center of wheel hub, **Fig. 8.**
3. Remove and discard nut from engine

10. Release pressure from spring and remove from spring compressor.
11. Reverse procedure to install, noting the following:
    a. Inspect spring, upper and lower spring seats, mount and insulator for damage. If spring coating is damaged, replace spring.
    b. Install new strut mounting nuts and bolts.

CONTROL ARM
REPLACE
Lower
REMOVAL

1. Ensure ignition switch is off in unlocked position.
2. Raise and support vehicle, then remove wheels.
3. Remove splash shields.
4. Disconnect stabilizer bar link from lower control arm and discard nut.
5. Disconnect strut from lower control arm, then discard nut and bolt.
6. Disconnect lower control arm from steering knuckle and discard nut.

7. Remove front lower control arm bolt and nut, then discard nut and bolt.
8. Remove two nuts and bolts, then loosen nut and bolt and turn steering gear rack to access lower control arm rear bolt, **Fig. 5.**
9. Remove and discard rear lower control arm nut and bolt.

INSTALLATION

1. Position lower control arm and install new caster adjustment cam bolt with cam lobe pointed downward, ensure cam is seated between cam guides on crossmember No. 1, **Fig. 6.**
2. Install nut. **Do not fully tighten nut until wheel alignment is performed.**
3. Install new camber adjustment cam bolt with cam lobe pointed downward, ensure cam is seated in groove of crossmember No. 2 and nut, **Fig. 7.**
4. Install nut. **Do not fully tighten nut until wheel alignment is performed.**
5. Connect lower ball joint to control arm. Ensure tapered washer is installed on ball joint.
6. Connect stabilizer link and strut to lower arm.
7. Install splash shields.
8. Tighten bolts and nuts loosened when positioning steering gear.

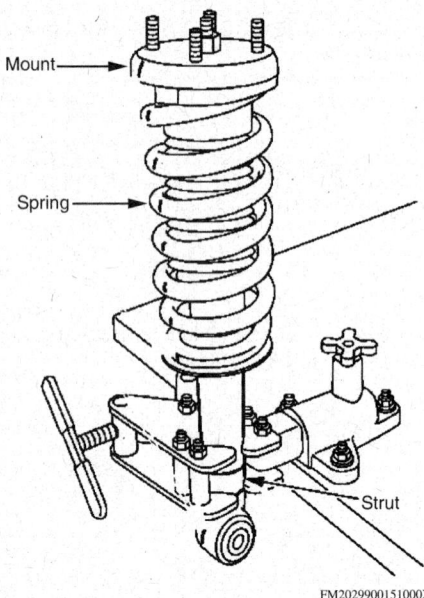

Mount

Spring

Strut

Fig. 4 Front strut components

FM2029900151000X

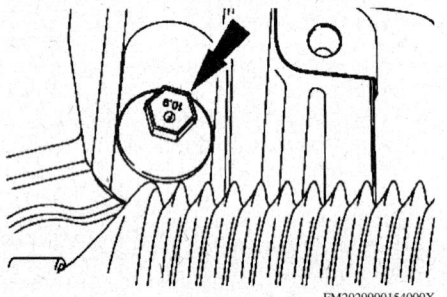

Fig. 7 Camber adjustment bolt installation

FM2029900154000X

compartment, **Fig. 10.**
4. Disconnect wiring harness and brackets to access control arm mounting bolts and nuts.
5. Remove upper control arm mounting nut and discard.
6. Disconnect stabilizer bar link from control arm and discard nut.
7. Remove and discard strut to lower control arm mounting bolt.
8. Remove strut to body mounting bolts, **Fig. 3. Do not remove strut center nut.**
9. Secure knuckle to body using suitable mechanics wire.
10. Disconnect upper ball joint from steering knuckle and discard nut.
11. Remove upper arm mounting bolts, nuts and upper arm. Discard mounting bolts and nuts.
12. Reverse procedure to install, noting the following:
    a. Ensure suspension is at recorded distance, before tightening control arm mounting bolts.
    b. When servicing suspension components, always use new nuts and bolts.

STEERING KNUCKLE

REPLACE

1. Raise and support vehicle.

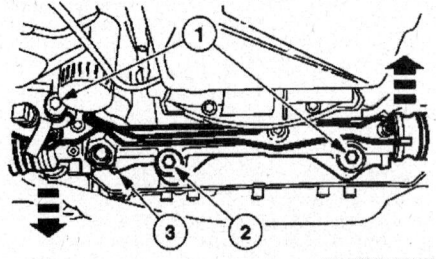

Fig. 5 Steering gear bolts

FM2029900152000X

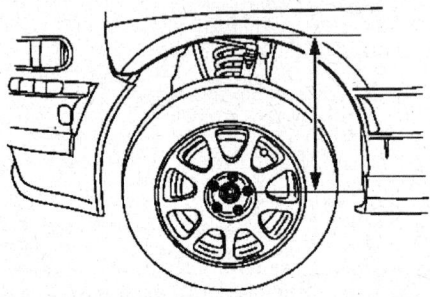

Fig. 8 Curb height measurement

FM2029900155000X

2. Remove front wheels.
3. Remove brake rotor as outlined in "Disc Brakes" chapter.
4. Remove inner fender splash shield and position aside.
5. Disconnect ABS wheel speed sensor and separate from wire retainers. **Do not remove ABS sensor from hub unless new sensor and wire are being installed.**
6. Remove wheel hub and bearing mounting bolts and discard, **Fig. 2.**
7. Remove wheel hub and bearing from knuckle. **Do not use slide hammer or strike back of wheel hub and bearing to remove. Hub and bearing should slide out from knuckle.**
8. Disconnect tie rod, upper control arm and lower control arm from steering knuckle and discard nuts.
9. Remove steering knuckle.
10. Reverse procedure to install, noting the following:
    a. Support steering knuckle using suitable jackstand during installation.
    b. Ensure knuckle bore is clean enough to allow hub and bearing to be seated by hand.
    c. Apply Motorcraft high temperature nickel anti-seize lubricant F6AZ-9L494-AA, or equivalent, to bearing carrier and wheel knuckle.
    d. When servicing suspension components always use new nuts and bolts.

STABILIZER BAR

REPLACE

1. Remove air cleaner.
2. Remove stabilizer bracket bolt, **Fig. 11.**
3. Raise and support vehicle, then remove front wheels.

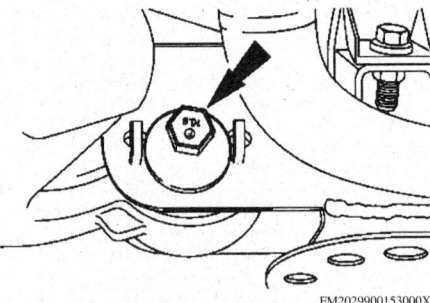

Fig. 6 Caster adjustment bolt installation

FM2029900153000X

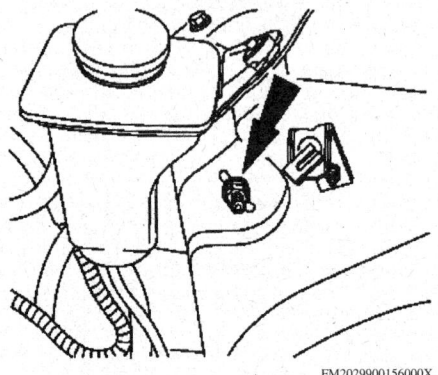

Fig. 9 Upper control arm mounting nut location

FM2029900156000X

4. Remove left, righthand and center splash shields.
5. Disconnect stabilizer bar link from control arm and stabilizer bar, discard nuts.
6. Disconnect strut from lefthand lower control arm, discard bolt and nut.
7. Disconnect lower control arm from lefthand steering knuckle, discard nut.
8. Remove heater water valve bracket and position valve aside.
9. Remove stabilizer bar brackets and bushings. Remove righthand front bolt first.
10. Remove stabilizer bar through lefthand wheel well.
11. Reverse procedure to install. When servicing suspension components, always use new nuts and bolts.

TIE ROD

REPLACE

Refer to "Power Steering" chapter for inner and outer tie rod replacement procedures.

POWER STEERING GEAR

REPLACE

1. Raise and support vehicle, then remove front wheels.
2. Disconnect tie rod ends from steering knuckles and discard nuts.
3. Disconnect power steering gear electrical connector.
4. Loosen steering shaft bolt.

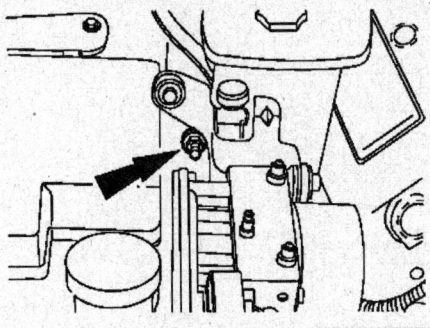

Fig. 10 Engine compartment nut location

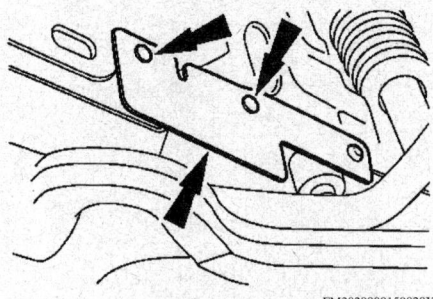

Fig. 12 Power steering pump shield (Part 2 of 2)

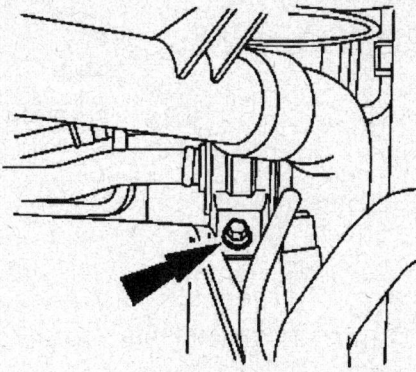

Fig. 11 Stabilizer bracket bolt replacement

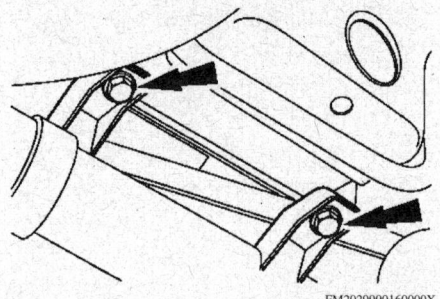

Fig. 13 Coolant tube bolt location

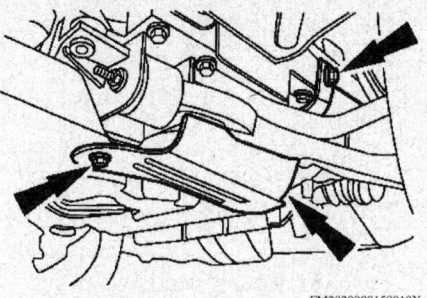

Fig. 12 Power steering pump shield (Part 1 of 2)

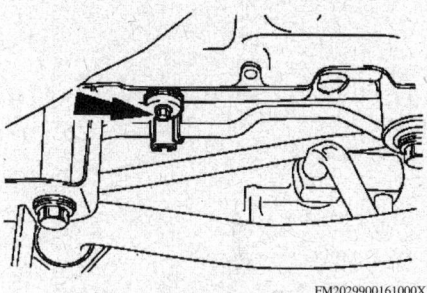

Fig. 14 Power steering line bracket

5. Remove pinch bolt and disconnect intermediate shaft.
6. Remove power steering hose bracket.
7. Disconnect power steering hoses from steering gear. Plug hose ends at gear.
8. Remove steering gear mounting nuts, bolts and gear. Discard mounting nuts and bolts.
9. Reverse procedure to install, noting the following:
   a. Install new seal to power steering lines using Teflon seal replacer set tool No. D90P-3517-A, or equivalent.
   b. When servicing suspension components, always use new nuts and bolts.
   c. Fill system and inspect for leaks. Ensure wheel alignment is within specifications.

POWER STEERING PUMP

REPLACE

3.0L Engine

1. Remove engine appearance cover.
2. Remove air cleaner and outlet tube.
3. Remove accessory drive belt.
4. Disconnect power steering reservoir to pump hose and drain fluid into suitable container.
5. Raise and support vehicle, then remove front wheels.
6. Remove lower power steering pump shield, **Fig. 12**.
7. Remove power steering hose bracket bolt, then disconnect hose from pump.
8. Remove mounting bolts and pump.

9. Reverse procedure to install, noting the following:
   a. Install new O-rings to power steering hoses using Teflon seal replacer set tool No. D90P-3517-A, or equivalent.
   b. Tighten upper pump mounting bolts after lower bolts are installed.
   c. Fill power steering system and inspect for leaks.

3.9L Engine

1. Remove engine appearance cover.
2. Remove air cleaner and outlet tube.
3. Remove coolant tube mounting bolts, **Fig. 13**.
4. Remove accessory drive belt.
5. Disconnect power steering reservoir to pump hose and drain fluid into suitable container.
6. Remove power steering reservoir mounting bolts and position reservoir aside.
7. Raise and support vehicle, then remove front wheels.
8. Remove power steering pump shields, **Fig. 12**.
9. Remove pump line bracket bolt, **Fig. 14**.
10. Disconnect power steering pump electrical connector and wire retainer.
11. Remove air conditioning compressor mounting bolts and position compressor aside.
12. Disconnect power steering pressure hose from pump.
13. Remove pump mounting bolts, **Fig. 15**.
14. Lower vehicle, then remove remaining pump mounting bolts and pump.

15. Reverse procedure to install, noting the following:
    a. Install new O-ring seals to power steering lines using Teflon seal replacer set tool No. D90P-3517-A, or equivalent.
    b. Tighten upper pump mounting bolts after lower bolts are installed.

POWER STEERING SYSTEM BLEED

1. Ensure power steering reservoir is filled to proper level.
2. Install vacuum tester tool No. 014-R1054, or equivalent, to reservoir, **Fig. 16**.
3. Start and run engine at idle speed.
4. Apply maximum vacuum for at least three minutes. Maintain vacuum with vacuum pump.
5. Remove vacuum tester.
6. Add Motorcraft Mercon multi-purpose ATF transmission fluid XT-2-QDX, or equivalent, fluid to bring reservoir to proper level.
7. Attach vacuum tester to reservoir and apply maximum vacuum. Cycle steering wheel from stop to stop every 30 seconds for 5 minutes. **Do not hold steering wheel against stops for more than 5 seconds.**
8. Remove vacuum tester and install reservoir cap.
9. Ensure fluid is at proper level and inspect system for leaks.
10. Repeat procedure.

POWER STEERING FLUID COOLER

REPLACE

1. Recover refrigerant as outlined in "Air

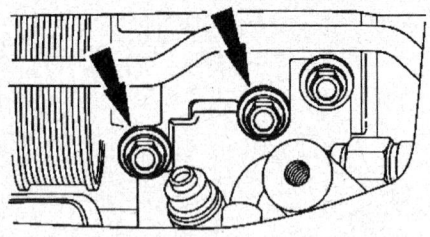

Fig. 15 Power steering pump bolts

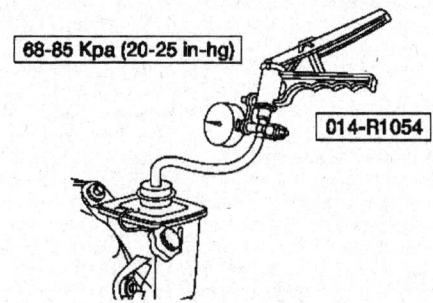

Fig. 16 Power steering vacuum bleed

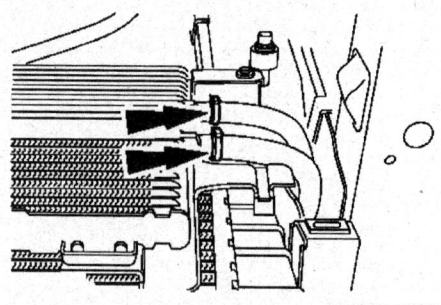

Fig. 17 Power steering fluid cooler

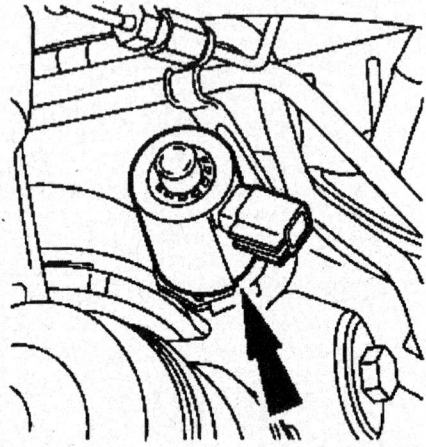

Fig. 18 Power steering control valve actuator

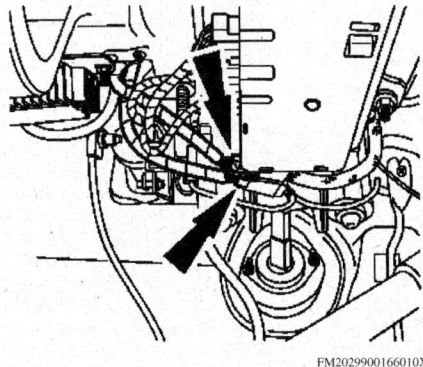

Fig. 19 Steering wheel rotation sensor replacement (Part 1 of 2)

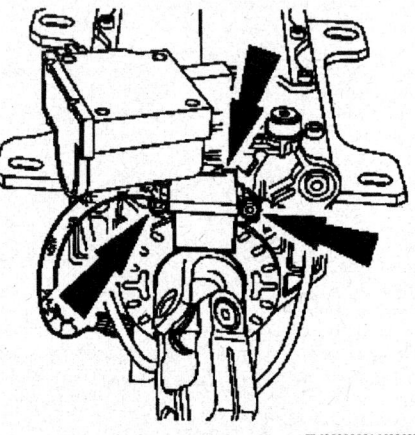

Fig. 19 Steering wheel rotation sensor replacement (Part 2 of 2)

Conditioning" chapter.

2. Remove left, righthand and center splash shields.
3. **On models equipped with 3.9L engine,** disconnect air intake tube and position aside.
4. **On all models,** disconnect air conditioning lines from condenser.
5. Support condenser, then remove condenser mounting bolts and condenser.
6. Remove and discard fluid cooler clamps, **Fig. 17.**
7. Disconnect fluid cooler hoses and drain into suitable container.
8. Remove mounting bolts and cooler.
9. Reverse procedure to install. Tighten fluid cooler clamps using CV boot clamp tool No. T95P-3514-A, or equivalent.

POWER STEERING CONTROL VALVE ACTUATOR
REPLACE

1. Raise and support vehicle.

2. Disconnect steering control valve electrical connector.
3. Remove power steering hose bracket and position aside.
4. Disconnect and plug power steering hoses.
5. Remove control valve actuator, **Fig. 18.**
6. Reverse procedure to install. Install new O-rings to power steering lines using Teflon seal replacer set tool No. D90P-3517-A, or equivalent.

STEERING WHEEL ROTATION SENSOR
REPLACE

1. Ensure wheels are in straight ahead position, then center steering wheel.
2. Remove driver air bag module as outlined in "Passive Restraint Systems" chapter.
3. Remove lower steering column opening finish panel and hood release.
4. Remove lefthand lower heater duct.
5. Pull carpet away from console tunnel and remove bracket bolts.

6. Remove steering column opening reinforcement.
7. Disconnect steering wheel rotation sensor and electric tilt/telescoping motor electrical connectors.
8. Disconnect lower steering column electrical connectors.
9. Secure steering column and shaft using suitable mechanics wire. **Ensure steering column and shaft do not turn.**
10. Remove and discard steering column shaft pinch bolt and disconnect shaft.
11. Support steering column, then remove and discard column locknuts.
12. Lower steering column, then remove sensor mounting screws and sensor, **Fig. 19.**
13. Reverse procedure to install. Install new steering column locknuts and pinch bolt.

TIGHTENING SPECIFICATIONS

Year	Component	Torque, Ft. Lbs.
2001–05	Air Conditioning Compressor	18
	Control Valve Actuator	22
	Engine Control Wiring Bracket	44①
	Heater Water Valve Bracket	44①
	Hub & Bearing To Knuckle	66
	Intermediate Shaft	18
	Intermediate Shaft To Gear Pinch Bolt	26
	Lower Arm To Frame	129
	Lower Arm To Knuckle	111
	Power Steering Cooler To Radiator	89①
	Power Steering Hose Brackets	89①
	Power Steering Pressure Hose	23
	Power Steering Return Hose To Gear	23
	Power Steering Pump	18
	Power Steering Reservoir, Lower	9
	Power Steering Reservoir, Upper	53①
	Radiator Tube To Engine	89①
	Stabilizer Bar Bracket	41
	Stabilizer Bar Link	41
	Steering Column Lock Nut	30
	Steering Column Opening Reinforcement	15
	Steering Column Shaft To Intermediate Shaft Pinch Bolt	26
	Steering Gear Lock Nut	76
	Steering Sensor Mounting Bolts	27①
	Strut To Body	21
	Strut To Lower Arm	129
	Tie Rod End To Knuckle	74
	Upper Control Arm To Body	35
	Upper Control Arm To Knuckle	66
	Upper Strut Rod To Upper Mount	37
	Wheel Lug Nut	100

① — Inch lbs.

Wheel Alignment

INDEX

PRELIMINARY INSPECTION

1. Inspect suspension and steering components for looseness and wear.
2. Inspect tires for similar tread and proper air pressure.
3. Ensure vehicle ride height is within specifications.

FRONT WHEEL ALIGNMENT

Caster & Camber

If vehicle is equipped with hex head bolts in lower control arm, new cam bolts and lock nuts must be installed before adjusting suspension. If new bolts are to be installed, refer to "Control Arm, Replace" in "Front Suspension & Steering" chapter for replacement procedure.

1. In order to turn camber and caster cams, loosen lower control arm mounting nuts, **Figs. 1 and 2.**
2. Turn caster adjustment bolt until caster is within specifications.
3. Turn camber adjustment bolt while supporting lower control arm by hand until camber is within specifications. Adjustments to camber may affect toe setting. Toe and camber may be adjusted at same time. Refer to "Toe" to adjust toe settings.
4. Tighten lower control arms and inspect alignment.

Toe

1. Start engine and center steering wheel.

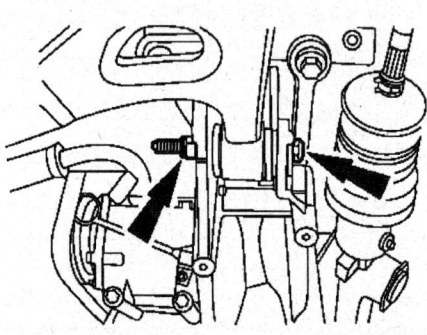

Fig. 1   Camber adjustment bolt

2. Turn engine off and hold steering wheel in straight ahead position by attaching suitable rigid link from steering wheel to brake pedal.
3. Remove tie rod boot clamps, then loosen jam nuts, **Fig. 3.**
4. Clean and lubricate nuts and tie rod threads.
5. Turn inner tie rod link to adjust to. Do not allow bellows to twist when tie rod is rotated.
6. Ensure toe is within specifications and tighten jam nuts.
7. Inspect alignment settings.

REAR WHEEL ALIGNMENT

Caster & Camber

Caster and camber are not adjustable on the rear suspension.

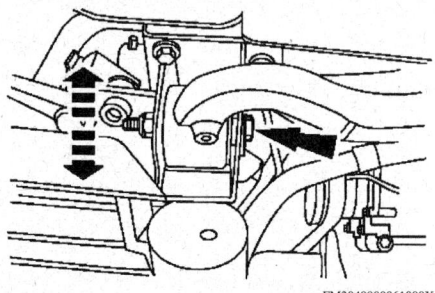

Fig. 2   Caster adjustment bolt

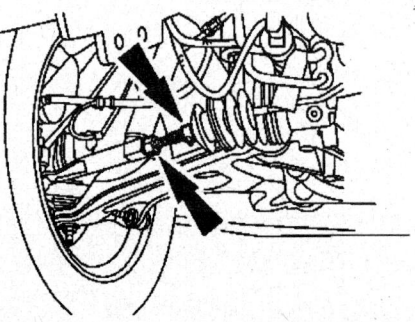

Fig. 3   Tie rod adjustment

Toe

1. Clean toe link threads and nut.
2. Loosen toe link jam nut and turn toe link until alignment is within specifications.
3. Tighten jam nut.
4. Ensure alignment is within specifications.

MUSTANG

NOTE: Refer To The Rear Of This Manual For Vehicle Manufacturer's Special Service Tool Suppliers.

INDEX OF SERVICE OPERATIONS

Specifications

GENERAL ENGINE SPECIFICATIONS

Year	Engine Liter (VIN)①	Fuel System	Bore & Stroke	Compression Ratio	Net H.P. @ RPM	Maximum Torque Ft. Lbs. @ RPM	Normal Oil Pressure, psi
2001	3.8L (4)	SEFI	3.81 × 3.39	9.4	190 @ 5250	220 @ 2750	40–125③
	4.6L (V) DOHC	SEFI	3.55 × 3.54	9.0	260 @ 5250	302 @ 4000	20–45④
	4.6L (X) SOHC	SEFI	3.55 × 3.54	9.9	320 @ 6000	317 @ 4750	20–45④
2002	3.8L (4)	SEFI	3.81 × 3.39	9.4	190 @ 5250	220 @ 2750	40–125③
	4.6L (X) SOHC	SEFI	3.55 × 3.54	9.9	260 @ 5250	302 @ 4000	20–45④
2003	3.8L (4)	SEFI	3.81 × 3.39	9.4	190 @ 5250	220 @ 2750	40–125③
	4.6L (R) DOHC	SEFI	3.55 × 3.54	10.1	305 @ 5800	320 @ 4200	20–45④
	4.6L (X) SOHC	SEFI	3.55 × 3.54	9.3	260 @ 5250	302 @ 4000	20–45④
	4.6L (Y) DOHC②	SEFI	3.55 × 3.54	8.5	390 @ 6000	390 @ 3500	20–45④
2004	3.8L (4)	SEFI	3.81 × 3.39	9.4	193 @ 5500	225 @ 2800	40–125③
	4.6L (R) DOHC	SEFI	3.55 × 3.54	10.1	305 @ 5800	320 @ 4200	20–45④
	4.6L (X) SOHC	SEFI	3.55 × 3.54	9.4	260 @ 5250	302 @ 4000	20–45④
2005	4.0L (N) SOHC	SEFI	3.95 x 3.32	9.7	210 @ 5250	240 @ 3500	15 @ 2000 RPM
	4.6L (H) SOHC	SEFI	3.55 x 3.54	9.8	300 @ 5750	320 @ 4500	75 @ 2000

DOHC — Double overhead cams, four valves per cylinder
SEFI — Sequential Multi-Port Electronic Fuel Injection
SOHC — Single overhead cam, two valves per cylinder
OHV — Overhead valve, two valves per cylinder

① — Eighth digit denotes engine code.
② — Supercharged.
③ — Engine hot @ 2500 RPM.
④ — Engine hot @ 1500 RPM.

TUNE UP SPECIFICATIONS

| Year & Engine (Code①) | Spark Plug Gap | Ignition Timing BTDC | | | | Curb Idle Speed | | Fast Idle Speed | | Fuel Pump Pressure, psi⑧ | Valve Lash, Inch |
		Firing Order Fig.	Man. Trans.	Auto. Trans.	Mark Fig.	Man. Trans.	Auto Trans.	Man. Trans.	Auto. Trans.		
2001											
3.8L (4)	.054	A②	10⑥	10⑥	⑦	⑤	⑤	⑤	⑤	35–55	④
4.6L (V) DOHC	.054	③	10⑥	10⑥	⑦	⑤	⑤	⑤	⑤	45–60	④
4.6L (X) SOHC	.054	③	10⑥	10⑥	⑦	⑤	⑤	⑤	⑤	30–45	④
2002											
3.8L (4)	.052–.056	②	⑥	⑥	⑦	⑤	⑤	⑤	⑤	35–50	④
4.6L (X) SOHC	.052–.056	③	⑥	⑥	⑦	⑤	⑤	⑤	⑤	35–50	④
2003											
3.8L (4)	.052–.056	②	⑥	⑥	⑦	⑤	⑤	⑤	⑤	35–50	④
4.6L (R) DOHC	.052–.056	③	⑥	⑥	⑦	⑤	⑤	⑤	⑤	35–50	④
4.6L (Y) DOHC	.052–.056	③	⑥	⑥	⑦	⑤	⑤	⑤	⑤	35–50	④
4.6L (X) SOHC	.052–.056	③	⑥	⑥	⑦	⑤	⑤	⑤	⑤	35–50	④
2004											
3.8L (4)	.052–.056	②	⑥	⑥	⑦	⑤	⑤	⑤	⑤	35–50	④
4.6L (R) DOHC	.052–.056	③	⑥	⑥	⑦	⑤	⑤	⑤	⑤	35–50	④
4.6L (X) SOHC	.052–.056	③	⑥	⑥	⑦	⑤	⑤	⑤	⑤	35–50	④

Continued

TUNE UP SPECIFICATIONS—Continued

Year & Engine (Code①)	Spark Plug Gap	Ignition Timing BTDC				Curb Idle Speed		Fast Idle Speed		Fuel Pump Pressure, psi⑧	Valve Lash, Inch
		Firing Order Fig.	Man. Trans.	Auto. Trans.	Mark Fig.	Man. Trans.	Auto Trans.	Man. Trans.	Auto. Trans.		
2005											
4.0L (N) SOHC	.052–.056	②	⑥	⑥	⑦	⑤	⑤	⑤	⑤	27–37	④
4.6L (H) SOHC	—	⑥	10⑥	10⑦	⑤	⑤	⑤	⑤	⑤	27–37	④

BTDC — Before Top Dead Center

① — Eighth digit denotes engine code.

② — Cylinder numbering front to rear, righthand bank, 1, 2, 3 ; lefthand bank, 4, 5, 6. Firing order 1-4-2-5-3-6.

③ — Cylinder numbering front to rear: righthand bank 1, 2, 3, 4; lefthand bank 5, 6, 7, 8. Firing order 1-3-7-2-6-5-4-8. Refer to **Fig. B** for ignition coil tower terminal numbering.

④ — Equipped w/hydraulic valve tappets.

⑤ — Idle speed controlled by an automatic idle speed control.

⑥ — Non-adjustable.

⑦ — Equipped w/crankshaft position sensor.

⑧ — Wrap shop towel around fitting to prevent fuel spillage, then connect suitable fuel pressure gauge to fuel diagnostic valve on fuel rail assembly. Gradually open fuel pressure gauge test valve to relieve fuel system pressure & drain fuel into suitable container. Close fuel pressure gauge test valve. Turn ignition On. Access output test mode on scan tool & operate fuel pump to obtain maximum fuel pressure. Fuel pump will operate for approximately 8 seconds. Inspect fuel pressure gauge reading.

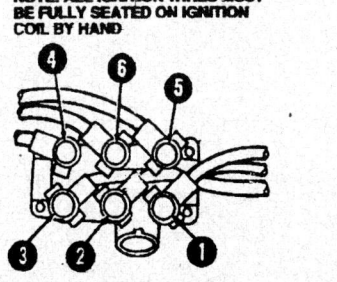

NOTE: ALL IGNITION WIRES MUST BE FULLY SEATED ON IGNITION COIL BY HAND

FM1138800242000X

Fig. A

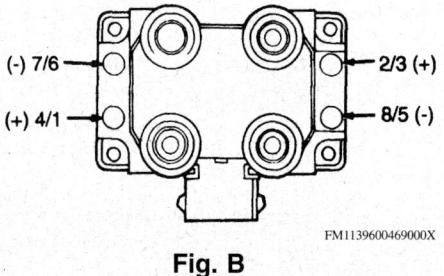

(-) 7/6   2/3 (+)
(+) 4/1   8/5 (-)

FM1139600469000X

Fig. B

FRONT WHEEL ALIGNMENT SPECIFICATIONS

Model	Caster Angle, Degrees①		Camber Angle, Degrees		Total Toe, Inches②		Toe Out On Turns, Degrees	
	Limits	Desired	Limits	Desired	Limits	Desired	Outer Wheel	Inner Wheel
2001								
All	+2.45 to +3.95	+3.2	-1.25 to +.25	-.5	.01 to +.25	+.13	—	—
2002								
All	+2.45 to +3.95	+3.2	-1.00 to -.20	-.6	-.01 to +.25	+.12	—	—
2003–04								
Base & GT	+2.45 to +3.95	+3.2	-1.25 to +.25	-.5	0 to +.26	+.13	—	—
Cobra	+2.45 to +3.95	+3.2	-1.30 to -.50	-.9	0 to +.26	+.13	—	—
2005								
All	+7.05 to +7.15	+7.10	-.25 to -1.25	-.75	-.10 to +.30	+.10	—	—

① — Difference side to side, lefthand minus righthand should not be more than .75°.

② — Toe-In (+). Toe-Out (−).

REAR WHEEL ALIGNMENT SPECIFICATIONS

Model	Caster Angle, Degrees	Camber Angle, Degrees		Toe-In, Inches	
		Limits	Desired	Limits	Desired
2001 Cobra	—	-.9 to -.5	-.7	+.06 to +.20	+.13
2003–04 Cobra	—	-1.0 to -.6	-.8	-.02 to +.18	+.08
2005	—	—	—	—	—

VEHICLE RIDE HEIGHT SPECIFICATIONS

Model	Year	Body Style	Manufacturer's Original Tire Size①	Measurement Points & Specifications②					
				Front③			Rear③		
				Dim.	Specification		Dim.	Specification	
					Inches	mm		Inches	mm
Mustang	2001	Base & GT	—	1	.2	4	2	5.00	128
		Cobra	—	1	.2	4	1	1.40	36
	2002	Base & GT	—	1	.2	4	2	5.00	128
	2003–04	Base & GT	—	1	.2	4	2	5.00	128
		Cobra	—	1	.2	4	2	1.40	36
	2005	Base	P215/65R16	1	1.5④	38⑤	2	4.5⑥	115⑦
		GT	P235/55ZR17	1	1.5④	38⑤	2	4.5⑥	115⑦

1 Dim. — Front suspension: Height from ground to center of lower control arm mounting bolt minus height from ground to bottom of steering knuckle

1 Dim. — Rear suspension: Height from ground to center of lower control arm mounting bolt minus height from ground to center of steering knuckle lower mounting bolt

2 Dim. — Rear axle arch center to body reinforcement at closest point

Dim. — Dimension

① — See door sticker or inside of glove compartment for manufacturer's original tire size specifications. If tires on vehicle do not match manufacturer's original tire size & measurement is not within limits, it will be required to refer to the "Non-Standard Tire & Wheel Size Adjustment To Ride Height Specification & Tire Size Adjustment Charts" in the front of this manual for approximate changes in ride height specifications.

② — Measurement is with fuel, radiator coolant and engine oil full, spare tire, jack, hand tools and mats in designated positions and tires properly inflated.

③ — Ride height side to side should be within .50 inch (13 mm). Ride height front to rear should be within .75 inch (19 mm).

④ — 1.2–1.8 inches.

⑤ — 30–46 mm.

⑥ — 4.2–4.8 inches.

⑦ — 107–123 mm

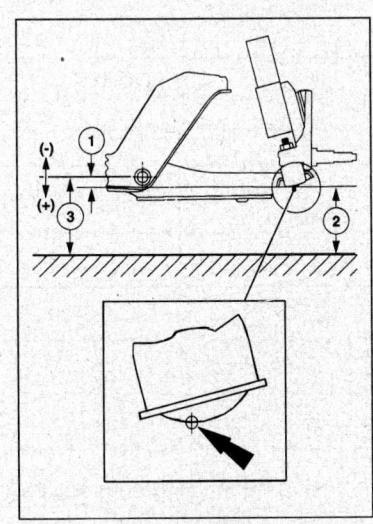

Item	Description
1	Ride height = B - A
2	Measurement A
3	Measurement B

FM2020100207000X

Fig. A Front ride height

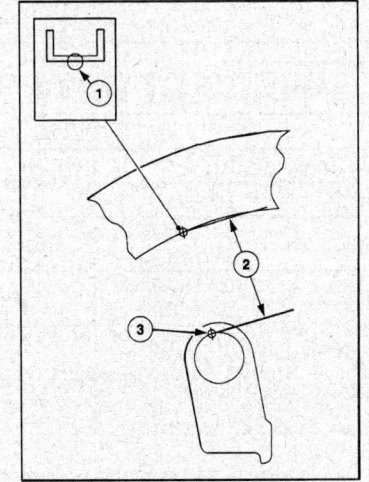

Item	Description
1	Body reinforcement
2	Ride height (shortest distance)
3	Rear axle

FM2030100158000X

Fig. B Rear ride height. Base & GT

Item	Description
1	Ride height = B - A
2	Measurement A
3	Measurement B

FM2030100159000X

Fig. C Rear ride height. Cobra

FLUID CAPACITIES & COOLING SYSTEM DATA

Year	Engine (VIN①)	Cooling Capacity, Qts. Less Air Conditioning	Cooling Capacity, Qts. With Air Conditioning	Coolant Type	Radiator Cap Relief Pressure, Lbs.	Thermo. Opening Temp. Deg. F	Fuel Tank Gals.	Engine Oil Refill Qts.②	Transmission Oil Man. Trans. Pints	Transmission Oil Auto. Trans. Qts.③	Rear Axle Oil Pints
2001	3.8L (4)	11.8	11.8	EG	13–18	189–196	15.7	5.0	5.6	5.0	3.25–3.50
	4.6L (V) DOHC	19.0	19.0	EG	13–18	192–199	15.7	6.0	6.6	5.0	2.60–2.90④
	4.6L (X) SOHC	19.2	19.2	EG	13–18	192–199	15.7	5.0	7.5	5.0	3.50–3.75④
2002	3.8L (4)	11.8	11.8	⑤	13–18	189–196	15.7	5.0	5.6	5.0	3.25–3.50
	4.6L (X) SOHC	14.1	14.1	⑤	13–18	189–196	15.7	5.0	7.5	5.0	3.50–3.75④
2003	3.8L (4)	11.8	11.8	⑤	13–18	189–196	15.7	5.0	5.6	5.0	3.50
	4.6L (R) DOHC	16.0	16.0	⑤	13–18	175–18	15.7	6.0	8.2	5.0	2.60–2.90
	4.6L (X) SOHC	14.1	14.1	⑤	13–18	192–199	15.7	5.0	7.5	5.0	4.00
	4.6L (Y) DOHC②	16.0	16.0	⑤	13–18	175–182	15.7	6.0		5.0	2.60–2.90
2004	3.8L (4)	11.8	11.8	⑤	13–18	189–196	15.7	5.0	5.6	5.0	3.50
	4.6L (R) DOHC	16.0	16.0	⑤	13–18	175–182	15.7	6.0	8.2	5.0	2.60–2.90
	4.6L (X) SOHC	14.1	14.1	⑤	13–18	192–199	15.7	5.0	7.5	5.0	4.00
2005	4.0L (N) SOHC	16.1	16.1	⑥	16	194–201	16.0	5.0	5.6	11.9	3.00④
	4.6L (H) SOHC	16.1	16.1	⑥	16	175–182	16.0	6.5	7.5	11.9	3.15④

EG — Ethylene Glycol
① — Eighth digit of Vehicle Identification Number (VIN) denotes engine code.
② — Includes filter.
③ — Approximate. Make final inspection w/dipstick.

④ — Models equipped with Traction-Lok axle, add 4 ounces of additive friction modifier.
⑤ — Always fill cooling system with same coolant that is present in the system. Do not mix coolant types. For models w/green coolant use ethylene glycol, Premium Engine

Coolant Fluid VC-4-A (in Oregon VC-5), or equivalent meeting Ford specifications ESE-M97B44-A.
⑥ — Motorcraft Premium Gold (Yellow) Engine Coolant VC-7-A (California, Oregon & New Mexico, VC-7-B), or equivalent.

LUBRICANT DATA

Year	Model	Lubricant Type Transmission Automatic	Lubricant Type Transmission Manual	Rear Axle	Power Steering	Brake System
2001–04	3.8L Engine	Mercon V	Mercon ATF XT-2-QDX	80W-90①	Mercon ATF XT-2-QDX	DOT 3
	4.6L Engine	Mercon V	Mercon ATF XT-2-QDX	75W-140②	Mercon ATF XT-2-QDX	DOT 3
2005	4.0L (N) SOHC	Mercon V	Mercon ATF XT-2-QDX	75W-140②	Mercon ATF XT-2-QDX	DOT 3
	4.6L (H) SOHC	Mercon V	Mercon ATF XT-2-QDX	75W-140②	Mercon ATF XT-2-QDX	DOT 3

① — Thermally Stable Rear Axle Lubricant XY-80W90-QL.
② — On models equipped w/Traction-

Lok axle, add 4 ounces of friction modifier C8AZ-19B546-A, or

equivalent meeting Ford specification EST-M2C118-A.

Electrical

NOTE: On Air Bag Equipped Models, Refer To "Air Bag System Precautions" Located In The Front Of This Manual For System Disarming & Arming Procedures.

NOTE: Refer To "Computer Relearn Procedures" Located In The Front Of This Manual When Battery Power To The Computer Has Been Interrupted.

NOTE: Prior To Performing Any Service Operations Listed In This Section, Consult The "Technical Service Bulletins" Section For Related Information.

INDEX

PRECAUTIONS

Air Bag Systems

Refer to "Air Bag System Precautions" in front of this manual for system disarming and arming procedures.

Battery Ground Cable

Prior to service, disconnect battery ground cable and isolate as required.

FUSE PANEL & FLASHER LOCATION

The fuse panel is located below and to the lefthand of the steering column near the brake pedal. To access these fuses, remove the panel cover.

There is also a power distribution and relay box located in the engine compartment, adjacent to the battery.

RELAY CENTER LOCATION

A relay and power distribution box is located under the hood. Ensure its cover is intact when filling fluid reservoirs or servicing the battery.

FUEL PUMP RELAY LOCATION

The fuel pump relay is located in the underhood relay and power distribution box.

STARTER

REPLACE

2001–04

1. Raise and support vehicle.
2. **On models equipped with 3.8L engine,** remove ground cable nut.

3. **On all models,** remove solenoid protective cap and wiring nuts. Position wiring aside.
4. Remove mounting bolts and starter motor.
5. Reverse procedure to install, noting the following:
   a. **Torque** starter mounting bolts to 17 ft. lbs.
   b. **Torque** solenoid B-terminal nut to 108 inch lbs.
   c. **Torque** solenoid terminal nut to 53 inch lbs.
   d. **On models equipped with 3.8L engine, torque** ground cable nut to 17 ft. lbs.
   e. **On models equipped with 4.6L engine, torque** HO2S bracket nut to 18 ft. lbs.

2005

4.0L ENGINE

1. Raise and support vehicle.

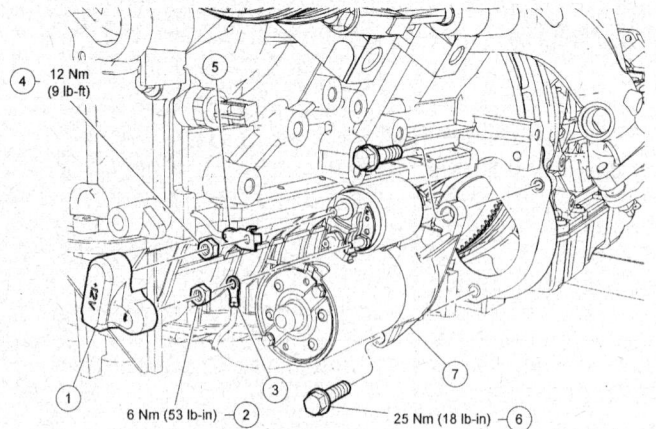

Item	Description
1	Starter solenoid terminal cover
2	Starter solenoid S-terminal nut
3	Starter solenoid S-terminal eyelet
4	Starter solenoid B+ terminal nut
5	Starter solenoid B+ terminal eyelet
6	Starter motor mounting bolt (2 required)
7	Starter motor

ARM0400000000594

Fig. 1 Starter replacement. 4.0L engine

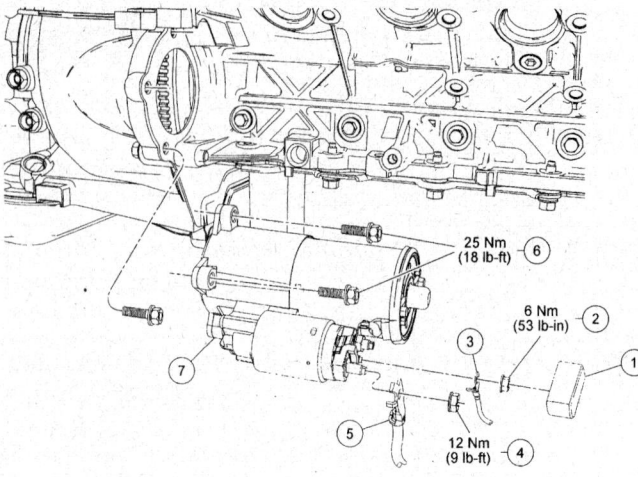

Item	Description
1	Starter solenoid terminal cover
2	Starter solenoid S-terminal nut
3	Starter solenoid S-terminal eyelet
4	Starter solenoid B+ terminal nut
5	Starter solenoid B+ terminal eyelet
6	Starter motor mounting bolt (3 required)
7	Starter motor

ARM0400000000524

Fig. 2 Starter motor replacement. 2005 4.6L engine

2. Remove starter solenoid terminal cap, **Fig. 1.**
3. Remove two terminal nuts and position starter solenoid wires aside.
4. Remove two mounting bolts and starter motor.
5. Reverse procedure to install, noting the following:
   a. **Torque** starter motor mounting bolts to 18 ft. lbs.
   b. **Torque** solenoid B+ terminal nut to 106 inch lbs.
   c. **Torque** solenoid S-terminal nut 53 inch lbs.

4.6L ENGINE

1. Ensure anti-theft system is deactivated.
2. Raise and support vehicle.
3. Remove starter solenoid terminal cap, **Fig. 2.**
4. Remove two nuts terminal nuts and position wires aside.
5. Remove three mounting bolts and starter motor.
6. Reverse procedure to install, noting the following:
   a. **Torque** mounting bolts to 18 ft. lbs.
   b. **Torque** B+ terminal nut to 106 inch lbs.
   c. **Torque** S terminal nut to 53 inch lbs.

ALTERNATOR
REPLACE
2001-04

1. Remove serpentine drive belt from alternator pulley. Leave belt in place to ease installation.
2. **On models equipped with 4.6L SOHC engine,** remove mounting bolts and alternator upper bracket, then disconnect alternator electrical connector by pressing tab. **Do not pull on tab.**
3. **On all models,** disconnect alternator electrical connections.
4. Remove mounting bolts and alternator.
5. Reverse procedure to install, noting the following:
   a. **On models equipped with 3.8L engine, torque** alternator lower mounting bolt to 35 ft. lbs., and upper bolt to 18 ft. lbs.
   b. **On models equipped with 4.6L engines, torque** alternator lower mounting bolts to 18 ft. lbs., and upper bolts to 89 inch lbs.
   c. **On all models, torque** battery positive cable nut to solenoid to 72 inch lbs.

2005
4.0L

1. Rotate tensioner counterclockwise and position front end accessory drive belt aside.
2. Disconnect alternator electrical connector.
3. Position boot aside, remove the nut and position B+ terminal aside.
4. Remove two mounting nuts and position shield aside.
5. Remove two stud nuts, mounting bolt and alternator.
6. Reverse procedure to install, noting the following:
   a. **Torque** B+ terminal nut to 71 inch lbs.
   b. **Torque** shield nuts to 26 ft. lbs.
   c. **Torque** stud nuts and mounting bolt to 35 ft. lbs.

4.6L SOHC 2005

1. Press lock tab, remove crankcase vent tube from air cleaner outlet pipe and position it aside.
2. Loosen clamp, remove air cleaner outlet pipe from throttle body and position it aside.
3. Rotate tensioner clockwise and position front end accessory drive belt aside.
4. Remove two mounting bolts.
5. Remove two outer bracket bolts and position alternator aside.
6. Remove two inner bracket bolts.
7. Remove harness locator and bracket.
8. Disconnect electrical connector.
9. Position B+ protective boot aside, then remove nut and position generator B+

terminal aside.
10. Remove alternator.
11. Reverse procedure to install, noting the following:
    a. **Torque** mounting bolts to 18 ft. lbs.
    b. **Torque** bracket bolts to 89 inch lbs.
    c. **Torque** terminal nut to 71 inch lbs.

IGNITION COIL PACK
REPLACE
2001-04
3.8L ENGINE

1. Disconnect electrical connectors.
2. Tag spark plug wires, squeeze locking tabs and disconnect. Position wires aside.
3. Record radio ignition interference capacitor location.
4. Remove mounting bolts and coil.
5. Reverse procedure to install, noting the following:
   a. Ensure radio ignition interference capacitor is located under proper coil mounting bolt.
   b. **Torque** coil mounting bolts to 53 inch lbs.
   c. Apply silicone brake caliper grease and dielectric compound No. D7AZ-19A331-A, or equivalent, to inside of each wire coil boot.

4.6L ENGINE

1. Remove air cleaner outlet tube.
2. Disconnect ignition coil.
3. Remove mounting bolt and ignition coil.
4. Reverse procedure to install, noting the following:
   a. Ensure ignition coil spring is correctly located inside boot and tip is not damaged.
   b. **Torque** mounting bolts to 89 inch lbs.

2005
4.0L ENGINE

1. Disconnect ignition coil electrical connector.
2. Disconnect six spark plug wires from ignition coil.
3. Remove four mounting bolts and ignition coil.
4. Reverse procedure to install. **Torque** mounting bolts to 53 inch lbs.

4.6L ENGINE

1. Disconnect ignition coil electrical connector.
2. Remove mounting bolts and ignition coil.
3. Reverse procedure to install, noting the following:
   a. Apply light film of suitable silicone brake caliper great and dielectric compound to inside of coil boots.
   b. **Torque** mounting bolts to 44 inch lbs.

IGNITION LOCK
REPLACE
2001-04
FUNCTIONING

1. Turn ignition to switch to Run position.
2. Remove ignition switch by depressing retaining pin with suitable drift punch in hole in upper steering column shroud under switch.
3. Reverse procedure to install. Ensure lock cylinder operates properly.

NON-FUNCTIONING

1. Remove driver's air bag module as outlined in "Passive Restraint Systems" chapter.
2. Remove and discard steering wheel mounting bolt.
3. Remove steering wheel using suitable puller tool.
4. Twist ignition switch lock cylinder cap with suitable locking-type pliers until it separates from ignition switch lock cylinder.
5. Center punch retaining pin with suitable small pilot punch through access hole in lower steering column shroud and drill it out with 1/8 inch diameter drill.
6. Drill down middle of key slot using 3/8 inch diameter bit approximately 1 3/4 inches until lock cylinder breaks loose.
7. Remove ignition switch lock cylinder.
8. Record positions of column lock gear, bearing and retainer.
9. Remove bearing retainer, steering column lock housing bearing, ignition switch lock cylinder and steering column lock gear.
10. Reverse procedures to install, noting the following:
    a. Repair steering column lock cylinder housing.
    b. Ensure components are properly aligned and oriented.
    c. Coat lock gear and housing with ignition lock grease No. F0AZ-19584-A, or equivalent.
    d. Install new steering wheel mounting bolt.
    e. **Torque** mounting bolt to 23–32 ft. lbs.

2005

1. Remove steering column cover.
2. Remove three mounting screws and lower steering column shroud.
3. Turn key to RUN position.
4. Insert suitable, small punch into hole and remove ignition lock cylinder.
5. Reverse procedure to install.

IGNITION SWITCH
REPLACE
2001-04

1. Remove mounting screws and steering column lower cover.

2. Remove mounting screws and instrument panel reinforcement.
3. Loosen mounting bolt and disconnect ignition switch electrical connector.
4. Ensure ignition switch is in OFF position.
5. Remove mounting screws and ignition switch.
6. Reverse procedure to install, noting the following:
   a. **Torque** ignition switch mounting screws to 53 inch lbs.
   b. **Torque** instrument panel reinforcement mounting screws to 80 inch lbs.
   c. **Torque** steering column lower cover mounting screws to 80 inch lbs.

2005

1. Disarm the supplemental restraint system as outlined under "Air Bag System Precautions" in front of this manual.
2. Remove upper steering column shroud by carefully pressing sides inward.
3. Remove three mounting screws and lower steering column shroud.
4. Disconnect ignition switch electrical connector, release two locking tabs and remove ignition switch.
5. Reverse procedure to install.

CLUTCH START SWITCH
REPLACE
2001-04

1. Disconnect clutch pedal position switch electrical connector.
2. Record switch's positioning.
3. Remove mounting bolt and switch.
4. Reverse procedure to install.

2005

1. Disconnect Clutch Pedal Position (CPP) switch electrical connector.
2. Release CPP switch from clutch pedal bracket.
3. Reverse procedure to install.

NEUTRAL SAFETY SWITCH
REPLACE

On these models the neutral safety switch is incorporated into the digital Transmission Range (TR) sensor.

1. Apply parking brake and place transmission in Neutral position.
2. Raise and support vehicle.
3. Disconnect TR sensor electrical connector.
4. Disconnect range selector cable.
5. Remove mounting bolts and TR sensor.
6. Reverse procedure to install, noting the following:
   a. Ensure shift lever shaft is in Neutral position.
   b. Align sensor slots using TR sensor

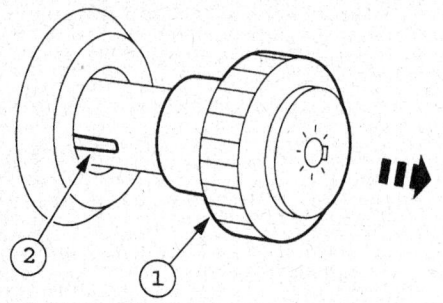

1. Knob
2. Slot

FM9019900384000X

Fig. 3 Headlamp switch knob replacement

alignment tool No. T97L-70010-A, or equivalent.
c. **Torque** sensor mounting bolts to 62–89 inch lbs.
d. Ensure starter cranks in Park or Neutral position, only.

HEADLAMP SWITCH
REPLACE

1. Pull headlamp switch to full ON position.
2. Pull and remove knob by inserting suitable thin tool into slot, **Fig. 3.**
3. Remove mounting screws and instrument cluster finish retaining panel.
4. Remove mounting screws and headlamp switch.
5. Disconnect headlamp switch electrical connector.
6. Reverse procedure to install.

STOP LIGHT SWITCH
REPLACE

1. Remove stop lamp switch linkage clip and retainer, **Fig. 4.**
2. Disconnect switch electrical connector and remove switch.
3. Reverse procedure to install.

MULTI-FUNCTION SWITCH
REPLACE
2001-04

1. Turn ignition to switch to Run position.
2. Remove ignition switch by depressing retaining pin with suitable drift punch in hole in upper steering column shroud under switch.
3. Remove tilt wheel handle.
4. Remove mounting screws, then the steering column upper and lower shrouds.
5. Remove multi-function switch mounting screws.
6. Disconnect electrical connectors and remove multi-function switch.
7. Reverse procedure to install. **Torque** multi-function switch mounting screws to 18–26 inch lbs.

2005

1. Remove steering wheel as outlined under "Steering Wheel, Replace."
2. Remove and discard steering wheel mounting bolt.
3. Remove steering wheel using suitable puller tool.
4. Remove upper steering column shroud by carefully pressing sides inward.
5. Remove three mounting screws and lower steering column shroud.
6. Disconnect four lower multifunction switch electrical connectors.
7. Disconnect upper multifunction switch electrical connector.
8. Remove four mounting screws and multifunction switch.
9. Reverse procedure to install.

STEERING WHEEL
REPLACE

1. Remove driver's air bag module as outlined in "Passive Restraint Systems" chapter.
2. Remove and discard steering wheel mounting bolt.
3. Remove steering wheel using suitable puller tool.
4. Reverse procedure to install, noting the following:
   a. Install new steering wheel mounting bolt.
   b. **On 2001–04 models, torque** mounting bolt to 23–32 ft. lbs.
   c. **On 2005 models, torque** mounting bolt to 43 ft. lbs.

INSTRUMENT CLUSTER
REPLACE
2001-04

1. Pull headlamp switch to full ON position.
2. Pull and remove knob by inserting suitable thin tool into slot, **Fig. 3.**
3. Remove mounting screws and instrument cluster finish retaining panel.
4. Remove mounting screws and cluster out.
5. Disconnect electrical connector.
6. Remove instrument cluster.
7. Reverse procedure to install.

2005

Prior to removal of the instrument cluster, upload the instrument cluster configuration information to a suitable diagnostic tool.
1. Disarm supplemental restraint system as outlined under "Air Bag System Precautions" in the front of this manual.
2. Remove instrument cluster finish panel.
3. Remove four mounting screws and instrument cluster, then disconnect electrical connector.
4. Reverse procedure to install.

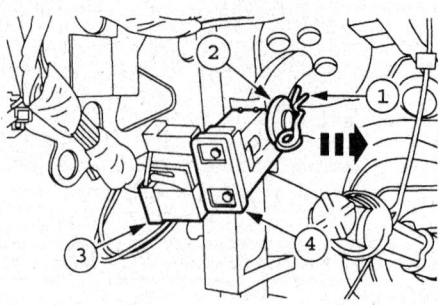

1. Linkage Clip
2. Retainer
3. Connector
4. Switch

FM9019900385000X

Fig. 4 Stop lamp switch replacement

RADIO
REPLACE

1. Remove instrument panel center finishing panel.
2. Remove mounting screws and radio.
3. Disconnect electrical connector and antenna lead-in cable.
4. Reverse procedure to install.

WIPER MOTOR
REPLACE
2001-04

The internal permanent magnets used in the windshield wiper motor are of a ceramic material. Care must be exercised in handling the motor to avoid damaging the magnets. **Do not strike or tap motor with a hammer or other object.**
1. Turn windshield wipers on. When blades reach full upright travel on glass, turn ignition switch Off.
2. Remove windshield wiper pivot arms and blades.
3. Remove cowl top vent grille.
4. Disconnect wiper motor adapter and connecting linkage clip from motor arm.
5. Remove linkage drive arm from windshield wiper motor.
6. Disconnect wiper motor electrical connector and remove motor to cowl mounting fasteners.
7. Remove wiper motor.
8. Reverse procedures to install. **Torque** wiper motor mounting screws to 10–12 ft. lbs.

2005

1. Remove two covers, two mounting nuts and two wiper pivot arms.
2. Remove four cowl vent screen pin-type retainers.
3. Remove right and lefthand cowl vent screen overlaps. Righthand screen overlaps left.
4. Remove three mounting bolts, windshield wiper mounting arm and pivot shaft.

5. Remove mounting bolt, then disconnect mounting arm and pivot shaft linkage from wiper motor output shaft.
6. Remove three mounting bolts and windshield wiper motor.
7. Reverse procedure to install, noting the following:
   a. **Torque** wiper motor mounting bolt to 11 ft. lbs.
   b. **Torque** arm mounting bolt to 13 ft. lbs. If reusing mounting bolt, apply suitable Threadlock to bolt.
   c. **Torque** windshield wiper mounting arm and pivot shaft mounting bolts to 62 inch lbs.

WIPER SWITCH
REPLACE
2001–04

1. Turn ignition to switch to Run position.
2. Remove ignition switch by depressing retaining pin with suitable drift punch in hole in upper steering column shroud under switch.
3. Remove tilt wheel handle.
4. Remove mounting screws, then the steering column upper and lower shrouds.
5. Remove multi-function switch mounting screws.
6. Disconnect electrical connectors and remove multi-function switch.
7. Reverse procedure to install. **Torque** multi-function switch mounting screws to 18–26 inch lbs.

2005

1. Remove two mounting screws, then the upper and lower steering column shrouds.
2. Remove two windshield wiper/washer switch mounting screws.
3. Disconnect electrical connector and remove windshield wiper/washer switch.
4. Reverse procedure to install.

WIPER TRANSMISSION
REPLACE
2001–04

1. Turn windshield wipers on. When blades reach full upright travel on glass, turn ignition Off.
2. Remove windshield wiper pivot arms and blades.
3. Remove cowl top vent grille.
4. Remove linkage drive arm from windshield wiper motor.
5. Lower hood, then remove mounting bolts and wiper transmission through righthand cowl chamber opening.
6. Reverse procedure to install, noting the following:
   a. Install retaining clip onto end of wiper transmission linkage.
   b. **Torque** transmission mounting bolts to 11 ft. lbs.
   c. Cycle wipers back to park position, then install arms and blades.

2005

1. Remove two covers, two mounting nuts and two wiper pivot arms.
2. Remove four cowl vent screen pin-type retainers.
3. Remove right and lefthand cowl vent screen overlaps. Righthand screen overlaps left.
4. Remove three mounting bolts, windshield wiper mounting arm and pivot shaft.
5. Reverse procedure to install. **Torque** windshield wiper mounting arm and pivot shaft mounting bolts to 62 inch lbs.

BLOWER MOTOR
REPLACE
2001–04

1. Disconnect jumper wire harness from main harness electrical connector.
2. Disconnect main harness at blower motor resistor.
3. Remove blower motor mounting screws.
4. Separate cover and motor.
5. Disconnect blower motor jumper harness.
6. Remove blower motor.
7. Reverse procedure to install.

2005

1. Disconnect blower motor electrical connector.
2. Remove three mounting screws and blower motor.
3. Remove clip and blower motor wheel.
4. Reverse procedure to install.

HEATER CORE
REPLACE
2001–04

1. Remove evaporator core housing as outlined under "Evaporator Core, Replace."
2. Remove foam sealing strip.
3. Remove mounting screws and heater core cover.
4. Remove heater core.
5. Reverse procedure to install.

2005

1. Recover refrigerant as outlined in "Air Conditioning" chapter.
2. Remove instrument panel as outlined in "Dash Panel Service" chapter.
3. Clamp off and disconnect heater core inlet and outlet hoses at core
4. Remove two nuts and disconnect evaporator core fitting.
5. Remove two exterior heater and evaporator core housing nuts at dash panel.
6. Disconnect antenna cable from heater and evaporator core housing.
7. Remove interior heater and evaporator core housing nut.

8. Remove heater and evaporator core housing.
9. Reverse procedure to install, noting the following:
   a. Install new O-ring seals.
   b. Lubricate refrigerant system with correct amount of suitable, clean PAG oil.
   c. **Torque** interior heater and evaporator core housing nut to 44 inch lbs.
   d. **Torque** exterior heater and evaporator core housing nuts to 62 inch lbs.
   e. Install new evaporator core O-ring seals and **torque** mounting nuts to 71 inch lbs.

EVAPORATOR CORE
REPLACE
2001–04

1. Recover refrigerant as outlined in "Air Conditioning" chapter.
2. Drain coolant into suitable container.
3. Remove instrument panel as outlined in "Dash Panel Service" chapter.
4. Place suitable container in heater water hose connections.
5. Disconnect heater hoses at underhood core fittings.
6. Disconnect vacuum connector near firewall.
7. Remove air conditioning accumulator.
8. Disconnect air conditioning liquid line.
9. Remove evaporator core housing nuts and screws at firewall.
10. Remove evaporator core housing bolts from inside passenger compartment.
11. Remove evaporator core housing.
12. Reverse procedure to install. **Torque** evaporator core housing bolts to 71 inch lbs.

2005

1. Recover refrigerant as outlined in "Air Conditioning" chapter.
2. Remove instrument panel as outline in "Dash Panel Service" chapter.
3. Clamp off and disconnect heater core inlet and outlet hoses at core
4. Remove two nuts and disconnect evaporator core fitting.
5. Remove two exterior heater and evaporator core housing nuts at dash panel.
6. Disconnect antenna cable from heater and evaporator core housing.
7. Remove interior heater and evaporator core housing nut.
8. Remove heater and evaporator core housing.
9. Reverse procedure to install, noting the following:
   a. Install new O-ring seals.
   b. Lubricate refrigerant system with correct amount of suitable, clean PAG oil.
   c. **Torque** interior heater and evaporator core housing nut to 44 inch lbs.
   d. **Torque** exterior heater and evaporator core housing nuts to 62 inch

lbs.
  e. Install new evaporator core O-ring seals and **torque** mounting nuts to 71 inch lbs.

TECHNICAL SERVICE BULLETINS

Repeated Heater Core Failure

On some of these models there may be repeated heater core leaks.

This condition may be caused by a chemical reaction (electrolysis).

To correct this condition, proceed as follows:

1. Place positive probe of suitable digital volt/ohm meter in engine coolant and negative probe on battery ground terminal.
2. Adjust engine to 2000 RPM.
3. If more than .4 volt is recorded, flush coolant and inspect voltage, again.
4. If voltage is still excessive, inspect body/battery grounds.
5. If condition still exists, add extra grounds to heater core and engine, as follows:
   a. Secure 16 gauge stranded copper wire to heater core inlet tube using suitable hose clamp.
   b. Secure other end of wire to existing body sheet metal fastener.
   c. Secure another extra ground between existing engine and body sheet metal fasteners.
   d. Ensure there is continuity between added grounds and battery ground terminal.
6. If condition still exists, install restrictor as follows:
   a. Cut line as close to engine block as possible.
   b. Install restrictor (part No. F1UZ-18D406-A) on inlet hose with arrow facing coolant flow direction (toward heater core).
   c. Secure with two suitable hose clamps.
7. Bleed cooling system trapped air as follows:
   a. Disconnect heater hose at right-hand front or rear of engine.
   b. Remove thermostat and housing.
   c. Fill engine with suitable coolant until mixture is seen at engine side heater hose connection.
   d. Connect heater hose, then install thermostat and housing.
   e. Fill degas bottle to coolant fill level mark.
   f. Fun engine to normal operating temperature.
   g. Select max heat and blower speeds.

3.8L Engine

NOTE: On Air Bag Equipped Models, Refer To "Air Bag System Precautions" Located In The Front Of This Manual For System Disarming & Arming Procedures.

NOTE: Refer To "Computer Relearn Procedures" Located In The Front Of This Manual When Battery Power To The Computer Has Been Interrupted.

NOTE: Prior To Performing Any Service Operations Listed In This Section, Consult The "Technical Service Bulletins" Section For Related Information.

INDEX

PRECAUTIONS

Air Bag Systems

Refer to "Air Bag System Precautions" in the front of this manual for system disarming and arming procedures.

Battery Ground Cable

Prior to service, disconnect battery ground cable and isolate as required.

Fuel System Pressure Relief

Fuel supply tubes will remain pressurized for long periods of time after engine shutdown. This pressure must be relieved before beginning fuel system service or personal injury and vehicle damage may occur. A valve is provided on the fuel injection supply manifold for this purpose.
1. Remove engine air cleaner.
2. Connect EFI/CFI fuel pressure gauge tool No. T80L-9974-B, or equivalent, to fuel pressure relief valve on fuel injection supply manifold.
3. Open manual valve on fuel pressure gauge tool to relieve fuel system pressure.

COMPRESSION PRESSURE

When inspecting cylinder compression, lowest cylinder must be within 75% of highest cylinder. Perform compression test with engine at normal operating temperature, spark plugs and air cleaner removed and the throttle propped wide open.

ENGINE MOUNT
REPLACE

Whenever self-locking mounting bolts and nuts are removed, they must be replaced with new self-locking bolts and nuts.
1. Remove fan shroud mounting screws and air tube from remote air cleaner.
2. Raise and support vehicle, then support engine using suitable jack and wood block placed below engine.
3. Remove insulator to front subframe through bolts, **Fig. 1.**
4. Disconnect shift linkage and raise engine enough to clear front subframe brackets.
5. Remove accessories and oil cooler line attaching clips from engine support brackets.
6. Remove mounting bolts, insulator and bracket.
7. Reverse procedure to install.

ENGINE
REPLACE

1. Recover air conditioning refrigerant as outlined in "Air Conditioning" chapter.
2. Drain coolant into suitable container.

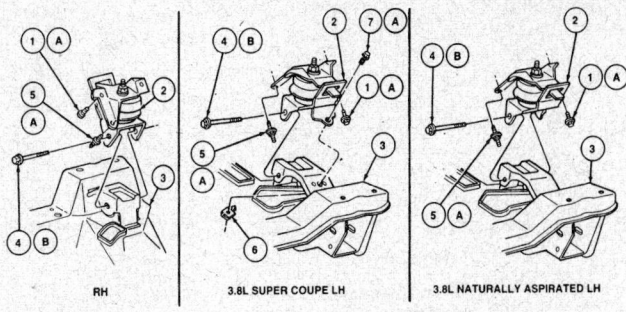

Item	Part Number	Description
1	N803098-S100	Bolt (2 Req'd)
2	6038	Front Engine Support Insulator
3	5C145	Front Sub-Frame
4	N805748-S36	Bolt
5	N805803-S36	Stud

Item	Part Number	Description
6	N805968-S36	U-Nut
7	N605918-S56	Bolt
A	—	Tighten to 34-47 N·m (25-35 Lb-Ft)
B	—	Tighten to 47-68 N·m (35-50 Lb-Ft)

FM1069100113000X

Fig. 1   Engine mount replacement

3. Relieve fuel system pressure as outlined under "Precautions."
4. Disconnect hood ground strap and underhood lamp electrical connector.
5. Mark hinge positions, then remove bolts and hood.
6. Disconnect vacuum hose near firewall.
7. Disconnect battery positive cable at alternator and alternator electrical connectors.
8. Disconnect power steering pump fluid lines and drain into suitable container.
9. Disconnect lower radiator hose at water pump.
10. Disconnect upper radiator hose at coolant outlet.
11. Remove coolant reservoir.
12. Disconnect accelerator cable.
13. Remove mounting bolt and position accelerator cable bracket aside.
14. Remove air cleaner and outlet tube.
15. Disconnect air conditioning manifold and tube.
16. Disconnect air conditioning compressor electrical connector.
17. Disconnect fuel supply line using fuel line disconnection set tool No. T90T-9550-S, or equivalent.
18. Disconnect vacuum hose at righthand rear corner of engine compartment.
19. Disconnect heater hoses at underhood core fittings and drain into suitable containers.
20. Disconnect 42-pin electrical connector at righthand rear corner of engine compartment and position wiring harness aside.
21. Disconnect vacuum tube and connector at rear of TBI.
22. Disconnect EVAP return tube.
23. Raise and support vehicle.
24. Remove ground cable nut.
25. Remove solenoid protective cap and wiring nuts. Position wiring aside.
26. Remove mounting bolts and starter motor.
27. Disconnect electrical connectors at lefthand and righthand O2 sensors.
28. Remove dual converter mounting nuts.
29. Remove lefthand and righthand exhaust manifold flange nuts.
30. Remove Y-pipe.

31. Disconnect engine ground strap.
32. Drain engine oil into suitable container.
33. **On models equipped with automatic transmission,** remove inspection cover and four torque converter to flexplate nuts. Discard nuts.
34. **On all models,** remove bellhousing upper and lower bolts.
35. **On models equipped with automatic transmission,** remove transmission fluid filler tube.
36. **On all models,** remove lefthand and righthand engine mount nuts.
37. Lower vehicle.
38. Support transmission using suitable floor jack and block of wood.
39. Install engine lifting brackets tool No. D94L-6001-A, or equivalent.
40. Connect spreader bar tool No. D93L-6001-A3, or equivalent, to brackets.
41. Remove engine, then mount on suitable stand using suitable crane or skyhook.
42. Reverse procedure to install, noting the following:
   a. **On models equipped with automatic transmission,** install four new torque converter to flexplate nuts.
   b. **On all models,** install oil pan drain plug and close radiator petcock.

INTAKE MANIFOLD
REPLACE

Upper

1. Remove air cleaner outlet tube.
2. Disconnect vacuum tube and Idle Air Control (IAC) solenoid, **Fig. 2.**
3. Disconnect Throttle Position (TP) sensor and EVAP return tube.
4. Disconnect accelerator cable from TBI and position aside.
5. Remove solenoid bracket bolts, **Fig. 3.**
6. Disconnect PCV tube and vacuum tubes.
7. Remove mounting bolts and position ignition coil aside.
8. Record remove upper intake manifold mounting bolts' locations.

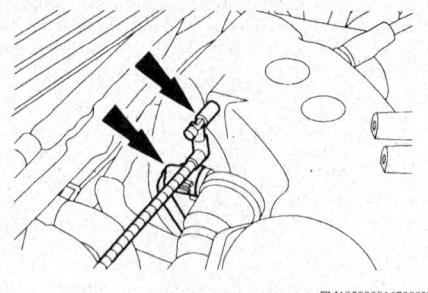

Fig. 2 Vacuum tube at upper intake manifold replacement

FM1059900167000X

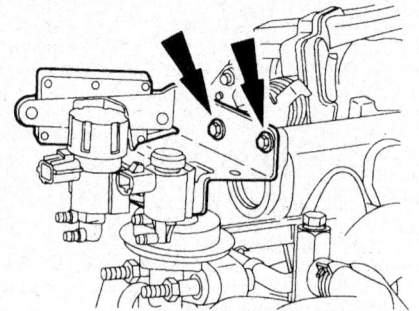

FM1059900168000X

Fig. 3 Solenoid bracket replacement

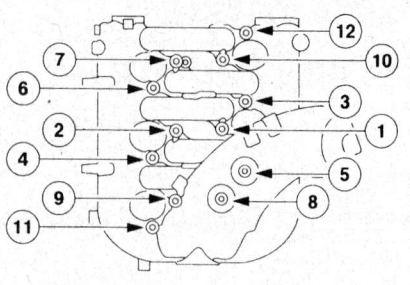

FM1059900169000X

Fig. 4 Upper intake manifold bolt tightening sequence

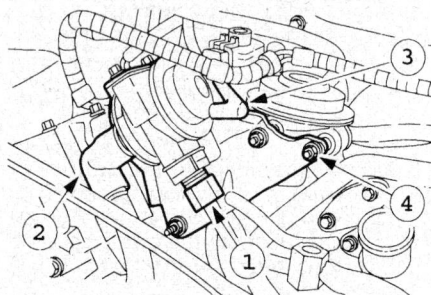

1. Tube Nut
2. Air Tube
3. Vacuum Tube
4. Nut

FM1059900170000X

Fig. 5 Exhaust air supply valve replacement

9. Remove upper intake manifold. Discard gasket.
10. Reverse procedure to install, noting the following:
    a. Install new upper to lower intake manifold gasket.
    b. Ensure mounting bolts are in original proper locations.
    c. **Torque** manifold mounting bolts in sequence to 89 inch lbs., **Fig. 4.**
    d. Final tighten bolts an additional 90° in sequence.

Lower

1. Drain coolant into suitable container.
2. Remove upper intake manifold as outlined under "Upper."
3. Relieve fuel system pressure as outlined under "Precautions."
4. Disconnect fuel pressure sensor electrical connector.
5. Disconnect fuel injection supply manifold.
6. Disconnect engine wiring harness and position it aside.
7. Disconnect heater hose at rear of engine.
8. Position spark plug wire loom aside and remove stud bolt.
9. Disconnect EGR valve vacuum tube.
10. **On models equipped with exhaust air supply valve,** proceed as follows:
    a. Loosen tube nut, **Fig. 5.**
    b. Disconnect air tube.
    c. Disconnect vacuum tube.
    d. Remove nuts.

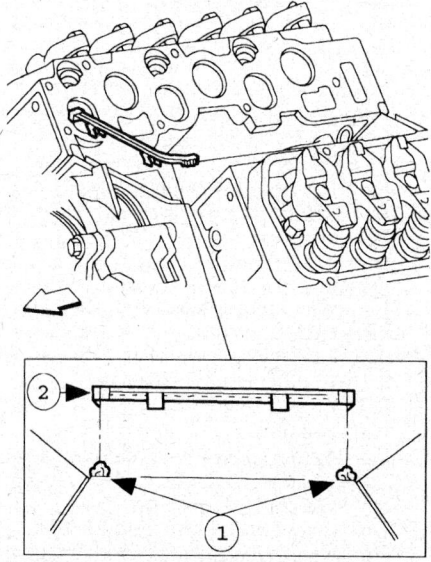

1. Sealant Beads
2. End Seals

FM1059900171000X

Fig. 6 Lower intake manifold end seals bead locations

11. **On all models,** loosen EGR hex tube nut and disconnect tube.
12. Disconnect radiator upper hose and bypass hose.
13. Disconnect electrical connectors.
14. Remove bypass tube bolt.
15. Remove mounting bolts, then the fuel injection supply manifold and injectors.
16. Record lower intake manifold mounting bolts' locations.
17. Remove mounting bolts and lower intake manifold. Discard gaskets and end seals.
18. Reverse procedure to install, noting the following:
    a. Apply beads of silicone gasket sealant No. F7AZ-19554-EA, or equivalent, to end seal mounting points, **Fig. 6.**
    b. Apply beads of sealant to lower intake manifold mounting locations, **Fig. 7.**
    c. **Install lower intake manifold within four minutes of sealant application.**
    d. Ensure manifold mounting bolts are installed in original locations.

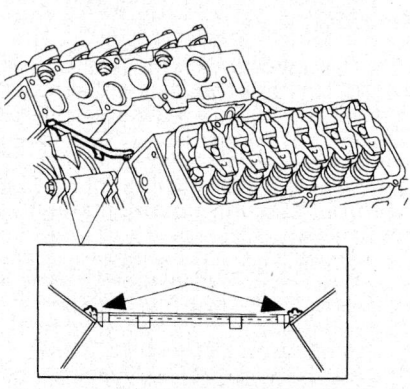

FM1059900172000X

Fig. 7 Lower intake manifold sealant bead locations

e. **Torque** manifold mounting bolts in sequence to 44 inch lbs., **Fig. 8.**
f. **Torque** mounting bolts to 89 inch lbs., in sequence.

EXHAUST MANIFOLD

REPLACE

Lefthand

1. Raise and support vehicle.
2. Remove lefthand manifold flange nuts and lower vehicle.
3. Remove engine oil dipstick tube.
4. **On models equipped with exhaust air supply valve,** loosen tube nut at front of exhaust manifold.
5. **On all models,** remove mounting nuts and exhaust manifold. Discard gasket.
6. Reverse procedure to install, noting the following:
    a. Install new exhaust manifold gasket.
    b. **Torque** exhaust manifold mounting nuts in sequence to 24 ft. lbs., **Fig. 9.**

Righthand

1. Remove air cleaner outlet tube.
2. Disconnect two TBI hoses, **Fig. 10.**
3. **On models equipped with exhaust air supply valve,** proceed as follows:
    a. Loosen tube nut, **Fig. 5.**
    b. Disconnect air tube.
    c. Disconnect vacuum tube.
    d. Remove nuts and valve.

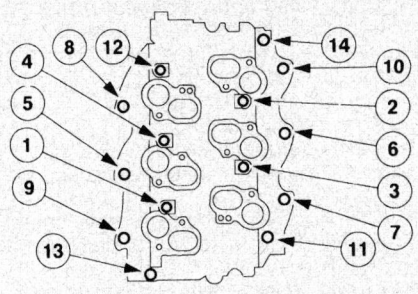

Fig. 8 Lower intake manifold bolt tightening sequence

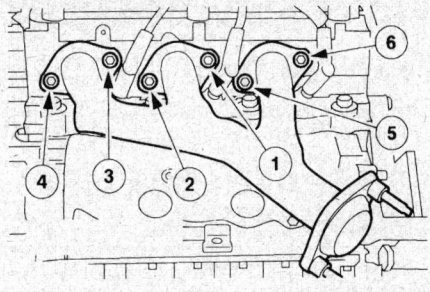

Fig. 9 Lefthand exhaust manifold tightening sequence

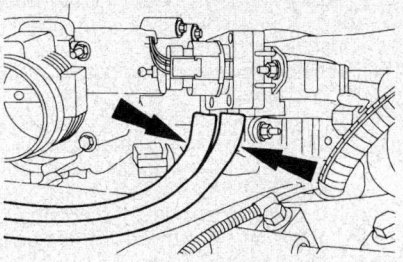

Fig. 10 TBI hose replacement

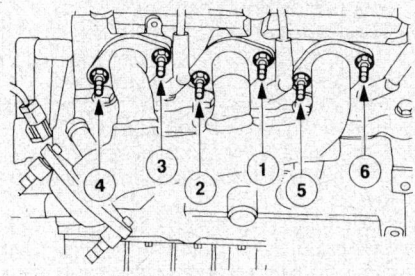

Fig. 11 Righthand exhaust manifold tightening sequence

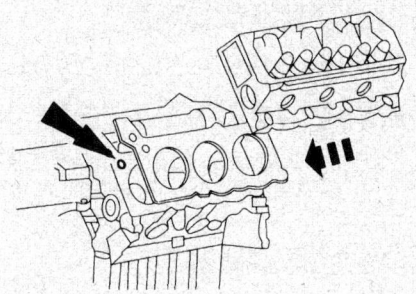

Fig. 12 Cylinder head gasket orientation

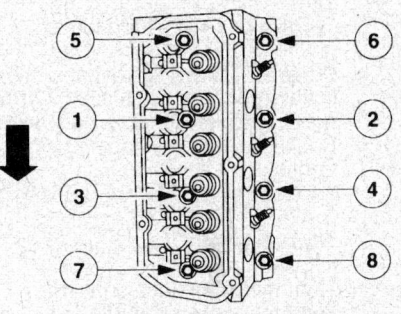

Fig. 13 Cylinder head bolt tightening sequence

4. **On all models,** loosen EGR hex tube nut, disconnect vacuum lines and remove tube.
5. Raise and support vehicle.
6. Remove righthand manifold flange nuts and lower vehicle.
7. **On models equipped with exhaust air supply valve,** loosen tube nut at front of righthand exhaust manifold.
8. **On all models,** remove mounting nuts and manifold. Discard gasket.
9. Reverse procedure to install, noting the following:
   a. Install new exhaust manifold gasket.
   b. **Torque** exhaust manifold mounting nuts in sequence to 24 ft. lbs., **Fig. 11.**

CYLINDER HEAD

REPLACE

Lefthand

1. Drain coolant into suitable container.
2. Remove exhaust manifold as outlined under "Exhaust Manifold, Replace."
3. Remove lower intake manifold as outlined under "Intake Manifold, Replace."
4. Mark locations and position spark plug wires aside.
5. Disconnect PCV valve.
6. Remove mounting bolts and position ignition coil aside.
7. Remove lefthand valve cover. Discard gasket.
8. Keeping in order for installation in original position, remove mounting bolts, rocker arms and pushrods.
9. Remove serpentine belt.
10. Remove power steering pump pulley

using pulley remover tool No. T69L-10300-B, or equivalent.
11. Remove power steering pump and alternator mounting brackets.
12. Remove exhaust manifold mounting studs.
13. Record long and short cylinder head bolts' locations.
14. Remove and discard cylinder head bolts.
15. Remove cylinder head.
16. Reverse procedure to install, noting the following:
   a. Install new head gaskets with small hole to front of engine, **Fig. 12.**
   b. Lubricate new cylinder head bolts with clean 5W-30 engine oil.
   c. Place cylinder head in position.
   d. Install new long cylinder head bolts, then the short ones.
   e. **Torque** cylinder head bolts in sequence to 15 ft. lbs., **Fig. 13.**
   f. **Torque** bolts in sequence to 30 ft. lbs.
   g. **Torque** bolts in sequence to 37 ft. lbs.
   h. **Perform following cylinder head bolt steps on each bolt before moving to next bolt in sequence.**
   i. Back off cylinder head bolts 2–3 turns
   j. **Torque** long bolt to 33 ft. lbs.
   k. **Torque** short bolt to 18 ft. lbs.
   l. Tighten bolt an additional 180°.
   m. **Torque** rocker arm bolts to 44 inch lbs.
   n. **Torque** arm bolts to 26 ft. lbs.
   o. Install TBI with new mounting gasket.
   p. **Torque** TBI mounting nuts and bolts to 80 inch lbs.

q. Tighten nuts and bolts an additional 85–90°.

Righthand

1. Drain coolant into suitable container.
2. Remove exhaust manifold as outlined under "Exhaust Manifold, Replace."
3. Remove lower intake manifold as outlined under "Intake Manifold, Replace."
4. Disconnect crankcase ventilation hose.
5. Disconnect transducer vacuum hoses.
6. **On models equipped with exhaust air supply valve** proceed as follows:
   a. Loosen tube nut.
   b. Disconnect air and vacuum tubes.
   c. Remove nuts valve.
7. **On all models,** disconnect and remove EGR tube.
8. Mark locations and position spark plug wires aside.
9. Remove air cleaner outlet tube.
10. Disconnect throttle and speed control cables.
11. Remove mounting nuts, bolts and TBI. Discard gasket.
12. Remove righthand valve cover. Discard gasket.
13. Remove serpentine belt.
14. Recover air conditioning refrigerant as outlined in "Air Conditioning" chapter.
15. Disconnect air conditioning manifold and tube.
16. Disconnect air conditioning compressor clutch electrical connector.
17. Remove air conditioning compressor mounting bracket.
18. Remove exhaust manifold mounting studs.
19. Record long and short cylinder head bolts' locations.

20. Remove and discard cylinder head bolts.
21. Remove cylinder head.
22. Reverse procedure to install, noting the following:
   a. Install new head gaskets with small hole to front of engine, **Fig. 12.**
   b. Lubricate new cylinder head bolts with clean 5W-30 engine oil.
   c. Place cylinder head in position.
   d. Install new long cylinder head bolts, then the short ones.
   e. **Torque** cylinder head bolts in sequence to 15 ft. lbs. **Fig. 13.**
   f. **Torque** bolts in sequence to 30 ft. lbs.
   g. **Torque** bolts in sequence to 37 ft. lbs.
   h. **Perform following cylinder head bolt steps on each bolt before moving to next bolt in sequence.**
   i. Back off cylinder head bolts 2–3 turns.
   j. **Torque** long bolt in sequence to 33 ft. lbs.
   k. **Torque** short bolt in sequence to 18 ft. lbs.
   l. Tighten bolt an additional 180°.
   m. **Torque** rocker arm bolts to 44 inch lbs.
   n. **Torque** bolts to 26 ft. lbs.
   o. Install TBI with new mounting gasket.
   p. **Torque** TBI mounting nuts and bolts to 80 inch lbs.
   q. Tighten nuts and bolts an additional 85–90°.

VALVE COVER
REPLACE

Lefthand

1. Mark and position spark plug wires aside.
2. Disconnect PCV valve.
3. Remove mounting bolts and position ignition coil aside.
4. Remove cover and discard gasket.
5. Reverse procedure to install.

Righthand

1. Mark and position spark plug wires aside.
2. Disconnect crankcase ventilation hose.
3. Disconnect transducer vacuum hoses.
4. **On models equipped with exhaust air supply valve,** proceed as follows:
   a. Loosen tube nut.
   b. Disconnect air and vacuum tubes.
   c. Remove nuts and valve.
5. **On all models,** disconnect and remove EGR tube.
6. Remove air cleaner outlet tube.
7. Disconnect throttle and speed control cables.
8. Remove mounting nuts, bolts and TBI. Discard gasket.
9. Remove cover and discard gasket.
10. Reverse procedure to install.

VALVE ARRANGEMENT
Front To Rear

Righthand Side ....I-E-I-E-I-E
Lefthand Side ....E-I-E-I-E-I

CAMSHAFT LOBE LIFT SPECIFICATIONS

Engine	Intake, Inch	Exhaust, Inch
3.8L	.257	.259

VALVE CLEARANCE SPECIFICATIONS

Correct valve clearance is .09–.19 inch.

VALVE ADJUSTMENT

This engine is equipped with hydraulic valve lash adjusters. No adjustment is required.

ROCKER ARMS
Removal

1. Remove valve covers.
2. Remove seat mounting bolts and rocker arms.

Installation

1. Lubricate rocker arms with engine assembly lubricant D9AZ-19579-D, or equivalent.
2. **Rocker arm seats must be fully seated in cylinder head and pushrods must be seated in rocker arm sockets prior to final tightening.**
3. Rotate crankshaft until valve tappet rests onto heel (base circle) of camshaft lobe.
4. Position rocker arms over pushrods.
5. Install rocker arm seats.
6. Tighten rocker arm seat mounting bolts.
7. Repeat procedure for each rocket arm.
8. Final tighten with camshaft in any position.
9. Install valve cover.

VALVE GUIDES

Valve guides consist of holes bored in the cylinder head. For service the guide holes can be reamed oversize to accommodate valves with oversize stems of .015 and .030 inch.

HYDRAULIC LIFTERS
REPLACE

Before replacing a lifter for noisy operation, ensure the noise is not caused by improper valve to rocker arm clearance or by worn rocker arms or pushrods.

Removal

1. Disconnect ignition wires at spark plugs using spark plug wire remover tool No. T74P-666-A, or equivalent.
2. Remove ignition wire routing clips from studs on valve cover mounting bolts. Lay ignition wires with routing clips toward front of engine.
3. Remove upper intake manifold as outlined under "Intake Manifold, Replace."
4. Remove valve covers and lower intake manifold as outlined under "Intake Manifold, Replace."
5. Loosen rocker arms seat mounting bolt sufficiently to allow rocker arm to be lifted off pushrod and rotated to one side.
6. Remove pushrods and mark for installation in original positions.
7. Remove four bolts holding two tappet guide plates and retainers in place (bolts are held captive in retainers).
8. Remove six valve tappet guide plates from adjacent valve tappets.
9. Remove lifters using suitable magnet and mark for installation in original positions.
10. If lift is stuck in bores because excessive varnish or gum deposits, rotate it back and forth using suitable claw-type tool.

Installation

1. Lean cylinder head and valve sealing surfaces using suitable solvent.
2. Lightly oil bolts and stud threads before installation, except those specifying special sealant.
3. Lubricate each lift and bore with engine assembly lubricant No. D9AZ-19579-D, or equivalent.
4. Install each lifer in bore from which it was removed.
5. If new lifters are being installed, inspect for free fit in bore.
6. Align flats on side of lifter and install six valve tappet guide plates between adjacent valve lifters (ensure word UP is showing).
7. Install two tappet guide plates and retainers, then tighten four captive bolts.
8. Dip each push rod end in engine assembly lubricant No. D9AZ-19579-D, or equivalent.
9. Install pushrods in original positions.
10. Lubricate rocker arms with engine assembly lubricant No. D9AZ-19579-D, or equivalent.
11. **Rocker arm seats must be fully seated in cylinder heads and pushrods must be seated in rocker arm sockets prior to final tightening.**
12. Rotate crankshaft until valve tappet rests onto heel (base circle) of camshaft lobe.
13. Position rocker arms over push rods.
14. Tighten rocker arm seat mounting bolts.
15. Repeat procedure for each rocket arm.
16. Final tighten with camshaft in any position.
17. Tighten rocker arm seat mounting bolts.
18. Repeat procedure for each rocket arm.
19. Final tighten with camshaft in any position.

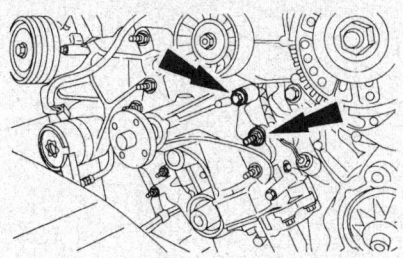

Fig. 14 Front cover capscrew location

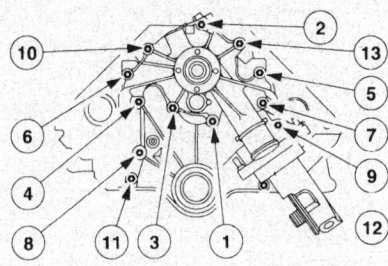

Fig. 17 Front cover bolt tightening sequence

20. Install lower intake manifold.
21. Install upper intake manifold.
22. Install routing clips and connect ignition wires to spark plugs.

FRONT COVER
REPLACE

1. Drain coolant into suitable container.
2. Remove serpentine belt.
3. Raise and support vehicle.
4. Rotate crankshaft pulley in engine's normal running direction until piston No. 1 reaches TDC mark.
5. Remove bolt and pulley using crankshaft pulley remover tool Nos. T58P-6316-D and T82L-6316-B, or equivalents.
6. Remove bolts and water pump pulley.
7. Remove power steering pump and bracket with hoses intact. Position pump aside.
8. Loosen nut and disconnect EGR valve tube.
9. Disconnect upper radiator and bypass hoses above front cover.
10. Disconnect connector, then remove mounting bolts and Camshaft Position (CMP) sensor.
11. Remove heater water outlet tube.
12. Ensure piston No. 1 is still at TDC.
13. Remove camshaft synchronizer mounting bolt, washer and sensor. **Oil pump intermediate shaft should be removed with synchronizer.**
14. Disconnect radiator lower hose at water pump.
15. Disconnect crankshaft position (CKP) sensor.
16. Remove engine front wiring harness pin-style retainer.
17. Record locations, types and sizes of

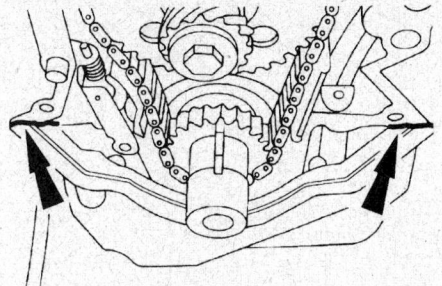

Fig. 15 Sealant application before gasket installation

front cover mounting bolts, nuts and screws. Pay attention to hidden cap screw, **Fig. 14.**
18. Slide front cover off alignment dowels. Discard gasket.
19. Reverse procedure to install, noting the following:
    a. Ensure gasket surfaces are clean and flat.
    b. Before installing front cover gasket, apply small portion of silicone gasket sealant No. F7AZ-19554-EA, or equivalent, **Fig. 15.**
    c. Install new front cover gasket.
    d. After installing front cover gasket, apply silicone gasket sealant to top of oil pan surface, **Fig. 16.**
    e. Install cover mounting bolts are in original positions.
    f. **Torque** cover mounting bolt No. 12 to 89 inch lbs., and remaining bolts in sequence to 18 ft. lbs., **Fig. 17.**
    g. Coat camshaft synchronizer gear with clean 10W-30 engine oil.
    h. Install synchro positioning tool No. 303-630, or equivalent, by rotating tool until it engages synchronizer housing notch and armature.
    i. Install synchronizer housing with tool's arrow at 54° from engine centerline, **Fig. 18.**

TIMING CHAIN
REPLACE

The front cover contains the oil pump gears and the water pump. If a new front cover is to be installed, remove water pump and oil pump gears from old front cover.

Removal

1. Remove front cover as outlined under "Front Cover, Replace."
2. Remove mounting bolt and camshaft position sensor drive gear.
3. Rotate crankshaft until timing marks and keyways align, **Fig. 19.**
4. Compress timing chain tensioner and install suitable retaining pin.
5. Remove camshaft sprocket, crankshaft sprocket and timing chain as an assembly.
6. Remove mounting bolts and timing chain tensioner.

Installation

1. Install timing chain tensioner.

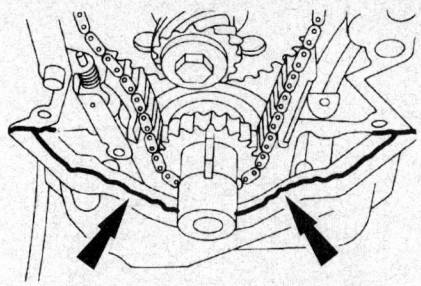

Fig. 16 Sealant application gasket installation

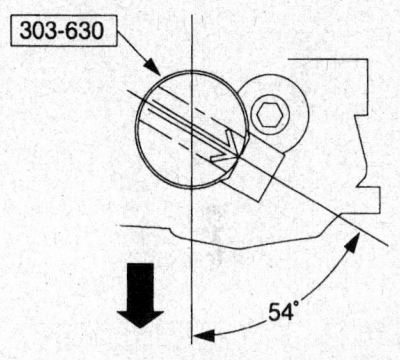

Fig. 18 Camshaft synchronizer installation

2. Rotate crankshaft so piston No. 1 is at TDC and key is at 12 o'clock position, **Fig. 20.**
3. Turn camshaft sprocket so timing mark is on bottom of balance shaft, **Fig. 21.**
4. Install timing chain, camshaft sprocket and crankshaft sprocket.
5. Ensure timing marks and keyways are aligned, **Fig. 19.**
6. Install camshaft position sensor drive gear.
7. Remove retaining pin from timing chain tensioner.
8. Install front cover as outlined under "Front Cover, Replace."

CAMSHAFT
REPLACE

1. Remove lifter as outlined under "Hydraulic Lifter, Replace."
2. Remove timing chain as outlined under "Timing Chain, Replace."
3. Remove radiator fan and shroud.
4. Remove camshaft key and engine balance shaft drive gear.
5. Remove mounting bolts and camshaft thrust plate.
6. Remove spacer and camshaft.
7. Reverse procedure to install. Lubricate camshaft with clean engine oil.

PISTON & ROD ASSEMBLY

When installed, piston and rod should

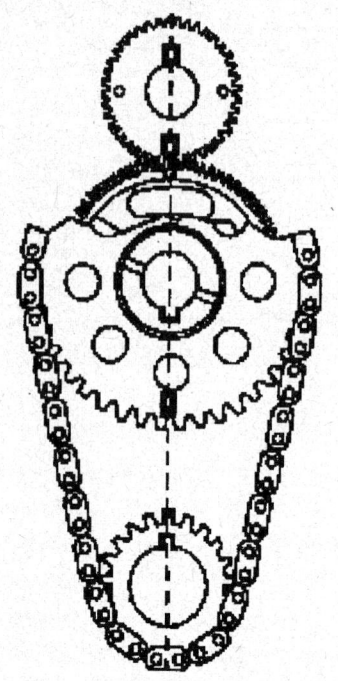

Fig. 19   Timing chain alignment marks

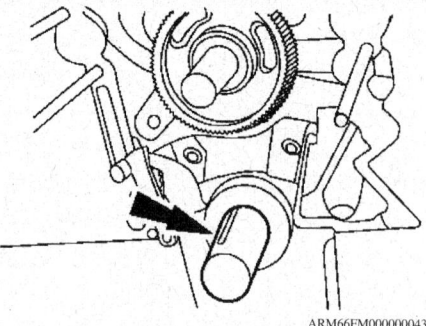

Fig. 20   Crankshaft key alignment

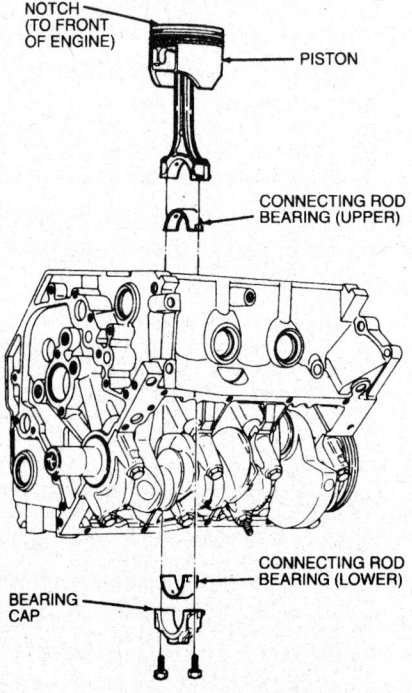

Fig. 22   Piston & rod assembly

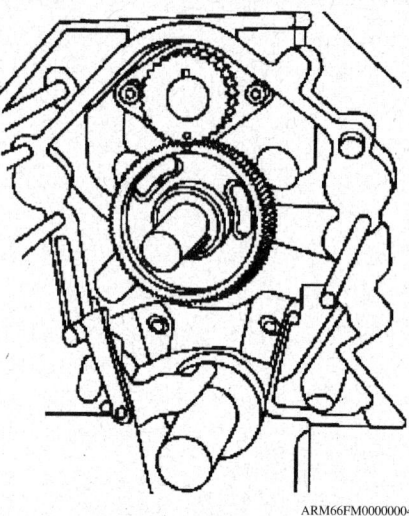

Fig. 21   Camshaft timing mark alignment

have the notch or arrow in piston head toward front of engine, **Fig. 22.** Side clearance between connecting rods at each crankshaft journal should be .0047–.0193 inch.

PISTONS, PINS & RINGS

Pistons are available in standard sizes and oversizes of .003, .020, .030 and .040 inch. Piston rings are available in standard sizes and oversizes of .020, .030 and .040 inch. Piston pins are available in standard size and oversizes of .001 and .002 inch.

MAIN & ROD BEARINGS

Main and rod bearings are available in standard sizes and undersizes of .001, .002, .010, .020 and .030 inch.

CRANKSHAFT REAR OIL SEAL

REPLACE

Removal

1. Remove transmission as outlined in **MOTOR's "Domestic Transmission Manual, In-Vehicle Service."**
2. Remove crankshaft rear oil seal using crankshaft rear seal remover tool No. T95T-6701-AR, or equivalent.

Installation

1. Lubricate new seal with clean engine oil.

2. Install crankshaft rear oil seal using crankshaft rear oil seal installation tool No. T95P-6701-EH, or equivalent.
3. Install transmission as outlined in **MOTOR's "Domestic Transmission Manual, In-Vehicle Service."**

OIL PAN

REPLACE

1. Remove air cleaner outlet tube.
2. Remove radiator upper sight shield and coolant reservoir.
3. Raise and support vehicle using engine lift bracket tool set No. D94L-6001-A and engine support tool No. 303-F072, or equivalents, and suitable hoist.
4. Remove lefthand and righthand engine mount nuts, then lower vehicle.
5. Raise engine with engine support, then raise and support vehicle.
6. Drain engine oil into suitable oil pan.
7. Remove solenoid protective cap and wiring nuts. Position wiring aside.
8. Remove mounting bolts and starter motor.

9. Remove ground cable nut.
10. Position wiring harness bracket aside.
11. Remove bellhousing lower bolts.
12. Remove oil pan bolts.
13. Support front subframe with suitable jack.
14. Remove four lower and two upper front subframe bolts.
15. Loosen two forward front subframe bolts.
16. Lower front subframe.
17. Remove oil pan. Empty residual oil into suitable container.
18. Reverse procedure to install, noting the following:
    a. Apply silicone gasket sealant No. F7AZ-19554-EA, or equivalent, to oil pan and block sealing surfaces, **Fig. 23. Assembly must occur within 15 minutes of sealer application.**
    b. Install oil and loosely install bolts.
    c. **Torque** oil pan mounting bolts in sequence to 44 inch lbs., **Fig. 24.**
    d. **Torque** mounting bolts in sequence to 89 inch lbs.

OIL PUMP

REPLACE

This procedure has been revised by a Technical Service Bulletin.

Some 2001 models built between Nov. 27, 2000, and May 30, 2001, may be equipped with a new Liquid Injection Sealing (LIS) oil pump. This oil pump cannot be repaired and must be replaced with suitable oil pump and O-ring.

1. Raise and support vehicle.
2. Drain engine oil into suitable container.
3. Remove engine oil filter.
4. Remove oil pump cover, mounting bolts and filter pad housing.
5. Separate oil pump drive and driven gears from cover. Discard O-ring.
6. Measure warpage across oil pump cover and front cover mounting surfaces, **Fig. 25.** If surface is warped more than .0016 inch, replace oil pump cover or front cover.

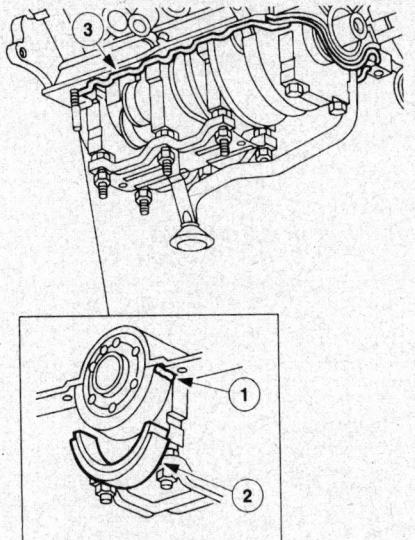

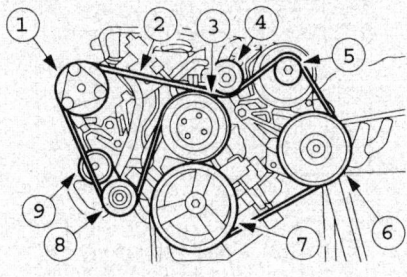

Fig. 23 Oil pan sealant locations

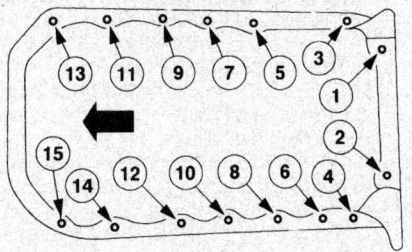

Fig. 24 Oil pan bolt tightening sequence

Refer to "Oil Pump, Replace" for procedure.

SERPENTINE DRIVE BELT

Conditions requiring belt replacement are excessive wear, rib chunk-out, severe glazing and frayed cords. Replace any belt exhibiting any one of these conditions. Cracks on rib side of a belt are considered acceptable.

If the belt has chunks missing from its ribs, it should be replaced. If two or more adjacent ribs have lost sections ½ inch or longer, or if missing chunks are creating a noise or vibration condition, replace the belt.

Belt Routing

Refer to **Fig. 26** for serpentine drive belt routing.

Belt Replacement

1. Lift or rotate automatic tensioner.
2. Remove belt.
3. Install new belt over pulleys. Ensure V-grooves make proper contact with pulley.
4. Rotate tensioner over belt.

COOLING SYSTEM BLEED

1. Remove vent plug, **Fig. 27**.
2. Fill radiator completely and install radiator cap.
3. Fill coolant reservoir and degas bottle to full cold mark.
4. Set heater control to full hot, high fan and set controls so air vents from dash vents.
5. Start and operate engine until fully warmed up while observing water temperature gauge as follows:
   a. If system is functioning properly, temperature will indicate normal and hot air will be felt at dash outlets.
   b. If system is not functioning properly, temperature gauge will not read and/or no hot air will be felt at dash vents.
6. If system is not functioning properly, allow engine to cool and repeat procedure.

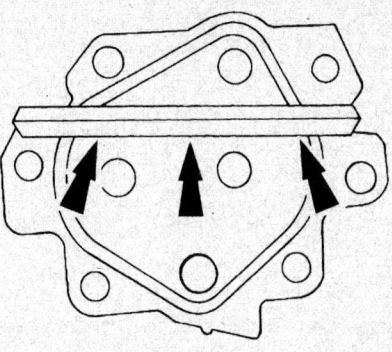

Fig. 25 Oil pump cover & front cover surface inspections

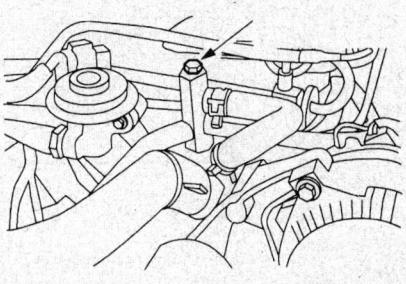

Fig. 27 Cooling system vent plug

7. If system is functioning properly, allow engine to cool and fill coolant reservoir to full cold mark.
8. Install vent plug.

THERMOSTAT
REPLACE

1. Partially drain cooling system into suitable container.
2. Disconnect upper radiator hose at thermostat housing.
3. Remove two mounting bolts, housing and gaskets.
4. Reverse procedure to install.

WATER PUMP
REPLACE

1. Drain coolant into suitable container.
2. Loosen water pump pulley bolts.
3. Remove serpentine belt.
4. Remove power steering pump pulley using pulley remover tool No. T69L-10300-B, or equivalent.
5. Remove bolts and water pump pulley.
6. Remove mounting bolts and position power steering pump aside with hoses attached.
7. Remove mounting bolts and power steering pump mounting bracket.
8. Disconnect radiator lower hose at water pump.
9. Remove mounting bolts and position power steering fluid reservoir aside with hoses attached.
10. Disconnect camshaft position (CMP) sensor electrical connector.
11. Remove mounting bolt and CMP sensor.

1. Air Conditioning Compressor
2. Belt
3. Water Pump
4. Idler
5. Alternator
6. Power Steering Pump
7. Crankshaft
8. Tensioner Pulley
9. Tensioner

Fig. 26 Serpentine drive belt routing

7. Remove front cover as outlined under "Front Cover, Replace."
8. Reverse procedure to install, noting the following:
   a. Clean components in suitable solvent.
   b. Lubricate oil pump components with clean 5W-30 engine oil.
   c. Assemble pressure relief valve ball and spring with new plug.

OIL PUMP SERVICE

This procedure has been revised by a Technical Service Bulletin.

Some 2001 models built between Nov. 27, 2000, and May 30, 2001, may be equipped with a new Liquid Injection Sealing (LIS) oil pump. The LIS oil pump has a blue paint stripe along righthand edge when viewed from above. This oil pump cannot be repaired and must be replaced with suitable oil pump and O-ring.

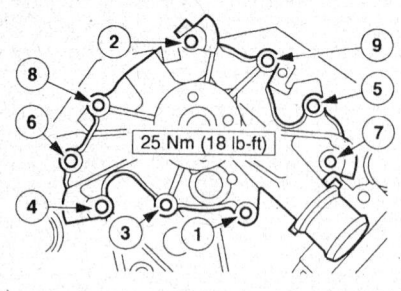

FM1069901053000X

Fig. 28   Water pump tightening sequence

12. Remove stud, bolts and nuts and water pump.
13. Reverse procedure to install, noting the following:
    a. Install new water pump gasket.
    b. Tighten stud, bolts and nuts in sequence to 18 ft. lbs., **Fig. 28.**

RADIATOR

REPLACE

1. Drain radiator and degas bottle coolant into suitable container.
2. Disconnect cooling fan motor electrical connector and separate fan harness from shroud.
3. Remove fan shroud lefthand and righthand mounting bolts.
4. Remove cooling fan, motor and shroud.
5. Remove radiator sight shield.
6. Disconnect radiator upper hose at radiator.
7. **On models equipped with automatic transmission,** remove lower and upper cooler tube fittings.
8. **On all models,** raise and support vehicle.
9. Disconnect radiator lower hose at radiator and lower vehicle.
10. Remove supports and radiator.
11. Reverse procedure to install.

FUEL PUMP

REPLACE

1. Relieve fuel pressure as outlined under "Precautions."
2. Drain fuel tank into suitable container.
3. Raise and support vehicle.
4. Mark lines to be installed in original positions.
5. Disconnect and cap fuel tank fuel and vent lines.

6. Remove exhaust pipe and shield to gain access to fuel tank.
7. Mark electrical connections to be installed in original positions.
8. Disconnect electrical connectors from fuel sender and pump.
9. Disconnect fuel filler tube.
10. Remove support straps and fuel tank.
11. Remove fuel pump by rotating lock ring counterclockwise using fuel tank sender wrench No. T74P-9275-A, or equivalent, **Fig. 29.**
12. Reverse procedure to install.

FUEL FILTER

REPLACE

1. Relieve fuel system pressure as outlined under "Precautions."
2. Raise and support vehicle.
3. Remove push connect fittings at both ends of filter.
4. Remove fuel filter from bracket by loosening worm gear clamp. Record direction of flow arrow as installed in bracket to ensure proper direction of fuel flow through replacement filter.
5. Reverse procedure to install.

TECHNICAL SERVICE BULLETINS

Fuel Pump Whining/ Buzzing Through Radio Speaker

2001

On some of these models there may be a whining or buzzing in speakers.

This condition may be caused by fuel pump electrical noise.

To correct this condition install an electronic noise Radio Frequency Interference (RFI) filter (part No. F1PZ-18B925-A) on fuel pump inside fuel tank, as follows:
1. Remove fuel pump sender from fuel tank as outlined under "Fuel Pump, Replace."
2. Cut fuel pump wires three inches from flange. Discard wires.
3. Connect RFI filter connectors to fuel pump spade terminal.
4. Cut and solder both RFI filter red and black wires to flange red and black wires.
5. Install suitable heat shrink tubing over solder connectors.

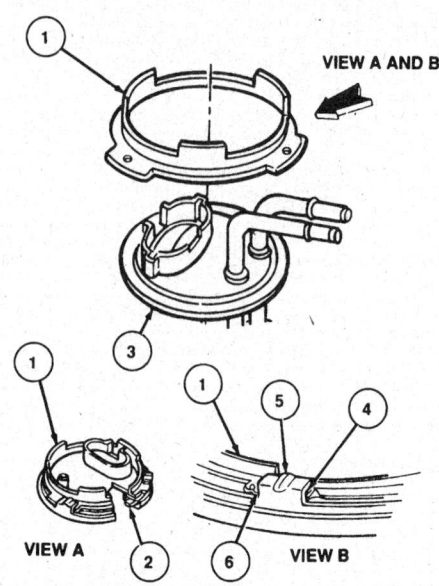

FM1029100137000A

Fig. 29   Fuel pump ring replacement

Item	Description
1	Fuel Pump Locking Retainer Ring
2	Fuel Pump Mounting Gasket
3	Fuel Pump Module
4	Stop
5	Tab
6	Detent

6. Secure RFI filter to fuel pump using suitable bundling strap.
7. Install fuel pump sender.

Righthand Exhaust Leak

1999-2004

On some of these models there may be a exhaust leak from the righthand exhaust pipe.

This condition may be caused by the inlet pipe.

To correct this condition, install new inlet pipe, condensation shield and exhaust hanger included in kit (manual transmission part No. 3R3Z-5H264-MT, or automatic transmission part No. 3R3Z-5H264-AT).

TIGHTENING SPECIFICATIONS

Year	Component	Torque/Ft. Lbs.
2001–04	Accelerator Cable Bracket	89①
	Air Conditioning Compressor Bracket, Bolt & Nut	35
	Air Conditioning Compressor Bracket, Stud	18
	Alternator Bracket	18
	Alternator Bracket To Head	30
	Alternator Positive Cable	89①
	Automatic Transmission Oil Cooler Tube Bracket	20
	Bulkhead 42-Pin Electrical Connector	89①
	Camshaft Position Sensor	27①
	Camshaft Synchronizer Drive Gear To Camshaft	33
	Camshaft Synchronizer To Front Cover	18
	Camshaft Thrust Plate	108①
	Connecting Rod Cap	18⑤
	Coolant Reservoir To Head	89①
	Coolant Reservoir To Bracket	80①
	Cooling System Vent Plug	108①
	Crankshaft Main Bearing	⑥
	Crankshaft Pulley	118
	Cylinder Head	④
	EGR Transducer Bracket	89①
	EGR Tube	30
	Engine Mount Ground Strap	20
	Engine Mount	52
	Engine Mount Bracket	52
	Engine Mount To Subframe Nut	85
	Engine To Transmission	30
	Exhaust Air Supply Tube	22
	Exhaust Air Supply Valve	89①
	Exhaust Manifold, Nut	⑦
	Exhaust Manifold, Stud	71①
	Fan Shroud	80①
	Flywheel	59
	Front Cover	⑧
	Front Subframe To Body	66
	Front Subframe To Shock Tower	85
	Fuel Supply Manifold	89①
	Hood Ground Strap	108①
	Hood Hinge	108①
	Ignition Coil To Intake Manifold	53①
	Intake Manifold, Lower	③
	Intake Manifold, Upper	③
	Main Bearing Bridge	24
	Motor Mount Bracket	52
	Motor Mount To Motor Mount	52
	Motor Mount To Subframe	85
	Oil Dipstick Tube	89①
	Oil Pan Baffle	35
	Oil Pan Drain Plug	19
	Oil Pan To Block	②
	Oil Pan To Bellhousing	33

Continued

TIGHTENING SPECIFICATIONS—Continued

Year	Component	Torque/Ft. Lbs.
2001–04	Oil Pickup Tube To Baffle	35
	Oil Pickup Tube To Block	18
	Oil Pump Cover To Front Cover	18
	Power Steering Pressure Tube	30
	Power Steering Pump	18
	Power Steering Pump Bracket	71①
	Power Steering Pump Bracket To Block	15
	Radiator Support	22
	Rocker Arm Pivot	④
	Steering Column Pinch	35
	Throttle Body	④
	Throttle Cable Bracket	89①
	Timing Chain Tensioner	108①
	Torque Converter	27
	Valve Cover	89①
	Valve Lifter Guide Plate	108①
	Water Outlet Tube	89①
	Water Pump Pulley	⑨
	Wire Harness	20
	42-Pin Connector	89①

① — Inch lbs.
② — Refer to "Oil Pan, Replace" for tightening specifications and sequence.
③ — Refer to "Intake Manifold, Replace" for tightening specifications and sequence.
④ — Refer to "Cylinder Head, Replace" for tightening specifications and sequence.
⑤ — Torque to 33 ft. lbs.; then final tighten additional 105°.
⑥ — Torque to 37 ft. lbs., then tighten an additional 90°.
⑦ — Refer to "Exhaust Manifold, Replace" for tightening specifications and sequence.
⑧ — Refer to "Front Cover, Replace" for tightening specifications and sequence.
⑨ — Refer to "Water Pump, Replace" for tightening specifications and sequence.

4.0L Engine

NOTE: On Air Bag Equipped Models, Refer To "Air Bag System Precautions" Located In The Front Of This Manual For System Disarming & Arming Procedures.

INDEX

PRECAUTIONS

Air Bag Systems

Refer to "Air Bag System Precautions" in front of this manual for system disarming and arming procedures.

Battery Ground Cable

Prior to service, disconnect battery ground cable and isolate as required.

Fuel System Pressure Relief

1. Remove fuel pump relay.
2. Start engine and allow it idle until is stalls.
3. Crank engine for approximately five seconds to ensure fuel injection supply manifold pressure has been released.
4. Turn ignition switch to OFF position.

COMPRESSION PRESSURE

1. Ensure crankcase oil is correct viscosity and correct level, and battery is fully charged.
2. Operate vehicle until engine at normal operating temperature.
3. Turn ignition switch to OFF position and remove all spark plugs.
4. Set throttle plates in wide-open position.
5. Install suitable compression gauge in cylinder No. 1.
6. Install suitable auxiliary start switch.
7. Turn ignition switch to ON position.
8. Crank engine at least five compression strokes using auxiliary starter switch.

9. Record highest reading and approximate number of compression strokes required to obtain highest reading.
10. Repeat test on each cylinder.
11. Compression pressures are within specifications is the lowest cylinder reading is at least 75% of highest.

ENGINE MOUNT
REPLACE

1. Raise and support vehicle.

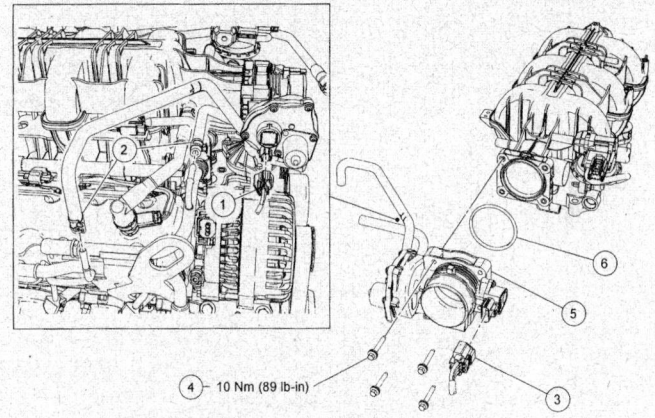

Item	Description
1	Throttle body (TB) electrical connector
2	TB coolant hoses (2 required)
3	Throttle position (TP) sensor electrical connector
4	TB bolts (4 required)
5	TB
6	TB gasket

4 — 10 Nm (89 lb-in)

ARM0400000000562

Fig. 1 Throttle body replacement

2. **If removing lefthand engine mount,** disconnect crankcase vent tube from air cleaner outlet pipe.
3. **On all engine mounts,** disconnect two throttle body electrical connectors, **Fig. 1.**
4. Disconnect two throttle body coolant hoses from coolant tube. Plug coolant hoses.
5. Remove four mounting bolts and throttle body.
6. Remove front end accessory drive

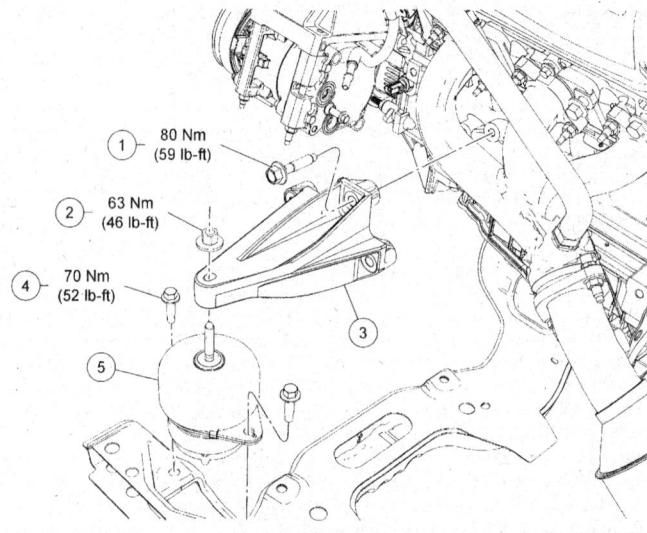

80 Nm
(59 lb-ft)

63 Nm
(46 lb-ft)

70 Nm
(52 lb-ft)

ARM0400000000554

Fig. 2   Engine mount replacement (Part 1 of 2). Lefthand

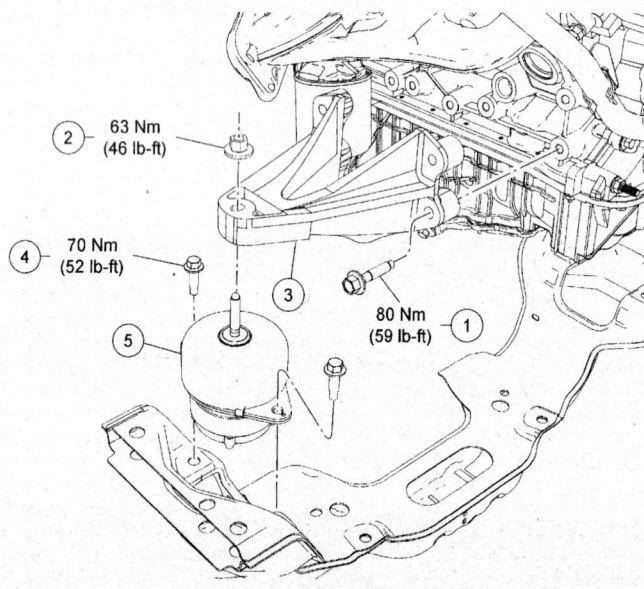

63 Nm
(46 lb-ft)

70 Nm
(52 lb-ft)

80 Nm
(59 lb-ft)

ARM0400000000563

Fig. 3   Engine mount replacement (Part 1 of 2). Righthand

Item	Description
1	LH engine mount bracket bolt (3 required)
2	LH engine mount bracket-to-engine mount nut
3	LH engine mount bracket
4	LH engine mount bolt (2 required)
5	LH engine mount

ARM0400000000555

Fig. 2   Engine mount replacement (Part 2 of 2). Lefthand

Item	Description
1	RH engine mount bracket bolt (3 required)
2	RH engine mount bracket-to-engine mount nut
3	RH engine mount bracket
4	RH engine mount bolt (2 required)
5	RH engine mount

ARM0400000000564

Fig. 3   Engine mount replacement (Part 2 of 2). Righthand

11. Drain cooling system into suitable container.
12. **On models equipped with automatic transmission,** remove transmission as outlined in **MOTOR's "Domestic Transmission Manual, In-Vehicle Service."**
13. **On models equipped with manual transmission,** remove clutch as outlined in **MOTOR's "Domestic Transmission Manual, In-Vehicle Service."**
14. **On all models,** disconnect two Heated Oxygen Sensor (HO2S) and two catalyst monitor sensor electrical connectors.
15. Remove four catalytic converter-to-exhaust manifold nuts.
16. Remove stud bolt, then disconnect and position aside.
17. Drain engine oil into suitable container.
18. Disconnect upper radiator hose from thermostat housing.
19. Disconnect lower radiator hose from water pump.
20. Remove mounting bolt and disconnect power steering supply hose bracket from Front Engine Accessory Drive (FEAD) bracket.
21. Remove mounting bolt and disconnect Power Steering Pressure (PSP) tube bracket from crossmember.
22. Disconnect PSP switch electrical connector.

bracket bolt and install engine lifting bracket tool No. D70P-6000, or equivalent.
7. Remove six pin-type retainers and radiator sight shield.
8. Support engine using suitable three-bar engine support tool.
9. Remove engine mount bracket-to-engine mount nut, **Figs. 2 and 3.**
10. Remove three mounting nuts and engine mount bracket.
11. Remove two mounting bolts and engine mount.
12. Reverse procedure to install.

ENGINE
REPLACE

1. Raise and support vehicle.

2. Remove fuel pump relay.
3. Start engine and allow it idle until is stalls.
4. Crank engine for approximately five seconds to ensure fuel injection supply manifold pressure has been released.
5. Turn ignition switch to OFF position.
6. Loosen clamp and disconnect a outlet pipe from air cleaner.
7. Disconnect Mass Air Flow (MAF) sensor electrical connector.
8. Remove mounting bolts and air cleaner assembly bolt. Ensure two rubber grommets are retained to air cleaner feet.
9. Mark hood hinge location for installation alignment.
10. Remove four bolts and hood.

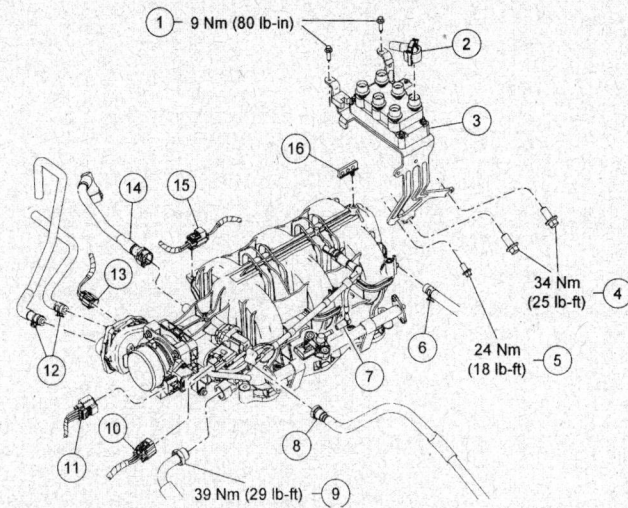

Item	Description
1	Ignition coil bracket upper bolts (2 required)
2	RH spark plug wire-to-ignition coil connectors (3 required)
3	Ignition coil and bracket assembly
4	Ignition coil bracket lower bolts (M12) (2 required)
5	Ignition coil bracket lower bolt (M8)
6	Brake booster vacuum hose
7	Vacuum harness fitting
8	Vapor tube
9	Exhaust gas recirculation (EGR) system module tube fitting

Item	Description
10	EGR system module electrical connector
11	Throttle position (TP) sensor electrical connector
12	Throttle body coolant hoses (2 required)
13	Throttle body electrical connector
14	Positive crankcase ventilation (PCV) tube
15	Knock sensor (KS) electrical connector
16	RH spark plug wire retainer

ARM0400000000566

Fig. 4   Intake manifold replacement (Part 1 of 2)

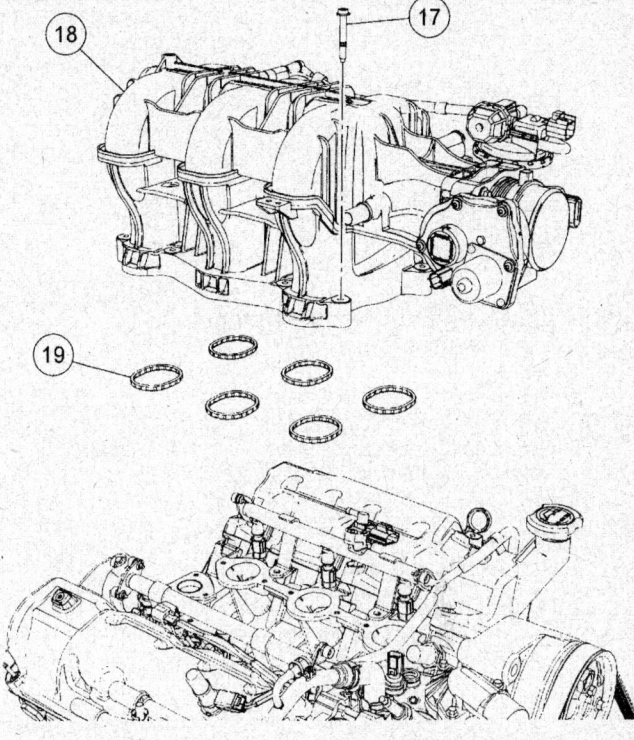

Item	Description
17	Intake manifold bolts (8 required)
18	Intake manifold
19	Intake manifold gaskets

ARM0400000000567

Fig. 4   Intake manifold replacement (Part 2 of 2)

23. Disconnect the air conditioning compressor and high pressure switch electrical connectors.
24. Disconnect two wiring retainers from FEAD bracket.
25. Disconnect fuel supply tube coupling.
26. Rotate accessory drive belt tensioner counterclockwise and remove accessory drive belt.
27. Remove three mounting bolts and power steering pump pulley.
28. Remove three mounting bolts and position power steering pump aside.
29. Remove three mounting bolts and stud bolt, then position FEAD bracket and air conditioning compressor aside.
30. Disconnect two heater hoses from coolant tube.
31. Disconnect heater hose bracket from righthand valve cover.
32. Remove three coolant tube bracket bolts.
33. Disconnect six spark plug wires from spark plugs using suitable spark plug wire remover.
34. Disconnect spark plug wire retainer from intake manifold.
35. Disconnect radio ignition interference

capacitor electrical connector.
36. Disconnect ignition coil electrical connector.
37. Remove two upper ignition coil bracket bolts.
38. Remove three lower ignition coil bracket bolts, then the ignition coil and spark plug wires.
39. Disconnect and remove crankcase vent tube from lefthand valve cover.
40. Disconnect brake booster vacuum hose from upper intake manifold.
41. Disconnect vapor tube from upper intake manifold.
42. Disconnect upper and lower Powertrain Control Module (PCM) electrical connectors.
43. Disconnect 16-pin electrical connector, two wiring retainers and three wiring harness retainers.
44. Remove power distribution box cover
45. Remove mounting bolt and disconnect power distribution box B+ terminal.
46. Disconnect pin type retainer from strut tower.
47. Disconnect power distribution box upper housing from lower housing.
48. Loosen bolt and disconnect 68-pin

connector from power distribution box.
49. Remove mounting bolt and disconnect ground cable from righthand strut tower.
50. Install suitable lifting brackets on cylinder heads.
51. Remove left and righthand engine mounts' nuts.
52. Remove engine using suitable spread bar.
53. Reverse procedure to install.

INTAKE MANIFOLD
REPLACE

1. Disconnect righthand spark plug wires from ignition coil and spark plug wire retainer from intake manifold, **Fig. 4.**
2. Remove two ignition coil bracket upper bolts and three lower bolts.
3. Position ignition coil and bracket aside.
4. Disconnect Exhaust Gas Recirculation (EGR) system module electrical connector.
5. Disconnect tube from EGR system module.
6. Disconnect brake booster vacuum hose from intake manifold.

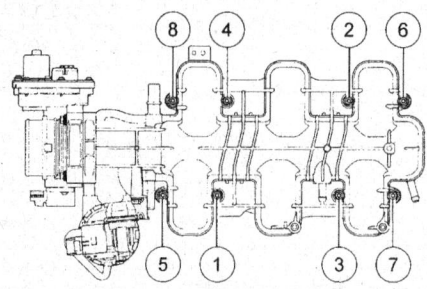

Fig. 5 Intake manifold tightening sequence

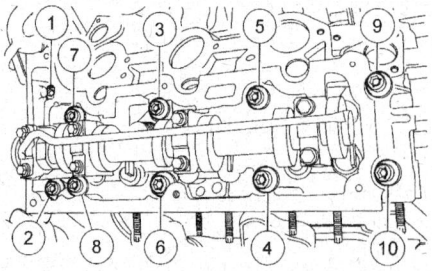

Fig. 6 Cylinder head removal sequence

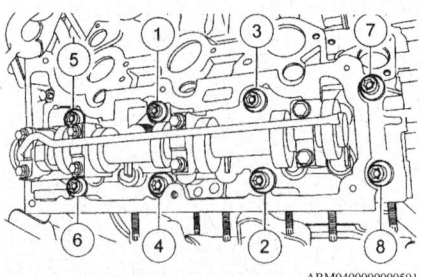

Fig. 7 Cylinder head tightening sequence

7. Disconnect vacuum tube from fuel rail pressure and temperature sensor.
8. Disconnect vapor tube from intake manifold.
9. Remove Positive Crankcase Ventilation (PCV) tube.
10. Disconnect Knock Sensor (KS) electrical connector retainer from intake manifold.
11. Disconnect Throttle Position (TP) sensor and throttle body electrical connectors.
12. Disconnect and plug two throttle body coolant hoses.
13. Remove eight mounting bolts and intake manifold.
14. Reverse procedure to install. Using sequence, **Fig. 5, torque** intake manifold mounting bolts to 89 inch lbs.

EXHAUST MANIFOLD
REPLACE

1. Raise and support vehicle.
2. Remove two catalytic converter-to-exhaust manifold nuts.
3. **If removing lefthand exhaust manifold,** disconnect Exhaust Gas Recirculation (EGR) system module tube.
4. **On all manifolds,** remove six nuts, exhaust manifold and gasket.
5. Reverse procedure to install.

CYLINDER HEAD
REPLACE

   Left and righthand camshaft timing procedure must be performed when either camshaft is serviced.
1. Raise and support vehicle.
2. Drain engine cooling system into suitable container.
3. Remove intake manifold as outlined under "Intake Manifold, Replace."
4. Remove valve covers as outlined under "Valve Cover, Replace."
5. Rotate crankshaft until camshaft for cylinder being serviced is at base circle.
6. Mark position of camshaft roller followers so they can be installed in original positions.
7. Remove camshaft roller followers using valve spring compressor tool No. T97T-6565-A, or equivalent.
8. Rotate accessory drive belt tensioner

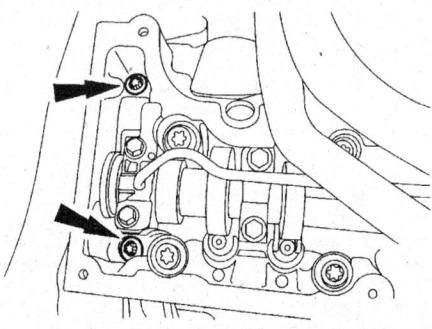

Fig. 8 M8 cylinder head bolts

counterclockwise and remove accessory drive belt.
9. **On righthand side,** proceed as follows:
   a. Disconnect alternator electrical connector, then remove mounting nut and disconnect B+ terminal.
   b. Disconnect pin-type retainer.
   c. Remove mounting bolt and accessory drive belt tensioner.
   d. Remove mounting nut, two bolts and alternator mounting bracket.
   e. Disconnect heater hose from thermostat housing.
   f. Disconnect Engine Coolant Temperature (ECT) sensor electrical connector.
   g. Disconnect upper radiator hose.
   h. Position coolant bypass hose clamp aside.
   i. Remove three mounting bolts and thermostat housing.
10. **On lefthand side,** proceed as follows:
   a. Remove mounting bolt and oil level indicator tube.
   b. Remove mounting bolt and disconnect power steering supply hose bracket from Front Engine Accessory Drive (FEAD) bracket.
   c. Remove mounting bolt and disconnect Power Steering Pressure (PSP) tube bracket from crossmember.
   d. Remove three mounting bolts and power steering pump pulley.
   e. Remove three mounting bolts and position power steering pump aside.
   f. Remove three mounting bolts, stud bolt and position FEAD bracket and air conditioning compressor aside.

   g. Remove mounting bolt and disconnect starter motor wiring retainer bracket.
   h. Remove ground strap bolt and disconnect wiring harness retainer from backside of cylinder head.
   i. Remove mounting bolt and disconnect starter motor wiring bracket.
11. **On all heads,** remove spark wire using suitable spark plug wire remover tool.
12. Remove four mounting bolts and fuel rail and injectors.
13. Separate fuel injectors from fuel rail and discard O-ring seals.
14. Remove four catalytic converter-to-manifold nuts.
15. Remove 12 mounting nuts, exhaust manifolds and gaskets.
16. **On righthand side,** proceed as follows:
   a. Remove righthand hydraulic chain tensioner.
   b. Install camshaft sprocket holding tool No. T97T-6256-B and adapter tool T97T-6256-A, or equivalents.
   c. Remove righthand camshaft bolt using torque wrench extension tool No. T97T-6256-F and camshaft sprocket nut socket tool No. 303-565, or equivalents.
   d. Remove righthand cassette bolt.
   e. Remove righthand camshaft sprocket from timing chain.
   f. Install suitable rubber band around cassette and timing chain.
17. **On lefthand side,** proceed as following:
   a. Remove lefthand hydraulic chain tensioner camshaft sprocket holding tool No. T97T-2656-B and adapter tool T97T-6256-A, or equivalents.
   b. Remove lefthand camshaft sprocket bolt.
   c. Remove lefthand cassette bolt.
   d. Remove lefthand camshaft sprocket from timing chain.
   e. Install suitable rubber band around cassette and timing chain.
18. **On all heads,** remove cylinder head bolts in sequence, **Fig. 6.**
19. Remove cylinder head with assistance and gaskets. **On righthand side, avoid contacting air conditioning tube.**
20. Reverse procedure to install, noting the following:
   a. Install new, torque-to-yield cylinder

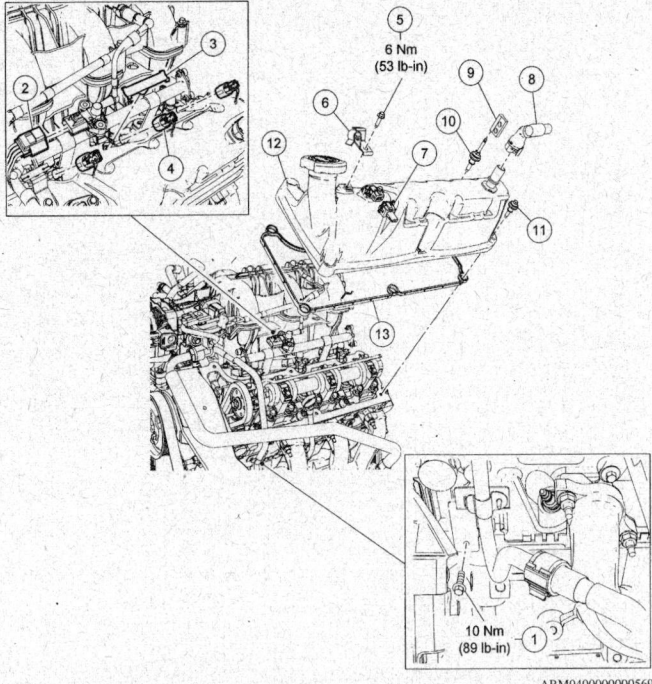

Fig. 9   Valve cover replacement (Part 1 of 2).
Lefthand

Item	Description
1	Fuel rail supply tube bracket-to-cylinder head bolt
2	Fuel rail pressure and temperature sensor electrical connector
3	Wiring harness retainer
4	Fuel injector electrical connector (3 required)
5	Fuel rail supply tube bracket
6	Fuel rail supply tube bracket-to-valve cover bolt
7	Camshaft position (CMP) sensor electrical connector
8	Crankcase ventilation tube
9	Spark plug wire retainer
10	LH valve cover stud bolt (3 required)
11	LH valve cover bolt (3 required)
12	LH valve cover
13	LH valve cover gasket

ARM0400000000570

Fig. 9   Valve cover replacement
(Part 2 of 2). Lefthand

head bolts.
b. Install eight new M12 bolts and tighten in sequence to 106 inch lbs., **Fig. 7.**
c. **Torque** head bolts to 18 ft. lbs.
d. Install two new M8 bolts and **torque** to 24 ft. lbs., **Fig. 8.**
e. Tighten eight M12 bolts an additional 90° in sequence.
f. Final tighten M12 bolts an additional 90° in sequence.

VALVE COVER
REPLACE
Lefthand

1. Disconnect ignition coil electrical connector, **Fig. 9.**
2. Disconnect six spark plug wires from ignition coil.
3. Remove four mounting bolts and ignition coil.
4. Remove fuel rail supply tube bracket-to-cylinder head bolt and cover bolt, then position fuel rail supply tube aside.
5. Disconnect crankcase ventilation tube from valve cover and position tube aside.
6. Disconnect Camshaft Position (CMP) sensor electrical connector.
7. Disconnect fuel rail pressure and temperature sensor electrical connector.
8. Disconnect three lefthand fuel injector electrical connectors.
9. Disconnect wiring retainer from valve cover stud bolt and position it aside.
10. Disconnect spark plug wire retainer from valve cover stud bolt.

11. Remove three mounting bolts, three stud bolts and lefthand valve cover.
12. Reverse procedure to install, tighten valve cover mounting bolts in sequence, **Fig. 10.**

Righthand

1. Remove Positive Crankcase Ventilation (PCV) tube and disconnect PCV valve electrical connector, **Fig. 11.**
2. Disconnect heater hose retainer from valve cover.
3. Remove wiring harness bracket bolt from back of righthand cylinder head and disconnect bracket from valve cover stud bolt.
4. Disconnect engine wiring and spark plug wiring retainers from two valve cover stud bolts.
5. Remove two mounting bolts, four stud bolts and righthand valve cover.
6. Reverse procedure to install.

CAMSHAFT ROLLER FOLLOWER
REPLACE

1. Remove valve covers as outlined under "Valve Cover, Replace."
2. Rotate crankshaft until camshaft for cylinder being serviced is at base circle.
3. Mark position of camshaft roller followers so they can be installed in original positions.
4. Remove camshaft roller followers using valve spring compressor tool No. T97T-6565-A, or equivalent.
5. Reverse procedure to install. Lubricate

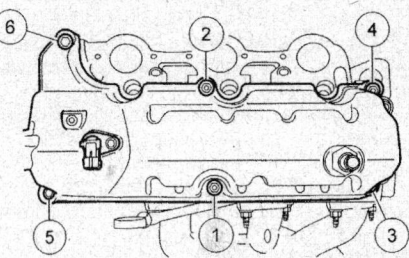

ARM0400000000571

Fig. 10   Valve cover tightening
sequence

camshaft roller followers with suitable, clean engine oil.

CAMSHAFT LOBE LIFT SPECIFICATIONS

Engine	Intake, Inch	Exhaust, Inch
4.0L	.259	.259

VALVE ADJUSTMENT

These engine are equipped with hydraulic valve lash adjusters. No valve adjustment is required.

HYDRAULIC LASH ADJUSTER
REPLACE

1. Mark position of camshaft roller followers so they can be installed in original positions.
2. Remove valve covers as outlined under "Valve Cover, Replace."

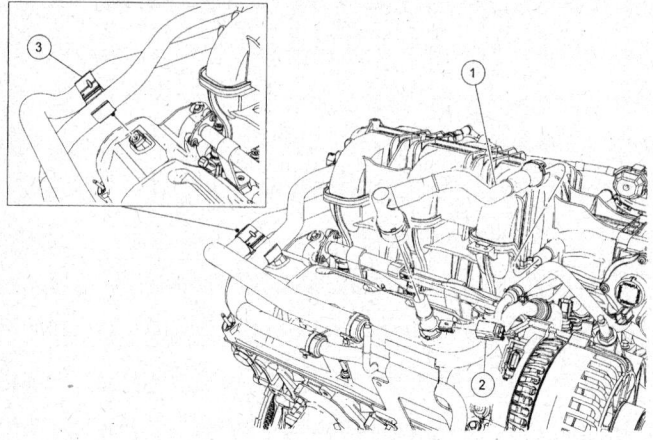

Item	Description
1	Positive crankcase ventilation (PCV) tube
2	PCV valve electrical connector
3	Heater hose retainer bracket

ARM0400000000572

Fig. 11   Valve cover replacement (Part 1 of 2). Righthand

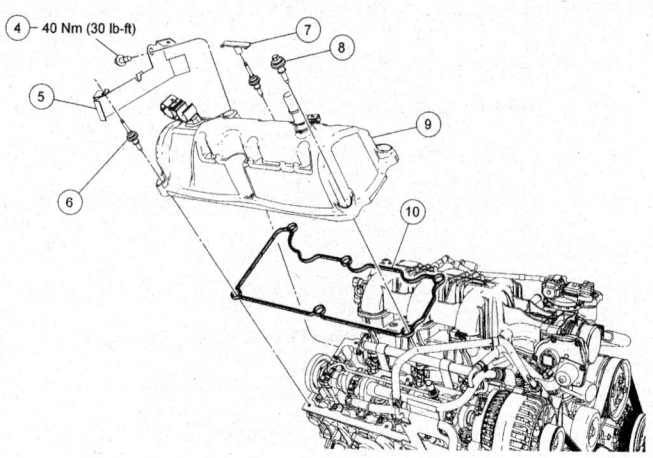

Item	Description
4	Wiring harness bracket bolt
5	Wiring harness bracket
6	RH valve cover stud bolt (4 required)
7	Wiring retainer
8	RH valve cover bolt (2 required)
9	RH valve cover
10	RH valve cover gasket

ARM0400000000573

Fig. 11   Valve cover replacement (Part 2 of 2). Righthand

3. Rotate crankshaft until camshaft for cylinder being serviced is at base circle.
4. Mark position of camshaft roller followers so they can be installed in original positions.
5. Remove camshaft roller followers using valve spring compressor tool No. T97T-6565-A, or equivalent.
6. Mark position of hydraulic lash adjusters so they can be installed in original positions.
7. Remove hydraulic lash adjusters.
8. Reverse procedure to install. Lubricate hydraulic lash adjusters and camshaft roller followers with suitable, clean engine oil

CRANKSHAFT DAMPER
REPLACE

1. Raise and support vehicle.
2. Disconnect crankcase vent tube from air cleaner outlet pipe.
3. Loosen two clamps and remove air cleaner outlet pipe.
4. Rotate accessory drive belt tensioner clockwise with suitable belt tensioner release tool and remove belt.
5. Remove crankshaft pulley bolt using suitable strap wrench.
6. Install crankshaft pulley bolt 2–3 turns, then remove crankshaft pulley using crankshaft vibration damper remover tool No. T74P-3616-A, or equivalent.
7. Reverse procedure to install, noting the following:
   a. Install crankshaft pulley using crankshaft vibration damper installer tool No. T74P-6316-B, or equivalent.
   b. **Torque** new torque-to-yield crankshaft pulley bolt to 33 ft. lbs.

c. Tighten pulley bolt an additional 85°.

FRONT COVER
REPLACE

1. Drain cooling system into suitable container.
2. Remove crankshaft pulley as outlined under "Crankshaft Damper, Replace."
3. Remove crankshaft front seal using crankshaft front oil seal remover tool No. T74P-6700-A and aligner tool No, T74P-6019-A, or equivalent.
4. Disconnect upper radiator hose, **Fig. 12.**
5. Disconnect water pump water heater and lower radiator hoses.
6. Remove mounting bolt and accessory drive belt idler pulley.
7. Disconnect Crankshaft Position (CKP) sensor and two 2 wiring retainers.
8. Remove five engine block cradle-to-engine front cover bolts.
9. Remove engine front cover five mounting bolts and 5 stud bolts.
10. Disconnect water pump coolant by-pass hose.
11. Remove engine front cover.
12. Drain engine oil into suitable container.
13. Reverse procedure to install, noting the following:
   a. Clean sealing area using suitable silicone gasket remover and metal surface prep.
   b. Apply suitable silicone gasket and sealant to oil pan and engine block mating surfaces, **Fig. 13.** Front cover must be secured within

four minutes of sealant application.
   c. Apply thread sealant to stud bolts and ensure bolts are installed in original positions.
   d. Loosely install five mounting bolts and five stud bolts, then align front cover using front cover aligner tool No. T74P-6019-A, or equivalent, and tighten bolts and stud bolts to 14 ft. lbs.

FRONT COVER SEAL
REPLACE

1. Remove crankshaft pulley as outlined under "Crankshaft Damper, Replace."
2. Remove crankshaft front seal using crankshaft front oil seal remover tool No. T74P-6700-A and aligner tool No, T74P-6019-A, or equivalent.
3. Reverse procedure to install using aligner tool and crankshaft vibration damper installer tool No. T74P-6316-B, or equivalent.

TIMING CHAIN
REPLACE

These engines have an interference fit design. If engine has jumped time cylinder heads must be removed to repair damage to valves and/or pistons.

At no time, when the timing chains are removed and the cylinder heads are installed, may the crankshaft and/or camshaft be rotated unless all rocker arms have been removed. Rotation may result in valve and/or piston damage.

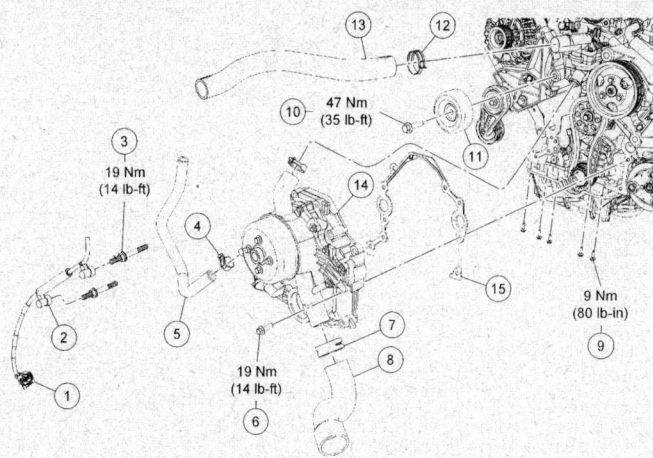

Item	Description
10	Accessory drive belt idler pulley bolt
11	Accessory drive belt idler pulley
12	Clamp
13	Upper radiator hose
14	Engine front cover
15	Engine front cover gasket

ARM0400000000584

Fig. 12 Front cover replacement (Part 2 of 2)

Item	Description		Item	Description
1	Crankshaft position (CKP) sensor electrical connector		5	Coolant hose
2	Wiring retainers (part of		6	Engine front cover bolt (5 required)
3	Engine front cover stud bolt (5 required)		7	Clamp
4	Clamp		8	Lower radiator hose
			9	Block cradle-to-engine front cover bolts (5 required)

ARM0400000000583

Fig. 12 Front cover replacement (Part 1 of 2)

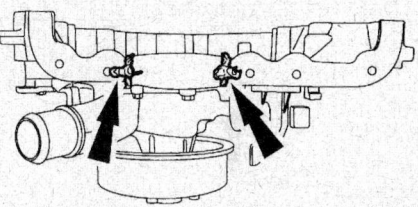

ARM0400000000586

Fig. 13 Oil pan & block silicone sealant (Part 2 of 2)

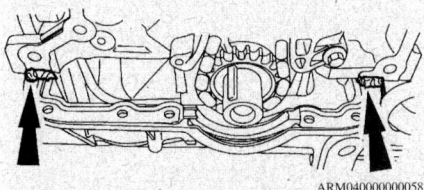

ARM0400000000585

Fig. 13 Oil pan & block silicone sealant (Part 1 of 2)

Left and righthand camshaft timing procedure must be performed when either camshaft is serviced.

1. Remove intake manifold as outlined under "Intake Manifold, Replace."
2. Remove engine front cover as outlined under "Front Cover, Replace."
3. Remove valve covers as outlined under "Valve Cover, Replace."
4. Rotate crankshaft until camshaft for cylinder being serviced is at base circle.
5. Mark position of camshaft roller followers so they can be installed in original positions.
6. Remove camshaft roller followers using valve spring compressor tool No. T97T-6565-A, or equivalent.
7. Turn crankshaft clockwise to position cylinder No. 1 at top dead center.
8. Remove lefthand hydraulic chain tensioner and camshaft sprocket bolt, **Fig. 14.**
9. Install camshaft sprocket holding tool No. T97T-6256-B, and adapter tool No. T97T-6256-A, or equivalent, on front of lefthand cylinder head.
10. Remove lefthand camshaft sprocket bolt.
11. Prevent crankshaft from turning using

crankshaft holding tool No. 303-674, or equivalent, and remove jackshaft sprocket bolt.
12. Remove two mounting bolts and primary chain tensioner.
13. Remove primary chain and sprockets as assembly.
14. Remove upper mounting bolt and lefthand cassette.
15. Reverse procedure to install, noting the following:
    a. Ensure camshaft chain sprockets are oriented correctly, **Fig. 15.**
    b. **Torque** jackshaft sprocket bolt to 33 ft. lbs.
    c. Tighten an additional 90°.

CAMSHAFT
REPLACE

These engines have an interference fit design. If engine has jumped time cylinder heads must be removed to repair damage to valves and/or pistons.

At no time, when the timing chains are removed and the cylinder heads are installed, may the crankshaft and/or camshaft be rotated unless all rocker arms have been removed. Rotation may result in valve and/or piston damage.

Left and righthand camshaft timing procedure must be performed when either camshaft is serviced.

1. Remove valve covers as outlined under "Valve Cover, Replace."
2. Rotate crankshaft until camshaft for cylinder being serviced is at base circle.
3. Mark position of camshaft roller followers so they can be installed in original positions.
4. Remove camshaft roller followers

using valve spring compressor tool No. T97T-6565-A, or equivalent.
5. Rotate crankshaft clockwise to position cylinder No. 1 at TDC and lock damper in place using crankshaft TDC timing tool No. T97T-6303-A, or equivalent. Ensure tool contacts engine block. **Do not rotate engine counterclockwise.**
6. **On righthand camshaft,** proceed as follows:
    a. Install camshaft sprocket holding tool No. T97T-6256-B, and adapter tool No. T97T-6256-A, or equivalent, on rear of righthand cylinder head.
    b. Loosen camshaft sprocket bolt using torque wrench extension tool No. T97T-6256-F, and camshaft sprocket nut socket tool No. T97T-6256-G, or equivalents. **Righthand camshaft sprocket is lefthand-threaded bolt.**
    c. Position righthand camshaft sprocket aside.
7. **On lefthand camshaft,** proceed as follows:
    a. Install camshaft sprocket holding tool No. T97T-6256-B, and adapter tool No. T97T-6256-A, or equivalent, on front of lefthand cylinder head.
    b. Loosen camshaft sprocket bolt using torque wrench extension tool No. T97T-6256-F, and camshaft sprocket nut socket tool No. T97T-6256-G, or equivalents.
    c. Position lefthand camshaft sprocket aside.
8. **On all camshafts,** mark camshaft bearing caps positions for installation

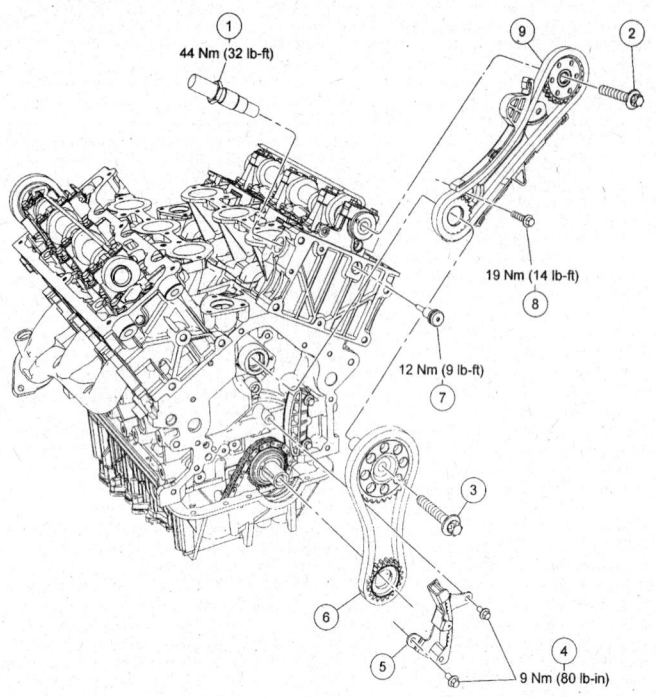

44 Nm (32 lb-ft)

19 Nm (14 lb-ft)

12 Nm (9 lb-ft)

9 Nm (80 lb-in)

Item	Description
1	Hydraulic chain tensioner
2	Camshaft sprocket bolt
3	Jackshaft sprocket bolt
4	Primary chain tensioner bolts (2 required)
5	Primary chain tensioner
6	Primary chain and sprocket assembly
7	Chain guide bolt
8	Chain guide bolt

Item	Description
9	Timing chain and guide assembly

ARM0400000000589

Fig. 14   Timing chain replacement

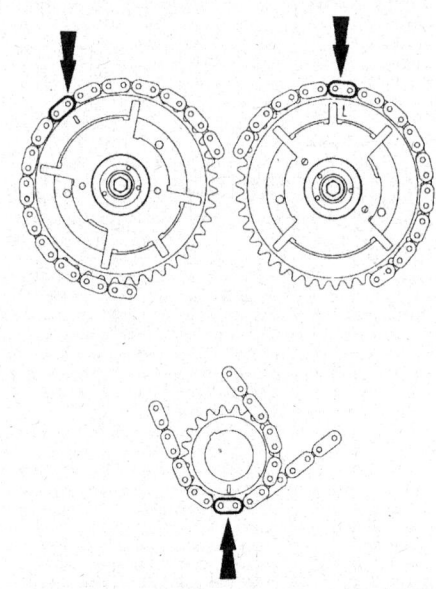

ARM0400000000590

Fig. 15   Camshaft chain sprocket orientation

in original positions.
9. Remove mounting bolts sequence, **Fig. 16.**
10. Remove bearing caps and oil supply tube, then the camshaft.
11. Reverse procedure to install, noting the following:
   a. Lubricate camshafts and camshaft bearing caps with suitable, clean engine oil.
   b. Ensure camshaft has free rotation.
   c. **Torque** camshaft bearing caps bolts in sequence to 53 inch lbs., **Fig. 17.**
   d. **Torque** bolts to 12 ft. lbs.

CAMSHAFT TIMING

Left and righthand camshaft timing procedure must be performed when either camshaft is serviced.
1. Remove valve covers as outlined under "Valve Cover, Replace."
2. Rotate crankshaft until camshaft for cylinder being serviced is at base circle.
3. Mark position of camshaft roller followers so they can be installed in original positions.
4. Remove camshaft roller followers

ARM0400000000587

Fig. 16   Camshaft bearing cap remove sequence

using valve spring compressor tool No. T97T-6565-A, or equivalent.
5. Rotate crankshaft clockwise to position cylinder No. 1 at TDC and lock damper in place using crankshaft TDC timing tool No. T97T-6303-A, or equivalent. Ensure tool contacts engine block. **Do not rotate engine counterclockwise.**
6. Install camshaft sprocket holding tool No. T97T-6256-B, and adapter tool No. T97T-6256-A, or equivalent, on rear of righthand cylinder head.

7. Loosen camshaft sprocket bolt using torque wrench extension tool No. T97T-6256-F, and camshaft sprocket nut socket tool No. T97T-6256-G, or equivalents. **Righthand camshaft sprocket is lefthand-threaded bolt.**
8. Loosen top two camshaft sprockets holding tool clamp bolts.
9. Position camshaft timing slots below centerline of camshaft **Camshaft timing slots are off-center.**
10. Install camshaft holding tool No. T97T-6303-C and adapter tool No. T97T-6256-D, or equivalents, on front of righthand cylinder head.
11. Remove righthand camshaft tensioner.
12. Install timing chain tensioner tool No. T97T-6K254-A, or equivalent.
13. Tighten camshaft sprocket bolt and holding tool clamp bolts.
14. Tighten camshaft bolt using torque wrench extension and camshaft sprocket nut socket tools.
15. Remove special tool.
16. Install new O-ring seal on tensioner and lubricate it with suitable, clean engine oil.
17. Install righthand camshaft tensioner.
18. Remove righthand cylinder head special tools.
19. Install camshaft sprocket holding tool No. T97T-6256-B, and adapter tool No. T97T-6256-A, or equivalent, on front of lefthand cylinder head.
20. Loosen camshaft sprocket bolt using torque wrench extension tool No. T97T-6256-F, and camshaft sprocket nut socket tool No. T97T-6256-G, or equivalents.
21. Loosen top two camshaft sprocket holding tool clamp bolts and allow camshaft sprocket to rotate freely
22. Position camshaft timing slots below

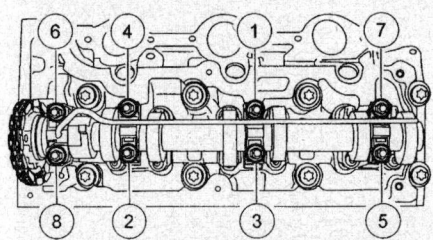

Fig. 17 Camshaft tightening sequence

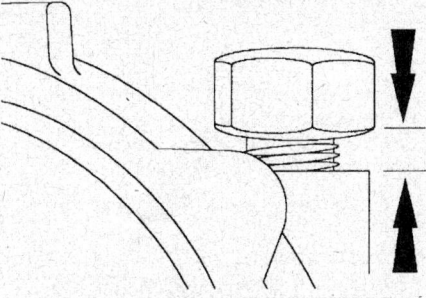

Fig. 18 Connecting rod nut removal

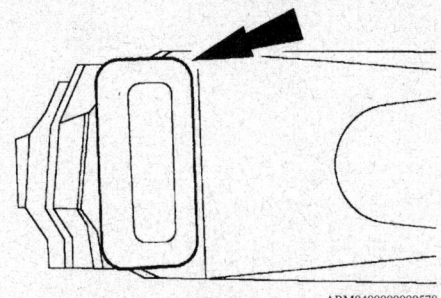

Fig. 19 Connecting rod bolt installation

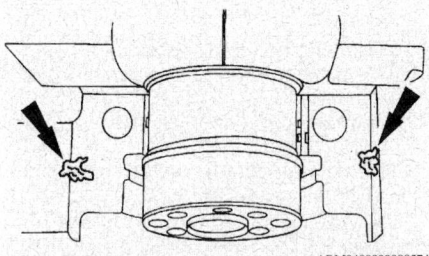

Fig. 20 Cylinder block sealant

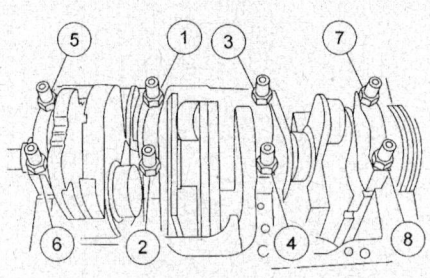
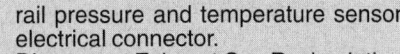

Fig. 21 Main bearing cap tightening sequence

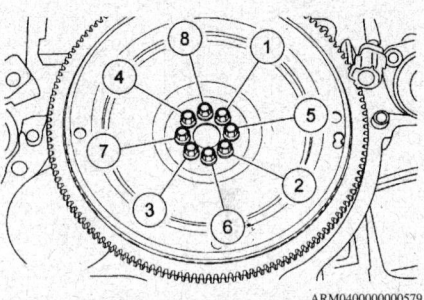

Fig. 22 Flexplate/flywheel tightening sequence

centerline of camshaft **Camshaft timing slots are off-center.**

23. Install camshaft holding tool No. T97T-6303-C and adapter tool No. T97T-6256-D, or equivalents, on rear of lefthand cylinder head.
24. Remove lefthand camshaft tensioner.
25. Install timing chain tensioner tool No. T97T-6K254-A, or equivalent.
26. Tighten camshaft sprocket bolt and holding tool clamp bolts.
27. Tighten camshaft bolt.
28. Remove special tool.
29. Install new O-ring seal on tensioner and lubricated with suitable, clean engine oil.
30. Install lefthand camshaft tensioner.
31. Remove special tools from lefthand cylinder head.
32. Install camshaft roller followers.

BALANCE SHAFT

REPLACE

Balance shaft is on engines equipped with manual transmission only.

Complete engine disassembly is required to access the balance shaft.

1. Remove engine as outlined under "Engine, Replace."
2. Remove eight mounting bolts and flexplate/flywheel.
3. Remove spacer plate and flexplate-to-crankshaft spacer.
4. Mount engine on suitable engine stand.
5. Disconnect alternator throttle body electrical connectors.
6. Remove mounting nut and disconnect alternator B+ terminal.
7. Disconnect wiring retainer coolant tube bracket.
8. Disconnect vacuum tubes, then fuel

rail pressure and temperature sensor electrical connector.

9. Disconnect Exhaust Gas Recirculation (EGR) system module and Throttle Position (TP) sensor electrical connectors.
10. Disconnect tube fitting from EGR system module.
11. Disconnect EGR tube fitting from lefthand exhaust manifold and remove the tube.
12. Disconnect two throttle body coolant hoses from coolant tube.
13. Disconnect Positive Crankcase Ventilation (PCV) tube fittings and remove the tube.
14. Disconnect Knock Sensor (KS) electrical connector and wiring retainer.
15. Remove eight mounting bolts and intake manifold.
16. Remove two fuel supply tube bracket bolts.
17. Disconnect Camshaft Position (CMP) electrical connector.
18. Disconnect oil pressure sensor electrical connector and wiring retainer.
19. Remove mounting bolt and belt tensioner.
20. Remove two mounting bolts, nu, alternator and bracket.
21. Disconnect Crankshaft Position (CKP) sensor electrical connector and two wiring retainers.
22. Disconnect Engine Coolant Temperature (ECT) sensor electrical connector.
23. Disconnect PCV valve electrical connector.
24. Disconnect fuel injector electrical connectors and wiring retainer from valve cover stud bolts.

25. Remove three bolts, disconnect wiring retainers and remove the main engine wiring harness.
26. Remove four mounting bolts, fuel rail and injectors.
27. Remove mounting and knock sensor.
28. Remove mounting bolt, then disconnect coolant bypass and heater hose from water pump.
29. Remove three mounting bolts, thermostat housing, hoses and coolant tube.
30. Remove three mounting bolts, three stud bolts and lefthand valve cover.
31. Remove two mounting bolts, four stud bolts and righthand valve cover.
32. Remove bolt and oil level indicator tube.
33. Remove six mounting nuts, lefthand exhaust manifold. and gasket.
34. Remove three mounting bolts and lefthand engine mount bracket.
35. Remove six mounting nuts, righthand exhaust manifold and gasket.
36. Remove four mounting bolts and righthand engine mount bracket.
37. Rotate crankshaft until cam lobe is in up position.
38. Mark each camshaft roller follower for installation in original position.
39. Remove camshaft roller followers using valve spring compressor tool No. T97T-6565-A, or equivalent.
40. Remove righthand hydraulic chain tensioner.
41. Install camshaft sprocket holding tool No. T97T-6256-B and adapter tool No. T97T-6256-A, or equivalent, on righthand cylinder head.
42. Remove righthand camshaft sprocket bolt. **Righthand camshaft sprocket**

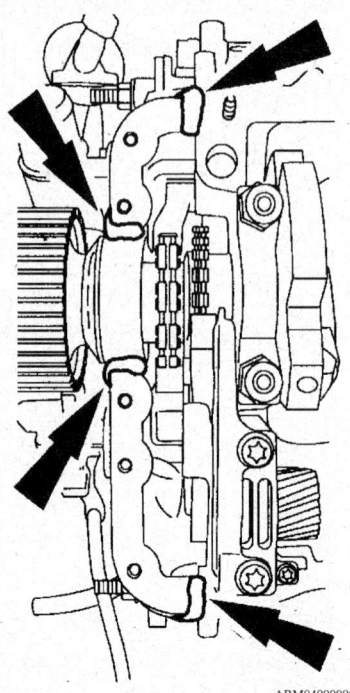

Fig. 23 Engine cradle silicone application (Part 1 of 2)

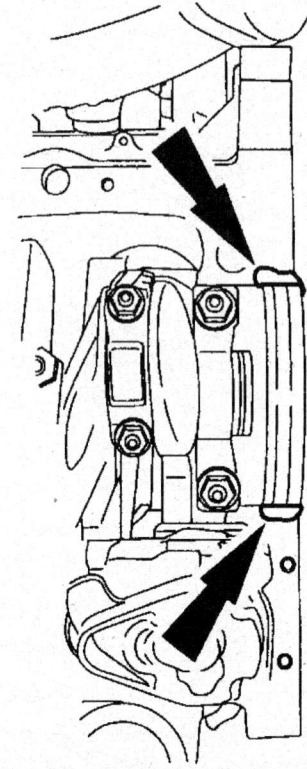

Fig. 23 Engine cradle silicone application (Part 2 of 2)

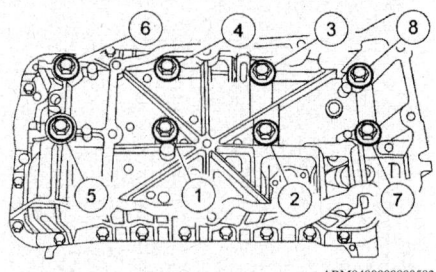

Fig. 24 Cylinder block cradle tightening sequence

bolt is lefthand-threaded bolt.
43. Remove righthand cassette bolt.
44. Remove righthand camshaft sprocket from timing chain.
45. Hold timing chain and cassette with suitable rubber band
46. Remove lefthand hydraulic chain tensioner.
47. Install camshaft sprocket holding tool No. T97T-6256-B and adapter tool No. T97T-6256-A, or equivalent, on left-hand cylinder head.
48. Remove lefthand camshaft sprocket bolt.
49. Remove lefthand cassette bolt.
50. Remove lefthand camshaft sprocket from timing chain.
51. Hold cassette and timing chain with suitable rubber band.
52. Remove mounting bolts in sequence, then the cylinder heads and gaskets, **Fig. 6.**
53. Remove mounting bolts and CKP sensor.
54. Remove mounting bolt and washer using suitable strap wrench, then the crankshaft pulley using crankshaft vibration damper remover tools Nos. T74P-3616-A and D85L-6000-A, or equivalent
55. Remove crankshaft front oil seal using crankshaft front oil seal remover tool No. T74P-6700-A, or equivalent.
56. Remove five cylinder block cradle-to-engine front cover bolts.
57. Remove five mounting bolts, five stud bolts and engine front cover.
58. Remove engine oil filter.
59. Remove mounting bolts and oil pan.
60. Remove mounting bolt, oil pump

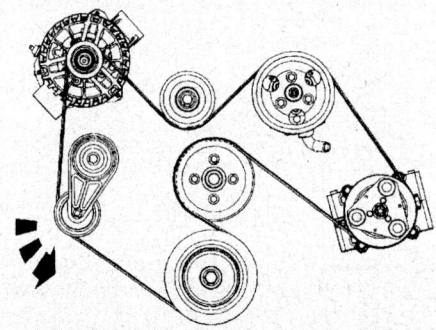

Fig. 25 Serpentine drive belt routing

screen cover and tube.
61. Record location of two silver-colored bolts with washer seals for installation in original positions.
62. Remove cylinder block cradle inner bolts and washers.
63. Remove two cylinder block cradle Torx bolts.
64. Remove 15 mounting bolts, two nuts and cylinder block cradle.
65. Remove two bolts, oil pump pickup tube and intermediate shaft.
66. Remove oil filter adapter.
67. Remove rear jackshaft plug.
68. Hold crankshaft using crankshaft socket tool No. 303-674, or equivalent.
69. Remove rear jackshaft sprocket-

retaining bolt and spacer.
70. Remove mounting bolt and righthand cassette.
71. Remove mounting bolt, retainer and oil pump drive.
72. Hold crankshaft using crankshaft socket tool No. 303-674, or equivalent.
73. Loosen front sprocket retaining bolt, then remove bolts and chain tensioner.
74. Remove chain guide.
75. Remove mounting bolt, jackshaft sprocket and chain.
76. Remove mounting bolt and lefthand cassette.
77. Remove thrust plate and jackshaft.
78. Install suitable pin in balance shaft tensioner.
79. Remove two mounting bolts and balance shaft tensioner.
80. Remove two mounting bolts and Balance Shaft Chain Guide.
81. **Do not remove balance shaft sprocket bolt.**
82. Remove balance shaft chain and crankshaft sprocket.
83. Remove two mounting and balance shaft.
84. Reverse procedure to install

PISTON & ROD ASSEMBLY

Position the piston with the indentation arrow toward the front of the cylinder block.
1. Install connecting rod bearings.
2. Install rubber hose pieces on connecting rod bolts to protect crankshaft.
3. Install pistons using suitable piston ring compressor tool rotating crankshaft as required.
4. Check clearance of each connecting rod bearing using old nuts and bolts.
5. Rotate crankshaft until piston is at bottom of its stroke.
6. For cylinders Nos. 1, 2 and 3, remove connecting rod nut at oil split hole side first
7. For cylinders Nos. 4, 5 and 6, remove opposite nut first.
8. Loosen first nut until face is approximately .08 inch over end of bolt, **Fig. 18.**
9. Tap on nut until bolt can be removed by hand.
10. Repeat previous steps for opposite bolt.

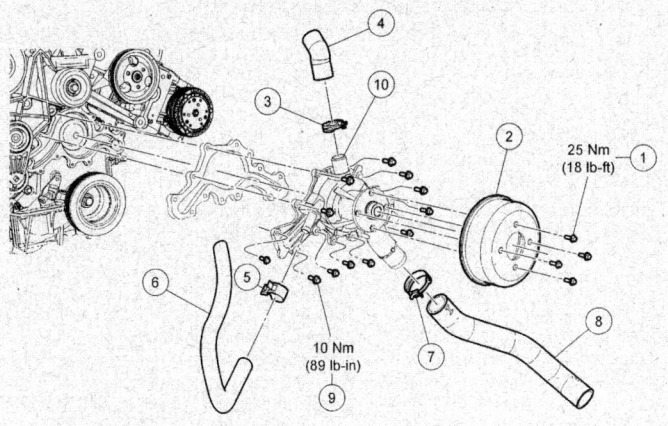

Item	Description
1	Coolant pump pulley bolt (4 required)
2	Coolant pump pulley
3	Hose clamp
4	Thermostat housing-to-coolant pump hose
5	Hose clamp
6	Heater hose
7	Hose clamp
8	Radiator-to-coolant pump hose
9	Coolant pump bolts (12 required)
10	Coolant pump

ARM0400000000593

Fig. 26 Water pump replacement

Item	Description		Item	Description
1	Power steering reservoir bolt		4	Upper degas bottle hose
2	Power steering reservoir		5	Degas bottle bolt (2 required)
3	Upper degas bottle hose clamp		6	Degas bottle

ARM0400000000559

Fig. 27 Degas bottle replacement

11. Install new bolts ensure head is parallel to sideward face of connecting rod, **Fig. 19.**
12. Install connecting rod cap in its original position.
13. Install and tighten connecting rod nuts finger-tight.
14. **Torque** connecting rod nuts to 15 ft. lbs.
15. Tighten bolts an additional 90°.

MAIN & ROD BEARINGS

1. Lubricate crankshaft main bearings with suitable, clean engine oil.
2. Install crankshaft main bearings and the thrust bearing.
3. Install lower main bearings in bearing caps.
4. Install crankshaft.
5. Apply silicone gasket and sealant to rear main bearing cap to cylinder block parting line, **Fig. 20. Cap must be secured within four minutes and seal application.**
6. Install main bearing caps in order in which they were removed.
7. **Torque** main bearing cap bolts in sequence to 26 ft. lbs, **Fig. 21.**
8. Tighten cap bolts an additional 57° in sequence.

CRANKSHAFT SEAL
REPLACE

1. Remove crankshaft pulley as outlined under "Crankshaft Damper, Replace."
2. Remove crankshaft front seal using crankshaft front oil seal remover tool No. T74P-6700-A and aligner tool No, T74P-6019-A, or equivalent.
3. Reverse procedure to install using aligner tool and crankshaft vibration damper installer tool No. T74P-6316-B, or equivalent.

CRANKSHAFT REAR OIL SEAL
REPLACE

1. **On models equipped with automatic transmission,** remove transmission as outlined in **MOTOR's "Domestic Transmission Manual, In-Vehicle Service."**
2. **On models equipped with manual transmission,** remove clutch as outlined in **MOTOR's "Domestic Transmission Manual, In-Vehicle Service."**
3. **On all models,** remove eight mounting bolts and flexplate/flywheel.
4. Remove spacer plate.
5. Remove crankshaft rear seal using oil seal remover too No. T92C-6700-CH, or equivalent. **Do not scratch or damage crankshaft rear seal running surface.**
6. Reverse procedure to install, noting the following:
   a. Lubricate crankshaft rear oil seal with suitable, clean engine oil
   b. Install seal using crankshaft rear oil seal tool No. T95T-6701-AR, or equivalent.
   c. **Torque** flexplate/flywheel mounting bolts in sequence to 115 inch lbs., **Fig. 22.**
   d. **Torque** mounting bolts in sequence to 52 ft. lbs.

OIL PAN
REPLACE

1. Raise and support vehicle.
2. Drain engine oil into suitable container.
3. Remove mounting bolts, oil pan and gasket.
4. Reverse procedure to install.

OIL PUMP
REPLACE

1. Raise and support vehicle.
2. Disconnect two throttle body electrical connectors, **Fig. 1.**
3. Disconnect two throttle body coolant hoses from coolant tube. Plug coolant hoses.
4. Remove four mounting bolts and throttle body.
5. Remove front end accessory drive bracket bolt and install engine lifting bracket tool No. D70P-6000, or equivalent.
6. Remove six pin-type retainers and radiator sight shield.
7. Support engine using suitable three-bar engine support tool.
8. Remove left and righthand engine mount nuts.
9. Drain engine oil into suitable container.
10. Remove mounting bolts, oil pan and gasket.
11. Remove mounting bolt, the oil pump screen and pickup tube.
12. Remove mounting bolt and disconnect steering column intermediate shaft from steering gear. **Do not allow**

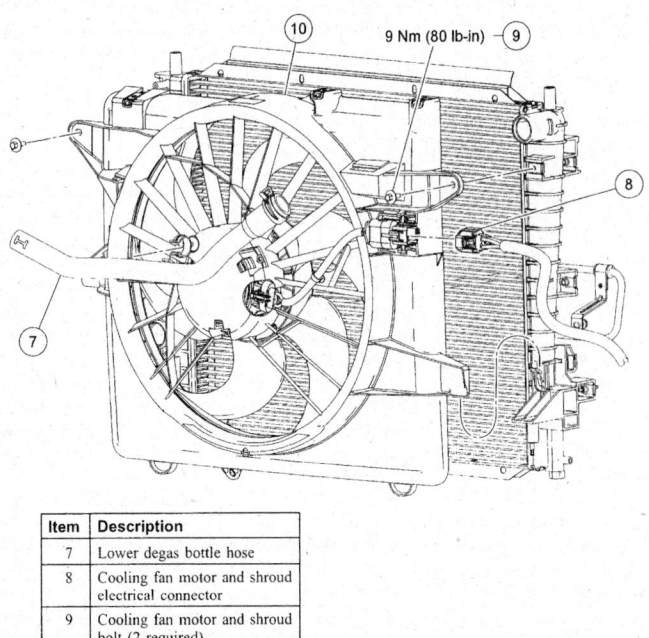

Item	Description
7	Lower degas bottle hose
8	Cooling fan motor and shroud electrical connector
9	Cooling fan motor and shroud bolt (2 required)
10	Cooling fan motor and shroud

ARM0400000000560

Fig. 28 Cooling fan motor & shroud replacement

Item	Description		Item	Description
1	Hose clamp		6	Lower radiator hose
2	Degas bottle-to-radiator hose		7	Radiator support bracket bolt (4 required)
3	Hose clamp		8	Radiator support bracket (2 required)
4	Upper radiator hose			
5	Hose clamp			

ARM0400000000557

Fig. 29 Radiator replace (Part 1 of 2)

steering wheel to rotate while steering column intermediate shaft is disconnected.

13. Remove two steering gear-to-crossmember bolts and disconnect gear from crossmember.
14. Record positions and remove two cylinder block cradle rear Torx bolts.
15. Remove 20 mounting bolts and two nuts along outside of cylinder block cradle.
16. Remove with cylinder block cradle inner bolts and two washer seals. **Record location two silver-colored bolts that have washer seals for installation in original position.**
17. Raise engine and remove lower block cradle.
18. Remove two mounting bolts and oil pump.
19. Reverse procedure to install, noting the following:
    a. Back set screws off until they are below cylinder block cradle boss.
    b. Clean gasket mating surfaces using suitable silicone gasket remover and metal surface prep.
    c. Apply silicone, **Fig. 23**. **Cylinder block cradle must be secured within four minutes of sealant application.**
    d. Position new gasket and cylinder block cradle.
    e. Install outer 20 mounting bolts, two nuts finger, two rear Torx bolts and two bell housing-to-cylinder block cradle bolts finger tight.
    f. **Torque** two bell housing-to-cylinder block cradle bolts to 35 ft. lbs.
    g. **Torque** outer 20 mounting bolts and two nuts to 89 inch lbs.
    h. **Torque** cylinder block cradle rear Torx bolts to 71 inch lbs.
    i. **Torque** eight inserts to 27 inch lbs.
    j. Install two silver-colored bolts and new washer seals finger tight.
    k. Install six remaining inner bolts finger tight.
    l. **Torque** eight inner bolts in sequence to 11 ft. lbs., **Fig. 24.**
    m. **Torque** bolts in sequence to 25 ft. lbs.

BELT TENSION DATA

These models are equipped with an automatic drive belt tensioner. No adjustment or maintenance is required.

SERPENTINE DRIVE BELT

Always use square drive tool in hole in tensioner to move tensioner. Never pry on tensioner pulley. When releasing drive belt tensioner, never allow tensioner to snap back. Damage to tensioner or personal injury could result.

Do not allow engine coolant to remain on serpentine belt or pulleys. If required, remove belt and flush with clean water.

Routing

Refer to **Fig. 25** for serpentine drive belt routing.

Replacement

Rotate the accessory drive belt tensioner clockwise with suitable belt tensioner release tool and remove the belt.

COOLING SYSTEM BLEED

1. Fill radiator through degas bottle until the coolant level is between the COOLANT FILL LEVEL marks.
2. Select maximum heater temperature and blower motor speed settings.
3. Position control to discharge air at air conditioning vents in instrument panel.
4. Start engine and allow to idle.
5. While engine is idling, feel for hot air at air conditioning vents.
6. **If air discharge remains cool and engine coolant temperature gauge does not move, engine coolant level is low and must be filled. Stop engine, allow it to cool and fill cooling system.**
7. Allow engine to idle until normal operating temperature is reached. Hot air should discharge from air conditioning vents.
8. Engine coolant temperature gauge should maintain stabilized reading in middle of NORMAL range.
9. Upper radiator hose should feel hot to touch.
10. Shut engine off and allow it to cool.
11. Check engine for coolant leaks.
12. Check and adjust engine coolant level in degas bottle.

THERMOSTAT

REPLACE

1. Drain cooling system into suitable container.
2. Disconnect crankcase vent tube from air cleaner outlet pipe.
3. Loosen two clamps and remove air cleaner outlet pipe.
4. Disconnect two throttle body electrical connectors, **Fig. 1.**

5. Disconnect two throttle body coolant hoses from coolant tube. Plug coolant hoses.
6. Remove four mounting bolts and throttle body.
7. Remove three upper mounting bolts and position thermostat housing aside.
8. Reverse procedure to install, using new thermostat O-ring seal and lubricate with suitable, clean engine coolant.

WATER PUMP
REPLACE

1. Drain engine coolant into suitable container.
2. Disconnect crankcase vent tube from air cleaner outlet pipe.
3. Loosen two clamps and remove air cleaner outlet pipe.
4. Loosen for water pump pulley mounting bolts, **Fig. 26.**
5. Rotate accessory drive belt tensioner clockwise with suitable belt tensioner release tool and remove belt.
6. Remove four mounting bolts and water pump pulley.
7. Disconnect thermostat housing-to-coolant pump hose and position aside.
8. Disconnect heater hose and position aside.
9. Disconnect radiator-to-coolant pump hose and position aside.
10. Remove 12 mounting bolts, water pump and gasket.
11. Reverse procedure to install using new gasket.

RADIATOR
REPLACE

1. Drain cooling system into suitable container.
2. Remove four push pin retainers and air deflector.
3. Disconnect crankcase vent tube from air cleaner outlet pipe.
4. Loosen two clamps and remove air cleaner outlet pipe.
5. Remove mounting bolt and position power steering reservoir aside, **Fig. 27.**
6. Remove two mounting bolts and position degas bottle aside.
7. Detach and position lower degas bottle hose aside.
8. Disconnect cooling fan motor and shroud electrical connector, **Fig. 28.**
9. Remove two mounting bolts, cooling fan motor and shroud.
10. Disconnect upper and lower radiator hoses from radiator, then position aside, **Fig. 29.**
11. Remove four mounting bolts and radiator support brackets.
12. Remove two power steering tubes and air conditioning condenser retaining nuts, then position power steering tubes aside.
13. Remove two condenser bolts and remove radiator.

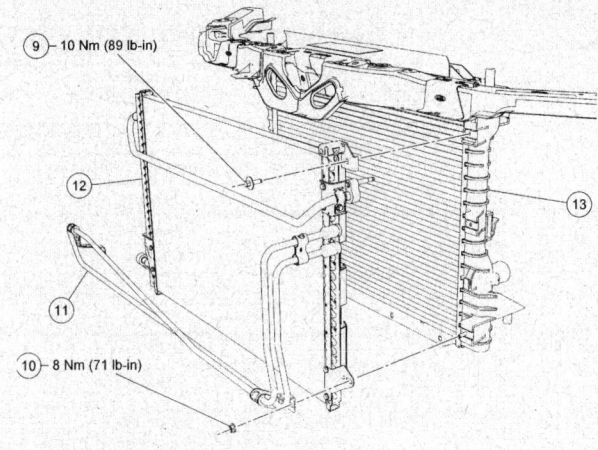

Item	Description
9	A/C condenser bolt (2 required)
10	Power steering tubes and A/C condenser retaining nut (2 required)
11	Power steering tubes
12	A/C condenser
13	Radiator

ARM0400000000558

Fig. 29   Radiator replace (Part 2 of 2)

14. Reverse procedure to install.

FUEL PUMP
REPLACE

1. Remove fuel pump relay.
2. Start engine and allow it idle until is stalls.
3. Crank engine for approximately five seconds to ensure fuel injection supply manifold pressure has been released.
4. Turn ignition switch to OFF position.
5. Remove fuel tank filler cap and insert suitable fuel tank drain hose into filler neck.
6. Insert chamfered end of hose into filler pipe through guide tube.
7. Attach suitable fuel recovery system to hose and remove fuel from tank. **Ensure to drain 1/8 of fuel capacity through filler pipe prior to removing pumps.**
8. Remove rear seat bottom and fuel pump module insulation padding.
9. Remove fuel pump module access cover.
10. Disconnect electrical connector and release fuel tube quick connect coupling on fuel pump module.
11. Remove fuel pump module lock retaining ring using suitable fuel tank locking wrench.
12. Position fuel pump module askew, then install suitable hose and fuel recovery system.
13. Completely drain fuel pump side of fuel tank.
14. Lift fuel pump module out of fuel tank allowing access to quick connect coupling.

15. Disconnect quick connect coupling from bottom of fuel pump module.
16. Remove fuel pump module. **Do not damage float arm.**
17. Reverse procedure to install, noting the following:
    a. Install new O-ring seal and lock ring.
    b. Apply suitable, clean engine oil to O-ring seal.
    c. Ensure alignment arrows on fuel pump module and fuel tank meet before tightening lock ring.

FUEL FILTER
REPLACE

1. Raise and support vehicle.
2. Remove fuel pump relay.
3. Start engine and allow it idle until is stalls.
4. Crank engine for approximately five seconds to ensure fuel injection supply manifold pressure has been released.
5. Turn ignition switch to OFF position.
6. Remove fuel bundle shield mounting bolts and nuts.
7. Remove fuel bundle shield pin-type retainer.
8. Release four mounting nuts and fuel bundle shield. **Nuts are encapsulated as part of fuel bundle shield and should only be removed as part of shield.**
9. Disconnect fuel tube quick connect couplings from both sides of fuel filter.
10. Release bracket mounting bolt and remove fuel filter.
11. Reverse procedure to install.

TIGHTENING SPECIFICATIONS

Year	Component	Torque/Ft. Lbs.
2005	Accessory Drive Belt Idler Pulley	35
	Air Cleaner Outlet Pipe	27①
	Air Conditioning Condenser	89①
	Alternator	35
	Balance Shaft	20
	Balance Shaft Chain Guide	89①
	Balance Shaft Tensioner	21
	Belt Tensioner	35
	Camshaft	⑦
	Camshaft Cassette, Lefthand Lower	106①
	Camshaft Cassette, Lefthand Upper	14①
	Camshaft Cassette, Righthand	89①
	Camshaft Sprocket	63
	Camshaft Sprocket Holding Tool	89①
	Camshaft Tensioner	32
	Catalytic Converter-To-Exhaust Manifold	30
	Connecting Rod	④
	Cooling Fan Motor & Shroud	80①
	Crankshaft Damper	②
	Crankshaft Position (CKP) Sensor	89①
	Cylinder Block Cradle	⑥
	Cylinder Head	⑩
	EGR System Module Tube	29
	Engine Lifting Bracket	35
	Engine Mount	52
	Engine Mount Bracket	57
	Engine Mount Bracket-To-Engine	46
	Exhaust Gas Recirculation (EGR) System Module Tube	29
	Exhaust Manifold	17
	Flexplate/Flywheel	⑤
	Front Cassette	14
	Front Cover	14
	Front End Accessory Drive (FEAD) Bracket	35
	Fuel Bundle Shield	62①
	Fuel Filter	44①
	Fuel Rail	17
	Fuel Rail Supply Tube Bracket, Lower	89①
	Fuel Rail Supply Tube Bracket, Upper	53①
	Ignition Coil & Bracket, M8	18
	Ignition Coil & Bracket, M12	25
	Ignition Coil Bracket Upper	89①
	Intake Manifold	89①
	Jackshaft	⑨
	Jackshaft Cassette, Righthand	107①
	Jackshaft Chain Guide	14
	Jackshaft Chain Tensioner	89①
	Jackshaft Rear Sprocket	15⑧
	Jackshaft Thrust Plate	97①
	Knock Sensor	15
	Main Bearings	③

Continued

4.0L ENGINE

TIGHTENING
SPECIFICATIONS—Continued

Year	Component	Torque/Ft. Lbs.
2005	Main Engine Wiring Harness	30
	Oil Filter Adapter	42
	Oil Level Indicator Tube	97①
	Oil Pan	80①
	Oil Pan Drain Plug	19
	Oil Pump	15
	Oil Pump Drive	14
	Oil Pump Intermediate Shaft	14
	Oil Pump Screen & Pickup Tube	97①
	Power Steering Reservoir	71①
	Radiator Support Bracket	22
	Steering Gear	86
	Steering Column Intermediate Shaft	18
	Thermostat Housing	89①
	Throttle Body	89①
	Timing Chain Tensioner, Primary	80①
	Water Pump	89①
	Water Pump Pulley	18

① — Inch pounds.
② — Refer to "Crankshaft Damper, Replace" for tightening specifications and sequence.
③ — Refer to "Main & Rod Bearings" for tightening specifications and sequence.
④ — Refer to "Piston & Rod Assembly" for tightening specifications and sequence.
⑤ — Refer to "Crankshaft Rear Oil Seal, Replace" for tightening specifications and sequence.
⑥ — Refer to "Oil Pump, Replace" for tightening specifications and sequence.
⑦ — Refer to "Camshaft, Replace" for tightening specifications and sequence.
⑧ — Tighten an additional 90°.
⑨ — Refer to "Timing Chain, Replace" for tightening specifications and sequence.
⑩ — Refer to "Cylinder Head, Replace" for tightening specifications and sequence.

4.6L DOHC Engine

NOTE: For Procedures Not Found In This Section, Refer To "4.6L DOHC Engine" Section In "Continental" Chapter.

NOTE: On Air Bag Equipped Models, Refer To "Air Bag System Precautions" Located In The Front Of This Manual For System Disarming & Arming Procedures.

NOTE: Refer To "Computer Relearn Procedures" Located In The Front Of This Manual When Battery Power To The Computer Has Been Interrupted.

NOTE: Prior To Performing Any Service Operations Listed In This Section, Consult The "Technical Service Bulletins" Section For Related Information.

INDEX

PRECAUTIONS

Air Bag Systems

Refer to "Air Bag System Precautions" in front of this manual for system disarming and arming procedures.

Battery Ground Cable

Prior to service, disconnect battery ground cable and isolate as required.

Fuel System Pressure Relief

Fuel supply tubes will remain pressurized for long periods of time after engine shutdown. This pressure must be relieved before beginning fuel system service or personal injury or damage to vehicle may occur. A valve is provided on fuel injection supply manifold for this purpose.

1. Connect EFI/CFI fuel pressure gauge tool No. T80L-9974-B, or equivalent, to fuel pressure relief valve on fuel injection supply manifold.
2. Place outlet hose of tool into suitable fuel container.
3. Open manual valve on fuel pressure gauge tool to relieve fuel system pressure.

COMPRESSION PRESSURE

When inspecting cylinder compression, lowest cylinder must be within 75% of highest cylinder. Perform compression test with engine at normal operating temperature, spark plugs and air cleaner removed and the throttle propped wide open.

ENGINE MOUNT

REPLACE

1. Install lift bracket tool No. D93P-6001-A3, or equivalent.
2. Install engine support tool No. 303-290-A, or equivalent.
3. Raise and support vehicle.
4. Remove solenoid protective cap and wiring nuts. Position wiring aside.
5. Remove mounting bolts and starter motor.
6. Remove engine mount nuts and lower vehicle.

7. Raise engine using support tool.
8. Raise vehicle and remove engine mount.
9. Reverse procedure to install.

ENGINE
REPLACE

1. Drain coolant into suitable container.
2. Recover air conditioning refrigerant as outlined in "Air Conditioning" chapter.
3. Remove air cleaner and outlet tube.
4. Relieve fuel system pressure as outlined under "Precautions."
5. Disconnect fuel lines.
6. Remove radiator upper hose.
7. Disconnect throttle and speed control cables, then the return spring.
8. Remove bracket mounting bolts, then the throttle and speed control cables aside.
9. Disconnect EVAP emissions return line.
10. Disconnect 16- and 42-pin electrical connectors.
11. Separate wiring harness at three firewall locations.
12. Disconnect TBI electrical connectors.
13. Disconnect HVAC vacuum supply hoses.
14. Place suitable container firewall fittings and disconnect heater hoses.
15. Remove nuts and wiring support bracket.
16. Disconnect electrical connectors near underhood power distribution box.
17. Slide underhood power distribution box access cover up, then remove nut and battery cables.
18. Disconnect low coolant sensor electrical connector.
19. Disconnect coolant hose at bypass tube.
20. Remove transmission shift lever knob.
21. Remove console panel shifter plate. Lift boot over lever.
22. Remove mounting bolts and shift lever.
23. Remove mounting screws inner boot.
24. Remove four mounting bolts and shifter.
25. Raise and support vehicle.
26. Remove front wheels and tires assemblies.
27. Disconnect front wheel speed sensor electrical connectors.
28. Remove mounting bolts and position front brake caliper aside with suitable wire or rope.
29. Remove mounting fasteners and three-way catalytic converter.
30. Disconnect air conditioning compressor inlet and outlet lines.
31. Position air conditioning muffler aside.
32. Raise and support vehicle.
33. Remove solenoid protective cap and wiring nuts. Position wiring aside.
34. Remove mounting bolts and starter motor.
35. Position wiring harness at front of engine aside.
36. Disconnect engine oil pressure sensor electrical connector.
37. Remove mounting nut and engine power ground cable.
38. Disconnect hose oil filter adapter.
39. Remove radiator lower hose.

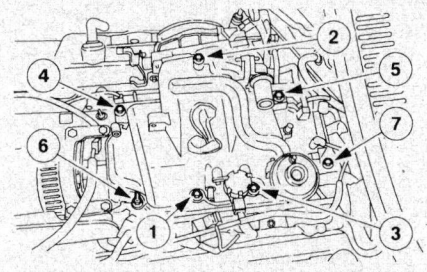

Fig. 1   Upper intake manifold bolt tightening sequence

FM1069901056000X

40. Disconnect clutch cable at transmission.
41. Disconnect power steering high pressure line.
42. Disconnect lower power steering line from fluid cooler.
43. Disconnect hose at power steering fluid reservoir.
44. Remove mounting bolt and power steering pump anti-rotation clip.
45. Disconnect power steering pump high pressure line fitting.
46. Separate steering shaft from steering gear, discarding bolt.
47. Remove pin-style retainers, then position lefthand and righthand splash shields aside.
48. Remove stabilizer bar clamp nuts.
49. Remove mounting bolts and inspection cover.
50. Remove exhaust air supply valve tube nuts at exhaust manifolds.
51. Position universal powertrain lift and extension.
52. Mark crossmember for installation alignment.
53. Remove crossmember to body and frame bolts.
54. Remove engine and transmission.
55. Install engine righthand lifting bracket tool No. D93P-6001-A1 and lefthand lifting bracket tool No. D93P-6002-A2, or equivalents.
56. Install suitable engine lifting crank or skyhook.
57. Remove motor mount nuts.
58. Disconnect transmission wiring.
59. Remove transmission to engine bolts.
60. Raise and separate engine from front A-frame.
61. Reverse procedure to install.

INTAKE MANIFOLD
REPLACE
2001
UPPER

1. Remove air cleaner outlet tube.
2. Disconnect accelerator and speed control cables, then the return spring.
3. Remove accelerator and speed control cable bracket bolts, then position cables aside.
4. Disconnect TPS electrical connector.
5. Disconnect EVAP emissions return hose.

6. Disconnect idle air control (IAC) valve electrical connector.
7. Disconnect differential pressure feedback EGR.
8. Disconnect main vacuum supply and EGR vacuum lines.
9. Disconnect differential pressure feedback EGR hoses.
10. Disconnect EGR valve to exhaust tube from EGR valve.
11. Disconnect EGR vacuum regulator solenoid vacuum lines and electrical connector.
12. Remove PCV valve and tube.
13. Remove upper intake manifold mounting bolts in sequence, **Fig. 1.**
14. Remove upper intake manifold. Discard gasket.
15. Reverse procedure to install, noting the following:
    a. Install new upper to lower intake gasket.
    b. **Torque** upper intake manifold mounting bolts in sequence to 89 inch lbs., **Fig. 1.**

LOWER

1. Remove upper intake manifold as outlined under "Upper.".
2. Relieve fuel system pressure as outlined under "Precautions."
3. Remove coolant bypass tube.
4. Remove serpentine drive belt from alternator pulley. Leave belt in place to ease installation.
5. Disconnect alternator electrical connections.
6. Remove mounting bolts and alternator.
7. Disconnect fuel pressure sensor electrical connector and vacuum line.
8. Disconnect fuel injector electrical connectors.
9. Separate fuel charging wiring from three injection supply manifold studs.
10. Remove lower intake manifold mounting bolts and studs in sequence, **Fig. 2.**
11. Remove lower intake manifold.
12. Reverse procedure to install, noting the following:
    a. Install new manifold mounting gaskets.
    b. **Torque** lower intake manifold mounting bolts in sequence to 89 inch lbs., **Fig. 2.**

2003-04
UPPER

Refer to "2001."

LOWER

1. Drain engine and supercharger coolant into suitable container.
2. Relieve fuel system pressure as outlined under "Precautions."
3. Remove radiator upper and lower hoses, then the supercharger degas hose.
4. Remove supercharger drive belt.
5. Disconnect coolant hose.
6. Remove air cleaner outlet tube.
7. Disconnect throttle position (TP) sensor and idle air control (IAC) valve

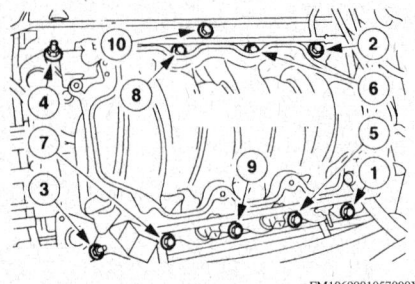

Fig. 2 Lower intake manifold tightening sequence. 2001

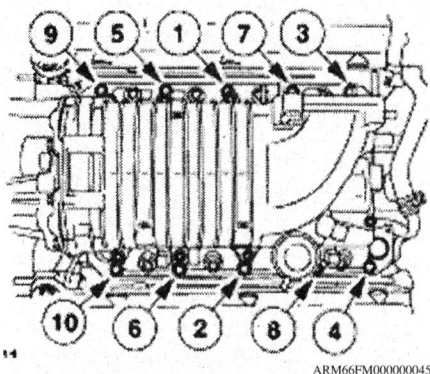

Fig. 3 Lower intake manifold tightening sequence. 2003–04

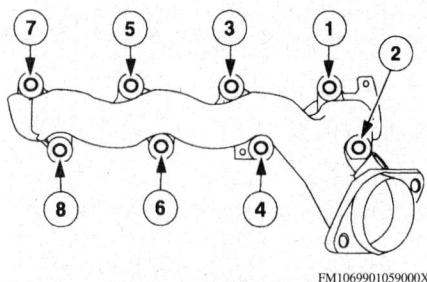

Fig. 4 Lefthand exhaust manifold nut tightening sequence

electrical connectors.

8. Disconnect vacuum hoses from lower intake manifold.
9. Disconnect fuel hose spring lock coupling.
10. Disconnect accelerator and speed control cables.
11. Remove accelerator cable bracket bolts, then release clip and position bracket and cables aside.
12. Disconnect electrical connector from fuel pulse damper, EGR regulator solenoid, super charger bypass vacuum solenoid and differential pressure feedback EGR system.
13. Disconnect vacuum hoses from differential pressure feedback EGR system.
14. Disconnect vacuum hoses from supercharger bypass vacuum solenoid and actuator.
15. Disconnect vacuum hoses from fuel pulse damper and EGR vacuum regulator solenoid.
16. Disconnect vacuum hoses from back of supercharger and position aside.
17. Remove mounting bolts and vacuum accessory bracket.
18. Disconnect exhaust manifold to EGR valve tube.
19. Disconnect barometric pressure sensor electrical connector and PCV ventilation hose.
20. Separate fuel charging wiring harness from fuel injection supply manifold in four places and position aside.
21. Remove ten mounting bolts, then the lower intake manifold, supercharger and fuel supply manifold as an assembly.
22. Reverse procedure to install, noting the following:
    a. Install new bypass tube O-rings and lubricate them with clean engine oil.
    b. Tighten intake manifold bolts in sequence, **Fig. 3**.

EXHAUST MANIFOLD

REPLACE

2001

1. Raise and support vehicle.
2. Disconnect exhaust pipe HO2S electrical connectors.
3. **If removing lefthand manifold,** disconnect EGR tube at manifold.
4. **On all models,** remove exhaust pipe flange to manifold bolts.

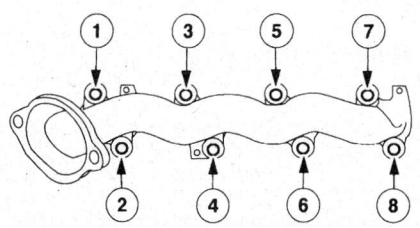

Fig. 5 Righthand exhaust manifold nut tightening sequence

5. Remove mounting nuts, manifold and gasket. Discard gasket.
6. Reverse procedure to install, noting the following:
    a. Install new manifold gaskets.
    b. **Torque** manifold mounting nuts in sequence to 15 ft. lbs., **Figs. 4 and 5.**

2003–04

RIGHTHAND

1. Raise and support vehicle, then remove dual converter Y-pipe.
2. Remove solenoid protective cap and wiring nuts. Position wiring aside.
3. Remove mounting bolts and starter motor.
4. Remove mounting nuts and exhaust manifold.
5. Reverse procedure to install with new exhaust manifold gasket. **Torque** mounting nuts in sequence to 18 ft. lbs., **Fig. 5.**

LEFTHAND

1. Position steering wheel straight ahead and lock.
2. Raise and support vehicle, then remove dual converter Y-pipe.
3. Remove and discard steering pinch bolt, then separate steering coupler.
4. Disconnect EGR tube at exhaust manifold.
5. Remove oil dipstick tube.
6. Remove mounting nuts and exhaust manifold.
7. Reverse procedure to install with new exhaust manifold gasket. **Torque**

mounting nuts in sequence to 18 ft. lbs., **Fig. 4.**

CYLINDER HEAD

REPLACE

2001

Refer to "4.6L DOHC Engine" section in "Continental" chapter.

2003–04

1. Remove intake manifold as outlined under "Intake Manifold, Replace."
2. Remove valve covers as outlined under "Valve Covers, Replace."
3. Remove exhaust manifolds as outlined under "Exhaust Manifold, Replace."
4. Remove timing chains as outlined under "Timing Chain, Replace."
5. Remove mounting bolts and cylinder head.
6. Reverse procedure to install, noting the following:
    a. Lubricate cylinder head bolts and threads with clean engine oil.
    b. **Torque** cylinder head bolts in sequence to 30 ft. lbs., **Fig. 6.**
    c. Tighten bolts an additional 90° in sequence.
    d. Loosen bolts at least of one full turn.
    e. **Torque** bolts in sequence to 30 ft. lbs.
    f. Tighten bolts an additional 90° in sequence.
    g. Tighten bolts an additional 90° in sequence.

VALVE COVER

REPLACE

2001

LEFTHAND

1. Turn engine off and depress brake pedal several times.
2. Disconnect brake fluid level sensor electrical connector.
3. Position suitable drain pan and disconnect brake fluid lines on lower side of master cylinder.
4. Position suitable drain pan and disconnect power steering fluid return line hose.

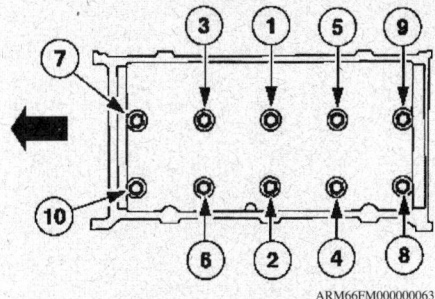

Fig. 6 Cylinder head tightening sequence. 2003-04

5. Disconnect power steering pressure lines at hydro-booster. Discard Teflon seals.
6. Remove self-locking pin in hydro-booster linkage.
7. Remove stop lamp switch and hydro-booster pushrod from brake pedal pin.
8. Remove hydro-booster mounting nuts at firewall.
9. Remove brake hydro-booster unit.
10. Disconnect clutch cable at clutch pedal and position aside.
11. Remove lefthand bank ignition coils.
12. Remove mounting bolts and valve cover.
13. Reverse procedure to install, noting the following:
    a. Apply .32 inch bead of silicone gasket sealant No. F7AZ-19554-EA, or equivalent, to valve cover sealing surfaces. **Install and tighten cover and mounting bolts within four minutes.**
    b. **Torque** valve cover bolts and studs in sequence to 89 inch lbs., **Fig. 7.**
    c. Install new power steering pressure line Teflon seals.
    d. Bleed brake and power steering fluid systems.

RIGHTHAND

1. Remove righthand bank ignition coils.
2. Relieve fuel system pressure as outlined under "Precautions."
3. Disconnect fuel lines.
4. Disconnect EVAP emissions return tube.
5. Remove mounting bolts and valve cover.
6. Reverse procedure to install, noting the following:
    a. Apply .32 inch bead of silicone gasket sealant No. F7AZ-19554-EA, or equivalent, to valve cover sealing surfaces. **Install and tighten cover and mounting bolts within four minutes.**
    b. **Torque** valve cover bolts and studs in sequence to 89 inch lbs., **Fig. 7.**

2003-04

LEFTHAND

1. Turn engine off and depress brake pedal several times.
2. Disconnect brake fluid level sensor electrical connector.
3. Position suitable drain pan and disconnect brake fluid lines on lower side of

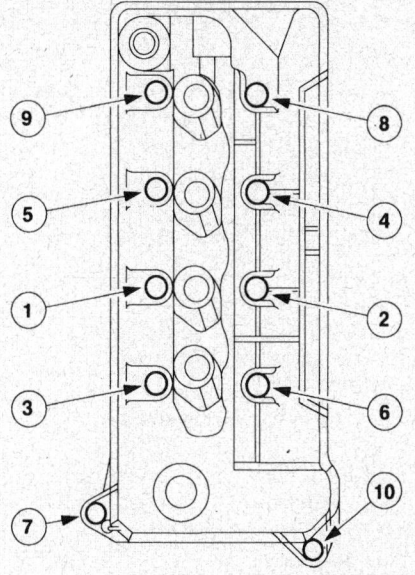

Fig. 7 Valve cover bolt tightening sequence

master cylinder.
4. Position suitable drain pan and disconnect power steering fluid return line hose.
5. Disconnect power steering pressure lines at hydro-booster. Discard Teflon seals.
6. Remove self-locking pin in hydro-booster linkage.
7. Remove stop lamp switch and hydro-booster pushrod from brake pedal pin.
8. Remove hydro-booster mounting nuts at firewall.
9. Remove brake hydro-booster unit.
10. Remove lefthand ignition coils.
11. Unclip wiring harness from power steering bracket.
12. Disconnect electrical connectors from fuel pulse damper, EGR vacuum regulator solenoid, supercharger bypass vacuum solenoid and differential pressure feedback EGR system.
13. Disconnect vacuum hoses from differential pressure feedback EGR system.
14. Disconnect vacuum hoses from supercharger bypass vacuum solenoid and actuator.
15. Disconnect vacuum hoses from fuel pulse damper and EGR vacuum regulator solenoid, then position vacuum harness aside.
16. Remove mounting bolts and vacuum accessory bracket.
17. Disconnect camshaft position (CMP) sensor electrical connector.
18. Remove mounting bolts and position power steering reservoir aside.
19. Remove mounting bolt and position oil dipstick tube aside.
20. Disconnect PCV valve and position aside.
21. Remove mounting bolts and valve cover.
22. Reverse procedure to install, noting the following:
    a. Apply bead of silicone gasket and sealant No. F7AZ-19554-EA, or

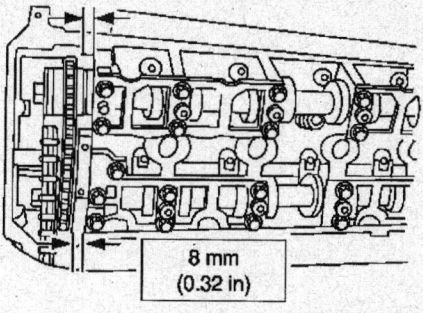

Fig. 8 Sealant application. 2003-04

equivalent, **Fig. 8.**
    b. **Install and tighten cover and mounting bolts within four minutes.**
    c. **Torque** valve cover bolts and studs in sequence to 89 inch lbs., **Fig. 7.**

RIGHTHAND

1. Remove righthand ignition coils.
2. Remove air conditioning condenser to evaporator tube.
3. Remove air conditioning manifold and tube.
4. Disconnect throttle position sensor and idle air control (IAC) valve electrical connectors.
5. Disconnect fuel hose spring lock coupling.
6. Disconnect accelerator and speed control cables.
7. Remove accelerator cable bracket bolts, then release clip and position bracket and cables aside.
8. Remove throttle body and spacer.
9. Remove mounting bolts and valve cover.
10. Reverse procedure to install, noting the following:
    a. Apply bead of silicone gasket and sealant No. F7AZ-19554-EA, or equivalent, **Fig. 8.**
    b. **Install and tighten cover and mounting bolts within four minutes.**
    c. **Torque** valve cover bolts and studs in sequence to 89 inch lbs., **Fig. 7.**

VALVE ARRANGEMENT

Front To Rear

Righthand Side. S-P-E-E-S-P-E-E-S-P-E-E-S-P-E-E①
Lefthand Side. E-E-P-S-E-E-P-S-E-E-P-S-E-E-P-S

①—S-Secondary Intake; P-Primary Intake; E-Exhaust.

CAMSHAFT LOBE LIFT SPECIFICATIONS

Engine	Intake, Inch	Exhaust, Inch
4.6L DOHC	.2200	.2186

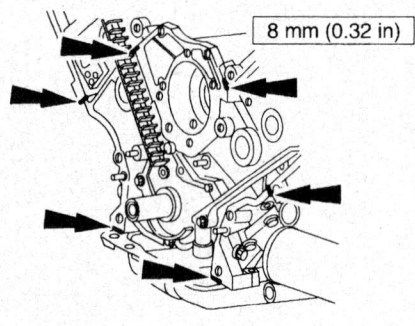

8 mm (0.32 in)

FM1069901063000X

Fig. 9 Front cover sealant application locations

VALVE ADJUSTMENT

These engine are equipped with hydraulic valve lash adjusters. No valve adjustment is required.

FRONT COVER

REPLACE

2001

1. Remove valve covers as outlined under "Valve Cover, Replace."
2. Drain coolant from radiator and degas bottle into suitable container.
3. Disconnect cooling fan motor electrical connector and separate fan harness from shroud.
4. Remove fan shroud lefthand and right-hand mounting bolts.
5. Remove cooling fan, motor and shroud.
6. Remove mounting bolts and water pump pulley.
7. Raise and support vehicle.
8. Drain engine oil into suitable container.
9. Remove mounting bolt and crankshaft pulley using puller tool No. T58P-6316-D, or equivalent.
10. Remove mounting nut and position air conditioning muffler aside.
11. Remove mounting bolts and position power steering pump aside.
12. Disconnect crankshaft position (CKP) sensor electrical connector.
13. Remove front oil pan to front cover bolts.
14. Remove crankshaft front oil seal using seal remover tool No. T74P-6700-A, or equivalent.
15. Lower vehicle.
16. Disconnect camshaft position (CMP) sensor electrical connector.
17. Remove serpentine belt idler pulley.
18. Mark locations for installation alignment, then remove front cover mounting bolts and studs.
19. Remove front cover. Discard gaskets.
20. Reverse procedure to install, noting the following:
    a. Apply silicone gasket sealer part No. F7AZ-19554-EA, or equivalent, **Fig. 9.**
    b. Install bolts and studs in original locations, **Fig. 10.**

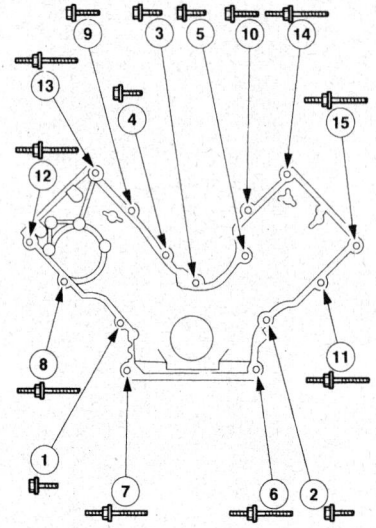

Item	Description
1	Bolt, Hex Flange Head Pilot, M8 x 1.25 x 53
2	Bolt, Hex Flange Head Pilot, M8 x 1.25 x 53
3	Bolt, Hex Flange Head Pilot, M8 x 1.25 x 53
4	Bolt, Hex Flange Head Pilot, M8 x 1.25 x 53
5	Bolt, Hex Flange Head Pilot, M8 x 1.25 x 53
6	Stud, Hex-Head Pilot, M8 x 1.5 x 1.5 x 103.1
7	Stud, Hex-Head Pilot, M8 x 1.5 x 1.5 x 103.1
8	Stud, Hex Pilot, M8 x 1.5 x 57.5
9	Screw and Washer, Hex Pilot, M8 x 1.5 x 57.5
10	Screw and Washer, Hex Pilot, M8 x 1.5 x 57.5
11	Stud and Washer, Hex-Head Pilot, M8 x 1.5 x M8 x 1.25 x 91.1
12	Stud and Washer, Hex-Head Pilot, M8 x 1.5 x M8 x 1.25 x 91.0
13	Stud and Washer, Hex-Head Pilot, M8 x 1.5 x M8 x 1.25 x 91.0
14	Stud and Washer, Hex-Head Pilot, M8 x 1.5 x M8 x 1.25 x 91.0
15	Stud and Washer, Hex-Head Pilot, M8 x 1.5 x M8 x 1.25 x 91.0

FM1069901065000X

Fig. 10 Front cover mounting locations. 2001

c. **Torque** oil pan to front cover bolts to 18 inch lbs.
d. **Torque** cover mounting bolts to 15 ft. lbs.
e. Final tighten mounting bolts an additional 60°.
f. Install new crankshaft pulley oil seal using installer and aligner tool No. T88T-6701-A, or equivalent.
g. Apply silicone gasket sealer to crankshaft pulley keyway slot.
h. **Install and tighten pulley and mounting bolt within four minutes.**

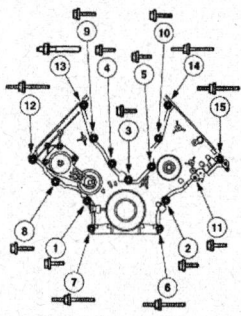

Item	Part Number	Description
1	N806177	Bolt, Hex Flange Head Pilot, M8 x 1.25 x 53
2	N806177	Bolt, Hex Flange Head Pilot, M8 x 1.25 x 53
3	N806177	Bolt, Hex Flange Head Pilot, M8 x 1.25 x 53
4	N806177	Bolt, Hex Flange Head Pilot, M8 x 1.25 x 53
5	N806177	Bolt, Hex Flange Head Pilot, M8 x 1.25 x 53
6	N806300	Stud, Hex Shldr Pilot, M8 x 1.25 x 1.25 x 91.1
7	N806300	Stud, Hex Shldr Pilot, M8 x 1.25 x 1.25 x 91.1
8	N806177	Bolt, Hex Flange Head Pilot, M8 x 1.25 x 53
9	N806177	Bolt, Hex Flange Head Pilot, M8 x 1.25 x 53
10	N806177	Bolt, Hex Flange Head Pilot, M8 x 1.25 x 53
11	N806177	Bolt, Hex Flange Head Pilot, M8 x 1.25 x 53
12	W706560	Stud, Hex Head Pilot, M8 x 1.25 x 65 — M8 x 1.25 x 16
13	N806300	Stud, Hex Shldr Pilot, M8 x 1.25 x 1.25 x 91.1
14	N806300	Stud, Hex Shldr Pilot, M8 x 1.25 x 1.25 x 91.1
15	N806300	Stud, Hex Shldr Pilot, M8 x 1.25 x 1.25 x 91.1

ARM66FM000000047

Fig. 11 Front cover bolt location & tightening sequence. 2003–04

i. Install crankshaft pulley using installer tool No. T74P-6316-B, or equivalent.
j. **Torque** crankshaft pulley bolt to 66 ft. lbs., then loosen one full turn.
k. **Torque** pulley bolt to 37 ft. lbs.
l. Final tighten bolt an additional 85–95°.

2003-04

1. Remove front seal as outlined under "Front Cover Seal, Replace."
2. Remove oil filter adapter.
3. Remove mounting bolts and position power steering pump aside.
4. Remove air conditioning muffler bracket nut.
5. Remove mounting bolts and position air conditioning compressor aside.
6. Disconnect crankshaft position sensor electrical connector.
7. Remove four front oil pan bolts.
8. Disconnect alternator electrical connectors.
9. Remove mounting bolts and alternator.
10. Remove alternator support bracket.
11. Drain coolant into suitable container.
12. Remove coolant bypass tube.
13. Remove valve covers as outlined under "Valve Cover, Replace."
14. Disconnect supercharger coolant hose and remove coolant hose mounting bolt.
15. Disconnect supercharger coolant hoses, then remove supercharger hose and tube.
16. Disconnect camshaft position sensor electrical connector and unclip wiring

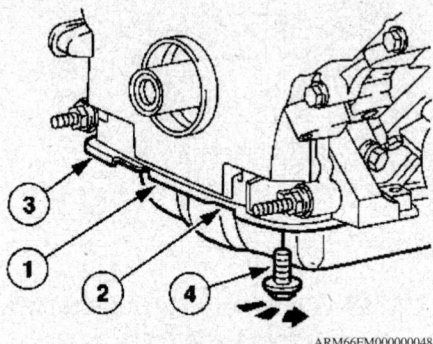

Fig. 12 Oil pan front bolts tightening sequence. 2003–04

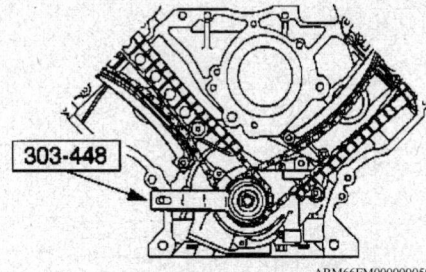

ARM66FM000000050

Fig. 13 Crankshaft holding tool installation. 2003–04

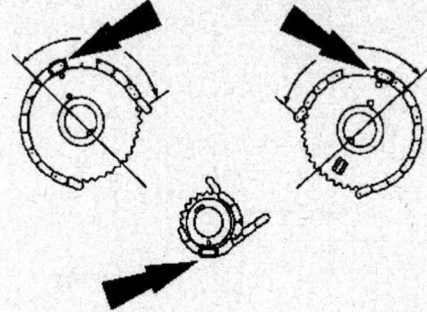

ARM66FM000000051

Fig. 14 Camshaft timing marks. 2003–04

harness from power steering bracket.

17. Disconnect power steering hoses and drain power steering fluid into suitable container.
18. Remove mounting bolts and power steering reservoir.
19. Remove mounting nut and position power steering hose aside.
20. Remove mounting bolts and super-charger belt idler support bracket.
21. Remove wiring harness bracket.
22. Remove water pump pulley.
23. Remove mounting bolts and engine front cover.
24. Reverse procedure to install, noting the following:
    a. Apply silicone gasket sealer part No. F7AZ-19554-EA, or equivalent, **Fig. 9**.
    b. Ensure front cover bolts and studs are installed in original locations, **Fig. 11**.
    c. Tighten front cover bolts in sequence, **Fig. 11**.
    d. **Torque** oil pan front bolts in sequence, to 18 inch lbs., **Fig. 12**.
    e. **Torque** pan front bolts in sequence to 15 ft. lbs.
    f. Tighten front bolts an additional 60° in sequence.

FRONT COVER SEAL

REPLACE

1. Remove cooling fan and supercharger drive belt.
2. Remove coolant hose bolt.
3. Raise and support vehicle.
4. Remove solenoid protective cap and wiring nuts. Position wiring aside.
5. Remove mounting bolts and starter motor.
6. Install flywheel lock tool No. 303-673, or equivalent.
7. Remove mounting bolts and alternator support bracket.
8. Remove stud and position coolant hose aside.
9. Remove auxiliary crankshaft pulley. Auxiliary crankshaft pulley is lefthand threaded.
10. Insert suitable square drive tool into square hole in tensioner arm and rotate tensioner away from belt.
11. Lift belt from pulley and slowly release tensioner.
12. Remove belt.
13. Remove crankshaft pulley using

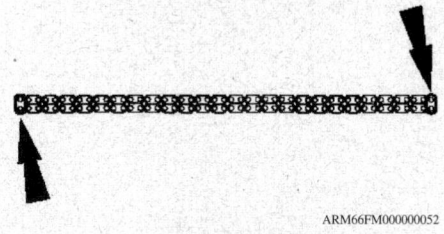

ARM66FM000000052

Fig. 15 Timing chain timing marks. 2003–04

crankshaft vibration damper remover tool No. T58P-6316-D, or equivalent.

14. Remove front seal using front seal remover tool No. T74P-6700-A, or equivalent.
15. Reverse procedure to install, noting the following:
    a. Lubricate engine front cover and front seal with clean engine oil.
    b. Install front seal using seal installer tool No. T88T-6701-A, or equivalent.
    c. Apply suitable sealant to Woodriff key slot on crankshaft pulley.
    d. Install crankshaft pulley using crankshaft vibration damper installer tool No. T74P-6316-B, or equivalent.
    e. **Torque** crankshaft pulley bolt to 66 ft. lbs.
    f. Loosen pulley bolt one full turn.
    g. **Torque** bolt to 37 ft. lbs.
    h. Tighten bolt an additional 85–95°.

TIMING CHAIN

REPLACE

2001

Refer to "4.6L DOHC Engine" section in "Continental" chapter.

2003–04

REMOVAL

Unless otherwise instructed, at no time when timing chains are removed and the cylinder heads are installed is the crankshaft or camshaft to be rotated.

1. Remove front cover as outlined under "Front Cover, Replace."
2. Remove crankshaft sensor ring from crankshaft.

3. Install crankshaft holding tool No. T93P-6303-A, or equivalent, **Fig. 13**.
4. Align camshaft timing marks, **Fig. 14**. Copper links on timing chain may not line up with timing marks on sprockets. If required, turn crankshaft one full turn clockwise.
5. Remove two mounting bolts, timing chain tensioner and arm.
6. Remove crankshaft holding tool.
7. Remove righthand timing chain from camshaft and crankshaft sprocket.
8. Remove lefthand timing chain from camshaft and crankshaft sprocket.
9. Remove mounting bolts and timing chain guides. **Bolts are different lengths and must be installed in original locations.**

INSTALLATION

1. Compress tensioner plunger using suitable soft jawed vise and install retaining clip to hold plunger.
2. If copper links are not visible, mark links on opposite ends of timing chain to use as timing marks, **Fig. 15**.
3. Install timing chain guides.
4. Rotate lefthand camshaft sprocket until timing mark is approximately at 12 o'clock position, **Fig. 14**.
5. Rotate righthand camshaft sprocket until timing mark is approximately at 11 o'clock position.
6. Install crankshaft holding tool No. T93P-6303-A, or equivalent, to position crankshaft. **Fig. 13**.
7. Remove crankshaft holding tool.
8. Install crankshaft sprocket with flange facing forward, **Fig. 16**.
9. Install lefthand timing chain onto crankshaft sprocket, aligning one copper link on timing chain with slot on crankshaft sprocket.
10. Install righthand timing chain onto crankshaft sprocket, aligning one copper link on timing chain with slot on crankshaft sprocket.
11. Ensure camshaft sprockets and timing chain copper links are aligned.
12. Install timing chain tensioners and arms.
13. Remove retaining clips from timing chain tensioners.
14. Install crankshaft sensor ring on crankshaft.
15. Install engine front cover as outlined under "Front Cover, Replace."

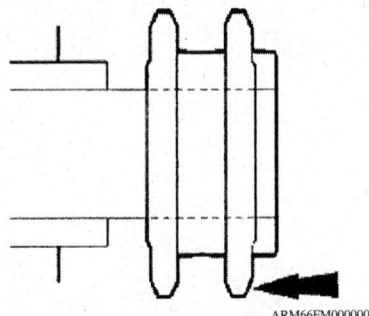

Fig. 16 Crankshaft sprocket installation. 2003–04

TIMING CHAIN TENSIONER BLEED

1. Position timing chain tensioner in suitable soft-jawed vise.
2. Lock ratchet stem mechanism position using suitable tool and slowly compress tensioner plunger by rotating vise handle. **Tensioner must be compressed slowly.**
3. When tensioner plunger bottoms in bore, continue holding ratchet lock mechanism and push ratchet mechanism down until flush with tensioner face.
4. While holding ratchet stem flush to tensioner face, release ratchet lock mechanism and install paper clip or suitable tool to lock tensioner in collapsed position.
5. **Do not remove paper clip or suitable tool until timing chain, tensioner arm, tensioner and timing chain guide are installed on engine.**

CAMSHAFT

REPLACE

2001

Refer to "4.6L DOHC Engine" section in "Continental" chapter.

2003–04

1. Remove valve covers as outlined under "Valve Cover, Replace."
2. Position piston being worked on at bottom of stroke and camshaft lobe at base of circle.
3. Compress valve spring and remove roller followers using valve spring compressor tool No. T93P-6565-AR, or equivalent.
4. Remove timing chains as outlined under "Timing Chain, Replace."
5. Install camshaft holding tool No. T93P-6256-AHR, or equivalent.
6. Remove exhaust camshaft sprocket, then the intake camshaft bolt, washer and spacer.
7. Remove camshaft holding tool.
8. Compress chain tensioner and install suitable lock pin.

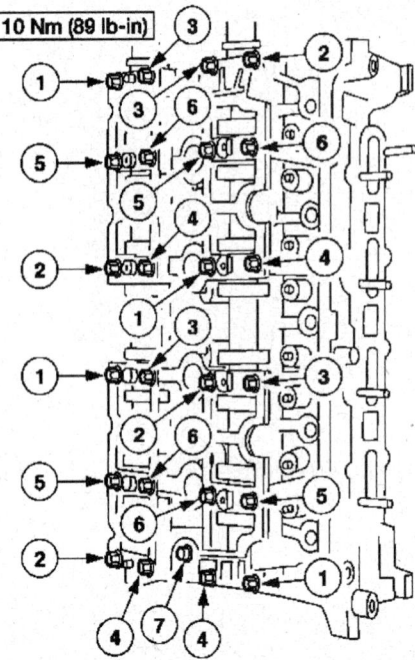

10 Nm (89 lb-in)

Fig. 17 Camshaft bearing cap tightening sequence. 2003–04

9. Remove chain, sprocket and intake camshaft sprocket spacer.
10. Remove chain tensioner bolts.
11. Remove bolts and camshaft bearings. Identify cap locations for installation alignment. **Outer exhaust cam bearing cap bolts are longer and must be installed in original location or engine damage may occur.**
12. Remove camshafts.
13. Reverse procedure to install, noting the following:
   a. Lubricate camshafts with clean engine oil.
   b. Tighten camshaft bearing caps in sequence to 89 inch lbs., **Fig. 17.**
   c. Install camshaft sprockets and chain as an assembly.
   d. Align timing marks to 12 o'clock position and index at 6 o'clock position, **Fig. 18.**
   e. **Torque** camshaft sprocket bolt to 30 ft. lbs., then tighten an additional 90°.

PISTON & ROD ASSEMBLY

1. Rod bearing cap bolts are torque-to-yield bolts, do not reuse bolts.
2. Install connecting rod to piston with marks facing toward front of engine.
3. Install piston with arrow facing toward front of engine.
4. **Torque** connecting rod bearing cap bolts to 18 ft. lbs.
5. **On models equipped less supercharger, torque** cap bolts to 33 ft. lbs.
6. **On models equipped with supercharger, torque** cap bolts to 59 ft. lbs.

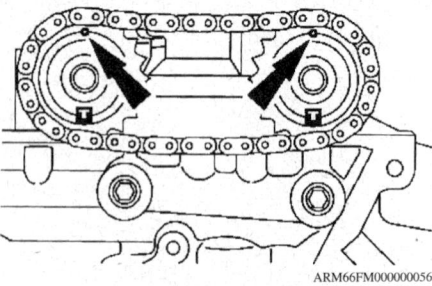

Fig. 18 Camshaft sprocket timing marks. 2003–04

7. **On all models,** final tighten bolts an additional 90°.

MAIN & ROD BEARINGS

2001

Refer to "4.6L DOHC Engine" section in "Continental" chapter.

2003–04

LESS SUPERCHARGER

1. **Torque** main bearing bolts in sequence to 89 inch lbs., **Fig. 19.**
2. **Torque** bearing bolts in sequence. to 18 ft. lbs.
3. **Torque** bolts in sequence to 30 ft. lbs.
4. Final tighten bolts an additional 90° in sequence.
5. **Torque** side bolts to 30 ft. lbs., then tighten an additional 90°.

WITH SUPERCHARGER

1. **Torque** vertical main bearing cap bolts in sequence to 30 ft. lbs., **Fig. 20.**
2. Tighten bolts an additional 85–95° in sequence.
3. **Torque** jackscrews against cylinder block in sequence to 44 inch lbs., **Fig. 21.**
4. **Torque** jackscrews against cylinder block in sequence to 89 inch lbs.
5. **Torque** main bearing cap side bolts in sequence to 15 ft. lbs., **Fig. 22.**

CRANKSHAFT SEAL

REPLACE

1. Remove transmission as outlined in **MOTOR's "Domestic Transmission Manual, In-Vehicle Service."**
2. Remove flywheel.
3. Remove crankshaft oil slinger using rear crankshaft slinger remover tool No. T-95P-6701-AH, or equivalent, and suitable slide hammer.
4. Remove crankshaft rear oil seal using rear crankshaft seal remover tool No. T95P-6701-BH, or equivalent, and suitable slide hammer.
5. Reverse procedure to install, noting the following:
   a. Install rear oil seal using crankshaft

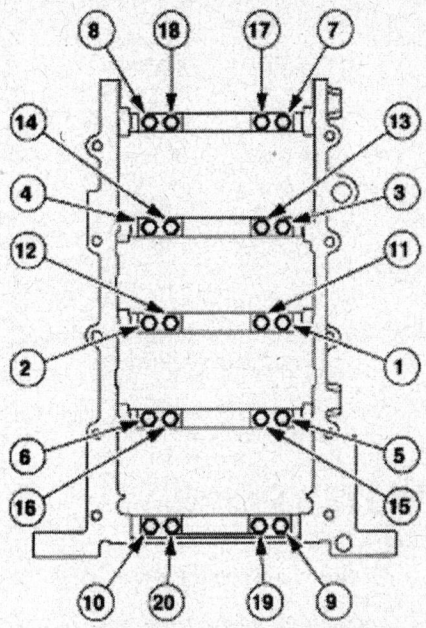

Fig. 19 Main bearing bolt tightening sequence. 2003–04 less supercharger

seal replacer tool No. T-95P-6701-AH and rear crankshaft seal adapter tool No. T-95P-6701-DH, or equivalents.

b. With rear crankshaft seal adapter still installed, use rear crankshaft slinger replacer and rear crankshaft seal replacer to install crankshaft oil slinger.

OIL PAN

REPLACE

2001

1. Remove air cleaner outlet tube.
2. Remove radiator sight shield.
3. Support engine using engine lifting bracket tool No. D93P-6001-A2 and engine support kit tool No. 303-F072, or equivalents.
4. Raise and support vehicle.
5. Remove lefthand and righthand engine mount nuts.
6. Lower vehicle and raise engine.
7. Raise and support vehicle.
8. Drain engine oil into suitable container.
9. Compress front coil springs using compressor tool No. D78P-5310-A, or equivalent.
10. Position suitable jack stand under subframe.
11. Remove four subframe side bolts.
12. Loosen front subframe bolts. **Do not completely remove bolts.**
13. Lower front subframe.
14. Remove mounting bolts and pan. **If gasket is in good condition it may be used again.**
15. Reverse procedure to install, noting the following:
    a. Apply silicone gasket sealant No. F7AZ-19554-EA, or equivalent, to rear oil seal retainer to block seal-

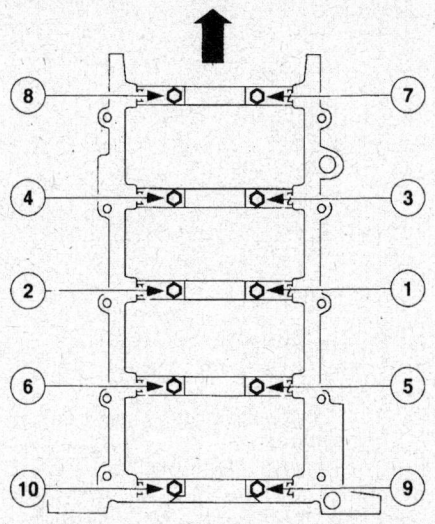

Fig. 20 Main bearing vertical cap bolt tightening sequence. 2003–04 supercharged engines

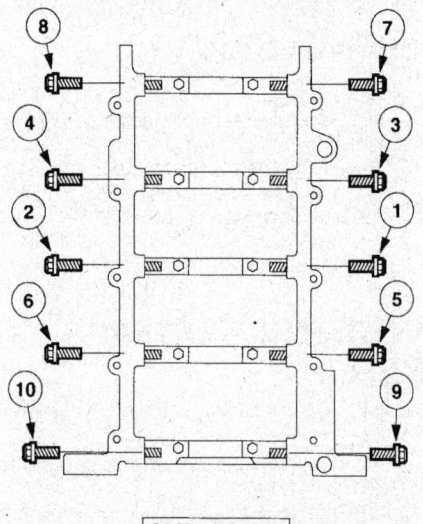

21 Nm (15 lb-ft)

ARM66FM000000059

Fig. 22 Main bearing cap side bolt tightening sequence. 2003–04 supercharged engines

ing surface and at front cover to block mating surface.
b. **Install and tighten oil pan and mounting bolts within four minutes.**
c. Move oil pan into position and loosely install bolts.
d. **Torque** pan bolts in sequence to 18 inch lbs., **Fig. 23.**
e. **Torque** bolts in sequence to 15 ft. lbs.
f. Final tighten bolts an additional 60° in sequence.

2003–04

1. Remove transmission.
2. Remove air cleaner outlet tube and radiator sight shield.
3. Remove accumulator to compressor

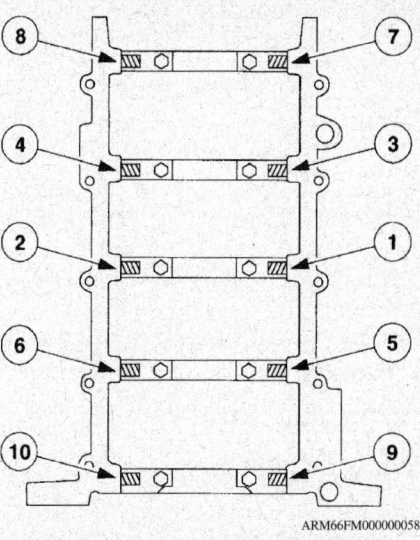

Fig. 21 Jackscrew tightening sequence. 2003–04 supercharged engines

manifold and tube.
4. Remove air conditioning line.
5. Install engine support tool No. 303-F072, or equivalent.
6. Raise and support vehicle.
7. Remove lefthand and righthand engine mount nuts, then lower vehicle.
8. Raise engine 2.5 inches using engine support tool.
9. Raise and support vehicle, then drain engine oil into suitable container.
10. Compress coil springs using coil spring compressor tool No. D78P-5310-A, or equivalent.
11. Position suitable jack stand under subframe.
12. Loosen but do not remove subframe bolts.
13. Lower subframe and remove brace.
14. Remove mounting nuts and position starter wiring harness aside.
15. Remove mounting bolts and oil pan.
16. Reverse procedure to install, noting the following:
    a. Apply silicone gasket sealant No. F7AZ-19554-EA, or equivalent, to rear oil seal retainer to block sealing surface and at front cover to block mating surface.
    b. **Install and tighten cover and mounting bolts within four minutes.**
    c. Move oil pan into position and loosely install bolts.
    d. **Torque** oil pan bolts in sequence to 18 inch lbs., **Fig. 23.**
    e. **Torque** pan bolts in sequence. to 15 ft. lbs.
    f. Final tighten bolts an additional 60° in sequence.

OIL PUMP

REPLACE

This procedure has been revised by a Technical Service Bulletin.
1. Remove valve covers as outlined under "Valve Cover, Replace."

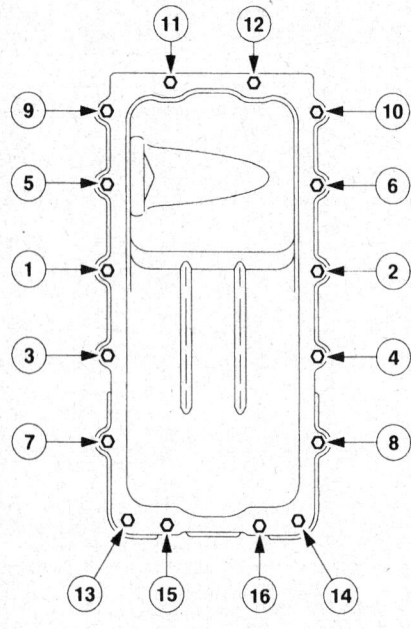

Fig. 23 Oil pan bolt tightening sequence

2. Remove front cover as outlined under "Front Engine Cover, Replace."
3. Remove oil pan as outlined under "Oil Pan, Replace."
4. Remove timing chains as outlined under "Timing Chain, Replace."
5. Remove mounting bolts and oil pump.
6. Reverse procedure to install, noting the following:
   a. Align oil pump inner rotor with flat of crankshaft.
   b. Prime oil pump and system prior to starting engine.

BELT TENSION DATA

These models are equipped with an automatic drive belt tensioner. No adjustment or maintenance is required.

SERPENTINE DRIVE BELT

Always use square drive tool in hole in tensioner to move tensioner. Never pry on tensioner pulley. When releasing drive belt tensioner, never allow tensioner to snap back. Damage to tensioner or personal injury could result.

Do not allow engine coolant to remain on serpentine belt or pulleys. If required, remove belt and flush with clean water.

Removal

1. Insert suitable square drive tool into square hole in tensioner arm and rotate tensioner away from belt.
2. Lift belt from pulley and slowly release tensioner.
3. Remove belt.

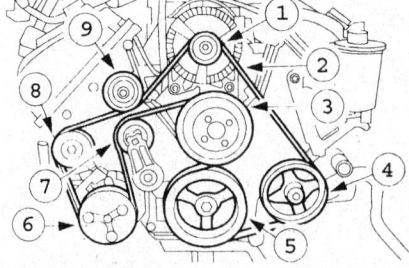

1. Alternator
2. Belt
3. Water Pump
4. Power Steering Pump
5. Crankshaft
6. Air Conditioning Compressor
7. Tensioner
8 & 9. Idler Pulleys

Fig. 24 Serpentine belt routing. 2001–04

Routing

Refer to **Fig. 24** for belt routing.

Installation

1. Route belt.
2. Ensure belt is properly seated in pulley grooves.
3. Insert suitable square drive tool into square hole in tensioner arm and rotate tensioner away from belt.
4. Position belt under tensioner and slowly release tensioner onto belt.

COOLING SYSTEM BLEED

1. Fill radiator completely full and install radiator cap.
2. Fill coolant reservoir and degas bottle to full cold mark.
3. Set heater control to full hot, high fan and set controls so air vents from dash vents.
4. Start and operate engine until fully warmed up while observing water temperature gauge.
5. If system is functioning properly, temperature will indicate normal and hot air will be felt at dash outlets.
6. If system is not functioning properly, temperature gauge will not read and/or no hot air will be felt at dash vents.
7. If system is not functioning properly, allow engine to cool and repeat procedure.
8. If system is functioning properly, allow engine to cool and fill coolant reservoir to full cold mark.

THERMOSTAT

REPLACE

1. Drain engine coolant into suitable container.
2. Remove thermostat housing bolts.
3. Remove thermostat and O-ring seal.
4. Reverse procedure to install. Thermo-

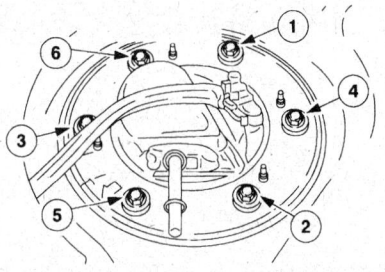

Fig. 25 Fuel tank sender unit bolt tightening sequence

stat is indexed and must be installed to original position.

WATER PUMP

REPLACE

1. Drain engine coolant into suitable container.
2. **On supercharged models,** remove supercharger drive belt.
3. **On all models,** loosen water pump pulley mounting bolts.
4. Insert suitable square drive tool into square hole in tensioner arm and rotate tensioner away from belt.
5. Lift belt from pulley and slowly release tensioner.
6. Remove belt.
7. Remove mounting bolts, water pump and gasket. Discard gasket.
8. Reverse procedure to install.

RADIATOR

REPLACE

1. Drain coolant from radiator and degas bottle into suitable container.
2. Disconnect cooling fan motor electrical connector and separate fan harness from shroud.
3. Remove fan shroud lefthand and right-hand mounting bolts.
4. Remove cooling fan, motor and shroud.
5. Remove radiator sight shield.
6. Disconnect radiator upper hose at radiator.
7. **On models equipped with automatic transmission,** remove lower and upper cooler tube fittings.
8. **On all models,** raise and support vehicle.
9. Disconnect radiator lower hose at radiator. Lower vehicle.
10. Remove supports and radiator.
11. Reverse procedure to install.

FUEL PUMP

REPLACE

1. Relieve fuel system pressure as outlined under "Precautions."
2. Drain fuel from fuel tank into suitable container using draining tool No. 310-F013 and storage tanker tool No. 164-R3202, or equivalents.
3. Raise and support vehicle.

4. Remove filler pipe mounting bolt and disconnect pipe hose connections to tank.
5. Disconnect fuel tank electrical connector.
6. Disconnect vapor tube fitting at left-hand front side of tank.
7. Place suitable jack stand under tank.
8. Remove front two bolts from fuel tank support straps and position lefthand strap aside.
9. Remove righthand rear bolt and support strap.
10. Partially lower tank and disconnect fuel lines using suitable spring lock coupler tools.
11. Cut pipe-to-tank grommet's outer edge and remove grommet.
12. Lower and remove tank. Move tank to suitable bench.
13. Remove sender unit orientation for installation alignment and remove mounting bolts.
14. Pull sender unit up until locking tabs are accessible. **Avoid damaging filter, float arm, tubing and wiring.**
15. Remove sender by reaching through opening and squeeze locking tabs together.
16. Reverse procedure to install, noting the following:
    a. Install mounting bolts hand tight and tighten in sequence, **Fig. 25.**
    b. Lubricate filler pipe check valve area and new tank-to-filler pipe grommet with Serfactant (Merpol), or equivalent.

FUEL FILTER
REPLACE

1. Relieve fuel system pressure as outlined under "Precautions."
2. Raise and support vehicle.
3. Remove push connector fittings from fuel filter ends using suitable spring lock coupler tools.
4. Loosen worm gear clamp and remove filter from bracket. Record flow arrow to ensure proper direction of fuel flow through filter.
5. Reverse procedure to install using new retainer clips in each fitting.

SUPERCHARGER
REPLACE

Refer to "Intake Manifold, Replace" for supercharger replacement.

TECHNICAL SERVICE BULLETINS

Fuel Pump Whining/ Buzzing Through Radio Speaker

2001

On some of these models there may be a whining or buzzing in speakers.

This condition may be caused by fuel pump electrical noise.

To correct this condition install an electronic noise Radio Frequency Interference (RFI) filter (part No. F1PZ-18B925-A) on fuel pump inside the fuel tank, as follows:

1. Remove fuel pump sender from fuel tank as outlined under "Fuel Pump, Replace."
2. Cut fuel pump wires three inches from flange. Discard wires.
3. Connect RFI filter connectors to fuel pump spade terminal.
4. Cut and solder both RFI filter red and black wires to flange red and black wires.
5. Install suitable heat shrink tubing over solder connectors.
6. Secure RFI filter to fuel pump using suitable bundling strap.
7. Install fuel pump sender.

TIGHTENING SPECIFICATIONS

Year	Component	Torque/Ft. Lbs.
2001–02	Accelerator Cable Bracket	72–96①
	Air Conditioning Compressor	18
	Air Conditioning Muffler	15
	Alternator	18
	Alternator Brace	89①
	Battery Cable To Alternator	89①
	Battery Cable Support Bracket	15
	Belt Idler Pulley	18
	Belt Tensioner	18
	Camshaft	81–95
	Camshaft Cover	89①
	Camshaft Position Sensor	89①
	Camshaft Sprocket	81–95
	Clutch Pressure Plate	26
	Connecting Rod	⑪
	Crankshaft Damper	114–121
	Crankshaft Position Sensor	89①
	Crankshaft Pulley	⑩
	Crankshaft Rear Seal Retainer	89①
	Cylinder Head	③
	Drive Belt Tensioner	18
	EGR Sensor Bracket	89①
	EGR Tube Connector	30–33
	EGR Vacuum Regulator Solenoid Bracket	89①
	EGR Valve	18
	EGR Tube To EGR Valve	26
	EGR Tube To Exhaust Manifold	30
	Engine Coolant Temperature Sensor	11
	Engine Mount, Nut	111
	Engine Mount To Block	52
	Exhaust Manifold	⑥
	Exhaust Pipe To Exhaust Manifold	20–30
	Flywheel	59
	Front Brake Caliper	23
	Front Cover	④
	Front Engine Mount	45–59
	Front Engine Mount Through Bolts	15–22
	Fuel Filer	27–44①
	Fuel Rail	89①
	Fuel Tank Sender	89①
	Heater Hose Fitting Studs To Manifold	18
	Idle Air Control Valve	89①
	Ignition Coil	53①
	Ignition Coil Cover	89①
	Intake Manifold	⑤
	Intake Manifold To Cylinder Head	53–64
	Main Bearing	⑧
	Oil Dipstick Tube	89①
	Oil Filter	37
	Oil Filter Adapter	15–22
	Oil Filter Adapter Insert	43
	Oil Inlet Tube To Main Bearing Cap	15–22
	Oil Inlet Tube To Oil Pump	72–108①
	Oil Pan	②
	Oil Pan Drain Plug	120①

Continued

4.6L DOHC ENGINE

TIGHTENING
SPECIFICATIONS—Continued

Year	Component	Torque/Ft. Lbs.
2001–02	Oil Pump	89①
	Oil Pump Screen Cover & Tube To Main Cap Stud Spacer	18
	Oil Pump Screen Cover & Tube To Pump	89①
	Oxygen Sensor	27–33
	Power Steering Pump	18
	Power Steering Reservoir	89①
	Powertrain Frame	73–100
	Pressure Plate	47①
	Rear Engine Mount, Bolt	50–70
	Rear Engine Mount, Nut	35–50
	Rear Engine Support	15–22
	Rear Seal Retainer	89①
	RFI Capacitor	89①
	Serpentine Belt Idler Pulley	18
	Serpentine Belt Tensioner	18
	Spark Plug	13
	Subframe	85
	Thermostat Housing	15–22
	Throttle Body	⑤
	Throttle Cable Bracket	89①
	Timing Chain Tensioner	18
	Torque Converter	22–25
	Transmission Filler Tube	35
	Transmission Shift Lever	27
	Transmission Shift Lever Inner Boot	89①
	Transmission Shift Lever Plate To Transmission	13
	Valve Cover	⑦
	Water Bypass Tube	72–96①
	Water Drain Plug	15
	Water Outlet	18
	Water Pump	18
	Water Pump Pulley	18
	Wheel Lug Nuts	95
	Wiring Harness	89①
2003–04	Accelerator Bracket	89①
	Air Conditioning Compressor	18
	Air Conditioning Muffler Nut	18
	Alternator	18
	Belt Idler Support Bracket	18
	Belt Idler Pulley	18
	Camshaft Cap	⑨
	Camshaft Sprocket	⑨
	Connecting Rod	⑪
	Coolant Bypass Tube	18
	Crankshaft Pulley	⑩
	Cylinder Head	③
	Drive Belt Tensioner	18
	Engine Mount Bolts	52
	Engine Mount Nuts	111
	Exhaust Manifold	⑥
	Front Cover	④
	Heater Water Inlet Tube	89①
	Heater Water Outlet Tube	18

Continued

TIGHTENING
SPECIFICATIONS—Continued

Year	Component	Torque/Ft. Lbs.
2003–04	Idler Pulley Bracket	18
	Intake Manifold	⑤
	Main Bearing Cap	⑧
	Oil Dipstick Tube	89①
	Oil Filter Adapter	18
	Oil Pan	②
	Oil Pump Screen Cover	89①
	Oil Pump Screen & Pickup Tube Spacer To Main Bearing Stud	18
	Oil Pump To Cylinder Block	89①
	Power Steering Hose Fitting	48
	Power Steering Hose Bracket	89①
	Power Steering Pump	18
	Power Steering Pump To Cylinder Block	18
	Primary Timing Chain Guide	89①
	Subframe Brace	30
	Thermostat Housing	18
	Throttle Body	⑤
	Throttle Body Spacer	18
	Timing Chain Tensioner (Primary)	18
	Timing Chain (Secondary)	89①
	Valve Cover	⑦
	Water Pump Pulley	18
	Water Pump To Cylinder Block	18

① — Inch pounds.
② — Refer to "Oil Pan, Replace" for tightening specifications and sequence.
③ — Refer to "Cylinder Head, Replace" for tightening specifications and sequence.
④ — Refer to "Front Cover, Replace" for tightening specifications and sequence.
⑤ — Refer to "Intake Manifold, Replace" for tightening specifications and sequence.
⑥ — Refer to "Exhaust Manifold, Replace" for tightening specifications and sequence.
⑦ — Refer to "Valve Cover, Replace" for tightening specifications and sequence.
⑧ — Refer to "Main & Rod Bearings" for tightening specifications and sequence.
⑨ — Refer to "Camshaft, Replace" for tightening specifications and sequence.
⑩ — Refer to "Front Cover Seal, Replace" for tightening specifications and sequence.
⑪ — Refer to "Piston & Rod Assembly" for tightening specifications and sequence.

4.6L SOHC (VIN X) Engine

NOTE: For Procedures Not Found In This Section, Refer To "4.6L DOHC Engine" Section.

NOTE: On Air Bag Equipped Models, Refer To "Air Bag System Precautions" Located In The Front Of This Manual For System Disarming & Arming Procedures.

NOTE: Refer To "Computer Relearn Procedures" Located In The Front Of This Manual When Battery Power To The Computer Has Been Interrupted.

NOTE: Prior To Performing Any Service Operations Listed In This Section, Consult The "Technical Service Bulletins" Section For Related Information.

INDEX

PRECAUTIONS

Air Bag Systems

Refer to "Air Bag System Precautions" in front of this manual for system disarming and arming procedures.

Battery Ground Cable

Prior to service, disconnect battery ground cable and isolate as required.

Fuel System Pressure Relief

Fuel supply tubes will remain pressurized for long periods of time after engine shutdown. This pressure must be relieved before beginning fuel system service or personal injury or damage to vehicle may occur. A valve is provided on fuel injection supply manifold for this purpose.

1. Connect EFI/CFI fuel pressure gauge tool No. T80L-9974-B, or equivalent, to fuel pressure relief valve on fuel injection supply manifold.
2. Place outlet hose of tool into suitable fuel container.
3. Open manual valve on fuel pressure gauge tool to relieve fuel system pressure.

COMPRESSION PRESSURE

When inspecting cylinder compression, lowest cylinder must be within 75% of highest cylinder. Perform compression test with engine at normal operating temperature, spark plugs and air cleaner removed and the throttle propped wide open.

ENGINE MOUNT

REPLACE

1. Install lift bracket tool No. D93P-6001-A3, or equivalent.

2. Install engine support tool No. 303-290-A, or equivalent.
3. Raise and support vehicle.
4. Remove solenoid protective cap and wiring nuts. Position wiring aside.
5. Remove mounting bolts and starter motor.
6. Remove engine mount nuts and lower vehicle.
7. Raise engine using support tool.
8. Raise vehicle and remove engine mount.
9. Reverse procedure to install.

ENGINE

REPLACE

1. Drain coolant into suitable container.
2. Recover air conditioning refrigerant as outlined in "Air Conditioning" chapter.
3. Mark hinge locations, then disconnect ground strap and underhood lamp electrical connector.
4. Remove hood and battery.
5. Remove air cleaner and outlet tube.
6. Remove degas bottle.

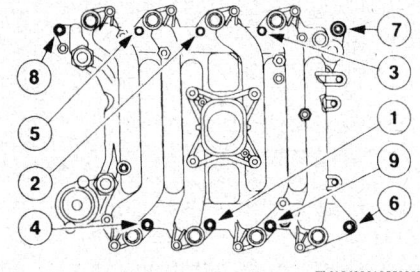

Fig. 1 Intake manifold bolt tightening sequence. 2001

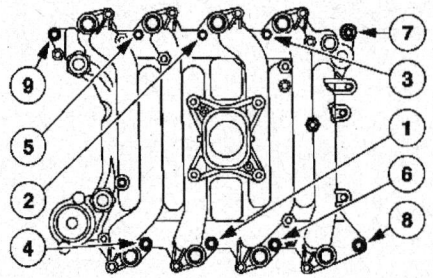

FM1060101426000X

Fig. 2 Intake manifold bolt tightening sequence. 2002–04

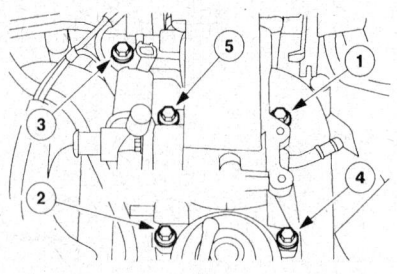

FM1069901066000X

Fig. 3 TBI bolt tightening sequence

7. Relieve fuel system pressure as outlined under "Precautions."
8. Disconnect fuel lines.
9. Disconnect radiator upper hose at water outlet.
10. Disconnect throttle and speed control cables, then the return spring.
11. Remove bracket mounting bolts, then position throttle and speed control cables aside.
12. Disconnect HVAC vacuum supply hoses.
13. Place suitable drain pan under firewall fittings and disconnect heater hoses.
14. Remove mounting bolt and disconnect bulkhead multi-pin electrical connector.
15. Separate wiring harness at three firewall locations.
16. Disconnect TBI electrical connectors.
17. Remove safety clip and disconnect manifold suction tube.
18. Disconnect air conditioning pressure cycling switch electrical connector.
19. Separate liquid tube from air conditioning condenser.
20. Disconnect power steering hose from fluid reservoir.
21. Disconnect engine to body or frame ground wires.
22. Disconnect fusible link and electrical connector near battery tray.
23. Disconnect ground connector near washer fluid reservoir.
24. Slide underhood power distribution box access cover up, then remove nut and battery cables.
25. Separate degas sensor electrical connector from battery tray.
26. Raise and support vehicle.
27. Disconnect HO2S electrical connectors.
28. Remove exhaust pipe to manifold flange nuts.
29. Remove solenoid protective cap and wiring nuts. Position wiring aside.
30. Remove mounting bolts and starter motor.
31. Remove nine bellhousing to engine bolts.
32. Disconnect engine to body lower ground strap.
33. Remove serpentine belt.
34. Position suitable drain pan under power steering pump.
35. Disconnect power steering fluid lines at pump.
36. Remove power steering pump pulley using power steering pump pulley re-

mover tool No. T69L-10300-B, or equivalent.
37. Remove mounting bolts and power steering pump.
38. Lower vehicle.
39. Remove safety clip and disconnect receiver-dryer suction tube.
40. Remove safety clip and disconnect evaporator core line.
41. Disconnect air conditioning line at rear of condenser.
42. Remove two nuts at righthand exhaust manifold.
43. Raise and support vehicle.
44. Remove six remaining righthand exhaust manifold nuts. **Do not remove exhaust manifold now.**
45. Lower vehicle.
46. Remove mounting bolts and alternator upper bracket, then disconnect alternator electrical connector by pressing tab. **Do not pull on tab.**
47. Disconnect alternator electrical connections.
48. Remove mounting bolts and alternator.
49. Install engine lifting bracket tool No. 303-639, or equivalent.
50. Raise engine using suitable crane or skyhook.
51. Remove righthand exhaust manifold from bottom of engine compartment.
52. Install engine lifting brackets tool No. 303-D074, or equivalent.
53. Support transmission with suitable floor jack and wooden block.
54. Connect spreader bar tool No. D93P-6001-A3, or equivalent, to suitable crane or skyhook.
55. Connect spreader bar to lifting brackets.
56. Raise engine slightly and disconnect transmission wiring pin at support bracket.
57. Remove engine.
58. If engine will be mounted on stand, remove rear seal as outlined under "Crankshaft Seal, Replace"
59. Reverse procedure to install.

INTAKE MANIFOLD
REPLACE

1. Drain coolant into suitable container.
2. Remove air cleaner outlet tube.
3. Relieve fuel system pressure as outlined under "Precautions."
4. Disconnect fuel lines.
5. Remove radiator upper hose.

6. Disconnect accelerator and speed control cables, then the return spring.
7. Remove accelerator and speed control cable bracket bolts, then position cables aside.
8. Remove breather tube at valve cover.
9. Disconnect EVAP emissions return line.
10. Disconnect differential pressure feedback EGR electrical connector.
11. Disconnect differential pressure feedback EGR transducer hoses.
12. Disconnect EGR vacuum regulator solenoid electrical connector and vacuum supply.
13. Remove EGR vacuum regulator solenoid bracket from intake manifold.
14. Disconnect EGR tube from EGR valve.
15. Remove PCV valve and hose.
16. Disconnect EGR valve vacuum lines.
17. Disconnect idle air control (IAC) valve electrical connector.
18. Disconnect main vacuum supply from TBI base adapter.
19. Disconnect TPS electrical connector.
20. Remove mounting bolts, TBI and adapter. Replace gasket.
21. Disconnect fuel pressure sensor electrical connector and fuel charging ground wire.
22. Disconnect ignition coil and fuel injector electrical connectors.
23. Disconnect HVAC vacuum supply lines and remove harness.
24. Remove four fuel supply manifold mounting studs.
25. Remove injectors and supply manifold.
26. Remove mounting bolts and ignition coils.
27. Remove mounting bolts and alternator upper bracket, then disconnect alternator electrical connector by pressing tab. **Do not pull on tab.**
28. Disconnect alternator electrical connections.
29. Remove mounting bolts and alternator.
30. Disconnect heater hose at rear of intake manifold.
31. Unclip harness at manifold and position engine wiring harness aside.
32. Disconnect coolant temperature sender electrical connector.
33. Remove thermostat housing, thermostat and O-ring.
34. Remove intake manifold mounting

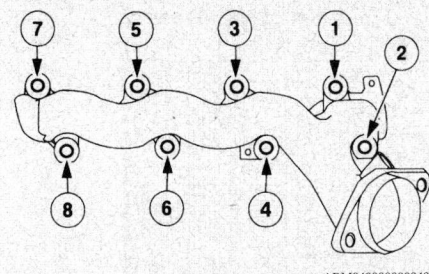

ARM0400000000495

Fig. 4 Lefthand exhaust manifold nut tightening sequence

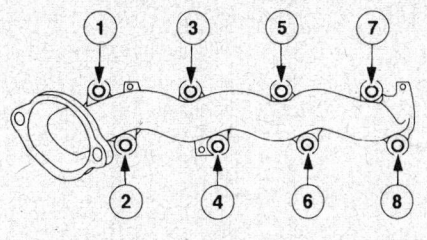

ARM040000000496

Fig. 5 Righthand exhaust manifold nut tightening sequence

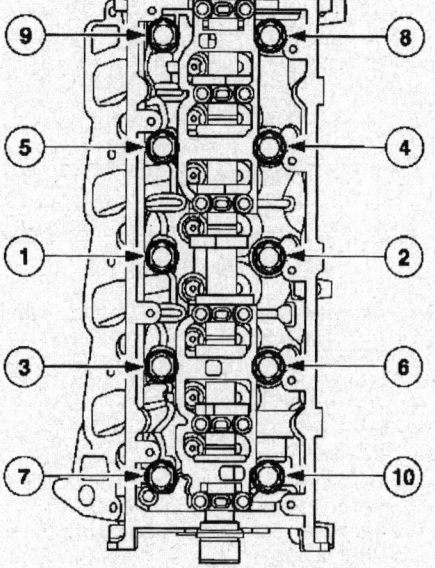

ARM66FM000000061

Fig. 7 Lefthand cylinder head tightening sequence

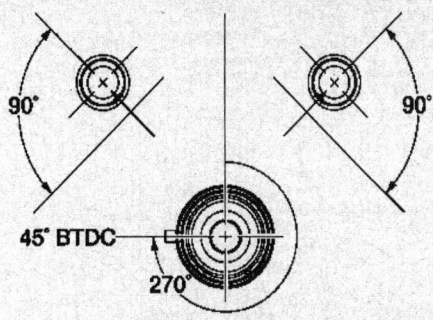

ARM66FM000000060

Fig. 6 Camshaft & Crankshaft keyway alignment

---

bolts in sequence, **Figs. 1 and 2. Gaskets can be used again if not damaged.**

35. Reverse procedure to install, noting the following:
   a. **Torque** intake manifold mounting bolts in sequence to 18 ft. lbs., **Figs. 1 and 2.**
   b. Tighten TBI mounting bolts in sequence to 89 inch lbs., **Fig. 3.**

EXHAUST MANIFOLD
REPLACE
2001

1. Raise and support vehicle.
2. Disconnect exhaust pipe HO2S electrical connectors.
3. Remove exhaust pipe flange to manifold bolts.
4. Remove mounting nuts, manifold and gasket. Discard gasket.
5. Reverse procedure to install, noting the following:
   a. Install new manifold gaskets.
   b. **Torque** manifold mounting nuts in sequence to 17–20 ft. lbs., **Figs. 4 and 5.**

2003–04
RIGHTHAND

1. Raise and support vehicle, then remove dual converter Y-pipe.
2. Remove solenoid protective cap and wiring nuts. Position wiring aside.
3. Remove mounting bolts and starter motor.
4. Remove mounting nuts and exhaust manifold.
5. Reverse procedure to install with new exhaust manifold gasket. **Torque** mounting nuts in sequence to 18 ft. lbs., **Fig. 5.**

LEFTHAND

1. Position steering wheel straight ahead and lock.
2. Raise and support vehicle, then remove dual converter Y-pipe.
3. Remove and discard steering pinch bolt, then separate steering coupler.
4. Disconnect EGR tube at exhaust manifold.
5. Remove oil dipstick tube.
6. Remove mounting nuts and exhaust manifold.

7. Reverse procedure to install with new exhaust manifold gasket. **Torque** mounting nuts in sequence to 18 ft. lbs., **Fig. 4.**

CYLINDER HEAD
REPLACE

1. Remove intake manifold as outlined under "Intake Manifold, Replace."
2. Remove timing chains as outlined under "Timing Chain, Replace."
3. Disconnect oxygen sensor electrical connectors and remove H-pipes.
4. Remove exhaust manifold as outlined under "Exhaust Manifold, Replace."
5. Remove oil dipstick tube.
6. Remove bolt and position water bypass tube aside.
7. Remove cylinder head bolts supporting lower bolts with rubber band.
8. Remove cylinder head.
9. Reverse procedure to install, noting the following:
   a. **Camshaft keyways must maintain 90° clocked position relative to valve cover rail, Fig. 6.**
   b. **Crankshaft keyway must be clocked at 270° (45° BTDC) be-**

fore installation of cylinder head, **Fig. 6.** Rotate crankshaft clockwise only.
   c. **Torque** cylinder head bolts in sequence to 30 ft. lbs., **Figs. 7 and 8.**
   d. Tighten head bolts an additional 90° in sequence.
   e. Loosen bolts at least of one full turn.
   f. **Torque** bolts to 30 ft. lbs., in sequence.
   g. Tighten an additional 90° in sequence.
   h. Tighten an additional 90° in sequence.

VALVE COVER
REPLACE
Lefthand

1. Remove bracket bolt and position oil dipstick tube aside.
2. Disconnect breather tube at valve cover grommet.
3. Disconnect engine wiring harness at valve cover retaining clips.
4. Remove bolts, studs and valve cover.
5. Reverse procedure to install, noting the following:
   a. Apply .32 inch bead of silicone gasket sealant No. F7AZ-19554-EA, or equivalent, to valve cover sealing surfaces.
   b. **Install and tighten cover and mounting bolts within four minutes.**
   c. **Torque** valve cover bolts and studs in sequence to 89 inch lbs., **Fig. 9.**

Righthand

1. Remove air cleaner outlet tube.
2. Relieve fuel system pressure as outlined under "Precautions."
3. Disconnect fuel lines.
4. Disconnect engine wiring harness at valve cover retaining clips.
5. Disconnect PCV valve and hose at valve cover grommet. Position them aside.
6. Remove bolts, studs and valve cover.
7. Reverse procedure to install, noting the following:
   a. Apply .32 inch bead of silicone gasket sealant No. F7AZ-19554-EA, or equivalent, to valve cover sealing surfaces.

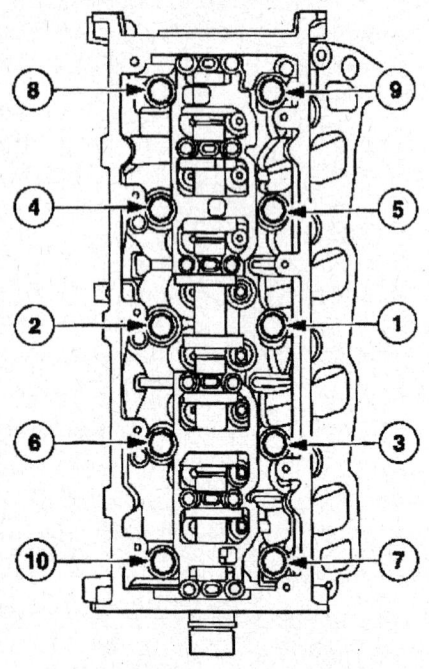

ARM66FM000000062

Fig. 8 Righthand cylinder head tightening sequence

b. **Install and tighten cover and mounting bolts within four minutes.**
c. **Torque** valve cover bolts and studs in sequence to 89 inch lbs., **Fig. 10.**

VALVE ARRANGEMENT

Front To Rear

Righthand Side.....................I-E-I-E-I-E-I-E
Lefthand Side ....E-I-E-I-E-I-E-I

CAMSHAFT LOBE LIFT SPECIFICATIONS

Engine	Intake, Inch	Exhaust, Inch
4.6L SOHC	.2591	.2597

VALVE ADJUSTMENT

These engine are equipped with hydraulic valve lash adjusters. No valve adjustment is required.

FRONT COVER

REPLACE

1. Remove mounting nuts and position RFI capacitor aside.
2. Remove valve covers as outlined under "Valve Cover, Replace."
3. Drain coolant from radiator and degas bottle into suitable container.
4. Disconnect cooling fan motor electrical connector and separate fan harness from shroud.
5. Remove fan shroud lefthand and righthand mounting bolts.
6. Remove cooling fan, motor and shroud.
7. Remove serpentine belt.

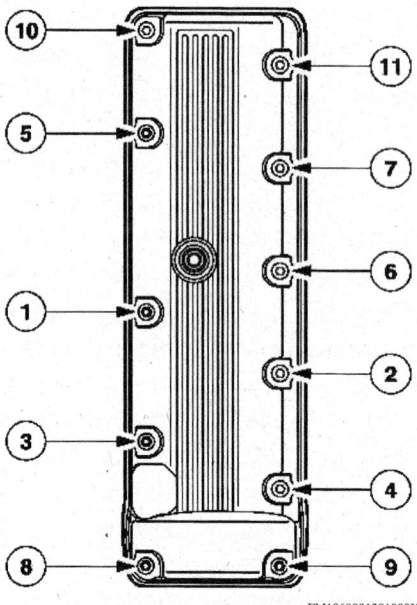

FM1060001201000X

Fig. 9 Lefthand valve cover bolt tightening sequence

8. Remove mounting bolts and water pump pulley.
9. Remove mounting nut and position air conditioning muffler aside.
10. Raise and support vehicle.
11. Drain engine oil into suitable container.
12. Position power steering pump aside.
13. Disconnect crankshaft position (CKP) sensor electrical connector.
14. Remove battery cable support nuts at front of engine.
15. Remove bolt and crankshaft pulley using puller tool No. T58P-6316-D, or equivalent.
16. Remove crankshaft front seal using seal remover tool No. T74P-6700-A, or equivalent.
17. Remove oil pan to front cover bolts.
18. Lower vehicle.
19. Position suitable drain pan under and remove power steering fluid reservoir.
20. Disconnect camshaft position (CMP) sensor electrical connector.
21. Remove serpentine belt idler pulley.
22. Mark locations for installation alignment, then remove front cover mounting bolts and studs.
23. Remove front cover. Discard gaskets.
24. Reverse procedure to install, noting the following:
   a. Apply silicone gasket sealer part No. F7AZ-19554-EA, or equivalent, **Fig. 9.**
   b. Ensure bolts and studs are in original locations, **Fig. 11.**
   c. **Torque** oil pan to front cover bolts to 18 inch lbs.
   d. **Torque** oil pan to cover mounting bolts to 15 ft. lbs.
   e. Final tighten mounting bolts an additional 60°.
   f. Install new crankshaft pulley oil seal using installer and aligner tool No. T88T-6701-A, or equivalent.
   g. Apply silicone gasket sealer to crankshaft pulley keyway slot.

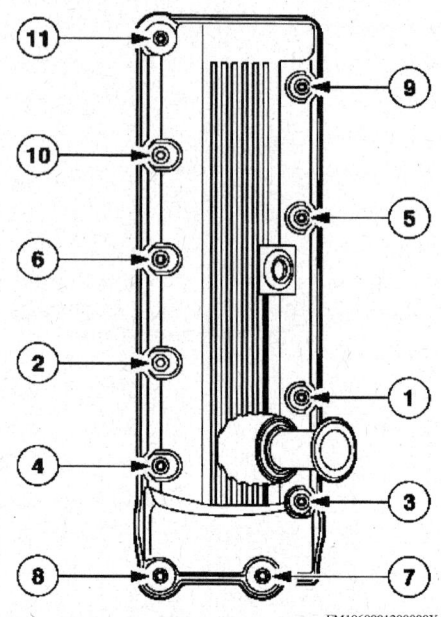

FM1060001200000X

Fig. 10 Righthand valve cover bolt tightening sequence

h. **Install and tighten pulley and mounting bolt within four minutes.**
i. Install crankshaft pulley using installer tool No. T74P-6316-B, or equivalent.
j. **Torque** crankshaft pulley bolt to 66 ft. lbs., then loosen one full turn.
k. **Torque** pulley bolt to 37 ft. lbs.
l. Final tighten bolt an additional 90°.

FRONT COVER SEAL

REPLACE

1. Insert suitable square drive tool into square hole in tensioner arm and rotate tensioner away from belt.
2. Lift belt from pulley and slowly release tensioner.
3. Remove belt.
4. Raise and support vehicle, then remove crankshaft pulley bolt.
5. Remove crankshaft pulley using crankshaft vibration damper remover tool No. T58P-6316-D, or equivalent.
6. Remove front seal using front seal remover tool No. T74P-6700-A, or equivalent.
7. Reverse procedure to install, noting the following:
   a. Lubricate engine front cover and front seal with clean engine oil.
   b. Install front seal using seal installer tool No. T88T-6701-A, or equivalent.
   c. Apply suitable sealant to Woodriff key slot on crankshaft pulley.
   d. Install crankshaft pulley using crankshaft vibration damper installer tool No. T74P-6316-B, or equivalent.
   e. **Torque** crankshaft pulley bolt to 66 ft. lbs.
   f. Loosen crankshaft pulley bolt one full turn.
   g. **Torque** pulley bolt to 37 ft. lbs.

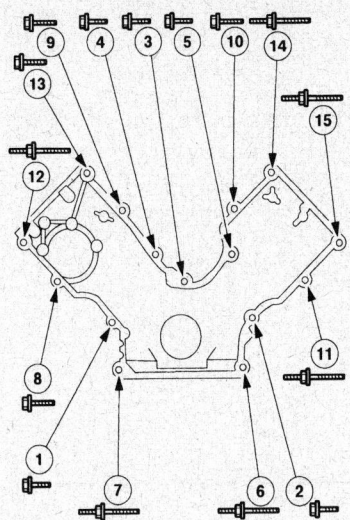

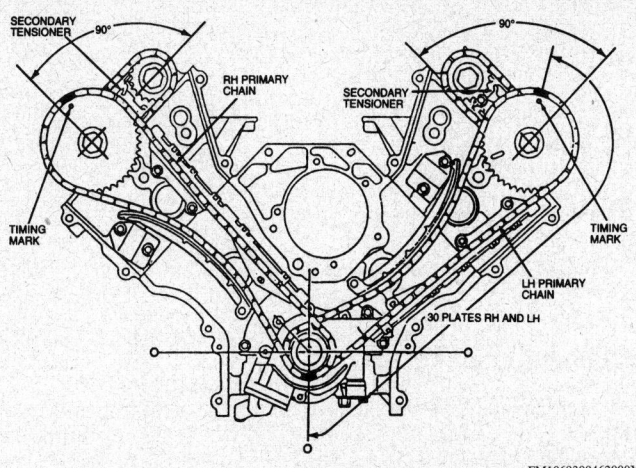

Fig. 12 Setting cylinder No. 1 to TDC. DOHC engine

Item	Description
1	Bolt, Hex Flange Head Pilot, M8 x 1.25 x 53
2	Bolt, Hex Flange Head Pilot, M8 x 1.25 x 53
3	Bolt, Hex Flange Head Pilot, M8 x 1.25 x 53
4	Bolt, Hex Flange Head Pilot, M8 x 1.25 x 53
5	Bolt, Hex Flange Head Pilot, M8 x 1.25 x 53
6	Stud, Hex-Head Pilot, M10 x 1.5 x 1.5 x 103.1
7	Stud, Hex-Head Pilot, M10 x 1.5 x 1.5 x 103.1
8	Screw and Washer, Hex Pilot, M10 x 1.5 x 57.5
9	Screw and Washer, Hex Pilot, M10 x 1.5 x 57.5
10	Screw and Washer, Hex Pilot, M10 x 1.5 x 57.5
11	Stud and Washer, Hex-Head Pilot, M10 x 1.5 x M8 x 1.25 x 109.6
12	Stud and Washer, Hex-Head Pilot, M10 x 1.5 x M8 x 1.25 x 109.6
13	Stud and Washer, Hex-Head Pilot, M10 x 1.5 x M8 x 1.25 x 109.6
14	Stud and Washer, Hex-Head Pilot, M10 x 1.5 x M8 x 1.25 x 109.6
15	Stud and Washer, Hex-Head Pilot, M10 x 1.5 x M8 x 1.25 x 109.6

FM1069901064000X

Fig. 11   Front cover mounting locations

h. Tighten bolt an additional 90°.

TIMING CHAIN

REPLACE

These engines have an interference fit design. If engine has jumped time cylinder heads must be removed to repair damage to valves and/or pistons.

At no time, when the timing chains are removed and the cylinder heads are installed, may the crankshaft and/or camshaft be rotated unless all rocker arms have been removed. Rotation may result in valve and/or piston damage.

Before loosening or tightening camshaft sprocket nuts and bolts, ensure camshaft positioning and locking devices are in place.

2001-02

PRIMARY

REMOVAL

1. Remove valve covers as outlined under "Valve Cover, Replace."
2. Remove rocker arms as outlined under "Hydraulic Lifters, Replace."
3. Remove front engine cover as outlined under "Front Engine Cover, Replace."
4. Remove oil pan.
5. Remove crankshaft position pulse wheel and rotate engine to cylinder No. 1 TDC, **Figs. 12 and 13.**
6. Install cam positioning tool No. T91P-6256-A, or equivalent on camshaft flats, **Fig. 14.**
7. Remove mounting bolts, righthand tensioner and arm.
8. Remove mounting bolts and righthand chain guide. **Record bolt lengths for installation.**
9. Remove righthand timing chain and crankshaft sprocket. **Record sprocket position for installation.**
10. Remove righthand camshaft gear mounting bolt, washer, gear and spacer.
11. Remove mounting bolts, lefthand tensioner and arm.
12. Remove mounting bolts and lefthand chain guide. **Record bolt lengths for later installation.**
13. Remove lefthand timing chain and crankshaft sprocket. **Record gear position for installation.**
14. Remove lefthand camshaft gear mounting bolt, washer, sprocket and spacer.

INSTALLATION

If engine has jumped time, ensure all repairs to engine components and/or valve train are completed. During timing chain installation ensure all rocker arm have been remove, if cam or crank should turn with rockers installed engine damage will result.

1. Rotate engine until keyway is 45° counterclockwise from vertical.
2. Install cam positioning tool No. T91P-6256-A, or equivalent, on camshaft flats, **Fig. 14.**
3. If removed, install primary timing chain cam sprockets onto camshaft, and hand tighten nuts.
4. Install lefthand timing chain onto camshaft sprocket and ensure one timing chain colored link is aligned with camshaft sprocket timing marks, **Fig. 15.**
5. Install lefthand timing chain onto crankshaft sprocket and ensure one timing chain colored link is aligned with camshaft sprocket timing marks. Ensure tapered boss of crankshaft sprocket is facing away from engine block, **Fig. 16.**
6. Bleed timing chain tensioner as outlined under "Timing Chain Tensioner Bleed."
7. Install lefthand chain rail, tensioner and arm.
8. Remove timing chain slack using suitable C-clamp across both timing chain rails and release timing chain tensioner.
9. Repeat procedures for righthand timing chain. Ensure crankshaft sprocket tapered boss faces toward engine block, **Fig. 16.**
10. Tighten camshaft sprocket nuts.
11. Install crankshaft position pulse wheel.
12. Install oil pan.
13. Install front engine cover as outlined under "Front Engine Cover, Replace."
14. Install rocker arms as outlined under "Hydraulic Lifters, Replace."
15. Install valve covers as outlined under "Valve Cover, Replace."

2003-04

REMOVAL

1. Remove engine front cover as outlined under "Front Cover, Replace."
2. Remove crankshaft sensor ring from crankshaft.

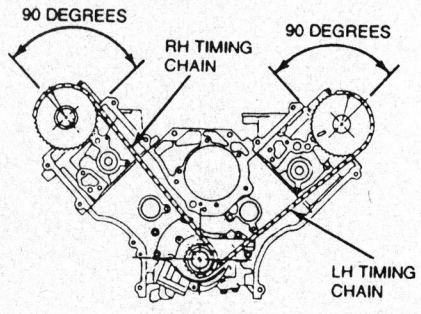

Fig. 13 Engine rotation to TDC

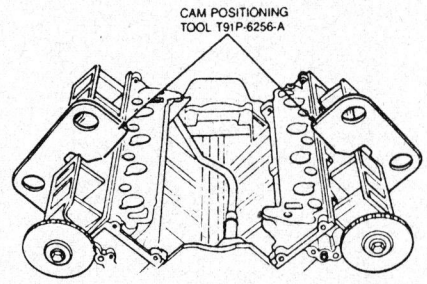

Fig. 14 Camshaft positioning tool

3. Disconnect eight ignition coil electrical connectors.
4. Remove mounting bolts and eight ignition coils.
5. Remove spark plugs.
6. Remove 16 roller followers using valve spring compressor tool No. T97P-6565-AH, or equivalent.
7. Remove mounting bolts, lefthand and righthand timing chain tensioners.
8. Remove lefthand and righthand timing chain tensioner arms from dowel pins.
9. Remove timing chains and crankshaft sprocket.
10. Remove mounting bolts and timing chain guides.
11. Install camshaft position aligner tool No. T96T-6256-B, or equivalent.
12. Remove mounting bolts and camshaft gears.

INSTALLATION

1. Compress tensioner plunger using suitable soft jawed vise.
2. While holding ratchet mechanism, push ratchet arm back into tensioner housing.
3. Install paper clip into hole in tensioner housing to hold ratchet and plunger in during installation.
4. If copper links are not visible, mark links on opposite ends of timing chain to use as timing marks, **Fig. 15.**
5. Install camshaft sprockets.
6. **Torque** bolts to 30 ft. lbs., then tighten an additional 90°.
7. Remove camshaft position aligner tool.
8. Position crankshaft with cylinder No. 1 at TDC using crankshaft holding tool No. T93P-6303-A, or equivalent.
9. Install crankshaft sprocket with flange facing forward, **Fig. 16.**
10. Install lefthand and righthand timing chain guides.
11. Install lefthand timing chain on crankshaft sprocket, aligning copper link with dot on crankshaft sprocket.
12. Install lefthand timing chain on camshaft sprocket, aligning copper link with dot on camshaft sprocket.
13. Install righthand timing chain on crankshaft sprocket, aligning copper link with dot on crankshaft sprocket.
14. Install righthand timing chain on camshaft sprocket, aligning copper link with dot on camshaft sprocket.
15. Ensure copper links are aligned with dots on crankshaft and camshaft

sprockets, **Fig. 17.**
16. Install lefthand and righthand timing chain tensioner arms on dowel pins. Lefthand tensioner arm has bump near dowel hole.
17. Install timing chain tensioners and remove paper clip.
18. Install 16 roller followers using valve spring compressor tool No. T97P-6565-AH, or equivalent.
19. Install spark plugs and ignition coils.
20. Install crankshaft sensor ring on crankshaft.
21. Install engine front cover as outlined under "Front Cover, Replace."

TIMING CHAIN TENSIONER BLEED

1. Position timing chain tensioner in suitable soft-jawed vise.
2. Lock ratchet stem mechanism position using suitable tool and slowly compress tensioner plunger by rotating vise handle. **Tensioner must be compressed slowly.**
3. When tensioner plunger bottoms in bore, continue holding ratchet lock mechanism and push ratchet mechanism down until flush with tensioner face.
4. While holding ratchet stem flush to tensioner face, release ratchet lock mechanism and install paper clip or suitable tool to lock tensioner in collapsed position.
5. **Do not remove paper clip or suitable tool until timing chain, tensioner arm, tensioner and timing chain guide are installed on engine.**

CAMSHAFT
REPLACE
2001-02

1. Remove timing chains as outlined under "Timing Chain, Replace."
2. Rotate crankshaft key counterclockwise 45° from vertical. Ensure pistons are below top of engine deck face. **Crankshaft must be in position prior to rotating camshafts or piston and/or valve damage may result if rocker arms have not been removed.**
3. Remove camshaft cap cluster mounting bolts, **Fig. 18.**
4. Tap upward, then remove cap and camshaft, **Fig. 19.**

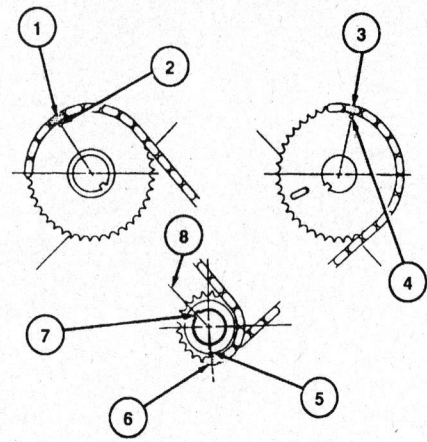

Item	Description
1	RH Camshaft Timing Chain Mark
2	RH Camshaft Sprocket Mark
3	LH Camshaft Timing Chain Mark
4	RH Camshaft Sprocket Mark
5	Crankshaft Sprocket Mark
6	Crankshaft Timing Chain Mark
7	Crankshaft Sprocket
8	Crankshaft Keyway Center Line

Fig. 15 Crankshaft to camshaft timing mark alignment

5. Reverse procedure to install.

2003-04

1. Remove rocker arms as outlined under "Rocker Arms, Replace."
2. Remove timing chain as outlined under "Timing Chain, Replace."
3. Remove bolt, then the camshaft sprocket and spacer.
4. Remove 13 camshaft bearing cap bolts.
5. Remove camshaft bearing cap ladders, then the camshaft.
6. Reverse procedure to install noting the following:
   a. Lubricate camshaft journals and bearing cap ladders with clean engine oil.
   b. Tighten bearing cap bolts in sequence, **Fig. 20.**

PISTON & ROD ASSEMBLY

Ensure side clearance between connecting rods and crankshaft journal is .00059–.01772 inch.

1. Assemble pistons, pins, bearings, caps, nuts and bolts in original positions.
2. Install pistons with notch to front of engine.
3. **Torque** connecting rod bearing cap bolts to 18 ft. lbs.

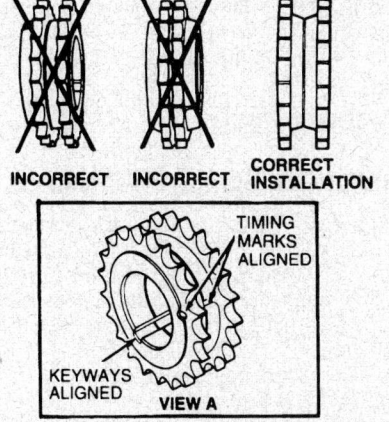

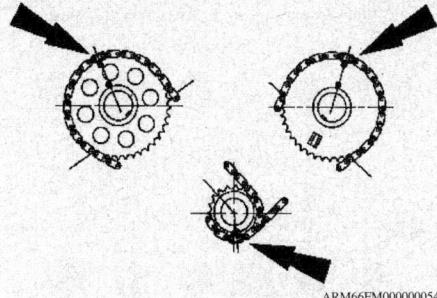

Fig. 17 Timing chain timing marks. 2003-04

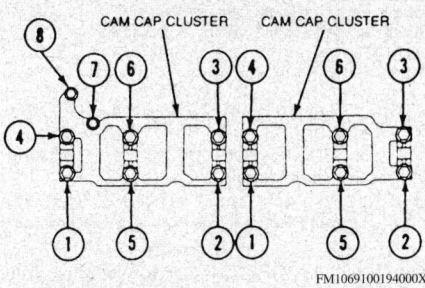

FM1069100194000X

Fig. 18 Camshaft cap cluster loosening & tightening sequence. 2001-02

Fig. 16 Crankshaft sprocket position

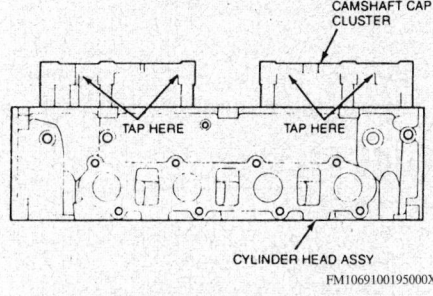

FM1069100195000X

Fig. 19 Camshaft cap cluster removal. 2001-02

4. **Torque** cap bolts to 30 ft. lbs.
5. Final tighten bolts an additional 90°.
6. Rotate crankshaft to ensure smooth operation.

MAIN & ROD BEARINGS

Refer to "2003-04" in "DOHC" for main bearing tightening sequences.

CRANKSHAFT SEAL

REPLACE

1. Remove transmission as outlined in **MOTOR's "Domestic Transmission Manual, In-Vehicle Service."**
2. Remove flywheel.
3. Remove crankshaft oil slinger using rear crankshaft slinger remover tool No. T-95P-6701-AH, or equivalent, and suitable slide hammer.
4. Remove crankshaft rear oil seal using rear crankshaft seal remover tool No. T95P-6701-BH, or equivalent, and suitable slide hammer.
5. Reverse procedure to install, noting the following:
   a. Install rear oil seal using crankshaft seal replacer tool No. T-95P-6701-AH and rear crankshaft seal adapter tool No. T-95P-6701-DH, or equivalents.
   b. With rear crankshaft seal adapter still installed, use rear crankshaft slinger replacer and rear crankshaft seal replacer to install crankshaft oil slinger.

OIL PAN

REPLACE

1. Remove air cleaner outlet tube.
2. Remove radiator sight shield.
3. Support engine with engine lifting bracket tool No. D93P-6001-A2 and support tool No. 303-290-A, or equivalents.
4. Raise and support vehicle.
5. Drain engine oil into suitable container.

6. Remove lefthand and righthand engine mount nuts.
7. Lower vehicle.
8. Raise engine using support tool.
9. Raise and support vehicle.
10. Compress front coil springs using compressor tool No. D78P-5310-A, or equivalent.
11. Position suitable jack stand under subframe.
12. Remove four engine mount bolts.
13. Loosen front subframe bolts. **Do not completely remove bolt.**
14. Lower front subframe.
15. Remove mounting bolts and pan. **If gasket is in good condition it may be used again.**
16. Reverse procedure to install, noting the following:
    a. Apply silicone gasket sealant No. F7AZ-19554-EA, or equivalent, to rear oil seal retainer to block sealing surface and at front cover to block mating surface.
    b. **Install and tighten cover and mounting bolts within four minutes.**
    c. Move oil pan into position and loosely install bolts.
    d. **Torque** oil pan bolts in sequence to 18 inch lbs.
    e. **Torque** pan bolts in sequence 15 ft. lbs.
    f. Final tighten bolts an additional 60° in sequence.

OIL PUMP

REPLACE

This procedure has been revised by a Technical Service Bulletin.
1. Remove valve covers as outlined under "Valve Cover, Replace."

2. Remove front cover as outlined under "Front Engine Cover, Replace."
3. Remove oil pan as outlined under "Oil Pan, Replace."
4. Remove timing chains as outlined under "Timing Chain, Replace."
5. Remove mounting bolts and oil pump.
6. Reverse procedure to install, noting the following:
   a. Align oil pump inner rotor with flat of crankshaft.
   b. Prime oil pump and system prior to starting engine.

BELT TENSION DATA

These models are equipped with an automatic drive belt tensioner. No adjustment or maintenance is required.

SERPENTINE DRIVE BELT

Always use square drive tool in hole in tensioner to move tensioner. Never pry on tensioner pulley. When releasing drive belt tensioner, never allow tensioner to snap back. Damage to tensioner or personal injury could result.

Do not allow engine coolant to remain on serpentine belt or pulleys. If required, remove belt and flush with clean water.

Removal

1. Insert suitable square drive tool into square hole in tensioner arm and rotate tensioner away from belt.
2. Lift belt from pulley and slowly release tensioner.
3. Remove belt.

Routing

Refer to "4.6L DOHC Engine" section for belt routing.

Installation

1. Route belt.
2. Ensure belt is properly seated in pulley grooves.
3. Insert suitable square drive tool into square hole in tensioner arm and rotate tensioner away from belt.
4. Position belt under tensioner and slowly release tensioner onto belt.

COOLING SYSTEM BLEED

1. Fill radiator completely full and install radiator cap.
2. Fill coolant reservoir and degas bottle to full cold mark.
3. Set heater control to full hot, high fan and set controls so air vents from dash vents.
4. Start and operate engine until fully warmed up while observing water temperature gauge.
5. If system is functioning properly, temperature will indicate normal and hot air will be felt at dash outlets.
6. If system is not functioning properly, temperature gauge will not read and/or no hot air will be felt at dash vents.
7. If system is not functioning properly, allow engine to cool and repeat procedure.
8. If system is functioning properly, allow engine to cool and fill coolant reservoir to full cold mark.

THERMOSTAT

REPLACE

1. Drain engine coolant into suitable container.
2. Remove mounting bolts and water outlet connection.
3. Position water outlet connection and upper radiator hose aside.
4. Remove thermostat and ring seal.
5. Reverse procedure to install.

WATER PUMP

REPLACE

1. Drain engine coolant into suitable container.
2. Loosen water pump pulley mounting bolts.
3. Insert suitable square drive tool into square hole in tensioner arm and rotate tensioner away from belt.
4. Lift belt from pulley and slowly release tensioner.
5. Remove belt.
6. Remove mounting bolts, water pump and gasket. Discard gasket.
7. Reverse procedure to install.

RADIATOR

REPLACE

Refer to "4.6L DOHC Engine" section for radiator replacement procedure

FUEL PUMP

REPLACE

Refer to "4.6L DOHC Engine" section for fuel pump replacement procedure

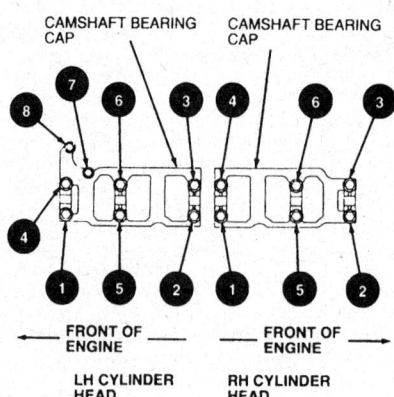

FM1069100139000X

Fig. 20 Camshaft cap cluster tightening sequence. 2003–04

FUEL FILTER

REPLACE

1. Relieve fuel system pressure as outlined under "Precautions."
2. Raise and support vehicle.
3. Remove push connector fittings from fuel filter ends using suitable spring lock coupler tools.
4. Loosen worm gear clamp and remove filter from bracket. Record flow arrow to ensure proper direction of fuel flow through filter.
5. Reverse procedure to install using new retainer clips in each fitting.

TECHNICAL SERVICE BULLETINS

Fuel Pump Whining/ Buzzing Through Radio Speaker

2001

On some of these models there may be a whining or buzzing in speakers.

This condition may be caused by fuel pump electrical noise.

To correct this condition install an electronic noise Radio Frequency Interference (RFI) filter (part No. F1PZ-18B925-A) on fuel pump inside the fuel tank, as follows:

1. Remove fuel pump sender from fuel tank as outlined under "Fuel Pump, Replace."
2. Cut fuel pump wires three inches from flange. Discard wires.
3. Connect RFI filter connectors to fuel pump spade terminal.
4. Cut and solder both RFI filter red and black wires to flange red and black wires.

5. Install suitable heat shrink tubing over solder connectors.
6. Secure RFI filter to fuel pump using suitable bundling strap.
7. Install fuel pump sender.

Engine Tick

2001–04 SOHC ENGINE

On some of these models with engines built before Sept. 17, 2003, there may be an engine tick noise at all temperatures during idle. The noise may be prevalent in the front wheel well area, but may be heard with the hood open.

This condition may be caused by the cylinder head valve guide area.

To correct this condition, proceed as follows:

1. Ensure noise is coming from back of cylinder head near exhaust ports by listening with suitable stethoscope.
2. Ensure noise is heard in wheel well or catalytic converter and from under vehicle.
3. Ensure there are no exhaust manifold leaks.
4. Ensure noise is present when canceling each cylinder by unplugging injectors one at a time.
5. Ensure camshaft spacers are in place.
6. Ensure cam sprocket is tightened.
7. Inspect hydraulic lash adjusters for spongy condition.
8. Ensure timing chain tensioner pin been removed.
9. Replace cylinder head and cam (lefthand, part No. 4L3Z-6049-AA; righthand part No. 4L3Z-4069-BA).

PCV Valve Area Oil Leak

2002 SOHC ENGINE

On some of these models there may be an oil leak coming from the camshaft/valve cover where the Positive Crankcase Ventilation (PCV) valve mounts.

This condition may be caused by stack up tolerance between the PCV valve and tube.

To correct this condition, proceed as follows:

1. Remove air cleaner outlet tube.
2. Disconnect PCV valve tube.
3. Install hose clamp (part No. 376240-S100) with worm gear down.
4. Install tube.
5. **Torque** hose clamp to 12–20 inch lbs.
6. Install air cleaner outlet tube.

TIGHTENING SPECIFICATIONS

Year	Component	Torque/Ft. Lbs.
2001–02	Accelerator Cable Bracket	72–96①
	Air Conditioning Compressor	18
	Air Conditioning Muffler	15
	Alternator	18
	Alternator Brace	89①
	Battery Cable To Alternator	89①
	Battery Cable Support Bracket	15
	Belt Idler Pulley	18
	Belt Tensioner	18
	Camshaft	81–95
	Camshaft Cover	89①
	Camshaft Position Sensor	89①
	Clutch Pressure Plate	26
	Connecting Rod	⑪
	Crankshaft Damper	114–121
	Crankshaft Position Sensor	89①
	Crankshaft Pulley	⑩
	Crankshaft Rear Seal Retainer	89①
	Cylinder Head	③
	Drive Belt Tensioner	18
	EGR Sensor Bracket	89①
	EGR Tube Connector	30–33
	EGR Vacuum Regulator Solenoid Bracket	89①
	EGR Valve	18
	EGR Tube To EGR Valve	26
	EGR Tube To Exhaust Manifold	30
	Engine Coolant Temperature Sensor	11
	Engine Mount, Nut	111
	Engine Mount To Block	52
	Exhaust Manifold	⑥
	Exhaust Pipe To Exhaust Manifold	20–30
	Flywheel	59
	Front Brake Caliper	23
	Front Cover	④
	Front Engine Mount	45–59
	Front Engine Mount Through Bolts	15–22
	Fuel Filer	27–44①
	Fuel Rail	89①
	Fuel Tank Sender	89①
	Heater Hose Fitting Studs To Manifold	18
	Idle Air Control Valve	89①
	Ignition Coil	53①
	Ignition Coil Cover	89①
	Intake Manifold	⑤
	Intake Manifold To Cylinder Head	53–64
	Main Bearing	⑧
	Oil Dipstick Tube	89①
	Oil Filter	11
	Oil Filter Adapter	15–22
	Oil Filter Adapter Insert	43
	Oil Inlet Tube To Main Bearing Cap	15–22
	Oil Inlet Tube To Oil Pump	72–108①
	Oil Pan	②
	Oil Pan Drain Plug	120①
	Oil Pump	89①

Continued

TIGHTENING
SPECIFICATIONS—Continued

Year	Component	Torque/Ft. Lbs.
2001–02	Oil Pump Screen Cover & Tube To Main Cap Stud Spacer	18
	Oil Pump Screen Cover & Tube To Pump	89①
	Oxygen Sensor	27–33
	Power Steering Pump	18
	Power Steering Reservoir	89①
	Powertrain Frame	73–100
	Pressure Plate	47①
	Rear Engine Mount, Bolt	50–70
	Rear Engine Mount, Nut	35–50
	Rear Engine Support	15–22
	Rear Seal Retainer	89①
	RFI Capacitor	89①
	Serpentine Belt Idler Pulley	18
	Serpentine Belt Tensioner	18
	Spark Plug	13
	Subframe	85
	Thermostat Housing	15–22
	Throttle Body	⑤
	Throttle Cable Bracket	89①
	Timing Chain Tensioner	18
	Torque Converter	18
	Transmission Filler Tube	35
	Transmission Shift Lever	27
	Transmission Shift Lever Inner Boot	89①
	Transmission Shift Lever Plate To Transmission	13
	Valve Cover	⑦
	Water Bypass Tube	72–96①
	Water Drain Plug	15
	Water Outlet	18
	Water Pump	18
	Water Pump Pulley	18
	Wheel Lug Nuts	95
	Wiring Harness	89①
2003–04	Accelerator Bracket	89①
	Air Conditioning Compressor	18
	Air Conditioning Muffler Nut	18
	Alternator	18
	Belt Idler Support Bracket	18
	Belt Idler Pulley	18
	Camshaft Cap	⑨
	Camshaft Sprocket	⑨
	Connecting Rod	⑪
	Coolant Bypass Tube	18
	Crankshaft Pulley	⑩
	Cylinder Head	③
	Drive Belt Tensioner	18
	Engine Mount Bolts	52
	Engine Mount Nuts	111
	Exhaust Manifold	⑥
	Front Cover	④
	Heater Water Inlet Tube	89①
	Heater Water Outlet Tube	18
	Idler Pulley Bracket	18

Continued

TIGHTENING
SPECIFICATIONS—Continued

Year	Component	Torque/Ft. Lbs.
2003–04	Intake Manifold	⑤
	Main Bearing Cap	⑧
	Oil Filter Adapter	18
	Oil Dipstick Tube	89①
	Oil Pan	②
	Oil Pump Screen Cover	89①
	Oil Pump Screen & Pickup Tube Spacer To Main Bearing Stud	18
	Oil Pump To Cylinder Block	89①
	Power Steering Hose Fitting	48
	Power Steering Hose Bracket	89①
	Power Steering Pump	18
	Power Steering Pump To Cylinder Block	18
	Primary Timing Chain Guide	89①
	Subframe Brace	30
	Thermostat Housing	18
	Throttle Body	⑤
	Throttle Body Spacer	18
	Timing Chain Tensioner (Primary)	18
	Timing Chain (Secondary)	89①
	Valve Cover	⑦
	Water Pump Pulley	18
	Water Pump To Cylinder Block	18

① — Inch pounds.
② — Refer to "Oil Pan, Replace" for tightening specifications and sequence.
③ — Refer to "Cylinder Head, Replace" for tightening specifications and sequence.
④ — Refer to "Front Cover, Replace" for tightening specifications and sequence.
⑤ — Refer to "Intake Manifold, Replace" for tightening specifications and sequence.
⑥ — Refer to "Exhaust Manifold, Replace" for tightening specifications and sequence.
⑦ — Refer to "Valve Cover, Replace" for tightening specifications and sequence.
⑧ — Refer to "Main & Rod Bearings" for tightening specifications and sequence.
⑨ — Refer to "Camshaft, Replace" for tightening specifications and sequence.
⑩ — Refer to "Front Cover Seal, Replace" for tightening specifications and sequence.
⑪ — Refer to "Piston & Rod Assembly" for tightening specifications and sequence.

4.6L SOHC (VIN Z) Engine

NOTE: For Procedures Not Found In This Section, Refer To "4.6L SOHC (VIN X) Engine" Section.

NOTE: On Air Bag Equipped Models, Refer To "Air Bag System Precautions" Located In The Front Of This Manual For System Disarming & Arming Procedures.

INDEX

PRECAUTIONS

Air Bag Systems

Refer to "Air Bag System Precautions" in front of this manual for system disarming and arming procedures.

Battery Ground Cable

Prior to service, disconnect battery ground cable and isolate as required.

Fuel System Pressure Relief

1. Remove fuel pump relay.
2. Start engine and allow it idle until is stalls.
3. Crank engine for approximately five seconds to ensure fuel injection supply manifold pressure has been released.
4. Turn ignition switch to OFF position.

COMPRESSION PRESSURE

1. Ensure crankcase oil is correct viscosity and correct level, and battery is fully charged.
2. Operate vehicle until engine at normal operating temperature.
3. Turn ignition switch to OFF position and remove all spark plugs.
4. Set throttle plates in wide-open position.
5. Install suitable compression gauge in cylinder No. 1.
6. Install suitable auxiliary start switch.
7. Turn ignition switch to ON position.
8. Crank engine at least five compression strokes using auxiliary starter switch.
9. Record highest reading and approximate number of compression strokes required to obtain highest reading.
10. Repeat test on each cylinder.
11. Compression pressures are within specifications is the lowest cylinder reading is at least 75% of highest.

ENGINE MOUNT
REPLACE

1. Raise and support vehicle.
2. Loosen clamp and disconnect air cleaner outlet pipe.
3. Disconnect Mass Air Flow (MAF) sensor electrical connector.
4. Remove mounting bolt and air cleaner. Ensure two rubber grommets are retained to feet.
5. Disconnect Throttle Position (TP) sensor and electronic throttle control electrical connectors, **Fig. 1.**
6. Remove mounting bolts, nuts and throttle body.
7. Remove fix pin-type retainers and radiator sight shield, **Fig. 2.**
8. Remove two outer bracket mounting bolts and two lower mounting nuts, then disconnect alternator electrical connector and pin-type retainer.
9. Position cover aside, then remove B+ terminal nut and alternator.
10. Support engine using suitable engine lifting brackets and three-bar engine support tools.
11. Remove left and righthand engine support insulator nuts, **Figs. 3 and 4.**
12. Raise engine approximately 1.57 inches.
13. Remove two mounting bolts and righthand engine support insulator.
14. Remove four mounting bolts and lefthand engine support engine support bracket.
15. Remove two mounting bolts and lefthand engine support insulator.
16. Reverse procedure to install.

ENGINE
REPLACE

1. Raise and support vehicle.
2. Remove fuel pump relay.
3. Start engine and allow it idle until is stalls.
4. Crank engine for approximately five seconds to ensure fuel injection supply manifold pressure has been released.
5. Turn ignition switch to OFF position.
6. Mark hood hinge location for installation alignment.
7. Remove four mounting bolts and hood.
8. Remove two cover, mounting nuts and wiper pivot arms.
9. Remove four cowl vent screen pin-type retainers.
10. Remove righthand, then the lefthand vent screen.
11. Loosen clamp and disconnect air cleaner outlet pipe.
12. Disconnect Mass Air Flow (MAF) sensor electrical connector.
13. Remove mounting bolt and air cleaner.

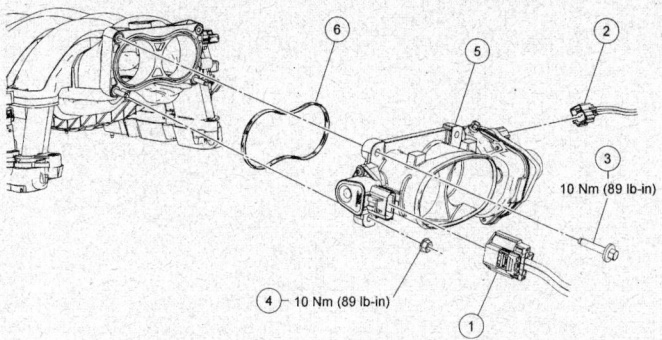

Item	Description
1	Electronic throttle control electrical connector
2	Throttle position (TP) sensor electrical connector
3	Throttle body bolts (2 required)
4	Throttle body nuts (2 required)
5	Throttle body
6	Throttle body gasket

ARM0400000000517

Fig. 1 Throttle body replacement

Item	Description		Item	Description
1	Pin-type retainer		6	Wiring harness pin-type retainer
2	Radiator sight shield		7	Generator nut (2 required)
3	B+ terminal nut		8	Generator bracket bolt (2 required)
4	B+ terminal cover		9	Generator
5	Generator electrical connector			

ARM0400000000519

Fig. 2 Alternator replacement (Part 2 of 2)

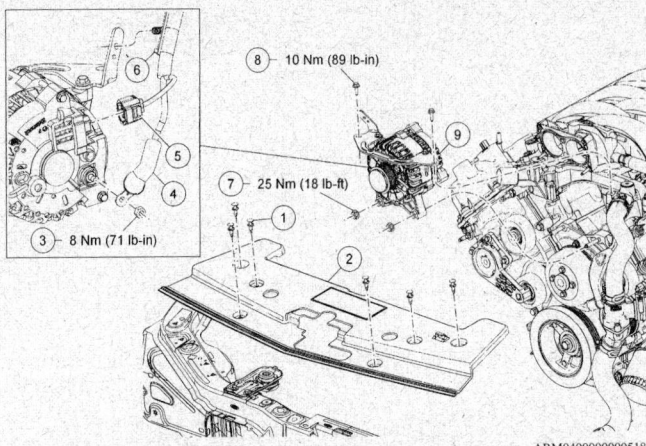

ARM0400000000518

Fig. 2 Alternator replacement (Part 1 of 2)

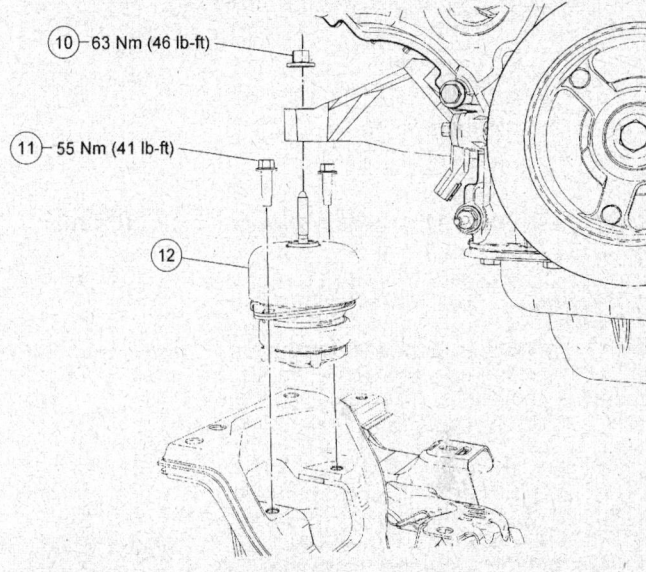

Item	Description
10	RH engine support insulator nut
11	RH engine support insulator bolt (2 required)
12	RH engine support insulator

ARM0400000000533

Fig. 3 Engine mounting replacement. Righthand

Ensure two rubber grommets are retained to feet.

14. Drain engine cooling system into suitable container.
15. Remove intake manifold as outlined under "Intake Manifold, Replace."
16. Remove four mounting bolts and position alternator support bracket aside, **Fig. 5.**
17. Disconnect, then position coolant crossover assembly-to-thermostat housing and assembly-to-radiator hoses aside.
18. Disconnect quick connect fitting, then position heater return and supply hose aside.
19. Remove two mounting bolts, coolant crossover and gasket.
20. Disconnect, the position upper and lower degas bottle hoses aside.
21. Remove two mounting bolts and degas bottle.
22. Remove fix pin-type retainers and radiator sight shield, **Fig. 2.**
23. Rotate accessory drive belt tensioner clockwise with suitable belt tensioner release tool and remove belt.
24. Disconnect air conditioning pressure transducer electrical connector.
25. Disconnect coolant hose from oil filter adapter.
26. Drain engine oil into suitable container.

27. Disconnect degas bottle hose from cooling fan.
28. Disconnect lower radiator hose from thermostat housing.
29. Remove thermostat housing and coolant hoses.
30. Disconnect oil temperature sensor electrical connector and two pin-type retainers.
31. Remove mounting nut and ground wire from stud bolt.
32. Disconnect pin-type retainer from air conditioning compressor.
33. Disconnect air conditioning clutch and Crankshaft Position (CKP) sensor electrical connectors.
34. Disconnect retainers and position wir-

ing harness aside.
35. Remove mounting bolt and three nuts, then position and support air conditioning compressor aside.
36. Remove two mounting nuts and power steering pulley shield.
37. Remove wiring harness retainer, nut and tube retaining clip from power steering stud bolt.
38. Remove three stud bolts, then position and support power steering pump aside.
39. Support engine using suitable engine lifting brackets and three-bar engine support tools. **Do not position engine support legs on fenders. Legs should be positioned on body**

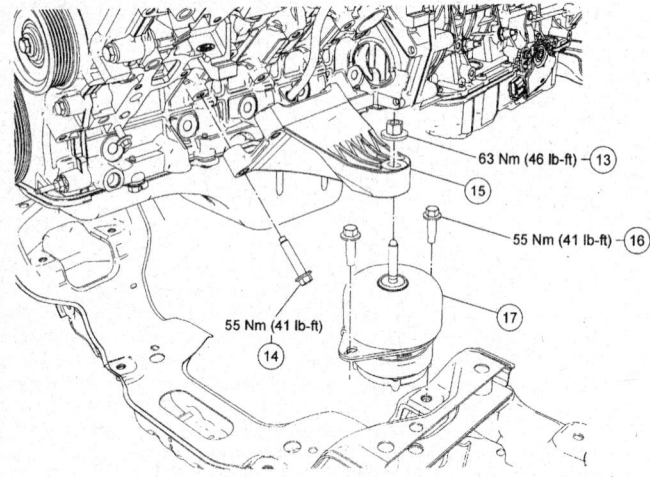

Item	Description
13	LH engine support insulator nut
14	LH engine support bracket bolt (4 required)
15	LH engine support bracket
16	LH engine support insulator bolt (2 required)
17	LH engine support insulator

ARM0400000000534

Fig. 4 Engine mount replacement. Lefthand

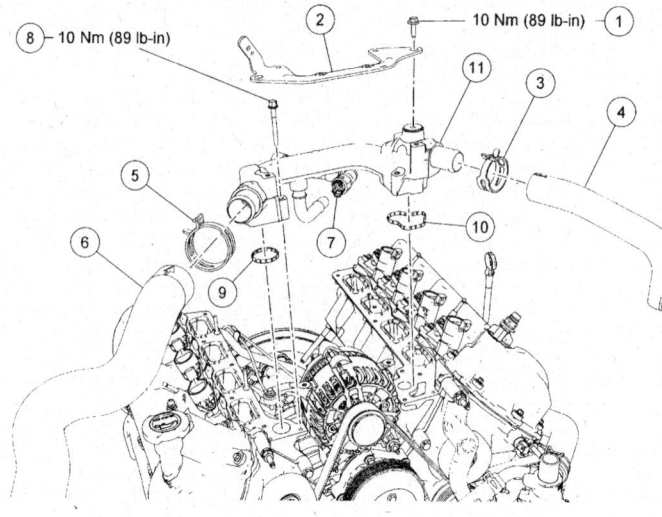

Item	Description
1	Alternator support bracket bolt (4 required)
2	Alternator support bracket
3	Hose clamp
4	Coolant crossover assembly-to-thermostat housing hose
5	Hose clamp
6	Coolant crossover assembly-to-radiator hose
7	Heater return and supply hose
8	Coolant crossover assembly bolt (2 required)
9	Gasket
10	Gasket
11	Coolant crossover assembly

ARM0400000000535

Fig. 5 Coolant crossover replacement

structure near suspension strut tower.

40. **On models equipped with automatic transmission,** proceed as follows:
    a. Remove mounting nut and position transmission cooler tube bracket aside.
    b. Remove transmission as outlined in **MOTOR's "Domestic Transmission Manual, In-Vehicle Service."**
41. **On models equipped with manual transmission,** remove clutch as outlined in **MOTOR's "Domestic Transmission Manual, In-Vehicle Service."**
42. **On all models,** remove four catalytic converter flange nuts.
43. Disconnect righthand Heated Oxygen Sensor (HO2S) electrical connector.
44. Disconnect left and righthand Catalyst Monitor Sensor (CMS).
45. Remove engine-to-transmission spacer plate.
46. Disconnect heater hoses.
47. Remove mounting bolt and ground strap from cowl. Disconnect pin-type retainer.
48. Disconnect alternator jumper harness electrical connector.
49. Remove two mounting nuts, then position alternator and harness aside.
50. Disconnect upper and lower Powertrain Control Module (PCM) electrical connectors.
51. Disconnect 16-pin electrical connector and two wiring retainers.
52. Remove power distribution box cover.
53. Disconnect power distribution box upper housing from lower housing.
54. Loosen bolt and disconnect 68-pin

connector from power distribution box.
55. Remove mounting nut, radio interference capacitor and J-bracket from engine front cover stud bolt.
56. Remove left and righthand engine support insulator nuts.
57. Attach suitable floor crane and engine lifting bracket modular tool No. 014-00073, or equivalent, to engine.
58. Remove three-bar support.
59. Remove engine.
60. Reverse procedure to install.

INTAKE MANIFOLD
REPLACE

1. Remove fuel pump relay.
2. Start engine and allow it idle until is stalls.
3. Crank engine for approximately five seconds to ensure fuel injection supply manifold pressure has been released.
4. Turn ignition switch to OFF position.
5. Disconnect crankcase vent tube from air cleaner outlet pipe.
6. Loosen two clamps and remove air cleaner outlet pipe.
7. Disconnect fuel supply tube spring lock coupling.

8. Disconnect two retainers from fuel rail stud bolts and position wiring harness aside.
9. Disconnect fuel rail pressure and temperature sensor electrical connector and vacuum hose.
10. Disconnect eight fuel injection electrical connectors.
11. Remove four fuel rail stud bolts.
12. Remove fuel rail and injectors.
13. Disconnect Evaporative Emissions (EVAP) tube from intake manifold and position it aside, **Fig. 6.**
14. Disconnect Positive Crankcase Ventilation (PCV) tube from intake manifold and position it aside.
15. Disconnect Throttle Position (TP) sensor and electronic throttle body electrical connectors.
16. Disconnect Charge Motion Control Valve (CMCV) electrical connector.
17. Disconnect wiring retainers from intake manifold stud bolt and CMCV bracket. Position wiring harness aside.
18. Disconnect vacuum hose from T fitting.
19. Remove nine mounting bolts, stud bolt, intake manifold and gasket.
20. Reverse procedure to install, noting the following:
    a. Install new gasket.

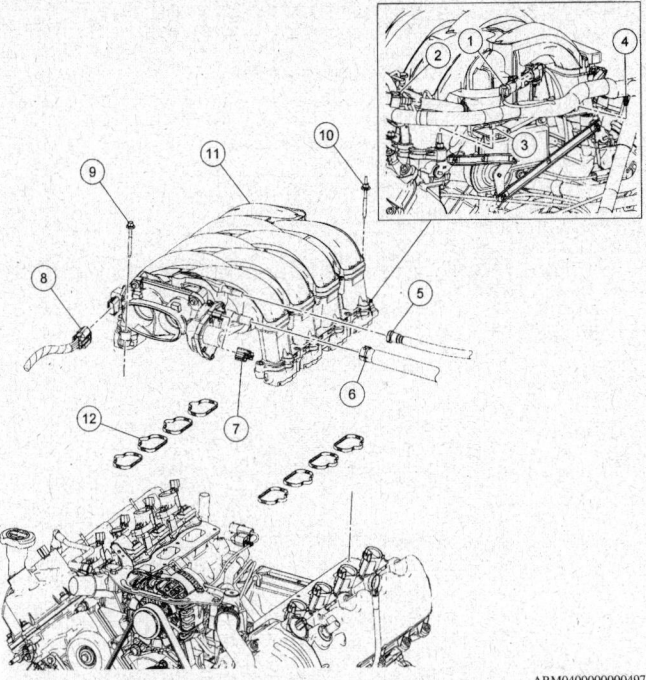

Fig. 6 Intake manifold replacement (Part 1 of 2)

ARM0400000000497

Item	Description
1	Charge motion control valve (CMCV) electrical connector
2	Vacuum hose T-fitting
3	Wiring harness retainer
4	Wiring harness pin-type retainer
5	Evaporative emissions
6	Positive crankcase ventilation (PCV) tube
7	Electronic throttle body electrical connector
8	Throttle position (TP) sensor electrical connector
9	Intake manifold bolt (9 required)
10	Intake manifold stud bolt
11	Intake manifold
12	Intake manifold gasket (8 required)

ARM0400000000498

Fig. 6 Intake manifold replacement (Part 2 of 2)

b. Tighten mounting bolts in sequence, **Fig. 7.**
c. Install new upper and lower fuel injector O-ring seals lubricated with suitable, clean engine oil.

EXHAUST MANIFOLD

REPLACE

Lefthand

1. Raise and support vehicle.
2. Loosen clamp and disconnect air cleaner outlet pipe.
3. Disconnect Mass Air Flow (MAF) sensor electrical connector.
4. Remove mounting bolt and air cleaner. Ensure two rubber grommets are retained to feet.
5. Disconnect Throttle Position (TP) sensor and electronic throttle control electrical connectors, **Fig. 1.**
6. Remove mounting bolts, nuts and throttle body.
7. Disconnect lefthand Heated Oxygen Sensor (HO2S) electrical connector and wiring harness retainer.
8. Remove two righthand catalytic converter to exhaust manifold nuts, **Fig. 8.**
9. Remove two lefthand converter-to-exhaust manifold nuts.
10. Remove fix pin-type retainers and radiator sight shield, **Fig. 2.**
11. Remove two outer bracket mounting bolts and two lower mounting nuts, then disconnect alternator electrical connector and pin-type retainer.
12. Position cover aside, then remove B+ terminal nut and alternator.
13. Support engine using suitable engine lifting brackets and three-bar engine support tools.

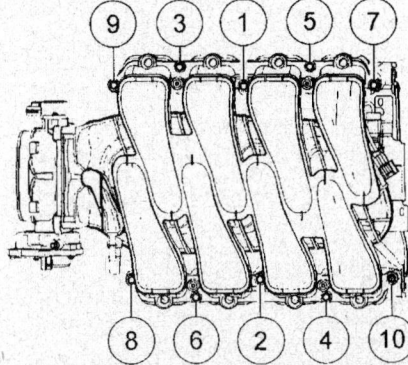

Fig. 7 Intake manifold tightening sequence

ARM0400000000499

14. Remove left and righthand engine support insulator nuts.
15. Raise engine approximately 1.57 inches.
16. Remove bolt and disconnect steering coupling. **Do not rotate steering wheel when steering column intermediate shaft is disconnected.**
17. Remove four bolts and lefthand engine support insulator bracket.
18. Remove eight nuts, exhaust manifold and gasket.
19. Reverse procedure to install, noting the following:
    a. Install new exhaust manifold gaskets.
    b. Tighten exhaust manifold mounting nuts in sequence, **Fig. 9.**

Righthand

1. Raise and support vehicle.

2. Loosen clamp and disconnect air cleaner outlet pipe.
3. Disconnect Mass Air Flow (MAF) sensor electrical connector.
4. Remove mounting bolt and air cleaner. Ensure two rubber grommets are retained to feet.
5. Disconnect Throttle Position (TP) sensor and electronic throttle control electrical connectors, **Fig. 1.**
6. Remove mounting bolts, nuts and throttle body.
7. Ensure anti-theft system is deactivated.
8. Raise and support vehicle.
9. Remove starter solenoid terminal cap.
10. Remove two nuts terminal nuts and position wires aside.
11. Remove three mounting bolts and starter motor.
12. Disconnect lefthand Heated Oxygen Sensor (HO2S) electrical connector and wiring harness retainer.
13. Remove two righthand catalytic converter to exhaust manifold nuts, **Fig. 10.**
14. Remove two lefthand catalytic converter-to-exhaust manifold nuts.
15. Remove six pin-type retainers and radiator sight shield, **Fig. 2.**
16. Remove two outer bracket mounting bolts and two lower mounting nuts, then disconnect alternator electrical connector and pin-type retainer.
17. Position cover aside, then remove B+ terminal nut and alternator.
18. Support engine using suitable engine lifting brackets and three-bar engine support tools.
19. Remove left and righthand engine support insulator nuts.

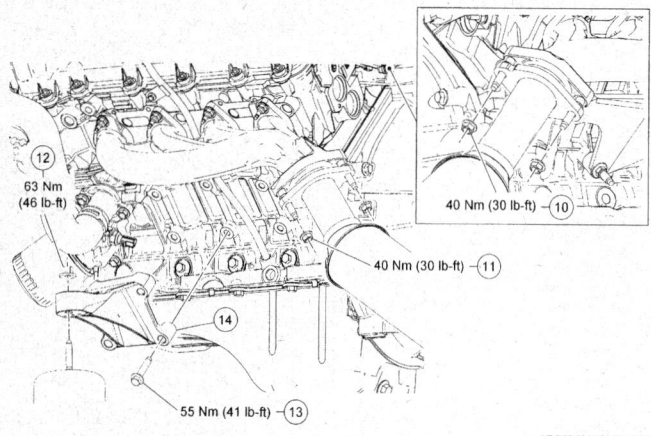

63 Nm
(46 lb-ft) — (12)

40 Nm (30 lb-ft) — (10)

40 Nm (30 lb-ft) — (11)

(14)

55 Nm (41 lb-ft) — (13)

ARM0400000000520

Fig. 8   Exhaust manifold replacement (Part 1 of 2). Lefthand

Item	Description	Item	Description
10	RH catalytic converter-to-exhaust manifold nuts (2 required)	13	LH engine support insulator bracket bolt (4 required)
11	LH catalytic converter-to-exhaust manifold nuts (2 required)	14	LH engine support insulator bracket
12	LH engine support insulator nut		

ARM0400000000521

Fig. 8   Exhaust manifold replacement (Part 2 of 2), Lefthand

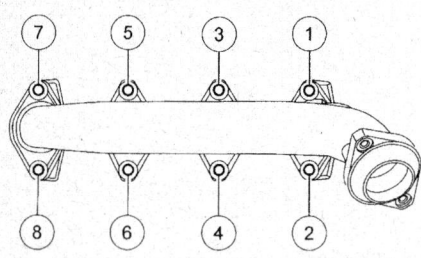

ARM0400000000522

Fig. 9   Exhaust manifold tightening sequence. Lefthand

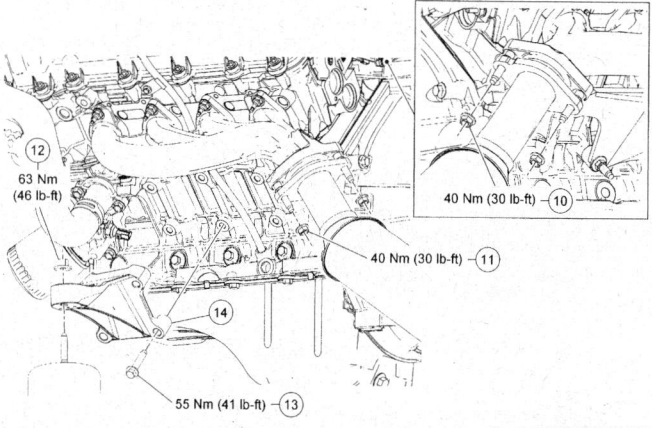

63 Nm
(46 lb-ft) — (12)

40 Nm (30 lb-ft) — (10)

40 Nm (30 lb-ft) — (11)

(14)

55 Nm (41 lb-ft) — (13)

ARM0400000000523

Fig. 10   Exhaust manifold replacement. Righthand

20. Raise engine approximately 1.57 inches.
21. Remove nut and ground wire from stud bolt.
22. **On models equipped with automatic transmission,** remove mounting nut and position transmission cooler tube bracket aside.
23. **On all models,** remove two bolts, two stud bolts and righthand engine support insulator bracket.
24. Remove eight nuts, exhaust manifold and gasket.
25. Reverse procedure to install, noting the following:
    a. Install new exhaust manifold gaskets.
    b. Tighten exhaust manifold mounting nuts in sequence, **Fig. 11.**

CYLINDER HEAD

REPLACE

1. Remove engine as outlined under "Engine. Replace."
2. Mount the engine on suitable work stand and remove special tools.
3. Disconnect left and righthand Camshaft Position (CMP) sensor electrical connectors.
4. Disconnect left and righthand Variable Camshaft Timing (VCT) solenoid electrical connectors.
5. Disconnect engine wiring harness pin-type retainers.

6. Remove mounting nut and righthand radio ignition interference capacitor.
7. Remove Positive Crankcase Ventilation (PCV) tubes from left and righthand valve covers.
8. Disconnect ignition coils' electrical connectors.
9. Disconnect two engine wiring harness retainers from righthand and lefthand valve cover studs.
10. Disconnect engine wiring harness pin-type retainers.
11. Disconnect Cylinder Head Temperature (CHT) sensor electrical connector and jumper harness electrical connector pin-type retainer.
12. Disconnect Knock Sensor (KS) electrical connector and pin-type retainer.
13. Disconnect lefthand Heated Oxygen Sensor (HO2S) electrical connector.
14. Disconnect engine wiring harness retainer from stud bolt.
15. Disconnect engine oil pressure sensor electrical connector.
16. Remove engine wiring harness.
17. Remove oil filter.
18. Remove mounting bolt and oil level indicator tube.
19. Remove mounting bolts, then the left and righthand CMP sensors.
20. Remove eight mounting bolts and ignition coils.
21. Loosen 29 mountings bolts and valve covers. **Mounting bolts are part of valve cover and should not be removed.**
22. Remove five mounting bolts, water pump pulley and righthand side acces-

sory drive belt idler pulley.
23. Remove crankshaft pulley mounting bolt and washer.
24. Remove crankshaft pulley using suitable three-jaw puller tool.
25. Remove four oil pan-to-engine front cover mounting bolts.
26. Record front cover mounting bolt locations for installation alignment.
27. Remove mounting bolts and front cover.
28. Remove crankshaft sensor ring.
29. Position crankshaft keyway at 12 o'clock position, **Fig. 12,** noting the following:
    a. If camshaft lobes are not exactly positioned, **Fig. 13,** crankshaft will require one full additional rotation to 12 o'clock position.
    b. Cylinder No. 1 camshaft exhaust lobe must be coming up on exhaust stroke.
    c. Ensure positioning of two intake lobes and exhaust lobe on cylinder No. 1.
30. Mark components for installation into original locations.
31. Remove only three roller followers righthand cylinder head using valve spring compressor tool No. 303-1039, or equivalent, **Fig. 14. Do not allow valve keepers to fall off valve or valve may drop into cylinder.**
32. Remove only three roller followers lefthand cylinder head using valve spring compressor tool No. 303-1039, or equivalent, **Fig. 15. Do not allow valve keepers to fall off valve or**

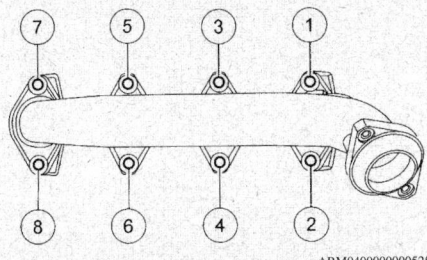

Fig. 11 Exhaust manifold tightening sequence. Righthand

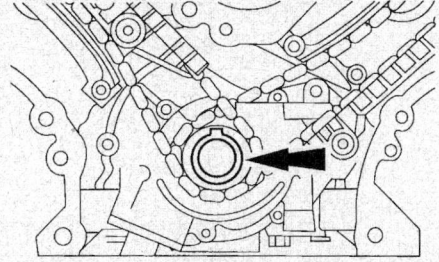

Fig. 12 Crankshaft keyway 12 o'clock position

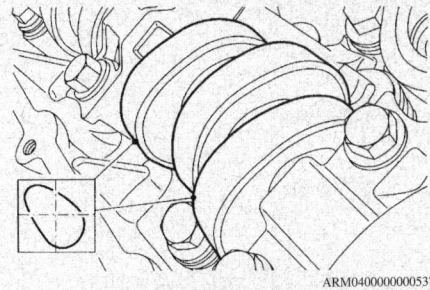

Fig. 13 Camshaft lobe positioning

valve may drop into cylinder.

33. Rotate crankshaft clockwise and position crankshaft keyway at 6 o'clock position. **Do not move crankshaft past 6 o'clock position.**
34. Remove mounting bolts, then the left and righthand timing chain tensioners and tensioner arms.
35. Remove righthand timing chain from camshaft and crankshaft sprockets.
36. Remove lefthand timing chain from the camshaft and crankshaft sprockets.
37. Remove two mounting bolts and both timing chain guides.
38. Remove mounting bolts, then the left and righthand camshaft phaser sprocket using camshaft phase locking tool No. 303-1046, or equivalent. **Only use hand tools.**
39. Mark camshaft bearing caps for installation original locations.
40. Remove camshaft bearing caps bolts in sequence, **Fig. 16.**
41. **Remove front thrust camshaft bearing cap straight upward from bearing towers.** Remove remaining bearing caps.
42. Remove camshaft.
43. Mark components for installation into original locations.
44. Remove all remaining roller followers.
45. Remove hydraulic lash adjusters.
46. Install cylinder head remover/installer tool No. T97T-6000-A, or equivalent.
47. Remove eight mounting nuts and exhaust manifold.
48. Remove nut and ground strap from lefthand cylinder head stud bolt.
49. Remove stud bolt and coolant tube from righthand cylinder head.
50. Place suitable, clean shop towels over exposed engine cavities.
51. Remove 20 mounting bolts, cylinder heads and gaskets.
52. Reverse procedure to install, noting the following:
    a. **Ensure all coolant residue and foreign material are cleaned from block surface and cylinder bore.**
    b. **Do not use sealing aids (aviation cement, copper spray and glue).** Gasket must be installed dry.
    c. **Cylinder head bolts are tighten-to-yield must be discarded and new bolts installed.**
    d. **Do not turn the crankshaft until instructed to do so.**
    e. Position cylinder head gaskets and cylinder heads over the dowels sing

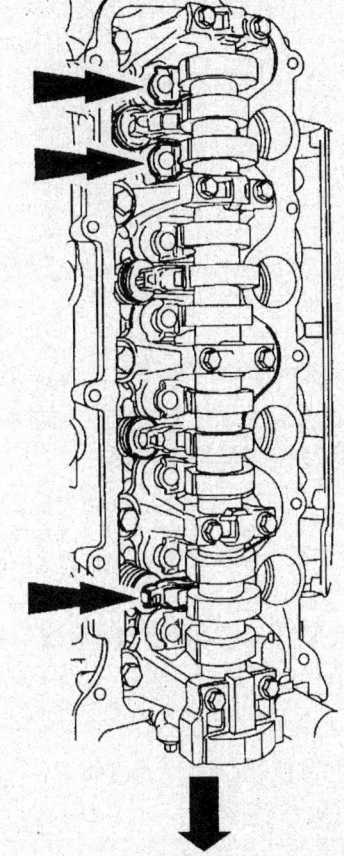

Fig. 14 Roller follower removal. Righthand

cylinder head alignment pin tools No. SR-015486, or equivalent, and install cylinder head bolts loosely.
f. **Torque** cylinder head bolts in sequence to 30 ft. lbs., **Fig. 17.**
g. Tighten head bolts an additional 90° in sequence.
h. Final tighten bolts an additional 90° in sequence.

VALVE COVER
REPLACE
Lefthand

1. Disconnect crankcase vent tube from

air cleaner outlet pipe.
2. Loosen two clamps and remove air cleaner outlet pipe.
3. Disconnect ignition coil electrical connector.
4. Remove mounting bolts and ignition coil.
5. Raise and support vehicle.
6. Disconnect Evaporative Emissions (EVAP) canister purge valve from bracket and position it aside, **Fig. 18.**
7. Remove oil level indicator and tube mounting bolt.
8. Remove oil level indicator tube and O-ring.
9. Disconnect EVAP tube from Intake manifold, **Fig. 19.**
10. Remove Positive Crankcase Ventilation (PCV) tube.
11. Disconnect Variable Camshaft Timing (VCT) solenoid electrical connector and two wiring harness pin-type retainers.
12. Disconnect two wiring harness retainers from valve cover stud bolts.
13. Loosen 15 mounting bolts, then remove valve cover and gasket. **Mounting bolts are part of valve cover and should not be removed.**
14. Clean cylinder head valve cover mating surfaces with suitable silicone gasket remover.
15. Clean valve cover gasket groove with soap and water, or suitable solvent.
16. Reverse procedure to install, noting the following:
    a. **Valve cover must be secured within four minutes of sealant application.**
    b. Apply .32 inch bead of suitable silicone gasket and sealant to where engine front cover meets cylinder head, **Fig. 20.**
    c. Tighten mounting bolts in sequence, **Fig. 21.**
    d. Lubricate new oil level indicator tube O-ring seal with suitable, clean engine oil.
    e. Apply light film of suitable silicone brake caliper great and dielectric compound to inside of coil boots.

Righthand

1. Disconnect ignition coil electrical connector.
2. Remove mounting bolts and ignition coil.

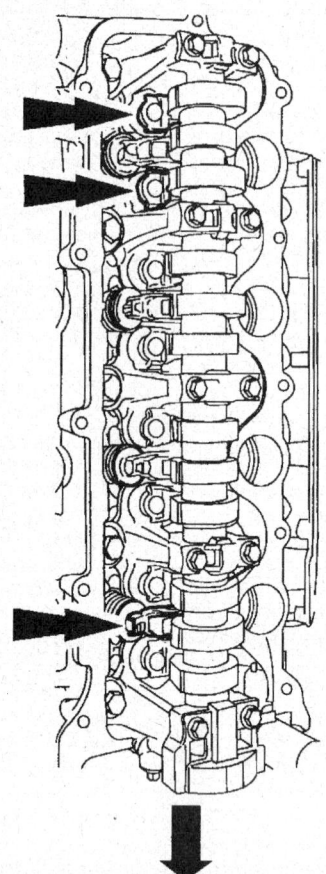

ARM0400000000539

Fig. 15 Roller follower removal. Lefthand

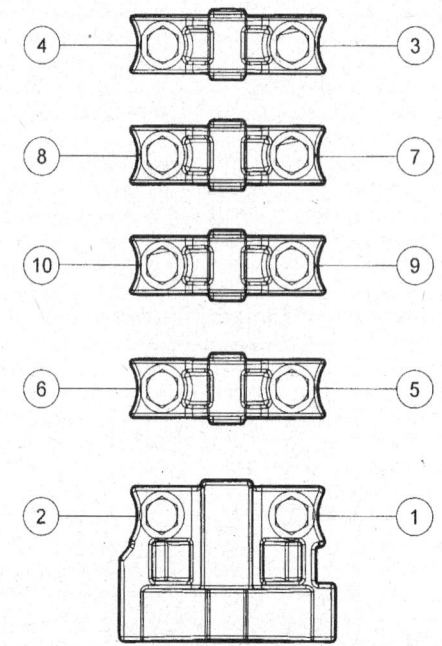

ARM0400000000540

Fig. 16 Camshaft bearing cap removal sequence

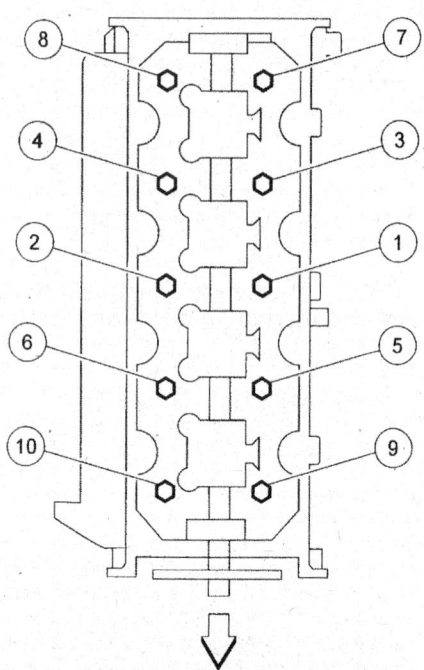

ARM0400000000541

Fig. 17 Cylinder head tightening sequence

3. Disconnect two wiring harness retainers from valve cover stud bolts.
4. Disconnect Variable Camshaft Timing (VCT) solenoid electrical connector, **Fig. 22.**
5. Disconnect Positive Crankcase Ventilation (PCV) tube.
6. Disconnect for wiring harness retainers from valve cover stud bolts.
7. Loosen 14 mounting bolts, then remove valve cover and gasket. **Mounting bolts are part of valve cover and should not be removed.**
8. Clean cylinder head valve cover mating surfaces with suitable silicone gasket remover.
9. Clean valve cover gasket groove with soap and water, or suitable solvent.
10. Reverse procedure to install, noting the following:
    a. **Valve cover must be secured within four minutes of sealant application.**
    b. Apply .32 inch bead of suitable silicone gasket and sealant to where engine front cover meets cylinder head, **Fig. 23.**
    c. Tighten mounting bolts in sequence, **Fig. 24.**
    d. Apply light film of suitable silicone brake caliper great and dielectric

compound to inside of coil boots.

CAMSHAFT LOBE LIFT SPECIFICATIONS

Engine	Intake, Inch	Exhaust, Inch
4.6L SOHC (VIN Z)	.217	.217

VALVE ADJUSTMENT

These engine are equipped with hydraulic valve lash adjusters. No valve adjustment is required.

HYDRAULIC LASH ADJUSTER
REPLACE

1. Remove camshafts as outlined under "Camshaft, Replace."
2. Rotate crankshaft until piston for valve being service is at top of stroke with intake and exhaust valves closed.
3. Compress spring and remove camshaft roller follower using valve spring compressor tool No. 303-1029, or equivalent.
4. Mark hydraulic lash adjusters for installation in original positions,
5. Remove hydraulic lash adjusters.
6. Reverse procedure to install.

CRANKSHAFT DAMPER
REPLACE

1. Raise and support vehicle.
2. Disconnect crankcase vent tube from air cleaner outlet pipe.

3. Loosen two clamps and remove air cleaner outlet pipe.
4. Rotate accessory drive belt tensioner clockwise with suitable belt tensioner release tool and remove belt.
5. Remove crankshaft pulley mounting bolt and washer.
6. Remove crankshaft pulley using suitable three-jaw puller tool.
7. Reverse procedure to install, noting the following:
    a. **Pulley must be secured within four minutes of sealant application.**
    b. Apply suitable silicone gasket and sealant to crankshaft pulley Woodruff key slot,
    c. Install crankshaft pulley using crankshaft vibration damper installer tool No. T74P-6316-B, or equivalent.
    d. **Torque** next crankshaft pulley bolt to 66 ft. lbs.
    e. Loosen crankshaft pulley bolt 360°.
    f. **Torque** pulley bolt to 37 ft. lbs.
    g. Tighten bolt an additional 90°.

FRONT COVER
REPLACE

1. Raise and support vehicle.
2. Drain engine oil into suitable container.
3. Drain engine coolant into suitable container.
4. Disconnect, the position upper and lower degas bottle hoses aside.
5. Remove two mounting bolts and degas bottle.
6. Rotate accessory drive belt tensioner

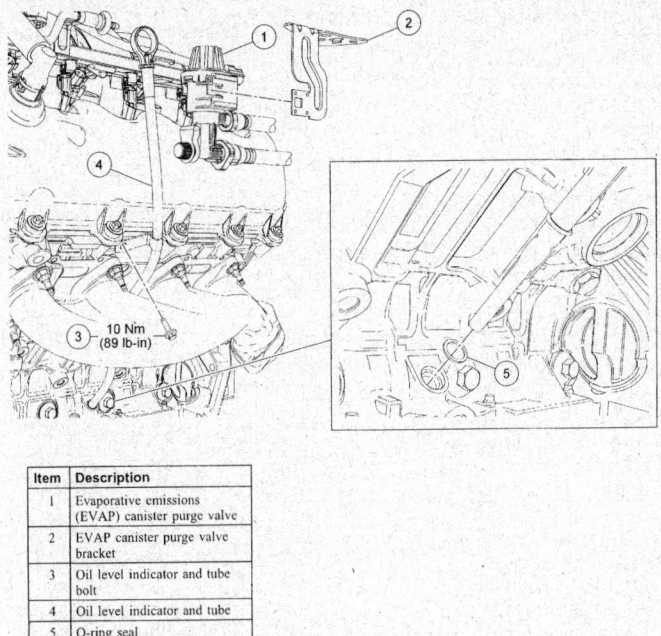

Item	Description
1	Evaporative emissions (EVAP) canister purge valve
2	EVAP canister purge valve bracket
3	Oil level indicator and tube bolt
4	Oil level indicator and tube
5	O-ring seal

ARM0400000000501

Fig. 18 Oil level indicator tube replacement

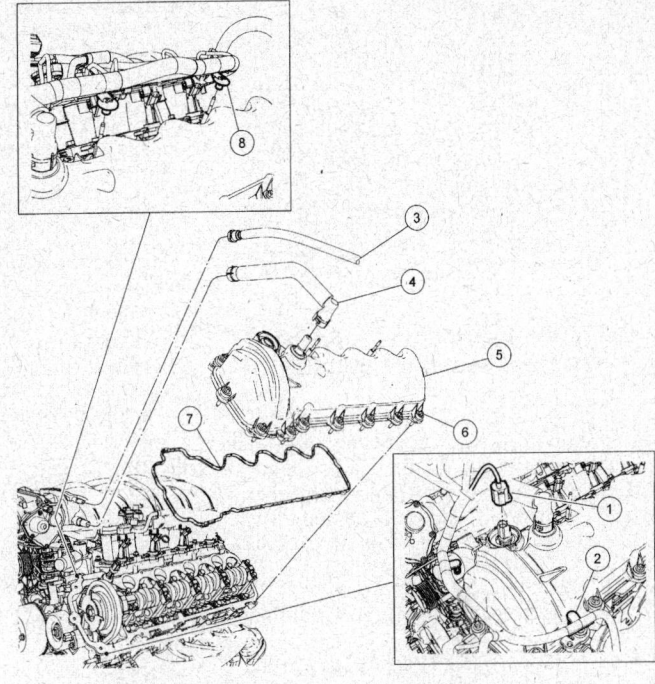

Item	Description		Item	Description
1	LH variable camshaft timing (VCT) solenoid electrical connector		6	LH valve cover bolts (15 required)
2	Engine wiring harness retainers (2 required)		7	LH valve cover gasket
3	Evaporative emissions (EVAP) tube		8	Engine wiring harness retainers (2 required)
4	Positive crankcase ventilation (PCV) tube			
5	LH valve cover			

ARM0400000000500

Fig. 19 Valve cover replacement. Lefthand

clockwise with suitable belt tensioner release tool and remove belt.

7. Remove mounting bolt and righthand belt idler pulley.
8. Remove valve covers as outlined under "Valve Cover, Replace."
9. Disconnect two coolant hoses from crossover, **Fig. 25.**
10. Remove mounting nut and position righthand radio ignition interference capacitor aside.
11. Disconnect righthand Camshaft Position (CMP) sensor electrical connector.
12. Remove mounting nut and position lefthand radio ignition interference capacitor aside.
13. Remove J bracket from engine front cover stud bolt.
14. Disconnect lefthand CMP sensor electrical connector.
15. Remover four mounting bolts and water pump pulley.
16. Remove two mounting nuts and power steering pulley shield.
17. Remove wiring harness, retainer, nut and tube clip from power steering stud bolt.
18. Remove three stud bolts and support power steering pump aside.
19. Disconnect Crankshaft Position (CKP) sensor connector.
20. Remove crankshaft pulley mounting bolt and washer.
21. Remove crankshaft pulley using suitable three-jaw puller tool.
22. Remove crankshaft seal using crankshaft front seal remover tool No. T74P-66700-A, or equivalent.
23. Remove four front oil pan mounting bolts.
24. Record front cover mounting bolt locations for installation alignment.
25. Remove mounting bolts, studs and front cover.
26. Clean mating surfaces with suitable silicone gasket remover.
27. Reverse procedure to install, noting the following:
    a. **Front cover must be secured within four minutes of sealant application.**
    b. Apply silicone gasket and sealant along cylinder head-to-cylinder block and oil pan-to-cylinder block surfaces, **Fig. 26.**
    c. Install new front cover gasket and tighten mounting bolts and studs in sequence to 15 ft. lbs., **Fig. 27.**
    d. Tighten bolts and studs an additional 60° in sequence.

FRONT COVER SEAL
REPLACE

1. Remove crankshaft pulley as outlined under "Crankshaft Damper, Replace."
2. Remove crankshaft seal using crankshaft front seal remover tool No. T74P-66700-A, or equivalent.
3. Reverse procedure to install, noting the following:
    a. Lubricate engine front cover and crankshaft front seal inner lip with suitable, clean engine oil.

b. Install seal using crankshaft front seal installer tool No. 303-635, front cover seal installer tool No. T88T-6701-A and crankshaft vibration damper installer tool No. T74P-6316-B, or equivalents.

TIMING CHAIN
REPLACE

These engines have an interference fit design. If engine has jumped time cylinder heads must be removed to repair damage to valves and/or pistons.

At no time, when the timing chains are removed and the cylinder heads are installed, may the crankshaft and/or camshaft be rotated unless all rocker arms have been removed. Rotation may result in valve and/or piston damage.

Before loosening or tightening camshaft sprocket nuts and bolts, ensure camshaft positioning and locking devices are in place.

Removal

1. Remove engine front cover as outlined under "Front Cover, Replace."
2. Remove crankshaft sensor ring.
3. Position crankshaft keyway at 12

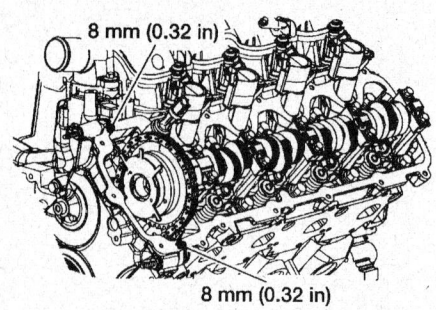

8 mm (0.32 in)

8 mm (0.32 in)

ARM0400000000502

Fig. 20 Valve cover silicone gasket & sealant. Lefthand

o'clock position, **Fig. 12,** noting the following:

a. If camshaft lobes are not exactly positioned, **Fig. 13,** crankshaft will require one full additional rotation to 12 o'clock position.

b. Cylinder No. 1 camshaft exhaust lobe must be coming up on exhaust stroke.

c. Ensure positioning of two intake lobes and exhaust lobe on cylinder No. 1.

4. Remove only three roller followers righthand cylinder head using valve spring compressor tool No. 303-1039, or equivalent, **Fig. 14. Do not allow valve keepers to fall off valve or valve may drop into cylinder.**

5. Remove only three roller followers lefthand cylinder head using valve spring compressor tool No. 303-1039, or equivalent, **Fig. 15. Do not allow valve keepers to fall off valve or valve may drop into cylinder.**

6. Rotate crankshaft clockwise and position crankshaft keyway at 6 o'clock position. **Do not move crankshaft past 6 o'clock position.**

7. Remove mounting bolts, then the left and righthand timing chain tensioners and tensioner arms.

8. Remove righthand timing chain from camshaft and crankshaft sprockets.

9. Remove lefthand timing chain from the camshaft and crankshaft sprockets.

10. Remove two mounting bolts and both timing chain guides.

11. Remove mounting bolts, then the left and righthand camshaft phaser sprocket using camshaft phase locking tool No. 303-1046, or equivalent. **Only use hand tools.**

12. Mark camshaft bearing caps for installation original locations.

13. Remove camshaft bearing caps bolts in sequence, **Fig. 16.**

14. **Remove front thrust camshaft bearing cap straight upward from bearing towers.** Remove remaining bearing caps.

15. Mark components for installation into original locations.

16. Remove all remaining roller followers.

INSTALLATION

1. Install camshafts as outlined under "Camshaft, Replace."

2. Install camshaft phaser sprockets and new mounting bolts finger tight.

3. **Torque** camshaft phaser sprocket bolts using camshaft phase locking tool No. 303-1046, or equivalent. to 30 ft. lbs. **Only use hand tools.**

4. Tighten sprocket bolts an additional 90°.

5. Install crankshaft sprocket, making sure the flange faces forward.

6. Rotate crankshaft to position crankshaft sprocket timing mark in 6 o'clock position, **Fig. 28.**

7. Compress tensioner plunger, using suitable vise.

8. Install suitable retaining clip to hold plunger in place.

9. If copper links are not visible, mark one 1 link on one end and one link on other end and use as timing marks.

10. Install timing chain guides and four mounting bolts.

11. Position lower end of lefthand (inner) timing chain on crankshaft sprocket, aligning timing mark on outer flange of crankshaft sprocket with single copper (marked) link on chain, **Fig. 29.**

12. Ensure upper half of timing chain is below tensioner arm dowel.

13. Position lefthand timing chain on camshaft sprocket. Ensure camshaft sprocket timing mark is aligned with copper (marked) chain link, **Fig. 30.**

14. Position lefthand timing chain tensioner arm on dowel pin, then install lefthand timing chain tensioner and mounting bolts. Lefthand timing chain tensioner arm has bump near dowel hole for identification.

15. Remove retaining clip from lefthand timing chain tensioner.

16. Position lower end of righthand (outer) timing chain on crankshaft sprocket, aligning timing mark on sprocket with single copper (marked) chain link, **Fig. 31.**

17. Lower half of timing chain must be positioned above tensioner arm dowel.

18. Position righthand timing chain on camshaft sprocket. Ensure camshaft sprocket timing mark is aligned with copper (marked) chain link, **Fig. 32.**

19. Position righthand timing chain tensioner arm on dowel pin, then install righthand timing chain tensioner and mounting bolts.

20. Remove retaining clip from righthand timing chain tensioner.

21. Righthand and lefthand camshaft phaser sprockets are similar. Righthand camshaft phaser sprocket has single timing mark to identify, while L timing mark identifies lefthand camshaft phaser sprocket. Ensure timing marks on sprockets align, **Fig. 33.**

22. Install crankshaft sensor ring.

23. Lubricate roller followers with suitable, clean engine oil.

24. Rotate engine to position camshaft lobes at base circle and install all camshaft roller followers.

25. Install engine front cover as outlined under "Front Cover, Replace."

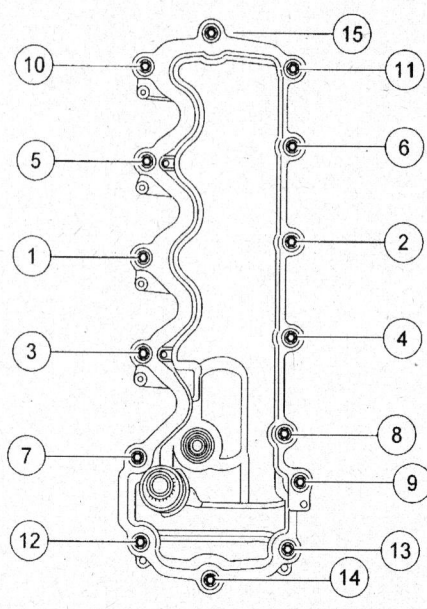

ARM0400000000503

Fig. 21 Valve cover tightening sequence. Lefthand

CAMSHAFT
REPLACE

These engines have an interference fit design. If engine has jumped time cylinder heads must be removed to repair damage to valves and/or pistons.

At no time, when the timing chains are removed and the cylinder heads are installed, may the crankshaft and/or camshaft be rotated unless all rocker arms have been removed. Rotation may result in valve and/or piston damage.

Before loosening or tightening camshaft sprocket nuts and bolts, ensure camshaft positioning and locking devices are in place.

If removing both camshafts, righthand camshaft must be removed first.

Righthand

1. Position crankshaft damper spoke at 12 o'clock position and timing mark indentation at 1 o'clock position, **Fig. 34.**

2. Remove righthand valve cover as outlined under "Valve Cover, replace."

3. Loosen and back off righthand camshaft phaser bolt one full turn.

4. Disconnect righthand Camshaft Position (CMP) sensor electrical connector.

5. Remove mounting bolt and righthand CMP sensor.

6. If camshaft lobes are not exactly positioned, **Fig. 13,** crankshaft will require one full additional rotation to 12 o'clock position.

7. Cylinder No. 1 camshaft exhaust lobe must be coming up on exhaust stroke.

8. Ensure positioning of two intake lobes and exhaust lobe on cylinder No. 1.

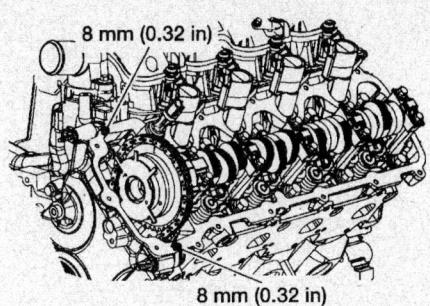

8 mm (0.32 in)

8 mm (0.32 in)

ARM0400000000505

Fig. 23 Valve cover silicone gasket & sealant. Righthand

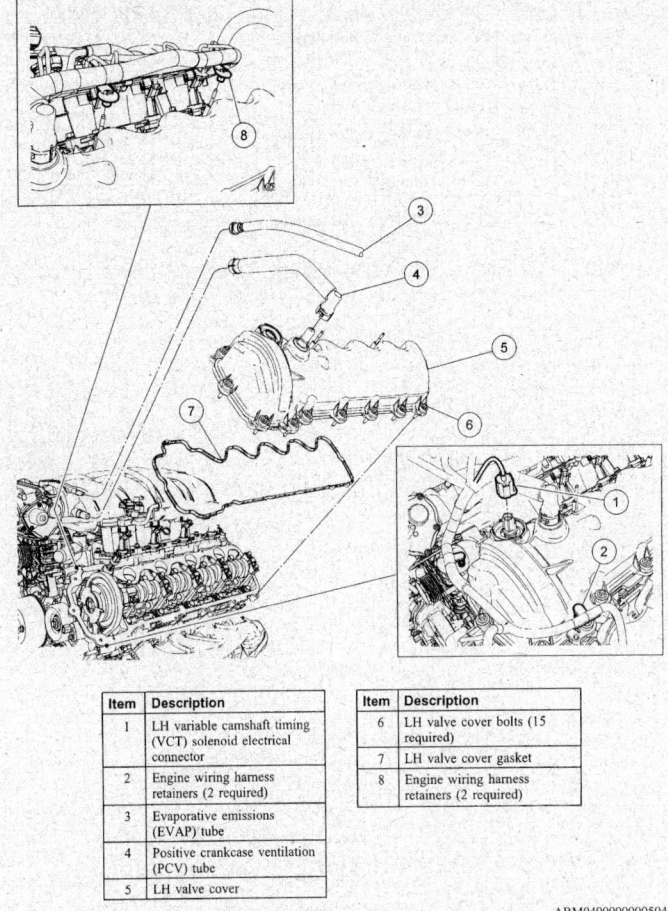

Item	Description
1	LH variable camshaft timing (VCT) solenoid electrical connector
2	Engine wiring harness retainers (2 required)
3	Evaporative emissions (EVAP) tube
4	Positive crankcase ventilation (PCV) tube
5	LH valve cover

Item	Description
6	LH valve cover bolts (15 required)
7	LH valve cover gasket
8	Engine wiring harness retainers (2 required)

ARM0400000000504

Fig. 22 Valve cover replacement. Righthand

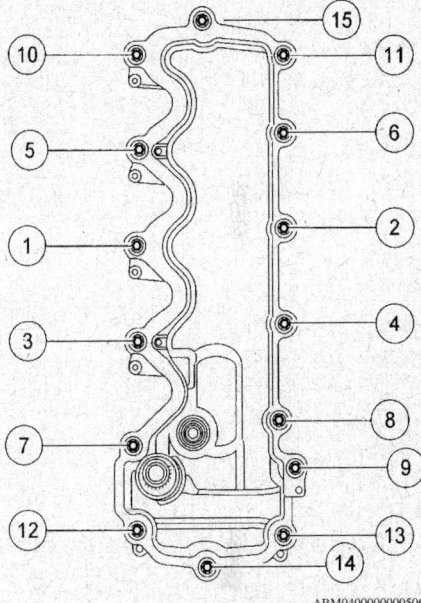

ARM0400000000506

Fig. 24 Valve cover tightening sequence. Righthand

9. Remove only three roller followers righthand cylinder head using valve spring compressor tool No. 303-1039, or equivalent, **Fig. 14. Do not allow valve keepers to fall off valve or valve may drop into cylinder.**
10. Rotate crankshaft clockwise, as viewed from front, positioning crankshaft damper spoke at 6 o'clock position and timing mark indentation at 7 o'clock position, **Fig. 35. Crankshaft cannot be moved past 6 o'clock position once set.**
11. Install timing chain wedge tool No. 303-636 and handle tool No. 303-637, or equivalents, square to timing chain and engine block, **Fig. 36.**
12. **If timing chain wedge is removed or out of placement, engine front cover must be removed and engine must be timed.**
13. Mark timing chain and camshaft phaser sprocket for installation alignment.
14. Mark camshaft bearing caps for installation original locations.
15. Remove camshaft bearing caps bolts in sequence, **Fig. 16.**
16. **Remove front thrust camshaft bearing cap straight upward from bearing towers.** Remove remaining bearing caps.
17. Remove mounting bolt and withdraw camshaft from phaser sprocket leaving sprocket in place.
18. Reverse procedure to install, noting the following:
    a. Lubricate camshaft and camshaft journals with suitable, clean engine oil.
    b. Ensure camshaft phaser sprocket and timing chain scribe marks are still in alignment.
    c. **Do not allow roller followers to move out of position when installing camshaft.**
    d. Install camshaft bearing caps in original locations.
    e. Lubricate camshaft bearing caps with suitable, clean engine oil.
    f. Position front camshaft bearing cap.
    g. Position remaining camshaft bearing caps.
    h. Install mounting bolts loosely.
    i. Tighten mounting bolts in sequence, **Fig. 37.**
    j. Remove special tools.

Lefthand

1. Position crankshaft damper spoke at 12 o'clock position and timing mark indentation at 1 o'clock position, **Fig. 34.**
2. Remove lefthand valve cover as outlined under "Valve Cover, replace."

3. Loosen and back off lefthand camshaft phaser bolt one full turn.
4. Disconnect lefthand Camshaft Position (CMP) sensor electrical connector.
5. Remove mounting bolt and lefthand CMP sensor.
6. If camshaft lobes are not exactly positioned, **Fig. 38,** crankshaft keyway will require one full additional rotation to 12 o'clock position.
7. Cylinder No. 5 cylinder must be coming up on exhaust stroke.
8. Ensure positioning of two intake lobes and exhaust lobe on cylinder No. .5.
9. Remove only three roller followers lefthand cylinder head using valve spring compressor tool No. 303-1039, or equivalent, **Fig. 15. Do not allow valve keepers to fall off valve or valve may drop into cylinder.**
10. Rotate crankshaft clockwise, as viewed from front, positioning crankshaft damper spoke at 6 o'clock position and timing mark indentation at 7

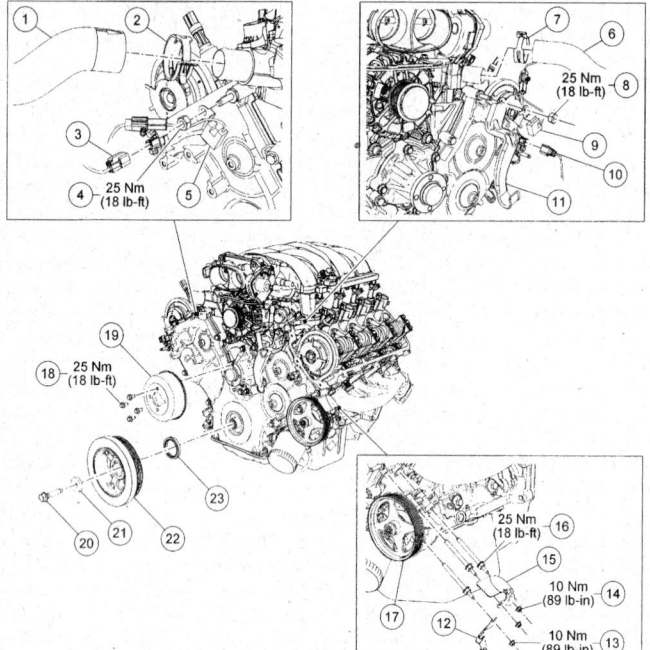

Item	Description
13	Power steering tube retaining clip nut
14	Power steering pulley shield nut (2 required)
15	Power steering pulley shield
16	Power steering pump stud bolt (3 required)
17	Power steering pump

Item	Description
18	Coolant pump pulley bolts (4 required)
19	Coolant pump pulley
20	Crankshaft pulley bolt
21	Crankshaft pulley bolt washer
22	Crankshaft pulley
23	Crankshaft front oil seal

ARM0400000000511

Fig. 25   Front cover replacement (Part 2 of 3)

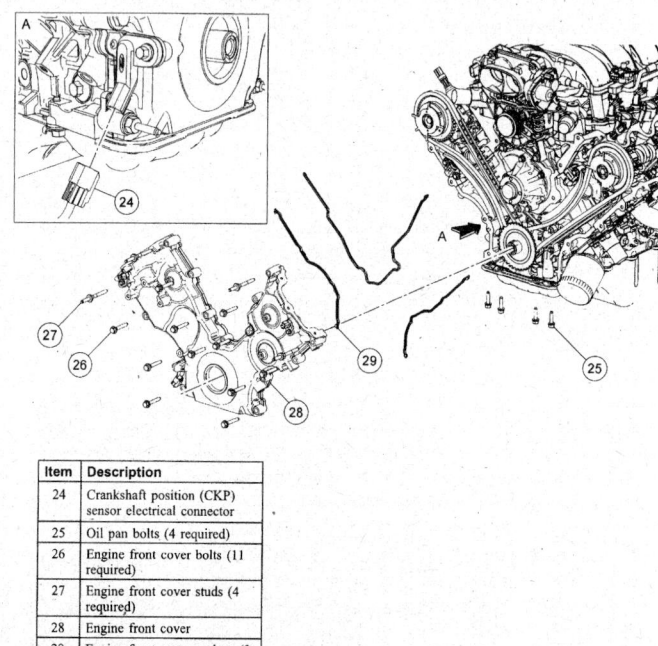

Item	Description
1	Coolant hose
2	Hose clamp
3	RH camshaft position (CMP) sensor electrical connector
4	RH radio ignition interference capacitor nut
5	RH radio ignition interference capacitor
6	Coolant hose

Item	Description
7	Hose clamp
8	LH radio ignition interference capacitor nut
9	LH radio ignition interference capacitor
10	LH CMP sensor electrical connector
11	J-bracket
12	Power steering tube retaining clip

ARM0400000000510

Fig. 25   Front cover replacement (Part 1 of 3)

Item	Description
24	Crankshaft position (CKP) sensor electrical connector
25	Oil pan bolts (4 required)
26	Engine front cover bolts (11 required)
27	Engine front cover studs (4 required)
28	Engine front cover
29	Engine front cover gaskets (3 required)

ARM0400000000512

Fig. 25   Front cover replacement (Part 3 of 3)

o'clock position, **Fig. 35. Crankshaft cannot be moved past 6 o'clock position once set.**

11. Install timing chain wedge tool No. 303-636 and handle tool No. 303-637, or equivalents, square to timing chain and engine block, **Fig. 39**.
12. **If timing chain wedge is removed or out of placement, engine front cover must be removed and engine must be timed.**
13. Mark timing chain and camshaft phaser sprocket for installation alignment.
14. Mark camshaft bearing caps for installation original locations.
15. Remove camshaft bearing caps bolts in sequence, **Fig. 16**.
16. **Remove front thrust camshaft bearing cap straight upward from bearing towers.** Remove remaining bearing caps.
17. Remove mounting bolt and withdraw camshaft from phaser sprocket leaving sprocket in place.
18. Reverse procedure to install, noting the following:
    a. Lubricate camshaft and camshaft journals with suitable, clean engine oil.
    b. Ensure camshaft phaser sprocket

and timing chain scribe marks are still in alignment.
    c. **Do not allow roller followers to move out of position when installing camshaft.**
    d. Install camshaft bearing caps in original locations.
    e. Lubricate camshaft bearing caps with suitable, clean engine oil.
    f. Position front camshaft bearing cap.
    g. Position remaining camshaft bearing caps.
    h. Install mounting bolts loosely.
    i. Tighten mounting bolts in sequence, **Fig. 37**.
    j. Remove special tools.

PISTON & ROD ASSEMBLY

The connecting rod must be installed into the connecting rod with identification markings toward the front, **Fig. 40**.
1. Lubricate piston and ring with suitable, clean engine oil.

2. Lubricate rod bearings with suitable, clean engine oil.
3. Install piston and connecting rod with upper connecting rod bearing in place using suitable piston ring compressor tool and connecting rod installer tools No. T93P-6136-A, or equivalent.
4. Once connecting rod is seated on crankshaft journal, remove special tools.
5. **The rod cap must be in same orientation as marked during disassembly.**
6. Position lower bearing and connecting rod, then install new bolts loosely.
7. **Torque** connecting rod bolts in sequence to 32 ft. lbs., **Fig. 41**.
8. Tighten bolts and additional 105° in sequence.

MAIN & ROD BEARINGS

1. Install crankshaft main bearings.
2. Install crankshaft upper main bearings into cylinder block.

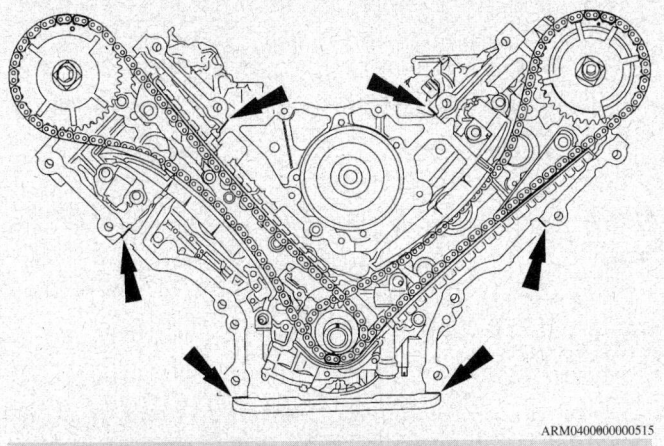

Fig. 26 Front cover sealing

ARM0400000000515

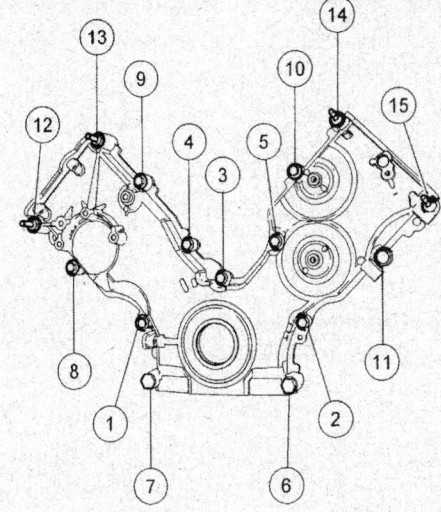

Item	Description	Item	Description
1	Bolt, Hex Flange Head Pilot, M8 x 1.25 x 53	10	Bolt, Hex Flange Head Pilot, M8 x 1.25 x 53
2	Bolt, Hex Flange Head Pilot, M8 x 1.25 x 53	11	Bolt, Hex Flange Head Pilot, M8 x 1.25 x 53
3	Bolt, Hex Flange Head Pilot, M8 x 1.25 x 53	12	Stud, Hex Shoulder Pilot, M8 x 1.25 x 1.25 x 91.1
4	Bolt, Hex Flange Head Pilot, M8 x 1.25 x 53	13	Stud, Hex Shoulder Pilot, M8 x 1.25 x 1.25 x 91.1
5	Bolt, Hex Flange Head Pilot, M8 x 1.25 x 53	14	Stud, Hex Shoulder Pilot, M8 x 1.25 x 1.25 x 91.1
6	Bolt, Hex Flange Head Pilot, M8 x 1.25 x 53	15	Stud, Hex Shoulder Pilot, M8 x 1.25 x 1.25 x 91.1
7	Bolt, Hex Flange Head Pilot, M8 x 1.25 x 53		
8	Bolt, Hex Flange Head Pilot, M8 x 1.25 x 53		
9	Bolt, Hex Flange Head Pilot, M8 x 1.25 x 53		

ARM0400000000516

Fig. 27 Front cover tightening sequence

3. Install crankshaft lower main bearings into bearing caps.
4. Ensure all oil passages are aligned.
5. Lubricate all main bearings with suitable, clean engine oil.
6. Lubricate crankshaft bearing journals with suitable, clean engine oil
7. Install crankshaft onto upper crankshaft main bearings.
8. **Oil groove on thrust washer must face toward rear of engine (against crankshaft thrust surface).**
9. Push crankshaft rearward and install rear crankshaft upper thrust washer at back of main boss No. 5.
10. Install rear (No. 5) main bearing cap.
11. Install crankshaft lower main bearings into main bearing caps and lubricate them with suitable, clean engine oil.
12. Locate main bearing cap on cylinder block and, keeping cap as square as possible, alternately draw cap down evenly using cap fasteners.
13. Push crankshaft forward to seat crankshaft thrust washer. Hold crankshaft in forward position.
14. Install vertical main bearing cap nuts and bolts, then tighten in sequence, **Fig. 42.**
15. **Torque** 1–20 in sequence to 89 inch lbs.
16. **Torque** 1–10 in sequence to 18 ft. lbs.
17. **Torque** 11–20 in sequence to 30 ft. lbs.
18. Tighten 1–20 an additional 90° in sequence.
19. Install cross-mounted main bearing cap bolts and tighten in sequence, **Fig. 43.**
20. **Torque** in sequence to 30 ft. lbs.
21. Tighten an additional 90° in sequence.
22. Inspect crankshaft end play.
23. Ensure crankshaft torque-to-turn does not exceed 53 inch lbs.

CRANKSHAFT SEAL

REPLACE

1. Remove crankshaft pulley as outlined under "Crankshaft Damper, Replace,"
2. Remove crankshaft seal using crankshaft front seal remover tool No. T74P-66700-A, or equivalent, **Fig. 44.**

3. Reverse procedure to install, noting the following:
   a. Lubricate engine front cover and crankshaft front seal inner lip with suitable, clean engine oil.
   b. Install seal using crankshaft front seal installer tool No. 303-635, front cover seal installer tool No. T88T-6701-A and crankshaft vibration damper installer tool No. T74P-6316-B, or equivalents.

CRANKSHAFT REAR OIL SEAL

REPLACE

1. Remove automatic transmission or manual transmission and clutch as outlined in **MOTOR's "Domestic Transmission Manual, In-Vehicle Service."**
2. Remove six mounting bolts and flywheel/flexplate, **Fig. 45.**
3. Remove engine-to-transmission spacer plate.
4. Remove crankshaft oil slinger using crankshaft rear oil seal slinger remover

tool No. T95P-6701-AH, or equivalent, and suitable impact slide hammer.
5. Remove crankshaft rear seal using crankshaft rear seal remover tool No. T95P-6701-EH, or equivalent, and suitable impact slide hammer.
6. Remove two oil pan-to-crankshaft rear seal retainer plate bolts.
7. Remove six mounting bolts and crankshaft rear seal retainer plate.
8. Clean sealing surfaces with suitable silicone gasket remover.
9. Reverse procedure to install, noting the following:
   a. **Rear crankshaft seal retainer plate must be secured within four minutes of sealant application.**
   b. Apply .16 inch bead of silicone gasket and sealant around crankshaft rear seal retainer plate sealing surface.
   c. Tighten mounting bolts in sequence, **Fig. 46.**
   d. Tighten flywheel/flexplate mounting bolts in sequence, **Fig. 47.**
   e. **Torque** retainer plate-to-oil pan bolts to 15 ft. lbs., then tighten an

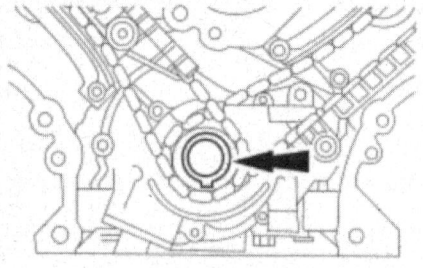

Fig. 28 Crankshaft keyway 6 o'clock position

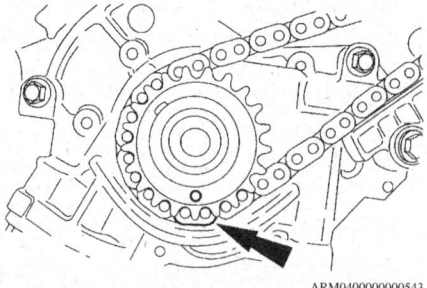

Fig. 29 Lefthand timing chain & crankshaft sprocket alignment

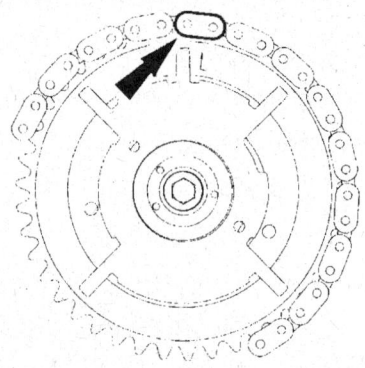

Fig. 30 Lefthand timing chain & camshaft sprocket alignment

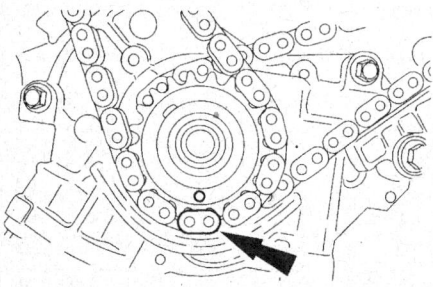

Fig. 31 Righthand timing chain & crankshaft sprocket alignment

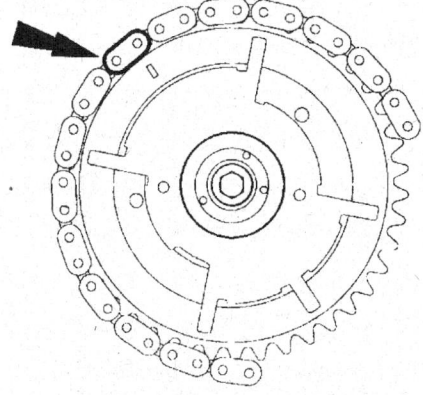

Fig. 32 Righthand timing chain & camshaft sprocket alignment

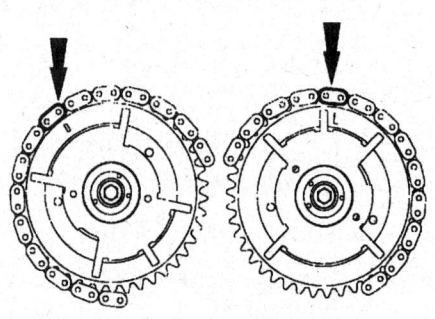

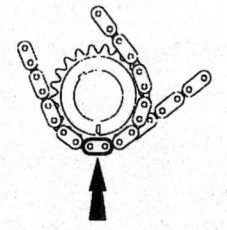

Fig. 33 Timing chain alignment

additional 60°.
   f. Lubricate crankshaft rear seal with suitable, clean engine oil, then install using crankshaft rear seal installer tools Nos. T95P-6701-BH and T95P-6701-DH, or equivalents.
   g. Install crankshaft real oil slinger using crankshaft rear oil slinger tool No. T95P-6501-BH, crankshaft rear seal installer tools Nos. T95P-6701-BH and T95P-6701-DH, or equivalents.

OIL PAN

REPLACE

1. Raise and support vehicle.
2. Drain engine oil into suitable container.
3. Loosen clamp and disconnect air cleaner outlet pipe.
4. Disconnect Mass Air Flow (MAF) sensor electrical connector.
5. Remove mounting bolt and air cleaner. Ensure two rubber grommets are retained to feet.
6. Disconnect Throttle Position (TP) sensor and electronic throttle control electrical connectors, **Fig. 1.**
7. Remove mounting bolts, nuts and throttle body.
8. Remove six pin-type retainers and radiator sight shield, **Fig. 2.**
9. Remove two outer bracket mounting bolts and two lower mounting nuts, then disconnect alternator electrical connector and pin-type retainer.
10. Position cover aside, then remove B+ terminal nut and alternator.
11. Support engine using suitable engine

lifting brackets and three-bar engine support tools.
12. Remove left and righthand engine support insulator nuts.
13. Raise engine approximately 1.57 inches.
14. Position suitable adjustable jack stand under subframe.
15. Mark position of four subframe mounting nuts and four mounting bolts for installation alignment.
16. Remove subframe mounting nuts and bolts.
17. Lower subframe approximately 1.96 inches.
18. Disconnect oil temperature sensor electrical connector and two pin-type retainers.
19. Remove six mounting bolts, oil pan and gasket. **Oil pan gasket is reusable if it is not damaged.**
20. Reverse procedure to install, noting the following:
   a. Clean oil pan mating surface with suitable silicone gasket remover and metal surface prep.
   b. **Oil pan must be secured within four minutes of sealant application.**
   c. Apply silicone gasket and sealant at crankshaft rear seal retainer plate-to-cylinder block sealing surface, **Fig. 48.**
   d. Apply silicone gasket and sealant at engine front cover-to-cylinder

block sealing surface, **Fig. 48.**
   e. Install gasket and the oil pan, then loosely install 16 mounting bolts.
   f. **Torque** oil pan mounting bolts in sequence to 18 inch lbs., **Fig. 49.**
   g. **Torque** pan mounting bolts in sequence to 15 ft. lbs.
   h. Tighten mounting bolts an additional 60° in sequence.

OIL PUMP

REPLACE

1. Remove oil pan as outlined under "Oil Pane, Replace."
2. Remove timing chain as outlined under "Timing Chain, Replace."
3. Remove mounting bolts, then the oil pump screen and pickup tube.
4. Remove three mounting bolts and oil pump.
5. Reverse procedure to install.

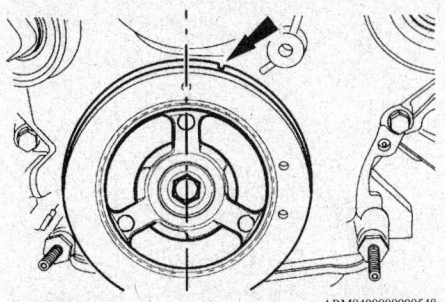

Fig. 34 Crankshaft damper position 12 o'clock position

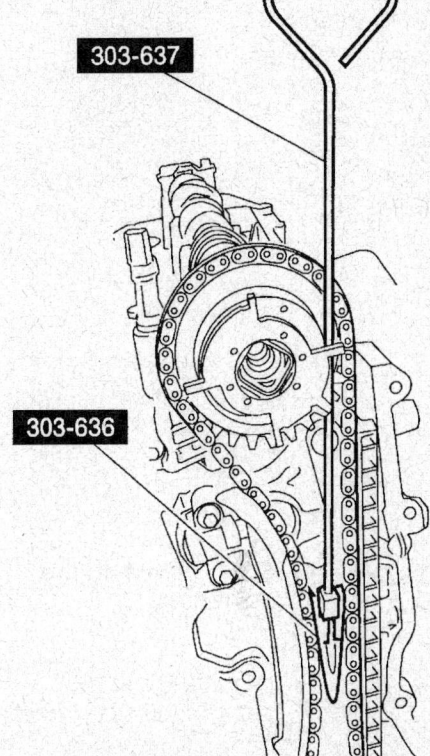

Fig. 35 Crankshaft damper position 6 o'clock position

BELT TENSION DATA

These models are equipped with an automatic drive belt tensioner. No adjustment or maintenance is required.

SERPENTINE DRIVE BELT

Always use square drive tool in hole in tensioner to move tensioner. Never pry on tensioner pulley. When releasing drive belt tensioner, never allow tensioner to snap back. Damage to tensioner or personal injury could result.

Do not allow engine coolant to remain on serpentine belt or pulleys. If required, remove belt and flush with clean water.

Routing

Refer to **Fig. 50** for serpentine drive belt routing.

Replacement

Rotate the accessory drive belt tensioner clockwise with suitable belt tensioner release tool and remove the belt.

COOLING SYSTEM BLEED

1. Fill radiator through degas bottle until the coolant level is between the COOLANT FILL LEVEL marks.
2. Select maximum heater temperature and blower motor speed settings.
3. Position control to discharge air at air conditioning vents in instrument panel.
4. Start engine and allow to idle.
5. While engine is idling, feel for hot air at air conditioning vents.
6. **If air discharge remains cool and engine coolant temperature gauge does not move, engine coolant level is low and must be filled. Stop engine, allow it to cool and fill cooling system.**
7. Allow engine to idle until normal operating temperature is reached. Hot air should discharge from air conditioning vents.
8. Engine coolant temperature gauge

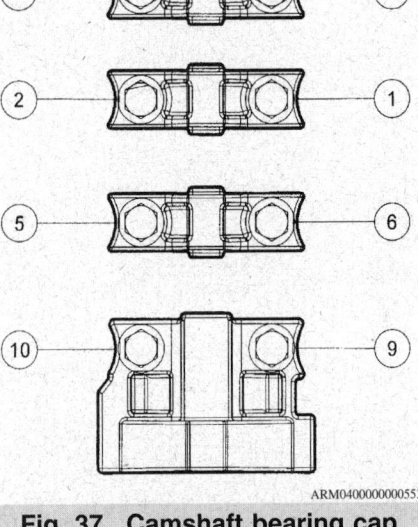

Fig. 37 Camshaft bearing cap tightening sequence

should maintain stabilized reading in middle of NORMAL range.
9. Upper radiator hose should feel hot to touch.
10. Shut engine off and allow it to cool.
11. Check engine for coolant leaks.
12. Check and adjust engine coolant level in degas bottle.

THERMOSTAT
REPLACE

1. Drain engine cooling system into suitable container.
2. Loosen clamp and disconnect air cleaner outlet pipe.
3. Remove two housing mounting bolts, thermostat. and O-ring seal.
4. Reverse procedure to install using new thermostat O-ring seal and lubricate with suitable, clean engine coolant.

WATER PUMP
REPLACE

1. Drain engine cooling system into suit-

Fig. 36 Timing chain wedge installation. Righthand

able container.
2. Loosen clamp and disconnect air cleaner outlet pipe.
3. Loosen four coolant pump pulley bolts, **Fig. 51.**
4. Rotate accessory drive belt tensioner clockwise with suitable belt tensioner release tool and remove belt.
5. Remove four mounting bolts and water pump pulley.
6. Remove four mounting bolts, water pump and O-ring seal.
7. Reverse procedure to install, install new coolant pump O-ring seal and lubricate with suitable, clean engine coolant.

RADIATOR
REPLACE

Refer to "4.0L Engine" for radiator replacement procedure

FUEL PUMP
REPLACE

Refer to "4.0L Engine" for fuel pump replacement procedure

FUEL FILTER
REPLACE

Refer to "4.0L Engine" for fuel pump replacement procedure

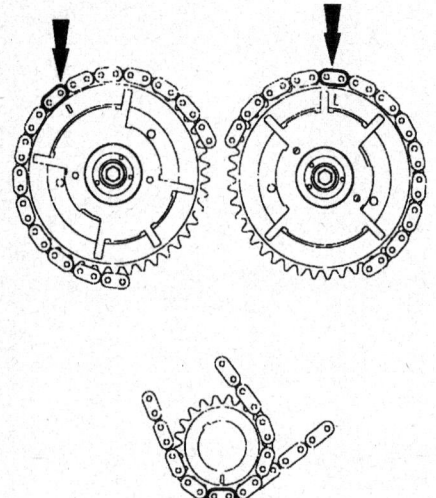

Fig. 38   Lefthand camshaft lobe positioning

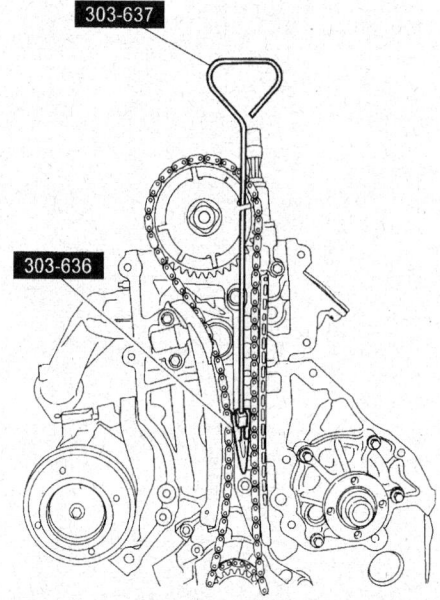

Fig. 39   Timing chain wedge installation. Lefthand

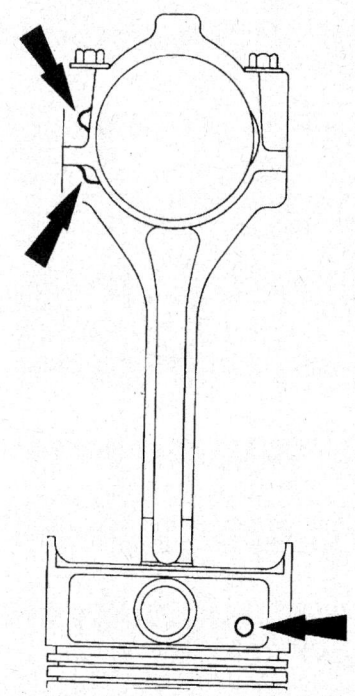

Fig. 40   Piston & connecting rod

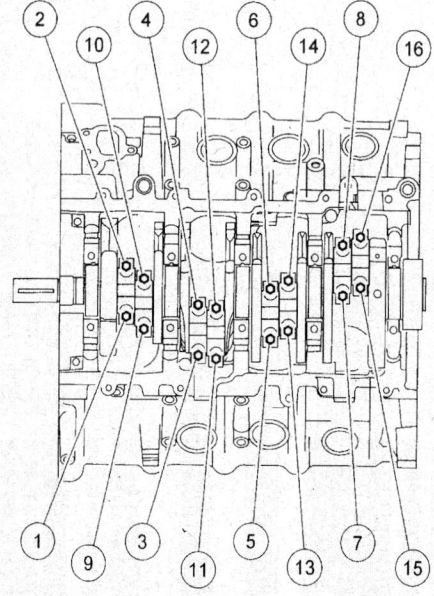

Fig. 41   Connecting rod bearing tightening sequence

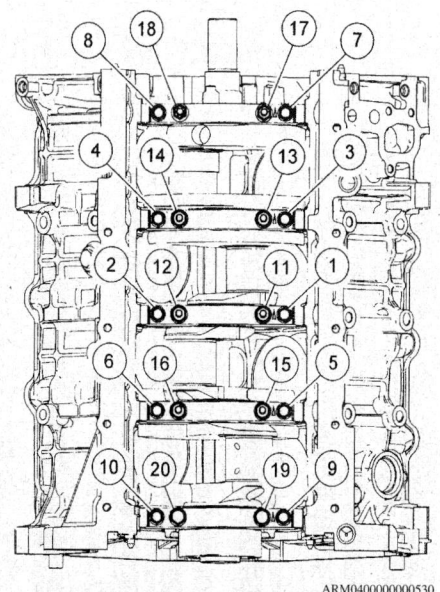

Fig. 42   Vertical main bearing cap tightening sequence

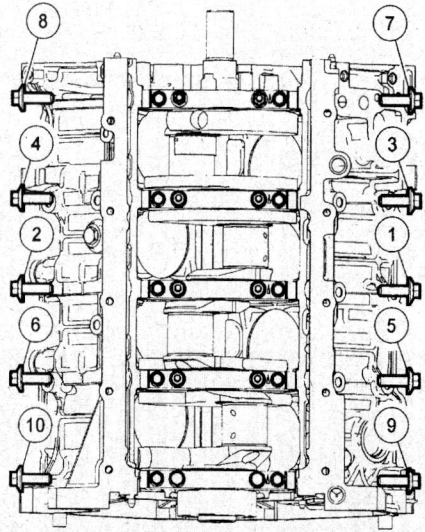

Fig. 43   Cross-mounted main bearing cap tightening sequence

4.6L SOHC (VIN Z) ENGINE

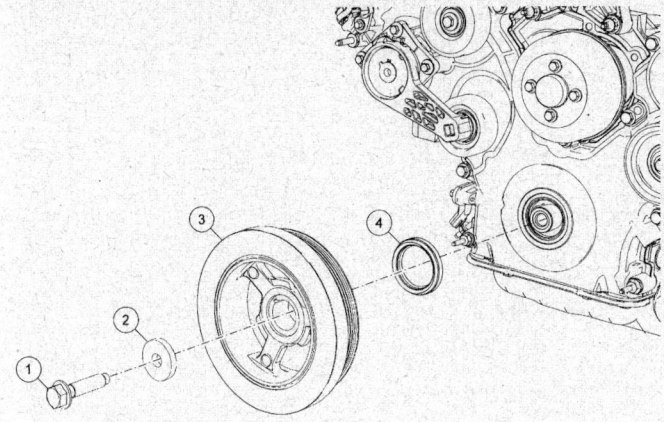

Item	Description
1	Crankshaft pulley bolt
2	Crankshaft pulley bolt washer
3	Crankshaft pulley
4	Crankshaft front oil seal

ARM0400000000513

Fig. 44   Front crankshaft seal replacement

Item	Description		Item	Description
1	Flywheel/flexplate bolts (6 required)		6	Crankshaft rear seal retainer plate
2	Flywheel/flexplate		7	Crankshaft rear seal retainer plate bolts (6 required)
3	Engine-to-transmission spacer plate		8	Oil pan bolts (2 required)
4	Crankshaft oil slinger			
5	Crankshaft rear seal			

ARM0400000000514

Fig. 45   Crankshaft rear oil seal replacement

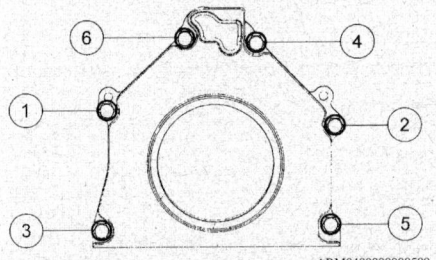

ARM0400000000509

Fig. 46   Rear crankshaft seal retaining plate tightening sequence

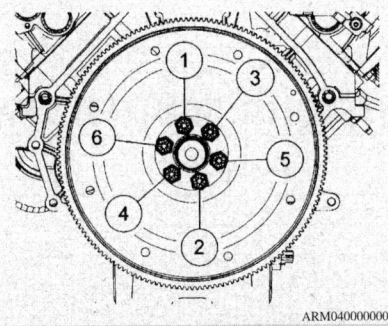

ARM0400000000508

Fig. 47   Flywheel/flexplate tightening sequence

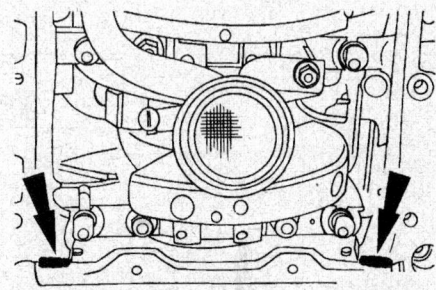

ARM0400000000526

Fig. 48   Oil pan sealing (Part 1 of 2)

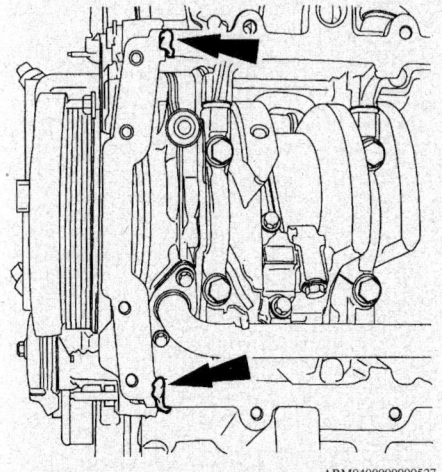

ARM0400000000527

Fig. 48   Oil pan sealing (Part 2 of 2)

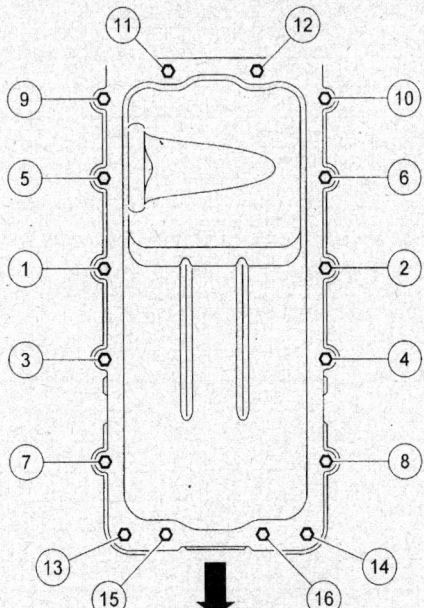

ARM0400000000528

Fig. 49   Oil pan tightening sequence

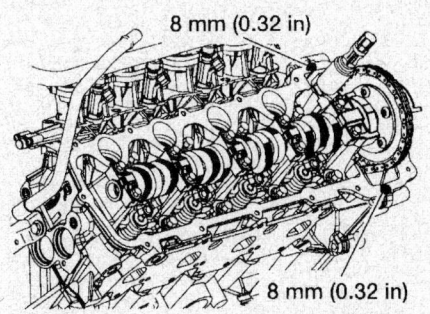

8 mm (0.32 in)

8 mm (0.32 in)

ARM0400000000507

Fig. 50   Serpentine drive belt routing

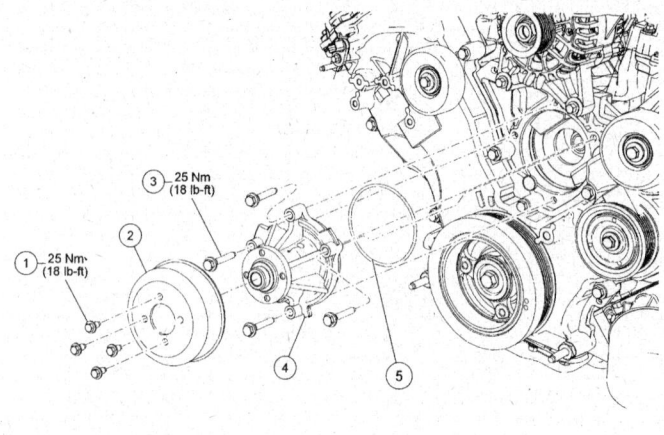

Item	Description
1	Coolant pump pulley bolts (4 required)
2	Coolant pump pulley
3	Coolant pump bolts (4 required)
4	Coolant pump
5	Coolant pump O-ring seal

ARM0400000000561

Fig. 51   Water pump replacement

TIGHTENING SPECIFICATIONS

Year	Component	Torque/Ft. Lbs.
2005	Air Cleaner	71①
	Air Cleaner Outlet Pipe.	27①
	Air Conditioning Compressor	18
	Air Conditioning Condenser	89①
	Alternator, Lower	18
	Alternator, Upper	89①
	Alternator B+ Terminal	71①
	Alternator Support Bracket	89①
	Belt Idler Pulley	18
	Camshaft Bearing Cap	89①
	Camshaft Phaser Sprocket	⑧
	Catalytic Converter-To-Exhaust Manifold	30
	Coolant Crossover	89①
	Cooling Fan Motor & Shroud	80①
	Connecting Rod	⑥
	Crankshaft Pulley	②
	Crankshaft Rear Seal Retainer Plate	89①
	Crankshaft Rear Seal Retainer Plate To Oil Pan	③
	Cylinder Head	⑦
	Degas Bottle	71①
	Engine Support Insulator, Bolt	41
	Engine Support Insulator, Nut	46
	Exhaust Manifold	41
	Flywheel/Flexplate	59
	Front Cover	④
	Fuel Bundle Shield	62①
	Fuel Filter	44①
	Fuel Rail	89①

Continued

TIGHTENING
SPECIFICATIONS—Continued

Year	Component	Torque/Ft. Lbs.
2005	Ground Wire	18
	Ignition Coil	44①
	Ignition Coil	53①
	Intake Manifold	89①
	Main Bearings	⑤
	Oil Level Indicator Tube	89①
	Oil Pan	⑨
	Oil Pan Drain Plug	19
	Oil Pump	89①
	Oil Pump Screen & Pickup Tube-To-Oil Pump	89①
	Power Steering Pulley Shield	89①
	Power Steering Pump	18
	Power Steering Tube	89①
	Radiator Support Bracket	22
	Radio Ignition Interference Capacitor	18
	Steering Coupling	18
	Thermostat	89①
	Throttle Body	89①
	Timing Chain Guide	89①
	Timing Chain Tensioner	18
	Transmission Cooler Tube Bracket	18
	Valve Cover	89①
	Valve Cover Wiring Harness Bracket	30
	Water Pump	18
	Water Pump Pulley	18

① — Inch pounds.
② — Refer to "Crankshaft Damper, Replace" for tightening specifications and sequence.
③ — Refer to "Crankshaft Rear Oil Seal, Replace" for tightening specifications and sequence.
④ — Refer to "Front Cover, Replace" for tightening specifications and sequence.
⑤ — Refer to "Main & Rod Bearings" for tightening specifications and sequence.
⑥ — Refer to "Piston & Rod Assembly" for tightening specifications and sequence.
⑦ — Refer to "Cylinder Head, Replace" for tightening specifications and sequence.
⑧ — Refer to "Timing Chain, Replace" for tightening specifications and sequence.
⑨ — Refer to "Pan Pan, Replace" for tightening specifications and sequence.

Rear Axle & Suspension

NOTE: On Air Bag Equipped Models, Refer To "Air Bag System Precautions" Located In The Front Of This Manual For System Disarming & Arming Procedures.

NOTE: Refer To "Computer Relearn Procedures" Located In The Front Of This Manual When Battery Power To The Computer Has Been Interrupted.

NOTE: Prior To Performing Any Service Operations Listed In This Section, Consult The "Technical Service Bulletins" Section For Related Information.

INDEX

PRECAUTIONS

Shock Absorber

These vehicles are equipped with gas pressurized shock absorbers which will extend unassisted. Do not apply heat or flame to shock absorber.

DESCRIPTION

Except Cobra

This rear axle is an integral design hypoid with center line of pinion set below center line of ring gear, **Figs. 1 and 2.** Semi-floating axle shafts are retained in housing by ball bearings and bearing retainers at axle ends.

The differential is mounted on two opposed tapered roller bearings which are retained in housing by removable caps. The differential bearing preload and drive gear backlash is adjusted by nuts located behind each differential bearing cup.

The drive pinion is mounted on two opposed tapered roller bearings. The pinion bearing preload is adjusted by a collapsible spacer on pinion shaft. The pinion and ring gear tooth contact is adjusted by shims between rear bearing cone and pinion gear.

Cobra

On these models the hypoid type axle has an 8.8 inch ring gear and a one-piece differential case, **Fig. 3.** Two opposed pinion bearings support the drive pinion gear in the differential housing. Two pinion gears engage the differential side gears with halfshaft splines.

REAR AXLE

REPLACE

2001–04

EXCEPT COBRA

1. Raise and support vehicle, then position safety stands under rear frame crossmember.
2. Drain axle lubricant into suitable container by removing axle housing cover.
3. Remove wheels, rear disc brake calipers and rear disc brake rotors as outlined in "Disc Brakes" chapter.
4. Remove lockpin and differential pinion shaft.
5. Remove rear brake anti-lock sensor.
6. Remove rear axle shaft U-washers by pushing axle shafts inward.
7. Remove axle shafts.
8. Remove brake junction block to axle housing cover bolt and brake hose support bracket from clips. Position hose aside.
9. Mark driveshaft centering socket yoke and rear axle universal joint flange for installation alignment.
10. Disconnect driveshaft at rear axle universal joint flange and wire it to underbody.
11. Support rear axle housing with suitable jackstands or hoist.
12. Disconnect rear brake hose from rear brake hose to rear axle housing clips.
13. Disconnect rear axle housing vent from rear axle housing.
14. Disconnect lower shock absorber studs from rear shock absorber lower mounting bracket.
15. Remove rear suspension arm and bushing nuts and bolts from axle housing rear bracket mountings.
16. Lower rear axle housing until rear springs are released and remove rear springs.
17. Remove rear suspension lower arm to rear axle housing nuts and bolts, then disconnect both rear suspension lower arms from rear axle housing.
18. Lower rear axle housing and remove it.
19. Reverse procedure to install, noting the following:

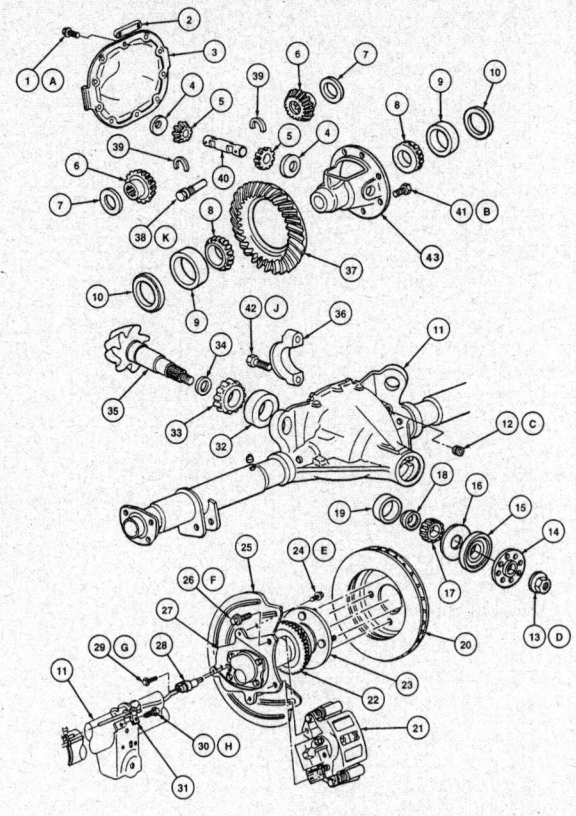

Item	Description
1	Bolt
2	Rear Axle Brake Line Clip
3	Axle Housing Cover
4	Differential Pinion Thrust Washer
5	Differential Pinion Gear
6	Differential Side Gear
7	Differential Side Gear Thrust Washer
8	Differential Bearing
9	Differential Bearing Cup
10	Differential Bearing Shim
11	Rear Axle Housing
12	Filler Plug
13	Pinion Nut
14	Rear Axle Universal Joint Flange
15	Rear Axle Drive Pinion Seal
16	Rear Axle Drive Pinion Shaft Oil Slinger
17	Differential Pinion Bearing
18	Differential Drive Pinion Collapsible Spacer
19	Differential Drive Pinion Bearing Cup
20	Rear Disc Brake Rotor
21	Rear Disc Brake Caliper
22	Rear Brake Anti-Lock Sensor Indicator
23	Axle Shaft Flange (Part of 4234)
24	Bolt (3 Req'd)
25	Rear Wheel Disc Brake Shield
26	Caliper Anchor Bolt
27	Left Hand Rear Disc Brake Adapter
	Right Hand Rear Disc Brake Adapter

Item	Description
28	Rear Brake Anti-Lock Sensor
29	Bolt
30	Bolt
31	Clip
32	Rear Axle Pinion Bearing Cup
33	Differential Pinion Bearing
34	Drive Pinion Bearing Adjustment Shim
35	Drive Pinion (Part of 4209)
36	Bearing Cap (Part of 4010)
37	Ring Gear (Part of 4209)
38	Differential Pinion Shaft Lock Pin
39	U-Washer
40	Differential Pinion Shaft
41	Rear Axle Differential Gear Case Bolt
42	Bolt (Part of 4010)
43	Differential Case
A	Tighten to 24-38 N·m (18-28 Lb-Ft)
B	Tighten to 95-115 N·m (70-85 Lb-Ft)
C	Tighten to 20-41 N·m (15-30 Lb-Ft)
D	Tighten to 190 N·m (140 Lb-Ft)
E	Tighten to 8-12 N·m (6-9 Lb-Ft)
F	Tighten to 87-119 N·m (64-87.7 Lb-Ft)
G	Tighten to 5-7 N·m (40-60 Lb-In)
H	Tighten to 10-14 N·m (7-10 Lb-Ft)
J	Tighten to 102-122 N·m (75-90 Lb-Ft)
K	Tighten to 20-41 N·m (15-30 Lb-Ft)

FM3039400270010X

FM3039400270020X

Fig. 1 Exploded view of integral rear axle (Part 1 of 2). 7.5 inch ring gear less Traction-Lock or except Cobra

Fig. 1 Exploded view of integral rear axle (Part 2 of 2). 7.5 inch ring gear less Traction-Lock or except Cobra

a. Tighten differential pinion shaft lockpin using stud and bearing mount tool No. E0AZ-19554-BA, or equivalent.
b. Tighten axle housing cover bolt in crosswise pattern.
c. Apply threadlock and sealer E0AZ-19554-AA, or equivalent, to rear axle housing vents threads.

COBRA

1. Park vehicle at curb height and on level ground.
2. Mark rear shock absorber positions relative to upper sleeves for installation alignment.
3. Raise and safely support vehicle, then remove rear wheel and tire assemblies.
4. Remove exhaust system.
5. Record transverse bar fastener for installation alignment.
6. Remove mounting nuts and pinion nose crossmember.
7. Mark driveshaft companion flange to pinion flange for installation alignment.
8. Remove and discard companion flange to pinion flange bolts.
9. Position driveshaft aside with suitable wire or rope.
10. Disconnect parking brake cables and conduits from parking brake lever and calipers.
11. Separate parking brake cables and conduits from knuckles.

12. Remove rear brake rotors.
13. Remove rear brake calipers and support brackets from knuckles as an assembly. Position calipers aside with suitable wire or rope.
14. Remove rear brake anti-lock sensors and position aside.
15. Support lower suspension arm and bushing with suitable jack stand.
16. Remove and discard lower suspension arm nuts and bolts.
17. Remove and discard toe link cotter pins and nuts.
18. Disconnect toe links from knuckles using separator tool No. T64P-3590-F, or equivalent.
19. Mark cam bolt to upper control arms and bushings for installation alignment.
20. Remove and discard lower control arm bushing nuts and bolts.
21. Disconnect knuckles from lower control arms.
22. Mark upper control arm cam bolts for installation alignment.
23. Remove and discard upper control arm bushing nuts and bolts.
24. Disconnect knuckles from upper control arms.
25. Separate CV joint from side gear using halfshaft removal tool No. 205-475, or equivalent, to overcome circlip. **Ensure tool fork crowns face away from differential housing. Position tool between CV joint and housing.**
26. Install seal protector tool No. 205-461,

or equivalent.
27. Remove halfshaft and knuckle assemblies.
28. Install differential plug tool No. T89P-4850-B, or equivalent, into housing bores.
29. Support differential housing with suitable transmission jack.
30. Remove differential to frame mounting bolts.
31. Lower and remove axle.
32. Reverse procedure to install, noting the following:
   a. Install seal protector tool No. 205-461, or equivalent, before install halfshafts.
   b. Ensure inboard CV joints circlips are properly seated.
   c. Ensure transverse bar is in place and bolt passes through it. **Do not tighten until vehicle is on ground and shock absorber marks are aligned.**
   d. Install new cam bolts and nuts at control arms and bushings. **Do not tighten until vehicle is on ground and shock absorber marks are aligned.**
   e. Apply high temperature nickel anti-seize lubricant part No. F6AZ-9L494-AA, or equivalent, to rear brake anti-lock sensors at axle housing contact points.
   f. Adjust wheel alignment.

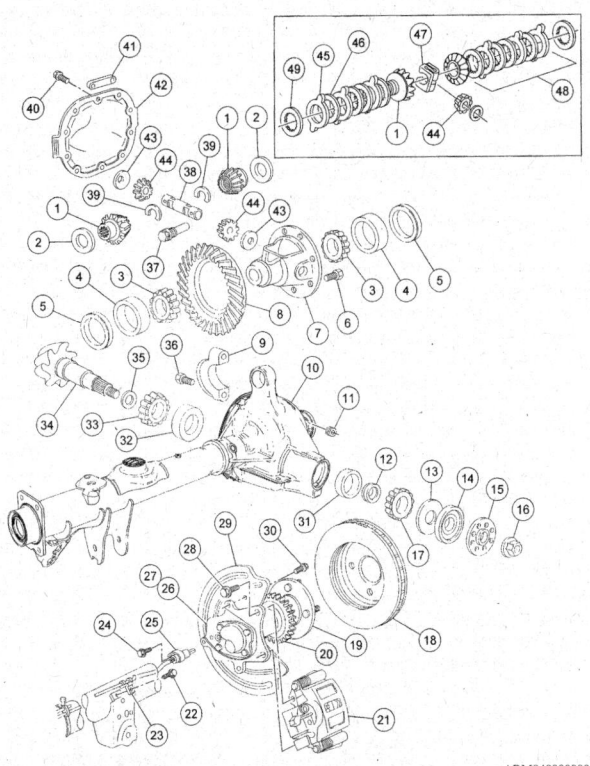

Fig. 2 Exploded view of integral rear axle (Part 1 of 2). 8.8 inch ring gear less Cobra

ARM0400000000595

Item	Description
1	Differential side gear
2	Differential side gear thrust washer
3	Differential bearing
4	Differential bearing cup
5	Differential bearing shim
6	Differential ring gear bolt (10 required)
7	Differential case
8	Differential ring gear (part of
9	Differential bearing cap (2 required
10	Axle housing
11	Filler plug
12	Drive pinion collapsible spacer
13	Drive pinion shaft oil slinger
14	Drive pinion seal
15	Pinion flange
16	Pinion nut
17	Drive pinion bearing (outer)
18	Brake disc
19	Axle shaft flange (2 required)
20	Anti-lock sensor indicator (2 required)
21	Disc brake caliper (2 required)
22	Brake line clip bolt
23	Brake line clip
24	Anti-lock sensor bolt (2 required)
25	Anti-lock sensor (2 required)
26	LH disc brake adapter
27	RH disc brake adapter
28	Disc brake caliper anchor bolt (4 required)
29	Brake disc shield (2 required)
30	Brake disc shield bolt (6 required)
31	Drive pinion bearing cup (outer)
32	Drive pinion bearing cup (inner)
33	Drive pinion bearing (inner)

Item	Description
34	Drive pinion gear
35	Drive pinion bearing adjustment shim
36	Differential bearing cap bolt (4 required
37	Differential pinion shaft lock bolt
38	Differential pinion shaft
39	Axle shaft U-washer
40	Differential housing cover bolt (10 required)
41	Axle identification tag
42	Differential housing cover
43	Differential pinion gear thrust washer
44	Differential pinion gear
45	Steel plate
46	Clutch disc
47	Differential clutch spring
48	Differential clutch pack
49	Rear axle differential clutch shim

ARM0400000000596

Fig. 2 Exploded view of integral rear axle (Part 2 of 2). 8.8 inch ring gear less Cobra

2005

1. Mark rear shock absorbers relative to their protective sleeve for installation alignment with vehicle on level ground and at curb height.
2. Raise and support vehicle.
3. Remove rear wheel and tire assemblies.
4. **On convertible models,** proceed as follows:
   a. Remove four rear support brace bolts.
   b. Remove two upper support brace bolts.
   c. Remove four front support brace bolts.
5. **On all models,** depress tabs of trackbar cover retaining clip using two screwdrivers through access hole and remove trackbar cover.
6. Remove mounting bolts, flag nuts and Trackbar.
7. Support and secure differential housing to suitable transmission jack.
8. Remove shock absorber mounting nuts and bolts.
9. Remove upper suspension arm mounting nut and bolt.
10. Lower axle slightly and remove springs.
11. Remove trailing arm mounting nuts and bolts.
12. Disconnect lower suspension arms from axle housing.
13. Lower and remove axle housing.
14. Reverse procedure to install, noting

the following:
   a. Raise suspension to reference mark before tightening suspension mounting nuts and bolts.
   b. Install new rear, upper and front support brace mounting bolts.
   c. Install new trackbar mounting bolts and flag nuts.
   d. Install new shock absorber mounting bolts and nuts
   e. Install new upper suspension and trailing arm mounting bolts and nuts.

REAR AXLE SHAFT

REPLACE

2001-04

EXCEPT COBRA

1. Raise and support vehicle, then remove rear wheel and tire assembly.
2. Remove brake drum as outlined in

"Drum Brakes" chapter or rear disc brake calipers and rear disc brake rotors as outlined in "Disc Brakes" chapter.
3. Remove axle housing cover and drain axle lubricant into suitable container.
4. Remove lockpin and differential pinion shaft.
5. Remove rear brake anti-lock sensor.
6. Push axle shaft flanged end toward vehicle center and remove C-lock from axle shaft button end.
7. Remove axle shaft from housing. **Do not damage oil seal.**
8. Reverse procedure to install.

COBRA

Refer to "Rear Axle, Replace" for rear axle shaft replacement procedure.

2005

1. Raise and support vehicle, then remove rear wheel and tire assembly.
2. Remove 10 differential cover mounting

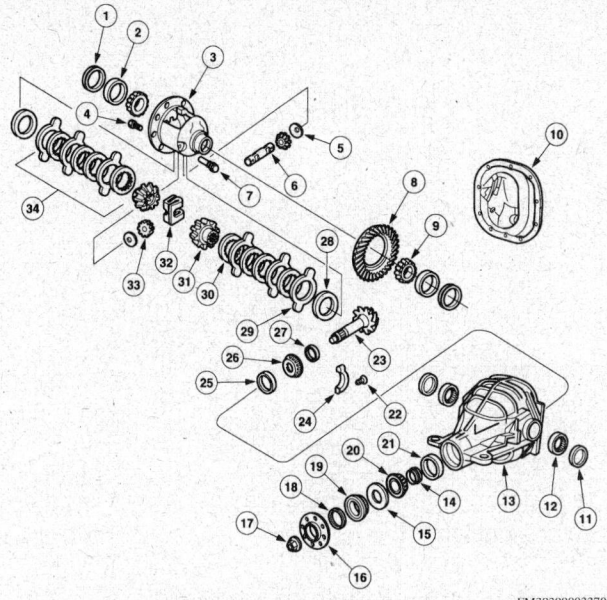

Item	Description
1	Differential bearing shim
2	Differential bearing cup
3	Differential case
4	Differential ring gear case bolt
5	Differential pinion thrust washer
6	Differential pinion shaft
7	Differential pinion shaft lock bolt
8	Differential ring gear
9	Differential bearing
10	Differential housing cover
11	Inboard CV joint stub shaft pilot bearing housing seal
12	Inboard CV joint stub shaft pilot bearing
13	Differential housing
14	Differential drive pinion collapsible spacer
15	Rear axle drive pinion shaft oil slinger
16	Rear axle pinion flange

Item	Description
17	Pinion nut
18	Drive pinion oil seal deflector
19	Rear axle drive pinion seal
20	Pinion bearing
21	Differential drive pinion bearing cup
22	Bolt
23	Drive pinion gear
24	Differential bearing cap
25	Rear axle pinion bearing cup
26	Pinion bearing
27	Drive pinion bearing adjustment shim
28	Rear axle differential clutch shim
29	Clutch plate
30	Clutch disc
31	Differential side gear
32	Differential clutch spring
33	Differential pinion gear
34	Differential clutch pack

Fig. 3   Exploded view of rear axle (Part 1 of 2). Cobra

Fig. 3   Exploded view of rear axle (Part 2 of 2). Cobra

bolts and drain lubricant from axle housing into suitable container.
3. Remove differential housing cover.
4. Remove two mounting bolts, then position and support disc brake caliper aside.
5. Remove disc brake pads.
6. Remove two mounting bolts and disc brake caliper anchor.
7. Remove brake disc.
8. Remove mounting bolt and anti-lock sensor from hub.
9. Remove lock bolt and differential pinion shaft.
10. Push in on axle shaft and U-washer.**Do not damage rubber O-ring in axle shaft grooves.**
11. Remove the axle shaft. **Do not damage axle shaft oil seal.**
12. Reverse procedure to install, noting the following:
    a. Lubricate lip of axle shaft oil seal with grease.
    b. If new differential pinion shaft lock bolt is unavailable, coat threads of old differential pinion shaft lock bolt with suitable Threadlock and Sealer.
    c. Install new differential pinion shaft lock bolt.
    d. Apply anti-seize lubricant to Anti-Lock Sensor body where it will contact .
    e. Apply new continuous bead of suitable silicone sealant to differential housing cover.
    f. **Differential housing cover must be installed within 15 minutes of application of silicone sealant.**

AXLE DAMPER
REPLACE
1. Raise vehicle and support rear axle, then remove rear wheel and tire assembly.

2. Remove axle damper front retaining pivot bolt and rear mounting nut, **Fig. 4.**
3. Remove damper and washers.
4. Reverse procedure to install.

PROPELLER SHAFT
REPLACE
2001-04
EXCEPT COBRA
REMOVAL
1. Mark rear driveshaft yoke and drive pinion flange relationship for installation alignment.
2. Disconnect rear U-joint from companion flange, **Fig. 5.**
3. Wrap tape around loose bearing caps to prevent them from falling off spider.
4. Pull driveshaft toward rear of vehicle until slip yoke clears transmission extension housing and seal.
5. Install suitable plug into extension housing to prevent lubricant leakage.

INSTALLATION
1. Lubricate slip yoke splines with suitable grease and remove transmission extension plug.
2. Inspect housing seal for damage.
3. Align slip yoke index mark with transmission output shaft mark and install driveshaft. **Do not allow slip yoke to bottom on output shaft with excessive force.**
4. Install driveshaft so index mark on rear flange is aligned with index mark on axle companion flange to ensure original driveline balance.
5. When installing new driveshaft, align factory made yellow paint mark at rear of driveshaft tube with factory made yellow paint mark on axle companion flange.

COBRA
1. Raise and support vehicle.
2. Remove exhaust hangers from rubber mounts.
3. Remove two mounting nuts on left-hand side exhaust flange.
4. Lower muffler pipe to clear flange and move muffler forward to disconnect third exhaust hanger.
5. Mark driveshaft companion flange to pinion flange for installation alignment.
6. Mark driveshaft yoke to transmission tailshaft for installation alignment.
7. Remove and discard companion flange to pinion flange bolts.
8. Lower driveshaft rear it clears axle housing.
9. Pull driveshaft rearward out of transmission.
10. Reverse procedure to install.

2005
4.0L ENGINE
1. Raise and support vehicle.
2. Mark driveshaft for installation alignment.
3. Remove eight driveshaft flange bolts, **Fig. 6.**
4. Disconnect driveshaft flanges from pilots and remove driveshaft using suitable tool, **Fig. 7. Driveshaft flanges fits tightly on pilots. Never hammer on driveshaft or any of its components to disconnect flanges from pilots. Pry only in area with suitable tool, to disconnect driveshaft flanges from flange pilots.**
5. Reverse procedure to install, noting the following:
    a. Install new mounting bolts.
    b. If new driveshaft flange bolts are not available, coat threads of original driveshaft flange bolts with Medium Strength Threadlocker TA-25,

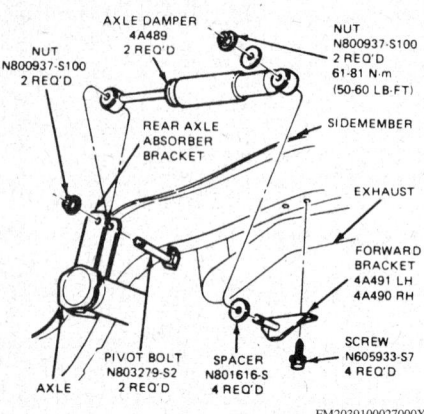

Fig. 4 Axle damper replacement

or equivalent meeting Ford specification WSK-M2G351-A5.

4.6L ENGINE

1. Raise and support vehicle.
2. Remove two exhaust hangers from rubber mounts.
3. Loosen two Exhaust Pipe nuts on left-hand side and disconnect lefthand muffler.
4. Lower muffler to clear exhaust pipe, then position muffler assembly forward and disconnect third exhaust hanger.
5. Mark driveshaft for installation alignment.
6. Remove six mounting bolts and washers, then disconnect Constant Velocity (CV) joint from pinion flange, **Fig. 8.**
7. Remove four driveshaft flange bolts.
8. Disconnect driveshaft flanges from transmission flange pilot, **Fig. 7. Driveshaft flanges fits tightly on pilots. Never hammer on driveshaft or any of its components to disconnect flanges from pilots. Pry only in area with suitable tool, to disconnect driveshaft flanges from flange pilots.**
9. Remove two center bearing bolts and spacers, then remove driveshaft.
10. Reverse procedure to install, noting the following:
    a. Install new mounting bolts.
    b. If new driveshaft flange bolts are not available, coat threads of original driveshaft flange bolts with Medium Strength Threadlocker TA-25, or equivalent meeting Ford specification WSK-M2G351-A5.
    c. Tighten CV joint bolts evenly in star pattern.

SHOCK ABSORBER
REPLACE
2001-04
EXCEPT COBRA

1. Open luggage compartment and remove rubber cap.
2. Remove shock absorber upper stud nut, washer and insulator.

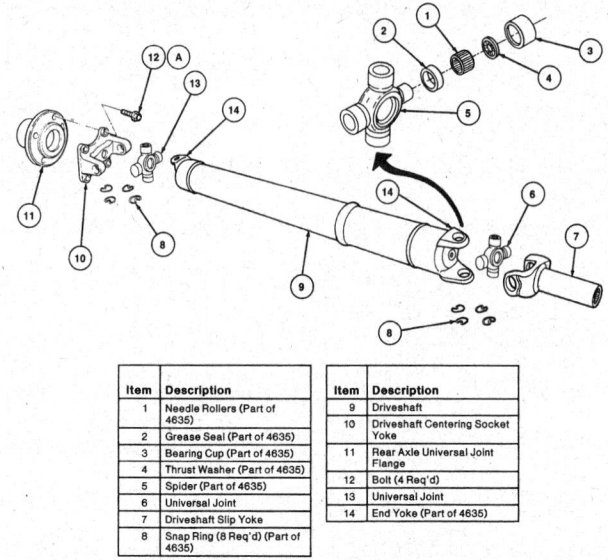

Item	Description
1	Needle Rollers (Part of 4635)
2	Grease Seal (Part of 4635)
3	Bearing Cup (Part of 4635)
4	Thrust Washer (Part of 4635)
5	Spider (Part of 4635)
6	Universal Joint
7	Driveshaft Slip Yoke
8	Snap Ring (8 Req'd) (Part of 4635)

Item	Description
9	Driveshaft
10	Driveshaft Centering Socket Yoke
11	Rear Axle Universal Joint Flange
12	Bolt (4 Req'd)
13	Universal Joint
14	End Yoke (Part of 4635)

Fig. 5 Driveshaft & universal joint replacement. Single Cardan type U-joint

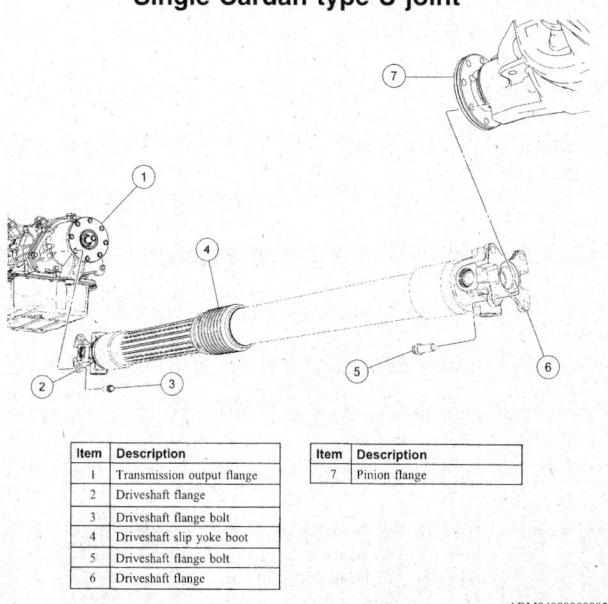

Item	Description
1	Transmission output flange
2	Driveshaft flange
3	Driveshaft flange bolt
4	Driveshaft slip yoke boot
5	Driveshaft flange bolt
6	Driveshaft flange

Item	Description
7	Pinion flange

Fig. 6 Drive shaft replacement. 2005 w/4.0L engine

3. Raise and support vehicle, then support rear axle.
4. Remove shock absorber lower stud nut, washer and insulator.
5. Compress shock absorber to clear upper shock tower.
6. Remove shock absorber.
7. Reverse procedure to install.

COBRA

1. Open luggage compartment and position carpet aside.
2. Remove and discard shock absorber mounting nut, washer and insulator.
3. Raise and support vehicle.
4. Remove and discard shock absorber lower mounting bolt and nut.

5. Remove shock absorber insulator and washer.
6. Reverse procedure to install, noting the following:
   a. Install new lower insulator and washer onto shock absorber.
   b. **Ensure hardened washer sits between lower control arm and bushing and absorber.**
   c. Install new upper insulator, washer and nut.

2005

1. Open luggage compartment lid and position carpet aside.
2. Raise and support vehicle.
3. Support the rear axle with a jack stand.

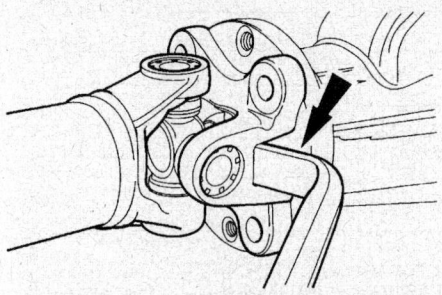

Fig. 7 Driveshaft flange pry area. 2005 w/4.0L engine

Do not support rear axle at differential housing. Do not allow axle to be supported by upper or lower control arms.

4. Remove mounting nut, washer and insulator assembly, **Fig. 9.**
5. **On models equipped with rear stabilizer bar,** proceed as follows:
   a. Remove both stabilizer bar link bolts and nuts.
   b. Position stabilizer bar to access shock absorber lower bolt.
6. **On all models,** remove lower bolt and nut, then remove shock absorber.
7. Reverse procedure to install using new mounting nuts and bolts.

COIL SPRING

REPLACE

2001–04

EXCEPT COBRA

1. Raise rear of vehicle and support at rear body crossmember.
2. Remove stabilizer bar, **Fig. 10.**
3. Lower axle housing until shock absorbers are fully extended. Support axle housing with suitable jack.
4. Support control arm with suitable jack under lower control arm rear pivot bolt. Remove pivot bolt.
5. Lower control arm until spring tension is relieved, then remove coil spring and insulator.
6. Reverse procedure to install. Tighten lower control arm pivot bolt with suspension at curb height.

COBRA

1. Raise and support vehicle.
2. Support No. 1 crossmember with suitable jack stand.
3. Remove rear tire and wheel assemblies.
4. Remove both mufflers.
5. Mark rear driveshaft yoke and drive pinion flange relationship for installation alignment.
6. Disconnect rear U-joint from companion flange, **Fig. 5.**
7. Wrap tape around loose bearing caps to prevent them from falling off spider.
8. Pull driveshaft toward rear of vehicle

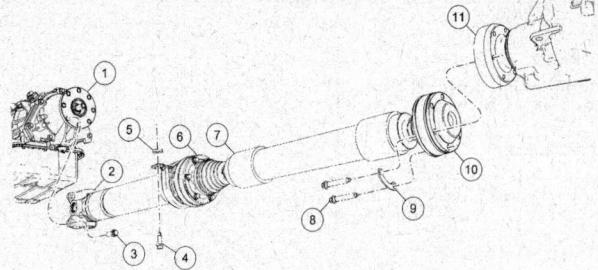

Item	Description
1	Transmission output flange
2	Driveshaft flange
3	Driveshaft flange bolt
4	Center bearing bolt
5	Spacer
6	Center bearing
7	Driveshaft assembly
8	Constant velocity (CV) joint bolts (6 required)
9	CV joint washer (3 required)
10	CV joint
11	Pinion flange

ARM0400000000599

Fig. 8 Drive shaft replacement. 2005 w/4.6L engine

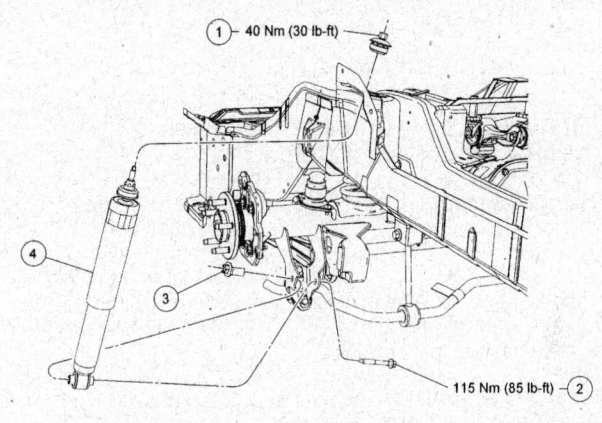

Item	Description		Item	Description
1	Upper nut, washer and insulator		3	Shock flag nut
2	Shock lower bolt (part of		4	Shock

ARM0400000000600

Fig. 9 Shock absorber replacement. 2005

until slip yoke clears transmission extension housing and seal.
9. Install suitable plug into extension housing to prevent lubricant leakage.
10. Disconnect parking brake cables and conduits at parking brake levers, rear brake calipers and rear knuckles.
11. Remove parking brake cable brackets at coil spring seats.
12. Remove rear brake line to axle mounting bolts and position lines aside.
13. Remove mounting bolts and rear wheel speed sensors.
14. Disconnect ABS sensor wiring harness at subframe.
15. Support lower control arms and bushings with suitable jack stands.
16. Discard shock absorber lower mounting nuts and bolts.
17. Lower control arms and bushings, then remove jack stands.
18. Support rear subframe using powertrain lift tool No. 014-00765, or equivalent.
19. Remove and discard subframe front mounting nuts.
20. Remove and discard subframe rear mounting nuts and bolts.
21. Lower subframe and allow it to pivot on its front bolts.
22. Remove springs and insulators.
23. Reverse procedure to install, noting the following:
   a. Install new lower insulator and washer onto shock absorber.
   b. **Ensure hardened washer sits between lower control arm and bushing and absorber.**

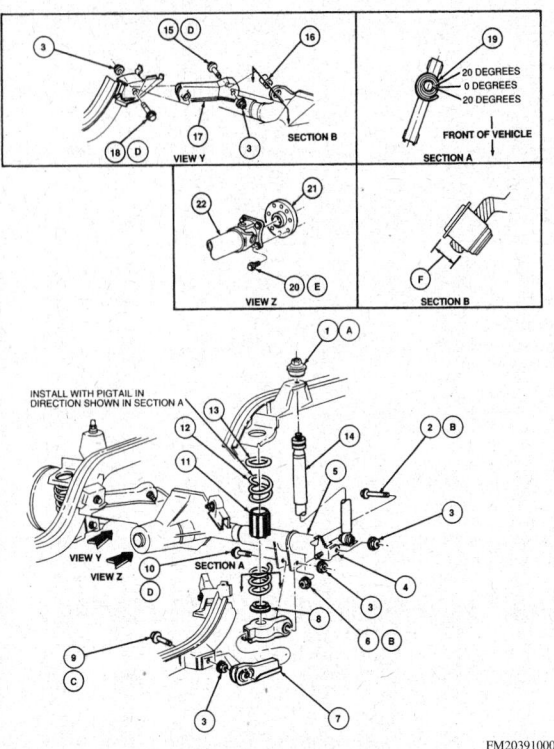

Item	Description
1	Nut, Insulator Assy (Part of 18198)
2	Bolt (2 Req'd)
3	Nut (2 Req'd)
4	Rear Shock Absorber Lower Mounting Bracket (2 Req'd)
5	Axle
6	Nut (2 Req'd)
7	Rear Suspension Lower Arm (2 Req'd)
8	Rear Spring Insulator (2 Req'd)
9	Bolt (2 Req'd)
10	Bolt
11	Rear Spring Damper (2 Req'd)
12	Rear Spring (2 Req'd)
13	Rear Spring Insulator (2 Req'd)
14	Rear Shock Absorber (2 Req'd)
15	Bolt (2 Req'd)

Item	Description
16	Rear Suspension Arm Bushing (2 Req'd)
17	Rear Suspension Arm and Bushing (2 Req'd)
18	Bolt (2 Req'd)
19	Pigtail
20	Bolt (4 Req'd)
21	Rear Axle Universal Joint Flange
22	Driveshaft
A	Tighten to 34-46 N·m (25-34 Lb-Ft)
B	Tighten to 76-103 N·m (57-75 Lb-Ft)
C	Tighten to 98-132 N·m (71-79 Lb-Ft)
D	Tighten to 98-132 N·m (71-79 Lb-Ft)
E	Tighten to 56-77 N·m (41-56 Lb-Ft)
F	Install to 35.5-36.5 mm (1.39-1.43 In)

FM2039100026020X

Fig. 10 Exploded view of rear suspension (Part 2 of 2). Except Cobra

FM2039100026010X

Fig. 10 Exploded view of rear suspension (Part 1 of 2). Except Cobra

c. Adjust wheel alignment.

2005

1. Mark rear shock absorber relative to protective sleeve with the vehicle in a static, level ground position for installation alignment.
2. Raise and support vehicle.
3. Support rear axle with suitable hi-lift jack .
4. **One models equipped with rear stabilizer bar,** proceed as follows:
   a. Remove both stabilizer bar link mounting bolts and nuts.
   b. Position stabilizer bar to gain access to shock absorber lower bolt.
5. **On all models,** remove shock absorber lower mounting bolt and nut.
6. Lower rear axle and remove spring, **Fig. 11.**
7. Reverse procedure to install, noting the following:
   a. Use new mounting nuts and bolts
   b. When installing new spring, ensure tag is toward axle.

CONTROL ARM

REPLACE

2001-04

EXCEPT COBRA

LOWER

1. Raise and support vehicle, then support body at rear crossmember.
2. Lower hoist until rear shock absorbers are fully extended and place suitable

transmission jack under lower arm to axle pivot bolt.
3. Remove and discard lower control arm front pivot bolt and nut, **Fig. 10.**
4. Remove control arm.
5. Reverse procedure to install.

UPPER

Removal

1. Raise rear of vehicle and support at rear body crossmember.
2. Remove rear and front pivot bolts, then the upper control arm.

Installation

1. Position upper control arm into side rail bracket and install front pivot bolt. **Do not tighten bolt now.**
2. Raise rear axle until upper control arm rear pivot bolt hole is aligned with hole in axle housing and install rear pivot bolt. **Do not tighten bolt now.**
3. Position suspension at curb height and tighten front pivot bolt.

COBRA

UPPER

1. Park vehicle at curb height and on level ground.
2. Mark rear shock absorber positions relative to upper sleeves.
3. Raise and support vehicle, then remove rear wheel and tire assemblies.
4. Remove rear brake rotor.
5. Remove coil springs as outlined under "Coil Spring, Replace."
6. Raise subframe into position, then remove and discard front bolts.
7. Mark upper control arm and bushing

cam bolt position for installation alignment.
8. Remove and discard upper control arm bushing nut and bolt.
9. Disconnect knuckle from upper control arm.
10. Remove and discard upper control arm nut and bolt.
11. Remove upper control arm.
12. Reverse procedure to install, noting the following:
    a. Install new cam bolts and nuts at control arms and bushings. **Do not tighten until vehicle is on ground and shock absorber marks are aligned.**
    b. Adjust wheel alignment.

LOWER

1. Park vehicle at curb height and on level ground.
2. Mark rear shock absorber positions relative to upper sleeves.
3. Mark transverse bar fastener for installation alignment.
4. Remove coil springs as outlined under "Coil Spring, Replace."
5. Disconnect lower control arm from knuckle. Discard nut and bolt.
6. Disconnect lower control arm from subframe. Discard nuts and bolts.
7. Reverse procedure to install, noting the following:
   a. Install lower control arm with new fasteners. **Do not tighten until vehicle is on ground and shock absorber marks are aligned.**
   b. Ensure transverse bar is in place and bolt passes through it. **Do not tighten until vehicle is on ground and shock absorber marks are aligned.**
   c. Adjust wheel alignment.

2005

LOWER

1. Raise and support vehicle, then remove tire and wheel assembly.
2. Remove clip and disconnect parking brake cable from rear caliper.
3. Remove parking brake cable bracket.

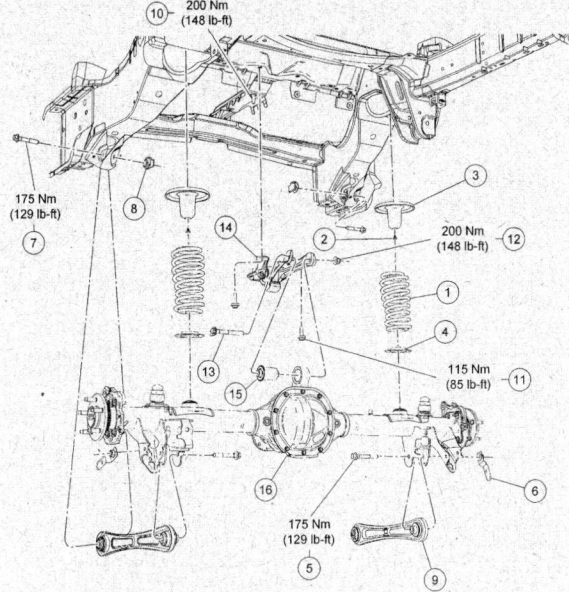

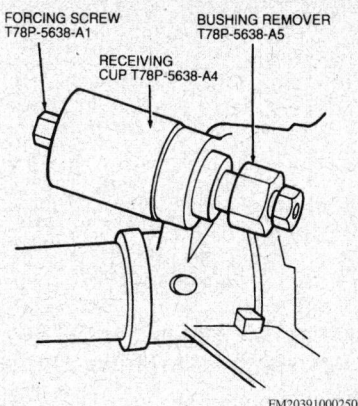

Fig. 12 Upper control arm axle bracket bushing removal. Except Cobra

Item	Description
1	Spring (2 required)
2	Pin-type fastener (2 required)
3	Upper insulator (2 required)
4	Lower insulator (2 required)
5	Lower control arm rear bolt (2 required)
6	Lower control arm rear nut (2 required)
7	Lower control arm front bolt (2 required)

Item	Description
8	Lower control arm front nut (2 required)
9	Lower control arm (2 required)
10	Upper control arm front bolt
11	Upper control arm rear bolt (2 required)
12	Upper control arm rear nut
13	Upper control arm flag bolt
14	Upper control arm
15	Upper control arm bushing
16	Rear axle assembly

ARM0400000000601

Fig. 11 Coil spring and control arm replacement. 2005

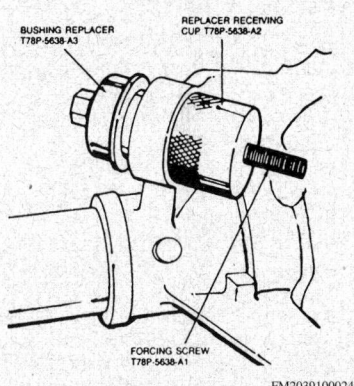

Fig. 13 Upper control arm axle bracket bushing installation. Except Cobra

4. Support rear axle with suitable jack stand. **Do not support rear axle at differential housing.**
5. Remove lower arm front mounting bolt and nut, **Fig. 11.**
6. Remove lower arm rear mounting bolt and flag nut.
7. Remove lower arm.
8. Reverse procedure to install, noting the following:
   a. Install new mounting nuts and bolts.
   b. Tighten lower arm mounting bolts while suspension is at curb height.

UPPER

1. Remove rear seat cushion.
2. Remove upper control arm front mounting bolt, **Fig. 11.**
3. Mark rear shock absorber relative to protective sleeve with vehicle in static, level ground position (curb height) for installation alignment.
4. Raise and support vehicle.
5. Place suitable safety support under fuel tank.
6. Remove two rear bolts and position both fuel tank support straps aside.
7. Partially lower fuel tank to access to upper control arm.
8. Remove two upper control arm rear mounting bolts, then the arm bushing

flag bolt and nut.
9. Remove upper control arm.
10. Reverse procedure to install using new mounting nuts and bolts.

CONTROL ARM BUSHING

REPLACE

2001-04

EXCEPT COBRA

1. Remove control arm as outlined under "Control Arm, Replace."
2. Remove bushing using bushing remover and installer set tool No. T78P-5638-A, or equivalent, **Fig. 12.**
3. Reverse procedure to install using suitable installer tool, **Fig. 13.**

COBRA

1. Remove upper control arm as outlined under "Control Arm, Replace."
2. Remove bushing using bushing remover and installer set tool No. T79P-5638-A, or equivalent.
3. Reverse procedure to install. Ensure bushing is properly installed, **Fig. 14.**

2005

1. Remove upper control arm as outlined under "Control Arm, Replace."
2. Remove upper arm bushing using C-frame and screw installer/remover tool T74P-4635-C, or equivalent.
3. Reverse proceed to install.

STABILIZER BAR

REPLACE

2001-04

EXCEPT COBRA

1. Raise and support rear of vehicle.
2. Remove four bolts attaching stabilizer bar to brackets on lower control arms.
3. Remove stabilizer bar.
4. Reverse procedure to install.

COBRA

1. Remove rear coil springs as outlined under "Coil Spring, Replace."
2. Raise subframe into position, then remove and discard its front bolts.
3. Lower subframe.
4. Remove stabilizer link and nuts. Discard nuts.
5. Remove stabilizer bar brackets and bolts. Discard bolts.

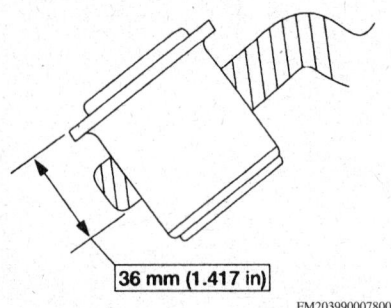

Fig. 14 Upper control arm bushing installation. Cobra

6. Remove stabilizer bar and bushings.
7. Reverse procedure to install.

2005

1. Raise and support vehicle.
2. Remove stabilizer bar link mounting bolts and nuts, **Fig. 15.**
3. Remove stabilizer bar bracket mounting nuts and studs.
4. Remove stabilizer bar and brackets.
5. Reverse procedure to install, noting the following:
   a. When installing new stabilizer bar, ensure tag is on lefthand side of vehicle.
   b. Stabilizer bar for convertible will have a B suffix in part number and it will have green-colored tag.
   c. Stabilizer bar for coupe will have an A suffix in part number and it will have yellow-colored tag.
   d. Install new mounting nuts and bolts.

LATERAL ROD

REPLACE

1. Raise and support vehicle.
2. Support rear axle with suitable jack stand. **Do not support rear axle at differential housing.**
3. Loosen panard rod-to-body mount nut, then remove lateral stiffener bar-to-body mount nut and flag bolt, **Fig. 16.**
4. Remove laterals stiffener bar-to-body bolts.
5. Remove panard rod arm support bracket.
6. Reverse procedure to install, noting the following:
   a. Tighten panard rod fasteners while suspension is at curb height.
   b. Install new mounting nuts and bolts.

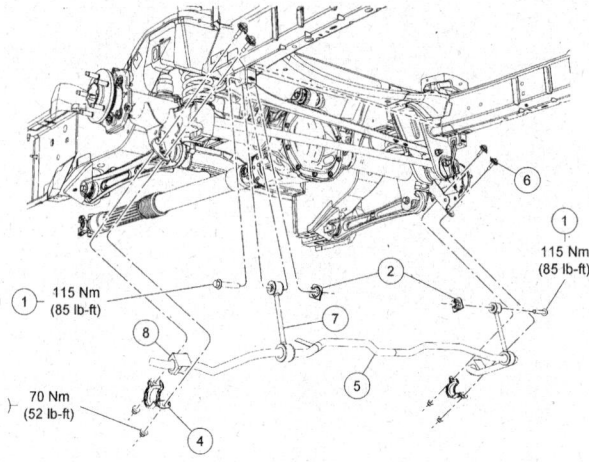

Item	Description
1	Link bolt (2 required)
2	Clip nut (2 required)
3	Bracket nut (4 required)
4	Stabilizer bar bracket (2 required)
5	Stabilizer bar

Item	Description
6	Clip studs (4 required)
7	Stabilizer bar link (2 required)
8	Stabilizer bar bushing (2 required)

Fig. 15 Stabilizer bar replacement. 2005

TECHNICAL SERVICE BULLETINS

Coastdown Rear Axle Whine

2001 MODELS w/3.8L ENGINE

On some of these models there may be a whining during coastdown from 60–35 mph. This noise disappears at less than 35 mph.

This condition may be caused by a variation in tooth contact between the differential ring gear and pinion, and by the original upper control arm bushings inability to isolate the noise.

To correct this condition, proceed as follows:

1. Raise and support vehicle.
2. Replace driveshaft, noting the following:
   a. **On models equipped with automatic transmission,** ensure driveshaft front yellow dot aligns with dot on transmission output shaft end.
   b. **On all models,** ensure driveshaft rear yellow dot aligns with corresponding pinion flange dot.
3. Remove two rear upper control arms.
4. Install two revised upper control arms (part No.1R3Z-5500-AA). **Do not tighten mounting bolts now.**
5. Place suitable screw-type jack at vehicle front under front crossmember just below steering gear. **Do not raise vehicle with jack stand.**
6. Raise axle as far as possible without raising vehicle using suitable transmission jack.
7. **Torque** two upper arm-to-frame bolts to 66 ft. lbs.
8. **Torque** two upper arm-to-axle bolts to 76 ft. lbs.

Rear Suspension Clunk Or Pop

2001–03 COBRA

On some of these models there may be a popping while turning into or out of an incline at speed of less than 15 mph. The steeper the incline the more noticeable the noise.

This condition may be caused by lateral movement of the stabilizer bar.

To correct this condition, proceed as follows:

1. Raise and support vehicle.
2. **Torque** stabilizer bar bracket bolts to 39–46 ft. lbs.
3. **Torque** stabilizer bar collar bolts to 67–103 inch lbs.
4. **Torque** lower shock absorber bolts to 83–113 ft. lbs.
5. **Torque** upper control arm bushing bolts to 56–76 ft. lbs.
6. **Torque** stabilizer bar link bolts to 30–40 ft. lbs.

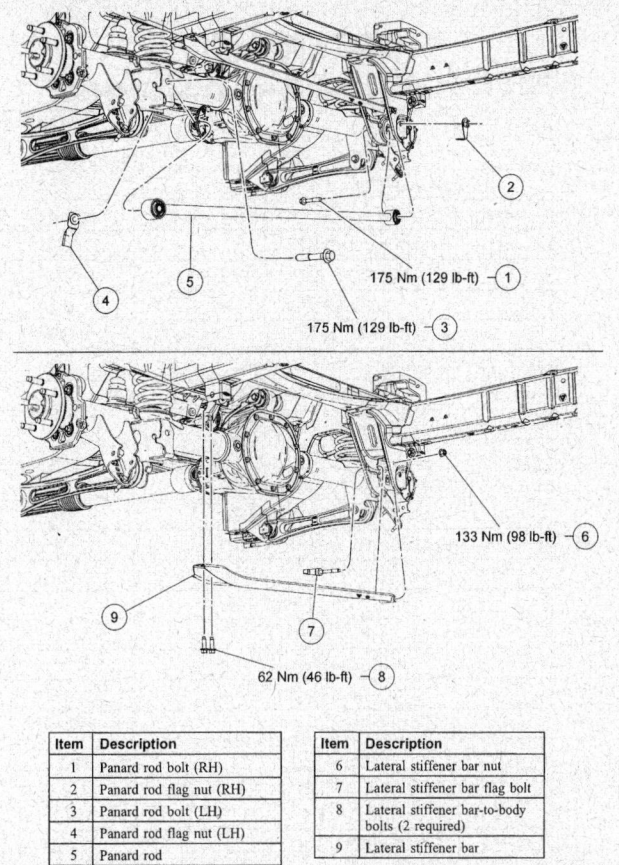

Item	Description	Item	Description
1	Panard rod bolt (RH)	6	Lateral stiffener bar nut
2	Panard rod flag nut (RH)	7	Lateral stiffener bar flag bolt
3	Panard rod bolt (LH)	8	Lateral stiffener bar-to-body bolts (2 required)
4	Panard rod flag nut (LH)	9	Lateral stiffener bar
5	Panard rod		

ARM0400000000603

Fig. 16 Panard rod replacement. 2005

TIGHTENING SPECIFICATIONS

Year	Component	Torque/Ft. Lbs.
2001–04	ABS Sensor	17
	Axle Damper	66
	Axle Damper Bracket	59
	Axle Shaft To Hub	240
	Bracket To Differential Housing	35
	Brake Fluid Line To Caliper	30
	Brake Rotor Dust Shield	89①
	Differential Insulator, Front	52
	Differential Insulator, Rear	76
	Differential Pinion Shaft Lockpin	15–30
	Driveshaft To Companion Flange	83
	Lower Control Arm	111
	Lower Control Arm & Bushing To Subframe (Cobra)	184
	Lower Control Arm & Bushing To Knuckle (Cobra)	85
	Lubricant Filler Plug	25
	Parking Brake Cable Bracket (Cobra)	11
	Parking Brake Cable Bracket (Except Cobra)	41
	Pinion Bumper	10
	Pinion Nose Crossmember	184

Continued

TIGHTENING
SPECIFICATIONS—Continued

Year	Component	Torque/Ft. Lbs.
2001–04	Shock Absorber, Lower (Cobra)	98
	Shock Absorber, Lower (Except Cobra)	59
	Shock Absorber, Upper	30
	Shock Absorber Clevis Bracket	80
	Stabilizer Bar	41
	Stabilizer Bar Link	35
	Subframe Rear Bracket	59
	Subframe To Body	76
	Subframe To Rear Bracket	76
	Toe Link	35
	Upper Control Arm (Cobra)	66
	Upper Control Arm To Axle	82
	Upper Control Arm To Frame	72
	Wheel Hub Retainer	251
	Wheel Lug Nuts	95
2005	Anti-Lock Sensor	62①
	Center Bearing	35
	Control Arm Bushing	148
	Control Arm, Lower	129
	Control Arm, Upper (Front)	148
	Control Arm, Upper (Rear)	85
	CV Joint	41
	Differential Filler Plug	22
	Differential Housing Cover	33
	Differential Pinion Shaft Lock	22
	Disc Brake Caliper Anchor	25
	Disc Brake Caliper Anchor	76
	Driveshaft Flange	76
	Exhaust Pipe	35
	Front Support Brace	46
	Laterals Stiffener Bar-To-Body	46
	Lateral Stiffener Bar-To-Body Mount	98
	Panard Rod-To-Body Mount	129
	Parking Brake Cable Bracket	26
	Shock Absorber, Lower	85
	Shock Absorber, Upper	30
	Stabilizer Bar Bracket	52
	Stabilizer Bar Link	85
	Rear Support Brace (Convertible)	46
	Rear Support Brace (Convertible)	46
	Trackbar	129
	Trailing Arm	129
	Upper Suspension Arm	129

① — Inch lbs.

Front Suspension & Steering

NOTE: On Air Bag Equipped Models, Refer To "Air Bag System Precautions" Located In The Front Of This Manual For System Disarming & Arming Procedures.

NOTE: Refer To "Computer Relearn Procedures" Located In The Front Of This Manual When Battery Power To The Computer Has Been Interrupted.

INDEX

PRECAUTIONS

Strut

These vehicles are equipped with gas pressurized strut which will extend unassisted. Do not apply heat or flame to shock absorber.

DESCRIPTION

The front suspension is of a modified McPherson strut design using shock struts and coil springs, **Fig. 1.** The springs are mounted between the lower control arm and a crossmember spring pocket.

WHEEL BEARING

ADJUST

Wheel bearings are not adjustable.

HUB & BEARING

REPLACE

2001-04

1. Raise and support vehicle, then remove wheel and tire assembly.
2. Remove and discard front hub cap grease seal.
3. Remove two mounting bolts and front disc brake caliper. **Do not let front disc brake caliper hang by front brake hose. Suspend it with suitable wire or rope.**

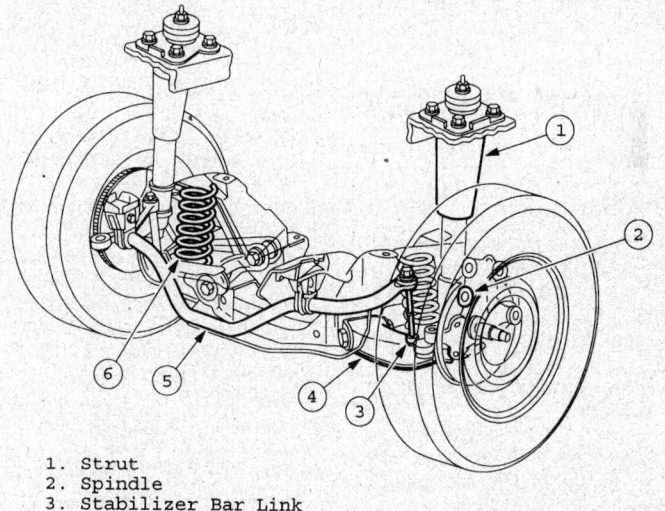

1. Strut
2. Spindle
3. Stabilizer Bar Link
4. Lower Control Arm
5. Stabilizer Bar
6. Spring

FM2029700167000X

Fig. 1 Exploded view of front suspension. 2001–04

4. Remove front disc brake rotor. Discard factory push-on nuts.
5. Remove and discard front axle wheel hub retainer.
6. Remove wheel hub and bearing. If assembly cannot be removed by hand, use front hub remover/replacer tool No. T81P-1104-C, or equivalent.
7. Reverse procedure to install. Install new wheel hub retainer and hub cap grease seal.

2005

1. Raise and support vehicle, then remove wheel and tire assembly.
2. Remove two mounting bolts, then position and support brake caliper and anchor plate aside, **Fig. 2. Never allow brake caliper and anchor plate to hang from brake flexible hose.**
3. Remove brake disc.

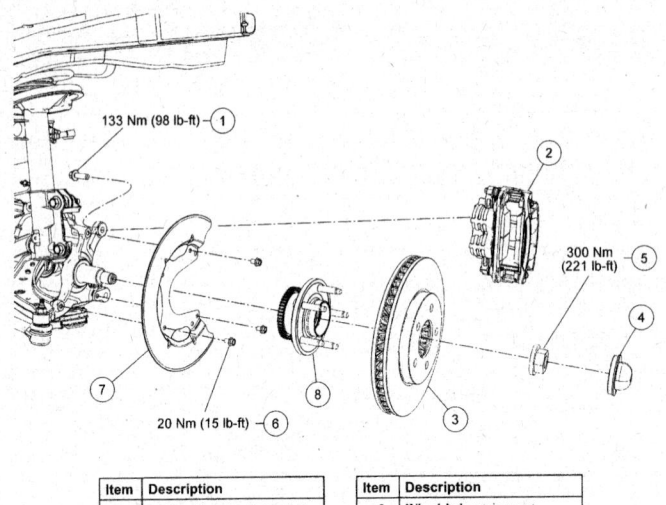

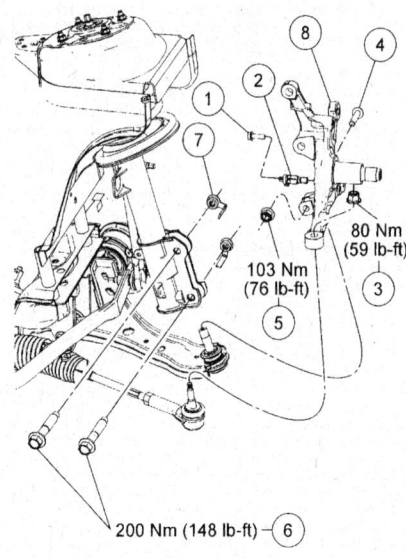

Item	Description
1	Brake caliper bracket bolt (2 required)
2	Brake caliper assembly
3	Brake disc
4	Wheel hub grease cap
5	Wheel hub retainer nut
6	Dust shield bolt (3 required)
7	Dust shield
8	Wheel hub assembly (ABS/non-ABS)

ARM0400000000604

Fig. 2 Front wheel bearing replacement. 2005

Item	Description
1	Wheel speed sensor bolt
2	Wheel speed sensor
3	Outer tie rod end nut
4	Wheel spindle pinch bolt
5	Wheel spindle pinch nut
6	Strut-to-wheel spindle bolt (2 required)
7	Strut-to-wheel spindle flag nut (2 required)
8	Wheel spindle (RH/LH)

ARM0400000000605

Fig. 3 Front wheel spindle replacement

4. Remove front hub cap grease seal.
5. Remove wheel hub retainer.
6. Remove front wheel hub and bearing.
7. Reverse procedure to install using new front hubcap grease seal and wheel hub retainer.

FRONT WHEEL SPINDLE
REPLACE
2001-04

1. Raise and support vehicle, then remove front wheel and tire assembly.
2. Remove front brake anti-lock sensor from spindle.
3. Remove disc brake caliper, rotor and dust shield.
4. Remove wheel hub and front stabilizer bar from lower arm.
5. Remove tie rod end from wheel spindle using tie rod end remover tool No. 3290-D, or equivalent. **Do not remove nut from ball joint stud now.**
6. Loosen ball joint nut one or two turns and tap spindle boss sharply to relieve stud pressure.
7. Compress front coil spring using suitable floor jack under front suspension lower arm as outlined under "Coil Spring, Replace."
8. Remove stud nut and front anti-lock sensor bracket.
9. Remove two mounting bolts and front wheel spindle.
10. Reverse procedures to install.

2005

1. Raise and support vehicle, then remove wheel and tire assembly.
2. Remove two mounting bolts, then position and support brake caliper and anchor plate aside, **Fig. 3. Never**

allow brake caliper and anchor plate to hang from brake flexible hose.
3. Remove brake disc.
4. Remove front hub cap grease seal.
5. Remove wheel hub retainer.
6. Remove front wheel hub and bearing.
7. Remove three mounting bolts and brake disc dust shield.
8. Remove mounting bolt and ABS sensor.
9. Remove brake line bracket bolt and disconnect ABS sensor wire from bracket.
10. Remove outer tie rod end nut.
11. Disconnect tie rod end from front wheel spindle using tie-rod end remover tool No. Tool-3290-D, or equivalent. **do not damage tie rod end dust boot.**
12. Support front suspension lower arm with suitable jack stand.
13. Remove pinch bolt and nut.
14. Separate lower control arm and wheel spindle. **Do not damage lower ball joint boot.**
15. Mark two strut-to-spindle bolts for installation alignment, then remove mounting bolts and nuts.
16. Remove wheel spindle.
17. Reverse procedure to install, noting the following:
    a. Install new outer tie rod end nut.
    b. Install new front hubcap grease seal and wheel hub retainer.

BALL JOINT INSPECTION

1. Raise and support front of vehicle.
2. Ensure front wheel hub and bearing are in good condition.
3. Place suitable jack stands under lower control arms.
4. Position suitable dial indicator between spindle and ball joint.
5. Grasp tire at top and bottom, then slowly move inward and outward.

6. Replace lower control arm if movement more than .031 inch.

BALL JOINT
REPLACE

On these models the ball joint and lower control arm must be replaced as an assembly.

COIL SPRING
REPLACE
2001-04

1. Park vehicle at curb height and on level ground.
2. Mark front strut positions to upper sleeves for installation alignment.
3. Raise and support vehicle.
4. Allowing front suspension lower arms to hang free, then remove wheel and tire assembly.
5. Remove brake caliper and support aside using suitable wire or rope.
6. Disconnect front wheel spindle connecting rod or end from front wheel spindle using tie rod end remover tool No. 3290-D, or equivalent.
7. Disconnect stabilizer bar link from lower control arm.

8. Remove mounting bolts and position steering gear so suspension arm bolt may be removed.
9. Compress coil spring using coil spring compressor tool No. D78P-5310-A, or equivalent.
10. Remove suspension arm-to-crossmember nuts and bolts.
11. Remove compression rod and coil spring.
12. Reverse procedure to install. Ensure lower spring end is positioned between two holes in lower control arm spring pocket.

2005

1. Raise and support vehicle, then remove wheel and tire assembly.
2. Remove mounting bolt and ABS sensor.
3. Remove brake line bracket bolt and disconnect ABS sensor wire from bracket.
4. Remove stabilizer bar link upper nut, **Fig. 4. Use hex-holding feature to prevent studs from turning while removing or installing stabilizer bar link nuts.**
5. Disconnect link from strut.
6. Support lower control arm using suitable jack stand.
7. Mark two strut bolts for installation alignment, then remove strut bolts and nuts.
8. Lower front suspension lower arm and remove four strut-to-body nuts.
9. Remove strut and spring.
10. Compress spring until tension is released from strut using suitable spring compressor.
11. Holding strut rod and remove strut upper nut.
12. Remove strut, dust boot, jounce bumper, washer and upper bearing.
13. Release tension and remove spring.
14. Reverse procedure to install, noting the following:
    a. Align notch on upper bearing with clevis at bottom of strut.
    b. Install new strut upper nut.
    c. Notch and arrow etched into upper bearing must face outboard side of vehicle.
    d. Install new stabilizer bar link upper nut.

STRUT
REPLACE
2001-04

1. Place ignition in unlocked position.
2. Raise and support vehicle.
3. Remove front wheel and tire assembly.
4. Remove disc brake caliper and position aside with suitable wire or rope.
5. Remove mounting bolt and ABS wheel speed sensor.
6. Disconnect ABS sensor wiring harness at bracket.
7. Support lower control arm with suitable jack stand.
8. Remove two strut to front wheel spindle mounting nuts.

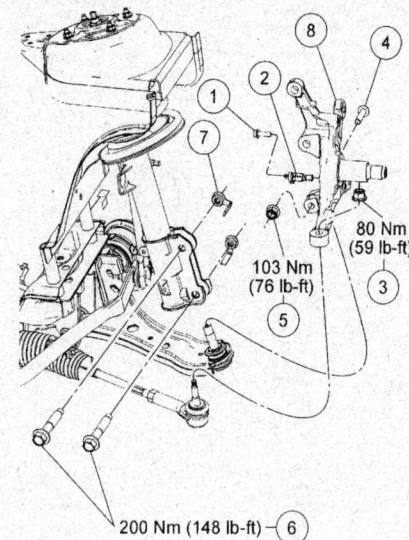

200 Nm (148 lb-ft) – ⑥

Item	Description
1	Wheel speed sensor bolt
2	Wheel speed sensor
3	Outer tie rod end nut
4	Wheel spindle pinch bolt
5	Wheel spindle pinch nut
6	Strut-to-wheel spindle bolt (2 required)
7	Strut-to-wheel spindle flag nut (2 required)
8	Wheel spindle (RH/LH)

ARM0400000000606

Fig. 4 Strut & coil spring replacement. 2005

9. Lower control arm and remove jack stand.
10. Lower vehicle.
11. Remove strut upper mounting nuts and bolts. Discard nuts.
12. Remove strut.
13. Reverse procedures to install.

2005

1. Raise and support vehicle, then remove wheel and tire assembly.
2. Remove mounting bolt and ABS sensor.
3. Remove brake line bracket bolt and disconnect ABS sensor wire from bracket.
4. Remove stabilizer bar link upper nut, **Fig. 4. Use hex-holding feature to prevent studs from turning while removing or installing stabilizer bar link nuts.**
5. Disconnect link from strut.
6. Support lower control arm using suitable jack stand.
7. Mark two strut bolts for installation alignment, then remove strut bolts and nuts.
8. Lower front suspension lower arm and remove four strut-to-body nuts.
9. Remove strut and spring.
10. Reverse procedure to install, noting

the following:
a. Notch and arrow etched into upper bearing must face outboard side of vehicle.
b. Install new stabilizer bar link upper nut.

CONTROL ARM
REPLACE
2001-04

1. Park vehicle at curb height and on level ground.
2. Mark front strut positions to upper sleeves for installation alignment.
3. Raise and support vehicle. Allowing front suspension lower arms to hang free.
4. Remove wheel and tire assembly.
5. Remove front disc brake caliper and position it aside with suitable wire or rope.
6. Remove front disc brake rotor and front disc brake rotor shield as outlined in "Disc Brakes" chapter.
7. Disconnect front wheel spindle connecting rod or end from front wheel spindle using tie rod end remover tool No. 3290-D, or equivalent.
8. Remove mounting bolts and steering gear so front suspension lower arm bolt is accessible.
9. Disconnect front stabilizer link from front suspension lower arm.
10. Loosen ball joint nut one or two turns and tap spindle boss sharply to relieve stud pressure. **Do not remove ball joint nut now.**
11. Compress spring using spring compressor tool No. D78P-5310-A, or equivalent.
12. Remove and discard ball joint stud nut.
13. Remove front shock absorber and spindle. Wire aside to obtain working room.
14. Remove and discard front suspension lower arm to crossmember nuts and bolts.
15. Remove front suspension lower arm and coil spring.
16. Reverse procedure to install, noting the following:
    a. Ensure spring end is positioned between two holes in front suspension lower arm pocket.
    b. Adjust wheel alignment.

2005

1. Raise and support vehicle, then remove wheel and tire assembly.
2. Remove pinch bolt and nut.
3. Separate lower control arm and wheel spindle.
4. Remove mounting bolts and position steering gear to access to lower control arm forward bolt.
5. Remove lower control arm forward bolt and nut, **Fig. 5. Do not damage steering gear boot while removing or installing lower control arm forward bolt.**
6. Remove lower control arm rearward nuts and flag bolts.

7. Remove lower control arm and bracket.
8. Remove three mounting and heat shield.
9. Reverse procedure to install, noting the following:
   a. Install new mounting bolts and nuts.
   b. To ease installation, position of lower control arm nut and flag bolt can be reversed to allow installation of nut from underneath vehicle.

STABILIZER BAR
REPLACE

2001-04

1. Raise and support vehicle.
2. Disconnect stabilizer bar from each link.
3. Remove insulator clamps, insulators and stabilizer bar.
4. Reverse procedure to install.

2005

1. Raise and support vehicle.
2. Remove both stabilizer bar link lower nuts, **Fig. 4. Use hex-holding feature to prevent studs from turning while removing or installing stabilizer bar link nuts. Boot seal must not be allowed to twist at all while tightening nut.**
3. Disconnect both links from stabilizer bar.
4. Remove four stabilizer bracket nuts.
5. Remove stabilizer bar and brackets.
6. Reverse procedure to install.

STABILIZER BAR BUSHING
REPLACE

2001-04

1. Raise and support vehicle.
2. Disconnect stabilizer bar from each link.
3. Remove insulator clamps, insulators and stabilizer bar.
4. Reverse procedure to install.

2005

1. Raise and support vehicle.
2. Disconnect stabilizer bar from each link.
3. Remove insulator clamps, insulators and stabilizer bar.
4. Coat front stabilizer bar and inside diameter of stabilizer bar bushing with suitable silicone spray lubricant.
5. Remove stabilizer bar bushing by sliding if off stabilizer bar.
6. Reverse procedure to install.

10 Nm (89 lb-in)
175 Nm (129 lb-ft)
175 Nm (129 lb-ft)

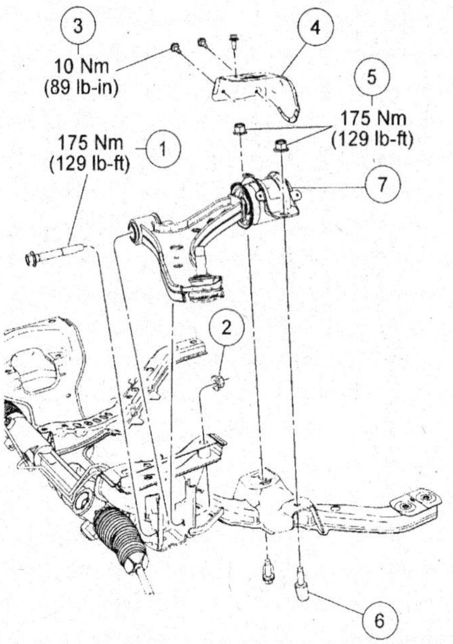

Item	Description
1	Lower control arm forward bolt
2	Lower control arm forward nut
3	Heat shield bolt (3 required)
4	Heat shield
5	Lower control arm rearward nut (2 required)
6	Lower control arm rearward flag bolt (2 required)
7	Lower control arm (LH/RH)

ARM0400000000607

Fig. 5 Lower control arm replacement. 2005

POWER STEERING GEAR
REPLACE

2001-04

1. Place front wheels in straight-ahead position. **Do not lock steering column.**
2. Raise and support vehicle, then remove front wheel and tire assemblies.
3. Remove tie rod end to spindle nut. Discard cotter pin.
4. Separate tie rod end from spindle using tie 'rod end separator tool No. 3290-D, or equivalent.
5. Remove and discard steering column intermediate shaft pinch bolt.
6. Lower vehicle.
7. Place front wheels in straight-ahead position and lock steering column. **Do not rotate steering wheel when lower column shaft is disconnected.**
8. Disconnect intermediate shaft coupling.
9. Remove steering gear mounting nuts, washers and bolts. Position gear forward.
10. Position drain pan to catch power steering lines' fluid,
11. Disconnect power steering hoses, remove and discard O-rings. Plug open ports.
12. Remove steering gear.
13. Reverse procedure to install, noting the following:
    a. Install new O-rings using seal replacement tool set No. D90P-3517-A, or equivalent.
    b. Install new shaft coupling pinch bolt.

2005

1. Place steering wheel in straight-ahead position and turn ignition switch to OFF position.
2. Raise and support vehicle.
3. Remove two nuts and disconnect tie-rod ends from wheel knuckles, **Fig. 6. Use hex holding feature to prevent the tie-rod end stud from turning.**
4. Remove steering column coupling-to-steering gear bolt and disconnect coupling from steering gear.
5. Remove power steering line clamp plate bolt , then disconnect power steering pressure and return lines. Allow fluid to drain into suitable container.
6. Remove two pressure line bracket-to-crossmember bolts and position pressure line aside.
7. Remove two mounting bolts and steering gear.
8. Reverse procedure to install. Install new O-ring seals.

POWER STEERING PUMP
REPLACE
2001-04
TYPE CII

1. Remove serpentine drive belt.
2. Position drain pan to catch power steering lines' fluid.
3. Disconnect power steering hose, remove and discard O-ring. Plug open ports.
4. Remove pump pulley using removal tool No. T69L-10300-B, or equivalent.
5. Remove mounting bolts and power steering pump.
6. Reverse procedure to install, noting the following:
   a. Install pump pulley using installer tool No. T65P-3A733-C, or equivalent.
   b. Install new O-ring using seal replacement tool set No. D90P-3517-A, or equivalent.

TYPE CIII

1. Remove serpentine drive belt.
2. Raise and support vehicle.
3. Remove pump pulley using removal tool No. T69L-10300-B, or equivalent.

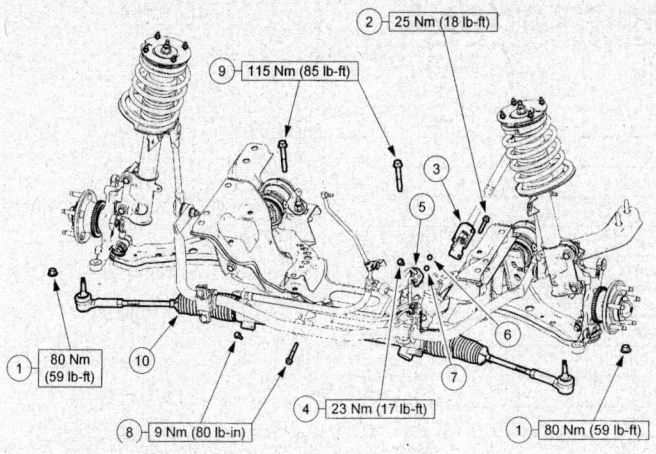

Fig. 6 Steering gear replacement. 2005

Item	Description
1	Tie-rod end nuts (2 required)
2	Steering column coupling-to-steering gear bolt
3	Steering column coupling
4	Power steering line clamp plate bolt
5	Power steering lines (pressure/return)
6	Pressure line O-ring seal
7	Return line O-ring seal
8	Pressure line bracket-to-crossmember bolts (2 required)
9	Steering gear bolts (2 required)
10	Steering gear

ARM0400000000608

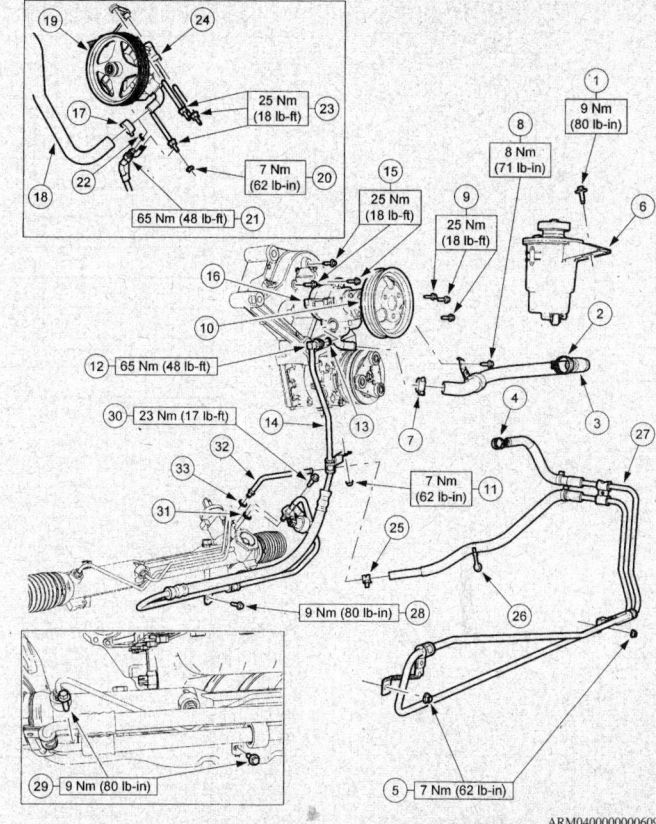

Fig. 7 Power steering pump replacement. 2005

ARM0400000000609

4. Remove mounting bolt and bracket.
5. Position drain pan to catch power steering lines' fluid.
6. Disconnect power steering hoses, remove and discard O-rings. Plug open ports.
7. Remove mounting bolts and power steering pump.
8. Reverse procedure to install, noting the following:
   a. Inspect pump pulley for paint marks in hub web area. **If two paint marks are visible, discard pulley and install new one.**
   b. If there is only one or no mark, mark web area and pulley.
   c. Install pump pulley using installer tool No. T91P-3A733-A, or equivalent.
   d. Install new O-ring using seal replacement tool set No. D90P-3517-A, or equivalent.

2005

4.0L ENGINE

1. Rotate tensioner counterclockwise and remove accessory drive belt from power steering pump pulley.
2. Remove three mounting bolts and power steering pump pulley, **Fig. 7.**
3. Disconnect clamp and suction hose from power steering pump.
4. Disconnect pressure line fitting.
5. Remove suction hose bracket bolt.
6. Remove three mounting bolts and power steering pump.
7. Reverse procedure to install. Install new Teflon seal on power steering pressure line fitting nut using Teflon seal replacer set tool No. D90P-3517-A, or equivalent.

4.6L ENGINE

1. Rotate tensioner counterclockwise

and remove accessory drive belt from the power steering pump pulley.
2. Raise and support vehicle.
3. Remove power steering pump pulley using pump pulley remover tool No. T69L-10300-B, or equivalent, **Fig. 7.**
4. Disconnect clamp and suction hose from power steering pump.
5. Disconnect pressure line fitting.
6. Remove pressure line bracket nut.
7. Remove three bolts and power steering pump.
8. Reverse procedure to install, noting the following:
   a. Install new Teflon seal on power steering pressure line fitting nut using Teflon seal replacer set tool No. D90P-3517-A, or equivalent.
   b. Install pulley using pump pulley replacer tool No. T91P-3A733-A, or equivalent.

TIGHTENING SPECIFICATIONS

Year	Component	Torque/Ft. Lbs.
2001–04	ABS Sensor	53①
	ABS Sensor Wire Bracket	21
	Ball Joint To Spindle	129
	Lower Control Arm	148
	Stabilizer Bar Bracket	52
	Stabilizer Bar Link	14
	Steering Gear To Crossmember	52
	Strut To Spindle	148
	Strut Upper Mount	30
	Strut, Upper	74
	Tie Rod To Spindle	41
	Wheel Hub & Bearing Retainer	258
	Wheel Lug Nuts	95
2005	Brake Caliper & Anchor Plate	86
	Brake Disc Dust Shield	15
	Brake Line Bracket	15
	Control Arm Pinch	76
	Heat Shield	89①
	Lower Control Arm	129
	Outer Tie Rod End	59
	Pinch Bolt	76
	Power Steering Line Clamp	17
	Power Steering Pump	18
	Power Steering Pump Pulley	18
	Power Steering Pump Pressure Line	48
	Power Steering Suction Hose Bracket	71①
	Pressure Line Bracket	62①
	Pressure Line Bracket-To-Crossmember	80①
	Stabilizer Bar Link	85
	Stabilizer Bracket	52
	Steering Column Coupling-To-Steering Gear	18
	Steering Gear	85
	Strut	148
	Strut-To-Body	35
	Strut-To-Spindle	148
	Strut, Upper Nit	46
	Wheel Hub Retainer	221

① — Inch lbs.

Wheel Alignment

INDEX

PRELIMINARY INSPECTION

1. Inspect tires for proper inflation and similar tread wear.
2. Inspect hub and bearing for excessive wear.
3. Inspect ball joints.
4. Inspect tie rod ends for excessive looseness.
5. Measure wheel and tire runout.
6. Inspect rack and pinion for looseness at frame.
7. Ensure proper strut operation.
8. Inspect suspension and steering components for damage.
9. Inspect vehicle ride height.

FRONT WHEEL ALIGNMENT

Basic Inspection

Inspect front wheel alignment under following curb load conditions:
1. Spare tire, wheel, jack and jack handle in proper positions.
2. Front seats in rearmost positions.
3. All other loading and aftermarket equipment removed.
4. All tires inflated to specified cold pressure.
5. All excessive mud, dirt and road deposit accumulation removed from chassis and underbody.

Caster

2001–04

Caster angle is preset during production and not adjustable. **However, if caster is still not within specifications by .6° after other sources have been inspected and corrected, perpendicular slot cutting is allowed at the tops of the strut towers. Each millimeter of adjustment will yield approximately .12° in caster change. Do not cut any slots longer than .2 inch in any direction.**

2005

If caster adjustment is required, slot the subframe and install cam bolts. This procedure should only be performed after all other possible sources have been inspected and corrected as required.

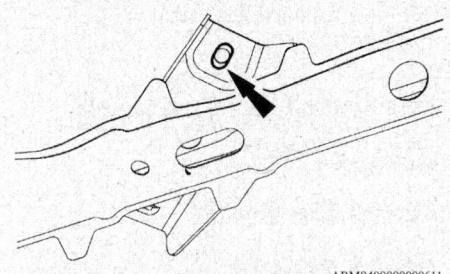

Fig. 1 Subframe hole elongating

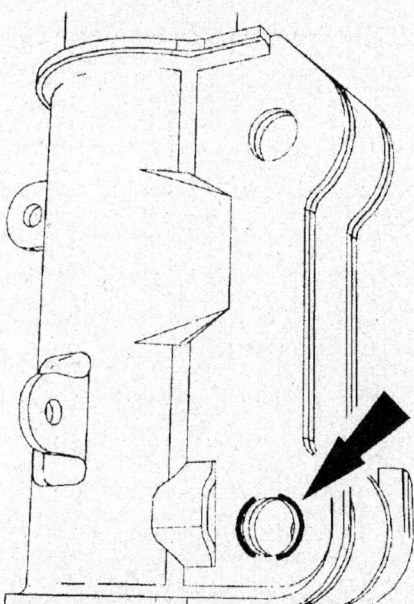

Fig. 2 Strut-to-wheel spindle lower mounting hole elongating

1. Remove front lower control arm as outlined in "Front Suspension & Steering" section.
2. Elongate lower control arm rear outboard mounting hole as indicated by etchings in subframe using suitable grinding tool, **Fig. 1.**
3. Do not elongate hole any more than indicated by etchings on subframe.
4. Remove any burrs, then clean and paint any exposed metal.
5. Install front lower control arm using cam bolt (part No. 4R33-2B236-BA)

and new nut in rear inboard mounting hole.
6. Do not tighten cam bolt until alignment has been corrected.
7. Adjust the front caster using cam bolt until it is within specifications
8. **Torque** nut 129 ft. lbs.

Camber

2001–04

1. Remove camber plate pop rivet.
2. Loosen two strut mount to body apron nuts and one strut mount to body apron bolt.
3. Move top of shock strut to bring camber angle within specifications.
4. **Pop rivet replacement is not required.**

2005

If caster adjustment is required, slot the strut at the lower mounting plate and install cam bolts. This procedure should only be performed after all other possible sources have been inspected and corrected as required.
1. Remove strut and spring as outlined in "Front Suspension & Steering" section.
2. Enlarge strut-to-wheel spindle lower mounting holes as indicated by etchings in strut lower mount using suitable grinding tool, **Fig. 2.**
3. Do not enlarge holes any more than indicated by etchings on strut mount.
4. Remove any burrs, then clean and paint any exposed metal.
5. Install strut and spring using cam bolts (part No. 4R33-2B236-AA) and new nuts in place of regular strut-to-wheel spindle bolts and flag nuts.
6. Do not tighten cam bolts until alignment has been corrected.
7. Adjust front camber using cam bolts until it is within specifications.
8. **Torque** nuts 148 ft. lbs.

Toe-In

1. Determine if steering shaft and steering wheel marks are in alignment and in top position.
2. Loosen clamp screw on tie rod bellows and free seal on rod to prevent bellows from twisting.
3. Loosen tie rod jam nut.

Item	Lefthand		Righthand		Total/Split	
	Limits	Desired	Limits	Desired	Limits	Desired
Front Camber Angle, Degrees	-1.000 to -.600	-.800	-1.200 to -.800	-1.000	0 to +.40	+.20
Front Caster Angle, Degrees	+2.900 to +3.300	+3.100	+3.100 to +3.500	+3.300	-.40 to 0	-.20
Front Toe-In	+.085 to +.165	+.125	+.085 to +.165	+.125	-.17 to +.33	+.25
Rear Camber	-1.000 to -.600	-.800	-1.000 to -.600	-.800	-.20 to +.20	0
Rear Toe-In	+.060 to +.140	+.100	+.060 to +.140	+.100	-.60 to +1.00	+.20

Fig. 3   2003 Cobra revised alignment specifications

4. Turn tie rod inner end to correct adjustment to specifications using suitable pliers, **Do not use pliers on tie rod threads.** Turning to reduce number of threads showing will increase toe-in. Turning in opposite direction will reduce toe-in.
5. Tighten nut.

REAR WHEEL ALIGNMENT

2001 Cobra

On these models the independent rear suspension alignment is adjustable for camber and toe. Performing preliminary inspections, then proceed as follows:

1. Loosen upper control arm pivot nuts.
2. Rotate bolts and cams until camber is within range.
3. Tighten nuts.
4. Loosen toe control jam nuts and rotate toe link until toe is within range.
5. Tighten nuts.

TECHNICAL SERVICE BULLETINS

Drift Or Pull

2003 COBRA

On some of these models there may be a steering drift/pull condition.

This condition may be caused by P275/40R17 tires that are particularly sensitive to road crown and truck ruts.

To correct this condition, proceed as follows:

1. Inspect front tires and ensure pressure is at 32 psi.
2. Inspect front suspension components for wear or play.
3. Inspect steering components for wear or play.
4. Inspect brakes for drag.
5. Align vehicle to revised specifications, **Fig. 3.**

SABLE & TAURUS

INDEX OF SERVICE OPERATIONS

Specifications

GENERAL ENGINE SPECIFICATIONS

Liter (Code①)	Fuel System	Bore & Stroke	Comp. Ratio	Net H.P. @ RPM	Maximum Torque/Ft. Lbs. @ RPM	Normal Oil Pressure, psi
3.0L OHV (U)	SFI	3.50 x 3.14	9.3:1	155 @ 4900	185 @ 3950	40–60②
3.0L DOHC (S)	SFI	3.50 x 3.13	10:1	200 @ 5700	200 @ 4400	11③

DOHC — Dual Overhead Cam
OHV — Overhead Valve
SFI — Sequential Fuel Injection

① — The eighth digit of the VIN denotes engine code.
② — At 2500 RPM w/engine at operat-ing temperature.
③ — At 1500 RPM with engine hot.

TUNE UP SPECIFICATIONS

Liter (Code①)	Spark Plug Gap	Ignition Timing, °BTDC Firing Order Fig. ②	Ignition Timing, °BTDC Man. Trans.	Ignition Timing, °BTDC Auto. Trans.	Ignition Timing, °BTDC Mark Fig.	Curb Idle Speed, RPM Man. Trans.	Curb Idle Speed, RPM Auto. Trans.	Fast Idle Speed, RPM Man. Trans.	Fast Idle Speed, RPM Auto. Trans.	Fuel Pump Pressure, psi	Valve Clear-ance
2001											
3.0L OHV (U)	.044	⑤	—	10⑦	⑧	—	④	—	④	35–55③	⑥
3.0L DOHC (S)	.054	⑨	—	⑦	⑧	—	④	—	④	35–55③	⑥
2002–05											
3.0L OHV (U)	.044	⑨	—	10⑦	—	—	④	—	④	⑩	⑥
3.0L DOHC (S)	.054	⑨	—	⑦	—	—	④	—	④	⑩	⑥

BTDC — Before Top Dead Center
D — Drive
① — The eighth digit of the VIN denotes engine code.
② — Before disconnecting wires from distributor cap or coil, determine location of wire, as position may have been altered from that mounting at end of this chart.
③ — Wrap shop towel around fitting to prevent fuel spillage, then connect suitable fuel pressure gauge to fuel diagnostic valve on fuel rail assembly. Gradually open fuel pressure gauge test valve to relieve fuel system pressure & drain fuel into suitable container. Close fuel pressure gauge test valve. Place ignition switch in ON position. Access output test mode on scan tool & operate fuel pump to obtain maximum fuel pressure. Fuel pump will operate for approximately 8 seconds. Inspect fuel pressure gauge reading.
④ — Idle speed is controlled by an automatic idle control system.
⑤ — Cylinder numbering front to rear, righthand bank, 1, 2, 3; lefthand bank, 4, 5, 6. Firing order 1-4-2-5-3-6, refer to **Fig. A,** for spark plug wire connections at distributor cap.
⑥ — Equipped w/hydraulic valve lifters; no provision for adjustment.
⑦ — Non-adjustable.
⑧ — Equipped w/crankshaft position sensor.
⑨ — Coil on plug ignition system. Cylinder numbering front to rear, righthand bank, 1, 2, 3 ; lefthand bank, 4, 5, 6. Firing order 1-4-2-5-3-6.
⑩ — Key on engine off, 37–45 psi. Key on engine running, 26–45 psi.

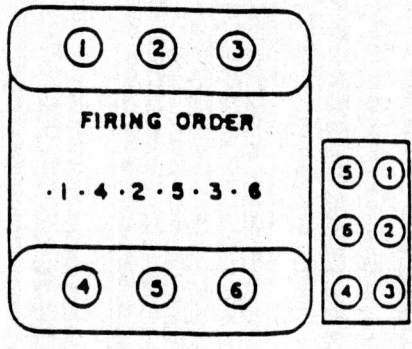

FM1139300273000X

Fig. A

FRONT WHEEL ALIGNMENT SPECIFICATIONS

Model	Caster Angle, Degrees		Camber Angle, Degrees		Total Toe, Inches		Ball Joint Wear
	Limits	Desired	Limits	Desired	Limits	Desired	
			Left	Left			
All	+2.8 to +4.8	+3.8	-1.1 to +.1	-.5	-.22 to +.02	-.1	①

① — Refer to "Ball Joint Inspection" in "Front Suspension & Steering" section.

REAR WHEEL ALIGNMENT SPECIFICATIONS

Model	Camber Angle, Degrees①		Total Toe-In, Inches	
	Limits	Desired	Limits	Desired
Sedan	-1.7 to -.3	-1.0	+.05 to +.23	+.18
Wagon	-.1 to +1.3	+.6	+.05 to +.23	+.18

① — Not adjustable.

VEHICLE RIDE HEIGHT SPECIFICATIONS

Model	Year	Body Style	Manufacturer's Original Tire Size	Measurement Points & Specifications					
				Front			Rear		
				Dim.	Specification		Dim.	Specification	
					Inches	mm		Inches	mm
Sable	2001–05	Sedan	①	E	27.89–28.27	703–723	G	27.22–27.60	686–706
		Wagon	①	E	27.80–28.15	700–720	G	27.47–27.85	692–712
Taurus	2001–05	Sedan	①	E	27.89–28.27	703–723	G	27.22–27.60	686–706
		Wagon	①	E	27.80–28.15	700–720	G	27.47–27.85	692–712

A Dim. — Distance from Front Rocker Panel to Ground

B Dim. — Distance from Rear Rocker Panel to Ground

E Dim. — Ground to Front Wheel Opening Through Centerline of Wheel

G Dim. — Ground to Rear Wheel Opening Through Centerline of Wheel

Dim. — Dimension

① — See door sticker or inside of glove box for manufacturer's original tire size specifications. If tires on vehicle do not match manufacturer's original tire size & measurement is not within limits, it will be required to refer to the Non-Standard Tire & Wheel Size Adjustment To Ride Height Specification & Tire Size Adjustment Charts.

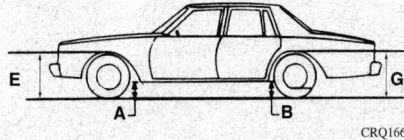

CRQ166

Fig. A   Dimensions A, B, E & G

FLUID CAPACITIES & COOLING SYSTEM DATA

Model	Engine Liter (Code①)	Coolant Capacity, Qts.	Coolant Type	Radiator Cap Relief Pressure, Lbs.	Thermo. Opening Temp. °F	Fuel Tank Gals.	Engine Oil Refill, Qts.②	Transaxle Capacity	
								Manual Trans., Pts.	Auto. Trans., Qts.④
2001									
All	3.0L OHV (U)	11.6	EG	13–18	175–182	16	4.5	—	③
	3.0L DOHC (S)	10.6	EG	13–18	175–182	16	5.5	—	③
2002									
All	3.0L OHV (U)	11.6	⑤	13–18	175–182	16	4.5	—	③
	3.0L DOHC (S)	10.6	⑤	13–18	175–182	16	5.5	—	③
2003–05									
All	3.0L OHV (U)	11.6	⑤	13–18	183–190	16	4.5	—	③
	3.0L DOHC (S)	10.6	⑤	13–18	183–190	16	5.5	—	③

EG — Ethylene Glycol

① — The eighth digit of the VIN denotes engine code.

② — Includes filter.

③ — Models w/AX4S transaxle, 12.25 qts.; models w/AX4N transaxle, 13.50 qts.

④ — Approximate; make final inspection w/dipstick.

⑤ — For models w/green coolant use ethylene glycol. For models w/orange coolant use coolant meeting Ford specifications.

LUBRICANT DATA

Year	Transaxle		Power Steering	Brake System
	Manual	**Automatic**		
2001–05	—	Mercon V	①	DOT 3

① — Motorcraft MERCON Multi-Purpose ATF part No. XT-2-QDX, or equivalent.

Electrical

NOTE: On Air Bag Equipped Models, Refer To "Air Bag System Precautions" Located In The Front Of This Manual For System Disarming & Arming Procedures.

NOTE: Refer To "Computer Relearn Procedures" Located In The Front Of This Manual When Battery Power To The Computer Has Been Interrupted.

INDEX

PRECAUTIONS

Air Bag Systems

Refer to "Air Bag System Precautions" in the front of this manual for system disarming and arming procedures.

Battery Ground Cable

Prior to service, disconnect battery ground cable and isolate as required.

FUSE PANEL & FLASHER LOCATION

The fuse panel is located under the instrument cluster or instrument panel, lefthand of the steering column. The combination turn signal/hazard flasher is located behind on the lefthand side instrument panel reinforcement above the fuse panel.

RELAY CENTER LOCATION

The relay panel/power distribution center is located at the front center of the engine compartment, attached to the radiator support. This panel contains the PCM relay, low fan control relay, high fan control relay and air conditioning WAC relay.

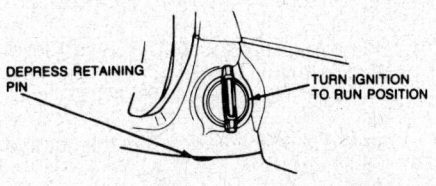

DEPRESS RETAINING PIN

TURN IGNITION TO RUN POSITION

FM9129100011000X

Fig. 1   Ignition lock cylinder replacement

FUEL PUMP RELAY LOCATION

The fuel pump relay is located at the front center of the engine compartment, in the power distribution center.

STARTER

REPLACE

The heavy gauge input lead connected to the starter solenoid is hot at all times. Ensure the protective cap is installed over the terminal and is replaced after service.

1. Raise and support vehicle.
2. Remove lower air deflector.
3. Remove starter solenoid safety cap.
4. Remove starter solenoid and ground stud cables.
5. Remove mounting bolts, stud and starter.
6. Reverse procedure to install.

ALTERNATOR

REPLACE

DOHC Engine

1. Remove accessory drive belt from alternator.
2. Remove mounting nut, then position engine control sensor wiring and hose bracket aside.
3. Loosen alternator pulley nut and remove inboard upper alternator mounting bolt.
4. Loosen outboard upper alternator bolt.
5. Disconnect electrical harness connector and output terminal wiring.
6. Raise and support vehicle, then remove wheel and tire assembly.
7. Remove alternator splash shield and outboard upper alternator bolt.
8. Remove lower alternator bolt.
9. Remove pulley nut and alternator.
10. Reverse procedure to install, noting the following:
    a. **Torque** alternator mounting bolts to 15–22 ft. lbs.
    b. **Torque** alternator output nut to 80–106 inch lbs.
    c. **Torque** alternator pulley nut to 60–100 ft. lbs.

OHV Engine

The alternator is not internally serviceable.

1. Disconnect integral alternator/voltage regulator electrical connectors.

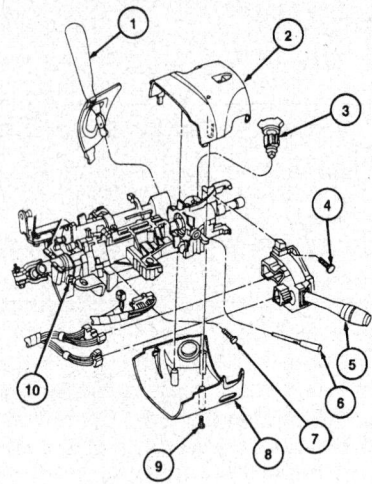

Fig. 2 Ignition switch replacement

Item	Description
1	Gearshift Lever
2	Upper Steering Column Shroud
3	Ignition Lock Assy
4	Screw (2 Req'd)
5	Multi-Function Switch
6	Tilt Steering Column Lock Lever
7	Screw
8	Steering Column Shroud
9	Screw (3 Req'd)
10	Ignition Switch

FM9129600018000X

2. Loosen alternator pivot bolt and remove mounting alternator brace bolt.
3. Disconnect accessory drive belt from alternator pulley.
4. Remove alternator brace.
5. Remove alternator pivot bolt and alternator/voltage regulator.
6. Reverse procedure to install, noting the following:
   a. **Torque** mounting nut and brace bolt to 15–22 ft. lbs.
   b. **Torque** alternator brace bolts to 72–96 inch lbs.
   c. **Torque** pivot bolt to 30–40 ft. lbs.
   d. **Torque** alternator output nut (B+) to 60–84 inch lbs.

IGNITION LOCK
REPLACE

1. Place ignition switch in RUN position.
2. Depress lock cylinder retaining pin with suitable 1/8 inch drill or drift punch while working through steering column lower shroud, **Fig. 1.**
3. Pull ignition lock cylinder from housing.
4. Reverse procedure to install. Ensure proper installation by rotating ignition switch through travel.

IGNITION SWITCH
REPLACE

1. Remove lower instrument panel steering column cover, **Fig. 2.**
2. Turn ignition lock to RUN position.
3. Disconnect ignition switch electrical connector.

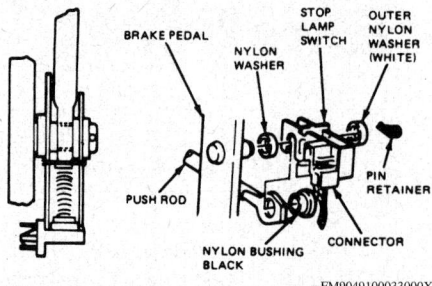

Fig. 3 Stop lamp switch replacement.

4. Remove mounting screws and ignition switch.
5. Reverse procedure to install, noting the following:
   a. Ensure ignition lock is in RUN position when installing ignition switch.
   b. **Torque** ignition switch mounting screws to 50–69 inch lbs.

NEUTRAL SAFETY SWITCH
REPLACE

Neutral safety switch functions are incorporated into the Transaxle Range (TR) sensor.
1. Place manual control lever in Neutral position.
2. Remove engine air cleaner and outlet tube.
3. Disconnect TR sensor electrical connector.
4. Remove manual control lever from transaxle.
5. Remove mounting bolts and TR sensor.
6. Reverse procedure to install, noting the following:
   a. Ensure manual control lever is in Neutral position.
   b. Install transaxle range sensor and mounting bolts loosely.
   c. Align position sensor using manual lever position sensor alignment tool No. T92P-70010-AH, or equivalent.
   d. **Torque** sensor mounting bolts to 84–106 inch lbs.
   e. **Torque** manual lever mounting bolts to 96–132 inch lbs.

HEADLAMP SWITCH
REPLACE

1. Pry headlamp switch housing from instrument panel.
2. Depress release button and pull headlamp switch away from instrument panel.
3. Disconnect electrical connectors and remove headlamp switch.
4. Reverse procedure to install.

STOP LIGHT SWITCH
REPLACE
Removal

1. Lift stop lamp switch harness wiring

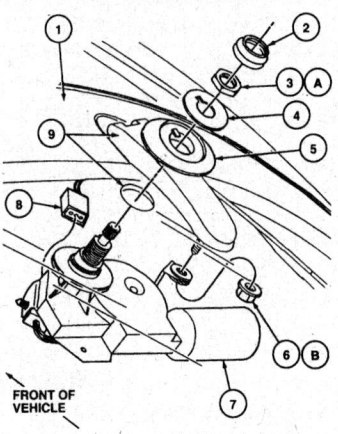

Item	Description
1	Liftgate
2	Windshield Wiper Output Arm Cover
3	Nut
4	Washer
5	Bezel
6	Nut and Washer
7	Windshield Wiper Motor
8	Rear Window Wiper / Washer Wire
9	Liftgate Window
A	Tighten to 15-20 N·m (11-15 Lb-Ft)
B	Tighten to 5-7 N·m (44-62 Lb-In)

FM9029600401000X

Fig. 4 Rear wiper motor replacement

connector locking tab and remove connector.
2. Remove hairpin retainer and white nylon washer.
3. Slide switch and pushrod assembly away from brake pedal.
4. Remove switch, **Fig. 3. Removing master cylinder pushrod, black bushing or one white bushing nearest brake pedal from brake pedal pin is not required.**

Installation

1. Position switch so U-shaped side is nearest brake pedal and directly over brake pedal pin. **Black bushing must be in position in pushrod eyelet with washer face on side away from pedal arm.**
2. Slide switch up and down to trap black plastic bushing and pushrod between two switch side plates.
3. Push switch and pushrod assembly towards brake pedal arm.
4. Install white nylon washer on pedal pin and hairpin retainer. **Do not substitute another type of pin retainer.**
5. Connect wire harness connector to switch and inspect brake lamps for proper operation. Brake lamps should illuminate with less than six pounds of force applied at brake pedal pad.

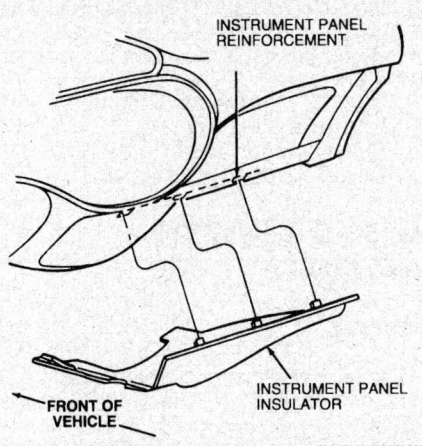

Fig. 5 Instrument panel insulator panel replacement

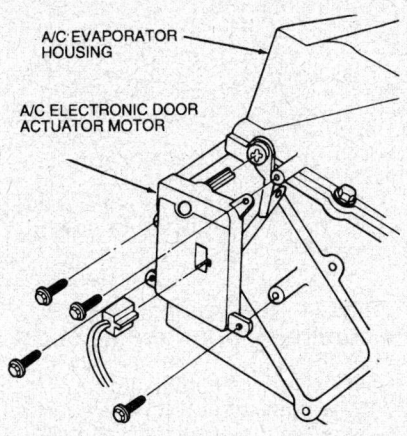

Fig. 6 Air conditioning electronic door actuator motor replacement

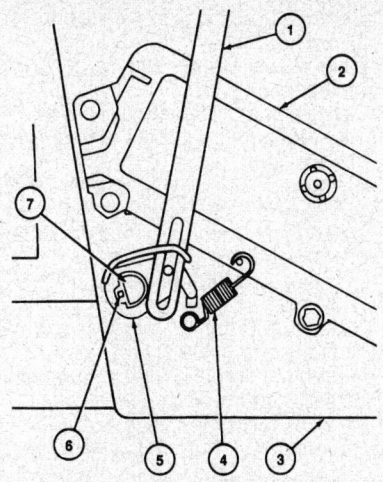

Item	Description
1	Metal Link
2	Heater Core Cover
3	A / C Evaporator Housing
4	Spring
5	Lever
6	Locking Ramp (Part of Secondary A / C Air Temperature Control Door Shaft)
7	Secondary A / C Air Temperature Control Door Shaft

Fig. 7 Spring & metal link replacement

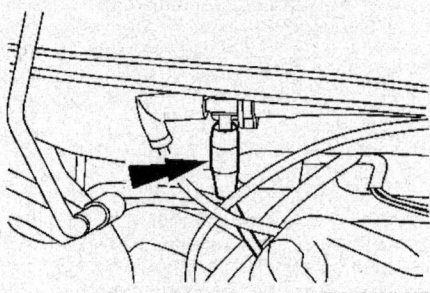

Fig. 8 Vacuum supply hose replacement

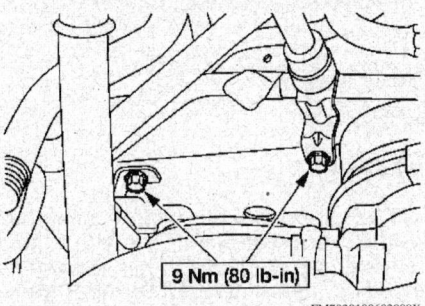

Fig. 9 Air conditioning clamp hold-down bolts replacement

   b. **Torque** tilt lever mounting screw to 6–8 inch lbs.

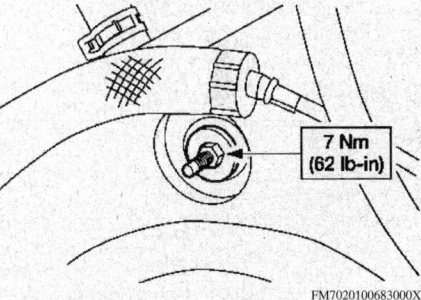

Fig. 10 Evaporator housing replacement

   d. **Torque** new steering wheel mounting bolt to 26–34 ft. lbs.

MULTI-FUNCTION SWITCH
REPLACE

1. **On models equipped with tilt steering column,** move column to lowest position, then remove tilt and key release levers.
2. **On all models,** place ignition switch in RUN position, then depress lock cylinder retaining pin with suitable ⅛ inch drill or drift punch while working through steering column lower shroud, **Fig. 1.**
3. Pull ignition lock cylinder from housing.
4. Rotate replacement lock cylinder to RUN position, depressing retaining pin and insert lock cylinder into housing. Ensure proper installation by rotating ignition switch through travel.
5. Remove upper and lower steering column shrouds.
6. Remove multi-function switch mounting screws and disconnect switch from casting.
7. Disconnect electrical connectors and remove switch.
8. Reverse procedure to install. noting the following:
   a. **Torque** multi-function switch mounting screws to 18–27 inch lbs.

STEERING WHEEL
REPLACE

1. Center front wheels to straight-ahead position.
2. Disconnect speed control wire harness from steering wheel.
3. Remove driver's side air bag module as outlined in "Passive Restraint Systems" chapter.
4. Remove and discard steering wheel mounting bolt.
5. Remove steering wheel using steering wheel puller tool No. T67L-3600-A, or equivalent. Route contact assembly wire harness through steering wheel as wheel is lifted off shaft.
6. Reverse procedure to install, noting the following:
   a. Ensure front wheels are in straight-ahead position.
   b. Route contact assembly wire harness through steering column opening at three o'clock position.
   c. Align steering shaft alignment marks.

INSTRUMENT CLUSTER
REPLACE
Analog
COLUMN SHIFT

1. Pull ignition lock cylinder from housing.
2. Rotate replacement lock cylinder to RUN position, depressing retaining pin and insert lock cylinder into housing. Ensure proper installation by rotating ignition switch through travel.

3. Remove upper and lower steering column shrouds.
4. Remove instrument panel steering column cover.
5. Remove integrated control panel.
6. Tilt steering wheel to its lowest possible position.
7. Remove instrument panel. finish panel.
8. Disconnect PRNDL cable loop from column shift selector tube.
9. Remove adjustment nut and PRNDL cable from bracket.
10. Remove mounting screws and pull cluster toward steering wheel.
11. Disconnect three electrical connectors behind instrument cluster.
12. Remove instrument cluster.
13. Reverse procedure to install.

FLOOR SHIFT

1. Pull ignition lock cylinder from housing.
2. Rotate replacement lock cylinder to RUN position, depressing retaining pin and insert lock cylinder into housing. Ensure proper installation by rotating ignition switch through travel.
3. Remove upper and lower steering column shrouds.
4. Remove mounting screws and instrument finish panel.
5. Tilt steering wheel to its lowest possible position.
6. Remove instrument cluster mounting screws and pull top of cluster toward steering wheel.
7. Disconnect three electrical connectors behind instrument cluster.
8. Remove instrument cluster.
9. Reverse procedure to install.

RADIO
REPLACE

Each audio control is part of the Integrated Control Panel (ICP) and cannot be repaired separately. On the sedan model, the CD changer is located in the lefthand side of the luggage compartment. On the wagon, it is located in the righthand side of the rear quarter panel. On the six-passenger model it is located in the center console.

Integrated Control Panel (ICP)

1. Release mounting clips by install radio removal tool No. T87P-19061-A, or equivalent, to face plate and pushing tool inward approximately 1–1½ inches. **Do not push tool with excessive force.**
2. Apply light even force on tool and remove radio.
3. **On models equipped with automatic temperature control,** disconnect sensor hose and elbow.
4. **On all models,** disconnect radio electrical connectors and antenna lead.
5. Reverse procedure to install.

Radio

1. **On sedan models,** remove lefthand

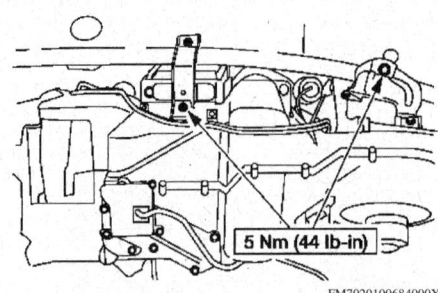

Fig. 11 Evaporator housing mounting support replacement

luggage compartment trim panel.
2. **On wagon models,** remove lefthand spare tire trim panel and spare tire.
3. **On all models,** disconnect wiring connectors and antenna lead in cable.
4. Remove mounting screws, nut and radio.
5. Reverse procedure to install.

WIPER MOTOR
REPLACE
Front

The wiper mounting arm and pivot shafts are connected with non-removable plastic ball joints. Except for the wiper motor, the entire wiper transmission assembly is non-serviceable.

1. **Record normal park positions of wiper arms and blades for installation alignment.**
2. Remove wiper arm mounting nuts from pivot shafts.
3. Turn ignition switch to ON position and wiper switch to LO.
4. Turn ignition switch to OFF position when arms and blades to move to straight up-and-down position.
5. Remove wiper arms from pivot shafts.
6. Turn eight plastic cowl vent screen nuts ¼ turn counterclockwise.
7. Remove clips mounting vent screen to inner panels.
8. Remove mounting screws and wiper assembly.
9. Reverse procedure to install, noting the following:
   a. Turn ignition switch to ON position and wiper control switch to Low or High.
   b. Turn wiper control switch to OFF position after wipers have cycled once or twice.
   c. **Torque** wiper assembly screws to 84–120 inch lbs.
   d. Install wiper arms and blades in their previously recorded park positions.
   e. **Torque** pivot arm nuts to 22–29 ft. lbs.

Rear

1. Open liftgate and remove window wiper motor cover, **Fig. 4.**
2. Disconnect rear window wiper/washer electrical connector.

3. Remove windshield wiper output arm cover.
4. Remove outside mounting nut, washer and bezel.
5. Remove wiper motor to liftgate window hinge mounting nut.
6. Remove wiper motor.
7. Reverse procedure to install.

WIPER SWITCH
REPLACE
Front

The windshield wiper switch is an integral component of the multi-function switch.

1. **On models equipped with tilt steering column,** move column to lowest position, then remove tilt and key release levers.
2. **On all models,** place ignition switch in RUN position, then depress lock cylinder retaining pin with suitable ⅛ inch drill or drift punch while working through steering column lower shroud, **Fig. 1.**
3. Pull ignition lock cylinder from housing.
4. Rotate replacement lock cylinder to RUN position, depressing retaining pin and insert lock cylinder into housing. Ensure proper installation by rotating ignition switch through travel.
5. Remove upper and lower steering column shrouds.
6. Remove multi-function switch mounting screws and disconnect switch from casting.
7. Disconnect electrical connectors and remove switch.
8. Reverse procedure to install. noting the following:
   a. **Torque** multi-function switch mounting screws to 18–27 inch lbs.
   b. **Torque** tilt lever mounting screw to 6–8 inch lbs.

Rear

1. Pull rear wiper/washer switch straight out of instrument panel.
2. Disconnect electrical connector and remove switch.
3. Reverse procedure to install.

WIPER TRANSMISSION
REPLACE

The wiper mounting arm and pivot shafts are connected with non-removable plastic ball joints. Except for the wiper motor, the entire wiper transmission assembly is non-serviceable.

1. **Record normal park positions of wiper arms and blades for installation alignment.**
2. Remove wiper arm mounting nuts from pivot shafts.
3. Turn ignition switch to ON position and wiper switch to LO.
4. Turn ignition switch to OFF position when arms and blades to move to straight up-and-down position.
5. Remove wiper arms from pivot shafts.

6. Turn eight plastic cowl vent screen nuts ¼ turn counterclockwise.
7. Remove clips mounting vent screen to inner panels.
8. Remove mounting screws and wiper assembly.
9. Reverse procedure to install, noting the following:
   a. Turn ignition switch to ON position and wiper control switch to Low or High.
   b. Turn wiper control switch to OFF position after wipers have cycled once or twice.
   c. **Torque** wiper assembly screws to 84–120 inch lbs.
   d. Install wiper arms and blades in their previously recorded park positions.
   e. **Torque** pivot arm nuts to 22–29 ft. lbs.

BLOWER MOTOR
REPLACE

1. Pull instrument panel insulator from lower righthand side instrument panel reinforcement, **Fig. 5.**
2. Disconnect blower motor electrical connector.
3. Remove mounting screws and blower motor from evaporator housing.
4. Reverse procedure to install.

CABIN AIR FILTER
REPLACE

1. Remove righthand cowl vent screen.

2. Remove water shield.
3. Remove cabin air filter.
4. Reverse procedure to install.

HEATER CORE
REPLACE

1. Drain coolant into suitable container.
2. Remove instrument panel as outlined in "Dash Panel Service" chapter.
3. Disconnect heater hoses from core. Plug heater core tubes.
4. Remove four electronic door actuator motor to evaporator housing mounting screws, **Fig. 6.**
5. Disconnect spring from heater core cover and remove it from lever, **Fig. 7.**
6. Gently depress locking ramp and remove lever from secondary air temperature control door end. **Do not bend any part of lever.**
7. Rotate primary air temperature door shaft downward, swing metal link and remove from pin.
8. Remove three mounting screws, heater core cover and seal from evaporator housing.
9. Remove heater core and seal by pushing on tubes.
10. Reverse procedure to install.

EVAPORATOR CORE
REPLACE

The evaporator core is serviced as a core and housing assembly. The evapora-

tor core, internal doors, seals and door linkage are included with the housing. Transfer the blower motor and wheel assembly, heater core and cover, dash panel seals and vacuum actuators to the new housing.
1. Recover refrigerant as outlined in "Air Conditioning" chapter.
2. Drain coolant into suitable container.
3. Remove instrument panel as outlined in "Dash Panel Service" chapter.
4. Remove righthand cowl vent screen and water shield.
5. Disconnect vacuum supply hose, **Fig. 8.**
6. Clamp heater hoses using suitable pinching pliers and disconnect hoses. Cap fittings.
7. Disconnect evaporator outlet spring lock coupling. Cap evaporator outlet tube and suction accumulator tube.
8. Remove air conditioning pipe clamps' hold-down bolts, **Fig. 9.**
9. Disconnect evaporator inlet spring lock coupling. Cap evaporator inlet tube and condenser to evaporator line tube.
10. Remove three evaporator housing mounting nuts, **Fig. 10.**
11. Remove heater outlet floor duct.
12. Remove evaporator housing support bracket mounting nuts, **Fig. 11.**
13. Remove heater/evaporator core housing.
14. Reverse procedure to install.

3.0L Engine

NOTE: On Air Bag Equipped Models, Refer To "Air Bag System Precautions" Located In The Front Of This Manual For System Disarming & Arming Procedures.

NOTE: Refer To "Computer Relearn Procedures" Located In The Front Of This Manual When Battery Power To The Computer Has Been Interrupted.

NOTE: Prior To Performing Any Service Operations Listed In This Section, Consult The "Technical Service Bulletins" Section For Related Information.

INDEX

PRECAUTIONS

Air Bag Systems

Refer to "Air Bag System Precautions" in the front of this manual for system disarming and arming procedures.

Flexible Fuel Models

Flexible Fuel (FF) vehicles use unique methanol-compatible components. Certain gasoline-only components may appear identical to these FF vehicle components.

Under no circumstances should these components be interchanged.

Fuel System Pressure Relief

When releasing fuel pressure on flexible fuel vehicles, use methanol resistant gloves and eye protection. Avoid prolonged skin contact with liquid or breathing of vapors.

If methanol fuel should be spilled on paint, flush immediately with cold water. **Do not wipe, or paint damage may occur.**

Fuel supply lines will remain pressurized for long periods of time after engine shutdown. This pressure must be relieved before any service is attempted. A valve is provided on the fuel rail assembly for this purpose.

1. Remove air cleaner assembly.
2. Connect pressure gauge tool No. T80L-9974-A or T80L-9974-B, or equivalent, onto fuel rail assembly fuel valve.
3. Open manual valve on pressure gauge tool.
4. To pressurize fuel system, proceed as follows:
   a. Install pressure gauge tool onto fuel rail pressure fitting.

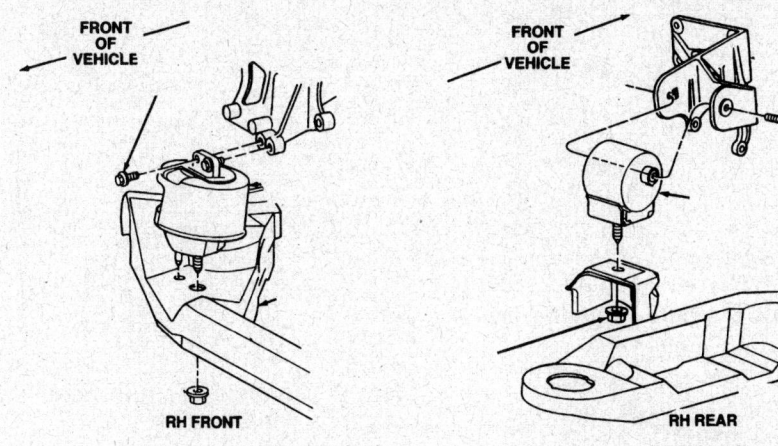

Fig. 1 Engine mount replacement. DOHC engine

b. Turn ignition switch to ON position for three seconds, 5–10 times until pressure gauge indicates 13 psi.

Battery Ground Cable

Prior to service, disconnect battery ground cable and isolate as required.

COMPRESSION PRESSURE

Perform compression inspection with engine at normal operating temperature, spark plugs removed and throttle wide open.

The lowest cylinder must be within 75 percent of the highest cylinder.

ENGINE MOUNT
REPLACE
Front

1. Raise and support vehicle.
2. Place suitable jack and wood block under engine block.
3. Remove lefthand and righthand front engine support insulator to subframe mounting nuts, **Figs. 1 and 2.**
4. Raise jack enough to remove load from support insulators.
5. Remove mounting bolts, then the lefthand and righthand engine support insulators.
6. Reverse procedure to install.

Engine & Transaxle

1. Raise and support vehicle. Remove lefthand front tire and wheel assembly.
2. Support transaxle with suitable transaxle jack.
3. Remove engine and transaxle support insulator to rear engine and transaxle bracket mounting nut, **Fig. 3.**
4. Remove two engine and transaxle support insulator to subframe through bolts.
5. Raise transaxle enough to remove

load from engine and transaxle support insulator.
6. Remove support insulator.
7. Reverse procedure to install.

ENGINE
REPLACE

1. Drain cooling system into suitable container.
2. Remove cowl vent screen and cowl vent extension.
3. Remove engine air cleaner and outlet tube.
4. Recover refrigerant as outlined in "Air Conditioning" chapter.
5. Relieve fuel system pressure as outlined in "Precautions."
6. Disconnect and position steering column input shaft coupling aside.
7. Remove snow shield, **Fig. 4.**
8. Disconnect accelerator and speed control actuator cables, then the throttle return spring from throttle body. Position accelerator cable bracket aside.
9. Disconnect chassis vacuum hose, **Fig. 5.**
10. Disconnect manual control lever cable from lever and bracket, then set it aside.
11. Disconnect 42-pin and transaxle range sensor electrical connectors.
12. Disconnect upper radiator and heater hoses from thermostat housing.
13. Remove battery.
14. Remove nut and ground strap electrical connector, **Fig. 6.**
15. Disconnect lefthand exhaust manifold flange.
16. Disconnect power steering return hose.
17. Disconnect alternator electrical connectors and position wire harness aside.
18. Disconnect air condition suction tube from accumulator drier.
19. Disconnect fuel supply hose.
20. Remove engine roll restrictor brace and restrictor.
21. Disconnect hose from degas bottle.
22. Disconnect heater water hose.

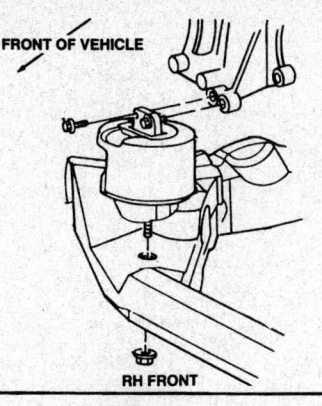

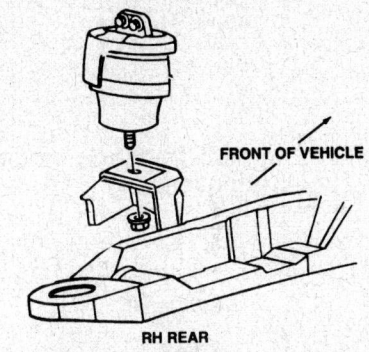

Fig. 2 Engine mount replacement. OHV engine

23. Disconnect electrical ground connectors, **Fig. 7.**
24. Disconnect evaporative emissions canister purge valve electrical connector.
25. Disconnect powertrain control module electrical connector.
26. Raise and support vehicle.
27. Remove valance panel.
28. Disconnect catalyst monitor sensor electrical connector.
29. Remove catalytic converters and Y-pipe assemblies.
30. Remove front wheels.
31. Disconnect air conditioning discharge tube.
32. Disconnect water pump lower radiator hose and radiator support bracket.
33. Disconnect lower radiator hose from radiator and degas bottle supply hose.
34. Disconnect transaxle oil cooler hose.
35. Disconnect wire harness electrical connector.
36. Disconnect auxiliary oil cooler.
37. Drain engine oil into suitable container.
38. Remove starter motor, engine rear plate and torque converter nuts.
39. Disconnect stabilizer links from stabilizer bar and separate lower control arms from steering knuckles.
40. Separate tie rod ends from steering knuckles.
41. Remove both halfshafts from steering knuckles.
42. Support engine with cradle tool No. 014-00765, or equivalent.
43. Remove four subframe to body bolts, **Fig. 8.**

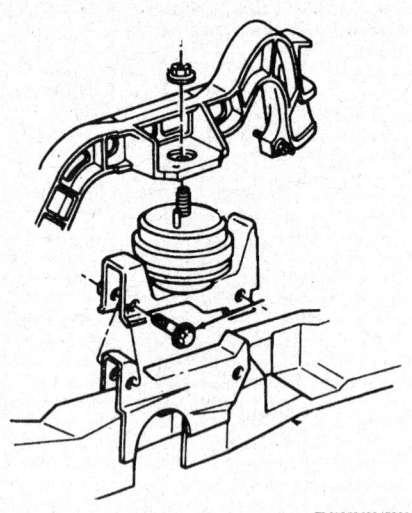

Fig. 3   Engine & transaxle mount replacement

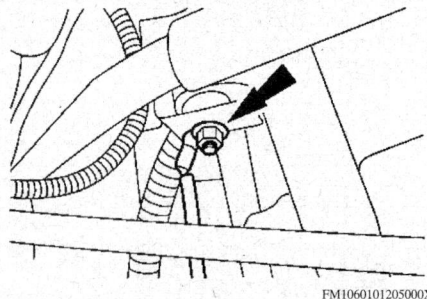

Fig. 6   Ground strap electrical connector replacement

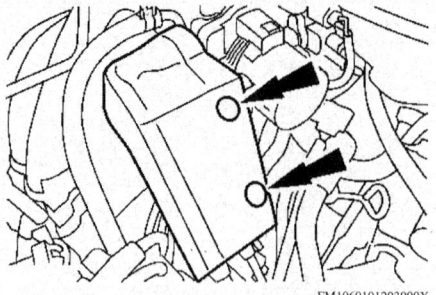

Fig. 4   Snow shield replacement

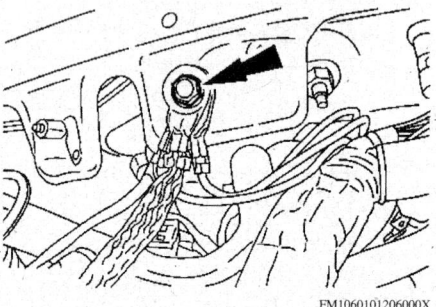

Fig. 7   Ground electrical connectors replacement

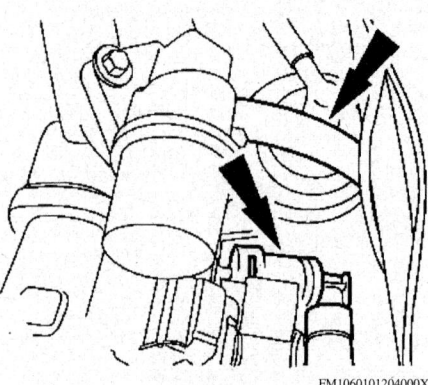

Fig. 5   Chassis vacuum hose replacement

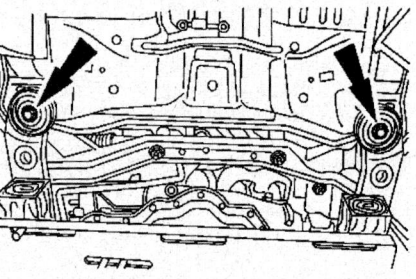

Fig. 8   Subframe to body bolts replacement

44. Lower engine, transaxle and subframe assembly.
45. Reverse procedure to install.

INTAKE MANIFOLD

REPLACE

DOHC Engine

UPPER

1. Remove air cleaner outlet tube.
2. Remove accelerator cable splash shield.
3. Disconnect throttle and cruise control cables.
4. Disconnect throttle position sensor and idle air control valve electrical connectors, then the harness from throttle body.
5. Disconnect Exhaust Gas Recirculation (EGR) vacuum regulator and vacuum supply hoses.
6. Disconnect PCV and EVAP vacuum hoses.
7. Remove EGR valve and vacuum regulator valve.
8. Remove eight mounting bolts and upper intake manifold.
9. Reverse procedure to install, noting the following:
   a. Install new gaskets.
   b. **Torque** upper intake manifold

mounting bolts to 89 inch lbs., in sequence, **Fig. 9.**

LOWER

1. Relieve fuel system pressure as outlined in "Precautions."
2. Remove upper intake manifold as outlined in "Upper."
3. Disconnect fuel line spring lock coupling.
4. Disconnect fuel injector electrical connectors.
5. Remove mounting bolts in sequence, **Fig. 10.**
6. Remove lower intake manifold.
7. Remove fuel rail and injectors.
8. Reverse procedure to install, noting the following:
   a. Install new gaskets.
   b. Lubricate new O-ring seals lightly with suitable motor oil. **Do not use silicone grease.**
   c. **Torque** bolts to 89 inch lbs., in sequence, **Fig. 11.**

OHV Engine

UPPER

1. Remove air cleaner and outlet tube.
2. Remove snow shield, then the accelerator and speed control actuator cables.
3. Remove throttle return spring from throttle body.
4. Remove accelerator cable bracket and position aside.
5. Disconnect vacuum hoses and evaporative emissions return tube.
6. Disconnect idle air control valve and throttle position sensor.
7. Disconnect engine wiring harness from intake manifold support bracket.

8. Remove upper intake manifold support bracket.
9. Disconnect Positive Crankcase Ventilation (PCV) tube from upper intake manifold.
10. Disconnect EGR tube from valve.
11. Disconnect vacuum tube from EGR valve.
12. Disconnect vacuum tube from upper intake manifold and Electronic Vacuum Regulator (EVR).
13. Disconnect electrical connector from EVR.
14. Disconnect wiring harness retaining clip and spark plug wire holder.
15. Remove mounting bolts and upper intake manifold.
16. Reverse procedure to install, noting the following:
    a. Hand tighten mounting bolts in sequence, **Fig. 12.**
    b. **Torque** mounting bolts to 89 inch lbs., in sequence.

LOWER

1. Disconnect fuel supply line.
2. Remove upper intake manifold as outlined in "Upper."
3. Remove both valve covers.
4. Disconnect engine control sensor wiring harness from fuel injectors.
5. Remove fuel injection supply manifold and fuel injectors as an assembly.
6. Disconnect heater hose and coolant temperature sender.
7. Disconnect engine coolant temperature sensor and degas bottle hose.
8. Disconnect upper radiator hose from thermostat housing.

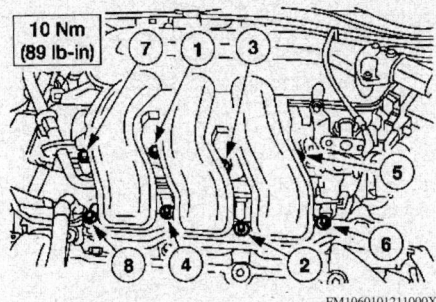

Fig. 9 Upper intake manifold bolt tightening sequence. DOHC engine

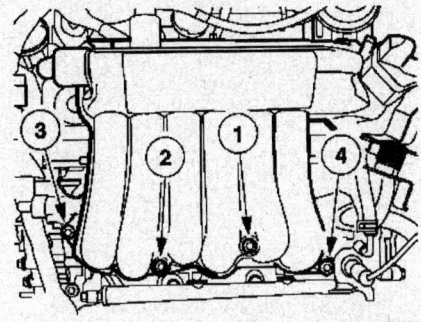

Fig. 12 Upper intake manifold bolt tightening sequence. OHV engine

9. Remove Camshaft Position (CMP) sensor.
10. Remove lower intake manifold.
11. Reverse procedure to install, noting the following:
   a. Apply a drop of silicone gasket and sealant at four cylinder block to cylinder head seams, **Fig. 13**.
   b. Position gaskets and end seals.
   c. **Torque** mounting bolts to 11 ft. lbs., in sequence, **Fig. 14**.
   d. **Torque** bolts to 24 ft. lbs., in sequence, **Fig. 14**.

EXHAUST MANIFOLD
REPLACE
DOHC Engine
LEFTHAND

1. Remove lefthand exhaust manifold to pipe nuts.
2. Remove coolant tube bracket bolt.
3. Disconnect lefthand heated oxygen sensor electrical connector from coolant tube.
4. Raise and support vehicle.
5. Remove pin type retainers, mounting bolts and front splash shield.
6. Remove lower exhaust manifold nuts.
7. Remove coolant tube lower bracket.
8. Lower vehicle.
9. Remove upper mounting nuts and exhaust manifold.
10. Reverse procedure to install, noting the following:

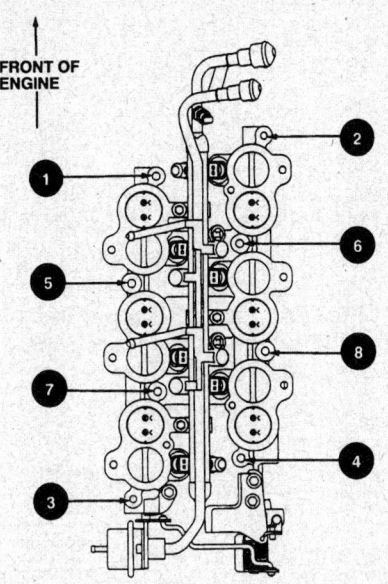

Fig. 10 Lower intake manifold bolt removal sequence. DOHC engine

   a. Install new exhaust manifold gasket.
   b. **Torque** nuts to 13–16 ft. lbs., in sequence, **Fig. 15**.
   c. **Torque** manifold to pipe nuts to 30 ft. lbs.

RIGHTHAND

1. Remove cowl panel grille.
2. Remove righthand valve cover.
3. Disconnect exhaust gas recirculation tube from exhaust manifold.
4. Raise and support vehicle.
5. Remove manifold to Y-pipe nuts.
6. Remove engine support insulator nut.
7. Lower vehicle.
8. Raise engine until exhaust manifold can be removed using suitable engine lifting device.
9. Remove nuts in sequence, **Fig. 16**.
10. Remove exhaust manifold.
11. Reverse procedure to install, noting the following:
   a. Install new exhaust manifold gasket.
   b. **Torque** exhaust manifold nuts to 13–16 ft. lbs., in sequence, **Fig. 17**.

OHV Engine
LEFTHAND

1. Disconnect heated oxygen sensor electrical connector.
2. Remove oil dipstick tube.
3. Disconnect power steering pressure line from power steering pump.
4. Remove nut from power steering line hold-down bracket and position hose aside.
5. Disconnect secondary air injection tube from exhaust manifold.
6. Separate dual converter Y-pipe from exhaust manifold.
7. Remove four exhaust manifold bolts

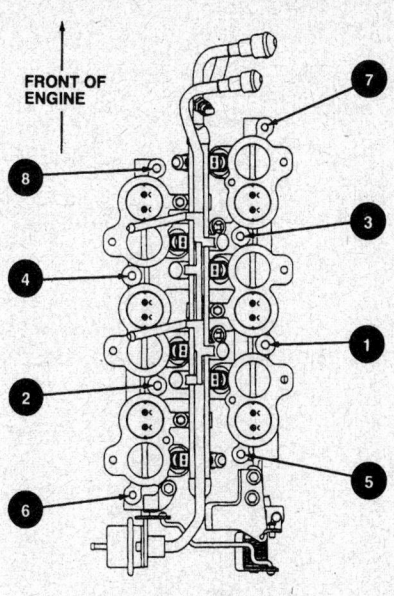

Fig. 11 Lower intake manifold bolt tightening sequence. DOHC engine

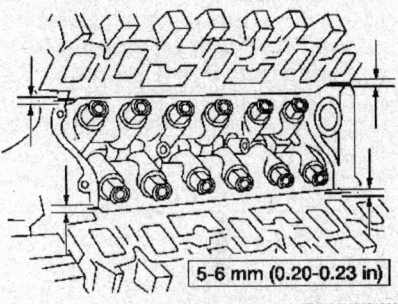

5-6 mm (0.20-0.23 in)

Fig. 13 Lower intake manifold silicone gasket sealant placement. OHV engine

and two stud bolts.
8. Remove exhaust manifold and gasket.
9. Reverse procedure to install, noting the following:
   a. Install new gasket.
   b. **Torque** mounting bolts to 89 inch lbs., in sequence, **Fig. 18**.
   c. **Torque** bolts to 16 ft. lbs., in sequence.

RIGHTHAND

1. Remove cowl vent screen and cowl extension.
2. Disconnect oxygen sensor electrical connector.
3. Remove exhaust manifold to exhaust gas recirculation tube.
4. Remove exhaust manifold heat shield.
5. Disconnect catalytic converter from exhaust manifold.
6. Remove six mounting bolts and exhaust manifold.
7. Reverse procedure to install, noting the following:
   a. Install new exhaust manifold gasket.
   b. **Torque** bolts to 89 inch lbs., in sequence, **Fig. 19**.

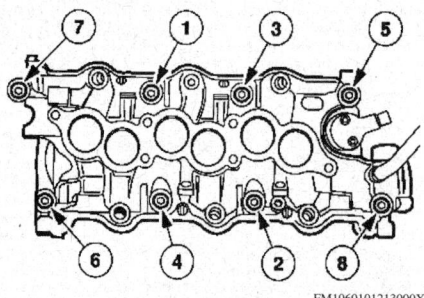

Fig. 14 Lower intake manifold bolt tightening sequence. OHV engine

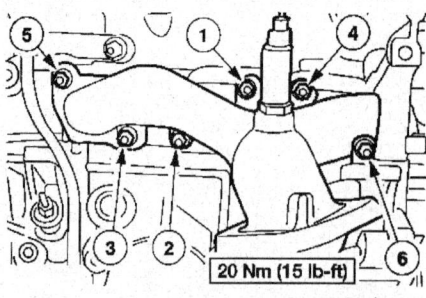

Fig. 15 Lefthand exhaust manifold tightening sequence. DOHC engines

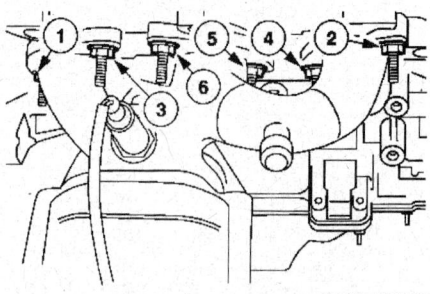

Fig. 16 Righthand exhaust manifold bolt loosening sequence. DOHC engine

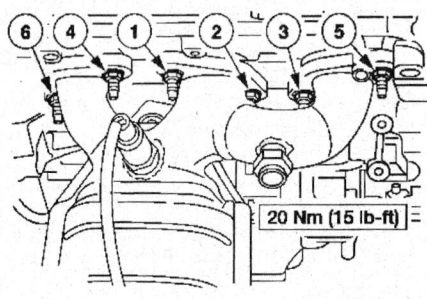

Fig. 17 Righthand exhaust manifold bolt tightening sequence. DOHC engine

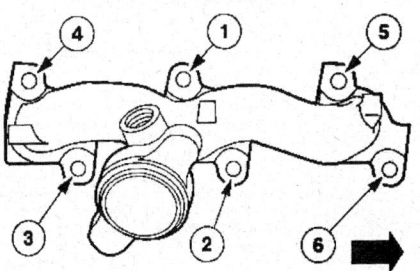

Fig. 18 Lefthand exhaust manifold bolt tightening sequence. OHV engine

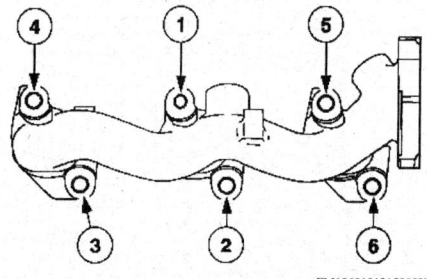

Fig. 19 Righthand exhaust manifold tightening sequence. OHV engine

c. **Torque** bolts to 16 ft. lbs., in sequence.

CYLINDER HEAD
REPLACE

DOHC Engine
LEFTHAND

1. Remove coolant bypass tube.
2. Remove exhaust manifold.
3. Remove water pump as outlined in "Water Pump, Replace."
4. Remove timing chain and gears as outlined in "Timing Chain, Replace."
5. Remove air cleaner outlet tube.
6. Remove accelerator cable splash shield.
7. Disconnect throttle and cruise control cables.
8. Disconnect throttle position sensor and idle air control valve electrical connectors, then the harness from throttle body.
9. Disconnect Exhaust Gas Recirculation (EGR) vacuum regulator and vacuum supply hoses.
10. Disconnect PCV and EVAP vacuum hoses.
11. Remove EGR valve and vacuum regulator valve.
12. Remove eight mounting bolts and upper intake manifold.
13. Remove both valve covers as outlined in "Valve Cover, Replace."
14. Remove camshaft journal cap bolts in sequence, **Fig. 20.**
15. Remove camshafts and rocker arms. Mark rocker arms for installation alignment.

16. Remove camshaft followers and hydraulic lash adjusters.
17. Remove exhaust manifold.
18. Remove cylinder head bolts in sequence, **Fig. 21.**
19. Remove cylinder head. Discard gasket and bolts.
20. Reverse procedure to install, noting the following:
    a. Install new head gasket and bolts. **Bolts are torque to yield design and cannot be reused.**
    b. **Torque** cylinder head bolts to 30 ft. lbs., in sequence, **Fig. 22.**
    c. Tighten head bolts and additional 90° in sequence.
    d. Loosen bolts one full turn.
    e. **Torque** cylinder head bolts to 30 ft. lbs., in sequence.
    f. Tighten bolts an additional 90° in sequence.
    g. Final tighten bolts an additional 90° in sequence.

RIGHTHAND

1. Remove coolant bypass tube.
2. Remove timing chain and gears as outlined in "Timing Chain, Replace."
3. Remove air cleaner outlet tube.
4. Remove accelerator cable splash shield.
5. Disconnect throttle and cruise control cables.
6. Disconnect throttle position sensor and idle air control valve electrical connectors, then the harness from throttle body.
7. Disconnect Exhaust Gas Recirculation (EGR) vacuum regulator and vacuum supply hoses.

8. Disconnect PCV and EVAP vacuum hoses.
9. Remove EGR valve and vacuum regulator valve.
10. Remove eight mounting bolts and upper intake manifold.
11. Remove both valve covers as outlined in "Valve Cover, Replace."
12. Remove camshaft journal cap bolts in sequence, **Fig. 20.**
13. Remove camshafts and rocker arms. Mark rocker arms for installation alignment.
14. Raise and support vehicle.
15. Remove righthand exhaust manifold to pipe bolts.
16. Lower vehicle.
17. Disconnect Exhaust Gas Recirculation (EGR) tube from exhaust manifold.
18. Remove camshaft followers and hydraulic lash adjusters.
19. Remove exhaust manifold as outlined in "Exhaust Manifold, Replace"
20. Remove cylinder head bolts in sequence, **Fig. 21.**
21. Remove cylinder head. Discard gasket and bolts.
22. Reverse procedure to install, noting the following:
    a. Install new head gasket and bolts. **Bolts are torque to yield design and cannot be reused.**
    b. **Torque** cylinder head bolts to 30 ft. lbs., in sequence, **Fig. 22.**
    c. Tighten head bolts and additional 90° in sequence.
    d. Loosen bolts one full turn.
    e. **Torque** cylinder head bolts to 30 ft. lbs., in sequence.
    f. Tighten bolts an additional 90° in sequence.

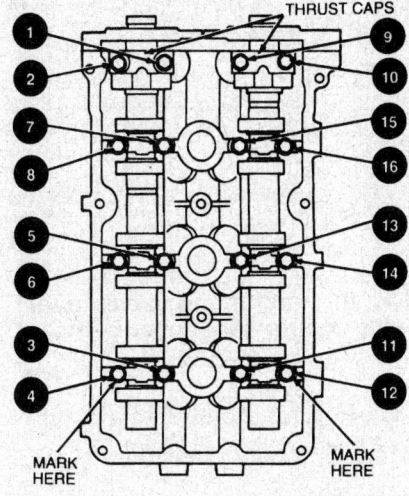

MARK HERE   MARK HERE

FM1069600487000X

Fig. 20 Camshaft journal cap bolt removal sequence. DOHC engine

g. Final tighten bolts an additional 90° in sequence.

OHV Engine

LEFTHAND

1. Remove lower intake manifold as outlined "Intake Manifold, Replace."
2. Remove accessory drive belt.
3. Remove engine anti-roll strut brace.
4. Disconnect alternator electrical connector.
5. Remove alternator.
6. Remove accessory drive belt idler and tensioner pulleys.
7. Remove spark plug wires.
8. Disconnect heated oxygen sensor electrical connector.
9. Remove oil dipstick tube.
10. Disconnect power steering pressure line from power steering pump.
11. Remove nut from power steering line hold-down bracket and position hose aside.
12. Disconnect secondary air injection tube from exhaust manifold.
13. Separate dual converter Y-pipe from exhaust manifold.
14. Remove four exhaust manifold bolts and two stud bolts.
15. Remove exhaust manifold and gasket.
16. Remove power steering pump and bracket assembly.
17. Remove eight mounting bolts and cylinder head.
18. Reverse procedure to install, noting the following:
    a. Installing new head gasket with V notch faces front of engine.
    b. **Torque** cylinder head bolts to 37 ft. lbs., in sequence, **Fig. 23.**
    c. Loosen cylinder head bolts one full turn in sequence.

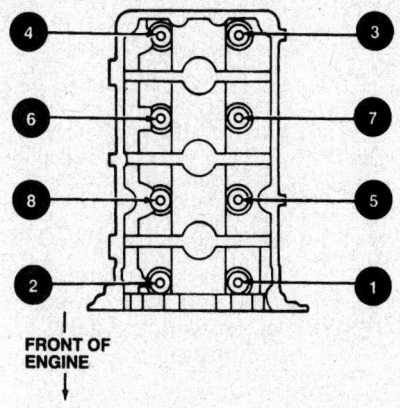

FRONT OF ENGINE

FM1069600488000X

Fig. 21 Cylinder head bolt removal sequence. DOHC engine

d. **Torque** head bolts to 22 ft. lbs., in sequence.
e. Tighten bolts an additional 90° in sequence.
f. Tighten bolts an additional 90° in sequence.

RIGHTHAND

1. Remove lower intake manifold as outlined in "Intake Manifold, Replace."
2. Disconnect Crankshaft Position (CKP) sensor electrical connector.
3. Disconnect oxygen sensor electrical connector.
4. Disconnect wire harness ground connections.
5. Disconnect Powertrain Control Module (PCM) electrical connectors.
6. Disconnect evaporative emissions canister purge valve electrical connector.
7. Position spark plug wires aside.
8. Disconnect Exhaust Gas Recirculation (EGR) tube.
9. Remove exhaust manifold heat shield.
10. Loosen exhaust manifold to catalytic converter bolts.
11. Remove six exhaust manifold to cylinder head bolts.
12. Disconnect engine wire harness locator.
13. Separate catalytic converter heat shield from cylinder head.
14. Remove eight mounting bolts and cylinder head.
15. Reverse procedure to install, noting the following:
    a. Installing new head gasket with V notch faces front of engine.
    b. **Torque** cylinder head bolts to 37 ft. lbs., in sequence, **Fig. 23.**
    c. Loosen cylinder head bolts one full turn in sequence.
    d. **Torque** head bolts to 22 ft. lbs., in sequence.
    e. Tighten bolts an additional 90° in sequence.
    f. Tighten bolts an additional 90° in sequence.

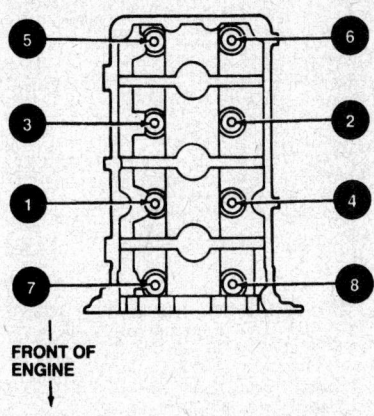

FRONT OF ENGINE

FM1069600490000X

Fig. 22 Cylinder head bolt tightening sequence. DOHC engine

VALVE COVER
REPLACE

DOHC Engine

LEFTHAND

1. Disconnect crankcase ventilation tube from valve cover.
2. Remove water pump drive belt cover.
3. Remove spark plug wire using a slight twisting motion to break seal.
4. Disconnect spark plug wire holder and position aside.
5. Disconnect wiring harness from valve cover and position aside.
6. Remove mounting bolts, studs and valve cover.
7. Reverse procedure to install, noting the following:
    a. Install new valve cover gasket.
    b. Apply 5 mm dot of silicone gasket sealant to front cover to cylinder head joints.
    c. **Torque** valve cover mounting bolts to 89 inch lbs., in sequence, **Fig. 24.**

RIGHTHAND

1. Remove upper intake manifold as outlined in "Intake Manifold, Replace."
2. Remove ignition coil and bracket.
3. Remove spark plug wires.
4. Disconnect differential pressure feedback exhaust gas recirculation electrical connector.
5. Remove wiring harness nut and position harness aside.
6. Disconnect crankcase ventilation tube from valve cover.
7. Remove mounting bolts, studs and valve cover.
8. Reverse procedure to install, noting the following:
    a. Install new valve cover gasket.
    b. Apply 5 mm dot of silicone gasket

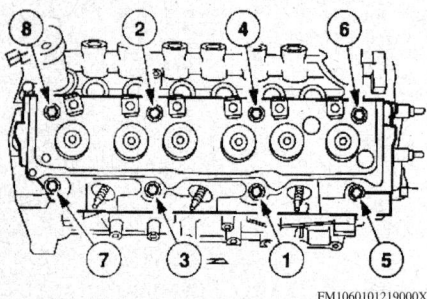

Fig. 23 Cylinder head bolt torque sequence. OHV engine

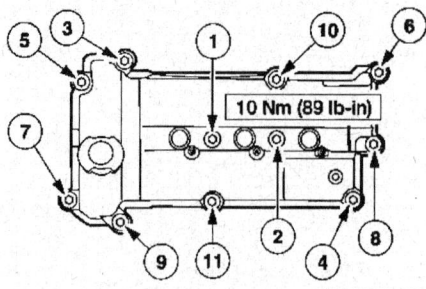

Fig. 24 Lefthand valve cover tightening sequence. DOHC engine

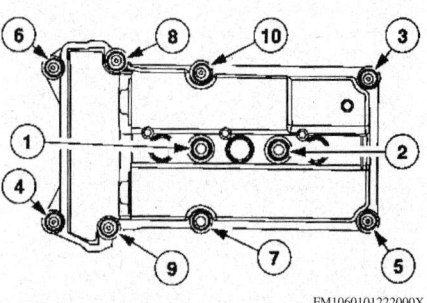

Fig. 25 Righthand valve cover tightening sequence. DOHC engine

and sealant to front cover cylinder head joints.

c. **Torque** valve cover mounting bolts to 89 inch lbs., in sequence, **Fig. 25**.

OHV Engine

LEFTHAND

1. Remove ignition coil.
2. Disconnect crankcase ventilation hose.
3. Position engine wiring harness from front and back of valve cover aside.
4. Remove radio suppressor.
5. Remove retainers and position spark plug wires aside.
6. Remove valve cover.
7. Reverse procedure to install, noting the following:
   a. **Do not clean valve cover with solvent.**
   b. Apply bead of silicone gasket and sealant in two places where cylinder head and intake manifold meet.

RIGHTHAND

1. Remove air cleaner outlet tube.
2. Remove accelerator cable splash shield.
3. Disconnect throttle and cruise control cables.
4. Disconnect throttle position sensor and idle air control valve electrical connectors, then the harness from throttle body.
5. Disconnect Exhaust Gas Recirculation (EGR) vacuum regulator and vacuum supply hoses.
6. Disconnect PCV and EVAP vacuum hoses.
7. Remove EGR valve and vacuum regulator valve.
8. Remove eight mounting bolts and upper intake manifold.
9. Position degas bottle aside.
10. Position fuel charge harness aside.
11. Position spark plug wires aside.
12. Remove valve cover.
13. Reverse procedure to install, noting the following:
    a. **Do not clean valve cover with solvent.**
    b. Apply bead of silicone gasket and sealant in two places where cylin-

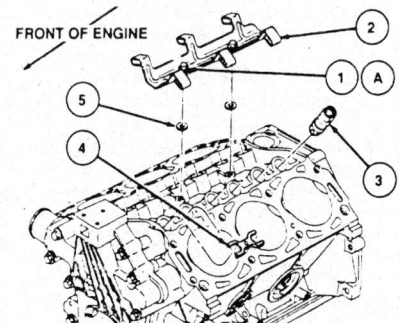

Item	Description
1A	Bolt (2 Req'd) (Part of 6K654)
2	Tappet Guide Plate and Retainer
3	Valve Tappet (12 Req'd)
4	Valve Tappet Guide Plate (6 Req'd)
5	Washer (2 Req'd) (Part of 6K564)
A	Tighten to 10-14 N·m (8-10 Lb·Ft)

Fig. 26 Roller lifter replace. OHV engine

der head and intake manifold meet.

VALVE ARRANGEMENT

OHV Engine

FRONT TO REAR
Righthand ....I-E-I-E-I-E
Lefthand ....E-I-E-I-E-I

CAMSHAFT LOBE LIFT SPECIFICATIONS

DOHC Engine

Exhaust.................................... .188 inch
Intake .... .188 inch

OHV Engine

Exhaust ....264 inch
Intake ....251 inch

VALVE CLEARANCE SPECIFICATIONS

OHV Engine

If any valve train component is replaced or if valve train components become intermixed, valve clearance will have to be inspected on those valves.

1. Apply pressure to push rod side of rocker arm until hydraulic lifter has bled down and bottomed out using suitable pry bar.
2. Ensure clearance between valve stem and rocker arm is .085–.185 inch.

VALVE ADJUSTMENT

Hydraulic valve lifters are used in this engine. No adjustment is required.

HYDRAULIC LIFTERS

REPLACE

OHV Engine

Before replacing a hydraulic valve lifter for noisy operation, ensure the noise is not caused by improper rocker arm to stem clearance, worn rocker arms, pushrods or valve tips.

1. Set engine to cylinder No. 1 TDC compression.
2. Remove intake manifold as outlined in "Intake Manifold, Replace."
3. Loosen remaining rocker arm fulcrum mounting bolts enough to swing rocker arm aside to allow pushrods to be removed and remove pushrods. Keep pushrods in order so they can be returned to original positions.
4. Remove mounting bolts and roller lifter guide retainer plate, **Fig. 26**.
5. Remove roller lifter guide from lifter pair by lifting straight up.
6. **If lifters are stuck in their bores by excessive varnish or gum buildup, use suitable claw type puller to remove roller lifters with a rocking and twisting motion.**
7. Place roller lifter lifters in rack so they can be installed in original positions.

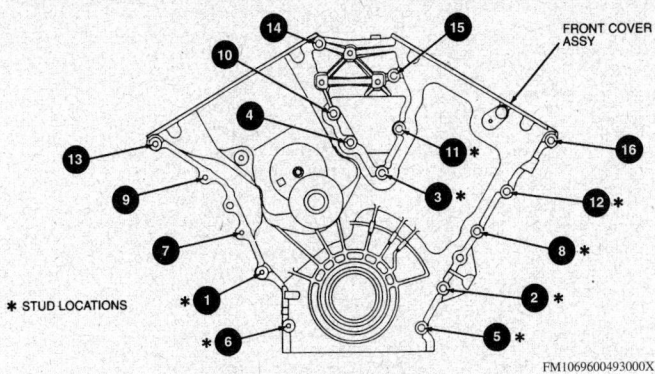

Fig. 27 Front cover bolt tightening sequence. DOHC engine

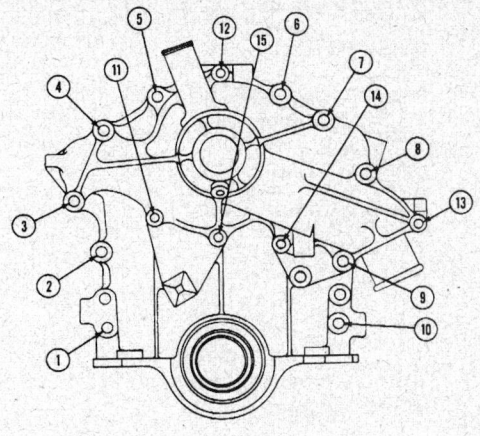

FASTENER AND HOLE NO.	FASTENERS		
	PART NO.	SIZE	FASTENER APPLICATION
1	N804113-S8	M8 x 1.25 x 43.5	F/C TO BLOCK
2	N804113-S100	M8 x 1.25 x 43.5	F/C TO BLOCK
3	N804811-S100	M8 x 1.25 x 70	W/P & F/C TO BLOCK
4	N804811-S8	M8 x 1.25 x 70	W/P & F/C TO BLOCK
5	N605909-S8	M8 x 1.25 x 42	F/C TO BLOCK
6	N804811-S8	M8 x 1.25 x 70	W/P & F/C TO BLOCK
7	N804811-S8	M8 x 1.25 x 70	W/P & F/C TO BLOCK
8	N804811-S8	M8 x 1.25 x 70	W/P & F/C TO BLOCK
9	N804811-S8	M8 x 1.25 x 70	W/P & F/C TO BLOCK
10	N605909-S8	M8 x 1.25 x 42	F/C TO BLOCK
11	N804168-S8	M6 x 1 x 25	W/P TO F/C
12	N804168-S8	M6 x 1 x 25	W/P TO F/C
13	N804168-S8	M6 x 1 x 25	W/P TO F/C
14	N804168-S8	M6 x 1 x 25	W/P TO F/C
15	N804168-S8	M6 x 1 x 25	W/P TO F/C

W/P — Water Pump Assy
F/C — Front Cover Assy
T/P — Timing Pointer

Fig. 28 Timing cover & water pump replacement. OHV engine

8. Reverse procedure to install, noting the following:
   a. Ensure word UP and/or button is facing upward when installing roller lifter guide plates.
   b. Lubricate lifters, lifter bores, rocker arms and pushrods with oil conditioner part No. D9AZ-19579-A, or suitable heavy engine oil.
   c. Starting with engine at cylinder No. 1 TDC compression.
   d. Rotate crankshaft one full turn clockwise.
   e. Install exhaust No. 2 and No. 5, intake No. 1 and No. 4 intake push rod, then the rocker arm assembly.
   f. **Torque** rocker arm mounting bolts to 6–11 ft. lbs.
   g. **Torque** mounting bolts 20–28 ft. lbs.
   h. Rotate crankshaft 1/3 turn clockwise.
   i. Install remaining push rod and rocker arm assemblies.
   j. **Torque** rocker arm mounting bolts to 6–11 ft. lbs.
   k. **Torque** mounting bolts 20–28 ft. lbs.
   l. Ensure rocker arm bolts are fully seated to their shoulder after tightening.
   m. If any valve train components were replaced or intermixed, inspect valve clearance as outlined in "Valve Clearance Specifications."

FRONT COVER
REPLACE
DOHC Engine

1. Remove lefthand and righthand valve covers as outlined in "Valve Cover, Replace."
2. Remove power steering pump.
3. Raise and support vehicle.
4. Remove righthand front wheel and inner splash shield.
5. Remove dual converter Y-pipe.
6. Drain engine oil into suitable container.
7. Remove engine to transaxle bracket.
8. Remove torque converter inspection cover.
9. Remove oil pan.
10. Remove mounting nut, then position

power steering pressure line and muffler aside.
11. Remove alternator, crankshaft pulley and Crankshaft Position (CKP) sensor.
12. Remove air conditioning compressor to front cover bracket.
13. Disconnect Camshaft Position (CMP) sensor.
14. Remove belt tensioner.
15. Remove engine cooling fan.
16. Install suitable engine support tool.
17. Remove upper air conditioning compressor bolts and position air conditioning compressor aside.
18. Lower vehicle.
19. Remove air conditioning bracket.
20. Remove mounting bolts, studs and front cover.
21. Reverse procedure to install, noting the following:
   a. Install new gaskets in front cover.
   b. Apply .24 inch bead of gasket and sealer to cylinder block to lower block and cylinder head mating surfaces. Front cover must be installed and bolts tightened within six minutes of applying sealant.
   c. **Torque** front cover mounting bolt to 18 ft. lbs., in sequence, **Fig. 27.**

OHV Engine

1. Drain coolant into suitable container.
2. Remove engine anti-roll strut brace.
3. Remove engine roll restrictor.
4. Remove coolant expansion tank.
5. Loosen water pump pulley bolts.

6. Raise and support vehicle.
7. Remove crankshaft damper.
8. Disconnect lower radiator hose.
9. Remove Crankshaft Position (CKP) sensor.
10. Raise and support vehicle.
11. Remove starter motor.
12. Remove engine rear plate.
13. Drain engine oil into suitable container.
14. Remove oil pan.
15. Remove alternator and support brace.
16. Remove accessory drive belt, drive belt idler pulley and drive belt tensioner.
17. Remove air conditioning compressor bracket.
18. Disconnect heater hose.
19. Remove water pump pulley.
20. Remove engine front cover and water pump as an assembly.
21. Reverse procedure to install, noting the following:
   a. Apply pipe sealant with Teflon to bolts No. 1, 2, 3, 6 and 7, **Fig. 28.**
   b. **Torque** front cover mounting bolts to 18 ft. lbs., in sequence, **Fig. 28.**

FRONT COVER SEAL
REPLACE
OHV Engine
REMOVAL

1. Loosen accessory drive belts and remove righthand front wheel.
2. Remove four crankshaft pulley to

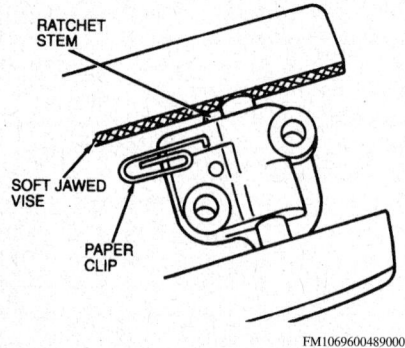

Fig. 29 Timing chain tensioner. DOHC engine

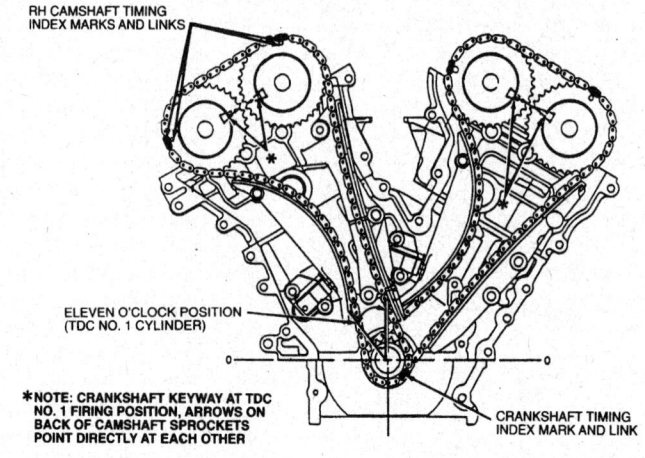

Fig. 30 Timing mark alignment. DOHC engine

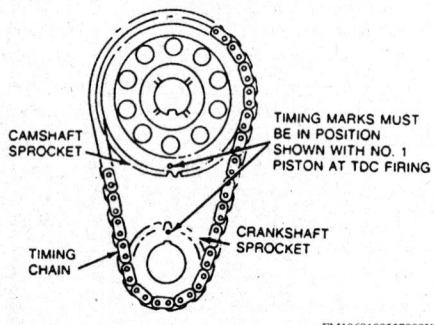

Fig. 31 Timing chain alignment. OHV engine

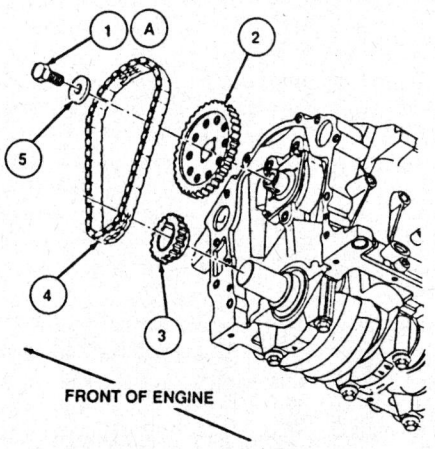

Item	Description
1A	Bolt
2	Camshaft Sprocket
3	Crankshaft Sprocket
4	Timing Chain Lubricate With Oil
5	Washer-Cam Sprocket
A	Tighten to 50-70 N-m (37-51 Lb-Ft)

Fig. 32 Timing chain installation. OHV engine

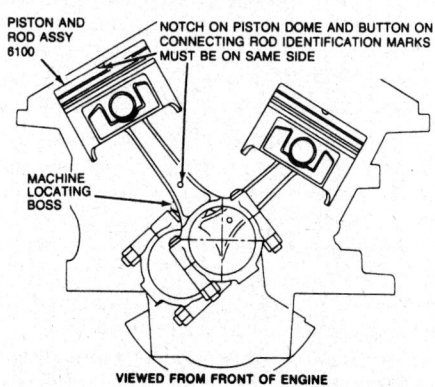

Fig. 33 Piston & rod assembly

damper mounting bolts, then the remove accessory drive belt and pulley.
3. Remove mounting bolt, and vibration damper using suitable puller.
4. Pry seal from front timing cover using flat bladed screwdriver, or other suitable tool. **Do not damage front cover or crankshaft.**

INSTALLATION

1. Lubricate replacement seal lip with suitable, clean engine oil and install seal with suitable seal installer.
2. Lubricate inner hub surface of vibration damper with suitable clean engine oil and apply RTV sealant to keyway of inner hub surface of vibration damper.
3. Install vibration damper and tighten mounting bolt.
4. Install crankshaft pulley and tighten bolts.
5. Install accessory drive belts and right-hand front wheel.

TIMING CHAIN
REPLACE

DOHC Engine

1. Remove engine front cover as outlined in "Front Cover, Replace."
2. Remove ignition pulse wheel.
3. Install damper bolt, remove spark plugs and rotate crankshaft clockwise to position crankshaft keyway in 11 o'clock position.
4. Ensure camshaft are correctly located

in cylinder No. 1 TDC position. If not, rotate crankshaft one additional turn and inspect.
5. Rotate crankshaft clockwise 120° to 3 o'clock position to place righthand camshafts in neutral position. Ensure camshafts are correctly positioned.
6. Remove righthand timing chain tensioner arm, timing chain guide and timing chain.
7. Rotate crankshaft clockwise two times to position crankshaft keyway in 11 o'clock position and ensure camshafts in neutral position.
8. Remove lefthand timing chain tensioner, tensioner arm and timing chain.
9. Remove crankshaft damper bolt.

10. Reverse procedure to install, noting the following:
   a. Position chain tensioner in suitable soft jawed vise.
   b. Hold chain tensioner ratchet lock mechanism away from ratchet stem with suitable small pick and slowly compress timing chain tensioner.
   c. Retain tensioner piston with .06 inch wire, or paper clip, **Fig. 29.**
   d. Ensure timing marks on sprockets and timing chain are aligned, **Fig. 30.**

OHV Engine

1. Remove front engine cover as outlined in "Front Cover, Replace"
2. Rotate crankshaft until piston No. 1 is at TDC and timing marks are aligned, **Fig. 31.**
3. Remove camshaft sprocket mounting bolt and washer.
4. Slide sprockets and timing chain forward, then remove as an assembly.
5. Reverse procedure to install, noting the following:
   a. Slide timing chain and sprockets on with timing marks aligned, **Fig. 32.**
   b. Camshaft bolt is special oil transferring part. **Do not replace with**

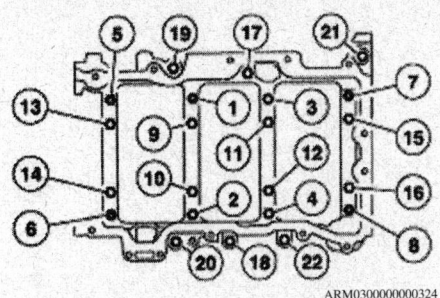

Fig. 34 Main bearing tighten sequence. DOHC engine

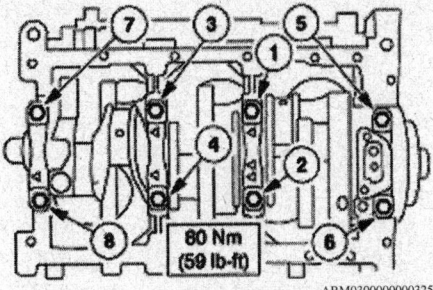

Fig. 35 Main bearing tightening sequence. OHV engine

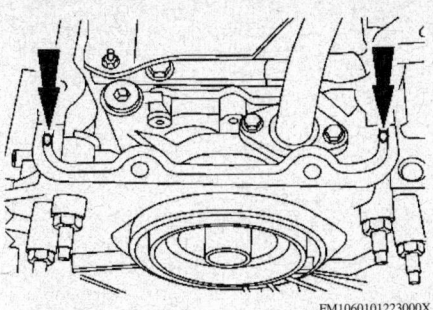

Fig. 36 Silicone gasket and sealer placement. DOHC engine

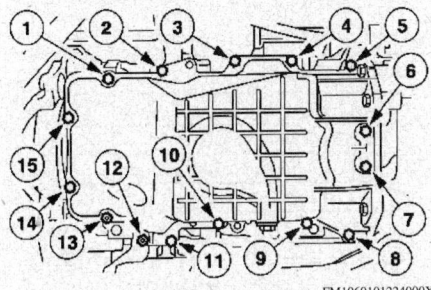

Fig. 37 Oil pan bolt tightening sequence. DOHC engine

standard bolt.

CAMSHAFT
REPLACE
DOHC Engine

1. Remove timing chain and gears as outlined in "Timing Chain, Replace."
2. Remove upper intake manifold as outlined in "Intake Manifold, Replace."
3. Remove both valve covers as outlined in "Valve Cover, Replace."
4. Remove camshaft journal cap bolts in sequence, **Fig. 20.**
5. Remove camshafts and rocker arms. Mark rocker arms for installation alignment.
6. Reverse procedure to install.

OHV Engine

1. Remove engine and mount in suitable work stand.
2. Remove front cover and timing chain as outlined in "Timing Chain, Replace."
3. Remove intake manifolds and hydraulic valve lifters as outlined in "Hydraulic Lifters, Replace."
4. Remove camshaft thrust plate and pull camshaft from cylinder block. **Do not damage bearings, journals and lobes.**
5. Reverse procedure to install. Lubricate lifters, lifter bores, rocker arms and pushrods with oil conditioner part No. D9AZ-19579-A, or suitable heavy engine oil.

PISTON & ROD ASSEMBLY

Assemble the rod to the piston with the notch on the piston dome on the same side as the button on the connecting rod identification marks. Assemble piston and rod assembly in engine with notch in dome facing front of engine, **Fig. 33.**

After installation, inspect connecting rod big end side clearance. Clearance should be .006–.014 inch.

MAIN & ROD BEARINGS

Main bearings are available in standard sizes and undersizes of .001 and .002 inch.

DOHC Engine
CONNECTING ROD

1. **Torque** connecting rod caps and bolts to 17 ft. lbs.
2. **Torque** caps and bolts to 32 ft. lbs.

MAIN BEARINGS

The bolts and studs vary in size and length. Ensure bolts and studs are installed in correct position.
1. **Torque** bolts and studs 1–8 to 18 ft. lbs., in sequence, **Fig. 34.**
2. **Torque** bolts and studs 9–16 to 30 ft. lbs.
3. Tighten bolts and studs 1–16 an additional 90° in sequence.
4. **Torque** bolts and studs 17–22 to 18 ft. lbs., in sequence.

OHV
MAIN BEARINGS

Torque bolts to 59 ft. lbs., in pairs sequence, **Fig. 35.**

CRANKSHAFT REAR OIL SEAL
REPLACE

1. Remove transaxle as outlined in MOTOR's **"Domestic Transmission Manual, In-Vehicle Service"** manual.
2. Remove flywheel.
3. Remove rear cover plate.
4. Punch hole into seal metal surface between lip and block using suitable tool.
5. Remove seal using slide hammer tool No. T77L-9533-B, or equivalent.
6. Coat crankshaft seal area and lip with suitable engine oil.

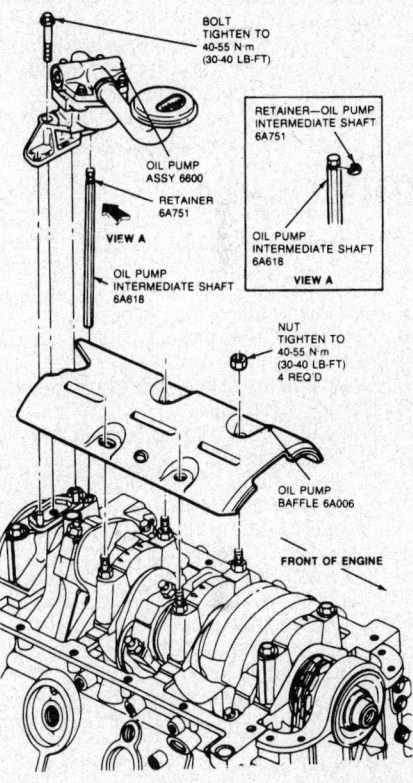

Fig. 38 Oil pump replacement. OHV engine

7. Install seal using tool No. T82L-6701-A, or equivalent.
8. Install rear cover plate and two dowels.
9. Install flywheel.
10. Install transaxle as outlined in **MOTOR's "Domestic Transmission Manual, In-Vehicle Service"** manual.

OIL PAN
REPLACE
DOHC Engine

1. Raise and support vehicle.
2. Remove righthand front wheel and inner splash shield.
3. Remove dual converter Y-pipe.
4. Drain engine oil into suitable container.
5. Remove engine to transaxle bracket.
6. Remove torque converter inspection cover.
7. Remove oil pan.

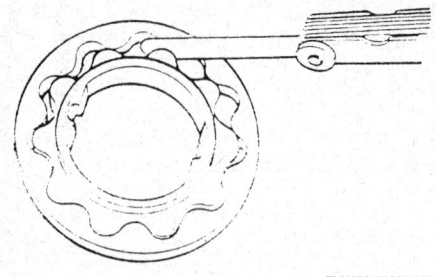

Fig. 39 Oil pump tip clearance. OHV engine

8. Reverse procedure to install, noting the following:
   a. Apply .40 inch diameter dot of suitable silicone gasket and sealer to areas indicated, **Fig. 36.**
   b. **Torque** oil pan mounting bolts to 18 ft. lbs., in sequence, **Fig. 37.**

OHV Engine

This procedure has been modified by a Technical Service Bulletin.
1. Raise and support vehicle.
2. Remove dual converter Y-pipe.
3. Remove starter motor.
4. Remove engine rear plate.
5. Drain engine oil into suitable container.
6. Remove oil pan.
7. Reverse procedure to install, noting the following:
   a. Apply bead of silicone gasket and sealant to front cover and in rear main bearing cap-to-block parting lines.
   b. Install new, longer mounting bolts (kit part No. 2U7Z-6710-AA, includes new gasket).
   c. **Torque** four corner mounting bolts to 106 inch lbs.
   d. **Torque** remaining 16 mounting bolts from back to front to 106 inch lbs.
   e. After engine has run and cooling fan cycles at least once, stop engine and **torque** mounting bolts to 106 inch lbs.

OIL PUMP
REPLACE

DOHC Engine

1. Remove timing chains as outlined in "Timing Chain, Replace."
2. Remove mounting bolts and oil pump from crankshaft.
3. Reverse procedure to install.

OHV Engine

1. Remove oil pan as outlined in "Oil Pan, Replace."
2. Remove oil pump mounting bolts, **Fig. 38.**
3. Remove oil pump and intermediate shaft.
4. Pull intermediate shaft from oil pump.
5. Reverse procedure to install. Ensure

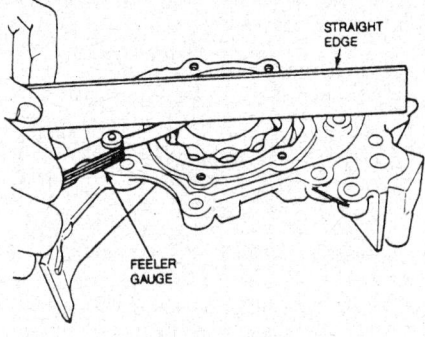

Fig. 40 Oil pump rotor endplay. OHV engine

intermediate shaft retainer clicks into position.

OIL PUMP SERVICE
OHV Engine

1. Wash all components in suitable solvent and dry with compressed air.
2. Ensure all dirt and particles are removed.
3. Inspect inner pump housing for wear or damage.
4. Inspect pump cover mating surface for wear. Scuff marks are normal. If surface is worn or grooved, replace pump.
5. Inspect rotor for nicks, burrs or score marks, and remove imperfections with suitable oil stone.
6. Measure inner tip to outer rotor tip clearance using suitable feeler gauge, **Fig. 39.** Clearance should be .0024–.0071 inch.
7. Install suitable straightedge and measure rotor endplay, **Fig. 40.** Clearance should be .0012–.0035 inch.
8. If any clearance does not meet specifications, replace oil pump.

BELT TENSION DATA

Belt	New, Lbs.	Used, Lbs.
Five-Rib	140–160	110–130
Six-Rib	①	①

① — Automatic tensioner.

SERPENTINE DRIVE BELT

Belt Routing

Refer to **Figs. 41 and 42,** for serpentine drive belt routing.

Belt, Replace

1. **On models equipped with DOHC engine,** rotate drive belt tensioner counterclockwise.
2. **On models equipped with OHV engine,** rotate drive belt tensioner clockwise.
3. **On all models,** remove serpentine drive belt.

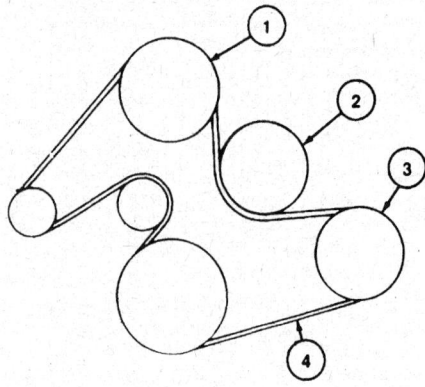

Item	Description
1	Power Steering Pump
2	Water Pump
3	A/C Compressor
4	Drive Belt

Fig. 41 Serpentine belt routing. DOHC engine

4. Reverse procedure to install. Ensure spring keeper releases.

COOLING SYSTEM BLEED

1. Select maximum blower motor and heater temperature settings.
2. Set controls to discharge air through instrument panel air conditioning vents.
3. Start engine and allow to idle until operating temperature is reached.
4. Hot air should now blow through air conditioning vents, temperature gauge should rest in NORMAL range and upper radiator hose should feel hot to touch. **If air discharge remains cool and engine coolant temperature gauge does not move, coolant level is low and must be filled, as follows:**
   a. Stop engine, allow to cool.
   b. Add coolant to bring level to top of Cold Fill mark on de-gas bottle.
   c. Start engine and allow it to idle. Feel for hot air at vents.
5. Stop engine and allow to cool. Inspect for leaks.
6. When engine coolant level indicator flashes, approximately one to 1 ½ quarts of coolant may now be added to de-gas bottle after proper refill.

THERMOSTAT
REPLACE

Removal

1. Drain cooling system into suitable container to below level of upper radiator hose.
2. Remove upper radiator hose.
3. Remove mounting bolts, then the housing and thermostat as an assembly. Discard gasket.

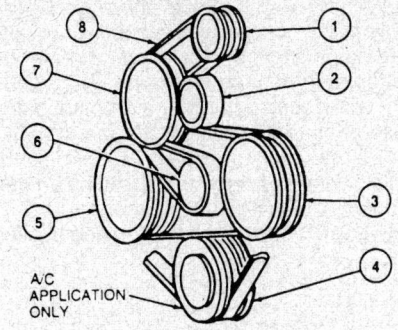

Item	Description
1	Generator
2	Drive Belt Tensioner
3	Power Steering Pump
4	A/C Compressor
5	Crankshaft Pulley
6	Idler Pulley
7	Water Pump
8	Drive Belt

FM1069500393000X

Fig. 42 Serpentine belt routing. OHV engine

Installation

1. Install thermostat into housing. Ensure jiggle valve is up in relation to housing.
2. Install gasket onto housing using bolts to hold position.
3. Install housing and thermostat assembly and mounting bolts.
4. Install upper radiator hose.
5. Fill and bleed cooling system as outlined in "Cooling System Bleed."

WATER PUMP

REPLACE

DOHC Engine

1. Raise and support vehicle.
2. Drain cooling system into suitable container.
3. Remove splash shield.
4. Disconnect water hose from bottom of water pump.
5. Remove radiator lower tube bolt.
6. Lower vehicle.
7. Remove air cleaner, battery and battery tray.
8. Remove water pump belt.
9. Remove radiator upper front tube bolt.
10. Disconnect upper radiator hose and engine vent hose.
11. Disconnect transaxle 10-pin connector.
12. Remove radiator bypass hose assembly.
13. Disconnect thermostat housing and position aside.
14. Disconnect hose from water pump.
15. Remove water pump.
16. Reverse procedure to install, noting the following:
    a. **Torque** water pump mounting bolts to 89 inch lbs.
    b. Tighten mounting bolts an additional 90°.

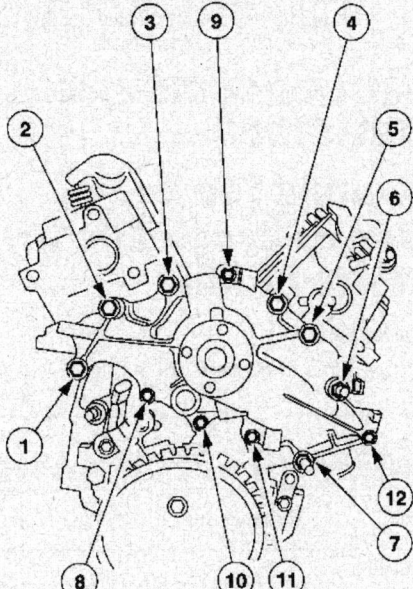

FM1060101225000X

Fig. 43 Water pump bolt tightening sequence. OHV engine

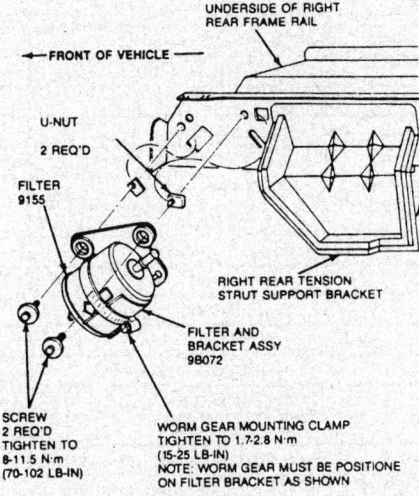

FM1029100143000X

Fig. 45 Fuel filter replacement

OHV Engine

1. Drain cooling system into suitable container.
2. Remove accessory drive belt.
3. Remove engine anti roll strut brace and strut.
4. Remove accessory drive belt tensioner.
5. Remove roll restrictor bracket.
6. Remove bolts and water pump pulley.
7. Disconnect water pump inlet hose and Crankshaft Position (CKP) sensor.
8. Remove support bracket.
9. Remove water pump.
10. Reverse procedure to install, noting the following:
    a. **Torque** numbers 1–7 to 18 ft. lbs., in sequence, **Fig. 43.**
    b. **Torque** numbers 8–12 to 89 inch lbs., in sequence.

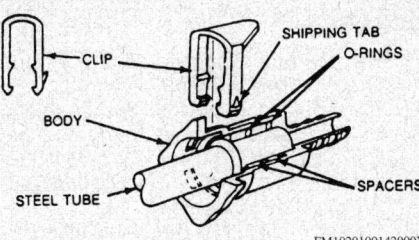

FM1029100142000X

Fig. 44 Push connect fitting removal

RADIATOR

REPLACE

1. Remove battery and battery tray.
2. Drain cooling system into suitable container.
3. Disconnect upper radiator hose.
4. Disconnect degas return hose.
5. Disconnect upper transaxle cooler line using suitable disconnect tool.
6. Remove air conditioning condenser mounting bolts.
7. Raise and support vehicle.
8. Disconnect lower radiator hose and transaxle cooler line.
9. Remove condenser to radiator mounting bolts.
10. Remove power steering cooler to radiator mounting bolts.
11. Remove nuts and radiator support bracket.
12. Remove radiator.
13. Reverse procedure to install.

FUEL PUMP

REPLACE

1. Relieve fuel system pressure as outlined in "Precautions."
2. **On models equipped with flexible fuel,** remove fuel from tank as follows:
    a. Remove foam and rubber protective cover from special quick disconnect fitting on fuel drain tube found on righthand side of fuel tank.
    b. Attach adapter hose tool No. 034-00020, or equivalent, to suitable fuel storage tank.
    c. Pump fuel from tank.
3. **On models equipped with nonflexible fuel,** remove fuel from fuel tank by pumping it out filler neck using suitable fuel storage tanker.
4. **On all models,** raise and support vehicle.
5. Disconnect and remove fuel filler neck.
6. Support fuel tank and remove tank support straps.
7. Lower fuel tank partially, then remove fuel lines, electrical connectors and vent lines.
8. Remove tank and place on suitable workbench.
9. Remove fuel pump locking ring by turning it counterclockwise.
10. Remove fuel pump, bracket and gasket assembly.
11. Reverse procedure to install.

FUEL FILTER
REPLACE

1. Relieve fuel system pressure as outlined in "Precautions."
2. Twist push connect fittings at each end of filter until they move freely on tube.
3. Bend and break shipping tab from hairpin clip and spread two clip legs approximately ⅛ inch, **Fig. 44.**
4. Remove clip from tube and fitting by pulling gently on triangular end.
5. Separate fitting and hose assembly from fuel filter.
6. Install retainer clips in each connect fitting.
7. Loosen worm gear mounting clip and remove filter from bracket, **Fig. 45.**
8. Reverse procedure to install.

TECHNICAL SERVICE BULLETINS

Cooling Fan Body Boom, Rough Idle Or Noise At Idle

2002-03

On some of these models built between April 1 and Oct. 1, 2002, there may be a cooling fan induced body boom, rough idle or unusual engine noise at idle when cooling fan is in high speed mode. The condition will occur with the air conditioning system on and ambient temperature of 80°F or more.

This condition may be caused by an out-of-balance cooling fan assembly.

To correct this condition, replace cooling fan.

TIGHTENING SPECIFICATIONS

Year	Component	Torque/Ft. Lbs.
DOHC ENGINE		
2001–05	Air Conditioning Compressor	18
	Alternator Mounting	18
	Ball Joint Nuts	59
	Camshaft Cap Bolt	89①
	Camshaft Oil Seal Retainer	89①
	Camshaft Position Sensor	89①
	Connecting Rod	⑩
	Crankshaft Position Sensor	89①
	Cylinder Head	②
	EGR Tube	30
	EGR Valve	18
	Engine Mount	52
	Exhaust Manifold	⑤
	Flexplate	59
	Front Cover	⑧
	Fuel Rail	89①
	Halfshaft	191
	Intake Manifold	④
	Knock Sensor	13
	Lefthand Engine Support Insulator, Bolt	52
	Lefthand Engine Support Insulator, Nut	66
	Main Bearing Cap	⑩
	Oil Pan	③
	Oil Pan To Transaxle	30
	Oil Pump	89①
	Oil Separator	89①
	Power Steering Pressure Line	27
	Power Steering Pump	18
	Righthand Engine Support Insulator, Nut	66
	Righthand Engine Support Insulator, Through Bolt	89
	Shifter Cable	13
	Spark Plugs	11
	Steering Shaft Pinch Bolt	18
	Subframe Bolts	76
	Timing Chain Guide	18
	Timing Chain Tensioner	18
	Torque Converter To Flex Plate	27
	Valve Cover	⑥
	Water Pump	⑨

Continued

3.0L ENGINE

TIGHTENING
SPECIFICATIONS—Continued

Year	Component	Torque/Ft. Lbs.
2001–05	Y-Pipe Nuts	30
	Y-Pipe To Exhaust Manifold	30

OHV ENGINE

Year	Component	Torque/Ft. Lbs.
2001–05	Accessory Drive Belt Tensioner	18
	Air Conditioning Compressor To Bracket	18
	Air Conditioning Compressor Bracket To Engine	35
	Air Conditioning Compressor Bracket Stabilizer	18
	Air Conditioning Manifold & Tube	89①
	Accelerator Cable Bracket	13
	Accessory Drive Belt Idler Pulley	35
	Accessory Drive Belt Tensioner Pulley	35
	Camshaft Position Sensor	18①
	Camshaft Sprocket	46
	Camshaft Synchronizer Clamp	18
	Camshaft Thrust Plate	89①
	Connecting Rod	26
	Crankshaft Damper	107
	Crankshaft Pulley	35
	Cylinder Head	②
	EGR Tube, Righthand Exhaust	30
	EGR Tube, EGR Valve	30
	EGR Valve	18
	Engine Rear Insulator To Front Subframe	40
	Engine Rear Insulator To Transaxle Bracket	72
	Engine Rear Plate	106①
	Engine Roll Restrictor	35
	Engine Roll Restrictor To Front Cover & Alternator	18
	Exhaust Manifold Heat Shield	89①
	Exhaust Manifold	⑤
	Flywheel	59
	Front Cover	⑧
	Fuel Injection Supply Manifold	89①
	Halfshaft To Steering Knuckle	190
	Intake Manifold	④
	Lower Control Arm To Steering Knuckle	59
	Main Bearing Cap	⑩
	Oil Filter Mounting Boss	25
	Oil Pan	③
	Oil Pan Drain Plug	10
	Oil Pump	35
	Power Steering Pressure Line	35
	Power Steering Pump Bracket	35
	Rocker Arm	⑦
	Righthand Engine Insulator To Front Subframe	66
	Righthand Engine Insulator Bracket To Transaxle	44
	Righthand Engine Insulator Through Bolt	89
	Secondary Air Injection Tube	30
	Spark Plugs	11
	Starter Motor	18

Continued

TIGHTENING SPECIFICATIONS—Continued

Year	Component	Torque/Ft. Lbs.
2001–05	Transaxle to Engine	37
	Valve Cover	106①
	Water Pump	⑨

① — Inch lbs.
② — Refer to "Cylinder Head, Replace" for tightening specifications and sequence.
③ — Refer to "Oil Pan, Replace" for tightening specifications and sequence.
④ — Refer to "Intake Manifold, Replace" for tightening specifications and sequence.
⑤ — Refer to "Exhaust Manifold, Replace" for tightening specifications and sequence.
⑥ — Refer to "Valve Cover, Replace" for tightening specifications and sequence.
⑦ — Refer to "Hydraulic Lifters, Replace" for tightening specifications and sequence.
⑧ — Refer to "Front Cover, Replace" for tightening specifications and sequence.
⑨ — Refer to "Water Pump, Replace" for tightening specifications and sequence.
⑩ — Refer to "Main & Rod Bearings" for tightening specifications and sequence.

Rear Suspension

NOTE: On Air Bag Equipped Models, Refer To "Air Bag System Precautions" Located In The Front Of This Manual For System Disarming & Arming Procedures.

NOTE: Refer To "Computer Relearn Procedures" Located In The Front Of This Manual When Battery Power To The Computer Has Been Interrupted.

INDEX

DESCRIPTION

Sedan

These models utilize an independent rear suspension. Each side consists of a McPherson strut, an upper mount and washers, two parallel lower control arms, a tension strut, a spindle and a stabilizer bar mounted on the strut.

The top of the McPherson strut is attached to the inner body side panel, while the lower end of the strut is attached to the spindle with a pinch clamp and bolt. The parallel lower control arms attach to the underbody with nuts and bolts. The tension strut attaches to the lower part of the spindle and to the underbody, **Fig. 1.**

Wagon

These models also utilize an independent rear suspension. Each side consists of an upper and lower control arm, a shock absorber, a two-piece spindle tension control strut and a coil spring.

The top of the shock absorber is attached to the body side panel by a rubber insulated top mount and to the lower control arms by two nuts. The upper control arm attaches to the crossmember and the upper part of the spindle. The lower control arm attaches to the underbody and lower part of the spindle. The coil spring operates against the lower control arm and is located inboard of the shock absorber, **Fig. 2.**

WHEEL BEARING

ADJUST

The rear wheel bearings are of a sealed cartridge design and are not adjustable.

REAR WHEEL SPINDLE

REPLACE

Sedan

1. Remove hub cap or wheel cover.
2. Measure distance from center of hub to lip of fender with vehicle in level static ground position.
3. Remove wheel hub and bearing.
4. Remove brake hose from shock absorber.
5. Remove rear anti-lock brake sensor.
6. **Do not allow brake components to hang from brake hose.**
7. Remove brake backing plate and support with suitable mechanics wire.
8. Remove lower control arm nuts, washers and flag bolts.
9. Remove and discard spindle pinch bolt.
10. Spread pinch joint with suitable large screwdriver.
11. Remove rear spindle.
12. Reverse procedure to install, noting the following:
    a. Cupped side of lower arm mounting washers must face away from bushing.
    b. Install nuts and bolts loosely.
    c. Position suitable floor jack under rear suspension and raise to previously measured height.
    d. Tighten suspension nuts and bolts.

Wagon

1. Remove hub cap or wheel cover.
2. Measure distance from center of hub to lip of fender with vehicle in a level static ground position.
3. Remove wheel hub and bearing.
4. Remove disc brake shield and anti-lock wheel sensor.

5. Place suitable jack stand under lower control arm and slightly raise suspension.
6. Remove and discard bolt and nut, **Fig. 3.**
7. Disconnect shock absorber, then remove washer and bushing.
8. Disconnect upper arm using suitable joint removal tool.
9. Remove wheel spindle. Discard nuts and flag bolts.
10. Reverse procedure to install, noting the following:
    a. Install new flag bolts, nuts and washers.
    b. Before tightening suspension nuts and bolts, raise suspension with suitable floor jack to previous height.

STRUT

REPLACE

1. Position suitable jack or hoist under vehicle, and raise just enough to contact body. **Do not raise vehicle by tension strut.**
2. Remove rear parcel shelf.
3. Raise and support vehicle. Remove tire and wheel assembly.
4. Remove brake differential valve to control arm mounting bolt.
5. Suspend control arm to body using suitable wire.
6. Remove brake hose to shock strut bracket mounting clip and position hose aside.
7. Remove U-bracket, stabilizer bar mounting nut, washer and insulator. Separate stabilizer bar from link.
8. Remove tension strut to spindle mounting nut, washer and insulator.
9. Separate spindle from tension strut by moving it rearward.
10. Remove strut to spindle pinch bolt.

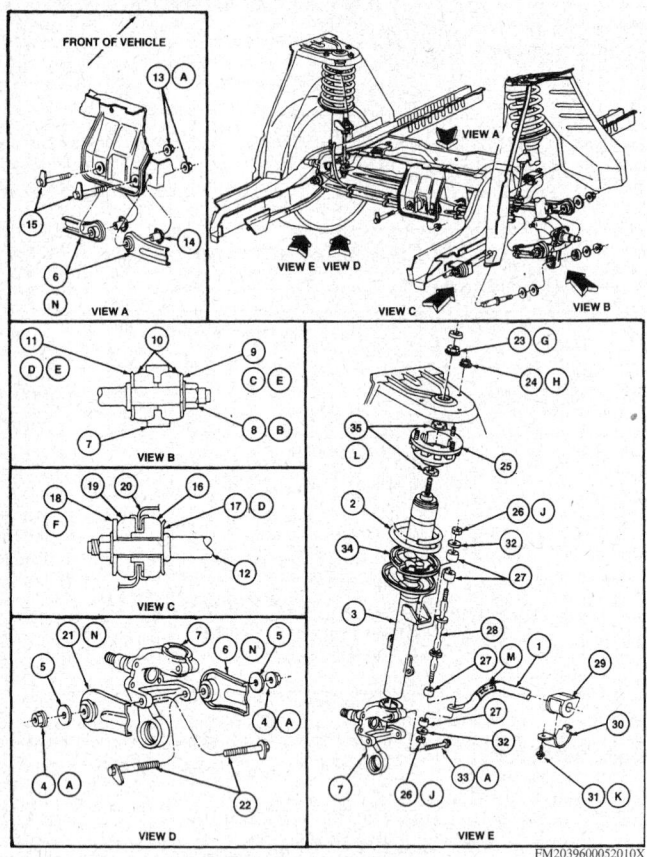

Fig. 1 Exploded view of rear suspension (Part 1 of 2). Sedan

Item	Description
1	Rear Stabilizer Bar
2	Rear Spring
3	Shock Absorber
4	Nut (4 Req'd)
5	Washer (4 Req'd)
6	Rear Lower Suspension Arm (2 Req'd)
7	Rear Wheel Spindle
8	Nut (4 Req'd)
9	Washer (2 Req'd)
10	Rear Suspension Tie Rod Bushing (4 Req'd)
11	Washer (2 Req'd)
12	Rear Suspension Tension Strut (2 Req'd)
13	Nut (4 Req'd)
14	Rear Suspension Arm Adjusting Cam Kit (4 Req'd)
15	Bolt (4 Req'd)
16	Rear Strut Body End Bushing Inner (2 Req'd)
17	Washer (2 Req'd)
18	Washer (2 Req'd)
19	Bushing - Outer (2 Req'd)
20	Body
21	Forward Lower Suspension Arm (2 Req'd)
22	Bolt (4 Req'd)
23	Nut (2 Req'd)
24	Nut (6 Req'd)
25	Rear Shock Absorber Bracket (2 Req'd)
26	Nut (4 Req'd)
27	Lower Suspension Arm Stabilizer Bar Insulator (8 Req'd)
28	Rear Stabilizer Bar Link (2 Req'd)
29	Lower Suspension Arm Stabilizer Bar Insulator (2 Req'd)
30	Stabilizer Bar Bracket (2 Req'd)
31	Bolt (2 Req'd)
32	Washer (4 Req'd)
33	Bolt (2 Req'd)
34	Rear Spring Center Mounting Insulator (Part of 18080)
35	Washer (2 Req'd)
A	Tighten to 68-92 N·m (50-68 Lb-Ft)
B	Tighten to 47-63 N·m (35-46 Lb-Ft)
C	Stamped Rear
D	Stamped This Side Out
E	Assemble N802855-S36 and N801335-S36 As Shown
F	Assemble 5B536 and 5B537 As Shown
G	Tighten to 53-71 N·m (39-53 Lb-Ft)
H	Tighten to 25-34 N·m (19-26 Lb-Ft)
J	Tighten to 7-9 N·m (62-79 Lb-In)
K	Tighten to 34-46 N·m (25-33 Lb-Ft)
L	Dished-Side Down
M	Color Code Must Be Installed on RH Side Of Vehicle
N	Arm Assemblies Must Be Installed As Shown. Trim Flange To Be Rearward On Front Arms And Left Rear Arm. Trim Flange To Be Forward On Right Rear Arm All Arms Are Stamped Bottom On Lower Surface

Fig. 1 Exploded view of rear suspension (Part 2 of 2). Sedan

11. Separate pinch joint using pry bar, or other suitable tool.
12. Remove strut from pinch joint then lower vehicle to allow removal of three strut to inner body mounting bolts.
13. Remove strut. **Do not stretch rear brake hose or kink steel brake line.**
14. Reverse procedure to install, noting the following:
   a. Install new mounting components.
   b. Tighten in order: stabilizer link to strut, strut pinch bolt, tension strut to spindle, stabilizer link to stabilizer bar, stabilizer bar U-bracket and strut top mount.

STRUT SERVICE

1. Remove mounting nut, washer, insulator and link.
2. Mark location of insulator to top mount for assembly alignment.
3. Place strut, spring and upper mount assembly in suitable spring compressor. Compress spring.
4. While preventing strut shaft from turning with suitable six-point deep well socket on top of shaft, remove mounting nut with oxygen sensor wrench tool No. T94P-9472-A, or equivalent. **Do not use vise grips or pliers to hold strut shaft.**
5. Loosen spring compressor tool, then remove top mount bracket assembly, spring insulator and spring, **Fig. 4.**
6. Reverse procedure to install. Ensure

spring is properly located in upper and lower spring seats, **Fig. 5.**

TENSION STRUT
REPLACE
Sedan

1. Raise vehicle on frame contact hoist using lift pads located rearward of front wheels and forward of rear wheels. Raise hoist only enough to contact body.
2. Working inside trunk, loosen, but do not remove, three strut to inner body mounting nuts.
3. Raise vehicle, and remove tire and wheel assembly.
4. Remove and discard tension strut to spindle mounting nut.
5. Remove and discard tension strut to body mounting nut.
6. While moving spindle rearward, remove tension strut.
7. Install new inner washers and bushings on both ends of tension strut, **Fig. 6.**

8. Install tension strut end into body bracket, outer bushing, washers and nut. **Do not tighten nut now.**
9. While moving spindle rearward, install tension strut in spindle, outer bushing, washer and nut.
10. Ensure bushings are properly seated in mountings, **Fig. 6.**
11. Support spindle with suitable jack stand, and working inside trunk, remove three strut to inner body mounting nuts. Install new nuts and tighten.
12. Remove jack stand, and install tire and wheel assembly.
13. Lower vehicle.

Wagon
REMOVAL

1. Raise vehicle on frame contact hoist.
2. Remove wheel and tension strut to lower control arm mounting nut and bolt.
3. Remove tension strut to body bracket mounting nut and bolt, and tension strut.

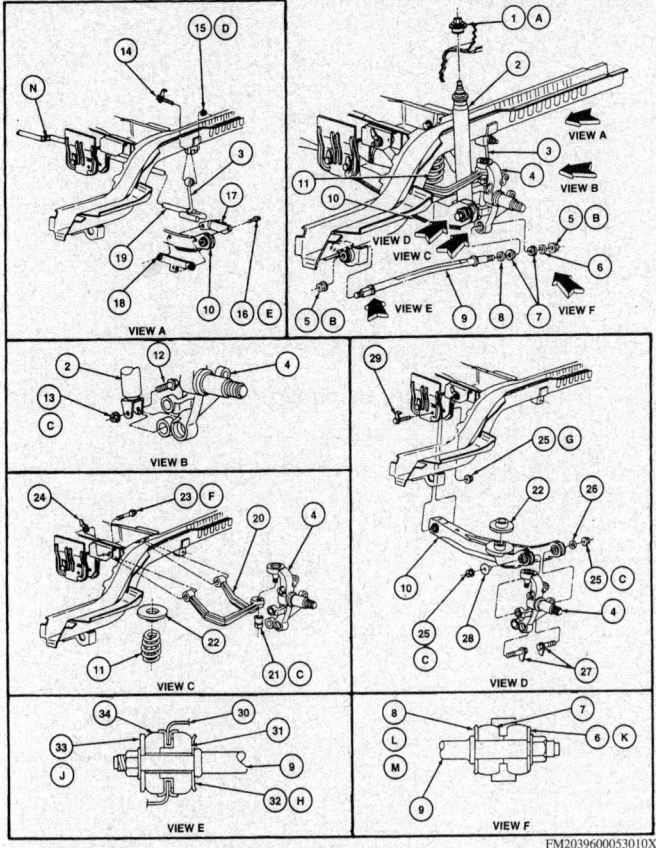

Fig. 2 Exploded view of rear suspension (Part 1 of 2). Wagon

Item	Description	Item	Description
1	Upper Shock Absorber Nut (2 Req'd)	26	Washer (2 Req'd)
2	Shock Absorber (2 Req'd)	27	Bolt (4 Req'd)
3	Rear Stabilizer Bar Link and Bushing	28	Rear Suspension Arm Adjusting Cam Kit (2 Req'd)
4	Rear Wheel Spindle	29	Bolt (2 Req'd)
5	Nut (4 Req'd)	30	Body
6	Washer (2 Req'd)	31	Rear Strut Body End Bushing Inner (2 Req'd)
7	Rear Suspension Tie Rod Bushing (4 Req'd)	32	Washer (2 Req'd)
8	Washer (2 Req'd)	33	Sleeve (2 Req'd)
9	Rear Suspension Tension Strut and Bushing (2 Req'd)	34	Bushing Outer(2 Req'd)
10	Rear Suspension Arm and Bushing	A	Tighten to 25-34 N·m (19-25 Lb-Ft)
11	Rear Spring (2 Req'd)	B	Tighten to 47-63 N·m (35-46 Lb-Ft)
12	Bolt (2 Req'd)	C	Tighten to 68-92 N·m (50-67 Lb-Ft)
13	Nut (2 Req'd)	D	Tighten to 60-80 N·m (45-59 Lb-Ft)
14	Bolt (2 Req'd)	E	Tighten to 19-26 N·m (14-19 Lb-Ft)
15	Nut (2 Req'd)	F	Tighten to 98-132 N·m (73-97 Lb-Ft)
16	Bolt (4 Req'd)	G	Tighten to 54-71 N·m (40-52 Lb-Ft)
17	Stabilizer Bar Bracket	H	Stamped "This Side Out"
18	Nut and Retainer Assembly (2 Req'd)	J	Assemble 5B536 and 5B537 As Shown
19	Rear Stabilizer Bar	K	Stamped "Rear"
20	Rear Suspension Arm and Bushing	L	Stamped "This Side Out"
21	Nut (2 Req'd)	M	Assemble N802855-S36 and N801335-S36 As Shown
22	Rear Spring Insulators (4 Req'd)	N	Color Code Must Be Installed On
23	Bolt (4 Req'd)		
24	Nut (4 Req'd)		
25	Nut (2 Req'd)		

Fig. 2 Exploded view of rear suspension (Part 2 of 2). Wagon

INSTALLATION

1. Insert front end of replacement torsion strut in body bracket, then install new mounting nut and bolt. **Do not tighten now.**
2. Position rear end of torsion strut in lower control arm, then install new mounting nut and bolt.
3. Tighten torsion strut to body bracket mounting nut and bolt.
4. Install wheel and tire assembly.

SHOCK ABSORBER
REPLACE

1. Raise and support rear of vehicle. **If a frame contact hoist is used, support lower control arm with floor jack. If a twin post lift is used, support body with floor jacks on lifting pads forward of tension strut body bracket.**
2. Remove tire and wheel assembly.
3. Loosen shock absorber to lower control arm mounting nuts. **Do not remove nuts now.**
4. Lower vehicle and remove rear compartment access panels.
5. Remove shock absorber top mounting nut, washer and insulator.
6. Raise and support vehicle.
7. Remove absorber to lower control arm mounting nuts and absorber. **Shock absorbers are gas filled and will require effort to collapse.**

8. **Do not grip shock absorber shafts with pliers or vise grips.**
9. Reverse procedure to install. **Use new bushing repair kit.**

COIL SPRING
REPLACE
Removal

1. Raise vehicle on frame contact hoist.
2. Raise lower control arm to normal curb height using suitable floor jack.
3. Remove tire and wheel assembly.
4. Remove brake hose bracket from body.
5. Remove shock absorber.
6. Install spring cage tool No. 164-R3555, or equivalent, on spring.
7. Remove and discard upper ball joint nut, then separate joint from spindle.
8. Slowly lower rear suspension arm and bushing, then remove spring and its insulators.

Installation

1. Install lower spring insulator on control arm. Ensure insulator is seated properly.
2. Position upper insulator on spring and install spring on lower control arm. Ensure spring is properly seated.
3. Slowly raise suspension arm and

bushing, guiding upper insulator onto upper spring seat on underbody.
4. Position upper ball joint into suspension arm and bushing.
5. Install shock absorber, stabilizer bar and bracket.
6. Remove spring cage tool.
7. Install brake hose bracket to body.
8. Install tire and wheel assembly.
9. Lower vehicle and inspect rear wheel alignment.

CONTROL ARM
REPLACE
Lower
SEDAN
REMOVAL

1. Raise and support vehicle. **Do not support tension strut and bushing.**
2. Disconnect brake proportioning valve from lefthand front control arm, parking brake cable and conduit from control arms.
3. Remove control arm to spindle mounting bolt, nut and washer.
4. Remove body bracket mounting bolt, nut and control arm.

INSTALLATION

1. Position control arm at body bracket, **Fig. 7.**

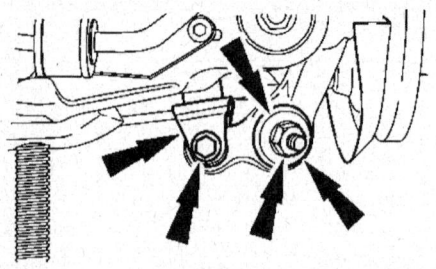

FM1060101226000X

Fig. 3 Rear spindle replacement. Wagon

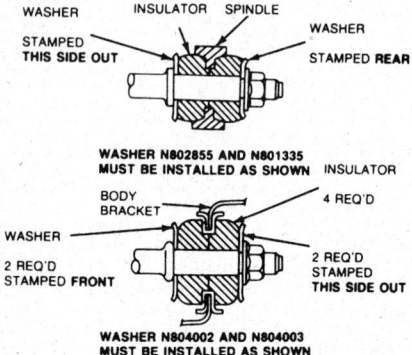

FM2039100032000X

Fig. 6 Tension strut bushing installation. Sedan

2. **Offset must face up** (the arms are stamped bottom on lower edge). Flange edge of righthand rear arm stamping must face front of vehicle. Other three must face rear of vehicle.
3. Control arms have two adjustment cams that fit inside bushings at control arm to body attachment. Cam is installed from rear on lefthand arm and from front on righthand arm.
4. Install new nut and bolt. **Do not tighten now.**
5. Position outer end of arm at spindle, then install new bolt, washer and nut.
6. Attach parking brake cables and brake proportioning valve to control arms.
7. Lower vehicle and inspect rear toe.

WAGON
REMOVAL
1. Raise and support rear of vehicle.
2. Remove tire and wheel assembly.
3. Remove rear spring as outlined in "Coil Spring, Replace."
4. Remove lower control arm to body bracket mounting bolt and control arm.

INSTALLATION
1. Position lower control arm in body bracket.
2. Install new nut and bolt with bolt head toward front of vehicle. **Do not tighten now.**
3. Install rear spring as outlined in "Coil Spring, Replace."
4. Support lower control arm at normal curb height and tighten control arm to body bracket mounting bolt.
5. Tighten lower control arm to spindle

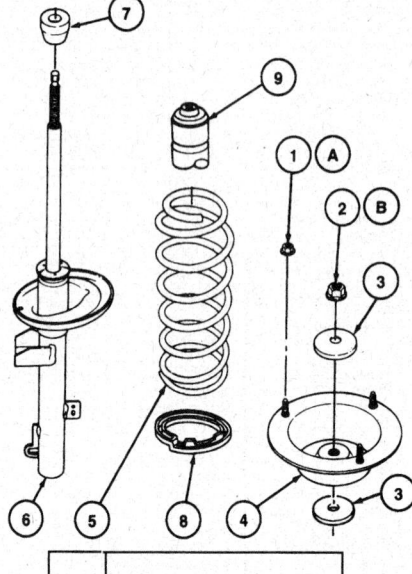

Item	Description
1	Nut (3 Req'd)
2	Nut
3	Washer (2 Req'd)
4	Rear Shock Absorber Bracket
5	Rear Spring
6	Shock Absorber
7	Rear Shock Absorber Jounce Bumper (Part of 18080)
8	Rear Spring Center Mounting insulator (Part of 18080)
9	Dust Boot (Part of 18080)
A	Tighten to 25-34 N·m (19-25 Lb-Ft)
B	Tighten to 53-71 N·m (39-53 Lb-Ft)

FM2039600054000X

Fig. 4 Exploded view of rear strut & spring

mounting bolt.
6. Install tire and wheel assembly.

Upper
REMOVAL
1. Raise and support vehicle.
2. Raise lower control arm to normal curb height using suitable floor jack.
3. Remove wheel and tire assembly, then the brake hose bracket from body.
4. Loosen spindle to lower and upper control arms mounting nuts.
5. Remove and discard upper ball joint nut.
6. Separate joint from spindle.
7. Remove upper control arms to body brackets mounting nuts and bolts. **Ensure spindle does not fall outward.**
8. Tilt upper part of spindle outward until upper control arms are clear of body brackets. Wire spindle in position.
9. Remove mounting nut and upper control arms.

INSTALLATION
1. Install upper control arms on spindle

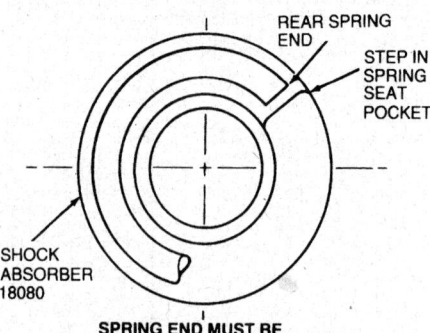

FM2039600055000X

Fig. 5 Spring & seat positioning

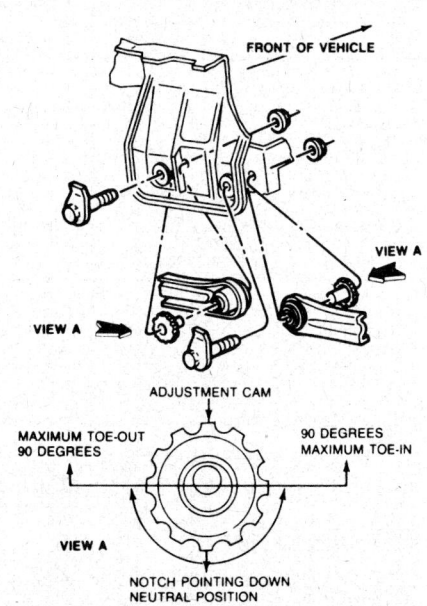

FM2039100033000X

Fig. 7 Lower control arm bushing & cam installation. Sedan

and install new nut. **Do not tighten now.**
2. Position upper control arms in body brackets, and install new nuts and bolts. Remove support wire.
3. Tighten control arms to spindle mounting nuts.
4. Install brake hose bracket on body, and tire and wheel assembly.
5. Remove floor jack and lower vehicle.
6. Inspect rear wheel alignment.

STABILIZER BAR
REPLACE
Sedan
1. Raise and support vehicle. **Do use tension strut and bushing for support.**
2. Remove stabilizer bar to link mounting nuts, washers and insulators from both sides.
3. Remove U-bracket mounting bolts and stabilizer bar.
4. Remove link to strut mounting nuts, washers and insulators.

5. Reverse procedure to install. Use new mounting components.

Wagon

1. Raise and support vehicle.
2. Place jack stands under rear suspension arm and bushings so bar links and bushings are neutralized.
3. Remove U-bracket mounting nuts and bolts from either side, and slide U-brackets and insulators from stabilizer bar.
4. Remove link to body bracket mounting nuts and bolts, then the stabilizer and link assemblies.
5. Slide link assemblies from stabilizer bar.
6. Reverse procedure to install. Use new mounting components.

TIGHTENING SPECIFICATIONS

Year	Component	Torque/Ft. Lbs.
SEDAN		
2001–05	Brake Hose Bracket	9–12
	Control Arm To Body	73–97
	Control Arm To Spindle	50–67
	Stabilizer Bar Link To Stabilizer Bar	60–84 ①
	Stabilizer Bar Link To Strut	60–84 ①
	Stabilizer U-Bracket To Body	25–34
	Strut Rod Nut	39–53
	Strut Top Mount To Body	19–26
	Strut To Spindle	50–67
	Strut To Top Mount	35–50
	Tension Strut To Body	35–50
	Tension Strut To Spindle	35–50
	Wheel Bearing	188–254
	Wheel Lug	85–105
WAGON		
2001–05	Brake Hose Bracket	9–12
	Lower Control Arm To Body	40–52
	Shock Absorber To Body	19–27
	Shock Absorber To Lower Suspension Arm	12–20
	Shock Absorber To Lower Suspension Spindle	50–67
	Spindle To Lower Control Arm	50–67
	Stabilizer Bar U-Bracket To Lower Suspension Arm	20–30
	Stabilizer Link	44–59
	Tension Strut To Body	35–46
	Tension Strut To Spindle	35–46
	Upper Ball Joint	50–68
	Upper Control Arms To Body	70–95
	Upper Control Arms To Spindle	150–190
	Upper Suspension Arm To Spindle	40–55
	Wheel Bearing	188–254
	Wheel Lug	85–105

① — Inch lbs.

Front Suspension & Steering

NOTE: On Air Bag Equipped Models, Refer To "Air Bag System Precautions" Located In The Front Of This Manual For System Disarming & Arming Procedures.

NOTE: Refer To "Computer Relearn Procedures" Located In The Front Of This Manual When Battery Power To The Computer Has Been Interrupted.

INDEX

DESCRIPTION

This suspension is a gas filled McPherson strut type, **Fig. 1.** The strut top mount consists of a rubber insulated bearing and seat and coil spring insulator. The top mount is attached to the body side apron by three bolts. The lower part of the strut is mounted in the steering knuckle and is retained by a pinch bolt. A forged lower control arm is attached to the subframe and to the steering knuckle. A tension strut is connected to the lower control arm and to the forward part of the subframe.

WHEEL BEARING
REPLACE

1. Turn ignition switch to OFF position and place steering column in unlocked position.
2. Remove wheel hub nut, then raise and support vehicle.
3. Remove cotter pin and nut from tie rod end stud. Discard cotter pin and nut.
4. Remove tie rod end from front wheel knuckle using tie rod end remover tool No. 3290-D, and tie rod adapter tool No. T81P-3504-W, or equivalents. **Do not use power tools to remove nut. Avoid damaging rod boot seal.**
5. Remove stabilizer bar link from front wheel knuckle.
6. Remove disc brake caliper and support it aside.
7. Remove anti-lock brake sensor.
8. Remove and discard lower ball joint nut.
9. Compress front coil spring until lower ball joint clears front suspension lower arm using Rotunda spring compressor tool No. 164-R-3571, or equivalent.
10. Push front axle from hub using suitable service tools.
11. Remove and discard three hub and bearing mounting bolts from front wheel knuckle.
12. **Wheel hub is not pressed into front wheel knuckle. Do not use slide hammer to remove stuck wheel hub. Do not strike back of inner bearing race.**
13. If bearing carrier is corroded to front wheel knuckle, apply rust penetrant part No. D7AZ-19A501-AA, or equivalent, to inboard and outboard wheel hub/knuckle mating surface and allow to soak. Pry wheel hub from knuckle assembly using suitable pry bar.
14. Reverse procedure to install, noting the following:
    a. If wheel hub is damaged, or if any endplay is detectable, replace wheel hub.
    b. Remove any foreign material from knuckle bearing bore.
    c. Lightly lubricate mating surfaces of bearing and front wheel knuckle.

BALL JOINT INSPECTION

1. Raise and support vehicle with wheels in full down position.
2. Grasp lower edge of tire, then move wheel assembly in and out.
3. As wheel is being moved, observe lower end of knuckle and lower control arm.
4. If movement is observed, replace lower control arm.

BALL JOINT
REPLACE

The ball joint must be replaced with the control arm as an assembly.

STRUT
REPLACE

1. Place ignition switch in OFF position and ensure steering wheel is not locked.
2. Remove hub nut and loosen three strut mounting nuts.

3. Raise and support vehicle. **Do not raise vehicle with lower control arm.**
4. Remove wheel and tire assembly.
5. Remove brake caliper and position it aside.
6. Remove brake rotor and tie rod end. **Do not use power tools to remove tie rod nut. Avoid damaging boot seal.**
7. Remove nut and stabilizer bar link from strut.
8. Remove lower control arm to steering knuckle pinch nut and bolt, slightly spread joint and remove lower control arm.
9. Press axle from hub using suitable hub remover/installer.
10. Wire axle shaft to body to maintain level position. **Do not allow axle shaft to move outward.**
11. Remove strut to steering knuckle pinch bolt and spread joint slightly.
12. Remove steering knuckle and hub.
13. Remove mounting nuts and strut.
14. Reverse procedure to install, noting the following:
    a. Tighten in following order: strut to steering knuckle pinch bolt, lower control arm to steering knuckle pinch bolt, stabilizer bar assembly to strut, tie rod end mounting nut and strut mounting nuts.
    b. Tighten hub nut with vehicle on ground.

COIL SPRING & STRUT SERVICE

1. Compress strut spring with Rotunda coil spring compressor tool No. 164-R3571, or equivalent.
2. Hold strut shaft with suitable box wrench and remove strut mounting nut using suitable crowfoot socket. **Do not allow strut shaft to rotate.**
3. Loosen compressor tool, then remove strut top mount bracket, bearing and seat assembly, and spring, **Fig. 2.**
4. Reverse procedure to install.

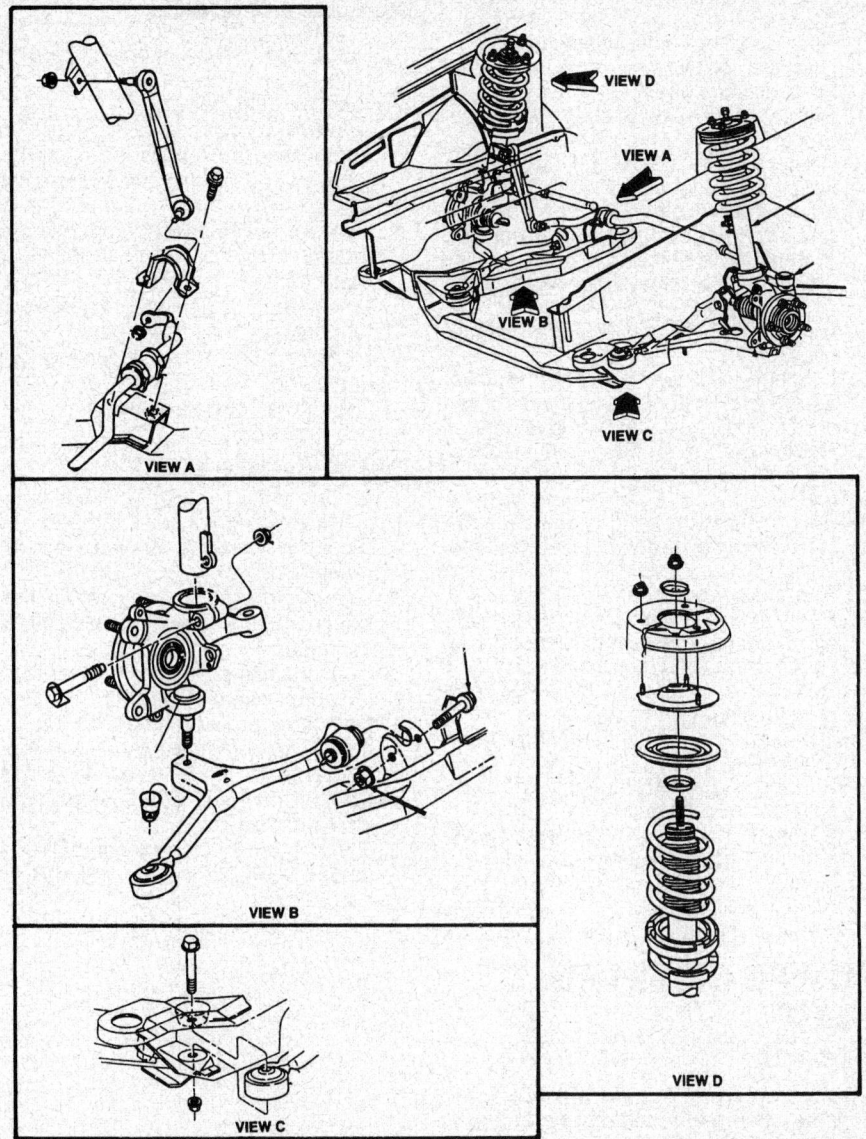

Fig. 1 Exploded view of front suspension

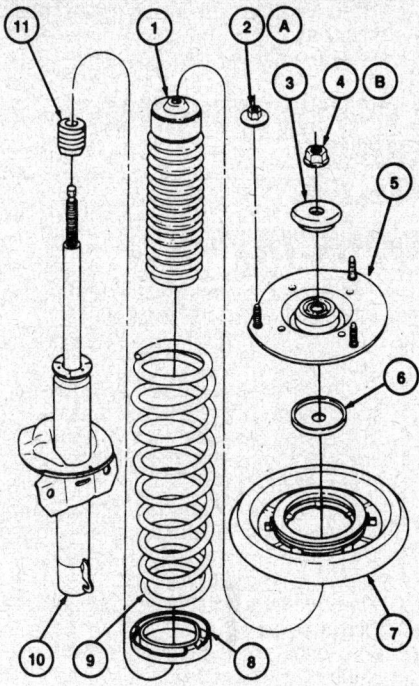

Item	Description
1	Dust Boot
2	Nut (3 Req'd)
3	Washer
4	Nut
5	Front Shock Absorber Mounting Bracket
6	Washer
7	Front Suspension Bearing and Seal
8	Front Spring Insulator
9	Front Coil Spring
10	Front Spring and Shock
11	Jounce Bumper
A	Tighten to 30-40 N·m (23-29 Lb-Ft)
B	Tighten to 53-72 N·m (40-53 Lb-Ft)

FM2029500087000X

Fig. 2 Exploded view of McPherson strut

CONTROL ARM

REPLACE

1. Turn ignition switch to OFF position and place steering column in unlocked position.
2. Raise and support vehicle.
3. Remove and discard lower ball joint nut.
4. Separate ball joint from knuckle using ball joint remover tool No. T96P-3010-A and tie rod end remover tool No. T81P-3504-W, or equivalents.
5. Compress front coil spring until lower ball joint clears front suspension lower arm using Rotunda spring compressor tool No. 164-R-3571, or equivalent.
6. Remove forward lower suspension arm mounting nut and bolt.
7. Remove rear lower suspension arm mounting nut, bolt and suspension arm.
8. Reverse procedure to install.

STEERING KNUCKLE

REPLACE

Wheel hub retainer is a torque prevailing design and cannot be reused. If loosened, retainer must be replaced.

1. Ensure steering wheel in unlocked position.
2. Remove hub cap or wheel cover, wheel hub retainer and washer. Discard retainer.
3. Remove steering knuckle tie rod end using suitable joint removal tool.
4. Remove anti-lock brake sensor.
5. Disconnect ABS sensor wire retainer and position sensor aside.
6. Remove knuckle to shock mounting bolt and nut. Discard nut.
7. Disconnect ball joint from lower arm using suitable joint removal tool.
8. Push lower arm down until ball joint is free from arm using suitable pry bar.
9. Press halfshaft from wheel bearing

and hub using front wheel hub installation tool No. T81P-1104-C, or equivalent.
10. Support halfshaft in level position.
11. Remove flag bolt and steering knuckle.
12. Reverse procedure to install.

STABILIZER BAR

REPLACE

1. Raise and support vehicle. Place safety stands behind front subframe.
2. Remove stabilizer bar link to strut mounting nuts.
3. Remove stabilizer bar link to bar mounting nuts.
4. Remove mounting bolts and move steering gear off subframe.
5. Support subframe with second set of safety stands and remove rear subframe mounting bolts.
6. Lower rear part of subframe to access to stabilizer bar mounting brackets.

7. Remove mounting brackets and stabilizer bar.
8. Reverse procedure to install.

POWER STEERING GEAR

REPLACE

DOHC Engine

1. Turn steering wheel ¼ turn and turn ignition switch to OFF position.
2. Remove both front wheel and tire assemblies.
3. Remove tie rod end jam nuts. Discard tie rod end cotter pins and nuts.
4. Record of turns required to remove tie rod ends from steering gear for installation alignment.
5. Remove tie rod ends from steering knuckle with suitable joint removal tool.
6. Remove tie rod ends.
7. Remove nuts and disconnect both stabilizer bar links from stabilizer bar.
8. Remove bolt and disconnect intermediate shaft coupling.
9. **Do not allow steering wheel to rotate while steering column intermediate shaft is disconnected.**
10. Remove catalytic converter.
11. Remove and discard both steering gear mounting nuts.
12. Remove bolts and lower rear of front subframe approximately 4 inches.
13. Disconnect power steering pressure switch and remove pressure hose.
14. Remove bracket/heat shield.
15. Remove power steering lines from steering gear.
16. Remove brackets, pipes and steering gear through lefthand fender well.
17. Reverse procedure to install.

OHV Engine

1. Turn steering wheel ½ turn to right-hand and turn ignition switch to OFF position.
2. Remove air cleaner outlet pipe.
3. Remove power steering pressure hose. Discard seals.
4. Remove intermediate shaft pinch bolt. Discard bolt.
5. Center steering wheel and turn ignition switch to OFF position.
6. **Do not allow steering wheel to rotate while steering column intermediate shaft is disconnected.**
7. Disconnect intermediate shaft from steering gear.
8. Remove front wheel and tire assemblies.
9. Loosen tie rod jam nuts, then remove tie rod end cotter pins and nuts. Discard tie rod end cotter pins and nuts.
10. Remove tie rod ends from steering knuckle using suitable joint removal tool.
11. Record number of turns required to remove tie rod ends for installation alignment.
12. Remove tie rod ends.
13. Remove nuts and disconnect both stabilizer bar links from stabilizer bar.
14. Remove catalytic converter.
15. Remove and discard steering gear mounting nuts.
16. Remove remaining steering gear brackets and pipes.
17. Support rear of front subframe with suitable jack stands.
18. Remove mounting bolts and lower subframe approximately four inches.
19. Remove steering gear through lefthand fender well.
20. Reverse procedure to install.

POWER STEERING PUMP

REPLACE

Power steering pumps are replaced only as complete assemblies. They have no serviceable components.

DOHC Engine

1. Drain and remove coolant recovery reservoir.
2. Remove drive belt.
3. Remove power steering reservoir pump hose from between pump and reservoir. Drain fluid into suitable container.
4. Remove pulley using pump pulley remover tool No. T69L-10300-B, or equivalent.
5. Disconnect power steering lefthand turn pressure hose from pump.
6. Remove three pump mounting bolts and pump.
7. Reverse procedure to install.

OHV Engine

1. Remove drive belt and alternator.
2. Drain and remove coolant recovery reservoir.
3. Remove power steering return hose from pump and drain fluid into suitable container.
4. Remove idler pulley from power steering pump support.
5. Remove power steering bracket mounting bolt from under tensioner mounting.
6. Remove power steering pump support with pump attached.
7. Remove pulley using pump pulley remover tool No. T69L-10300-B, or equivalent.
8. Reverse procedure to install.

TIGHTENING SPECIFICATIONS

Year	Component	Torque/Ft. Lbs.
2001–05	Control Arm Pivot Bolt	72–97
	Control Arm To Subframe	72–97
	Hub Nut	170–202
	Stabilizer Bar Bracket To Subframe	22–39
	Stabilizer Bar Link To Stabilizer Bar	35–48
	Stabilizer Bar Link To Shock Strut	57–75
	Steering Gear	85–100
	Strut Top Mount To Body	30–40
	Strut To Top Mount	39–53
	Strut To Knuckle	72–97
	Tension Strut To Control Arm	70–95
	Tension Strut To Subframe	70–95
	Tie Rod End To Steering Knuckle	35–46
	Wheel Lug	85–105

Wheel Alignment

INDEX

PRELIMINARY INSPECTION

1. Ensure tires are inflated to proper pressure.
2. Inspect tires for wear patterns that may indicate improper wheel alignment, tire imbalance or damage because bulges or separations.
3. Inspect suspension for modifications such as trailer towing equipment or heavy duty handling components.
4. Inspect vehicle for signs of overloading or sagging. Ensure luggage compartment does not contain heavy objects.
5. Road test vehicle to isolate area of concern.

FRONT WHEEL ALIGNMENT

Caster & Camber

Caster is not adjustable. If caster is not be within specifications, inspect vehicle for suspension component damage, deteriorated bushings or distorted body mounting points.

1. Loosen subframe to body mounting bolts.
2. Install ¾ inch outside diameter pipe, or similar tool, into lefthand front subframe and body alignment holes, **Fig. 1.**
3. Align lefthand front subframe and body alignment holes and slightly tighten lefthand front subframe mounting bolt.
4. Repeat previous alignment steps on righthand front alignment holes.
5. Inspect lefthand front alignment again.
6. Tighten subframe mounting bolts.
7. Center punch spot welds on both strut alignment plates and loosen strut mounting nuts, **Fig. 2.**
8. Remove spot welds using Rotunda Spot-Eze, or equivalent. **Do not drill deeper than thickness of alignment plates.**
9. Remove strut mounting nuts and alignment plates.
10. Remove burrs from strut towers and alignment plates. Paint all exposed metal on strut towers and alignment plates.

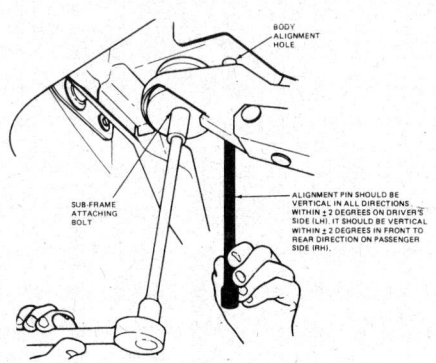

Fig. 1   Front suspension alignment

FM2049100028000X

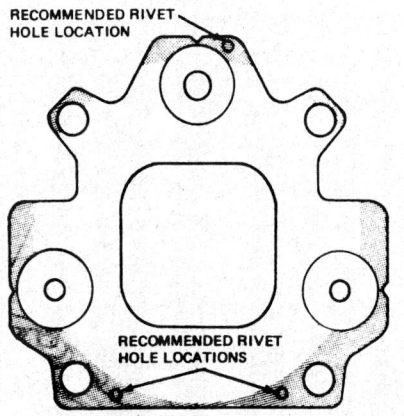

DRILL THREE (3) HOLES IN ALIGNMENT PLATE FOR 1/8 INCH RIVETS.

DRILL IN SHADED AREA ONLY.

FM2049100030000X

Fig. 3   Rivet hole location

11. Install alignment plates and loosely install strut mounting nuts.
12. Align front end and tighten strut mounting nuts.
13. Drill three ⅛ inch holes through alignment plates and strut towers, then paint exposed metal, **Fig. 3. Do not drill deeper than ⅜ inch into strut tower.**
14. Install three ⅛ inch diameter pop rivets with grip range of ¼ inch into alignment plate/strut tower.

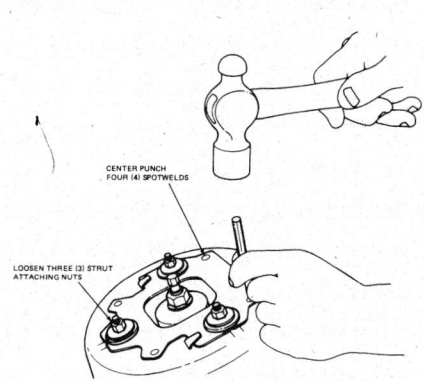

FM2049100029000X

Fig. 2   Alignment plate loosening

Toe-In

1. Lock steering wheel in straight ahead position using suitable steering wheel holder.
2. Loosen and slide small outer clamps from off steering boot.
3. Loosen tie rod adjusting, then adjust lefthand and righthand tie rods until each wheel has half desired total toe specification.
4. Tighten tie rod adjusting nuts and install clamps.
5. Remove steering wheel holding tool.

REAR WHEEL ALIGNMENT

Caster & Camber

The caster and camber angles are factory set and cannot be adjusted. However, rear camber adjustment kit part No. E7DZ-5K751-B, or an equivalent, may be installed to allow for adjustment.

Toe-In

On sedan models, toe-in is adjusted by rotating the cams located inside the rear inner lower control arm bushings.

On wagon models, toe-in is adjusted by rotating the cams located inside the outer lower control arm bushings.

FOCUS

NOTE: Refer To The Rear Of This Manual For Manufacturer's Special Service Tool Suppliers.

INDEX OF SERVICE OPERATIONS

FOCUS

Specifications

GENERAL ENGINE SPECIFICATIONS

Year	Engine Liter (Code①)	Fuel System	Bore x Stroke, Inches	Comp. Ratio	Net HP @ RPM	Maximum Torque, Ft. Lbs. @ RPM	Oil Pressure, psi
2001	2.0L DOHC (3)	SFI	3.34 x 3.46	9.6:1	130 @ 5300	127 @ 3750	②
	2.0L SOHC (P)	SFI	3.34 x 3.46	9.35:1	110 @ 5000	125 @ 3750	③
2002	2.0L DOHC (3)	SFI	3.34 x 3.46	9.6:1	130 @ 5500	135 @ 4500	②
	2.0L SOHC (P)	SFI	3.34 x 3.46	9.35:1	110 @ 5000	125 @ 3750	③
2003–04	2.0L DOHC (3)	SFI	3.34 x 3.46	9.6:1	130 @ 5300	135 @ 4500	②
	2.0L DOHC SVT (5)	SFI	3.34 x 3.46	10.2:1	170 @ 7000	145 @ 5500	②
	2.0L SOHC (P)	SFI	3.34 x 3.46	9.35:1	110 @ 5000	125 @ 3750	③
2005	2.0L (N) DOHC	SFI	3.34 x 3.45	10.0:1	130 @ 4500	129 @ 45000	29–39
	2.3L (Z) DOHC	SFI	3.44 x 3.70	9.7:1	151 @ 5750	154 @ 4250	29–39

SFI — Sequential Electronic Fuel Injection
① — The eighth digit of the VIN denotes engine code.

② — Pressure at normal operating temperature should be 18.9–36.3 psi @ 800–850 RPM and 53.7–79.8 psi @ 4000 RPM.

③ — Pressure at normal operating temperature should be 34.8–65.3 psi @ 2000 RPM.

TUNE UP SPECIFICATIONS

Year & Engine (Code①)	Spark Plug Gap	Ignition Timing BTDC				Curb Idle Speed⑩		Fast Idle Speed⑩		Fuel Pump Pressure, psi.	Valve Lash, Inch
		Firing Order Fig.④	Man. Trans.	Auto. Trans.	Mark Fig.	Man. Trans.	Auto. Trans.	Man. Trans.	Auto. Trans.		
2001											
2.0L DOHC (3)	.054	③	②	②	⑧	⑨	⑨	⑨	⑨	35–55⑦	⑥
2.0L SOHC (P)	.054	③	②	②	⑧	⑨	⑨	⑨	⑨	35–55⑦	⑤
2002–04											
2.0L DOHC (3 & 5)	.052–.056	③	②	②	—	⑨	⑨	⑨	⑨	30–65	⑥
2.0L SOHC (P)	.044	③	②	②	—	⑨	⑨	⑨	⑨	30–65	⑤
2005											
2.0L DOHC (N)	.049–.053	③	②	②	—	⑨	⑨	⑨	⑨	30–65	⑪
2.3L (Z) DOHC	.049–.053	③	②	—	—	⑨	—	⑨	—	30–65	⑪

BTDC — Before Top Dead Center
N — Neutral
① — The eighth digit of the VIN denotes engine code.
② — Non-adjustable.
③ — Cylinder numbering from front to rear of engine, 1-2-3-4. Firing order, 1-3-4-2.
④ — Before disconnecting wires from distributor cap or coil unit, deter-

mine location of ignition wires, as position may have been altered from that outlined at end of this chart.
⑤ — Equipped w/hydraulic lash adjusters.
⑥ — Measured at 59–77°F. Intake, .0043–.0071 inch; exhaust, .0106–.0134 inch.

⑦ — Wrap shop towel around fitting to prevent fuel spillage, then connect suitable fuel pressure gauge to fuel diagnostic valve on fuel rail assembly. Gradually open fuel pressure gauge test valve to relieve fuel system pressure & drain fuel into suitable container. Close fuel pressure gauge test valve. Place ignition switch in On position. Access output test mode on scan tool & operate fuel pump to obtain maximum fuel pressure. Fuel pump will operate for approximately 8 seconds. Inspect fuel pressure gauge reading.

⑧ — Equipped w/crankshaft position sensor.
⑨ — Idle speed controlled by an automatic idle speed control.
⑩ — When adjusting idle speed, set parking brake & chock drive wheels.

⑪ — Intake, .008–.011 inch; exhaust, .010–.023 inch.

FRONT WHEEL ALIGNMENT SPECIFICATIONS

| Year | Vehicle | Caster Angle, Degrees | | Camber Angle, Degrees | | Toe-In, Inches | |
		Limits	Desired	Limits	Desired	Limits	Desired
2001	Coupe & Sedan	+1.93 to +3.93	+2.93	-1.85 to +.65	-.60	-.13 to +.13	0
	Wagon	+1.44 to +3.50	+2.47	-1.87 to +.63	-.62	-.13 to +.13	0
2002	Coupe & Sedan	+1.97 to +4.09	+3.03	-1.82 to +.70	-.56	-.10 to +.10	0
	Wagon	+1.87 to +3.89	+2.88	-1.89 to +.63	-.63	-.10 to +.10	0
2003–04	Coupe & Sedan	+1.97 to +4.09	+3.03	-1.82 to +.70	-.56	-.10 to +.10	0
	SVT	+1.97 to +4.09	+3.03	-1.82 to +.70	-.56	-.13 to +.13	0
	Wagon	+1.87 to +3.89	+2.88	-1.89 to +.63	-.63	-.10 to +.10	0
2005	All	+1.75 to +3/75	+2.75	-1.75 to +.75	-.50	-.20 to +2.0	0

REAR WHEEL ALIGNMENT SPECIFICATIONS

| Year | Vehicle | Camber, Degrees | | Toe-In, Inches | |
		Limits	Desired	Limits	Desired
2001	Coupe & Sedan	-2.18 to +.32	-.93	+.15 to +.35	+.25
	Wagon	-1.86 to +.64	-.61	+.07 to +.27	+.17
2002	Coupe & Sedan	-2.33 to +.30	-1.02	+.15 to +.35	+.25
	Wagon	-2.22 to +.34	-.94	+.15 to +.35	+.25
2003–04	Coupe & Sedan	-2.33 to +.30	-1.02	+.15 to +.35	+.25
	SVT	-2.33 to +.30	-1.02	+.25 to +.29	+.27
	Wagon	-2.22 to +.34	-.94	+.15 to +.35	+.25
2005	Sedan	-2.27 to +.23	-1.02	+.30 to +.70	+.50
	Wagon	-2.19 to +.31	-.94	+.30 to +.70	+.50

FLUID CAPACITIES & COOLING SYSTEM DATA

| Year | Engine (Code①) | Coolant Capacity, Qts. | Coolant Type | Radiator Cap Relief Pressure, lbs. | Thermo. Opening Temp., Deg. F | Fuel Tank, Gals. | Engine Oil Refill, Qts.② | Transmission Fluid | |
								Man. Trans., Pts	Auto. Trans., Qts.
2001	2.0L DOHC (3)	6.1	EG	14.4–17.6	194–201	13.2	4.5	4.0	6.9
	2.0L SOHC (P)	6.1	EG	14.4–17.6	188–195	13.2	4.0	4.9	6.9
2002–04	2.0L DOHC (3)	6.1	③	14.4–17.6	194–201	13.2	4.5	4.0	6.9
	2.0L DOHC (5)	6.1	③	14.4–17.6	194–201	13.2	4.5	3.6	—
	2.0L SOHC (P)	6.1	③	14.4–17.6	188–195	13.2	4.0	4.9	6.9
2005	2.0L DOHC (H)	6.1	④	17.4–21.7	194	14.0	4.5	3.3	7.0
	2.3L (Z) DOHC	7.6	④	17.4–21.7	194	14.0	4.5	3.3	7.0

EG — Ethylene Glycol
① — The eighth digit of the VIN denotes engine code.
② — Including oil filter.

③ — For models w/green coolant use ethylene glycol. For models w/orange coolant use coolant meeting Ford specifications.

④ — Motorcraft Premium Gold Engine Coolant VC-7-A (Oregan, VC-7-B), or equivalent, (yellow).

LUBRICANT DATA

Year	Transmission		Power Steering	Brake System	Hydraulic Clutch Fluid
	Manual	Automatic			
	IB5	MTX 75				
2001–04	①	②	Mercon V XT-5-QM	③	DOT 3④	DOT 3
2005	—	②	Mercon V XT-5-QM	Mercon (ATF) XT-2-QDX	DOT 3	DOT 3

① — Transaxle fluid meeting Ford specification WSD-M2C200-C.
② — Transaxle fluid meeting Ford specification ESD-M2C186-A.

③ — Power steering fluid meeting Ford specification WSA-M2C195-A.
④ — The use of super DOT 4 brake fluid meeting Ford specification

Delta ESD-M6C57-A is recommended for all vehicles equipped with manual transaxles.

Electrical

NOTE: On Air Bag Equipped Models, Refer To "Air Bag System Precautions" Located In The Front Of This Manual For System Disarming & Arming Procedures.

NOTE: Refer To "Computer Relearn Procedures" Located In The Front Of This Manual When Battery Power To The Computer Has Been Interrupted.

NOTE: Prior To Performing Any Service Operations Listed In This Section, Consult The "Technical Service Bulletins" Section For Related Information.

INDEX

PRECAUTIONS
Air Bag Systems

Refer to "Air Bag System Precautions" in the front of this manual for system disarming and arming procedures.

Battery Ground Cable

Prior to service, disconnect battery ground cable and isolate as required.

Electrostatic Discharge

Electronic modules are sensitive to electrical charges. Ensure modules are not exposed to these charges.

FUSE PANEL & FLASHER LOCATION

The central junction box is located in the lefthand footwell, **Fig. 1.**

The fuse box is located under the lefthand side of instrument panel, **Fig. 2.**

FUEL PUMP RELAY LOCATION

The fuel pump relay is located in the battery junction box in the engine compartment, **Fig. 3.**

STARTER
REPLACE
DOHC Engine
VINS N & Z

1. Ensure transmission is in Neutral position, then raise and support vehicle.
2. Remove terminal nuts and disconnect starter motor wiring.
3. Remove mounting nut and disconnect Power Steering Pressure (PSP) tube brackets from stud bolts.
4. Remove mounting bolts and starter motor.
5. Reverse procedure to install, noting the following:
   a. **Torque** starter motor mounting bolts to 18 ft. lbs.
   b. **Torque** PSP tube bracket nut to 10 ft. lbs.

VIN 3

1. Disconnect Mass Air Flow (MAF) sensor.
2. Disconnect breather pipe.
3. Disconnect air cleaner outlet tube from throttle body and remove air cleaner.
4. Remove starter motor upper mounting bolts.
5. Raise and support vehicle.
6. Disconnect starter motor electrical connector.

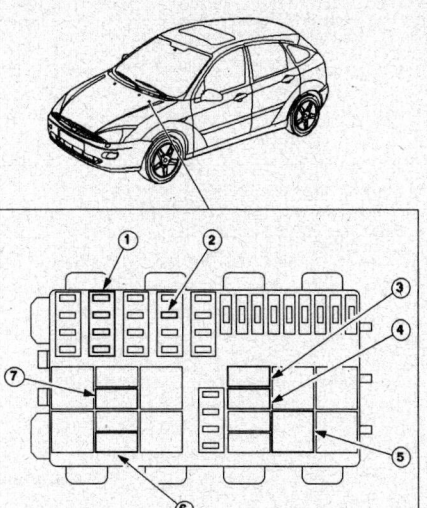

Fig. 1   Central junction box (Part 1 of 2)

Item	Description
1	Fuse F16 (10 A) for dipped beam, left
2	Fuse F17 (10 A) for dipped beam, right
3	Fuse F26 (10 A) main beam, left
4	Fuse F27 (10 A) main beam, right
5	Fuse F22 (15 A) - Dipped beam /daytime running lights
6	Main beam relay
7	Dipped beam relay
8	Headlamp washer system relay
9	Brake light relay
10	Daytime running lights relay

FM9049900301020X

Fig. 1   Central junction box (Part 2 of 2)

7. Remove lower mounting bolts and starter motor.
8. Reverse procedure to install, noting the following:
   a. **Torque** starter motor mounting bolts to 26 ft. lbs.
   b. **Torque** starter motor power connection nut to 106 inch lbs.
   c. **Torque** starter solenoid connection nut to 53 inch lbs.

VIN 5

1. Remove intake manifold as outlined under "Intake Manifold, Replace" in "2.0L (VINs 3 & 5) DOHC Engines" section.
2. Disconnect starter motor electrical connectors.

3. Remove mounting bolts and starter motor.
4. Reverse procedure to install, noting the following:
   a. **Torque** starter motor mounting bolts to 26 ft. lbs.
   b. **Torque** starter motor power connection nut to 106 inch lbs.
   c. **Torque** starter solenoid connection nut to 53 inch lbs.

SOHC Engine

1. Remove air cleaner outlet tube.
2. Remove starter motor mounting bolts.
3. Raise and support vehicle.
4. Disconnect starter motor electrical connector.
5. Remove starter motor.
6. Reverse procedure to install, noting the following:
   a. **Torque** starter motor mounting bolts to 26 ft. lbs.
   b. **Torque** starter motor power connection nut to 106 inch lbs.
   c. **Torque** starter solenoid connection nut to 53 inch lbs.

ALTERNATOR
REPLACE
DOHC Engine

1. Remove drive belt.
2. Remove cover and disconnect electrical connectors.
3. Remove mounting bolt and secure coolant expansion tank aside.
4. Secure power steering reservoir aside.
5. Remove mounting bolt and secure engine wiring bracket aside.
6. Disconnect ground cable.
7. Remove mounting nuts and secure evaporative emission canister purge valve aside.
8. Remove righthand mounting bolt and fully loosen lefthand bolt. Lefthand bolt cannot be remove at this time.
9. Remove alternator.
10. Reverse procedure to install, noting the following:
    a. **Torque** alternator mounting bolts to 18 ft. lbs.
    b. **Torque** electrical connector nut to 71 inch lbs.

SOHC Engine

1. Remove cooling fan motor and shroud.
2. Remove drive belt.
3. Remove power steering pipe support brackets.
4. Remove exhaust manifold heat shield.
5. Raise and support vehicle.
6. Disconnect alternator electrical connectors.
7. Remove alternator lower mounting bolt.
8. Lower vehicle.
9. Remove clip and two upper mounting bolts.
10. Remove alternator.
11. Reverse procedure to install, noting the following:

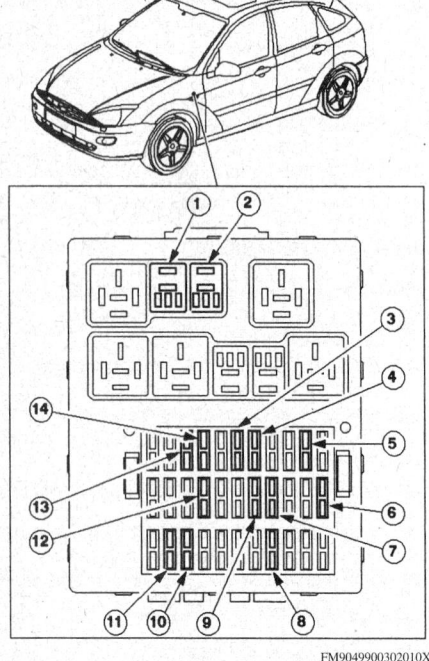

Fig. 2   Fuse box (Part 1 of 2)

a. **Torque** alternator mounting bolts to 35 ft. lbs.
b. **Torque** electrical connector nut to 71 inch lbs.

Item	Description
1	Rear wiper relay
2	Windscreen wiper relay
3	Fuse F35 (7,5 A) - Interior lights
4	Fuse F36 (7,5 A) - Interior lights
5	Fuse F39 (10A) - reversing lights
8	Fuse F59 (7,5 A) - Direction indicators, electronic module
9	Fuse F47 (7,5A) - left-hand side lights
10	Fuse F54 (15 A) - Brake light
11	Fuse F53 (10A) - reversing lights
12	Fuse F44 (20 A) - Fog lamps
13	Fuse F32 (10 A) for instrument cluster illumination
14	Fuse F33 (15 A) - Hazard warning lights switch

FM9049900302020X

Fig. 2   Fuse box (Part 2 of 2)

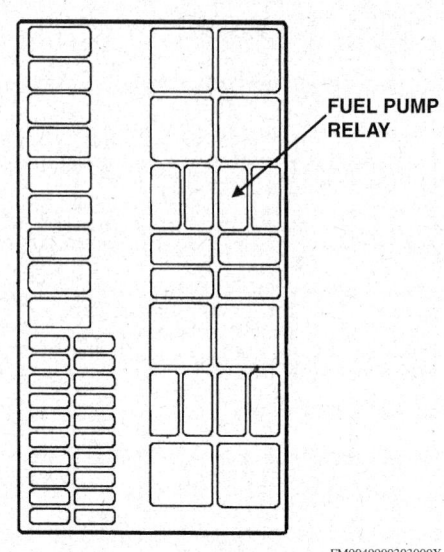

FUEL PUMP RELAY

FM9049900303000X

Fig. 3   Battery junction box

IGNITION COIL
REPLACE
DOHC Engine

1. Remove ignition coil cover.
2. Disconnect spark plug wires and electrical connectors from ignition coil.
3. Remove mounting bolts and ignition coil.
4. Reverse procedure to install. **Torque** mounting bolts to 53 inch lbs.

SOHC Engine

1. Disconnect spark plug wires from ignition coil.
2. Disconnect electrical connectors from ignition coil and capacitor.
3. Remove mounting bolts, ignition coil, capacitor and bracket.
4. Reverse procedure to install. **Torque** mounting bolts to 88 inch lbs.

IGNITION LOCK
REPLACE

1. Remove mounting screws, fastener and instrument panel lower panel.
2. Disconnect steering column upper shroud using suitable thin bladed screwdriver to release clip on each side.
3. Remove audio control switch using suitable thin bladed screwdriver to release locking tang and disconnect electrical connector.
4. Release locking lever, then remove

mounting screws and steering column lower shroud.
5. Disconnect electrical connector, then remove mounting screw and passive anti-theft system transceiver.
6. Insert key and turn ignition switch to accessory position No. 1.
7. Depress detent using suitable thin bladed screwdriver.
8. Remove lock cylinder.
9. Reverse procedure to install.

IGNITION SWITCH
REPLACE

1. Remove mounting screws, fastener and instrument panel lower panel.
2. Disconnect steering column upper shroud using suitable thin bladed screwdriver to release clip on each side.
3. Release locking lever, then remove mounting screws, ignition key and steering column lower shroud.
4. Disconnect electrical connectors.
5. Release clips and remove ignition switch.
6. Reverse procedure to install.

NEUTRAL SAFETY SWITCH
REPLACE

1. Disconnect Transmission Range (TR) sensor electrical connector and selector lever cable.
2. Remove manual control lever. **Shift**

lever must be held while loosening manual shaft lever.
3. Remove mounting bolts and TR sensor.
4. Reverse procedure to install, noting the following:
   a. Align TR sensor using alignment tool No. 307-415, or equivalent.
   b. **Torque** mounting bolts to 88 inch lbs.

HEADLAMP SWITCH
REPLACE

1. Remove lefthand side lower footwell trim.
2. Remove mounting screws and disconnect lamp switch bezel.
3. Remove mounting screws and disconnect electrical connectors.
4. Remove headlamp switch.
5. Reverse procedure to install.

STEERING WHEEL
REPLACE

1. Remove air bag module as outlined in "Passive Restraint Systems" chapter.
2. Ensure steering wheel is centered.
3. Remove ignition key to lock steering in position.
4. Disconnect speed control electrical connector.
5. Remove mounting bolt and steering wheel.
6. Reverse procedure to install, noting the following:
   a. Ensure air bag sliding contact is centralized.
   b. **Torque** steering wheel mounting bolt to 37 ft. lbs.
   c. Turn steering wheel counterclockwise to ensure location.

INSTRUMENT CLUSTER
REPLACE

1. Disconnect instrument cluster bezel.
2. Disconnect luggage compartment release switch electrical connector and remove instrument cluster bezel.

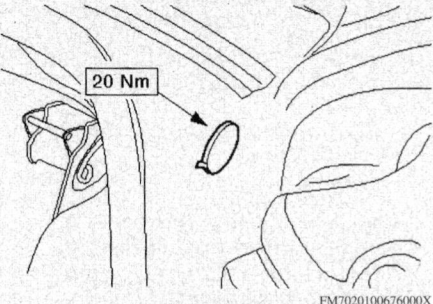

Fig. 4 Cross-vehicle blind bolt replacement

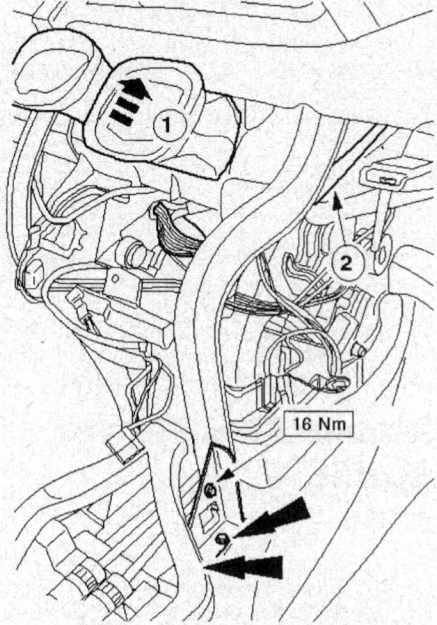

Fig. 7 Cross-vehicle beam replacement

3. Remove instrument cluster mounting screws.
4. Release locking tang and disconnect electrical connector.
5. Remove instrument cluster. **Instrument cluster must be kept upright to avoid leaking silicone liquid from gauges.**
6. Reverse procedure to install.

RADIO
REPLACE

1. Install radio remover tools No. T87P-19061-A, or equivalent, into locating holes until they click into place.
2. Pull tools gently left and right until locking tangs release.
3. Slide radio out of instrument panel.
4. Disconnect electrical connectors and remove radio.
5. Reverse procedure to install.

WIPER MOTOR
REPLACE
Front

1. Ensure wiper motor is in park position.

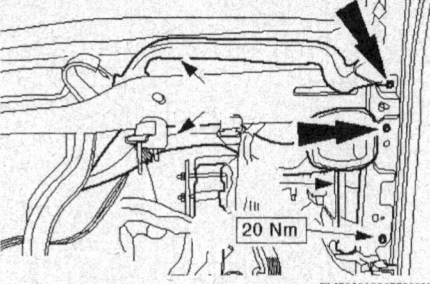

Fig. 5 Ventilation hoses & wiring harness replacement

2. Lift plastic caps and loosen wiper arm mounting nuts approximately two turns.
3. Disconnect wiper arms from taper and position aside.
4. Remove mounting nuts and wiper arms.
5. Remove caps, mounting bolts and air cowl grille.
6. Remove wiper motor protective cap and disconnect electrical connector.
7. Remove mounting bolts, wiper motor and linkage.
8. Mark lever to assembly plate position for installation alignment.
9. Remove mounting nut and bolts, then the wiper motor from plate and lever.
10. Reverse procedure to install, noting the following:
    a. Ensure wiper motor is in park position.
    b. **Torque** wiper motor mounting bolts to 71 inch lbs.
    c. **Torque** linkage bolt to 15 ft. lbs.
    d. Fit guide pins before fitting mounting bolts when installing wiper linkage.
    e. Ensure wiper blades do not touch air cowl griller or molding.

Rear

1. Ensure wiper motor is in park position.
2. Lift plastic caps and loosen wiper arm mounting nuts approximately two turns.
3. Disconnect wiper arms from taper and position aside.
4. Remove mounting nuts and wiper arms.
5. Remove two mounting bolts, 10 clips and cover.
6. Disconnect wiper motor electrical connector and ground lead.
7. Remove mounting bolts and wiper motor from bracket.
8. Reverse procedure to install, noting the following:
    a. Ensure wiper motor is in park position.
    b. **Torque** wiper motor mounting bolts to 71 inch lbs.

BLOWER MOTOR
REPLACE

1. Remove righthand footwell lower trim.
2. Open glove compartment.

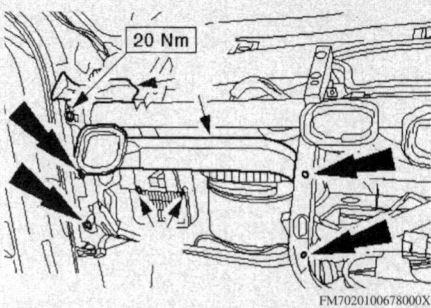

Fig. 6 Central junction box and ventilation hose replacement

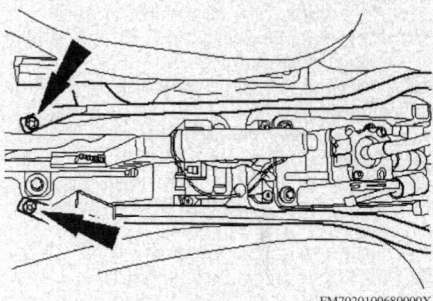

Fig. 8 Rear footwell ventilation hoses replacement

3. Disconnect hose and remove footwell vent air duct.
4. Close glove compartment.
5. Disconnect electrical connector.
6. Remove mounting screws and blower motor.
7. Reverse procedure to install.

CABIN AIR FILTER
REPLACE

1. Position wipers vertically.
2. Disconnect two clips, then remove mounting bolt and righthand air cowl grille.
3. Open service flap and remove cabin air filter.
4. Reverse procedure to install, noting the following:
    a. Ensure filter is installed in correct direction flow.
    b. Clean grille rubber edging between wiper motor and filter housing.
    c. Install new air cowl grille gasket.
    d. Ensure air cowl grille gasket for windscreen is seated correctly.

HEATER CORE
REPLACE

1. Install radio remover tools No. T87P-19061-A, or equivalent, into locating holes until they click into place.
2. Pull tools gently left and right until locking tangs release.
3. Slide radio out of instrument panel.
4. Disconnect electrical connectors and remove radio.
5. Recover air conditioning refrigerant as outlined in "Air Conditioning" chapter.
6. Drain cooling system into suitable container.

7. Remove instrument panel as outlined in "Dash Panel Service" chapter.
8. Disconnect heat exchanger take off connection coolant hoses.
9. Disconnect evaporator refrigerant lines using suitable air conditioning fitting removal tool.
10. Remove cap and mounting bolt, **Fig. 4.**
11. Remove ventilation hoses and mounting screws, then disconnect wiring harnesses from beam, **Fig. 5.**
12. Remove ventilation hoses and mounting screws, then disconnect junction box from cross-vehicle beam, **Fig. 6.**
13. Remove ventilation hose and disconnect wiring harnesses from beam.
14. Remove bracket and cross-vehicle beam, **Fig. 7.**
15. Remove rear footwell ventilation hoses, **Fig. 8.**
16. Disconnect wiring harnesses from heater housing.
17. Remove heater housing mounting nuts from passenger and engine compartments.
18. Remove heater housing.
19. Reverse procedure to install.

EVAPORATOR CORE

REPLACE

Refer to "Heater Core, Replace" for evaporator core replacement.

TECHNICAL SERVICE BULLETINS

Horn Inoperative

2001-03

On some of these models the horn may not operate.

This condition may be caused by water ingestion and internal horn corrosion.

To correct this condition, install revised horn and bracket (P/N 3M5Z-13832-BA) onto mounting surface opposite radiator support bracket, **Fig. 9.** **Torque** mounting bolt to 106 inch lbs.

Ignition Lock Difficult To Turn

2001-02

On some of these models the ignition lock may be difficult to turn, or the key may not be inserted or stick.

This condition may be caused by the ignition lock cylinder.

To correct this condition, proceed as follows:

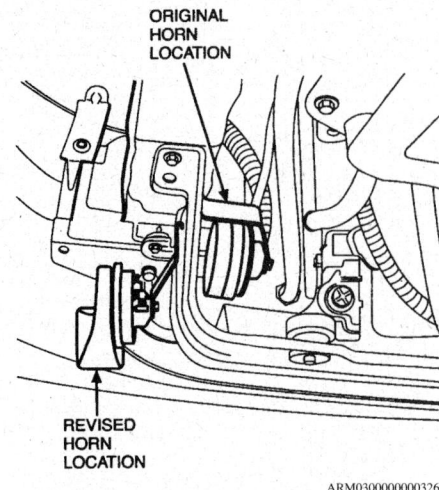

ORIGINAL HORN LOCATION

REVISED HORN LOCATION

ARM0300000000326

Fig. 9   Horn replacement

1. Remove steering wheel as outlined under "Steering Wheel, Replace."
2. Disconnect electrical connector, then remove mounting screw and Passive Anti-Theft System (PATS) transceiver.
3. Draw line through middle of cylinder face 90° to key slot.
4. Drill .157 inch pilot hole .118 inch deep, .118 inch down from slot.
5. Drill .394 inch hole 1.378 inches deep.
6. Remove lockbar from hole.
7. Turn cylinder while depressing retainer pin and remove it.
8. Install lock cylinder repair kit (P/N XS4Z-11582-AA).

Loss of Intermittent Wiper Or Park Function

2002-05

On some of these models the wipers may intermittently be inoperative, one sweep function may stop in the middle of glass when the stalk is released or the wipers may jump when parked from intermittent mode.

This condition may be caused by the wiper relay.

To correct this condition, replace the wiper relay.

Turn Signal Lamp Function Does Not Cancel

2001-02

On some of these models the turn signal function may not cancel after turning.

This condition may be caused by the sliding contact.

To correct this condition, install a spacer during sliding contact replacement, as follows:

1. Turn accessories and ignition switch to OFF position.
2. Remove cover from central junction box below lefthand side of instrument panel, then the Restraints Control Module (RCM) fuse.
3. Turn ignition switch to ON position and ensure air bag indicator remains lit (no flashing).
4. Turn ignition switch to OFF position.
5. Disconnect and isolate battery ground cable. Wait at least one minute before proceeding to next step.
6. Rotate steering wheel as required to undo driver air bag module captive bolts.
7. Disconnect driver air bag module retaining clips.
8. Carefully remove air bag module from steering wheel.
9. Disconnect electrical connector.
10. Remove the air bag module sliding contact as outlined under "Air Bag Slip Ring/Sliding Contact, Replace" in "Passive Restraint Systems" chapter.
11. Install .035 inch spacer (P/N W709947-S300) onto steering column.
12. Install new air bag sliding contact.

Inoperative Blower Motor

2000-03

On some of these models there may be an inoperative heater blower motor resistor, blower motor or blown blower motor fuse.

This condition may be caused by water entering the climate control heater blower motor case.

To correct this condition, proceed as follows:

1. If blower motor resistor is inoperative, replace resistor and blower motor.
2. If blower motor is inoperative or fuse is blown, replace blower motor.
3. **On models built before Jan. 2, 2003,** if there are visible gaps between windshield and cowl grille, replace cowl grille.
4. **On all models,** remove cowl panel. If there are gaps between the cabin air filter housing gasket and sheet metal plenum, repair bent studs or slot housing to allow it to center on studs.
5. Repair sheet metal flanges as required.
6. Replace cabin air filter gasket as required.
7. If not water leaks are found, replace cabin air filter.

2.0L (VINs 3 & 5) DOHC Engines

NOTE: On Air Bag Equipped Models, Refer To "Air Bag System Precautions" Located In The Front Of This Manual For System Disarming & Arming Procedures.

NOTE: Refer To "Computer Relearn Procedures" Located In The Front Of This Manual When Battery Power To The Computer Has Been Interrupted.

NOTE: Prior To Performing Any Service Operations Listed In This Section, Consult The "Technical Service Bulletins" Section For Related Information.

INDEX

PRECAUTIONS

Air Bag Systems

Refer to "Air Bag System Precautions" in the front of this manual for system disarming and arming procedures.

Battery Ground Cable

Prior to service, disconnect battery ground cable and isolate as required.

Fuel System Pressure Relief

1. Remove fuel pump fuse.
2. Start engine and idle until engine stalls.
3. Crank engine for approximately five seconds to ensure fuel supply manifold pressure has been relieved.
4. Install fuel pump fuse.

Quick Disconnect Hoses

R-CLIP

When working with R-clip type connections, do not use tools to disconnect, **Fig. 1.**
Use of tools may deform clip components and could cause leaks.
To disconnect, proceed as follows:
1. Bend shipping tab downward.
2. Spread R-clip and push clip into fitting.
3. Separate fitting from tube.
To connect, proceed as follows:
1. Inspect fitting and tube for damage and ensure connections are clean.
2. Apply light coat of suitable, clean engine oil to male end of tube.
3. Insert R-clip into fitting.
4. Align tube and fitting, then insert tube into fitting and push together until click is heard.
5. Pull on connection to ensure it is fully engaged.

SPRING LOCK

When working with spring lock type connections, spring lock tool set No. T84L-19623-B, or equivalent, must be used to disconnect fittings, **Fig. 2.**
When connecting spring lock type fittings, proceed as follows:
1. Inspect and clean both coupling ends.
2. Lubricate fuel line O-ring seals with suitable, clean engine oil.
3. When connection is made, pull on line to ensure it is fully engaged.

VAPOR TUBE

To disconnect vapor tube connections, squeeze fitting and disconnect vapor tube from fitting, **Fig. 3.**
To connect, proceed as follows:
1. Ensure fittings are clean and free from damage.
2. Push tube onto fitting until it snaps into place.
3. Pull on connection to verify fitting is secure.

COMPRESSION PRESSURE

1. Ensure crankcase oil is of correct viscosity and at correct level.
2. Ensure battery is fully charged and engine is at normal operating temperature.
3. Turn ignition switch to OFF position.
4. Remove spark plugs.
5. Set throttle plates to wide open position.
6. Install suitable compression gauge in cylinder No. 1.
7. Install auxiliary starter switch in starting circuit.
8. With ignition switch off, use to crank engine at least five compression strokes using auxiliary starter switch.
9. Record number of compression strokes required to reach highest reading and record highest reading.

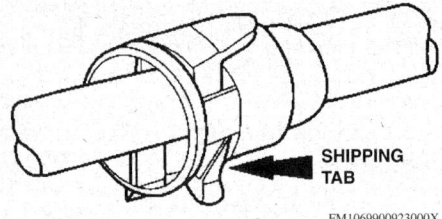

Fig. 1 R-clip connection

10. Repeat test on each cylinder, cranking engine same number of compression strokes.
11. Lowest cylinder reading must be within 75% of highest reading.

ENGINE
REPLACE
VIN 3

1. Relieve fuel system pressure as outlined under "Precautions."
2. Ensure engine is cool, then open coolant expansion tank.
3. Remove battery and tray, then disconnect ground cable.
4. Disconnect Mass Air Flow (MAF) sensor, Positive Crankcase Ventilation (PCV) hose and intake hose from air cleaner housing.
5. Remove air cleaner housing.
6. Disconnect body ground cables.
7. Remove air cleaner intake hose from core support.
8. Raise and support vehicle.
9. Drain engine coolant into suitable container. Install drain plug.
10. Drain engine oil into suitable container. Install drain plug.
11. Partially lower vehicle.
12. Loosen lefthand and righthand suspension strut center nuts five turns. Prevent strut piston rod from turning by using suitable Allen key.
13. Loosen lefthand and righthand front wheel nuts.
14. **On models equipped with manual transaxle,** proceed as follows:
    a. Move shift lever to neutral position.
    b. Remove shift lever cover.
    c. Attach gearshift alignment tool No. T97P-7025-A, or equivalent, to gearshift lever.
15. **On all models,** disconnect speed control and accelerator cables.
16. Disconnect ignition coil, radio interference filter and heated oxygen sensor connectors.
17. Disconnect cooling fan, duel injector, alternator and engine harness connectors.
18. **On models equipped with manual transaxle,** disconnect clutch slave cylinder high pressure line.
19. **On all models,** raise and support vehicle.
20. **On models equipped with manual transaxle,** disconnect reverse lamp switch.
21. **On all models,** disconnect Vehicle Speed Sensor (VSS) and Crankshaft Position (CKP) sensor.

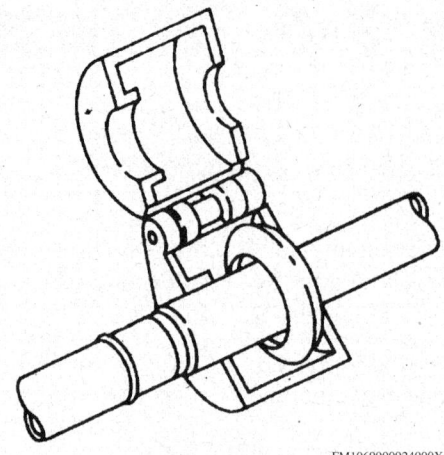

Fig. 2 Spring lock connection

22. Remove air deflector and cooling fan.
23. Partially lower vehicle.
24. Disconnect engine and brake servo vacuum hoses.
25. Disconnect fuel lines and coolant hoses.
26. **On models equipped with automatic transaxle,** proceed as follows:
    a. Disconnect selector lever cable from transaxle.
    b. Remove oil filler pipe/selector cable bracket.
    c. Mark location of transaxle cooling lines for installation alignment, then remove.
27. **On models equipped with manual transaxle,** proceed as follows:
    a. Disconnect shift cable from gear lever.
    b. Pretension abutment collars by turning counterclockwise and remove cable assembly from bracket.
    c. Disconnect selector cable from selector lever.
    d. Pretension abutment collars by turning counterclockwise and remove cable assembly from bracket.
    e. Release adjustment mechanism by pressing inward.
28. **On all models,** raise and support vehicle.
29. Remove drive belt cover.
30. Disconnect Power Steering Pressure (PSP) switch and remove accessory drive belt.
31. **On models equipped with air conditioning,** remove compressor from mounting bracket, and attach it to radiator crossmember.
32. **On all models,** disconnect coolant hose and remove power steering pump bolts.
33. Lower vehicle, then disconnect coolant expansion tank and position aside.
34. Remove power steering reservoir and position aside.
35. Disconnect bracket of power steering high pressure pipe.
36. Remove power steering pump.
37. Raise and support vehicle.
38. Remove flexible exhaust pipe.
39. Remove engine roll restrictor.
40. Remove mounting bolts and discon-

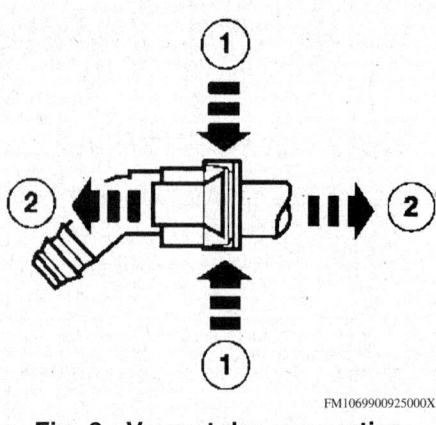

Fig. 3 Vapor tube connection

nect lower ball joint from steering knuckle.
41. Disconnect intermediate shaft bearing cap and discard nuts and bearing cap. **Do not bend inner joint more than 18° or outer joint more than 45°.**
42. Pull intermediate shaft with front half-shaft from transmission and support using suitable mechanics wire.
43. Remove lefthand driveshaft from transaxle and support using suitable mechanics wire.
44. Install plug tool No. T81P-4026-A, or equivalent, to both sides of differential.
45. Place suitable assembly table with wooden blocks under vehicle.
46. Lower vehicle until engine and transmission assembly is on assembly stand.
47. Secure engine and transmission assembly to assembly stand using suitable safety strap.
48. Remove rear and front engine mounts.
49. Raise and support vehicle.
50. Install engine lift brackets tool No. T70P-6000 and spreader bar tool No. D93P-6001-A3, or equivalents to engine.
51. Attaching suitable lifting crane to spreader bar.
52. Remove starter motor and ground cable.
53. Remove engine to transmission mounting bolts and separate engine from transmission.
54. Reverse procedure to install noting the following:
    a. When installing driveshafts, use new snap rings, center bearing caps and bolts.
    b. Install righthand, then lefthand half-shaft.

VIN 5

1. Relieve fuel system pressure as outlined under "Precautions."
2. Ensure engine is cool, then open coolant expansion tank.
3. Remove battery, then battery tray.
4. Disconnect upper clip on air cleaner outlet tube.
5. Disconnect Mass Air Flow (MAF) sensor electrical connector and breather pipe from air cleaner housing.
6. Remove air cleaner.

7. Disconnect ground cable from inner fender.
8. Remove air cleaner intake hose and resonator.
9. Raise and support vehicle.
10. Drain engine coolant into suitable container. Install drain plug.
11. Drain engine oil into suitable container. Install drain plug.
12. Partially lower vehicle.
13. Loosen lefthand and righthand suspension strut center nuts five turns. Use suitable Allen key to prevent strut piston rod from turning.
14. Disconnect speed control and accelerator cables from throttle body.
15. Remove electronic ignition coil cover.
16. Disconnect fuel injector wiring harness.
17. Disconnect ground cable from engine lifting eye.
18. Disconnect alternator electrical connector.
19. Disconnect high pressure line from clutch slave cylinder.
20. Raise and support vehicle.
21. Disconnect Vehicle Speed Sensor (VSS).
22. Disconnect reverse lamp switch electrical connector.
23. Partially lower vehicle.
24. Disconnect engine vacuum hoses from intake manifold.
25. Release quick release coupling and disconnect brake booster pipe from intake manifold.
26. Disconnect fuel lines and coolant hoses.
27. Disconnect shift and selector cables from selector levers.
28. Disconnect retaining bracket from transaxle.
29. Raise and support vehicle.
30. Remove drive belt cover, rotate tensioner clockwise. Remove accessory drive belt.
31. **On models equipped with air conditioning,** remove compressor from mounting bracket, and attach to radiator crossmember.
32. **On all models,** disconnect radiator lower coolant hose from radiator.
33. Disconnect coolant hose from oil cooler.
34. Lower vehicle, disconnect coolant expansion tank and position aside.
35. Ensure road wheels are in straight ahead position and lock them in position.
36. Disconnect steering column from steering gear pinion extension.
37. Drain power steering reservoir into suitable container.
38. Remove power steering reservoir and position aside.
39. Raise and support vehicle.
40. Remove flexible exhaust pipe.
41. Remove front tire and wheel assemblies.
42. Loosen tie-rod end mounting nut on both sides. **Leave tie-rod end mounting nuts in place.**
43. Disconnect tie-rod end from wheel knuckle on both sides using tie-rod end remover tool No. TOOL-3290-D, or equivalent. **Protect ball joint seal**

with soft cloth. Discard tie-rod end mounting nuts.
44. Disconnect stabilizer bar connecting link from stabilizer bar on both sides. Use 5 mm Allen Key to prevent ball joint from rotating.
45. Remove heat shields.
46. Disconnect lower arm ball joint from wheel knuckle on both sides. **Protect ball joint seal with soft cloth.**
47. Remove engine support insulator to transaxle center mounting bolt.
48. Remove steering gear heat shield.
49. Disconnect power steering line to clamp.
50. Remove power steering line clamp mounting bolt.
51. Rotate power steering clamp clockwise. Drain oil into suitable container.
52. Support crossmember with suitable transmission jack.
53. Remove c mounting bolts and crossmember.
54. Disconnect intermediate shaft bearing cap and discard nuts and bearing cap. **Do not bend inner joint more than 18° or outer joint i more than 45°.**
55. Pull intermediate shaft with front halfshaft from transmission and support using suitable mechanics wire.
56. Remove lefthand driveshaft from transaxle using halfshaft remover tool No. T86P-3514-A, or equivalent. Support it aside using mechanics wire and discard snap ring.
57. Place suitable assembly table with wooden blocks under vehicle.
58. Lower vehicle until engine and transmission assembly is on assembly stand.
59. Secure engine and transmission assembly to assembly stand using suitable safety strap.
60. Remove rear and front engine mounts.
61. Raise and support vehicle.
62. Install engine lift brackets tool No. T70P-6000 and spreader bar tool No. D93P-6001-A3, or equivalents, to engine.
63. Attaching suitable lifting crane to spreader bar.
64. Remove catalyst monitor sensor.
65. Support catalytic convertor and remove support bracket.
66. Remove heated oxygen sensor.
67. Disconnect catalytic convertor from exhaust manifold. Discard gaskets and nuts.
68. Remove engine to transmission upper mounting bolts.
69. Disconnect ground cable from transaxle.
70. Remove starter motor and secure aside.
71. Remove engine to transmission mounting bolts, then separate engine from transmission.
72. Reverse procedure to install. noting the following:
    a. Install new exhaust flange gasket and nuts.
    b. Installing new front driveshaft snap rings, center bearing caps and bolts.
    c. Install righthand, then lefthand halfshaft.

d. Bleed hydraulic clutch system.

INTAKE MANIFOLD
REPLACE

VIN 3

1. Relieve fuel system pressure as outlined under "Precautions."
2. Remove alternator.
3. Disconnect Mass Air Flow (MAF) sensor electrical connector, crankcase ventilation hose and air intake hose from air cleaner housing.
4. Remove air cleaner housing.
5. Disconnect accelerator and speed control cables from throttle body.
6. Remove fuel pressure sensor.
7. Remove Exhaust Gas Recirculation (EGR) valve and EGR pipe bracket.
8. Disconnect vacuum hoses from throttle body.
9. Disconnect fuel injector and Camshaft Position (CMP) sensor electrical connectors.
10. Remove fuel line from throttle body.
11. Remove engine lifting eye.
12. Remove intake manifold studs from front of engine.
13. Remove intake manifold mounting bolts, nuts and intake manifold.
14. Reverse procedure to install.

VIN 5

1. Relieve fuel system pressure as outlined under "Precautions."
2. Raise and support vehicle.
3. Remove intake manifold lower mounting bolt.
4. Lower vehicle.
5. Disconnect inner cable from throttle body.
6. Disconnect Vehicle Speed Sensor (VSS) from throttle body.
7. Remove retaining clip and disconnect inner cable from throttle body.
8. Rotate outer cable.
9. Disconnect accelerator from throttle body.
10. Remove air cleaner outlet tube.
11. Disconnect fuel injector electrical connectors.
12. Remove fuel injection supply manifold.
13. Disconnect upper clip on air cleaner outlet tube.
14. Disconnect Mass Air Flow (MAF) Sensor and breather pipe from air cleaner housing.
15. Remove air cleaner housing.
16. Disconnect throttle Position Sensor (TPS) electrical connector.
17. Rotate Intake Manifold Runner Control (IMRC) lever.
18. Remove IMRC actuator cable.
19. Release IMRC actuator cable locking tangs.
20. Disconnect IRMC actuator from intake manifold.
21. Disconnect vacuum hoses from throttle body.
22. Release quick release coupling and pull out brake booster pipe.
23. Disconnect brake booster pipe from intake manifold.

24. Remove fuel line from throttle body.
25. Separate two sections of intake manifold.
26. Remove manifold inner section mounting nuts and bolt.
27. Remove intake manifold inner section retaining stud.
28. Remove intake manifold section.
29. Reverse procedure to install.

EXHAUST MANIFOLD
REPLACE
VIN 3

1. Raise and support vehicle.
2. Remove catalyst bracket and disconnect heated oxygen sensor electrical connectors.
3. Lower vehicle and remove heat shield from side of engine.
4. Disconnect Mass Air Flow (MAF) sensor.
5. Disconnect Positive Crankcase Ventilation (PCV) hose.
6. Disconnect air inlet hose and remove air cleaner housing.
7. Remove Exhaust Gas Recirculation (EGR) tube.
8. Remove catalytic converter to exhaust manifold mounting bolts.
9. Remove manifold to cylinder head mounting bolts and exhaust manifold.
10. Reverse procedure to install.

VIN 5

1. Remove oil dipstick.
2. Disconnect cooling fan motor electrical connectors.
3. Remove two pin-type retainers.
4. Raise and support vehicle.
5. Disconnect radiator top clip. then remove cooling fan motor and shroud.
6. Raise vehicle and support.
7. Remove heat shield lower mounting bolts.
8. Disconnect exhaust manifold from catalytic converter.
9. Lower vehicle.
10. Remove exhaust manifold heat shield.
11. Remove exhaust manifold and discard gaskets.
12. Reverse procedure to install.

CYLINDER HEAD
REPLACE
VIN 3

1. Raise and support vehicle.
2. Drain engine coolant into suitable container. Install drain plug after draining.
3. Release quick release coupling and disconnect brake booster pipe from intake manifold.
4. Disconnect oil pressure switch connector.
5. Lower vehicle and remove intake manifold as outlined under "Intake Manifold, Replace."
6. Remove exhaust manifold heat shield, then catalytic converter to exhaust manifold mounting bolts.

7. Remove thermostat housing mounting bolts, then thermostat housing.
8. Remove power steering pipe bracket and oil dipstick tube.
9. Disconnect bracket from power steering pump.
10. Loosen lefthand side bolt and remove righthand side bolt of alternator.
11. Remove upper bolt from alternator bracket.
12. Remove timing belt as outlined under "Timing Belt, Replace."
13. Remove air intake pipe.
14. To prevent camshaft pulley from turning, attach camshaft pulley remover tool No. T74P-6256-B, or equivalent, to camshaft pulley.
15. Remove camshaft pulleys mounting bolts, then camshaft pulleys.
16. Remove camshaft bearing cap mounting bolts in several steps in sequence, **Fig. 4.**
17. Remove oil seals and camshafts.
18. Remove cylinder head mounting bolts in sequence, **Fig. 5.**
19. Remove cylinder head.
20. Reverse procedure to install, noting the following:
    a. **Torque** new cylinder head bolts in sequence to 15 ft. lbs., **Fig. 6.**
    b. **Torque** head bolts in sequence to 30 ft. lbs.
    c. Tighten bolts an additional 90° in sequence.

VIN 5

1. Relieve fuel system pressure as outlined under "Precautions."
2. Relieve cooling system pressure by turning expansion tank cap ¼ turn. Remove cap when pressure has been released.
3. Raise and support vehicle.
4. Drain cooling system into suitable container.
5. Install radiator drain plug after draining coolant.
6. Release quick release coupling and disconnect brake booster pipe from intake manifold.
7. Disconnect oil pressure switch electrical connector.
8. Lower vehicle.
9. Remove air cleaner.
10. Disconnect accelerator cable from throttle body.
11. Disconnect vacuum hoses from intake manifold.
12. Disconnect fuel injector wiring harness.
13. Disconnect Camshaft Position (CMP) sensor electrical connector.
14. Disconnect fuel lines and ground cable.
15. Remove exhaust manifold as outlined under "Exhaust Manifold, Replace."
16. Disconnect thermostat housing.
17. Disconnect power steering pipe bracket from cylinder head.
18. Disconnect power steering pump bracket from cylinder head and cylinder block.
19. Loosen lefthand bolt and remove righthand alternator mounting bolt.
20. Disconnect wiring harness from Elec-

tronic Ignition (EI) coil and from Engine Coolant Temperature (ECT) sensor.
21. Remove alternator bracket upper mounting bolt.
22. Remove timing belt as outlined under "Timing Belt, Replace."
23. Hold camshafts by hexagon with an open ended wrench to prevent them from rotating.
24. Remove mounting bolts camshaft pulleys.
25. Remove oil feed flange and discard camshaft oil seals and oil feed flange oil seal.
26. Remove camshaft bearing cap mounting bolts in several steps in sequence, **Fig. 4.**
27. Remove camshaft.
28. Remove cylinder head mounting bolts in sequence, **Fig. 5.**
29. Remove cylinder head.
30. Reverse procedure to install, noting the following:
    a. **Torque** new torque-to-yield cylinder head bolts in sequence to 15 ft. lbs., **Fig. 6.**
    b. **Torque** head bolts in sequence to 30 ft. lbs.
    c. Tighten bolts an additional 90° in sequence.

VALVE COVER
REPLACE

1. Remove air inlet hose from throttle body and air cleaner housing.
2. Remove upper timing belt cover mounting bolts. Do not remove timing belt cover.
3. Disconnect spark plug connectors and crankcase ventilation hose.
4. Remove valve cover mounting bolts from outside to inside, working diagonally.
5. Remove valve cover.
6. Reverse procedure to install, noting the following:
    a. **Torque** valve cover mounting bolts to 18 ft. lbs., from inside to outside, working diagonally.
    b. **Torque** mounting bolts to 62 ft. lbs., from inside to outside, working diagonally.

VALVE CLEARANCE SPECIFICATIONS

Valve	Clearance, Inches①
Intake	.0043–.0071
Exhaust	.0106–.0134

① — At 59–77°F.

VALVE ADJUSTMENT

1. Remove air inlet hose from throttle body and air cleaner housing.
2. Remove upper timing belt cover mounting bolts. Do not remove timing belt cover.
3. Disconnect spark plug connectors and crankcase ventilation hose.

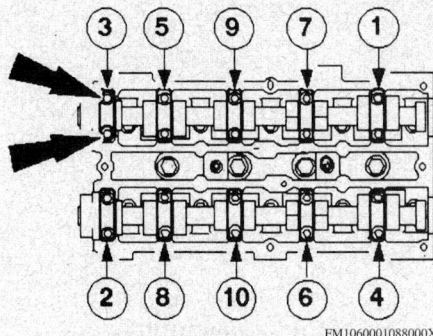

FM1060001088000X

Fig. 4 Camshaft bearing cap bolt loosening sequence

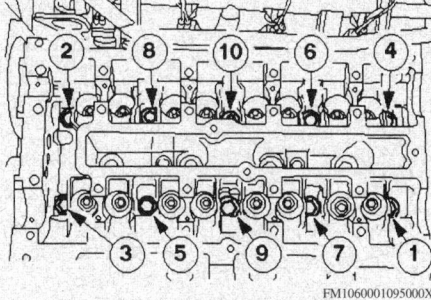

FM1060001095000X

Fig. 5 Cylinder head bolt loosening sequence

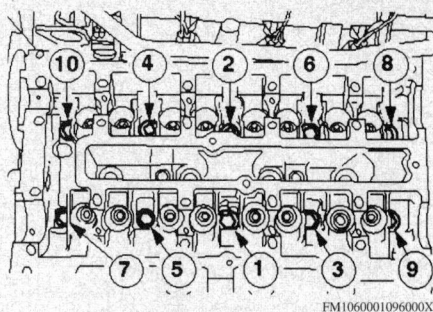

FM1060001096000X

Fig. 6 Cylinder head bolt tightening sequence

4. Remove valve cover mounting bolts from the outside to the inside, working diagonally.
5. Remove valve cover.
6. Turn crankshaft to cylinder No. 1 Top Dead Center (TDC).
7. Measure valve clearance on cylinder No. 1, using suitable feeler gauge.
8. Rotate engine 180°, then measure valve clearance on cylinder No. 3.
9. Rotate engine 180°, then measure valve clearance on cylinder No. 4.
10. Rotate engine 180°, then measure valve clearance on cylinder No. 2.
11. If valve adjustment is required, remove camshafts as outlined under "Camshaft, Replace."
12. Each tappet is marked with number that indicates its thickness in millimeters.
13. To determine correct size tappet required, add tappet size to measured clearance.
14. Select and install a tappet that will bring clearance within specifications. Refer to "Valve Clearance Specifications."
15. Install camshafts as outlined under "Camshaft, Replace."

CRANKSHAFT DAMPER
REPLACE

1. Move serpentine belt tensioner in clockwise to relieve accessory belt tension.
2. Remove serpentine belt.
3. Remove crankshaft pulley/vibration damper.
4. Reverse procedure to install.

TIMING BELT
REPLACE
Removal

1. Loosen righthand front wheel lug nuts.
2. Raise and support vehicle.
3. Remove righthand front tire and wheel assembly.
4. Remove serpentine drive belt cover.
5. Loosen water pump pulley bolts.
6. Move serpentine belt tensioner in clockwise to relieve accessory belt tension.
7. Remove serpentine belt.
8. Remove water pump pulley.

9. Remove serpentine drive belt idler pulley.
10. Remove crankshaft pulley mounting bolt.
11. Remove crankshaft pulley using suitable puller tool.
12. Remove lower portion of engine front cover.
13. Lower vehicle.
14. Remove fasteners and position coolant expansion tank aside.
15. Disconnect power steering fluid reservoir and position it aside with hose attached.
16. Position suitable floor jack and wooden block under engine oil pan.
17. Mark engine front support insulator mounting position for installation alignment.
18. Take pressure off engine front support insulator by raising floor jack slightly. Remove insulator.
19. Remove upper timing belt cover mounting bolts.
20. Remove center cover and front engine mounting bracket bolts.
21. Remove timing belt cover upper and center portions.
22. Remove engine appearance cover.
23. Mark spark plug wires, and disconnect them at spark plugs.
24. Disconnect crankcase ventilation hose.
25. Remove mounting bolts working diagonally from outside to inside and valve cover.
26. Remove spark plugs.
27. Rotate crankshaft until cylinder No. 1 is approximately at TDC position.
28. Record timing belt tensioner alignment marks and loosen tensioner bolt.
29. Rotate belt tensioner clockwise to release tension.
30. Loosen belt tensioner bolt four turns and disconnect tensioner.
31. Remove timing belt.

Installation

1. Loosen exhaust camshaft sprocket and intake camshaft sprocket using holding tool No. T74P-6256-B, or equivalent, to prevent camshaft sprockets from turning when loosening bolts.
2. Rotate crankshaft until cylinder No. 1 reaches TDC, **Fig. 7.**
3. Remove engine block slide blanking plug and install timing peg tool No.

T97P-6000-A, or equivalent, **Fig. 8.**
4. Hold camshafts by hexagons and turn them in direction of engine rotation.
5. Install camshaft alignment tool No. T94P-6256-CH, or equivalent, **Fig. 9.**
6. Ensure crankshaft is still resting against timing peg. **Do not rotate crankshaft.**
7. With timing belt tensioner bolt backed out four full turns, position tensioner so location tab is at approximately four o'clock position, **Fig. 10.** Line up hex key slot in tensioner adjusting washer with pointer which is located behind pulley.
8. Starting at crankshaft and working counterclockwise, install timing belt.
9. Rotate timing belt tensioner locating tab counterclockwise and insert locating tab into slot in rear timing cover.
10. Position hex key slot in tensioner adjusting washer to 4 o'clock position.
11. Tighten tensioner bolt enough to seat tensioner firmly against rear timing belt cover, but still loose enough to allow tensioner adjusting washer to be rotated with 6 mm hex wrench.
12. Rotate adjusting washer counterclockwise until notch in pointer is centered over index line on locating tab using 6 mm hex wrench. During adjustment pointer will move in clockwise direction.
13. While holding adjusting washer in position, tighten tensioner mounting bolt.
14. After tightening tensioner bolt, ensure tensioner pointer is still aligned with index line. If not, repeat previous steps.
15. Prevent camshaft sprockets from turning, by using holding tool No. T74P-6256-B, or equivalent. Tighten intake and exhaust camshaft sprockets.
16. Remove timing peg.
17. Remove camshaft locking tool.
18. Rotate crankshaft two revolutions in direction of engine rotation to cylinder No. 1 TDC compression stroke.
19. Install timing peg and ensure crankshaft timing is properly set.
20. Ensure camshaft timing is properly set by installing aligning tool No. T94P-6256-CH, or equivalent, onto camshafts. If aligning tool refuses to fit into both slots, loosen tensioner and both camshaft sprocket bolts, then tension timing belt again.
21. Remove alignment tool from camshafts and timing peg for crankshaft.

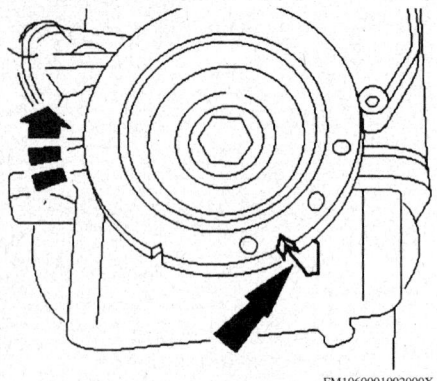

FM1060001092000X

Fig. 7 Crankshaft timing mark alignment

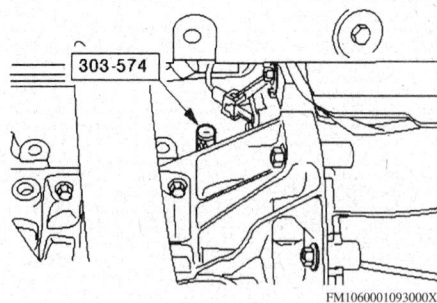

FM1060001093000X

Fig. 8 Crankshaft TDC timing peg installation

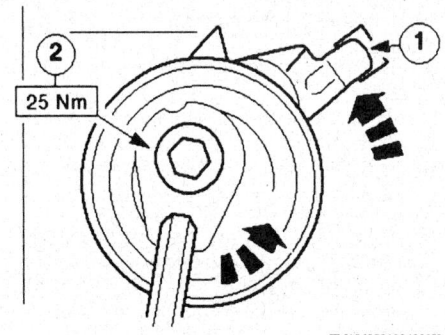

FM1060001094000X

Fig. 10 Timing belt tensioner alignment

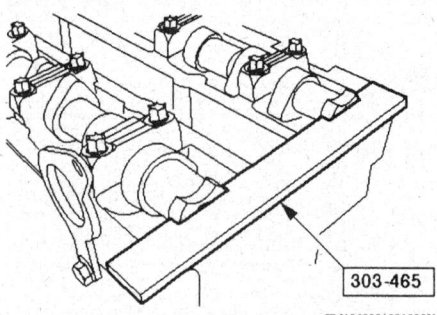

FM1060001091000X

Fig. 9 Camshaft alignment

Install blanking plug in crankshaft timing peg hole.
22. Install valve cover.
23. Install spark plugs.
24. Connect crankcase ventilation hose.
25. Connect spark plug wires.
26. Install engine appearance cover.
27. Install center and upper portions of engine front cover and engine support bracket.
28. Raise floor jack slightly and install engine support insulator.
29. Install coolant expansion tank.
30. Raise and support vehicle.
31. Install lower portion of timing belt cover.
32. Install crankshaft pulley.
33. Install serpentine belt idler and water pump pulleys.
34. Rotate serpentine belt tensioner clockwise and install belt.
35. Tighten water pump pulley bolts.
36. Install serpentine drive belt cover.
37. Install righthand front tire and wheel assembly.
38. Lower vehicle.
39. Tighten righthand front wheel lug nuts.
40. **Some abnormal drive symptoms may appear for approximately 10 miles while vehicle relearns its adaptive strategy.**

CAMSHAFT
REPLACE
Removal

1. Remove air intake pipe.
2. Disconnect accelerator and speed control cables from throttle body.
3. Remove timing belt as outlined under "Timing Belt, Replace."
4. Prevent camshaft pulley from turning, by installing camshaft pulley remover tool No. T74P-6256-B, or equivalent, to camshaft pulley.
5. Remove mounting bolts and camshaft pulleys.
6. Remove camshaft bearing cap mounting bolts in several steps in sequence, **Fig. 4.**
7. Remove oil seals and camshafts.

Installation

1. Camshaft bearing caps have identification numbers stamped on outer face. Apply suitable sealant to bearing caps marked 0 and 5, **Fig. 11.**
2. Turn crankshaft to approximately 60° Before Top Dead Center (BTDC) on cylinder No. 1.
3. Lubricate camshafts and bearing caps with suitable, clean engine oil.
4. Place camshafts into position so none of cams are at full lift.
5. Tighten camshaft bearing cap bolts evenly ½ turn at a time in sequence, **Fig. 12.**
6. **Torque** bolts in sequence to 88 inch lbs.
7. **Torque** bolts in sequence to 14 ft. lbs.
8. Lubricate camshaft and new camshaft oil seal lip with suitable, clean engine oil, then install oil seal.
9. Install camshaft timing pulleys. **Do not tighten pulley bolts fully at this time. Pulleys must be able to turn freely on camshafts.**
10. Install timing belt as outlined under "Timing Belt, Replace."
11. Connect accelerator and speed control cables to throttle body.
12. Install air intake pipe.

CRANKSHAFT SEAL
REPLACE

1. Remove crankshaft timing belt as outlined under "Timing Belt, Replace."
2. Remove crankshaft pulley hub.

3. Remove timing belt thrust washer. Record position of thrust washer for installation alignment.
4. Remove crankshaft front oil seal using oil seal remover tool No. T81P-6700-A, or equivalent.
5. Reverse procedure to install. Lubricate new oil seal and crankshaft running surface with suitable, clean engine oil.

CRANKSHAFT REAR OIL SEAL
REPLACE

1. Remove transaxle as outlined in **MOTOR's "Domestic Transmission, In-Vehicle Service"** manual.
2. **On models with manual transaxle,** remove clutch pressure plate and clutch disc as outlined in **MOTOR's "Domestic Transmission, In-Vehicle Service"** manual.
3. **On all models,** remove flywheel using flywheel locking tool No. T74P-6375-A, or equivalent.
4. Remove crankshaft rear seal using seal remover tool No. T92C-6700-CH, or equivalent.
5. Reverse procedure to install. Install oil seal using crankshaft rear oil installer tool No. T88P-6701B-1, or equivalent.

OIL PAN
REPLACE

1. **On 2002–04 models,** remove catalytic converter.
2. **On all models,** raise and support vehicle, then drain engine oil into suitable container.
3. Remove oil pan mounting bolts.
4. Separate oil pan from lower crankcase with suitable sharp tool.
5. Reverse procedure to install, noting the following:
   a. Install 10 M6 X 20 studs into dead end bores, **Fig. 13.**
   b. Apply suitable sealant to oil pan mating surface.
   c. **Install oil pan within 10 minutes of applying sealant.**
   d. **Torque** oil pan bolts in sequence to 53 inch lbs., **Fig. 14.**
   e. **Torque** bolts in sequence to 89 inch lbs.

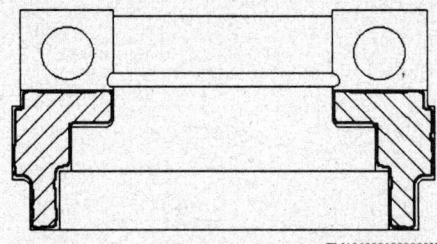

Fig. 11 Camshaft bearing cap sealant application

FM1060001089000X

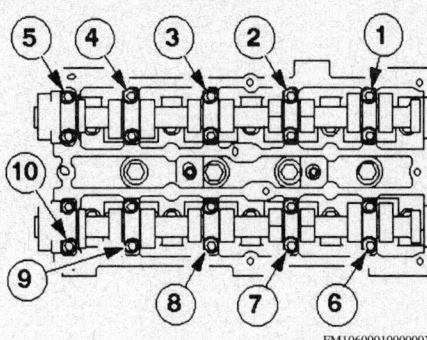

FM1060001090000X

Fig. 12 Camshaft bearing cap bolt tightening sequence

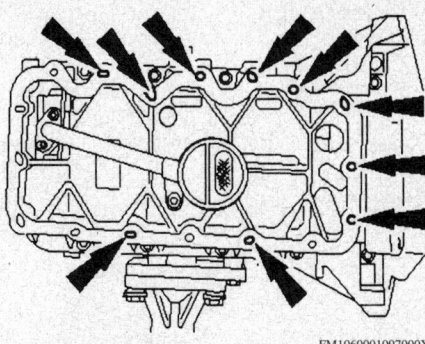

FM1060001097000X

Fig. 13 Lower crankcase dead end bore stud installation

SERPENTINE DRIVE BELT

Routing

Refer to **Figs. 15 and 16,** for serpentine belt routing.

Replace

1. Raise and support vehicle.
2. Remove drive belt cover.
3. Loosen bolts on coolant pump pulley.
4. Rotate belt tensioner counterclockwise, and remove belt.
5. Reverse procedure to install.

THERMOSTAT
REPLACE

1. Drain engine cooling system into suitable container.
2. Disconnect thermostat housing coolant hoses.
3. Remove mounting bolts and thermostat housing.
4. Remove thermostat and discard rubber seal.
5. Reverse procedure to install.

WATER PUMP
REPLACE

1. Drain engine cooling system into suitable container.
2. Loosen water pump pulley mounting bolts.
3. Remove drive belt cover.
4. Loosen bolts on coolant pump pulley.
5. Rotate belt tensioner counterclockwise, and remove belt.
6. Remove water pump pulley.
7. Remove timing belt as outlined under "Timing Belt, Replace."
8. Remove timing belt idler pulley.
9. Disconnect water pump hose.
10. Remove lower and upper mounting bolts, then water pump.
11. Remove and discard water pump sealing ring.
12. Reverse procedure to install.

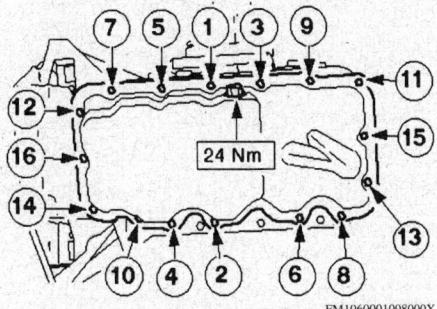

FM1060001098000X

Fig. 14 Oil pan bolt tightening sequence

RADIATOR
REPLACE

1. Disconnect cooling fan motor electrical connectors.
2. Remove two pin-type retainers.
3. Raise and support vehicle.
4. Disconnect radiator top clip. then remove cooling fan motor and shroud.
5. Drain coolant into suitable container.
6. Remove four pin-type retainers from radiator air deflector.
7. Lower vehicle and disconnect upper radiator hose.
8. Raise and support vehicle.
9. **On models equipped with air conditioning,** support condenser and transaxle oil cooler.
10. **On all models,** disconnect radiator upper coolant hose.
11. Disconnect radiator lower coolant hoses.
12. Disconnect horn electrical connector.
13. Remove mounting bolts and radiator support bracket bolts.
14. Remove radiator.
15. Reverse procedure to install.

FUEL PUMP
REPLACE

1. Relieve fuel system pressure as outlined under "Precautions."
2. Drain fuel tank into suitable container.
3. Disconnect exhaust pipe from rear hanger insulator.

4. Disconnect center muffler from hanger.
5. Remove mounting nuts and disconnect exhaust pipe from remaining hangers. Position exhaust pipe aside.
6. Remove heat shield.
7. Disconnect fuel tank vent and filler pipes.
8. Disconnect inline fuel coupling as outlined under "Precautions."
9. Disconnect evaporative emission pipe and rollover valve connector.
10. Support fuel tank with suitable jack, then remove support strap bolt.
11. Partially lower tank and disconnect rollover valve hose.
12. Disconnect fuel pump electrical connector.
13. Disconnect fuel pressure sensor electrical connector.
14. Remove fuel tank.
15. Pull red fuel line clip fully towards fuel pump module.
16. Disconnect fuel supply line from module, by holding red fuel line clip against fuel pump module and firmly pulling line.
17. Remove locking ring using fuel tank sender unit wrench tool No. 310-069, or equivalent.
18. Rotate fuel pump module counterclockwise and remove it from tank. **Do not damage float or arm.**
19. Reverse procedure to install, noting the following:
    a. **Ensure red fuel line clip i clicks into place.**
    b. **Ensure that fuel line is fully seated by pulling on line. Clip should move slightly away from module and fuel line should not be able to be removed.**
    c. Ensure new fuel pump module seal is seated correctly on fuel tank prior to tightening locking ring.

FUEL FILTER
REPLACE

1. Relieve fuel system pressure as outlined under "Precautions."
2. Raise and support vehicle.

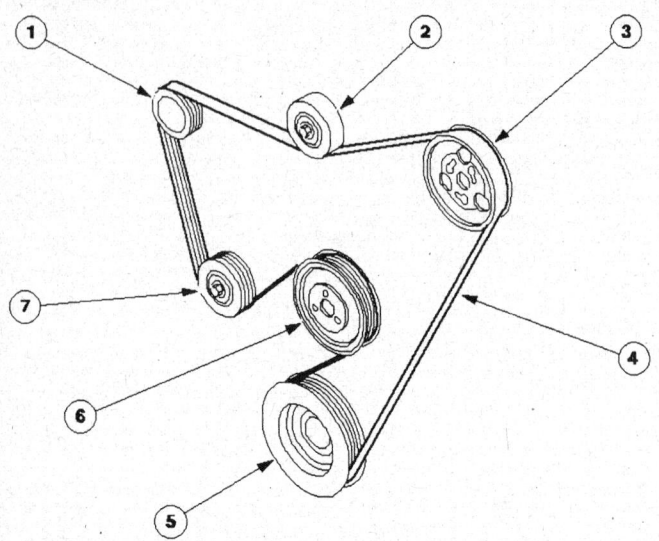

Fig. 15 Serpentine drive belt routing. Less air conditioning

FM1060001106000X

Item	Description
1	Generator pulley
2	Belt idler pulley
3	Power steering pump pulley
4	Accesory drive belt
5	Crankshaft pulley
6	Water pump pulley
7	Belt tensioner

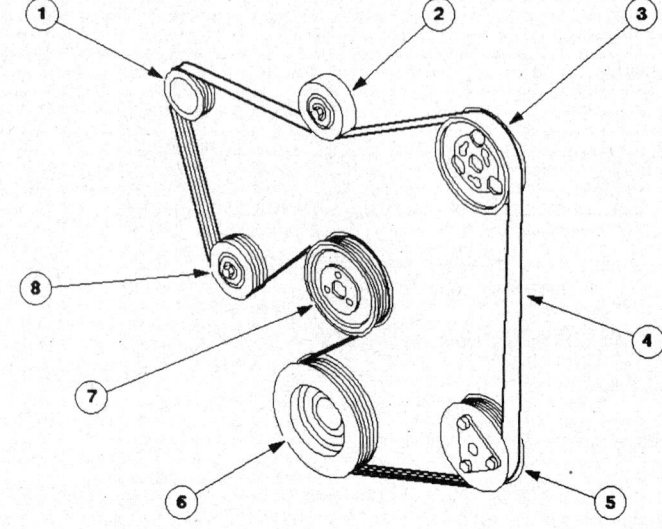

Fig. 16 Serpentine drive belt routing. With air conditioning

FM1060001107000X

Item	Description
1	Generator pulley
2	Belt idler pulley
3	Power steering pump pulley
4	Accessory drive belt
5	A/C compressor pulley
6	Crankshaft pulley
7	Water pump pulley
8	Belt tensioner

3. Disconnect evaporative emission pipe.
4. Remove fuel filter outlet pipe and disconnect inlet pipe.
5. Remove fuel filter and bracket.
6. Separate filter from bracket.
7. Reverse procedure to install.

TECHNICAL SERVICE BULLETINS

Rough, Rolling Or High Idle Or Stall

2002 SVT

On some of these models the engine may have a rough idle, rolling idle, stall, high idle or backfire after a cold start. There may also be a hesitation or surge at steady cruise.

This condition may be caused by the intake manifold separating at the rubber boots.

To correct this condition, proceed as follows:

1. Inspect intake manifold boots and clamps.
2. If they are loose, not in position or separated, remove fuel rail and injectors as an assembly.
3. Disconnect hooking clips and remove clamps.
4. Unscrew worm drive clamps (P/N W525939-S300) into C shape.
5. Place new clamps around boots in original hooking clips' positions.
6. **Torque** clamps to 31–39 inch lbs.
7. Install fuel rail with injectors.

TIGHTENING SPECIFICATIONS

Year	Component	Torque, Ft. Lbs.
2001–04	Alternator	18
	Alternator Bracket	48
	Camshaft Bearing Cap	③
	Camshaft Pulleys	50
	Catalytic Converter	35
	Clutch Pressure Plate	21
	Connecting Rod Bearing Cap	②
	Crankcase Ventilation Pipe Bracket	17
	Crankshaft Belt Pulley	85
	Cylinder Block Oil Gallery Blanking Plugs	17
	Cylinder Head	⑦
	Drive Belt Idler Pulley	30
	Driveplate	83
	EGR Pipe To Ignition Coil Bracket	53①
	EGR Valve	18
	Engine Roll Restrictor	35
	Exhaust Manifold Heat Shield	89①
	Exhaust Manifold Nuts	12
	Exhaust Manifold Studs	44①
	Flywheel	83
	Front Engine Lifting Eye	35
	Front Engine Mounting To Engine	59
	Fuel Pump Module	59
	Fuel Rail	89①
	Idler Pulley	17
	Ignition Coil Bracket	15
	Intake Manifold, Bolts & Nuts	13
	Intake Manifold, Studs	44①
	Lower Crankcase To Cylinder Block	16
	Main Bearing	⑤
	Oil Drain Plug	18
	Oil Intake Pipe To Oil Pump	89①
	Oil Pan	④
	Oil Pressure Switch	20
	Oil Pump	96①
	Power Steering Pump	18
	Rear Crankshaft Oil Seal Carrier	13
	Rear Engine Lifting Eye	35
	Rear Engine Mounting To Body	35
	Spark Plugs	11
	Starter Motor To Transmission	26
	Thermostat Housing	15
	Timing Belt Cover	89①
	Timing Belt Tensioner	18
	Transaxle Oil Drain Plug	33
	Valve Cover	⑥
	Water Pump Pulley	18
	Wheel Lug Nuts	63

① — Inch lbs.
② — Torque to 26 ft. lbs., then tighten an additional 90°.
③ — Refer to "Camshaft, Replace" for tightening specifications and sequence.
④ — Refer to "Oil Pan, Replace" for tightening specifications and sequence.
⑤ — Torque to 18 ft. lbs., then tighten an additional 60°.
⑥ — Refer to "Valve Cover, Replace" for tightening specifications and sequence.
⑦ — Refer to "Cylinder Head, Replace" for tightening specifications and sequence.

2.0L (VIN P) SOHC Engine

NOTE: On Air Bag Equipped Models, Refer To "Air Bag System Precautions" Located In The Front Of This Manual For System Disarming & Arming Procedures.

NOTE: Refer To "Computer Relearn Procedures" Located In The Front Of This Manual When Battery Power To The Computer Has Been Interrupted.

INDEX

PRECAUTIONS

Air Bag Systems

Refer to "Air Bag System Precautions" in the front of this manual for system disarming and arming procedures.

Battery Ground Cable

Prior to service, disconnect battery ground cable and isolate as required.

Fuel System Pressure Relief

1. Remove fuel pump fuse.
2. Start engine and idle until engine stalls.
3. Crank engine for approximately five seconds to ensure fuel supply manifold pressure has been relieved.
4. Install fuel pump fuse.

Quick Disconnect Hoses

R-CLIP

When working with R-clip type connections, do not use tools to disconnect, **Fig. 1.** Use of tools may deform clip components and could cause leaks.

To disconnect, proceed as follows:
1. Bend shipping tab downward.
2. Spread R-clip and push clip into fitting.
3. Separate fitting from tube.

To connect, proceed as follows:
1. Inspect fitting and tube for damage and ensure connections are clean.

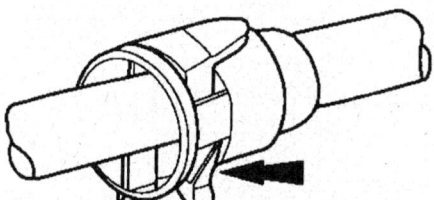

Fig. 1 R-clip connection

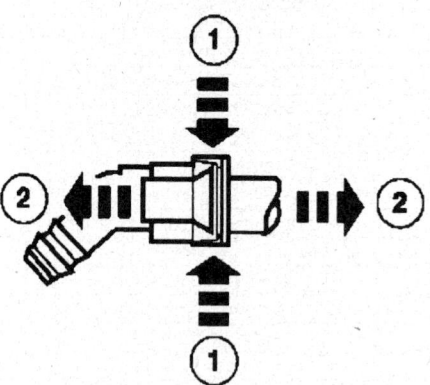

Fig. 3 Vapor tube connection

2. Apply light coat of suitable, clean engine oil to male end of tube.
3. Insert R-clip into fitting.
4. Align tube and fitting, then insert tube into fitting and push together until click is heard.
5. Pull on connection to ensure it is fully engaged.

SPRING LOCK

When working with spring lock type connections, spring lock tool set No. T84L-

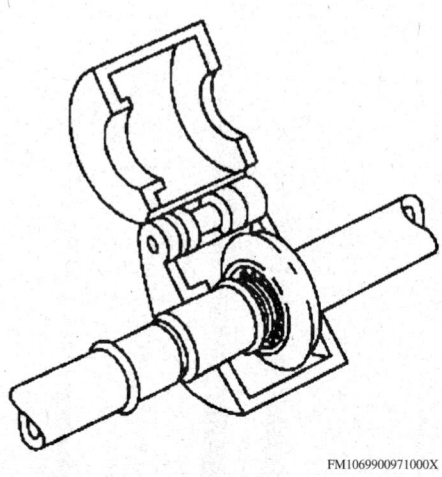

Fig. 2 Spring lock connection

19623-B, or equivalent, must be used to disconnect fittings, **Fig. 2.**

When connecting spring lock type fittings, proceed as follows:
1. Inspect and clean both coupling ends.
2. Lubricate fuel line O-ring seals with suitable, clean engine oil.
3. When connection is made, pull on line to ensure it is fully engaged.

VAPOR TUBE

To disconnect vapor tube connections, squeeze fitting and disconnect vapor tube from fitting, **Fig. 3.**

To connect, proceed as follows:
1. Ensure fittings are clean and free from damage.
2. Push tube onto fitting until it snaps into place.

3. Pull on connection to verify fitting is secure.

COMPRESSION PRESSURE

1. Ensure crankcase oil is of correct viscosity and at correct level.
2. Ensure battery is fully charged and engine is at normal operating temperature.
3. Turn ignition switch to OFF position.
4. Remove spark plugs.
5. Set throttle plates to wide open position.
6. Install suitable compression gauge in cylinder No. 1.
7. Install auxiliary starter switch in starting circuit.
8. With ignition switch off, use to crank engine at least five compression strokes using auxiliary starter switch.
9. Record number of compression strokes required to reach highest reading and record highest reading.
10. Repeat test on each cylinder, cranking engine same number of compression strokes.
11. Lowest cylinder reading must be within 75 percent of highest reading.

ENGINE
REPLACE

Automatic Transaxle

1. Relieve fuel system pressure as outlined under "Precautions."
2. Open coolant expansion tank.
3. Disconnect ground lead and remove battery tray.
4. Disconnect chassis ground cable.
5. Drain coolant into suitable container.
6. Loosen strut piston nuts five turns on both sides using suitable Allen wrench to prevent rod from turning.
7. Disconnect Mass Air Flow (MAF) sensor electrical connector and intake air hose, then remove air cleaner housing from rubber bushing.
8. Remove air cleaner intake pipe, then the accelerator and speed control cables.
9. Disconnect power steering pump pressure switch, alternator and heated oxygen sensor electrical connectors.
10. Disconnect both Powertrain Control Module (PCM) connectors.
11. Remove EVAP, brake servo, delta pressure feedback electronic system sensor and EGR valve vacuum hoses.
12. Disconnect intake manifold vacuum hoses.
13. Disconnect fuel hose and drain excess fuel into suitable container.
14. Disconnect intake manifold coolant hose.
15. Remove water pump and coolant pipe coolant hoses, then disconnect coolant expansion tank and position it aside.
16. Remove power steering reservoir and position it aside.
17. Remove radiator fan.

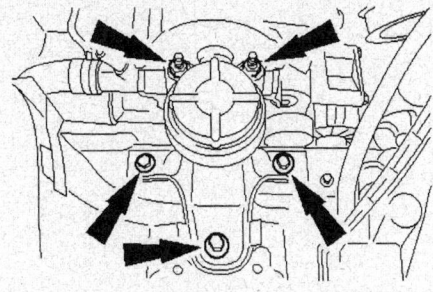

Fig. 4 Engine front mount replacement

18. Remove starter motor upper mounting bolts.
19. Remove accessory drive belt.
20. Remove power steering pump pulley using universal flange holding wrench tool No. 15-031A, or equivalent.
21. Remove power steering pump and position it aside.
22. Remove alternator and alternator bracket.
23. Remove coolant pipe bolt.
24. Raise and support vehicle.
25. Disconnect both lower suspension arms.
26. Disconnect oxygen sensor electrical connectors and remove drive belt cover.
27. **On models equipped with air conditioning,** remove compressor and tie it to radiator crossmember.
28. **On all models,** disconnect exhaust pipe.
29. Remove cover bolts and disconnect torque converter from engine drive plate.
30. Remove transaxle lower flange bolts.
31. Disconnect righthand front drive halfshaft from intermediate shaft.
32. Remove lefthand front drive halfshaft from tripod housing.
33. Remove intermediate shaft and secure aside with suitable cable tie.
34. Disconnect electrical connectors and remove starter motor.
35. Remove crankshaft pulley, righthand engine support insulator, then the lefthand and righthand transaxle flange bolts.
36. Lower vehicle.
37. Disconnect fuel line and drain excess fuel into suitable container.
38. Support transaxle with suitable jack. **Install wooden block between jack and transaxle.**
39. Relieve support insulators' pressure by raising engine slightly with suitable engine lifting device.
40. Remove engine front mounting, **Fig. 4.**
41. Disconnect Crankshaft Position (CKP) sensor electrical connector.
42. Remove upper transaxle flange bolts and separate engine from transaxle.
43. Remove engine.
44. Hold torque converter in transaxle using torque converter holding tool No. T96T-7902-A, or equivalent.
45. Reverse procedure to install.

Manual Transaxle

1. Relieve fuel system pressure as outlined under "Precautions."
2. Open coolant expansion tank.
3. Disconnect ground lead and remove battery tray.
4. Disconnect chassis ground cable.
5. Drain coolant into suitable container.
6. Loosen strut piston nuts five turns on both sides using suitable Allen wrench to prevent rod from turning.
7. Disconnect Mass Air Flow (MAF) sensor electrical connector and intake air hose, then remove air cleaner housing from rubber bushing.
8. Remove air cleaner intake pipe, then the accelerator and speed control cables.
9. Disconnect power steering pump pressure switch, alternator and heated oxygen sensor electrical connectors.
10. Disconnect both Powertrain Control Module (PCM) connectors.
11. Disconnect Vehicle Speed Sensor (VSS) and reverse lamp switch electrical connectors.
12. Remove high pressure pipe from clutch slave cylinder.
13. Remove EVAP, brake servo, delta pressure feedback electronic system sensor and EGR valve vacuum hoses.
14. Disconnect intake manifold vacuum hoses.
15. Disconnect intake manifold coolant hose.
16. Remove water pump and coolant pipe coolant hoses, then disconnect coolant expansion tank and position it aside.
17. Remove accessory drive belt.
18. Remove power steering pump pulley using universal flange holding wrench tool No.15-031-A, or equivalent.
19. Remove power steering pump and position it aside.
20. Remove powers steering reservoir and position it aside.
21. Remove radiator fan, catalytic converter, flexible exhaust pipe and drive belt cover.
22. Remove shift and selector cable covers, then the cables.
23. **On models equipped with air conditioning,** remove compressor and tie it to radiator crossmember.
24. **On all models,** remove righthand engine support insulator,
25. Remove both lower suspension arms.
26. Remove righthand front drive halfshaft from intermediate shaft. **Do not bend Inner joint more than 18° or outer joint more than 45°.**
27. Remove lefthand front drive halfshaft from tripod housing.
28. Position suitable engine assembly stand with wooden blocks under vehicle.
29. Lower vehicle until engine and transaxle assembly is on engine stand.
30. Remove engine rear mount, **Fig. 5.**
31. Remove front engine mount, **Fig. 4.**
32. Secure engine and transaxle assembly with suitable restraining strap to assembly table.
33. Raise vehicle, then pull assembly

Fig. 5 Rear engine mount replacement

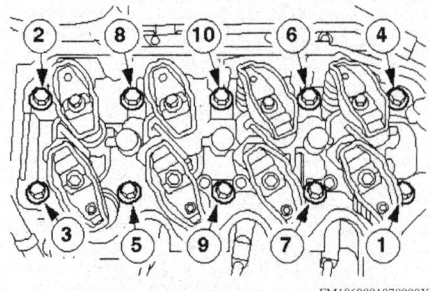

Fig. 6 Cylinder head bolt loosening sequence

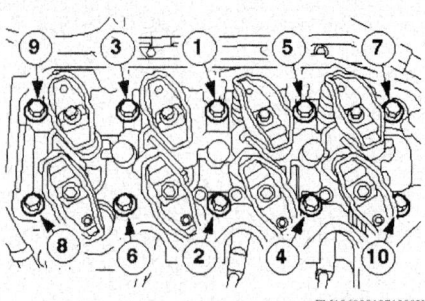

Fig. 7 Cylinder head bolt tightening sequence

stand forward with engine and transaxle assembly.
34. Separate engine from transaxle using suitable lifting device.
35. Reverse procedure to install.

INTAKE MANIFOLD
REPLACE

1. Relieve fuel system pressure as outlined under "Precautions."
2. Raise and support vehicle.
3. Remove intake manifold bracket.
4. Disconnect Mass Air Flow (MAF) sensor, electrical connector.
5. Remove intake hose and air cleaner housing from rubber bushing.
6. Disconnect accelerator and speed control cables, then the plastic clips and position cables aside.
7. Disconnect Positive Crankcase Ventilation (PCV) hoses.
8. Remove EVAP system, brake servo, Delta pressure feedback electronic system sensor and EGR valve vacuum hoses.
9. Remove EGR valve.
10. Clamp coolant hoses to prevent leakage and remove from intake manifold.
11. Remove vacuum hose assembly.
12. Disconnect Throttle Position Sensor (TP) and Idle Air Control (IAC) valve.
13. Remove mounting bolt and oil dipstick tube bracket.
14. Remove intake manifold upper support bracket.
15. Disconnect fuel injector electrical connectors from intake manifold.
16. Disconnect Intake Manifold Runner Control (IMRC) electrical connector.
17. Disconnect Camshaft Position (CMP) sensor.
18. Disconnect ignition coil electrical connector.
19. Disconnect fuel lines from fuel rail.
20. Remove intake manifold retainers and position manifold to rear of engine compartment.
21. Remove two studs and Intake Manifold Runner Control (IMRC) manifolds.
22. Remove intake manifold.
23. Reverse procedure to install. **Torque** intake manifold mounting bolts and nuts 89 inch lbs., then tighten an additional 180°.

EXHAUST MANIFOLD
REPLACE

1. Disconnect Mass Air Flow (MAF) elec-

trical connector.
2. Disconnect air intake hose.
3. Remove air cleaner housing from rubber bushing.
4. Disconnect heated oxygen sensor electrical connector.
5. Remove power steering high pressure tube.
6. Remove exhaust manifold heat shield.
7. Remove EGR tube at exhaust manifold, then loosen tube nut approximately three turns at valve.
8. Remove catalytic converter.
9. Remove mounting nuts and exhaust manifold.
10. Reverse procedure to install.

CYLINDER HEAD
REPLACE

1. Disconnect Mass Air Flow (MAF) sensor and intake air hose, then remove air cleaner housing from rubber bushing.
2. Disconnect battery ground cable and remove battery tray.
3. Disconnect accelerator and speed control cables, then the plastic clips and position cables aside.
4. Disconnect both Powertrain Control Module (PCM) connectors.
5. Disconnect heated oxygen sensor electrical connector.
6. Disconnect EVAP, brake servo, delta pressure feedback electronic system sensor and EGR valve vacuum hoses.
7. Remove nut and oil dipstick tube bracket.
8. Drain coolant into suitable container and remove thermostat housing coolant hoses.
9. Disconnect fuel line and drain excess fuel into suitable container.
10. Raise and support vehicle.
11. Disconnect knock sensor and oil pressure sensor electrical connectors.
12. Remove intake manifold bracket.
13. Remove catalyst monitor sensor electrical connector.
14. Lower vehicle.
15. Remove power steering high pressure tube.
16. Remove exhaust manifold heat shield.
17. Remove catalytic converter from exhaust manifold.
18. Remove timing belt as outlined under "Timing Belt, Replace."
19. Disconnect Crankshaft Position (CKP) sensor electrical connector.

20. Disconnect PCV and fresh air hoses.
21. Remove valve cover.
22. Loosen cylinder head bolts in sequence, **Fig. 6.**
23. Remove cylinder head.
24. Reverse procedure to install, noting the following:
    a. Lubricate cylinder head bolts with suitable, clean engine oil.
    b. **Torque** new torque-to-yield cylinder head bolts in sequence to 37 ft. lbs., **Fig. 7.**
    c. Back head bolts off ½ turn.
    d. **Torque** cylinder head bolts in sequence to 37 ft. lbs.
    e. Tighten head bolt an additional 90° in sequence.
    f. Final tighten bolts an additional 90° in sequence.

VALVE ADJUSTMENT

Valve clearance is hydraulically controlled and is not adjustable.

TIMING BELT
REPLACE

Removal

1. Remove mounting bolt and expansion tank aside with hose attached.
2. Disconnect power steering reservoir and position aside with hose attached.
3. Turn engine accessory drive belt tensioner clockwise and remove drive belt.
4. Raise and support vehicle.
5. Remove mounting screws and drive belt cover.
6. Lower vehicle.
7. Disconnect cables from spark plugs. Mark cables for installation alignment.
8. Remove two spark plug cable separators from valve cover.
9. Remove spark plugs. Note location of spark plugs so can be installed at same cylinders.
10. Position suitable jack under engine oil pan. Place wooden block between oil pan and jack.
11. Relieve weight from engine mounts by raising jack slightly.
12. Remove mounting bolts, nuts and front engine mount.
13. Remove three mounting bolts and timing belt lower cover.
14. Remove four mounting bolts and front engine mounting bracket.

15. Align crankshaft and camshaft sprocket timing marks, **Fig. 8.**
16. Insert 8 mm hex head wrench into tensioner pulley bore, then rotate timing belt tensioner ¼ turn counterclockwise.
17. Insert ⅛ inch drill bit, or similar item, through timing belt tensioner pulley hole to hold pulley in place.
18. Remove timing belt from crankshaft and camshaft sprockets.

Installation

1. Ensure crankshaft and camshaft sprocket timing marks are aligned, **Fig. 8.**
2. Install new timing belt in counterclockwise direction, over crankshaft sprocket, over camshaft sprocket, under timing belt tensioner, then over water pump sprocket. **Keep belt span taut between crankshaft and camshaft sprockets.**
3. Remove item holding timing belt tensioner pulley in position and allow tensioner to tension timing belt.
4. Rotate crankshaft two turns in normal direction of rotation.
5. Inspect crankshaft and camshaft sprocket timing marks for proper alignment, **Fig. 8.** If marks are improperly aligned, timing belt must be removed and installed.
6. Install front engine mounting bracket.
7. Install timing belt lower cover.
8. Install front engine mounting.
9. Remove jack and wooden block supporting engine.
10. Install spark plugs.
11. Install two spark plug cable wire separators to valve cover.
12. Apply suitable silicone grease to inside of spark plug connector boot, then spark plugs cables to spark plugs.
13. Raise and support vehicle.
14. Install crankshaft pulley.
15. Position accessory drive belt on crankshaft pulley.
16. Install drive belt cover.
17. Lower vehicle.
18. Install accessory drive belt.
19. Install power steering reservoir.
20. Install coolant expansion tank and mounting bolt.

CAMSHAFT
REPLACE

1. Disconnect battery ground cable and remove battery tray.
2. Disconnect Mass Air Flow (MAF) sensor and air cleaner outlet pipe, then remove air cleaner housing from rubber bushing.
3. Remove air cleaner intake pipe.
4. Remove ignition coil.
5. Disconnect PCV hoses.
6. Remove valve cover and rocker arms.
7. Remove plate retainers, plates and valve tappets. Keep tappets in order for reassembly.
8. Remove timing belt as outlined under "Timing Belt, Replace."

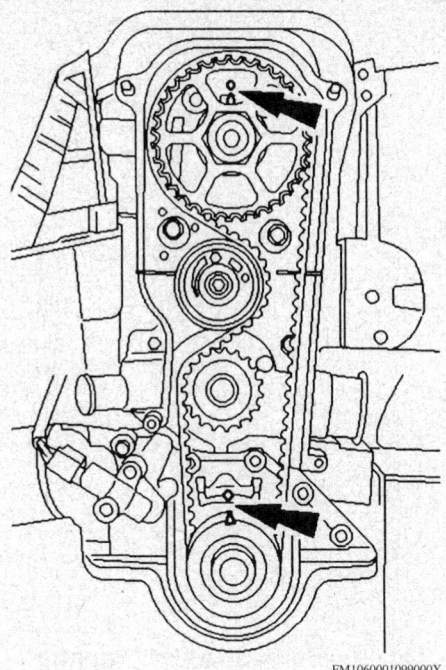

FM1060001099000X

Fig. 8 Timing mark alignment

9. Remove camshaft timing belt pulley using wrench tool No. T74P-6256-B, or equivalent.
10. Remove and camshaft oil seal using seal remover tool No. T92C-6700-CH, or equivalent.
11. Support engine with suitable engine lifting device.
12. Remove rear engine mount.
13. Disconnect air cleaner housing bracket and position it aside.
14. Remove camshaft thrust plate.
15. Remove and discard blanking plug from rear of cylinder head.
16. Remove camshaft from rear of cylinder head.
17. Reverse procedure to install, noting the following:
    a. Coat cylinder head bore with suitable, clean engine oil prior to camshaft installation.
    b. Install camshaft through rear of cylinder head.
    c. Install new camshaft oil seal using oil seal installer tool No. T81P-6292-A, or equivalent, and draw seal into place with timing belt pulley bolt.
    d. Install camshaft timing pulley. using camshaft pulley wrench tool No. T74P-6256-B, or equivalent.

CRANKSHAFT SEAL
REPLACE

1. Remove timing belt as outlined under "Timing Belt, Replace."
2. Support engine using suitable floor jack and wooden block under oil pan.
3. Support engine using engine support tool Nos. 303-290, 303-050, 303-290-01 and 303-290-03, or equivalents.
4. Remove floor jack.
5. Raise and support vehicle.
6. Remove crankshaft timing belt pulley.

7. Remove crankshaft seal using seal remover tool No. T92C-6700-CH, or equivalent.
8. Reverse procedure to install, noting the following:
    a. Lubricate new crankshaft seal and crankshaft surface with suitable, clean engine oil.
    b. Install crankshaft front seal using seal installer tool No. 303-164, or equivalent.

CRANKSHAFT REAR OIL SEAL
REPLACE

1. Remove transaxle as outlined in **MOTOR's "Domestic Transmission, In-Vehicle Service"** manual.
2. **On models equipped with manual transaxle,** remove clutch pressure plate and clutch disc as outlined in **MOTOR's "Domestic Transmission, In-Vehicle Service"** manual.
3. **On all models,** remove flywheel using flywheel locking tool No. T74P-6375-A, or equivalent.
4. Remove crankshaft rear seal using seal remover tool No. T92C-6700-CH, or equivalent.
5. Reverse procedure to install. Install oil seal using crankshaft rear oil installer tool No. T88P-6701B-1, or equivalent.

OIL PAN
REPLACE

1. Remove three-way catalytic converter.
2. Remove mounting bolts and two exhaust brackets.
3. Remove mounting bolts and intake manifold bracket.
4. Remove bolts and axle shaft bracket clamp.
5. Remove mounting bolts and axle shaft bracket.
6. Remove coolant tube mounting bolt.
7. Drain engine oil into suitable container.
8. Record oil pan stud bolts locations for installation alignment.
9. Remove mounting bolts and oil pan.
10. Reverse procedure to install, noting the following:
    a. Apply .12 inch wide bead of suitable silicone gasket sealant at oil pump to block joints and crankshaft rear seal retainer to block joints.
    b. **Oil pan must be installed within 10 minutes of sealant application.**
    c. Ensure press fit tabs fully engage in oil pan gasket channel.
    d. **Torque** oil pan bolts in sequence to 18 ft. lbs., **Fig. 9.**

OIL PUMP
REPLACE

1. Remove timing belt as outlined under "Timing Belt, Replace."
2. Support engine using suitable floor jack and wooden block under oil pan.
3. Support engine using engine support tool Nos. 303-290, 303-050, 303-290-01 and 303-290-03, or equivalents.

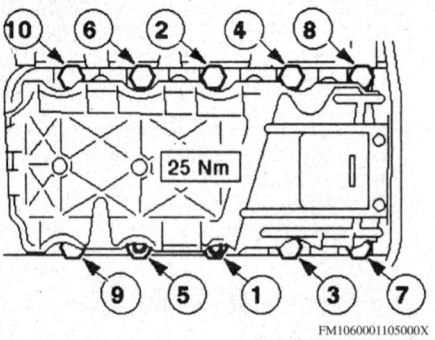

Fig. 9   Oil pan fastener tightening sequence

FM1060001105000X

4. Remove floor jack.
5. Remove crankshaft timing belt pulley.
6. Remove three-way catalytic converter.
7. Remove mounting bolts and two exhaust brackets.
8. Remove mounting bolts and intake manifold bracket.
9. Remove bolts and axle shaft bracket clamp.
10. Remove mounting bolts and axle shaft bracket.
11. Remove coolant tube mounting bolt.
12. Drain engine oil into suitable container.
13. Record oil pan stud bolts locations for installation alignment.
14. Remove mounting bolts and oil pan.
15. Remove Crankshaft Position (CKP) sensor.
16. Remove two mounting bolts, oil pump screen cover and tube.
17. Remove mounting bolts and oil pump.
18. Reverse procedure to install noting the following:
    a. Install oil pump seal using crankshaft front oil seal installer tool No. T81P-6700-A, or equivalent.
    b. Install new gasket.

SERPENTINE DRIVE BELT

Routing

Refer to **Figs. 10 and 11,** for serpentine drive belt routing.

Replace

1. Raise and support vehicle.
2. Remove serpentine drive belt splash shield.
3. Lower vehicle.
4. Rotate tensioner clockwise using suitable ⅜ inch drive breaker bar.
5. Remove serpentine drive belt.
6. Reverse procedure to install.

FM1060001080000X

Fig. 10   Serpentine belt routing. Less air conditioning

Tensioner

1. Raise and support vehicle.
2. Remove serpentine drive belt splash shield.
3. Lower vehicle.
4. Rotate tensioner clockwise using suitable ⅜ inch drive breaker bar.
5. Remove serpentine drive belt.
6. Remove power steering pipe to exhaust manifold bracket nuts and position pipe aside.
7. Remove mounting bolts and exhaust manifold heat shield.
8. Remove mounting bolts and serpentine drive belt tensioner.
9. Reverse procedure to install.

THERMOSTAT
REPLACE

1. Drain coolant into suitable container.
2. Disconnect thermostat housing coolant hoses.
3. Remove mounting bolts and thermostat housing.
4. Reverse procedure to install. Install new O-rings.

WATER PUMP
REPLACE

1. Drain cooling system into suitable container.
2. Remove timing belt as outlined under "Timing Belt, Replace."
3. Remove timing belt tensioner.

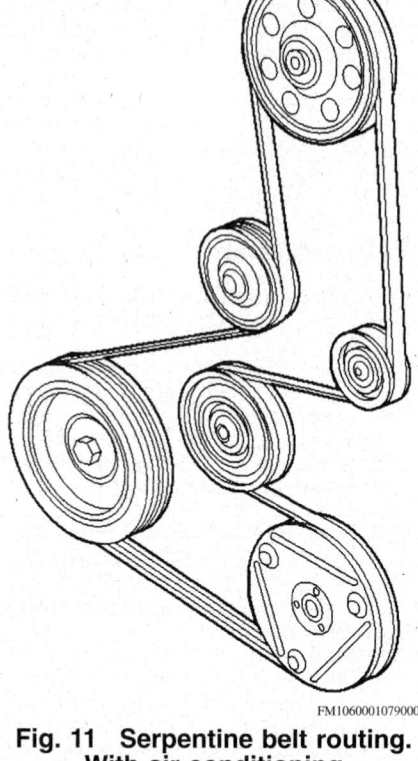

FM1060001079000X

Fig. 11   Serpentine belt routing. With air conditioning

4. Disconnect coolant hoses.
5. Remove water pump.
6. Reverse procedure to install. using new gasket.

RADIATOR
REPLACE

Refer to "Radiator, Replace" in "2.0L (VINs 3 & 5) DOHC Engines" section for radiator replacement procedure.

FUEL PUMP
REPLACE

Refer to "Fuel Pump, Replace" in "2.0L (VINs 3 & 5) DOHC Engines" section for fuel pump replacement procedure.

FUEL FILTER
REPLACE

1. Relieve fuel system pressure as outlined under "Precautions."
2. Raise and support vehicle.
3. Disconnect evaporative emission pipe.
4. Remove fuel filter outlet pipe and disconnect inlet pipe.
5. Remove fuel filter and bracket.
6. Separate filter from bracket.
7. Reverse procedure to install.

TIGHTENING SPECIFICATIONS

Year	Component	Torque/Ft. Lbs.
2001–04	Accessory Drive Bracket	35
	Air Conditioning Compressor	18
	Alternator	35
	Battery Tray	18
	Camshaft Position Sensor	18
	Camshaft Pulley	77
	Camshaft Thrust Plate	89①
	Catalytic Converter To Exhaust Manifold	30
	Crankshaft Position Sensor	53①
	Crankshaft Pulley	89
	Cylinder Head	②
	EGR Manifold Tube To Exhaust Manifold	53①
	EGR Valve To EGR Manifold Tube	18
	EGR Valve To Intake Manifold	53①
	Engine Oil Drain Plug	18
	Engine Roll Restrictor To Subframe	35
	Engine Roll Restrictor To Transaxle	35
	Exhaust Manifold	20
	Flexible Exhaust Pipe	35
	Front Engine Mounting To Body	35
	Front Engine Mounting To Engine	59
	Intake Manifold	③
	Intake Manifold Bracket	89①
	Intermediate Shaft Bracket	35
	Knock Sensor	10
	Lefthand Transaxle Flange Bolts	35
	Lower Ball Joint To Spindle Carrier	35
	Lower Transaxle Flange Bolts	35
	Oil Intake Pipe To Oil Pump	89①
	Oil Pan Baffle	18
	Oil Pan	④
	Oil Pump	10
	Oil Pump Tube	89①
	Power Steering Pump	17
	Radiator Bracket	19
	Rear Crankshaft Oil Seal Retainer	18
	Rear Engine Mounting (Nut On Transaxle Mounting Bracket)	98
	Rear Engine Mounting To Body	35
	Rocker Arms	18
	Starter Motor To Transaxle	26
	Thermostat Housing	10
	Timing Belt Cover (Lower)	89①
	Timing Belt Cover (Upper)	35
	Timing Belt Tensioner	18
	Upper Transaxle Flange Bolts	35
	Valve Cover Bolts	80①
	Water Pump	18
	Wheel Lug Nuts	63

① — Inch lbs.
② — Refer to "Cylinder Head, Replace" for tightening specifications and sequence.
③ — Refer to "Intake Manifold, Replace" for tightening specifications and sequence.
④ — Refer to "Oil Pan, Replace" for tightening specifications and sequence.

2.0L (VIN N) & 2.3L (VIN Z) DOHC Engines

NOTE: On Air Bag Equipped Models, Refer To "Air Bag System Precautions" Located In The Front Of This Manual For System Disarming & Arming Procedures.

NOTE: Refer To "Computer Relearn Procedures" Located In The Front Of This Manual When Battery Power To The Computer Has Been Interrupted.

INDEX

PRECAUTIONS

Air Bag Systems

Refer to "Air Bag System Precautions" in the front of this manual for system disarming and arming procedures.

Battery Ground Cable

Prior to service, disconnect battery ground cable and isolate as required.

Fuel System Pressure Relief

1. Remove fuel pump fuse.
2. Start engine and idle until engine stalls.
3. Crank engine for approximately five seconds to ensure fuel supply manifold pressure has been relieved.
4. Install fuel pump fuse.

Quick Disconnect Hoses

R-CLIP

When working with R-clip type connections, do not use tools to disconnect. Use of tools may deform clip components and could cause leaks.

DISCONNECT

1. Bend shipping tab downward.
2. Spread R-clip and push clip into fitting.
3. Separate fitting from tube.

CONNECT

1. Inspect fitting and tube for damage and ensure connections are clean.
2. Apply light coat of suitable, clean engine oil to male end of tube.
3. Insert R-clip into fitting.
4. Align tube and fitting, then insert tube into fitting and push together until click is heard.
5. Pull on connection to ensure it is fully engaged.

SPRING LOCK

When working with spring lock type connections, spring lock tool set No. T84L-19623-B, or equivalent, must be used to disconnect fittings.

When connecting spring lock type fittings, proceed as follows:
1. Inspect and clean both coupling ends.
2. Lubricate fuel line O-ring seals with suitable, clean engine oil.
3. When connection is made, pull on line to ensure it is fully engaged.

VAPOR TUBE

To disconnect vapor tube connections, squeeze fitting and disconnect vapor tube from fitting.

To connect, proceed as follows:

1. Ensure fittings are clean and free from damage.
2. Push tube onto fitting until it snaps into place.
3. Pull on connection to verify fitting is secure.

COMPRESSION PRESSURE

1. Ensure crankcase oil is of correct viscosity and at correct level.
2. Ensure battery is fully charged and engine is at normal operating temperature.
3. Turn ignition switch to OFF position.
4. Remove spark plugs.
5. Set throttle plates to wide open position.
6. Install suitable compression gauge in cylinder No. 1.
7. Install auxiliary starter switch in starting circuit.
8. With ignition switch off, use to crank engine at least five compression strokes using auxiliary starter switch.
9. Record number of compression strokes required to reach highest reading and record highest reading.
10. Repeat test on each cylinder, cranking engine same number of compression strokes.
11. Lowest cylinder reading must be within 75% of highest reading.

ENGINE MOUNT

REPLACE

1. Remove mounting bolts and position expansion tank aside.
2. Support engine using three-bar engine support tool No. 303-F072, or equivalent.
3. Remove mounting nuts, bolts and engine mount.
4. Remove procedure to install.

ENGINE

REPLACE

1. Ensure transmission is in Neutral position, then raise and support vehicle.
2. Relieve fuel system pressure as outlined under "Precautions."
3. Remove battery, then the mounting bolts and tray.
4. Recover air conditioning refrigerant as outlined in "Air Conditioning" chapter.
5. Drain engine cooling system into suitable container.
6. Drain engine oil into suitable container.
7. Remove mounting bolts and accessory drive belt splash shield.
8. Turn tensioner clockwise and remove accessory drive belt.
9. Remove mounting nuts and disconnect catalytic converter from muffler.
10. Remove mounting bolts and catalytic converter support bracket.
11. Remove mounting bolts and position catalytic converter heat shield aside.
12. Disconnect exhaust sensor electrical connector.
13. Disconnect upper exhaust sensor electrical connector and retainer.
14. Disconnect Secondary Air Injection (AIR) hose.
15. Remove catalytic converter-to-engine mounting nuts, then position converter aside using suitable mechanics wire. Remove gasket.
16. Loosen clamp and disconnect air cleaner outlet pipe vent tube.
17. Remove mounting bolts and disconnect air intake resonator from grommets. Remove resonator and outlet pipe.
18. Disconnect evaporative emissions hose pin-type retainer.
19. Remove mounting screw, pin-type retainer and accelerator control snow shield.
20. Disconnect accelerator and speed control cables from throttle body.
21. Remove mounting bolts, then position accelerator and speed control cables and bracket aside.
22. Disconnect quick release coupling from fuel rail and position fuel tube aside.
23. Disconnect evaporative emissions tube.
24. Disconnect AIR hose and vacuum regulator electrical connector.
25. Depress quick release locking ring and disconnect power brake booster vacuum tube.
26. Disconnect Exhaust Gas Recirculation (EGR) valve electrical connector.

27. Disconnect upper radiator, heater and coolant vent hoses from coolant bypass.
28. Remove mounting bolt and ground eyelet.
29. Disconnect fuel charging wiring harness electrical connectors and retainer.
30. Disconnect power distribution wiring harness.
31. Disconnect wiring harness retainers.
32. Remove mounting nut and power distribution wiring harness eyelet.
33. Disconnect three main engine wiring harness electrical connectors. Disconnect connectors from bracket.
34. **On models equipped with manual transaxle,** proceed as follows:
    a. Disconnect shifter cable from transaxle.
    b. Disconnect selector cable from lever.
    c. Disconnect shifter cable from retaining bracket, turning abutment sleeves counterclockwise.
    d. Disconnect selector cable from retaining bracket, turning abutment sleeves counterclockwise.
    e. Remove clip and clutch slave cylinder supply tube. Position tube aside using suitable cable ties.
    f. Disconnect back-up lamp switch electrical connector.
35. **On models equipped with 2.0L engine and automatic transaxle,** proceed as follows:
    a. Disconnect and position shifter cable aside.
    b. Disconnect transaxle cooler lines.
36. **On all models,** disconnect heater hose from "T" fitting and position it aside.
37. Disconnect hoses from coolant expansion tank.
38. Remove mounting bolt and coolant expansion tank.
39. Remove power steering pump pulley using power steering pump pulley remover tool No. T69L-10300-8, or equivalent.
40. Disconnect Power Steering Pressure (PSP) switch electrical connector.
41. Disconnect PSP tube.
42. Remove mounting bolts and position power steering pump aside.
43. Disconnect cooling fan electrical connectors.
44. Disconnect top clips and remove cooling fan.
45. Disconnect lower radiator hose.
46. Remove mounting bolt and ground cable.
47. Remove alternator cooling pipe.
48. Disconnect starter motor electrical terminals.
49. Remove mounting bolts and disconnect power steering pressure tube brackets from stud bolts.
50. Disconnect air conditioning compressor electrical connector.
51. Remove three compressor mounting bolts.
52. Lower compressor, then remove fourth mounting bolt and compressor.
53. Disconnect lefthand brake hose from

support bracket.
54. Remove covers, mounting bolts and lefthand caliper. Support caliper aside.
55. Loosen lefthand strut and spring top mount nuts four turns.
56. Remove mounting nut and disconnect lefthand stabilizer bar at strut.
57. Remove lefthand and righthand tie-end nuts.
58. Disconnect tie-rods from knuckles using tie-rod end remover tool, No. 393-050, or equivalent.
59. Remove mounting bolts and disconnect both lower control arms from knuckles.
60. Remove mounting nuts and intermediate shaft bearing bracket.
61. Remove intermediate shaft and righthand front drive halfshaft. Position aside shaft using suitable mechanics wire.
62. Install transaxle plug tools No. T88C-7025-AH, or equivalent, into transaxle housing.
63. Remove lefthand front drive halfshaft using front drive halfshaft remover tool No. D93P-1175-B, or equivalent. Position shaft aside using suitable mechanics's wire.
64. Remove mounting bolts and transaxle roll restrictor.
65. Remove three mounting bolts and starter motor.
66. Remove start isolator.
67. Remove two lower bell housing bolts.
68. Remove two oil pan-to-bell housing mounting bolts.
69. Attach engine to suitable lift table using universal adaptor bracket tools No. 014-0001, or equivalent.
70. Remove mounting mount nuts.
71. Remove transaxle mount center nut.
72. Lower engine and transaxle.
73. **On models equipped with manual transaxle,** disconnect Vehicle Speed Sensor (VSS) electrical connector.
74. **On models equipped with 2.0L engine and automatic transaxle,** proceed as follows:
    a. Mark one stud and flexplate from installation alignment.
    b. Remove four torque converter mounting nuts.
    c. Disconnect Output Shaft Speed (OSS) sensor electrical connector.
    d. Disconnect Turbine Shaft Speed (TSS) sensor electrical connector.
    e. Disconnect solenoid body and Transmission Range (TR) sensor electrical connectors.
75. **On all models,** lower engine to within inches of floor.
76. Remove engine from lift table using suitable engine crane and spreader bar tool No. D93P-6001-A3, or equivalent.
77. Remove remaining bell housing bolts and separate engine and transaxle.
78. Remove dowel pins.
79. Lock torque converter in place using torque converter holding tool No. T96T-7902-A, or equivalent.
80. Reverse procedure to install, noting the following:
    a. Install new dowel pins.

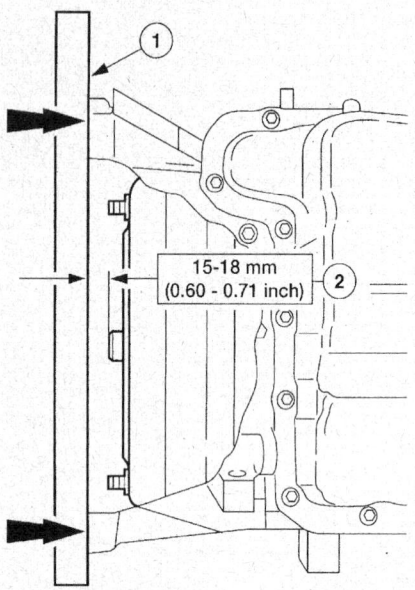

1- Straightedge
2- Torque converter centering spigot

ARM0400000000482

Fig. 1 Torque converter installation depth. 2.0L (VIN N) engine

b. Ensure transaxle flange and torque converter centering spigot clearance is .60–.71 inch, **Fig. 1.**
c. Install new front driveshaft snap rings.
d. Install new air conditioning compressor manifold and tube O-ring seals.
e. Install new power steering pump union O-ring seal.
f. Install new catalytic converter flange if it is wrapped more than .0295 inch.
g. Install catalytic converter flange using new gasket and mounting nuts.
h. Tighten catalytic converter flange mounting nuts in sequence, **Fig. 2.**
i. Install new catalytic converter to muffler gasket and mounting nuts.

INTAKE MANIFOLD
REPLACE

1. Ensure transmission is in Neutral position, then raise and support vehicle.
2. Disconnect dual electric cooling fan electrical connector.
3. Remove cooling fan motors and shroud from bracket, then lower assembly from vehicle.
4. Remove lower intake manifold mounting bolt.
5. Loosen clamps, then disconnect and remove air cleaner outlet pipe.
6. Disconnect evaporative emissions hose pin-type retainer.
7. Remove mounting screw, pin-type retainer and accelerator control snow shield.

8. Disconnect accelerator and speed control cables from throttle body.
9. Remove mounting bolts, then position accelerator and speed control cables and bracket aside.
10. Disconnect Throttle Position (TP) sensor electrical connector and wiring harness pin-type retainer.
11. Disconnect Idle Air Control (IAC) valve electrical connector and wiring harness pin-type retainer.
12. Disconnect evaporative emissions hose.
13. Depress quick release locking ring and disconnect power brake booster vacuum tube.
14. Disconnect fuel rail pressure and temperature sensor vacuum hose.
15. Disconnect wiring harness pin-type retainer.
16. Disconnect Intake Manifold Runner Control (IMRC) actuator electrical connector.
17. Disconnect Manifold Absolute Pressure (MAP) sensor electrical connector.
18. **On models equipped with 2.0L engine,** proceed as follows:
    a. Disconnect Secondary Air Injection (AIR) vacuum supply hose.
    b. Disconnect swirl control valve electrical connector.
19. **On models equipped with 2.3L engine,** disconnect swirl control valve electrical connectors and pin-type retainers.
20. **On all models,** remove mounting bolt and oil dipstick tube.
21. Mark mounting bolts for installation alignment.
22. Remove seven intake manifold mounting bolts.
23. Raise intake manifold and disconnect Knock Sensor (KS) electrical connector.
24. Disconnect Positive Crankcase Ventilation (PCV) hose.
25. Remove intake manifold.
26. Remove Exhaust Gas Recirculation (EGR) tube.
27. Reverse procedure to install, noting the following:
    a. Install new intake manifold gaskets.
    b. **On models equipped with 2.3L engine,** use 6-inch long, 5/16 inch diameter hose to install lower center mounting bolt.

CYLINDER HEAD
REPLACE

1. Drain cooling system into suitable container.
2. Remove camshaft as outlined under "Camshaft, Replace."
3. Relieve fuel system pressure as outlined under "Precautions."
4. Disconnect quick release coupling from fuel rail and position fuel tube aside.
5. Disconnect fuel injector electrical connector.
6. Disconnect fuel rail pressure and temperature sensor electrical connector, then the vacuum tube.

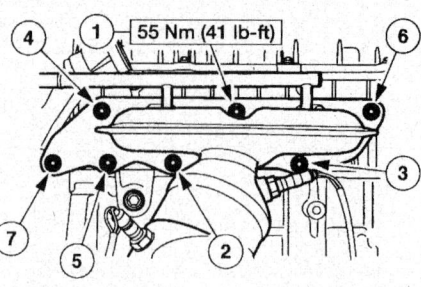

ARM0400000000493

Fig. 2 Catalytic converter flange tightening sequence. 2.0L (VIN N) & 2.3L (VIN Z) DOHC engines

7. Remove mounting bolts, fuel rail, injectors and spacers.
8. Remove intake manifold as outlined under "Intake Manifold, Replace."
9. **On models equipped with 2.0L engine,** proceed as follows:
    a. Disconnect Secondary Air Injection (AIR) vacuum regulator electrical connector and vacuum hose.
    b. Disconnect AIR control valve hoses.
    c. Disconnect upper exhaust sensor electrical connector and retainer.
10. **On all models,** remove mounting nuts and disconnect catalytic converter from muffler.
11. Remove mounting bolts and catalytic converter support bracket.
12. Remove four mounting bolts and catalytic converter heat shield.
13. Disconnect exhaust sensor electrical connector.
14. Remove mounting nuts and position catalytic converter aside using suitable mechanic's wire.
15. Remove Exhaust Gas Recirculation (EGR) valve electrical connector.
16. Disconnect coolant bypass hoses.
17. Remove mounting bolts, coolant bypass and gasket.
18. Disconnect EGT coolant hose.
19. Remove mounting bolts, cylinder head and gasket.
20. Reverse procedure to install, noting the following:
    a. Apply suitable silicone gasket and sealant, **Fig. 3.**
    b. Tighten new torque-to-yield bolts in five steps using sequence, **Fig. 4.** First step, **torque** bolts to 44 inch lbs.; second step, **torque** bolts to 11 ft. lbs.; third step, **torque** bolts to 33 ft. lbs.; fourth step, tighten bolts an additional 90°; fifth step, tighten bolts an additional 90.°
    c. Install new fuel injector O-ring seals lubricated with suitable, clean engine oil.

VALVE COVER
REPLACE

1. Disconnect Camshaft Position (CMP) sensor electrical connector.
2. Lift connector boot and disconnect Cylinder Head Temperature (CHT) sensor electrical connector.

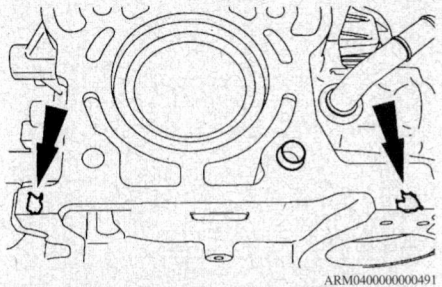

Fig. 3 Head silicone gasket & sealant installation

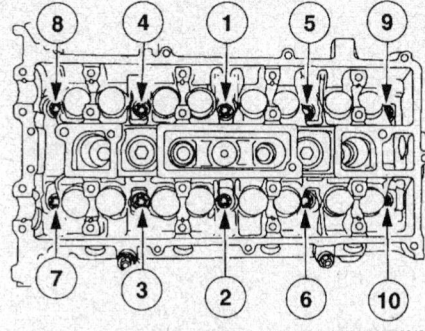

Fig. 4 Cylinder head bolt tightening sequence

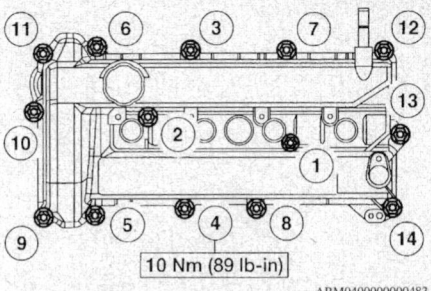

10 Nm (89 lb-in)

Fig. 5 Valve cover bolt tightening sequence

3. Disconnect coil-on-plug electrical connectors.
4. Remove mounting bolts, the rotate and remove ignition coils.
5. Disconnect breather tube.
6. Disconnect fuel rail pressure and temperature sensor, then the fuel injector electrical connectors. Disconnect wiring harness retainers.
7. Remove mounting bolt and position radio interference capacitor bracket aside.
8. Disconnect Heated Oxygen Sensor (HO2S) electrical connector.
9. Disconnect wiring harness retainer and position it aside.
10. Remove mounting bolts and valve cover.
11. Reverse procedure to install. Tighten valve cover attaching bolts as follows:
   a. Refer to tightening sequence, **Fig. 5.**
   b. **Torque** bolts to 18 ft. lbs.
   c. **Torque** bolts to 62 ft. lbs.

CAMSHAFT LOBE LIFT SPECIFICATIONS

Engine	Lobe Lift, Inch	
	Intake	Exhaust
2.0L	.324	.307
2.3L	.324	.307

VALVE CLEARANCE SPECIFICATIONS

Valve	Clearance, Inch
Intake	.008–.011
Exhaust	.010–.023

VALVE ADJUSTMENT

1. Remove valve cover as outlined under "Valve Cover, Replace."
2. Measure and record each valve clearance at base circle with lobe pointed away from tappet.
3. Select tappets based on (tappet thickness = measured clearance + base tappet thickness - most desirable thickness.)
4. Tappets are mark with digits following decimal, For example, tappet marked .650 is 3.650 mm thick.

CRANKSHAFT DAMPER
REPLACE

Removal

1. Disconnect dual electric cooling fan electrical connector.
2. Remove cooling fan motors and shroud from bracket, then lower assembly from vehicle.
3. Remove mounting bolts and accessory drive belt splash shield.
4. Turn tensioner clockwise and remove accessory drive belt.
5. Remove valve cover as outlined under "Valve Cover, Replace."
6. Remove mounting bolts and position expansion tank aside.
7. Remove battery, then the mounting bolts and tray.
8. Turn crankshaft pulley clockwise and position piston No. 1 at TDC.
9. Install camshaft alignment plate too No. T94P-6256-CH, or equivalent, in slots at rear of both camshafts. If timing slots are offset, rotate crankshaft pulley clockwise one complete revolution.
10. Install crankshaft timing peg tool No. 303-507, or equivalent.
11. Support engine using three-bar engine support tool No. 303-F072, or equivalent.
12. Remove transaxle mount center nut.
13. Remove engine mount nuts.
14. Loosen lower transaxle mount nuts.
15. Lower engine for clearance.
16. Install drive pinion flange holding fixture tool No. T78P-4851-A, or equivalent.
17. Remove mounting bolt, special tool and crankshaft pulley.

Installation

1. Apply suitable, clean engine oil to seal area.
2. Install crankshaft pulley and new damper bolt finger tight.
3. Install standard .23 by .7 inch bolt through pulley into front cover.
4. Hold crankshaft pulley in place using holding fixture tool No. T78P-4851-A, or equivalent.
5. **Torque** damper bolt to 74 ft. lbs., then tighten an additional 90°.

6. Remove standard bolt.
7. Remove crankshaft timing peg tool.
8. Remove camshaft alignment plate.
9. Turn engine two complete revolutions clockwise until piston No. 1 is at TDC.
10. Install crankshaft timing peg tool.
11. Attempt to install standard .23 by .7 inch bolt through pulley into front cover. If bolt cannot be installed, engine is timed correctly.
12. Inspect camshaft positions with camshaft alignment plate. If plate cannot be installed, engine is timed correctly.
13. Remove standard bolt and special tools.
14. Raise engine.
15. Install engine mount nuts, then the transaxle mount center nut.
16. Tighten lower transaxle mount nuts.
17. Install battery tray and coolant expansion tank.
18. Install valve cover and accessory drive belt.
19. Install fan and shroud.

FRONT COVER
REPLACE

1. Remove crankshaft pulley as outlined under "Crankshaft Damper, Replace."
2. Disconnect Crankshaft Position (CKP) sensor electrical connector and wiring harness pin-type retainer.
3. Disconnect Power Steering Pressure (PSP) electrical connector.
4. Remove mounting nut and disconnect PSP tube bracket.
5. Disconnect PSP tube.
6. Remove four mounting bolts and position power steering pump aside.
7. Remove mounting bolts and water pump pulley.
8. Remove mounting bolt and accessory drive belt idler pulley.
9. Remove mounting bolts and front cover.
10. Reverse procedure to install, noting the following:
   a. **Front cover must be installed and bolts tighten within four minutes of applying silicone gasket and sealant.**
   b. Apply .098 inch bead of suitable silicone gasket and sealant to cylinder head and oil pan joint areas.
   c. Apply .098 inch bead of suitable silicone gasket and sealant to front cover, **Fig. 6.**

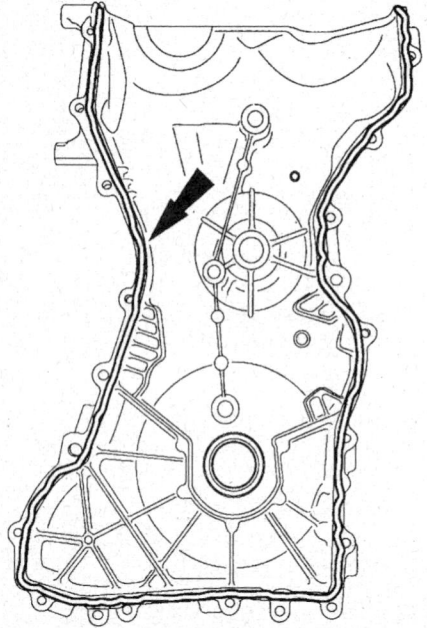

Fig. 6   Front cover sealant application

ARM0400000000484

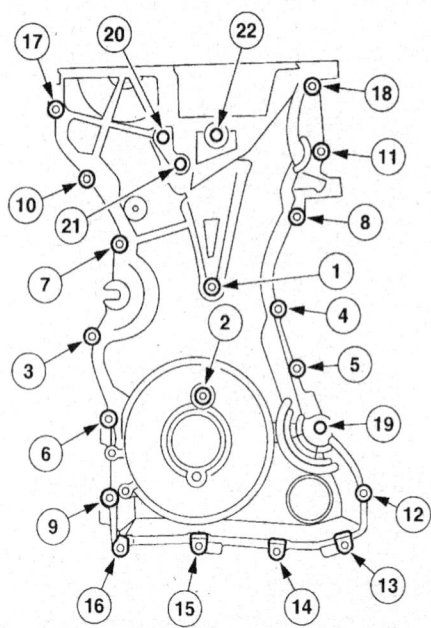

Fig. 7   Front cover tightening sequence

ARM0400000000485

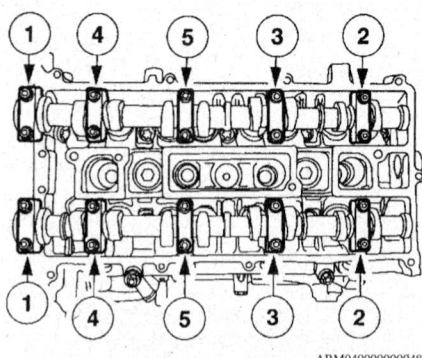

ARM0400000000486

Fig. 8   Camshaft removal sequence

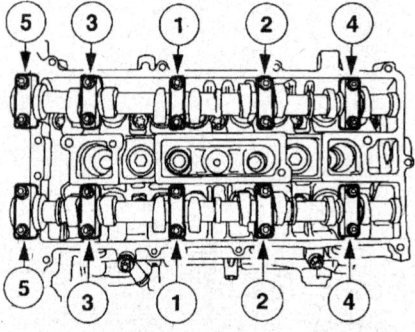

ARM0400000000487

Fig. 9   Camshaft bearing cap bolt tightening sequence

   d. Tighten mounting bolts in sequence, **Fig. 7.**
   e. Install new PSP tube O-ring.

TIMING CHAIN

REPLACE

1. Ensure transmission is in Neutral position, then raise and support vehicle.
2. Relieve fuel system pressure as outlined under "Precautions."
3. Remove cooling fan motors and shroud from bracket, then lower assembly from vehicle.
4. Turn tensioner clockwise and remove accessory drive belt.
5. Remove valve cover as outlined under "Valve Cover, Replace."
6. Disconnect hoses from coolant expansion tank.
7. Remove mounting bolt and coolant expansion tank.
8. Remove battery, then the mounting bolts and tray.
9. Disconnect Crankshaft Position (CKP) sensor electrical connector and wiring harness pin-type retainers.
10. Remove crankshaft pulley as outlined under "Crankshaft Damper, Replace."
11. Remove mounting bolts and accessory belt tensioner.
12. Remove front cover as outlined under "Front Cover, Replace."
13. Compress timing chain tensioner and hold in place by installing suitable paper clip into hole.
14. Remove mounting bolts and timing chain tensioner.
15. Remove mounting bolts and righthand timing chain guide.
16. Remove timing chain.
17. Remove mounting bolts and lefthand timing chain guide.

CAMSHAFT

REPLACE

1. Remove valve cover as outlined under "Valve Cover, Replace."
2. Measure and record each valve clearance at base circle with lobe pointed away from tappet.
3. Remove timing chain and sprockets as outlined under "Timing Chain, Replace."
4. Remove camshaft alignment plate tool.
5. Mark position of camshaft lobes on cylinder No. 1 for installation alignment.
6. Loosen camshaft bearing cap bolts one turn at a time in sequence, **Fig. 8.**

7. Repeat one turn removal sequence until all camshaft bearing cap tension is removed.
8. Remove bearing caps and camshaft.
9. Reverse procedure to install, noting the following:
   a. Lubricate camshaft journals and bearing caps with suitable, clean engine oil.
   b. Tighten camshaft bearing cap bolts one turn at a time until tight in sequence, **Fig. 9.**
   c. **Torque** bolts in sequence to 61 inch lbs.
   d. **Torque** bolts in sequence to 12 ft. lbs.

18. Prevent camshaft rotation by holding at flats, then remove mounting bolts and camshaft sprockets.
19. Reverse procedure to install. Do not tighten camshaft sprockets mounting bolts until after guides, timing chain and tensioner have been installed.

CRANKSHAFT SEAL

REPLACE

1. Remove crankshaft pulley as outlined under "Crankshaft Damper, Replace."
2. Remove crankshaft front oil seal using front oil seal remover tool No. T92C-6700-CH, or equivalent. **Do not damage front cover or crankshaft.**
3. Reverse procedure to install, noting the following:
   a. Lubricate new seal with suitable, clean engine oil.
   b. Use front oil seal installer tool No. T74P-6150-A, or equivalent.

CRANKSHAFT REAR OIL SEAL

REPLACE

1. Ensure transmission is in Neutral position, then raise and support vehicle.
2. Remove automatic transaxle or manual transaxle and clutch as outlined in **MOTOR's "Domestic Transmission, In-Vehicle Service"** manual.
3. Lock flywheel/flexplate in position using locking tool No. T74P-8375-A. or equivalent.
4. Remove mounting bolts and flywheel/flexplate.
5. Drain engine oil into suitable container.
6. Remove engine oil dipsticks, then the mounting bolt and tube.
7. Disconnect pin-type retainers and position wiring harness aside.
8. Remove mounting bolts and oil pan.

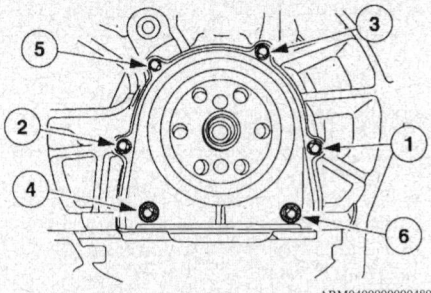

ARM0400000000489

Fig. 10 Crankshaft rear main oil seal tighten sequence

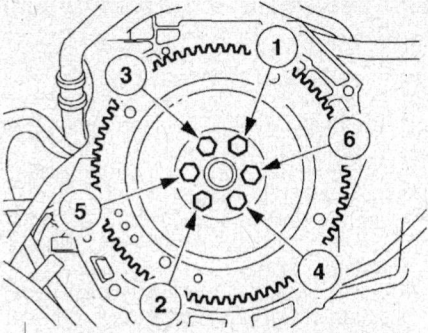

ARM0400000000490

Fig. 11 Flywheel/flexplate bolt tightening sequence

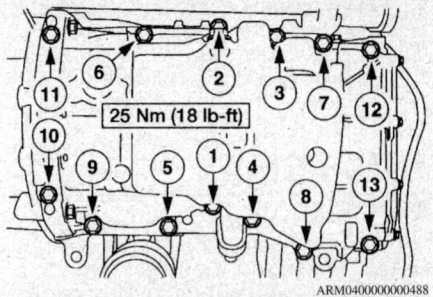

ARM0400000000488

Fig. 12 Oil pan bolt tightening sequence

9. Remove mounting bolts and crankshaft rear oil seal.
10. Reverse procedure to install, noting the following:
   a. Install seal using crankshaft rear main oil seal installer tool No. T88P-6701-B1, or equivalent.
   b. Tighten bolts in sequence, **Fig. 10.**
   c. Tighten flywheel/flexplate mounting bolts in three steps using sequence, **Fig. 11.** First step, **torque** bolts 37 ft. lbs.; second step, **torque** bolts to 50 ft. lbs.; third step, **torque** bolts to 83 ft. lbs.

OIL PAN
REPLACE

1. Ensure transmission is in Neutral position, then raise and support vehicle.
2. Drain engine oil into suitable container.
3. Remove engine oil dipsticks, then the mounting bolt and tube.
4. Disconnect pin-type retainers and position wiring harness aside.
5. Remove mounting bolts and oil pan.
6. Reverse procedure to install, noting the following:
   a. **Oil pan must be installed and bolts tightened within four minutes of applying silicone gasket and sealant.**
   b. Apply .098 inch bead of suitable silicone gasket and sealant to oil pan.
   c. Tighten mounting bolts in sequence, **Fig. 12.**

SERPENTINE DRIVE BELT
Routing

Refer to **Fig. 13,** for serpentine belt routing.

Replace

1. Ensure transmission is in Neutral position, then raise and support vehicle.
2. Remove mounting bolts and accessory drive belt splash shield.
3. Turn tensioner clockwise and remove accessory drive belt.
4. Reverse procedure to install.

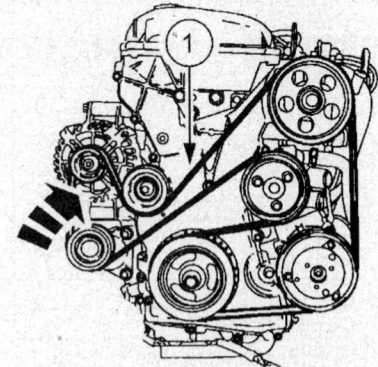

1- ACCESSORY DRIVE BELT

ARM0400000000494

Fig. 13 Serpentine drive belt routing

COOLING SYSTEM BLEED

1. Disconnect heater inlet hose from engine.
2. Fill cooling system through inlet hose using suitable funnel until coolant starts trickling from engine.
3. Connect heater inlet hose.
4. Ensure heater temperature control is in HOT position.
5. Ensure blower switch and air conditioning switched are OFF.
6. Fill degas bottle to MAX mark with engine off.
7. Start and run engine for two fan cycles.
8. Allow engine to cool, then inspect and adjust coolant level to MAX mark.

THERMOSTAT
REPLACE

1. Ensure transmission is in Neutral position, then raise and support vehicle.
2. Remove cooling fan motors and shroud from bracket, then lower assembly from vehicle.
3. Remove mounting bolts, cover and air conditioning compressor drive belt.
4. Disconnect compressor field coil electrical connector.
5. Remove mounting bolts and position power steering line aside.

6. Remove three mounting bolts and position air conditioning compressor aside.
7. Drain cooling system into suitable container.
8. Disconnect clamps and remove thermostat housing hoses.
9. Remove mounting bolts, housing and thermostat.
10. Reverse procedure to install. Lubricate housing O-ring with clean engine oil.

WATER PUMP
REPLACE

1. Ensure transmission is in Neutral position, then raise and support vehicle.
2. Remove mounting bolts and accessory drive belt splash shield.
3. Turn tensioner clockwise and remove accessory drive belt.
4. Drain cooling system into suitable container.
5. Remove mounting bolts and water pump pulley.
6. Remove mounting bolts and water pump.
7. Reverse procedure to install. Install new O-ring lubricated with suitable, clean engine oil.

RADIATOR
REPLACE

1. Ensure transmission is in Neutral position, then raise and support vehicle.
2. Disconnect dual electric cooling fans electrical connector.
3. Drain cooling system into suitable container.
4. Remove cooling fan motors and shroud from retainer bracket, then lower and remove.
5. Disconnect horn electrical connector.
6. Disconnect clamps, then the radiator upper and lower hoses.
7. Remove push-pins and lower radiator splash shield.
8. **On models equipped with air conditioning,** disconnect and support condenser aside.
9. **On all models,** disconnect radiator support bracket wiring harness retaining clip.
10. **On models equipped with automatic transaxle,** disconnect fluid cooler from two righthand and one lefthand bracket. Support cooler aside.

11. **On all models,** remove mounting bolts and lower core support.
12. Remove radiator.
13. Reverse procedure to install.

FUEL PUMP
REPLACE

1. Ensure transmission is in Neutral position, then raise and support vehicle.
2. Relieve fuel system pressure as outlined under "Precautions."
3. Drain fuel tank into suitable container.
4. Disconnect fuel pump module electrical connector.
5. Remove heat shield mounting nut.

6. Loosen clamp and disconnect filler pipe.
7. Press quick release tabs, then disconnect vent and fuel feed hoses.
8. Support fuel tank with suitable high-lift jack using suitable packing material to prevent damage to tank.
9. Remove mounting bolt and position fuel tank straps aside.
10. Remove fuel tank.
11. Press quick release tab and disconnect fuel tube.
12. Turn lock ring counterclockwise using suitable fuel pump lock ring remover and remove fuel pump module.
13. Reverse procedure to install, noting the following:
    a. Install new locking ring and seal.

b. Lubricate fuel tube fittings with clean engine oil.

FUEL FILTER
REPLACE

1. Ensure transmission is in Neutral position, then raise and support vehicle.
2. Relieve fuel system pressure as outlined under "Precautions."
3. Press quick release tabs, then disconnect filter inlet and outlet tubes.
4. Loosening mounting bolt and remove fuel filter.
5. Reverse procedure to install. Lubricate fuel tube fittings with clean engine oil.

TIGHTENING SPECIFICATIONS

Year	Component	Torque, Ft. Lbs.
2005	Accelerator & Speed Control Cables' Bracket	89①
	Accelerator Control Snow Shield	89①
	Accessory Belt Tensioner	18
	Accessory Drive Belt Idler Pulley	18
	Air Cleaner Pipe	35①
	Air Conditioning Compressor	18
	Air Conditioning Compressor Manifold	15
	Bell Housing	35
	Caliper	21
	Camshaft	③
	Catalytic Converter Flange	41
	Catalytic Converter Heat Shield	89①
	Catalytic Converter Support Bracket;	35
	Catalytic Converter-To-Muffler;	35
	Coil	89①
	Coolant Expansion Tank	89①
	Crankshaft Damper	②
	Crankshaft Pulley	②
	Crankshaft Rear Oil Seal	89①
	Cylinder Head	⑤
	EGR Tube	41
	Flexplate	④
	Flywheel	④
	Front Cover, 8 mm	89①
	Front Cover, 13 mm	35
	Fuel Rail	18
	Fuel Tank Strap	18
	Ground Bolt	35
	Ground Eyelet	89①
	Intake Manifold	18
	Intermediate Shaft Bearing Bracket	18
	Lower Control Arm To Knuckle	37
	Motor Mount	59
	Oil Indicator Tube	89①

2005		
Oil Pan	18
Oil Pan Drain Plug	21
Power Distribution Harness Eyelet	89①
Power Steering Pressure Tube	44
Radiator Bracket	18
Radio Interference Capacitor Bracket	89①
Stabilizer Bar	37
Starter Motor	18
Strut & Spring Top Mount	18
Thermostat Housing	89①
Tie Rod End	35
Timing Chain Guide	89①
Timing Chain Sprocket	48
Timing Chain Tensioner	89①
Torque Converter	26
Transaxle Mount	98
Transaxle Roll Restrictor	35
Valve Cover	89①
Water Pump	89①
Water Pump Pulley	18

① — Inch lbs.
② — Refer to "Crankshaft Damper, Replace" for tightening specifications and sequence.
③ — Refer to "Camshaft, Replace" for tightening specifications and sequence.
④ — Refer to "Crankshaft Rear Oil Seal, Replace" for tightening specifications and sequence.
⑤ — Refer to "Cylinder Head, Replace" for tightening specifications and sequence.

Rear Suspension

NOTE: On Air Bag Equipped Models, Refer To "Air Bag System Precautions" Located In The Front Of This Manual For System Disarming & Arming Procedures.

NOTE: Refer To "Computer Relearn Procedures" Located In The Front Of This Manual When Battery Power To The Computer Has Been Interrupted.

INDEX

PRECAUTIONS

Air Bag Systems

Refer to "Air Bag System Precautions" in the front of this manual for system disarming and arming procedures.

Battery Ground Cable

Prior to service, disconnect battery ground cable and isolate as required.

DESCRIPTION

Refer to **Figs. 1 and 2,** for exploded view of rear suspension.

HUB & BEARING

REPLACE

1. Release parking brake, then remove tire and wheel assembly.
2. Remove dust cap.
3. **On models equipped with rear disc brakes,** proceed as follows:
   a. Disconnect caliper parking brake cable.
   b. Disconnect brake caliper and anchor plate from wheel knuckle.
   c. Suspend brake caliper and anchor plate aside.
   d. Remove brake disc.
4. **On all models,** remove mounting nut and wheel hub.
5. **On models equipped with Anti-Lock Brake System (ABS),** remove ABS sensor ring.
6. **On all models,** remove circlip and press out bearing using suitable drift.
7. Reverse procedures to install noting the following:
   a. Install new bearing using axle bearing installer tool No. T80T-4000N, or equivalent.
   b. **On models equipped with ABS,** install new ABS sensor ring. Ensure

ABS sensor ring is pressed on slowly and squarely.
   c. **On models equipped with rear drum brakes,** rotate drum in opposite direction when tightening wheel hub mounting nut.
   d. **On models equipped with rear disc brakes,** rotate hub assembly 10 times in opposite direction when tightening wheel hub mounting nut.

REAR WHEEL SPINDLE

REPLACE

1. Release parking brake adjuster.
2. Loosen wheel nuts, then raise and support vehicle Remove tire and wheel assembly.
3. **On models equipped with anti-lock brakes,** disconnect wheel speed sensor.
4. **On models equipped with rear disc brakes,** proceed as follows:
   a. Disconnect caliper parking brake cable.
   b. Disconnect brake caliper and anchor plate from wheel knuckle.
   c. Suspend brake caliper and anchor plate aside.
   d. Remove brake disc.
5. **On all models equipped with rear drum brakes,** remove mounting nut, and wheel hub.
6. **On models equipped with Anti-lock Brake System (ABS),** ensure ABS sensor ring is not knocked or damaged and is kept free from metallic fragments when removing brake drum.
7. **On all models,** remove wheel spindle.
8. Reverse procedures to install noting the following:
   a. Install new bearing using axle bearing installer tool No. T80T-4000N, or equivalent.
   b. **On models equipped with ABS,** install new ABS sensor ring. Ensure ABS sensor ring is pressed on slowly and squarely.

   c. **On models equipped with rear drum brakes,** rotate drum in opposite direction when tightening wheel hub mounting nut.
   d. **On models equipped with rear disc brakes,** rotate hub assembly 10 times in opposite direction when tightening wheel hub mounting nut.

SHOCK ABSORBER

REPLACE

Coupe & Sedan

1. Raise and support vehicle.
2. Remove luggage compartment interior trim panel.
3. Remove shock absorber upper mounting nut using suitable spanner to prevent piston rod from rotating.
4. Remove lower mounting bolt and shock absorber.
5. Reverse procedure to install. Final suspension component tightening must be performed with vehicle weight on road wheels.

Wagon

1. Raise and support vehicle, then remove rear tire and wheel assembly.
2. When removing lefthand shock absorber, disconnect exhaust system from rear hanger insulator and remove exhaust heat shield.
3. Support lower arm using suitable transmission jack,
4. Remove shock absorber upper mounting bolt.
5. Remove lower mounting bolt and shock absorber.
6. Reverse procedure to install. Final suspension component tightening must be performed with vehicle weight on road wheels.

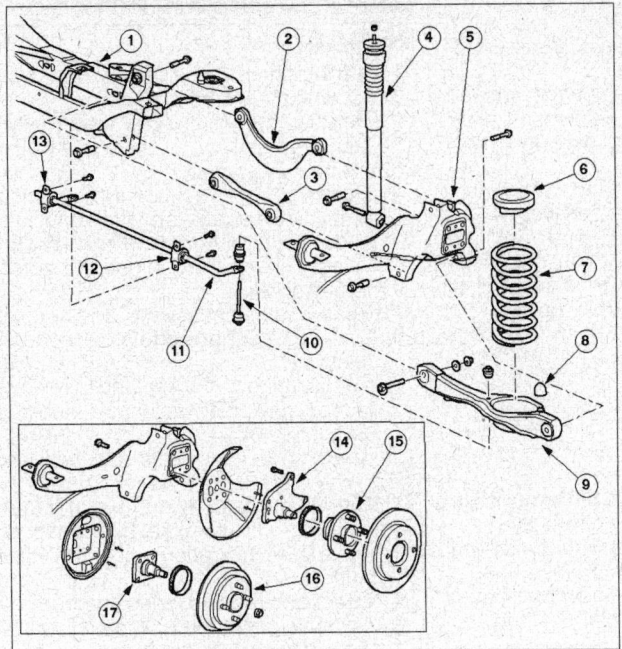

Fig. 1 Rear suspension. Coupe & sedan

Item	Description
1	Crossmember
2	Upper arm
3	Front lower arm
4	Shock absorber assembly
5	Tie-bar and knuckle
6	Spring pad
7	Spring
8	Bump stop
9	Rear lower arm
10	Stabilizer bar link
11	Stabilizer bar
12	Stabilizer bar bushing
13	Stabilizer bar bushing clamp
14	Wheel spindle (disc brakes)
15	Wheel hub (disc brakes)
16	Drum and hub assembly (drum brakes)
17	Wheel spindle (drum brakes)

FM2039900095000X

Item	Description
1	Crossmember
2	Upper arm
3	Front lower arm
4	Shock absorber
5	Tie-bar and knuckle
6	Spring pad
7	Spring
8	Rear lower arm
9	Stabilizer bar
10	Stabilizer bar bushing
11	Stabilizer bar bushing clamp
12	Wheel spindle (disc brakes)
13	Wheel hub (disc brakes)
14	Drum and hub assembly (drum brakes)
15	Wheel spindle (drum brakes)

FM2039900096000X

Fig. 2 Rear suspension. Wagon

COIL SPRING
REPLACE
Coupe & Sedan

1. Remove rear tire and wheel.
2. Compress coil spring. using suitable compressor tool.
3. Disconnect shock absorber from wheel knuckle.
4. Mark position of coil spring compressor to coil spring for installation alignment.
5. Remove coil spring. **Coil spring is under extreme tension.**
6. If coil spring is to be removed from coil spring compressor, mark position of coil spring compressor to coil spring to aid installation.
7. Reverse procedure to install noting the following:
   a. Final tightening of shock absorber lower mounting bolt should be carried out when vehicle weight is on road wheels.
   b. Ensure top seat mounting is installed, and spring ends butt correctly against upper and lower spring seats.

Wagon

1. Remove rear tire and wheel assembly.
2. Disconnect stabilizer bar from rear lower arms.
3. Raise rear lower arm 1.25 inches using suitable transmission jack.
4. Disconnect rear lower arm from wheel knuckle.
5. Lower and remove transmission jack.
6. With the aid of another technician, pull stabilizer bar away from rear lower arm, lower rear lower arm and remove spring. **Coil spring is under extreme tension.**

7. Reverse procedure to install noting the following:
   a. Final tightening of shock absorber lower mounting bolt should be carried out when vehicle weight is on road wheels.
   b. Ensure top seat mounting is installed, and spring ends butt correctly against upper and lower spring seats.

CONTROL ARM
REPLACE
Lower
FRONT

1. Remove coil spring as outlined under "Coil Spring, Replace."
2. Set suspension ride height as outlined in "Wheel Alignment" section.
3. Record position of arm for installation alignment.
4. Remove mounting bolts and front lower arm.
5. Reverse procedures to install. Final tightening of rear suspension components should be carried out at ride height setting.

REAR

1. Remove coil spring as outlined under "Coil Spring, Replace"
2. Set suspension ride height as outlined in "Wheel Alignment" section.
3. Mark position of rear lower arm adjustment cam on crossmember for installation alignment.
4. Remove mounting bolts and rear lower arm.
5. Reverse procedure to install. Final tightening of rear suspension components should be carried out at ride height setting.

Upper

1. Remove coil spring as outlined under "Coil Spring, Replace."
2. Set suspension ride height as outlined in "Wheel Alignment" section.
3. Record position of upper arm for installation alignment.
4. Remove outer bolt and disconnect upper arm from wheel knuckle.
5. Remove inner bolt and upper arm.
6. Reverse procedures to install. Final tightening of rear suspension components should be carried out at ride height setting.

TIE-BAR
REPLACE

1. **On models equipped with rear disc brakes,** remove brake disc shield.
2. **On models equipped with rear drum brakes,** remove brake drum.
3. **On all models,** disconnect rear brake hose using suitable clamp, then the pipe at union.
4. Disconnect parking brake sleeve and cable.
5. Disconnect cable guide, then pull cable and guide through tie-bar.
6. Set suspension ride height as outlined in "Wheel Alignment" section.
7. Remove shock absorber lower mounting bolt, then the outer mount bolts and front lower arm.
8. Remove rear lower arm bolts.
9. Remove spring using suitable coil spring compressor.
10. Disconnect and remove upper arm.
11. Remove front mounting bolts and tie-bar.
12. Reverse procedures to install noting the following:
    a. Bleed brake system.
    b. Inspect rear wheel alignment.

REAR CROSSMEMBER
REPLACE

1. Set suspension ride height as outlined in "Wheel Alignment" section.
2. Remove mounting bolts, clamps and stabilizer bar.
3. Remove bushings.
4. Remove rear lower arms, front lower arms and upper arms as outlined under "Control Arm, Replace." Ensure wheel knuckles are supported before removing arms.
5. Support exhaust system, and bracket.
6. **On 2001 sedan models,** proceed as follows:
   a. Disconnect EVAP and emission canister vent solenoid electrical connector.
   b. Remove vent pipes and emission canister.
7. **On all models,** support rear crossmember with suitable jack, then remove three mounting bolts from either side.
8. Lower and remove crossmember.
9. Reverse procedures to install noting the following:
   a. Do not lower suspension from ride height.
   b. Inspect rear wheel alignment.

STABILIZER BAR
REPLACE

1. Set suspension ride height as outlined in "Wheel Alignment" section.
2. Remove mounting bolts, clamps and remove stabilizer bar.
3. Remove bushings.
4. Reverse procedures to install noting the following:
   a. Ensure bushing nipple is on left-hand side when installing onto stabilizer bar.
   b. Apply water to clamp to assist installation.

TIGHTENING SPECIFICATIONS

Year	Component	Torque, Ft. Lbs.
2001–05	Control Arm	85
	Crossmember	85
	EVAP Canister	84①
	Lug Nut	94
	Spindle Bolt	49
	Shock Absorber, Lower	85
	Shock Absorber, Top	13
	Stabilizer Bar Link	11
	Stabilizer Bracket	35
	Tie Bar	85
	Wheel Hub Nut	173
	Wheel Speed Sensor	84①

① — Inch lbs.

Front Suspension & Steering

NOTE: On Air Bag Equipped Models, Refer To "Air Bag System Precautions" Located In The Front Of This Manual For System Disarming & Arming Procedures.

NOTE: Refer To "Computer Relearn Procedures" Located In The Front Of This Manual When Battery Power To The Computer Has Been Interrupted.

NOTE: Prior To Performing Any Service Operations Listed In This Section, Consult The "Technical Service Bulletins" Section For Related Information.

INDEX

PRECAUTIONS

Air Bag Systems

Refer to "Air Bag System Precautions" in the front of this manual for system disarming and arming procedures.

Battery Ground Cable

Prior to service, disconnect battery ground cable and isolate as required.

DESCRIPTION

Refer to **Fig. 1,** for exploded view of front suspension.

WHEEL BEARING

ADJUST

Wheel bearing cannot be adjusted.
1. Raise and support vehicle.
2. Rock tire and wheel assembly at top and bottom to inspect for bearing looseness.
3. Spin wheel quickly by hand. Ensure wheel turns smoothly without noise from bearing.
4. Remove tire and wheel assembly, then brake caliper anchor plate.
5. Position dial indicator gauge bracket and gauge Nos. 100-D004 and 100-D005, or equivalent, against wheel hub, then push and pull wheel hub.
6. If end play exists, replace bearing.

HUB & BEARING

REPLACE

1. Remove knuckle as outlined under "Steering Knuckle, Replace."
2. Remove wheel hub and outer bearing race using bearing puller No. 205-D064, or equivalent, and suitable drift, **Fig. 2.**
3. Remove bearing circlip.
4. Remove inner bearing using suitable drift.
5. Reverse procedure to install. Install new bearing using bearing cup installer No. 205-139, or equivalent.

BALL JOINT

REPLACE

1. Raise and support vehicle, then remove tire and wheel assembly.
2. Remove mounting bolt and ball joint from knuckle.
3. Reverse procedure to install.

COIL SPRING

REPLACE

1. Raise and support vehicle, then remove tire and wheel assembly.
2. Remove knuckle as outlined under "Steering Knuckle, Replace."
3. Remove mounting nuts, strut and spring assembly.
4. Compress coil spring using suitable compressor tool.
5. Remove thrust bearing nut using suitable Allen key to prevent piston rod rotation.

6. Disassemble strut and spring assembly, **Fig. 3.**
7. Reverse procedure to assemble.

STRUT

REPLACE

1. Raise and support vehicle, then remove tire and wheel assembly.
2. Remove knuckle as outlined under "Steering Knuckle, Replace."
3. Remove mounting nuts, strut and spring assembly.
4. Reverse procedure to install.

COIL SPRING & STRUT SERVICE

1. Compress coil spring using suitable compressor tool.
2. Remove thrust bearing nut using suitable Allen key to prevent piston rod rotation.
3. Disassemble strut and spring assembly, **Fig. 3.**
4. Reverse procedure to assemble.

CONTROL ARM

REPLACE

1. Raise and support vehicle, then remove tire and wheel assembly.
2. Remove mounting bolt and ball joint from knuckle.
3. Remove mounting bolts and lower arm.
4. Reverse procedure to install, noting the following.

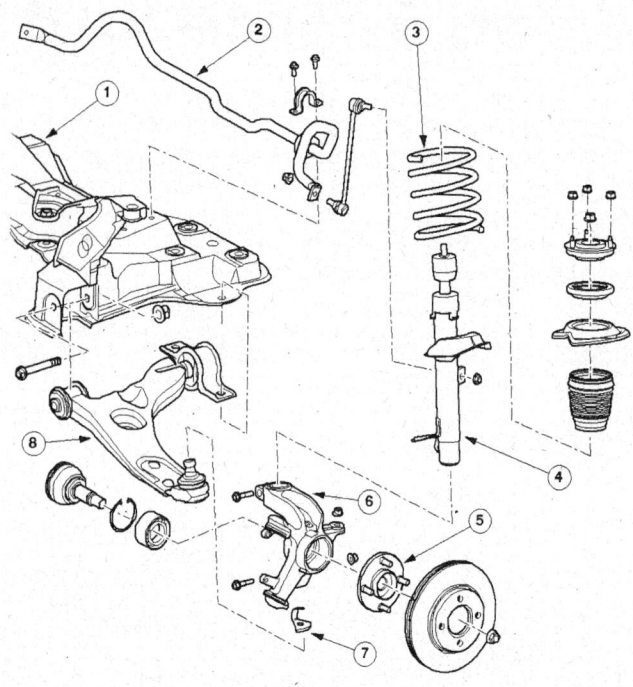

Fig. 1   Exploded view of front suspension (Part 1 of 2)

FM2020000172010X

Item	Description
1	Crossmember
2	Stabilizer bar
3	Spring
4	Strut
5	Wheel hub
6	Wheel knuckle
7	Lower arm ball joint heat shield
8	Lower arm

FM2020000172020X

Fig. 1   Exploded view of front suspension (Part 2 of 2)

g. Raise crossmember, engaging guide pins into chassis aligning holes.

a. Install lower arm nuts, bolts and washers.
b. **Torque** nut 1 to 74 ft. lbs., **Fig. 4.**
c. Tighten nut 1 an additional 60°.
d. **Torque** nut 2 to 89 ft. lbs.
e. **Torque** bolt 3 to 89 ft. lbs.
f. Tighten bolt 3 an additional 90°.
g. Ensure bolt 3 is **torqued** to 125–170 ft. lbs.

STEERING KNUCKLE
REPLACE

1. Loosen wheel hub mounting nut.
2. Loosen wheel nuts.
3. Loosen strut tower nuts at least five turns.
4. Raise and support vehicle, then remove tire and wheel assembly.
5. Disconnect brake hose from support bracket.
6. Disconnect wheel speed sensor, then remove and support brake caliper aside.
7. Remove brake rotor.
8. Remove tie rod end using tie rod end remover tool No. TOOL-3290-D, or equivalent.
9. Remove ball joint from knuckle.
10. Remove hub mounting nut.
11. Separate wheel hub from halfshaft using puller tools Nos. 204-067 and 204-069, or equivalents. **Ensure halfshaft does not disconnected from inner constant velocity joint.**
12. Remove pinch bolt and knuckle from strut.
13. Reverse procedure to install.

STABILIZER BAR
REPLACE

1. Center and lock steering wheel in position.
2. Disconnect steering column shaft from pinion extension.
3. Raise and support vehicle, then remove tire and wheel assemblies.
4. Remove tie rod end nuts, then using tie rod end remover No. TOOL-3290-D, or equivalent.
5. Disconnect tie rod ends from knuckles.
6. Disconnect stabilizer bar links.
7. Remove ball joints from knuckles.
8. Remove support insulator to transaxle center bolt, **Fig. 5.**
9. Support crossmember using suitable transmission jack.
10. Remove six crossmember mounting bolts, **Fig. 6.**
11. Lower crossmember.
12. Remove bolts, clamps and stabilizer bar.
13. Reverse procedure to install, noting the following:
    a. Install bushings onto stabilizer bar. **Do not use lubricant.**
    b. Support stabilizer bar to design height, **Fig. 7.**
    c. **Torque** clamp lower mounting bolts to 37 ft. lbs.
    d. **Torque** clamp upper mounting bolts to 52 ft. lbs.
    e. Insert alignment tool No. 502-002, or equivalent, guide pins through crossmember alignment holes, **Fig. 8.**
    f. Slide locking plates into grooves and tighten guide pin sleeve.

TIE ROD
REPLACE

1. Remove steering gear as outlined under "Power Steering Gear, Replace."
2. Remove tie rod end and locknut.
3. Remove steering gear boot.
4. Rotate pinion to expose rack gear teeth.
5. Secure steering gear in suitable vise.
6. Remove tie rod using suitable pipe wrench.
7. Remove thread locking compound.
8. Reverse procedure to install. Apply thread locking compound to new tie rod inner threads.

TIE ROD END
REPLACE

1. Raise and support vehicle, then remove tire and wheel assembly.
2. Loosen tie rod end lock nut, then remove mounting nut.
3. Disconnect tie rod end from knuckle using tie rod end remover tool No. TOOL-3290-D, or equivalent.
4. Note number of turns required to remove tie rod end.
5. Remove tie rod end and lock nut.
6. Reverse procedure to install. Inspect toe.

POWER STEERING GEAR
REPLACE

1. Center and lock steering wheel into position.
2. Remove instrument panel lower cover.
3. Disconnect steering column shaft from pinion extension.
4. Raise and support vehicle, then remove front tire and wheel assemblies.

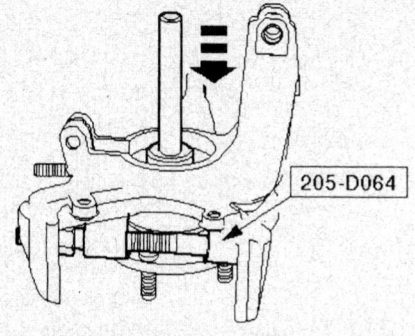

Fig. 2 Hub & outer race removal

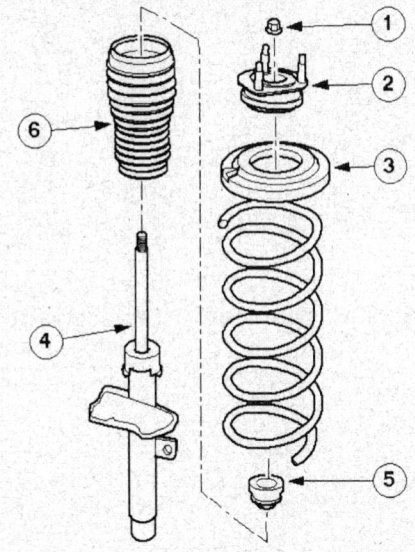

Fig. 3 Exploded view of strut & spring.

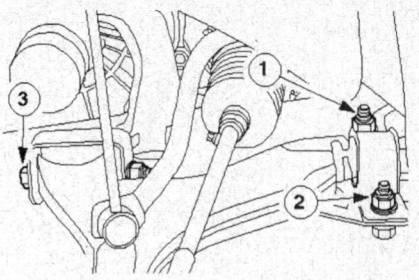

Fig. 4 Lower arm tightening sequence

5. Remove tie rod ends from knuckles using tie rod end removal tool No. TOOL-3290-D, or equivalent.
6. Disconnect stabilizer bar links from struts.
7. Disconnect fluid cooler hose using coupling tool No. 310-041, or equivalent. Drain fluid into suitable container.
8. Remove support insulator to transaxle center bolt, **Fig. 5.**
9. Remove steering gear heat shield.
10. Disconnect support clamp and remove steering gear hoses. Drain fluid into suitable container.
11. Support crossmember using suitable transmission jack.
12. Remove six mounting bolts and lower crossmember, **Fig. 6.**
13. Remove steering column coupling shaft and floor seal.
14. Move floor seal upwards.
15. Remove mounting bolts and steering gear.
16. Reverse procedure to install, noting the following:
    a. Insert alignment tool No. 502-002, or equivalent, guide pins through crossmember alignment holes, **Fig. 8.**
    b. Slide locking plates into grooves and tighten guide pin sleeve.
    c. Raise crossmember, engaging guide pins into chassis aligning holes.

POWER STEERING PUMP
REPLACE

2.0L DOHC Engine
VINS N & Z

1. Turn tensioner clockwise and remove accessory drive belt.
2. Disconnect Power Steering Pressure (PSP) switch electrical connector.
3. Remove clamp, disconnect steering fluid suction line from pump. Drain fluid into suitable container.
4. Disconnect power steering pressure line fitting nut.
5. Raise and support vehicle.
6. Remove mounting nuts and position power steering pressure line bracket aside.

7. Remove power steering pump lower mounting bolts.
8. Lower vehicle.
9. Remove upper mounting bolts and power steering pump.
10. Reverse procedure to install.

VIN 3

1. Remove accessory drive belt, then raise and support vehicle.
2. Disconnect fluid cooler hose using coupling tool No. 310-041, or equivalent. Drain fluid into suitable container.
3. Disconnect power steering pump line.
4. Lower vehicle, then disconnect pressure line support brackets.
5. Disconnect speed control cable.
6. Disconnect Power Steering Pressure (PSP) switch electrical connector.
7. Disconnect power steering pump hose. Drain fluid into suitable container.
8. Remove four mounting bolts power steering pump.
9. Remove PSP switch.
10. Reverse procedure to install. Install new O-ring seal onto pressure line using Teflon seal installer tool No. D90P-3517-A, or equivalent.

VIN 5

1. Remove accessory drive belt.
2. Disconnect fender splash shield from front bumper cover.
3. Remove righthand headlamp assembly lower mounting bolt.
4. Disconnect power steering fluid cooler line from cooler using coupling tool No. 310-041, or equivalent.
5. Disconnect power steering pump line.
6. Remove power steering pump lower mounting bolts.
7. Lower vehicle.
8. Remove radiator grille.
9. Remove righthand headlamp assembly.

10. Disconnect power steering pump hose.
11. Disconnect power steering line from engine and position aside.
12. Remove power steering pump.
13. Reverse procedure to install. Install new O-ring seal onto power steering pump to steering gear line union using Teflon seal installer tool No. D90P-3517-A, or equivalent.

2.0L SOHC Engine

1. Rotate tensioner in a clockwise direction using suitable ½ square drive breaker bar.
2. Disconnect serpentine drive belt from power steering pump pulley.
3. Remove power steering pump pulley mounting nut.
4. Remove power steering pump pulley mounting nut. using flange holding tool wrench tool No. T78P-4851-A, or equivalent.
5. Remove power steering pump pulley.
6. Disconnect power steering pump fluid reservoir hose. Drain fluid into suitable container.
7. Disconnect power steering high-pressure line from power steering pump. Drain fluid into suitable container.
8. Remove power steering pump.
9. Remove power steering fluid reservoir to power steering pump hose union.
10. Reverse procedure to install. Install new O-ring seal onto power steering pump to steering gear line union using Teflon seal installer tool No. D90P-3517-A, or equivalent.

POWER STEERING SYSTEM BLEED

1. Fill power steering fluid reservoir to MAX mark with suitably, fresh power steering fluid.
2. Start engine and slowly turn wheel from lock to lock once. Ensure fluid level does not fall below MIN mark as air could enter system. **Do not hold steering wheel against lock stops for more than five seconds.**
3. Stop engine and inspect system for leaks.
4. Inspect and adjust reservoir fluid level.
5. Maintain a vacuum of 15 inches Hg. using vacuum tool No. 416-D002, or equivalent. If vacuum decreases more

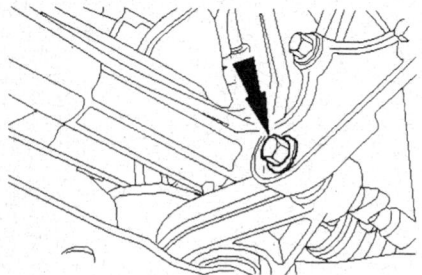

Fig. 5 Support insulator bolt replacement

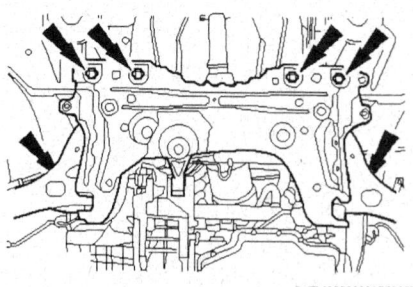

Fig. 6 Crossmember replacement

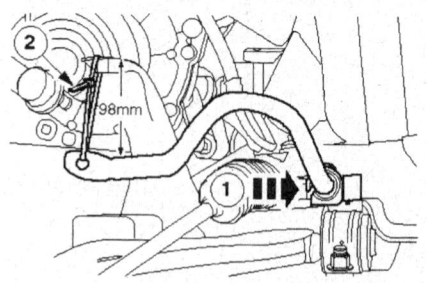

Fig. 7 Stabilizer bar design height setting

than 2 inches Hg in five minutes, inspect for leaks.

6. Start engine and turn wheel from lock to lock once, then turn it to righthand just off lock stop.
7. Stop engine and apply vacuum of 15 inches Hg. Maintain vacuum for five minutes until air is evacuated from system.
8. Release vacuum, then repeat previous two steps, turning wheel to left, just off stop lock.
9. Remove vacuum tool and adjust reservoir fluid level.
10. Start engine and turn wheel from lock to lock. If there is excessive noise, repeat procedure.
11. If noise level is still unacceptable, allow vehicle to stand overnight and repeat procedure.

POWER STEERING FLUID COOLER

REPLACE

1. Disconnect coolant expansion tank and position aside.
2. Remove power steering fluid reservoir hose. Drain fluid into suitable container.
3. Disconnect hose from bracket, then raise and support vehicle.
4. Remove radiator splash shield.
5. Disconnect fluid cooler hose using

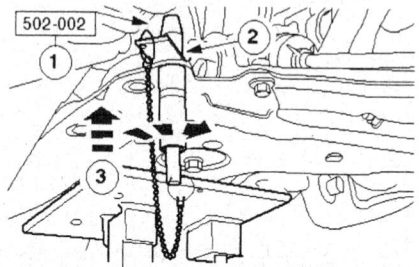

Fig. 8 Crossmember alignment

coupling tool No. 310-041, or equivalent. Drain fluid into suitable container.
6. Remove fluid cooler.
7. Reverse procedure to install.

TECHNICAL SERVICE BULLETINS

Front Suspension Creaking, Crunching, Grinding Or Rattle

2001-04

On some of these models there may be a front suspension creaking, crunching, grinding or rattle at slow speeds or while turning.

This condition may be caused by stabilizer bar and links, spring's rubber sleeve or upper strut bearing.

To correct this condition, proceed as follows:

1. Grasp stabilizer bar end links and shake them along link direction and transverse in inboard/outboard directions.
2. If there is no looseness, proceed to next step. If there is looseness, proceed as follows:
   a. Inspect link end joints.
   b. If joints are not severely corroded, **torque** nut to 36 ft. lbs.
   c. If joints are still loose or are severely corroded, replace link (P/N YS4Z-5K484-AA).
3. Inspect upper spring seat contact. If spring is positioned properly, proceed to next step. If spring is out of position, proceed as follows:
   a. Remove original sleeve.
   b. Install new rubber sleeve (P/N 1S4Z-8484-AA) starting from top of spring coil.
4. Remove strut(s) and inspect for misaligned upper strut bearing.
5. If bearing is misaligned, replace it (P/N YS4Z-18198-AAA) into existing rubber top mount on existing strut.
6. Relieve fuel system pressure as outlined under "Precautions."If clicking or popping is from front strut, install service spring end cap (P/N 4S4Z-5L302-AA) on top spring tip.

TIGHTENING SPECIFICATIONS

Year	Component	Torque, Ft. Lbs..
2001–05	Caliper To Knuckle	21
	Column Shaft To Pinion	26
	Crossmember, Front	85
	Crossmember, Rear	148
	Fluid Cooler	44①
	Hose Clamps	17
	Hub Nut	233
	Knuckle To Strut Pinch Bolt	66
	Lower Arm To Knuckle Pinch Bolt	37
	Power Steering Pump	18
	Pressure Line To Pump Union	48
	Pressure Line Support Bracket	②
	PSP Switch	15
	Speed Sensor	80①
	Stabilizer Bar Link	37
	Steering Gear	59
	Steering Gear Heat Shield	53①
	Strut	18
	Strut Thrust Bearing	35
	Support Insulator Center Bolt	37
	Tie Rod End	35
	Wheel Lug Nuts	63

① — Inch lbs.
② — DOHC engine, 18 ft. lbs. SOHC engine, 44 inch lbs.

Wheel Alignment

NOTE: Prior To Performing Any Service Operations Listed In This Section, Consult The "Technical Service Bulletins" Section For Related Information.

INDEX

PRELIMINARY INSPECTION

1. Inspect suspension components for damage or wear.
2. Inflate tires to specifications.
3. Ensure vehicle is at curb weight.
4. Ensure spare tire, jack and vehicle tools are in proper locations.
5. Remove luggage and additional items.
6. Jounce vehicle to bring suspension to normal design height setting.

RIDE HEIGHT

Coupe & Sedan

1. Raise and support vehicle.
2. Fabricate .787 inch wide and 4.448 inches long spacer.
3. Remove bump stop.
4. Position spacer and raise rear control arm using suitable floor jack and wooden block.
5. Space should be between rear lower arm and crossmember in vertical plane, **Fig. 1.**

Wagon

1. Raise and support vehicle.
2. Fabricate .787 inch wide and 6.181 inches long spacer.
3. Position spacer and raise rear control arm using suitable floor jack and wooden block.
4. Space should be between rear lower arm and crossmember in vertical plane, **Fig. 2.**

FRONT WHEEL ALIGNMENT

Caster & Camber

On these models, caster and camber are not adjustable.

Toe

1. Inspect toe setting.

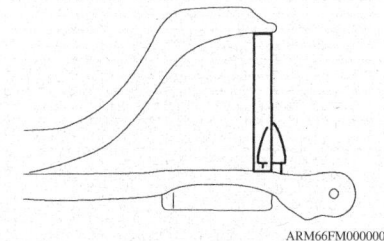

Fig. 1   Spacer position. Coupe & sedan

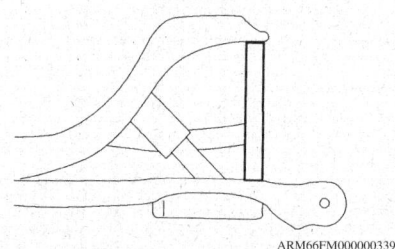

Fig. 2   Spacer position. Wagon

2. Loosen tie-rod end locknuts.
3. Remove steering gear boot outer clamps.
4. Rotate tie-rods an equal amount in either clockwise or counterclockwise direction.
5. **Torque** tie-rod end locknuts to 46 ft. lbs.
6. Install steering gear boot outer clamps.
7. Ensure toe is set to specifications.

REAR WHEEL ALIGNMENT

Camber

On these models, camber is not adjustable.

Toe

1. Inspect toe setting.
2. Raise and support vehicle.
3. Set suspension to ride height as outlined under "Ride Height Specifications."
4. Loosen rear lower arm cam bolt nut.

5. **Torque** rear lower arm cam bolt nut to 71 inch lbs.
6. Lower suspension from ride height.
7. Install coil spring as outlined under "Coil Spring, Replace" in "Rear Suspension" section.
8. Lower vehicle and bounce vehicle to ensure suspension is in its normal resting position.
9. Rotate bolt and eccentric washer until proper toe setting is reached.
10. Raise and support vehicle.
11. **Torque** rear lower arm cam bolt nut to 85 ft. lbs.
12. Lower vehicle.
13. Ensure toe setting is with specifications.

TECHNICAL SERVICE BULLETINS

Rear Tire Inner Edge Wear

On some of these models the rear tire may have inner edge wear.

This condition may be caused by rear camber beyond negative end of specifications (maximum on wagon models is -2.2°; on coupe and sedan models, -2.3°.

To correct this condition install revised +1° rear upper control arms kit (P/N 3S4Z-1A154-AA) as follows:

1. **On wagon models,** remove lower mounting bolt and position shock absorber aside.
2. **On all models,** remove inboard upper control arm mounting bolt and arm.
3. Install upper control arm and new inboard upper control arm bolt.
4. **On wagon models,** install shock absorber and lower mounting bolt.
5. **On all models,** position upper control arm in wheel knuckle and install new outboard upper control arm bolt.
6. **Final tighten of rear suspension component(s) when suspension is at load and at ride height.**
7. Inspect alignment.

FIVE HUNDRED, FREESTYLE & MONTEGO

NOTE: Refer To The Rear Of This Manual For Vehicle Manufacturer's Special Service Tools.

INDEX OF SERVICE OPERATIONS

Specifications

GENERAL ENGINE SPECIFICATIONS

Year/Engine (VIN)①	Fuel System	Bore & Stroke	Comp. Ratio	Net H.P. @ RPM	Maximum Torque/Ft. Lbs. @ RPM	Normal Oil Pressure, psi
2005						
3.0L (1)	SFI	3.50 x 3.13	10:1	200 @ 5700	200 @ 4400	11②

DOHC — Dual Overhead Cam
SFI — Sequential Fuel Injection

① — The eighth digit of the VIN denotes engine code.

② — At 1500 RPM with engine hot.

TUNE UP SPECIFICATIONS

Liter (Code①)	Spark Plug Gap	Ignition Timing, °BTDC			Curb Idle Speed, RPM		Fast Idle Speed, RPM		Fuel Pump Pressure, psi	Valve Clearance
		Firing Order Fig. ②	Man. Trans.	Auto. Trans.	Mark Fig.	Man. Trans.	Auto. Trans.	Man. Trans.	Auto. Trans.	
2005										
3.0L (1)	.054	③	—	⑦	⑧	—	④	—	④	⑤	⑥

BTDC — Before Top Dead Center

① — The eighth digit of the VIN denotes engine code.

② — Before disconnecting wires from distributor cap or coil, determine location of wire, as position may have been altered from that mounting at end of this chart.

③ — Coil on plug ignition system. Cylinder numbering front to rear, **Fig. A** righthand bank, 1, 2, 3 ; lefthand bank, 4, 5, 6. Firing order 1-4-2-5-3-6.

④ — Idle speed is controlled by an automatic idle control system.

⑤ — Key on engine off, 37–45 psi. Key on engine running, 26–45 psi.

⑥ — Equipped w/hydraulic valve lifters; no provision for adjustment.

⑦ — Non-adjustable.

⑧ — Equipped w/crankshaft position sensor.

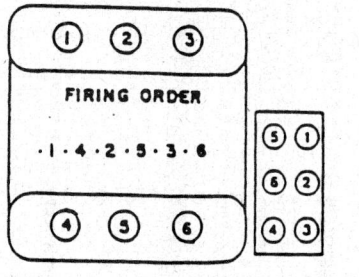

FM1139300273000X

Fig. A

FRONT WHEEL ALIGNMENT SPECIFICATIONS

Model	Caster Angle, Degrees		Camber Angle, Degrees		Total Toe, Degrees		Ball Joint Wear
	Limits	Desired	Limits	Desired	Limits	Desired	
Five Hundred & Montego (AWD)	+2.75 to +4.25	+3.50	−1.5 to +.15	−.60	−.40 to +.40	+.20	①
Five Hundred & Montego (FWD)	+2.55 to +4.05	+3.30	−1.5 to +.15	−.60	−.22 to +.02	−.10	①
Freestyle (AWD)	+2.25 to +3.75	+3.00	−1.07 to +1.07.	−.32	−.40 to +.40	+.20	①
Freestyle (FWD)	+2.35 to +3.85	+3.10	−1.03 to +1.03	−.28	−.22 to +.02	−.10	①

AWD — All Wheel Drive
FWD — Front Wheel Drive

① — Refer to "Ball Joint Inspection" in "Front Suspension & Steering" section.

REAR WHEEL ALIGNMENT SPECIFICATIONS

Model	Camber Angle, Degrees①		Total Toe-In, Degrees	
	Limits	Desired	Limits	Desired
Five Hundred & Montego (AWD)	−1.05 to +1.45	+.70	−.01 to +.30	+.10
Five Hundred & Montego (FWD)	−.75 to +0.75	+.75	−.01 to +.30	+.10
Freestyle (AWD	+.75 to −.75	−.0	−.01 to +.30	+.10
Freestyle (FWD)	−.18 to +1.32	−.57	−.01 to +.30	+.10

AWD — All Wheel Drive   FWD — Front Wheel Drive   ① — Not adjustable.

VEHICLE RIDE HEIGHT SPECIFICATIONS

Model	Year	Manufacturer's Original Tire Size	Measurement Points & Specifications					
			Front			Rear		
			Dim.	Specification		Dim.	Specification	
				Inches	mm		Inches	mm
Five Hundred & Montego (AWD)	2005	①	E	—	—	G	—	—
Five Hundred & Montego (FWD)	2005	①	E	—	—	G	—	—
Freestyle (AWD)	2005	①	E	—	—	G	—	—
Freestyle (FWD)	2005	①	E	—	—	G	—	—

AWD — All Wheel Drive
FWD — Front Wheel Drive
A Dim. — Distance from Front Rocker Panel to Ground
B Dim. — Distance from Rear Rocker Panel to Ground
E Dim. — Ground to Front Wheel Opening Through Centerline of Wheel

G Dim. — Ground to Rear Wheel Opening Through Centerline of Wheel
Dim. — Dimension
① — See door sticker or inside of glove box for manufacturer's original tire size specifications. If tires on vehicle do not match manufacturer's original tire size & measure-

ment is not within limits, it will be required to refer to the Non-Standard Tire & Wheel Size Adjustment To Ride Height Specification & Tire Size Adjustment Charts.

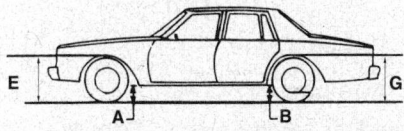

Fig. A   Dimensions A, B, E & G

FLUID CAPACITIES & COOLING SYSTEM DATA

Model	Engine Liter (VIN) ①	Coolant Capacity, Qts.	Coolant Type	Radiator Cap Relief Pressure, Lbs.	Thermo. Opening Temp. °F	Fuel Tank Gals.	Engine Oil Refill, Qts.②	Transaxle Capacity	
								Transfer Case., Pts.	Auto. Trans., Qts.④
2005									
All	3.0L (1)	⑥	⑤	13–18	180–203	19	6.0	2	③

CVT — Continuously Variable Chain Type transaxle.

① — The eighth digit of the VIN denotes engine code.

② — Includes filter.

③ — Models w/CVT transaxle, 10.0 qts.; models w/6 speed transaxle; 7.40 qts.

④ — Approximate; make final inspection w/dipstick.

⑤ — Motorcraft premium gold part No.

VC-7–A, or equivalent. In California and Oregon use Motorcraft premium gold part No. VC-7–B, or equivalent.

⑥ — Less auxiliary heater 10.6 quarts.; with auxiliary heater 12.7 quarts.

LUBRICANT DATA

Year	Transaxle		Power Steering	Brake System
	Manual/Transfer Case	Automatic		
2005	②	Mercon V	①	DOT 3

① — Motorcraft MERCON Multi-Purpose ATF part No. XT-2-QDX, or equivalent.

② — SAE 80W-90 premium rear axle lubricant part No. XY-80W-90–QL, or equivalent.

Electrical

NOTE: On Air Bag Equipped Models, Refer To "Air Bag System Precautions" Located In The Front Of This Manual For System Disarming & Arming Procedures.

NOTE: Refer To "Computer Relearn Procedures" Located In The Front Of This Manual When Battery Power To The Computer Has Been Interrupted.

INDEX

PRECAUTIONS

Air Bag Systems

Refer to "Air Bag System Precautions" in the front of this manual for system disarming and arming procedures.

Battery Ground Cable

Prior to service, disconnect battery ground cable and isolate as required.

FUSE PANEL & FLASHER LOCATION

The engine compartment power distribution center is located on the front lefthand side of the engine compartment. The fuse panel is located under the instrument panel, left of the steering column. The combination turn signal/hazard flasher is located behind the lefthand side of the instrument panel reinforcement, in the Smart Junction Box (SJB).

FUEL PUMP RELAY LOCATION

The fuel pump relay is located at the front left of the engine compartment near the battery, in the power distribution center.

STARTER
REPLACE

The heavy gauge input lead connected to the starter solenoid is hot at all times. Ensure the protective cap is installed over the terminal and is replaced after service.
1. Raise and support vehicle.
2. Remove lower air deflector.
3. Remove starter solenoid safety cap.
4. Remove starter solenoid and ground stud cables.
5. Remove mounting bolts, stud and starter.
6. Reverse procedure to install.

ALTERNATOR
REPLACE

1. Remove accessory drive belt from alternator.
2. Remove mounting nut, then position engine control sensor wiring and hose bracket aside.
3. Loosen alternator pulley nut and remove inboard upper alternator mounting bolt.
4. Loosen outboard upper alternator bolt.
5. Disconnect electrical harness connector and output terminal wiring.
6. Raise and support vehicle, then remove wheel and tire assembly.
7. Remove alternator splash shield and outboard upper alternator bolt.
8. Remove lower alternator bolt.
9. Remove pulley nut and alternator.

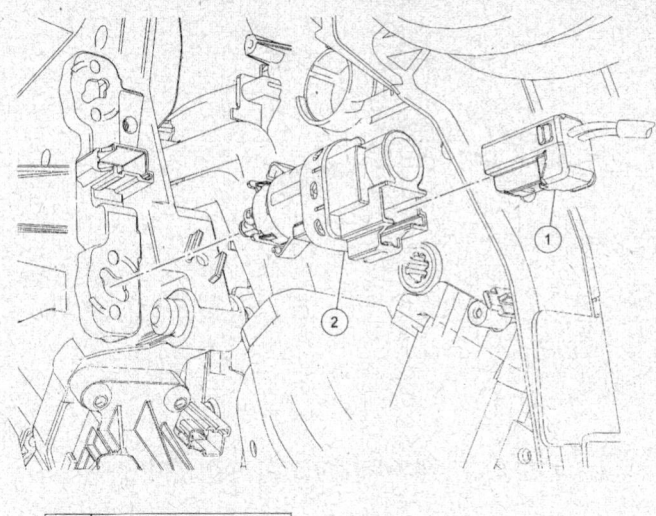

Item	Description
1	Electrical connector
2	Brake pedal position (BPP) switch

ARM0400000000457

Fig. 1   Brake light switch replacement

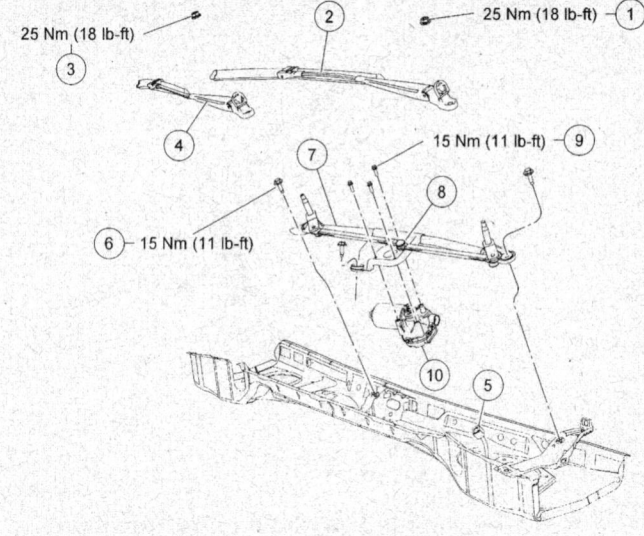

Item	Description		Item	Description
1	Wiper pivot arm nut		7	Wiper mounting arm and pivot shaft assembly
2	LH wiper arm		8	Wiper pivot arm linkage
3	Wiper pivot arm nut		9	Wiper motor bolt
4	RH wiper arm		10	Wiper motor
5	Electrical connector			
6	Wiper mounting arm and pivot shaft bolts (3 required)			

ARM0400000000458

Fig. 2   Front wiper motor replacement

10. Reverse procedure to install, noting the following:
    a. **Torque** alternator mounting bolts to 15–22 ft. lbs.
    b. **Torque** alternator output nut to 80–106 inch lbs.
    c. **Torque** alternator pulley nut to 60–100 ft. lbs.

IGNITION LOCK
REPLACE

1. Place ignition switch in RUN position.
2. Depress lock cylinder retaining pin with suitable ⅛ inch drill or drift punch while working through steering column lower shroud.
3. Pull ignition lock cylinder from housing.
4. Reverse procedure to install. Ensure proper installation by rotating ignition switch through it's travel range.

IGNITION SWITCH
REPLACE

1. Remove lower instrument panel steering column cover.
2. Turn ignition lock to RUN position.
3. Disconnect ignition switch electrical connector.
4. Remove mounting screws and ignition switch.
5. Reverse procedure to install, noting the following:
    a. Ensure ignition lock is in RUN position when installing ignition switch.
    b. **Torque** ignition switch mounting screws to 50–69 inch lbs.

NEUTRAL SAFETY SWITCH
REPLACE

Neutral safety switch functions are incorporated into the Transaxle Range (TR) sensor.
1. Place manual control lever in Neutral position.
2. Remove engine air cleaner and outlet tube.
3. Disconnect TR sensor electrical connector.
4. Remove manual control lever from transaxle.
5. Remove mounting bolts and TR sensor.
6. Reverse procedure to install, noting the following:
    a. Ensure manual control lever is in Neutral position.
    b. Install transaxle range sensor and mounting bolts loosely.
    c. Align position sensor using manual lever position sensor alignment tool No. T92P-70010-AH, or equivalent.
    d. **Torque** sensor mounting bolts to 84–106 inch lbs.
    e. **Torque** manual lever mounting bolts to 96–132 inch lbs.

HEADLAMP SWITCH
REPLACE

1. Pry headlamp switch housing from instrument panel.

2. Depress release button and pull headlamp switch away from instrument panel.
3. Disconnect electrical connectors and remove headlamp switch.
4. Reverse procedure to install.

STOP LIGHT SWITCH
REPLACE

1. Lift stop lamp switch harness wiring connector locking tab and remove connector, **Fig. 1**.
2. Push inward on brake light switch locking tabs, then pull switch straight back to remove from mounting bracket.
3. Reverse procedure to install.

MULTI-FUNCTION SWITCH
REPLACE

1. **On models equipped with tilt steering column,** move column to lowest position, then remove tilt and key release levers.
2. **On all models,** place ignition switch in RUN position, then depress lock cylinder retaining pin with suitable ⅛ inch drill or drift punch while working through steering column lower shroud.
3. Pull ignition lock cylinder from housing.
4. Rotate replacement lock cylinder to RUN position, depressing retaining pin and insert lock cylinder into housing.

Fig. 3 Rear wiper arm pivot nut replacement

ARM0400000000459

Fig. 4 Rear wiper motor replacement

ARM0400000000460

Ensure proper installation by rotating ignition switch through travel.

5. Remove upper and lower steering column shrouds.
6. Remove multi-function switch mounting screws and disconnect switch from casting.
7. Disconnect electrical connectors and remove switch.
8. Reverse procedure to install, noting the following:
   a. **Torque** multi-function switch mounting screws to 18–27 inch lbs.
   b. **Torque** tilt lever mounting screw to 6–8 inch lbs.

STEERING WHEEL
REPLACE

1. Place front wheels in straight-ahead position.
2. Disconnect speed control wire harness from steering wheel.
3. Remove driver's side air bag module as outlined in "Passive Restraints" chapter.
4. Remove and discard steering wheel mounting bolt.
5. Remove steering wheel using steering wheel puller tool No. T67L-3600-A, or equivalent. Route contact assembly wire harness through steering wheel as wheel is lifted off shaft.
6. Reverse procedure to install, noting the following:
   a. Ensure front wheels are in straight-ahead position.
   b. Route contact assembly wire harness through steering column opening at three o'clock position.
   c. Align steering shaft alignment marks.
   d. **Torque** new steering wheel mounting bolt to 26–34 ft. lbs.

INSTRUMENT CLUSTER
REPLACE

1. Remove instrument finish panel mounting screws, then the finish panel

2. Tilt steering wheel to its lowest possible position.
3. Remove instrument cluster mounting screws and pull top of cluster toward steering wheel.
4. Disconnect electrical connectors behind instrument cluster.
5. Remove instrument cluster.
6. Reverse procedure to install.

RADIO
REPLACE

1. Remove instrument panel center finish panel retaining screws, then the finish panel.
2. Remove two radio to instrument panel mounting screws.
3. Pull radio outward to access electrical connectors.
4. Disconnect electrical connectors and antenna lead.
5. Remove radio from instrument panel.
6. Reverse procedure to install.

WIPER MOTOR
REPLACE

Front

The wiper mounting arm and pivot shafts are connected with non-removable plastic ball joints. Except for the wiper motor, the entire wiper transmission assembly is non-serviceable.

1. Note normal park position of wiper arms and blades for installation alignment.
2. Remove wiper arm mounting nuts from pivot shafts, **Fig. 2.**
3. Turn ignition switch to ON position and wiper switch to LO.
4. Turn ignition switch to OFF position when arms and blades to move to straight up-and-down position.
5. Remove wiper arms from pivot shafts.
6. Turn eight plastic cowl vent screen nuts ¼ turn counterclockwise.

7. Remove clips mounting vent screen to inner panels.
8. Remove pivot shaft assembly mounting screws and wiper assembly.
9. Reverse procedure to install, noting the following:
   a. Turn ignition switch to ON position and wiper control switch to Low or High.
   b. Turn wiper control switch to OFF position after wipers have cycled once or twice.
   c. **Torque** pivot shaft assembly to 11 ft. lbs.
   d. Install wiper arms and blades in their previously recorded park positions.
   e. **Torque** pivot arm nuts to 18 ft. lbs.

Rear

1. Open pivot arm nut cover, **Fig. 3,** then remove rear wiper arm pivot nut and wiper arm blade assembly.
2. Open liftgate and remove trim panel using suitable trim tool to release trim retaining clips.
3. Remove liftgate trim panel.
4. Disconnect wiper motor electrical connector, **Fig. 4.**
5. Remove three wiper motor mounting bolts, then the wiper motor.
6. Reverse procedure to install, noting the following:
   a. **Torque** wiper motor mounting bolts to 53 inch lbs.
   b. **Torque** wiper pivot nut to 13 ft. lbs.

WIPER SWITCH
REPLACE

Front

Refer to "Multi-Function Switch, Replace," for procedure.

Rear

1. Pull rear wiper/washer switch straight out of instrument panel.
2. Disconnect electrical connector and remove switch.
3. Reverse procedure to install.

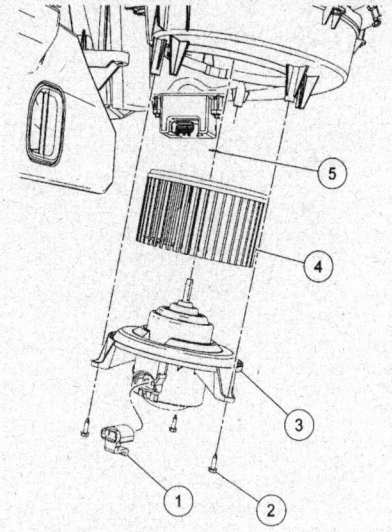

Item	Description
1	Blower motor electrical connector
2	Blower motor screws (3 required)
3	Blower motor
4	Blower motor wheel
5	Blower motor wheel clip

ARM0400000000461

Fig. 5 Blower motor replacement

WIPER TRANSMISSION
REPLACE

The wiper mounting arm and pivot shafts are connected with non-removable plastic ball joints. Except for the wiper motor, the entire wiper transmission assembly is non-serviceable.

For wiper transmission replacement procedure refer to "Wiper Motor, Replace."

BLOWER MOTOR
REPLACE

1. Pull instrument panel insulator from lower righthand side of instrument panel reinforcement, **Fig. 5.**
2. Disconnect blower motor electrical connector.
3. Remove mounting screws and blower motor from evaporator housing.
4. Remove blower motor wheel retaining clip, then the wheel.
5. Reverse procedure to install.

CABIN AIR FILTER
REPLACE

1. Remove righthand cowl vent screen.
2. Remove water shield.
3. Remove cabin air filter.
4. Reverse procedure to install.

HEATER CORE
REPLACE

1. Drain coolant into suitable container.
2. Remove instrument panel as outlined

Item	Description
1	Heater tube bracket screw (2 required)
2	LH temperature blend door actuator screw (3 required)
3	LH temperature blend door actuator electrical connector
4	LH temperature blend door actuator
5	Heater core cover screw (3 required)
6	Heater core cover
7	Heater core
8	Evaporator discharge air temperature sensor electrical connector

ARM0400000000462

Fig. 6 Heater core replacement

in "Dash Panel Service" chapter.
3. Disconnect heater hoses from core. Plug heater core tubes.
4. Remove dash panel seal from heater core.
5. Remove heater core bracket mounting screws and bracket, **Fig. 6.**
6. Remove evaporator discharge air temperature sensor electrical sensor.
7. Disconnect lefthand temperature blend door actuator electrical connector.
8. Remove lefthand temperature blend door actuator mounting screws and actuator.
9. Remove three heater core cover mounting screws and seal from evaporator housing, **Fig. 6.**
10. Remove heater core and seal by pushing on tubes.
11. Reverse procedure to install.

EVAPORATOR CORE
REPLACE

The evaporator core is serviced as a core and housing assembly. The evaporator core, internal doors, seals and door linkage are included with the housing. Transfer the blower motor and wheel assembly, heater core and cover, dash panel seals and vacuum actuators to the new housing.

1. Recover refrigerant as outlined in "Air Conditioning" chapter.
2. Drain coolant into suitable container.
3. Remove instrument panel as outlined in "Dash Panel Service" chapter.
4. Remove righthand cowl vent screen and water shield.
5. Disconnect vacuum supply hose.
6. Clamp heater hoses using suitable pinching pliers and disconnect hoses. Cap fittings.
7. Disconnect evaporator outlet spring lock coupling. Cap evaporator outlet tube and suction accumulator tube, **Fig. 7.**
8. Remove air conditioning pipe clamps' hold-down bolts.
9. Disconnect evaporator inlet spring lock coupling. Cap evaporator inlet tube and condenser to evaporator line tube.
10. Remove three evaporator housing mounting nuts.
11. Remove heater outlet floor duct.
12. Remove evaporator housing support bracket mounting nuts.
13. Remove heater/evaporator core housing and core, **Fig. 8.**
14. Reverse procedure to install. **Torque** housing mounting bolts to 80 inch lbs.

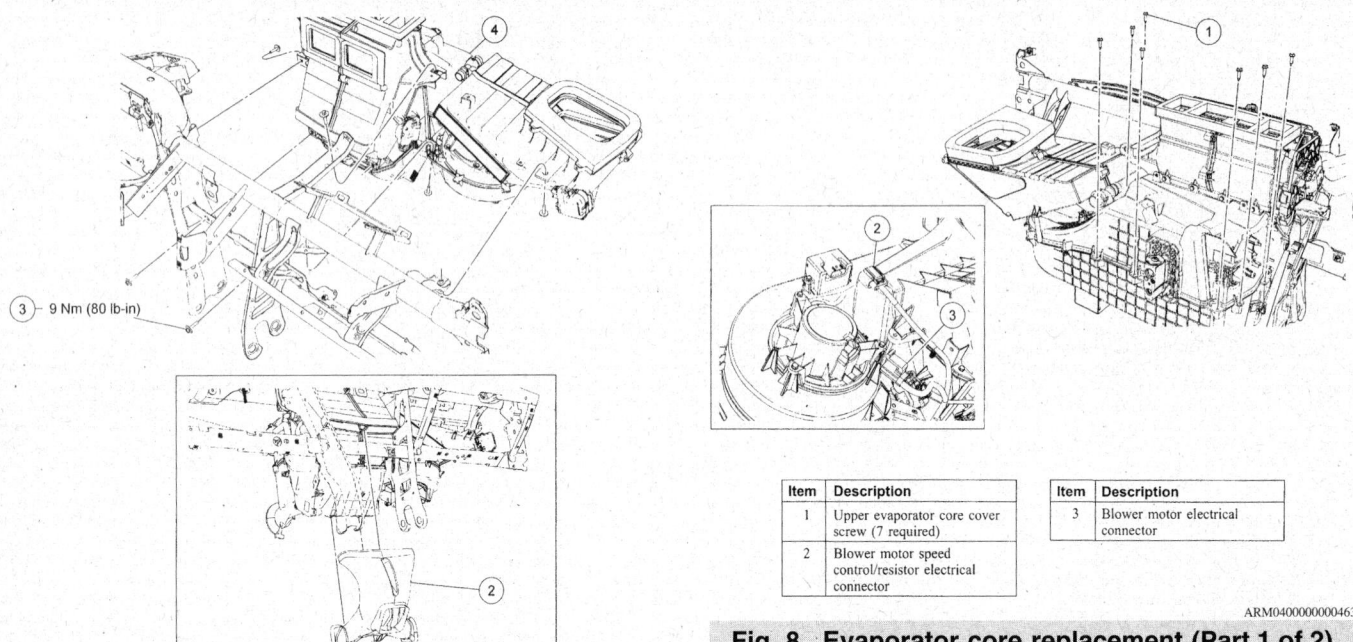

Item	Description
1	Upper evaporator core cover screw (7 required)
2	Blower motor speed control/resistor electrical connector

Item	Description
3	Blower motor electrical connector

ARM0400000000463

Fig. 8   Evaporator core replacement (Part 1 of 2)

1. Floor duct screws
2. Floor duct
3. Heater core and evaporator core housing bolts
4. Heater core and evaporator core housing assembly

ARM0400000000465

Fig. 7   Evaporator core & heater core housing assembly replacement

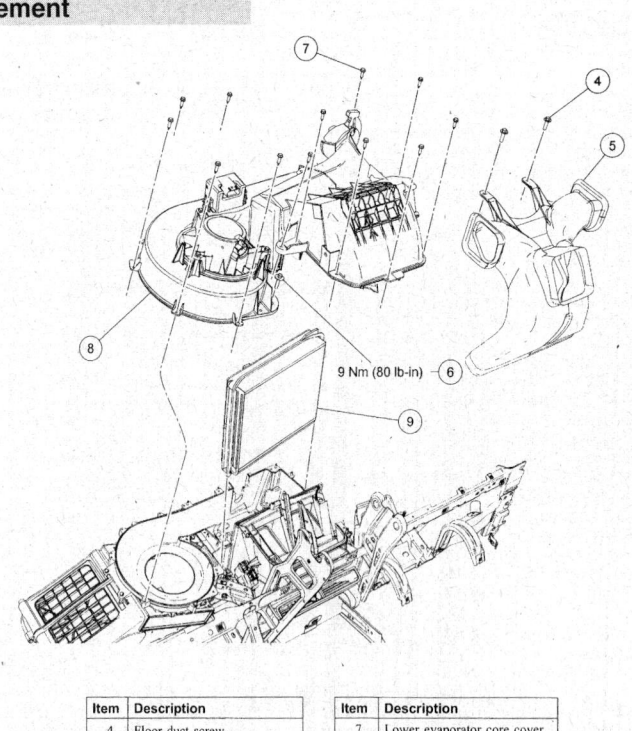

Item	Description
4	Floor duct screw
5	Floor duct
6	Heater core and evaporator core housing bolt

Item	Description
7	Lower evaporator core cover screw (13 required)
8	Lower evaporator core cover
9	Evaporator core

ARM0400000000464

Fig. 8   Evaporator core replacement (Part 2 of 2)

3.0L Engine

NOTE: On Air Bag Equipped Models, Refer To "Air Bag System Precautions" Located In The Front Of This Manual For System Disarming & Arming Procedures.

NOTE: Refer To "Computer Relearn Procedures" Located In The Front Of This Manual When Battery Power To The Computer Has Been Interrupted.

NOTE: Prior To Performing Any Service Operations Listed In This Section, Consult The "Technical Service Bulletins" Section For Related Information.

INDEX

PRECAUTIONS

Air Bag Systems

Refer to "Air Bag System Precautions" in the front of this manual for system disarming and arming procedures.

Flexible Fuel Models

Flexible Fuel (FF) vehicles use unique methanol-compatible components. Certain gasoline-only components may appear identical to these FF vehicle components. Under no circumstances should these components be interchanged.

Fuel System Pressure Relief

When releasing fuel pressure on flexible fuel vehicles, use methanol resistant gloves and eye protection. Avoid prolonged skin contact with liquid or breathing of vapors.

If methanol fuel should be spilled on paint, flush immediately with cold water. **Do not wipe, or paint damage may occur.**

Fuel supply lines will remain pressurized for long periods of time after engine shutdown. This pressure must be relieved before any service is attempted. A valve is provided on the fuel rail assembly for this purpose.

1. Remove air cleaner assembly.
2. Connect pressure gauge tool No. T80L-9974-A or T80L-9974-B, or equivalent, onto fuel rail assembly fuel valve.
3. Open manual valve on pressure gauge tool.
4. To pressurize fuel system, proceed as follows:
   a. Install pressure gauge tool onto fuel rail pressure fitting.
   b. Turn ignition switch to ON position for three seconds, 5–10 times until pressure gauge indicates 13 psi.

Battery Ground Cable

Prior to service, disconnect battery ground cable and isolate as required.

COMPRESSION PRESSURE

Perform compression inspection with engine at normal operating temperature, spark plugs removed and throttle wide open.

The lowest cylinder must be within 75 percent of the highest cylinder.

ENGINE MOUNT
REPLACE

Front

1. Raise and support vehicle.
2. Place suitable jack and wood block under engine block.
3. Remove lefthand and righthand front engine support insulators to subframe mounting nuts.
4. Raise jack enough to remove load from support insulators.
5. Remove mounting bolts, then the lefthand and righthand engine support insulators.
6. Reverse procedure to install.

Engine & Transaxle

1. Raise and support vehicle, then remove lefthand front tire and wheel assembly.

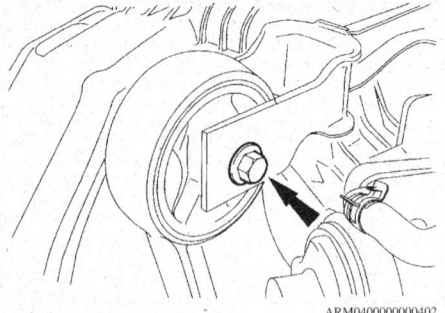

Fig. 1   Roll restrictor bolt removal

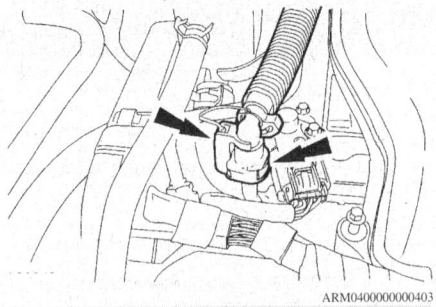

Fig. 2   Fuel supply line removal

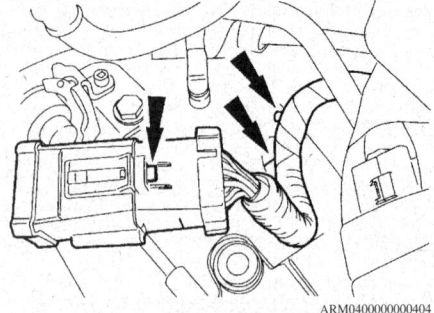

Fig. 3   Transaxle electrical harness disconnected

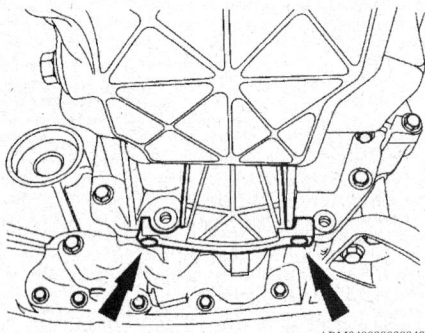

Fig. 4   Torque converter access plug location

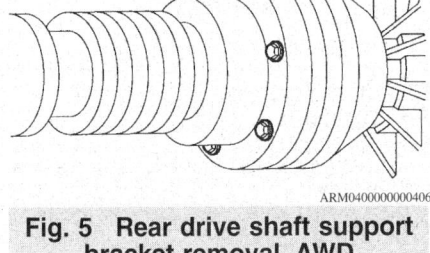

Fig. 5   Rear drive shaft support bracket removal. AWD

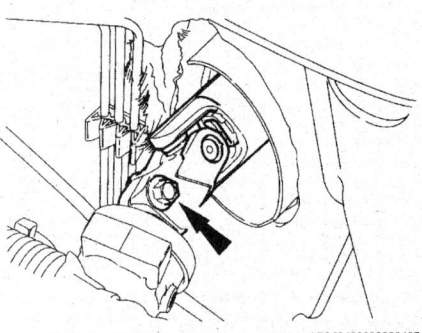

Fig. 6   Intermediate steering shaft removal

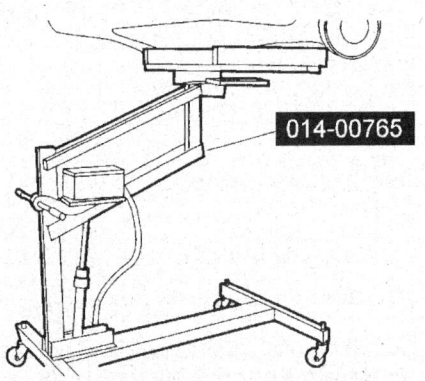

014-00765

Fig. 7   Powertrain supported

2. Support transaxle with suitable transaxle jack.
3. Remove engine and transaxle support insulator to rear engine and transaxle bracket mounting nut.
4. Remove two engine and transaxle support insulator to subframe through bolts.
5. Raise transaxle enough to remove load from engine and transaxle support insulator.
6. Remove support insulator.
7. Reverse procedure to install.

ENGINE
REPLACE

1. Drain engine coolant and oil into suitable container.
2. Relieve fuel system pressure as outlined in "Precautions."
3. Recover refrigerant as outlined in "Air Conditioning" chapter.
4. Remove righthand and lefthand halfshafts as outlined in "Front Wheel Drive Axles" chapter.
5. Remove cowl vent screen and cowl vent extension.
6. Remove engine air cleaner and outlet tube.
7. Disconnect and position steering column input shaft coupling aside.
8. Disconnect accelerator and speed control actuator cables, then the throttle return spring from throttle body. Position accelerator cable bracket aside.
9. Remove exhaust flex pipe, then the lefthand and righthand catalytic converters.
10. Remove and discard roller restrictor cross brace bolt, **Fig. 1.**
11. Disconnect manual control lever cable from lever and bracket, then position it bracket aside.
12. Remove and discard four roll restrictor cross brace bolts, then the cross brace.
13. Remove lefthand and righthand ground straps located on top of fenders.
14. Disconnect redundant clip, press inward on quick release coupling button, **Fig. 2,** then disconnect fuel supply line from fuel rail.
15. Disconnect fuel vapor tube from purge valve.
16. Disconnect two powertrain control module electrical connectors and position wiring conduit aside.
17. Disconnect power steering reservoir hose and hose retainer clips.
18. Disconnect shift cable from transaxle lever.
19. Disconnect transaxle 16 pin electrical connector, **Fig. 3,** then disconnect harness from shift cable bracket.
20. Remove shift cable retaining bracket and position bracket/cable assembly aside.
21. Disconnect heater and throttle body coolant hoses.
22. Disconnect upper, lower and bypass coolant hoses.
23. Remove all engine component electrical connectors, **Mark connector locations for installation.**
24. Disconnect A/C compressor manifold tube assembly.
25. Disconnect A/C tubes from condenser, position tube assembly aside.
26. Disconnect transaxle and power steering cool lines.
27. Remove two pin type retainers from torque converter access plug, **Fig. 4,** remove and four torque converter retaining nuts.
28. Remove three engine to transaxle bolts, then the lefthand catalytic converter bracket.
29. **On models equipped with AWD,** remove driveshaft support bracket.
30. **On models equipped with AWD,** remove driveshaft to rear axle mounting bolts, **Fig. 5,** then position driveshaft aside.
31. **On all models,** disconnect outer tie rods from wheel knuckles.
32. Remove and discard steering column

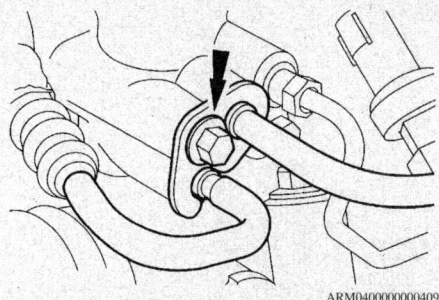

Fig. 8 Power steering pressure tubes removal

ARM0400000000409

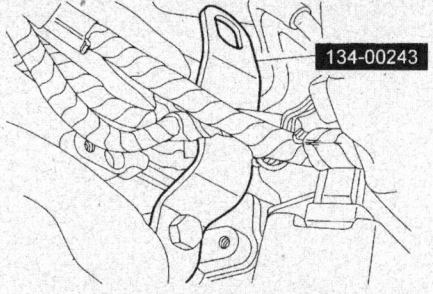

ARM0400000000410

Fig. 9 Engine removal eye hook tool installation. Righthand head

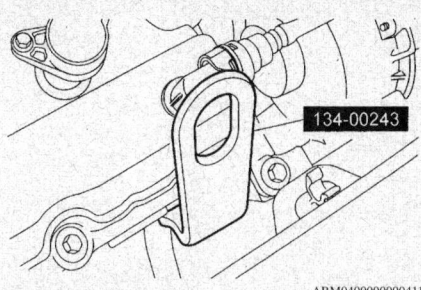

ARM0400000000411

Fig. 10 Engine removal eye hook tool installation. Lefthand head

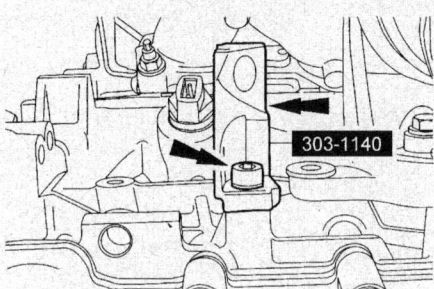

ARM0400000000412

Fig. 11 Lower engine lifting bracket installed

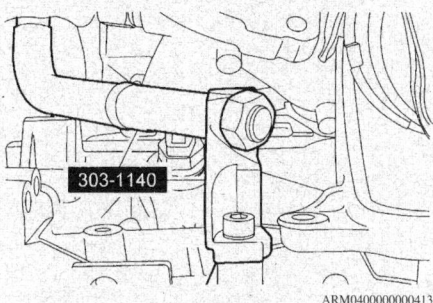

ARM0400000000413

Fig. 12 Upper engine lifting bracket installed

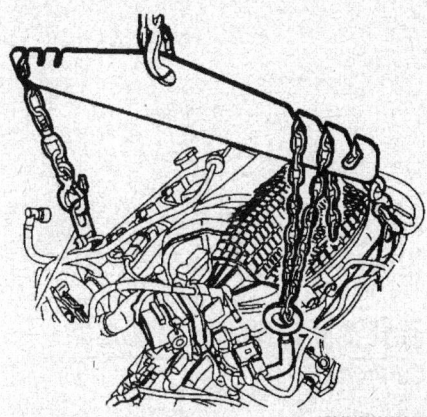

ARM0400000000414

Fig. 13 Engine lifting crane installed

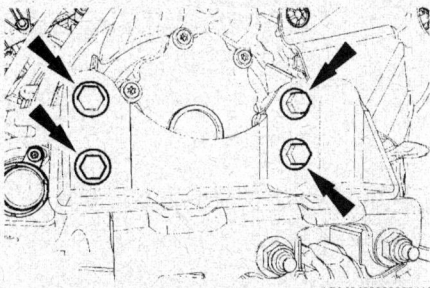

ARM0400000000415

Fig. 14 Insulator bolt removal. CVT transaxle

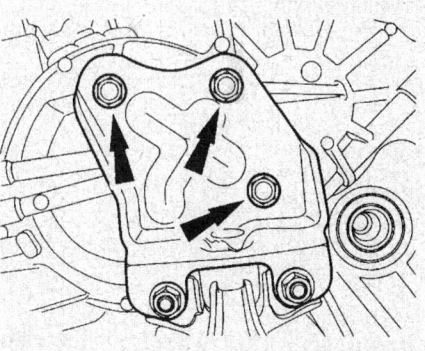

ARM0400000000416

Fig. 15 Insulator bolt removal. 6 speed transaxle

intermediate shaft to steering gear lock nut and bolt, **Fig. 6.** Separate intermediate shaft from steering gear.
33. Support powertrain and subframe using powertrain support/lift tool No. 014–00765, or equivalent, **Fig. 7.**
34. Remove six rear subframe bolts, then the subframe brackets.
35. Remove two front subframe bolts and washers.
36. Using powertrain support/lift tool No. 014–00765, or equivalent, slowly lower powertrain and subframe far enough to access and remove the following components from subframe:
   a. Disconnect Power Steering Pressure (PSP) switch electrical connector.
   b. Remove power steering pressure tubes, **Fig. 8.**
   c. Disconnect righthand catalyst monitor sensor electrical connector and twp-pin type retainers from subframe.
   d. **On models equipped with CVT**

transaxle, transaxle disconnect transaxle to bulkhead electrical connector, then disconnect wiring harness retainers from transaxle and subframe.
   e. Remove roll restrictor bracket, then the roll restrictor.
   f. Disconnect starter motor electrical connectors.
   g. Remove starter motor.
   h. Disconnect transaxle to frame ground cable.
   i. **On models equipped with six speed transaxle,** disconnect Transaxle Control Module (TCM) electrical connector.
   j. Remove four roll restrictor bracket bolts, then the roll restrictor.
   k. Disconnect starter motor electrical connectors.
   l. Remove starter motor.
   m. Remove transaxle to frame ground cable.
37. **On all models,** Install engine installation, removal eye hooks tool No. 134–00243, or equivalent, to righthand cylinder head, **Fig. 9.**
38. Install engine installation, removal eye hooks tool No. 134–00243, or equivalent, to lefthand cylinder head, **Fig. 10.**
39. Install upper and lower engine lifting brackets tool No. 303–1140, or equivalent, **Figs. 11 and 12,** to transaxle housing.
40. Support powertrain assembly, **Fig. 13,** using suitable engine lift crane.
41. Remove front transaxle stabilizer bolt.
42. Remove exhaust heat shields.
43. Remove righthand and lefthand upper engine insulator retaining nuts.
44. **On models equipped with CVT tran-**

saxle, remove four transaxle insulator bracket bolts, **Fig. 14.**
45. **On models equipped with six speed transaxle,** remove three transaxle insulator bracket bolts, **Fig. 15.**
46. **On all models,** use suitable engine crane, **Fig. 13,** to lift powertrain assembly from subframe.
47. Lower powertrain and support transaxle using suitable wooden blocks.
48. Remove transaxle to engine mounting bolts, then separate engine from transaxle.
49. Reverse procedure to install. Replace all discarded bolts and nuts with OEM replacements.

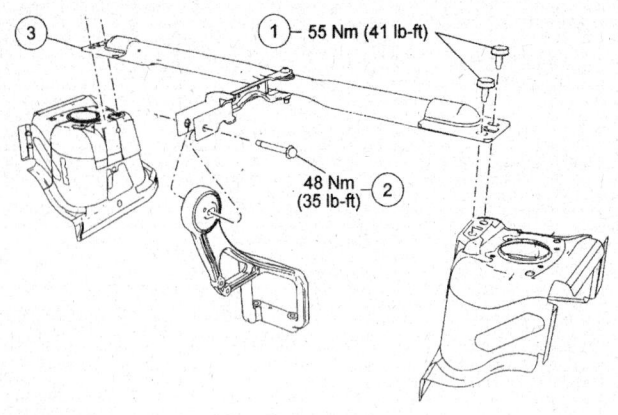

Item	Description
1	Transaxle roll restrictor cross brace bolts (4 required)
2	Transaxle roll restrictor bolt

Item	Description
3	Transaxle roll restrictor cross brace

ARM0400000000417

Fig. 16 Upper intake manifold replacement (Part 1 of 3)

INTAKE MANIFOLD
REPLACE
Upper

Refer to, **Fig. 16,** for component descriptions and locations when servicing upper intake manifold.

1. Relieve fuel system pressure as outlined in "Precautions."
2. Drain engine coolant into suitable container.
3. Remove air cleaner outlet tube.
4. Remove and discard transaxle roll restrictor cross brace bolts, then the cross brace.
5. Disconnect EVAP canister purge valve tube, then disconnect retaining clamp and position tube aside.
6. Disconnect PVC valve and brake booster vacuum harness tubes.
7. Disconnect EGR system module electrical connector and vacuum tube.
8. Disconnect and plug PCV and throttle body coolant hoses.
9. Disconnect throttle body electrical connector.
10. Remove and discard four upper manifold to lower manifold retaining screws.
11. Remove eight upper intake manifold mounting bolts.
12. Reverse procedure to install, noting the following:
    a. Replace all discarded bolts and nuts with OEM replacements.
    b. **Torque** intake mounting bolts to 89 inch lbs., in sequence, **Fig. 17.**

Lower

Refer to, **Fig. 18,** for component descriptions and locations when servicing upper intake manifold.

1. Relieve fuel system pressure as outlined in "Precautions."
2. Remove upper intake manifold as out-

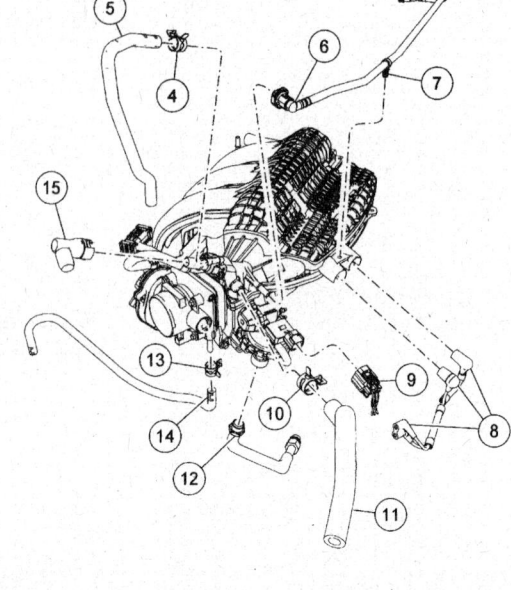

Item	Description
4	Positive crankcase ventiliation (PCV) coolant hose clamp
5	PCV coolant hose
6	Evaporative emissions (EVAP) canister purge valve tube
7	EVAP canister purge valve tube retainer
8	Vacuum tube fittings (3 required)
9	Exhaust gas recirculation (EGR) system module electrical connector

Item	Description
10	Brake booster vacuum hose clamp
11	Brake booster vacuum hose
12	EGR system module tube fitting
13	Throttle body coolant hose clamp
14	Throttle body coolant hose
15	PCV tube

ARM0400000000418

Fig. 16 Upper intake manifold replacement (Part 2 of 3)

lined in "Intake Manifold, Replace"
3. Disconnect fuel supply tube redundant clip, press inward on quick release coupling button, **Fig. 2,** then disconnect fuel supply line from fuel rail.
4. Disconnect fuel injector electrical connectors.
5. Remove lower intake manifold mounting bolts.
6. Remove lower intake manifold.
7. Remove fuel rail and injectors from manifold.
8. Reverse procedure to install, noting the following:
    a. Install new gaskets and O-rings.
    b. Lubricate new O-ring seals lightly with suitable motor oil. **Do not use silicone grease.**
    c. **Torque** bolts to 89 inch lbs., in sequence, **Fig. 19.**

EXHAUST MANIFOLD
REPLACE
Lefthand

1. Drain engine coolant into suitable container.

2. Disconnect coolant hose retainers from cooling fan shroud, then position hoses aside.
3. Disconnect cooling fan electrical connector.
4. Remove lefthand exhaust manifold to exhaust pipe nuts, **Fig. 20.**
5. Remove coolant tube bracket bolt, then the bracket.
6. Disconnect heated oxygen sensor electrical connector from coolant tube.
7. Raise and support vehicle.
8. Remove front splash shield pin type retainers and mounting bolts, then the splash shield.
9. Remove lower exhaust manifold mounting nuts.
10. Remove coolant tube lower bracket.
11. Lower vehicle.
12. Remove upper mounting nuts and exhaust manifold.
13. Reverse procedure to install, noting the following:
    a. Install new exhaust manifold gasket.
    b. **Torque** nuts to 13–16 ft. lbs., in sequence, **Fig. 21.**
    c. **Torque** manifold to pipe nuts to 30 ft. lbs.,

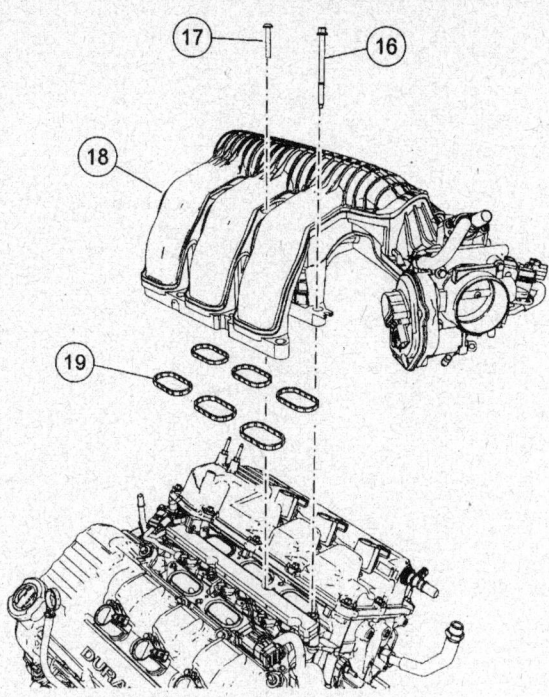

Item	Description
16	Upper intake manifold bolts (8 required)
17	Upper intake manifold-to-lower intake manifold screw (4 required)
18	Upper intake manifold
19	Upper intake manifold gaskets (6 required)

ARM0400000000419

Fig. 16   Upper intake manifold replacement (Part 3 of 3)

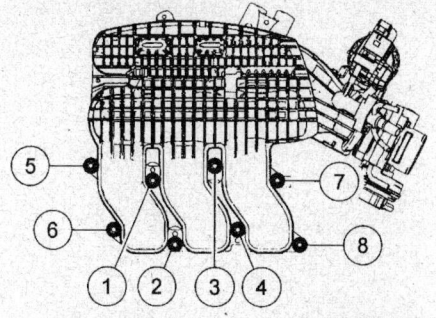

ARM0400000000420

Fig. 17   Upper intake manifold bolt tightening sequence

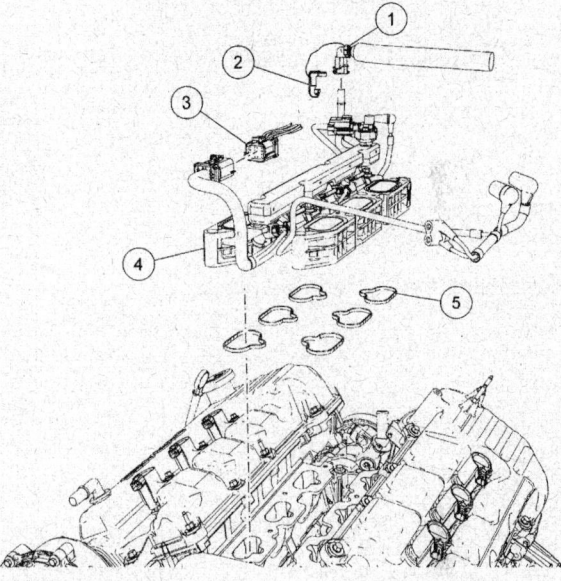

Item	Description
1	Fuel tube
2	Fuel tube redundant clip
3	Fuel charging wiring harness electrical connector

Item	Description
4	Lower intake manifold
5	Lower intake manifold gaskets (6 required)

ARM0400000000421

Fig. 18   Lower intake manifold replacement

Righthand

1. Remove righthand catalytic converter,
2. Disconnect exhaust gas recirculation tube, **Fig. 22,** from exhaust manifold.
3. Raise and support vehicle.
4. Disconnect HO2S sensor connector.
5. Remove three manifold heat shield retaining bolts, then the heat shield.
6. Remove six exhaust manifold mounting nuts, then the manifold.
7. Reverse procedure to install, noting the following:
   a. Install new exhaust manifold gasket.
   b. **Torque** exhaust manifold nuts to 15 ft. lbs., in sequence, **Fig. 23.**

CYLINDER HEAD

REPLACE

Lefthand

1. Drain engine coolant into suitable container.
2. Remove coolant bypass tube.
3. Remove oil level indicator and tube.

4. Remove exhaust manifold as outlined in "Exhaust Manifold, Replace"
5. Remove water pump as outlined in "Water Pump, Replace."
6. Remove timing chain and gears as outlined in "Timing Chain, Replace."
7. Remove air cleaner outlet tube.
8. Remove accelerator cable splash shield.
9. Disconnect throttle and cruise control cables.
10. Disconnect throttle position sensor and idle air control valve electrical connectors, then disconnect harness from throttle body and intake manifold.
11. Disconnect Exhaust Gas Recirculation (EGR) vacuum regulator and vacuum supply hoses.
12. Disconnect PCV and EVAP vacuum hoses.
13. Remove EGR valve and vacuum regulator valve.

14. Remove upper and lower intake manifolds as outlined in "Intake Manifold, Replace."
15. Remove both valve covers as outlined in "Valve Cover, Replace."
16. Remove camshafts and rocker arms as outlined in "Camshaft, Replace."
17. Remove camshaft followers and hydraulic lash adjusters as outlined in "Hydraulic Liters, Replace."
18. Remove cylinder head bolts in sequence, **Fig. 24.**
19. Remove cylinder head. Discard gasket and bolts.
20. Reverse procedure to install, noting the following:
   a. Install new head gasket and bolts. **Bolts are torque to yield design and cannot be reused.**
   b. Tighten cylinder head bolts in six steps in sequence, **Fig. 25,** as follows:

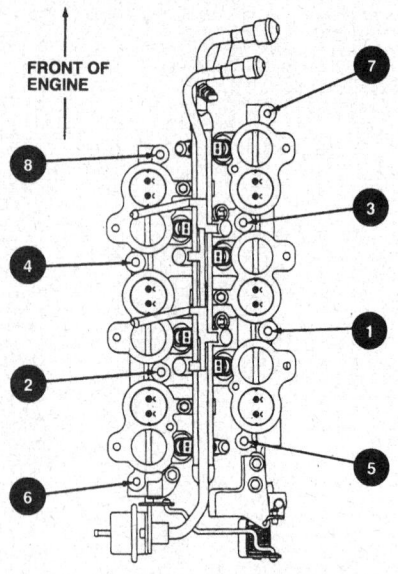

Fig. 19 Lower intake manifold bolt tightening sequence

c. Step one, **torque** cylinder head bolts to 30 ft. lbs.
d. Step two, tighten head bolts and additional 90° in sequence.
e. Step three, loosen all bolts one full turn.
f. Step four, **torque** cylinder head bolts to 30 ft. lbs., in sequence.
g. Step five, tighten bolts an additional 90° in sequence.
h. Step six, tighten bolts an additional 90° in sequence.

Righthand

1. Remove coolant bypass tube.
2. Remove timing chain and gears as outlined in "Timing Chain, Replace."
3. Remove air cleaner outlet tube.
4. Remove accelerator cable splash shield.
5. Disconnect throttle and cruise control cables.
6. Disconnect throttle position sensor and idle air control valve electrical connectors, then harness from throttle body and intake manifold.
7. Disconnect Exhaust Gas Recirculation (EGR) vacuum regulator and vacuum supply hoses.
8. Disconnect PCV and EVAP vacuum hoses.
9. Remove EGR valve and vacuum regulator valve.
10. Remove upper and lower intake manifolds as outlined in "Intake Manifold, Replace."
11. Remove both valve covers as outlined in "Valve Cover, Replace."
12. Remove camshaft journal cap bolts as outlined in "Camshaft, Replace."
13. Remove camshafts and rocker arms.

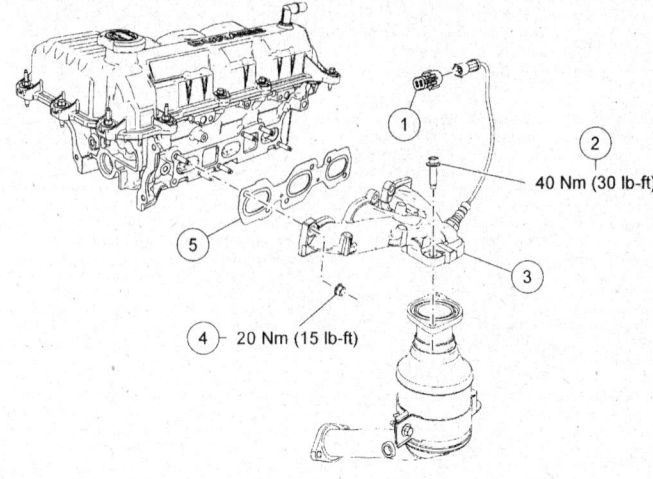

Item	Description
1	Heated oxygen sensor (HO2S) electrical connector
2	LH exhaust manifold-to-catalytic converter bolts (2 required)
3	LH exhaust manifold
4	LH exhaust manifold nut (6 required)
5	LH exhaust manifold gasket

Fig. 20 Lefthand exhaust manifold replacement

Mark rocker arms for installation alignment.
14. Raise and support vehicle.
15. Remove exhaust manifold to pipe bolts.
16. Lower vehicle.
17. Disconnect Exhaust Gas Recirculation (EGR) tube from exhaust manifold.
18. Remove camshaft followers and hydraulic lash adjusters as outlined in "Hydraulic Liters, Replace."
19. Remove exhaust manifold as outlined in "Exhaust Manifold, Replace"
20. Remove cylinder head bolts in sequence, **Fig. 26.**
21. Remove cylinder head. Discard gasket and bolts.
22. Reverse procedure to install, noting the following:
    a. Install new head gasket and bolts. **Bolts are torque to yield design and cannot be reused.**
    b. Tighten cylinder head bolts in six steps in sequence, **Fig. 27,** as follows:
    c. Step one, **torque** cylinder head bolts to 30 ft. lbs.
    d. Step two, tighten head bolts and additional 90° in sequence.
    e. Step three, loosen bolts one full turn.
    f. Step four, **torque** cylinder head bolts to 30 ft. lbs., in sequence.
    g. Step five, tighten bolts an additional 90° in sequence.
    h. Step six, tighten bolts an additional 90° in sequence.

VALVE COVER
REPLACE
Lefthand

1. Disconnect crankcase ventilation tube from valve cover, **Fig. 28.**
2. Disconnect ignition coil electrical connector.
3. Remove ignition coil mounting bolts, then coil.
4. Remove three wiring conduit mounting nuts, then position conduit aside.
5. Remove oil level indicator.
6. Disconnect wiring harness from valve cover and position aside.
7. Remove mounting bolts, studs and valve cover.
8. Reverse procedure to install, noting the following:
    a. Install new valve cover gasket.
    b. Apply 5 mm dot of silicone gasket sealant to front cover to cylinder head joints.
    c. **Torque** valve cover mounting bolts to 89 inch lbs., in sequence, **Fig. 29.**

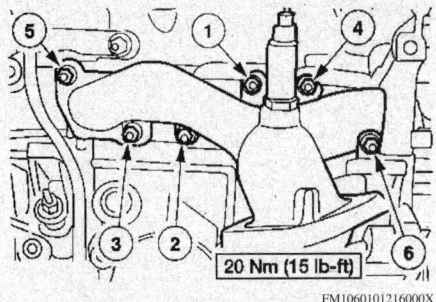

FM1060101216000X

Fig. 21 Lefthand exhaust manifold tightening sequence

Righthand

1. Remove upper intake manifold as outlined in "Intake Manifold, Replace."
2. Remove ignition coil and bracket, **Fig. 30.**
3. Remove power steering pressure tube to reservoir bracket mounting bolts, then position pressure tube aside.
4. Remove power steering fluid reservoir bolts, then the reservoir.
5. Remove wiring harness nut and position harness aside.
6. Disconnect crankcase ventilation tube from valve cover.
7. Remove mounting bolts, studs and valve cover.
8. Reverse procedure to install, noting the following:
   a. Install new valve cover gasket.
   b. Apply 5 mm dot of silicone gasket and sealant to front cover cylinder head joints.
   c. **Torque** valve cover mounting bolts to 89 inch lbs., in sequence, **Fig. 31.**

CAMSHAFT LOBE LIFT SPECIFICATIONS

Exhaust......................................388 inch
Intake ....388 inch

VALVE ADJUSTMENT

Hydraulic valve lifters are used in this engine. No adjustment is required.

HYDRAULIC LIFTERS
REPLACE

1. Remove valve covers as outlined in "Valve Cover, Replace."
2. Remove spark plugs.
3. Remove righthand splash shield.
4. Rotate crankshaft until camshaft lobe is pointing directly away from roller follower.
5. Remove hydraulic roller lifter using lifter removal tool N. 303–473, or equivalent, **Fig. 32**
6. Reverse procedure to install. Lubricate camshaft followers using clean suitable engine oil.

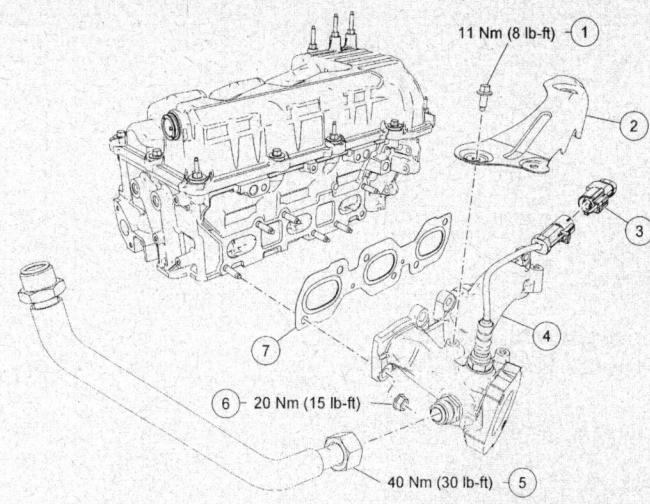

Item	Description
1	RH exhaust manifold heat shield (2 required)
2	RH exhaust manifold heat shield
3	Heated oxygen sensor (HO2S) electrical connector
4	RH exhaust manifold
5	Exhaust gas recirculation (EGR) system module tube fitting
6	RH exhaust manifold nut (6 required)
7	RH exhaust manifold gasket

ARM0400000000440

Fig. 22 Righthand exhaust manifold replacement

FRONT COVER
REPLACE

1. Drain engine coolant and oil into suitable container.
2. Remove lefthand and righthand valve covers as outlined in "Valve Cover, Replace."
3. Remove power steering pump.
4. Raise and support vehicle.
5. Remove righthand front wheel and inner splash shield.
6. Remove dual converter Y-pipe.
7. Disconnect upper, lower, bypass and heater hoses from front of engine.
8. Remove engine to transaxle bracket.
9. Remove torque converter inspection cover.
10. Remove oil pan as outlined in "Oil Pan, Replace."
11. Remove mounting nut, then position power steering pressure line and muffler aside.
12. Remove alternator, crankshaft pulley and Crankshaft Position (CKP) sensor.
13. Remove air conditioning compressor to front cover bracket.
14. Disconnect Camshaft Position (CMP) sensor.
15. Remove belt tensioner.
16. Disconnect cooling fan electrical connectors.
17. Remove engine cooling fan/shroud mounting bolts, then the cooling fan/shroud assembly
18. Install suitable engine support tool.
19. Remove upper air conditioning compressor bolts and position compressor aside.
20. Lower vehicle.
21. Remove air conditioning line retaining bracket.
22. Remove front engine cover mounting bolts and studs, then the engine cover.
23. Reverse procedure to install, noting the following:
   a. Install new front cover gaskets.
   b. Apply .24 inch bead of gasket sealer to cylinder block, lower front engine block and cylinder head mating surfaces. Front cover must be installed and bolts tightened within four minutes of applying sealant.
   c. **Torque** front cover mounting bolt to 18 ft. lbs., in sequence, **Fig. 33.**

FRONT COVER SEAL
REPLACE
Removal

1. Loosen accessory drive belts and remove righthand front wheel.
2. Remove four crankshaft pulley to

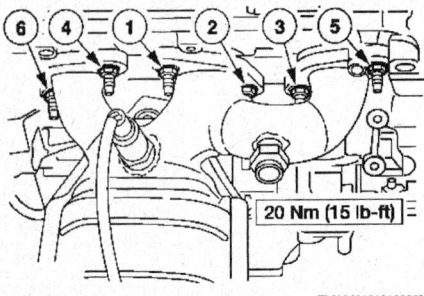

Fig. 23 Righthand exhaust manifold bolt tightening sequence

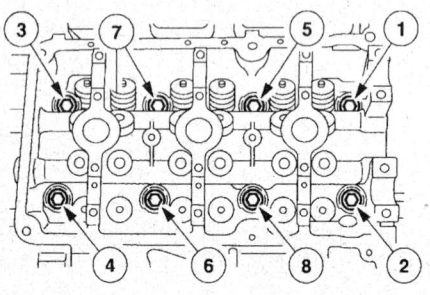

Fig. 26 Righthand exhaust manifold bolt loosening sequence

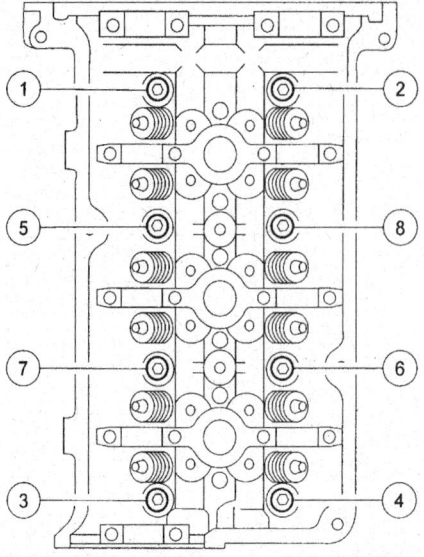

Fig. 24 Lefthand cylinder head bolt removal sequence

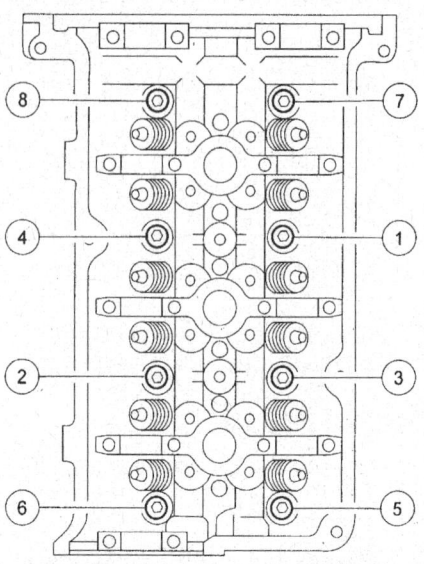

Fig. 25 Lefthand cylinder head bolt tightening sequence

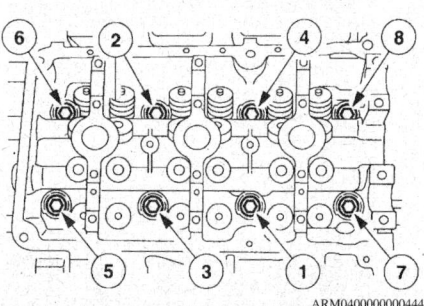

Fig. 27 Lefthand cylinder head bolt tightening sequence

damper mounting bolts, then the remove accessory drive belt and pulley.
3. Remove mounting bolt, and vibration damper using suitable puller.
4. Pry seal from front timing cover using flat bladed screwdriver, or other suitable tool. **Do not damage front cover or crankshaft.**

Installation

1. Lubricate replacement seal lip with suitable, clean engine oil and install seal with suitable seal installer.
2. Lubricate inner hub surface of vibration damper with suitable clean engine oil and apply RTV sealant to keyway of inner hub surface of vibration damper.
3. Install vibration damper and tighten mounting bolt.
4. Install crankshaft pulley and tighten bolts.
5. Install accessory drive belts and righthand front wheel.

TIMING CHAIN
REPLACE

1. Remove engine front cover as outlined in "Front Cover, Replace."
2. Remove ignition pulse wheel.
3. Remove spark plugs, Install damper bolt, then rotate crankshaft clockwise to position crankshaft keyway in 11 O'clock position.
4. Ensure camshafts are correctly located in cylinder No. 1 TDC position. If not, rotate crankshaft one additional turn and inspect.
5. Rotate crankshaft clockwise 120° to 3 O'clock position to place righthand

camshafts in neutral position. Ensure camshafts are correctly positioned, **Fig. 34.**
6. Remove righthand timing chain tensioner arm, timing chain guide and timing chain.
7. Rotate crankshaft clockwise two times to position crankshaft keyway in 11 O'clock position and ensure camshafts in neutral position.
8. Remove lefthand timing chain tensioner, tensioner arm and timing chain.
9. Remove crankshaft damper bolt.
10. Reverse procedure to install, noting the following:
    a. Position chain tensioner in suitable soft jawed vise.
    b. Hold chain tensioner ratchet lock mechanism away from ratchet stem with suitable small pick and slowly compress timing chain tensioner.
    c. Retain tensioner piston with .05 inch wire, or paper clip, **Fig. 35.**
    d. Ensure timing marks on sprockets and timing chain are aligned, **Fig. 34.**
    e. Verify timing and component alignment as shown, **Fig. 36. Failure to verify correct timing drive component alignment will result in server engine damage.**

CAMSHAFT
REPLACE

When servicing camshafts refer to **Figs. 37 and 38,** for component identifications and locations

Removal
LEFTHAND

1. Remove timing chain and gears as outlined in "Timing Chain, Replace."

2. Remove upper intake manifold as outlined in "Intake Manifold, Replace."
3. Remove valve covers as outlined in "Valve Cover, Replace."
4. Remove three camshaft oil seal retaining bolts, then the retaining plate and seal.
5. Press oil seal from retaining plate using suitable press.
6. Remove camshaft journal cap bolts in sequence, **Fig. 39.**
7. Remove camshafts and rocker arms. Mark rocker arms for installation alignment.

RIGHTHAND

1. Remove timing chain and gears as outlined in "Timing Chain, Replace."
2. Remove upper intake manifold as outlined in "Intake Manifold, Replace."
3. Remove both valve covers as outlined in "Valve Cover, Replace."
4. Remove camshaft journal cap bolts in sequence, **Fig. 40.**
5. Remove camshaft bearings and thrust caps.
6. Remove camshafts and rocker arms. Mark rocker arms for installation alignment.

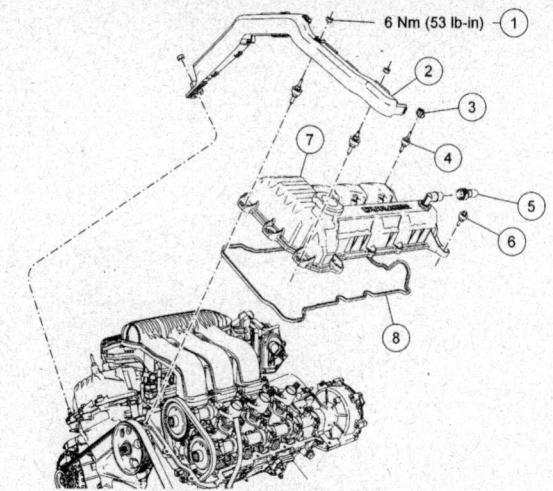

Item	Description
1	Wiring conduit-to-valve cover stud bolt nuts (3 required)
2	Wiring conduit
3	Wiring retainers (3 required)

Item	Description
4	Valve cover stud bolts (8 required)
5	Crankcase ventilation tube
6	Valve cover bolts (6 required)
7	Valve cover
8	Valve cover gasket

ARM0400000000434

Fig. 28 Lefthand valve cover replacement

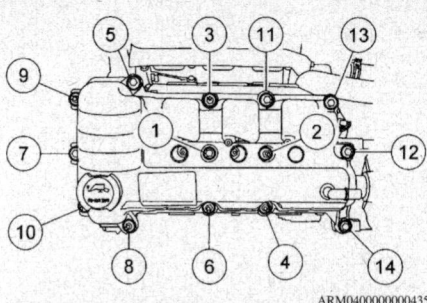

ARM0400000000435

Fig. 29 Lefthand valve cover tightening sequence

Installation

LEFTHAND

1. Lubricate camshafts and bearings using suitable clean engine oil.
2. Align camshafts as shown, **Fig. 41.**
3. Install rocker arms and thrust caps.
4. **Torque** thrust cap bolts to 89 inch lbs. in sequence, **Fig. 42.**
5. Install camshaft oil seal using seal installation tool No. 303–463, or equivalent, **Fig. 43.**
6. Install oil seal retaining plate.
7. Install timing chain and gears as outlined in "Timing Chain, Replace."
8. Install upper intake manifold as outlined in "Intake Manifold, Replace."
9. Install valve covers as outlined in "Valve Cover, Replace."

RIGHTHAND

1. Lubricate camshafts and bearings using suitable clean engine oil.
2. Align camshafts as shown, **Fig. 44.**
3. Install rocker arms and thrust caps.
4. **Torque** thrust cap bolts to 89 inch lbs. in sequence, **Fig. 40.**
5. Install timing chain and gears as outlined in "Timing Chain, Replace."
6. Install upper intake manifold as outlined in "Intake Manifold, Replace."
7. Install both valve covers as outlined in "Valve Cover, Replace."

PISTON & ROD ASSEMBLY

The piston and rod assemblies in these engines are not serviceable, should failure occur a short block will be required.

MAIN & ROD BEARINGS

The main and rod bearings in these engines are not serviceable, should failure occur a short block will be required.

CRANKSHAFT REAR OIL SEAL

REPLACE

1. Remove transaxle as outlined in **MOTOR's "Domestic Transmission Manual, In-Vehicle Service"** manual.
2. Remove mounting bolts, then the flywheel.
3. Remove rear cover plate.
4. Punch hole into seal metal surface between lip and block using suitable tool.
5. Remove seal using slide hammer tool No. T77L-9533-B, or equivalent.
6. Coat crankshaft seal area and lip with suitable engine oil.
7. Install seal using seal replacement tool No. T82L-6701-A, or equivalent.
8. Install rear cover plate and two dowels.
9. Install flywheel.
10. Install transaxle as outlined in **MOTOR's "Domestic Transmission Manual, In-Vehicle Service"** manual.

OIL PAN

REPLACE

1. Raise and support vehicle.
2. Drain engine oil into suitable container.
3. Remove righthand front wheel and inner splash shield.
4. Remove dual converter Y-pipe.
5. Remove engine to transaxle bracket.

6. Remove torque converter inspection cover.
7. Remove oil pan mounting bolts, then the oil pan.
8. Reverse procedure to install, noting the following:
   a. Apply .40 inch diameter dot of suitable silicone gasket and sealer to areas indicated, **Fig. 45.**
   b. **Torque** oil pan mounting bolts to 18 ft. lbs., in sequence, **Fig. 46.**

OIL PUMP

REPLACE

1. Remove timing chains as outlined in "Timing Chain, Replace."
2. Remove oil pump mounting bolts in sequence, **Fig. 47.**
3. Remove oil pump and gasket.
4. Reverse procedure to install, noting the following:
   a. Install new oil pump gasket.
   b. **Torque** oil pump bolts to 89 inch lbs. in sequence, **Fig. 48.**
   c. Install timing chains as outlined in "Timing Chain, Replace."

OIL PUMP SERVICE

Oil pump is serviced as an assembly and must be replaced if failure occurs.

BELT TENSION DATA

Belt	New, Lbs.	Used, Lbs.
Five-Rib	140–160	110–130
Six-Rib	①	①

① — Automatic tensioner.

SERPENTINE DRIVE BELT

Belt Routing

Refer to **Figs. 49,** for serpentine drive belt routing.

Belt, Replace

1. Remove accessory drive belt splash shield, **Fig. 50.**
2. Rotate drive belt tensioner counterclockwise.
3. Remove serpentine drive belt.
4. Reverse procedure to install.

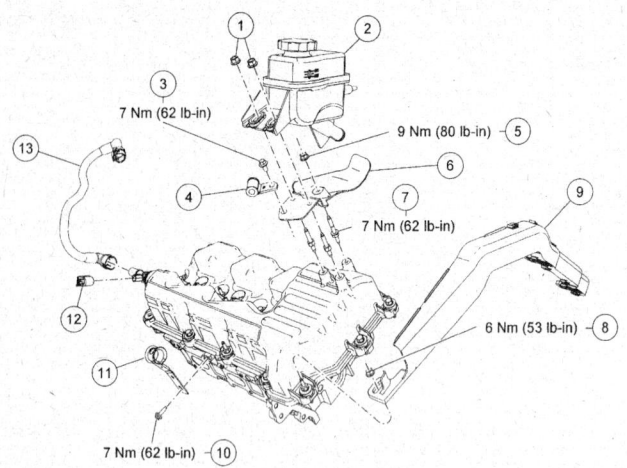

7 Nm (62 lb-in)

9 Nm (80 lb-in) — 5

7 Nm (62 lb-in)

6 Nm (53 lb-in) — 8

7 Nm (62 lb-in) — 10

Item	Description
1	Power steering reservoir nuts (2 required)
2	Power steering fluid reservoir
3	Power steering pressure (PSP) tube retainer bracket bolt
4	PSP tube retainer bracket
5	Power steering fluid reservoir bracket nut
6	Power steering fluid reservoir bracket
7	Power steering fluid reservoir bracket stud bolts (3 required)

Item	Description
8	Wiring conduit nuts (3 required)
9	Wiring conduit (part of
10	PSP tube retainer bracket bolt
11	PSP tube retainer bracket
12	Positive crankcase ventilation (PCV) valve electrical connector
13	PCV tube

Item	Description
14	Wiring retainers (2 required)
15	Valve cover stud bolts (5 required)
16	Valve cover bolts (9 required)
17	Valve cover
18	Valve cover gasket

ARM0400000000437

Fig. 30 Righthand valve cover replacement (Part 2 of 2)

ARM0400000000436

Fig. 30 Righthand valve cover replacement (Part 1 of 2)

COOLING SYSTEM BLEED

1. Select maximum blower motor and heater temperature settings.
2. Set controls to discharge air through instrument panel air conditioning vents.
3. Start engine and allow to idle until operating temperature is reached.
4. Hot air should now blow through air conditioning vents, temperature gauge should rest in NORMAL range and upper radiator hose should feel hot to touch.
5. If hot air does not blow through vents or temperature gauge is not in NORMAL range, proceed as follows:
   a. Stop engine, allow to cool.
   b. Add coolant to bring level to top of Cold Fill mark on de-gas bottle.
   c. Start engine and allow it to idle. Feel for hot air at vents.
6. Stop engine and allow to cool. Inspect for leaks.
7. When engine coolant level indicator flashes, approximately one to 1 ½ quarts of coolant may now be added to de-gas bottle after proper refill.

THERMOSTAT
REPLACE
Removal

1. Drain cooling system into suitable con-

tainer to below level of upper radiator hose.
2. Remove upper radiator hose.
3. Remove three thermostat housing bolts, **Fig. 51,** then separate upper and lower thermostat housings.
4. Remove thermostat from housing and discard gasket.

Installation

1. Align thermostat bridge with alignment marks in lower housing, **Fig. 52,** then install lower thermostat housing into upper housing.
2. Install gasket onto housing using bolts to hold position.
3. Install lower housing onto upper housing, **Fig. 52.**
4. Install and **torque** mounting bolts to 89 inch. lbs.
5. Install upper radiator hose.
6. Fill and bleed cooling system as outlined in "Cooling System Bleed."

WATER PUMP
REPLACE

1. Raise and support vehicle.
2. Drain engine coolant into suitable container.
3. Remove air cleaner assembly.
4. Disconnect water hose from bottom of water pump.
5. Remove radiator lower coolant tube bolt.
6. Lower vehicle.

7. Remove water pump belt.
8. Remove radiator upper front coolant tube bolt.
9. Disconnect upper radiator hose and engine vent hose.
10. Disconnect transaxle 10-pin connector.
11. Remove radiator bypass hose assembly.
12. Disconnect thermostat housing and position aside, **Fig. 53.**
13. Remove water pump mounting bolts, then the water pump..
14. Reverse procedure to install, noting the following:
   a. Tighten water pump mounting bolts in four steps as follows:
   b. Step one, **torque** water pump center bolt to 35 inch lbs.
   c. Step two, **torque** water pump outer mounting bolts to 89 inch lbs.
   d. Step three, tighten mounting bolts an additional 90°.
   e. Step four, **torque** water pump center bolt to 18 ft. lbs.

RADIATOR
REPLACE

1. Drain cooling system into suitable container.
2. Remove battery and battery tray.
3. Disconnect upper radiator hose.
4. Disconnect degas bottle return hose.
5. Disconnect upper transaxle cooler line using suitable disconnect tool.
6. Remove air conditioning condenser mounting bolts.
7. Raise and support vehicle.
8. Disconnect lower radiator hose and transaxle cooler line.

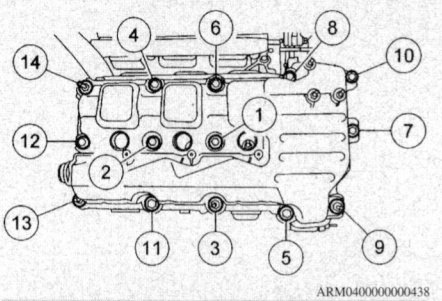

Fig. 31 Righthand valve cover tightening sequence

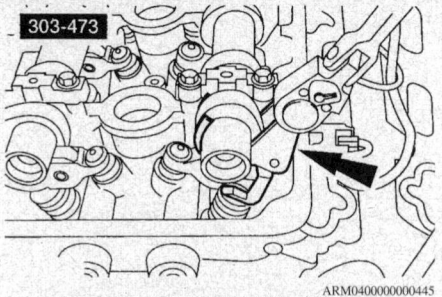

Fig. 32 Hydraulic roller lifter replacement

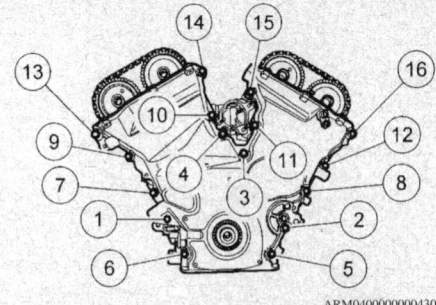

Fig. 33 Front cover bolt tightening sequence

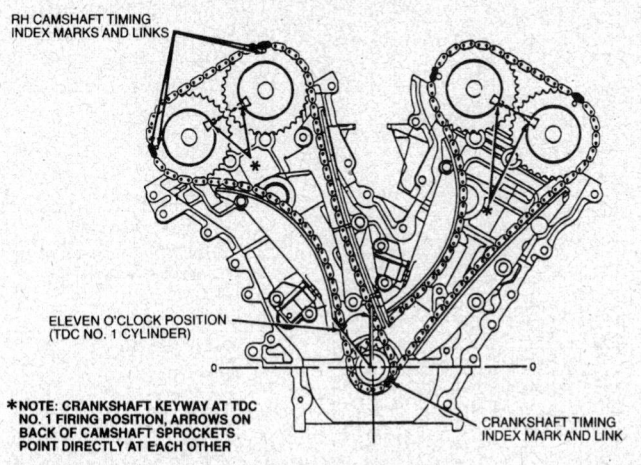

Fig. 34 Timing mark alignment

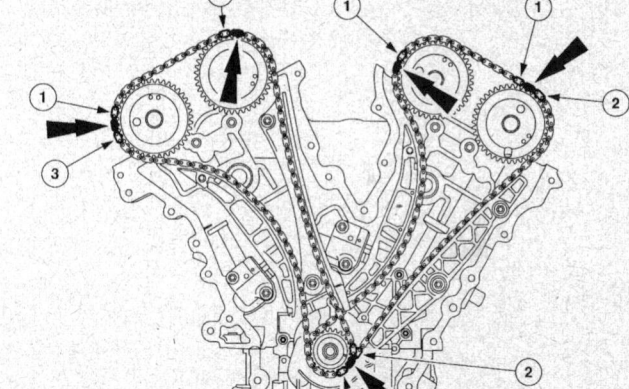

Fig. 35 Timing chain tensioner

1. There should be: 12 chain links between the camshaft timing mark
2. There should be: 27 chain links between the camshaft and crankshaft timing marks
3. There should be: 30 chain links between the camshaft and crankshaft timing marks

Fig. 36 Timing drive component alignment

9. Remove condenser to radiator mounting bolts.
10. Remove power steering cooler to radiator mounting bolts.
11. Remove nuts and radiator support bracket.
12. Remove radiator.
13. Reverse procedure to install.

FUEL PUMP
REPLACE

1. Relieve fuel system pressure as outlined in "Precautions."
2. **On Five Hundred and Montego models,** release rear seat lower cushion latches, then pull upward to remove seat cushion.
3. **On Freestyle models,** position second row seat rearward. Remove seat latching bracket bolts and brackets, then the rear seat.
4. **On all models,** remove fuel pump module access cover.
5. Clean surrounding area of fuel pump module mounting flange and quick connect fittings, **Fig. 54.**
6. Disconnect fuel pump module electrical connector.
7. Disconnect fuel supply and fuel vapor tubes quick connect coupling from fuel pump module.

8. Remove fuel pump locking ring by turning it counterclockwise using lock ring tool No. ST2803–A. or equivalent.
9. Remove fuel pump, bracket and gasket assembly.
10. Reverse procedure to install. Ensure alignment arrows on fuel pump module and fuel tank meet before tightening lock ring.

FUEL FILTER
REPLACE

1. Relieve fuel system pressure as outlined in "Precautions."

2. Twist push connect fittings at each end of filter until they move freely on tube.
3. Bend and break shipping tab from hairpin clip and spread two clip legs approximately ⅛ inch.
4. Remove clip from tube and fitting by pulling gently on triangular end.
5. Separate fitting and hose assembly from fuel filter.
6. Install retainer clips in each connect fitting.
7. Loosen worm gear mounting clip and remove filter from bracket.
8. Reverse procedure to install.

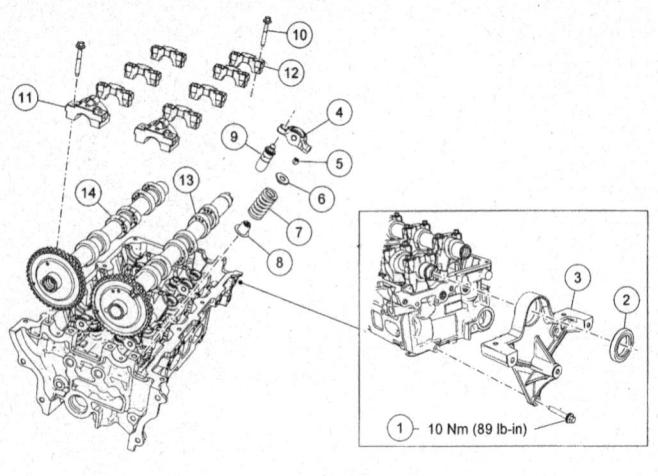

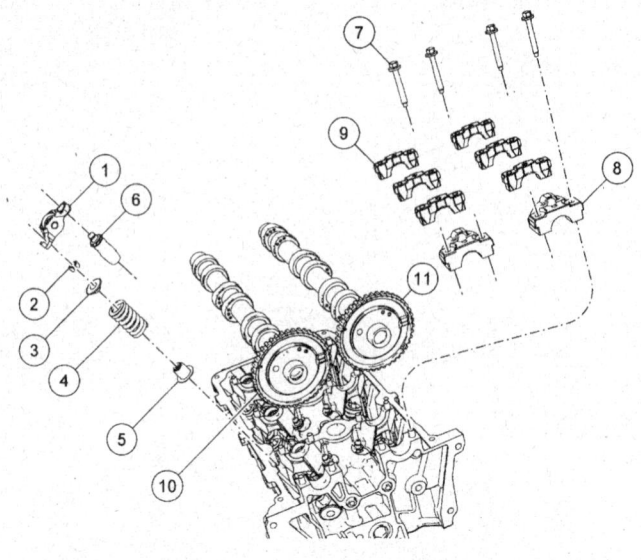

Item	Description
1	Camshaft oil seal retainer bolts (3 required)
2	Camshaft oil seal
3	Camshaft oil seal retainer
4	Roller follower
5	Valve spring retainer key
6	Valve spring retainer
7	Valve spring
8	Valve stem seal

Item	Description
9	Hydraulic lash adjuster
10	Camshaft bearing cap bolts (16 required)
11	Camshaft bearing thrust cap (2 required)
12	Camshaft bearing cap (7 required)
13	Exhaust camshaft
14	Intake camshaft

ARM0400000000428

Fig. 37 Exploded view of lefthand camshafts & rocker arms

Item	Description
1	Roller follower
2	Valve spring retainer key
3	Valve spring retainer
4	Valve spring
5	Valve stem seal
6	Hydraulic lash adjuster
7	Camshaft bearing cap bolts (16 required)

Item	Description
8	Camshaft bearing thrust cap (2 required)
9	Camshaft bearing cap (6 required)
10	Exhaust camshaft
11	Intake camshaft

ARM0400000000429

Fig. 38 Exploded view of righthand camshafts & rocker arms

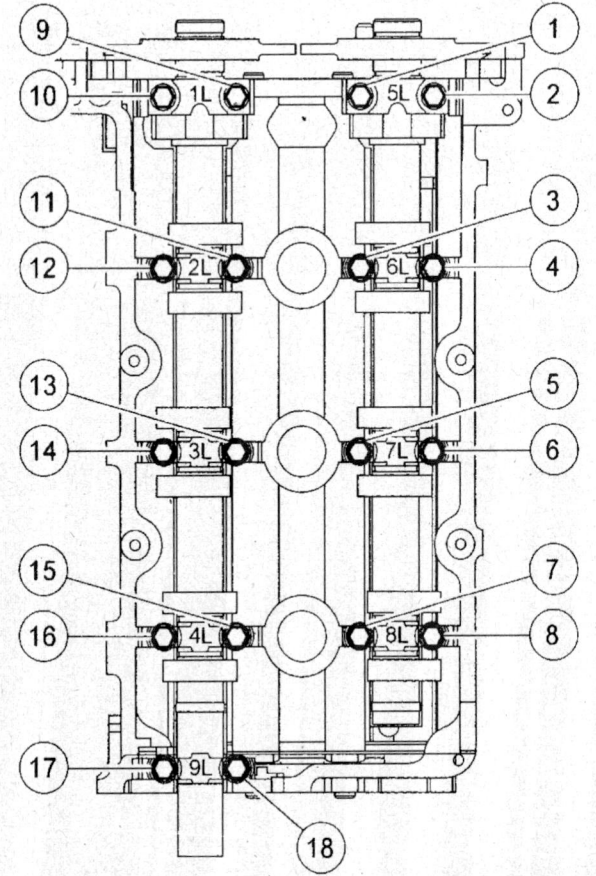

ARM0400000000424

Fig. 39 Lefthand camshaft loosening sequence

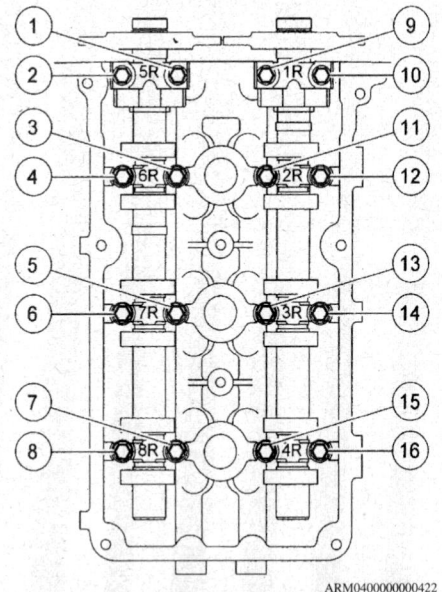

ARM0400000000422

Fig. 40 Righthand camshafts thrust cap bolt loosening & tightening sequence

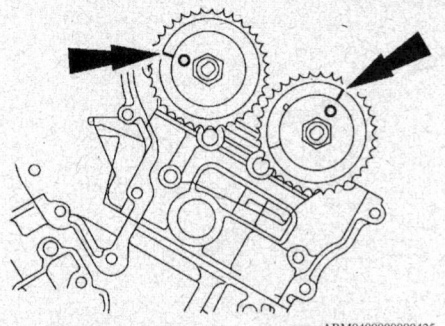

ARM0400000000425

Fig. 41   Lefthand camshafts alignment

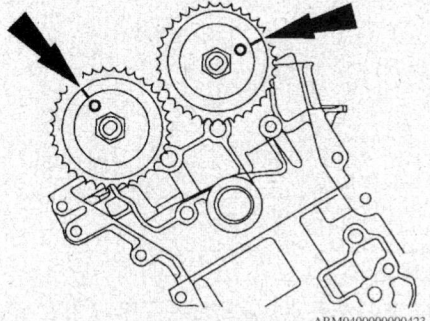

ARM0400000000423

Fig. 44   Righthand camshafts alignment

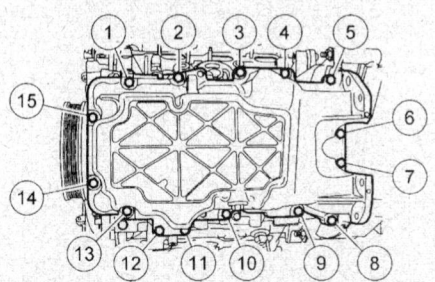

ARM0400000000447

Fig. 46   Oil pan bolt tightening sequence

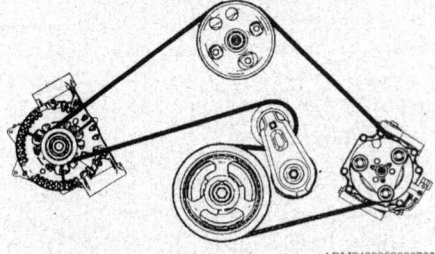

ARM0400000000732

Fig. 49   Serpentine belt routing

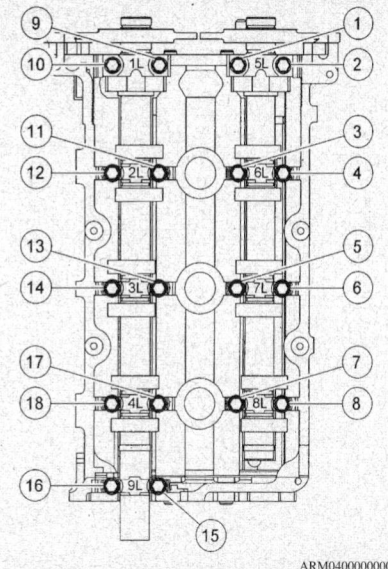

ARM0400000000426

Fig. 42   Lefthand camshafts thrust cap bolt tightening sequence

ARM0400000000448

Fig. 47   Oil pump bolt loosening sequence

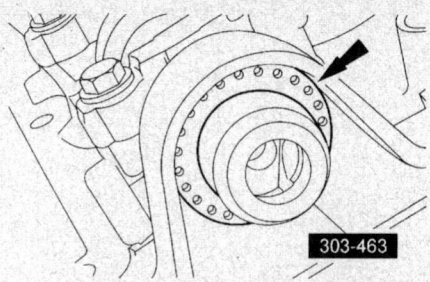

303-463

ARM0400000000427

Fig. 43   Camshaft oil seal installation

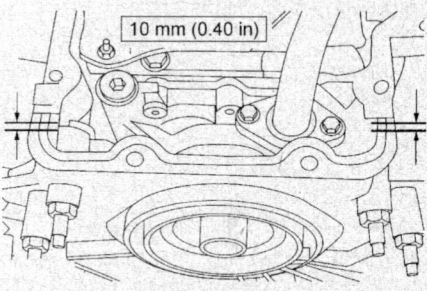

10 mm (0.40 in)

ARM0400000000446

Fig. 45   Silicone gasket & sealer placement

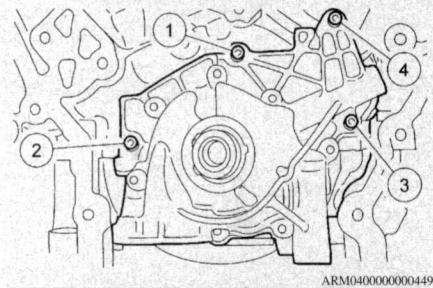

ARM0400000000449

Fig. 48   Oil pump bolt tightening sequence

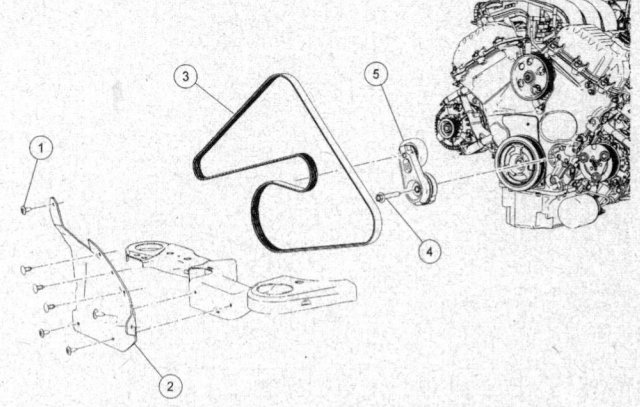

Item	Description
1	Pin-type retainer (7 required)
2	Splash shield
3	Accessory drive belt
4	Accessory drive belt tensioner bolt (part of 6B209)
5	Accessory drive belt tensioner

ARM0400000000733

Fig. 50   Exploded view of serpentine drive belt system

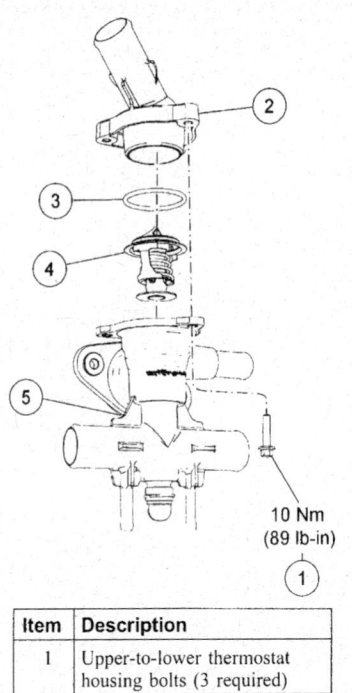

Item	Description
1	Upper-to-lower thermostat housing bolts (3 required)
2	Lower thermostat housing
3	Thermostat O-ring seal
4	Thermostat
5	Upper thermostat housing

ARM0400000000450

Fig. 51   Thermostat replacement

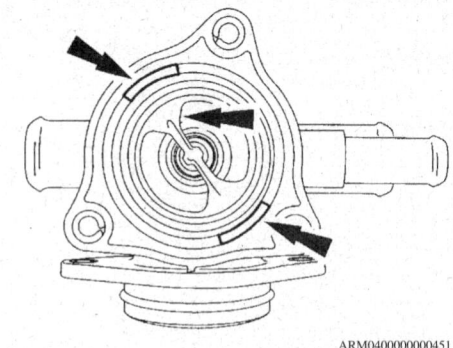

ARM0400000000451

Fig. 52   Thermostat replacement

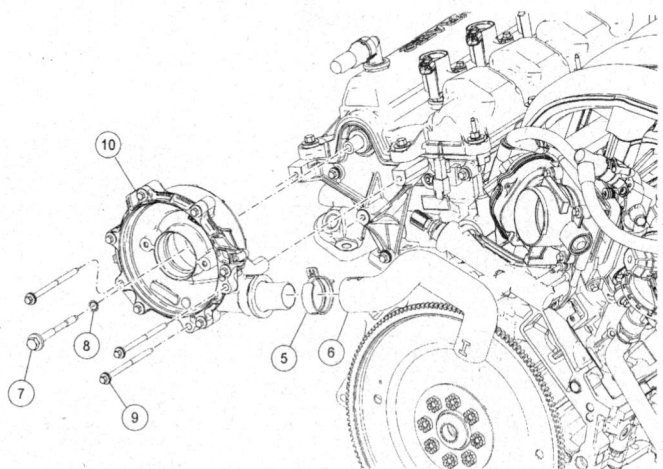

Item	Description
5	Coolant pump hose clamp
6	Coolant pump hose
7	Center coolant pump bolt
8	Center coolant pump bolt sealing washer
9	Outer coolant pump bolts (3 required)
10	Coolant pump

ARM0400000000453

Fig. 53   Water pump replacement (Part 2 of 2)

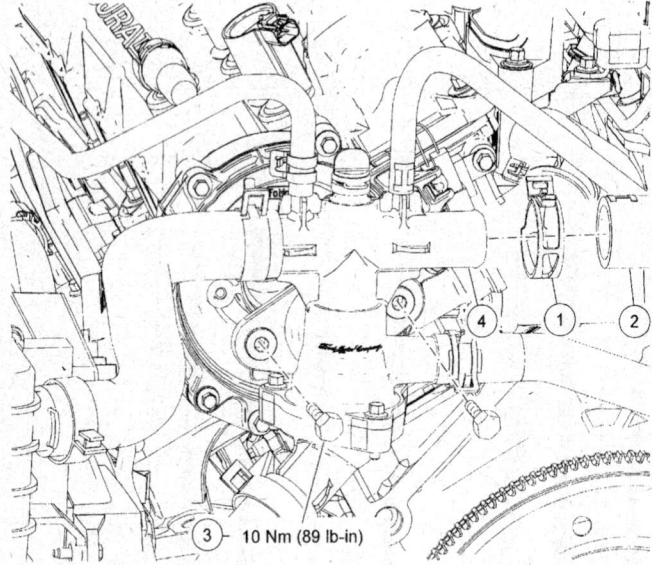

Item	Description		Item	Description
1	Thermostat housing-to-bypass tube hose clamp		3	Thermostat housing bolt (2 required)
2	Thermostat housing-to-bypass tube hose		4	Thermostat housing

ARM0400000000452

Fig. 53   Water pump replacement (Part 1 of 2)

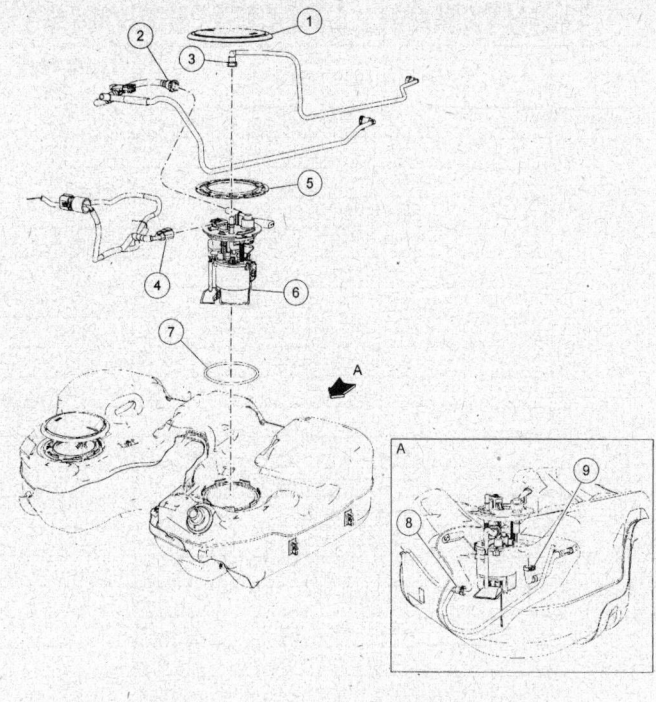

Item	Description
1	Fuel pump module access cover
2	Fuel vapor control tube assembly valve quick connect coupling
3	Fuel supply tube quick release coupling
4	Fuel pump module electrical connector

Item	Description
5	Fuel pump module lock ring
6	Fuel pump module
7	Fuel pump module O-ring seal
8	Fuel transfer supply tube quick connect coupling
9	Fuel vapor tube quick connect coupling

ARM0400000000456

Fig. 54 Fuel pump replacement

TIGHTENING SPECIFICATIONS

Year	Component	Torque/Ft. Lbs.
2005	Accessory Drive Belt Tensioner Bolt	33
	Air Conditioning Compressor	18
	Alternator Mounting	18
	Ball Joint Nuts	59
	Camshaft Cap Bolt	89①
	Camshaft Position Sensor	89①
	Camshaft Oil Seal Retainer	89①
	Crankshaft Position Sensor	89①
	Cylinder Head	②
	EGR Tube	30
	EGR Valve	18
	Engine Mount	52
	Exhaust Manifold	⑤
	Flexplate	59
	Front Cover	⑧
	Fuel Rail	89①
	Halfshaft	191
	Intake Manifold	④
	Knock Sensor	13
	Lefthand Engine Support Insulator, Bolt	52
	Lefthand Engine Support Insulator, Nut	66
	Oil Pan	③
	Oil Pan To Transaxle	30
	Oil Pump	89①
	Oil Separator	89①
	Power Steering Pressure Line	27
	Power Steering Pump Nuts	18
	Righthand Engine Support Insulator, Nut	66
	Righthand Engine Support Insulator, Through Bolt	89
	Shifter Cable	13
	Spark Plugs	11
	Steering Shaft Pinch Bolt	18
	Subframe Bolts	76
	Timing Chain Guide	18
	Timing Chain Tensioner	18
	Torque Converter To Flex Plate	27
	Valve Cover	⑥
	Water Pump	⑦
	Y-Pipe Nuts	30
	Y-Pipe To Exhaust Manifold	30

① — Inch lbs.
② — Refer to "Cylinder Head, Replace" for tightening specifications and sequence.
③ — Refer to "Oil Pan, Replace" for tightening specifications and sequence.
④ — Refer to "Intake Manifold, Replace" for tightening specifications and sequence.
⑤ — Refer to "Exhaust Manifold, Replace" for tightening specifications and sequence.
⑥ — Refer to "Valve Cover, Replace" for tightening specifications and sequence.
⑦ — Refer to "Water Pump, Replace" for tightening specifications and sequence.
⑧ — Refer to "Front Cover, Replace" for tightening specifications and sequence.

NOTE: On Air Bag Equipped Models, Refer To "Air Bag System Precautions" Located In The Front Of This Manual For System Disarming & Arming Procedures.

NOTE: Refer To "Computer Relearn Procedures" Located In The Front Of This Manual When Battery Power To The Computer Has Been Interrupted.

INDEX

DESCRIPTION

These models utilize an independent rear suspension. Each side consists of an upper and lower control arm, a shock absorber, a two-piece spindle tension control shock and a coil spring.

The top of the shock absorber is attached to the body side panel by a rubber insulated top mount and to the lower control arms by two nuts. The upper control arm attaches to the crossmember and the upper part of the spindle. The lower control arm attaches to the underbody and lower part of the spindle. The coil spring operates against the lower control arm and is located inboard of the shock absorber, **Fig. 1.**

HUB & BEARING
REPLACE

1. Remove hub cap or wheel cover.
2. Remove tire/wheel assembly
3. Remove caliper mounting bolts, then the caliper. Position caliper aside and secure to frame using suitable wire.
4. **On models equipped with AWD,** remove and discard axle shaft nut. Using suitable hub removal tool, **Fig. 2,** press axle shaft out of hub and bearing assembly.
5. **On all models,** remove wheel bearing and hub to knuckle retaining bolts.
6. Remove wheel hub and bearing.
7. Reverse procedure to install.

WHEEL BEARING
ADJUST

The rear wheel bearings are of a sealed cartridge design and are not adjustable.

SHOCK ABSORBER
REPLACE

After removal discard all suspension component mounting bolts and nuts. Replace discarded fasteners.

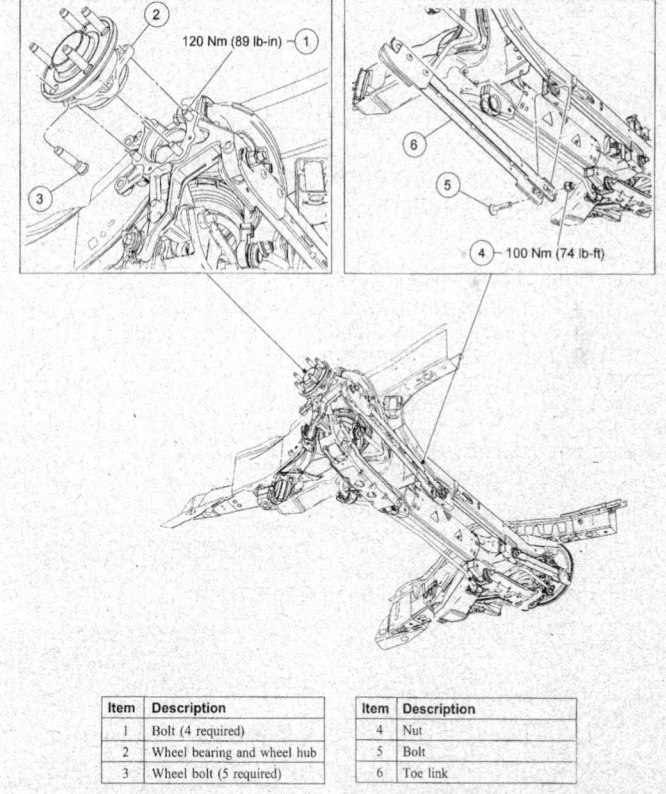

Item	Description
1	Bolt (4 required)
2	Wheel bearing and wheel hub
3	Wheel bolt (5 required)

Item	Description
4	Nut
5	Bolt
6	Toe link

ARM0400000000466

Fig. 1 Exploded view of rear suspension (Part 1 of 4)

1. Measure and record distance from center of hub to lip of fender with vehicle in a level static ground position (curb height), **Fig. 3.**
2. Remove interior trim panel to access upper shock absorber mounting nut, then remove nut.
3. Raise and support vehicle, then remove tire/wheel assembly.
4. Remove brake caliper mounting bolts, position caliper aside and secure to frame using suitable wire.
5. Position a V-topped transmission jack under knuckle at trailing arm attachment point.
6. Raise wheel knuckle until toe link is parallel to ground, **Fig. 4.**
7. Remove trailing arm to knuckle mounting bolt.
8. Lower transmission jack, then remove

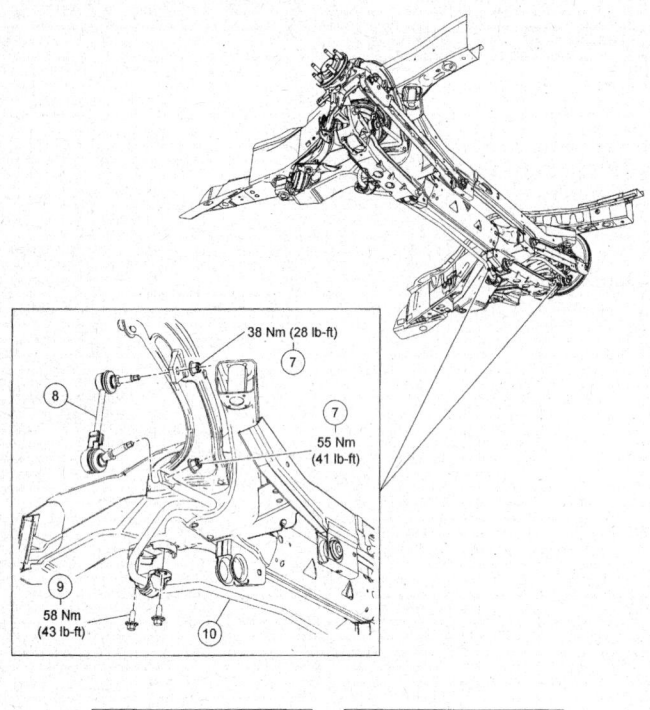

Item	Description	Item	Description
7	Nut	9	Bolt (4 required)
8	Stabilizer bar link	10	Stabilizer bar

ARM0400000000467

Fig. 1 Exploded view of rear suspension (Part 2 of 4)

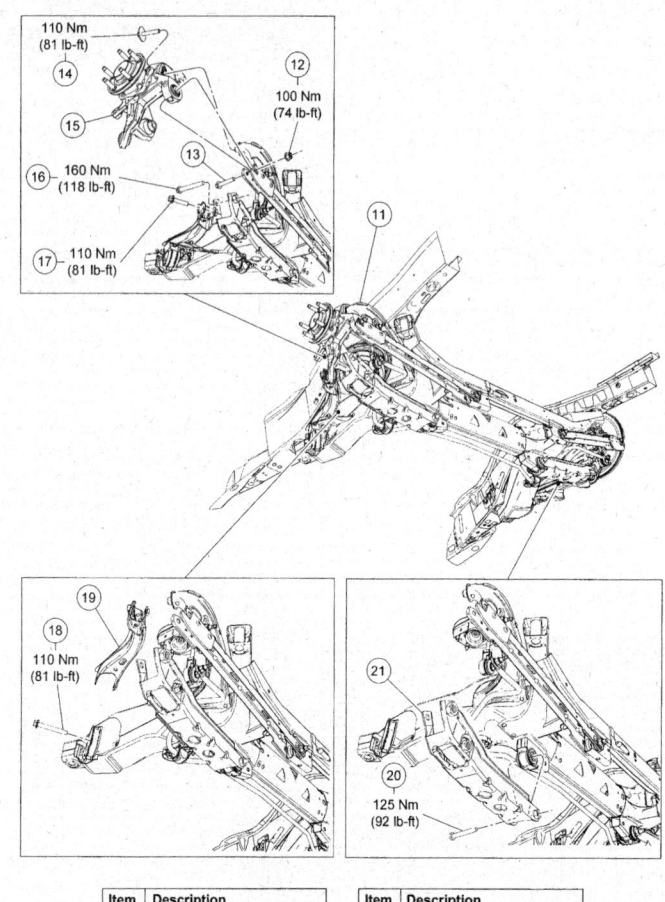

Item	Description	Item	Description
11	Upper arm	17	Bolt
12	Nut	18	Bolt
13	Bolt	19	Trailing arm
14	Bolt	20	Bolt
15	Wheel knuckle	21	Lower arm
16	Bolt		

ARM0400000000468

Fig. 1 Exploded view of rear suspension (Part 3 of 4)

trailing arm to subframe mounting bolt.

9. Position V-topped transmission jack under lower shock absorber mount, then raise jack enough to compress shock absorber and spring.

10. Remove lower arm to knuckle mounting bolt.

11. Loosen lower arm to subframe bolt.

12. Lower and remove transmission jack.

13. Remove lower shock absorber to lower arm bolt.

14. While holding shock absorber and spring, swing lower arm downward to access and remove shock absorber and spring.

15. Reverse procedure to install, noting the following:

   a. Tape coil spring to upper rubber spring seat to ensure proper alignment of spring on seat.

   b. Before tightening suspension nuts and bolts, raise suspension with suitable floor jack to previously measured height, **Fig. 3.**

COIL SPRING

REPLACE

Refer to "Shock Absorber, Replace" for coil spring replacement procedure.

CONTROL ARM

REPLACE

After removal discard all suspension component mounting bolts and nuts. Replace discarded fasteners.

Lower

1. Measure and record distance from center of hub to lip of fender with vehicle in a level static ground position (curb height), **Fig. 3.**

2. Raise and support rear of vehicle.

3. Remove tire and wheel assembly.

4. Remove rear spring as outlined in "Coil Spring, Replace."

5. Remove lower control arm to body bracket mounting bolt and control arm.

6. Reverse procedure to install, noting the following:

   a. Tape coil spring to upper rubber spring seat to ensure proper alignment of spring on seat.

   b. Before tightening suspension nuts and bolts, raise suspension with suitable floor jack to previously measured height, **Fig. 3.**

Upper

REMOVAL

The front and rear control arm bushings must be replaced in pairs.

1. Raise and support vehicle.

2. Remove rear subframe, **Fig. 5.**

3. Raise lower control arm to normal curb height using suitable floor jack.

4. Remove wheel and tire assembly, then the brake hose bracket from body.

5. Remove front and rear upper arm to subframe mounting bolts.

6. Remove stabilizer bar link to upper

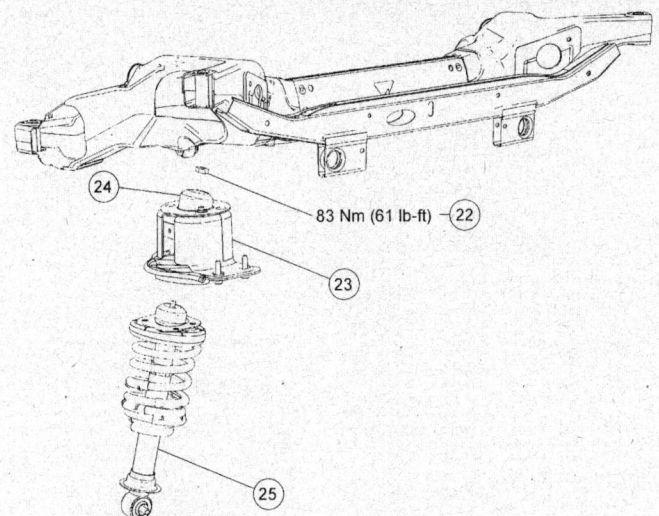

83 Nm (61 lb-ft)

Item	Description
22	Upper shock absorber nut
23	Upper shock mount
24	Bushing
25	Shock absorber/spring

ARM0400000000469

Fig. 1 Exploded view of rear suspension (Part 4 of 4)

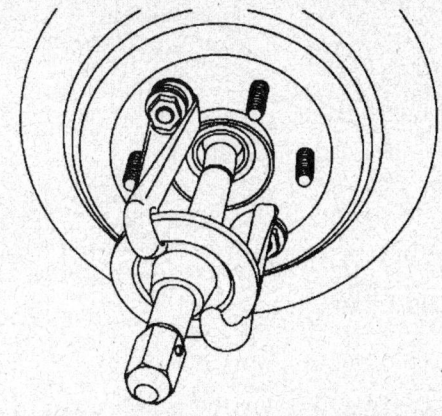

ARM0400000000471

Fig. 2 Hub & bearing removal. AWD models

ARM0400000000470

Fig. 3 Static ground position (curb height) measurement

arm nut, then separate link from upper arm.

7. Remove upper arm to knuckle mounting bolt.
8. Remove upper arm and upper arm front bushing from subframe using bushing replacement tool No. 204–357, or equivalent, **Fig. 6.**
9. Remove front upper arm rear bushing from arm using jaw puller tool No. 205–D072 and 205–D064, or equivalents, **Fig. 7.**
10. Remove rear bushing from subframe using draw bar bushing tool No. 205–098, or equivalent, **Fig. 8.**
11. Remove upper arm from subframe.

INSTALLATION

1. Install rear bushing into subframe using draw bar bushing tool No. 205–098, or equivalent, **Fig. 8.** Install bushing to correct depth in subframe using opposite side bushing as a guide, **Fig. 9.**
2. Position upper arm bushing on wheel knuckle ball stud and into rear bushing, then insert forward part of upper arm into front subframe bore.
3. Loosely install rear upper arm to subframe bolt.
4. Hold upper and adjust it to correct specifications, **Fig. 10,** then tighten bolt to specifications.
5. Install rear upper arm to subframe bolt.
6. Install front upper arm bushing into subframe using bushing replacement tool No. 204–357, or equivalent, **Fig. 6,** while an assistant hold upper arm in center of bushing bore.
7. Install front bushing into subframe

using draw bar bushing tool No. 205–098, or equivalent, **Fig. 8. Install bushing to correct depth in subframe using opposite side bushing as a guide.**
8. Install front arm to subframe bolt.
9. Install upper arm to knuckle bolts.
10. Install stabilized bar link and nut on upper arm.
11. Install rear subframe, **Fig. 5.** Align subframe to body following alignment specification, **Fig. 11.**

KNUCKLE
REPLACE

After removal, discard all suspension component mounting bolts and nuts. Replace discarded fasteners.

1. Measure and record distance from center of hub to lip of fender with vehicle in a level static ground position (curb height), **Fig. 3.**
2. Remove tire/wheel assembly
3. Remove hub and bearing as outlined under "Hub & Bearing, Replace."
4. Remove disc brake shield and antilock wheel sensor.

5. Place suitable jack stand under lower control arm and slightly raise suspension.
6. Remove trailing arm to knuckle mounting bolt.
7. Remove toe link to knuckle mounting bolt.
8. Remove shock absorber/spring assembly to lower control arm mounting bolt.
9. Remove upper and lower subframe to knuckle mounting bolts.
10. Remove wheel knuckle.
11. Reverse procedure to install, noting the following:
    a. Install new flag bolts, nuts and washers.
    b. Before tightening suspension nuts and bolts, raise suspension with suitable floor jack to previously measured height, **Fig. 3.**

TRAILING ARM
REPLACE

After removal discard all suspension component mounting bolts and nuts. Replace discarded fasteners.

1. Measure and record distance from

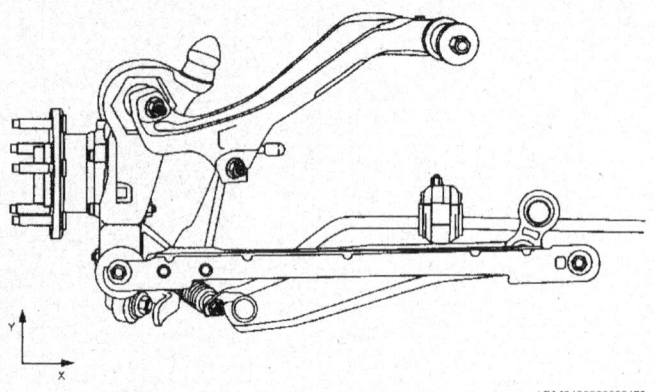

Fig. 4   Toe link in parallel position

ARM0400000000472

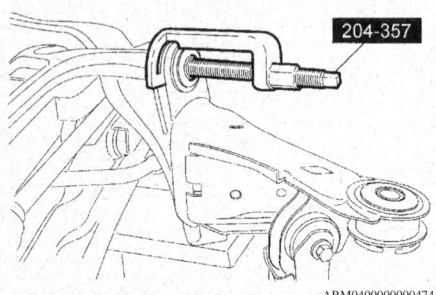

204-357

Fig. 6   Subframe front bushing removal

ARM0400000000474

center of hub to lip of fender with vehicle in a level static ground position (curb height), **Fig. 3.**
2. Raise and support vehicle.
3. Remove trailing arm to knuckle mounting bolt.
4. Remove trailing arm to subframe mounting bolt.
5. Remove trailing arm.
6. Reverse procedure to install. Before tightening suspension nuts and bolts, raise suspension with suitable floor jack to previously measured height, **Fig. 3.**

STABILIZER BAR
REPLACE
AWD

After removal discard all suspension component mounting bolts and nuts. Replace discarded fasteners.
1. Raise and support vehicle. **Do use tension strut and bushing for support.**
2. Lower exhaust system from rear of flex pipe by disconnecting insulators.
3. Remove tire/wheel assemblies.
4. Remove lefthand and righthand brake caliper mounting bolts, then position calipers side and secure to frame using suitable wire.
5. Remove and discard lefthand and righthand axle shaft retaining nuts.

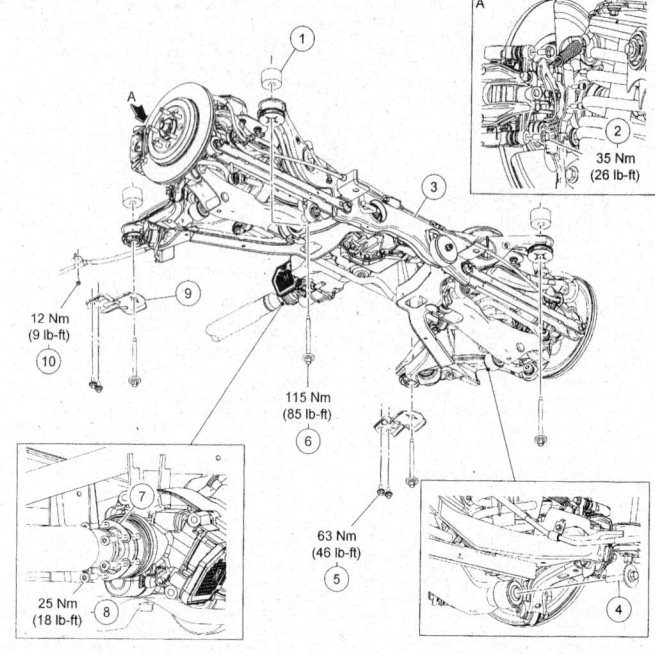

12 Nm (9 lb-ft)

115 Nm (85 lb-ft)

63 Nm (46 lb-ft)

25 Nm (18 lb-ft)

35 Nm (26 lb-ft)

1. Rear subframe to under body spacers, FWD Freestyl only
2. Rear caliper pins
3. Rear subframe assembly
4. Rear Shock to lower control arm bolts
5. Rear subframe assembly
6. Rear subframe mounting bolts
7. Driveshaft washers, AWD only
8. Driveshaft bolts, AWD only
9. Rear subframe bracket
10. Park brake cable routing bolt

ARM0400000000473

Fig. 5   Exploded view of rear subframe

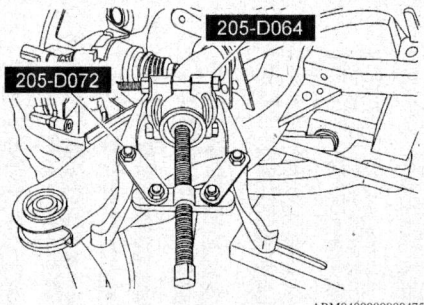

205-D064

205-D072

ARM0400000000475

Fig. 7   Upper control arm bushing removal

6. Press axle shafts out of hubs using suitable hub removal press.
7. Remove lefthand and righthand upper control arm to knuckle bolts.
8. Remove lefthand and righthand trailing arm to knuckle bolt, then loosen trailing arm to subframe bolt.
9. Remove lefthand and righthand lower shock to lower control arm nut, then the lower control arm.
10. Loosen lefthand and righthand toe link to subframe bolts, allow both knuckles to hang in a downward position.

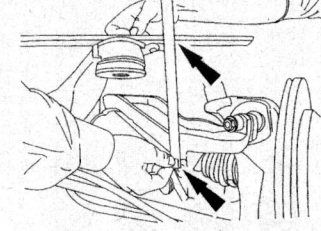

Vehicle	Ride Height Specification
Freestyle 2WD	163 mm (6.4 in)
Five Hundred/Montego 2WD	147 mm (5.7 in)
Freestyle AWD	158 mm (6.2 in)
Five Hundred/Montego AWD	138 mm (5.4 in)

ARM0400000000476

Fig. 8   Subframe rear bushing replacement

11. Remove subframe cross brace bolts, then the cross brace, **Fig. 12.**
12. Remove stabilizer bar link to stabilizer bar nuts.

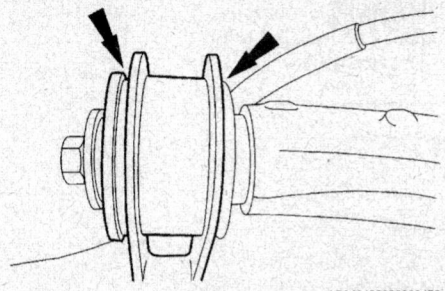

Fig. 9 Control arm bushing depth verification

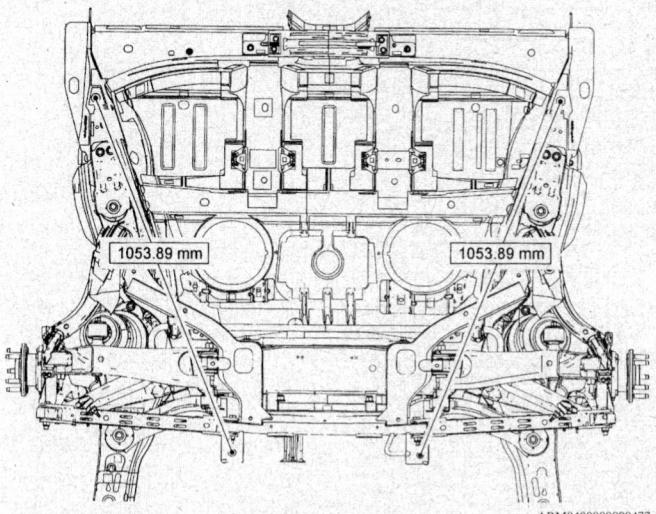

Fig. 11 Rear subframe alignment specifications

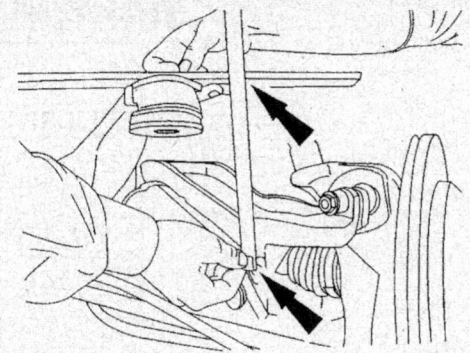

Vehicle	Ride Height Specification
Freestyle 2WD	163 mm (6.4 in)
Five Hundred/Montego 2WD	147 mm (5.7 in)
Freestyle AWD	158 mm (6.2 in)
Five Hundred/Montego AWD	138 mm (5.4 in)

ARM0400000000478

Fig. 10 Ride height specifications & measurement points

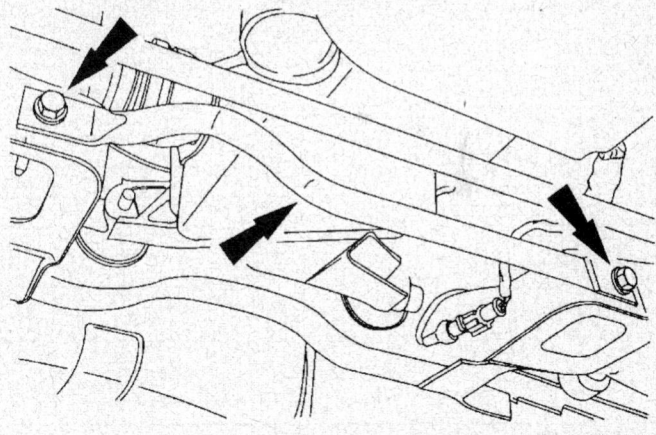

ARM0400000000480

Fig. 12 Subframe cross brace removal

13. Remove stabilizer to subframe bracket bolts.
14. Remove stabilizer bar and link assembly.
15. Reverse procedure to install.

FWD

After removal discard all suspension component mounting bolts and nuts. Replace discarded fasteners.
1. Raise and support vehicle.
2. Place jack stands under rear suspension arm and bushings so bar links and bushings are neutralized.
3. Lower exhaust system from rear of flex pipe by disconnecting insulators.
4. Remove stabilizer bar link to stabilizer bar mounting nuts.
5. Remove stabilizer bar bracket to subframe mounting bolts.
6. Remove stabilizer bar and link assembly.
7. Reverse procedure to install.

TOE LINK
REPLACE

After removal discard all suspension component mounting bolts and nuts. Replace discarded fasteners.
1. Raise and support vehicle.
2. Measure and record distance from center of hub to lip of fender with vehicle in a level static ground position (curb height), **Fig. 3.**

3. Remove tire/wheel assembly.
4. Remove wheel speed sensor wire retainer and wire from toe link.
5. Remove toe link to knuckle bolt.
6. Remove toe link to subframe nut and bolt.
7. Reverse procedure to install. Before tightening suspension nuts and bolts, raise suspension with suitable floor jack to previously measured height, **Fig. 3.**

TIGHTENING SPECIFICATIONS

Year	Component	Torque/Ft. Lbs.
ALL WHEEL DRIVE		
2005	Axle Shaft Nut	148
	Brake Hose Bracket Bolt	9–12
	Disc Brake Shield Bolt	10
	Lower Arm To Wheel Knuckle Bolt	66
	Lower arm To Subframe Bolt	98
	Lower Shock Absorber To Mount Nut	61
	Stabilizer Bar Bracket Bolt	43
	Stabilizer Bar Link To Stabilizer Bar Bolt	41
	Subframe Cross Brace Bolts	46
	Toe Link To Subframe Bolt	74
	Toe Link To Wheel Knuckle Bolt	74
	Trailing Arm To Subframe Bolt	81
	Trailing Arm To Wheel Knuckle Bolt	77
	Upper Arm To Wheel Knuckle Nut	77
	Upper Shock Absorber To Mount Housing Bolt	22
	Upper Arm To Subframe Bolt	81
	Wheel Lug	85–105
FRONT WHEEL DRIVE		
2005	Axle Shaft Nut	148
	Brake Hose Bracket Bolt	9–12
	Disc Brake Shield Bolt	10
	Lower Arm To Wheel Knuckle Bolt	92
	Lower arm To Subframe Bolt	118
	Lower Shock Absorber To Mount Nut	61
	Stabilizer Bar Bracket Bolt	43
	Stabilizer Bar Link To Stabilizer Bar Bolt	41
	Toe Link To Subframe Bolt	74
	Toe Link To Wheel Knuckle Bolt	74
	Trailing Arm To Subframe Bolt	81
	Trailing Arm To Wheel Knuckle Bolt	77
	Upper Arm To Wheel Knuckle Nut	81
	Upper Shock Absorber To Mount Housing Bolt	22
	Upper Arm To Subframe Bolt	81
	Wheel Lug	85–105

NOTE: On Air Bag Equipped Models, Refer To "Air Bag System Precautions" Located In The Front Of This Manual For System Disarming & Arming Procedures.

NOTE: Refer To "Computer Relearn Procedures" Located In The Front Of This Manual When Battery Power To The Computer Has Been Interrupted.

INDEX

DESCRIPTION

This suspension is a gas filled McPherson strut type. The strut top mount consists of a rubber insulated bearing and seat and coil spring insulator. The top mount is attached to the body side apron by three bolts. The lower part of the strut is mounted in the steering knuckle and is retained by a pinch bolt. A forged lower control arm is attached to the subframe and to the steering knuckle. A tension strut is connected to the lower control arm and to the forward part of the subframe.

WHEEL BEARING
REPLACE

1. Turn ignition switch to OFF position and place steering column in unlocked position.
2. Remove wheel hub nut, then raise and support vehicle.
3. Remove cotter pin and nut from tie rod end stud. Discard cotter pin and nut.
4. Remove tie rod end from front steering knuckle using tie rod end remover tool No. 3290-D, and tie rod adapter tool No. T81P-3504-W, or equivalents. **Do not use power tools to remove nut. Avoid damaging rod boot seal.**
5. Remove stabilizer bar link from front wheel knuckle.
6. Remove disc brake caliper and support it aside.
7. Remove anti-lock brake sensor.
8. Remove and discard lower ball joint nut.
9. Compress front coil spring until lower ball joint clears front suspension lower arm using Rotunda spring compressor tool No. 164-R-3571, or equivalent.
10. Push front axle from hub using suitable service tools.
11. Remove and discard four hub and bearing mounting bolts, **Fig. 1**, from front steering knuckle.
12. **Wheel hub is not pressed into front wheel knuckle. Do not use slide**

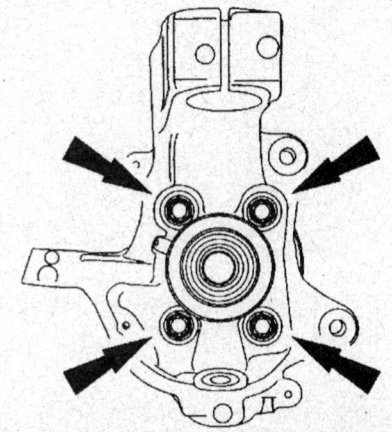

ARM0400000000481

Fig. 1 Hub & bearing removal

hammer to remove stuck wheel hub. Do not strike back of inner bearing race.
13. If bearing carrier is corroded to front steering knuckle, apply rust penetrant part No. D7AZ-19A501-AA, or equivalent, to inboard and outboard steering knuckle to hub mating surface and allow to soak. Pry wheel hub from knuckle assembly using suitable pry bar.
14. Reverse procedure to install, noting the following:
   a. If wheel hub is damaged, or if any endplay is detectable, replace wheel hub.
   b. Remove any foreign material from knuckle bearing bore.
   c. Lightly lubricate mating surfaces of bearing and front wheel knuckle.

BALL JOINT INSPECTION

1. Raise and support vehicle with wheels in full down position.

2. Grasp lower edge of tire, then move wheel assembly in and out.
3. As wheel is being moved, observe lower end of knuckle and lower control arm
4. If movement is observed, replace lower control arm.

BALL JOINT
REPLACE

The ball joint must be replaced with the control arm as an assembly.

STRUT
REPLACE

1. Place ignition switch in OFF position and ensure steering wheel is not locked.
2. Remove hub nut and loosen four strut upper mounting plate retaining nuts, **Fig. 2.**
3. Raise and support vehicle. **Do not raise vehicle with lower control arm.**
4. Remove wheel and tire assembly.
5. Remove brake caliper and position it aside.
6. Remove brake rotor and tie rod end to knuckle retaining nut. **Do not use power tools to remove tie rod nut. Avoid damaging boot seal.**
7. Remove nut and stabilizer bar link from strut.
8. Remove wheel speed sensor from knuckle.
9. Remove lower strut to wheel knuckle pinch nut and bolt, **Fig. 3,** then slightly spread joint and remove lower control arm.
10. Press axle from hub using suitable hub remover/installer.
11. Wire axle shaft to body to maintain level position. **Do not allow axle shaft to move outward.**
12. Remove strut to steering knuckle pinch bolt and spread joint slightly.
13. Remove steering knuckle and hub.
14. Remove mounting nuts and strut.

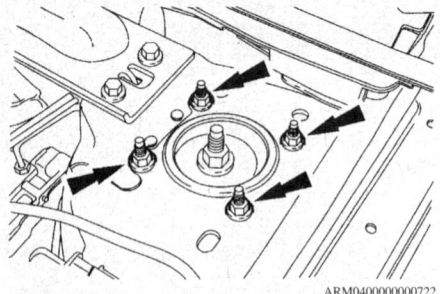

Fig. 2 Strut upper mounting plate removal

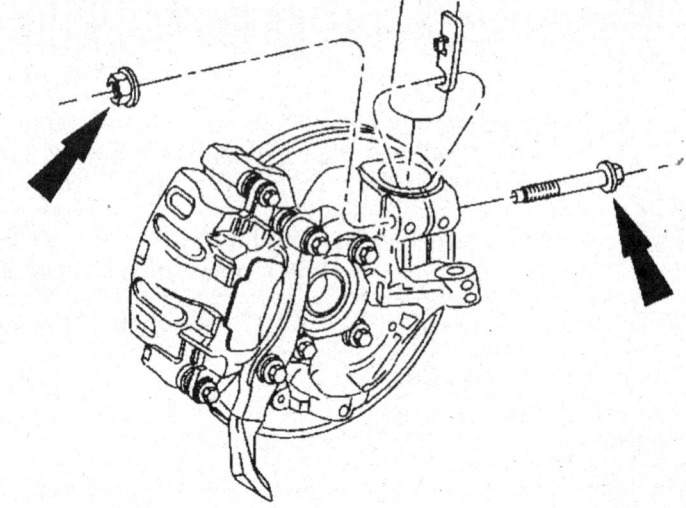

Fig. 3 Strut to wheel knuckle pinch bolt removal

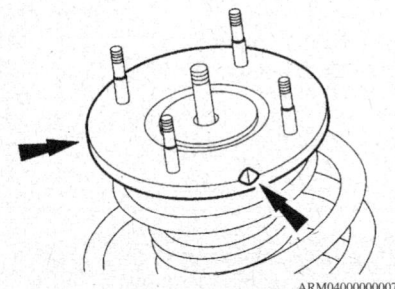

Fig. 4 Upper strut mount outboard alignment

15. Reverse procedure to install, noting the following:
    a. Tighten in following order: strut to wheel knuckle pinch bolt, lower control arm to steering knuckle pinch bolt, stabilizer bar assembly to strut, tie rod end mounting nut and strut mounting nuts.
    b. Tighten hub nut with vehicle on ground.

COIL SPRING & STRUT SERVICE

Disassemble

1. Compress strut spring with Rotunda coil spring compressor tool No. 164-R3571, or equivalent.
2. Hold strut shaft with suitable box wrench and remove strut mounting nut using suitable crowfoot socket. **Do not allow strut shaft to rotate.**
3. Loosen compressor tool, then remove strut top mount bracket, bearing and seat assembly, and spring.

Assemble

1. Position notch and arrow on upper strut mount outboard opposite locator on strut tab, **Fig. 4.**
2. Position notch and arrow on upper strut mount inboard aligned with locator tab on strut, **Fig. 5.**
3. Compress strut spring with Rotunda coil spring compressor tool No. 164-R3571, or equivalent.
4. Install spring over strut into lower seat, then install upper strut mounting plate

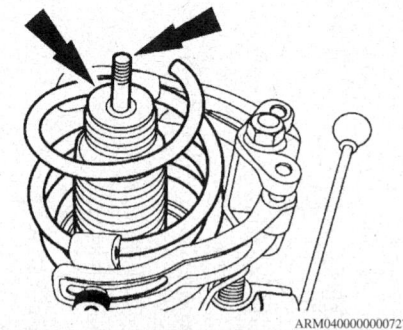

Fig. 5 Upper strut mount inboard alignment

with spring seat. Ensure spring is correctly seated in both upper and lower spring seats.
5. Hold strut shaft with suitable box wrench and install upper strut mounting plate retaining nut using suitable crowfoot socket. **Do not allow strut shaft to rotate.**
6. Install strut spring assembly with upper strut mount alignment arrow facing outward away from vehicle, **Fig. 6.**

CONTROL ARM
REPLACE

1. Turn ignition switch to OFF position and place steering column in unlocked position.
2. Raise and support vehicle.
3. Remove and discard lower ball joint nut.
4. Separate ball joint from steering knuckle using ball joint remover tool No. T96P-3010-A and tie rod end remover tool No. T81P-3504-W, or equivalents.
5. Compress front coil spring until lower ball joint clears front suspension lower arm using Rotunda spring compressor tool No. 164-R-3571, or equivalent.
6. Remove forward lower suspension arm mounting nut and bolt.

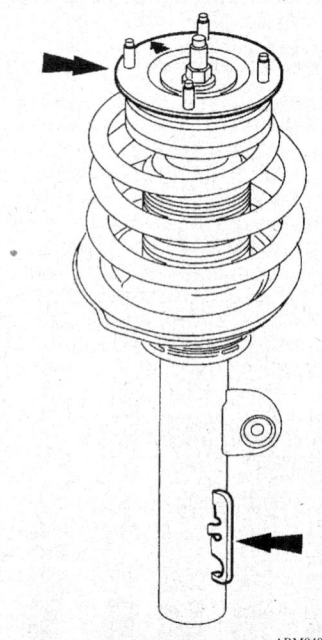

Fig. 6 Strut assembly installation alignment

7. Remove rear lower control arm mounting nut, bolt and control arm.
8. Reverse procedure to install.

STEERING KNUCKLE
REPLACE

Wheel hub retainer is a torque prevailing design and cannot be reused. If loosened, retainer must be replaced.
1. Ensure steering wheel is in unlocked position.
2. Remove wheel cover, wheel hub retainer and washer. Discard retainer.
3. Remove steering knuckle tie rod end using suitable ball joint removal tool.
4. Remove anti-lock brake wheel speed sensor.

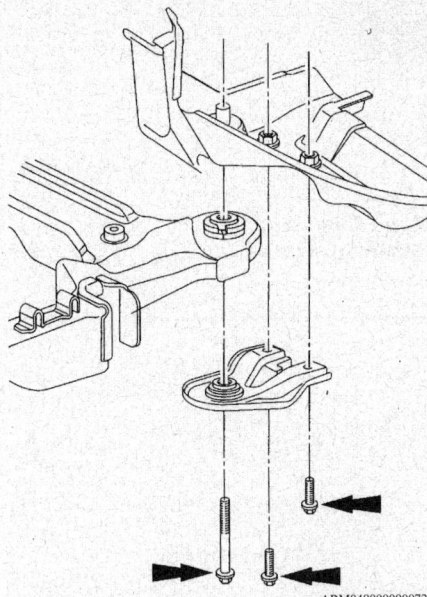

Fig. 7 Subframe lowered

5. Disconnect ABS sensor wire retainer and position sensor aside.
6. Remove knuckle to shock mounting bolt and nut. Discard nut.
7. Disconnect ball joint from lower arm using suitable joint removal tool.
8. Push lower arm down until ball joint is free from arm using suitable pry bar.
9. Press halfshaft from wheel bearing and hub using front wheel hub installation tool No. T81P-1104-C, or equivalent.
10. Support halfshaft in level position.
11. Remove flag bolt and steering knuckle.
12. Reverse procedure to install.

STABILIZER BAR
REPLACE

1. Raise and support vehicle. Place safe-

ty stands behind front subframe.
2. Remove stabilizer bar link to strut and bar mounting nuts.
3. Remove mounting bolts and move steering gear off of subframe.
4. Support subframe with safety stands and remove rear subframe mounting bolts.
5. Lower rear part of subframe approximately two inches to access to stabilizer bar mounting brackets, **Fig. 7**.
6. Remove mounting brackets and stabilizer bar, **Fig. 8**.
7. Reverse procedure to install.

POWER STEERING GEAR
REPLACE

1. Turn steering wheel ¼ turn and turn ignition switch to OFF position.
2. Remove both front wheel and tire assemblies.
3. Remove tie rod end jam nuts. Discard tie rod end cotter pins and nuts.
4. Record number of turns required to remove tie rod ends from steering gear for installation reference.
5. Remove tie rod ends from steering knuckle with suitable joint removal tool.
6. Remove tie rod ends.
7. Remove nuts and disconnect both stabilizer bar links from stabilizer bar.
8. Remove bolt and disconnect intermediate shaft coupling. **Do not allow steering wheel to rotate while steering column intermediate shaft is disconnected.**
9. Remove catalytic converter.
10. Remove and discard both steering gear mounting nuts.
11. Remove bolts and lower rear of front subframe approximately four inches.
12. Disconnect power steering pressure switch and remove pressure hose.
13. Remove bracket/heat shield.

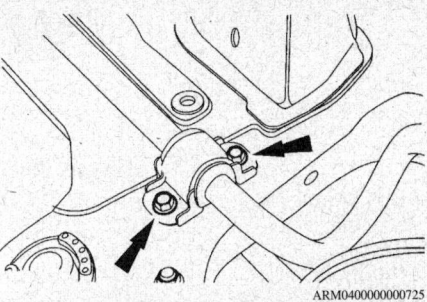

Fig. 8 Stabilizer bar mounting bracket removal

14. Remove power steering lines from steering gear.
15. Remove brackets, pipes and steering gear through lefthand fender well.
16. Reverse procedure to install.

POWER STEERING PUMP
REPLACE

The power steering pump can only be replaced as a complete assembly. The pump has no serviceable components.
1. Drain and remove coolant recovery reservoir.
2. Remove drive belt.
3. Remove power steering reservoir pump hose from between pump and reservoir. Drain fluid into suitable container.
4. Remove pulley using pump pulley remover tool No. T69L-10300-B, or equivalent.
5. Disconnect power steering lefthand turn pressure hose from pump.
6. Remove three pump mounting bolts and pump.
7. Reverse procedure to install.

TIGHTENING SPECIFICATIONS

Year	Component	Torque/Ft. Lbs.
2005	Axle Shaft Wheel Hub Nut	148
	Lower Arm Ball Joint Nut	85
	Lower Arm Bushing To Subframe Bolts	73
	Lower Arm To Subframe Bolt	111
	Rear Subframe To Body Bolts	111
	Stabilizer Bar Bracket bolts	37
	Stabilizer Bar Link To Stabilizer Bar Nut	41
	Stabilizer Bar Link To Strut Nut	41
	Strut & Spring Mounting Bracket Bolts	37
	Strut & Spring Top Mounting Nut	59
	Subframe To Body Bolts	148
	Tie Rod To Steering Knuckle Nut	85
	Wheel Bearing & Hub To Steering Knuckle Bolts	81
	Wheel Speed Sensor Retaining Nut	10

Wheel Alignment

INDEX

PRELIMINARY INSPECTION

1. Ensure tires are inflated to proper pressure.
2. Inspect tires for wear patterns that may indicate improper wheel alignment, tire imbalance or damage because bulges or separations.
3. Inspect suspension for modifications such as trailer towing equipment or heavy duty handling components.
4. Inspect vehicle for signs of overloading or sagging. Ensure luggage compartment does not contain heavy objects.
5. Road test vehicle to isolate area of concern.

FRONT WHEEL ALIGNMENT

Camber

1. Raise and support vehicle.
2. Remove upper strut mount nuts. **Do not rotate strut mount to any other position than 180° from it's original position, Fig. 1.** Arrow on top of strut must be pointed to three O-clock or nine O-clock positions.
3. Push strut downward and rotate it 180 degrees. When rotated 180 degrees from original position, camber changes by +.05 degrees.
4. Install strut mount nuts, **torque** nuts to 20 FT. lbs.
5. Inspect alignment for proper specifications as outlined in "Specifications."

Caster

Caster is not adjustable. If caster is not within specifications, inspect vehicle for suspension component damage, deteriorated bushings or distorted body mounting points.

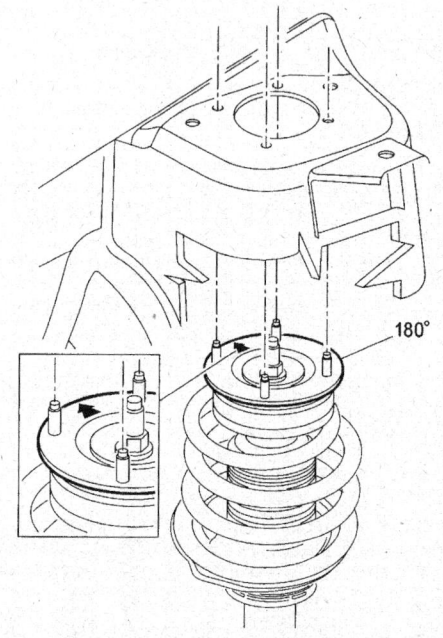

ARM0400000000729

Fig. 1   Strut rotated 180° from original position

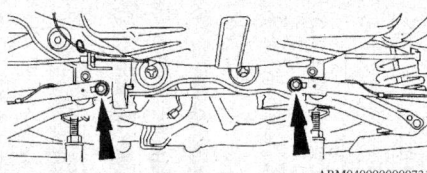

ARM0400000000731

Fig. 3   Rear toe-in adjustment

Toe-In

1. Start engine and center steering wheel.
2. Turn ignition to Off position, then lock steering wheel in straight ahead posi-

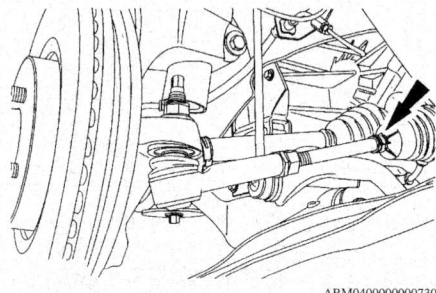

ARM0400000000730

Fig. 2   Steering gear bellows clamps

tion using suitable steering wheel holder.
3. Remove steering gear bellows clamps, **Fig. 2.**
4. Loosen tie rod jam nut, then adjust left-hand and righthand tie rods until each wheel has half desired total toe specification. **Do not allow steering bellows to become twisted.**
5. Tighten tie rod adjusting nuts and install clamps.
6. Remove steering wheel holding tool.

REAR WHEEL ALIGNMENT

Caster & Camber

The caster and camber angles are factory set and cannot be adjusted.

Toe-In

Loosen toe link jam nut, **Fig. 3,** approximately one full turn.

Adjust toe-in by rotating the toe link bolt from the opposite side. Rotate to link bolt to achieve the correct specifications as outlined in "Specifications.". **Torque** toe link nut to 74 ft. lbs.

AIR CONDITIONING

TABLE OF CONTENTS

System Testing

NOTE: On Air Bag Equipped Models, Refer To "Air Bag System Precautions" Located In The Front Of This Manual For System Disarming & Arming Procedures.

NOTE: Refer To "Computer Relearn Procedures" Located In The Front Of This Manual When Battery Power To The Computer Has Been Interrupted.

INDEX

PRECAUTIONS

Battery Ground Cable

Prior to service, disconnect battery ground cable and isolate as required.

Safety

Protective goggles should be worn when opening any refrigerant lines. A bottle of sterile mineral oil and a quantity of weak boric acid solution must always be kept nearby when servicing air conditioning system. **If liquid coolant does touch eyes, immediately use a few drops of sterile mineral oil to wash them out, then wash eyes clean with weak boric acid solution. Seek a doctor's aid immediately even though irritation may have ceased.**

Freon refrigerant used in vehicle A/C systems will usually be in a vapor state when being handled in a repair shop. But if a portion of liquid coolant should come in contact with hands or face, note that its temperature momentarily will be at least 22° below zero.

When inspecting a system for leaks with a torch type leak detector, do not breathe vapors coming from flame. Do not recover refrigerant in area of a live flame. A poisonous phosgene gas is produced when refrigerant is burned. While a small amount of this gas produced by a leak detector is not harmful unless inhaled directly at flame.

Never allow temperature of refrigerant drums to exceed 125°F. Resultant increase in temperature will cause a corresponding increase in pressure which may cause safety plug to release or drum to burst.

If it is required to heat a drum of refrigerant when charging a system, drum should be placed in water that is no hotter than 125°F. Never use a blowtorch, or other open flame. If possible, a pressure release mechanism should be attached before drum is heated.

Cleanliness

Air conditioning systems are extremely sensitive to moisture and dirt. Importance of clean working conditions is extremely important, as smallest particle of foreign matter in an air conditioning system will contaminate refrigerant, causing rust, ice or damage to compressor. For this reason, all replacement components are sold in vacuum sealed containers and should not be opened until they are to be installed in system. If, for any reason, a part has been removed from its container for any length of time, part must be completely flushed remove any dust or moisture that may have accumulated during storage. In cases of collision repairs where system has been open for any length of time, entire system must be purged completely and a new receiver-drier must be installed because element of existing unit will have become saturated and unable to remove any moisture from system once system is recharged.

When making gauge connections, purge gauge lines first by cracking charging valve and allowing a small amount of refrigerant to flow through lines, then connect lines immediately.

Cleanliness is especially important when servicing compressors because of very close tolerances used in these units. Consequently, repairs to compressor itself should not be attempted unless all proper tools are at hand and a virtually spotless work area is provided.

AIR CONDITIONING

IMPORTANT — TEST REQUIREMENTS

The following test conditions must be established to obtain accurate pressure readings:

- Run engine at 1500 rpm for 10 minutes.
- Operate A/C system on max A/C (recirculating air).
- Run blower at max speed.
- Stabilize in car temperature @ 70°F to 80°F (21°C to 22°C).

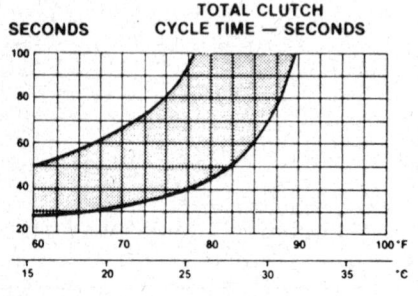

TOTAL CLUTCH CYCLE TIME — SECONDS

AMBIENT TEMPERATURES

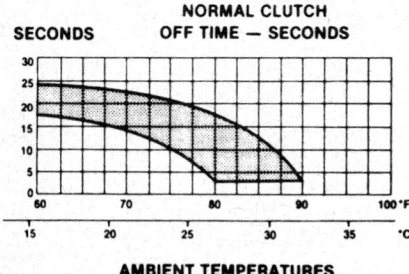

NORMAL CLUTCH OFF TIME — SECONDS

AMBIENT TEMPERATURES

NORMAL CENTER REGISTER DISCHARGE TEMPERATURES

CENTER REGISTER DISCHARGE AIR TEMPERATURES °F/°C

AMBIENT TEMPERATURES

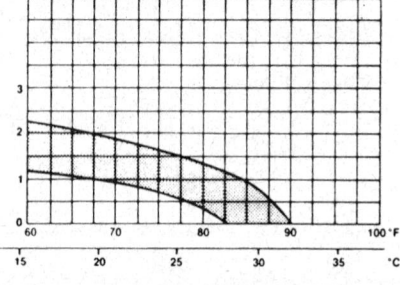

NORMAL CLUTCH CYCLE RATE PER MINUTE

CYCLES/MINUTE

AMBIENT TEMPERATURES

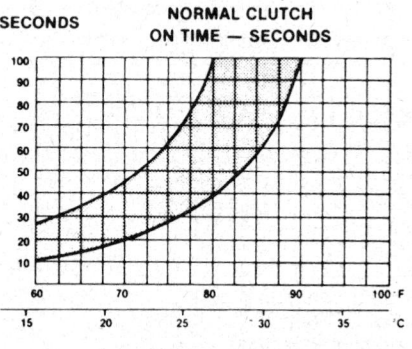

NORMAL CLUTCH ON TIME — SECONDS

AMBIENT TEMPERATURES

NORMAL FIXED ORIFICE TUBE CYCLING CLUTCH REFRIGERANT SYSTEM PRESSURES

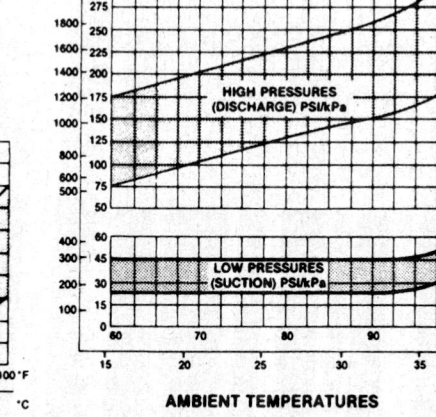

HIGH PRESSURES (DISCHARGE) PSI/kPa

LOW PRESSURES (SUCTION) PSI/kPa

AMBIENT TEMPERATURES

FM7029100026000X

Fig. 1 Refrigerant pressure & temperature charts. Except Escort & ZX2

General Service

Use care when disconnecting or connecting refrigerant lines; always use a back-up wrench and be careful not to overtighten any connection. Overtightening may result in a line or flare seat distortion and a system leak.

When making pressure inspections on systems having service valves, ensure valve is in intermediate position. If turned in too far, hose connection will be closed, a position used for isolating compressor. When closing gauge port, do not overtighten valve or damage to seat will result.

After disconnecting gauge lines, inspect valve areas to ensure service valves are correctly seated and Schraeder valves, if used, are not leaking.

EXERCISE SYSTEM

An important fact most vehicle owners ignore is that A/C system must be used periodically. Vehicle manufacturers caution that when air conditioner is not used regularly, particularly during cold months, it should be turned on for a few minutes once every two or three weeks while engine is running. This keeps system in good operating condition.

Inspecting out system for effects of disuse before onset of summer is one of most important aspects of A/C system servicing.

First clean out condenser core, mounted in most cases at front of vehicle's radiator. All obstructions, such as leaves, bugs, and dirt, must be removed, as they will reduce heat transfer and impair efficiency of system. Ensure space between condenser and radiator also is free of foreign matter.

Ensure evaporator water drain is open. Evaporator cools and dehumidifies air before it enters car.

PERFORMANCE TEST
Except Escort & ZX2

Refrigerant system problems are diagnosed by inspecting refrigerant pressures and clutch cycle rate and times. Compare pressures and cycle time to charts, **Fig. 1.** Conditional requirements for refrigerant system tests must be satisfied to obtain accurate pressure readings. If findings do not fall between lines on respective charts, **Fig. 2,** determine specific cause of improper readings.

After required repairs have been performed, take pressure readings while meeting conditional requirements to ensure problem has been corrected.

Visual inspection of system may determine problems with refrigerant system. By making a visual inspection, some of following problems can be diagnosed: obstructed air passages, broken belts, disconnected or broken wires, loose or broken mounting brackets and refrigerant leaks.

A refrigerant leak will usually appear as an oily residue at leakage point in system.

Escort & ZX2

1. Connect manifold gauge set to system.
2. Start engine and turn on A/C system.
3. As soon as system is stabilized, record high and low pressures as outlined by manifold gauges.
4. Low side pressure should be 35–50 psi. High side pressure should be 178–235 psi. As low pressure drops, high pressure should rise.
5. When clutch disengages, low side pressure should rise and high side pressure should drop.
6. Determine A/C clutch cycle rate per minute (one cycle is A/C clutch On time plus Off time).
7. Record A/C Off time in seconds.
8. Record A/C On time in seconds.
9. Record center duct temperature.
10. Determine and record ambient temperature.
11. Compare test readings with applicable chart, **Fig. 1.**

LEAK TEST

R-134a systems require use of special service equipment designed specifically for R-134a systems. R-12 servicing equipment cannot be used on R-134a systems.

Testing refrigerant system for leaks is one of most important phases of troubleshooting. One or more of methods outlined will prove useful in detecting leaks or inspecting connections if service work is performed. Before beginning any leak test, attach a manifold gauge set and note pressure. If little or no pressure is indicated, a partial charge must be installed. Inspect all connections, compressor head gasket, oil filler plug and compressor shaft seal for leaks.

NOTE: System test requirements must be met to obtain accurate test readings for evaluation. Refer to the normal refrigerant system pressure/temperature and the normal clutch cycle ratio and times charts.

High (Discharge) Pressure	Low (Suction) Pressure	Clutch Cycle Time			Component — Causes
		Rate	On	Off	
High	High	Continuous Run			Condenser — Inadequate Airflow
High	Normal to High				Engine Overheating
Normal to High	Normal				Air in Refrigerant / Refrigerant Overcharge (a) / Humidity or Ambient Temp Very High (b)
Normal	High				Fixed Orifice Tube — Missing / O Rings Leaking/Missing
Normal	High	Slow	Long	Long	Clutch Cycling Switch — High Cut In
Normal	Normal	Slow or No Cycle	Long or Continuous	Normal or No Cycle	Moisture in Refrigerant System / Excessive Refrigerant Oil
		Fast	Short	Short	Clutch Cycling Switch — Low Cut In or High Cut Out
Normal	Low	Slow	Long	Long	Clutch Cycling Switch — Low Cut Out
Normal to Low	High	Continuous Run			Compressor — Low Performance
Normal to Low	Normal to High				A/C Suction Line — Partially Restricted or Plugged (c)
Normal to Low	Normal	Fast	Short	Normal	Evaporator — Restricted Airflow
			Short to Very Short	Normal to Long	Condenser fixed orifice Tube or A/C Liquid Line — Partically Restricted or Plugged
			Short to Very Short	Short to Very Short	Low Refrigerant Charge
			Short to Very Short	Long	Evaporator Core — Partially Restricted or Plugged
Normal to Low	Normal	Continuous Run			A/C Suction Line — Partially Restricted or Plugged (d) / Clutch Cycling Switch — Sticking Closed
Low	Normal	Very Fast	Very Short	Very Short	Clutch Cycling Switch — Cycling Range Too Close
Erratic Operation or Compressor Not Running	—	—	—		Clutch Cycling Switch — Dirty Contacts or Sticking Open / Poor Connection at A/C Clutch Connector or Clutch Cycling Switch Connector / A/C Electrical Circuit Erratic

Additional Possible Cause Components Associated with Inadequate Compressor Operation

- Compressor Drive Belt — Loose
- Compressor Clutch — Slipping
- Clutch Coil Open — Shorted or Loose Mounting
- Control Assembly Switch — Dirty Contacts or Sticking Open
- Clutch Wiring Circuit — High Resistance Open or Blown Fuse

Additional Possible Cause Components Associated with a Damaged Compressor

- Compressor Clutch — Seized
- Clutch Cycling Switch — Sticking Closed
- Suction Accumulator Drier — Refngerant Oil Bleed Hole Plugged
- Refrigerant Leaks

(a) Compressor may make noise on initial run. This is slugging condition caused by excessive liquid refrigerant.
(b) Compressor clutch may not cycle in ambient temperatures above 80°F depending on humidity conditions.
(c) Low pressure reading will be normal to high if pressure is taken at accumulator and if restriction is downstream of service access valve.
(d) Low pressure reading will be low if pressure is taken near the compressor and restriction is upstream of service access valve.

FM7029100028000X

Fig. 2 Refrigerant system pressure evaluation chart. Except Escort & ZX2

Electronic Detectors

There are a number of electronic leak detectors available to perform leak tests. Refer to operating instructions for unit being used and observe these general procedures:

1. Move detector probe one inch per second in areas of suspected leaks.
2. Position probe below test point, as refrigerant gas is heavier than air.
3. Ensure to inspect service access gauge port valve fittings, particularly when valve caps are missing, as dirt accumulations can destroy sealing area of valve core when manifold gauge set is attached. Replace missing valve caps after cleaning valve core area. **Valve caps should only be finger tightened. Using pliers to tighten valve caps may distort sealing surface of valve.**
4. Inspect for leaks in manifold gauge set and hoses, as well as rest of system.

Flame-Type (Halide) Detectors

When using flame-type detectors, avoid inhaling fumes produced by burn- ing refrigerant. **Do not use this type detector where concentrations of combustible or explosive gases, dusts or vapors may exist.**

1. Adjust detector flame as low as possible to obtain maximum sensitivity. Ensure copper element is cherry red and not burned away. Flame will be almost colorless.
2. Slowly move detector along areas of suspected leaks. A slight leak will cause flame to change to a bright yellow-green color. A significant leak will be indicated by a brilliant blue flame. Position detector under areas being tested as refrigerant gas is heavier than air. **Presence of dust in pickup hose may cause a change in color of flame. If not recognized, a false diagnosis could be made. Store leak detector in a clean place and ensure hose is free of dust before leak testing.**
3. Inspect for leaks in manifold gauge set and hoses, as well as rest of system.
4. Use a small fan to ventilate areas where leak detector indicates refrigerant constantly. These areas are contaminated with refrigerant and must be ventilated before leak can be pinpointed.

Fluid Leak Detectors

Apply leak detector solution around joints to be tested. A cluster of bubbles will form immediately if there is a leak. A white foam that forms after a short while will indicate an extremely small leak. In some confined areas such as sections of evaporator and condenser, electronic leak detectors will be more useful.

Tracer Dye

R-134a fluorescent tracer dye has been added to the A/C systems of new vehicles. Leak inspections can be performed with an ultraviolet lamp and is an acceptable alternative to using an electronic leak detector. The fluorescent lifespan of the leak tracer dye is 500 hours of A/C system use, after which another injection of dye is required. A/C system pressure must be above 80 psi for the operation. Scan all components, fittings and lines of the A/C system with Rotunda Ultraviolet Lamp 164-R0721, or equivalent, the exact location of the leak or leaks can be pinpointed by the bright yellow-green glow of the tracer dye. Since more than one leak may exist in the system, always inspect each component.

After the leak is serviced, the traces of dye can be removed from the previously leaking areas by using any general purpose oil solvent. Verify the service by operation the A/C system for a short while and reinspecting the system with the UV lamp. Rotunda Fluoro-Lite for R-134a/PAG A/C Systems 164-R3712, or equivalent, may be introduced into the A/C system using Rotunda R-134a Fluorescent Tracer Dye Injector 164-R2610, or equivalent. Inject the dye while charging the system and inspect for leaks as follows:

1. Adjust quick disconnect valve on dye injector to maximum counterclockwise (closed) position.
2. Remove plug from end of dye injector reservoir and fill reservoir with ¼ ounces of Rotunda Fluoro-Lite for R-134a/PAG A/C Systems 164-R3712, or equivalent.
3. Replace plug, then tighten securely.
4. Attach low-side quick disconnect from either the manifold gauge set or the charging station to the plug on the dye injector.
5. Install dye injector quick disconnect valve to high-pressure service port on vehicle.
6. Adjust all quick disconnect valves to maximum clockwise (open) position.
7. Charge vehicle with required amount of refrigerant , then flow of refrigerant through dye injector will inject dye into vehicle system.
8. When vehicle charging is complete, close dye injector and high-side quick disconnect valves and remove quick disconnects from vehicle.
9. Recover refrigerant from dye injector and close low-side quick disconnect valve.
10. Remove dye injector from low-side quick disconnect valve. The dye injector should only be connected to charging/recovery station when dye is to be injected. The dye injector has a one-way check valve that will prevent system refrigerant recovery and evacuation.
11. Inspect system for leaks using Rotunda Ultraviolet Lamp 164-R0721 or equivalent.

DISCHARGING SYSTEM

Use of refrigerant recovery and recycling stations allows recovery and reuse of refrigerant after contaminants and moisture have been removed.

When using a recovery or recycling station, follow manufacturer's operating instructions, noting following:

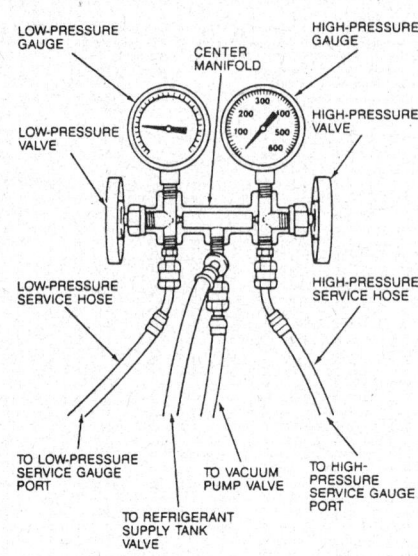

Fig. 3   Refrigerant system service connections

1. **Use extreme caution and observe all safety and service precautions related to use of refrigerants.**
2. Connect refrigerant recycling station hose(s) to vehicle A/C service port(s) and recovery station inlet fitting. Hoses used should have shutoff devices or check valves within 12 inches of hose ends to minimize introduction of air into recycling station and to minimize amount of refrigerant released when hose(s) is disconnected.
3. Turn recycling station On to start recovery process. Allow recycling station to pump refrigerant from A/C system until station pressure gauge indicates vacuum.
4. After vehicle A/C system has been evacuated, close station inlet valve, if equipped.
5. Turn station Off. On some stations pump will automatically be turned Off by a low pressure switch.
6. Allow vehicle A/C system to remain closed for approximately two minutes. Observe vacuum level indicated on gauge. If pressure does not rise, disconnect recycling station hose(s).
7. If system pressure rises, repeat steps 3 through 6 until vacuum level remains stable for two minutes.
8. Service A/C system as required, then evacuate and recharge A/C system.

SYSTEM EVACUATION

Vacuum pumps suitable for removing air and moisture from A/C systems are commercially available. A specification for system pump down used here is 28–29 ½ inches vacuum. This reading can be attained at or near sea level only. For each 1000 feet of altitude, reading will be one inch of vacuum less than standard specification given. For example, at 5000 feet elevation, only 23–24 ½ inches of vacuum can be obtained. **System must be completely discharged before it can be evacuated. Damage to vacuum pump will result if pressurized refrigerant is allowed to enter pump assembly.**

1. Connect vacuum pump to gauge manifold. With gauges connected into system, remove cap from vacuum hose connector. Install center hose from gauge manifold to vacuum pump connector. Mid position high and low side compressor service valve (if used). Open high and low side gauge manifold hand valves.
2. Operate vacuum pump a minimum of 30 minutes for air and moisture removal. Watch compound gauge to see that system pumps down into a vacuum. System will reach 28–29 ½ inches Hg. vacuum in a maximum of five minutes. If system does not pump down, inspect all connections and leak test if required.
3. Close gauge manifold hand valves and shutoff vacuum pump.
4. Inspect ability of system to hold vacuum. Watch compound gauge to see that gauge does not rise at a faster rate than one inch vacuum every four or five minutes. If compound gauge rises at too rapid a rate, install partial charge and leak test. Then discharge system as outlined above.
5. If system holds vacuum, charge system with refrigerant.

CHARGING SYSTEM

R-134a systems require use of special service equipment designed specifically for R-134a systems. R-12 servicing equipment cannot be used on R-134a systems.

Refer to "A/C Specifications" for refrigerant capacities.

When charging from small cans, do not open manifold gauge set high pressure (discharge) gauge valve, as this can cause containers to explode.

1. Connect manifold gauge set, then set valves closed to center hose, disconnect vacuum pump from manifold gauge set, **Fig. 3.**
2. Connect center hose of manifold gauge set to refrigerant supply.
3. Purge air from center hose by loosening hose at manifold gauge set and open refrigerant drum valve. When refrigerant escapes from hose, tighten center hose connection at manifold gauge set.

4. On vehicles so equipped, disconnect wire harness connector at clutch cycling pressure switch. Install jumper wire across terminals of connector.
5. On all models, open manifold gauge set low side valve and allow refrigerant to enter system. Refrigerant can must be kept upright if vehicle low pressure service gauge port is not on suction accumulator/drier or suction accumulator fitting.
6. When system stops drawing refrigerant in, start engine and set control lever to A/C position and blower switch to Hi position to draw remaining refrigerant into system.
7. When specified weight of refrigerant is in system, close gauge set low pressure valve and refrigerant supply valve.
8. On vehicles so equipped, remove jumper wire from clutch cycling pressure switch connector and connect connector to pressure switch.
9. On all models, operate system until pressures stabilize to inspect operation and system pressures. During high ambient temperatures, a high volume fan may be required to blow air through radiator and condenser to cool engine and prevent excessive refrigerant system pressures.
10. When charging is complete and system operating pressures are normal, disconnect manifold gauge set from vehicle and install protective caps on service gauge port valves.

System Service

NOTE: On Air Bag Equipped Models, Refer To "Air Bag System Precautions" Located In The Front Of This Manual For System Disarming & Arming Procedures.

NOTE: Refer To "Computer Relearn Procedures" Located In The Front Of This Manual When Battery Power To The Computer Has Been Interrupted.

INDEX

OIL CHARGE

Ford FS-10 Swash Plate Compressor

A new service replacement compressor contains no refrigerant oil.
1. Drain and measure oil from old compressor.
2. Drain oil from new compressor into clean measuring device.
3. If 3–5 oz. were drained from old compressor, add equal amount plus 1 oz. of new oil to new compressor.
4. If more than 5 oz. were drained from old compressor, add equal amount of new oil to new compressor.
5. If less then 3 oz. was drained from old compressor, add 3 oz. to new compressor.
6. When other air conditioning system components are replaced, add the following quantities of refrigerant oil:
   a. Accumulator, same amount drained from old accumulator plus 2 oz.
   b. Evaporator core, 3 oz.
   c. Condenser, 1 oz.
7. Add 2 oz. of new oil after replacing other system components such as hoses, evaporator core orifice, cycling switch, compressor pressure relief valve and pressure cutoff switch, or following minor repairs such O-ring, port, compressor shaft seal and hose leaks.

Ford SC-90V Variable Scroll Compressor

A new service replacement compressor contains 7 oz. of refrigerant oil.

1. Drain and measure oil from old compressor.
2. Drain oil from new compressor into clean measuring device.
3. If 3–5 oz. were drained from old compressor, add equal amount plus 1 oz. of new oil to new compressor.
4. If more than 5 oz. were drained from old compressor, add equal amount of new oil to new compressor.
5. If less then 3 oz. was drained from old compressor, add 3 oz. to new compressor.
6. When other air conditioning system components are replaced, add the following quantities of refrigerant oil:
   a. Accumulator, same amount drained from old accumulator plus 2 oz.
   b. Evaporator core, 1 oz.
   c. Condenser, 1 oz.
7. Add .75 oz. of new oil after replacing other system components such as hoses, evaporator core orifice, cycling switch, compressor pressure relief valve and pressure cutoff switch, or following minor repairs such O-ring, port, compressor shaft seal and hose leaks.

Ford SC100 Variable Scroll Compressor

A new service replacement compressor contains no refrigerant oil.
1. Drain and measure oil from old compressor.
2. Drain oil from new compressor into clean measuring device.
3. If 3–5 oz. were drained from old compressor, add equal amount plus 1 oz. of new oil to new compressor.
4. If more than 5 oz. were drained from old compressor, add equal amount of new oil to new compressor.
5. If less then 3 oz. was drained from old compressor, add 3 oz. to new compressor.
6. When other air conditioning system components are replaced, add the following quantities of refrigerant oil:
   a. Accumulator, same amount drained from old accumulator plus 2 oz.
   b. Condenser, same amount drained from old accumulator plus 2 oz.
   c. Expansion valve, same amount drained from old accumulator.
   d. Evaporator core, same amount drained from old accumulator plus 1.5 oz.
7. Add 2 oz. of new oil after replacing other system components such as hoses, evaporator core orifice, cycling switch, compressor pressure relief valve and pressure cutoff switch, or following minor repairs such O-ring, port, compressor shaft seal and hose leaks.

Ford SC115 Fixed Scroll Compressor

Refer to "Ford FS-10 Swash Plate 10-Cylinder Compressor."

Ford VS-90

Refer to "Ford FS-10 Swash Plate 10-Cylinder Compressor."

OIL LEVEL CHECK

Oil level of these compressors should be inspected whenever refrigerant has been lost due to leakage or through normal system servicing.

Specifications

INDEX

A/C SPECIFICATIONS

Year	Compressor Model	Refrigerant		Refrigerant Oil		Compressor Clutch Air Gap, Inch
		Capacity, Lbs.	Type	Viscosity	Total System Capacity, Oz. ①	
CONTINENTAL						
2001–02	Ford FS-10	2.38	R-134a	②	7.00	.014–.033
COUGAR						
2001–02	Ford FS-10	③	R-134a	②	6.76	.014–.033
CROWN VICTORIA						
2001–05	Ford SC115	2.38	R-134a	②	7.50	.014–.030
ESCORT						
2001–02	Ford FS-10	1.75	R-134a	②	7.00	.014–.033
FIVE HUNDRED, FREESTYLE & MONTEGO						
2005	Ford SC100	2.42④	R-134a	②	7.50⑤	.014–.030
FOCUS						
2001–02	Ford FS-10	③	R-134a	②	6.76	.014–.033
2003–05	Ford FS-10	2.20	R-134a	②	7.00	.014–.030
GRAND MARQUIS						
2001–05	Ford SC115	2.38	R-134a	②	7.50	.014–.030
LS						
2001–02	Ford VS-90	1.75	R-134a	②	7.00	.014–.033
2003–05	Ford SC-90V	1.75	R-134a	②	7.00	.014–.030
MARAUDER						
2003–04	Ford SC115	2.38	R-134a	②	7.50	.014–.030
MUSTANG						
2001–02	Ford FS-10	2.17	R-134a	②	8.60	.014–.030
2003–04	Ford FS-10	2.13	R-134a	②	8.60	.014–.030
2005	Ford FS-10	2.60	R-134a	②	7.00	.014–.030
SABLE						
2001–02	Ford FS-10	2.11	R-134a	②	6.60	.014–.030
2003–05	Ford FS-10	2.13	R-134a	②	6.60	.014–.030
TAURUS						
2001–02	Ford FS-10	2.11	R-134a	②	6.60	.014–.030
2003–05	Ford FS-10	2.13	R-134a	②	6.60	.014–.030
THUNDERBIRD						
2002–05	Ford SC-90V	1.75	R-134a	②	7.00	.014–.033
TOWN CAR						
2001–05	Ford FS-10	2.38	R-134a	②	7.50	.014–.030
ZX2						
2001–02	Ford FS-10	1.50	R-134a	②	6.60	.014–.030
2003	Ford FS-10	1.50	R-134a	②	7.00	.014–.030

① — Oil level inches cannot be inspected.

② — Motorcraft YN-12C PAG (Polyalkaline Glycol), or equivalent.

③ — See label on vehicle.

④ — With auxiliary climate control, 3.20 lbs.

⑤ — With auxiliary climate control, 9.00 ounces

CHARGING VALVE LOCATION

Model	High Pressure Fitting	Low Pressure Fitting
Continental	High Pressure Line From Compressor	Accumulator
Cougar	High Pressure Line From Compressor	Low Pressure Line From Compressor
Crown Victoria	High Pressure Line From Compressor	Accumulator
Escort	High Pressure Line From Compressor	Low Pressure Line From Compressor
Five Hundred, Freestyle & Montego	High Pressure Line From Compressor Near Condenser Fitting	Accumulator Line Near Evaporator Fitting
Focus	High Pressure Line From Compressor	Low Pressure Line Form Compressor
Grand Marquis	High Pressure Line From Compressor	Accumulator
LS	High Pressure Line From Compressor	Accumulator
Mustang	High Pressure Line From Compressor Near Condenser Fitting	Accumulator Line Near Evaporator Fitting
Sable	High Pressure Line From Compressor	Accumulator
Taurus	High Pressure Line From Compressor	Accumulator
Thunderbird	High Pressure Line From Compressor	Accumulator
Town Car	High Pressure Line From Compressor	Accumulator
ZX2	High Pressure Line From Compressor	Low Pressure Line From Compressor

BELT TENSION

Engine	New, Lbs.	Used, Lbs.
2.0L	①	①
2.5L	①	①
3.0L	②	③
3.8L	①	①
3.9L	①	①
4.0L	①	①
4.6L	①	①

① — Drive belt tension is not adjustable. Drive belt tensioner automatically adjusts tensioner.

② — 5-rib belt, 140-160 lbs.; 6-rib belt, belt tension is not adjustable; drive belt tensioner automatically adjusts tensioner.

③ — 5-rib belt, 110-130 lbs., 6-rib belt, belt tensioner automatically adjusts tensioner.

COOLING FANS

TABLE OF CONTENTS

Electric Cooling Fans

NOTE: On Air Bag Equipped Models, Refer To "Air Bag System Precautions" Located In The Front Of This Manual For System Disarming & Arming Procedures.

NOTE: Refer To "Computer Relearn Procedures" Located In The Front Of This Manual When Battery Power To The Computer Has Been Interrupted.

NOTE: "Wire Color Code Identification And Symbol Identification" Located At The Front Of This Manual Can Be Used As An Aid When Using Wiring Circuits Found In This Section.

INDEX

PRECAUTIONS

Air Bag Systems

Refer to "Air Bag System Precautions" in the front of this manual for system disarming and arming procedures.

Battery Ground Cable

Prior to service, disconnect battery ground cable and isolate as required.

Coolant

Do not mix standard (green) coolant with extended life (orange) coolant.

DESCRIPTION

Continental

The electric drive cooling fan system consists of a fan and a two-speed electric motor. The fan motor will only run when ignition switch is in Run position.

Cooling fan is controlled during engine operation by the Integrated Relay Control Module (IRCM) and EEC module. These controls activate the fan at low speed when engine temperature reaches approximately 215°F, or when air conditioning is on and vehicle does not provide enough air flow. Fan will continue to run until engine temperature drops to approximately 210°F.

Cooling fan will run at high speed when fan has been operating at low speed, but engine temperature is still more than 230°F, or during idle when engine temperature has reached approximately 236°F. Cooling fan will begin to operate at low speed when engine temperature drops to approximately 224°F. Cooling fan does not cycle with air conditioning.

Cougar

The cooling fan system consists of a fan blade with a two-speed cooling fan motor. Vehicles with the 2.0L engine have a single cooling fan motor and fan blade system, vehicles with the 2.5L engine have dual cooling fan motors and fan blades.

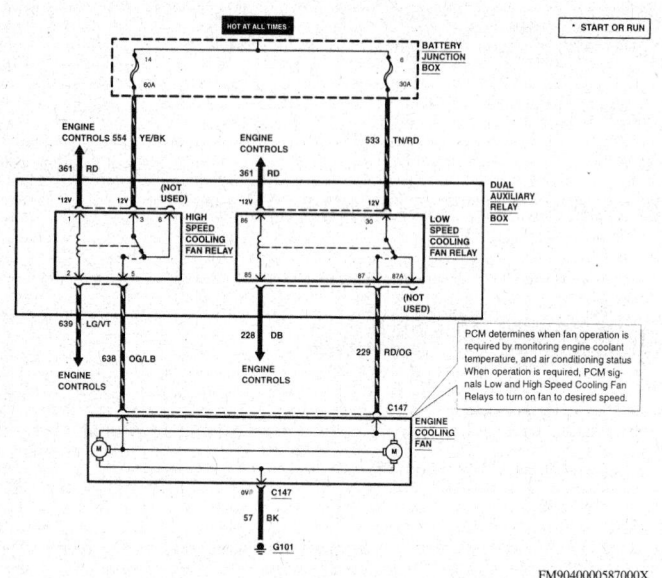

Fig. 1 Wiring diagram. 2001 Continental

FM9040000587000X

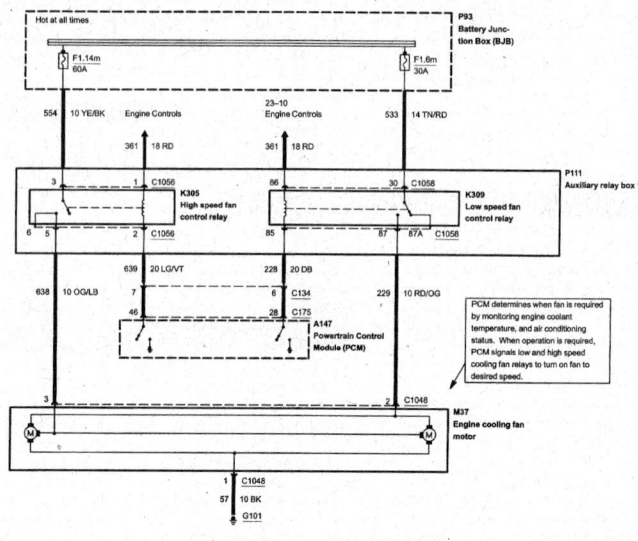

FM9040202018000X

Fig. 2 Wiring diagram. 2002 Continental

The cooling fan motors operate only when the ignition switch is in the Run position, preventing cooling fan motor operation after the ignition switch is turned to the Off position.

Crown Victoria, Grand Marquis, Marauder & Town Car

Auxiliary cooling fan motor runs continuously when air conditioning is on and does not cycle on/off with air conditioning clutch. Fan will shut off at speeds more than 45 mph when coolant temperature is less than 220°F. Auxiliary cooling fan will also operate when temperatures are more than 220°F even with air conditioning off.

Escort & ZX2

The cooling fan is controlled by a Constant Control Relay Module (CCRM), Powertrain Control Module (PCM) and Engine Coolant Temperature (ECT) sensor. The fan comes on when engine temperature is at 221°F and when the air conditioning is turned on.

Five Hundred, Freestyle & Montego

The cooling fans are controlled by a fan control module. The fan control module receives a variable signal from the powertrain control module (PCM).

The cooling fan motors operate only when the ignition switch is in the Run position, preventing cooling fan motor operation after the ignition switch is turned to the Off position.

Focus

The cooling fan is controlled by the engine management system and an increase in coolant temperature may cause the fan to operate even with the ignition in the Off position.

Mustang

This system consists of a dual-speed fan, which operates only when ignition switch is in the run position. Cooling fan is controlled during vehicle operation by the Constant Control Relay Module (CCRM) and Powertrain Control Module (PCM). Cooling fan operates when coolant temperature reaches 221°F, or with air conditioning on and vehicle speed less than 43 mph. Fan will continue to run until coolant temperature drops to 200°F, or vehicle speed reaches at least 48 mph.

Sable & Taurus

Electric cooling fan system consists of two electrical fans, CCRM, PCM, air conditioning cycling switch and air conditioning clutch coil circuit. The cooling fan motors operate only when ignition switch is in the RUN position, preventing cooling fan from operating after the ignition switch is turned Off. **The electric cooling fan may come on at any time without warning with ignition switch in the RUN position, even if the engine is not running.**

SYSTEM DIAGNOSIS & TESTING

The LS and Thunderbird models are equipped with hydraulic cooling fans. Refer to "Hydraulic Cooling Fans" section for diagnostic procedures and testing on these models.

Perform visual inspection prior to performing any diagnosis and testing procedures.

1. Inspect coolant level and condition.
2. Inspect condition of radiator, thermostat and hoses.
3. Inspect for fan blade interference.
4. Inspect for proper mounting of fan motor.
5. Inspect for proper fan blade attachment to motor.
6. Inspect for blown fuses.
7. Inspect wiring harnesses for damaged wires and poor or corroded connectors.
8. Ensure battery is fully charged.

Wiring Diagrams

Refer to **Figs. 1 through 23,** for wiring diagrams.

Symptoms

Refer to **Figs. 24 through 32,** for symptoms.

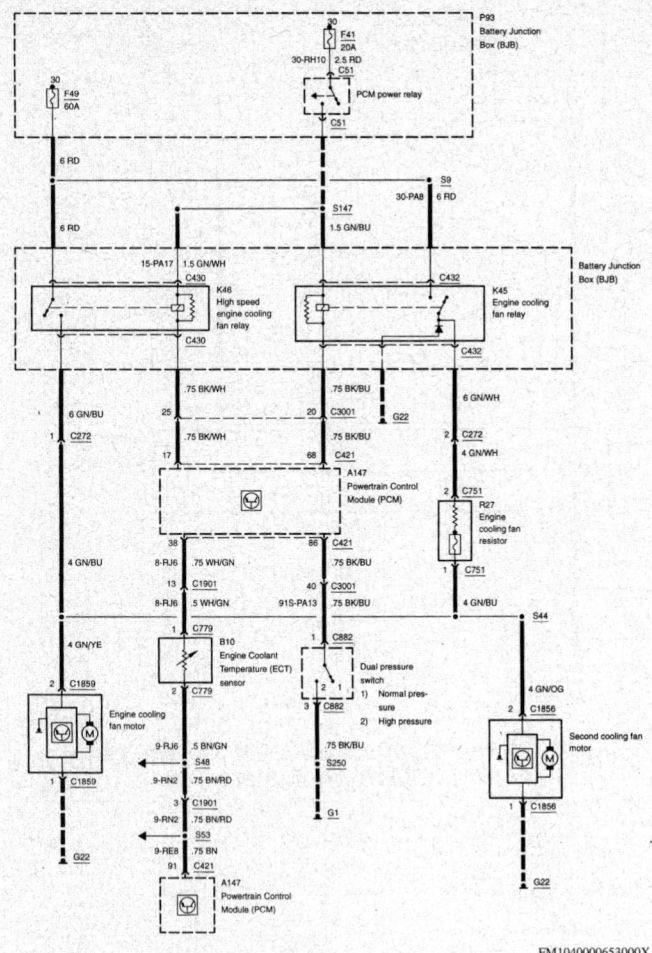

Fig. 3 Wiring diagram. Cougar w/2.0L engine

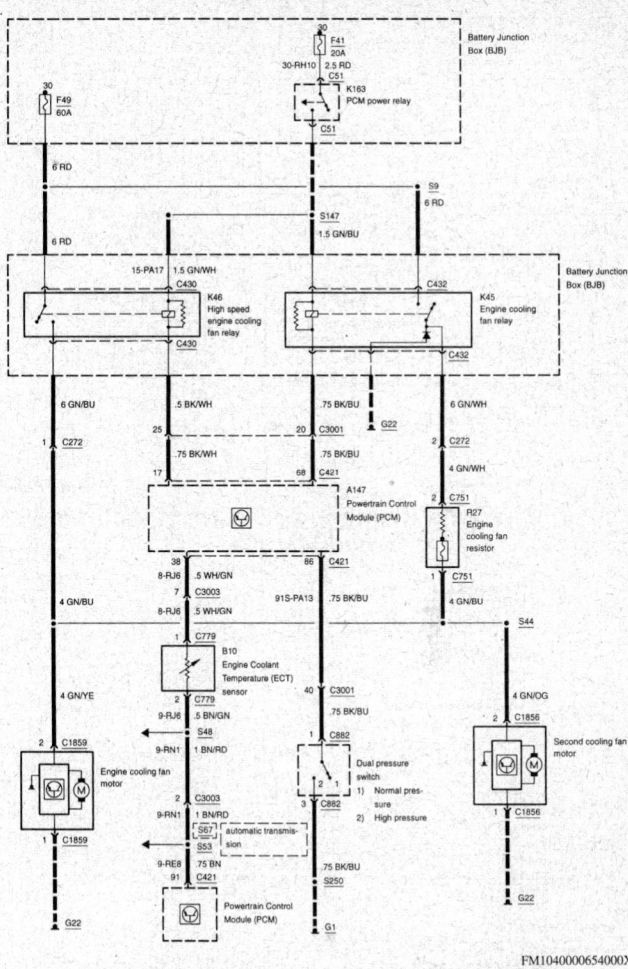

Fig. 4 Wiring diagram. Cougar w/2.5L engine

Symptom Related Tests

CONTINENTAL

Refer to **Figs. 33 through 36,** for symptom related tests.

COUGAR

Refer to **Figs. 37 through 40,** symptom related tests.

CROWN VICTORIA, GRAND MARQUIS, MARAUDER & TOWN CAR

Refer to **Figs. 41 through 44,** for symptom related tests.

ESCORT & ZX2

Refer to **Figs. 45 through 50,** for symptom related tests.

FIVE HUNDRED, FREESTYLE & MONTEGO

Refer to **Figs. 51 through 53,** for symptom related tests.

FOCUS

Refer to **Figs. 54 through 60,** for symptom related Tests

MUSTANG

Refer to **Figs. 61 through 64,** for symptom related tests.

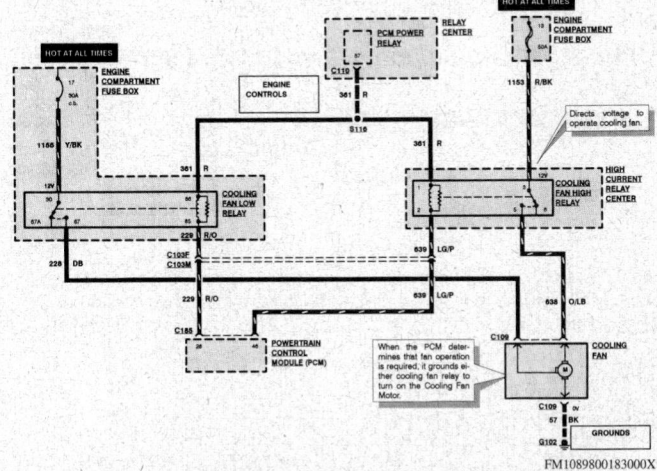

Fig. 5 Wiring diagram. 2001 Crown Victoria & Grand Marquis

SABLE & TAURUS

Refer to **Figs. 65 through 70,** for symptom related tests.

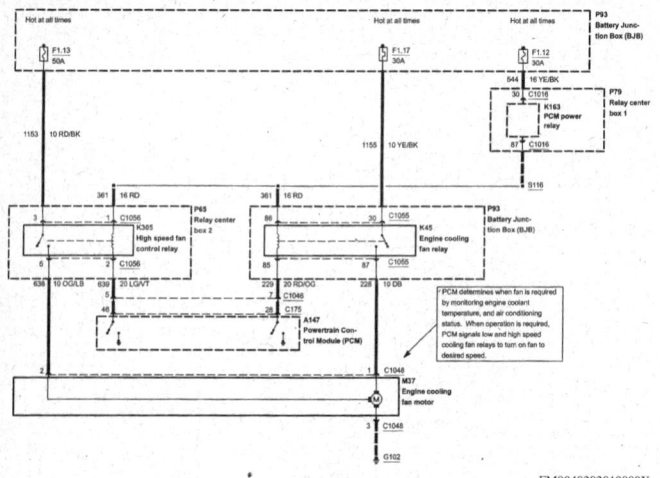

Fig. 6 Wiring diagram. 2002 Crown Victoria & Grand Marquis

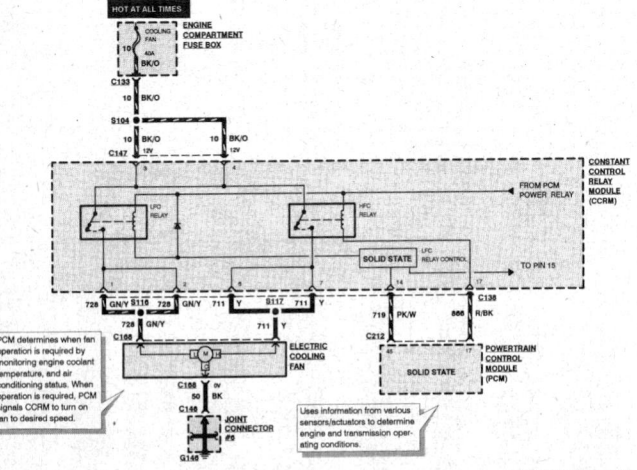

Fig. 8 Wiring diagram (Part 1 of 2). Escort & ZX2

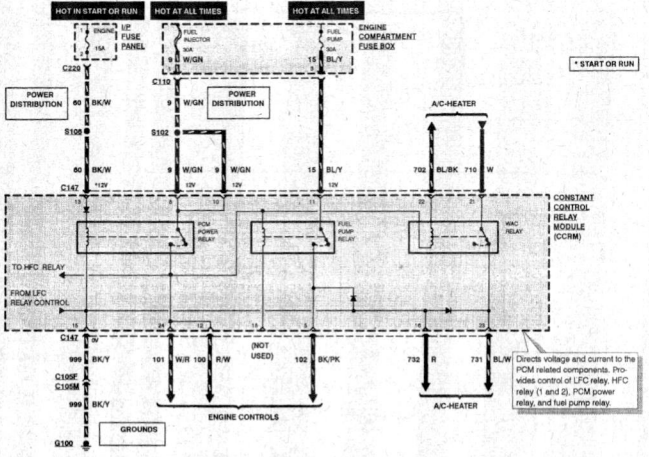

Fig. 8 Wiring diagram (Part 2 of 2). Escort & ZX2

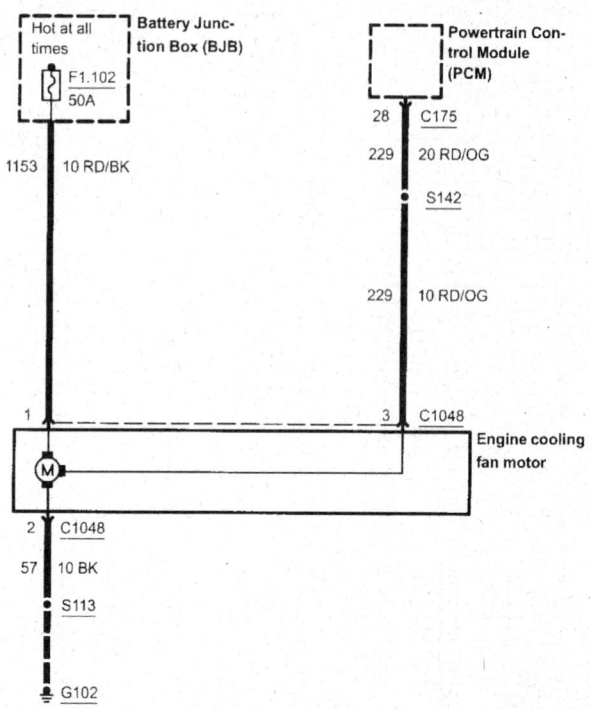

Fig. 7 Wiring diagram. 2003–05 Crown Victoria, Grand Marquis & Marauder

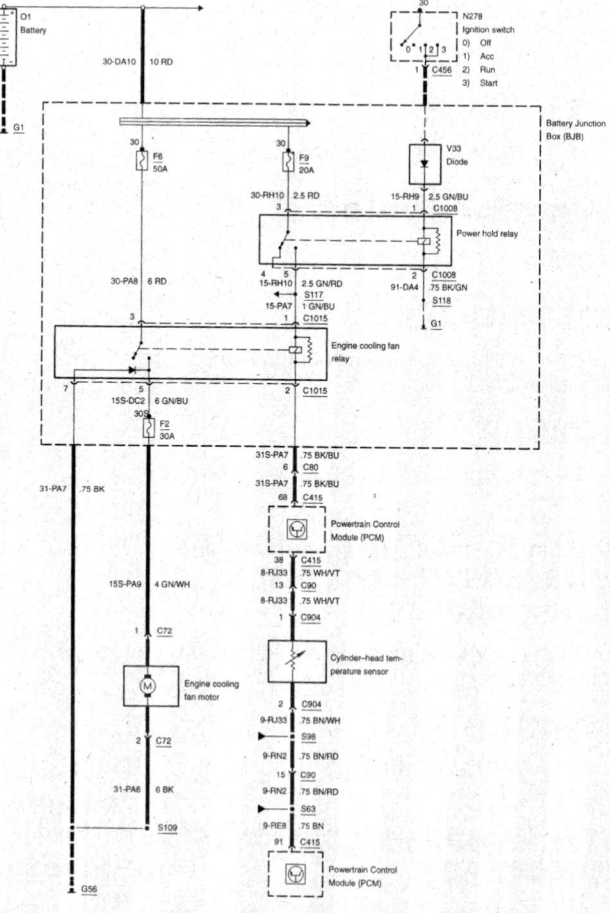

Fig. 9 Wiring diagram. 2001 Focus DOHC less air conditioning

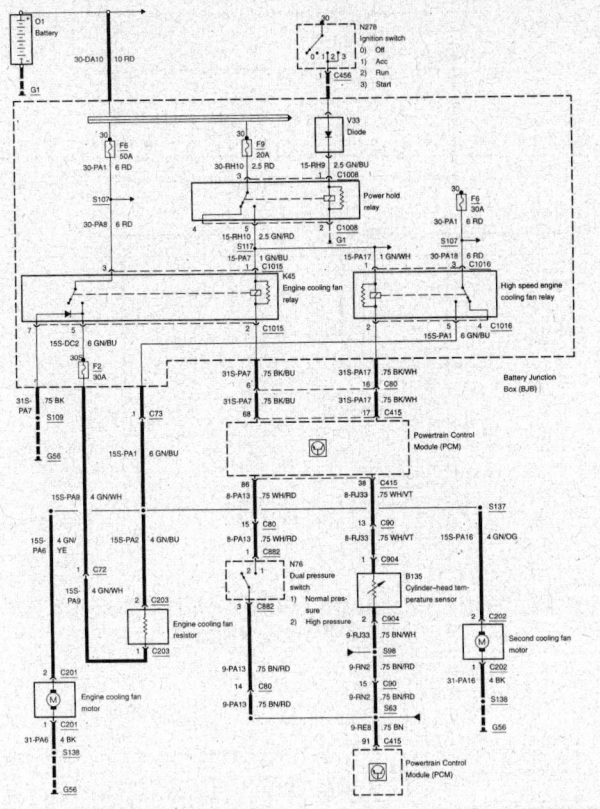

Fig. 10 Wiring diagram. 2001 Focus DOHC w/air conditioning

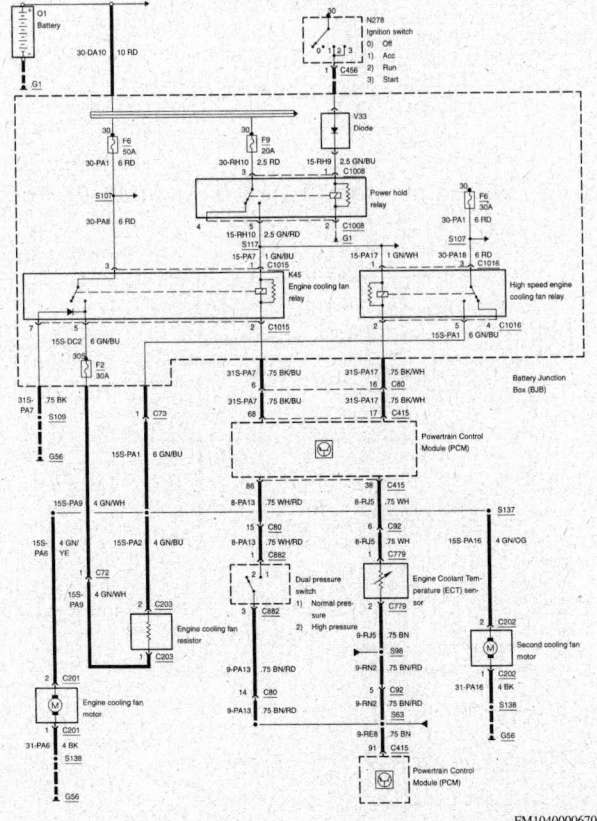

Fig. 12 Wiring diagram. 2001 Focus SOHC w/air conditioning

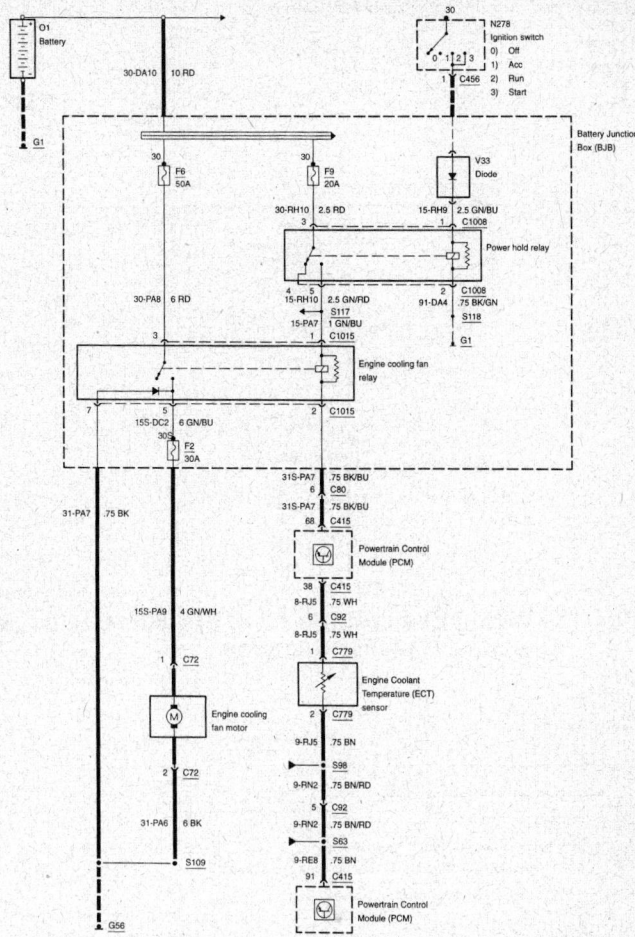

Fig. 11 Wiring diagram. 2001 Focus SOHC less air conditioning

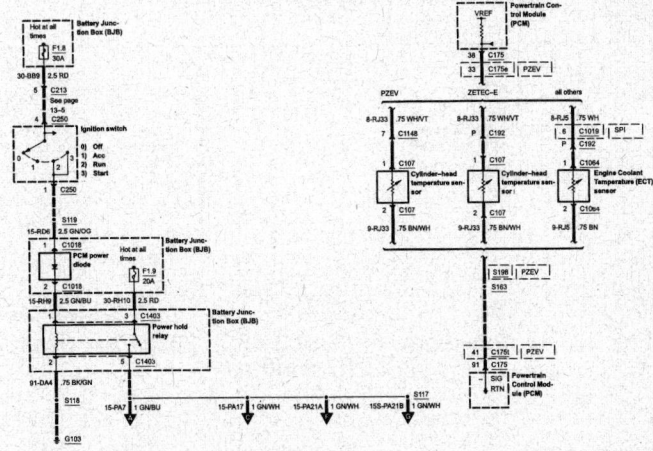

Fig. 13 Wiring diagram (Part 1 of 5). 2002–05 Focus

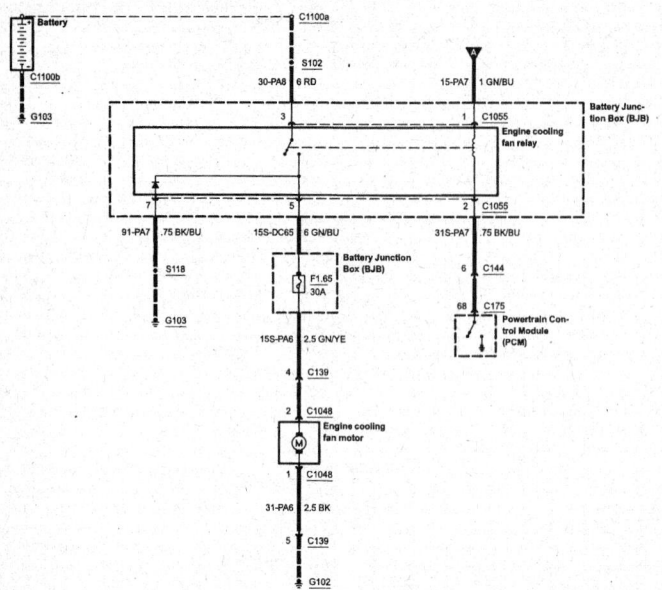

Fig. 13   Wiring diagram (Part 2 of 5). 2002–05 Focus w/DOHC engine

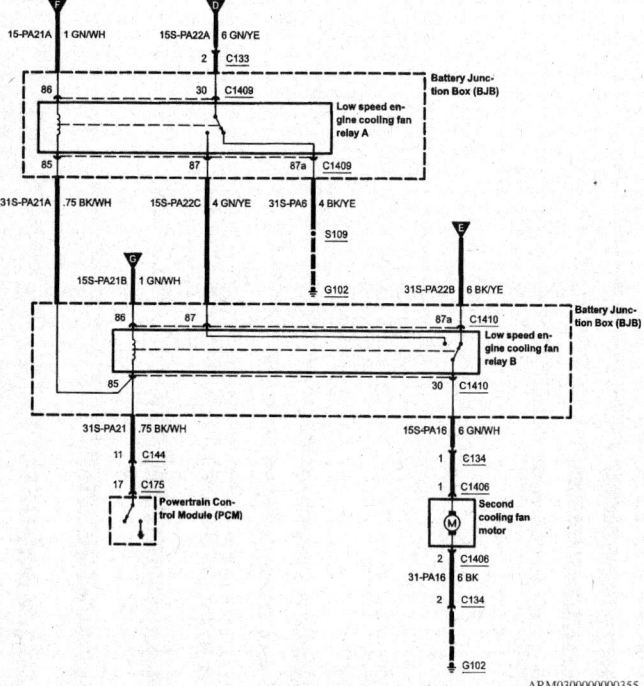

Fig. 13   Wiring diagram (Part 3 of 5). 2002–05 Focus w/SOHC engine

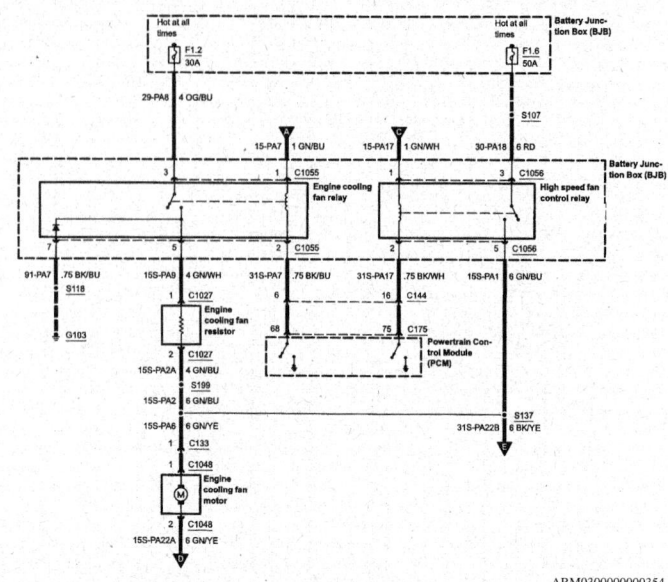

Fig. 13   Wiring diagram (Part 2 of 5). 2002–05 Focus w/SOHC engine

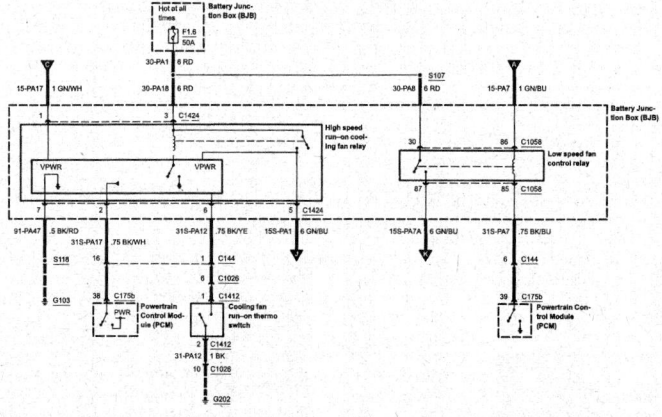

Fig. 13   Wiring diagram (Part 4 of 5). 2002–05 Focus

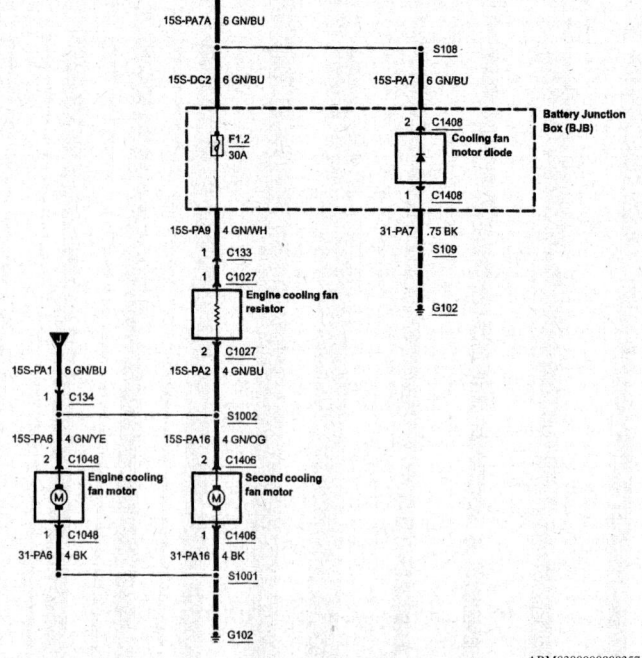

Fig. 13   Wiring diagram (Part 5 of 5). 2002–05 Focus

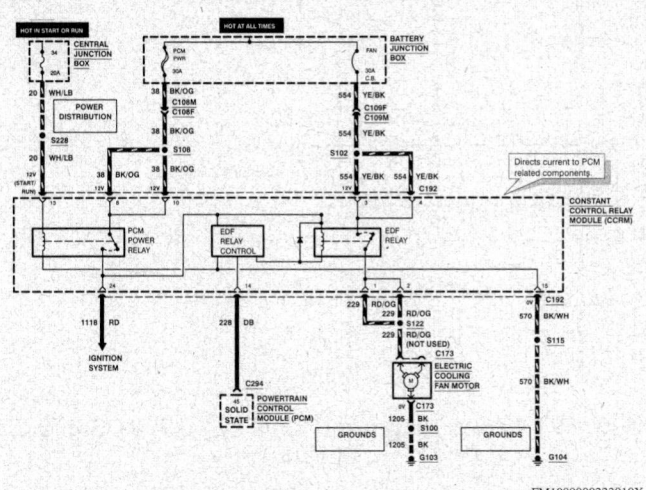

Fig. 14 Wiring diagram. 2001 Mustang w/3.8L engine

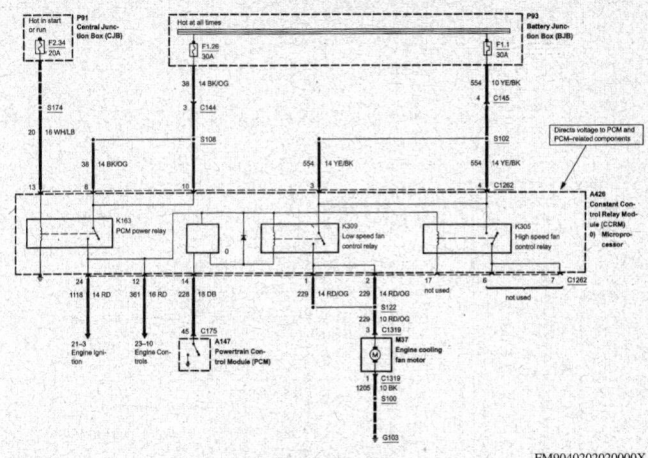

Fig. 15 Wiring diagram. 2002–04 Mustang w/3.8L engine

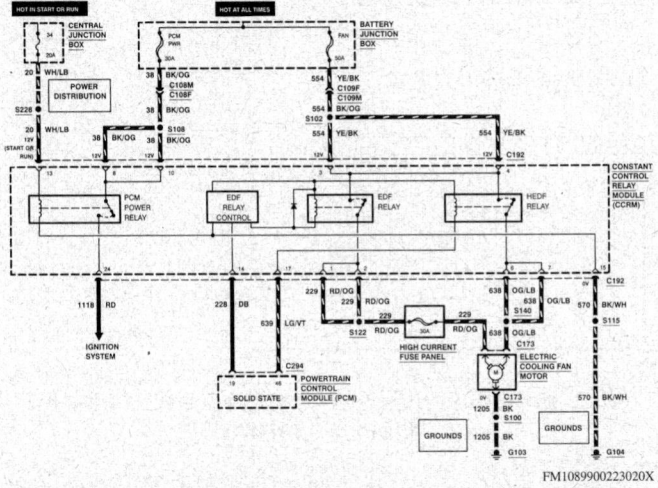

Fig. 16 Wiring diagram. 2001–04 Mustang w/4.6L engine

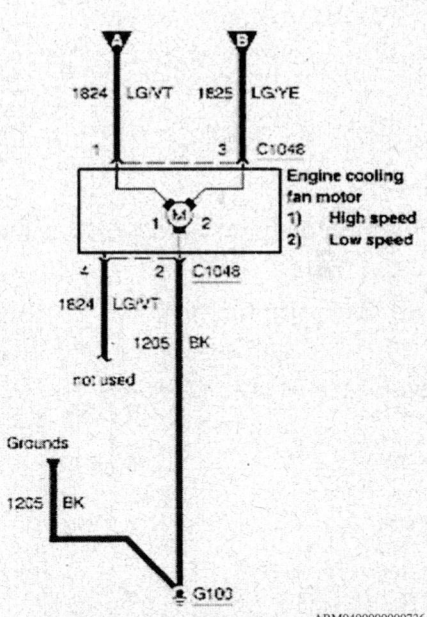

Fig. 17 Wiring diagram (Part 2 of 2). 2005 Mustang

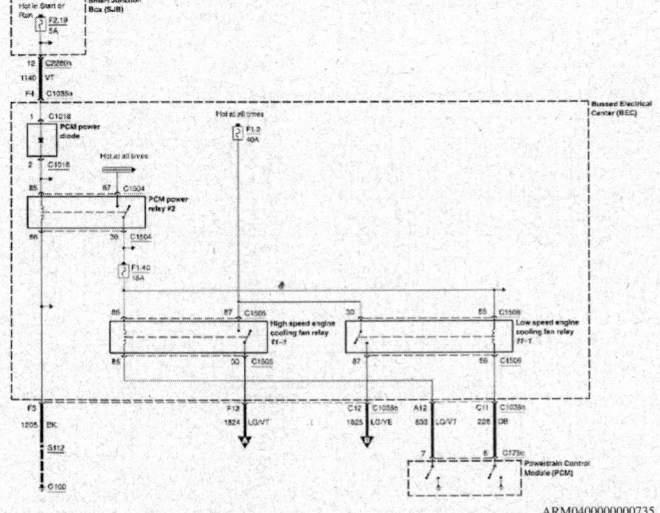

Fig. 17 Wiring diagram (Part 1 of 2). 2005 Mustang

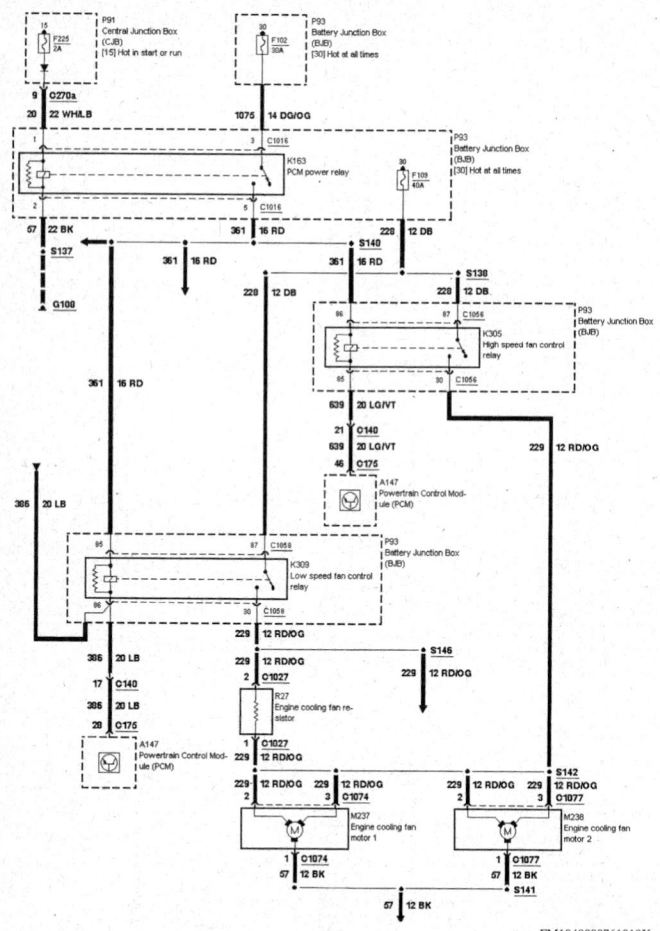

Fig. 18   Wiring diagram (Part 1 of 3). 2001 Sable & Taurus

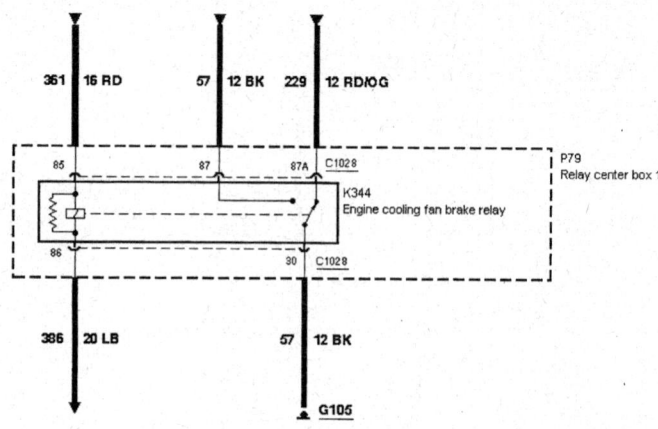

Fig. 18   Wiring diagram (Part 2 of 3). 2001 Sable & Taurus

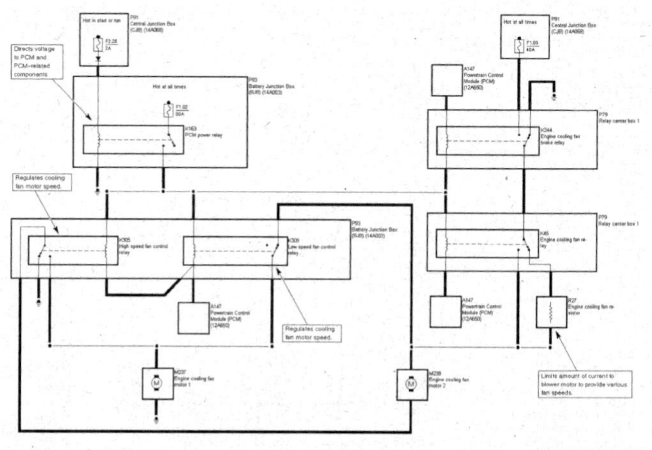

Fig. 19   Cooling Fan Wiring Diagram. 2002–05 Sable & Taurus

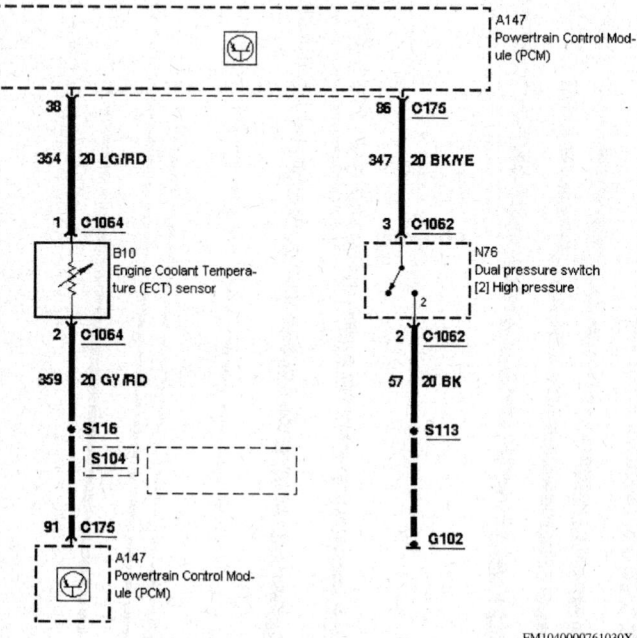

Fig. 18   Wiring diagram (Part 3 of 3). 2001 Sable & Taurus

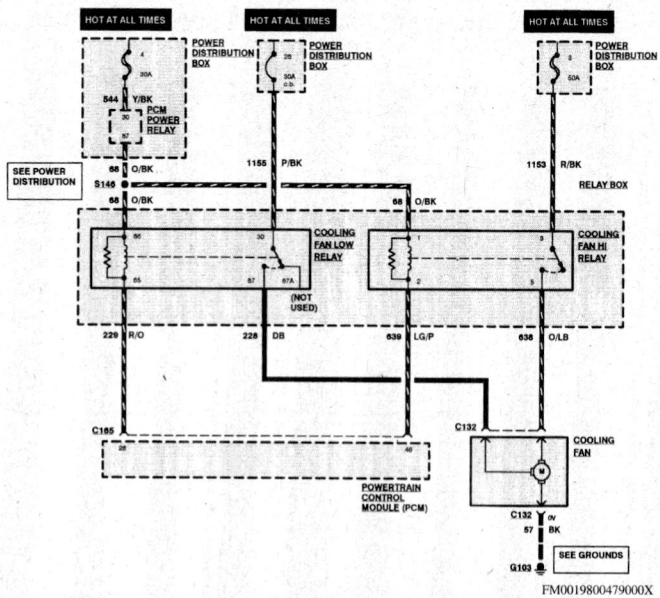

Fig. 20   Wiring diagram. 2001 Town Car

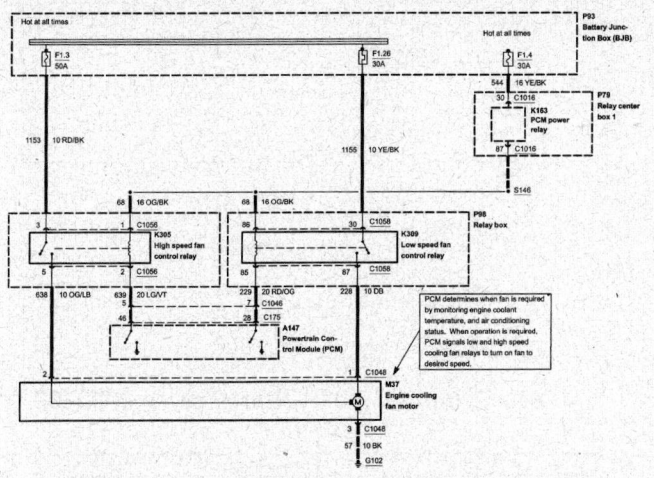

Fig. 21   Wiring diagram. 2002 Town Car

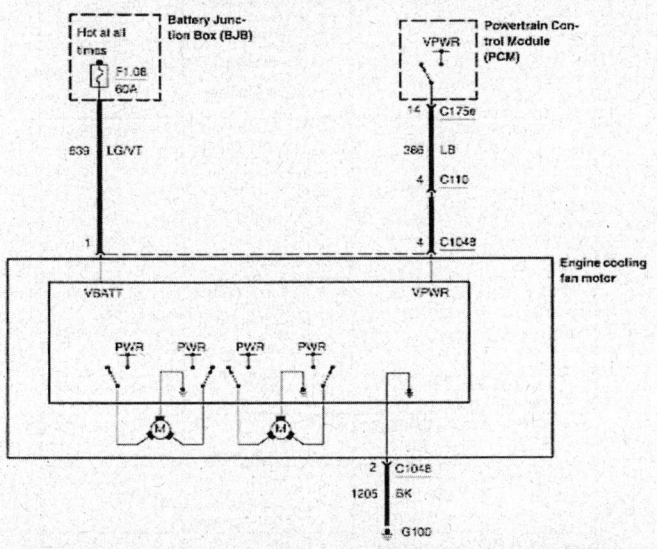

Fig. 23   Wiring diagram. Five Hundred, Freestyle & Montego

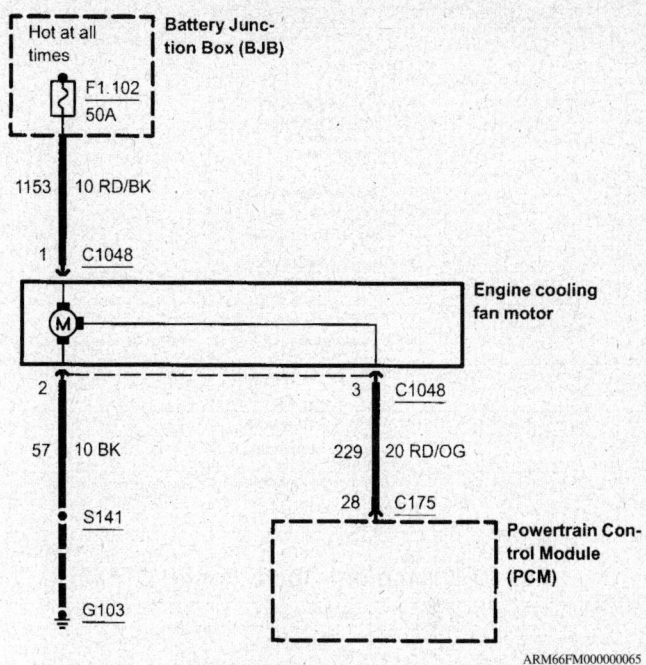

Fig. 22   Wiring diagram. 2003–05 Town Car

Condition	Possible Source	Action
• Loss of engine coolant	• Radiator. • Thermostat housing assembly. • Heater control valve. • Oil cooler. • PCV heater system. • Throttle body adapter heating. • Water pump seal. • Radiator hoses. • Heater hoses. • Heater core. • Engine gaskets. • Degas bottle.	• GO to Pinpoint Test A.
• The engine overheats	• Water thermostat. • Airlock in the system. • Water pump. • Internal engine coolant leak. • Radiator. • Radiator airflow obstruction. • Heater core. • Cooling fan. • Pressure relief cap.	• GO to Pinpoint Test B.
• The engine does not reach normal operating temperature	• Water thermostat.	• GO to Pinpoint Test C.
• The block heater does not operate correctly	• Block heater power cable. • Block heater.	• GO to Pinpoint Test D.

FM1080000303000X

Fig. 24   Symptoms Chart. Continental

Condition	Possible Sources	Action
• Loss of coolant	• Hoses. • Hose connections. • Radiator. • Water pump. • Heater core. • Gaskets. • Engine casting cracks. • Engine block core plugs.	• GO to Pinpoint Test A.

FM1080000263010X

Fig. 25   Symptom Chart (Part 1 of 2). Cougar

Condition	Possible Sources	Action
• The engine overheats	• Engine coolant. • Thermostat. • Fuse. • Circuit. • Fan motor. • Engine coolant temperature (ECT) sensor. • Powertrain control module (PCM).	• GO to Pinpoint Test B.
• The engine does not reach normal operating temperature	• Thermostat. • Electric fans.	• GO to Pinpoint Test C.
• Engine block heater does not operate properly	• Block heater power cable. • Block heater.	• GO to Pinpoint Test D.

FM1080000263020X

Fig. 25   Symptom Chart (Part 2 of 2). Cougar

Condition	Possible Source	Action
• Loss of Engine Coolant	• Radiator. • Water pump seal. • Radiator hoses. • Heater hoses. • Heater core. • Engine gaskets. • Degas bottle.	• GO to Pinpoint Test A.
• The Engine Overheats	• Water thermostat. • Water pump. • Internal engine coolant leak. • Radiator. • Heater core. • Cooling fan. • Pressure relief cap.	• GO to Pinpoint Test B.
• The Engine Does Not Reach Normal Operating Temperature	• Water thermostat.	• GO to Pinpoint Test C.
• The Block Heater Does Not Operate Properly	• Block heater power cable. • Block heater.	• GO to Pinpoint Test D.

FM1089900304000X

Fig. 26   Symptoms Chart. Crown Victoria, Grand Marquis, Marauder & Town Car

Condition	Possible Source	Action
• Loss of Coolant	• Hoses and hose connections. • Radiator. • Water pump. • Heater core. • Gaskets. • Engine casting cracks. • Engine block core plugs.	• GO to Pinpoint Test A.
• Engine Overheats	• Engine coolant weak, contaminated or low. • Thermostat. • Fuse. • Constant control relay module. • Circuit. • Fan motor. • Engine coolant temperature sensor. • Powertrain control module.	• GO to Pinpoint Test B.
• Engine Does Not Reach Normal Operating Temperature	• Thermostat.	• REPLACE the thermostat.
• Engine Block Heater Does Not Operate Properly	• Power cord. • Engine block heater.	• REPLACE the power cord. • REPLACE the engine block heater.
• Engine Cooling Fan Operates Continuously	• Constant control relay module. • Circuit. • Powertrain control module.	• Diagnose circuit as necessary.
• Engine Cooling Fan Low Speed Inoperative	• Constant control relay module. • Circuit. • Powertrain control module. • Fan motor.	• Diagnose circuit as necessary.
• Engine Cooling Fan High Speed Inoperative	• Constant control relay module. • Circuit. • Powertrain control module. • Fan motor.	• Diagnose circuit as necessary.

FM1089600130000A

Fig. 27   Symptom Chart. Escort & ZX2

Condition	Possible Sources	Action
• The engine does not reach normal operating temperature	• Thermostat. • Electric fans.	• GO to Pinpoint Test C.

FM1080000271020X

Fig. 28   Symptom Chart (Part 2 of 2). 2000–02 Focus

Condition	Possible Source	Action
• Loss of coolant	• Radiator. • Water pump seal. • Radiator hoses. • Heater hoses. • Heater core. • Engine gaskets. • Degas bottle or coolant expansion tank.	• GO to Pinpoint Test A.
• The engine overheats	• Water thermostat. • Water pump. • Internal engine coolant leak. • Radiator. • Heater core. • Cooling fan. • Pressure relief cap or radiator cap.	• GO to Pinpoint Test B.
• The engine does not reach normal operating temperature	• Water thermostat.	• GO to Pinpoint Test C.
• The block heater does not operate correctly	• Block heater power cable. • Block heater.	• GO to Pinpoint Test D.

FM1089900203000X

Fig. 30   Symptom Chart. Mustang

Condition	Possible Source	Action
• Loss of engine coolant	• Radiator. • Thermostat housing assembly. • Heater control valve. • Oil cooler. • PCV heater system. • Throttle body adapter heating. • Water pump seal. • Radiator hoses. • Heater hoses. • Heater core. • Engine gaskets. • Degas bottle.	• GO to Pinpoint Test A.

FM1080000275010X

Fig. 31   Symptom Chart (Part 1 of 2). Sable & Taurus

Condition	Possible Source	Action
• The engine overheats	• Water thermostat. • Airlock in the system. • Water pump. • Internal engine coolant leak. • Radiator. • Radiator airflow obstruction. • Heater core. • Cooling fan. • Pressure relief cap.	• GO to Pinpoint Test B.
• The engine does not reach normal operating temperature	• Water thermostat.	• GO to Pinpoint Test C.
• The block heater does not operate correctly	• Block heater power cable. • Block heater.	• GO to Pinpoint Test D.

FM1080000275020X

Fig. 31   Symptom Chart (Part 2 of 2). Sable & Taurus

Condition	Possible Sources	Action
• Loss of coolant	• Hoses. • Hose connections. • Radiator. • Water pump. • Coolant expansion tank. • Heater core. • Gaskets. • Engine casting cracks. • Engine block core plugs.	• GO to Pinpoint Test A.
• The engine overheats	• Engine coolant loss. • Towing weight exceeded. • System restriction. • Blocked radiator grille. • Thermostat. • Fuse. • Circuit. • Fan motor. • Water pump. • Accessory drive belt. • Cylinder head temperature (CHT) sensor. • Powertrain control module (PCM).	• GO to Pinpoint Test B.

FM1080000271010X

Fig. 28   Symptom Chart (Part 1 of 2). 2000–02 Focus

Condition	Possible Sources	Action
• Loss of coolant	• Hoses. • Hose connections. • Radiator. • Coolant pump. • Coolant expansion tank. • Heater core. • Gaskets. • Engine casting cracks. • Engine block core plugs.	• Go To Pinpoint Test A.
• The engine overheats	• Engine coolant loss. • Towing weight exceeded. • System restriction. • Blocked radiator grille. • Thermostat. • Fuse. • Circuit. • Fan motor. • Coolant pump. • Accessory drive belt. • Cylinder head temperature (CHT) sensor. • Powertrain control module (PCM).	• Go To Pinpoint Test B.
• The engine does not reach normal operating temperature	• Thermostat.	• Go To Pinpoint Test C.
• The cooling fan(s) is inoperative	• Fuse(s). • Circuitry. • Cooling fan motor.	• Go To Pinpoint Test D.
• The cooling fans are on at all times	• Fuse(s). • Circuitry. • Low speed fan relay. • High speed fan relay.	• Go To Pinpoint Test E.
• The cooling fans operate in one speed only	• Fuse(s). • Circuitry. • Low speed fan relay. • High speed fan relay. • Cooling fan resistor.	• Go To Pinpoint Test F.
• The run on fan (ROF) is inoperative	• Fuse(s). • Circuitry. • High speed fan relay. • ROF thermo-switch.	• Go To Pinpoint Test G.
• The LH fan operates only in high speed and the RH fan operates only in low speed	• Circuitry.	• REPAIR splice S1002 for an open.

ARM0300000000329

Fig. 29   Symptom Chart. 2003–05 Focus

Condition	Possible Sources	Action
• The engine overheats	• Low coolant level. • Thermostat. • Airlock in the system. • Coolant pump. • Internal engine coolant leak. • Radiator. • Radiator airflow obstruction. • Cooling fan. • Pressure relief cap.	• GO to Pinpoint Test A. • GO to Pinpoint Test B.
• The engine does not reach normal operating temperature	• Thermostat.	• GO to Pinpoint Test C.
• The block heater does not operate correctly	• Block heater power cable. • Block heater.	• CHECK continuity in all three power cable circuits. If any circuit measures greater than 5 ohms, INSTALL a new power cable. • INSTALL a new block heater.
• The cooling fans are inoperative	• Circuitry. • Fan control module. • Cooling fan motor(s).	• Refer to MOTOR's Domestic Engine Performance & Driveability manual.

ARM0400000000737

Fig. 32   Symptom Chart. Five Hundred, Freestyle & Montego

DIAGNOSTIC CHART INDEX

Test	Description	Page No.	Fig. No.
CONTINENTAL			
Test A	Loss Of Coolant	11-12	33
Test B	Engine Overheats	11-12	34
Test C	Engine Does Not Reach Normal Operating Temperature	11-13	35
Test D	Block Heater Does Not Operate Properly	11-13	36
COUGAR			
Test A	Loss Of Coolant	11-13	37
Test B	Engine Overheats	11-13	38
Test C	Engine Does Not Reach Normal Operating Temperature	11-14	39
Test D	Engine Block Heater Does Not Operate Correctly	11-14	40
CROWN VICTORIA, GRAND MARQUIS, MARAUDER & TOWN CAR			
Test A	Loss Of Coolant	11-14	41
Test B	Engine Overheats	11-15	42
Test C	Engine Does Not Reach Normal Operating Temperature	11-16	43
Test D	Block Heater Does Not Operate Properly	11-16	44
ESCORT			
Test A	Loss Of Coolant	11-16	45
Test B	Engine Overheats	11-16	46
Test D	Block Heater Does Not Operate Properly	11-16	47
Test C	Engine Does Not Reach Normal Operating Temperature	11-17	48
FIVE HUNDRED, FREESTYLE & MONTEGO			
Test A	Loss Of Coolant	11-17	51
Test B	Engine Overheats	11-18	52
Test C	Engine Does Not Reach Normal Operating Temperature	11-18	53
MUSTANG			
Test A	Loss Of Coolant	11-20	61
Test B	Engine Overheats	11-21	62
Test C	Engine Does Not Reach Normal Operating Temperature	11-21	63
Test D	Block Heater Does Not Operate Correctly	11-21	64
SABLE & TAURUS			
Test A	Loss Of Coolant	11-22	65
Test B	Engine Overheats	11-22	66
Test C	Engine Does Not Reach Normal Operating Temperature	11-23	67
Test D	Block Heater Does Not Operate Correctly	11-23	68
Test D	Cooling Fans Are Inoperative	11-23	69
Test E	Cooling Fans Stay On At All Times	11-25	70
2001 FOCUS			
Test A	Loss Of Coolant	11-18	54
Test B	Engine Overheats	11-18	55
Test C	Engine Does Not Reach Normal Operating Temperature	11-18	56
2003–05 FOCUS			
Test A	Loss Of Coolant	11-18	54
Test B	Engine Overheats	11-18	55
Test C	Engine Does Not Reach Normal Operating Temperature	11-18	56
Test D	Cooling Fan(s) Inoperative	11-18	57
Test E	Cooling Fans Are On At All Times	11-19	58
Test F	Cooling Fans Operate In One Speed Only	11-19	59
Test G	Run On Fan Is Inoperative	11-20	60
2001 ZX2			
Test A	Loss Of Coolant	11-16	45
Test B	Engine Overheats	11-16	46
Test D	Block Heater Does Not Operate Properly	11-16	47
Test C	Engine Does Not Reach Normal Operating Temperature	11-17	48
2002–03 ZX2			
Test A	Loss Of Coolant	11-17	49
Test B	Engine Overheats	11-17	50

COOLING FANS

TEST CONDITIONS	TEST DETAILS/RESULTS/ACTIONS
A1 CHECK THE ENGINE COOLANT LEVEL	
NOTE: Allow the engine to cool before checking the engine coolant level.	
[1]	[2] Visually check the engine coolant level at the degas bottle. • Is the engine coolant level within specification? → Yes GO to A2. → No REFILL the engine coolant as necessary. GO to A6.

FM1089800299010X

Fig. 33 Test A: Loss Of Coolant (Part 1 of 4).
Continental

TEST CONDITIONS	TEST DETAILS/RESULTS/ACTIONS
A5 PRESSURE TEST THE ENGINE COOLING SYSTEM	
	[1] Pressure test the engine cooling system; refer to the Component Tests in this section. • Does the engine cooling system leak? → Yes REPAIR or REPLACE leaking components. TEST the system for normal operation. → No The cooling system is operational. RETURN to the Symptom Chart.
A6 CHECK THE COOLANT RECOVERY SYSTEM	
	[1] ⚠ WARNING: Never remove the pressure relief cap under any conditions while the engine is operating. Failure to follow these instructions could result in damage to the cooling system or engine and/or personal injury. To avoid having scalding hot coolant or steam blow out of the cooling system, use extreme care when removing the pressure relief cap from a hot degas bottle. Wait until the engine has cooled, then wrap a thick cloth around the pressure relief cap and turn it slowly one turn (counterclockwise). Step back while the pressure is released from the cooling system. When certain all the pressure has been released, remove the pressure relief cap (still with a cloth). Allow the engine to cool. [2] Remove the pressure relief cap. [3] Inspect the pressure relief cap for foreign material between the sealing gasket and the diaphragm. • Is the pressure relief cap OK? → Yes GO to A7. → No CLEAN or REPLACE the pressure relief cap. TEST the system for normal operation. GO to A1.

FM1089800299030X

Fig. 33 Test A: Loss Of Coolant (Part 3 of 4).
Continental

TEST CONDITIONS	TEST DETAILS/RESULTS/ACTIONS
A7 CHECK THE DEGAS BOTTLE	
	[1] NOTE: The engine must be cool when coolant is added to the degas bottle. Add coolant to the degas bottle until fluid is between the coolant fill level marks. • Does the degas bottle leak? → Yes REPLACE the degas bottle. TEST the system for normal operation. → No PERFORM Pressure Test in this section; REPAIR as necessary. TEST the system for normal operation.

FM1089800299040X

Fig. 33 Test A: Loss Of Coolant (Part 4 of 4).
Continental

TEST CONDITIONS	TEST DETAILS/RESULTS/ACTIONS
A2 CHECK THE PRESSURE RELIEF CAP	
	[1] Perform the pressure relief cap test; • Is pressure relief cap OK? → Yes GO to A3. → No REPLACE the damaged pressure relief cap. TEST the system for normal operation.
A3 CHECK THE ENGINE COOLANT FOR INTERNAL LEAK	
[1]	[2] Inspect the engine coolant in degas bottle for signs of transmission fluid or engine oil. • Is oil or transmission fluid evident in coolant? → Yes If engine oil is evident, REPAIR engine as necessary. If transmission fluid is evident, INSTALL a new radiator as necessary. → No GO to A4.
A4 CHECK THE ENGINE AND THE TRANSMISSION FOR COOLANT	
	[1] Remove the oil level dipsticks (6750) from the engine and the transmission. • Is coolant evident in oil or transmission fluid? → Yes If coolant is in engine, REPAIR engine as necessary. If coolant is in transmission, REPAIR or REPLACE the radiator as necessary. → No GO to A5.

FM1089800299020X

Fig. 33 Test A: Loss Of Coolant (Part 2 of 4).
Continental

TEST CONDITIONS	TEST DETAILS/RESULTS/ACTIONS
B1 CHECK THE ENGINE COOLANT LEVEL	
NOTE: If the engine is hot, allow the engine to cool before proceeding.	
[1]	[1] ⚠ WARNING: Never remove the pressure relief cap under any conditions while the engine is operating. Failure to follow these instructions could result in damage to the cooling system or engine and/or personal injury. To avoid having scalding hot coolant or steam blow out of the cooling system, use extreme care when removing the pressure relief cap from a hot degas bottle. Wait until the engine has cooled, then wrap a thick cloth around the pressure relief cap and turn it slowly one turn (counterclockwise). Step back while the pressure is released from the cooling system. When certain all the pressure has been released, remove the pressure relief cap (still with a cloth). [2] Check the engine coolant level at the degas bottle. • Is the engine coolant OK? → Yes GO to B2. → No REFILL the engine coolant at the degas bottle. GO to Pinpoint Test A.

FM1089800300010X

Fig. 34 Test B: Engine Overheats (Part 1 of 3).
Continental

11-12

ELECTRIC COOLING FANS

TEST CONDITIONS	TEST DETAILS/RESULTS/ACTIONS
B2 CHECK THE COOLANT CONDITION	
	[1] Check the coolant for contaminants such as rust, corrosion, or discoloration. • Is the coolant condition OK? → **Yes** GO to **B3**. → **No** FLUSH the engine cooling system; TEST the system for normal operation.
B3 CHECK FOR AN AIRFLOW OBSTRUCTION	
	[1] Inspect the A/C condenser core (19712) and radiator for obstructions such as leaves or dirt. • Is there an obstruction? → **Yes** REMOVE the obstruction. CLEAN the A/C condenser core and radiator. TEST the system for normal operation. → **No** GO to **B4**.
B4 CHECK THE HEATER CORE OPERATION	
	[1] Install the pressure relief cap.

FM1089800300020X

Fig. 34   Test B: Engine Overheats (Part 2 of 3). Continental

TEST CONDITIONS	TEST DETAILS/RESULTS/ACTIONS
B4 CHECK THE HEATER CORE OPERATION (Continued)	
	[3] As the engine starts to heat up, feel the inlet and outlet heater water hoses (18472). They should feel approximately the same after three or four minutes. • Is the heater water hose approximately the same temperature as the inlet heater water hose? → **Yes** GO to **B5**. → **No** TURN the engine off. REPAIR or REPLACE heater core. the system for normal operation.
B5 CHECK THE WATER THERMOSTAT OPERATION	
	[1] Start the engine and allow the engine to run for ten minutes. [2] Feel the inlet and outlet heater water hoses and the underside of the upper radiator hose (8260). • Are the upper radiator hose and the heater water hoses cold? → **Yes** REPLACE the water thermostat; TEST the system for normal operation. → **No** GO to **B6**.
B6 CHECK THE COOLING FAN OPERATION	
	[1] Perform the Electric Coolant Fan Test Powertrain Control/Emissions Diagnosis • Is the cooling fan operation OK? → **Yes** diagnosis and testing of the engine. → **No** REPLACE the fan component determined; TEST the system for normal operation.

FM1089800300030X

Fig. 34   Test B: Engine Overheats (Part 3 of 3). Continental

Test Step	Result	▶	Action to Take
C1 CHECK ENGINE TEMPERATURE • Start engine and allow to RUN for 10 minutes. • Feel inlet and outlet heater water hoses and underside of upper radiator hose. • Are upper radiator hose and heater water hoses cold?	Yes	▶	REPLACE water thermostat RETEST system.
	No	▶	Diagnose instrument cluster.

FM1089600159000X

Fig. 35   Test C: Engine Does Not Reach Normal Operating Temperature. Continental

CONDITIONS	DETAILS/RESULTS/ACTIONS
A1: VISUAL INSPECTION	
	[1] Visually inspect for loss of coolant. • Is the engine cooling system leaking? → **Yes** REPAIR the components in question. → **No** CARRY OUT the Pressure Test.

FM1080000264000X

Fig. 37   Test A: Loss Of Coolant. Cougar

CONDITIONS	DETAILS/RESULTS/ACTIONS
B1: CHECK COOLANT	
⚠ **WARNING:** Never remove the expansion tank cap under any circumstances while the engine is operating. Failure to follow these instructions may result in damage to the cooling system of the engine and/or personal injury. To avoid having scalding hot water or steam blow out of the cooling system, use extreme care when removing the expansion tank cap from a hot cooling system. Wait until the engine has cooled, then wrap a thick cloth around the expansion tank cap and turn it slowly until the pressure begins to release, step back while the pressure is released from the cooling system. When certain all the pressure has been released (still with a cloth) turn and remove the expansion tank cap. Failure to follow these instructions may result in personal injury.	

FM1080000265010X

Fig. 38   Test B: Engine Overheats (Part 1 of 2). Cougar

TEST CONDITIONS	TEST DETAILS/RESULTS/ACTIONS
D1 CHECK THE POWER CABLE	
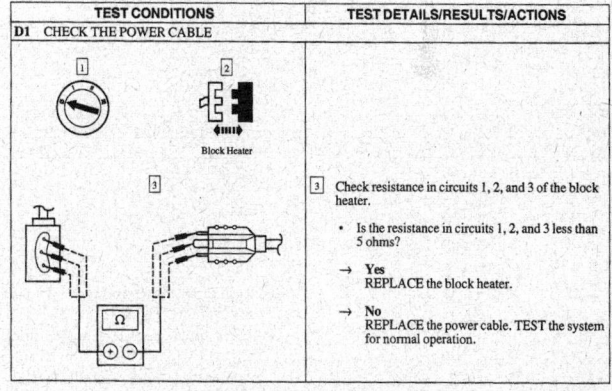	[3] Check resistance in circuits 1, 2, and 3 of the block heater. • Is the resistance in circuits 1, 2, and 3 less than 5 ohms? → **Yes** REPLACE the block heater. → **No** REPLACE the power cable. TEST the system for normal operation.

FM1089800302000X

Fig. 36   Test D: Block Heater Does Not Operate Properly. Continental

CONDITIONS	DETAILS/RESULTS/ACTIONS
	[1] Inspect the coolant level and condition. • Is the coolant OK? → **Yes** GO TO **B2** → **No** If coolant is weak or contaminated, FLUSH and REFILL with new coolant as necessary. If the coolant is low, REFILL the system and CARRY OUT the Component Test.
B2: CHECK THERMOSTAT	
	[1] Carry out the component test in this section. • Is the thermostat OK? → **Yes** Diagnose cooling system. → **No** INSTALL a new thermostat.

FM1080000265020X

Fig. 38   Test B: Engine Overheats (Part 2 of 2). Cougar

CONDITIONS	DETAILS/RESULTS/ACTIONS
C1: CHECK THERMOSTAT	
	1 Carry out the component test in this section.
	• Is the thermostat OK?
	→ Yes
	Diagnose cooling system.
	→ No
	INSTALL a new thermostat.
	FM1080000266000X

Fig. 39 Test C: Engine Does Not Reach Normal Operating Temperature. Cougar

CONDITIONS	DETAILS/RESULTS/ACTIONS
	3 Check for broken, cracked or cut wires.
	• Are the connector and wires OK?
	→ Yes
	GO TO D2
	→ No
	REPAIR or INSTALL as necessary. GO TO D2
D2: CHECK CONTINUITY OF ELECTRICAL CONNECTOR AND WIRE	
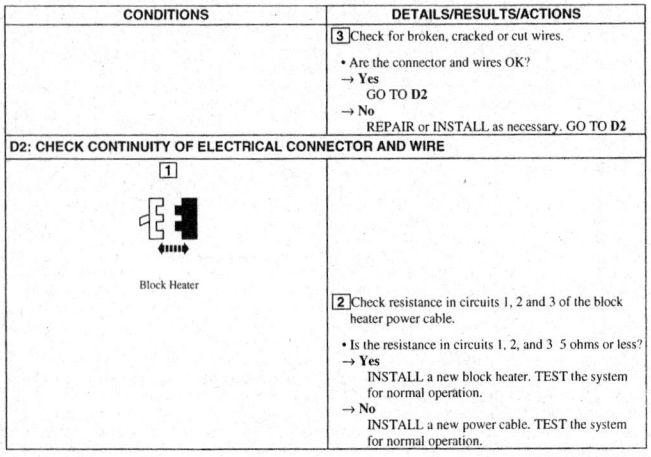 Block Heater	2 Check resistance in circuits 1, 2 and 3 of the block heater power cable.
	• Is the resistance in circuits 1, 2, and 3 5 ohms or less?
	→ Yes
	INSTALL a new block heater. TEST the system for normal operation.
	→ No
	INSTALL a new power cable. TEST the system for normal operation.
	FM1080000267020X

Fig. 40 Test D: Engine Block Heater Does Not Operate Correctly (Part 2 of 2). Cougar

TEST CONDITIONS	TEST DETAILS/RESULTS/ACTIONS
A2 CHECK THE PRESSURE RELIEF CAP	
	1 Perform the pressure relief cap test; refer to the Component Tests in this section.
	• Is pressure relief cap OK?
	→ Yes
	GO to A3.
	→ No
	REPLACE the damaged pressure relief cap. TEST the system for normal operation.
A3 CHECK THE ENGINE COOLANT FOR INTERNAL LEAK	
	2 Inspect the engine coolant in degas bottle for signs of transmission fluid or engine oil.
	• Is oil or transmission fluid evident in coolant?
	→ Yes
	If engine oil is evident, REPAIR engine as necessary. If transmission fluid is evident, REPAIR or REPLACE the radiator as necessary.
	→ No
	GO to A4.
A4 CHECK THE ENGINE AND THE TRANSMISSION FOR COOLANT	
	1 Remove the oil level dipsticks from the engine and the transmission.
	• Is coolant evident in oil or transmission fluid?
	→ Yes
	If coolant is in engine, REPAIR engine as necessary. If coolant is in transmission, REPAIR or REPLACE the radiator as necessary.
	→ No
	GO to A5.
	FM1089900305020X

Fig. 41 Test A: Loss Of Coolant (Part 2 of 4). Crown Victoria, Grand Marquis, Marauder & Town Car

CONDITIONS	DETAILS/RESULTS/ACTIONS
D1: CHECK ELECTRICAL CONNECTOR AND WIRE	
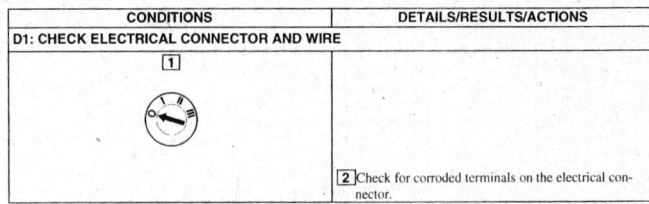	
	2 Check for corroded terminals on the electrical connector.
	FM1080000267010X

Fig. 40 Test D: Engine Block Heater Does Not Operate Correctly (Part 1 of 2). Cougar

TEST CONDITIONS	TEST DETAILS/RESULTS/ACTIONS
A1 CHECK THE ENGINE COOLANT LEVEL	
NOTE: Allow the engine to cool before checking the engine coolant level.	
	2 Visually check the engine coolant level at the degas bottle.
	• Is the engine coolant level within specification?
	→ Yes
	GO to A2.
	→ No
	REFILL the engine coolant as necessary. GO to A6.
	FM1089900305010X

Fig. 41 Test A: Loss Of Coolant (Part 1 of 4). Crown Victoria, Grand Marquis, Marauder & Town Car

TEST CONDITIONS	TEST DETAILS/RESULTS/ACTIONS
A5 PRESSURE TEST THE ENGINE COOLING SYSTEM	
	1 Pressure test the engine cooling system; refer to the Component Tests in this section.
	• Does the engine cooling system leak?
	→ Yes
	REPAIR or REPLACE leaking components. TEST the system for normal operation.
	→ No
	The cooling system is operational. RETURN to the Symptom Chart.
A6 CHECK THE COOLANT RECOVERY SYSTEM	
	1 ⚠ WARNING: Never remove the pressure relief cap under any conditions while the engine is operating. Failure to follow these instructions could result in damage to the cooling system or engine and/or personal injury. To avoid having scalding hot coolant or steam blow out of the cooling system, use extreme care when removing the pressure relief cap from a hot degas bottle. Wait until the engine has cooled, then wrap a thick cloth around the pressure relief cap and turn it slowly one turn (counterclockwise). Step back while the pressure is released from the cooling system. When certain all the pressure has been released, remove the pressure relief cap (still with a cloth). Allow the engine to cool.
	2 Remove the pressure relief cap.
	3 Inspect the pressure relief cap for foreign material between the sealing gasket and the diaphragm.
	• Is the pressure relief cap OK?
	→ Yes
	GO to A7.
	→ No
	CLEAN or REPLACE the pressure relief cap. TEST the system for normal operation. GO to A1.
	FM1089900305030X

Fig. 41 Test A: Loss Of Coolant (Part 3 of 4). Crown Victoria, Grand Marquis, Marauder & Town Car

TEST CONDITIONS	TESTDETAILS/RESULTS/ACTIONS
A7 CHECK THE DEGAS BOTTLE	
	1 **NOTE:** The engine must be cool when coolant is added to the degas bottle. Add coolant to the degas bottle until fluid is between the coolant fill level marks. • Does the degas bottle leak? → **Yes** REPLACE the degas bottle. TEST the system for normal operation. → **No** PERFORM the cooling system pressure test; REPAIR as necessary. TEST the system for normal operation.

FM1089900305040X

Fig. 41   Test A: Loss Of Coolant (Part 4 of 4). Crown Victoria, Grand Marquis, Marauder & Town Car

TEST CONDITIONS	TESTDETAILS/RESULTS/ACTIONS
B2 CHECK THE COOLANT CONDITION	
	1 Check the coolant for contaminants such as rust, corrosion, or discoloration. • Is the coolant condition OK? → **Yes** GO to **B3**. → **No** FLUSH the engine cooling system; TEST the system for normal operation.
B3 CHECK FOR AN AIRFLOW OBSTRUCTION	
	1 Inspect the A/C condenser core and radiator for obstructions such as leaves or dirt. • Is there an obstruction? → **Yes** REMOVE the obstruction. CLEAN the A/C condenser core and radiator. TEST the system for normal operation. → **No** GO to **B4**.
B4 CHECK THE HEATER CORE OPERATION	
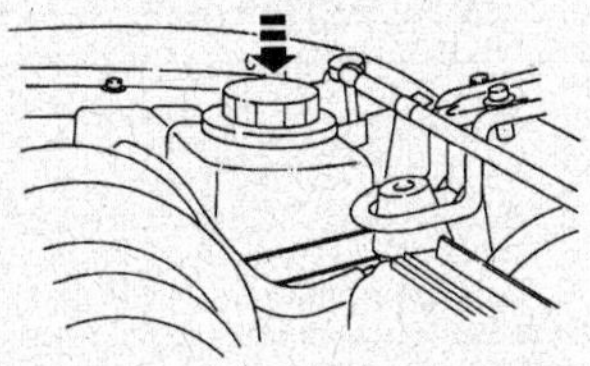 	1 Install the pressure relief cap.

FM1089900306020X

Fig. 42   Test B: Engine Overheats (Part 2 of 3). Crown Victoria, Grand Marquis, Marauder & Town Car

TEST CONDITIONS	TESTDETAILS/RESULTS/ACTIONS
B1 CHECK THE ENGINE COOLANT LEVEL	
NOTE: If the engine is hot, allow the engine to cool before proceeding.	
	1 ⚠ **WARNING: Never remove the pressure relief cap under any conditions while the engine is operating. Failure to follow these instructions could result in damage to the cooling system or engine and/or personal injury. To avoid having scalding hot coolant or steam blow out of the cooling system, use extreme care when removing the pressure relief cap from a hot degas bottle. Wait until the engine has cooled, then wrap a thick cloth around the pressure relief cap and turn it slowly one turn (counterclockwise). Step back while the pressure is released from the cooling system. When certain all the pressure has been released, remove the pressure relief cap (still with a cloth).** 2 Check the engine coolant level at the degas bottle. • Is the engine coolant OK? → **Yes** GO to **B2**. → **No** REFILL the engine coolant at the degas bottle. GO to Pinpoint Test A.

FM1089900306010X

Fig. 42   Test B: Engine Overheats (Part 1 of 3). Crown Victoria, Grand Marquis, Marauder & Town Car

TEST CONDITIONS	TESTDETAILS/RESULTS/ACTIONS
B4 CHECK THE HEATER CORE OPERATION (Continued)	
	3 As the engine starts to heat up, feel the inlet and outlet heater water hoses. They should feel approximately the same after three or four minutes. • Is the heater water hose approximately the same temperature as the inlet heater water hose? → **Yes** GO to **B5**. → **No** TURN the engine off. REPAIR or REPLACE heater core. TEST the system for normal operation.
B5 CHECK THE WATER THERMOSTAT OPERATION	
	1 Start the engine and allow the engine to run for ten minutes. 2 Feel the inlet and outlet heater water hoses and the underside of the upper radiator hose. • Are the upper radiator hose and the heater water hoses cold? → **Yes** REPLACE the water thermostat. TEST the system for normal operation. → **No** GO to **B6**.
B6 CHECK THE COOLING FAN OPERATION	
	1 Perform the cooling fan component tests; refer to the Component Tests in this section. • Is the cooling fan operation OK? → **Yes** GO to diagnosis and testing of the engine. → **No** REPLACE the fan component determined; TEST the system for normal operation.

FM1089900306030X

Fig. 42   Test B: Engine Overheats (Part 3 of 3). Crown Victoria, Grand Marquis, Marauder & Town Car

TEST CONDITIONS	TEST DETAILS/RESULTS/ACTIONS
C1 CHECK THE ENGINE TEMPERATURE	
1 2	1 Start the engine and allow the engine to idle for ten minutes. 2 Feel the inlet and heater water hoses and the underside of the upper radiator hose. • Are the upper radiator hose and the heater water hoses cold? → **Yes** REPLACE the water thermostat; TEST the system for normal operation. → **No** GO to diagnosis and testing of the engine coolant temperature gauge.

FM1089900307000X

Fig. 43   Test C: Engine Does Not Reach Normal Operating Temperature. Crown Victoria, Grand Marquis, Marauder & Town Car

TEST CONDITIONS	TEST DETAILS/RESULTS/ACTIONS
A1 VISUAL INSPECTION	
1	2 Visually inspect for evidence of coolant leakage. • Is (are) there any visible coolant leak(s)? → **Yes** REPAIR the component(s) in question. REFER to the appropriate section. → **No** PERFORM the Pressure Test.

FM1089600131000X

Fig. 45   Test A: Loss Of Coolant. Escort & 2001 ZX2

TEST CONDITIONS	TEST DETAILS/RESULTS/ACTIONS
B2 CHECK THERMOSTAT	
	1 Perform the thermostat operation component test • Is the thermostat OK? → **Yes** → **No** REPLACE the thermostat.

FM1089600132020X

Fig. 46   Test B: Engine Overheats (Part 2 of 2). Escort & 2001 ZX2

TEST CONDITIONS	TESTDETAILS/RESULTS/ACTIONS
D1 CHECK THE POWER CABLE	
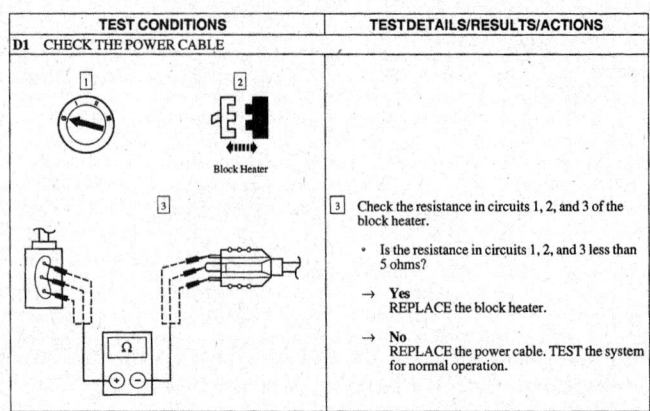	3 Check the resistance in circuits 1, 2, and 3 of the block heater. • Is the resistance in circuits 1, 2, and 3 less than 5 ohms? → **Yes** REPLACE the block heater. → **No** REPLACE the power cable. TEST the system for normal operation.

FM1089900308000X

Fig. 44   Test D: Block Heater Does Not Operate Properly. Crown Victoria, Grand Marquis, Marauder & Town Car

TEST CONDITIONS	TEST DETAILS/RESULTS/ACTIONS
B1 CHECK COOLANT	
	1 Inspect the coolant level and quality. • Is the coolant OK? → **Yes** GO to **B2**. → **No** If coolant is weak or contaminated, FLUSH and REPLACE as necessary. If the coolant is low, REFILL the system and PERFORM the Pressure Test.

FM1089600132010X

Fig. 46   Test B: Engine Overheats (Part 1 of 2). Escort & 2001 ZX2

TEST CONDITIONS	TEST DETAILS/RESULTS/ACTIONS
D1 CHECK POWER CABLE	
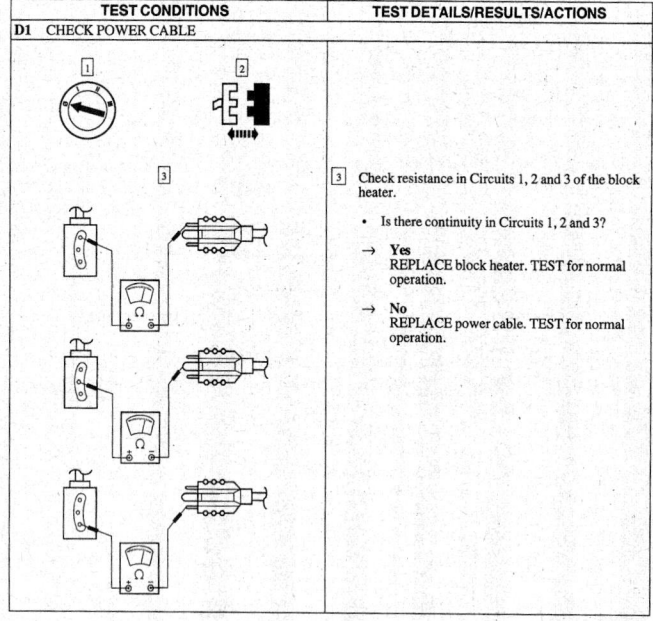	3 Check resistance in Circuits 1, 2 and 3 of the block heater. • Is there continuity in Circuits 1, 2 and 3? → **Yes** REPLACE block heater. TEST for normal operation. → **No** REPLACE power cable. TEST for normal operation.

FM1089700176000X

Fig. 47   Test D: Block Heater Does Not Operate Properly. Escort & ZX2

TEST CONDITIONS	TEST DETAILS/RESULTS/ACTIONS
C1 CHECK ENGINE TEMPERATURE	
	⃞ **Test Thermostat** • Is the thermostat OK? → **Yes** REFER to the Symptom Chart in this section. → **No** REPLACE the water thermostat. TEST for normal operation.

FM1089700175000X

Fig. 48   Test C: Engine Does Not Reach Normal Operating Temperature. Escort & ZX2

Test Step	Result / Action to Take
B1 CHECK COOLANT	
⚠ **WARNING: Never remove the pressure relief cap while the engine is operating or when the cooling system is hot. Failure to follow these instructions can result in damage to the cooling system or engine or personal injury. To avoid having scalding hot coolant or steam blow out of the degas bottle when removing the pressure relief cap, wait until the engine has cooled, then wrap a thick cloth around the pressure relief cap and turn it slowly. Step back while the pressure is released from the cooling system. When you are sure all the pressure has been released (still with a cloth) turn and remove the pressure relief cap.** • Inspect the coolant level and quality. • **Is the coolant OK?**	**Yes** GO to B2 . **No** If coolant is weak or contaminated, FLUSH and REPLACE as necessary. If the coolant is low, REFILL the system and PERFORM the Pressure Test.
B2 CHECK THE COOLANT CONDITION	
• Check the coolant for dirt, rust or contamination. • **Is the coolant condition OK?**	**Yes** GO to B3 . **No** FLUSH the engine cooling system. TEST the system for normal operation.
B3 CHECK FOR AN AIRFLOW OBSTRUCTION	
• Inspect the A/C condenser core and radiator for obstructions such as leaves and dirt. • **Is there an obstruction?**	**Yes** REMOVE the obstruction. CLEAN the A/C condenser core and radiator. TEST the system for normal operation. **No** GO to B4 .
B4 CHECK THERMOSTAT	
• Carry out the thermostat mechanical component test in this section. • **Is the thermostat OK?**	**Yes** GO to Symptom Chart **No** INSTALL a new thermostat.

ARM0300000000328

Fig. 50   Test B: Engine Overheats. 2002–03 ZX2

Test Step	Result / Action to Take
A1 CHECK THE ENGINE COOLANT LEVEL	
⚠ **WARNING: Never remove the pressure relief cap while the engine is operating or when the cooling system is hot. Failure to follow these instructions can result in damage to the cooling system or engine or personal injury. To avoid having scalding hot coolant or steam blow out of the degas bottle when removing the pressure relief cap, wait until the engine has cooled, then wrap a thick cloth around the pressure relief cap and turn it slowly. Step back while the pressure is released from the cooling system. When you are sure all the pressure has been released, turn and remove the pressure relief cap (still with a cloth).** **NOTE:** Allow the engine to cool before checking the engine coolant level. • Key in OFF position. • Visually check the engine coolant level at the degas bottle. • **Is the engine coolant level within specification?**	**Yes** GO to **A2**. **No** REFILL the engine coolant as necessary. GO to **A2**.

ARM0400000000738

Fig. 51   Test A: Loss Of Engine Coolant (Part 1 of 2). Five Hundred, Freestyle & Montego

Test Step	Result / Action to Take
A1 VISUAL INSPECTION	
⚠ **WARNING: To avoid personal injury, do not unscrew the coolant pressure relief cap while the engine is operating or hot. The cooling system is under pressure; steam and hot liquid can release forcefully when the cap is loosened slightly.** • Key in OFF position. • Visually inspect for evidence of coolant leakage. • **Is (are) there any visible coolant leak(s)?**	**Yes** REPAIR the component(s) in question. **No** GO to A2.
A2 TEST THE PRESSURE RELIEF CAP	
⚠ **WARNING: To avoid personal injury, do not unscrew the coolant pressure relief cap while the engine is operating or hot. The cooling system is under pressure; steam and hot liquid can release forcefully when the cap is loosened slightly.** • Allow the engine to cool. • Remove the pressure relief cap. • Inspect the pressure relief cap for foreign material between the sealing gasket and the diaphragm. • **Is the pressure relief cap OK?**	**Yes** REFER to Component Tests, Pressure Relief Cap. GO to A3 **No** CLEAN or INSTALL a new pressure relief cap. TEST the system for normal operation. GO to A3 .
A3 CHECK THE ENGINE COOLANT FOR INTERNAL LEAK	
⚠ **WARNING: To avoid personal injury, do not unscrew the coolant pressure relief cap while the engine is operating or hot. The cooling system is under pressure; steam and hot liquid can release forcefully when the cap is loosened slightly.** • Key in OFF position. • Inspect the engine coolant in the degas bottle for signs of engine oil. • **Is oil evident in the coolant?**	**Yes** If engine oil is evident, **No** GO to A4 .
A4 CHECK THE ENGINE FOR COOLANT	
• Remove the oil level indicators from the engine. • **Is coolant evident in the oil?**	**Yes** If coolant is in the engine, REFER to Section 303-00 . **No** GO to A5 .
A5 CHECK THE DEGAS BOTTLE	
⚠ **WARNING: To avoid personal injury, do not unscrew the coolant pressure relief cap while the engine is operating or hot. The cooling system is under pressure; steam and hot liquid can release forcefully when the cap is loosened slightly.** • **NOTE:** The engine must be cool when coolant is added to the degas bottle. • Add coolant to the degas bottle until fluid is between the coolant fill level marks. • **Does the degas bottle leak?**	**Yes** INSTALL a new degas bottle. TEST the system for normal operation. **No** GO to A6 .
A6 PRESSURE TEST THE ENGINE COOLING SYSTEM	
• Pressure test the engine cooling system. Refer to the Component Tests in this section. • **Does the engine cooling system leak?**	**Yes** REPAIR or INSTALL new components. TEST the system for normal operation. **No** The cooling system is operational.

ARM0300000000327

Fig. 49   Test A: Loss Of Coolant. 2002–03 ZX2

	Test Step	Result / Action to Take
A2	INSPECT THE DEGAS BOTTLE PRESSURE RELIEF CAP	
	⚠ **WARNING: Never remove the pressure relief cap while the engine is operating or when the cooling system is hot. Failure to follow these instructions can result in damage to the cooling system or engine or personal injury. To avoid having scalding hot coolant or steam blow out of the degas bottle when removing the pressure relief cap, wait until the engine has cooled, then wrap a thick cloth around the pressure relief cap and turn it slowly. Step back while the pressure is released from the cooling system. When you are sure all the pressure has been released, turn and remove the pressure relief cap (still with a cloth).** • Remove the pressure relief cap. • Inspect the pressure relief cap for foreign material between the sealing gasket and the diaphragm. • Test the pressure relief cap. Refer to component tests in this section. • **Is the pressure relief cap OK?**	**Yes** GO to A3. **No** CLEAN or INSTALL a new pressure relief cap. TEST the system for normal operation.
A3	CHECK THE ENGINE COOLANT FOR INTERNAL LEAK	
	⚠ **WARNING: Never remove the pressure relief cap while the engine is operating or when the cooling system is hot. Failure to follow these instructions can result in damage to the cooling system or engine or personal injury. To avoid having scalding hot coolant or steam blow out of the degas bottle when removing the pressure relief cap, wait until the engine has cooled, then wrap a thick cloth around the pressure relief cap and turn it slowly. Step back while the pressure is released from the cooling system. When you are sure all the pressure has been released, turn and remove the pressure relief cap (still with a cloth).** • Inspect the engine coolant in the degas bottle for signs of engine oil. • **Is oil evident in the coolant?**	**Yes** Diagnose engine oil in coolant. **No** GO to A4.
A4	CHECK THE ENGINE FOR COOLANT	
	• Remove the oil level dipsticks from the engine. • **Is coolant evident in the oil?**	**Yes** Diagnose coolant in engine. **No** GO to A5.
A5	PRESSURE TEST THE ENGINE COOLING SYSTEM	
	• Pressure test the engine cooling system. Refer to the Component Tests in this section. • **Does the engine cooling system leak?**	**Yes** REPAIR or INSTALL new components. TEST the system for normal operation. **No** The cooling system is operational. GO to Symptom Chart.

ARM0400000000739

Fig. 51   Test A: Loss Of Engine Coolant (Part 2 of 2). Five Hundred, Freestyle & Montego

Test Step	Result / Action to Take
B1 CHECK THE ENGINE COOLANT LEVEL	
NOTE: If the engine is hot, allow the engine to cool before proceeding. • Key in OFF position. ⚠ WARNING: Never remove the pressure relief cap while the engine is operating or when the cooling system is hot. Failure to follow these instructions can result in damage to the cooling system or engine or personal injury. To avoid having scalding hot coolant or steam blow out of the degas bottle when removing the pressure relief cap, wait until the engine has cooled, then wrap a thick cloth around the pressure relief cap and turn it slowly. Step back while the pressure is released from the cooling system. When you are sure all the pressure has been released, turn and remove the pressure relief cap (still with a cloth). Check the engine coolant level at the degas bottle. • **Is the engine coolant OK?**	**Yes** GO to B2. **No** REFILL the engine coolant at the degas bottle. GO to Pinpoint Test A.
B2 CHECK THE COOLANT CONDITION	
• Check the coolant for dirt, rust or contamination. • **Is the coolant condition OK?**	**Yes** GO to B3. **No** FLUSH the engine cooling system. REFER to Cooling System Draining, Filling and Bleeding in this section. TEST the system for normal operation.
B3 CHECK FOR AN AIRFLOW OBSTRUCTION	
• Inspect the A/C condenser core and radiator for obstructions such as leaves or dirt. • **Is there an obstruction?**	**Yes** REMOVE the obstruction. CLEAN the A/C condenser core and radiator. TEST the system for normal operation. **No** GO to B4.
B4 CHECK THE THERMOSTAT OPERATION	
• Key in START position. Start the engine and allow the engine to run for 10 minutes. • Key in OFF position. • Feel the upper and lower radiator hose. • **Are the upper and lower radiator hoses cold?**	**Yes** CARRY OUT the thermostat component tests. **No** GO to B5.
B5 CHECK THE COOLING FAN OPERATION	
• Using the diagnostic tool, cycle the cooling fans to the HIGH and LOW positions. • **Do the cooling fans operate?**	**Yes** Refer to MOTOR's Domestic Engine Performance & Driveability manual. **No** Refer to MOTOR's Domestic Engine Performance & Driveability manual.

ARM0400000000740

Fig. 52   Test B: Engine Overheats. Five Hundred, Freestyle & Montego

CONDITIONS	DETAILS/RESULTS/ACTIONS
A1: CHECK FOR COOLANT LEAKS	

	① Visually inspect for loss of coolant.
	
	• Is the engine cooling system leaking?
	→ **Yes**
	   REPAIR the components in question.
	
	→ **No**
	   CARRY OUT the Pressure Test.

FM1080000272000X

Fig. 54   Test A: Loss Of Coolant. Focus

CONDITIONS	DETAILS/RESULTS/ACTIONS
B2: CHECK THERMOSTAT	

	① Carry out the component test.
	
	• Is the thermostat OK?
	→ **Yes**
	   Diagnose cooling system.
	
	→ **No**
	   INSTALL a new thermostat.

FM1080000273020X

Fig. 55   Test B: Engine Overheats (Part 2 of 2). Focus

CONDITIONS	DETAILS/RESULTS/ACTIONS
C1: CHECK THERMOSTAT	

	① Carry out the component test in this section.
	
	• Is the thermostat OK?
	→ **Yes**
	   Diagnose cooling system.
	
	→ **No**
	   INSTALL a new thermostat.

FM1080000274000X

Fig. 56   Test C: Engine Does Not Reach Normal Operating Temperature. Focus

Test Step	Result / Action to Take
C1 CHECK THE ENGINE TEMPERATURE	
• Key in START position. Start the engine and allow the engine to idle for 10 minutes. • Key in OFF position. Feel the upper and lower radiator hoses. • **Are the upper and lower radiator hoses cold?**	**Yes** CARRY OUT the thermostat component tests. **No** Diagnose engine coolant temperature gauge.

ARM0400000000741

Fig. 53   Test C: Engine Does Not Reach Normal Operating Temperature. Five Hundred, Freestyle & Montego

CONDITIONS	DETAILS/RESULTS/ACTIONS
B1: CHECK COOLANT	

⚠WARNING: Never remove the expansion tank cap under any circumstances while the engine is operating. Failure to follow these instructions may result in damage to the cooling system of the engine and may cause personal injury. To avoid having scalding hot water or steam blow out of the cooling system, use extreme care when removing the expansion tank cap from a hot cooling system. Wait until the engine has returned to outside air temperature, then wrap a thick cloth around the expansion tank cap and turn it slowly until the pressure begins to release, step back while the pressure is released from the cooling system. When certain all the pressure has been released (still with a cloth) turn and remove the expansion tank cap. Failure to follow these instructions may result in personal injury.	① Inspect the coolant level and condition.
	
	• Is the coolant OK?
	→ **Yes**
	   GO TO B2
	→ **No**
	   If coolant is weak or contaminated, FLUSH and REFILL with new coolant as necessary. If the coolant is low, REFILL the system and CARRY OUT the Component Test.

FM1080000273010X

Fig. 55   Test B: Engine Overheats (Part 1 of 2). Focus

Test Step	Result / Action to Take
NOTE: Before carrying out the following test, diagnose any PCM DTCs.	
D1 CHECK FOR FAN OPERATION	
• Key in ON position. • Enter the following diagnostic mode on the diagnostic tool: Low Speed Fan Relay Active Command. • Command the low speed fan relay ON. • **Does either fan operate?**	**Yes** GO to D3. **No** GO to D2.
D2 CHECK CIRCUIT 31-PA6 (BK) FOR GROUND	
• Key in OFF position. • Disconnect: LH Cooling Fan C1048. • Measure the resistance between the LH cooling fan C1048 pin 1, circuit 31-PA6 (BK) and ground. 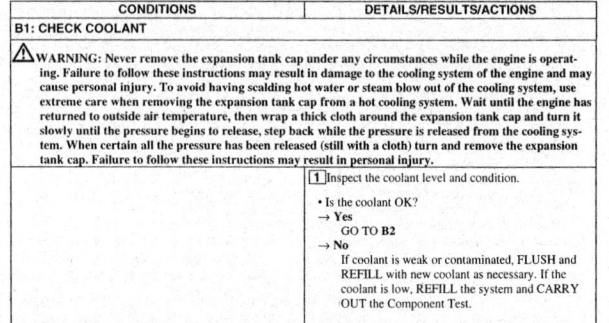 • Is the resistance less than 5 ohms?	**Yes** REPAIR circuit 30-PA1 (RD) for an open. TEST the system for normal operation. **No** REPAIR circuit 31-PA6 (BK) for an open. TEST the system for normal operation.
D3 CHECK CIRCUIT 31-PA6 (BK) OR CIRCUIT 31-PA16 (BK) FOR GROUND	
• Key in OFF position. • Disconnect: Inoperative Cooling Fan. • Measure the resistance between the inoperative cooling fan (LH) C1048 pin 1, circuit 31-PA6 (BK) or (RH) C1406 pin 1, circuit 31-PA16 (BK) and ground. • Is the resistance less than 5 ohms?	**Yes** GO to D4. **No** REPAIR circuit 31-PA6 (BK) or 31-PA16 (BK) for an open. TEST the system for normal operation.
D4 CHECK FOR VOLTAGE TO COOLING FAN MOTOR	
• Key in ON position. • Enter the following diagnostic mode on the diagnostic tool: Low Speed Fan Relay Active Command. • Command the high speed fan relay ON. • Measure the voltage between the inoperative cooling fan (LH) C1048 pin 2, circuit 15S-PA6 (GN/YE) or (RH) C1406 pin 2, circuit 15S-PA16 (GN/OG) and ground. • Is the voltage greater than 10 volts?	**Yes** INSTALL a new cooling fan motor. TEST the system for normal operation. **No** REPAIR circuit 15S-PA6 (GN/YE) or 15S-PA16 (GN/OG) for an open. TEST the system for normal operation.

ARM0300000000330

Fig. 57   Test D: Cooling Fan(s) Inoperative. 2003–05 Focus

NOTE: Before carrying out the following test, diagnose any PCM DTCs.

Test Step	Result / Action to Take
E1 CHECK THE FAN SPEED	
• Key in ON position. • Do the fans run continuously in LOW speed?	Yes GO to E2 . No GO to E3 .
E2 CHECK CIRCUIT 15S-PA9 (GN/WH)/15S-PA7A (GN/BU) FOR A SHORT TO VOLTAGE	
• Key in OFF position. • Disconnect: Low Speed Fan Relay. • Key in ON position. • Do the fans run continuously in LOW speed?	Yes REPAIR circuit 15S-PA9 (GN/WH)/15S-PA7A (GN/BU) for a short to voltage. TEST the system for normal operation. No INSTALL a new low speed fan relay. TEST the system for normal operation.
E3 CHECK CIRCUIT 15S-PA6 (GN/YE)/15S-PA1 (GN/BU) OR 15S-PA16 (GN/OG)/15S-PA2 (GN/BU) FOR A SHORT TO VOLTAGE	
• Key in OFF position. • Disconnect: High Speed Fan Relay. • Key in ON position. • Do the fans run continuously?	Yes REPAIR circuit 15S-PA6 (GN/YE)/15S-PA1 (GN/BU) or 15S-PA16 (GN/OG)/15S-PA2 (GN/BU) for a short to voltage. TEST the system for normal operation. No INSTALL a new high speed fan relay. TEST the system for normal operation.

ARM0300000000331

Fig. 58   Test E: Cooling Fans Are On At All Times. 2003–05 Focus

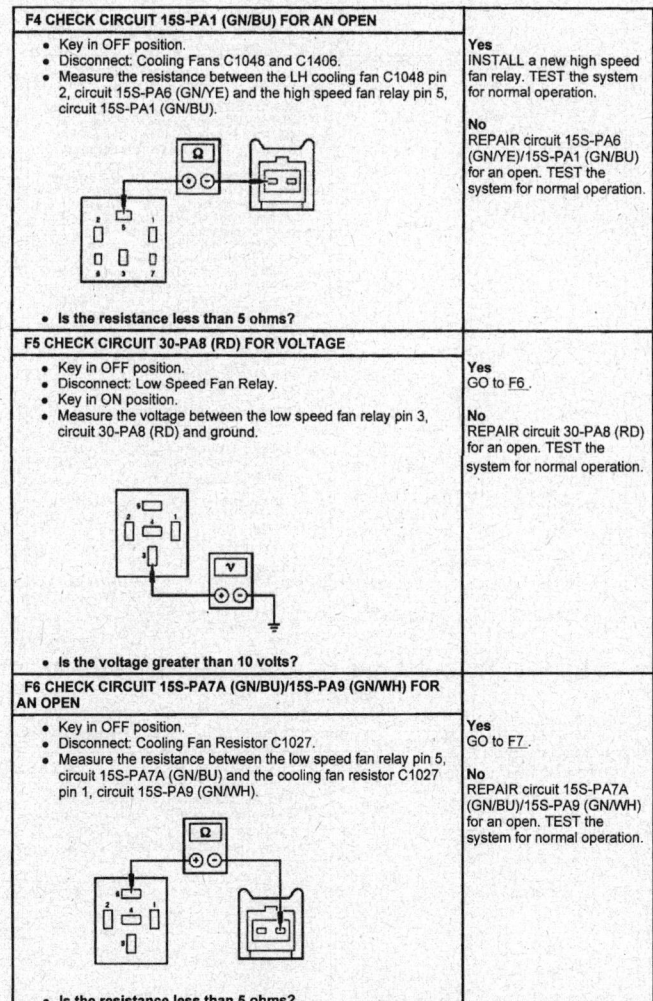

F4 CHECK CIRCUIT 15S-PA1 (GN/BU) FOR AN OPEN	
• Key in OFF position. • Disconnect: Cooling Fans C1048 and C1406. • Measure the resistance between the LH cooling fan C1048 pin 2, circuit 15S-PA6 (GN/YE) and the high speed fan relay pin 5, circuit 15S-PA1 (GN/BU). • Is the resistance less than 5 ohms?	Yes INSTALL a new high speed fan relay. TEST the system for normal operation. No REPAIR circuit 15S-PA6 (GN/YE)/15S-PA1 (GN/BU) for an open. TEST the system for normal operation.
F5 CHECK CIRCUIT 30-PA8 (RD) FOR VOLTAGE	
• Key in OFF position. • Disconnect: Low Speed Fan Relay. • Key in ON position. • Measure the voltage between the low speed fan relay pin 3, circuit 30-PA8 (RD) and ground. • Is the voltage greater than 10 volts?	Yes GO to F6 . No REPAIR circuit 30-PA8 (RD) for an open. TEST the system for normal operation.
F6 CHECK CIRCUIT 15S-PA7A (GN/BU)/15S-PA9 (GN/WH) FOR AN OPEN	
• Key in OFF position. • Disconnect: Cooling Fan Resistor C1027. • Measure the resistance between the low speed fan relay pin 5, circuit 15S-PA7A (GN/BU) and the cooling fan resistor C1027 pin 1, circuit 15S-PA9 (GN/WH). • Is the resistance less than 5 ohms?	Yes GO to F7 . No REPAIR circuit 15S-PA7A (GN/BU)/15S-PA9 (GN/WH) for an open. TEST the system for normal operation.

ARM0300000000333

Fig. 59   Test F: Cooling Fans Operate In One Speed Only (Part 2 of 3). 2003–05 Focus

NOTE: Before carrying out the following test, diagnose any PCM DTCs.

Test Step	Result / Action to Take
F1 CHECK FOR FAN LOW SPEED OPERATION	
• Key in ON position. • Enter the following diagnostic mode on the diagnostic tool: Low Speed Fan Relay Active Command. • Command the low speed fan relay ON. • Command the high speed fan relay ON. • Do the fans operate in low speed only?	Yes GO to F2 . No GO to F5 .
F2 CHECK CIRCUIT 91-PA47 (BK/RD) FOR GROUND	
• Key in OFF position. • Disconnect: High Speed Fan Relay. • Measure the resistance between the high speed fan relay pin 6, circuit 91-PA47 (BK/RD) and ground. • Is the resistance less than 5 ohms?	Yes GO to F3 . No REPAIR circuit 91-PA47 (BK/RD) for an open. TEST the system for normal operation.
F3 CHECK CIRCUIT 30-PA18 (RD) FOR VOLTAGE	
• Key in ON position. • Measure the voltage between the high speed fan relay pin 3, circuit 30-PA18 (RD) and ground. • Is the voltage greater than 10 volts?	Yes GO to F4 . No REPAIR circuit 30-PA18 (RD) for an open. TEST the system for normal operation.

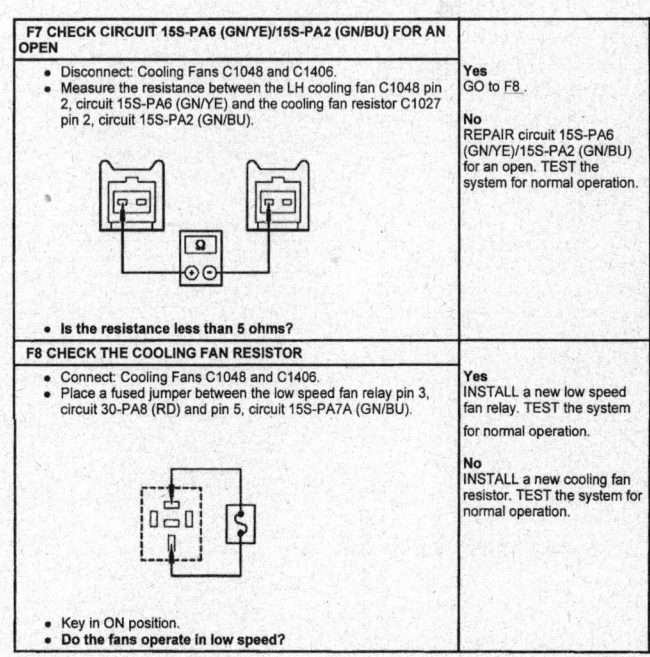

ARM0300000000332

Fig. 59   Test F: Cooling Fans Operate In One Speed Only (Part 1 of 3). 2003–05 Focus

F7 CHECK CIRCUIT 15S-PA6 (GN/YE)/15S-PA2 (GN/BU) FOR AN OPEN	
• Disconnect: Cooling Fans C1048 and C1406. • Measure the resistance between the LH cooling fan C1048 pin 2, circuit 15S-PA6 (GN/YE) and the cooling fan resistor C1027 pin 2, circuit 15S-PA2 (GN/BU). • Is the resistance less than 5 ohms?	Yes GO to F8 . No REPAIR circuit 15S-PA6 (GN/YE)/15S-PA2 (GN/BU) for an open. TEST the system for normal operation.
F8 CHECK THE COOLING FAN RESISTOR	
• Connect: Cooling Fans C1048 and C1406. • Place a fused jumper between the low speed fan relay pin 3, circuit 30-PA8 (RD) and pin 5, circuit 15S-PA7A (GN/BU). • Key in ON position. • Do the fans operate in low speed?	Yes INSTALL a new low speed fan relay. TEST the system for normal operation. No INSTALL a new cooling fan resistor. TEST the system for normal operation.

ARM0300000000334

Fig. 59   Test F: Cooling Fans Operate In One Speed Only (Part 3 of 3). 2003–05 Focus

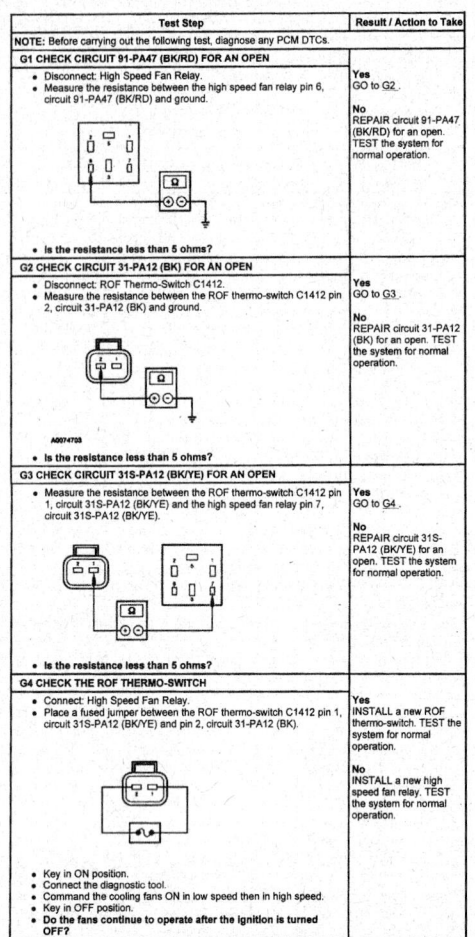

Test Step	Result / Action to Take
NOTE: Before carrying out the following test, diagnose any PCM DTCs.	
G1 CHECK CIRCUIT 91-PA47 (BK/RD) FOR AN OPEN	
• Disconnect: High Speed Fan Relay. • Measure the resistance between the high speed fan relay pin 6, circuit 91-PA47 (BK/RD) and ground. • Is the resistance less than 5 ohms?	**Yes** GO to G2. **No** REPAIR circuit 91-PA47 (BK/RD) for an open. TEST the system for normal operation.
G2 CHECK CIRCUIT 31-PA12 (BK) FOR AN OPEN	
• Disconnect: ROF Thermo-Switch C1412. • Measure the resistance between the ROF thermo-switch C1412 pin 2, circuit 31-PA12 (BK) and ground. • Is the resistance less than 5 ohms?	**Yes** GO to G3. **No** REPAIR circuit 31-PA12 (BK) for an open. TEST the system for normal operation.
G3 CHECK CIRCUIT 31S-PA12 (BK/YE) FOR AN OPEN	
• Measure the resistance between the ROF thermo-switch C1412 pin 1, circuit 31S-PA12 (BK/YE) and the high speed fan relay pin 7, circuit 31S-PA12 (BK/YE). • Is the resistance less than 5 ohms?	**Yes** GO to G4. **No** REPAIR circuit 31S-PA12 (BK/YE) for an open. TEST the system for normal operation.
G4 CHECK THE ROF THERMO-SWITCH	
• Connect: High Speed Fan Relay. • Place a fused jumper between the ROF thermo-switch C1412 pin 1, circuit 31S-PA12 (BK/YE) and pin 2, circuit 31-PA12 (BK).	**Yes** INSTALL a new ROF thermo-switch. TEST the system for normal operation. **No** INSTALL a new high speed fan relay. TEST the system for normal operation.
• Key in ON position. • Connect the diagnostic tool. • Command the cooling fans ON in low speed then in high speed. • Key in OFF position. • Do the fans continue to operate after the ignition is turned OFF?	

ARM0300000000335

Fig. 60 Test G: Run On Fan Is Inoperative. 2003–05 Focus

TEST CONDITIONS	TESTDETAILS/RESULTS/ACTIONS
A2 CHECK THE PRESSURE RELIEF CAP	
	1 Carry out the Cap—3.8L or Cap—4.6L test • Is pressure relief/radiator cap OK? → **Yes** GO to A3. → **No** INSTALL a new pressure relief/radiator cap. TEST the system for normal operation.
A3 CHECK THE ENGINE COOLANT FOR INTERNAL LEAK	
	2 Inspect the engine coolant in degas bottle/coolant expansion tank for signs of transmission fluid or engine oil. • Is oil or transmission fluid evident in the coolant? → **Yes** If engine oil is evident If transmission fluid is evident, REPAIR or INSTALL a new radiator as necessary. → **No** GO to A4.
A4 CHECK THE ENGINE AND THE TRANSMISSION FOR COOLANT	
	1 Remove the oil level dipstick from the engine and the transmission. • Is coolant evident in the oil or transmission fluid? → **Yes** If coolant is in engine If coolant is in transmission, REPAIR or INSTALL a new radiator as necessary. → **No** GO to A5.

FM1089900204020X

Fig. 61 Test A: Loss Of Coolant (Part 2 of 4). Mustang

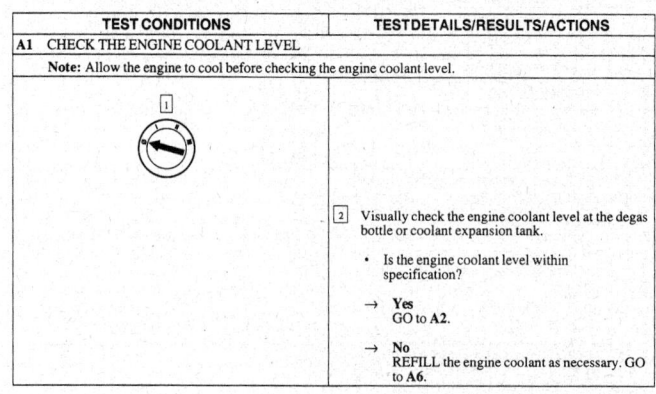

TEST CONDITIONS	TESTDETAILS/RESULTS/ACTIONS
A1 CHECK THE ENGINE COOLANT LEVEL	
Note: Allow the engine to cool before checking the engine coolant level.	
	2 Visually check the engine coolant level at the degas bottle or coolant expansion tank. • Is the engine coolant level within specification? → **Yes** GO to A2. → **No** REFILL the engine coolant as necessary. GO to A6.

FM1089900204010X

Fig. 61 Test A: Loss Of Coolant (Part 1 of 4). Mustang

TEST CONDITIONS	TESTDETAILS/RESULTS/ACTIONS
A5 PRESSURE TEST THE ENGINE COOLING SYSTEM	
	1 Pressure test the engine cooling system; go to Component Tests in this section. • Does the engine cooling system leak? → **Yes** REPAIR or install new components. TEST the system for normal operation. → **No** The cooling system is operational. RETURN to the Symptom Chart.
A6 CHECK THE COOLANT RECOVERY SYSTEM	
	1 ⚠ WARNING: Never remove the pressure relief cap/radiator cap under any conditions while the engine is operating. Failure to follow these instructions could result in damage to the cooling system or engine and/or personal injury. To avoid having scalding hot coolant or steam blow out of the cooling system, use extreme care when removing the pressure relief cap from a hot degas bottle or the radiator cap from the radiator. Wait until the engine has cooled, then wrap a thick cloth around the pressure relief cap and turn it slowly one turn (counterclockwise) or with a thick cloth around the radiator cap turn the radiator cap (counterclockwise) slowly to the first pressure stop, step back while the pressure is released from the cooling system. When certain all the pressure has been released, remove the pressure relief cap/radiator cap (still with a cloth). Allow the engine to cool. 2 Remove the pressure relief cap/radiator cap. 3 Inspect the pressure relief cap/radiator cap for foreign material between the sealing gasket and the diaphragm. • Is the pressure relief cap/radiator cap OK? → **Yes** GO to A7. → **No** CLEAN the pressure relief cap/radiator cap or INSTALL a new cap. TEST the system for normal operation. GO to A1.

FM1089900204030X

Fig. 61 Test A: Loss Of Coolant (Part 3 of 4). Mustang

TEST CONDITIONS	TESTDETAILS/RESULTS/ACTIONS
A7 CHECK THE DEGAS BOTTLE/COOLANT EXPANSION TANK	
	1 Note: The engine must be cool when coolant is added to the degas bottle/coolant expansion tank. Add coolant to the degas bottle/coolant expansion tank until the fluid is between the coolant fill level marks. • Does the degas bottle/coolant expansion tank leak? → **Yes** INSTALL a new degas bottle/coolant expansion tank. TEST the system for normal operation. → **No** CARRY out the cooling system pressure test; REPAIR as necessary. TEST the system for normal operation.

FM1089900204040X

Fig. 61 Test A: Loss Of Coolant (Part 4 of 4). Mustang

TEST CONDITIONS	TESTDETAILS/RESULTS/ACTIONS
B1 CHECK THE ENGINE COOLANT LEVEL	
Note: If the engine is hot, allow the engine to cool before proceeding.	
☐1	☐1 ⚠ **WARNING:** Never remove the pressure relief cap/radiator cap under any conditions while the engine is operating. Failure to follow these instructions could result in damage to the cooling system or engine and/or personal injury. To avoid having scalding hot coolant or steam blow out of the cooling system, use extreme care when removing the pressure relief cap from a hot degas bottle or the radiator cap from the radiator. Wait until the engine has cooled, then wrap a thick cloth around the pressure relief cap and turn it slowly one turn (counterclockwise) or with a thick cloth around the radiator cap turn the radiator cap (counterclockwise) slowly to the first pressure stop. Step back while the pressure is released from the cooling system. When certain all the pressure has been released, remove the pressure relief cap/radiator cap (still with a cloth).
	☐2 Check the engine coolant level at the degas bottle/coolant expansion tank. • Is the engine coolant OK? → **Yes** GO to **B2**. → **No** REFILL the engine coolant at the degas bottle/coolant expansion tank. GO to Pinpoint Test A.
B2 CHECK THE COOLANT CONDITION	
☐1	☐1 Check the coolant for contaminants such as rust, corrosion, or discoloration. • Is the coolant condition OK? → **Yes** GO to **B3**. → **No** FLUSH the engine cooling system; TEST the system for normal operation.

FM1089900205010X

Fig. 62 Test B: Engine Overheats (Part 1 of 3). Mustang

TEST CONDITIONS	TESTDETAILS/RESULTS/ACTIONS
B5 CHECK THE WATER THERMOSTAT OPERATION (Continued)	
☐2	☐2 Feel the inlet and outlet heater water hoses and the underside of the upper radiator hose. • Are the upper radiator hose and the heater water hoses cold? → **Yes** INSTALL a new water thermostat; TEST the system for normal operation. → **No** GO to **B6**.
B6 CHECK THE COOLING FAN OPERATION	
☐1	☐1 Carry out the cooling fan component tests; go to Component Tests. • Is the cooling fan operation OK? → **Yes** TEST the system for normal operation. → **No** INSTALL a new fan component determined; TEST the system for normal operation.

FM1089900205030X

Fig. 62 Test B: Engine Overheats (Part 3 of 3). Mustang

TEST CONDITIONS	TESTDETAILS/RESULTS/ACTIONS
C1 CHECK THE ENGINE TEMPERATURE (Continued)	
☐2	☐2 Feel the inlet and heater water hoses and the underside of the upper radiator hose. • Are the upper radiator hose and the heater water hoses cold? → **Yes** INSTALL a new water thermostat; TEST the system for normal operation. → **No** For diagnosis and testing of the engine coolant temperature gauge

FM1089900206020X

Fig. 63 Test C: Engine Does Not Reach Normal Operating Temperature (Part 2 of 2). Mustang

TEST CONDITIONS	TESTDETAILS/RESULTS/ACTIONS
B3 CHECK FOR AN AIRFLOW OBSTRUCTION	
	☐1 Inspect the A/C condenser core and radiator for obstructions such as leaves or dirt. • Is there an obstruction? → **Yes** REMOVE the obstruction. CLEAN the A/C condenser core and radiator. TEST the system for normal operation. → **No** GO to **B4**.
B4 CHECK THE HEATER CORE OPERATION	
☐2	☐1 Install the pressure relief cap/radiator cap.
	☐3 As the engine starts to heat up, feel the inlet and outlet heater water hoses. They should feel approximately the same after three or four minutes. • Is the outlet heater water hose approximately the same temperature as the inlet heater water hose? → **Yes** GO to **B5**. → **No** TURN the engine off. REPAIR or INSTALL a new heater core. TEST the system for normal operation.
B5 CHECK THE WATER THERMOSTAT OPERATION	
☐1	☐1 Start the engine and allow the engine to run for ten minutes.

FM1089900205020X

Fig. 62 Test B: Engine Overheats (Part 2 of 3). Mustang

TEST CONDITIONS	TESTDETAILS/RESULTS/ACTIONS
C1 CHECK THE ENGINE TEMPERATURE	
☐1	☐1 Start the engine and allow the engine to idle for ten minutes.

FM1089900206010X

Fig. 63 Test C: Engine Does Not Reach Normal Operating Temperature (Part 1 of 2). Mustang

TEST CONDITIONS	TESTDETAILS/RESULTS/ACTIONS
D1 CHECK THE POWER CABLE	
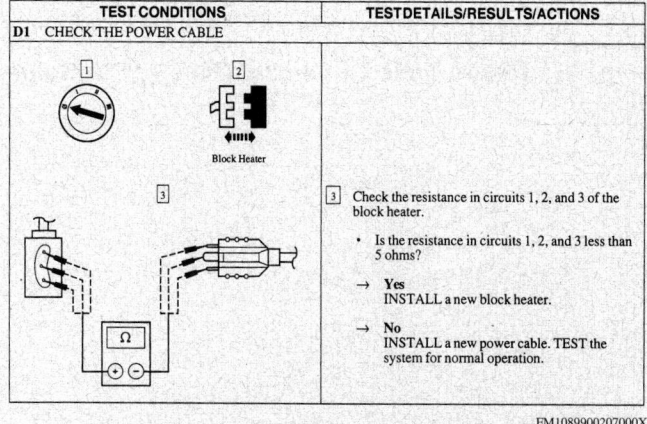	☐3 Check the resistance in circuits 1, 2, and 3 of the block heater. • Is the resistance in circuits 1, 2, and 3 less than 5 ohms? → **Yes** INSTALL a new block heater. → **No** INSTALL a new power cable. TEST the system for normal operation.

FM1089900207000X

Fig. 64 Test D: Block Heater Does Not Operate Correctly. Mustang

TEST CONDITIONS	TEST DETAILS/RESULTS/ACTIONS
A1 CHECK THE ENGINE COOLANT LEVEL	
Note: Allow the engine to cool before checking the engine coolant level.	

[1]	[2] Visually check the engine coolant level at the degas bottle.
	
	• Is the engine coolant level within specification?
	
	→ **Yes**
	    GO to **A2**.
	
	→ **No**
	    REFILL the engine coolant as necessary. GO to **A6**.

FM1080000276010X

Fig. 65   Test A: Loss Of Coolant (Part 1 of 3). Sable & Taurus

TEST CONDITIONS	TEST DETAILS/RESULTS/ACTIONS
A4 CHECK THE ENGINE FOR COOLANT	

	[1] Remove the oil level dipsticks from the engine.
	
	• Is coolant evident in the oil?
	
	→ **Yes**
	    If coolant is in the engine, diagnose engine.
	
	→ **No**
	    GO to **A5**.

A5 PRESSURE TEST THE ENGINE COOLING SYSTEM	

	[1] Pressure test the engine cooling system.
	
	• Does the engine cooling system leak?
	
	→ **Yes**
	    REPAIR or INSTALL new components. TEST the system for normal operation.
	
	→ **No**
	    The cooling system is operational. RETURN to the Symptom Chart.

A6 CHECK THE DEGAS BOTTLE	

	[1] **Note:** The engine must be cool when coolant is added to the degas bottle.
	Add coolant to the degas bottle until fluid is between the coolant fill level marks.
	
	• Does the degas bottle leak?
	
	→ **Yes**
	    INSTALL a new degas bottle. TEST the system for normal operation.
	
	→ **No**
	    Carry out the cooling system pressure test. REFER to the Component Tests REPAIR as necessary. TEST the system for normal operation.

FM1080000276030X

Fig. 65   Test A: Loss Of Coolant (Part 3 of 3). Sable & Taurus

TEST CONDITIONS	TEST DETAILS/RESULTS/ACTIONS
A2 TEST THE DEGAS BOTTLE PRESSURE RELIEF CAP	

	[1] ⚠ **WARNING: To avoid personal injury, do not unscrew the coolant pressure relief cap while the engine is on or hot. The cooling system is under pressure; steam and hot liquid can come out forcefully when the cap is loosened slightly.**
	Allow the engine to cool.
	
	[2] Remove the pressure relief cap.
	
	[3] Inspect the pressure relief cap for foreign material between the sealing gasket and the diaphragm.
	
	• Is the pressure relief cap OK?
	
	→ **Yes**
	    REFER to Component Tests Pressure Test.
	
	→ **No**
	    CLEAN or INSTALL a new pressure relief cap. TEST the system for normal operation. GO to **A1**.

A3 CHECK THE ENGINE COOLANT FOR INTERNAL LEAK	

[1]	[2] Inspect the engine coolant in the degas bottle for signs of engine oil.
	
	• Is oil evident in the coolant?
	
	→ **Yes**
	    If engine oil is evident, diagnose engine.
	
	→ **No**
	    GO to **A4**.

FM1080000276020X

Fig. 65   Test A: Loss Of Coolant (Part 2 of 3). Sable & Taurus

TEST CONDITIONS	TEST DETAILS/RESULTS/ACTIONS
B1 CHECK THE ENGINE COOLANT LEVEL	
Note: If the engine is hot, allow the engine to cool before proceeding.	

[1]	[1] ⚠ **WARNING: To avoid personal injury, do not unscrew the coolant pressure relief cap while the engine is operating or hot. The cooling system is under pressure; steam and hot liquid can come out forcefully when the cap is loosened slightly.**
	Check the engine coolant level at the degas bottle.
	
	• Is the engine coolant OK?
	
	→ **Yes**
	    GO to **B2**.
	
	→ **No**
	    REFILL the engine coolant at the degas bottle. GO to Pinpoint Test A.

B2 CHECK THE COOLANT CONDITION	

	[1] Check the coolant for contaminants such as rust, corrosion, or discoloration.
	
	• Is the coolant condition OK?
	
	→ **Yes**
	    GO to **B3**.
	
	→ **No**
	    FLUSH the engine cooling system. TEST the system for normal operation.

B3 CHECK FOR AN AIRFLOW OBSTRUCTION	

	[1] Inspect the A/C condenser core and radiator for obstructions such as leaves or dirt.
	
	• Is there an obstruction?
	
	→ **Yes**
	    REMOVE the obstruction. CLEAN the A/C condenser core and radiator. TEST the system for normal operation.
	
	→ **No**
	    GO to **B4**.

FM1080000277010X

Fig. 66   Test B: Engine Overheats (Part 1 of 3). Sable & Taurus

TEST CONDITIONS	TESTDETAILS/RESULTS/ACTIONS
B4 CHECK THE HEATER CORE OPERATION	
①	① Start the engine.
	② As the engine starts to heat up, feel the inlet and outlet heater water hoses. They should feel approximately the same after three or four minutes.
	• Is the outlet heater water hose approximately the same temperature as the inlet heater water hose?
	→ **Yes** GO to **B5**.
	→ **No** TURN the engine off. REPAIR or INSTALL a new heater core. TEST the system for normal operation.
B5 CHECK THE WATER THERMOSTAT OPERATION	
①	① Start the engine and allow the engine to run for 10 minutes.
②	② Turn the engine off.
③	③ Feel the upper and lower radiator hose.
	• Are the upper and lower radiator hoses cold?
	→ **Yes** CARRY OUT thermostat component tests.
	→ **No** GO to **B6**.

FM1080000277020X

Fig. 66   Test B: Engine Overheats (Part 2 of 3). Sable & Taurus

TEST CONDITIONS	TESTDETAILS/RESULTS/ACTIONS
C1 CHECK THE ENGINE TEMPERATURE	
①	① Start the engine and allow the engine to idle for 10 minutes.
②	② Feel the upper and lower radiator hoses.
	• Are the upper and lower radiator hoses cold?
	→ **Yes** CARRY OUT thermostat component tests.
	→ **No** INSPECT engine coolant temperature gauge.

FM1080000278000X

Fig. 67   Test C: Engine Does Not Reach Normal Operating Temperature. Sable & Taurus

TEST CONDITIONS	TESTDETAILS/RESULTS/ACTIONS
D1 CHECK THE POWER CABLE (Continued)	
③	③ Check the resistance in circuits 1, 2, and 3 of the block heater.
	• Is the resistance in circuits 1, 2, and 3 less than 5 ohms?
	→ **Yes** INSTALL a new block heater.
	→ **No** INSTALL a new power cable. TEST the system for normal operation.

FM1080000279020X

Fig. 68   Test D: Block Heater Does Not Operate Correctly (Part 2 of 2). Sable & Taurus

TEST CONDITIONS	TESTDETAILS/RESULTS/ACTIONS
B6 CHECK THE COOLING FAN OPERATION	
①	① Carry out the cooling fan component tests.
	• Is the cooling fan operation OK?
	→ **Yes** Diagnsoe engine cooling.
	→ **No** INSTALL new the fan component determined. TEST the system for normal operation.

FM1080000277030X

Fig. 66   Test B: Engine Overheats (Part 3 of 3). Sable & Taurus

TEST CONDITIONS	TESTDETAILS/RESULTS/ACTIONS
D1 CHECK THE POWER CABLE	
① ② Block Heater	

FM1080000279010X

Fig. 68   Test D: Block Heater Does Not Operate Correctly (Part 1 of 2). Sable & Taurus

CONDITIONS	DETAILS/RESULTS/ACTIONS
D1 CHECK FAN CONTROL FAULT PIDS TO VERIFY FAN CONTROL PRIMARY CIRCUITS	
①	② Verify A/C is OFF, and engine temperature is below the temperature where the cooling fan would come on.
③	③ Access the LFCF, MFCF and HFCF PIDs.
	• Does the LFCF, MFCF and HFCF PID indicate a fault (or YES)?
	→ **Yes** REFER to MOTOR's "Domestic Engine Performance & Driveability Manual".
	→ **No** GO to **D2**.
D2 CHECK OPERATION OF THE COOLING FANS	
①	① Using the diagnostic tool, command the cooling fans on HIGH and LOW.
	• Do the cooling fans operate?
	→ **Yes** GO to **D3**.
	→ **No** If the driver and passenger side cooling fans do not operate at any speed, GO to **D4**.
	If the driver/passenger side cooling fans do not operate at LOW speed, GO to **D8**.
	If the driver side cooling fan does not operate at HIGH speed, GO to **D8**.
	If the passenger side cooling fan does not operate at HIGH speed, GO to **D12**.

ARM0300000000336

Fig. 69   Test D: Cooling Fans Are Inoperative (Part 1 of 8). Sable & Taurus

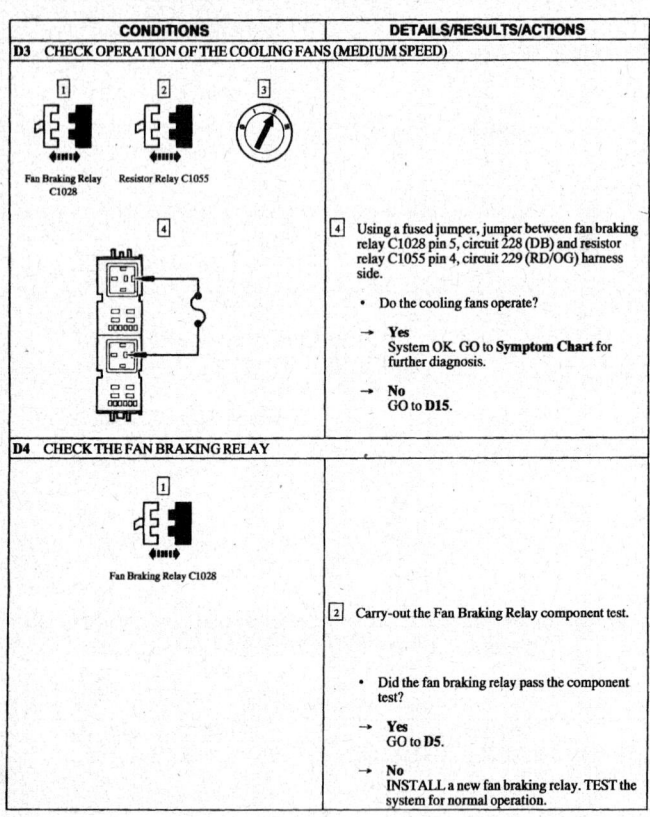

CONDITIONS	DETAILS/RESULTS/ACTIONS
D3 CHECK OPERATION OF THE COOLING FANS (MEDIUM SPEED)	
	4 Using a fused jumper, jumper between fan braking relay C1028 pin 5, circuit 228 (DB) and resistor relay C1055 pin 4, circuit 229 (RD/OG) harness side. • Do the cooling fans operate? → **Yes** System OK. GO to **Symptom Chart** for further diagnosis. → **No** GO to **D15**.
D4 CHECK THE FAN BRAKING RELAY	
	2 Carry-out the Fan Braking Relay component test. • Did the fan braking relay pass the component test? → **Yes** GO to **D5**. → **No** INSTALL a new fan braking relay. TEST the system for normal operation.

ARM0300000000337

Fig. 69   Test D: Cooling Fans Are Inoperative (Part 2 of 8). Sable & Taurus

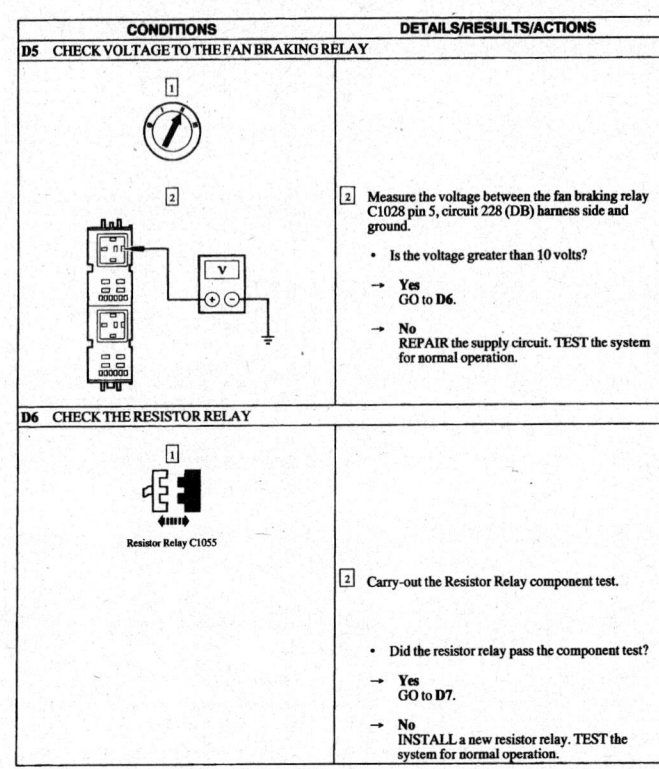

CONDITIONS	DETAILS/RESULTS/ACTIONS
D5 CHECK VOLTAGE TO THE FAN BRAKING RELAY	
	2 Measure the voltage between the fan braking relay C1028 pin 5, circuit 228 (DB) harness side and ground. • Is the voltage greater than 10 volts? → **Yes** GO to **D6**. → **No** REPAIR the supply circuit. TEST the system for normal operation.
D6 CHECK THE RESISTOR RELAY	
	2 Carry-out the Resistor Relay component test. • Did the resistor relay pass the component test? → **Yes** GO to **D7**. → **No** INSTALL a new resistor relay. TEST the system for normal operation.

ARM0300000000338

Fig. 69   Test D: Cooling Fans Are Inoperative (Part 3 of 8). Sable & Taurus

CONDITIONS	DETAILS/RESULTS/ACTIONS
D7 CHECK VOLTAGE TO THE RESISTOR RELAY	
	3 Measure the voltage between the resistor relay C1055 pin 3, circuit 3850 (LG/VT) harness side and ground. • Is the voltage greater than 10 volts? → **Yes** CONNECT the resistor relay C1055. GO to **D8**. → **No** REPAIR the circuit. TEST the system for normal operation.
D8 CHECK VOLTAGE TO THE DRIVER SIDE COOLING FAN	
	3 Measure the voltage between the driver side cooling fan C1077, circuit 229 (RD/OG) harness side and ground. • Is the voltage greater than 10 volts? → **Yes** GO to **D9**. → **No** REPAIR the circuit. TEST the system for normal operation.

ARM0300000000339

Fig. 69   Test D: Cooling Fans Are Inoperative (Part 4 of 8). Sable & Taurus

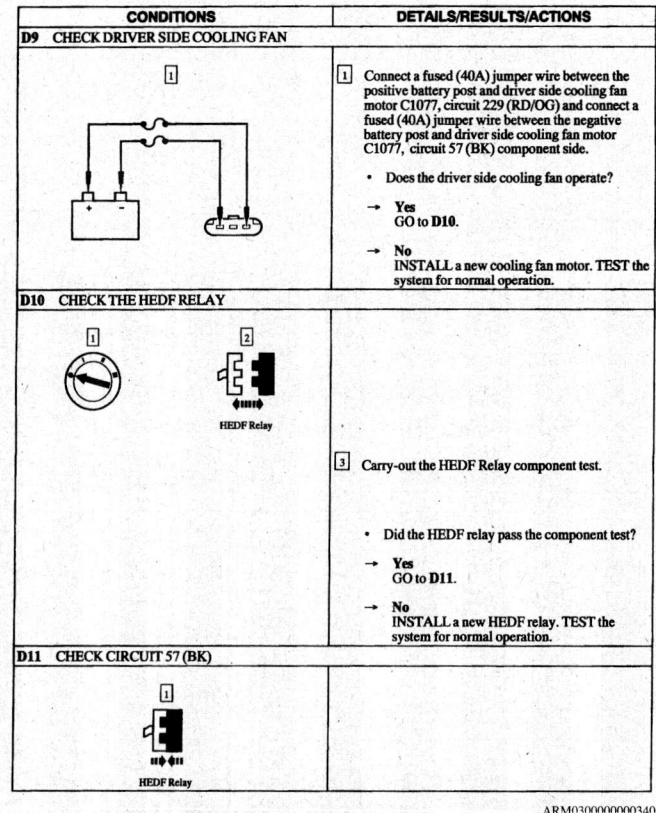

CONDITIONS	DETAILS/RESULTS/ACTIONS
D9 CHECK DRIVER SIDE COOLING FAN	
	1 Connect a fused (40A) jumper wire between the positive battery post and driver side cooling fan motor C1077, circuit 229 (RD/OG) and connect a fused (40A) jumper wire between the negative battery post and driver side cooling fan motor C1077, circuit 57 (BK) component side. • Does the driver side cooling fan operate? → **Yes** GO to **D10**. → **No** INSTALL a new cooling fan motor. TEST the system for normal operation.
D10 CHECK THE HEDF RELAY	
	3 Carry-out the HEDF Relay component test. • Did the HEDF relay pass the component test? → **Yes** GO to **D11**. → **No** INSTALL a new HEDF relay. TEST the system for normal operation.
D11 CHECK CIRCUIT 57 (BK)	

ARM0300000000340

Fig. 69   Test D: Cooling Fans Are Inoperative (Part 5 of 8). Sable & Taurus

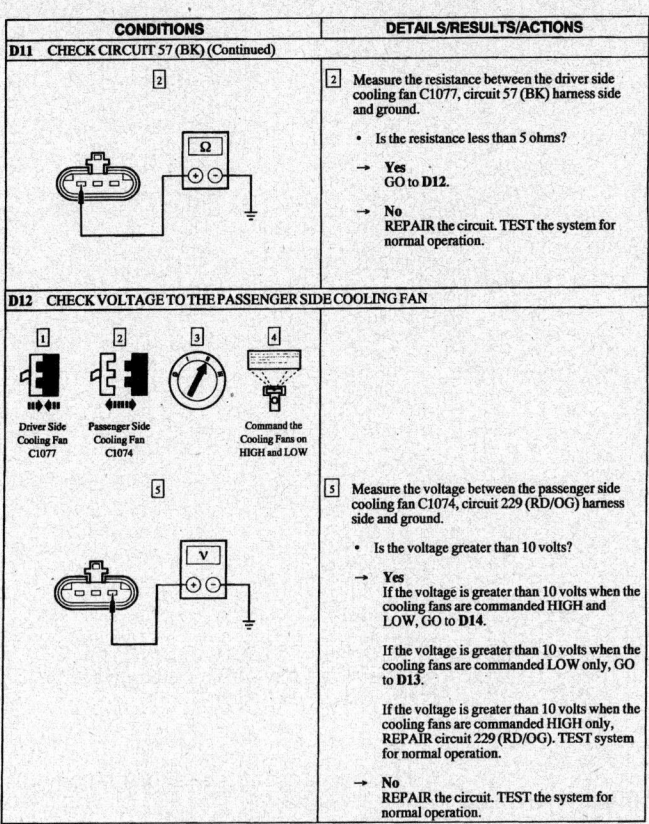

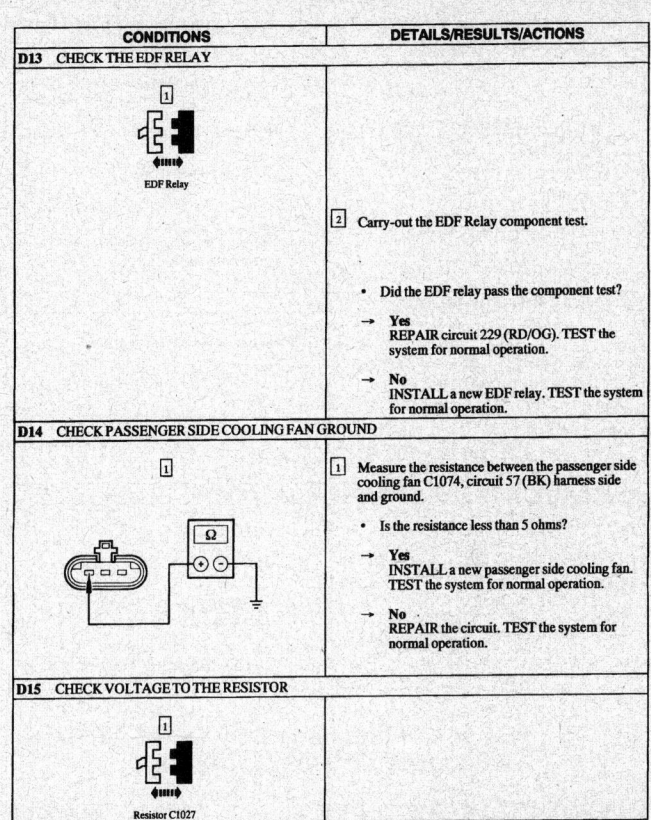

CONDITIONS	DETAILS/RESULTS/ACTIONS
D11 CHECK CIRCUIT 57 (BK) (Continued)	
[2]	[2] Measure the resistance between the driver side cooling fan C1077, circuit 57 (BK) harness side and ground. • Is the resistance less than 5 ohms? → **Yes** GO to **D12**. → **No** REPAIR the circuit. TEST the system for normal operation.
D12 CHECK VOLTAGE TO THE PASSENGER SIDE COOLING FAN	
[1] Driver Side Cooling Fan C1077 [2] Passenger Side Cooling Fan C1074 [3] [4] Command the Cooling Fans on HIGH and LOW [5]	[5] Measure the voltage between the passenger side cooling fan C1074, circuit 229 (RD/OG) harness side and ground. • Is the voltage greater than 10 volts? → **Yes** If the voltage is greater than 10 volts when the cooling fans are commanded HIGH and LOW, GO to **D14**. If the voltage is greater than 10 volts when the cooling fans are commanded LOW only, GO to **D13**. If the voltage is greater than 10 volts when the cooling fans are commanded HIGH only, REPAIR circuit 229 (RD/OG). TEST system for normal operation. → **No** REPAIR the circuit. TEST the system for normal operation.

ARM0300000000341

Fig. 69 Test D: Cooling Fans Are Inoperative (Part 6 of 8). Sable & Taurus

CONDITIONS	DETAILS/RESULTS/ACTIONS
D13 CHECK THE EDF RELAY	
[1] EDF Relay [2]	[2] Carry-out the EDF Relay component test. • Did the EDF relay pass the component test? → **Yes** REPAIR circuit 229 (RD/OG). TEST the system for normal operation. → **No** INSTALL a new EDF relay. TEST the system for normal operation.
D14 CHECK PASSENGER SIDE COOLING FAN GROUND	
[1]	[1] Measure the resistance between the passenger side cooling fan C1074, circuit 57 (BK) harness side and ground. • Is the resistance less than 5 ohms? → **Yes** INSTALL a new passenger side cooling fan. TEST the system for normal operation. → **No** REPAIR the circuit. TEST the system for normal operation.
D15 CHECK VOLTAGE TO THE RESISTOR	
[1] Resistor C1027	

ARM0300000000342

Fig. 69 Test D: Cooling Fans Are Inoperative (Part 7 of 8). Sable & Taurus

CONDITIONS	DETAILS/RESULTS/ACTIONS
D15 CHECK VOLTAGE TO THE RESISTOR (Continued)	
[2]	[2] Measure the voltage between the resistor C1027 pin 1, circuit 229 (RD/OG) harness side and ground. • Is the voltage greater than 10 volts? → **Yes** GO to **D16**. → **No** REPAIR the circuit. TEST the system for normal operation.
D16 CHECK CIRCUIT 229 (RD/OG) FOR AN OPEN	
[1] Driver Side Cooling Fan Motor C1077 [2]	[2] Measure the resistance between the resistor C1027 pin 2, circuit 229 (RD/OG) and driver side cooling fan motor C1077 circuit 229 (RD/OG) harness side. • Is the resistance less than 5 ohms? → **Yes** INSTALL a new resistor. TEST the system for normal operation. → **No** REPAIR the circuit. TEST the system for normal operation.

ARM0300000000343

Fig. 69 Test D: Cooling Fans Are Inoperative (Part 8 of 8). Sable & Taurus

CONDITIONS	DETAILS/RESULTS/ACTIONS
E1 CHECK THE A/C HIGH PRESSURE SWITCH INPUT TO PCM	
[1] [3]	[2] Verify the A/C is OFF. [3] Monitor the A/C high pressure switch ACP PID. • Does the A/C high pressure switch ACP PID read CLOSED? → **Yes** GO to **E2**. → **No** GO to **E4**.
E2 CHECK A/C HIGH PRESSURE SWITCH	
[1] A/C High Pressure Switch C1062 [2]	[2] Monitor the A/C high pressure switch ACP PID. • Does the A/C high pressure switch ACP PID read CLOSED? → **Yes** GO to **E3**. → **No** If the A/C system is working correctly, INSTALL a new A/C high pressure switch. If the A/C system is not working correctly,
E3 CHECK CIRCUIT 347 (BK/YE) FOR A SHORT TO GROUND	
[1] [2] PCM C175	

ARM0300000000358

Fig. 70 Test E: Cooling Fans Stay On At All Times (Part 1 of 2). Sable & Taurus

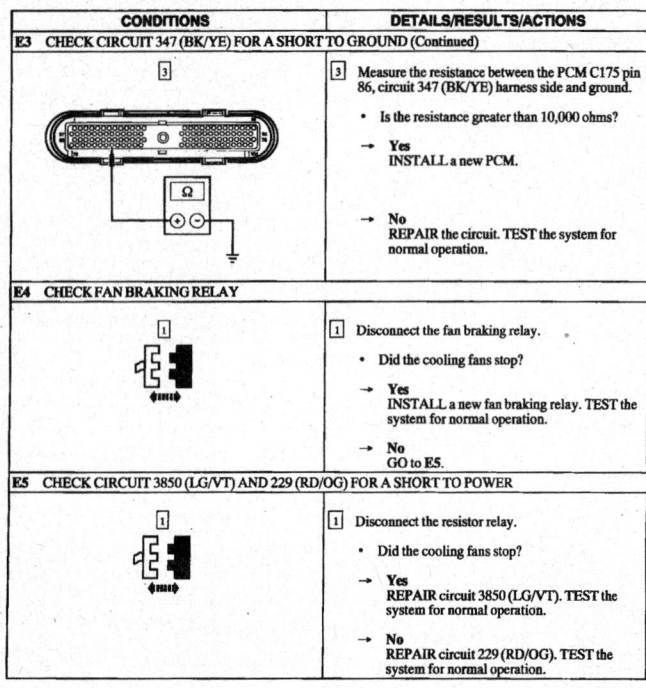

CONDITIONS	DETAILS/RESULTS/ACTIONS
E3 CHECK CIRCUIT 347 (BK/YE) FOR A SHORT TO GROUND (Continued)	

3 Measure the resistance between the PCM C175 pin 86, circuit 347 (BK/YE) harness side and ground.

- Is the resistance greater than 10,000 ohms?
- → **Yes**
  INSTALL a new PCM.
- → **No**
  REPAIR the circuit. TEST the system for normal operation.

E4 CHECK FAN BRAKING RELAY

1 Disconnect the fan braking relay.
- Did the cooling fans stop?
- → **Yes**
  INSTALL a new fan braking relay. TEST the system for normal operation.
- → **No**
  GO to E5.

E5 CHECK CIRCUIT 3850 (LG/VT) AND 229 (RD/OG) FOR A SHORT TO POWER

1 Disconnect the resistor relay.
- Did the cooling fans stop?
- → **Yes**
  REPAIR circuit 3850 (LG/VT). TEST the system for normal operation.
- → **No**
  REPAIR circuit 229 (RD/OG). TEST the system for normal operation.

ARM0300000000359

Fig. 70 Test E: Cooling Fans Stay On At All Times (Part 2 of 2). Sable & Taurus

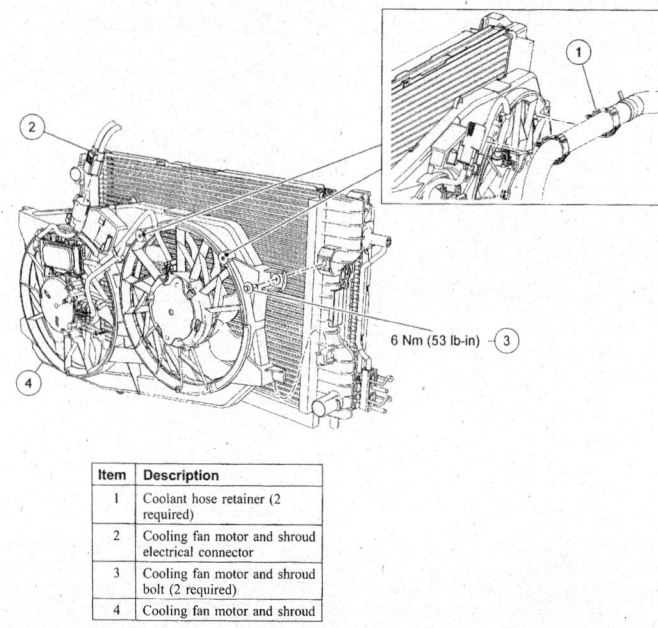

6 Nm (53 lb-in) - 3

Item	Description
1	Coolant hose retainer (2 required)
2	Cooling fan motor and shroud electrical connector
3	Cooling fan motor and shroud bolt (2 required)
4	Cooling fan motor and shroud

ARM0400000000744

Fig. 71 Cooling fan replacement. Five Hundred, Freestyle & Montego

COMPONENT REPLACEMENT

Constant Control Relay Module/ Integrated Relay Control Module (CCRM/IRCM)

CONTINENTAL

1. Remove radiator as outlined in "Radiator, Replace" in "4.6L Engine" section of "Continental & Town Car" chapter.
2. Remove mounting bolts and cooling fan motor/blade/shroud assembly.
3. Remove fan blade mounting clips and blades.
4. Remove motor mounting screws and motors.
5. Remove Constant Control Relay Module (CCRM).
6. Reverse procedure to install. **Torque** CCRM mounting screws to 40–56 inch lbs. and shroud mounting bolts to 24–48 ft. lbs.

MUSTANG

1. **On models equipped with 3.8L engine,** remove righthand inner fender splash shield.
2. **On all models,** disconnect CCRM and remove CCRM mounting nuts.
3. Reverse procedure to install, noting the following:
   a. **On models equipped with 3.8L engine,** torque CCRM mounting nuts to 12–17 inch lbs.

b. **On models equipped with 4.6L engine, torque** CCRM mounting nuts to 36 inch lbs.

SABLE & TAURUS

1. Disconnect engine control sensor wiring from module connector.
2. Release clips and module from battery tray.
3. Reverse procedure to install. **Torque** engine control sensor connector to 12–18 inch lbs.

Cooling Fan Motor

CONTINENTAL

1. Remove radiators as outlined in "Radiator, Replace" in "4.6L Engine" section of "Continental" chapter.
2. Remove mounting bolts and cooling fan motor/blade/shroud assembly.
3. Remove fan blade mounting clips and blades.
4. Remove motor mounting screws and motors.
5. Remove Constant Control Relay Module (CCRM).
6. Reverse procedure to install. **Torque** CCRM mounting screws to 40–56 inch lbs. and shroud mounting bolts to 24–48 ft. lbs.

COUGAR

2.0L ENGINE

1. Raise and support vehicle.
2. Remove lower radiator splash shield.
3. Disconnect fan motor connector.
4. Disconnect fan resistor connector and wiring harness.
5. Remove air conditioning accumulator bolts and place to one side.
6. Lower vehicle.

7. Disconnect air conditioning compressor connector.
8. Disconnect heated oxygen sensor connector and wiring harness.
9. Disconnect air conditioning tube from mounting bracket.
10. Remove mounting nut and fan shroud.
11. Reverse procedure to install.

2.5L ENGINE

1. Drain coolant into suitable container.
2. Remove radiator.
3. Raise and support vehicle.
4. Disconnect cooling fan connector and wiring harness.
5. Disconnect remaining electrical connectors and remaining harnesses.
6. Remove fan.
7. Reverse procedure to install.

CROWN VICTORIA, GRAND MARQUIS, MARAUDER & TOWN CAR

1. Drain coolant from degas bottle into suitable container.
2. Disconnect degas bottle supply and overflow hoses.
3. Remove mounting bolt and degas bottle.
4. Disconnect fan motor connector.
5. Remove two mounting, fan blade, motor and shroud.
6. Reverse procedure to install.

ESCORT & ZX2

Fan motor, blade and shroud are not serviced separately.

1. Remove air cleaner outlet tube.
2. Disconnect fan motor and upstream heated oxygen sensor electrical connectors.
3. Remove mounting bolts, fan blade and shroud assembly.
4. Reverse procedure to install.

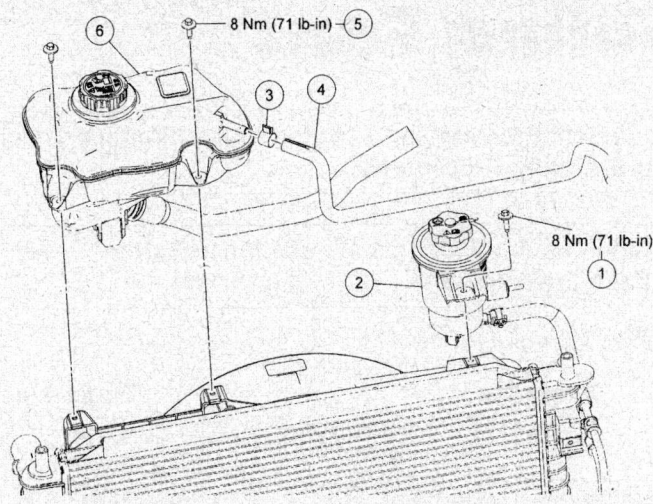

Item	Description
1	Power steering reservoir bolt
2	Power steering reservoir
3	Upper degas bottle hose clamp

Item	Description
4	Upper degas bottle hose
5	Degas bottle bolt (2 required)
6	Degas bottle

ARM0400000000742

Fig. 72   Cooling fan replacement (Part 1 of 2). 2005 Mustang

Item	Description
7	Lower degas bottle hose
8	Cooling fan motor and shroud electrical connector
9	Cooling fan motor and shroud bolt (2 required)
10	Cooling fan motor and shroud

ARM0400000000743

Fig. 72   Cooling fan replacement (Part 2 of 2). 2005 Mustang

FIVE HUNDRED, FREESTYLE & MONTEGO

1. Disconnect two coolant hose retainers from shroud, **Fig. 71.**
2. Disconnect cooling fan electrical connector.
3. Remove cooling fan/shroud assembly mounting bolts, then the fan assembly.
4. Reverse procedure to install. **Torque** fan/shroud mounting bolts to 53 inch lbs.

FOCUS

1. Disconnect cooling fan electrical connectors and two pin type retainers.
2. Raise and support vehicle.
3. Remove cooling fan motor and shroud.
4. Reverse procedure to install.

MUSTANG

2001-04

1. Remove degas bottle or coolant expansion tank.
2. Disconnect electrical connector and separate fan harness from shroud.
3. Remove mounting bolts, fan, motor and shroud.
4. Reverse procedure to install. **Torque** mounting bolts to 89 inch lbs.

2005

1. Remove air cleaner outlet pipe.
2. Remove power steering fluid reservoir mounting bolt, **Fig. 72,** then position reservoir aside.

3. Remove two degas bottle mounting bolts, then position bottle aside.
4. Disconnect cooling fan motor electrical connector.
5. Remove cooling fan/shroud assembly mounting bolts, then the fan assembly.
6. Reverse procedure to install. **Torque** cooling fan mounting bolts to 80 inch lbs.

SABLE & TAURUS

1. Drain engine coolant into suitable container.
2. Remove distribution box and set aside.
3. Disconnect cooling fan electrical connectors.
4. Remove retainers and cooling fan.
5. Reverse procedure to install.

Hydraulic Cooling Fans

NOTE: On Air Bag Equipped Models, Refer To "Air Bag System Precautions" Located In The Front Of This Manual For System Disarming & Arming Procedures.

NOTE: Refer To "Computer Relearn Procedures" Located In The Front Of This Manual When Battery Power To The Computer Has Been Interrupted.

INDEX

PRECAUTIONS

Air Bag Systems

Refer to "Air Bag System Precautions" in the front of this manual for system disarming and arming procedures.

Battery Ground Cable

Prior to service, disconnect battery ground cable and isolate as required.

DESCRIPTION

The hydraulic cooling fan is controlled by the Powertrain Control Module (PCM) via the hydraulic fan solenoid. The fan motor operates only when the engine is running.

The cooling fan operates at 2200–2400 RPM. Operating pressure is 900 psi, with a maximum pressure of 1200 psi. The fans operating flow rate is 3.75–4.25 gallons per minute.

SYSTEM DIAGNOSIS & TESTING

Perform visual inspection prior to performing any diagnosis and testing procedures. Inspect the following:
1. Leaks.
2. Restricted airflow through condenser/radiator.
3. Damaged hoses.
4. Loose/damaged hose clamps.
5. Damaged water gasket.
6. Damaged head gaskets.
7. Damaged water pump.
8. Damaged radiator.
9. Damaged degas bottle.
10. Damaged heater core.
11. Hydraulic cooling fan system:
    a. Fluid level.
    b. Hydraulic line or joint leaks.
    c. Kinked hydraulic lines.
12. Damaged cylinder head temperature sensor.
13. Damaged wiring.
14. Hydraulic cooling fan pump solenoid/solenoid wiring.

Wiring Diagrams

Refer to **Fig. 1,** for wiring diagram.

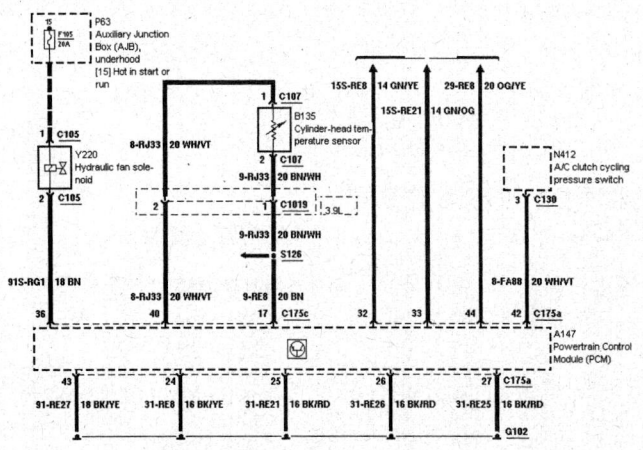

Fig. 1   Wiring diagram. LS

Condition	Possible Sources	Action
Loss of engine coolant	• Radiator. • Thermostat housing assembly. • Auxiliary water pump. • Heater control valve. • Oil cooler. • PCV heater system. • Throttle body adapter heating. • Water pump seal. • Radiator hoses. • Heater hoses. • Heater core. • Engine gaskets. • Degas bottle.	• GO to Pinpoint Test A.
The engine overheats	• Water thermostat. • Airlock in the system. • Water pump. • Internal engine coolant leak. • Radiator. • Radiator airflow obstruction. • Heater core. • Cooling fan. • Pressure relief cap.	• GO to Pinpoint Test B.
The engine does not reach normal operating temperature	• Water thermostat.	• GO to Pinpoint Test C.

Fig. 2   Symptoms (Part 1 of 2)

Symptoms

Refer to **Fig. 2,** for symptoms.

Diagnostic Tests

Refer to **Figs. 3 through 6,** for symptom related tests.

Condition	Possible Sources	Action
• The block heater does not operate correctly	• Block heater power cable. • Block heater.	• DISCONNECT the power cable from the heater. • CHECK the resistance in all three power cable circuits. If the resistance is greater than 5 ohms in any circuit, INSTALL a new power cable. If the resistance is less than 5 ohms in all three circuits, INSTALL a new block heater.
• Noisy cooling fan operation	• Incorrect fluid level. • Kinked or leaking line. • Blocked reservoir screen. • Hydraulic motor. • Hydraulic pump.	• REFILL fluid to specified level. CHECK for leaks and retest. • INSTALL a new line. RETEST and CHECK for leaks. • REFER to Component Tests

ARM0300000000361

Fig. 2 Symptoms (Part 2 of 2)

DIAGNOSTIC CHART INDEX

Test	Description	Page No.	Fig. No.
Test A	Loss Of Coolant	11-29	3
Test B	Engine Overheats	11-30	4
Test C	Inspect Engine Temperature	11-31	5
Test D	Inspect Power Cable	11-31	6

A1   CHECK THE ENGINE COOLANT LEVEL

Note:
Allow the engine to cool before checking the engine coolant level.

1

2   Visually check the engine coolant level at the degas bottle.

●   **Is the engine coolant level within specification?**

➔ **Yes**

Go to «A2».

➔ **No**

REFILL the engine coolant as necessary. Go to «A6».

FM1089900209010X

Fig. 3   Test A: Loss Of Coolant (Part 1 of 6)

A3   CHECK THE ENGINE COOLANT FOR INTERNAL LEAK

1

2   Inspect the engine coolant in the degas bottle for signs of engine oil.

●   **Is oil evident in the coolant?**

➔ **Yes**

If engine oil is evident, inspect engine.

➔ **No**

Go to «A4».

FM1089900209030X

Fig. 3   Test A: Loss Of Coolant (Part 3 of 6)

A2   DEGAS BOTTLE PRESSURE RELIEF CAP

1   ⚠ **WARNING:**
Never remove the pressure relief cap under any conditions while the engine is operating. Failure to follow these instructions could result in damage to the cooling system or engine and/or personal injury. To avoid having scalding hot coolant or steam blow out of the cooling system, use extreme care when removing the pressure relief cap from a hot degas bottle. Wait until the engine has cooled, then wrap a thick cloth around the pressure relief cap and turn it slowly one turn (counterclockwise). Step back while the pressure is released from the cooling system. When certain all the pressure has been released, remove the pressure relief cap (still with a cloth).

Allow the engine to cool.

2   Remove the pressure relief cap.

3   Inspect the pressure relief cap for foreign material between the sealing gasket and the diaphragm.

●   **Is the pressure relief cap OK?**

➔ **Yes**

REFER to Component Tests.

➔ **No**

CLEAN or INSTALL a new pressure relief cap. TEST the system for normal operation. Go to «A1».

FM1089900209020X

Fig. 3   Test A: Loss Of Coolant (Part 2 of 6)

A4   CHECK THE ENGINE FOR COOLANT

1   Remove the oil level indicator from the engine.

●   **Is coolant evident in the oil?**

➔ **Yes**

If coolant is in the engine, inspect engine.

➔ **No**

Go to «A5».

FM1089900209040X

Fig. 3   Test A: Loss Of Coolant (Part 4 of 6)

COOLING FANS

A5   PRESSURE TEST THE ENGINE COOLING SYSTEM

1   Pressure test the engine cooling system

- ● **Does the engine cooling system leak?**

- → **Yes**

    REPAIR or INSTALL new components. TEST the system for normal operation.

- → **No**

    The cooling system is operational. RETURN to the Symptom Chart.

FM1089900209050X

Fig. 3   Test A: Loss Of Coolant (Part 5 of 6)

B1   CHECK THE ENGINE COOLANT LEVEL

Note:
If the engine is hot, allow the engine to cool before proceeding.

1

⚠ **WARNING:**
Never remove the pressure relief cap under any conditions while the engine is operating. Failure to follow these instructions could result in damage to the cooling system or engine and/or personal injury. To avoid having scalding hot coolant or steam blow out of the cooling system, use extreme care when removing the pressure relief cap from a hot degas bottle. Wait until the engine has cooled, then wrap a thick cloth around the pressure relief cap and turn it slowly one turn (counterclockwise). Step back while the pressure is released from the cooling system. When certain all the pressure has been released, remove the pressure relief cap (still with a cloth).

2   Check the engine coolant level at the degas bottle.

- ● **Is the engine coolant OK?**

- → **Yes**

    Go to «B2».

- → **No**

    REFILL the engine coolant at the degas bottle. GO to «Pinpoint Test A».

FM1089900210010X

Fig. 4   Test B: Engine Overheats (Part 1 of 6)

B3   CHECK FOR AN AIRFLOW OBSTRUCTION

1   Inspect the A/C condenser core and radiator for obstructions such as leaves or dirt.

- ● **Is there an obstruction?**

- → **Yes**

    REMOVE the obstruction. CLEAN the A/C condenser core and radiator. TEST the system for normal operation.

- → **No**

    Go to «B4».

FM1089900210030X

Fig. 4   Test B: Engine Overheats (Part 3 of 6)

A6   CHECK THE DEGAS BOTTLE

1   **Note:**
The engine must be cool when coolant is added to the degas bottle.

Add coolant to the degas bottle until fluid is between the coolant fill level marks.

- ● **Does the degas bottle leak?**

- → **Yes**

    INSTALL a new degas bottle. TEST the system for normal operation.

- → **No**

    CARRY OUT the cooling system pressure test.
    REPAIR as necessary. TEST the system for normal operation.

FM1089900209060X

Fig. 3   Test A: Loss Of Coolant (Part 6 of 6)

B2   CHECK THE COOLANT CONDITION

1   Check the coolant for contaminants such as rust, corrosion, or discoloration.

- ● **Is the coolant condition OK?**

- → **Yes**

    Go to «B3».

- → **No**

    FLUSH the engine cooling system.
    TEST the system for normal operation.

FM1089900210020X

Fig. 4   Test B: Engine Overheats (Part 2 of 6)

B4   CHECK THE HEATER CORE OPERATION

1   Install the pressure relief cap.

2

3   As the engine starts to heat up, feel the inlet and outlet heater water hoses. They should feel approximately the same after three or four minutes.

- ● **Is the outlet heater water hose approximately the same temperature as the inlet heater water hose?**

- → **Yes**

    Go to «B5».

- → **No**

    TURN the engine off. REPAIR or INSTALL a new heater core.
    TEST the system for normal operation.

FM1089900210040X

Fig. 4   Test B: Engine Overheats (Part 4 of 6)

B5   CHECK THE WATER THERMOSTAT OPERATION

1

Start the engine and allow the engine to run for 10 minutes.

2

3   Feel the upper and lower radiator hoses.

● **Are the upper and lower radiator hoses cold?**

→ **Yes**

INSTALL a new water thermostat. TEST the system for normal operation.

→ **No**

Go to «B6».

FM1089900210050X

Fig. 4   Test B: Engine Overheats (Part 5 of 6)

C1   CHECK THE ENGINE TEMPERATURE

1

Start the engine and allow the engine to idle for 10 minutes.

2

Feel the upper and lower radiator hoses.

● **Are the upper and lower radiator hoses cold?**

→ **Yes**

INSTALL a new water thermostat. TEST the system for normal operation.

→ **No**

Diagnose and test the engine coolant temperature gauge.

FM1089900211000X

Fig. 5   Test C: Inspect Engine Temperature

B6   CHECK THE COOLING FAN OPERATION

1

Carry out the cooling fan component tests

● **Is the cooling fan operation OK?**

→ **Yes**

Refer to MOTOR's "DOMESTIC ENGINE PERFORMANCE & DRIVEABILITY MANUAL."

→ **No**

INSTALL a new fan component as necessary. TEST the system for normal operation.

FM1089900210060X

Fig. 4   Test B: Engine Overheats (Part 6 of 6)

D1   CHECK THE POWER CABLE

1

2   *Block Heater*

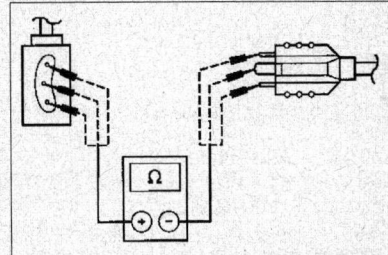

3

Check the resistance in circuits 1, 2, and 3 of the block heater.

● **Are the resistances in circuits 1, 2, and 3 less than 5 ohms?**

→ **Yes**

INSTALL a new block heater. TEST the system for normal operation.

→ **No**

INSTALL a new power cable. TEST the system for normal operation.

FM1089900212000X

Fig. 6   Test D: Inspect Power Cable

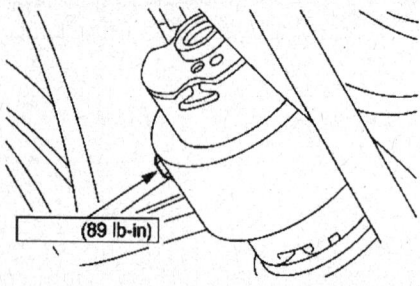

Fig. 7 Electric water pump replacement. LS w/3.9L engine & Thunderbird

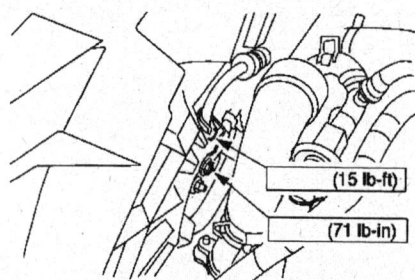

Fig. 8 Cooling fan high pressure line replacement. LS & Thunderbird

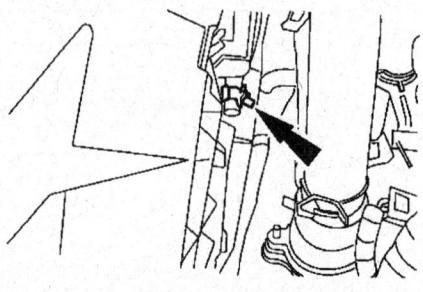

Fig. 9 Return line replacement. LS & Thunderbird

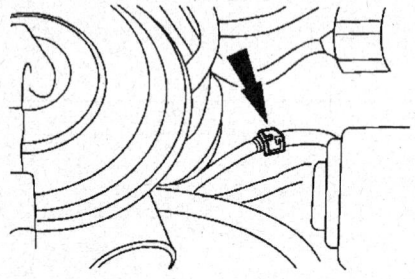

Fig. 10 Fan shroud return line separation. LS & Thunderbird

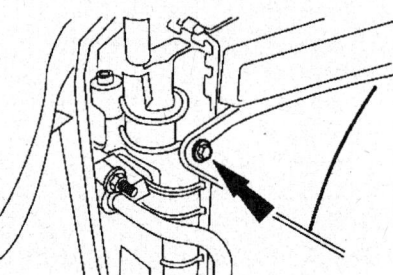

Fig. 11 Fan shroud mounting bolts replacement. LS & Thunderbird

COMPONENT REPLACEMENT

Cooling Fan Motor

1. Drain engine cooling system into suitable container.
2. Remove upper radiator sight shield.
3. Remove air cleaner outlet tube.
4. Remove mounting bolts and radiator support brackets.
5. Remove upper radiator hose.
6. Remove mounting bolt and position receiver drier aside.
7. **On models equipped with 3.9L engine,** remove mounting bolt and position electric water pump aside, **Fig. 7.**
8. **On all models,** disconnect high pressure cooling fan line, **Fig. 8.**
9. Disconnect return hose, **Fig. 9.**
10. Separate return hose from fan shroud and position aside, **Fig. 10.**
11. Remove mounting bolts and fan shroud, **Fig. 11.**
12. Support air conditioning condenser with suitable mechanics wire.
13. Raise and support vehicle.
14. Remove mounting screws, then the left and righthand splash shields.
15. Remove radiator air deflector.
16. Disconnect lower radiator hose.
17. Remove radiator condenser mounting bolts.
18. Remove mounting bolts and condenser support brackets.
19. Remove radiator.
20. Reverse procedure to install, noting the following:
    a. **Torque** radiator condenser mounting bolts to 89 inch lbs.
    b. **Torque** lower radiator hose clamp to 10 ft. lbs.
    c. **Torque** cooling fan high pressure line mounting bolt to 15 ft. lbs.
    d. **Torque** cooling fan high pressure line bracket mounting bolt to 71 inch lbs.
    e. **Torque** electric water pump mounting bolt to 89 inch lbs.
    f. **Torque** receiver drier mounting bolt 96 inch lbs.
    g. **Torque** upper radiator support mounting bolts to 89 inch lbs.

STARTER MOTORS
Ford Motorcraft Starters

NOTE: On Air Bag Equipped Models, Refer To "Air Bag System Precautions" Located In The Front Of This Manual For System Disarming & Arming Procedures.

NOTE: Refer To "Computer Relearn Procedures" Located In The Front Of This Manual When Battery Power To The Computer Has Been Interrupted.

NOTE: "Electrical Symbol & Wire Color Code Identification" Located In The Front Of This Manual May Be Used As An Aid When Using Wiring Circuits Found In This Section.

INDEX

GENERAL INFORMATION

Solenoid Switches

The solenoid switch on a cranking motor not only closes the circuit between the battery and the cranking motor but also shifts the drive pinion into mesh with the engine flywheel ring gear. This is done by means of a linkage between the solenoid switch plunger and the shift lever on the cranking motor.

There are two windings in the solenoid; a pull-in winding and a hold-in winding. Both windings are energized when the external control switch is closed. They produce a magnetic field which pulls the plunger in so that the drive pinion is shifted into mesh, and the main contacts in the solenoid switch are closed to connect the battery directly to the cranking motor. Closing the main switch contacts shorts out the pull-in winding since this winding is connected across the main contacts. The magnetism produced by the hold-in winding is sufficient to hold the plunger in, and shorting out the pull-in winding reduces drain on the battery. When the control switch is opened, it disconnects the hold-in winding from the battery. When the hold-in winding is disconnected from the battery, the shift lever spring withdraws the plunger from the

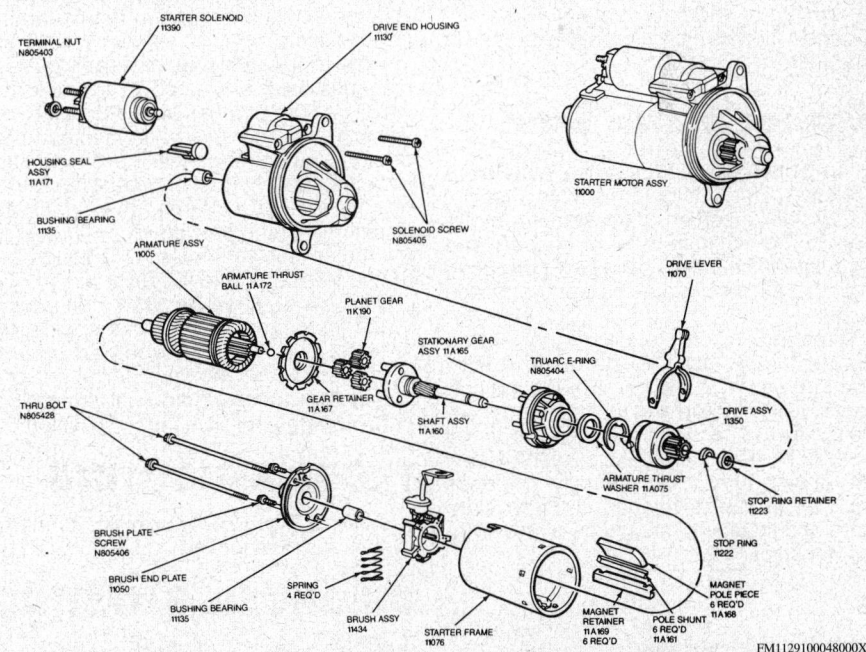

Fig. 1 Exploded view of Ford Motorcraft gear reduced permanent magnet starter motor

solenoid, opening the solenoid switch contacts and at the same time withdrawing the drive pinion from mesh. Proper operation of the switch depends on maintaining a defi-

nite balance between the magnetic strength of the pull-in and hold-in windings.

This balance is established in the design by the size of the wire and the number of

Condition	Possible Source	Action
• The Engine Does Not Crank or the Relay Clicks	• Battery. • Starter motor (11002). • Starter motor relay. • Ignition switch. • Damaged fuse. • Anti-theft system. • Circuitry.	• GO to Pinpoint Test A.
• The Engine Cranks Slowly	• Battery. • Starter motor. • Circuitry.	• PERFORM the Starter Motor—Voltage Drop Test
• Unusual Starter Noise	• Starter mounting. • Flywheel/ring gear. • Starter motor.	• GO to Pinpoint Test B.

FM1120100592010X

Fig. 2 Starting system troubleshooting (Part 1 of 2). Continental

Condition	Possible Sources	Action
•Engine does not crank but relay clicks	•Battery. •Starter motor •Relay. •Circuit	•GO to Pinpoint Test A.
•Engine does not crank and relay does not click	•Battery. •Fuse. •Relay. •Circuit. •Starter motor. •Ignition switch.	•GO to Pinpoint Test B.
•Engine cranks slowly	•Battery. •Circuitry. •Starter motor.	•GO to Pinpoint Test C.
•Unusual starter motor noise	•Starter motor. •Flywheel ring gear.	•CHECK flywheel ring gear. •INSPECT starter motor for alignment, cracked case. Make sure the mounting bolts are tightened. If necessary, INSTALL a new starter motor.
•The starter spins but the engine does not crank	•Starter motor.	•INSPECT the flywheel ring gear for missing teeth. CHECK starter motor for correct mounting. If concern persists, INSTALL a new starter motor.

FM1120100600000X

Fig. 3 Starting system troubleshooting. Cougar

turns specified. An open circuit in the hold-in winding or attempts to crank with a discharged battery will cause the switch to chatter.

Starter Motor Service

To obtain full performance data on a starting motor or to determine the cause of abnormal operation, the starting motor should be submitted to a no-load and torque test. These tests are best performed with the starter mounted on a starter bench tester.

From a practical standpoint, however, a simple torque test may be made quickly with the starter in the car. Ensure the battery is fully charged and that the starter circuit wires and terminals are in good condition, then operate the starter to see if the engine turns over normally. If it does not, the torque developed is below standard and the starter should be removed for further inspecting.

DESCRIPTION

This type of starter motor has the starter solenoid mounted on the starter housing, **Fig. 1.** The starter relay connects battery power to the starter solenoid, causing it to energize. On models equipped with manual transmission, a clutch switch in the starter control circuit prevents operation unless the clutch pedal is depressed. On models equipped with automatic transmission, a neutral safety switch in the starter control

circuit prevents operation of the starter unless the selector lever is in the Neutral or Park position.

When the starter solenoid is energized, a magnetic field is created in the solenoid windings. The plunger core is drawn to the solenoid coil and a lever connected to the drive assembly engages the drive pinion gear into the flywheel ring gear. When the plunger is all the way in, its contact disc closes the circuit between the battery and the motor feed terminals. This sends current to the motor and the drive pinion gear cranks the flywheel to start the engine. When the current flows to the engine, the solenoid pull-in coil is bypassed and the hold-in coil keeps the drive pinion gear engaged with the flywheel until the ignition switch is released from the On position.

TROUBLESHOOTING

Refer to **Figs. 2 through 10,** for starter system troubleshooting.

DIAGNOSIS & TESTING
Motor Feed Circuit Voltage Drop Test

1. Ensure battery is fully charged.
2. Disconnect inertia fuel shutoff switch.
3. Connect remote starter switch between starter solenoid S terminal and battery positive.
4. Connect suitable multi-meter positive lead to battery positive post, and negative lead to starter M terminal, **Fig. 11.**

Condition	Possible Source	Action
• The Starter Spins But The Engine Does Not Crank	• Starter motor • Damaged flywheel/ring gear teeth.	• INSPECT the starter motor mounting and engagement. REPLACE the starter motor. • INSPECT the flywheel/ring gear for damaged, missing or worn teeth. REPAIR as required.

FM1120100592020X

Fig. 2 Starting system troubleshooting (Part 2 of 2). Continental

Condition	Possible Source	Action
• The Engine Does Not Crank	• Battery. • Starter motor. • Starter motor solenoid relay switch. • Starter motor relay. • Ignition switch (11572). • Damaged fuse. • Anti-theft system. • Circuitry.	• GO to Pinpoint Test A.
• The Engine Cranks in Reverse and Other Forward Gears	• Shift linkage (Adjustment). • Digital Transmission Range (TR) Sensor.	
• The Engine Cranks Slowly	• Battery. • Starter motor. • Circuitry.	• PERFORM the Starter Motor—Voltage Drop Test REFER to Starter Motor—Voltage Drop

FM1120100612010X

Fig. 4 Starting system troubleshooting (Part 1 of 2). Crown Victoria, Grand Marquis & Marauder

5. Engage remote starter switch and measure voltage.
6. Measurement should be approximately .5 volts.
7. If measurement is .5 volts or less, refer to "Motor Ground Circuit Voltage Drop Test."
8. If measurement is more than .5 volts, move multi-meter negative lead to starter solenoid B terminal and repeat test.
9. If measurement at B terminal is less than .5 volt, inspect starter solenoid connections or solenoid contacts.
10. Remove cables from B, S and M terminals, clean, install and perform voltage drop test, again.
11. If voltage drop measurement is still more than .5 volts when inspected at M terminal, or less than .5 volts when inspected at B terminal, replace starter.
12. If voltage drop reading is still more than .5 volts at B terminal after terminal cleaning, replace positive battery cable.

Motor Ground Circuit Voltage Drop Test

1. Disconnect inertia fuel cutoff switch.
2. Connect remote starter switch between starter solenoid S terminal and battery positive terminal.
3. Connect suitable multi-meter positive lead to starter motor housing and negative lead to negative battery terminal, **Fig. 12.**
4. Engage remote starter switch and crank engine.
5. Measurement should be approximately .2 volts, or less.
6. If voltage drop is more than .2 volts, clean negative cable connections at battery and body connections and re-test.
7. If voltage drop is more than .2 volts, proceed as follows:

Condition	Possible Source	Action
• Unusual Starter Noise	• Starter mounting. • Flywheel/ring gear. • Starter motor.	• GO to Pinpoint Test B.
• The Starter Spins But the Engine Does Not Crank	• Starter motor. • Damaged flywheel/ring gear teeth.	• INSPECT the starter motor mounting and engagement. REPAIR as required. • INSPECT the flywheel/ring gear for damaged, missing or worn teeth. REPAIR as required.

FM1120100612020X

Fig. 4 Starting system troubleshooting (Part 2 of 2). Crown Victoria, Grand Marquis & Marauder

Condition	Possible Source	Action
• Starter Spins but Engine Does Not Crank	• Starter motor. • Damaged flywheel/ring gear teeth.	• INSPECT the starter motor mounting and engagement. REPAIR as necessary. • INSPECT the flywheel/ring gear for damaged, missing or worn teeth. REPAIR as necessary.
• Engine Cranks With Clutch Pedal Not Applied (Manual)	• Starter clutch pedal position switch.	• REPLACE the starter clutch pedal position switch.

FM1120100635020X

Fig. 5 Starting system troubleshooting (Part 2 of 2). Escort & ZX2

a. Determine which way the current is flowing in cable, then connect multi-meter positive cable to end nearest battery positive.
b. Connect multi-meter negative lead to terminal at other end of cable.
c. Crank engine.
d. Measurement should be approximately .2 volts. or less.
e. If voltage drop is too high, clean terminal ends and perform test again.
f. If voltage drop reading is still too high, replace cable.
g. If measurement is less than .2 volts and engine cranks slowly, replace starter motor.

Load Test

1. Ensure battery is fully charged.
2. Set parking brake and shift transaxle/transmission to Neutral position.
3. Disconnect ignition coil electrical connector.
4. Connect suitable starter, alternator, battery regulator electrical tester.
5. Connect remote starter switch across starter relay S terminal and battery terminal.
6. Turn ignition key to Run position.
7. Crank engine with remote starter switch and measure voltage.
8. Stop cranking engine and turn carbon pile rheostat until voltmeter indicates same reading as obtained in previous step.
9. Ammeter will indicate starter current draw under load.
10. Compare amperage indicated with specifications listed in "Starter Specifications."

No Load Test

1. Remove starter motor.
2. Connect suitable battery, alternator battery regulator electrical tester to fully charged battery and remote starter switch to starter motor.
3. Engage remote starter switch.
4. Ensure pinion shifts to crank position and starter motor operates smoothly.
5. While starter motor is operating, inspect voltmeter and ammeter readings.
6. Voltmeter should read approximately 11 volts and amperage should be not more than 70 amps.
7. If voltage is lower than specified or amperage is higher than specified, refer to **Fig. 13.**

Symptom Related Test

CONTINENTAL

Refer to **Figs. 14 and 15,** for starting system symptom related test.

COUGAR

Refer to **Figs. 16 through 18,** for starting system symptom related test.

CROWN VICTORIA, GRAND MARQUIS & MARAUDER

Refer to **Figs. 19 and 20,** for starting system symptom related test.

Condition	Possible Source	Action
• The Engine Cranks Slowly	• Battery. • Starter motor. • Circuitry.	• CARRY OUT the starter motor-motor feed circuit and/or the starter motor-ground circuit test.
• The Engine Does Not Crank or the Relay Clicks	• Battery. • Starter motor. • Circuitry.	• GO to Pinpoint Test A.
• Unusual Starter Noise	• Starter mounting. • Starter motor. • Improper starter drive engagement.	• GO to Pinpoint Test B.

FM1120100635010X

Fig. 5 Starting system troubleshooting (Part 1 of 2). Escort & ZX2

Condition	Possible Sources	Action
•Engine does not crank but relay clicks	•Battery. •Starter motor •Relay. •Circuit.	•GO to Pinpoint Test A.
•Engine does not crank and relay does not click	•PATS. •Battery. •Fuse. •Relay. •Circuit. •Starter motor. •Ignition switch. •Ignition switch (manual transaxle only)	•GO to Pinpoint Test B.
•Engine cranks slowly	•Battery. •Circuit. •Starter motor.	•GO to Pinpoint Test C.
•Unusual starter motor noise	•Starter motor. •Flywheel ring gear.	•CHECK flywheel ring gear. •INSPECT starter motor for alignment, cracked case. Make sure the mounting bolts are tightened. If necessary, INSTALL a new starter motor.

FM1120100685010X

Fig. 6 Starting system troubleshooting (Part 1 of 2). Focus

ESCORT & ZX2

Refer to **Figs. 21 and 22,** for starting system symptom related test.

FOCUS

Refer to **Figs. 23 through 25,** for starting system symptom related test.

LS & THUNDERBIRD

Refer to **Figs. 26 and 27,** for starting system symptom related test.

MUSTANG

Refer to **Figs. 28 and 29,** for starting system symptom related test.

FIVE HUNDRED, FREESTYLE, MONTEGO, SABLE & TAURUS

Refer to **Figs. 30 and 31,** for starting system symptom related test.

TOWN CAR

Refer to **Figs. 32 and 33,** for starting system symptom related test.

Condition	Possible Sources	Action
• The starter spins but the engine does not crank	• Starter motor.	• INSPECT the flywheel ring gear for missing teeth. CHECK starter motor for correct mounting. If concern persists, INSTALL a new starter motor.

FM1120100685020X

Fig. 6 Starting system troubleshooting (Part 2 of 2). Focus

Condition	Possible Source	Action
• The engine does not crank	• Battery. • BJB fuse ignition switch (40A). • CJB Fuse 6 (20A). • Starter motor (11002). • Ignition switch (11572). • Circuitry. • Starter motor relay. • Clutch pedal position (CPP) switch.	• GO to Pinpoint Test A.
• The engine cranks slowly	• Battery. • Starter motor. • Ignition switch. • Circuitry.	• CARRY OUT The Starter Motor-Voltage Drop Test Component Test.
• Unusual starter noise	• Starter motor mounting. • Starter motor. • Incorrect starter drive engagement.	• GO to Pinpoint Test B.
• The starter spins but the engine does not crank	• Starter Motor • Damaged flywheel/ring gear teeth.	• INSPECT the starter motor mounting and engagement. REPAIR as necessary. • INSPECT the flywheel/ring gear for damaged, missing or worn teeth. REPAIR as necessary.

FM1120100659000X

Fig. 8 Starting system troubleshooting. Mustang

Condition	Possible Source	Action
• The Engine Does Not Crank	• Battery. • Starter motor. • Starter motor solenoid relay switch. • Starter motor relay. • Ignition switch (11572). • Damaged fuse. • Anti-theft system. • Circuitry.	• GO to Pinpoint Test A.
• The Engine Cranks in Reverse and Other Forward Gears	• Shift linkage (Adjustment). • Digital Transmission Range (TR) Sensor.	• **Diagnose transmission shift linkage & digital sensor**
• The Engine Cranks Slowly	• Battery. • Starter motor. • Circuitry.	• PERFORM the Starter Motor—Voltage Drop Test Component Test.

FM1120100682010X

Fig. 10 Starting system troubleshooting (Part 1 of 2). Town Car

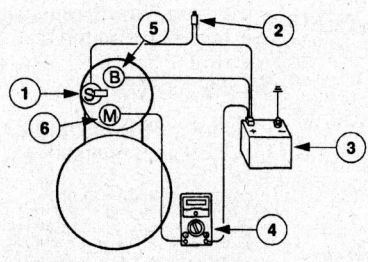

Item	Part Number	Description
1	—	S-Terminal
2	—	Remote Starter Switch
3	10653	Battery
4	—	Rotunda 73 Digital Multimeter
5	—	B-Terminal
6	—	M-Terminal

FM1120100598000X

Fig. 11 Starter motor feed circuit voltage drop test

Condition	Possible Source	Action
• The engine cranks slowly	• Battery. • Ignition switch. • Starter motor. • Circuitry.	• CARRY OUT the starter motor-motor feed circuit and/or the starter motor-ground circuit test.
• The engine does not crank	• Battery. • Central junction box (CJB) fuse F201 (5A). • Auxiliary junction box (AJB) fuse F121 (30A). • Battery junction box (BJB) fuse F422 (20A). • Ignition switch. • Starter relay. • Anti-theft system. • Circuitry.	• GO to Pinpoint Test A.
• Unusual starter noise	• Starter motor. • Starter motor mounting. • Incorrect starter motor drive engagements.	• GO to Pinpoint Test B.
• The starter spins but the engine does not crank	• Starter motor. • Broken flywheel/ring gear teeth.	• INSPECT the starter motor mounting and engagement. • INSPECT the flywheel/ring gear for broke, missing or worn teeth. REPAIR as necessary.
• Engine cranks with clutch pedal not applied (manual transmission)	• Starter clutch pedal position (CPP) switch.	• INSTALL a new clutch pedal position (CPP) switch.

FM1120100652000X

Fig. 7 Starting system troubleshooting. LS & Thunderbird

Condition	Possible Source	Action
• The engine does not crank	• Battery. • Open fuse. • Starter motor. • Ignition switch. • Digital transmission range (TR) sensor. • Circuitry. • Starter motor relay. • Anti-theft system.	• GO to Pinpoint Test A.
• The engine cranks slowly	• Battery. • Starter motor. • Ignition switch. • Circuitry.	• CARRY OUT the starter motor component test.
• Unusual starter noise	• Starter motor mounting. • Starter motor. • Incorrect starter drive engagement.	• GO to Pinpoint Test B.
• The starter spins but the engine does not crank	• Starter motor. • Damaged flywheel/ring gear teeth.	• INSPECT the starter motor mounting and engagement. • INSPECT the flywheel/ring gear for damaged, missing or worn teeth. REPAIR as necessary.

FM1120100672000X

Fig. 9 Starting system troubleshooting. Five Hundred, Freestyle, Montego, Sable & Taurus

Condition	Possible Source	Action
• Unusual Starter Noise	• Starter mounting. • Flywheel/ring gear. • Starter motor.	• GO to Pinpoint Test B.
• The Starter Spins But the Engine Does Not Crank	• Starter motor. • Damaged flywheel/ring gear teeth.	• INSPECT the starter motor mounting and engagement. REPAIR as required. • INSPECT the flywheel/ring gear for damaged, missing or worn teeth. REPAIR as required.

FM1120100682020X

Fig. 10 Starting system troubleshooting (Part 2 of 2). Town Car

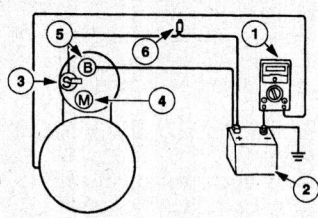

Item	Part Number	Description
1	—	Rotunda 73 Digital Multimeter
2	10653	Battery
3	—	S-Terminal
4	—	M-Terminal
5	—	B-Terminal
6	—	Remote Starter Switch

FM1120100599000X

Fig. 12 Starter motor ground circuit voltage drop test

Condition	Possible Sources	Action
•Normal current and speed	•Battery. •Switches. •Wiring.	•RECHECK battery, switches and wiring, including voltage drop tests, if cranking starter motor operation on engine is slow or sluggish.
•Current flow with test circuit switch open	•Solenoid contacts.	•TEST and, if necessary, INSTALL a new solenoid assembly.
•Failure to operate with very little or no current	•Solenoid winding.	•INSPECT and TEST solenoid assembly.
	•Field circuit.	•INSPECT and TEST frame and field coil assembly.
	•Armature coil or commutator bars.	•INSPECT armature.
	•Brush springs or brushes.	•INSPECT brushes and brush springs.
•Failure to operate with high current	•Bearing or drivetrain.	•INSPECT bearing, armature, driveshaft and related drive parts.

FM1120100604010X

Fig. 13 Starter motor no load test results
(Part 1 of 2)

Condition	Possible Sources	Action
	•Terminals or fields.	•INSPECT and TEST frame and field coil assembly, solenoid assembly and brush installations for shorts.
•Low speed with high current	•Bushings, gear reduction unit, armature shaft, pole shoe or driveshaft.	•INSPECT bearing, armature, driveshaft and gear reduction gears.
	•Armature.	•INSPECT and TEST armature.
	•Armature or fields.	•INSPECT and TEST frame and field coil assembly and armature.
•Low speed with normal or low current	•Connections, leads or commutator.	•INSPECT internal wiring, electrical connections and armature commutator.
	•Solenoid winding.	•INSPECT and TEST solenoid assembly.
	•Field circuit.	•INSPECT and TEST frame and field coil assembly.
	•Armature coils or commutator bars.	•INSPECT armature.
	•Brush springs or brushes.	•INSPECT brushes and brush springs.
•High speed with high current	•Fields.	•INSPECT and TEST field and frame assembly.

FM1120100604020X

Fig. 13 Starter motor no load test results
(Part 2 of 2)

DIAGNOSTIC CHART INDEX

TEST CONDITIONS	TEST DETAILS/RESULTS/ACTIONS
A1 CHECK THE BATTERY	
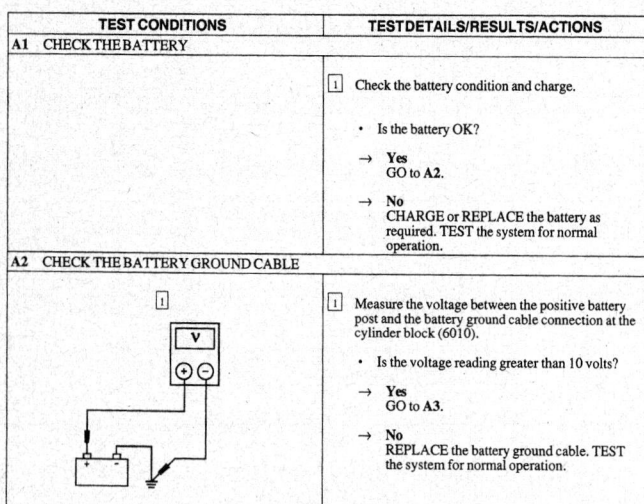	① Check the battery condition and charge. • Is the battery OK? → **Yes** GO to **A2**. → **No** CHARGE or REPLACE the battery as required. TEST the system for normal operation.
A2 CHECK THE BATTERY GROUND CABLE	
①	① Measure the voltage between the positive battery post and the battery ground cable connection at the cylinder block (6010). • Is the voltage reading greater than 10 volts? → **Yes** GO to **A3**. → **No** REPLACE the battery ground cable. TEST the system for normal operation.

FM1120100596010X

Fig. 14   Test A: Engine Does Not Crank Or Relay Clicks (Part 1 of 10). Continental

TEST CONDITIONS	TEST DETAILS/RESULTS/ACTIONS
A5 CHECK THE STARTER MOTOR	
①	① Connect one end of a jumper wire to the B terminal of the starter motor and momentarily connect the other end of the starter solenoid S terminal. • Does the starter motor engage and the engine crank? → **Yes** GO to **A6**. → **No** REPLACE the starter motor. TEST the system for normal operation.
A6 CHECK START INPUT TO THE STARTER MOTOR	
① Starter S Connector ③	② Hold the ignition switch to the START position. ③ Measure the voltage at the starter motor solenoid S connector. • Is the voltage reading greater than 10 volts? → **Yes** CLEAN the starter solenoid S terminal and connector. CHECK the wiring and the starter motor for a loose or intermittent connection. TEST the system for normal operation. → **No** GO to **A7**.

FM1120100596030X

Fig. 14   Test A: Engine Does Not Crank Or Relay Clicks (Part 3 of 10). Continental

TEST CONDITIONS	TEST DETAILS/RESULTS/ACTIONS
A3 CHECK THE STARTER MOTOR GROUND	
①	① Measure the voltage between the battery positive post and the starter motor case. • Is the voltage greater than 10 volts? → **Yes** GO to **A4**. → **No** CLEAN the starter motor mounting flange and make sure the starter motor is properly mounted. TEST the system for normal operation.
A4 CHECK THE POWER SUPPLY TO THE STARTER MOTOR	
①	② Measure the voltage at the starter motor B terminal. • Is the voltage reading greater than 10 volts? → **Yes** GO to **A5**. → **No** REPLACE the positive battery cable. TEST the system for normal operation.

FM1120100596020X

Fig. 14   Test A: Engine Does Not Crank Or Relay Clicks (Part 2 of 10). Continental

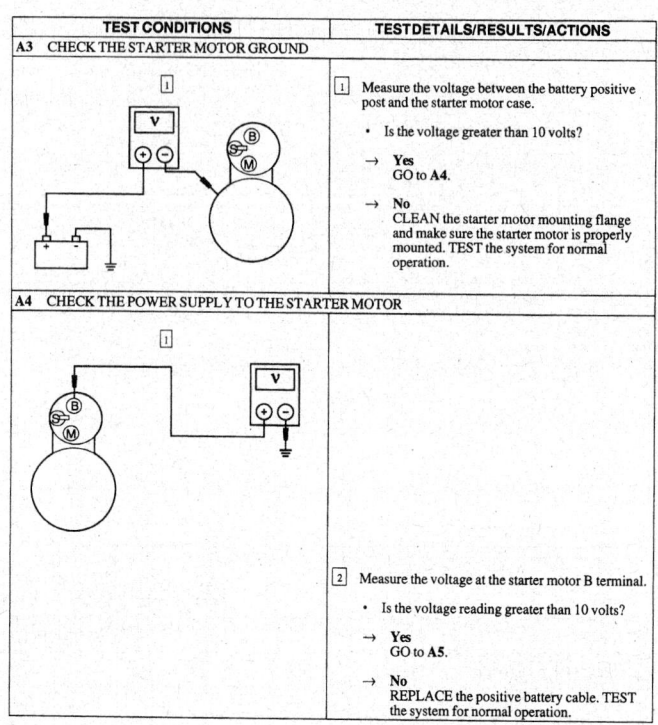

TEST CONDITIONS	TEST DETAILS/RESULTS/ACTIONS
A7 CHECK THE START INPUT TO THE STARTER RELAY	
① ② Starter Relay ④	③ Hold the ignition switch in the START position. ④ Measure the voltage at the starter relay connector Pin 86, Circuit 1093 (T/R). • Is the voltage reading greater than 10 volts? → **Yes** GO to **A8**. → **No** GO to **A12**.
A8 CHECK THE BATTERY SUPPLY TO THE STARTER RELAY	
① ②	② Measure the voltage at the starter relay connector Pin 30, Circuit 113 (Y/LB). • Is the voltage reading greater than 10 volts? → **Yes** GO to **A9**. → **No** REPAIR the open in Circuit 113 (Y/LB). TEST the system for normal operation.

FM1120100596040X

Fig. 14   Test A: Engine Does Not Crank Or Relay Clicks (Part 4 of 10). Continental

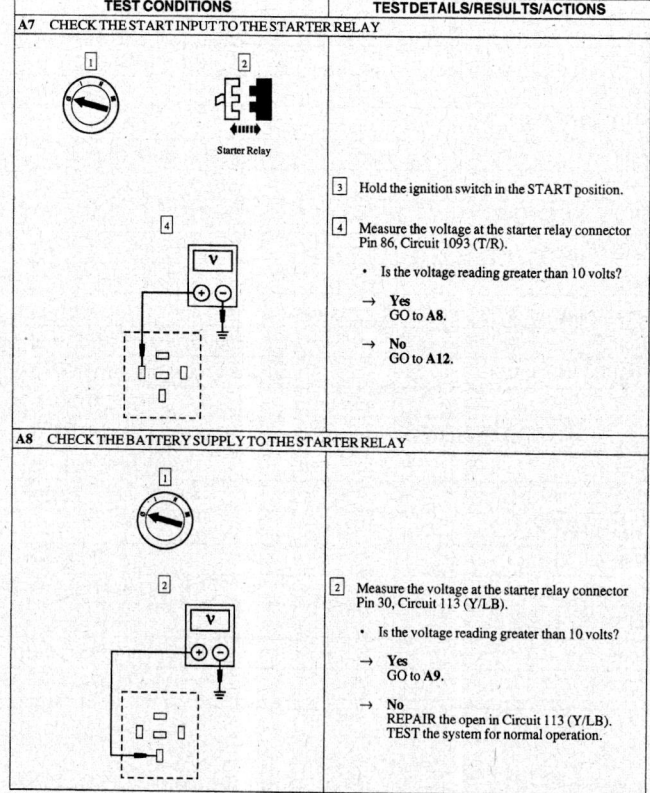

TEST CONDITIONS	TESTDETAILS/RESULTS/ACTIONS
A9 CHECK THE STARTER RELAY GROUND	

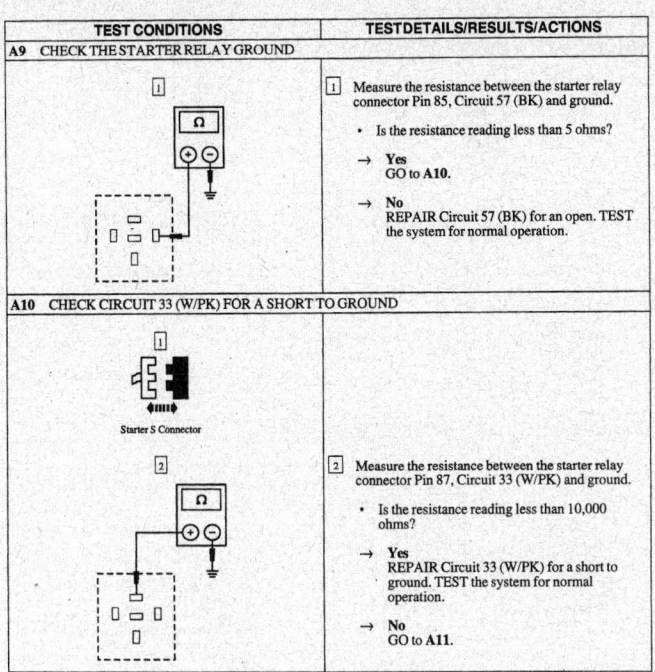

① Measure the resistance between the starter relay connector Pin 85, Circuit 57 (BK) and ground.

- Is the resistance reading less than 5 ohms?

→ **Yes**
GO to **A10**.

→ **No**
REPAIR Circuit 57 (BK) for an open. TEST the system for normal operation.

TEST CONDITIONS	TESTDETAILS/RESULTS/ACTIONS
A10 CHECK CIRCUIT 33 (W/PK) FOR A SHORT TO GROUND	

Starter S Connector

② Measure the resistance between the starter relay connector Pin 87, Circuit 33 (W/PK) and ground.

- Is the resistance reading less than 10,000 ohms?

→ **Yes**
REPAIR Circuit 33 (W/PK) for a short to ground. TEST the system for normal operation.

→ **No**
GO to **A11**.

FM1120100596050X

Fig. 14   Test A: Engine Does Not Crank Or Relay Clicks (Part 5 of 10). Continental

TEST CONDITIONS	TESTDETAILS/RESULTS/ACTIONS
A14 CHECK THE SUPPLY TO THE IGNITION SWITCH	

Ignition Switch C236

② Measure the voltage at the ignition switch connector Pin C236-B4, Circuit 38 (BK/O).

- Is the voltage reading greater than 10 volts?

→ **Yes**
GO to **A15**.

→ **No**
REPAIR Circuit 38 (BK/O) for an open. TEST the system for normal operation.

TEST CONDITIONS	TESTDETAILS/RESULTS/ACTIONS
A15 CHECK CIRCUIT 32 (R/LB) FOR AN OPEN	

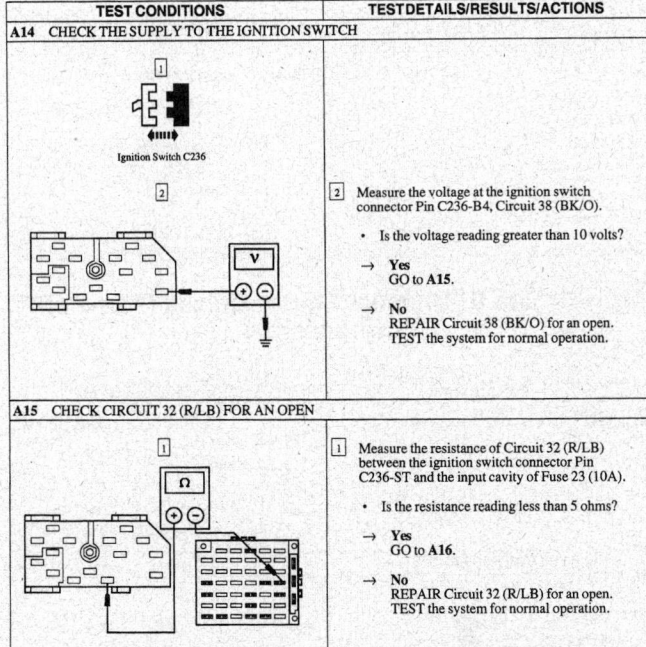

① Measure the resistance of Circuit 32 (R/LB) between the ignition switch connector Pin C236-ST and the input cavity of Fuse 23 (10A).

- Is the resistance reading less than 5 ohms?

→ **Yes**
GO to **A16**.

→ **No**
REPAIR Circuit 32 (R/LB) for an open. TEST the system for normal operation.

FM1120100596070X

Fig. 14   Test A: Engine Does Not Crank Or Relay Clicks (Part 7 of 10). Continental

TEST CONDITIONS	TESTDETAILS/RESULTS/ACTIONS
A11 CHECK CIRCUIT 33 (W/PK) FOR AN OPEN	

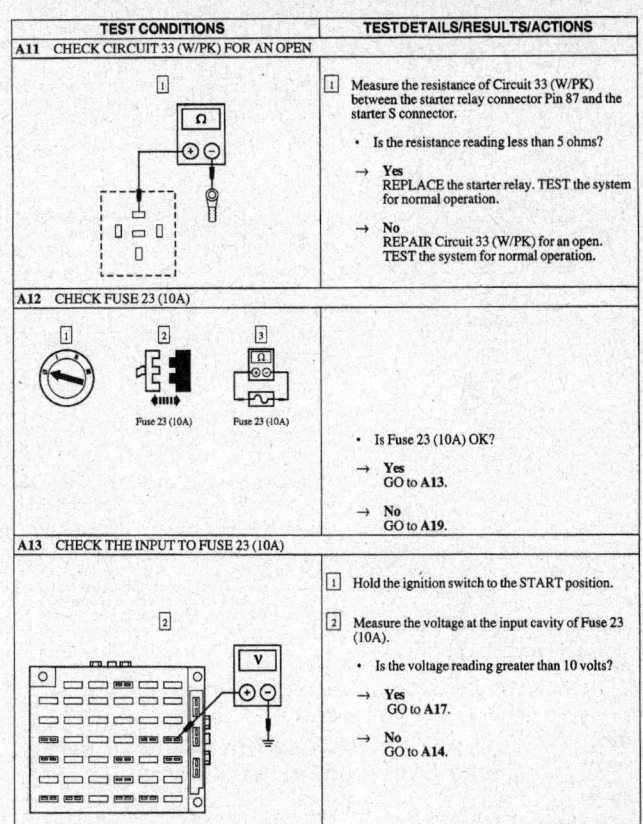

① Measure the resistance of Circuit 33 (W/PK) between the starter relay connector Pin 87 and the starter S connector.

- Is the resistance reading less than 5 ohms?

→ **Yes**
REPLACE the starter relay. TEST the system for normal operation.

→ **No**
REPAIR Circuit 33 (W/PK) for an open. TEST the system for normal operation.

TEST CONDITIONS	TESTDETAILS/RESULTS/ACTIONS
A12 CHECK FUSE 23 (10A)	

Fuse 23 (10A)   Fuse 23 (10A)

- Is Fuse 23 (10A) OK?

→ **Yes**
GO to **A13**.

→ **No**
GO to **A19**.

TEST CONDITIONS	TESTDETAILS/RESULTS/ACTIONS
A13 CHECK THE INPUT TO FUSE 23 (10A)	

① Hold the ignition switch to the START position.

② Measure the voltage at the input cavity of Fuse 23 (10A).

- Is the voltage reading greater than 10 volts?

→ **Yes**
GO to **A17**.

→ **No**
GO to **A14**.

FM1120100596060X

Fig. 14   Test A: Engine Does Not Crank Or Relay Clicks (Part 6 of 10). Continental

TEST CONDITIONS	TESTDETAILS/RESULTS/ACTIONS
A16 CHECK CIRCUIT 32 (R/LB) FOR A SHORT TO GROUND	

① Measure the resistance between the ignition switch connector Pin C236-ST, Circuit 32 (R/LB) and ground.

- Is the resistance reading less than 10,000 ohms?

→ **Yes**
REPAIR Circuit 32 (R/LB) for a short to ground. TEST the system for normal operation.

→ **No**
REPLACE the ignition switch. TEST the system for normal operation.

TEST CONDITIONS	TESTDETAILS/RESULTS/ACTIONS
A17 CHECK CIRCUIT 1290 (W/O) FOR AN OPEN	

Digital TR C180

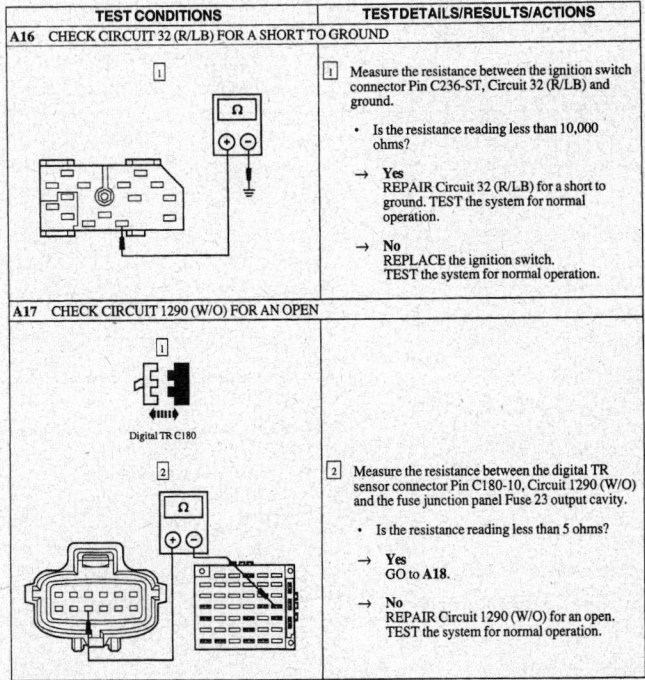

② Measure the resistance between the digital TR sensor connector Pin C180-10, Circuit 1290 (W/O) and the fuse junction panel Fuse 23 output cavity.

- Is the resistance reading less than 5 ohms?

→ **Yes**
GO to **A18**.

→ **No**
REPAIR Circuit 1290 (W/O) for an open. TEST the system for normal operation.

FM1120100596080X

Fig. 14   Test A: Engine Does Not Crank Or Relay Clicks (Part 8 of 10). Continental

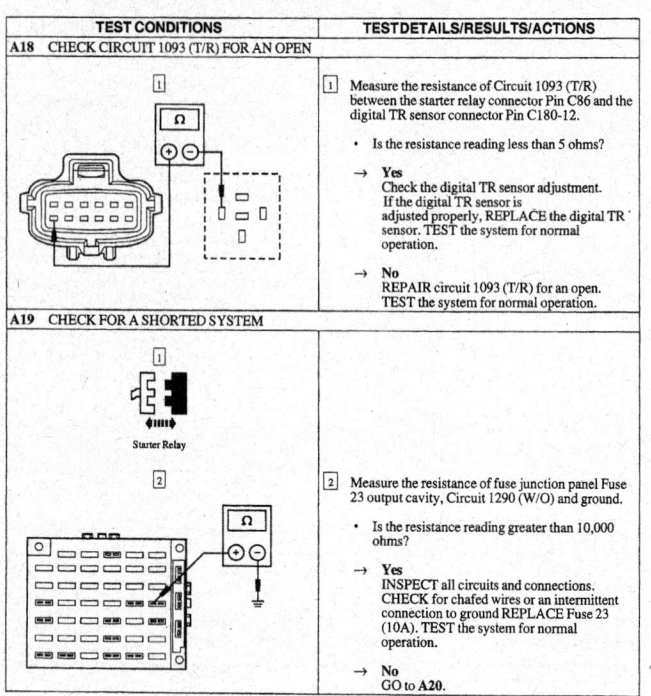

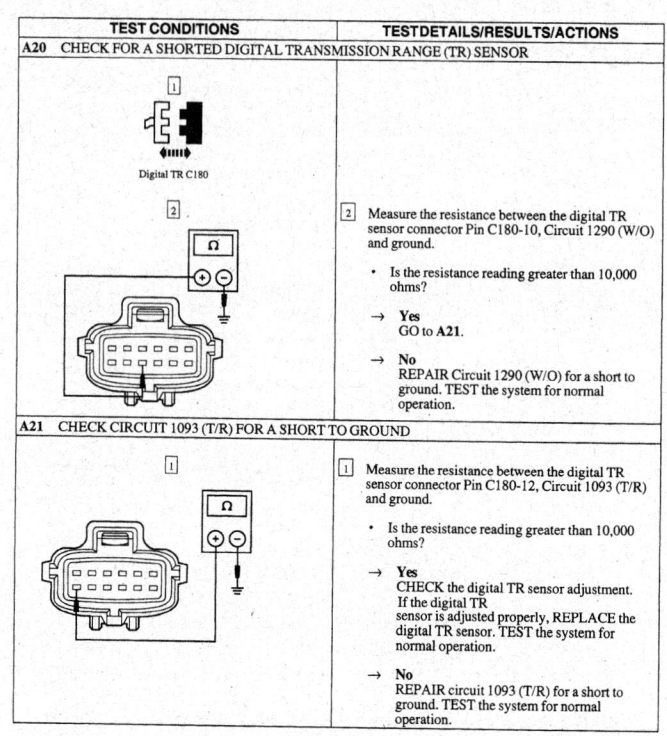

TEST CONDITIONS	TESTDETAILS/RESULTS/ACTIONS
A18 CHECK CIRCUIT 1093 (T/R) FOR AN OPEN	**1** Measure the resistance of Circuit 1093 (T/R) between the starter relay connector Pin C86 and the digital TR sensor connector Pin C180-12. • Is the resistance reading less than 5 ohms? → **Yes** Check the digital TR sensor adjustment. If the digital TR sensor is adjusted properly, REPLACE the digital TR sensor. TEST the system for normal operation. → **No** REPAIR circuit 1093 (T/R) for an open. TEST the system for normal operation.
A19 CHECK FOR A SHORTED SYSTEM	**2** Measure the resistance of fuse junction panel Fuse 23 output cavity, Circuit 1290 (W/O) and ground. • Is the resistance reading greater than 10,000 ohms? → **Yes** INSPECT all circuits and connections. CHECK for chafed wires or an intermittent connection to ground REPLACE Fuse 23 (10A). TEST the system for normal operation. → **No** GO to **A20**.

FM1120100596090X

Fig. 14   Test A: Engine Does Not Crank Or Relay Clicks (Part 9 of 10). Continental

TEST CONDITIONS	TESTDETAILS/RESULTS/ACTIONS
A20 CHECK FOR A SHORTED DIGITAL TRANSMISSION RANGE (TR) SENSOR	**2** Measure the resistance between the digital TR sensor connector Pin C180-10, Circuit 1290 (W/O) and ground. • Is the resistance reading greater than 10,000 ohms? → **Yes** GO to **A21**. → **No** REPAIR Circuit 1290 (W/O) for a short to ground. TEST the system for normal operation.
A21 CHECK CIRCUIT 1093 (T/R) FOR A SHORT TO GROUND	**1** Measure the resistance between the digital TR sensor connector Pin C180-12, Circuit 1093 (T/R) and ground. • Is the resistance reading greater than 10,000 ohms? → **Yes** CHECK the digital TR sensor adjustment. If the digital TR sensor is adjusted properly, REPLACE the digital TR sensor. TEST the system for normal operation. → **No** REPAIR circuit 1093 (T/R) for a short to ground. TEST the system for normal operation.

FM1120100596100X

Fig. 14   Test A: Engine Does Not Crank Or Relay Clicks (Part 10 of 10). Continental

TEST CONDITIONS	TESTDETAILS/RESULTS/ACTIONS
B1 CHECK STARTER MOUNTING	**1** Inspect the starter mounting bolts and brackets for looseness. • Is the starter motor mounted properly? → **Yes** GO to **B2**. → **No** Install the starter motor properly; TEST the system for normal operation.
B2 CHECK FOR ENGINE NOISE	**2** Engage the starter motor and verify the noise is due to the starter operation. **3** Connect a remote starter switch between the starter solenoid B and S terminals. • Is the noise due to the starter motor engagement? → **Yes** GO to **B3**. → **No** Diagnose engine mechainical noise.
B3 CHECK FOR UNUSUAL WEAR	**1** Remove the starter motor

FM1120100597010X

Fig. 15   Test B: Unusual Starter Noises (Part 1 of 2). Continental

TEST CONDITIONS	TESTDETAILS/RESULTS/ACTIONS
B3 CHECK FOR UNUSUAL WEAR (Continued)	**2** Inspect the ring gear for damaged or worn teeth. • Is the noise due to ring gear tooth damage? → **Yes** REPLACE the ring gear. EXAMINE the starter pinion teeth. If damaged, REPLACE the starter motor. TEST the system for normal operation. → **No** REPLACE the starter motor. TEST the system for normal operation.

FM1120100597020X

Fig. 15   Test B: Unusual Starter Noises (Part 2 of 2). Continental

CONDITIONS	DETAILS/RESULTS/ACTIONS
A1: CHECK THE BATTERY	**1** Check the battery. • Is the battery OK? → **Yes** GO TO **A2** → **No** INSTALL a new battery. TEST the system for normal operation.
A2: CHECK THE STARTER RELAY	**2** Carry out the ISO mini relay component test. • Is the relay OK? → **Yes** GO TO **A3** → **No** INSTALL a new starter relay. TEST the system for normal operation.

FM1120100601010X

Fig. 16   Test A: Engine Does Not Crank & Relay Clicks (Part 1 of 2). Cougar

CONDITIONS	DETAILS/RESULTS/ACTIONS
A3: CHECK VOLTAGE TO STARTER RELAY	

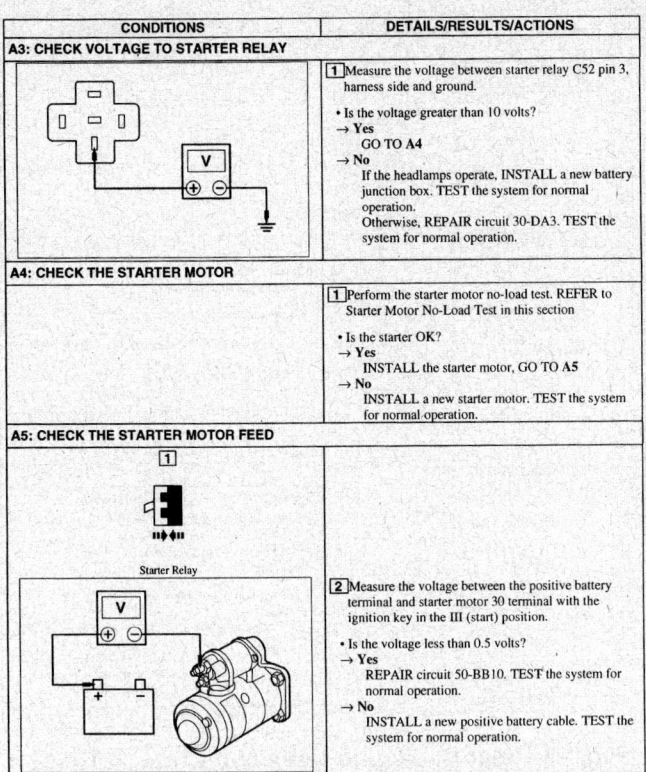

CONDITIONS	DETAILS/RESULTS/ACTIONS

A3: CHECK VOLTAGE TO STARTER RELAY	[1] Measure the voltage between starter relay C52 pin 3, harness side and ground.
	
	• Is the voltage greater than 10 volts?
	→ **Yes**
	  GO TO **A4**
	→ **No**
	  If the headlamps operate, INSTALL a new battery junction box. TEST the system for normal operation.
	  Otherwise, REPAIR circuit 30-DA3. TEST the system for normal operation.

A4: CHECK THE STARTER MOTOR	[1] Perform the starter motor no-load test. REFER to Starter Motor No-Load Test in this section
	
	• Is the starter OK?
	→ **Yes**
	  INSTALL the starter motor, GO TO **A5**
	→ **No**
	  INSTALL a new starter motor. TEST the system for normal operation.

A5: CHECK THE STARTER MOTOR FEED	[2] Measure the voltage between the positive battery terminal and starter motor 30 terminal with the ignition key in the III (start) position.
	
	• Is the voltage less than 0.5 volts?
	→ **Yes**
	  REPAIR circuit 50-BB10. TEST the system for normal operation.
	→ **No**
	  INSTALL a new positive battery cable. TEST the system for normal operation.

FM1120100601020X

Fig. 16   Test A: Engine Does Not Crank & Relay Clicks (Part 2 of 2). Cougar

CONDITIONS	DETAILS/RESULTS/ACTIONS

B1: CHECK THE BATTERY	[1] Check the battery.
	
	• Is the battery OK?
	→ **Yes**
	  GO TO **B2**
	→ **No**
	  INSTALL a new battery. TEST the system for normal operation.

B2: CHECK SWITCHED POWER TO THE STARTER RELAY	[2] Measure the voltage between starter relay C52 pin 2, harness side and ground with the ignition key in the III (start) position.
	
	• Is the voltage greater than 10 volts?
	→ **Yes**
	  GO TO **B3**
	→ **No**
	  GO TO **B4**

B3: CHECK GROUND SIGNAL FOR THE STARTER RELAY	[1] Measure the resistance between starter relay C52 pin 1, harness side and ground with the ignition key in the III (start) position.
	
	• Is the resistance less than 5 ohms?
	→ **Yes**
	  INSTALL a new starter relay. TEST the system for normal operation.
	→ **No**
	  If manual transmission, GO TO **B6**
	  If automatic transmission, GO TO **B9**

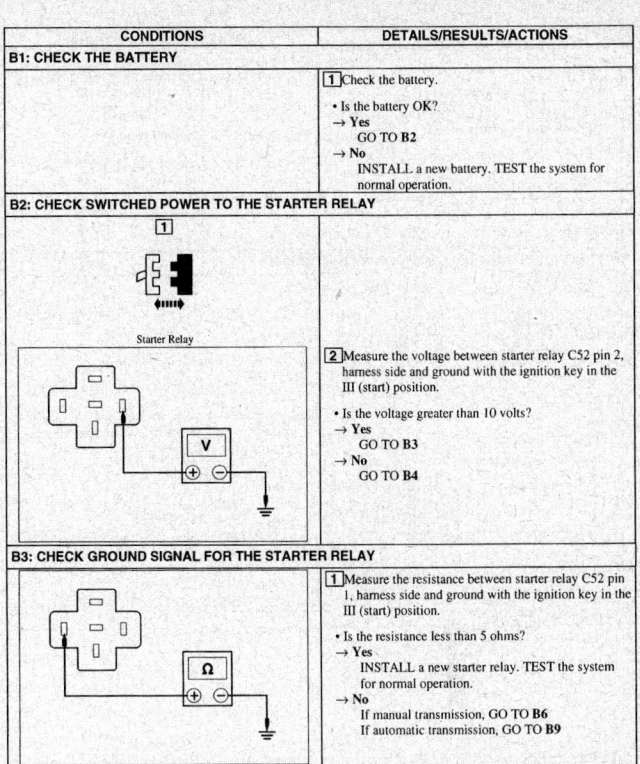

FM1120100602010X

Fig. 17   Test B: Engine Does Not Crank & Relay Does Not Click (Part 1 of 5). Cougar

CONDITIONS	DETAILS/RESULTS/ACTIONS

B4: CHECK DIODE	[2] Measure the voltage between the diode C61 pin 1, harness side and ground with the ignition key in the III (start) position
	
	• Is the voltage greater than 10 volts?
	→ **Yes**
	  INSTALL a new diode. TEST the system for normal operation.
	→ **No**
	  GO TO **B5**

B5: CHECK CIRCUIT 50 BB11 FOR OPEN	[2] Measure the resistance between ignition switch C456 pin 5, circuit 50-BB11 (GY/WH), harness side and diode C61 pin 1, harness side.
	
	• Is the resistance less than 5 ohms?
	→ **Yes**
	  INSTALL a new ignition switch. TEST the system for normal operation.
	→ **No**
	  REPAIR the circuit. TEST the system for normal operation.

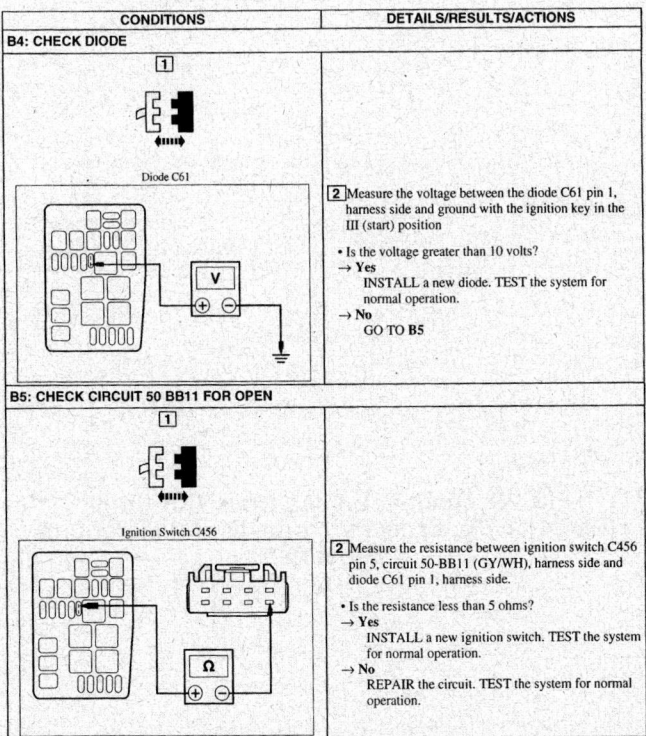

FM1120100602020X

Fig. 17   Test B: Engine Does Not Crank & Relay Does Not Click (Part 2 of 5). Cougar

CONDITIONS	DETAILS/RESULTS/ACTIONS

B6: CHECK CIRCUIT TO CLUTCH PEDAL	[3] Measure the voltage between start inhibit switch C1919 pin 2, circuit 31S-BB12 (BK/YE), harness side and ground with the ignition key in the III (start) position.
	
	• Is the voltage greater than 10 volts?
	→ **Yes**
	  GO TO **B7**
	→ **No**
	  REPAIR the circuit. TEST the system for normal operation.

B7: CHECK START INHIBIT SWITCH	[1] Measure the resistance between the start inhibit switch pin 1 and pin 2, component side. Note the reading with the clutch pedal pressed in and with the pedal released.
	
	• Is the resistance less than 5 ohms with the clutch pedal pressed, and greater than 10,000 ohms with the pedal released?
	→ **Yes**
	  GO TO **B8**
	→ **No**
	  ADJUST the start inhibit switch. REPEAT this Pinpoint Test, if necessary INSTALL a new start inhibit switch. TEST the system for normal operation.

B8: CHECK CIRCUIT 31 - BB6	

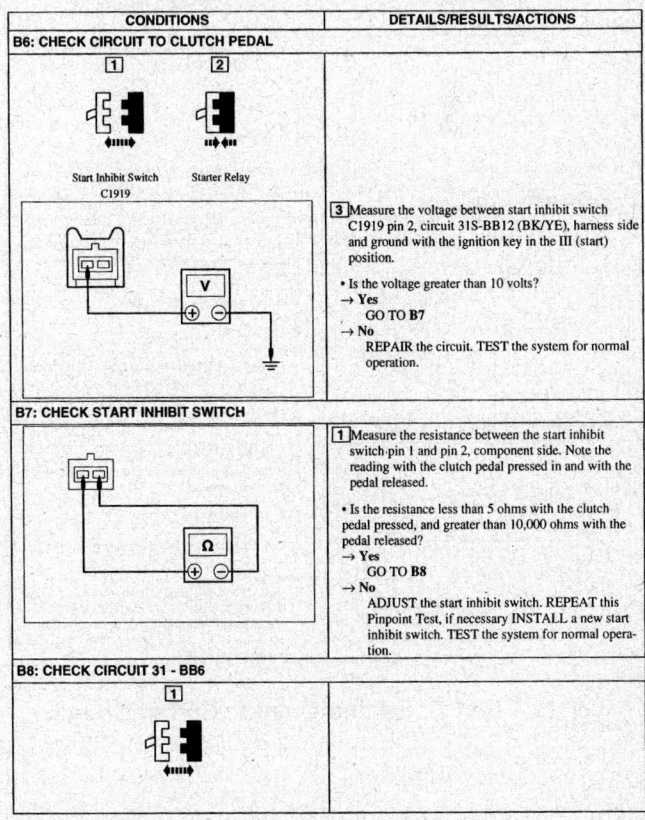

FM1120100602030X

Fig. 17   Test B: Engine Does Not Crank & Relay Does Not Click (Part 3 of 5). Cougar

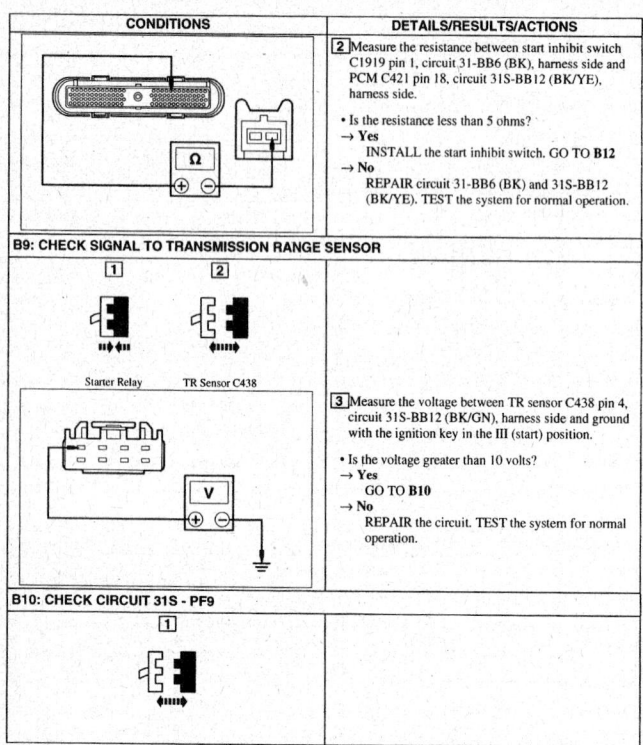

CONDITIONS	DETAILS/RESULTS/ACTIONS

	2 Measure the resistance between start inhibit switch C1919 pin 1, circuit 31-BB6 (BK), harness side and PCM C421 pin 18, circuit 31S-BB12 (BK/YE), harness side.
	
	• Is the resistance less than 5 ohms?
	→ Yes
	  INSTALL the start inhibit switch. GO TO **B12**
	→ No
	  REPAIR circuit 31-BB6 (BK) and 31S-BB12 (BK/YE). TEST the system for normal operation.

B9: CHECK SIGNAL TO TRANSMISSION RANGE SENSOR	

	3 Measure the voltage between TR sensor C438 pin 4, circuit 31S-BB12 (BK/GN), harness side and ground with the ignition key in the III (start) position.
	
	• Is the voltage greater than 10 volts?
	→ Yes
	  GO TO **B10**
	→ No
	  REPAIR the circuit. TEST the system for normal operation.

B10: CHECK CIRCUIT 31S - PF9	

Fig. 17   Test B: Engine Does Not Crank & Relay Does Not Click (Part 4 of 5). Cougar

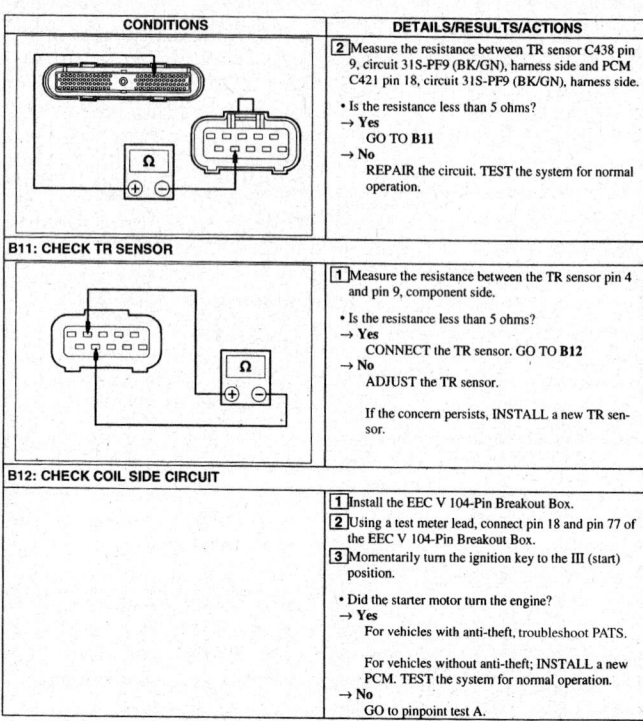

CONDITIONS	DETAILS/RESULTS/ACTIONS

	2 Measure the resistance between TR sensor C438 pin 9, circuit 31S-PF9 (BK/GN) and PCM C421 pin 18, circuit 31S-PF9 (BK/GN), harness side.
	
	• Is the resistance less than 5 ohms?
	→ Yes
	  GO TO **B11**
	→ No
	  REPAIR the circuit. TEST the system for normal operation.

B11: CHECK TR SENSOR	

	1 Measure the resistance between the TR sensor pin 4 and pin 9, component side.
	
	• Is the resistance less than 5 ohms?
	→ Yes
	  CONNECT the TR sensor. GO TO **B12**
	→ No
	  ADJUST the TR sensor.
	
	If the concern persists, INSTALL a new TR sensor.

B12: CHECK COIL SIDE CIRCUIT	

	1 Install the EEC V 104-Pin Breakout Box.
	2 Using a test meter lead, connect pin 18 and pin 77 of the EEC V 104-Pin Breakout Box.
	3 Momentarily turn the ignition key to the III (start) position.
	
	• Did the starter motor turn the engine?
	→ Yes
	  For vehicles with anti-theft, troubleshoot PATS.
	
	  For vehicles without anti-theft; INSTALL a new PCM. TEST the system for normal operation.
	→ No
	  GO to pinpoint test A.

FM1120100602050X

Fig. 17   Test B: Engine Does Not Crank & Relay Does Not Click (Part 5 of 5). Cougar

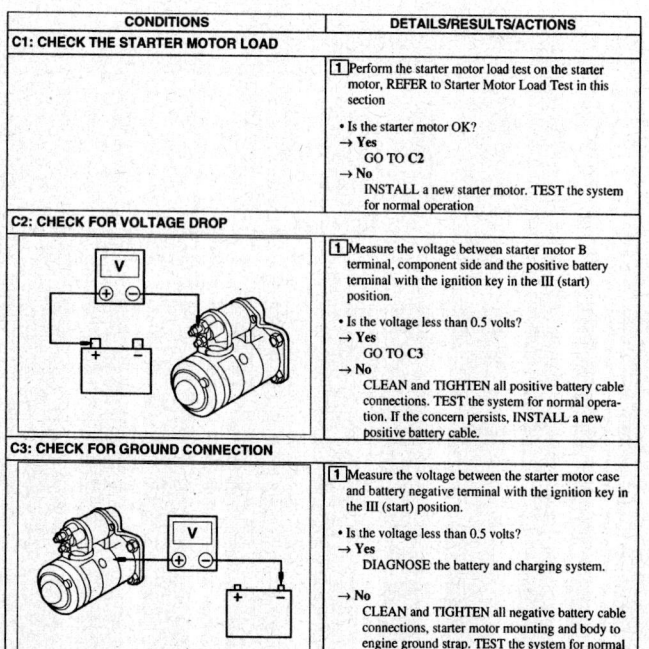

CONDITIONS	DETAILS/RESULTS/ACTIONS
C1: CHECK THE STARTER MOTOR LOAD	

	1 Perform the starter motor load test on the starter motor, REFER to Starter Motor Load Test in this section
	
	• Is the starter motor OK?
	→ Yes
	  GO TO **C2**
	→ No
	  INSTALL a new starter motor. TEST the system for normal operation

C2: CHECK FOR VOLTAGE DROP	

	1 Measure the voltage between starter motor B terminal, component side and the positive battery terminal with the ignition key in the III (start) position.
	
	• Is the voltage less than 0.5 volts?
	→ Yes
	  GO TO **C3**
	→ No
	  CLEAN and TIGHTEN all positive battery cable connections. TEST the system for normal operation. If the concern persists, INSTALL a new positive battery cable.

C3: CHECK FOR GROUND CONNECTION	

	1 Measure the voltage between the starter motor case and battery negative terminal with the ignition key in the III (start) position.
	
	• Is the voltage less than 0.5 volts?
	→ Yes
	  DIAGNOSE the battery and charging system.
	
	→ No
	  CLEAN and TIGHTEN all negative battery cable connections, starter motor mounting and body to engine ground strap. TEST the system for normal operation. If the concern persists, INSTALL a new negative battery cable.

FM1120100603000X

Fig. 18   Test C: Engine Cranks Slowly. Cougar

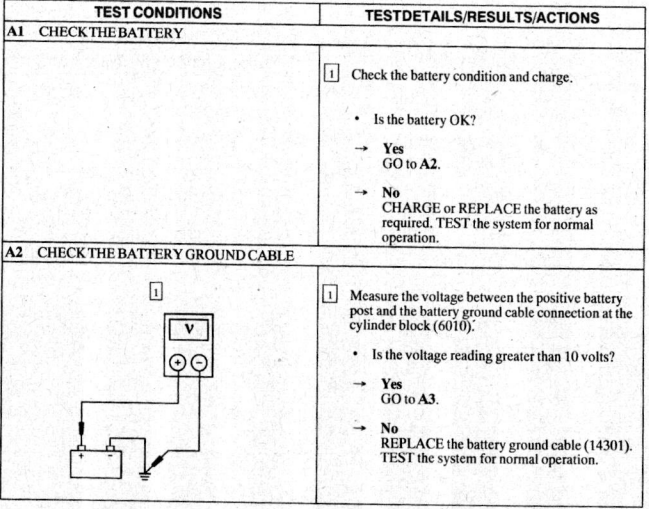

TEST CONDITIONS	TESTDETAILS/RESULTS/ACTIONS
A1 CHECK THE BATTERY	

	1 Check the battery condition and charge.
	
	• Is the battery OK?
	→ Yes
	  GO to **A2**.
	
	→ No
	  CHARGE or REPLACE the battery as required. TEST the system for normal operation.

A2 CHECK THE BATTERY GROUND CABLE	

	1 Measure the voltage between the positive battery post and the battery ground cable connection at the cylinder block (6010).
	
	• Is the voltage reading greater than 10 volts?
	
	→ Yes
	  GO to **A3**.
	
	→ No
	  REPLACE the battery ground cable (14301). TEST the system for normal operation.

FM1120100613010X

Fig. 19   Test A: Engine Does Not Crank (Part 1 of 13). Crown Victoria, Grand Marquis & Marauder

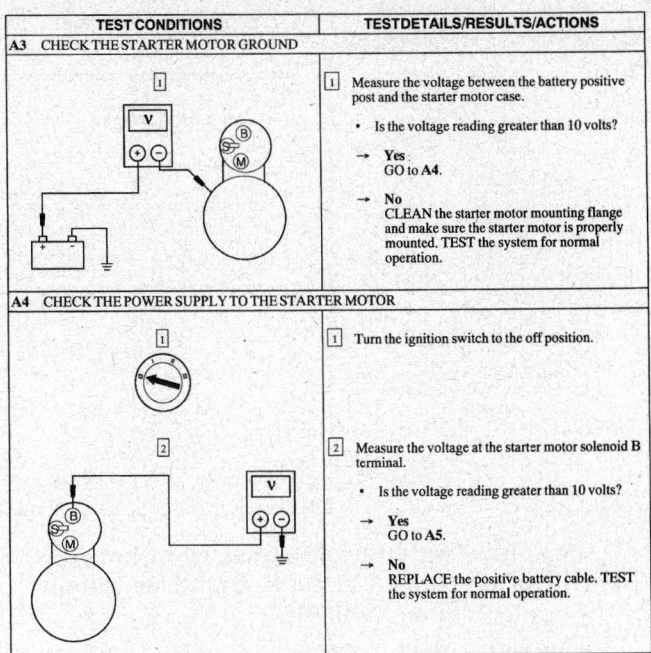

TEST CONDITIONS	TESTDETAILS/RESULTS/ACTIONS
A3 CHECK THE STARTER MOTOR GROUND	① Measure the voltage between the battery positive post and the starter motor case. • Is the voltage reading greater than 10 volts? → **Yes** GO to **A4**. → **No** CLEAN the starter motor mounting flange and make sure the starter motor is properly mounted. TEST the system for normal operation.
A4 CHECK THE POWER SUPPLY TO THE STARTER MOTOR	① Turn the ignition switch to the off position. ② Measure the voltage at the starter motor solenoid B terminal. • Is the voltage reading greater than 10 volts? → **Yes** GO to **A5**. → **No** REPLACE the positive battery cable. TEST the system for normal operation.

FM1120100613020X

Fig. 19   Test A: Engine Does Not Crank (Part 2 of 13). Crown Victoria, Grand Marquis & Marauder

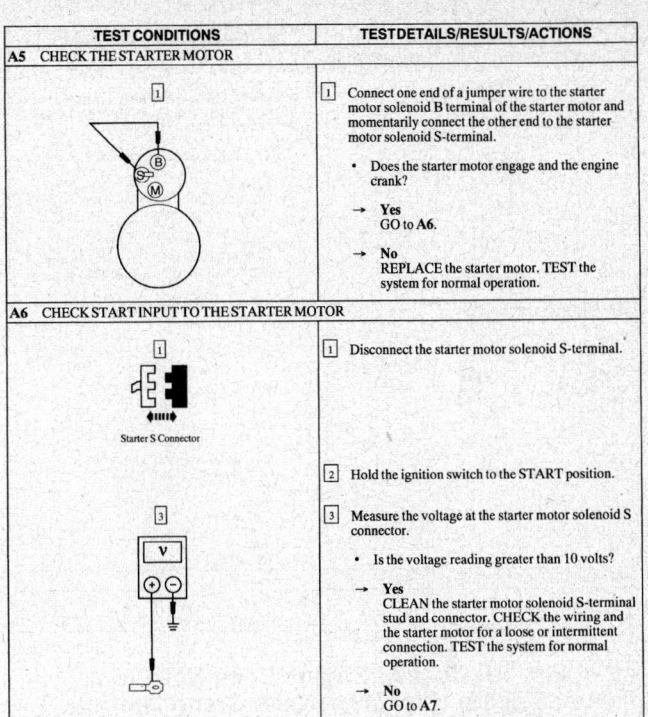

TEST CONDITIONS	TESTDETAILS/RESULTS/ACTIONS
A5 CHECK THE STARTER MOTOR	① Connect one end of a jumper wire to the starter motor solenoid B terminal of the starter motor and momentarily connect the other end to the starter motor solenoid S-terminal. • Does the starter motor engage and the engine crank? → **Yes** GO to **A6**. → **No** REPLACE the starter motor. TEST the system for normal operation.
A6 CHECK START INPUT TO THE STARTER MOTOR	① Disconnect the starter motor solenoid S-terminal. ② Hold the ignition switch to the START position. ③ Measure the voltage at the starter motor solenoid S connector. • Is the voltage reading greater than 10 volts? → **Yes** CLEAN the starter motor solenoid S-terminal stud and connector. CHECK the wiring and the starter motor for a loose or intermittent connection. TEST the system for normal operation. → **No** GO to **A7**.

FM1120100613030X

Fig. 19   Test A: Engine Does Not Crank (Part 3 of 13). Crown Victoria, Grand Marquis & Marauder

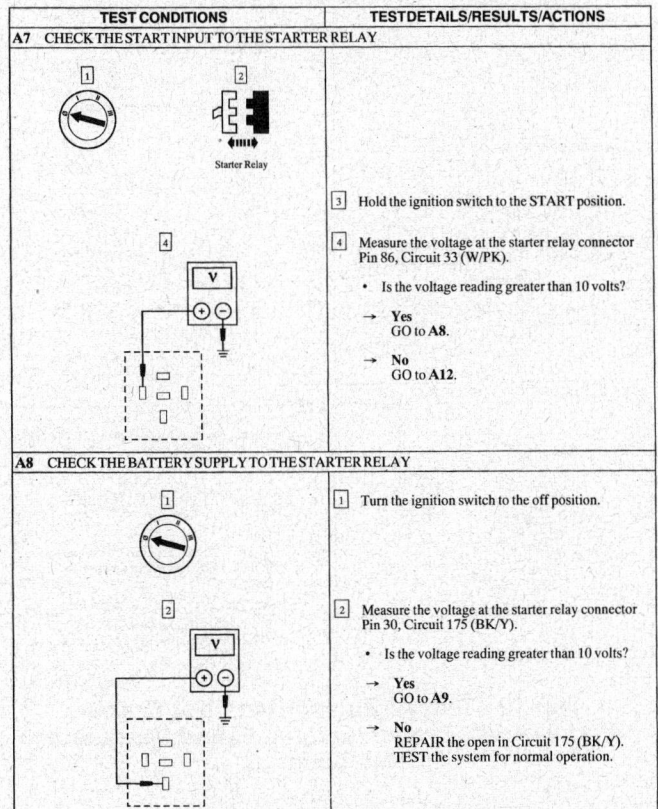

TEST CONDITIONS	TESTDETAILS/RESULTS/ACTIONS
A7 CHECK THE START INPUT TO THE STARTER RELAY	③ Hold the ignition switch to the START position. ④ Measure the voltage at the starter relay connector Pin 86, Circuit 33 (W/PK). • Is the voltage reading greater than 10 volts? → **Yes** GO to **A8**. → **No** GO to **A12**.
A8 CHECK THE BATTERY SUPPLY TO THE STARTER RELAY	① Turn the ignition switch to the off position. ② Measure the voltage at the starter relay connector Pin 30, Circuit 175 (BK/Y). • Is the voltage reading greater than 10 volts? → **Yes** GO to **A9**. → **No** REPAIR the open in Circuit 175 (BK/Y). TEST the system for normal operation.

FM1120100613040X

Fig. 19   Test A: Engine Does Not Crank (Part 4 of 13). Crown Victoria, Grand Marquis & Marauder

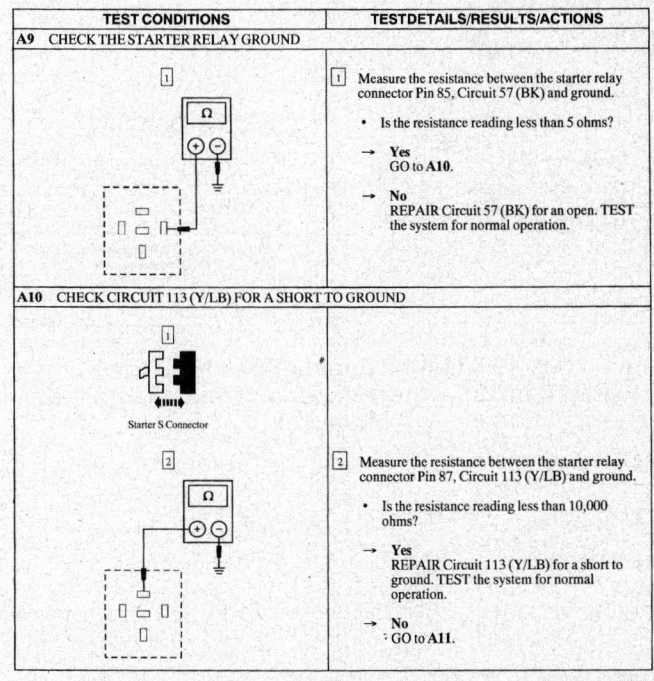

TEST CONDITIONS	TESTDETAILS/RESULTS/ACTIONS
A9 CHECK THE STARTER RELAY GROUND	① Measure the resistance between the starter relay connector Pin 85, Circuit 57 (BK) and ground. • Is the resistance reading less than 5 ohms? → **Yes** GO to **A10**. → **No** REPAIR Circuit 57 (BK) for an open. TEST the system for normal operation.
A10 CHECK CIRCUIT 113 (Y/LB) FOR A SHORT TO GROUND	② Measure the resistance between the starter relay connector Pin 87, Circuit 113 (Y/LB) and ground. • Is the resistance reading less than 10,000 ohms? → **Yes** REPAIR Circuit 113 (Y/LB) for a short to ground. TEST the system for normal operation. → **No** GO to **A11**.

FM1120100613050X

Fig. 19   Test A: Engine Does Not Crank (Part 5 of 13). Crown Victoria, Grand Marquis & Marauder

TEST CONDITIONS	TESTDETAILS/RESULTS/ACTIONS
A11 CHECK CIRCUIT 113 (Y/LB) FOR AN OPEN	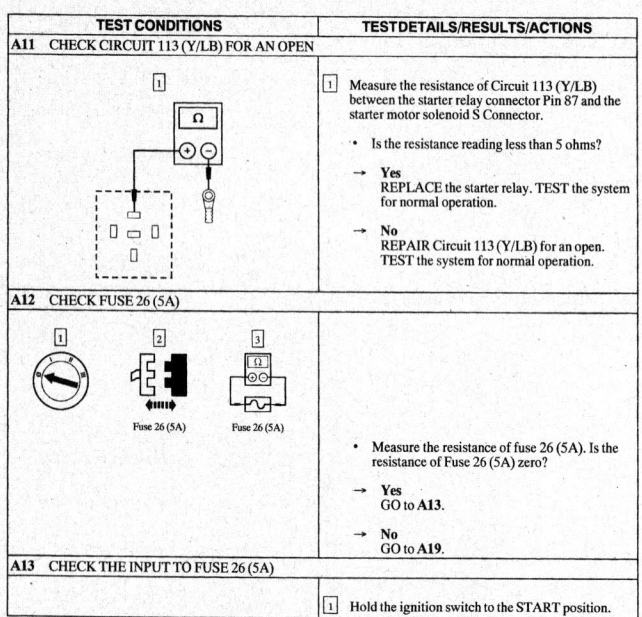 1 Measure the resistance of Circuit 113 (Y/LB) between the starter relay connector Pin 87 and the starter motor solenoid S Connector. • Is the resistance reading less than 5 ohms? → **Yes** REPLACE the starter relay. TEST the system for normal operation. → **No** REPAIR Circuit 113 (Y/LB) for an open. TEST the system for normal operation.
A12 CHECK FUSE 26 (5A)	• Measure the resistance of fuse 26 (5A). Is the resistance of Fuse 26 (5A) zero? → **Yes** GO to **A13**. → **No** GO to **A19**.
A13 CHECK THE INPUT TO FUSE 26 (5A)	1 Hold the ignition switch to the START position.

FM1120100613060X

Fig. 19   Test A: Engine Does Not Crank (Part 6 of 13). Crown Victoria, Grand Marquis & Marauder

TEST CONDITIONS	TESTDETAILS/RESULTS/ACTIONS
A14 CHECK THE SUPPLY TO THE IGNITION SWITCH	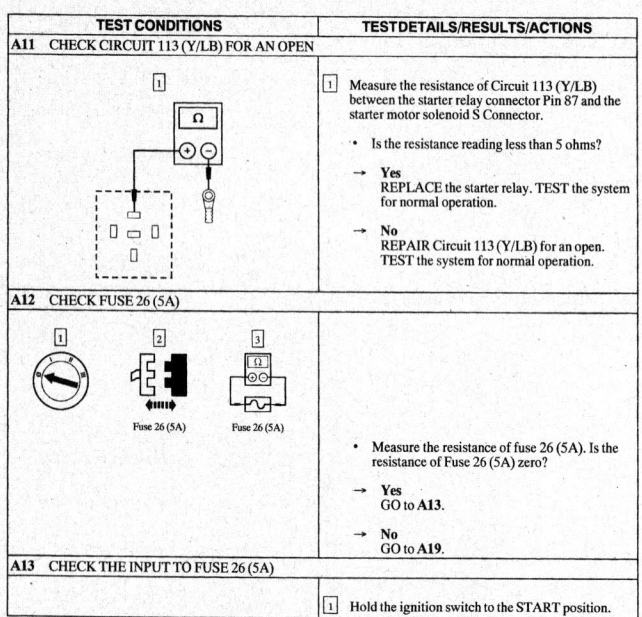 Ignition Switch C292 2 Measure the voltage at the ignition switch connector Pin C292-B4, Circuit 37 (Y). • Is the voltage reading greater than 10 volts? → **Yes** GO to **A15**. → **No** REPAIR Circuit 37 (Y) for an open. TEST the system for normal operation.

FM1120100613080X

Fig. 19   Test A: Engine Does Not Crank (Part 8 of 13). Crown Victoria, Grand Marquis & Marauder

TEST CONDITIONS	TESTDETAILS/RESULTS/ACTIONS
A13 CHECK THE INPUT TO FUSE 26 (5A) (Continued)	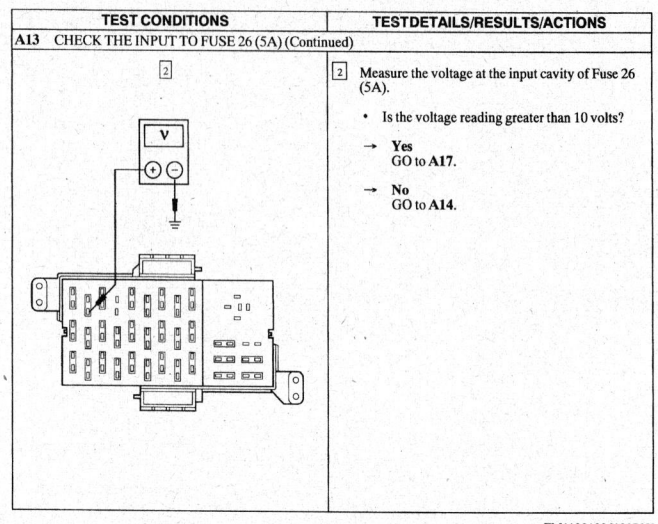 2 Measure the voltage at the input cavity of Fuse 26 (5A). • Is the voltage reading greater than 10 volts? → **Yes** GO to **A17**. → **No** GO to **A14**.

FM1120100613070X

Fig. 19   Test A: Engine Does Not Crank (Part 7 of 13). Crown Victoria, Grand Marquis & Marauder

TEST CONDITIONS	TESTDETAILS/RESULTS/ACTIONS
A15 CHECK CIRCUIT 32 (R/LB) FOR AN OPEN	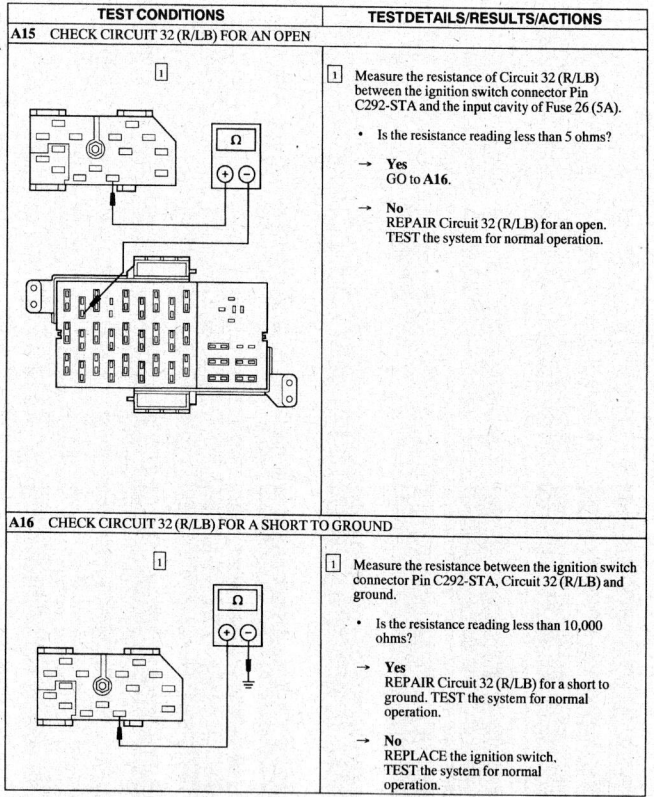 1 Measure the resistance of Circuit 32 (R/LB) between the ignition switch connector Pin C292-STA and the input cavity of Fuse 26 (5A). • Is the resistance reading less than 5 ohms? → **Yes** GO to **A16**. → **No** REPAIR Circuit 32 (R/LB) for an open. TEST the system for normal operation.
A16 CHECK CIRCUIT 32 (R/LB) FOR A SHORT TO GROUND	1 Measure the resistance between the ignition switch connector Pin C292-STA, Circuit 32 (R/LB) and ground. • Is the resistance reading less than 10,000 ohms? → **Yes** REPAIR Circuit 32 (R/LB) for a short to ground. TEST the system for normal operation. → **No** REPLACE the ignition switch. TEST the system for normal operation.

FM1120100613090X

Fig. 19   Test A: Engine Does Not Crank (Part 9 of 13). Crown Victoria, Grand Marquis & Marauder

TEST CONDITIONS	TESTDETAILS/RESULTS/ACTIONS
A17 CHECK CIRCUIT 262 (BR/PK) FOR AN OPEN	

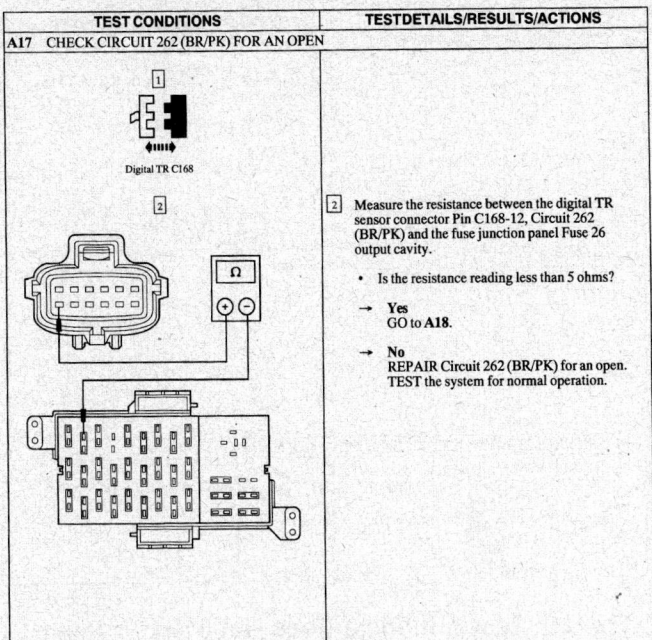

2. Measure the resistance between the digital TR sensor connector Pin C168-12, Circuit 262 (BR/PK) and the fuse junction panel Fuse 26 output cavity.

- Is the resistance reading less than 5 ohms?

→ **Yes**
GO to **A18**.

→ **No**
REPAIR Circuit 262 (BR/PK) for an open. TEST the system for normal operation.

FM1120100613100X

Fig. 19 Test A: Engine Does Not Crank (Part 10 of 13). Crown Victoria, Grand Marquis & Marauder

TEST CONDITIONS	TESTDETAILS/RESULTS/ACTIONS
A19 CHECK FOR A SHORTED SYSTEM	

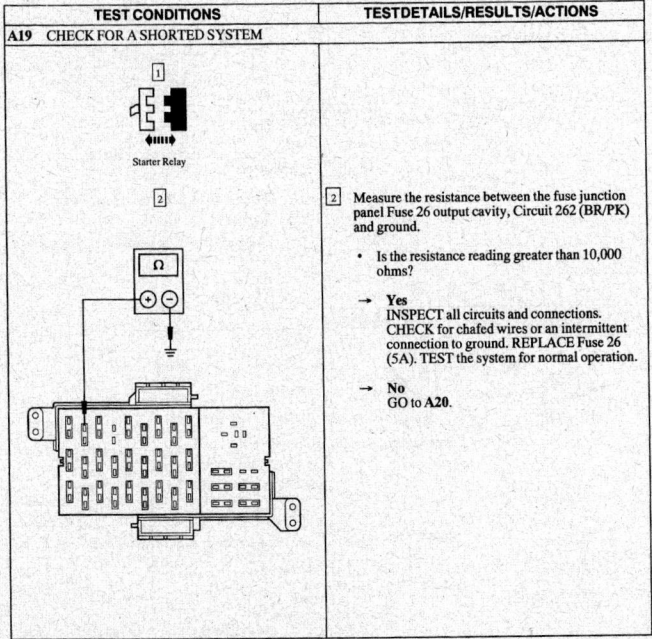

2. Measure the resistance between the fuse junction panel Fuse 26 output cavity, Circuit 262 (BR/PK) and ground.

- Is the resistance reading greater than 10,000 ohms?

→ **Yes**
INSPECT all circuits and connections. CHECK for chafed wires or an intermittent connection to ground. REPLACE Fuse 26 (5A). TEST the system for normal operation.

→ **No**
GO to **A20**.

FM1120100613120X

Fig. 19 Test A: Engine Does Not Crank (Part 12 of 13). Crown Victoria, Grand Marquis & Marauder

TEST CONDITIONS	TESTDETAILS/RESULTS/ACTIONS
A18 CHECK CIRCUIT 33 (W/PK) FOR AN OPEN	

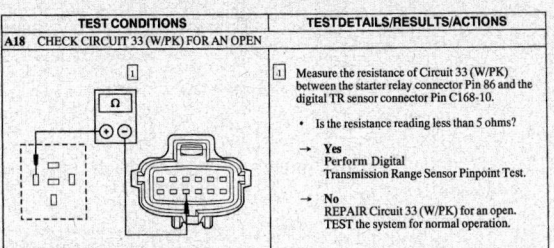

1. Measure the resistance of Circuit 33 (W/PK) between the starter relay connector Pin 86 and the digital TR sensor connector Pin C168-10.

- Is the resistance reading less than 5 ohms?

→ **Yes**
Perform Digital Transmission Range Sensor Pinpoint Test.

→ **No**
REPAIR Circuit 33 (W/PK) for an open. TEST the system for normal operation.

FM1120100613110X

Fig. 19 Test A: Engine Does Not Crank (Part 11 of 13). Crown Victoria, Grand Marquis & Marauder

TEST CONDITIONS	TESTDETAILS/RESULTS/ACTIONS
A20 CHECK CIRCUIT 262 (BR/PK) FOR A SHORT TO GROUND	

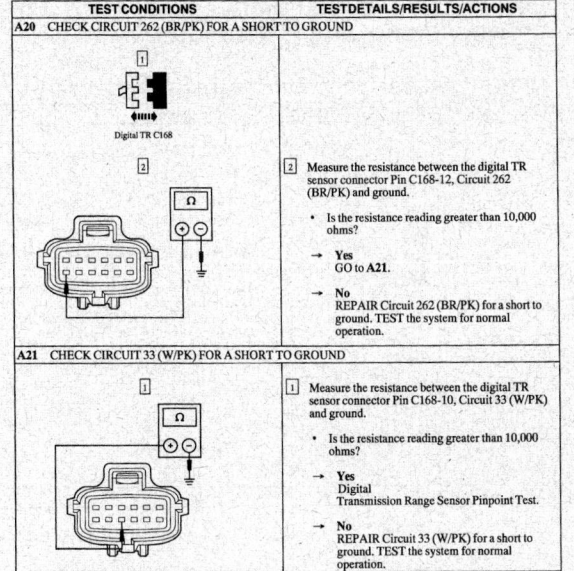

2. Measure the resistance between the digital TR sensor connector Pin C168-12, Circuit 262 (BR/PK) and ground.

- Is the resistance reading greater than 10,000 ohms?

→ **Yes**
GO to **A21**.

→ **No**
REPAIR Circuit 262 (BR/PK) for a short to ground. TEST the system for normal operation.

TEST CONDITIONS	TESTDETAILS/RESULTS/ACTIONS
A21 CHECK CIRCUIT 33 (W/PK) FOR A SHORT TO GROUND	

1. Measure the resistance between the digital TR sensor connector Pin C168-10, Circuit 33 (W/PK) and ground.

- Is the resistance reading greater than 10,000 ohms?

→ **Yes**
Digital Transmission Range Sensor Pinpoint Test.

→ **No**
REPAIR Circuit 33 (W/PK) for a short to ground. TEST the system for normal operation.

FM1120100613130X

Fig. 19 Test A: Engine Does Not Crank (Part 13 of 13). Crown Victoria, Grand Marquis & Marauder

TEST CONDITIONS	TESTDETAILS/RESULTS/ACTIONS
B1 CHECK THE STARTER MOUNTING	

1. Inspect the starter motor mounting bolts and brackets for looseness.

- Is the starter motor mounted properly?

→ **Yes**
GO to **B2**.

→ **No**
INSTALL the starter motor properly; TEST the system for normal operation.

TEST CONDITIONS	TESTDETAILS/RESULTS/ACTIONS
B2 CHECK FOR ENGINE NOISE	

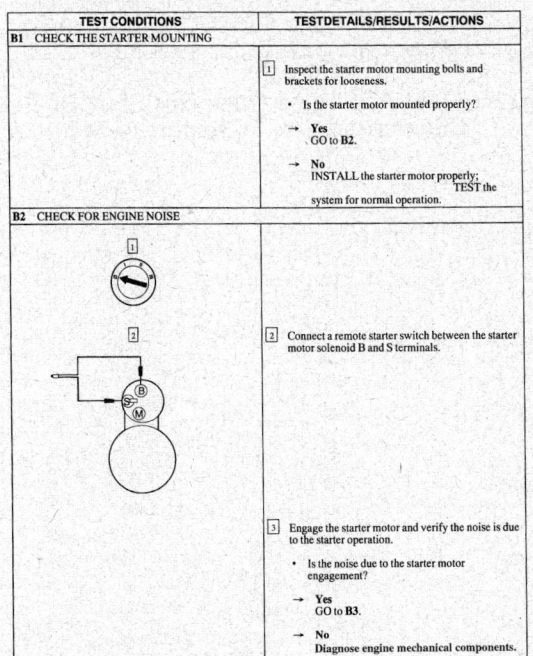

2. Connect a remote starter switch between the starter motor solenoid B and S terminals.

3. Engage the starter motor and verify the noise is due to the starter operation.

- Is the noise due to the starter motor engagement?

→ **Yes**
GO to **B3**.

→ **No**
Diagnose engine mechanical components.

FM1120100614010X

Fig. 20 Test B: Unusual Starter Noise (Part 1 of 2). Crown Victoria, Grand Marquis & Marauder

TEST CONDITIONS	TEST DETAILS/RESULTS/ACTIONS
B3 CHECK FOR UNUSUAL WEAR	
	[1] Remove the starter motor.
	[2] Inspect the ring gear for damaged or worn teeth.
	• Is the noise due to flywheel ring gear (6384) tooth damage?
	→ **Yes** REPLACE the flywheel ring gear. EXAMINE the starter pinion teeth. If damaged, REPLACE the starter motor. TEST the system for normal operation.
	→ **No** REPLACE the starter motor. TEST the system for normal operation.

FM1120100614020X

Fig. 20   Test B: Unusual Starter Noise (Part 2 of 2). Crown Victoria, Grand Marquis & Marauder

TEST CONDITIONS	TEST DETAILS/RESULTS/ACTIONS
A3 CHECK THE START SIGNAL TO THE STARTER MOTOR (Continued)	
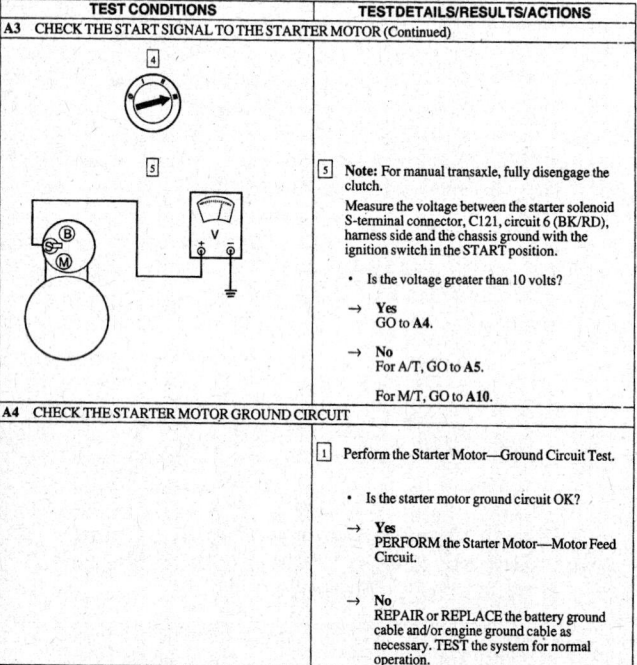	[5] **Note:** For manual transaxle, fully disengage the clutch. Measure the voltage between the starter solenoid S-terminal connector, C121, circuit 6 (BK/RD), harness side and the chassis ground with the ignition switch in the START position.
	• Is the voltage greater than 10 volts?
	→ **Yes** GO to **A4**.
	→ **No** For A/T, GO to **A5**. For M/T, GO to **A10**.
A4 CHECK THE STARTER MOTOR GROUND CIRCUIT	
	[1] Perform the Starter Motor—Ground Circuit Test.
	• Is the starter motor ground circuit OK?
	→ **Yes** PERFORM the Starter Motor—Motor Feed Circuit.
	→ **No** REPAIR or REPLACE the battery ground cable and/or engine ground cable as necessary. TEST the system for normal operation.

FM1120100636020X

Fig. 21   Test A: Engine Does Not Start Or Relay Clicks (Part 2 of 6). Escort & ZX2

TEST CONDITIONS	TEST DETAILS/RESULTS/ACTIONS
A1 CHECK THE BATTERY CONNECTIONS	
	[1] Inspect the battery terminals for loose or corroded connections.
	• Are the battery terminals clean and tight?
	→ **Yes** GO to **A2**.
	→ **No** CLEAN and TIGHTEN the battery cable connections. TEST the system for normal operation.
A2 CHECK THE BATTERY	
	[1] Check the battery.
	• Is the battery OK?
	→ **Yes** GO to **A3**.
	→ **No** CHARGE or REPLACE the battery.
A3 CHECK THE START SIGNAL TO THE STARTER MOTOR	
[1] [2] [3] Starter Solenoid C121	[3] Vehicle in PARK (A/T) or NEUTRAL (M/T).

FM1120100636010X

Fig. 21   Test A: Engine Does Not Start Or Relay Clicks (Part 1 of 6). Escort & ZX2

TEST CONDITIONS	TEST DETAILS/RESULTS/ACTIONS
A5 CHECK THE LINKAGE ADJUSTMENT	
	[1] Check the transaxle linkage adjustment.
	• Is the linkage adjustment OK?
	→ **Yes** GO to **A6**.
	→ **No** ADJUST the linkage. TEST the system for normal operation.
A6 VERIFY THE TRANSMISSION RANGE (TR) SWITCH ADJUSTMENT	
	[1] Verify the transmission range (TR) switch adjustment.
	• Does the TR switch need adjustment?
	→ **Yes** ADJUST the TR switch. TEST the system for normal operation.
	→ **No** GO to **A7**.
A7 CHECK THE VOLTAGE TO THE TR SWITCH	
[1] [2] TR Switch C122 [3]	[3] Measure the voltage between the TR switch connector C122 pin 9, circuit 5 (RD), harness side and ground while turning the ignition to START.
	• Is the voltage greater than 10 volts?
	→ **Yes** GO to **A8**.
	→ **No** REPAIR the circuit or the starter clutch pedal position (SCPP) switch. TEST the system for normal operation.

FM1120100636030X

Fig. 21   Test A: Engine Does Not Start Or Relay Clicks (Part 3 of 6). Escort & ZX2

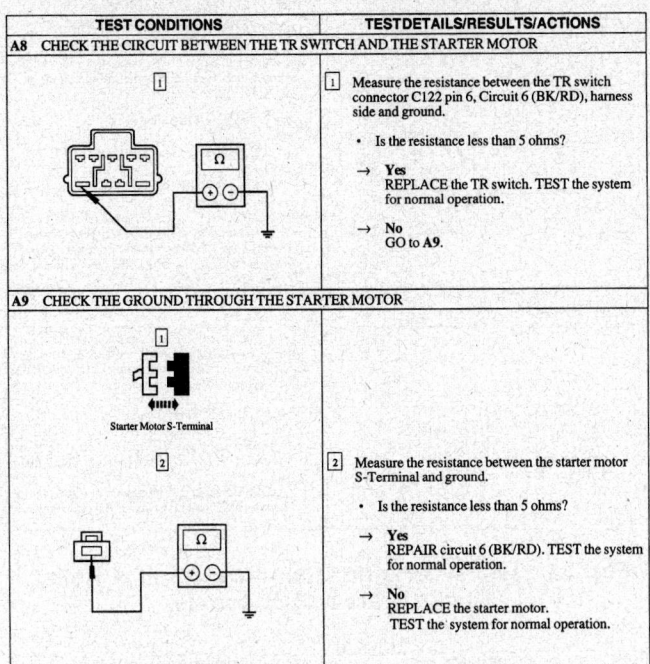

TEST CONDITIONS	TESTDETAILS/RESULTS/ACTIONS
A8 CHECK THE CIRCUIT BETWEEN THE TR SWITCH AND THE STARTER MOTOR	1 Measure the resistance between the TR switch connector C122 pin 6, Circuit 6 (BK/RD), harness side and ground. • Is the resistance less than 5 ohms? → **Yes** REPLACE the TR switch. TEST the system for normal operation. → **No** GO to **A9**.
A9 CHECK THE GROUND THROUGH THE STARTER MOTOR Starter Motor S-Terminal	2 Measure the resistance between the starter motor S-Terminal and ground. • Is the resistance less than 5 ohms? → **Yes** REPAIR circuit 6 (BK/RD). TEST the system for normal operation. → **No** REPLACE the starter motor. TEST the system for normal operation.

FM1120100636040X

Fig. 21   Test A: Engine Does Not Start Or Relay Clicks (Part 4 of 6). Escort & ZX2

TEST CONDITIONS	TESTDETAILS/RESULTS/ACTIONS
A12 CHECK THE GROUND THROUGH THE STARTER MOTOR S-Terminal C121	2 Measure the resistance between starter motor S-Terminal C121 and ground. • Is the resistance less than 5 ohms? → **Yes** REPAIR the circuit. TEST the system for normal operation. → **No** REPLACE the starter motor. TEST the system for normal operation.

FM1120100636060X

Fig. 21   Test A: Engine Does Not Start Or Relay Clicks (Part 6 of 6). Escort & ZX2

TEST CONDITIONS	TESTDETAILS/RESULTS/ACTIONS
B2 INSPECT THE STARTER MOTOR (Continued)	2 Inspect the starter motor for damage. • Is the starter motor damaged? → **Yes** REPLACE the starter motor. TEST the system for normal operation. → **No** Diagnose engine mechanical components.

FM1120100637020X

Fig. 22   Test B: Unusual Starter Noise (Part 2 of 2). Escort & ZX2

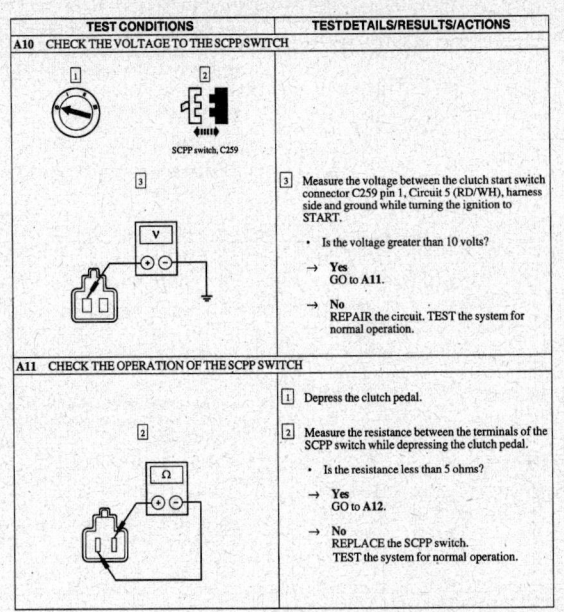

TEST CONDITIONS	TESTDETAILS/RESULTS/ACTIONS
A10 CHECK THE VOLTAGE TO THE SCPP SWITCH SCPP switch, C259	3 Measure the voltage between the clutch start switch connector C259 pin 1, Circuit 5 (RD/WH), harness side and ground while turning the ignition to START. • Is the voltage greater than 10 volts? → **Yes** GO to **A11**. → **No** REPAIR the circuit. TEST the system for normal operation.
A11 CHECK THE OPERATION OF THE SCPP SWITCH	1 Depress the clutch pedal. 2 Measure the resistance between the terminals of the SCPP switch while depressing the clutch pedal. • Is the resistance less than 5 ohms? → **Yes** GO to **A12**. → **No** REPLACE the SCPP switch. TEST the system for normal operation.

FM1120100636050X

Fig. 21   Test A: Engine Does Not Start Or Relay Clicks (Part 5 of 6). Escort & ZX2

TEST CONDITIONS	TESTDETAILS/RESULTS/ACTIONS
B1 CHECK THE STARTER MOTOR MOUNTING	1 Check the starter motor mounting bolts for looseness. 2 Check the starter motor for proper alignment. • Is the starter motor mounted properly? → **Yes** GO to **B2**. → **No** REINSTALL the starter motor properly. TEST the system for normal operation.
B2 INSPECT THE STARTER MOTOR	1 Remove the starter motor.

FM1120100637010X

Fig. 22   Test B: Unusual Starter Noise (Part 1 of 2). Escort & ZX2

CONDITIONS	DETAILS/RESULTS/ACTIONS
A1: CHECK THE BATTERY	1 Check the battery. Carry out the battery capacity test using a scan tool. • Is the battery OK? → **Yes** GO TO **A2** → **No** INSTALL a new battery. TEST the system for normal operation.
A2: CHECK THE STARTER RELAY Starter Relay	2 Carry out the ISO mini relay component test. For additional information refer to the wiring diagrams. • Is the relay OK? → **Yes** GO TO **A3** → **No** INSTALL a new starter relay. TEST the system for normal operation.
A3: CHECK VOLTAGE TO STARTER RELAY CIRCUIT 50-BB17 (GY/OG)	

FM1120100686010X

Fig. 23   Test A: Engine Does Not Crank & Relay Clicks (Part 1 of 3). Focus

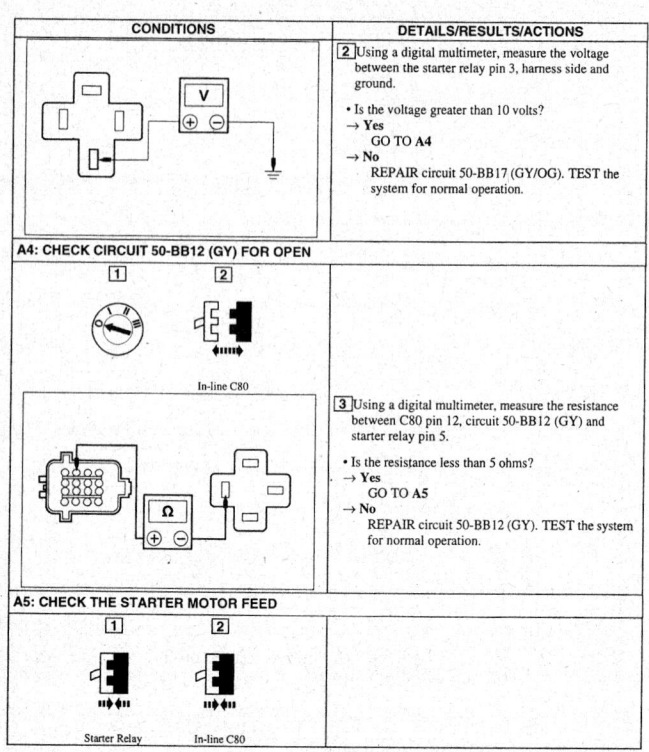

CONDITIONS	DETAILS/RESULTS/ACTIONS

	2 Using a digital multimeter, measure the voltage between the starter relay pin 3, harness side and ground.
	• Is the voltage greater than 10 volts?
	→ **Yes**
	  GO TO **A4**
	→ **No**
	  REPAIR circuit 50-BB17 (GY/OG). TEST the system for normal operation.

A4: CHECK CIRCUIT 50-BB12 (GY) FOR OPEN	

In-line C80	**3** Using a digital multimeter, measure the resistance between C80 pin 12, circuit 50-BB12 (GY) and starter relay pin 5.
	• Is the resistance less than 5 ohms?
	→ **Yes**
	  GO TO **A5**
	→ **No**
	  REPAIR circuit 50-BB12 (GY). TEST the system for normal operation.

A5: CHECK THE STARTER MOTOR FEED	
Starter Relay In-line C80	

FM1120100686020X

Fig. 23   Test A: Engine Does Not Crank & Relay Clicks (Part 2 of 3). Focus

CONDITIONS	DETAILS/RESULTS/ACTIONS
B1: CHECK CONDITION OF PATS SYSTEM	

	1 Observe the PATS warning indicator.
	• Does the indicator flash when attempting to start the vehicle?
	→ **Yes**
	  Fault within the PATS system.
	→ **No**
	  GO TO **B2**

FM1120100687010X

Fig. 24   Test B: Engine Does Not Crank & Relay Does Not Click (Part 1 of 5). Focus

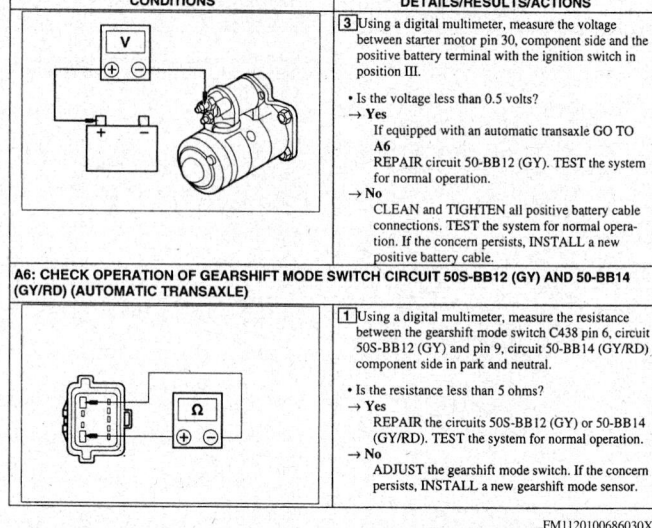

CONDITIONS	DETAILS/RESULTS/ACTIONS

	3 Using a digital multimeter, measure the voltage between starter motor pin 30, component side and the positive battery terminal with the ignition switch in position III.
	• Is the voltage less than 0.5 volts?
	→ **Yes**
	  If equipped with an automatic transaxle GO TO **A6**
	  REPAIR circuit 50-BB12 (GY). TEST the system for normal operation.
	→ **No**
	  CLEAN and TIGHTEN all positive battery cable connections. TEST the system for normal operation. If the concern persists, INSTALL a new positive battery cable.

A6: CHECK OPERATION OF GEARSHIFT MODE SWITCH CIRCUIT 50S-BB12 (GY) AND 50-BB14 (GY/RD) (AUTOMATIC TRANSAXLE)	

	1 Using a digital multimeter, measure the resistance between the gearshift mode switch C438 pin 6, circuit 50S-BB12 (GY) and pin 9, circuit 50-BB14 (GY/RD) component side in park and neutral.
	• Is the resistance less than 5 ohms?
	→ **Yes**
	  REPAIR the circuits 50S-BB12 (GY) or 50-BB14 (GY/RD). TEST the system for normal operation.
	→ **No**
	  ADJUST the gearshift mode switch. If the concern persists, INSTALL a new gearshift mode sensor.

FM1120100686030X

Fig. 23   Test A: Engine Does Not Crank & Relay Clicks (Part 3 of 3). Focus

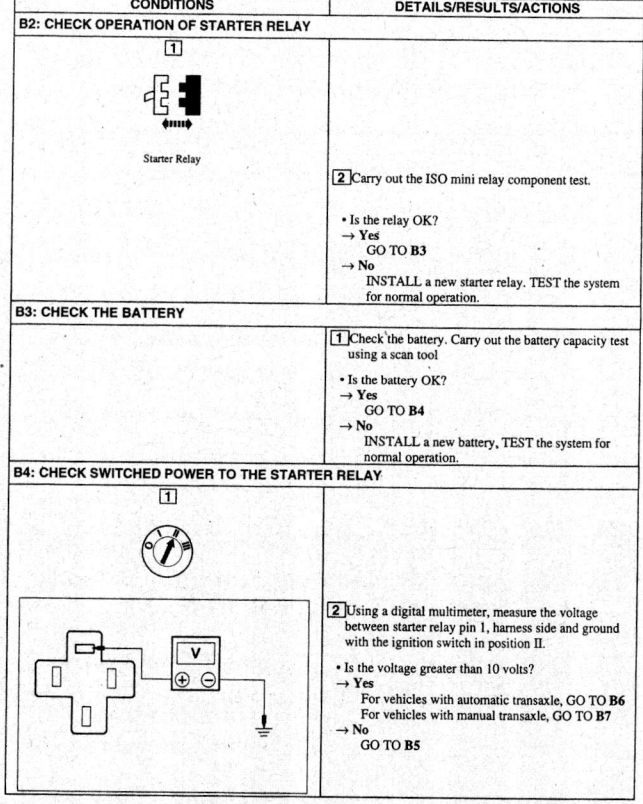

CONDITIONS	DETAILS/RESULTS/ACTIONS
B2: CHECK OPERATION OF STARTER RELAY	

Starter Relay	**2** Carry out the ISO mini relay component test.
	• Is the relay OK?
	→ **Yes**
	  GO TO **B3**
	→ **No**
	  INSTALL a new starter relay. TEST the system for normal operation.

B3: CHECK THE BATTERY	

	1 Check the battery. Carry out the battery capacity test using a scan tool
	• Is the battery OK?
	→ **Yes**
	  GO TO **B4**
	→ **No**
	  INSTALL a new battery. TEST the system for normal operation.

B4: CHECK SWITCHED POWER TO THE STARTER RELAY	

	2 Using a digital multimeter, measure the voltage between starter relay pin 1, harness side and ground with the ignition switch in position II.
	• Is the voltage greater than 10 volts?
	→ **Yes**
	  For vehicles with automatic transaxle, GO TO **B6**
	  For vehicles with manual transaxle, GO TO **B7**
	→ **No**
	  GO TO **B5**

FM1120100687020X

Fig. 24   Test B: Engine Does Not Crank & Relay Does Not Click (Part 2 of 5). Focus

CONDITIONS	DETAILS/RESULTS/ACTIONS
B5: CHECK FUSE 8 (30A)	
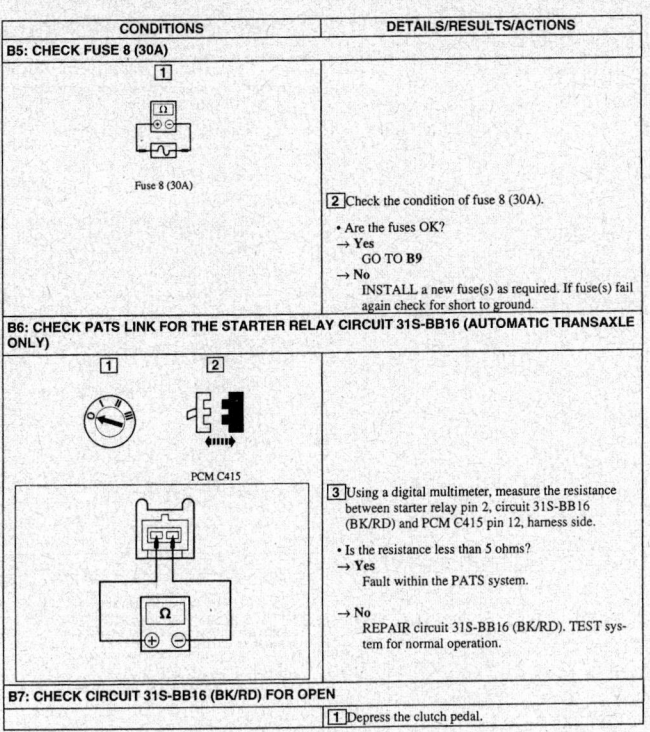 Fuse 8 (30A)	2 Check the condition of fuse 8 (30A). • Are the fuses OK? → **Yes** GO TO **B9** → **No** INSTALL a new fuse(s) as required. If fuse(s) fail again check for short to ground.
B6: CHECK PATS LINK FOR THE STARTER RELAY CIRCUIT 31S-BB16 (AUTOMATIC TRANSAXLE ONLY)	
PCM C415	3 Using a digital multimeter, measure the resistance between starter relay pin 2, circuit 31S-BB16 (BK/RD) and PCM C415 pin 12, harness side. • Is the resistance less than 5 ohms? → **Yes** Fault within the PATS system. → **No** REPAIR circuit 31S-BB16 (BK/RD). TEST system for normal operation.
B7: CHECK CIRCUIT 31S-BB16 (BK/RD) FOR OPEN	
	1 Depress the clutch pedal.

FM1120100687030X

Fig. 24   Test B: Engine Does Not Crank & Relay Does Not Click (Part 3 of 5). Focus

CONDITIONS	DETAILS/RESULTS/ACTIONS
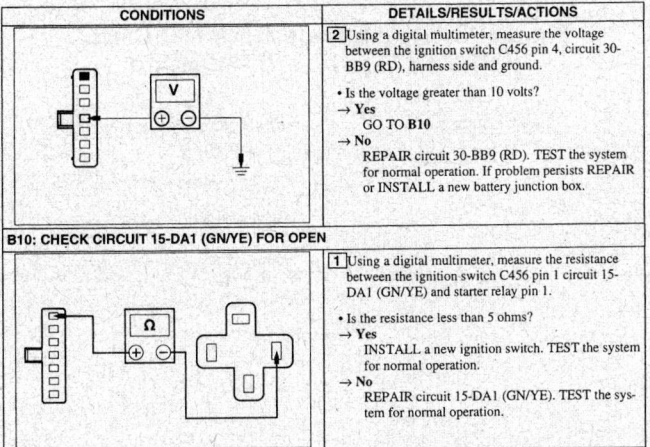	2 Using a digital multimeter, measure the voltage between the ignition switch C456 pin 4, circuit 30-BB9 (RD), harness side and ground. • Is the voltage greater than 10 volts? → **Yes** GO TO **B10** → **No** REPAIR circuit 30-BB9 (RD). TEST the system for normal operation. If problem persists REPAIR or INSTALL a new battery junction box.
B10: CHECK CIRCUIT 15-DA1 (GN/YE) FOR OPEN	
	1 Using a digital multimeter, measure the resistance between the ignition switch C456 pin 1 circuit 15-DA1 (GN/YE) and starter relay pin 1. • Is the resistance less than 5 ohms? → **Yes** INSTALL a new ignition switch. TEST the system for normal operation. → **No** REPAIR circuit 15-DA1 (GN/YE). TEST the system for normal operation.

FM1120100687050X

Fig. 24   Test B: Engine Does Not Crank & Relay Does Not Click (Part 5 of 5). Focus

CONDITIONS	DETAILS/RESULTS/ACTIONS
C1: CHECK THE STARTER MOTOR LOAD	
	1 Carry out the starter motor load test on the starter motor. • Is the starter motor OK? → **Yes** GO TO **C2** → **No** INSTALL a new starter motor. TEST the system for normal operation

FM1120100688010X

Fig. 25   Test C: Engine Cranks Slowly (Part 1 of 2). Focus

CONDITIONS	DETAILS/RESULTS/ACTIONS
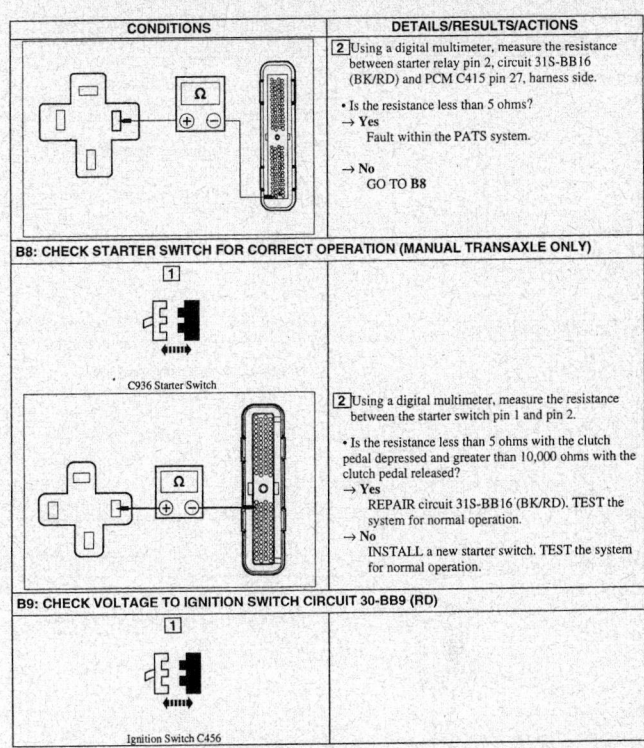 C936 Starter Switch	2 Using a digital multimeter, measure the resistance between starter relay pin 2, circuit 31S-BB16 (BK/RD) and PCM C415 pin 27, harness side. • Is the resistance less than 5 ohms? → **Yes** Fault within the PATS system. → **No** GO TO **B8**
B8: CHECK STARTER SWITCH FOR CORRECT OPERATION (MANUAL TRANSAXLE ONLY)	
	2 Using a digital multimeter, measure the resistance between the starter switch pin 1 and pin 2. • Is the resistance less than 5 ohms with the clutch pedal depressed and greater than 10,000 ohms with the clutch pedal released? → **Yes** REPAIR circuit 31S-BB16 (BK/RD). TEST the system for normal operation. → **No** INSTALL a new starter switch. TEST the system for normal operation.
B9: CHECK VOLTAGE TO IGNITION SWITCH CIRCUIT 30-BB9 (RD)	
Ignition Switch C456	

FM1120100687040X

Fig. 24   Test B: Engine Does Not Crank & Relay Does Not Click (Part 4 of 5). Focus

CONDITIONS	DETAILS/RESULTS/ACTIONS
C2: CHECK FOR VOLTAGE DROP	
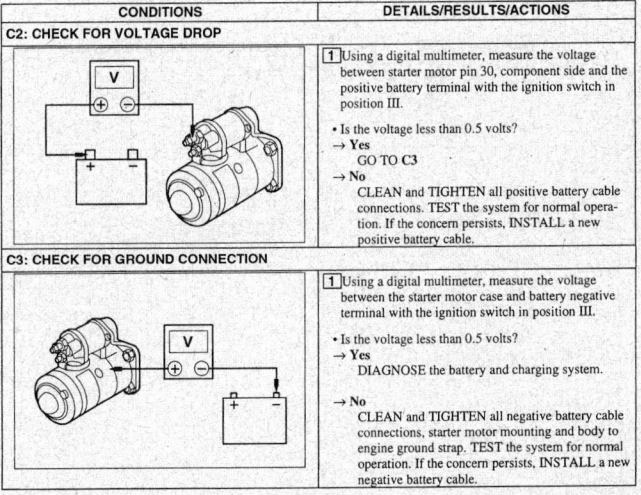	1 Using a digital multimeter, measure the voltage between starter motor pin 30, component side and the positive battery terminal with the ignition switch in position III. • Is the voltage less than 0.5 volts? → **Yes** GO TO **C3** → **No** CLEAN and TIGHTEN all positive battery cable connections. TEST the system for normal operation. If the concern persists, INSTALL a new positive battery cable.
C3: CHECK FOR GROUND CONNECTION	
	1 Using a digital multimeter, measure the voltage between the starter motor case and battery negative terminal with the ignition switch in position III. • Is the voltage less than 0.5 volts? → **Yes** DIAGNOSE the battery and charging system. → **No** CLEAN and TIGHTEN all negative battery cable connections, starter motor mounting and body to engine ground strap. TEST the system for normal operation. If the concern persists, INSTALL a new negative battery cable.

FM1120100688020X

Fig. 25   Test C: Engine Cranks Slowly (Part 2 of 2). Focus

TEST CONDITIONS	TESTDETAILS/RESULTS/ACTIONS
A1 CHECK FOR INSTRUMENT CLUSTER DIAGNOSTIC TEST CODES	
	1 **Note:** The instrument cluster PATS DTCs are the only DTCs of concern in this step. Only repair retrieved non-PATS DTCs if a customer concern is reported. Carry out the instrument cluster self-test. • Were any PATS DTCs retrieved from the instrument cluster? → **Yes** Diagnose the PATS DTCs. → **No** GO to **A2**.
A2 CHECK THE BATTERY	
	1 Check the battery condition and charge. • Is the battery OK? → **Yes** GO to **A3**. → **No** CHARGE or INSTALL a new battery as necessary. TEST the system for normal operation.
A3 CHECK THE BATTERY GROUND CABLE	
	1 Measure the voltage between the positive battery post and the battery ground cable connection on the engine. • Is the voltage greater than 10 volts? → **Yes** GO to **A4**. → **No** INSTALL a new battery ground cable. TEST the system for normal operation.

FM1120100653010X

Fig. 26   Test A: Engine Does Not Crank (Part 1 of 17). LS & Thunderbird

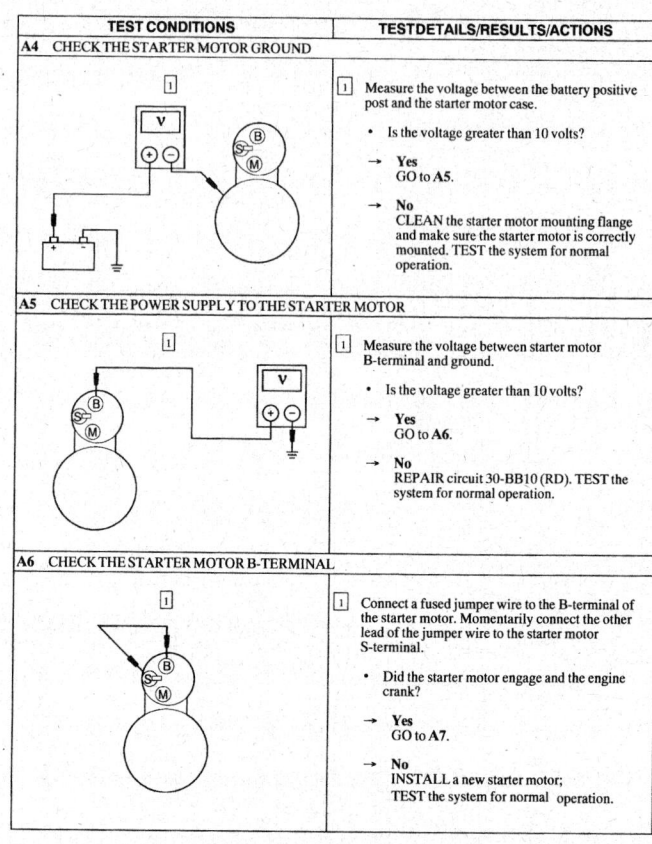

TEST CONDITIONS	TESTDETAILS/RESULTS/ACTIONS
A4 CHECK THE STARTER MOTOR GROUND	
	1 Measure the voltage between the battery positive post and the starter motor case. • Is the voltage greater than 10 volts? → **Yes** GO to **A5**. → **No** CLEAN the starter motor mounting flange and make sure the starter motor is correctly mounted. TEST the system for normal operation.
A5 CHECK THE POWER SUPPLY TO THE STARTER MOTOR	
	1 Measure the voltage between starter motor B-terminal and ground. • Is the voltage greater than 10 volts? → **Yes** GO to **A6**. → **No** REPAIR circuit 30-BB10 (RD). TEST the system for normal operation.
A6 CHECK THE STARTER MOTOR B-TERMINAL	
	1 Connect a fused jumper wire to the B-terminal of the starter motor. Momentarily connect the other lead of the jumper wire to the starter motor S-terminal. • Did the starter motor engage and the engine crank? → **Yes** GO to **A7**. → **No** INSTALL a new starter motor; TEST the system for normal operation.

FM1120100653020X

Fig. 26   Test A: Engine Does Not Crank (Part 2 of 17). LS & Thunderbird

TEST CONDITIONS	TESTDETAILS/RESULTS/ACTIONS
A7 CHECK THE START INPUT TO THE STARTER MOTOR	
1 Starter motor C197 **2** **3**	**2** Measure the voltage between starter motor C197, circuit 50-BB12 (GY/BK), harness side and ground while holding the ignition switch in the START position. • Is the voltage greater than 10 volts in START? → **Yes** CLEAN the starter motor S-terminal and connector. CHECK the wiring and the starter motor for a loose or intermittent connection. TEST the system for normal operation. → **No** GO to **A8**.
A8 CHECK THE START INPUT TO THE STARTER RELAY	
1 Starter relay	**2** For manual transmissions, depress the clutch pedal position (CPP) switch.

FM1120100653030X

Fig. 26   Test A: Engine Does Not Crank (Part 3 of 17). LS & Thunderbird

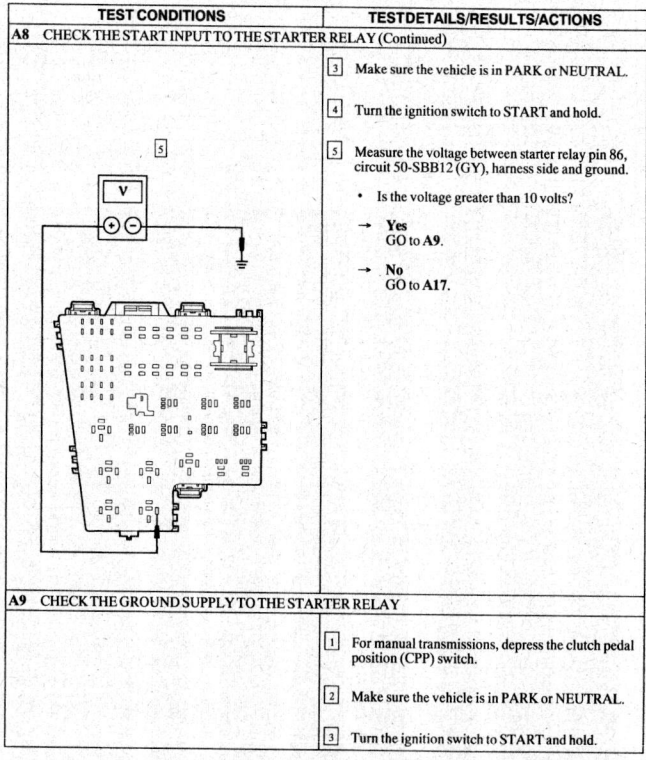

TEST CONDITIONS	TESTDETAILS/RESULTS/ACTIONS
A8 CHECK THE START INPUT TO THE STARTER RELAY (Continued)	
	3 Make sure the vehicle is in PARK or NEUTRAL.
	4 Turn the ignition switch to START and hold.
	5 Measure the voltage between starter relay pin 86, circuit 50-SBB12 (GY), harness side and ground. • Is the voltage greater than 10 volts? → **Yes** GO to **A9**. → **No** GO to **A17**.
A9 CHECK THE GROUND SUPPLY TO THE STARTER RELAY	
	1 For manual transmissions, depress the clutch pedal position (CPP) switch.
	2 Make sure the vehicle is in PARK or NEUTRAL.
	3 Turn the ignition switch to START and hold.

FM1120100653040X

Fig. 26   Test A: Engine Does Not Crank (Part 4 of 17). LS & Thunderbird

TEST CONDITIONS	TEST DETAILS/RESULTS/ACTIONS
A9 CHECK THE GROUND SUPPLY TO THE STARTER RELAY (Continued)	

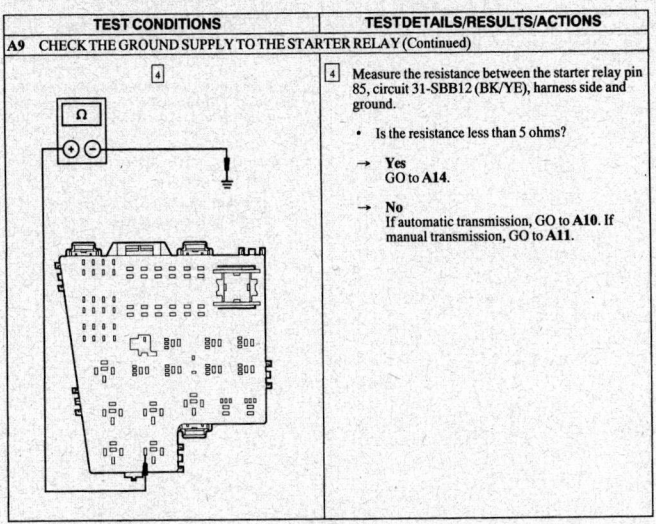

4 Measure the resistance between the starter relay pin 85, circuit 31-SBB12 (BK/YE), harness side and ground.

- Is the resistance less than 5 ohms?

→ **Yes**
GO to **A14**.

→ **No**
If automatic transmission, GO to **A10**. If manual transmission, GO to **A11**.

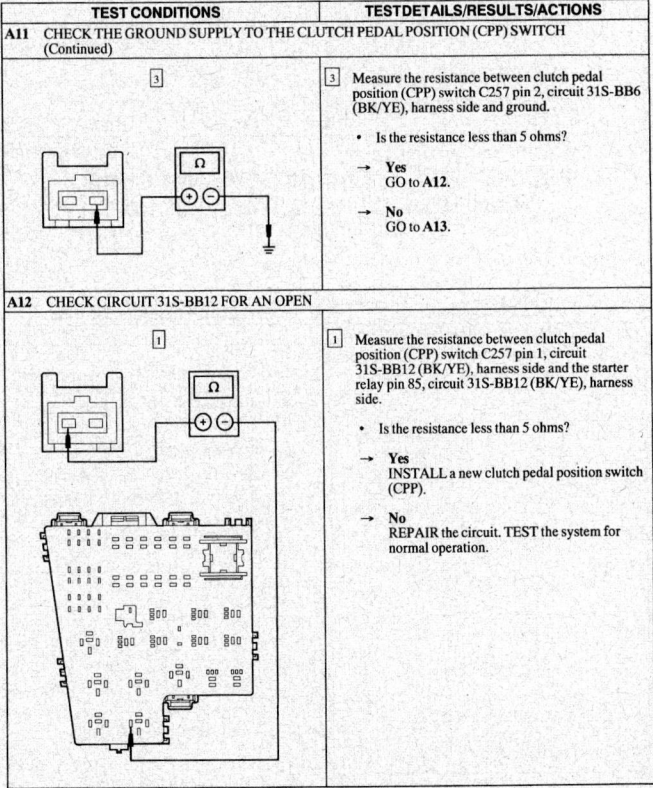

FM1120100653050X

**Fig. 26   Test A: Engine Does Not Crank
(Part 5 of 17). LS & Thunderbird**

TEST CONDITIONS	TEST DETAILS/RESULTS/ACTIONS
A11 CHECK THE GROUND SUPPLY TO THE CLUTCH PEDAL POSITION (CPP) SWITCH (Continued)	

3 Measure the resistance between clutch pedal position (CPP) switch C257 pin 2, circuit 31S-BB6 (BK/YE), harness side and ground.

- Is the resistance less than 5 ohms?

→ **Yes**
GO to **A12**.

→ **No**
GO to **A13**.

TEST CONDITIONS	TEST DETAILS/RESULTS/ACTIONS
A12 CHECK CIRCUIT 31S-BB12 FOR AN OPEN	

1 Measure the resistance between clutch pedal position (CPP) switch C257 pin 1, circuit 31S-BB12 (BK/YE), harness side and the starter relay pin 85, circuit 31S-BB12 (BK/YE), harness side.

- Is the resistance less than 5 ohms?

→ **Yes**
INSTALL a new clutch pedal position switch (CPP).

→ **No**
REPAIR the circuit. TEST the system for normal operation.

FM1120100653070X

**Fig. 26   Test A: Engine Does Not Crank
(Part 7 of 17). LS & Thunderbird**

TEST CONDITIONS	TEST DETAILS/RESULTS/ACTIONS
A10 CHECK THE CIRCUIT 31S-BB12 FOR AN OPEN	

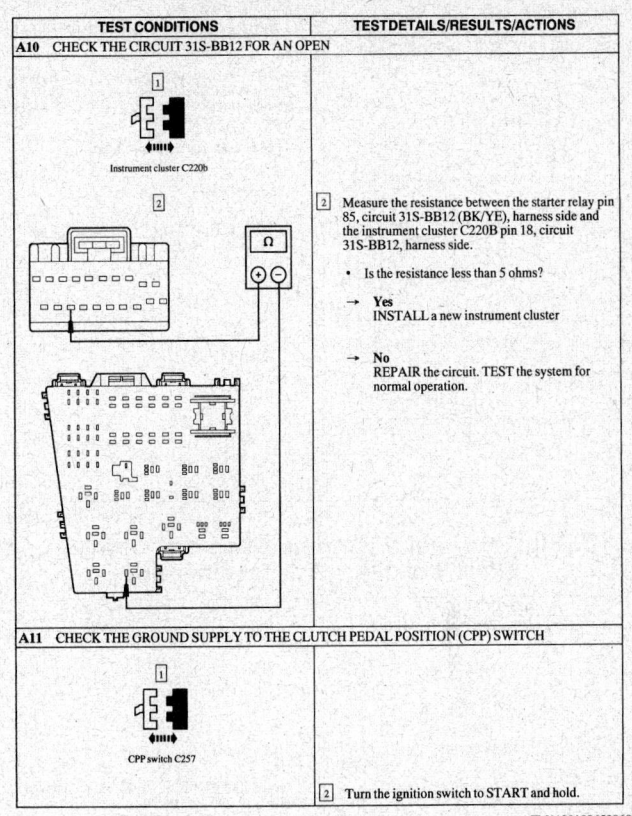

Instrument cluster C220b

2 Measure the resistance between the starter relay pin 85, circuit 31S-BB12 (BK/YE), harness side and the instrument cluster C220B pin 18, circuit 31S-BB12, harness side.

- Is the resistance less than 5 ohms?

→ **Yes**
INSTALL a new instrument cluster

→ **No**
REPAIR the circuit. TEST the system for normal operation.

TEST CONDITIONS	TEST DETAILS/RESULTS/ACTIONS
A11 CHECK THE GROUND SUPPLY TO THE CLUTCH PEDAL POSITION (CPP) SWITCH	

CPP switch C257

2 Turn the ignition switch to START and hold.

FM1120100653060X

**Fig. 26   Test A: Engine Does Not Crank
(Part 6 of 17). LS & Thunderbird**

TEST CONDITIONS	TEST DETAILS/RESULTS/ACTIONS
A13 CHECK CIRCUIT(S) 31S-BB12 AND 31S-BB6 FOR AN OPEN	

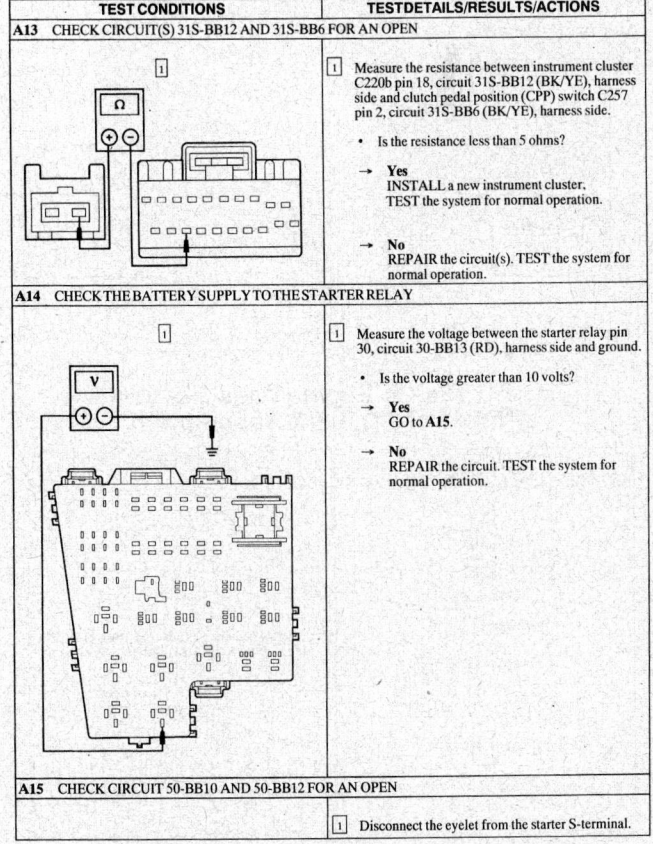

1 Measure the resistance between instrument cluster C220b pin 18, circuit 31S-BB12 (BK/YE), harness side and clutch pedal position (CPP) switch C257 pin 2, circuit 31S-BB6 (BK/YE), harness side.

- Is the resistance less than 5 ohms?

→ **Yes**
INSTALL a new instrument cluster. TEST the system for normal operation.

→ **No**
REPAIR the circuit(s). TEST the system for normal operation.

TEST CONDITIONS	TEST DETAILS/RESULTS/ACTIONS
A14 CHECK THE BATTERY SUPPLY TO THE STARTER RELAY	

1 Measure the voltage between the starter relay pin 30, circuit 30-BB13 (RD), harness side and ground.

- Is the voltage greater than 10 volts?

→ **Yes**
GO to **A15**.

→ **No**
REPAIR the circuit. TEST the system for normal operation.

TEST CONDITIONS	TEST DETAILS/RESULTS/ACTIONS
A15 CHECK CIRCUIT 50-BB10 AND 50-BB12 FOR AN OPEN	

1 Disconnect the eyelet from the starter S-terminal.

FM1120100653080X

**Fig. 26   Test A: Engine Does Not Crank
(Part 8 of 17). LS & Thunderbird**

TEST CONDITIONS	TEST DETAILS/RESULTS/ACTIONS
A15 CHECK CIRCUIT 50-BB10 AND 50-BB12 FOR AN OPEN (Continued)	

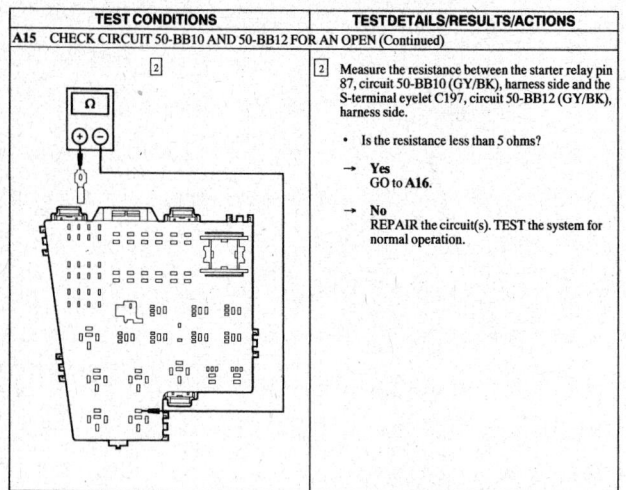	[2] Measure the resistance between the starter relay pin 87, circuit 50-BB10 (GY/BK), harness side and the S-terminal eyelet C197, circuit 50-BB12 (GY/BK), harness side.
	
	• Is the resistance less than 5 ohms?
	
	→ **Yes**
	    GO to **A16**.
	
	→ **No**
	    REPAIR the circuit(s). TEST the system for normal operation.

FM1120100653090X

Fig. 26   Test A: Engine Does Not Crank (Part 9 of 17). LS & Thunderbird

TEST CONDITIONS	TEST DETAILS/RESULTS/ACTIONS
A18 CHECK THE START INPUT TO FUSE 1	

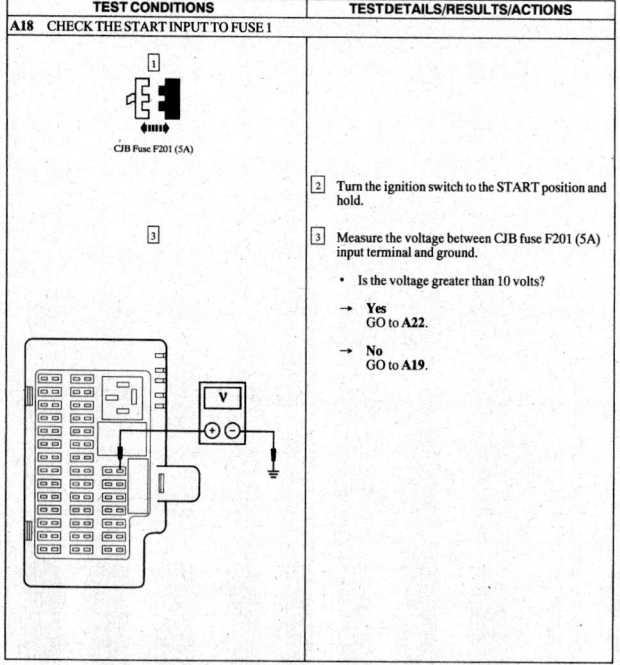	[2] Turn the ignition switch to the START position and hold.
	
	[3] Measure the voltage between CJB fuse F201 (5A) input terminal and ground.
	
	• Is the voltage greater than 10 volts?
	
	→ **Yes**
	    GO to **A22**.
	
	→ **No**
	    GO to **A19**.

FM1120100653110X

Fig. 26   Test A: Engine Does Not Crank (Part 11 of 17). LS & Thunderbird

TEST CONDITIONS	TEST DETAILS/RESULTS/ACTIONS
A19 CHECK THE BATTERY INPUT TO THE IGNITION SWITCH	

Ignition switch C250	[2] Measure the voltage between ignition switch C250 pin 1, circuit 30-BB9 (RD), harness side and ground.
	
	• Is the voltage greater than 10 volts?
	
	→ **Yes**
	    GO to **A20**.
	
	→ **No**
	    REPAIR the circuit. TEST the system for normal operation.

FM1120100653120X

Fig. 26   Test A: Engine Does Not Crank (Part 12 of 17). LS & Thunderbird

TEST CONDITIONS	TEST DETAILS/RESULTS/ACTIONS
A16 CHECK CIRCUIT 50-BB10 AND 50-BB12 FOR A SHORT TO GROUND	

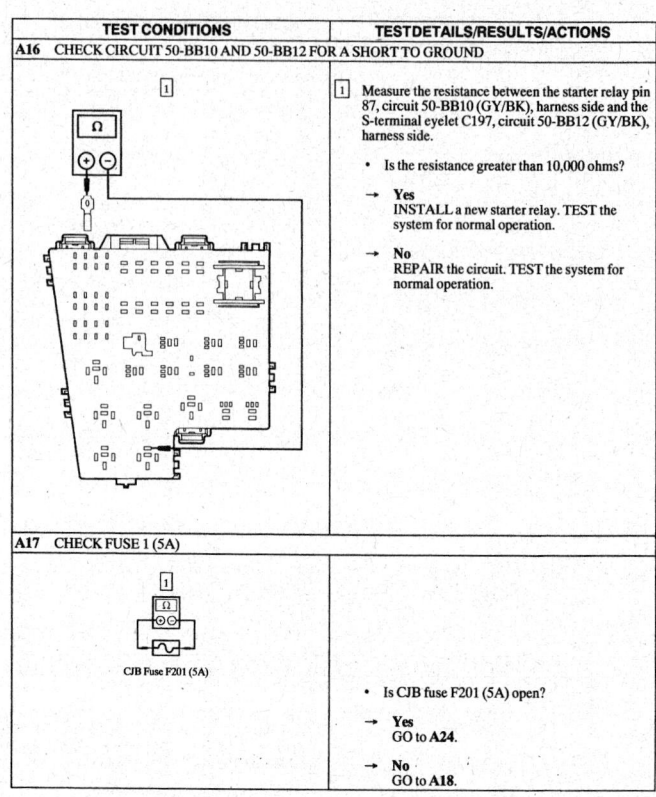	[1] Measure the resistance between the starter relay pin 87, circuit 50-BB10 (GY/BK), harness side and the S-terminal eyelet C197, circuit 50-BB12 (GY/BK), harness side.
	
	• Is the resistance greater than 10,000 ohms?
	
	→ **Yes**
	    INSTALL a new starter relay. TEST the system for normal operation.
	
	→ **No**
	    REPAIR the circuit. TEST the system for normal operation.

A17 CHECK FUSE 1 (5A)	

CJB Fuse F201 (5A)	• Is CJB fuse F201 (5A) open?
	
	→ **Yes**
	    GO to **A24**.
	
	→ **No**
	    GO to **A18**.

FM1120100653100X

Fig. 26   Test A: Engine Does Not Crank (Part 10 of 17). LS & Thunderbird

TEST CONDITIONS	TEST DETAILS/RESULTS/ACTIONS
A20 CHECK CIRCUIT 50-DD5 FOR AN OPEN	

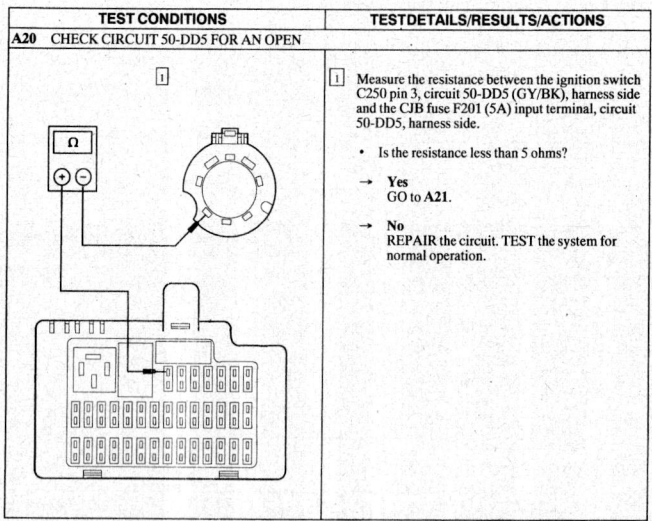	[1] Measure the resistance between the ignition switch C250 pin 3, circuit 50-DD5 (GY/BK), harness side and the CJB fuse F201 (5A) input terminal, circuit 50-DD5, harness side.
	
	• Is the resistance less than 5 ohms?
	
	→ **Yes**
	    GO to **A21**.
	
	→ **No**
	    REPAIR the circuit. TEST the system for normal operation.

FM1120100653130X

Fig. 26   Test A: Engine Does Not Crank (Part 13 of 17). LS & Thunderbird

TEST CONDITIONS	TESTDETAILS/RESULTS/ACTIONS
A21 CHECK CIRCUIT 50-DD5 FOR A SHORT TO GROUND	

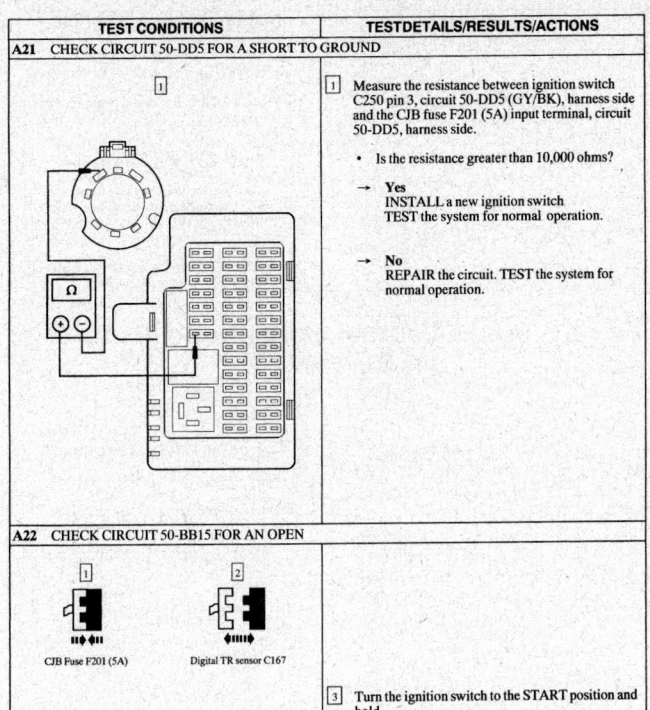

1 Measure the resistance between ignition switch C250 pin 3, circuit 50-DD5 (GY/BK), harness side and the CJB fuse F201 (5A) input terminal, circuit 50-DD5, harness side.

- Is the resistance greater than 10,000 ohms?

→ **Yes**
INSTALL a new ignition switch
TEST the system for normal operation.

→ **No**
REPAIR the circuit. TEST the system for normal operation.

TEST CONDITIONS	
A22 CHECK CIRCUIT 50-BB15 FOR AN OPEN	

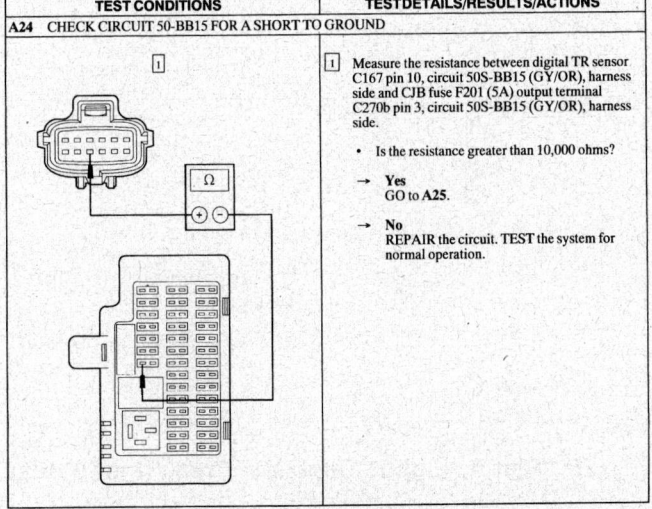

CJB Fuse F201 (5A)   Digital TR sensor C167

3 Turn the ignition switch to the START position and hold.

FM1120100653140X

**Fig. 26   Test A: Engine Does Not Crank
(Part 14 of 17). LS & Thunderbird**

TEST CONDITIONS	TESTDETAILS/RESULTS/ACTIONS
A22 CHECK CIRCUIT 50-BB15 FOR AN OPEN (Continued)	

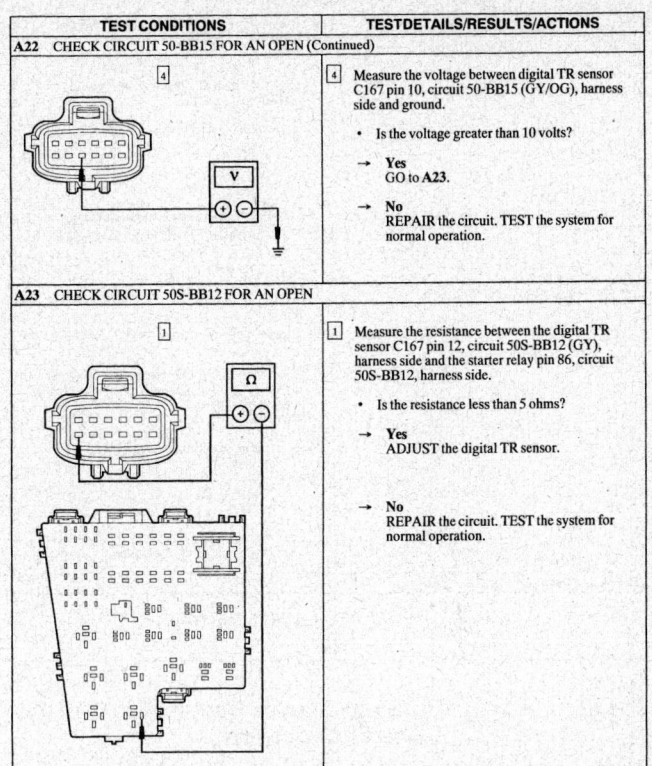

4 Measure the voltage between digital TR sensor C167 pin 10, circuit 50-BB15 (GY/OG), harness side and ground.

- Is the voltage greater than 10 volts?

→ **Yes**
GO to **A23**.

→ **No**
REPAIR the circuit. TEST the system for normal operation.

A23 CHECK CIRCUIT 50S-BB12 FOR AN OPEN	

1 Measure the resistance between the digital TR sensor C167 pin 12, circuit 50S-BB12 (GY), harness side and the starter relay pin 86, circuit 50S-BB12, harness side.

- Is the resistance less than 5 ohms?

→ **Yes**
ADJUST the digital TR sensor.

→ **No**
REPAIR the circuit. TEST the system for normal operation.

FM1120100653150X

**Fig. 26   Test A: Engine Does Not Crank
(Part 15 of 17). LS & Thunderbird**

TEST CONDITIONS	TESTDETAILS/RESULTS/ACTIONS
A24 CHECK CIRCUIT 50-BB15 FOR A SHORT TO GROUND	

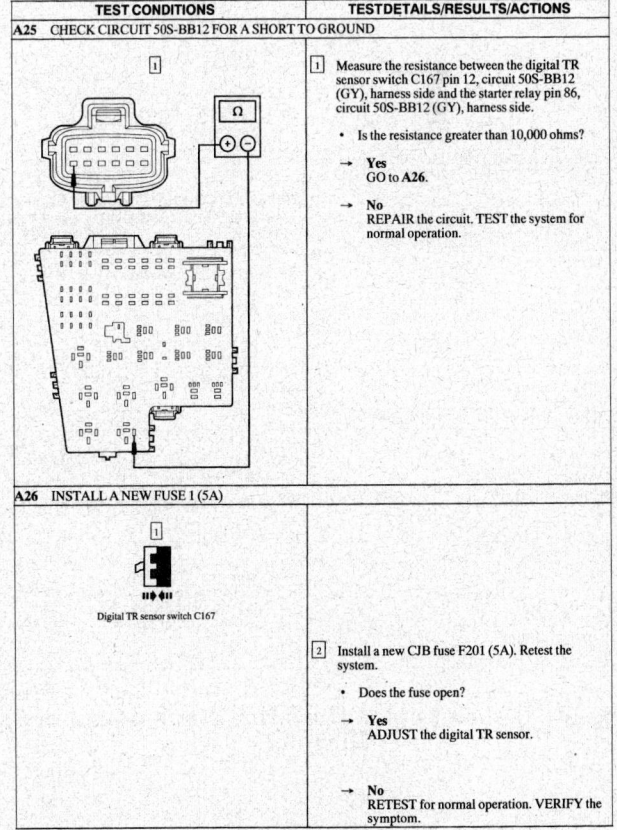

1 Measure the resistance between digital TR sensor C167 pin 10, circuit 50-BB15 (GY/OR), harness side and CJB fuse F201 (5A) output terminal C270b pin 3, circuit 50S-BB15 (GY/OR), harness side.

- Is the resistance greater than 10,000 ohms?

→ **Yes**
GO to **A25**.

→ **No**
REPAIR the circuit. TEST the system for normal operation.

FM1120100653160X

**Fig. 26   Test A: Engine Does Not Crank
(Part 16 of 17). LS & Thunderbird**

TEST CONDITIONS	TESTDETAILS/RESULTS/ACTIONS
A25 CHECK CIRCUIT 50S-BB12 FOR A SHORT TO GROUND	

1 Measure the resistance between the digital TR sensor switch C167 pin 12, circuit 50S-BB12 (GY), harness side and the starter relay pin 86, circuit 50S-BB12 (GY), harness side.

- Is the resistance greater than 10,000 ohms?

→ **Yes**
GO to **A26**.

→ **No**
REPAIR the circuit. TEST the system for normal operation.

A26 INSTALL A NEW FUSE 1 (5A)	

Digital TR sensor switch C167

2 Install a new CJB fuse F201 (5A). Retest the system.

- Does the fuse open?

→ **Yes**
ADJUST the digital TR sensor.

→ **No**
RETEST for normal operation. VERIFY the symptom.

FM1120100653170X

**Fig. 26   Test A: Engine Does Not Crank
(Part 17 of 17). LS & Thunderbird**

TEST CONDITIONS	TEST DETAILS/RESULTS/ACTIONS
B1 CHECK THE STARTER MOUNTING	

	1 Inspect the starter motor mounting bolts and brackets for looseness.
	
	• Is the starter motor mounted correctly?
	
	→ **Yes**
	     GO to **B2**.
	
	→ **No**
	     INSTALL the starter motor correctly.
	     TEST the system for normal operation.

B2 CHECK FOR ENGINE NOISE	

	1 Turn the ignition switch to the OFF position.
	
	2 Connect a fused jumper wire from the B-terminal to the S-terminal of the starter motor. Engage the starter motor and verify the noise is due to the starter operation.
	
	• Is the noise due to the starter motor engagement?
	
	→ **Yes**
	     GO to **B3**.
	
	→ **No**
	     Diagnose Engine Mechanical Components

B3 CHECK FOR UNUSUAL WEAR	
	1 Remove the starter motor.

FM1120100654010X

Fig. 27   Test B: Unusual Starter Noise (Part 1 of 2). LS & Thunderbird

TEST CONDITIONS	TEST DETAILS/RESULTS/ACTIONS
A1 CHECK THE BATTERY	

	1 Check the battery condition and charge.
	
	• Is the battery OK?
	
	→ **Yes**
	     GO to **A2**.
	
	→ **No**
	     CHARGE or install a new battery as necessary. TEST the system for normal operation.

A2 CHECK THE BATTERY GROUND CABLE	

	1 Measure the voltage between the positive battery post and the battery ground cable connection at the cylinder block or the starter motor mounting stud bolt, Circuit 2057 (BK).
	
	• Is the voltage greater than 10 volts?
	
	→ **Yes**
	     GO to **A3**.
	
	→ **No**
	     INSTALL a new battery ground cable. TEST the system for normal operation.

A3 CHECK THE STARTER MOTOR GROUND	

	1 Measure the voltage between the battery positive post and the starter motor case.
	
	• Is the voltage greater than 10 volts?
	
	→ **Yes**
	     GO to **A4**.
	
	→ **No**
	     CLEAN the starter motor mounting flange and make sure the starter motor is correctly mounted. TEST the system for normal operation.

FM1120100660010X

Fig. 28   Test A: Engine Does Not Crank (Part 1 of 9). Mustang

TEST CONDITIONS	TEST DETAILS/RESULTS/ACTIONS
B3 CHECK FOR UNUSUAL WEAR (Continued)	

	2 Inspect the ring gear for damaged or worn teeth.
	
	• Is the noise due to flywheel ring gear tooth damage?
	
	→ **Yes**
	     INSTALL a new flywheel ring gear.
	     EXAMINE the starter pinion teeth. If damaged, INSTALL a new starter motor. TEST the system for normal operation.
	
	→ **No**
	     INSTALL a new starter motor. TEST the system for normal operation.

FM1120100654020X

Fig. 27   Test B: Unusual Starter Noise (Part 2 of 2). LS & Thunderbird

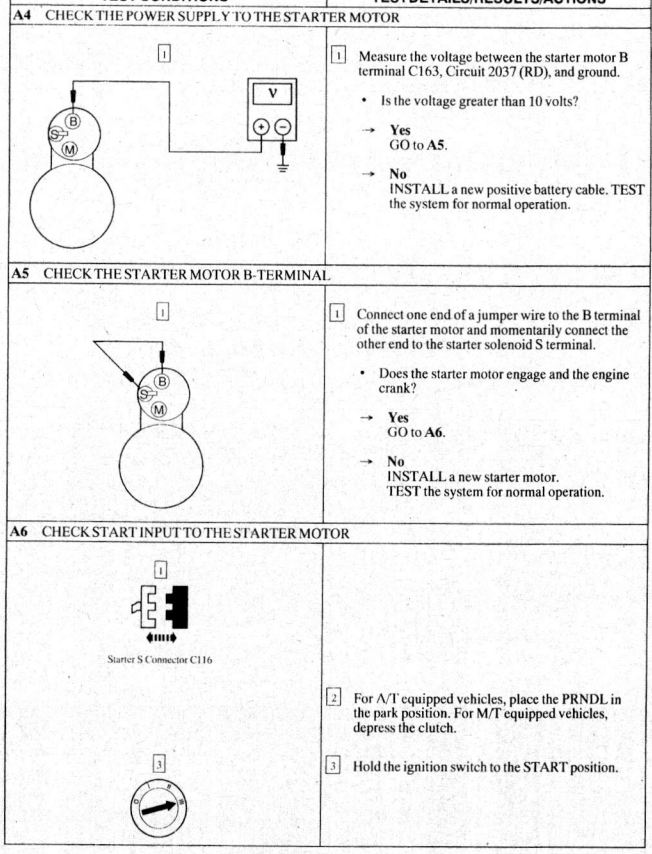

TEST CONDITIONS	TEST DETAILS/RESULTS/ACTIONS
A4 CHECK THE POWER SUPPLY TO THE STARTER MOTOR	

	1 Measure the voltage between the starter motor B terminal C163, Circuit 2037 (RD), and ground.
	
	• Is the voltage greater than 10 volts?
	
	→ **Yes**
	     GO to **A5**.
	
	→ **No**
	     INSTALL a new positive battery cable. TEST the system for normal operation.

A5 CHECK THE STARTER MOTOR B-TERMINAL	

	1 Connect one end of a jumper wire to the B terminal of the starter motor and momentarily connect the other end to the starter solenoid S terminal.
	
	• Does the starter motor engage and the engine crank?
	
	→ **Yes**
	     GO to **A6**.
	
	→ **No**
	     INSTALL a new starter motor.
	     TEST the system for normal operation.

A6 CHECK START INPUT TO THE STARTER MOTOR	
Starter S Connector C116	**2** For A/T equipped vehicles, place the PRNDL in the park position. For M/T equipped vehicles, depress the clutch. **3** Hold the ignition switch to the START position.

FM1120100660020X

Fig. 28   Test A: Engine Does Not Crank (Part 2 of 9). Mustang

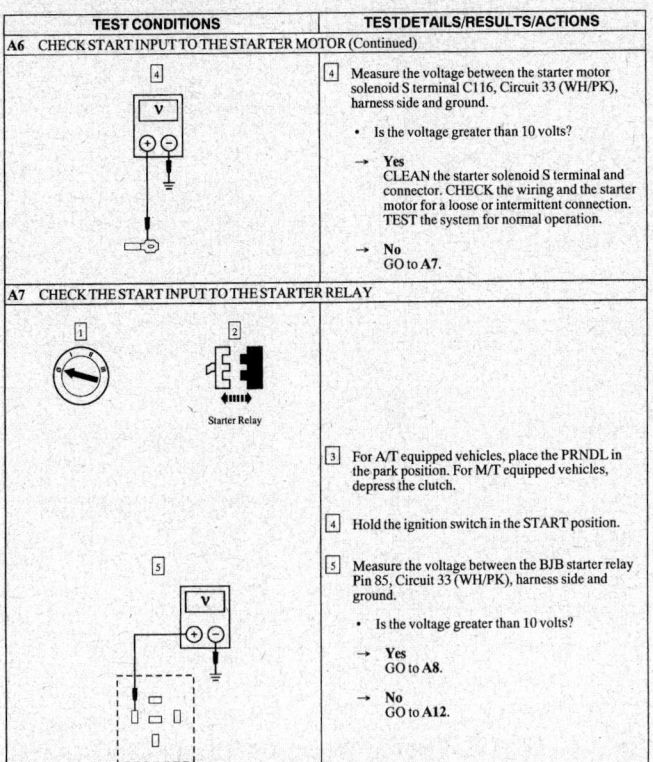

TEST CONDITIONS	TESTDETAILS/RESULTS/ACTIONS
A6 CHECK START INPUT TO THE STARTER MOTOR (Continued)	
[4]	[4] Measure the voltage between the starter motor solenoid S terminal C116, Circuit 33 (WH/PK), harness side and ground. • Is the voltage greater than 10 volts? → **Yes** CLEAN the starter solenoid S terminal and connector. CHECK the wiring and the starter motor for a loose or intermittent connection. TEST the system for normal operation. → **No** GO to **A7**.
A7 CHECK THE START INPUT TO THE STARTER RELAY	
[1] [2] Starter Relay	[3] For A/T equipped vehicles, place the PRNDL in the park position. For M/T equipped vehicles, depress the clutch. [4] Hold the ignition switch in the START position. [5] Measure the voltage between the BJB starter relay Pin 85, Circuit 33 (WH/PK), harness side and ground. • Is the voltage greater than 10 volts? → **Yes** GO to **A8**. → **No** GO to **A12**.
[5]	

FM1120100660030X

Fig. 28   Test A: Engine Does Not Crank (Part 3 of 9). Mustang

TEST CONDITIONS	TEST DETAILS/RESULTS/ACTIONS
A10 CHECK CIRCUIT 262 (BN/PK) FOR A SHORT TO GROUND	
[1]	[1] Measure the resistance between the BJB starter relay Pin 87, Circuit 262 (BN/PK), harness side and ground. • Is the resistance greater than 10,000 ohms? → **Yes** GO to **A11**. → **No** REPAIR the circuit. TEST the system for normal operation.
A11 CHECK CIRCUIT 262 (BN/PK) FOR AN OPEN	
[1]	[1] Measure the resistance between the BJB starter relay Pin 87, Circuit 262 (BN/PK), harness side and the starter solenoid S connector C116, Circuit 33 (WH/PK), harness side. • Is the resistance less than 5 ohms? → **Yes** INSTALL a new starter relay. TEST the system for normal operation. → **No** REPAIR the circuit. TEST the system for normal operation.
A12 CHECK THE START INPUT TO THE CLUTCH PEDAL POSITION (CPP) SWITCH	
[1] [2] CPP Switch C255 (M/T) or Jumper Connector C253 (A/T)	[2] Hold the ignition switch to the START position.

FM1120100660050X

Fig. 28   Test A: Engine Does Not Crank (Part 5 of 9). Mustang

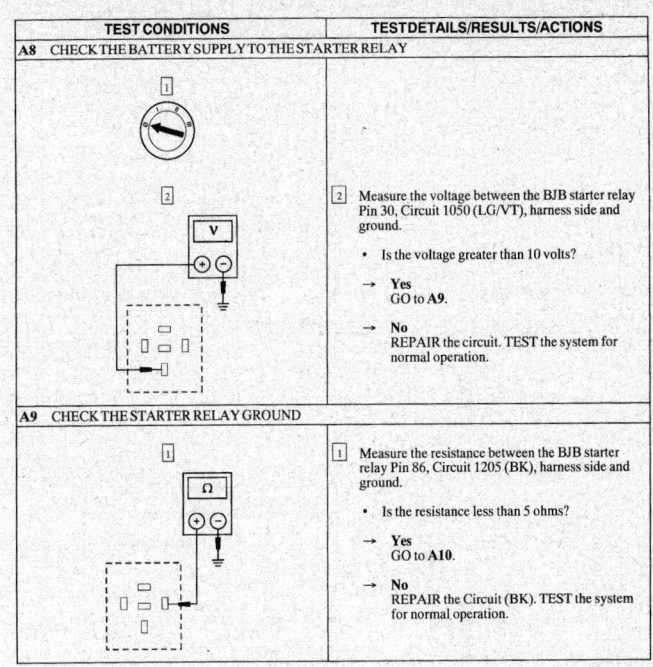

TEST CONDITIONS	TESTDETAILS/RESULTS/ACTIONS
A8 CHECK THE BATTERY SUPPLY TO THE STARTER RELAY	
[1] [2]	[2] Measure the voltage between the BJB starter relay Pin 30, Circuit 1050 (LG/VT), harness side and ground. • Is the voltage greater than 10 volts? → **Yes** GO to **A9**. → **No** REPAIR the circuit. TEST the system for normal operation.
A9 CHECK THE STARTER RELAY GROUND	
[1]	[1] Measure the resistance between the BJB starter relay Pin 86, Circuit 1205 (BK), harness side and ground. • Is the resistance less than 5 ohms? → **Yes** GO to **A10**. → **No** REPAIR the Circuit (BK). TEST the system for normal operation.

FM1120100660040X

Fig. 28   Test A: Engine Does Not Crank (Part 4 of 9). Mustang

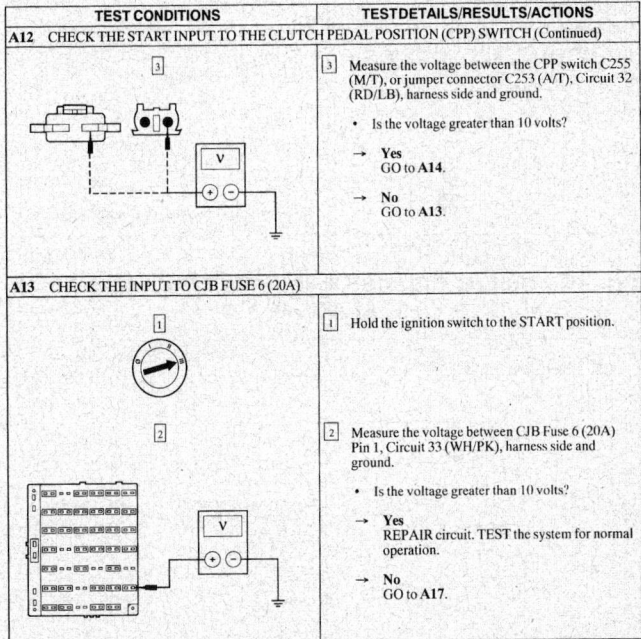

TEST CONDITIONS	TESTDETAILS/RESULTS/ACTIONS
A12 CHECK THE START INPUT TO THE CLUTCH PEDAL POSITION (CPP) SWITCH (Continued)	
[3]	[3] Measure the voltage between the CPP switch C255 (M/T), or jumper connector C253 (A/T), Circuit 32 (RD/LB), harness side and ground. • Is the voltage greater than 10 volts? → **Yes** GO to **A14**. → **No** GO to **A13**.
A13 CHECK THE INPUT TO CJB FUSE 6 (20A)	
[1] [2]	[1] Hold the ignition switch to the START position. [2] Measure the voltage between CJB Fuse 6 (20A) Pin 1, Circuit 33 (WH/PK), harness side and ground. • Is the voltage greater than 10 volts? → **Yes** REPAIR circuit. TEST the system for normal operation. → **No** GO to **A17**.

FM1120100660060X

Fig. 28   Test A: Engine Does Not Crank (Part 6 of 9). Mustang

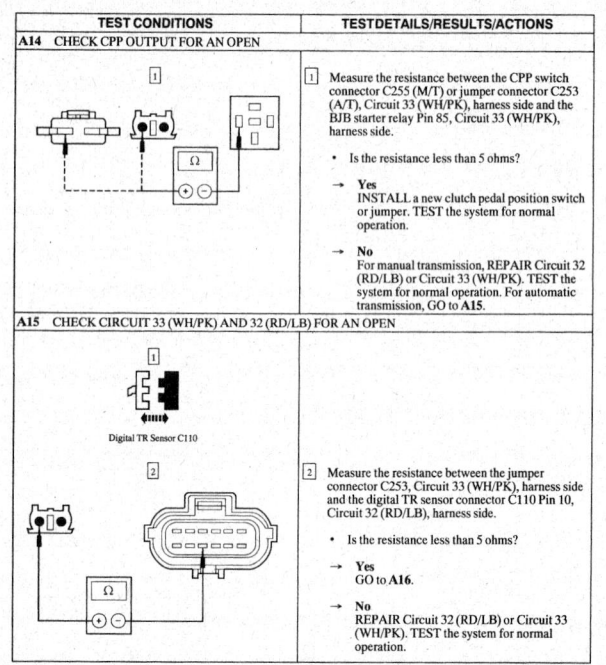

TEST CONDITIONS	TEST DETAILS/RESULTS/ACTIONS
A14 CHECK CPP OUTPUT FOR AN OPEN	
①	① Measure the resistance between the CPP switch connector C255 (M/T) or jumper connector C253 (A/T), Circuit 33 (WH/PK), harness side and the BJB starter relay Pin 85, Circuit 33 (WH/PK), harness side. • Is the resistance less than 5 ohms? → **Yes** INSTALL a new clutch pedal position switch or jumper. TEST the system for normal operation. → **No** For manual transmission, REPAIR Circuit 32 (RD/LB) or Circuit 33 (WH/PK). TEST the system for normal operation. For automatic transmission, GO to **A15**.
A15 CHECK CIRCUIT 33 (WH/PK) AND 32 (RD/LB) FOR AN OPEN	
① Digital TR Sensor C110	② Measure the resistance between the jumper connector C253, Circuit 33 (WH/PK), harness side and the digital TR sensor connector C110 Pin 10, Circuit 32 (RD/LB), harness side. • Is the resistance less than 5 ohms? → **Yes** GO to **A16**. → **No** REPAIR Circuit 32 (RD/LB) or Circuit 33 (WH/PK). TEST the system for normal operation.

FM1120100660070X

Fig. 28 Test A: Engine Does Not Crank (Part 7 of 9). Mustang

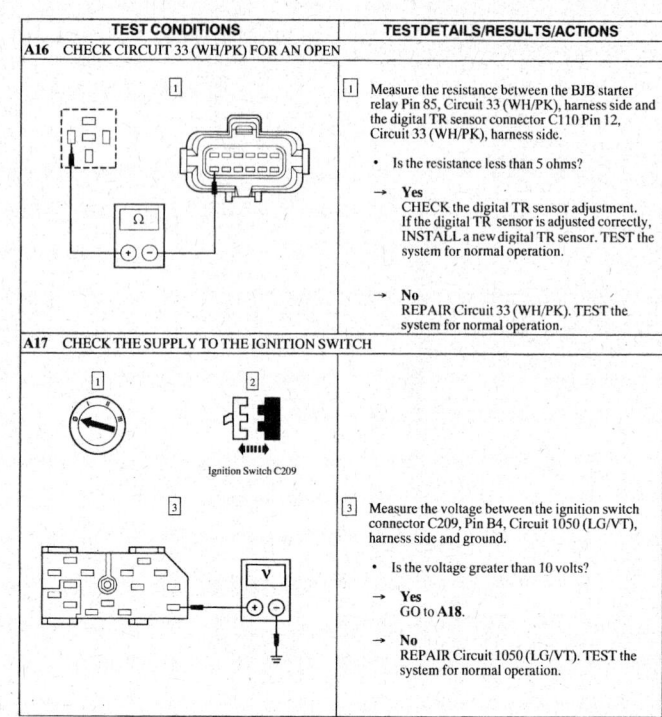

TEST CONDITIONS	TEST DETAILS/RESULTS/ACTIONS
A16 CHECK CIRCUIT 33 (WH/PK) FOR AN OPEN	
①	① Measure the resistance between the BJB starter relay Pin 85, Circuit 33 (WH/PK), harness side and the digital TR sensor connector C110 Pin 12, Circuit 33 (WH/PK), harness side. • Is the resistance less than 5 ohms? → **Yes** CHECK the digital TR sensor adjustment. If the digital TR sensor is adjusted correctly, INSTALL a new digital TR sensor. TEST the system for normal operation. → **No** REPAIR Circuit 33 (WH/PK). TEST the system for normal operation.
A17 CHECK THE SUPPLY TO THE IGNITION SWITCH	
① ② Ignition Switch C209 ③	③ Measure the voltage between the ignition switch connector C209, Pin B4, Circuit 1050 (LG/VT), harness side and ground. • Is the voltage greater than 10 volts? → **Yes** GO to **A18**. → **No** REPAIR Circuit 1050 (LG/VT). TEST the system for normal operation.

FM1120100660080X

Fig. 28 Test A: Engine Does Not Crank (Part 8 of 9). Mustang

TEST CONDITIONS	TEST DETAILS/RESULTS/ACTIONS
A18 CHECK CIRCUIT 33 (WH/PK) FOR AN OPEN	
①	① Measure the resistance between the ignition switch connector C209 Pin STA, Circuit 33 (WH/PK), harness side and CJB Fuse 6 (20A) Pin 1, Circuit 33 (WH/PK) harness side. • Is the resistance less than 5 ohms? → **Yes** INSTALL a new ignition switch. TEST the system for normal operation. → **No** REPAIR the circuit. TEST the system for normal operation.

FM1120100660090X

Fig. 28 Test A: Engine Does Not Crank (Part 9 of 9). Mustang

TEST CONDITIONS	TEST DETAILS/RESULTS/ACTIONS
B1 CHECK STARTER MOUNTING	
	① Inspect the starter mounting bolts and brackets for looseness. • Is the starter motor mounted correctly? → **Yes** GO to **B2**. → **No** INSTALL the starter motor correctly. TEST the system for normal operation.

FM1120100661010X

Fig. 29 Test B: Unusual Starter Noise (Part 1 of 3). Mustang

TEST CONDITIONS	TEST DETAILS/RESULTS/ACTIONS
B2 CHECK FOR ENGINE NOISE	
① ② (B) (S)(M)	② Connect a remote starter switch between the starter solenoid B and S terminals. ③ Engage the starter motor and verify the noise is due to the starter operation. • Is the noise due to the starter motor engagement? → **Yes** GO to **B3**. → **No** continue the diagnosis.
B3 CHECK FOR UNUSUAL WEAR	
	① Remove the starter motor.

FM1120100661020X

Fig. 29 Test B: Unusual Starter Noise (Part 2 of 3). Mustang

TEST CONDITIONS	TEST DETAILS/RESULTS/ACTIONS
B3 CHECK FOR UNUSUAL WEAR (Continued)	
	② Inspect the ring gear. • Is the noise due to ring gear tooth damage? → **Yes** INSTALL a new ring gear. EXAMINE the starter pinion teeth. If damaged, INSTALL a new starter motor. normal operation. → **No** INSTALL a new starter motor. TEST the system for normal operation.

FM1120100661030X

Fig. 29 Test B: Unusual Starter Noise (Part 3 of 3). Mustang

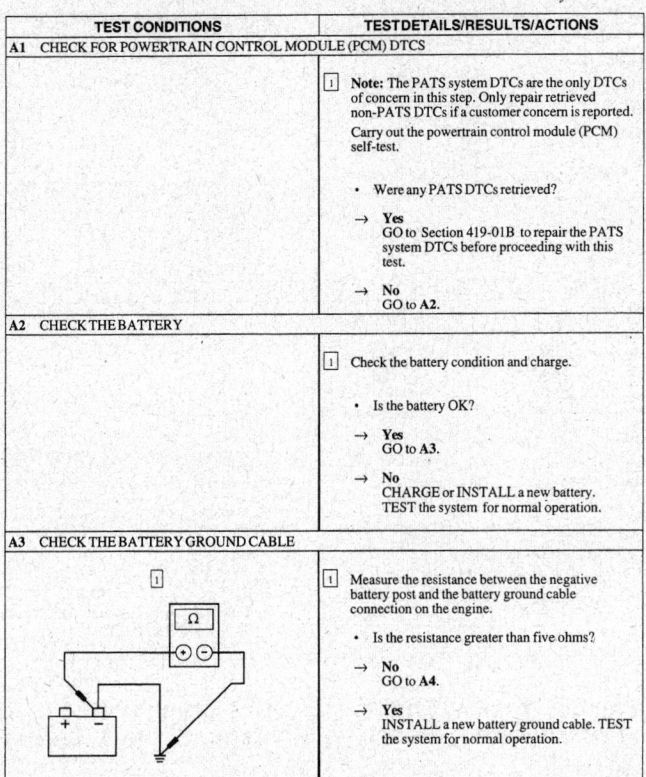

TEST CONDITIONS	TESTDETAILS/RESULTS/ACTIONS
A1 CHECK FOR POWERTRAIN CONTROL MODULE (PCM) DTCS	

	1 **Note:** The PATS system DTCs are the only DTCs of concern in this step. Only repair retrieved non-PATS DTCs if a customer concern is reported. Carry out the powertrain control module (PCM) self-test.
	
	• Were any PATS DTCs retrieved?
	
	→ **Yes**
	  GO to Section 419-01B to repair the PATS system DTCs before proceeding with this test.
	
	→ **No**
	  GO to **A2**.

A2 CHECK THE BATTERY	

	1 Check the battery condition and charge.
	
	• Is the battery OK?
	
	→ **Yes**
	  GO to **A3**.
	
	→ **No**
	  CHARGE or INSTALL a new battery. TEST the system for normal operation.

A3 CHECK THE BATTERY GROUND CABLE	

	1 Measure the resistance between the negative battery post and the battery ground cable connection on the engine.
	
	• Is the resistance greater than five ohms?
	
	→ **No**
	  GO to **A4**.
	
	→ **Yes**
	  INSTALL a new battery ground cable. TEST the system for normal operation.

FM1120100673010X

Fig. 30   Test A: Engine Does Not Crank (Part 1 of 8). Five Hundred, Freestyle, Montego, Sable & Taurus

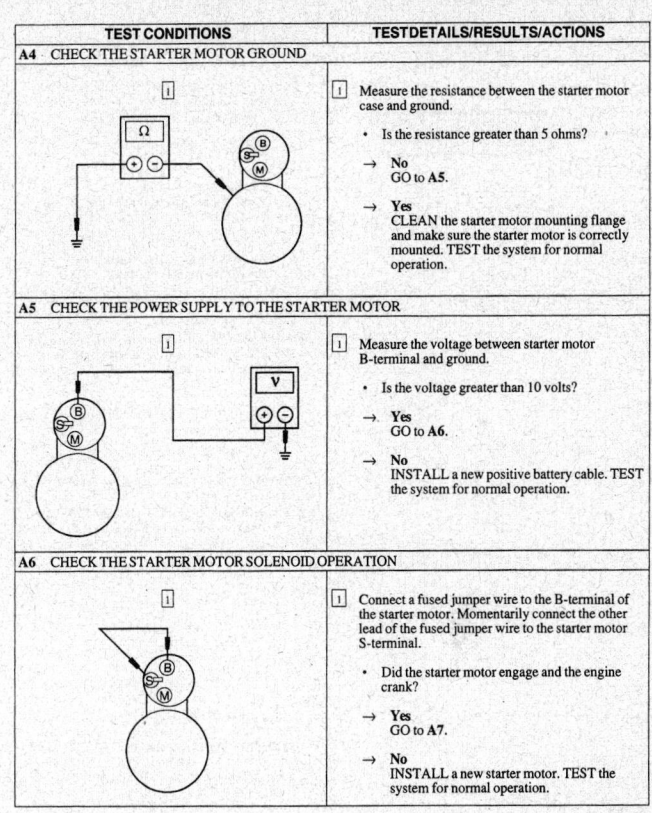

TEST CONDITIONS	TESTDETAILS/RESULTS/ACTIONS
A4 CHECK THE STARTER MOTOR GROUND	

	1 Measure the resistance between the starter motor case and ground.
	
	• Is the resistance greater than 5 ohms?
	
	→ **No**
	  GO to **A5**.
	
	→ **Yes**
	  CLEAN the starter motor mounting flange and make sure the starter motor is correctly mounted. TEST the system for normal operation.

A5 CHECK THE POWER SUPPLY TO THE STARTER MOTOR	

	1 Measure the voltage between starter motor B-terminal and ground.
	
	• Is the voltage greater than 10 volts?
	
	→ **Yes**
	  GO to **A6**.
	
	→ **No**
	  INSTALL a new positive battery cable. TEST the system for normal operation.

A6 CHECK THE STARTER MOTOR SOLENOID OPERATION	

	1 Connect a fused jumper wire to the B-terminal of the starter motor. Momentarily connect the other lead of the fused jumper wire to the starter motor S-terminal.
	
	• Did the starter motor engage and the engine crank?
	
	→ **Yes**
	  GO to **A7**.
	
	→ **No**
	  INSTALL a new starter motor. TEST the system for normal operation.

FM1120100673020X

Fig. 30   Test A: Engine Does Not Crank (Part 2 of 8). Five Hundred, Freestyle, Montego, Sable & Taurus

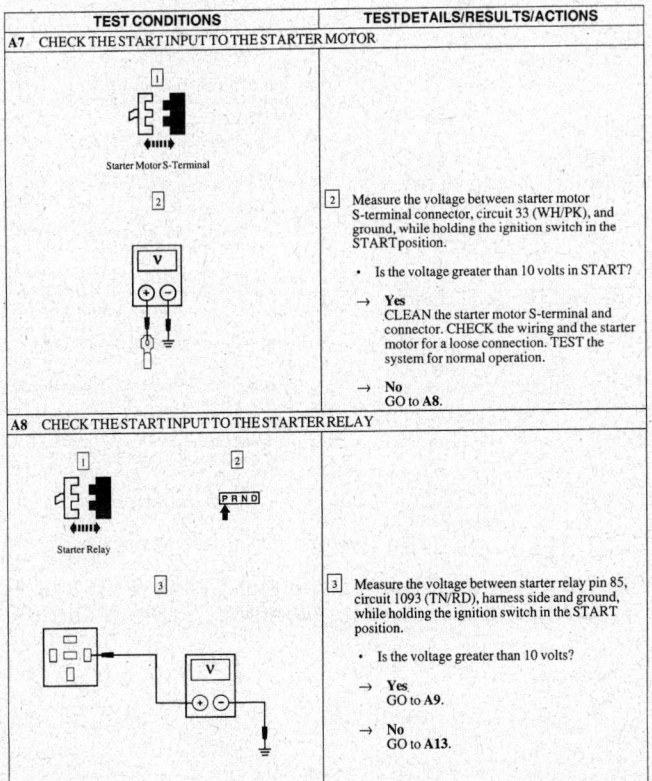

TEST CONDITIONS	TESTDETAILS/RESULTS/ACTIONS
A7 CHECK THE START INPUT TO THE STARTER MOTOR	

Starter Motor S-Terminal	2 Measure the voltage between starter motor S-terminal connector, circuit 33 (WH/PK), and ground, while holding the ignition switch in the START position.
	
	• Is the voltage greater than 10 volts in START?
	
	→ **Yes**
	  CLEAN the starter motor S-terminal and connector. CHECK the wiring and the starter motor for a loose connection. TEST the system for normal operation.
	
	→ **No**
	  GO to **A8**.

A8 CHECK THE START INPUT TO THE STARTER RELAY	

Starter Relay	3 Measure the voltage between starter relay pin 85, circuit 1093 (TN/RD), harness side and ground, while holding the ignition switch in the START position.
	
	• Is the voltage greater than 10 volts?
	
	→ **Yes**
	  GO to **A9**.
	
	→ **No**
	  GO to **A13**.

FM1120100673030X

Fig. 30   Test A: Engine Does Not Crank (Part 3 of 8). Five Hundred, Freestyle, Montego, Sable & Taurus

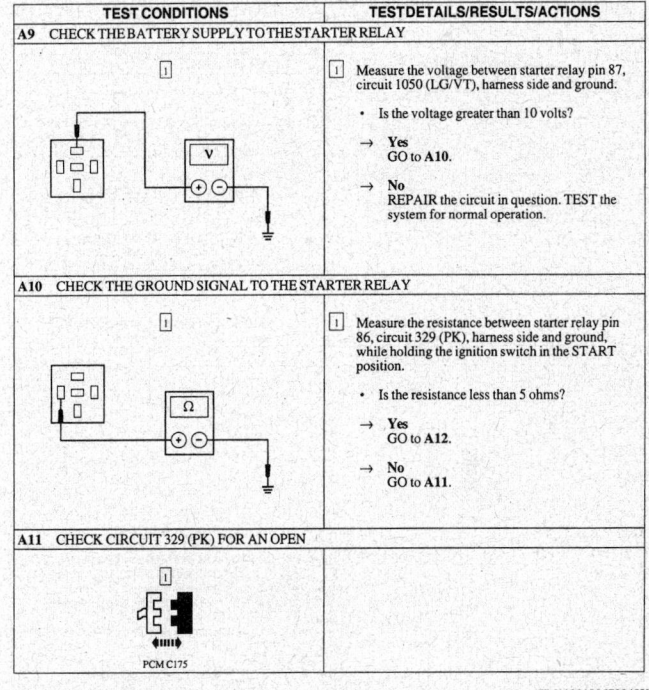

TEST CONDITIONS	TESTDETAILS/RESULTS/ACTIONS
A9 CHECK THE BATTERY SUPPLY TO THE STARTER RELAY	

	1 Measure the voltage between starter relay pin 87, circuit 1050 (LG/VT), harness side and ground.
	
	• Is the voltage greater than 10 volts?
	
	→ **Yes**
	  GO to **A10**.
	
	→ **No**
	  REPAIR the circuit in question. TEST the system for normal operation.

A10 CHECK THE GROUND SIGNAL TO THE STARTER RELAY	

	1 Measure the resistance between starter relay pin 86, circuit 329 (PK), harness side and ground, while holding the ignition switch in the START position.
	
	• Is the resistance less than 5 ohms?
	
	→ **Yes**
	  GO to **A12**.
	
	→ **No**
	  GO to **A11**.

A11 CHECK CIRCUIT 329 (PK) FOR AN OPEN	
PCM C175	

FM1120100673040X

Fig. 30   Test A: Engine Does Not Crank (Part 4 of 8). Five Hundred, Freestyle, Montego, Sable & Taurus

TEST CONDITIONS	TESTDETAILS/RESULTS/ACTIONS
A11 CHECK CIRCUIT 329 (PK) FOR AN OPEN (Continued)	

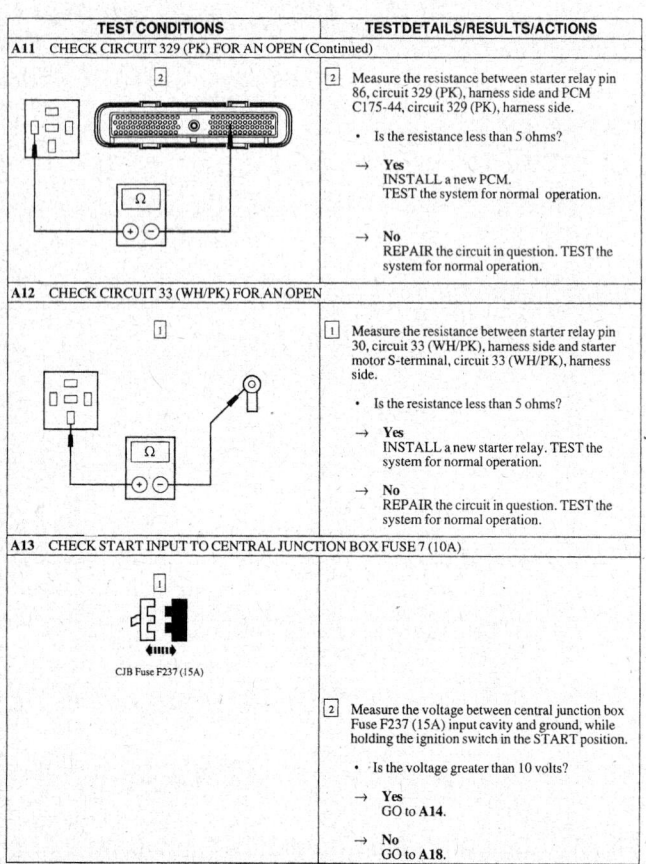

	2 Measure the resistance between starter relay pin 86, circuit 329 (PK), harness side and PCM C175-44, circuit 329 (PK), harness side.
	• Is the resistance less than 5 ohms?
	→ **Yes** INSTALL a new PCM. TEST the system for normal operation.
	→ **No** REPAIR the circuit in question. TEST the system for normal operation.

TEST CONDITIONS	TESTDETAILS/RESULTS/ACTIONS
A12 CHECK CIRCUIT 33 (WH/PK) FOR AN OPEN	
	1 Measure the resistance between starter relay pin 30, circuit 33 (WH/PK), harness side and starter motor S-terminal, circuit 33 (WH/PK), harness side.
	• Is the resistance less than 5 ohms?
	→ **Yes** INSTALL a new starter relay. TEST the system for normal operation.
	→ **No** REPAIR the circuit in question. TEST the system for normal operation.
A13 CHECK START INPUT TO CENTRAL JUNCTION BOX FUSE 7 (10A)	
	2 Measure the voltage between central junction box Fuse F237 (15A) input cavity and ground, while holding the ignition switch in the START position.
	• Is the voltage greater than 10 volts?
	→ **Yes** GO to **A14**.
	→ **No** GO to **A18**.

FM1120100673050X

Fig. 30 Test A: Engine Does Not Crank (Part 5 of 8). Five Hundred, Freestyle, Montego, Sable & Taurus

TEST CONDITIONS	TESTDETAILS/RESULTS/ACTIONS
A16 CHECK CIRCUIT 1093 (TN/RD) FOR AN OPEN	

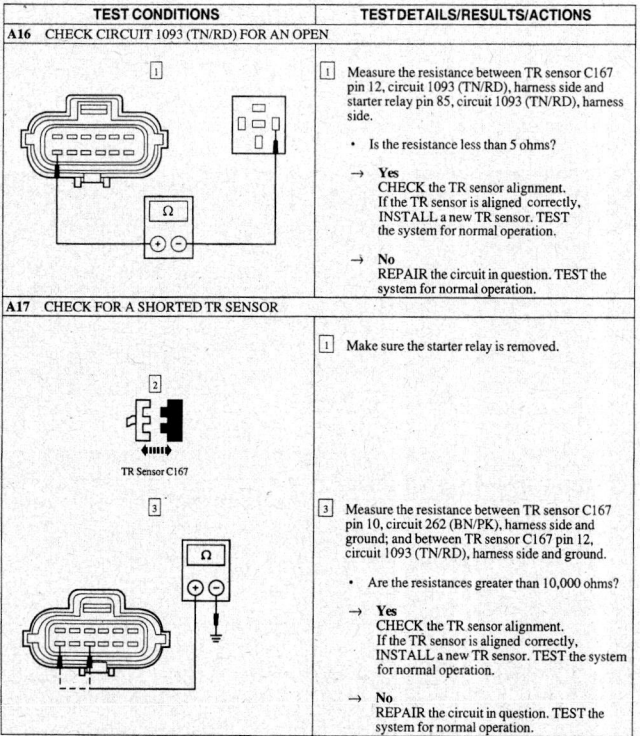

	1 Measure the resistance between TR sensor C167 pin 12, circuit 1093 (TN/RD), harness side and starter relay pin 85, circuit 1093 (TN/RD), harness side.
	• Is the resistance less than 5 ohms?
	→ **Yes** CHECK the TR sensor alignment. If the TR sensor is aligned correctly, INSTALL a new TR sensor. TEST the system for normal operation.
	→ **No** REPAIR the circuit in question. TEST the system for normal operation.
A17 CHECK FOR A SHORTED TR SENSOR	
	1 Make sure the starter relay is removed.
	3 Measure the resistance between TR sensor C167 pin 10, circuit 262 (BN/PK), harness side and ground; and between TR sensor C167 pin 12, circuit 1093 (TN/RD), harness side and ground.
	• Are the resistances greater than 10,000 ohms?
	→ **Yes** CHECK the TR sensor alignment. If the TR sensor is aligned correctly, INSTALL a new TR sensor. TEST the system for normal operation.
	→ **No** REPAIR the circuit in question. TEST the system for normal operation.

FM1120100673070X

Fig. 30 Test A: Engine Does Not Crank (Part 7 of 8). Five Hundred, Freestyle, Montego, Sable & Taurus

TEST CONDITIONS	TESTDETAILS/RESULTS/ACTIONS
A14 CHECK FOR A SYSTEM SHORT TO GROUND	

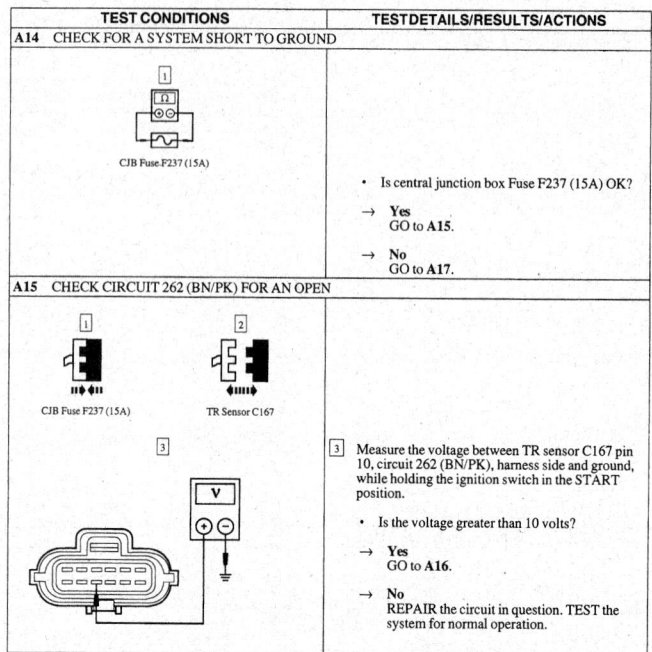

	• Is central junction box Fuse F237 (15A) OK?
	→ **Yes** GO to **A15**.
	→ **No** GO to **A17**.
A15 CHECK CIRCUIT 262 (BN/PK) FOR AN OPEN	
	3 Measure the voltage between TR sensor C167 pin 10, circuit 262 (BN/PK), harness side and ground, while holding the ignition switch in the START position.
	• Is the voltage greater than 10 volts?
	→ **Yes** GO to **A16**.
	→ **No** REPAIR the circuit in question. TEST the system for normal operation.

FM1120100673060X

Fig. 30 Test A: Engine Does Not Crank (Part 6 of 8). Five Hundred, Freestyle, Montego, Sable & Taurus

TEST CONDITIONS	TESTDETAILS/RESULTS/ACTIONS
A18 CHECK THE POWER SUPPLY TO THE IGNITION SWITCH	

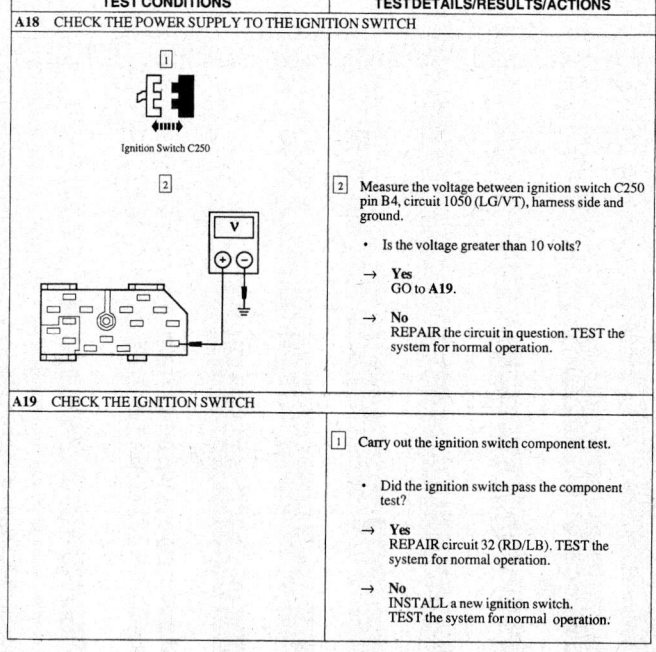

	2 Measure the voltage between ignition switch C250 pin B4, circuit 1050 (LG/VT), harness side and ground.
	• Is the voltage greater than 10 volts?
	→ **Yes** GO to **A19**.
	→ **No** REPAIR the circuit in question. TEST the system for normal operation.
A19 CHECK THE IGNITION SWITCH	
	1 Carry out the ignition switch component test.
	• Did the ignition switch pass the component test?
	→ **Yes** REPAIR circuit 32 (RD/LB). TEST the system for normal operation.
	→ **No** INSTALL a new ignition switch. TEST the system for normal operation.

FM1120100673080X

Fig. 30 Test A: Engine Does Not Crank (Part 8 of 8). Five Hundred, Freestyle, Montego, Sable & Taurus

TEST CONDITIONS	TESTDETAILS/RESULTS/ACTIONS
B1 CHECK STARTER MOUNTING	
	[1] Inspect the starter mounting bolts and brackets for looseness. • Is the starter motor mounted correctly? → **Yes** GO to **B2**. → **No** INSTALL the starter motor correctly. TEST the system for normal operation.
B2 CHECK FOR ENGINE NOISE	
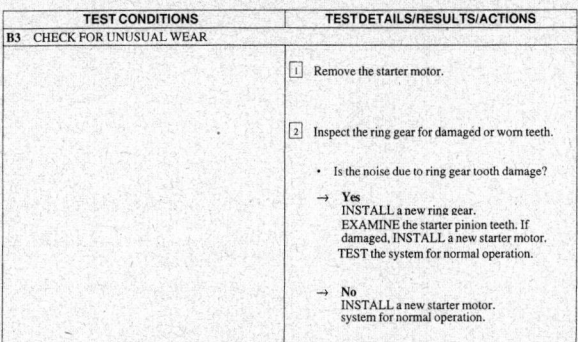	[2] Connect a remote starter switch between the starter solenoid B and S terminals. [3] Engage the starter motor and verify the noise is due to the starter operation. • Is the noise due to the starter motor engagement? → **Yes** GO to **B3**. → **No** Diagnose engine mechanical components

FM1120100674010X

Fig. 31   Test B: Unusual Starter Noise (Part 1 of 2). Five Hundred, Freestyle, Montego, Sable & Taurus

TEST CONDITIONS	TESTDETAILS/RESULTS/ACTIONS
A1 CHECK THE BATTERY	
	[1] Check the battery condition and charge. • Is the battery OK? → **Yes** GO to **A2**. → **No** CHARGE or REPLACE the battery as required. TEST the system for normal operation.
A2 CHECK THE BATTERY GROUND CABLE	
	[1] Measure the voltage between the positive battery post and the battery ground cable connection at the cylinder block (6010). • Is the voltage reading greater than 10 volts? → **Yes** GO to **A3**. → **No** REPLACE the battery ground cable (14301). TEST the system for normal operation.

FM1120100683010X

Fig. 32   Test A: Engine Does Not Crank (Part 1 of 12). Town Car

TEST CONDITIONS	TESTDETAILS/RESULTS/ACTIONS
B3 CHECK FOR UNUSUAL WEAR	
	[1] Remove the starter motor. [2] Inspect the ring gear for damaged or worn teeth. • Is the noise due to ring gear tooth damage? → **Yes** INSTALL a new ring gear. EXAMINE the starter pinion teeth. If damaged, INSTALL a new starter motor. TEST the system for normal operation. → **No** INSTALL a new starter motor. system for normal operation.

FM1120100674020X

Fig. 31   Test B: Unusual Starter Noise (Part 2 of 2). Five Hundred, Freestyle, Montego, Sable & Taurus

TEST CONDITIONS	TESTDETAILS/RESULTS/ACTIONS
A3 CHECK THE STARTER MOTOR GROUND	
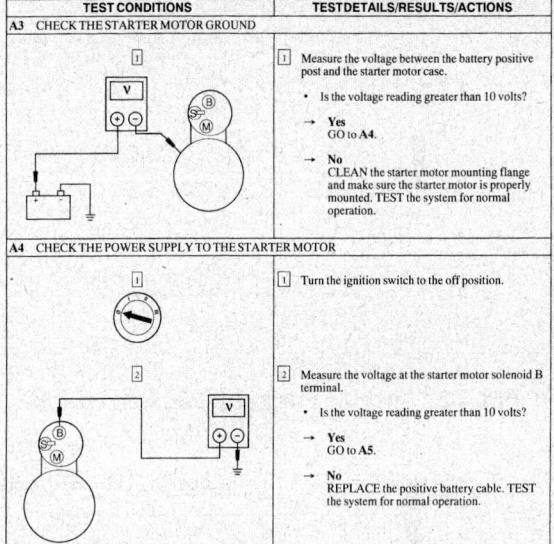	[1] Measure the voltage between the battery positive post and the starter motor case. • Is the voltage reading greater than 10 volts? → **Yes** GO to **A4**. → **No** CLEAN the starter motor mounting flange and make sure the starter motor is properly mounted. TEST the system for normal operation.
A4 CHECK THE POWER SUPPLY TO THE STARTER MOTOR	
	[1] Turn the ignition switch to the off position. [2] Measure the voltage at the starter motor solenoid B terminal. • Is the voltage reading greater than 10 volts? → **Yes** GO to **A5**. → **No** REPLACE the positive battery cable. TEST the system for normal operation.

FM1120100683020X

Fig. 32   Test A: Engine Does Not Crank (Part 2 of 12). Town Car

TEST CONDITIONS	TESTDETAILS/RESULTS/ACTIONS
A5 CHECK THE STARTER MOTOR	
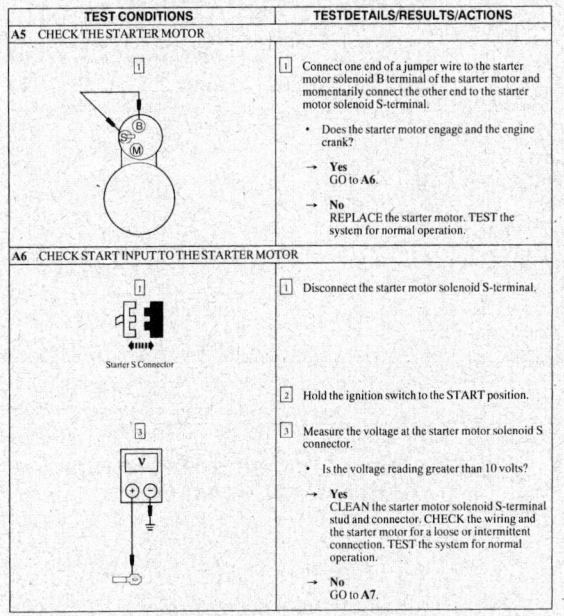	[1] Connect one end of a jumper wire to the starter motor solenoid B terminal of the starter motor and momentarily connect the other end to the starter motor solenoid S-terminal. • Does the starter motor engage and the engine crank? → **Yes** GO to **A6**. → **No** REPLACE the starter motor. TEST the system for normal operation.
A6 CHECK START INPUT TO THE STARTER MOTOR	
	[1] Disconnect the starter motor solenoid S-terminal. [2] Hold the ignition switch to the START position. [3] Measure the voltage at the starter motor solenoid S connector. • Is the voltage reading greater than 10 volts? → **Yes** CLEAN the starter motor solenoid S-terminal stud and connector. CHECK the wiring and the starter motor for a loose or intermittent connection. TEST the system for normal operation. → **No** GO to **A7**.

FM1120100683030X

Fig. 32   Test A: Engine Does Not Crank (Part 3 of 12). Town Car

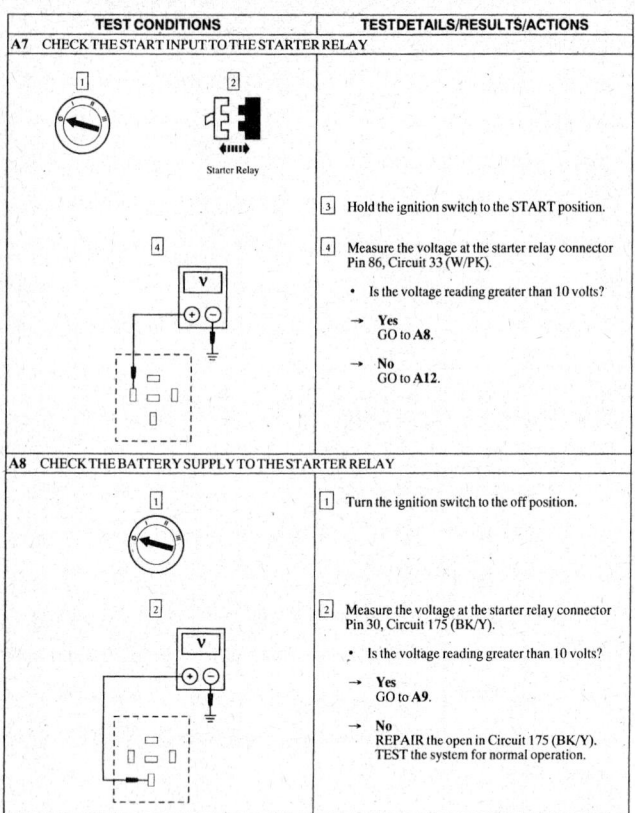

Fig. 32   Test A: Engine Does Not Crank (Part 4 of 12). Town Car

TEST CONDITIONS	TESTDETAILS/RESULTS/ACTIONS
A7 CHECK THE START INPUT TO THE STARTER RELAY	
	3 Hold the ignition switch to the START position.
	4 Measure the voltage at the starter relay connector Pin 86, Circuit 33 (W/PK).
	• Is the voltage reading greater than 10 volts?
	→ **Yes** GO to **A8**.
	→ **No** GO to **A12**.
A8 CHECK THE BATTERY SUPPLY TO THE STARTER RELAY	
	1 Turn the ignition switch to the off position.
	2 Measure the voltage at the starter relay connector Pin 30, Circuit 175 (BK/Y).
	• Is the voltage reading greater than 10 volts?
	→ **Yes** GO to **A9**.
	→ **No** REPAIR the open in Circuit 175 (BK/Y). TEST the system for normal operation.

FM1120100683040X

TEST CONDITIONS	TESTDETAILS/RESULTS/ACTIONS
A11 CHECK CIRCUIT 113 (Y/LB) FOR AN OPEN	
	1 Measure the resistance of Circuit 113 (Y/LB) between the starter relay connector Pin 87 and the starter motor solenoid S Connector.
	• Is the resistance reading less than 5 ohms?
	→ **Yes** REPLACE the starter relay. TEST the system for normal operation.
	→ **No** REPAIR Circuit 113 (Y/LB) for an open. TEST the system for normal operation.
A12 CHECK FUSE 26 (5A)	
	• Measure the resistance of fuse 26 (5A). Is the resistance of Fuse 26 (5A) zero?
	→ **Yes** GO to **A13**.
	→ **No** GO to **A19**.
A13 CHECK THE INPUT TO FUSE 26 (5A)	
	1 Hold the ignition switch to the START position.

FM1120100683060X

Fig. 32   Test A: Engine Does Not Crank (Part 6 of 12). Town Car

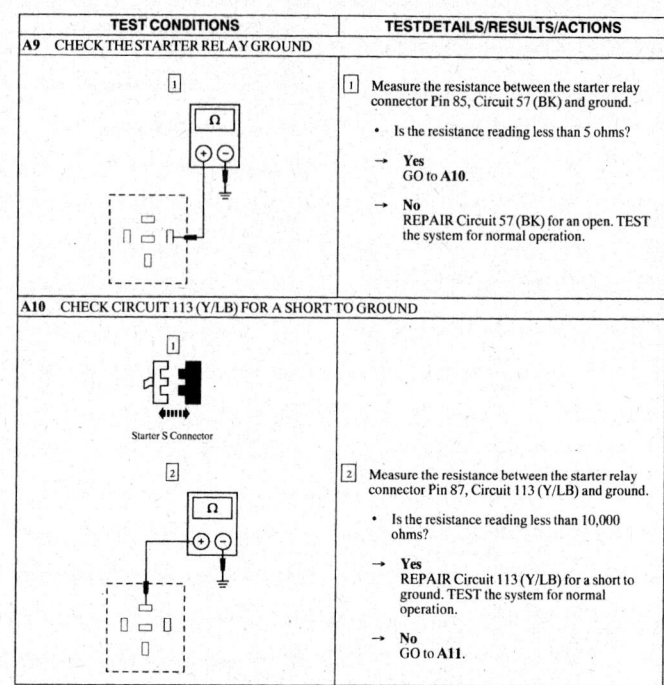

TEST CONDITIONS	TESTDETAILS/RESULTS/ACTIONS
A9 CHECK THE STARTER RELAY GROUND	
	1 Measure the resistance between the starter relay connector Pin 85, Circuit 57 (BK) and ground.
	• Is the resistance reading less than 5 ohms?
	→ **Yes** GO to **A10**.
	→ **No** REPAIR Circuit 57 (BK) for an open. TEST the system for normal operation.
A10 CHECK CIRCUIT 113 (Y/LB) FOR A SHORT TO GROUND	
	2 Measure the resistance between the starter relay connector Pin 87, Circuit 113 (Y/LB) and ground.
	• Is the resistance reading less than 10,000 ohms?
	→ **Yes** REPAIR Circuit 113 (Y/LB) for a short to ground. TEST the system for normal operation.
	→ **No** GO to **A11**.

FM1120100683050X

Fig. 32   Test A: Engine Does Not Crank (Part 5 of 12). Town Car

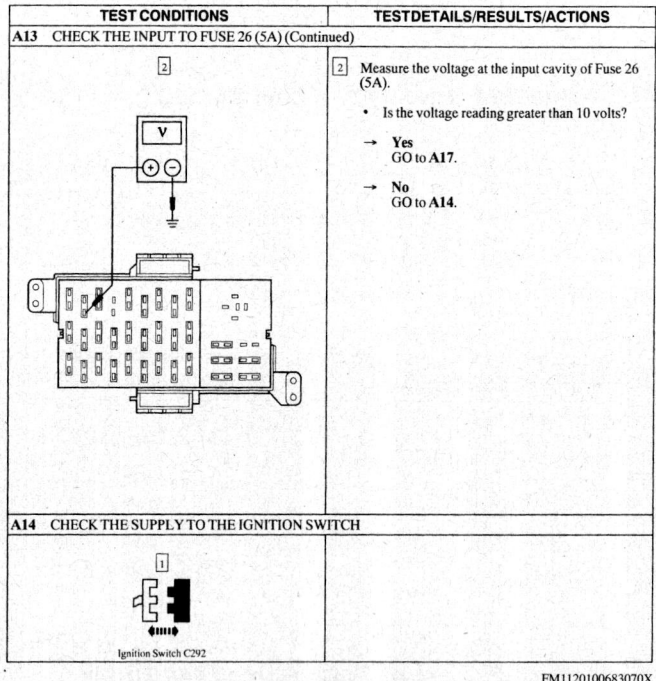

TEST CONDITIONS	TESTDETAILS/RESULTS/ACTIONS
A13 CHECK THE INPUT TO FUSE 26 (5A) (Continued)	
	2 Measure the voltage at the input cavity of Fuse 26 (5A).
	• Is the voltage reading greater than 10 volts?
	→ **Yes** GO to **A17**.
	→ **No** GO to **A14**.
A14 CHECK THE SUPPLY TO THE IGNITION SWITCH	

FM1120100683070X

Fig. 32   Test A: Engine Does Not Crank (Part 7 of 12). Town Car

TEST CONDITIONS	TESTDETAILS/RESULTS/ACTIONS
A14 CHECK THE SUPPLY TO THE IGNITION SWITCH (Continued)	
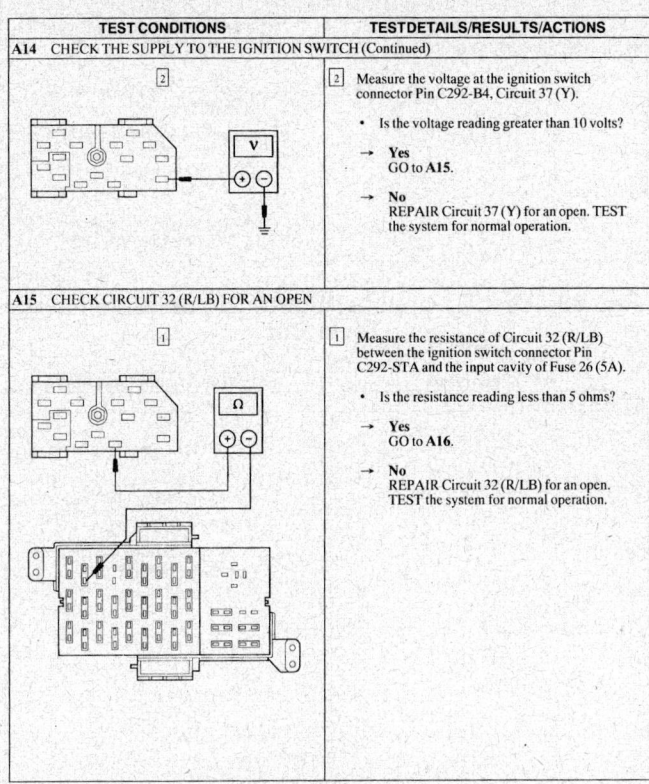	☐2 Measure the voltage at the ignition switch connector Pin C292-B4, Circuit 37 (Y). • Is the voltage reading greater than 10 volts? → **Yes** GO to **A15**. → **No** REPAIR Circuit 37 (Y) for an open. TEST the system for normal operation.
A15 CHECK CIRCUIT 32 (R/LB) FOR AN OPEN	
	☐1 Measure the resistance of Circuit 32 (R/LB) between the ignition switch connector Pin C292-STA and the input cavity of Fuse 26 (5A). • Is the resistance reading less than 5 ohms? → **Yes** GO to **A16**. → **No** REPAIR Circuit 32 (R/LB) for an open. TEST the system for normal operation.

FM1120100683080X

**Fig. 32 Test A: Engine Does Not Crank
(Part 8 of 12). Town Car**

TEST CONDITIONS	TESTDETAILS/RESULTS/ACTIONS
A17 CHECK CIRCUIT 262 (BR/PK) FOR AN OPEN (Continued)	
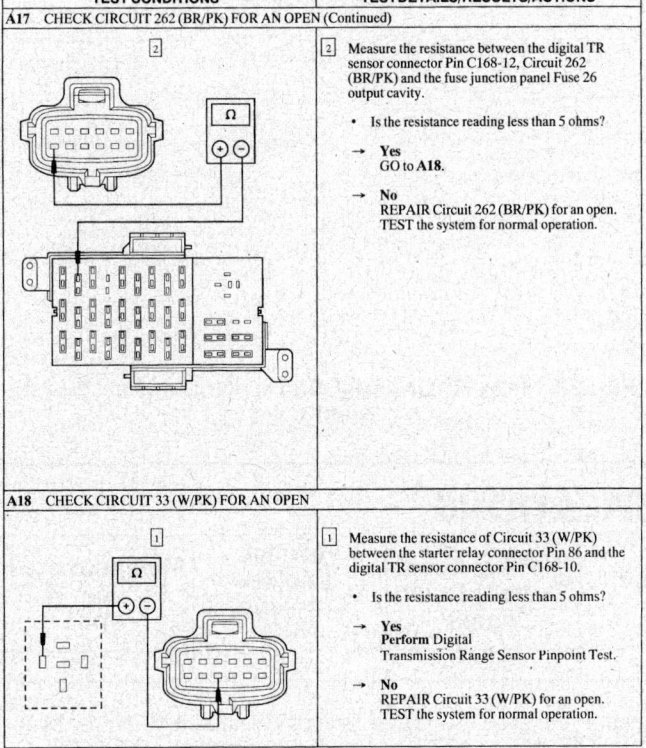	☐2 Measure the resistance between the digital TR sensor connector Pin C168-12, Circuit 262 (BR/PK) and the fuse junction panel Fuse 26 output cavity. • Is the resistance reading less than 5 ohms? → **Yes** GO to **A18**. → **No** REPAIR Circuit 262 (BR/PK) for an open. TEST the system for normal operation.
A18 CHECK CIRCUIT 33 (W/PK) FOR AN OPEN	
	☐1 Measure the resistance of Circuit 33 (W/PK) between the starter relay connector Pin 86 and the digital TR sensor connector Pin C168-10. • Is the resistance reading less than 5 ohms? → **Yes** **Perform** Digital Transmission Range Sensor Pinpoint Test. → **No** REPAIR Circuit 33 (W/PK) for an open. TEST the system for normal operation.

FM1120100683100X

**Fig. 32 Test A: Engine Does Not Crank
(Part 10 of 12). Town Car**

TEST CONDITIONS	TESTDETAILS/RESULTS/ACTIONS
A16 CHECK CIRCUIT 32 (R/LB) FOR A SHORT TO GROUND	
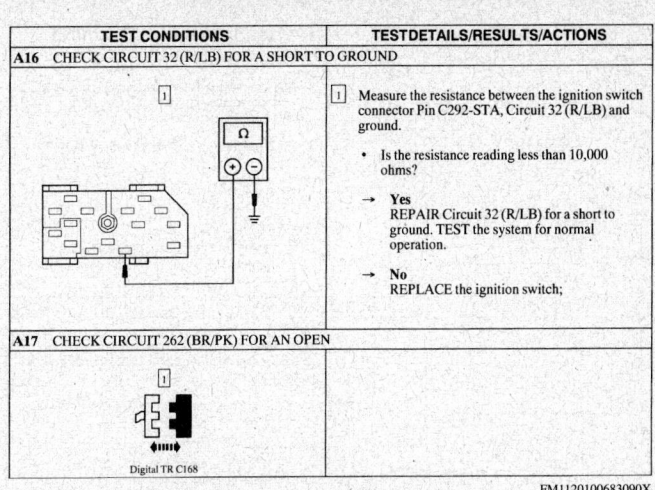	☐1 Measure the resistance between the ignition switch connector Pin C292-STA, Circuit 32 (R/LB) and ground. • Is the resistance reading less than 10,000 ohms? → **Yes** REPAIR Circuit 32 (R/LB) for a short to ground. TEST the system for normal operation. → **No** REPLACE the ignition switch;
A17 CHECK CIRCUIT 262 (BR/PK) FOR AN OPEN	
Digital TR C168	

FM1120100683090X

**Fig. 32 Test A: Engine Does Not Crank
(Part 9 of 12). Town Car**

TEST CONDITIONS	TESTDETAILS/RESULTS/ACTIONS
A19 CHECK FOR A SHORTED SYSTEM	
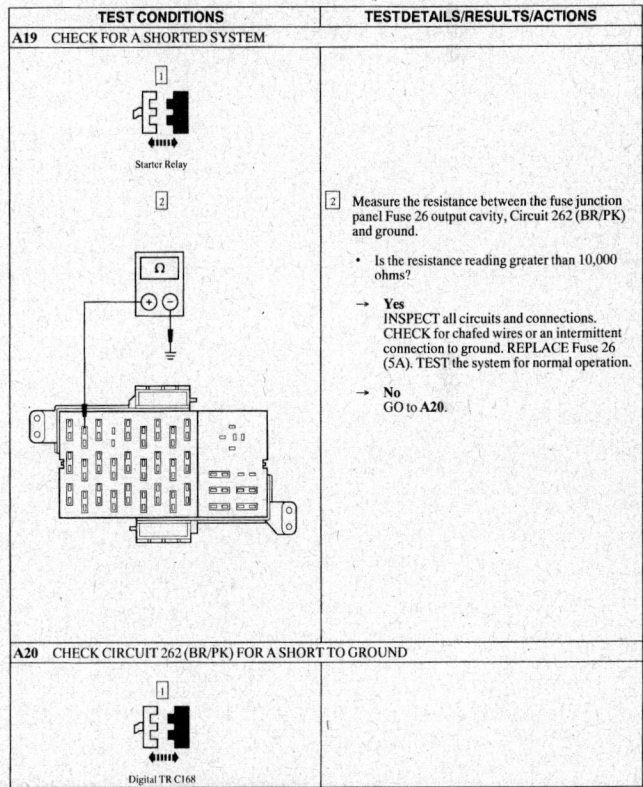 Starter Relay	☐2 Measure the resistance between the fuse junction panel Fuse 26 output cavity, Circuit 262 (BR/PK) and ground. • Is the resistance reading greater than 10,000 ohms? → **Yes** INSPECT all circuits and connections. CHECK for chafed wires or an intermittent connection to ground. REPLACE Fuse 26 (5A). TEST the system for normal operation. → **No** GO to **A20**.
A20 CHECK CIRCUIT 262 (BR/PK) FOR A SHORT TO GROUND	
Digital TR C168	

FM1120100683110X

**Fig. 32 Test A: Engine Does Not Crank
(Part 11 of 12). Town Car**

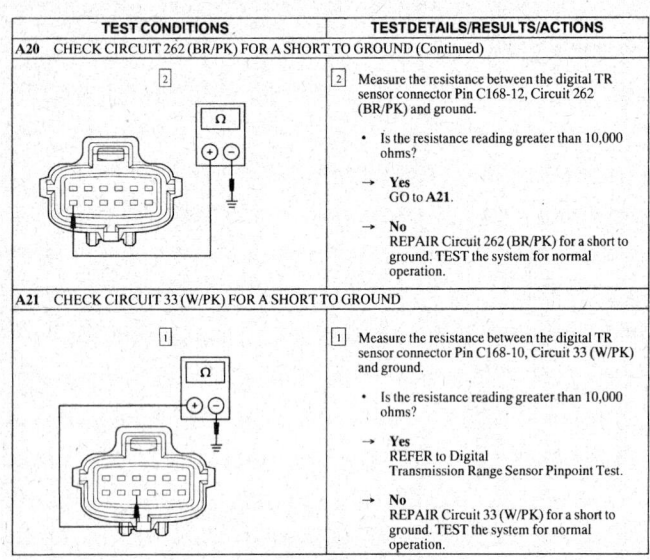

TEST CONDITIONS	TESTDETAILS/RESULTS/ACTIONS
A20 CHECK CIRCUIT 262 (BR/PK) FOR A SHORT TO GROUND (Continued)	
	2 Measure the resistance between the digital TR sensor connector Pin C168-12, Circuit 262 (BR/PK) and ground. • Is the resistance reading greater than 10,000 ohms? → **Yes** GO to **A21**. → **No** REPAIR Circuit 262 (BR/PK) for a short to ground. TEST the system for normal operation.
A21 CHECK CIRCUIT 33 (W/PK) FOR A SHORT TO GROUND	
	1 Measure the resistance between the digital TR sensor connector Pin C168-10, Circuit 33 (W/PK) and ground. • Is the resistance reading greater than 10,000 ohms? → **Yes** REFER to Digital Transmission Range Sensor Pinpoint Test. → **No** REPAIR Circuit 33 (W/PK) for a short to ground. TEST the system for normal operation.

FM1120100683120X

Fig. 32   Test A: Engine Does Not Crank (Part 12 of 12). Town Car

TEST CONDITIONS	TESTDETAILS/RESULTS/ACTIONS
B1 CHECK THE STARTER MOUNTING	
	1 Inspect the starter motor mounting bolts and brackets for looseness. • Is the starter motor mounted properly? → **Yes** GO to **B2**. → **No** INSTALL the starter motor properly; TEST the system for normal operation.

FM1120100684010X

Fig. 33   Test B: Unusual Starter Noise (Part 1 of 2). Town Car

TEST CONDITIONS	TESTDETAILS/RESULTS/ACTIONS
B2 CHECK FOR ENGINE NOISE	
	2 Connect a remote starter switch between the starter motor solenoid B and S terminals.
	3 Engage the starter motor and verify the noise is due to the starter operation. • Is the noise due to the starter motor engagement? → **Yes** GO to **B3**. → **No** **Diagnose engine mechanical components**
B3 CHECK FOR UNUSUAL WEAR	
	1 Remove the starter motor;
	2 Inspect the ring gear for damaged or worn teeth. • Is the noise due to flywheel ring gear (6384) tooth damage? → **Yes** REPLACE the flywheel ring gear. EXAMINE the starter pinion teeth. If damaged, REPLACE the starter motor. TEST the system for normal operation. → **No** REPLACE the starter motor. TEST the system for normal operation.

FM1120100684020X

Fig. 33   Test B: Unusual Starter Noise (Part 2 of 2). Town Car

STARTER SPECIFICATIONS

Starter Frame Dia., Inch	Brush Spring Tension, Ounces	No Load, Amps	Max Load, Amps	Normal Load Current Draw, Amps	Normal Engine Cranking, RPM	Minimum Stall, Ft. Lbs. @ 5 Volts
3.0	64	60–80	③	130–190	①	②

① — Escort, Five Hundred, Freestyle, Montego & ZX2, 200–250 RPM; Mustang, 100–140 RPM; Except

Escort, Five Hundred, Freestyle, Montego, Mustang & ZX2, 140–220 RPM.

② — Escort & ZX2, 10.0 ft. lbs.; except Escort & ZX2, 14.7 ft. lbs.

③ — Except Mustang, 800 amps; Mustang, 400 amps.

ALTERNATORS
Ford Motorcraft Alternator

NOTE: On Air Bag Equipped Models, Refer To "Air Bag System Precautions" Located In The Front Of This Manual For System Disarming & Arming Procedures.

NOTE: Refer To "Computer Relearn Procedures" Located In The Front Of This Manual When Battery Power To The Computer Has Been Interrupted.

NOTE: "Electrical Symbol & Wire Color Code Identification" Located In The Front Of This Manual May Be Used As An Aid When Using Wiring Circuits Found In This Section.

INDEX

PRECAUTIONS

Air Bag Systems

Refer to "Air Bag System Precautions" in the front of this manual for system disarming and arming procedures.

Battery Ground Cable

Prior to service, disconnect battery ground cable and isolate as required.

General

1. Ensure proper battery polarity when servicing units. Reversed polarity will damage rectifiers and regulators.
2. If booster battery is used for starting, ensure proper polarity.
3. When fast charger is used to charge battery, vehicle battery cables should be disconnected unless fast charger is equipped with special alternator protector, in which case vehicle battery cables need not be disconnected. A fast charger should never be used to start vehicle as damage to rectifiers will result.
4. Unless system includes load relay or field relay, grounding alternator output terminal will damage alternator and/or circuits. This is true even when system is not in operation since circuit breaker is not used and battery voltage is applied to alternator output terminal at all times. Field or load relay acts as circuit breaker in that it is controlled by ignition switch.
5. Before starting any on vehicle tests of alternator or regulator, battery should be inspected and circuit inspected for faulty wiring or insulation, loose or corroded connections and poor ground circuits.
6. Ensure alternator belt tension is tight enough to prevent slipping under load.
7. To prevent damage to system, ignition should be in Off position and battery ground cable disconnected before making any test connections.
8. Vehicle battery must be fully charged or fully charged battery may be installed for test purposes.

DESCRIPTION

The electrical charging system is a negative ground system consisting of an Integral Alternator/Voltage Regulator (IGR), charge indicator, storage battery and required wiring and cables.

The I circuit, or ignition circuit is used to turn on the alternator regulator. This circuit is powered up with the ignition in the Run position. The circuit also turns the indicator lamp on if there is a fault in the charging system.

The A circuit, or the battery sense circuit, is used to sense battery voltage. This circuit also supplies power to the alternator stator and coil. With the system functioning normally, alternator output current is determined by voltage at the A circuit (battery sense voltage). The A circuit voltage is compared to a set voltage inside the regulator to maintain the proper alternator output. The set voltage will vary with temperature and is typically higher in the winter than in the summer, allowing for better battery recharge in the winter and reducing the chance of overcharging the battery in the summer.

The S circuit, or stator and coil circuit, is used to feed back a voltage signal from the alternator to the regulator. This voltage is typically ½ battery voltage and is used by the regulator to turn off the indicator.

If an ammeter is used in the charging

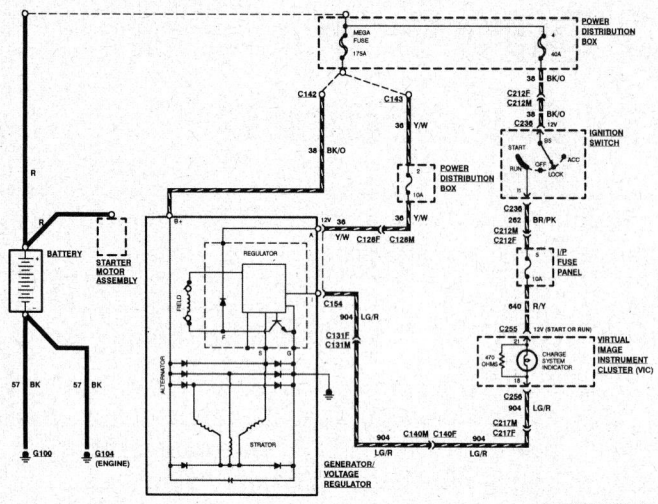

Fig. 1   Wiring diagram. 2001 Continental

Fig. 2   Wiring diagram. 2002 Continental

system, the regulator 1 terminal and the alternator stator terminal are not used. When the ignition is turned On, the field relay closes and electrical current passes through the regulator A terminal and is metered to the alternator field. When the engine is started, the alternator field rotates causing the alternator to operate.

Closing the ignition switch energizes the warning lamp or ammeter and turns on the regulator output stage. The alternator receives maximum field current and is ready to generate an output voltage. As the alternator rotor speed increases, the output and stator terminal voltages increase from zero to the system regulation level determined by the regulator setting. When the ignition is turned Off, the solid state relay circuit turns the output stage off, interrupting the current flow through the regulator so there is no current drain on the battery.

DIAGNOSIS & TESTING

Wiring Diagrams

Refer to **Fig. 1 through 24,** for charging system wiring diagram.

No-Load Test

CONTINENTAL, FIVE HUNDRED, FREESTYLE, MONTEGO, SABLE, TAURUS & TOWN CAR

1. Switch Rotunda alternator tester tool No. 010-00725, or equivalent, to voltmeter function.
2. Connect voltmeter positive lead to alternator B+ terminal and negative lead to ground.
3. Turn all electrical accessories off.
4. With engine running at 2000 RPM, measure alternator output voltage.
5. Measurement should be 13–15 volts.
6. If voltage is not as specified, refer to "Symptom Related Tests."

COUGAR, CROWN VICTORIA, ESCORT, FOCUS, GRAND MARQUIS, LS, MARAUDER, MUSTANG, THUNDERBIRD & ZX2

1. Connect voltmeter leads across battery terminals.
2. Measure base voltage.
3. Start and run engine at 1500 RPM with no electrical load.
4. Voltage should be 14.1–15.1 volts.
5. If voltage increase is less than 2.5 volts over base voltage, refer to "Load Test."
6. If there is no voltage increase or voltage increase is more than 2.5 volts, refer to "Symptom Related Tests."

Load Test

COUGAR, CROWN VICTORIA, ESCORT, FOCUS, FIVE HUNDRED, FREESTYLE, GRAND MARQUIS, LS, MARAUDER, MONTEGO, MUSTANG, SABLE, TAURUS, THUNDERBIRD & ZX2

1. Connect leads of voltmeter across battery terminals.
2. Measure base voltage.
3. With engine running, turn on air conditioner, set blower motor to high speed and headlamps to high beam position.
4. Increase engine speed to approximately 2000 RPM.
5. Voltage should increase at least .5 volts above base voltage.
6. If voltage does not increase, refer to "Symptom Related Tests."
7. If voltage increases as specified, charging system is operating properly.

CONTINENTAL & TOWN CAR

1. Turn off lamps and electrical components.

2. Apply parking brake and place transmission in Neutral position.
3. Switch Rotunda alternator tester tool No. 010-00725, or equivalent, to ammeter function.
4. Connect positive and negative leads to battery.
5. Connect current probe to alternator B+ output lead.
6. With engine running at 2000 RPM, adjust tester load bank to determine output of alternator.
7. Alternator output should be more than 87 amps at 2000 RPM.
8. If alternator output is not as specified, refer to "Symptom Related Tests."

Drain Test

A periodic pulsing of up to .080 amp is caused by the Integrated Control Panel (ICP) and is considered normal. However, no production vehicle should have a continuous draw of more than .050 amp.

Inspect for current drains on battery in excess of 50 milliamperes with all the electrical accessories off and the vehicle at rest. **Do not perform these tests on a recently recharged lead-acid battery. Explosive gases can cause personal injury.**

CLAMP ON DC AMMETER TEST

1. Connect 12-volt test lamp in series with battery positive terminal. If test lamp glows, drain exists.
2. Use clamp-type current probe to battery positive or ground terminal. Ensure probe is properly calibrated to prevent false readings.
3. Connect inline ammeter between battery positive or ground post, and its respective cable.
4. Turn ignition switch to Off position.
5. Ensure electrical loads are off.
6. Ensure engine compartment lamp operates properly, then disconnect lamp.
7. Clamp meter clip securely around positive or battery ground. **Do not start vehicle with clip on cable.**
8. Measure current. Reading should be less than .05 amp.

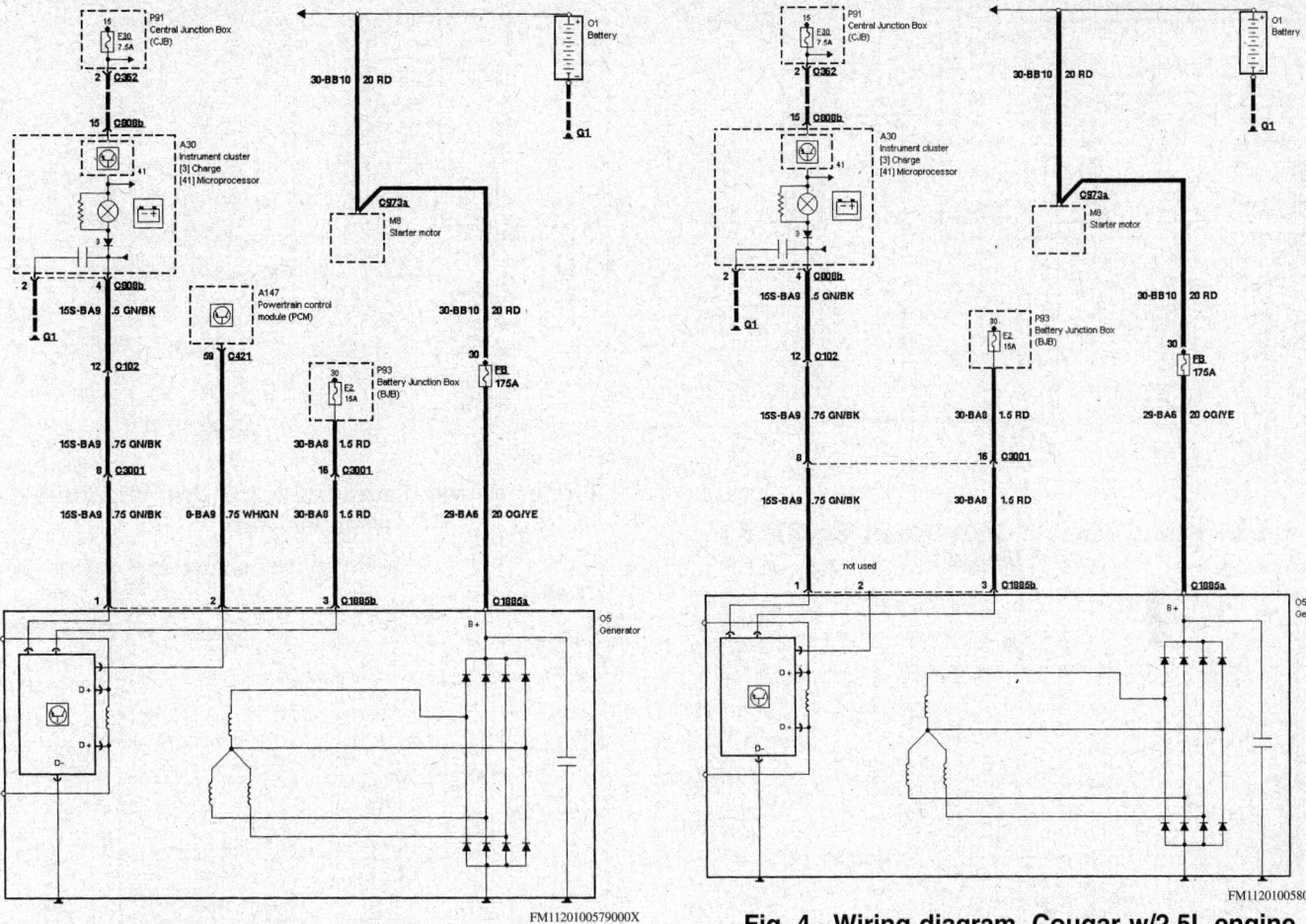

Fig. 3   Wiring diagram. Cougar w/2.0L engine

Fig. 4   Wiring diagram. Cougar w/2.5L engine

9. If current reading is more .05 amps, there is constant drain.
10. Possible sources of current drain are vehicle lamps such as engine compartment, glove compartment or luggage compartment .
11. If drain is not caused by vehicle lamps, remove fuses one at a time until cause of drain is located.
12. If drain is still undetermined, disconnect leads at starter relay one at a time to find offending circuit.

INLINE MULTIMETER TEST

This test will require a digital volt amp ohmmeter with an appropriate ampere scale.
1. Drive vehicle at least five minutes at more than 30 mph to turn on and exercise vehicle systems.
2. Turn ignition switch to Off position.
3. Allow vehicle to sit with key off at least 40 minutes to allow modules to time out and power down.
4. Ensure electrical loads are turned off.
5. Connect suitable fused jumper wire between battery ground cable and negative battery post to prevent modules from resetting and to catch capacitive drains.
6. Disconnect battery ground cable without breaking jumper wire connection.
7. Ensure engine compartment lamp operates properly, then disconnect lamp.

8. Measure battery voltage. If measurement is less than 11.5 volts, charge battery to more than 11.5 volts.
9. Set ammeter to DC amperage scale **Do not crank engine with ammeter connected.**
10. Current reading should be less than .05 amp.
11. If reading is .2–.9 amp, drain may be present.
12. Possible sources of current drain are vehicle lamps such as engine compartment, glove compartment or luggage compartment.
13. If drain is not caused by vehicle lamps, remove fuses one at a time until cause is located.
14. If cause of drain is still undetermined, disconnect leads at starter relay one at a time to find offending circuit.

BATTERY CABLE DISCONNECTED TEST

1. Connect suitable 12-volt test lamp in series with battery positive terminal. If test lamp glows, drain exists.
2. Use clamp type current probe to battery positive or ground terminal. Ensure probe is properly calibrated to prevent false readings.
3. Connect inline ammeter between battery positive or ground post and its respective cable.
4. Without starting engine, turn ignition

switch to On position for a few seconds, then Off.
5. **On models equipped with illuminated entry lamps,** wait one minute for those lamps to turn off.
6. **On all models,** connect ammeter and read amperage,
7. Current reading should be less than .05 amp.
8. If reading is more than .05 amp after few minutes and drain did not show up in previous tests, drain is most likely caused by faulty electronic component.
9. Remove fuses and disconnect starter leads one at a time to locate offending circuit.

ELECTRONIC DRAINS WHICH SHUT OFF w/BATTERY CABLE DISCONNECTED TEST

1. Perform "Inline Multimeter Test."
2. Ensure doors are closed and accessories are turned off.
3. Turn ignition to Run position for a moment without starting engine, then turn ignition switch to Off position.
4. **On models equipped with illuminated entry lamps,** wait few minutes for those lamps to turn off.
5. **On all models,** connect ammeter and record amperage drain.
6. Current drain reading should not be

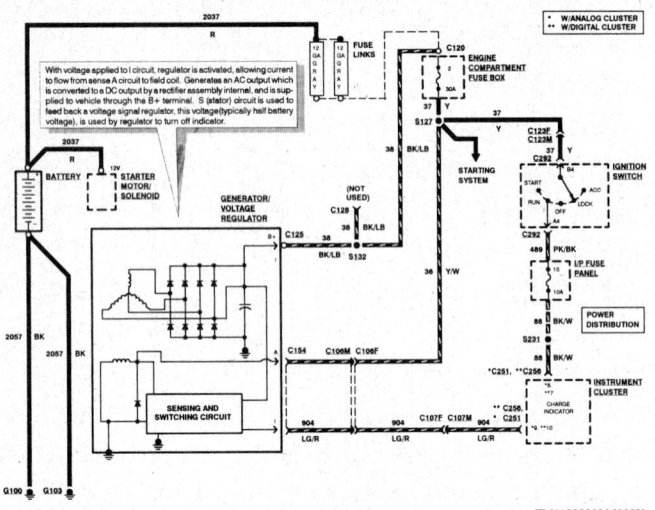

Fig. 5   Wiring diagram. 2001 Crown Victoria & Grand Marquis

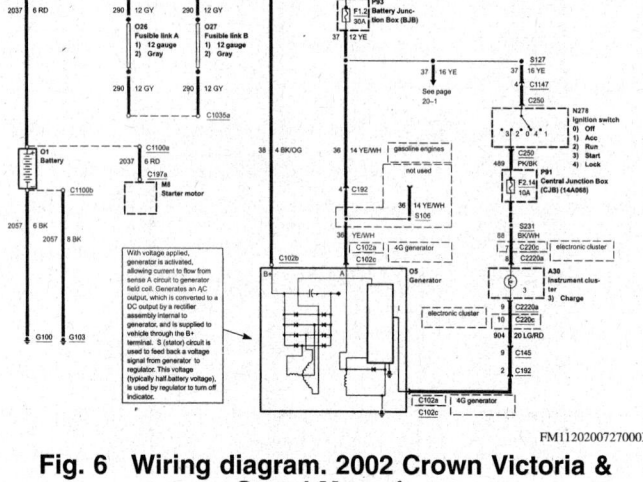

Fig. 6   Wiring diagram. 2002 Crown Victoria & Grand Marquis

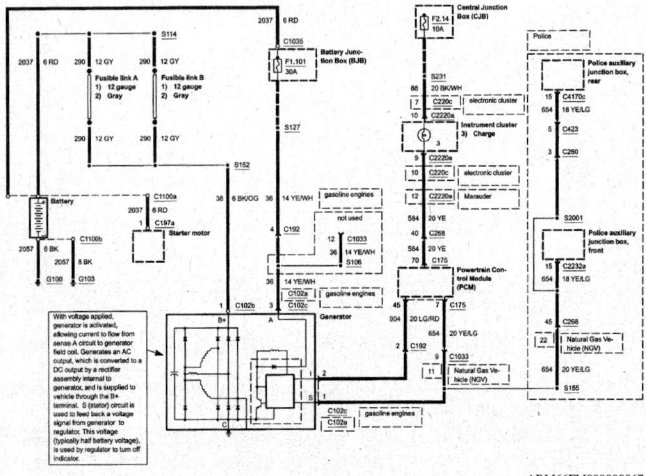

Fig. 7   Wiring diagram. Marauder, 2003–05 Crown Victoria & Grand Marquis

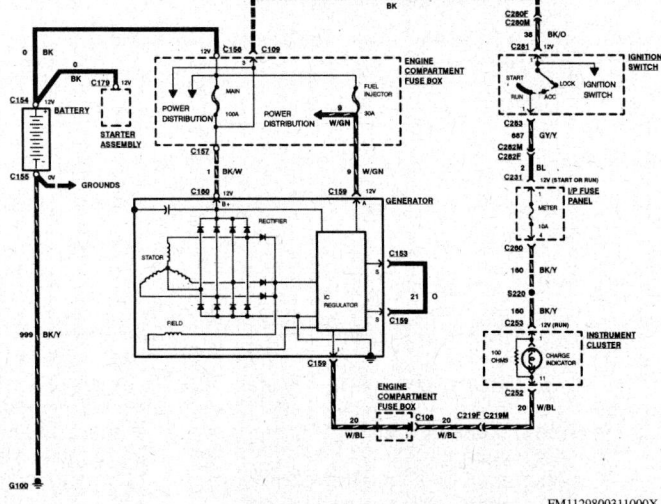

Fig. 8   Wiring diagram. Escort & ZX2

more than .05 amp.

7. If drain exceeds specifications after few minutes and if this drain did not appear in previous tests, it is most likely caused by an inoperative electronic component. Remove fuses from battery/central junction box one at a time to locate offending circuit.

Symptoms

Refer to **Figs. 25 through 38,** for symptoms.

Symptom Related Tests

CONTINENTAL

Refer to **Figs. 39 through 58,** for symptom related tests.

COUGAR

Refer to **Figs. 59 and 60,** for symptom related tests.

CROWN VICTORIA, GRAND MARQUIS & MARAUDER

Refer to **Figs. 61 through 84,** for symptom related tests.

ESCORT & ZX2

Refer to **Figs. 85 through 91,** for symptom related tests.

FIVE HUNDRED, FREESTYLE & MONTEGO

Refer to **Figs. 92 through 98,** for symptom related tests.

FOCUS

Refer to **Figs. 99 and 100,** for symptom related tests.

LS & THUNDERBIRD

Refer to **Figs. 101 through 108,** for symptom related tests.

MUSTANG

Refer to **Figs. 109 through 131,** for symptom related tests.

SABLE & TAURUS

Refer to **Figs. 132 through 147,** for symptom related tests.

TOWN CAR

Refer to **Figs. 148 through 175,** for symptom related tests.

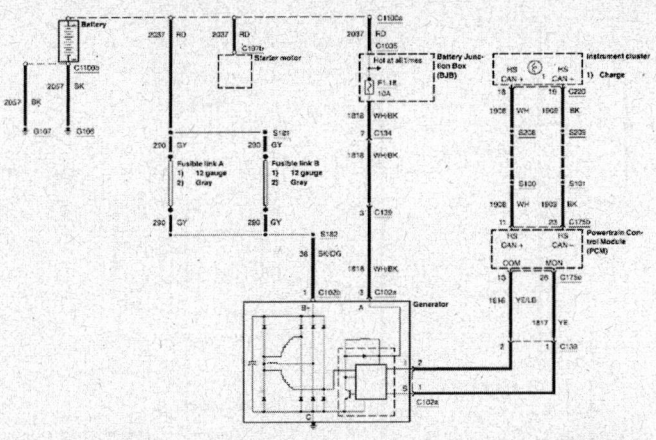

Fig. 9   Wiring diagram. Five Hundred, Freestyle & Montego

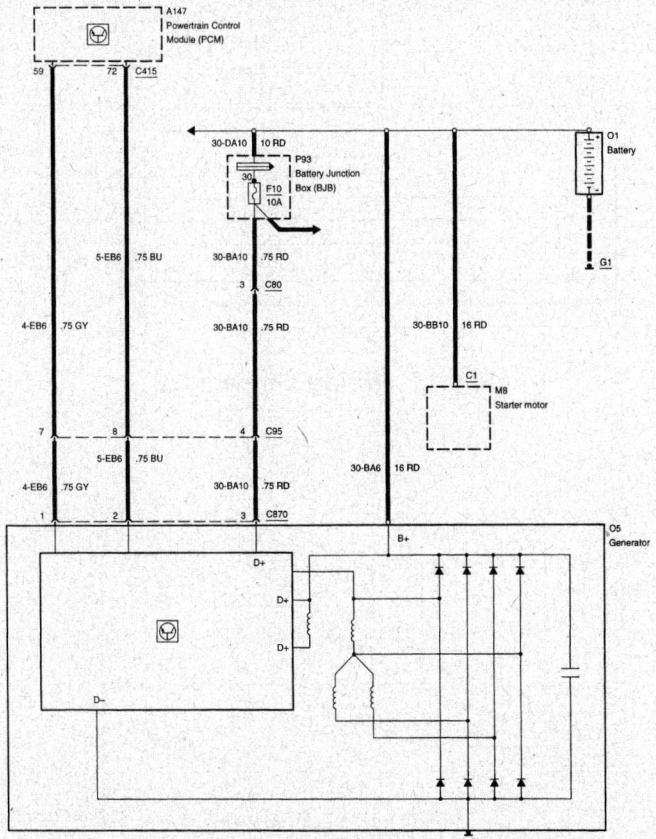

Fig. 11   Wiring diagram. 2001–02 Focus w/2.0L SOHC engine

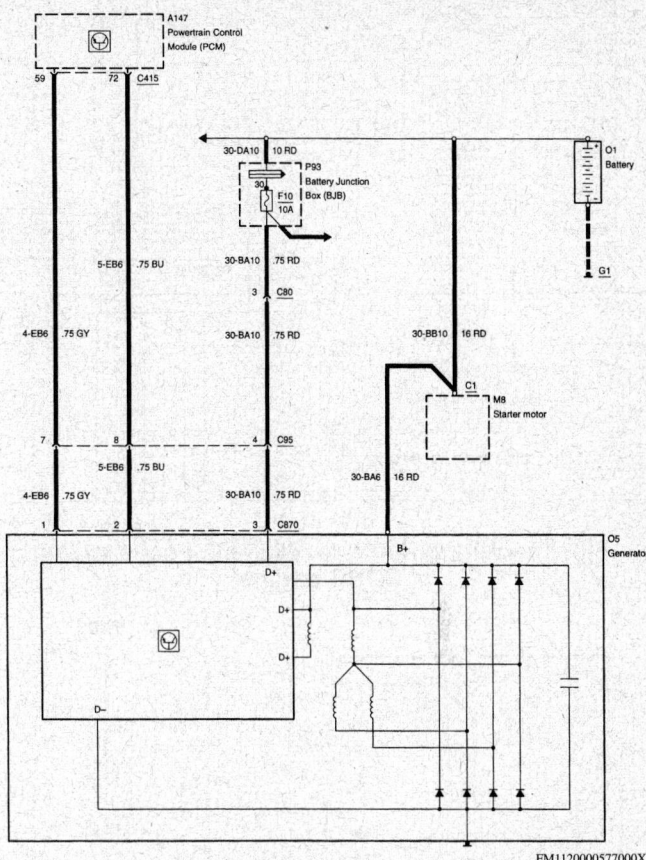

Fig. 10   Wiring diagram. 2001–02 Focus w/2.0L DOHC engine

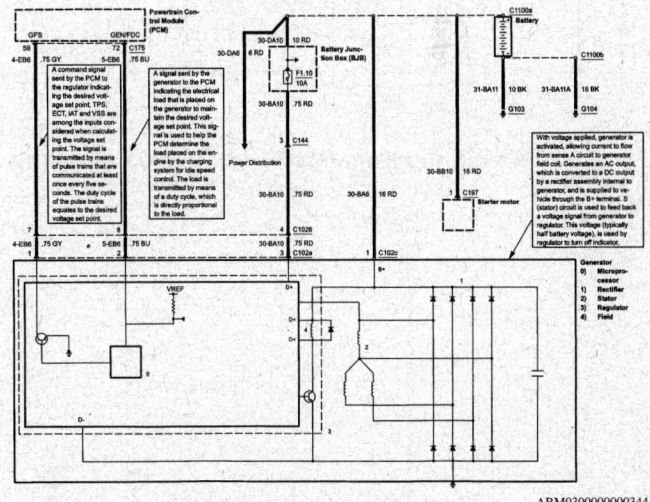

Fig. 12   Wiring diagram. 2003–05 Focus w/2.0L DOHC engine

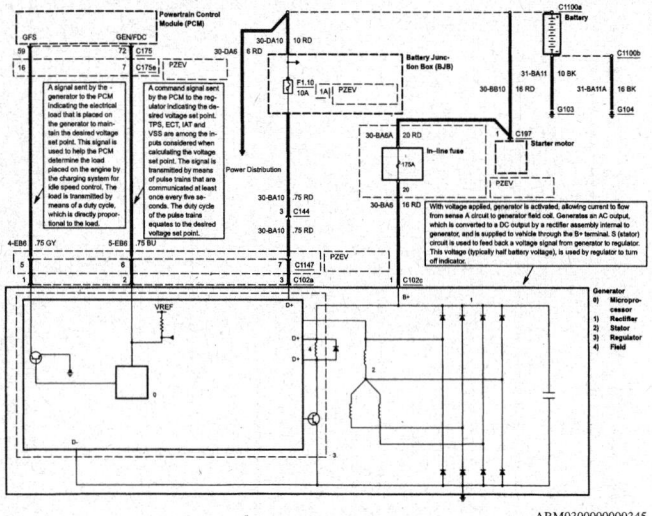

Fig. 13 Wiring diagram. 2003–05 Focus w/2.0L SOHC engine

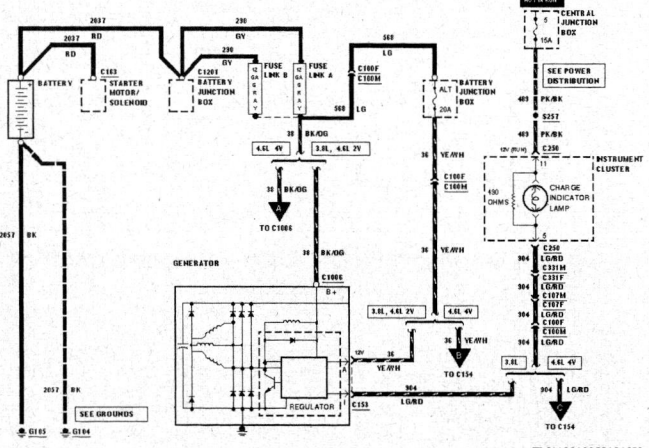

Fig. 15 Wiring diagram (Part 1 of 2). 2001 Mustang

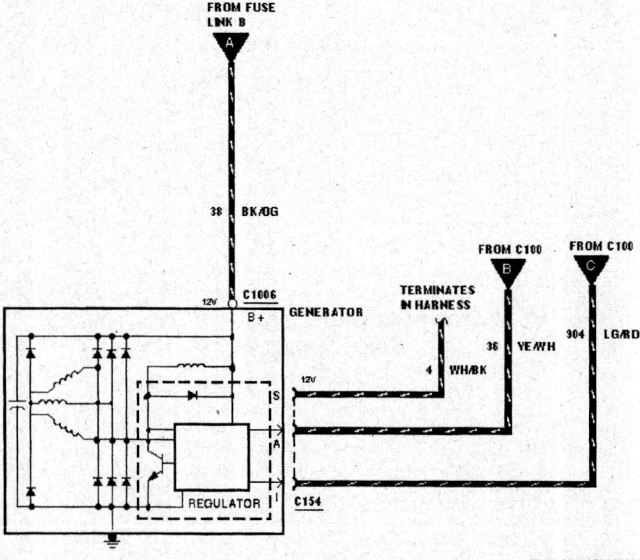

Fig. 15 Wiring diagram (Part 2 of 2). 2001 Mustang

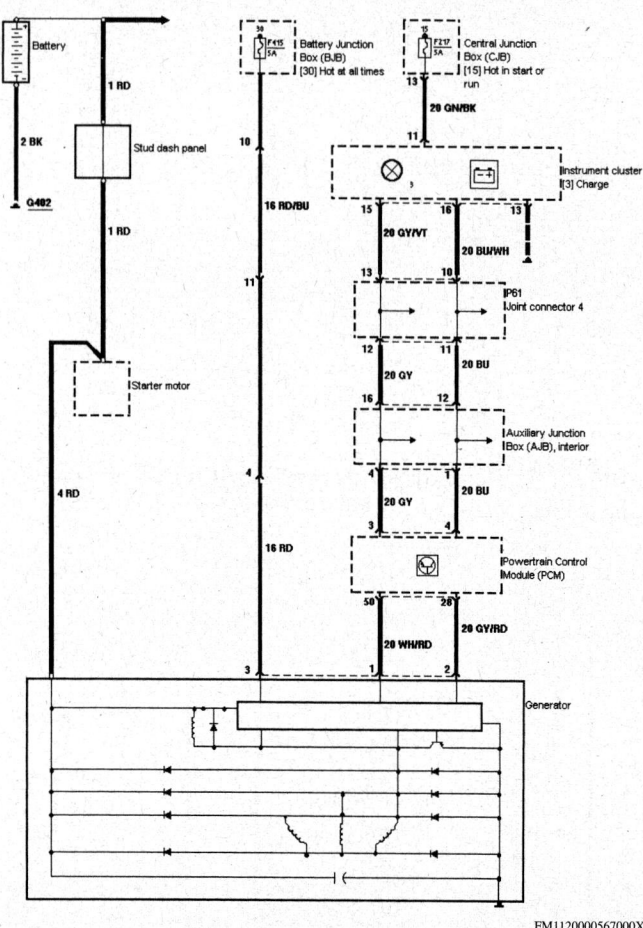

Fig. 14 Wiring diagram. LS

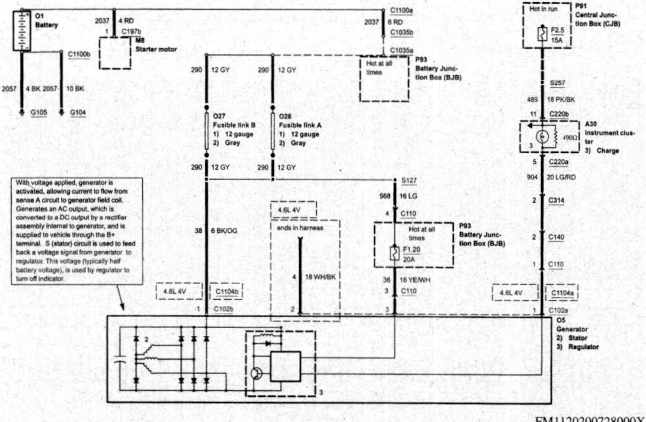

Fig. 16 Wiring diagram. 2002–04 Mustang

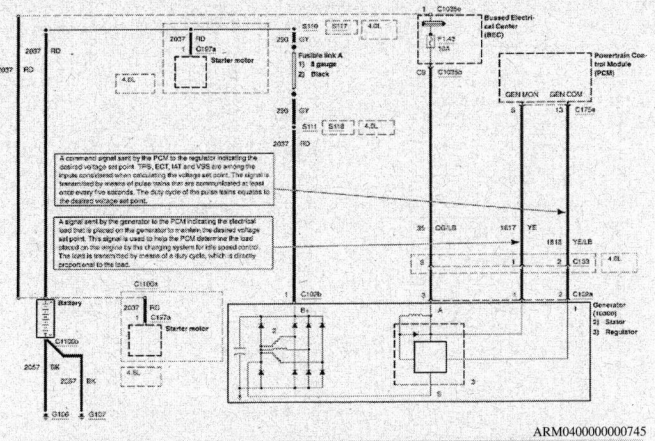

Fig. 17 Wiring diagram. 2005 Mustang

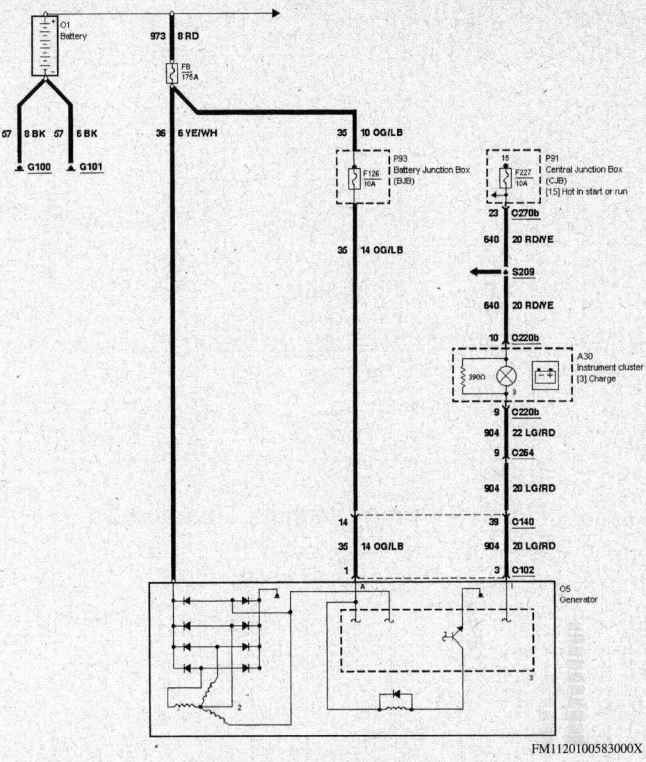

Fig. 18 Wiring diagram. 2000–01 Sable & Taurus w/3.0L DOHC engine

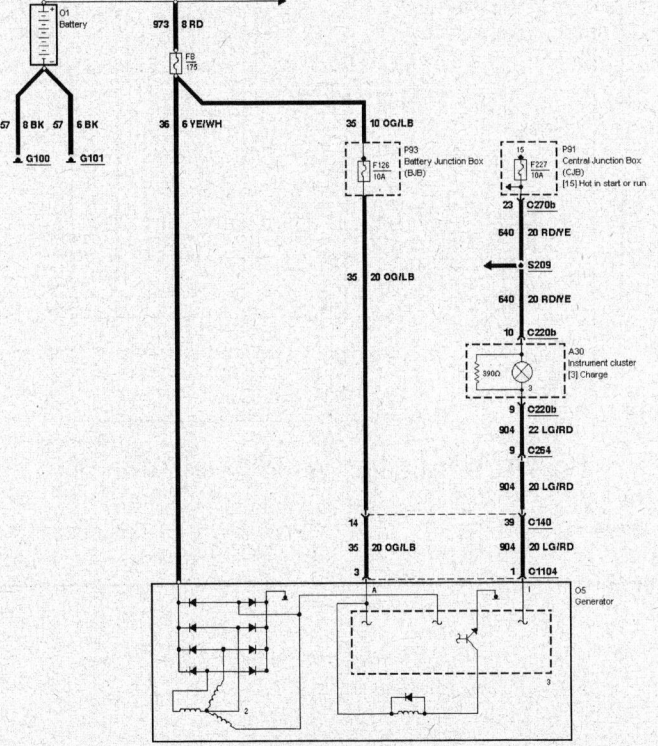

Fig. 19 Wiring diagram. 2000–01 Sable & Taurus w/3.0L OHV engine

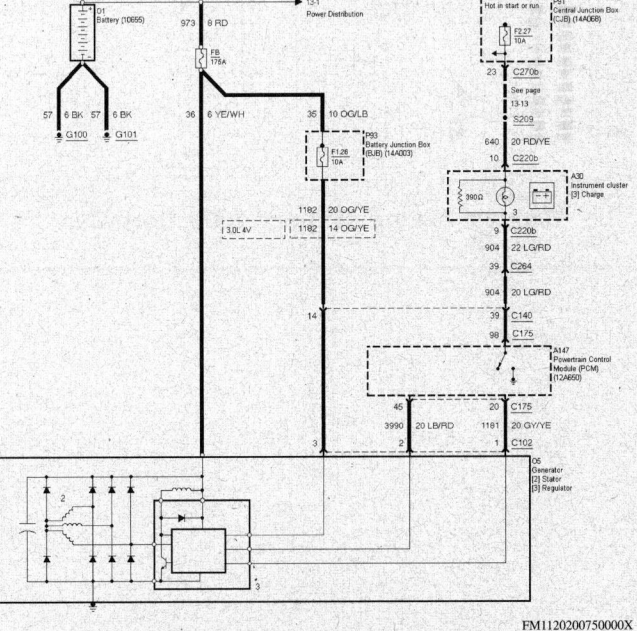

Fig. 20 Wiring Diagram. 2002–04 Sable & Taurus

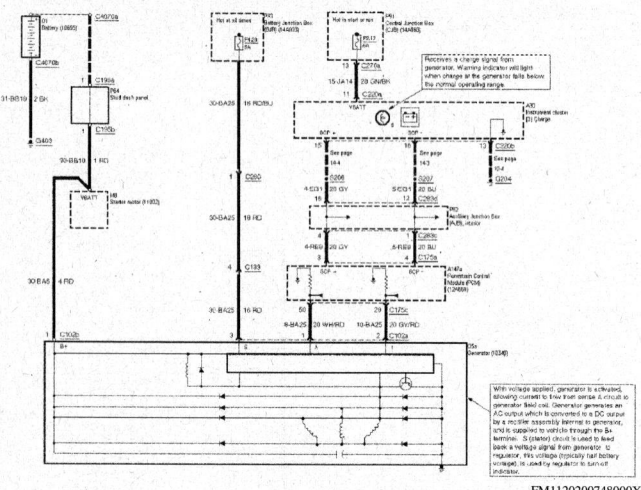

Fig. 21   Wiring Diagram. Thunderbird

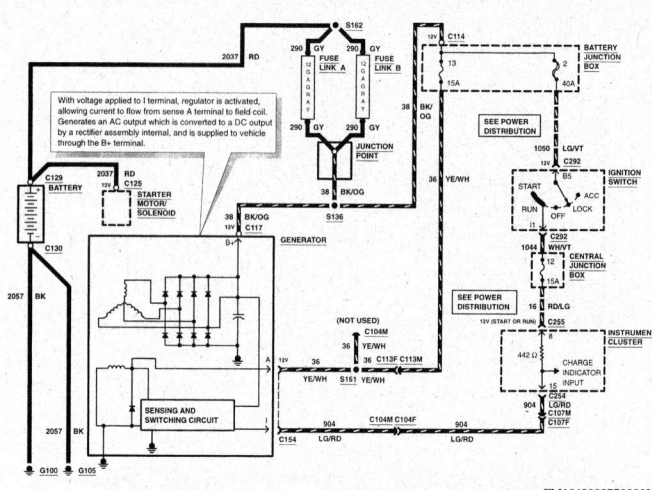

Fig. 22   Wiring diagram. 2000–01 Town Car

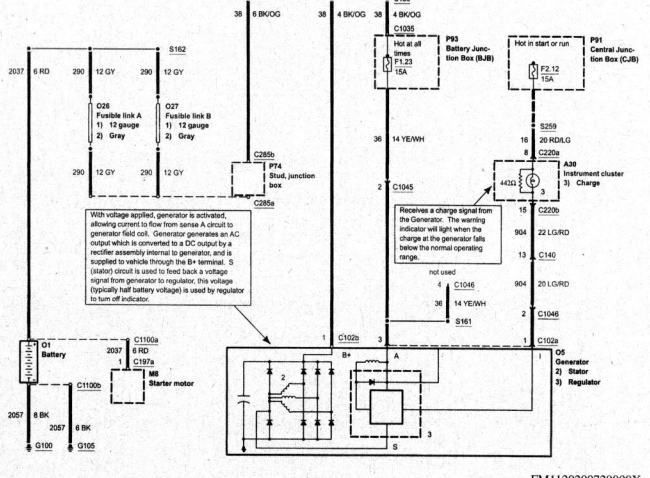

Fig. 23   Wiring diagram. 2002 Town Car

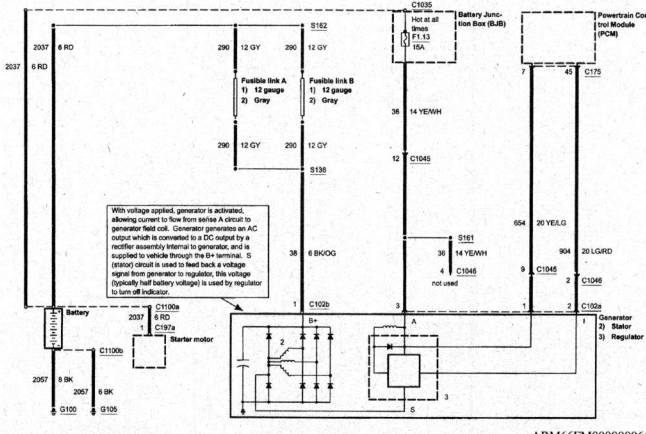

Fig. 24   Wiring diagram. 2003–04 Town Car

DIAGNOSTIC CHART INDEX

Continued

DIAGNOSTIC CHART INDEX—Continued

Test	Description	Page No.	Fig. No.
ESCORT & ZX2			
Test B	Warning Indicator Stays On	13-33	86
Test C	Warning Indicator Flickers/Intermittent	13-34	87
Test D	Alternator Is Noisy	13-34	88
Test E	Radio Interference	13-35	89
Test F	Battery Does Not Hold A Charge	13-35	90
Test G	System Does Not Charge	13-35	91
FIVE HUNDRED, FREESTYLE & MONTEGO			
Test A	Battery Is Discharged Or Battery Voltage Is Low	13-35	92
Test B	Charging System Warning Indicator Is On w/Engine Running, Engine Voltage Does Not Increase	13-36	93
Test C	System Overcharges, Battery Voltage Is More Than 15.5 Volts	13-36	94
Test D	Charging System Warning Indicator Is On w/Engine Running, System Increases Voltage	13-37	95
Test E	Charging System Warning Indicator Is Off w/Ignition Switch In Run Position & Engine Off	13-37	96
Test F	Alternator Is Noisy	13-37	97
Test G	Radio Interference	13-37	98
FOCUS			
—	Symptoms	13-13	30
Test A	Charging System Warning Indicator Is On w/Engine Running	13-38	99
Test B	Radio Interference	13-38	100
LS & THUNDERBIRD			
—	Symptoms	13-14	31
Test A	Battery Is Discharged Or Battery Voltage Is Low	13-38	101
Test B	Charging System Warning Indicator Is On w/Engine Running, Charging System Voltage Does Not Increase	13-39	102
Test C	Charging System Overcharges, Battery Voltage Is More Than 15	13-40	103
Test D	Charging System Warning Indicator Is On w/Engine Running & Battery Increases Voltage	13-41	104
Test E	Charging System Warning Indicator Is Off w/Ignition Switch In Run Position & Engine Is Off	13-42	105
Test F	Charging System Warning Indicator Flickers Or Is Intermittent	13-43	106
Test G	Alternator Is Noisy	13-44	107
Test H	Radio Interference	13-45	108
MARAUDER, 2003–05 CROWN VICTORIA & GRAND MARQUIS			
—	Symptoms	13-13	28
Test A	Battery Is Discharged Or Battery Voltage Is Low	13-30	77
Test B	Charging System Warning Indicator Is On w/Engine Running, Engine Voltage Does Not Increase	13-30	78
Test C	System Overcharges, Battery Voltage More Than 15	13-31	79
Test D	Charging System Warning Indicator Is On w/Engine Running, System Increases Voltage	13-31	80
Test E	Charging System Warning Indicator Is Off w/Ignition Switch In Run Position & Engine Off	13-32	81
Test F	Charging System Warning Indicator Lamp Flickers Or Is Intermittent	13-32	82
Test G	Alternator Is Noisy	13-32	83
Test H	Radio Interference	13-33	84
2001 MUSTANG w/3.8L ENGINE			
—	Symptoms	13-14	32
Test A	System Does Not Charge	13-45	109
Test B	System Overcharging	13-46	110
Test C	Indicator Lamp Remains Lit w/Engine Running	13-46	111
Test D	Indicator Lamp Does Not Light	13-46	112
Test E	Indicator Lamp Flickers Or Lights Intermittently	13-46	113
Test F	Alternator Noisy	13-47	114
Test G	Radio Interference	13-47	115

Continued

DIAGNOSTIC CHART INDEX—Continued

Test	Description	Page No.	Fig. No.
2001 MUSTANG w/4.6L ENGINE			
—	Symptoms	13-14	33
Test H	System Does Not Charge	13-48	116
Test I	System Overcharging	13-48	117
Test J	Indicator Lamp Lights, Engine Running	13-48	118
Test K	Indicator Lamp Does Not Light	13-48	119
Test L	Indicator Lamp Flickers or Lights Intermittently	13-49	120
Test M	Alternator is Noisy	13-49	121
Test N	Radio Interference	13-49	122
Test O	Battery Discharged or Voltage Low	13-50	123
2002–05 MUSTANG			
—	Symptoms	13-14	34
Test A	Battery Is Charged Or Voltage Is Low	13-50	124
Test B	Charging System Warning Indicator Is On w/Engine Running, Battery Voltage Does Not Increase	13-50	125
Test C	System Overcharges, Battery Voltage Is More Than 15	13-51	126
Test D	Charging System Warning Indicator Is On w/Engine Running & Battery Increases Voltage	13-52	127
Test E	Charging System Warning Indicator Is Off w/Ignition Switch In Run Position & Engine Off	13-52	128
Test F	Charging System Warning Indicator Lamp Flickers Or Is Intermittent	13-52	129
Test G	Alternator Is Noisy	13-53	130
Test H	Radio Interference	13-54	131
2001 SABLE & TAURUS			
—	Symptoms	13-15	35
Test A	Battery Is Discharged Or Voltage Is Low	13-54	132
Test B	Charge Indicator Lights w/Engine Running, System Voltage Does Not Increase	13-54	133
Test C	System Overcharges	13-56	134
Test D	Charge Indicator Lights w/Engine Running, System Voltage Increases	13-56	135
Test E	Charge Indicator Off w/Ignition In Run Position & Engine Off	13-56	136
Test F	Indicator Flickers/Intermittent	13-57	137
Test H	Radio Interference	13-57	139
2002–05 SABLE & TAURUS			
—	Symptoms	13-15	36
Test A	Battery Is Discharged Or Voltage Is Low	13-58	140
Test B	Charging System Warning Indicator Is On w/Engine Running, System Voltage Does Not Increase	13-58	141
Test C	System Overcharges, Battery Voltage More Than 15 Volts	13-59	142
Test D	Charging System Warning Indicator Is On w/Engine Running, System Increases Voltage	13-59	143
Test E	Charging System Warning Indicator Is Off w/Ignition Switch In Run Position & Engine Off	13-60	144
Test F	Charging System Warning Indicator Lamp Flickers Or Is Intermittent	13-61	145
Test G	Alternator Is Noisy	13-62	146
Test G	Alternator Is Noisy	13-57	138
Test H	Radio Interference	13-62	147
2001 TOWN CAR			
—	Symptoms	13-15	37
Test A	Warning Indicator Lights w/Engine Running, Battery Voltage Does Not Increase	13-62	148
Test B	Warning Indicator Is Off w/Ignition In Run Position & Engine Off	13-63	149
Test C	Warning Indicator Is On w/Engine Running & Battery Voltage Increase	13-63	150
Test D	Warning Indicator Off w/Ignition In Run Position & Engine Off	13-64	151
Test E	Warning Indicator Operates Properly But Battery Voltage Does Not Increase	13-64	152
Test F	Battery Is Dead Or Will Not Stay Charged Or Low Battery Or Alternator Voltage	13-64	153
Test G	Warning Indicator Flickers Or Is Intermittent	13-65	154
Test H	System Overcharges, Battery Voltage More Than 15	13-65	155
Test J	Battery Leakage Or Damage	13-66	156
Test K	Voltage Gauge Reads High Or Low	13-66	157

Continued

DIAGNOSTIC CHART INDEX—Continued

Condition	Possible Source	Action
• The Charging System Warning Indicator is ON with the Engine Running (The Battery Voltage Does Not Increase)	• A Circuit 35 (O/LB). • A Circuit in-line mini-fuse. • B+ Circuit 36 (Y/W). • B+ mega fuse. • I Circuit 904 (LG/R). • Voltage regulator. • Generator	• GO to Pinpoint Test A.
• The Charging System Warning Indicator is OFF with the Ignition Switch in the RUN Position and the Engine OFF (Battery Voltage Does Not Increase)	• Voltage regulator connector. • I Circuit 904 (LG/R). • Fuse 19 (10A). • Voltage regulator. • Loose or damaged generator. • Harness connector.	• GO to Pinpoint Test B.
• The Charging System Warning Indicator is ON with the Engine Running and the Battery Voltage Increases	• Generator. • Voltage regulator.	• GO to Pinpoint Test C.

FM1129800244010X

Fig. 25 Symptoms (Part 1 of 2). 2001 Continental

Condition	Possible Source	Action
• The Charging System Warning Indicator is OFF with the Ignition Switch in the RUN Position and the Engine OFF (Battery Voltage Increases)	• Charging system warning indicator lamp bulb. • Instrument cluster. • Generator. • Voltage regulator.	• GO to Pinpoint Test D.
• The Charging System Warning Indicator Operates Correctly but the Battery Voltage Does Not Increase	• B+ Circuit 36 (Y/W). • B+ mega fuse. • Loose or damaged harness connector. • Battery cables. • Generator. • Voltage regulator.	• GO to Pinpoint Test E.
• The Battery is Dead or Will Not Stay Charged or Low Battery or Generator Voltage	• Corroded terminal(s). • Loose connection(s). • High key-off load. • Generator. • Voltage regulator.	• GO to Pinpoint Test F.
• The Charging System Warning Indicator Flickers/Is Intermittent	• Loose connection(s). • In-line mini-fuse A Circuit loose. • Fuse 19 (10A) I Circuit loose. • Voltage regulator.	• GO to Pinpoint Test G.
• The System Overcharges (Battery Voltage Greater Than 15.5 Volts)	• A Circuit 35 (O/LB). • Generator (low output). • Voltage regulator. • I Circuit 904 (LG/R).	• GO to Pinpoint Test H.
• Battery Leakage or Damage	• A Circuit 35 (O/LB). • Generator. • Voltage regulator. • Battery.	• GO to Pinpoint Test J.
• The Voltage Gauge Reads High or Low	• Generator (low output) • Voltage regulator. • Voltage gauge. • Instrument cluster/wiring.	• GO to Pinpoint Test K.
• The Generator is Noisy	• Loose bolts/brackets. • Drive belt. • Generator/Pulley.	• GO to Pinpoint Test L.
• Radio Interference	• Generator. • Wiring/routing. • In-vehicle entertainment system.	• GO to Pinpoint Test M.

FM1129800244020X

Fig. 25 Symptoms (Part 2 of 2). 2001 Continental

Condition	Possible Sources	Action
Battery is discharged or voltage is low	• Corroded terminal(s). • Loose connection(s). • High key-off current drain(s). • Battery. • Generator.	• GO to Pinpoint Test A.
The charging system warning indicator is on with the engine running (the system voltage does not increase)	• Circuitry. • Voltage regulator. • Generator.	• GO to Pinpoint Test B.
The system overcharges (battery voltage greater than 15.5 volts)	• Circuitry. • Voltage regulator. • Generator.	• GO to Pinpoint Test C.
The charging system warning indicator is on with the engine running and the system increases voltage	• Circuitry. • Instrument cluster. • Voltage regulator. • Generator.	• GO to Pinpoint Test D.

FM1120200731010X

Fig. 26 Symptoms (Part 1 of 2). 2002 Continental

Condition	Possible Sources	Action
The charging system warning indicator is off with the ignition switch in the RUN position and the engine off	• Bulb. • Circuitry. • Instrument cluster. • Voltage regulator. • Generator.	• GO to Pinpoint Test E.
The charging system warning indicator flickers or is intermittent	• Corroded terminal(s). • Fuse(s). • Circuitry. • Voltage regulator. • Generator.	• GO to Pinpoint Test F.
The generator is noisy	• Bolts or brackets. • Drive belt. • Generator or pulley.	• GO to Pinpoint Test G.
Radio interference	• Generator. • Circuitry. • In-vehicle entertainment system.	• GO to Pinpoint Test H.

FM1120200731020X

Fig. 26 Symptoms (Part 2 of 2). 2002 Continental

Condition	Possible Sources	Action
Charging System Warning Indicator Is On, Intermittent Or Flickers w/Engine Running	Accessory Drive Belt Fuse No. 7 (20A) Wiring Circuit Alternator	Refer To "Pinpoint test A"
Charging System Warning Indicator Is Off W/Ignition In Run Position & Engine Off	Bulb Circuit Alternator	—
Radio Interference	Circuit Alternator	Refer To "Pinpoint Test B: Radio Interference"
System Overcharges	Alternator	—

Fig. 27 Symptoms. Cougar

Condition	Possible Source	Action
The System Overcharges	• Voltage drop in circuit A. • Generator. • Regulator.	• GO to Pinpoint Test A.
The Charging System Warning Indicator Stays On	• Open A circuit. • Shorted I circuit. • Open/high resistance S circuit. • Regulator. • Generator.	• GO to Pinpoint Test B.
The Charging System Warning Indicator Is Inoperative	• Circuitry. • Instrument cluster.	• INSPECT Instrument Cluster & Panel Lighting.
The Charging System Warning Indicator Flickers/Is Intermittent	• Circuitry. • Generator.	• GO to Pinpoint Test C.
Generator Is Noisy	• Drive belt. • Generator. • Related components.	• GO to Pinpoint Test D.

FM1129800227010X

Fig. 29 Symptoms (Part 1 of 2). Escort & ZX2

Condition	Possible Source	Action
Battery is discharged or voltage is low	• Corroded terminal(s). • Loose connection(s). • High key-off current drain(s). • Battery. • Generator.	• GO to Pinpoint Test A.
The charging system warning indicator is on with the engine running (the system voltage does not increase)	• Circuitry. • Voltage regulator. • Generator.	• GO to Pinpoint Test B.
The system overcharges (battery voltage greater than 15.5 volts)	• Circuitry. • Voltage regulator. • Generator.	• GO to Pinpoint Test C.
The charging system warning indicator is on with the engine running and the system increases voltage	• Circuitry. • Instrument cluster. • Voltage regulator. • Generator.	• GO to Pinpoint Test D.
The charging system warning indicator is off with the ignition switch in the RUN position and the engine off	• Bulb. • Circuitry. • Instrument cluster. • Voltage regulator. • Generator.	• GO to Pinpoint Test E.
The charging system warning indicator flickers or is intermittent	• Corroded terminal(s). • Fuse(s). • Circuitry. • Voltage regulator. • Generator.	• GO to Pinpoint Test F.
The generator is noisy	• Bolts or brackets. • Drive belt. • Generator or pulley.	• GO to Pinpoint Test G.
Radio interference	• Generator. • Circuitry. • In-vehicle entertainment system.	• GO to Pinpoint Test H.

FM1120000541000X

Fig. 28 Symptoms. Crown Victoria, Grand Marquis & Marauder

Condition	Possible Source	Action
Radio Interference	• Generator. • Regulator. • Other components.	• GO to Pinpoint Test E.
The Battery Does Not Hold a Charge	• Battery drain. • Circuitry. • Regulator. • Generator. • Battery.	• GO to Pinpoint Test F.
The System Does Not Charge	• Drive Belt. • Generator. • Circuitry.	• GO to Pinpoint Test G.

FM1129800227020X

Fig. 29 Symptoms (Part 2 of 2). Escort & ZX2

Condition	Possible Sources	Action
Charging System Warning Indicator Is On w/Engine Running	Accessory Drive Belt Battery Junction Box Fuse No. 10 (10A) Wiring Circuit Alternator	Refer To "Pinpoint test A"
Charging System Warning Indicator Is Off w/Ignition On & Engine Off	Bulb Circuit Alternator	—
Radio Interference	Circuit Alternator	Refer To "Pinpoint Test B"
System Overcharges	Alternator	—

Fig. 30 Symptoms. Focus

Condition	Possible Sources	Action
• The battery is discharged or battery voltage is low	• Circuitry. • High key-off current drain(s). • Battery. • Generator.	• GO to Pinpoint Test A.
• The charging system warning indicator is on with the engine running (the charging system voltage does not increase)	• Generator. • Rear battery junction box (BJB) fuse 20 (5A). • Circuitry.	• GO to Pinpoint Test B.
• The charging system overcharges (battery voltage is greater than 15.5 volts)	• Rear BJB fuse 20 (5A). • Circuitry. • Generator.	• GO to Pinpoint Test C.
• The charging system warning indicator is on with the engine running and the battery increases voltage	• Rear BJB fuse 20 (5A). • Generator. • Instrument cluster. • Powertrain control module(PCM). • Circuitry.	• GO to Pinpoint Test D.
• The charging system warning indicator is off with the ignition switch in the RUN position and the engine off	• Generator connector unplugged C102a. • Battery. • Circuitry. • Instrument cluster. • PCM.	• GO to Pinpoint Test E.
• The charging system warning indicator flickers or is intermittent	• Rear BJB fuse 20 (5A). • Generator connector unplugged (C102a). • Circuitry. • Generator.	• GO to Pinpoint Test F.
• The generator is noisy	• Loose bolts/brackets. • Drive belt. • Generator/pulley.	• GO to Pinpoint Test G.
• Radio interference	• Generator. • Wiring/routing. • In-vehicle entertainment system.	• GO to Pinpoint Test H.

FM1120200791000X

Fig. 31   Symptoms. LS & Thunderbird

Condition	Possible Source	Action
• Radio interference	• Generator. • Wiring or routing. • In-vehicle entertainment system.	• GO to Pinpoint Test G.
• The voltage gauge (if equipped) is inaccurate	• Generator. • Voltage regulator. • Voltage gauge. • Instrument cluster. • Wiring.	• Repair as required.
• Battery is discharged or voltage is low	• Corroded terminal(s). • Loose connection(s). • High key-off current drains. • Battery. • Generator.	• GO to Pinpoint Test O.

FM1120000550020X

Fig. 32   Symptoms (Part 2 of 2). 2001 Mustang w/3.8L engine

Condition	Possible Source	Action
• The charging system warning indicator lamp flickers or is intermittent	• Corroded terminals. • Connections. • Fuses. • Generator.	• GO to Pinpoint Test L.
• The generator is noisy	• Bolts or brackets. • Drive belt. • Generator or pulley.	• GO to Pinpoint Test M.
• Radio interference	• Harness routing. • In-vehicle entertainment system. • A Circuit 36 (YE/WH).	• GO to Pinpoint Test N.
• Voltage gauge (if equipped) is inaccurate.	• Generator. • Voltage regulator. • Voltage gauges. • Instrument cluster. • Wiring.	• REPAIR as required.
• Battery is discharged or voltage is low	• Corroded terminal(s). • Loose connection(s). • High key-off current drains. • Battery. • Generator.	• GO to Pinpoint Test O.

FM1120000551020X

Fig. 33   Symptoms (Part 2 of 2). 2001 Mustang w/4.6L engine

Condition	Possible Source	Action
• The battery is not being charged by generator	• Voltage regulator connector. • Charging system warning indicator lamp bulb. • Voltage regulator. • Generator. • Connections.	• GO to Pinpoint Test A.
• Battery overcharging (voltage is greater than 15.5 volts)	• S Circuit 4 (WH/BK). • Generator. • Voltage regulator.	• GO to Pinpoint Test B.
• The charging system warning indicator is on with the engine running (system is charging)	• I Circuit 904 (LG/RD). • Instrument cluster. • S Circuit 4 (WH/BK). • Generator. • Voltage regulator.	• GO to Pinpoint Test C.
• The charging system indicator lamp does not come on	• I Circuit 904 (LG/RD). • Connections. • Battery cables. • Generator. • Voltage regulator. • Instrument panel. • Indicator lamp.	• GO to Pinpoint Test D.
• The charging system warning indicator flickers or is intermittent	• Connections. • I Circuit fuse loose CJB Fuse 5 (15A). • A Circuit fuse loose. • Generator. • Voltage regulator.	• GO to Pinpoint Test E.
• The generator is noisy	• Bolts or brackets. • Drive belt. • Generator or pulley.	• GO to Pinpoint Test F.

FM1120000550010X

Fig. 32   Symptoms (Part 1 of 2). 2001 Mustang w/3.8L engine

Condition	Possible Source	Action
• The battery is not being charged by the generator	• Fuse links. • I Circuit 904 (LG/RD). • I Circuit fuse (20A). • Generator. • Charging system warning indicator lamp bulb. • Harness connector.	• GO to Pinpoint Test H.
• Battery overcharging (voltage greater than 15.5 volts)	• Generator.	• GO to Pinpoint Test I.
• The charging system warning indicator lamp is on with the engine running (system is charging)	• I Circuit 904 (LG/RD). • Instrument cluster. • Generator.	• GO to Pinpoint Test J.
• The charging system warning indicator lamp does not come on	• Lamp bulb. • Instrument cluster. • I Circuit 904 (LG/RD). • Harness connector. • Generator.	• GO to Pinpoint Test K.

FM1120000551010X

Fig. 33   Symptoms (Part 1 of 2). 2001 Mustang w/4.6L engine

Condition	Possible Sources	Action
• Battery is discharged or voltage is low	• Circuitry. • High key-off current drain(s). • Battery. • Generator.	• GO to Pinpoint Test A.
• The charging system warning indicator is on with the engine running (the system voltage does not increase)	• Circuitry. • Voltage regulator. • Generator.	• GO to Pinpoint Test B.
• The system overcharges (the battery voltage is greater than 15.5 volts)	• Circuitry. • Voltage regulator. • Generator.	• GO to Pinpoint Test C.
• The charging system warning indicator is on with the engine running and the battery increases voltage	• Circuitry. • Instrument cluster. • Voltage regulator. • Generator.	• GO to Pinpoint Test D.
• The charging system warning indicator is off with the ignition switch in the RUN position and the engine off	• Bulb. • Circuitry. • Instrument cluster. • Voltage regulator. • Generator.	• GO to Pinpoint Test E.
• The charging system warning indicator flickers or is intermittent	• Central junction box (CJB) fuse 5 (15A). • Generator connector unplugged (C102a). • Circuitry. • Generator.	• GO to Pinpoint Test F.
• The generator is noisy	• Bolts or brackets. • Drive belt. • Generator or pulley.	• GO to Pinpoint Test G.
• Radio interference	• Generator. • Circuitry. • In-vehicle entertainment system.	• GO to Pinpoint Test H.

FM1120200761000X

Fig. 34   Symptoms. 2002–05 Mustang

Condition	Possible Source	Action
• System Does Not Charge	• Ignition switch OFF battery drain. • Circuitry. • Voltage regulator. • Generator. • Battery. • Battery connections. • Drive belt.	• GO to Pinpoint Test A.
• System Overcharges (Battery Boils Over)	• Circuitry. • Poor ground. • Voltage regulator. • Generator.	• GO to Pinpoint Test B.
• Indicator Lamp Stays On, Engine Running	• Circuitry. • Voltage regulator. • Generator.	• GO to Pinpoint Test C.
• Indicator Lamp Stays On, Ignition Switch OFF	• Circuitry. • Improper lamp circuit wiring. • Instrument cluster.	• GO to Pinpoint Test D.

FM1129800218010X

Fig. 35 Symptoms (Part 1 of 2). 2001 Sable & Taurus

Condition	Possible Sources	Action
• Battery is discharged or voltage is low	• Circuitry. • High key-off current drain(s). • Battery. • Generator.	• GO to Pinpoint Test A.
• The charging system warning indicator is on with the engine running (the system voltage does not increase)	• Generator. • BJB fuse 2 (10A). • Circuitry.	• GO to Pinpoint Test B.
• The system overcharges (battery voltage greater than 15 volts)	• BJB fuse 2 (10A). • Circuitry. • Generator.	• GO to Pinpoint Test C.
• The charging system warning indicator is on with the engine running (the system increases voltage)	• BJB fuse 2 (10A). • Generator. • Instrument cluster. • PCM. • Circuitry.	• GO to Pinpoint Test D.
• The charging system warning indicator is off with the ignition switch in the RUN position and the engine off	• Generator connector unplugged (C102). • Battery. • Circuitry. • Instrument cluster. • PCM.	• GO to Pinpoint Test E.
• The charging system warning indicator flickers or is intermittent	• BJB fuse 2 (10A). • Generator connector unplugged (C102). • Circuitry. • Generator.	• GO to Pinpoint Test F.
• The generator is noisy	• Loose bolts/brackets. • Drive belt. • Generator/pulley.	• GO to Pinpoint Test G.
• Radio interference	• Generator. • Wiring/routing. • In-vehicle entertainment system.	• GO to Pinpoint Test H.

FM1120200770000X

Fig. 36 Symptoms. 2002–05 Sable & Taurus

Condition	Possible Source	Action
• The Charging System Warning Indicator Operates Correctly but the Battery Voltage Does Not Increase	• B+ Circuit 38 (B/O). • B+ fuse links. • Loose or damaged harness connector. • Battery cables. • Generator. • Voltage regulator.	• GO to Pinpoint Test E.
• The Battery is Dead or Will Not Stay Charged or Low Battery or Generator Voltage	• Corroded terminal(s). • Loose connection(s). • High key-off load.	• GO to Pinpoint Test F.
• The Charging System Warning Indicator Flickers or Is Intermittent	• Loose connection(s). • In-line mini-fuse A Circuit loose. • I Circuit fuse(s). • Generator.	• GO to Pinpoint Test G.
• The System Overcharges (Battery Voltage Greater Than 15.5 Volts)	• A Circuit. • Generator. • I Circuit.	• GO to Pinpoint Test H.
• Battery Leakage or Damage	• A Circuit. • Generator. • Battery.	• GO to Pinpoint Test J.
• The Voltage Gauge Reads High or Low	• Generator. • Voltage gauge. • Instrument cluster/wiring.	• GO to Pinpoint Test K.
• The Generator is Noisy	• Loose bolts/brackets. • Drive belt. • Generator/Pulley.	• GO to Pinpoint Test L.
• Radio Interference	• Generator. • Wiring/routing. • In-vehicle entertainment system.	• GO to Pinpoint Test M.

FM1129800284020X

Fig. 37 Symptoms (Part 2 of 2). 2001 Town Car

Condition	Possible Source	Action
• Indicator Lamp Does Not Come On	• Circuitry. • Burned out indicator bulb. • Poor ground. • Voltage regulator. • Generator.	• GO to Pinpoint Test E.
• Indicator Lamp Flickers / Intermittent	• Loose connection to generator, voltage regulator or power distribution box. • Circuitry. • Loose brush holder screw. • Voltage regulator. • Generator.	• GO to Pinpoint Test F.
• Generator Noisy	• Accessory drive belt. • Accessory brackets. • Bent pulley. • Generator. • Other accessories.	• GO to Pinpoint Test G.
• Radio Interference	• Voltage regulator. • Generator. • Other components.	• GO to Pinpoint Test H.

FM1129800218020X

Fig. 35 Symptoms (Part 2 of 2). 2001 Sable & Taurus

Condition	Possible Source	Action
• The Charging System Warning Indicator is ON with the Engine Running (The Battery Voltage Does Not Increase)	• A Circuit. • A Circuit in-line mini-fuse. • B+ Circuit 38 (B/O). • B+ fuse links. • I Circuit 904 (LG/R) • Generator	• GO to Pinpoint Test A.
• The Charging System Warning Indicator is OFF with the Ignition Switch in RUN and the Engine OFF (Battery Voltage Does Not Increase When the Engine is Running).	• Voltage regulator connector. • I Circuit 904 (LG/R) • I Circuit fuse(s). • Charging system warning indicator lamp bulb. • Loose or damaged generator. • Harness connector.	• GO to Pinpoint Test B.
• The Charging System Warning Indicator is ON with the Engine Running and the Battery Voltage Increases	• Generator.	• GO to Pinpoint Test C.
• The Charging System Warning Indicator is OFF with the Ignition Switch in RUN and the Engine OFF (Battery Voltage Increases When the Engine is Running).	• Charging system warning indicator lamp bulb. • Instrument cluster. • Generator.	• GO to Pinpoint Test D.

FM1129800284010X

Fig. 37 Symptoms (Part 1 of 2). 2001 Town Car

Condition	Possible Sources	Action
• Battery is discharged or voltage is low	• Corroded terminal(s). • Loose connection(s). • High key-off current drain(s). • Battery. • Generator.	• GO to Pinpoint Test A.
• The charging system warning indicator is on with the engine running (the system voltage does not increase)	• Circuitry. • Voltage regulator. • Generator.	• GO to Pinpoint Test B.
• The system overcharges (battery voltage greater than 15.5 volts)	• Circuitry. • Voltage regulator. • Generator.	• GO to Pinpoint Test C.
• The charging system warning indicator is on with the engine running and the system increases voltage	• Circuitry. • Instrument cluster. • Voltage regulator. • Generator.	• GO to Pinpoint Test D.
• The charging system warning indicator is off with the ignition switch in the RUN position and the engine off	• Bulb. • Circuitry. • Instrument cluster. • Voltage regulator. • Generator.	• GO to Pinpoint Test E.
• The charging system warning indicator flickers or is intermittent	• Corroded terminal(s). • Fuse(s). • Circuitry. • Voltage regulator. • Generator.	• GO to Pinpoint Test F.
• The generator is noisy	• Bolts or brackets. • Drive belt. • Generator or pulley.	• GO to Pinpoint Test G.
• Radio interference	• Generator. • Circuitry. • In-vehicle entertainment system.	• GO to Pinpoint Test H.

FM1120200779000X

Fig. 38 Symptoms. 2002–05 Town Car

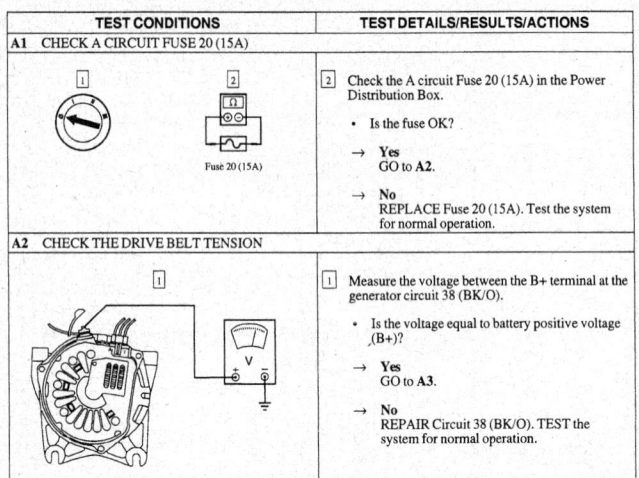

TEST CONDITIONS	TEST DETAILS/RESULTS/ACTIONS

A1 CHECK A CIRCUIT FUSE 20 (15A)	2 Check the A circuit Fuse 20 (15A) in the Power Distribution Box.
	• Is the fuse OK?
	→ **Yes**
	  GO to **A2**.
	→ **No**
	  REPLACE Fuse 20 (15A). Test the system for normal operation.

A2 CHECK THE DRIVE BELT TENSION	1 Measure the voltage between the B+ terminal at the generator circuit 38 (BK/O).
	• Is the voltage equal to battery positive voltage (B+)?
	→ **Yes**
	  GO to **A3**.
	→ **No**
	  REPAIR Circuit 38 (BK/O). TEST the system for normal operation.

FM1129800245010X

Fig. 39   Test A: Warning Indicator Is On, Engine Running (Part 1 of 3). 2001 Continental

TEST CONDITIONS	TEST DETAILS/RESULTS/ACTIONS

A4   CHECK I CIRCUIT 904 (LG/R) FOR AN OPEN
 	
 Generator Connector C154
	3 **NOTE:** The voltage regulator must be connected to the wiring harness for this test.
	Measure the voltage between the voltage regulator I-terminal, Circuit 904 (LG/R) and ground.
	• Is the voltage greater than 1 volt?
	→ **Yes**
	  GO to **A5**.
	→ **No**
	  REPAIR Circuit 904 (LG/R) as necessary. TEST the system for normal operation.

A5 CHECK GENERATOR OUTPUT	2 With the engine running, ground the F pin on the generator/regulator.
	• Does the battery voltage increase and the charging system warning indicator turn off?
	→ **Yes**
	  REPLACE the generator. TEST the system for normal operation.
	→ **No**
	  REPLACE the generator. TEST the system for normal operation.

FM1129800245030X

Fig. 39   Test A: Warning Indicator Is On, Engine Running (Part 3 of 3). 2001 Continental

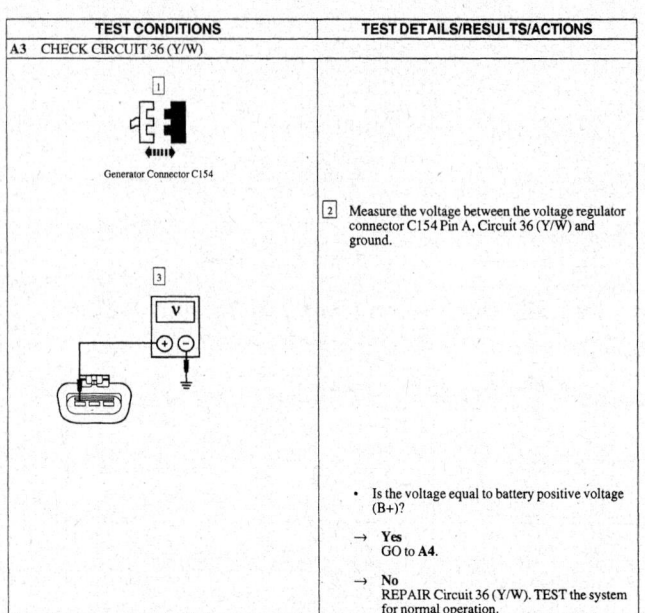

TEST CONDITIONS	TEST DETAILS/RESULTS/ACTIONS

A3   CHECK CIRCUIT 36 (Y/W)
 	
 Generator Connector C154
	2 Measure the voltage between the voltage regulator connector C154 Pin A, Circuit 36 (Y/W) and ground.
	
	• Is the voltage equal to battery positive voltage (B+)?
	→ **Yes**
	  GO to **A4**.
	→ **No**
	  REPAIR Circuit 36 (Y/W). TEST the system for normal operation.

FM1129800245020X

Fig. 39   Test A: Warning Indicator Is On, Engine Running (Part 2 of 3). 2001 Continental

TEST CONDITIONS	TEST DETAILS/RESULTS/ACTIONS

B1   CHECK GENERATOR CONNECTOR C154
 	
 Generator Connector C154
	2 Check the generator connector C154 for bent or damaged pins.
	• Is the connector OK?
	→ **Yes**
	  GO to **B2**.
	→ **No**
	  REPAIR connector C154 as necessary. TEST the system for normal operation.

B2 CHECK GENERATOR GROUNDS	1 Check all ground connections between the generator, voltage regulator, and battery.
	• Are the ground connections OK?
	→ **Yes**
	  GO to **B3**.
	→ **No**
	  REPAIR connections as necessary. TEST the system for normal operation.

FM1129800246010X

Fig. 40   Test B: Warning Indicator Is Off w/Ignition In Run Position & Engine Off (Part 1 of 2). 2001 Continental

TEST CONDITIONS	TEST DETAILS/RESULTS/ACTIONS
B3 CHECK VOLTAGE AT I CIRCUIT 904 (LG/R)	

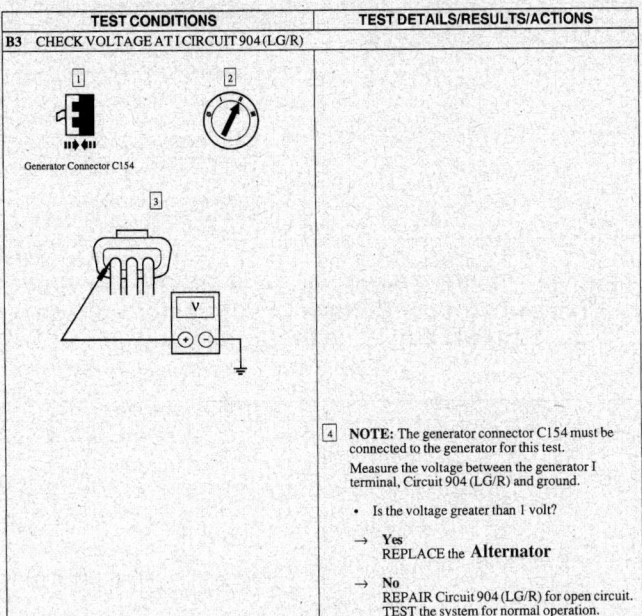

Generator Connector C154

4. **NOTE:** The generator connector C154 must be connected to the generator for this test.

Measure the voltage between the generator I terminal, Circuit 904 (LG/R) and ground.

- Is the voltage greater than 1 volt?

→ **Yes**
REPLACE the **Alternator**

→ **No**
REPAIR Circuit 904 (LG/R) for open circuit. TEST the system for normal operation.

FM1129800246020X

Fig. 40 Test B: Warning Indicator Is Off w/Ignition In Run Position & Engine Off (Part 2 of 2). 2001 Continental

TEST CONDITIONS	TEST DETAILS/RESULTS/ACTIONS
C3 CHECK WARNING INDICATOR OPERATION	

Generator Connector C154

4. With the engine running at idle, check the Warning Indicator.

- Is the warning indicator on?

→ **Yes**
REPAIR connector C154, I Circuit 904 (LG/R) as necessary. TEST the system for normal operation.

→ **No**
GO to Pinpoint Test D.

FM1129800247020X

Fig. 41 Test C: Warning Indicator Is On w/Engine Running & Battery Voltage Increases (Part 2 of 2). 2001 Continental

TEST CONDITIONS	TEST DETAILS/RESULTS/ACTIONS
D1 CHECK CHARGING SYSTEM WARNING INDICATOR OPERATION	

3. Ground the generator connector C154 I circuit with the key ON and the engine OFF.

- Is the warning indicator on?

→ **Yes**
REPLACE the generator. TEST for normal operation.

→ **No**
REPAIR connector C154 I Circuit 904 (LG/R) as necessary. TEST for normal operation.

FM1129800248000X

Fig. 42 Test D: Warning Indicator Is Off w/Ignition In Run Position & Engine Off. 2001 Continental

TEST CONDITIONS	TEST DETAILS/RESULTS/ACTIONS
C1 CHECK CONNECTOR C154	

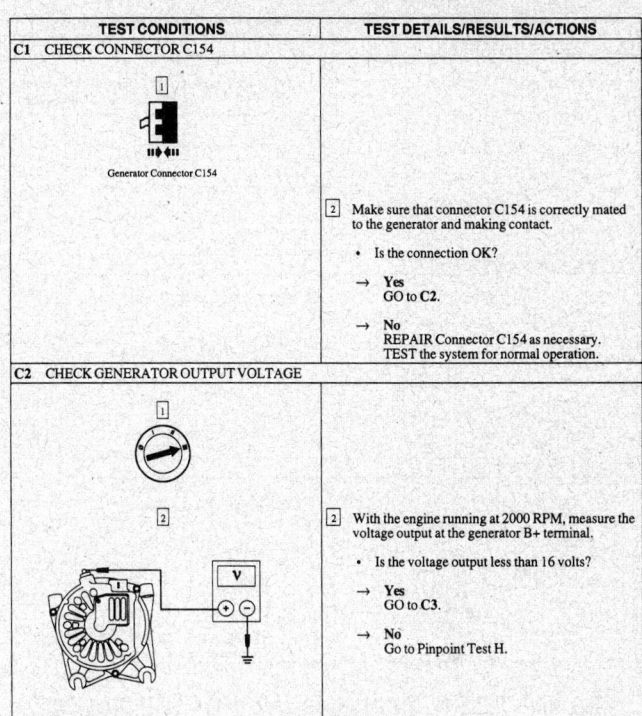

Generator Connector C154

2. Make sure that connector C154 is correctly mated to the generator and making contact.

- Is the connection OK?

→ **Yes**
GO to **C2**.

→ **No**
REPAIR Connector C154 as necessary. TEST the system for normal operation.

TEST CONDITIONS	TEST DETAILS/RESULTS/ACTIONS
C2 CHECK GENERATOR OUTPUT VOLTAGE	

2. With the engine running at 2000 RPM, measure the voltage output at the generator B+ terminal.

- Is the voltage output less than 16 volts?

→ **Yes**
GO to **C3**.

→ **No**
Go to Pinpoint Test H.

FM1129800247010X

Fig. 41 Test C: Warning Indicator Is On w/Engine Running & Battery Voltage Increases (Part 1 of 2). 2001 Continental

TEST CONDITIONS	TEST DETAILS/RESULTS/ACTIONS
E1 CHECK CIRCUIT 36 (Y/W) VOLTAGE	

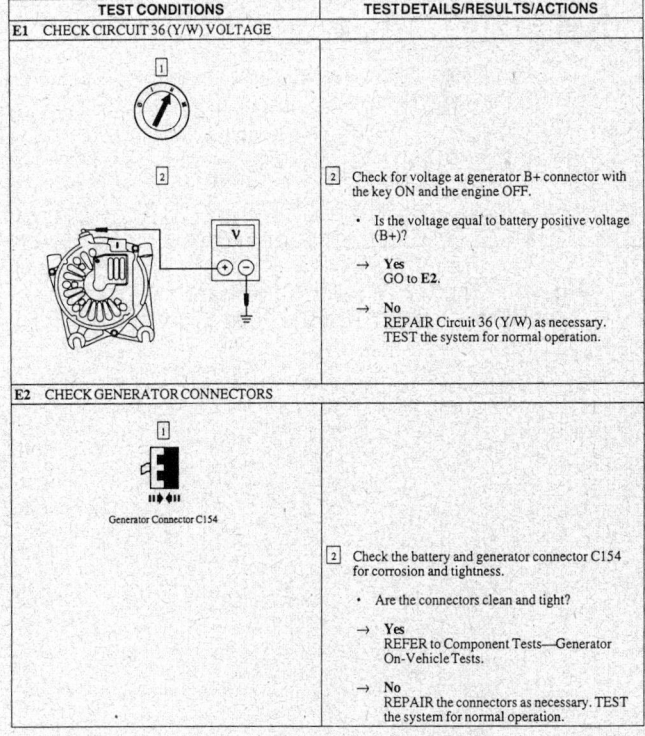

2. Check for voltage at generator B+ connector with the key ON and the engine OFF.

- Is the voltage equal to battery positive voltage (B+)?

→ **Yes**
GO to **E2**.

→ **No**
REPAIR Circuit 36 (Y/W) as necessary. TEST the system for normal operation.

TEST CONDITIONS	TEST DETAILS/RESULTS/ACTIONS
E2 CHECK GENERATOR CONNECTORS	

Generator Connector C154

2. Check the battery and generator connector C154 for corrosion and tightness.

- Are the connectors clean and tight?

→ **Yes**
REFER to Component Tests—Generator On-Vehicle Tests.

→ **No**
REPAIR the connectors as necessary. TEST the system for normal operation.

FM1129800249000X

Fig. 43 Test E: Warning Indicator Operates Properly But Battery Voltage Does Not Increase. 2001 Continental

TEST CONDITIONS	TEST DETAILS/RESULTS/ACTIONS
F1 CHECK BATTERY DRAIN	
	1️⃣ Make sure that all interior lights and switches are off and all doors are closed. Perform battery drain test. • Is the drain greater than 0.5 amps? → **Yes** Go to Component Tests, Battery—Drain Testing. → **No** GO to F2.
F2 CHECK GENERATOR OUTPUT	
	1️⃣ Check generator output. • Is the generator OK? → **Yes** GO to F3. → **No** REPLACE the generator. TEST the system for normal operation.
F3 CHECK BATTERY CONDITION	
	1️⃣ Check the battery capacity. • Is the battery OK? → **Yes** GO to F4. → **No** REPLACE the battery. TEST the system for normal operation.

FM1129800250010X

Fig. 44   Test F: Battery Is Dead Or Will Not Stay Charged Or Low Battery Or Alternator Voltage (Part 1 of 2). 2001 Continental

TEST CONDITIONS	TEST DETAILS/RESULTS/ACTIONS
G1 CHECK POWER TO CIRCUITS 36 (Y/W) AND 904 (LG/R)	
1️⃣ 2️⃣ 3️⃣ Fuse 20 (15A) Fuse 5 (10A)	4️⃣ Check Fuse 5 (10A) and the Fuse 20 (15A). • Are the fuses OK? → **Yes** GO to G2. → **No** REPAIR as necessary. TEST the system for normal operation.

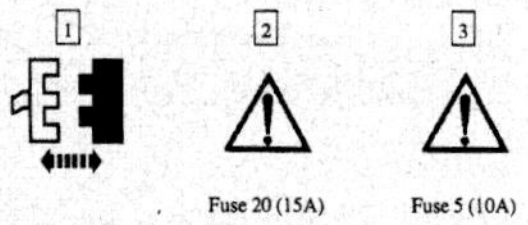

FM1129800251010X

Fig. 45   Test G: Warning Indicator Flickers/ Intermittent (Part 1 of 2). 2001 Continental

TEST CONDITIONS	TEST DETAILS/RESULTS/ACTIONS
F4 CHECK OTHER SYSTEMS FOR DRAINS	
	1️⃣ Check for drains from electronic modules. • Are electronic modules OK? → **Yes** RECHARGE the battery. TEST the system for normal operation. → **No** REPLACE the defective module as necessary. TEST the system for normal operation.

FM1129800250020X

Fig. 44   Test F: Battery Is Dead Or Will Not Stay Charged Or Low Battery Or Alternator Voltage (Part 2 of 2). 2001 Continental

TEST CONDITIONS	TEST DETAILS/RESULTS/ACTIONS
G2 CHECK FIELD CIRCUIT	
1️⃣ 2️⃣ V	2️⃣ Using an insulated probe measure voltage at test point F at rear of generator. • Is the voltage equal to battery voltage? → **Yes** GO to G3. → **No** REPLACE the generator. TEST the system for normal operation.
G3 CHECK THE WARNING SYSTEM INDICATOR OPERATION	
1️⃣	2️⃣ With the engine running, increase engine speed. Check the indicator operation and for battery voltage increase. • Does the voltage increase above 15 volts or the indicator flicker? → **Yes** REPAIR Circuit 36 (Y/W) or Circuit 904 (LG/R) as necessary. TEST the system for normal operation. → **No** REPLACE the generator. TEST the system for normal operation.

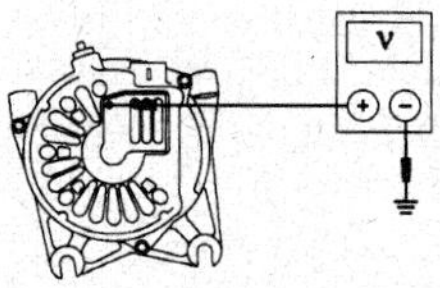

FM1129800251020X

Fig. 45   Test G: Warning Indicator Flickers/ Intermittent (Part 2 of 2). 2001 Continental

TEST CONDITIONS	TEST DETAILS/RESULTS/ACTIONS
H1 CHECK FOR VOLTAGE DROP	

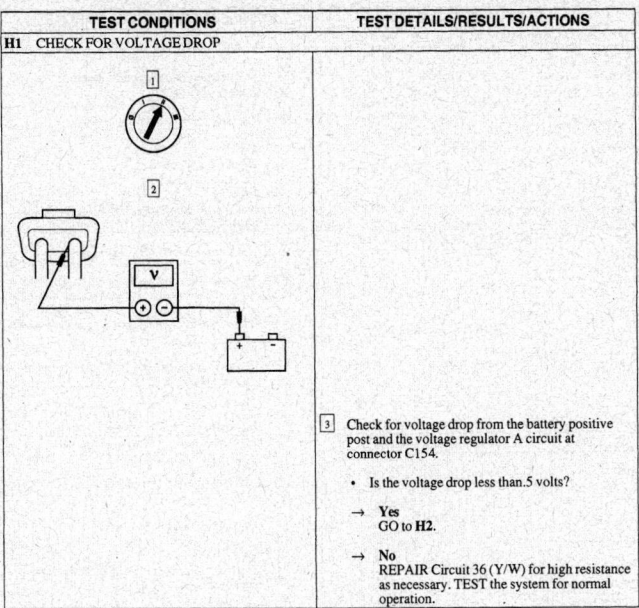

3. Check for voltage drop from the battery positive post and the voltage regulator A circuit at connector C154.

- Is the voltage drop less than .5 volts?

→ **Yes**
  GO to **H2**.

→ **No**
  REPAIR Circuit 36 (Y/W) for high resistance as necessary. TEST the system for normal operation.

FM1129800252010X

Fig. 46   Test H: System Overcharges, Battery Voltage More Than 15.5 Volts (Part 1 of 4). 2001 Continental

TEST CONDITIONS	TEST DETAILS/RESULTS/ACTIONS
H2 CHECK BATTERY VOLTAGE	

3. With the engine running turn off all accessories. Increase the engine speed and monitor the voltage at the battery.

- Does battery voltage remain less than 15 volts?

→ **Yes**
  GO to **H3**.

→ **No**
  GO to **H5**.

FM1129800252020X

Fig. 46   Test H: System Overcharges, Battery Voltage More Than 15.5 Volts (Part 2 of 4). 2001 Continental

TEST CONDITIONS	TEST DETAILS/RESULTS/ACTIONS
H3 CHECK GENERATOR FOR LOW VOLTAGE	

3. With the ignition switch OFF, use an insulated probe to measure the voltage at the voltage regulator F terminal.

- Does the voltage equal battery voltage?

→ **Yes**
  GO to **H4**.

→ **No**
  REPLACE the generator. TEST the system for normal operation.

FM1129800252030X

Fig. 46   Test H: System Overcharges, Battery Voltage More Than 15.5 Volts (Part 3 of 4). 2001 Continental

H4 CHECK THE WARNING SYSTEM INDICATOR OPERATION	

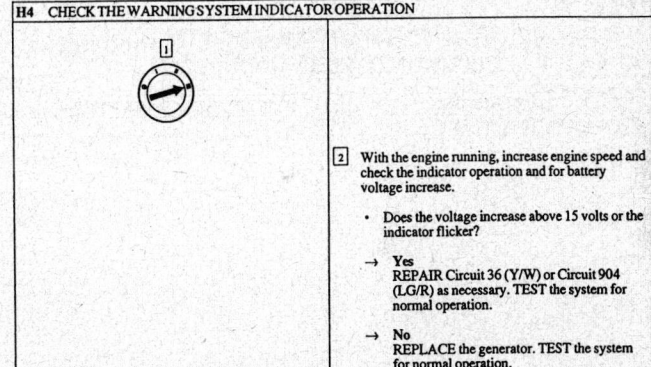

2. With the engine running, increase engine speed and check the indicator operation and for battery voltage increase.

- Does the voltage increase above 15 volts or the indicator flicker?

→ **Yes**
  REPAIR Circuit 36 (Y/W) or Circuit 904 (LG/R) as necessary. TEST the system for normal operation.

→ **No**
  REPLACE the generator. TEST the system for normal operation.

FM1129800252040X

Fig. 46   Test H: System Overcharges, Battery Voltage More Than 15.5 Volts (Part 4 of 4). 2001 Continental

TEST CONDITIONS	TEST DETAILS/RESULTS/ACTIONS
J1 CHECK FOR ACID LEAKAGE DAMAGE	
	1 Check for Acid damage to vehicle harness and to the body. • REPAIR damaged areas as necessary. → **Yes** REPAIR damaged areas as necessary. → **No** GO to **J2**.
J2 CHECK CHARGING SYSTEM FOR OVERCHARGING	
1 2	3 With the engine running turn off all accessories. Increase the engine speed and monitor the voltage at the battery. • Does battery voltage increase more than 15 volts? → **Yes** Go to Pinpoint Test H. → **No** GO to **J3**.

FM1129800253010X

Fig. 47 Test J: Battery Leakage Or Damage (Part 1 of 2). 2001 Continental

TEST CONDITIONS	TEST DETAILS/RESULTS/ACTIONS
J3 CHECK BATTERY MOUNTING	
	1 Make sure the battery is properly mounted and level in the battery tray. • Is the battery properly mounted? → **Yes** GO to **J4**. → **No** REPAIR as necessary. TEST the system for normal operation.
J4 CHECK FOR BATTERY CONTACT	
	1 Make sure that there are no fasteners or other parts contacting the battery case causing excess pressure. • Is there anything contacting the battery case? → **Yes** REPAIR as necessary. TEST the system for normal operation. → **No** GO to **J5**.
J5 CHECK BATTERY CASE FOR DAMAGE	
	1 Check the battery case for defects such as cracks or poor seals. • Is the battery OK? → **Yes** System is OK. Test the system for normal operation. → **No** REPLACE the battery. TEST the system for normal operation.

FM1129800253020X

Fig. 47 Test J: Battery Leakage Or Damage (Part 2 of 2). 2001 Continental

TEST CONDITIONS	TEST DETAILS/RESULTS/ACTIONS
K1 CHECK BATTERY VOLTAGE	
1 2	3 With the engine running turn off all accessories. Increase the engine speed and monitor the voltage at the battery. • Is the battery voltage more than 15 volts? → **Yes** Go to Pinpoint Test H. → **No** GO to **K2**.

FM1129800254010X

Fig. 48 Test K: Voltage Gauge Reads High Or Low (Part 1 of 2). 2001 Continental

TEST CONDITIONS	TEST DETAILS/RESULTS/ACTIONS
K2 CHECK VOLTAGE GAUGE OPERATION	
1	2 With the engine running monitor the voltage gauge reading and the battery voltage. • Are the voltage readings consistent? → **Yes** System is operating normally. → **No** Inspect instrument cluster.

FM1129800254020X

Fig. 48 Test K: Voltage Gauge Reads High Or Low (Part 2 of 2). 2001 Continental

TEST CONDITIONS	TEST DETAILS/RESULTS/ACTIONS
L1 CHECK FOR ACCESSORY DRIVE NOISE	
	1 Check the drive belt to make sure it is properly installed and aligned. • Is the drive belt OK? → **Yes** GO to **L2**. → **No** REPAIR the accessory drive belt as required. RETEST the system.

FM1129800255010X

Fig. 49 Test L: Alternator Is Noisy (Part 1 of 2). 2001 Continental

TEST CONDITIONS	TEST DETAILS/RESULTS/ACTIONS
L2 CHECK THE GENERATOR MOUNTING	
	1 Check the generator and generator mounting brackets for loose bolts or misalignment. • Is the generator mounted correctly? → **Yes** REPLACE the generator. RETEST the system. → **No** INSTALL the generator to specifications. RETEST the system.

FM1129800255020X

Fig. 49 Test L: Alternator Is Noisy (Part 2 of 2). 2001 Continental

TEST CONDITIONS	TEST DETAILS/RESULTS/ACTIONS
M1 CHECK FOR RADIO INTERFERENCE	
	2 Tune the radio to a station where the interference is present.
	• Is the interference present with the generator Connector C154 removed?
	→ **Yes** LOCATE the cause of the radio interference. RETEST the system.
	→ **No** REPLACE the generator. RETEST the system.

FM1129800256000X

Fig. 50 Test M: Radio Interference. 2001 Continental

CONDITIONS	DETAILS/RESULTS/ACTIONS
A2 CHECK FOR GENERATOR OUTPUT	
	1 Carry out the Generator On-Vehicle Load/No-Load Tests.
	• Is the generator OK?
	→ **Yes** GO to **A3**.
	→ **No** GO to Pinpoint Test B.
A3 CHECK FOR CURRENT DRAINS	
	1 Carry out the Battery — Drain Test.
	• Are there any excessive current drains?
	→ **Yes** REPAIR as necessary. TEST the system for normal operation.
	→ **No** GO to **A4**.
A4 CHECK FOR CURRENT DRAINS WHICH SHUT OFF WHEN THE BATTERY IS DISCONNECTED	
	1 Carry out the Battery — Electronic Drains Which Shut Off When the Battery Cable is Disconnected Test.
	• Are there any current drains which shut off when the battery is disconnected?
	→ **Yes** REPAIR as necessary. TEST the system for normal operation.
	→ **No** GO to Pinpoint Test B.

FM1120200732020X

Fig. 51 Test A: Battery Is Discharged Or Voltage Is Low (Part 2 of 2). 2002 Continental

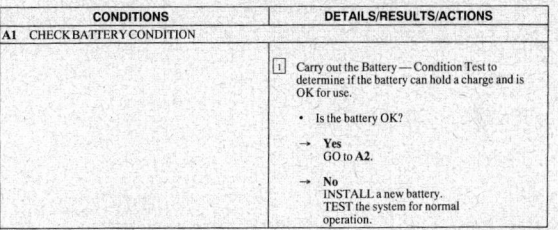

CONDITIONS	DETAILS/RESULTS/ACTIONS
A1 CHECK BATTERY CONDITION	
	1 Carry out the Battery — Condition Test to determine if the battery can hold a charge and is OK for use.
	• Is the battery OK?
	→ **Yes** GO to **A2**.
	→ **No** INSTALL a new battery. TEST the system for normal operation.

FM1120200732010X

Fig. 51 Test A: Battery Is Discharged Or Voltage Is Low (Part 1 of 2). 2002 Continental

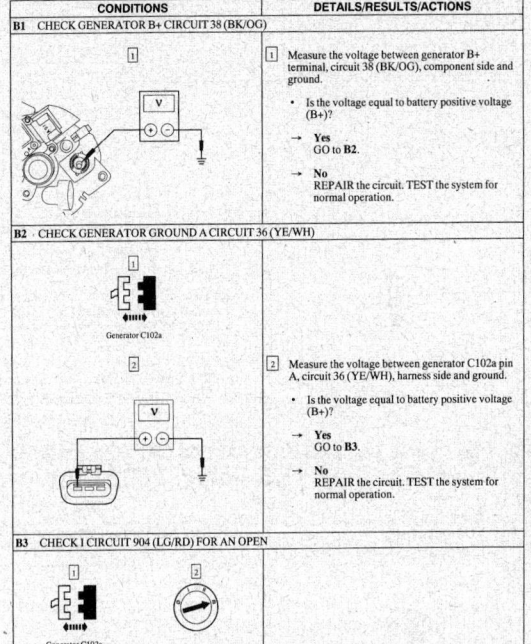

Fig. 52 Test B: Charging System Warning Indicator Is On w/Engine Running, System Voltage Does Not Increase (Part 1 of 2). 2002 Continental

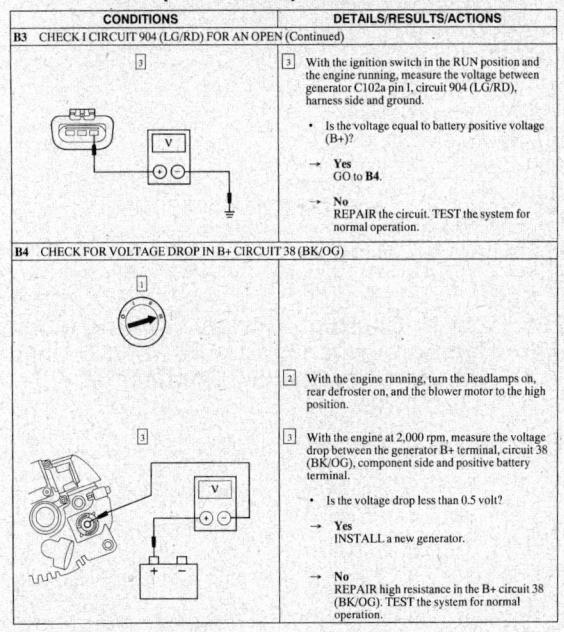

Fig. 52 Test B: Charging System Warning Indicator Is On w/Engine Running, System Voltage Does Not Increase (Part 2 of 2). 2002 Continental

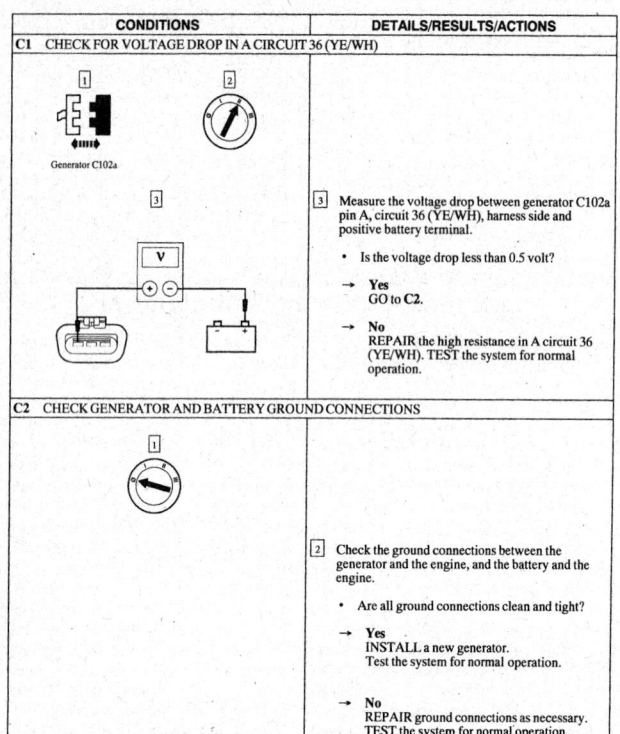

CONDITIONS	DETAILS/RESULTS/ACTIONS
C1 CHECK FOR VOLTAGE DROP IN A CIRCUIT 36 (YE/WH)	
Generator C102a	3 Measure the voltage drop between generator C102a pin A, circuit 36 (YE/WH), harness side and positive battery terminal. • Is the voltage drop less than 0.5 volt? → **Yes** GO to **C2**. → **No** REPAIR the high resistance in A circuit 36 (YE/WH). TEST the system for normal operation.
C2 CHECK GENERATOR AND BATTERY GROUND CONNECTIONS	
	2 Check the ground connections between the generator and the engine, and the battery and the engine. • Are all ground connections clean and tight? → **Yes** INSTALL a new generator. Test the system for normal operation. → **No** REPAIR ground connections as necessary. TEST the system for normal operation.

FM1120200734000X

Fig. 53   Test C: System Overcharges (Battery Voltage Is More Than 15.5 Volts). 2002 Continental

CONDITIONS	DETAILS/RESULTS/ACTIONS
E1 CHECK THE CHARGING SYSTEM WARNING INDICATOR LAMP	
Generator C102a	2 With the engine off, connect a fused (15A) jumper wire between the generator C102a pin I, circuit 904 (LG/RD), harness side and ground.

FM1120200736010X

Fig. 55   Test E: Charging System Warning Indicator Is Off w/Ignition Switch In Run Position & Engine Off (Part 1 of 2). 2002 Continental

CONDITIONS	DETAILS/RESULTS/ACTIONS
D1 CHECK I CIRCUIT 904 (LG/RD) FOR SHORT TO GROUND	
Generator C102a	2 With the ignition switch in the RUN position, check the charging system warning indicator. • Is the charging system warning indicator illuminated? → **Yes** REPAIR generator I circuit 904 (LG/RD) for a short to ground. TEST the system for normal operation. → **No** INSTALL a new generator. TEST the system for normal operation.

FM1120200735000X

Fig. 54   Test D: Charging System Warning Indicator Is On w/Engine Running & System Increases Voltage. 2002 Continental

CONDITIONS	DETAILS/RESULTS/ACTIONS
E1 CHECK THE CHARGING SYSTEM WARNING INDICATOR LAMP (Continued)	
	• Is the charging system warning indicator lamp illuminated? → **Yes** INSTALL a new generator. TEST the system for normal operation. → **No** Diagnosis and test the instrument cluster.

FM1120200736020X

Fig. 55   Test E: Charging System Warning Indicator Is Off w/Ignition Switch In Run Position & Engine Off (Part 2 of 2). 2002 Continental

CONDITIONS	DETAILS/RESULTS/ACTIONS
F1 CHECK FOR LOOSE CONNECTIONS	
	1 Check all generator, battery, and power distribution connections for looseness, corrosion, loose or bent terminals, or loose eyelets. • Are all connections clean and tight? → **Yes** GO to **F2**. → **No** REPAIR as necessary. TEST the system for normal operation.
F2 CHECK FUSE CONNECTIONS	
	1 With the engine running, check BJB fuse 13 (15A) in A circuit 36 (YE/WH) and the CJB fuse 12 (15A) in I circuit 904 (LG/RD) for looseness by wiggling the fuse and noting the charging system warning indicator lamp operation. • Does the charging system warning indicator flicker? → **Yes** REPAIR loose fuse connection(s) as necessary. TEST the system for normal operation. → **No** GO to **F3**.

FM1120200737010X

Fig. 56   Test F: Charging System Warning Indicator Lamp Flickers Or Is Intermittent (Part 1 of 2). 2002 Continental

CONDITIONS	DETAILS/RESULTS/ACTIONS

F3 CHECK A CIRCUIT 36 (YE/WH) CONNECTIONS

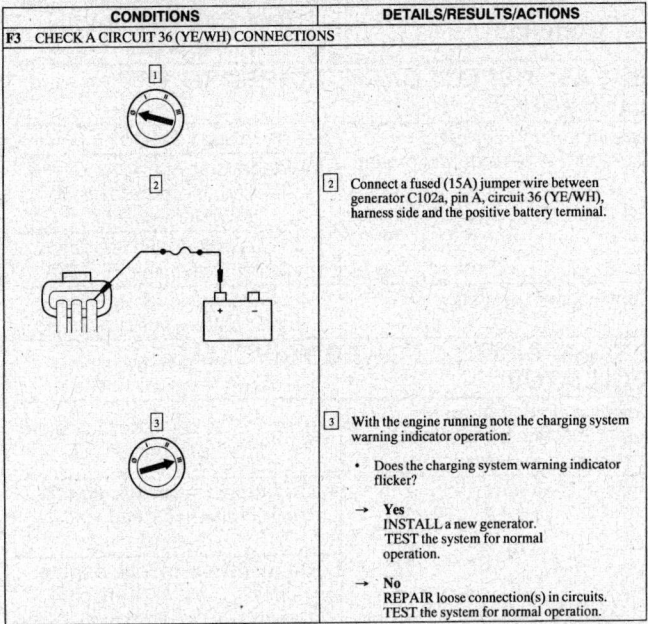

2 Connect a fused (15A) jumper wire between generator C102a, pin A, circuit 36 (YE/WH), harness side and the positive battery terminal.

3 With the engine running note the charging system warning indicator operation.

- Does the charging system warning indicator flicker?

→ **Yes**
INSTALL a new generator. TEST the system for normal operation.

→ **No**
REPAIR loose connection(s) in circuits. TEST the system for normal operation.

FM1120200737020X

Fig. 56   Test F: Charging System Warning Indicator Lamp Flickers Or Is Intermittent (Part 2 of 2). 2002 Continental

CONDITIONS	DETAILS/RESULTS/ACTIONS

G4 CHECK GENERATOR FOR MECHANICAL NOISE

Generator C102a

4 Turn all accessories OFF. With the engine running, use a stethoscope or equivalent listening device to probe the generator for unusual mechanical noise.

- Is the generator the noise source?

→ **Yes**
INSTALL a new generator. TEST the system for normal operation.

→ **No**
Diagnose the source of engine noise.

FM1120200738020X

Fig. 57   Test G: Alternator Is Noisy (Part 2 of 2). 2002 Continental

CONDITIONS	DETAILS/RESULTS/ACTIONS

G1 CHECK FOR ACCESSORY DRIVE NOISE

1 Check the accessory drive belt for damage and correct installation. Check the accessory mounting brackets and generator pulley for looseness or misalignment.

- Is the accessory drive OK?

→ **Yes**
GO to G2.

→ **No**
REPAIR as necessary. TEST the system for normal operation.

G2 CHECK GENERATOR MOUNTING

1 Check the generator mounting for loose bolts or misalignment.

- Is the generator mounted correctly?

→ **Yes**
GO to G3.

→ **No**
REPAIR as necessary. TEST the system for normal operation.

G3 CHECK GENERATOR FOR ELECTRICAL NOISE

Generator C102a

3 With the engine running, turn the headlamps on, rear defroster on, and the blower motor to the high position.

- Is the noise still present?

→ **Yes**
GO to G4.

→ **No**
INSTALL a new generator. TEST the system for normal operation.

FM1120200738010X

Fig. 57   Test G: Alternator Is Noisy (Part 1 of 2). 2002 Continental

CONDITIONS	DETAILS/RESULTS/ACTIONS

H1 VERIFY GENERATOR IS SOURCE OF RADIO INTERFERENCE

1 With the engine running, tune the radio to a station where the interference is present.

2 Tune the radio to a station where the interference is present.

Generator C102a

FM1120200739010X

Fig. 58   Test H: Radio Interference (Part 1 of 2). 2002 Continental

CONDITIONS	DETAILS/RESULTS/ACTIONS

H1 VERIFY GENERATOR IS SOURCE OF RADIO INTERFERENCE (Continued)

- Is the interference present with the generator disconnected?

→ **Yes**
Diagnose and test in-vehicle entertainment system.

→ **No**
INSTALL a new generator. TEST the system for normal operation.

FM1120200739020X

Fig. 58   Test H: Radio Interference (Part 2 of 2). 2002 Continental

Test Condition	Test Details/Results/Actions
TEST A1: INSPECT BATTERY	
Inspect battery capacity	If battery capacity is not at normal operating range, replace battery
Inspect system operation	—
TEST A2: INSPECT CHARGING SYSTEM	
Perform "Load Test"	If alternator output is not as specified, refer to "Test A3: Inspect For A Good Ground"
TEST A3: INSPECT FOR A GOOD GROUND	
Measure voltage between alternator case and battery ground terminal	If voltage is less than .5 volts, refer to "Test A4: Inspect Battery Cable"
	If voltage is more than .5 volts, clean and tighten alternator mounting bolts, engine to body ground strap and battery round cable
Inspect system operation	If voltage is still not as specified, replace battery ground cable
TEST A4: INSPECT BATTERY CABLE	
Measure voltage between alternator B+ terminal and battery positive terminal	Voltage should be less than .5 volts.
	If voltage is as specified, refer to "Test A5: Inspect Battery Feed To Alternator"
	If voltage is not as specified, clean and tighten battery positive cable connections
Inspect system operation	If voltage is still not as specified, replace battery positive cable

Fig. 59   Test A: Charging System Warning Indicator Is On w/Engine Running (Part 1 of 2). Cougar

Test Condition	Test Details/Results/Actions
TEST A5: INSPECT BATTERY FEED TO THE ALTERNATOR	
Measure voltage between alternator B+ terminal and ground	Battery voltage should be present
	If voltage is as specified, refer to "Test A6: Inspect Power To Voltage Regulator"
	If voltage is not as specified, inspect fusible link FB 175A
Inspect system operation	If voltage is not as specified, repair battery positive cable
TEST A6: INSPECT POWER TO VOLTAGE REGULATOR	
Measure voltage between alternator connector pin No. 3 harness side and ground	There should be 10 volts or more present
If voltage is as specified	**On models with 2.0L engine,** replace alternator and inspect system
	On models with 2.5L engine, refer to "Test A7: Charging System Warning Indicator Is On w/Engine Running"
	On all models, if voltage is not as specified, inspect fuse No. F7 and charging system
TEST A7: INSPECT OUTPUT FEEDBACK TO REGULATOR	
Measure resistance between alternator connector pin No. 2 harness side and pin No. 1 harness side	Resistance should be less than 5 ohm
	If resistance is as specified, replace alternator and inspect system
	If resistance is not as specified, repair circuit and inspect system

Fig. 59   Test A: Charging System Warning Indicator Is On w/Engine Running (Part 2 of 2). Cougar

Test Condition	Test Details/Results/Actions
Test B1: Isolate The Alternator	
Remove accessory drive belt	—
Run engine for a few seconds with radio turned on	If radio interference is still present, inspect audio entertainment system for faults
	If radio interference is not present, clean and tighten battery clamps and alternator mounting bolts
	If interference is still present, replace alternator

Fig. 60   Test B: Radio Interference. Cougar

TEST CONDITIONS	TESTDETAILS/RESULTS/ACTIONS
A1 CHECK BATTERY CONDITION	
	[1] Carry out the Battery — Condition Test to determine if the battery can hold a charge and is OK for use. • Is the battery OK? → **Yes** GO to A2. → **No** INSTALL a new battery. TEST the system for normal operation.
A2 CHECK FOR GENERATOR OUTPUT	
	[1] Carry out the On-Vehicle Generator Load/No-Load Tests. • Is the generator OK? → **Yes** GO to A3. → **No** GO to Pinpoint Test B.
A3 CHECK FOR CURRENT DRAINS	
	[1] Carry out the Battery — Drain Test. • Are there any excessive current drains? → **Yes** REPAIR as necessary. TEST the system for normal operation. → **No** GO to A4.

FM1120000542010X

Fig. 61   Test A: Battery Discharged or Voltage Low (Part 1 of 2). 2001 Crown Victoria & Grand Marquis

TEST CONDITIONS	TESTDETAILS/RESULTS/ACTIONS
A4 CHECK FOR CURRENT DRAINS WHICH SHUT OFF WHEN THE BATTERY IS DISCONNECTED	
	1 Carry out the Battery — Electronic Drains Which Shut Off When the Battery Cable is Disconnected Test. • Are there any current drains which shut off when the battery is disconnected? → Yes REPAIR as necessary. TEST the system for normal operation. → No GO to Pinpoint Test B.

FM1120000542020X

Fig. 61   Test A: Battery Discharged or Voltage Low (Part 2 of 2). 2001 Crown Victoria & Grand Marquis

TEST CONDITIONS	TESTDETAILS/RESULTS/ACTIONS
B2 CHECK GENERATOR GROUND A CIRCUIT 36 (YE/WH)	
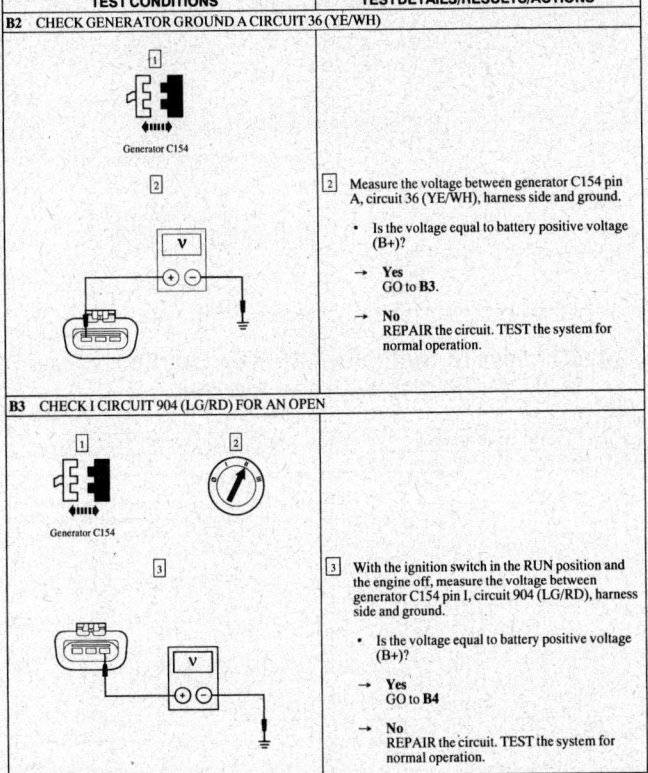	2 Measure the voltage between generator C154 pin A, circuit 36 (YE/WH), harness side and ground. • Is the voltage equal to battery positive voltage (B+)? → Yes GO to B3. → No REPAIR the circuit. TEST the system for normal operation.
B3 CHECK I CIRCUIT 904 (LG/RD) FOR AN OPEN	
	3 With the ignition switch in the RUN position and the engine off, measure the voltage between generator C154 pin I, circuit 904 (LG/RD), harness side and ground. • Is the voltage equal to battery positive voltage (B+)? → Yes GO to B4 → No REPAIR the circuit. TEST the system for normal operation.

FM1120000543020X

Fig. 62   Test B: Indicator Stays On, Engine Running (Part 2 of 3). 2001 Crown Victoria & Grand Marquis

TEST CONDITIONS	TESTDETAILS/RESULTS/ACTIONS
B1 CHECK GENERATOR B+ CIRCUIT 38 (BK/OG)	
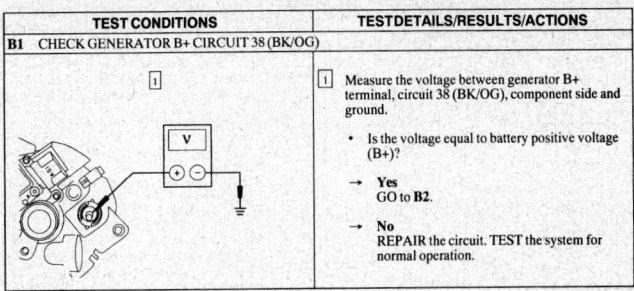	1 Measure the voltage between generator B+ terminal, circuit 38 (BK/OG), component side and ground. • Is the voltage equal to battery positive voltage (B+)? → Yes GO to B2. → No REPAIR the circuit. TEST the system for normal operation.

FM1120000543010X

Fig. 62   Test B: Indicator Stays On, Engine Running (Part 1 of 3). 2001 Crown Victoria & Grand Marquis

TEST CONDITIONS	TESTDETAILS/RESULTS/ACTIONS
B4 CHECK FOR VOLTAGE DROP IN B+ CIRCUIT 38 (BK/OG)	
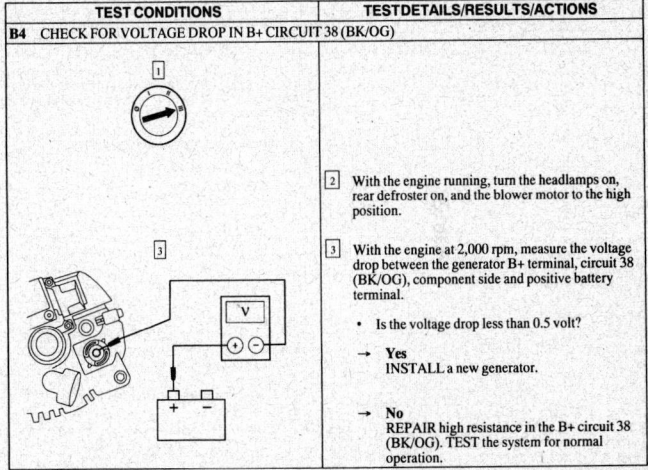	2 With the engine running, turn the headlamps on, rear defroster on, and the blower motor to the high position. 3 With the engine at 2,000 rpm, measure the voltage drop between the generator B+ terminal, circuit 38 (BK/OG), component side and positive battery terminal. • Is the voltage drop less than 0.5 volt? → Yes INSTALL a new generator. → No REPAIR high resistance in the B+ circuit 38 (BK/OG). TEST the system for normal operation.

FM1120000543030X

Fig. 62   Test B: Indicator Stays On, Engine Running (Part 3 of 3). 2001 Crown Victoria & Grand Marquis

TEST CONDITIONS	TESTDETAILS/RESULTS/ACTIONS
C1 CHECK FOR VOLTAGE DROP IN A CIRCUIT 36 (YE/WH)	
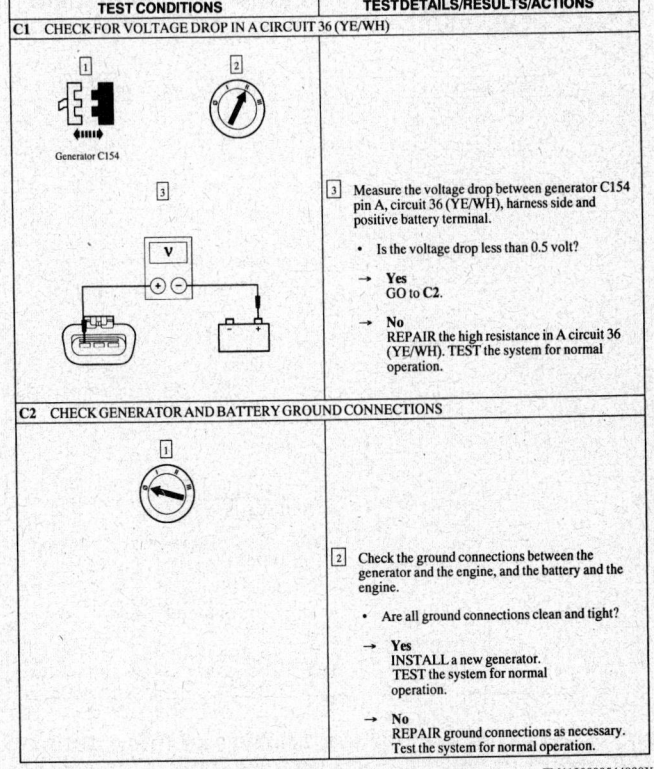	3 Measure the voltage drop between generator C154 pin A, circuit 36 (YE/WH), harness side and positive battery terminal. • Is the voltage drop less than 0.5 volt? → Yes GO to C2. → No REPAIR the high resistance in A circuit 36 (YE/WH). TEST the system for normal operation.
C2 CHECK GENERATOR AND BATTERY GROUND CONNECTIONS	
	2 Check the ground connections between the generator and the engine, and the battery and the engine. • Are all ground connections clean and tight? → Yes INSTALL a new generator. TEST the system for normal operation. → No REPAIR ground connections as necessary. Test the system for normal operation.

FM1120000544000X

Fig. 63   Test C: System Overcharges. 2001 Crown Victoria & Grand Marquis

TEST CONDITIONS	TEST DETAILS/RESULTS/ACTIONS
D1 CHECK I CIRCUIT 904 (LG/RD) FOR SHORT TO GROUND	
[diagram] Generator C154	☐2 With the ignition switch in the RUN position, check the charging system warning indicator. • Is the charging system warning indicator illuminated? → **Yes** REPAIR generator I circuit 904 (LG/RD) for a short to ground. TEST the system for normal operation. → **No** INSTALL a new generator. TEST the system for normal operation.

FM1120000545000X

Fig. 64 Test D: Indicator Stays On, Engine Running. 2001 Crown Victoria & Grand Marquis

TEST CONDITIONS	TEST DETAILS/RESULTS/ACTIONS
F1 CHECK FOR LOOSE CONNECTIONS	
	☐1 Check all generator, battery, and power distribution connections for looseness, corrosion, loose or bent terminals, or loose eyelets. • Are all connections clean and tight? → **Yes** GO to **F2**. → **No** REPAIR as necessary. TEST the system for normal operation.
F2 CHECK FUSE CONNECTIONS	
[diagram]	☐1 With the engine running, check BJB fuse 2 (30A) in A circuit 36 (YE/WH) and the CJB fuse 15 (10A) in I circuit 904 (LG/RD) for looseness by wiggling the fuse and noting the charging system warning indicator lamp operation. • Does the charging system warning indicator flicker? → **Yes** REPAIR loose fuse connection(s) as necessary. TEST the system for normal operation. → **No** GO to **F3**.

FM1120000547010X

Fig. 66 Test F: Indicator Flickers or Intermittent (Part 1 of 2). 2001 Crown Victoria & Grand Marquis

TEST CONDITIONS	TEST DETAILS/RESULTS/ACTIONS
F3 CHECK A CIRCUIT 36 (YE/WH) CONNECTIONS	
[diagram]	☐2 Connect a fused (15A) jumper wire between generator C154, pin A, circuit 36 (YE/WH), harness side and the positive battery terminal. ☐3 With the engine running note the charging system warning indicator operation. • Does the charging system warning indicator flicker? → **Yes** INSTALL a new generator. TEST the system for normal operation. → **No** REPAIR loose connection(s) in circuits. TEST the system for normal operation.

FM1120000547020X

Fig. 66 Test F: Indicator Flickers or Intermittent (Part 2 of 2). 2001 Crown Victoria & Grand Marquis

TEST CONDITIONS	TEST DETAILS/RESULTS/ACTIONS
E1 CHECK THE CHARGING SYSTEM WARNING INDICATOR LAMP	
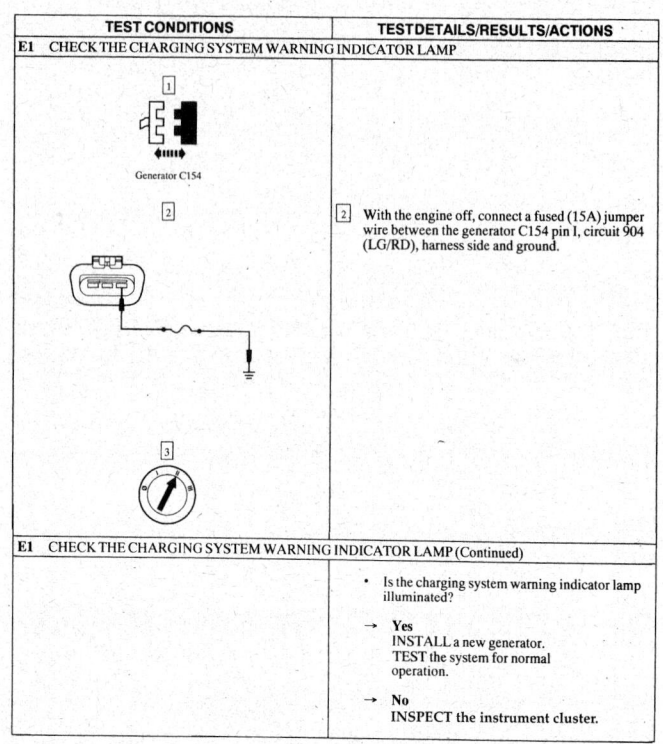	☐2 With the engine off, connect a fused (15A) jumper wire between the generator C154 pin I, circuit 904 (LG/RD), harness side and ground.
E1 CHECK THE CHARGING SYSTEM WARNING INDICATOR LAMP (Continued)	
	• Is the charging system warning indicator lamp illuminated? → **Yes** INSTALL a new generator. TEST the system for normal operation. → **No** INSPECT the instrument cluster.

FM1120000546000X

Fig. 65 Test E: Indicator Off, Key On. 2001 Crown Victoria & Grand Marquis

TEST CONDITIONS	TEST DETAILS/RESULTS/ACTIONS
G1 CHECK FOR ACCESSORY DRIVE NOISE	
	☐1 Check the accessory drive belt for damage and correct installation. Check the accessory mounting brackets and generator pulley for looseness or misalignment. • Is the accessory drive OK? → **Yes** GO to **G2**. → **No** REPAIR as necessary. TEST the system for normal operation.
G2 CHECK GENERATOR MOUNTING	
	☐1 Check the generator mounting for loose bolts or misalignment. • Is the generator mounted correctly? → **Yes** GO to **G3**. → **No** REPAIR as necessary. TEST the system for normal operation.
G3 CHECK GENERATOR FOR ELECTRICAL NOISE	
[diagram] Generator C154	☐3 With the engine running, turn the headlamps on, rear defroster on, and the blower motor to the high position. • Is the noise still present? → **Yes** GO to **G4**. → **No** INSTALL a new generator. TEST the system for normal operation.

FM1120000548010X

Fig. 67 Test G: Alternator Is Noisy (Part 1 of 2). 2001 Crown Victoria & Grand Marquis

TEST CONDITIONS	TEST DETAILS/RESULTS/ACTIONS
G4 CHECK GENERATOR FOR MECHANICAL NOISE	
[1] [2] [3] Generator C154	[4] Turn all accessories OFF. With the engine running, use a stethoscope or equivalent listening device to probe the generator for unusual mechanical noise. • Is the generator the noise source? → **Yes** INSTALL a new generator. TEST the system for normal operation. → **No** INSPECT for source of engine noise.

FM1120000548020X

Fig. 67   Test G: Alternator Is Noisy (Part 2 of 2). 2001 Crown Victoria & Grand Marquis

CONDITIONS	DETAILS/RESULTS/ACTIONS
A1 CHECK BATTERY CONDITION	
	[1] Carry out the Battery — Condition Test to determine if the battery can hold a charge and is OK for use. • Is the battery OK? → **Yes** GO to A2. → **No** INSTALL a new battery. TEST the system for normal operation.

FM1120200740010X

Fig. 69   Test A: Battery Is Discharged Or Voltage Is Low (Part 1 of 2). 2002 Crown Victoria & Grand Marquis

CONDITIONS	DETAILS/RESULTS/ACTIONS
A2 CHECK FOR GENERATOR OUTPUT	
	[1] Carry out the On-Vehicle Generator Load/No-Load Tests. • Is the generator OK? → **Yes** GO to A3. → **No** GO to Pinpoint Test B.
A3 CHECK FOR CURRENT DRAINS	
	[1] Carry out the Battery — Drain Test. • Are there any excessive current drains? → **Yes** REPAIR as necessary. TEST the system for normal operation. → **No** GO to A4.
A4 CHECK FOR CURRENT DRAINS WHICH SHUT OFF WHEN THE BATTERY IS DISCONNECTED	
	[1] Carry out the Battery — Electronic Drains Which Shut Off When the Battery Cable is Disconnected Test. Refer to Component Tests in this section. • Are there any current drains which shut off when the battery is disconnected? → **Yes** REPAIR as necessary. TEST the system for normal operation. → **No** GO to Pinpoint Test B.

FM1120200740020X

Fig. 69   Test A: Battery Is Discharged Or Voltage Is Low (Part 2 of 2). 2002 Crown Victoria & Grand Marquis

TEST CONDITIONS	TEST DETAILS/RESULTS/ACTIONS
H1 VERIFY GENERATOR IS SOURCE OF RADIO INTERFERENCE	
[1] [3] [4] [5] Generator C154	[1] With the engine running, tune the radio to a station where the interference is present. [2] Tune the radio to a station where the interference is present.
H1 VERIFY GENERATOR IS SOURCE OF RADIO INTERFERENCE (Continued)	
	• Is the interference present with the generator disconnected? → **Yes** INSPECT the in-vehicle entertainment system. → **No** INSTALL a new generator. TEST the system for normal operation.

FM1120000549000X

Fig. 68   Test H: Radio Interference. 2001 Crown Victoria & Grand Marquis

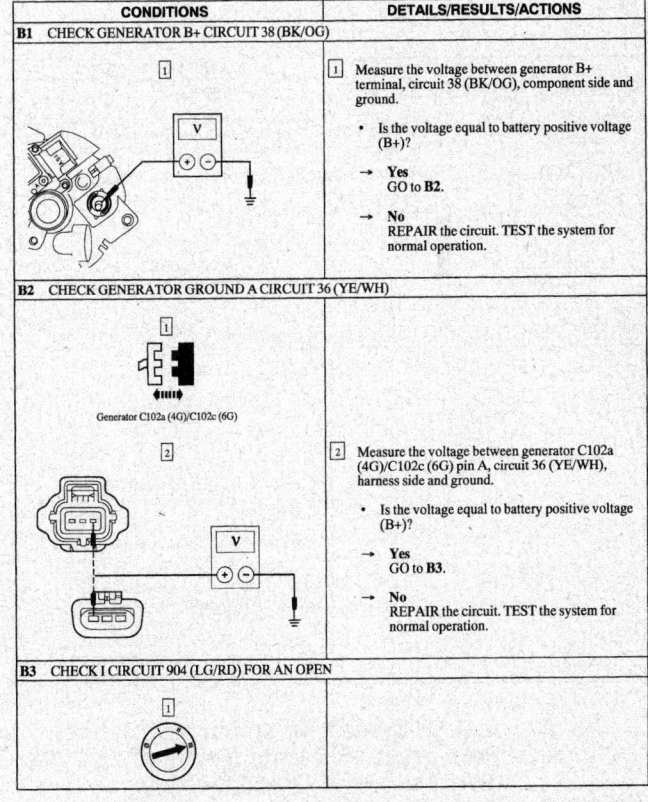

CONDITIONS	DETAILS/RESULTS/ACTIONS
B1 CHECK GENERATOR B+ CIRCUIT 38 (BK/OG)	
[1]	[1] Measure the voltage between generator B+ terminal, circuit 38 (BK/OG), component side and ground. • Is the voltage equal to battery positive voltage (B+)? → **Yes** GO to B2. → **No** REPAIR the circuit. TEST the system for normal operation.
B2 CHECK GENERATOR GROUND A CIRCUIT 36 (YE/WH)	
[1] Generator C102a (4G)/C102c (6G) [2]	[2] Measure the voltage between generator C102a (4G)/C102c (6G) pin A, circuit 36 (YE/WH), harness side and ground. • Is the voltage equal to battery positive voltage (B+)? → **Yes** GO to B3. → **No** REPAIR the circuit. TEST the system for normal operation.
B3 CHECK I CIRCUIT 904 (LG/RD) FOR AN OPEN	
[1]	

FM1120200741010X

Fig. 70   Test B: Charging System Warning Indicator Is On w/Engine Running, Engine Voltage Does Not Increase (Part 1 of 2). 2002 Crown Victoria & Grand Marquis

CONDITIONS	DETAILS/RESULTS/ACTIONS
B3 CHECK I CIRCUIT 904 (LG/RD) FOR AN OPEN (Continued)	
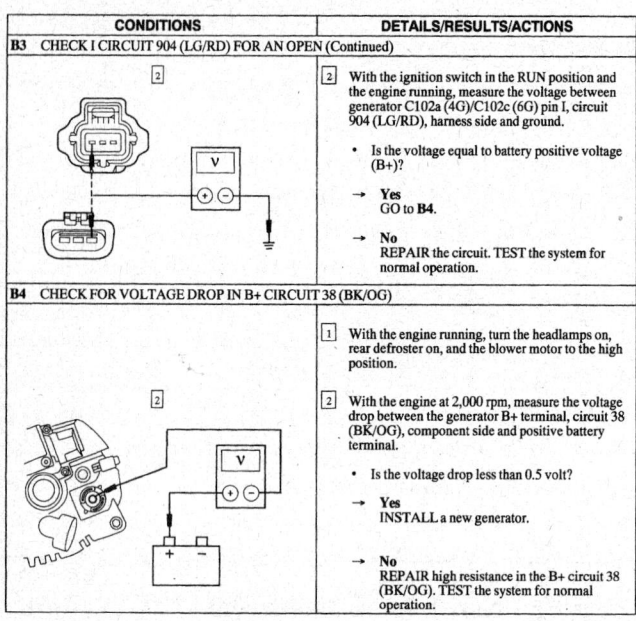 ②	With the ignition switch in the RUN position and the engine running, measure the voltage between generator C102a (4G)/C102c (6G) pin I, circuit 904 (LG/RD), harness side and ground. • Is the voltage equal to battery positive voltage (B+)? → **Yes** GO to **B4**. → **No** REPAIR the circuit. TEST the system for normal operation.
B4 CHECK FOR VOLTAGE DROP IN B+ CIRCUIT 38 (BK/OG)	
②	① With the engine running, turn the headlamps on, rear defroster on, and the blower motor to the high position. ② With the engine at 2,000 rpm, measure the voltage drop between the generator B+ terminal, circuit 38 (BK/OG), component side and positive battery terminal. • Is the voltage drop less than 0.5 volt? → **Yes** INSTALL a new generator. → **No** REPAIR high resistance in the B+ circuit 38 (BK/OG). TEST the system for normal operation.

FM1120200741020X

Fig. 70 Test B: Charging System Warning Indicator Is On w/Engine Running, Engine Voltage Does Not Increase (Part 2 of 2). 2002 Crown Victoria & Grand Marquis

CONDITIONS	DETAILS/RESULTS/ACTIONS
C1 CHECK FOR VOLTAGE DROP IN A CIRCUIT 36 (YE/WH) (Continued)	
③	③ Measure the voltage drop between generator C102a (4G)/C102c (6G) pin A, circuit 36 (YE/WH), harness side and positive battery terminal. • Is the voltage drop less than 0.5 volt? → **Yes** GO to **C2**. → **No** REPAIR the high resistance in A circuit 36 (YE/WH). TEST the system for normal operation.
C2 CHECK GENERATOR AND BATTERY GROUND CONNECTIONS	
①	② Check the ground connections between the generator and the engine, and the battery and the engine. • Are all ground connections clean and tight? → **Yes** INSTALL a new generator. TEST the system for normal operation. → **No** REPAIR ground connections as necessary. Test the system for normal operation.

FM1120200742020X

Fig. 71 Test C: System Overcharges, Battery Voltage Is More Than 15.5 Volts (Part 2 of 2). 2002 Crown Victoria & Grand Marquis

CONDITIONS	DETAILS/RESULTS/ACTIONS
C1 CHECK FOR VOLTAGE DROP IN A CIRCUIT 36 (YE/WH)	
① ② Generator C102a (4G)/C102c (6G)	

FM1120200742010X

Fig. 71 Test C: System Overcharges, Battery Voltage Is More Than 15.5 Volts (Part 1 of 2). 2002 Crown Victoria & Grand Marquis

CONDITIONS	DETAILS/RESULTS/ACTIONS
D1 CHECK I CIRCUIT 904 (LG/RD) FOR SHORT TO GROUND	
① ②	② With the ignition switch in the RUN position, check the charging system warning indicator. • Is the charging system warning indicator illuminated? → **Yes** REPAIR generator I circuit 904 (LG/RD) for a short to ground. TEST the system for normal operation. → **No** INSTALL a new generator. TEST the system for normal operation.

FM1120200743000X

Fig. 72 Test D: Charging System Warning Indicator Is On w/Engine Running & System Increases Voltage. 2002 Crown Victoria & Grand Marquis

CONDITIONS	DETAILS/RESULTS/ACTIONS
E1 CHECK THE CHARGING SYSTEM WARNING INDICATOR LAMP	
① ② ③	② With the engine off, connect a fused (15A) jumper wire between the generator C102a (4G)/C102c (6G) pin I, circuit 904 (LG/RD), harness side and ground.

FM1120200744010X

Fig. 73 Test E: Charging System Warning Indicator Is Off w/Ignition Switch In Run Position & Engine Off (Part 1 of 2). 2002 Crown Victoria & Grand Marquis

CONDITIONS	DETAILS/RESULTS/ACTIONS
E1 CHECK THE CHARGING SYSTEM WARNING INDICATOR LAMP (Continued)	
	• Is the charging system warning indicator lamp illuminated? → **Yes** INSTALL a new generator. TEST the system for normal operation. → **No** Test the instrument cluster.

FM1120200744020X

Fig. 73 Test E: Charging System Warning Indicator Is Off w/Ignition Switch In Run Position & Engine Off (Part 2 of 2). 2002 Crown Victoria & Grand Marquis

CONDITIONS	DETAILS/RESULTS/ACTIONS
F1 CHECK FOR LOOSE CONNECTIONS	

	☐1 Check all generator, battery, and power distribution connections for looseness, corrosion, loose or bent terminals, or loose eyelets.
	
	• Are all connections clean and tight?
	
	→ **Yes**
	  GO to **F2**.
	
	→ **No**
	  REPAIR as necessary. TEST the system for normal operation.

F2 CHECK FUSE CONNECTIONS	

☐1	☐1 With the engine running, check BJB fuse 2 (30A) in A circuit 36 (YE/WH) and the CJB fuse 14 (10A) in I circuit 904 (LG/RD) for looseness by wiggling the fuse and noting the charging system warning indicator lamp operation.
	
	• Does the charging system warning indicator flicker?
	
	→ **Yes**
	  REPAIR loose fuse connection(s) as necessary. TEST the system for normal operation.
	
	→ **No**
	  GO to **F3**.

FM1120200745010X

Fig. 74 Test F: Charging System Warning Indicator Flickers Or Is Intermittent (Part 1 of 2). 2002 Crown Victoria & Grand Marquis

CONDITIONS	DETAILS/RESULTS/ACTIONS
F3 CHECK A CIRCUIT 36 (YE/WH) CONNECTIONS	

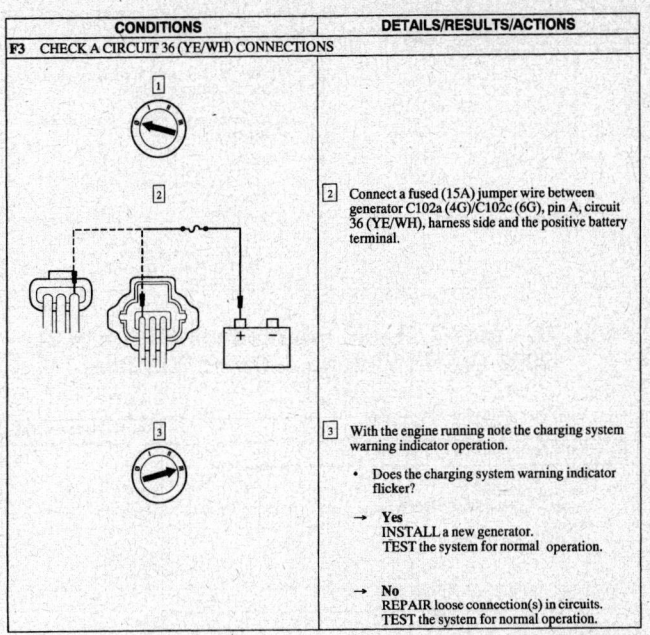	☐2 Connect a fused (15A) jumper wire between generator C102a (4G)/C102c (6G), pin A, circuit 36 (YE/WH), harness side and the positive battery terminal.
	
	☐3 With the engine running note the charging system warning indicator operation.
	
	• Does the charging system warning indicator flicker?
	
	→ **Yes**
	  INSTALL a new generator. TEST the system for normal operation.
	
	→ **No**
	  REPAIR loose connection(s) in circuits. TEST the system for normal operation.

FM1120200745020X

Fig. 74 Test F: Charging System Warning Indicator Flickers Or Is Intermittent (Part 2 of 2). 2002 Crown Victoria & Grand Marquis

CONDITIONS	DETAILS/RESULTS/ACTIONS
G1 CHECK FOR ACCESSORY DRIVE NOISE	

	☐1 Check the accessory drive belt for damage and correct installation. Check the accessory mounting brackets and generator pulley for looseness or misalignment.
	
	• Is the accessory drive OK?
	
	→ **Yes**
	  GO to **G2**.
	
	→ **No**
	  REPAIR as necessary. TEST the system for normal operation.

G2 CHECK GENERATOR MOUNTING	

	☐1 Check the generator mounting for loose bolts or misalignment.
	
	• Is the generator mounted correctly?
	
	→ **Yes**
	  GO to **G3**.
	
	→ **No**
	  REPAIR as necessary. TEST the system for normal operation.

G3 CHECK GENERATOR FOR ELECTRICAL NOISE	

Generator C102a (4G)/C102c (6G)	☐3 With the engine running, listen for the concern. Use a stethoscope or equivalent listening device, if necessary.
	
	• Is the noise still present?
	
	→ **Yes**
	  GO to **G4**.
	
	→ **No**
	  INSTALL a new generator. TEST the system for normal operation.

FM1120200746010X

Fig. 75 Test G: Alternator Is Noisy (Part 1 of 2). 2002 Crown Victoria & Grand Marquis

CONDITIONS	DETAILS/RESULTS/ACTIONS
G4 CHECK GENERATOR FOR MECHANICAL NOISE	

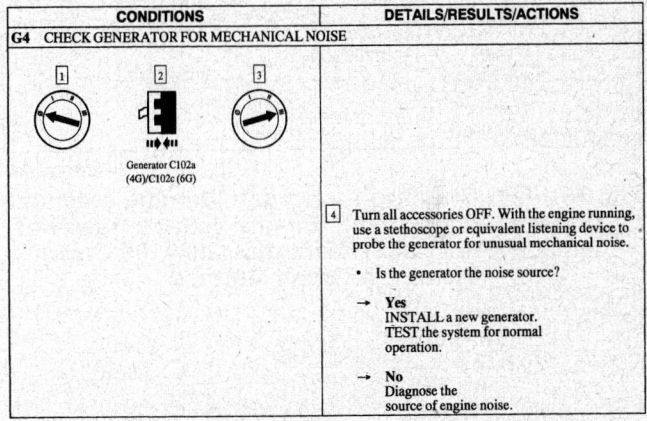
Generator C102a (4G)/C102c (6G)
	☐4 Turn all accessories OFF. With the engine running, use a stethoscope or equivalent listening device to probe the generator for unusual mechanical noise.
	
	• Is the generator the noise source?
	
	→ **Yes**
	  INSTALL a new generator. TEST the system for normal operation.
	
	→ **No**
	  Diagnose the source of engine noise.

FM1120200746020X

Fig. 75 Test G: Alternator Is Noisy (Part 2 of 2). 2002 Crown Victoria & Grand Marquis

CONDITIONS	DETAILS/RESULTS/ACTIONS
H1 VERIFY GENERATOR IS SOURCE OF RADIO INTERFERENCE	
	☐2 With the engine running, tune the radio to a station where the interference is present.

FM1120200747010X

Fig. 76 Test H: Radio Interference (Part 1 of 2). 2002 Crown Victoria & Grand Marquis

CONDITIONS	DETAILS/RESULTS/ACTIONS
H1 VERIFY GENERATOR IS SOURCE OF RADIO INTERFERENCE (Continued)	
	6 Tune the radio to a station where the interference is present, with the engine running. • Is the interference present with the generator disconnected? → **Yes** Test the in-vehicle entertainment system. → **No** INSTALL a new generator. TEST the system for normal operation.

FM1120200747020X

Fig. 76 Test H: Radio Interference (Part 2 of 2). 2002 Crown Victoria & Grand Marquis

Test Step	Result / Action to Take
B1 CHECK THE FAULT CODES IN THE PCM	
• Connect the diagnostic tool. • Key in ON position. • Use the recorded PCM DTCs from the continuous and on-demand self-test. • Are any DTCs recorded?	**Yes** REFER to PCM Diagnostic Trouble Code (DTC) Index. **No** GO to B2 .
B2 CHECK CIRCUIT 904 (LG/RD)	
• Key in OFF position. • Disconnect the diagnostic tool. • Disconnect: Generator C102a (4G), C102c (6G). • Key in ON position. • Measure the voltage between the generator C102a (4G), C102c (6G) pin 2, circuit 904 (LG/RD), harness side and ground. • Is the voltage 0 volts?	**Yes** GO to B3 . **No** GO to B4 .

ARM66FM000000069

Fig. 78 Test B: Charging System Warning Indicator Is On w/Engine Running, Engine Voltage Does Not Increase (Part 1 of 2). Marauder, 2003–05 Crown Victoria & Grand Marquis

Test Step	Result / Action to Take
A1 CHECK BATTERY CONDITION	
• Carry out the Battery — Condition Test to determine if the battery can hold a charge and is OK for use. • Is the battery OK?	**Yes** GO to A2 . **No** INSTALL a new battery. TEST the system for normal operation.
A2 CHECK THE GENERATOR OUTPUT	
• Carry out the Generator On-Vehicle Test—Load Test and No-Load Test. • Is the generator OK?	**Yes** GO to A3 . **No** Go To Pinpoint Test B .
A3 CHECK FOR CURRENT DRAINS	
• Carry out the Battery — Drain Testing. • Are there any excessive current drains?	**Yes** REPAIR as necessary. TEST the system for normal operation. **No** Go To Pinpoint Test B .

ARM66FM000000068

Fig. 77 Test A: Battery Is Discharged Or Battery Voltage Is Low. Marauder, 2003–05 Crown Victoria & Grand Marquis

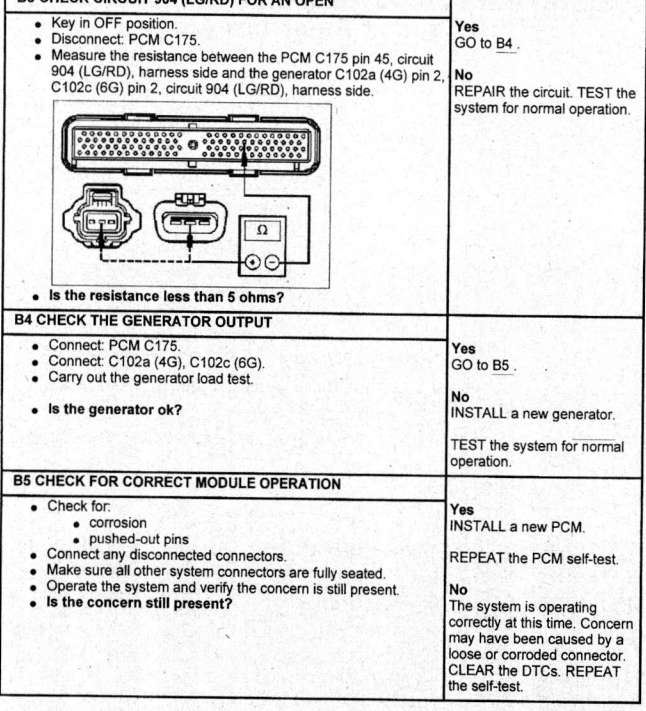

Test Step	Result / Action to Take
B3 CHECK CIRCUIT 904 (LG/RD) FOR AN OPEN	
• Key in OFF position. • Disconnect: PCM C175. • Measure the resistance between the PCM C175 pin 45, circuit 904 (LG/RD), harness side and the generator C102a (4G) pin 2, C102c (6G) pin 2, circuit 904 (LG/RD), harness side. • Is the resistance less than 5 ohms?	**Yes** GO to B4 . **No** REPAIR the circuit. TEST the system for normal operation.
B4 CHECK THE GENERATOR OUTPUT	
• Connect: PCM C175. • Connect: C102a (4G), C102c (6G). • Carry out the generator load test. • Is the generator ok?	**Yes** GO to B5 . **No** INSTALL a new generator. TEST the system for normal operation.
B5 CHECK FOR CORRECT MODULE OPERATION	

• Check for:
   • corrosion
   • pushed-out pins
 • Connect any disconnected connectors.
 • Make sure all other system connectors are fully seated.
 • Operate the system and verify the concern is still present.
 • Is the concern still present?
	Yes
	 INSTALL a new PCM.
	 REPEAT the PCM self-test.
	
	 No
	 The system is operating correctly at this time. Concern may have been caused by a loose or corroded connector. CLEAR the DTCs. REPEAT the self-test.

ARM66FM000000070

Fig. 78 Test B: Charging System Warning Indicator Is On w/Engine Running, Engine Voltage Does Not Increase (Part 2 of 2). Marauder, 2003–05 Crown Victoria & Grand Marquis

Test Step	Result / Action to Take
C1 CHECK THE FAULT CODES IN THE PCM	
• Connect the diagnostic tool. • Key in ON position. • Use the recorded PCM DTCs from the continuous and on-demand self-test. • **Are any DTCs recorded?**	**Yes** REFER to PCM Diagnostic Trouble Code (DTC) Index. **No** GO to C2.
C2 CHECK THE BATTERY VOLTAGE	
• Key in OFF position. • Disconnect the diagnostic tool. • Key in START position. • With the engine running and all accessories turned off, measure the voltage at the battery while varying the engine rpm. 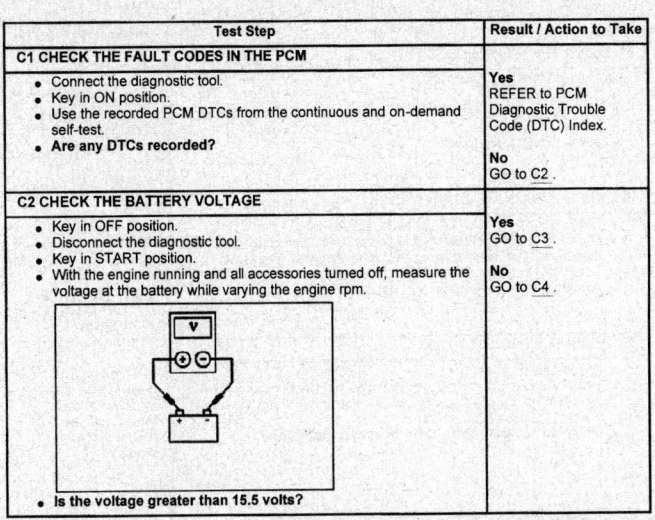 • **Is the voltage greater than 15.5 volts?**	**Yes** GO to C3. **No** GO to C4.

ARM66FM000000071

Fig. 79 Test C: System Overcharges, Battery Voltage More Than 15.5 Volts (Part 1 of 2). Marauder, 2003–05 Crown Victoria & Grand Marquis

Test Step	Result / Action to Take
C3 CHECK CIRCUIT 36 (YE/WH)	
• Measure the voltage between the generator C102a (4G) pin 3, C102c (6G) pin 3, circuit 36 (YE/WH), harness side and ground. 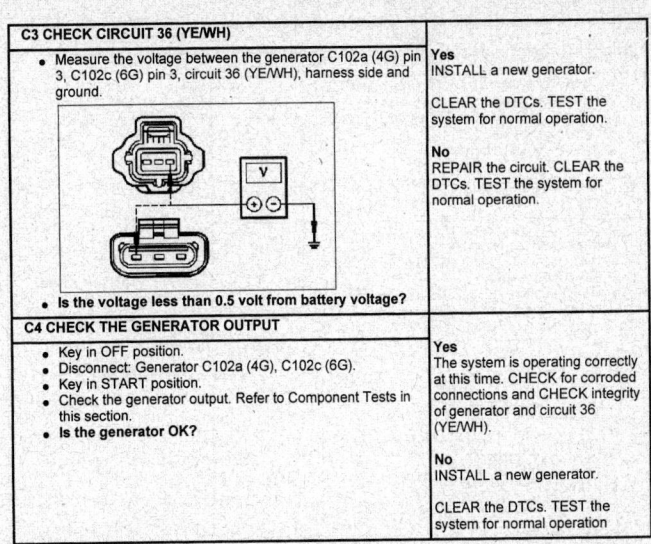 • **Is the voltage less than 0.5 volt from battery voltage?**	**Yes** INSTALL a new generator. CLEAR the DTCs. TEST the system for normal operation. **No** REPAIR the circuit. CLEAR the DTCs. TEST the system for normal operation.
C4 CHECK THE GENERATOR OUTPUT	
• Key in OFF position. • Disconnect: Generator C102a (4G), C102c (6G). • Key in START position. • Check the generator output. Refer to Component Tests in this section. • **Is the generator OK?**	**Yes** The system is operating correctly at this time. CHECK for corroded connections and CHECK integrity of generator and circuit 36 (YE/WH). **No** INSTALL a new generator. CLEAR the DTCs. TEST the system for normal operation

ARM66FM000000072

Fig. 79 Test C: System Overcharges, Battery Voltage More Than 15.5 Volts (Part 2 of 2). Marauder, 2003–05 Crown Victoria & Grand Marquis

Test Step	Result / Action to Take
D1 CHECK THE FAULT CODES IN THE PCM	
• Connect the diagnostic tool. • Key in ON position. • Use the recorded PCM DTCs from the continuous and on-demand self-test. • **Are any DTCs recorded?**	**Yes** REFER to PCM Diagnostic Trouble Code (DTC) Index. **No** GO to D2.
D2 CHECK THE SYSTEM FOR OVERCHARGING	
• Key in OFF position. • Disconnect the diagnostic tool. • Key in START position. • With the engine running and all accessories off, measure the voltage at the battery terminals while varying the engine rpm. • **Is the voltage greater than 15.5 volts?**	**Yes** Go To Pinpoint Test C. **No** GO to D3.

ARM66FM000000073

Fig. 80 Test D: Charging System Warning Indicator Is On w/Engine Running, System Increases Voltage (Part 1 of 2). Marauder, 2003–05 Crown Victoria & Grand Marquis

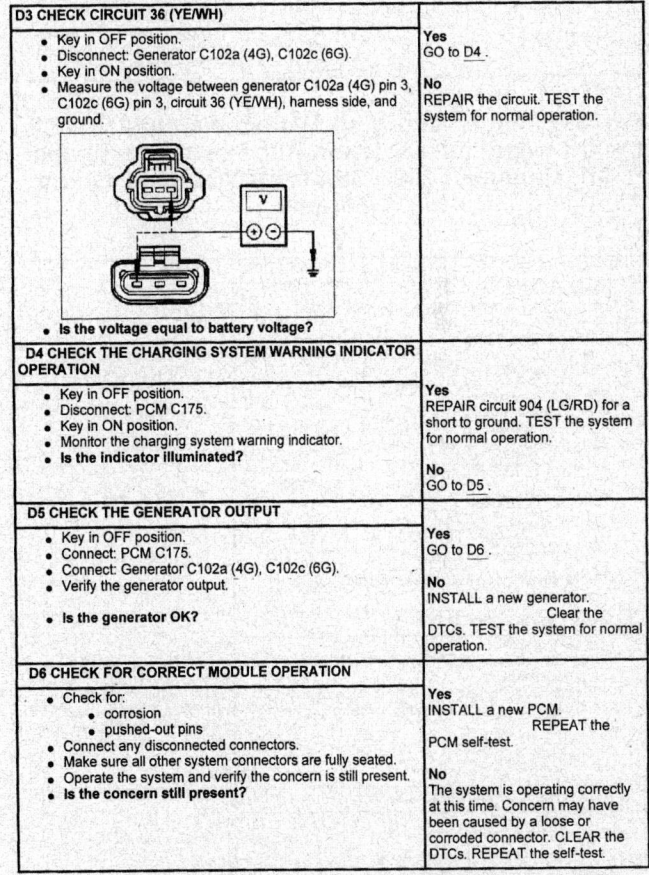

Test Step	Result / Action to Take
D3 CHECK CIRCUIT 36 (YE/WH)	
• Key in OFF position. • Disconnect: Generator C102a (4G), C102c (6G). • Key in ON position. • Measure the voltage between generator C102a (4G) pin 3, C102c (6G) pin 3, circuit 36 (YE/WH), harness side, and ground. • **Is the voltage equal to battery voltage?**	**Yes** GO to D4. **No** REPAIR the circuit. TEST the system for normal operation.
D4 CHECK THE CHARGING SYSTEM WARNING INDICATOR OPERATION	
• Key in OFF position. • Disconnect: PCM C175. • Key in ON position. • Monitor the charging system warning indicator. • **Is the indicator illuminated?**	**Yes** REPAIR circuit 904 (LG/RD) for a short to ground. TEST the system for normal operation. **No** GO to D5.
D5 CHECK THE GENERATOR OUTPUT	
• Key in OFF position. • Connect: PCM C175. • Connect: Generator C102a (4G), C102c (6G). • Verify the generator output. • **Is the generator OK?**	**Yes** GO to D6. **No** INSTALL a new generator. Clear the DTCs. TEST the system for normal operation.
D6 CHECK FOR CORRECT MODULE OPERATION	
• Check for: • corrosion • pushed-out pins • Connect any disconnected connectors. • Make sure all other system connectors are fully seated. • Operate the system and verify the concern is still present. • **Is the concern still present?**	**Yes** INSTALL a new PCM. REPEAT the PCM self-test. **No** The system is operating correctly at this time. Concern may have been caused by a loose or corroded connector. CLEAR the DTCs. REPEAT the self-test.

ARM66FM000000074

Fig. 80 Test D: Charging System Warning Indicator Is On w/Engine Running, System Increases Voltage (Part 2 of 2). Marauder, 2003–05 Crown Victoria & Grand Marquis

Test Step	Result / Action to Take
E1 CHECK THE FAULT CODES IN THE PCM • Connect the diagnostic tool. • Key in ON position. • Use the recorded PCM DTCs from the continuous and on-demand self-test. • **Are any DTCs recorded?**	**Yes** REFER to PCM Diagnostic Trouble Code (DTC) Index. **No** GO to E2 .
E2 CHECK THE CHARGING SYSTEM WARNING INDICATOR OPERATION • Key in OFF position. • Disconnect the diagnostic tool. • Disconnect: Generator C102a (4G), C102c (6G). • Key in ON position. • With the engine off, connect a fused (15A) jumper wire between the generator C102a (4G) pin 2, C102c (6G) pin 2, circuit 904 (LG/RD), harness side and ground. • **Does the charging system warning indicator illuminate?**	**Yes** INSTALL a new generator. TEST the system for normal operation. **No** GO to E3 .

E3 CHECK FOR CORRECT MODULE OPERATION
• Check for:
  • corrosion
  • pushed-out pins
• Connect any disconnected connectors.
• Make sure all other system connectors are fully seated.
• Operate the system and verify the concern is still present.
• **Is the concern still present?**
	Yes
	INSTALL a new PCM. REPEAT the PCM self-test.
	
	No
	The system is operating correctly at this time. Concern may have been caused by a loose or corroded connector. CLEAR the DTCs. REPEAT the self-test.

ARM66FM000000075

Fig. 81 Test E: Charging System Warning Indicator Is Off w/Ignition Switch In Run Position & Engine Off. Marauder, 2003–05 Crown Victoria & Grand Marquis

Test Step	Result / Action to Take
F5 CHECK THE WARNING SYSTEM INDICATOR OPERATION • Key in OFF position. • Disconnect: Generator C102a (4G), C102c (6G). • Key in ON position. • Connect a fused jumper wire between generator C102a (4G) pin 2, C102c (6G) pin 2, circuit 904 (LG/RD), harness side and ground. • **Does the charging system warning indicator illuminate?**	**Yes** GO to F6 . **No** REPAIR the circuit. TEST the system for normal operation.
F6 CHECK THE PCM OPERATION • Key in OFF position. • Connect: Generator C102a (4G), C102c (6G). • Key in ON position. • Monitor the charging system warning indicator operation. • **Is the charging system warning indicator illuminated?**	**Yes** The PCM is operating correctly. RECHECK the generator circuits (including the generator) for intermittent shorts or opens. TEST the system for normal operation. **No** GO to F7 .

F7 CHECK FOR CORRECT MODULE OPERATION
• Check for:
  • corrosion
  • pushed-out pins
• Connect any disconnected connectors.
• Make sure all other system connectors are fully seated.
• Operate the system and verify the concern is still present.
• **Is the concern still present?**
	Yes
	INSTALL a new PCM. REPEAT the PCM self-test.
	
	No
	The system is operating correctly at this time. Concern may have been caused by a loose or corroded connector. CLEAR the DTCs. REPEAT the self-test.

ARM66FM000000077

Fig. 82 Test F: Charging System Warning Indicator Lamp Flickers Or Is Intermittent (Part 2 of 2). Marauder, 2003–05 Crown Victoria & Grand Marquis

Test Step	Result / Action to Take
F1 CHECK THE FAULT CODES IN THE PCM • Connect the diagnostic tool. • Key in ON position. • Use the recorded PCM DTCs from the continuous and on-demand self-test. • **Are any DTCs recorded?**	**Yes** REFER to PCM Diagnostic Trouble Code (DTC) Index. **No** GO to F2 .
F2 CHECK FOR LOOSE CONNECTIONS • Disconnect: Generator C102a (4G), C102c (6G). • Check all generator, battery, and power distribution connections for looseness, corrosion, loose or bent terminals, or loose eyelets. • Connect: Generator C102a (4G), C102c (6G). • **Are all connections clean and tight?**	**Yes** GO to F3 . **No** REPAIR as necessary. TEST the system for normal operation.
F3 CHECK FUSE CONNECTIONS • Key in START position. • With the engine running, check BJB fuse 101 (30A) in circuit 37 (YE) for looseness by wiggling the fuse and noting the charging system warning indicator lamp operation. • **Does the charging system warning indicator flicker?**	**Yes** REPAIR loose fuse connection(s) as necessary. TEST the system for normal operation. **No** GO to F4 .
F4 CHECK THE BATTERY VOLTAGE • Key in START position. • With the engine running, and all accessories turned off, measure the voltage at the battery while varying the engine rpm. • **Is the voltage greater than 15.5 volts?**	**Yes** Go To Pinpoint Test C . **No** GO to F5 .

ARM66FM000000076

Fig. 82 Test F: Charging System Warning Indicator Lamp Flickers Or Is Intermittent (Part 1 of 2). Marauder, 2003–05 Crown Victoria & Grand Marquis

Test Step	Result / Action to Take
G1 CHECK FOR ACCESSORY DRIVE NOISE • Check the accessory drive belt for damage and correct installation. • Check the accessory mounting brackets and generator pulley for looseness or misalignment. • **Is the accessory drive OK?**	**Yes** If equipped with a one-way clutch (OWC) pulley, GO to G2 . If not equipped with a OWC pulley, GO to G3 . **No** REPAIR as necessary. TEST the system for normal operation.
G2 CHECK ONE-WAY CLUTCH (OWC) PULLEY • With the front-end accessory drive (FEAD) belt removed, spin the OWC pulley in a clockwise direction, then reverse the direction of the pulley by spinning it in a counterclockwise direction. • **Does the OWC pulley engage with the rotor when spun in a clockwise direction and free-wheel when spun in a counterclockwise direction with minimal noise as compared to a known good vehicle?**	**Yes** GO to G3 . **No** INSTALL a new generator assembly with OWC pulley. TEST the system for normal operation.
G3 CHECK GENERATOR MOUNTING • Check the generator mounting for loose bolts or misalignment. • **Is the generator mounted correctly?**	**Yes** GO to G4 . **No** REPAIR as necessary. TEST the system for normal operation.

ARM66FM000000078

Fig. 83 Test G: Alternator Is Noisy (Part 1 of 2). Marauder, 2003–05 Crown Victoria & Grand Marquis

G4 CHECK GENERATOR FOR ELECTRICAL NOISE	
• Disconnect: Generator C102a (4G), C102c (6G). • Key in START position. • With the engine running. • **Is the noise still present?**	**Yes** GO to G5. **No** INSTALL a new generator. TEST the system for normal operation.
G5 CHECK GENERATOR FOR MECHANICAL NOISE	
• Key in OFF position. • Key in START position. • Turn all accessories OFF. With the engine running, use a stethoscope or equivalent listening device to probe the generator for unusual mechanical noise. • **Is the generator the noise source?**	**Yes** INSTALL a new generator. TEST the system for normal operation. **No** diagnose the source of the engine noise.

ARM66FM000000079

Fig. 83 Test G: Alternator Is Noisy (Part 2 of 2). Marauder, 2003–05 Crown Victoria & Grand Marquis

TEST CONDITIONS	TEST DETAILS/RESULTS/ACTIONS
A1 CHECK CIRCUIT 9 (W/GN) FOR VOLTAGE	
	② Measure the voltage between voltage regulator terminal A, circuit 9 (W/GN), and the battery positive post. • Is the voltage less than 0.25 volts? → **Yes** GO to A2. → **No** REPAIR circuit 9 (W/GN). TEST the system for normal operation.

FM1129800228010X

Fig. 85 Test A: System Overcharges (Part 1 of 2). Escort & ZX2

TEST CONDITIONS	TEST DETAILS/RESULTS/ACTIONS
B1 CHECK SYSTEM VOLTAGE	
	① Perform No-Load Test in this section. • Is the system voltage below the specified range (undercharging)? → **Yes** GO to B2. → **No** REPAIR circuit 20 (W/BL) for short to ground. TEST the system for normal operation.
B2 CHECK CIRCUIT 9 (W/GN) FOR OPEN	
	② Measure the voltage between voltage regulator terminal A and ground. • Is the voltage equal to battery voltage? → **Yes** GO to B3. → **No** REPAIR circuit 9 (W/GN). TEST the system for normal operation.

FM1129800229010X

Fig. 86 Test B: Warning Indicator Stays On (Part 1 of 4). Escort & ZX2

Test Step	Result / Action to Take
H1 VERIFY GENERATOR IS SOURCE OF RADIO INTERFERENCE	
• Key in START position. • Start and run the engine. • Tune the radio to a station where the interference is present. • Key in OFF position. • Disconnect: Generator C102a (4G), C102c (6G). • Key in START position. • **Is the interference present with the generator disconnected?**	**Yes** diagnose and test the in-vehicle entertainment system. **No** INSTALL a new generator. TEST the system for normal operation.

ARM66FM000000080

Fig. 84 Test H: Radio Interference. Marauder, 2003–05 Crown Victoria & Grand Marquis

TEST CONDITIONS	TEST DETAILS/RESULTS/ACTIONS
A2 CHECK CIRCUIT 21 (O) FOR OPEN	
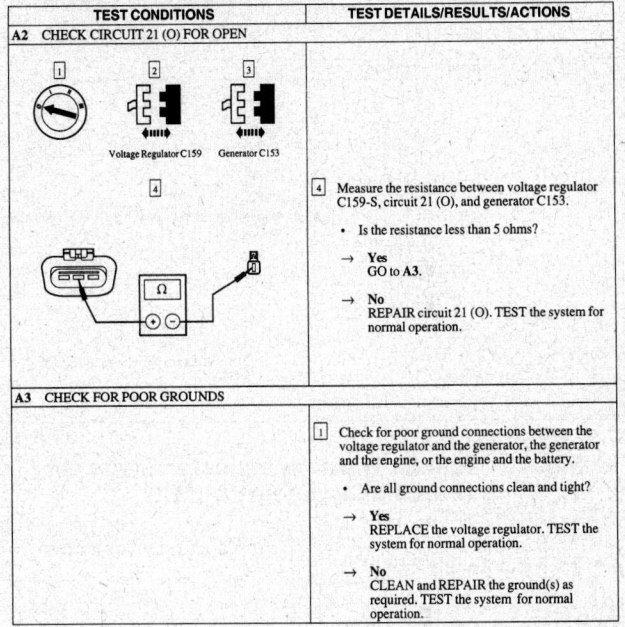	④ Measure the resistance between voltage regulator C159-S, circuit 21 (O), and generator C153. • Is the resistance less than 5 ohms? → **Yes** GO to A3. → **No** REPAIR circuit 21 (O). TEST the system for normal operation.
A3 CHECK FOR POOR GROUNDS	
	① Check for poor ground connections between the voltage regulator and the generator, the generator and the engine, or the engine and the battery. • Are all ground connections clean and tight? → **Yes** REPLACE the voltage regulator. TEST the system for normal operation. → **No** CLEAN and REPAIR the ground(s) as required. TEST the system for normal operation.

FM1129800228020X

Fig. 85 Test A: System Overcharges (Part 2 of 2). Escort & ZX2

TEST CONDITIONS	TEST DETAILS/RESULTS/ACTIONS
B3 CHECK CIRCUIT 20 (W/BL) FOR OPEN	
	• Is the warning indicator lamp on? → **Yes** REPAIR circuit 20 (W/BL). TEST the system for normal operation. → **No** GO to B4.
B4 VERIFY CIRCUIT 21 (O) OPERATES	
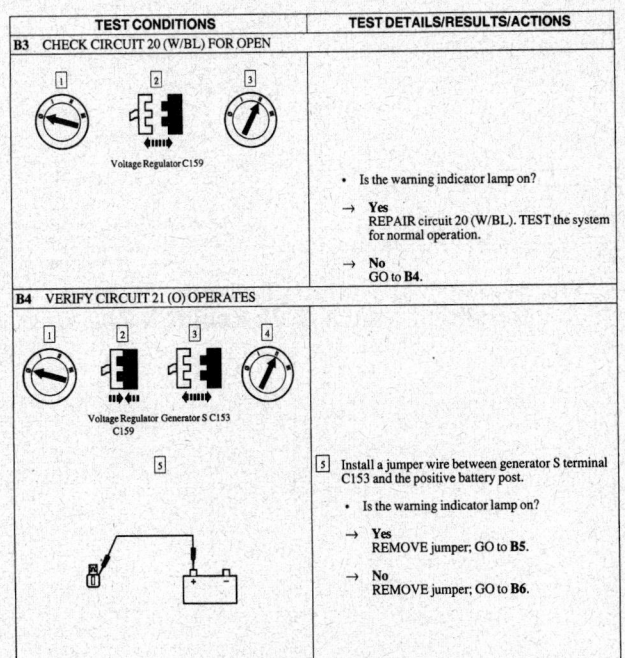	⑤ Install a jumper wire between generator S terminal C153 and the positive battery post. • Is the warning indicator lamp on? → **Yes** REMOVE jumper; GO to B5. → **No** REMOVE jumper; GO to B6.

FM1129800229020X

Fig. 86 Test B: Warning Indicator Stays On (Part 2 of 4). Escort & ZX2

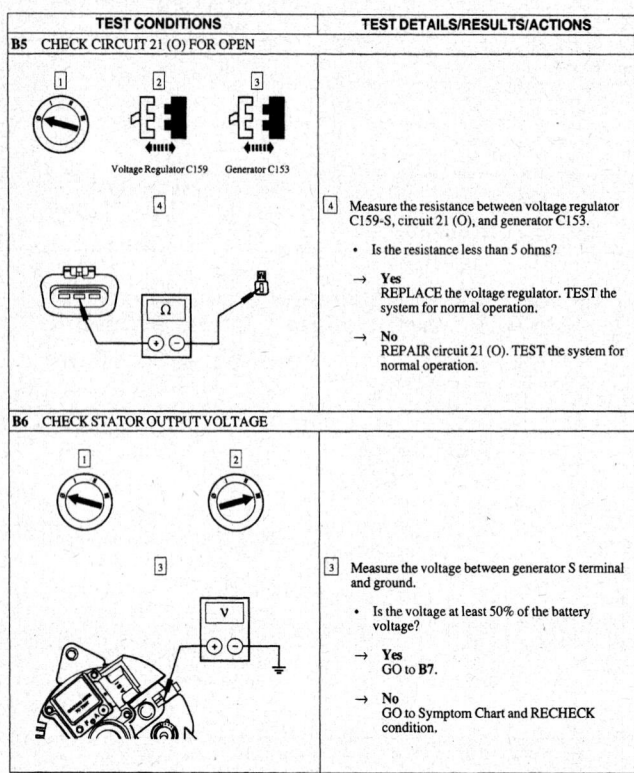

TEST CONDITIONS	TEST DETAILS/RESULTS/ACTIONS
B5 CHECK CIRCUIT 21 (O) FOR OPEN	

Voltage Regulator C159   Generator C153

4 Measure the resistance between voltage regulator C159-S, circuit 21 (O), and generator C153.

- Is the resistance less than 5 ohms?

→ **Yes**
REPLACE the voltage regulator. TEST the system for normal operation.

→ **No**
REPAIR circuit 21 (O). TEST the system for normal operation.

TEST CONDITIONS	TEST DETAILS/RESULTS/ACTIONS
B6 CHECK STATOR OUTPUT VOLTAGE	

3 Measure the voltage between generator S terminal and ground.

- Is the voltage at least 50% of the battery voltage?

→ **Yes**
GO to B7.

→ **No**
GO to Symptom Chart and RECHECK condition.

FM1129800229030X

Fig. 86   Test B: Warning Indicator Stays On (Part 3 of 4). Escort & ZX2

TEST CONDITIONS	TEST DETAILS/RESULTS/ACTIONS
C1 CHECK FOR LOOSE CONNECTIONS	

2 Check the following connections for corrosion, loose or bent pins and/or terminals, or loose eyelets:
— Voltage regulator connector.
— Generator S terminal connector.
— Generator B+ eyelet.
— Power distribution box eyelets.
— Battery cables.

- Are all connections clean and tight?

→ **Yes**
GO to C2.

→ **No**
REPAIR or CLEAN connections as required. TEST the system for normal operation.

FM1129800230010X

Fig. 87   Test C: Warning Indicator Flickers/ Intermittent (Part 1 of 2). Escort & ZX2

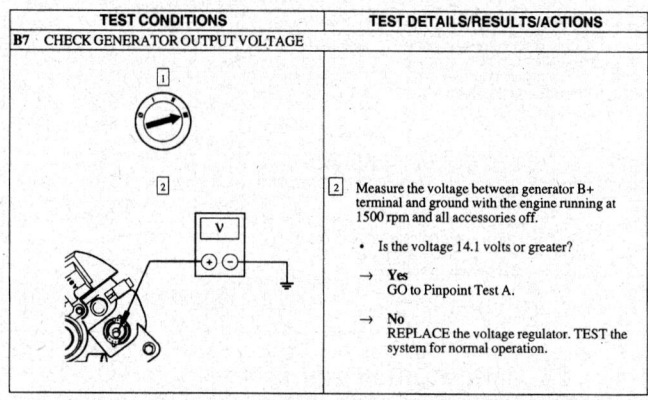

TEST CONDITIONS	TEST DETAILS/RESULTS/ACTIONS
B7 CHECK GENERATOR OUTPUT VOLTAGE	

2 Measure the voltage between generator B+ terminal and ground with the engine running at 1500 rpm and all accessories off.

- Is the voltage 14.1 volts or greater?

→ **Yes**
GO to Pinpoint Test A.

→ **No**
REPLACE the voltage regulator. TEST the system for normal operation.

FM1129800229040X

Fig. 86   Test B: Warning Indicator Stays On (Part 4 of 4). Escort & ZX2

TEST CONDITIONS	TEST DETAILS/RESULTS/ACTIONS
C2 CHECK BRUSH HOLDER SCREWS	

1 Check voltage regulator brush holder screws (test points A and F).

- Are the brush holder screws tight?

→ **Yes**
GO to C3.

→ **No**
TEST the system for normal operation.

| **C3** CHECK FOR GROUNDED SLIP RING | |

Voltage Regulator C159

2 Remove the voltage regulator from the generator housing.

3 Measure the resistance between each generator slip ring and generator housing.

- Is the resistance between any slip ring and generator housing 200 ohms or less?

→ **Yes**
CLEAN the slip rings and MEASURE the resistance of the slip rings again. If still less than 200 ohms, REPLACE the generator. TEST the system for normal operation.

→ **No**
REPLACE the voltage regulator. TEST the system for normal operation.

FM1129800230020X

Fig. 87   Test C: Warning Indicator Flickers/ Intermittent (Part 2 of 2). Escort & ZX2

TEST CONDITIONS	TEST DETAILS/RESULTS/ACTIONS
D1 CHECK FOR ACCESSORY DRIVE NOISE	

1 Check the drive belt for damage and verify correct installation

2 Check the accessory mounting brackets for loose bolts or misalignment.

FM1129800231010X

Fig. 88   Test D: Alternator Is Noisy (Part 1 of 2). Escort & ZX2

TEST CONDITIONS	TEST DETAILS/RESULTS/ACTIONS
D1 CHECK FOR ACCESSORY DRIVE NOISE (Continued)	3 Check for a bent pulley. • Is the accessory drive belt system OK? → **Yes** GO to **D2**. → **No** Inspect accessory drive system and repair as necessary.
D2 SUBSTITUTE KNOWN GOOD GENERATOR 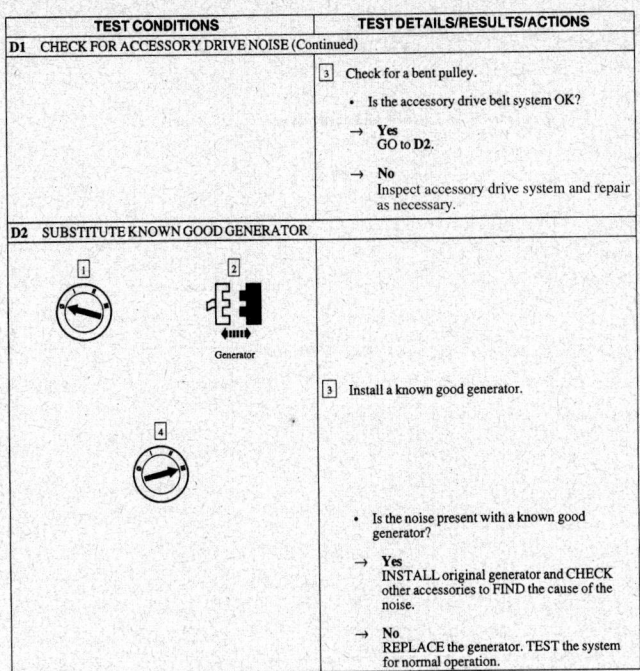	3 Install a known good generator. • Is the noise present with a known good generator? → **Yes** INSTALL original generator and CHECK other accessories to FIND the cause of the noise. → **No** REPLACE the generator. TEST the system for normal operation.

FM1129800231020X

Fig. 88   Test D: Alternator Is Noisy (Part 2 of 2). Escort & ZX2

TEST CONDITIONS	TEST DETAILS/RESULTS/ACTIONS
F1 CHECK BATTERY	2 Inspect condition of battery. • Is the battery OK? → **Yes** GO to **F2**. → **No** REPLACE the battery. TEST the system for normal operation.

FM1129800233010X

Fig. 90   Test F: Battery Does Not Hold A Charge (Part 1 of 2). Escort & ZX2

TEST CONDITIONS	TEST DETAILS/RESULTS/ACTIONS
G1 CHECK DRIVE BELT TENSION	1 Inspect the drive belt tension • Is the drive belt tension correct? → **Yes** GO to **G2**. → **No** REPLACE the drive belt or drive belt tensioner. TEST the system for normal operation.
G2 CHECK SYSTEM VOLTAGE	1 Perform No-Load Test. • Is the system voltage below the specified range (undercharging)? → **Yes** GO to Pinpoint Test B. → **No** Perform Drain Testing in this section. REPAIR the system in question. TEST the system for normal operation.

FM1129800234000X

Fig. 91   Test G: System Does Not Charge. Escort & ZX2

TEST CONDITIONS	TEST DETAILS/RESULTS/ACTIONS
E1 VERIFY RADIO INTERFERENCE 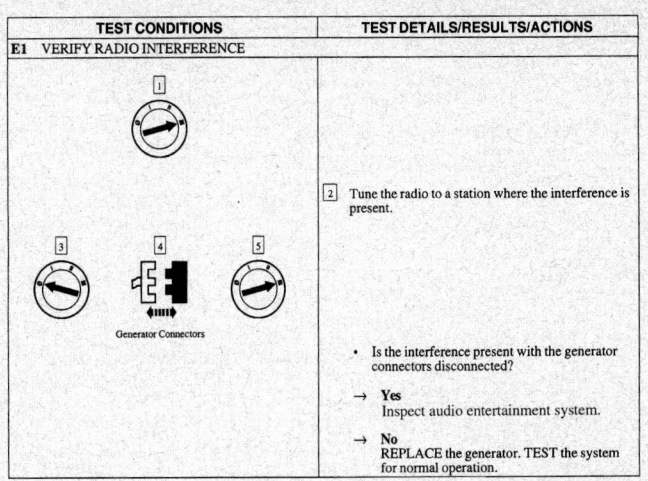 Generator Connectors	2 Tune the radio to a station where the interference is present. • Is the interference present with the generator connectors disconnected? → **Yes** Inspect audio entertainment system. → **No** REPLACE the generator. TEST the system for normal operation.

FM1129800232000X

Fig. 89   Test E: Radio Interference. Escort & ZX2

TEST CONDITIONS	TEST DETAILS/RESULTS/ACTIONS
F2 CHECK FOR KEY-OFF DRAIN	1 Perform the Drain Testing. • Is the drain less than 0.05 amps? → **Yes** GO to Pinpoint Test G. → **No** REPAIR the system in question. TEST the system for normal operation.

FM1129800233020X

Fig. 90   Test F: Battery Does Not Hold A Charge (Part 2 of 2). Escort & ZX2

Test Step	Result / Action to Take
A1 CHECK THE BATTERY CONDITION • Carry out the Battery — Condition Test to determine if the battery can hold a charge and is OK for use. • Does the battery pass the condition test?	**Yes** GO to **A2**. **No** INSTALL a new battery.
A2 CHECK THE GENERATOR OUTPUT • Carry out the Generator On-Vehicle Load Test and No Load Test. Refer to Component Tests in this section. • Does the generator pass the component tests?	**Yes** GO to **A3**. **No** INSTALL a new generator
A3 CHECK FOR CURRENT DRAINS • Carry out the Battery — Drain Test. • Are any excessive current drains present?	**Yes** REPAIR as necessary. TEST the system for normal operation. **No** GO to **A4**.
A4 CHECK THE VEHICLE GROUNDS • Key in START position. • With the engine running, measure the voltage drop between the generator housing and the negative battery terminal. • Is the voltage drop less than 0.1 volt?	**Yes** GO to **A5**. **No** CHECK the engine ground, generator ground and the battery ground for corrosion. TEST the system for normal operation.
A5 CHECK THE VOLTAGE DROP IN THE B+ CIRCUIT • With the engine running, measure the voltage drop between the generator B+ C102b, circuit 38 (BK/OG) and the positive battery terminal. • Is the voltage drop less than 0.1 volt?	**Yes** VERIFY if the customer left any component(s) on or if there is an intermittent excessive battery draw. TEST the system for normal operation. **No** CHECK for any corrosion in the positive battery cable and/or connections. REPAIR as necessary. TEST the system for normal operation.

ARM0400000000747

Fig. 92   Test A: Battery Or Battery Voltage Is Low. Five Hundred, Freestyle & Montego

Test Step	Result / Action to Take
B1 CHECK THE DTCs IN THE PCM • Check the recorded PCM DTCs from the continuous and on-demand self-tests. • **Are any PCM DTCs recorded?**	**Yes** REFER to MOTOR's Domestic Engine Performanc & Driveability manual. **No** GO to **B2**.
B2 CHECK THE GENERATOR B+ CIRCUIT FOR VOLTAGE • Key in OFF position. • Measure the voltage between the generator C102b, circuit 38 (BK/OG) and ground. 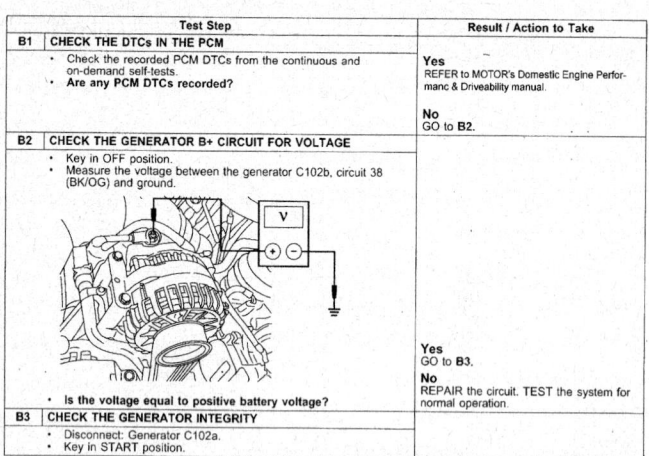 • **Is the voltage equal to positive battery voltage?**	**Yes** GO to **B3**. **No** REPAIR the circuit. TEST the system for normal operation.
B3 CHECK THE GENERATOR INTEGRITY • Disconnect: Generator C102a. • Key in START position.	

Fig. 93 Test B: Charging System Warning Indicator Is On w/Engine Running & Battery Voltage Does Not Increase (Part 1 of 3). Five Hundred, Freestyle & Montego

ARM0400000000748

Test Step	Result / Action to Take
B3 CHECK THE GENERATOR INTEGRITY (Continued) • **NOTE:** If the generator communication lines are disconnected, DTC P0622 may set, and the generator self-excites if it is operated at approximately 2,000 engine rpm for a momentary period of time. It then operates in a default mode at 13.5 volts until the engine is turned off. • With the engine running at approximately 2,000 rpm, measure the battery voltage. • **Is the battery voltage approximately 13.5 volts?**	**Yes** GO to **B4**. **No** INSTALL a new generator.
B4 CHECK CIRCUIT 1816 (YE/LB) FOR AN OPEN OR SHORT TO GROUND • Key in OFF position. • Disconnect: PCM C175e. • Measure the resistance between the generator C102a-2, circuit 1816 (YE/LB), harness side and the PCM C175e-13, circuit 1816 (YE/LB), harness side; and between the generator C102a-2, circuit 1816 (YE/LB), harness side and ground. • **Is the resistance less than 5 ohms between the generator and the PCM, and greater than 10,000 ohms between the generator and ground?**	**Yes** GO to **B5**. **No** REPAIR the circuit. TEST the system for normal operation.

ARM0400000000749

Fig. 93 Test B: Charging System Warning Indicator Is On w/Engine Running & Battery Voltage Does Not Increase (Part 2 of 3). Five Hundred, Freestyle & Montego

Test Step	Result / Action to Take
B5 CHECK CIRCUIT 1817 (YE) FOR AN OPEN OR SHORT TO GROUND • Measure the resistance between the generator C102a-1, circuit 1817 (YE), harness side and the PCM C175e-26, circuit 1817 (YE), harness side; and between the generator C102a-1, circuit 1817 (YE), harness side and ground. • **Is the resistance less than 5 ohms between the generator and the PCM, and greater than 10,000 ohms between the generator and ground?**	**Yes** GO to **B6**. **No** REPAIR the circuit. TEST the system for normal operation.

B6 CHECK FOR CORRECT PCM OPERATION
• Disconnect all of the PCM connectors.
• Check for:
  • corrosion
  • pushed-out pins
• Connect all of the PCM connectors and make sure they seat correctly.
• Operate the system and verify the concern is still present.
• **Is the concern still present?**
	Yes
	INSTALL a new PCM.
	
	No
	The system is operating correctly at this time. The concern may have been caused by a loose or corroded connector. CLEAR the DTCs. REPEAT the self-test. TEST the system for normal operation.

ARM0400000000750

Fig. 93 Test B: Charging System Warning Indicator Is On w/Engine Running & Battery Voltage Does Not Increase (Part 3 of 3). Five Hundred, Freestyle & Montego

Test Step	Result / Action to Take
C1 CHECK THE DTCs IN THE PCM • Check the recorded PCM DTCs from the continuous and on-demand self-tests. • **Are any PCM DTCs recorded?**	**Yes** REFER to MOTOR's Domestic Engine Performanc & Driveability manual. **No** GO to **C2**.
C2 CHECK THE BATTERY VOLTAGE • Key in START position. • With the engine running and all the accessories turned off, measure the voltage at the battery while varying the engine RPM. • **Is the voltage greater than 15.5 volts?**	**Yes** GO to **C3**. **No** GO to **C4**.
C3 CHECK THE VOLTAGE IN CIRCUIT 1818 (WH/BK) • Key in OFF position. • Disconnect: Generator C102a. • Measure the voltage between the generator C102a-3, circuit 1818 (WH/BK), harness side and ground. • **Is the voltage within 0.5 volt of battery voltage?**	**Yes** CONNECT the generator C102a. GO to **C4**. **No** REPAIR the circuit for high resistance. TEST the system for normal operation.
C4 CHECK THE GENERATOR PIDs • Connect the diagnostic tool. • Key in START position. • Enter the following diagnostic mode on the diagnostic tool: Monitor PCM PIDs. • With the engine running, monitor the generator output fault PID in the PCM. • **Does the PID read YES?**	**Yes** GO to **C5**. **No** GO to **C6**.
C5 CHECK THE GENERATOR INTEGRITY • Key in OFF position. • Disconnect: Generator C102a. • Key in START position.	

ARM0400000000751

Fig. 94 Test C: Charging System Overcharges (Part 1 of 2). Five Hundred, Freestyle & Montego

Test Step		Result / Action to Take
C5	**CHECK THE GENERATOR INTEGRITY (Continued)**	
	• **NOTE:** If the generator communication lines are disconnected, DTC P0622 may be set, and the generator self-excites if it is operated at approximately 2,000 engine rpm for a momentary period of time. It then operates in a default mode at 13.5 volts until the engine is turned off. • With the engine running at approximately 2,000 rpm, measure the battery voltage.	**Yes** GO to **C6**. **No** INSTALL a new generator.
	• **Is the battery voltage approximately 13.5 volts?**	
C6	**CHECK FOR CORRECT PCM OPERATION**	**Yes** INSTALL a new PCM.

	• Disconnect all of the PCM connectors.
	• Check for:
	  • corrosion
	  • pushed-out pins
	• Connect all of the PCM connectors and make sure they seat correctly.
	• Operate the system and verify the concern is still present.
	• **Is the concern still present?**
		No
		The system is operating correctly at this time. The concern may have been caused by a loose or corroded connector. CLEAR the DTCs. REPEAT the self-test. TEST the system for normal operation.

ARM0400000000752

Fig. 94 Test C: Charging System Overcharges (Part 2 of 2). Five Hundred, Freestyle & Montego

Test Step		Result / Action to Take
E1	**CHECK THE CHARGING SYSTEM WARNING INDICATOR OPERATION**	
	• Key in ON position. • Enter the following diagnostic mode on the diagnostic tool: Instrument Cluster Active Commands. • Using the instrument cluster Active Commands, turn on the charging system warning indicator. • **Is the charging system warning indicator on?**	**Yes** GO to **E2**. **No** Diagnose the charging system warning indicator.
E2	**CHECK FOR CORRECT PCM OPERATION**	**Yes** INSTALL a new PCM.

	• Disconnect all of the PCM connectors.
	• Check for:
	  • corrosion
	  • pushed-out pins
	• Connect all of the PCM connectors and make sure they seat correctly.
	• Operate the system and verify the concern is still present.
	• **Is the concern still present?**
		No
		The system is operating correctly at this time. The concern may have been caused by a loose or corroded connector. CLEAR the DTCs. REPEAT the self-test. TEST the system for normal operation.

ARM0400000000754

Fig. 96 Test E: Charging System Warning Indicator Is Off w/Ignition Switch In Run Position & Engine Off. Five Hundred, Freestyle & Montego

Test Step		Result / Action to Take
F1	**CHECK FOR ACCESSORY DRIVE NOISE AND MOUNTING BRACKETS**	
	• Key in OFF position. • Check the accessory drive belt for damage and correct installation. Refer to Section 303-05. • Check the accessory mounting brackets and generator pulley for looseness or misalignment. • **Is the accessory drive OK?**	**Yes** GO to **F2**. **No** REPAIR as necessary. TEST the system for normal operation.

ARM0400000000755

Fig. 97 Test F: Alternator Is Noisy (Part 1 of 2). Five Hundred, Freestyle & Montego

Test Step		Result / Action to Take
D1	**CHECK THE DTCs IN THE PCM**	
	• Check the recorded PCM DTCs from the continuous and on-demand self-tests. • **Are any PCM DTCs recorded?**	**Yes** REFER to MOTOR's Domestic Engine Performance & Driveability manual. **No** GO to **D2**.
D2	**CHECK THE SYSTEM FOR OVERCHARGING**	
	• Key in START position. • With the engine running and all accessories off, measure the voltage at the battery terminals while varying the engine RPM.	
	• **Is the voltage greater than 15.5 volts?**	**Yes** GO to Pinpoint Test C. **No** GO to **D3**.
D3	**CHECK THE CHARGING SYSTEM WARNING INDICATOR OPERATION**	
	• Enter the following diagnostic mode on the diagnostic tool: PCM PIDs. • With the engine running, monitor the generator output fault PID in the PCM. • **Does the PID read YES?**	**Yes** GO to **D4**. **No** Diagnose the charging system warning indicator.
D4	**CHECK THE GENERATOR OUTPUT**	
	• Verify the generator output. • **Does the generator pass the component tests?**	**Yes** GO to **D5**. **No** INSTALL a new generator.
D5	**CHECK FOR CORRECT PCM OPERATION**	**Yes** INSTALL a new PCM.

	• Disconnect all of the PCM connectors.
	• Check for:
	  • corrosion
	  • pushed-out pins
	• Connect all of the PCM connectors and make sure they seat correctly.
	• Operate the system and verify the concern is still present.
	• **Is the concern still present?**
		No
		The system is operating correctly at this time. The concern may have been caused by a loose or corroded connector. CLEAR the DTCs. REPEAT the self-test. TEST the system for normal operation.

ARM0400000000753

Fig. 95 Test D: Charging System Warning Indicator Is On w/Engine Running & Battery Increases Voltage. Five Hundred, Freestyle & Montego

Test Step		Result / Action to Take
F2	**CHECK THE GENERATOR FOR EXCESSIVE ELECTRICAL NOISE**	
	• Disconnect: Generator C102b. • Key in START position. • With the engine running, determine if the generator is still noisy. • **Is the noise still present?**	**Yes** GO to **F3**. **No** INSTALL a new generator.
F3	**CHECK THE GENERATOR FOR MECHANICAL NOISE**	
	• Turn all the accessories off. With the engine running, use a stethoscope or equivalent listening device to probe the generator for unusual mechanical noise. • **Is the generator the noise source?**	**Yes** INSTALL a new generator. **No** Diagnose the source of the engine noise.

ARM0400000000756

Fig. 97 Test F: Alternator Is Noisy (Part 2 of 2). Five Hundred, Freestyle & Montego

Test Step		Result / Action to Take
G1	**VERIFY THE GENERATOR IS THE SOURCE OF THE RADIO INTERFERENCE**	
	NOTE: If the original equipment manufactured (OEM) audio unit has been replaced with an aftermarket unit, the vehicle may not pass this test. Return the vehicle to OEM condition before following this pinpoint test. • Key in START position. • With the engine running, tune the radio to a station where the interference is present. • Key in OFF position. • Disconnect: Generator C102b. • Key in START position. • With the engine running, determine if the interference is still present. • **Is the interference present with the generator disconnected?**	**Yes** Diagnose netertainment system. **No** INSTALL a new generator.

ARM0400000000757

Fig. 98 Test G: Radio Interference. Five Hundred, Freestyle & Montego

Test Condition	Test Details/Results/Actions
TEST A1: INSPECT BATTERY	
Inspect battery capacity	If battery capacity is not at normal operating range, replace battery
Inspect system operation	—
TEST A2: INSPECT CHARGING SYSTEM	
Perform "Load Test"	If alternator output is not as specified, refer to "Test A3: Inspect For A Good Ground"
TEST A3: INSPECT FOR A GOOD GROUND	
Measure voltage between alternator case and battery ground terminal	If voltage is less than .5 volts, refer to "Test A4: Inspect Battery Cable"
	If voltage is more than .5 volts, clean and tighten alternator mounting bolts, engine to body ground strap and battery ground cable
Inspect system operation	—
TEST A4: INSPECT BATTERY CABLE	
Measure voltage between alternator B+ terminal and battery positive terminal	Voltage should be less than .5 volts
	If voltage is as specified, refer to "Test A5: Inspect Battery Feed To Alternator"
	If voltage is not as specified, clean and tighten battery positive cable connections
Inspect system operation	If voltage is still not as specified, replace battery positive cable
TEST A5: INSPECT BATTERY FEED TO ALTERNATOR	
Measure voltage between alternator B+ terminal and ground	Battery voltage should be present
	If voltage is as specified, refer to "Test A6: Inspect Power To Voltage Regulator"
	If voltage is not as specified, inspect fusible links and fuses and replace as required
Inspect system operation	If voltage is not as specified, repair battery positive cable
TEST A6: INSPECT POWER TO VOLTAGE REGULATOR	
Measure voltage between alternator connector pin No. 3 harness side and ground	Battery voltage should be present
	If voltage is as specified, replace alternator and inspect system once again
	If voltage is not as specified, inspect fuse No. F10 and repair circuit 30-BA10

Fig. 99   Test A: Charging System Warning Indicator Is On w/Engine Running. Focus

Test Condition	Test Details/Results/Actions
Test B1: Isolate The Alternator	
Remove accessory drive belt	—
Run engine for a few seconds with radio turned on	If radio interference is still present, inspect audio entertainment system for faults
	If radio interference is not present, clean and tighten battery clamps and alternator mounting bolts
	If interference is still present, replace alternator

Fig. 100   Test B: Radio Interference. Focus

CONDITIONS	DETAILS/RESULTS/ACTIONS
A1 CHECK THE GENERATOR OUTPUT	
	1 Carry out the On-Vehicle Generator Load/No Load Tests. • **Is the generator OK?** → **Yes** GO to A2 . → **No** GO to Pinpoint Test B .
A2 CHECK FOR CURRENT DRAINS	
	1 Carry out the Battery — Drain Test. • **Are there any excessive current drains?** → **Yes** REPAIR as necessary. TEST the system for normal operation. → **No** GO to A3 .
A3 CHECK FOR CURRENT DRAINS WHICH SHUT OFF WHEN THE BATTERY IS DISCONNECTED	
	1 Carry out the Battery — Electronic Drains Which Shut Off When the Battery Cable is Disconnected Test. • **Are there any current drains which shut off when the battery is disconnected?** → **Yes** REPAIR as necessary. TEST the system for normal operation. → **No** GO to Pinpoint Test B .

FM1120200792000X

Fig. 101   Test A: Battery Is Discharged Or Battery Voltage Is Low. LS & Thunderbird

CONDITIONS	DETAILS/RESULTS/ACTIONS

B1 CHECK THE FAULT CODES IN THE PCM

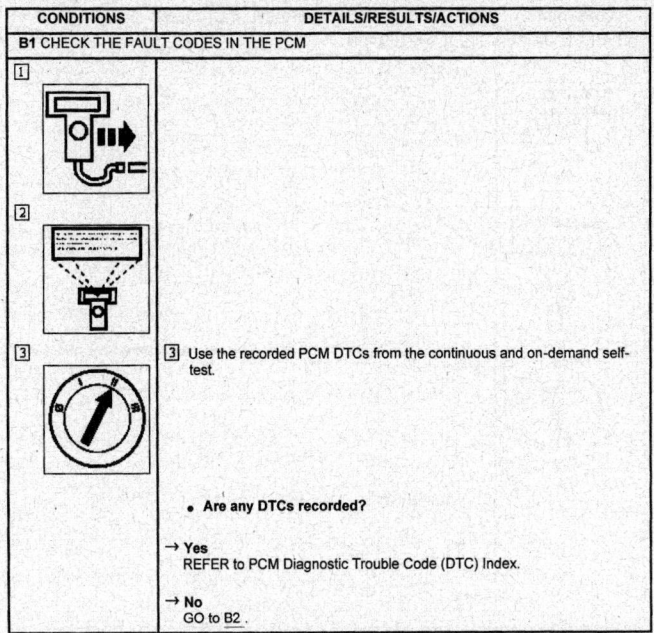

3 Use the recorded PCM DTCs from the continuous and on-demand self-test.

• Are any DTCs recorded?

→ Yes
REFER to PCM Diagnostic Trouble Code (DTC) Index.

→ No
GO to B2 .

FM1120200793010X

Fig. 102   Test B: Charging System Warning Indicator Is On w/Engine Running, Charging System Voltage Does Not Increase (Part 1 of 5). LS & Thunderbird

B3 CHECK CIRCUIT 10-BA25 (GY/RD) FOR AN OPEN

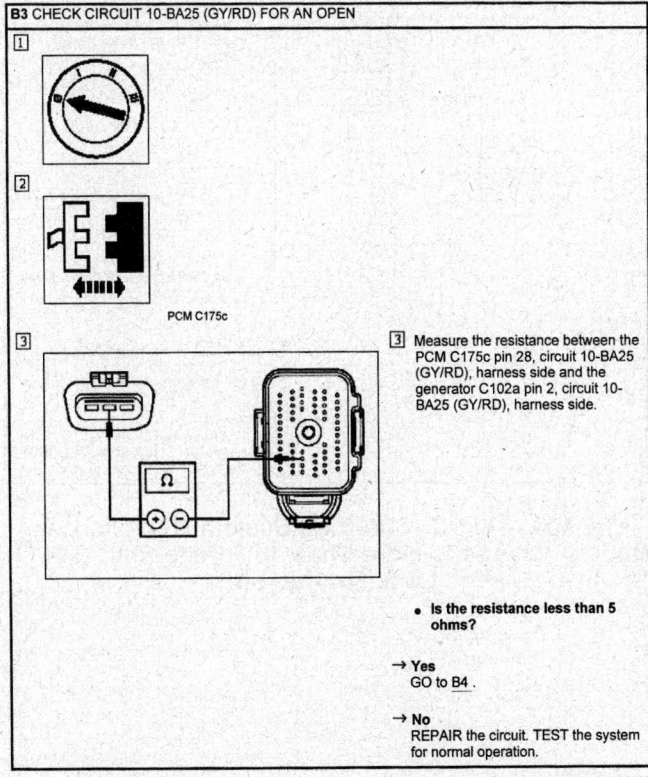

PCM C175c

3 Measure the resistance between the PCM C175c pin 28, circuit 10-BA25 (GY/RD), harness side and the generator C102a pin 2, circuit 10-BA25 (GY/RD), harness side.

• Is the resistance less than 5 ohms?

→ Yes
GO to B4 .

→ No
REPAIR the circuit. TEST the system for normal operation.

FM1120200793030X

Fig. 102   Test B: Charging System Warning Indicator Is On w/Engine Running, Charging System Voltage Does Not Increase (Part 3 of 5). LS & Thunderbird

B2 CHECK CIRCUIT 10-BA25 (GY/RD)

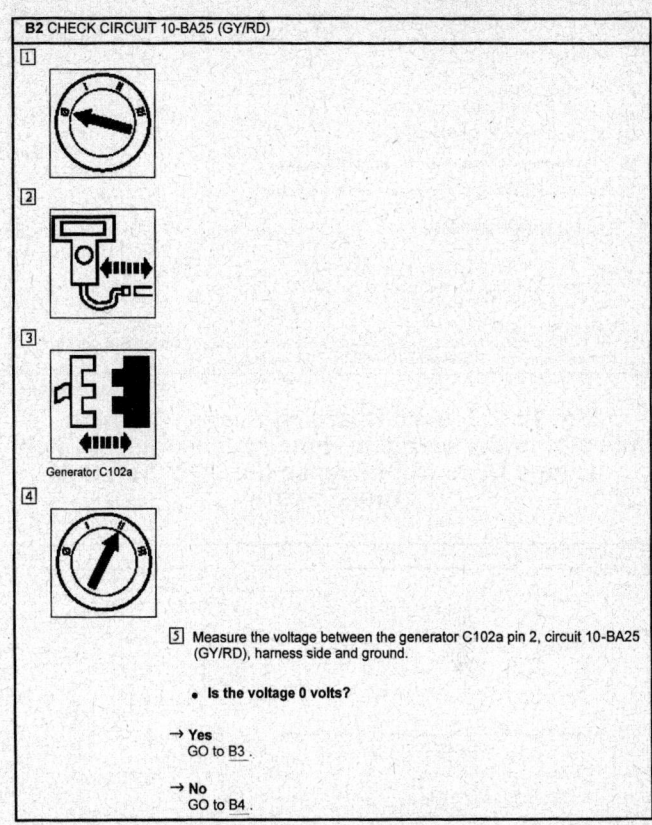

Generator C102a

5 Measure the voltage between the generator C102a pin 2, circuit 10-BA25 (GY/RD), harness side and ground.

• Is the voltage 0 volts?

→ Yes
GO to B3 .

→ No
GO to B4 .

FM1120200793020X

Fig. 102   Test B: Charging System Warning Indicator Is On w/Engine Running, Charging System Voltage Does Not Increase (Part 2 of 5). LS & Thunderbird

B4 CHECK THE GENERATOR OUTPUT

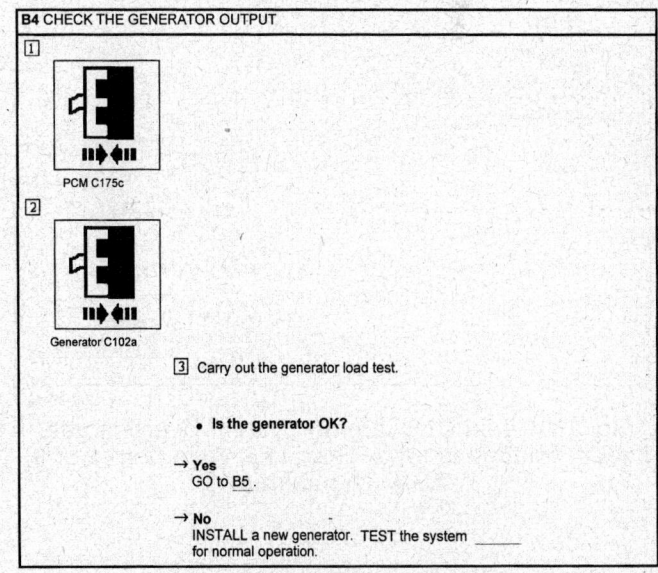

PCM C175c

Generator C102a

3 Carry out the generator load test.

• Is the generator OK?

→ Yes
GO to B5 .

→ No
INSTALL a new generator. TEST the system _____ for normal operation.

FM1120200793040X

Fig. 102   Test B: Charging System Warning Indicator Is On w/Engine Running, Charging System Voltage Does Not Increase (Part 4 of 5). LS & Thunderbird

B5 CHECK FOR CORRECT MODULE OPERATION

1. Check for:

   - corrosion
   - pushed-out pins

2. Connect any disconnected connectors.

3. Make sure all other system connectors are fully seated.

4. Operate the system and verify the concern is still present.

   - **Is the concern still present?**

   → **Yes**
   INSTALL a new PCM. REPEAT the PCM self-test.

   → **No**
   The system is operating correctly at this time. Concern may have been caused by a loose or corroded connector. CLEAR the DTCs. REPEAT the self-test.

   FM1120200793050X

Fig. 102   Test B: Charging System Warning Indicator Is On w/Engine Running, Charging System Voltage Does Not Increase (Part 5 of 5). LS & Thunderbird

C2 CHECK THE GENERATOR OUTPUT

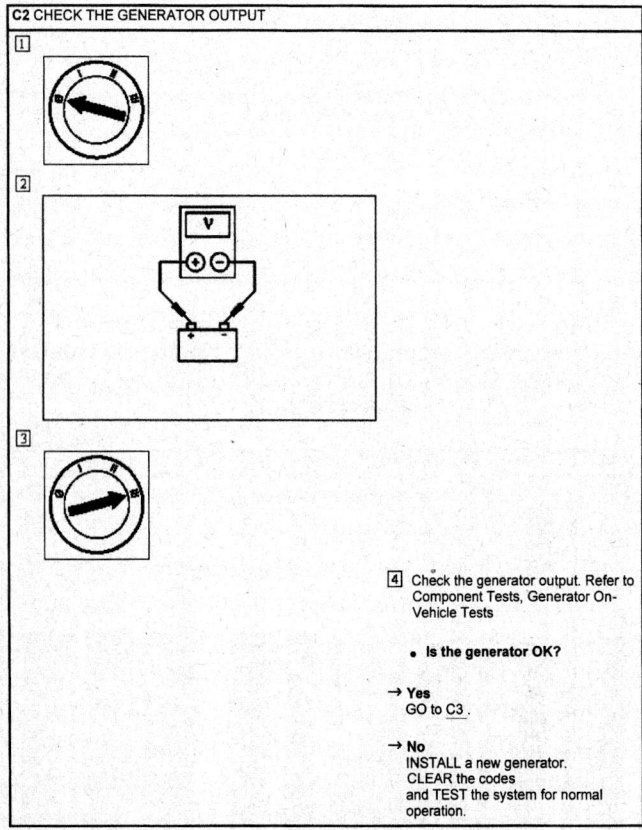

4. Check the generator output. Refer to Component Tests, Generator On-Vehicle Tests

   - **Is the generator OK?**

   → **Yes**
   GO to C3 .

   → **No**
   INSTALL a new generator.
   CLEAR the codes
   and TEST the system for normal operation.

   FM1120200794020X

Fig. 103   Test C: Charging System Overcharges, Battery Voltage Is More Than 15.5 Volts (Part 2 of 3). LS & Thunderbird

CONDITIONS	DETAILS/RESULTS/ACTIONS

C1 CHECK THE FAULT CODES IN THE PCM

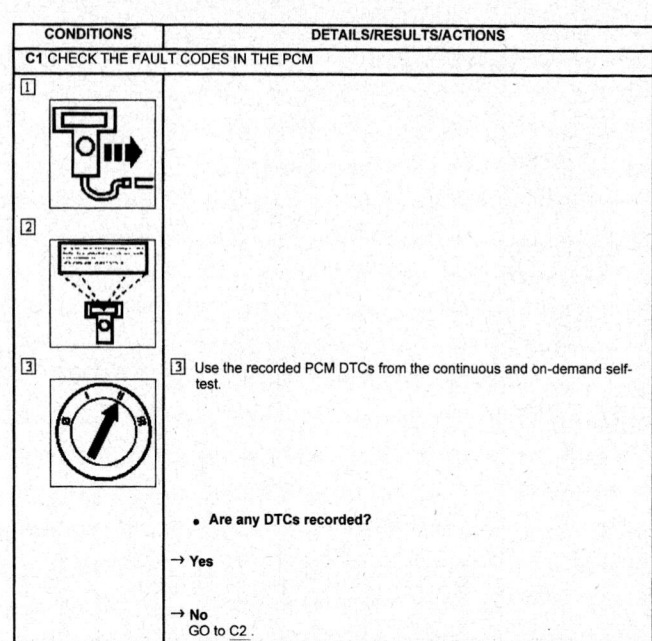

3. Use the recorded PCM DTCs from the continuous and on-demand self-test.

   - **Are any DTCs recorded?**

   → **Yes**

   → **No**
   GO to C2 .

   FM1120200794010X

Fig. 103   Test C: Charging System Overcharges, Battery Voltage Is More Than 15.5 Volts (Part 1 of 3). LS & Thunderbird

C3 CHECK CIRCUIT 30-BA25 (RD)

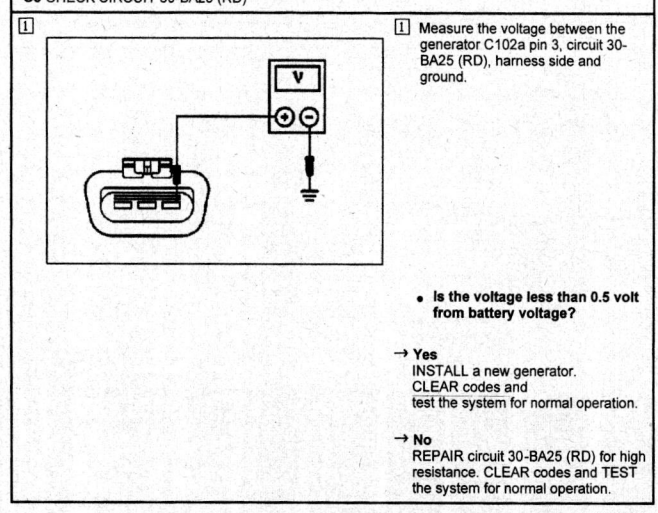

1. Measure the voltage between the generator C102a pin 3, circuit 30-BA25 (RD), harness side and ground.

   - **Is the voltage less than 0.5 volt from battery voltage?**

   → **Yes**
   INSTALL a new generator.
   CLEAR codes and
   test the system for normal operation.

   → **No**
   REPAIR circuit 30-BA25 (RD) for high resistance. CLEAR codes and TEST the system for normal operation.

   FM1120200794030X

Fig. 103   Test C: Charging System Overcharges, Battery Voltage Is More Than 15.5 Volts (Part 3 of 3). LS & Thunderbird

CONDITIONS	DETAILS/RESULTS/ACTIONS

D1 CHECK THE FAULT CODES IN THE PCM

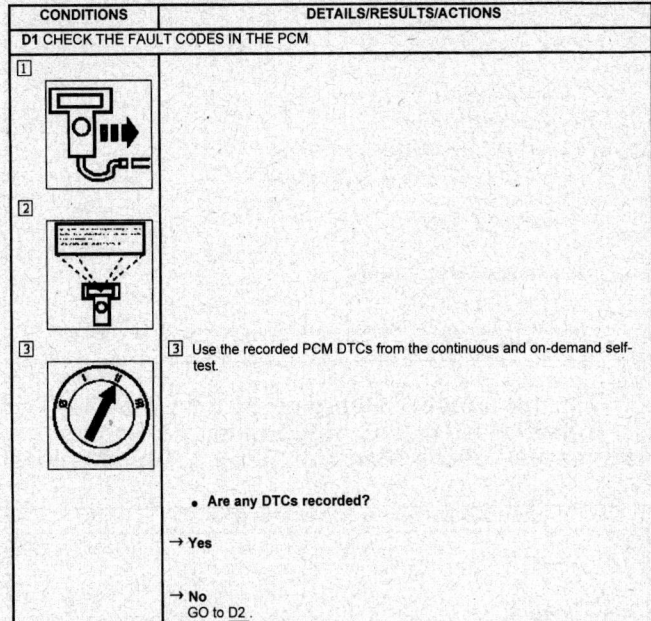

3 Use the recorded PCM DTCs from the continuous and on-demand self-test.

- Are any DTCs recorded?

→ Yes

→ No
GO to D2.

FM1120200795010X

Fig. 104 Test D: Charging System Warning Indicator Is On w/Engine Running & Battery Increases Voltage (Part 1 of 6). LS & Thunderbird

D3 CHECK CIRCUIT 30-BA25 (RD)

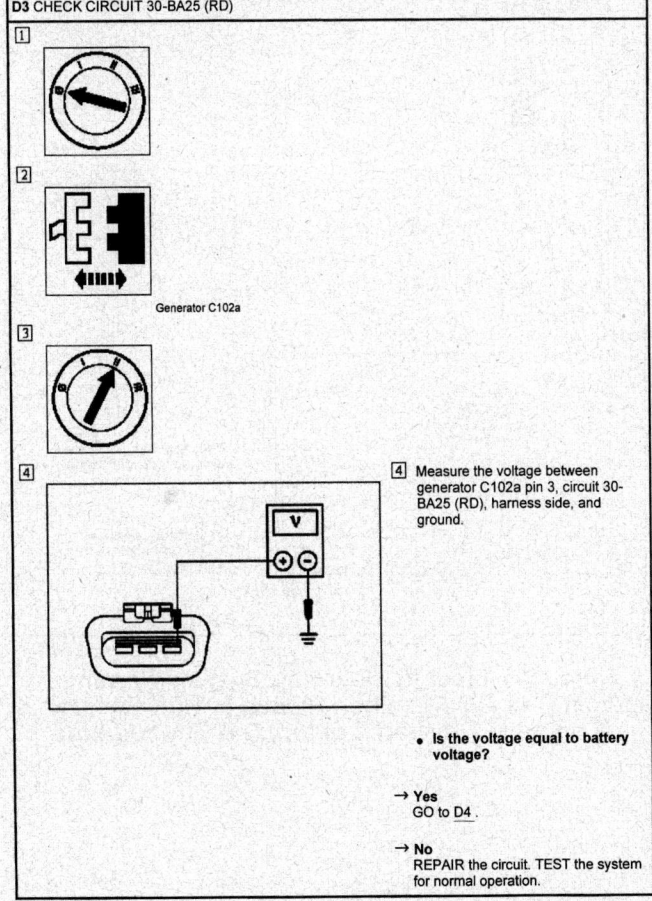

Generator C102a

4 Measure the voltage between generator C102a pin 3, circuit 30-BA25 (RD), harness side, and ground.

- Is the voltage equal to battery voltage?

→ Yes
GO to D4.

→ No
REPAIR the circuit. TEST the system for normal operation.

FM1120200795030X

Fig. 104 Test D: Charging System Warning Indicator Is On w/Engine Running & Battery Increases Voltage (Part 3 of 6). LS & Thunderbird

D2 CHECK THE SYSTEM FOR OVERCHARGING

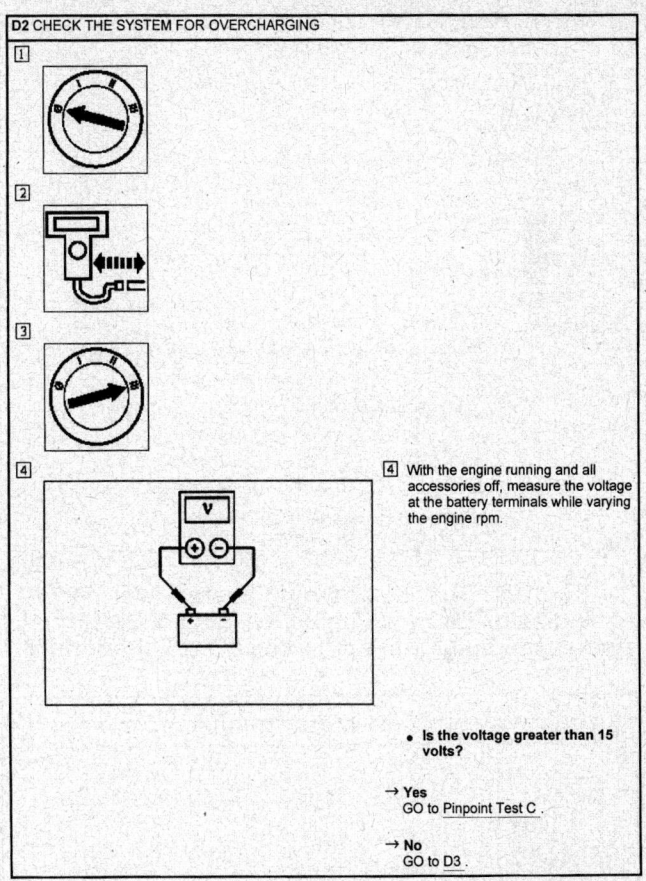

4 With the engine running and all accessories off, measure the voltage at the battery terminals while varying the engine rpm.

- Is the voltage greater than 15 volts?

→ Yes
GO to Pinpoint Test C.

→ No
GO to D3.

FM1120200795020X

Fig. 104 Test D: Charging System Warning Indicator Is On w/Engine Running & Battery Increases Voltage (Part 2 of 6). LS & Thunderbird

D4 CHECK THE CHARGING SYSTEM WARNING INDICATOR OPERATION

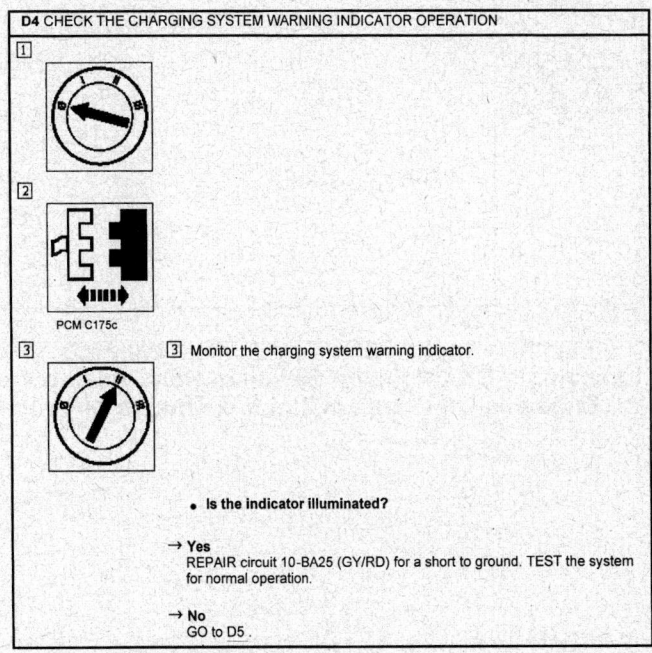

PCM C175c

3 Monitor the charging system warning indicator.

- Is the indicator illuminated?

→ Yes
REPAIR circuit 10-BA25 (GY/RD) for a short to ground. TEST the system for normal operation.

→ No
GO to D5.

FM1120200795040X

Fig. 104 Test D: Charging System Warning Indicator Is On w/Engine Running & Battery Increases Voltage (Part 4 of 6). LS & Thunderbird

D5 CHECK THE GENERATOR OUTPUT

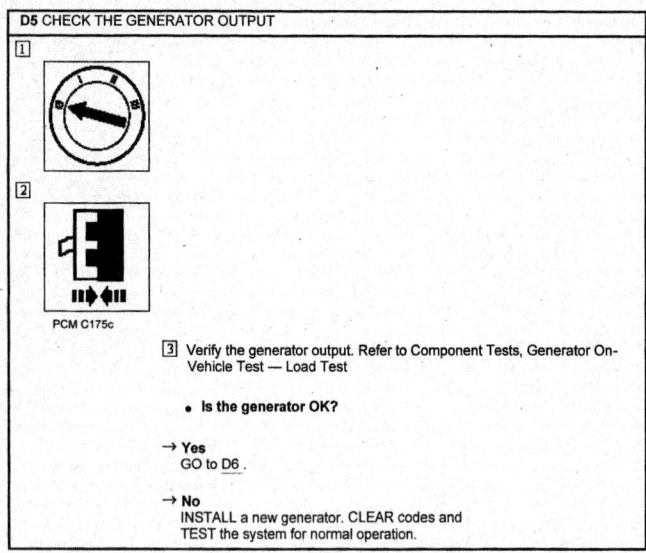

PCM C175c

3. Verify the generator output. Refer to Component Tests, Generator On-Vehicle Test — Load Test

- **Is the generator OK?**

→ **Yes**
GO to D6 .

→ **No**
INSTALL a new generator. CLEAR codes and TEST the system for normal operation.

FM1120200795050X

Fig. 104   Test D: Charging System Warning Indicator Is On w/Engine Running & Battery Increases Voltage (Part 5 of 6). LS & Thunderbird

D6 CHECK FOR CORRECT MODULE OPERATION

1. Check for:

- corrosion
- pushed-out pins

2. Connect any disconnected connectors.

3. Make sure all other system connectors are fully seated.

4. Operate the system and verify the concern is still present.

- **Is the concern still present?**

→ **Yes**
INSTALL a new PCM. REPEAT the PCM self-test.

→ **No**
The system is operating correctly at this time. Concern may have been caused by a loose or corroded connector. CLEAR the DTCs. REPEAT the self-test.

FM1120200795060X

Fig. 104   Test D: Charging System Warning Indicator Is On w/Engine Running & Battery Increases Voltage (Part 6 of 6). LS & Thunderbird

CONDITIONS	DETAILS/RESULTS/ACTIONS

E1 CHECK THE FAULT CODES IN THE PCM

3. Use the recorded PCM DTCs from the continuous and on-demand self-test.

- **Are any DTCs recorded?**

→ **Yes**

→ **No**
GO to E2 .

FM1120200796010X

Fig. 105   Test E: Charging System Warning Indicator Is Off w/Ignition Switch In Run Position & Engine Is Off (Part 1 of 3). LS & Thunderbird

E2 CHECK THE CHARGING SYSTEM WARNING INDICATOR OPERATION

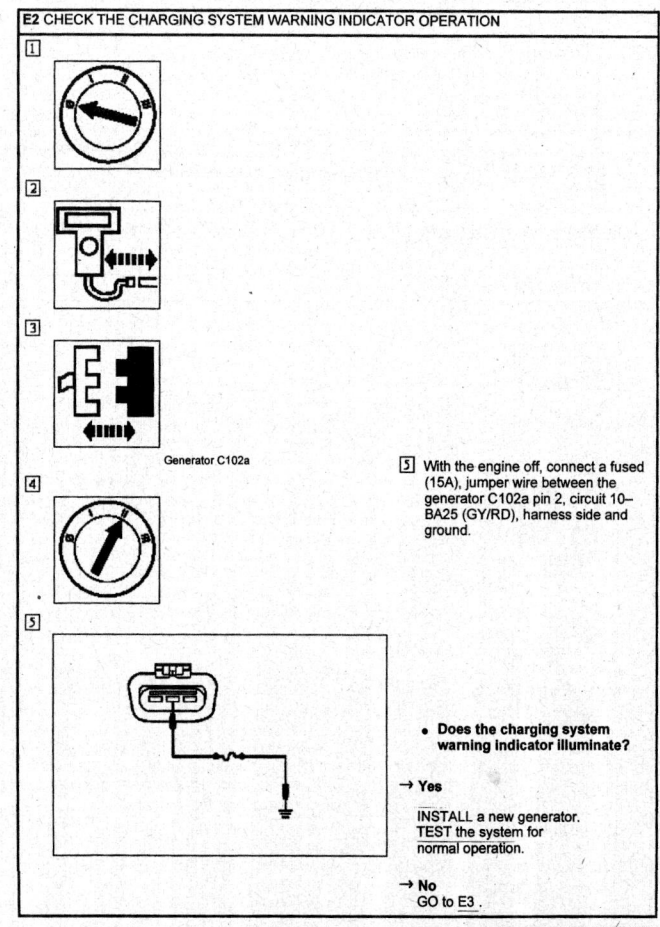

Generator C102a

5. With the engine off, connect a fused (15A) jumper wire between the generator C102a pin 2, circuit 10–BA25 (GY/RD), harness side and ground.

- **Does the charging system warning indicator illuminate?**

→ **Yes**
INSTALL a new generator. TEST the system for normal operation.

→ **No**
GO to E3 .

FM1120200796020X

Fig. 105   Test E: Charging System Warning Indicator Is Off w/Ignition Switch In Run Position & Engine Is Off (Part 2 of 3). LS & Thunderbird

E3 CHECK FOR CORRECT MODULE OPERATION

1. Check for:
   - corrosion
   - pushed-out pins
   - open circuit or grounded circuit on circuit 10-BA25 (GY/RD)

2. Connect any disconnected connectors.

3. Make sure all other system connectors are fully seated.

4. Operate the system and verify the concern is still present.

- **Is the concern still present?**

→ **Yes**
INSTALL a new PCM. REPEAT the PCM self-test.

→ **No**
The system is operating correctly at this time. Concern may have been caused by a loose or corroded connector. CLEAR the DTCs. REPEAT the self-test.

FM1120200796030X

Fig. 105 Test E: Charging System Warning Indicator Is Off w/Ignition Switch In Run Position & Engine Is Off (Part 3 of 3). LS & Thunderbird

---

F2 CHECK FOR LOOSE CONNECTIONS

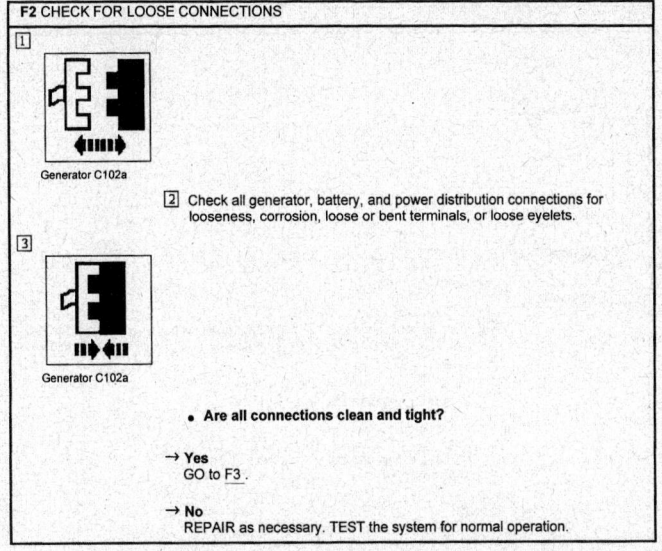

Generator C102a

Generator C102a

2. Check all generator, battery, and power distribution connections for looseness, corrosion, loose or bent terminals, or loose eyelets.

- **Are all connections clean and tight?**

→ **Yes**
GO to F3.

→ **No**
REPAIR as necessary. TEST the system for normal operation.

FM1120200797020X

Fig. 106 Test F: Charging System Warning Indicator Flickers Or Is Intermittent (Part 2 of 6). LS & Thunderbird

---

F3 CHECK FUSE CONNECTION

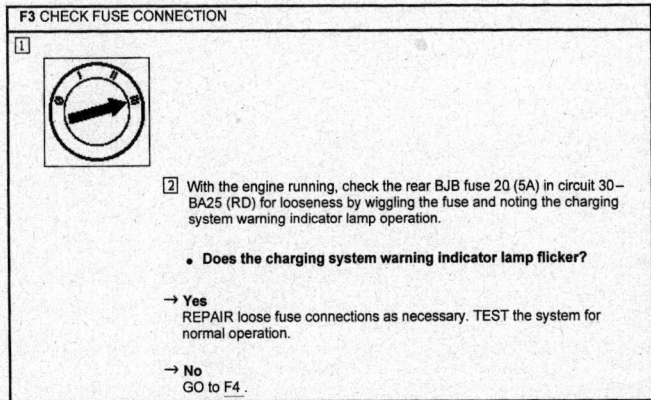

2. With the engine running, check the rear BJB fuse 20 (5A) in circuit 30–BA25 (RD) for looseness by wiggling the fuse and noting the charging system warning indicator lamp operation.

- **Does the charging system warning indicator lamp flicker?**

→ **Yes**
REPAIR loose fuse connections as necessary. TEST the system for normal operation.

→ **No**
GO to F4.

FM1120200797030X

Fig. 106 Test F: Charging System Warning Indicator Flickers Or Is Intermittent (Part 3 of 6). LS & Thunderbird

---

CONDITIONS	DETAILS/RESULTS/ACTIONS

F1 CHECK THE FAULT CODES IN THE PCM

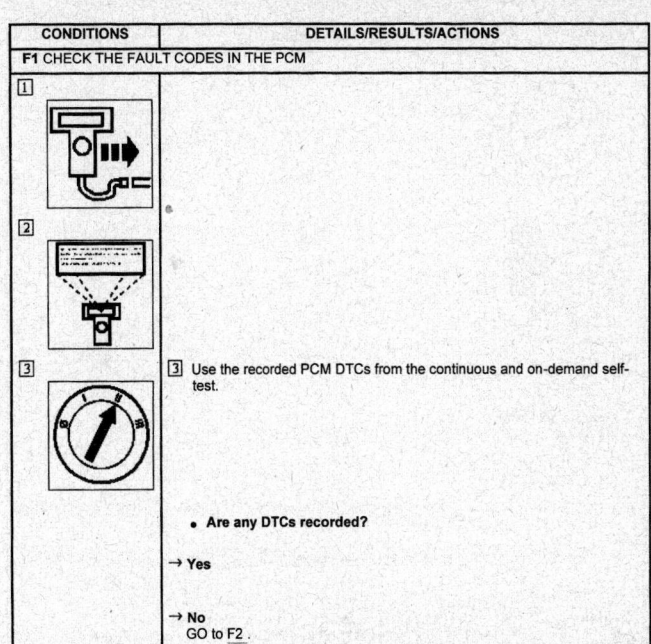

3. Use the recorded PCM DTCs from the continuous and on-demand self-test.

- **Are any DTCs recorded?**

→ **Yes**

→ **No**
GO to F2.

FM1120200797010X

Fig. 106 Test F: Charging System Warning Indicator Flickers Or Is Intermittent (Part 1 of 6). LS & Thunderbird

---

F4 CHECK THE BATTERY VOLTAGE

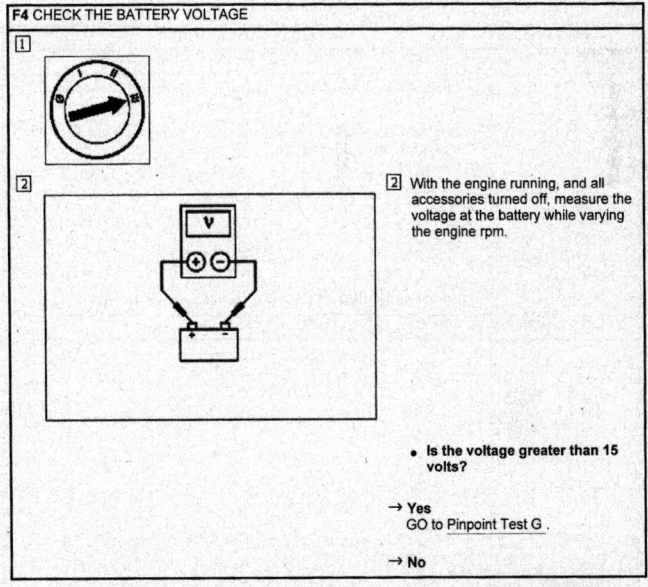

2. With the engine running, and all accessories turned off, measure the voltage at the battery while varying the engine rpm.

- **Is the voltage greater than 15 volts?**

→ **Yes**
GO to Pinpoint Test G.

→ **No**

FM1120200797040X

Fig. 106 Test F: Charging System Warning Indicator Flickers Or Is Intermittent (Part 4 of 6). LS & Thunderbird

F5 CHECK THE WARNING SYSTEM INDICATOR OPERATION

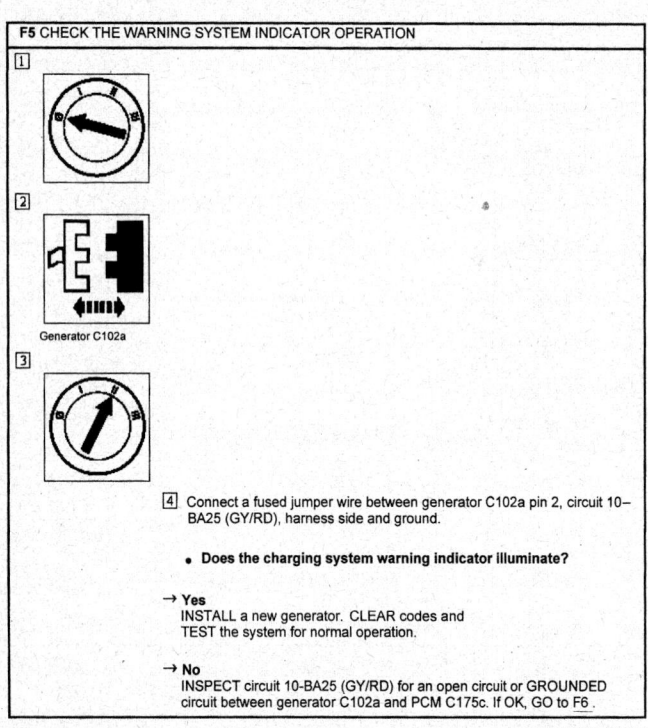

Generator C102a

4 Connect a fused jumper wire between generator C102a pin 2, circuit 10–BA25 (GY/RD), harness side and ground.

- **Does the charging system warning indicator illuminate?**

→ **Yes**
INSTALL a new generator. CLEAR codes and TEST the system for normal operation.

→ **No**
INSPECT circuit 10-BA25 (GY/RD) for an open circuit or GROUNDED circuit between generator C102a and PCM C175c. If OK, GO to F6 .

FM1120200797050X

Fig. 106 Test F: Charging System Warning Indicator Flickers Or Is Intermittent (Part 5 of 6). LS & Thunderbird

CONDITIONS	DETAILS/RESULTS/ACTIONS
G1 CHECK FOR ACCESSORY DRIVE NOISE AND MOUNTING BRACKETS	

1 Check the accessory drive belt for damage and correct installation.

2 Check the accessory mounting brackets and generator pulley for looseness or misalignment.

- **Is the accessory drive OK?**

→ **Yes**
GO to G2 .

→ **No**
REPAIR as necessary. TEST the system for normal operation.

G2 CHECK GENERATOR FOR ELECTRICAL NOISE

Generator C102a

3 With the engine running.

- **Is the noise still present?**

→ **Yes**
GO to G3 .

→ **No**
INSTALL a new generator. TEST the system for normal operation.

FM1120200798010X

Fig. 107 Test G: Alternator Is Noisy (Part 1 of 2). LS & Thunderbird

F6 CHECK FOR CORRECT MODULE OPERATION

1 Check for:

  - corrosion
  - pushed-out pins

2 Connect any disconnected connectors.

3 Make sure all other system connectors are fully seated.

4 Operate the system and verify the concern is still present.

- **Is the concern still present?**

→ **Yes**
INSTALL a new PCM. REPEAT the PCM self-test.

→ **No**
The system is operating correctly at this time. Concern may have been caused by a loose or corroded connector. CLEAR the DTCs. REPEAT the self-test.

FM1120200797060X

Fig. 106 Test F: Charging System Warning Indicator Flickers Or Is Intermittent (Part 6 of 6). LS & Thunderbird

G3 CHECK GENERATOR FOR MECHANICAL NOISE

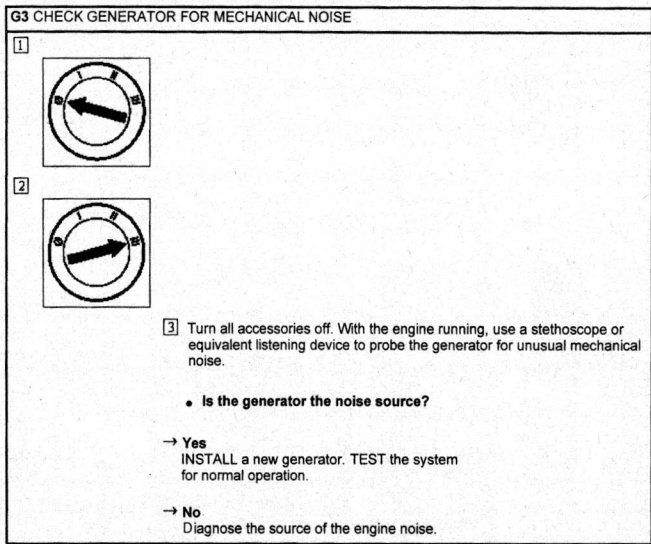

3 Turn all accessories off. With the engine running, use a stethoscope or equivalent listening device to probe the generator for unusual mechanical noise.

- **Is the generator the noise source?**

→ **Yes**
INSTALL a new generator. TEST the system for normal operation.

→ **No**
Diagnose the source of the engine noise.

FM1120200798020X

Fig. 107 Test G: Alternator Is Noisy (Part 2 of 2). LS & Thunderbird

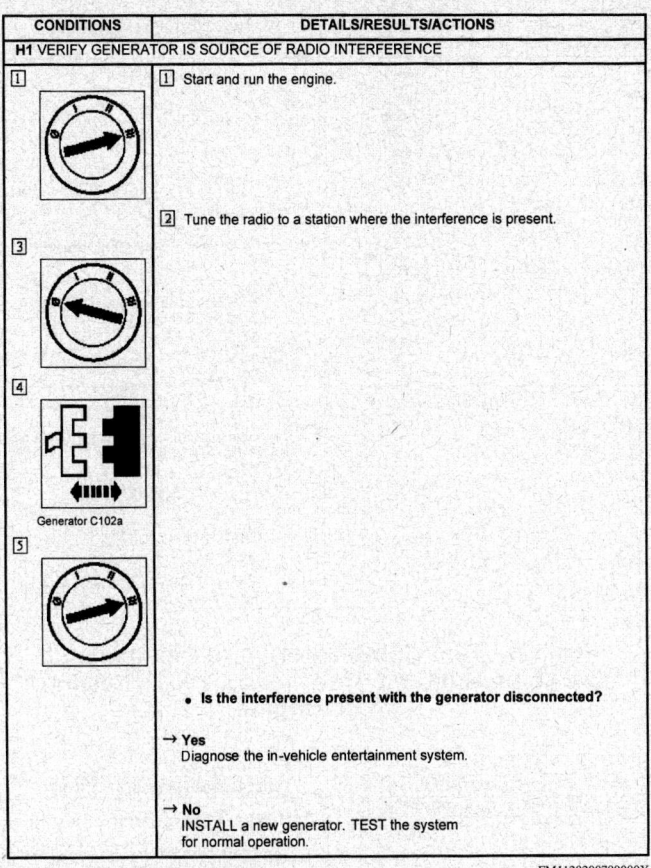

CONDITIONS	DETAILS/RESULTS/ACTIONS
H1 VERIFY GENERATOR IS SOURCE OF RADIO INTERFERENCE	
1	1 Start and run the engine.
	2 Tune the radio to a station where the interference is present.
3	
4 Generator C102a	
5	• Is the interference present with the generator disconnected? → Yes Diagnose the in-vehicle entertainment system. → No INSTALL a new generator. TEST the system for normal operation.

FM1120200799000X

Fig. 108   Test H: Radio Interference. LS & Thunderbird

TEST CONDITIONS	TESTDETAILS/RESULTS/ACTIONS
A3 CHECK I CIRCUIT 904 (LG/RD)	
1 2 Generator C154 3	3 With the key ON, engine OFF, measure the voltage by backprobing between generator C154 Pin I, Circuit 904 (LG/RD) harness side and ground. • Is the voltage equal to battery B+? → Yes GO to A4. → No REPAIR circuit. TEST the system for normal operation.
A4 CHECK FOR VOLTAGE DROP IN B+ CIRCUIT 38 (BK/OG)	
1	1 Measure the voltage drop between the B+ terminal on the generator and the battery positive post. • Is the voltage drop less than 0.5 volt? → Yes GO to A5. → No REPAIR high resistance in the B+ circuit. TEST the system for normal operation.

FM1120000552020X

Fig. 109   Test A: System Does Not Charge (Part 2 of 3). 2001 Mustang w/3.8L Engine

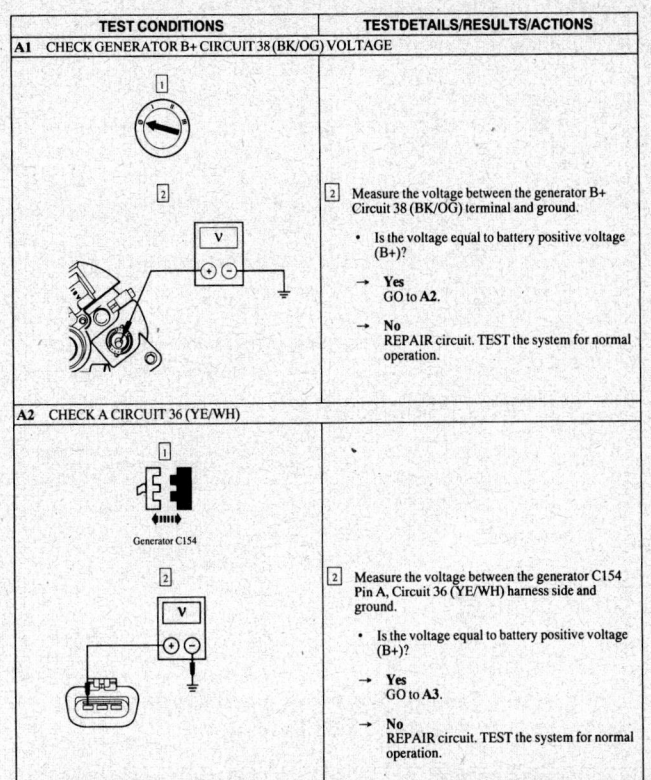

TEST CONDITIONS	TESTDETAILS/RESULTS/ACTIONS
A1 CHECK GENERATOR B+ CIRCUIT 38 (BK/OG) VOLTAGE	
1	2 Measure the voltage between the generator B+ Circuit 38 (BK/OG) terminal and ground. • Is the voltage equal to battery positive voltage (B+)? → Yes GO to A2. → No REPAIR circuit. TEST the system for normal operation.
A2 CHECK A CIRCUIT 36 (YE/WH)	
1 Generator C154 2	2 Measure the voltage between the generator C154 Pin A, Circuit 36 (YE/WH) harness side and ground. • Is the voltage equal to battery positive voltage (B+)? → Yes GO to A3. → No REPAIR circuit. TEST the system for normal operation.

FM1120000552010X

Fig. 109   Test A: System Does Not Charge (Part 1 of 3). 2001 Mustang w/3.8L Engine

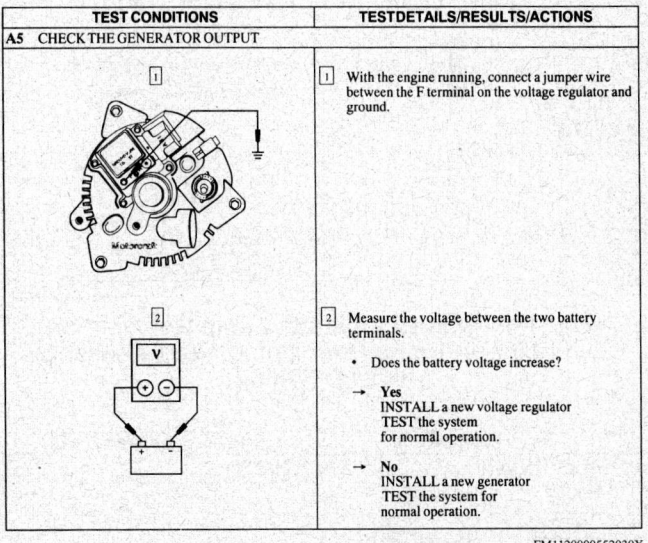

TEST CONDITIONS	TESTDETAILS/RESULTS/ACTIONS
A5 CHECK THE GENERATOR OUTPUT	
1	1 With the engine running, connect a jumper wire between the F terminal on the voltage regulator and ground.
2	2 Measure the voltage between the two battery terminals. • Does the battery voltage increase? → Yes INSTALL a new voltage regulator TEST the system for normal operation. → No INSTALL a new generator TEST the system for normal operation.

FM1120000552030X

Fig. 109   Test A: System Does Not Charge (Part 3 of 3). 2001 Mustang w/3.8L Engine

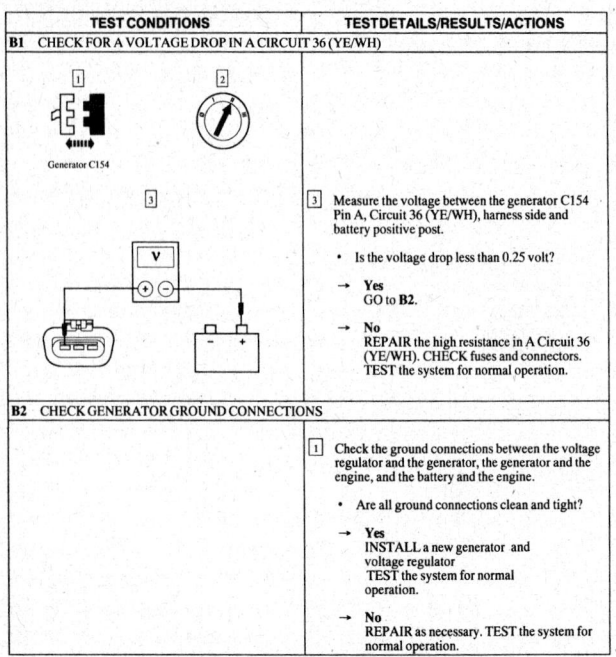

TEST CONDITIONS	TESTDETAILS/RESULTS/ACTIONS
B1 CHECK FOR A VOLTAGE DROP IN A CIRCUIT 36 (YE/WH)	
	3 Measure the voltage between the generator C154 Pin A, Circuit 36 (YE/WH), harness side and battery positive post. • Is the voltage drop less than 0.25 volt? → **Yes** GO to **B2**. → **No** REPAIR the high resistance in A Circuit 36 (YE/WH). CHECK fuses and connectors. TEST the system for normal operation.
B2 CHECK GENERATOR GROUND CONNECTIONS	
	1 Check the ground connections between the voltage regulator and the generator, the generator and the engine, and the battery and the engine. • Are all ground connections clean and tight? → **Yes** INSTALL a new generator and voltage regulator TEST the system for normal operation. → **No** REPAIR as necessary. TEST the system for normal operation.

FM1120000553000X

Fig. 110   Test B: System Overcharging. 2001 Mustang w/3.8L Engine

TEST CONDITIONS	TESTDETAILS/RESULTS/ACTIONS
C3 CHECK GENERATOR FOR LOW VOLTAGE	
	2 With the engine running at 2,000 rpm, measure the voltage between generator C153, Circuit 4 (WH/BK), harness side and ground. • Is the voltage greater than 5 volts? → **Yes** INSTALL a new voltage regulator TEST the system for normal operation. → **No** INSTALL a new generator TEST the system for normal operation.

FM1120000554020X

Fig. 111   Test C: Indicator Lamp Remains Lit w/Engine Running (Part 2 of 2). 2001 Mustang w/3.8L Engine

TEST CONDITIONS	TESTDETAILS/RESULTS/ACTIONS
D1 CHECK CHARGING SYSTEM WARNING INDICATOR LAMP	
	3 With the engine OFF, connect a fused 15A jumper wire between generator C154 Pin 1, Circuit 904 (LG/RD), harness side and ground. • Is the charging system warning indicator lamp on? → **Yes** INSTALL a new voltage regulator TEST the system for normal operation. → **No** INSPECT lamp as required.

FM1120000555000X

Fig. 112   Test D: Indicator Lamp Does Not Light. 2001 Mustang w/3.8L Engine

TEST CONDITIONS	TESTDETAILS/RESULTS/ACTIONS
C1 CHECK I CIRCUIT 904 (LG/RD) FOR SHORT TO GROUND	
	3 Turn the key ON, engine OFF. • Is the charging system warning indicator lamp on? → **Yes** REPAIR the short to ground in I Circuit 904 (LG/RD). TEST the system for normal operation. → **No** GO to **C2**.
C2 INSPECT GENERATOR S C153	
	1 Inspect generator C153 to make sure it is correctly mated to the generator and making contact with the S terminal. • Is the generator C153 OK? → **Yes** GO to **C3**. → **No** REPAIR as necessary. TEST the system for normal operation.

FM1120000554010X

Fig. 111   Test C: Indicator Lamp Remains Lit w/Engine Running (Part 1 of 2). 2001 Mustang w/3.8L Engine

TEST CONDITIONS	TESTDETAILS/RESULTS/ACTIONS
E1 CHECK FOR LOOSE CONNECTIONS	
	1 Check all generator, battery, and power distribution connections for looseness, corrosion, loose or bent terminals, or loose eyelets. • Are all connections clean and tight? → **Yes** GO to **E2**. → **No** REPAIR as necessary. TEST the system for normal operation.
E2 CHECK FUSES/FUSE LINKS	
	1 With the engine running, check fuses in A Circuit 36 (YE/WH) and I Circuit 904 (LG/RD), and fuse links, Circuit 38 (GY), for looseness by wiggling the fuse and noting the charging system warning indicator lamp. • Did the charging system warning indicator lamp flicker? → **Yes** REPAIR loose fuse connections as necessary. TEST the system for normal operation. → **No** GO to **E3**.
E3 CHECK A CIRCUIT 36 (YE/WH) CONNECTIONS	
	1 Connect a fused 20A jumper wire by back probing between generator C154 Pin A, Circuit 36 (YE/WH) and battery positive post.

FM1120000556010X

Fig. 113   Test E: Indicator Lamp Flickers Or Lights Intermittently (Part 1 of 3). 2001 Mustang w/3.8L Engine

TEST CONDITIONS	TEST DETAILS/RESULTS/ACTIONS
E3 CHECK A CIRCUIT 36 (YE/WH) CONNECTIONS (Continued)	
2	2 With the engine running, check the charging system warning indicator lamp. • Does the charging system warning indicator lamp flicker? → **Yes** GO to **E4**. → **No** REPAIR loose connections in circuits. TEST the system for normal operation.
E4 INSPECT GENERATOR S C153	
	1 Check the generator S connector C153 to make sure it is correctly mated to the generator and making good contact with the S terminal on the generator. • Is generator C153 (S connector) OK? → **Yes** GO to **E5**. → **No** REPAIR as necessary. TEST the system for normal operation.
E5 CHECK GENERATOR BRUSHES	
2	1 Remove the generator from the vehicle. 2 Measure the resistance between the A and F terminals on the voltage regulator. • Is the resistance less than 5 ohms? → **Yes** INSTALL a new generator TEST the system for normal operation. → **No** GO to **E6**.

FM1120000556020X

Fig. 113 Test E: Indicator Lamp Flickers Or Lights Intermittently (Part 2 of 3). 2001 Mustang w/3.8L Engine

TEST CONDITIONS	TEST DETAILS/RESULTS/ACTIONS
F1 CHECK FOR ACCESSORY DRIVE NOISE	
	1 Check the accessory drive belt for damage and correct installation. Check the accessory mounting brackets and generator pulley for looseness or misalignment. • Is the accessory drive OK? → **Yes** GO to **F2**. → **No** REPAIR as necessary. TEST the system for normal operation.
F2 CHECK GENERATOR MOUNTING	
	1 Check the generator mounting for loose bolts or misalignment. • Is the generator mounted correctly? → **Yes** GO to **F3**. → **No** REPAIR as necessary. TEST the system for normal operation.
F3 CHECK GENERATOR FOR ELECTRICAL NOISE	
1 2 Generator C154	3 With the engine running, turn the headlights ON, rear defroster ON, and the blower motor to HI. • Is the noise still present? → **Yes** GO to **F4**. → **No** INSTALL a new generator (10346). TEST the system for normal operation.

FM1120000557010X

Fig. 114 Test F: Alternator Noisy (Part 1 of 2). 2001 Mustang w/3.8L Engine

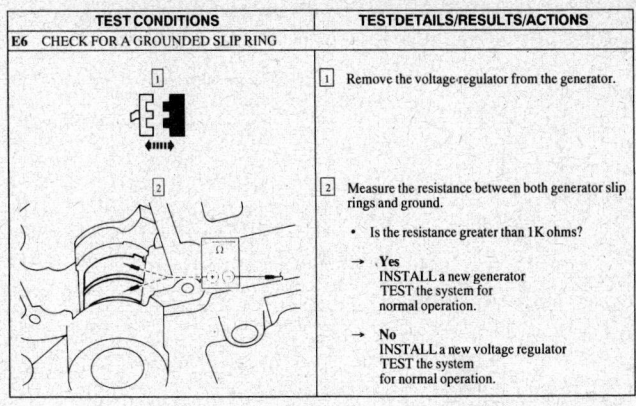

TEST CONDITIONS	TEST DETAILS/RESULTS/ACTIONS
E6 CHECK FOR A GROUNDED SLIP RING	
1	1 Remove the voltage regulator from the generator.
2	2 Measure the resistance between both generator slip rings and ground. • Is the resistance greater than 1K ohms? → **Yes** INSTALL a new generator TEST the system for normal operation. → **No** INSTALL a new voltage regulator TEST the system for normal operation.

FM1120000556030X

Fig. 113 Test E: Indicator Lamp Flickers Or Lights Intermittently (Part 3 of 3). 2001 Mustang w/3.8L Engine

TEST CONDITIONS	TEST DETAILS/RESULTS/ACTIONS
F4 CHECK GENERATOR FOR MECHANICAL NOISE	
1 Generator C154	2 Turn all accessories OFF. With the engine running, use a stethoscope or equivalent listening device to probe the generator for unusual mechanical noise. • Is the generator the noise source? → **Yes** INSTALL a new generator TEST the system for normal operation. → **No** diagnose the source of engine noise.

FM1120000557020X

Fig. 114 Test F: Alternator Noisy (Part 2 of 2). 2001 Mustang w/3.8L Engine

TEST CONDITIONS	TEST DETAILS/RESULTS/ACTIONS
G1 VERIFY GENERATOR IS SOURCE OF RADIO INTERFERENCE	
1	1 Start and run the engine.
	2 Tune the radio to a station where the interference is present.
3 4 5 Generator C154	• Is the interference present with the generator disconnected? → **Yes** INSPECT the in-vehicle entertainment system. → **No** INSTALL a new generator (10346). TEST the system for normal operation.

FM1120000558000X

Fig. 115 Test G: Radio Interference. 2001 Mustang w/3.8L Engine

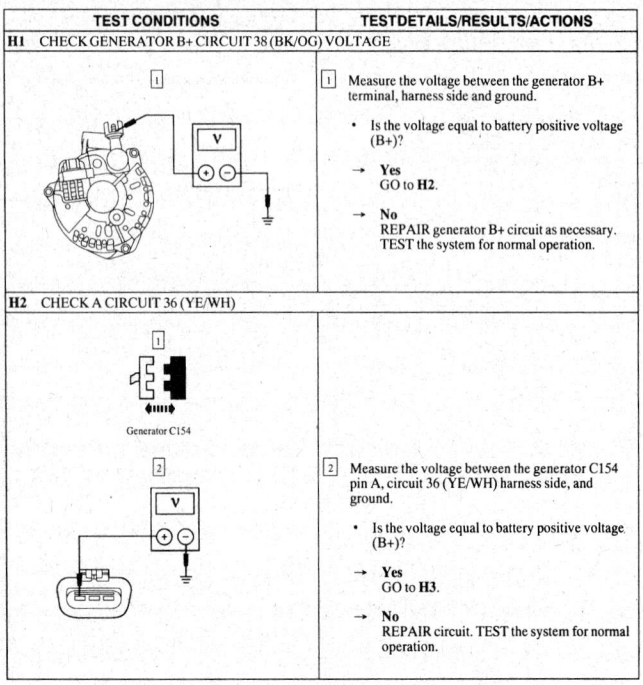

TEST CONDITIONS	TESTDETAILS/RESULTS/ACTIONS
H1 CHECK GENERATOR B+ CIRCUIT 38 (BK/OG) VOLTAGE	
	1 Measure the voltage between the generator B+ terminal, harness side and ground. • Is the voltage equal to battery positive voltage (B+)? → **Yes** GO to **H2**. → **No** REPAIR generator B+ circuit as necessary. TEST the system for normal operation.
H2 CHECK A CIRCUIT 36 (YE/WH)	
Generator C154	2 Measure the voltage between the generator C154 pin A, circuit 36 (YE/WH) harness side, and ground. • Is the voltage equal to battery positive voltage (B+)? → **Yes** GO to **H3**. → **No** REPAIR circuit. TEST the system for normal operation.

FM1120000559010X

Fig. 116   Test H: System Does Not Charge (Part 1 of 2). 2001 Mustang w/4.6L Engine

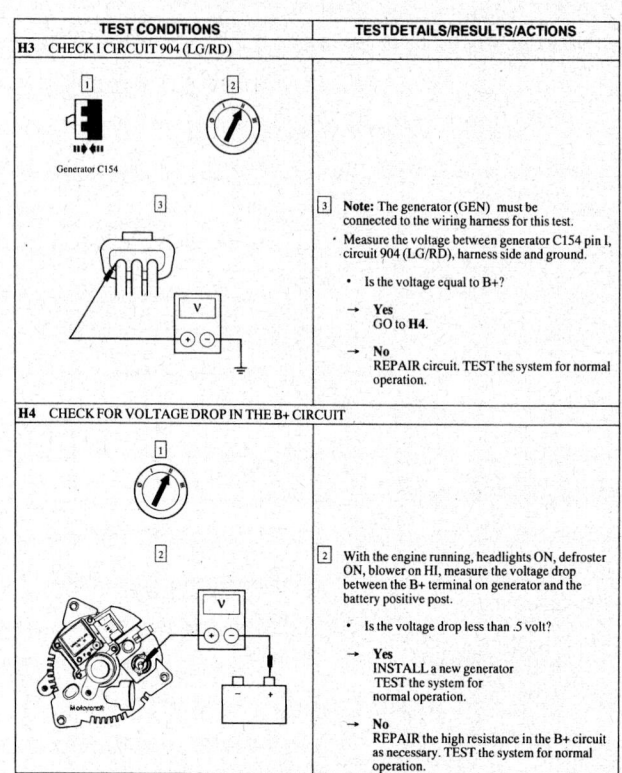

TEST CONDITIONS	TESTDETAILS/RESULTS/ACTIONS
H3 CHECK I CIRCUIT 904 (LG/RD)	
Generator C154	3 **Note:** The generator (GEN) must be connected to the wiring harness for this test. • Measure the voltage between generator C154 pin I, circuit 904 (LG/RD), harness side and ground. • Is the voltage equal to B+? → **Yes** GO to **H4**. → **No** REPAIR circuit. TEST the system for normal operation.
H4 CHECK FOR VOLTAGE DROP IN THE B+ CIRCUIT	
	2 With the engine running, headlights ON, defroster ON, blower on HI, measure the voltage drop between the B+ terminal on generator and the battery positive post. • Is the voltage drop less than .5 volt? → **Yes** INSTALL a new generator TEST the system for normal operation. → **No** REPAIR the high resistance in the B+ circuit as necessary. TEST the system for normal operation.

FM1120000559020X

Fig. 116   Test H: System Does Not Charge (Part 2 of 2). 2001 Mustang w/4.6L Engine

TEST CONDITIONS	TESTDETAILS/RESULTS/ACTIONS
I1 CHECK FOR A VOLTAGE DROP IN A CIRCUIT 36 (YE/WH)	
Generator C154	3 With the key ON, engine OFF, measure the voltage between generator C154, pin A, circuit 36 (YE/WH), harness side and battery positive post. • Is the voltage drop less than 0.25 volt? → **Yes** GO to **I2**. → **No** REPAIR circuit. TEST the system for normal operation.
I2 CHECK GROUND CONNECTIONS	
	1 Check ground connections between the generator and the engine, and the battery and the engine. • Are all ground connections clean and tight? → **Yes** INSTALL a new generator TEST the system for normal operation. → **No** REPAIR as necessary. TEST the system for normal operation.

FM1120000560000X

Fig. 117   Test I: System Overcharging. 2001 Mustang w/4.6L Engine

TEST CONDITIONS	TESTDETAILS/RESULTS/ACTIONS
J1 CHECK FOR SHORTED I CIRCUIT	
Generator C154	• Is the charging system warning indicator lamp on? → **Yes** REPAIR generator I circuit 904 (LG/RD) for a short to ground as necessary. TEST the system for normal operation. → **No** INSTALL a new generator TEST the system for normal operation.

FM1120000561000X

Fig. 118   Test J: Indicator Lamp Lights, Engine Running. 2001 Mustang w/4.6L Engine

TEST CONDITIONS	TESTDETAILS/RESULTS/ACTIONS
K1 CHECK CHARGING SYSTEM INDICATOR LAMP	
Generator C154	3 With the key ON and the engine OFF, connect a jumper wire between generator C154 pin I, circuit 904 (LG/RD), harness side and ground. • Is the charging system warning indicator lamp on? → **Yes** INSTALL a new generator (10346). TEST the system for normal operation. → **No**

FM1120000562000X

Fig. 119   Test K: Indicator Lamp Does Not Light. 2001 Mustang w/4.6L Engine

TEST CONDITIONS	TESTDETAILS/RESULTS/ACTIONS
L1 CHECK FOR LOOSE CONNECTIONS	

	[1] Check all generator, battery, and power distribution connections for looseness, corrosion, loose or bent terminals, or loose eyelets.
	
	• Are all connections clean and tight?
	
	→ **Yes**
	   GO to **L2**.
	
	→ **No**
	   TEST the system for normal operation.

L2 CHECK FUSES AND FUSE LINKS	

	[1] With the engine running, check the fuses for A circuit 36 (YE/WH) and I circuit 904 (LG/RD), and circuit 38 (GY) fuse links for looseness by wiggling the fuse/fuse link and noting the charging system warning indicator lamp operation.
	
	• Did the charging system warning indicator lamp flicker?
	
	→ **Yes**
	   REPAIR loose fuse connections as necessary. TEST the system for normal operation.
	
	→ **No**
	   GO to **L3**.

FM1120000563010X

Fig. 120   Test L: Indicator Lamp Flickers or Lights Intermittently (Part 1 of 2). 2001 Mustang w/4.6L Engine

TEST CONDITIONS	TESTDETAILS/RESULTS/ACTIONS
L3 CHECK A CIRCUIT 36 (YE/WH) CONNECTIONS	

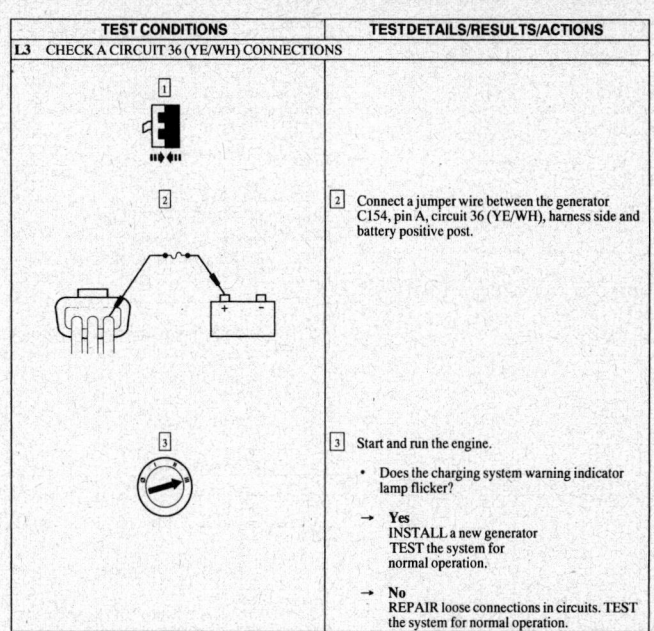	[2] Connect a jumper wire between the generator C154, pin A, circuit 36 (YE/WH), harness side and battery positive post.
	
	[3] Start and run the engine.
	
	• Does the charging system warning indicator lamp flicker?
	
	→ **Yes**
	   INSTALL a new generator
	   TEST the system for normal operation.
	
	→ **No**
	   REPAIR loose connections in circuits. TEST the system for normal operation.

FM1120000563020X

Fig. 120   Test L: Indicator Lamp Flickers or Lights Intermittently (Part 2 of 2). 2001 Mustang w/4.6L Engine

TEST CONDITIONS	TESTDETAILS/RESULTS/ACTIONS
M1 CHECK FOR ACCESSORY DRIVE NOISE	

	[1] Check the accessory drive (serpentine) belt for damage and to verify correct installation. Check the accessory mounting brackets for loose bolts or misalignment. Check for a bent generator pulley.
	
	• Is the accessory drive OK?
	
	→ **Yes**
	   GO to **M2**.
	
	→ **No**
	   continue diagnosis and testing of the accessory drive system or REPAIR as necessary. TEST the system for normal operation.

M2 CHECK GENERATOR MOUNTING	

	[1] Check the generator mounting for loose bolts or misalignment.
	
	• Is the generator mounted correctly?
	
	→ **Yes**
	   GO to **M3**.
	
	→ **No**
	   REPAIR as necessary. TEST the system for normal operation.

M3 CHECK GENERATOR FOR ELECTRICAL NOISE	
[1] [2] With the engine running, turn the headlights ON, rear defroster ON, and blower motor to HI. [3] Generator C154	

FM1120000564010X

Fig. 121   Test M: Alternator is Noisy (Part 1 of 2). 2001 Mustang w/4.6L Engine

TEST CONDITIONS	TESTDETAILS/RESULTS/ACTIONS
M3 CHECK GENERATOR FOR ELECTRICAL NOISE (Continued)	

	• Is the noise still present with the generator disconnected?
	
	→ **Yes**
	   GO to **M4**.
	
	→ **No**
	   INSTALL a new generator TEST the system for normal operation.

M4 CHECK GENERATOR FOR MECHANICAL NOISE	

[1]
Generator C154
	[2] Turn all accessories OFF. With the engine running, use a stethoscope or other listening device, to listen to the generator for unusual mechanical noise.
	
	• Is the generator the noise source?
	
	→ **Yes**
	   INSTALL a new generator TEST the system for normal operation.
	
	→ **No**
	   diagnose the source of engine noise.

FM1120000564020X

Fig. 121   Test M: Alternator is Noisy (Part 2 of 2). 2001 Mustang w/4.6L Engine

TEST CONDITIONS	TESTDETAILS/RESULTS/ACTIONS
N1 VERIFY GENERATOR FOR SOURCE OF RADIO INTERFERENCE	

	[1] With the engine running, tune the radio to station where interference is present and disconnect generator C154.
	
	• Is radio interference still present with the generator C154 disconnected?
	
	→ **Yes**
	   diagnose the cause of the radio interference.
	
	→ **No**
	   INSTALL a new generator TEST the system for normal operation.

FM1120000565000X

Fig. 122   Test N: Radio Interference. 2001 Mustang w/4.6L Engine

TEST CONDITIONS	TESTDETAILS/RESULTS/ACTIONS
O1 CHECK BATTERY CONDITION	
	① Carry out the Battery — Condition Test to determine if the battery can hold a charge and is OK for use. • Is the battery OK? → **Yes** GO to O2. → **No** INSTALL a new battery. TEST the system for normal operation.
O2 CHECK FOR GENERATOR OUTPUT	
	① Carry out the On-Vehicle Generator Load/No-Load Test. • Is the generator OK? → **Yes** GO to O3. → **No** GO to Pinpoint Test B.
O3 CHECK FOR CURRENT DRAINS	
	① Carry out the Battery — Drain Test. • Are there any excessive current drains? → **Yes** REPAIR as necessary. TEST the system for normal operation. → **No** GO to O4.

FM1120000566010X

Fig. 123   Test O: Battery Discharged or Voltage Low (Part 1 of 2). 2001 Mustang w/4.6L Engine

CONDITIONS	DETAILS/RESULTS/ACTIONS
A1 CHECK BATTERY CONDITION	
	① Carry out the Battery—Condition Test to determine if the battery can hold a charge and is OK for use. • Is the battery OK? → **Yes** GO to A2. → **No** INSTALL a new battery. TEST the system for normal operation.
A2 CHECK THE GENERATOR OUTPUT	
	① Carry out the On-Vehicle Generator Load/No Load Test. • Is the generator OK? → **Yes** GO to A3. → **No** GO to Pinpoint Test B.
A3 CHECK FOR CURRENT DRAINS	
	① Carry out the Battery—Drain Test. • **Are there any excessive current drains?** → **Yes** REPAIR as necessary. TEST the system for normal operation. → **No** GO to A4.
A4 CHECK FOR CURRENT DRAINS WHICH SHUT OFF WHEN THE BATTERY IS DISCONNECTED	
	① Carry out the Battery—Electronic Drains Which Shut Off When the Battery Cable is Disconnected Test. Refer or Component Tests • **Are there any current drains which shut off when the battery is disconnected?** → **Yes** REPAIR as necessary. TEST the system for normal operation. → **No** GO to Pinpoint Test B.

FM1120200762000X

Fig. 124   Test A: Battery Is Charged Or Voltage Is Low. 2002–05 Mustang

TEST CONDITIONS	TESTDETAILS/RESULTS/ACTIONS
O4 CHECK FOR CURRENT DRAINS WHICH SHUT OFF WHEN THE BATTERY IS DISCONNECTED	
	① Carry out the Battery — Electronic Drains Which Shut Off When the Battery Cable is Disconnected Test. • Are there any current drains which shut off when the battery is disconnected? → **Yes** REPAIR as necessary. TEST the system for normal operation. → **No** If 3G generator, GO to Pinpoint Test A. If 4G or 6G generator, GO to Pinpoint Test H.

FM1120000566020X

Fig. 123   Test O: Battery Discharged or Voltage Low (Part 2 of 2). 2001 Mustang w/4.6L Engine

CONDITIONS	DETAILS/RESULTS/ACTIONS
B1 CHECK GENERATOR B+ CIRCUIT 38 (BK/OG)	
① 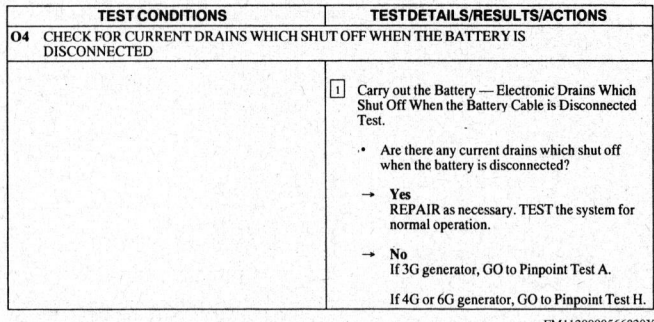 Generator B+ C1104b (4.6L 4V) or C102b (3.8L or 4.6L 2V) ② 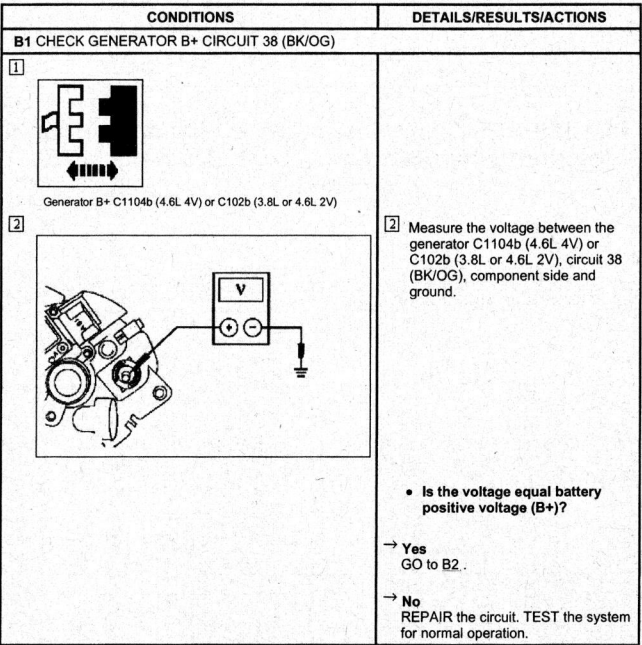	② Measure the voltage between the generator C1104b (4.6L 4V) or C102b (3.8L or 4.6L 2V), circuit 38 (BK/OG), component side and ground. • **Is the voltage equal battery positive voltage (B+)?** → **Yes** GO to B2. → **No** REPAIR the circuit. TEST the system for normal operation.

FM1120200763010X

Fig. 125   Test B: Charging System Warning Indicator Is On w/Engine Running, Battery Voltage Does Not Increase (Part 1 of 4). 2002–05 Mustang

B2 CHECK GENERATOR A CIRCUIT 36 (YE/WH)

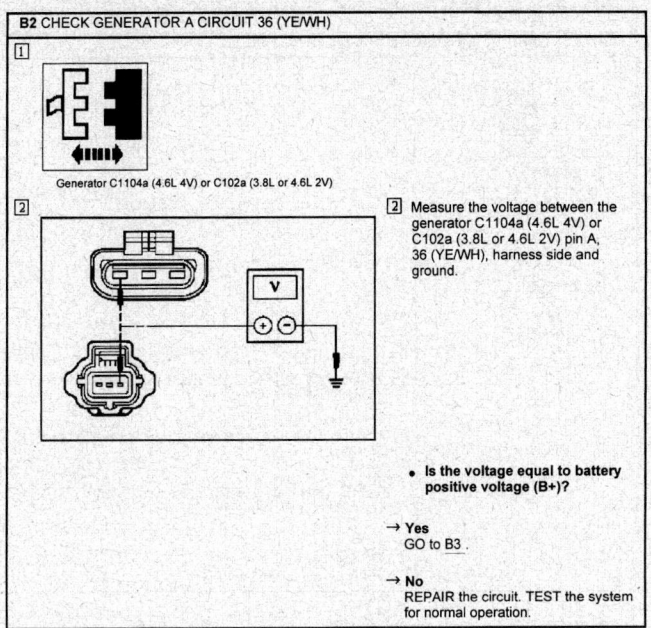

Generator C1104a (4.6L 4V) or C102a (3.8L or 4.6L 2V)

2 Measure the voltage between the generator C1104a (4.6L 4V) or C102a (3.8L or 4.6L 2V) pin A, 36 (YE/WH), harness side and ground.

• Is the voltage equal to battery positive voltage (B+)?

→ Yes
GO to B3.

→ No
REPAIR the circuit. TEST the system for normal operation.

FM1120200763020X

Fig. 125   Test B: Charging System Warning Indicator Is On w/Engine Running, Battery Voltage Does Not Increase (Part 2 of 4). 2002–05 Mustang

B3 CHECK I CIRCUIT 904 (LG/RD) FOR AN OPEN

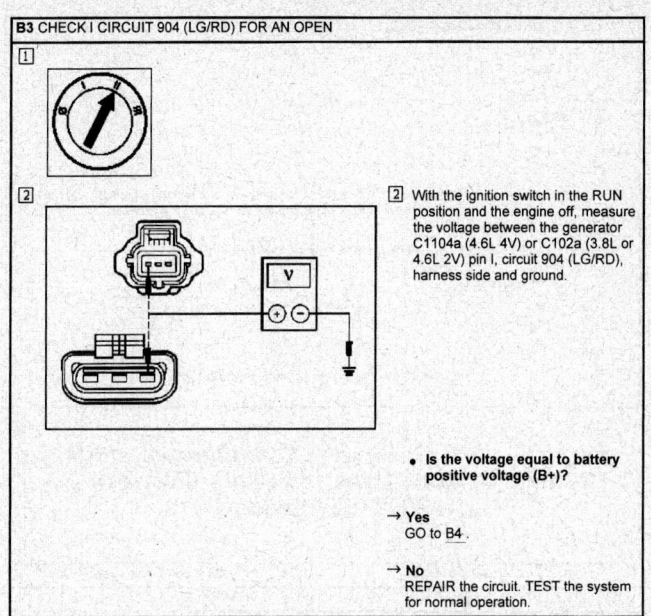

2 With the ignition switch in the RUN position and the engine off, measure the voltage between the generator C1104a (4.6L 4V) or C102a (3.8L or 4.6L 2V) pin I, circuit 904 (LG/RD), harness side and ground.

• Is the voltage equal to battery positive voltage (B+)?

→ Yes
GO to B4.

→ No
REPAIR the circuit. TEST the system for normal operation.

FM1120200763030X

Fig. 125   Test B: Charging System Warning Indicator Is On w/Engine Running, Battery Voltage Does Not Increase (Part 3 of 4). 2002–05 Mustang

B4 CHECK FOR VOLTAGE DROP IN B+ CIRCUIT 38 (YE/WH)

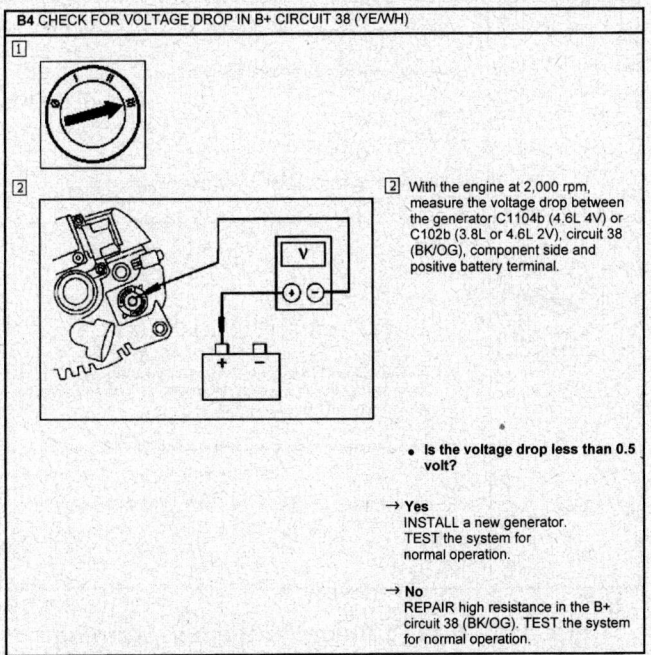

2 With the engine at 2,000 rpm, measure the voltage drop between the generator C1104b (4.6L 4V) or C102b (3.8L or 4.6L 2V), circuit 38 (BK/OG), component side and positive battery terminal.

• Is the voltage drop less than 0.5 volt?

→ Yes
INSTALL a new generator. TEST the system for normal operation.

→ No
REPAIR high resistance in the B+ circuit 38 (BK/OG). TEST the system for normal operation.

FM1120200763040X

Fig. 125   Test B: Charging System Warning Indicator Is On w/Engine Running, Battery Voltage Does Not Increase (Part 4 of 4). 2002–05 Mustang

CONDITIONS	DETAILS/RESULTS/ACTIONS
C1 CHECK FOR VOLTAGE DROP IN A CIRCUIT 36 (YE/WH)	

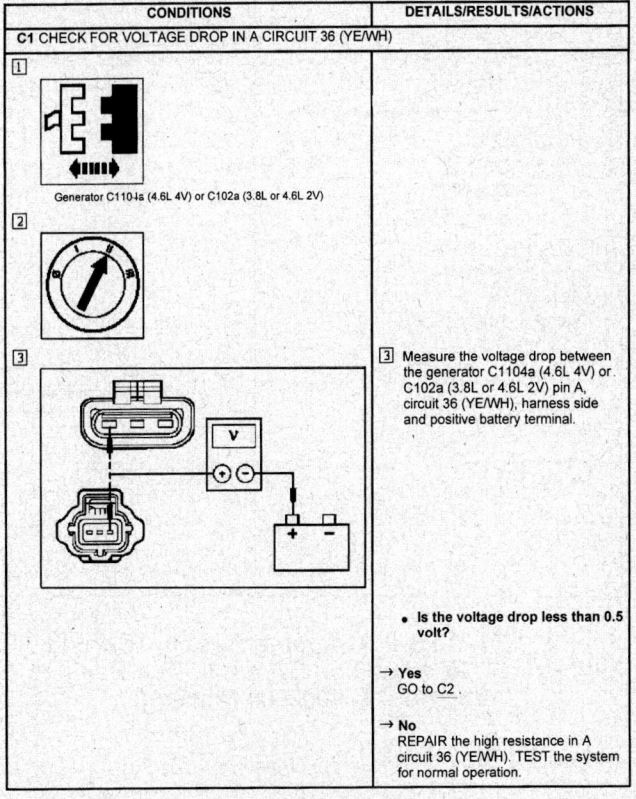

Generator C1104a (4.6L 4V) or C102a (3.8L or 4.6L 2V)

3 Measure the voltage drop between the generator C1104a (4.6L 4V) or C102a (3.8L or 4.6L 2V) pin A, circuit 36 (YE/WH), harness side and positive battery terminal.

• Is the voltage drop less than 0.5 volt?

→ Yes
GO to C2.

→ No
REPAIR the high resistance in A circuit 36 (YE/WH). TEST the system for normal operation.

FM1120200764010X

Fig. 126   Test C: System Overcharges, Battery Voltage Is More Than 15.5 Volts (Part 1 of 2). 2002–05 Mustang

C2 CHECK GENERATOR AND BATTERY GROUND CONNECTIONS

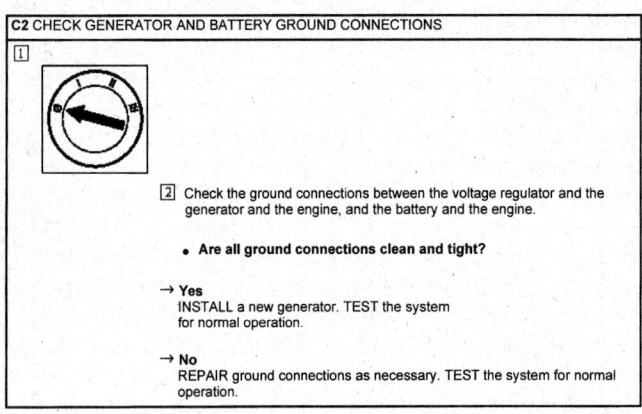

2. Check the ground connections between the voltage regulator and the generator and the engine, and the battery and the engine.

- **Are all ground connections clean and tight?**

→ **Yes**
INSTALL a new generator. TEST the system for normal operation.

→ **No**
REPAIR ground connections as necessary. TEST the system for normal operation.

FM1120200764020X

Fig. 126 Test C: System Overcharges, Battery Voltage Is More Than 15.5 Volts (Part 2 of 2). 2002–05 Mustang

CONDITIONS	DETAILS/RESULTS/ACTIONS
E1 CHECK THE CHARGING SYSTEM WARNING INDICATOR LAMP	

1.

Generator C1104a (4.6L 4V) or C102a (3.8L or 4.6L 2V)

2.

3.

2. With the engine off, connect a fused (15A) jumper wire between the generator C1104a (4.6L 4V) or C102a (3.8L or 4.6L 2V) pin I, circuit 904 (LG/RD), harness side and ground.

- **Is the charging system warning indicator lamp illuminated?**

→ **Yes**
INSTALL a new generator. TEST the system for normal operation.

→ **No**
Diagnose and Test the instrument cluster.

FM1120200766000X

Fig. 128 Test E: Charging System Warning Indicator Is Off w/Ignition Switch In Run Position & Engine Off. 2002–05 Mustang

CONDITIONS	DETAILS/RESULTS/ACTIONS
D1 CHECK I CIRCUIT 904 (LG/RD) FOR A SHORT TO GROUND	

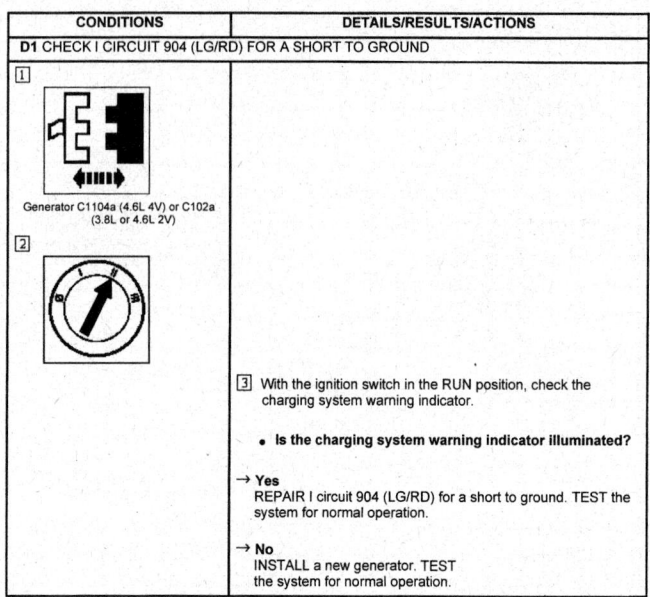

Generator C1104a (4.6L 4V) or C102a (3.8L or 4.6L 2V)

3. With the ignition switch in the RUN position, check the charging system warning indicator.

- **Is the charging system warning indicator illuminated?**

→ **Yes**
REPAIR I circuit 904 (LG/RD) for a short to ground. TEST the system for normal operation.

→ **No**
INSTALL a new generator. TEST the system for normal operation.

FM1120200765000X

Fig. 127 Test D: Charging System Warning Indicator Is On w/Engine Running & Battery Increases Voltage. 2002–05 Mustang

CONDITIONS	DETAILS/RESULTS/ACTIONS
F1 CHECK FOR LOOSE CONNECTIONS	

1. Check all generator, battery, and power distribution connections for looseness, corrosion, loose or bent terminals, or loose eyelets.

- **Are all connections clean and tight?**

→ **Yes**
GO to F2.

→ **No**
REPAIR as necessary. TEST the system for normal operation.

| **F2 CHECK FUSE** | |

1.

2. With the engine running, check battery junction box (BJB) fuse 20 (20A) in A circuit 36 (YE/WH) for looseness by wiggling the fuse and noting the charging system warning indicator lamp operation.

- **Does the charging system warning indicator lamp flicker?**

→ **Yes**
REPAIR loose fuse connections as necessary. TEST the system for normal operation.

→ **No**
GO to F3.

FM1120200767010X

Fig. 129 Test F: Charging System Warning Indicator Lamp Flickers Or Is Intermittent (Part 1 of 2). 2002–05 Mustang

F3 CHECK A CIRCUIT 36 (YE/WH) CONNECTIONS

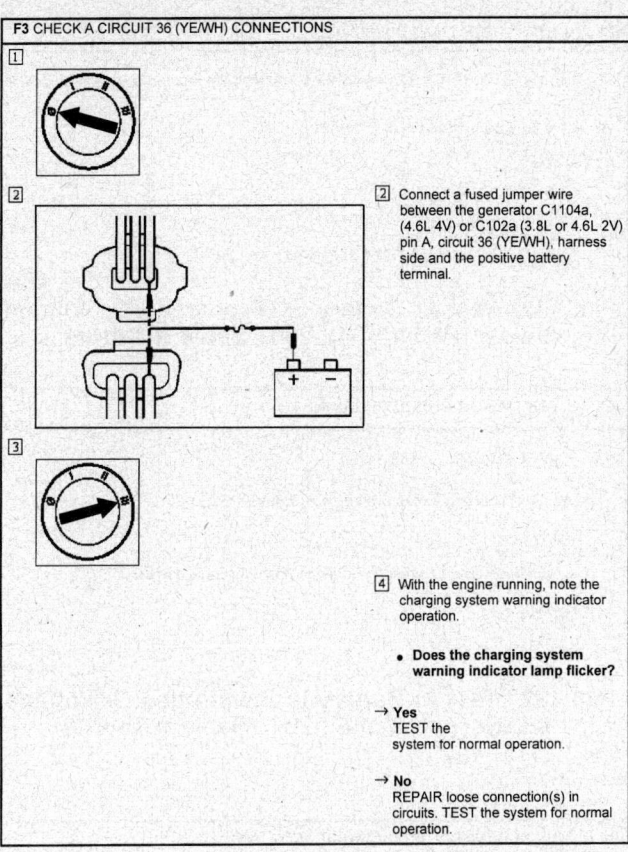

2 Connect a fused jumper wire between the generator C1104a, (4.6L 4V) or C102a (3.8L or 4.6L 2V) pin A, circuit 36 (YE/WH), harness side and the positive battery terminal.

4 With the engine running, note the charging system warning indicator operation.

- **Does the charging system warning indicator lamp flicker?**

→ **Yes**
TEST the system for normal operation.

→ **No**
REPAIR loose connection(s) in circuits. TEST the system for normal operation.

FM1120200767020X

Fig. 129   Test F: Charging System Warning Indicator Lamp Flickers Or Is Intermittent (Part 2 of 2). 2002–05 Mustang

G3 CHECK GENERATOR FOR ELECTRICAL NOISE

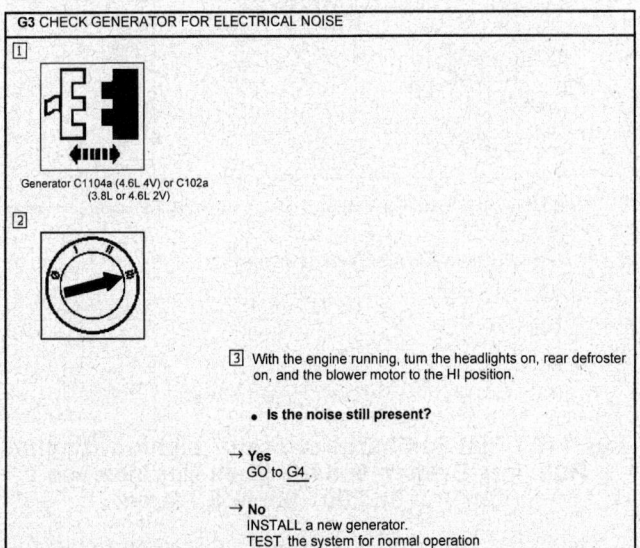

Generator C1104a (4.6L 4V) or C102a (3.8L or 4.6L 2V)

3 With the engine running, turn the headlights on, rear defroster on, and the blower motor to the HI position.

- **Is the noise still present?**

→ **Yes**
GO to G4.

→ **No**
INSTALL a new generator. TEST the system for normal operation

FM1120200768020X

Fig. 130   Test G: Alternator Is Noisy (Part 2 of 3). 2002–05 Mustang

CONDITIONS	DETAILS/RESULTS/ACTIONS
G1 CHECK FOR ACCESSORY DRIVE NOISE	

1 Check the accessory drive belt for damage and correct installation. Check the accessory mounting brackets and generator pulley for looseness or misalignment.

- **Is the accessory drive OK?**

→ **Yes**
GO to G2.

→ **No**
REPAIR as necessary.
TEST the system for normal operation.

G2 CHECK GENERATOR MOUNTING

1 Check the generator mounting for loose bolts or misalignment.

- **Is the generator mounted correctly?**

→ **Yes**
GO to G3.

→ **No**
REPAIR as necessary. TEST the system for normal operation.

FM1120200768010X

Fig. 130   Test G: Alternator Is Noisy (Part 1 of 3). 2002–05 Mustang

G4 CHECK GENERATOR FOR MECHANICAL NOISE

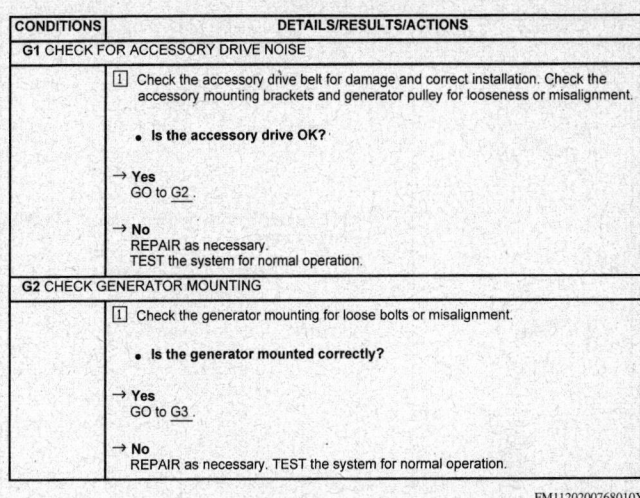

Generator C1104a (4.6L 4V) or C102a (3.8L or 4.6L 2V)

4 Turn all accessories off. With the engine running, use a stethoscope or equivalent listening device to probe the generator for unusual mechanical noise.

- **Is the generator the noise source?**

→ **Yes**
INSTALL a new generator.

→ **No**
diagnose the source of engine noise.

FM1120200768030X

Fig. 130   Test G: Alternator Is Noisy (Part 3 of 3). 2002–05 Mustang

CONDITIONS	DETAILS/RESULTS/ACTIONS
H1 VERIFY GENERATOR IS SOURCE OF RADIO INTERFERENCE	

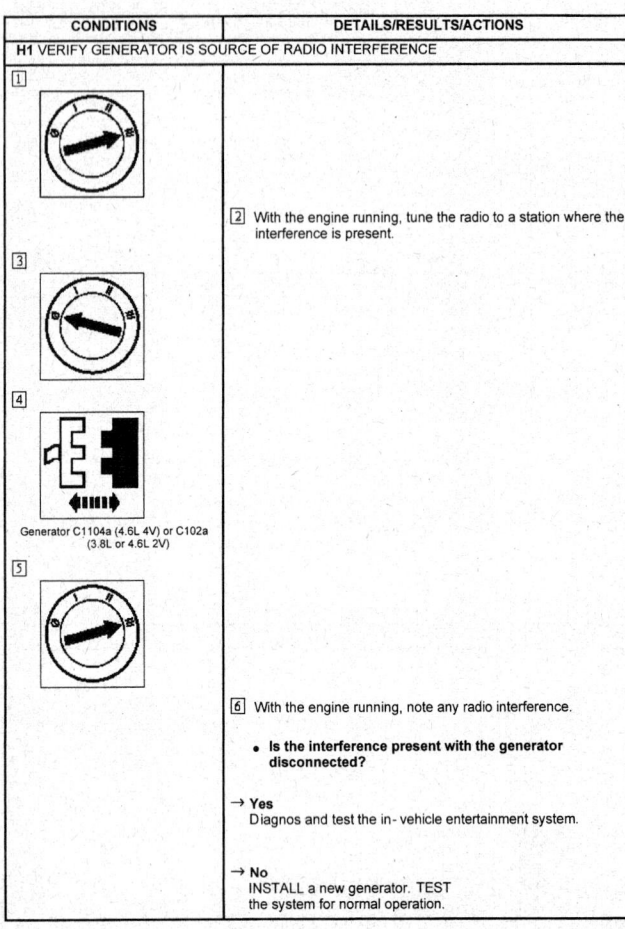

② With the engine running, tune the radio to a station where the interference is present.

Generator C1104a (4.6L 4V) or C102a (3.8L or 4.6L 2V)

⑥ With the engine running, note any radio interference.

● **Is the interference present with the generator disconnected?**

→ **Yes**
Diagnos and test the in- vehicle entertainment system.

→ **No**
INSTALL a new generator. TEST the system for normal operation.

FM1120200769000X

Fig. 131   Test H: Radio Interference. 2002–05 Mustang

A2   CHECK THE GENERATOR OUTPUT

1   Carry out the On — Vehicle Generator Load/No Load Test.

● **Is the generator OK?**

→ **Yes**
Go to «A3».

→ **No**
GO to «Pinpoint Test B».

FM1120100584020X

Fig. 132   Test A: Battery Is Discharged Or Voltage Is Low (Part 2 of 4). 2001 Sable & Taurus

---

A4   CHECK FOR CURRENT DRAINS WHICH SHUT OFF WHEN THE BATTERY IS DISCONNECTED

1   Carry out the Battery — Electronic Drains Which Shut Off When the Battery Cable is Disconnected Test.

● **Are there any current drains which shut off when the battery is disconnected?**

→ **Yes**
REPAIR as necessary. TEST the system for normal operation.

→ **No**
GO to «Pinpoint Test B».

FM1120100584040X

Fig. 132   Test A: Battery Is Discharged Or Voltage Is Low (Part 4 of 4). 2001 Sable & Taurus

---

A1   CHECK THE BATTERY CONDITION

1   Carry out the Battery - Capacity Test to determine if the battery can hold a charge and is OK for use.

● **Is the battery OK?**

→ **Yes**
Go to «A2».

→ **No**
INSTALL a new battery. TEST the system for normal operation.

FM1120100584010X

Fig. 132   Test A: Battery Is Discharged Or Voltage Is Low (Part 1 of 4). 2001 Sable & Taurus

---

A3   CHECK FOR CURRENT DRAINS

1   Carry out the Battery - Drain Test.

● **Are there any excessive current drains?**

→ **Yes**
REPAIR as necessary. TEST the system for normal operation.

→ **No**
Go to «A4».

FM1120100584030X

Fig. 132   Test A: Battery Is Discharged Or Voltage Is Low (Part 3 of 4). 2001 Sable & Taurus

---

B1   CHECK GENERATOR B+ CIRCUIT 36 (YE/WH)

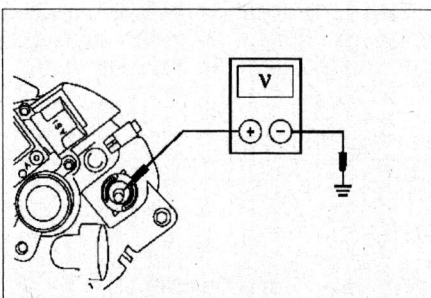

1

Measure the voltage between generator B+ terminal, circuit 36 (YE/WH), component side and ground.

● **Is the voltage equal to battery positive voltage (B+)?**

→ **Yes**
Go to «B2».

→ **No**
REPAIR the circuit. TEST the system for normal operation.

FM1120100585010X

Fig. 133   Test B: Charge Indicator Lights w/Engine Running, System Voltage Does Not Increase (Part 1 of 5). 2001 Sable & Taurus

B2   CHECK GENERATOR A CIRCUIT 35 (OG/LB)

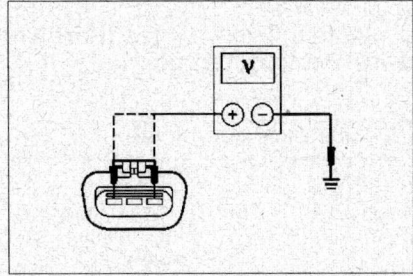

Generator C102a (4V) or C1104 (2V)

Measure the voltage between generator C102a (4V) or C1104 (2V) pin A, circuit 35 (OG/LB), harness side and ground.

- Is the voltage equal to battery positive voltage (B+)?

→ Yes

   Go to «B3».

→ No

   Repair the circuit. Test system for normal operation.

FM1120100585020X

Fig. 133   Test B: Charge Indicator Lights w/Engine Running, System Voltage Does Not Increase (Part 2 of 5). 2001 Sable & Taurus

With the ignition switch in the RUN position and the engine running, measure the voltage between generator C102a (4V) or C1104 (2V) pin I, circuit 904 (LG/RD), harness side and ground.

- Is the voltage equal to battery positive voltage (B+)?

→ Yes

   Go to «B4».

→ No

   REPAIR the circuit. TEST the system for normal operation.

FM1120100585040X

Fig. 133   Test B: Charge Indicator Lights w/Engine Running, System Voltage Does Not Increase (Part 4 of 5). 2001 Sable & Taurus

B3   CHECK I CIRCUIT 904 (LG/RD) FOR AN OPEN

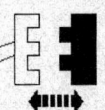

1   Generator C102a (4V) or C1104 (2V)

2

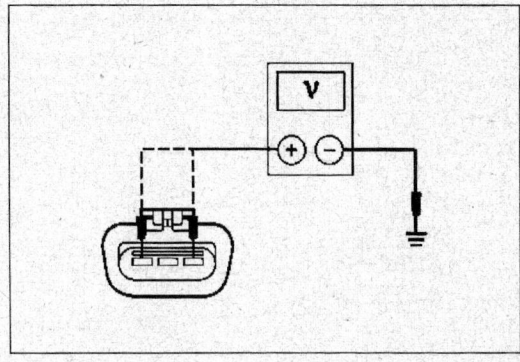

3

FM1120100585030X

Fig. 133   Test B: Charge Indicator Lights w/Engine Running, System Voltage Does Not Increase (Part 3 of 5). 2001 Sable & Taurus

B4   CHECK FOR VOLTAGE DROP IN B+ CIRCUIT 36 (YE/WH)

1

2   With the engine running, turn the headlamps on, rear defroster on, and the blower motor to the high position.

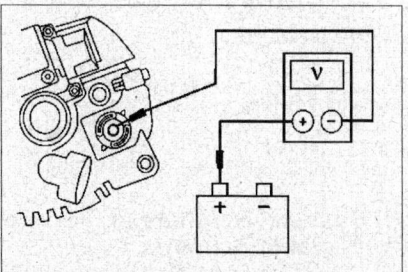

3   With the engine at 2,000 rpm, measure the voltage drop between the generator B+ terminal, circuit 36 (YE/WH), component side and positive battery terminal.

- Is the voltage drop less than 0.5 volt?

→ Yes

   INSTALL a new generator. TEST the system for normal operation.

→ No

   REPAIR high resistance in the B+ circuit 36 (YE/WH). TEST the system for normal operation.

FM1120100585050X

Fig. 133   Test B: Charge Indicator Lights w/Engine Running, System Voltage Does Not Increase (Part 5 of 5). 2001 Sable & Taurus

C1   **CHECK FOR VOLTAGE DROP IN A CIRCUIT 35 (OG/LB)**

1   *Generator C102a (4V) or C1104 (2V)*

2

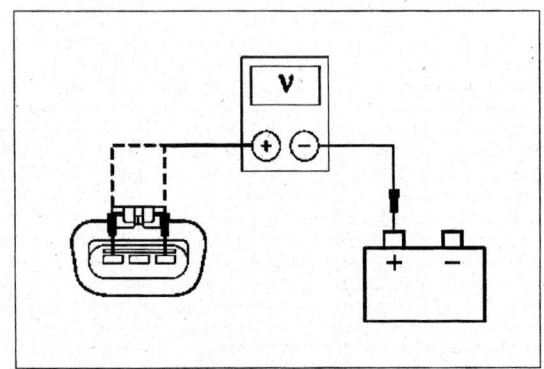

3

FM1120100586010X

Fig. 134   Test C: System Overcharges (Part 1 of 3). 2001 Sable & Taurus

C2   **CHECK GENERATOR AND BATTERY GROUND CONNECTIONS**

1

2   Check the ground connections between the voltage regulator and the generator (3.0L 2V engine only), the generator and the engine, and the battery and the engine.

- **Are all ground connections clean and tight?**

→ **Yes**

INSTALL a new generator. TEST the system for normal operation.

→ **No**

REPAIR ground connections as necessary. TEST the system for normal operation.

FM1120100586030X

Fig. 134   Test C: System Overcharges (Part 3 of 3). 2001 Sable & Taurus

Measure the voltage drop between generator C102a (4V) or C1104 (2V) pin A, circuit 35 (OG/LB), harness side and positive battery terminal.

- **Is the voltage drop less than 0.5 volt?**

→ **Yes**

Go to «C2».

→ **No**

REPAIR the high resistance in A circuit 35 (OG/LB). TEST the system for normal operation.

FM1120100586020X

Fig. 134   Test C: System Overcharges (Part 2 of 3). 2001 Sable & Taurus

D1   **CHECK I CIRCUIT 904 (LG/RD) FOR SHORT TO GROUND**

1   *Generator C102a (4V) or C1104 (2V)*

2

3   With the ignition switch in the RUN position, check the charging system warning indicator.

- **Is the charging system warning indicator illuminated?**

→ **Yes**

REPAIR I circuit 904 (LG/RD) for a short to ground. TEST the system for normal operation.

→ **No**

INSTALL a new generator; TEST the system for normal operation.

FM1120100587000X

Fig. 135   Test D: Charge Indicator Lights w/Engine Running, System Voltage Increases. 2001 Sable & Taurus

E1   **CHECK THE CHARGING SYSTEM WARNING INDICATOR LAMP**

1   *Generator C102a (4V) or C1104 (2V)*

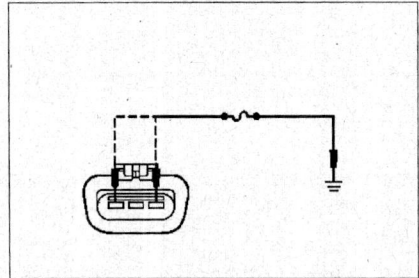

2

With the engine off, connect a fused (15A) jumper wire between the generator C102a (4V) or C1104 (2V) pin I, circuit 904 (LG/RD), harness side and ground.

FM1120100588010X

Fig. 136   Test E: Charge Indicator Off w/Ignition In Run Position & Engine Off (Part 1 of 2). 2001 Sable & Taurus

3

- **Is the charging system warning indicator lamp illuminated?**

➔ **Yes**

INSTALL a new generator. TEST the system for normal operation.

➔ **No**

Diagnose instrument cluster fault condition.

FM1120100588020X

Fig. 136   Test E: Charge Indicator Off w/Ignition In Run Position & Engine Off (Part 2 of 2). 2001 Sable & Taurus

| F2 | CHECK FUSE CONNECTIONS |

1

With the engine running, check the BJB fuse F126 (30A) in A circuit 35 (OG/LB) and the CJB fuse F227 (10A) in I circuit 904 (LG/RD) for looseness by wiggling the fuse and noting the charging system warning indicator operation.

- **Does the charging system warning indicator flicker?**

➔ **Yes**

REPAIR loose fuse connection(s) as necessary. TEST the system for normal operation.

➔ **No**

Go to «F3».

FM1120100589020X

Fig. 137   Test F: Indicator Flickers/Intermittent (Part 2 of 4). 2001 Sable & Taurus

3

With the engine running, note the charging system warning indicator operation.

- **Does the charging system warning indicator flicker?**

➔ **Yes**

INSTALL a new generator. TEST the system for normal operation.

➔ **No**

REPAIR loose connection(s) in circuits. TEST the system for normal operation.

FM1120100589040X

Fig. 137   Test F: Indicator Flickers/Intermittent (Part 4 of 4). 2001 Sable & Taurus

Test Step		Result	►	Action to Take
G1	**CHECK FOR ACCESSORY DRIVE BELT NOISE**			
• Check the drive belt to make sure that it is installed properly and is not damaged.		Yes	►	GO to **G2**.
		No	►	SERVICE accessory drive belt as required. RETEST system.
• **Is drive belt OK?**				
G2	**CHECK GENERATOR MOUNTING**			
• Check the generator and generator mounting bracket for loose bolts or misalignment condition.		Yes	►	If noise is still present, REPLACE generator. RETEST system.
• **Is generator mounted correctly?**		No	►	INSTALL generator to specifications. RETEST system.

FM1129800225000X

Fig. 138   Test G: Alternator Is Noisy. Sable & Taurus

| F1 | CHECK FOR LOOSE CONNECTIONS |

1   Check all generator, battery, and power distribution connections for looseness, corrosion, loose or bent terminals, or loose eyelets.

- **Are all connections clean and tight?**

➔ **Yes**

Go to «F2».

➔ **No**

REPAIR as necessary. TEST the system for normal operation.

FM1120100589010X

Fig. 137   Test F: Indicator Flickers/Intermittent (Part 1 of 4). 2001 Sable & Taurus

| F3 | CHECK A CIRCUIT 35 (OG/LB) CONNECTIONS |

1

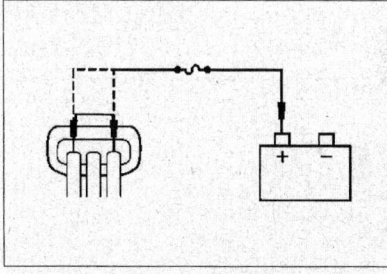

2

Connect a fused (15A) jumper wire between generator C102a (4V) or C1104 (2V) pin A, circuit 35 (OG/LB) and the positive battery terminal.

FM1120100589030X

Fig. 137   Test F: Indicator Flickers/Intermittent (Part 3 of 4). 2001 Sable & Taurus

| H1 | VERIFY GENERATOR IS SOURCE OF RADIO INTERFERENCE |

1

2   With the engine running, tune the radio to a station where the interference is present.

3

4   *Generator C102a (4V) or C1104 (2V)*

5

FM1120100590010X

Fig. 139   Test H: Radio Interference (Part 1 of 2). 2001 Sable & Taurus

6   With the engine running, note any radio interference.

● **Is the radio interference present with the generator disconnected?**

→ **Yes**

TEST the in-vehicle entertainment system.

→ **No**

INSTALL a new generator. TEST the system for normal operation.

FM1120100590020X

Fig. 139   Test H: Radio Interference (Part 2 of 2). 2001 Sable & Taurus

CONDITIONS	DETAILS/RESULTS/ACTIONS
B1 CHECK THE FAULT CODES IN THE PCM	
	③ Use the recorded PCM DTCs from the continuous and on-demand self-test. • Are any DTCs recorded? → **Yes** REFER to PCM Diagnostic Trouble Code (DTC) Index. → **No** GO to **B2**.
B2 CHECK CIRCUIT 3990 (LB/RD)	
Generator C102 (4V) or C1104 (2V)	⑤ Measure the voltage between the generator C102 (4V) or C1104 (2V) pin 2, circuit 3990 (LB/RD), harness side and ground. • Is the voltage 0 volts? → **Yes** GO to **B3**. → **No** GO to **B4**.
B3 CHECK CIRCUIT 3990 (LB/RD) FOR AN OPEN	

FM1120200772010X

Fig. 141   Test B: Charging System Warning Indicator Is On w/Engine Running, System Voltage Does Not Increase (Part 1 of 3). 2002–05 Sable & Taurus

CONDITIONS	DETAILS/RESULTS/ACTIONS
A1 CHECK THE GENERATOR OUTPUT	
	① Carry out the On-Vehicle Generator Load/No Load Tests. • Is the generator OK? → **Yes** GO to **A2**. → **No** GO to Pinpoint Test B.
A2 CHECK FOR CURRENT DRAINS	
	① Carry out the Battery — Drain Test. • Are there any excessive current drains? → **Yes** REPAIR as necessary. TEST the system for normal operation. → **No** GO to **A3**.
A3 CHECK FOR CURRENT DRAINS WHICH SHUT OFF WHEN THE BATTERY IS DISCONNECTED	
	① Carry out the Battery — Electronic Drains Which Shut Off When the Battery Cable is Disconnected Test. • Are there any current drains which shut off when the battery is disconnected? → **Yes** REPAIR as necessary. TEST the system for normal operation. → **No** GO to Pinpoint Test B.

FM1120200771000X

Fig. 140   Test A: Battery Is Discharged Or Voltage Is Low. 2002–05 Sable & Taurus

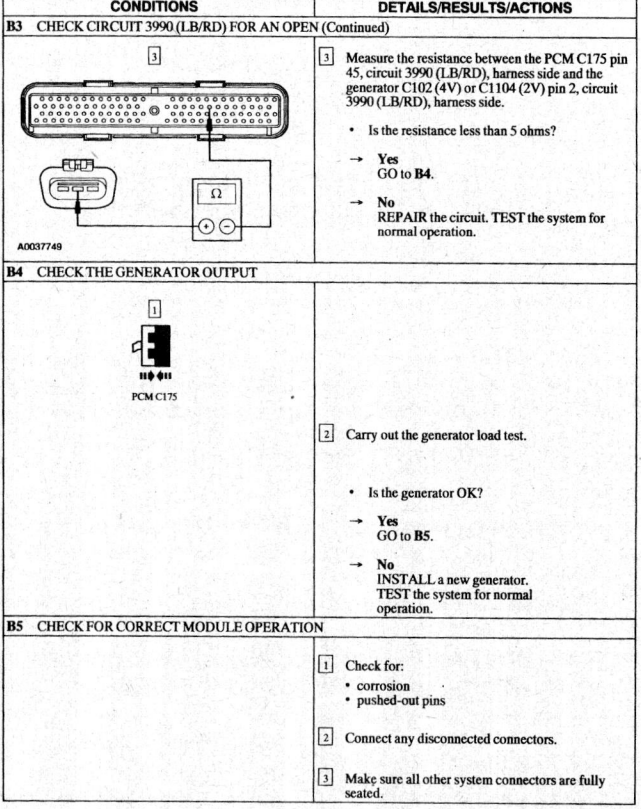

CONDITIONS	DETAILS/RESULTS/ACTIONS
B3 CHECK CIRCUIT 3990 (LB/RD) FOR AN OPEN (Continued)	
A0037749	③ Measure the resistance between the PCM C175 pin 45, circuit 3990 (LB/RD), harness side and the generator C102 (4V) or C1104 (2V) pin 2, circuit 3990 (LB/RD), harness side. • Is the resistance less than 5 ohms? → **Yes** GO to **B4**. → **No** REPAIR the circuit. TEST the system for normal operation.
B4 CHECK THE GENERATOR OUTPUT	
PCM C175	② Carry out the generator load test. • Is the generator OK? → **Yes** GO to **B5**. → **No** INSTALL a new generator. TEST the system for normal operation.
B5 CHECK FOR CORRECT MODULE OPERATION	
	① Check for: • corrosion • pushed-out pins ② Connect any disconnected connectors. ③ Make sure all other system connectors are fully seated.

FM1120200772020X

Fig. 141   Test B: Charging System Warning Indicator Is On w/Engine Running, System Voltage Does Not Increase (Part 2 of 3). 2002–05 Sable & Taurus

CONDITIONS	DETAILS/RESULTS/ACTIONS
B5 CHECK FOR CORRECT MODULE OPERATION (Continued)	
	4 Operate the system and verify the concern is still present. • Is the concern still present? → **Yes** INSTALL a new PCM. CLEAR the DTCs. REPEAT the PCM self-test. → **No** The system is operating correctly at this time. Concern may have been caused by a loose or corroded connector. CLEAR the DTCs. REPEAT the self-test.

FM1120200772030X

Fig. 141   Test B: Charging System Warning Indicator Is On w/Engine Running, System Voltage Does Not Increase (Part 3 of 3). 2002–05 Sable & Taurus

CONDITIONS	DETAILS/RESULTS/ACTIONS
C2 CHECK THE BATTERY VOLTAGE (Continued)	
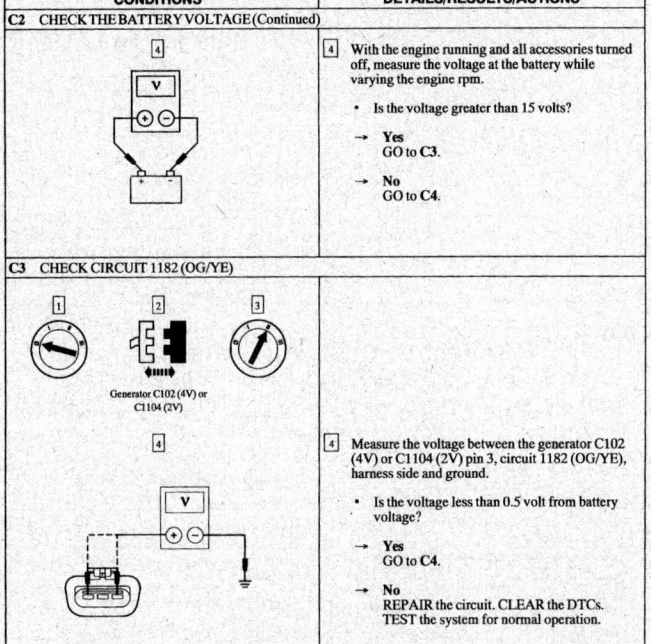	**4** With the engine running and all accessories turned off, measure the voltage at the battery while varying the engine rpm. • Is the voltage greater than 15 volts? → **Yes** GO to **C3**. → **No** GO to **C4**.
C3 CHECK CIRCUIT 1182 (OG/YE)	
Generator C102 (4V) or C1104 (2V)	**4** Measure the voltage between the generator C102 (4V) or C1104 (2V) pin 3, circuit 1182 (OG/YE), harness side and ground. • Is the voltage less than 0.5 volt from battery voltage? → **Yes** GO to **C4**. → **No** REPAIR the circuit. CLEAR the DTCs. TEST the system for normal operation.

FM1120200773020X

Fig. 142   Test C: System Overcharges, Battery Voltage More Than 15 Volts (Part 2 of 3). 2002–05 Sable & Taurus

CONDITIONS	DETAILS/RESULTS/ACTIONS
C1 CHECK THE FAULT CODES IN THE PCM	
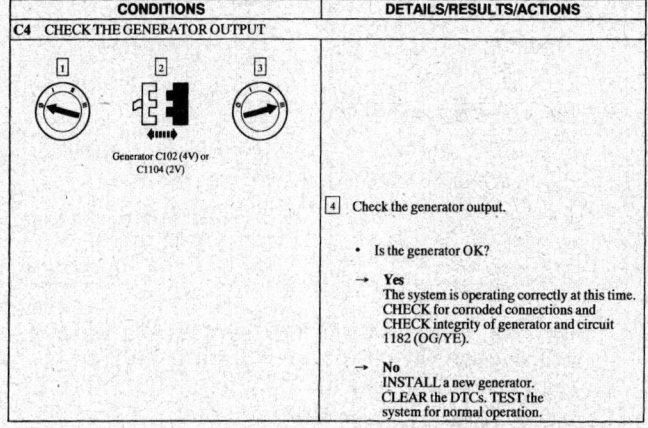	**3** Use the recorded PCM DTCs from the continuous and on-demand self-test. • Are any DTCs recorded? → **Yes** REFER to PCM Diagnostic Trouble Code (DTC) Index. → **No** GO to **C2**.
C2 CHECK THE BATTERY VOLTAGE	

FM1120200773010X

Fig. 142   Test C: System Overcharges, Battery Voltage More Than 15 Volts (Part 1 of 3). 2002–05 Sable & Taurus

CONDITIONS	DETAILS/RESULTS/ACTIONS
C4 CHECK THE GENERATOR OUTPUT	
Generator C102 (4V) or C1104 (2V)	**4** Check the generator output. • Is the generator OK? → **Yes** The system is operating correctly at this time. CHECK for corroded connections and CHECK integrity of generator and circuit 1182 (OG/YE). → **No** INSTALL a new generator. CLEAR the DTCs. TEST the system for normal operation.

FM1120200773030X

Fig. 142   Test C: System Overcharges, Battery Voltage More Than 15 Volts (Part 3 of 3). 2002–05 Sable & Taurus

CONDITIONS	DETAILS/RESULTS/ACTIONS
D1 CHECK THE FAULT CODES IN THE PCM	
	3 Use the recorded PCM DTCs from the continuous and on-demand self-test. • Are any DTCs recorded? → **Yes** REFER to PCM Diagnostic Trouble Code (DTC) Index. → **No** GO to **D2**.
D2 CHECK THE SYSTEM FOR OVERCHARGING	

FM1120200774010X

Fig. 143   Test D: Charging System Warning Indicator Is On w/Engine Running, System Increases Voltage (Part 1 of 3). 2002–05 Sable & Taurus

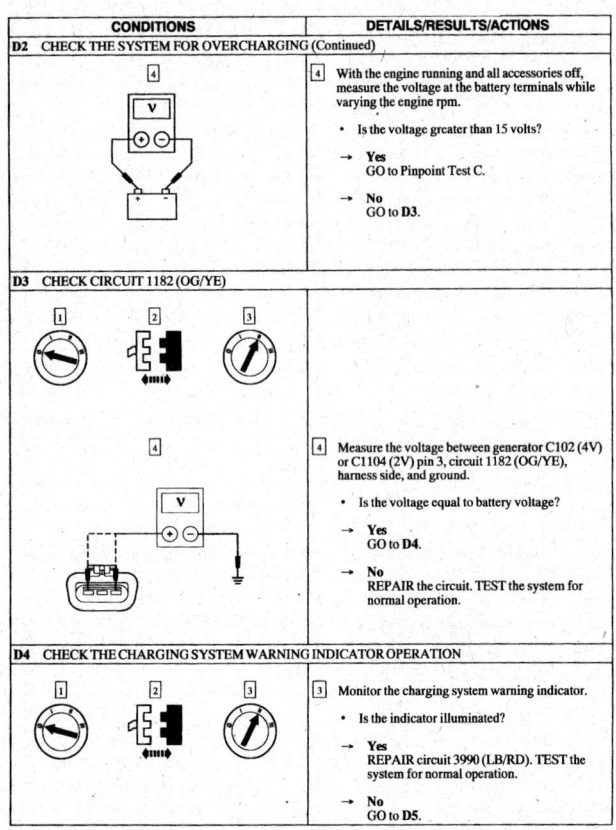

CONDITIONS	DETAILS/RESULTS/ACTIONS
D2 CHECK THE SYSTEM FOR OVERCHARGING (Continued)	
[4]	[4] With the engine running and all accessories off, measure the voltage at the battery terminals while varying the engine rpm. • Is the voltage greater than 15 volts? → **Yes** GO to Pinpoint Test C. → **No** GO to **D3**.
D3 CHECK CIRCUIT 1182 (OG/YE)	
[1] [2] [3] [4]	[4] Measure the voltage between generator C102 (4V) or C1104 (2V) pin 3, circuit 1182 (OG/YE), harness side, and ground. • Is the voltage equal to battery voltage? → **Yes** GO to **D4**. → **No** REPAIR the circuit. TEST the system for normal operation.
D4 CHECK THE CHARGING SYSTEM WARNING INDICATOR OPERATION	
[1] [2] [3]	[3] Monitor the charging system warning indicator. • Is the indicator illuminated? → **Yes** REPAIR circuit 3990 (LB/RD). TEST the system for normal operation. → **No** GO to **D5**.

FM1120200774020X

Fig. 143 Test D: Charging System Warning Indicator Is On w/Engine Running, System Increases Voltage (Part 2 of 3). 2002–05 Sable & Taurus

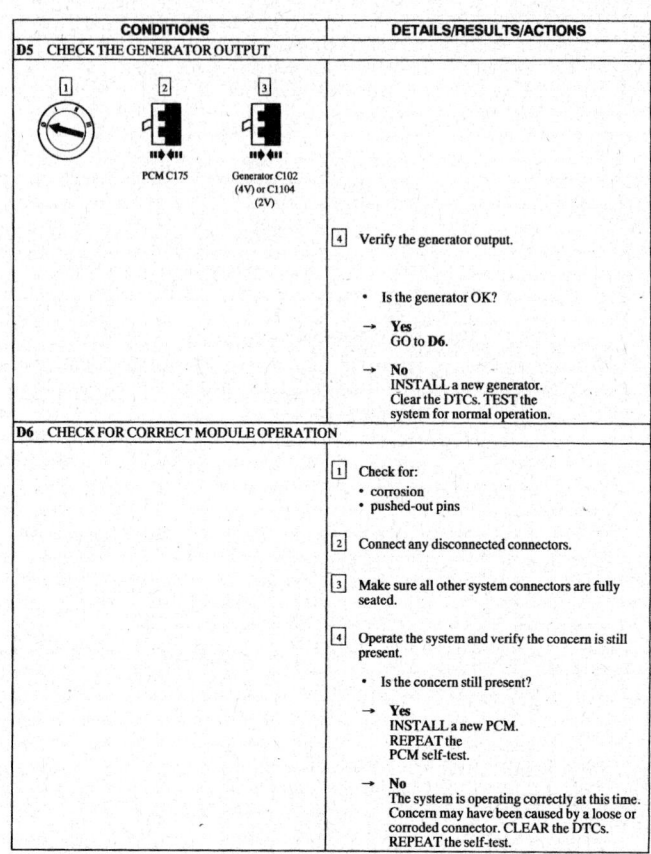

CONDITIONS	DETAILS/RESULTS/ACTIONS
D5 CHECK THE GENERATOR OUTPUT	
[1] [2] [3] PCM C175 Generator C102 (4V) or C1104 (2V) [4]	[4] Verify the generator output. • Is the generator OK? → **Yes** GO to **D6**. → **No** INSTALL a new generator. Clear the DTCs. TEST the system for normal operation.
D6 CHECK FOR CORRECT MODULE OPERATION	
	[1] Check for: • corrosion • pushed-out pins [2] Connect any disconnected connectors. [3] Make sure all other system connectors are fully seated. [4] Operate the system and verify the concern is still present. • Is the concern still present? → **Yes** INSTALL a new PCM. REPEAT the PCM self-test. → **No** The system is operating correctly at this time. Concern may have been caused by a loose or corroded connector. CLEAR the DTCs. REPEAT the self-test.

FM1120200774030X

Fig. 143 Test D: Charging System Warning Indicator Is On w/Engine Running (System Increases Voltage, (Part 3 of 3). 2002–05 Sable & Taurus

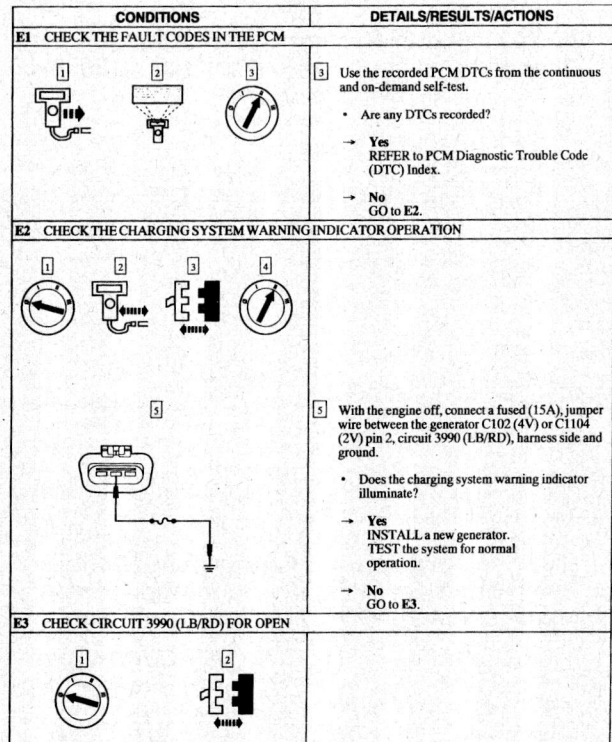

CONDITIONS	DETAILS/RESULTS/ACTIONS
E1 CHECK THE FAULT CODES IN THE PCM	
[1] [2] [3]	[3] Use the recorded PCM DTCs from the continuous and on-demand self-test. • Are any DTCs recorded? → **Yes** REFER to PCM Diagnostic Trouble Code (DTC) Index. → **No** GO to **E2**.
E2 CHECK THE CHARGING SYSTEM WARNING INDICATOR OPERATION	
[1] [2] [3] [4] [5]	[5] With the engine off, connect a fused (15A) jumper wire between the generator C102 (4V) or C1104 (2V) pin 2, circuit 3990 (LB/RD), harness side and ground. • Does the charging system warning indicator illuminate? → **Yes** INSTALL a new generator. TEST the system for normal operation. → **No** GO to **E3**.
E3 CHECK CIRCUIT 3990 (LB/RD) FOR OPEN	
[1] [2]	

FM1120200775010X

Fig. 144 Test E: Charging System Warning Indicator Is Off w/Ignition Switch In Run Position & Engine Off (Part 1 of 2). 2002–05 Sable & Taurus

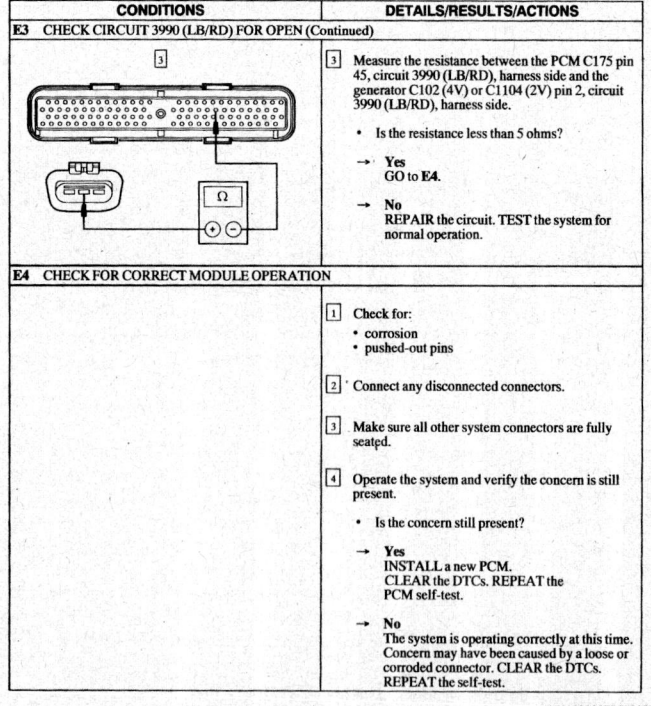

CONDITIONS	DETAILS/RESULTS/ACTIONS
E3 CHECK CIRCUIT 3990 (LB/RD) FOR OPEN (Continued)	
[3]	[3] Measure the resistance between the PCM C175 pin 45, circuit 3990 (LB/RD), harness side and the generator C102 (4V) or C1104 (2V) pin 2, circuit 3990 (LB/RD), harness side. • Is the resistance less than 5 ohms? → **Yes** GO to **E4**. → **No** REPAIR the circuit. TEST the system for normal operation.
E4 CHECK FOR CORRECT MODULE OPERATION	
	[1] Check for: • corrosion • pushed-out pins [2] Connect any disconnected connectors. [3] Make sure all other system connectors are fully seated. [4] Operate the system and verify the concern is still present. • Is the concern still present? → **Yes** INSTALL a new PCM. CLEAR the DTCs. REPEAT the PCM self-test. → **No** The system is operating correctly at this time. Concern may have been caused by a loose or corroded connector. CLEAR the DTCs. REPEAT the self-test.

FM1120200775020X

Fig. 144 Test E: Charging System Warning Indicator Is Off w/Ignition Switch In Run Position & Engine Off (Part 2 of 2). 2002–05 Sable & Taurus

CONDITIONS	DETAILS/RESULTS/ACTIONS
F1 CHECK THE FAULT CODES IN THE PCM	

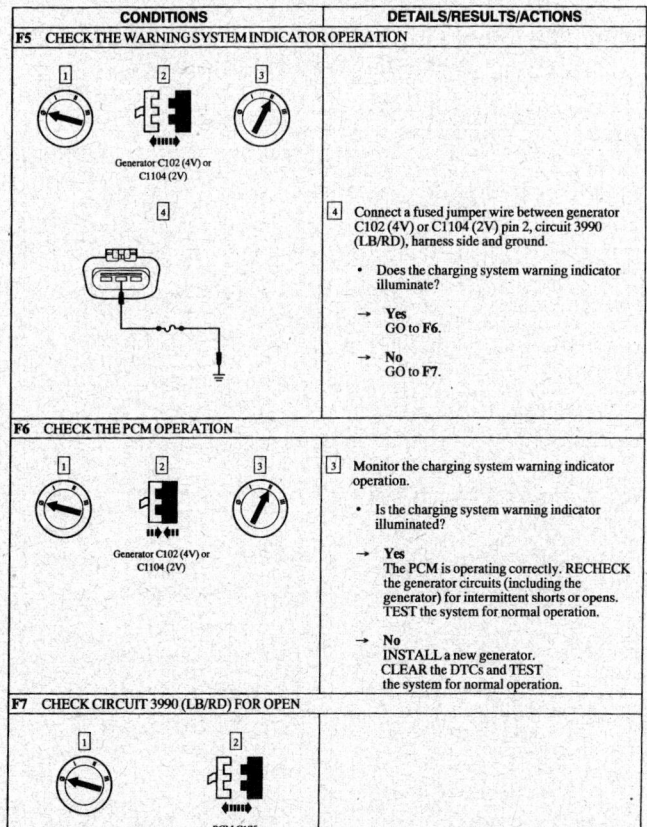	③ Use the recorded PCM DTCs from the continuous and on-demand self-test.
	
	• Are any DTCs recorded?
	
	→ **Yes**
	  Diagnose Trouble Code
	
	→ **No**
	  GO to **F2**.

F2 CHECK FOR LOOSE CONNECTIONS	

Generator C102 (4V) or C1104 (2V)
 	
Generator C102 (4V) or C1104 (2V)
	② Check all generator, battery, and power distribution connections for looseness, corrosion, loose or bent terminals, or loose eyelets.
	
	• Are all connections clean and tight?
	
	→ **Yes**
	  GO to **F3**.
	
	→ **No**
	  REPAIR as necessary. TEST the system for normal operation.

FM1120200776010X

Fig. 145   Test F: Charging System Warning Indicator Lamp Flickers Or Is Intermittent (Part 1 of 4). 2002–05 Sable & Taurus

CONDITIONS	DETAILS/RESULTS/ACTIONS
F3 CHECK FUSE CONNECTION	

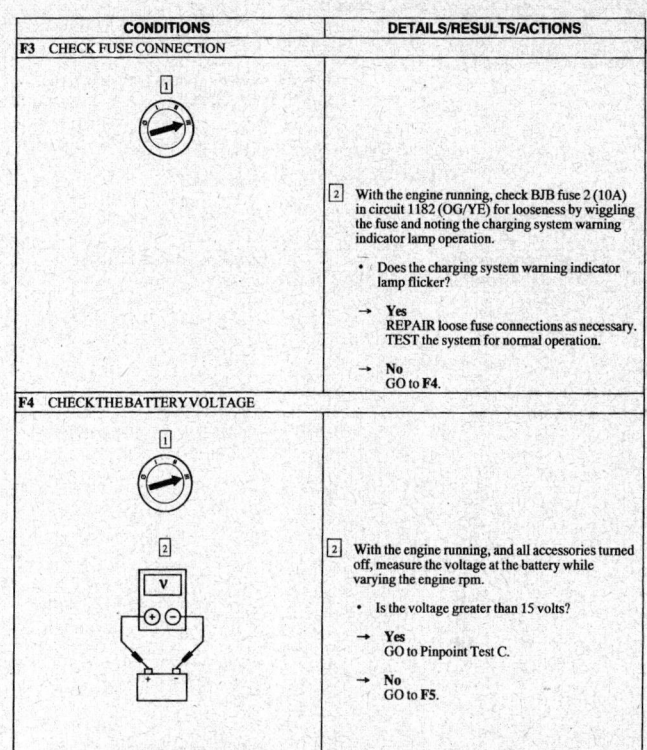	② With the engine running, check BJB fuse 2 (10A) in circuit 1182 (OG/YE) for looseness by wiggling the fuse and noting the charging system warning indicator lamp operation.
	
	• Does the charging system warning indicator lamp flicker?
	
	→ **Yes**
	  REPAIR loose fuse connections as necessary. TEST the system for normal operation.
	
	→ **No**
	  GO to **F4**.

F4 CHECK THE BATTERY VOLTAGE	

	② With the engine running, and all accessories turned off, measure the voltage at the battery while varying the engine rpm.
	
	• Is the voltage greater than 15 volts?
	
	→ **Yes**
	  GO to Pinpoint Test C.
	
	→ **No**
	  GO to **F5**.

FM1120200776020X

Fig. 145   Test F: Charging System Warning Indicator Lamp Flickers Or Is Intermittent (Part 2 of 4). 2002–05 Sable & Taurus

CONDITIONS	DETAILS/RESULTS/ACTIONS
F5 CHECK THE WARNING SYSTEM INDICATOR OPERATION	

Generator C102 (4V) or C1104 (2V)	④ Connect a fused jumper wire between generator C102 (4V) or C1104 (2V) pin 2, circuit 3990 (LB/RD), harness side and ground.
	
	• Does the charging system warning indicator illuminate?
	
	→ **Yes**
	  GO to **F6**.
	
	→ **No**
	  GO to **F7**.

F6 CHECK THE PCM OPERATION	

Generator C102 (4V) or C1104 (2V)	③ Monitor the charging system warning indicator operation.
	
	• Is the charging system warning indicator illuminated?
	
	→ **Yes**
	  The PCM is operating correctly. RECHECK the generator circuits (including the generator) for intermittent shorts or opens. TEST the system for normal operation.
	
	→ **No**
	  INSTALL a new generator. CLEAR the DTCs and TEST the system for normal operation.

F7 CHECK CIRCUIT 3990 (LB/RD) FOR OPEN	
PCM C175	

FM1120200776030X

Fig. 145   Test F: Charging System Warning Indicator Lamp Flickers Or Is Intermittent (Part 3 of 4). 2002–05 Sable & Taurus

CONDITIONS	DETAILS/RESULTS/ACTIONS
F7 CHECK CIRCUIT 3990 (LB/RD) FOR OPEN (Continued)	

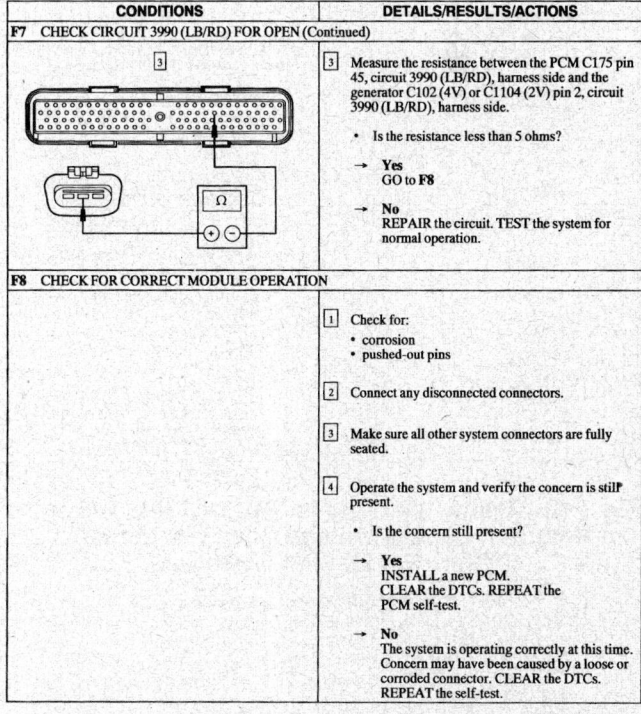	③ Measure the resistance between the PCM C175 pin 45, circuit 3990 (LB/RD), harness side and the generator C102 (4V) or C1104 (2V) pin 2, circuit 3990 (LB/RD), harness side.
	
	• Is the resistance less than 5 ohms?
	
	→ **Yes**
	  GO to **F8**
	
	→ **No**
	  REPAIR the circuit. TEST the system for normal operation.

F8 CHECK FOR CORRECT MODULE OPERATION	

	① Check for:
	• corrosion
	• pushed-out pins
	
	② Connect any disconnected connectors.
	
	③ Make sure all other system connectors are fully seated.
	
	④ Operate the system and verify the concern is still present.
	
	• Is the concern still present?
	
	→ **Yes**
	  INSTALL a new PCM. CLEAR the DTCs. REPEAT the PCM self-test.
	
	→ **No**
	  The system is operating correctly at this time. Concern may have been caused by a loose or corroded connector. CLEAR the DTCs. REPEAT the self-test.

FM1120200776040X

Fig. 145   Test F: Charging System Warning Indicator Lamp Flickers Or Is Intermittent (Part 4 of 4). 2002–05 Sable & Taurus

CONDITIONS	DETAILS/RESULTS/ACTIONS
G1 CHECK FOR ACCESSORY DRIVE NOISE AND MOUNTING BRACKETS	
	1 Check the accessory drive belt for damage and correct installation

FM1120200777010X

Fig. 146   Test G: Alternator Is Noisy (Part 1 of 2). 2002–05 Sable & Taurus

CONDITIONS	DETAILS/RESULTS/ACTIONS
H1 VERIFY GENERATOR IS SOURCE OF RADIO INTERFERENCE	
1	**1** Start and run the engine.
	2 Tune the radio to a station where the interference is present.
3 **4** **5** Generator C102 (4V) or C1104 (2V)	• Is the interference present with the generator disconnected? → **Yes** Diagnosis and test the in-vehicle entertainment system. → **No** INSTALL a new generator. TEST the system for normal operation.

FM1120200778000X

Fig. 147   Test H: Radio Interference. 2002–05 Sable & Taurus

TEST CONDITIONS	TEST DETAILS/RESULTS/ACTIONS
A1 CHECK A CIRCUIT GENERATOR (10A) MINI FUSE	
1 **2** Generator Mini Fuse (10A)	**2** Check the generator (10A) A Circuit Mini Fuse in the power distribution box. • Is the fuse OK? → **Yes** GO to **A2**. → **No** REPLACE the Generator Mini Fuse (10A). TEST the system for normal operation.
A2 CHECK GENERATOR OUTPUT CIRCUIT	
1	**1** Measure the voltage at the B+ terminal of the generator, Circuit 38 (BK/O). • Is the voltage equal to battery positive voltage (B+)? → **Yes** GO to **A3**. → **No** REPAIR generator output Circuit 38 (BK/O) or fusible links Circuit 290 (GY). TEST the system for normal operation.

FM1129800285010X

Fig. 148   Test A: Warning Indicator Lights w/Engine Running, Battery Voltage Does Not Increase (Part 1 of 3). 2001 Town Car

CONDITIONS	DETAILS/RESULTS/ACTIONS
G1 CHECK FOR ACCESSORY DRIVE NOISE AND MOUNTING BRACKETS (Continued)	
	2 Check the accessory mounting brackets and generator pulley for looseness or misalignment. • Is the accessory drive OK? → **Yes** GO to **G2**. → **No** REPAIR as necessary. TEST the system for normal operation.
G2 CHECK GENERATOR FOR ELECTRICAL NOISE	
1 **2** Generator C102 (4V) or C1104 (2V)	• Is the noise still present? → **Yes** GO to **G3**. → **No** INSTALL a new generator. TEST the system for normal operation.
G3 CHECK GENERATOR FOR MECHANICAL NOISE	
1 **2**	**3** Turn all accessories off. With the engine running, use a stethoscope or equivalent listening device to probe the generator for unusual mechanical noise. • Is the generator the noise source? → **Yes** INSTALL a new generator. TEST the system for normal operation. → **No** Diagnose source of engine noise.

FM1120200777020X

Fig. 146   Test G: Alternator Is Noisy (Part 2 of 2). 2002–05 Sable & Taurus

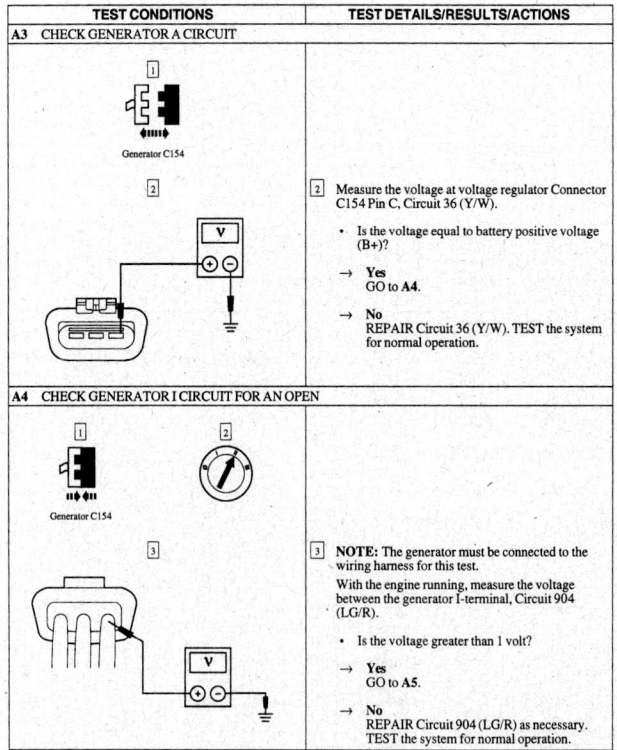

TEST CONDITIONS	TEST DETAILS/RESULTS/ACTIONS
A3 CHECK GENERATOR A CIRCUIT	
1 Generator C154 **2**	**2** Measure the voltage at voltage regulator Connector C154 Pin C, Circuit 36 (Y/W). • Is the voltage equal to battery positive voltage (B+)? → **Yes** GO to **A4**. → **No** REPAIR Circuit 36 (Y/W). TEST the system for normal operation.
A4 CHECK GENERATOR I CIRCUIT FOR AN OPEN	
1 **2** Generator C154 **3**	**3** **NOTE:** The generator must be connected to the wiring harness for this test. With the engine running, measure the voltage between the generator I-terminal, Circuit 904 (LG/R). • Is the voltage greater than 1 volt? → **Yes** GO to **A5**. → **No** REPAIR Circuit 904 (LG/R) as necessary. TEST the system for normal operation.

FM1129800285020X

Fig. 148   Test A: Warning Indicator Lights w/Engine Running, Battery Voltage Does Not Increase (Part 2 of 3). 2001 Town Car

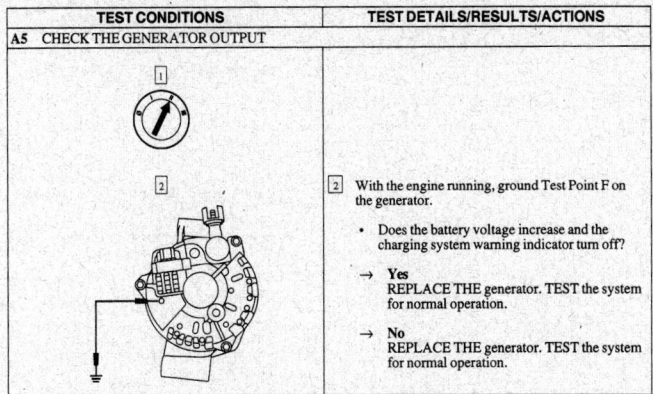

TEST CONDITIONS	TEST DETAILS/RESULTS/ACTIONS
A5 CHECK THE GENERATOR OUTPUT	

② With the engine running, ground Test Point F on the generator.

- Does the battery voltage increase and the charging system warning indicator turn off?

→ **Yes**
REPLACE THE generator. TEST the system for normal operation.

→ **No**
REPLACE THE generator. TEST the system for normal operation.

FM1129800285030X

Fig. 148   Test A: Warning Indicator Lights w/Engine Running, Battery Voltage Does Not Increase (Part 3 of 3). 2001 Town Car

TEST CONDITIONS	TEST DETAILS/RESULTS/ACTIONS
B2 CHECK THE GENERATOR GROUNDS	

① Check all the ground connections between the generator and the battery.

- Are all the ground connections OK?

→ **Yes**
GO to **B3**.

→ **No**
REPAIR the connections as necessary. TEST the system for normal operation.

TEST CONDITIONS	TEST DETAILS/RESULTS/ACTIONS
B3 CHECK THE VOLTAGE AT THE GENERATOR I CIRCUIT	

Generator C154

③ **NOTE:** The generator Connector C154 must be connected to the generator test.
With engine running, measure the voltage at the generator I terminal, Circuit 904 (LG/R).

- Is the voltage greater than 1 volt?

→ **Yes**
REPLACE the generator.

→ **No**
REPAIR Circuit 904 (LG/R) for an open circuit. TEST the system for normal operation.

FM1129800286020X

Fig. 149   Test B: Warning Indicator Is Off w/Ignition In Run Position & Engine Off (Part 2 of 2). 2001 Town Car

TEST CONDITIONS	TEST DETAILS/RESULTS/ACTIONS
B1 CHECK GENERATOR CONNECTOR C154	

Generator C154

② Check generator Connector C154 for bent or damaged pins.

- Is the connector OK?

→ **Yes**
GO to **B2**.

→ **No**
REPAIR Connector C154 as necessary. TEST the system for normal operation.

FM1129800286010X

Fig. 149   Test B: Warning Indicator Is Off w/Ignition In Run Position & Engine Off (Part 1 of 2). 2001 Town Car

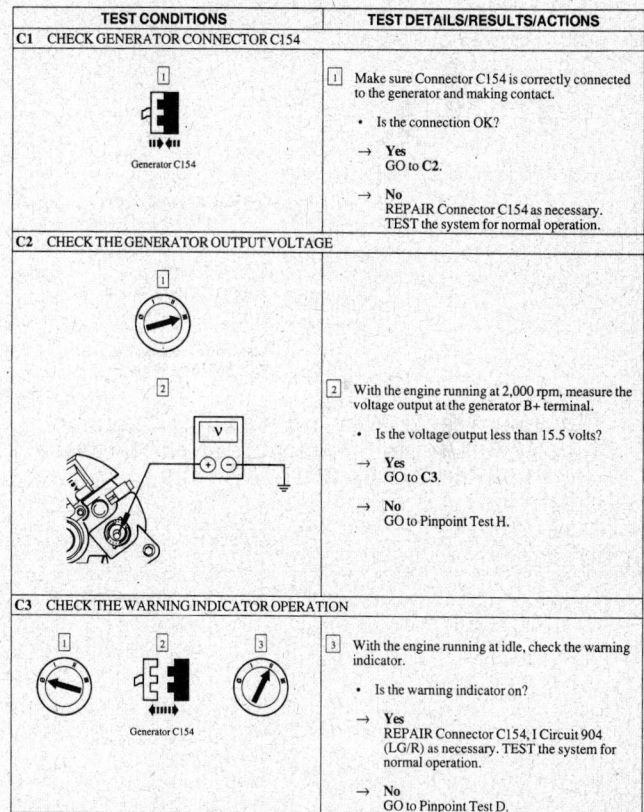

TEST CONDITIONS	TEST DETAILS/RESULTS/ACTIONS
C1 CHECK GENERATOR CONNECTOR C154	

Generator C154

① Make sure Connector C154 is correctly connected to the generator and making contact.

- Is the connection OK?

→ **Yes**
GO to **C2**.

→ **No**
REPAIR Connector C154 as necessary. TEST the system for normal operation.

TEST CONDITIONS	TEST DETAILS/RESULTS/ACTIONS
C2 CHECK THE GENERATOR OUTPUT VOLTAGE	

② With the engine running at 2,000 rpm, measure the voltage output at the generator B+ terminal.

- Is the voltage output less than 15.5 volts?

→ **Yes**
GO to **C3**.

→ **No**
GO to Pinpoint Test H.

TEST CONDITIONS	TEST DETAILS/RESULTS/ACTIONS
C3 CHECK THE WARNING INDICATOR OPERATION	

Generator C154

③ With the engine running at idle, check the warning indicator.

- Is the warning indicator on?

→ **Yes**
REPAIR Connector C154, I Circuit 904 (LG/R) as necessary. TEST the system for normal operation.

→ **No**
GO to Pinpoint Test D.

FM1129800287000X

Fig. 150   Test C: Warning Indicator Is On w/Engine Running & Battery Voltage Increase. 2001 Town Car

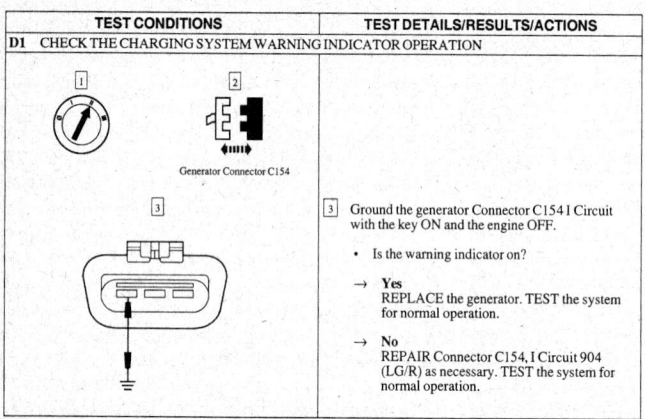

TEST CONDITIONS	TEST DETAILS/RESULTS/ACTIONS
D1 CHECK THE CHARGING SYSTEM WARNING INDICATOR OPERATION	

3 Ground the generator Connector C154 I Circuit with the key ON and the engine OFF.

- Is the warning indicator on?

→ **Yes**
REPLACE the generator. TEST the system for normal operation.

→ **No**
REPAIR Connector C154, I Circuit 904 (LG/R) as necessary. TEST the system for normal operation.

FM1129800288000X

Fig. 151   Test D: Warning Indicator Off w/Ignition In Run Position & Engine Off. 2001 Town Car

TEST CONDITIONS	TEST DETAILS/RESULTS/ACTIONS
E2 CHECK THE GENERATOR CONNECTORS	

3 Check the battery connections and generator Connector C154 for corrosion and tightness.

- Are the connectors clean and tight?

→ **Yes**
REFER to Lead and No Lead Tests in this section.

→ **No**
REPAIR the connectors as necessary. TEST the system for normal operation.

FM1129800289020X

Fig. 152   Test E: Warning Indicator Operates Properly But Battery Voltage Does Not Increase (Part 2 of 2). 2001 Town Car

TEST CONDITIONS	TEST DETAILS/RESULTS/ACTIONS
F1 CHECK FOR DRAINS ON THE BATTERY	

2 Make sure all the interior lights and switches are off and all doors are closed. Perform the Battery Drain Test; refer to Component Tests, Battery—Drain Testing

- Is the drain greater than .05 amps?

→ **Yes**
Go to Component Tests—Battery—Drain Testing.

→ **No**
GO to **F2**.

FM1129800290010X

Fig. 153   Test F: Battery Is Dead Or Will Not Stay Charged Or Low Battery Or Alternator Voltage (Part 1 of 2). 2001 Town Car

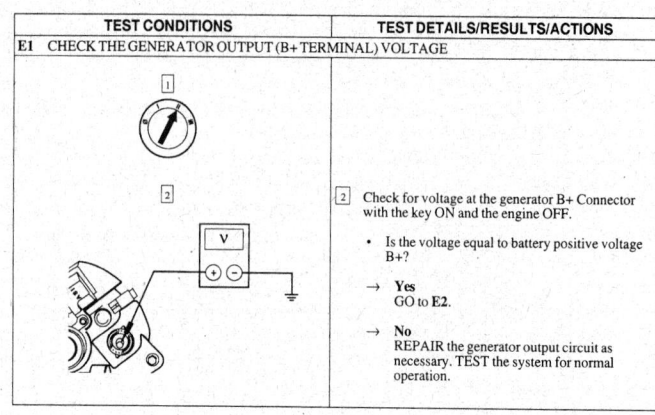

TEST CONDITIONS	TEST DETAILS/RESULTS/ACTIONS
E1 CHECK THE GENERATOR OUTPUT (B+ TERMINAL) VOLTAGE	

2 Check for voltage at the generator B+ Connector with the key ON and the engine OFF.

- Is the voltage equal to battery positive voltage B+?

→ **Yes**
GO to E2.

→ **No**
REPAIR the generator output circuit as necessary. TEST the system for normal operation.

FM1129800289010X

Fig. 152   Test E: Warning Indicator Operates Properly But Battery Voltage Does Not Increase (Part 1 of 2). 2001 Town Car

TEST CONDITIONS	TEST DETAILS/RESULTS/ACTIONS
F2 CHECK THE GENERATOR OUTPUT	

1 Check the generator output; refer to Component Tests, Alternator On-Vehicle Tests in this section.

- Is the generator OK?

→ **Yes**
GO to F3.

→ **No**
REPLACE the generator. TEST the system for normal operation.

| F3   CHECK THE BATTERY CONDITION | |

1 Check the battery capacity

- Is the battery OK?

→ **Yes**
GO to F4.

→ **No**
REPLACE the battery. TEST the system for normal operation.

| F4   CHECK OTHER SYSTEMS FOR DRAINS | |

1 Check for drains from the electronic modules; refer to Component Test, Battery—Electronic Drains Which Shut Off When the Battery Cable is Disconnected

- Are all the electronic modules OK?

→ **Yes**
RECHARGE the battery. TEST the system for normal operation.

→ **No**
REPLACE the damaged module as necessary. TEST the system for normal operation.

FM1129800290020X

Fig. 153   Test F: Battery Is Dead Or Will Not Stay Charged Or Low Battery Or Alternator Voltage (Part 2 of 2). 2001 Town Car

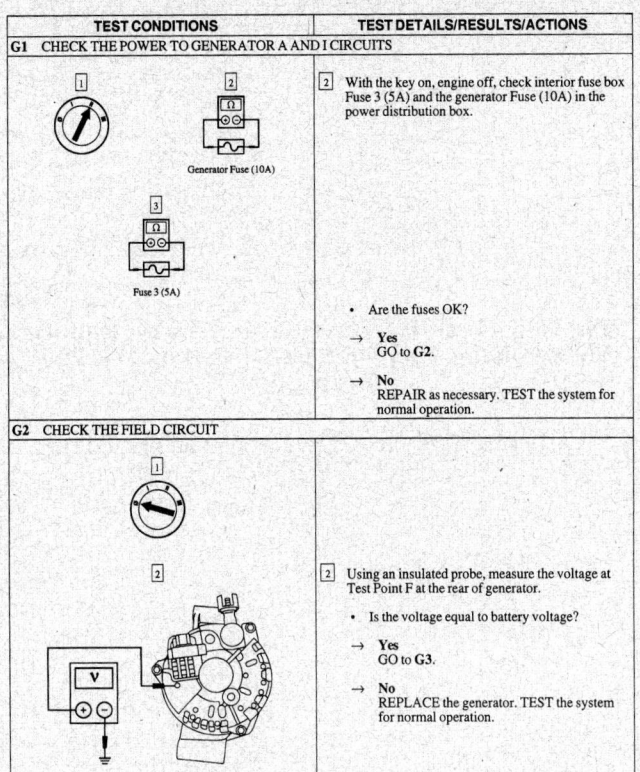

TEST CONDITIONS	TEST DETAILS/RESULTS/ACTIONS
G1 CHECK THE POWER TO GENERATOR A AND I CIRCUITS	

2 With the key on, engine off, check interior fuse box Fuse 3 (5A) and the generator Fuse (10A) in the power distribution box.

• Are the fuses OK?

→ **Yes**
GO to **G2**.

→ **No**
REPAIR as necessary. TEST the system for normal operation.

TEST CONDITIONS	TEST DETAILS/RESULTS/ACTIONS
G2 CHECK THE FIELD CIRCUIT	

2 Using an insulated probe, measure the voltage at Test Point F at the rear of generator.

• Is the voltage equal to battery voltage?

→ **Yes**
GO to **G3**.

→ **No**
REPLACE the generator. TEST the system for normal operation.

FM1129800291010X

Fig. 154 Test G: Warning Indicator Flickers Or Is Intermittent (Part 1 of 2). 2001 Town Car

TEST CONDITIONS	TEST DETAILS/RESULTS/ACTIONS
H1 CHECK FOR A VOLTAGE DROP	

2 With key on, engine off, check for voltage drop from the battery positive post and the generator A circuit at Connector C154.

• Does the voltage drop less than 0.5 volts? .

→ **Yes**
GO to **H2**.

→ **No**
REPAIR Circuit 36 (Y/W) for high resistance as necessary. TEST the system for normal operation.

FM1129800292010X

Fig. 155 Test H: System Overcharges, Battery Voltage More Than 15.5 Volts (Part 1 of 4). 2001 Town Car

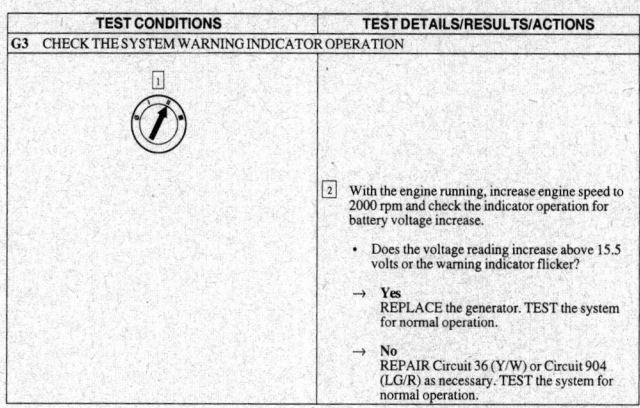

TEST CONDITIONS	TEST DETAILS/RESULTS/ACTIONS
G3 CHECK THE SYSTEM WARNING INDICATOR OPERATION	

2 With the engine running, increase engine speed to 2000 rpm and check the indicator operation for battery voltage increase.

• Does the voltage reading increase above 15.5 volts or the warning indicator flicker?

→ **Yes**
REPLACE the generator. TEST the system for normal operation.

→ **No**
REPAIR Circuit 36 (Y/W) or Circuit 904 (LG/R) as necessary. TEST the system for normal operation.

FM1129800291020X

Fig. 154 Test G: Warning Indicator Flickers Or Is Intermittent (Part 2 of 2). 2001 Town Car

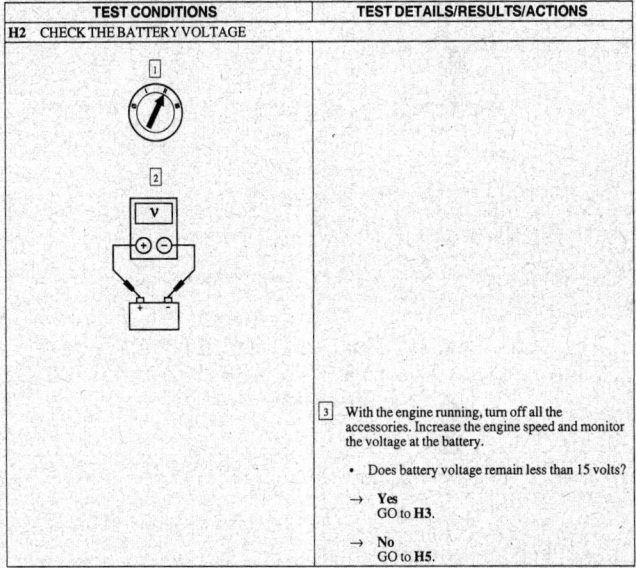

TEST CONDITIONS	TEST DETAILS/RESULTS/ACTIONS
H2 CHECK THE BATTERY VOLTAGE	

3 With the engine running, turn off all the accessories. Increase the engine speed and monitor the voltage at the battery.

• Does battery voltage remain less than 15 volts?

→ **Yes**
GO to **H3**.

→ **No**
GO to **H5**.

FM1129800292020X

Fig. 155 Test H: System Overcharges, Battery Voltage More Than 15.5 Volts (Part 2 of 4). 2001 Town Car

TEST CONDITIONS	TEST DETAILS/RESULTS/ACTIONS
H3 CHECK THE GENERATOR FOR LOW VOLTAGE	
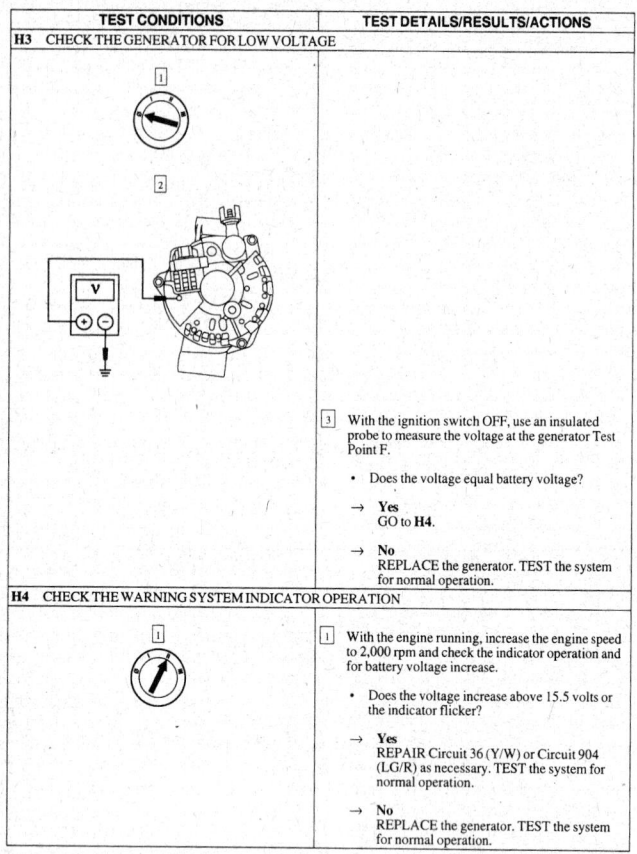	**3** With the ignition switch OFF, use an insulated probe to measure the voltage at the generator Test Point F. • Does the voltage equal battery voltage? → **Yes** GO to **H4**. → **No** REPLACE the generator. TEST the system for normal operation.
H4 CHECK THE WARNING SYSTEM INDICATOR OPERATION	
	1 With the engine running, increase the engine speed to 2,000 rpm and check the indicator operation and for battery voltage increase. • Does the voltage increase above 15.5 volts or the indicator flicker? → **Yes** REPAIR Circuit 36 (Y/W) or Circuit 904 (LG/R) as necessary. TEST the system for normal operation. → **No** REPLACE the generator. TEST the system for normal operation.

FM1129800292030X

Fig. 155   Test H: System Overcharges, Battery Voltage More Than 15.5 Volts (Part 3 of 4). 2001 Town Car

TEST CONDITIONS	TEST DETAILS/RESULTS/ACTIONS
J1 CHECK FOR ACID LEAKAGE DAMAGE	
	1 Check for acid damage to the vehicle harnesses and to the body. • Is there acid damage? → **Yes** REPAIR the damaged areas as necessary. → **No** GO to **J2**.
J2 CHECK THE CHARGING SYSTEM FOR OVERCHARGING	
	1 With the engine running, turn off all the accessories. Increase the engine speed and monitor the voltage at the battery.

FM1129800293010X

Fig. 156   Test J: Battery Leakage Or Damage (Part 1 of 3). 2001 Town Car

TEST CONDITIONS	TEST DETAILS/RESULTS/ACTIONS
J5 CHECK THE BATTERY CASE FOR DAMAGE	
	1 Check the battery case for defects such as cracks or poor seals. • Is the battery OK? → **Yes** The system is OK. TEST the system for normal operation. → **No** REPLACE the battery. TEST the system for normal operation.

FM1129800293030X

Fig. 156   Test J: Battery Leakage Or Damage (Part 3 of 3). 2001 Town Car

TEST CONDITIONS	TEST DETAILS/RESULTS/ACTIONS
H5 CHECK THE VOLTAGE REGULATOR OPERATION	
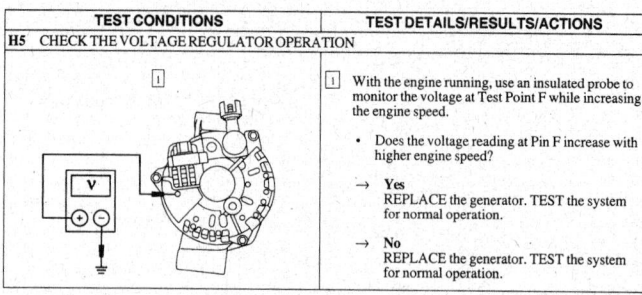	**1** With the engine running, use an insulated probe to monitor the voltage at Test Point F while increasing the engine speed. • Does the voltage reading at Pin F increase with higher engine speed? → **Yes** REPLACE the generator. TEST the system for normal operation. → **No** REPLACE the generator. TEST the system for normal operation.

FM1129800292040X

Fig. 155   Test H: System Overcharges, Battery Voltage More Than 15.5 Volts (Part 4 of 4). 2001 Town Car

TEST CONDITIONS	TEST DETAILS/RESULTS/ACTIONS
J2 CHECK THE CHARGING SYSTEM FOR OVERCHARGING (Continued)	
	• Does battery voltage increase more than 15.5 volts? → **Yes** GO to Pinpoint Test H. → **No** GO to **J3**.
J3 CHECK THE BATTERY MOUNTING	
	1 Make sure the battery is properly mounted and level in the battery tray. • Is the battery properly mounted? → **Yes** GO to **J4**. → **No** REPAIR as necessary. TEST the system for normal operation.
J4 CHECK FOR BATTERY CONTACT	
	1 Make sure there are no fasteners or other parts contacting the battery case causing excess pressure. • Is there anything contacting the battery case? → **Yes** REPAIR as necessary. TEST the system for normal operation. → **No** GO to **J5**.

FM1129800293020X

Fig. 156   Test J: Battery Leakage Or Damage (Part 2 of 3). 2001 Town Car

TEST CONDITIONS	TEST DETAILS/RESULTS/ACTIONS
K1 CHECK BATTERY VOLTAGE	
	2 With the engine running, turn off all the accessories. Increase the engine speed to 2,000 rpm and monitor the voltage at the battery. • Is the battery voltage more than 15.5 or less than 13 volts? → **Yes** GO to Pinpoint Test H for readings higher than 15.5 volts. GO to Pinpoint Test F for readings less than 13 volts. → **No** GO to **K2**.

FM1129800294010X

Fig. 157   Test K: Voltage Gauge Reads High Or Low (Part 1 of 2). 2001 Town Car

TEST CONDITIONS	TEST DETAILS/RESULTS/ACTIONS
K2 CHECK THE VOLTAGE GAUGE OPERATION	
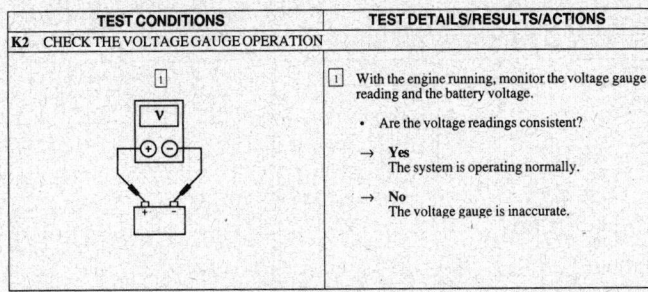	1 With the engine running, monitor the voltage gauge reading and the battery voltage. • Are the voltage readings consistent? → **Yes** The system is operating normally. → **No** The voltage gauge is inaccurate.

FM1129800294020X

Fig. 157   Test K: Voltage Gauge Reads High Or Low (Part 2 of 2). 2001 Town Car

TEST CONDITIONS	TEST DETAILS/RESULTS/ACTIONS
M1 VERIFY THERE IS RADIO INTERFERENCE	
	1 Start and run the engine.
	2 Tune the radio to a station where the interference is present.
	3 Turn the engine off.
	4 Disconnect the generator Connector C176.
	5 Start and run the engine. • Is the interference present with the generator disconnected? → **Yes** INSPECT the in-vehicle entertainment system. → **No** GO to **M2**.
M2 SUBSTITUTE A KNOWN GOOD GENERATOR	
	1 Turn the engine off.
	2 Install a known good generator.

FM1129800296010X

Fig. 159   Test M: Radio Interference (Part 1 of 2). 2001 Town Car

TEST CONDITIONS	TEST DETAILS/RESULTS/ACTIONS
L1 CHECK FOR ACCESSORY DRIVE NOISE	
	1 Check the drive belt for damage and verify installation
	2 Check the accessory mounting brackets for loose bolts or misalignment.
	3 Check for a bent generator pulley.
	4 Check other accessories for a bent, misaligned or loose pulley. • Is the accessory drive OK? → **Yes** REPLACE the generator. TEST the system for normal operation. → **No** INSPECT the accessory drive system.

FM1129800295000X

Fig. 158   Test L: Alternator Is Noisy. 2001 Town Car

TEST CONDITIONS	TEST DETAILS/RESULTS/ACTIONS
M2 SUBSTITUTE A KNOWN GOOD GENERATOR (Continued)	
	3 Start and run the engine. • Is there radio interference with a known good generator? → **Yes** INSTALL the original generator and INSPECT the in-vehicle entertainment system. → **No** REPLACE the generator. TEST the system for normal operation.

FM1129800296020X

Fig. 159   Test M: Radio Interference (Part 2 of 2). 2001 Town Car

CONDITIONS	DETAILS/RESULTS/ACTIONS
A1 CHECK BATTERY CONDITION	
	1 Carry out the Battery — Condition Test to determine if the battery can hold a charge and is OK for use. • **Is the battery OK?** → **Yes** GO to A2. → **No** INSTALL a new battery. TEST the system for normal operation.
A2 CHECK FOR GENERATOR OUTPUT	
	1 Carry out the Generator On-Vehicle Load/No-Load Tests. • **Is the generator OK?** → **Yes** GO to A3. → **No** GO to Pinpoint Test B.
A3 CHECK FOR CURRENT DRAINS	
	1 Carry out the Battery — Drain Test. • **Are there any excessive current drains?** → **Yes** REPAIR as necessary. TEST the system for normal operation. → **No** GO to A4.

FM1120200780010X

Fig. 160   Test A: Battery Is Discharged Or Voltage Is Low (Part 1 of 2). 2002 Town Car

A4 CHECK FOR CURRENT DRAINS WHICH SHUT OFF WHEN THE BATTERY IS DISCONNECTED

1. Carry out the Battery — Electronic Drains Which Shut Off When the Battery Cable is Disconnected Test.

- **Are there any current drains which shut off when the battery is disconnected?**

→ **Yes**
REPAIR as necessary. TEST the system for normal operation.

→ **No**
GO to Pinpoint Test B .

FM1120200780020X

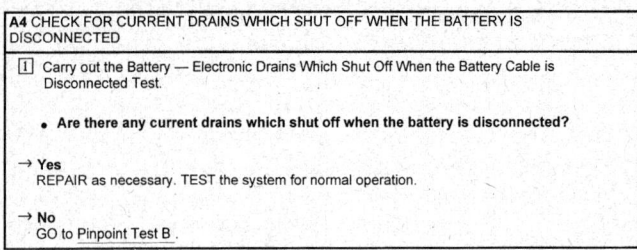

Fig. 160   Test A: Battery Is Discharged Or Voltage Is Low (Part 2 of 2). 2002 Town Car

B2 CHECK GENERATOR GROUND A CIRCUIT 36 (YE/WH)

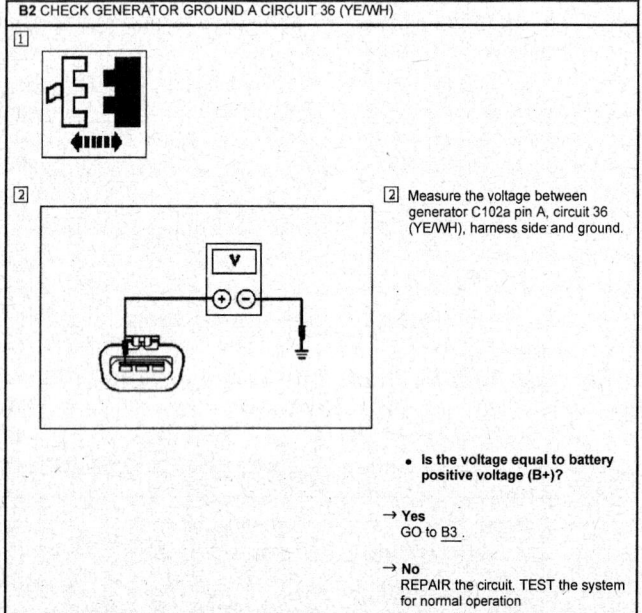

2. Measure the voltage between generator C102a pin A, circuit 36 (YE/WH), harness side and ground.

- **Is the voltage equal to battery positive voltage (B+)?**

→ **Yes**
GO to B3 .

→ **No**
REPAIR the circuit. TEST the system for normal operation

FM1120200781020X

Fig. 161   Test B: Charging System Warning Indicator Is On w/Engine Running, System Voltage Does Not Increase (Part 2 of 4). 2002 Town Car

CONDITIONS	DETAILS/RESULTS/ACTIONS
B1 CHECK GENERATOR B+ CIRCUIT 38 (BK/OG)	

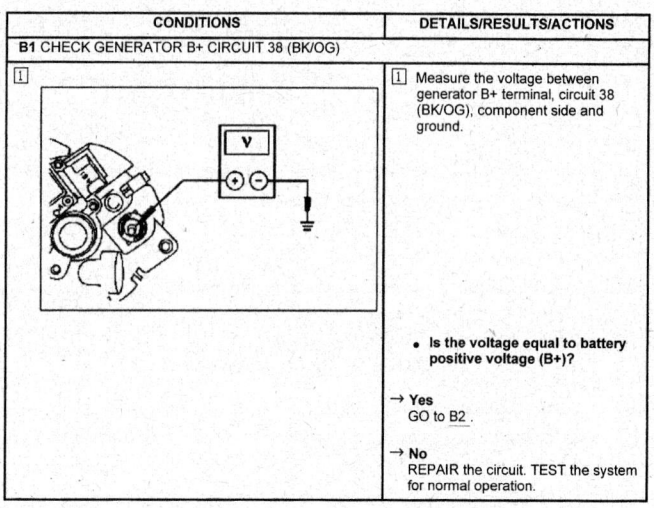

1. Measure the voltage between generator B+ terminal, circuit 38 (BK/OG), component side and ground.

- **Is the voltage equal to battery positive voltage (B+)?**

→ **Yes**
GO to B2 .

→ **No**
REPAIR the circuit. TEST the system for normal operation.

FM1120200781010X

Fig. 161   Test B: Charging System Warning Indicator Is On w/Engine Running, System Voltage Does Not Increase (Part 1 of 4). 2002 Town Car

B3 CHECK I CIRCUIT 904 (LG/RD) FOR AN OPEN

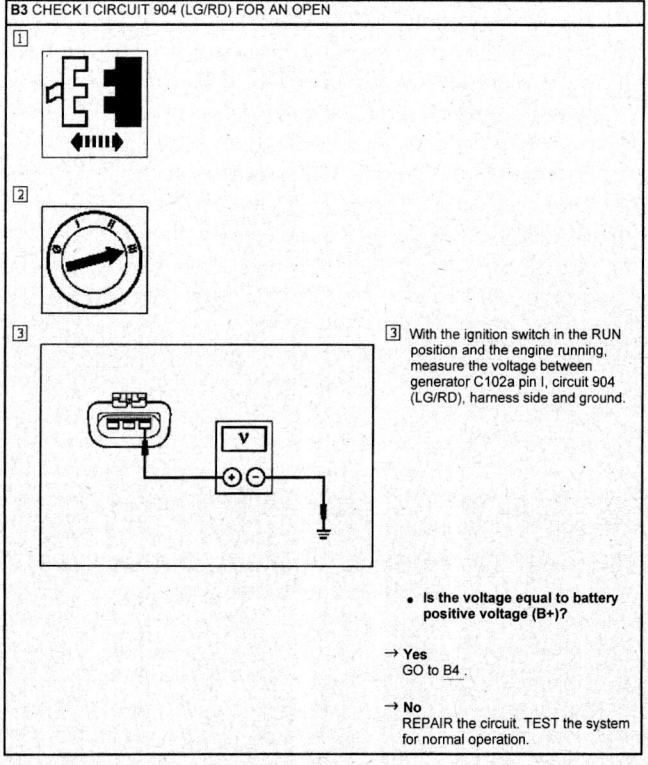

3. With the ignition switch in the RUN position and the engine running, measure the voltage between generator C102a pin I, circuit 904 (LG/RD), harness side and ground.

- **Is the voltage equal to battery positive voltage (B+)?**

→ **Yes**
GO to B4 .

→ **No**
REPAIR the circuit. TEST the system for normal operation.

FM1120200781030X

Fig. 161   Test B: Charging System Warning Indicator Is On w/Engine Running, System Voltage Does Not Increase (Part 3 of 4). 2002 Town Car

B4 CHECK FOR VOLTAGE DROP IN B+ CIRCUIT 38 (BK/OG)

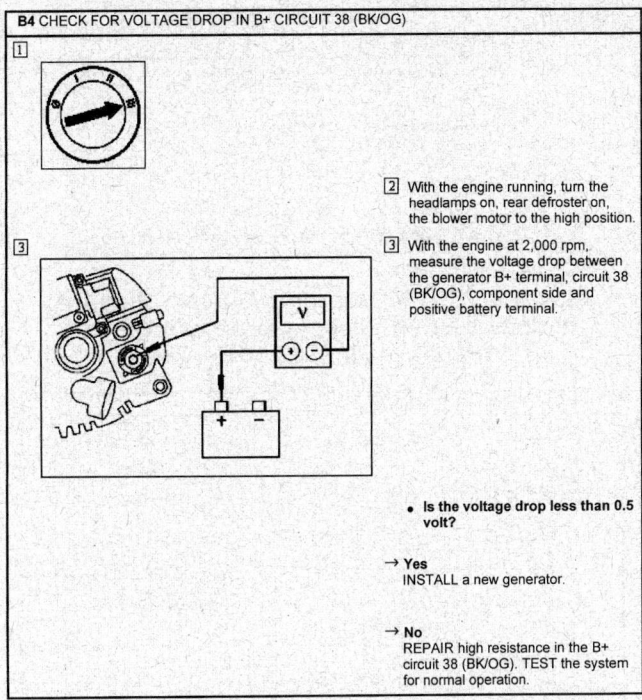

☑ With the engine running, turn the headlamps on, rear defroster on, the blower motor to the high position.

☑ With the engine at 2,000 rpm, measure the voltage drop between the generator B+ terminal, circuit 38 (BK/OG), component side and positive battery terminal.

- Is the voltage drop less than 0.5 volt?

→ **Yes**
INSTALL a new generator.

→ **No**
REPAIR high resistance in the B+ circuit 38 (BK/OG). TEST the system for normal operation.

FM1120200781040X

Fig. 161   Test B: Charging System Warning Indicator Is On w/Engine Running, System Voltage Does Not Increase (Part 4 of 4). 2002 Town Car

C2 CHECK GENERATOR AND BATTERY GROUND CONNECTIONS

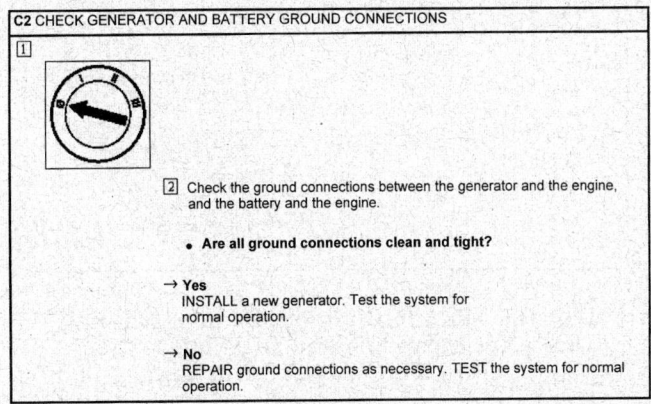

☑ Check the ground connections between the generator and the engine, and the battery and the engine.

- Are all ground connections clean and tight?

→ **Yes**
INSTALL a new generator. Test the system for normal operation.

→ **No**
REPAIR ground connections as necessary. TEST the system for normal operation.

FM1120200782020X

Fig. 162   Test C: System Overcharges, Battery Voltage Is More Than 15.5 Volts (Part 2 of 2). 2002 Town Car

CONDITIONS	DETAILS/RESULTS/ACTIONS

C1 CHECK FOR VOLTAGE DROP IN A CIRCUIT 36 (YE/WH)

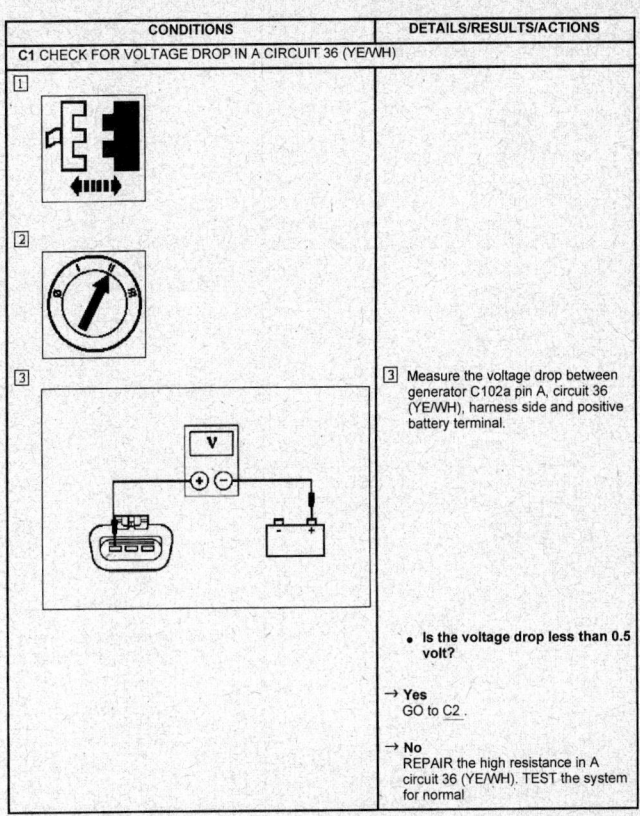

☑ Measure the voltage drop between generator C102a pin A, circuit 36 (YE/WH), harness side and positive battery terminal.

- Is the voltage drop less than 0.5 volt?

→ **Yes**
GO to C2 .

→ **No**
REPAIR the high resistance in A circuit 36 (YE/WH). TEST the system for normal

FM1120200782010X

Fig. 162   Test C: System Overcharges, Battery Voltage Is More Than 15.5 Volts (Part 1 of 2). 2002 Town Car

CONDITIONS	DETAILS/RESULTS/ACTIONS

D1 CHECK I CIRCUIT 904 (LG/RD) FOR SHORT TO GROUND

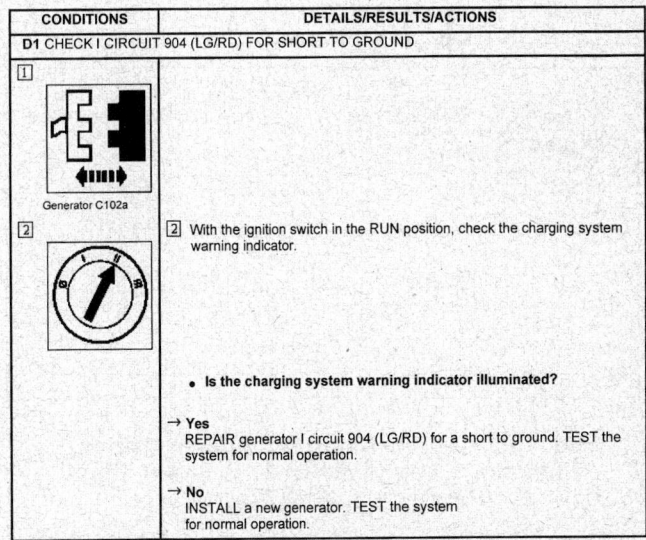

Generator C102a

☑ With the ignition switch in the RUN position, check the charging system warning indicator.

- Is the charging system warning indicator illuminated?

→ **Yes**
REPAIR generator I circuit 904 (LG/RD) for a short to ground. TEST the system for normal operation.

→ **No**
INSTALL a new generator. TEST the system for normal operation.

FM1120200783000X

Fig. 163   Test D: Charging System Warning Indicator Is On w/Engine Running & System Increases Voltage. 2002 Town Car

CONDITIONS	DETAILS/RESULTS/ACTIONS

E1 CHECK THE CHARGING SYSTEM WARNING INDICATOR LAMP

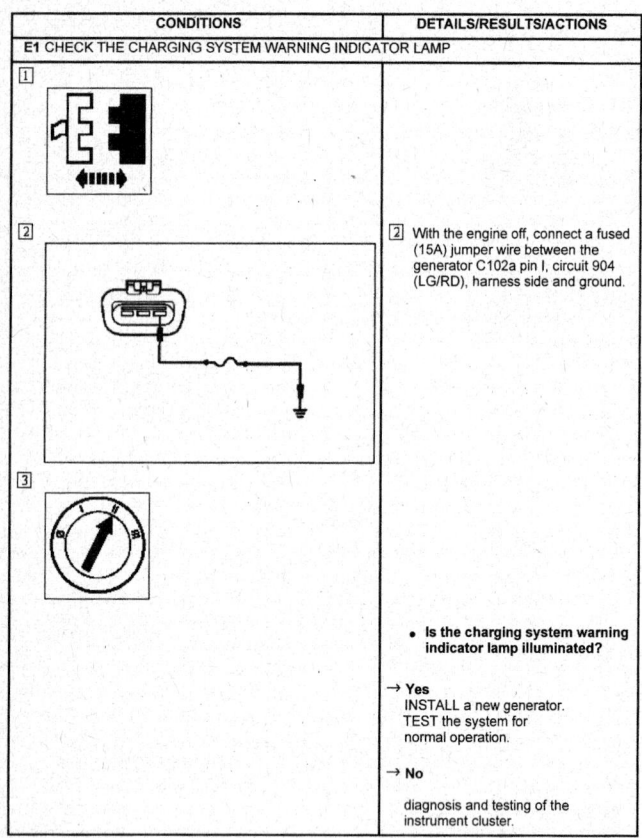

2. With the engine off, connect a fused (15A) jumper wire between the generator C102a pin I, circuit 904 (LG/RD), harness side and ground.

- **Is the charging system warning indicator lamp illuminated?**

→ **Yes**
INSTALL a new generator. TEST the system for normal operation.

→ **No**

diagnosis and testing of the instrument cluster.

FM1120200784000X

Fig. 164   Test E: Charging System Warning Indicator Is Off w/Ignition Switch In Run Position & Engine Off. 2002 Town Car

F2 CHECK FUSE CONNECTIONS

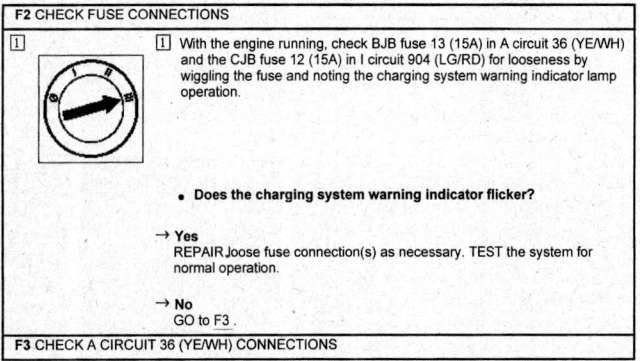

1. With the engine running, check BJB fuse 13 (15A) in A circuit 36 (YE/WH) and the CJB fuse 12 (15A) in I circuit 904 (LG/RD) for looseness by wiggling the fuse and noting the charging system warning indicator lamp operation.

- **Does the charging system warning indicator flicker?**

→ **Yes**
REPAIR loose fuse connection(s) as necessary. TEST the system for normal operation.

→ **No**
GO to F3.

F3 CHECK A CIRCUIT 36 (YE/WH) CONNECTIONS

FM1120200785020X

Fig. 165   Test F: Charging System Warning Indicator Lamp Flickers Or Is Intermittent (Part 2 of 3). 2002 Town Car

CONDITIONS	DETAILS/RESULTS/ACTIONS

F1 CHECK FOR LOOSE CONNECTIONS

1. Check all generator, battery, and power distribution connections for looseness, corrosion, loose or bent terminals, or loose eyelets.

- **Are all connections clean and tight?**

→ **Yes**
GO to F2.

→ **No**
REPAIR as necessary. TEST the system for normal operation.

FM1120200785010X

Fig. 165   Test F: Charging System Warning Indicator Lamp Flickers Or Is Intermittent (Part 1 of 3). 2002 Town Car

F3 CHECK A CIRCUIT 36 (YE/WH) CONNECTIONS

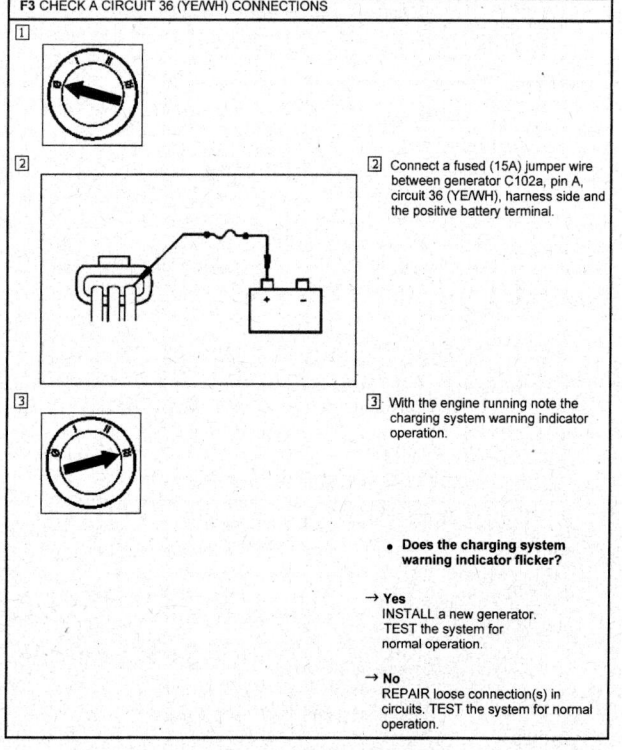

2. Connect a fused (15A) jumper wire between generator C102a, pin A, circuit 36 (YE/WH), harness side and the positive battery terminal.

3. With the engine running note the charging system warning indicator operation.

- **Does the charging system warning indicator flicker?**

→ **Yes**
INSTALL a new generator. TEST the system for normal operation.

→ **No**
REPAIR loose connection(s) in circuits. TEST the system for normal operation.

FM1120200785030X

Fig. 165   Test F: Charging System Warning Indicator Lamp Flickers Or Is Intermittent (Part 3 of 3). 2002 Town Car

CONDITIONS	DETAILS/RESULTS/ACTIONS

G1 CHECK FOR ACCESSORY DRIVE NOISE

1. Check the accessory drive belt for damage and correct installation. Check the accessory mounting brackets and generator pulley for looseness or misalignment.

- **Is the accessory drive OK?**

→ **Yes**
GO to G2.

→ **No**
REPAIR as necessary. Diagnosis and testing of the accessory drive system. TEST the system for normal operation.

G2 CHECK GENERATOR MOUNTING

1. Check the generator mounting for loose bolts or misalignment.

- **Is the generator mounted correctly?**

→ **Yes**
GO to G3.

→ **No**
REPAIR as necessary. TEST the system for normal operation.

FM1120200786010X

Fig. 166   Test G: Alternator Is Noisy (Part 1 of 3). 2002 Town Car

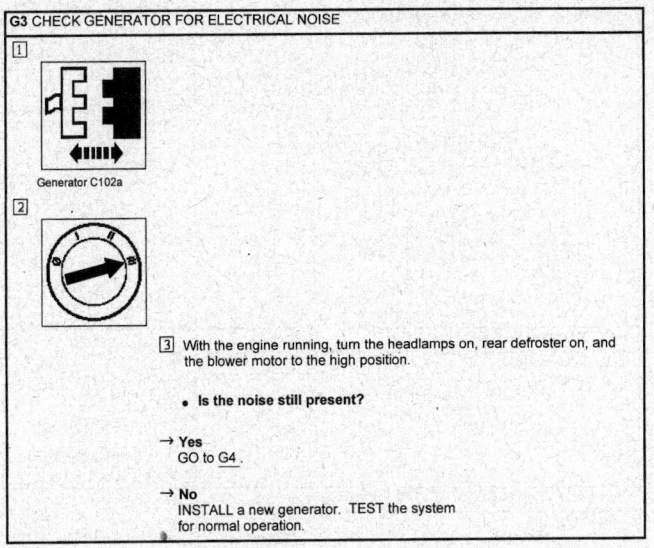

G3 CHECK GENERATOR FOR ELECTRICAL NOISE

Generator C102a

③ With the engine running, turn the headlamps on, rear defroster on, and the blower motor to the high position.

- **Is the noise still present?**

→ **Yes**
GO to G4 .

→ **No**
INSTALL a new generator. TEST the system for normal operation.

FM1120200786020X

Fig. 166   Test G: Alternator Is Noisy (Part 2 of 3). 2002 Town Car

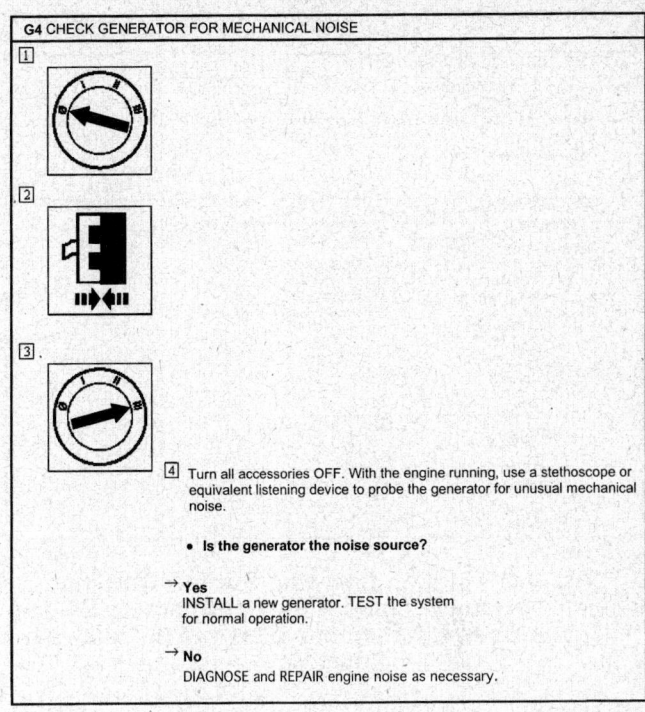

G4 CHECK GENERATOR FOR MECHANICAL NOISE

④ Turn all accessories OFF. With the engine running, use a stethoscope or equivalent listening device to probe the generator for unusual mechanical noise.

- **Is the generator the noise source?**

→ **Yes**
INSTALL a new generator. TEST the system for normal operation.

→ **No**
DIAGNOSE and REPAIR engine noise as necessary.

FM1120200786030X

Fig. 166   Test G: Alternator Is Noisy (Part 3 of 3). 2002 Town Car

CONDITIONS	DETAILS/RESULTS/ACTIONS
H1 VERIFY GENERATOR IS SOURCE OF RADIO INTERFERENCE	

① With the engine running, tune the radio to a station where the interference is present.

② Tune the radio to a station where the interference is present.

Generator C102a

- **Is the interference present with the generator disconnected?**

→ **Yes**
Diagnosis and testing of the in-vehicle entertainment system.

→ **No**
INSTALL a new generator. TEST the system for normal operation.

FM1120200787000X

Fig. 167   Test H: Radio Interference. 2002 Town Car

Test Step	Result / Action to Take
A1 CHECK BATTERY CONDITION	
• Carry out the Battery — Condition Test to determine if the battery can hold a charge and is OK for use. • **Is the battery OK?**	**Yes** GO to A2 . **No** INSTALL a new battery. TEST the system for normal operation.
A2 CHECK THE GENERATOR OUTPUT	
• Carry out the Generator On-Vehicle Tests—Load Test and No Load Test. • **Is the generator OK?**	**Yes** GO to A3 . **No** Go To Pinpoint Test B .
A3 CHECK FOR CURRENT DRAINS	
• Carry out the Battery — Drain Testing. • **Are there any excessive current drains?**	**Yes** REPAIR as necessary. TEST the system for normal operation. **No** Go To Pinpoint Test B .

ARM66FM000000162

Fig. 168   Test A: Battery Is Discharged Or Battery Voltage Is Low. 2003–05 Town Car

Test Step	Result / Action to Take
B1 CHECK THE FAULT CODES IN THE PCM	
• Connect the diagnostic tool. • Key in ON position. • Use the recorded PCM DTCs from the continuous and on-demand self-test. • **Are any DTCs recorded?**	**Yes** REFER to PCM Diagnostic Trouble Code (DTC) Index. **No** GO to B2 .
B2 CHECK CIRCUIT 904 (LG/RD)	
• Key in OFF position. • Disconnect the diagnostic tool. • Disconnect: Generator C1104a (4G), C102a (6G). • Key in ON position. • Measure the voltage between the generator C1104a (4G) pin 2, C102a (6G) pin 2, circuit 904 (LG/RD), harness side and ground. • **Is the voltage 0 volts?**	**Yes** GO to B3 . **No** GO to B4 .

ARM66FM000000163

Fig. 169 Test B: Charging System Warning Indicator Is On w/Engine Running, Charging System Voltage Does Not Increase (Part 1 of 2). 2003–05 Town Car

Test Step	Result / Action to Take
C1 CHECK THE FAULT CODES IN THE PCM	
• Connect the diagnostic tool. • Key in ON position. • Use the recorded PCM DTCs from the continuous and on-demand self-test. • **Are any DTCs recorded?**	**Yes** REFER to PCM Diagnostic Trouble Code (DTC) Index. **No** GO to C2 .
C2 CHECK THE BATTERY VOLTAGE	
• Key in OFF position. • Disconnect the diagnostic tool. • Key in START position. • With the engine running and all accessories turned off, measure the voltage at the battery while varying the engine rpm. • **Is the voltage greater than 15.5 volts?**	**Yes** GO to C3 . **No** GO to C4 .

ARM66FM000000165

Fig. 170 Test C: Charging System Overcharges, Battery Voltage More Than 15.5 Volts (Part 1 of 2). 2003–05 Town Car

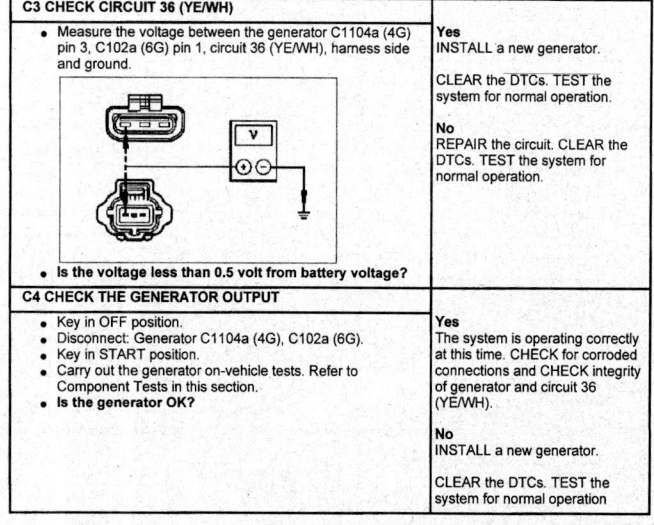

Test Step	Result / Action to Take
B3 CHECK CIRCUIT 904 (LG/RD) FOR AN OPEN	
• Key in OFF position. • Disconnect: PCM C175. • Measure the resistance between the PCM C175 pin 45, circuit 904 (LG/RD), harness side and the generator C1104a (4G) pin 2, C102a (6G) pin 2, circuit 904 (LG/RD), harness side. • **Is the resistance less than 5 ohms?**	**Yes** GO to B4 . **No** REPAIR the circuit. TEST the system for normal operation.
B4 CHECK THE GENERATOR OUTPUT	
• Connect: PCM C175. • Connect: C1104a (4G), C102a (6G). • Carry out the generator on-vehicle tests-load test. • **Is the generator OK?**	**Yes** GO to B5 . **No** INSTALL a new generator. TEST the system for normal operation.
B5 CHECK FOR CORRECT MODULE OPERATION	

• Check for:
  • corrosion
  • pushed-out pins
• Connect any disconnected connectors.
• Make sure all other system connectors are fully seated.
• Operate the system and verify the concern is still present.
• **Is the concern still present?**
	Yes
	INSTALL a new PCM.
	
	REPEAT the PCM self-test.
	
	No
	The system is operating correctly at this time. Concern may have been caused by a loose or corroded connector. CLEAR the DTCs. REPEAT the self-test.

ARM66FM000000164

Fig. 169 Test B: Charging System Warning Indicator Is On w/Engine Running, Charging System Voltage Does Not Increase (Part 2 of 2). 2003–05 Town Car

Test Step	Result / Action to Take
C3 CHECK CIRCUIT 36 (YE/WH)	
• Measure the voltage between the generator C1104a (4G) pin 3, C102a (6G) pin 1, circuit 36 (YE/WH), harness side and ground. • **Is the voltage less than 0.5 volt from battery voltage?**	**Yes** INSTALL a new generator. CLEAR the DTCs. TEST the system for normal operation. **No** REPAIR the circuit. CLEAR the DTCs. TEST the system for normal operation.
C4 CHECK THE GENERATOR OUTPUT	
• Key in OFF position. • Disconnect: Generator C1104a (4G), C102a (6G). • Key in START position. • Carry out the generator on-vehicle tests. Refer to Component Tests in this section. • **Is the generator OK?**	**Yes** The system is operating correctly at this time. CHECK for corroded connections and CHECK integrity of generator and circuit 36 (YE/WH). **No** INSTALL a new generator. CLEAR the DTCs. TEST the system for normal operation

ARM66FM000000166

Fig. 170 Test C: Charging System Overcharges, Battery Voltage More Than 15.5 Volts (Part 2 of 2). 2003–05 Town Car

Test Step	Result / Action to Take
D1 CHECK THE FAULT CODES IN THE PCM • Connect the diagnostic tool. • Key in ON position. • Use the recorded PCM DTCs from the continuous and on-demand self-test. • **Are any DTCs recorded?**	**Yes** REFER to PCM Diagnostic Trouble Code (DTC) Index. **No** GO to D2 .
D2 CHECK THE SYSTEM FOR OVERCHARGING • Key in OFF position. • Disconnect the diagnostic tool. • Key in START position. • With the engine running and all accessories off, measure the voltage at the battery terminals while varying the engine rpm. • **Is the voltage greater than 15.5 volts?**	**Yes** Go To Pinpoint Test C . **No** GO to D3 .
D3 CHECK CIRCUIT 36 (YE/WH) • Key in OFF position. • Disconnect: Generator C1104a (4G), C102a (6G). • Key in ON position. • Measure the voltage between generator C1104a (4G) pin 3, C102a (6G) pin 1, circuit 36 (YE/WH), harness side, and ground. • **Is the voltage equal to battery voltage?**	**Yes** GO to D4 . **No** REPAIR the circuit. TEST the system for normal operation.

ARM66FM000000167

Fig. 171   Test D: Charging System Warning Indicator Is On w/Engine Running & Battery Increases Voltage (Part 1 of 2). 2003–05 Town Car

Test Step	Result / Action to Take
E1 CHECK THE FAULT CODES IN THE PCM • Connect the diagnostic tool. • Key in ON position. • Use the recorded PCM DTCs from the continuous and on-demand self-test. • **Are any DTCs recorded?**	**Yes** REFER to PCM Diagnostic Trouble Code (DTC) Index. **No** GO to E2 .
E2 CHECK THE CHARGING SYSTEM WARNING INDICATOR OPERATION • Key in OFF position. • Disconnect the diagnostic tool. • Disconnect: Generator C1104a (4G), C102a (6G). • Key in ON position. • With the engine off, connect a fused (15A) jumper wire between the generator C1104a (4G) pin 2, C102a (6G) pin 2, circuit 904 (LG/RD), harness side and ground. • **Does the charging system warning indicator illuminate?**	**Yes** INSTALL a new generator. TEST the system for normal operation. **No** GO to E3 .

E3 CHECK FOR CORRECT MODULE OPERATION
 • Check for:
   • corrosion
   • pushed-out pins
 • Connect any disconnected connectors.
 • Make sure all other system connectors are fully seated.
 • Operate the system and verify the concern is still present.
 • **Is the concern still present?**
	Yes
	 INSTALL a new PCM. REPEAT the PCM self-test.
	 No
	 The system is operating correctly at this time. Concern may have been caused by a loose or corroded connector. CLEAR the DTCs. REPEAT the self-test.

ARM66FM000000169

Fig. 172   Test E: Charging System Warning Indicator Is Off w/Ignition Switch In Run Position & Engine Is Off. 2003–05 Town Car

Test Step	Result / Action to Take
D4 CHECK THE CHARGING SYSTEM WARNING INDICATOR OPERATION • Key in OFF position. • Disconnect: PCM C175. • Key in ON position. • Monitor the charging system warning indicator. • **Is the indicator illuminated?**	**Yes** REPAIR circuit 904 (LG/RD) for a short to ground. TEST the system for normal operation. **No** GO to D5 .
D5 CHECK THE GENERATOR OUTPUT • Key in OFF position. • Connect: PCM C175. • Connect: Generator C1104a (4G), C102a (6G). • Carry out generator on-vehicle tests. • **Is the generator OK?**	**Yes** GO to D6 . **No** INSTALL a new generator. Clear the DTCs. TEST the system for normal operation.

D6 CHECK FOR CORRECT MODULE OPERATION
 • Check for:
   • corrosion
   • pushed-out pins
 • Connect any disconnected connectors.
 • Make sure all other system connectors are fully seated.
 • Operate the system and verify the concern is still present.
 • **Is the concern still present?**
	Yes
	 INSTALL a new PCM. REPEAT the PCM self-test.
	 No
	 The system is operating correctly at this time. Concern may have been caused by a loose or corroded connector. CLEAR the DTCs. REPEAT the self-test.

ARM66FM000000168

Fig. 171   Test D: Charging System Warning Indicator Is On w/Engine Running & Battery Increases Voltage (Part 2 of 2). 2003–05 Town Car

Test Step	Result / Action to Take
F1 CHECK THE FAULT CODES IN THE PCM • Connect the diagnostic tool. • Key in ON position. • Use the recorded PCM DTCs from the continuous and on-demand self-test. • **Are any DTCs recorded?**	**Yes** REFER to PCM Diagnostic Trouble Code (DTC) Index. **No** GO to F2 .
F2 CHECK FOR LOOSE CONNECTIONS • Disconnect: Generator C1104a (4G), C102a (6G). • Check all generator, battery, and power distribution connections for looseness, corrosion, loose or bent terminals, or loose eyelets. • Connect: Generator C1104a (4G), C102a (6G). • **Are all connections clean and tight?**	**Yes** GO to F3 . **No** REPAIR as necessary. TEST the system for normal operation.
F3 CHECK FUSE CONNECTION • Key in START position. • With the engine running, check BJB fuse 13 (15A) in circuit 36 (YE/WH) for looseness by wiggling the fuse and noting the charging system warning indicator lamp operation. • **Does the charging system warning indicator lamp flicker?**	**Yes** REPAIR loose fuse connections as necessary. TEST the system for normal operation. **No** GO to F4 .
F4 CHECK THE BATTERY VOLTAGE • Key in START position. • With the engine running, and all accessories turned off, measure the voltage at the battery while varying the engine rpm. • **Is the voltage greater than 15.5 volts?**	**Yes** Go To Pinpoint Test C . **No** GO to F5 .

ARM66FM000000170

Fig. 173   Test F: Charging System Warning Indicator Lamp Flickers Or Is Intermittent (Part 1 of 2). 2003–05 Town Car

Fig. 173 (Test F)

F5 CHECK THE WARNING SYSTEM INDICATOR OPERATION	
• Key in OFF position. • Disconnect: Generator C1104a (4G), C102a (6G). • Key in ON position. • Connect a fused jumper wire between generator C1104a (4G) pin 2, C102a (6G) pin 2, circuit 904 (LG/RD), harness side and ground. 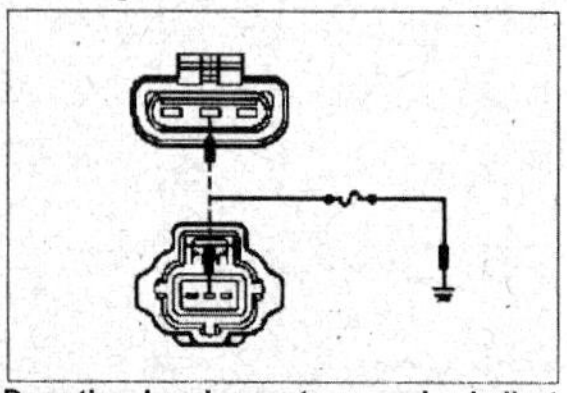 • **Does the charging system warning indicator illuminate?**	**Yes** GO to F6 . **No** REPAIR the circuit. TEST the system for normal operation.
F6 CHECK THE PCM OPERATION	
• Key in OFF position. • Connect: Generator C1104a (4G), C102a (6G). • Key in ON position. • Monitor the charging system warning indicator operation. • **Is the charging system warning indicator illuminated?**	**Yes** The PCM is operating correctly. RECHECK the generator circuits (including the generator) for intermittent shorts or opens. TEST the system for normal operation. **No** GO to F7 .
F7 CHECK FOR CORRECT MODULE OPERATION	
• Check for: ○ corrosion ○ pushed-out pins • Connect any disconnected connectors. • Make sure all other system connectors are fully seated. • Operate the system and verify the concern is still present. • **Is the concern still present?**	**Yes** INSTALL a new PCM. REPEAT the PCM self-test. **No** The system is operating correctly at this time. Concern may have been caused by a loose or corroded connector. CLEAR the DTCs. REPEAT the self-test.

ARM66FM000000171

Fig. 173   Test F: Charging System Warning Indicator Lamp Flickers Or Is Intermittent (Part 2 of 2). 2003–05 Town Car

Fig. 174 (Test G)

Test Step	Result / Action to Take
G1 CHECK FOR ACCESSORY DRIVE NOISE AND MOUNTING BRACKETS	
• Check the accessory drive belt for damage and correct installation • Check the accessory mounting brackets and generator pulley for looseness or misalignment. • **Is the accessory drive OK?**	**Yes** GO to G2 . **No** REPAIR as necessary. TEST the system for normal operation.
G2 CHECK GENERATOR FOR ELECTRICAL NOISE	
• Disconnect: Generator C1104a (4G), C102a (6G). • Key in START position. • With the engine running, • **Is the noise still present?**	**Yes** GO to G3 . **No** INSTALL a new generator. TEST the system for normal operation.
G3 CHECK GENERATOR FOR MECHANICAL NOISE	
• Key in OFF position. • Key in START position. • With the engine running, use a stethoscope or equivalent listening device to probe the generator for unusual mechanical noise. • **Is the generator the noise source?**	**Yes** INSTALL a new generator. TEST the system for normal operation. **No** diagnose the source of the engine noise.

ARM66FM000000172

Fig. 174   Test G: Alternator Is Noisy. 2003–05 Town Car

Fig. 175 (Test H)

Test Step	Result / Action to Take
H1 VERIFY GENERATOR IS SOURCE OF RADIO INTERFERENCE	
• Key in START position. • Start and run the engine. • Tune the radio to a station where the interference is present. • Key in OFF position. • Disconnect: Generator C1104 (4G), C102a (6G). • Key in START position. • **Is the interference present with the generator disconnected?**	**Yes** diagnose and test the in-vehicle entertainment system. **No** INSTALL a new generator. TEST the system for normal operation.

ARM66FM000000173

Fig. 175   Test H: Radio Interference. 2003–05 Town Car

ALTERNATOR SPECIFICATIONS

Model	Year	Engine	Model	Amp Rating
Continental	2001–02	4.6L	F8OU-CA	130
Cougar	2001–02	2.0L & 2.5L	—	—
Crown Victoria	2001–05	4.6L	F6LU-CA	130
Escort	2001–03	2.0L DOHC	—	95
		2.0L SOHC	—	75
Five Hundred	2005	3.0L		120
Focus	2001–05	2.0L	—	—
Freestyle	2005	3.0L	—	120
Grand Marquis	2001–05	4.6L	F6LU-CA	130
LS	2001–05	3.0L	XR8U-AC	105
		3.9L	XR8U-CD	105
Marauder	2003–04	4.6L	F6LU-CA	130
Montego	2005	3.0L	—	120
Mustang	2001–05	3.8L	1R3U-BA	110
		4.0L	—	135
		4.6L DOHC	F6ZU-BE	120
		4.6L SOHC	XR3U-AB	110
Sable	2001–05	3.0L DOHC	XF2V-BC	125
		3.0L OHV	XF2V-AB	110
Taurus	2001–05	3.0L DOHC	XF2V-BC	125
		3.0L OHV	XF2V-AB	110
Thunderbird	2002–05	3.9L	XR8U-CD	105
Town Car	2000–05	4.6L	F6LU-CA	130
ZX2	2001–03	2.0L DOHC		95

STEERING COLUMNS

NOTE: On Air Bag Equipped Models, Refer To "Air Bag System Precautions" Located In The Front Of This Manual For System Disarming & Arming Procedures.

NOTE: Refer To "Computer Relearn Procedures" Located In The Front Of This Manual When Battery Power To The Computer Has Been Interrupted.

NOTE: Models Equipped With "Automatic Ride Control System" Utilize A Steering Sensor Located On The Steering Column Assembly. For Sensor Replacement, Refer To "Automatic Ride Control System" In The "Active Suspension" Section.

NOTE: Prior To Performing Any Service Operations Listed In This Section, Consult The "Technical Service Bulletins" Section For Related Information.

INDEX

PRECAUTIONS

Air Bag Systems

Refer to "Air Bag System Precautions" in the front of this manual for system disarming and arming procedures.

Battery Ground Cable

Prior to service, disconnect battery ground cable and isolate as required. Allow one minute for back-up power supply to be depleted.

DESCRIPTION

The steering column used on models equipped with air bags is of a modular construction and features easy to service electrical switches. The washer/wiper switch and the combination turn signal/hazard/horn/flash-to-pass/dimmer switch are attached with self-tapping screws.

These models are equipped with either a brush type or a clockspring type slip ring. Removal and installation procedures for the two types are the same except where noted.

Fasteners used on steering column components must be replaced after removal. The fasteners are coated with an epoxy adhesive and cannot be used again.

Whenever the steering column is removed or is separated from the steering gear, the steering column must be in locked position to prevent the steering wheel from being rotated accidentally and damaging the air bag slip ring.

The LS and Thunderbird models are equipped with a power tilt/telescopic steering column of modular construction. It has easy-to-service electrical switches. This column is equipped with an electric tilt and telescopic mechanism that allows the steering wheel angle and length to be adjusted to suit the driver.

On models equipped with the memory package, the steering wheel position is stored in memory the same way as driver seat position and retrieved as a personality feature. The steering column is controlled by the instrument cluster module.

STEERING COLUMN

REPLACE

Continental

1. Ensure wheels are in straight-ahead position.
2. Remove steering wheel as outlined in "Electrical" section of "Continental & Town Car" chassis chapter.
3. Remove instrument panel lower trim cover and air bag sliding contact as outlined in "Passive Restraint Systems" chapter.
4. Remove tilt wheel handle and shank by unscrewing it from column and removing mounting screws.
5. Rotate ignition switch lock cylinder to RUN position, press lock cylinder retaining pin through access hole and remove lock cylinder.
6. Remove four upper and lower steering column shrouds.
7. Remove instrument panel reinforcement brace.
8. Disconnect shift cable and bracket from steering column, then the transaxle shift cable loop from shift tube hook.
9. Remove mounting screws and position multi-function switch aside.
10. Remove ignition switch mounting screw and disconnect wiring.
11. Remove front mounting nuts and steering column impact absorber.
12. Remove steering column lower yoke pinch bolt.
13. Remove and discard rear column mounting nuts, then lower and support column.

14. Disconnect parking brake release vacuum hose extensions at parking brake release switch or remove vacuum release assembly.
15. Disconnect shift cable and bracket from selector lever pivot.
16. Remove shift cable and bracket from lower column mounting.
17. Remove mounting screws and shift lock actuator.
18. Reverse procedure to install.

Cougar

1. Remove driver's side instrument panel lower cover.
2. Center and lock steering wheel.
3. Remove steering column upper and lower shrouds.
4. Disconnect flexible coupling. Discard pinch bolt.
5. Disconnect electrical connectors on left and righthand sides of steering column.
6. Cut cable tie and disconnect air bag control module electrical connector.
7. Disconnect wiring harnesses.
8. Remove mounting bolt and slide outwards to disengage retaining tab.
9. Reverse procedure to install.

Crown Victoria, Grand Marquis, Marauder & Town Car

1. Ensure wheels are in straight-ahead position.
2. Remove air bag sliding contact.
3. Disconnect multi-function switch electrical connectors.
4. Remove mounting screws and multi-function switch.
5. Remove instrument panel reinforcement brace.
6. Disconnect ignition switch electrical connector.
7. Disconnect brake shift interlock solenoid connector.
8. Remove Passive Anti-Theft System (PATS) sensor ring.
9. Remove shift cable and bracket from steering column.
10. Remove and discard lower steering column shaft pinch bolt.
11. Disconnect lower steering column shaft from steering column lower yoke.
12. Remove and discard steering column mounting nuts, then lower steering column to floor.
13. Disconnect parking brake release vacuum hose extension from parking brake release switch.
14. Disconnect, then position shift cable and bracket aside.
15. Remove steering column.
16. Reverse procedure to install.

Escort & ZX2

1. Remove steering wheel as outlined in "Electrical" section of "Escort & ZX2" chassis chapter.
2. Remove mounting screws, then the upper and lower steering column shrouds.
3. Loosen mounting nut, then remove hood latch control handle and cable. Position aside.
4. Remove mounting screws and release instrument panel steering column cover.
5. Disconnect headlamp switch electrical connector and remove instrument panel steering column cover.
6. Disconnect steering column electrical connectors and remove retainer plate.
7. Remove mounting bolts and lower steering column tube.
8. Remove steering column input shaft coupling to steering gear input shaft pinch bolt. Discard bolt.
9. Remove support bracket mounting nuts and steering column.
10. Reverse procedure to install.

Five Hundred, Freestyle & Montego

Do not allow the steering column to rotate while the intermediate shaft is disconnected, damage to the clockspring may result.
1. Ensure wheels are in straight-ahead position, then remove ignition key.
2. Remove instrument panel lower trim cover.
3. Remove upper and lower steering column shrouds, **Fig. 1.**
4. Disconnect intermediate shaft to steering column retaining bolt, then disconnect shaft from column.
5. Disconnect ignition switch, multi-function switch and anti-theft system transceiver electrical connectors.
6. Disconnect wire harness to steering column 2-pin type retainers, then position harness aside.
7. Remove four steering column to instrument panel mounting bolts.
8. Remove steering column.
9. Reverse procedure to install. Ensure intermediate shaft boot bearing clamp does not contact boot after installation, **Fig. 2.**

Focus

1. Ensure wheels are in straight-ahead position.
2. Remove ignition key.
3. Remove mounting screws, release fastener and disconnect instrument panel lower panel.
4. Disconnect hood release cable and data link electrical connector, then remove instrument panel lower panel.
5. Remove steering column upper shroud using suitable thin bladed screwdriver to release clips on each side.
6. Release steering column locking lever, then remove mounting screws and steering column lower shroud.
7. Disconnect Passive Anti-Theft System (PATS) transceiver, wiper/washer switch and air bag sliding contact/speed control on righthand side of steering column.
8. Disconnect ignition switch and turn signal/flash-to-pass switch electrical connectors on lefthand side of steering column.
9. Disconnect steering column wiring harness by releasing locating pin.
10. Remove mounting bolt and disconnect steering column shaft from steering gear pinion extension.
11. Remove mounting bolts and steering column.
12. Reverse procedure to install.

LS & Thunderbird

1. Ensure wheels are in straight-ahead position.
2. Remove driver's air bag module and air bag sliding contact as outlined in "Passive Restraint Systems" chapter.
3. Remove steering wheel as outlined in "Electrical" section of "LS & Thunderbird" chassis chapter.
4. Remove steering column shaft pinch bolt and separate intermediate shaft from steering column yoke. Discard pinch bolt.
5. Disconnect electronic steering sensor and steering column release motor electrical connectors.
6. **On models equipped with automatic transmission,** remove and discard locknuts while supporting steering column.
7. **On models equipped with manual transmission,** remove and discard locknuts while supporting steering column. Lower steering column and disconnect lock actuator electrical connector.
8. **On all models,** remove steering column.
9. Reverse procedure to install.

Mustang

1. Remove steering wheel as outlined in "Electrical" section of "Mustang" chassis chapter.
2. Remove steering column lower yoke to lower steering column shaft mounting bolt.
3. Remove ignition switch lock cylinder as outlined in "Electrical" section of "Mustang" chassis chapter.
4. Remove steering column opening cover, reinforcement and instrument panel cross brace.
5. Remove upper and lower steering column shrouds.
6. Disconnect ignition switch and key warning buzzer electrical connectors.
7. Remove mounting screws and position multi-function switch aside.
8. Remove nuts mounting steering shaft tube boot to dash panel.
9. Remove mounting nuts and lower steering column to clear mounting bolts.
10. **On models equipped with automatic transmission,** remove ignition/shifter interlock cable.
11. **On all models,** remove steering column.
12. Reverse procedure to install.

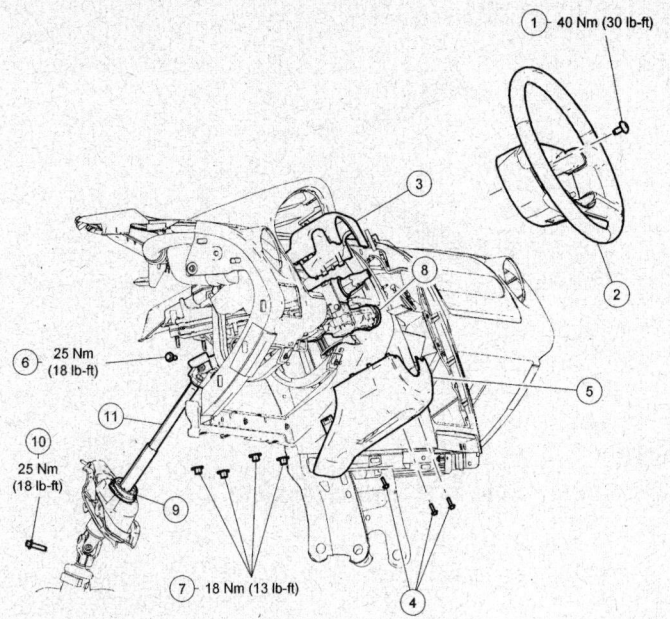

1 - 40 Nm (30 lb-ft)

6 - 25 Nm (18 lb-ft)

10 - 25 Nm (18 lb-ft)

7 - 18 Nm (13 lb-ft)

1. Steering wheel bolt
2. Steering wheel
3. Upper steering column shroud
4. Lower steering column shroud screws
5. Lower steering column shroud
6. Intermediate shaft to steering column bolt
7. Steering column nuts
8. Steering column
9. Intermediate shaft boot bearing clamp
10. Intermediate shaft to steering gear bolt
11. Intermediate shaft

ARM0400000000758

Fig. 1   Exploded view of steering column. Five Hundred, Freestyle & Montego

Sable & Taurus

Do not remove steering wheel or air bag module as an assembly unless the column is locked or the steering column gear input shaft coupling is secured to keep it from turning.

1. Ensure wheels are in straight-ahead position.
2. Remove steering wheel as outlined in "Electrical" section of "Sable & Taurus" chassis chapter.
3. Remove steering column intermediate shaft coupling to steering column lower yoke mounting bolt.
4. Remove lower instrument panel steering column cover.
5. Push in on release pin by inserting suitable tool into access hole located in bottom of lower steering column shroud, then rotate ignition cylinder clockwise to Run position and remove cylinder.
6. Remove lower and upper steering column shrouds.
7. Remove mounting screws and position Passive Anti-Theft System (PATS) transceiver aside.

8. **On models equipped with column shift,** disconnect and slide shift control selector lever boot toward end of control lever. Remove control lever by removing retaining pin.
9. **On models equipped with overdrive lock-out switch on column lever,** disconnect wiring connector at bottom of steering column and remove wiring from column with control lever.
10. **On all models,** disconnect wiring connectors for ignition switch, horn, speed control, interlock switch and air bag module.
11. Remove mounting screws and position multi-function switch aside.
12. Remove shift indicator cable from shifter tube.
13. Remove shifter indicator retainer mounting screw from column adjustment cable.
14. Remove mounting nuts and lower steering column.
15. **On models equipped with console shift,** disconnect BTSI electrical connector.
16. **On all models,** remove steering column.

17. Reverse procedure to install. Adjust shift indicator cable.

STEERING COLUMN SERVICE

Continental

1. **Record steering column lock gear, bearing and retainer position for assembly alignment.**
2. Remove bearing retainer, lock housing bearing and lock gear, **Fig. 3.**
3. Disconnect electrical connector, then remove mounting screws and shock absorber electronic steering sensor.
4. Remove steering column lower bearing spring and sensor ring.
5. Remove steering column bearing tolerance ring from shaft.
6. Remove mounting bolts and ignition switch.
7. Remove lock cylinder housing pivot screws.
8. Pry up on steering column locking levers using fabricated tool and remove column position spring. **Steering column position spring is under tension and may come out with great force.**
9. Remove turn signal cancel cam and snap ring.
10. Remove steering column upper bearing spring and sleeve.
11. Slide steering column shaft in toward steering column lock cylinder housing and out.
12. Slide steering column bearing tolerance ring off steering column shaft.
13. Remove column bearing from steering column lock cylinder housing using suitable punch.
14. Remove mounting screws and parking brake release switch.
15. Remove mounting bolts and brake shift interlock solenoid.
16. Remove mounting bolts, clamps and shift tube.
17. Remove mounting bolts, transaxle selector lever arm and support.
18. Remove gearshift selector tube spring and drive out shift tube gearshift lever pin.
19. Remove gearshift lever and column shift selector lever plunger. Replace lever plunger if it is bent.
20. Remove gearshift lever socket bushings and transaxle control selector lever spring clip.
21. Drive out steering column lock lever pin and remove steering column lock pawl.
22. Remove lower steering column bearing and sleeve.
23. Remove mounting bolts and steering column lower bearing retainer.
24. Remove upper and lower steering column actuators.
25. Reverse procedure to assemble.

Cougar

1. Remove mounting screws and air bag module.
2. Disconnect wiring harness connectors for air bag module and speed control.
3. Remove steering wheel mounting bolt.
4. Remove steering wheel. **Do not damage air bag sliding contact harness during removal.**
5. Prevent accidental rotation by applying tape across air bag sliding contact stator and rotor.
6. Remove lock cylinder, ignition switch and combination switch as outlined in "Electrical" section of "Cougar" chassis chapter.
7. Remove lower steering shaft bearing retainer, **Fig. 4.**
8. Remove lower steering shaft.
9. Reverse procedure to install.

Crown Victoria, Grand Marquis, Marauder & Town Car

1. **Record positions of steering column lock gear, bearing and retainer for assembly alignment.**
2. Remove bearing retainer, lock housing bearing and lock gear, **Fig. 5.**
3. Disconnect electrical connector, then remove screws and shock absorber electronic steering sensor.
4. Remove steering column lower bearing spring and sensor ring.
5. Remove steering column bearing tolerance ring from column shaft.
6. Remove mounting bolts and ignition switch.
7. Remove lock cylinder housing pivot screws.
8. Pry up on steering column locking levers using fabricated tool and remove column position spring. **Steering column position spring is under tension and may come out with great force.**
9. Remove turn signal cancel cam and snap ring.
10. Remove steering column upper bearing spring and sleeve.
11. Slide steering column shaft in toward steering column lock cylinder housing and out.
12. Slide steering column bearing tolerance ring off steering column shaft.
13. Remove column bearing from steering column lock cylinder housing using suitable punch.
14. Remove mounting screws and parking brake release switch.
15. Remove mounting bolts and brake shift interlock solenoid.
16. Remove mounting bolts, clamps and shift tube.
17. Remove mounting bolts, transaxle selector lever arm and support.
18. Remove gearshift selector tube spring and drive out shift tube gearshift lever pin.
19. Remove gearshift lever and column shift selector lever plunger. Replace lever plunger if it is bent.

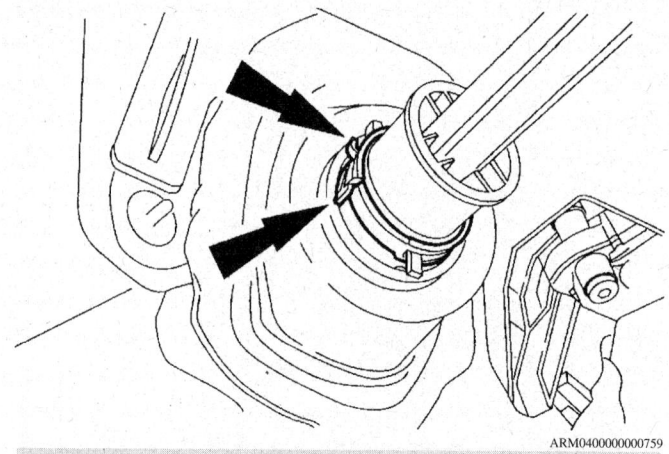

ARM0400000000759

Fig. 2 Intermediate shaft bearing boot clamp position. Five Hundred, Freestyle & Montego

20. Remove gearshift lever socket bushings and transaxle control selector lever spring clip.
21. Drive out steering column lock lever pin and remove steering column lock pawl.
22. Remove lower steering column bearing and sleeve.
23. Remove mounting bolts and steering column lower bearing retainer.
24. Remove upper and lower steering column actuators.
25. Reverse procedure to assemble.

Escort, ZX2 & Focus

The steering column is serviced as an assembly. If service other than the air bag clockspring, combination switch or ignition switch assembly is required, the steering column must be replaced, **Fig. 6.**

Five Hundred, Freestyle & Montego

The steering column is serviced as an assembly. If service other than the air bag clockspring, combination switch or ignition switch assembly is required, the steering column must be replaced, **Fig. 1.**

LS & Thunderbird

DISASSEMBLE

1. Place steering column in suitable vise.
2. **On models equipped with manual transmission,** proceed as follows:
   a. Remove shear bolts' heads using suitable drill motor with 3/8 inch drill bit.
   b. Remove steering wheel lock actuator. **Do not damage actuator.**
   c. Remove steering column upper shaft assembly shear bolts using suitable locking pliers.
3. **On all models,** remove electronic steering sensor, **Fig. 7.**
4. Disconnect steering column release motor (telescopic) electrical connector.

5. Connect telescopic release motor electrical terminals using suitable 1 amp 12 volt battery charger and telescope column out until it is fully extended. **Do not telescope steering column manually.**
6. Connect steering column release motor (telescopic) electrical connector.
7. Replace steering column release motor if it is damaged or inoperable before installing telescoping steering column.
8. Remove mounting screws and steering column release motors. **Do not disconnect steering column release motors' harness electrical connectors.**
9. Remove mounting bolts, steering column outer housing cover plate, outer housing and column track.
10. Remove steering column connector link.
11. Install spring compressor tool No. 211-201, or equivalent, on steering column position spring and tighten by hand.
12. Remove spring mounting bolts.
13. Release spring tension using spring compressor tool, then remove spring and tool.
14. Separate front and rear halves of steering column upper shaft and column inner housing. Upper shaft sensor ring and coupler are serviced as an assembly.
15. Remove rear half of steering column upper shaft from support.
16. Remove steering column telescopic actuator. **Curl strap on steering column actuator must not be bent or altered.** Replace steering column telescopic actuator if curl strap is damaged.
17. Remove column track from support and potentiometer.
18. Remove steering column release pin and place inner housing in suitable vise.
19. Remove steering column tilt actuator, inner track bearing retainers and column tracks.
20. Remove steering column tube flange

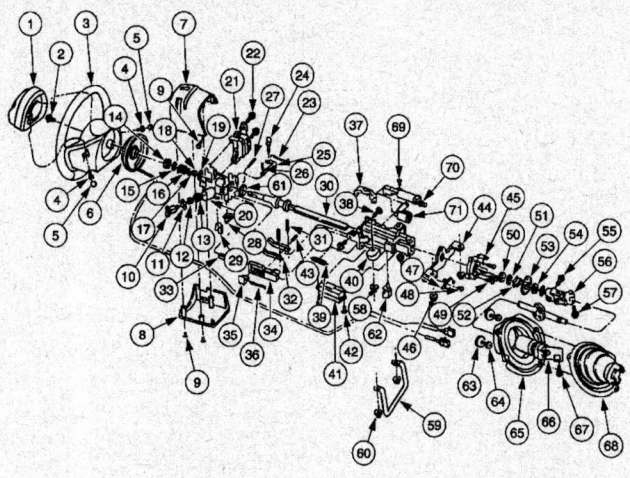

Item	Part Number	Description
1	043B13	Driver Air Bag Module
2	N804385-S100	Steering Wheel Bolt
3	3600 *	Steering Wheel
4	N808324-S424	Air Bag Module Retaining Screws
5	3L518	Steering Wheel Spoke Cover
6	14A664	Air Bag Sliding Contact — Assy
7	3530	Steering Column Shroud — (Upper)
8	3530	Steering Column Shroud — (Lower)
9	55929	Shroud Retaining Screws
10	11582	Ignition Switch Lock Cylinder
11	3C610	Bearing Retainer
12	3E700	Steering Column Lock Housing Bearing
13	3E717	Steering Column Lock Gear
14	13318	Turn Indicator Cancel Cam
15	3C610	Snap Ring
16	3520	Steering Column Upper Bearing Spring
17	3518	Steering Column Bearing Sleeve

FM6049900123010X

Fig. 3 Exploded view of steering column (Part 1 of 3). Continental

18	3L539	Steering Column Bearing Tolerance Ring
19	3517	Steering Column Bearing — (Small)
20	3511	Steering Column Lock Cylinder Housing
21	13K359	Multi-Function Switch
22	390345-S36	Screws
23	3D655	Steering Column Position Spring
24	3F609	Tilt Wheel Handle and Shank
25	3D544	Steering Column Release Lever
26	N805857	Steering Column Lock Actuator Lever Pin
27	N806157	Pin-Lock Cam Pivot
28	3E695	Steering Column Lock Cam
29	14A163	Wiring Harness Retainer — (Upper)
30	3524	Steering Shaft Assy
31	3B664	Steering Column Locking Lever Spring
32	3B661 (RH), 3D653 (LH)	Steering Column Locking Lever
33	3E715	Steering Column Lock Lever Actuator — (Upper)
34	3E715	Steering Column Lock Lever Actuator — (Lower)
35	3E691	Steering Column Lock Pawl — (Shaft)
36	3E696	Steering Column Lock Spring — (Shaft)
37	14A099	Wiring Shield
38	N806582	Tilt Pivot Screws
39	3D655	Steering Column Position Spring
40	3F723	Steering Actuator Housing
41	11572	Ignition Switch
42	N805858	Screws
43	3F530	Steering Column Lock Actuator Lever Pin
44	3668	Steering Column Lower Mounting Bracket
45	3D681	Steering Column Lower Bearing Retainer
46	N806423-S56	Column Mounting Nuts
47	14A206	Wire Connector Bracket
48	N804409	Screw
49	N805859	Lower Bearing Housing Retaining Screws
50	3518	Steering Column Bearing Sleeve — (Lower)
51	3517	Steering Column Bearing — (Lower)
52	3L539	Steering Column Bearing Tolerance Ring
53	3C131	Suspension Height Sensor Control Ring

FM6049900123020X

Fig. 3 Exploded view of steering column (Part 2 of 3). Continental

and upper bearing retainer.

21. Remove column upper bearing spring and sleeve.
22. Spread steering column upper bearing tolerance ring using suitable flat blade screwdriver and slide it out of column upper shaft.
23. Remove front half of steering column upper shaft.
24. Drive out small and large steering column tube bearing assemblies using suitable brass drifts.

ASSEMBLE

1. Install large and small steering column tube bearings using suitable bearing installer tools.
2. Slide steering shaft into tilt housing and install steering column upper bearing tolerance ring.
3. Install column bearing sleeve and upper bearing spring.
4. Install steering column upper bearing retainer, tube flange and mounting bolts.
5. Position steering column tilt actuator and install mounting bolts.
6. Install steering column release pin, potentiometer and mounting screws.
7. Install steering column telescopic actuator and mounting nuts.
8. Install steering column track on support. Apply Premium Long-Life Grease part No. XG-1-C, or equivalent, to steering column track bearing surface.
9. Attach steering column tracks and inner track bearings to steering column inner housing.
10. Apply Premium Long-Life Grease to column track bearings and steering column tracks' bearing surface.
11. Install rear half of steering column upper shaft into steering column support and mounting bolts.
12. Join front and rear halves of steering column upper shaft and steering column inner housing in column support housing.
13. Position steering column spring.
14. Compress spring until actuator telescopic assembly bolt until holes align using compressor tool No. 211-201, or equivalent, Install mounting bolts and remove tool.
15. Install steering column connector link and column track on outer housing. Apply grease to bearing surface of steering column track.
16. Ensure steering column inner track bearing retainers are properly staged.
17. Install steering column outer housing and housing cover plate. Hand tighten loosely.
18. Ensure steering column inner track bearings are properly staged. **Steering column inner track bearings must be installed against rear column inner housing track bearing retaining end. Inner housing must be installed in fully extended (out) position.**
19. Apply Threadlock 262 part No. E2FZ-19554-B, or equivalent, to threads and

54	3520	Steering Column Upper Bearing Spring
55	N803942-S100	Bolt – Flange Yoke
56	3N725	Steering Column Lower Yoke
57	N803942	Bolt
58	N806423-S56	Upper Column Mounting Nuts
59	3E644	Steering Column Absorber
60	N801555	Nuts
61	3517	Steering Column Bearing – (Large)
62	14A163	Wiring Harness Retainer – (Lower)
63	N804326	Nut (2 Req'd)
64	N804795-S2	Nut (3 Req'd)
65	3513	Steering Column Opening Weather Seal
66	3A525	Steering Column Intermediate Shaft Coupling
67	N806349-S100	Bolt
68	3513	Steering Column Opening Weather Seal – (Secondary)
69	N806038-S2	Screw
70	3F719	Ignition/Shifter Interlock Cable
71	7H178	Bracket

FM6049900123030X

Fig. 3 Exploded view of steering column (Part 3 of 3). Continental

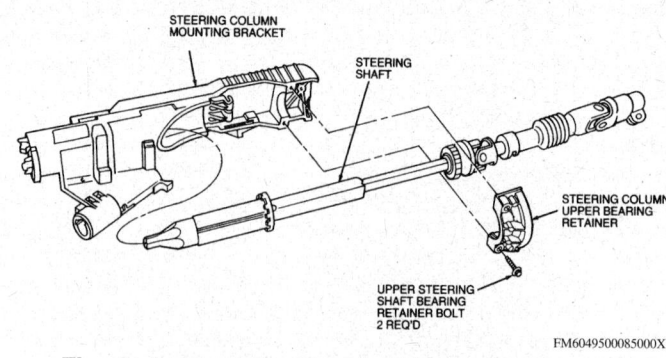

Fig. 4 Lower steering shaft removal. Cougar

Item	Description	Item	Description
9	Steering Column Release Lever Pin	35	Steering Column Bearing
10	Steering Column Release Lever	36	Steering Column Retaining Nuts
11	Tilt Wheel Handle and Shank	37	Wiring Harness Retainer
12	Column Shift Selector Lever Plunger	38	Steering Actuator Housing
13	Gearshift Lever	39	Steering Column Lock Lever Pin
14	Steering Column Shaft	40	Ignition Switch
15	Transmission Control Selector Lever Plunger Spring	41	Steering Column Position Spring
16	Gearshift Lever Pin	42	Steering Column Lock Lever
17	Transmission Column Shift Selector Tube	43	Steering Column Position Lock Spring
18	Tilt Column Pivot Screw	44	Steering Column Locking Lever
19	Transmission Control Selector Lever Spring Clip	45	Steering Column Lock Lever Actuator
20	Gearshift Tube Bushing Clamp	46	Steering Column Lock Spring
21	Brake Shift Interlock Solenoid	47	Steering Column Lock Pawl
22	Gearshift Lever Socket Bushing	48	Steering Column Lock Actuator
23	Transmission Shift Selector Position Insert	49	Steering Column Lock Cam
24	Transmission Selector Lever Arm and Support	50	Steering Column Tilt Flange Bumper
25	Shift Cable and Bracket	51	Wiring Harness Retainer
26	Gearshift Lever	52	Shroud Screws
27	Steering Column Lock Pawl	53	Steering Column Shroud
28	Gearshift Lever Pin	54	Steering Column Lock Gear
29	Steering Column Instrument Panel Bracket	55	Steering Column Lock Housing Bearing
30	Steering Column Lower Bearing Retainer	56	Bearing Retainer
31	Steering Column Bearing Sleeve	57	Ignition Switch Lock Cylinder
32	Steering Column Bearing Tolerance Ring	58	Passive Anti-Theft System (PATS) Sensor Ring
33	Steering Column Bearing Spring	59	Steering Column Bearing Tolerance Ring
34	Suspension Height Sensor Control Ring	60	Steering Column Upper Bearing Spring
		61	Bearing Retainer
		62	Turn Indicator Cancel Cam

FM6049900124020X

Fig. 5 Exploded view of steering column (Part 2 of 2). Crown Victoria, Grand Marquis, Marauder & Town Car

Item	Description	Item	Description
1	Air Bag Sliding Contact	5	Steering Column Bearing
2	Cellular Phone Voice Activated-Microphone	6	Steering Column Lock Cylinder Housing
3	Steering Column Shroud	7	Multi-Function Switch
4	Steering Column Bearing Sleeve	8	Pin

FM6049900124010X

Fig. 5 Exploded view of steering column (Part 1 of 2). Crown Victoria, Grand Marquis, Marauder & Town Car

28. **On models equipped with manual transmission,** install steering wheel lock actuator and new shear bolts.

Mustang

DISASSEMBLE

1. Remove steering column lower yoke and upper bearing spring, then the suspension height sensor control ring and upper bearing tolerance ring, **Fig. 8.**
2. Remove turn indicator cancel cam by pushing up with suitable flat-bladed screwdriver. **Record flush surface direction.**

tighten mounting bolts.

20. Install steering column release motors and mounting screws.
21. Disconnect steering column telescopic release motor electrical connector.
22. Connect motor electrical connector terminals to suitable 1 amp 12-volt battery charger and test column for normal operation.
23. Connect steering column telescopic release motor electrical connector.
24. Disconnect steering column tilt release motor electrical connector.
25. Connect motor electrical connector terminals to battery charger and test column for normal operation.
26. Connect steering column tilt release motor electrical connector.
27. Install electronic steering sensor with screws.

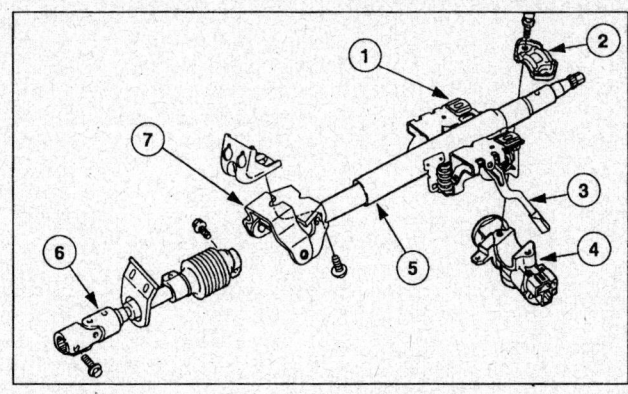

Item	Description
1	Steering Column Upper Mounting Bracket
2	Ignition Switch Lock Cylinder Bracket
3	Tilt Lever (If Equipped)
4	Lock Cylinder

Item	Description
5	Steering Column
6	Steering Column Intermediate Shaft Coupling
7	Steering Column Support Bracket

FM6049700096000X

Fig. 6 Exploded view of steering column. Escort, ZX2 & Focus

3. Remove ignition switch, steering column bearing retainer and spring.
4. Remove steel steering column upper bearing tolerance ring and bearing sleeve.
5. Remove ignition switch bore plastic steering column upper bearing retainer.
6. Remove metal steering column lock housing bearing from ignition switch bore and steering column lock gear.
7. Remove pivot bolts and lock cylinder housing. **Steering column position spring will release when bolts are removed.**
8. Remove steering gear input worm gear and rack from steering column tube.
9. Remove steering column lock lever actuator and steering actuator housing.
10. Remove lower steering column tube bearing and steering column lower bearing retainer.
11. Remove tilt position lever using suitable drift.
12. Remove steering column lock lefthand lever and steering column locking lever springs.

ASSEMBLE

1. Install steering gear input worm gear and rack into steering actuator housing.
2. Install lower steering column tube bearing and steering column instrument panel clamp.
3. Install suspension height sensor control and upper bearing tolerance rings.
4. Install steering column upper bearing spring and lower yoke to steering gear input worm gear and rack.
5. Position steering column lock lever actuator and steering actuator housing in lock cylinder housing.
6. Spray actuators with multi-purpose

grease part No. DOAZ-19584-AA, or equivalent.
7. Position actuator cam in lock cylinder housing and install cam pivot pin with small hammer. Tap pin in until flush with lock cylinder housing.
8. Install one steering column locking lever spring and righthand steering column locking lever with steering column lock actuator lever pin.
9. Tap steering column lock actuator lever pin into place while driving out drift.
10. Support steering actuator housing in suitable vise and drive steering column lock actuator lever pin flush with steering actuator housing.
11. Place two nuts or spacers to hold steering column lock lefthand lever/righthand steering column locking lever away from steering actuator housing.
12. Lubricate pivot bolts with multi-purpose grease part No. DOAZ-19584-AA, or equivalent.
13. Position steering column position spring on lock cylinder housing, then install lock cylinder housing and pivot bolts.
14. Install steel steering column upper bearing tolerance ring and tube bearing sleeve over steering column.
15. Install steering column upper bearing spring and new steering retainer on top side of spring using ¾ inch by ⅔ inch PVC pipe.
16. Install turn indicator cancel cam flush with surface facing up.
17. Install ignition switch.
18. Align pin from ignition switch with slot in lock/column and position slot in lock/column with index mark on casting.
19. Install steering column and coat lock gear with multi-purpose grease part No. DOAZ-19584-AA, or equivalent.

20. Install metal steering column lock housing bearing and coat lock gear with multi-purpose grease.
21. Install steering column upper bearing retainer.

Sable & Taurus

CONSOLE SHIFT

1. Remove mounting screws and ignition switch.
2. Record steering column lock gear, bearing and retainer positions for installation alignment, **Fig. 9.**
3. Remove bearing retainer, lock housing bearing and lock gear.
4. Remove lower bearing spring and sensor ring.
5. Remove lower bearing tolerance ring from shaft.
6. Remove tilt pivot mounting screws.
7. Remove lock cylinder housing and shaft assembly from actuator housing by prying up on lock actuator lever using suitable fabricated tool, **Fig. 10.**
8. Remove position spring. **Steering column position spring is under tension and can come out with great force.**
9. Remove turn indicator cancel cam.
10. Remove snap ring, upper bearing spring and sleeve.
11. Slide steering column shaft in toward lock cylinder housing and steering column bearing tolerance ring from steering column shaft, then remove shaft.
12. Remove lower bearing from lock cylinder housing using suitable punch.
13. Remove lock cylinder housing bearing using suitable punch.
14. Remove lower bearing and sleeve.
15. Remove mounting bolts and lower bearing retainer.
16. Remove upper and lower lock lever actuators.
17. Remove ignition lock cylinder lockout lever and lock actuator lever return spring.
18. Remove pin and lock actuator lever, then the pin and locking lever cam using suitable pin punch.
19. Remove pin, tilt locking levers and springs using suitable pin punch. **Do not remove tilt lock levers if not required.**
20. Reverse procedure to install, noting the following:
    a. Lock lever with two teeth is installed on lefthand side.
    b. Lubricate lock lever actuator with ignition lock grease part No. F0AZ-19584-A, or equivalent.
    c. Lower bearing UP position must face forward.
    d. Install steering column bearing so inner race is visible using suitable bearing installer tool or socket.
    e. Lubricate tilt pivot bushings and mounting screws with ignition lock grease.
    f. Ensure upper and lower lock actuators are aligned.
    g. Align ignition switch with actuator housing slot and index mark.
    h. Ensure narrow section of lock gear

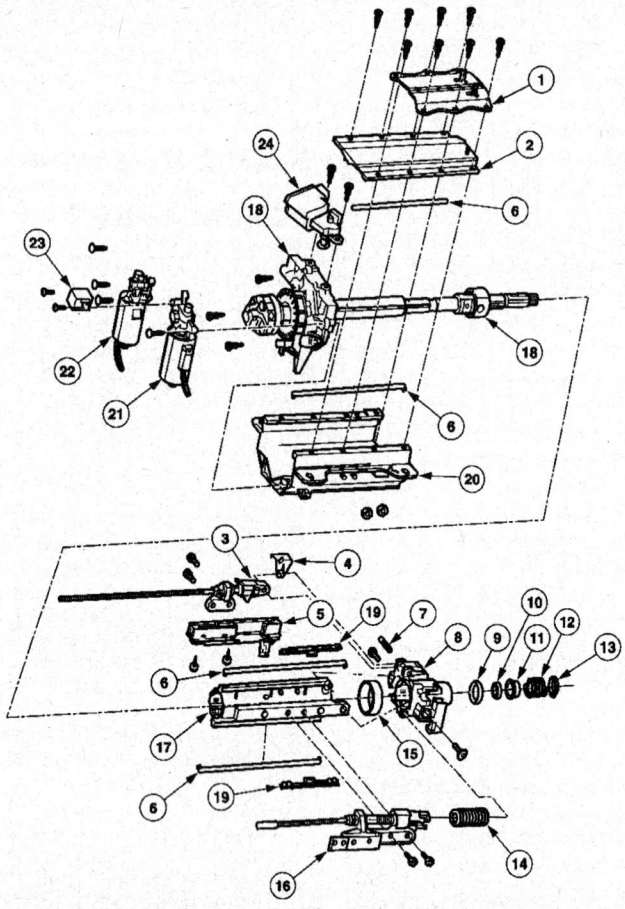

Item	Part Number	Description
1	3F790	Steering column outer housing plate
2	3F789	Steering column outer housing
3	3F797	Steering column actuator assembly (tilt)

FM6049900122010X

Fig. 7 Exploded view of steering column (Part 1 of 2). LS & Thunderbird

4	3A517	Steering column connector link
5	14A605	Steering column potentiometer assembly
6	3B628	Steering column track
7	3D545	Steering column release pin
8	3511	Steering column tube flange
9	3517	Steering column tube bearing assembly
10	3L539	Steering column upper bearing tolerance ring
11	3518	Steering column bearing sleeve
12	3520	Steering column upper bearing spring
13	97663	Steering column upper bearing retainer
14	3D655	Steering column position spring
15	3517	Steering column tube bearing assembly
16	3F797	Steering column actuator assembly (telescopic)
17	3F791	Steering column inner housing
18	3524	Steering column upper shaft assembly
19	3F795	Steering column inner track bearing retainer assembly
20	3B718	Steering column support assembly
21	3D538	Steering column release motor assembly (telescopic)
22	3D538	Steering column release motor assembly (tilt)
23	18B015	Steering wheel absorber electronic steering sensor
24	3K772	Steering wheel lock actuator (manual transmission only)

FM6049900122020X

Fig. 7 Exploded view of steering column (Part 2 of 2). LS & Thunderbird

keyhole is in 1 o'clock position with tab inboard at 3 o'clock position.
  i. Coat lock gear with ignition lock grease.
  j. Lubricate lock housing bearing with ignition lock grease and rotate counterclockwise.
  k. Ensure upper bearing retainer firmly engages lock housing retention tabs.

COLUMN SHIFT

1. Disconnect steering column opening gearshift lever seal, then remove retaining pin and gearshift lever.
2. Record steering column lock gear, bearing and retainer prior positions for assembly alignment, **Fig. 11**.
3. Remove steering column lock housing bearing and gear.
4. **On models equipped with fixed steering column,** remove steering column shaft bottom snap ring.
5. **On models equipped with tilt steering column,** remove steering column lower bearing spring and sensor ring.
6. **On all models,** remove steering column bearing tolerance ring.
7. Remove lock cylinder housing pivot mounting screws.
8. Pry steering column locking levers up using suitable fabricated tool, **Fig. 10**.
9. Remove lock cylinder housing and steering column shaft from steering actuator housing.
10. **On models equipped with tilt steering column,** remove steering column position spring. **Steering column position spring is under tension and can come out with great force.**
11. **On all models,** remove turn indicator cancel cam by prying up flush surface

using suitable flat-blade screwdriver.
12. Remove snap ring, upper bearing spring and sleeve.
13. Slide steering column shaft in toward steering column lock cylinder housing, then remove bearing tolerance ring and shaft.
14. Remove steering column upper bearing from lock cylinder housing using suitable punch.
15. **On models equipped with tilt steering column,** remove steering column lower bearing from lock cylinder housing using suitable punch.
16. **On all models,** remove mounting screws and plastic harness retainer.
17. Remove mounting bolts, brake shift interlock solenoid and transaxle shift position insert.
18. Remove mounting bolts, clamps and shift tube.
19. Remove mounting bolts and transaxle shift arm assembly.
20. Remove gearshift lever spring from shift tube.
21. Drive pin out and remove gearshift lever from shift tube.
22. Remove column shift selector lever

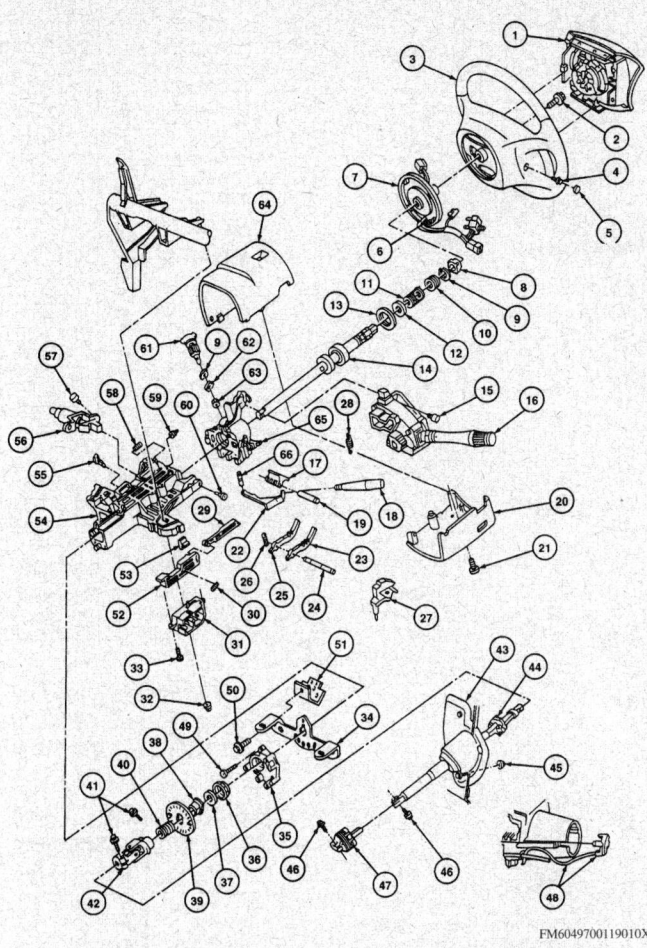

Item	Description		Item	Description
1	Driver Air Bag Module		35	Steering Column Lower Bearing Retainer
2	Steering Wheel Bolt		36	Steering Column Bearing Sleeve
3	Steering Wheel		37	Steering Column Bearing (Lower)
4	Air Bag Module Retaining Screws (2 Req'd)		38	Steering Column Bearing Tolerance Ring (Lower)
5	Steering Wheel Spoke Cover (2 Req'd)		39	Suspension Height Sensor Control Ring
6	Locking Tabs		40	Steering Column Upper Bearing Spring
7	Air Bag Sliding Contact		41	Bolt - Flange Yoke
8	Turn Indicator Cancel Cam		42	Steering Column Lower Yoke
9	Snap Ring		43	Steering Column Tube Boot
10	Steering Column Upper Bearing Spring		44	Lower Steering Column Shaft
11	Steering Column Bearing Sleeve (Upper)		45	Nut
12	Steering Column Bearing (Upper)(Small)		46	Bolt
13	Steering Column Bearing (Large)		47	Steering Column Intermediate Shaft Coupling
14	Steering Shaft Assy		48	Ignition Key Warning Switch Terminal and Wire
15	Screw		49	Lower Bearing Housing Retaining Screw
16	Multi-Function Switch		50	Screw
17	Steering Column Lock Cam		51	Wire Connector Bracket
18	Tilt Wheel Handle and Shank		52	Steering Column Lock Lever Actuator (Lower)
19	Pin - Lock Cam Pivot		53	Steering Column Lock Pawl
20	Steering Column Shroud (Lower)		54	Steering Actuator Housing
21	Shroud Retaining Screws		55	Steering Column Lock Actuator Cover
22	Steering Column Release Lever		56	Ignition / Shifter Interlock Cable
23	Steering Column Lock RH Lever		57	Screw
24	Steering Column Lock Actuator Lever Pin		58	Steering Column Position Spring
25	Steering Column Lock Left Hand Lever		59	Steering Column Tilt Flange Bumper
26	Steering Column Locking Lever Spring		60	Tilt Pivot Screws
27	Wiring Shield		61	Ignition Switch Lock Cylinder
28	Steering Column Position Spring		62	Steering Column Lock Housing Bearing
29	Steering Column Lock Lever Actuator		63	Steering Column Lock Gear
30	Steering Column Lock Spring (Shaft)		64	Steering Column Shroud (Upper)
31	Ignition Switch		65	Steering Column Lock Cylinder Housing
32	Lower Column Mounting Nuts		66	Steering Column Lock Actuator Lever Pin
33	Screw			
34	Steering Column Mounting Bracket			

FM6049700119020X

Fig. 8 Exploded view of steering column (Part 2 of 2). Mustang

FM6049700119010X

Fig. 8 Exploded view of steering column (Part 1 of 2). Mustang

plunger. Replace lever plunger if it is bent.

23. Remove gearshift lever socket bushings and transaxle control selector lever spring clip.
24. Drive out steering column lock lever pin and remove steering column lock pawl.
25. Remove mounting screws and ignition switch.
26. Remove steering column lower bearing and sleeve.
27. Remove mounting bolts and steering column lower bearing retainer.
28. Remove steering column upper and lower lock actuator.
29. Reverse procedure to install, noting the following:
   a. Lubricate steering column lock actuators, and coat lock pawl and pin surfaces with ignition lock grease part No. F0AZ-19584-A, or equivalent.
   b. Steering column lower bearing UP position must face engine.
   c. Install steering column lower bearing and sleeve so inner race is visible.
   d. Align ignition switch with steering column slot and index mark.
   e. Coat gearshift lever socket bushings and column shift selector plunger with steering gear grease part No. C3AZ-19578-A, or equivalent.
   f. Coat gearshift selector tube spring with steering gear grease.
   g. Install upper and large steering column bearings so inner race is visible with suitable bearing installer tool or socket.
   h. Lubricate lock cylinder housing bushings and mounting screws with rust penetrant and inhibitor part No. F2AZ-19A501-A, or equivalent.
   i. Ensure upper and lower steering column lock actuators are aligned.
   j. Narrow section of lock gear keyhole must be in 1 o'clock position with tab inboard at 3 o'clock position.
   k. Coat steering column lock gear with ignition lock grease.
   l. Rotate lock gear counterclockwise.
   m. Lubricate steering column lock housing bearing with ignition lock grease.
   n. Ensure steering column lock housing bearing engages housing retention tabs.

TECHNICAL SERVICE BULLETINS

Steering Column Pop/Click

2001-02 LS & 2002 THUNDERBIRD

On some of these models there may be a pop or click from the steering column while turning.

This condition may be caused by a lack of lubricant at the upper tilt shaft to bearing surface.

To correct this condition, lubricate the surface area with suitable multi-purpose XG-4 grease.

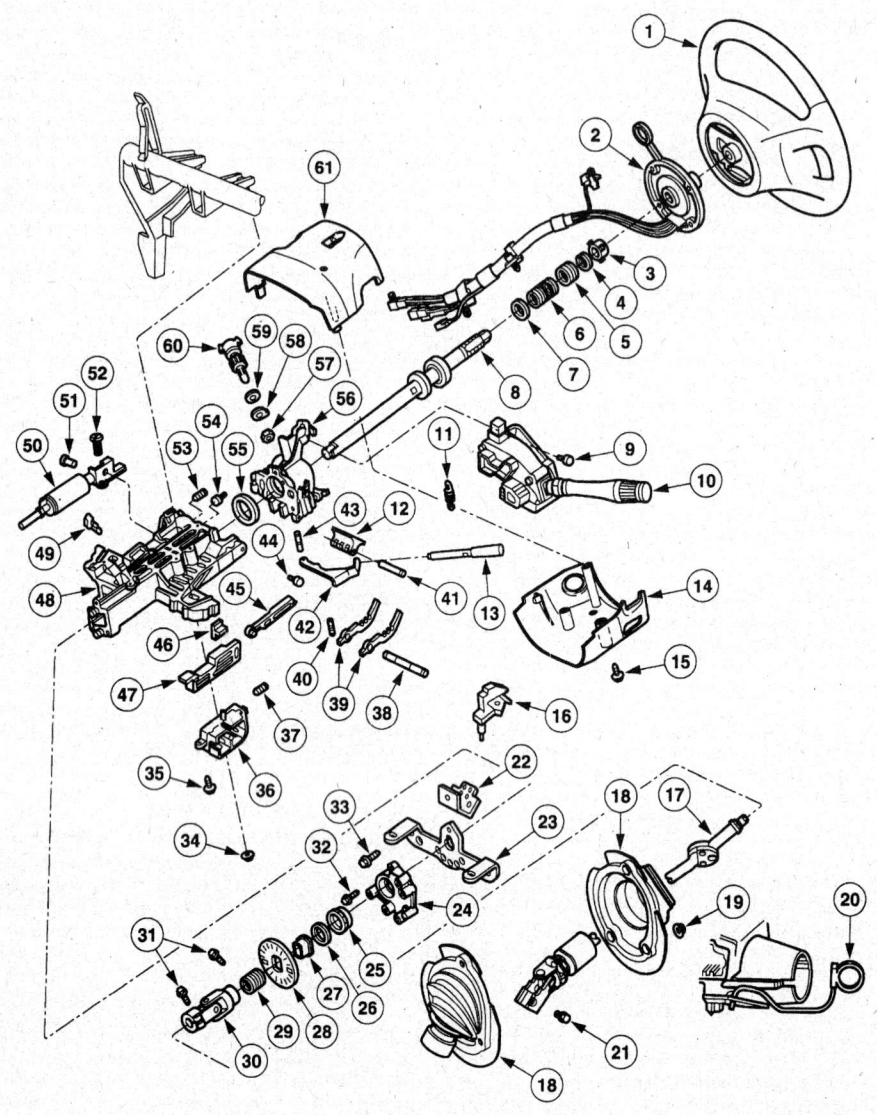

Item	Description
1	Steering wheel
2	Air bag sliding contact
3	Turn indicator cancel cam
4	Snap ring
5	Bearing spring
6	Upper bearing sleeve
7	Upper bearing (small)
8	Shaft assembly
9	Screw
10	Multi-function switch
11	Lock lever spring return
12	Lock cam
13	Tilt wheel handle
14	Lower shroud
15	Shroud retaining screws
16	Wiring shield
17	Intermediate shaft
18	Tube boot
19	Nut
20	Perimeter anti-theft system (PATS)sensor
21	Bolt
22	Wire connector bracket
23	Mounting bracket
24	Bearing retaining
25	Bearing sleeve
26	Lower bearing
27	Lower bearing tolerance ring
28	Sensor ring
29	Bearing spring
30	Coupling
31	Bolt — flange yoke

Item	Description
32	Bearing housing retaining screw
33	Screw
34	Steering column mounting lower nuts
35	Screw
36	Ignition switch
37	Lock spring (shaft)
38	Lock actuator lever pin
39	Lock actuator lever
40	Lock lever spring (2 req'd)
41	Lock cam pivot pin
42	Release lever
43	Lock actuator lever pin
44	Tilt pivot screws
45	Lock lever upper actuator
46	Lock pawl
47	Lock lever lower actuator
48	Actuator housing
49	Lock actuator cover
50	Ignition/shifter interlock cable
51	Screw
52	Screw
53	Position spring
54	Tilt flange bumper
55	Lower bearing (large)
56	Lock cylinder housing
57	Lock gear
58	Lock housing bearing
59	Bearing retainer
60	Ignition switch lock cylinder
61	Upper shroud

FM6040000131020X

Fig. 9 Exploded view of steering column (Part 2 of 2). Sable & Taurus w/console shift

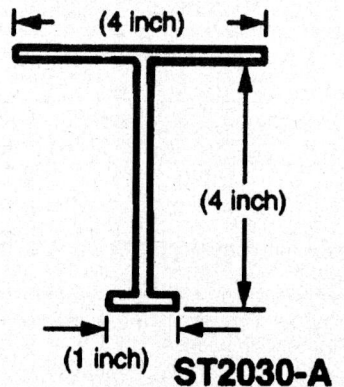

ST2030-A

FM6040000133000X

Fig. 10 Steering column locking lever fabricated tool dimensions. Sable & Taurus

FM6040000131010X

Fig. 9 Exploded view of steering column (Part 1 of 2). Sable & Taurus w/console shift

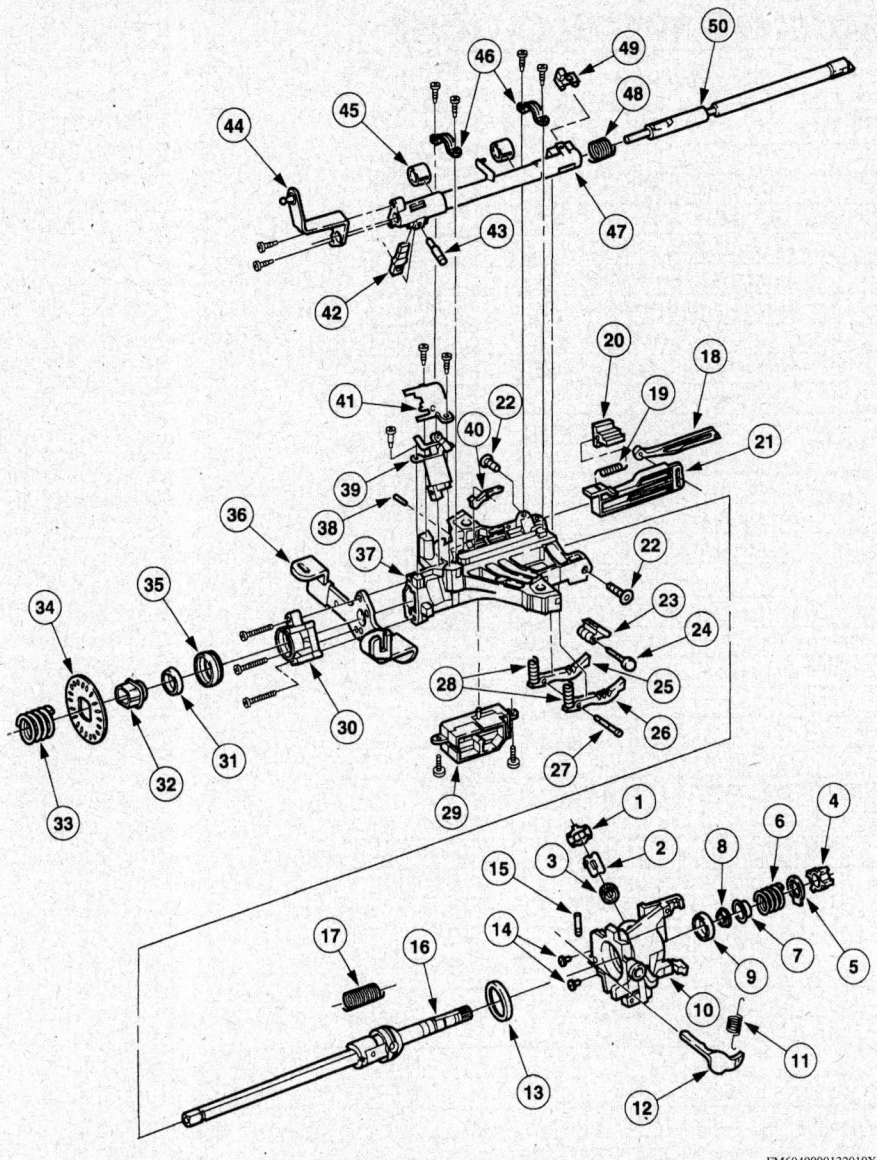

Item	Description	Item	Description
1	Steering column upper bearing retainer	27	Steering column lock lever actuator pin
2	Steering column lock housing bearing	28	Steering column locking lever spring
3	Steering column lock gear	29	Ignition switch
4	Turn indicator cancel cam	30	Steering column lower bearing retainer
5	Snap ring	31	Steering column bearing
6	Steering column upper bearing spring	32	Lower steering column bearing tolerance ring
7	Steering column bearing sleeve	33	Steering column bearing spring
8	Steering column upper bearing tolerance ring	34	Suspension height sensor control ring
9	Upper steering column bearing (small)	35	Steering column bearing sleeve
10	Lock cylinder housing	36	Steering column lower mounting bracket
11	Steering column release lever spring	37	Steering actuator housing
12	Steering column release lever	38	Steering column lock lever pin (shifter)
13	Upper steering column bearing (large)	39	Brake shift interlock solenoid
14	Lock cylinder housing bumper	40	Steering column lock pawl (shifter)
15	Tilt release lever pivot pin	41	Transmission shift selector position insert
16	Steering shaft assy	42	Transmission gearshift lever
17	Steering column position spring	43	Transmission gearshift lever pin
18	Upper lock actuator assy	44	Shift arm assy
19	Steering column lock spring	45	Gearshift lever socket bushing
20	Steering column lock pawl	46	Gearshift tube bushing clamp
21	Lower lock actuator assy	47	Transmission column shift selector tube
22	Tilt pivot screws	48	Gearshift selector tube spring
23	Steering column lock cam	49	Transmission control selector lever spring clip
24	Steering column lock cam pivot pin	50	Column shift selector lever plunger
25	Steering column locking lever (RH)		
26	Steering column locking lever (LH)		

FM6040000132020X

Fig. 11 Exploded view of steering column (Part 2 of 2). Sable & Taurus w/column shift

FM6040000132010X

Fig. 11 Exploded view of steering column (Part 1 of 2). Sable & Taurus w/column shift

TIGHTENING SPECIFICATIONS

Year	Component	Torque/Ft. Lbs.
CONTINENTAL		
2001–02	Clockspring	18–26①
	Driver's Air Bag Module	108①
	Ignition Switch	47–64①
	Lower Column Bearing	62–97①
	Multi-Function Switch	18–26①
	Shift Cable & Bracket	62–97①
	Shift Selector Tube	62–97①
	Steering Actuator Housing Pivot	14–19
	Steering Column Boot	45–53①
	Steering Column Impact Absorber	10–14
	Steering Column	10–12
	Steering Column Trim Shroud	6–8①
	Steering Column Yoke	19–25
	Steering Wheel	23–25
COUGAR		
2001–02	Driver's Air Bag Module	44①
	Flexible Coupling To Steering Column	18
	Flexible Coupling To Steering Gear	14
	Lower Bearing Retainer Collar	17
	Steering Column	18
	Steering Wheel	37
CROWN VICTORIA, GRAND MARQUIS & MARAUDER		
2001–05	Brake Shift Interlock Solenoid	80①
	Driver's Air Bag Module	108①
	Ignition Switch	53①
	Lock Cylinder Housing	16
	Lower Steering Column Shaft, Lower	35
	Lower Steering Column Shaft, Upper	22
	Parking Brake Release Switch	27①
	Shift Tube	80①
	Shock Absorber Electronic Steering Sensor	9①
	Steering Column Lower Bearing	80①
	Steering Column Support	11
	Steering Wheel	30
	Transmission Range Indicator	27①
	Transmission Selector Lever Arm & Support	11
ESCORT & ZX2		
2001–03	Driver's Air Bag Module	70–103①
	Ignition/Shifter Interlock Cable Mounting Bracket	35–53①
	Steering Column Input Shaft Coupling To Steering Gear Input Shaft	30–36
	Steering Column Shaft To Steering Column Gear Input Shaft Coupling	30–36
	Steering Column Support Bracket	89–106①
	Steering Column Upper Mounting Bracket	80–124①
	Steering Wheel	34–46

TIGHTENING
SPECIFICATIONS—Continued

Year	Component	Torque/Ft. Lbs.
FIVE HUNDRED, FREESTYLE & MONTEGO		
2005	Column Shroud Screws	62①
	Multi-Function Switch Screws	18①
	Shift Tube Bolts	80①
	Steering Column Coupler Bolts	18
	Steering Column Nuts	11
	Steering Column Shaft Bolts	18
	Steering Wheel Bolt	30
FOCUS		
2001–05	Air Bag Module	44①
	Hood Release Cable	15
	Steering Column	10
	Steering Column Shaft	21
	Steering Wheel	37
LS		
2001–05	Driver's Air Bag Module	108①
	Electronic Steering Sensor	27①
	Steering Column	13
	Steering Column Actuator Telescopic Bolt	11
	Steering Column Actuator Telescopic Nut	13
	Steering Column Actuator Tilt, Bolt	11
	Steering Column Actuator Tilt, Nut	13
	Steering Column Outer Housing Cover Plate	10
	Steering Column Release Motor	27①
	Steering Column Tube Flange Pivot Bolts	17
	Steering Column Upper Shaft	10
	Steering Shaft Pinch Bolt	22
	Steering Wheel (2000–01)	30
	Steering Wheel (2002–04)	38
	Steering Wheel Lock Actuator Mounting	108①
MUSTANG		
2001–05	Air Bag Sliding Contact	18–26
	Air Bag Sliding Contact	18–26
	Driver's Air Bag Module	36–53①
	Ignition Switch	45–61①
	Interlock Cable	14–17①
	Intermediate Shaft Coupler	19
	Lock Cylinder	17
	Steering Column Gear Input Shaft Coupling To Column Shaft	30–40
	Steering Column Gear Input Shaft Coupling To Gear Pinch	19–25
	Steering Column Lower Bearing	80①
	Steering Column Lower Mount	62–97①
	Steering Column Mount	10–12
	Steering Column Pivot	14–19
	Steering Column Tube Boot	71–88①
	Steering Wheel	23–32

Continued

TIGHTENING
SPECIFICATIONS—Continued

Year	Component	Torque/Ft. Lbs.
SABLE & TAURUS		
2001–05	Brake Shift Interlock Solenoid	80①
	Ignition Switch	54①
	Instrument Panel Opening Cover Support	11
	Lock Cylinder Housing	17
	Shift Tube	80①
	Steering Column	11
	Steering Column Coupler	18
	Steering Column Finish Panel	62①
	Steering Column Lower Bearing	80①
	Steering Column Shaft	36
	Steering Wheel Pinion Shaft	13
	Transaxle Selector Lever Arm & Support	11
THUNDERBIRD		
2002–05	Driver's Air Bag Module	108①
	Electronic Steering Sensor	27①
	Steering Column	13
	Steering Column Actuator Telescopic Bolt	11
	Steering Column Actuator Telescopic Nut	13
	Steering Column Actuator Tilt, Bolt	11
	Steering Column Actuator Tilt, Nut	13
	Steering Column Outer Housing Cover Plate	10
	Steering Column Release Motor	27①
	Steering Column Tube Flange Pivot Bolts	17
	Steering Column Upper Shaft	10
	Steering Shaft Pinch Bolt	22
	Steering Wheel	38
	Steering Wheel Lock Actuator Mounting	108①
TOWN CAR		
2001–05	Brake Shift Interlock Solenoid	80①
	Ignition Switch	62①
	Lock Cylinder Housing	16
	Parking Brake Release Switch	27①
	Shift Tube	80①
	Shock Absorber Electronic Steering Sensor	13①
	Steering Column Lower Bearing	80①
	Steering Column Support	11
	Steering Wheel	30
	Transmission Range Indicator	80①
	Transmission Selector Arm & Support	11
	Upper Intermediate Shaft To Lower Intermediate Shaft	22
	Upper Intermediate Steering Shaft To Steering Column Shaft	22

① — Inch lbs.

POWER STEERING

TABLE OF CONTENTS

Power Steering Pressure Specifications

Vehicle	Engine	Minimum Flow, GPM①	Minimum Relief Pressure, psi	Maximum Relief Pressure, psi	Pump Model②	Maximum Free Flow, GPM @ RPM
Continental	4.6L	1.70	1300	1480	CII	2.7 @ 1500
Cougar	2.0L & 2.5L	1.13	1200	1380	Atsugi Vane-Type	2.4 @ 2500
Crown Victoria	4.6L	1.40	1200	1380	CII	3.2 @ 2500
Escort	2.0L	1.15	1117	1247	CIII	2.4 @ 1500
Five Hundred	3.0L	1.15	1450	1580	CIII	③
Focus	2.0L DOHC	1.15	1117	1247	CIII	2.4 @ 1500
	2.0L SOHC	1.15	1117	1247	CIII	2.4 @ 1500
Freestyle	3.0L	1.15	1450	1580	CIII	③
Grand Marquis	4.6L	1.40	1200	1380	CII	3.2 @ 2500
LS	3.0L	1.40	1400	1530	CII	2.4 @ 1500
	3.9L	1.40	1400	1530	CII	2.4 @ 1500
Marauder	4.6L	1.40	1400	1530	CII	3.2 @ 2500
Montego	3.0L	1.15	1450	1580	CIII	③
Mustang	3.8L	0.90	1050	1230	CII	2.6 @ 1500
	4.0L	1.30	1400	1530	CIII	2.2 @ 2150
	4.6L	1.25	1200	1380	CIII	2.6 @ 1500
Sable & Taurus	3.0L OHV	1.15	1400	1530	CII	2.8 @ 1500
	3.0L DOHC	1.15	1400	1530	CIII	2.8 @ 1500
Thunderbird	3.9L	1.40	1400	1530	CII	2.6 @ 1500
Town Car	4.6L	1.40	1200	1380	CII	3.2 @ 2500
ZX2	2.0L	1.15	1117	1247	CIII	2.4 @ 1500

GPM — Gallons per minute
① — Flow is dependent on pump model, engine RPM & pulley ratio. Engine idle speed must be within specifications when measuring minimum flow.

② — Power steering pump identification tag is located on the reservoir body.

③ — Maximum flow @ curb idle 2.8 GPM.

Application Chart

Model	Year	Power Steering Pump		Power Steering Gear		Power Steering Assist	
		Type	Page No.	Type	Page No.	Type	Page No.
Continental	2001–02	Ford Model CII Slipper-Type Pump	14-3	Ford Integral Rack & Pinion Steering Gear	14-9	—	—
Cougar	2001–02	Atsugi Vane-Type Pump	14-3	Ford Integral Rack & Pinion Steering Gear	14-9	—	—
Crown Victoria	2001–05	Ford Model CII Slipper-Type Pump	14-3	Ford Torsion Bar Power Steering Gear	14-16	Ford Variable Assist Electronic Variable Orifice (EVO) System	14-20
Escort	2001–03	Ford CIII Vane-Type Pump	14-7	Ford Integral Rack & Pinion Steering Gear	14-9	—	—
Five Hundred	2005	Ford CIII Vane-Type Pump	14-7	Ford Integral Rack & Pinion Steering Gear	14-9	—	—
Focus	2001–05	①	—	Focus Rack & Pinion Steering Gear	14-7	—	—
Freestyle	2005	Ford CIII Vane-Type Pump	14-7	Ford Integral Rack & Pinion Steering Gear	14-9	—	—
Grand Marquis	2000–04	Ford Model CII Slipper-Type Pump	14-3	Ford Torsion Bar Power Steering Gear	14-16	Ford Variable Assist Electronic Variable Orifice (EVO) System	14-20
LS	2001–05	Ford Model CII Slipper-Type Pump	14-3	Ford Integral Rack & Pinion Steering Gear	14-9	Ford Variable Assist Power Steering (VAPS) System	14-34
Marauder	2003–04	Ford Model CII Slipper-Type Pump	14-3	Ford Torsion Bar Power Steering Gear	14-16	Ford Variable Assist Electronic Variable Orifice (EVO) System	14-20
Montego	2005	Ford CIII Vane-Type Pump	14-7	Ford Integral Rack & Pinion Steering Gear	14-9	—	—
Mustang	2001–04	②	—	Ford Integral Rack & Pinion Steering Gear	14-9	—	—
Sable	2001–05	③	—	Ford Integral Rack & Pinion Steering Gear	14-9	—	—
Taurus	2001–05	③	—	Ford Integral Rack & Pinion Steering Gear	14-9	—	—
Town Car	2001	Ford CIII Vane-Type Pump	14-7	Ford Torsion Bar Power Steering Gear	14-16	Ford Variable Assist Electronic Variable Orifice (EVO) System	14-20
	2002–05	Ford Model CII Slipper-Type Pump	14-3	Ford Torsion Bar Power Steering Gear	14-16	Ford Variable Assist Electronic Variable Orifice (EVO) System	14-20
Thunderbird	2002–05	Ford Model CII Slipper-Type Pump	14-3	Ford Integral Rack & Pinion Steering Gear	14-9	Ford Variable Assist Power Steering (VAPS) System	14-34
ZX2	2001–03	Ford CIII Vane-Type Pump	14-7	Ford Integral Rack & Pinion Steering Gear	14-9	—	—

① — 2.0L DOHC engine, Ford CIII Vane-Type Pump; 2.0L SOHC engine, Focus Power Steering Pump.

② — 3.8L engine, Ford Model CII Slipper-Type Pump; 4.6L engine, Ford CIII Vane-Type Pump.

③ — 3.0L DOHC engine, Atsugi Vane-Type Pump; 3.0L OHV engine, Ford Model CII Slipper-Type Pump.

Atsugi Vane-Type Pump

NOTE: These Pumps Are Not Serviceable. If Service Is Required, Pump Must Be Replaced.

Focus Power Steering Pump

NOTE: These Pumps Are Not Serviceable. If Service Is Required, Pump Must Be Replaced.

Ford Model CII Slipper-Type Pump

NOTE: On Air Bag Equipped Models, Refer To "Air Bag System Precautions" Located In The Front Of This Manual For System Disarming & Arming Procedures.

NOTE: Refer To "Computer Relearn Procedures" Located In The Front Of This Manual When Battery Power To The Computer Has Been Interrupted.

INDEX

PRECAUTIONS

Air Bag Systems

Refer to "Air Bag System Precautions" in the front of this manual for system disarming and arming procedures.

Battery Ground Cable

Prior to service, disconnect battery ground cable and isolate as required.

DESCRIPTION

The Ford model CII power steering pump is a belt driven 10-slipper type pump incorporating a fiberglass filled nylon reservoir. The reservoir is attached to the rear side of the aluminum pump housing assembly. The pump body is encased within the housing and reservoir assembly. The pump design incorporates a pump pressure fitting which allows the pump pressure line to swivel. A pressure sensitive identification tag is attached to the reservoir body. This tag indicates the basic model number and the suffix.

TROUBLESHOOTING

Power Steering Pump Leaks

1. Excessive fluid fill.
2. Dipstick missing, loose, damaged or missing O-ring.
3. Broken or cracked fluid reservoir.
4. Loose or damaged hose fittings.
5. Shaft seal not pressed flush with housing surface.
6. Shaft seal damage.
7. Rotor shaft damage, helical grooving or OD has an axial scratch.
8. Shaft bushing worn.
9. Plugged drain back hole.
10. Damaged or missing reservoir O-ring.
11. Damaged or missing outlet fitting O-rings.
12. Excessive pump assembly bracket vibration.
13. Plate and bushing reservoir seal groove damage, metal chips or foreign material in seal groove.
14. Faulty outlet fitting.

Power Steering Pump Noise, Moan Or Whine

1. Fluid aeration.
2. Low fluid.
3. Hose grounded.
4. Steering column grounded.
5. Valve cover O-ring or baffle missing or damaged.
6. Interference between components in pumping elements.
7. Loose or poor bracket alignment.
8. Cam contour damaged.

SYSTEM SERVICE

Power Steering Pump

DISASSEMBLE

1. Remove pulley, **Fig. 1**.

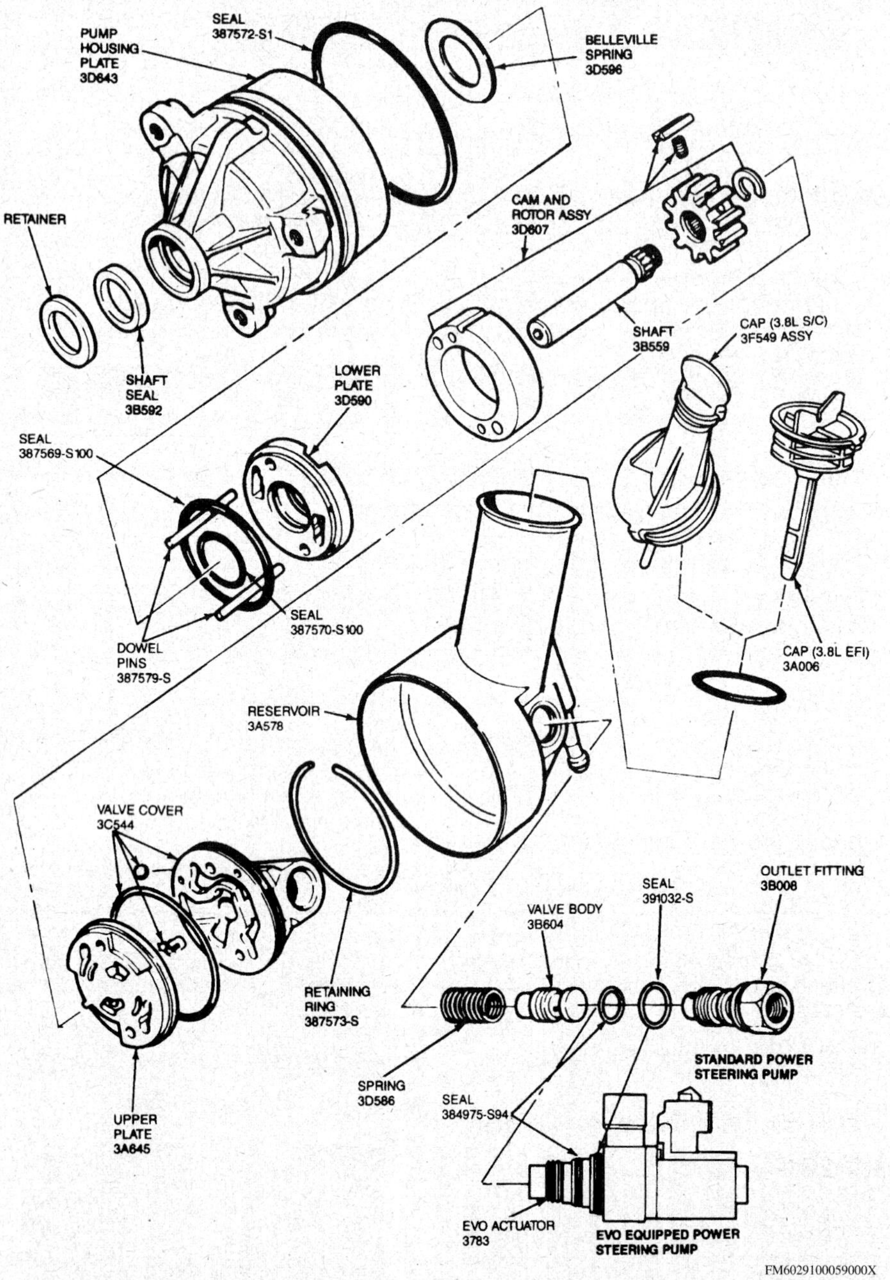

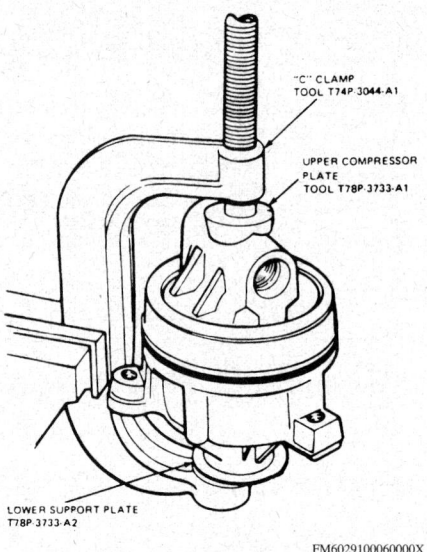

Fig. 1 Exploded view of Ford Model CII power steering pump

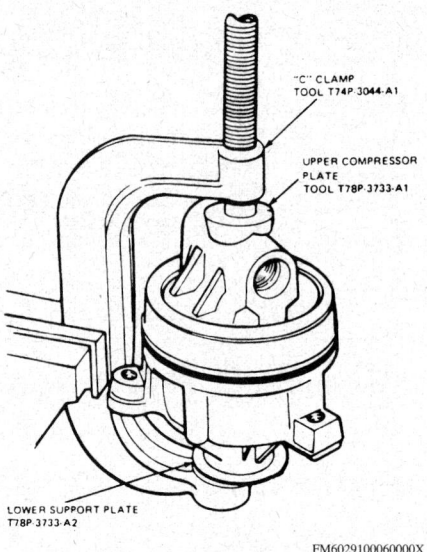

FM60291000060000X

Fig. 2 Positioning pump in C-clamp

recessed notch on insert cam is facing upward.

4. With rotor extended upward approximately half out of cam, insert spring into rotor pocket, **Fig. 4.**
5. Install slipper to compress spring and slipper with groove facing cam, **Fig. 5.**
6. Repeat pervious steps on slipper cavity beneath opposite inlet recess.
7. While holding cam stationary, index rotor left or right one space, then install another spring and slipper until all 10 rotor cavities have been filled. Ensure when turning rotor that springs and slippers remain in position.
8. Apply Loctite No. 242 or 271 adhesive, or equivalent, to outside diameter of seal and Locquic NF or T primer, or equivalent to seal bore in housing.
9. Install rotor shaft seal using seal driver tool No. T78P-3733-A3, or equivalent.
10. Drive seal into bore until properly seated using suitable plastic mallet.
11. Position pump plate on flat surface with pulley side facing downward.
12. Install two dowel pins and spring into housing. **Spring must be inserted with dished surface facing upward.**
13. Lubricate inner and outer O-ring seals with suitable power steering fluid, then install seals on lower pressure plate.
14. Install lower pressure plate into housing and over dowel pin with O-ring seals facing toward front of pump.
15. Position assembly on C-clamp.
16. Seat outer O-ring seal by placing seal driver tool No. T78P-3733-A3, or equivalent, into rotor shaft hole and press on lower plate lightly until it bottoms in pump housing. This will seat outer O-ring seal.
17. Install cam, rotor and slippers and rotor shaft assembly into pump housing over dowel pins.
18. When installing assembly into pump housing, stepped holes must be used for dowel pins and notch in cam insert must be toward reservoir and approximately 180° opposite square mounting

2. Remove outlet fitting, flow control valve and flow control valve spring from pump, then the reservoir.
3. Place suitable C-clamp in vise.
4. Position lower support plate tool No. T78P-3733-A2, or equivalent, over pump rotor shaft.
5. Install upper compressor plate tool No. T78P-3733-A1, or equivalent, into upper portion of C-clamp.
6. While holding compressor tool, place pump assembly into C-clamp with rotor shaft facing downward, **Fig. 2.**
7. Tighten C-clamp until slight bottoming of valve cover is observed.
8. Through small hole located on side of pump housing, insert suitable drift and push inward on valve cover snap ring.
9. While pushing inward on snap ring, place screwdriver under snap ring

edge and remove ring from housing, **Fig. 3.**
10. Loosen C-clamp, then remove lower support plate tool and pump.
11. Remove pump valve cover and O-ring.
12. Remove rotor shaft, upper plate, cam and rotor, then the two dowel pins.
13. Remove lower plate and spring by tapping housing on flat surface.
14. Remove rotor shaft seal using suitable screwdriver.

ASSEMBLE

1. Position rotor on rotor shaft splines with triangle detent on rotor counterbore facing upward.
2. Install snap ring into groove on end of rotor shaft.
3. Position insert cam over rotor. Ensure

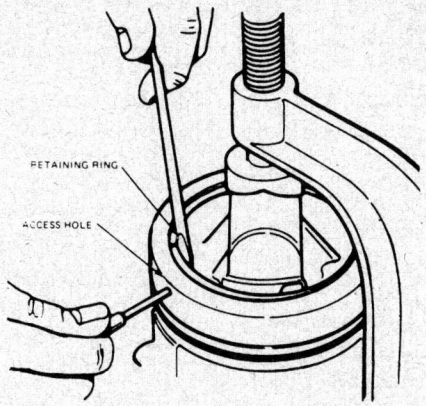

Fig. 3   Valve cover retaining ring removal

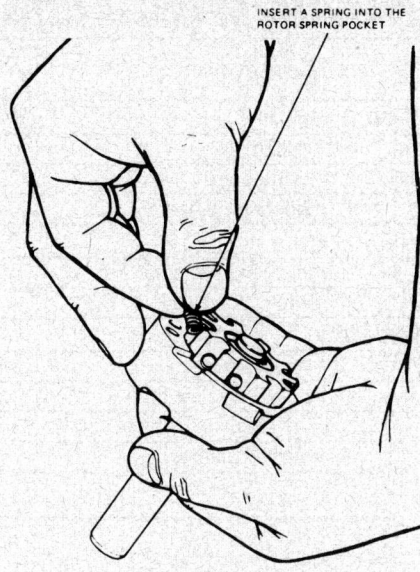

Fig. 4   Slipper springs installation

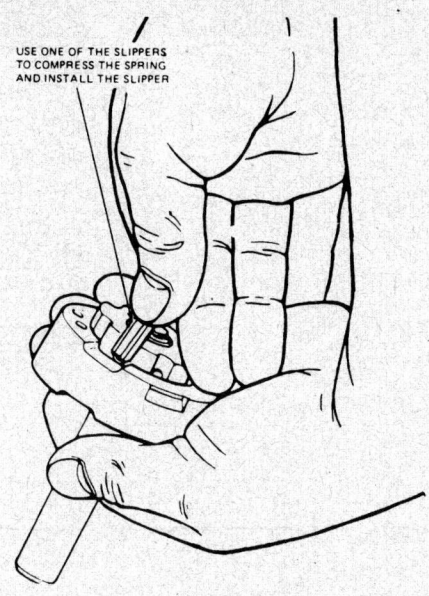

Fig. 5   Slipper installation

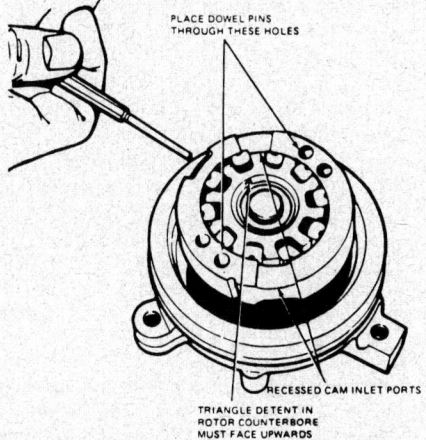

Fig. 6   Assembling cam, slippers & rotor

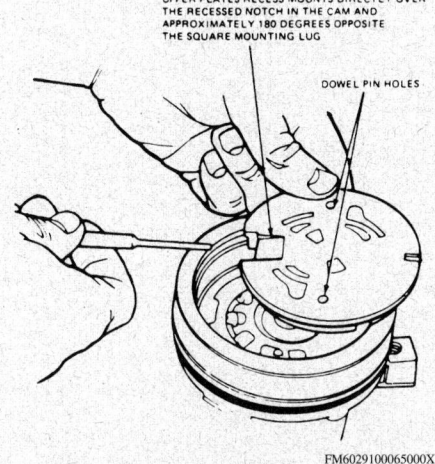

Fig. 7   Upper pressure plate installation

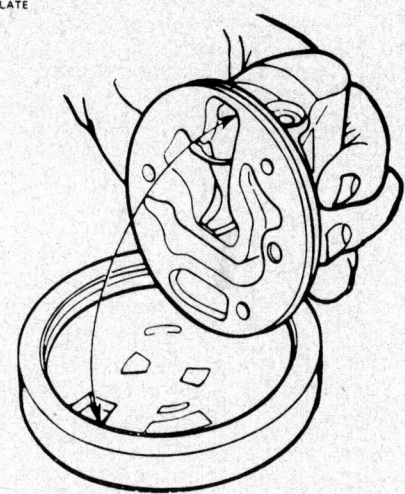

Fig. 8   Valve cover installation

lug on housing, **Fig. 6.**

19. Position upper pressure plate over dowel pins with recess directly over recessed notch on cam insert and approximately 180° opposite square mounting lug, **Fig. 7.**
20. Lubricate O-ring seal with suitable power steering fluid, then position O-ring on valve cover. Ensure plastic baffle is securely in position on valve cover. Coat of petroleum jelly may be used to hold baffle in position.
21. Insert valve cover over dowel pins. Ensure outlet fitting hole in valve cover is aligned with square mounting lug on housing, **Fig. 8.**

22. Place assembly in C-clamp and compress valve cover into pump housing until snap ring groove on housing is exposed.
23. Install valve cover snap ring in pump housing. Ensure snap ring ends are near access hole in pump housing.
24. Remove pump from C-clamp.
25. Lubricate O-ring seal with suitable power steering fluid and place it on pump housing.
26. Install reservoir on pump housing.
27. Install flow control valve and spring

into valve cover.
28. Lubricate O-ring seals with suitable power steering fluid and lace them on outlet fitting.
29. Install outlet fitting on valve cover.
30. Tighten outlet fitting.
31. **Do not cock flow control valve when installing.**
32. **Do not force valve forward.**

TIGHTENING SPECIFICATIONS

Year	Component	Torque/Ft. Lbs.
CONTINENTAL		
2001–02	Hose Fitting	31–39
	Reservoir	54–61①
	Steering Pump	15–22
MUSTANG		
2001–05	Power Steering Pump	38
	Pressure Line Fitting	30
SABLE & TAURUS		
2001–05	Hose Bracket	89①
	Pressure Hose Fitting	27
	Return Line	27
	Support Bracket	35

① — Inch lbs.

Ford CIII Vane-Type Pump

NOTE: These Pumps Are Not Serviceable. If Service Is Required, Pump Must Be Replaced.

ZUA Vane-Type Pump

NOTE: These Pumps Are Not Serviceable. If Service Is Required, Pump Must Be Replaced.

Focus Rack & Pinion Steering Gear

NOTE: On Air Bag Equipped Models, Refer To "Air Bag System Precautions" Located In The Front Of This Manual For System Disarming & Arming Procedures.

NOTE: Refer To "Computer Relearn Procedures" Located In The Front Of This Manual When Battery Power To The Computer Has Been Interrupted.

INDEX

PRECAUTIONS

Air Bag Systems

Refer to "Air Bag System Precautions" in the front of this manual for system disarming and arming procedures.

Battery Ground Cable

Prior to service, disconnect battery ground cable and isolate as required.

DESCRIPTION

The steering gear is operated and controlled by the hydraulic fluid supplied by the power steering pump.

The rack and pinion is held in position by two mounting brackets and rubber bushings. The gear uses an integral piston and rack design to provide power assisted steering control.

SYSTEM SERVICE

Steering Gear Bushing

REPLACE

1. Remove steering gear as outlined in "Front Suspension & Steering" section of "Focus" chassis chapter.

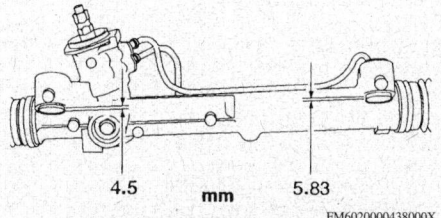

4.5   mm   5.83

FM6020000438000X

Fig. 1 Steering gear bushing installation depths

2. Remove insulator bushings using bushing remover and installer tool No. 205-297 and wheel hub installer tool No. 204-148, or equivalents.
3. If housing is damaged, replace steering gear.
4. Reverse procedure to install, noting the following:
   a. Lubricate new bushings with suitable rubber lubricant.
   b. Install new bushings to proper depth using bushing and hub installer tools, **Fig. 1.**

Power Steering System Bleed

1. Fill reservoir to MAX mark with proper power steering fluid. Inspect level when fluid is cold.
2. Ensure fluid in reservoir does not drop below MIN mark.
3. Start engine and slowly turn steering wheel once from lock to lock.
4. Stop engine and examine all hose connections, steering gear boots, valve body and steering pump for external leaks.
5. Inspect power steering fluid reservoir fluid level and adjust fluid level.
6. Apply 15 inches of vacuum using hand vacuum pump tool No. D95L-7559-A, or equivalent.
7. Observe vacuum gauge reading. If it decreases by more than two inches in five minutes inspect power steering system for leaks.
8. Start engine and slowly turn steering wheel from lock to lock once, then turn to right, but just off lock stop.
9. Stop engine and apply 15 inches of vacuum for at least minutes until air is evacuated from system.
10. Release vacuum at pump tool.
11. Repeat bleed procedure, but this time turn steering wheel to left, just off lock stop.
12. Remove vacuum pump and adjust reservoir level.
13. Start engine and turn steering wheel from lock to lock.
14. Repeat bleed procedure if there is excessive noise.
15. If noise level is still excessive, allow vehicle to sit overnight, then repeat bleed procedure next day.

TIGHTENING SPECIFICATIONS

Year	Component	Torque/Ft. Lbs.
2001–05	Crossmember, Front	85
	Crossmember, Rear	148
	Fluid Cooler	44①
	Power Steering Pressure (PSP) Switch	15
	Pressure Line To Pump Union	48
	Power Steering Gear Hose Clamps	17
	Power Steering Pump	17
	Pressure Line Support Bracket (DOHC Engine)	18
	Pressure Line Support Bracket (SOHC Engine)	44①
	Stabilizer Bar Link	37
	Steering Column Shaft Coupling	18
	Steering Column Shaft To Pinion	26
	Steering Gear	59
	Steering Gear Heat Shield	53①
	Support Insulator	37
	Tie Rod End	35
	Wheel Lug Nuts	63

① — Inch lbs.

Ford Integral Rack & Pinion Steering Gear

NOTE: On Air Bag Equipped Models, Refer To "Air Bag System Precautions" Located In The Front Of This Manual For System Disarming & Arming Procedures.

NOTE: Refer To "Computer Relearn Procedures" Located In The Front Of This Manual When Battery Power To The Computer Has Been Interrupted.

NOTE: Also Refer To "Ford Variable Assist Electronic Variable Orifice (EVO) System" For Cougar Models Equipped With EVO System.

INDEX

PRECAUTIONS

Air Bag Systems

Refer to "Air Bag System Precautions" in the front of this manual for system disarming and arming procedures.

Battery Ground Cable

Prior to service, disconnect battery ground cable and isolate as required.

DESCRIPTION

These power rack and pinion steering gears are hydraulic-mechanical units, using an integral piston and rack to provide power assisted steering control. Internal valve controls pump flow and pressure as required during operation, **Figs. 1 through 3.** The unit consists of a rotary hydraulic control valve connected to the input shaft and a boost cylinder integral with the rack.

Operation

The rotary control valve utilizes the relative rotational position of the input shaft and valve sleeve to control fluid flow. As the steering wheel is turned, the resistance of the wheels and weight of the vehicle cause a torsion bar to deflect. This deflection changes position of rotary valve and sleeve ports, thereby directing fluid under pressure to the proper end of the power cylinder. The pressure differential acting on the piston attached to the rack provides the power assist.

The control valve is forced back to a centered position by the torsion bar when steering effort is removed. Pressure is then equalized on each side of the piston and the front wheels tend to return to a straight ahead position.

TROUBLESHOOTING

Refer to **Fig. 4,** for troubleshooting procedure.

DIAGNOSIS & TESTING

Pressure Test

During the following procedure, power steering system pressure may exceed 1200 psi. Confirm proper tool fit prior to performing test. Exercise extreme.
1. Prior to performing pump flow and pressure tests, ensure following conditions exist:
   a. Proper pump reservoir fluid level.
   b. Proper tire air pressure.
   c. Proper pump belt tension.
   d. Proper model and vehicle pump application.
   e. Proper size pulleys on pump and engine.
   f. Ensure system is not damaged or leaking, repair as required.
2. Disconnect pump high pressure line and connect suitable analyzer hose adapter, **Figs. 5 through 8.**
3. Thread other analyzer adapter to pump.
4. Connect analyzer hose to adapters. **Torque** connections to 15 ft. lbs.
5. Adjust power steering fluid, start engine and allow to run approximately two minutes. Ensure idle is set to specifications.
6. Measure flow in gallons per minute at 165–175°F.
7. Measure pressure at 165–175°F and idle with gate fully open.
8. If gallon per minute flow is below specifications, pump may require service. Continue test, measuring flow and relief pressure.
9. If pressure is more than 150 psi, inspect hoses for restrictions.
10. Partially close gate valve to build up 740 psi, observe and record flow at 165–175°F.
11. Completely close and partially open gate valve three times. **Do not allow valve to remain closed for more than five seconds.** Observe and record pressure.
12. If pressure is above specifications, pump flow control valve should be removed and cleaned or replaced.
13. Fully open gate valve and increase engine speed to approximately 2500 RPM. Observe and record flow.

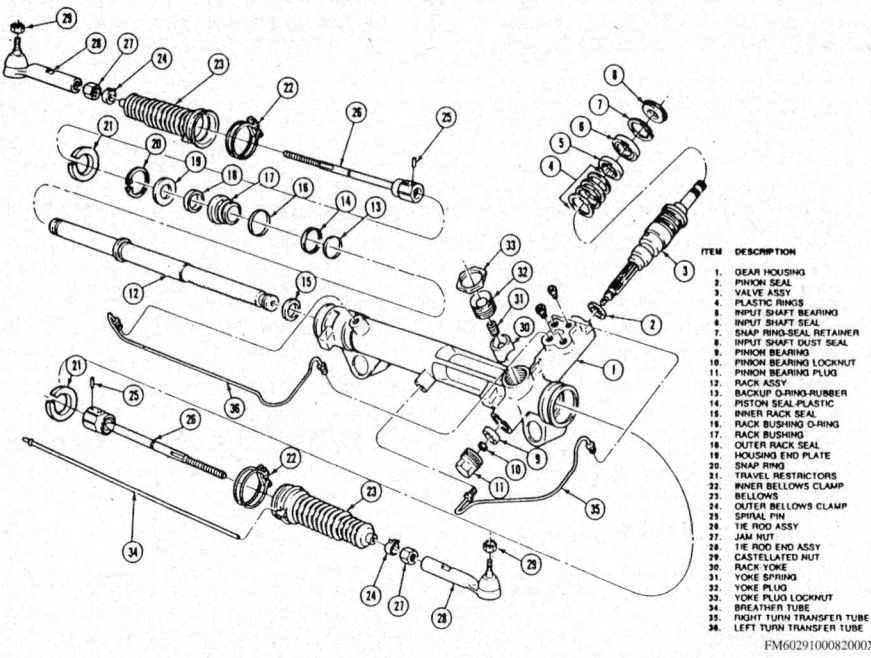

Fig. 1 Exploded view of steering gear. Cougar & Mustang

ITEM	DESCRIPTION
1.	GEAR HOUSING
2.	PINION SEAL
3.	VALVE ASSY
4.	PLASTIC RINGS
5.	INPUT SHAFT BEARING
6.	INPUT SHAFT SEAL
7.	SNAP RING-SEAL RETAINER
8.	INPUT SHAFT DUST SEAL
9.	PINION BEARING
10.	PINION BEARING LOCKNUT
11.	PINION BEARING PLUG
12.	RACK ASSY
13.	BACKUP O-RING-RUBBER
14.	PISTON SEAL-PLASTIC
15.	INNER RACK SEAL
16.	RACK BUSHING O-RING
17.	RACK BUSHING
18.	OUTER RACK SEAL
19.	HOUSING END PLATE
20.	SNAP RING
21.	TRAVEL RESTRICTORS
22.	INNER BELLOWS CLAMP
23.	BELLOWS
24.	OUTER BELLOWS CLAMP
25.	SPIRAL PIN
26.	TIE ROD ASSY
27.	JAM NUT
28.	TIE ROD END ASSY
29.	CASTELLATED NUT
30.	RACK YOKE
31.	YOKE SPRING
32.	YOKE PLUG
33.	YOKE PLUG LOCKNUT
34.	BREATHER TUBE
35.	RIGHT TURN TRANSFER TUBE
36.	LEFT TURN TRANSFER TUBE

FM6029100082000X

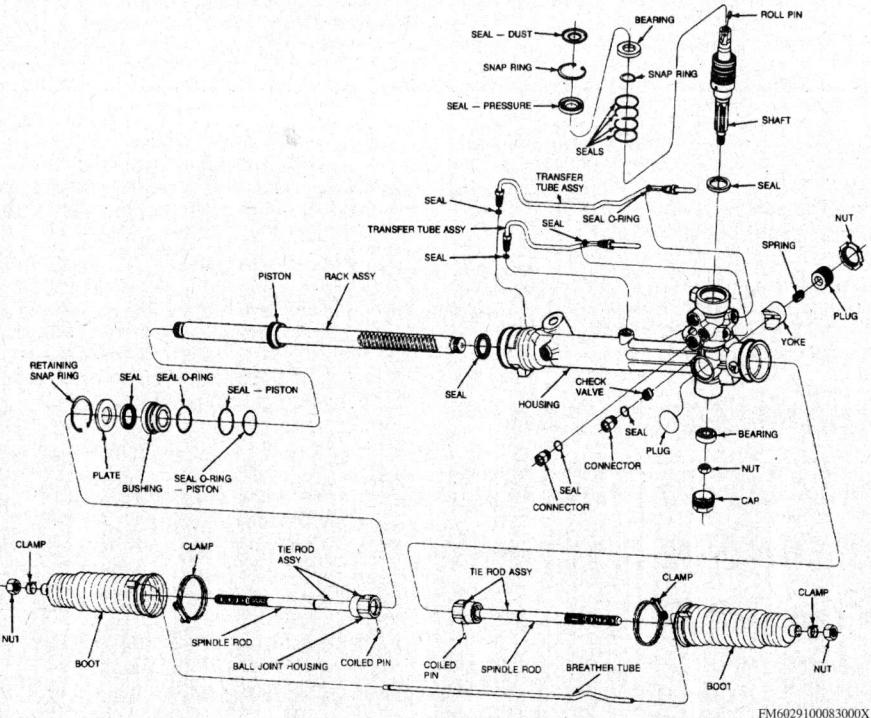

Fig. 2 Exploded view of steering gear. Continental, Sable & Taurus

FM6029100083000X

14. If flow exceeds maximum per-minute free flow, pump flow control valve should be removed and cleaned or replaced.

15. Inspect idle speed. With engine at idle, turn steering wheel to left and right-hand stops, then record pressure and flow at stops.

16. Pressure at both stops should be approximately same as maximum pump output pressure. Flow should drop below .5 gallons per minute.

17. If pressure is not within specifications, there may be excessive internal leakage is indicated. Remove and disassemble steering gear, replace worn or damaged components and inspect rack piston and valve seals for damage.

18. Turn steering wheel slightly in both directions and quickly release wheel. Pressure should move from normal backpressure and snap back as wheel is released. If needle returns slowly or sticks, steering gear rotary valve is sticking.

19. Flush power steering system.

20. If fault still exists, inspect ball joint and linkage.

SYSTEM SERVICE
Adjustments
STEERING GEAR

Rack yoke bearing preload is the only service adjustment required. This adjustment is performed with the steering gear removed from the vehicle. Refer to the appropriate chassis chapter for steering gear replacement procedure.

1. Clean steering gear's exterior, then install two long bolts and washers through bushings and attach to bench fixture tool No. T57L-500-B, or equivalent.

2. **Do not remove external pressure lines unless damaged or leaking.**

3. Drain power steering fluid into suitable container by rotating input shaft from lock to lock two times using pinion shaft torque adapter tool No. T74P-3504-R, or equivalent. Cover ports on valve housing with clean shop cloth while draining gear.

4. Position suitable inch pound torque wrench and pinion shaft adapter tool on input shaft splines.

5. Loosen yoke plug locknut using pinion housing yoke locknut wrench tool No. T78P-3504-H, or equivalent, then loosen yoke plug using a ¾ inch socket wrench, **Fig. 9.**

6. Clean yoke plug threads. **torque** yoke plug to 40–50 inch lbs., with rack at center of travel.

7. Back off yoke plug approximately ⅛ turn until torque required to rotate input shaft is 7–18 inch lbs.

8. While holding yoke plug in position, tighten locknut.

9. Measure input shaft rotating torque after tightening locknut using pinion housing yoke locknut wrench tool No. T78P-3504-H, or equivalent.

10. If external pressure lines were removed, they must be replaced with new ones. Remove copper seals from the pressure ports prior to installing new lines.

11. Remove steering gear from holding fixture and install external pressure lines.

Component Service

STEERING GEAR

The steering gear on these models is not serviceable and must be replaced as an assembly.

TIE ROD ENDS, BELLOWS & BALL JOINT SOCKETS

CONTINENTAL, FIVE HUNDRED, FREESTYLE, MONTEGO, MUSTANG, SABLE & TAURUS

Disassemble

1. Install two long bolts and washers through bushings and attach gear to holding fixture tool No. T57L-500-B, or equivalent.
2. Loosen jam nuts, then remove tie rod ends and jam nuts.
3. Remove four clamps attaching bellows to tie rods and gear housing.
4. Drain power steering fluid into suitable container.
5. Remove bellows with breather tube. **Do not damage bellows.**
6. If pinion is to be removed, remove pinion.
7. Thread point of roll pin remover tool No. T78P-3504-N, or equivalent, into roll pin on ball socket and hand tighten.
8. Remove roll pins, **Fig. 10.**
9. If pinion was not removed, remove gear housing from holding fixture and place it on bench.
10. Position rack so several teeth are exposed. Hold rack using suitable adjustable wrench on end teeth while loosening ball sockets with nut wrench tool No. T74P-3504-U, or equivalent, **Fig. 11.**

Assemble

This procedure has been revised by a Technical Service Bulletin.
1. **On models equipped with tie rods retained by rivet or pin,** proceed as follows:
   a. **If pinion was not removed from housing, these steps must be performed with steering gear removed from holding fixture and positioned on bench.**
   b. Install tie rod and ball socket assemblies onto rack.
   c. Hold one ball socket with 1 5/16 inch wrench while tightening other ball socket, using nut wrench tool No. T74P-3504-U, or equivalent.
   d. Both ball socket assemblies will be torqued simultaneously.
   e. Support ball housing using suitable wooden block and install roll pins by tapping lightly with suitable plastic mallet.
   f. If pinion was removed, install pinion.
   g. Thoroughly clean rack and housing bore.
   h. Apply suitable lubricant to bellows clamp under cut on tie rod, then install bellows and breather tube.
   i. Install clamps retaining bellows to

steering gear securing clamp using tool No. T63P-9171-A, or equivalent.
   j. Install clamps retaining bellows to tie rods, jam nuts and tie rod ends.
2. **On models equipped with tie rods not retained by rivet or pin,** proceed as follows:
   a. Turn rack to lefthand stop, then place suitable adjustable wrench on rack to prevent turning during tightening procedures.
   b. Install tie rod to rack.
   c. Install rack boots, then secure to rack body and tie rod using suitable clamps.
   d. Install tie rod end jam nuts and tie rod ends to tie rods.

COUGAR, LS & THUNDERBIRD

1. Secure steering gear in holding fixture tool No. T57L-500-B, or equivalent.
2. Loosen tie rod end jam nuts, then remove tie rod ends and jam nuts from tie rods. Record turns required to remove tie rod ends.

3. Remove clamps and rack boots.
4. Place suitable adjustable wrench only on rack end teeth, then, loosen and remove tie rods using suitable pipe wrench. **Do not allow rack to turn in gear.**
5. Reverse procedure to install.

ESCORT & ZX2

1. Raise and support vehicle.
2. Disconnect tie rod ends from knuckle using separator tool No. T85M-3395-A, or equivalent.
3. Loosen tie rod end jam nuts, then remove tie rod ends and jam nuts from tie rods. **Record turns required to remove tie rod ends.**
4. Remove clamps and rack boots.
5. Place suitable 20 mm crowfoot wrench, or equivalent, on end of rack.
6. Remove tie rods using tie rod socket tool No. C3AZ-19578-A, or equivalent. **Do not allow rack to turn in gear.**
7. Reverse procedure to install.

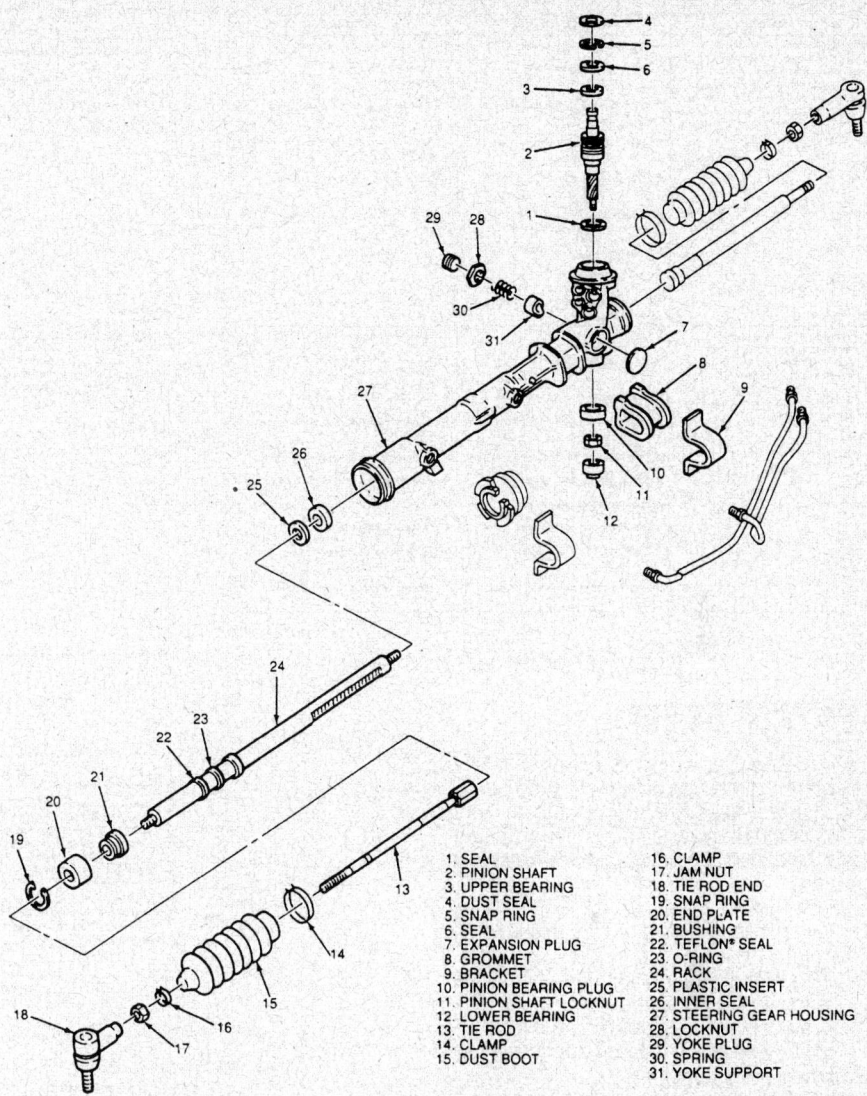

1. SEAL	16. CLAMP
2. PINION SHAFT	17. JAM NUT
3. UPPER BEARING	18. TIE ROD END
4. DUST SEAL	19. SNAP RING
5. SNAP RING	20. END PLATE
6. SEAL	21. BUSHING
7. EXPANSION PLUG	22. TEFLON® SEAL
8. GROMMET	23. O-RING
9. BRACKET	24. RACK
10. PINION BEARING PLUG	25. PLASTIC INSERT
11. PINION SHAFT LOCKNUT	26. INNER SEAL
12. LOWER BEARING	27. STEERING GEAR HOUSING
13. TIE ROD	28. LOCKNUT
14. CLAMP	29. YOKE PLUG
15. DUST BOOT	30. SPRING
	31. YOKE SUPPORT

FM6029100084000X

Fig. 3   Exploded view of steering gear. Escort & ZX2

CONDITION	POSSIBLE SOURCE	ACTION
• Wander — Vehicle wander is a condition where the vehicle wanders side to side on the roadway when it is driven straight ahead while the steering wheel is held in a firm position. Evaluation should be conducted on a level road (little road crown).	• Improper wheel alignment.	• Set alignment to specification.
	• Loose outer tie rod ends.	• Replace outer tie rod end assemblies.
	• Inner tie rod ball housing loose or worn.	• Replace inner tie rod assemblies.
	• Gear assembly mounting loose.	• Tighten mounting bolts to specification.
	• Loose suspension struts or ball joints.	• Adjust or replace as required.
	• Column intermediate shaft connecting bolts loose.	• Tighten bolts to specification.
	• Loose wheel bearings.	• Service as required.
	• Column intermediate shaft joints loose or worn.	• Replace intermediate shaft.
• Feedback — (Rattle, chuckle, knocking noises in the steering gear. Feedback is a condition where roughness is felt in the steering wheel by the driver when the vehicle is driven over rough pavement.	• Column U-joints loose.	• Replace if bad.
	• Loose outer tie rod ends.	• Replace outer tie rod end assemblies.
	• Loose/worn inner tie rod ball.	• Replace inner tie rod assemblies.
	• Gear assembly mounting loose.	• Tighten mounting bolts to specification.
	• Loose pinion bearing cap.	• Tighten cap to specification.
	• Loose pinion bearing locknut.	• Tighten locknut to specification.
	• Piston disengaged or loose on rack.	• Replace rack assembly.
	• Steering gear yoke worn.	• Replace yoke assembly.
	• Column intermediate shaft connecting bolts loose.	• Tighten bolts to specification.
	• Loose suspension struts on ball joints.	• Adjust or replace as necessary.

FM6029100087010X

Fig. 4   Troubleshooting (Part 1 of 3)

CONDITION	POSSIBLE SOURCE	ACTION
• Poor Returnability — Sticky Feel — Poor returnability is noticed when the steering fails to return to center following a turn without manual effort from the driver. In addition, when the driver returns the steering to center, it may have a sticky or catchy feel.	• Misaligned steering column or column flange rubbing steering wheel and/or flange.	• Align column.
	• Check rotational torque of intermediate shaft joints.	• If binding, replace intermediate shaft.
	• Improper wheel alignment.	• Set to specification.
	• Tight inner tie rod ball joints.	• Replace inner tie rod as required.
	• Binding in valve assembly.	• Replace input shaft valve assembly.
	• Bent or damaged rack.	• Replace rack assembly.
	• Bent or damaged sub-frame.	• Replace as necessary.
	• Column bearing binding.	• Replace bearing.
	• Tight suspension struts or lower control arm ball joints.	• Adjust or replace as required.
	• Contamination in system.	• Flush power steering system.
	• Deformed engine mounts.	• Replace as necessary.
• Heavy Steering Efforts (Poor or loss of assist) — A heavy effort and poor assist condition is recognized by the driver while turning corners and especially while parking. A road test will verify this condition	• Leakage/loss of fluid.	• external leakage service.
	• Low pump fluid.	• Fill as necessary.
	• Pump external leakage.	• Service
	• Improper drive belt tension.	• Readjust belt tension.
	• Hose or cooler external leakage.	• Replace as necessary.
	• Improper engine idle speed.	• Readjust idle.
	• Pulley loose or warped.	• Replace pulley.
	• Pump/flow pressure not to specification.	
	• Hose/cooler line restrictions.	• Clear or replace as required.
	• Valve plastic ring cut or twisted.	• Replace ring.
	• Damaged/worn plastic piston ring.	• Replace ring.
	• Loose/missing rubber backup piston O-ring.	• Replace/install O-ring.
	• Loose rack piston.	• Replace rack assembly.
	• Gear assembly oil passages restricted.	• Clear/service as required.
	• Bent/damaged rack assembly.	• Replace rack assembly.

FM6029100087020X

Fig. 4   Troubleshooting (Part 2 of 3)

CONDITION	POSSIBLE SOURCE	ACTION
• Hissing Sound There is some noise in all power steering systems. One of the most common is a hissing sound most evident at standstill parking. There is no relationship between this noise and the performance of the steering gear. **CAUTION:** Do not hold steering wheel at full lock more than five seconds, as damage to power steering pump may result.	• Hiss may be expected when the steering wheel is at the end of travel or when turning at standstill.	• Hiss is a normal characteristic of rotary steering gears and in no way affects steering. Do not replace the rack assembly unless the hiss is extremely objectionable. A replacement rack will also exhibit a slight noise and is not always a cure for the condition. Investigate for a grounded column or a loose boot at the dash panel. Any metal-to-metal contact will transmit valve hiss into the passenger compartment through the steering column. Verify clearance between flexible coupling components. Ensure steering column shaft and gear are aligned so flexible coupling rotates in a flat plane and is not distorted as shaft rotates.

FM6029100087030X

Fig. 4   Troubleshooting (Part 3 of 3)

SYSTEM BLEED

Air trapped in power steering system may be removed with power steering pump air evacuator assembly vacuum tester tool No. 021-00014, or equivalent. **Do not use engine vacuum to purge power steering system.**

1. Remove reservoir cap.
2. Inspect and adjust fluid level to cold fill mark.
3. Disconnect ignition coil wire, then raise and support front wheels.
4. Crank engine with starter motor and inspect fluid level. **Do not turn steering wheel.**
5. If fluid level has dropped, fill reservoir to cold fill mark, crank engine with starter motor while turning steering wheel lock to lock. Inspect fluid level.
6. Install air evacuator rubber stopper tightly to pump reservoir and connect coil wire.
7. With engine at idle, apply 15 inches maximum vacuum to pump reservoir for at least three minutes.
8. As air purges from system, vacuum will decrease. Maintain adequate vacuum.
9. Release vacuum and remove source. If fluid level has dropped, fill to cold fill mark.
10. With engine at idle, apply 15 inches maximum vacuum to pump reservoir, then turn steering wheel from lock to lock every 30 seconds for approximately five minutes. **Do not hold steering wheel on stops when turning.** Maintain adequate vacuum.
11. Release vacuum and remove equipment.
12. Adjust power steering fluid and install cap.

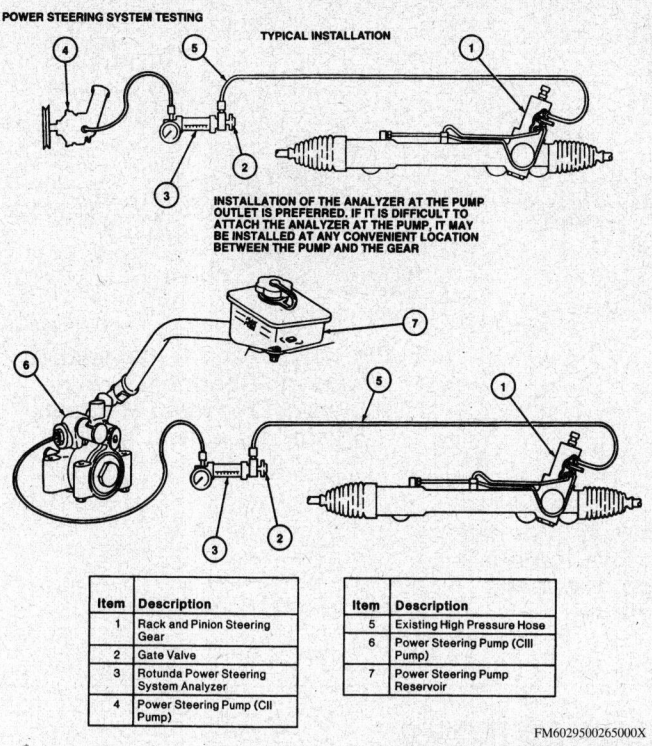

POWER STEERING SYSTEM TESTING

TYPICAL INSTALLATION

INSTALLATION OF THE ANALYZER AT THE PUMP OUTLET IS PREFERRED. IF IT IS DIFFICULT TO ATTACH THE ANALYZER AT THE PUMP, IT MAY BE INSTALLED AT ANY CONVENIENT LOCATION BETWEEN THE PUMP AND THE GEAR.

FM6029500265000X

Item	Description		Item	Description
1	Rack and Pinion Steering Gear		5	Existing High Pressure Hose
2	Gate Valve		6	Power Steering Pump (CIII Pump)
3	Rotunda Power Steering System Analyzer		7	Power Steering Pump Reservoir
4	Power Steering Pump (CII Pump)			

Fig. 5   Pressure test connections. Mustang

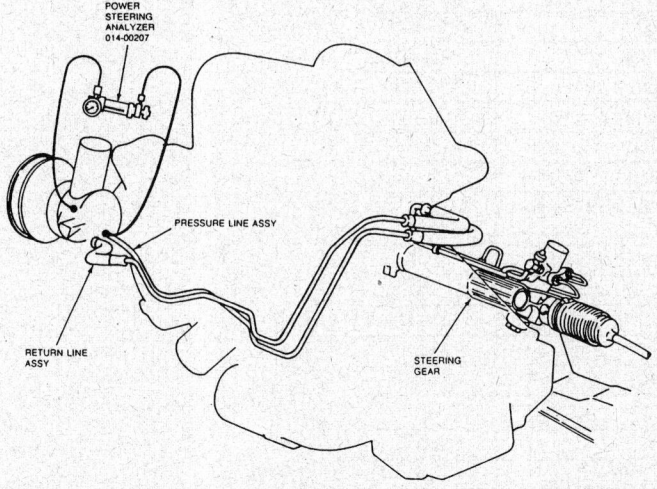

POWER STEERING ANALYZER 014-00207

PRESSURE LINE ASSY

RETURN LINE ASSY

STEERING GEAR

FM6029100090000X

Fig. 7   Pressure test connections. Sable & Taurus

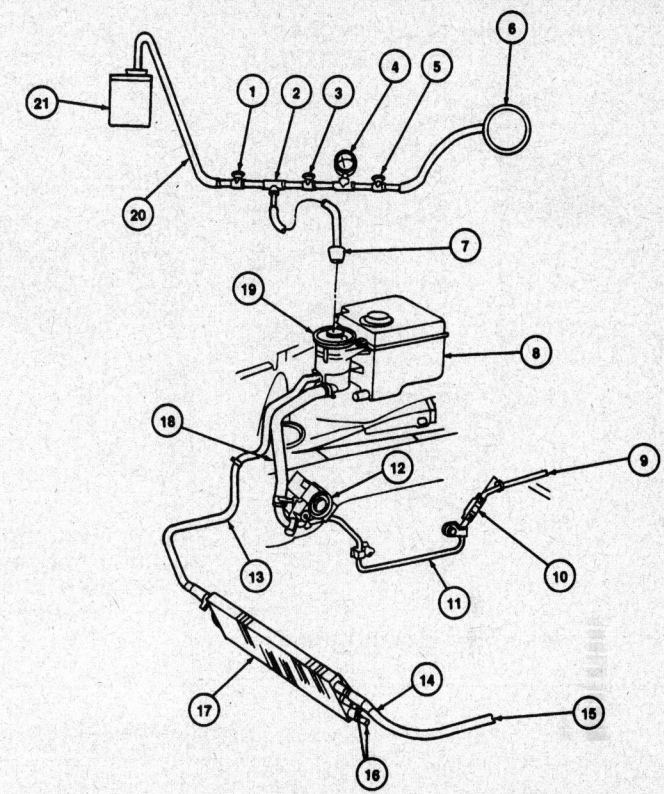

Item	Description		Item	Description
1	Valve No. 1		11	Power Steering Pressure Hose
2	Tee		12	Power Steering Pump
3	Valve No. 2		13	Oil Cooler-To-Reservoir Hose
4	0 to 30 Inch Vacuum Gauge		14	Power Steering Return Hose
5	Valve No. 3		15	From Power Steering Gear
6	Vacuum Source		16	Transmission Fluid Cooler Ports
7	No. 7 Stopper		17	Combination Power Steering and Automatic Transmission Fluid Cooler
8	Radiator Coolant Recovery Reservoir		18	Power Steering Reservoir Pump Hose
9	Power Steering Left Turn Pressure Hose (To Auxiliary Actuator)			
10	Intermediate Connection			

FM6029500266000X

Fig. 6   Pressure test connections. Continental

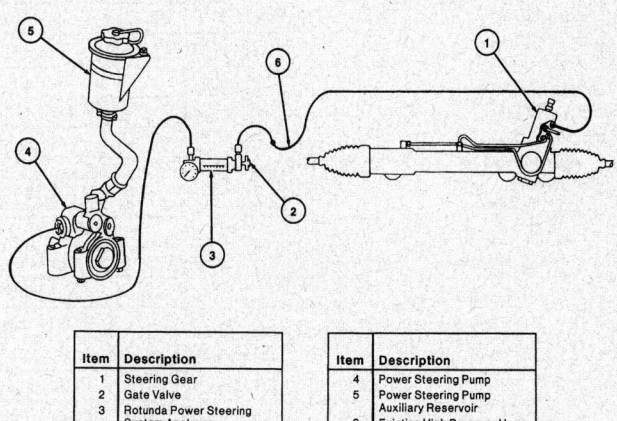

Item	Description		Item	Description
1	Steering Gear		4	Power Steering Pump
2	Gate Valve		5	Power Steering Pump Auxiliary Reservoir
3	Rotunda Power Steering System Analyzer		6	Existing High Pressure Hose

FM6029400202000X

Fig. 8   Pressure test connections. Cougar

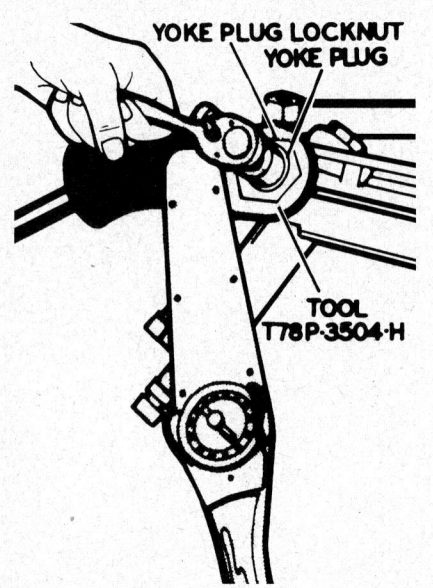

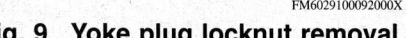

Fig. 9 Yoke plug locknut removal

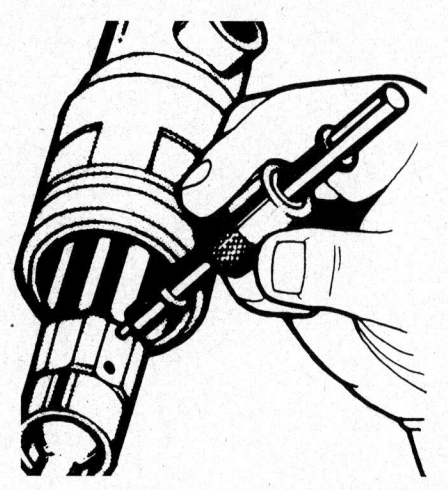

Fig. 10 Roll pin removal from ball socket. Continental, Five Hundred, Freestyle, Montego, Mustang, Sable & Taurus

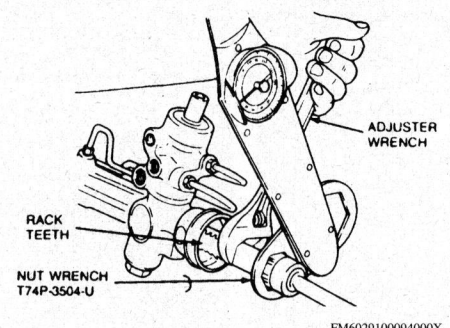

Fig. 11 Tie rod & ball socket removal. Continental, Five Hundred, Freestyle, Montego, Mustang, Sable & Taurus

TIGHTENING SPECIFICATIONS

Year	Component	Torque/Ft. Lbs.
CONTINENTAL		
2001–02	Bellows Clamp	20–30①
	Gear Hose Fittings	24–30
	Gear Housing Return Line	20–25
	Gear To Crossmember	100–144
	Intermediate Shaft To Steering Column	15–24
	Intermediate Shaft To Steering Gear	30–38
	Pressure Line Fitting To Actuator Banjo Bolt	22–28
	Pump Pressure Line Fitting	42–54
	Tie Rod Ball Socket To Rack	②
	Tie Rod End Jam Nut	35–48
	Tie Rod End To Spindle Arm	35–47
	VAPS Actuator	24–30
COUGAR		
2001–02	Bellows Clamp	25①
	Flexible Coupling Pinch Bolt	21
	Gear Hose Fittings	23
	Gear Housing Return Line	23
	Gear Cover Plate	37
	Gear To Crossmember	101
	Pump Pressure Line Fitting	48
	Tie Rod End Jam Nut	45
	Tie Rod End To Spindle Arm	21
ESCORT & ZX2		
2001–03	Air Conditioning Compressor	15–22
	High Pressure Line To Housing Flare Nut	21–25
	Return Line To Housing Flare Nut	21–25
	Tie Rod End Jam Nuts	25–37
	Tie Rod To Rack	40–50

Continued

TIGHTENING
SPECIFICATIONS—Continued

Year	Component	Torque/Ft. Lbs.
FIVE HUNDRED, FREESTYLE & MONTEGO		
2005	Power Steering Line Clamp Plate Bolt	15
	Pressure Line Bracket To Engine	89①
	Pressure Line Fitting	48
	Pressure Line Fitting To Pump Adapter	48
	Return Line Bracket To Frame Bolts	89①
	Steering Gear Mounting Nuts	86
	Steering Pump Mounting Nuts	18
	Tie Rod End Jam Nuts	59
	Tie Rod End Nuts	66
LS & THUNDERBIRD		
2001–05	Hose Bracket To Steering Gear	89①
	Steering Gear To Frame	46③
	Steering Gear Fluid Lines	23
	Steering Shaft To Gear Pinch Bolt	26
	Tie Rod To Steering Knuckle	74
	Tie Rod To Rack	88
MUSTANG		
2001–05	Front Wheel Spindle Tie Rod	74
	Pressure Line Fitting	48
	Steering Gear	35
	Steering Intermediate Shaft Coupling Pinch Bolt	25
	Tie Rod End Castellated Nut	11
	Tie Rod End Jam Nut	41
SABLE & TAURUS		
2001–05	Bellows Clamp	20–30①
	Gear Hose Fittings	15–25
	Gear Housing Return Line	24–30
	Gear To Crossmember	85–100
	Intermediate Shaft To Steering Column	15–25
	Intermediate Shaft To Steering Gear	30–38
	Pressure Line Fitting To Actuator Banjo Bolt	22–28
	Pump Pressure Line Fitting	42–54
	Tie Rod Ball Socket To Rack	66–81
	Tie Rod End Jam Nut	35–50
	Tie Rod End To Spindle Arm	35–47
	VAPS Actuator	24–30

① — Inch lbs.
② — Tie rod retained w/pin or rivet, 55–65 ft. lbs., tie rod not retained by a pin or rivet, 68–81 ft. lbs.
③ — Discard and replace nuts.

Ford Torsion Bar Power Steering Gear

NOTE: On Air Bag Equipped Models, Refer To "Air Bag System Precautions" Located In The Front Of This Manual For System Disarming & Arming Procedures.

NOTE: Refer To "Computer Relearn Procedures" Located In The Front Of This Manual When Battery Power To The Computer Has Been Interrupted.

NOTE: Also Refer To "Ford Variable Assist Electronic Variable Orifice (EVO) System," For Models Equipped With EVO System.

INDEX

PRECAUTIONS

Air Bag Systems

Refer to "Air Bag System Precautions" in the front of this manual for system disarming and arming procedures.

Battery Ground Cable

Prior to service, disconnect battery ground cable and isolate as required.

DESCRIPTION

The power steering unit is a torsion bar type of hydraulic-assisted system, **Fig. 1.** This system furnishes power to reduce the amount of turning effort required at the steering wheel. It also reduces road shock and vibrations.

The unit includes a worm and one piece rack-piston which is meshed to the gear teeth on the steering sector shaft. The unit also includes a hydraulic valve, valve actuator, input shaft and torsion bar assembly which are mounted on the end of the worm shaft and operated by a twisting action of the torsion bar.

The gear unit is designed with the one piece rack-piston, worm and sector shaft in the one housing and the valve spool in an attaching housing. This makes internal fluid passages possible between valve and cyl-

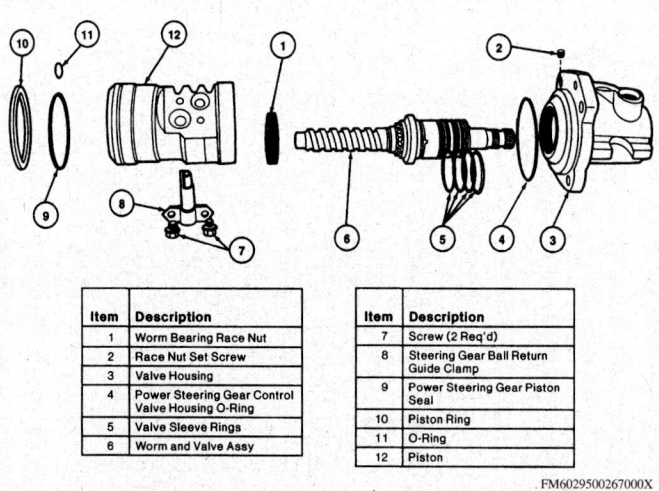

Item	Description
1	Worm Bearing Race Nut
2	Race Nut Set Screw
3	Valve Housing
4	Power Steering Gear Control Valve Housing O-Ring
5	Valve Sleeve Rings
6	Worm and Valve Assy

Item	Description
7	Screw (2 Req'd)
8	Steering Gear Ball Return Guide Clamp
9	Power Steering Gear Piston Seal
10	Piston Ring
11	O-Ring
12	Piston

FM6029500267000X

Fig. 1 Exploded view of Ford power steering gear

inder, thus eliminating all external lines and hoses except the pressure and return hoses between pump and gear.

The power cylinder is an integral part of the gear housing. The piston is double acting in that fluid pressure may be applied to either of its sides.

Operation

The operation of the hydraulic control valve spool is governed by the twisting of a torsion bar. All effort applied to the steering

wheel is transmitted directly through the input shaft and torsion bar to the worm and piston. Any resistance to the turning of the front wheels results in twisting of the bar. The twisting of the bar increases as the front wheel turning effort increases. The control valve spool, actuated by the twisting of the torsion bar, directs fluid to the side of the piston where hydraulic assistance is required.

As the torsion bar twists, its radial motion is transferred into axial motion by three helical threads. Thus, the valve is moved off

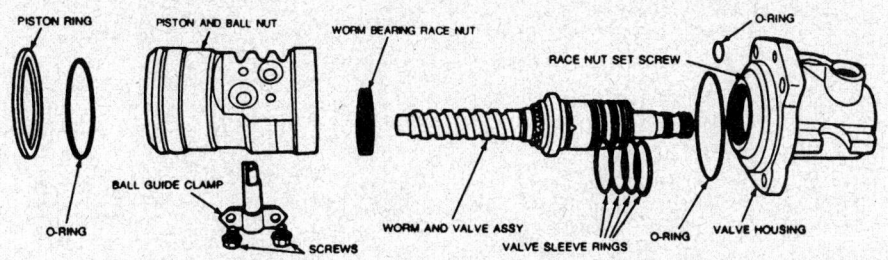

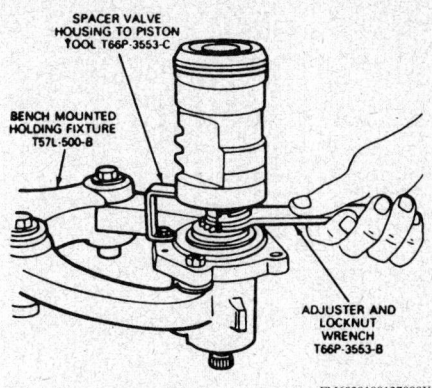

Fig. 2   Exploded view of ball nut & valve housing

FM6029100126000X

Fig. 3   Input shaft removal

FM6029100127000X

center, and fluid is directed to one side of the piston or the other.

TROUBLESHOOTING

Steering Drift/Wander

1. Tire size and pressure.
2. Loose or worn tie rod ends or ball joints.
3. Steering gear mounting insulators or retaining bolts loose or damaged.
4. Loose front suspension lower arm struts.
5. Steering column gear input shaft coupling connecting bolts loose.
6. Steering gear input shaft coupling joints lose or worn.
7. Improper wheel alignment.
8. Excessive toe-in.
9. Excessive friction between components.

Pulls To One Side

1. Improper tire pressure.
2. Improper tire size or type.
3. Vehicle is unevenly loaded.
4. Improper wheel alignment.
5. Damaged front or rear suspension components.
6. Steering gear valve effort out of adjustment.
7. Front or rear brakes operating improperly.
8. Bent rear axle housing, damaged or sagging front coil springs or damaged or worn rear suspension component.
9. loose or damaged rear suspension retaining fasteners.

Feedback (Rattle, Chuckle or Knocking Noises From Steering Gear)

1. Steering column gear input shaft coupling joints loose or worn.
2. Loose tie rod ends.
3. Steering gear retaining bolts loose or damaged.

4. Loose suspension bushings, fasteners or ball joints.
5. Improper steering gear adjustment.

Poor Returnability, Sticky Feel

1. Improper tire pressure, tire size or tire type.
2. Misaligned steering column or column flange.
3. Steering column gear input shaft universal joints binding.
4. Steering column tube boot tears.
5. Binding or damaged tie rod ends.
6. Damaged or worn front suspension components.
7. Improper wheel alignment.
8. Column bearing binding.
9. Contamination in system.
10. Improper steering gear adjustment.

Heavy Steering Effort, Poor Assist or Loss Of Assist

1. Contamination of system by foreign objects in power steering oil reservoir or metallic particles in fluid being generated by cam pack discrepancies.
2. Low power steering fluid.
3. Steering gear assembly internal or external leak.
4. Improper drive belt tension.
5. Hose or cooler external leak or internal restriction.
6. Improper engine idle speed.
7. Power steering pump pulley loose or warped.
8. Power steering pump flow or pressure not to specifications.
9. Improper steering gear adjustments.
10. System contamination.
11. EVO power steering control valve actuator sticking.

Power Steering Pump Leaks At EVO Control Valve Actuator

1. Damaged power steering control valve actuator ring.

2. EVO power steering control valve actuator electrical connector damaged.
3. EVO power steering control valve actuator damaged.

Noisy Pump

SWISH TYPE NOISE

A swish type noise may be created by the flow of excessive fluid into the bypass port of the pump valve housing with temperatures below 130°. This is a normal condition and will diminish when fluid temperature increases.

1. Low fluid level and possible leak.

CLICKING TYPE NOISE

1. Excessive power steering pump wear.

MOAN OR WHINE TYPE NOISE

1. Fluid aeration.
2. Power steering pump loose or misaligned with engine.
3. Low fluid.
4. Hose or steering column grounded.
5. Damaged internal components.

SYSTEM SERVICE

Adjustments

MESH LOAD

Perform the following adjustment with the steering gear and fluid lines disconnected from the vehicles steering system components.

1. Rotate input shaft either right or left to stop.
2. Rotate shaft in opposite direction and count number of turns.
3. Rotate shaft back one half number of turns counted.
4. Measure torque required to rotate input shaft 45° either side of center using suitable inch pounds torque

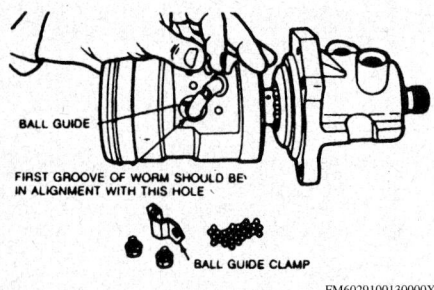

Fig. 4   Piston assembly on worm shaft

wrench. If torque reading is not 12–16 inch lbs., turn sector shaft adjusting screw to adjust mesh load.

Component Service
OVERHAUL
GEAR
Disassemble

1. Hold steering gear over drain pan in inverted position and cycle input shaft six times to drain remaining fluid.
2. Install gear in bench mounting fixture tool No. T57L-500-B, or equivalent, using suitable mounting pads for support.
3. Remove locknut from adjusting screw.
4. Turn input shaft to either stop and back approximately 1 5/8 turns to center gear. **Input shaft spline indexing flat should be facing downward.**
5. Remove sector shaft cover bolts.
6. Tap lower end of sector shaft with suitable soft-faced hammer to loosen it, then lift cover and shaft from housing as a unit. Discard O-ring.
7. Turn sector shaft cover counterclockwise off adjuster screw.
8. Remove valve housing mounting bolts.
9. Lift valve housing from gear housing while holding piston to prevent it from rotating off worm shaft.
10. Remove valve housing and lube passage O-rings.
11. Remove valve housing mounting bolts and ID tag, while holding piston separate valve housing from housing. Remove and discard O-rings.
12. With piston held, remove ball clamp screws and guide clamp, **Fig. 2.**
13. With finger over ball guide opening, turn piston so ball guide faces downward over clean container. Allow guide tubes to drop into container.
14. Rotate input shaft from stop to stop, until all balls fall from piston, then remove valve assembly from piston. **Ensure all balls have been removed. Worm may no longer be removed from piston.**
15. Install valve body to bench mounting fixture tool No. T57L-500-B, or equivalent, then loosen valve housing race nut lockscrew.
16. Remove worm bearing race using adjuster locknut wrench tool No. T66P-3553-B and spacer valve housing tool

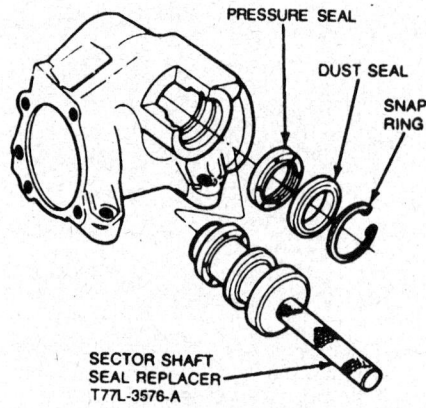

Fig. 5   Exploded view of steering gear housing

No. T66P-3553-C, or equivalents.
17. Slide input shaft, worm and valve assembly from valve housing, **Fig. 3.**

Assemble

1. Install worm and valve in housing.
2. Install retaining nut in housing, then tighten nut using adjuster and locknut wrench tool No. T66P-3553, or equivalent. Because length of tool required to tighten nut will affect torque wrench reading, the following formula for determining torque must be used: torque (using tool T66P-3553-B, or equivalent) equals (length of torque wrench X 72 ft. lbs., length of torque wrench + 5.5 inches).
3. Install race nut screw and tighten.
4. Place piston on bench with ball guide holes facing up.
5. Insert worm shaft into piston so first groove is in alignment with hole nearest to center of piston, **Fig. 4.**
6. Place ball guide into piston. Place balls in guide (27 minimum), turning worm clockwise (viewed from input end of shaft). If all balls have not been fed into guide upon reaching righthand stop, rotate input shaft in one direction and then in the other while installing balls. After balls have been installed, do not rotate input shaft or piston more than 3½ turns off righthand stop.
7. Secure guides to ball nut with clamp and tighten.
8. Apply petroleum jelly to piston seal.
9. Place new O-ring on valve housing.
10. Slide piston and valve into gear housing. **Do not damage seal.**
11. Align lube passage in valve housing with one in gear housing, place O-ring in gear housing oil passage hole, then identification tag and install. **Do not tighten mounting bolts at this time.**
12. Rotate ball nut so teeth are in same plane as sector teeth. Tighten valve housing mounting bolts.
13. Position sector shaft cover O-ring in gear housing. Turn input shaft to center piston.
14. Apply petroleum jelly to sector shaft journal, then position sector shaft and cover into gear housing.
15. Install air conditioner line mounting

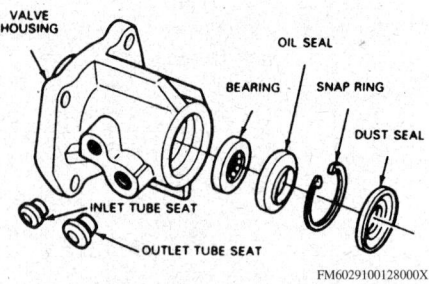

Fig. 6   Exploded view of valve housing

bracket and two sector shaft cover bolts.
16. Attach an inch pound torque wrench to input shaft and adjust mesh load as outlined in "Adjustments."

GEAR HOUSING

1. Remove lower end housing snap ring, **Fig. 5.**
2. Remove and discard dust and pressure seals using puller attachment tool No. T58L-101-B, or equivalent. **Bearing is not serviceable and must be replaced as an assembly.**
3. Lubricate new pressure, dust seal and sector shaft seal bore.
4. Install dust seal on sector shaft using seal replacer tool No. T77L-3576-A, or equivalent, with seal raised lip toward tool.
5. Install pressure seal with lip away from tool. Pressure seal flat side should be against flat side of dust deal.
6. Install tool to sector shaft bore, then drive tool until seals clear snap ring grooves. **Do not bottom seal against bearing.**
7. Install snap ring in housing groove.

REPLACEMENT
VALVE HOUSING
Disassemble

1. Remove and discard dust seal using puller attachment tool No. T58L-101-B, or equivalent, **Fig. 6.**
2. Remove snap ring from valve housing and turn fixture so valve housing is upside down.
3. Install bearing remover tool No. T65P-3524-A2 and installer tool No. T65P-3524-A3, or equivalents, to valve body opposite oil seal.
4. Gently tap bearing and seal from housing. Discard seal. **Do not damage housing valve bore.**
5. If damaged, remove oil inlet and outlet tube seats with rack bushing holding tool No. T74P-3504-L, or equivalent.

Assemble

1. Coat tube seats with petroleum jelly and position them in housing.
2. Install and tighten tube nuts to press seats to proper location using brass tube seat replacer tool No. T74P-3504-M, or equivalent.
3. Coat bearing and seal surface in housing with film of petroleum jelly.

4. Install bearing with metal side that covers rollers facing downward, then seat bearing using bearing installer tool No. T65P-3524-A, or equivalent. Inspect for smooth bearing operation.
5. Dip new oil seal in suitable premium power steering fluid and place it in housing with metal side of seal facing outward.
6. Drive seal into housing until outer edge of seal does not quite clear snap ring.
7. Place snap ring in housing, then drive on ring until snap ring seats in its groove to properly locate seal.
8. Apply coating of suitable multipurpose grease between seals.
9. Place dust seal in housing with dished side (rubber side) facing outward.
10. Drive dust seal in place so that it is located behind undercut in input shaft when it is installed.

WORM & VALVE SLEEVES

1. Cut valve sleeve rings from valve sleeve, then position worm end in suitable soft jawed vice.
2. Install four valve sleeve rings using tool kit No. T75L-3517-A1, or equivalent.
3. Ensure sleeve ring turn freely in grooves after installation.

PISTON & BALL NUT

1. Remove plastic ring and O-ring from piston and ball nut.
2. Dip new O-ring in suitable premium power steering fluid, then lubricate and install on piston and ball nut.
3. Install new Teflon ring on piston and ball nut. **Do not stretch ring more than needed.**

INSPECTION

VALVE SPOOL CENTERING INSPECTION

The out of and in-vehicle valve centering inspection are same except the torque and simultaneous pressure reading must be made at the left and righthand stops instead of either side of center.
1. Install satiable 2000 psi pressure gauge in pressure line between pump outlet port and steering gear inlet port. Ensure valve on gauge is in fully open position.
2. Inspect and adjust fluid level in reservoir.
3. Start engine and cycle steering wheel from stop to stop to bring steering lubricant up to normal operating temperature.
4. Stop engine and inspect reservoir. Adjust fluid level.
5. With engine running at fast idle speed (1000 RPM) and steering wheel centered, attach an inch pound torque wrench to steering wheel nut.
6. Apply sufficient torque to wrench in each direction (either side of center) to get gauge reading of 250 psi.
7. Torque reading should be same in both directions. If difference exceed 4 inch lbs., replace shaft and control assemblies.

TIGHTENING SPECIFICATIONS

Year	Component	Torque/Ft. Lbs.
2001–05	Ball Return Guide Clamp	42–70①
	Flex Coupling To Gear Input Shaft	20–30
	Gear To Side Rail	50–65
	Hose Clamps	12–24①
	Mesh Load Adjusting Screw Locknut	35–45
	Piston End Cap	70–110
	Pitman Arm To Sector Shaft	200–250
	Pressure Hose To Gear	16–25
	Race Nut Setscrew	15–25①
	Return Hose To Gear	16–25
	Sector Shaft Cover	55–70
	Valve Housing To Gear Housing	30–45

① — Inch lbs.

Ford Variable Assist Electronic Variable Orifice (EVO) System

NOTE: On Air Bag Equipped Models, Refer To "Air Bag System Precautions" Located In The Front Of This Manual For System Disarming & Arming Procedures.

NOTE: Refer To "Computer Relearn Procedures" Located In The Front Of This Manual When Battery Power To The Computer Has Been Interrupted.

NOTE: "Electrical Symbol & Wire Color Code Identification" Located In The Front Of This Manual May Be Used As An Aid When Using Wiring Circuits Found In This Section.

INDEX

PRECAUTIONS

Air Bag Systems

Refer to "Air Bag System Precautions" in the front of this manual for system disarming and arming procedures.

Battery Ground Cable

Prior to service, disconnect battery ground cable and isolate as required.

DESCRIPTION

The electronic variable orifice system is designed to vary the flow from the power steering pump based on vehicle speed and the rate of steering wheel rotation, **Fig. 1.** The system provides full assist at low speed for light parking effort and minimum assist at high speed for good road feel and directional stability. In the event of system failure, full assist is provided.

TROUBLESHOOTING

Crown Victoria, Grand Marquis, Marauder & Town Car

Refer to **Figs. 2 through 5,** for troubleshooting procedures.

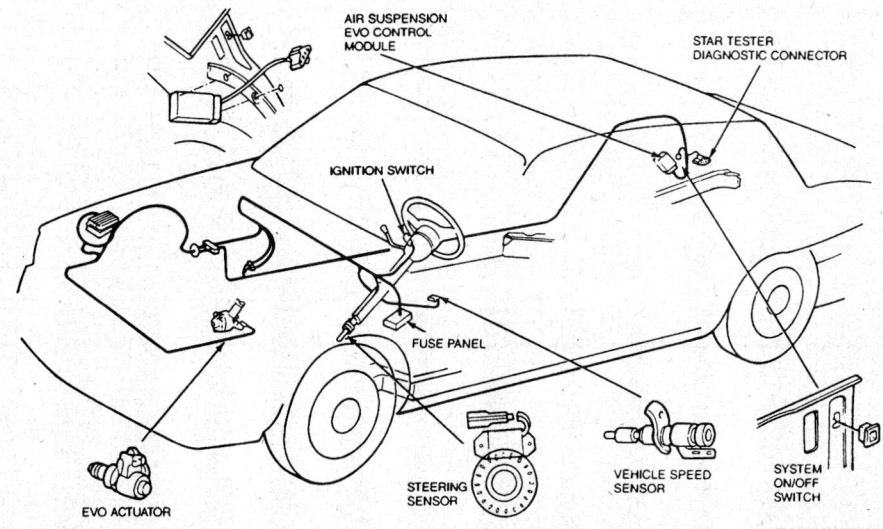

Fig. 1 Electronic variable orifice system component locations

DIAGNOSIS & TESTING

Pinpoint Tests

CROWN VICTORIA, GRAND MARQUIS & MARAUDER

On 2000–02 models, diagnosis and testing requires the use of a Super Star II hand held diagnostic tester, Rotunda model No. 007-0041A, or equivalent, and suitable digital volt/ohm meter.

On 2003–05 models, diagnosis and testing requires the use of Worldwide diagnostic tester, Rotunda model No. 418-F224 or New Generation Star, Rotunda model No. 418-F052, or equivalent.

Refer to **MOTOR's "Domestic Engine Performance & Driveability Manual"** for trouble code index.

If vehicle is equipped with air suspension, perform the "Auto Test." procedure.

Refer to **Fig. 6,** for symptom chart and **Figs. 7 through 19,** for system diagnosis and testing.

TOWN CAR

Refer to **Fig. 20,** for symptom chart and **Figs. 21 through 26,** for pinpoint tests.

Condition	Possible Source	Action
• NOTE: Evaluation should be conducted on a level road (little road crown) Steering Drift / Wander — Condition Where the Vehicle Wanders Side-To-Side on the Roadway When it is Driven Straight Ahead While the Steering Wheel is Held in a Firm Position	• Check tire size and pressure.	• Be sure tire sizes are correct and ADJUST tire pressures.
	• Check if vehicle is unevenly loaded or overloaded.	• ADJUST load.
	• Loose / worn tie rod ends or ball socket.	• REPLACE tie rod end assembly as necessary.
	• Steering gear mounting insulators and / or retaining bolts loose or damaged.	• REPLACE bolts.
	• Loose front suspension lower arm struts or ball joint(s).	• REPLACE arm and ball joint assembly.
	• Steering gear input shaft coupling connecting bolts loose.	• TIGHTEN at gear and at column.
	• Steering column gear input shaft coupling joints loose / worn.	• REPLACE steering column intermediate shaft coupling assembly.
	• Improper wheel alignment.	• ADJUST as required.
	• Excessive friction between components.	• REFER to Sensitive Steering Diagnostic and Service Procedure.
	• Excessive toe-in.	• CHECK alignment.
• Pulls to One Side — A Condition Where the Vehicle Tends to Pull to One Side When Driven on a Level Surface	• Improper tire pressure.	• ADJUST tire pressure.
	• Improper tire size or different type.	• REPLACE as required.
	• Vehicle is unevenly or excessively loaded.	• ADJUST load.
	• Improper wheel alignment.	• ADJUST as required.
	• Damaged front suspension components.	• REFER to front suspension replacement.
	• Damaged rear suspension components.	• REFER to rear suspension replacement.
	• Steering gear valve effort out of balance.	• PLACE transmission in NEUTRAL while driving and TURN engine off (coasting). If vehicle does not pull with the engine off, REPLACE the steering gear valve assembly. If vehicle does drift with engine off CROSS switch front tire / wheel assemblies. —If vehicle pulls to opposite side, CROSS switch tire / wheel assemblies that were on the rear to same side on the front. —If vehicle pull direction is not changed, CHECK front suspension components and wheel alignment.
	• Check front and rear brakes for proper operation.	• ADJUST if necessary.
	• Check for bent rear axle housing and for damaged or sagging front coil springs in the front and / or rear suspension.	• REPLACE if necessary.
	• Check for damaged air spring in the front and / or rear suspension.	• REPLACE if necessary.
	• Check rear suspension for loose / worn rear shock absorber struts, suspension arm retaining fasteners.	• TIGHTEN all retaining fasteners.

FM6029600224020X

Fig. 2 Steering systems symptom chart (Part 1 of 3). 01–02 Crown Victoria, Grand Marquis & Town Car

Condition	Possible Source	Action
• Heavy Steering Efforts, Poor Assist or Loss of Assist — Condition Recognized by the Driver While Turning Corners and During Parking Maneuvers	• Low power steering pump fluid.	• FILL as required and CHECK for system leaks.
	• Steering gear assembly external or internal leak.	
	• Power steering pump external leak.	• REPLACE power steering pump.
	• Improper drive belt tension.	• ADJUST drive belt tension.
	• Hose or cooler external leak.	• SERVICE / REPLACE as necessary.
	• Improper engine idle speed.	• ADJUST idle.
	• Power steering pump pulley loose or warped.	• REPLACE power steering pump pulley.
	• Power steering pump flow / pressure not to specifications.	
	• Hose or cooler line restriction.	• CLEAN or REPLACE as necessary.
	• Check steering gear adjustments.	
	• System contamination.	• INSPECT system for foreign objects, kinked hose, etc. —FLUSH system.
	• EVO power steering control valve actuator sticking.	• Vehicles with air suspension, GO to Pinpoint Test B. • Vehicles without air suspension, GO to Pinpoint Test A.
• Fluid Leakage	• Overfilled system.	• CORRECT fluid level as required.
	• Component leak.	• LOCATE suspect component, and
• Power Steering Pump Leaks, EVO Power Steering Control Valve Actuator	• Damaged EVO power steering control valve actuator ring.	• Vehicles without air suspension, GO to Pinpoint Test A. Vehicles with air suspension, GO to Pinpoint Test B.
	• EVO power steering control valve actuator electrical connector damaged.	
	• EVO power steering control valve actuator damaged.	

FM6029600224040X

Fig. 2 Steering systems symptom chart (Part 3 of 3). 2001–02 Crown Victoria, Grand Marquis & Town Car

Condition	Possible Source	Action
• Feedback (Rattle, Chuckle, Knocking Noises in Steering Gear) — Condition Where Roughness is Felt in the Steering Wheel by the Driver When the Vehicle is Driven Over Rough Pavement	• Steering column gear input shaft coupling joints loose / worn.	• REPLACE steering column intermediate shaft coupling assembly.
	• Loose tie rod ends.	• REPLACE tie rod ends.
	• Steering gear retaining bolts loose or damaged.	• REPLACE retaining bolts and tighten.
	• Steering column gear input shaft coupling connecting bolts loose.	• TIGHTEN bolts to specification at steering gear and at steering column intermediate shaft coupling.
	• Loose suspension bushings / fasteners or ball joints.	• TIGHTEN suspension fasteners, REPLACE worn bushings, or REPLACE ball joints.
	• Check steering gear adjustments.	
	• Check steering column conditions.	
• Poor Returnability, Sticky Feel — Condition Noticed When the Steering Fails to Return to Center Following a Turn Without Manual Effort From the Driver. In Addition, When the Driver Returns the Steering Wheel to Center, it May Have a Sticky or Catchy Feel	• Improper tire pressure.	• ADJUST tire pressures.
	• Improper tire size or incorrect type.	• REPLACE as required.
	• Misaligned steering column or column flange rubbing steering wheel and / or flange.	• ALIGN steering column.
	• Steering column gear input shaft coupling universal joints binding.	• REPLACE steering column intermediate shaft coupling assembly.
	• Check for steering column tube boot tears and / or evidence of binding or damage to tie rod ends.	• REPLACE as necessary.
	• Damaged / worn front suspension components.	• INSPECT control arm ball joints.
	• Improper wheel alignment.	• ADJUST toe as required.
	• Column bearing binding.	• REPLACE bearing.
	• Contamination in system.	• FLUSH power steering system as outlined under Cleaning and Inspection.
	• Check steering gear adjustments.	
• Light Steering Efforts at All Vehicle Speeds	• Electronic variable orifice (EVO actuator).	• Vehicles with air suspension, GO to Pinpoint Test B1. Vehicles without air suspension, GO to Pinpoint Test DTC 28.
• Excessive Steering Effort While Making Quick Maneuvers at High Speed	• Steering sensor.	• Vehicles with air suspension, GO to Pinpoint Test B. Vehicles without air suspension, GO to Pinpoint Test DTC 33.

FM6029600224030X

Fig. 2 Steering systems symptom chart (Part 2 of 3). 2001–02 Crown Victoria, Grand Marquis & Town Car

Condition	Possible Sources	Action
• No communication with the front electronics module	• Circuit. • Module.	• REFER to MOTOR's "Domestic Engine Performance & Driveability Manual"
• Hard steering or lack of assist	• Seized lower steering column shaft U-joints.	• INSTALL a new lower steering column shaft.
	• Damaged, fractured steering column bearing(s).	• REPAIR the steering column.
	• Power steering pump.	• Check Pump Flow.
	• Suspension components.	• Inspect for suspension system
	• Steering gear internal leakage.	• Check Pump Flow.
• Excessive steering pump noise	• Power steering pump.	• Check Pump Flow.
• Excessive steering wheel play	• Damaged, loose, or worn tie-rod end (3290).	• Inspect Steering Linkage Component
	• Loose, worn or damaged tie-rod (3280).	
	• Damaged/worn steering gear.	• INSTALL a new steering gear.
	• Loose, worn or damaged steering column bearing(s).	• INSTALL new steering column bearing(s).
	• Loose or damaged lower steering column shaft U-joint(s).	• INSTALL a new lower steering column shaft.
• Wander	• Unevenly loaded or overloaded vehicle.	• INFORM the customer of incorrect vehicle loading.
	• Loose, worn or damaged tie-rod.	
	• Loose, worn or damaged tie-rod ends.	
	• Loose or damaged steering gear mounting bolts.	• INSTALL new bolts or TIGHTEN the bolts.
	• Loose lower steering column shaft U-joint bolts.	• TIGHTEN the bolts.
	• Loose, worn or damaged lower steering column shaft U-joints.	• INSTALL a new lower steering column shaft.
	• Loose, worn or damaged steering column bearing(s).	• INSTALL new steering column bearings.

ARM66FM000000242

Fig. 3 Steering systems symptom chart (Part 1 of 2). Marauder & 2003–05 Crown Victoria, Grand Marquis & Town Car

Condition	Possible Sources	Action
• Drift/pull	• Unevenly loaded or overloaded vehicle. • Wheel alignment.	• INFORM the customer of incorrect vehicle loading. • ADJUST as required.
	• Loose, worn or damaged tie-rod. • Loose, worn or damaged tie-rod ends.	• INSPECT steering components • INSPECT
	• The steering gear valve effort out of balance.	• CHECK valve operation.
	• Check the brake system for correct operation. • Incorrect frame/underbody alignment.	• CORRECT as required.
• Feedback	• Loose, worn or damaged tie-rod. • Loose, worn or damaged tie-rod ends. • Loose or damaged steering gear insulators or bolts. • Loose lower steering column shaft U-joint bolts. • Loose suspension bushings, fasteners or ball joints. • Worn or damaged steering column bearing(s).	• INSPECT • INSPECT • INSTALL new bolts or TIGHTEN the retaining bolts. • TIGHTEN the bolts. • INSTALL new as necessary. • INSTALL new steering column bearing(s).
• Poor returnability/sticky steering	• Binding lower steering column shaft U-joints. • Loose, worn or damaged front wheel spindle tie-rod. • Loose, worn or damaged tie-rod ends. • Suspension components. • Binding steering column bearing(s).	• INSTALL a new lower steering column shaft. • INSPECT • INSPECT • INSTALL new steering column bearing(s).
• Shimmy	• Loose, worn or damaged tie-rod end. • Loose, worn or damaged tie-rod. • Suspension components.	• INSPECT • INSPECT • INSPECT

ARM66FM000000243

Fig. 3 Steering systems symptom chart (Part 2 of 2). Marauder & 2003–05 Crown Victoria, Grand Marquis & Town Car

Condition	Possible Source	Action
• Power Steering Pump / Remote Power Steering Oil Reservoir Leaks	• Excessive fluid fill. • Fluid cap missing, loose, damaged or missing O-ring. • Loose or damaged hose fittings. • Leakage at shaft seal or any visible point on pump.	• ADJUST fluid to proper level. • SERVICE or REPLACE, if required. • SERVICE or REPLACE. • REPLACE power steering pump.
• Power Steering Pump — No or Poor Assist	• Contamination can be caused by foreign objects in the power steering oil reservoir or power steering pump or metallic particles being generated by cam pack discrepancies.	• Thoroughly flush system when installing a serviced or new power steering pump.
• Moan or Whine Type Noise	• Fluid aeration. • Power steering pump loose or misaligned on engine. • Low fluid. • Hose grounded. • Steering column grounded. • Damaged internal components.	• PURGE the power steering system to reduce aeration noise. • TIGHTEN or ALIGN as required. • CHECK fluid level. • CHECK for hose being grounded. • CHECK steering column tube alignment. • REPLACE power steering pump.

FM6029600225020X

Fig. 4 Power steering pump noise symptom chart (Part 2 of 2). 2001–02 Crown Victoria, Grand Marquis & Town Car

Condition	Possible Source	Action
• Drive Belt Squeal (Particularly at Full Steering Wheel Travel and Stand Still Parking)	• Loose drive belt.	• ADJUST drive belt tension to specification.
• Chirp Noise in Steering Pump	• Loose or worn drive belt.	• ADJUST drive belt tension to specification or REPLACE drive belt.
• Power Steering Pump Noisy	• Low fluid level and possible leak.	• REFILL to specified level. PURGE air from system. CHECK for leaks. SERVICE as required.
• Swish Type Noise	• A noise created by the flow of excessive fluid into the bypass port of the pump valve housing (with temperature below 55°C (130°F). The shearing effect of the cooler (heavier) fluid is not detrimental to power steering pump operation.	• A normal condition. Noise will diminish with fluid temperature increase.
• Clicking Type Noise	• Excessive power steering pump wear.	• REPLACE power steering pump.

FM6029600225010X

Fig. 4 Power steering pump noise symptom chart (Part 1 of 2). 2001–02 Crown Victoria, Grand Marquis & Town Car

Condition	Possible Sources	Action
• Power steering pump noisy	• Low fluid level and possible leakage. • Plugged reservoir filter. • Power steering pump.	• FILL reservoir to specified level. CHECK for leaks. REPAIR as necessary. • INSTALL a new reservoir; • INSTALL a new power steering pump;

ARM66FM000000244

Fig. 5 Power steering pump noise symptom chart. Marauder & 2003–05 Crown Victoria, Grand Marquis & Town Car

DIAGNOSTIC CHART INDEX

Test/Code	Description	Page No.	Fig. No.
CROWN VICTORIA, GRAND MARQUIS & MARAUDER			
—	Symptom chart	15-23	6
Test A	No Communication w/EVO Control Module	15-23	7
Test B	No Communication w/Air Suspension Control Module	15-24	8
Test C	Unable To Enter Auto Test — EVO Control Module	15-24	9
Test D	Unable To Enter Auto Test– Air Suspension Control Module	15-24	10
Test E	EVO Actuator	15-25	11
Code 16	EVO Actuator Shorted	15-25	11
Code 17	EVO Actuator Shorted or Open	15-25	11
Code 18	EVO Actuator Resistance Out Of Range	15-25	11
Code 27	EVO Actuator Circuit Open	15-26	12
Code 28	EVO Actuator Circuit Shorted	15-26	13
Code 29	EVO Actuator Circuit High Side Shorted To Ground	15-27	14
Code 30	EVO Actuator Circuit Shorted To Battery	15-27	15
Code 31	EVO Actuator Circuit Low Side Shorted To Ground	15-27	16
Code 33	Steering Rotation Not Detected	15-28	17
Code 35	Vehicle Speed Above 15 mph Not Detected	15-28	18
Code 74	Steering Rotation Not Detected	15-29	19
TOWN CAR			
—	Symptom Chart	15-30	20
Test A	Steering Sensor Circuit Failure	15-30	21
Test B	Steering VAPS II Circuit Loop Failure	15-31	22
Test C	Steering Is Very Difficult/Very Easy	15-32	23
Test D	Steering Does Not Vary w/Increased Wheel Rotation	15-32	24
Test E	Steering Does Not Vary w/Vehicle Speed	15-33	25
Test F	No Communication w/Rear Air Suspension Control Module	15-33	26
Code C1441	Steering Sensor Circuit Failure	15-30	21
Code C1442	Steering Sensor Circuit Failure	15-30	21
Code C1897	Steering VAPS II Circuit Loop Failure	15-31	22

Condition	Possible Source	Action
• No communication with the EVO control module	• CJB Fuse: — 5 (15A). • Battery junction box (BJB) Fuse: — 8 (30A). • Circuitry. • EVO control module.	• GO to Pinpoint Test A.
• No communication with the air suspension control module	• CJB Fuse: — 5 (15A). • BJB Fuse: — 8 (30A). • Circuitry. • Air suspension control module.	• GO to Pinpoint Test B.
• Unable to enter auto test — EVO control module	• CJB Fuse: — 5 (15A). • BJB Fuse: — 8 (30A). • Circuitry. • EVO control module.	• GO to Pinpoint Test C.
• Unable to enter auto test — air suspension control module	• CJB Fuse: — 5 (15A). • BJB Fuse: — 8 (30A). • Circuitry. • Air suspension control module.	• GO to Pinpoint Test D.
• Steering very difficult/very easy	• Power steering pump actuator valve. • Circuitry open/shorted. • EVO control module. • Air suspension control module.	• PERFORM actuator output test and steering wheel sensor test. PERFORM Pinpoint Test E (with air suspension).
• Steering does not vary with increased wheel rotation	• Steering wheel rotation sensor inoperative. • Open/shorted circuitry.	• PERFORM Steering Wheel Sensor Test. PERFORM Pinpoint Test E (with air suspension).

FM6029900334000X

Fig. 6 Symptom chart. Crown Victoria, Grand Marquis & Marauder

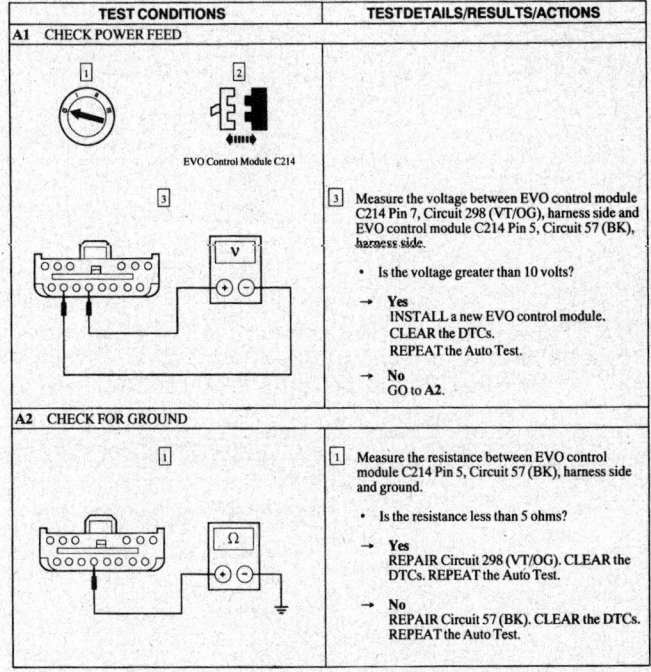

FM6029900335000X

Fig. 7 Test A: No Communication w/EVO Control Module. Crown Victoria, Grand Marquis & Marauder

TEST CONDITIONS	TEST DETAILS/RESULTS/ACTIONS
B1 CHECK CIRCUIT 1053 (LB/PK) AND CIRCUIT 298 (VT/OG) FOR AN OPEN	

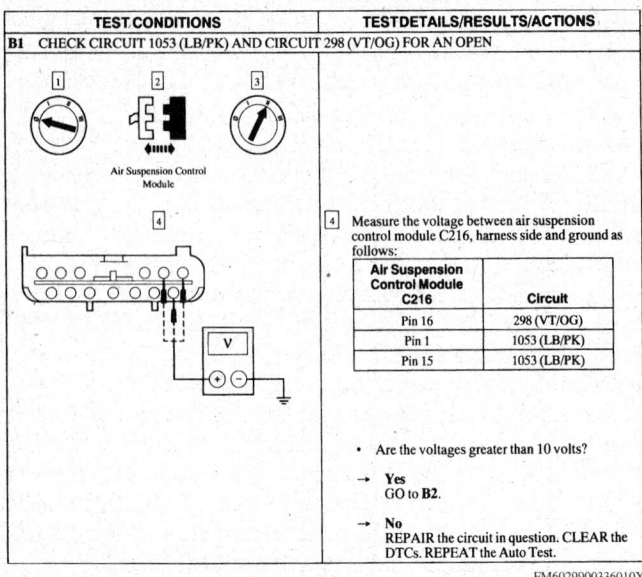

4. Measure the voltage between air suspension control module C216, harness side and ground as follows:

Air Suspension Control Module C216	Circuit
Pin 16	298 (VT/OG)
Pin 1	1053 (LB/PK)
Pin 15	1053 (LB/PK)

- Are the voltages greater than 10 volts?

→ **Yes**
GO to **B2**.

→ **No**
REPAIR the circuit in question. CLEAR the DTCs. REPEAT the Auto Test.

FM6029900336010X

Fig. 8   Test B: No Communication w/Air Suspension Control Module. (Part 1 of 4). Crown Victoria, Grand Marquis & Marauder

TEST CONDITIONS	TEST DETAILS/RESULTS/ACTIONS
B4 CHECK CIRCUIT 419 (DG/LG) FOR VOLTAGE AT THE AIR SUSPENSION TEST CONNECTOR	

1. Measure the voltage between air suspension test connector C459 Pin 4, Circuit 419 (DG/LG), harness side and ground.

- Is the voltage greater than 10 volts?

→ **Yes**
GO to **B5**.

→ **No**
REPAIR the circuit. CLEAR the DTCs. REPEAT the Auto Test.

TEST CONDITIONS	
B5 CHECK CIRCUIT 844 (GY/RD)	

1. Measure the resistance between air suspension control module C215 Pin 9, Circuit 844 (GY/RD), harness side and air suspension test connector C459 Pin 5, Circuit 844 (GY/RD), harness side; and between air suspension control module C215 Pin 9, Circuit 844 (GY/RD), harness side and ground.

- Is the resistance less than 5 ohms between air suspension control module and air suspension test connector; and greater than 10,000 ohms between air suspension control module and ground?

→ **Yes**
GO to **B6**.

→ **No**
REPAIR the circuit. CLEAR the DTCs. REPEAT the Auto Test.

FM6029900336030X

Fig. 8   Test B: No Communication w/Air Suspension Control Module. (Part 3 of 4). Crown Victoria, Grand Marquis & Marauder

TEST CONDITIONS	TEST DETAILS/RESULTS/ACTIONS
C1 CHECK COMMUNICATION TO THE EVO CONTROL MODULE	

1. Check communication between the Super Star II Tester and the EVO control module.

- Does the Super Star II Tester communicate?

→ **Yes**
INSTALL a new EVO control module. REPEAT the Auto Test.

→ **No**
GO to Pinpoint Test A.

FM6029900337000X

Fig. 9   Test C: Unable To Enter Auto Test — EVO Control Module. Crown Victoria, Grand Marquis & Marauder

TEST CONDITIONS	TEST DETAILS/RESULTS/ACTIONS
B2 CHECK CIRCUIT 57 (BK) AND CIRCUIT 676 (PK/OG) FOR AN OPEN	

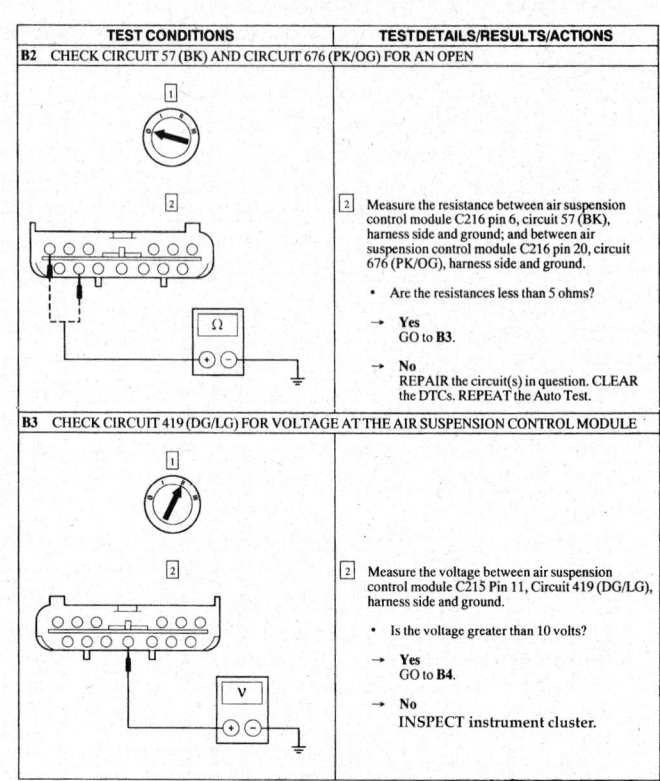

2. Measure the resistance between air suspension control module C216 pin 6, circuit 57 (BK), harness side and ground; and between air suspension control module C216 pin 20, circuit 676 (PK/OG), harness side and ground.

- Are the resistances less than 5 ohms?

→ **Yes**
GO to **B3**.

→ **No**
REPAIR the circuit(s) in question. CLEAR the DTCs. REPEAT the Auto Test.

B3 CHECK CIRCUIT 419 (DG/LG) FOR VOLTAGE AT THE AIR SUSPENSION CONTROL MODULE	

2. Measure the voltage between air suspension control module C215 Pin 11, Circuit 419 (DG/LG), harness side and ground.

- Is the voltage greater than 10 volts?

→ **Yes**
GO to **B4**.

→ **No**
INSPECT instrument cluster.

FM6029900336020X

Fig. 8   Test B: No Communication w/Air Suspension Control Module. (Part 2 of 4). Crown Victoria, Grand Marquis & Marauder

TEST CONDITIONS	TEST DETAILS/RESULTS/ACTIONS
B6 CHECK CIRCUIT 432 (BK/PK)	

1. Measure the resistance between air suspension control module C215 Pin 8, Circuit 432 (BK/PK), harness side and air suspension test connector C459 Pin 2, Circuit 432 (BK/PK), harness side; and between air suspension control module C215 Pin 9, Circuit 432 (BK/PK), harness side and ground.

- Is the resistance less than 5 ohms between air suspension control module and air suspension test connector; and greater than 10,000 ohms between air suspension control module and ground?

→ **Yes**
INSTALL a new air suspension control module. REPEAT the Auto Test.

→ **No**
REPAIR the circuit. CLEAR the DTCs. REPEAT the Auto Test.

FM6029900336040X

Fig. 8   Test B: No Communication w/Air Suspension Control Module. (Part 4 of 4). Crown Victoria, Grand Marquis & Marauder

TEST CONDITIONS	TEST DETAILS/RESULTS/ACTIONS
D1 CHECK COMMUNICATION TO THE AIR SUSPENSION CONTROL MODULE	

1. Check communication between the Super Star II Tester and the air suspension control module.

- Does the Super Star II Tester communicate?

→ **Yes**
INSTALL a new air suspension control module. REPEAT the Auto Test.

→ **No**
GO to Pinpoint Test B.

FM6029900338000X

Fig. 10   Test D: Unable To Enter Auto Test — Air Suspension Control Module. Crown Victoria & Grand Marquis

TEST CONDITIONS	TEST DETAILS/RESULTS/ACTIONS
E1 EVO ACTUATOR VALVE CHECK (DTC 16)	

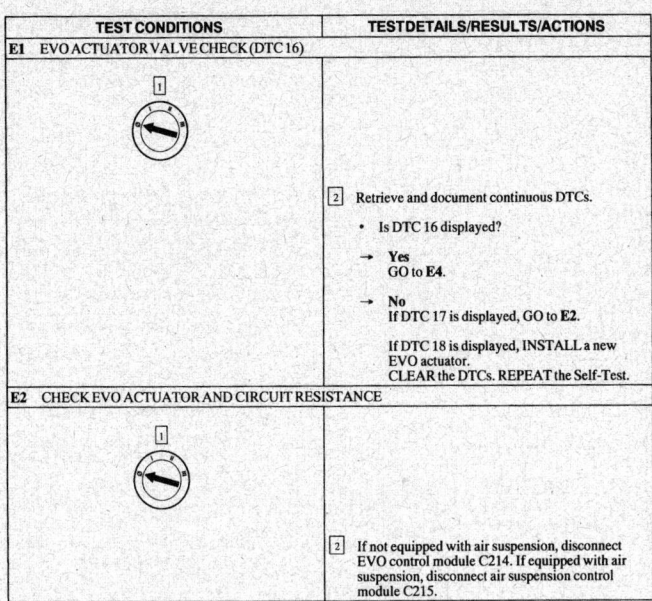

2. Retrieve and document continuous DTCs.
- Is DTC 16 displayed?
  → **Yes**
     GO to **E4**.
  → **No**
     If DTC 17 is displayed, GO to **E2**.
     If DTC 18 is displayed, INSTALL a new EVO actuator. CLEAR the DTCs. REPEAT the Self-Test.

TEST CONDITIONS	TEST DETAILS/RESULTS/ACTIONS
E2 CHECK EVO ACTUATOR AND CIRCUIT RESISTANCE	

2. If not equipped with air suspension, disconnect EVO control module C214. If equipped with air suspension, disconnect air suspension control module C215.

FM6029900339010X

Fig. 11 Test E — Code 16: EVO Actuator Shorted; Code 17: EVO Actuator Shorted or Open; Code 18: EVO Actuator Resistance Out Of Range (Part 1 of 6). Crown Victoria, Grand Marquis & Marauder

TEST CONDITIONS	TEST DETAILS/RESULTS/ACTIONS
E3 CHECK CIRCUITS 86 (GY/OG) AND 87 (TN/YE)	

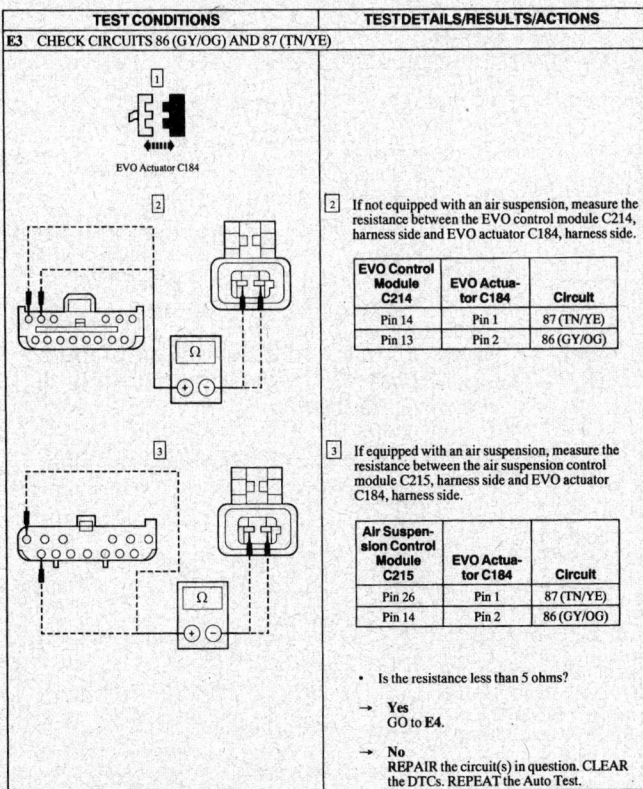

EVO Actuator C184

2. If not equipped with an air suspension, measure the resistance between the EVO control module C214, harness side and EVO actuator C184, harness side.

EVO Control Module C214	EVO Actuator C184	Circuit
Pin 14	Pin 1	87 (TN/YE)
Pin 13	Pin 2	86 (GY/OG)

3. If equipped with an air suspension, measure the resistance between the air suspension control module C215, harness side and EVO actuator C184, harness side.

Air Suspension Control Module C215	EVO Actuator C184	Circuit
Pin 26	Pin 1	87 (TN/YE)
Pin 14	Pin 2	86 (GY/OG)

- Is the resistance less than 5 ohms?
  → **Yes**
     GO to **E4**.
  → **No**
     REPAIR the circuit(s) in question. CLEAR the DTCs. REPEAT the Auto Test.

FM6029900339030X

Fig. 11 Test E — Code 16: EVO Actuator Shorted; Code 17: EVO Actuator Shorted or Open; Code 18: EVO Actuator Resistance Out Of Range (Part 3 of 6). Crown Victoria, Grand Marquis & Marauder

TEST CONDITIONS	TEST DETAILS/RESULTS/ACTIONS
E2 CHECK EVO ACTUATOR AND CIRCUIT RESISTANCE	

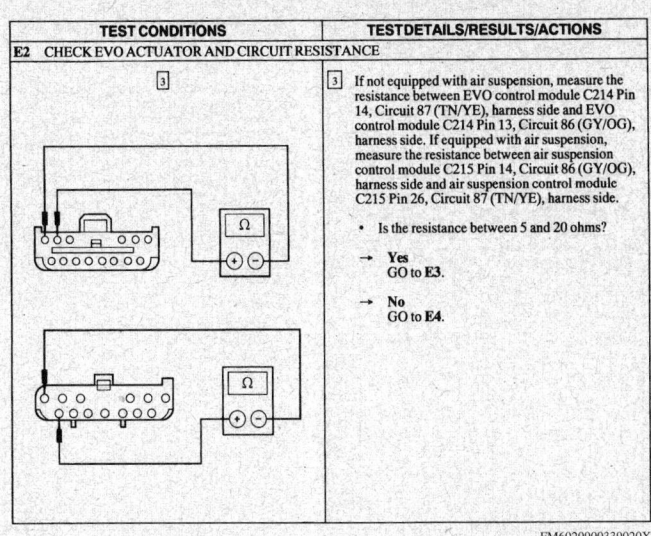

3. If not equipped with air suspension, measure the resistance between EVO control module C214 Pin 14, Circuit 87 (TN/YE), harness side and EVO control module C214 Pin 13, Circuit 86 (GY/OG), harness side. If equipped with air suspension, measure the resistance between air suspension control module C215 Pin 14, Circuit 86 (GY/OG), harness side and air suspension control module C215 Pin 26, Circuit 87 (TN/YE), harness side.

- Is the resistance between 5 and 20 ohms?
  → **Yes**
     GO to **E3**.
  → **No**
     GO to **E4**.

FM6029900339020X

Fig. 11 Test E — Code 16: EVO Actuator Shorted; Code 17: EVO Actuator Shorted or Open; Code 18: EVO Actuator Resistance Out Of Range (Part 2 of 6). Crown Victoria, Grand Marquis & Marauder

TEST CONDITIONS	TEST DETAILS/RESULTS/ACTIONS
E4 CHECK EVO ACTUATOR RESISTANCE	

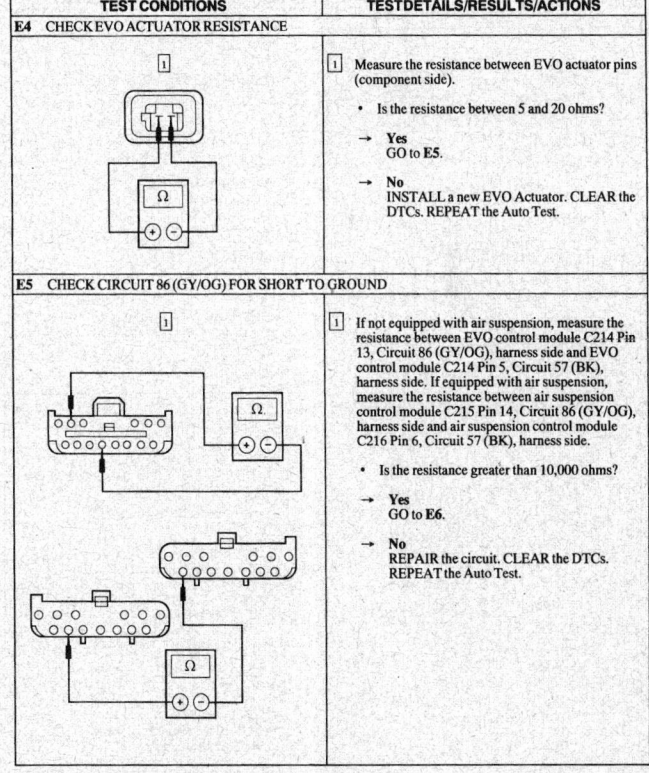

1. Measure the resistance between EVO actuator pins (component side).

- Is the resistance between 5 and 20 ohms?
  → **Yes**
     GO to **E5**.
  → **No**
     INSTALL a new EVO Actuator. CLEAR the DTCs. REPEAT the Auto Test.

TEST CONDITIONS	TEST DETAILS/RESULTS/ACTIONS
E5 CHECK CIRCUIT 86 (GY/OG) FOR SHORT TO GROUND	

1. If not equipped with air suspension, measure the resistance between EVO control module C214 Pin 13, Circuit 86 (GY/OG), harness side and EVO control module C214 Pin 5, Circuit 57 (BK), harness side. If equipped with air suspension, measure the resistance between air suspension control module C215 Pin 14, Circuit 86 (GY/OG), harness side and air suspension control module C216 Pin 6, Circuit 57 (BK), harness side.

- Is the resistance greater than 10,000 ohms?
  → **Yes**
     GO to **E6**.
  → **No**
     REPAIR the circuit. CLEAR the DTCs. REPEAT the Auto Test.

FM6029900339040X

Fig. 11 Test E — Code 16: EVO Actuator Shorted; Code 17: EVO Actuator Shorted or Open; Code 18: EVO Actuator Resistance Out Of Range (Part 4 of 6). Crown Victoria, Grand Marquis & Marauder

TEST CONDITIONS	TESTDETAILS/RESULTS/ACTIONS
E6 CHECK CIRCUIT 87 (TN/YE) FOR SHORT TO GROUND	

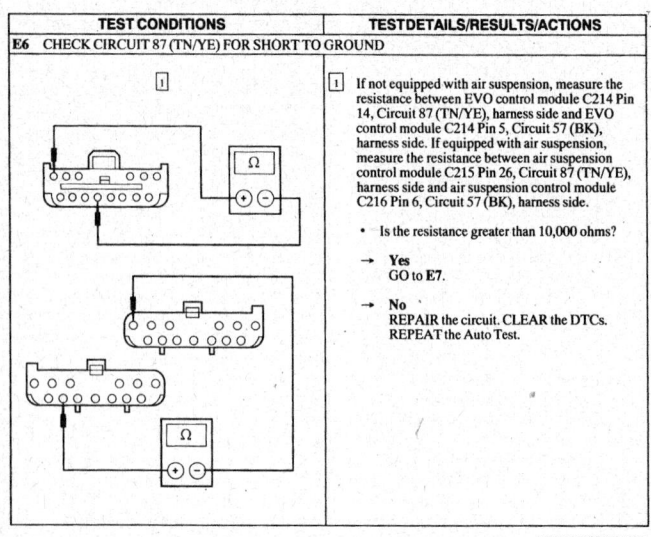

| | 1 If not equipped with air suspension, measure the resistance between EVO control module C214 Pin 14, Circuit 87 (TN/YE), harness side and EVO control module C214 Pin 5, Circuit 57 (BK), harness side. If equipped with air suspension, measure the resistance between air suspension control module C215 Pin 26, Circuit 87 (TN/YE), harness side and air suspension control module C216 Pin 6, Circuit 57 (BK), harness side. • Is the resistance greater than 10,000 ohms? → Yes GO to E7. → No REPAIR the circuit. CLEAR the DTCs. REPEAT the Auto Test. |

FM6029900339050X

Fig. 11 Test E — Code 16: EVO Actuator Shorted; Code 17: EVO Actuator Shorted or Open; Code 18: EVO Actuator Resistance Out Of Range (Part 5 of 6). Crown Victoria, Grand Marquis & Marauder

TEST CONDITIONS	TESTDETAILS/RESULTS/ACTIONS
F1 CHECK EVO ACTUATOR FOR AN OPEN	

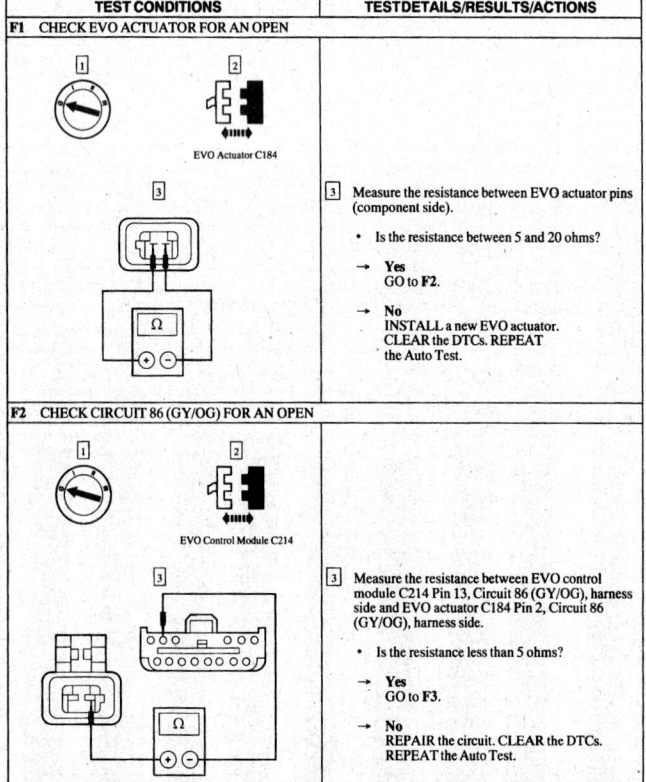

	3 Measure the resistance between EVO actuator pins (component side). • Is the resistance between 5 and 20 ohms? → Yes GO to F2. → No INSTALL a new EVO actuator. CLEAR the DTCs. REPEAT the Auto Test.
F2 CHECK CIRCUIT 86 (GY/OG) FOR AN OPEN	
	3 Measure the resistance between EVO control module C214 Pin 13, Circuit 86 (GY/OG), harness side and EVO actuator C184 Pin 2, Circuit 86 (GY/OG), harness side. • Is the resistance less than 5 ohms? → Yes GO to F3. → No REPAIR the circuit. CLEAR the DTCs. REPEAT the Auto Test.

FM6029900340010X

Fig. 12 Code 27: EVO Actuator Circuit Open (Part 1 of 2). Crown Victoria, Grand Marquis & Marauder

TEST CONDITIONS	TESTDETAILS/RESULTS/ACTIONS
E7 CHECK FOR SHORT TO BATTERY	

| | 2 If not equipped with air suspension, measure the voltage between EVO control module C214 Pin 13, Circuit 86 (GY/OG), harness side and ground; and between EVO control module C214 Pin 14, Circuit 87 (TN/YE), harness side and ground. If equipped with air suspension, measure the voltage between air suspension control module C215 Pin 14, Circuit 86 (GY/OG), harness side and ground; and between air suspension control module C215 Pin 26, Circuit 87 (TN/YE), harness side and ground. • Are the resistances greater than 10,000 ohms? → Yes If not equipped with air suspension, INSTALL a new EVO control module. CLEAR the DTCs. REPEAT the Auto Test. If equipped with air suspension, INSTALL a new air suspension module. CLEAR the DTCs. REPEAT the Auto Test. → No REPAIR the circuit(s) in question. CLEAR the DTCs. REPEAT the Auto Test. |

FM6029900339060X

Fig. 11 Test E — Code 16: EVO Actuator Shorted; Code 17: EVO Actuator Shorted or Open; Code 18: EVO Actuator Resistance Out Of Range (Part 6 of 6). Crown Victoria, Grand Marquis & Marauder

TEST CONDITIONS	TESTDETAILS/RESULTS/ACTIONS
F3 CHECK CIRCUIT 87 (TN/YE) FOR AN OPEN	

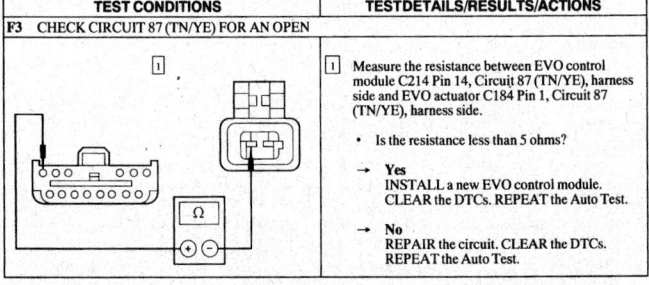

| | 1 Measure the resistance between EVO control module C214 Pin 14, Circuit 87 (TN/YE), harness side and EVO actuator C184 Pin 1, Circuit 87 (TN/YE), harness side. • Is the resistance less than 5 ohms? → Yes INSTALL a new EVO control module. CLEAR the DTCs. REPEAT the Auto Test. → No REPAIR the circuit. CLEAR the DTCs. REPEAT the Auto Test. |

FM6029900340020X

Fig. 12 Code 27: EVO Actuator Circuit Open (Part 2 of 2). Crown Victoria, Grand Marquis & Marauder

TEST CONDITIONS	TESTDETAILS/RESULTS/ACTIONS
G1 CHECK EVO ACTUATOR FOR A SHORT	

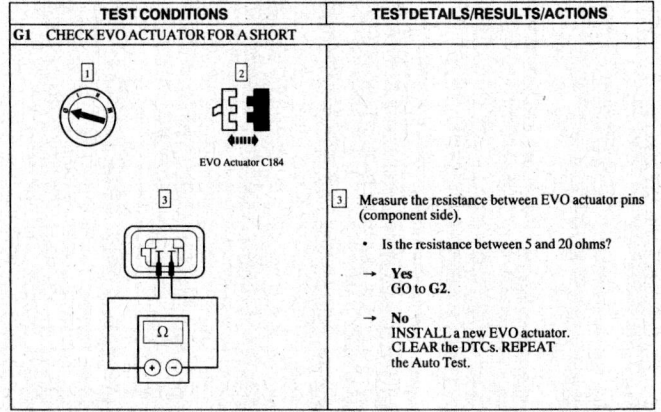

| | 3 Measure the resistance between EVO actuator pins (component side). • Is the resistance between 5 and 20 ohms? → Yes GO to G2. → No INSTALL a new EVO actuator. CLEAR the DTCs. REPEAT the Auto Test. |

FM6029900341010X

Fig. 13 Code 28: EVO Actuator Circuit Shorted (Part 1 of 3). Crown Victoria, Grand Marquis & Marauder

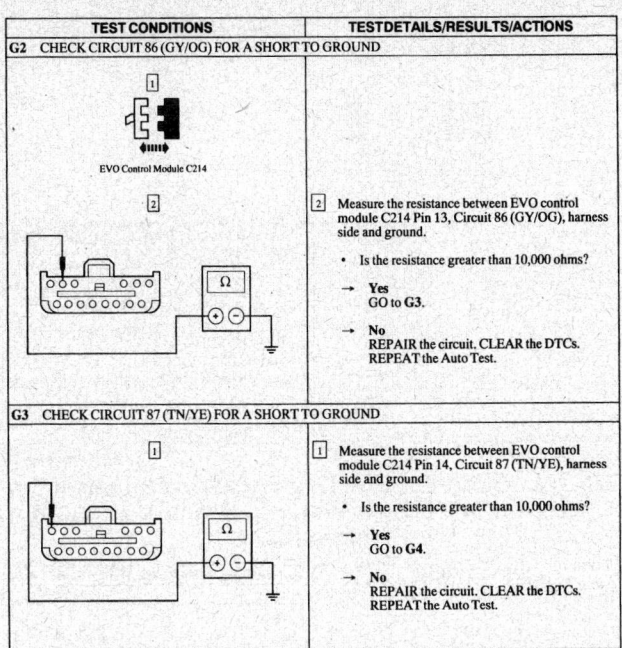

TEST CONDITIONS	TESTDETAILS/RESULTS/ACTIONS
G2 CHECK CIRCUIT 86 (GY/OG) FOR A SHORT TO GROUND	

EVO Control Module C214

2   Measure the resistance between EVO control module C214 Pin 13, Circuit 86 (GY/OG), harness side and ground.

- Is the resistance greater than 10,000 ohms?
  - → **Yes**   GO to **G3**.
  - → **No**   REPAIR the circuit. CLEAR the DTCs. REPEAT the Auto Test.

TEST CONDITIONS	TESTDETAILS/RESULTS/ACTIONS
G3 CHECK CIRCUIT 87 (TN/YE) FOR A SHORT TO GROUND	

1   Measure the resistance between EVO control module C214 Pin 14, Circuit 87 (TN/YE), harness side and ground.

- Is the resistance greater than 10,000 ohms?
  - → **Yes**   GO to **G4**.
  - → **No**   REPAIR the circuit. CLEAR the DTCs. REPEAT the Auto Test.

FM6029900341020X

Fig. 13   Code 28: EVO Actuator Circuit Shorted (Part 2 of 3). Crown Victoria, Grand Marquis & Marauder

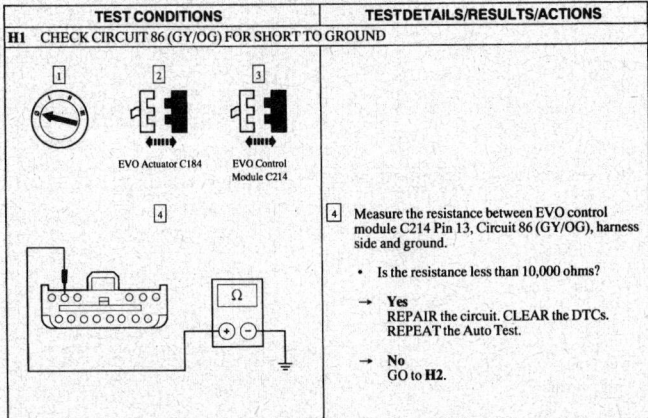

TEST CONDITIONS	TESTDETAILS/RESULTS/ACTIONS
H1 CHECK CIRCUIT 86 (GY/OG) FOR SHORT TO GROUND	

EVO Actuator C184   EVO Control Module C214

4   Measure the resistance between EVO control module C214 Pin 13, Circuit 86 (GY/OG), harness side and ground.

- Is the resistance less than 10,000 ohms?
  - → **Yes**   REPAIR the circuit. CLEAR the DTCs. REPEAT the Auto Test.
  - → **No**   GO to **H2**.

FM6029900342010X

Fig. 14   Code 29: EVO Actuator Circuit High Side Shorted To Ground (Part 1 of 2). Crown Victoria, Grand Marquis & Marauder

TEST CONDITIONS	TESTDETAILS/RESULTS/ACTIONS
I1 CHECK CIRCUIT 86 (GY/OG) FOR SHORT TO BATTERY	

EVO Actuator C184   EVO Control Module C214

4   Measure the voltage between EVO control module C214 Pin 13, Circuit 86 (GY/OG), harness side and ground.

- Is voltage present?
  - → **Yes**   REPAIR the circuit. CLEAR the DTCs. REPEAT the Auto Test.
  - → **No**   GO to **I2**.

FM6029900343010X

Fig. 15   Code 30: EVO Actuator Circuit Shorted To Battery (Part 1 of 2). Crown Victoria, Grand Marquis & Marauder

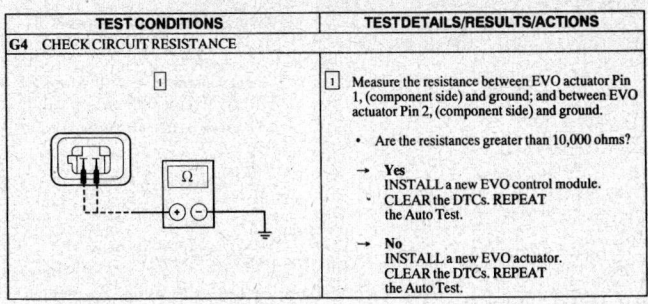

TEST CONDITIONS	TESTDETAILS/RESULTS/ACTIONS
G4 CHECK CIRCUIT RESISTANCE	

1   Measure the resistance between EVO actuator Pin 1, (component side) and ground; and between EVO actuator Pin 2, (component side) and ground.

- Are the resistances greater than 10,000 ohms?
  - → **Yes**   INSTALL a new EVO control module. CLEAR the DTCs. REPEAT the Auto Test.
  - → **No**   INSTALL a new EVO actuator. CLEAR the DTCs. REPEAT the Auto Test.

FM6029900341030X

Fig. 13   Code 28: EVO Actuator Circuit Shorted (Part 3 of 3). Crown Victoria, Grand Marquis & Marauder

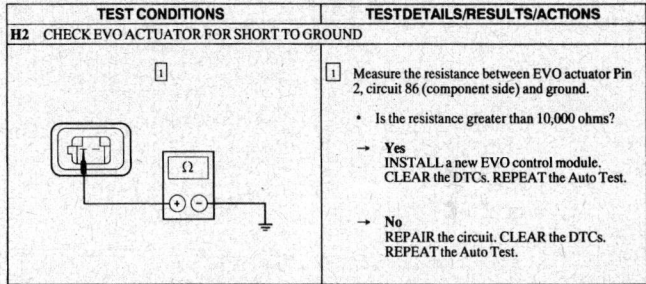

TEST CONDITIONS	TESTDETAILS/RESULTS/ACTIONS
H2 CHECK EVO ACTUATOR FOR SHORT TO GROUND	

1   Measure the resistance between EVO actuator Pin 2, circuit 86 (component side) and ground.

- Is the resistance greater than 10,000 ohms?
  - → **Yes**   INSTALL a new EVO control module. CLEAR the DTCs. REPEAT the Auto Test.
  - → **No**   REPAIR the circuit. CLEAR the DTCs. REPEAT the Auto Test.

FM6029900342020X

Fig. 14   Code 29: EVO Actuator Circuit High Side Shorted To Ground (Part 2 of 2). Crown Victoria, Grand Marquis & Marauder

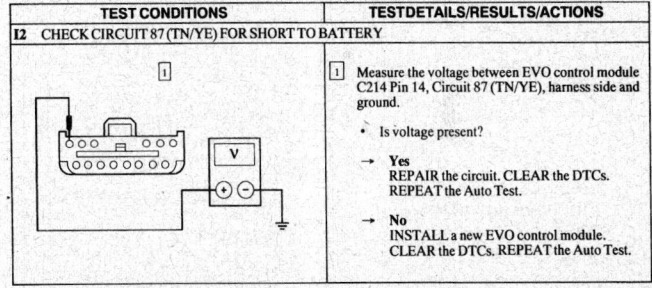

TEST CONDITIONS	TESTDETAILS/RESULTS/ACTIONS
I2 CHECK CIRCUIT 87 (TN/YE) FOR SHORT TO BATTERY	

1   Measure the voltage between EVO control module C214 Pin 14, Circuit 87 (TN/YE), harness side and ground.

- Is voltage present?
  - → **Yes**   REPAIR the circuit. CLEAR the DTCs. REPEAT the Auto Test.
  - → **No**   INSTALL a new EVO control module. CLEAR the DTCs. REPEAT the Auto Test.

FM6029900343020X

Fig. 15   Code 30: EVO Actuator Circuit Shorted To Battery (Part 2 of 2). Crown Victoria, Grand Marquis & Marauder

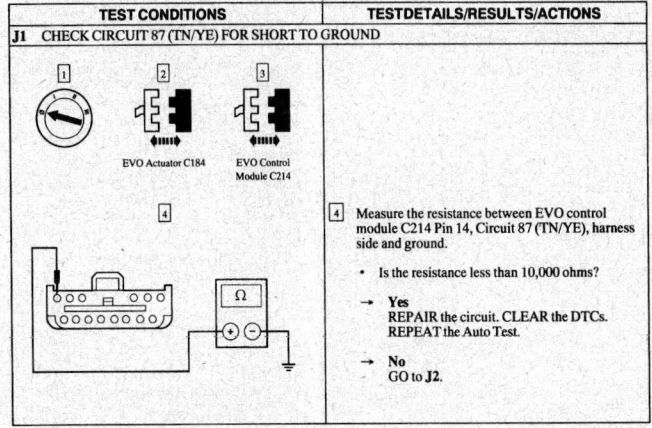

TEST CONDITIONS	TESTDETAILS/RESULTS/ACTIONS
J1 CHECK CIRCUIT 87 (TN/YE) FOR SHORT TO GROUND	

EVO Actuator C184   EVO Control Module C214

4   Measure the resistance between EVO control module C214 Pin 14, Circuit 87 (TN/YE), harness side and ground.

- Is the resistance less than 10,000 ohms?
  - → **Yes**   REPAIR the circuit. CLEAR the DTCs. REPEAT the Auto Test.
  - → **No**   GO to **J2**.

FM6029900344010X

Fig. 16   Code 31: EVO Actuator Circuit Low Side Shorted To Ground (Part 1 of 2). Crown Victoria, Grand Marquis & Marauder

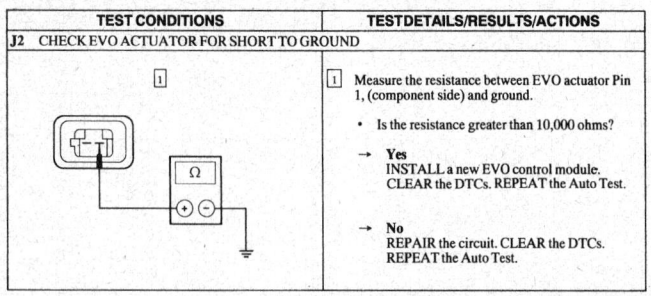

TEST CONDITIONS	TESTDETAILS/RESULTS/ACTIONS
J2 CHECK EVO ACTUATOR FOR SHORT TO GROUND	
1	1 Measure the resistance between EVO actuator Pin 1, (component side) and ground.
	• Is the resistance greater than 10,000 ohms?
	→ **Yes** INSTALL a new EVO control module. CLEAR the DTCs. REPEAT the Auto Test.
	→ **No** REPAIR the circuit. CLEAR the DTCs. REPEAT the Auto Test.

FM6029900344020X

Fig. 16   Code 31: EVO Actuator Circuit Low Side Shorted To Ground (Part 2 of 2). Crown Victoria, Grand Marquis & Marauder

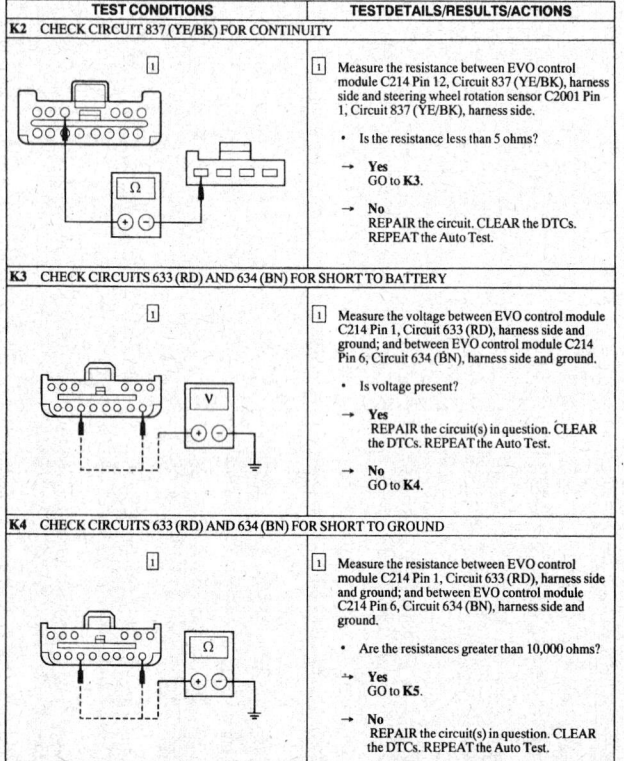

TEST CONDITIONS	TESTDETAILS/RESULTS/ACTIONS
K2 CHECK CIRCUIT 837 (YE/BK) FOR CONTINUITY	
1	1 Measure the resistance between EVO control module C214 Pin 12, Circuit 837 (YE/BK), harness side and steering wheel rotation sensor C2001 Pin 1, Circuit 837 (YE/BK), harness side.
	• Is the resistance less than 5 ohms?
	→ **Yes** GO to **K3**.
	→ **No** REPAIR the circuit. CLEAR the DTCs. REPEAT the Auto Test.
K3 CHECK CIRCUITS 633 (RD) AND 634 (BN) FOR SHORT TO BATTERY	
1	1 Measure the voltage between EVO control module C214 Pin 1, Circuit 633 (RD), harness side and ground; and between EVO control module C214 Pin 6, Circuit 634 (BN), harness side and ground.
	• Is voltage present?
	→ **Yes** REPAIR the circuit(s) in question. CLEAR the DTCs. REPEAT the Auto Test.
	→ **No** GO to **K4**.
K4 CHECK CIRCUITS 633 (RD) AND 634 (BN) FOR SHORT TO GROUND	
1	1 Measure the resistance between EVO control module C214 Pin 1, Circuit 633 (RD), harness side and ground; and between EVO control module C214 Pin 6, Circuit 634 (BN), harness side and ground.
	• Are the resistances greater than 10,000 ohms?
	→ **Yes** GO to **K5**.
	→ **No** REPAIR the circuit(s) in question. CLEAR the DTCs. REPEAT the Auto Test.

FM6029900345020X

Fig. 17   Code 33: Steering Rotation Not Detected (Part 2 of 4). Crown Victoria, Grand Marquis & Marauder

TEST CONDITIONS	TESTDETAILS/RESULTS/ACTIONS
K6 CHECK STEERING WHEEL ROTATION SENSOR	
5	5 **Note:** Touch 73 Digital Multimeter leads together to be sure the audio (beep) function is operational.
	Note: The 73 Digital Multimeter should beep several times while rotating the steering wheel.
	Connect 73 Digital Multimeter leads between EVO control module C214 Pin 1, Circuit 633 (RD), harness side and ground; and between EVO control module C214 Pin 6, Circuit 634 (BN), harness side and ground. Listen for an audible beep while turning the steering wheel one quarter turn in each direction.
	• Does 73 Digital Multimeter beep multiple times in each direction?
	→ **Yes** INSTALL a new EVO control module. CLEAR the DTCs. REPEAT the Auto Test.
	→ **No** INSTALL a new steering wheel rotation sensor. CLEAR the DTCs. REPEAT the Auto Test.

FM6029900345040X

Fig. 17   Code 33: Steering Rotation Not Detected (Part 4 of 4). Crown Victoria, Grand Marquis & Marauder

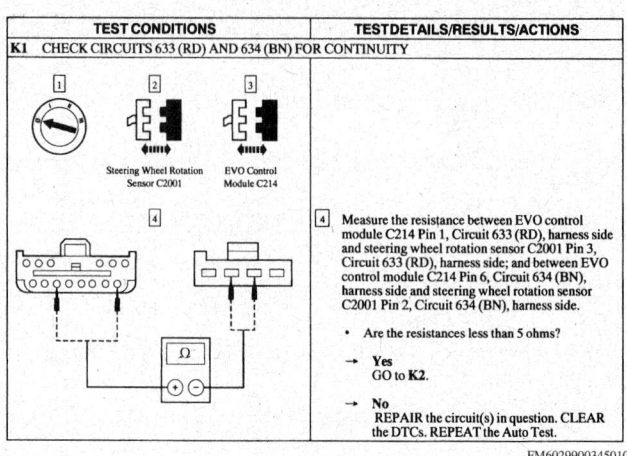

TEST CONDITIONS	TESTDETAILS/RESULTS/ACTIONS
K1 CHECK CIRCUITS 633 (RD) AND 634 (BN) FOR CONTINUITY	
1 2 3	4 Measure the resistance between EVO control module C214 Pin 1, Circuit 633 (RD), harness side and steering wheel rotation sensor C2001 Pin 3, Circuit 633 (RD), harness side; and between EVO control module C214 Pin 6, Circuit 634 (BN), harness side and steering wheel rotation sensor C2001 Pin 2, Circuit 634 (BN), harness side.
4	• Are the resistances less than 5 ohms?
	→ **Yes** GO to **K2**.
	→ **No** REPAIR the circuit(s) in question. CLEAR the DTCs. REPEAT the Auto Test.

FM6029900345010X

Fig. 17   Code 33: Steering Rotation Not Detected (Part 1 of 4). Crown Victoria, Grand Marquis & Marauder

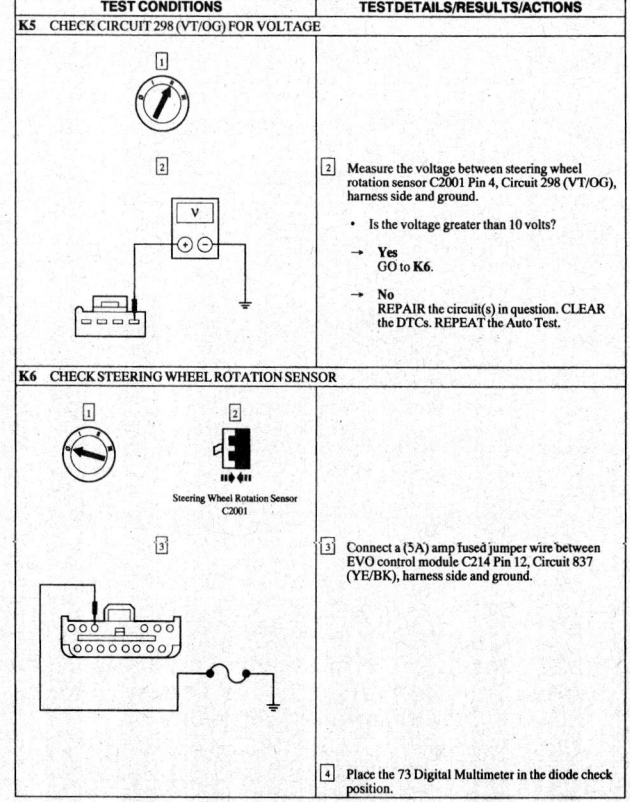

TEST CONDITIONS	TESTDETAILS/RESULTS/ACTIONS
K5 CHECK CIRCUIT 298 (VT/OG) FOR VOLTAGE	
1	2 Measure the voltage between steering wheel rotation sensor C2001 Pin 4, Circuit 298 (VT/OG), harness side and ground.
2	• Is the voltage greater than 10 volts?
	→ **Yes** GO to **K6**.
	→ **No** REPAIR the circuit(s) in question. CLEAR the DTCs. REPEAT the Auto Test.
K6 CHECK STEERING WHEEL ROTATION SENSOR	
1 2	3 Connect a (5A) amp fused jumper wire between EVO control module C214 Pin 12, Circuit 837 (YE/BK), harness side and ground.
3	
	4 Place the 73 Digital Multimeter in the diode check position.

FM6029900345030X

Fig. 17   Code 33: Steering Rotation Not Detected (Part 3 of 4). Crown Victoria, Grand Marquis & Marauder

TEST CONDITIONS	TESTDETAILS/RESULTS/ACTIONS
L1 CHECK SPEEDOMETER OPERATION	
	1 Drive the vehicle and check for correct speedometer operation.
	• Does the speedometer indicate vehicle speeds above 24 km/h (15 mph)?
	→ **Yes** GO to **L2**.
	→ **No** INSPECT instrument cluster. CLEAR the DTCs. REPEAT the Auto Test.

FM6029900346010X

Fig. 18   Code 35: Vehicle Speed Above 15 mph Not Detected (Part 1 of 2). Crown Victoria, Grand Marquis & Marauder

TEST CONDITIONS	TEST DETAILS/RESULTS/ACTIONS
L2 CHECK CIRCUIT 676 (PK/OG) FOR AN OPEN	

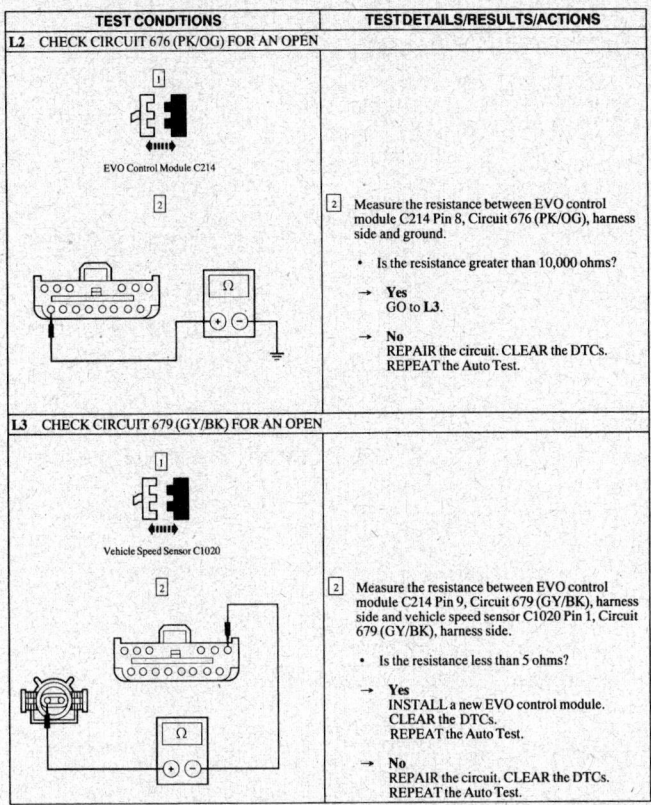

EVO Control Module C214

	2 Measure the resistance between EVO control module C214 Pin 8, Circuit 676 (PK/OG), harness side and ground. • Is the resistance greater than 10,000 ohms? → **Yes** GO to **L3**. → **No** REPAIR the circuit. CLEAR the DTCs. REPEAT the Auto Test.

TEST CONDITIONS	TEST DETAILS/RESULTS/ACTIONS
L3 CHECK CIRCUIT 679 (GY/BK) FOR AN OPEN	

Vehicle Speed Sensor C1020

	2 Measure the resistance between EVO control module C214 Pin 9, Circuit 679 (GY/BK), harness side and vehicle speed sensor C1020 Pin 1, Circuit 679 (GY/BK), harness side. • Is the resistance less than 5 ohms? → **Yes** INSTALL a new EVO control module. CLEAR the DTCs. REPEAT the Auto Test. → **No** REPAIR the circuit. CLEAR the DTCs. REPEAT the Auto Test.

FM6029900346020X

Fig. 18 Code 35: Vehicle Speed Above 15 mph Not Detected (Part 2 of 2). Crown Victoria, Grand Marquis & Marauder

TEST CONDITIONS	TEST DETAILS/RESULTS/ACTIONS
M3 CHECK CIRCUIT 837 (YE/BK) FOR GROUND	

	1 Measure the resistance between steering wheel rotation sensor C2001 Pin 1, Circuit 837 (YE/BK), harness side and ground. • Is the resistance greater than 10,000 ohms? → **Yes** GO to **M4**. → **No** REPAIR the circuit. CLEAR the DTCs. REPEAT the Auto Test.

TEST CONDITIONS	TEST DETAILS/RESULTS/ACTIONS
M4 CHECK CIRCUITS 633 (RD) AND 634 (BN) FOR SHORT TO BATTERY	

	1 Measure the voltage between air suspension control module C216 Pin 18, Circuit 633 (RD), harness side and ground; and between air suspension control module C216 Pin 19, circuit 634 (BN), harness side and ground. • Is voltage present? → **Yes** REPAIR the circuit(s) in question. CLEAR the DTCs. REPEAT the Auto Test. → **No** GO to **M5**.

TEST CONDITIONS	TEST DETAILS/RESULTS/ACTIONS
M5 CHECK CIRCUITS 633 (RD) AND 634 (BN) FOR SHORT TO GROUND	

	1 Measure the resistance between air suspension control module C216 Pin 18, Circuit 633 (RD), harness side and ground; and between air suspension control module C216 Pin 19, Circuit 634 (BN), harness side and ground. • Are the resistances greater than 10,000 ohms? → **Yes** GO to **M6**. → **No** REPAIR the circuit(s) in question. CLEAR the DTCs. REPEAT the Auto Test.

FM6029900347020X

Fig. 19 Code 74: Steering Rotation Not Detected (Part 2 of 4). Crown Victoria, Grand Marquis & Marauder

TEST CONDITIONS	TEST DETAILS/RESULTS/ACTIONS
M1 CHECK CIRCUITS 633 (RD) AND 634 (BN) FOR CONTINUITY	

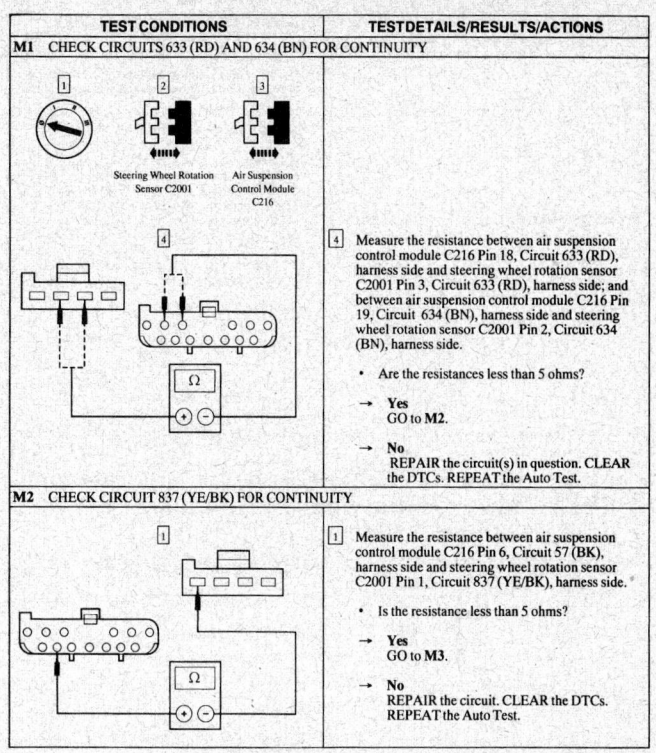

Steering Wheel Rotation Sensor C2001   Air Suspension Control Module C216

	4 Measure the resistance between air suspension control module C216 Pin 18, Circuit 633 (RD), harness side and steering wheel rotation sensor C2001 Pin 3, Circuit 633 (RD), harness side; and between air suspension control module C216 Pin 19, Circuit 634 (BN), harness side and steering wheel rotation sensor C2001 Pin 2, Circuit 634 (BN), harness side. • Are the resistances less than 5 ohms? → **Yes** GO to **M2**. → **No** REPAIR the circuit(s) in question. CLEAR the DTCs. REPEAT the Auto Test.

TEST CONDITIONS	TEST DETAILS/RESULTS/ACTIONS
M2 CHECK CIRCUIT 837 (YE/BK) FOR CONTINUITY	

	1 Measure the resistance between air suspension control module C216 Pin 6, Circuit 57 (BK), harness side and steering wheel rotation sensor C2001 Pin 1, Circuit 837 (YE/BK), harness side. • Is the resistance less than 5 ohms? → **Yes** GO to **M3**. → **No** REPAIR the circuit. CLEAR the DTCs. REPEAT the Auto Test.

FM6029900347010X

Fig. 19 Code 74: Steering Rotation Not Detected (Part 1 of 4). Crown Victoria, Grand Marquis & Marauder

TEST CONDITIONS	TEST DETAILS/RESULTS/ACTIONS
M6 CHECK CIRCUIT 298 (VT/OG) FOR VOLTAGE	

	2 Measure the voltage between steering wheel rotation sensor C2001 Pin 4, Circuit 298 (VT/OG), harness side and ground. • Is the voltage greater than 10 volts? → **Yes** GO to **M7**. → **No** REPAIR the circuit(s) in question. CLEAR the DTCs. REPEAT the Auto Test.

TEST CONDITIONS	TEST DETAILS/RESULTS/ACTIONS
M7 CHECK STEERING WHEEL ROTATION SENSOR	

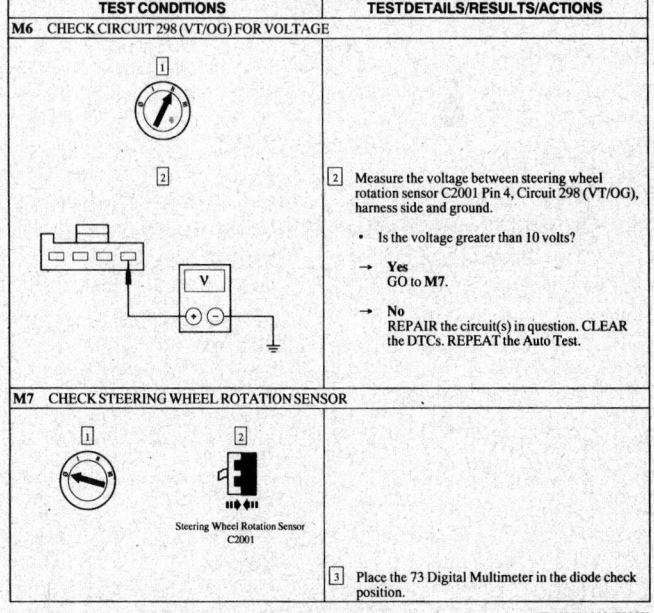

Steering Wheel Rotation Sensor C2001

	3 Place the 73 Digital Multimeter in the diode check position.

FM6029900347030X

Fig. 19 Code 74: Steering Rotation Not Detected (Part 3 of 4). Crown Victoria, Grand Marquis & Marauder

TEST CONDITIONS	TEST DETAILS/RESULTS/ACTIONS
M7 CHECK STEERING WHEEL ROTATION SENSOR	
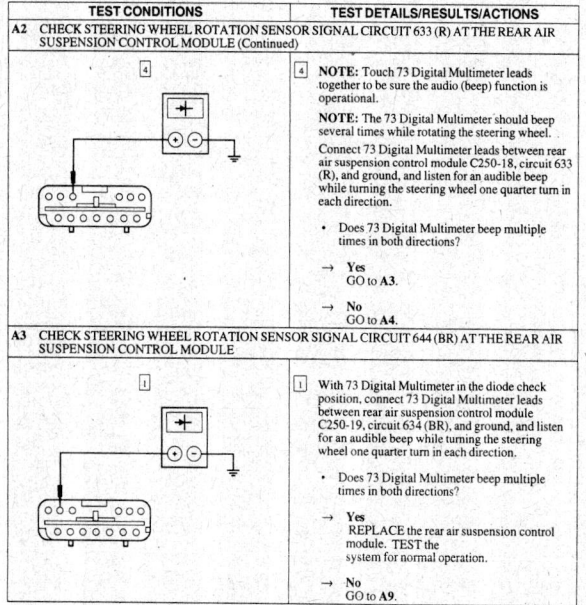	**4** Note: Touch 73 Digital Multimeter leads together to be sure the audio (beep) function is operational. Note: The 73 Digital Multimeter should beep several times while rotating the steering wheel. Connect 73 Digital Multimeter leads between air suspension control module C216 Pin 18, Circuit 633 (RD), harness side and ground; and between air suspension control module C216 Pin 19, Circuit 634 (BN), harness side and ground. Listen for an audible beep while turning the steering wheel one quarter turn in each direction. • Does 73 Digital Multimeter beep multiple times in each direction? → **Yes** INSTALL a new EVO control module. CLEAR the DTCs. REPEAT the Auto Test. → **No** INSTALL a new steering wheel rotation sensor. CLEAR the DTCs. REPEAT the Auto Test.

FM6029900347040X

Fig. 19   Code 74: Steering Rotation Not Detected (Part 4 of 4). Crown Victoria, Grand Marquis & Marauder

Condition	Possible Source	Action
Steering Is Very Difficult/Very Easy	• Power steering pump. • Power steering linkage. • Steering gear.	• GO to Pinpoint Test C.
Steering Does Not Vary With Increased Wheel Rotation	• Power steering pump. • Power steering hose(s).	• GO to Pinpoint Test D.
Steering Does Not Vary With Vehicle Speed	• Circuitry. • Rear Air suspension control module.	• GO to Pinpoint Test E.
No Communication With The Module — Rear Air Suspension Control Module	• Fuse. • Circuitry. • Rear Air suspension control module.	• GO to Pinpoint Test F.
Power Steering Pump Noisy	• Low fluid level and possible leakage. • Plugged reservoir filter. • Power steering pump.	• REFILL to specified level. Refer to Final Fill. CHECK for leaks. REPAIR and/or REPLACE as necessary. REPLACE the reservoir • REPLACE the power steering pump
System Back Pressure	• Power steering pump. • Power steering gear. • Hoses or fittings. • Power steering pump.	• REFER to Pump Flow And Pressure Test.

FM6029800289000X

Fig. 20   Symptom chart. Town Car

TEST CONDITIONS	TEST DETAILS/RESULTS/ACTIONS
A1 CHECK FUSE JUNCTION PANEL FUSE 8 (10A)	
Fuse Junction Panel Fuse 8 (10A)	• Is the fuse OK? → **Yes** GO to A2. → **No** REPLACE the fuse. TEST the system for normal operation. If the fuse fails again, CHECK for short to ground. REPAIR as necessary. TEST the system for normal operation.
A2 CHECK STEERING WHEEL ROTATION SENSOR SIGNAL CIRCUIT 633 (R) AT THE REAR AIR SUSPENSION CONTROL MODULE	
Rear Air Suspension Control Module	**3** Place the 73 Digital Multimeter in the diode check position.

FM6029800290010X

Fig. 21   Test A, Codes C1441 & C1442: Steering Sensor Circuit Failure (Part 1 of 5). Town Car

TEST CONDITIONS	TEST DETAILS/RESULTS/ACTIONS
A2 CHECK STEERING WHEEL ROTATION SENSOR SIGNAL CIRCUIT 633 (R) AT THE REAR AIR SUSPENSION CONTROL MODULE (Continued)	
4	**4** NOTE: Touch 73 Digital Multimeter leads together to be sure the audio (beep) function is operational. NOTE: The 73 Digital Multimeter should beep several times while rotating the steering wheel. Connect 73 Digital Multimeter leads between rear air suspension control module C250-18, circuit 633 (R), and ground, and listen for an audible beep while turning the steering wheel one quarter turn in each direction. • Does 73 Digital Multimeter beep multiple times in both directions? → **Yes** GO to A3. → **No** GO to A4.
A3 CHECK STEERING WHEEL ROTATION SENSOR SIGNAL CIRCUIT 644 (BR) AT THE REAR AIR SUSPENSION CONTROL MODULE	
1	**1** With 73 Digital Multimeter in the diode check position, connect 73 Digital Multimeter leads between rear air suspension control module C250-19, circuit 634 (BR), and ground, and listen for an audible beep while turning the steering wheel one quarter turn in each direction. • Does 73 Digital Multimeter beep multiple times in both directions? → **Yes** REPLACE the rear air suspension control module. TEST the system for normal operation. → **No** GO to A9.

FM6029800290020X

Fig. 21   Test A, Code C1441, C1442: Steering Sensor Circuit Failure (Part 2 of 5). Town Car

TEST CONDITIONS	TEST DETAILS/RESULTS/ACTIONS
A4 CHECK STEERING WHEEL ROTATION SENSOR C184 FOR POWER AND GROUND	
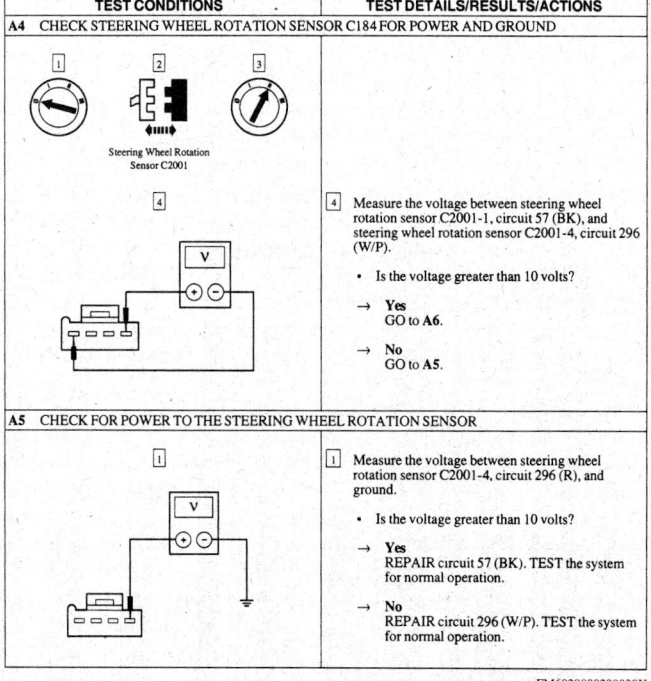 Steering Wheel Rotation Sensor C2001	**4** Measure the voltage between steering wheel rotation sensor C2001-1, circuit 57 (BK), and steering wheel rotation sensor C2001-4, circuit 296 (W/P). • Is the voltage greater than 10 volts? → **Yes** GO to A6. → **No** GO to A5.
A5 CHECK FOR POWER TO THE STEERING WHEEL ROTATION SENSOR	
1	**1** Measure the voltage between steering wheel rotation sensor C2001-4, circuit 296 (R), and ground. • Is the voltage greater than 10 volts? → **Yes** REPAIR circuit 57 (BK). TEST the system for normal operation. → **No** REPAIR circuit 296 (W/P). TEST the system for normal operation.

FM6029800290030X

Fig. 21   Test A, Code C1441, C1442: Steering Sensor Circuit Failure (Part 3 of 5). Town Car

FORD VARIABLE ASSIST ELECTRONIC VARIABLE ORIFICE (EVO) SYSTEM

TEST CONDITIONS	TEST DETAILS/RESULTS/ACTIONS
A6 CHECK CIRCUIT 633 (R) FOR SHORT TO POWER	

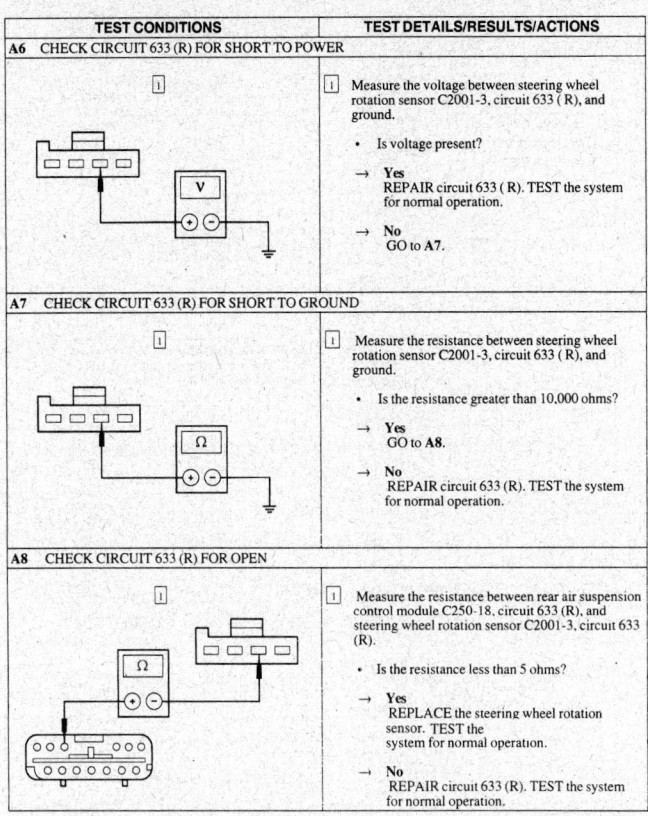

A6 (continued)

☐ Measure the voltage between steering wheel rotation sensor C2001-3, circuit 633 (R), and ground.

- Is voltage present?
- → **Yes**
  REPAIR circuit 633 (R). TEST the system for normal operation.
- → **No**
  GO to **A7**.

A7 CHECK CIRCUIT 633 (R) FOR SHORT TO GROUND

☐ Measure the resistance between steering wheel rotation sensor C2001-3, circuit 633 (R), and ground.

- Is the resistance greater than 10,000 ohms?
- → **Yes**
  GO to **A8**.
- → **No**
  REPAIR circuit 633 (R). TEST the system for normal operation.

A8 CHECK CIRCUIT 633 (R) FOR OPEN

☐ Measure the resistance between rear air suspension control module C250-18, circuit 633 (R), and steering wheel rotation sensor C2001-3, circuit 633 (R).

- Is the resistance less than 5 ohms?
- → **Yes**
  REPLACE the steering wheel rotation sensor. TEST the system for normal operation.
- → **No**
  REPAIR circuit 633 (R). TEST the system for normal operation.

FM6029800290040X

Fig. 21 Test A, Code C1441, C1442: Steering Sensor Circuit failure (Part 4 of 5). Town Car

TEST CONDITIONS	TEST DETAILS/RESULTS/ACTIONS
A9 CHECK CIRCUIT 634 (BR) FOR SHORT TO POWER	

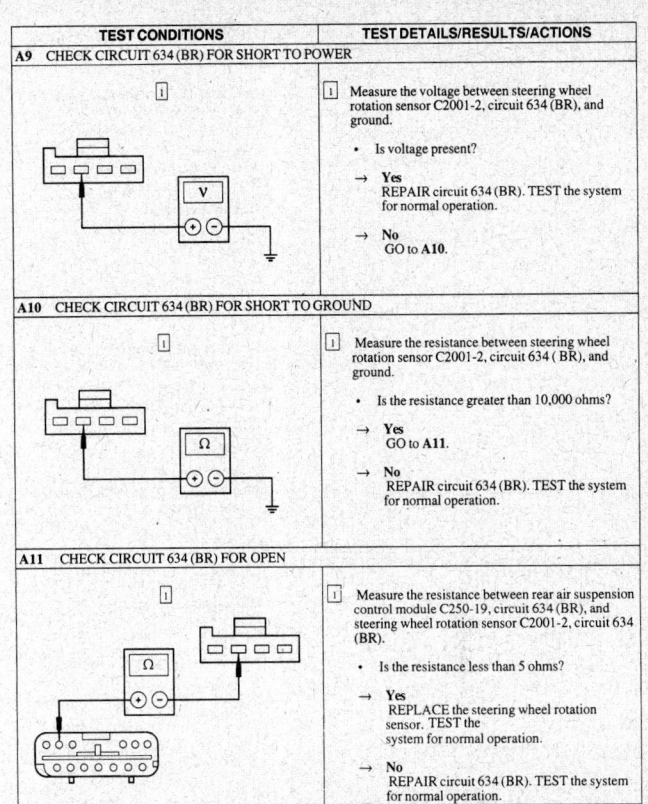

A9 (continued)

☐ Measure the voltage between steering wheel rotation sensor C2001-2, circuit 634 (BR), and ground.

- Is voltage present?
- → **Yes**
  REPAIR circuit 634 (BR). TEST the system for normal operation.
- → **No**
  GO to **A10**.

A10 CHECK CIRCUIT 634 (BR) FOR SHORT TO GROUND

☐ Measure the resistance between steering wheel rotation sensor C2001-2, circuit 634 (BR), and ground.

- Is the resistance greater than 10,000 ohms?
- → **Yes**
  GO to **A11**.
- → **No**
  REPAIR circuit 634 (BR). TEST the system for normal operation.

A11 CHECK CIRCUIT 634 (BR) FOR OPEN

☐ Measure the resistance between rear air suspension control module C250-19, circuit 634 (BR), and steering wheel rotation sensor C2001-2, circuit 634 (BR).

- Is the resistance less than 5 ohms?
- → **Yes**
  REPLACE the steering wheel rotation sensor. TEST the system for normal operation.
- → **No**
  REPAIR circuit 634 (BR). TEST the system for normal operation.

FM6029800290050X

Fig. 21 Test A, Code C1441, C1442: Steering Sensor Circuit Failure (Part 5 of 5). Town Car

TEST CONDITIONS	TEST DETAILS/RESULTS/ACTIONS
B1 CHECK THE POWER STEERING CONTROL VALVE ACTUATOR	

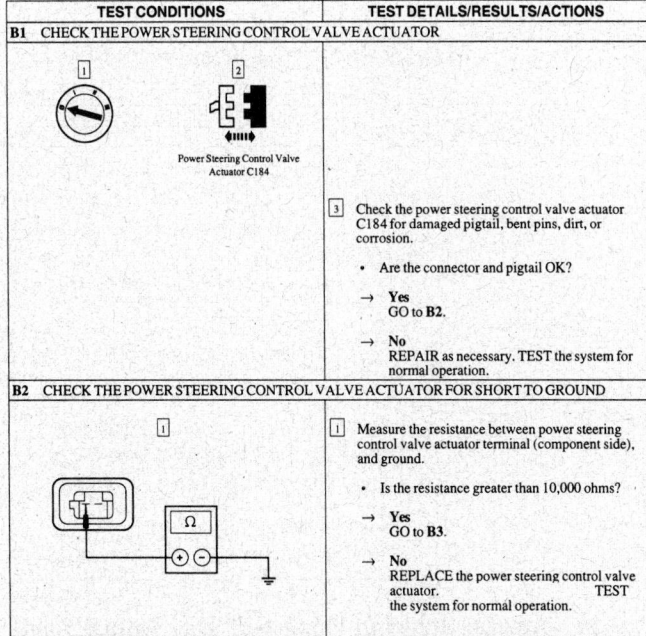

Power Steering Control Valve Actuator C184

☐ Check the power steering control valve actuator C184 for damaged pigtail, bent pins, dirt, or corrosion.

- Are the connector and pigtail OK?
- → **Yes**
  GO to **B2**.
- → **No**
  REPAIR as necessary. TEST the system for normal operation.

B2 CHECK THE POWER STEERING CONTROL VALVE ACTUATOR FOR SHORT TO GROUND

☐ Measure the resistance between power steering control valve actuator terminal (component side), and ground.

- Is the resistance greater than 10,000 ohms?
- → **Yes**
  GO to **B3**.
- → **No**
  REPLACE the power steering control valve actuator. TEST the system for normal operation.

FM6029800291010X

Fig. 22 Test A, Code C1441, C1442: Steering VAPS II Circuit Loop Failure (Part 1 of 4). Town Car

TEST CONDITIONS	TEST DETAILS/RESULTS/ACTIONS
B3 CHECK THE POWER STEERING CONTROL VALVE ACTUATOR RESISTANCE	

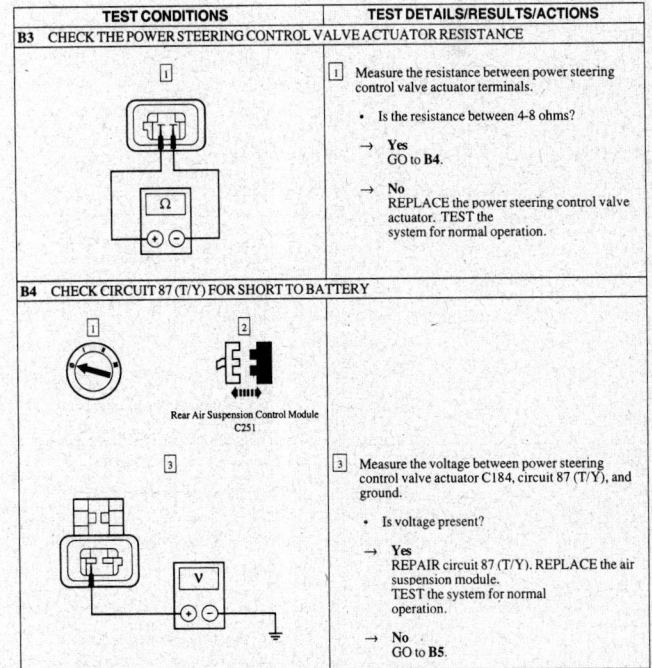

☐ Measure the resistance between power steering control valve actuator terminals.

- Is the resistance between 4-8 ohms?
- → **Yes**
  GO to **B4**.
- → **No**
  REPLACE the power steering control valve actuator. TEST the system for normal operation.

B4 CHECK CIRCUIT 87 (T/Y) FOR SHORT TO BATTERY

Rear Air Suspension Control Module C251

☐ Measure the voltage between power steering control valve actuator C184, circuit 87 (T/Y), and ground.

- Is voltage present?
- → **Yes**
  REPAIR circuit 87 (T/Y). REPLACE the air suspension module. TEST the system for normal operation.
- → **No**
  GO to **B5**.

FM6029800291020X

Fig. 22 Test B, Code C1897: Steering VAPS II Circuit Loop Failure (Part 2 of 4). Town Car

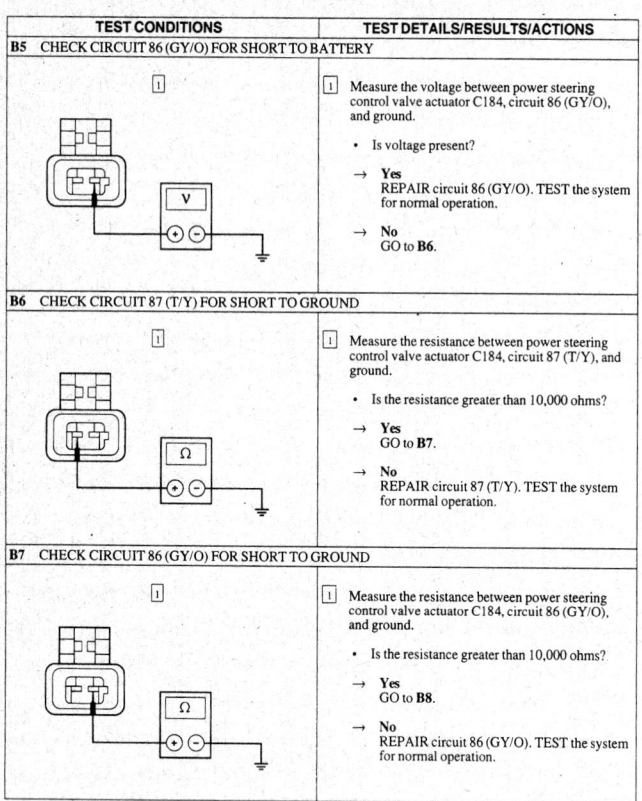

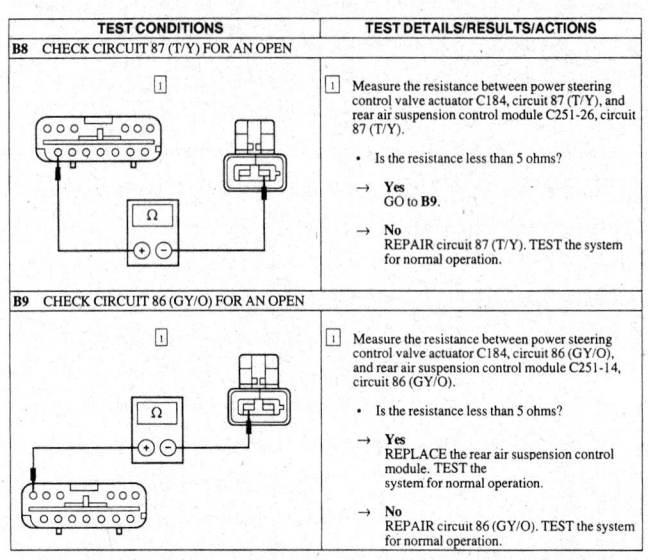

TEST CONDITIONS	TEST DETAILS/RESULTS/ACTIONS
B5 CHECK CIRCUIT 86 (GY/O) FOR SHORT TO BATTERY	① Measure the voltage between power steering control valve actuator C184, circuit 86 (GY/O), and ground. • Is voltage present? → **Yes** REPAIR circuit 86 (GY/O). TEST the system for normal operation. → **No** GO to **B6**.
B6 CHECK CIRCUIT 87 (T/Y) FOR SHORT TO GROUND	① Measure the resistance between power steering control valve actuator C184, circuit 87 (T/Y), and ground. • Is the resistance greater than 10,000 ohms? → **Yes** GO to **B7**. → **No** REPAIR circuit 87 (T/Y). TEST the system for normal operation.
B7 CHECK CIRCUIT 86 (GY/O) FOR SHORT TO GROUND	① Measure the resistance between power steering control valve actuator C184, circuit 86 (GY/O), and ground. • Is the resistance greater than 10,000 ohms? → **Yes** GO to **B8**. → **No** REPAIR circuit 86 (GY/O). TEST the system for normal operation.

FM6029800291030X

Fig. 22   Test B, Code C1897: Steering VAPS II Circuit Loop Failure (Part 3 of 4). Town Car

TEST CONDITIONS	TEST DETAILS/RESULTS/ACTIONS
B8 CHECK CIRCUIT 87 (T/Y) FOR AN OPEN	① Measure the resistance between power steering control valve actuator C184, circuit 87 (T/Y), and rear air suspension control module C251-26, circuit 87 (T/Y). • Is the resistance less than 5 ohms? → **Yes** GO to **B9**. → **No** REPAIR circuit 87 (T/Y). TEST the system for normal operation.
B9 CHECK CIRCUIT 86 (GY/O) FOR AN OPEN	① Measure the resistance between power steering control valve actuator C184, circuit 86 (GY/O), and rear air suspension control module C251-14, circuit 86 (GY/O). • Is the resistance less than 5 ohms? → **Yes** REPLACE the rear air suspension control module. TEST the system for normal operation. → **No** REPAIR circuit 86 (GY/O). TEST the system for normal operation.

FM6029800291040X

Fig. 22   Test B, Code C1897: Steering VAPS II Circuit Loop Failure (Part 4 of 4). Town Car

TEST CONDITIONS	TEST DETAILS/RESULTS/ACTIONS
C4 CHECK THE STEERING GEAR (Continued)	② Check the steering gear mounting fasteners for loose bolts. • Is the steering gear OK? → **Yes** If condition still exists, GO to the Symptom Chart. → **No** TIGHTEN and/or REPLACE the steering gear; TEST the system for normal operation.

FM6029800292020X

Fig. 23   Test C: Steering Is Very Difficult/Very Easy (Part 2 of 2). Town Car

TEST CONDITIONS	TEST DETAILS/RESULTS/ACTIONS
C1 CHECK THE POWER STEERING PUMP (Continued)	
① Ignition ON, Engine Running ② Check power steering pump for leaks by turning steering Wheel and observing pump	③ Perform the Pump Flow and Pressure Test; go to Component Tests. • Is the power steering pump OK? → **Yes** GO to **C2**. → **No** REPLACE the power steering pump TEST the system for normal operation.
C2 CHECK THE STEERING LINKAGE	① Visually check the steering linkage while an assistant rotates the steering wheel from stop to stop. • Does the steering linkage move smoothly from stop to stop? → **Yes** GO to **C3**. → **No** REPLACE the damaged steering linkage component(s) TEST the system for normal operation.
C3 CHECK THE STEERING ASSEMBLY	① Check the ball joints for worn surfaces. • Are the ball joints OK ? → **Yes** GO to **C4**. → **No** REPLACE worn ball joints. TEST the system for normal operation.
C4 CHECK THE STEERING GEAR	① Visually check the steering gear operation while an assistant rotates the steering wheel from stop to stop.

FM6029800292010X

Fig. 23   Test C: Steering Is Very Difficult/Very Easy (Part 1 of 2). Town Car

TEST CONDITIONS	TEST DETAILS/RESULTS/ACTIONS
D1 CHECK THE POWER STEERING PUMP	② Check the power steering pump for leaks by rotating the steering wheel while watching the power steering pump. ③ Perform the Pump Flow and Pressure Test; go to Component Tests. • Is the power steering pump OK? → **Yes** INSPECT for kinked lines or hoses from the power steering pump. REPLACE lines or hoses as necessary. TEST the system for normal operation. → **No** REPLACE the power steering pump. TEST the system for normal operation.

FM6029800293000X

Fig. 24   Test D: Steering Does Not Vary w/Increased Wheel Rotation. Town Car

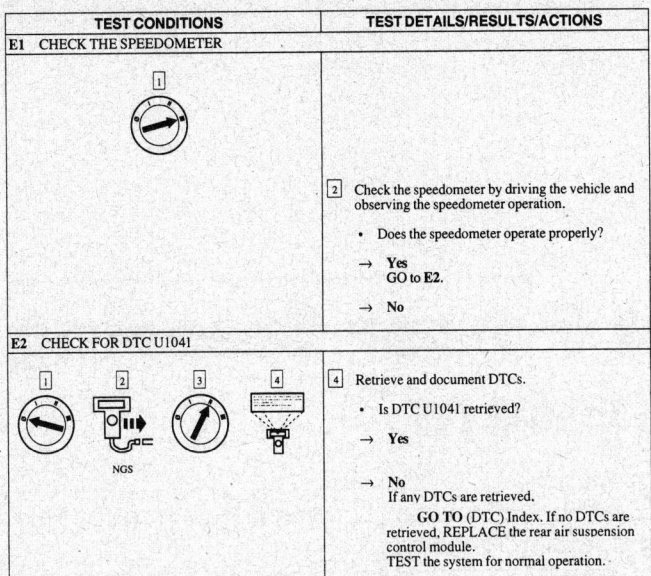

Fig. 25 Test E: Steering Does Not Vary w/Vehicle Speed. Town Car

TEST CONDITIONS	TEST DETAILS/RESULTS/ACTIONS
F3 CHECK CIRCUIT 418 (DG/Y) FOR AN OPEN	1 Measure the voltage between rear air suspension control module C250-1, circuit 418 (DG/Y), and ground. • Is the voltage greater than 10 volts? → **Yes** GO to **F4.** → **No** REPAIR circuit 418 (DG/Y). TEST the system for normal operation.
F4 CHECK CIRCUIT 57 (BK) FOR AN OPEN	2 Measure the resistance between rear air suspension control module C250-6, circuit 57 (BK), and ground. • Is the resistance less than 5 ohms? → **Yes** → **No** REPAIR circuit 57 (BK). TEST the system for normal operation.

FM6029800295020X

Fig. 26 Test F: No Communication w/Rear Air Suspension Control Module (Part 2 of 2). Town Car

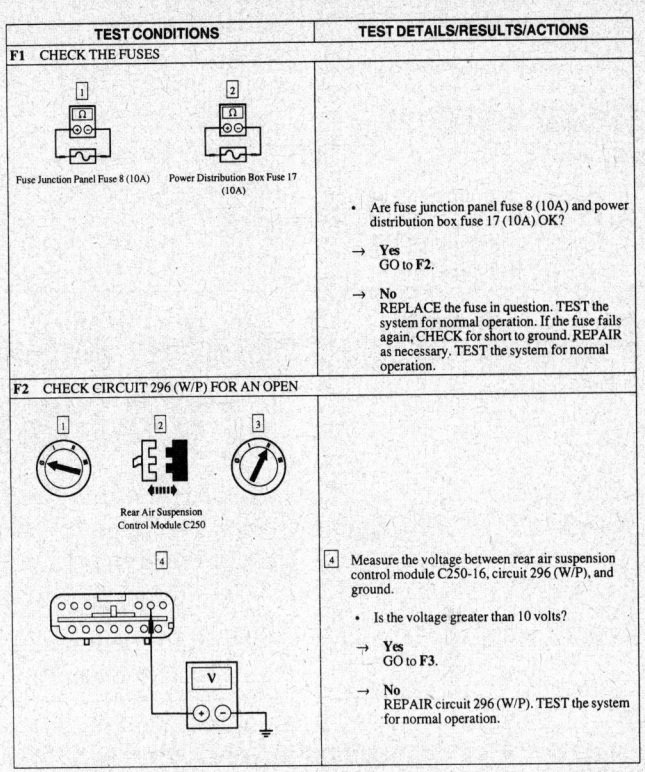

Fig. 26 Test F: No Communication w/Rear Air Suspension Control Module (Part 1 of 2). Town Car

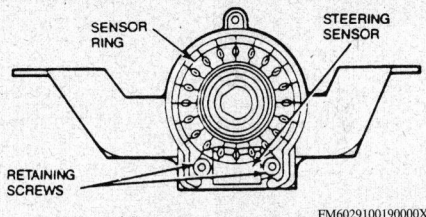

FM6029100190000X

Fig. 27 Steering sensor replacement

5. Reverse procedure to install.

CONTROL MODULE
REPLACE

The EVO control module and air suspension modules are one unit.
1. Turn air suspension switch to Off position.
2. **On 2001–02 models,** proceed as follows:
   a. Remove lower dash panel.
   b. Disconnect lamp from panel.
   c. Disconnect wiring.
   d. Remove module mounting screws.
3. **On all models,** pull module out to access connectors.
4. Disconnect each electrical connectors.
5. Reverse procedure to install. **Torque** mounting nuts to 60–84 inch lbs.

CONTROL VALVE ACTUATOR
REPLACE

1. Raise and support vehicle.
2. Remove engine oil filter.
3. Disconnect power steering auxiliary actuator electrical connector.
4. Remove mounting screw and power steering auxiliary actuator.

STEERING SENSOR
REPLACE

1. **On 2001–02 models,** remove sound panel, finish panel and knee bolster and bracket from under steering column.
2. **On all models,** disconnect sensor electrical connector.
3. Remove sensor electrical connector from bracket under instrument panel.
4. Remove two mounting screws and sensor, **Fig. 27.**
5. Reverse procedure to install.

STEERING SENSOR RING
REPLACE

1. Remove steering column as outlined in "Steering Columns" chapter.

2. Remove steering shaft and sensor ring.
3. Reverse procedure to install.

SPEED SENSOR
REPLACE

1. Raise and support vehicle.
2. Remove clip mounting bolt, speed sensor and driven gear.

3. Disconnect sensor electrical connector.
4. Remove retainer and driven gear.

5. Reverse procedure to install. Ensure internal O-ring is seated in sensor housing.

Ford Variable Assist Power Steering (VAPS) System

NOTE: On Air Bag Equipped Models, Refer To "Air Bag System Precautions" Located In The Front Of This Manual For System Disarming & Arming Procedures.

NOTE: Refer To "Computer Relearn Procedures" Located In The Front Of This Manual When Battery Power To The Computer Has Been Interrupted.

NOTE: "Electrical Symbol & Wire Color Code Identification" Located In The Front Of This Manual May Be Used As An Aid When Using Wiring Circuits Found In This Section.

INDEX

PRECAUTIONS
Air Bag Systems

Refer to "Air Bag System Precautions" in the front of this manual for system disarming and arming procedures.

Battery Ground Cable

Prior to service, disconnect battery ground cable and isolate as required.

DESCRIPTION

The Variable Assist Power Steering (VAPS) System uses the Front Electronics Module (FEM) to improve steering characteristics. The VAPS system begins operation when engine speed exceeds 100 RPM.

The level of assist provided by the VAPS system depends on vehicle speed. The faster the vehicle speed, the less assist provided by the VAPS system. Vehicle speed is determined by the FEM and is based on Pulse Width Modulated (PWM) current sent to the control valve actuator.

Engine RPM is provided to the FEM by the Powertrain Control Module (PCM) through the Standard Corporate Protocol (SCP). Vehicle speed is provided through the ABS system.

TROUBLESHOOTING
Hard Steering Or Lack Of Assist

1. Seized lower steering column shaft U-joint.
2. Damaged or fractured steering column bearings.
3. Power steering pump.
4. Suspension components.
5. Steering gear internal leakage.

Excessive Steering Pump Noise

Power steering pump failure.

Excessive Steering Wheel Play

1. Damaged, loose or worn tie-rod.
2. Damaged or worn steering gear.
3. Loose, worn or damaged steering column bearings.
4. Loose, worn or damaged lower steering column shaft U-joint.

Steering Wander

1. Unevenly loaded or overloaded vehicle.
2. Loose, worn or damaged tie-rod.
3. Loose or damaged steering gear mounting bolts.
4. Loose lower steering column shaft U-joint bolts or joints.
5. Loose, worn or damaged steering column bearings.
6. Suspension components.

Drift/Pull

1. Unevenly loaded or overloaded vehicle.
2. Loose, worn or damaged tie-rod.
3. Wheel alignment.
4. Suspension components.
5. Steering gear valve effort out of balance.
6. Inspect brake system for correct operation.
7. Incorrect frame or underbody alignment.

Feedback

1. Loose, worn or damaged tie-rod.
2. Loose, worn or damaged steering gear insulators or bolts.
3. Loose lower steering column shaft U-joint bolts.
4. Loose suspension bushings, fasteners or ball joints.
5. Worn or damaged steering column bearings.

Poor Returnability/ Sticky Steering

1. Binding lower steering column shaft U-joints.
2. Loose, worn or damaged tie-rod ends.
3. Suspension components.
4. Binding steering column bearings.

Shimmy

1. Loose, worn or damaged tie-rod.

2. Suspension components.

Power Steering Pump Noisy

1. Low fluid level and possible leakage.
2. Plugged reservoir.
3. Power steering pump.

DIAGNOSIS & TESTING

Accessing Diagnostic Trouble Codes

Diagnosing and testing requires the use of a New Generation Star (NGS) scan tool

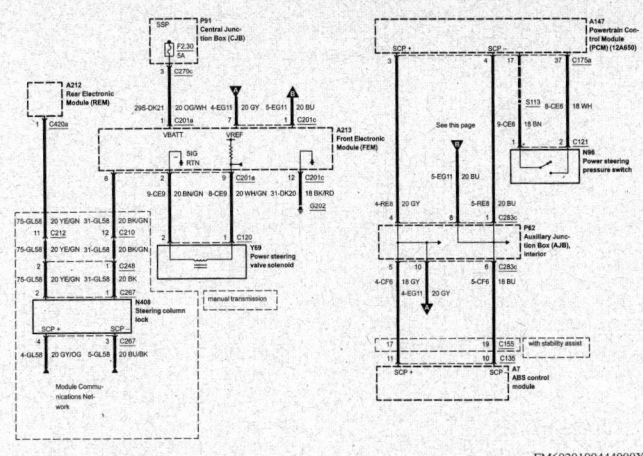

FM6020100444000X

Fig. 1   VAPS wiring diagram. LS & Thunderbird

No. 418-F052, or equivalent and suitable digital volt/ohm meter. The Data Link Connector (DLC) is located under the instrument panel, between the steering column and radio.

Wiring Diagrams

Refer to **Fig. 1,** for wiring diagram.

Pinpoint Tests

Refer to **Figs. 2 through 4,** for pinpoint tests.

DIAGNOSTIC CHART INDEX

Test/Code	Description	Page No.	Fig No.
Test A	VAPS Solenoid Actuator Output Circuit Short To Ground	15-36	2
Test B	VAPS Solenoid Actuator Return Circuit Failure	15-36	3
Test C	Front Electronics Module Does Not Respond To Diagnostic Tool	15-37	4
Code C1924	VAPS Solenoid Actuator Output Circuit Short To Ground	15-36	2
Code C1925	VAPS Solenoid Actuator Return Circuit Failure	15-36	3

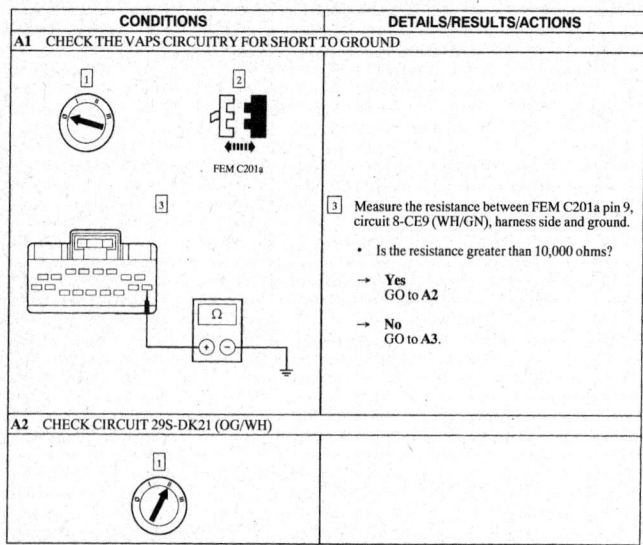

CONDITIONS	DETAILS/RESULTS/ACTIONS
A1 CHECK THE VAPS CIRCUITRY FOR SHORT TO GROUND	
FEM C201a	3 Measure the resistance between FEM C201a pin 9, circuit 8-CE9 (WH/GN), harness side and ground. • Is the resistance greater than 10,000 ohms? → **Yes** GO to **A2** → **No** GO to **A3**.
A2 CHECK CIRCUIT 29S-DK21 (OG/WH)	

FM6020100446010X

Fig. 2 Test A, Code C1924: VAPS Solenoid Actuator Output Circuit Short To Ground (Part 1 of 2)

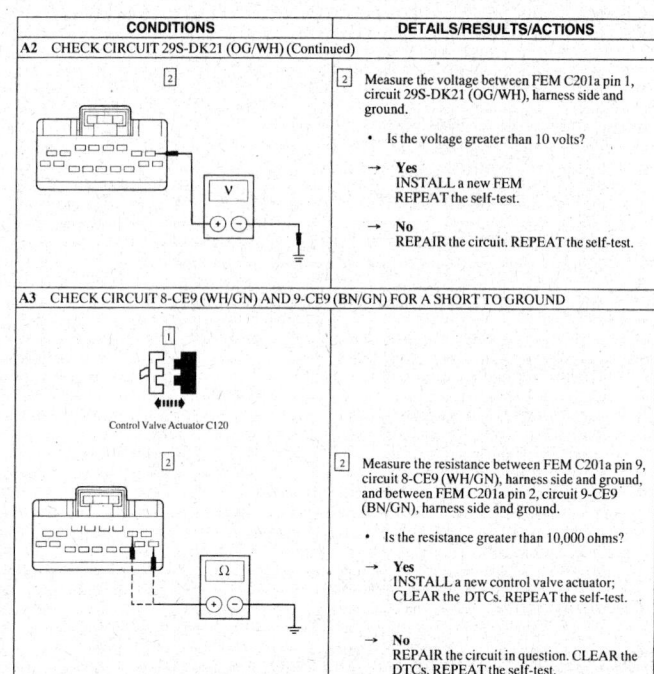

CONDITIONS	DETAILS/RESULTS/ACTIONS
A2 CHECK CIRCUIT 29S-DK21 (OG/WH) (Continued)	
	2 Measure the voltage between FEM C201a pin 1, circuit 29S-DK21 (OG/WH), harness side and ground. • Is the voltage greater than 10 volts? → **Yes** INSTALL a new FEM REPEAT the self-test. → **No** REPAIR the circuit. REPEAT the self-test.
A3 CHECK CIRCUIT 8-CE9 (WH/GN) AND 9-CE9 (BN/GN) FOR A SHORT TO GROUND	
Control Valve Actuator C120	2 Measure the resistance between FEM C201a pin 9, circuit 8-CE9 (WH/GN), harness side and ground, and between FEM C201a pin 2, circuit 9-CE9 (BN/GN), harness side and ground. • Is the resistance greater than 10,000 ohms? → **Yes** INSTALL a new control valve actuator; CLEAR the DTCs. REPEAT the self-test. → **No** REPAIR the circuit in question. CLEAR the DTCs. REPEAT the self-test.

FM6020100446020X

Fig. 2 Test A, Code C1924: VAPS Solenoid Actuator Output Circuit Short To Ground (Part 2 of 2)

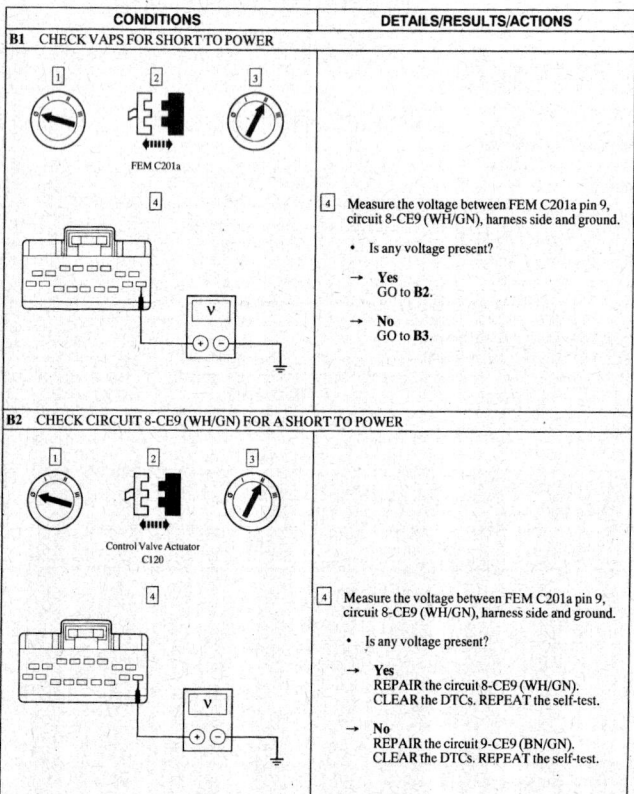

CONDITIONS	DETAILS/RESULTS/ACTIONS
B1 CHECK VAPS FOR SHORT TO POWER	
FEM C201a	4 Measure the voltage between FEM C201a pin 9, circuit 8-CE9 (WH/GN), harness side and ground. • Is any voltage present? → **Yes** GO to **B2**. → **No** GO to **B3**.
B2 CHECK CIRCUIT 8-CE9 (WH/GN) FOR A SHORT TO POWER	
Control Valve Actuator C120	4 Measure the voltage between FEM C201a pin 9, circuit 8-CE9 (WH/GN), harness side and ground. • Is any voltage present? → **Yes** REPAIR the circuit 8-CE9 (WH/GN). CLEAR the DTCs. REPEAT the self-test. → **No** REPAIR the circuit 9-CE9 (BN/GN). CLEAR the DTCs. REPEAT the self-test.

FM6020100447010X

Fig. 3 Test B, Code C1925: VAPS Solenoid Actuator Return Circuit Failure (Part 1 of 3)

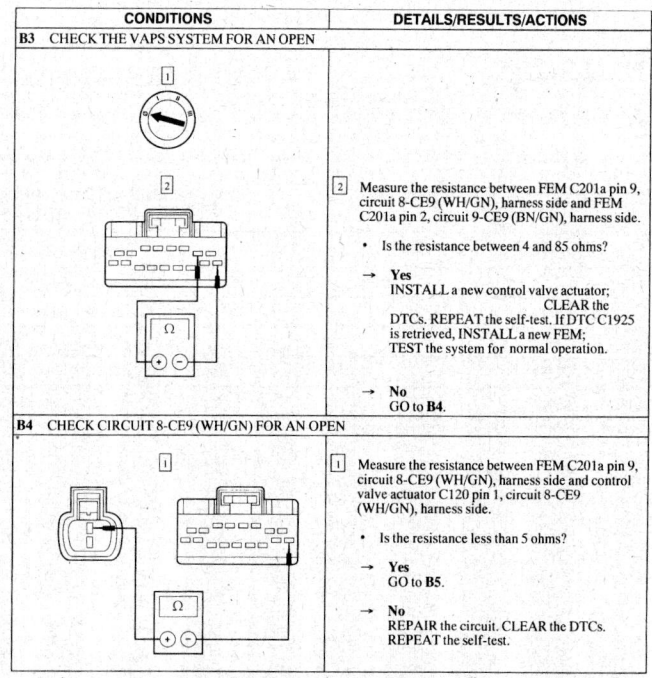

CONDITIONS	DETAILS/RESULTS/ACTIONS
B3 CHECK THE VAPS SYSTEM FOR AN OPEN	
	2 Measure the resistance between FEM C201a pin 9, circuit 8-CE9 (WH/GN), harness side and FEM C201a pin 2, circuit 9-CE9 (BN/GN), harness side. • Is the resistance between 4 and 85 ohms? → **Yes** INSTALL a new control valve actuator; CLEAR the DTCs. REPEAT the self-test. If DTC C1925 is retrieved, INSTALL a new FEM; TEST the system for normal operation. → **No** GO to **B4**.
B4 CHECK CIRCUIT 8-CE9 (WH/GN) FOR AN OPEN	
	1 Measure the resistance between FEM C201a pin 9, circuit 8-CE9 (WH/GN), harness side and control valve actuator C120 pin 1, circuit 8-CE9 (WH/GN), harness side. • Is the resistance less than 5 ohms? → **Yes** GO to **B5**. → **No** REPAIR the circuit. CLEAR the DTCs. REPEAT the self-test.

FM6020100447020X

Fig. 3 Test B, Code C1925: VAPS Solenoid Actuator Return Circuit Failure (Part 2 of 3)

CONDITIONS	DETAILS/RESULTS/ACTIONS

B5 CHECK CIRCUIT 9-CE9 (BN/GN) FOR AN OPEN

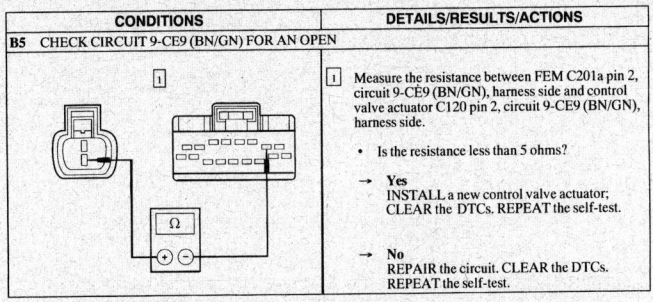

1. Measure the resistance between FEM C201a pin 2, circuit 9-CE9 (BN/GN), harness side and control valve actuator C120 pin 2, circuit 9-CE9 (BN/GN), harness side.

- Is the resistance less than 5 ohms?

→ **Yes**
INSTALL a new control valve actuator; CLEAR the DTCs. REPEAT the self-test.

→ **No**
REPAIR the circuit. CLEAR the DTCs. REPEAT the self-test.

FM6020100447030X

Fig. 3 Test B, Code C1925: VAPS Solenoid Actuator Return Circuit Failure (Part 3 of 3))

CONDITIONS	DETAILS/RESULTS/ACTIONS

B2 CHECK FOR OPEN BETWEEN DLC C251 AND FEM C201c — SCP (+)

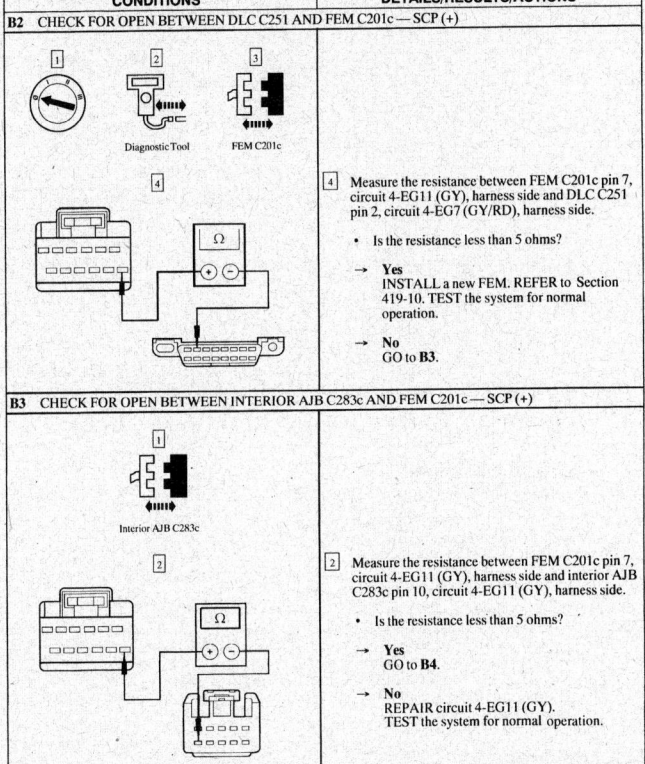

4. Measure the resistance between FEM C201c pin 7, circuit 4-EG11 (GY), harness side and DLC C251 pin 2, circuit 4-EG7 (GY/RD), harness side.

- Is the resistance less than 5 ohms?

→ **Yes**
INSTALL a new FEM. REFER to Section 419-10. TEST the system for normal operation.

→ **No**
GO to **B3**.

B3 CHECK FOR OPEN BETWEEN INTERIOR AJB C283c AND FEM C201c — SCP (+)

2. Measure the resistance between FEM C201c pin 7, circuit 4-EG11 (GY), harness side and interior AJB C283c pin 10, circuit 4-EG11 (GY), harness side.

- Is the resistance less than 5 ohms?

→ **Yes**
GO to **B4**.

→ **No**
REPAIR circuit 4-EG11 (GY). TEST the system for normal operation.

FM6020100448020X

Fig. 4 Test C: Front Electronics Module Does Not Respond To Diagnostic Tool (Part 2 of 6)

CONDITIONS	DETAILS/RESULTS/ACTIONS

B1 CHECK FEM C201c FOR DAMAGE

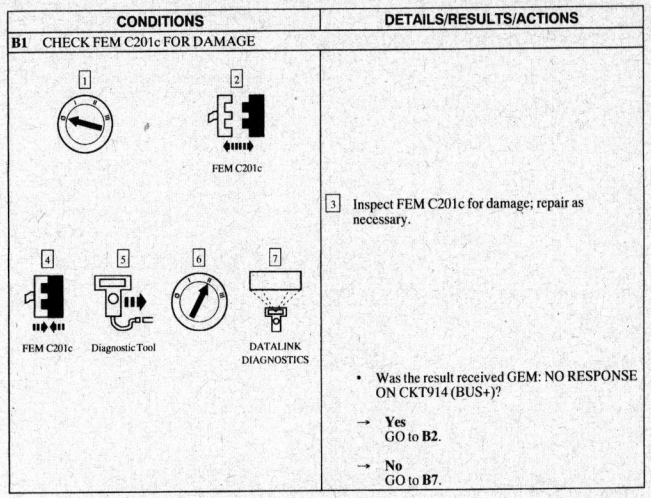

3. Inspect FEM C201c for damage; repair as necessary.

- Was the result received GEM: NO RESPONSE ON CKT914 (BUS+)?

→ **Yes**
GO to **B2**.

→ **No**
GO to **B7**.

FM6020100448010X

Fig. 4 Test C: Front Electronics Module Does Not Respond To Diagnostic Tool (Part 1 of 6)

CONDITIONS	DETAILS/RESULTS/ACTIONS

B4 CHECK FOR OPEN BETWEEN INTERIOR AJB C283c AND INTERIOR AJB C283d — SCP (+)

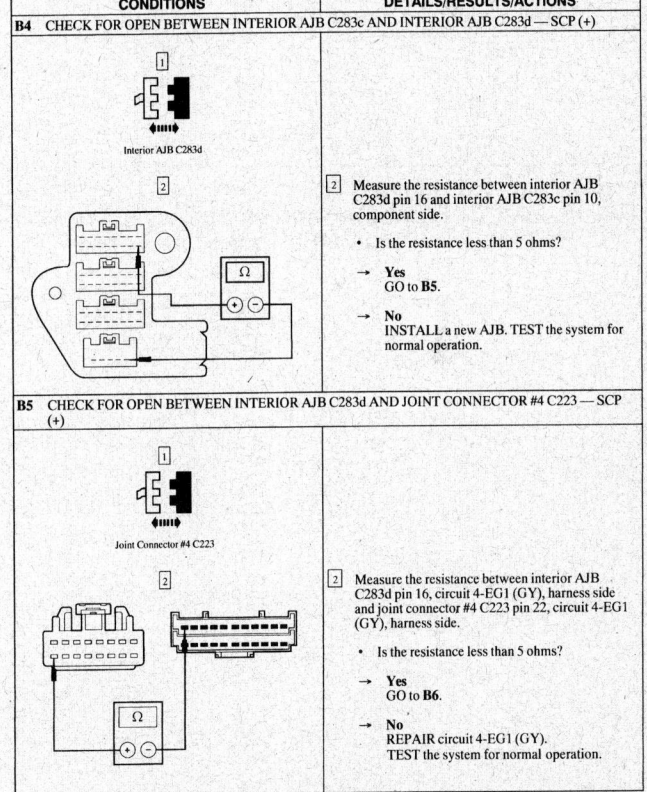

2. Measure the resistance between interior AJB C283d pin 16 and interior AJB C283c pin 10, component side.

- Is the resistance less than 5 ohms?

→ **Yes**
GO to **B5**.

→ **No**
INSTALL a new AJB. TEST the system for normal operation.

B5 CHECK FOR OPEN BETWEEN INTERIOR AJB C283d AND JOINT CONNECTOR #4 C223 — SCP (+)

2. Measure the resistance between interior AJB C283d pin 16, circuit 4-EG1 (GY), harness side and joint connector #4 C223 pin 22, circuit 4-EG1 (GY), harness side.

- Is the resistance less than 5 ohms?

→ **Yes**
GO to **B6**.

→ **No**
REPAIR circuit 4-EG1 (GY). TEST the system for normal operation.

FM6020100448030X

Fig. 4 Test C: Front Electronics Module Does Not Respond To Diagnostic Tool (Part 3 of 6)

POWER STEERING

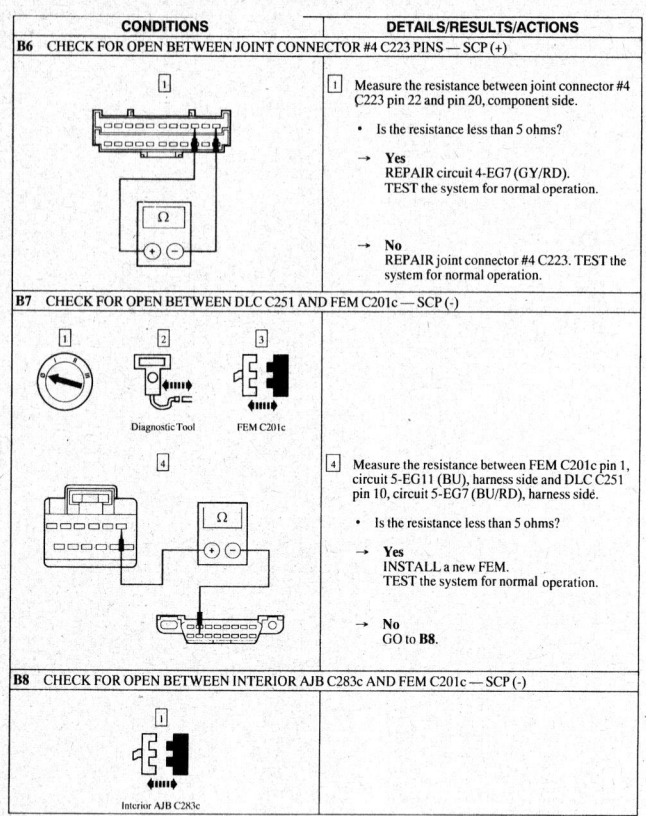

CONDITIONS	DETAILS/RESULTS/ACTIONS
B6 CHECK FOR OPEN BETWEEN JOINT CONNECTOR #4 C223 PINS — SCP (+)	**1** Measure the resistance between joint connector #4 C223 pin 22 and pin 20, component side. • Is the resistance less than 5 ohms? → **Yes** REPAIR circuit 4-EG7 (GY/RD). TEST the system for normal operation. → **No** REPAIR joint connector #4 C223. TEST the system for normal operation.
B7 CHECK FOR OPEN BETWEEN DLC C251 AND FEM C201c — SCP (-)	**4** Measure the resistance between FEM C201c pin 1, circuit 5-EG11 (BU), harness side and DLC C251 pin 10, circuit 5-EG7 (BU/RD), harness side. • Is the resistance less than 5 ohms? → **Yes** INSTALL a new FEM. TEST the system for normal operation. → **No** GO to **B8**.
B8 CHECK FOR OPEN BETWEEN INTERIOR AJB C283c AND FEM C201c — SCP (-)	

FM6020100448040X

Fig. 4 Test C: Front Electronics Module Does Not Respond To Diagnostic Tool (Part 4 of 6)

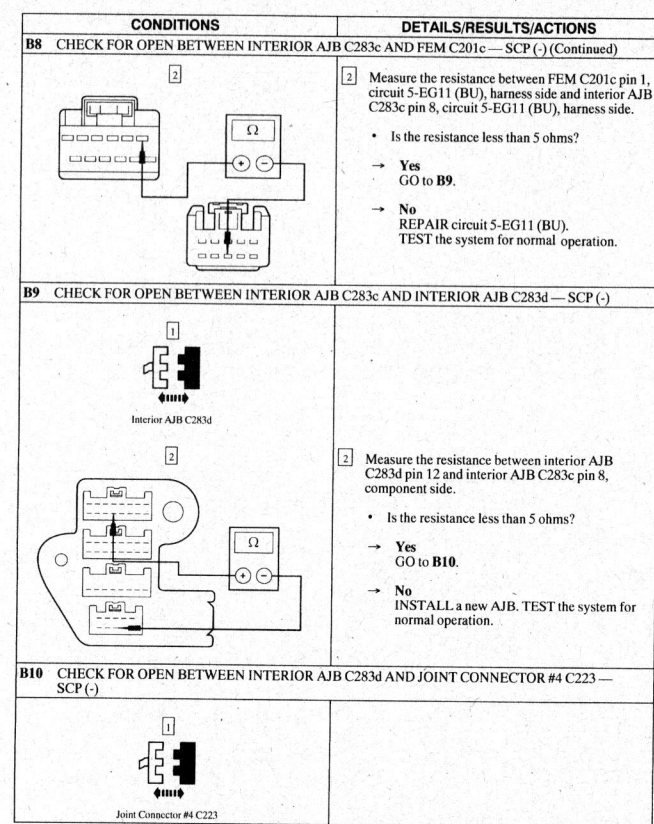

CONDITIONS	DETAILS/RESULTS/ACTIONS
B8 CHECK FOR OPEN BETWEEN INTERIOR AJB C283c AND FEM C201c — SCP (-) (Continued)	**2** Measure the resistance between FEM C201c pin 1, circuit 5-EG11 (BU), harness side and interior AJB C283c pin 8, circuit 5-EG11 (BU), harness side. • Is the resistance less than 5 ohms? → **Yes** GO to **B9**. → **No** REPAIR circuit 5-EG11 (BU). TEST the system for normal operation.
B9 CHECK FOR OPEN BETWEEN INTERIOR AJB C283c AND INTERIOR AJB C283d — SCP (-)	**2** Measure the resistance between interior AJB C283d pin 12 and interior AJB C283c pin 8, component side. • Is the resistance less than 5 ohms? → **Yes** GO to **B10**. → **No** INSTALL a new AJB. TEST the system for normal operation.
B10 CHECK FOR OPEN BETWEEN INTERIOR AJB C283d AND JOINT CONNECTOR #4 C223 — SCP (-)	

FM6020100448050X

Fig. 4 Test C: Front Electronics Module Does Not Respond To Diagnostic Tool (Part 5 of 6)

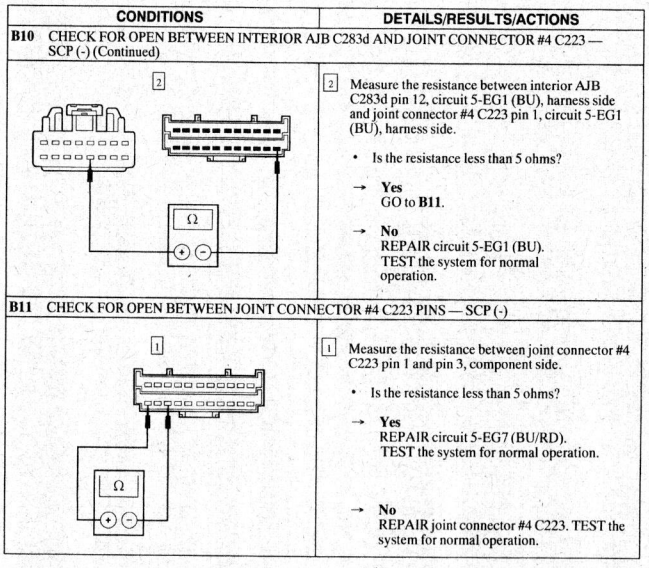

CONDITIONS	DETAILS/RESULTS/ACTIONS
B10 CHECK FOR OPEN BETWEEN INTERIOR AJB C283d AND JOINT CONNECTOR #4 C223 — SCP (-) (Continued)	**2** Measure the resistance between interior AJB C283d pin 12, circuit 5-EG1 (BU), harness side and joint connector #4 C223 pin 1, circuit 5-EG1 (BU), harness side. • Is the resistance less than 5 ohms? → **Yes** GO to **B11**. → **No** REPAIR circuit 5-EG1 (BU). TEST the system for normal operation.
B11 CHECK FOR OPEN BETWEEN JOINT CONNECTOR #4 C223 PINS — SCP (-)	**1** Measure the resistance between joint connector #4 C223 pin 1 and pin 3, component side. • Is the resistance less than 5 ohms? → **Yes** REPAIR circuit 5-EG7 (BU/RD). TEST the system for normal operation. → **No** REPAIR joint connector #4 C223. TEST the system for normal operation.

FM6020100448060X

Fig. 4 Test C: Front Electronics Module Does Not Respond To Diagnostic Tool (Part 6 of 6)

DISC BRAKES

TABLE OF CONTENTS

Front Disc Brakes

NOTE: On Air Bag Equipped Models, Refer To "Air Bag System Precautions" Located In The Front Of This Manual For System Disarming & Arming Procedures.

NOTE: Refer To "Computer Relearn Procedures" Located In The Front Of This Manual When Battery Power To The Computer Has Been Interrupted.

INDEX

PRECAUTIONS

Air Bag Systems

Refer to "Air Bag System Precautions" in the front of this manual for system disarming and arming procedures.

Battery Ground Cable

Prior to service, disconnect battery ground cable and isolate as required.

System Depressurizing

On models equipped with anti-lock brakes, hydraulic system must be depressurized prior to disconnecting any hydraulic lines or fittings, by pumping the brake pedal at least 25 times with ignition in Off position.

DESCRIPTION

Dual Piston Calipers

The caliper consists of a sliding bridge

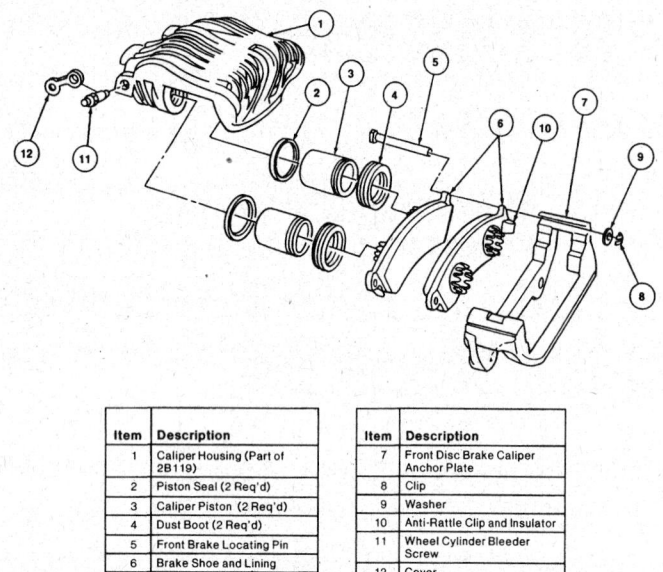

Item	Description	Item	Description
1	Caliper Housing (Part of 2B119)	7	Front Disc Brake Caliper Anchor Plate
2	Piston Seal (2 Req'd)	8	Clip
3	Caliper Piston (2 Req'd)	9	Washer
4	Dust Boot (2 Req'd)	10	Anti-Rattle Clip and Insulator
5	Front Brake Locating Pin	11	Wheel Cylinder Bleeder Screw
6	Brake Shoe and Lining	12	Cover

FM4079500073000X

Fig. 1 Exploded view of dual piston disc brake caliper. Mustang Cobra

type caliper housing with dual pistons, caliper mounting frame and inner and outer friction pad assemblies, **Figs. 1 and 2.** The caliper is located into and slides on the anchor frame by its thrust face and a locating pin and clip. The friction pads are retained into the anchor frame by the caliper sliding bridge assembly and use an anti-rattle spring clip to reduce brake noise. The friction pads are retained into the sliding bridge assembly by clips located on the back of the friction pad.

Lefthand and righthand caliper and inner and outer lefthand and righthand friction pads are unique and cannot be interchanged. When servicing this system, mark all components with location marks for later reference and assembly.

Single Piston Calipers

The caliper consists of a pin sliding caliper housing, inner and outer shoe and lining assemblies and a single piston, **Figs. 3 and 4.** The caliper slides on two pins which also act as mounting bolts between caliper and the combination anchor plate and spindle. The outer brake shoe and lining assembly is longer than the inner brake shoe and lining assembly. Inner and outer shoe and lining assemblies are attached to the caliper by spring clips riveted to the shoe surfaces. The inner shoe is attached to the caliper by installing the spring clip to the inside of the caliper piston. The outer shoe clips directly to the caliper housing. A wear indicator is incorporated, which emits a noise when the lining is worn to a point for required replacement. Lefthand and righthand inner and outer shoes are not interchangeable.

TROUBLESHOOTING
Brake Roughness
THICKNESS VARIATION

If roughness or vibration is encountered during highway operation or if pedal pumping is experienced at low speeds, the disc may have excessive thickness variation. Measure the disc at 12 points with a micrometer at a radius approximately one inch from edge of disc. If thickness measurements vary by more than .0005 inch, replace the disc.

LATERAL RUNOUT

Excessive lateral runout of braking disc may cause a knocking back of the pistons, possibly creating increased pedal travel and vibration when brakes are applied.

WHEEL BEARING LOOSENESS

Adjust the wheel bearings as outlined in "Front Steering & Suspension" in appropriate chassis chapter before measuring lateral runout. The adjustment is important and will be required at the completion of the test to prevent bearing failure.

Brake Booster Operation Test

1. Inspect hydraulic system for leaks or insufficient fluid.
2. With transmission in park, stop engine.
3. Apply brakes several times to release system vacuum.
4. Depress brake pedal and hold in applied position.
5. Start engine and note whether brake pedal moves downward under constant foot pressure.
6. If no pedal movement is felt, brake booster system is inoperative.
7. Remove vacuum hose from power brake booster valve.
8. Inspect for vacuum at valve end of hose with engine at idle speed and transmission in neutral.
9. Ensure unused vacuum ports are properly capped and vacuum hoses are not cracked or deteriorated.
10. If manifold vacuum is present and no pedal movement is noted during testing, replace power brake booster.
11. Operate engine at least 10 seconds at fast idle. Stop engine and let vehicle stand for 10 minutes.
12. Apply brake pedal with approximately 20 ft. lbs., force.
13. Pedal feel should be same as that noted with engine operating.
14. If bake pedal feels hard (no power assist), replace check valve and repeat test.
15. If brake pedal still feels hard after check valve replacement, replace power brake booster.
16. If pedal movement feels spongy, bleed hydraulic system to remove air.

Brake Master Cylinder
NORMAL CONDITIONS

The following conditions are considered normal and are not indications the brake master cylinder is faulting:
1. Slight turbulence in brake master cylinder reservoir fluid occurring when brake pedal is released. Turbulence occurs as brake fluid returns to master cylinder after releasing brakes.
2. Trace of brake fluid on booster shell below master cylinder mounting flange. This condition results from lubricating action of master cylinder wiping seal.

ABNORMAL CONDITIONS

Prior to performing any diagnosis, ensure brake system warning indicator is functional.

Diagnostic procedures use brake pedal feel, warning indicator illumination and brake fluid level indicators in diagnosing brake system problems. The following conditions are considered abnormal:
1. **Brake pedal goes down fast.** Inspect for external or internal leak.
2. **Brake pedal eases down slowly.** Inspect for internal or external leak.
3. **Brake pedal is low or feels spongy.** Proceed as follows:
   a. Inspect fluid level in brake master cylinder reservoir.

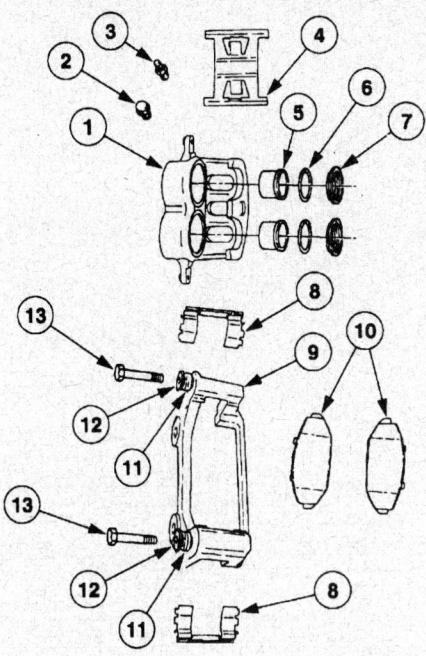

Fig. 2 Exploded view of dual piston disc brake caliper (Part 1 of 2). Crown Victoria, Grand Marquis, LS, Thunderbird & Town Car

b. Inspect brake master cylinder reservoir cap vent holes for clogging.
c. Inspect rear brake adjustment.
d. Inspect for air in hydraulic system.
4. **Brake pedal effort is excessive.** Inspect for binding or obstructed brake pedal linkage or insufficient power brake booster vacuum.
5. **Rear brakes lock up during light brake pedal application.** Inspect for wrong tire pressure, worn tires, grease or fluid on brake linings, damaged linings, improperly adjusted parking brakes or damaged brake pressure control valve.
6. **Brake pedal effort is erratic.** Inspect for power brake booster fault, extreme caliper piston knock back or improperly installed disc brake shoe or lining.
7. **Brake warning indicator is on.** Inspect for low fluid level, ignition wire routing too close to fluid level indicator or float assembly damage.

BYPASS CONDITION INSPECTION

1. Inspect fluid level in brake master cylinder reservoir.
2. Observe fluid level in brake master cylinder. If, after several brake applications fluid level remains same, measure wheel turning torque required to rotate wheels with brakes applied as follows:
   a. Place transmission in neutral.
   b. Raise vehicle on hoist.
   c. Apply brakes slowly to at least of 100 ft. lbs., and hold for approximately 15 seconds.
   d. With brakes still applied, exert 75 ft.

lbs., of torque on one front wheel and one rear wheel.
   e. If either wheel rotates, inspect internal components of brake master cylinder.

NON-PRESSURE LEAKS

An empty brake master cylinder reservoir condition may be caused by either of the following non-pressure external leaks:
1. Inspect for an external leak that may occur at the brake master cylinder reservoir cap because of improper positioning of gasket and cap.
2. Inspect for a leak at the brake master cylinder reservoir mounting grommets. Install new grommets if required.

BRAKE SYSTEM BLEED

Pressure bleeding is recommended for all hydraulic disc brake systems.

Do not reuse brake fluid drained from the hydraulic system when bleeding the brakes. Ensure disc brake pistons are returned to their normal positions and the shoe and lining assemblies are properly seated.

Do not shake the pressure bleeder tank while air is being added or after it has been pressurized. This will prevent air from the tank getting into the lines. Do not move the tank during the bleeding operation. The tank should be kept at least one third full.

On models equipped with power brakes, exhaust the vacuum in the power unit by pumping the brake pedal several times with the engine Off.

On vehicles equipped with disc brakes and master cylinders without proportioners or pressure control valves located in the master cylinder outlet port, the brake metering valve or combination valve must be held in position using suitable tool.

On vehicles equipped with plastic reservoirs, do not exceed 25 psi bleeding pressure.

When bleeding without pressure, open the bleed valve three quarters of a turn, depress the pedal a full stroke, close the bleeder and allow the pedal to return slowly to its released position. Repeat until no more air is visible in fluid.

Discard drained or bled brake fluid. Do not spill fluid on vehicle surfaces, brake fluid will damage painted finishes.

Flushing is essential if there is water, mineral oil or other contaminants in the lines, and whenever new components are installed in the hydraulic system. Fluid contamination is usually indicated by swollen and deteriorated cups and other rubber components.

If air has entered system because of low fluid levels, or removal of master cylinder brake lines, all four wheels will require bleeding. If a line is disconnected at only one cylinder, then only that cylinder needs to be bled.

Master cylinders equipped with bleeder valves should be bled first before the wheel cylinders are bled. In all cases where a master cylinder has been overhauled, it must be bled. Where there is no bleeder

Item	Part Number	Description
1	2B120	Disc brake caliper
2	2L126	Bleeder screw cap
3	2208	Bleeder screw
4	2B164	Anti-rattle spring
5	2196	Caliper piston
6	2B115	Piston seal
7	2207	Piston dust boot
8	2L200	Shoe slipper
9	2B292	Front disc brake caliper anchor plate
10	2001	Brake pads
11	2A492	Guide pin boot
12	2B296	Guide pin
13	2N386	Caliper bolt

FM4079800099020X

Fig. 2 Exploded view of dual piston disc brake caliper (Part 2 of 2). Crown Victoria, Grand Marquis, LS, Thunderbird & Town Car

valve, leave the lines loose, then actuate the brake pedal to expel the air. Tighten lines and repeat until no air is visible in expelled fluid.

System Priming

When a new master cylinder is installed or if the brake system has been partially or completely emptied, fluid may not flow from the bleeder screws during normal bleeding. It may be required to prime the system using the following procedure:
1. Remove brake lines from master cylinder.
2. Install short brake lines in master cylinder and position them back into the reservoir. Ensure short brake line ends are submerged in reservoir brake fluid.
3. Fill reservoir with recommended brake fluid, then cover master cylinder fluid reservoir with shop towel.
4. Pump brakes until clear, bubble-free fluid comes out of both brake lines. If any brake fluid spills on paint, wash it off immediately with water.
5. Remove short brake lines, then install original brake lines.
6. Bleed each brake line at master cylinder using the following procedure:
   a. Have assistant pump brake pedal 10 times, then hold firm pressure on pedal.
   b. Open rearmost brake line fittings until stream of brake fluid comes out. Have assistant maintain pressure on brake pedal until brake line fitting is tightened.
   c. Repeat this operation until clear, bubble-free fluid comes out from around tube fitting.
   d. Repeat bleeding operation at front brake line fitting.
7. If any of brake lines or calipers have been removed, it may be required to prime system by gravity bleeding.

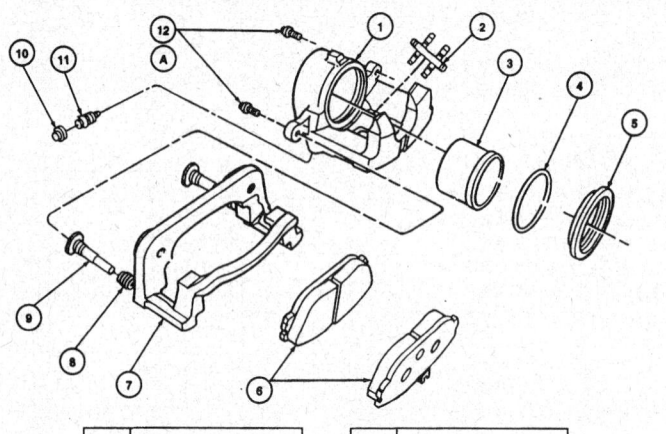

Item	Description
1	Disc Brake Caliper
2	Disc Brake Pad Anti-Rattle Clip
3	Caliper Piston
4	Brake Piston Seal
5	Front Disc Brake Caliper Boot
6	Brake Shoe and Lining
7	Front Disc Brake Caliper Anchor Plate

Item	Description
8	Locating Pin Boots
9	Disc Brake Caliper Locating Pin
10	Bleed Screw Cap
11	Wheel Cylinder Bleeder Screw
12	Caliper Guide Pin Bolt
A	Tighten to 28-36 N-m (21-26 Lb-Ft) (Tighten Bottom Caliper Guide Pin Bolt First)

FM4079500072000X

Fig. 3 Exploded view of single piston disc brake caliper. Continental, Cougar, Five Hundred, Freestyle, Montego, Mustang (except Cobra), Sable & Taurus

Item	Description
1	Boot
2	Piston Seal
3	Piston
4	Dust Seal
5	Snap Ring

Item	Description
6	Disc Brake Caliper
7	Boot
8	Brake Caliper Bleeder Screw
9	Brake Caliper Bleeder Screw Cap
10	Front Caliper Sleeve

FM4079500074000X

Fig. 4 Exploded view of single piston disc brake caliper. Escort & ZX2

Gravity bleed system after master cylinder is primed and bled. To prime system using gravity method, proceed as follows:

a. Fill master cylinder with manufacturer recommended brake fluid or equivalent.

b. Loosen both rear bleeder screws and leave open until clear brake fluid flows out. **Inspect reservoir fluid level frequently. Do not allow fluid level to drop below halfway.**

c. Tighten rear bleeder screws.

d. Loosen bleeder screw on front caliper and leave open until clear fluid flows out. **Bleed front calipers one side at a time.**

8. After master cylinder has been primed, lines bled at master cylinder and brake system primed, resume normal brake system bleeding at each wheel.

Wheel Bleeding Sequence

Rear Wheel Drive...............RR-LR-RF-LF
Front Wheel Drive ....RR-LF-LR-RF

INSPECTION

Remove wheels and inspect brake disc, caliper and linings. Inspect wheel bearings and repack if required.

If the caliper is cracked or fluid leakage through the casting is evident, it must be replaced as a unit.

If caliper is removed when installing new components, clean all components in alcohol, then wipe dry using lint-free cloths. Blow out drilled passages and bores with compressed air. Inspect dust boots for punctures or tears, replace as required.

Inspect piston bores in both housings for scoring or pitting. Bores showing light scratches or corrosion can be cleaned with crocus cloth. Bores with deep scratches or scoring may be honed, provided the diameter of the bore is not increased more than .002 inch. If the bore does not clean up within this specification, replace the caliper. **Black stains on the bore walls are caused by piston seals and do not adversely affect caliper performance.**

When using a hone, install the hone baffle before honing the bore. The baffle is used to protect the hone stones from damage. Use extreme care in cleaning the caliper after honing. Remove all dust and grit by flushing the caliper with alcohol. Wipe the caliper dry with a clean lint-free cloth, then repeat cleaning procedure.

BRAKE DISC SERVICE

Disc brake service is critical because of the close tolerances required in machining the brake disc to ensure proper brake operation.

Maintaining close control of the shape of the rubbing surfaces is required to prevent brake roughness. In addition, the surface finish must be non-directional and maintained at a micro-inch finish. This is required to avoid pulls and erratic performance, and to promote long lining life and equal lining wear of both the lefthand and righthand brakes.

Do not attempt to refinish the rubbing surfaces unless precision equipment, capable of measuring in micro inches (millionths of an inch), is available.

To inspect the disc lateral runout, mount a dial indicator, so the indicator's plunger contacts the disc one inch from the outer edge, **Fig. 5.** If the total indicated runout exceeds specifications, install a new disc.

To inspect parallelism (thickness variation), mount dial indicators so the plunger contacts the rotor approximately one inch from the outer edge, **Fig. 6.** If parallelism exceeds specifications, replace the rotor.

BRAKE PAD SERVICE

On models with anti-lock brakes, the brake hydraulic system must be depressurized before disconnecting any hydraulic lines or fittings. Depressurize the system by pumping the brake pedal at least 25 times with the ignition in the Off position.

Continental, Cougar, Crown Victoria, Five Hundred, Freestyle, Grand Marquis, LS, Marauder, Montego, Sable, Taurus, Thunderbird & Town Car

REMOVAL

1. Remove brake fluid until reservoir is half full.

2. **On models equipped with air suspension,** turn air suspension service switch to Off position.

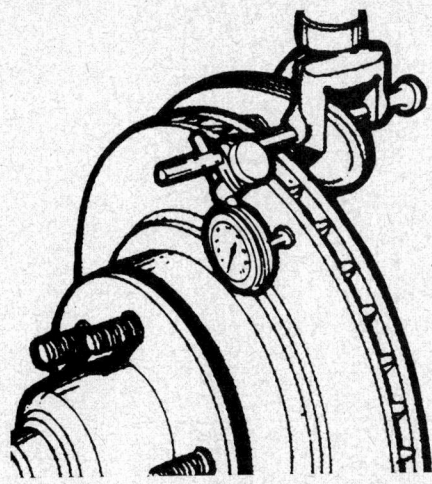

Fig. 5 Rotor lateral runout inspection

FM40791000009000X

3. **On all models,** raise and support front of vehicle, then remove tire and wheel assembly.
4. Remove two caliper anchor bracket mounting bolts and discard.
5. Lift front disc brake caliper anchor plate away from rotor using rotating motion.
6. Remove outer brake shoe from disc brake caliper by sliding brake shoe away from outer leg to disconnect it from anchor plate.
7. Remove inner brake shoe and lining assembly by sliding brake shoe away from piston disconnecting it from caliper anchor plate.
8. Suspend caliper from inner fender housing with suitable wire.

INSTALLATION

Some models have pistons made of phenolic material. **Do not seat these pistons in bore by applying C-clamp directly to piston.** Use extra care during to prevent damage to the piston. Metal or sharp objects should not come into direct contact with the piston.

1. Seat caliper piston in bore using suitable C-clamp and block of 2¾ x 1 inch and approximately ¾ inch thick wood. Remove C-clamp and wooden block.
2. Install caliper anchor plate with caliper guide pin bolts. Tighten lower bolt first, then the upper bolt.
3. Ensure anti-rattle spring and clip are seated in caliper lining inspection opening. Anti-rattle clips must be installed from lining side.
4. Engage brake shoe and lining in anchor plate by first engaging the side opposite anti-rattle clip.
5. Press other end of brake shoe and lining to compress disc brake pad anti-rattle clip, then engage brake shoe lining in front anchor plate.
6. Inspect caliper and anchor plate to ensure brake shoes and linings are properly installed.
7. Position caliper and anchor plate over rotor. Install two new caliper anchor bracket bolts.

8. Inspect caliper locating pin and pin boots. If caliper locating pin is binding, remove and clean.
9. Install tire and wheel assembly, then lower vehicle.
10. **On models equipped with air suspension,** turn air suspension service switch to On position.
11. **On all models,** fill master cylinder, then pump brake pedal several times to position brake linings before moving vehicle.

Escort & ZX2
REMOVAL

1. Raise and support vehicle, then remove tire and wheel assembly.
2. Remove springs and brake pad retaining pins, **Fig. 7.**
3. Remove brake pads and shims.

INSTALLATION

1. Push piston fully back into caliper bore.
2. Apply grease between shims and brake pad guide plates.
3. Position brake pads and shims into caliper.
4. Install springs and two brake pad retaining pins.
5. Install tire and wheel assembly.

Focus
REMOVAL

1. Raise and support vehicle, then remove tire and wheel assembly.
2. Disconnect brake hose from front strut support bracket.
3. Remove outer brake pad retaining clip.
4. Remove covers and bolts, then pull caliper outwards to release piston.
5. Support brake caliper from wire hook. **Do not allow caliper to hang from brake hose.**
6. Lift outer pad retaining clip over spring retaining lugs, then remove outer and inner brake pads.

INSTALLATION

1. Fully retract caliper piston into caliper.
2. Install inner, then outer brake pads.
3. Push outer retaining clip over spring retaining lugs.
4. Install caliper, bolts and covers.
5. Install brake hose onto support bracket.
6. Install outer pad retaining clip.
7. Install tire and wheel assemblies, then inspect brake fluid level.

Mustang
COBRA

Brake components are not interchangeable. Ensure each component is installed in it's original location.

REMOVAL

1. Remove approximately ½ of brake fluid from master cylinder reservoir.
2. Raise and support vehicle, then remove tire and wheel assemblies. **Do**

FM40791000010000X

Fig. 6 Rotor parallelism (thickness variation) inspection

not damage disc brake shields or bleeder screws.
3. Remove clip and washer, then the caliper locating pin.
4. Lift caliper with pads from anchor frame.
5. Secure assembly aside with suitable wire or tie wrap.
6. Mark inner and outer friction pads for installation alignment. Remove pads.

INSPECTION

Inspect caliper piston and caliper pin boots for damage.

Inspect rotor for wear and runout. Minor glazing of surfaces can be removed by hand sanding with medium grit sandpaper.

INSTALLATION

1. Clean sliding and contact surfaces of brake components.
2. Remove protective paper from adhesive insulator material on friction pads. **Do not to contaminate adhesive surface.**
3. Install pads into caliper. Ensure correct pad is fully seated into proper caliper position.
4. Compress pistons into caliper using suitable C-clamp. Ensure sufficient clearance exists to allow pads to fit over rotor.
5. Place caliper into position on anchor frame, then install locating pin, washer and clip.
6. Install tire and wheel assemblies. **Do not damage brake shields or bleeder screws.**
7. Lower vehicle. Pump brake pedal until firm pedal is achieved.

EXCEPT COBRA

Refer to "Continental, Cougar, Crown Victoria, Grand Marquis, LS, Marauder, Sable, Taurus, Thunderbird & Town Car" for brake pad service procedure.

CALIPER SERVICE
Replacement

On models with anti-lock brakes, the

brake booster system must be depressurized before disconnecting any hydraulic lines or fittings. Depressurize the system by pumping the brake pedal at least 25 times with the ignition in the Off position.

CONTINENTAL, COUGAR, CROWN VICTORIA, FIVE HUNDRED, FREESTYLE, GRAND MARQUIS, LS, MARAUDER, MONTEGO, SABLE, TAURUS, THUNDERBIRD & TOWN CAR

Before removing calipers, mark left and righthand calipers so they can be installed in their original position.

1. **On models equipped with air suspension,** turn air suspension service switch to Off position.
2. **On all models,** raise and support front of vehicle, then remove tire and wheel assembly.
3. Loosen brake tube fitting connecting brake tube to fitting on frame. Plug brake tube.
4. Remove retaining clip from brake hose and bracket, then disconnect brake hose from caliper.
5. Remove caliper locating pins.
6. Lift caliper from rotor and spindle anchor plate assembly.
7. **On models equipped with phenolic caliper piston,** do not pry directly against piston.
8. **On all models,** reverse procedure to install, noting the following:
   a. Install caliper over rotor with outer shoe against rotor braking surface to prevent pinching piston boot between inner brake shoe and piston. **Ensure calipers are installed in proper position.**
   b. Bleed brake system as outlined in "Brake System Bleed."
   c. Pump brake pedal several times to position brake shoes before moving vehicle.
   d. Turn air suspension switch to ON position.

ESCORT & ZX2

1. Raise and support vehicle, then remove brake pads as outlined in "Brake Pad Service."
2. Clamp center of brake flex hose to prevent brake fluid leakage using suitable needle nose vise grips.
3. Remove banjo bolt retaining brake flex hose to caliper.
4. Disconnect brake hose from caliper and discard two copper washers.
5. Remove two mounting bolts and caliper.
6. Reverse procedure to install, noting the following:

a. Install new copper sealing washers.
b. Bleed brakes as outlined in "Brake System Bleed."

FOCUS

1. Raise and support vehicle, then remove front tire and wheel assemblies.
2. Disconnect brake hose from support bracket on front strut.
3. Loosen brake hose fitting on caliper.
4. Remove front brake pads as outlined in "Brake Pad Service."
5. Disconnect front caliper from brake hose. Cap brake hose.
6. Reverse procedure to install. Bleed brakes as outlined in "Brake System Bleed."

MUSTANG

COBRA

Brake components are unique and are not interchangeable. Ensure each component is installed in its original location.

1. Remove brake pads as outlined in "Brake Pad Service."
2. Remove brake flex hose from caliper and discard copper sealing washers.
3. Remove two mounting bolts and lift caliper/anchor frame assembly off rotor.
4. Reverse procedure to install, noting the following:
   a. Use new copper sealing washers.
   b. Bleed brakes as outlined in "Brake System Bleed."

EXCEPT COBRA

Refer to "Continental, Cougar, Crown Victoria, Grand Marquis, LS, Marauder, Sable, Taurus, Thunderbird & Town Car" for caliper replacement procedure.

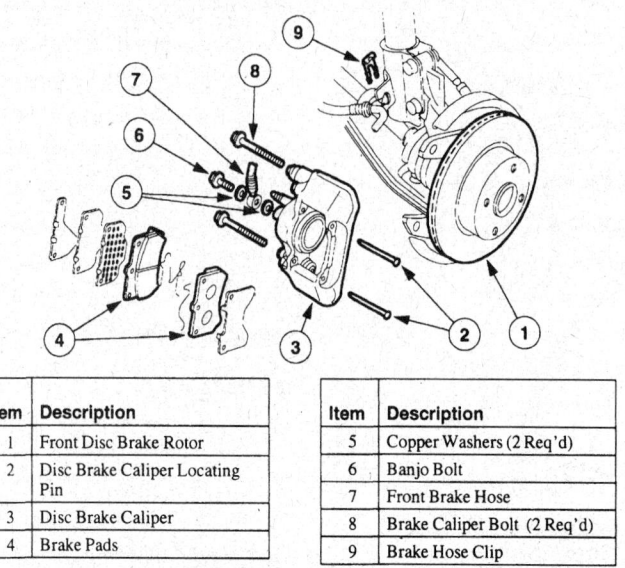

Item	Description	Item	Description
1	Front Disc Brake Rotor	5	Copper Washers (2 Req'd)
2	Disc Brake Caliper Locating Pin	6	Banjo Bolt
3	Disc Brake Caliper	7	Front Brake Hose
4	Brake Pads	8	Brake Caliper Bolt (2 Req'd)
		9	Brake Hose Clip

FM4079500075000X

Fig. 7 Front disc brake assembly. Escort & ZX2

Overhaul

CONTINENTAL, COUGAR, CROWN VICTORIA, FIVE HUNDRED, FREESTYLE, GRAND MARQUIS, LS, MARAUDER, MONTEGO, SABLE, TAURUS, THUNDERBIRD & TOWN CAR

DISASSEMBLE

1. Position fiber block and shop towels between caliper piston and caliper housing, then apply compressed air to caliper brake line fitting bore to force piston from caliper.
2. Remove dust boot, **Fig. 3.**
3. Remove piston seal from cylinder and discard.

INSPECTION

1. Inspect piston for scratches, scoring or damage.
2. Inspect caliper bore for scratches, scoring or corrosion. Light scratches or slight corrosion can be polished out using crocus cloth.
3. Ensure bleeder screw and bleeder screw bore hole in caliper are fully open.
4. Inspect caliper bushings for corrosion and dust boot retaining ring for damage or tension loss. Replace components as required.

ASSEMBLE

1. Lubricate piston seal with suitable, clean brake fluid, then install seal in caliper bore. **Ensure seal is firmly seated in groove.**
2. Install new dust boot in outer groove of caliper bore.
3. Coat clean brake fluid and install piston in caliper bore.
4. Spread dust boot over piston as it is installed, then seat dust boot in piston groove.

ESCORT & ZX2

DISASSEMBLE

1. Remove front caliper sleeves and dust boots.
2. Remove cap and caliper bleed screw.
3. Remove snap ring and caliper piston dust seal.
4. Position wood block or shop towels between caliper and piston, then apply air pressure to brake hose fitting to remove piston from caliper. Use only enough air pressure to ease piston from caliper bore. **Keep hands and fingers away from piston.**

INSPECTION

1. Inspect piston for scratches, scoring or damage.
2. Inspect caliper bore for scratches, scoring or corrosion. Light scratches or slight corrosion can be polished out using crocus cloth.
3. Ensure bleeder screw and bleeder screw bore hole in caliper are fully open.
4. Inspect caliper bushings for corrosion and dust boot retaining ring for damage or tension loss.

ASSEMBLE

1. Lubricate piston seal with suitable brake fluid and position seal in caliper bore groove.
2. Lubricate piston and caliper bore with suitable brake fluid.

FOCUS

DISASSEMBLE

1. Place block of wood or some shop towels between brake caliper piston and housing.
2. Remove caliper piston using compressed air applied to caliper.
3. Remove and discard caliper dust seal and piston seal.
4. Inspect caliper piston and piston bore for pitting or scoring.
5. Replace damaged or scored components.

ASSEMBLE

1. Lubricate piston bore, piston seal and caliper piston with DOT 3 brake fluid.
2. Install new caliper seal into machined

---

groove in piston bore.
3. Install new dust seal onto caliper piston.
4. Install caliper piston into caliper bore.
5. Seat dust seal and install caliper.

MUSTANG

COBRA

Disassemble

1. Drain remaining brake fluid from caliper into suitable container.
2. Position fiber block and shop towels between caliper pistons and caliper housing.
3. Apply compressed air to caliper brake line fitting bore to force pistons from caliper.
4. Remove dust boots from caliper.
5. Remove piston seals from cylinder and discard.

Inspection

1. Inspect pistons for scratches, scoring or damage.
2. Inspect caliper bores for scratches, scoring or corrosion. Light scratches or slight corrosion can be polished out using crocus cloth.
3. Ensure bleeder screw and bleeder screw bore hole in caliper are fully open.

Assemble

1. Lubricate piston seals with suitable, clean brake fluid, then install seals in caliper bore. **Ensure seals are firmly seated in groove.**
2. Install new dust boots in outer groove of caliper bore.
3. Coat pistons with clean brake fluid and install pistons in caliper bore.
4. Install dust boots over piston as they are installed, then seat dust boots in piston groove.

EXCEPT COBRA

Refer to "Continental, Cougar, Crown Victoria, Grand Marquis, LS, Marauder, Sable, Taurus, Thunderbird & Town Car" for caliper overhaul procedure.

ROTOR

REPLACE

This procedure has been revised by a Technical Service Bulletin.

On Continental, Sable and Taurus models, the disc rotor is a hat section-type of composite steel and cast iron. A Rotunda Rotor Mounting Adapter tool No. 054-00032, or equivalent, is required for use on the brake lathe for refinishing. **Failure to use the adapter will result in gouging the brake disc, making it unfit for use.**

On Continental, Sable and Taurus models, if service is required, install the new full cast front disc rotors, part No.

F10Y-1125-B, in pairs only. **Never install a full cast rotor on one side of the vehicle with a composite rotor on the other side.**

On all models if caliper does not require servicing, do not disconnect brake hose or remove caliper. Position caliper aside with wire or tie straps.

If excessive force must be used to remove the rotor, then it should be inspected for lateral runout before installation.

Removal

1. **On models equipped with air suspension,** turn service switch to Off position.
2. **On all models,** raise and support vehicle, then remove tire and wheel assembly. **Do not damage or interference with caliper bleeder screw fitting and brake rotor shield.**
3. Remove caliper anchor bracket bolts.
4. Position caliper aside with suitable wire or tie straps. **Prevent deformation of rotor and nicking, scratching or contaminating brake lining and rotor surfaces.**
5. Remove front rotor from hub assembly by pulling it off hub studs, noting the following:
   a. If excessive force is required to remove rotor, inspect rotor for lateral runout prior to installation.
   b. If additional force is required to remove front disc brake rotor, apply suitable rust penetrant and inhibitor on front and rear rotor/hub mating surfaces.
   c. Strike rotor between studs with suitable plastic hammer.
   d. If rotor still will not come off, install three-jaw puller tool No. D80L-1013-A, or equivalent, and remove rotor.

Installation

1. If front disc brake rotor is being replaced, remove protective coating from new rotor with suitable carburetor cleaner.
2. If original rotor is being installed, ensure rotor braking and mounting surfaces are clean.
3. Apply suitable lubricant to pilot diameter of front disc brake rotor, then install rotor on wheel hub assembly.
4. Install caliper and caliper anchor bracket bolts on rotor.
5. Install tire and wheel assembly. **Tighten wheel hub bolt nuts with torque wrench in star pattern.**
6. Lower vehicle, then pump brake pedal to position brake linings prior to moving vehicle.
7. Turn air suspension service switch to On position.
8. Road test vehicle.

DISC BRAKE SPECIFICATIONS

Model	Year	Front Disc Brake						Rear Disc Brake					
		Brake Lining Wear Limit, Inch [1]	Rotor Thickness, Inch			Thickness Variation Parallelism Inch	Lateral Run Out (T.I.R.) Inch	Brake Lining Wear Limit, Inch [2]	Rotor Thickness, Inch			Thickness Variation Parallelism Inch	Lateral Run Out (T.I.R.) Inch
			Nominal	Min. Refinish	Discard Limit [3]				Nominal	Min. Refinish	Discard Limit [3]		
Continental	2001–02	.039	1.024	—	.974	.00035	.003	.039	.550	—	.502	.0004	.004
Cougar	2001–02	—	.950	—	.870	.00060	.003	—	.790	—	.710	.0006	.003
Crown Victoria	2001–02	.039	1.063	—	1.010	.00035	.002	.039	.550	—	.510	.0004	.002
	2003–05	.039	1.063	—	1.037	—	—	.039	—	—	.790	—	.003
Escort	2001	.080	.870	.820	.790	—	.002	.040	.350	—	.280	—	.002
Five Hundred	2005	.039	1.024	—	.974	.00040	.002	.039	.550	—	.502	.0004	.004
Focus	2001	.059	.870	—	.790	.00080	.002	—	—	—	—	—	—
	2002–05	.059	[4]	—	.870	.00080	.002	.059	.390	—	.350	.0008	
Freestyle	2005	.039	1.024	—	.974	.00040	.002	.039	.550	—	.502	.0004	.004
Grand Marquis	2001–02	.039	1.063	—	1.010	.00035	.002	.039	.550	—	.510	.0004	.002
	2003–05	.039	1.063	—	1.037	—	—	.039	—	—	.790	—	.003
LS	2001–05	.080	1.181	—	1.120	.00040	.004	.040	.787	—	.740	.0004	.004
Marauder	2003–05	.039	1.063	—	1.037	—	—	.039	—	—	.790	—	.003
Montego	2005	.039	1.024	—	.974	.00040	.002	.039	.550	—	.502	.0004	.004
Mustang	2001	.080	1.063	—	1.010	.00035	.002	.039	.550	—	.502	.0004	.002
	2002–05	.080	[5]	—	[6]	.00035	.002	.039	.550	—	.502	.0004	.004
Sable	2001	.039	1.063	—	1.010	.00040	.002	.039	.550	—	.502	.0004	.004
	2002–05	.039	1.024	—	.974	.00040	.002	.039	.550	—	.502	.0004	.004
Taurus	2001	.039	1.063	—	1.010	.00040	.002	.039	.550	—	.502	.0004	.004
	2002–05	.039	1.024	—	.974	.00040	.002	.039	.550	—	.502	.0004	.004
Thunderbird	2002–05	.079	—	—	1.120	.00040	.004	.039	—	—	.740	.0004	.004
Town Car	2000–02	.039	1.063	—	1.010	.00035	.002	.039	.550	—	.510	.0004	.002
	2003–05	.039	1.063	—	1.037	—	—	.039	—	—	.790	—	.003
ZX2	2001–03	.080	.870	.820	.790	—	.002	.040	.350	.310	.280	—	.002

[1] — With 16 inch wheels.

[2] — Above rivet head or backing plate. Original equipment type brake lining.

[3] — Discard thickness is stamped on rotor.

[4] — Models w/2.0L DOHC engine, .950 inch; w/2.0L SOHC engine, .870 inch.

[5] — Except Cobra, 1.020 inch; Cobra, 1.100 inch.

[6] — Except Cobra, .970 inch; Cobra, 1.040 inch.

TIGHTENING SPECIFICATIONS

Year/Model	Component	Torque/Ft. Lbs.
CONTINENTAL		
2001–02	Brake Hose	16–44
	Front Brake Master Cylinder Tube Fitting	18
	Front Caliper Bleeder Screw	84①
	Locating Pin	18–25
	Rear Brake Master Cylinder Tube Fitting	13
	Rear Caliper Bleeder Screw	84①
	Wheel Caliper Bleeder Screw	71①
	Wheel Lug Nut	65–88
COUGAR		
2001–02	Brake Hose To Caliper Union	11
	Caliper To Knuckle	21
	Wheel Lug Nuts	94
CROWN VICTORIA, GRAND MARQUIS, MARAUDER & TOWN CAR		
2001–02	Brake Hose	16–44
	Locating Pin	40–60
	Wheel Lug Nut	85–105
2003–05	Brake Hose	41
	Caliper	32
	Caliper Bleeder Screw	15
	Wheel Lug Nut	95
ESCORT & ZX2		
2001–03	Brake Hose	16–44
	Caliper	36–43
	Locating Pin	18–25
	Wheel Lug Nut	74–100
FOCUS		
2001–05	Brake Hose To Caliper Union	11
	Caliper To Knuckle	21
	Wheel Lug Nut	94
LS		
2001–05	Brake Hose	16–44
	Wheel Lug Nut	100
FIVE HUNDRED, FREESTYLE & MONTEGO		
2005	Brake Hose	108①
	Caliper Bolts	44
	Wheel Lug Nuts	85–104
MUSTANG		
2001–02	Brake Hose	16–44
	Locating Pin	45–65
	Wheel Lug Nut	85–105
2003–05	Brake Hose	30
	Caliper	23
	Caliper Bleeder Screw	7
	Wheel Lug Nuts	95
SABLE & TAURUS		
2001–05	Brake Hoses	16–44
	Locating Pin	18–25
	Wheel Lug Nuts	85–104

① — Inch lbs.

Rear Disc & Parking Brakes

> **NOTE:** On Air Bag Equipped Models, Refer To "Air Bag System Precautions" Located In The Front Of This Manual For System Disarming & Arming Procedures.

> **NOTE:** Refer To "Computer Relearn Procedures" Located In The Front Of This Manual When Battery Power To The Computer Has Been Interrupted.

INDEX

PRECAUTIONS

Air Bag Systems

Refer to "Air Bag System Precautions" in the front of this manual for system disarming and arming procedures.

Battery Ground Cable

Prior to service, disconnect battery ground cable and isolate as required.

System Depressurizing

On models equipped with anti-lock brakes, hydraulic system must be depressurized prior to disconnecting any hydraulic lines or fittings, by pumping the brake pedal at least 25 times with ignition in Off position.

DESCRIPTION

Continental, Cougar, Five Hundred, Freestyle, LS, Montego, Mustang, Sable & Taurus

Sliding caliper rear disc brakes are used on these models. The caliper is basically the same as the larger front wheel caliper. However, a parking brake mechanism and a larger inner brake shoe anti-rattle spring have been added.

The parking brake lever, located at the rear of the caliper, is actuated by a cable system similar to rear drum brake applications. When the parking brake is applied, the cable rotates the lever and operating shaft, driving the caliper piston and brake shoe assembly against the rotor. An automatic adjuster in the assembly compensates for lining wear and maintains proper clearance in the parking brake mechanism.

The cast iron rotors are ventilated by curved fins located between the braking surfaces and are designed to cause the rotor to act as an air pump when the vehicle is traveling forward. The rotors are not interchangeable and are identified by a Right or Left marking cast inside the hat section of the rotor. The rotor is secured to the axle flange in the same manner as a rear brake drum. A splash shield is bolted to a forged axle adapter to protect the inboard rotor surface.

Crown Victoria, Grand Marquis, Marauder & Town Car

The rear disc brake system uses a pin slider-type caliper, and a cast iron rotor bolted to the rear axle shaft flange. The caliper has a phenolic piston with a seal and a press-in type dust boot.

The inner pads are interchangeable left to right and use a three-finger clip fit inside the caliper piston. The outer pads are interchangeable left to right and use a dual-purpose clip which holds the brake pads on the caliper housing and also prevents caliper rattle.

The flanges on both inner and outer pads slide on a machined surfaces of the brake adapter.

Escort & ZX2

The self-adjusting rear disc brake system consists of a disc rotor and a single piston caliper. The brake pads are held in position between the caliper and the rotor by two guides, two shims and an anti rattle spring. It is not required to remove the caliper completely to replace the brake pads; they can be removed simply by pivoting the caliper on its mounting bracket. **On some models it may be required to disconnect the parking brake cable to allow full caliper rotation.**

During normal operation, hydraulic pressure from the master cylinder pushes the piston forward and applies pressure on the inboard brake pad. This pressure also causes the caliper to slide inward on the guide pins. As the brakes are applied, the square cut piston seal distorts. When the brake pedal is released, The square cut seal returns the piston to its normal position. If the piston moves no further than the square cut deformation limit, no self-adjustment takes place. If piston movement is greater than the deformation limit of the square cut seal, the piston and sleeve nut will travel on the threads of the spindle. This is because the loosened adjuster spring allows the sleeve nut to rotate. When the brake pedal is released, the piston returns the amount the square cut seal was deformed but it does not return to its original position. This is because the tightened adjuster spring does not allow the sleeve nut to rotate and travel on the thread. The piston can adjust outward from the caliper housing but it cannot move inward.

The parking brake cable is attached to the caliper at the operating lever. When the parking brake is applied, the operating lever pushes the connecting link against the piston which forces application of the brake pads. When the parking brake is released, pressure against the piston is released and the brake pads return to their normal position.

TROUBLESHOOTING

If roughness or vibration is encountered during highway operation or if pedal pumping is experienced at low speeds, the disc may have excessive thickness variation. Measure the disc at 12 points with a micrometer at a radius approximately one inch from the edge of the disc. If thickness measurements vary by more than .0005 inch, replace the rotor.

Excessive lateral runout of braking disc may cause a knocking back of the pistons, possibly creating increased pedal travel and vibration when brakes are applied.

Adjust the wheel bearings before inspecting the runout. The readjustment is very important and will be required at the completion of the test to prevent bearing failure. Adjust the wheel bearings as outlined in "Front Suspension & Steering" in appropriate chassis chapter.

BRAKE SYSTEM BLEED

Pressure bleeding is recommended for all hydraulic disc brake systems.

Do not use brake fluid drained from the hydraulic system when bleeding the brakes. Ensure disc brake pistons are returned to their normal positions and the shoe and lining assemblies are properly seated. Before driving the vehicle, inspect the brake operation.

Do not shake the pressure bleeder tank while air is being added or after it has been pressurized. This will prevent air from the tank getting into the lines. Set the tank in the required location, then bring the air hose to the tank. Do not move the tank during the bleeding operation. The tank should be kept at least one third full.

On models equipped with power brakes, exhaust the vacuum in the power unit by pumping the brake pedal several times with the engine Off before starting to bleed the system.

On vehicles equipped with disc brakes and master cylinders without proportioners or pressure control valves located in the master cylinder outlet port, the brake metering valve or combination valve must be held in position using suitable tool.

On vehicles equipped with plastic reservoirs, do not exceed 25 psi bleeding pressure.

When bleeding without pressure, open the bleed valve three quarters of a turn, depress the brake pedal a full stroke, then close the bleeder valve and allow the pedal to return slowly to its released position. Repeat as required until fluid is free of air bubbles.

Discard drained or bled brake fluid. Brake fluid will damage painted finishes. Do not spill fluid on vehicle surfaces.

Flushing is essential if there is water, mineral oil or other contaminants in the lines, and whenever new components are installed in the hydraulic system. Fluid contamination is usually indicated by swollen and deteriorated cups and other rubber components.

Bleeding is required on all four wheels if air has entered the system because of low fluid level or the line or lines have been disconnected. If a line is disconnected at any one wheel cylinder, only that cylinder needs to be bled.

Master cylinders equipped with bleeder valves should be bled first before the wheel cylinders are bled. In all cases where a master cylinder has been overhauled, it must be bled. Where there is no bleeder valve, this can be done by leaving the lines loose, actuating the brake pedal to expel the air then tightening the lines.

After overhauling a dual master cylinder used in conjunction with disc brakes, air may be trapped between the master cylinder pistons. Bleed the cylinder before installing it on the vehicle.

System Priming

When a new master cylinder is installed or the brake system is partially or completely emptied, fluid may not flow from the bleeder screws during normal bleeding. If required, prime the system using the following procedure:

1. Remove brake lines from master cylinder.
2. Install short brake lines in master cylinder and position them back into the reservoir. Ensure short brake line ends are submerged in reservoir brake fluid.
3. Fill reservoir with recommended brake fluid, then cover master cylinder fluid reservoir with shop towel.
4. Pump brakes until clear, bubble-free fluid comes out of both brake lines. **If any brake fluid spills on paint, wash it off immediately with water.**
5. Remove short brake lines, then reinstall original brake lines.
6. Bleed each brake line at master cylinder as follows:
   a. Have assistant pump brake pedal 10 times, then hold firm pressure on pedal.
   b. Open rearmost brake line fittings with tubing wrench until stream of brake fluid comes out. Have assistant maintain pressure on brake pedal until brake line fitting is tightened.
   c. Repeat until clear, bubble-free fluid comes out from around tube fitting.
   d. Repeat bleeding operation at front brake line fitting.
7. If any of brake lines or calipers have been removed, it may be helpful to prime system by gravity bleeding. This should be done after master cylinder is primed and bled. To prime system using gravity method, use following procedure:
   a. Fill master cylinder with manufacturer's recommended brake fluid, or equivalent.
   b. Loosen both rear bleeder screws and leave open until clear brake fluid flows out. **Inspect reservoir fluid level frequently. Do not allow fluid level to drop below halfway.**
   c. Tighten rear bleeder screws.
   d. Loosen bleeder screw on front caliper and leave open until clear fluid flows out. **Bleed front calipers one side at a time.**
8. After master cylinder has been primed, lines bled at master cylinder and brake system primed, resume normal brake

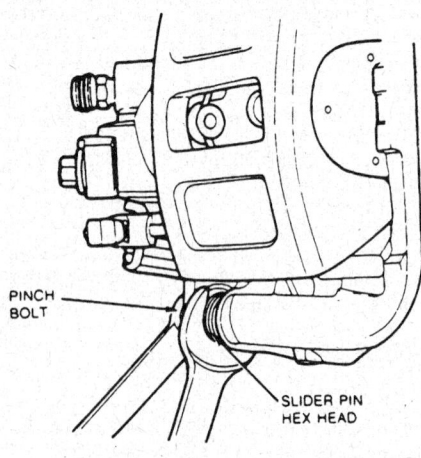

Fig. 1   Slider pin removal. Continental, Cougar, Five Hundred, Freestyle, Montego, Mustang, Sable & Taurus

system bleeding at each wheel.

Wheel Bleeding Sequence

Rear Wheel Drive..............RR-LR-RF-LF
Front Wheel Drive ....RR-LF-LR-RF

INSPECTION

Remove wheels and inspect brake disc, calipers and linings.

If the caliper is cracked or fluid leakage through the casting is evident, it must be replaced as a unit.

If caliper was removed when installing new components, clean all components in alcohol, then wipe dry using lint-free cloths. Using an air hose, blow out drilled passages and bores. Inspect dust boots for punctures or tears. If punctures or tears are evident, install new boots during assembly.

Inspect piston bores in both housings for scoring or pitting. Bores showing light scratches or corrosion can usually be cleaned with crocus cloth. Bores with deep scratches or scoring may be honed, provided the diameter of the bore is not increased more than .002 inch. If the bore does not clean up within this specification, a new caliper housing should be installed. Black stains on the bore walls are caused by piston seals and will not adversely affect caliper performance.

When using a hone, install the hone baffle before honing the bore. The baffle is used to protect the hone stones from damage. Use extreme care in cleaning the caliper after honing. Remove all dust and grit by flushing the caliper with alcohol. Wipe the caliper dry with a clean lint-free cloth, then repeat cleaning procedure.

BRAKE DISC SERVICE

Disc brake service is critical because of the close tolerances required in machining the brake disc to ensure proper brake operation.

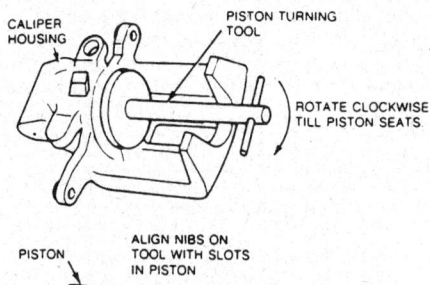

Fig. 2   Caliper piston seating. Continental, Cougar, Five Hundred, Freestyle, Montego, Mustang, Sable & Taurus

Maintaining close control of the shape of the rubbing surfaces is required to prevent brake roughness. In addition, the surface finish must be non-directional and maintained at a micro-inch finish. This is required to avoid pulls and erratic performance and promote long lining life and equal lining wear of both the lefthand and righthand brakes.

Do not attempt to refinish the rubbing surfaces unless precision equipment, capable of measuring in micro inches (millionths of an inch) is available.

To inspect the disc lateral runout, mount a dial indicator on a convenient part, such as a steering knuckle, tie rod, or caliper housing, so the indicator's plunger contacts the disc one inch from the outer edge. If the total indicated runout exceeds specifications, install a new disc.

To inspect parallelism (thickness variation), mount dial indicators so the plunger contacts the rotor approximately one inch from the outer edge. If parallelism exceeds specifications, replace the rotor.

BRAKE PAD SERVICE

On models with anti-lock brakes, the brake system power booster must be depressurized before disconnecting any hydraulic lines or fittings. Depressurize the system by pumping the brake pedal at least 25 times with the ignition in the Off position.

After performing any service work, obtain a firm brake pedal before moving the vehicle.

Continental, Cougar, Five Hundred, Freestyle, Montego, Mustang, Sable & Taurus

REMOVAL

1. **On models equipped with air suspension,** turn service switch Off position.

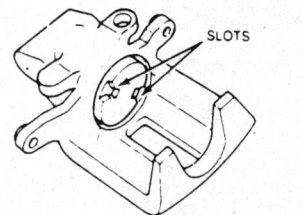 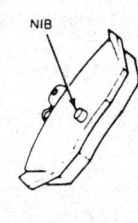

Fig. 3   Caliper piston to brake pad nib positioning. Continental, Cougar, Five Hundred, Freestyle, Montego, Mustang, Sable & Taurus

2. **On all models,** raise and support rear of vehicle, then remove tire and wheel assembly.
3. Remove brake hose bracket to shock unit bracket screw.
4. Remove retaining clip, then disconnect parking brake cable from lever.
5. Remove upper pinch bolt using open end wrench to hold slider pin in position, **Fig. 1**. Loosen, but do not lower, slider pin pinch bolt.
6. Rotate caliper away from rotor, then remover inner and outer brake pads and anti-rattle springs from anchor plate.

INSTALLATION

1. Rotate caliper piston clockwise until fully seated using rear caliper piston adjuster tool No. T87P-2588-A, or equivalent, **Fig. 2**.
2. Position one of two piston slots so it will engage nib on rear of brake pad, **Fig. 3**.
3. Position inner and outer brake pads on anchor plate, then install anti-rattle springs.
4. Rotate caliper over brake rotor. Ensure brake pads and anti-rattle springs are properly positioned, **Fig. 4**.
5. Apply suitable thread sealer and locking compound to pinch bolt threads. Install pinch bolts, while holding slider pin in position with suitable open end wrench.
6. Position parking brake cable to lever and install retaining clip.
7. Position brake hose and bracket to shock unit bracket and install mounting bolt.
8. Install tire and wheel assembly, then lower vehicle.
9. **On models equipped with air suspension,** turn service switch to On position.
10. **On all models,** cycle brake pedal several times to position brake pads and caliper piston.

Crown Victoria, Grand Marquis, Marauder & Town Car

REMOVAL

1. **On models equipped with air suspension,** turn service switch to Off position.

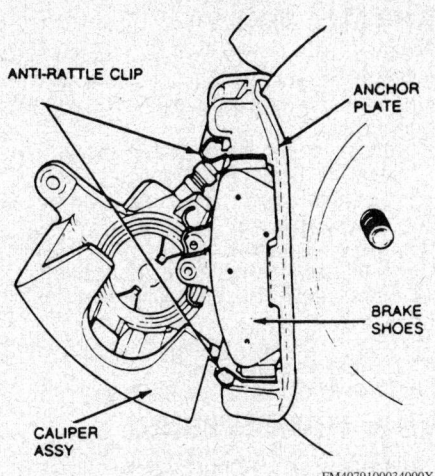

Fig. 4 Anti-rattle clip positioning. Continental, Cougar, Five Hundred, Freestyle, Montego, Mustang, Sable & Taurus

2. **On all models,** remove master cylinder cap and inspect fluid level in reservoir. Remove brake fluid until reservoir is half full.
3. Raise and support vehicle, then remove tire and wheel assembly.
4. Remove caliper as outlined in "Caliper Service."
5. Remove inner and outer brake linings.

INSTALLATION

1. Inspect both rotor braking surfaces. Minor scoring or buildup of lining material does not require machining or replacement of the rotor assembly. Hand sand glaze from both rotor braking surfaces using garnet paper 100-A (medium grit) or aluminum oxide 150-J (medium).
2. Suspend caliper inside fender housing with suitable wire or tie straps. **Do not damage caliper or stretch brake hose.**
3. **Prevent damaging plastic piston. Metal or sharp objects should not come in direct contact with piston surface or damage will result.**
4. Seat caliper piston in piston bore using suitable C-clamp and wood block approximately 2¾ inch x 1 inch and at least ¾ inch thick.
5. Remove all rust buildup from inside of caliper legs (outer shoe contact area).
6. Install inner shoe and lining assembly in caliper piston(s). **Do not bend shoe clips during installation.**
7. Install outer pad in caliper. Ensure clips are properly seated.
8. Install caliper as outlined in "Caliper Service."
9. Install tire and wheel assemblies, and lower vehicle.
10. **On models equipped with air suspension,** turn service switch to On position.

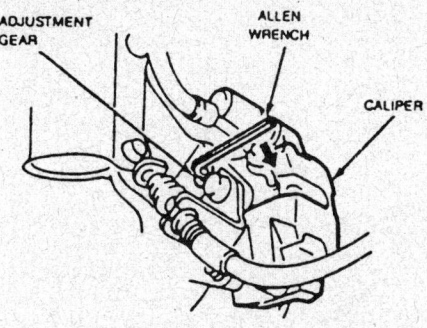

Fig. 5 Rear disc brake adjustment gear location. Escort & ZX2

Escort & ZX2
REMOVAL

1. Remove approximately two thirds of brake fluid from master cylinder.
2. Raise and support vehicle, then remove tire and wheel assembly.
3. Loosen adjusting nut and remove cable housing from bracket and parking lever.
4. Turn brake adjuster screw counterclockwise with suitable Allen wrench to pull caliper piston inward, **Fig. 5.** Turn brake adjuster screw until it stops to fully retract caliper piston.
5. Remove lower caliper mounting bolt, then pivot caliper to clear brake pads, **Fig. 6.**
6. Remove caliper and support aside with suitable wire from strut.
7. Remove anti-rattle springs from disc pads, then the disc pads, anti-rattle shims and retaining clips, **Fig. 7.** If disc pads and anti-rattle shims are to be used again, they must be installed in original positions.
8. Remove and resurface rotor. **Rotor must be machined while it is bolted to hub. Rotor and hub are mounted as an assembly on lathe to decrease possibility of rotor runout.**

INSTALLATION

1. Install disc pad retaining clips, then position anti-rattle shims on disc pads.
2. Position disc pads into caliper anchor bracket.
3. Install anti-rattle springs into disc pads.
4. Lubricate guide pin bushings with high temperature grease part No. D7AZ-19590-A, or equivalent.
5. Install caliper on guide pin, then pivot caliper over brake disc pads.
6. Install caliper mounting bolt and tighten.
7. Bleed brake system.
8. Position parking brake cable into parking brake lever and bracket.
9. Adjust parking brake cable so there is no clearance between cable end and parking brake lever.

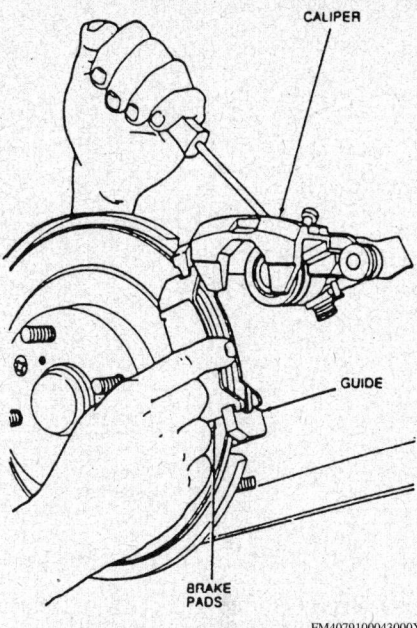

Fig. 6 Rear caliper rotating into position for brake pad replacement. Escort & ZX2

10. Tighten parking brake cable locknut.
11. Install tire and wheel assembly.

LS & Thunderbird

1. Raise and support vehicle, then remove tire and wheel assembly.
2. Remove mounting bolts and caliper. **Do not allow caliper to hang from brake hose.**
3. Remove brake pads.
4. Measure brake disc and resurface as required. **Use hub-mount brake lathe if required to machine brake disc.**
5. Compress disc brake piston and adjuster into disc brake caliper using rear caliper piston adjuster tool No. T87P-2588-A, or equivalent.
6. Reverse procedure to install.

CALIPER SERVICE
Replacement

CONTINENTAL, COUGAR, FIVE HUNDRED, FREESTYLE, MONTEGO, MUSTANG, SABLE & TAURUS

REMOVAL

1. Raise and support rear of vehicle, then remove tire and wheel assembly.
2. Disconnect brake hose from caliper.
3. Remove retaining clip and disconnect parking brake cable from lever arm.
4. Remove pinch bolts using open end wrench to hold slider pin in position.

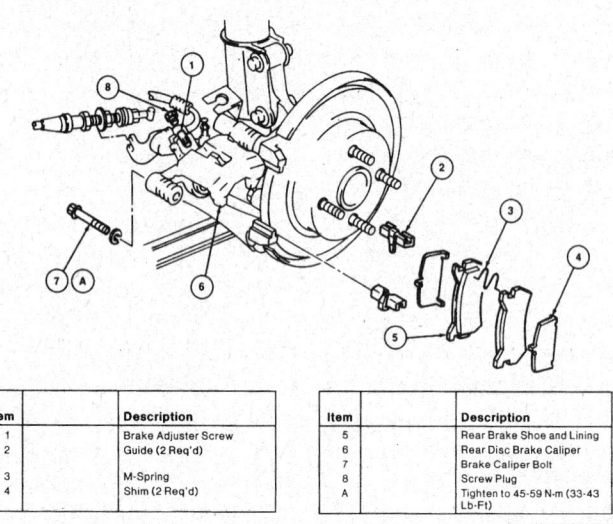

Item	Description
1	Brake Adjuster Screw
2	Guide (2 Req'd)
3	M-Spring
4	Shim (2 Req'd)

Item	Description
5	Rear Brake Shoe and Lining
6	Rear Disc Brake Caliper
7	Brake Caliper Bolt
8	Screw Plug
A	Tighten to 45-59 N·m (33-43 Lb-Ft)

FM4079300067000X

Fig. 7 Rear brake pad replacement. Escort & ZX2

5. Lift caliper from anchor plate, then remove slider pins and boots.

INSTALLATION

1. Apply suitable silicone dielectric compound to slider pins and inside of boots.
2. Place slider pins and boots on anchor plate, then position caliper on anchor plate. Ensure brake pads and anti-rattle springs are properly positioned.
3. Apply suitable sealer and thread locking compound to threads, then install pinch bolts.
4. Tighten pinch bolts using open end wrench to hold slider pin in position.
5. Attach parking brake cable to lever arm and install retaining clip.
6. Connect brake hose to caliper using replacement washers.
7. Bleed brake system as outlined in "Brake System Bleed."
8. Install tire and wheel assembly.
9. Cycle brake pedal several times to position brake pads and caliper piston.

CROWN VICTORIA, GRAND MARQUIS, MARAUDER & TOWN CAR

Visually inspect caliper. If the caliper housing is leaking, it should be replaced. If a seal is leaking, the caliper must be disassembled and new seals and dust boot installed. If a piston is seized in the bore, replace caliper. Care must be taken when removing plastic piston.

REMOVAL

1. **On models equipped with air suspension,** turn service switch to Off position.
2. **On all models,** raise and support vehicle, then remove tire and wheel assembly.
3. Remove flexible brake hose mounting bolt from caliper. Plug hose and caliper fitting.
4. Remove caliper locating pins using Torx drive bit tool No. D79P-2100-T40, or equivalent.

5. Lift caliper off rotor and anchor plate using rotating motion. **Do not pry directly against plastic piston.**

INSTALLATION

1. Retract piston fully into piston bore and position caliper above rotor with anti-rattle spring located on lower adapter support arm.
2. Install caliper over rotor with rotating motion. Ensure inner shoe is properly positioned.
3. Install caliper locating pins. **Caliper locating pins must be inserted and started by hand.**
4. Tighten locating pins.
5. Remove plugs from caliper fittings, then install flexible brake hose on caliper with new gasket on each side of fitting outlet.
6. Insert mounting bolt through washers and fittings.
7. Bleed brake system as outlined in "Brake System Bleed."
8. Pump brake pedal to position brake linings before moving vehicle.
9. **On models equipped with air suspension,** turn service switch to On position.

ESCORT & ZX2

REMOVAL

1. Remove tire and wheel assembly, then the brake pads as outlined in "Brake Pad Service."
2. Remove brake flex hose clip from strut bracket.
3. Remove brake flex hose to caliper banjo bolt.
4. Remove and discard two copper washers sealing flex hose banjo fitting.
5. Remove lower caliper bolt.
6. Remove upper caliper guide pin dust cap to gain access to Allen head guide pin using cold chisel.
7. Loosen and remove upper caliper guide pin using suitable Allen wrench.
8. Lift caliper off rotor.

INSTALLATION

Before installation, remove upper and lower guide pin bushings and lubricate with high temperature grease D7AZ-19590-A, or equivalent.

1. Install brake pads and shims as outlined in "Brake Pad Service."
2. Position caliper over rotor and install mounting bolts.
3. Install two new copper washers and banjo bolt on flex hose banjo fitting.
4. Position flex hose on caliper and install banjo bolt.
5. Bleed brake system as outlined in "Brake System Bleed."
6. Install tire and wheel assembly.

LS & THUNDERBIRD

1. Raise and support vehicle, then remove tire and wheel assembly.
2. Disconnect parking brake cable end from parking brake lever arm.
3. Remove parking brake cable and conduit.
4. Remove mounting bolts, flow bolt and caliper.
5. Discard copper washers.
6. Reverse procedure to install using new copper washers.
7. Bleed brake system.

Overhaul

CONTINENTAL, COUGAR, FIVE HUNDRED, FREESTYLE, MONTEGO, MUSTANG, SABLE & TAURUS

DISASSEMBLE

1. Remove caliper as outlined in "Caliper Service."
2. Position caliper in suitable soft-jawed vise.
3. Remove from caliper bore using tool No. T75P-2588-B, or equivalent, to rotate caliper piston counterclockwise.
4. Remove piston dust boot and seal from caliper piston bore.
5. Remove snap ring retaining pushrod to caliper. Use care when removing, snap ring and spring cover are under spring load.
6. Remove spring cover, spring, washer, key plate and pushrod and strut pin from caliper.
7. Remove O-ring from pushrod.
8. Remove parking brake lever return spring, then the brake lever stop bolt and pull lever from caliper.

CLEANING & INSPECTION

1. Clean all metal components with Isopropyl alcohol.
2. Use compressed air to clean out passages and grooves.
3. Inspect caliper bore for damage and excessive wear.
4. Inspect caliper piston for pitting, scoring or worn plating.

ASSEMBLE

1. Apply light coating of suitable silicone dielectric compound to parking brake

lever bore and parking brake lever seal. Position seal into caliper bore.
2. Apply suitable silicone dielectric compound to parking brake lever shaft. Install shaft into caliper housing bore.
3. Install O-ring into groove on pushrod, then apply suitable silicone dielectric compound to recesses in pushrod.
4. Place strut pin into caliper housing and recess of parking brake lever shaft.
5. Position pushrod into caliper housing bore. Ensure strut pin is properly located between shaft recesses and recess at end of pushrod.
6. Position key plate over pushrod, so washer nib is located in hole in caliper housing.
7. Install flat washer, spring and spring cage into caliper bore.
8. Install snap ring using rear caliper spring compressor set No. T87P-2588-P, or equivalent. Ensure snap ring is properly seated in recess.
9. Lubricate replacement piston seal with suitable, clean brake fluid. Install seal into caliper bore groove.
10. Lubricate piston and dust boot with clean brake fluid, then install dust boot into caliper bore.
11. Position piston into dust boot, seating dust boot in piston groove.
12. Turn piston in clockwise direction until piston is fully seated in caliper bore using rear caliper spring compressor set No. T75P-2588-B, or equivalent, **Fig. 2.**
13. Position one of two slots on piston so it will engage nib on rear of disc pad when caliper is installed, **Fig. 3.**
14. Install caliper as outlined in "Caliper Service."

CROWN VICTORIA, GRAND MARQUIS, MARAUDER & TOWN CAR

Visually inspect caliper. If the caliper housing is leaking, it should be replaced. If a seal is leaking, the caliper must be disassembled and new seals and dust boot installed. If a piston is seized in the bore, replace the caliper. Care must be taken when removing the plastic piston.

DISASSEMBLE

1. **On models equipped with air suspension,** turn service switch to Off position.
2. **On all models,** remove caliper from mounting bracket.
3. Remove outer pad by slipping down caliper leg until clip is disconnected, then inner pad by pulling it straight out of piston.
4. Place shop towels between caliper piston and caliper bridge. **Do not place fingers between these areas.**
5. If air pressure is not available, slowly apply brake pedal until caliper piston is forced from bore. This method can only be done one caliper at a time.

6. If air pressure is to be used, use following procedure:
   a. Disconnect flexible hose from caliper and remove caliper.
   b. Apply light air pressure to brake hose inlet until piston is free from caliper. **Do not use shop pressure if it cannot be adjusted down 15–30 psi.**
7. Remove seal and dust boot from caliper.

CLEANING & INSPECTION

Clean all metal components with Isopropyl alcohol. Dry grooves and passageways with compressed air. Ensure caliper bore and component components are cleaned thoroughly. Inspect cylinder bore and piston for damage or excessive wear.

Examine piston for surface irregularities or small chips and cracks. Minor surface imperfections are allowable, provided they do not enter the dust boot groove area. Replace piston if damaged.

ASSEMBLE

1. Coat new seal and dust boot with suitable, clean brake fluid, then install in caliper.
2. Coat piston with suitable, clean brake fluid, then place piston in caliper and push firmly into bore.
3. With piston seated, completely seat piston using suitable C-clamp and block of wood approximately 2¾ inch x 1 inch x ¾ inch thick.
4. Ensure dust boot is tight in boot groove on piston and in caliper.
5. Install brake pads as outlined in "Brake Pad Service," then the caliper.

ESCORT & ZX2
DISASSEMBLE

1. Remove caliper as outlined in "Caliper Service."
2. Open bleeder screw and drain brake fluid from caliper through brake flex hose fitting into suitable container. Close bleeder screw.
3. Remove caliper guide bushing and dust boots.
4. Pry retaining spring off dust boot with suitable screwdriver, then remove piston.
5. Remove and discard dust boot.
6. Remove piston seal from caliper and discard. **Use plastic or wooden pick to remove seal. Metal tools can scratch or nick seal groove.**
7. Remove stopper snap ring.
8. Remove adjusting spindle, stopper and connecting link. Separate adjuster spindle and stopper.
9. Remove O-ring from adjuster spindle. Discard O-ring.
10. Remove parking brake return spring, then operating lever nut and lockjaws.
11. Mark relationship between operating lever and shaft, then remove lever from shaft.
12. Remove seal from caliper housing.

13. Remove shaft from caliper housing, then the needle bearings.

INSPECTION

1. Inspect caliper bore, piston seal groove and piston for cuts, deep scratches and pitting. Piston and piston bore may be lightly polished with crocus cloth. If deep scratches cannot be removed, replace caliper.
2. Caliper seal groove must be free of deep scratches which would prevent seal from operating properly.
3. Inspect upper guide pin and lower guide pin bushing for wear.
4. Inspect bushing dust boots for damage or poor sealing.

ASSEMBLE

1. Lubricate needle bearings with orange grease included in caliper rebuilding kit part No. FOJY-2221-A.
2. Align opening in bearing with bore in caliper housing, then install needle bearings.
3. Install operating shaft into caliper housing.
4. Install operating lever. Align marks made during removal.
5. Install lockjaws nut.
6. Install connecting link into operating shaft.
7. Install O-ring onto adjuster spindle, then position stopper onto adjuster spindle so pin will align with caliper housing.
8. Install adjuster spindle in caliper by aligning adjuster spindle pins with caliper holes.
9. Install parking brake return spring.
10. Lubricate new piston seal with suitable brake fluid and install in caliper groove.
11. Lubricate caliper bore and caliper piston with brake fluid.
12. Install dust boot in caliper bore.
13. Install piston in caliper bore by rotating piston until seated.
14. Install upper and lower guide pin dust boots.
15. Install caliper upper guide pin and lower guide pin bushing.
16. Install caliper as outlined in "Caliper Service."

LS & THUNDERBIRD

1. Remove brake caliper as outlined in "Caliper Service."
2. Drain brake fluid from caliper into suitable container.
3. Secure brake caliper in suitable vise.
4. Turn brake piston counterclockwise with rear caliper piston adjuster tool No. T87P-2588-A, or equivalent.
5. Remove brake piston from caliper bore.
6. Remove and discard piston dust boot and piston seal from caliper bore.
7. Reverse procedure to assemble, noting the following:
   a. Install new seals and dust boots.

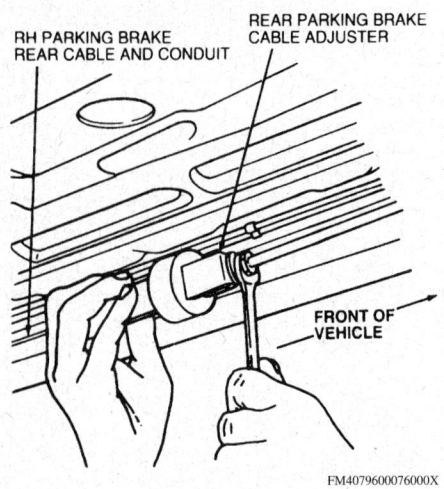

Fig. 8 Park brake adjustment. Five Hundred, Freestyle, Montego, Sable & Taurus

b. Use new brake fluid when assembling and bleeding brake system.

ROTOR
REPLACE

Continental, Cougar, Five Hundred, Freestyle, Montego, Mustang, Sable & Taurus

REMOVAL

1. Remove rear disc brake caliper as outlined in "Caliper Service." **Do not disconnect flexible hose unless caliper requires service.**
2. Support caliper with suitable wire or tie strap so flexible hose is not stretched or twisted.
3. Remove rear disc support bracket to wheel knuckle bolts.
4. Remove rear disc support bracket and brake shoes and linings.
5. Remove two nuts and rotor.

INSTALLATION

1. If installing new rotor, remove protective coating from rotor with suitable carburetor cleaner.
2. Lubricate rear hub pilot diameter with suitable grease.
3. Install rotors on axle shaft flange, then the two mounting nuts.
4. Install inner and outer brake shoes and linings in rear disc support bracket.
5. Clean rear disc support bracket and bolt threads, then add one drop of suitable sealer to each bolt.
6. Install caliper/rear support bracket to rear wheel knuckle.
7. Install bolts and tighten.

8. Install inner and outer brake shoes and linings as outlined in "Brake Pad Service."
9. Install rear disc brake caliper as outlined in "Caliper Service."

Crown Victoria, Grand Marquis, Marauder & Town Car
REMOVAL

1. Raise and support vehicle, then remove tire and wheel assembly.
2. Remove rear disc brake caliper as outlined in "Caliper Service." **Do not disconnect flexible hose unless caliper requires service.**
3. Position caliper aside and support with suitable wire or tie strap.
4. Remove rotor push nuts, then the disc brake rotor. If additional force is required, use following procedure:
   a. Apply rust penetrant and inhibitor part No. D7AZ-19A501-AA, or equivalent, to rotor/flange mating surface.
   b. Install three-jaw puller tool No. D80L-1013-A, or equivalent.
   c. Remove rear disc brake rotor. **If excessive force is required to remove rotor, it should be inspected for lateral runout prior to installation.**

INSTALLATION

1. If installing new rotor, remove protective coating with suitable carburetor cleaner.
2. If installing original rotor, ensure rotor braking and mounting surfaces are clean.
3. Install rotor and push nuts.
4. Install caliper as outlined in "Caliper Service."
5. Install tire and wheel assembly, then lower vehicle.
6. Pump brake pedal to position brake shoes and linings before moving vehicle and road testing.

Escort & ZX2

1. Raise and support vehicle, then remove tire and wheel assembly.
2. Remove rear brake shoe and lining as outlined in "Brake Pad Service."
3. Remove two rear disc brake rotor screws.
4. Pivot rear disc brake caliper on rear disc support bracket and remove rotor using suitable screwdriver.
5. Reverse procedure to install.

LS & Thunderbird

1. Remove support bracket.
2. Remove and discard pushups.
3. Remove brake disc.
4. Reverse procedure to install.

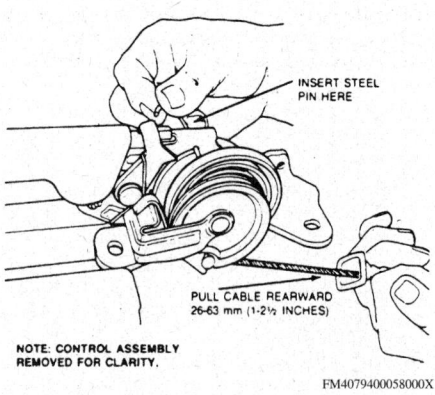

NOTE: CONTROL ASSEMBLY REMOVED FOR CLARITY.

Fig. 9 Self-adjuster reel rotation. Mustang

PARKING BRAKE SERVICE
Parking Brake Linings, Replace

CROWN VICTORIA, GRAND MARQUIS, MARAUDER & TOWN CAR

1. Remove tire and wheel assembly.
2. Remove brake rotor.
3. Remove spring and brake shoe adjusting screw.
4. Remove brake shoe hold down springs.
5. Remove parking bake shoe and linings.
6. Reverse procedure to install noting the following:
   a. Lubricate brake shoe contact point before installation with silicone brake caliper grease and dielectric compound part No. D7AZ-19A331-A, or equivalent.
   b. Adjust rear brake shoe and lining diameter to .020 inch less than inside diameter of drum portion of rear brake using suitable brake adjusting gauge.
   c. Adjust parking brake cable tension.

ADJUSTMENTS
Parking Brake

COUGAR, CROWN VICTORIA, GRAND MARQUIS, MARAUDER & TOWN CAR

1. Apply parking brake control fully with 100 lbs., foot pedal effort, then release brake control.
2. Place transmission in Neutral position, then raise and support vehicle.
3. With parking brake control in Off position, grasp pensioner around housing.

4. Unlock clip by pulling downward with suitable hook tool place into rounded end of clip and support pensioner.
5. Tensioner spring will take up cable slack and load cables, while holding pensioner, lock clip by pushing up on bottom of clip. If clip does not slide up move assembly slightly to align closest groove on adjuster rod to clip.
6. Examine pensioner for remaining cable take up capability. If none is present, inspect all cables, parking brake control and brackets for possible damage or deflection.

CONTINENTAL

1. Fully release parking brake control, then raise and support vehicle.
2. Pull parking brake cable adjuster clip downward. Tensioner spring will take up cable slack and load cables.
3. Push up on bottom of clip to lock adjustment. If clip does not slide up, move assembly slightly to align closest groove on parking brake cable adjuster rod with clip.
4. Apply 157 lbs., of force to parking brake control for 20 minutes.

5. Repeat previous steps, then lower vehicle and ensure operation of parking brake.

ESCORT & ZX2

1. Start engine and shift transaxle into Reverse position.
2. With vehicle moving in Reverse, depress brake pedal several times.
3. Shift into Park position and stop engine.
4. Remove parking brake console.
5. Turn adjusting nut until parking brake lever stroke is 5–7 notches when pulled with force of 22 lbs.
6. Install parking brake console.

FIVE HUNDRED, FREESTYLE, MONTEGO, SABLE & TAURUS

1. Ensure parking brake control is fully released, then raise and support vehicle.
2. **Torque** adjusting nut against rear parking brake cable adjuster until cable tension is 34–46 lbs., using Rotunda cable tension gauge tool No. 014-R1056, or equivalent, **Fig. 8.**

3. Apply parking brake control fully, then release.
4. Ensure cable tension is still within specification and there is no drag on rear brakes.
5. Lower vehicle and ensure operation of parking brake.

MUSTANG

1. Place parking brake control in released position.
2. Remove console top panel by pry finish panel up from retaining clips and disconnect electrical connectors.
3. Raise and support vehicle with assistant inside.
4. Have another assistant pull parking brake cable and equalizer rearward approximately 1–2 ½ inches to rotate self-adjuster reel backward, **Fig. 9.**
5. Insert steel locking through holes in lever and parking brake control assembly to lock ratchet wheel in cable-released position. **Do not remove steel locking until rear cable and conduit are connected to parking brake cable and equalizer.**

DISC BRAKE SPECIFICATIONS
Rotor Specifications

Refer to "Front Disc Brakes" for disc specifications.

Caliper Specifications

Model	Year	Caliper Bore Diameter Inch
FRONT		
Continental	2001–02	①
Cougar	2001–02	①
Crown Victoria	2001–05	①
Escort & ZX2	2001–03	2.120①
Five Hundred	2005	①
Focus	2001–05	①
Freestyle	2005	①
Grand Marquis	2001–05	①
LS	2001–05	①
Marauder	2003–05	①
Montego	2005	①
Mustang	2001–05	①
Sable & Taurus	2001–05	①
Thunderbird	2001–05	①
Town Car	2001–05	①
REAR		
Continental	2001–02	①
Cougar	2001–02	①
Crown Victoria	2001–05	①
Escort & ZX2	2001–03	1.190①
Five Hundred	2005	①
Freestyle	2005	①
Grand Marquis	2001–05	①
LS	2001–05	①
Marauder	2003–05	①
Montego	2005	①
Mustang	2001–02	1.500
	2003–05	①
Sable & Taurus	2001–05	①
Thunderbird	20012–053	①
Town Car	20010–054	①

① — Replace brake caliper if there is scoring or damage to caliper cylinder. Do not hone cylinder.

TIGHTENING SPECIFICATIONS

Year/ Model	Component	Torque/Ft. Lbs.
CONTINENTAL		
2001–02	Anchor Plate	64–88
	Brake Adapter	44–60
	Brake Hose Bracket To Shock	8–11
	Brake Hose To Caliper, Banjo	30–40
	Brake Pin	23–26
	Caliper	23–28
	Disc Brake Shield	80–106①
	Rear Caliper Bleeder Screw	12–18
COUGAR		
2001–02	Anchor Plate	89
	Backing Plate	37
	Caliper Brake Hose Union	120①
	Caliper Locating Bolt	30
	Rear Brake Cylinder Brake Tube Union	10
	Rear Wheel Cylinder	108①
	Rear Hub Nut	214
	Shield	17
	Wheel Lug Nut	94
CROWN VICTORIA, GRAND MARQUIS, MARAUDER & TOWN CAR		
2001–02	Anchor Plate To Spindle	125–169
	Brake Hose To Caliper, Banjo	30–44
	Caliper, Front	32
	Caliper, Rear	18
	Caliper Bleed Screw	80–106①
	Caliper Locating Pin	22–30
	Hydraulic Tube Connection	9–11
	Rear Caliper Anchor Plate	45–55
	Wheel Lug	85–105
2003–05	Anchor Plate To Spindle	118
	Brake Hose To Caliper, Banjo	41
	Caliper Bleed Screw	15
	Rear Caliper Anchor Plate	50
	Wheel Lug	95
ESCORT & ZX2		
2001–03	Brake Hose To Caliper, Banjo	16–22
	Caliper	33–43
	Parking Brake Cable Lockout	14–21
	Screw Plug	9–12
	Wheel Lug	74–100
FIVE HUNDRED, FREESTYLE & MONTEGO		
2005	Anchor Plate, Front	74
	Anchor Plate, Rear	81
	Bleeder Screw, Front	96①
	Bleeder Screw, Rear	89①
	Brake Disc Shield, Front	96①
	Brake Disc Shield, Rear	10
	Caliper Bolts, Front	44
	Caliper Bolts, Rear	23
	Flex Hose, Front	108①
	Flex Hose, Rear	18
	Line Fitting	13
	Parking Brake Cable Bracket Bolt	108①
	Upper Control Arm Parking Brake Cable Bracket Nut	27

Continued

TIGHTENING
SPECIFICATIONS—Continued

Year/ Model	Component	Torque/Ft. Lbs.
LS & THUNDERBIRD		
2001–05	Anchor Plate	76
	Axle Shaft	221
	Caliper	26
	Caliper Bleeder Screw	60–120①
	Caliper Flow Bolt	35
	Master Cylinder Tube Fitting	11–15
	Support Bracket	36
	Wheel Lug	100
MUSTANG		
2001–02	Anchor Plate Nut	64–88
	Brake Hose To Axle	18–24
	Brake Hose To Caliper, Banjo	20–30
	Brake Pin Retainer	30–35
	Disc Brake Adapter	30–40
	Limiting Bolt	60–84①
	Parking Brake Cable To Axle Bracket	23–26
	Rear Disc Shield	80–106①
	Rear Disc Shield Support Bracket	64–88
	Wheel Lug	85–105
2003–05	Anchor Plate	85
	Brake Hose To Axle	24
	Brake Hose To Caliper, Banjo	30
	Caliper, Front	23
	Caliper, Rear	25
	Limiting Bolt	84①
	Parking Brake Cable To Axle Bracket	25
	Rear Disc Shield	89①
	Rear Disc Shield Support Bracket	76
	Wheel Lug	95
SABLE & TAURUS		
2001–05	Anchor Plate	64–88
	Axle Nut	188–254
	Brake Adapter	44–60
	Brake Hose Bracket To Shock	8–11
	Brake Hose To Caliper, Banjo	30–40
	Brake Pin mounting bolt	23–26
	Disc Brake Shield	72–108①
	Hub Nut	188–254
	Park Brake Lever Limit Bolt	60–84①
	Rear Anti-Lock Sensor	36–60①

① — Inch lbs.

DRUM BRAKES

TABLE OF CONTENTS

Cougar, Sable & Taurus

NOTE: On Air Bag Equipped Models, Refer To "Air Bag System Precautions" Located In The Front Of This Manual For System Disarming & Arming Procedures.

NOTE: Refer To "Computer Relearn Procedures" Located In The Front Of This Manual When Battery Power To The Computer Has Been Interrupted.

INDEX

PRECAUTIONS

Air Bag Systems

Refer to "Air Bag System Precautions" in the front of this manual for system disarming and arming procedures.

Battery Ground Cable

Prior to service, disconnect battery ground cable and isolate as required.

Safety Precautions

When working on or around brake assemblies, care must be taken to prevent breathing asbestos dust, as many manufacturers incorporate asbestos fibers in the production of brake linings. During routine service operations the amount of asbestos dust from brake lining wear is at a low level, due to a chemical breakdown during use. A few precautions will minimize exposure. **Do not sand or grind brake linings unless suitable local exhaust ventilation equipment is used to prevent excessive asbestos exposure.**

1. Wear suitable respirator approved for asbestos dust use during all repair procedures.
2. When cleaning brake dust from brake components, use vacuum cleaner with highly efficient filter system. If suitable vacuum cleaner is not available, use water-soaked rag. **Do not use compressed air or dry brush to clean brake components.**
3. Keep work area clean, using same equipment as for cleaning brake components.
4. Properly dispose of rags and vacuum cleaner bags by placing them in plastic bags.
5. **Never use gasoline, kerosene, alcohol, motor oil, transmission fluid, or any fluid containing mineral oil to clean brake system components. These fluids will damage rubber caps and seals. If system contamination is suspected, inspect brake fluid in reservoir for dirt, discoloration, or separation (breakdown) of brake fluid into distinct layers. Drain and flush hydraulic system with clean brake fluid if contamination is suspected.**

INSPECTION

1. Inspect components for damage and unusual wear.
2. Inspect wheel cylinders. Boots which are torn, cut, or heat damaged indicate need for wheel cylinder replacement. Fluid spilling from boot center hole, or wetness around wheel cylinder ends indicates cup leakage and need for wheel cylinder replacement. **A small amount of fluid is always present and is considered normal, acting as lubricant for cylinder pistons.**
3. Inspect backing plate for evidence of seal leakage. If leakage exists, refer to appropriate chassis chapter for axle seal replacement procedure.
4. Inspect backing plate bolts and ensure they are tight.
5. Inspect adjuster screw operation. If satisfactory, lightly lubricate adjusting screw and washer with suitable brake lubricant. If operation is unsatisfactory, replace.
6. Clean rust and dirt from shoe contact surfaces on backing plate using fine emery cloth or other suitable abrasive.

BRAKE SERVICE

Removal

1. Raise and support rear of vehicle, then remove tire and wheel assembly.
2. Remove retainer push nuts and slide drum off hub, **Fig. 1.**
3. If drum is stuck to hub, use suitable hammer to lightly tap on face of drum in flange mounting area to release.
4. If brake lining is dragging on brake drum, back off brake adjustment by holding adjustment lever off and loosen star wheel, **Fig. 2.**
5. Remove hub nut cover and discard.
6. Remove hub nut and discard. Slide hub and one-piece bearing off spindle.
7. Install suitable wheel cylinder piston retainer tool.

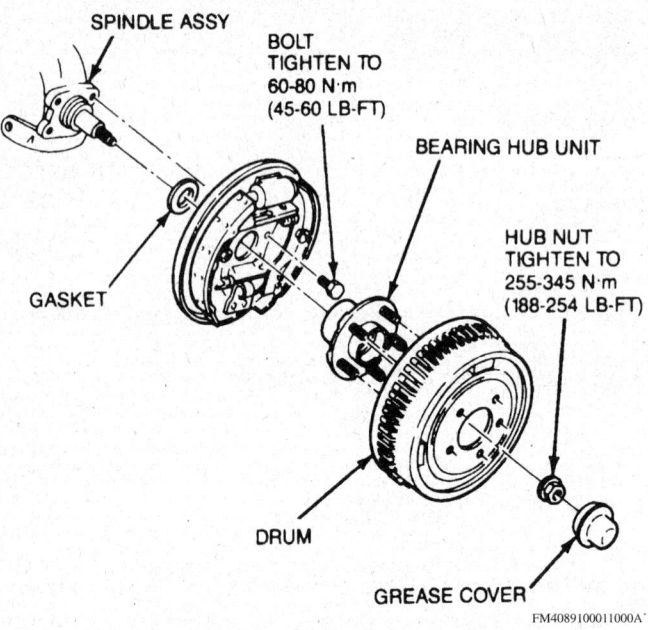

SPINDLE ASSY

BOLT TIGHTEN TO 60-80 N·m (45-60 LB-FT)

BEARING HUB UNIT

HUB NUT TIGHTEN TO 255-345 N·m (188-254 LB-FT)

GASKET

DRUM

GREASE COVER

FM4089100011000A

Fig. 1   Drum & hub assembly

BOOT

PISTON AND INSERT

CUP   SPRING EXPANDER

PISTON AND INSERT

WHEEL CYLINDER

WHEEL CYLINDER ATTACHING SCREW

ACCESS HOLE COVER

ADJUSTER SCREW RETRACTING SPRING

WHEEL CYLINDER

SHOE HOLD-DOWN PIN

ADJUSTING PIVOT NUT

PARKING BRAKE LEVER PIN

CUP

SHOE ADJUSTMENT ACCESS HOLE

ADJUSTING SCREW

WASHER

BOOT

BACKING PLATE ASSY

LEADING SHOE AND LINING

BRAKE LINING INSPECTION ACCESS HOLE

WASHER

ADJUSTER SOCKET

225 AND 250mm (8.85 AND 9.84 INCHES) BRAKE

PARKING LEVER RETAINING CLIP

LOWER RETRACTING SPRING

TRAILING SHOE AND LINING

ADJUSTER LEVER

SHOE HOLD-DOWN SPRING ASSY

PARKING BRAKE LEVER

FM4089100010000X

Fig. 2   Drum brake assembly

8. Remove shoe hold-down springs and pins.
9. Lift shoes, springs and adjuster off backing plate and wheel cylinder. **Do not bend adjusting lever.**
10. Remove parking brake cable from parking brake lever.
11. Remove retracting springs from lower shoe attachments and upper shoe to adjusting lever attachment points.
12. Disconnect shoes and adjuster mechanism.
13. Clean dirt from drum, backing plate and other components. **Do not use compressed air or dry brush to clean brake components. Clean brake components with water-soaked rag or suitable vacuum cleaner to minimize airborne dust.**

Installation

1. Lightly lubricate backing plate shoe contact surfaces with suitable brake lubrication.
2. Apply thin uniform coat of suitable brake lubricant to adjuster screw threads and socket end of adjusting screw.
3. Install stainless steel washer over socket end of adjusting screw.
4. Install socket, turn adjusting screw fully into adjusting pivot nut and back off ½ turn.
5. Assemble parking brake lever to trailing shoe and lining by installing spring washer and new horseshoe retaining clip. Crimp clip until it securely retains lever to shoe.
6. Attach parking brake cable to lever.

7. Attach lower shoe retracting spring to leading and trailing shoe assemblies, then install on backing plate. Stretch retracting spring as shoes are installed downward over anchor plate to inside of retaining plate.
8. Install adjuster screw assembly between leading shoe slot and slot in trailing shoe and parking brake lever. Adjuster socket end slot must fit into trailing shoe and parking brake lever. **Adjuster socket blade is marked R or L for righthand and lefthand brake assemblies. The adjuster blade must be installed with letter R or L in upright position (facing wheel cylinder) on proper side to ensure deeper of two slots in adjuster sockets fits into parking brake lever.**
9. Assemble adjuster lever in groove located in parking brake lever pin and into slot of adjuster socket that fits into trailing shoe web.
10. Attach upper retracting spring to leading shoe slot and stretch other end of spring into notch on adjuster lever using suitable tool. **If adjuster lever does not contact star wheel after installing spring, adjuster socket may be improperly installed.**
11. Install hub to spindle and tighten new hub nut. Install new hub nut cover.
12. Install brake drum to hub, then the drum retainer push nuts.
13. Install tire and wheel assembly.
14. If any hydraulic connections have been opened, bleed system as outlined in "Hydraulic Brake System" chapter.
15. Adjust parking brake as outlined in

"Adjustments."
16. Inspect hydraulic lines and connections for leakage.
17. Adjust master cylinder fluid level.
18. Inspect brake pedal for proper feel and return.
19. Lower vehicle and road test. **Do not severely apply brakes immediately after installation of new linings. Brakes must be used moderately during first several hundred miles of operation to ensure proper burnishing of linings.**

ADJUSTMENTS
Service Brakes

Although the brakes are self-adjusting, an initial adjustment is required after a brake repair.

1. Determine inside diameter of brake drum surface using brake shoe gauge tool No. D81L-1103-A, or equivalent.
2. Adjust brake shoe diameter to fit gauge.
3. Hold automatic adjusting lever out of engagement while rotating adjusting screw.
4. Ensure screw rotates freely.
5. Install brake drum, then the tire and wheel assembly.

Parking Brake

1. Ensure parking brake lever is released.
2. With transmission in Neutral, raise and support vehicle.
3. Tighten parking brake nut against brake equalizer until rear brakes drag.
4. Loosen nut until rear brakes are fully released.
5. Lower vehicle and inspect parking brake operation.

DRUM BRAKE SPECIFICATIONS

Model	Year	Brake Lining Wear Limit, Inch③	Brake Drum Inside Diameter, Inches			Drum Runout Limit, Inch	Drum Maximum Out Of Roundness, Inch
			Nominal	Maximum Refinish	Maximum Inside Diameter (Discard Limit)①		
Cougar	2001–02	②	9.00	—	9.04	—	—
Sable	2001–05	②	8.86	—	8.92	.005	—
Taurus	2001–05	②	8.86	—	8.92	.005	—

① — Maximum brake drum inside diameter (discard limit) is stamped on drum.

② — Wear limit, riveted lining, 1/32 inch above rivet head; bonded lining, 1/16 inch lining thickness.

③ — Above rivet head or shoe. Original equipment type brake linings.

TIGHTENING SPECIFICATIONS

Year	Component	Torque/Ft. Lbs.
COUGAR		
2001–02	ABS Sensor	120①
	Axle Nut	214
	Backing Plate	37
	Brake Hose	10
	Hub Nut	214
	Wheel Cylinder	108①
	Wheel Lug Nuts	94
SABLE & TAURUS		
2001–05	ABS Sensor	72–96①
	Axle Nut	188–254
	Brake Backing Plate To Spindle	45–59
	Brake Hose	12–14
	Hub Nut	188–254
	Parking Brake Stop Bolt	96–108①
	Wheel Cylinder	9–13
	Wheel Lug Nuts	85–104

① — Inch lbs.

DRUM BRAKES

Escort & ZX2

NOTE: On Air Bag Equipped Models, Refer To "Air Bag System Precautions" Located In The Front Of This Manual For System Disarming & Arming Procedures.

NOTE: Refer To "Computer Relearn Procedures" Located In The Front Of This Manual When Battery Power To The Computer Has Been Interrupted.

INDEX

PRECAUTIONS

Air Bag Systems

Refer to "Air Bag System Precautions" in the front of this manual for system disarming and arming procedures.

Battery Ground Cable

Prior to service, disconnect battery ground cable and isolate as required.

Safety Precautions

When working on or around brake assemblies, care must be taken to prevent breathing asbestos dust. Many manufacturers incorporate asbestos fibers in the production of brake linings. During routine service operations, the amount of asbestos dust from brake lining wear is at a low level due to a chemical breakdown during use. **Do not sand or grind brake linings unless suitable local exhaust ventilation equipment is used to prevent excessive asbestos exposure.**

1. Wear suitable respirator approved for asbestos dust use during all repair procedures.
2. When cleaning brake dust from brake components, use vacuum cleaner with highly efficient filter system. If suitable vacuum cleaner is not available, use water-soaked rag. **Do not use compressed air or dry brush to clean brake components.**
3. Keep work area clean, using same equipment as for cleaning brake components.
4. Properly dispose of rags and vacuum cleaner bags by placing them in plastic bags.
5. **Never use gasoline, kerosene, alcohol, motor oil, transmission fluid, or any fluid containing mineral oil to clean brake system components. These fluids will damage rubber caps and seals. If system contamination is suspected, inspect brake**

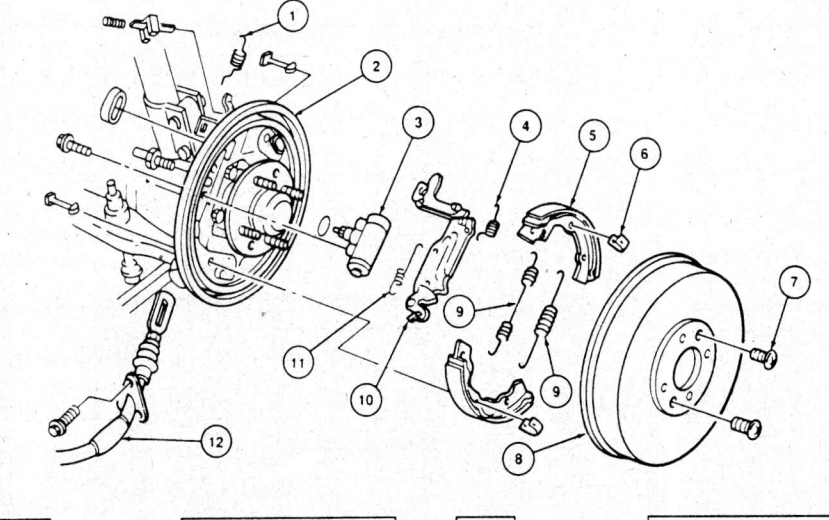

Fig. 1 Exploded view of drum brake

Item	Description
1	Parking Brake Link Spring
2	Brake Backing Plate
3	Rear Wheel Cylinder
4	Right Hand Anti-Rattle Spring
5	Rear Brake Shoe and Lining
6	Brake Shoe Hold Down Spring
7	Screw

Item	Description
8	Brake Drum
9	Brake Shoe Retracting Spring
10	Parking Brake Actuating Lever
11	Rear Brake Adjusting Quadrant Spring
12	Parking Brake Rear Cable and Conduit

FM4089400016000X

fluid in reservoir for dirt, discoloration, or separation (breakdown) of brake fluid into distinct layers. Drain and flush hydraulic system with clean brake fluid if contamination is suspected.

INSPECTION

1. Inspect components for damage and unusual wear.
2. Inspect wheel cylinders. Boots which are torn, cut, or heat damaged indicate need for wheel cylinder replacement. Fluid spilling from boot center hole, or wetness around wheel cylinder ends indicates cup leakage and need for

wheel cylinder replacement. **A small amount of fluid is always present and is considered normal, acting as lubricant for cylinder pistons.**

3. Inspect backing plate for evidence of seal leakage. If leakage exists, refer to appropriate chassis chapter for axle seal replacement procedure.
4. Inspect backing plate bolts and ensure tightness.
5. Inspect adjuster screw operation. If satisfactory, lightly lubricate adjusting screw and washer with suitable brake lubricant. If operation is unsatisfactory, replace.

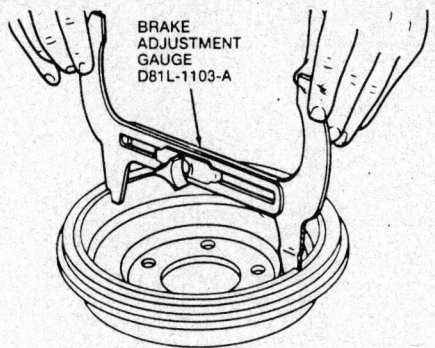

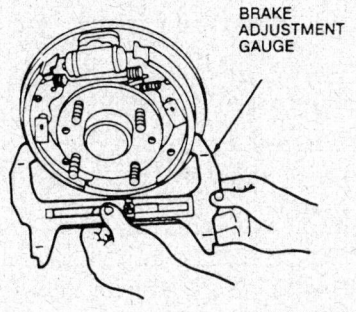

Fig. 2 Drum brake & shoe lining measurements

6. Clean rust and dirt from shoe contact surfaces on backing plate using fine emery cloth or other suitable abrasive.

BRAKE SERVICE
Removal

1. Raise and support vehicle, then remove wheel and tire assembly.
2. Remove screws and brake drum.

3. Remove wheel hub as outlined in "Escort & ZX2" chassis chapter.
4. Remove brake shoe retracting springs using suitable screwdriver to push in and twist spring to disengage it from pin, **Fig. 1.**
5. Remove righthand anti-rattle spring.
6. Push, turn and remove brake shoe hold down springs.
7. Remove primary rear shoe and lining from backing plate, then the secondary shoe and lining.

Installation

1. If rear shoes and linings are to be used again, ensure they meet specifications.
2. Clean backing plate with suitable brake vacuum, then lubricate shoe and lining contact points and areas where shoes and linings ride with Motorcraft WA-10 lubricant, or equivalent.
3. If new shoes and linings are being installed, resurface drums to remove glazing and ensure an equal friction surface from side to side. Resurfacing will also correct out-of-round and bell conditions.
4. Position secondary rear shoe and lining on backing plate, then install one shoe hold-down spring.
5. Position primary rear shoe and lining on backing plate, then install other shoe hold-down spring.
6. Install righthand anti-rattle spring, then the upper and lower shoe retracting springs.
7. Measure drum, shoes and linings with brake adjustment gauge tool No. D81L-1103-A, or equivalent, **Fig. 2.**
8. Adjust shoes and linings to same measurement of drum using suitable screwdriver into knurled quadrant of rear quad operating lever stopper.
9. Install wheel hub as outlined in "Escort

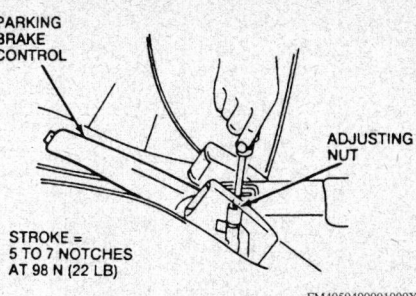

Fig. 3 Parking brake adjustment

& ZX2" chassis chapter.
10. Install drum and screws.
11. Install wheel and tire assembly.

ADJUSTMENTS
Parking Brake

1. Start engine and move shift control selector lever into Reverse position.
2. With vehicle moving in Reverse, press and release brake pedal several times.
3. Move shift control selector lever into Park position and stop engine.
4. Position both front seats to rearmost position and remove front console screws.
5. Recline both front seats and remove rear console screws.
6. Unbuckle safety belts. With parking brake control engaged, remove console.
7. Turn adjusting nut until control stroke is 5–7 notches when pulled with 22 lbs., of force, **Fig. 3.**
8. Feed safety belt ends through proper holes and install console over parking brake control.
9. Install console screws and return both seats to original positions.

DRUM BRAKE SPECIFICATIONS

| Model | Year | Brake Lining Wear Limit, Inch② | Brake Drum Inside Diameter, Inches | | | Drum Runout Limit, Inch | Drum Maximum Out Of Roundness, Inch |
			Nominal	Maximum Refinish	Maximum Inside Diameter (Discard Limit)①		
9" Drum	2001–03	.040	9.00	—	9.06	—	—

① — Maximum brake drum inside diameter (discard limit) is stamped on drum.

② — Above rivet head or shoe. Original equipment type brake linings.

TIGHTENING SPECIFICATIONS

Year	Component	Torque/Ft. Lbs.
2001–03	Axle Nut	130–174
	Backing Plate	33–43
	Bleeder Screws	53–77①
	Brake Drum Screws	84–120①
	Cable Bracket To Backing Plate	14–19
	Hose	12–16
	Hub Nut	130–174
	Rear Wheel Cylinder	84–108①
	Wheel Lug	74–100

① — Inch lbs.

Focus

NOTE: On Air Bag Equipped Models, Refer To "Air Bag System Precautions" Located In The Front Of This Manual For System Disarming & Arming Procedures.

NOTE: Refer To "Computer Relearn Procedures" Located In The Front Of This Manual When Battery Power To The Computer Has Been Interrupted.

INDEX

PRECAUTIONS

Air Bag Systems

Refer to "Air Bag System Precautions" in the front of this manual for system disarming and arming procedures.

Battery Ground Cable

Prior to service, disconnect battery ground cable and isolate as required.

Safety Precautions

When working on or around brake assemblies, care must be taken to prevent breathing asbestos dust. Many manufacturers incorporate asbestos fibers in the production of brake linings. During routine service operations, the amount of asbestos dust from brake lining wear is at a low level due to a chemical breakdown during use. **Do not sand or grind brake linings unless suitable local exhaust ventilation equipment is used to prevent excessive asbestos exposure.**

1. Wear suitable respirator approved for asbestos dust use during all repair procedures.
2. When cleaning brake dust from brake components, use vacuum cleaner with highly efficient filter system. If suitable vacuum cleaner is not available, use water-soaked rag. **Do not use compressed air or dry brush to clean brake components.**
3. Keep work area clean, using same equipment as for cleaning brake components.
4. Properly dispose of rags and vacuum cleaner bags by placing them in plastic bags.
5. **Never use gasoline, kerosene, alcohol, motor oil, transmission fluid, or any fluid containing mineral oil to clean brake system components. These fluids will damage rubber caps and seals. If system contamination is suspected, inspect brake fluid in reservoir for dirt, discoloration, or separation (breakdown) of brake fluid into distinct layers. Drain and flush hydraulic system with clean brake fluid if contamination is suspected.**

INSPECTION

1. Inspect components for damage and unusual wear.
2. Inspect wheel cylinders. Boots which are torn, cut, or heat damaged indicate need for wheel cylinder replacement. Fluid spilling from boot center hole or wetness around wheel cylinder ends indicates cup leakage and need for wheel cylinder replacement. **A small amount of fluid is always present and is considered normal, acting as lubricant for cylinder pistons.**
3. Inspect backing plate for evidence of seal leakage. If leakage exists, refer to "Focus" chassis chapter for axle seal replacement procedure.
4. Inspect backing plate bolts and ensure they are tight.
5. Inspect adjuster screw operation. If satisfactory, lightly lubricate adjusting screw and washer with suitable brake lubricant. If operation is unsatisfactory, replace.
6. Clean rust and dirt from shoe contact surfaces on backing plate using fine emery cloth or other suitable abrasive.

BRAKE SERVICE

Removal

1. Release parking brake.
2. Raise and support vehicle, then remove tire and wheel assemblies.

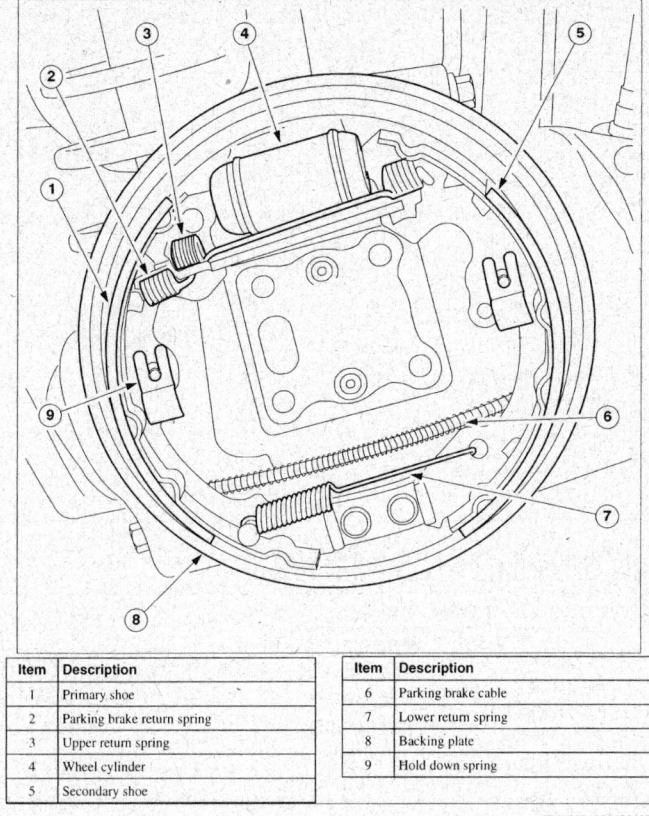

Item	Description
1	Primary shoe
2	Parking brake return spring
3	Upper return spring
4	Wheel cylinder
5	Secondary shoe

Item	Description
6	Parking brake cable
7	Lower return spring
8	Backing plate
9	Hold down spring

FM4080100043000X

Fig. 1 Rear brake spring locations

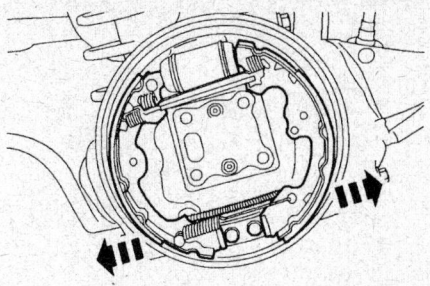

FM4080100044000X

Fig. 2 Brake shoe removal

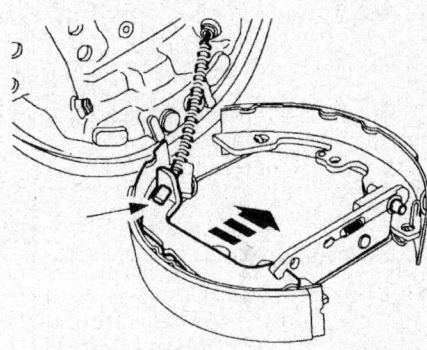

FM4080100045000X

Fig. 3 Parking brake cable removal

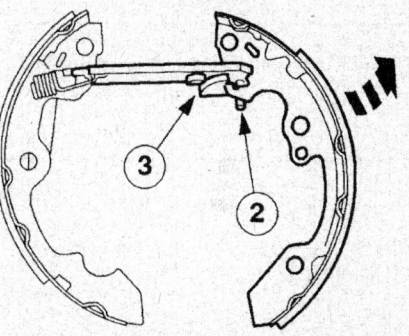

FM4080100046000X

Fig. 4 Primary brake shoe removal

3. **On models equipped with anti-lock brakes,** remove wheel speed sensor.
4. **On all models,** remove brake drum and wheel hub.
5. Remove brake shoe hold down springs and pins, **Fig. 1.**
6. Disconnect brake shoes from wheel cylinders. Hold wheel cylinder pistons in place with suitable rubber bands.
7. Remove shoes from anchor block, **Fig. 2.**
8. Push parking brake lever inward and remove cable, **Fig. 3.**
9. Remove lower and upper return springs.
10. Remove primary shoe from strut and brake shoe adjuster, **Fig. 4.**
11. Remove secondary shoe from support, **Fig. 5. Support spring is under pressure.**
12. Remove parking brake return spring.

Installation

1. Clean, inspect and apply Silicone dielectric compound to backing plate contact points.
2. Install parking brake return spring, then the strut support and move upward.
3. Install strut to primary brake shoe, push shoe inwards and rotate adjuster fully clockwise, **Fig. 6.**
4. Install upper and lower return springs.
5. Push parking brake lever inward and connect parking brake cable.
6. Remove rubber band holding wheel cylinders in place.

7. Install brake shoes to wheel cylinder to anchor block.
8. Install hold down springs, then the brake drum and wheel hub assembly.
9. **On models equipped with anti-lock brake system,** install wheel speed sensor.
10. **On all models,** install tire and wheel assemblies.
11. Operate brake pedal to achieve automatic brake adjustment.

ADJUSTMENTS
Service Brakes

These models are equipped with self adjusting brake mechanisms and require no adjustment. The brakes are adjusted as required whenever the service brakes are applied.

Parking Brake

1. Remove clip and parking brake boot.
2. Ensure rear brakes are not hot when adjusting.
3. Release parking brake to its lowest position.
4. Remove clip and loosen parking brake cable adjustment nut until there is no tension in cable.
5. Apply and release brake pedal to ensure brakes are adjusted correctly.
6. Raise and support vehicle.
7. Ensure parking brake cable is correctly routed in its clips.

8. Lower vehicle.
9. Raise parking brake control lever up four notches.
10. Tighten parking brake cable adjustment nut until increased torque is felt.
11. Apply and release handbrake lever several times with sufficient force to settle parking brake system.
12. Release parking brake lever to its lowest position.
13. Inspect movement of plunger in righthand and lefthand backing plates while moving lever up and down, **Fig. 7.**
14. Total movement of both righthand and lefthand plungers added together should be .039–.315 inch.
15. If further adjustment is required, adjust cable using parking brake cable adjustment nut.
16. Install parking brake adjustment nut clip and control lever boot.

DRUM BRAKES

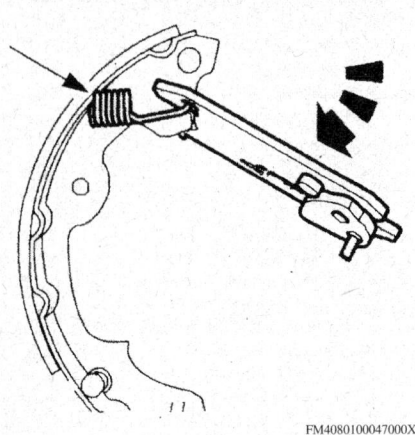

Fig. 5 Secondary brake shoe removal

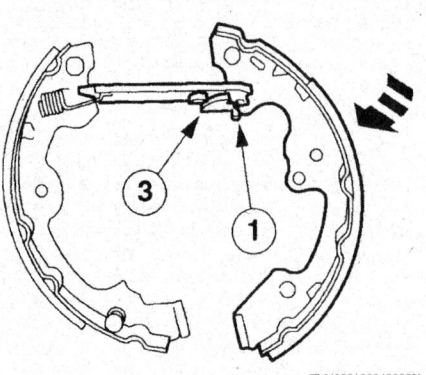

Fig. 6 Primary brake shoe to strut assembly

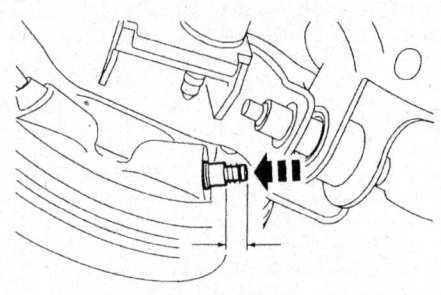

Fig. 7 Parking brake cable plunger inspection

DRUM BRAKE SPECIFICATIONS

| Year | Brake Lining Wear Limit, Inch② | Brake Drum Inside Diameter, Inches | | Maximum Inside Diameter (Discard Limit)① | Drum Runout Limit, Inch | Drum Maximum Out Of Roundness, Inch |
		Nominal	Maximum Refinish			
2001–05	.039	7.99	—	8.03	—	—

① — Maximum brake drum inside diameter (discard limit) is stamped on drum.

② — Above rivet head or shoe. Original equipment type brake linings.

TIGHTENING SPECIFICATIONS

Year	Component	Torque/Ft. Lbs.
2001–05	Brake Drum & Wheel Hub Nuts	49
	Brake Pipe To Wheel Cylinder	71①
	Wheel Cylinder To Backing Plate	108①
	Wheel Lug Nuts	94
	Wheel Speed Sensor	80①

① — Inch lbs.

HYDRAULIC BRAKE SYSTEMS

NOTE: On Air Bag Equipped Models, Refer To "Air Bag System Precautions" Located In The Front Of This Manual For System Disarming & Arming Procedures.

NOTE: Refer To "Computer Relearn Procedures" Located In The Front Of This Manual When Battery Power To The Computer Has Been Interrupted.

INDEX

PRECAUTIONS

Air Bag Systems

Refer to "Air Bag System Precautions" in the front of this manual for system disarming and arming procedures.

Battery Ground Cable

Prior to service, disconnect battery ground cable and isolate as required.

DESCRIPTION

This system operates on the same principles as conventional front and rear split systems using primary and secondary master cylinders moving simultaneously to exert hydraulic pressure on their respective systems, **Fig. 1.**

The hydraulic brake lines on this system, however, have been diagonally split front to rear (left front to right rear and right front to left rear) in place of separate lines to the front and rear wheels.

In the event of a system failure this would cause the remaining good system to do all the braking on one front wheel and the opposite rear wheel, thus maintaining 50% of the total braking force. The hydraulic pressure loss would result in a pressure differential in the system and cause a warning light on the dashboard to glow as in front and rear split systems.

Brake Warning Light Systems

When a pressure differential occurs be-tween the front and rear brake systems, the valves will shuttle toward the side with the low pressure. Movement of the differential valve forces the switch plunger upward over the tapered shoulder of the valve to close the switch contacts and light the dual brake warning lamp, signaling a brake system failure.

The valve assembly consists of two valves in a common bore that are spring loaded toward the centered position. The spring-loaded switch contact plunger rests on top of the valves in the centered position. When a pressure differential occurs between the front and rear brake systems, the valves will shuttle the side with the low pressure. The spring-loaded switch plunger is triggered and the ground circuit for the warning light is completed, lighting the lamp.

As pressure falls in one system, the other system's normal pressure forces the piston to the inoperative side, contacting the switch terminal, causing the warning light on the instrument panel to glow.

On front wheel drive models, a fluid level indicator replaces the pressure differential valve used in previous brake systems. It is contained inside the body of the master cylinder plastic reservoir and activates the brake warning light when fluid level is low.

TESTING WARNING LIGHT SYSTEMS

If the parking brake light is connected into the service brake warning light system, the brake warning light will flash only when the parking brake is applied with the ignition turned ON. The same light will also glow should one of the two service brake systems fail when the brake pedal is applied.

To test the system, turn the ignition on and apply the parking brake. If the lamp fails to light, inspect for a burned out bulb, disconnected socket, a broken or disconnected wire at the switch.

To test the brake warning system, raise the vehicle and open a wheel bleeder valve while a helper depresses the brake pedal and observes the warning light on the instrument panel. If the bulb fails to light, inspect for a burned out bulb, disconnected socket, or a broken or disconnected wire at the switch. If the bulb is not burned out, and wire continuity is proven, replace the brake warning switch.

Combination Valve

The combination valve is a metering valve, failure warning switch, and a proportioned in one assembly and is used on disc brake applications. The metering valve delays front disc braking until the rear drum brake shoes contact the drum. The failure warning switch is actuated in event of front or rear brake system failure, in turn activating a dash warning lamp. The proportioned balances front to rear braking action during rapid deceleration.

Combination valves used on diagonally split brake systems do not use metering valves instead two proportioning valves are used.

METERING VALVE

When the brakes are not applied, the metering valve permits the brake fluid to flow through the valve, thus allowing the fluid to expand and contract with temperature changes.

When the brakes are initially applied, the metering valve, stem moves to the left, preventing fluid to flow through the valve to the

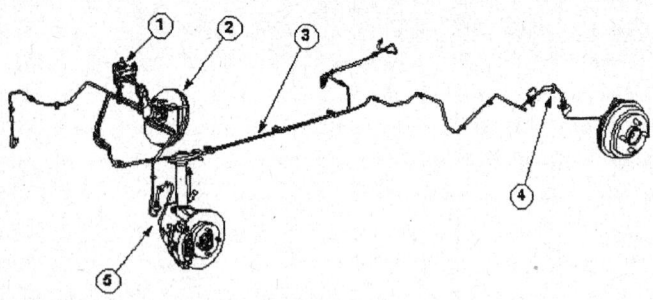

Item	Description
1	Brake fluid reservoir
2	Brake booster and master cylinder
3	Brake hydraulic tubes
4	Rear brake hose
5	Front brake hose

ARM66FM000000402

Fig. 1   Diagonally split brake system

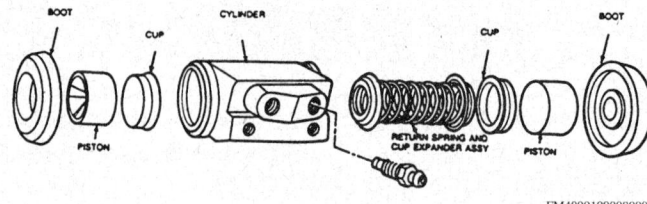

FM4099100008000X

Fig. 2   Exploded view of typical wheel cylinder

front disc brakes. This is accomplished by the smooth end of the metering valve stem contacting the metering valve seal lip at 4–30 psi. The metering valve spring holds the retainer against the seal until a predetermined pressure is produced at the valve inlet port which overcomes the spring pressure and permits hydraulic pressure to actuate the front disc brakes. The increased pressure into the valve is metered through the valve seal, to the front disc brakes, producing an increased force on the diaphragm. The diaphragm then pulls the pin, in turn pulling the retainer and reduces the spring pressure on the metering valve seal. Eventually, the pressure reaches a point at which the spring is pulled away by the diaphragm pin and retainer, leaving the metering valve unrestricted, permitting full pressure to pass through the metering valve.

On some applications, two- or three-way combination valves are used. The three-way combination valve consists of a metering valve, failure warning switch and a proportioned mounted in an aluminum body. The two-way combination valve consists of a failure warning switch and a proportioned. On models equipped with metering valves, the metering valve release rod must be pushed in during bleeding operations on the front wheels.

FAILURE WARNING SWITCH

If the rear brake system fails, the front system pressure forces the switch piston to one side. The switch pin is then forced up into the switch, completing the electrical circuit and activates the dash warning lamp.

When repairs are made and pressure returns to the system, the piston moves to the left, resetting the switch. The detent on the piston requires approximately 100–450 psi to permit full reset of the piston. In event of front brake system failure, the piston moves to the left and the same sequence of events is followed as for rear system failure except the piston resets to the right.

PROPORTIONER OR PRESSURE CONTROL VALVE

During rapid deceleration, a portion of vehicle weight is transferred to the front wheels. This resultant loss of weight at rear wheels must be compensated for to avoid early rear wheel skid. The proportioned or pressure control valve reduces rear brake system pressure, delaying rear wheel skid. When the proportioned or pressure control valve is incorporated in the combination valve assembly, pressure developed within the valve acts against the large end of the piston, overcoming the spring pressure, moving the piston. The piston then contacts the stem seat and restricts line pressure through the valve.

During normal braking operation, the proportioned or pressure control valve is not functional. Brake fluid flows into the proportioned or pressure control valve between the piston center hole and the valve stem, through the stop plate and to the rear brakes. Spring pressure loads the piston during normal braking, causing it to rest against the stop plate.

On diagonally split brake systems, two proportioners or pressure control valves are used. One controls the left rear brake, the other the right rear brake. On front wheel drive models less power brakes, the proportioners or pressure control valves are located in the combination valve. On front wheel drive models with power brakes, the proportioners or pressure control valves are installed in the master cylinder rear brake outlet ports.

Brake Distribution Valve & Switch

This switch assembly which is used on some diagonally split brake systems, is connected to the outlet ports of the master cylinder and also to the brake warning light that warns the driver if either the primary or secondary brake system has failed.

When hydraulic pressure is equal in both primary and secondary brake systems, the switch remains centered. If pressure fails in one of the systems, hydraulic pressure moves the piston toward the inoperative side. The shoulder of the piston contacts the switch terminal, providing a ground and lighting the warning lamp.

Proportioning Valve & Switch

DESCRIPTION

The proportioning valve provides balanced braking action between front and rear brakes under a wide range of braking conditions. The valve regulates the hydraulic pressure applied to the rear wheel cylinders, thus limiting rear braking action when high pressures are required at the front brakes. In this manner, premature rear wheel skid is prevented.

TESTING

When a premature rear wheel slide is obtained on a brake application, it usually is an indication that the fluid pressure to the rear wheels is above the 50% reduction ratio for the rear line pressure and that fault has occurred within the proportioning valve.

To test the valve, install gauge set in brake line between master cylinder and proportioning valve, and at output end of proportioning valve and brake line as outlined. Ensure all joints are fluid tight.

Have a helper exert pressure on brake pedal (holding pressure). Obtain a reading on master cylinder output of approximately 700 psi. While pressure is being held as above, reading on valve outlet should be 550–610 psi. If the pressure readings do not meet these specifications, the valve should be removed and a new valve installed.

COMPONENT REPLACEMENT

Master Cylinder

CONTINENTAL, CROWN VICTORIA, GRAND MARQUIS, MARAUDER, MUSTANG & TOWN CAR

1. Depress brake pedal several times to exhaust system vacuum.
2. Disconnect master cylinder brake lines and electrical connectors.
3. Disconnect hydraulic control unit supply hose at master cylinder. Secure hose aside.

4. Remove two mounting bolts, then secure proportioning valve and tubes aside.
5. Remove mounting nuts and master cylinder.
6. Reverse procedure to install.

COUGAR

1. Apply brake pedal several times to exhaust system vacuum.
2. Disconnect brake warning switch, then remove master cylinder primary and secondary outlet ports' brake tubes.
3. **On models equipped with manual transaxle,** disconnect hydraulic clutch master cylinder hose and drain brake fluid into suitable container.
4. **On all models,** remove brake lines.
5. Remove two mounting nuts and master cylinder.
6. Reverse procedure to install.

ESCORT & ZX2

1. **On models equipped with manual transaxle,** disconnect clutch master cylinder hose from brake master cylinder reservoir.
2. **On all models,** disconnect master cylinder fluid level sensor and brake tubes.
3. Cap brake tubes and master cylinder ports.
4. Remove two mounting nuts master cylinder.
5. Reverse procedure to install.

FOCUS

1. Disconnect electrical connector and remove filler cap.
2. Raise and support vehicle, remove front tire and wheel assemblies.
3. Drain brake fluid into suitable container.
4. Lower vehicle and install brake fluid cap.
5. Remove air cleaner and tube.
6. Disconnect electrical connector, then remove retaining screw and central box.
7. Disconnect brake fluid feed tube and remove remaining brake tubes.
8. Remove brake booster vacuum hose.
9. Remove master cylinder.
10. Reverse procedure to install.

LS & THUNDERBIRD

1. Disconnect fluid level sensor connector.
2. Remove mounting nuts and hose, then position Vapor Management Valve (VMV) aside.
3. Disconnect brake tubes.
4. Disconnect brake master cylinder IVD solenoid electrical connector.
5. Remove brake master cylinder mounting nuts.
6. Disconnect, then position fuel line and vapor management hose aside.
7. Remove brake master cylinder.
8. Reverse procedure to install. Bleed brake system.

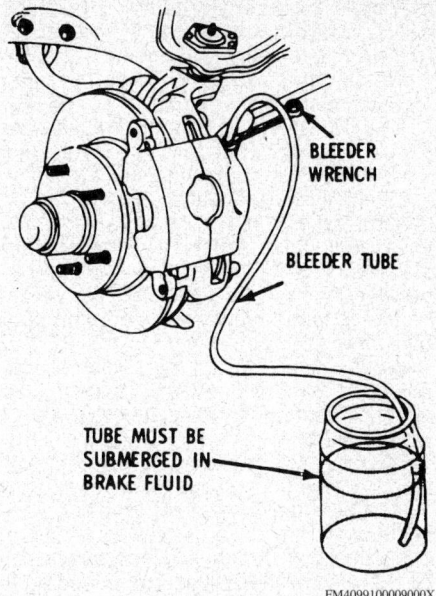

BLEEDER WRENCH

BLEEDER TUBE

TUBE MUST BE SUBMERGED IN BRAKE FLUID

FM40991000009000X

Fig. 3 Hydraulic brake system flushing

FIVE HUNDRED, FREESTYLE, MONTEGO, SABLE & TAURUS

1. Disconnect brake fluid level sensor electrical connector.
2. Loosen fittings and disconnect brake tubes from master cylinder.
3. Remove mounting bolts and master cylinder
4. Reverse procedure to install. Bleed system.

Wheel Cylinders

REMOVAL

1. Remove wheel, drum and brake shoes.
2. Disconnect hydraulic line at wheel cylinder. **Do not pull metal line away from cylinder.** Line will separate from cylinder when cylinder is moved away from brake backing plate.
3. Remove mounting screws and cylinder from brake plate.

INSTALLATION

1. Wipe end of hydraulic line to remove any foreign matter.
2. Place hydraulic cylinder in position. Enter tubing into cylinder and start connecting fitting.
3. Secure cylinder to backing plate and then complete tightening of tubing fitting.
4. Install brake shoes, drum and wheel.
5. Bleed system as outlined in "Brake System Bleed."

COMPONENT SERVICE

Master Cylinder

DISASSEMBLE

1. Clean outside of master cylinder thoroughly. Drain brake fluid from master cylinder into suitable container.
2. Remove stop bolt and pressure control valves.
3. Pry up and remove reservoir from master cylinder body.
4. Remove fluid control valve.
5. Depress primary piston and remove snap ring from retaining groove at open end of bore.
6. Remove primary and secondary piston assemblies from master cylinder. If secondary piston does not come out, apply air pressure to secondary outlet port to remove.

INSPECTION

1. Wash components in clean brake fluid only. Use an air hose to blow out all passages, orifices and valve holes.
2. Air dry and place components on clean paper or lint-free cloth.
3. Inspect master cylinder bore for scoring, rust, pitting or etching. Any of these conditions will require housing replacement.
4. Inspect master cylinder pistons for scoring, pitting or distortion. Replace piston if any of these conditions exist.
5. If either master cylinder housing or piston is replaced, clean new components with clean brake fluid and blow out all passages with air hose.
6. Examine reservoirs for foreign matter and inspect all passages for restrictions. If there is any suspicion of contamination or evidence of corrosion, completely flush hydraulic system.
7. When overhauling a master cylinder, use all components contained in repair kit.
8. Dip all cups, seals, pistons, springs, check valves and retainers in clean brake fluid and place in clean pan or on clean paper.
9. Wash hands with soap and water only to prevent contamination of rubber components from oil, kerosene or gasoline.
10. During assembly, dip all components in clean brake fluid.
11. Inspect through side outlet of dual master cylinder housing to ensure cup lips do not hang up on edge of hole or turn back, which would result in faulty operation. Piece of $\frac{3}{16}$ inch rod with an end rounded off will help guide cups past hole.
12. Inspect aluminum master cylinder bore for corrosion. If corroded, replace master cylinder. **Do not hone or use abrasives on bore.**

ASSEMBLE

1. Coat replacement piston assemblies in clean heavy duty DOT 3 brake fluid.
2. Install secondary piston into bore, spring end first.
3. Install primary piston, spring end first.
4. Depress primary piston and install snap ring.
5. **On all models except Escort and ZX2,** install fluid control valve and **torque** to 96–120 inch lbs.
6. **On Escort and ZX2 models,** install

fluid control valve and **torque** to 33–39 ft. lbs.

7. **On all models,** install stop bolt and pressure control valves.
8. Lubricate new reservoir grommets with brake fluid and install in master cylinder body.
9. Install reservoir into new grommets.
10. Fill and bench bleed master cylinder.

Wheel Cylinders

1. Refer to **Fig. 2,** when serving wheel cylinders.
2. Place all components, except cylinder casting in clean brake fluid. Wipe cylinder walls with clean brake fluid.
3. Examine cylinder bore. A scored bore may be honed providing diameter is not increased more than .005 inch. Replace worn or damaged components from repair kit.
4. Wash hands with soap and water only, as oil, kerosene or gasoline will contaminate rubber components.
5. Lubricate cylinder wall and rubber cups with brake fluid.
6. Install springs, cups, pistons and boots in housing.

BRAKE SYSTEM BLEED

Pressure bleeding is recommended for all hydraulic brake systems. Ensure all dirt and contaminants are removed from master cylinder area prior to removing reservoir cap.

To prevent air from the pressure tank getting into the lines, do not shake the tank while air is being added to the tank or after it has been pressurized. Set the tank in the required location, bring the air hose to the tank, and do not move it during the bleeding operation. The tank should be kept at least one-third full.

On vehicles equipped with disc brakes and master cylinders without proportioners or pressure control valves located in the master cylinder outlet port, the brake metering valve or combination valve must be held in position using suitable tool.

If air does get into the fluid, releasing the pressure will cause the bubbles to increase in size, rise to the top of the fluid, and escape. Pressure should not be greater than about 35 psi.

On vehicles equipped with plastic reservoirs, do not exceed 25 psi during bleeding pressure.

When bleeding without pressure, open the bleed valve three-quarters of a turn, depress the pedal a full stroke, then allow the pedal to return slowly to its released position. It is suggested that after the pedal has been depressed to the end of its stroke, the bleeder valve should be closed before the start of the return stroke. On models with power brakes, first reduce the vacuum in

the power unit to zero by pumping the brake pedal several times with the engine off before starting to bleed the system.

Pressure bleeding eliminates the need for pedal pumping.

Discard drained or bled brake fluid. Care should be taken not to spill brake fluid, since this can damage the finish of the car.

Flushing is essential if there is water, mineral oil or other contaminants in the lines, and whenever new components are installed in the hydraulic system. Fluid contamination is usually indicated by swollen and deteriorated cups and other rubber components.

Wheel cylinders on disc brakes are equipped with bleeder valves, and are bled in the same manner as wheel cylinders for drum brakes.

Bleeding is required on all four wheels if air has entered the system because of low fluid level, or the line or lines have been disconnected. If a line is disconnected at any one wheel cylinder, that cylinder only need be bled. On brake reline jobs, bleeding is advisable to remove any air or contaminants.

Master cylinders equipped with bleeder valves should be bled first before the wheel cylinders are bled. In all cases where a master cylinder has been overhauled, it must be bled. Where there is no bleeder valve, this can be done by leaving the lines loose, actuating the brake pedal to expel the air and then tightening the lines.

After overhauling a dual master cylinder used in conjunction with disc brakes, it is advisable to bleed the cylinder before installing it on the car. The reason for this recommendation is that air may be trapped between the master cylinder pistons because there is only one residual pressure valve (check valve) used in these units.

System Priming

When a new master cylinder has been installed or the brake system emptied or partially emptied, fluid may not flow from the bleeder screws during normal bleeding. It may be required to prime the system using the following procedure:

1. Remove brake lines from master cylinder.
2. Install short brake lines in master cylinder and position them back into reservoir, ensure short brake line ends are submerged in reservoir brake fluid.
3. Fill reservoir with recommended brake fluid, then cover master cylinder fluid reservoir with shop towel.
4. Pump brakes until clear, bubble free fluid comes out of both brake lines. **If any brake fluid spills on paint, wash it off immediately with water.**
5. Remove short brake lines, then reinstall original brake lines.
6. Bleed each brake line at master cylinder using the following procedure:
   a. Have assistant pump brake pedal

ten times, then hold firm pressure on pedal.
   b. Open rearmost brake line fittings with a tubing wrench until a stream of brake fluid comes out. Have assistant maintain pressure on brake pedal until brake line fitting is tightened again.
   c. Repeat this operation until clear, bubble free fluid comes out from around tube fitting.
   d. Repeat this bleeding operation at front brake line fitting.
7. If any of brake lines or calipers have been removed, it may be helpful to prime system by gravity bleeding. this should be done after the master cylinder is primed and bled. To prime the system using the gravity method, proceed as follows:
   a. Fill master cylinder with recommended brake fluid.
   b. Loosen both rear bleeder screws and leave them open until clear brake fluid flows out. **Inspect reservoir fluid level frequently; do not allow fluid level to drop below half full.**
   c. Tighten rear bleeder screws.
   d. Loosen bleeder screw on front caliper, leave open until clear fluid flows out. **Bleed front calipers one side at a time.**
8. After master cylinder has been primed, lines bled at master cylinder and brake system primed, normal brake system bleeding can be resumed at each wheel.

Wheel Bleeding Sequence

Rear Wheel Drive..............RR-LR-RF-LF
Front Wheel Drive ....RR-LF-LR-RF

HYDRAULIC BRAKE SYSTEM FLUSH

Whenever new brake components are installed in the hydraulic system, it is recommended that the entire hydraulic system be thoroughly flushed with clean brake fluid.

It may sometime become required to flush out the system due to the presence of mineral oil, kerosene, gasoline, etc., which will cause swelling of rubber piston cups and valves and render them inoperative.

Flushing is performed at each wheel in the same manner as the bleeding operation except that the bleeder valve is opened 1½ turns and the fluid is forced through the lines and bleeder valve until it emerges clear in color, **Fig. 3.** Approximately one quart of clean brake fluid is required to flush the hydraulic system. After completing the flushing operation at all bleeder valves, inspect to ensure the master cylinder is filled to the proper level.

POWER BRAKE UNITS

NOTE: On Models Equipped With Anti-Lock Brakes, Refer To "Anti-Lock Brake" Section.

NOTE: On Air Bag Equipped Models, Refer To "Air Bag System Precautions" Located In The Front Of This Manual For System Disarming & Arming Procedures.

NOTE: Refer To "Computer Relearn Procedures" Located In The Front Of This Manual When Battery Power To The Computer Has Been Interrupted.

INDEX

APPLICATION CHART

Model	Year	Power Brake Booster System
Continental	2001–02	Dual Diaphragm
Cougar	2001–02	Single Diaphragm
Crown Victoria	2001–05	Bendix Tandem Diaphragm
Escort	2001–03	Single Diaphragm
Five Hundred	2005	Dual Diaphragm
Freestyle	2005	Dual Diaphragm
Focus	2001–05	Single Diaphragm
Grand Marquis	2001–05	Bendix Tandem Diaphragm
LS	2001–05	Dual Diaphragm
Marauder	2003–04	Bendix Tandem Diaphragm
Mustang	2001–05	①
Montego	2005	Dual Diaphragm
Sable	2001–05	Bendix Single Diaphragm
Taurus	2001–05	Bendix Single Diaphragm
Thunderbird	2002–05	Dual Diaphragm
Town Car	2001–05	Bendix Tandem Diaphragm
ZX2	2001–03	Single Diaphragm

① — 3.8L and 4.0L engines, Bendix Tandem Diaphragm. 4.6L engine, Bendix Hydro-Boost system.

PRECAUTIONS

Air Bag Systems

Refer to "Air Bag System Precautions" in the front of this manual for system disarming and arming procedures.

Battery Ground Cable

Prior to service, disconnect battery ground cable and isolate as required.

DESCRIPTION

Bendix Diaphragm System

These units are of the vacuum suspended system. Some units are of the single diaphragm system, while others are of the tandem diaphragm system. Both single piston and double piston or split system master cylinders are used.

The vacuum suspended diaphragm system units utilize engine manifold vacuum and atmospheric pressure for its power. It consists of three basic elements combined into a single power unit. The three basic elements of the single diaphragm system are:

1. Vacuum power section which includes front and rear shell, power diaphragm, return spring and pushrod.
2. Control valve, built integral with power diaphragm and connected through valve rod to brake pedal, controls degree of brake application or release in accordance with pressure applied to brake pedal.
3. Hydraulic master cylinder, attached to vacuum power section which contains all elements of conventional brake master cylinder except for pushrod, supplies fluid under pressure to wheel brakes in proportion to pressure applied to brake pedal.

Upon application of the brakes, the valve rod and plunger move to the lefthand in the power diaphragm to close the vacuum port and open the atmospheric port to admit air through the air cleaner and valve at the rear diaphragm chamber. With vacuum present in the rear chamber, a force is developed to move the power diaphragm, hydraulic pushrod and hydraulic piston or pistons to close the compensating port or ports and force fluid under pressure through the residual check valve or valves and lines into the front and rear wheel cylinders to actuate the brakes.

As pressure is developed within the master cylinder a counter force acting through the hydraulic pushrod and reaction disc against the vacuum power diaphragm

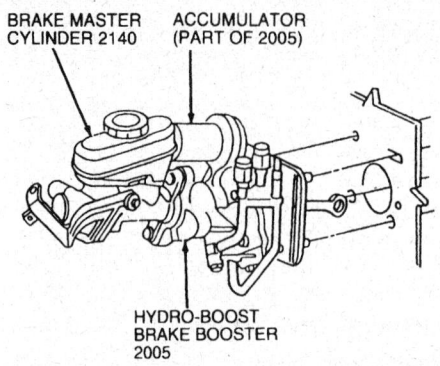

BRAKE MASTER CYLINDER 2140   ACCUMULATOR (PART OF 2005)

HYDRO-BOOST BRAKE BOOSTER 2005

FM4099600012000X

Fig. 1 Bendix Hydro-Boost

and valve plunger sets up a reaction force opposing the force applied to the valve rod and plunger. This reaction force tends to close the atmospheric port and reopen the vacuum port. Since this force is in opposition to the force applied to the brake pedal by the driver it gives the driver a feel of the amount of brake applied. The proportion of reactive force applied to the valve plunger through the reaction disc is designed into the Master-Vac to ensure maximum power consistent with maintaining pedal feel. The reaction force is in direct proportion to the hydraulic pressure developed within the brake system.

Bendix Hydro-Boost System

The Bendix Hydro-Boost System is a hydraulically operated booster with fluid provided by the power steering pump, **Fig. 1.** If power steering fluid flow is interrupted, a reserve accumulator system stores enough fluid under pressure to provide at least two power-assisted stops. Manual brake application is permitted if the reserve system is depleted.

The Hydro-Boost booster, power steering pump and hydraulic hoses are all serviced separately. If the booster becomes inoperative or is damaged, it must be replaced as an assembly.

Vacuum Assist Diaphragm System

The vacuum assist diaphragm assembly multiplies the force exerted on the master cylinder piston in order to increase the hydraulic pressure delivered to the wheel cylinders while decreasing the effort required to obtain acceptable stopping performance.

Vacuum assist units get their energy by opposing engine vacuum to atmospheric pressure. A piston, cylinder and flexible diaphragm utilize this energy to provide brake

assistance. The diaphragm is balanced with engine vacuum until the brake pedal is depressed, allowing atmospheric pressure to unbalance the unit and apply force to the brake system.

Brakes will operate even if the power unit fails. This means the conventional brake system and the power assist system are completely separate. Troubleshooting conventional and power assist systems are exactly the same until the power unit is reached. As with conventional hydraulic brakes, a spongy pedal still means air is trapped in the hydraulic system. Power brakes give higher line pressure, making leaks more critical.

TROUBLESHOOTING

Power brake operation concerns should be handled as if two separate systems exist.

1. Inspect for faults in hydraulic system first.
2. If hydraulic system is satisfactory, inspect power brake circuit.
3. Press brake pedal firmly and then start engine.
4. Pedal should fall away slightly and less pressure should be needed to maintain pedal in any position.
5. Install of suitable pressure gauge in brake hydraulic system.
6. Record pressure with engine off and power unit not operating.
7. Maintain pedal height, start engine and record measurement.
8. There should be substantial pressure increase in second measurement.
9. Pedal travel should be kept strictly to specifications.
10. Measure manifold vacuum or inspect operation of external vacuum pump if power unit is not giving enough assistance. On emission controlled engines, manifold vacuum readings may be less than 15 inches Hg. at idle.
11. If manifold vacuum is abnormally low, tune engine and then inspect power brakes.
12. Loose vacuum lines and clogged air intake filters will cut down brake efficiency.
13. Most units have check valve that retains some vacuum in system when engine is off. Vacuum gauge inspection of this valve will tell when it is restricted, stuck open or closed.
14. Failure of brakes to release in most instances is caused by tight or misaligned connection between power unit and brake linkage.
15. If this connection is free, look for broken piston, diaphragm or bellows and return spring.
16. Loosen connection between master cylinder and brake booster.

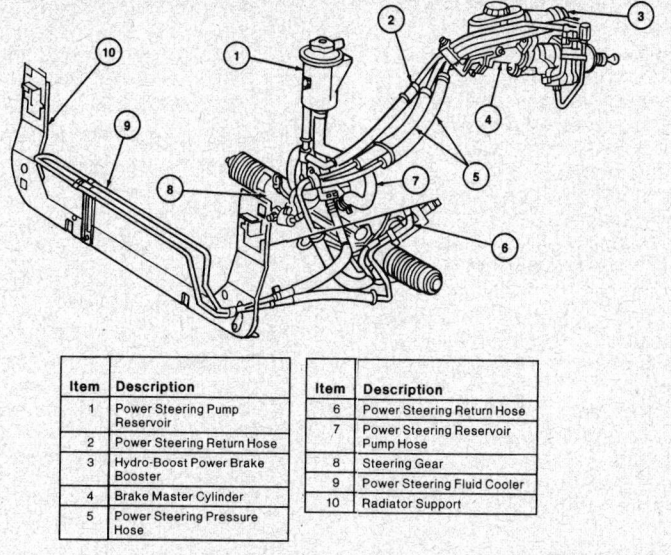

FM4099600013000X

Fig. 2 Hydro-Boost system fluid distribution. Mustang w/4.6L engine

Item	Description	Item	Description
1	Power Steering Pump Reservoir	6	Power Steering Return Hose
2	Power Steering Return Hose	7	Power Steering Reservoir Pump Hose
3	Hydro-Boost Power Brake Booster	8	Steering Gear
4	Brake Master Cylinder	9	Power Steering Fluid Cooler
5	Power Steering Pressure Hose	10	Radiator Support

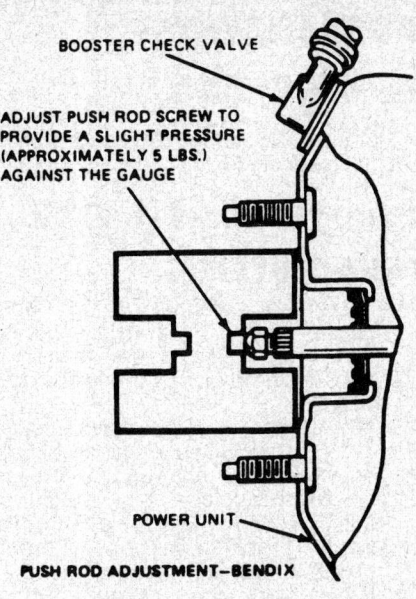

FM4099100010000X

Fig. 3 Master cylinder pushrod adjustment. Bendix system vacuum booster

17. If brakes release, trouble is in power unit; if brakes still will not release, look for restricted brake line or similar difficulties in regular hydraulic circuit.
18. Residual pressure check valve is usually located immediately under brake line connection on hydraulic assist power brakes.
19. This valve maintains slight hydraulic pressure within brake lines and wheel cylinders to give better pedal response. If it is sticking, brakes may not release.
20. Power brakes that have hard pedal are usually suffering from milder form of same ills that cause complete power unit failure. Collapsed or leaking vacuum lines or insufficient manifold vacuum, as well as punctured diaphragms or bellows and leaky piston seals, all lead to weak power unit operation.
21. Steady hiss when brake is held down means vacuum leak that will cause poor power unit operation.
22. Do not immediately condemn power unit if brakes grab. Proceed as follows:
    a. Look for greasy linings, scored rotors or drums.
    b. Investigate power unit.
    c. Inspect for damaged reaction control. Reaction control is usually made up of diaphragm, spring and valves that tends to resist pedal action. It is put in system to give the pedal feel.
23. **On models equipped with Bendix Hydro-Boost system,** proceed as follows:
    a. Ensure engine is in off position.

b. Press and release brake pedal several times to relieve all hydraulic pressure from booster.
c. Depress and hold pedal with light pressure.
d. Start engine and note pedal reaction.
e. If it does not fall slightly and hold, press and release pedal several times, then depress and hold with medium foot pressure.
f. If the pedal now moves toward floor, inspect for brake fluid leakage at master cylinder, brake hoses and all connections, **Fig. 2.**
g. Idle engine, then depress and hold brake pedal for no more than five seconds with heavy foot pressure.
h. If booster shows any signs of fluid leakage, it must be replaced.
24. **On all models,** operating engine at idle, then depress and hold brake pedal for not less than five seconds with heavy foot pressure or holding steering wheel at full stop.
25. Turn ignition switch to Off position and wait 8–12 hours.
26. Depress brake pedal and inspect for reserve.
27. If no reserve is present, booster is faulty.

Bendix Diaphragm System
HARD PEDAL OR NO ASSIST

1. Air cleaner element clogged.

2. Control valve faulty.
3. Faulty diaphragm.
4. Worn or distorted reaction plate or levers.
5. Cracked or broken power piston or levers.
6. Internal or external leaks.

BRAKES GRAB

1. Control valve faulty or sticking.
2. Bind in linkage.
3. Reaction diaphragm leaking.
4. Worn or distorted levers or plate.

NO OR SLOW RELEASE

1. Pushrod adjustment improper.
2. Linkage binding.
3. Return spring faulty.

Bendix Hydro-Boost System
NO POWER ASSIST

1. Power steering pump drive belt slipping or worn.
2. Power steering pump fluid level improper.
3. Linkage binding.
4. Hydro-Boost unit failure.

ERRATIC BOOSTER OPERATION, BINDING, GRABBING OR STICKING

1. Supply hose leakage or obstructions.
2. Hydro-Boost unit seal leakage.

ADJUSTMENTS

Escort & ZX2

Refer to "Hydraulic Brake Systems" chapter for pushrod adjustment procedure.

Except Escort & ZX2

BENDIX SYSTEM

1. Disconnect master cylinder from booster leaving brake lines connected and secure cylinder aside.
2. Start engine and operate engine at idle speed.
3. With engine running, position gauge over pushrod. Gauge should bottom against booster housing with force of approximately five lbs. applied to pushrod, **Fig. 3. Ensure pushrod is properly seated in booster when performing gauge inspection.**
4. If force required to seat gauge is more than five lbs., shorten length of pushrod.
5. If force required to seat gauge is less than five lbs., lengthen pushrod.
6. Install master cylinder and remove reservoir cover.
7. With engine running, observe fluid surface in reservoir when brakes are applied and released rapidly. If no movement is observed on fluid surface, pushrod is adjusted too long.

SINGLE DIAPHRAGM BOOSTER

1. Remove master cylinder.
2. Position master cylinder gauge T87C-2500-A, or equivalent, on end of master cylinder.
3. Loosen setscrew and push gauge plunger against bottom of primary piston.
4. While holding gauge in position, tighten setscrew.
5. Invert gauge and place over brake booster pushrod. Measurement should be zero.
6. If clearance is not zero, loosen pushrod locknut and adjust pushrod.
7. Reverse procedure to install.

POWER BRAKE UNIT SERVICE

Power Booster, Replace

CONTINENTAL

1. Remove battery and disconnect speed control actuator electrical connector.
2. Remove two mounting nuts and speed control actuator cable, then position aside.
3. Remove two strut tower brace nuts and brace.
4. Remove windshield wiper motor and rubber grommet from lower cowl panel.
5. Remove mounting nut, bolts and lower cowl panel.
6. Disconnect power brake booster check valve and master cylinder.
7. Remove mounting nut and evaporative emission canister purge valve.
8. Disconnect EVAP electrical connector and vacuum hoses.
9. Remove push-pins and instrument close out panel.
10. Remove retaining pin, then slide stop lamp switch and booster push rod from brake pedal pin.
11. Remove mounting nuts and power brake booster.
12. Reverse procedure to install, noting the following:
    a. Ensure proper clearance between pushrod and master cylinder as outlined in "Adjustments."
    b. Bleed brake system as outlined in "Hydraulic Brake Systems" chapter.
    c. **Torque** booster to dash panel mounting nuts to 19–25 ft. lbs.

COUGAR

2.0L ENGINE

1. Remove air cleaner, Mass Air Flow (MAF) sensor and outlet tube.
2. Disconnect engine wiring harness electrical connector.
3. **On models equipped with automatic transaxle,** remove automatic transaxle fluid dipstick.
4. **On all models,** remove master cylinder as outlined "Hydraulic Brake Systems" chapter.
5. Remove brake booster actuator rod retaining clip.
6. Disconnect vacuum hose from brake booster. **Do not pull on accelerator speed control cable.**
7. Remove brake booster.
8. Reverse procedure to install, noting the following:
    a. Bleed brake system.
    b. Ensure that brake booster connecting rod is correctly positioned through bulkhead rubber boot.

2.5L ENGINE

1. Remove air cleaner and outlet tube.
2. Remove master cylinder as outlined "Hydraulic Brake Systems" chapter.
3. Disconnect vacuum hose from brake booster.
4. Remove brake booster actuator rod retaining clip.
5. **On models equipped with automatic transaxle,** remove automatic transaxle fluid dipstick.
6. **On all models,** remove brake booster nuts.
7. Remove master cylinder brake lines from control unit.
8. Disconnect booster electrical connectors.
9. **On models equipped with automatic transaxle,** disconnect gear selector cable and bracket.
10. **On all models,** disconnect starter motor power cable.
11. Relieve fuel system pressure as outlined in "Precautions" section of appropriate engine section of chassis chapter.
12. Disconnect fuel flow and return lines.
13. Remove brake booster.
14. Reverse procedure to install.

CROWN VICTORIA, GRAND MARQUIS, MARAUDER & TOWN CAR

1. Disconnect fluid level sensor connector.
2. Position speed control cable aside.
3. Disconnect power brake booster check valve.
4. Remove brake master cylinder mounting nuts.
5. Remove wiring harness bracket and position aside.
6. Remove brake master cylinder and position aside.
7. Remove push-pins and instrument close-out panel.
8. Remove stoplight switch retaining pin.
9. Slide stoplight switch and booster push rod off brake pedal pin.
10. Remove mounting nuts and power brake booster.
11. Reverse procedure to install. **Torque** mounting nuts to 16–21 ft. lbs.

ESCORT & ZX2

Pump brake pedal several times to exhaust any vacuum in the booster.

1. Remove master cylinder as outlined in "Hydraulic Brake Systems" chapter.
2. Disconnect rubber hose connecting intake manifold to power brake unit.
3. Remove instrument panel steering column cover.
4. Remove spring clip in brake pedal clevis pin.
5. Remove clevis pin and brake pedal pushrod.
6. Remove mounting nuts power brake unit.
7. Reverse procedure to install, noting the following:
    a. Ensure proper clearance between pushrod and master cylinder exists as outlined in "Adjustments."
    b. **Torque** booster to dash panel mounting nuts to 14–19 ft. lbs.
    c. **Torque** master cylinder mounting nuts to 8–12 ft. lbs.

FOCUS

1. Remove master cylinder as outlined in "Hydraulic Brake Systems" chapter.
2. **On models equipped with speed control,** disconnect electrical connector and remove speed control unit.
3. **On all models,** remove brake tubes from bulkhead retainers.
4. Disconnect hydraulic control unit electrical connector.
5. Disconnect brake lines from hydraulic control unit. Cap all fittings.
6. Remove brake booster actuating rod from brake pedal.
7. Remove mounting nuts and brake booster.
8. Reverse procedure to install.

LS & THUNDERBIRD

1. Remove mounting nuts and wiper

arms, then disconnect washer hose.
2. Remove push-pins, rubber trim and cowl cover.
3. Remove mounting nut and position vacuum hose bracket aside.
4. Remove cowl brace center and end bolts, then the bracket.
5. Disconnect coolant reservoir return hose.
6. Remove brake master cylinder.
7. Disconnect power brake booster check valve and electrical connector.
8. Remove coolant reservoir mounting bolts and disconnect hose.
9. Remove coolant reservoir.
10. Remove clip and brake pedal pin.
11. Remove mounting nuts and power brake booster.
12. Reverse procedure to install.

MUSTANG

3.8L ENGINE

2001-02

Pump brake pedal several times to exhaust any vacuum in the booster.
1. Remove air cleaner.
2. Disconnect manifold vacuum hose from power booster check valve.
3. Disconnect hydraulic lines from master cylinder. Cap open lines and ports.
4. Remove mounting nuts and master cylinder.
5. **On models equipped with manual transmission,** remove routing bracket and position clutch cable aside.
6. **On all models,** disconnect accelerator cable at dash pane, pedal and shaft. Position cable aside to gain maneuvering room for brake booster.
7. Disconnect electrical connector from stop lamp switch.
8. Remove hairpin retainer, then idle stop lamp switch off brake pedal pin just far enough for switch outer hole to clear pin.
9. Lower switch away from pin.
10. Slide brake master cylinder pushrod bushing off brake pedal pin.
11. Remove booster-to-dash panel mounting nuts.
12. **On models equipped with speed control,** disconnect control amplifier from lower outboard booster stud and position aside.
13. **On all models,** move booster forward until booster studs clear dash panel, then raise front of unit and remove.
14. Reverse procedure to install, noting the following:
    a. Ensure proper clearance between pushrod and master cylinder exists as outlined in "Adjustments."
    b. Bleed brake system as outlined in "Hydraulic Brake Systems" chapter.
    c. **Torque** booster to dash panel

mounting nuts and master cylinder to booster locking nuts to 15–23 ft. lbs.

2003-05

1. Remove air cleaner housing.
2. Remove mounting nuts and position master cylinder aside.
3. Discharge accumulator by depress brake pedal several times with engine off.
4. Disconnect booster vacuum hose.
5. Remove stop lamp self-locking pin.
6. Remove stop lamp switch and brake booster push rod from brake pedal pin.
7. Remove mounting nuts and power brake booster.
8. Reverse procedure to install. **Torque** power brake booster and brake master cylinder mounting nuts to 19 ft. lbs.

4.6L ENGINE

Do not carry the booster by the accumulator.

Do not drop booster on accumulator. Keep the accumulator away from excessive heat, fire or incineration.

Before disposal, drill a $\frac{1}{16}$ inch diameter hole in the accumulator can's end to relieve the high pressure nitrogen gas pressure. Wear safety glasses while performing this operation.

Do not activate the booster when the master cylinder has been removed.

2001-02

1. Apply brake pedal several times to discharge accumulator.
2. Remove brake lines from proportioning valve's primary and secondary ports.
3. Disconnect fluid level sensor.
4. **On models equipped with automatic transmission,** disconnect shift interlock cable.
5. **On models equipped with manual transmission,** disconnect clutch cable from master cylinder routing bracket.
6. **On all models,** remove hose routing bracket from master cylinder.
7. Disconnect power steering pressure hoses and return line from Hydro-Boost unit. Position hoses aside.
8. Remove brake lamp switch electrical connector.
9. Loosen four booster mounting nuts and brake pedal support bracket to cowl bolt.
10. Remove hairpin retainer. Slide stop lamp switch off brake pedal pin far enough for switch outer arm to clear pin, then remove switch.
11. Slide brake master cylinder pushrod bushing off brake pedal pin.
12. Remove booster to firewall mounting nuts.

13. Move booster and master cylinder forward and upward until booster's studs clear firewall. Remove unit.
14. Reverse procedure to install, noting the following:
    a. **Torque** booster to firewall nuts to 16–21 ft. lbs.
    b. **Torque** brake pedal support bracket to cowl bolt to 14–19 ft. lbs.
    c. **Torque** brake line fittings in ports to 11–17 ft. lbs.
    d. **Torque** power steering pressure hoses and return line to booster tubes to 10–15 ft. lbs., **Fig. 2.**
    e. Bleed brake system.

2003-05

1. Apply brake pedal several times to discharge accumulator.
2. Disconnect brake fluid level sensor electrical connector.
3. Disconnect brake lines.
4. Disconnect power steering return and pressure lines.
5. Remove self-locking pin.
6. Remove stop lamp switch and brake booster push rod from brake pedal pin.
7. Remove mounting nuts and power brake booster.
8. Reverse procedure to install, noting the following:
    a. Install new Teflon seals on power steering pressure fittings.
    b. **Torque** booster nuts to 19 ft. lbs.
    c. **Torque** power steering pressure lines to 14 ft. lbs.
    d. **Torque** brake lines to 13 ft. lbs.

FIVE HUNDRED, FREESTYLE, MONTEGO, 2001-05 SABLE & TAURUS

2001-05

1. Disconnect Mass Air Flow (MAF) sensor and breather tubes.
2. Disconnect outlet tube from throttle body.
3. Remove cover and position engine air cleaner housing aside.
4. Remove wiper mounting arm and pivot shaft.
5. Remove brake master cylinder as outlined in "Hydraulic Brake Systems" chapter.
6. Disconnect electrical connector and remove mounting nuts, then position speed control module and bracket aside.
7. Disconnect manual control lever cable from transmission range sensor, then remove manual cable bracket and nut.
8. Remove mounting bolts and position manual cable bracket aside.
9. Remove vacuum outlet manifold.

POWER BRAKE UNITS

10. Disconnect vacuum check valve from brake booster.
11. Remove retainer strap and position heater hose aside.
12. Remove wiring harnesses and connectors from brake booster.
13. Remove steering column opening cover.
14. Disconnect stoplight switch electrical connector, then remove retainer and push rod off pin.
15. Remove stoplight switch, washer and bushing.
16. Remove and discard brake booster mounting nuts.
17. Remove brake booster.
18. Reverse procedure to install, noting the following:
    a. Adjust pushrod as outlined in "Adjustments."
    b. Install new brake booster mounting nuts.

Overhaul

Overhaul is not required. Replace power brake unit as an assembly. In some instances, the only service required is replacement of the check valve, grommet and pushrod adjustment.

FRONT WHEEL DRIVE AXLES

TABLE OF CONTENTS

Continental

NOTE: On Air Bag Equipped Models, Refer To "Air Bag System Precautions" Located In The Front Of This Manual For System Disarming & Arming Procedures.

NOTE: Refer To "Computer Relearn Procedures" Located In The Front Of This Manual When Battery Power To The Computer Has Been Interrupted.

INDEX

PRECAUTIONS

Air Bag Systems

Refer to "Air Bag System Precautions" in the front of this manual for system disarming and arming procedures.

Battery Ground Cable

Prior to service, disconnect battery ground cable and isolate as required.

DESCRIPTION

Each front wheel driveshaft employs Constant Velocity (CV) joints at both inboard (differential side) and outboard (wheel side) for vehicle operating smoothness. The CV joints are connected by an intermediate shaft which is splined at both ends and retained in the inboard and outboard CV joints by snap rings, **Fig. 1.**

Inboard CV joint is permanently retained by the intermediate driveshaft. The service components of the CV joint include the shaft and the driveshaft joint boot. The joint and outboard boot will need to be removed to replace the boot, joint or shaft.

TROUBLESHOOTING

Refer to **Fig. 2,** for troubleshooting.

DRIVESHAFT

REPLACE

If removing both left and righthand driveshafts, install plugs tool No. T81P-1177B, or equivalent.

Install a new hub retainer nut, lower control arm to steering knuckle mounting bolt and nut and a new inboard CV joint stub shaft snap ring.

Removal

1. Turn air suspension system switch Off and discharge air from both front air springs.
2. Raise and support vehicle, then remove tire and wheel assemblies.
3. Remove hub retainer nut and washer. Discard nut.
4. Prevent halfshaft from turning by installing steel pin in brake disc.
5. Remove mounting bolt at strut assembly and position stabilizer bar link aside.
6. Remove ball joint to steering knuckle mounting nut. **Discard nut.**

7. Separate lower ball joint from steering knuckle using suitable suspension arm puller.
8. Remove anti-lock brake sensor from steering knuckle.
9. Remove height sensor link at lower arm ball stud.
10. Separate outboard CV joint from hub using front hub remover tool Nos. T81P-1104-A, T83P-1104-BH1, T86P-1104-A1 and T81P-1104-C, or equivalents. **Do not use hammer to separate outboard CV joint stub shaft from hub.**
11. Turn steering hub and support strut aside.
12. Remove CV joint from transaxle using CV joint puller tool No. T86P-3514-A2 and impact slide hammer tool No. D79P-100-A, or equivalents.
13. Suspend shaft end from conventional underbody component with suitable length of wire. **Do not allow shaft to hang unsupported.**
14. Remove driveshaft.

Installation

1. Install new snap ring onto inboard CV joint stub shaft intermediate driveshaft. **Outboard CV joint stub shaft does not have snap ring.** Start one end in

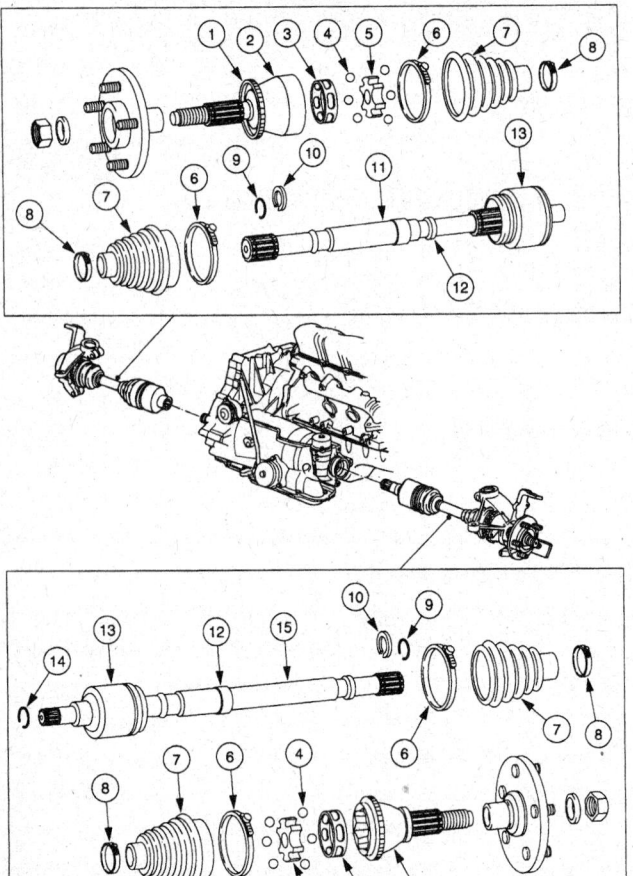

Item	Description	Item	Description
1	Front Brake Anti-Lock Sensor Indicator	9	Circlip
2	Front Wheel Driveshaft Joint	10	Stop Ring
3	Ball Cage	11	Interconnecting Shaft
4	Balls (6 Req'd)	12	Halfshaft Identification Label
5	Race	13	Inboard CV Joint Housing
6	Front Wheel Driveshaft Joint Boot Clamp (Large)	14	Circlip
7	Front Wheel Driveshaft Joint Boot	15	Interconnecting Shaft
8	Front Wheel Driveshaft Joint Boot Clamp (Small)		

FM3039500309020X

Fig. 1 Exploded view of driveshaft assemblies (Part 2 of 2)

FM3039500309010X

Fig. 1 Exploded view of driveshaft assemblies (Part 1 of 2)

groove and work ring over stub shaft end and into groove

2. Align inboard CV joint stub shaft or link shaft and differential splines.
3. Push CV joint into differential until snap ring seats in differential side gear using suitable plastic mallet to seat snap ring. **Do not damage differential oil seal.**
4. Align outboard CV joint stub shaft and hub splines.
5. Push shaft into hub as far as possible.
6. Temporarily attach rotor to hub with washers and two wheel lug nuts.
7. Prevent rotor from turning during CV joint installation by install steel rod into rotor and rotate clockwise to contact steering knuckle.
8. Install hub nut washer and new hub retainer nut. Manually thread retainer onto CV joint shaft as far as possible.
9. Connect control arm to steering knuckle using new lower ball joint to steering knuckle mounting nut.
10. Connect stabilizer bar link to stabilizer bar.
11. Connect ride height sensor link.
12. Install anti-lock sensor link into control arm.
13. Install tire and wheel assembly, then lower vehicle and turn air suspension switch on.

DRIVESHAFT SERVICE
Outboard Joint

CV joint components are matched during manufacturing and cannot be interchanged with components from another joint. Do not intermix or substitute components between joints.

DISASSEMBLE

1. Clamp driveshaft into suitable vise. Do not allow vise jaws to contact boot or clamp.
2. Cut large boot clamp and peel it away from boot.
3. Support intermediate driveshaft in suitable soft jaw vise and angle CV joint to expose inner bearing race.
4. Disconnect internal snap ring and separate CV joint from intermediate driveshaft by tapping inner bearing race using suitable brass drift and hammer. Remove boot.
5. Inspect CV joint grease for contamination. If CV joints are operating satisfactorily and grease does not appear to be contaminated, add grease and replace boot. If grease appears contaminated or has gritty feeling, inspect for worn components.

6. Remove snap ring located near end of shaft. Discard snap ring. New snap ring is supplied with boot replacement kit and CV joint. **Stop ring located just below snap ring should only be removed if it is damaged.**
7. Clamp CV joint stub shaft in suitable vise with outer facing pointing upward. **Do not damage dust seal.**
8. Press inner race down until it tilts enough to allow removal of ball. Remove ball.
9. Repeat until all six balls are removed.
10. Pivot cage and inner race assembly until it is facing straight up and down in outer race.
11. Align cage windows with outer race lands while pivoting bearing race.
12. With cage pivoted and aligned, lift assembly from outer race.
13. Rotate inner race up and out of cage.

ASSEMBLE

1. Apply light coat of CV grease No. E43Z-19590-A, or equivalent, onto inner and outer ball races
2. Install inner race into bearing cage.
3. Install inner race and cage assembly into outer race.
4. Install assembly vertically and pivot 90° into position.
5. Align bearing cage and inner race with outer race.
6. Tilt inner race and cage, then install ball. Repeat until all six balls are installed.
7. Left and righthand intermediate driveshafts are not same end-for-end. Outboard end is shorter from end of shaft to end of boot groove than inboard end. Ensure proper inboard and outboard CV joint to shaft installation, **Fig. 3.**
8. Install CV joint boot after removing stop ring.
9. Ensure boot is properly seated in its groove and clamp into position.
10. Install stop ring. If not removed, ensure stop ring is properly seated in groove.
11. Install new snap ring supplied with service kit in groove nearest end of shaft.
12. **Do not overexpand or twist snap ring.**
13. Pack CV joint and boot with 6.3 ounces grease supplied in service kit.
14. With boot peeled back, position CV

joint on shaft and tap into position. **CV joint is completely seated when snap ring locks in groove cut into CV joint inner race. Inspect for snap ring seating by trying to pull joint from shaft.**

15. Remove excess grease from CV joint external surfaces.
16. Position boot over CV joint.
17. Ensure boot is seated in its groove and clamp in position.

Dust Seal

1. Gently and evenly tap around dust seal until unseated using suitable hammer.
2. Install dust seal using seal installation tool Nos. T83T-3132-A1 and T86P-1104-A4, or equivalents. **Dust seal flange must face outboard.**

Speed Indicator Ring

1. Remove outboard CV joint as outlined in "Outboard Joint."
2. Remove speed indicator ring using press tool No. T88P-2020-A, or equivalent, and suitable press.
3. Reverse procedure to install. Ring is properly installed when bottomed out in tool.

Inboard Joint

Inboard CV joint is permanently retained to intermediate driveshaft. The service CV joint includes shaft and driveshaft joint boot. Joint and outboard boot will require removal to replace the boot, joint or shaft.

DISASSEMBLE

1. Cut and remove boot clamps, then slide boot back on shaft.
2. Remove stop ring and driveshaft bearing retainer circlip.
3. Slide boot off intermediate driveshaft.

ASSEMBLE

1. Install driveshaft boot on intermediate driveshaft and position boot to allow for inboard joint housing installation.
2. Position boot in small boot groove.
3. Install small boot clamp using boot clamp replacement tool No. T95P-3514-A, or equivalent. Tighten tool through bolt until tool is in closed position.
4. Fill inboard joint housing with Ford High Temperature CV Joint Grease part No. E43Z-19590-A, or equivalent.

Condition	Possible Source
• Clicking, Popping or Grinding Noises While Turning	• Inadequate or contaminated lube in outboard front wheel driveshaft joint or inboard front wheel driveshaft joint. • Another component contacting halfshaft assembly. • Worn, damaged or improperly installed wheel bearings, brakes, suspension or steering components.
• Vibration at Highway Speeds	• Out of balance front wheels or tires. • Out of round front tires. • Improperly seated outboard front wheel driveshaft joint in front wheel hub.
• Shudder Vibration During Acceleration	• Excessively high front wheel driveshaft joint operating angles caused by improper ride height. • Excessively worn or damaged inboard front wheel driveshaft and joint or outboard front wheel driveshaft joint.
• Front Wheel Drive Shaft Joint Pullout	• Inboard driveshaft bearing retainer circlip missing or not properly seated in differential side gear. • Engine / transaxle assembly mispositioned. • Frame rail or shock tower out of position or damaged. • Front suspension components worn or damaged.

FM3039500310000X

Fig. 2 Troubleshooting chart

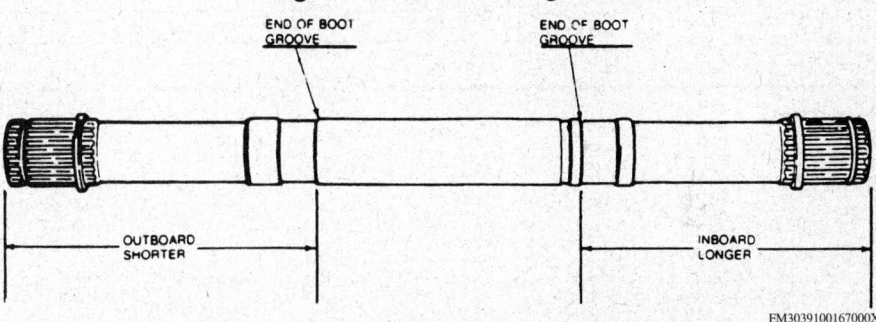

FM3039100167000X

Fig. 3 Interconnecting shaft identification

5. Spread remaining grease evenly inside driveshaft joint boot for total combined fill of 16 ¾ ounces.
6. Remove excess grease from CV joint external surfaces.
7. Position boot over joint, then move joint inward and outward to specified length, **Fig. 4.**
8. Allow trapped air to escape from boot by inserting dull tip screwdriver blade between boot and outer bearing race.
9. Locate clamp tabs in slots. Hand tighten clamps.
10. Ensure boot is properly seated in its groove and clamp is in position.
11. Tighten tool through bolt using boot clamp replacement tool No. T95P-3514-A, or equivalent, until tool is in closed position.
12. Work CV joint through several angles through its full travel range. Joint should compress, extend and flex smoothly.

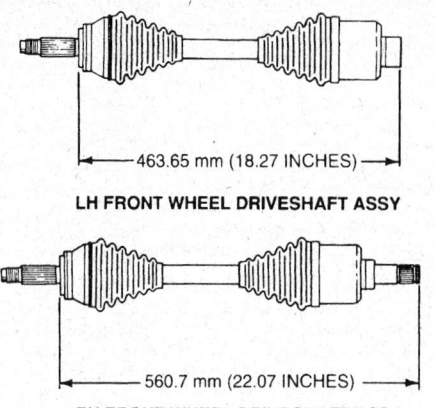

463.65 mm (18.27 INCHES)

LH FRONT WHEEL DRIVESHAFT ASSY

560.7 mm (22.07 INCHES)

RH FRONT WHEEL DRIVESHAFT ASSY

FM3039600274000X

Fig. 4   Driveshaft assembled lengths

TIGHTENING SPECIFICATIONS

Year	Component	Torque/Ft. Lbs.
2001–02	ABS Sensor	84①
	Ball Joint	46
	Hub Nut	184
	Stabilizer Bar Link	67
	Wheel Lug Nut	95

① — Inch lbs.

Cougar

NOTE: On Air Bag Equipped Models, Refer To "Air Bag System Precautions" Located In The Front Of This Manual For System Disarming & Arming Procedures.

NOTE: Refer To "Computer Relearn Procedures" Located In The Front Of This Manual When Battery Power To The Computer Has Been Interrupted.

INDEX

PRECAUTIONS

Air Bag Systems

Refer to "Air Bag System Precautions" in the front of this manual for system disarming and arming procedures.

Battery Ground Cable

Prior to service, disconnect battery ground cable and isolate as required.

DESCRIPTION

The front drive halfshafts transmit torque from the engine to the wheels. In order to allow vertical movement of the wheels and engine, the front drive halfshafts operate at varying lengths and angles. The tripod joints allow for changes in driveshaft length during axial movements.

To reduce running friction, the front drive halfshafts are fitted with Constant Velocity (CV) joints at both ends. Tripod joints (with tripod, running rollers and tripod housing) are fitted on the transaxle side. Fix joints (with ball star, ball cage and ball shell) are fitted on the wheel side. The lefthand tripod joint is secured in the differential with a snap ring. The intermediate shaft (righthand side) is not secured in the differential, but is secured by the intermediate shaft bearing bracket. The tripod joint of the right-hand front drive halfshaft is secured in the intermediate shaft with a snap ring. The outboard constant velocity joints are attached to the wheel hubs.

TROUBLESHOOTING

Clicking, Popping or Grinding Noises While Turning

1. Another component contacting half-shaft.

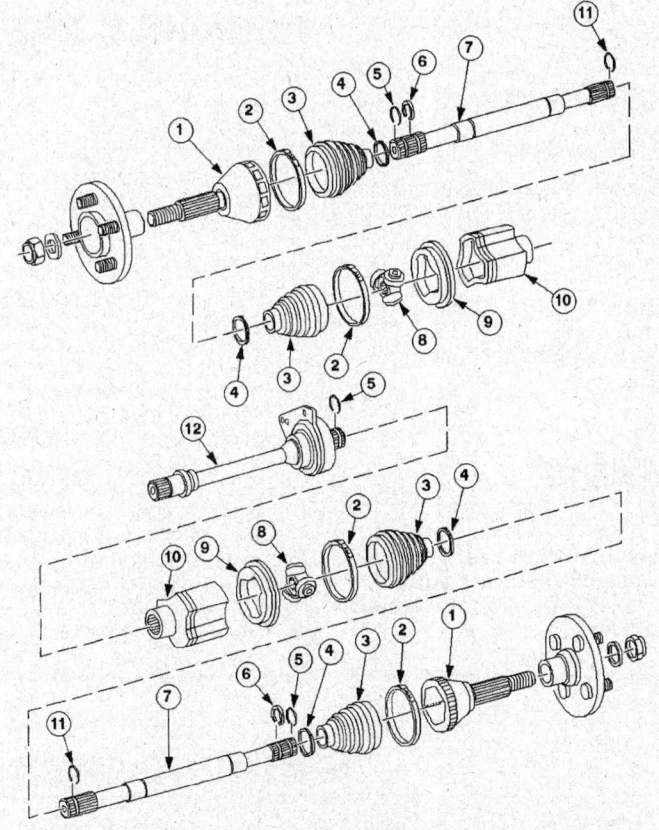

Fig. 1 Exploded view of driveshafts (Part 1 of 2)

2. Inadequate or contaminated lube in outboard/inboard front wheel halfshaft joint.
3. Inspect wheel bearings, brakes, suspension or steering components.

Vibration At Highway Speeds

1. Out of balance front wheels or tires.

2. Out of round tires.
3. Incorrectly seated outboard front wheel halfshaft joint in front wheel hub.

Shudder Vibration During Acceleration

1. Excessively high CV joint operating angles caused by incorrect ride height.
2. Excessively worn or damaged inboard

Item	Part Number	Description
1	-	Fix joint
2	-	Boot clamp (large)
3	-	Boot
4	-	Boot clamp (small)
5	-	Halfshaft joint snap ring
6	-	Snap ring
7	-	Front drive halfshaft
8	-	Tripod
9	-	Tripod housing insert
10	-	Tripod housing
11	-	Halfshaft joint snap ring
12	-	Intermediate shaft

FM3039900320020X

Fig. 1   Exploded view of driveshafts (Part 2 of 2)

front wheel halfshaft joint or outboard front wheel halfshaft joint.

Halfshaft Joint Pullout

1. Inboard halfshaft bearing retainer circlip missing or not correctly seated in differential side gear.
2. Engine/transaxle assembly misaligned.
3. Frame rail or strut tower out of position or damaged.
4. Front suspension components worn or damaged.

DRIVESHAFT

REPLACE

Install new driveshaft bearing retainer circlips, new hub retainer nut, lower control arm to steering knuckle mounting bolt and nut.

Lefthand & Righthand

1. Loosen suspension strut locknut five turns.
2. Loosen driveshaft stub nut and front wheel nuts.
3. Raise and support vehicle, then remove tire and wheel assemblies
4. Remove driveshaft stub nut.
5. Remove fender splash shields.
6. Remove lower ball joint to steering knuckle pinch bolt and nut, then separate ball joint from steering knuckle using suitable pry bar.
7. Disconnect ABS wiring harness bracket from suspension strut.
8. Remove driveshaft from wheel hub using front hub removal tool No. T81P1104C, or equivalent.
9. Disconnect driveshaft from transaxle using halfshaft removal tool No. T86P3514A, or equivalent.
10. Install suitable transaxle plug into lefthand driveshaft opening.
11. Remove driveshaft.
12. Reverse procedure to install.

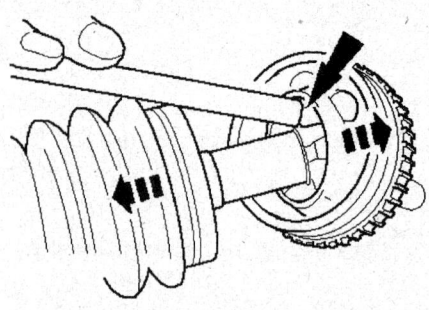

FM3039900321000X

Fig. 2   Driveshaft joint removal

Intermediate

1. Remove righthand driveshaft as outlined in "Lefthand & Righthand."
2. Remove intermediate driveshaft support bearing bracket mounting bolts. **Do not bend inner CV joint by more than 18°.**
3. Disconnect intermediate driveshaft from transaxle using halfshaft removal tool No. T86P3514A, or equivalent.
4. Insert suitable transaxle plug into driveshaft opening.
5. Reverse procedure to install.

DRIVESHAFT SERVICE

1. Cut small and large boot clamps, **Fig. 1.** Discard clamps
2. Slide boot back and pull out tripod joint.
3. Remove snap ring and tripod using suitable puller.
4. Loosen driveshaft joint at wheel end.
5. Cut and remove boot clamps.
6. Slide boot back.
7. Unseat driveshaft joint from snap ring seat using suitable brass drift, **Fig. 2.**
8. Remove driveshaft joint.
9. Remove snap ring.
10. Remove stop ring.
11. Pull off boot.
12. Reverse procedure to install, noting the following:
    a. Install new snap rings and boot clamps.
    b. Pack tripod joint with 6 ounces of suitable high temperature CV joint grease.

TIGHTENING SPECIFICATIONS

Year	Component	Torque/Ft. Lbs.
2001–02	Ball Joint	63
	Hub Nut	214
	Stabilizer Link	35
	Support Bearing Bracket	20
	Tie Rod	19
	Upper Strut Mount	34
	Wheel Lug Nuts	95

Escort & ZX2

NOTE: On Air Bag Equipped Models, Refer To "Air Bag System Precautions" Located In The Front Of This Manual For System Disarming & Arming Procedures.

NOTE: Refer To "Computer Relearn Procedures" Located In The Front Of This Manual When Battery Power To The Computer Has Been Interrupted.

INDEX

PRECAUTIONS

Air Bag Systems

Refer to "Air Bag System Precautions" in the front of this manual for system disarming and arming procedures.

Battery Ground Cable

Prior to service, disconnect battery ground cable and isolate as required.

TROUBLESHOOTING

Noise & Vibration On Turns

1. Cut or damaged CV joint boots, resulting in contaminated lube in outboard or inboard joints.
2. Loose joint clamps.
3. Worn, damaged or improperly installed wheel bearings.
4. Halfshaft connecting component.

Vibration At Highway Speeds

1. Front wheels or tires out of balance.
2. Front tires out of round.

Shudder Or Vibration On Acceleration

1. Excessively worn or damaged inboard or outboard CV joint.
2. Excessively high CV joint operating angles caused by improper ride height.

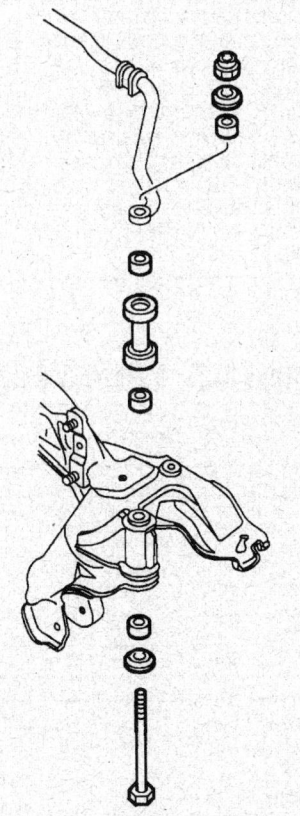

FM3039800319000X

Fig. 1 Stabilizer bar removal

Halfshaft Or CV Joint Pull-Out

ENGINE OR TRANSAXLE MISALIGNED

Engine mount damage.

FRONT SUSPENSION COMPONENTS WORN OR DAMAGED

Worn bushings or bent front suspension components

IMPROPERLY INSTALLED OR MISSING RETAINERS

CV joint circlip missing or not properly seated in transaxle side gear.

DRIVESHAFT

REPLACE

1. Raise and support vehicle, then remove front tire and wheel assembly.
2. Raise staked portion of front axle wheel hub retainer.
3. Remove and discard front axle wheel hub retainer.
4. Remove cotter pin and tie rod end nut.
5. Separate tie rod end from steering knuckle using suitable tie rod remover.
6. Remove front stabilizer bar end nut, **Fig. 1.**
7. Remove front stabilizer bar end bolt.
8. Remove upper front stabilizer bar end retainer.
9. Remove front stabilizer bar end bushings above and below front stabilizer bar.
10. Remove front stabilizer bar end bushing.
11. Remove front stabilizer bar end bushings above and below front subframe.
12. Remove lower front stabilizer bar end retainer.
13. Remove ball joint nut and pinch bolt.
14. Separate front suspension lower arm ball joint from steering knuckle.
15. Pull driveshaft and joint from steering knuckle.
16. Releasing front wheel driveshaft and

| Model | Transaxle | Length, Inches | |
		Lefthand	Righthand
Except ZX2	Automatic	24.96	35.93
	Manual	24.87	36.59
ZX2	Automatic	24.47	36.59
	Manual	24.49	24.49

Fig. 2 Halfshaft specifications

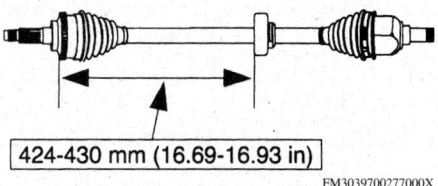

424-430 mm (16.69-16.93 in)

FM3039700277000X

Fig. 3 Righthand damper installation

joint from differential side gears by inserting suitable pry bar between front wheel driveshaft and joint and transaxle case, then pry outward.

17. **On ZX2 models equipped with manual transaxles,** proceed as follows:
   a. Remove bolts from center support bearing.
   b. Lower driveshaft assembly and remove halfshaft from differential side gears.
   c. Separate driveshaft and joint from center support bearing and halfshaft.

18. **On all models,** reverse procedure to install.

DRIVESHAFT SERVICE

CV Joint

DISASSEMBLE

1. Secure driveshaft in suitable soft-jawed vise.
2. Remove ABS sensor ring from joint housing suitable punch. Discard sensor.

3. Remove clamps and slide boot back to expose joint.
4. Mark joint to shaft for reference for assembly alignment, then installation, then separate outboard joint use suitable soft-face hammer to gently tapping it from shaft.
5. Remove and discard bearing retainer circlip.
6. Remove snap ring from outboard side of shaft.
7. Wrap outboard shaft splines with suitable tape before sliding boot from shaft.

ASSEMBLE

1. Clean and inspect outboard bearings and cage for grit in grease, or any signs of cracking or pitting.
2. Lubricate outboard joint bearings with Ford CV Joint Grease part No. E43Z-19590-A, or equivalent.
3. Wrap outboard shaft splines with suitable tape and install boot.
4. Install snap ring on outboard side of shaft.
5. Install new bearing retainer circlip.
6. Install joint onto shaft using suitable

soft-face hammer.
7. Remove excess grease on mating surfaces and slide boot forward onto joint.
8. Ensure proper halfshaft lengths, **Fig. 2.**
9. After adjusting boot spacing, remove excess air trapped in boot with suitable dull screwdriver.
10. Install new boot clamps using pliers tool No. D87P-1098-A, or equivalent.
11. Install new ABS sensor indicator using replacer tool No. T94P-20202-B, or equivalent.

Dynamic Damper Bearing

1. Remove outboard driveshaft joint.
2. Remove and discard damper retaining clamp, then remove damper.
3. Install damper, **Fig. 3.** Install new retainer.
4. Install driveshaft.

TIGHTENING SPECIFICATIONS

Year	Component	Torque/Ft. Lbs.
2001–03	Ball Joint Pinch Bolt	32–43
	Center Support Bearing	32–46
	Crossmember	69–93
	Dynamic Damper Bearing	31–46
	Hub Nut	174–235
	Tie Rod End	32–41
	Wheel Lug Nut	74–100

Focus

NOTE: On Air Bag Equipped Models, Refer To "Air Bag System Precautions" Located In The Front Of This Manual For System Disarming & Arming Procedures.

NOTE: Refer To "Computer Relearn Procedures" Located In The Front Of This Manual When Battery Power To The Computer Has Been Interrupted.

PRECAUTIONS

Air Bag Systems

Refer to "Air Bag System Precautions" in the front of this manual for system disarming and arming procedures.

Battery Ground Cable

Prior to service, disconnect battery ground cable and isolate as required.

TROUBLESHOOTING

Clicking, Popping or Grinding Noises While Turning

1. Another component contacting halfshaft.
2. Inadequate or contaminated lube in outboard/inboard front wheel halfshaft joint.
3. Wheel bearings, brakes, suspension or steering components.

Vibration At Highway Speeds

1. Out of balance front wheels or tires.
2. Out of round tires.
3. Incorrectly seated outboard front wheel halfshaft joint in front wheel hub.

Shudder Vibration During Acceleration

1. Excessively high CV joint operating angles caused by incorrect ride height.
2. Excessively worn or damaged inboard front wheel halfshaft joint or outboard front wheel halfshaft joint.

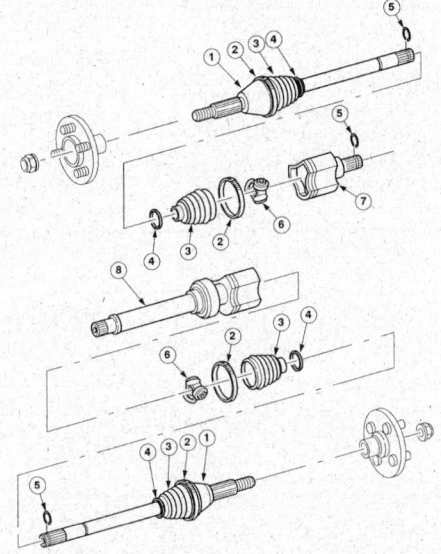

FM3030000338010X

Fig. 1 Exploded view of driveshaft (Part 1 of 2)

Halfshaft Joint Pullout

1. Inboard halfshaft bearing retainer circlip missing or not correctly seated in differential side gear.
2. Engine/transaxle assembly misaligned.
3. Frame rail or strut tower out of position or damaged.
4. Front suspension components worn or damaged.

DRIVESHAFT

REPLACE

1. Loosen suspension strut locknut five turns.

Item	Description
1	Fixed ball joint with front drive halfshaft
2	Clamping strap (large)
3	Boot
4	Clamping strap (small)
5	Snap-ring - CV joint, transmission end
6	Tripod star with constant velocity rollers
7	Tripode housing
8	Intermediate shaft with intermediate shaft bearing

FM3030000338020X

Fig. 1 Exploded view of driveshaft (Part 2 of 2)

2. Loosen driveshaft stub nut and front wheel nuts.
3. Raise and support vehicle, then remove front tire and wheel assembly.
4. Remove driveshaft stub nut.
5. Remove bolt and disconnect lower arm ball joint.
6. Remove hub nut and press halfshaft stub out from wheel hub using suitable puller. Mark nut usage. **Hub nut can be reused four times.**
7. Disconnect driveshaft from transaxle.
8. Remove driveshaft.
9. Reverse procedure to install.

DRIVESHAFT SERVICE

1. Hold intermediate shaft in suitable vise, then separate and discard clamping straps. Push back boot along shaft.
2. Pull apart tripod joint, then remove grease and tripod snap ring, **Fig. 1.**
3. Remove tripod using tool No. T81P-1104C, or equivalent, then the boot.
4. Separate and discard clamping straps. Remove boot over transaxle side and accessible grease.
5. Reverse procedure to assemble.

TIGHTENING SPECIFICATIONS

Year	Component	Torque/Ft. Lbs.
2001–05	Ball Joint	63
	Driveshaft Nut	214
	Gaiter Clamps	15
	Hub Nut	214
	Suspension Strut Nut	35

Five Hundred, Freestyle, Montego

NOTE: On Air Bag Equipped Models, Refer To "Air Bag System Precautions" Located In The Front Of This Manual For System Disarming & Arming Procedures.

NOTE: Refer To "Computer Relearn Procedures" Located In The Front Of This Manual When Battery Power To The Computer Has Been Interrupted.

INDEX

PRECAUTIONS

Air Bag Systems

Refer to "Air Bag System Precautions" in the front of this manual for system disarming and arming procedures.

Battery Ground Cable

Prior to service, disconnect battery ground cable and isolate as required.

TROUBLESHOOTING

Noise & Vibration On Turns

1. Cut or damaged CV joint boots, resulting in contaminated lube in outboard or inboard CV joints.
2. Loose CV joint clamps.
3. Worn, damaged or improperly installed wheel bearings.
4. Foreign object contacting driveshaft assembly.

Shudder Or Vibration On Acceleration

1. Excessively worn or damaged inboard or outboard CV joint.
2. Excessively high CV joint operating angles caused by improper ride height.

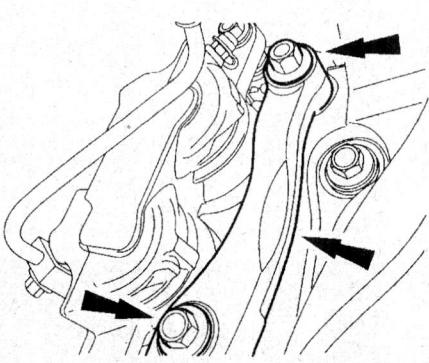
ARM0400000000760

Fig. 1 Caliper anchor removal

Vibration At Highway Speeds

1. Front wheels or tires out of balance.
2. Improperly seated outboard CV joint in front wheel hub.
3. Bent intermediate driveshaft.
4. Front tires out of round.

Driveshaft Or CV Joint Pull-Out

1. Inboard CV joint circlip missing or improperly seated in transaxle side gear.
2. Engine or transaxle improperly positioned. Inspect engine mounts.
3. Frame rail or strut tower improperly po-

sitioned or damaged.
4. Front suspension components worn or damaged.

DRIVESHAFT

REPLACE

Lefthand

1. Remove and discard front axle retainer nut.
2. Raise and support vehicle.
3. Support suspension at steering stop using suitable jack stand.
4. Remove brake caliper anchor mounting bolts, **Fig. 1,** then position caliper and anchor assembly aside. Secure assembly to suspension using suitable wire.
5. Press halfshaft from wheel hub using wheel hub removal tool No. D93P-1175–B, or equivalent.
6. Remove and discard lower ball joint retaining nut, then disconnect ball joint from lower control arm.
7. Separate halfshaft from wheel hub.
8. **On models equipped with six speed transaxle,** remove halfshaft from transaxle using slide hammer tool No. T50T-100–A and halfshaft removal plate No. T89P-3415–B, or equivalents.
9. **On models equipped with CVT transaxle,** remove halfshaft from transaxle using slide hammer tool No. T50T-100–A and halfshaft removal plate No. T86P-3514–A, or equivalents.

10. **On all models,** inspect halfshaft seal replace if necessary.
11. Reverse procedure to install, noting the following:
    a. Install new driveshaft bearing retainer circlip.
    b. **Do not damage seal when installing driveshaft joints into transaxle.**
    c. Ensure bearing retainer circlip is properly seated in transaxle.
    d. Use old axle hub nut and washer to seat halfshaft into wheel hub.
    e. Install tighten new front axle retaining nut to specification in a continuous rotation. **Stopping rotation during installation will cause nylon lock to seat incorrectly. Causing incorrect torque reading and lead to bearing failure.**
    f. Install new ball joint nut.

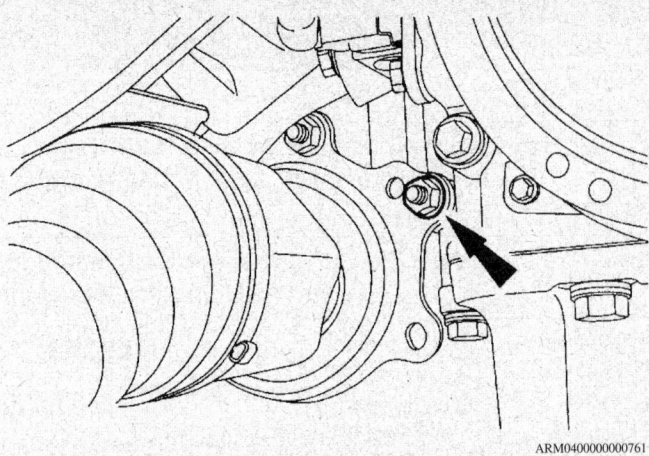

Fig. 2 Righthand halfshaft removal

Righthand

1. Remove and discard front axle retainer nut.
2. Raise and support vehicle.
3. Support suspension at steering stop using suitable jack stand.
4. Remove brake caliper anchor mounting bolts, **Fig. 1,** then position caliper and anchor assembly aside. Secure assembly to suspension using suitable mechanic's wire.
5. Press halfshaft from wheel hub using wheel hub removal tool No. D93P-1175–B, or equivalent.
6. Remove and discard lower ball joint retaining nut, then disconnect ball joint from lower control arm.
7. Separate halfshaft from wheel hub.
8. Remove two halfshaft to transaxle bearing mounting nuts, **Fig. 2.**
9. Remove halfshaft assembly.
10. **On all models,** inspect halfshaft seal, replace if necessary.
11. Reverse procedure to install, noting the following:
    a. Install halfshaft to transaxle mounting bolts.
    b. Install new ball joint nut.
    c. Use old axle hub nut and washer to seat halfshaft into wheel hub.
    d. Install tighten new front axle retaining nut to specification in a continuous rotation. **Stopping rotation during installation will cause nylon lock to seat incorrectly. Causing incorrect torque reading and lead to bearing failure.**

DRIVESHAFT SERVICE

Driveshafts are not serviceable and should be replaced as an assembly.

TIGHTENING SPECIFICATIONS

Year	Component	Torque/Ft. Lbs.
2005	Ball Joint Nut	59
	Caliper Anchor Bolts	74
	Halfshaft To Transaxle Nuts	20
	Hub Nut	184①
	Lower Suspension Arm Nut	59
	Wheel Lug Nut	85

① — Tighten new hub to specification in one continuous rotation. Stopping will cause nylon lock to set causing incorrect torque readings.

Sable & Taurus

> **NOTE:** On Air Bag Equipped Models, Refer To "Air Bag System Precautions" Located In The Front Of This Manual For System Disarming & Arming Procedures.

> **NOTE:** Refer To "Computer Relearn Procedures" Located In The Front Of This Manual When Battery Power To The Computer Has Been Interrupted.

INDEX

PRECAUTIONS

Air Bag Systems

Refer to "Air Bag System Precautions" in the front of this manual for system disarming and arming procedures.

Battery Ground Cable

Prior to service, disconnect battery ground cable and isolate as required.

TROUBLESHOOTING

Noise & Vibration On Turns

1. Cut or damaged CV joint boots, resulting in contaminated lube in outboard or inboard CV joints.
2. Loose CV joint clamps.
3. Worn, damaged or improperly installed wheel bearings.
4. Foreign object contacting driveshaft assembly.

Shudder Or Vibration On Acceleration

1. Excessively worn or damaged inboard or outboard CV joint.
2. Excessively high CV joint operating angles caused by improper ride height.

Vibration At Highway Speeds

1. Front wheels or tires out of balance.
2. Improperly seated outboard CV joint in front wheel hub.

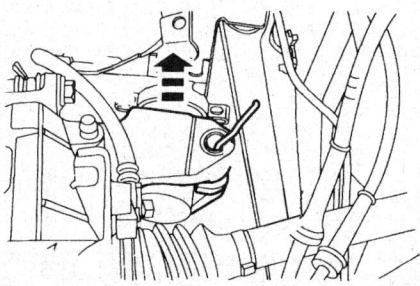

FM3030100392000X

Fig. 1 Steering knuckle positioned on strut

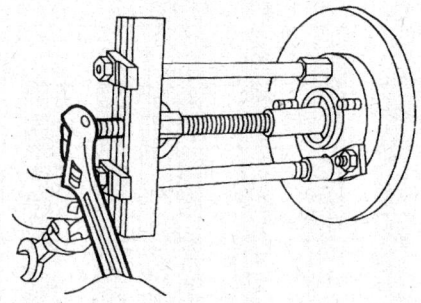

FM3030100393000X

Fig. 2 Outer CV Joint removal from hub

3. Bent intermediate driveshaft.
4. Front tires out of round.

Driveshaft Or CV Joint Pull-Out

1. Inboard CV joint circlip missing or improperly seated in transaxle side gear.
2. Engine or transaxle improperly positioned. Inspect engine mounts.
3. Frame rail or strut tower improperly po-

sitioned or damaged.
4. Front suspension components worn or damaged.

DRIVESHAFT

REPLACE

1. Raise and support vehicle, then remove front tire and wheel assemblies.
2. Remove and discard front axle retainer nut and washer.
3. Remove anti-lock brake sensor wiring harness retaining clip from bracket on lower end of strut assembly.
4. Remove sensor from mounting bracket. Discard nut and position sensor aside.
5. Remove lower strut to steering knuckle mounting bolt and nut, then separate steering knuckle from strut.
6. Position knuckle on strut body and secure it to strut using suitable wire, **Fig. 1.**
7. Pull upward on knuckle to raise it approximately ½ inch on strut body and secure it to strut with suitable wire.
8. Remove and discard nut from lower ball joint.
9. Loosen ball joint in lower control arm using suitable suspension arm puller.
10. Release lower ball joint by prying down on control arm using suitable pry bar through opening in lower control arm and under frame.
11. Separate outer CV joint from hub using suitable front wheel hub removal tool, **Fig. 2. Do not use hammer to drive joint from hub.**
12. **Do not allow driveshaft to hang from inner joint.**
13. Remove inner joint from transaxle.
14. Reverse procedure to install, noting the following:
    a. Install new front axle retainer nut.

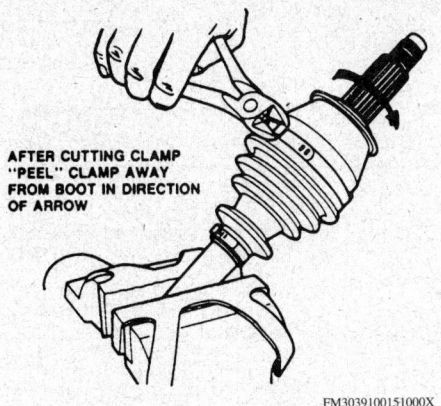

AFTER CUTTING CLAMP "PEEL" CLAMP AWAY FROM BOOT IN DIRECTION OF ARROW

FM3039100151000X

Fig. 3 Boot clamp removal

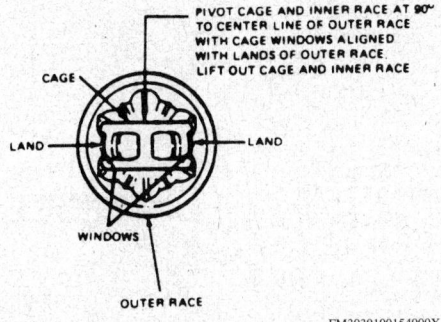

PIVOT CAGE AND INNER RACE AT 90° TO CENTER LINE OF OUTER RACE WITH CAGE WINDOWS ALIGNED WITH LANDS OF OUTER RACE. LIFT OUT CAGE AND INNER RACE

CAGE

LAND   LAND

WINDOWS

OUTER RACE

FM3039100154000X

Fig. 6 Cage & inner race removal

b. Install new driveshaft bearing retainer circlip.
c. Instal new ball joint nut.
d. **Do not damage seal when installing driveshaft joints into transaxle.**
e. Ensure proper engagement of lefthand driveshaft inner joint spline into transaxle side gears.
f. Ensure bearing retainer circlip is properly seated.
g. Ensure proper engagement of transaxle shaft spline into righthand inner CV joint.
h. Ensure bearing retainer circlip is properly seated.

DRIVESHAFT SERVICE
Outboard Joint & Boot

During manufacturing, CV joint components are matched. Components cannot be interchanged with another joint's components. If a joint component is faulty, entire joint should be replaced.

DISASSEMBLE

1. Position driveshaft in suitable soft jaw vise **Do not allow vise to contact CV joint boot or clamps.**
2. Cut large boot clamp using suitable side cutting pliers and peel away from boot.
3. Roll boot back over driveshaft, **Fig. 3.**
4. Turn driveshaft over in vise and angle

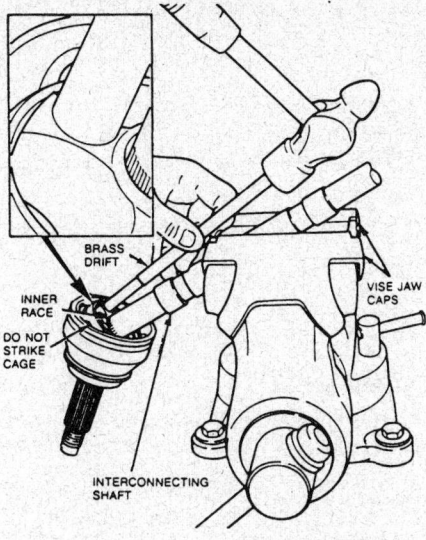

BRASS DRIFT

INNER RACE

DO NOT STRIKE CAGE

VISE JAW CAPS

INTERCONNECTING SHAFT

FM3039100152000X

Fig. 4 Internal snap ring removal

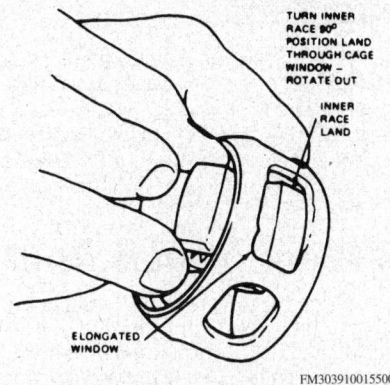

TURN INNER RACE 90° POSITION LAND THROUGH CAGE WINDOW – ROTATE OUT

INNER RACE LAND

ELONGATED WINDOW

FM3039100155000X

Fig. 7 Inner race replacement

CV joint so inner bearing race is exposed, **Fig. 4.**
5. Disconnect internal snap ring by rapping inner bearing race using suitable brass drift and hammer.
6. Separate CV joint from driveshaft and remove boot.
7. Inspect CV joint grease for contamination. If grease appears contaminated or has a gritty feeling, inspect for worn components. If grease is not contaminated and joint was operating satisfactorily, add grease and replace boot.
8. Remove and discard circlip from end of shaft. Inspect stop ring located below circlip.
9. Clamp CV joint stub axle in suitable soft jaw vise. **Do not damage dust seal.**
10. Push CV joint inner race down until it tilts enough to allow ball removal, **Fig. 5.** If inner race is tight, it can be tilted by tapping inner race with wooden dowel and hammer. **Do not hit cage.**
11. Remove balls from cage. If balls are tight, use blunt screwdriver to pry balls from cage.
12. Pivot cage and inner race assembly until it is straight up, **Fig. 6.**
13. Align cage windows with outer race lands while pivoting bearing cage, then lift out cage and inner race.

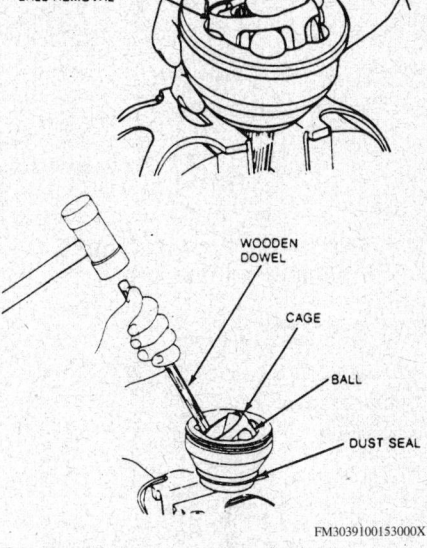

CAGE AND INNER RACE TILTED FOR BALL REMOVAL

WOODEN DOWEL

CAGE

BALL

DUST SEAL

FM3039100153000X

Fig. 5 CV joint ball removal

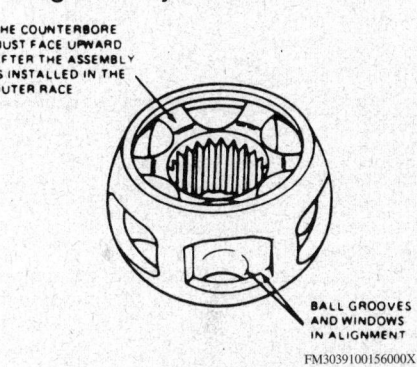

THE COUNTERBORE MUST FACE UPWARD AFTER THE ASSEMBLY IS INSTALLED IN THE OUTER RACE

BALL GROOVES AND WINDOWS IN ALIGNMENT

FM3039100156000X

Fig. 8 Inner race & cage assembly

14. Rotate inner race up and out of cage, **Fig. 7.**

INSPECTION

If any components are cracked, broken, severely pitted, worn or otherwise unserviceable, replace CV joint.

If any components appear polished, do not replace joint as this is a normal condition.

If anti-lock brake sensor wheel's teeth are chipped or cracked, install replacement sensor wheel.

ASSEMBLE

1. Apply light coating of Ford CV joint grease No. E2FZ-19590-A, or equivalent, on inner and outer races.
2. Install inner race in bearing cage.
3. Install inner race and cage in outer race, **Fig. 8.**
4. Install CV joint assembly into outer race and pivot 90° into position, **Fig. 9.**
5. Align bearing cage and inner race with outer race, then tilt inner race and install remaining five balls.
6. Determine which end of driveshaft is for outboard CV joint. The outboard joint side has a shorter end of boot

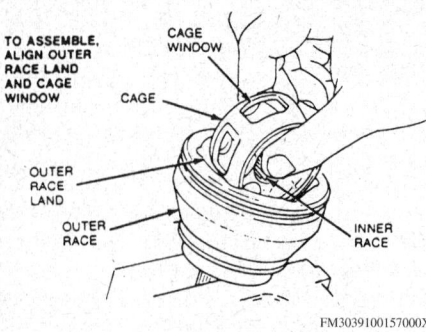

Fig. 9   CV joint assembly installation into outer race

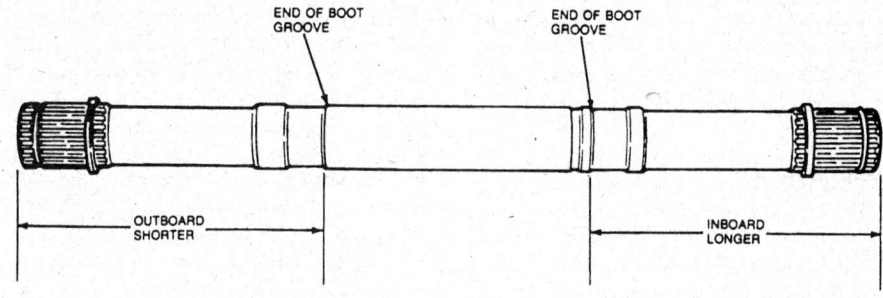

Fig. 10   Driveshaft end identification

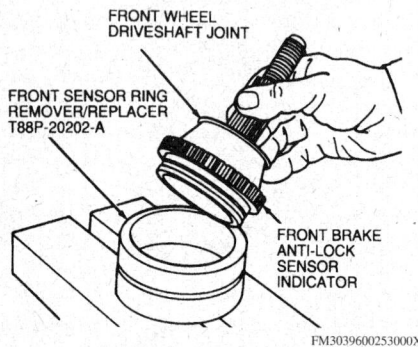

Fig. 11   Anti-Lock brake sensor wheel removal

groove to end of shaft dimension, **Fig. 10.**

7. Install CV joint boot and small boot clamp.
8. Install stop ring. If stop ring was not removed, ensure it is seated properly in groove.
9. Install new circlip.
10. Pack CV joint with Ford CV joint grease No. E2FZ-19590-A, or equivalent. Spread remaining grease evenly inside CV boot.
11. With boot peeled back, position CV joint on driveshaft and tap into position with suitable plastic hammer. Joint is properly seated when circlip locks into position. Inspect for proper retention by attempting to pull off joint.
12. Remove excess grease from external surfaces, then position boot over joint.
13. Ensure boot is seated in its groove and install clamp.

Anti-Lock Brake Sensor Wheel

DISASSEMBLE

1. Remove outer CV joint as outlined in "Outboard Joint & Boot."
2. Place CV joint into removal tool No. T88P-20202-A, or equivalent, **Fig. 11.**
3. Push CV joint out of sensor wheel using suitable press.
4. **Do not damage sensor wheel teeth.**

INSPECTION

If anti-lock brake sensor wheel's teeth are chipped or cracked, install replacement sensor wheel.

ASSEMBLE

1. Position sensor wheel onto remover t.
2. Position CV joint into sensor wheel and tool.
3. Push joint into sensor wheel using replacer tool No. T88P-20202-A, or equivalent, until joint bottoms in tool
4. **Do not damage sensor wheel teeth.**

Dust Seal

1. Remove seal using suitable light duty hammer and screwdriver to tap evenly around seal, **Fig. 12.**
2. Install dust seal using spindle/axle seal tool No. T83T-3132-A1, and dust seal installer tool No. T83P-3425-AH, or equivalents.

Inboard Joint & Boot

The tripod is an integral part of the intermediate driveshaft and inboard CV joint housing and are not repairable and must be replace with new components if damaged. Only inner driveshaft boot can be replaced, **Figs. 13 and 14.**

Three types of boots and CV joints are used, **Fig. 15.** These components are not interchangeable. Always use matching type when replacing components.

DISASSEMBLE

1. Remove large and small boot clamp, then remove inner joint outer housing.
2. If boot replacement is required, remove outer CV joint as outlined in "Outboard Joint & Boot," then remove outer joint stop ring.
3. Remove old boot by sliding off outboard end of driveshaft.

ASSEMBLE

1. Slide new boot onto shaft and into position groove of shaft from outer end of driveshaft.
2. Position new small boot clamp onto boot from outer end of driveshaft and tighten clamp.
3. **On models equipped with Ford CV joints,** fill inner CV joint and boot with 5.88 ounces of suitable CV joint grease.
4. **On models equipped with GKN CV joints,** fill inner CV joint and boot with 16.75 ounces of suitable CV joint grease.
5. **On all models,** install outer joint stop ring, then outer CV joint as outlined in

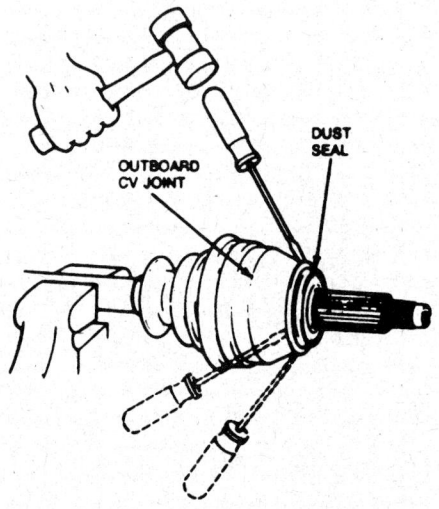

Fig. 12   Dust seal removal

"Outboard Joint & Boot."

6. Position inner joint outer housing onto tripod and install large end of boot onto joint outer housing.
7. Ensure boot is not stretched or collapsed. Allow air pressure to equalize using suitable blunt flat tool to pry up boot lip.
8. Ensure driveshaft length is proper, **Fig. 16.**
9. Clean excess grease from outside of boot.
10. Position new large boot clamp onto boot and tighten clamp.
11. Position clamp replacement tool No. T95P-3514-A, or equivalent, on clamp ear and tighten tool through bolt until tool is in closed position.

Intermediate Shaft

1. Clamp intermediate shaft in suitable vise with driveshaft supported.
2. Separate intermediate shaft from driveshaft using puller adapter tool No. T86P-3514-A and slide hammer tool No. D79P-100-A, or equivalents, **Fig. 17.**
3. Pry seal from link shaft with suitable screwdriver.
4. Position intermediate shaft in suitable arbor press and press off bearing.
5. Reverse procedure to install. Coat shaft splines with Ford CV joint grease No. E2FZ-19590-A, or equivalent.

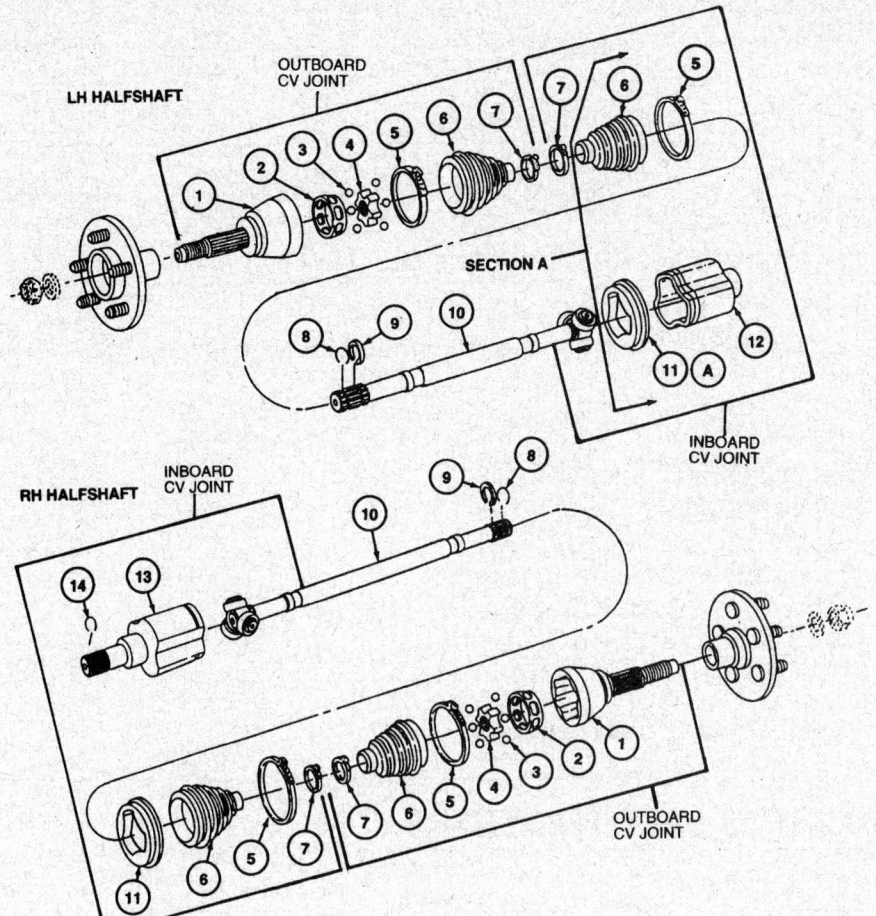

Item	Description
1	Front Wheel Driveshaft Joint
2	Ball Cage
3	Balls (6 required)
4	Inner Race
5	Front Wheel Driveshaft Joint Boot Clamp (Large)
6	Front Wheel Driveshaft Joint Boot
7	Front Wheel Driveshaft Joint Boot Clamp (Small)
8	Circlip
9	Stop Ring
10	Interconnecting Shaft
11	Tri-Lobe Insert
12	LH Inboard CV Joint Housing
13	RH Inboard CV Joint Housing
14	Circlip
A	Part Used Only With Ford Design Conventional Boot

FM3039600254020X

Fig. 13 Exploded view of driveshaft assemblies (Part 2 of 2)

FM3039600254010X

Fig. 13 Exploded view of ford driveshaft assemblies (Part 1 of 2)

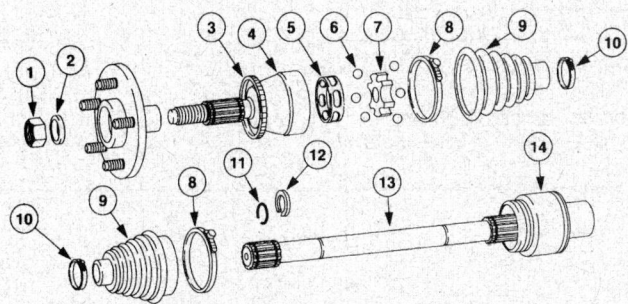

Item	Description		Item	Description
1	Front axle wheel hub retainer		10	Front wheel driveshaft joint boot clamp (small)
2	Washer		11	Circlip
3	Front brake anti-lock sensor indicator		12	Stop ring
4	Front wheel driveshaft joint		13	Interconnecting shaft (part of 3B437)
5	Ball cage (part of 3B413)		14	Inboard CV joint housing assembly
6	Balls (6 req'd) (part of 3B413)		15	Inboard CV joint housing assembly
7	Race (part of 3B413)		16	Interconnecting shaft (part of 3B436)
8	Front wheel driveshaft joint boot clamp (large)			
9	Front wheel driveshaft joint boot			

FM3030100394020X

Fig. 14 Exploded view of driveshaft assemblies (Part 2 of 2). GKN

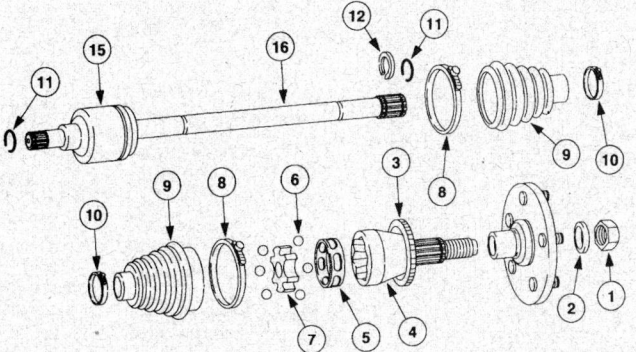

FM3030100394010X

Fig. 14 Exploded view of driveshaft assemblies (Part 1 of 2). GKN

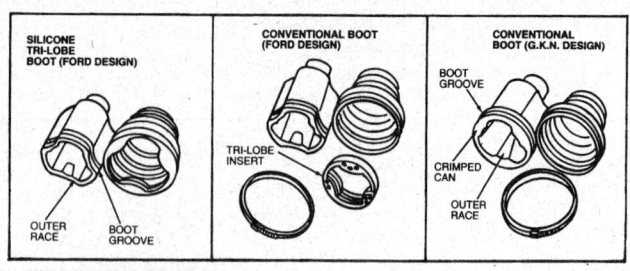

NOTE: HALFSHAFTS ARE SUPPLIED BY FORD AND G.K.N. CHECK LABEL ON SHAFT FOR MANUFACTURER. ALTHOUGH THE DESIGNS ARE SIMILAR, THERE IS NOT INTERCHANGEABILITY OF BOOTS BETWEEN THE THREE DESIGNS.

FM3039600255000X

Fig. 15 CV joint & boot types

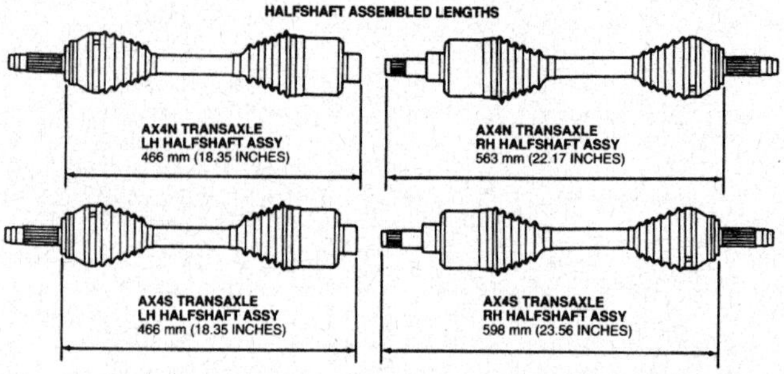

FM3039600256000X

Fig. 16 Driveshaft assembled length

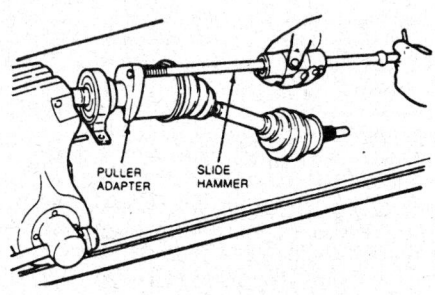

FM3039100165000X

Fig. 17 Link shaft removal

TIGHTENING SPECIFICATIONS

Year	Component	Torque/Ft. Lbs.
2001–05	Ball Joint Nut	59
	Hub Nut	184②
	Knuckle To Strut Bolt & Nut	108①
	Lower Suspension Arm Nut	59
	Stabilizer Bar Joint Nut	65
	Wheel Lug Nut	85

① — Inch lbs.
② — Tighten new hub to specification in one continuous rotation. Stopping will cause nylon lock to set causing incorrect torque readings.

DRIVE AXLES

NOTE: On Air Bag Equipped Models, Refer To "Air Bag System Precautions" Located In The Front Of This Manual For System Disarming & Arming Procedures.

NOTE: Refer To "Computer Relearn Procedures" Located In The Front Of This Manual When Battery Power To The Computer Has Been Interrupted.

NOTE: Prior To Performing Any Service Operations Listed In This Section, Consult The "Technical Service Bulletins" Section For Related Information.

INDEX

IDENTIFICATION

Rear Axle Tag

The plant code on the axle identification tag identifies the axle assembly, **Fig. 1.** The plant code will not change as long as that particular axle assembly never undergoes an external design change. If an internal design change is made to an axle during its production life and that internal change affects service components interchangeability, a dash and numerical suffix will be added to the plant code, **Fig. 2.**

Information on axle ratio, differential type and ring gear diameter may also be found on this tag.

Vehicle Certification Label

Information on axle ratio and differential type may be found on the vehicle certification label, which is affixed to the lefthand front door lock panel or door pillar. A code

found in the AX or AXLE box on the label will identify the originally installed axle, **Fig. 3.**

TROUBLESHOOTING

Except Five Hundred, Freestyle & Montego w/AWD

Refer to **Fig. 4,** for rear axle troubleshooting symptoms.

Five Hundred, Freestyle & Montego

To access Diagnostic Trouble Codes (DTC) connect a suitably programed scan tool to the Diagnostic Link Connector (DLC) located under the lefthand side of the instrument panel, then follow scan tool manufacturer's instructions.

Refer to **Fig. 5,** for AWD rear axle DTC interpretations & troubleshooting. If scan

tool returns the message, No communication with the Differential Electronic Module (DEM), refer to **Fig. 6.**

Axle Noise

NOISE ACCEPTABILITY

Drive axles produce a certain amount of noise. Some noise is acceptable and may be audible at certain speeds or under various driving conditions, such as a newly paved blacktop road. The slight noise is in no way detrimental to rear axle operation and may be considered normal.

With Traction-Lok limited slip differential, slight chatter noise on slow, tight turns after extended highway driving is considered acceptable and has no detrimental effect on the axle's locking function.

GEAR NOISE

Gear noise is the typical howling or whining of the ring gear and pinion because of an improper gear pattern, gear damage or improper bearing preload. It can occur at

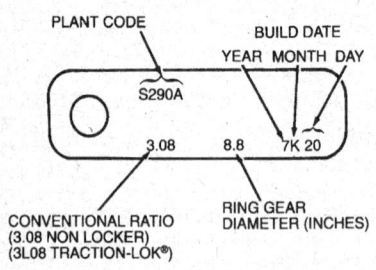

Fig. 1 Rear axle identification tag

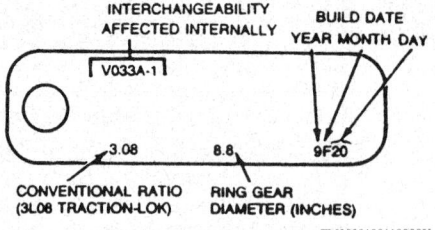

Fig. 2 Internally modified rear axle identification tag

Axle Code	Differential Type	Gear Ratio
EXCEPT FIVE HUNDRED, FRESTYLE & MONTEGO		
E	Traction-Lok	3.27
F	Conventional	3.45
K	Traction-Lok	3.55
M	Traction-Lok	2.73
R	Traction-Lok	3.45
W	Traction-Lok	3.73
Y	Conventional	3.08
Z	Traction-Lok	3.08
2	Conventional	3.55
5	Conventional	3.27
6	Conventional	3.73
8	Conventional	2.73
FIVE HUNDRED & MONTEGO		
1	Traction-Lok	3.46
2	Traction-Lok	4.98
3	Traction-Lok	5.19
FREESTYLE		
3A	Traction-Lok	5.19
CD	Traction-Lok	5.54

Fig. 3 Drive axle identification

various speeds and driving conditions or it can be continuous.

CHUCKLE

Chuckle is a particular rattling noise that sounds like a stick against the spokes of a bicycle wheel. It occurs while decelerating from 40 mph and can be heard all the way to a stop. The frequency varies with the vehicle's speed.

KNOCK

Knock is very similar to chuckle, though it may be louder and occurs on acceleration or deceleration.

CLUNK

Clunk may be a metallic noise heard when the automatic transmission is engaged in Reverse or Drive or it may occur when the throttle is applied or released. It is caused by backlash somewhere in the driveline or loose suspension components.

BEARING WHINE

Bearing whine is a high pitched sound similar to a whistle. It is usually caused by faulting pinion bearings, which are operating at driveshaft speed. Bearing noise occurs at all driving speeds. This distinguishes it from gear whine, which usually comes and goes as speed changes.

BEARING RUMBLE

Bearing rumble sounds like marbles being tumbled. This condition is usually caused by a faulting wheel bearing. The lower pitch is because the wheel bearing turns at only about one third of driveshaft speed. In addition, wheel bearing noise may be high pitched, similar to gear noise but will be evident in all four driving modes.

CHATTER ON CORNERING

Chattering noise when cornering is a condition where the whole rear end vibrates only when the vehicle is moving. The vibration is plainly felt as well as heard. In conventional axles, extra differential thrust washers cause a partial lockup condition which creates this chatter. Chatter noise on Traction-Lok axles can usually be traced to erratic movement between adjacent clutch plates and can be corrected with a lubricant change.

CLICK AT ENGAGEMENT

Click at engagement is a condition on axles of a slight noise, distinct from a clunk that happens in Reverse or Drive engagement. It can be corrected by installing a slinger between the companion flange and front pinion bearing.

Leakage Conditions

Most rear axle leakage conditions can be corrected without a tear-down. However, it is important to clean the leaking area enough to identify the exact source of the leak.

A plugged or seized jiggle cap vent will cause excessive seal lip wear because of internal pressure buildup. When a leak occurs, inspect cap by pressing down on it with index finger. If the cap moves up and down freely, it is working properly. If it does not move freely, it must be replaced.

Inspect axle lubricant level, which should be $9/16$ inch below bottom of filler hole.

DRIVE PINION SEAL

If the drive pinion seal leaks, it is usually because of improper installation or because of poor quality of the seal journal surface. Any damage to the seal bore, such as dings, dents and gouges, will distort the seal casing and allow leakage past the outer edge of the seal.

PINION NUT

Some models may experience oil leakage past the threads of the pinion nut. The condition can be corrected by removing the nut and applying pipe sealant with Teflon part No. D8AZ-19554-A, or equivalent, on the pinion threads and nut face. **Ensure the proper procedure for setting the bearing preload is followed when the nut is installed.**

POROUS CASTING

The differential carrier may leak through small pockets in the metal. These pockets (casting leakage) are caused by gas bubbles in the casting process.

Because the axle's sound characteristics may be changed if torn down to replace the carrier, servicing the porosity is preferable. Below are two recommended procedures that may be employed to fix a porous axle:

1. Peen small amount of body lead into hole and seal pocket with suitable epoxy sealer metallic plastic.
2. In larger pockets, drill shallow hole and tap it for small setscrew.
3. Install setscrew and seal it over with suitable epoxy sealer metallic plastic.

AXLE VENT

There have been some occurrences of lubricant leaking through the axle vent. This may be caused by a clogged or sticking axle vent cap. If this is the case, the vent assembly should be replaced. Use Stud and Bearing Mount part No. EOAZ-19554-BA, or equivalent, on vent's threads to ensure retention.

Vibration Conditions

Few vibration conditions are caused by the axle. Most rear end vibration is caused by the tires or driveline angle.

Vehicles equipped with a Traction-Lok differential will always have both wheels driving. If only one wheel is raised off the floor and the rear axle is driven by the engine, the wheel on the floor could drive the vehicle off the safety stand. Ensure both rear wheels are raised off the floor.

TIRES

Some vehicles are equipped with directional tires. See tire rotation arrows on tire sidewall. If a directional tire is removed for service, it must be mounted in its original location.

Do not balance the rear wheels and tires while they are mounted on the vehicle. Use only an off-vehicle wheel and tire balancer.

A vibration can sometimes be corrected by properly rotating or inflating the tires. The best tires should be placed on the rear to minimize vibration, especially on vehicles with rear coil springs.

DRIVELINE ANGLE

An improper driveline (pinion) angle can

Condition	Possible Sources	Action
• Traction-Lok® does not work in snow, mud or on ice	• Differential.	• CARRY OUT the Traction-Lok® Differential Operation Check REPAIR as necessary.
• Lubricant leaking from the pinion seal or axle shaft oil seals	• Vent.	• CLEAN the axle housing vent.
	• Damage in the seal contact area or dust slinger on the pinion flange dust shield.	• INSTALL new pinion flange and the pinion seal if damage is found.
• Differential side gears/pinion gears are scored	• Insufficient lubrication.	• INSTALL new gears. FILL the axle to specification.
	• Incorrect or contaminated lubricant type.	• INSTALL new gears. CLEAN and REFILL the axle to specification.
• Axle overheating	• Lubricant level too low.	• CHECK the lubricant level. FILL the axle to specification.
	• Incorrect or contaminated lubricant type.	• INSPECT the axle for damage. REPAIR as necessary. CLEAN and REFILL the axle to specification.
	• Bearing preload adjusted too tight.	• CHECK the ring and pinion for damage. INSPECT the ring and pinion wear pattern. ADJUST the preload as necessary.
	• Excessive gear wear.	• INSPECT all the axle gears for wear or damage. INSTALL new components as necessary.
	• Incorrect ring gear backlash.	• INSPECT the ring gear for scoring. INSPECT the ring and pinion wear pattern. ADJUST the ring gear backlash as necessary.
• Broken gear teeth on the ring gear or pinion	• Overloading the vehicle.	• INSTALL a new ring and pinion.
• Axle shaft broken	• Overloading the vehicle.	• INSTALL a new axle shaft.
	• Misaligned axle shaft tube.	• INSPECT the axle for damage. CHECK axle shaft tube alignment. INSTALL a new axle shaft.

FM3030100370000X

Fig. 4 Troubleshooting chart. Except Five Hundred, Freestyle & Montego w/AWD

DTC Code	Description	Action
P0562	System Voltage Low	Check Charging System
P0563	System voltage High	Check Charging System
P0602	Powertrain Control Module PCM Programing Error	Install New Differential Electronic Module (DEM)
P0606	ECM/PCM Processor	Install New Differential Electronic Module (DEM)
P0610	Control Module Vehicle Option Error	Reconfigure Differential Electronic Module (DEM)
P0932	Hydraulic Pressure Sensor Circuit	Install New Axle Oil Temperature Sensor
P0937	Hydraulic Oil Temperature Sensor Circuit	Install New Rear Axle Oil Temperature Sensor
P0939	Hydraulic Oil Temperature Sensor Circuit, Low Input	Install New Rear Axle Oil Temperature Sensor
P0940	Hydraulic Oil Temperature Sensor Circuit, High Input	Install New Rear Axle Oil Temperature Sensor
P0960	Pressure Control Solenoid A Control Circuit Open	Install New Active On-Demand Coupling Oil Pump
P0961	Pressure Control Solenoid A Control Circuit Range Performance	Install New Active On-Demand Coupling Oil Pump
P1889	Oil Pressure Pump Performance	Install New Active On-Demand Coupling Oil Pump

Fig. 5 DTC interpretations & troubleshooting chart. Five Hundred, Freestyle & Montego w/AWD

often be detected by the driving condition when vibration occurs.
1. Vibration during coasting from 35–45 mph is often caused by high pinion angle.
2. Vibration during acceleration from 35–45 mph may indicate lower than specified pinion angle.

Traction-Lok Differential Operation Inspection

A Traction-Lok differential can be inspected for proper operation without removing it from the axle housing using procedure outlined below:
1. Raise and support one rear wheel, then remove wheel cover.
2. Install adapter for Traction-Lok differential tool No. T59L-4204-A, or equivalent, and suitable torque wrench.
3. Rotate axle shaft. **Ensure transmission is in Neutral, one wheel is on floor and other rear wheel is raised off floor.**
4. Breakaway torque required to start ro-

tation should be at least 20 ft. lbs. Initial breakaway torque may be higher than continuous turning torque. This is normal.
5. Axle shaft should turn with even pressure throughout inspection without slipping or binding. If torque reading is less than specified, inspect differential for improper assembly.

DISASSEMBLE

Crown Victoria, Grand Marquis, Marauder, Mustang & Town Car

DIFFERENTIAL CASE

1. Raise and support rear of vehicle, then loosen axle housing cover bolts and drain lubricant into suitable container, **Figs. 7 and 8.**
2. Wipe excess lubricant from inside axle housing and visually inspect components for wear and/or damage.

3. Rotate gears and inspect for roughness, indicating damaged bearings or gears.
4. Inspect and record ring gear back face runout using suitable dial indicator mounted on axle housing cover flange. Maximum back face runout is .004 inch.
5. Remove rear axles and propeller shaft. Refer to "Rear Axle & Suspension" section of appropriate chassis chapter for procedures.
6. Scribe reference marks on differential bearing caps for assembly alignment and loosen bearing cap bolts. **Observe and record direction arrows are facing on bearing caps. Arrows must installed facing in original direction.**
7. Pry differential case, bearing cups and shims out of housing until loose in bearing caps using suitable tool.
8. Remove bearing caps and differential assembly. Mark side cups and shims for assembly alignment.

DRIVE PINION

1. Scribe reference mark between drive pinion and companion flange.
2. Remove pinion nut and pinion flange using holding tool No. T78P-4851-A, or equivalent.
3. Drive pinion out of front bearing cone and remove from rear of axle housing using suitable soft faced hammer.
4. Remove oil seal, front bearing cone

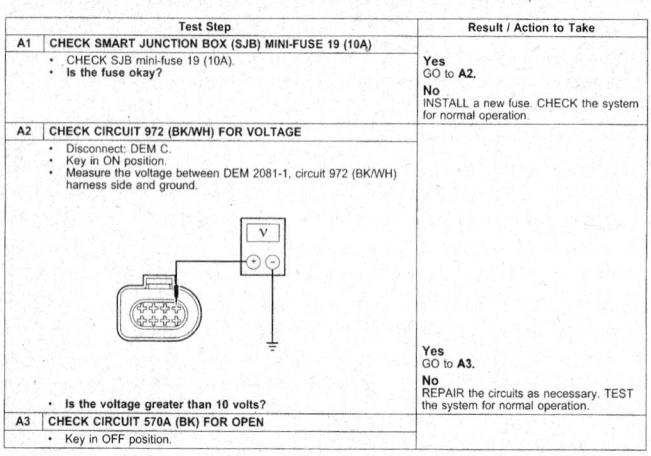

Fig. 6 Test A: No communication with DEM (Part 1 of 2). Five Hundred, Freestyle & Montego

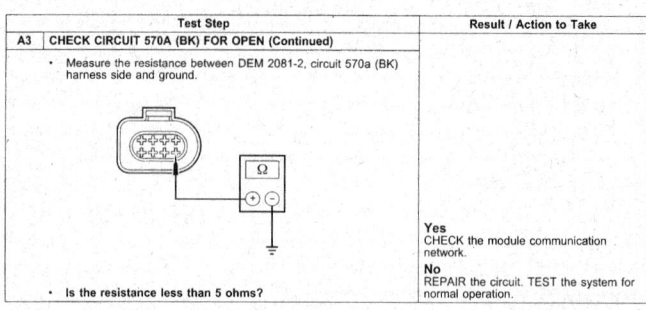

Fig. 6 Test A: No communication with DEM (Part 2 of 2). Five Hundred, Freestyle & Montego

and roller from pinion housing.

5. Remove rear pinion bearing using suitable arbor press and adapters.
6. Measure and record thickness of shim which is found under rear bearing cone.
7. Remove pinion bearing cups from pinion housing with suitable brass drift.
8. Install cups using suitable bearing cup installer. Cups are not properly installed if .015 feeler gauge can be installed between cup and bottom of bore at any point around cup.
9. **If any bearing cups are replaced, respective cone and roller must also be replaced.**

Five Hundred, Freestyle & Montego

DIFFERENTIAL CASE

The differential is not serviceable, should internal failure occur it will be necessary to replace the differential assembly.

DRIVE PINION FLANGE & OUTER PINION SEAL

REMOVAL

1. Place index marks on driveshaft to rear axle pinion flange, Power Take Off (PTO) flange and center bearing bracket for installation reference.
2. Remove and discard front and rear driveshaft flange bolts, **Fig. 9.**
3. Remove and discard drive pinion flange nut.
4. Remove drive pinion flange.
5. Remove outer drive pinion seal using suitable screwdriver or seal removal pry bar.

INSTALLATION

1. Install outer drive pinion seal using halfshaft seal installer tool No. 205–814, or equivalent, **Fig. 10.**
2. Install drive pinion flange and nut. **Torque** pinion flange nut to 74 ft. lbs.
3. Install drive shaft, **Fig. 9,** noting the following:

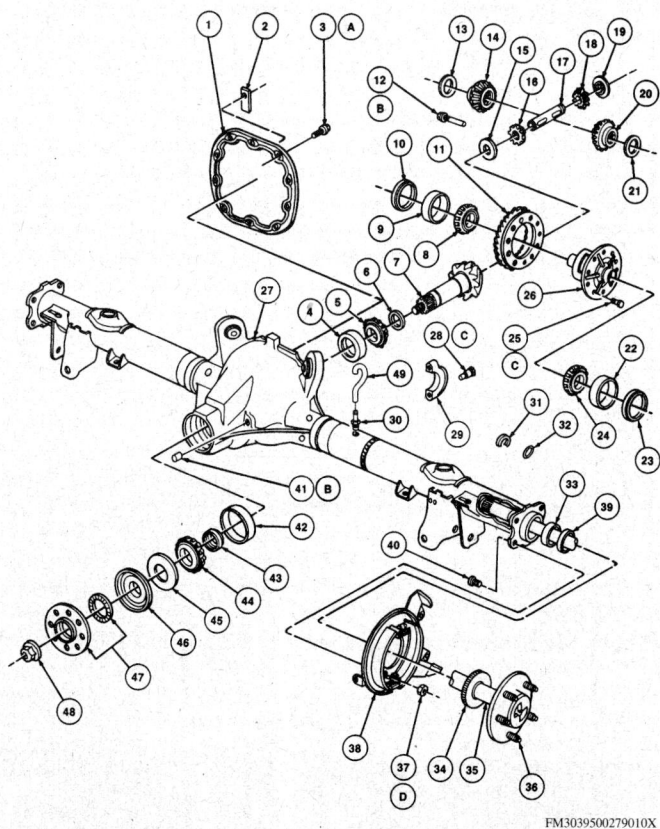

Fig. 7 Exploded view of 8.8 inch rear axles (Part 1 of 2). Crown Victoria, Grand Marquis, Marauder & Town Car

a. Align center bearing bracket, front and rear flange index marks made during removal.
b. **Torque** driveshaft to flange bolts to 18 ft. lbs.
c. **Torque** center bearing bolts to 15 ft. lbs.
d. **Torque** center bearing bracket bolts to 18 ft. lbs.
e. **Torque** exhaust support brace bolts to 22 ft. lbs.

INNER DRIVE PINION SEAL

1. Remove active on-demand coupling as outlined under "Active On-Demand Coupling."
2. Drive pinion inner seal is a two piece design, remove and discard both pieces using suitable screwdriver or seal

removal pry bar.

3. Reverse procedure to install, noting the following:
a. Install both seals as an assembly using seal installation tool No. 205–812, or equivalent, **Fig. 11.**
b. If seals become misaligned in there bore during installation, install new seals.

ACTIVE ON-DEMAND COUPLING

REMOVAL

1. Drain active on-demand coupling fluid into suitable container.
2. Disconnect Differential Electronic Module (DEM) electrical connector, **Fig. 12.**

Item	Description	Item	Description
1	Axle Housing Cover	28	Bolt
2	I.D. Tag	29	Differential Bearing Cap (Part of 4010)
3	Axle Housing Cover Bolt	30	Rear Axle Housing Vent
4	Rear Axle Pinion Bearing Cup	31	U-Washer
5	Differential Pinion Bearing	32	Rear Axle Shaft O-Ring
6	Drive Pinion Bearing Adjustment Shim	33	Rear Wheel Bearing
7	Drive Pinion (Part of 4209)	34	Rear Brake Anti-Lock Sensor Indicator
8	Differential Bearing (RH)	35	Axle Shaft
9	Differential Bearing Cup	36	Lug Bolt
10	Differential Bearing Shim	37	Nut
11	Ring Gear (Part of 4209)	38	Rear Wheel Disc Brake Adapter
12	Differential Pinion Shaft Lock Pin	39	Inner Wheel Bearing Oil Seal
13	Differential Side Gear Thrust Washer	40	Bolt
14	Differential Side Gear	41	Fill Plug
15	Differential Pinion Thrust Washer	42	Differential Drive Pinion Bearing Cup
16	Differential Pinion Gear	43	Differential Drive Pinion Collapsible Spacer
17	Differential Pinion Shaft	44	Differential Pinion Bearing
18	Differential Pinion Gear	45	Rear Axle Drive Pinion Shaft Oil Slinger
19	Differential Pinion Thrust Washer	46	Rear Axle Drive Pinion Seal
20	Differential Side Gear	47	Rear Axle Universal Joint Flange
21	Differential Side Gear Thrust Washer	48	Drive Pinion Nut
22	Differential Bearing	49	Formed Vent Hose
23	Differential Bearing Shim	A	Tighten to 38-52 N·m (28-38 Lb-Ft)
24	Differential Bearing (LH)	B	Tighten to 20-41 N·m (15-30 Lb-Ft)
25	Rear Axle Differential Gear Case Bolt	C	Tighten to 95-115 N·m (70-85 Lb-Ft)
26	Differential Case	D	Tighten to 27-40 N·m (20-30 Lb-Ft)
27	Rear Axle Housing		

FM3039500279020X

Fig. 7 Exploded view of 8.8 inch rear axles (Part 2 of 2). Crown Victoria, Grand Marquis, Marauder & Town Car

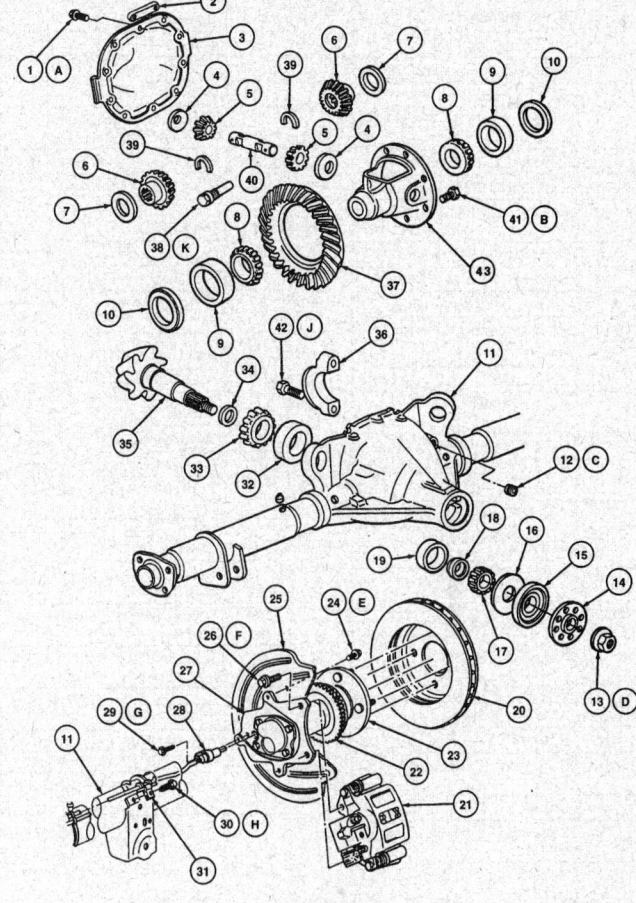

FM3039800326010X

Fig. 8 Exploded view of 7½ & 8.8 inch rear axles (Part 1 of 2). Mustang

3. Remove four active on-demand coupling mounting bolts, **Fig. 13. Record bolt locations before removal, bolt length varies and need to be install in the correct locations.**
4. Remove active on-demand coupling.

INSTALLATION

1. Clean and inspect axle assembly cavity for foreign material.
2. Install new coupling seal.
3. Install coupling and mounting bolts, torque mounting bolts to 35 ft. lbs. **Ensure mounting bolts are installed in correct positions, as marked during removal.**
4. Connect DEM electrical connector.
5. Fill active on-demand coupling with Volvo transmission oil part No. 116–1641, or equivalent, to bottom of fill hole, **Fig. 14.**

ACTIVE ON-DEMAND COUPLING OIL PUMP

1. Remove drive pinion flange as outlined under "Drive Pinion Flange & Outer Pinion Seal."
2. Disconnect active on-demand coupling oil pump electrical connector.
3. Remove oil pump to coupling mount-

ing bolts, **Fig. 15.**
4. Remove active on-demand coupling oil pump.
5. Reverse procedure to install. **Torque** oil pump mounting bolts to 53 inch lbs.

DIFFERENTIAL ELECTRONIC MODULE (DEM)
REMOVAL

Differential electronic module, solenoid valve and oil temperature sensor are calibrated together and must be replaced as a set.

1. Remove active on-demand coupling as outlined under "Active On-Demand Coupling."
2. Remove two DEM mounting bolts, **Fig. 16,** then the DEM.
3. Remove and discard spacer plate, **Fig. 17.**
4. Remove solenoid valve and discard O-ring seals, **Fig. 18.**
5. Remove and discard solenoid valve seat seal, **Fig. 19.**
6. Remove and discard oil temperature sensor seal.

INSTALLATION

1. Lubricate all seals with Volvo transmis-

sion fluid part No. 116–1641, or equivalent, before installation.
2. Install new spacer plate, **Fig. 17.**
3. Install new temperature sensor seal.
4. Install new solenoid valve seal, **Fig. 19.**
5. Install new solenoid valve O-ring seals, **Fig. 18.**
6. Install solenoid valve and oil temperature sensor into DEM.
7. Install active on demand coupling spacer plate and DEM onto active on-demand coupling. **Torque** DEM mounting bolts to 53 inch lbs.
8. Flash DEM with most current software.

LS & Thunderbird

Do not damage aluminum rear axle housing.

1. Remove differential housing cover.
2. Install dial indicator with bracket tool No. 4201-G, or equivalent.
3. Measure and record ring gear runout, **Fig. 20.**
4. Attach housing spreader adapters tool No. T93P-4000-A, or equivalent, to rear axle housing with four cover bolts.
5. Attach housing spreader adapters to holding fixture tool No. T57L-500-B, or equivalent, with two ⅜ inch x 1-½ inch bolts.

Item	Description
1	Axle Housing Cover Bolt
2	Rear Axle Brake Line Clip
3	Axle Housing Cover
4	Differential Pinion Thrust Washer
5	Differential Pinion Gear
6	Differential Side Gear
7	Differential Side Gear Thrust Washer
8	Differential Bearing
9	Differential Bearing Cup
10	Differential Bearing Shim
11	Rear Axle Housing
12	Filler Plug
13	Pinion Nut
14	Rear Axle Universal Joint Flange
15	Rear Axle Drive Pinion Seal
16	Rear Axle Drive Pinion Shaft Oil Slinger
17	Differential Pinion Bearing
18	Differential Drive Pinion Collapsible Spacer
19	Differential Drive Pinion Bearing Cup
20	Rear Disc Brake Rotor
21	Rear Disc Brake Caliper
22	Rear Brake Anti-Lock Sensor Indicator
23	Axle Shaft Flange
24	Bolt (3 Req'd)
25	Rear Wheel Disc Brake Shield
26	Caliper Anchor Bolt
27	Left Hand Rear Disc Brake Adapter
28	Rear Brake Anti-Lock Sensor

Item	Description
29	Bolt
30	Bolt
31	Clip
32	Rear Axle Pinion Bearing Cup
33	Differential Pinion Bearing
34	Drive Pinion Bearing Adjustment Shim
35	Drive Pinion
36	Bearing Cap
37	Ring Gear
38	Differential Pinion Shaft Lock Pin
39	U-Washer
40	Differential Pinion Shaft
41	Rear Axle Differential Gear Case Bolt
42	Bearing Cap Bolt
43	Differential Case
A	Tighten to 38-52 N·m (28-38 Lb-Ft)
B	Tighten to 95-115 N·m (70-84 Lb-Ft)
C	Tighten to 20-41 N·m (15-30 Lb-Ft)
D	Tighten to 190 N·m (140 Lb-Ft)
E	Tighten to 8-12 N·m (70-106 Lb-In)
F	Tighten to 87-119 N·m (65-87 Lb-Ft)
G	Tighten to 4.5-6.8 N·m (40-60 Lb-In)
H	Tighten to 10-14 N·m (89-123 Lb-In)
J	Tighten to 102-122 N·m (76-89 Lb-Ft)
K	Tighten to 20-41 N·m (15-30 Lb-Ft)

FM3039800326020X

Fig. 8   Exploded view of 7½ & 8.8 inch rear axles (Part 2 of 2). Mustang

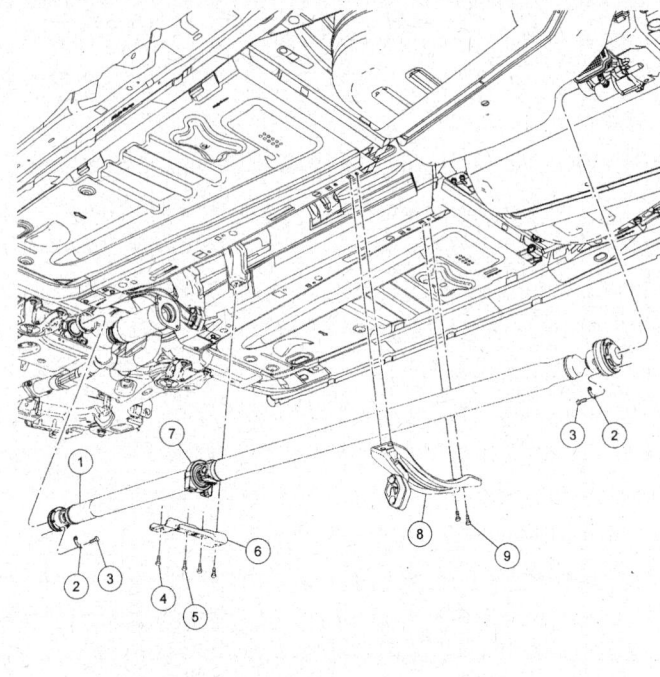

Item	Description
1	Driveshaft assembly
2	Driveshaft flange washer (6 required)
3	Driveshaft flange bolts (12 required)
4	Center bearing bracket bolts (2 required)

Item	Description
5	Center bearing bolts (2 required)
6	Center bearing bracket
7	Center bearing
8	Exhaust support brace
9	Exhaust support brace bolts (4 required) (part of

ARM0400000000764

Fig. 9   Driveshaft replacement. Five Hundred, Freestyle & Montego

6. Install differential carrier spreader tool No. T4000-E, or equivalent, onto housing spreader adapters with spreader pins aligned with housing spreader adapters holes.

7. **On models equipped with aluminum axle,** proceed as follows:
   a. Install dial indicator tool and attach clutch housing alignment adapter tool No. T75L-4201-A, or equivalent, to dial indicator with tip positioned in spreader adapter hole.
   b. Tighten and loosen housing spreader adapter screw to normalize housing spreader adapters prior to final dial indicator reading. **Overspreading can damage rear axle housing.**
   c. Adjust dial indicator to zero and tighten housing spreader screw until rear axle housing is spread to .030 inch. Remove dial indicator.

8. **On models equipped with nodular iron axle,** housing spreader adapters are used to give the rear axle housing stability. **Do not spread rear axle housing.**

9. **On all models,** mark position of bearing caps as arrows may not be visible. Bearing caps must be installed in original locations and positions.

10. Remove mounting bolts and bearing caps.

11. **On models equipped with aluminum axle,** proceed as follows:
    a. Position wood blocks on top and bottom of differential.
    b. Pry differential case and bearing shims out of rear axle housing, **Fig. 21.**
    c. Remove special tool.

12. **On models equipped with nodular iron axle,** remove differential case.

13. **On all models,** remove 10 ring gear bolts.

14. Drive ring gear off using suitable punch in bolt holes. **Do not damage bolt hole threads.**

15. Remove differential bearing using two-jaw puller tool No. D97L-4221-A and step plate tool No. D83T-4205-C2, or equivalents.

16. Repeat procedure on other side.

17. Remove differential lock bolt, pinion shaft, gears and side gears.

18. Install suitable torque wrench on pinion nut and record torque required to maintain rotation of drive pinion gear through several revolutions.

19. Install flange holding tool No. 205-478, or equivalent. **Ensure to install cotter key in special tool.**

20. Remove pinion nut using suitable breaker bar. **Discard pinion nut.**

21. Mark pinion flange in relation to drive pinion stem for assembly alignment.

22. Remove pinion flange using flange remover tool No. 307-408l, or equivalent.

23. Install pinion thread protector tool No. 205-460, or equivalent.

24. Drive pinion out of front bearing cone using suitable soft-faced hammer. Remove pinion through rear of housing.

25. Remove rear axle drive pinion shaft oil slinger, pinion seal and collapsible spacer.

26. Position pinion bearing cone remover tool No. T71P-4621-B, or equivalent, under pinion bearing.

27. Remove pinion bearing using suitable press.

28. Remove front pinion bearing.

29. Measure and record thickness of drive pinion bearing adjustment shim found under differential pinion bearing.

30. Remove drive pinion bearing adjustment shim.

31. Remove damaged rear axle pinion bearing cups from rear axle housing using pinion outer bearing cup remover tool No. 205-482 and pinion inner bearing cup remover tool No. 205-481, or equivalents.

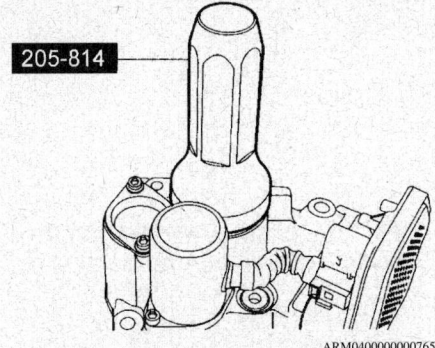

Fig. 10 Outer drive pinion seal installation. Five Hundred, Freestyle & Montego

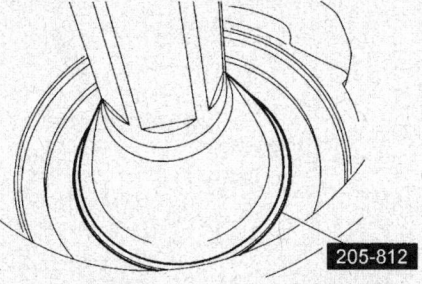

Fig. 11 Inner drive pinion seal installation. Five Hundred, Freestyle & Montego

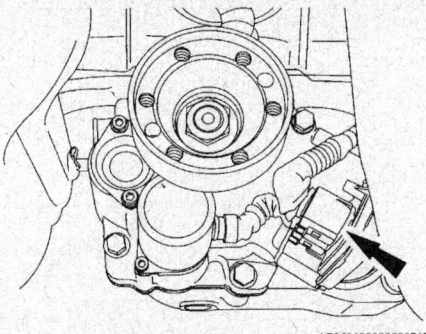

Fig. 12 Differential Electronic Module (DEM) connector location. Five Hundred, Freestyle & Montego

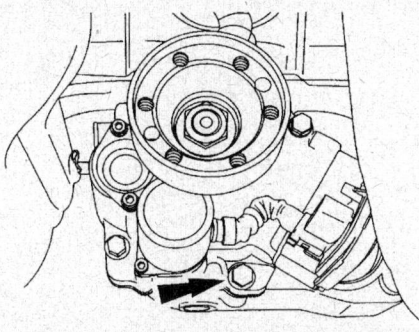

Fig. 13 Active on-demand coupling removal. Five Hundred, Freestyle & Montego

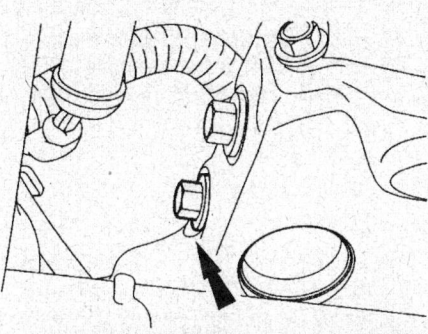

Fig. 14 Active on-demand coupling oil fill hole location. Five Hundred, Freestyle & Montego

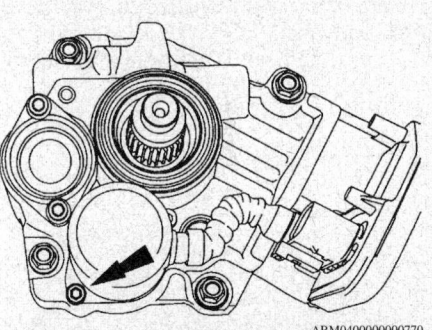

Fig. 15 Active on-demand coupling oil pump replacement. Five Hundred, Freestyle & Montego

SUBASSEMBLY SERVICE

Conventional Differential

CROWN VICTORIA, GRAND MARQUIS, MARAUDER, MUSTANG & TOWN CAR

DIFFERENTIAL CASE BEARINGS

1. If differential bearings are to be replaced, remove and replace with suitable puller.
2. If ring gear backlash measured during removal exceeded .015 inch, proceed as follows:
   a. Install differential bearing cups on cones, then the differential case in rear housing with drive pinion removed.
   b. Install .265 inch shim on lefthand side of case.
   c. Install bearing cap and hand tighten bolts.
   d. Install progressively larger shims on righthand side of case until largest shim selected can be installed with slight drag.
   e. Install bearing cap and **torque** bolts to 70–85 ft. lbs.
3. Rotate differential several turns in either direction to ensure free rotation and to seat bearings.
4. Inspect ring gear back face runout using suitable dial indicator mounted to axle housing.
5. Ring gear back face runout should be within .004 inch. If ring gear back face runout is within specifications, original reading was caused by insufficient differential bearing preload. If ring gear back face runout is still not within specifications, proceed as follows:
   a. Inspect differential case runout. It should be within .004 inch.
   b. If runout is within specifications, ring gear is out of specifications and should be replaced.
   c. If runout is not within specifications, differential case is damaged and should be replaced.
6. Remove differential case from axle housing, then the ring gear.
7. Install differential case less ring gear in housing.
8. Inspect differential case runout. Runout should be within .004 inch. If runout is within specifications, ring gear is out of specifications and should be replaced. If runout is not within specifications, differential case is damaged and should be replaced.

DRIVE PINION DEPTH DETERMINATION

Prior to determining drive pinion depth, clean pinion bearing cups and differential bearing pedestals thoroughly to ensure an accurate reading. Apply only light oil film to bearing assemblies to avoid false readings.

1. Assemble aligning adapter, gauge disc and gauge block to tool No. T79P-4020-A, or equivalent, **Fig. 22**.
2. Place rear pinion bearing over aligning adapter, then install tool and bearing in rear pinion bearing cup in pinion housing bore.
3. Place front pinion bearing over screw in front pinion bearing cup and assemble tool handle onto screw.
4. **Torque** handle to 20 inch lbs. Ensure tool is mounted securely between front and rear bearings.
5. Rotate gauge block several half turns to ensure bearings are seated properly. Rotational torque should be 20 inch lbs., with new bearings. Set gauge block at an angle approximately 45° from horizontal, **Fig. 23**.
6. Install gauge tube in differential bearing mounts, then the bearing caps and bolts.
7. install pinion shims between gauge block and gauge tube. Proper shim will fit with slight drag. **Do not force shim between block and tube. Do not use shims that are bent, dirty, nicked or mutilated as gauge.**
8. Record proper shim size and remove tool from axle housing.
9. Remove rear pinion bearing using suitable arbor press and adapters.

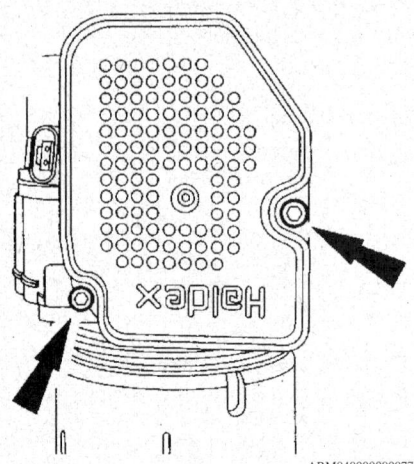

Fig. 16 Differential Electronic Module (DEM) mounting bolt locations. Five Hundred, Freestyle & Montego

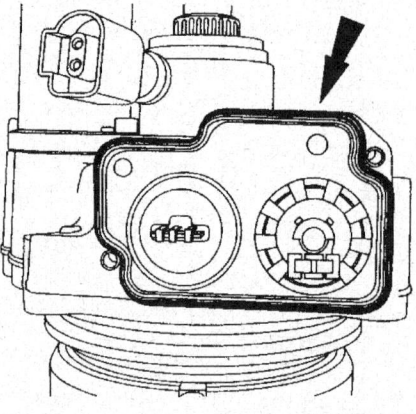

Fig. 17 Differential Electronic Module (DEM) spacer plate. Five Hundred, Freestyle & Montego

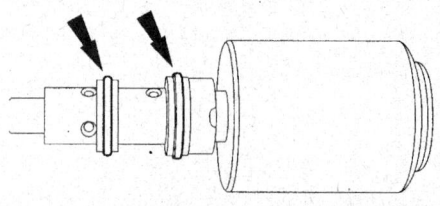

Fig. 18 Differential Electronic Module (DEM) solenoid valve & O-ring seals. Five hundred, Freestyle & Montego

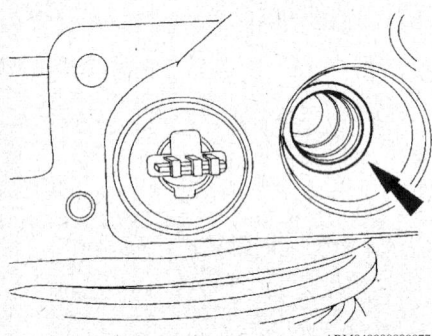

Fig. 19 Differential Electronic Module (DEM) solenoid valve seat seal. Five Hundred, Freestyle & Montego

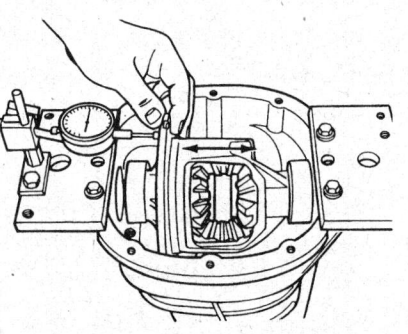

Fig. 20 Differential case end play measurement

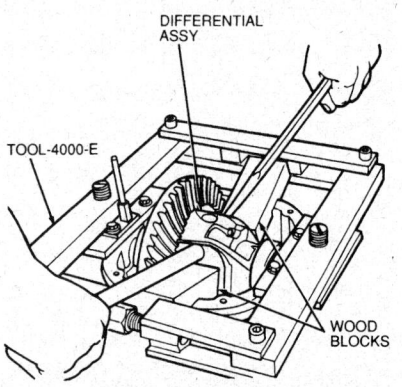

Fig. 21 Differential case removal

10. Install previously determined shim on pinion shaft and bearing using arbor press. **Rear pinion bearing used to determine drive pinion depth must be used in final assembly.**

DRIVE PINION INSTALLATION

1. Lubricate pinion bearings with suitable axle lubricant, then install pinion shaft and rear bearing, collapsible spacer and front bearing.
2. Install slinger and pinion oil seal, then install pinion flange in seal and hold firmly in place against front bearing.
3. From rear of housing, install pinion shaft into flange.
4. Install pinion yoke nut. While holding pinion flange, tighten nut only enough to remove bearing endplay.
5. When there is an increase in pinion nut turning effort stop tightening pinion nut.
6. Rotate pinion several times in both directions to seat bearings.
7. Continue to tighten pinion nut in very small increments.
8. Measure pinion rotational torque occasionally. Rotating torque must not exceed 20 inch lbs. **Do not exceed**

specified preload torque. **Do not loosen pinion nut if preload torque is exceeded. If preload torque is exceeded, remove pinion nut, yoke, oil seal, slinger and collapsible spacer. Replace collapsible spacer and oil seal and repeat procedure.**

LS & THUNDERBIRD

Do not damage aluminum rear axle housing.
1. Lubricate differential side gear thrust washers with Premium Long-Life Grease XG-1-C, or equivalent.
2. Install differential side gears in differential case.
3. Lubricate differential pinion thrust washers with Premium Long-Life Grease XG-1-C, or equivalent.
4. Install differential pinion gears with differential pinion thrust washers in differential case.
5. If new pinion shaft lock bolt is unavailable, coat threads with Threadlock and Sealer EOAZ-19554-AA, or equivalent, prior to installation.
6. Install differential pinion shaft and new pinion shaft lock bolt.
7. Install differential bearing on differential case using differential side bearing replacer tool No. T57L-4221-A2, or equivalent. Repeat for other side.
8. Start two of ring gear bolts through dif-

ferential case and into ring gear to ensure ring gear bolt holes align with differential case bolt holes correctly then press ring gear on differential case.
9. Install ring gear bolts. Apply Stud and Bearing Mount EOAZ-19554-BA, or equivalent, to bolts.
10. With pinion removed, place differential case/gear subassembly with differential bearing and rear axle pinion bearing cups in rear axle housing.
11. Install differential bearing shim of thickness shown on lefthand side of differential case.
12. Install lefthand bearing cap hand tight.
13. Apply pressure toward lefthand side to fully seat differential bearing cup.
14. Install progressively larger differential bearing shims on righthand side until largest differential bearing shim selected can be assembled with slight drag feel.
15. Install righthand bearing cap and **torque** bearing caps to 77 ft. lbs.
16. Rotate differential assembly to ensure it rotates freely.
17. Install dial indicator with bracket tool No. T4201-C, or equivalent.
18. Measure and record ring gear runout, **Fig. 20.**
19. If runout is .003 inch, original out-of-specification runout was caused by insufficient bearing preload.
20. If runout is more than .003 inch, proceed as follows:
    a. Remove differential case.
    b. Remove ring gear.

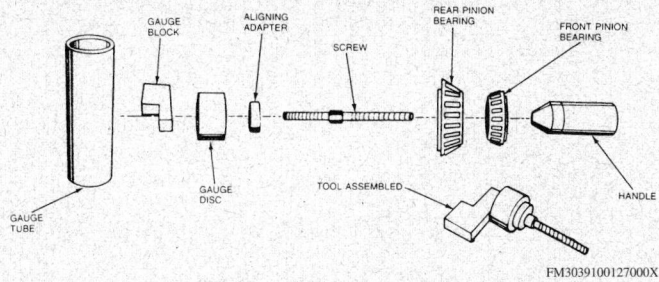

Fig. 22 Rear axle pinion depth gauge

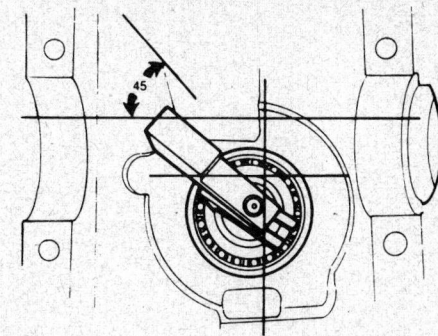

Fig. 23 Pinion depth gauge block installation

c. Install differential case without ring gear.

d. Rotate differential case to correctly seat differential bearings.

e. Measure differential case flange runout using dial indicator.

f. If runout is .003 inch, install new ring gear and pinion.

g. If runout is more than .003 inch, ring gear is true. Concern is because of either damaged differential case or differential bearings.

h. Inspect differential bearings.

i. If differential bearings are not damaged, install new differential case and differential bearings.

j. Measure runout with new differential case and differential bearings.

21. Install new inner rear axle pinion bearing cup in rear axle housing using pinion inner bearing cup tool No. 205-480 and cup replacer tool No. T71P-4616-A, or equivalents.

22. Install new outer rear axle pinion bearing cup in rear axle housing using cup replacer tools.

23. Coat new rear axle pinion bearing cup with SAE 5W-30 Super Premium Motor Oil XO-5W30-QSP, or equivalent.

24. Position rear axle pinion bearing cup on handle tool No. T76P-4020-A11, screw tool No. T76P-4020-A9, pinion depth gauge aligner tool No. 205-477, pinion depth gauge disc tool No. 205-476, and gauge block tool No. T76P-4020-A10, or equivalent, **Fig. 22.**

25. Position bearing cup replacer in rear axle housing and tighten special tool to fully seat rear axle pinion bearing cup in bore.

26. Apply light film of SAE 75W140 Synthetic Rear Axle Lubricant F1TZ-19580-B, or equivalent, on front differential pinion bearing and rear differential pinion bearing assemblies.

27. Thread handle onto screw and **torque** to 20 inch lbs.

28. Rotate gauge block tool several half turns to correctly seat pinion bearings, **Fig. 23. Gauge block tool must be offset to obtain an accurate reading.**

29. Position gauge tube tool No. T93P-4020-A, or equivalent, on differential bearing seat of rear axle housing.

30. Install differential bearing caps and cap bolts. **Torque** cap bolts to 77 ft. lbs.

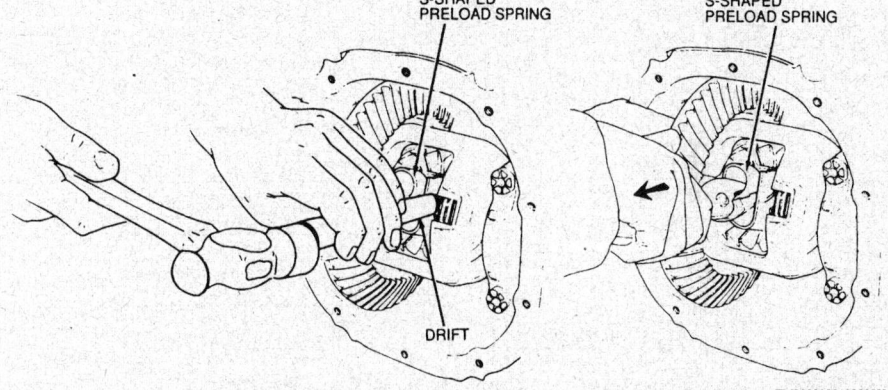

Fig. 24 C-clips S shaped preload spring removal. Traction-Lok

31. Slight drag should be felt for correct shim selection. Remove special tool.

32. Same pinion bearings and drive pinion bearing adjustment shim used in drive pinion shim selection procedure must be used in final axle assembly.

33. Position drive pinion bearing adjustment shim, pinion bearing, and bearing/seal service plate tool No. T75L-1165-B and universal bearing puller tool No. T53T-4621-C, or equivalents, on pinion stem.

34. Firmly seat drive pinion bearing adjustment shim and pinion bearing on pinion stem using suitable press.

35. Install front pinion bearing, rear axle drive pinion shaft oil slinger and rear axle drive pinion seal.

36. Ensure pinion stem splines are free of burrs. Remove burrs using fine crocus cloth working in rotational motion.

37. Install new drive pinion collapsible spacer on pinion stem against pinion stem shoulder.

38. Install drive pinion and drive pinion collapsible spacer into rear axle housing.

39. Master bearings are marked LH and RH.

40. Remove differential bearings and install righthand master bearing tool No. T93P-4222-B and lefthand master bearing tool No. T93P-4222-A, or equivalents, on differential case.

41. Lubricate rear axle pinion flange splines using SAE 75W140 Synthetic Rear Axle Lubricant F1TZ-19580-B, or equivalent.

42. Align rear axle pinion flange with drive pinion shaft and install rear axle pinion flange. Disregard scribe marks if new rear axle pinion flange is being installed.

43. With drive pinion in place in rear axle housing, install rear axle pinion flange using pinion flange installer tool No. 205-479 and flange holding tool No. 205-478, or equivalents.

44. Tighten pinion nut using flange holding tool No. 205-478, or equivalent. **Ensure to install cotter key in special tool.**

45. Rotate pinion occasionally to ensure differential pinion bearings seat correctly.

46. Take frequent differential pinion bearing torque preload readings by rotating pinion with suitable torque wrench. Preload **torque** should be 8–10 inch lbs., with used bearings or 16–28 inch lbs., with new bearings.

47. **Do not loosen pinion nut to reduce preload. If it is required to reduce preload, install new collapsible spacer and pinion nut.**

48. **On models equipped with aluminum axle,** proceed as follows:

a. Place differential case and dial indicator into rear axle housing. Position dial indicator on outside mounting hole.

b. Attach dial indicator with indicator tip positioned on machined surface of differential case flange.

c. Move differential case to lefthand and righthand as far as possible.

d. Repeat procedure until consistent

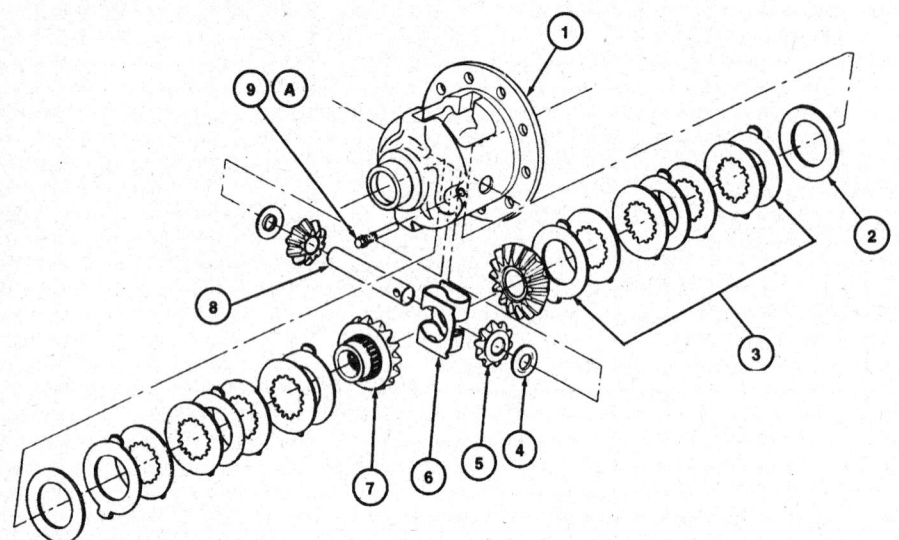

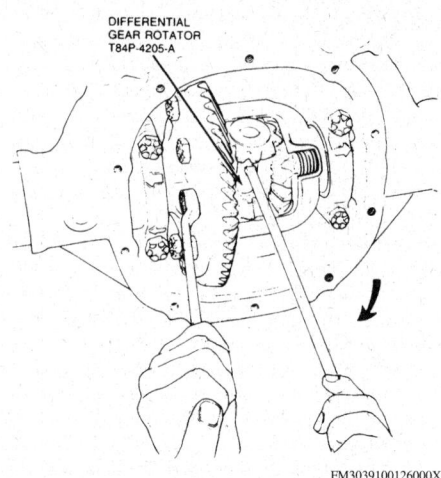

Fig. 26 Pinion gear removal & installation. Traction-Lok

Item	Description
1	Differential Case
2	Rear Axle Differential Clutch Shim
3	Differential Clutch Pack
4	Differential Pinion Thrust Washer
5	Differential Pinion Gear

Item	Description
6	Differential Clutch Spring
7	Differential Side Gear
8	Differential Pinion Shaft
9	Differential Pinion Shaft Lock Pin
A	Tighten to 20-41 N·m (15-30 Lb-Ft)

Fig. 25 Exploded view of Traction-Lok

reading is obtained.
e. Record reading.
f. Remove special tool and differential case from rear axle housing.

Traction-Lok Limited Slip Differential

EXCEPT FIVE HUNDRED, FREESTYLE & MONTEGO

For differential case and ring gear runout inspections and differential bearing replacement, refer to "Conventional Differential."

1. Remove and discard ring gear to differential case mounting bolts.
2. Tap on ring gear using a suitable mallet and remove ring gear from case.
3. Remove pinion shaft lock screw and pinion shaft.
4. Remove preloaded S shaped spring, **Fig. 24. S shaped spring is under tension.**
5. Rotate pinion gears and thrust washers using 12-inch socket extension installed into pinion gear rotator tool No. T80P-4205-A, or equivalent, until they can be removed through access hole.
6. Remove lefthand and righthand side gears, clutch packs and shims, **Fig. 25.** Record order and side removed from, then tag for assembly alignment.
7. Apply suitable lubricant to clutch plates, then install lefthand side gear, clutch pack and new shim into differential case. Repeat procedure for right-

hand hand side.
8. Install pinion gears and thrust washers 180° apart and in contact with side gears.
9. Align gears with pinion shaft bore using 12-inch socket extension installed in pinion shaft rotator, **Fig. 26.**
10. Install S shaped preload spring into differential using soft faced hammer.

FIVE HUNDRED, FREESTYLE & MONTEGO

These vehicles have no serviceable sub-assemblies, should internal failure occur it will be necessary to replace the differential assembly.

CLEANING & INSPECTION

Conventional Differential

Clean all components in suitable solvent. Dry all components except bearings with compressed air or shop towels. Allow bearings to air dry or use shop towels. **Do not use compressed air to dry bearings.**

Inspect differential bearings and cups for wear, pitting, galling, flat spots or cracks. Any bearing or cup showing any signs of wear or damage must be replaced. Bearings and respective cups must be replaced as an assembly only. Do not attempt to interchange bearings and cups as bearing life will be affected.

Inspect non-machined differential case surfaces for nicks and burrs which can be removed with an oil stone or fine tooth file. Inspect pinion shaft bore to ensure it is not elongated or worn. If damage is evident, differential case must be replaced. Inspect machined differential surfaces and counterbores. They must be smooth and free of nicks, gouges, cracks and other visible damage. If damage is evident, differential case must be replaced.

Inspect pinion shaft for excessive wear, scoring or galling. Ensure shaft is smooth and concentric. If any wear or damage is evident, replace the shaft. Inspect pinion shaft lockpin for damage and to ensure it has a snug fit in the differential case. Replace lockpin or case as required.

Inspect pinion and ring gears for worn or chipped teeth, cracks, damaged bearing journals or mounting bolt threads. If any of the above are evident, replace ring gear and pinion as a matched set.

Inspect pinion and side gears. Gears must exhibit a uniform contact pattern without any signs of cracks, wear, scoring or galling. If any of the above are evident, replace all the gears. Inspect thrust washers for wear and replace as required.

Inspect pinion and ring gears for worn or chipped teeth, cracks, damaged bearing journals or mounting bolt threads. If any of the above are evident, replace ring gear and pinion as a matched set.

Inspect axle shaft C-locks (if equipped) for signs of cracks or wear and replace as required.

Traction-Lok Limited Slip Differential

The cleaning and inspection of these units is the same as for conventional differentials except that cleaning solvent should not be allowed to contact the clutch plates. The clutch plates should be wiped clean only. In addition, the following steps should be performed which only apply to the Traction-Lok differential.

Visually inspect clutch packs, side gears, pinion gears and pinion shaft for damage or wear.

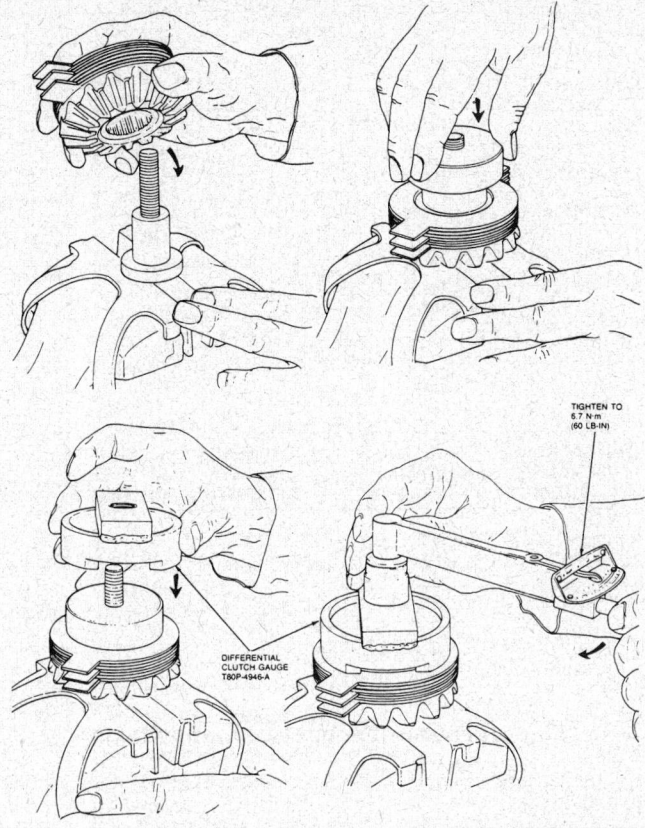

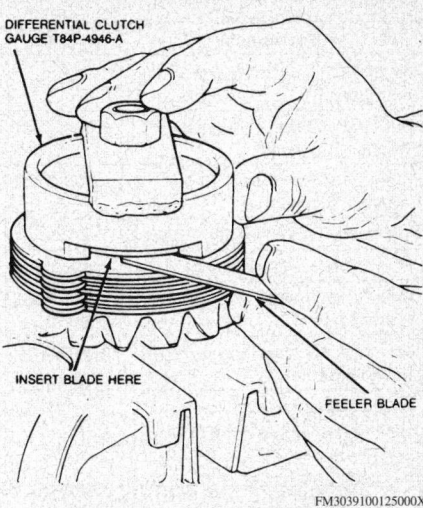

Fig. 28 Shim thickness measurement using tool No. T80P-4946-A, or equivalent. Traction-Lok

Fig. 27 Shim thickness measuring. Traction-Lok

Place each clutch pack without shims into tool No. T80P-4946-A, or equivalent, **Fig. 27.** Torque nut to 60 inch lbs. Determine thickness of new shims by installing thickest feeler blade possible between clutch pack and too, then note size for use during assembly, **Fig. 28.**

ASSEMBLE

Crown Victoria, Grand Marquis, Marauder, Mustang & Town Car

1. Install replacement ring gear. Apply suitable locking compound to new bolts and **torque** to 70–85 ft. lbs.
2. Apply suitable axle lubricant to differential bearing bores.
3. Place differential bearing cups on bearings and set differential assembly in axle housing. **If ring gear and pinion gear have punch marks, assemble ring gear in carrier so marked tooth on pinion is indexed between marked teeth of ring gear.**
4. Mount suitable dial indicator on axle housing cover flange and measure ring gear backlash. refer to **Fig. 29,** for specifications.
5. If backlash is within specifications, increase both lefthand and righthand side shims by .006 inch to provide

proper differential bearing preload. Ensure shims are fully seated and case assembly turns freely.
6. If backlash is not within specifications, correct by increasing thickness of one shim and decreasing thickness on other shim by same amount. Refer to **Fig. 30,** for approximate shim change.
7. If backlash measured more than zero, add .020 inch to righthand side of case and subtract .020 inch from lefthand side of case, then inspect backlash again.
8. If backlash now ranges within specifications, install shims and bearing caps.
9. **Torque** bearing cap bolts to 70–85 ft. lbs., then rotate differential case assembly several turns in both directions.
10. Inspect tooth mesh contacting pattern using suitable white marking compound applied to ring gear. **Tooth mesh contacting pattern can be improved by installing propeller shaft and axle assemblies and rotating both tires in drive and coast direction.**
11. Contacting pattern should be within primary area of ring gear tooth surface avoiding narrow contact with outer perimeter of tooth. Inspect pattern on drive (pull) side of ring gear. If serious error is determined, inspect pinion shim selection.
12. Install axle housing cover, driveshaft and axle assemblies.
13. Fill rear axle assembly with suitable

axle lubricant .
14. **On models equipped with 7½ inch Traction-Lok differential,** subtract 3 ounces of axle lubricant and replace with 3 ounces of Friction Modifier part No. C8AZ-19546-A, or equivalent.

LS & Thunderbird

1. Draw-file differential ring gear mounting surface to remove any nicks or burrs.
2. Place ring gear onto differential case, then hand start three bolts to align ring gear holes and differential case.
3. Place differential case and ring gear onto press bed blocks with ring gear teeth facing down.
4. Press ring gear into place
5. Install remaining ring gear bolts and **torque** to 77 ft. lbs.
6. **On models equipped with aluminum axle,** proceed as follows:
   a. Place differential case, lefthand master bearing tool No. T93P-4222-A, righthand master bearing tool No. T93P-4222-B, or equivalents, and ring gear into rear axle housing.
   b. Ring gear bolt heads inside rear axle housing may interfere. If so, remove 3–5 bolts to provide clearance.
   c. Attach dial indicator with indicator tip positioned on machined surface of case flange.
   d. Rock ring gear to allow full mesh with pinion gear.
   e. With gears in full mesh, set dial indicator to zero.
   f. Move differential case as far as possible and record reading.
   g. Record reading for differential bearing shim selection procedure.
   h. Remove dial indicator and differential case from rear axle housing.
   i. Stand height of both differential bearings must be measured prior to installation.

Description	inches
Maximum Runout of Backface of Ring Gear	0.004
Differential Side Gear Thrust Washer Thickness	0.030-0.032
Differential Pinion Gear Thrust Washer Thickness	0.030-0.032
Maximum Differential Case Runout	0.003
Nominal Pinion Locating Shim	0.030
Backlash Between Ring Gear and Pinion Teeth	0.008-0.015
Maximum Backlash Variation Between Teeth	0.004
Maximum Radial Runout of Companion Flange in Assembly	0.010 TIR

FM3039400281000X

Fig. 29 Rear axle specifications & tolerances

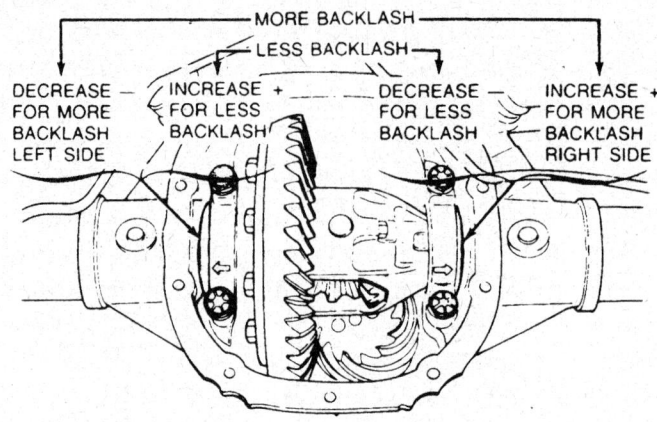

BACKLASH CHANGE REQUIRED	THICKNESS CHANGE REQUIRED	BACKLASH CHANGE REQUIRED	THICKNESS CHANGE REQUIRED
.001	.002	.009	.012
.002	.002	.010	.014
.003	.004	.011	.014
.004	.006	.012	.016
.005	.006	.013	.018
.006	.008	.014	.018
.007	.010	.015	.020
.008	.010		

FM3039100129000X

Fig. 30 Rear axle backlash adjustment

j. Place bearing preload tool No. T93P-4220-AR, or equivalent, base in suitable soft-jawed vise with bearing mounting surface above vise jaws.

k. Position differential bearing on bearing preload tool base.

l. Attach bolt, spring, washers and spacer. Tighten bolt.

m. Mark differential bearings, lefthand and righthand before measuring.

n. Invert bearing preload tool No. T93P-4220-AR, or equivalent, and clamp bolt head in suitable vise.

o. Position suitable depth micrometer flat on differential bearing.

p. Measure stand height of both differential bearings and record for differential bearing shim selection.

q. Press lefthand and righthand differential bearing on differential case.

r. Install differential carrier spreader tool No. T4000-E, or equivalent, and dial indicator.

s. **Overspreading may damage rear axle housing.**

t. Tighten and loosen housing spreader adapter screw to normalize housing spreader adapters prior to final dial indicator reading.

u. Adjust dial indicator to zero and tighten differential carrier spreader screw to spread rear axle housing to .030 inch.

v. Remove dial indicator.

7. **On all models,** apply light coating of Premium Long-Life Grease XG-1-C, or equivalent, to differential bearing shim to help hold in place.

8. Select correct size lefthand side differential bearing shim as follows:
   a. Add end play and bearing height.
   b. Subtract backlash.
   c. Round off initial thickness to nearest shim thickness.

9. Add end play and bearing height.

10. Add backlash.

11. Round off initial thickness to nearest shim thickness.

12. Install differential bearing shims in rear axle housing.

13. Position differential bearing cups on differential bearings.

14. Lower differential case in place between differential bearing shims.

15. Install bearing caps in original positions and **torque** bolts to 77 ft. lbs.

16. Tighten bearing cap bolts prior to releasing housing spreader.

17. Remove differential carrier spreader and move dial indicator to 12 o'clock position.

18. Position indicator needle centrally on drive tooth and zero indicator.

19. Turn ring gear without turning pinion gear.

20. Record indicator reading.

21. Measure ring gear backlash at four places to obtain consistent reading.

22. If backlash is not .004 inch, correct by increasing thickness of one differential bearing shim and decreasing thickness of other differential bearing shim by the same amount.

23. Ensure machined surfaces on both rear axle housing and differential housing cover are clean and free of oil before installing new silicone sealant.

24. Inside of rear axle must be covered when cleaning machined surface to prevent contamination.

25. Apply new continuous bead of Silicone Rubber D6AZ-19562-AA, or equivalent, sealant to differential housing cover.

26. Install differential housing cover.

27. Install rear axle and refill.

TECHNICAL SERVICE BULLETINS

Axle Bearing Or Shaft Wear

2003 CROWN VICTORIA, GRAND MARQUIS & TOWN CAR

On some of these models built before Jan. 1, 2003, the rear axle shaft and or axle bearing may prematurely wear.

This condition may be caused by excessive load, temperature and inadequate lubrication.

To correct this condition, install rear axle bearing service kit (part No. 3W1Z-4A109-AA) according to kit's instructions.

ENGINE REBUILDING SPECIFICATIONS

NOTE: For Engine Tightening Specifications, Refer To The Engine Section In The Appropriate Chassis Chapter Of This Manual.

INDEX

CYLINDER HEAD, VALVE GUIDE & VALVE SEATS

All Measurements Given In Inches, Unless Otherwise Specified.

Engine Liter (VIN①)	Year	Cylinder Head Warpage Limit	Valve Guides Bore Diameter	Valve Guides Stem to Guide Clearance Intake	Valve Guides Stem to Guide Clearance Exhaust	Seat Angle °	Valve Seats Seat Width Intake	Valve Seats Seat Width Exhaust	Run-Out	Seat Insert Bore Diameter Intake	Seat Insert Bore Diameter Exhaust
2.0L DOHC (3)⑥	2001–05	②	.2386	.0007–.0026	.0007–.0026	45.00	—	—	—	—	—
2.0L DOHC (3 & 5)⑧	2001–05	.0039	—	.0007–.0025	.0007–.0025	—	—	—	—	—	—
2.0L SOHC (P)	2001–05	⑦	.3174–.3187	.0008–.0027	.0019–.0037	45.50	.0591–.0910	.0591–.0910	.0025	1.572–1.573	1.572–1.573
2.5L DOHC (G & L)	2001–02	②	—	.0007–.0027	.0017–.0037	44.75	.0433–.0551	.0433–.0551	.0010	—	—
3.0L DOHC (S)③	2001–05	.0047	—	.0009–.0026	.0014–.0031	44.50–45.00	.0433–.0551	.0551–.0669	.0008	—	—
3.0L DOHC (S)④	2001–05	②	—	.0007–.0027	.0018–.0037	44.75	.0433–.0551	.0551–.0669	.0020	—	—
3.0L DOHC (1)	2005	—	.2360–.2370	.0007–.0027	.0018–.0037	44.50–45.00	.0430–.0550	.0550–.0660	.001	—	—
3.0L OHV (U & 2)	2001–05	.0031	.2763–.2772	.0010–.0028	.0015–.0033	45.00	.0591–.0787	.0787–.0984	.0031–.0039	—	—
3.8L OHV (4)	2001–03	.0071	.2763–.2773	.0008–.0027	.0015–.0033	44.75	.0591–.0787	.0591–.0787	.0030	—	—
3.9L DOHC (A)	2001–05	.0031	—	.0009	.0012	⑨	.0394	.0787	.0016	—	—
4.0L SOHC (N)	2005	.0030	.2760–.2762	.0001–.0002	.0001–.0003	45.00	.0500–.0830	.0610–.0950	.0020	—	—
4.6L DOHC (V & Y)	2001–05	⑤	.2762–.2773	.0008–.0027	.0018–.0037	45.00	.0709–.0866	.0709–.0866	.0020	—	—
4.6L SOHC (X)	2001–05	.0039	—	.0008–.0027	.0018–.0037	45.00	.0512–0591	.0512–0591	.0020	—	—
4.6L SOHC (W & 9)	2001–05	.0039	—	.0008–.0027	.0018–.0037	45.00	.0709–.0866	.0709–.0866	.0020	—	—

DOHC — Dual Overhead Cam
OHV — Overhead Valve
SOHC — Single Overhead Cam
① — Eighth digit Vehicle Identification Number (VIN) denotes engine code.

② — .0020 inch for each 5.91 inches of length.
③ — LS.
④ — Sable & Taurus.
⑤ — VIN R, .0059 inch; VIN W & Y, .0039 inch.

⑥ — Cougar, Escort & ZX2.
⑦ — .0016 inch for every 1.26 inches or .0033 inch for every 6.14 inches length.
⑧ — Focus.
⑨ — Intake, 14°; Exhaust, 13°.

VALVE SPRINGS

All Measurements Given In Inches, Unless Otherwise Specified.

Engine Liter (VIN①)	Year	Free Length	Installed Height	Installed Pressure Lbs. @ Inches		Comp. Pressure Lbs. @ Inches		Out Of Square Limit
				Intake	Exhaust	Intake	Exhaust	
2.0L DOHC (3) ⑤⑦	2001–05	1.7010	1.3460	32.5 @ 1.3460	40.5 @ 1.3460	82.1 @ .9880	94.9 @ 1.0275	—
2.0L DOHC (3 & 5)⑥	2001–05	—	—	—	—	—	—	—
2.0L SOHC (P)⑥	2001–05	2.0630	1.5560	18.7 @ 1.1520	18.7 @ 1.1520	78.7 @ 1.5560	78.7 @ 1.5560	⑨
2.5L DOHC (G & L)	2001–02	④	—	—	—	—	—	.0640
3.0L DOHC (S)③	2001–05	1.7400	1.3150	37.1–41.6 @ 1.3150	37.1–41.6 @ 1.3150	85.0–94.9 @ .9650	85.0–94.9 @ .9650	—
3.0L DOHC (S)②	2001–05	1.8430	1.5740	51.3 @ 1.5740	51.3 @ 1.5740	152.9 @ 1.1890	152.9 @ 1.1890	⑩
3.0L DOHC (1)	2005	1.8400	1.6528–1.7389	53.95 @ 2.6900	53.95 @ 2.6900	156 @ 1.1800	156 @ 1.1800	⑩
3.0L OHV (U & 2)	2001–05	1.8268	1.6528–1.7389	64.1–72.6 @ 1.5953	64.1–72.6 @ 1.5953	192.6–217.4 @ 1.1709	192.6–217.4 @ 1.1709	⑩
3.8L OHV (4)	2001–05	—	1.6024	78.7 @ 1.6024	78.7 @ 1.6024	224.8 @ 1.1496	224.8 @ 1.1496	—
3.9L DOHC (A)	2001–05	—	—	—	—	—	—	—
4.0L SOHC (N)	2005	1.7000	1.5690–1.6090	72.0 @ 1.5690	72.0 @ 1.5690	202.8–224.9 @ 1.413–1.445	202.8–224.9 @ 1.413–1.445	1.5°
4.6L DOHC (R, V & Y)	2000–04	1.6598	1.4228	65.0 @ 1.4228	65.0 @ 1.4228	159.9 @ 1.0311	159.9 @ 1.0311	⑧
4.6L SOHC (X)	2001–05	2.0380–2.1642	1.6650–1.6890	63.6–72.1 @ 1.6756	63.6–72.1 @ 1.6756	161.9–179.8 @ 1.1339	161.9–179.8 @ 1.1339	⑩
4.6L SOHC (W & 9)	2001–05	1.9764	1.5984–1.7165	61.2–68.8 @ 1.5748	61.2–68.8 @ 1.5748	142.3–157.7 @ 1.1102	142.3–157.7 @ 1.1102	2.5°

DOHC — Dual Overhead Cam
OHV — Overhead Valve
SOHC — Single Overhead Cam
① — Eighth digit Vehicle Identification Number (VIN) denotes engine code.
② — Sable & Taurus.

③ — LS.
④ — Intake, 1.729 inches; exhaust, 1.847 inches.
⑤ — Escort
⑥ — Focus.
⑦ — Cougar & ZX2

⑧ — 2001–02, 10% force loss @ specified height; 2003–05, 2%.
⑨ — Service limit, 5% force loss @ specified height.
⑩ — Service limit, 10% force loss @ specified height.

VALVES

All Measurements Given In Inches, Unless Otherwise Specified.

Engine Liter (VIN①)	Year	Valves					
		Stem Diameter		Run Out	Face Angle, Degrees	Clearance	
		Intake	Exhaust			Intake	Exhaust
2.0L DOHC (3)⑦⑨	2001–05	.2374	.2374	.0014	45.00	.0043–.0071②	.01068–.0134②
2.0L DOHC (3 & 5)⑧	2001–05	—	—	—	—	.0043–.0071⑩	.0106–.0134⑩
2.0L SOHC (P)⑦	2001–05	.3159–.3167	.3149–.3156	—	45.60	⑥	⑥
2.0L SOHC (P)⑧	2001–05	.3159–.3167	.3152–.3156	—	45.50	⑥	⑥
2.5L DOHC (G & L)	2001–02	.2350–.2358	.2343–.2350	—	45.50	.0190–.0430	.0190–.0430
3.0L DOHC (S)⑤	2001–05	.2156–.2162	.2151–.2157	.0016	45.50	.0069–.0089	.0128–.0148
3.0L DOHC (S)④	2001–05	.2352–.2360	.2343–.2350	.0020	45.50	.0197–.0437②	.0197–.0437②
3.0L DOHC (1)	2005	.2350–.2358	.2343–.2350	.0010	45.25–45.75	⑥	⑥
3.0L OHV (U & 2)	2001–05	.2744–.2752	.2740–.2748	.0020	45.00	.0878–.1878②	.0878–.1878②

Continued

VALVES—Continued

All Measurements Given In Inches, Unless Otherwise Specified.

Engine Liter (VIN①)	Year	Valves					
		Stem Diameter		Run Out	Face Angle, Degrees	Clearance	
		Intake	Exhaust			Intake	Exhaust
3.8L OHV (4)	2001–05	.2738–.2751	.2728–.2741	.00197	45.67	.0890–.1890②	.0890–.1890②
3.9L DOHC (A)	2001–05	.1959–.1960	.1951–.1957	.0016	45.00	—	—
4.0L DOHC (N)	2005	.2740–.2750	.2730–.2740	.0010	45.00	⑥	⑥
4.6L DOHC (R & Y)	2003–05	.2746–.2754	.2736–.2744	.0020	45.50	.0315–.0472②	.0315–.0472②
4.6L DOHC (V)	2001–05	.2746–.2753	.2736–.2744	.0011	45.50	②③	②③
4.6L SOHC (X, W & 9)	2001–05	.2746–.2753	.2736–.2744	.0020	45.50	.0177–.0335②	.0177–.0335②

DOHC — Dual Overhead Cam
OHV — Overhead Valve
SOHC — Single Overhead Cam
① — Eighth digit Vehicle Identification Number (VIN) denotes engine code.

② — With cylinder @ top dead center, hold steady pressure on lifter until fully collapsed to check clearance.
③ — Continental, .0018–.0033 inch; Mustang, .1798–.2698 inch; Marauder, .0315–.0472 inch.
④ — Sable & Taurus.

⑤ — LS.
⑥ — Not adjustable, zero lash hydraulic lifters used.
⑦ — Escort.
⑧ — Focus.
⑨ — Cougar & ZX2.
⑩ — @ 59–77°F.

CAMSHAFT

All Measurements Given In Inches unless Otherwise Specified.

Engine Liter (VIN①)	Year	Camshaft Journal Diameter	Camshaft Bearing Inside Diameter	Camshaft Bearing Clearance	Camshaft Endplay	Lifter Bore Diameter	Lifter Diameter	Lifter To Bore Clearance
2.0L DOHC (3) ②	2001–05	1.0220–1.0228	—	.0008–.0028	.0031–.0087	—	—	—
2.0L DOHC (3 & 5)⑤	2001–05	—	1.0220–1.0228	.0008–.0028	.0031–.0087	—	—	—
2.0L SOHC (P)	2001–05	1.8007–1.8017	1.8030–1.8040	.0013–.0033	.0008–.0079	.8701–.8858	.8740–.8745	.0009–.0026
2.5L DOHC (G & L)	2001–02	1.0600–1.0610	1.0620–1.0630	.0010–.0029	.0010–.0064	—	.6290–.6294	.0007–.0027
3.0L DOHC (S)③	2001–05	1.0603–1.604	—	.0010–.0059	.0028–.0109	—	—	—
3.0L DOHC (S) ④	2001–05	1.0605–1.0615	1.0625–1.0635	.0010–.0048	.0075	—	.6294–.6299	.0007–.0027
3.0L DOHC (1)	2005	1.0610–1.0600	1.0625–1.0635	.0010–.0029	.0009–.0064	—	6290–.6294	.0007–.0027
3.0L OHV (U & 2)	2001–05	2.0074–2.0084	2.0094–2.0104	.0010–.0030	.0001	.8752–.8767	.8742	.0007–.0027
3.8L OHV (4)	2001–05	2.0525–2.0543	2.0670–2.0740	.0010–.0030	.0010–.0069	.8752–.8767	.8738–.8745	.0007–.0027
3.9L DOHC (A)	2001–05	—	—	—	—	—	—	—
4.0L DOVC (N)	2005	1.0990–1.1010	1.1020–1.1040	.0020–.0040	.0030–.0070	—	—	—
4.6L DOHC (R, V & Y)	2001–05	1.0605–1.0615	1.0625–1.0635	.0010–.0030	.0011–.0075	—	.6294–.6299	.0006–.0027
4.6L SOHC (X, W & 9)	2001–05	1.0602–1.0615	1.0625–1.0634	.0010–.0030	.0012–.0075	—	.6294–.6299	.0007–.0027

DOHC — Dual Overhead Cam
OHV — Overhead Valve
SOHC — Single Overhead Cam

① — Eighth digit Vehicle Identification Number (VIN) denotes engine code.
② — Cougar, Escort & ZX2.

③ — LS.
④ — Sable & Taurus.
⑤ — Focus.

CRANKSHAFT, BEARINGS & RODS

All Measurements Given In Inches, Unless Otherwise Specified.

Engine Liter (VIN①)	Year	Crankshaft			Bearing Clearance			Connecting Rods		
		Main Bearing Journal Diameter	Connecting Rod Journal Diameter	Crankshaft Endplay	Max. Out of Round All	Max. Taper	Main Bearings	Connecting Rod Bearings	Pin Bore Diameter	Side Clearance
2.0L DOHC (3 & 5)	2001–05	2.2827–2.2835	1.8461–1.8468	.0035–.0102	—	—	.0004–.0022	.0006–.0028	.7855–.7867	.0036–.0126
2.0L SOHC (P)	2001–05	2.2827–2.2835	1.8460–1.8468	.0039–.0118	.0003	.0003	.0008–.0026	.0008–.0026	.8098–.8114	.0036–.0140
2.5L DOHC (G & L)	2001–02	2.4670–2.2790	1.9670–1.9680	.0040–.0090	—	—	.0009–.0017	.0010–.0025	.8270–.8280	.0039–.0118
3.0L DOHC (S)④	2001–05	2.4690–2.4800	1.9673–1.9681	.0043–.0091	—	—	—	.0011–.0018	—	.0039–.0138
3.0L DOHC (S)②	2001–05	2.4790–2.4800	1.9673–1.9681	.0053–.0100	—	.—	—	.0011–.0026	.8274–.8280	.0039–.0118
3.0L DOHC (1)	2005	2.4790–2.4800	1.9673–1.9681	.0050–.0100	.0082	.0003	—	.001–.0025	.8273–.8275	.0039–.0118
3.0L OHV (U & 2)	2001–04	2.5190–2.5198	2.1253–2.1261	.00390–.0079	.0003	.0024	.0009–.0027	.0009–.0027	.9096–.9112	.0059–.0142
3.8L OHV (4)	2001–03	2.5190–2.5198	2.3103–2.3111	.0039–.0079	.0006	.0003	.0005–.0023	.0009–.0027	.9031–.9047	.0047–.0193
3.9L DOHC (A)	2001–05	—	—	—	—	—	—	—	—	—
4.0L SOHC (N)	2005	2.243–2.244	2.125–2.126	.002–.0126	.0003	.0003	.0003–.0024	.0003–.0024	.943–.944	.0036–.0106
4.6L DOHC (R)	2003–05	2.6567–2.6577	2.0859–2.2396	.0051–.0119	.0020	.0020	.0010–.0020	.0006–.0027	.8666–.8671	.0059–.0197
4.6L DOHC (V)	2001–05	③	2.0859–2.2396	.0051–.0119	.0020	.0020	.0010–.0020	.0011–.0027	.8666–.8671	.0059–.0197
4.6L DOHC (Y)	2003–05	2.6572	2.2396.–2.2388	.0051–.0119	.0020	.0020	.0009–.0022	.0011–.0027	.8666–.8671	.0059–.0197
4.6L SOHC (W & 9)	2001–05	2.6568–2.6576	2.0859–2.0867	.0119	.0020	.0002	.0009–.0026	.0008–.0023	.8666–.8671	.0059–.0177
4.6L SOHC (X)	2001–05	2.6568–2.6576	2.0859–2.0867	.0030–.0148	.0020	—	.0010–.0020	.0011–.0027	.8666–.8671	.0049–.0197

DOHC — Dual Overhead Cam

OHV — Overhead Valve

SOHC — Single Overhead Cam

① — Eighth digit Vehicle Identification Number (VIN) denotes engine code.

② — Sable & Taurus.

③ — Continental, 2.6576–2.6765 inches; Marauder & Mustang, 2.6567–2.6577 inches.

④ — LS.

BALANCE SHAFT

All Measurements Given In Inches, Unless Otherwise Specified.

Engine Liter (VIN①)	Year	Balance Shaft Bore		Balance Shaft		
		Inside Bore Diameter	End Play	Journal Diameter	End Play	Runout
3.8L OHV (4)	2001–03	2.1915–2.1924	.0030–.0060	2.0505–2.0515	.0030–.0079	.0010

OHV — Overhead Valve

① — Eighth digit Vehicle Identification Number (VIN) denotes engine code.

PISTONS, PINS & RINGS

All Measurements Given In Inches, Unless Otherwise Specified.

Engine Liter (VIN①)	Year	Piston Diameter (Std.)	Piston Clearance	Piston Pin Diameter	Pin To Piston Clearance	Piston End Ring Gap		Piston Ring Side Clearance	
						Comp.	Oil	Comp.	Oil
2.0L DOHC (3)⑱	2001–02	㉝	.0004–.0012	⑤	.0004–.0006	㉒	.00590–.02560	㉕	⑭
2.0L DOHC (3)⑬	2001–05	㉔	.0004–.0012	⑤	.0004–.0006	㉒	.00590–.02560	㉕	⑭
2.0L DOHC (3 & 5)⑩	2001–05	㉘	.0004–.0012	㉚	.0006–.0019	.0118–.0197	.01570–05510	—	—
2.0L SOHC (P)	2001–05	3.3374–3.3386	.0008–.0028	.8119–.8122	.0003–.0005	.0098–.0110	.00160–.06610	.0016–.0031	.0016–.0035
2.5L DOHC (G & L)	2001–02	⑥	.0005–.0009	.8278–.8279	.0001–.0005	⑦	.00600–.02500	⑧	⑭
3.0L (S)⑨	2001–05	㉖	.0005–.0009	.8272–.8273	-.0002 to .0001	⑯	.00590–.03540	—	—
3.0L DOHC (S)⑫	2001–05	㉖㉜	.0005–.0009	.8272–.8273	-.0002 to .0001	⑦	.00590–.03540	⑧	.0039
3.0L DOHC (1)	2005	㉞	.0007–.0016	.8271–.8273	—	㉟	.0059–.0255	—	—
3.0L OHV (U & 2)	2001–05	⑪	.0012–.0022	.9119–.9124	.0002–.0005	.00098–.0197	00098–.04920	.0016–.0037	—
3.8L OHV (4)	2001–03	⑮	.0007–.0017	.9031–.9047	.0004–.0007	.0575	⑭	.0012–.0031	—
3.9L DOHC (A)	2001–05	—	—	—	—	—	—	—	—
4.0L DOHC (N)	2005	3.952–3.9528	.0012–.0020	㊱	.0004–.0006	.0008–.0018	.0016–.0024	—	—
4.6L DOHC (R)	2001–05	⑲	-.0004 to +.0010	.8662–.8663	-.0002 to .0001	㉒	.00590–.02560	⑰	⑭
4.6L DOHC (V)㉓	2001–02	㉗	-.0004 to +.0010	.8662–.8663	-.0002 to +.0001	㉒	.00590–.02560	.0012–.0027	⑭
4.6L DOHC (V)㉑	2001–05	⑲	-.0004 to +.0010	.8662–.8663	-.0002 to +.0001	㉒	.00590–.02600	㉙	⑭
4.6L DOHC (Y)	2003–05	3.5504–3.5507	-.0004 to +.0010	.8658–.8659	.0002–.0005	④	.02560	⑧	.0019–.0079
4.6L SOHC (X)	2001–05	②	-.0020 to +.0010	.8662–.8663	-.0002 to +.0005	㉛	.00590–.02560	③	⑭
4.6L SOHC (W)	2001–02	⑳	—	.8659–.8660	.0004–.0006	.002–.006	.00600–.01200	—	—
	2003–05	⑳	-.0002–.0010	.8659–.8660	.0004–.0006	.0598–.0606	.11930–.12030	.0008–.0024	.0012–.0028
4.6L SOHC (9)	2001–02	⑳	—	.8662–.8663	.0002	.0059–.0118	.00590–.01180	—	—

DOHC — Dual Overhead Cam
OHV — Overhead Valve
SOHC — Single Overhead Cam

① — Eighth digit Vehicle Identification Number (VIN) denotes engine code.
② — Code red, 3.5506–3.5514 inches; Code blue, 3.5510–3.5518 inches; Code yellow, 3.5514–3.5522 inches.
③ — Top, .0020–.0035 inch; bottom, .0012–.0031 inch.
④ — Top, .0012 inch ; bottom, .0020 inch
⑤ — Code white, .8120–.8135 inch; Code red, .8120–.8121 inch; Code blue, .8121–.8122 inch.
⑥ — Grade 1, 3.2436–3.2444 inch; Grade 2, 3.2440–3.2449 inch; Grade 3, 3.2444–3.2452 inch.
⑦ — Top, .0039–.0197 inch; bottom, .0106–.0256 inch.
⑧ — Top, .0016–.0031 inch; bottom, .0011–.0027 inch.
⑨ — LS.
⑩ — Focus.

⑪ — Code red, 3.5024–3.5031 inch; Code blue, 3.5035–3.5041 inch; Code yellow, 3.5045–3.5051 inch.
⑫ — Sable & Taurus.
⑬ — Escort & ZX2.
⑭ — Snug fit.
⑮ — Code red, 3.8103–3.8108 inch; Code blue, 3.8108–3.8113 inch; Code yellow, 3.8113–3.8118 inch.
⑯ — Top, .0039–.0197 inch; bottom, .0106–.0256 inch.
⑰ — Top, .0004–.0009 inch; bottom, .0012–.0031 inch
⑱ — Cougar.
⑲ — Code red, 3.5499–3.5507 inch; Code blue, 3.5504–3.5510 inch; Code yellow, 3.5511–3.5515 inch.
⑳ — Code red, 3.5508–3.5514 inch; Code blue, 3.5513–3.5520 inch; Code yellow, 3.5518–3.5524 inch.
㉑ — Marauder & Mustang.
㉒ — Top, .0059–.0118 inch; bottom, .0118–.0217 inch.
㉓ — Continental.
㉔ — Class 1, 3.3378–3.3385 inch; Class 2, 3.3573–3.3358 inch.

㉕ — Top, .0016–.0028 inch; bottom, .0008–.0020 inch.
㉖ — Coated: Grade 1, 3.5035–3.5043 inch; Grade 2, 3.5039–3.5048 inch; Grade 3, 3.5043–3.5051 inch.
㉗ — Code red, 3.5495–3.5505 inches; Code blue, 3.5504–3.5510 inches; Code yellow, 3.5509–3.5515 inches.
㉘ — Grade 1, 3.3374–3.3378 inch; Grade 2, 3.3378–3.3382 inch; Grade 3, 3.3382–3.3386 inch.
㉙ — 2000–02, Top, .0004–.0009 inch; bottom, .0012–.0031 inch; 2003–04, Top, .0003–.0009 inch; bottom, .0118–.0031 inch
㉚ — Code white, .7873–7874 inch; Code red, .8120–.8121 inch.
㉛ — Top .0051–.0110 inch; bottom, .0118–.0217 inch.
㉜ — Uncoated: Grade 1, 3.5028–3.5031 inches; Grade 2, 3.5031–3.5036 inches; Grade 3, 3.5043–3.5051 inches.

㉝ — Grade 1, 3.3392–3.3395 inch;
Grade 2, 3.3395–3.3399 inch;
Grade 3, 3.3399–3.3403 inch.

㉞ — Coated: Grade 1, 3.5035–3.5043
inch; Grade 2, 3.5039–3.5048 inch;
Grade 3, 3.5043–3.5051 inch.

Uncoated: Grade 1, 3.5027–3.5031
inch; Grade 2, 3.5030–3.5036 inch;
Grade 3, 3.5035–3.5039 inch.

㉟ — Top, .0039–.0098 inch; Bottom,
.0059–.0255 inch.

㊱ — Code red, .9446–.9448 inch; Code
blue, .9448–.9449 inch.

CYLINDER BLOCK

All Measurements Given In Inches, Unless Otherwise Specified.

Engine Liter (VIN①)	Year	Cylinder Bore Diameter (Std.)	Cylinder Bore Taper Max.	Cylinder Bore Out of Round Max.
2.0L DOHC (3)	2001–05	⑦	—	—
2.0L SOHC (P)	2001–05	3.3386	.0005	.0010
2.5L DOHC (G & L)	2000–02	③	.0002	.0007
3.0L DOHC (S)	2001–05	⑤	.0008	.0006
3.0L DOHC (1)	2005	⑧	.0008	.0007
3.0L OHV (U & 2)	2001–05	3.5039	.0020	.0010
3.8L OHV (4)	2001–05	3.8115	.0020	.0020
3.9L DOHC (A)	2001–05	—	—	—
4.0L DOHC (N)	2005	3.9530	.0001	.0001
4.6L DOHC (R)	2003–05	—	.0002	.0006–.0008
4.6L DOHC (V)	2001–05	—	.0002	②
4.6L DOHC (Y)	2003–05	3.5511–3.5527	.0006	.0006
4.6L SOHC (X)	2001–02	⑥	.0276	.0276
	2003–04	④	.0276	.0276
4.6L SOHC (W & 9)	2001–02	⑥	.0010	.0015
	2003–05	3.5516–3.5522	.0005	.0006

DOHC — Dual Overhead Cam

OHV — Overhead Valve

SOHC — Single Overhead Cam

① — Eighth digit Vehicle Identification Number (VIN) denotes engine code.

② — 2000–02, .0008 inch; 2003–04 .0006 inch.

③ — Grade 1, 3.2465–3.2469; Grade 2, 3.2469–3.2473; Grade 3, 3.2473–3.2477.

④ — Code red, 3.5512–3.5516 inches; Code blue, 3.5516–3.5520 inches; Code yellow 3.5520–3.5524 inches.

⑤ — Grade 1, 3.5039–3.5043 inches; Grade 2, 3.5043–3.5047 inches; Grade 3, 3.5047–3.5051 inches.

⑥ — Code red, 3.5539–3.5544 inches; Code blue, 3.5544–3.5549 inches; Code yellow, 3.5549–3.5554 inches.

⑦ — Grade 1, 3.3386–3.3390 inches; Grade 2, 3.3390–3.3394 inches; Grade 3, 3.3394–3.3398 inches.

⑧ — Grade 1, 3.5043–3.5047 inch; Grade 2, 3.5043–3.5047 inch; Grade 3, 3.5047–3.5051 inch.

OIL PUMP

All Measurements Given In Inches, Unless Otherwise Specified.

Engine Liter (VIN①)	Year	Rotor Backlash	Rotor To Body Clearance	Rotor Endplay②	Driveshaft To Pump Body Clearance	Relief Valve To Body Clearance	Relief Spring Pressure Lbs./Inches
2.0L DOHC (3)④	2001–05	—	—	—	—	—	—
2.0L SOHC (P)	2001–05	—	.0029–.0063	.0005–.0035	—	.0008–.0031	9.3–10.3 @ 1.11
2.5L DOHC (G & L)④	—	—	—	—	—	—	—
3.0L DOHC (S)④	2001–05	—	—	—	—	—	—
3.0L DOHC (1)④	2005	—	—	—	—	—	—
3.0L OHV (U & 2)④	2001–05	—	—	—	—	—	—
3.8L OHV (4)	2001–05	.0080–.0012	.0020–.0055	.0005–.0055	③	.0017–.0029	15.2–17.1 @ 1.20
3.9L DOHC (A)④	2001–05	—	—	—	—	—	—
4.0L DOHC (N)④	2005	—	—	—	—	—	—
4.6L DOHC (R, V & Y) & SOHC (W, X & 9)④	2001–05	—	—	—	—	—	—

DOHC — Dual Overhead Cam

OHV — Overhead Valve

SOHC — Single Overhead Cam

① — Eighth digit Vehicle Identification Number (VIN) denotes engine code.

② — Measured between pump cover mounting surface & end of gear, using straightedge & feeler gauge.

③ — Driver shaft to body clearance, .0015–.0030 inch; idler shaft to idler clearance, .0005–.0017 inch.

④ — Replace as an assembly.

GENERAL MOTORS CORP.

GENERAL MOTORS CORP.

ALERO, GRAND AM & MALIBU

INDEX OF SERVICE OPERATIONS

Specifications

GENERAL ENGINE SPECIFICATIONS

Engine Liter	Fuel Injection System	Bore & Stroke	Compression Ratio	Net H.P. @ RPM②	Maximum Torque Ft. Lbs. @ RPM	Normal Oil Pressure psi
2001						
2.4L	SFI	3.54 × 3.70	9.5:1	150 @ 5600	155 @ 4400	④
3.1L	SFI	3.51 × 3.31	9.6:1	170 @ 5200	190 @ 4000	⑤
3.4L	SFI	3.62 × 3.31	9.5:1	170 @ 4800	195 @ 4000	⑤
3.4L③	SFI	3.62 × 3.31	9.5:1	175 @ 5200	205 @ 4000	⑤
2002–03						
2.2L	SFI	3.38 x 3.38	10:1	140 @ 5600	150 @ 4000	50–80①
3.1L	SFI	3.51 × 3.31	9.6:1	170 @ 5200	190 @ 4000	⑤
3.4L	SFI	3.62 × 3.31	9.5:1	170 @ 4800	195 @ 4000	⑤
3.4L③	SFI	3.62 × 3.31	9.5:1	175 @ 5200	205 @ 4000	⑤
2004–05						
2.2L	SFI	3.38 x 3.38	10.0:1	140 @ 5600	150 @ 4000	50–80①
3.4L	SFI	3.62 × 3.31	9.5:1	170 @ 4800	195 @ 4000	⑤
3.4L③	SFI	3.62 × 3.31	9.5:1	175 @ 5200	205 @ 4000	⑤
3.5L	SFI	3.70 x 3.31	9.8:1	200 @ 5400	220 @ 3200	60①

SFI — Sequential Fuel Injection
① — Oil Pressure @ 1000 RPM.
② — Ratings are as installed in vehicle.
③ — Ram air.
④ — 10 psi minimum @ 900 RPM; 30 psi minimum @ 3000 RPM.
⑤ — 15 psi @1100 RPM.

TUNE UP SPECIFICATIONS

Year & Engine	Spark Plug Gap, Inch	Ignition Timing, ° BTDC			Curb Idle Speed RPM③		Fast Idle Speed RPM		Fuel Pump Pressure, psi	Valve Lash
		Firing Order	Man. Trans.	Auto. Trans.	Mark Fig.	Man. Trans.	Auto. Trans.	Man. Trans.	Auto Trans.	

Year & Engine	Spark Plug Gap	Firing Order	Man. Trans.	Auto. Trans.	Mark Fig.	Man. Trans.	Auto. Trans.	Man. Trans.	Auto. Trans.	Fuel Pump Pressure	Valve Lash
2001											
2.4L	.050	1-3-4-2	①	①	⑤	④	④	④	④	48–55②	⑥
3.1L	.060	1-2-3-4-5-6	①	①	⑤	④	④	④	④	48–55②	⑥
3.4L	.060	1-2-3-4-5-6	—	①	⑤	—	④	—	④	48–55②	⑥
2002–05											
2.2L	.042	1-3-4-2	①	①	⑤	④	④	④	④	50–60	⑥
3.1L	.060	1-2-3-4-5-6	①	①	⑤	④	④	④	④	48–55②	⑥
3.4L	.060	1-2-3-4-5-6	—	①	⑤	—	④	—	④	48–55②	⑥
3.5L	.060	1-2-3-4-5-6	—	①	⑤	—	④	—	④	50–60	②

BTDC — Before Top Dead Center
① — Ignition timing is controlled by Powertrain Control Module (PCM).
② — Disconnect and isolate battery ground cable. Loosen fuel filler cap. Remove fuel pressure connection cap. Wrap shop towel around fuel pressure connection while connecting pressure gauge tool No. J-34730-1A, or equivalent. Connect battery ground cable and inspect fuel pressure with ignition On, but engine not running.
③ — P: Park. When adjusting idle speed, set parking brake & block drive wheels.
④ — Idle speed is controlled by an idle air control (IAC) valve or an idle speed control (ISC) motor.
⑤ — Equipped with crankshaft position sensor.
⑥ — Vehicle is equipped w/hydraulic valve lifters. No adjustment is required.

ALERO, GRAND AM & MALIBU

FRONT WHEEL ALIGNMENT SPECIFICATIONS

Model	Caster Angle, Degrees		Camber Angle, Degrees		Total Toe, Degrees	Ball Joint Wear
	Limits	Desired	Limits	Desired		
2001–03						
All	+3.10 to +5.10	+4.10	−1.20 to +.80	−.20	−.15 to +.35	①
2004–05						
Alero & Grand Am②	+3.35 to +4.85	+4.10	-.70 to +.70	.00	-.06 to +.34	①
Alero & Grand Am③	+3.35 to +4.85	+4.10	-.70 to +.70	.00	.00 to +.40	①
Malibu	+2.75 to +3.75	+3.25	-1.50 to -.50	-1.00	-.20 to +.20	①

① — Refer to "Front Suspension & Steering" section for ball joint inspection procedure.

② — With 15 inch wheels.
③ — With 16 inch wheels.

REAR WHEEL ALIGNMENT SPECIFICATIONS

Model	Camber Angle, Degrees		Total Toe, Degrees	Thrust Angle, Degrees
	Limits	Desired		
2001–03				
All	−.70 to +.30	−.20	−.26 to +.14	−.20 to +.20
2004–05				
Alero & Grand Am	-.40 to +.40	.00	-.10 to +.30	-.20 to +.20
Malibu	-1.30 to -.30	-.80	-.40 to .00	-.15 to +.15

VEHICLE RIDE HEIGHT SPECIFICATIONS

Model	Year	Body Style	Manufacturer's Original Tire Size	Front Dim.	Front Spec. Inches	Front Spec. mm	Rear Dim.	Rear Spec. Inches	Rear Spec. mm
Alero & Grand Am	2001–03	All	②	A	31.5	800	B	22.31	666
				C	9.37	238	D	9.56	243
	2004–05	All	②	C	9.33	237	D	9.61	244
Malibu	2001–03	All	②	C	9.33	237	D	9.61	244
	2004–05	All①	②	C	9.00	229	D	9.40	239
		All③	②	C	9.30	235	D	9.60	245

A Dim. — Measurement From Front Wheel Center to Check Point On Rocker Panel.
B Dim. — Measurement From Rear Wheel Center to Check Point On Rocker Panel.

C Dim. — Ground to Rocker Panel, Front.
D Dim. — Ground to Rocker Panel, Rear.
Dim. — Dimension.
① — 15 inch wheels.

② — See door sticker or inside of glove box for manufacturer's original tire size specifications.

③ — 16 inch wheels.

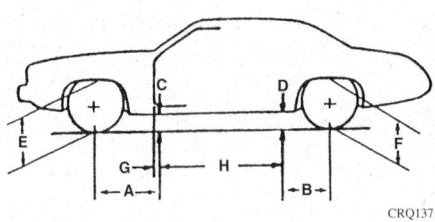

CRQ137

Fig. A

FLUID CAPACITIES & COOLING SYSTEM DATA

Year	Engine	Coolant Capacity, Qts.	Coolant Type	Surge Tank Cap Relief Pressure, psi	Thermo. Opening Temp. Deg. F	Fuel Tank Gals.	Engine Oil Refill Qts.	Transaxle Oil	
								5 Speed Manual Transaxle Pts.	Auto. Transaxle Qts.①
ALERO & GRAND AM									
2001	2.4L	10.0	Dex-Cool	15	185	14.3	4.0	3.6	②
	3.4L	12.5	Dex-Cool	15	195	14.3	4.0	3.6	②
2002	2.2L	10.0	Dex-Cool	15	195	14.1	4.0	3.6	②
	3.4L	12.5	Dex-Cool	15	195	14.3	4.0	3.6	②
2003	2.2L	8.6	Dex-Cool	15	195	14.1	5.0	3.6	②
	3.4L	13.6	Dex-Cool	15	195	14.1	4.5	3.6	②
2004–05	2.2L	8.6	Dex-Cool	15	195	14.1	5.0	3.6	②
	3.4L	13.6	Dex-Cool	15	195	14.1	4.0	3.6	②
MALIBU									
2001–03	3.1L	13.6	Dex-Cool	15	195	14.3	4.5	—	②
2004–05	2.2L	6.7	Dex-Cool	15	195	16.5	5.0	—	②
	3.5L	10.0	Dex-Cool	15	195	16.5	4.0	—	②

① — Approximate. Make final inspection w/dipstick.

② — Oil pan removal, 6.9 qts.; overhaul, 9.5 qts.; dry 12.9 qts.

LUBRICANT DATA

Year	Model	Lubricant Type				
		Transaxle		Clutch Hydraulic System	Power Steering System	Brake System
		Automatic	Manual			
2001–05	All	Dexron III	Dexron III	DOT 3	①	DOT 3

① — Power Steering Fluid, GM part No. 1052884 (pint), 1050017 (quart), or equivalent.

Electrical

NOTE: On Air Bag Equipped Models, Refer To "Air Bag System Precautions" Located In The Front Of This Manual For System Disarming & Arming Procedures.

NOTE: Refer To "Computer Relearn Procedures" Located In The Front Of This Manual When Battery Power To The Computer Has Been Interrupted.

INDEX

PRECAUTIONS

Air Bag Systems

Refer to "Air Bag System Precautions" in the front of this manual for system disarming and arming procedures.

Battery Ground Cable

Prior to service, disconnect battery ground cable and isolate as required.

FUSE PANEL & FLASHER LOCATION

The lefthand instrument panel fuse block is located behind the lefthand side of the instrument panel. The righthand instrument panel fuse block is located behind the righthand side of the instrument panel. The underhood fuse block is located on the lefthand side of the engine compartment. The turn signal and hazard flasher module is an internal component of the hazard switch located behind the center of the instrument panel.

FUEL PUMP RELAY LOCATION

The fuel pump relay is located in the engine compartment relay center on the lefthand side of the engine compartment.

RELAY CENTER LOCATION

Relays are located in all the fuse and junction blocks, refer to "Fuse Panel & Flasher Location" for relay center locations.

STARTER

REPLACE

2.2L & 3.1L Engines

1. Raise and support vehicle.
2. Remove mounting bolts and lower starter.
3. Disconnect starter electrical connectors and remove starter.
4. Reverse procedure to install, noting the following:

   a. **On models equipped with 2.2L engine, torque** starter mounting bolts to 30 ft. lbs.
   b. **On models equipped with 3.1L engine, torque** starter mounting bolts to 37 ft. lbs.

2.4L Engine

1. Remove air inlet duct from throttle body.
2. Remove starter upper mounting bolt.
3. Raise and support vehicle.
4. Remove shrouding and closeout panels.
5. Remove starter lower mounting bolt.
6. Position engine wiring harness aside.
7. Move starter to access solenoid wiring and remove starter electrical wiring.
8. Remove starter.
9. Reverse procedure to install, noting the following:

   a. **Torque** cable to solenoid nut to 108 inch lbs.
   b. **Torque** lower mounting bolt to 66 ft. lbs.
   c. **Torque** upper mounting bolt to 66 ft. lbs.

Fig. 1 Ignition coil & control module replacement. 2.4L engine

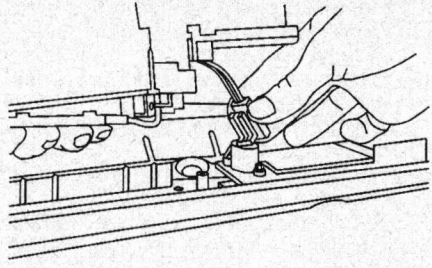

Fig. 2 Coil harness electrical connector connection. 2.4L engine

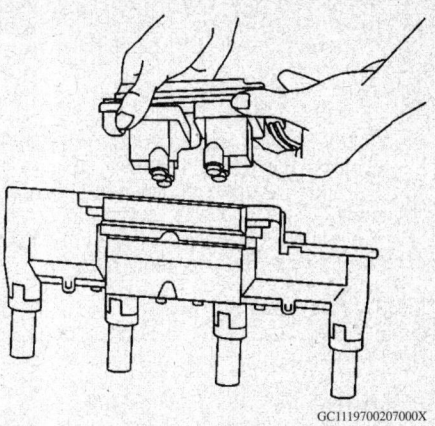

Fig. 3 Ignition coil replacement. 2.4L engine

3.4L Engine

REMOVAL

1. Raise and support vehicle.
2. Remove flywheel inspection cover.
3. Remove starter electrical connectors.
4. Remove mounting bolts and starter.

INSTALLATION

1. Tighten solenoid BAT terminal nut next to cap while starter is still on bench.
2. Connect solenoid electrical terminal.
3. **Torque** solenoid battery terminal inside nut to 84 inch lbs.
4. Install electrical connectors to starter.
5. **Torque** solenoid battery terminal outside nut to 84 inch lbs.
6. **Torque** solenoid S terminal outside nut to 22 inch lbs.
7. Install starter onto engine and **torque** mounting bolts to 32 ft. lbs.
8. Install inspection cover and **torque** bolts to 84 inch lbs.

ALTERNATOR
REPLACE
2.2L & 2.4L Engines

1. Remove serpentine drive belt using tool No. J-37059, or equivalent, to rotate tensioner.
2. Remove mounting bolts and studs.
3. Disconnect electrical leads and remove alternator.
4. Reverse procedure to install, noting the following:
   a. **On models equipped with 2.2L engine, torque** alternator mounting bolts to 16 ft. lbs.
   b. **On all models, torque** alternator electrical connector to 15 ft. lbs.
   c. **On models equipped with 2.4L engine, torque** alternator mounting bolts to 37 ft. lbs.

3.1L Engine

1. Remove serpentine drive belt.
2. Disconnect alternator electrical connectors and power steering line clip.
3. Remove alternator rear brace.
4. Disconnect alternator air inlet connector.
5. Remove mounting bolts, nuts and alternator.
6. Reverse procedure to install. **Torque** mounting bolts to 18 ft. lbs., and nut to 37 ft. lbs.

3.4L Engine

1. Remove cruise control module.
2. Remove engine mount.
3. Rotate serpentine drive belt tensioner in clockwise direction and remove belt using suitable ⅜ inch breaker bar.
4. Disconnect alternator electrical connectors and power steering line clip.
5. Remove mounting bolts, nuts and alternator.
6. Reverse procedure to install, noting the following:
   a. **Torque** alternator mounting bolts to 37 ft. lbs.
   b. **Torque** alternator mounting nuts to 22 ft. lbs.
   c. **Torque** engine mount to body bolt to 96 ft. lbs.
   d. **Torque** engine mount to body nut to 49 ft. lbs.
   e. **Torque** engine mount bracket support bolts to 96 ft. lbs.

COIL PACK
REPLACE
2.2L Engine

1. Turn ignition to Off position.
2. Disconnect mounting screws and Ignition Control Module (ICM).
3. Reverse procedure to install. **Torque** ICM mounting screws to 13 ft. lbs.

2.4L Engine
REMOVAL

1. Remove accelerator and cruise control cables from hold-down clip.
2. Remove fuel line retainer clip bolt.
3. Disconnect electronic Ignition Control Module (ICM) 11-pin electrical connector.

4. Remove ICM and coil to camshaft housing bolts, **Fig. 1.**
5. If spark plug boots adhere to plugs, twist and pull upward on retainers using remover tool No. J-36011, or equivalent.
6. Remove coil and ICM.
7. Remove housing to cover screws. Ensure ground strap remains in place.
8. Disconnect coil harness electrical connector and remove housing from cover, **Fig. 2.**
9. Remove ignition coil(s), **Fig. 3.**
10. Disconnect coil electrical connectors.
11. Remove contact springs from housing.
12. Remove coil seals.

INSTALLATION

1. Install new seals into ignition coils.
2. Install contact springs into housing using petroleum jelly to keep them in place.
3. Connect coil electrical connector.
4. Install coils into housing.
5. Connect ground strap.
6. Connect coil(s) electrical connector to ICM, ensuring ground strap stays in place.
7. Install housing to cover.
8. Install housing to cover screws. **Torque** to 35 inch lbs.
9. Install spark plug boots and retainers to housing.
10. Install coil and ICM to engine, carefully aligning boots to plug terminals.
11. Coat coil and ICM to camshaft housing bolts with GM Loctite sealant part No. 12346004, or equivalent.
12. Install bolts with isolator washer rubber sides facing down and **torque** to 16 ft. lbs.
13. Connect ICM 11-pin electrical connector.
14. Install fuel line retainer clip bolt.
15. Install accelerator and cruise control cables into hold-down clip.

3.1L Engine

1. Disconnect ignition control module electrical connectors.
2. Remove spark plug wires from ignition coils.
3. Remove mounting screws and ignition coils.

4. Reverse procedure to install. **Torque** mounting screws to 40 inch lbs.

3.4L Engine

1. Tag spark plug wires routing and disconnect them from ignition coils.
2. Remove mounting screws and ignition coils.
3. Reverse procedure to install. **Torque** mounting screws to 40 inch lbs.

IGNITION LOCK
REPLACE
Alero

1. Remove ignition switch bezel using suitable flatbladed screwdriver.
2. Remove radio as outlined under "Radio, Replace."
3. Insert key and turn ignition switch lock cylinder to On position.
4. Remove ignition lock cylinder while rotating.
5. Reverse procedure to install.

Grand Am

1. Apply parking brake and place shift lever in the LOW position.
2. Remove ignition switch bezel with a suitable flat-bladed tool.
3. Disengage accessory trim plate from center of instrument panel.
4. Disconnect accessory trim plate electrical connectors, then remove cigar lighter from trim plate.
5. Remove accessory switch mounting plate bracket bolts and bracket.
6. Remove accessory trim plate from center of instrument panel.
7. Insert key and turn ignition switch lock cylinder to On position.
8. Depress ignition lock cylinder detent with a suitable L-shaped hex wrench, then pull lock cylinder out with key.
9. Reverse procedure to install.

Malibu

Refer to "Ignition Switch, Replace" for lock cylinder replacement.

IGNITION SWITCH
REPLACE
Alero

1. Remove radio as outlined under "Radio, Replace."
2. Remove instrument panel cluster as outlined under "Instrument Cluster, Replace."
3. Remove ignition switch mounting bolts.
4. Position ignition switch to cluster opening for access.
5. Remove mounting bolts and ignition switch bracket.
6. Install key and turn lock cylinder to On position.
7. Depress transaxle park lock cable retainer to release cable.

8. Remove ignition switch lock cylinder by depressing retaining tab and pulling cylinder out with key.
9. Disconnect ignition switch pass lock electrical connector.
10. Disconnect ignition switch electrical connectors.
11. Remove ignition switch through cluster opening.
12. Reverse procedure to install. **Torque** mounting bolts to 53 inch lbs.

Grand Am

1. Remove instrument cluster as outlined under "Instrument Cluster, Replace.".
2. Remove mounting bolts and ignition switch.
3. Disconnect electrical connectors.
4. Disconnect ignition lock cable from switch.
5. Insert key into ignition lock cylinder and turn to Run position.
6. Depress cylinder release plunger and remove cylinder by pulling key.
7. Reverse procedure to install.

Malibu

1. Remove lefthand sound insulator, ignition switch trim ring and accessory trim plates, then the instrument cluster.
2. Remove mounting bolts, electrical connectors and console trim plate.
3. Remove ignition lock cable from shift lever and bracket at console front.
4. Remove ignition switch.
5. Reverse procedure to install. **Torque** ignition switch mounting bolts to 18 inch lbs.

CLUTCH START SWITCH
REPLACE

1. Disconnect switch electrical connector.
2. Remove mounting nuts and switch.
3. Reverse procedure to install. Inspect switch for proper operation.

NEUTRAL SAFETY SWITCH
REPLACE
Removal

1. Disconnect switch electrical connector.
2. Remove mounting nut and shift linkage.
3. Remove shift linkage lever.
4. Mark switch position for installation alignment.
5. Remove mounting screws and switch.

Installation

1. Place shift shaft in Neutral position and align flats on shaft with those on switch.
2. Loosely install switch with marks properly aligned.
3. If original switch is being installed, proceed as follows:

a. Insert 3/32 inch drill bit into switch adjustment hole.
b. Move switch until drill bit drops to depth of 9/64 inch.
c. **Torque** switch mounting screws to 18 ft. lbs.
d. Remove drill bit.
4. New switches are pinned in Neutral position. If installation is difficult, ensure shift shaft is in Neutral. **Do not rotate switch.**
5. **Torque** switch mounting screws to 18 ft. lbs.

HEADLAMP SWITCH
REPLACE

Refer to "Multi-Function Switch, Replace" for replacement procedure.

STOP LIGHT SWITCH
REPLACE
Removal

1. Remove lefthand side instrument panel insulator.
2. Disconnect stop lamp switch electrical connector.
3. Remove switch retainer by grasping and turning 90° counterclockwise and pulling toward rear of vehicle.
4. Remove stop lamp switch.

Installation

1. Insert stop lamp switch into retainer until switch body has seated onto retainer.
2. Pull brake pedal upward against its internal stop.
3. Adjust switch so its plunger extends no more than .78 inch beyond threaded portion when brake pedal is fully released.
4. Rotate switch 90° clockwise until it locks into position.
5. Connect switch electrical connector.

MULTI-FUNCTION SWITCH
REPLACE
Alero & Grand Am

1. Remove steering column trim panels.
2. Remove multi-function switch mounting screws.
3. Disconnect switch electrical connectors.
4. Remove switch from steering column.
5. Reverse procedure to install.

Malibu

1. Remove horn pad and steering wheel as outlined under "Steering Wheel, Replace."
2. Position spark plug boot, or other suitable device, over tilt lever and remove steering column tilt lever using suitable locking pliers.

3. Remove steering column upper and lower covers, then the dampener.
4. Remove mounting screw and switch, **Fig. 4.**
5. Reverse procedure to install.

TURN SIGNAL SWITCH
REPLACE

Refer to "Multi-Function Switch, Replace" for replacement procedure.

STEERING WHEEL
REPLACE

1. Disarm driver's air bag module as outlined in "Air Bag System Precautions."
2. Remove mounting screws for horn pad or air bag module.
3. **On models equipped with radio controls,** remove wire protector plate connector.
4. **On all models,** remove horn pad or air bag module and horn lead, then the steering wheel retainer and nut.
5. Remove steering wheel using puller tool No. J-1859-A and legs tool No. J-42120, or equivalent.
6. Reverse procedure to install, noting the following:
   a. **Torque** steering wheel nut to 27–30 ft. lbs.
   b. **Torque** air bag module screws to 89 inch lbs.

INSTRUMENT CLUSTER
REPLACE

1. Remove steering column covers.
2. Remove instrument panel cluster trim plate mounting screws then the trim plate.
3. Remove instrument cluster to instrument panel mounting screws.
4. Disconnect cluster electrical connectors and remove instrument cluster.
5. Reverse procedure to install.

RADIO
REPLACE

Alero & Grand Am

1. Remove accessory trim plate.
2. Remove radio mounting screws.
3. Pull radio rearward.
4. Disconnect electrical connectors and antenna lead-in.
5. Reverse procedure to install.

Malibu

1. Remove ignition key trim cover using suitable flat-bladed pry tool.
2. Pull accessory trim plate to rear and remove.
3. Remove mounting screws and pull radio to rear.
4. Disconnect electrical connectors and antenna lead-in.
5. Remove radio.

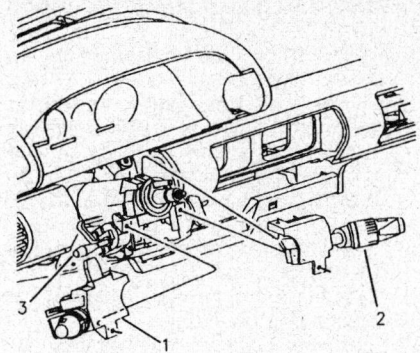

1 HEADLAMP/TURN SIGNAL/CRUISE CONTROL HAZARD SWITCH
2 WINDSHIELD WIPER/WASHER SWITCH
3 TILT LEVER (IF EQUIPPED)

GC9049200112000A

Fig. 4 Multi-function switch replacement. Malibu

6. Reverse procedure to install.

WIPER MOTOR
REPLACE

Alero & Grand Am

1. Remove wiper arms from shafts.
2. Remove cowl air inlet grille.
3. Disconnect wiper motor electrical connector.
4. Remove three wiper drive system mounting screws.
5. Remove wiper transmission from crank arm using separator tool No. J-39232, or equivalent.
6. Remove two mounting screws and motor.
7. Reverse procedure to install, noting the following:
   a. **Torque** motor to tube frame mounting screws to 89 inch lbs.
   b. Install transmission assembly onto crank arm using installer tool No. J-39529, or equivalent.
   c. **Torque** drive system module mounting screws to 89 inch lbs.

Malibu

1. Remove wiper arm and blade.
2. Remove cowl cover.
3. Disconnect drive link from crank arm using wiper transmission separator tool No. J-39232, or equivalent.
4. Disconnect wiper motor electrical connectors.
5. Remove mounting screws and wiper motor.
6. Reverse procedure to install, noting the following:
   a. **Torque** motor mounting screws to 84 inch lbs.
   b. Connect drive link to crank arm

WIPER SWITCH
REPLACE

Refer to "Multi-Function Switch, Replace" for replacement procedure.

WIPER TRANSMISSION
REPLACE

Alero & Grand Am

1. Remove wiper arms from transmission shafts.
2. Remove air inlet screen from cowl panel.
3. Disconnect wiper motor electrical connector.
4. Remove mounting screws and wiper transmission.
5. Disconnect motor crank arm from transmission using separator tool No. J-39232, or equivalent.
6. Remove transmission cap.
7. Remove four mounting screws and transmission from tube frame.
8. Remove three grommets from tube frame and transmission.
9. Remove motor from tube frame.
10. Reverse procedure to install, noting the following:
    a. **Torque** wiper transmission to tube frame screws to 79 inch lbs.
    b. Install transmission onto crank arm using installer tool No. J-39529, or equivalent.
    c. **Torque** wiper transmission mounting screws to 79 inch lbs.

Malibu

1. Remove wiper arm and blades.
2. Remove cowl cover and disconnect wiper motor connector.
3. Remove mounting screws and wiper drive system module.
4. Remove wiper motor as outlined under "Wiper Motor, Replace."
5. Remove caps, wiper motor grommets and transmission.
6. Reverse procedure to install. **Torque** mounting screws to 72 inch lbs.

BLOWER MOTOR
REPLACE

The blower motor and fan are located in the lower righthand corner of the Heating, Ventilation and Air Conditioning (HVAC) module. The fan and motor are serviced only as a complete assembly.

1. Remove righthand closeout panel and insulator.
2. **On Alero and Grand Am models,** position Body Control Module (BCM) aside.
3. **On all models,** disconnect blower motor electrical connectors.

4. Remove mounting screws, blower motor and fan.
5. Reverse procedure to install. **Torque** blower motor mounting screws to 45 inch lbs.

HEATER CORE
REPLACE

Alero & Grand Am

1. Drain coolant into suitable container.
2. Recover A/C refrigerant as outlined in "Air Conditioning" chapter.
3. Raise and support vehicle.
4. Remove evaporator hose assembly nut from evaporator.
5. Remove evaporator hose assembly from evaporator.
6. Remove and discard seal washers.
7. Remove inlet and outlet heater hoses from heater core.
8. Remove drain tube elbow from evaporator block heater case plate
9. Remove nuts holding heater case plate for heater pipes.
10. Remove heater case plate and seals for heater pipes.
11. Remove nuts holding heater case plate for evaporator block.
12. Remove heater case plate and seal for evaporator block.
13. Remove nut for HVAC module assembly bracket.
14. Lower vehicle.
15. Pull door weatherstrip from windshield side upper garnish molding, as required.
16. Remove windshield side upper garnish molding by disconnecting clips.
17. Remove defroster grill by disconnecting retainers using suitable small flat bladed tool.
18. Remove instrument panel endcaps by pulling outward.
19. Remove righthand sound insulator and disconnect heater hose form duct.
20. Remove mounting screws and lefthand sound insulator.
21. Remove mounting screws under glove compartment door and open door.
22. Remove pocket mounting screws and glove compartment. Disconnect compartment lamp electrical connector.
23. Remove passenger's air bag module.
24. Position front seats to most rearward position.
25. Position emergency brake lever to full up position.
26. Position gear selector to NEUTRAL position.
27. Release front floor console trim plate using suitable small flat bladed tool.
28. Remove trim plate by rotating 90° and guiding it over shift handle.
29. Position shift lever fully rearward.
30. Remove mounting screws and console cupholder.
31. Remove ignition switch bezel using suitable small flat blade tool.
32. Remove instrument panel accessory trim plate by pulling from storage compartment to release retainers.
33. Disconnect cigarette lighter and hazard warning switch electrical connectors.
34. Remove cigarette lighter fuse and element.
35. Remove cigarette lighter socket by placing one side of T portion of cigarette lighter socket remover tool No. J-42059, or equivalent, into tab window and then other should be angled into opposite tab window.
36. Pull lighter socket straight out and remove tool.
37. Disconnect cigarette lighter socket electrical connector.
38. Remove cigarette lighter retainer.
39. Remove mounting screws and hazard warning switch retainer bracket.
40. Remove flasher and switch from switch retainer bracket using suitable small flat bladed tool to depress and release flasher retainers, while pressing flasher and switch.
41. Remove flasher and switch from switch retainer bracket.
42. Remove lower steering column trim cover mounting screws.
43. Remove upper column trim cover by tilting up and unsnapping from lower column trim cover hinges.
44. Remove tilt steering wheel lever by pulling retaining pin and snapping out.
45. Remove lower column trim cover.
46. Remove lower and upper mounting screws, then the instrument panel cluster trim plate.
47. Remove mounting screws and instrument panel cluster. Disconnect electrical connector.
48. Remove mounting screws and radio. Disconnect instrument panel wiring harness and antenna cable connectors.
49. Remove steering wheel as outlined under "Steering Wheel, Replace."
50. Remove steering column as outlined in "Steering Columns" chapter.
51. Position shift lever fully rearward.
52. Remove mounting screws, then the cupholder by lifting up and rearward to clear storage compartment.
53. Disconnect storage compartment lamp from cupholder.
54. Lift up front floor console armrest and remove rubber mat from storage compartment.
55. Remove storage compartment rear mounting bolts.
56. Remove center bolts from console sides.
57. Remove covers using suitable small flat bladed tool at front edge, then the front mounting screws.
58. Remove bracket front mounting nuts.
59. Remove floor console by pulling up and rearward, guiding emergency brake lever boot over emergency brake lever.
60. Remove ignition switch mounting bolts. Position ignition switch for ease of removal.
61. Remove ignition switch mounting bolts and bracket.
62. Insert key and turn ignition switch lock cylinder to ACC position.
63. Depress retainer and remove transaxle park/lock cable.
64. Remove ignition switch lock cylinder by depressing retaining tab and pulling cylinder out with key.
65. Disconnect pass lock and ignition switch electrical connectors.
66. Remove ignition switch.
67. Remove fog lamp/dimmer switch/vent trim plate using suitable small flat bladed tool. Disconnect electrical connectors.
68. Remove fog lamp switch using suitable small flat bladed tool on back side to release retainer tabs.
69. Remove instrument panel upper bolt covers.
70. Disconnect electrical junction box electrical connections.
71. Remove instrument panel to cross vehicle beam mounting screws.
72. Remove instrument panel.
73. Remove heater-A/C (HVAC) module support bracket.
74. Remove bolts from bracket attaching cross vehicle beam to HVAC module.
75. Remove cross vehicle beam to left-hand hinge pillar attaching bolts.
76. Remove cross vehicle beam to right-hand hinge pillar attaching bolts.
77. Remove cross vehicle beam from vehicle.
78. Remove daytime running lights (DRL) sensor wiring harness clip from HVAC module assembly.
79. Disconnect instrument panel lamp dimmer switch electrical connector.
80. Remove wiring harness clips from HVAC module assembly bracket.
81. Disconnect vacuum hose from vacuum tank.
82. Disconnect blower motor resistor and blower motor electrical connectors.
83. Disconnect temperature actuator electrical connector.
84. Remove HVAC module assembly.
85. Turn HVAC module assembly over.
86. Remove heater core case cover.
87. Remove heater core bracket and screw.
88. Remove heater core.
89. Reverse procedure to install, noting the following:
    a. **Torque** core mounting clamps to 12 inch lbs.
    b. **Torque** cover screws to 12 inch lbs.
    c. **Torque** floor air outlet screws to 12 inch lbs.
    d. Close radiator petcock, fill cooling system and inspect for leaks.

Malibu

1. Drain coolant into suitable container.
2. Remove heater hoses and drain tube.
3. Remove windshield side upper garnish molding by pulling windshield side upper garnish molding rearward to release tabs.
4. Remove defroster grille by unsnapping and lifting upward.
5. Remove end caps pulling outward in finger pull area.
6. Remove mounting screws under glove compartment door.
7. Open door and remove mounting screws inside pocket.
8. Disconnect glove compartment lamp

switch electrical connection.

9. Remove glove compartment.
10. Remove push pins and lefthand halve of lefthand side sound insulator.
11. Remove mounting bolts and righthand halve of lefthand side sound insulator.
12. Remove push pin and righthand side of righthand side sound insulator.
13. Remove mounting bolts and lefthand side of righthand side sound insulator.
14. Remove passenger's air bag module.
15. Remove driver's air bag module.
16. Remove steering wheel as outlined under "Steering Wheel, Replace."
17. Disconnect electrical connectors.
18. Remove mounting screw and multi-function switch, then disconnect electrical connectors.
19. Remove steering column stalks.
20. Remove mounting screws and instrument panel cluster trim plate by gently prying out using suitable small flat bladed tool.
21. Disconnect dimmer and hazard warning switches electrical connectors.
22. Remove ignition switch trim cover by prying off with suitable small flat bladed tool.
23. Remove accessory trim plate by gently prying with suitable small flat bladed tool to disconnect retainers.
24. Disconnect cigarette lighter electrical connector.
25. Remove cigarette lighter housing from trim plate.
26. Remove mounting screws and instrument cluster by pull rearward. Disconnect electrical connector.
27. Recover air conditioning refrigerant as outlined in "Air Conditioning" chapter.
28. Raise and support vehicle.
29. Drain engine coolant into suitable container.
30. Remove righthand wheel housing splash shield.
31. Remove evaporator hose nut from accumulator using suitable back-up wrench. Discard O-ring seal.
32. Remove mounting bolt and evaporator hose from condenser. Discard O-ring seal.
33. Remove mounting nut and evaporator hose from evaporator. Discard O-ring seal.
34. Unfasten two mounting clips and evaporator hose.
35. Lower vehicle.
36. Disconnect heater hose from heater pipe by squeezing quick-connect tabs.
37. Remove heater hose with quick-connect.
38. Remove heater hose and clamps from heater core.
39. Raise and support vehicle.

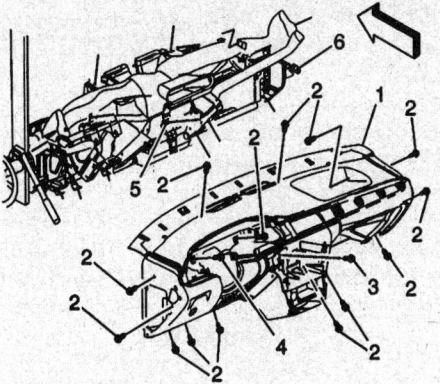

(1) Instrument Panel Assembly
(2) Screws (Tighten Last in Random Order)
(3) Screw (Tighten 1st)
(4) Screw (Tighten 2nd)
(5) Locator Pin
(6) Tie Bar Assembly

GC9149700134000X

Fig. 5 Exploded view of instrument panel. Malibu

40. Remove evaporator block heater case plate drain tube elbow.
41. Remove mounting nuts, heater pipes' heater case plate and seals.
42. Remove mounting nuts, evaporator block heater case plate and seal.
43. Remove HVAC module bracket mounting nut.
44. Lower vehicle.
45. Remove mounting bolts and radio.
46. Disconnect radio electrical connectors and antenna lead.
47. Remove mounting nuts and pull tape player out to access electrical connector.
48. Disconnect electrical connector and remove tape player.
49. Remove ignition switch mounting bolts and disconnect electrical connectors.
50. Insert key into ignition switch key cylinder, rotate key to RUN position.
51. Depress park lock cable tab and remove cable from ignition switch housing.
52. Press cylinder release plunger located at four o'clock position on ignition switch housing.
53. Pull cylinder from ignition switch housing using key.
54. Disconnect Pass Key electrical connector.
55. Remove ignition switch.
56. Position front seat forward and remove seat adjuster mounting bolts.
57. Disconnect lefthand side seat belt wiring harness.
58. Disconnect lefthand side power seat

electrical connector, as required.
59. Manually tilt forward, disconnect floor pan hooks and remove front seats.
60. Fold console compartment up.
61. Remove gear shift lever handle by pulling retainer pin and upward on handle.
62. Remove console trim plate by gently pry upward to disconnect retainers.
63. Remove rear cupholder.
64. Remove mounting screws and console.
65. Remove ashtray.
66. Remove instrument panel to tie bar mounting screws, **Fig. 5.**
67. Remove instrument panel.
68. Remove instrument panel and console as outlined in "Dash Panel Service."
69. Remove heater outlet, mounting screw and heater core cover.
70. Remove mounting clamps and heater core.
71. Reverse procedure to install.

EVAPORATOR CORE
REPLACE
Alero & Grand Am

1. Recover air conditioning refrigerant as outlined in "Air Conditioning" chapter.
2. Remove heater core as outlined under "Heater Core, Replace."
3. Remove evaporator core bracket.
4. Remove evaporator core.
5. Reverse procedure to install, noting the following:
   a. **Torque** evaporator mounting screws to 12 inch lbs.
   b. **Torque** heater core shroud and straps screws to 12 inch lbs.
   c. **Torque** heater cover screws to 12 inch lbs.
   d. **Torque** floor duct screws to 12 inch lbs.
   e. **Torque** evaporator hose fitting bolt to 18 ft. lbs.
   f. **On all models,** evacuate and charge refrigerant system.

Malibu

1. Recover air conditioning refrigerant as outlined in "Air Conditioning" chapter.
2. Drain coolant into suitable container.
3. Remove HVAC assembly as outlined under "Heater Core, Replace."
4. Remove thermal expansion valve screw, then the thermal expansion valve.
5. Remove and discard sealing washers
6. Remove evaporator core.
7. Reverse procedure to install. Use new sealing washers.

2.2L Engine

NOTE: On Air Bag Equipped Models, Refer To "Air Bag System Precautions" Located In The Front Of This Manual For System Disarming & Arming Procedures.

NOTE: Refer To "Computer Relearn Procedures" Located In The Front Of This Manual When Battery Power To The Computer Has Been Interrupted.

INDEX

PRECAUTIONS

Air Bag Systems

Refer to "Air Bag System Precautions" in the front of this manual for system disarming and arming procedures.

Battery Ground Cable

Prior to service, disconnect battery ground cable and isolate as required.

Fuel System Pressure Relief

1. Disconnect battery ground cable and isolate as required.
2. Install fuel pressure gauge tool No. J34730-1A, or equivalent.
3. Install bleed hose into suitable container and open valve to bleed system pressure.
4. Disconnect fuel pressure gauge from fuel pressure connection.

COMPRESSION PRESSURE

When inspecting cylinder compression, the engine should be at room temperature, the throttle should be open, the spark plugs removed and the battery at full charge. The lowest reading cylinder should not be less than 70% of the highest and no cylinder reading should be less than 100 psi. Turn ignition key until engine cranks through four compression cycles per cylinder. Normal compression builds up quickly and evenly to specified compression on each cylinder.

ENGINE MOUNT
REPLACE

1. Remove cruise control module.
2. Support engine with suitable wooden block and suitable floor jack positioned below oil pan.
3. Remove engine mount mounting nuts.
4. Remove engine mount to bracket bolts.
5. Remove engine mount.
6. Reverse procedure to install.

ENGINE
REPLACE

Automatic Transaxle

1. Open and support hood. Install suitable protective covering over fenders. Mark upper hood hinge location to hood with suitable grease pencil. Remove hood with assistance.
2. Remove air cleaner resonator to accelerator bracket bolt.
3. Remove throttle body resonator, air cleaner intake duct and vent hose.
4. Remove accelerator cable and cruise control cable.
5. Disconnect brake booster hose.
6. Remove power steering pump.
7. Disconnect fuel lines.
8. Drain coolant into suitable container.
9. Remove radiator inlet hose.

10. Remove surge tank to cylinder head hose.
11. Disconnect surge tank to radiator outlet hose.
12. Remove radiator outlet hose.
13. Remove inlet and outlet heater hoses.
14. Remove surge tank outlet hose mounting bolt to intake manifold.
15. Disconnect electrical connectors to engine components.
16. Remove engine electrical harness.
17. Remove upper transmission bellhousing mounting bolts.
18. Raise and support vehicle.
19. Remove front fender liner.
20. Rotate drive belt tensioner clockwise.
21. Remove serpentine drive belt.
22. Remove air conditioning compressor.
23. Remove crankshaft balancer bolt using harmonic balancer holder tool No. J38122-A, or equivalent, to ensure crankshaft does not rotate while loosening mounting bolt.
24. Remove crankshaft balancer.
25. Disconnect alternator electrical connectors.
26. Disconnect starter motor electrical connectors.
27. Drain engine oil into suitable container.
28. Disconnect front exhaust pipe from manifold.
29. Raise and support vehicle.
30. Remove mounting bolts and lower starter.
31. Disconnect starter electrical connectors and remove starter.
32. Remove flywheel to torque converter bolts.
33. Remove lower transmission bellhousing bolts.
34. Remove transmission to engine brace.

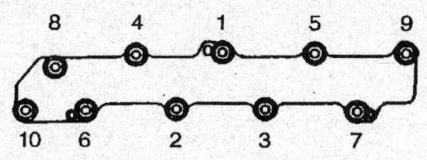

Fig. 1 Exhaust manifold tightening sequence

35. Lower vehicle.
36. Install engine bracket tool No. J42451, or equivalent, to righthand rear side of cylinder head.
37. Install suitable engine hoist to engine.
38. Remove cruise control module.
39. Support engine with suitable wooden block and suitable floor jack positioned below oil pan.
40. Remove engine mount mounting nuts.
41. Remove engine mount to bracket bolts.
42. Remove engine mount.
43. Remove upper transmission bellhousing bolts.
44. Separate engine from transmission.
45. Remove engine.
46. Reverse procedure to install.

Manual Transaxle

1. Open and support hood. Install suitable protective covering over fenders. Mark upper hood hinge location to hood with suitable grease pencil. Remove hood with assistance.
2. Remove air cleaner resonator to accelerator bracket bolt.
3. Disconnect accelerator and cruise cables.
4. Disconnect brake booster hose.
5. Remove power steering pump.
6. Disconnect engine fuel lines.
7. Disconnect transmission shift control cables from bracket.
8. Disconnect clutch actuator cylinder line.
9. Drain engine coolant into suitable container.
10. Remove engine radiator inlet hose.
11. Remove cylinder head surge tank hose.
12. Disconnect surge tank outlet hose to radiator.
13. Remove surge tank outlet hose to intake manifold.
14. Remove radiator outlet hose to engine.
15. Remove inlet and outlet heater hoses.
16. Disconnect electrical connectors to engine sensors and switches.
17. Remove engine harness and set aside.
18. Raise and support vehicle.
19. Remove drive axles and front crossmember as outlined under appropriate transaxle chapter in **MOTOR's** "Domestic Transmission Manual, In-Vehicle Service."
20. Remove front fender liner.
21. Rotate drive belt tensioner clockwise.
22. Remove serpentine drive belt.
23. Remove air conditioning compressor.
24. Disconnect alternator and starter electrical connectors.

25. Drain engine oil into suitable container.
26. Disconnect front exhaust pipe from manifold.
27. Support front of engine using suitable block of wood at oil pan, lower vehicle onto engine support table.
28. Remove cruise control module.
29. Remove engine mount mounting nuts.
30. Remove engine mount to bracket bolts.
31. Remove engine mount.
32. Remove transmission mount mounting bolts to frame.
33. Raise vehicle from engine and transmission.
34. Install engine lift bracket tool No. J42451, or equivalent, to righthand rear of cylinder head.
35. Install suitable engine hoist to engine.
36. Remove transmission bellhousing mounting bolts.
37. Remove engine from transmission and mount it to suitable engine stand.
38. Reverse procedure to install.

INTAKE MANIFOLD
REPLACE

1. Remove air inlet duct and resonator.
2. Disconnect IAC, TPS and MAP sensor.
3. Disconnect EVAP and PCV hose.
4. Disconnect purge solenoid tube and brake booster hose.
5. Remove oil dipstick tube bolt.
6. Disconnect accelerator and cruise control cables.
7. Remove throttle body and fuel rail.
8. Remove KS connector from intake manifold.
9. Remove mounting nuts, bolts and intake manifold.
10. Reverse procedure to install.

EXHAUST MANIFOLD
REPLACE

1. Remove exhaust manifold heat shield.
2. Remove oxygen sensor.
3. Raise and support vehicle.
4. Remove manifold to exhaust flex decoupler mounting bolts.
5. Pull down and back on exhaust pipe in order to disconnect pipe from exhaust manifold.
6. Lower vehicle.
7. Remove exhaust manifold to cylinder head mounting nuts.
8. Remove exhaust manifold, clean sealing surfaces.
9. Reverse procedure to install. **Torque** exhaust manifold to cylinder head mounting nuts to 106 inch lbs., in sequence, **Fig. 1**.

CYLINDER HEAD
REPLACE

1. Remove air inlet duct and resonator.
2. Disconnect IAC, TPS and MAP sensor.
3. Disconnect EVAP and PCV hose.
4. Disconnect purge solenoid tube and brake booster hose.
5. Remove oil dipstick tube bolt.
6. Disconnect accelerator and cruise control cables.

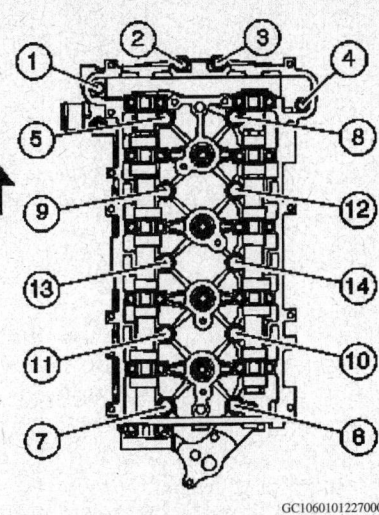

Fig. 2 Cylinder head bolt loosening

7. Remove throttle body and fuel rail.
8. Remove KS connector from intake manifold.
9. Remove mounting nuts, bolts and intake manifold.
10. Remove power steering pump.
11. Remove exhaust manifold heat shield.
12. Remove oxygen sensor.
13. Raise and support vehicle.
14. Remove manifold to exhaust flex decoupler mounting bolts.
15. Pull down and back on exhaust pipe in order to disconnect pipe from exhaust manifold.
16. Lower vehicle.
17. Remove exhaust manifold to cylinder head mounting nuts.
18. Remove exhaust manifold, clean sealing surfaces.
19. Remove timing chain as outlined under "Timing Chain, Replace."
20. Drain coolant system into suitable container.
21. Remove cylinder head bolts in sequence, **Fig. 2**. Discard bolts.
22. Remove cylinder head and gasket.
23. Reverse procedure to install, noting the following:
    a. Install new cylinder head bolts.
    b. **Torque** cylinder head bolts to 22 ft. lbs., in sequence, **Fig. 3**.
    c. Tighten head bolts an additional 155°.
    d. **Torque** front cylinder head bolts to 26 ft. lbs., **Fig. 4**.

VALVE COVER
REPLACE

1. Loosen vent hose clamp at air cleaner resonator, air cleaner intake duct clamp at air cleaner outlet resonator.
2. Loosen air cleaner outlet resonator to throttle body clamp, located forward of accelerator cable bracket. Remove air cleaner resonator to accelerator bracket bolt.
3. Remove throttle body resonator, air cleaner intake duct and vent hose.
4. Disconnect accelerator and cruise

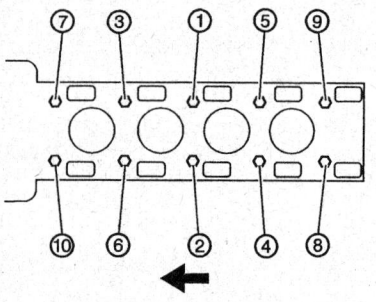

Fig. 3   Cylinder head bolt tightening sequence

control cables from throttle body, then the bracket.
5. Remove PCV valve.
6. Remove fuel line brackets and brake booster hose pipe from brackets.
7. Remove mounting screw, ignition coil and Ignition Control Module (ICM).
8. Remove ground strap.
9. Remove mounting bolts and camshaft cover.
10. Reverse procedure to install.

VALVE ADJUSTMENT

This engine is equipped with hydraulic valve lash adjusters. No adjustment is required.

VALVE LASH ADJUSTERS
REPLACE

Refer to "Camshaft, Replace" for valve lash adjuster replacement procedure.

CRANKSHAFT DAMPER
REPLACE

1. Raise and support vehicle.
2. Remove front tire and wheel assembly.
3. Remove front fender liner.
4. Rotate drive belt tensioner clockwise.
5. Remove serpentine drive belt.
6. Prevent crankshaft from rotating by install harmonic balancer holder tool No. J38122A, or equivalent.
7. Remove mounting bolt and crankshaft balancer. Discard bolt.
8. Reverse procedure to install.

FRONT COVER
REPLACE

1. Raise and support vehicle.
2. Remove front fender liner.
3. Rotate drive belt tensioner clockwise.
4. Remove serpentine drive belt.
5. Remove crankshaft balancer bolt using harmonic balancer holder tool No. J38122-A, or equivalent, to ensure crankshaft does not rotate while loosening mounting bolt.
6. Remove crankshaft balancer.
7. Remove engine front cover to water pump bolts, **Fig. 5**.
8. Remove remaining engine front cover mounting bolts.

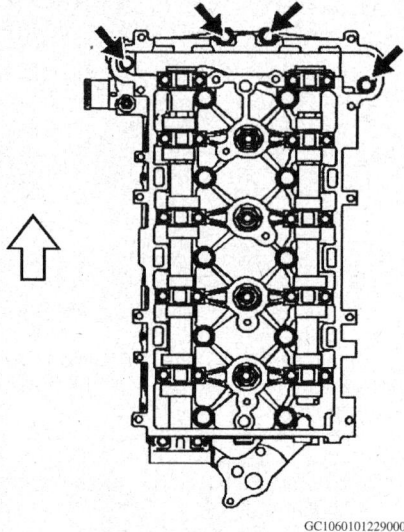

Fig. 4   Front cylinder head bolt tightening

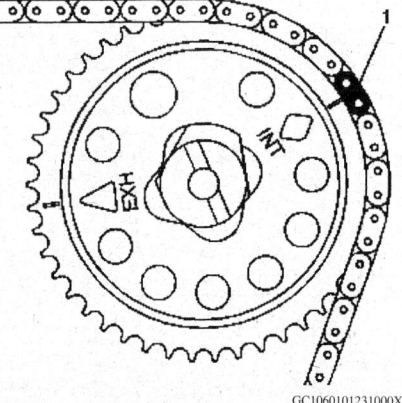

Fig. 6   Timing chain copper link alignment

9. Remove engine front cover gasket.
10. Reverse procedure to install.

TIMING CHAIN
REPLACE
Removal

1. Loosen vent hose clamp at air cleaner resonator, air cleaner intake duct clamp at air cleaner outlet resonator.
2. Loosen air cleaner outlet resonator to throttle body clamp, located forward of accelerator cable bracket. Remove air cleaner resonator to accelerator bracket bolt.
3. Remove throttle body resonator, air cleaner intake duct and vent hose.
4. Disconnect accelerator and cruise control cables from throttle body, then the bracket.
5. Remove PCV valve.
6. Remove fuel line brackets and brake booster hose pipe from brackets.
7. Remove mounting screw, ignition coil and Ignition Control Module (ICM).
8. Remove ground strap.

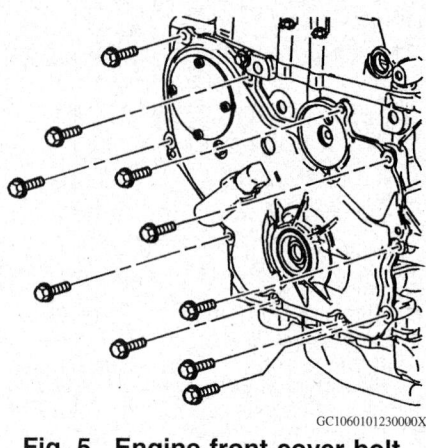

Fig. 5   Engine front cover bolt replacement

9. Remove mounting bolts and camshaft cover.
10. Raise and support vehicle.
11. Remove front fender liner.
12. Rotate drive belt tensioner clockwise.
13. Remove serpentine drive belt.
14. Remove crankshaft balancer bolt using harmonic balancer holder tool No. J38122-A, or equivalent, to ensure crankshaft does not rotate while loosening mounting bolt.
15. Remove crankshaft balancer.
16. Remove engine front cover to water pump bolts, **Fig. 5**.
17. Remove remaining engine front cover mounting bolts.
18. Remove engine front cover gasket.
19. Rotate engine until crankshaft sprocket mark aligns with second silver link at five o'clock position.
20. Lower vehicle.
21. Ensure intake camshaft sprocket INT diamond is aligned with copper link at two o'clock position, **Fig. 6**.
22. Ensure exhaust camshaft sprocket EXH triangle is aligned with silver link at 10 o'clock position, **Fig. 7**.
23. Remove timing chain tensioner.
24. Remove fixed timing chain guide access plug.
25. Remove fixed timing chain guide, **Fig. 8**.
26. Remove upper timing chain guide, **Fig. 9**.
27. Remove exhaust camshaft sprocket bolt and camshaft sprocket using suitable 24mm wrench to hold camshafts, **Fig. 10**.
28. Remove timing chain tensioner guide, **Fig. 11**.
29. Remove intake camshaft sprocket bolt, intake camshaft sprocket and timing chain through top of cylinder head, **Fig. 12**.
30. Remove crankshaft sprocket, balance shaft drive chain tensioner and adjustable balance shaft chain guide.
31. Remove small balance shaft drive chain guide.
32. Remove upper balance shaft drive chain guide, **Fig. 13**.
33. Remove balance shaft drive chain, **Fig. 14**.

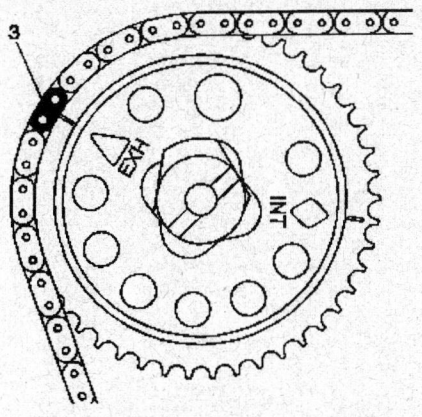

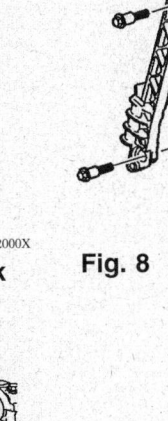

Fig. 7 Timing chain silver link alignment

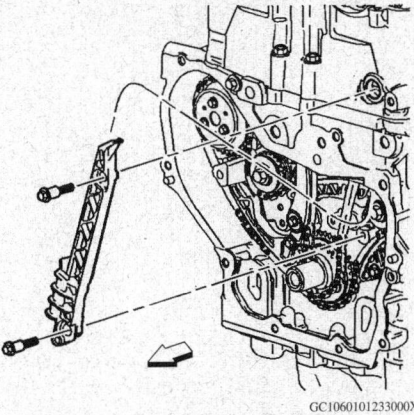

Fig. 8 Fixed timing chain guide replacement

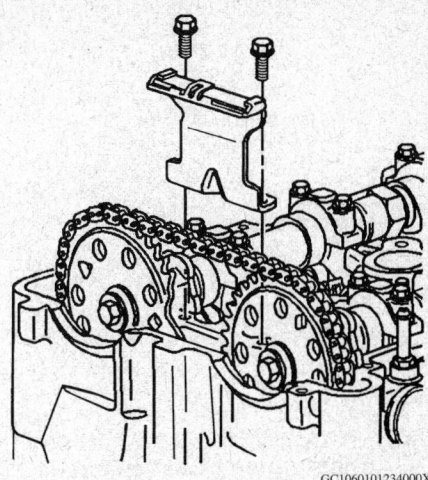

Fig. 9 Upper timing chain guide replacement

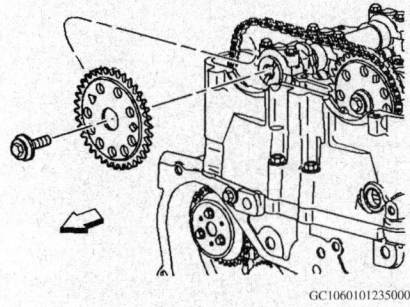

Fig. 10 Exhaust camshaft bolt & sprocket replacement

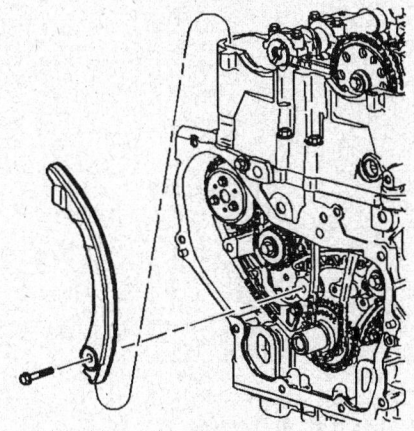

Fig. 11 Timing chain tensioner guide replacement

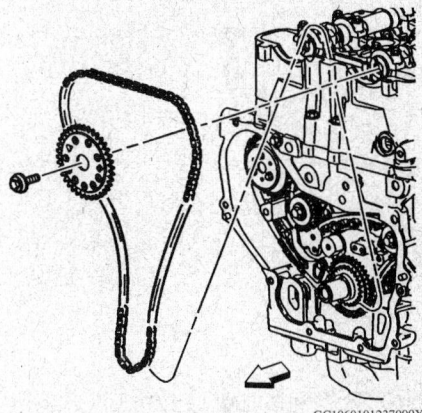

Fig. 12 Camshaft bolt, sprocket & timing chain replacement

Installation

1. Install upper balance shaft chain guide.
2. Install balance shaft drive chain with colored links lined up on marks on balance shaft drive sprockets and crankshaft sprocket, **Fig. 15.**
3. Place copper link so it aligns with intake side balance shaft sprocket timing mark, **Fig. 15.**
4. Move clockwise around chain, place first chrome link inline with timing mark on crankshaft drive sprocket, five o'clock position, **Fig. 15.**
5. Install chain on water pump drive sprocket, **Fig. 15.**
6. Align last chrome link with timing mark on exhaust side balance shaft drive sprocket, **Fig. 15.**
7. Install small balance shaft chain guide.
8. Tighten balance shaft chain guide bolts.
9. Install adjustable balance shaft drive chain guide.
10. Turn tensioner plunger 90° in its bore and compress plunger until paper clip can be inserted through hole in plunger body and into hole in tensioner plunger, **Fig. 16.**
11. Install timing chain tensioner.
12. Remove paper clip from balance shaft drive chain tensioner.
13. Install crankshaft sprocket with timing mark at five o'clock position, **Fig. 17.**
14. Lower timing chain through opening in

top of cylinder head and ensure chain installs around both sides of cylinder block bosses.
15. Install intake camshaft sprocket with INT diamond at two o'clock position, **Fig. 6.**
16. Hand tighten new intake camshaft sprocket bolt.
17. Install timing chain around crankshaft sprocket with second silver link aligning with timing mark.
18. Install timing chain around intake camshaft sprocket with copper link aligning with INT diamond.
19. Install timing chain tensioner guide through opening in top of cylinder head.
20. Install exhaust camshaft sprocket with timing chain silver link at EXH triangle aligned ten o'clock position, **Fig. 7.**
21. Install suitable 24mm wrench to rotate camshaft slightly, until exhaust sprocket aligns with camshaft.
22. Hand tighten new exhaust camshaft sprocket bolt.
23. Install fixed timing chain guide.
24. Apply sealant, GM part No. 12345382, or equivalent, compound to thread and install timing chain guide bolt access hole plug.
25. Install timing chain upper guide.
26. Measure timing chain tensioner when

fully compressed, tensioner will measure 2.83 inch.
27. Install timing chain tensioner.
28. Install suitable rubber tipped tool, place tool down through camshaft drive to contact timing chain, release tensioner using sharp contact downwards.
29. Install suitable 24mm wrench to hold camshaft, **Fig. 18,** and **torque** bolt to 63 ft. lbs., then tighten an additional 30°.
30. Install valve cover.
31. Raise and support vehicle.
32. Install front engine cover.
33. Lower vehicle.

CAMSHAFT
REPLACE

1. Loosen vent hose clamp at air cleaner resonator, air cleaner intake duct clamp at air cleaner outlet resonator.
2. Loosen air cleaner outlet resonator to throttle body clamp, located forward of accelerator cable bracket. Remove air cleaner resonator to accelerator bracket bolt.
3. Remove throttle body resonator, air cleaner intake duct and vent hose.

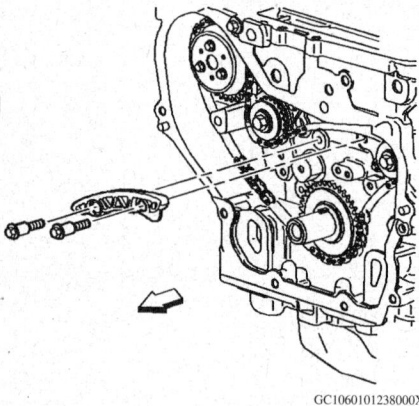

Fig. 13 Upper balance shaft drive chain guide replacement

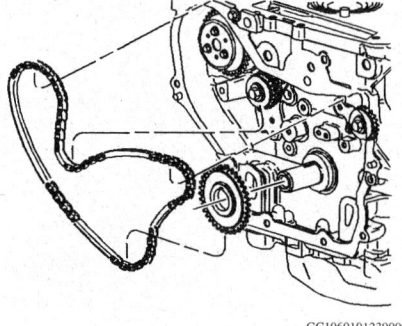

GC1060101239000X

Fig. 14 Balance shaft drive chain replacement

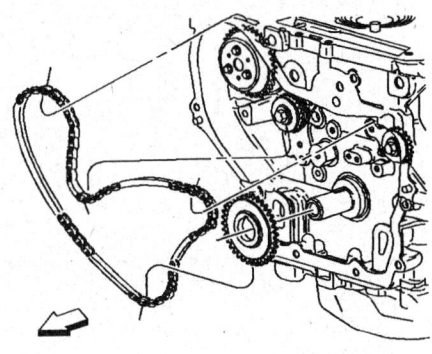

GC1060101240000X

Fig. 15 Timing chain installation

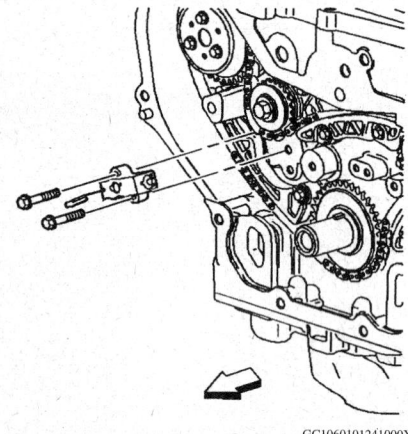

GC1060101241000X

Fig. 16 Tensioner plunger & body installation

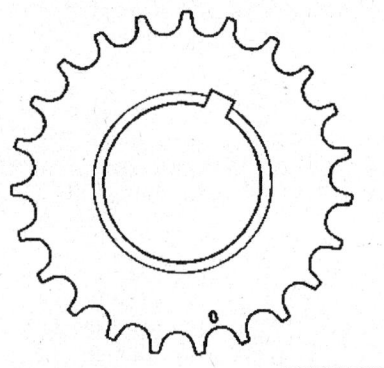

GC1060101242000X

Fig. 17 Crankshaft sprocket timing mark

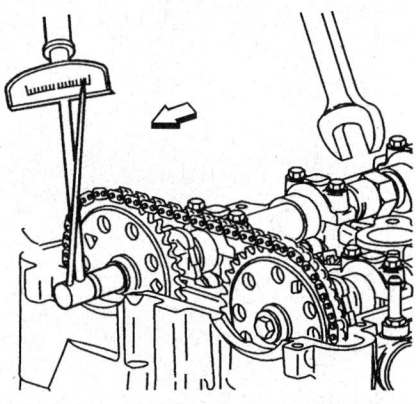

GC1060101243000X

Fig. 18 Camshaft tightening

4. Disconnect accelerator and cruise control cables from throttle body, then the bracket.
5. Remove PCV valve.
6. Remove fuel line brackets and brake booster hose pipe from brackets.
7. Remove mounting screw, ignition coil and Ignition Control Module (ICM).
8. Remove ground strap.
9. Remove mounting bolts and camshaft cover.
10. Remove upper timing chain guide.
11. Remove both intake and exhaust camshaft sprocket bolts using camshaft sprocket holding tool No. J43655, or equivalent.
12. Slide camshaft sprockets forward.
13. **On intake side,** remove power steering pump.
14. **On both sides,** mark bearing caps for installation reference.
15. Remove bearing caps.
16. Remove exhaust and intake camshafts.
17. Remove camshaft roller followers.
18. Remove hydraulic element lash adjusters.
19. Reverse procedure to install, noting the following:
   a. Lubricate valve tips using suitable lubricant.
   b. Ensure alignment notches are aligned with camshaft sprocket.

c. **Torque** camshaft bearing cap bolts in three increments to 89 inch lbs.
d. Apply anaerobic sealer bead, GM part No. 1052942, or equivalent, to rear intake camshaft bearing cap.
e. **Torque** camshaft sprocket bolts to 63 ft. lbs., then tighten an additional 30°.

PISTON & ROD ASSEMBLY

When installing piston and rod assemblies into cylinder block, ensure arrow on top of piston faces toward front of engine. Ensure flat area on bottom of piston aligns with small dimple above connecting rod crankshaft bearing bore.

PISTONS, PINS & RINGS

Pistons and rings are available in standard size and oversize. Pistons and pins are serviced as an assembly.

MAIN & ROD BEARINGS

Main and rod bearings are available in standard size only.

CRANKSHAFT SEAL
REPLACE

1. Raise and support vehicle.
2. Remove front tire and wheel assembly.
3. Remove front fender liner.
4. Rotate drive belt tensioner clockwise.
5. Remove serpentine drive belt.
6. Prevent crankshaft from rotating by install harmonic balancer holder tool No. J38122A, or equivalent.
7. Remove mounting bolt and crankshaft balancer. Discard bolt.
8. Remove front oil seal using suitable flat bladed tool.
9. Reverse procedure to install, using camshaft front main seal installer tool No. J35268A, or equivalent.

CRANKSHAFT REAR OIL SEAL
REPLACE

1. Remove transaxle as outlined in **MOTOR's "Domestic Transmission Manual, In-Vehicle Service."**
2. Remove flywheel or flexplate.
3. Remove crankshaft rear oil seal using suitable flat bladed tool.
4. Reverse procedure to install.

OIL PAN
REPLACE

1. Raise and support vehicle.
2. Drain engine oil into suitable container.

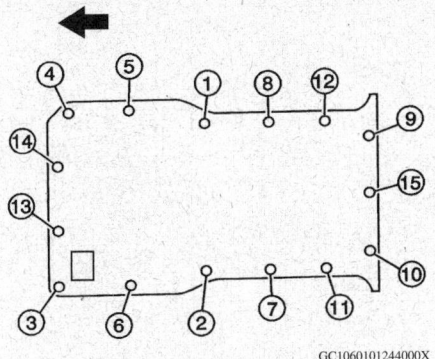

Fig. 19 Oil pan bolt loosening sequence

3. Remove engine mount strut bracket.
4. Remove front fender liner.
5. Rotate drive belt tensioner clockwise.
6. Remove serpentine drive belt.
7. Remove lower air conditioning compressor bolts.
8. Loosen upper air conditioning compressor bolts.
9. Remove oil pan bolts in sequence, **Fig. 19.**
10. Remove oil pan.
11. Reverse procedure to install. **Torque** oil pan mounting bolts to 18 ft. lbs., in reverse of loosening sequence, **Fig. 19.**

OIL PUMP
REPLACE

1. Raise and support vehicle.
2. Drain engine oil into suitable container.
3. Remove engine mount strut bracket.
4. Remove front fender liner.
5. Rotate drive belt tensioner clockwise.
6. Remove serpentine drive belt.
7. Remove lower air conditioning compressor bolts.
8. Loosen upper air conditioning compressor bolts.
9. Remove oil pan bolts in sequence, **Fig. 19.**
10. Remove oil pan.
11. Remove oil pump and drive shaft extension, **Fig. 20.**
12. Reverse procedure to install.

BELT TENSION DATA

1. Turn Off accessories.
2. Bring engine to operating temperature.
3. Turn engine Off.
4. Read belt tension using belt tension gauge tool No. J23600B, or equivalent, halfway between alternator and power steering pump.
5. Start engine and allow temperature to stabilize for 15 seconds.
6. Turn engine Off.
7. Install 15mm socket, apply clockwise force to tensioner pulley bolt.
8. Release force and measure belt tension without disturbing tensioner position.
9. Install 15mm socket, apply counterclockwise force to tensioner pulley bolt and raise pulley to eliminate tension.
10. Slowly lower pulley to belt and mea-

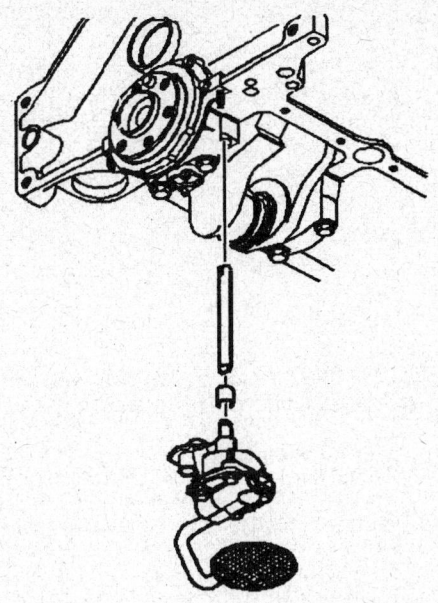

Fig. 20 Oil pump replacement

sure belt tension without disturbing tensioner position.
11. Average out readings.
12. If average is less than 30–50 lbs., replace belt tensioner.

SERPENTINE DRIVE BELT

1. Raise and support vehicle .
2. Remove front fender liner.
3. Rotate drive belt tensioner clockwise.
4. Remove drive belt, **Fig. 21.**
5. Reverse procedure to install.

COOLING SYSTEM BLEED

1. Slowly add mixture of 50/50 DEX-COOL and clean water to cooling system until coolant level reaches and maintains top of surge tank label.
2. Install surge tank cap.
3. Start engine, run at 2000–2500 RPM until engine reaches normal operating temperature.
4. Allow engine to idle for three minutes.
5. Shut engine Off.
6. Top off coolant.
7. Inspect cooling system for leaks.

THERMOSTAT
REPLACE

1. **On models equipped with automatic transmission,** remove exhaust manifold as outlined under "Exhaust Manifold, Replace."
2. **On all models,** drain cooling system into suitable container.
3. Remove thermostat housing to water pump feed pipe.
4. Remove thermostat.
5. Reverse procedure to install.

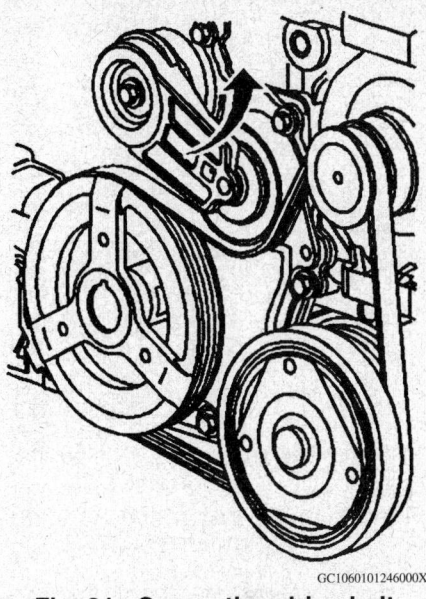

Fig. 21 Serpentine drive belt replacement

WATER PUMP
REPLACE

1. **On models equipped with automatic transmission,** remove exhaust manifold as outlined under "Exhaust Manifold, Replace."
2. **On all models,** drain cooling system into suitable container.
3. Raise and support vehicle.
4. Remove righthand front tire and wheel.
5. Remove front fender liner.
6. Remove water pump sprocket from timing cover access plate, **Fig. 22.**
7. Remove water pump sprocket bolts by holding sprocket using water pump sprocket holding tool No. J43651, or equivalent.
8. Remove engine block to water pump and engine front cover to water pump mounting bolts, **Fig. 23.**
9. Remove feed pipes thermostat to water pump.
10. Remove mounting bolts and water pump, **Fig. 24.**
11. Reverse procedure to install.

RADIATOR
REPLACE

Alero & Grand Am

1. Remove battery and tray.
2. Recover air conditioning refrigerant as outlined in "Air Conditioning" chapter.
3. Drain engine cooling system into suitable container.
4. Remove upper radiator hose.
5. Remove upper transaxle cooler line.
6. Remove coolant surge tank hose.
7. Remove condenser inlet fitting from discharge hose.
8. Disconnect cooling fan electrical connector.
9. Raise and support vehicle.
10. Remove lower cover panel.

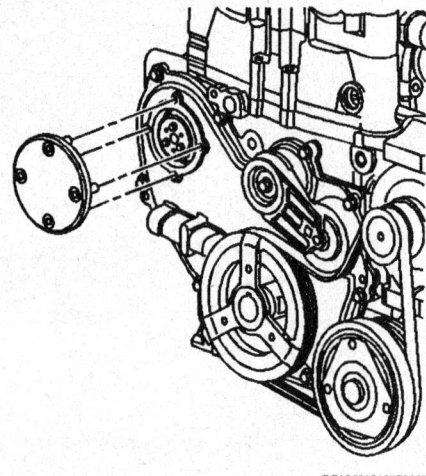

GC1060101247000X

Fig. 22   Water pump access plate replacement

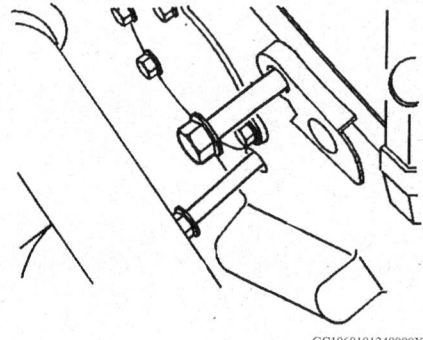

GC1060101248000X

Fig. 23   Water pump, engine block & front cover bolt replacement

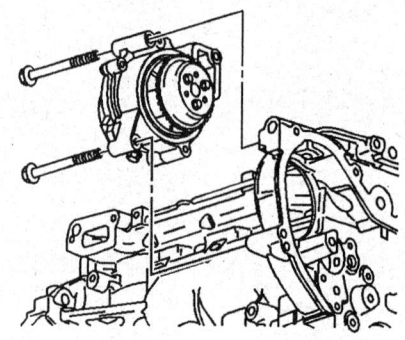

GC1060101249000X

Fig. 24   Water pump bolt replacement

11. Remove lower radiator hose from radiator.
12. Remove lower transaxle cooler line.
13. Remove evaporator line to condenser outlet.
14. Remove lower radiator mounting panel.
15. Remove radiator, fan and condenser as an assembly.
16. Reverse procedure to install.

Malibu

1. Drain engine coolant.
2. Remove lefthand headlamp assembly attaching bolts.
3. Lift headlamp assembly to unseat tabs on bottom edge of fender.
4. Disconnect headlamp assembly electrical connector and remove assembly from vehicle.
5. Remove righthand headlamp assembly attaching bolts.
6. Lift headlamp assembly to unseat tabs on bottom edge of fender.
7. Disconnect headlamp assembly electrical connector and remove assembly from vehicle.
8. Loop a suitable rope around upper two tabs of condenser, then tie rope around upper engine compartment tie bar.
9. Remove upper radiator support bracket bolts and support brackets.
10. Remove surge tank outlet hose from radiator.
11. Remove radiator inlet hose from radiator.
12. Raise and support vehicle.
13. Remove lower radiator air deflector retainers and the deflector.
14. Remove front fender liner retainers and fender liner.
15. Remove righthand and lefthand radiator air deflector retainers and deflectors.
16. Remove radiator outlet hose from radiator.
17. Place a suitable drain pan under transaxle cooler lines, then remove cooler

lines from transaxle.
18. Remove lower radiator support bracket bolts and support brackets.
19. Remove radiator lower mounts.
20. Remove and discard condenser mounting bolts from radiator.
21. Push upward on radiator and downward on condenser to unsnap condenser mounting tabs from radiator clips.
22. Remove and discard condenser mounting nuts from radiator.
23. Remove radiator air side seals.
24. Remove radiator, cooling fan shroud and transaxle cooler line assembly.
25. Remove transaxle cooler lines from radiator.
26. Pry upward on fan shroud tabs, then remove cooling fan and shroud assembly from radiator.
27. Reverse procedure to install.

FUEL PUMP
REPLACE
Alero & Grand Am

The fuel pump is part of the fuel sender assembly and must be replaced as a complete unit.
1. Drain fuel tank into suitable container.
2. Raise and support vehicle.
3. Disconnect quick-connect fitting at fuel filter.
4. Disconnect fuel return pipe quick connect fitting.
5. Remove rubber exhaust hangers, allow exhaust system to rest on rear axle.
6. Remove exhaust heat shield.
7. Loosen clamp and disconnect fuel tank filler hose.
8. Disconnect EVAP Emission (EVAP) canister vapor pipe.
9. Disconnect electrical harness from multi-way rear body connector and fuel strap.
10. Support fuel tank with aid of an assistant, disconnect fuel tank retaining straps and lower fuel tank.
11. Disconnect wiring harness from fuel sender and fuel tank pressure sensor.
12. Rotate retaining ring, press down and remove fuel sender.
13. Reverse procedure to install.

Malibu

1. Relieve fuel system pressure as outlined under "Precautions."
2. Drain fuel tank.
3. Raise and support vehicle.
4. Disconnect fuel pump module electrical harness connector from vehicle underbody wiring harness.
5. Disconnect EVAP vent valve solenoid harness electrical connector from vehicle underbody wiring harness.
6. Remove ABS wiring harness from retainer on EVAP canister.
7. Disconnect fuel feed and purge lines from fuel and brake line bundle on righthand side of vehicle.
8. Cap or plug fuel tank feed and vapor lines to prevent fuel loss or contamination.
9. Disconnect fuel filler pipe jumper hose from fuel tank.
10. Disconnect vapor recirculation line that runs parallel to fuel filler pipe jumper hose.
11. Remove exhaust pipe and muffler insulators from underbody hangers, then support exhaust system with suitable jackstand.
12. Support fuel tank with a suitable jackstand.
13. Remove lefthand and righthand fuel tank strap bolts.
14. Carefully lower righthand side of tank until is clear of frame rail, then remove tank toward righthand side of vehicle.
15. Remove fuel pump module assembly from fuel tank using fuel sender lock ring wrench tool No. J 45722, or equivalent.
16. Reverse procedure to install.

FUEL FILTER
REPLACE

1. Relieve fuel system pressure.
2. Raise and support vehicle.
3. Disconnect fuel filter fitting using suitable back-up wrench.
4. Disconnect fuel filter quick connect fitting.
5. Remove fuel filter.
6. Reverse procedure to install.

TIGHTENING SPECIFICATIONS

Year	Component	Torque/Ft. Lbs.
2001–05	Accelerator & Cruise Control Cable	89①
	Accelerator Pedal	22
	Access Hole Plug	30
	Access Plate	18①
	Air Cleaner Clamps	44①
	Air Cleaner Outlet Resonator	89①
	Alternator	15
	Alternator Electrical Connector	13
	Balance Shaft Chain Guide	89①
	Battery Terminal	13
	Bell Housing	66
	Blower Motor	45①
	Camshaft Bearing Cap Bolts	89①
	Camshaft	③
	Camshaft Cover	89①
	Chain Tensioner	89①
	Condenser To Inlet Discharge Hose	18
	Condenser To Radiator	44①
	Crankshaft Balancer	④
	Crankshaft Position Sensor	71①
	Cylinder Head	②
	Drive Belt Tensioner	33
	Engine Coolant Temperature Sensor	89①
	Engine Front Cover To Water Pump	15
	Engine Mount	49
	Engine To Transmission Brace	53
	Evaporator Core Bracket	9①
	EVAP Canister Purge Valve Mounting Bracket	71①
	EVAP Canister	89①
	EVAP Line	18
	Exhaust Manifold Heat Shield	18
	Exhaust Manifold	⑥
	Fixed Timing Chain Guide	89①
	Flywheel	⑤
	Front Cover	15
	Front Cover To Water Pump	15
	Fuel Filler Hose Clamp	27①
	Fuel Filler Pipe	89①
	Fuel Filter Fitting	20
	Fuel Line Bracket	89①
	Fuel Pipe	53①
	Fuel Pipe Retainer	89①
	Fuel Rail Pipe Fittings	89①
	Fuel Tank Retaining Strap	26
	Ground Strap	89①
	Heated Oxygen Sensor No. 1	22
	Heated Oxygen Sensor No. 2	30
	Heater Core Bracket	9①
	Heater Core Case	9①
	Heater Core Cover	9①
	ICM, Bolt	89①

Continued

TIGHTENING
SPECIFICATIONS—Continued

Year	Component	Torque/Ft. Lbs.
2001–05	ICM, Screw	13①
	Idle Air Control Valve	27①
	Ignition Switch	53①
	Ignition Switch Bracket	53①
	Intake Manifold	89①
	Knock Sensor	18
	Lower Radiator Mounting Panel	89①
	Manifold To Flex Decoupler	26
	Multi-Function Switch	35①
	Oil Pan	⑦
	Park Neutral Switch	18
	Power Steering Pump	19
	Pump To Rear Bearing Cap	30
	Radiator Drain Cock	18①
	Rear Intake Camshaft Bearing Cap	18
	Spark Plugs	15①
	Starter Motor	30
	Steering Wheel	27
	Throttle Body	89①
	Throttle Position Sensor	18①
	Timing Chain Tensioner	55
	Timing Chain Tensioner Guide	89①
	Timing Chain Upper Guide	89①
	Transaxle Oil Cooler Line	22
	Upper Air Cleaner Cover	27①
	Water Pump Drain Plug	16①
	Water Pump Feed Pipes	18①
	Water Pump Sprocket To Water Pump	89①
	Wiper Drive Module	89①
	Wiper Motor	89①

① — Inch lbs.
② — Refer to "Cylinder Head, Removal" for tightening specifications and sequence.
③ — **Torque** to 63 ft. lbs., then tighten additional 30°.
④ — **Torque** to 74 ft. lbs., then tighten additional 75°.
⑤ — **Torque** to 39 ft. lbs., then tighten additional 25°.
⑥ — Refer to "Exhaust Manifold, Removal" for tightening
specifications and sequence.
⑦ — Refer to "Oil Pan, Removal" for tightening specifications
and sequence.

2.4L Engine

NOTE: On Air Bag Equipped Models, Refer To "Air Bag System Precautions" Located In The Front Of This Manual For System Disarming & Arming Procedures.

NOTE: Refer To "Computer Relearn Procedures" Located In The Front Of This Manual When Battery Power To The Computer Has Been Interrupted.

INDEX

PRECAUTIONS

Air Bag Systems

Refer to "Air Bag System Precautions" in the front of this manual for system disarming and arming procedures.

Battery Ground Cable

Prior to service, disconnect battery ground cable and isolate as required.

Fuel System Pressure Relief

Failure to relieve system pressure prior to disconnecting fuel system components may cause fire or personal injury.

1. Loosen fuel tank filler cap to relieve tank pressure.
2. Raise and support vehicle.
3. Disconnect fuel pump electrical connector.
4. Lower vehicle.
5. Start and operate engine until fuel supply is consumed.
6. Crank engine for approximately three seconds to relieve remaining pressure.
7. Disconnect battery ground cable and connect fuel pump connector.

COMPRESSION PRESSURE

When inspecting cylinder compression, the engine should be at room temperature, the throttle should be open, the spark plugs removed and the battery at or near full charge. The lowest reading cylinder should not be less than 70% of the highest and no cylinder reading should be less than 100 psi. Turn ignition key until engine cranks through four compression cycles. Normal compression builds up quickly and evenly to specified compression on each cylinder.

ENGINE MOUNT
REPLACE

Front Mount

1. Remove coolant recovery tank mounting bolt and position tank aside with hoses connected.
2. Raise engine off mount using engine support tool No. J-28467-360, or equivalent.
3. Remove mount to body mounting nuts.
4. Remove engine bracket to mount mounting bolts.
5. Remove engine mount.
6. Reverse procedure to install.

Strut

1. Raise and support vehicle.
2. Remove righthand front splash shield.

3. Remove mounting bolts and engine mount strut, **Fig. 1.**
4. Reverse procedure to install.

ENGINE
REPLACE

Alero & Grand Am

1. Relieve fuel system pressure as outlined under "Precautions."
2. Drain coolant into suitable container.
3. Drain engine oil using approved containers and methods.
4. Remove fuel rail and air cleaner intake duct.
5. Disconnect and remove ignition coil and module.
6. Disconnect Camshaft Position Sensor (CMP) electrical connector.
7. Remove mounting bolts, then position power steering pump aside with lines and hoses attached.
8. Disconnect oil pressure sender electrical connector.
9. Remove air intake duct bracket and cruise control assembly, then position aside.
10. Install engine support fixture tool No. J-28467-360, or equivalent.
11. Remove engine mount.
12. Disconnect vacuum hose at fuel pressure regulator.
13. Raise engine using support fixture J hook.

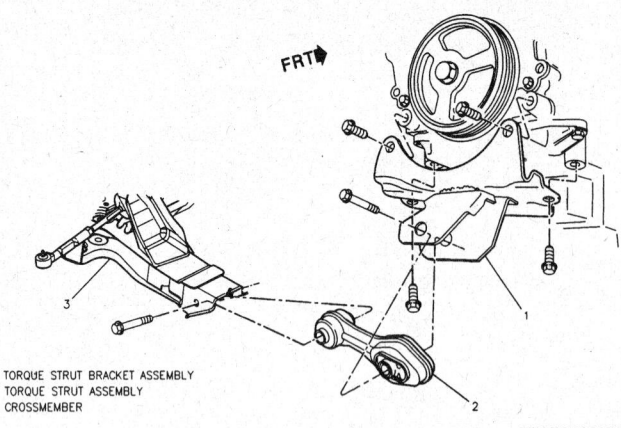

Fig. 1 Engine mount strut & bracket

1 TORQUE STRUT BRACKET ASSEMBLY
2 TORQUE STRUT ASSEMBLY
3 CROSSMEMBER

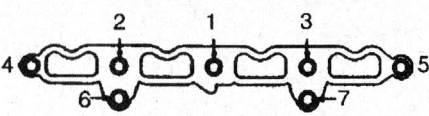

Fig. 2 Intake manifold tightening sequence

14. Remove engine mount bracket and lower engine.
15. Raise and support vehicle.
16. Remove serpentine drive belt using tensioner tool No. J-36018, or equivalent.
17. Remove front tires and wheels, then the righthand front splash shield.
18. Remove harmonic balancer using puller tool No. J-24420-C, or equivalent.
19. Lower vehicle.
20. Disconnect MAP, IAT and EGR sensors' electrical connectors, then the EVAP canister connector.
21. Remove alternator.
22. Remove and discard accelerator cable.
23. Position cruise control cable aside to avoid damage.
24. Remove accelerator cable bracket and starter motor.
25. Remove exhaust brace bolt from exhaust manifold and exhaust manifold heat shield.
26. Disconnect exhaust pipe at manifold.
27. Remove intake coolant pipe.
28. Remove torque converter bolts.
29. Raise and support vehicle.
30. Remove O2 sensor.
31. Remove mounting bolts and position air conditioning compressor aside with lines attached.
32. Remove oil pan to bellhousing bolts.
33. Remove transaxle mount.
34. Remove transaxle to engine mounting bolts.
35. Support engine with suitable lifting device.
36. Raise engine and separate it from transaxle.
37. If mounting engine onto stand, remove flexplate mounting bolts and flexplate.
38. Reverse procedure to install. If flexplate was removed, install it and its bolts. Tighten bolts evenly while holding flexplate in place with holder tool No. J-38122, or equivalent.

Malibu

1. Relieve fuel system pressure as outlined under "Precautions."
2. Recover air conditioning refrigerant as outlined in "Air Conditioning" chapter.
3. Drain coolant into suitable container.
4. Disconnect heater hose at thermostat housing.
5. Disconnect radiator upper inlet hose.
6. Remove air cleaner.
7. Remove coolant fan.
8. Disconnect compressor/condenser hose assembly at compressor and discard O-rings.
9. Disconnect vacuum hoses from front of engine.
10. Disconnect alternator, air conditioning compressor, injector harness, Idle Air Control (IAC) and Throttle Position (TP) sensors at throttle body, Manifold Air Pressure (MAP) and Intake Air Temperature (IAT) sensors, EVAP Canister Purge solenoid, starter solenoid and ground cables.
11. Disconnect battery ground cable from transaxle and electronic ignition coil and module ASM, then two engine coolant temperature sensors and oil pressure sensor/switch connectors.
12. Disconnect oxygen and Crankshaft Position (CSP) sensors, then the back-up lamp switch and camshaft position sensor.
13. Disconnect throttle body power brake vacuum hose.
14. Disconnect throttle cable and bracket.
15. Remove power steering bolts and pump. Position pump aside with lines attached.
16. Disconnect fuel lines.
17. Disconnect shift cables.
18. Remove exhaust manifold and heat shield.
19. Disconnect radiator lower outlet hose.
20. Install engine support fixture No. J-28467-360, or equivalent.
21. Remove coolant recovery tank mounting bolt and position tank aside with hoses attached.
22. Raise engine off mount using engine support tool No. J-28467-360, or equivalent.
23. Remove mount to body mounting nuts.
24. Remove engine bracket to mount mounting bolts.
25. Remove engine mount.
26. Raise and support vehicle.
27. Remove front wheel and tire assemblies.
28. Remove righthand splash shield.
29. Disconnect vehicle speed and sensors, starter solenoid and front ABS wheel speed sensor electrical connectors.
30. Remove righthand front splash shield.
31. Remove mounting bolts and engine mount strut, Fig. 1.
32. Remove transaxle mount.
33. Separate ball joints from steering knuckles.
34. Remove suspension supports, crossmember and stabilizer shaft as an assembly.
35. Remove heater outlet hose from radiator outlet pipe.
36. Remove flywheel housing cover.
37. Lower engine onto suitable support.
38. Mark threads on support fixture hooks for installation alignment and remove engine support fixture J-hooks.
39. Raise vehicle slowly off engine and transaxle. Engine/transaxle assembly may have to be move rearward to clear intake manifold.
40. Separate engine from transaxle.
41. Reverse procedure to install.

INTAKE MANIFOLD
REPLACE

1. Remove air cleaner duct.
2. Disconnect electrical connectors at MAP, IAT and EVAP sensors and fuel injector harness.
3. Disconnect vacuum hoses from fuel regulator and EVAP canister purge solenoid to canister.
4. Remove throttle cable bracket.
5. Disconnect throttle body coolant lines.
6. Remove stud-ended alternator mount bolt.
7. Remove EGR adapter pipe.
8. Raise and support vehicle.
9. Remove intake manifold support brace and lower vehicle.
10. Remove manifold mounting nuts, bolts, manifold and gasket, Fig. 2.
11. Reverse procedure to install. Torque intake manifold mounting bolts and nuts to 19 ft. lbs., in sequence, Fig. 2.

EXHAUST MANIFOLD
REPLACE

1. Disconnect oxygen sensor electrical connector.
2. Raise and support vehicle.
3. Remove exhaust manifold brace to manifold bolts.
4. Remove upper heat shield.
5. Remove mounting nuts and disconnect exhaust pipe from manifold by pulling it down and back. Do not bend exhaust flex coupler more than 3° in any direction.
6. Lower vehicle and remove exhaust

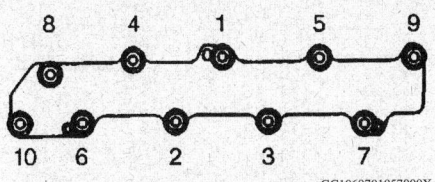

Fig. 3 Exhaust manifold installation & bolt tightening sequence

manifold to cylinder head mounting nuts, manifold, seals and gaskets.
7. Reverse procedure to install. **Torque** exhaust manifold mounting nuts to 41 ft. lbs., in sequence, **Fig. 3.**

CYLINDER HEAD

REPLACE

1. Drain coolant into suitable container.
2. Remove air cleaner duct.
3. Disconnect heater inlet and throttle body hoses from coolant outlet.
4. Disconnect power brake vacuum hose.
5. Disconnect MAP, IAT, CMP sensor and EVAP canister purge solenoid electrical connectors.
6. Remove alternator stud-ended bolt.
7. Disconnect vacuum hoses from fuel regulator and EVAP canister purge solenoid to canister.
8. Remove throttle cable bracket.
9. Disconnect throttle body coolant lines.
10. Remove EGR adapter pipe.
11. Raise and support vehicle.
12. Remove intake manifold support brace and lower vehicle.
13. Remove manifold mounting nuts, bolts, manifold and gasket, **Fig. 2.**
14. Install alternator stud-ended bolt.
15. Install engine support tool No. J-28467-360, or equivalent.
16. Disconnect oxygen sensor electrical connector.
17. Remove exhaust manifold brace to manifold bolts.
18. Remove upper heat shield.
19. Remove mounting nuts and disconnect exhaust pipe from manifold by pulling it down and back. **Do not bend exhaust flex coupler more than 3° in any direction.**
20. Lower vehicle and remove exhaust manifold to cylinder head mounting nuts, manifold, seals and gaskets.
21. Remove electrical connectors, mounting bolts and ignition coil and module.
22. Siphon as much power steering fluid as possible from reservoir.
23. **On models equipped with variable effort steering,** disconnect variable effort steering electrical connector.
24. **On all models,** place suitable drain pan in position and disconnect power steering pump lines.
25. Remove mounting bolts power steering pump.
26. Remove fuel pressure regulator vacuum line and fuel injector harness connectors.
27. Remove fuel line retaining clamp and

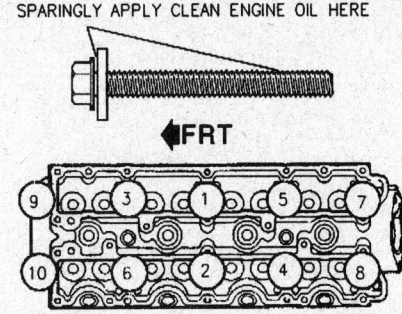

A TIGHTEN THE BOLTS TO THE FOLLOWING N•m (LB. FT.) SPECIFICATION IN SEQUENCE:
BOLTS 1 THROUGH 8: 40 N•m (30 LB. FT.)
BOLTS 9 AND 10: 35 N•m (26 LB. FT.)
B THEN TURN ALL 10 BOLTS AN ADDITIONAL 90 DEGREES IN SEQUENCE

Fig. 4 Cylinder head bolt tightening sequence

fuel rail mounting bolts on top of intake camshaft housing.
28. Cover injector openings and injector nozzles.
29. Remove fuel rail with lines attached and position aside.
30. **On Alero and Grand Am models,** proceed as follows:
   a. Remove timing chains as outlined under "Timing Chain, Replace."
   b. Remove timing sprockets.
   c. Remove water pump as outlined under "Water Pump, Replace."
31. **On Malibu models,** disconnect timing chain housing at intake camshaft housing. **Do not remove.**
32. **On all models,** remove intake and exhaust camshaft housings.
33. Remove valve lifters.
34. Disconnect oil pressure switch and ECT sensor electrical connectors.
35. Remove transaxle fluid level indicator tube.
36. Disconnect upper radiator hose and ECT sensor connectors.
37. Remove mounting bolts in reverse of tightening sequence, **Fig. 4.**
38. Reverse procedure to install. Tighten cylinder head mounting bolts using torque angle meter tool No. J-36660, or equivalent, **Fig. 4.**

CAMSHAFT LOBE LIFT SPECIFICATIONS

Engine/VIN	Int., Inch	Exh., Inch
2.4L/T	.354	.346

VALVE ADJUSTMENT

These engines are equipped with hydraulic valve lash adjusters. No adjustment is required.

VALVE GUIDES

Valve guides are an integral component of the cylinder head and are not removable.

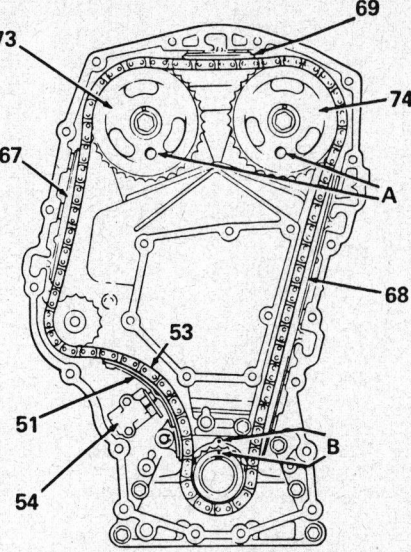

A. CAMSHAFT TIMING ALIGNMENT PIN LOCATIONS
B. CRANKSHAFT GEAR TIMING MARKS
51. SHOE ASM. TIMING CHAIN TENSIONER
53. TIMING CHAIN
54. TENSIONER, TIMING CHAIN
67. GUIDE – R.H. TIMING CHAIN
68. GUIDE – L.H. TIMING CHAIN
69. GUIDE – UPPER TIMING CHAIN
73. SPROCKET, EXHAUST CAMSHAFT
74. SPROCKET, INTAKE CAMSHAFT

Fig. 5 Valve timing marks

If valve stem clearance becomes excessive, the valve guide should be reamed to the next oversize and the appropriate oversize valves installed.

VALVE LASH ADJUSTERS

REPLACE

These engines use hydraulic valve lash adjusters. The valve lash adjusters can be replaced after camshaft and housing are removed. Refer to "Camshaft, Replace."

FRONT COVER

REPLACE

1. Drain coolant into suitable container.
2. Remove coolant reservoir or surge tank.
3. Remove serpentine drive belt.
4. Attach engine support tool Nos. J-28467-360 and J-28467-400, or equivalents, onto alternator stud-ended bolt.
5. Remove front cover upper mounting screws.
6. Remove engine mount and bracket adapter. Discard adapter bolts.
7. Raise and support vehicle.
8. Remove righthand front wheel and tire assembly, then the righthand splash shield.
9. Hold balancer in position using harmonic balancer tool No. J-38122, or equivalent, remove mounting bolt and balancer using puller tool No. J-24420-C, or equivalent.
10. Remove front cover lower mounting bolt.

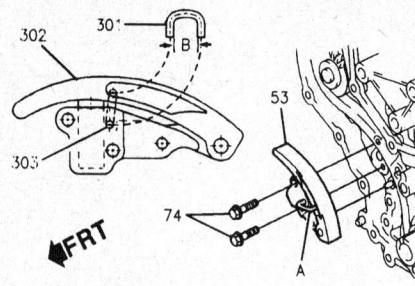

A AFTER INSTALLATION, REMOVE ANTI-RELEASE
FROM TENSIONER ASM. TO RELEASE TENSIONER
B 13 mm (1/2 INCH)

53 TIMING CHAIN TENSIONER AND SHOE ASSEMBLY
74 BOLTS – 10 N m (89 LBS. IN.)
301 ANTI-RELEASE KEEPER – FABRICATED
FROM HEAVY GAGE WIRE OR STEEL ROD
302 SHOE
303 RESET ACCESS HOLE

GC1069600656000X

Fig. 6   Timing chain tensioner spring & retainer

11. Lower vehicle.
12. Remove front cover and gaskets.
13. Reverse procedure to install, noting the following:
    a. **Components will not tighten properly if improper bolts are used.**
    b. **Torque** engine mount bracket adapter bolts to 81 ft. lbs., then tighten an additional 90°.

TIMING CHAIN
REPLACE
Removal

1. Remove front cover as outlined under "Front Cover, Replace."
2. Rotate crankshaft in clockwise direction until camshaft sprocket timing dowel pin holes line up with timing chain housing holes, **Fig. 5.**
3. Remove timing chain guides.
4. Raise and support vehicle.
5. Ensure timing chain slack is above tensioner, then remove tensioner, **Fig. 6.**
6. Disconnect timing chain from tensioner show grooves and remove shoe using suitable screwdriver under timing chain while pulling shoe outward.
7. If removing tensioner shoe is difficult, proceed as follows:
    a. Lower vehicle.
    b. Hold intake camshaft sprocket in position with camshaft sprocket wrench tool No. J-39579, or equivalent.
    c. Remove sprocket bolt and washer.
    d. Remove washer and install bolt into camshaft by hand.
    e. Position suitable three-jaw puller into intake camshaft sprocket relief holes and remove sprocket. Do not pry on camshaft sprocket as damage to sprocket or timing chain housing may result.

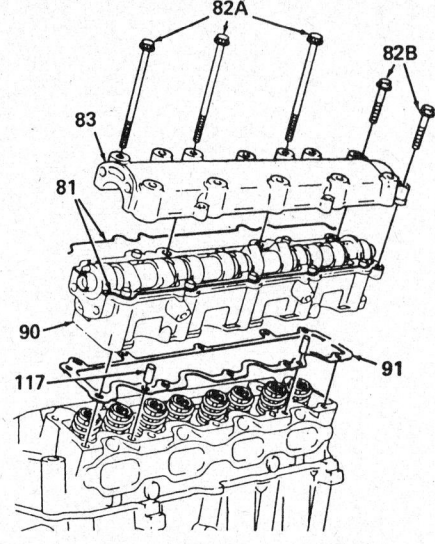

81. SEALS, CAMSHAFT HOUSING TO CAMSHAFT HOUSING COVER (EACH SEAL IS DIFFERENT)
82A. BOLT, CAMSHAFT HOUSING TO CYLINDER HEAD
82B. BOLT, CAMSHAFT HOUSING COVER TO CAMSHAFT HOUSING
83. COVER, CAMSHAFT
90. CAMSHAFT HOUSING (INTAKE SHOWN)
91. GASKET, CAMSHAFT HOUSING TO CYLINDER HEAD
117. DOWEL PIN (2)

GC1069100422000X

Fig. 7   Camshaft housing & cover

8. Remove mounting bolts and tensioner. **Tensioner is spring loaded.**
9. Mark timing chain and crankshaft sprocket for installation.
10. Remove timing chain.

Installation

Do not interchange timing chains between model years on this engine. There are differences in the sprockets. The links' shape matches the sprockets. Ensure the crankshaft sprocket and timing chain are assembled in the same orientation as they were removed.

1. Apply adhesive sealant compound part No. 12345493, or equivalent, on camshaft sprocket bolt.
2. Hold camshaft sprocket in position with camshaft sprocket tool No. J-39579, or equivalent, then tighten mounting bolt and washer.
3. Position camshafts using camshaft sprocket timing alignment pin tools No. J-36800, or equivalent, through camshaft sprockets' into timing chain housing holes, **Fig. 5.**
4. If camshafts are out of position and must be rotated more than 1/8 turn, proceed as follows:
    a. Rotate crankshaft clockwise to 90° off TDC.
    b. Position camshafts and install dowels.
    c. Rotate crankshaft counterclockwise back to TDC. **Rotating crankshaft clockwise to TDC will damage valves and pistons.**
5. Place timing chain over exhaust camshaft sprocket, coolant pump or idler

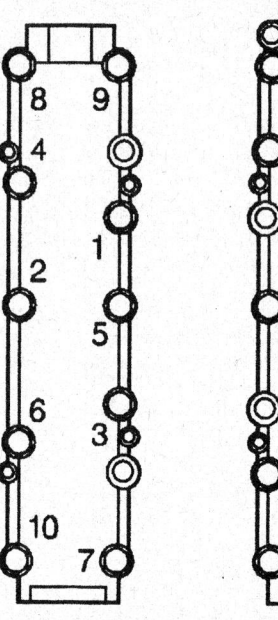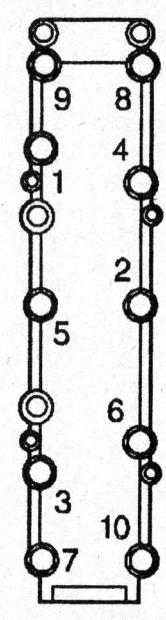

GC1069701058000X

Fig. 8   Camshaft housing bolt tightening sequence

sprocket and crankshaft sprocket.
6. Remove intake camshaft timing pin and attach camshaft sprocket tool No. J-39579, or equivalent.
7. Rotate intake camshaft sprocket counterclockwise with tool until timing chain can be installed over sprocket.
8. Release tool. Timing chain tension between camshaft sprockets should tighten.
9. Timing pin should easily fit through intake camshaft sprocket timing hole into timing chain housing timing hole. If timing pin does not fit easily, repeat procedure.
10. With timing pins installed, raise and support vehicle.
11. With timing chain slack between intake camshaft sprocket and crankshaft sprocket, timing marks on crankshaft and engine block should be aligned. If crankshaft timing marks are not aligned, move timing chain one tooth forward or rearward to remove slack, then align marks.
12. **On Malibu models,** proceed as follows:
    a. Load tensioner to zero position by forming keeper out of heavy gauge wire.
    b. Apply slight force on tensioner blade to compress plunger.
    c. Insert small screwdriver into reset access hole and pry ratchet pawl away from ratchet teeth while forcing plunger completely in hole.
    d. Install keeper between access hole and blade.
    e. Install tensioner to chain housing and inspect plunger installation again. Ensure long end is toward crankshaft.
13. **On Alero and Grand Am models,** proceed as follows:
    a. Assemble tensioner plunger and body.

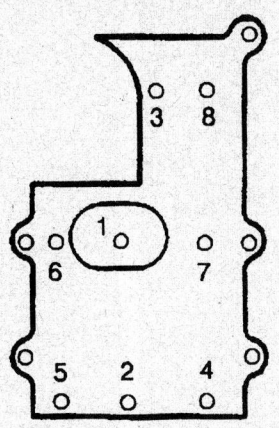

Fig. 9 Balance shaft housing bolt tightening sequence

b. With tensioner plunger fully extended, rotate tensioner with plunger down on flat surface.
c. Press down on tensioner body until plunger full seats in body.
d. Install tensioner onto timing chain housing.
e. Apply hand pressure to tensioner shoe until locking tab seats into stud groove.
f. Install tensioner bolts and tighten.
g. Release plunger.
h. Press plunger's face firmly down using suitable flat-bladed screwdriver, or similar tool, until plunger releases from rear of tensioner shoe. **Do not damage face.**
14. **On all models,** lower vehicle enough to remove alignment dowel pins.
15. Rotate crankshaft two revolutions clockwise.
16. Align crankshaft keyway with cylinder block alignment mark and insert timing pins through camshaft sprockets into timing chain housing timing holes.
17. Timing pins should slide easily through timing holes. If timing pins cannot be easily inserted, repeat procedure to properly time engine.
18. Install timing chain guides and front cover.

CAMSHAFT
REPLACE

Whenever camshaft housing to cylinder head mounting bolts are loosened, the camshaft housing to cylinder head gasket must be replaced.

Intake

1. Drain coolant into suitable container.
2. Disconnect ignition coil and module electrical connectors.
3. Remove mounting bolts and pull upward on ignition coil and module, **Fig. 1.** If connectors are stuck to spark plugs, remove them pulling straight upward using spark plug connector remover tool No. J-36011, or equivalent.
4. Disconnect camshaft position electrical sensor.

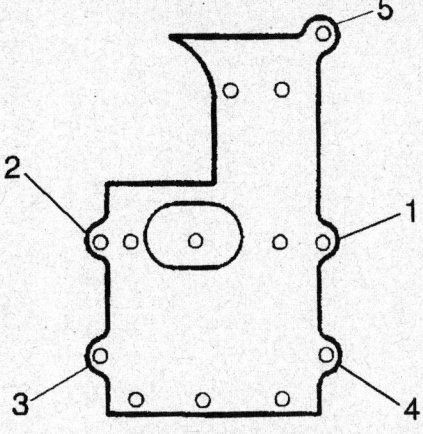

Fig. 10 Balance shaft housing to block bolt tightening sequence

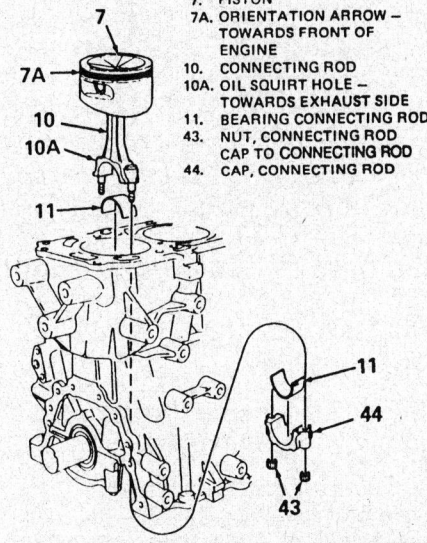

```
7.   PISTON
7A.  ORIENTATION ARROW –
     TOWARDS FRONT OF
     ENGINE
10.  CONNECTING ROD
10A. OIL SQUIRT HOLE –
     TOWARDS EXHAUST SIDE
11.  BEARING CONNECTING ROD
43.  NUT, CONNECTING ROD
     CAP TO CONNECTING ROD
44.  CAP, CONNECTING ROD
```

Fig. 12 Piston & rod assembly

5. Remove power steering pump and position aside with hoses attached.
6. Disconnect vacuum line from fuel pressure regulator and fuel injector wiring harness electrical connector.
7. Remove fuel line bracket from top of intake camshaft housing.
8. Remove fuel rail mounting bolts and fuel rail. Leave fuel lines attached and position fuel rail over master cylinder. Cover openings in cylinder head and injector nozzles.
9. Disconnect timing chain housing at intake camshaft housing. **Do not remove.**
10. Remove front cover as outlined under "Front Cover, Replace."
11. Raise and support vehicle.
12. Disconnect heater hose at thermostat housing and drain cylinder block completely into suitable container.
13. Remove timing chain tensioner and timing chain as outlined under "Timing Chain, Replace."
14. Remove water pump mounting nuts as outlined under "Water Pump, Replace."

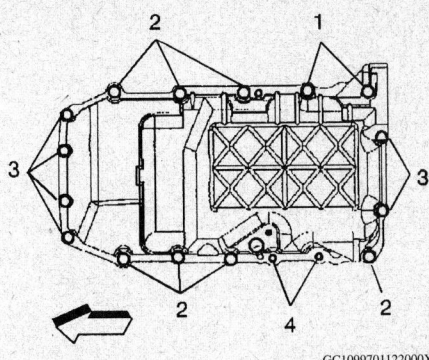

Fig. 11 Oil pan bolt replacement

15. Remove timing chain housing to block bolts and oil pan to front cover bolts.
16. Remove lowest front cover retaining stud.
17. Lower vehicle.
18. Remove camshaft sprocket mounting bolts and washers while holding sprockets with camshaft sprocket tool No. J-39579, or equivalent.
19. Remove camshaft sprockets. They are identical and interchangeable.
20. Remove chain housing to camshaft housing bolts. Do not remove timing chain housing.
21. Remove camshaft housing cover mounting bolts, **Fig. 7.**
22. Record gaskets' positions.
23. Loosen camshaft housing to cylinder head mounting bolts in reverse of tightening sequence, **Fig. 8.**
24. Leave two camshaft housing to cylinder head mounting bolts loosely installed.
25. Thread four camshaft housing to cylinder head bolts into tapped camshaft housing cover holes and push cover off housing.
26. Remove loosely installed bolts.
27. Record gasket positions, then remove and discard gasket.
28. Loosely install one camshaft housing to cylinder head bolt to retain housing during camshaft and lifter removal.
29. Record timing chain sprocket dowel pin position for assembly and remove camshaft. **Do not damage journals.**
30. Remove valve lash adjuster. Keep adjusters in order for assembly. Store them in upside down position on level surface in clean engine oil to minimize lifter bleed-down.
31. Remove camshaft housing and gasket.
32. Reverse procedure to install, noting the following:
    a. Lubricate entire camshaft and valve lash adjusters with lubricant part No. 12345501, or equivalent.
    b. Apply suitable sealant to threads of camshaft housing, cover retaining, ignition coil and module mounting bolts.
    c. **Torque** camshaft housing to cylinder head bolts to 16 ft. lbs., in sequence, **Fig. 8.**
    d. Tighten head bolts an additional 90°.
    e. **Torque** camshaft housing cover to

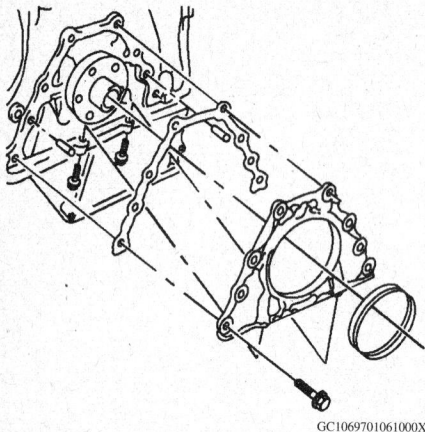

GC1069701061000X

Fig. 13 Crankshaft rear oil seal replacement

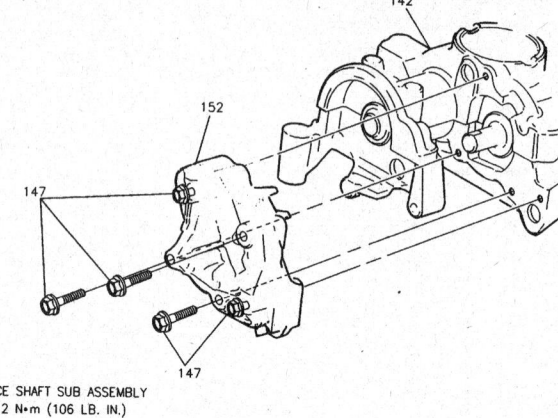

142 BALANCE SHAFT SUB ASSEMBLY
147 BOLT 12 N•m (106 LB. IN.)
152 OIL PUMP SUB ASSEMBLY

GC1069600658000A

Fig. 14 Oil pump replacement

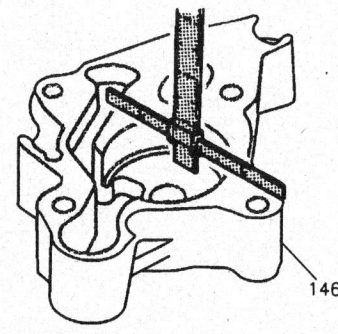

146 BODY, OIL PUMP

GC1069600662000A

Fig. 15 Gerotor cavity depth measurement

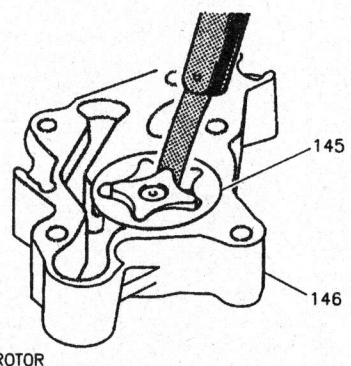

145 GEROTOR
146 BODY, OIL PUMP

GC1069600660000A

Fig. 16 Inner gear tip clearance measurement

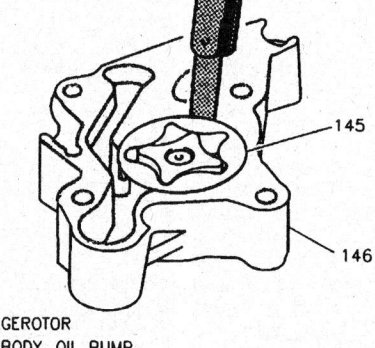

145 GEROTOR
146 BODY, OIL PUMP

GC1069600661000A

Fig. 17 Outer gerotor diameter clearance measurement

camshaft housing bolts to 16 ft. lbs.
f. Tighten housing bolts an additional 30°.
g. Apply ¼ inch bead of sealer part No. 12346286, or equivalent, onto joint at end of camshaft housing halves before installing power steering pump and face seal.
h. Apply pipe sealant part No. 1052080, or equivalent, onto ignition coil and module cover bolts.
i. If new camshaft was installed, add engine oil supplement part No. 1052367, or equivalent, to engine oil.

Exhaust

1. Drain coolant into suitable container.
2. Disconnect ignition coil and module electrical connectors.
3. Remove mounting bolts, then pull upward on ignition coil and module, **Fig. 1.** If connectors are stuck to spark plugs, pull straight upward to remove them using spark plug connector remover tool No. J-36011, or equivalent.
4. Disconnect oil pressure switch electrical connector.
5. Remove front cover as outlined under "Front Cover, Replace."
6. Raise and support vehicle.
7. Disconnect heater hose at thermostat housing and drain cylinder block com-

pletely into suitable container.
8. Disconnect timing chain housing at exhaust camshaft housing . **Do not remove.**
9. Remove transaxle fluid level indicator tube from exhaust camshaft cover and position it aside.
10. Lower vehicle.
11. Remove exhaust camshaft housing cover and gasket.
12. Loosen camshaft housing to cylinder head mounting bolts in reverse order of tightening sequence, **Fig. 8.**
13. Leave two camshaft housing to cylinder head mounting bolts loosely installed.
14. Thread four camshaft housing to cylinder head bolts into tapped camshaft housing cover holes and push cover off housing.
15. Remove loosely installed bolts.
16. Record gasket positions, then remove and discard gasket.
17. Loosely install one camshaft housing to cylinder head bolt to retain housing during camshaft and lifter removal.
18. Record timing chain sprocket dowel pin position for assembly and remove camshaft. **Do not damage journals.**
19. Remove valve lash adjuster. Keep them in order for assembly. Store them in upside down position, on level sur-

face in clean engine oil to prevent lifter bleed-down.
20. Remove camshaft housing and gasket.
21. Reverse procedure to install, noting the following:
a. Lubricate entire camshaft and valve lash adjusters with lubricant part No. 12345501, or equivalent.
b. Apply suitable sealant to threads of camshaft housing, cover retaining, ignition coil and module mounting bolts.
c. **Torque** camshaft housing to cylinder head bolts to 11 ft. lbs., in sequence, **Fig. 8.**
d. Tighten head bolts an additional 90°.
e. **Torque** camshaft housing cover to camshaft housing bolts to 11 ft. lbs.
f. Tighten housing bolts an additional 30°.
g. Tighten timing chain housing to engine and camshaft housing mounting bolts.
h. Apply pipe sealant part No. 1052080, or equivalent, on camshaft housing and threads of cover retainer bolt.
i. If new camshaft was installed, add engine oil supplement part No.

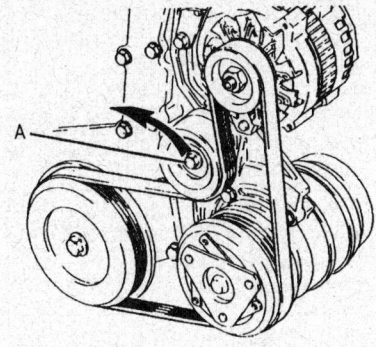

A ROTATE TENSIONER IN DIRECTION
OF ARROW TO REMOVE OR INSTALL BELT.

GC1069100427000A

Fig. 18 Serpentine belt replacement

1052367, or equivalent, to engine oil.

Valve Lifter Break-In

If new lifters have been installed or if they bled down while the engine was disassembled some excessive noise might be heard when first starting up again. This is normal and no engine damage should occur. To purge trapped air from the lifters, proceed as follows:
1. Start engine and allow it to idle and warm up for five minutes.
2. Increase engine speed to 2000 RPM until lifter noise disappears.
3. Return engine to idle for another five minutes or perform road test.

BALANCE SHAFT

REPLACE

Removal

1. Remove oil pan as outlined in "Oil Pan, Replace."
2. Remove mounting nut, bolt and balance shaft chain cover.
3. Loosen but do not remove balance shaft chain tensioner.
4. Remove oil pump and cover.
5. Rotate engine crankshaft until No. 1 piston is at TDC.
6. Prevent balance shafts from turning using balance shaft holding tool No. J-41088, or equivalent.
7. Mark driven sprocket's surface for installation alignment, then remove lefthand threaded driven sprocket bolt.
8. Loosen balance shaft housing bolts.
9. Remove mounting bolts and balance shaft housing.
10. Remove bolts and separate housing.
11. Remove balance shaft and gear, then the bearings, bolts and thrust plate.

Installation

1. Install thrust plate and tighten bolts.
2. Mount suitable dial indicator and measure shaft endplay at rear side of shafts.

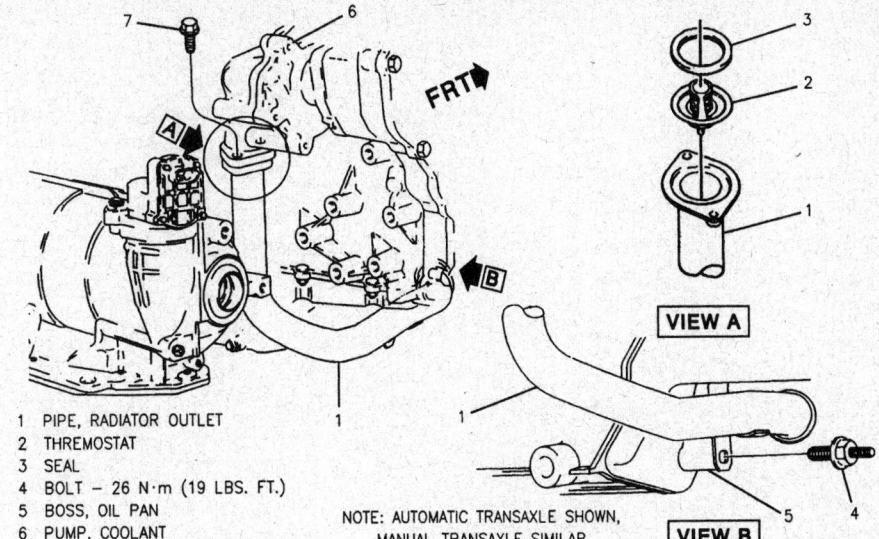

1 PIPE, RADIATOR OUTLET
2 THREMOSTAT
3 SEAL
4 BOLT – 26 N·m (19 LBS. FT.)
5 BOSS, OIL PAN
6 PUMP, COOLANT
7 BOLT – 14 N·m (10 LBS. FT.)

NOTE: AUTOMATIC TRANSAXLE SHOWN, MANUAL TRANSAXLE SIMILAR

GC1089600279000A

Fig. 19 Thermostat replacement

3. If endplay is not within .0073–.0179 inch, inspect and replace thrust plate.
4. Install balance shaft and gear subassemblies. Ensure gear timing marks are properly aligned.
5. Apply thread locker part No. 12345493, or equivalent, to mounting bolts and install housing.
6. **Torque** housing bolt Nos. 1, 2, 4, 5, 6 and 7 to 11 ft. lbs., in sequence, **Fig. 9.**
7. Tighten housing bolts an additional 40°.
8. **Torque** housing bolt Nos. 3 and 8 to 84 inch lbs., then tighten an additional 40°.
9. **Torque** housing bolt Nos. 1, 2 and 4 to 18 ft. lbs., in sequence, **Fig. 10.**
10. Tighten bolt Nos. 1, 2 and 4 an additional 70°.
11. **Torque** bolt No. 3 to 30 inch lbs., then tighten an additional 60°.
12. **Torque** bolt No. 5 to 39 ft. lbs.
13. Rotate balance shafts and ensure they spin freely.
14. Ensure piston No. 1 is at TDC.
15. Prevent shaft rotation by installing balance shaft holder tool No. J-41088, or equivalent.
16. **Torque** balance shaft driven sprocket bolt to 22 ft. lbs., then tighten an additional 45°. **Bolt is lefthand threaded and must be tightened by rotating counterclockwise.**
17. Adjust balance shaft chain tension with three lbs. of force to .040 inch using suitable brass feeler gauge between guide and chain.
18. **Torque** balance shaft chain tensioner bolt to 10 ft. lbs.
19. Install balance shaft chain cover and **torque** bolt to 10 ft. lbs.
20. Install oil pan with new gasket, **Fig. 11.**

PISTON & ROD ASSEMBLY

Assemble piston to rod with arrow on pis-

ton toward front of engine and oil squirt hole on rod toward exhaust side of engine, **Fig. 12.**
Upon installation, use a suitable feeler gauge to measure connecting rod side clearance, which should be .0059–.0177 inch.

PISTONS, PINS & RINGS

Pistons and rings are available in standard size and oversize. Pistons and pins are serviced as an assembly.

MAIN & ROD BEARINGS

Main and rod bearings are available in standard size only.

CRANKSHAFT REAR OIL SEAL

REPLACE

1. Remove transaxle as outlined in **MOTOR's "Domestic Transmission Manual, In-Vehicle Service."**
2. Remove mounting bolts and flywheel using holder tool No. J-38122, or equivalent.
3. Remove oil pan to crankshaft rear seal housing mounting bolts.
4. Remove mounting screws, crankshaft rear seal housing and gasket, **Fig. 13.**
5. Support crankshaft rear seal housing on two wooden blocks of equal thickness with crankshaft side facing upward and drive seal out through transaxle side of housing.
6. Reverse procedure to install, noting the following:
   a. If aluminum carrier oil pan top silicone strips across top at cylinder block and seal housing three-way

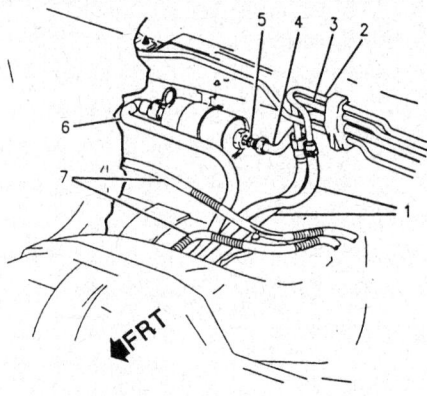

GC1029102737000X

Fig. 21 Fuel filter replacement

1 HOSE – PART OF FUEL SENDER
2 FUEL VAPOR PIPE
3 FUEL RETURN PIPE
4 FUEL FEED PIPE
5 FUEL FEED PIPE NUT –
   27 N·m (20 LBS. FT.)
6 HOSE – PART OF FUEL SENDER
7 ABS AND FUEL SENDER HARNESS

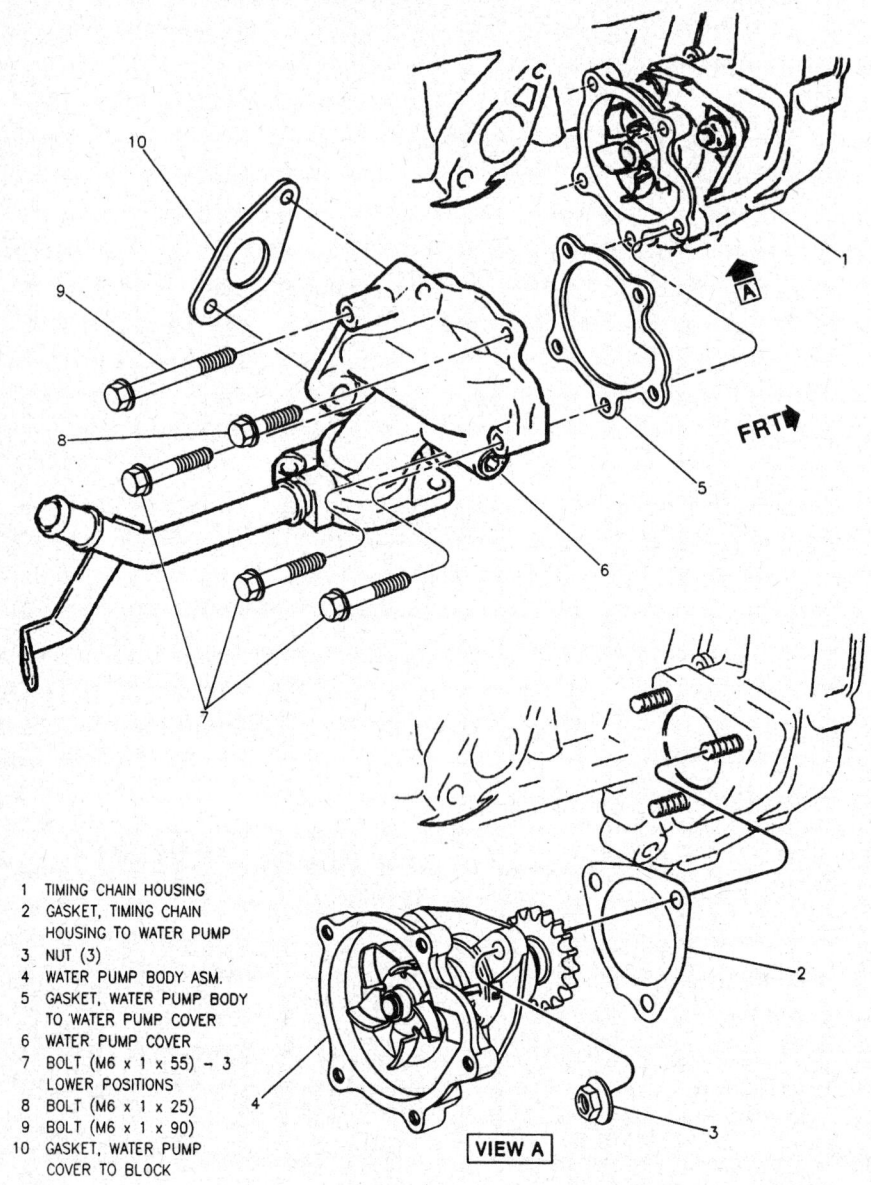

1 TIMING CHAIN HOUSING
2 GASKET, TIMING CHAIN
   HOUSING TO WATER PUMP
3 NUT (3)
4 WATER PUMP BODY ASM.
5 GASKET, WATER PUMP BODY
   TO WATER PUMP COVER
6 WATER PUMP COVER
7 BOLT (M6 x 1 x 55) – 3
   LOWER POSITIONS
8 BOLT (M6 x 1 x 25)
9 BOLT (M6 x 1 x 90)
10 GASKET, WATER PUMP
   COVER TO BLOCK

VIEW A

GC1089700446000X

Fig. 20 Water pump replacement

joint are damaged they can be restored to original dimensions using silicone sealant part No. 12345739, or equivalent.

b. Lubricate seal lips with engine oil prior to installing housing.

c. Press newt seal into housing using rear crankshaft seal installer No. J-36005, or equivalent.

d. If using old flywheel to crankshaft bolts, coat threads with adhesive sealant compound part No. 12345493, or equivalent.

OIL PAN
REPLACE

1. Drain crankcase and cooling system into approved containers.
2. Support engine using engine support fixture tool No. J-28467-360, or equivalent.

3. Remove flywheel housing inspection cover.
4. Remove righthand front wheel and tire assembly, then the splash shield.
5. Remove serpentine drive belt.
6. Remove air conditioning compressor lower mounting bolts and support compressor with hoses attached.
7. **On Alero and Grand Am models,** remove engine to transaxle brace.
8. **On all models,** remove engine mount strut bracket bolts and position bracket aside.
9. Raise engine approximately 1½ inches.
10. Remove bolts and radiator outlet pipe.
11. Remove exhaust manifold brace.
12. Remove oil pan to flywheel cover nut and bolt.
13. **On Alero and Grand Am models,** remove flywheel cover stud for clearance.
14. **On all models,** remove radiator outlet

pipe from lower radiator hose and oil pan.

15. Disconnect oil level sensor electrical connector.
16. Remove mounting bolts and oil pan.
17. Reverse procedure to install, noting the following:
    a. **Torque** M8 × 1.25 × 80 bolts (1) to 18 ft. lbs., **Fig. 11.**
    b. **Torque** M8 × 1.25 × 22 bolts (2) to 18 ft. lbs.
    c. **Torque** M6 × 1.00 × 25 bolts (3) to 108 inch lbs.
    d. **Torque** bolt (4) to 19 ft. lbs.

OIL PUMP
REPLACE

1. Remove oil pan as outlined under "Oil Pan, Replace."
2. Remove balance shaft chain cover.
3. Remove balance shaft chain tensioner.
4. Remove oil pump cover, mounting bolts and pump, **Fig. 14.**
5. Reverse procedure to install, noting the following:
    a. **Torque** cover to balance shaft housing bolts to 40 ft. lbs.
    b. Adjust balance shaft tension as outlined under "Balance Shaft, Replace."

OIL PUMP SERVICE

1. Remove oil pan as outlined under "Oil Pan, Replace."
2. Remove balance shaft chain cover.
3. Remove balance shaft chain tensioner.
4. Remove oil pump cover, mounting bolts and pump, **Fig. 14.**
5. Disassemble pump gerotor cover from housing.
6. Remove pump from balance shaft housing.
7. Disassemble pressure relief valve.
8. Remove roll pin with punch.

9. Pry out remaining bottom half of valve using suitable tool.
10. Clean components in suitable cleaning solvent. Remove varnish, sludge and dirt.
11. Inspect pump cover and housing for cracks, scoring, porous or damaged casting, damaged threads, excessive wear or galling.
12. Inspect relief valve for physical damage.
13. Inspect gerotor for chipping, galling or excessive wear.
14. Measure gerotor cavity depth, **Fig. 15.**
15. Depth should be .6023–.6043 inch.
16. Measure inner gerotor tip clearance, **Fig. 16,** which should be .0059 inch maximum.
17. Measure outer gerotor diameter clearance, **Fig. 17.**
18. Diameter clearance should be .0019–.0059 inch.
19. Replace any worn component if any measurement is not within specifications.

BELT TENSION DATA

1. Turn off accessories.
2. Bring engine to operating temperature.
3. Turn engine off.
4. Measure belt tension halfway between alternator and power steering pump using tension gauge tool No. J-23600-B or equivalent.
5. Start engine and allow temperature to stabilize for 15 seconds.
6. Turn engine off.
7. Apply clockwise force to tensioner pulley bolt.
8. Release force and measure belt tension without disturbing tensioner position.
9. Apply counterclockwise force to tensioner pulley bolt and raise pulley to eliminate tension.
10. Slowly lower pulley to belt and measure belt tension without disturbing tensioner position.
11. Average out three readings.
12. If average reading is less than 30–50 lbs., replace belt tensioner.

SERPENTINE DRIVE BELT

Refer to **Fig. 18,** for drive belt replacement. **Use a tight fitting 13 mm wrench at least 18 inches long.**

COOLING SYSTEM BLEED

After filling cooling system, start engine and allow it to reach operating temperature with surge tank pressure cap removed. Air will bleed through surge cap opening. Adjust coolant to proper level and install surge tank pressure cap.

THERMOSTAT
REPLACE

1. Drain coolant into suitable container until level falls below thermostat.
2. Remove exhaust manifold heat shield.
3. Remove inlet housing bolt through exhaust manifold.
4. Raise and support vehicle.
5. **On Alero and Grand Am models,** proceed as follows:
   a. Remove coolant inlet housing stud from oil pan.
   b. Remove tire and wheel.
   c. Remove splash shield.
   d. Remove transaxle to engine block brace.
6. **On all models,** remove radiator outlet pipe stud.
7. Remove second coolant inlet housing bolt and inlet housing.
8. Remove thermostat, **Fig. 19.**
9. Reverse procedure to install, noting the following:
   a. **Torque** coolant inlet housing stud to oil pan to 19 ft. lbs.
   b. **Torque** coolant inlet housing bolts through exhaust manifold to 10 ft. lbs.
   c. Bring engine to operating temperature and inspect for leaks.

WATER PUMP
REPLACE

1. Drain coolant into suitable container.
2. Remove serpentine drive belt.
3. Compress tensioner and hold while removing tensioner mounting bolts and tensioner.
4. Disconnect electrical connectors.
5. Remove exhaust manifold heat shields.
6. Remove heat wrap from heater hose.
7. Disconnect heater hoses.
8. Remove coolant inlet housing bolt through exhaust manifold.
9. Raise and support vehicle.
10. Remove exhaust manifold brace mounting bolt.
11. Remove exhaust pipe to manifold studs.
12. **On Alero and Grand Am models,** remove heater outlet pipe bracket to transmission bolt.
13. **On all models,** pull down and back on exhaust pipe to disconnect it from manifold bolts. **Do not rotate flex coupling more than 3°.**
14. Remove radiator outlet pipe from oil pan and transaxle. Leave lower radiator hose attached and pull down gently on radiator outlet pipe to disconnect it from water pump. Leave outlet pipe hanging.
15. Lower vehicle and remove brake vacuum pipe from cam housing.
16. Remove mounting nuts, exhaust manifold, seals and gaskets.
17. Remove engine front cover as outlined under "Front Cover, Replace."
18. Compress timing chain tensioner.
19. Remove cover bolts, timing chain housing nuts, water pump and cover, **Fig. 20.**

20. Reverse procedure to install, noting the following:
   a. Install cover and pump bolts hand tight.
   b. Lubricate coolant inlet pipe O-ring with clean antifreeze and slide pipe into pump cover. Hand tighten bolts.
   c. Tighten cover and pump bolts.

RADIATOR
REPLACE
Alero & Grand Am

1. Recover air conditioning refrigerant as outlined in "Air Conditioning" chapter.
2. Drain coolant into suitable container.
3. Remove battery and battery tray.
4. Remove upper radiator hose.
5. Remove upper transaxle cooler line.
6. Remove coolant surge tank hose.
7. Remove condenser inlet fitting from discharge hose.
8. Disconnect cooling fan electrical connector.
9. Raise and support vehicle.
10. Remove lower closeout panel.
11. Remove lower radiator hose from radiator.
12. Remove lower transaxle cooler line.
13. Remove evaporator line from condenser outlet.
14. Remove radiator lower mounting panel.
15. Remove Condenser Radiator Fan Module (CRFM).
16. Remove condenser and fan shroud from radiator.
17. Reverse procedure to install,

Malibu

1. Recover air conditioning refrigerant as outlined in "Air Conditioning" chapter.
2. Drain coolant into suitable container.
3. Remove upper radiator hose and transaxle cooler line, then the surge tank hose.
4. Remove condenser inlet fitting from discharge hose and lower transaxle cooler line.
5. Disconnect cooling fan electrical connector.
6. Raise and support vehicle.
7. Remove lower closeout panel, lower radiator hose and evaporator line.
8. Remove lower radiator mounting plate and condenser fan radiator module.
9. Remove condenser, fan shroud and radiator.
10. Reverse procedure to install.

FUEL PUMP
REPLACE

The fuel pump is a component of the fuel sender and must be replaced as a complete unit.

1. Relieve fuel system pressure as outlined under "Precautions."
2. Drain tank into suitable container.
3. Disconnect electrical connectors.
4. Remove ground wire mounting screw from underbody.

5. Disconnect hoses from tank meter, filler and vent pipes.
6. Support fuel tank and disconnect fuel tank retaining straps.
7. Remove fuel tank.
8. Modular fuel sender might spring up from its original position. Have suitable shop towel ready to absorb spills. Tip assembly slightly to avoid float damage.
9. Remove fuel tank sending unit and pump by holding it down, then removing lockring using lockring tool No. J-39765, or equivalent.
10. Reverse procedure to install, noting the following:
    a. Install new O-ring on sender tank flange.
    b. Align tab on front of fuel sender with slot on front of retainer lockring.
    c. Slowly apply pressure to top of spring loaded sender until sender aligns flush with tank retainer.
    d. Insert lockring into proper slots.
    e. Turn ignition switch to On position for two seconds.
    f. Turn ignition switch to Off position for 10 seconds.
    g. Turn ignition On.
    h. Inspect for fuel leaks.

FUEL FILTER
REPLACE

The fuel filter is located below the rear of the vehicle, rearward of the fuel tank.
1. Relieve fuel system pressure as outlined under "Precautions."
2. Raise and support vehicle.
3. Remove fuel filter fitting, **Fig. 21.**
4. Grasp filter and one nylon fuel connection line fitting, then twist quick connect fitting ¼ turn in each direction to loosen dirt in fitting.
5. Clean dirt from quick connect fitting.
6. Depress quick connect fitting plastic tabs of male end connector and pull apart.
7. Remove fuel filter.
8. Reverse procedure to install, noting the following:
    a. Apply few drops of clean engine oil to male pipe ends before connection to reduce risk of leakage and fire.
    b. Turn ignition switch to On position for two seconds.
    c. Turn ignition switch to Off position for 10 seconds.
    d. Turn ignition On.
    e. Inspect for fuel leaks.

TIGHTENING SPECIFICATIONS

Year	Component	Torque/Ft. Lbs.
2001–05	Balance Shaft Cover	10
	Balance Shaft Housing	⑤
	Balance Shaft Mounting	⑤
	Balance Shaft Sprocket	⑤
	Camshaft Housing & Cover	⑦
	Camshaft Position Sensor	89①
	Camshaft Sprocket To Cam	52
	Connecting Rod	②
	Coolant Inlet To Oil Pan	19
	Coolant Inlet To Water Pump	10
	Coolant Outlet To Cylinder Head	19
	Crankshaft Balancer To Crankshaft	③
	Crankshaft Bearing Cap Bolts	⑨
	Crankshaft Position Sensor	80①
	Cylinder Head	④
	Engine Mount Bracket	99
	Engine Mount To Bracket	46
	Engine Mount To Body	49
	Exhaust Camshaft Housing Rear Cover	⑦
	Exhaust Manifold Brace To Manifold	⑪
	Exhaust Manifold Brace To Oil Pan	19
	Exhaust Manifold Heat Shield	10
	Exhaust Manifold To Cylinder Head, Nut	41
	Exhaust Manifold To Cylinder Head, Stud	11
	Exhaust Manifold To Oil Pan	19
	Exhaust Manifold Studs To Manifold	19
	Exhaust Pipe To Manifold	26
	Flexplate To Clutch Cover	22
	Flexplate To Converter	46
	Flexplate To Crankshaft	⑥
	Front Cover To Timing Chain Housing	9
	Fuel Filter Fitting	20
	Fuel Pipe Bracket To Camshaft Housing	⑧
	Fuel Pipe To Fuel Rail	22
	Fuel Rail To Camshaft Housing	19
	Ignition Coil & Module	16
	Intake Manifold Brace	19

TIGHTENING
SPECIFICATIONS—Continued

Year	Component	Torque/Ft. Lbs.
2001–05	Intake Manifold To Cylinder Head, Nut	⑩
	Intake Manifold To Cylinder Head, Stud	96①
	Knock Sensor	15
	Oil/Air Separator To Intake Manifold	19
	Oil/Air Separator To Block	19
	Oil Filter Connector To Block	21
	Oil Pan	17
	Oil Pan, Second Set	106①
	Oil Pan Drain Plug	19
	Oil Pan Studs	19
	Oil Passage Plug	22
	Oil Passage Plugs, 1/8 × 27	89①
	Oil Passage Plugs, 1/4 × 18	15
	Oil Passage Plugs, 3/8 × 18	22
	Oil Pump To Balance Shaft Housing, Long Bolt (Alero & Grand Am)	106①
	Oil Pump To Balance Shaft Housing, Short Bolt (Alero & Grand Am)	89①
	Oxygen Sensor To Exhaust Manifold	31
	Radiator	89①
	Rear Crankshaft Seal Housing To Block	108①
	Spark Plugs	13
	Starter	66
	Thermostat Housing	19
	Throttle Body To Intake Manifold	89①
	Timing Chain Housing To Block Or Camshaft Housing	19
	Timing Chain Housing To Block, Stud	21
	Timing Chain Tensioner To Housing & Block	89①
	Transaxle To Block, Bolt	44
	Transaxle To Block, Nut	49
	Transaxle To Block, Stud	115①
	Water Pump Cover	10
	Water Pump Cover To Block	19
	Water Pump To Timing Chain Housing	19

① — Inch lbs.
② — **Torque** to 18 ft. lbs., then tighten an additional 80°.
③ — **Torque** to 129 ft. lbs., then tighten an additional 90°.
④ — Refer to "Cylinder Head, Replace" for tightening specifications and sequence.
⑤ — Refer to "Balance Shaft, Replace" for tightening specifications and sequence.
⑥ — **Torque** to 22 ft. lbs., then tighten an additional 45°.
⑦ — Refer to "Camshaft, Replace" for tightening specifications and sequence.
⑧ — **Torque** to 11 ft. lbs., then tighten an additional 30°.
⑨ — **Torque** to 15 ft. lbs, then tighten an additional 90°.
⑩ — Refer to "Intake Manifold, Replace" for tightening specifications and sequence.
⑪ — Refer to "Exhaust Manifold, Replace" for tightening specifications and sequence.

3.1L Engine

NOTE: On Air Bag Equipped Models, Refer To "Air Bag System Precautions" Located In The Front Of This Manual For System Disarming & Arming Procedures.

NOTE: For Procedures Not Found In This Section, Refer To "3.1L Engine" Section In The "Century, Grand Prix, Impala, Intrigue, Lumina, Monte Carlo & Regal" Chapter.

NOTE: Refer To "Computer Relearn Procedures" Located In The Front Of This Manual When Battery Power To The Computer Has Been Interrupted.

INDEX

PRECAUTIONS

Air Bag Systems

Refer to "Air Bag System Precautions" in the front of this manual for system disarming and arming procedures.

Battery Ground Cable

Prior to service, disconnect battery ground cable and isolate as required.

Fuel System Pressure Relief

Failure to relieve system pressure prior to disconnecting fuel system components may cause fire or personal injury.
1. Loosen fuel tank filler cap to relieve tank pressure.
2. Raise and support vehicle.
3. Disconnect fuel pump electrical connector.
4. Lower vehicle.
5. Start and operate engine until fuel supply is consumed.
6. Crank engine for approximately three seconds to relieve remaining pressure.
7. Disconnect battery ground cable and connect fuel pump connector.

COMPRESSION PRESSURE

When inspecting cylinder compression, the throttle should be open, the spark plugs removed and the battery at or near full charge. The lowest reading cylinder should not be less than 70% of the highest and no

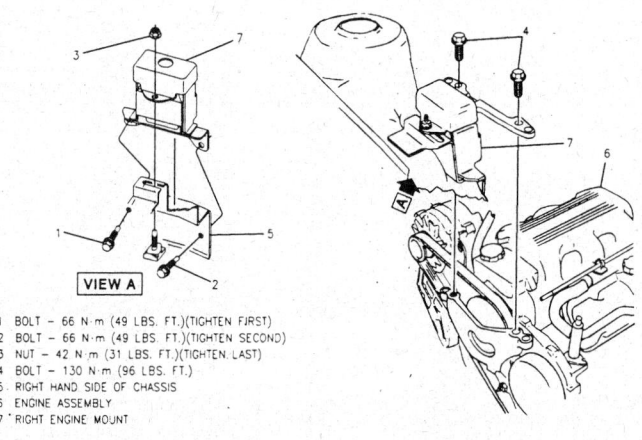

1. BOLT — 66 N·m (49 LBS. FT.)(TIGHTEN FIRST)
2. BOLT — 66 N·m (49 LBS. FT.)(TIGHTEN SECOND)
3. NUT — 42 N·m (31 LBS. FT.)(TIGHTEN LAST)
4. BOLT — 130 N·m (96 LBS. FT.)
5. RIGHT HAND SIDE OF CHASSIS
6. ENGINE ASSEMBLY
7. RIGHT ENGINE MOUNT

GC1069500596000X

Fig. 1 Engine mount replacement

cylinder reading should be less than 100 psi. Turn ignition key until engine cranks through four compression cycles. Normal compression builds up quickly and evenly to specified compression on each cylinder.

ENGINE MOUNT

REPLACE

1. Support engine by oil pan and remove engine mount to engine mount bracket support bolts, **Fig. 1.**
2. Remove engine mount to body bolts and nut.
3. Remove engine mount
4. Reverse procedure to install.

Strut

1. Raise and support vehicle.
2. Remove righthand splash shield.
3. Remove mounting bolts and engine mount strut , **Fig. 2.**

4. Reverse procedure to install.

ENGINE

REPLACE

1. Relieve fuel system pressure as outlined under "Precautions."
2. Remove upper half of air cleaner and throttle body duct.
3. Drain coolant into suitable container.
4. Disconnect upper radiator hose from engine and position aside.
5. Disconnect lower radiator hose from engine and position aside.
6. Disconnect coolant inlet line from surge tank.
7. Disconnect vacuum modulator, EVAP canister purge and power brake booster vacuum hoses.
8. Disconnect heater outlet hose from water pump.
9. Remove serpentine drive belt.

10. Disconnect accelerator and cruise control cable from throttle linkage.
11. Disconnect electrical connectors at electronic ignition, heated oxygen sensor, injector harness, IAC, throttle position sensor, engine coolant temperature sensor, PNP switch, transaxle shift solenoid, TCC solenoid and EGR and battery ground cable at transaxle.
12. Remove serpentine drive belt.
13. Disconnect alternator electrical connectors and power steering line clip.
14. Remove alternator rear brace.
15. Disconnect alternator air inlet connector.
16. Remove mounting bolts, nuts and alternator.
17. Disconnect power steering lines at power steering pump.
18. Disconnect fuel lines.
19. Remove cooling fan.
20. Disconnect shift cable linkage and cable from mounting bracket. Transaxle should be in low gear for better accessibility.
21. Disconnect transaxle vent tube from transaxle.
22. Disconnect vacuum hose at vacuum reservoir.
23. Remove engine support fixture.
24. Loosen but do not remove upper two air conditioning compressor bolts.
25. Raise and support vehicle.
26. Remove front tire and wheel assemblies.
27. Remove lefthand and righthand splash shields.
28. Raise and support vehicle.
29. Remove righthand splash shield.
30. Remove mounting bolts and engine mount strut, **Fig. 2**.
31. Remove both front ABS speed sensor connectors and harness from suspension supports.
32. Remove both ball joints.
33. Remove suspension support.
34. Remove drive axles from transaxle and support.
35. Remove oil filter and adapter.
36. Remove transaxle converter cover.
37. Remove mounting bolts and lower starter.
38. Disconnect starter electrical connectors and remove starter.
39. Disconnect knock sensor, front crankshaft position sensor, side crankshaft position sensor, oil level sensor, VSS and transaxle ground cable.
40. Disconnect heater hoses.
41. Remove air conditioning compressor lower bolts and position compressor aside.
42. Remove vacuum reserve tank.
43. Remove exhaust pipe from manifold and position aside.
44. Remove engine mount strut bracket.
45. Disconnect transaxle cooling lines at radiator.
46. Remove fluid level indicator and tube.
47. Lower vehicle and engine/transaxle onto suitable table.
48. Remove transaxle mount to body bolts, **Fig. 1**.

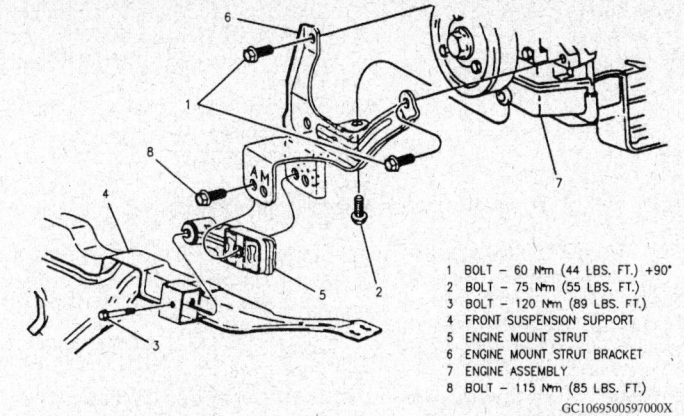

1 BOLT – 60 Nm (44 LBS. FT.) +90°
2 BOLT – 75 Nm (55 LBS. FT.)
3 BOLT – 120 Nm (89 LBS. FT.)
4 FRONT SUSPENSION SUPPORT
5 ENGINE MOUNT STRUT
6 ENGINE MOUNT STRUT BRACKET
7 ENGINE ASSEMBLY
8 BOLT – 115 Nm (85 LBS. FT.)
GC1069500597000X

Fig. 2 Engine mount strut bolt replacement

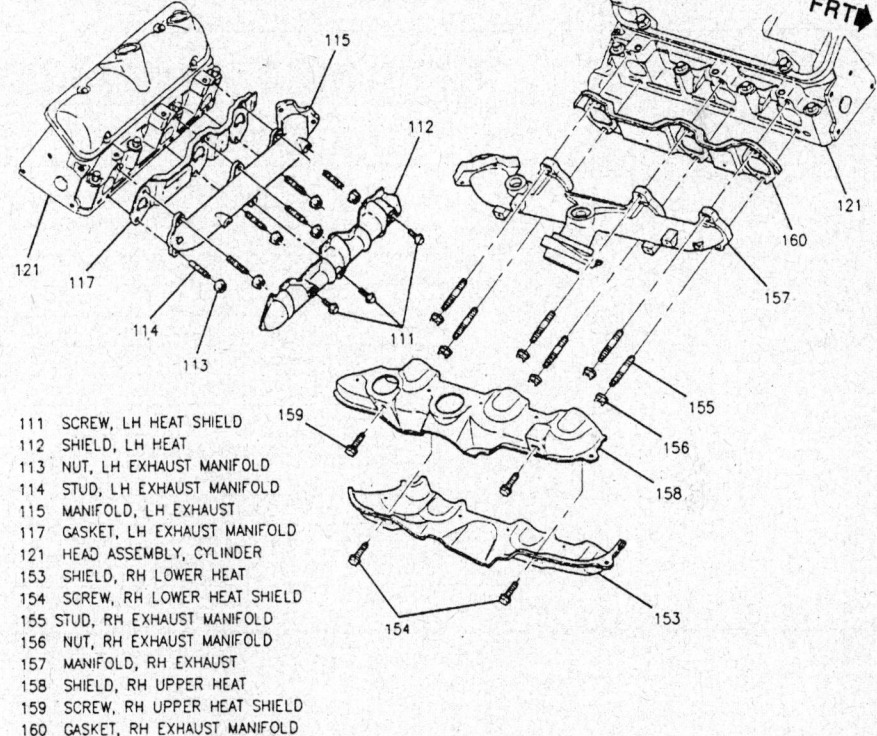

111 SCREW, LH HEAT SHIELD
112 SHIELD, LH HEAT
113 NUT, LH EXHAUST MANIFOLD
114 STUD, LH EXHAUST MANIFOLD
115 MANIFOLD, LH EXHAUST
117 GASKET, LH EXHAUST MANIFOLD
121 HEAD ASSEMBLY, CYLINDER
153 SHIELD, RH LOWER HEAT
154 SCREW, RH LOWER HEAT SHIELD
155 STUD, RH EXHAUST MANIFOLD
156 NUT, RH EXHAUST MANIFOLD
157 MANIFOLD, RH EXHAUST
158 SHIELD, RH UPPER HEAT
159 SCREW, RH UPPER HEAT SHIELD
160 GASKET, RH EXHAUST MANIFOLD

GC1069500600000X

Fig. 3 Exhaust manifold replacement

49. Remove intermediate bracket from righthand engine mount support bracket.
50. Raise and support vehicle, leaving powertrain on table.
51. Separate engine and transaxle.
52. Reverse procedure to install. After connecting engine to transaxle, loosely install serpentine drive belt to hold components in place.

INTAKE MANIFOLD
REPLACE
Upper

1. Disconnect vacuum lines.
2. Remove electrical connector, mounting screws and MAP sensor.
3. Remove pipe, bolts, EGR valve and gaskets.
4. Remove spark plug wires.
5. Remove mounting nuts, bolts and electronic ignition control module.
6. Remove mounting nuts, studs, upper intake manifold and gasket.
7. Reverse procedure to install.

Lower

1. Remove fuel feed and return pipe mounting bolt and clip.
2. Remove mounting bolts and fuel injector rail.
3. Remove mounting nut and heater inlet pipe.
4. Remove mounting bolts and lower intake manifold.

5. Reverse procedure to install.

EXHAUST MANIFOLD

REPLACE

Lefthand

1. Remove upper half of air cleaner and throttle cable duct.
2. Partially drain coolant into suitable container and disconnect radiator hose from thermostat housing.
3. Disconnect coolant bypass pipe at coolant pump and from exhaust manifold.
4. Remove exhaust crossover heat shield.
5. Remove exhaust crossover pipe from manifold.

6. Disconnect secondary ignition wires from spark plugs.
7. Remove exhaust manifold heat shield, **Fig. 3.**
8. Remove mounting nuts and exhaust manifold.
9. Reverse procedure to install.

Righthand

1. Remove upper half of air cleaner and throttle cable duct.
2. Remove exhaust crossover heat shield.
3. Remove crossover at exhaust manifold.
4. Remove heated oxygen sensor.
5. Disconnect EGR pipe at exhaust manifold.
6. Raise and support vehicle.

7. Remove transaxle oil fill tube and level indicator.
8. Remove exhaust pipe from exhaust manifold.
9. Disconnect exhaust pipe from converter flange and support converter.
10. Remove converter heat shield from body.
11. Remove exhaust manifold heat shield.
12. Remove mounting nuts and exhaust manifold, **Fig. 3.**
13. Reverse procedure to install.

RADIATOR

REPLACE

Refer to "2.4L Engine" section for radiator replacement procedure.

TIGHTENING SPECIFICATIONS

Year	Component	Torque/Ft. Lbs.
2001–05	Accelerator Cable Bracket	89①
	Coolant Drain Plug	14
	Coolant Outlet	18
	Drive Belt Tensioner	37
	Engine Mount Strut	52
	Engine Mount To Body, Bolt	49
	Engine Mount To Body, Nut	31
	Exhaust Manifold	12
	Exhaust Manifold Heat Shield	84①
	Lower Intake Manifold	10
	Oil Filter	9–10
	Upper Intake Manifold	18
	Water Pump	89①
	Water Pump Pulley	18

① — Inch lbs.

3.4L Engine

NOTE: On Air Bag Equipped Models, Refer To "Air Bag System Precautions" Located In The Front Of This Manual For System Disarming & Arming Procedures.

NOTE: Refer To "Computer Relearn Procedures" Located In The Front Of This Manual When Battery Power To The Computer Has Been Interrupted.

INDEX

PRECAUTIONS

Air Bag Systems

Refer to "Air Bag System Precautions" in the front of this manual for system disarming and arming procedures.

Battery Ground Cable

Prior to service, disconnect battery ground cable and isolate as required.

Fuel System Pressure Relief

Failure to relieve system pressure prior to disconnecting fuel system components may cause fire or personal injury.
1. Loosen fuel tank filler cap to relieve tank pressure.
2. Raise and support vehicle.
3. Disconnect fuel pump electrical connector.
4. Lower vehicle.
5. Start and operate engine until fuel supply is consumed.
6. Crank engine for approximately three seconds to relieve remaining pressure.
7. Disconnect and isolate battery ground cable, then connect fuel pump electrical connector.

COMPRESSION PRESSURE

When inspecting cylinder compression, the throttle should be open, the spark plugs removed and the battery at or near full charge. The lowest reading cylinder should not be less than 70% of the highest and no cylinder reading should be less than 100 psi. Crank engine until it runs through four compression cycles. Normal compression builds up quickly and evenly to specified compression on each cylinder.

ENGINE MOUNT

REPLACE

1. Support engine with suitable wooden block and suitable floor jack positioned below oil pan.
2. Remove cruise control module.
3. Remove engine mount to bracket support bolts.
4. Remove engine mount to body bolts.
5. Remove engine mount.
6. Reverse procedure to install.

Strut

1. Raise and support vehicle.
2. Remove righthand splash shield.
3. Remove mounting bolts and engine mount strut bolts.
4. Reverse procedure to install. **Torque** strut bolts to 74 ft. lbs., then tighten an additional 90°.

ENGINE

REPLACE

1. Relieve fuel system pressure as outlined under "Precautions."
2. Drain coolant into suitable container.
3. Remove engine air cleaner.
4. Remove hood.
5. Remove serpentine belt.
6. Remove hoses from surge tank.
7. Remove cruise control module.
8. Remove engine wiring harness from upper side of engine and position it aside.
9. Disconnect throttle and cruise control cables. **Manufacturer recommends throttle cable replacement when engine is removed and installed.**
10. Raise and support vehicle.
11. Remove starter motor.
12. Remove air conditioning compressor with lines attached and position aside.
13. Disconnect engine lower wiring harness and position it aside.
14. Disconnect catalytic converter flange from rear exhaust manifold.
15. Remove inspection cover.

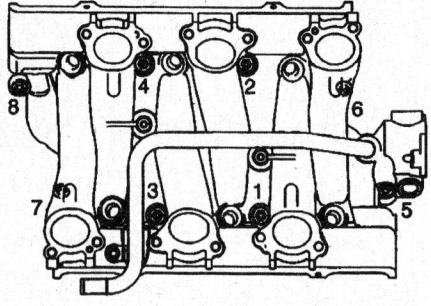

Fig. 1 Lower intake manifold bolt tightening sequence

GC1059900123000X

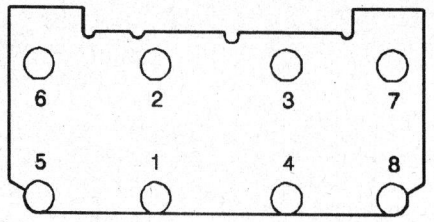

GC1059900124000X

Fig. 2 Cylinder head bolt tightening sequence

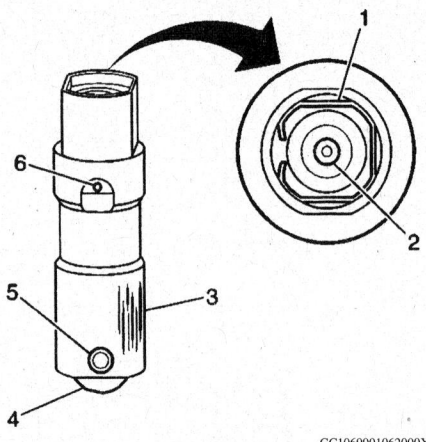

GC1069901062000X

Fig. 3 Valve lifter inspection locations

16. Remove torque converter to flexplate bolts.
17. Remove engine splash shields.
18. Remove transaxle to engine brace.
19. Remove two outer transaxle mounting bolts.
20. Disconnect upper and lower radiator hoses.
21. Lower vehicle.
22. Disconnect engine fuel lines.
23. Disconnect vacuum hoses at brake booster.
24. Disconnect heater hoses.
25. Install engine support fixture tool No. J-28467-360, or equivalent.
26. Raise engine.
27. Remove engine mount and adapter.
28. Remove power steering pump.
29. Install suitable engine lifting device.
30. Remove engine support fixture.
31. Remove transaxle to engine bolts.
32. Carefully remove engine.
33. If mounting engine onto suitable stand, remove flexplate mounting bolts and flexplate.
34. Reverse procedure to install.

INTAKE MANIFOLD
REPLACE
Upper

1. Drain coolant into suitable container.
2. Remove upper half of air cleaner.
3. Remove EGR valve.
4. Remove brake vacuum pipe at plenum.
5. Disconnect fuel pressure regulator vacuum hose from regulator and at PCV valve.
6. Mark and disconnect spark plug wires at plugs.
7. Remove spark plug wires from plenum harness.
8. Remove electronic ignition coil and module.
9. Remove EVAP canister purge solenoid.
10. Disconnect TP and IAC sensor electrical connectors.
11. Disconnect injector harness.
12. Disconnect ECT and CMP sensor electrical connectors.
13. Disconnect vacuum modulator.
14. Disconnect MAP sensor vacuum line and electrical connector.
15. Remove mounting bolts and MAP sensor.

16. Remove mounting bolts and upper intake manifold with gaskets.
17. Reverse procedure to install.

Lower
REMOVAL

1. Relieve fuel system pressure as outlined under "Precautions."
2. Remove upper intake manifold as outlined under "Upper."
3. Remove fuel lines at fuel rail and bracket, then the rail with injectors.
4. Support engine with suitable wooden block and suitable floor jack positioned below oil pan.
5. Remove cruise control module.
6. Remove engine mount to bracket support bolts.
7. Remove engine mount to body bolts.
8. Remove engine mount.
9. Remove mounting bolts and position power steering pump aside.
10. Remove heater inlet pipe from coolant outlet housing.
11. Remove heater bypass at coolant pump and at cylinder head.
12. Remove radiator hose at heater outlet housing.
13. Remove water outlet housing.
14. Remove valve covers as outlined under "Valve Cover, Replace."
15. Remove lower intake manifold bolts. **Keep washers in original positions on center bolts.**
16. Remove lower intake manifold.
17. Loosen rocker arm bolts.
18. Remove pushrods, keeping them in order. Intakes have yellow stripes and are 5.75 inches long. Exhausts have green stripes and are six inches long.
19. Remove intake manifold gaskets.

INSTALLATION

1. Clean gasket material from mating surfaces.
2. Remove excess RTV sealer from front and rear block ridges.
3. Clean sealing surfaces using suitable degreasing compound.
4. Place .079–.118 inch bead of RTV sealer part No. 12345739, or equivalent, on each manifold-to-block contact ridge.
5. Install new manifold gaskets.
6. Coat pushrod ends with prelube part No. 1052356, or equivalent.
7. Install pushrods in proper sequence. Intakes have yellow stripes and are 5.75 inches long. Exhausts have green stripes and are six inches long.

8. Install rocker arm bolts. **Torque** to 14 ft. lbs., then tighten an additional 30°.
9. Place lower intake manifold in position.
10. Apply sealant part No. 12345382, or equivalent, to lower intake manifold bolt threads.
11. **Torque** vertical bolts to 10 ft. lbs., in sequence, **Fig. 1. Always tighten vertical bolts before horizontals.**
12. **Torque** horizontal bolts to 10 ft. lbs., in sequence, **Fig. 1. Always tighten horizontal bolts after verticals.**
13. Install valve covers.
14. Install heater outlet housing.
15. Install heater inlet pipe to thermostat housing.
16. Install fuel lines to fuel rail and bracket.
17. Install upper intake manifold as outlined under "Upper"
18. Start engine and inspect for leaks.

EXHAUST MANIFOLD
REPLACE
Lefthand

1. Partially drain coolant into suitable container.
2. Remove complete air cleaner and throttle body duct.
3. Remove exhaust crossover heat shield.
4. Remove crossover pipe at exhaust manifold.
5. Remove upper radiator hose from thermostat housing.
6. Tag, disconnect and position front spark plug wires aside.
7. Remove exhaust manifold heat shield.
8. Remove mounting nuts and exhaust manifold.
9. Reverse procedure to install. Install new gasket.

Righthand

1. Remove complete air cleaner and throttle body duct.
2. Remove O2 sensors using socket tool No. J-39194-B, or equivalent.
3. Remove exhaust crossover heat shield.
4. Disconnect EGR pipe from manifold.

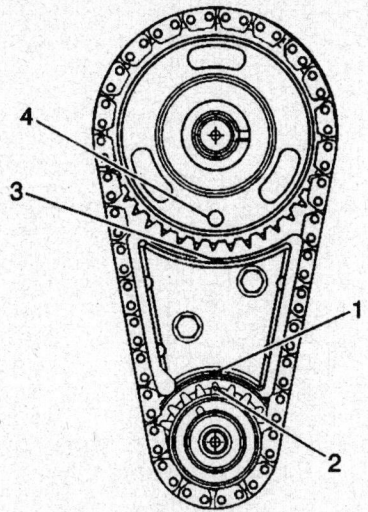

1. DAMPER LOWER TIMING MARK
2. CRANKSHAFT TIMING MARK
3. DAMPER UPPER TIMING
4. CAMSHAFT GEAR

GC1059900125000X

Fig. 4   Timing mark alignment

5. Remove exhaust crossover pipe from manifold.
6. Remove exhaust manifold heat shield.
7. Remove mounting nuts and exhaust manifold.
8. Reverse procedure to install. Install new gasket.

CYLINDER HEAD

REPLACE

Front

REMOVAL

1. Relieve fuel system pressure as outlined under "Precautions."
2. Drain coolant into suitable container.
3. Remove upper half of engine air cleaner.
4. Remove TBI unit duct.
5. Remove exhaust crossover.
6. Remove upper and lower intake manifolds as outlined under "Intake Manifold, Replace."
7. Remove valve cover as outlined under "Valve Cover, Replace."
8. Remove rocker arm bolts, pivot balls and arms.
9. Remove pushrods, keeping them in order. Intakes have yellow stripes and are 5.75 inches long. Exhausts have green stripes and are six inches long.
10. Remove front exhaust manifold as outlined under "Exhaust Manifold, Replace."
11. Remove mounting bolts and cylinder head.

INSTALLATION

1. Clean mating surfaces of head, block and intake manifold.

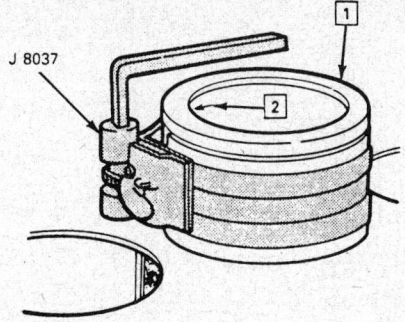

1 PISTON
2 ARROW TOWARDS FRONT OF ENGINE

GC1069100455000X

Fig. 5   Piston marking

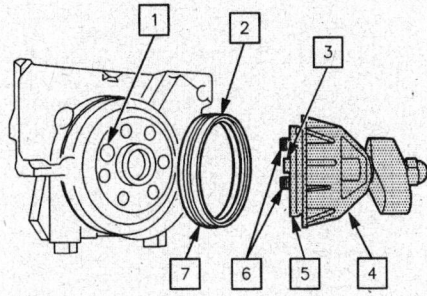

1 ALIGNMENT HOLE
2 DUST LIP
3 DOWEL PIN
4 COLLAR
5 MANDRIL
6 ATTACHING SCREWS
7 SEAL

GC1069701063000X

Fig. 7   Rear main seal installation

2. Clean cylinder head bolts and threads.
3. Place head gasket into position over dowel pins with "THIS SIDE UP" notice properly oriented.
4. Carefully place head into position.
5. Coat head bolt threads with sealer part No. 1052080, or equivalent.
6. **Torque** head bolts to 33 ft. lbs., in sequence, **Fig. 2.**
7. Tighten head bolts an additional 90°.
8. Install intake manifold gaskets.
9. Install pushrods in proper sequence. Intakes have yellow stripes and are 5.75 inches long. Exhausts have green stripes and are six inches long.
10. **Torque** rocker arms, pivot balls and bolts to 14 ft. lbs., then tighten an additional 30°.
11. Install intake manifolds as outlined under "Intake Manifold, Replace."
12. Install exhaust manifold as outlined under "Exhaust Manifold, Replace."
13. Install crossover pipe and heat shield.
14. Fill cooling system.
15. Install TBI unit duct.
16. Install upper half of air cleaner.

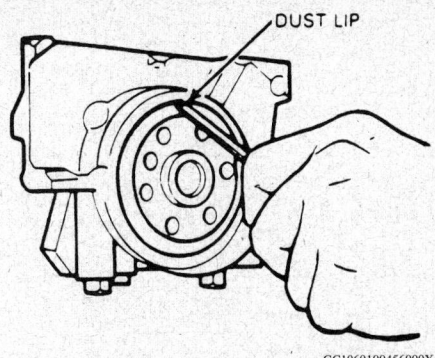

GC1069100456000X

Fig. 6   Rear main seal replacement

17. Start engine and inspect for leaks.

Rear

REMOVAL

1. Relieve fuel system pressure as outlined under "Precautions."
2. Drain coolant into suitable container.
3. Remove exhaust crossover pipe.
4. Raise and support vehicle.
5. Remove rear exhaust manifold as outlined under "Exhaust Manifold, Replace."
6. Lower vehicle.
7. Support engine with suitable wooden block and suitable floor jack positioned below oil pan.
8. Remove cruise control module.
9. Remove engine mount to bracket support bolts.
10. Remove engine mount to body bolts.
11. Remove engine mount.
12. Rotate belt tensioner in clockwise direction using suitable ⅜ inch breaker bar.
13. Remove serpentine belt.
14. Remove valve cover as outlined under "Valve Cover, Replace."
15. Remove rocker arm bolts, pivot balls and arms.
16. Remove pushrods, keeping them in order. Intakes have yellow stripes and are 5.75 inches long. Exhausts have green stripes and are six inches long.
17. Remove upper and lower intake manifolds as outlined under "Intake Manifold, Replace."
18. Remove mounting bolts and cylinder head.

INSTALLATION

1. Clean mating surfaces of head, block and intake manifold.
2. Clean cylinder head bolts and threads.
3. Place head gasket into position over dowel pins with "THIS SIDE UP" notice properly oriented.
4. Carefully place head into position.
5. Coat head bolt threads with sealer part No. 1052080, or equivalent.
6. **Torque** head bolts to 33 ft. lbs., in sequence, **Fig. 2.**
7. Tighten head bolts an additional 90°.

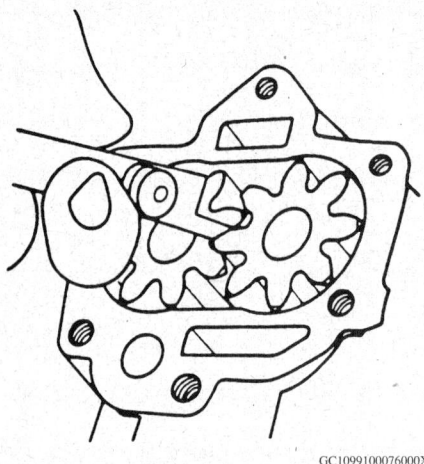

Fig. 8 Oil pump gear lash measurement

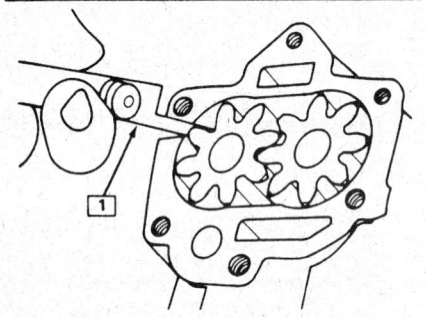

Fig. 11 Gear side clearance measurement

8. Install intake manifold gaskets.
9. Install pushrods in proper sequence. Intakes have yellow stripes and are 5.75 inches long. Exhausts have green stripes and are six inches long.
10. **Torque** rocker arms, pivot balls and bolts to 14 ft. lbs., then tighten an additional 30°.
11. Install intake manifolds as outlined under "Intake Manifold, Replace."
12. Install valve cover with new gasket.
13. Connect spark plug wires.
14. Install serpentine belt.
15. Raise and support vehicle.
16. Install exhaust manifold as outlined under "Exhaust Manifold, Replace."
17. Install crossover pipe and heat shield.
18. Fill cooling system.
19. Install TBI unit duct.
20. Install upper half of air cleaner.
21. Start engine and inspect for leaks.

VALVE COVER
REPLACE
Front

1. Partially drain coolant into suitable container.
2. Remove rear ignition wire harness and spark plug wires at spark plugs.
3. Remove heater bypass intake.

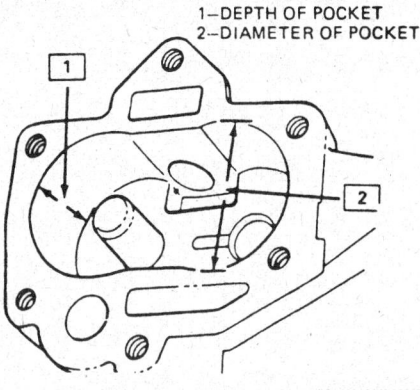

Fig. 9 Oil pump gear pocket measurement

4. Disconnect PCV vacuum hose.
5. Remove mounting bolts and valve cover. If cover is stubborn, break it loose by tapping it lightly with palm of hand or suitable soft rubber mallet.
6. Reverse procedure to install, noting the following:
   a. Install new cover gasket and grommets.
   b. Apply sealer part No. 12346192, or equivalent, in cover notch.

Rear

1. Remove cruise control module.
2. Remove engine mount.
3. Rotate serpentine drive belt tensioner in clockwise direction and remove belt using suitable ⅜ inch breaker bar.
4. Disconnect alternator electrical connectors and power steering line clip.
5. Remove mounting bolts, nuts and alternator.
6. Remove alternator bracket.
7. Remove rear bank spark plug wires.
8. Remove ignition coils and bracket.
9. Remove purge and vacuum canister solenoids.
10. Remove vacuum hose from rear bank valve cover grommet.
11. Remove serpentine belt tensioner.
12. Remove mounting bolts and valve cover. If cover is stubborn, break it loose by tapping it lightly with palm of hand or suitable soft rubber mallet.
13. Reverse procedure to install, noting the following:
   a. Install new cover gasket and grommets.
   b. Apply sealer part No. 12345739, or equivalent, at cylinder head to lower intake manifold joints.

VALVE ARRANGEMENT
Front To Rear

Cowl side ....E-I-E-I-I-E
Radiator side ....E-I-I-E-I-E

VALVE LIFTERS

Roller type valve lifters are must be replaced whenever the camshaft is replaced, **Fig. 3.**

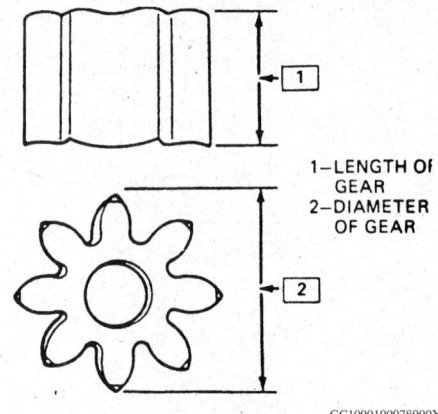

Fig. 10 Oil pump gear measurement

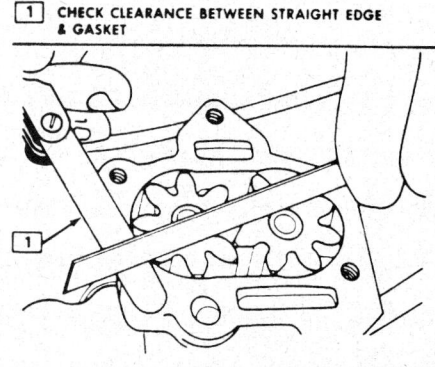

Fig. 12 Oil pump end clearance measurement

Inspect the lifters and look for a bent or broken clip (1), worn pushrod socket (2), scuffed or worn sides (3), flat spots on the roller (4), a loose or damaged pin, (5) a plugged oil hole (6) or worn or damaged roller bearing. Ensure the roller can rotate freely with no binding or rough operation. If the lifter show side wear the block lifter bores should also be inspected for damage or wear. Replace any lifter which does not pass these inspections.

Valve lifters must be kept in order for installation in original positions.

CAMSHAFT LOBE LIFT SPECIFICATIONS

Intake .... .2727
Exhaust... .2727

VALVE ADJUSTMENT

These engines are equipped with hydraulic valve lash adjusters. No adjustment is required.

PUSH RODS

1. Remove rocker arm covers and rocker arms. Identify components for installation in original positions.
2. Remove rocker arm pivot balls and rocker arms, then the pushrods, noting the following:

a. Intakes have yellow stripes and are 5.75 inches long.
b. Exhausts have green stripes and are six inches long.

3. Reverse procedure to install, noting the following:
   a. Ensure pushrods seat in lifters.
   b. Coat bearing surfaces of rocker arms and pivot balls with Molykote part No. 1052356, or equivalent lubricant.

FRONT COVER
REPLACE

1. Recover air conditioning refrigerant as outlined in "Air Conditioning" chapter.
2. Drain coolant into suitable container.
3. Install engine support tool No. J-28467-360, or equivalent.
4. Support engine with suitable wooden block and suitable floor jack positioned below oil pan.
5. Remove cruise control module.
6. Remove engine mount to bracket support bolts.
7. Remove engine mount to body bolts.
8. Remove engine mount.
9. Remove engine mount bracket support.
10. Rotate belt tensioner in clockwise direction using suitable 3/8 inch breaker bar.
11. Remove serpentine belt.
12. Remove complete engine air cleaner.
13. Remove TBI unit tube.
14. Disconnect power steering lines at power steering pump, allowing fluid to drain into suitable container.
15. Loosen upper two air conditioning compressor mounting bolts.
16. Disconnect alternator electrical connectors and power steering line clip.
17. Remove mounting bolts, nuts and alternator.
18. Remove alternator bracket.
19. Raise and support vehicle.
20. Drain engine oil using approved methods and equipment.
21. Remove righthand front tire and wheel.
22. Remove righthand front splash shield.
23. Remove flexplate inspection cover.
24. Remove harmonic balancer using puller tool No. J-24420-C, or equivalent.
25. Remove serpentine belt tensioner.
26. Disconnect righthand front wheel speed sensor electrical connector and wiring harness from suspension support.
27. Remove lower ball joint cotter pin and nut.
28. **On models equipped with ABS,** position wheel speed sensor wiring aside.
29. **On all models,** separate lower ball joint from steering knuckle using ball joint separator tool No. J-43828, or equivalent.
30. Locate center of rivet body and mark with suitable center punch.
31. Drill pilot holes completely through rivets. **Avoid damaging CV joint boots.**
32. Drill final holes through rivets to ensure proper fitting of new ball joint.
33. Remove stabilizer shaft link mounting nut.

34. Remove ball joint from knuckle and lower control arm.
35. Remove righthand stabilizer shaft from righthand suspension support and control arm.
36. Remove righthand suspension support.
37. Separate righthand outer tie rod from knuckle.
38. Remove air conditioning compressor to oil pan bolts.
39. Remove oil filter and adapter.
40. Remove flywheel inspection cover.
41. Remove starter electrical connectors.
42. Remove mounting bolts and starter.
43. Remove lower mounting bolts and position air conditioning compressor aside.
44. Remove evaporator to accumulator air conditioning line.
45. Remove righthand front and righthand rear engine cradle bolts.
46. Remove oil pan.
47. Remove CKP sensor.
48. Remove front cover lower bolts.
49. Lower vehicle.
50. Remove coolant bypass to coolant pump and manifold.
51. Remove radiator hose to coolant outlet housing.
52. Remove front cover mounting bolts.
53. Carefully remove front cover.
54. Remove and discard front cover crankshaft oil seal using suitable flat bladed tool.
55. Reverse procedure to install, noting the following:
    a. Clean gasket mating surfaces using suitable degreaser.
    b. Lubricate new front cover crankshaft oil seal with clean engine oil.
    c. Install crankshaft oil seal with lip facing engine using crankshaft seal installer and centering tool No. J-36468, or equivalent.
    d. Apply RTV sealer part No. 1052080, or equivalent, to both sides of front cover gasket's lower tabs.
    e. Fill cooling system, power steering reservoir and crankcase.
    f. Start engine and inspect for leaks.

FRONT COVER SEAL
REPLACE

1. Raise and support vehicle.
2. Remove righthand front tire and wheel.
3. Remove righthand front splash shield.
4. Remove crankshaft balancer using torsional dampener remover tool No. J-24420-C, or equivalent.
5. Remove crankshaft key.
6. Pry out seal using suitable tool, being careful not to damage crankshaft or front cover.
7. Reverse procedure to install, noting the following:
   a. Install new key if old one is damaged or worn.
   b. Lubricate new seal with clean engine oil and insert in front cover with lip facing engine.
   c. Drive seal into place using front cover alignment and oil seal installer tool No. J-35468, or equivalent.

TIMING CHAIN
REPLACE
Removal

1. Remove engine front cover as outlined under "Front Cover, Replace."
2. Turn engine in normal direction of rotation until piston No. 1 reaches TDC. This is cylinder No. 4 firing position.
3. Align camshaft gear timing mark, **Fig. 4,** with mark on top of chain damper and crankshaft gear timing mark with damper's lower mark.
4. Remove camshaft gear mounting bolt.
5. Remove camshaft gear and timing chain.
6. Remove crankshaft gear using puller tool No. J-5825-A, or equivalent. If gear is stubborn, gently tap lower edge with suitable plastic mallet to dislodge it.

Installation

1. Apply prelube part No. 12345501, or equivalent, to crankshaft gear thrust surface.
2. Install crankshaft gear using installer tool No. J-38612, or equivalent.
3. Install timing chain damper.
4. Ensure timing gear and damper marks are properly aligned.
5. Hold camshaft gear with chain hanging down.
6. Install chain to crankshaft gear.
7. Align camshaft dowel with camshaft gear dowel hole.
8. Draw camshaft gear onto camshaft by tightening mounting bolt.
9. Install front cover.
10. Fill cooling system, power steering reservoir and crankcase.
11. Start engine and inspect for leaks.

CAMSHAFT
REPLACE

1. Remove engine as outlined under "Engine, Replace."
2. Remove valve lifters.
3. Remove front cover.
4. Remove timing chain and gears.
5. Remove camshaft.
6. Reverse procedure to install, noting the following:
   a. If installing new camshaft, also install new valve lifters. **Do not install old lifters with new camshaft.**
   b. Coat camshaft lobes with engine oil supplement part No. 12345501, or equivalent.
   c. Lubricate camshaft journals with engine oil.

PISTON & ROD ASSEMBLY

When installing piston and rod assemblies into cylinder block, ensure arrow on top of piston faces toward front of engine,

Fig. 5. Ensure flat area on bottom of piston aligns with the small dimple above the connecting rod crankshaft bearing bore.

MAIN & ROD BEARINGS

Engine bearings are of the precision insert type. They are available for service usage in standard and various undersizes.

To determine proper replacement insert size, bearing clearance must be measured as follows:

1. Measure crankshaft journal diameter in several places, approximately 90° apart and average the measurements.
2. Measure taper and runout, which should be .0002 inch maximum.
3. Install bearing inserts, then tighten rod and main bearing cap bolts.
4. Measure connecting rod I.D. same direction as length of rod.
5. Select suitable set of inserts to provide specified clearance limits. **Do not mix inserts of different nominal size in same bearing bore.** If clearance limits cannot be met, crankshaft journal must be conditioned and undersize bearing inserts installed.

CRANKSHAFT REAR OIL SEAL

REPLACE

Removal

1. Support engine using engine support fixture tool No. J-28467-360 and fixture adapters tool No. J-28467-90, or equivalents.
2. Remove transaxle as outlined in **MOTOR's "Domestic Transmission Manual, In-Vehicle Service."**
3. Remove flexplate.
4. Remove seal by inserting tool through dust lip at angle, then prying seal out by moving tool handle toward end of crankshaft pilot, repeating around circumference of seal, **Fig. 6. Do not damage crankshaft O.D. surface or chamfer.**

Installation

1. Inspect I.D. of bore for nicks or burrs.
2. Inspect crankshaft for burrs or nicks on surface which contacts seal.
3. Apply clean engine oil to new seal I.D. and O.D.
4. Slide seal over mandrel until seal rear bottoms squarely against rear main bearing seal installer tool No. J-34686, or equivalent, collar, **Fig. 7.**
5. Align tool and crankshaft dowel pins by hand, then **torque** mounting screws to 45 inch lbs., **Fig. 7.**
6. Push seal into bore by turning tool T handle until collar is tight against case.
7. Loosen tool T hand until it stops, then remove mounting screws.
8. Ensure seal is seated squarely in bore.
9. Install flexplate and transaxle.

OIL PAN

REPLACE

1. Recover air conditioning refrigerant as outlined in "Air Conditioning" chapter.
2. Drain coolant into suitable container.
3. Support engine with suitable wooden block and suitable floor jack positioned below oil pan.
4. Remove cruise control module.
5. Remove engine mount to bracket support bolts.
6. Remove engine mount to body bolts.
7. Remove engine mount.
8. Rotate belt tensioner in clockwise direction using suitable ⅜ inch breaker bar.
9. Remove serpentine belt.
10. Install engine support tool No. J-28467-360, or equivalent.
11. Raise and support vehicle.
12. Drain engine oil using approved methods and equipment.
13. Remove righthand front tire and wheel.
14. Remove righthand front splash shield.
15. Remove righthand front wheel speed sensor harness from righthand front suspension support.
16. Separate righthand front ball joint from control arm.
17. Separate righthand outer tie rod end from knuckle.
18. Remove air conditioning compressor and position aside with hoses attached.
19. Remove evaporator to accumulator line.
20. Remove flexplate inspection cover.
21. Remove righthand front and rear engine cradle bolts.
22. Remove harmonic balancer using puller tool No. J-24420-C, or equivalent.
23. Remove starter motor.
24. Remove mounting bolts and oil pan.
25. Reverse procedure to install, noting the following:
    a. Clean oil pan flanges and rail, front cover, rear main cap, and bolt holes.
    b. Install new gasket.
    c. If installing rear main cap, install sealer part No. 1052080, or equivalent, on cap's outer gasket grooves' tabs.

OIL PUMP

REPLACE

1. Remove oil pan as outlined under "Oil Pan, Replace."
2. Remove mounting bolt, oil pump and drive shaft extension.
3. Reverse procedure to install.

OIL PUMP SERVICE

Disassemble

1. Drain pump oil into suitable container.
2. Remove pump driveshaft.
3. **Do not remove pickup tube from cover unless it is broken or loose.**
4. Remove pump cover and pump gears.
5. Remove pressure regulator valve and spring. If valve is stuck, soak pump housing in carburetor cleaning solvent. **Pressure regulator valve spring may be under pressure. Remove retaining pin carefully.**
6. Clean sludge, oil and varnish from components. Varnish may be removed by soaking in carburetor cleaning solvent.

Inspection

1. Inspect pump housing and cover for casting imperfections, cracks or damaged threads. **Do not attempt to repair pump housing.** Replace spring.
2. Inspect idler gear shaft. If loose in housing, replace pump.
3. Inspect pressure regulator valve for scoring or sticking. Burrs may be removed with fine oil stone.
4. Inspect pressure regulator valve spring for loss of tension or bending.
5. Inspect suction pipe and screen for looseness if permanently pressed into pump body. If pipe is loose or has been removed, pump body cover must be replaced. Inspect for broken wire mesh or screen.
6. Inspect gears for chipping, galling or wear.
7. Measure gear lash in several positions, **Fig. 8.** Lash should be .0037–.0077 inch.
8. Measure pump housing gear pocket depth, **Fig. 9.** Depth should be 1.202–1.204 inches.
9. Measure pump housing gear pocket diameter, **Fig. 9.** Pump housing diameter should be 1.503–1.505 inches.
10. Measure pump gear diameters, **Fig. 10.** Diameter should be 1.498–1.500 inches.
11. Measure pump gear side clearance, **Fig. 11.** Clearance should be .001–.003 inch.
12. Measure oil pump end clearance, **Fig. 12.** Clearance should be .002–.005 inch.

Assemble

1. Lubricate internal components with clean engine oil.
2. Install pump gears.
3. Install cover and gasket. **Use only original equipment gaskets because gasket thickness is critical to proper pump operation.**
4. Install pressure spring retaining pin, ensuring it is properly secured.
5. If installing new pickup screen and tube, apply sealer part No. 1050026, or equivalent, to tube. Drive new tube into position using plastic hammer and tube installer tool No. J-21882, or equivalent.

BELT TENSION DATA

Belt tension is maintained automatically by a spring tensioned idler pulley. Serpentine belt adjustment is not required.

If belt slippage is indicated and belt tensioner indicator is within normal operating range, measure belt tension as follows:

1. Bring engine to operating temperature and turn ignition switch to Off position.
2. Measure belt tension halfway between alternator and power steering pump using belt tension gauge tool No. J-23600-B, or equivalent.
3. Run engine for 15 seconds with accessories turned Off.
4. Apply clockwise force to tensioner pulley arm using ⅜ inch breaker bar.
5. Release force and immediately measure belt tension without disturbing tensioner position.
6. Apply counterclockwise force to tensioner pulley arm using suitable breaker bar and raise pulley arm to release tension.
7. Slowly lower pulley to belt and measure tension without disturbing tensioner position.
8. Average out three belt tension measurements, which should be 30–50 lbs.
9. If belt tension is not as specified, replace belt tensioner.

SERPENTINE DRIVE BELT

1. Support engine with suitable wooden block and suitable floor jack positioned below oil pan.
2. Remove cruise control module.
3. Remove engine mount to bracket support bolts.
4. Remove engine mount to body bolts.
5. Remove engine mount.
6. Rotate belt tensioner in clockwise direction using suitable ⅜ inch breaker bar.
7. Remove serpentine belt.
8. Reverse procedure to install. Route belt around power steering pump pulley last of all.

COOLING SYSTEM BLEED

1. Close radiator petcock.
2. If engine block drain plugs were removed, coat threads with pipe sealer part No. 12346004, or equivalent.
3. Open coolant air bleed valve located on top of thermostat bypass heater pipe. **Close this valve as soon as continuous coolant stream flows from it.**
4. Fill surge tank to base of filler neck.
5. Start engine while pressure cap is still off.
6. Operate engine until upper radiator hose starts to feel hot.

7. Adjust surge tank coolant level to Full Cold line.
8. **On models equipped with intermittent low coolant lamp,** this lamp may occasionally light during some extreme driving conditions. This might be eliminated by removing surge tank cap and adding coolant to level just at or above Full Cold line when system is cold.
9. **On all models,** install surge tank cap hand tight.

THERMOSTAT
REPLACE

1. Drain coolant into suitable container.
2. Remove complete engine air cleaner.
3. Remove surge tank line from coolant outlet.
4. Remove mounting bolts and coolant outlet.
5. Remove thermostat.
6. Reverse procedure to install.

WATER PUMP
REPLACE

1. Drain coolant into suitable container.
2. Support engine with suitable wooden block and suitable floor jack positioned below oil pan.
3. Remove cruise control module.
4. Remove engine mount to bracket support bolts.
5. Remove engine mount to body bolts.
6. Remove engine mount.
7. Rotate belt tensioner in clockwise direction using suitable ⅜ inch breaker bar.
8. Remove serpentine belt.
9. Remove mounting bolts and water pump pulley.
10. Remove mounting bolts and water pump.
11. Reverse procedure to install.

RADIATOR
REPLACE

Refer to "2.4L Engine" section for radiator replacement procedure.

FUEL PUMP
REPLACE

The fuel pump is a component of the fuel sender and must be replaced as a complete unit.
1. Relieve fuel system pressure as outlined under "Precautions."
2. Drain tank into suitable container.
3. Disconnect electrical connectors.

4. Remove ground wire mounting screw from underbody.
5. Disconnect hoses from tank meter, filler and vent pipes.
6. Support fuel tank and disconnect fuel tank retaining straps.
7. Remove fuel tank.
8. Modular fuel sender might spring up from its original position. Have suitable shop towel ready to absorb spills. Tip assembly slightly to avoid float damage.
9. Remove fuel tank sending unit and pump by holding it down, then removing lockring using lockring tool No. J-39765, or equivalent.
10. Reverse procedure to install, noting the following:
    a. Install new O-ring on sender tank flange.
    b. Align tab on front of fuel sender with slot on front of retainer lockring.
    c. Slowly apply pressure to top of spring loaded sender until sender aligns flush with tank retainer.
    d. Insert lockring into proper slots.
    e. Turn ignition switch to On position for two seconds.
    f. Turn ignition switch to Off position for 10 seconds.
    g. Turn ignition On.
    h. Inspect for fuel leaks.

FUEL FILTER
REPLACE

The fuel filter is located below the rear of the vehicle, rearward of the fuel tank.
1. Relieve fuel system pressure as outlined under "Precautions."
2. Raise and support vehicle.
3. Remove fuel filter fitting.
4. Grasp filter and one nylon fuel connection line fitting, then twist quick connect fitting ¼ turn in each direction to loosen dirt in fitting.
5. Clean dirt from quick connect fitting.
6. Depress quick connect fitting plastic tabs of male end connector and pull apart.
7. Remove fuel filter.
8. Reverse procedure to install, noting the following:
    a. Apply few drops of clean engine oil to male pipe ends before connection to reduce risk of leakage and fire.
    b. Turn ignition switch to On position for two seconds.
    c. Turn ignition switch to Off position for 10 seconds.
    d. Turn ignition On.
    e. Inspect for fuel leaks.

TIGHTENING SPECIFICATIONS

Year	Component	Torque/Ft. Lbs.
2001–05	Accelerator Cable Bracket	89①
	Alternator Bracket & Front Engine Lift Hook	37
	CKP Sensor To Front Cover	89①
	CKP Sensor To Block	96①
	CKP Sensor Wiring Bracket	37
	CMP Sensor	89①
	Camshaft Sprocket	103
	Camshaft Thrust Plate	89①
	Connecting Rod Bearing Cap	⑤
	Coolant Drain Plug	14
	Coolant Outlet	19
	Crankshaft Balancer	76
	Crankshaft Oil Deflector	18
	Cylinder Head	②
	ECT Sensor	17
	EGR Valve To Valve Pipe	18
	EGR Valve Adapter Pipe To Exhaust Manifold	18
	Engine Mount Bracket	43
	Engine Mount, Lower	32
	Engine Mount, Upper	35
	Engine Mount Strut	35
	Engine Mount Strut & Lift Bracket, Lefthand Rear	52
	Engine Mount Strut Bracket, Righthand	37
	Engine Mount Strut Bracket, Upper Radiator Support	21
	Exhaust Manifold Heat Shield	89①
	Exhaust Manifold, Nut	12
	Exhaust Manifold, Stud	13
	Exhaust Crossover	18
	Flexplate	52
	Front Cover, Large Bolt	41
	Front Cover, Medium Bolt	35
	Front Cover, Small Bolt	15
	Fuel Feed Pipe To Injector Rail	13
	Fuel Injector Rail	89①
	Fuel Pipe Bracket	37
	Fuel Pipe Clip	72①
	Fuel Return Pipe To Fuel Injector Rail	13
	HO2S	31
	Heater Inlet Pipe	18
	Ignition Coil Bracket	18
	Intake Manifold, Lower	⑦
	Intake Manifold, Upper	18
	Main Bearing Cap Bolts	③
	Oil Cooler Connector	37
	Oil Cooler Hose Fitting	14
	Oil Cooler Pipe Bracket	89①
	Oil Filter Fitting	29
	Oil Filter	10
	Oil Gallery Plugs, ¼ Inch	14
	Oil Gallery Plugs, ⅜ Inch	24
	Oil Dipstick	18

Continued

3.4L ENGINE

TIGHTENING
SPECIFICATIONS—Continued

Year	Component	Torque/Ft. Lbs.
2001–05	Oil Level Sensor	89①
	Oil Pan	⑥
	Oil Pan Drain Plug	18
	Oil Pressure Indicator Switch	10
	Oil Pump To Block	30
	Oil Pump Cover	89①
	Oil Pump Drive Clamp	27
	Rocker Arm	④
	Rocker Arm Cover	89①
	Serpentine Drive Belt Shield	89①
	Serpentine Drive Belt Tensioner	37
	Spark Plugs	20
	Thermostat Bypass Pipe To Cylinder Head	18
	Thermostat Bypass Pipe To Front Cover	108①
	Thermostat Bypass Pipe To Throttle Body	18
	Thermostat Housing	19
	Timing Chain Damper	15
	Valve Lifter Guide	89①
	Water Pump To Front Cover	89①
	Water Pump Pulley	18

① — Inch lbs.
② — Refer to "Cylinder Head, Replace" for tightening specifications and sequence.
③ — **Torque** to 37 ft. lbs., then tighten an additional 77°.
④ — **Torque** to 14 ft. lbs., then tighten an additional 30°.
⑤ — **Torque** to 15 ft. lbs., tighten an additional 75°.
⑥ — **Torque** mounting bolts to 18 ft. lbs. **Torque** side bolts to 37 ft. lbs.
⑦ — Refer to "Intake Manifold, Replace" for tightening specifications and sequence.

3.5L Engine

NOTE: On Air Bag Equipped Models, Refer To "Air Bag System Precautions" Located In The Front Of This Manual For System Disarming & Arming Procedures.

NOTE: Refer To "Computer Relearn Procedures" Located In The Front Of This Manual When Battery Power To The Computer Has Been Interrupted.

INDEX

PRECAUTIONS

Air Bag Systems

Refer to "Air Bag System Precautions" in the front of this manual for system disarming and arming procedures.

Battery Ground Cable

Prior to service, disconnect battery ground cable and isolate as required.

Fuel System Pressure Relief

Failure to relieve system pressure prior to disconnecting fuel system components may cause fire or personal injury.
1. Loosen fuel tank filler cap to relieve tank pressure.
2. Raise and support vehicle.
3. Disconnect fuel pump electrical connector.
4. Lower vehicle.
5. Start and operate engine until fuel supply is consumed.
6. Crank engine for approximately three seconds to relieve remaining pressure.
7. Disconnect and isolate battery ground cable, then connect fuel pump electrical connector.

COMPRESSION PRESSURE

When inspecting cylinder compression, the throttle should be open, the spark plugs removed and the battery at or near full charge. The lowest reading cylinder should not be less than 70% of the highest and no cylinder reading should be less than 100 psi. Crank engine until it runs through four compression cycles. Normal compression builds up quickly and evenly to specified compression on each cylinder.

ENGINE MOUNT

REPLACE
1. Raise and support vehicle.
2. Remove righthand tire and wheel assembly.
3. Remove splash shield from under engine.
4. Remove engine mount to engine mount bracket nuts.
5. Remove engine mount to frame nuts.
6. Raise engine with a suitable jackstand.
7. Remove motor mount from vehicle.
8. Reverse procedure to install.

ENGINE MOUNT STRUT

REPLACE
1. Remove air cleaner assembly.
2. Remove engine mount strut to engine attaching bolts.

3. Rotate engine mount strut to a vertical position.
4. Remove engine mount strut to body attaching bolts, then the strut from vehicle.
5. Reverse procedure to install.

ENGINE

REPLACE
1. Relieve fuel system pressure as outlined under "Precautions."
2. Drain coolant into suitable container.
3. Drain engine oil.
4. Remove engine air cleaner assembly.
5. Mark engine hinge locations for installation reference, then remove hood.
6. Remove serpentine belt.
7. Remove engine mount strut as outlined under "Engine Mount Strut, Replace."
8. Disconnect the following electrical connectors:
   a. Knock sensor.
   b. Camshaft Position (CMP) sensor.
   c. Crankshaft Position (CKP) sensor.
   d. Oxygen sensor.
   e. Manifold Absolute Pressure (MAP) sensor.
   f. EGR valve.
   g. Evaporative (EVAP) emission canister purge solenoid.
   h. Electronic throttle control.
   i. Ignition coil.
   j. Body wiring harness to engine harness.
9. Raise and support vehicle.

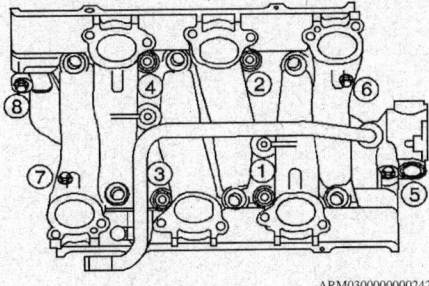

ARM0300000000242

Fig. 1   Lower intake manifold bolt tightening sequence

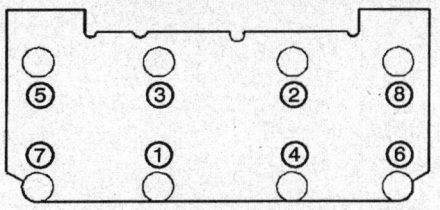

ARM0300000000243

Fig. 2   Cylinder head bolt tightening sequence

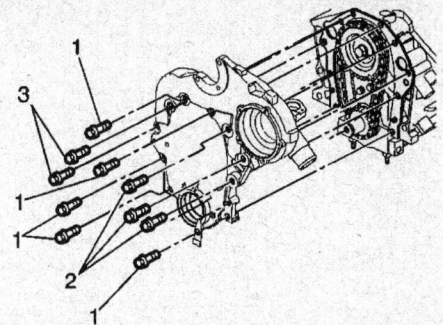

ARM0300000000244

Fig. 3   Front cover bolt identification

10. Remove exhaust crossover pipe retaining nuts, then the pipe.
11. Remove engine wiring harness grounds from transaxle.
12. Remove engine mount lower nuts.
13. Remove torque converter covers and starter motor.
14. Remove A/C compressor from mount. **Do not discharge A/C system refrigerant.**
15. Remove torque converter attaching bolts.
16. Remove transaxle support brace.
17. Remove lower transaxle to engine attaching bolts.
18. Remove radiator outlet hose from engine.
19. Lower vehicle and support transaxle with a suitable lifting device.
20. Remove heater inlet and outlet hoses from engine.
21. Remove vacuum and brake booster hoses from upper intake manifold.
22. Remove fuel lines from fuel rail.
23. Remove radiator inlet hose from engine.
24. Install a suitable engine lifting device to engine.
25. Remove upper transaxle to engine attaching bolts.
26. Remove engine from vehicle.
27. Reverse procedure to install.

INTAKE MANIFOLD

REPLACE

Upper

1. Remove vacuum hoses for the following :
   a. EVAP canister purge valve.
   b. Manifold vacuum.
   c. Brake booster.
   d. Heater and air conditioning source.
2. Disconnect the following electrical connectors:
   a. EGR valve.
   b. Mass Air Flow (MAF) sensor.
   c. Intake Air Temperature (IAT) sensor.
   d. Electronic throttle control.
   e. EVAP canister purge valve.
3. Remove air cleaner intake duct.
4. Drain cooling system.
5. Remove spark plug wires from lefthand spark plugs.
6. Remove Camshaft Position (CMP) sensor, lefthand side spark plug and engine wiring harnesses.

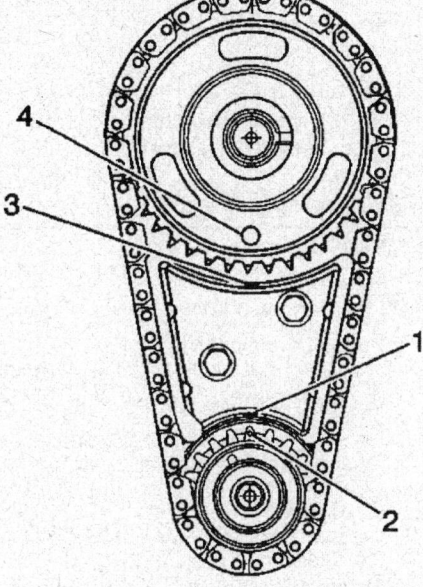

ARM0300000000245

Fig. 4   Timing mark alignment

7. Remove ignition coil bracket with coils.
8. Remove EVAP canister purge valve, MAP sensor and bracket, then the EGR valve.
9. Remove upper intake manifold bolts and stud.
10. Remove upper intake manifold and gaskets.
11. Reverse procedure to install.

Lower

1. Relieve fuel system pressure as outlined under "Precautions."
2. Remove upper intake manifold as outlined under "Upper."
3. Remove lefthand and righthand valve covers as outlined under "Valve Cover, Replace."
4. Disconnect Engine Coolant Temperature (ECT) sensor wiring harness.
5. Disconnect fuel injector and MAP sensor wiring harnesses.
6. Disconnect fuel injector electrical connectors.
7. Remove fuel lines at fuel rail and bracket, then the rail with injectors.
8. Disconnect heater inlet pipe with heater hose from lower intake manifold and position aside.
9. Remove radiator inlet hose from engine.
10. Disconnect thermostat bypass hose from bypass pipe and lower intake manifold.

11. Remove water outlet and thermostat.
12. Remove lower intake manifold bolts, then the manifold.
13. Remove valve rocker arms and pushrods as outlined in "Rocker Arms, Replace."
14. Remove lower intake manifold gaskets and seals.
15. Reverse procedure to install, noting the following:
    a. With gaskets and seals in place, apply a small drop (.31–.39 inch) of suitable RTV sealant to four corners of intake manifold block joints.
    b. Install new intake manifold bolts, apply sealer GM part No. 12345382, or equivalent, to bolt threads.
    c. Using sequence outlined in **Fig. 1,** tighten bolts in three steps. First step, **torque** all bolts to 62 inch lbs.; second step, **torque** bolts 1, 2, 3 and 4 to 115 inch lbs.; third step, **torque** bolts 5, 6, 7 and 8 to 18 ft. lbs.

EXHAUST MANIFOLD

REPLACE

Lefthand

1. Remove oxygen sensor.
2. Remove spark plugs.
3. Remove exhaust heat shield attaching bolts, then the heat shield.
4. Remove exhaust manifold retaining nuts, then the manifold and gasket.
5. Reverse procedure to install.

Righthand

1. Remove oxygen sensor.
2. Remove spark plug wires and spark plugs.
3. Remove EGR pipe to manifold and EGR valve attaching bolts, then the EGR pipe.
4. Remove exhaust heat shield attaching bolts, then the heat shield.
5. Remove exhaust manifold retaining nuts, then the manifold and gasket.
6. Reverse procedure to install.

CYLINDER HEAD

REPLACE

1. Raise and support vehicle.

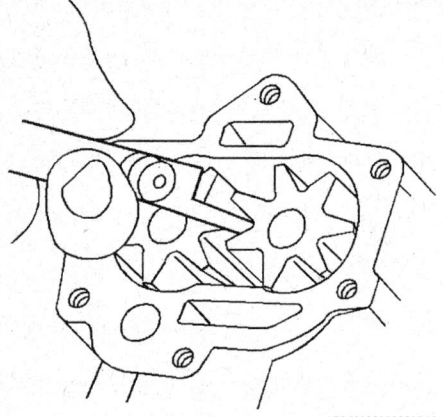

Fig. 5   Oil pump gear lash
measurement

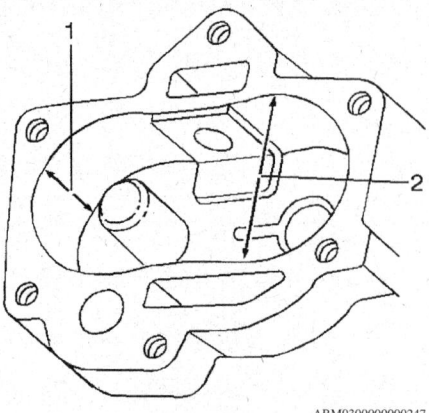

Fig. 6   Oil pump gear pocket
measurement

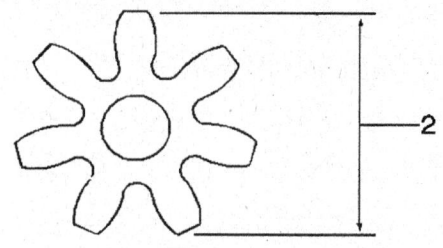

Fig. 7   Oil pump gear
measurement

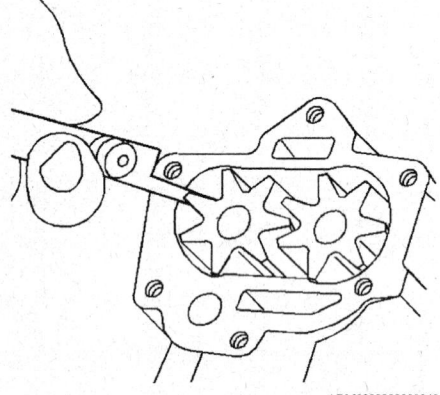

Fig. 8   Gear side clearance
measurement

2. Drain cooling system and engine oil.
3. Lower vehicle, then remove lower intake manifold as outlined under "Intake Manifold, Replace."
4. Remove valve rocker arms and push rods as outlined under "Rocker Arms, Replace."
5. Remove exhaust crossover pipe, then the oil dipstick tube.
6. Remove spark plug wires and spark plugs.
7. **On right cylinder head,** remove fuel line bracket attaching bolt and fuel line bracket.
8. **On right or left cylinder head,** remove exhaust manifold as outlined under "Exhaust Manifold, Replace."
9. Remove and discard cylinder head bolts.
10. Remove cylinder head and gasket.
11. Reverse procedure to install, noting the following:
    a. Replace cylinder head bolts with new torque to yield bolts. **Do not reuse bolts.**
    b. Clean cylinder head and cylinder block mating surfaces.
    c. Using sequence, **Fig. 2, torque** cylinder head bolts to 44 ft. lbs., then tighten an additional 95.°

VALVE COVER
REPLACE
Left

1. Partially drain cooling system.
2. Remove front ignition wiring harness at upper intake manifold and spark plugs.
3. Remove thermostat bypass pipe.
4. Disconnect PCV vacuum hose.
5. Remove valve cover bolts and the valve cover.
6. Reverse procedure to install, noting the following:
   a. Remove any old gasket material and sealer from cylinder head and valve cover mating surfaces.
   b. Install a new gasket and bolt grommets.
   c. Ensure gasket is seated in notch on valve cover.
   d. Apply sealer part No. 12378521, or equivalent, into groove on valve cover.

Right

1. Remove serpentine drive belt as outlined under "Serpentine Belt."
2. Remove alternator as outlined under "Alternator, Replace" in the "Electrical" section.
3. Remove alternator bracket.
4. Remove spark plug wires.
5. Disconnect vacuum hoses from EVAP purge valve, then remove purge valve.
6. Remove ignition coil bracket with coils, then the bracket studs.
7. Remove vacuum hose from valve cover grommet.
8. Remove valve cover bolts and the valve cover.
9. Reverse procedure to install, noting the following:
   a. Remove any old gasket material and sealer from cylinder head and valve cover mating surfaces.
   b. Install a new gasket and bolt grommets.

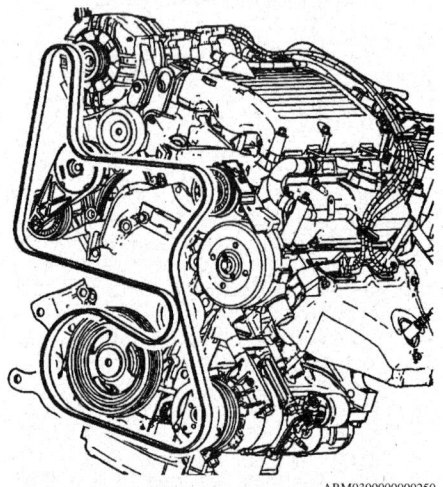

Fig. 9   Serpentine belt routing

   c. Ensure gasket is seated in notch on valve cover.
   d. Apply sealer part No. 12378521, or equivalent, into groove on valve cover.

CAMSHAFT LOBE LIFT SPECIFICATIONS
Intake .... .2727
Exhaust... .2727

VALVE ADJUSTMENT

These engines are equipped with hydraulic valve lash adjusters. No adjustment is required.

ROCKER ARMS
REPLACE

1. Remove valve cover as outlined under "Valve Cover, Replace."
2. Remove rocker arm bolts.
3. Remove rocker arms and push rods. Keep rocker arms and push rods in order, so they can be installed in the same location.
4. Reverse procedure to install, noting the following:
   a. Coat ends of pushrods with lubricant part No. 1052356, or equivalent.
   b. Ensure pushrods are installed in

their correct position. Intake push-rods are identified with yellow stripes and are 5¾ inches long. Exhaust pushrods are identified with green stripes and are 6 inches long.

c. Ensure pushrods are seated in lifter.

PUSH RODS

Refer to "Rocker Arms, Replace" for pushrod replacement.

HYDRAULIC LIFTERS

REPLACE

1. Remove lower intake manifold as outlined under "Intake Manifold, Replace."
2. Remove rocker arms and pushrods as outlined under "Rocker Arms, Replace."
3. Remove intake manifold oil splash shield.
4. Remove lifter guide bolts, lifter guides and lifters.
5. Reverse procedure to install, noting the following:
   a. Clean all gasket surfaces with a suitable degreaser.
   b. Coat valve lifters with prelube part No. 1052367, or equivalent.
   c. Install lifters into same location from which they were removed.

CRANKSHAFT BALANCER

REPLACE

1. Remove drive belt as outlined under "Serpentine Drive Belt."
2. Raise and support vehicle.
3. Remove righthand front tire and wheel assembly.
4. Remove righthand splash shield.
5. Place suitable jackstands under frame.
6. Loosen lefthand frame bolts, then remove righthand side frame bolts.
7. Lower righthand side of frame enough to access crankshaft balancer.
8. Remove torque converter covers.
9. Install flywheel holder tool No. J 37096, or equivalent, to hold flywheel in place.
10. Remove crankshaft balancer bolt and washer.
11. Remove crankshaft balancer with puller tool No. J 41816, or equivalent.
12. Reverse procedure to install.

FRONT COVER

REPLACE

1. Drain cooling system and engine oil.
2. Remove drive belt and tensioner.
3. Remove oil pan as outlined under "Oil Pan, Replace."
4. Remove crankshaft balancer as outlined under "Crankshaft Balancer, Replace."
5. Remove thermostat bypass pipe and radiator outlet hose from front cover.
6. Remove water pump as outlined under "Water Pump, Replace."

7. Remove Crankshaft Position (CKP) sensor wiring harness bracket attaching bolt, then the bracket.
8. Remove engine front cover attaching bolts, then the cover and gasket.
9. Reverse procedure to install, noting the following:
   a. Apply suitable sealant part No. 12346004, or equivalent, to both sides of engine cover gasket.
   b. Install front cover bolts.
   c. **Torque** front cover bolts identified as (1) in **Fig. 3,** to 20 ft. lbs.
   d. **Torque** front cover bolts identified as (2 & 3) in **Fig. 3,** to 41 ft. lbs.

TIMING CHAIN

REPLACE

Removal

1. Remove engine front cover as outlined under "Front Cover, Replace."
2. Align camshaft gear timing mark, **Fig. 4,** with mark on top of chain dampener and crankshaft gear timing mark with dampener's lower mark.
3. Remove camshaft gear mounting bolt.
4. Remove camshaft gear and timing chain.
5. Remove crankshaft dampener using puller tool No. J-5825-A, or equivalent.

Installation

1. Install crankshaft gear using installer tool No. J-38612, or equivalent.
2. Install timing chain damper.
3. Ensure timing gear and damper marks are properly aligned.
4. Hold camshaft gear with chain hanging down and install chain to crankshaft gear.
5. Align camshaft gear timing mark, **Fig. 4,** with mark on top of chain dampener and crankshaft gear timing mark with dampener's lower mark.
6. Align camshaft dowel with camshaft gear dowel hole.
7. Draw camshaft gear onto camshaft by tightening mounting bolt.
8. Install front cover.
9. Fill cooling system, power steering reservoir and crankcase.
10. Start engine and inspect for leaks.

CAMSHAFT

REPLACE

1. Remove lower intake manifold as outlined under "Intake Manifold, Replace."
2. Remove valve lifters as outlined under "Hydraulic Lifters, Replace."
3. Remove timing chain and gears as outlined under "Timing Chain, Replace."
4. Remove Camshaft Position (CMP) sensor retaining bolt, then the sensor.
5. Remove camshaft thrust plate.
6. Install camshaft sprocket bolt into camshaft finger tight, then carefully rotate and remove camshaft.
7. Reverse procedure to install, noting the following:

a. If installing new camshaft, install new valve lifters. **Do not install old lifters with new camshaft.**
b. Coat camshaft lobes with prelube part No. 12345501, or equivalent.
c. Lubricate camshaft journals with clean engine oil.

PISTON & ROD ASSEMBLY

When installing piston and rod assemblies into cylinder block, ensure arrow on top of piston faces toward front of engine.

MAIN & ROD BEARINGS

Engine bearings are of the precision insert type. They are available for service usage in standard and various undersizes.

To determine proper replacement insert size, bearing clearance must be measured as follows:

1. Measure crankshaft journal diameter in several places, approximately 90° apart and average the measurements.
2. Measure taper and runout, which should be .0002 inch maximum.
3. Install bearing inserts, then tighten rod and main bearing cap bolts.
4. Measure connecting rod I.D. same direction as length of rod.
5. Select suitable set of inserts to provide specified clearance limits. **Do not mix inserts of different nominal size in same bearing bore.** If clearance limits cannot be met, crankshaft journal must be conditioned and undersize bearing inserts installed.

CRANKSHAFT SEAL

REPLACE

Front

1. Remove crankshaft balancer as outlined under "Crankshaft Balancer, Replace."
2. Remove crankshaft key from keyway.
3. Pry out oil seal using a large screwdriver.
4. Reverse procedure to install. Coat new seal with clean engine oil.

CRANKSHAFT REAR OIL SEAL

REPLACE

Removal

1. Support engine using engine support fixture tool No. J-28467-360 and fixture adapters tool No. J-28467-90, or equivalents.
2. Remove transaxle as outlined in **MOTOR's** "Domestic Transmission Manual, In-Vehicle Service."
3. Remove flexplate.
4. Remove seal by inserting tool through dust lip at angle, then prying seal out by moving tool handle toward end of

crankshaft pilot, repeating around circumference of seal, **Do not damage crankshaft O.D. surface or chamfer.**

Installation

1. Inspect I.D. of bore for nicks or burrs.
2. Inspect crankshaft for burrs or nicks on surface which contacts seal.
3. Apply clean engine oil to new seal I.D. and O.D.
4. Push seal into bore of seal installation tool No. J 34686, or equivalent.
5. Turn tool T handle until collar is tight against case.
6. Loosen tool T handle until it stops, then remove mounting screws.
7. Ensure seal is seated squarely in bore.
8. Install flexplate and transaxle.

OIL PAN
REPLACE

1. Raise and support vehicle.
2. Drain engine oil.
3. Remove righthand front tire and wheel assembly.
4. Remove splash shield.
5. Remove wheel speed sensor harness from righthand suspension support.
6. Separate righthand front ball joint from steering knuckle as outlined in "Front Suspension & Steering" section.
7. Remove lower closeout panel.
8. Remove A/C compressor mounting bolts, then position compressor aside.
9. Remove engine to transaxle support braces.
10. Disconnect oil level sensor electrical connector.
11. Remove brake line to frame retainers.
12. Support engine with a suitable wooden block and floor jack positioned below oil pan.
13. Remove engine mount to body bolts.
14. Loosen lefthand engine cradle bolts.
15. Remove righthand front and rear engine cradle bolts.
16. Remove starter motor.
17. Remove mounting bolts and oil pan.
18. Reverse procedure to install, noting the following:
    a. Clean oil pan flanges and rail, front cover, rear main cap, and bolt holes.
    b. Install new gasket.
    c. If installing rear main cap, install sealer part No. 1052080, or equivalent, on cap outer gasket groove tabs.

OIL PUMP
REPLACE

1. Remove oil pan as outlined under "Oil Pan, Replace."
2. Remove mounting bolt, oil pump and drive shaft extension.
3. Reverse procedure to install.

OIL PUMP SERVICE

Disassemble

1. Remove pump driveshaft and driveshaft retainer.

2. Remove pump cover and pump gears.
3. Match mark gear teeth for assembly reference.
4. Clean sludge, oil and varnish from components. Varnish may be removed by soaking in carburetor cleaning solvent.

Inspection

1. Inspect pump housing and cover for casting imperfections, cracks or damaged threads. **Do not attempt to repair pump housing.** Replace spring.
2. Inspect idler gear shaft. If loose in housing, replace pump.
3. Inspect pressure regulator valve for scoring or sticking. Burrs may be removed with fine oil stone.
4. Inspect pressure regulator valve spring for loss of tension or bending.
5. Inspect suction pipe and screen for looseness if permanently pressed into pump body. If pipe is loose or has been removed, pump body cover must be replaced. Inspect for broken wire mesh or screen.
6. Inspect gears for chipping, galling or wear.
7. Measure gear lash in several positions, **Fig. 5.**
8. Measure pump housing gear pocket depth, **Fig. 6.** Depth should be 1.202–1.204 inches.
9. Measure pump housing gear pocket diameter, **Fig. 6.**
10. Measure pump gear diameter, **Fig. 7.**
11. Measure pump gear side clearance, **Fig. 8.**

Assemble

1. Lubricate internal components with clean engine oil.
2. Install pump gears.
3. Install cover and gasket.
4. Install pressure spring retaining pin, ensure pin is properly secured.

SERPENTINE DRIVE BELT

1. Remove air cleaner assembly.
2. Remove engine mount strut as outlined under "Engine Mount Strut, Replace."
3. Rotate belt tensioner in clockwise direction using suitable ⅜ inch breaker bar.
4. Remove serpentine belt.
5. Reverse procedure to install. Refer to **Fig. 9,** for belt routing.

COOLING SYSTEM BLEED

1. Close radiator petcock.
2. If engine block drain plugs were removed, coat threads with pipe sealer part No. 12346004, or equivalent.
3. Open coolant air bleed valve located on top of thermostat housing. **Close this valve as soon as continuous coolant stream flows from it.**
4. Fill surge tank to base of filler neck.

5. Start engine while pressure cap is still off.
6. Operate engine until upper radiator hose starts to feel hot.
7. Adjust surge tank coolant level to Full Cold line.
8. Install surge tank cap hand tight.

THERMOSTAT
REPLACE

1. Remove air cleaner inlet duct.
2. Partially drain cooling system.
3. Remove radiator inlet hose from water outlet housing.
4. Remove water outlet housing attaching bolts and outlet housing.
5. Remove thermostat.
6. Reverse procedure to install.

WATER PUMP
REPLACE

1. Drain coolant into suitable container.
2. Remove serpentine belt as outlined under "Serpentine Belt.".
3. Remove mounting bolts and water pump pulley.
4. Remove mounting bolts, water pump and gasket.
5. Reverse procedure to install.

RADIATOR
REPLACE

1. Drain engine coolant.
2. Remove lefthand headlamp assembly attaching bolts.
3. Lift headlamp assembly to unseat tabs on bottom edge of fender.
4. Disconnect headlamp assembly electrical connector and remove assembly from vehicle.
5. Remove righthand headlamp assembly attaching bolts.
6. Lift headlamp assembly to unseat tabs on bottom edge of fender.
7. Disconnect headlamp assembly electrical connector and remove assembly from vehicle.
8. Loop a suitable rope around upper two tabs of condenser, then tie rope around upper engine compartment tie bar.
9. Remove upper radiator support bracket bolts and support brackets.
10. Remove surge tank outlet hose from radiator.
11. Remove radiator inlet hose from radiator.
12. Raise and support vehicle.
13. Remove lower radiator air deflector retainers and the deflector.
14. Remove front fender liner retainers and fender liner.
15. Remove righthand and lefthand radiator air deflector retainers and deflectors.
16. Remove radiator outlet hose from radiator.
17. Place a suitable drain pan under transaxle cooler lines, then remove cooler lines from transaxle.
18. Remove lower radiator support bracket bolts and support brackets.

19. Remove radiator lower mounts.
20. Remove and discard condenser mounting bolts from radiator.
21. Push upward on radiator and downward on condenser to unsnap condenser mounting tabs from radiator clips.
22. Remove and discard condenser mounting nuts from radiator.
23. Remove radiator air side seals.
24. Remove radiator, cooling fan shroud and transaxle cooler line assembly.
25. Remove transaxle cooler lines from radiator.
26. Pry upward on fan shroud tabs, then remove cooling fan and shroud assembly from radiator.
27. Reverse procedure to install.

FUEL PUMP
REPLACE

1. Relieve fuel system pressure as outlined under "Precautions."
2. Drain fuel tank.
3. Raise and support vehicle.
4. Disconnect fuel pump module electrical harness connector from vehicle underbody wiring harness.
5. Disconnect EVAP vent valve solenoid harness electrical connector from vehicle underbody wiring harness.
6. Remove ABS wiring harness from retainer on EVAP canister.
7. Disconnect fuel feed and purge lines from fuel and brake line bundle on righthand side of vehicle.
8. Cap or plug fuel tank feed and vapor lines to prevent fuel loss or contamination.
9. Disconnect fuel filler pipe jumper hose from fuel tank.
10. Disconnect vapor recirculation line that runs parallel to fuel filler pipe jumper hose.
11. Remove exhaust pipe and muffler insulators from underbody hangers, then support exhaust system with suitable jackstand.
12. Support fuel tank with a suitable jackstand.
13. Remove lefthand and righthand fuel tank strap bolts.
14. Carefully lower righthand side of tank until is clear of frame rail, then remove tank toward righthand side of vehicle.
15. Remove fuel pump module assembly from fuel tank using fuel sender lock ring wrench tool No. J 45722, or equivalent.
16. Reverse procedure to install.

TIGHTENING SPECIFICATIONS

Year	Component	Torque/Ft. Lbs.
2004–05	Camshaft Position Sensor Bolt	89①
	Camshaft Sprocket Bolt	103
	Camshaft Thrust Plate	89①
	Connecting Rod Bearing Cap Bolt	②
	Coolant Drain Plug	14
	Coolant Temperature Sensor	17
	Crankshaft Balancer Bolt	③
	Crankshaft Main Bearing Cap Bolt	④
	Cylinder Head Bolts	⑤
	Drive Belt Tensioner Bolt	37
	EGR Valve Assembly Bolt	22
	EGR Valve Pipe Bolt (Exhaust Manifold)	89①
	EGR Valve Pipe Bolt (EGR)	18
	Engine Mount Strut To A/C Bracket Bolt	37
	Engine Mount Strut To Alternator Bracket	37
	Engine Mount Strut To Lift Bracket Bolt	52
	Engine Mount Strut To Support Bracket Bolt	18
	Engine Oil Pressure Switch	12
	Engine Wiring Harness Bracket	115①
	EVAP Purge Valve Bolt	12
	Exhaust Manifold Heat Shield Bolt	89①
	Exhaust Manifold Nut	12
	Flywheel Bolt	52
	Front Cover (Large & Medium Bolts)	41
	Front Cover (Small Bolts)	20
	Fuel Feed Pipe To Injector Rail Bolt	89①
	Fuel Injector Rail Bolt	89①
	Heater Inlet Pipe Nut	18
	Ignition Coil Bracket Bolt	18
	Intake Manifold Coolant Pipe Bolt	89①
	Intake Manifold (Lower)	⑥
	Intake Manifold (Upper)	18
	Knock Sensor	18
	Main Bearing Cap Bolt	④
	MAP Sensor	89①
	Oil Filter Adapter Bolt	18

Continued

TIGHTENING
SPECIFICATIONS—Continued

Year	Component	Torque/Ft. Lbs.
2004–06	Oil Filter	22
	Oil Filter Bypass Hole Plug	14
	Oil Filter Fitting	29
	Oil Dipstick Tube Bolt	18
	Oil Pan Bolt	18
	Oil Pan Drain Plug	18
	Oil Pan Side Bolt	37
	Oil Pump Cover Bolt	89①
	Oil Pump Drive Clamp Bolt	27
	Oil Pump Mounting Bolt	30
	Oxygen Sensor	31
	PCV Tube Clip Bolt	89①
	Rocker Arm Bolt	24
	Spark Plug	15
	Thermostat Bypass Pipe To Front Cover	89①
	Thermostat Bypass Pipe To Throttle Body	89①
	Throttle Body Bolt	89①
	Timing Chain Dampener Bolt	15
	Valve Lifter Guide Bolt	89①
	Valve Rocker Arm Bolt	24
	Valve Cover Bolts	89①
	Water Outlet Bolt	18
	Water Pump Bolt	89①
	Water Pump Pulley Bolt	18

① — Inch lbs.
② — 18 ft. lbs., plus an additional 110.°
③ — 52 ft. lbs., plus an additional 70.°
④ — 37 ft. lbs., plus an additional 77.°
⑤ — Refer to "Cylinder Head, Replace" for tightening procedure.
⑥ — Refer to "Intake Manifold, Replace" for tightening procedure.

Rear Axle & Suspension

INDEX

DESCRIPTION

The rear suspension, **Fig. 1**, uses coil springs over struts and lightweight aluminum knuckles. Each wheel is mounted to a tri-link independent suspension system. The three links include the inverted U-channel trailing arms and front and rear stamped lateral links.

The knuckles are machined aluminum castings. **Do not use hammers or pry bars to loosen any components.**

HUB & BEARING

REPLACE

1. Raise and support vehicle.
2. Remove wheel and tire assembly.
3. **On models equipped with rear drum brakes,** proceed as follows:
   a. Remove brake drum. **Do not hammer on drum.**
   b. Disconnect ABS wheel sensor electrical connector.
   c. Remove mounting bolts, then the hub and bearing assembly. **Partially remove hub and bearing assembly prior to removing upper rear hub mounting bolt.**
4. **On models equipped with rear disc brakes,** proceed as follows:
   a. Remove brake rotor as outlined in "Disc Brakes" chapter.
   b. Disconnect parking brake cable from parking brake lever.
   c. Disconnect ABS wheel sensor electrical connector.
   d. Remove mounting bolts and hub assembly from knuckle.
   e. Remove rear Torx head bolts, then the hub assembly from backing plate.
5. **On all models,** reverse procedure to install.

SUPPORT ASSEMBLY

REPLACE

1. Raise and support vehicle.
2. Remove rear wheels and tires.
3. Remove exhaust system.
4. Remove lower control arms as outlined under "Control Arms, Replace."
5. Remove upper control arm to support assembly attaching bolts and nuts.
6. Remove toe links as outlined under "Toe Links, Replace."

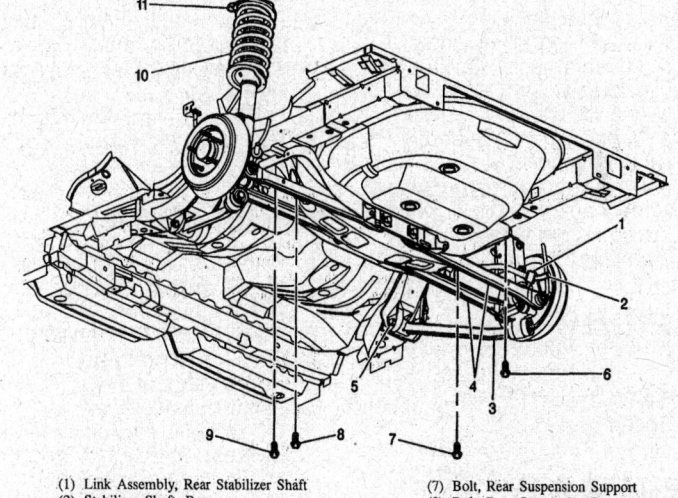

(1) Link Assembly, Rear Stabilizer Shaft
(2) Stabilizer Shaft, Rear
(3) Arm, Rear Suspension Trailing
(4) Link, Lateral
(5) Bolt, Rear Suspension Support
(6) Bolt, Rear Suspension Support
(7) Bolt, Rear Suspension Support
(8) Bolt, Rear Suspension Support
(9) Bolt, Rear Suspension Support
(10) Spring, Coil
(11) Mount, Upper Strut

GC2039700141000X

Fig. 1 Exploded view of rear suspension

7. Remove stabilizer shaft to knuckle attaching bolts.
8. Remove vehicle wiring harness from support assembly retaining clips.
9. Place a suitable jack stand under support assembly.
10. Remove support assembly to body attaching bolts.
11. Remove support assembly from vehicle.
12. Reverse procedure to install.

STRUT

REPLACE

Do not hammer or pry on the machined aluminum knuckle casting or any of the components attached to it.
1. Raise and support vehicle.
2. Remove tire and wheel assembly.
3. Scribe knuckle to strut position for installation alignment.
4. Open luggage compartment and remove strut mount nut.
5. Remove mounting bolts from wheelwell.
6. Remove mounting bolts and strut knuckle.
7. Reverse procedure to install.

STRUT SERVICE

Disassemble

1. Position strut compressor tool No. J-34013-B in holding fixture J-3289-20 with adapter tool No. J-34013-88, or equivalents.
2. Compress strut to approximately half of its height. **Do not bottom spring or damper rod.**
3. Remove nut from strut dampener shaft and position alignment rod tool No. J-34013-27, or equivalent, on dampener shaft. Position dampener shaft down through bearing cap while compressing coil spring using guide rod tool.
4. Remove strut components.

Assemble

1. Install bearing cap.
2. Mount strut to strut compressor tool using bottom locking pin only.
3. Extend dampener shaft and install dampener rod clamp tool No. J-34013-20, or equivalent.
4. Install spring over dampener.

5. Swing strut assembly up and install upper locking pin.
6. Install upper insulator, dust shield, bumper and upper spring seat. Flat on upper spring seat should face in same direction as centerline of strut knuckle
7. Compress strut using guide rod tool until dampener shaft threads are visible. Remove guide rod tool and install mounting nut.
8. While holding dampener shaft in position with suitable wrench, tighten mounting nut.
9. Remove dampener rod clamp tool.

SHOCK ABSORBER
REPLACE

1. Raise and support vehicle.
2. Remove tire and wheel assembly.
3. Place a suitable jack stand under knuckle assembly, then raise jack to relieve spring tension.
4. Remove lower shock absorber to knuckle attaching bolt.
5. Remove upper shock absorber to support assembly attaching bolt, then the shock absorber from vehicle.
6. Reverse procedure to install.

COIL SPRING
REPLACE

Refer to "Strut Service" for coil spring replacement procedures.

CONTROL ARM
REPLACE

Lower

1. Raise and support vehicle.
2. Remove wheel and tire assembly.
3. Remove coil spring as outlined under "Coil Spring, Replace."
4. Remove lower control arm to support assembly attaching bolt and nut.
5. Remove lower control arm from vehicle.
6. Reverse procedure to install.

Upper

1. Raise and support vehicle.
2. Remove wheel and tire assembly.
3. Disconnect ABS harness connector and position aside. Note position of harness for installation reference.

4. Remove upper control arm to support assembly attaching bolt.
5. Remove upper control arm to knuckle bolt and nut.
6. Remove upper control arm from vehicle through wheelwell opening.
7. Reverse procedure to install.

KNUCKLE
REPLACE
Removal

1. Raise and support vehicle, then remove tire and wheel assembly.
2. Scribe strut to knuckle position for installation reference.
3. Remove rear lateral link nut, bolt, washer and drum or rotor.
4. Remove ABS electrical connector and rear wheel hub.
5. Remove trailing arm from knuckle.
6. Remove strut nuts and bolts.
7. Remove knuckle.

Installation

1. Install knuckle onto vehicle.
2. Install strut to knuckle nuts and bolts. Hand tighten bolts.
3. Install stabilizer shaft link.
4. Install trailing arm to knuckle bolt, washer and bushing.
5. Install hub assembly.
6. **On models equipped with rear disc brakes,** connect parking brake cable to parking brake lever.
7. **On all models,** install rotor or drum.
8. Install lateral links to knuckle nut, bolt and washer.
9. Connect wheel speed sensor harness.
10. Tighten strut to knuckle bolts.
11. Install tire and wheel.
12. Lower vehicle.
13. Inspect rear wheel alignment.

REAR CROSSMEMBER
REPLACE

1. Raise and support vehicle, then remove tire and wheel assemblies.
2. Remove tailpipe.
3. Remove brake lines and parking brake cables from crossmember.
4. Remove link bolts.
5. Remove mounting nuts and insulator brackets.
6. Remove stabilizer shaft.

7. Disconnect rear wheel speed sensor electrical connectors and position harness aside.
8. If removing front lateral line and trailing arm, remove ABS wire harness.
9. Remove knuckle bolt, nut and washer. Push bolt forward enough for removal clearance.
10. Remove crossmember nut, then the rear lateral link and trailing arm.
11. Remove bolt from EVAP canister.
12. Support crossmember with suitable jack stands.
13. Remove mounting bolts and rear crossmember.
14. Reverse procedure to install.

TRAILING ARM
REPLACE

1. Raise and support vehicle.
2. Remove trailing arm knuckle bolt, washer and bushing.
3. Remove body bolt and trailing arm.
4. Reverse procedure to install.

STABILIZER SHAFT
REPLACE

1. Raise and support vehicle, then remove tire and wheel assemblies.
2. Remove link bolts.
3. Remove mounting nuts and insulator brackets.
4. Remove stabilizer shaft.
5. Reverse procedure to install.

LATERAL LINK
REPLACE

1. Raise and support vehicle, then remove tire and wheel assembly.
2. If removing front lateral line and trailing arm, remove ABS wire harness.
3. Remove knuckle bolt, nut and washer. Push bolt forward enough for removal clearance.
4. Remove crossmember nut and rear lateral link and trailing arm.
5. Reverse procedure to install.

TOE LINK
REPLACE

1. Raise and support vehicle.
2. Remove tire and wheel assembly.
3. Remove toe link to steering knuckle attaching bolt.
4. Remove toe link to support assembly attaching bolt and nut, then the toe link from vehicle.
5. Reverse procedure to install.

TIGHTENING SPECIFICATIONS

Year	Component	Torque/Ft. Lbs.
2010–05	Crossmember	89
	Disc Brake Caliper To Bracket	81
	Disc Brake Caliper To Knuckle	85
	Lateral Link To Crossmember	89
	Lateral Link To Knuckle	89
	Stabilizer Shaft Bracket	39
	Stabilizer Shaft Link	51
	Strut Nut	89
	Strut To Body	18
	Strut To Knuckle	89
	Trailing Arm To Body	①
	Trailing Arm To Knuckle	51
	Wheel Hub To Knuckle	70
	Wheel Lug Nuts	100

① — **Torque** to 48 ft. lbs, then tighten an additional 120°.

Front Suspension & Steering

INDEX

PRECAUTIONS

Air Bag Systems

Refer to "Air Bag System Precautions" in the front of this manual for system disarming and arming procedures.

Battery Ground Cable

Prior to service, disconnect battery ground cable and isolate as required.

DESCRIPTION

The front suspension on these vehicles, **Fig. 1,** is of the strut and spring design. The lower control arms pivot from the lower side rails through rubber bushings. The upper end of the strut is isolated by a rubber mount incorporating a bearing for wheel turning. The tie rods connect to the steering arm on the strut, below the spring seat. The lower end of the steering knuckle pivots on a ball stud which is retained to the lower control arm by rivets and is secured to the steering knuckle with a nut and cotter pin. The sealed wheel bearings are integral with the hub and are serviced as an assembly.

WHEEL BEARING
REPLACE

1. Raise and support vehicle.
2. Remove wheel and tire assembly.
3. Insert suitable drift punch into caliper and rotor to prevent turning and remove axle shaft nut and washer, **Fig. 2.**
4. Remove caliper mounting bolts and brake caliper with brake hose attached. Suspend caliper from underbody using suitable wire. **Do not allow caliper to hang from brake hose.**
5. Remove brake rotor, then the hub and bearing assembly mounting bolts, **Fig. 3.**
6. Remove hub and bearing assembly.
7. Reverse procedure to install. Inspect and adjust front wheel alignment.

BALL JOINT INSPECTION

Ball joints must be replaced if any looseness is detected in the joint or the seal is cut.

To inspect the ball joints, raise the front of the vehicle allowing the suspension to hang free. Grasp the tire at the top and bottom and move the top of tire with an in-and-out motion. Look for any horizontal movement of the steering knuckle relative to the front lower control arm.

If the ball stud is disconnected from the steering knuckle and any looseness is detected or if the ball stud can be twisted in its socket using hand pressure, replace the ball joint.

Ball stud tightness in the steering knuckle boss should also be inspected when inspecting the ball joint. This may be done by shaking the wheel and feeling for movement of the stud end or castellated nut at the knuckle boss. Inspecting the torque at the castellated nut is an alternative method of inspecting for wear. A loose nut can indicate a bent stud or an opened-up hole in the knuckle boss. Worn or damaged ball joints and knuckles must be replaced.

BALL JOINT
REPLACE

1. Raise and support vehicle.
2. Remove tire and wheel assembly.
3. Remove lower ball joint cotter pin and nut.
4. **On models equipped with ABS,** position wheel speed sensor wiring aside.
5. **On all models,** separate lower ball joint from steering knuckle using ball joint separator tool No. J-43828, or equivalent, **Fig. 4.**
6. Locate center of rivet body and mark with suitable center punch.
7. Drill pilot holes completely through rivets. **Avoid damaging CV joint boots.**
8. Drill final holes through rivets to ensure proper fitting of new ball joint.
9. Remove stabilizer shaft link mounting nut.
10. Remove ball joint from knuckle and lower control arm.

11. Reverse procedure to install using bolts provided in service package.

COIL SPRING
REPLACE

Refer to "Strut Service" for coil spring replacement.

STRUT
REPLACE

1. Remove strut body mounting nuts and bolt.
2. Raise and support vehicle.
3. Place jack stands under front crossmember and lower vehicle slightly so it rests on stands, not on control arms.
4. Remove wheel and tire. Install modified outer seal protector tool No. J-34754, or equivalent,
5. Remove tie rod end cotter pin and nut, then disconnect tie rod from strut using tie rod puller tool No. J-24319-01, or equivalent.
6. Remove brake line bracket.
7. Scribe alignment marks on strut flange, **Fig. 5.**
8. Remove mounting bolts and strut, **Fig. 1. Do no damage spring coating.**
9. Reverse procedure to install. Inspect and adjust wheel alignment.

STRUT SERVICE

Disassemble

1. Position strut compressor tool No. J-34013-B in holding fixture J-3289-20 with adapter tool No. J-34013-88, or equivalents.
2. Compress strut to approximately half of its height. **Do not bottom spring or damper rod.**
3. Remove nut from strut dampener shaft and position alignment rod tool No. J-34013-27, or equivalent, on dampener shaft. Position dampener shaft down through bearing cap while compressing coil spring using guide rod tool.
4. Remove strut components, **Fig. 6.**

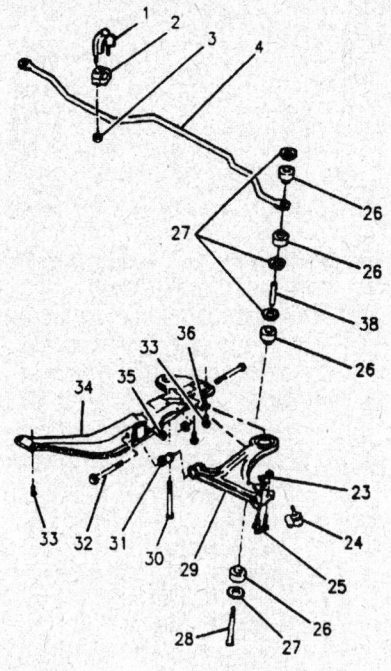

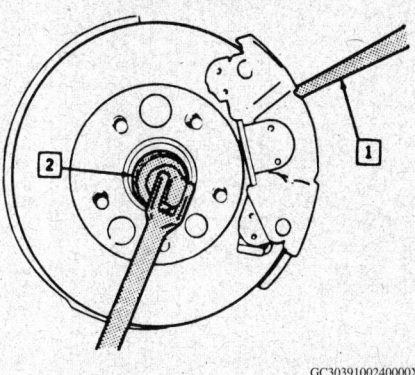

1. DRIFT PUNCH
2. 6 POINT DEEP WELL SOCKET

GC3039100240000X

Fig. 2   Drive axle shaft nut removal

1 CLAMP, STABILIZER SHAFT
2 INSULATOR, STABILIZER SHAFT
3 NUT
4 STABILIZER SHAFT
5 BOLT
6 NUT
7 NUT, STRUT DAMPENER SHAFT
8 RATE WASHER
9 STRUT MOUNT
10 UPPER SPRING SEAT
11 UPPER SPRING INSULATOR
12 DUST TUBE ASSEMBLY
13 SPRING
14 LOWER SPRING INSULATOR
15 STRUT
16 NUT
17 WASHER
18 BOLT
19 HUB AND BEARING ASSEMBLY

20 STEERING KNUCKLE
21 NUT, BALL JOINT
22 COTTER PIN
23 NUT
24 BALL JOINT
25 BOLT
26 INSULATOR, STABILIZER LINK
27 WASHER, STABILIZER LINK
28 BOLT, STABILIZER LINK
29 CONTROL ARM
30 BOLT
31 BUSHING, CONTROL ARM

32 BOLT
33 BOLT
34 SUSPENSION SUPPORT
35 NUT
36 WASHER
37 BOLT
38 SPACER, STABILIZER LINK

GC2029700271000X

Fig. 1   Exploded view of front suspension

Assemble

1. Install bearing cap.
2. Mount strut to strut compressor tool using bottom locking pin only.
3. Extend dampener shaft and install dampener rod clamp tool No. J-34013-20, or equivalent.
4. Install spring over dampener.
5. Swing strut assembly up and install upper locking pin.
6. Install upper insulator, dust shield, bumper and upper spring seat. Flat on upper spring seat should face in same direction as centerline of strut knuckle, **Fig. 7.**
7. Compress strut using guide rod tool until dampener shaft threads are visible. Remove guide rod tool and install mounting nut.
8. While holding dampener shaft in position with suitable wrench, tighten mounting nut.
9. Remove dampener rod clamp tool.

CONTROL ARM
REPLACE
Removal

1. Raise and support vehicle. Remove wheel and tire assembly.
2. Disconnect stabilizer bar at lower control arm and control arm support.
3. Remove ball joint cotter pin and nut.
4. Separate ball joint from steering knuckle with ball joint separator tool No. J-43828, or equivalent.
5. Remove mounting bolts, support and control arm as an assembly, **Fig. 8.**

Installation

1. Install control arm into position and hand tighten rear mounting bolt.
2. Install and hand tighten front mounting bolt.
3. Install stabilizer shaft link.
4. Install lower ball joint to knuckle.
5. Raise vehicle slightly, then remove jack stands.
6. Install tire and wheel.
7. Lower vehicle to ground, then tighten, in order, control arm front and rear mounting bolts.
8. Inspect and adjust front wheel alignment.

STEERING KNUCKLE
REPLACE

1. Raise and support vehicle.
2. Remove wheel and tire.
3. Remove front drive shaft as outlined in "Front Wheel Drive Axles" chapter.
4. Remove mounting bolts and steering knuckle.
5. Reverse procedure to install.

STABILIZER BAR
REPLACE

1. Raise and support vehicle, allowing control arms to hang free.
2. Remove front wheels and tires.
3. Remove stabilizer shaft links.
4. Separate tie rod ends from knuckles using separator tool No. J-24319-01, or equivalent.
5. Remove transaxle rear mount bolt.
6. Remove power steering line bracket from crossmember.
7. Disconnect stabilizer bar from control arms and suspension support, **Fig. 9.**
8. Loosen suspension support front, then remove rear and center mounting bolts. Lower support enough to allow stabilizer bar removal.
9. Remove stabilizer bar with insulators.
10. Reverse procedure to install. Tighten lefthand rear, righthand rear, lefthand front and righthand front crossmember mounting bolts in order.

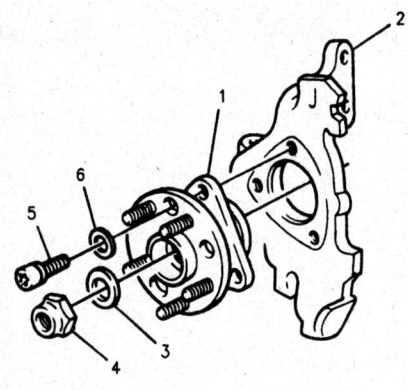

1 HUB AND BEARING ASSEMBLY
2 STEERING KNUCKLE
3 WASHER
4 DRIVE AXLE NUT
5 HUB AND BEARING RETAINING BOLT
6 WASHER

GC3039700369000X

Fig. 3 Front hub & wheel bearing replacement

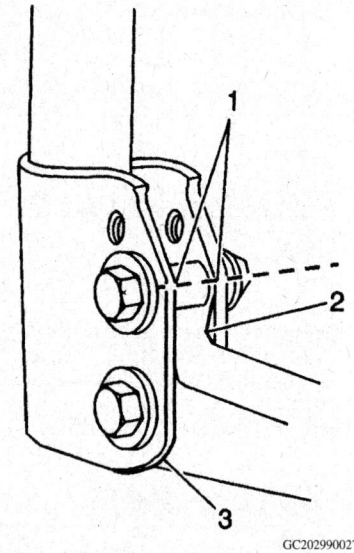

GC2029900274000X

Fig. 6 Exploded view of strut

TIE ROD END
REPLACE

Inner

1. Raise and support vehicle.
2. Remove tire and wheel assembly.
3. Remove outer tie rod as outlined under "Outer."
4. Remove steering gear as outlined under "Power Steering Gear, Replace."
5. Remove steering gear boot.
6. Slide shock damper toward steering gear, then remove inner tie rod from steering gear using two suitable wrenches.

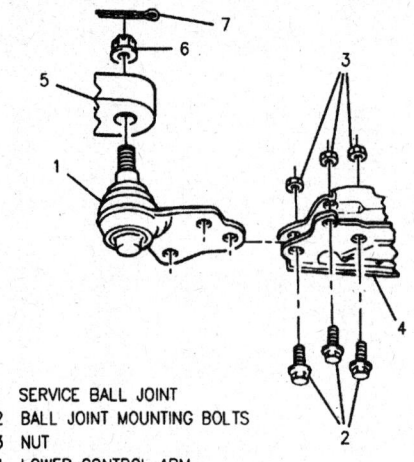

1 SERVICE BALL JOINT
2 BALL JOINT MOUNTING BOLTS
3 NUT
4 LOWER CONTROL ARM
5 STEERING KNUCKLE
6 NUT
7 PIN

GC2029700272000X

Fig. 4 Lower ball joint replacement

7. Reverse procedure to install. Adjust front end alignment as required, refer to "Wheel Alignment" section.

Outer

1. Raise and support vehicle.
2. Remove tire and wheel assembly.
3. Loosen outer tie rod end jam nut.
4. Remove outer tie rod end to steering knuckle retaining nut.
5. Separate tie rod end from knuckle with tie rod separator tool No. J 24319-B, or equivalent.
6. Remove outer tie rod end from inner tie rod end.
7. Reverse procedure to install. Adjust front end alignment as required, refer to "Wheel Alignment" section.

POWER STEERING GEAR
REPLACE

1. Carefully siphon fluid from power steering reservoir.
2. Raise and support vehicle, then remove front tires and wheels.
3. Remove stabilizer shaft links from control arms.
4. Remove tie rods from knuckles using separator tool No. J-24319-01, or equivalent.
5. Remove intermediate shaft lower pinch bolt.
6. Support rear of crossmember with suitable jack stands.
7. Remove stabilizer shaft.
8. Remove steering gear mounting bolts.
9. **On Malibu models,** proceed as follows:
   a. Remove transaxle mount-to-crossmember bolt.
   b. Remove rear crossmember to body bolts to provide pipe and hose removal clearance.
   c. Loosen front crossmember bolts.

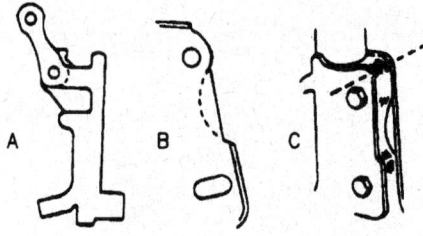

A SCRIBE KNUCKLE ALONG LOWER OUTBOARD STRUT RADIUS
B SCRIBE STRUT FLANGE ON INBOARD SIDE ALONG CURVE OF KNUCKLE
C SCRIBE ACROSS STRUT/KNUCKLE INTERFACE

GC2029700273000X

Fig. 5 Strut & knuckle alignment marks

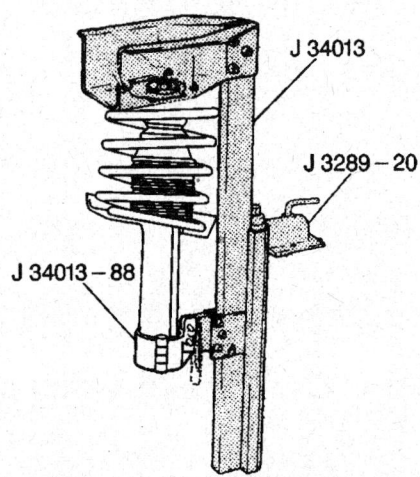

GC2029700275000X

Fig. 7 Strut replacement

10. **On all models,** remove steering gear mounting bolts.
11. Place suitable drain pan below steering gear and disconnect gear power steering fluid hoses.
12. Remove steering gear through left-hand wheel opening.
13. Reverse procedure to install.

POWER STEERING PUMP
REPLACE

2.2L Engine

1. Remove air cleaner outlet duct.
2. Remove relay center push in retainer.
3. Disconnect relay battery feed cable from upper air cleaner cover retaining clips.
4. Remove push in retainer from air cleaner assembly to battery tray, then the air cleaner assembly.
5. Disconnect evaporative emission (EVAP) canister purge valve harness connector, then the vacuum pipe from EVAP canister purge valve.

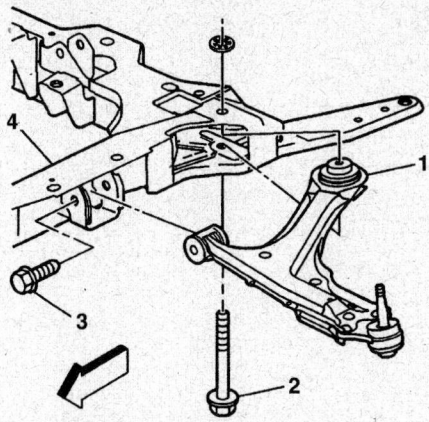

1 ARM
2 REAR MOUNTING BOLT
3 FRONT MOUNTING BOLT
4 CROSSMEMBER

GC2029700276000X

Fig. 8 Lower control arm replacement

6. Disconnect purge pipe from EVAP canister purge valve.
7. Remove EVAP canister purge valve and bracket, then the EVAP canister purge valve from purge bracket.
8. Remove power steering pressure hose as follows:
   a. Raise vehicle using a suitable lift.
   b. **On models equipped with automatic transaxles,** remove front exhaust pipe as outlined under "Exhaust Manifold, Replace" in "2.2L Engine" section.
   c. **On all models,** remove power steering pressure hose from power steering gear, then the power steering pressure hose from power steering pump pipe and hose from vehicle.
   d. Lower vehicle.
9. Remove power steering return hose as follows:
   a. Remove upper air cleaner assembly.
   b. Remove clamp and power steering return hose from power steering pump.
   c. Raise vehicle using suitable lift.
   d. **On models equipped with automatic transaxles,** remove front ex-

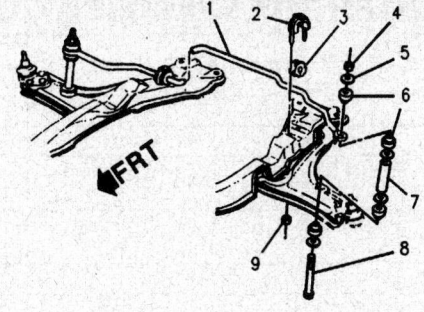

1 SHAFT, STABILIZER
2 CLAMP
3 INSULATOR, STABILIZER SHAFT
4 NUT
5 WASHER
6 INSULATOR, STABILIZER LINK
7 SPACER
8 BOLT
9 NUT

GC2029700277000X

Fig. 9 Stabilizer bar replacement

   haust pipe as outlined under "Exhaust Manifold, Replace" in "2.2L Engine" section.
   e. **On all models,** remove power steering return hose from vehicle.
10. Remove power steering pump attaching bolts, then the power steering pump from vehicle.
11. Reverse procedure to install.

2.4L Engine

1. Siphon as much power steering fluid as possible from reservoir.
2. **On models equipped with variable effort steering,** disconnect variable effort steering electrical connector.
3. **On all models,** place suitable drain pan in position and disconnect power steering pump lines, **Fig. 10.**
4. Remove mounting bolts power steering pump.
5. Reverse procedure to install.

3.1L & 3.4L Engines

1. Siphon as much power steering fluid as possible from reservoir.

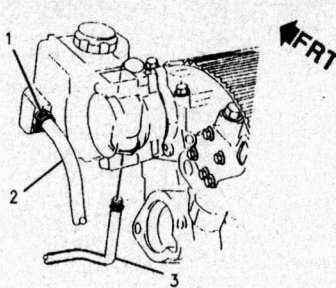

INLET HOSE — NON EVO

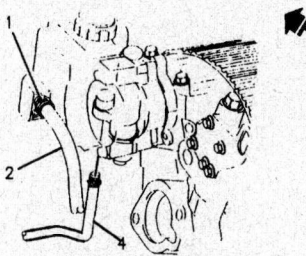

INLET HOSE EVO

1 CLAMP, HOSE
2 HOSE, OUTLET
3 HOSE, INLET (NON EVO)
4 HOSE, INLET (EVO)

GC6039700056000A

Fig. 10 Power steering pump replacement. 2.4L engine

2. Remove engine mount as outlined under "Engine Mount, Replace" in appropriate "Engine" section.
3. Remove serpentine belt as outlined under "Serpentine Drive Belt" in appropriate "Engine" section.
4. Remove alternator bracket retaining hose nut.
5. Remove power steering pump bolts.
6. Place suitable drain pan in position and disconnect power steering pump lines at pump.
7. Remove pump.
8. Remove transfer pulley.
9. Reverse procedure to install.

TIGHTENING SPECIFICATIONS

Year	Component	Torque/Ft. Lbs.
2001–05	Axle Nut	284
	Ball Joint To Knuckle (Alero)	41
	Control Arm To Frame, Front Bushing (Alero)	79
	Control Arm To Frame, Rear Bushing (Alero)	81
	Disc Brake Caliper	85
	Disc Brake Caliper To Bracket	23
	Driveshaft Nut	284
	Hub & Bearing Assembly	70
	Hub Nut	284
	Power Steering Line Fittings	20
	Power Steering Pump (2.2L & 2.4L Engine)	19
	Power Steering Pump (3.1L & 3.4L Engines)	25
	Stabilizer Shaft To Control Arm	13
	Stabilizer Shaft Bushing Clamp To Crossmember Support	49
	Stabilizer Shaft Link to Control Arm	13
	Steering Gear	89
	Steering Gear Mounting Clamp	22
	Steering Column Upper & Lower Pinch Bolt	16
	Steering Knuckle To Strut	133
	Strut To Body	18
	Strut Rod	52
	Tie Rod End To Steering Knuckle	15
	Tie Rod Jam Nut	50
	Transaxle Mount (Alero)	89
	Wheel Lug Nuts	100

Wheel Alignment

INDEX

PRELIMINARY INSPECTION

Ensure tires are properly inflated.

Before measuring and setting front wheel alignment, rest front wheels on turn plates.

Before setting rear toe, rest rear wheels on slider plates or turn plates.

Before setting any alignment angle, jounce the vehicle three times at each end to establish trim height.

Special adapters are available for using magnetic hub gauge at rear wheels. Depending on type of equipment used, these may not be required. After removing hub cap and bearing cap, hub gauge will snap into place on brake drum. Magnetic mounting toe gauges may also be installed in the same manner.

Always perform wheel alignment on level alignment rack. Before doing alignment, proceed as follows:

1. Inspect for worn suspension components.
2. Inspect standing curb height.
3. Remove heavy weights from trunk.
4. Inspect wheel bearings for excessive freeplay.
5. Ensure gas tank is full.
6. Place front seats in full rear position.
7. Inspect rear toe adjustment.
8. Always road test vehicle after adjusting alignment, noting the following:
   a. If vehicle still pulls, switch front tires.
   b. If vehicle pulls in same direction, inspect alignment and rear tracking.
   c. If vehicle pulls in opposite direction, rotate tires and road test.

FRONT WHEEL ALIGNMENT

Caster

Caster angle is not adjustable. If caster angle is not within specifications, **Fig. 1**, inspect suspension support for improper alignment and suspension components for damage.

Camber

Toe setting is the only adjustment normally required. In special circumstances such as damage because of road hazard or collision, the camber angle may be adjusted by modifying the strut, **Fig. 1**.

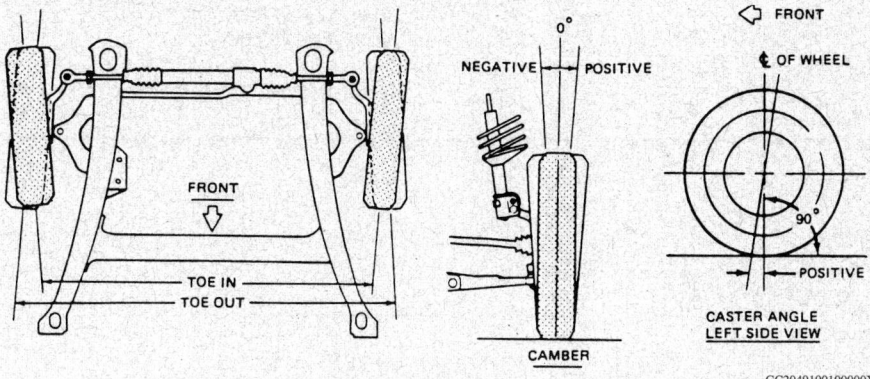

Fig. 1 Caster, camber & toe angles

1 STRUT IN VISE
2 BEFORE FILING
3 AFTER FILING

GC2049700155000X

Fig. 2 Strut bracket modification for camber adjustment

1. **With strut on vehicle,** disconnect strut from steering knuckle.
2. **With strut off vehicle,** secure strut bottom in suitable vise.
3. **On all models,** enlarge bottom holes in outer flanges with suitable round file, until holes in outer flanges match slots in inner flanges, **Fig. 2**.
4. Install or connect strut to steering knuckle and install bolts hand tight.
5. Grasp top of tire firmly and move tire inboard or outboard until proper camber reading is obtained. Tighten mounting bolts enough to retain camber setting.
6. Remove wheel and tire assembly, then tighten strut to steering knuckle mounting bolts.

Toe

The toe is controlled by tie rod position, **Fig. 1**.

A ADJUST TOE SETTING HERE
B LOOSEN LOCKNUT TO ADJUST TOE, RETIGHTEN
1 OUTER TIE ROD
2 STRUT DAMPER

GC2049700145000X

Fig. 3 Toe adjustment

1. Ensure front wheels are in straight-ahead position.
2. Loosen jam nut, **Fig. 3**.
3. Turn adjuster to obtain proper toe setting.
4. **Torque** jam nut to 50 ft. lbs.

REAR WHEEL ALIGNMENT

After front wheel alignment has been inspected or adjusted, rear wheel alignment angles should be inspected if vehicle still does not track properly, or if excessive rear tire wear is present. Rear wheels should be parallel to and the same distance from the vehicle centerline.

Rear wheel alignment is not adjustable. If alignment angles are not within specification, inspect for bent or damaged suspension arms, components or underbody.

THRUST ANGLE

The vehicle is steered by the front wheels. The path the rear wheels follow is the thrust angle, **Fig. 4.** In an ideal setting, the thrust angle would be aligned with the vehicle centerline.

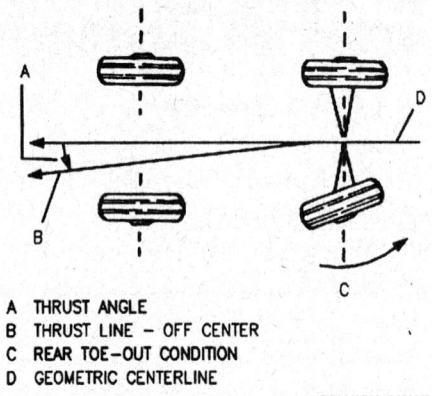

A   THRUST ANGLE
B   THRUST LINE – OFF CENTER
C   REAR TOE-OUT CONDITION
D   GEOMETRIC CENTERLINE

GC2049700156000X

Fig. 4   Thrust angle

AURORA

NOTE: Refer To The Rear Of This Manual For Manufacturer's Special Service Tool Supplies.

INDEX OF SERVICE OPERATIONS

Specifications

GENERAL ENGINE SPECIFICATIONS

Engine Liter/VIN Code①	Fuel System	Bore & Stroke	Compression Ratio	Net H.P. @ RPM②	Maximum Torque Ft. Lbs. @ RPM	Normal Oil Pressure, psi
2001–02						
3.5L/H	SFI	3.52 X 3.62	9.3	215 @ 5600	230 @ 4400	③
4.0L/C	SFI	3.43 X 3.31	10.0	250 @ 5600	260 @ 4000	④
2003						
4.0L/C	SFI	3.43 X 3.31	10.0	250 @ 5600	260 @ 4000	④

① — Eighth digit of VIN denotes engine code.

② — Ratings are net-as installed in vehicle.

③ — 35 psi @ 600 RPM, 80 psi @ 3600 RPM.

④ — 5 psi @ idle speed, 35 psi @ 2000 RPM.

TUNE UP SPECIFICATIONS

Engine Liter/VIN Code①	Spark Plug Gap	Firing Order	Wire Connections Fig.	Idle Speed	Fuel Pump Pressure, psi⑤	Valve Clearance, Inch
2001–02						
3.5L/H	.050	②	—	⑥	48–55	③
4.0L/C	.050	④	A	⑥	48–55	③
2003						
4.0L/C	.050	④	A	⑥	48–55	③

① — Eighth digit of VIN denotes engine code.

② — Cylinder numbering from lefthand to righthand as viewed front of vehicle, front bank 2, 4, 6; rear bank 1, 3, 5. Firing order, 1-2-3-4-5-6.

③ — Equipped w/hydraulic valve lifters; no adjustment required.

④ — Cylinder numbering from lefthand to righthand as viewed from front of vehicle, front bank 2, 4, 6, 8; rear bank 1, 3, 5, 7. Firing order, 1-2-7-3-4-5-6-8.

⑤ — With shop towel wrapped around fuel pressure gauge & fuel pressure test port to prevent spillage, connect fuel pressure gauge to fuel pressure test port. Inspect fuel pressure w/ignition key in On position and engine not running.

⑥ — Idle speed is controlled by Idle Speed Control Actuator.

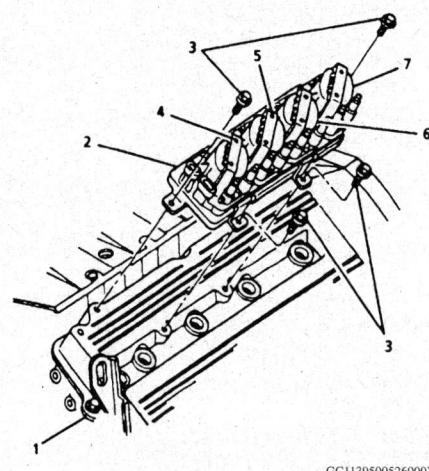

GC1139500526000X

Fig. A

FRONT WHEEL ALIGNMENT SPECIFICATIONS

Year	Model	Caster Angle, Degrees		Camber Angle, Degrees		Total Toe, Degree	Steering Angle, Degrees	Ball Joint Wear
		Limits	Desired	Limits	Desired			
2001	②	+5.5 to +6.5	+6	-.7 to +.3	-.2	0 to +.4	-3 to +3	①
	③	+4.5 to +5.5	+5	-.7 to +.3	-.2	0 to +.4	-3 to +3	①
2002–03	All	+4.5 to +5.5	+5	-.7 to +.3	-.2	0 to +.4	-3 to +3	①

① — Refer to "Ball Joint Inspection" in "Front Suspension & Steering" section.

② — VIN 14103349 or less.

③ — VIN 14103350 or greater.

REAR WHEEL ALIGNMENT SPECIFICATIONS

Year	Model	Camber Angle, Degrees		Total Toe, Degrees	Thrust Angle, Degrees
		Limits	Desired		
2001–03	All	-.8 to +.2	-.3	0 to +.4	-.1 to +.1

VEHICLE RIDE HEIGHT SPECIFICATIONS

Model	Year	Body Style	Manufacturer's Original Tire Size	Measurement Points & Specifications ①③					
				Front			Rear		
				Dim.	Specification		Dim.	Specification	
					Inches	mm		Inches	mm
Aurora	2001–03	All	②	Z	1.20–2.00	30–50	D	3.00–3.80	76–96

Dim. — Dimension

D Dim. — Rear suspension measurement from front outboard control arm bolt center line to bottom of control arm wheel bearing and hub face

Z Dim. — Front suspension measurement from front pivot bolt center line to lower corner of lower ball joint

① — ±.39 inch (10 mm) front to rear & side to side.

② — See door sticker or inside of glove compartment for manufacturers original tire size specifications.

③ — Measurement is with fuel, radiator coolant and engine oil full, spare tire, jack, hand tools and mats in designated positions and tires properly inflated.

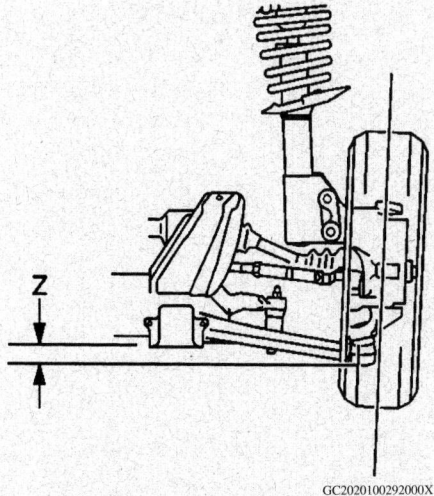

GC2020100292000X

Fig. A   Front suspension

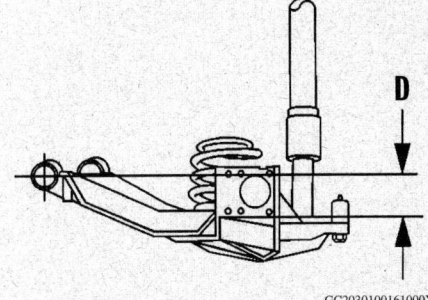

GC2030100161000X

Fig. B   Rear suspension

FLUID CAPACITIES & COOLING SYSTEM DATA

Model	Engine Liter/VIN Code①	Coolant Capacity, Qts.	Coolant Type	Radiator Cap Relief Pressure, Lbs.	Thermo Opening Temp.	Fuel Tank, Gallons	Engine Oil Refill, Qts. ④	Auto Transaxle, Qts.
2001–02								
Aurora	3.5L/H	10.0	DEX-COOL②	15	195	18.5	6.0	⑤
	4.0L/C	13.0	DEX-COOL②	15	185	17.5	7.0	③
2003								
Aurora	4.0L/C	13.0	DEX-COOL②	15	185	17.5	7.0	③

① — Eighth digit of VIN denotes engine code.

② — DEX-COOL, or equivalent, silicant-free antifreeze conforming to GM specification No. 6277M.

③ — Drain & refill, 11 qts.; overhaul, 12.6 qts.; total dry, 15 qts.

④ — With filter change.

⑤ — Drain & refill, 7.4 qts.; overhaul, 10 qts.; total dry 13.4 qts.

LUBRICANT DATA

Year	Model	Lubricant Type			
		Automatic Transaxle	Power Steering System	Supercharger	Brake System
2001–03	All	Dexron III	GM Part No. 1052884	Synthetic Oil GM Part No. 12345982	DOT 3

Electrical

NOTE: On Air Bag Equipped Models, Refer To "Air Bag System Precautions" Located In The Front Of This Manual For System Disarming & Arming Procedures.

NOTE: Refer To "Computer Relearn Procedures" Located In The Front Of This Manual When Battery Power To The Computer Has Been Interrupted.

NOTE: Prior To Performing Any Service Operations Listed In This Section, Consult The "Technical Service Bulletins" Section For Related Information.

INDEX

PRECAUTIONS

Air Bag Systems

Refer to "Air Bag System Precautions" in the front of this manual for system disarming and arming procedures.

Battery Ground Cable

Prior to service, disconnect battery ground cable and isolate as required.

FUSE PANEL & FLASHER LOCATION

The rear fuse block is located behind the righthand side of the rear seat. The underhood fuse block is located on the front righthand side of the engine compartment.

The turn signal/hazard lamp control module is located behind the lefthand side of the instrument panel, above the Data Link Connector (DLC).

FUEL PUMP RELAY LOCATION

The fuel pump relay is located behind the righthand side of the rear seat, in the rear fuse block.

RELAY CENTER LOCATION

Relays are located in the rear and underhood fuse blocks, refer to "Fuse Panel & Flasher Location."

STARTER
REPLACE
3.5L Engine

1. Raise and support vehicle.
2. Remove lower air deflector.
3. Remove mounting bolts and torque converter cover.
4. Disconnect battery cable and starter solenoid S terminal wires.
5. Remove starter mounting bolts and starter.
6. Reverse procedure to install, noting the following:
   a. **Torque** starter motor mounting bolts to 37 ft. lbs.
   b. **Torque** nut on solenoid battery terminal to 89 inch lbs.
   c. **Torque** nut on solenoid S terminal to 22 inch lbs.

4.0L Engine

1. Remove intake manifold as outlined

under "Intake Manifold, Replace" in "4.0L Engine" section.
2. Disconnect starter solenoid "S" and battery terminals electrical connectors.
3. Remove mounting bolts and starter.
4. Reverse procedure to install, noting the following:
   a. **Torque** inner nuts on solenoid terminals to 72 inch lbs.
   b. **Torque** "S" terminal nut to 26 inch lbs.
   c. **Torque** battery terminal nut to 72 inch lbs.
   d. **Torque** starter mounting bolts to 22 ft. lbs.

ALTERNATOR
REPLACE
3.5L Engine

1. Remove accessory drive belt.
2. Remove headlamp/fascia panel support brackets.
3. Remove radiator support brackets and air cleaner.
4. Position PCM aside.
5. Remove upper tie bar mounting bolts and upper tie bar.
6. Disconnect cooling fan motor electrical connectors.
7. Remove clips attaching wiring harness to fan shroud.

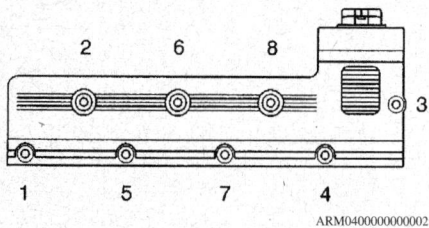

Fig. 1 Ignition control module removal sequence. 4.0L engine

8. Raise and support vehicle, then remove lower air deflector.
9. Remove transaxle oil cooler line mounting bolt and clip from fan shroud.
10. Lower vehicle and slide plastic cap off of upper quick connect joint, then disconnect upper transaxle oil cooler line from radiator.
11. Remove shroud mounting bolts and cooling fan.
12. Disconnect alternator electrical connectors.
13. Remove mounting bolt and drive belt idler pulley.
14. Remove alternator upper mounting bolts, then position alternator to access two upper air conditioning compressor mounting bolts.
15. Raise and support vehicle.
16. Remove air conditioning compressor upper mounting bolts and loosen rear compressor mounting nut.
17. Remove front air conditioning compressor mounting nut.
18. Position air conditioning compressor away from engine block.
19. Lower vehicle and remove alternator.
20. Reverse procedure to install, noting the following:
    a. **Torque** air conditioning compressor mounting bolts and front nut to 37 ft. lbs., then the rear nut to 18 ft. lbs.
    b. **Torque** idler pulley bolt to 37 ft. lbs.
    c. **Torque** alternator mounting bolts to 37 ft. lbs.
    d. **Torque** alternator battery output terminal nut to 111 inch lbs.

4.0L Engine

1. Release accessory drive belt tensioner.
2. Remove power steering pump and alternator drive belt.
3. Raise and support vehicle.
4. Drain cooling system into suitable container and lower vehicle.
5. Remove radiator as outlined under "Radiator, Replace" in "4.0L Engine" section.
6. Disconnect alternator electrical connectors.
7. Loosen lower and remove upper alternator mounting bolts.
8. Remove lower bolt and alternator.
9. Reverse procedure to install. **Torque** alternator mounting bolts to 37 ft. lbs.

COIL PACK
REPLACE

3.5L Engine
LEFTHAND

1. Remove two fuel injector sight shield front mounting nuts.
2. Lift front of sight shield up and slide from engine bracket.
3. Remove oil dipstick tube, then the PCV valve and feed tube from lefthand camshaft cover.
4. Remove ignition coil.
5. Reverse procedure to install.

RIGHTHAND

1. Remove automatic transaxle filler tube.
2. Remove fuel injector sight shield front mounting nuts.
3. Lift front of sight shield up and slide from engine bracket.
4. Remove mounting bolts and fuel injector sight shield bracket.
5. Disconnect PCV feed tube and engine wiring harness clips from front of camshaft cover. Position wiring harness aside.
6. Disconnect oxygen sensor electrical connector and remove connector end from camshaft cover.
7. Remove ignition coil.
8. Reverse procedure to install.

4.0L Engine

1. Remove fuel injector sight shield.
2. Disconnect ignition control module electrical connector.
3. Remove secondary air valve electrical connector, then the valve.
4. Remove ignition coil mounting bolts in sequence, **Fig. 1.**
5. Reverse procedure to install, noting the following:
    a. Tighten ignition coil mounting bolts using numbered sequence in, **Fig. 2.**
    b. **Torque** mounting bolts to 80 inch lbs.

IGNITION LOCK
REPLACE

1. Apply parking brake and remove radio as outlined under "Radio, Replace."
2. Insert ignition key and turn ignition switch to RUN position.
3. Locate ignition lock cylinder release button through radio opening in instrument panel.
4. Depress and hold ignition lock cylinder retaining tab (righthand lower side of ignition switch) using suitable flat-bladed screwdriver.
5. Pull lock cylinder from of instrument panel.
6. Remove lock cylinder reader/exciter ring.

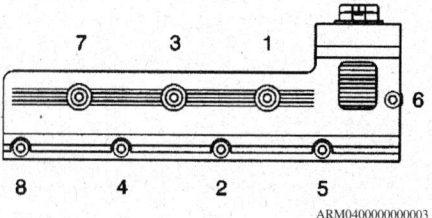

Fig. 2 Ignition coil module tightening sequence

7. Reverse procedure to install.

IGNITION SWITCH
REPLACE

1. Remove ignition lock cylinder as outlined under "Ignition Lock, Replace."
2. Remove ignition switch mounting screws.
3. Push and release retaining tab at rear of ignition switch.
4. Disconnect ignition switch electrical connectors, then remove bulb from side of switch.
5. Remove ignition switch through radio opening.
6. Reverse procedure to install. **Torque** ignition switch mounting screws to 80 inch lbs.

NEUTRAL SAFETY SWITCH
REPLACE

The transaxle range function is controlled by an internal transaxle mode switch. Refer to **MOTOR's "Domestic Transmission Manual, In-Vehicle Service"** for automatic transmission mode switch replacement.

STOP LIGHT SWITCH
REPLACE

1. Remove closeout panel from under lefthand side of instrument panel.
2. Turn switch counterclockwise and remove from brake pedal support.
3. Disconnect brake switch electrical connector and remove.
4. Reverse procedure to install.

MULTI-FUNCTION SWITCH
REPLACE

1. Tilt steering column to center position.
2. Remove tilt lever by pulling straight out.
3. Lock steering column by inserting steering column lock pin tool No. J 42640, or equivalent, into steering column access hole.
4. Remove steering wheel as outlined under "Steering Wheel, Replace."
5. Remove lefthand instrument panel

end cap by gently prying on rear edge to release retainers, then pull end cap rearward.

6. Remove knee bolster compartment by pulling past holding tab and lifting upward.
7. Remove knee bolster by unsnapping and pulling down and rearward.
8. Remove lefthand closeout insulator panel retaining screws, then the panel from instrument panel retainer.
9. Remove heater temperature sensor from closeout insulator panel by turning counterclockwise ¼ turn.
10. Disconnect lower instrument panel courtesy lamp electrical connector.
11. Remove closeout insulator panel by sliding rearward.
12. Remove knee bolster bracket mounting screws from instrument panel and steering column support, then the knee bolster bracket.
13. Remove steering column bracket mounting screws to carrier, then the bracket.
14. Disconnect steering column main body wiring harness electrical connector, then reposition seal.
15. Remove upper shaft pinch bolt, **Fig. 3.**
16. Support steering column.
17. Hold studs, then remove mounting nuts from steering column to instrument panel and upper support.
18. Remove steering column and mount in suitable vise.
19. Remove mounting screws, then the lower trim cover.
20. Remove one TORX head screw, then the upper trim cover and closeout trim cover.
21. Disconnect wire harness assembly from retainer strap.
22. Disconnect multi-function switch electrical connector from clockspring connector.
23. Disconnect two multi-function switch connectors from bulkhead connector by sliding outward.
24. Remove two pan head screws, then the multi-function switch assembly.
25. Reverse procedure to install.

STEERING WHEEL
REPLACE

1. Remove air bag as outlined in "Passive Restraints Systems" chapter.
2. Disconnect electrical connector from steering wheel.
3. Remove weight block from base of steering wheel, if equipped.
4. Remove steering wheel mounting nut, place match marks on shaft and steering wheel.
5. Remove steering wheel using pulling tools No. J 42578, and J 1859-A, or equivalents.
6. Reverse procedure to install. **Torque** steering wheel mounting nut to 30 ft. lbs.

INSTRUMENT CLUSTER
REPLACE

1. Lower tilt steering column to lowest position.

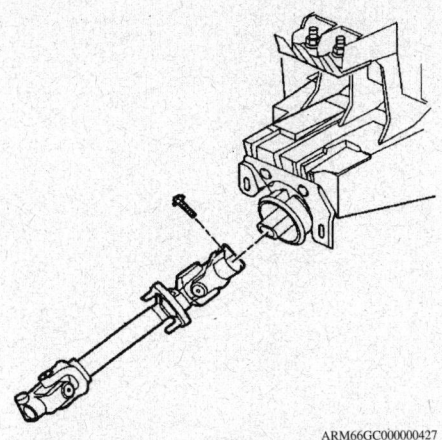

ARM66GC000000427

Fig. 3 Steering column upper intermediate shaft removal

2. Remove ignition lock cylinder bezel.
3. Remove lefthand instrument panel endcap.
4. Remove instrument panel center trim plate.
5. Remove righthand instrument panel endcap.
6. Open glove compartment door and remove righthand accessory trim plate to instrument panel mounting screws.
7. Remove instrument panel righthand accessory trim plate.
8. Remove mounting screws and instrument cluster upper trim cover.
9. Remove lefthand instrument panel air deflector.
10. Remove instrument cluster trim plate mounting screws.
11. Disconnect trim plate electrical connectors and remove instrument panel trim plate.
12. Remove instrument cluster mounting screws.
13. Disconnect cluster electrical connectors and remove cluster.
14. Reverse procedure to install.

RADIO
REPLACE

1. Remove instrument panel center trim plate by pulling rearward to disengage retainers.
2. Depress spring clip retainers on sides of radio.
3. Pull radio outward and disconnect antenna lead and electrical connectors.
4. Remove radio.
5. Reverse procedure to install.

WIPER MOTOR
REPLACE

1. Ensure wiper arms are in PARK position.
2. Remove mounting nuts and wiper arms.
3. Push air inlet grill panel retainers though grill panel.
4. Disconnect washer hose and remove air inlet grill panel.
5. Remove mounting bolts, nuts and windshield frame reinforcement.

6. Rotate wiper transmission linkage until motor crank arm is opposite PARK position.
7. Remove plenum hole harness grommet.
8. Disconnect wiper motor electrical connector, then push harness and grommet through hole.
9. Remove mounting screws and wiper system drive module.
10. Separate drive link from crank arm using separator tool No. J 39232, or equivalent.
11. Remove mounting screws then the wiper motor.
12. Reverse procedure to install.

BLOWER MOTOR
REPLACE

1. Remove righthand instrument panel sound insulator panel.
2. Remove glove compartment door to glove compartment mounting screws.
3. Remove mounting screws and glove compartment.
4. Remove Dash Integration Module (DIM) from bracket.
5. Remove mounting screws and DIM bracket .
6. Disconnect blower motor electrical connector.
7. Remove mounting screws and blower motor.
8. Reverse procedure to install.

CABIN AIR FILTER
REPLACE

Under normal operating conditions the cabin air filter should be replaced every 12 months or 15,000 miles. In dusty areas change the cabin air filter as required.

1. Open hood.
2. Lift up cabin air filter access cover located on air inlet panel.
3. Remove cabin air filter element from housing, **Fig. 4.**
4. Install new cabin air filter into filter housing.
5. Close cabin air filter access cover.
6. Close hood.

HEATER CORE
REPLACE

1. Recover air conditioning refrigerant as outlined in "Air Conditioning" chapter.
2. Drain cooling system.
3. Remove heater core hoses.
4. Remove instrument panel lefthand and righthand sound insulators.
5. Remove tray insert, then the center console lefthand and righthand trim plates.
6. Disconnect shifter and park lock cables.
7. Disconnect console main wiring harness connector.
8. Open glove compartment door and remove instrument panel to console mounting screw.
9. Remove console to instrument panel and console to floor mounting screws.
10. Slide console rearward and remove it.

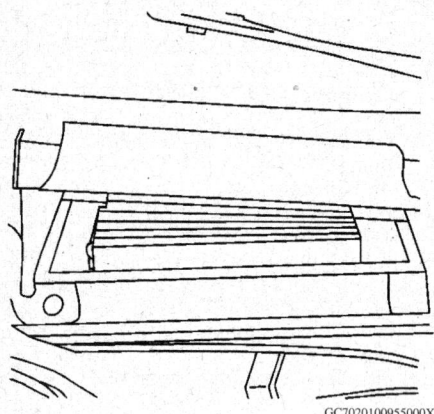

Fig. 4 Cabin air filter replacement

11. Remove auxiliary air distribution duct adapter.
12. Remove mounting screws and air distributor duct.
13. Remove mounting screws and heater core heat shield.
14. Remove mounting screws and heater core cover.
15. Remove mounting screw, strap and heater core.
16. Reverse procedure to install.

EVAPORATOR CORE
REPLACE

1. Recover air conditioning refrigerant as outlined in "Air Conditioning" chapter.
2. Remove evaporator hose nut and disconnect evaporator hose.
3. Drain cooling system into suitable container and remove heater core hoses. Plug heater core and evaporator openings.
4. Remove lefthand and righthand lower dash panel sound insulators.
5. Remove center instrument panel trim plate.
6. Remove center console trim plate screw and pull up on rear of console trim plate to disengage clips.
7. Disconnect center console trim plate electrical connectors and remove trim plate.
8. Remove console compartment.
9. Remove lefthand and righthand console side trim panels.
10. Disconnect shift cable and park lock cable.
11. Disconnect console main wiring harness connector.

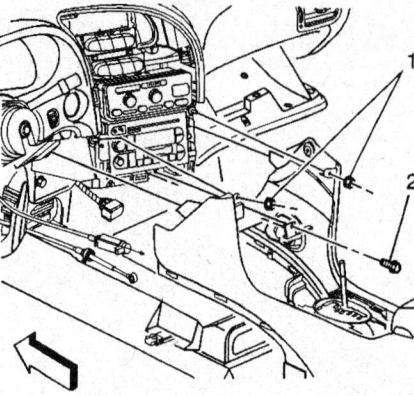

Fig. 5 Center console replacement (Part 1 of 2)

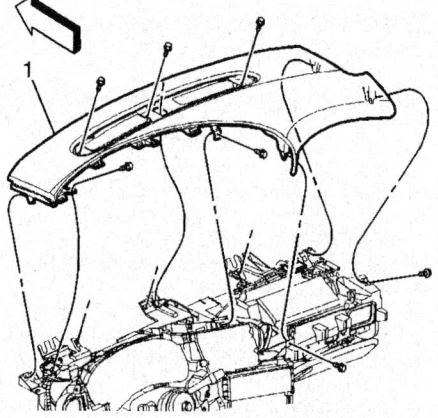

Fig. 6 Upper trim pad replacement

12. Open glove compartment and remove mounting screw.
13. Remove remaining mounting screws and console, **Fig. 5.**
14. Remove instrument panel endcaps.
15. Remove lefthand and righthand windshield garnish moldings, then the defroster grille.
16. Remove righthand instrument panel trim panel and instrument cluster trim plate.
17. Remove carrier bolts and instrument panel upper trim pad, **Fig. 6.**
18. Remove steering column as outlined in "Steering Columns" chapter.
19. Remove steering column support.
20. Disconnect instrument panel electrical harnesses.

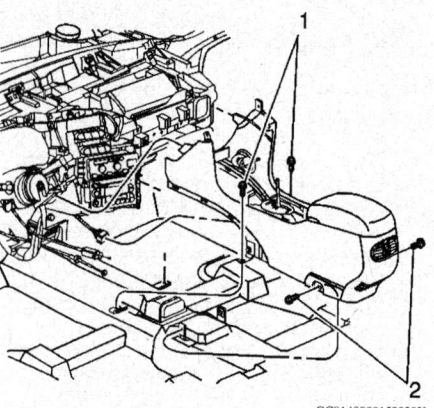

Fig. 5 Center console replacement (Part 2 of 2)

21. Remove instrument panel center support brackets.
22. Remove brackets and instrument panel.
23. Remove instrument panel lower support bracket.
24. Remove defroster duct mounting screws, nut and defroster duct.
25. Remove screws and air distributor duct.
26. Disconnect blower control module and instrument panel to HVAC module electrical connectors.
27. Remove mounting nuts and HVAC module.
28. Remove heater core and evaporator tubes' seal.
29. Remove upper HVAC evaporator case and evaporator core.
30. Reverse procedure to install.

TECHNICAL SERVICE BULLETINS

Intermittent No Start Or No Crank
2001 AURORA

On some of these models there may be an intermittent no start or no crank condition.

This condition may be caused by plastic particles interfering with the ignition switch electrical contacts.

To correct this condition, install improved ignition switch (part No. 25721650).

3.5L Engine

NOTE: On Air Bag Equipped Models, Refer To "Air Bag System Precautions" Located In The Front Of This Manual For System Disarming & Arming Procedures.

NOTE: Refer To "Computer Relearn Procedures" Located In The Front Of This Manual When Battery Power To The Computer Has Been Interrupted.

NOTE: Refer To "3.5L Engine" Section In The "Century, Grand Prix, Impala, Intrigue, Lumina, Monte Carlo & Regal" Chapter For Procedures Not Covered In This Section.

NOTE: Prior To Performing Any Service Operations Listed In This Section, Consult The "Technical Service Bulletins" Section For Related Information.

INDEX

PRECAUTIONS

Air Bag Systems

Refer to "Air Bag System Precautions" in the front of this manual for system disarming and arming procedures.

Battery Ground Cable

Prior to service, disconnect battery ground cable and isolate as required.

Fuel Pressure Relief

1. Turn ignition off and remove fuel pump relay.
2. Loosen fuel filler cap.
3. Remove mounting nuts and intake manifold top cover.
4. Connect suitable fuel pressure gauge and wrap connection with suitable shop towel to prevent fuel leakage.
5. Install suitable bleed hose into suitable container and open pressure valve to bleed system pressure.

COMPRESSION PRESSURE

Refer to "3.5L Engine" section in the "Century, Grand Prix, Impala, Intrigue, Lumina, Monte Carlo & Regal" chapter.

ENGINE MOUNT

REPLACE

1. Support engine using engine support fixture tool No. J 28467, or equivalent.
2. Remove mounting bolts and front engine mount support bracket.
3. Raise and support vehicle.
4. Remove engine mount to frame mounting nut.
5. Lower vehicle and remove engine mount.
6. Reverse procedure to install.

ENGINE

REPLACE

1. Relieve fuel system pressure as outlined under "Precautions."
2. Remove accessory drive belt.
3. Remove fuel injector sight shield.
4. Remove power steering pump and position aside. **Do not disconnect power steering pressure lines.**
5. Remove throttle body air intake duct.
6. Disconnect fuel rail lines and position aside.
7. Disconnect fuel vapor line.
8. Disconnect throttle and cruise cables with mounting bracket.
9. Disconnect brake vacuum booster hose from engine.
10. Disconnect air conditioning vacuum hose from engine.
11. Disconnect wiring harness connectors from engine and transaxle.
12. Drain cooling system into suitable container and remove radiator inlet hose from engine.
13. Disconnect transaxle fluid lines from radiator.
14. Remove thermostat housing and disconnect surge tank inlet hose.
15. Disconnect heater hoses from engine.
16. Raise and support vehicle.
17. Drain engine oil into suitable container and disconnect AIR pump outlet pipe from AIR crossover pipe.
18. Remove alternator as outlined in "Electrical" section.
19. Remove air conditioning compressor mounting bolts and nuts. Position compressor aside. **Do not discharge air conditioning system.**
20. Remove torque converter cover and starter motor.
21. Scribe alignment marks on flywheel and torque converter.
22. Remove torque converter to flywheel mounting bolts.
23. Remove lower transaxle to engine mounting bolts.
24. Remove front tire and wheel assemblies.
25. Remove inner fender splash shields.
26. Remove wheel speed sensor harness conduits from lower control arm retainers.
27. Remove tie rod ends from steering knuckle as outlined in "Front Suspension & Steering" section.
28. Remove lower ball joints from steering knuckles as outlined in "Front Suspension & Steering" section.
29. Remove intermediate steering shaft pinch bolt and disconnect intermediate shaft from steering gear.
30. Support engine/transaxle frame using frame table tool No. J 39580, or equivalent.
31. Lower vehicle slightly so frame table is

supporting engine/transaxle assembly.

32. Secure vehicle to hoist and remove frame to body mounting bolts.
33. Raise and support vehicle.
34. Remove frame table with engine/transaxle frame.
35. Remove transaxle to engine bracket.
36. Remove upper engine to transaxle mounting bolts and separate engine from transaxle.
37. Reverse procedure to install.

INTAKE MANIFOLD
REPLACE

Refer to "3.5L Engine" section in the "Century, Grand Prix, Impala, Intrigue, Lumina, Monte Carlo & Regal" chapter.

RADIATOR
REPLACE

1. Remove headlamp/fascia panel support brackets.
2. Remove radiator support brackets and air cleaner.
3. Position PCM aside.
4. Remove mounting bolts and upper tie bar.
5. Disconnect cooling fan motor electrical connectors.
6. Remove clips attaching wiring harness to fan shroud.
7. Raise and support vehicle, then remove lower air deflector.
8. Remove transaxle oil cooler line mounting bolt and clip from fan shroud.
9. Lower vehicle and slide plastic cap off

of upper quick connect joint, then disconnect upper transaxle oil cooler line from radiator.
10. Remove cooling fan shroud mounting bolts and cooling fan.
11. Disconnect upper and lower radiator hoses.
12. Remove upper radiator seal and headlamps.
13. Remove two condenser mounting bolts and lift condenser out of its lower mounting.
14. Remove radiator.
15. Reverse procedure to install.

FUEL PUMP
REPLACE

1. Relieve fuel system pressure as outlined under "Precautions."
2. Drain fuel tank to at least ¾ of full tank.
3. Remove spare tire cover, jack and spare tire.
4. Remove luggage compartment floor trim.
5. Remove mounting screws and fuel sender access panel.
6. Cover fuel pipe fittings with suitable shop towel to prevent spillage.
7. Remove quick-connect fittings air fuel sender.
8. Disconnect fuel sender and fuel pressure sensor electrical connectors.
9. Remove fuel sender retaining ring using fuel sender locknut wrench tool No. J 39765, or equivalent.
10. Remove fuel tank sender.
11. Reverse procedure to install.

FUEL FILTER
REPLACE

1. Relieve fuel system pressure as outlined under "Precautions."
2. Raise and support vehicle.
3. Disconnect quick-connect fitting at inlet end of inline fuel filter.
4. Remove outlet end threaded fitting and of filter. Drain remaining fuel into suitable container.
5. Reverse procedure to install.

TECHNICAL SERVICE BULLETINS

High Temperature Gauge Reading Or Overheating In Cold Weather
2001

On some of these models the temperature gauge may have higher than normal readings or the engine may overheat in cold weather. This condition may occur while idling or driving slowly in traffic when temperature is less than 32°F, with the heater control set to maximum heat and fan.

This condition may be caused by the thermostat not providing adequate coolant flow.

To correct this condition, install enhanced thermostat (part No. 12570247).

TIGHTENING SPECIFICATIONS

Year	Component	Torque, Ft. Lbs.
2001–02	Accelerator Cable Bracket	84①
	Air Conditioning Compressor, Front Nut	37
	Air Conditioning Compressor, Hose Fittings	15
	Air Conditioning Compressor, Mounting Bolt	37
	Air Conditioning Compressor, Rear Nut	18
	Air Conditioning Condenser	115①
	Alternator	37
	Ball Joint	41
	Camshaft Bearing Caps	44③
	Camshaft Position Sensor	84①
	Camshaft Sprocket	18②
	Connecting Rod	⑥
	Coolant Temperature Sensor	15
	Cylinder Head	⑤
	EGR to Crossover Pipe	44
	Engine Frame Insulator	12
	Engine Front Cradle	141
	Engine To Transaxle	55
	EVAP Canister Purge Solenoid	72①
	Exhaust Manifold	18

Continued

TIGHTENING
SPECIFICATIONS—Continued

Year	Component	Torque, Ft. Lbs.
2001–02	Exhaust Manifold, Crossover Stud	18
	Exhaust Manifold, Stud	53①
	Flywheel To Torque Converter	44
	Front Cover	11
	Front Cover Coolant Drain Plug	96①
	Front Engine Mount	52
	Front Lift Bracket, Hex Bolt	37
	Front Lift Bracket, Internal Drive Bolt	18
	Fuel Injector Sight Shield	27①
	Idler Pulley	37
	Intake Manifold	60①
	Intermediate Shaft Pinch Bolt	35
	Lower Control Arm	117
	Lower Crankcase	④
	Oil Gallery Plug	41
	Oil Level Sensor	84①
	Oil Pan	18
	Oxygen Sensor	30
	Power Steering Pump	25
	Stabilizer Shaft Link	13
	Steering Rack	48
	Thermostat Housing	80①
	Throttle Body	108①
	Tie Rod	55
	Timing Chain Tensioner	18
	Timing Chain Tensioner Shoe	22
	Transaxle Mount Bracket	37
	Transaxle Mount	48
	Transaxle To Engine	55
	Valve Cover	84①
	Water Pump	11
	Water Pump Pulley	108①
	Water Outlet Housing	84①

① — Inch lbs.
② — Tighten an additional 45°.
③ — Tighten an additional 30°.
④ — Refer to "Main & Rod Bearings" for tightening procedure.
⑤ — Refer to "Cylinder Head, Replace" for tightening procedure.
⑥ — Torque 22 ft. lbs.; loosen completely; torque to 18 ft. lbs. Final tighten an additional 110°.

4.0L Engine

NOTE: On Air Bag Equipped Models, Refer To "Air Bag System Precautions" Located In The Front Of This Manual For System Disarming & Arming Procedures.

NOTE: Refer To "Computer Relearn Procedures" Located In The Front Of This Manual When Battery Power To The Computer Has Been Interrupted.

NOTE: Prior To Performing Any Service Operations Listed In This Section, Consult The "Technical Service Bulletins" Section For Related Information.

INDEX

PRECAUTIONS

Air Bag Systems

Refer to "Air Bag System Precautions" in the front of this manual for system disarming and arming procedures.

Battery Ground Cable

Prior to service, disconnect battery ground cable and isolate as required.

Camshaft Timing & Timing Chain

With the timing chain removed or loosened, avoid turning the camshaft or crankshaft. If movement is required, exercise extreme caution to avoid valve damage caused by piston contact.

Fuel System Pressure Relief

After relieving fuel system pressure, a small amount of fuel may be released when servicing fuel pipes or connections. In order to reduce the risk of personal injury, cover fuel pipe fittings with shop towel before disconnecting to catch any fuel that may leak.

1. Loosen fuel filler cap to relieve tank pressure.
2. Connect suitable fuel pressure gauge to fuel pressure test connector. **Wrap suitable shop towel around connection to avoid fuel spillage.**
3. Insert bleed hose into suitable container and open valve to bleed system.
4. Drain any fuel remaining in fuel gauge into suitable container.

COMPRESSION PRESSURE

When inspecting compression, the lowest cylinder must be within 70 percent of the highest cylinder with a minimum pressure of 100 psi. Perform compression test with engine at normal operating temperature, spark plugs removed and throttle wide open.

ENGINE MOUNT

REPLACE

Righthand

1. Ensure ignition switch is in OFF position.
2. Raise and support vehicle.
3. Remove mounting nut from front engine mount to frame.
4. Support engine using support fixture tool No. J 28467-B, or equivalent.
5. Remove lefthand and righthand front tire and wheel assemblies.
6. Disconnect lefthand and righthand stabilizer bar link bolts.
7. Separate lefthand and righthand ball joints from steering knuckles using ball joint separator tool No. J 43828, or equivalent.
8. Remove lefthand front fascia extension.
9. Remove position pin from Electronic Brake Control Module (EBCM) electrical connector, then rotate connector tab to unlock.
10. Disconnect electrical connector, then position EBCM aside.

11. Remove retainers, then the front air deflector.
12. Rotate stabilizer bar downward.
13. Remove electrical harness clip and mounting bolts, then the power steering gear heat shield.
14. Remove all power steering hose brackets from frame.
15. Remove mounting fasteners from front and rear transmission mounts to frame.
16. Remove mounting fasteners from frame, then secure rack and pinion to body of vehicle.
17. Support engine frame using suitable jackstands.
18. Remove insulator fasteners, then lower engine frame.
19. Remove mounting nut from front engine mount bracket, then the front engine mount.
20. Reverse procedure to install.

Lefthand

1. Raise and support vehicle.
2. Remove righthand front wheel assembly.
3. Support engine assembly using a suitable jack.
4. Remove mounting nut from engine mount to engine mount bracket.
5. Lower engine slightly.
6. Remove mounting nut and bolt from righthand engine mount to frame rail.
7. Remove two mounting nuts, then the righthand engine mount.
8. Reverse procedure to install.

ENGINE
REPLACE

1. Recover refrigerant as outlined in "Air Conditioning" chapter.
2. Disconnect brake booster vacuum hose from connection, then position aside.
3. Disconnect fuel inlet and return quick-connect fittings at fuel rail and secure to air inlet grille.
4. Disconnect hose from EVAP canister valve and secure to air inlet grille.
5. Remove air cleaner assembly and intake manifold sight shield.
6. Remove battery cable from remote positive terminal and secure to top of engine.
7. Disconnect secondary AIR relay from bracket and secure to top of engine.
8. Disconnect Power Control Module (PCM), C101 and engine harness electrical connectors, then secure to top of engine.
9. Remove engine ground cable mounting bolt from righthand side body frame rail.
10. Remove cruise control cable from throttle body bracket and lever.
11. Remove accelerator control cable from throttle body.
12. Remove shift cable from bracket and manual shift lever, then position aside.
13. Drain cooling system into suitable container.
14. Remove upper radiator hose from coolant crossover and position aside.

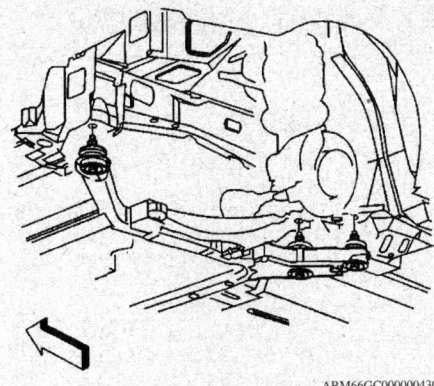

ARM66GC000000430

Fig. 1   Engine frame

15. Remove lower radiator hose from thermostat housing and position aside.
16. Disconnect coolant hose from overflow reservoir.
17. Disconnect heater hoses from heater pipes.
18. Remove two master cylinder brake pipes from Brake Pressure Modulator Valve (BPMV), then plug open outlet ports and mark location of brake pipes to (BPMV) for use during installation.
19. Remove upper transaxle oil cooler pipe mounting bolt from fan shroud.
20. Slide plastic cap off upper transaxle oil cooler pipe quick connect fitting.
21. Disconnect upper transaxle oil cooler pipe from radiator using quick connect tool No. J 41623-B, or equivalent.
22. Disconnect lower transaxle oil cooler pipe fitting from radiator.
23. Lock steering column using lock pin tool No. J 42640, or equivalent, with wheels straight ahead.
24. Remove righthand and lefthand side strut tower mounting bolts.
25. Raise and support vehicle.
26. Remove lefthand exhaust manifold as outlined under "Exhaust Manifold, Replace."
27. Remove both front wheels.
28. Disconnect front wheel speed sensor electrical leads from body frame rail.
29. Remove mounting retainers, then the front air deflector.
30. Remove mounting retainers, then the righthand and lefthand fascia extensions.
31. Disconnect inlet hose from secondary AIR pump.
32. Loosen both front brake pipe bracket to body frame rail mounting nuts.
33. Disconnect and carefully pull front brake pipes from retainers at body frame rails.
34. Disconnect two rear brake pipes at rear of engine frame, then plug open outlet ports.
35. Disconnect A/C pressure sensor.
36. Disconnect A/C discharge and suction hoses from compressor, then secure to cooling fan assembly.
37. Remove pinch bolt and steering gear from intermediate shaft.
38. Drill out center of rivets to remove oxygen sensor heat shield from floor panel, then disconnect sensor at pigtail.

39. Remove brace between engine oil pan and transaxle case.
40. Remove mounting bolts and engine to transaxle brace, then the torque converter cover.
41. Place matching marks on flywheel to torque converter.
42. Remove torque converter to flywheel mounting bolts.
43. Position engine support table tool No. J 39580, or suitable jack stands under engine frame and lower vehicle.
44. Place suitable block of wood between front of engine oil pan and the engine frame.
45. Remove lefthand engine to engine mount bracket mounting nut.
46. Remove transaxle mount to mount bracket mounting nut.
47. Remove six frame to body mounting bolts, **Fig. 1.**
48. Raise vehicle carefully to clear supported engine/transaxle assembly.
49. Drain engine oil, then remove oil filter.
50. Loosen heater inlet hose clamp and remove hose from heater pipe using suitable hose clamp pliers.
51. Remove inlet pipe mounting nut from transaxle.
52. Squeeze quick connect tabs on inlet pipe, then pull outward on inlet heater pipe to remove.
53. Loosen heater outlet hose clamp and remove hose from heater pipe using suitable hose clamp pliers.
54. Remove outlet pipe mounting nut from transaxle.
55. Loosen clamp from back side of thermostat housing to remove outlet pipe assembly.
56. Disconnect intermediate hose from secondary AIR valve at bank two.
57. Remove mounting nut from intermediate hose to secondary AIR valve at bank one.
58. Remove mounting nut from coil cassette ground wire to lefthand side cylinder head.
59. Disconnect engine wiring harness from engine.
60. Disconnect power steering hose from pump reservoir.
61. Remove power steering return hose mounting bolt from cylinder head.
62. Remove power steering pressure hose from pump.
63. Remove mounting nut from pressure hose to lefthand side engine mount.
64. Remove four lefthand side engine mount bracket mounting bolts, then the bracket.
65. Remove mounting bolt from rear transaxle brace to transaxle.
66. Remove mounting nuts from rear transaxle brace to stud located on lefthand side cylinder head.
67. Remove mounting bolts from front transaxle brace to the transaxle and lefthand side cylinder head.
68. Remove mounting nuts from vehicle speed sensor heat shield to transaxle.
69. Remove mounting bolts from center transaxle brace to the engine and transaxle.
70. Install lift bracket tool No. J 42504, or equivalent to cylinder head.

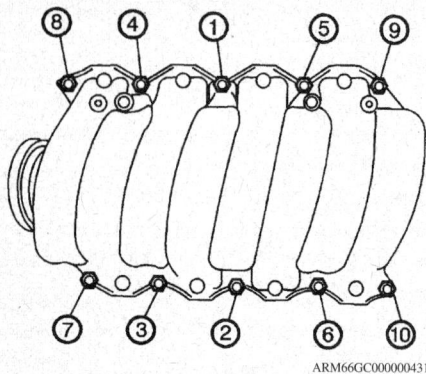

Fig. 2 Intake manifold tightening sequence

ARM66GC000000431

71. Install suitable lift chain to lift brackets, then attach to a suitable engine lift.
72. Remove mounting nut from righthand side engine mount to frame.
73. Remove mounting bolts from engine to transaxle.
74. Raise engine from supported frame and transaxle assembly.
75. Remove righthand side engine mount bracket.
76. Reverse procedure to install.

INTAKE MANIFOLD
REPLACE

1. Remove two mounting nuts from fuel injector sight shield, then lift front of shield and pull forward to release rear tab from bracket.
2. Disconnect electrical connectors from coil modules located in camshaft covers.
3. Disconnect PCV valve air tube, then the PCV fresh air tube from camshaft cover.
4. Disconnect fuel regulator vacuum tube.
5. Disconnect vacuum tubes from AIR solenoid.
6. Disconnect brake booster vacuum hose from intake manifold.
7. Disconnect fuel inlet and return quick connect fittings at fuel rail.
8. Remove fuel rail bracket mounting nut at rear lift bracket.
9. Remove two pushnuts from engine coolant heater wire, then position heater wire aside.
10. Carefully position coolant reservoir pipe away from fuel rail studs.
11. Disconnect eight electrical connectors from fuel injectors.
12. Remove four mounting bolts and lift fuel rail/injector assembly from intake manifold.
13. Loosen plenum duct clamp at rear of intake manifold.
14. Remove 10 mounting bolts from intake manifold to cylinder heads.
15. Remove intake manifold by lifting upward from front of manifold assembly.
16. Reverse procedure to install. Using sequence, **Fig. 2, torque** intake manifold bolts to 89 inch lbs.

EXHAUST MANIFOLD
REPLACE
Righthand

1. Disconnect heated oxygen sensor from sensor pigtail.
2. Lock steering column with wheels in straight ahead position using steering lock pin tool No. J 42640, or equivalent.
3. Raise and support vehicle.
4. Remove four mounting nuts from catalytic converter to exhaust manifold rear pipe, then position exhaust system rearward.
5. Remove and discard catalytic converter gasket.
6. Remove two mounting bolts from exhaust manifold rear pipe to righthand side exhaust manifold, **Fig. 3.**
7. Remove two mounting bolts from exhaust manifold rear pipe to exhaust manifold front pipe.
8. Remove rear manifold pipe and gasket, then the front manifold pipe seal. Discard gasket and seal.
9. Remove exhaust manifold flange seal retainer.
10. Remove two mounting nuts from secondary AIR tube and exhaust manifold.
11. Remove AIR tube and gasket. Discard gasket.
12. Disconnect post heated oxygen sensor wiring harness retainer from power steering gear heat shield.
13. Remove two mounting bolts, then the heat shield.
14. Remove rearward mounting nut from vehicle speed sensor heat shield.
15. Loosen forward mounting nut to remove heat shield.
16. Remove intermediate shaft pinch bolt. Disconnect shaft from steering gear.
17. Remove mounting nut from righthand side engine mount to mount bracket.
18. Remove mounting nut from transaxle mount to mount bracket.
19. Support rear of engine frame with suitable screw jack.
20. Remove four mounting bolts from rearward engine frame to body.
21. Lower screw jack allowing rear of engine frame to lower.
22. Remove mounting bolts, then the righthand exhaust manifold and gasket. Discard gasket.
23. Reverse procedure to install.

Lefthand

1. Remove two mounting nuts from secondary AIR tube to exhaust manifold, then remove tube and gasket. Discard gasket.
2. Remove front engine mount as outlined under "Engine Mount, Replace."
3. Remove two upper mounting bolts to front engine mount bracket and cylinder head.
4. Remove two mounting nuts from front engine mount bracket to engine block.
5. Remove mounting bolt and transaxle support brace.
6. Raise and support vehicle.

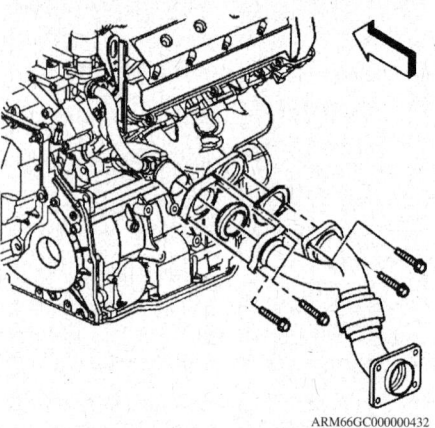

ARM66GC000000432

Fig. 3 Righthand exhaust manifold replace

7. Remove two mounting bolts from lefthand exhaust manifold to front exhaust manifold pipe.
8. Remove mounting bolts, then the lefthand exhaust manifold and gasket. Discard gasket.
9. Remove manifold pipe seal and flange seal retainer.
10. Reverse procedure to install.

CYLINDER HEAD
REPLACE
Lefthand

1. Remove lefthand exhaust manifold as outlined under "Exhaust Manifold, Replace."
2. Drain cooling system into suitable container.
3. Remove air cleaner assembly.
4. Remove fuel injector sight shield.
5. Disconnect brake booster vacuum tube from water housing crossover.
6. Disconnect fuel regulator vacuum tube.
7. Disconnect secondary AIR solenoid vacuum tube.
8. Relieve fuel system pressure as outlined under "Precautions."
9. Disconnect MAF electrical connector from sensor.
10. Remove air cleaner intake duct.
11. Remove PCV valve fresh air tube.
12. Remove cruise control and accelerator cables from accelerator controls cable bracket and throttle body lever.
13. Disconnect Idle Air Control (IAC) valve electrical connector from IAC valve.
14. Disconnect Throttle Position Sensor (TPS) electrical connector from TPS.
15. Remove fuel feed and return lines from retainer on accelerator controls cable bracket.
16. Remove transaxle shift cable clip from accelerator controls cable bracket.
17. Remove throttle body from water crossover.
18. Disconnect coolant reservoir inlet hose from fitting.
19. Disconnect fuel rail bracket mounting nut from rear lift bracket.
20. Remove coolant reservoir inlet fitting.

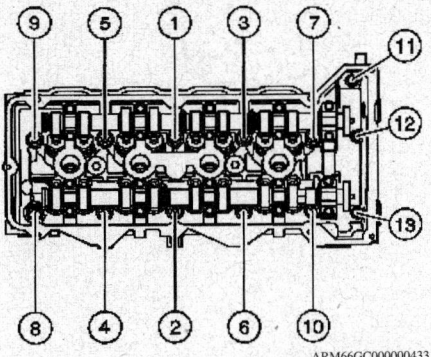

Fig. 4 Lefthand cylinder head bolt tightening sequence

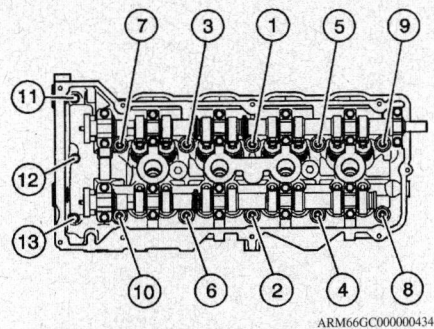

ARM66GC000000434

Fig. 5 Righthand cylinder head bot tightening sequence

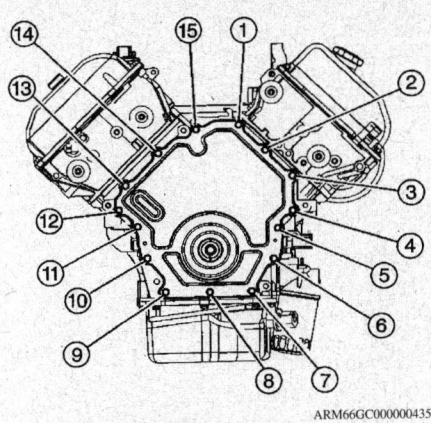

ARM66GC000000435

Fig. 6 Front cover tightening sequence. 2001–03

21. Remove rear lift bracket mounting bolt and bracket.
22. Remove EGR valve.
23. Disconnect EGR inlet pipe mounting nut from front exhaust manifold pipe.
24. Remove EGR inlet pipe mounting bolt and flange from water crossover. Discard EGR inlet pipe.
25. Remove evaporator canister purge valve.
26. Disconnect MAP sensor electrical connector, then remove sensor.
27. Remove radiator inlet hose from water housing crossover.
28. Remove radiator outlet hose from thermostat housing.
29. Remove water pump as outlined under "Water Pump, Replace."
30. Remove two mounting bolts from water pump belt tensioner to water crossover.
31. Disconnect cable harness clip from water housing crossover and position aside.
32. Disconnect heater hose from water housing crossover. Remove water housing crossover.
33. Remove intake manifold as outlined under "Intake Manifold, Replace."
34. Remove valve cover as outlined under "Valve Cover, Replace."
35. Remove engine front cover as outlined under "Front Cover, Replace."
36. Remove secondary camshaft drive chain as outlined under "Timing Chain, Replace, Camshaft Secondary Drive Chain."
37. Disconnect ECT sensor electrical connector.
38. Remove mounting nut from coil cassette ground wire to cylinder head.
39. Remove mounting bolt from exhaust crossover pipe to cylinder head.
40. Raise and support vehicle.
41. Remove mounting bolt from front transaxle brace to cylinder head.
42. Loosen mounting bolts from transaxle brace to transaxle.
43. Remove mounting bolt from rear transaxle brace to cylinder head.
44. Lower vehicle.
45. Remove mounting nuts from rear transaxle brace to cylinder head.
46. Remove three M6 external drive mounting bolts from front of cylinder head.
47. Remove 10 M11 internal drive cylinder

head bolts. Discard M11 bolts.
48. Remove lefthand side cylinder head. Ensure no dowel pins are stuck in head.
49. Reverse procedure to install, noting the following:
   a. Clean remaining gasket material from cylinder head and cylinder head mating surface.
   b. **Extreme care must be taken when cleaning aluminum gasket surfaces to prevent damage to sealing surfaces.**
   c. **Use only suitable plastic, wood or dull gasket scrapers. Chemical agents can be used to dissolve gasket materials following manufacturers recommendations.**
   d. **Torque** cylinder head bolts to 30 ft. lbs., in sequence, **Fig. 4.**
   e. Tighten M11 head bolts an additional 70° in sequence using torque angle meter tool No. J 3666-A, or equivalent.
   f. Tighten bolts an additional 60° in sequence.
   g. Final tighten bolts an additional 60°.
   h. **Torque** M6 head bolts to 106 inch lbs.

Righthand

1. Remove righthand exhaust manifold as outlined under "Exhaust Manifold, Replace."
2. Remove drive belt as outlined under "Serpentine Drive Belt, Replace."
3. Remove radiator as outlined under "Radiator, Replace."
4. Disconnect alternator wiring harness electrical connector.
5. Reposition protective boot, then remove mounting nut from alternator output battery terminal and disconnect positive lead.
6. Loosen lower mounting bolt from alternator.
7. Remove remaining three mounting bolts, then the alternator.
8. Drain cooling system into suitable container.
9. Remove air cleaner assembly.
10. Remove fuel injector sight shield.
11. Disconnect brake booster vacuum tube from water housing crossover.
12. Disconnect fuel regulator vacuum tube.

13. Disconnect secondary AIR solenoid vacuum tube.
14. Relieve fuel system pressure as outlined under "Precautions."
15. Disconnect MAF electrical connector from sensor.
16. Remove air cleaner intake duct.
17. Remove PCV valve fresh air tube.
18. Remove cruise control and accelerator cables from accelerator controls cable bracket.
19. Remove cruise and accelerator control cables from throttle body lever.
20. Disconnect Idle Air Control (IAC) valve electrical connector from IAC valve.
21. Disconnect Throttle Position Sensor (TPS) electrical connector from TPS.
22. Remove fuel feed and return lines from retainer on accelerator controls cable bracket.
23. Remove transaxle shift cable clip from accelerator controls cable bracket.
24. Remove throttle body from water crossover.
25. Disconnect coolant reservoir inlet hose from fitting.
26. Disconnect fuel rail bracket mounting nut from rear lift bracket.
27. Remove coolant reservoir inlet fitting.
28. Remove rear lift bracket mounting bolt and bracket.
29. Remove EGR valve.
30. Disconnect EGR inlet pipe mounting nut from front exhaust manifold pipe.
31. Remove EGR inlet pipe mounting bolt and flange from water crossover. Discard EGR inlet pipe.
32. Remove evaporator canister purge valve.
33. Disconnect MAP sensor electrical connector, then remove sensor.
34. Remove radiator inlet hose from water housing crossover.
35. Remove radiator outlet hose from thermostat housing.
36. Remove water pump as outlined under "Water Pump, Replace."
37. Remove two mounting bolts from water pump belt tensioner to water crossover.
38. Disconnect cable harness clip from water housing crossover and position aside.
39. Disconnect heater hose from water housing crossover. Remove water

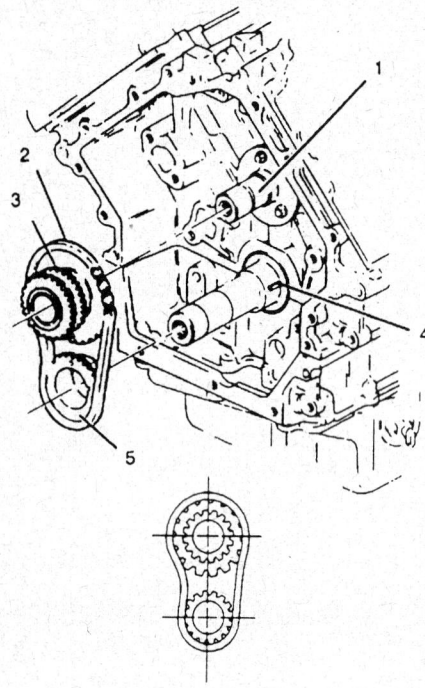

1 INTERMEDIATE SHAFT
2 PRIMARY CHAIN
3 INTERMEDIATE SHAFT SPROCKET
4 CRANKSHAFT SPROCKET KEY
5 SPROCKET

GC1069500607000X

Fig. 7   Primary drive chain replacement

housing crossover.
40. Remove intake manifold as outlined under "Intake Manifold, Replace."
41. Remove valve cover as outlined under "Valve Cover, Replace."
42. Remove engine front cover as outlined under "Front Cover, Replace."
43. Remove secondary camshaft drive chain as outlined under "Timing Chain, Replace."
44. Remove mounting bolt from power steering return hose to cylinder head.
45. Remove three M6 external drive mounting bolts from front of cylinder head.
46. Remove 10 M11 internal drive cylinder head bolts. Discard M11 bolts.
47. Remove righthand side cylinder head. Ensure no dowel pins are stuck in head.
48. Reverse procedure to install, noting the following:
   a. Clean remaining gasket material from cylinder head and cylinder head mating surface.
   b. **Extreme care must be taken when cleaning aluminum gasket surfaces to prevent damage to sealing surfaces.**
   c. **Use only suitable plastic, wood or dull gasket scrapers. Chemical agents can be used to dissolve gasket materials following manufacturers recommendations.**
49. **Torque** cylinder head bolts to 30 ft.

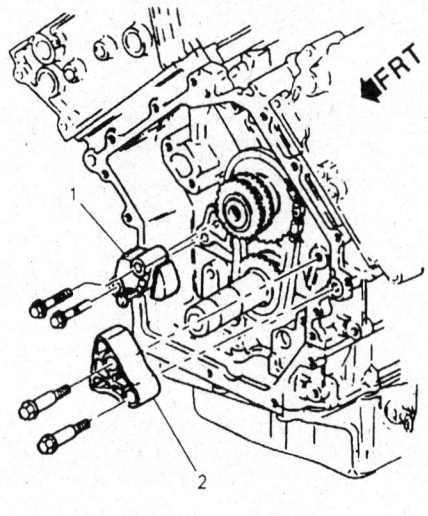

1 PRIMARY CHAIN TENSIONER
2 PRIMARY CHAIN GUIDE

GC1069500608000X

Fig. 8   Primary chain tensioner replacement

lbs., in sequence, **Fig. 5.**
   a. Tighten M11 head bolts an additional 70° in sequence using torque angle meter tool No. J 36660-A, or equivalent.
   b. Tighten bolts an additional 60° in sequence.
   c. Final tighten bolts an additional 60°.
   d. **Torque** M6 head bolts to 106 inch lbs.

VALVE COVER
REPLACE
Righthand

1. Remove two mounting nuts, then the intake manifold sight shield.
2. Disconnect PCV dirty air tube from orifice tube.
3. Disconnect oxygen sensor wire.
4. Disconnect vacuum tubes from secondary AIR vent solenoid.
5. Disconnect secondary AIR vent solenoid electrical connector.
6. Remove secondary AIR control valve bracket.
7. Remove mounting nut from secondary AIR tube.
8. Remove ignition coil cassette.
9. Remove ignition control module.
10. Remove spark plug boots.
11. Disconnect cable harness clips at front of camshaft cover and position harness aside.
12. Remove nine camshaft cover mounting bolts, then the cover.
13. Discard camshaft cover perimeter seals and spark plug seals if damaged or if seal comes out of groove in cover during removal.
14. Reverse procedure to install, noting the following:
   a. **Prevent camshaft cover seal ex-**

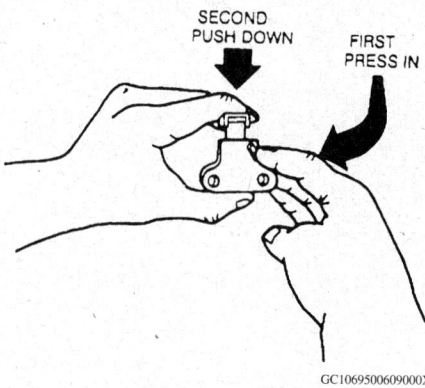

GC1069500609000X

Fig. 9   Rotating tensioner release lever

posed section from being damaged by cylinder head casting edge.

Lefthand

1. Remove two mounting nuts, then the intake manifold sight shield.
2. Partially drain cooling system into suitable container.
3. Remove radiator inlet hose from water housing crossover.
4. Disconnect PCV fresh air tube from camshaft cover.
5. Remove ignition coil cassette.
6. Remove ignition control module.
7. Remove spark plug boots.
8. Disconnect cable harness clips at front of camshaft cover and position harness aside.
9. Remove secondary AIR valve bracket mounting nut closest to center of engine.
10. Pry outward slightly on secondary AIR valve bracket. Remove water pump drive belt shield mounting nuts and bolts.
11. Disconnect water pump drive belt.
12. Loosen two mounting bolts from water pump belt tensioner to water crossover.
13. Remove water pump belt tensioner.
14. Remove plastic cap from end of intake camshaft.
15. Remove water pump drive pulley from intake camshaft using water pump drive pulley remover tool No. J 38825, or equivalent.
16. Remove three camshaft seal mounting bolts. Discard seal.
17. Remove nine camshaft cover mounting bolts.
18. Lift camshaft drive end of cover and pull rearward to clear water pump drive shaft.
19. Discard camshaft cover perimeter seals and spark plug seals if damaged or if seal comes out of groove in cover during removal.
20. Reverse procedure to install, noting the following:
   a. **Prevent camshaft cover seal exposed section from being damaged by cylinder head casting edge.**
   b. Insert intake camshaft end through

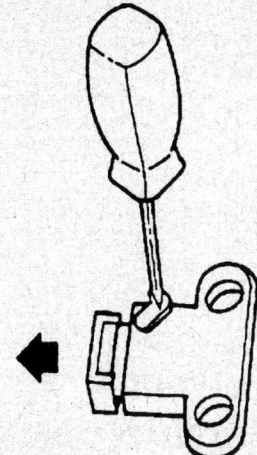

1 RELEASE TO FIRST CLICK
2 INSTALL LOCK PIN

GC1069500610000X

Fig. 10 Locking tensioner

hole in cover.
c. Work cover into position pivoting down allowing cover to clear camshaft drive chain and align bolt holes.
d. Refer to "Cooling System Bleed."

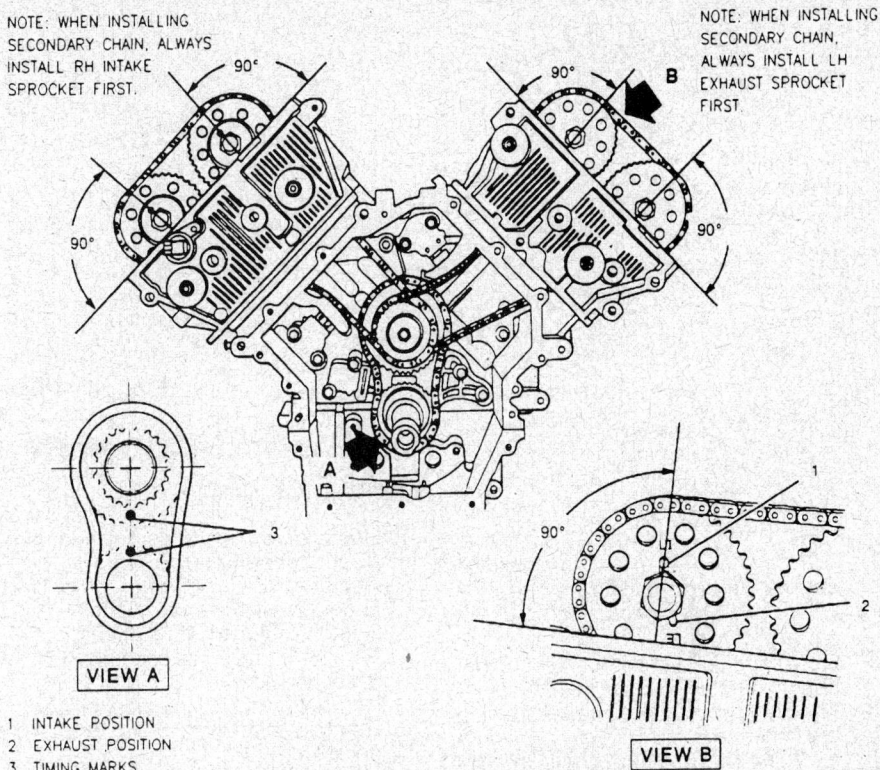

NOTE: WHEN INSTALLING SECONDARY CHAIN, ALWAYS INSTALL RH INTAKE SPROCKET FIRST.

NOTE: WHEN INSTALLING SECONDARY CHAIN, ALWAYS INSTALL LH EXHAUST SPROCKET FIRST.

VIEW A

1 INTAKE POSITION
2 EXHAUST POSITION
3 TIMING MARKS

VIEW B

GC1069500611000X

Fig. 11 Setting camshaft timing

VALVE CLEARANCE SPECIFICATIONS

These engines are equipped with hydraulic valve lifters. Valve clearance should be zero.

VALVE ADJUSTMENT

These engines are equipped with hydraulic valve lifters. No adjustment is required.

VALVE GUIDES

Inspect valve stem to valve guide clearance. Clearance should be .005 inch or less. Service valves are available in standard size (.235 inch). If clearance is excessive and new standard size valve stem will not bring clearance within specifications, cylinder head must be replaced.

HYDRAULIC LIFTERS
REPLACE

If camshafts remain in cylinder head, some valves will always be held open and cylinder head cannot be set on workbench with cylinder head face down. Damage to valves and/or gasket surface will result.

Do not mix cam bearing caps between positions or heads. Each cap must be assembled in the position from which it was removed and in the original orientation (arrow points toward front of engine).
1. Remove cylinder head as outlined under "Cylinder Head, Replace."
2. Place matchmarks on bearing caps.
3. Remove intake and exhaust cam-

shafts by alternately loosening each cam bearing cap bolt two turns at a time until valve spring pressure is completely released.
4. Remove valve lifters and arrange them so they may be installed in original position.
5. Reverse procedure to install, noting the following:
   a. Lubricate camshaft bearing journals with engine oil prior to installation.
   b. Alternately tighten camshaft bearing cap bolts one turn at a time to specifications.

CRANKSHAFT DAMPER
REPLACE

1. Remove accessory drive belt as outlined under "Serpentine Drive Belt, Replace."
2. Raise and support vehicle.
3. Remove righthand front wheel assembly.
4. Remove righthand front fascia extension.
5. Remove brace between engine oil pan and transaxle case.
6. Remove torque converter cover.
7. Install flywheel holder tool No. J 44214, or equivalent to engine block.
8. Remove crankshaft damper mounting bolt.
9. Install crankshaft damper remover tool No. J 41816, or equivalent to remove damper.
10. Reverse procedure to install, noting the following:

a. Press crankshaft damper in place using damper installer tool No. J 41998-B.
b. Clean damper bolt threads.
c. Apply clean engine oil to damper bolts threads.
d. **Torque** crankshaft damper mounting bolt to 37 ft. lbs.
e. Tighten crankshaft damper bolt an additional 120° using torque angle meter tool No. J 36660, or equivalent.

FRONT COVER
REPLACE

1. Remove accessory drive belt as outlined under "Serpentine Drive Belt, Replace."
2. Remove drive belt tensioner mounting bolt and tensioner.
3. Remove drive belt idler pulley mounting bolt and pulley.
4. Remove crankshaft damper as outlined under "Crankshaft Damper, Replace."
5. Raise and support vehicle.
6. Support engine assembly with suitable jack.
7. Remove mounting nut from engine mount to mount bracket.
8. Remove mounting nut from power steering hose to engine mount bracket.
9. Remove mounting bolts from engine mount bracket to engine and position bracket aside.
10. Remove front engine mounting bolts, cover and gasket.

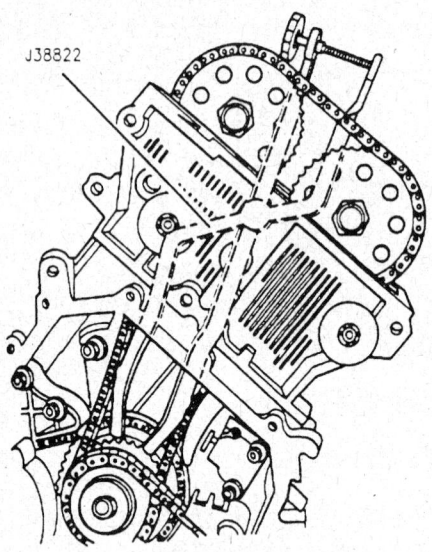

Fig. 12 Holding drive chain tension

11. Front cover gasket is reusable, do not discard unless gasket is damaged.
12. Reverse procedure to install, noting the following:
    a. Place small amount of sealant GM P/N 12345739 or equivalent at split line of upper and lower crankcases.
13. **Torque** front cover mounting bolts in sequence to 89 inch lbs., **Fig. 6.**

FRONT COVER SEAL
REPLACE

Crankshaft front oil seal is not a serviceable part. Front cover and oil seal sold as an assembly. Replace front cover as outlined under "Front Cover, Replace."

TIMING CHAIN
REPLACE

Camshaft Primary Drive Chain

1. Remove front cover as outlined under "Front Cover, Replace."
2. Remove oil pump as outlined under "Oil Pump, Replace."
3. Remove valve covers as outlined under "Valve Cover, Replace."
4. Remove timing chain tensioners and camshaft sprockets.
5. Remove secondary drive chains as outlined under "Camshaft Secondary Drive Chain."
6. Remove intermediate shaft sprocket bolt, then slide gears and primary drive chain off crankshaft and intermediate shaft, **Fig. 7.**
7. Reverse procedure to install. Set camshaft timing as outlined under "Setting Camshaft Timing."

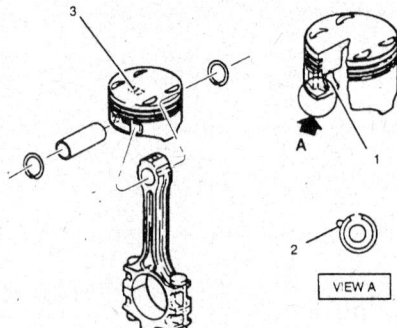

1. RETAINER GROOVE
2. REMOVAL ACCESS SLOT
3. ORIENTATION ARROW

VIEW A

GC1069500613000X

Fig. 13 Piston & rod assembly

Camshaft Secondary Drive Chain

1. Remove front cover as outlined under "Front Cover, Replace."
2. Remove valve covers as outlined under "Valve Cover, Replace."
3. Remove bolts and tensioners.
4. Remove chain guide access plugs noting O-ring seal.
5. Remove camshaft position sensor.
6. Remove mounting bolts and chain guides.
7. Remove mounting bolts and slide sprockets off camshafts.
8. Remove sprockets and secondary drive chain together. Leave intermediate sprocket in place.
9. Reverse procedure to install, set camshaft timing as outlined under "Setting Camshaft Timing."

TIMING CHAIN TENSIONER
REPLACE

Removal

1. Remove front cover as outlined under "Front Cover, Replace."
2. Remove transaxle to oil pan brace.
3. Lock flywheel using flywheel holder tool No. J 39411, or equivalent.
4. Remove mounting bolts and tensioner, **Fig. 8.**

Installation

1. Rotate ratchet release lever counterclockwise and hold, **Fig. 9.**
2. Collapse tensioner retainer shoe and hold.
3. Release ratchet lever and slowly release shoe pressure.
4. Hold tensioner shoe at first click hold, insert suitable pin through hole and release lever, **Fig. 10.**
5. Ensure release lever is facing you, install tensioner and bolts. Tighten to specifications.
6. Remove retaining pin allowing tensioner shoe to extend.
7. Remove flywheel holding tool and install pan brace.
8. Install front cover.

SETTING CAMSHAFT TIMING

This engine is an interference fit engine. The engine is not free spinning and pistons will strike valves if crankshaft is rotated with camshaft drive disconnected or if camshafts are not properly timed.

1. Remove valve covers as outlined under "Valve Cover, Replace."
2. Remove front engine mount as outlined under "Engine Mount, Replace."
3. Support front of engine and remove front cover as outlined under "Front Cover, Replace."
4. Remove three chain tensioners. Chain tensioners may remain in installed position, but must be fully retracted.
5. Remove oil pump as outlined under "Oil Pump, Replace."
6. Install crankshaft sprocket drive key. If required, tap into place using suitable small hammer until key bottoms in shaft.
7. Rotate crankshaft until piston No. 1 is at Top Dead Center (TDC) and sprocket drive key is at approximately one o'clock position using suitable socket.
8. Align crankshaft and intermediate shaft sprockets and install with primary drive chain, **Fig. 11.** Rotate crankshaft as required to engage crankshaft key in sprocket without changing timing marks relationship.
9. Install bolt and tighten intermediate sprocket mounting bolt to specification.
10. Install primary chain tensioner and release tensioner shoe as outlined under "Timing Chain Tensioner, Replace."
11. Lock crankshaft into position using flywheel holding tool No. J 39411, or equivalent.
12. If required, install secondary camshaft drive chain guides and access plugs.
13. Route lefthand cylinder head secondary drive chain over inner row of intermediate shaft teeth and chain guide.
14. Install lefthand exhaust cam sprocket to chain so camshaft drive pin engages sprocket notch marked LE. There should be no slack in lower chain section and cam drive pin must be perpendicular to cylinder head face. Camshaft drive pin must be perpendicular to cylinder head face.

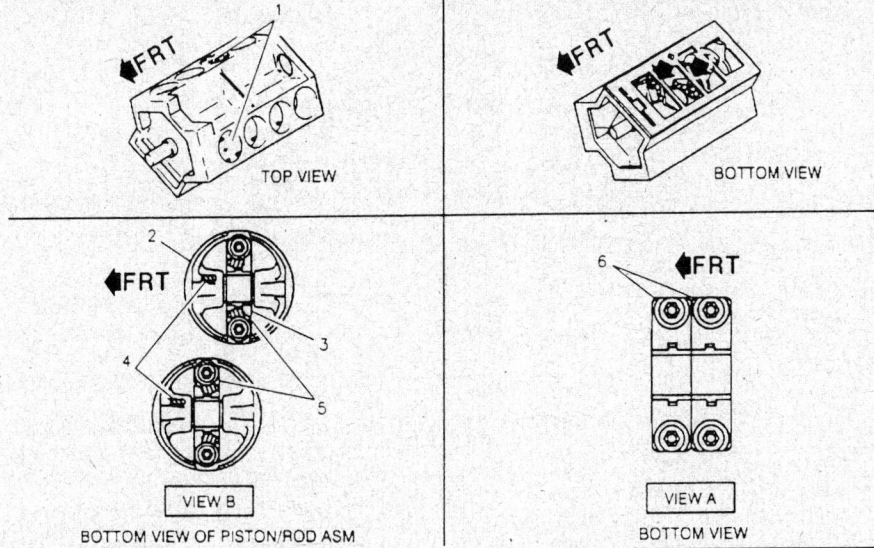

1 PISTON ARROW TOWARD CHAIN CASE ON BOTH SIDES
2 PISTON
3 ROD CAP
4 LOCATER LUGS INDICATE PISTON FRONT TOWARDS ENGINE FRONT
5 BEARING CAP NOTCHES POINT TOWARD EACH OTHER ON PAIRED RODS
6 ROD CAPS

GC1069500614000X

Fig. 14 Piston installation

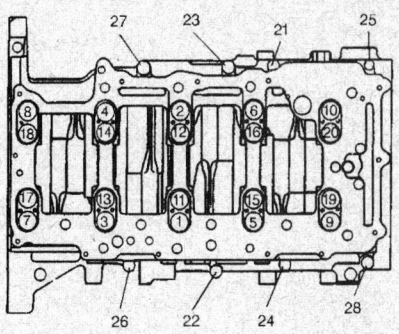

GC10699000001044

Fig. 15 Main bearing bolt tightening sequence

15. Install intake cam sprocket into chain so sprocket notch marked LI engages cam drive pin. Pin must be perpendicular to cylinder head face. A hex is cast into camshaft behind lobes for cylinder No. 2 so open end wrench may be used to provide minor camshaft positioning.
16. Loosely install intake and exhaust cam sprocket mounting bolts.
17. Install chain tensioner and release tension on shoe as outlined under "Timing Chain Tensioner, Replace."
18. Route secondary drive chain for righthand cylinder head over outer row of intermediate shaft teeth.
19. Install righthand exhaust cam sprocket to chain so camshaft drive pin engages sprocket notch marked RI. There should be no slack in lower chain section and cam drive pin must be perpendicular to cylinder head face. Camshaft drive pin must be perpendicular to cylinder head face.
20. Install intake cam sprocket into chain so sprocket notch marked RE engages cam drive pin. Pin must be perpendicular to cylinder head face. A hex is cast into camshaft behind lobes for cylinder No. 1 so open end wrench may be used to provide minor camshaft positioning.
21. Ensure RE sprocket contains camshaft position sensor pickup and install camshaft position sensor.
22. Loosely install intake and exhaust cam sprocket mounting bolts.
23. Install chain tensioner and release tension on shoe as outlined under "Timing Chain Tensioner, Replace."
24. Install oil pump as outlined under "Oil

Pump, Replace."
25. Install front cover as outlined under "Front Cover, Replace."
26. Install valve covers as outlined under "Valve Cover, Replace."
27. Install front engine mount as outlined under "Engine Mount, Replace."

CAMSHAFT
REPLACE

1. Remove valve cover as outlined under "Valve Cover, Replace."
2. Set engine at piston No. 1 TDC and align timing marks to correct position.
3. Secure cam sprocket to timing chain using tie-raps through cam sprocket holes. Use two tie-raps per sprocket. **Sprocket to chain relationship must be maintained throughout this procedure or camshaft timing will be lost and require further engine disassembly for timing.**
4. Working behind sprockets, install cam chain holder J 38822, or equivalent, so it is positioned between chain tensioner and chain guide, **Fig. 12.**
5. Apply tension to tool by tightening tension adjusting screw. **When using cam chain holder tool on righthand cylinder bank, remove wiper motor to gain clearance.**
6. Remove camshaft sprocket bolts. Record relative location of cam drive pins in ends of camshafts.
7. Work sprockets off camshaft using chain play.
8. Alternately loosening each cam bearing cap bolt two turns at a time until valve spring pressure is completely re-

leased. **Do not mix cam bearing caps between positions or heads. Each cap must be assembled in position from which it was removed and in original orientation (arrow points toward front of engine).**
9. Remove camshafts.
10. Reverse procedure to install.

PISTON & ROD ASSEMBLY

Refer to **Fig. 13,** for piston and rod assembly. Refer to **Fig. 14,** for piston installation.

MAIN & ROD BEARINGS

Shell type main bearings of steel backed aluminum are used at all positions. The upper and lower bearing halves are interchangeable except for the upper bearing in the No. 3 position as this is the thrust bearing. Maximum crankshaft endplay is .019 inch.

With the crankcase disassembled the main bearing clearance can be measured using suitable plastic gauging material as follows:

1. Wipe oil from crankshaft journals and bearing inserts.
2. Place plastic gauging material across journals to be measured.
3. Install lower crankcase and oil manifold.
4. Install main bearing bolts and tighten bolts to specifications in sequence, **Fig. 15.**
5. Determine clearance by comparing width of flattened plastic gauging material with measurement increments on plastic gauging package.
6. If bearing clearance is more than .0025 inch and new bearings do not reduce clearance to .0006–.0020 inch, new crankshaft is required. Undersized bearings are not available and no crankshaft grinding is allowed.

CRANKSHAFT REAR OIL SEAL
REPLACE

1. Remove transaxle as outlined in **MOTOR's** "Domestic Transmission

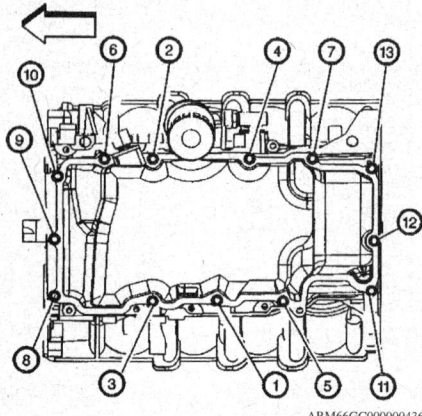

Fig. 16 Oil pan bolts tightening sequence

Manual, In-Vehicle Service."
2. Install crankshaft rear oil seal removal tool No. J 42841, or equivalent.
3. Install eight 1.0 inch self-drilling screws into seal using guide holes in removal tool.
4. Remove oil seal removal tool mounting bolts.
5. Tighten center screw on removal tool to pull seal from end of crankshaft.
6. Reverse procedure to install, noting the following:
   a. Place small amount of RTV sealant at crankcase split line across end of upper and lower crankcase seal.
   b. Lubricate rear main seal with clean engine oil prior to installation.

OIL PAN
REPLACE

1. Remove rear exhaust manifold pipe as outlined under "Exhaust Manifold, Replace."
2. Remove transaxle as outlined in **MOTOR's "Domestic Transmission Manual, In-Vehicle Service."**
3. Drain engine oil into suitable container.
4. Disconnect engine oil level sensor electrical connector, then the sensor from oil pan.
5. Remove mounting bolts and oil pan.
6. Reverse procedure to install, noting the following:
   a. Gasket is reusable unless damaged.
   b. **Do not remove gasket from oil pan groove unless replacement is required.**
   c. If replacing gasket do not expose new gasket to oil before inserting gasket into pan groove, gasket will expand when exposed to oil and will not stay in pan groove.
7. **Torque** oil pan mounting bolts to 89 inch lbs., using sequence, **Fig. 16.**

OIL PUMP
REPLACE

1. Remove engine front cover as outlined under "Front Cover, Replace."
2. Remove three mounting bolts and

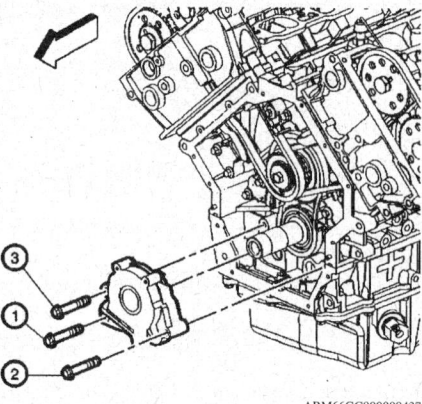

Fig. 17 Oil pump tightening sequence

slide oil pump assembly off nose of crankshaft with drive collar in place.
3. Reverse procedure to install, noting the following:
   a. Apply upward pressure on pump while tightening mounting bolts.
   b. **Torque** oil pump mounting bolts in sequence to 89 inch lbs., **Fig. 17.**
   c. Tighten mounting bolts in sequence an additional 35° using torque angle tool No. J 36660-A, or equivalent.

OIL PUMP SERVICE
Disassemble

1. Remove drive spacer and screws holding pump housing halves together.
2. Remove inner (drive) and outer (driven) rotors out of housing and mark mating surfaces for assembly.
3. Remove pressure relief valve cap retaining pin and plug without damaging O-ring seal.
4. Slide pressure relief valve spring and piston out of bore.

Assemble

1. Install inner and outer rotors to pump cover in same position as they were removed (dimples out). Chamfered edge of outer rotor must be face down (closest to engine rear).
2. Install pressure relief valve piston, spring and retaining cap in pump housing.
3. Pack housing with suitable white petroleum jelly.
4. Assemble housing and cover over locating dowel.
5. Insert ⅜ inch drill in pump mounting hole on opposite side to aid in alignment of housing and cover.
6. Install screws and tighten to specifications.

SERPENTINE DRIVE BELT
Belt, Replace

1. Release belt tension, then remove belt

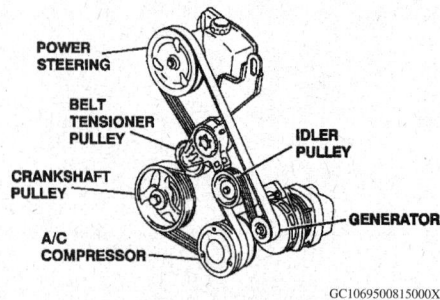

Fig. 18 Serpentine drive belt routing

from power steering and alternator pulleys.
2. Twist belt to get between tensioner and front cover, then between power steering pulley and engine mount bracket.
3. Raise and support vehicle.
4. Turn wheel to extreme righthand and remove righthand splash shield.
5. Remove belt from crankshaft and air conditioning compressor pulleys. Twist belt to get between idler pulley and engine mount bracket.
6. Lower vehicle.
7. Twisting new belt to get past front cover, install belt around power steering pump pulley, **Fig. 18.** Allow belt to hang free.
8. Twist belt to get between tensioner and front cover, wrap belt around alternator.
9. Remove belt from power steering pulley and set aside.
10. Raise and support vehicle.
11. Twist belt to get between tensioner and front cover, wrap belt around crankshaft and air conditioning compressor pulleys.
12. Install righthand side splash shield and lower vehicle.
13. Position belt around power steering pulley and release tensioner.

COOLING SYSTEM BLEED

This engine does not require a cooling system bleed procedure. However, when adding coolant, If other than GM Goodwrench DEX–COOL or HAVOLINE DEX–COOL is added to cooling system, engine coolant will require changing at 30,000 miles or 24 months. **Do not use cooling system seal tabs, or similar compounds. They may restrict coolant flow and cause overheating or cooling system damage.** To ensure sufficient engine cooling, freezing and corrosion protection, maintain proper protection level at –34°F or lower.

THERMOSTAT
REPLACE

1. Drain cooling system.
2. Remove air intake duct.
3. Disconnect thermostat housing radiator hose.
4. Remove mounting bolts and thermostat housing, **Fig. 19.**

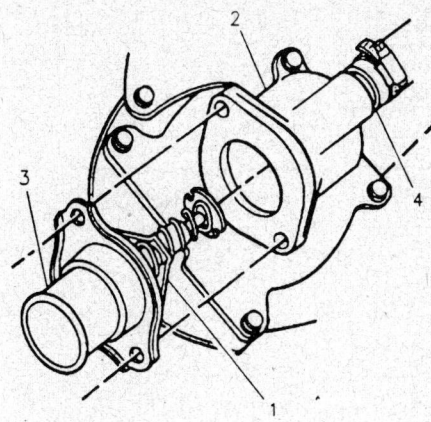

1 THERMOSTAT
2 THERMOSTAT HOUSING
3 COOLANT PUMP INLET
4 THERMOSTAT BY-PASS HOSE

GC1089500248000X

Fig. 19 Thermostat replacement

5. Remove thermostat.
6. Reverse procedure install. Refer to "Cooling System Bleed."

WATER PUMP
REPLACE

1. Drain engine coolant.
2. Remove air intake duct.
3. Remove coolant pump drive belt cover and belt.
4. Remove lower radiator and bypass hoses, then the water pump cover.
5. Remove water pump, seal and gasket by turning coolant remover/installer tool No. J 38816, or equivalent, clockwise, **Fig. 20.**
6. Reverse procedure to install. Refer to "Cooling System Bleed."

RADIATOR
REPLACE

1. Remove upper tie bar.
2. Drain cooling system into suitable container.
3. Remove upper and lower radiator hoses from radiator.
4. Remove upper transaxle oil cooler line retainer and bolt from fan shroud.
5. Slide plastic cap off quick connect joint.
6. Disconnect upper transaxle oil cooler line from radiator using quick connect tool No. J 41623-B, or equivalent.
7. Disconnect cooling fan motors wiring harness electrical connectors.
8. Remove retaining clips from harness to fan shroud.
9. Disconnect two retainers from A/C discharge hose.

10. Remove two fan shroud mounting bolts.
11. Lift cooling fan assembly off lower mountings of radiator and position towards righthand side of vehicle to remove.
12. Disconnect lower transaxle oil cooler line from radiator.
13. Remove upper radiator seal.
14. Remove headlamp mounting bolts.
15. Carefully pry straight forward in center area of headlamp to unsnap ball stud from socket.
16. Slide headlamp assembly straight forward and disconnect connector from forward lamp wiring harness.
17. Remove two condenser mounting bolts.
18. Lift condenser upward slightly to release lower feet from lower mountings located at front of radiator.
19. Remove radiator by lifting up and out of vehicle.
20. Reverse procedure to install. Refer to "Cooling System Bleed."

FUEL PUMP
REPLACE

1. Relieve fuel system pressure as outlined under "Precautions."
2. Drain fuel tank to at least ¾ of full tank.
3. Remove spare tire cover, jack and spare tire.
4. Remove luggage compartment floor trim.
5. Remove mounting screws and fuel sender access panel.
6. Cover fuel pipe fittings with suitable shop towel to prevent spillage.
7. Remove quick-connect fittings air fuel sender.
8. Disconnect fuel sender and fuel pressure sensor electrical connectors.
9. Remove fuel sender retaining ring using fuel sender locknut wrench tool No. J 39765, or equivalent.
10. Remove fuel tank sender.
11. Reverse procedure to install.

FUEL FILTER
REPLACE

1. Relieve fuel system pressure as outlined under "Precautions."
2. Raise and support vehicle.
3. Disconnect quick-connect fitting at inlet end of in-line fuel filter.
4. Disconnect threaded fitting at fuel filter outlet. Drain remaining fuel into suitable container.
5. Remove fuel pipe O-ring.
6. Reverse procedure to install.

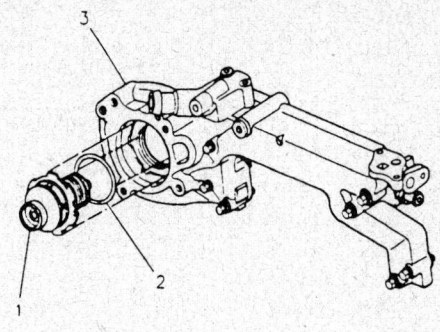

1 WATER PUMP ASSEMBLY
2 O-RING SEAL
3 WATER PUMP HOUSING ASSEMBLY

GC1089500249000X

Fig. 20 Coolant pump replacement

TECHNICAL SERVICE BULLETINS

Cold Engine Knock Or Tick
2001-02

On some of these models there may be a tick/knock noise. This may be an upper engine ticking or a deep low knock similar to main bearing knock. These noises are more often heard during engine start up after a long, cold soak. The noise may or may not diminish as engine reaches normal operating temperature. The knock may appear to be loudest at exhaust manifolds. These noises do not change when disconnecting spark plugs or disabling individual fuel injectors.

This condition may be caused by combustion chamber carbon deposits.

To correct this condition, proceed as follows:

1. Start engine and bring coolant temperature to more than 200°F on instrument panel gauge (220°F on scan tool).
2. **Do not raise engine above normal idle speed.**
3. Disconnect PCV hose from valve and slowly spray Top Engine Cleaner, part No. 1052626, or equivalent, into hose.
4. Raise engine speed to approximately 2000 RPM until white smoke comes from exhaust pipe.
5. Shut engine off.
6. Allow vehicle to set at least 20 minutes, preferably overnight.
7. Start engine and remove remaining top cleaner by increasing engine speed to 2000 RPM until white smoke diminishes.

TIGHTENING SPECIFICATIONS

Year	Component	Torque/Ft. lbs.
2001–03	Belt Idler Pulley	37
	Belt Tensioner	37
	Camshaft Bearing Cap	106⑦
	Camshaft Drive Chain Tensioner	18
	Camshaft Sprocket	44
	Connecting Rod Bearing Cap	⑥
	Crankshaft Damper	37②
	Cylinder Head	④
	Exhaust Manifold To Cylinder Head	18
	Flywheel To Converter	③
	Front Cover	89⑦
	Intake Manifold	89⑦
	Intermediate Sprocket	44
	Main Bearing Cap	15①
	Oil Filter Adapter	12
	Oil Manifold	89⑦
	Oil Pan	89⑦
	Oil Pump	89⑦⑤
	Oxygen Sensor	30
	Primary Chain Tensioner	18
	Valve Cover	89⑦

① — Refer to "Main & Rod Bearings" for tightening sequence.
② — Tighten an additional 120°.
③ — Tighten an additional 50°.
④ — Refer to "Cylinder Head, Replace" for tightening specifications and sequence.
⑤ — Tighten an additional 35°.
⑥ — Torque 22 ft. lbs., then back to zero, then 18 ft. lbs., plus an additional 110°.
⑦ — Inch lbs.

Rear Suspension

NOTE: On Air Bag Equipped Models, Refer To "Air Bag System Precautions" Located In The Front Of This Manual For System Disarming & Arming Procedures.

NOTE: Refer To "Computer Relearn Procedures" Located In The Front Of This Manual When Battery Power To The Computer Has Been Interrupted.

INDEX

DESCRIPTION

These models utilize an independent rear suspension that is secured to the vehicle body at four points, **Fig. 1.** Control arms, a stabilizer bar and adjustment links are connected to the rear suspension support assembly to provide side to side stability and to allow for rear toe adjustment.

The Electronic Level Control (ELC) system employs rear air adjustable shocks which are anchored at the control arms and allow the system to maintain proper vehicle ride height under various load conditions. The shocks are not manually adjustable and must be replaced if they lose resistance or begin leaking fluid.

The rear wheel bearings have been integrated into the hubs to eliminate the necessity of adjustments and periodic maintenance. This integral hub and bearing also incorporates a wheel speed sensor ring for anti-lock brake operation.

HUB & BEARING
REPLACE

1. Raise and support vehicle.
2. Remove wheel and disc brake caliper. **It is not required to disconnect hydraulic line from caliper. Support caliper from frame to prevent hydraulic line damage.**
3. Remove brake rotor and ABS sensor wire connector.
4. Remove bolts, then lift hub and bearing.
5. Remove brake shield from control arm, **Fig. 2.**
6. Reverse procedure to install. Tighten bolts and wheel lug nuts to specifications.

WHEEL BEARING
ADJUST

Because the hub and bearing are integral components, the bearing is not adjustable. If the bearing requires service, the entire hub assembly must be replaced.

REAR SUSPENSION
REPLACE

1. Raise and support vehicle. Remove rear wheels and disconnect exhaust system components as required to provide clearance.
2. Remove rear springs as outlined under "Coil Spring, Replace."
3. Remove brake calipers from control arms. **It is not required to disconnect hydraulic line at caliper; support caliper from frame to prevent hydraulic line damage.**
4. Disconnect parking brake cables at calipers and at rear suspension support.
5. Disconnect rear suspension support electrical connectors from electrical harness, then the Electronic Level Control (ELC) electrical connector and vent hose.
6. Disconnect ELC air tube from ELC compressor and support rear suspension using suitable jack, **Fig. 3.**
7. Remove support bracket to body bolts from each side of vehicle.
8. Remove front and rear anchor bolts and lower rear suspension support.
9. Reverse procedure to install. Tighten mounting bolts and nuts to specifications.

SHOCK ABSORBER
REPLACE

1. Raise and support vehicle.
2. Remove wheel and support control arm using suitable jack stand.
3. Disconnect Electronic Level Control (ELC) air tube from shock absorber and remove shock to control arm bolts, **Fig. 4.**
4. Remove luggage compartment trim as required to gain access to shock absorber upper mounting nuts and shock upper cover.
5. Remove upper mounting nuts, reinforcement and shock absorber.

6. Reverse procedure to install. Tighten mounting bolts and nuts to specifications.

COIL SPRING
REPLACE

1. Raise and support vehicle so control arm hangs freely, then remove wheel.
2. Support control arm using suitable jack and disconnect Electronic Level Control (ELC) air tube from shock absorber.
3. Disconnect shock absorber at control arm, then remove adjustment link to knuckle cotter pin and slotted nut.
4. Separate adjustment link from knuckle using universal steering linkage puller tool No. J 24319-B, or equivalent, and slowly lower control arm until it bottoms on rear suspension support.
5. Pry under lower coil spring insulator and remove spring with insulator, **Fig. 5,** then, if required, remove jounce bumper by pulling downward.
6. Reverse procedure to install. Tighten mounting bolts and nuts to specifications.

CONTROL ARM
REPLACE

1. Remove rear suspension support as outlined under "Rear Suspension, Replace."
2. If lefthand control arm is being replaced, remove Electronic Level Control (ELC) height sensor link.
3. Remove stabilizer link bolt and nut and disconnect ABS electrical connector.
4. Remove hub and bearing as outlined under "Hub & Bearing, Replace."
5. Remove adjustment link mounting nut, then separate from lower control arm using puller tool No. J 24319-B, or equivalent.
6. Remove control arm to rear suspension support mounting bolt and nut.
7. Reverse procedure to install, noting the following:

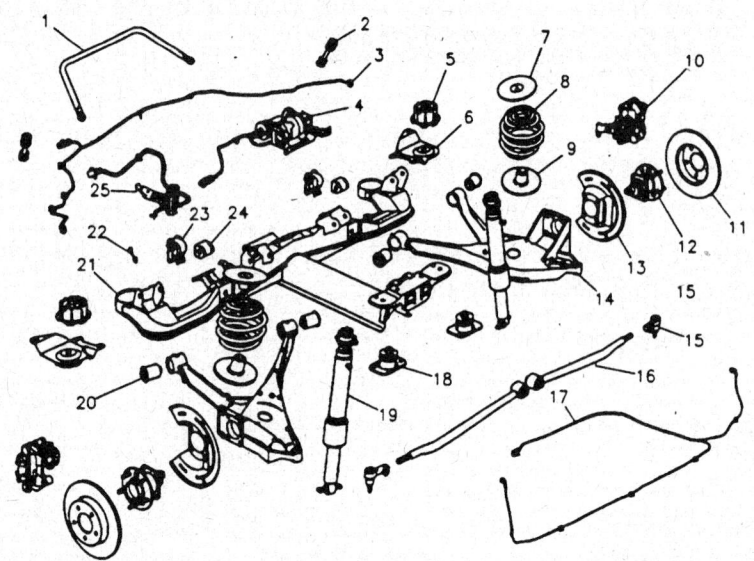

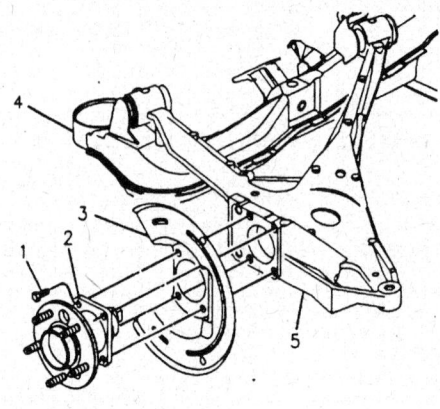

1	STABILIZER BAR	9	LOWER SPRING INSULATOR	18	REAR BODY MOUNT
2	STABILIZER BAR LINK	10	BRAKE CALIPER	19	SHOCK
3	ABS ELECTRICAL HARNESS	11	BRAKE ROTOR	20	CONTROL ARM BUSHING
4	ELC COMPRESSOR	12	HUB AND BEARING	21	REAR SUSPENSION SUPPORT ASSEMBLY
5	FORWARD BODY MOUNT	13	BRAKE SHIELD	22	ELC HEIGHT SENSOR LINK
6	SUPPORT BRACKET	14	CONTROL ARM	23	STABILIZER BAR CLAMP
7	JOUNCE BUMPER	15	OUTER ADJUSTMENT LINK	24	STABILIZER BAR INSULATOR
8	SPRING	16	INNER ADJUSTMENT LINK	25	ELC HEIGHT SENSOR
		17	ELC AIR LINE		

GC2039500107000X

Fig. 1 Exploded view of rear suspension

a. Tighten control arm nuts with vehicle weight resting on rear wheels.
b. Tighten mounting bolts and nuts to specifications.

CONTROL ARM BUSHING
REPLACE
Removal

1. Remove control arm as outlined under "Control Arm, Replace" and assemble bushing replacement tools, **Fig. 6.**
2. Tighten nut until bushing is driven from control arm and remove bushing replacement tools.

Installation

1. Start new bushing into control arm with flat on bushing positioned vertically and rearward.
2. Assemble bushing tools, **Fig. 6,** and tighten bolt until bushing is seated fully in control arm.
3. Remove bushing tools and install control arm as outlined under "Control Arm, Replace."

STABILIZER SHAFT
REPLACE

1. Raise and support vehicle. Remove wheels and disconnect Electronic Level Control (ELC) height sensor link at control arm.
2. Remove bolts and position ELC height sensor aside.
3. Remove stabilizer shaft link bolt, nut, retainer and insulators from control arm, **Fig. 7.**
4. Remove clamp bolt and bend open end of clamp upward and remove stabilizer shaft and insulators.
5. Reverse procedure to install, noting the following:
   a. Ensure stabilizer shaft is centered before tightening clamp bolt.
   b. Tighten mounting bolts and nuts to specifications.

ADJUSTMENT LINK
REPLACE
Inner

1. Raise and support vehicle.

1	BOLT
2	HUB & BEARING
3	BRAKE SHIELD
4	REAR SUSPENSION SUPPORT ASSEMBLY
5	CONTROL ARM

GC2039500108000X

Fig. 2 Hub & bearing replacement

2. Remove wheel and loosen pinch bolt.
3. Support exhaust and rear suspension support using suitable wood block at least seven inches long.
4. Remove exhaust hangers and rear suspension support mounting bolts.
5. Lower support and exhaust together.
6. Remove cam bolt, nut and adjustment link.
7. Remove inner link from outer link. Record number of turns for installation reference.
8. Reverse procedure to install. Inspect and adjust rear toe as outlined in "Wheel Alignment."

Outer

1. Raise and support vehicle. Remove wheel.
2. Loosen pinch bolt.
3. Remove cotter pin and slotted hex nut.
4. Separate adjustment link from knuckle using puller tool No. J 24319-B, or equivalent. **Do not drive wedge between joint and attached part.**
5. Remove outer from inner link. Record number of turns for assembly.
6. Reverse procedure to install. Inspect and adjust rear toe as outlined under "Wheel Alignment."

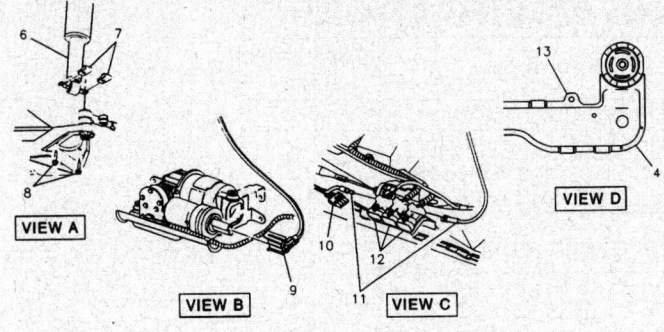

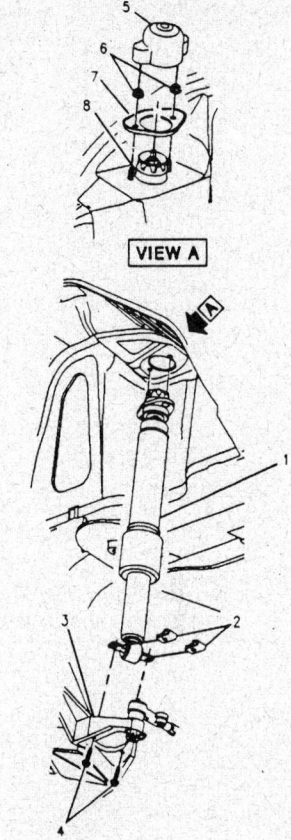

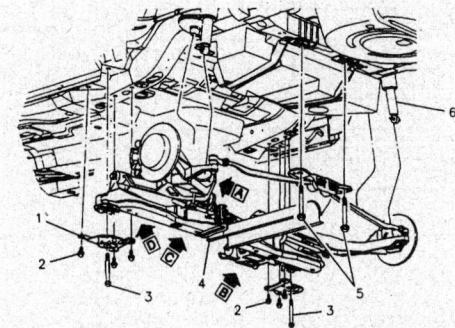

1 SUPPORT BRACKET	8 BOLT 24 N•m (18 LB. FT.)
2 BOLT 86 N•m (63 LB. FT.)	9 ELC AIR LINE
3 BOLT 191 N•m (141 LB. FT.)	10 ELC COMPRESSOR ELECTRICAL CONNECTOR
4 REAR SUSPENSION SUPPORT ASSEMBLY	11 ELC COMPRESSOR VENT TUBE
5 BOLT 165 N•m (122 LB. FT.)	12 ELECTRICAL CONNECTORS, (ELC HEIGHT
6 SHOCK	SENSOR, FUEL PUMP, ABS HARNESS)
7 U–NUT	13 GAUGE HOLE

GC2039500109000X

Fig. 3 Rear suspension replacement

1 SHOCK
2 U-NUTS
3 CONTROL ARM
4 BOLTS 24 N•m (18 LB. FT.)
5 COVER
6 NUTS 20 N•m (15 LB. FT.)
7 REINFORCEMENT
8 MOUNT, UPPER

GC2039500110000X

Fig. 4 Shock absorber replacement

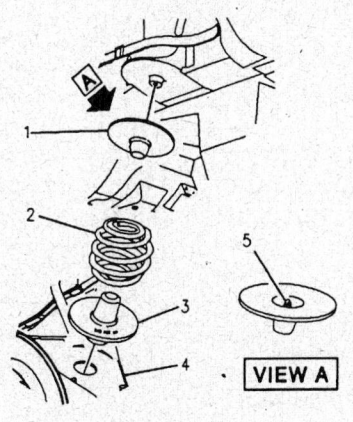

1 JOUNCE BUMPER
2 SPRING
3 LOWER SPRING INSULATOR
4 CONTROL ARM
5 RETAINER

GC2039500111000X

Fig. 5 Coil spring replacement

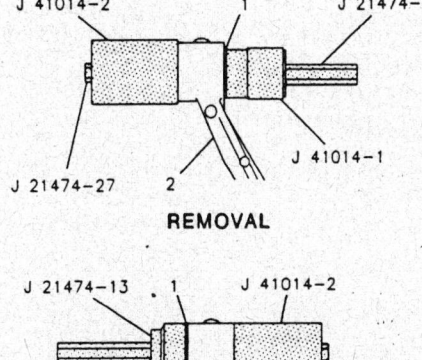

REMOVAL

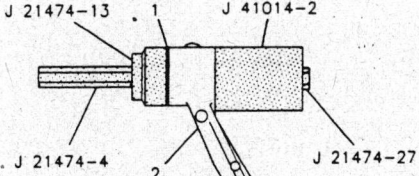

INSTALLATION

1 BUSHING
2 CONTROL ARM

GC2039500112000X

Fig. 6 Control arm bushing replacement tool installation

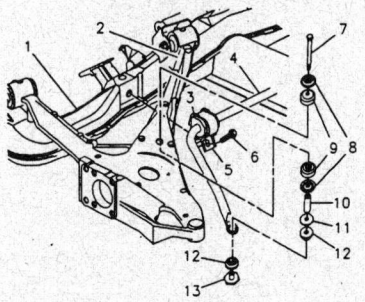

1 REAR SUSPENSION SUPPORT ASSEMBLY	7 BOLT, 13 N•m (115 LB. IN.)
2 CONTROL ARM	8 RETAINER, UPPER
3 INSULATOR, STABILIZER SHAFT	9 INSULATOR, UPPER
	10 SLEEVE
4 SHAFT, STABILIZER	11 RETAINER, LOWER
5 CLAMP, STABILIZER SHAFT	12 INSULATOR, LOWER
6 BOLT, 33 N•m (24 LB. IN.)	13 NUT

GC2039500113000X

Fig. 7 Stabilizer shaft replacement

TIGHTENING SPECIFICATIONS

Year	Component	Torque/Ft. Lbs.
2001–03	Adjustment Link Pinch Bolt	36
	Adjustment Link To Control Arm	55
	Adjustment Link To Rear Suspension Support	55
	Control Arm	78
	ELC Height Sensor	60①
	Hub & Bearing	52
	Rear Body	38
	Rear Suspension Support Bracket	63
	Rear Suspension Support To Body Rear	141
	Shock Absorber To Control Arm	18
	Shock Tower	15
	Stabilizer Link	11
	Stabilizer Shaft Clamp	24
	Stabilizer Shaft Link	115①
	Wheel Lug Nuts	100

① — Inch lbs.

Front Suspension & Steering

NOTE: On Air Bag Equipped Models, Refer To "Air Bag System Precautions" Located In The Front Of This Manual For System Disarming & Arming Procedures.

NOTE: Refer To "Computer Relearn Procedures" Located In The Front Of This Manual When Battery Power To The Computer Has Been Interrupted.

NOTE: Prior To Performing Any Service Operations Listed In This Section, Consult The "Technical Service Bulletins" Section For Related Information.

INDEX

HUB & BEARING

REPLACE

1. Raise and support vehicle, then remove tire and wheel assembly.
2. Insert suitable drift punch or screwdriver into caliper and rotor to prevent rotor from turning.
3. Remove drive axle nut, **Fig. 1.**
4. Remove caliper to steering knuckle bolts and support caliper using mechanics wire.
5. Remove brake rotor.
6. Disconnect ABS front wheel speed sensor connector and unclip from dust shield.
7. Remove hub and bearing mounting bolts and dust shield.
8. Place transmission in P position.
9. Separate hub and bearing from axle using front hub spindle remover tool No. J 28733-B, or equivalent.
10. Reverse procedure to install. Apply thin layer of grease to knuckle bore.

BALL JOINT INSPECTION

1. Raise front of vehicle.
2. Allow suspension to hang free.
3. Grasp tire at top and bottom and move it in and out.
4. Replace ball joint if any horizontal movement in knuckle relative to control arm is detected.
5. Replace ball joint if ball stud is disconnected from knuckle and looseness is detected or ball stud twists in its socket while using hand pressure.
6. Inspect for ball stud tightness in knuckle boss by shaking wheel and feeling for movement in stud end or nut. If any movement is detected, replace worn or damaged ball joints and knuckles.

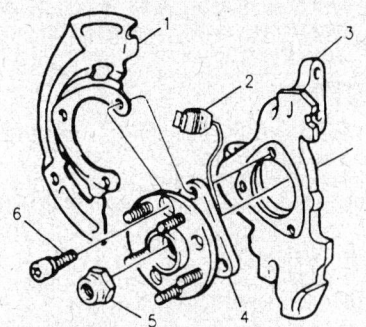

1. DUST SHIELD
2. WHEEL SPEED SENSOR CONNECTOR
3. STEERING KNUCKLE
4. HUB AND BEARING
5. NUT, DRIVE AXLE, 145 N·m (107 LB. FT.)
6. RETAINING BOLT, 95 N·m (75 LB. FT.)

GC2029500207000X

Fig. 1 Hub & bearing replacement

BALL JOINT

REPLACE

The ball joint is part of the lower control arm and cannot be serviced separately. Refer to "Control Arm, Replace" for replacement procedure.

STRUT

REPLACE

Care should be taken to avoid chipping or cracking the spring coating. Failure to observe may result in spring breakage.
1. Remove strut to body mounting bolts.
2. Raise and support vehicle with control arms hanging free.
3. Remove tire and wheel assembly.

4. Disconnect ABS front wheel speed sensor connector.
5. Remove speed sensor bracket from strut.
6. Remove brake line bracket from left-hand strut.
7. Chisel position mark across strut to knuckle interface, **Fig. 2.**
8. Scribe strut flange on inboard side along curve of knuckle, **Fig. 2.**
9. Scribe knuckle along lower outboard strut radius, **Fig. 2.**
10. Remove strut-to-knuckle bolts. **Knuckle must be retained after strut-to-knuckle bolts have been moved. Failure to observe this may cause ball joint and/or drive axle damage.**
11. Remove strut.
12. Reverse procedure to install: Adjust wheel alignment as outlined in "Wheel Alignment" section.

STRUT SERVICE

1. Place strut in strut compressor tool No. J 34013-B, or equivalent.
2. Compress spring slightly and remove strut shaft nut while holding strut shaft using suitable open-end wrench.
3. Loosen compressor screw while guiding strut shaft out of assembly.
4. Disassemble strut assembly as required, **Fig. 3.**
5. Reverse procedure to assemble.

CONTROL ARM

REPLACE

1. Raise and support vehicle with control arms hanging free.
2. Remove wheel and tire assembly.
3. Remove stabilizer link to control arm bolt.

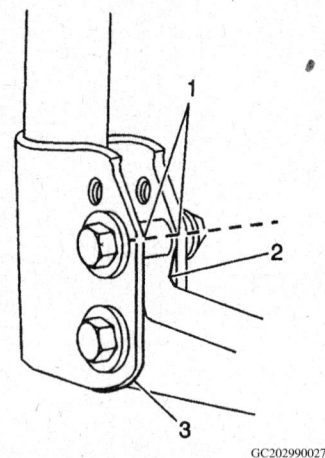

Fig. 2 Strut to knuckle position

4. Remove cotter pin and loosen nut from ball stud.
5. Separate ball joint from knuckle using ball joint separator tool No. J 43828, or equivalent.
6. Remove mounting bolts and control arm.
7. Reverse procedure to install, noting the following:
   a. **Torque** lower ball joint nut to 89 inch lbs., plus additional 180°.
   b. Tighten nut up to, but do not exceed an additional 60°, for cotter pin alignment.
   c. **Do not back off nut for cotter pin alignment.**

STEERING KNUCKLE
REPLACE

1. Raise and support vehicle.
2. Remove wheel and tire assembly.
3. Remove wheel bearing and hub as outlined under "Hub & Wheel Bearing, Replace."
4. Mark relationship of strut to knuckle as outlined under "Strut, Replace."
5. Separate ball joint from steering knuckle as outlined under "Lower Control Arm, Replace."
6. Remove strut to knuckle bolts and steering knuckle.
7. Reverse procedure to install. Adjust wheel alignment as outlined in "Wheel Alignment" section.

STABILIZER BAR
REPLACE

1. Raise and support vehicle with control arms hanging free.
2. Remove front wheels and tires.
3. Remove lefthand and righthand stabilizer link bolts.
4. Remove lefthand and righthand stabilizer bar brackets.
5. Separate lefthand tie rod end from knuckle using puller tool No. J 24319-B, or equivalent.
6. Remove exhaust pipe from manifold and immediate exhaust hangers and lower exhaust pipe.

7. Turn lefthand strut completely to left, then guide stabilizer shaft out lefthand side of vehicle between body and strut.
8. Remove stabilizer shaft out from under vehicle.
9. Reverse procedure to install.

TIE ROD
REPLACE
INNER

1. Remove steering gear as outlined under "Power Steering Gear, Replace."
2. Remove outer tie rod.
3. Remove inner tie rod jam nut and end clamp.
4. Remove boot clamp using side cutters and discard.
5. Mark breather tube location on steering gear for assembly.
6. Remove rack and pinion boot and breather tube.
7. Loosen inner tie rod shock dampener and slide back on rack.
8. Hold rack in suitable vice.
9. Turn inner tie rod housing counterclockwise using one wrench on rack assembly flats and another on inner tire rod housing flats, then remove it.
10. Reverse procedure to install. Gap between rack and housing stakes should be .01 inch.

OUTER

1. Remove cotter pin and hex slotted nut.
2. Loosen jam nut.
3. Remove outer tie rod from steering knuckle using universal steering linkage puller tool No. N 24319-01, or equivalent.
4. Remove outer from inner tie rod.
5. Reverse procedure to install.

POWER STEERING GEAR
REPLACE

1. Place front wheels in straight ahead position, then the ignition switch in Off position.
2. Lock steering column, using lock pin tool No. J 42640, or equivalent.
3. Raise and support vehicle, then remove front tire and wheel assemblies.
4. Remove stabilizer bar links, then rotate bar downward.
5. Remove electrical harness retainer and mounting bolts, then the steering gear heat shield.
6. Disconnect intermediate shaft lower pinch bolt, then separate shaft from power steering gear. **Failure to disconnect intermediate shaft from rack and pinion stub shaft can result in damage to steering gear and/or intermediate shaft which can cause loss of steering control.**
7. Remove lefthand side instrument panel insulator, then reposition dust seal.

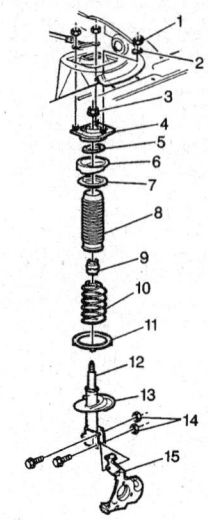

(1) Nut (3)
(2) Washer
(3) Torque Prevailing Nut
(4) Strut Mount
(5) Bearing
(6) Upper Spring Seat
(7) Upper Insulator
(8) Strut Shield
(9) Strut Bumper
(10) Spring
(11) Lower Insulator
(12) Strut
(13) Lower Spring Seat
(14) Torque Prevailing Nut (2)
(15) Steering Knuckle

Fig. 3 Exploded view of strut

8. Remove upper pinch bolt and disconnect intermediate shaft from steering column.
9. Remove intermediate steering shaft.
10. Remove lefthand and righthand outer tie rod mounting nuts and separate tie rods from steering knuckles, using separator tool No. J 24319-B, or equivalent.
11. Remove power steering pressure and return hoses from steering gear.
12. **On models equipped with variable effort steering,** disconnect variable effort steering electrical connector.
13. **On all models,** remove lefthand side stabilizer bar bracket bolts, then the bracket.
14. Pry upwards on stabilizer bar to remove insulator.
15. Remove power steering gear mounting bolts, then the steering gear through lefthand wheel opening.
16. Reverse procedure to install.

POWER STEERING PUMP
REPLACE

1. Remove drive belt as outlined under "Serpentine Drive Belt, Replace" in "4.0L Engine" section.
2. Place suitable drain pan under vehicle.
3. Remove power steering pressure line, then the return hose from power steering pump.
4. Remove bracket mounting bolt, then the power steering pump assembly.
5. Reverse procedure to install. Tighten all nuts and bolts to specification.

TIGHTENING SPECIFICATIONS

Year	Component	Torque Ft. Lbs.
2001–03	Ball Joint To Knuckle	③
	Brake LIne & Speed Sensor Bracket	13
	Control Arm Bolt	117
	Control Arm Nut	93
	Drive Axle Nut	118
	Hub & Bearing To Knuckle	70
	Intermediate Steering Shaft Pinch Bolt	35
	Stabilizer Bar Bracket Bolt	35
	Stabilizer Link Nut	13
	Steering Gear Heat Shield Bolt	89②
	Steering Gear Hose Connections	22
	Steering Gear Mount Bolt	70
	Steering Pump Mount Bolt	18
	Strut Mount To Body Nut	35
	Strut To Knuckle Bolt	136
	Tie Rod Nut	22①
	Wheel Lug Nuts	100

① — Rotate additional 180°.
② — Inch lbs.
③ — Refer to "Control Arm, Replace."

Wheel Alignment

INDEX

PRELIMINARY INSPECTION

Inspect tires for proper inflation.

Inspect tie rods for lateral end motion relative to the steering knuckle and tie rod end seals for any visible signs of damage. Replace tie rod end if either of these conditions exist.

Inspect runout of wheels and tires.

Inspect trim height. If out of specifications, correct before alignment. Inspect shocks, rack and pinion and control arms for looseness and proper operation. Replace any damaged steering/suspension components.

If any excess weight is normally carried in the trunk of vehicle, alignment is recommended with load in place.

* Ensure vehicle is level.

FRONT WHEEL ALIGNMENT

Caster

1. Remove top strut nuts and washers.
2. Raise and support front of vehicle to separate strut from inner wheel housing.
3. Drill two ¹²/₃₂ inch holes at front and rear of oval strut mounting hole on lefthand and righthand strut towers, **Fig. 1,** and file excess metal to create slotted holes. **Paint exposed metal with rust resistant paint or primer.**
4. Lower front of vehicle.
5. Install strut mounting nuts, but do not tighten at this time.
6. Adjust caster by moving top of strut towards front or rear. A .040 inch position change at tower will change caster approximately .1°.
7. When caster is within specifications, **torque** strut mounting nuts to 35 ft. lbs.

Camber

1. Loosen both strut to steering knuckle nuts and install camber adjusting tool No. J 39601, J 29862, or equivalents, and set camber to specifications, **Fig. 2.**
2. **Torque** strut to steering knuckle bolts to 136 ft. lbs.

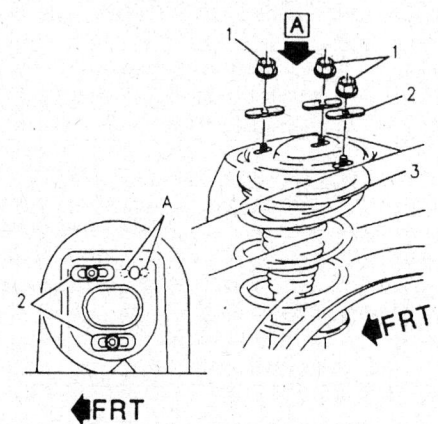

A DRILL 13/32 IN. HOLES
1 NUT, 47 N•m (35 LB. FT.)
2 WASHERS
3 STRUT

GC2049500108000X

Fig. 1   Front caster adjustment

Toe

1. Loosen lock nuts on tie rod ends. **Ensure boots are not twisted or damaged during adjustment.**
2. Rotate inner tie rod to adjust toe to specifications, **Fig. 2.**
3. **Torque** lock nuts to 47 ft. lbs.

REAR WHEEL ALIGNMENT

Make lefthand and righthand toe adjustments separately, per wheel.
1. Loosen inner adjustment link cam nut, **Fig. 3.**
2. Rotate cam bolt using suitable wrench or socket, then adjust toe to specifications.
3. **Torque** cam nut to 55 ft. lbs.

VEHICLE RIDE HEIGHT

Refer to "Specifications" section while inspecting vehicle ride height. Ensure vehicle

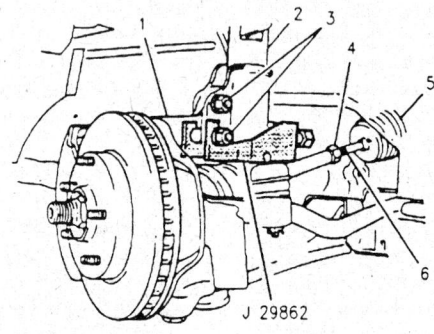

J 29862

1 KNUCKLE
2 STRUT
3 NUT, 185 N•m (136 LB. FT.)
4 LOCK NUT, 64 N•m (47 LB. FT.)
5 BOOT
6 INNER TIE ROD

GC2049500109000X

Fig. 2   Camber & toe adjustment

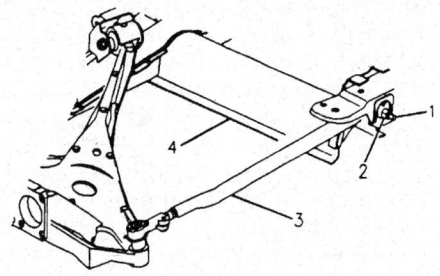

1 CAM BOLT
2 NUT, 75 N•m (55 LB. FT.)
3 INNER ADJUSTMENT LINK
4 REAR SUSPENSION SUPPORT ASSEMBLY

GC2049500110000X

Fig. 3   Rear toe adjustment

is on level ground and fuel tank is full. Ensure no extra weight is in passenger compartment or trunk.

On vehicle equipped with electronic level control (ELC), ensure ELC is functioning properly.
1. Place front seat to rear position.
2. Bounce vehicle three times at front and rear to normalize suspension.
3. Make measurement D, C, S and Z.
4. Refer to "Specifications" section for specifications.

BONNEVILLE, LESABRE & PARK AVENUE

NOTE: Refer To The Rear Of This Manual For Vehicle Manufacturer's Special Service Tool Suppliers.

INDEX OF SERVICE OPERATIONS

Specifications

GENERAL ENGINE SPECIFICATIONS

Year/Engine	VIN Code①	Fuel System	Bore & Stroke	Compression Ratio	Net H.P. @ RPM②	Maximum Torque Ft. Lbs. @ RPM	Normal Oil Pressure psi
2001–04							
3800	K	SFI	3.80 × 3.40	9.4:1	205 @ 5200	230 @ 4000	60③
3800	1	SFI	3.80 × 3.40	8.5:1	240 @ 5200	280 @ 3200	60③
2005							
3800	K	SFI	3.80 × 3.40	9.4:1	205 @ 5200	230 @ 4000	60③
4.6L	I	SFI	3.66 × 3.31	10.0:1	275 @ 5600	300 @ 4000	35④

MFI — Multi-Point Fuel Injection
SFI — Sequential Port Fuel Injection
① — The eighth digit denotes engine code.

② — Ratings are net as installed in vehicle.
③ — At 1850 RPM using SAE 10W-30 motor oil.

④ — At 2000 RPM.

TUNE UP SPECIFICATIONS

Engine/VIN Code①	Spark Plug Gap	Ignition Timing			Curb Idle Speed	Fast Idle Speed	Fuel Pump Pressure	Valve Clearance, Inch
		Firing Order Fig.②	°BTDC	Mark Fig.				
2001–04								
3800/K & 1	.060	⑥	⑦	⑧	③	③	53–59⑤	④
2005								
3800/K	.060	⑥	⑦	⑧	③	③	48–54⑤	④
4.6L/I	.050	⑨	⑦	⑧	③	③	41–47⑤	④

BTDC — Before Top Dead Center
① — The eighth digit of the Vehicle Identification Number (VIN) denotes engine code.
② — Before removing wires from distributor cap, determine location of No. 1 wire in cap, as distributor position may have been altered from that illustrated at end of this chart.
③ — Idle speed is controlled by an idle speed control (ISC) motor or an idle air control (IAC) valve.
④ — Equipped w/hydraulic valve lifters. There is no provision for adjustment.
⑤ — With shop towel wrapped around fuel pressure valve to prevent fuel spillage, connect a suitable fuel pressure gauge to fuel pressure valve. Measure fuel pressure w/ignition On, but engine not running.
⑥ — Cylinder numbering lefthand to righthand as viewed in Figs. A & B from front of vehicle, front bank, 1, 3, 5; rear bank, 2, 4, 6. Firing order 1-6-5-4-3-2. Two different types computer controlled coil ignition systems are used. Refer to

Figs. A and B, for spark plug wire connections at coil unit.
⑦ — Computer controlled. No adjustment.
⑧ — Equipped w/Crankshaft Position Sensor.
⑨ — Cylinder numbering from lefthand to righthand as viewed from front of vehicle, front bank, 2, 4, 6, 8; rear bank, 1, 3, 5, 7. Firing order 1-2-7-3-4-5-6-8.

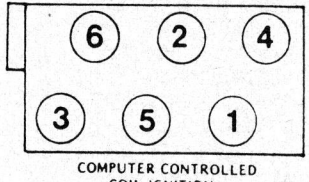

COMPUTER CONTROLLED COIL IGNITION
GC1139100129000X

Fig. A

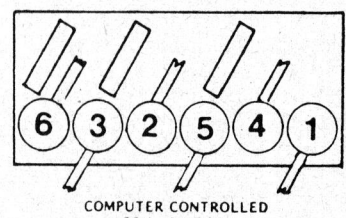

COMPUTER CONTROLLED COIL IGNITION
GC1139100130000X

Fig. B

FRONT WHEEL ALIGNMENT SPECIFICATIONS

Year	Model	Caster Angle, Degrees		Camber Angle, Degrees				Total Toe, Degrees	Ball Joint Wear
		Limits	Desired	Limits		Desired			
				Left	Right	Left	Right		
2001–05	All	+4.5 to +5.5	+5	–.7 to +.3	–.7 to +.3	–.2	–.2	+.2	①

① — Refer to "Ball Joint Inspection" in "Front Suspension & Steering" section.

REAR WHEEL ALIGNMENT SPECIFICATIONS

Year	Model	Camber Angle, Degrees		Total Toe, Degrees	Thrust Angle, Degrees	Ball Joint Wear
		Limits	Desired			
2001–05	All	–.8 to +.2	–.3	+.2	–.1 to +.1	①

① — Refer to "Ball Joint Inspection" in "Rear Suspension" section.

VEHICLE RIDE HEIGHT SPECIFICATIONS

Model	Year	Body Style	Manufacturer's Original Tire Size	Measurement Points & Specifications①③					
				Rear			Front		
				Dim.	Specification		Dim.	Specification	
					Inches	mm		Inches	mm
Bonneville	2001–05	All	②	D	3.00–3.80	76.00–96.00	Z	1.20–2.00	30.00–50.00
Lesabre	2001–05	All	②	D	3.00–3.80	76.20–96.52	Z	1.20–2.00	30.48–50.80
Park Ave	2001–05	All	②	D	3.00–3.80	76.20–96.52	Z	1.20–2.00	30.48–50.80

A Dim. — Measurement From Front Wheel Center to Inspection Point On Rocker Panel

B Dim. — Measurement From Rear Wheel Center to Inspection Point On Rocker Panel

C Dim. — Ground to Rocker Panel, Front

D Dim. — 2001–05 Models, Lowest Point On Ball Joint Housing Minus Grease Fitting To Centerline Of Rear Bushing.

E Dim. — Ground to Front Underbody Points

F Dim. — Ground to Rear Underbody Points

Z Dim. — Pivot bolt center line down to lower corner of lower ball joint.

Dim. — Dimension

① — ±.39 in (10 mm) front to rear & side to side.

② — See door sticker or inside of glove box for manufacturers original tire size specifications. If tires on vehicle do not match manufacturers original tire size & measurement is not within limits, it will be required to refer to the Non-Standard Tire & Wheel Size Adjustment To Ride Height Specification & Tire Size Adjustment Charts.

③ — Measurement is with fuel, radiator coolant and engine oil full, spare tire, jack, hand tools and mats in designated positions and tires properly inflated.

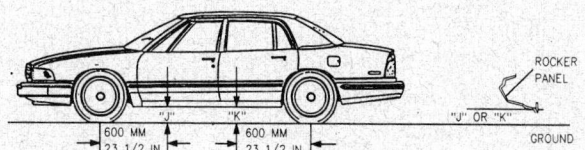

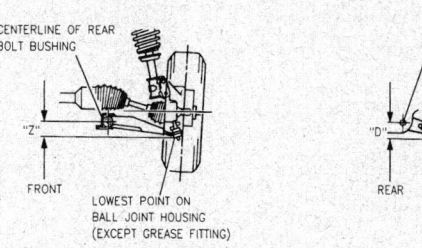

Fig. A   Ride height measurement locations. 2001–05

FLUID CAPACITIES & COOLING SYSTEM DATA

Year	Model	Engine	Coolant Capacity, Qts.	Coolant Type	Radiator Cap Relief Pressure, Lbs.	Thermo. Opening Temp.	Fuel Tank Gals.	Engine Oil Refill Qts.	Auto. Transaxle Qts.①
2001–05	All	3800	10	Dex-Cool	③	188	18.5	4.5②	④

① — Approximate. Make final inspection w/dipstick.

② — With filter.

③ — Relief pressure specification is stamped on cap.

④ — Drain and refill 7.4 qts.; overhaul 10 qts.; dry 13.4 qts.

LUBRICANT DATA

Year	Model	Lubricant Type		
		Automatic Transaxle	Power Steering	Brake System
2001–05	All	Dexron III	Power Steering Fluid①	DOT 3

① — GM part No. 1052884, or equivalent.

Electrical

NOTE: On Air Bag Equipped Models, Refer To "Air Bag System Precautions" Located In The Front Of This Manual For System Disarming & Arming Procedures.

NOTE: Refer To "Computer Relearn Procedures" Located In The Front Of This Manual When Battery Power To The Computer Has Been Interrupted.

INDEX

PRECAUTIONS

Air Bag Systems

Refer to "Air Bag System Precautions" in the front of this manual for system disarming and arming procedures.

Battery Ground Cable

Prior to service, disconnect battery ground cable and isolate as required.

FUSE PANEL & FLASHER LOCATION

Bonneville & LeSabre

The rear fuse panel is located under the drivers side rear seat. The engine compartment fuse panel is on the righthand side of the engine compartment.

Park Avenue

The instrument panel fuse panel is located under the righthand side and near the rear of the instrument panel. The rear fuse panel is located under the passengers side rear seat. The engine compartment fuse panels are on the righthand side of the engine compartment.

The combined turn signal and hazard flasher module is attached to the lighting control module (LCM) bracket under the instrument panel.

RELAY CENTER LOCATION

The relays are located in the fuse panels. Refer to "Fuse Panel & Flasher Location" for appropriate locations.

FUEL PUMP RELAY LOCATION

Bonneville & LeSabre

The fuel pump relay is located in the rear fuse panel.

Park Avenue

The fuel pump relay is located in the engine compartment fuse panel.

STARTER

REPLACE

Park Avenue & LeSabre

When removing starter, note if any shims are used between the starter and mounting surface. If shims are used, install in their original locations.

If starter is noisy during cranking, remove one .015 inch double shim or add one .015 inch single shim to the outer bolt. If starter makes a high pitched whine after engine starts, add .015 inch double shims until noise ceases.

1. Raise and support vehicle.
2. Remove starter braces, shields or other components as required.
3. Support starter, then remove mounting bolts.
4. Lower starter, then disconnect solenoid wires and battery cable.
5. Remove starter from vehicle.
6. Reverse procedure to install, noting the following:
   a. **Torque** starter mounting bolts to 32 ft. lbs.
   b. **Torque** solenoid terminal nut to 22 inch lbs.

Bonneville

3.8L

1. Raise and support vehicle.
2. Remove torque converter cover.
3. Disconnect starter electrical connections.
4. Remove starter motor mounting bolts, then the starter.

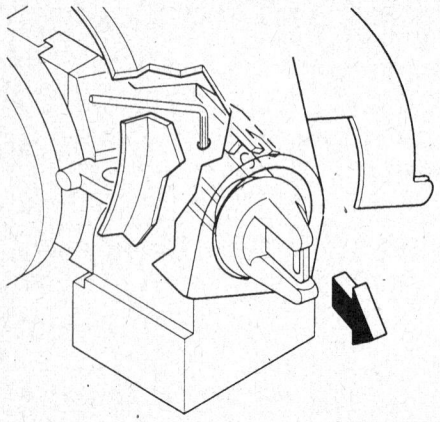

GC9049700157000X

Fig. 1 Lock cylinder removal. LeSabre & Park Avenue

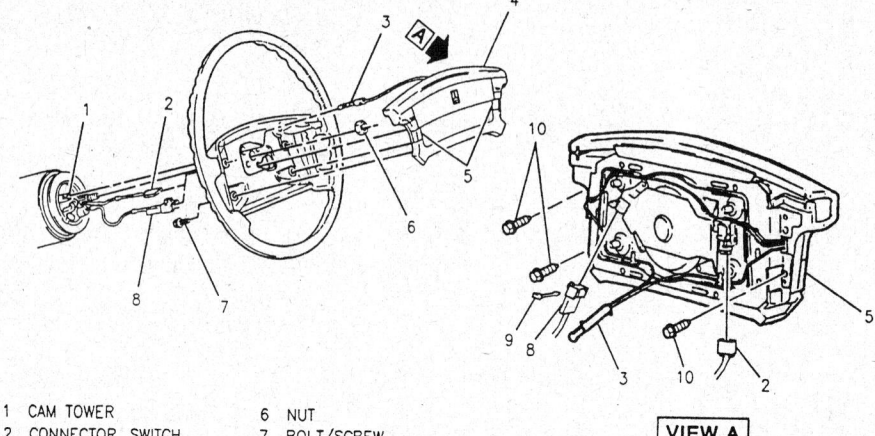

1	CAM TOWER	6	NUT
2	CONNECTOR, SWITCH	7	BOLT/SCREW
3	HORN CONTACT LEAD	8	CONNECTOR, SIR INFLATOR MODULE
4	INFLATOR MODULE	9	RETAINER, CPA
5	SWITCH ASM	10	BOLT/SCREW

GC6049100144000X

Fig. 2 Driver's air bag assembly

5. Reverse procedure to install, noting the following:
   a. **Torque** starter mounting bolts to 32 ft. lbs.
   b. **Torque** solenoid electrical connection to 22 inch lbs.

4.6L

1. Disconnect knock sensor electrical connections, then remove knock sensor.
2. Remove 2 starter motor retaining bolts.
3. Remove starter by sliding forward, then disconnect starter electrical connections.
4. Reverse procedure to install, noting the following:
   a. **Torque** starter motor mounting bolts to 22 ft. lbs.
   b. **Torque** knock sensor to 15 ft. lbs.
   c. **Torque** solenoid terminal nut to 30 inch lbs.

COIL PACK
REPLACE

1. Tag electrical connectors and spark plug wires to ensure proper installation, then disconnect them from ignition control module.
2. Remove screws securing ignition coils to ignition module, then the coils.
3. Reverse procedure to install. **Torque** attaching screws to 40 inch lbs.

IGNITION LOCK
REPLACE

Bonneville

1. Apply parking brake.
2. Remove instrument cluster trim bezel.
3. Remove radio.
4. Insert key and turn ignition switch to RUN position.
5. Look through radio opening to locate release button on side of switch.
6. Depress and hold lock cylinder retaining tab using suitable flat bladed tool and pull out to remove ignition cylinder.
7. Remove theft deterrent module.

8. Reverse procedure to install.

LeSabre & Park Avenue

REMOVAL

1. Remove steering wheel as outlined under "Steering Wheel, Replace."
2. Disconnect SIR wiring harness from wiring protector and wire harness strap.
3. Lower or remove steering column from vehicle.
4. **On models equipped with tilt column,** remove tilt lever.
5. **On all models,** remove column lower and upper shrouds.
6. Insert ignition key and hold in Start position.
7. Push on lock cylinder retaining tab using a 1/16 inch hex wrench, **Fig. 1.**
8. Release key to Run position and pull lock cylinder from lock module assembly.

INSTALLATION

1. Install upper shroud. **Torque** mounting screws to 12 inch lbs.
2. Install lower shroud, ensuring slots on lower shroud engage with tabs on upper shroud.
3. Install lower shroud mounting screws. **Torque** both screws to 53 inch lbs.
4. Install shift and multi-function lever seals to column shrouds.
5. Install tilt lever.
6. Raise or install steering column into vehicle.
7. Insert key into lock cylinder.
8. Ensure sector in lock module assembly is in Run position.
9. Align locking tabs, position tab with slots in lock module assembly and push cylinder into position.
10. Install lock cylinder through upper shroud and into lock module assembly.

IGNITION SWITCH
REPLACE

1. Remove lock cylinder assembly as outlined under "Ignition Lock, Replace."
2. Remove ignition switch retaining screws.
3. Depress retaining tab on rear of ignition switch and remove switch through radio opening.
4. Disconnect electrical connectors and ignition switch bulb.
5. Disconnect shift/park lock cable.
6. Reverse procedure to install. **Torque** ignition switch retaining screws to 80 inch lbs.

NEUTRAL SAFETY SWITCH
REPLACE

The transmission internal mode switch (IMS) is located within the transmission and controlled through the PCM.

BACK-UP LAMP SWITCH
REPLACE

Park Avenue

The back-up lamp switch is incorporated with the PERIM LP relay located in the I/P fuse panel and controlled by the PCM.

Bonneville & LeSabre

The back-up lamp switch is incorporated in the rear integration module (RIM) located behind the rear seat back and is controlled by the PCM.

HEADLAMP SWITCH
REPLACE

Refer to "Multi-Function Switch, Replace" for procedure.

MULTI-FUNCTION SWITCH
REPLACE

1. Remove steering wheel and tilt lever.
2. Remove two Torx screws from lower shroud, then tilt shroud down and slide back to disengage locking tabs.
3. Remove shroud protector.
4. Remove two Torx screws from upper shroud, then the shroud.
5. Remove instrument panel trim panel.
6. Remove two Torx screws from multi-function switch.
7. Disconnect multi-function switch electrical connectors, then remove switch.
8. Reverse procedure to install.

TURN SIGNAL SWITCH
REPLACE

Refer to "Multi-Function Switch, Replace" for procedure.

DIMMER SWITCH
REPLACE

Refer to "Multi-Function Switch, Replace" for procedure.

STEERING WHEEL
REPLACE

1. Remove driver's air bag module retaining screws from back of steering wheel.
2. Remove module from steering wheel, then disconnect horn contact by pushing slightly and twisting counterclockwise.
3. Remove connector position assurance, then disconnect coil assembly electrical connector, **Fig. 2.**
4. Remove steering wheel retaining nut.
5. Remove wheel using puller tool No. J1859-A and bolts No. J42578, or equivalents.
6. Reverse procedure to install, noting the following:
   a. **Torque** steering wheel nut to 30 ft. lbs.
   b. Ensure all wiring and electrical connectors are properly routed to avoid pinching.
   c. **Torque** driver's air bag module mounting screws to 27 inch lbs.

INSTRUMENT CLUSTER
REPLACE

Bonneville

1. Lower steering column to its lowest position.
2. Remove ignition lock cylinder bezel.
3. Remove Driver Information Center (DIC) switch.
4. Remove instrument cluster trim plate push-in fasteners.
5. Remove cluster trim plate by carefully pulling rearward and releasing clips.
6. Disconnect DIC switch electrical connector.

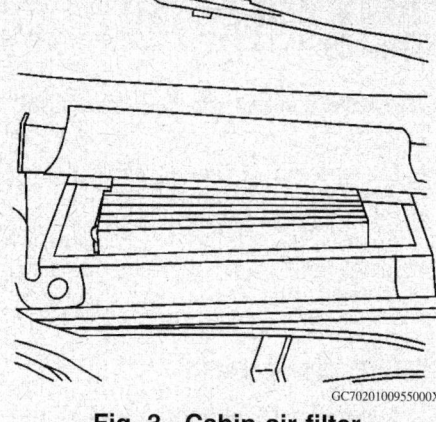

GC7020100955000X

Fig. 3   Cabin air filter replacement. Bonneville & LeSabre

7. Release instrument cluster pins, then pull cluster rearward and to right.
8. Disconnect all cluster electrical connectors.
9. Reverse procedure to install, noting the following:
   a. Ensure trim plate is fully seated to instrument panel. This is critical to proper functioning of automatic A/C control in-vehicle sensor.
   b. Ensure all electrical connectors are securely connected.
   c. Push instrument cluster pins into their corresponding locations. An audible snap will be heard when cluster is fully seated.

LeSabre & Park Avenue

1. Carefully pry defroster grill away from instrument panel.
2. Disconnect sunload sensor from grill, then remove grill from instrument panel.
3. Remove righthand and lefthand windshield garnish moldings.
4. Remove instrument panel upper trim pad attaching screws, then the upper trim pad from instrument panel.
5. Lower steering column to its lowest position.
6. Remove instrument cluster trim plate bezel to instrument panel attaching screws.
7. Disengage four upper cluster trim plate bezel retaining clips, then the bottom clips.
8. Disconnect trim bezel driver information center switch electrical connector, then remove trim plate bezel from instrument panel.
9. Remove four instrument cluster pins, then pull cluster rearward to remove.
10. Reverse procedure to install.

RADIO
REPLACE

1. Remove instrument panel cluster trim plate.
2. **On Bonneville & LeSabre models,**

depress spring clips on each side of radio.
3. **On Park Avenue models,** remove radio mounting screws.
4. **On all models,** pull radio rearward, then disconnect electrical connectors and antenna lead-in cable.
5. Reverse procedure to install.

WIPER MOTOR
REPLACE

Bonneville & LeSabre

1. Remove wiper arms.
2. Remove cowl cover panel.
3. Remove attaching bolts to windshield frame reinforcement, then the reinforcement.
4. Rotate wiper arm linkage from park 180° to opposite position.
5. Remove harness grommet from plenum.
6. Disconnect wiper motor harness connector.
7. Push harness and grommet through hole in plenum.
8. Remove attaching screws to wiper motor drive motor module.
9. Remove wiper drive system motor module.
10. Remove drive link from wiper motor cranks arm using tool No. J39232, or equivalent.
11. Remove wiper motor retaining screws, then the wiper motor from drive motor module.
12. Reverse procedure tom install, noting the following:
    a. **Torque** wiper drive system module screws to 71 inch lbs.
    b. **Torque** windshield reinforcement screws to 80 inch lbs.

Park Avenue

1. Disconnect electrical connectors.
2. Remove wiper motor attaching screws.
3. Place wiper arms 6–8 inches up on windshield.
4. Remove wiper motor, then disconnect drive link from crank arm.
5. Reverse procedure to install. **Torque** screws to 70 inch lbs.

WIPER SWITCH
REPLACE

Bonneville

1. **Make note of lefthand closeout and sound insulator panel fastener positions before removal. Improper installation may lead to possible accelerator or brake pedal binding.**
2. Remove instrument panel lefthand insulator.
3. Remove knee bolster and bracket.
4. Remove steering column bracket bolts. Disconnect electrical connectors from bracket.
5. Remove steering column bracket.
6. Remove steering column trim covers.

7. Remove wire harness assembly from wire restraint clips.
8. Disconnect wiper switch electrical connectors.
9. Depress switch locking tabs.
10. Pull switch assembly out of mounting bracket.
11. Reverse procedure to install, noting the following:
    a. Ensure all electrical connectors and wiring are properly routed to avoid pinching.
    b. Install new wire harness straps.
    c. Install steering column bracket and bolts. **Torque** bolts to 18 inch lbs.
    d. Install bolts and screws to knee bolster bracket at steering column support. **Torque** to 89 inch lbs.
    e. Install bolts and screws to knee bolster bracket at instrument panel. **Torque** to 18 inch lbs.
    f. Ensure lefthand closeout and insulator panel is properly positioned and fasteners are in original locations. **Torque** to 17 inch lbs.

LeSabre & Park Avenue

Refer to "Multi-Function Switch, Replace" for procedure.

WIPER TRANSMISSION
REPLACE

Refer to "Wiper Motor, Replace" for wiper transmission replacement procedure.

BLOWER MOTOR
REPLACE

1. Remove fasteners at rear edge of insulator to disengage from lower instrument panel.
2. Pry out retainers to release panel.
3. Turn heater temperature sensor 1/4 turn to release and allow to remain connected to its wire.
4. Disconnect electrical connectors, then slide insulator panel rearward to disengage.
5. Remove Dash Integration Module (DIM) from bracket, then the bracket.
6. Disconnect blower motor electrical connector.
7. Remove blower motor retaining screws, then lower the motor and rotate counterclockwise to remove from vehicle.
8. Reverse procedure to install. **Torque** screws to 12–15 inch lbs.

CABIN AIR FILTER
REPLACE
Bonneville & LeSabre

1. Open hood.
2. Lift up cabin air filter access cover located on air inlet panel.
3. Remove cabin air filter element from filter housing, **Fig. 3.**
4. Install new cabin air filter into filter housing.
5. Close cabin air filter access cover.

Park Avenue

1. **Make note of lefthand closeout and sound insulator panel fastener positions before removal. Improper installation may lead to possible accelerator or brake pedal binding.**
2. Disconnect courtesy lamp, DSIR and heater temperature sensor electrical connectors at closeout panel.
3. Remove lefthand closeout and sound insulator panel.
4. Remove filter access cover by pushing down, then pulling out.
5. Remove tape on first filter.
6. Remove first filter by pulling filter tab.
7. Remove tape on second filter.
8. Remove second filter by pulling filter tab.
9. Remove third filter by pulling filter tab.
10. Reverse procedure to install, noting the following:
    a. Lubricate new filter guides with suitable spray silicon for ease in installation. Keep filters as straight as possible.
    b. Install first filter into HVAC assembly. Use tab or a long screwdriver to raise filter so leading edge catches on holding rib inside filter case.
    c. Install second filter in first filter tab.
    d. Slide second filter into remaining channels of first filter.
    e. Slide third filter into remaining channels of second filter.
    f. Fold second filter tab down and third filter tab up over second.
    g. Install filter access cover.
    h. Ensure lefthand closeout and insulator panel is properly positioned and fasteners are in original locations. **Torque** to 17 inch lbs.

HEATER CORE
REPLACE

1. Drain cooling system into suitable container.

2. Remove fuel injector sight shield.
3. **Make note of lefthand closeout and sound insulator panel fastener positions before installation. Improper installation may lead to possible accelerator or brake pedal binding.**
4. From inside of vehicle, remove righthand and lefthand side sound insulators.
5. **On models equipped with rear A/C,** remove front console assembly and auxiliary air distribution duct adapter.
6. **On all models,** remove instrument panel lower trim plate.
7. Remove air distributor duct screws (righthand side screw is difficult to remove and may be lefthand out during reassembly), then the air duct.
8. Remove heater core shield and cover.
9. Remove retaining screw and strap from heater core.
10. Remove heater core.
11. Reverse procedure to install. Ensure lefthand closeout and insulator panel is properly positioned and fasteners are in original locations. **Torque** to 17 inch lbs.

EVAPORATOR CORE
REPLACE

1. Recover A/C refrigerant as outlined in "Air Conditioning" chapter.
2. Remove evaporator hose nut, then disconnect evaporator hose connection at evaporator.
3. Remove heater hoses from heater core, then pinch off hoses to minimize leakage of coolant.
4. Raise and support vehicle.
5. Remove drain tube from A/C module.
6. Lower vehicle.
7. **Make note of lefthand closeout and sound insulator panel fastener positions before removal. Improper installation may lead to possible accelerator or brake pedal binding.**
8. Remove instrument panel assembly.
9. Remove defroster duct and air distributor duct.
10. Disconnect blower control module connection and instrument panel to HVAC module connection.
11. Remove HVAC module retaining nuts, then the module assembly.
12. Remove seal from around heater core and evaporator tubes.
13. Remove upper A/C evaporator case, then the evaporator core.
14. Reverse procedure to install. Ensure lefthand closeout and insulator panel is properly positioned and fasteners are in original locations. **Torque** to 17 inch lbs.

3800 Engine

NOTE: On Air Bag Equipped Models, Refer To "Air Bag System Precautions" Located In The Front Of This Manual For System Disarming & Arming Procedures.

NOTE: Refer To "Computer Relearn Procedures" Located In The Front Of This Manual When Battery Power To The Computer Has Been Interrupted.

INDEX

PRECAUTIONS

Air Bag Systems

Refer to "Air Bag System Precautions" in the front of this manual for system disarming and arming procedures.

Battery Ground Cable

Prior to service, disconnect battery ground cable and isolate as required.

Fuel System Pressure Relief

After relieving fuel system pressure, a small amount of fuel may be released when servicing fuel pipes or connections. In order to reduce the risk of personal injury, cover fuel pipe fittings with a suitable shop towel before disconnecting to catch any fuel that may leak.

1. Loosen fuel filler cap to relieve tank pressure.
2. Connect fuel pressure gauge tool No. J34370-1, or equivalent, to fuel pressure connection. Wrap fitting in suitable shop towel.
3. Install bleed hose to suitable container, then open valve and bleed off pressure.

4. Disconnect fuel pressure gauge, then drain gauge in suitable container.

COMPRESSION PRESSURE

When measuring compression, lowest cylinder must be within 70 percent of the highest cylinder with a minimum pressure of 100 psi. Perform compression test with engine at normal operating temperature, spark plugs removed and throttle wide open.

ENGINE MOUNT

REPLACE

Bonneville & LeSabre

1. Raise and support vehicle.
2. Support engine with suitable jack.
3. Remove righthand engine mount to engine mount bracket retaining nut.
4. Lower engine slightly.
5. Remove engine mount to frame attaching bolt.
6. Remove engine mount to frame retaining nuts, then remove the mount.
7. Reverse procedure to install, noting the following:
   a. **Torque** engine mount to frame retaining nuts to 52 ft. lbs.
   b. **Torque** engine mount to engine

mount bracket retaining nut to 59 ft. lbs.

Park Avenue

2001–02

1. Remove fuel injector sight shield.
2. Install suitable engine support fixture.
3. Remove engine mount to engine mount bracket nuts, studs and spacers.
4. **On models equipped with supercharger,** remove supercharger drive belt tensioner.
5. **On all models,** remove power steering pump and position aside.
6. Disconnect coil pack assembly and position aside.
7. Remove water pump pulley.
8. Remove engine mount bracket, engine mount nuts and bolts, then the engine mount.
9. Reverse procedure to install.

2003–05

Refer to "Bonneville & LeSabre" for engine mount replacement procedure.

ENGINE

REPLACE

1. Scribe alignment marks on hood for installation reference, then remove hood.

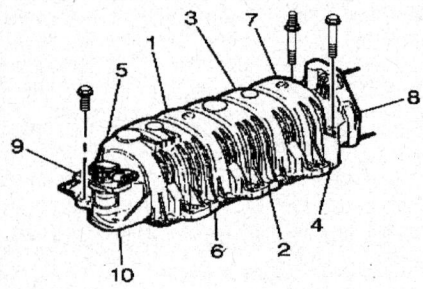

Fig. 1 Upper intake manifold. VIN K

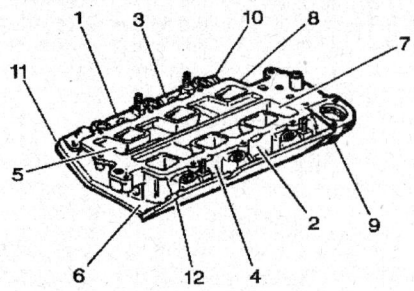

Fig. 2 Intake manifold tightening sequence. VIN K

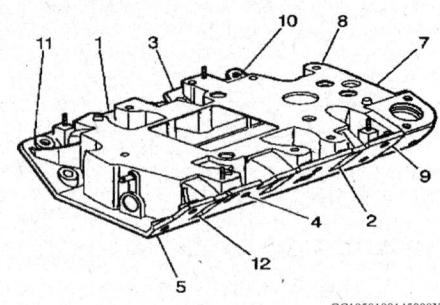

Fig. 3 Intake manifold tightening sequence. VIN 1

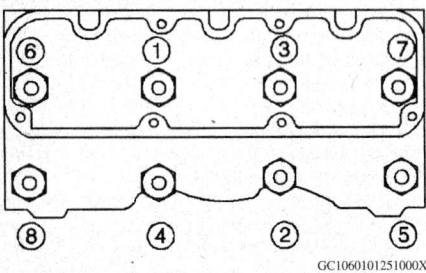

Fig. 4 Cylinder head tightening sequence

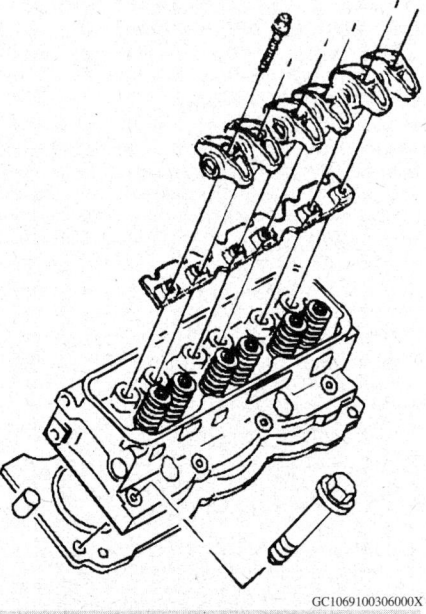

Fig. 5 Rocker arm assembly

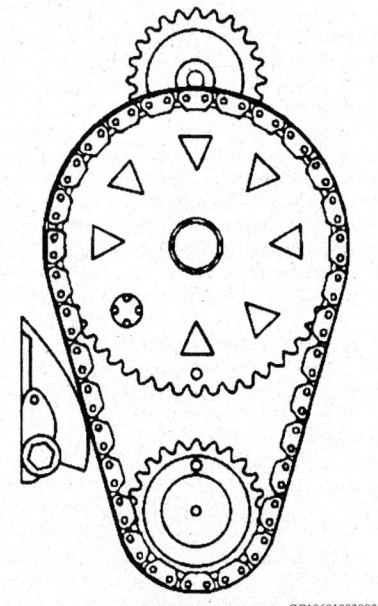

Fig. 6 Timing gear alignment marks

2. Remove fuel injector sight shield.
3. Disconnect vacuum brake booster hose from connections and position aside.
4. Disconnect fuel feed and return lines and secure to air inlet grill.
5. Remove EVAP purge valve solenoid and secure hose to air inlet grill.
6. Disconnect accelerator cable and cruise cable from throttle body bracket.
7. Disconnect cruise module electrical connector.
8. Remove retaining nuts, then cruise control module.
9. Rotate drive belt tensioner counter-clockwise to release belt tension, then remove belt.
10. Raise and support vehicle.
11. Remove battery ground cable and engine wire harness ground bolt from engine block.
12. Disconnect electrical connectors from A/C compressor clutch, oil level, knock, A/C pressure sensors and engine block heater.
13. Disconnect wire harness from retainer clip on back of A/C compressor.
14. Remove torque converter cover.
15. Remove starter as outlined under "Starter, Replace" in "Electrical" section.
16. Remove flywheel to torque converter bolts.
17. Disconnect electrical connectors to oil pressure, vehicle speed and knock sensors.
18. Remove transaxle brace to transaxle mounting bolts.
19. Remove retaining nuts on exhaust manifold pipe to righthand exhaust manifold, then remove pipe and position aside. Do not reuse gasket.
20. Remove righthand side front fascia extension.
21. Remove A/C compressor mounting

bolts, then position compressor aside.
22. Lower vehicle.
23. Remove PCM mounting bolt from left-hand side front of cylinder head.
24. Disconnect electrical connectors on lefthand side of engine from fuel injectors, ignition harness, ECT, TP, MAF sensors and IAC valve.
25. Disconnect electrical connectors on righthand side of engine from fuel injectors, EGR valve, MAP and O2 sensors then the alternator.
26. Secure engine harness to air inlet grill.
27. Remove alternator.
28. Remove air cleaner intake duct.
29. Install suitable engine support fixture.
30. Remove front power steering pump mounting bolts.
31. Raise and support vehicle.
32. Remove remaining power steering pump mounting bolt, then position pump aside.
33. Remove righthand side engine mount bracket.
34. Remove righthand lower engine to transaxle mounting bolt.
35. Drain cooling system into suitable container.
36. Lower vehicle.
37. Remove coolant inlet hose from water

pump using tool No. J38185, or equivalent, then remove coolant outlet hose from thermostat using same tool.
38. Remove heater hoses from drive belt tensioner retainers.
39. Support transaxle using suitable block of wood between floor jack and transaxle.
40. Remove engine support fixture.
41. Install suitable engine lift chain to engine lift bracket and attach to engine lift devise.
42. Remove remaining engine to transaxle mounting bolts.
43. Gently raise engine from vehicle, then drain engine oil into suitable container.
44. Remove transaxle brace to engine mounting bolts.
45. Remove exhaust manifold pipe.
46. Reverse procedure to install.

INTAKE MANIFOLD
REPLACE

VIN K
UPPER

1. Relieve fuel pressure as outlined under "Precautions."

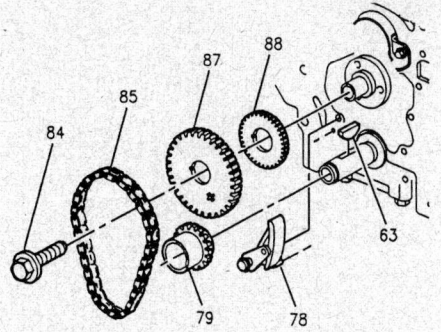

63 KEY
78 DAMPER ASSEMBLY
79 CRANKSHAFT SPROCKET
84 BOLT
85 TIMING CHAIN
87 CAMSHAFT SPROCKET
88 CAMSHAFT GEAR

GC1069100310000X

Fig. 7 Timing chain & sprockets

2. Remove fuel injector sight shield and air intake duct.
3. Remove spark plug wires on righthand (rear) side of engine and position aside.
4. Remove fuel rail, then exhaust manifold heat shield.
5. Remove throttle cable bracket to cylinder head mounting bolt.
6. Remove throttle body support bracket.
7. Remove upper intake manifold attaching bolts, then the manifold, **Fig. 1.**
8. Reverse procedure to install. Tighten bolts and nuts in sequence.

LOWER

The two bolts which mount the lower intake manifold to the cylinder head are accessible only after removing the upper intake manifold. The bolts are located in the righthand front and the lefthand rear corners of the lower intake manifold.
1. Relieve fuel pressure as outlined under "Precautions."
2. Remove fuel injector sight shield and air intake duct.
3. Remove spark plug wires on righthand (rear) side of engine and position aside.
4. Remove fuel rail, then exhaust manifold heat shield.
5. Remove throttle cable bracket to cylinder head mounting bolt.
6. Remove throttle body support bracket.
7. Remove upper intake manifold attaching bolts, then the manifold, **Fig. 1.**
8. Drain cooling system into suitable container, then remove upper radiator hose from coolant outlet.
9. Remove alternator and set aside.
10. Remove drive belt tensioner.
11. Remove EGR valve outlet pipe.
12. Remove intake manifold bolts, then the manifold.
13. Reverse procedure to install, noting the following:
    a. Clean cylinder block, heads and intake manifold sealing surface of all oil using a suitable solvent.
    b. Remove adhesive compound from

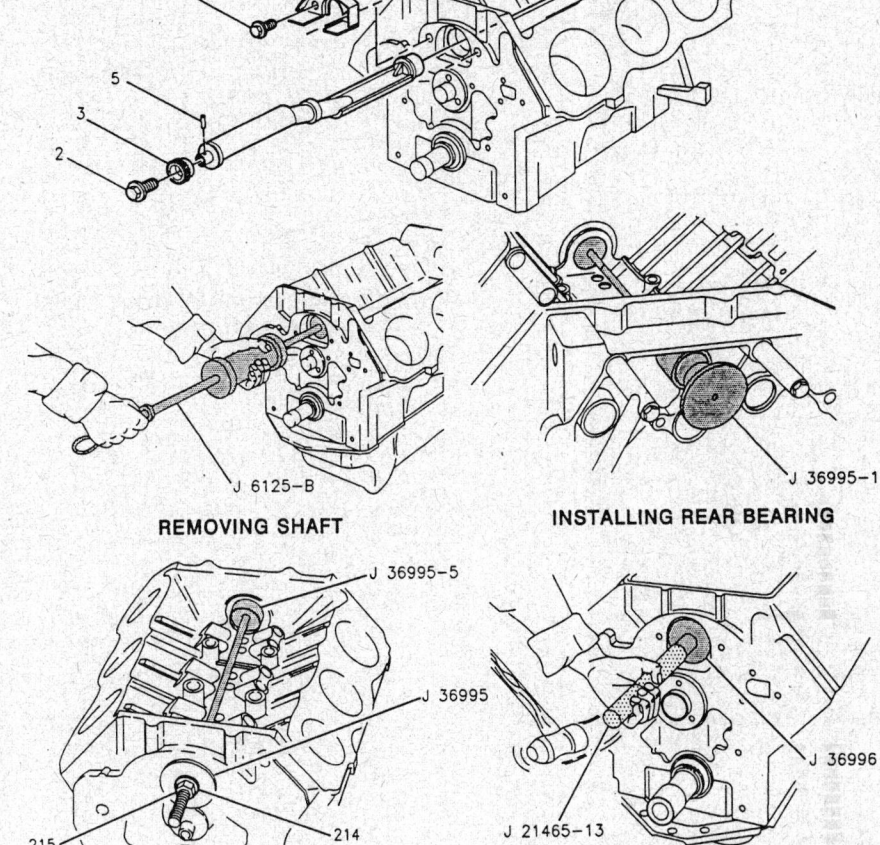

REMOVING SHAFT

INSTALLING REAR BEARING

REMOVING REAR BEARING

INSTALLING SHAFT

2	BOLT	7	RETAINER	215	NUT
3	BALANCE SHAFT GEAR	8	PLUG		
5	PIN	9	BEARING		
6	BOLT	214	WASHER		

GC1069100311000X

Fig. 8 Balance shaft service

intake manifold bolts and bolt holes.
c. Apply thread lock compound part No. 12345493, or equivalent, to intake manifold bolt threads prior to installation.
d. Tighten intake manifold bolts in sequence, **Fig. 2.**

VIN 1

The two bolts which fasten the lower intake manifold to the cylinder head are accessible only after removing the upper intake manifold. The bolts are located in the righthand front and the lefthand rear corners of the lower intake manifold.
1. **On models equipped with supercharger,** remove supercharger as outlined under "Supercharger, Replace."
2. **On all models,** relieve fuel pressure as outlined under "Precautions."
3. Remove fuel injector sight shield.

4. Remove plastic engine cover and air intake duct.
5. Disconnect manifold vacuum source, then drain cooling system into suitable container.
6. Disconnect righthand spark plug wires and position aside.
7. Remove fuel rail, then exhaust manifold heat shield.
8. Disconnect upper radiator and bypass hoses from coolant outlet.
9. Disconnect throttle position sensor and idle air control valve, then the fuel injectors and MAP sensor electrical connectors.
10. Remove EGR outlet pipe.
11. Remove throttle and cruise control cables.
12. Remove throttle bracket with power steering reservoir and set aside.
13. Mark running direction with suitable felt pen or chalk, then remove inner accessory drive belt.

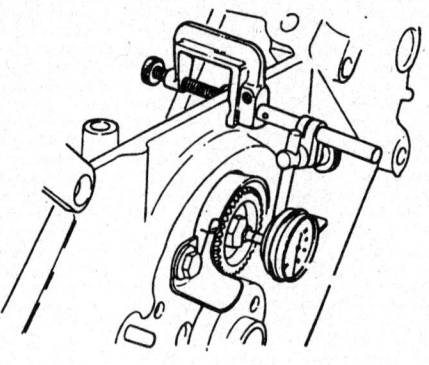

Fig. 9 Balance shaft endplay measurement

Fig. 10 Balance shaft front radial play measurement

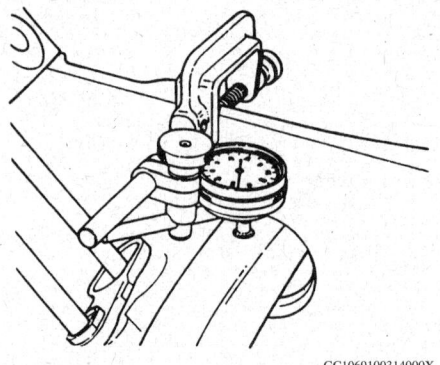

Fig. 11 Balance shaft rear radial play measurement

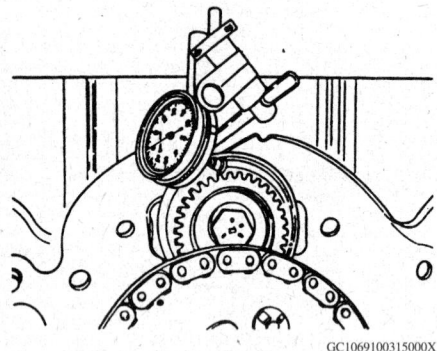

Fig. 12 Balance shaft gear lash inspection

14. Disconnect heater hose from intake manifold.
15. Remove tensioner bracket to supercharger retaining stud using standard double nut procedure.
16. Remove intake manifold attaching bolts, then the manifold.
17. Reverse procedure to install, noting the following:
   a. Clean cylinder block, heads and intake manifold sealing surface of all oil using a suitable solvent.
   b. Remove adhesive compound from intake manifold bolts and bolt holes.
   c. Apply thread lock compound part No. 12345493, or equivalent, to intake manifold bolt threads prior to installation.
   d. Tighten intake manifold bolts in sequence, **Fig. 3.**

EXHAUST MANIFOLD
REPLACE
Lefthand

Inspect the EGR outlet pipe for leaks whenever the pipe is removed from the righthand hand exhaust manifold. If a leak exists, replace the EGR adapter.

1. Disconnect spark plug wires from the spark plugs.
2. Remove oil level dipstick and tube.
3. Remove engine lift bracket.

59 PUMP OUTER GEAR
59 PUMP INNER GEAR
60 OIL PUMP COVER
64 SCREW
72 FRONT COVER

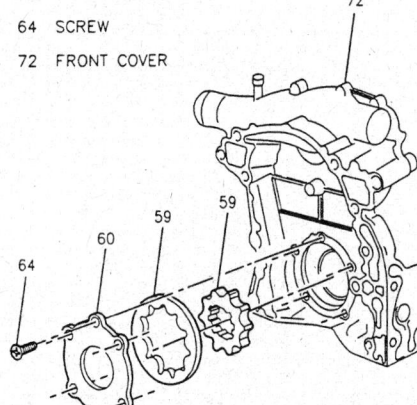

Fig. 13 Oil pump assembly

4. Remove bolts attaching lefthand exhaust manifold to crossover pipe.
5. Remove exhaust manifold bolts, then the manifold. Do not reuse gasket.
6. Reverse procedure to instal. **Torque** exhaust manifold bolts to 22 ft. lbs.

Righthand

1. Remove fuel injector sight shield.
2. Disconnect oxygen sensor electrical connector.
3. Remove righthand side spark plugs
4. Remove brake booster heat shield retaining nuts, then the heat shield.
5. Remove exhaust crossover to righthand side exhaust manifold bolts.
6. Remove transaxle filler tube.
7. Raise and support vehicle.
8. Remove exhaust manifold pipe.
9. Remove fuel injector sight shield bracket.
10. Remove righthand engine lift bracket.
11. Remove EGR inlet pipe to righthand side exhaust manifold retaining bolt.
12. Remove exhaust manifold bolts, then exhaust manifold. Do not reuse gasket.
13. Remove exhaust crossover pipe seal.

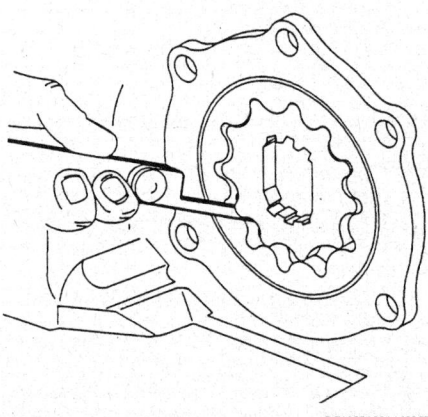

Fig. 14 Oil pump inner gear tip clearance inspection

Do not reuse seal.
14. Reverse procedure to install. **Torque** exhaust manifold bolts to 22 ft. lbs.

CYLINDER HEAD
REPLACE

1. Relieve fuel pressure as outlined under "Precautions."
2. Remove intake manifolds as outlined under "Intake Manifold, Replace."
3. Remove exhaust manifold as outlined under "Exhaust Manifold, Replace."
4. Remove appropriate valve cover.
5. Remove all wiring or brackets as required.
6. Remove rocker arm assemblies, guide plate and pushrods.
7. Remove and discard cylinder head attaching bolts, then the cylinder head.
8. Reverse procedure to install, noting the following:
   a. Clean all gasket mating surfaces and cylinder head bolt holes in block.
   b. Clean threads in block with appropriate tap.
   c. Apply suitable sealant to new bolt threads.
   d. Install new head gasket with arrow pointing towards front of engine.
   e. **Torque** cylinder head bolts to 37 ft. lbs., in sequence, **Fig. 4.**

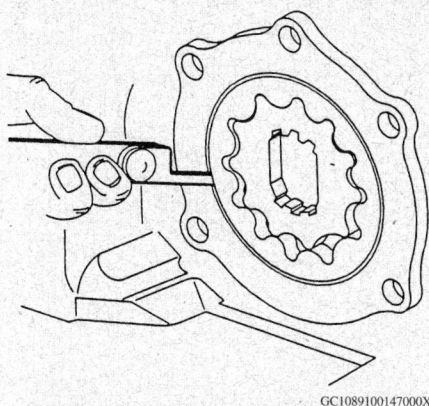

Fig. 15 Oil pump outer gear diameter clearance inspection

f. Tighten bolts an additional 120° in sequence.

CAMSHAFT LOBE LIFT SPECIFICATIONS

Engine	Year	Int.	Exh.
3800	All	.242	.234

VALVE CLEARANCE SPECIFICATIONS

These engines are equipped with hydraulic valve lifters. Valve clearance should be zero.

VALVE ADJUSTMENT

These engines are equipped with hydraulic valve lifters. There is no provision for adjustment.

ROCKER ARMS

Rocker arms are pedestal mounted over support plates, **Fig. 5.** To replace rocker arms, remove valve cover, pedestal retaining bolt(s), pedestal and the rocker arm. Replace rocker arms and pedestals as an assembly if they are damaged or excessively worn. If rocker arms are to be used again, they must be installed in original position.

VALVE GUIDES

The valve guides are an integral part of the cylinder head and cannot be replaced. If excessive valve stem clearance is noted, the valve guide must be reamed and an oversize valve guide installed. Valves are available in an oversize of .010 inch.

FRONT COVER
REPLACE

1. Remove righthand engine mount and bracket.
2. Remove drive belt tensioner as outlined under "Belt Tensioner, Replace."
3. Remove crankshaft balancer, sensor shield and crankshaft sensor.
4. Remove oil pan to front cover bolts.

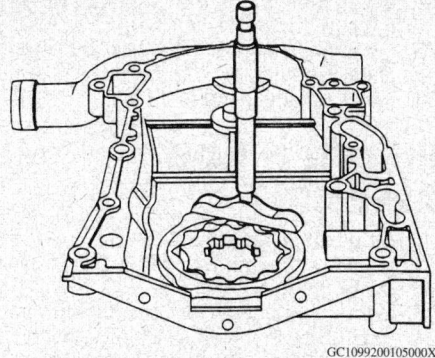

Fig. 16 Oil pump gear end clearance inspection

5. Remove engine front cover attaching bolts, then the front cover.
6. Inspect timing chain for overall in-and-out movement, which should not exceed one inch.
7. Inspect sprockets for visible signs of wear or damage.
8. Clean gasket mating surfaces at timing chain cover and cylinder block.
9. If oil pan gasket is excessively swollen, oil pan must be removed and gasket replaced.
10. Reverse procedure to install, noting the following:
    a. Apply sealer No. 12346004, or equivalent, to bolt threads.
    b. Install engine front cover bolts.
    c. **Torque** front cover bolts to 15 ft. lbs., then tighten front cover bolts an additional 40°
    d. Install oil pan to front engine cover bolts and **torque** to 124 inch lbs.
    e. Install crankshaft sensor and shield. **Do not adjust crankshaft sensor.**
    f. Crankshaft sensor bolt is designed to permanently stretch when installed. **Do not install a standard bolt. Components will not be tightened properly if improper bolt is used.**

TIMING CHAIN
REPLACE

1. Remove front cover as outlined under "Front Cover, Replace."
2. Align timing marks on sprockets, **Fig. 6,** so they are as close together as possible.
3. Remove timing chain dampener.
4. Remove camshaft sprocket bolts, **Fig. 7.**
5. Remove camshaft sprocket and chain, then crankshaft sprocket.
6. Reverse procedure to install, noting the following:
    a. Ensure No. 1 piston is at TDC.
    b. Assemble timing chain on sprockets with their timing marks aligned, **Fig. 6.**
    c. Tighten camshaft sprocket bolts.

CAMSHAFT
REPLACE

1. Relieve fuel pressure as outlined

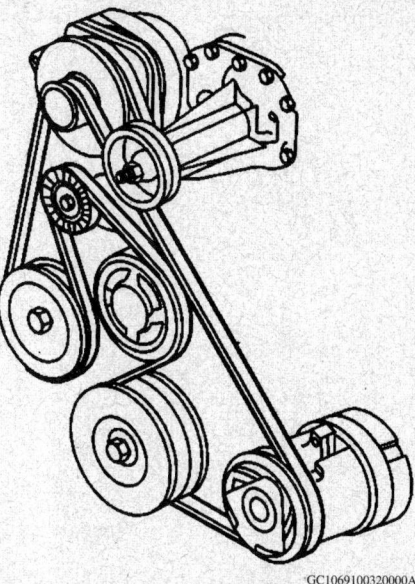

Fig. 17 Serpentine belt routing & replacement. VIN 1

under "Precautions."
2. Remove intake manifold as outlined under "Intake Manifold, Replace."
3. Remove valve cover, rocker arms, pushrods and valve lifters.
4. Remove crankshaft pulley and crankshaft sensor cover.
5. Remove front cover, timing chain and sprockets.
6. Remove camshaft thrust plate and camshaft. **Avoid marring bearing surface when removing or installing camshaft.**
7. Reverse procedure to install. Coat camshaft and valve lifters with prelube part No. 1052365, or equivalent, prior to installation.

BALANCE SHAFT
REPLACE
Removal

1. Remove engine as outlined under "Engine, Replace."
2. Remove flexplate, then the intake manifold as outlined under "Intake Manifold, Replace."
3. Remove lifter guide retainer, then the front cover.
4. Remove balance shaft drive gear bolt, **Fig. 8,** then the camshaft sprocket and timing chain.
5. Remove balance shaft retainer bolts, retainer and gear.
6. Remove balance shaft using slide hammer tool No. J6125-1B, or equivalent. **The balance shaft and both bearings are serviced as a complete package. Use only proper tools for bearing and shaft removal and installation. Inspect balance shaft drive gear and camshaft drive gear for nicks and burrs.**
7. Remove balance shaft rear plug.
8. Remove balance shaft rear bearing

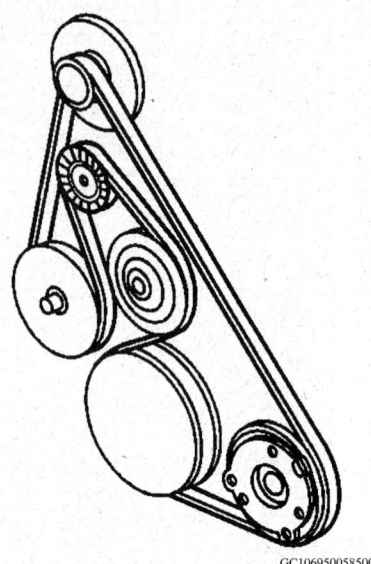

GC1069500585000A

Fig. 18   Serpentine belt routing & replacement. VIN K

using replacement tool No. J36995-5, or equivalent.

Installation

1. Dip balance shaft rear bearing in clean engine oil.
2. Install bearing with rolled edge facing into engine and manufacturers markings facing flexplate side using balance shaft bearing replacement tool No. J36995-1, or equivalent.
3. Dip balance shaft front bearing into clean engine oil.
4. Install balance shaft into block using installer tool Nos. J21465-13 and J36996, or equivalent.
5. Temporarily install balance shaft bearing retainer and bolts.
6. Install balance shaft drive gear.
7. Apply suitable sealant to bolt, then install and tighten.
8. Install balance shaft rear plug.
9. Measure balance shaft endplay, **Fig. 9,** which should not exceed .008 inch.
10. Measure balance shaft radial play at rear, **Figs. 10 and 11.** Radial play should be .0005–.0047 inch.
11. With camshaft sprocket temporarily installed, turn camshaft so timing mark is straight down.
12. With camshaft sprocket and camshaft gear removed, turn balance shaft so timing mark on gear points straight down.
13. Install camshaft gear, aligning marks on balance shaft gear and camshaft gear by turning balance shaft, **Fig. 6.**
14. Turn crankshaft so No. 1 piston is at TDC.
15. Install timing chain and camshaft sprocket.
16. Measure gear lash, **Fig. 12,** at four places, every ¼ turn. Gear lash should be .002–.005 inch.
17. Install balance shaft front bearing retainer and bolts, then tighten.

18. Install front cover, then the lifter guide retainer.
19. Install intake manifold, then the flexplate. Tighten flexplate bolts.
20. Install engine in vehicle.

PISTON & ROD ASSEMBLY

1. Coat piston pin with oil.
2. Install one piston pin retainer into retainer groove.
3. Install connecting rod and piston pin, rod can be installed in either direction.
4. Push piston pin in until it bottoms against installed piston pin retainer.
5. Ensure piston moves freely.

PISTONS, PINS & RINGS

Pistons and ring are available in standard sizes and oversizes of .010. Piston pins are supplied with piston and are available in standard size only.

To inspect piston fit in bore, measure bore diameter using suitable telescoping gauges and record reading. Measure piston across skirt at a point ¾ inch below piston pin center line and record reading. Subtract piston diameter from bore diameter and compare to specified clearance.

MAIN & ROD BEARINGS

Main and rod bearings are available in standard sizes and a variety of undersizes.
1. Lubricate crankshaft to main bearing contact areas with clean engine oil or engine assembly lubricant.
2. **Torque** all bolts to 52 ft. lbs., in equal increments.
3. Loosen all bolts 360°.
4. **Torque** all bolts to 15 ft. lbs.
5. **Torque** all bolts to 30 ft. lbs.
6. Tighten bolts an additional 35°.
7. Tighten bolts an additional 35°.
8. Final, tighten bolts an additional 40°.
9. Apply thread lock compound part No. 12345493, or equivalent, to side main bolts.
10. Install side main bolts and **torque** to 11 ft. lbs.
11. Tighten main bolts an additional 45°.
12. Install connecting rod bearings and bearing caps.
13. **Torque** cap bolts to 20 ft. lbs., then tighten an additional 50°.
14. Pry connecting rod back and forth, then inspect for binding.

CRANKSHAFT SEAL
REPLACE
Removal

1. Remove transaxle assembly and flexplate.
2. Pry out seal using a suitable screwdriver or other flat bladed tool.
3. Clean surfaces and inspect for visual

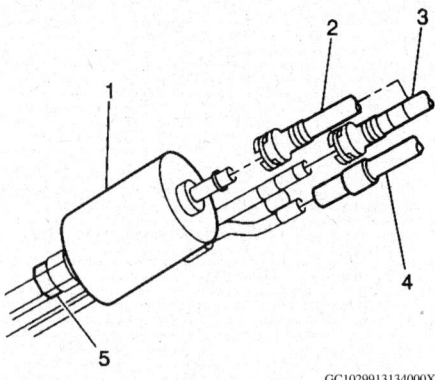

GC1029913134000X

Fig. 19   Fuel filter replacement

damage or excessive wear. Repair or replace components as required.

Installation

1. Apply clean engine oil to both sides of new seal.
2. Slide seal over mandrel of rear main oil seal installer tool No. J38196, or equivalent, until back of seal bottoms squarely against collar of tool.
3. Attach main seal oil installer tool to crankshaft by hand or **torque** attaching screws to 54 inch lbs.
4. Turn tool T-handle so that collar pushes seal into bore.
5. Turn handle until collar is tight against case.
6. Loosen T-handle until it comes to a stop, then remove attaching screws.

OIL PAN
REPLACE

1. Raise vehicle and drain engine oil into suitable container.
2. Remove flexplate inspection cover.
3. Remove engine mount as outlined under "Engine Mount, Replace."
4. Remove oil level sensor located in oil pan before oil pan is removed. Damage to sensor will occur if pan is removed with sensor installed.
5. Remove oil filter.
6. Remove oil pan, then the pickup screen.
7. Remove old oil pan gasket.
8. Clean oil pan and cylinder block mating surfaces.
9. Reverse procedure to install.

OIL PUMP
REPLACE
Removal

1. Remove front cover as outlined under "Front Cover, Replace."
2. Remove oil filter adapter, pressure regulator valve and spring.
3. Remove oil pump cover and gears, **Fig. 13.**

Installation

1. Lubricate all gears with clean engine oil, then install gears in housing.

2. Pack pump cavity with suitable petroleum jelly.
3. Install pump cover. Tighten cover mounting screws.
4. Install pressure regulator valve and spring.
5. Install oil filter adapter using a new gasket. Tighten oil filter adapter attaching bolts.
6. Install front cover on engine. **Ensure inner pump gear is properly engaged on crankshaft sprocket during front cover installation.**

OIL PUMP SERVICE

Inspection

1. Inspect pump cover and housing for cracks, scoring, porous or damaged casting, damaged threads or excessive wear or galling. Replace as required.
2. Inspect pressure regulator valve for scoring, burrs or sticking in valve bore. Replace as required.
3. Inspect pressure regulator valve spring for tension loss or bending. Replace spring as required.
4. Inspect gears for chipping galling or excessive wear. Replace as required.

Assembly & Installation

1. Measure oil pump inner gear tip clearance, **Fig. 14.** Maximum clearance should be .006 inch.
2. Measure oil pump outer gear diameter clearance, **Fig. 15,** which should be .008–.015 inch.
3. Measure oil pump gear end clearance with gear dropped in housing, **Fig. 16,** which should be .0001–.0035 inch.
4. Measure pressure regulator valve for valve to bore clearance of .0015–.0030 inch.

BELT TENSION DATA

This engine is equipped with an automatic belt tensioner.

SERPENTINE DRIVE BELT

Belt Routing

Refer to **Figs. 17 and 18,** for serpentine drive belt routing.

Belt Tensioner, Replace

VIN 1

1. Remove supercharger belt.
2. Remove ignition module.
3. Remove tensioner bolts, then the tensioner.
4. Reverse procedure to install.

VIN K

1. Raise and support vehicle.
2. Remove lower splash shield, then drain coolant into suitable container.
3. Install front splash shield, lower vehicle.
4. Remove alternator and heater hoses.
5. Remove drive belt tensioner.
6. Reverse procedure to install. Tighten tensioner bolts.

COOLING SYSTEM
BLEED

1. Fill cooling system and install radiator cap.
2. Start engine and run at 2000–2500 RPM until engine reaches operating temperature.
3. Allow engine return to idle and run for 3 minutes.
4. Shut engine off and allow to cool.
5. Inspect coolant level and top off as needed.

THERMOSTAT
REPLACE

1. Remove engine cover.
2. With engine cool, drain engine coolant below thermostat level.
3. Disconnect radiator hose from thermostat housing.
4. Remove thermostat housing, gasket and thermostat.
5. Reverse procedure to install, noting the following:
   a. Ensure thermostat gasket sealing surfaces are thoroughly clean prior to installation.
   b. Install thermostat with new gasket.
   c. Tighten thermostat housing retaining bolt(s).
   d. Fill and bleed cooling system as outlined under "Cooling System Bleed."

WATER PUMP
REPLACE
VIN K Engine

1. Drain coolant into suitable container.
2. Rotate drive belt tension counterclockwise and remove drive belt.
3. Remove water pump pulley.
4. Remove water pump mounting bolts, note their locations, then remove water pump.
5. Clean gasket mating surfaces.
6. Reverse procedure to install, noting the following:
   a. **Torque** water pump short bolts to 11 ft. lbs.
   b. **Torque** water pump long bolts to 22 ft. lbs.

VIN 1 Engine

1. Drain coolant into suitable container.
2. Remove supercharger and accessory drive belts.

3. Remove supercharger belt idler pulley bolt, then the pulley.
4. Remove water pump pulley mounting bolts, then the pulley.
5. Remove water pump mounting bolts, noting their location, then the water pump.
6. Clean gasket mating surfaces.
7. Reverse procedure to install, noting the following:
   a. **Torque** short water pump bolts to 11 ft. lbs.
   b. **Torque** long water pump bolts to 22 ft. lbs.

RADIATOR
REPLACE

1. Drain engine coolant into suitable container.
2. Remove upper radiator seal.
3. **On Park Avenue models,** remove upper two bolts from hood latch support.
4. **On all models,** remove upper radiator support bar.
5. Disconnect and plug coolant overflow hose from radiator.
6. Disconnect upper and lower radiator hoses from radiator and position out of way.
7. Remove bolt from transmission oil cooler pipe clip at lower radiator tie bar.
8. Remove cooling fans.
9. Disconnect transmission fluid cooler lines from radiator using coupling tool No. J41623-B, or equivalent. Position lines aside.
10. Disconnect overflow hose from radiator.
11. **The bolt retaining the condenser to radiator end tank is of a special length and must be used upon installation. Use of other bolts may damage radiator end tank.**
12. Remove condenser mounting bolts, then separate condenser from radiator and remove radiator from vehicle.
13. Reverse procedure to install, noting the following:
    a. **The bolt retaining the condenser to radiator end tank is of a special length and must be used upon installation. Use of other bolts may damage radiator end tank.**
    b. Fill radiator with proper coolant.
    c. Bleed cooling system as outlined under "Cooling System Bleed."
    d. Start engine, then inspect for and correct any leakage.

FUEL PUMP
REPLACE

1. Clean fuel pipe connections, hose connections and surrounding areas to prevent fuel system contamination.
2. Do not handle fuel sender/pump assembly by fuel pipes or damage to pipe joints could occur.
3. Relieve fuel system pressure as outlined in "Precautions."
4. Drain fuel from tank into a suitable storage unit.

5. Remove spare tire cover, jack and spare tire.
6. Remove rear compartment floor trim.
7. Remove fuel sender/pump access panel.
8. Remove quick connect fittings and electrical connector at fuel sender/pump assembly.
9. Remove electrical connector at fuel tank pressure sensor.
10. Remove fuel sender/pump retaining ring and assembly retaining cam with fuel sender locknut wrench tool No. J39765, or equivalent.
11. Remove fuel sender/pump from vehicle.
12. Reverse procedure to install, noting the following:
    a. Replace fuel sender O-rings during installation to avoid damaging sender assembly.
    b. Attach fuel lines with original type fasteners and hardware.
    c. **Do not repair sections of fuel pipe.**
    d. Upon completion of repairs, turn ignition On for two seconds, then Off for 10 seconds.

e. Turn ignition back On and inspect for leaks.

FUEL FILTER
REPLACE

1. Relieve fuel pressure as outlined under "Precautions."
2. Raise and support vehicle using a suitable lift.
3. Remove quick-connect fitting at fuel feed line (2), **Fig. 19.**
4. Remove threaded connection (5) at in-line fuel filter.
5. Inspect fuel lines and O-rings for cuts, swelling, cracks and distortion.
6. Inspect fuel return line and fuel vent pipe.
7. Drain any remaining fuel into suitable container.
8. Reverse procedure to install. Tighten fuel filter outlet nut.

SUPERCHARGER
REPLACE

1. Relieve fuel pressure as outlined under "Precautions."
2. Remove engine cover.

3. Remove injector sight shield.
4. Remove supercharger belt.
5. Disconnect vacuum brake booster hose from vacuum connections and position aside.
6. Remove evaporative emission canister purge valve, then secure hose to air inlet grille.
7. Remove alternator brace.
8. Disconnect righthand side spark plug wires from ignition module and position aside.
9. Disconnect electrical connectors from fuel injectors.
10. Remove MAP sensor bracket.
11. Remove fuel rail mounting bolts and the fuel rail with injectors.
12. Remove boost control solenoid.
13. Remove throttle body nuts.
14. Remove supercharger.
15. Reverse procedure to install, noting the following:
    a. Clean intake manifold and supercharger mating surfaces.
    b. **Do not use any sealer on supercharger gasket.**
    c. Tighten supercharger mounting bolts.

TIGHTENING SPECIFICATIONS

Year	Component	Torque/Ft. Lbs.
2001–05	Accessory Drive Belt Tensioner	37
	Alternator Support Through Alternator	36
	Alternator Support To Cylinder Head	36
	Balance Shaft Gear Bolt	16①
	Balance Shaft Retainer	22
	Boost Control Solenoid Retaining Nut	71②
	Bypass Valve Actuator Bolts	18
	Camshaft Sensor To Front Cover	89②
	Camshaft Sprocket Bolts	74⑤
	Connecting Rod Bolts	20④
	Coolant Plug	13
	Coolant Temperature Sensor To Intake	15
	Crankshaft Balancer	110⑥
	Crankshaft Sensor Clamp Bolt	40②
	Crankshaft Sensor To Front Cover	22
	Cylinder Block Drain Plug	13
	Cylinder Head To Block	③
	EGR Pipe To EGR Valve	22
	EGR Pipe To Exhaust Manifold	21
	EGR Valve Adapter	37
	EGR Valve To Intake Manifold Adapter	22
	Engine Mount To Cylinder Block	70
	Engine Mount To Frame Rail	52
	Engine Mount To Mount Bracket	59
	ESC Knock Sensor	14
	Exhaust Manifold To Cylinder Head	22
	Exhaust Pipe To Exhaust Manifold	18
	Flexplate Cover To Transaxle	10
	Flexplate To Crankshaft	11④
	Front Cover To Block	22
	Fuel Rail Hold-Down Bolts & Nuts	89②
	Fuel Filter Outlet Nut	22
	Fuel Injector Rail Stud	18
	Heater Hose Fitting To Intake	11
	Ignition Module To Alternator Support	18
	Intake Manifold To Cylinder Head	11
	Intake Manifold (Upper) To Lower Manifold	89②
	Main Bearing Cap Bolts	⑦
	Oil Dipstick Tube	14
	Oil Filter Adapter To Front Cover	11④
	Oil Galley Plugs	22
	Oil Level Sensor To Oil Pan	15
	Oil Pan Drain Plug	22
	Oil Pan To Block	10
	Oil Pan To Front Cover	10
	Oil Pressure Switch	12
	Oil Pump Cover To Front Cover	98②
	Oil Screen Housing To Cylinder Block	11
	O₂ Sensor	31
	Pulley Assembly To Crankshaft	111⑥
	Righthand Exhaust Manifold To Lefthand Exhaust Manifold	15
	Rocker Arm Cover	89②
	Rocker Arm Pedestal	11⑤

Continued

TIGHTENING SPECIFICATIONS—Continued

Year	Component	Torque/Ft. Lbs.
2001–05	Spark Plug	11
	Starter Motor	32
	Supercharger To Lower Intake Manifold	17
	Thermostat Housing	15
	Throttle Cable Bracket	35②
	Timing Chain Damper	16
	Torque Converter To Flexplate	46
	Transaxle To Engine Block	55
	Valve Lifter Guide Bolts	22
	Water Pump Pulley	116②

① — Rotate an additional 70°.
② — Inch lbs.
③ — Refer to "Cylinder Head, Replace."
④ — Rotate an additional 50°.
⑤ — Rotate an additional 90°.
⑥ — Rotate an additional 76°.
⑦ — Refer to "Crankshaft, Replace."

NOTE: Refer To "4.6L Engine" In "Deville, Eldorado & Seville" Chapter For Procedures Not Covered In This Section.

NOTE: On Air Bag Equipped Models, Refer To "Air Bag System Precautions" Located In The Front Of This Manual For System Disarming & Arming Procedures.

NOTE: Refer To "Computer Relearn Procedures" Located In The Front Of This Manual When Battery Power To The Computer Has Been Interrupted.

INDEX

PRECAUTIONS

Air Bag Systems

Refer to "Air Bag System Precautions" in the front of this manual for system disarming and arming procedures.

Battery Ground Cable

Prior to service, disconnect battery ground cable and isolate as required.

Fuel System Pressure Relief

A small amount of fuel may be released when servicing fuel connections even after pressure is released. Cover all fuel connections with shop towel before servicing.
1. Disconnect and isolate battery ground cable.
2. Remove intake manifold top cover.
3. Loosen fuel tank filler cap.
4. Install fuel pressure gauge tool No, J-34760-1A, or equivalent, to fuel pressure connection. Wrap shop towel around fitting while connecting gauge.
5. Install approved bleed hose into approved container, then open valve on gauge to relieve system pressure.

ENGINE MOUNT

REPLACE

Front

1. Install suitable engine support fixture.
2. Raise and support vehicle.
3. Remove front engine mount to engine frame retaining nut.
4. Remove engine frame.

5. Remove front engine mount to engine mount bracket retaining nut.
6. Remove engine mount.
7. Reverse procedure to install.

Right

1. Raise and support vehicle.
2. Remove righthand side front wheel.
3. Support engine with suitable jack stand.
4. Remove engine mount to engine mount bracket retaining nut.
5. Lower jack allowing engine to lower slightly then remove jack.
6. Remove engine mount to frame mounting bolts and nuts.
7. Lower vehicle.
8. Remove surge tank and position aside, then remove the frame rail retaining nuts.
9. Raise and support vehicle.
10. Push up on frame rail bolts to clear mount as it's tilted away from vehicle and remove mount.
11. Reverse procedure to install.

ENGINE

REPLACE

1. Recover air condition refrigerant as outlined in "Air Conditioning" chapter.
2. Disconnect vacuum booster hose connections and position aside.
3. Disconnect fuel supply and return quick connect fittings at fuel rail and secure to air inlet grill.
4. Disconnect EVAP purge valve hose and secure to air inlet grill.
5. Remove upper filler panel and air cleaner assembly.
6. Remove fuel injector sight shield.
7. Remove positive battery cable to remote positive terminal retaining nut then secure to top of engine.

8. Remove secondary air injection relay from bracket and secure to top of engine.
9. Disconnect electrical connectors from PCM, C101 and engine electrical harness.
10. Remove battery ground cable mounting bolt from righthand frame rail.
11. Disconnect cruise control and accelerator cables from throttle body. Do not reuse accelerator cable.
12. Disconnect shift cable from manual shift lever and bracket then position aside.
13. Drain coolant into suitable container.
14. Disconnect water housing crossover to surge tank inlet hose.
15. Disconnect heater pipe to surge tank outlet hose.
16. Disconnect heater hoses from heater pipes.
17. Disconnect brake lines from master cylinder. Plug open outlet ports.
18. Remove upper transaxle oil cooler line mounting bolt, then disconnect upper and lower oil cooler lines from radiator.
19. Ensure wheels are straight then lock steering column using lockpin tool No. J-42640, or equivalent.
20. Remove lefthand and righthand strut tower bolts.
21. Raise and support vehicle.
22. Remove rear exhaust manifold pipe.
23. Disconnect electrical connectors from wheel speed and brake pad wear sensors.
24. Remove air deflector and front fascia extensions.
25. Disconnect air inlet hose from air pump.
26. Disconnect front brake lines from frame rail and rear brake lines at rear of engine frame.
27. Disconnect A/C pressure sensor.
28. Disconnect A/C suction and discharge

lines from compressor and secure to cooling fan.

29. Remove intermediate shaft pinch bolt then remove steering gear from intermediate shaft.
30. Disconnect electrical connector from oxygen sensor.
31. Remove and discard engine oil cooler quick-connect fittings from oil filter adapter with oil lines still attached and position aside. **Quick-connect fittings must be replaced whenever they are removed from adapter.**
32. Remove brace between oil pan and transaxle, then remove torque converter cover.
33. Mark flywheel to torque orientation then remove mounting bolts.
34. Lower vehicle onto engine support tool No. J-39580, four suitable jack stands.
35. Remove righthand side engine mount to engine mount bracket retaining nut.
36. Remove lefthand transaxle mount to transaxle mount bracket retaining nut.
37. Secure front hoist pads to vehicle.
38. Remove six body to frame mounting bolts.
39. Slowly raise vehicle ensuring powertrain and subframe clear all wiring, hoses and lines.
40. Drain engine oil into suitable container.
41. Remove heater pipes.
42. Disconnect intermediate hose from air valve 1 and retaining nut on intermedi-

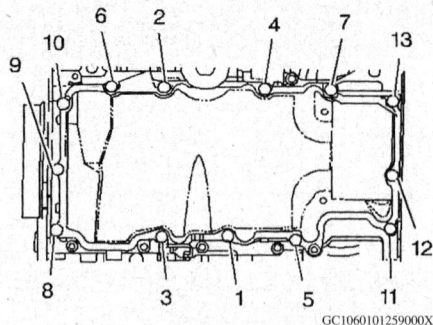

Fig. 1   Oil pan bolt tightening sequence

GC1060101259000X

ate hose to air valve 2.
43. Remove coil ground retaining nut from righthand cylinder head.
44. Disconnect engine harness from engine.
45. Disconnect power steering lines from steering pump and reservoir.
46. Remove power steering return line retaining bolt from cylinder head.
47. Remove righthand side engine mount bracket mounting bolts then the bracket.
48. Remove front and rear transaxle braces.
49. Remove engine to transaxle center

brace mounting bolts.
50. Install engine lift chain to engine lift brackets and attach to suitable engine lift devise.
51. Remove front engine mount to engine frame retaining nut.
52. Remove engine to transaxle mounting bolts.
53. Raise engine from transaxle and subframe.
54. Reverse procedure to install.

OIL PAN
REPLACE

1. Raise and support vehicle.
2. Drain oil into suitable container.
3. Remove catalytic converter to exhaust manifold pipe mounting bolts. Do not reuse seal.
4. Remove exhaust manifold pipe.
5. Disconnect oil level sensor electrical connector, then remove sensor.
6. Remove oil pan mounting bolts, then the pan. Oil pan gasket is reusable unless damaged.
7. Reverse procedure to install. Using sequence, **Fig. 1, torque** oil pan mounting bolts to 89 inch lbs.

TIGHTENING SPECIFICATIONS

Year	Component	Torque, Ft. Lbs.
2005	Engine Left Bracket To Cylinder Head	35
	Engine Lift Bracket To Water Crossover	17
	Engine Mount	52
	Engine Mount Bracket	37
	Engine To Transaxle	55
	Frame Mounting Bolt	141
	Oil Pan	①
	Transaxle Mount	37

① — Refer to "Oil Pan, Replace" for tightening sequence and specification.

Rear Suspension

NOTE: On Air Bag Equipped Models, Refer To "Air Bag System Precautions" Located In The Front Of This Manual For System Disarming & Arming Procedures.

NOTE: Refer To "Computer Relearn Procedures" Located In The Front Of This Manual When Battery Power To The Computer Has Been Interrupted.

INDEX

DESCRIPTION

The rear suspension components include independent control arms, springs, and struts for each rear wheel. This allows vertical movement of one rear wheel without any effect on the other. A suspension adjustment link on each arm provides for toe adjustment and minimal alignment variation during suspension movement. A stabilizer shaft minimizes body roll.

The bottom of each shock absorber mounts to the suspension knuckle. The top of each shock attaches to a reinforced body area. These shocks are non-adjustable and cannot be refilled. Replace any shock absorber if it suffers from loss of resistance, physical damage or fluid leakage.

Some models are equipped with Electronic Level Control (ELC) which utilizes air adjustable shocks and maintains the rear trim height under a variety of load conditions.

A single unit sealed hub and bearing is bolted to the rear knuckle and does not require wheel bearing adjustments or periodic maintenance. There is an integral speed sensor ring on the inboard side of the bearing for anti-lock brake functions. The wheel speed sensor is incorporated within the knuckle.

HUB & BEARING
REPLACE
Drum Brakes

1. Raise and support rear of vehicle.
2. Remove wheel assembly and brake drum. **Do not hammer on drum as bearing damage may occur.**
3. Disconnect ABS sensor wire.
4. Remove four hub and bearing assembly mounting bolts. **These four bolts also support brake assembly. When removing these bolts, support brake assembly with suitable wire. Do not let brake line or ABS electrical wire support weight.**

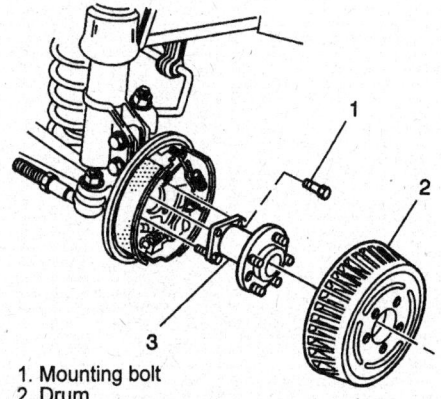

1. Mounting bolt
2. Drum
3. Hub & bearing assembly

GC2030100162000X

Fig. 1 Hub & bearing assembly

5. Remove hub and bearing assembly from axle, **Fig. 1.**
6. Reverse procedure to install. Tighten mounting bolts and wheel lug nuts.

Disc Brakes

1. Raise and support rear of vehicle.
2. Remove wheel and tire assembly.
3. Remove caliper and position aside.
4. Remove rotor, then disconnect wheel speed sensor electrical connector.
5. Remove four hub and bearing assembly mounting bolts.
6. Remove hub and bearing assembly, then the brake shield.
7. Clean control arm face and bore to remove any debris.
8. Reverse procedure to install. Tighten mounting bolts and wheel lug nuts.

STRUT
REPLACE

1. Raise and support vehicle, then remove tire and wheel.
2. Support lower control arm with suitable jack stand.
3. Disconnect air line from strut.

4. Remove strut lower mounting bolts, **Fig. 2.**
5. Remove luggage compartment trim to access strut tower mounting nuts, **Fig. 3.**
6. Remove strut tower mounting nuts and upper reinforcement, then the strut from vehicle.
7. Reverse procedure to install. Tighten mounting nuts and wheel lug nuts.

COIL SPRING
REPLACE

1. Raise and support vehicle.
2. Remove rear wheels and tires.
3. Support control arm with suitable jack stand.
4. Disconnect air line from shock.
5. Remove strut to control arm mounting bolts.
6. Remove cotter pin and slotted hex nut from tie rod.
7. Separate tie rod from lower control arm using linkage puller tool No. J24319-B, or equivalent.
8. Slowly lower control arm until it bottoms on support assembly.
9. Pry under lower spring insulator and remove spring with insulator.
10. Remove upper insulator by pulling downward.
11. Reverse procedure to install.

BALL JOINT INSPECTION

The ball joint has a visual wear indicator. Inspecting the condition of the ball joint is a simple procedure but must be followed accurately to prevent unrequired ball joint replacement.

The vehicle must be supported by the wheels during inspection to ensure vehicle weight is properly loading the ball joints.

The ball joint is inspected for wear by visual observation alone. Wear is indicated by retraction of the ½ inch diameter nipple into the ball joint cover (the ball joint grease fitting is threaded into this nipple).

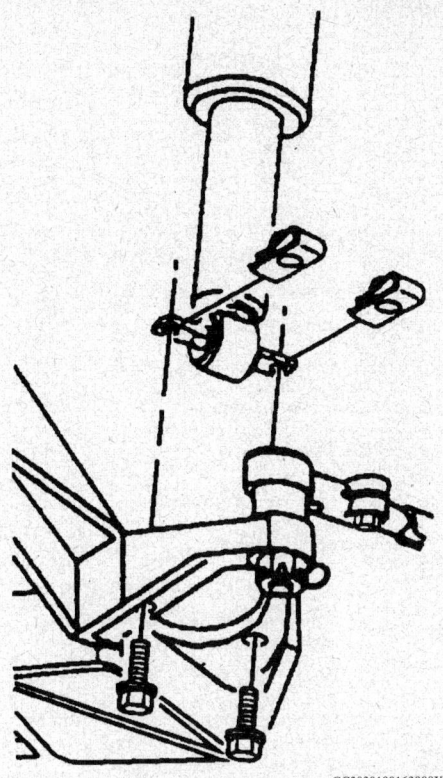

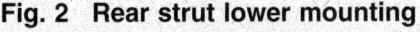

Fig. 2 **Rear strut lower mounting**

The nipple protrudes .050 inch beyond the surface of the ball joint cover on a new unworn joint. Normal wear will result in the surface of this nipple retracting very slowly inward. The ball joint should be replaced if the nipple is flush or below the cover surface, **Fig. 4**.

Ball stud tightness in the knuckle boss should also be inspected when inspecting the ball joint. This may be done by shaking the wheel and feeling for movement of the stud end or castellated nut at the knuckle boss.

Inspecting the fastener tightness at the castellated nut is an alternative method of inspecting (a loose nut can indicate a bent stud or an "opened up" hole in the knuckle boss). If worn, the ball joint and knuckle must be replaced.

If the ball joint is separated from the knuckle for suspension service, the ball joint seal should be inspected for damage. A damaged seal will cause joint failure. If seal damage is found the ball joint should be replaced.

BALL JOINT
REPLACE

The ball joint cannot be serviced separately, refer to "Control Arm, Replace" for replacement procedure.

CONTROL ARM
REPLACE

1. Raise and support vehicle, then re-

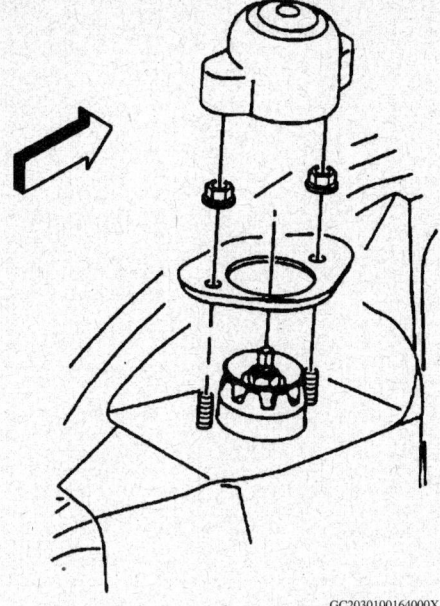

Fig. 3 **Strut tower mounting nuts**

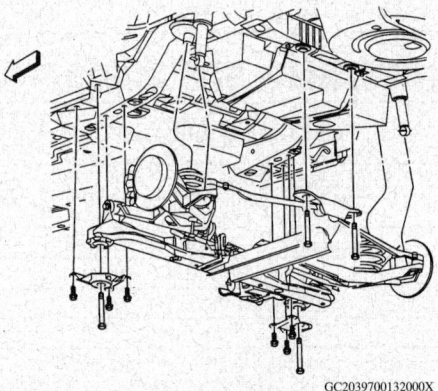

Fig. 5 **Rear suspension support assembly removal**

move rear tires and wheels.
2. Remove exhaust system as required.
3. Remove coil springs as outlined under "Coil Spring, Replace."
4. Remove rear brake calipers from control arms, then parking brake cables from calipers.
5. Disconnect electrical connectors from wiring harness.
6. Disconnect Electronic Level Control (ELC) electrical connector and vent hose.
7. Remove ELC air tube from compressor.
8. Support rear suspension support assembly with suitable jack.
9. Remove three bolts per side securing support assembly brackets to vehicle body, **Fig. 5**.
10. Remove front and rear suspension support assembly bolts, then support assembly.
11. On lefthand control arm, remove Elec-

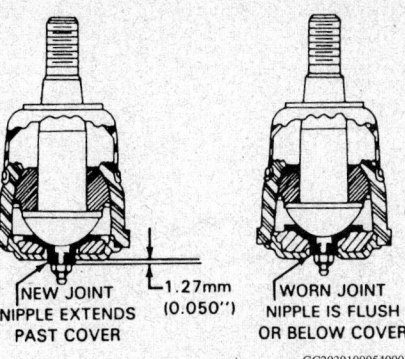

Fig. 4 **Ball joint inspection**

tronic Level Control height sensor.
12. Remove stabilizer link bolts and nuts.
13. Remove ABS electrical connectors.
14. Remove hub and bearing as outlined under "Hub & Bearing, Replace."
15. Remove bolt and nut securing control arm to rear suspension support assembly, then the control arm.
16. Reverse procedure to install.

TIE ROD
REPLACE

1. Raise and support vehicle.
2. Remove wheel assembly, cotter key and castle nut, **Fig. 6**.
3. Disconnect outer tie rod/adjustment from lower control arm or knuckle using steering linkage puller tool No. J24319-01, or equivalent. **Do not use a wedge when disconnecting tie rod/adjustment from lower control arm or knuckle since seal damage will occur.**
4. Remove rod/link assembly from lower control arm.
5. Reverse procedure to install, noting the following:
   a. Tighten link retaining nut.
   b. Tighten ball stud castellated nut.
   c. Install cotter pin retaining castellated nut, tightening nut to insert pin through hole in stud. **Do not loosen nut to align slots with hole.**

STABILIZER BAR
REPLACE

1. Raise and support vehicle.
2. Remove rear wheels and tires.
3. Disconnect ELC height sensor link from control arm.
4. Remove stabilizer shaft support bolt, nut, retainer, sleeve and insulators from lower control arm or knuckle bracket, **Fig. 7**.
5. Remove bushing clip bolt.
6. Bend open end of support assembly downward.
7. Remove stabilizer shaft and bushings.
8. Reverse procedure to install.

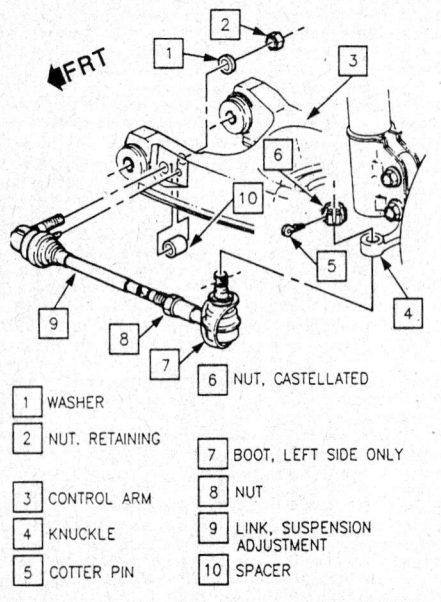

1. WASHER
2. NUT, RETAINING
3. CONTROL ARM
4. KNUCKLE
5. COTTER PIN
6. NUT, CASTELLATED
7. BOOT, LEFT SIDE ONLY
8. NUT
9. LINK, SUSPENSION ADJUSTMENT
10. SPACER

GC2039100053000X

Fig. 6 Tie rod/adjustment link installation

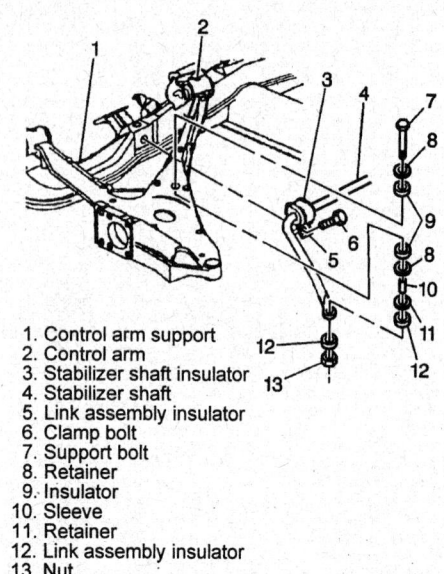

1. Control arm support
2. Control arm
3. Stabilizer shaft insulator
4. Stabilizer shaft
5. Link assembly insulator
6. Clamp bolt
7. Support bolt
8. Retainer
9. Insulator
10. Sleeve
11. Retainer
12. Link assembly insulator
13. Nut

GC2030100165000X

Fig. 7 Stabilizer bar & bushing assembly

TIGHTENING SPECIFICATIONS

Year	Component	Torque/Ft. Lbs.
BONNEVILLE & LESABRE		
2001–05	Adjustment Link Pinch Bolt	38
	Adjustment Link To Suspension Support	67
	Control Arm Nuts	78
	Hub & Bearing Bolts	52
	Rear Body Mount Bolts	38
	Rear Suspension Support To Body Front Bolts	141
	Rear Suspension Support To Body Rear Bolts	191
	Stabilizer Shaft Clamp Bolt	24
	Stabilizer Shaft Link Nut	11
	Strut To Control Arm Bolts	18
	Strut Tower Mounting Nut	15
	Wheel Lug Nuts	100
PARK AVENUE		
2001–05	Adjustment Link Pinch Bolt	36
	Adjustment Link Retaining Bolt	67
	Body Mount Bolt	38
	Control Arm Nut	78
	Hub Mounting Bolts	52
	Shock To Control Arm Bolts	18
	Shock Tower Mounting Nut	15
	Stabilizer Shaft Clamp Bolt	24
	Stabilizer Shaft Link Bolt	10
	Suspension Support Assembly To Body Front Bolts	141
	Suspension Support Assembly To Body Rear Bolts	141
	Suspension Support Assembly To Bracket Bolts	63
	Tie Rod Pinch Bolt	36
	Wheel Lug Nuts	100

NOTE: On Air Bag Equipped Models, Refer To "Air Bag System Precautions" Located In The Front Of This Manual For System Disarming & Arming Procedures.

NOTE: Refer To "Computer Relearn Procedures" Located In The Front Of This Manual When Battery Power To The Computer Has Been Interrupted.

INDEX

PRECAUTIONS
Air Bag Systems

Refer to "Air Bag System Precautions" in the front of this manual for system disarming and arming procedures.

Battery Ground Cable

Prior to service, disconnect battery ground cable and isolate as required.

DESCRIPTION

The front suspension is of the McPherson design, **Fig. 1.** The control arm pivots from the cradle and is mounted in rubber bushings. The upper end of the strut is isolated by a rubber mount and contains a bearing to allow for rotation. The lower end of the steering knuckle pivots on a ball joint riveted to the control arm. The ball joint is mounted to the steering knuckle with a castle nut and cotter pin. **Do not use a hammer to remove components from the steering knuckle.**

HUB & BEARING
REPLACE

1. Place transaxle selector lever in Park.
2. Raise and support vehicle, then remove tire and wheel assembly.
3. Clean and lubricate drive axle threads.
4. Insert a suitable drift into caliper and rotor to prevent assembly from rotating, then remove hub nut and washer. Discard hub nut.
5. Remove caliper bracket mounting bolts, caliper and bracket assembly and rotor. Secure assembly aside taking care not to stretch or damage brake hose.
6. Disconnect ABS front wheel speed sensor connector and unclip connector from dust shield.

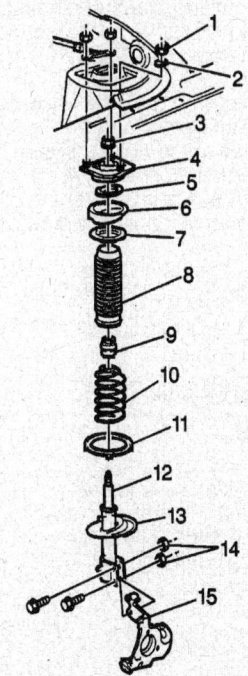

1. Control arm support
2. Control arm
3. Stabilizer shaft insulator
4. Stabilizer shaft
5. Link assembly insulator
6. Clamp bolt
7. Support bolt
8. Retainer
9. Insulator
10. Sleeve
11. Retainer
12. Link assembly insulator
13. Nut

GC2020100301000X

Fig. 1 Exploded view of front suspension

7. Remove hub and bearing retaining bolts and dust shield, **Fig. 2.**
8. Separate hub and bearing from drive axle using front hub spindle removal tool No. J28733-B, or equivalent, **Fig. 3.**
9. Clean face and bore of knuckle to remove any debris before assembly.

10. Reverse procedure to install, noting the following:
   a. Fill area between seal and bearing assembly with GM lubricant part No. 12377985, or equivalent.
   b. **Do not use old hub nut. Always install a new one.**

BALL JOINT INSPECTION

Ball joints must be replaced if any looseness is detected or ball joint seal is cut or damaged.

To inspect ball joints, raise the front of the vehicle, allowing suspension to hang freely. Grasp the tire at the top and bottom, then move the top of the tire in an in-and-out motion. Inspect for any horizontal movement of the knuckle relative to the control arm. If the ball stud is disconnected from the knuckle and looseness is detected or if the ball stud can be twisted using finger pressure, replace the ball joint.

Ball stud tightness in the knuckle boss should also be inspected. This may be done by shaking the wheel and feeling for movement of the stud end or nut at the knuckle boss. Worn or damaged ball joints and knuckles must be replaced.

BALL JOINT
REPLACE

The ball joint is serviced only with the control arm and cannot be serviced separately. Refer to "Control Arm, Replace" for replacement procedure.

STRUT
REPLACE

1. **On models equipped with CCR,** disconnect CCR connector.
2. **On all models,** remove three strut mount to body bolts or nuts.
3. Raise and support vehicle.
4. Remove wheel and tire.

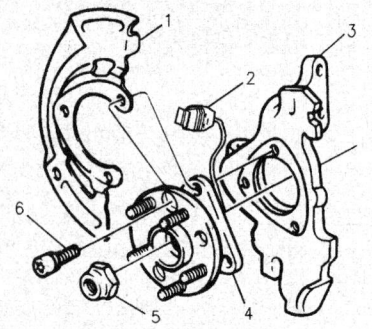

1 DUST SHIELD	4 HUB AND BEARING
2 WHEEL SPEED	5 NUT, DRIVE AXLE
SENSOR CONNECTOR	6 RETAINING BOLT
3 STEERING KNUCKLE	

GC2029300228000X

Fig. 2 Hub & bearing assembly

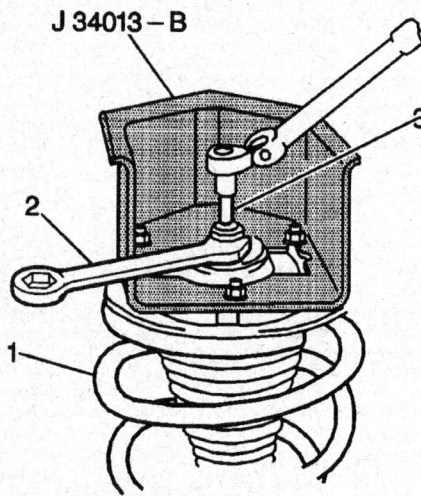

1. Coil spring
2. 24 MM wrench
3. Driver tool

GC2020100305000X

Fig. 5 Coil spring compression

5. Remove ABS front wheel speed sensor connector.
6. Remove speed sensor bracket from strut.
7. Remove brake line bracket from strut.
8. Retain knuckle in position to prevent damage to ball joint and/or drive axle.
9. Remove strut to knuckle bolts.
10. Remove strut from vehicle.
11. Reverse procedure to install. Avoid cracking or chipping spring coating when handling front suspension coil spring.

STRUT SERVICE

1. Remove strut as outlined under "Strut, Replace."
2. Mount strut in compressor tool No. J34013-B and holding fixture tool No. J3289-20, or equivalents, **Fig. 4.**
3. Rotate compressor forcing screw until spring compresses slightly, **Fig. 5.**

---

1. J-28733
2. TURN FORCING SCREW UNTIL AXLE SPLINES ARE JUST LOOSE

GC2029100117000X

Fig. 3 Separating drive axle from hub

4. Hold damper shaft from rotating and remove nut from top of strut assembly, **Fig. 6.**
5. Guide damper shaft from assembly using alignment rod tool No. J34013-38, or equivalent, **Fig. 7.**
6. Loosen compressor forcing screw while guiding damper shaft from assembly. Continue to loosen nut until strut damper and spring can be removed.
7. Reverse procedure to assemble, noting the following:
   a. When assembling spring, flat on upper spring seat must face outward 90° from centerline of vehicle or when mounted in strut compressor.
   b. Seat faces in same direction as steering knuckle mounting flange.

CONTROL ARM
REPLACE

1. Raise and support vehicle.
2. Remove wheel and tire.
3. Disconnect stabilizer link to control arm bolt, **Figs. 8 and 9.**
4. Remove cotter pin and loosen nut from ball joint stud.
5. Remove ball joint from steering knuckle using a suitable ball joint separator tool.
6. Remove control arm mounting bolts, then the control arm from the frame, **Figs. 10 and 11.**
7. Reverse procedure to install, noting the following:
   a. Install control arm to frame and loosely install mounting bolts, washers and nuts. **Do not tighten control arm nuts at this time.** Weight of vehicle must be supported by control arms so that vehicle design trim heights are obtained before tightening control arm mounting bolts.
   b. Install all remaining control arm hardware, then lower vehicle to ground.
   c. Inspect trim height.
   d. Tighten control arm nuts.

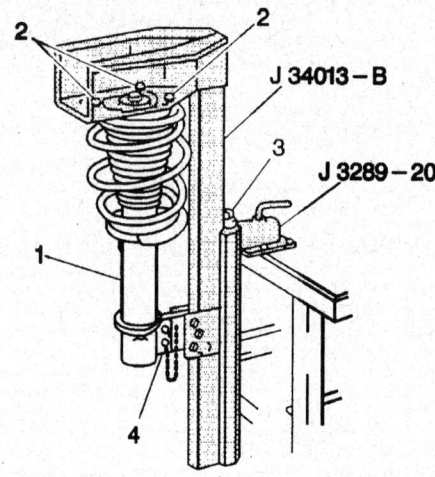

J 34013 - B
J 3289 - 20

1. Strut
2. Nuts
3. Strut compressor
4. Locking pins

GC2020100304000X

Fig. 4 Strut disassembly

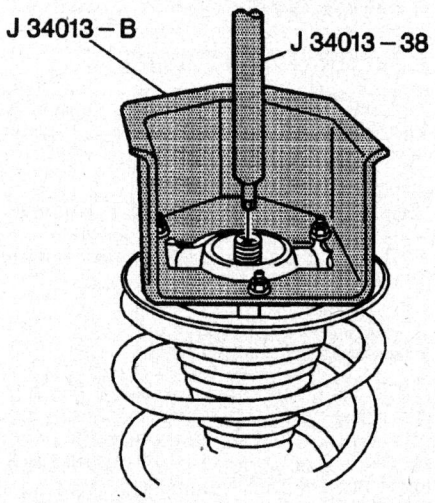

J 34013 - B   J 34013 - 38

GC2020100306000X

Fig. 6 Strut shaft nut removal

STABILIZER BAR
REPLACE

1. Raise and support vehicle and place jack stands under cradle. **Vehicle weight should not be placed on control arms.**
2. Remove wheel and tire assembly.
3. Install drive axle boot protectors.
4. Remove nuts, washers, bushings and bolt securing stabilizer shaft to each control arm, **Fig. 12.**
5. Remove stabilizer bar mounting bolts, two bolts from each side.
6. Disconnect tie rods from steering knuckles.
7. Remove exhaust pipe between exhaust manifold and catalytic converter.
8. Rotate righthand side strut assembly completely to left.
9. Slide stabilizer bar to righthand over steering knuckle and pull downward on

---

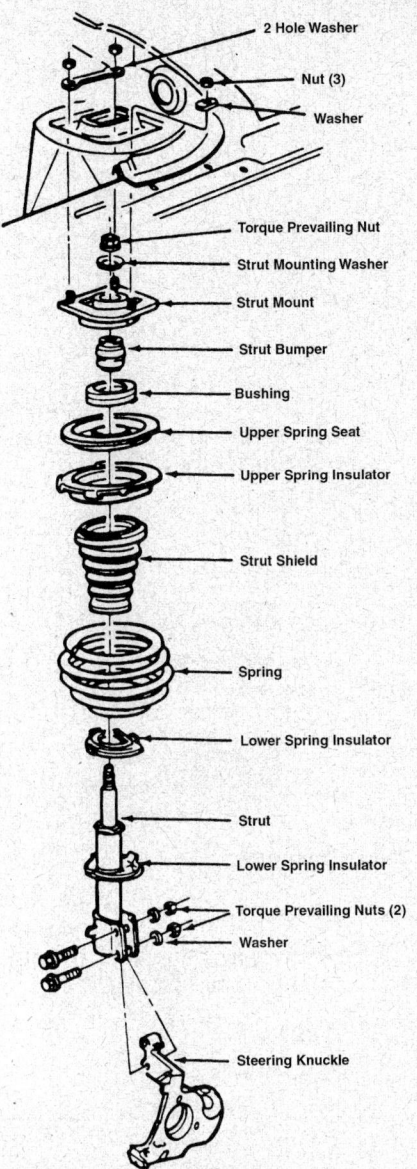

Fig. 7 Exploded view of strut assembly

lefthand side until stabilizer bar clears cradle, **Fig. 13**.
10. Reverse procedure to install.

POWER STEERING GEAR
REPLACE

1. Ensure front wheels are in straight-ahead position.
2. Lock steering column using lock pin tool No. J42640, or equivalent, **Fig. 14**.
3. Raise and support vehicle with weight resting on suspension.
4. Remove front tire and wheel assemblies.

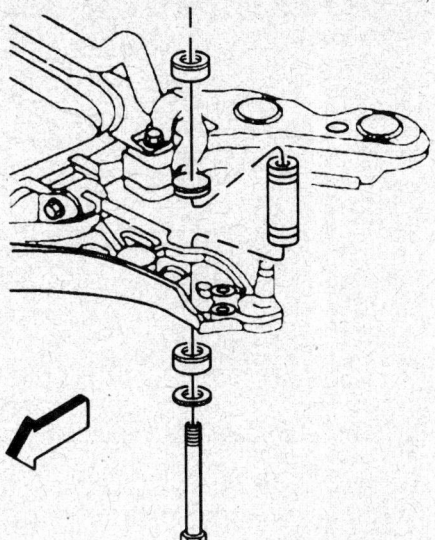

Fig. 8 Stabilizer link to control arm bolt. Park Avenue

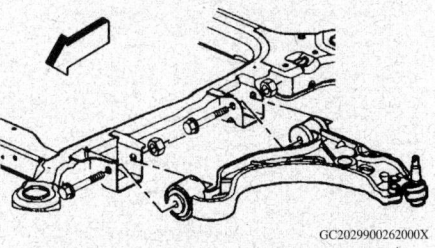

Fig. 10 Lower control arm replacement. Park Avenue

5. Remove steering gear heat shield.
6. Disconnect intermediate shaft from steering gear stub shaft.
7. Disconnect both tie rod ends from steering knuckles using separator tool No. J24319-B, or equivalent.
8. Remove line retainers and disconnect hydraulic lines from steering gear.
9. Disconnect speed sensitive steering electrical connectors from steering gear.
10. Remove steering gear attaching bolts, **Fig. 15**.
11. Remove steering gear from vehicle by sliding out of side.
12. Reverse procedure to install.

POWER STEERING PUMP
REPLACE

1. Remove air cleaner if required.
2. Mark running direction with suitable felt pen or chalk, then remove accessory drive belt.
3. Raise and support vehicle.
4. Position a suitable drain pan under power steering fluid lines at pump.
5. Disconnect fluid lines and electrical connectors from pump.

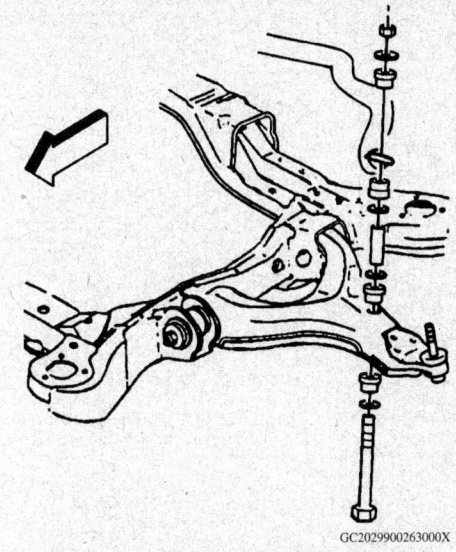

Fig. 9 Stabilizer shaft to control arm bolt. Bonneville & LeSabre

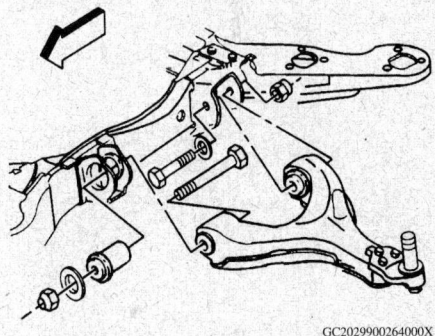

Fig. 11 Lower control arm replacement. Bonneville & LeSabre

6. If required, disconnect righthand outer tie rod end from steering knuckle using tie rod removal tool No. J24319-B, or equivalent.
7. **On Park Avenue models,** remove pump mounting bolts, then the pump from underneath vehicle.
8. **On all models,** lower vehicle.
9. **On Bonneville and LeSabre models,** remove pump mounting bolts, then the power steering pump.
10. **On all models,** reverse procedure to install, noting the following:
   a. If new pump does not include pulley, remove pulley from old pump using removal tool No. J25034-C, or equivalent, then install onto new pump using installer tool No. J25033-C, or equivalent. Ensure axial tolerance on pump shaft meets specifications, **Fig. 16**.
   b. Ensure all electrical connectors and wiring are properly routed to avoid pinching.
   c. Fill and bleed power steering system.

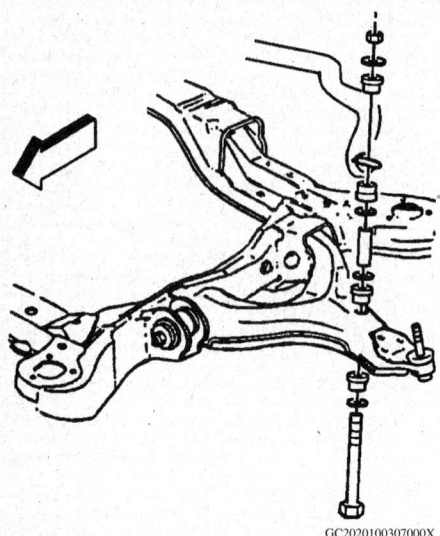

Fig. 12 Stabilizer bar bushing assembly

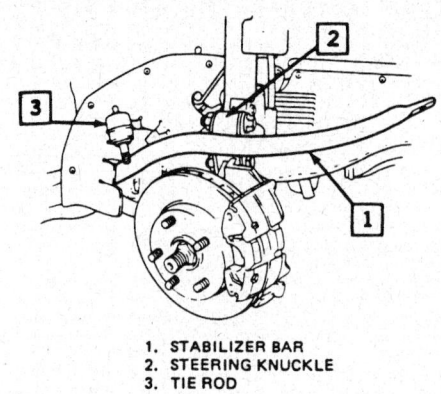

1. STABILIZER BAR
2. STEERING KNUCKLE
3. TIE ROD

Fig. 13 Stabilizer bar replacement

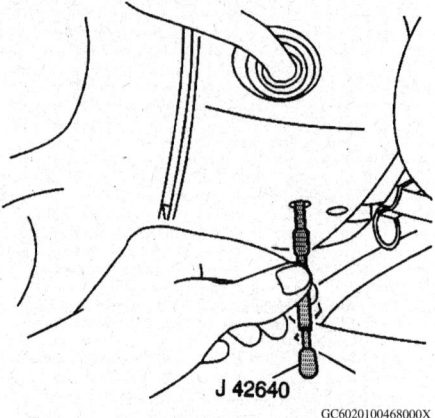

J 42640

Fig. 14 Steering column locked in straight-ahead position

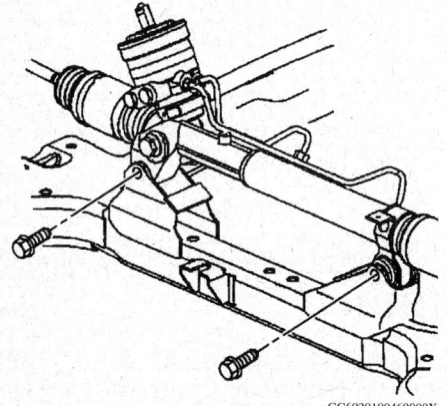

Fig. 15 Steering gear replacement

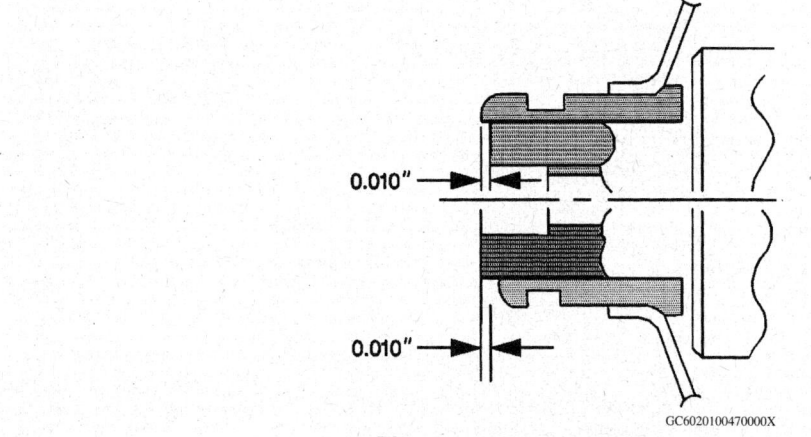

0.010"

0.010"

Fig. 16 Power steering pump pulley axial installation

TIGHTENING SPECIFICATIONS

Year	Component	Torque/Ft. Lbs.
BONNEVILLE & LESABRE		
2001–05	Ball Joint To Knuckle	50
	Brake Bracket To Strut	13
	Brake Caliper To Knuckle	38
	Brake Caliper Bracket To Knuckle	136
	Control Arm Bolts	117
	Control Arm Front Nut	93
	Cross Brace Assembly Through-Bolts	27
	Drive Axle Nut	118
	Hub And Bearing To Knuckle	70
	Inner Tie Rod	74
	Intermediate Shaft Pinch Bolt	33
	Power Steering Gear Hose Fittings To Pump And Steering Gear	20
	Power Steering Gear Mounting Bolts	48
	Power Steering Inlet/Outlet Hose Retainer Bolts	53①
	Power Steering Outer Hose Retaining Clamp Nuts	15
	Power Steering Pump Mounting Bolts	20
	Rack And Pinion Adjuster Plug Nut	50
	Rack And Pinion Cylinder End Fittings	20
	Stabilizer Shaft Bracket Bolt	35
	Stabilizer Shaft Link Nut	13
	Strut Mount Nut	55
	Strut Mount To Body Nuts	35
	Strut To Knuckle Nuts	136
	Tie Rod Locknut	50
	Tie Rod To Knuckle Castle Nut	35–52
	Wheel Speed Sensor Bracket To Strut	13
	Wheel Lug Nut	100

TIGHTENING
SPECIFICATIONS—Continued

Year	Component	Torque/Ft. Lbs.
PARK AVENUE		
2001–05	Ball Joint Mounting Nuts	50
	Ball Joint To Knuckle	50
	Brake Bracket To Strut	13
	Brake Caliper To Knuckle	38
	Control Arm Front Nut	93
	Control Arm Rear Bolt	117
	Cross Brace Assembly Through-Bolts	27
	Drive Axle Nut	107
	Hub & Bearing To Knuckle	70
	Intermediate Steering Shaft Pinch Bolt	35
	Outer Tie Rod Retaining Nut (2000)	35②
	Outer Tie Rod Retaining Nut (2001–04)	55
	Power Steering Gear Hose Fittings To Pump & Steering Gear	20
	Power Steering Inlet/Outlet Hose Retainer Bolts	53①
	Power Steering Outer Hose Retaining Clamp Nuts	15
	Power Steering Pump Mounting Bolts	20
	Stabilizer Shaft Bracket Bolt (2000)	30
	Stabilizer Shaft Bracket Bolt (2001–04)	35
	Stabilizer Shaft Link Bolt	11
	Stabilizer Shaft Link Nut (2000)	13
	Steering Gear Mounting Bolts	48
	Strut Mount Nut	55
	Strut Mount To Body Nuts	35
	Strut To Knuckle Nuts	136
	Tie Rod End To Knuckle Nut	35
	Wheel Lug Nuts	100
	Wheel Speed Sensor Bracket To Strut	13

① — Inch lbs.
② — Torque nut for cotter pin alignment to 52 ft. lbs., maximum.

Wheel Alignment

INDEX

PRECAUTIONS

Air Bag Systems

Refer to "Air Bag System Precautions" in the front of this manual for system disarming and arming procedures.

PRELIMINARY INSPECTION

1. Inspect tires for proper inflation and similar tread wear.
2. Inspect hub and bearing for excessive wear. Repair as required.
3. Inspect ball joints and tie rod ends for excessive looseness.
4. Measure wheel and tire runout.
5. Inspect vehicle ride height.
6. Inspect rack and pinion for looseness at frame.
7. Ensure proper strut operation.
8. Inspect control arm bushings.
9. Inspect stabilizer shaft for loose or missing components.
10. Inspect suspension and steering components for damage. Replace as required.

FRONT WHEEL ALIGNMENT

Caster

1. Loosen cross brace assembly through-bolts, **Fig. 1**.
2. Remove inboard strut nuts, then the brace assembly.
3. Remove remaining nut over oval strut mounting hole.
4. Lift front of vehicle by body to separate strut from inner wheelhouse.
5. Remove two guide pins and file to make slotted holes.
6. File excess metal to elongate original holes, then paint exposed metal with primer.
7. Lower front of vehicle.
8. Place cross brace assembly on inboard strut studs and install strut attaching nuts.
9. Set caster to specifications by moving top of strut forward or backward. A .040

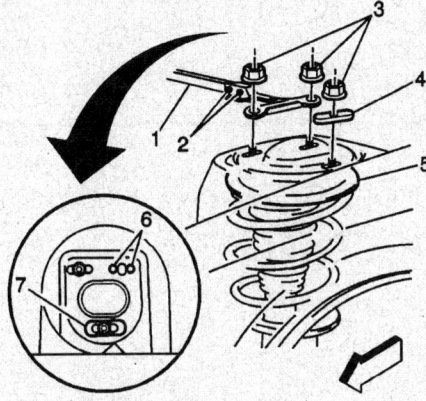

1. Strut housing tie bar
2. Through bolts
3. Nuts
4. Washers
5. Strut
6. New drilled holes
7. Washers

GC2040100169000X

Fig. 1   Cross brace removal

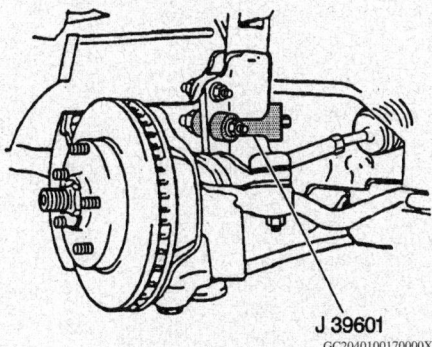

J 39601
GC2040100170000X

Fig. 2   Camber adjustment tool installation

inch position change at the tower is approximately equal to a .1° caster change.
10. Tighten strut attaching nuts and cross brace bar through-bolts.

Camber

1. Loosen both strut to knuckle attaching nuts.
2. Install camber adjusting tool No. J39601, or equivalent, **Fig. 2**.

3. Inspect camber, and if it does not meet specifications, proceed as follows:
   a. Raise and support vehicle, then remove tire and wheel.
   b. Drive upper and lower bolt and nut out of strut and knuckle. **Do not turn bolts. This will damage serrated shoulders.**
   c. Separate strut from knuckle.
   d. File inner metal plate to outside plate diameter using a suitable round file or die grinder.
   e. File excess metal to create slotted holes.
   f. Paint exposed metal with suitable rust preventive paint or primer.
   g. Connect strut to knuckle. **Do not tighten bolts just yet.**
   h. Install camber adjusting tool No. J39601, or equivalent, to bottom strut bolt.
   i. Tighten upper strut to knuckle nut.
   j. Remove adjusting tool, then tighten lower strut to knuckle attaching nuts.
   k. Inspect camber once again. Adjust as required.

Toe

1. Loosen locknuts on both inner tie rods, **Fig. 3**.
2. Adjust toe to specifications by rotating inner tie rod.
3. Tighten locknuts.
4. Inspect toe setting once again. Adjust as required.

REAR WHEEL ALIGNMENT

When inspecting rear wheel alignment, the electronic leveling system must have the superlift struts inflated with residual pressure only.

Place a weight in luggage compartment. Turn ignition On and move transmission selector from Park to Reverse position and back. This will activate the compressor. Turn ignition Off and remove weight from luggage compartment. Wait 30 seconds for the system to exhaust. Roll vehicle forward one complete wheel rotation. Jounce vehicle before inspecting alignment.

Camber

Rear camber is not adjustable. If rear camber does not meet specifications inspect for worn or damaged suspension components and replace as required.

Toe

Toe adjustment is made by loosening the locknut at tie rod end and turning inner tie rod to set toe to specifications.

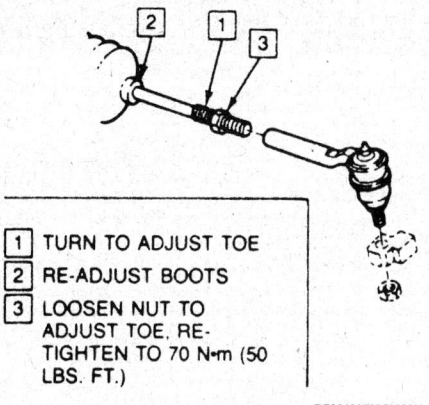

1 TURN TO ADJUST TOE
2 RE-ADJUST BOOTS
3 LOOSEN NUT TO ADJUST TOE. RE-TIGHTEN TO 70 N·m (50 LBS. FT.)

GC2049100059000X

Fig. 3 Toe adjustment

CAMARO & FIREBIRD

INDEX OF SERVICE OPERATIONS

Specifications

GENERAL ENGINE SPECIFICATIONS

Year	Engine		Fuel System	Bore & Stroke	Comp-ression Ratio	Net Brake H.P. @ RPM②	Maximum Torque	Normal Oil Pressure, psi
	Liter	VIN Code①						
2001–02	3800	K	SFI	3.80 x 3.40	9.4	200 @ 5200	225 @ 4000	⑤
	5.7L⑥	G	SFI	3.90 x 3.62	10.1	310 @ 5200	340 @ 4000	③
	5.7L④	G	SFI	3.90 x 3.62	10.1	325 @ 5200	350 @ 4000	③

SFI — Sequential Fuel Injection
① — The eighth digit of the VIN denotes engine code.
② — Ratings are net-as installed in vehicle.

③ — Minimum, 6 psi @ 1000 RPM; 18 psi @ 2000 RPM; 24 psi @ 4000 RPM.
④ — Models w/ram air.

⑤ — Minimum of 60 psi @ 1850 RPM w/10W-30 motor oil.
⑥ — Models less ram air.

TUNE UP SPECIFICATIONS

Year & Engine Liter (VIN Code)①	Spark Plug Gap	Ignition Timing BTDC				Curb Idle Speed②		Fast Idle Speed		Fuel Pump Pressure, psi	Valve Clearance, Inch
		Firing Order Fig.③	Man. Trans.	Auto. Trans.	Mark	Man. Trans.	Auto. Trans.	Man. Trans.	Auto. Trans.		
2001–02											
3800 (K)	.060	⑥	④	④	⑧	⑤	⑤	⑤	⑤	48–55	⑦
5.7L (G)	.060	⑨	④	④	⑧	⑤	⑤	⑤	⑤	55–60	⑦

BTDC — Before Top Dead Center
D — Drive
N — Neutral
① — The eighth digit of Vehicle Identification Number (VIN) denotes engine code.
② — When adjusting idle speed, set parking brake & block drive wheels.
③ — Before disconnecting wires from distributor cap, determine location

of No. 1 wire in cap, as distributor position may have been altered from that outlined at the end of this chart.
④ — Computer controlled, no adjustment.
⑤ — Idle speed is controlled by an Idle Speed Control (ISC) motor, Idle Air Control (IAC) valve or Idle Load Compensator (ILC).

⑥ — Cylinder numbering lefthand to righthand as viewed from front of vehicle: Front bank, 1, 3, 5; rear bank, 2, 4, 6. Firing order: 1-6-5-4-3-2. Refer to **Fig. A,** for spark plug wire connections at coil unit.
⑦ — Equipped w/hydraulic lifters.
⑧ — Equipped w/crankshaft sensor.
⑨ — Refer to **Fig. B,** for cylinder numbering. Firing order: 1-8-7-2-6-5-4-3.

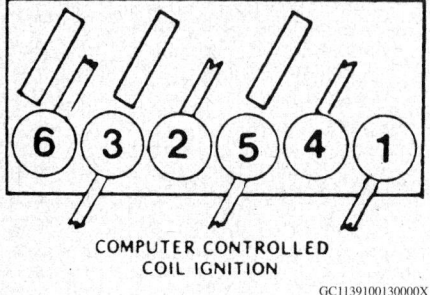

COMPUTER CONTROLLED COIL IGNITION

GC1139100130000X

Fig. A

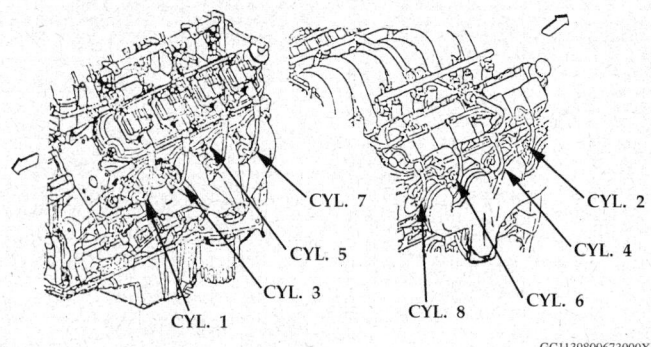

CYL. 7
CYL. 5
CYL. 3
CYL. 1
CYL. 2
CYL. 4
CYL. 6
CYL. 8

GC1139800673000X

Fig. B

FRONT WHEEL ALIGNMENT SPECIFICATIONS

| Year | Caster Angle, Degrees | | Camber Angle, Degrees | | Total Toe, Degrees | Ball Joint Wear | |
	Limits	Desired	Limits	Desired		Lower	Upper
2001–02	+4.5 to +5.5	+5	-.1 to +.9	+.4	-.2 to +.2	②	①

① — Deflection on dial indicator, when positioned against wheel rim, should not exceed .125 inch while moving top of wheel in & out.

② — While reading dial indicator, pry between lower control arm & steering knuckle. Vertical movement should not exceed .046875 inches.

REAR WHEEL ALIGNMENT SPECIFICATIONS

| Year | Camber Angle, Degrees | | Total Toe, Degrees | | Thrust Angle |
	Limits	Desired	Limits	Desired	
2001–02	-.6 to +.6	0	-.3 to +.3	0	-.15 to +.15

VEHICLE RIDE HEIGHT SPECIFICATIONS

Model	Year	Body Style	Manufacturer's Original Tire Size	Measurement Points & Specifications ① ③					
				Front			Rear		
				Dim.	Specification		Dim.	Specification	
					Inches	mm		Inches	mm
Camaro & Firebird	2001–02	All	②	A	32.62	828	B	17.25	438
				C	8.00	204	D	8.19	208

A Dim. — Measurement From Front Wheel Center to Check Point On Rocker Panel

B Dim. — Measurement From Rear Wheel Center to Check Point On Rocker Panel

C Dim. — Ground to Rocker Panel, Front

D Dim. — Ground to Rocker Panel, Rear

Dim. — Dimension

① — ±.39 in (10 mm) front to rear & side to side.

② — See door sticker or inside of glove box for manufacturer's original tire size specifications.

③ — Measurement is with fuel, radiator coolant and engine oil full, spare tire, jack, hand tools and mats in designated positions and tires properly inflated.

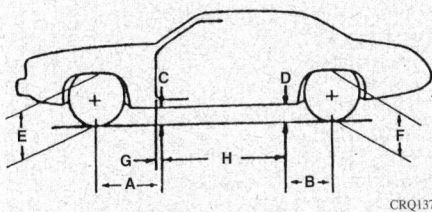

CRQ137

Fig. A

FLUID CAPACITIES & COOLING SYSTEM DATA

| Year | Engine Liter (VIN) ① | Coolant Capacity, Qts. | Coolant Type | Radiator Cap Relief Pressure, psi | Thermo. Opening Temp. °F | Fuel Tank, Gals. | Engine Oil Refill Qts. | Transmission Oil | | Rear Axle, Pts. ⑥ |
								Man Trans., Pts.	Auto. Trans., Qts. ②	
2001–02	3800 (K)	④	Dex-Cool	18	195	16.8	4.0 ③	6.8	12.2	3.5
	5.7L (G)	⑤	Dex-Cool	18	180	16.8	5.8 ③	8.0	15.1	3.5

① — The eighth digit of Vehicle Identification Number (VIN) denotes engine code.

② — Approximate, make final inspection w/dipstick.

③ — With filter change.

④ — Auto. trans., 12.3 qts.; Man. trans., 12.5 qts.

⑤ — Auto. trans., 15.1 qts.: Man. trans., 15.3 qts.

⑥ — All models require 4 oz. of limited differential additive lubricant part No. 1052358, or equivalent.

LUBRICANT DATA

Year	Lubricant Type				
	Transmission		Rear Axle	Power Steering System	Brake System
	Manual	Automatic			
2001–02	Dexron III	Dexron III	75W-90 GL-5①	Power Steering Fluid②	DOT 3

① — Limited slip differentials also require 4 oz. of lubricant additive (GM part No. 1052358, or equivalent).

② — Meeting GM specification 9985010.

Electrical

NOTE: On Air Bag Equipped Models, Refer To "Air Bag System Precautions" Located In The Front Of This Manual For System Disarming & Arming Procedures.

NOTE: Refer To "Computer Relearn Procedures" Located In The Front Of This Manual When Battery Power To The Computer Has Been Interrupted.

INDEX

PRECAUTIONS

Air Bag Systems

Refer to "Air Bag System Precautions" in the front of this manual for system disarming and arming procedures.

Battery Ground Cable

Prior to service, disconnect battery ground cable and isolate as required.

FUSE PANEL & FLASHER LOCATION

The instrument panel fuse block is attached to a bracket on the lefthand front hinge pillar and is accessed through a removable panel on the instrument panel carrier. The vehicle speed sensor (VSS) and hazard lamp flasher are attached to the relay center (convenience center), located on the lefthand side of the steering column. The turn signal flasher is mounted behind the instrument panel to the righthand of the steering column on the driver knee bolster bracket.

FUEL PUMP RELAY LOCATION

The fuel pump relay is located on the lefthand side of the engine compartment, in the No. 2 engine compartment relay center, **Fig. 1.**

RELAY CENTER LOCATION

The No. 1 and 2 relay centers are located in the engine compartment, on the lefthand fenderwell.

STARTER

REPLACE

This vehicle was designed for starter mounting without shims. If single or double shims have been added to correct a noise or engagement problem, they should be reinstalled in their original positions to ensure proper pinion to flywheel assembly engagement.

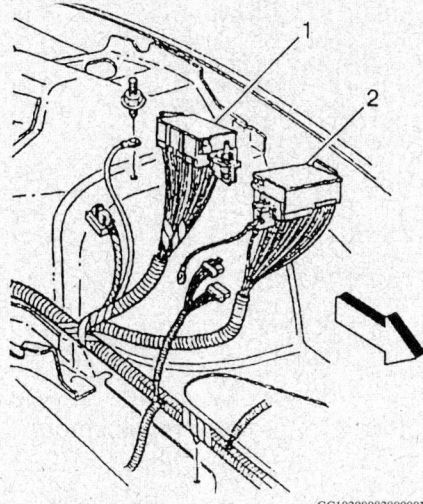

Fig. 1   Fuel pump relay location

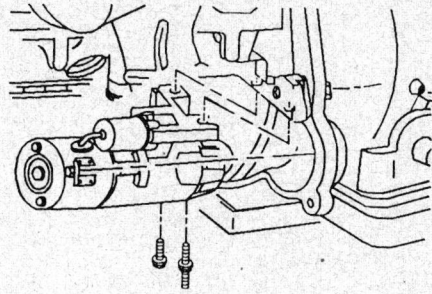

Fig. 2   Starter motor replacement. 3800 engine

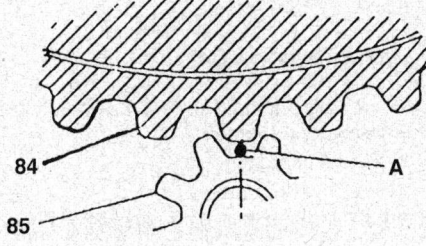

A   INSERT WIRE GAGE HERE TO CHECK
84   FLYWHEEL ASSEMBLY
85   PINION, STARTER DRIVE

Fig. 4   Flywheel assembly to pinion clearance inspection

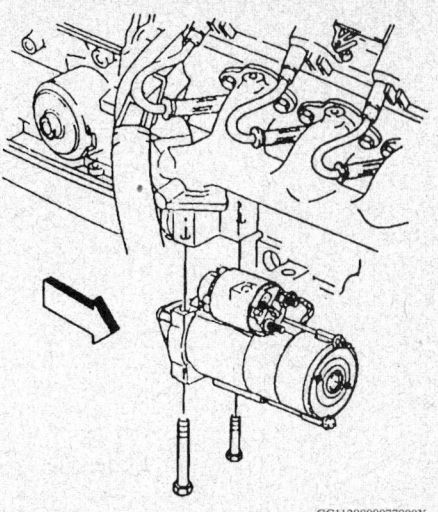

Fig. 3   Starter motor replacement. 5.7L engine

Removal

1. Raise and support vehicle.
2. **On models equipped with 5.7L engine,** remove lefthand catalytic converter.
3. **On models equipped with 3800 engine,** remove starter shield.
4. **On all models,** remove starter motor attaching bolts and lower starter motor assembly, **Figs. 2 and 3.**
5. Disconnect electrical connectors from starter motor assembly, then remove starter motor assembly.

Installation

Before connecting electrical connectors, tighten inner nuts on the solenoid terminals. If the nuts are not tight, the solenoid cap may be damaged during installation of connectors.

1. Connect electrical connectors to starter motor assembly, then **torque** BAT terminal nut to 84 inch lbs., and S terminal nut to 18 inch lbs.
2. Install starter motor assembly.
3. **On models equipped with 3800 engine, torque** starter bolt to 35 ft. lbs., and stud to 33 ft. lbs.
4. **On models equipped with 5.7L engine, torque** starter bolts to 37 ft. lbs.
5. **On all models,** measure pinion to flywheel clearance, **Fig. 4,** adding shims if required. Clearance should be .010–.160 inch.
6. **On models equipped with 3800 engine,** install starter shield.
7. **On all models,** connect exhaust to manifolds, then lower vehicle.

ALTERNATOR
REPLACE
3800 Engine

1. Remove serpentine drive belt as outlined under "Serpentine Drive Belt" in "3800 Engine" section.
2. Disconnect electrical connector from

alternator and battery positive terminal from "BAT" terminal.
3. Remove charcoal canister solenoid from alternator brace.
4. Remove bolt attaching alternator to rear brace, **Fig. 5.**
5. Remove bolts attaching alternator to drive belt tensioner.
6. Reverse procedure to install, noting the following:
   a. **Torque** mounting bolt (8) to 20 ft. lbs., and mounting bolt (11) to 38 ft. lbs.
   b. **Torque** rear brace bolt to 22 ft. lbs.

5.7L Engine

1. Remove accessory drive belt as outlined under "Serpentine Drive Belt" in "5.7L Engine" section.
2. Raise and support vehicle.
3. Remove alternator rear bracket bolt, **Fig. 6.**
4. Remove alternator mounting bolts.
5. Disconnect alternator electrical connectors, then remove from vehicle.
6. Reverse procedure to install. **Torque** mounting bolts to 37 ft. lbs., and bracket to 18 ft. lbs.

COIL PACK
REPLACE

1. Remove spark plug wire harness from coil pack/ignition control module.
2. Disconnect electrical harness from coil pack/ignition control module.
3. Remove coil pack/ignition control

module attaching bolts, then the coil pack/control module.
4. Reverse procedure to install.

IGNITION LOCK
REPLACE

1. Remove steering wheel as outlined under "Steering Wheel, Replace."
2. Remove turn signal switch as outlined under "Turn Signal Switch, Replace."
3. Remove buzzer switch retaining clip, then the buzzer switch.
4. Place ignition switch in Lock position.
5. Remove lock cylinder retaining screw, **Fig. 7.**
6. Disconnect terminal electrical connector at bulkhead connection to provide slack.
7. Remove wiring connector from steering column.
8. Attach a suitable length of mechanic wire to ignition lock electrical connector for use during installation. Detach wire retaining clip, then carefully pull ignition lock wiring through housing shroud, steering column and lock housing cover.
9. Remove lock cylinder.
10. Reverse procedure to install. Ensure lock cylinder wiring is properly routed through steering column. **Torque** lock cylinder retaining screw to 22 inch lbs.

IGNITION SWITCH
REPLACE
Removal

1. Remove lefthand instrument panel sound insulator assembly, then the instrument panel driver knee bolster assembly and deflector.
2. Ensure steering column lock and ignition switch are in Lock position, then remove steering column upper support nuts and lower column assembly.
3. Disconnect electrical connectors from

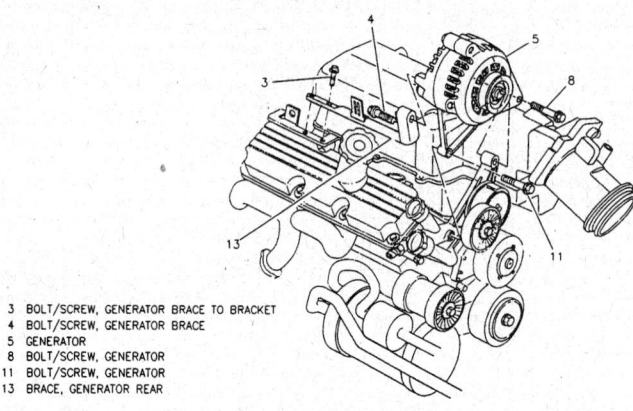

3 BOLT/SCREW, GENERATOR BRACE TO BRACKET
4 BOLT/SCREW, GENERATOR BRACE
5 GENERATOR
8 BOLT/SCREW, GENERATOR
11 BOLT/SCREW, GENERATOR
13 BRACE, GENERATOR REAR

GC1129600065000X

Fig. 5 Alternator replacement. 3800 engine

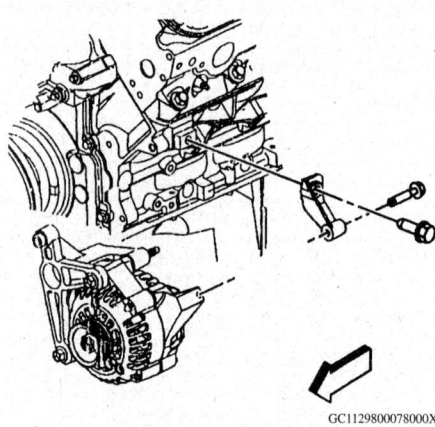

GC1129800078000X

Fig. 6 Alternator replacement. 5.7L engine

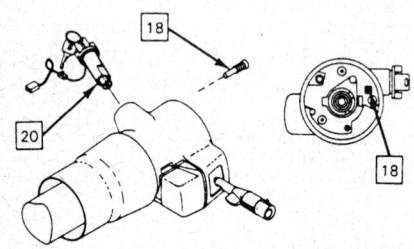

| 18 | LOCK RETAINING SCREW |
| 20 | VATS LOCK CYLINDER SET |

GC9129100016000X

Fig. 7 Ignition lock cylinder replacement

dimmer switch assembly and ignition switch, then remove dimmer switch actuator rod.

4. Remove dimmer switch assembly, then the ignition switch actuator rod.
5. Remove ignition switch, then disconnect automatic transmission park lock cable assembly, if equipped.

Installation

1. Connect automatic transmission park lock cable assembly, if equipped, then ensure ignition switch, steering column lock and ignition cylinder assembly are in Lock position.
2. Install ignition switch to jacket, then connect ignition switch actuator rod to ignition switch.
3. **Torque** ignition switch mounting screws to 22 inch lbs.
4. Install dimmer switch assembly, then adjust by pressing switch mechanism slightly to insert a 3/32 inch drill bit and moving dimmer switch assembly to remove tool.
5. **Torque** dimmer switch mounting screws to 35 inch lbs.
6. Install dimmer switch actuator rod, then connect electrical connectors to dimmer switch assembly and ignition switch.
7. Raise column assembly and install upper support nuts.
8. Install instrument panel driver knee bolster assembly and deflector, then

the lefthand instrument panel sound insulator assembly.

CLUTCH START SWITCH
REPLACE

1. Remove instrument panel driver knee bolster.
2. Disconnect clutch pedal position switch electrical connector.
3. Remove clutch pedal position switch from pedal bracket.
4. Reverse procedure to install.

NEUTRAL SAFETY SWITCH
REPLACE
Removal

1. Remove floor console, then disconnect electrical connectors from switch.
2. Place shift lever in Neutral position of detent plate, then remove switch attaching screws and switch, **Fig. 8**.

Installation

1. Ensure the shift lever is in Neutral, then position switch on shift lever making sure pin on shaft is in slot of switch.
2. If reinstalling existing switch, rotate switch to align service adjustment hole with carrier tang hole. Insert a 3/32 inch gauge pin and rotate switch until pin drops in to a depth of 19/32 inch. **Torque** switch attaching nut to 18 inch lbs., then remove gauge pin.
3. If installing a new switch, **torque** attaching nuts to 18 inch lbs., then move shift lever out of Neutral to shear pin which is a component of new switch.
4. Reconnect electrical connectors to switch, then apply parking brake and start engine. Inspect back-up lights and seat belt warning system for proper operation and ensure engine will start only in Park or Neutral.
5. Turn ignition off and install floor console.

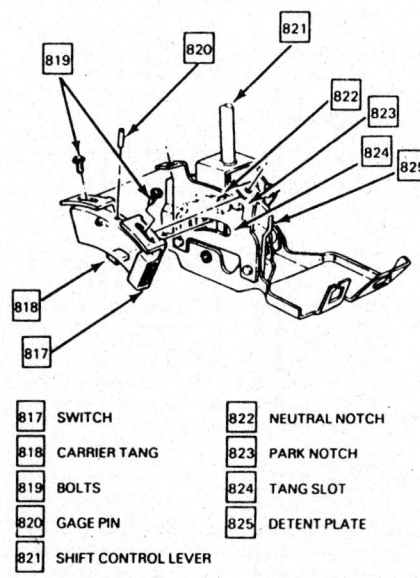

817	SWITCH	822	NEUTRAL NOTCH
818	CARRIER TANG	823	PARK NOTCH
819	BOLTS	824	TANG SLOT
820	GAGE PIN	825	DETENT PLATE
821	SHIFT CONTROL LEVER		

GC9049100061000X

Fig. 8 Neutral safety switch replacement

HEADLAMP SWITCH
REPLACE

1. **On Camaro models,** remove switch assembly from bezel assembly, **Fig. 9**.
2. **On Firebird models,** remove switch assembly from carrier, **Fig. 10**.
3. **On all models,** disconnect electrical connector from switch assembly.
4. Reverse procedure to install.

STOP LIGHT SWITCH
REPLACE

1. Remove lefthand instrument panel sound insulator assembly, then disconnect electrical connectors, **Fig. 11**.
2. Remove release switch assembly, stop lamp and TCC switch assembly and clutch switch assembly, or clutch anticipate switch assembly, if equipped, from pedal assembly with bracket.
3. Install release switch assembly, stop lamp and TCC switch assembly and

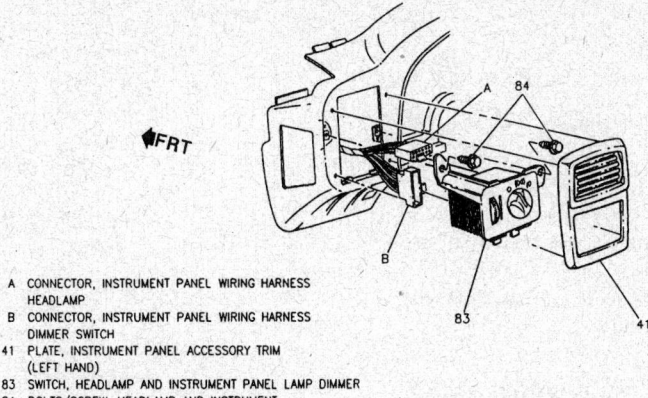

A CONNECTOR, INSTRUMENT PANEL WIRING HARNESS
  HEADLAMP
B CONNECTOR, INSTRUMENT PANEL WIRING HARNESS
  DIMMER SWITCH
41 PLATE, INSTRUMENT PANEL ACCESSORY TRIM
  (LEFT HAND)
83 SWITCH, HEADLAMP AND INSTRUMENT PANEL LAMP DIMMER
84 BOLTS/SCREW, HEADLAMP AND INSTRUMENT
  PANEL LAMP DIMMER SWITCH

GC9049800163000X

Fig. 9   Headlamp switch replacement. Camaro

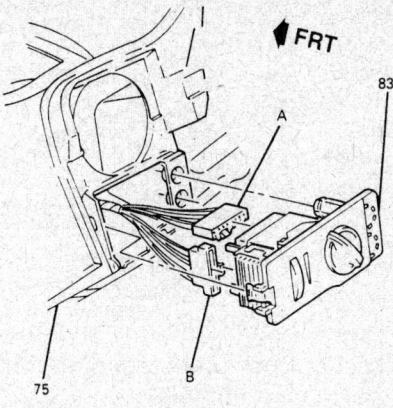

A CONNECTOR, INSTRUMENT PANEL WIRING HARNESS
  ELECTRICAL
B CONNECTOR, INSTRUMENT PANEL WIRING HARNESS
  ELECTRICAL
75 CARRIER, INSTRUMENT PANEL
83 SWITCH ASSEMBLY, HEADLAMP AND INSTRUMENT
  PANEL LAMP DIMMER

GC9049300058000X

Fig. 10   Headlamp switch replacement. Firebird

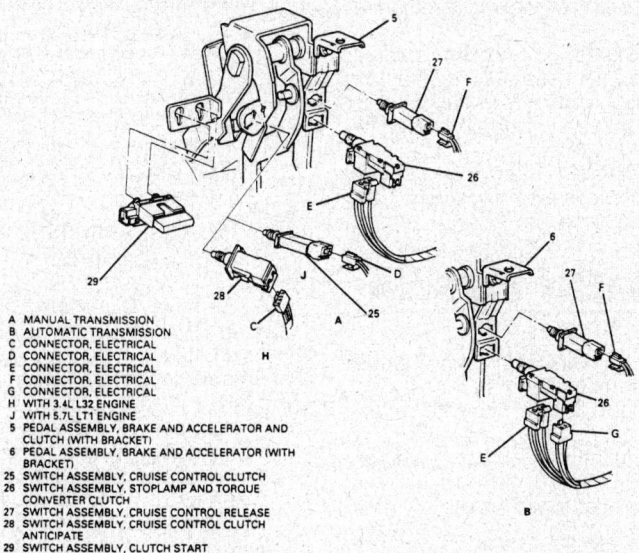

A MANUAL TRANSMISSION
B AUTOMATIC TRANSMISSION
C CONNECTOR, ELECTRICAL
D CONNECTOR, ELECTRICAL
E CONNECTOR, ELECTRICAL
F CONNECTOR, ELECTRICAL
G CONNECTOR, ELECTRICAL
H WITH 3.4L L32 ENGINE
J WITH 5.7L LT1 ENGINE
5 PEDAL ASSEMBLY, BRAKE AND ACCELERATOR AND
  CLUTCH (WITH BRACKET)
6 PEDAL ASSEMBLY, BRAKE AND ACCELERATOR (WITH
  BRACKET)
25 SWITCH ASSEMBLY, CRUISE CONTROL CLUTCH
26 SWITCH ASSEMBLY, STOPLAMP AND TORQUE
  CONVERTER CLUTCH
27 SWITCH ASSEMBLY, CRUISE CONTROL RELEASE
28 SWITCH ASSEMBLY, CRUISE CONTROL CLUTCH
  ANTICIPATE
29 SWITCH ASSEMBLY, CLUTCH START

GC9049300060000X

Fig. 11   Stop lamp switch replacement

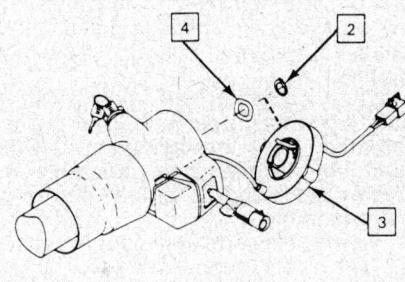

2 RETAINING RING
3 COIL ASSEMBLY
4 WAVE WASHER

GC9049100062000X

Fig. 12   Coil assembly removal

clutch switch assembly, or clutch antic-ipate switch assembly, if equipped, to pedal assembly with bracket.
4. Connect electrical connectors, then adjust switches as follows:
  a. Depress brake pedal assembly or clutch pedal assembly and insert release switch assembly, stop lamp and TCC switch assembly and clutch switch assembly, or clutch anticipate switch assembly into pedal assembly with bracket until retainer is fully seated.
  b. Slowly pull brake or clutch pedal assembly rearward with a force of 50 lbs. until click sounds can no longer be heard.
  c. Measure release switch assembly and stop lamp and TCC switch assembly contacts, should be open 1 inch or less of pedal assembly travel, and should occur at the same time or before onset of braking.
5. Install lefthand instrument panel sound insulator assembly.

TURN SIGNAL SWITCH
REPLACE

1. Remove steering wheel as outlined under "Steering Wheel, Replace."
2. Place ignition switch in Lock position to retain coil assembly in the centered position.
3. Remove coil assembly retaining ring, **Fig. 12.**
4. Lift coil assembly from steering shaft and allow to hang from wire, then remove wave washer.
5. Install a suitable tool, compress lock plate and remove snap ring (C-ring on tilt models), **Fig. 13.**
6. Remove lock plate, turn signal cancel-ing cam and upper bearing spring, inner race seat and inner race.
7. Place turn signal lever in righthand turn position, then remove multi-function lever and hazard warning flasher knob.
8. Remove turn signal switch lever at-taching screw, then remove lever.
9. Remove turn signal switch attaching screws.
10. Disconnect turn signal switch electrical connector at lower portion of steering column.
11. Remove turn signal switch wiring pro-tector cover from steering column, **Fig. 14.**
12. Carefully pull turn signal switch wiring up and out of steering column.
13. Reverse procedure to install. If coil as-sembly has become uncentered, refer to **Fig. 15,** for centering procedure.

DIMMER SWITCH
REPLACE

Refer to "Ignition Switch, Replace" for Dimmer Switch replacement.

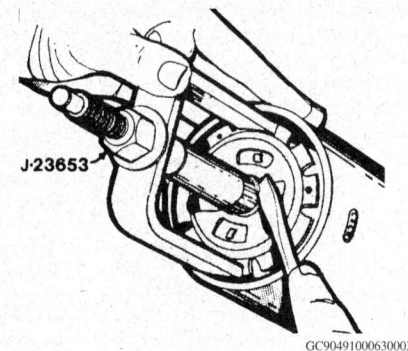

Fig. 13   Lock plate retaining ring removal

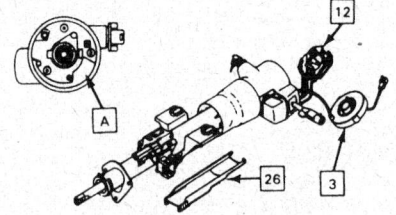

A   6 O'CLOCK POSITION: HARNESS THROUGH HERE
3   COIL ASSEMBLY
12   TURN SIGNAL AND HAZARD WARNING SWITCH
26   WIRING PROTECTOR

Fig. 14   Turn signal switch removal

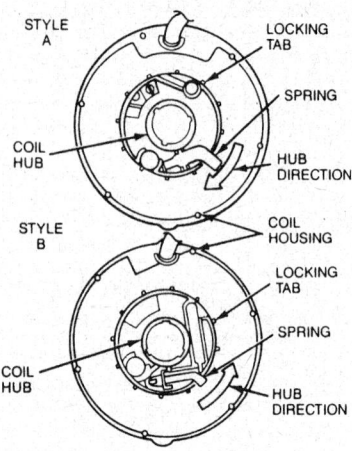

Perform the following steps to center coil assembly:

A. Remove coil assembly.
B. Hold coil assembly with clear bottom up to see coil ribbon.
C. NOTE: There are two different styles of coils. One rotates clockwise and the other rotates counterclockwise.
D. While holding coil assembly, depress spring lock to rotate hub in direction of arrow until it stops.
E. The coil ribbon should be wound up snug against center hub.
F. Rotate coil hub in opposite direction approximately two and a half (2-1/2) turns. Release spring lock between locking tabs in front of arrow.

Fig. 15   Coil assembly centered position

STEERING WHEEL
REPLACE

Removal

When removing steering wheel, use only specified puller. Do not hammer on end of steering column shaft. Hammering on shaft may damage plastic injections, affecting column assembly rigidity.

When attaching specified puller to steering wheel, use caution to prevent threading bolts through steering wheel hub into Supplemental Inflatable Restraint (SIR) coil assembly, damaging coil assembly.

1. Remove screws from back of steering wheel assembly using a No. 30 Torx driver, then the inflatable restraint steering wheel module assembly from steering wheel assembly.
2. Disconnect SIR coil assembly electrical connector and retainer from inflatable restraint steering wheel module assembly.
3. **On Firebird models,** disconnect radio control switch electrical connector from inflatable restraint steering wheel module assembly, if equipped.
4. **On all models,** disconnect horn lead from column assembly.
5. Remove steering wheel using steering wheel puller tool No. J1859-A and steering wheel puller bolts tool No. J38720, or equivalents.

Installation

1. Route SIR coil assembly electrical connector to steering wheel, then install steering wheel, aligning block tooth on steering wheel with block tooth on steering column shaft within one female serration.
2. Install nut and **torque** to 32 ft. lbs.
3. Connect horn lead to column assembly.
4. **On Firebird models,** connect radio control switch electrical connector from inflatable restraint steering wheel module assembly, if equipped.
5. **On all models,** connect SIR coil assembly electrical connector and retainer to inflatable restraint steering wheel module assembly.

6. Secure SIR coil assembly electrical connector to steering wheel by inserting thick section of wire into existing retainers.
7. Position inflatable restraint steering wheel module assembly to steering wheel, ensure wiring is not exposed or trapped between module assembly and steering wheel.
8. Install inflatable restraint steering wheel module assembly screws and **torque** to 25 inch lbs.

INSTRUMENT CLUSTER
REPLACE

1. Disconnect instrument panel upper trim panel assembly from lower windshield support, then remove from carrier.
2. Remove instrument cluster assembly from carrier, **Fig. 16.**
3. Reverse procedure to install.

RADIO
REPLACE

1. Remove accessory trim plate, **Fig. 17.**
2. Remove radio bracket bolts, **Fig. 18.**
3. Remove radio from instrument panel, then disconnect antenna cable and electrical connectors.
4. Reverse procedure to install noting the following:
   a. **On Firebird models,** install radio bracket bolts in following order; lower left, upper right, upper left.
   b. **On all models, torque** radio bracket bolts to 16 inch lbs.

WIPER MOTOR
REPLACE

Removal

1. Remove wiper arm and blade assemblies as follows:
   a. Operate wipers at lowest delay setting, then shut Off wipers at inner wipe (end of sweep) position.
   b. Mark windshield at tip of blade assembly to aid installation, then lift wiper arm nut cover and remove nut.

   c. Remove wiper arm from linkage drive shaft using wiper arm puller J39637.
2. Remove lefthand cowl panel and hood seal.
3. Disconnect washer hose assembly from lefthand cowl panel, then the electrical connector from wiper motor assembly.
4. Remove screw and nut from lefthand linkage assembly, **Fig. 19,** then disconnect socket of righthand linkage assembly from ball of lefthand linkage assembly using wiper linkage separator tool No. J39232, or equivalent.
5. Remove lefthand linkage assembly, then the screw from wiper motor assembly.
6. Pull wiper motor assembly free from slots of bracket, then disconnect socket of righthand linkage assembly from crank arm ball of wiper motor assembly using wiper linkage separator.

Installation

When installing wiper motor assembly, ensure crank arm is in inner wipe position. Crank arm drive pin must be engaged in cam pocket.

1. Press socket of righthand linkage assembly into engagement with crank arm ball of wiper motor assembly using wiper linkage installer tool No. J39529, or equivalent.
2. Install wiper motor assembly with two locator pads pressed fully into slots of bracket, then the mounting screw and **torque** to 96 inch lbs.
3. Install lefthand linkage assembly without attaching components, then press socket of righthand linkage assembly

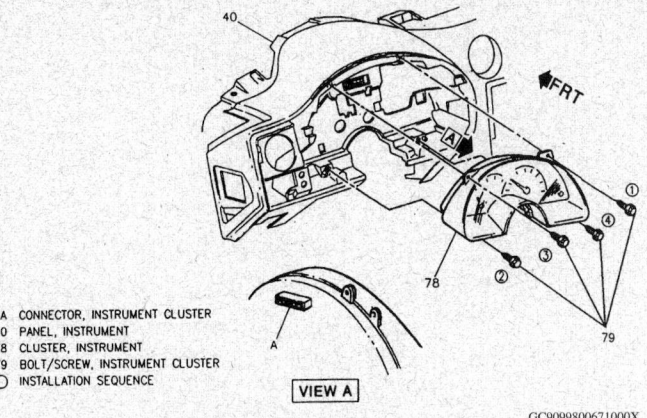

A CONNECTOR, INSTRUMENT CLUSTER
40 PANEL, INSTRUMENT
78 CLUSTER, INSTRUMENT
79 BOLT/SCREW, INSTRUMENT CLUSTER
○ INSTALLATION SEQUENCE

VIEW A

GC9099800671000X

Fig. 16 Instrument cluster

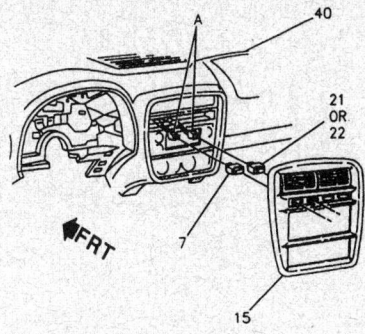

A CONNECTORS, INSTRUMENT PANEL
    WIRING HARNESS
7 SWITCH, FOG LAMP
15 PLATE, INSTRUMENT PANEL
    ACCESSORY TRIM
21 SWITCH, TRACTION CONTROL
22 SWITCH, SECOND GEAR START
40 PANEL, INSTRUMENT

GC9099800672000X

**Fig. 17 Accessory trim plate
removal**

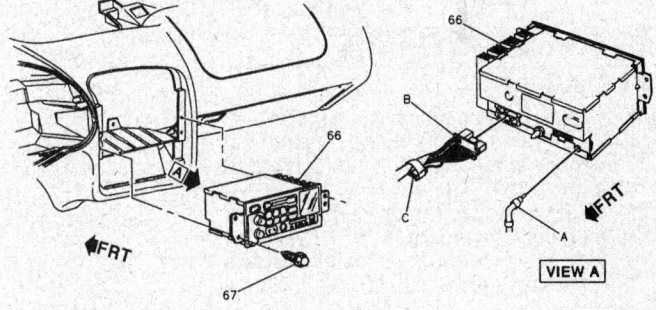

A CABLE, ANTENNA
B CONNECTOR, INSTRUMENT PANEL WIRING HARNESS
C CONNECTOR, REMOTE COMPACT DISC
66 RADIO, AM/FM STEREO AND CLOCK
67 BOLT/SCREW, RADIO BRACKET

VIEW A

GC9099800673000X

Fig. 18 Radio replacement

into engagement with ball of lefthand linkage assembly using wiper linkage installer.

4. Attach lefthand linkage assembly with screw and nut and **torque** to 90 inch lbs.
5. Connect electrical connector to wiper motor assembly, then the washer hose assembly to lefthand cowl panel and washer nozzle.
6. Install lefthand cowl panel and hood seal.
7. Install wiper arm and blade assemblies as follows:
   a. Install wiper arm and blade assembly onto linkage drive shaft, with tip of blade assembly aligned with mark made at removal.
   b. Install nut on linkage drive shaft and **torque** to 24 ft. lbs., while holding wiper arm.
   c. Close nut cover, then run wipers and inspect for proper wipe pattern. Turn wipers Off and inspect for correct park position.

WIPER SWITCH
REPLACE

1. **On models equipped with cruise control,** remove tilt wheel release lever and access cover, then disconnect electrical connectors.
2. **On all models,** remove wiper switch by grasping firmly and pulling straight out.
3. Reverse procedure to install, noting the following:
   a. Ensure wiper switch is in Off position before installing.
   b. Position tilt lever ± 5° from centerline of column assembly.

WIPER TRANSMISSION
REPLACE
Removal

1. Remove wiper arm and blade assemblies as follows:
   a. Operate wipers at lowest delay setting, then turn wipers Off at inner wipe (end of sweep) position.
   b. Mark windshield at tip of blade as-

sembly to aid installation, then lift wiper arm nut cover and remove nut.
   c. Remove wiper arm from linkage drive shaft using wiper arm puller tool No. J39637, or equivalent.
2. Remove lefthand cowl panel and hood seal, then disconnect washer hose assembly from lefthand cowl panel.
3. Remove screw and nut from lefthand linkage assembly, **Fig. 19,** then disconnect socket of righthand linkage assembly from ball of lefthand linkage assembly using wiper linkage separator tool No. J39232, or equivalent.
4. Remove lefthand linkage assembly, then the screws securing righthand linkage assembly.
5. Disconnect socket of righthand linkage assembly from crank arm ball of wiper motor assembly using wiper linkage separator, then remove righthand linkage assembly from slotted plenum access hole.

Installation

1. Install righthand linkage assembly from slotted plenum access hole, then the screws securing righthand linkage assembly finger tight.

2. Align righthand linkage assembly, then press socket of righthand linkage assembly into engagement with crank arm ball of wiper motor assembly using wiper linkage installer tool No. J39529, or equivalent.
3. Install lefthand linkage assembly without attaching components, then press socket of righthand linkage assembly into engagement with ball of lefthand linkage assembly using wiper linkage installer.
4. Attach lefthand linkage assembly with screw and nut and **torque** to 90 inch lbs.
5. Connect washer hose assembly to lefthand cowl panel and washer nozzle.
6. Install lefthand cowl panel and hood seal.
7. Install wiper arm and blade assemblies as follows:
   a. Install wiper arm and blade assembly onto linkage drive shaft, with tip of blade assembly aligned with mark made at removal.
   b. Install nut on linkage drive shaft and **torque** to 24 ft. lbs., while holding wiper arm.
   c. Close nut cover, then run wipers and inspect for proper wipe pattern.

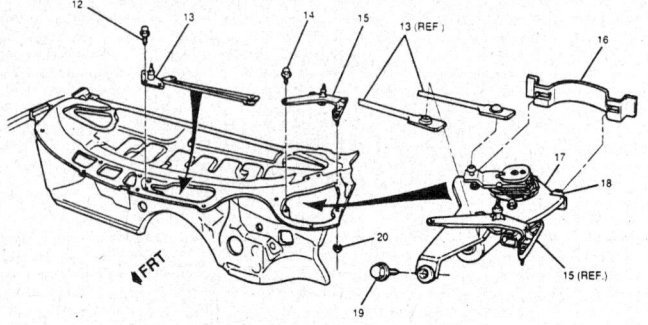

A CRANK ARM DRIVE PIN IN CAM POCKET
12 SCREW (3), 10 N·m (7.5 LB. FT.)
13 LINKAGE ASSEMBLY, RH
14 SCREW, 10 N·m (7.5 LB. FT.)
15 LINKAGE ASSEMBLY, LH
16 BRACKET, WIPER MOTOR
17 MOTOR ASSEMBLY, WIPER
18 PAD, LOCATOR (2)
19 SCREW, 10 N·m (7.5 LB. FT.)
20 NUT, 10 N·m (7.5 LB. FT.)

GC9099300207000X

Fig. 19 Windshield wiper motor/transmission assembly

Shut off wipers and inspect for correct park position.

BLOWER MOTOR

REPLACE

1. Ensure ignition switch is in Off position, then remove righthand instrument panel sound insulator assembly and side trim panel.
2. Remove blower motor mounting bolts, then the blower motor.
3. Reverse procedure to install. **Torque** mounting bolts to 20 inch lbs.

HEATER CORE

REPLACE

1. Drain engine coolant into suitable container.
2. Remove heater hoses and pipes.
3. Remove heater core tube clamp and shroud seal.
4. Slide heater rear case downward in order to disengage upper case clip, then remove heater rear case.
5. Remove glove compartment door.
6. Remove heater core clamp, then the heater core.
7. Reverse procedure to install.

EVAPORATOR CORE

REPLACE

1. Evacuate A/C as outlined under "Air Conditioning" chapter.
2. Drain engine coolant into suitable container.
3. Remove righthand instrument panel sound insulator panel assembly, then disconnect heater hoses at heater core assembly.
4. Remove instrument panel compartment, then the heater core as outlined under "Heater Core, Replace."
5. Remove evaporator temperature sensor assembly, **Fig. 20,** then disconnect temperature control cable assembly at temperature valve case assembly.
6. Remove bolts (located in engine compartment) from temperature valve case assembly, then the temperature valve case assembly by sliding downward to disengage upper case clip.
7. Remove thermostatic expansion valve assembly.
8. Install a small hand saw, remove perforated section of evaporator module assembly as one piece and retain for reuse.
9. Remove bolts retaining evaporator, then the evaporator from module assembly by sliding evaporator to lefthand and pulling out through opening cut in module.

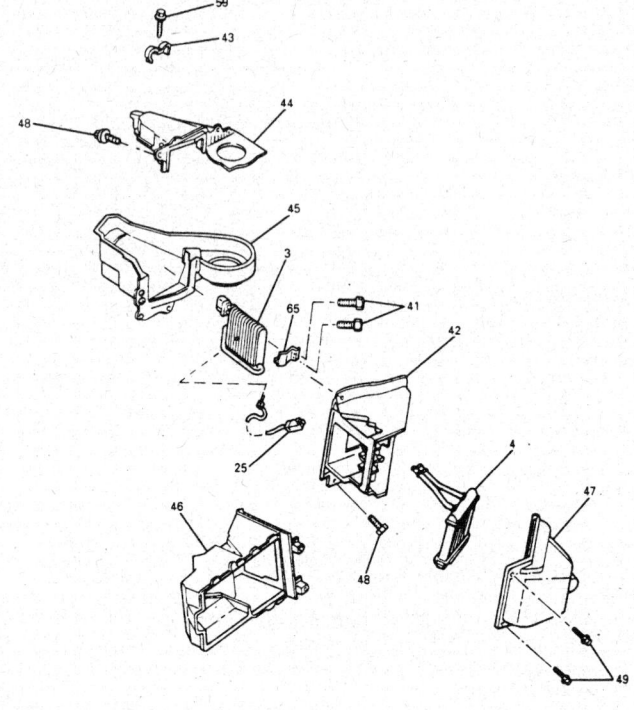

3 EVAPORATOR, AIR CONDITIONING
4 CORE ASSEMBLY, HEATER
25 SENSOR ASSEMBLY, AIR CONDITIONING EVAPORATOR TEMPERATURE
41 BOLT/SCREW, AIR CONDITIONING EVAPORATOR
42 CASE ASSEMBLY, TEMPERATURE VALVE
43 CLAMP, HEATER CORE TUBE
44 CASE, AIR CONDITIONING EVAPORATOR UPPER
45 CASE, AIR CONDITIONING EVAPORATOR LOWER
46 CASE, AIR DISTRIBUTOR UPPER
47 COVER, HEATER AND AIR CONDITIONING EVAPORATOR CASE
48 BOLT/SCREW, TEMPERATURE VALVE CASE ASSEMBLY
49 BOLT/SCREW, HEATER AND AIR CONDITIONING EVAPORATOR CASE COVER
59 BOLT/SCREW, HEATER CORE TUBE CLAMP
65 CLAMP, AIR CONDITIONING EVAPORATOR

GC7029300056000X

Fig. 20 Evaporator core replacement

10. Reverse procedure to install, noting the following:
    a. If replacing evaporator, transfer condensate screen to new evaporator and add 3 fluid ounces of polyalkalene glycol (PAG) synthetic refrigerant oil to new evaporator.
    b. Apply sealer No. 3012078, or equivalent, between evaporator upper and lower case just behind thermostatic expansion valve assembly to prevent air entry from engine compartment.
    c. Use epoxy glue to adhere perforated section of module assembly to module assembly.
    d. Fill radiator and bleed cooling system.
    e. Partially charge system and perform a leak test, then recover refrigerant and evacuate and charge system.

3800 Engine

NOTE: For Procedures Not Found In This Section, Refer To The "3800 Engine" In The "Bonneville, Eighty Eight, LeSabre, LSS & Park Avenue" Chapter.

NOTE: On Air Bag Equipped Models, Refer To "Air Bag System Precautions" Located In The Front Of This Manual For System Disarming & Arming Procedures.

NOTE: Refer To "Computer Relearn Procedures" Located In The Front Of This Manual When Battery Power To The Computer Has Been Interrupted.

INDEX

PRECAUTIONS

Air Bag Systems

Refer to "Air Bag System Precautions" in the front of this manual for system disarming and arming procedures.

Battery Ground Cable

Prior to service, disconnect battery ground cable and isolate as required.

Fuel System Pressure Relief

Refer to the "3800 Engine" in the "Bonneville, Eighty Eight, LeSabre, LSS & Park Avenue" chapter for fuel system pressure relief procedure.

Engine Support

When raising the engine for any reason, do not use a jack under the oil pan, crankshaft balancer or any sheet metal, this may result in damage to engine. Always use universal support fixture tool No. J28467-A and engine support adapter tool No. J41044, or equivalents.

COMPRESSION PRESSURE

When inspecting compression, lowest cylinder must be within 70 percent of the highest cylinder with a minimum pressure

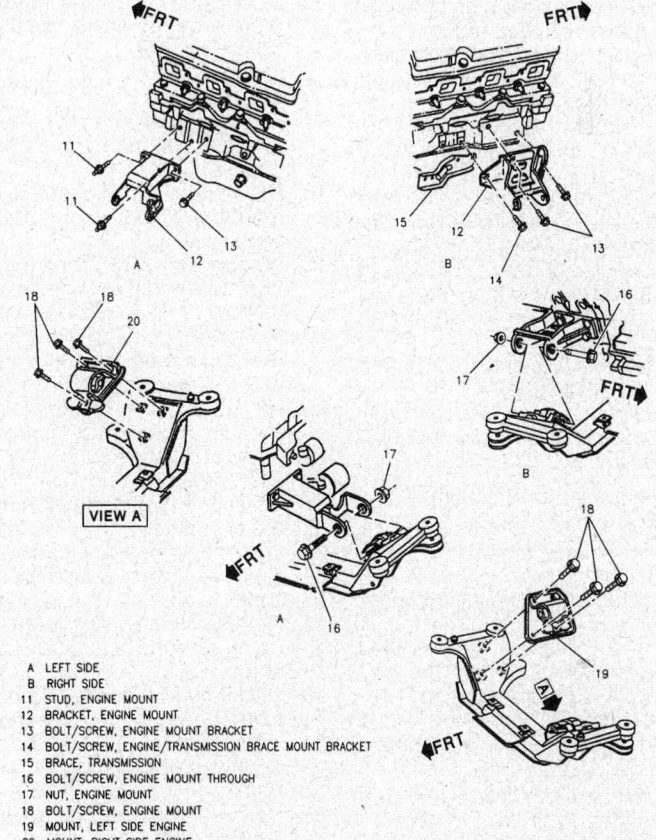

A LEFT SIDE
B RIGHT SIDE
11 STUD, ENGINE MOUNT
12 BRACKET, ENGINE MOUNT
13 BOLT/SCREW, ENGINE MOUNT BRACKET
14 BOLT/SCREW, ENGINE/TRANSMISSION BRACE MOUNT BRACKET
15 BRACE, TRANSMISSION
16 BOLT/SCREW, ENGINE MOUNT THROUGH
17 NUT, ENGINE MOUNT
18 BOLT/SCREW, ENGINE MOUNT
19 MOUNT, LEFT SIDE ENGINE
20 MOUNT, RIGHT SIDE ENGINE

GC1069600663000X

Fig. 1 Engine mount fasteners

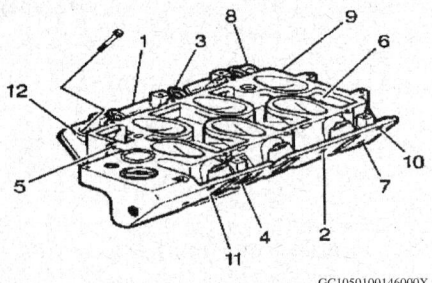

Fig. 2 Upper intake manifold tightening sequence

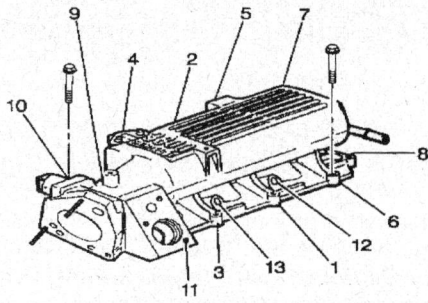

Fig. 3 Lower intake manifold tightening sequence

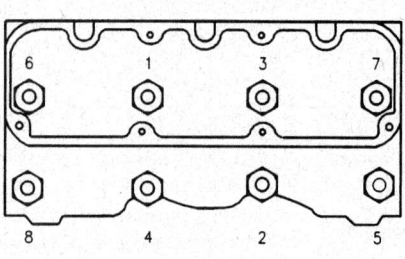

Fig. 4 Cylinder head bolt tightening sequence

of 100 psi. Perform compression test with engine at normal operating temperature, spark plugs removed and throttle wide open.

ENGINE MOUNT
REPLACE

1. Remove alternator as outlined under "Alternator, Replace" in "Electrical" section, then the ignition control module.
2. Raise and support vehicle using suitable lift.
3. Disconnect exhaust catalytic converter system.
4. Remove engine mount nuts.
5. Disconnect transmission oil cooler lines, if required.
6. Loosen air conditioning compressor and slide forward, if required.
7. Install universal support fixture tool No. J28467-A along with engine support adapter tool No. J41044, or equivalents, and support engine to allow for engine mount bolts/bracket removal and raise engine.
8. Remove engine mount bolts and screws, then remove mounts from engine cradle.
9. Remove engine bracket bolts and screws, then studs and brackets.
10. Reverse procedure to install, noting following:
   a. **Torque** bolts and screws (13) and studs (11), **Fig. 1**, to 74 ft. lbs.
   b. **Torque** bolts and screws (14) to 37 ft. lbs., and engine mount bolts (18) to 43 ft. lbs.

ENGINE
REPLACE

1. Recover refrigerant as outlined under "Air Conditioning" chapter.
2. Relieve fuel pressure as outlined under "Precautions."
3. Disconnect A/C compressor and condenser hose from accumulator.
4. Raise and support vehicle and remove front wheels.
5. Drain coolant and engine oil into suitable containers.
6. Disconnect 3-way catalytic converter.
7. Disconnect transmission converter and front fascia lower deflectors.
8. Disconnect stabilizer bar bushing bolts and transmission fluid cooler lines from radiator.
9. Remove radiator inlet hose, shift linkage from transmission and propeller shaft.
10. Disconnect rear axle torque arm from transmission and steering gear coupling shaft from rack and pinion assembly.
11. Disconnect power steering gear inlet and outlet hoses from power steering gear.
12. Disconnect starter motor and electrical ground strap from engine block.
13. Disconnect A/C compressor and condenser hoses.
14. Remove battery ground cable from rear of A/C compressor and engine coolant heater cord from block.
15. Lower vehicle, remove serpentine belt as outlined in "Serpentine Drive Belt," then any remaining hoses/brackets from tensioner.
16. Remove air cleaner outlet rear duct and resonator duct.
17. Remove fuel lines at fuel rail and cruise/accelerator cables from throttle body.
18. Disconnect radiator outlet hose from thermostat housing and brake booster vacuum hose.
19. Disconnect ABS combination valve from brake lines, clips and hydraulic modulator.
20. Remove righthand body hinge pillar trim panel and the three (blue, black and white) wiring harness connectors.
21. Disconnect the forward lamp wiring harness connectors and PCM and place on top of engine.
22. Disconnect engine wiring harness in passenger compartment and place on top of engine.
23. Disconnect positive lead at alternator.
24. Remove lower shock bolt from lower control arm.
25. Remove upper control arm ball stud from steering knuckle and secure struts.
26. Disconnect electrical connectors to wheel speed sensor at engine frame.
27. Install tool No. J39580, or equivalent, position lift table under engine and frame.
28. Remove engine frame to transmission support bolts.
29. Raise vehicle from engine, transmission and engine frame.
30. Remove transmission.
31. **On models equipped with manual transmission,** remove clutch.
32. **On all models,** remove engine mount through-bolt and separate engine from engine frame.
33. Reverse procedure to install, noting the following:
   a. When installing wiring harness back through front of dash, the rubber grommet must be installed correctly. If grommet is torn or damaged, it must be replaced.
   b. Align wheels as outlined in "Alignment."

INTAKE MANIFOLD
REPLACE

Upper

1. Remove righthand side spark plug wires, then manifold vacuum source.
2. Remove rear alternator mounting bracket bolts.
3. Remove EGR outlet pipe bolt and nut, then separate from intake manifold.
4. Remove throttle body and gasket.
5. Remove fuel rail with injectors attached.
6. Remove upper intake manifold and gasket.
7. Reverse procedure to install, noting the following:
   a. **Torque** vertical bolts in sequence, **Fig. 2,** to 11 ft. lbs.
   b. **Torque** water outlet bolts in sequence, **Fig. 2,** to 20 ft. lbs.
   c. **Torque** side bolts in sequence, **Fig. 2,** to 22 ft. lbs.

Lower

To remove the lower intake manifold, the upper manifold must be removed first.
1. Remove upper intake manifold as outlined in the "Upper" section of this manual to access two hidden bolts.
2. Remove lower intake manifold bolts, then manifold.
3. Reverse procedure to install, noting the following:
   a. Use a suitable thread locking compound on intake manifold bolts prior to assembly.
   b. Tighten bolts to 11 ft. lbs., in sequence, **Fig. 3.**

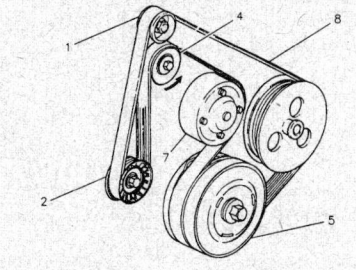

A INDICATOR MARK
B MINIMUM TOLERANCE BELT READING
C MAXIMUM TOLERANCE BELT READING
1 PULLEY, GENERATOR
2 PULLEY, DRIVE BELT IDLER
3 PULLEY, AIR CONDITIONING COMPRESSOR
4 TENSIONER, DRIVE BELT
5 PULLEY, CRANKSHAFT
6 PULLEY, POWER STEERING PUMP
7 PULLEY, WATER PUMP
8 BELT, SERPENTINE DRIVE

WITHOUT AIR CONDITIONING

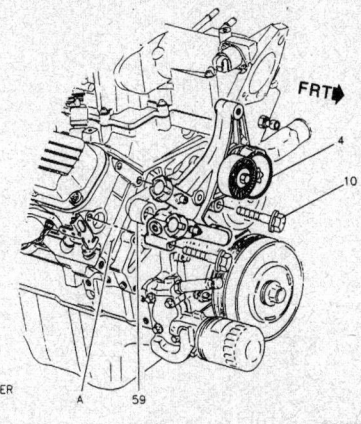

4   TENSIONER, DRIVE BELT
10 BOLT/SCREW, DRIVE BELT TENSIONER
59 COVER, ENGINE FRONT

GC1069600672000X

Fig. 6 Serpentine belt tensioner

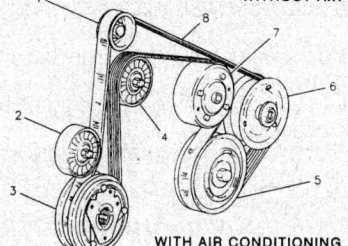

WITH AIR CONDITIONING

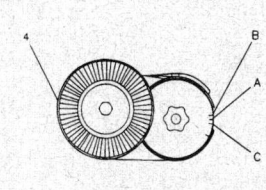

GC1069600671000X

Fig. 5 Serpentine belt routing

EXHAUST MANIFOLD
REPLACE
Righthand

1. Remove exhaust manifold heat shield nuts, then the shield.
2. Raise and support vehicle using a suitable lift.
3. Remove exhaust catalytic converter pipe.
4. Remove heated oxygen sensor electrical connector from bracket.
5. Lower vehicle and remove exhaust manifold studs and bolts, then the manifold.
6. Remove exhaust manifold gasket and clean cylinder head mating surface.
7. Reverse procedure to install.

Lefthand

1. Remove EGR valve adapter from exhaust manifold.
2. Remove oil dipstick and tube.
3. Remove exhaust manifold heat shield.
4. Raise and support vehicle using a suitable lift.
5. Remove exhaust catalytic converter pipe and oxygen sensor connector.
6. Disconnect spark plug wires and lower vehicle.
7. Remove exhaust manifold and gasket, then clean mating surfaces.
8. Reverse procedure to install, noting the following:
   a. Install new exhaust manifold gasket.
   b. Inspect EGR outlet tube for leaks.

CYLINDER HEAD
REPLACE

1. Remove upper and lower intake manifolds as outlined under "Intake Manifold, Replace."
2. Remove exhaust manifold as outlined under "Exhaust Manifold, Replace."

3. Remove rocker arm covers, rocker arms and push rods.
4. Remove and discard cylinder head bolts.
5. Remove cylinder head.
6. Reverse procedure to install, noting the following:
   a. Clean threads in block with proper size tap.
   b. Install new head gasket with the lefthand gasket, marked "L" and an arrow, pointing forward. The righthand gasket has just the arrow marking. These head gaskets are not interchangeable.
   c. **Torque** new cylinder head bolts to 37 ft. lbs., in sequence, **Fig. 4.**
   d. Tighten each bolt in sequence an additional 120°.

CRANKSHAFT DAMPER
REPLACE

1. Remove drive belt as outlined under "Serpentine Drive Belt," then raise and support vehicle using a suitable lift.
2. Remove starter motor as outlined under "Starter, Replace" in "Electrical" section, then transmission braces.
3. Remove transmission access cover.
4. Hold flywheel using tool No. J37096, or equivalent.
5. Remove crankshaft balancer/damper bolt and washer. **Note the relationship of the balancer/damper and crankshaft key as the balancer is removed.**
6. Remove crankshaft balancer using puller tool No. J38197, or equivalent. **The crankshaft damper is serviced as an assembly, do not separate pulley from balancer hub.**
7. Reverse procedure to install. Lubricate balancer and crankshaft mating surface with clean motor oil.

FRONT COVER
REPLACE

1. Drain engine oil and coolant into suit-

able containers.
2. Disconnect IAT sensor electrical connector.
3. Remove air intake duct.
4. Loosen water pump pulley bolts.
5. Remove drivebelt tensioner.
6. Install puller No. J25034–B, or equivalent, remove power steering pulley.
7. Place suitable container under power steering pump, then disconnect inlet and return hoses from pump.
8. Remove power steering pump, then raise and support vehicle.
9. Remove crankshaft damper as outlined under "Crankshaft Damper, Replace."
10. Disconnect CKP sensor electrical connector, then remove CKP sensor shield.
11. Remove CKP sensor, then the oil pan to front cover bolts.
12. Loosen oil pans bolts slightly to lower oil pan as an installation aid for front cover.
13. Lower vehicle, then remove water pump pulley.
14. Remove radiator outlet hose from front cover.
15. Remove front cover mounting studs and bolts.
16. Remove front cover and gasket.
17. Remove components from front cover as required if replacing cover.
18. Reverse procedure to install, noting the following:
   a. Apply sealant No. 12346004, or equivalent, to threads of front cover bolts and studs.
   b. **Torque** front cover bolts to 15 ft. lbs.
   c. Tighten bolts and studs an additional 40°.

BALANCE SHAFT
REPLACE

1. Remove drive belt as outlined under "Serpentine Drive Belt."
2. Raise and support vehicle using a suitable lift.
3. Remove starter motor as outlined under "Starter Motor, Replace" in "Electrical" section.
4. Remove transmission as outlined in **MOTOR's "Domestic Transmission**

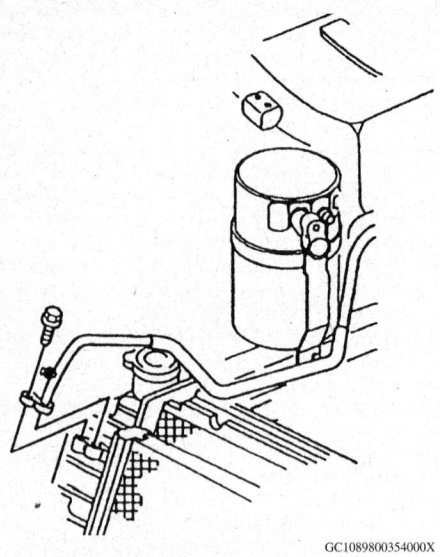

Fig. 7 Evaporator line removal

Manual, In-Vehicle Service," then the clutch and flywheel.
5. Remove crankshaft balancer bolt from balancer.
6. Remove crankshaft balancer using crankshaft balancer puller tool No. J38197A, or equivalent.
7. Remove key from crankshaft.
8. Reverse procedure to install, noting the following:
   a. Lubricate seal surface of crankshaft balancer with suitable engine oil.
   b. Perform crankshaft position system variation learn procedure as outlined under "Computer Relearn Procedures" in the front of this manual.

OIL PAN
REPLACE

1. Remove ignition coils.
2. Install engine support fixture tool No. J28467-A, or equivalent.
3. Raise and support vehicle using a suitable lift.
4. Drain engine oil into suitable container, then remove torque converter cover.
5. Remove exhaust crossover pipe.
6. Remove engine mount through bolts.
7. Raise engine using support fixture.
8. Remove oil level sensor, then the oil pan bolts.
9. Lower rear of oil pan, then rotate outward and remove pan.
10. Reverse procedure to install.

SERPENTINE DRIVE BELT

Cracks appearing perpendicular to the belt ribs indicate normal wear. If sections of rib are missing or if the belt is slipping, the belt must be replaced. The belt tensioner has a wear indicator, and if it is out of limits, either the belt or tensioner must be replaced.
1. Install suitable ratchet and socket, push tensioner clockwise and remove serpentine belt, **Fig. 5**.
2. Reverse procedure to install.

BELT TENSIONER
REPLACE

1. Drain engine coolant into suitable container.
2. Remove drive belt as outlined under "Serpentine Drive Belt."
3. Remove transmission oil dipstick and oil filler neck from rocker arm cover.
4. Remove manifold absolute pressure (MAP) sensor from alternator bracket and remove alternator.
5. Remove heater hoses from belt drive tensioner.
6. Remove belt drive tensioner, **Fig. 6**.
7. Reverse procedure to install.

RADIATOR
REPLACE

1. Recover refrigerant as outlined under "Air Conditioning" chapter.
2. Drain cooling system into suitable container, then remove radiator hoses.
3. Remove upper evaporator tube bracket bolt, **Fig. 7**.
4. Remove evaporator tube from condenser.
5. Remove upper and lower oil cooler lines from radiator.
6. Remove condenser tube from condenser, **Fig. 8**.
7. Remove overflow hose from radiator.
8. Remove air intake duct and air cleaner assembly, then disconnect cooling fan electrical connectors.
9. Remove electric cooling fans, then the coolant level indicator module.
10. Remove radiator and condenser.
11. Reverse procedure to install.

FUEL PUMP
REPLACE

1. Relieve fuel system pressure as outlined under "Precautions."

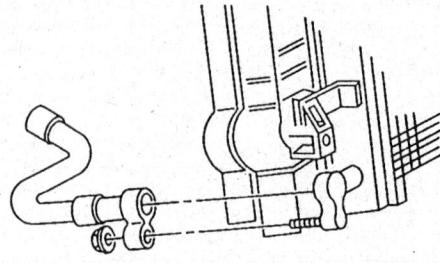

Fig. 8 Condenser tube removal

2. Raise and support vehicle using a suitable lift.
3. Drain fuel tank into suitable container, then remove.
4. Remove fuel sender retaining nuts, retaining ring, sender seal (discard seal) and sender assembly.
5. Reverse procedure to install, noting the following:
   a. **Always replace fuel sender seal when servicing sending unit. Do not handle fuel sender assembly by the sender pipes, as this may damage the solder joints.**
   b. Clean fuel sender assembly sealing surfaces.
   c. Fuel pump strainer must be in horizontal position. Ensure fuel pump strainer does not block full travel of float arm.
   d. Gently fold strainer over itself and insert into fuel tank making sure strainer is not damaged or trapped by sump walls.
   e. Inspect for leaks.

FUEL FILTER
REPLACE

1. Relieve fuel system pressure as outlined under "Precautions" then raise and support vehicle using a suitable lift.
2. Clean all inline fuel filter connections to avoid contaminating fuel system.
3. Remove quick-connect fitting at filter inlet using quick disconnect tool No. J37088-A, or equivalent, then the threaded fitting from filter outlet. Slide fuel filter from bracket.
4. Reverse procedure to install, noting the following:
   a. Inspect fuel pipe O-ring for cuts, nicks, swelling or distortion and replace, if required.
   b. Inspect for leaks.

TIGHTENING SPECIFICATIONS

Year	Component	Torque/Ft. Lbs.
2001–02	Balance Shaft Gear	16③
	Balance Shaft Retainer	22
	Camshaft Position Sensor	84⑧
	Camshaft Sprocket	⑩
	Connecting Rod Bearing Cap	20⑦
	Coolant Outlet	20
	Crankshaft Balancer	⑨
	Crankshaft Main Bearing Bolt	⑪
	Crankshaft Main Bearing Side Bolt	11④
	Crankshaft Position Sensor Stud	22
	Cylinder Head	①
	Drive Belt Tensioner	37
	EGR Valve Nut	21
	Engine Coolant Temperature Sensor	10
	Engine Front Cover	11⑥
	Engine Mount Bolts	43
	Engine Mount Through Bolt	70
	Engine Mount Through Bolt Nut	59
	Engine Oil Pressure Sensor	10
	ESC Knock Sensor	13
	Exhaust Manifold	22
	Flywheel Bolts (New)	11⑦
	Lower Intake Manifold	11
	Oil Pan	10
	Oil Pump Cover	96⑧
	Oxygen Sensor	31
	Throttle Body	84⑧
	Timing Chain Dampener	16
	Upper Intake Manifold (Two Side Bolts)	22
	Upper Intake Manifold (Two Water Outlet Bolts)	20
	Upper Intake Manifold (10 Vertical Bolts)	11
	Valve Lifter Guide Retainer	22
	Valve Rocker Arm	11⑤
	Water Pump	11 ②

① — Refer to "Cylinder Head, Replace."
② — Tighten an additional 80.°
③ — Tighten an additional 70.°
④ — Tighten an additional 45.°
⑤ — Tighten an additional 90.°
⑥ — Tighten an additional 40°
⑦ — Tighten an additional 50.°
⑧ — Inch lbs.
⑨ — Models equipped w/manual transmission, 111 ft. lbs., plus an additional 114.°
⑩ — 74 ft. lbs., plus an additional 90.°
⑪ — **Torque** cap bolts to 51 ft. lbs., to seat bearings, then loosen each bolt 1 turn. **To ensure cap seats properly, do not tighten at each bolt completely at one time. Make several passes until specified torque is achieved. Torque** to 30 ft. lbs., using a suitable torque angle meter, tighten in following steps; 35°, an additional 35°, then an additional 40.°

5.7L Engine

NOTE: For Procedures Not Found In This Section, Refer To The "5.7L VIN G Engine" Section In The "Corvette" Chapter.

NOTE: On Air Bag Equipped Models, Refer To "Air Bag System Precautions" Located In The Front Of This Manual For System Disarming & Arming Procedures.

NOTE: Refer To "Computer Relearn Procedures" Located In The Front Of This Manual When Battery Power To The Computer Has Been Interrupted.

INDEX

PRECAUTIONS

Air Bag Systems

Refer to "Air Bag System Precautions" in the front of this manual for system disarming and arming procedures.

Battery Ground Cable

Prior to service, disconnect battery ground cable and isolate as required.

Fuel System Pressure Relief

Before servicing any electrical component, the ignition key must be in the Off or Lock position and all electrical loads must be Off.
1. Turn ignition to Off position.
2. Loosen fuel filler cap in order to relieve fuel tank vapor pressure.
3. Connect J34730-1A fuel pressure gauge to fuel pressure valve.
4. Wrap a shop towel around fitting while connecting gauge in order to avoid spillage.
5. Install bleed hose of the gauge into an approved container.
6. Open valve on gauge to bleed system pressure.
7. The fuel connections are now safe for servicing.
8. Drain any fuel remaining in gauge into an approved container.

COMPRESSION PRESSURE

When inspecting compression, lowest cylinder must be within 70 percent of the highest cylinder with a minimum pressure of 100 psi. Perform compression test with engine at normal operating temperature, spark plugs removed and throttle wide open.

ENGINE MOUNT

REPLACE

Lefthand

1. Disconnect MAF and IAT sensor electrical connectors.
2. Remove air duct from throttle body and air cleaner box.
3. Support engine using engine fixture tool Nos. 42451, 28467, 36462 and 41044, or equivalents.
4. Raise and support vehicle, then remove lefthand catalytic converter.
5. Remove engine mount bracket to crossmember bolts.
6. Lower vehicle.
7. Raise lefthand side of engine using fixture tools.
8. Raise and support vehicle, then remove engine mount heat shield.
9. Remove engine mount bracket to block studs.
10. Remove engine mount from vehicle, then separate upper and lower mounts.
11. Reverse procedure to install.

Righthand

1. Support engine using support tool Nos. J42451, J41044 and J36462, or equivalent.
2. Raise and support vehicle using suitable lift.
3. Remove starter as outlined in "Electrical" section.
4. Remove battery ground cable from engine block.
5. Remove engine mount bracket to crossmember attaching bolts, then lower vehicle.
6. Raise righthand side of engine using support tool.
7. Raise and support vehicle using suitable lift.
8. Remove engine mount to bracket bolts, then the mount from vehicle.
9. Reverse procedure to install.

ENGINE

REPLACE

The engine and transmission are removed as an assembly.
The accelerator control cable must be replaced whenever the engine is removed.
1. Disconnect IAT and MAF sensor electrical connectors.
2. Remove air intake duct resonator.

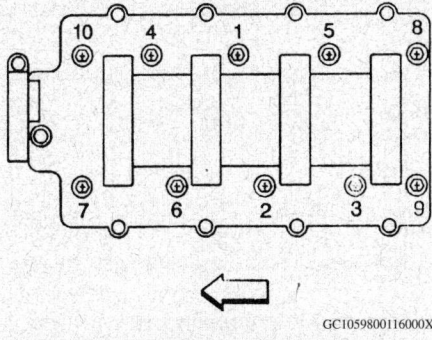

GC1059800116000X

Fig. 1   Intake manifold tightening sequence

3. Recover refrigerant as outlined under "Air Conditioning" chapter.
4. Relieve fuel system pressure as outlined under "Precautions" then raise and support vehicle using suitable lift.
5. Drain engine oil into suitable container, then remove front wheel and tire assemblies.
6. Drain engine coolant into suitable container, then remove righthand catalytic converter.
7. **On models equipped with manual transmission,** drain transmission fluid.
8. **On all models,** remove driveshaft and torque arm.
9. Remove starter motor.
10. **On models equipped with automatic transmission,** remove transmission range select cable.
11. **On models equipped with manual transmission,** remove clutch actuator line using special tool No. 36221, or equivalent.
12. **On all models,** remove lefthand side front air deflector.
13. Remove stabilizer bar brackets.
14. Remove intermediate steering shaft bolt and shaft from rack.
15. Remove ground bolt and straps from front rail.
16. Disconnect front wheel speed sensors.
17. Remove condenser hose bolt from A/C compressor.
18. Remove fuel line heat shield, then remove brake lines from retainer clip.
19. Lower vehicle, then remove A/C compressor hose from accumulator.
20. Remove inlet and outlet heater hoses from water pump.
21. Disconnect fuel line from fuel rail and vapor line from purge valve.
22. Remove accelerator and cruise control cables from throttle lever.
23. Remove accelerator and cruise control cables from servo adjuster as required.
24. Remove inlet hose from water pump.
25. Remove outlet hose from engine.
26. Remove brake booster vacuum hose, then disconnect two front brake lines from brake pressure modulator valve.
27. Disconnect forward lamp wiring harness from engine wiring harness.
28. Disconnect engine harness vacuum tube from bottom of vacuum check valve.

29. Disconnect PCM electrical connectors, then remove PCM.
30. Remove righthand side insulator panel, then hinge pillar trim panel.
31. Disconnect engine wiring harness from instrument panel harness.
32. Remove engine harness through front of dash.
33. **On models equipped with automatic transmission,** remove floor shift control.
34. **On models equipped with manual transmission,** remove shift control.
35. **On all models,** raise and support vehicle.
36. Remove righthand and lefthand lower shock bolts.
37. Remove cotter pins and nuts from righthand and lefthand upper ball joints.
38. Separate upper control arms from knuckles using separator tool No. 39549, or equivalent.
39. Remove both steering knuckles, then place engine support tool No. 39580, or equivalent, under vehicle.
40. Lower vehicle until crossmember is resting on support fixture.
41. Place engine wiring harness on top of engine.
42. Remove front crossmember bolts.
43. Remove transmission support bolts.
44. Raise vehicle to remove engine and transmission from vehicle.
45. Secure crossmember to support fixture.
46. Separate engine and transmission.
47. Reverse procedure to install.

INTAKE MANIFOLD
REPLACE

1. Drain cooling system into suitable container, then disconnect fuel lines from rail.
2. Disconnect IAT and MAF sensor electrical connectors.
3. Remove air intake duct.
4. Disconnect throttle body electrical connectors.
5. Remove accessory drive belt, then disconnect EGR valve connector.
6. Remove EGR valve tube.
7. Remove accelerator and cruise control cables from throttle lever.
8. Remove accelerator and cruise control cable bracket.
9. Disconnect fuel injector electrical connectors.
10. Disconnect MAP sensor electrical connector and vacuum hose.
11. Disconnect knock sensor and all remaining intake manifold electrical connectors.
12. Remove PCV tube, then the fresh air hose from throttle body.
13. Remove throttle body coolant hoses, then the EVAP purge tube.
14. Remove canister purge valve and bracket.
15. Remove intake manifold bolts, then the fuel rail stop bracket.
16. Remove intake manifold and gaskets.
17. Reverse procedure to install noting the following:
    a. Install new intake manifold gaskets.

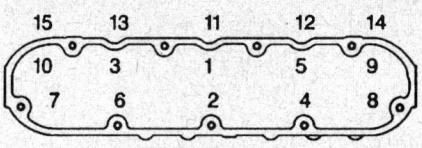

GC1069800912000X

Fig. 2   Cylinder head bolt tightening sequence

b. Apply GM threadlock partn No. 12345383, or equivalent to intake manifold bolts.
c. **Torque** intake manifold bolts to 44 inch lbs., in sequence, **Fig. 1.**
d. **Torque** intake manifold bolts to 90 inch lbs., in sequence, **Fig. 1.**

EXHAUST MANIFOLD
REPLACE
Lefthand

1. Loosen AIR hose clamps and remove hose assembly.
2. Do not remove check valve from AIR pipe unless service is needed.
3. Remove air pipe with check valve, bolts and gasket from lefthand exhaust manifold.
4. Remove spark plug wires from spark plugs. Do not remove from ignition coils unless required.
5. Do not remove oxygen sensor from exhaust manifold unless required.
6. Remove exhaust manifold bolts and gasket. Discard gasket.
7. Remove heat shield and bolts from manifold.
8. Reverse procedure to install.

Righthand

1. Do not remove EGR valve from pipe assembly unless service is required.
2. Remove EGR pipe and gasket from exhaust manifold.
3. With mild force, pull EGR pipe from intake manifold.
4. Remove O-ring seal from EGR valve pipe and discard.
5. Do not remove check valve from AIR pipe unless service is required.
6. Remove AIR pipe with check valve, from righthand exhaust manifold.
7. Remove spark plug wires from spark plugs. Do not remove wires from ignition coils unless required.
8. Do not remove oxygen sensor from exhaust manifold unless service is required.
9. Remove manifold and gasket, discard gasket.
10. Remove heat shield from manifold.
11. Reverse procedure to install.

CYLINDER HEAD
REPLACE
Lefthand

1. Remove intake manifold as outlined under "Intake Manifold, Replace."
2. Remove vapor vent tube from engine.

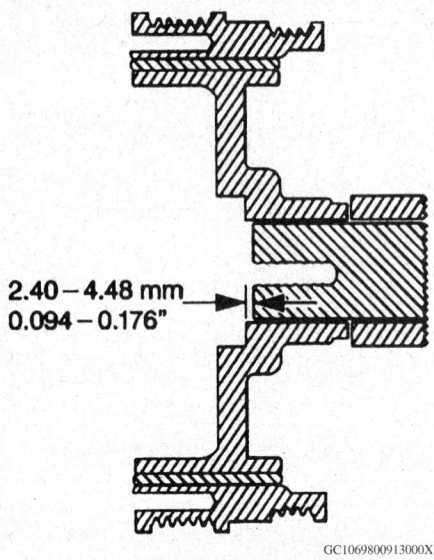

2.40 – 4.48 mm
0.094 – 0.176"

GC1069800913000X

Fig. 3 Crankshaft damper installation

3. Remove power steering pump pulley using a suitable puller.
4. Remove power steering pump and bracket.
5. Remove rocker arms, pedestals and pushrods.
6. Remove exhaust manifold as outlined under "Exhaust Manifold, Replace."
7. Remove ground straps from rear of cylinder head.
8. Remove spark plugs.
9. Remove cylinder head bolts, then the cylinder head. Discard M11 head bolts.
10. Reverse procedure to install noting the following:
    a. Clean cylinder head bolt holes, then ensure locating pins are in proper position.
    b. Ensure new gasket is installed facing proper direction.
    c. Install new M11 cylinder head bolts, then apply GM threadlock partn No. 12345382, or equivalent to M8 cylinder head bolts and install. M11 cylinder head bolts are identified as 1–10 and M8 bolts are 11–15, **Fig. 2.**
    d. **Torque** M11 head bolts to 22 ft. lbs., in sequence, **Fig. 2.**
    e. Tighten M11 cylinder head bolts an additional 90° in sequence .
    f. Tighten M11 head bolts 1–8 an additional 90° and bolts 9 and 10 an additional 50°.
    g. **Torque** M8 head bolts to 22 ft. lbs., in sequence.

Righthand

1. Remove intake manifold as outlined under "Intake Manifold, Replace."
2. Remove vapor vent tube from engine.
3. Remove exhaust manifold as outlined under "Exhaust Manifold, Replace."
4. Remove rocker arms, pedestals and pushrods.
5. Remove spark plugs.
6. Remove cylinder head bolts, then the cylinder head. Discard M11 head bolts.

7. Reverse procedure to install noting the following:
    a. Clean cylinder head bolt holes, then ensure locating pins are in proper position.
    b. Ensure new gasket is installed facing proper direction.
    c. Install new M11 cylinder head bolts, then apply GM threadlock part No. 12345382, or equivalent to M8 cylinder head bolts and install. M11 cylinder head bolts are identified as 1–10 and M8 bolts are 11–15, **Fig. 2.**
    d. **Torque** M11 head bolts to 22 ft. lbs., in sequence, **Fig. 2.**
    e. Tighten M11 cylinder head bolts an additional 90° in sequence.
    f. Tighten M11 head bolts 1–8 an additional 90° and bolts 9 and 10 an additional 50°.
    g. **Torque** M8 head bolts to 22 ft. lbs., in sequence.

VALVE COVER
REPLACE
Lefthand

1. Remove fuel lines from vehicle.
2. Remove PCV hose, then disconnect ignition coil main harness connector.
3. Remove spark plug wires, then the AIR hose and pipe.
4. Remove connector position assurance clip.
5. Remove valve cover bolts, then the valve cover.
6. Reverse procedure to install

Righthand

1. Remove AIR hose and pipe.
2. Disconnect ignition coil main harness.
3. Remove spark plug wires, then the valve cover bolts and valve cover.
4. Reverse procedure to install.

CAMSHAFT LOBE LIFT SPECIFICATIONS

Engine	Int., Inch	Exh., Inch
5.7L	.292	.292

VALVE ADJUSTMENT

This engine is equipped with hydraulic lifters, no adjustment is required.

CRANKSHAFT DAMPER
REPLACE

1. Remove accessory drive belts.
2. Raise and support vehicle, then remove starter.
3. Remove righthand torque converter cover, then the transmission oil cooler lines from radiator.
4. Remove power steering cooler if equipped.
5. Install flywheel holder tool No. J42386.
6. Remove crankshaft balancer bolt.

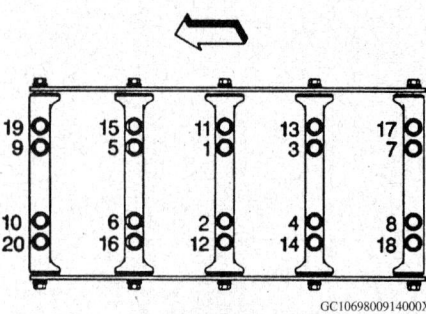

GC1069800914000X

Fig. 4 Main bearing tightening sequence

7. Install puller tool Nos. J41816 and J41816-2, or equivalent, then remove damper.
8. Reverse procedure to install, noting the following:
    a. Install crankshaft damper using pulley installation tool No. J41665, or equivalent.
    b. Transfer pulley weights if applicable.
    c. **Torque** crankshaft damper to 240 ft. lbs., using old damper bolt.
    d. Remove and discard damper bolt, then ensure nose of crankshaft extends .094–.176 inch into balancer bore, **Fig. 3.**
    e. If measurement is not as specified, repeat installation procedure.
    f. **Torque** new crankshaft damper bolt to 37 ft. lbs., then an additional 240 ft. lbs., then a final 140° using torque angle meter tool No. J36660, or equivalent.

FRONT COVER
REPLACE

1. Raise and support vehicle.
2. Remove cooling fan electrical connectors.
3. Drain engine coolant and engine oil into suitable containers.
4. Lower vehicle, then disconnect IAT and MAF sensors.
5. Remove air intake duct, then the accessory drive belts.
6. Remove coolant hoses from water pump and thermostat housing.
7. Remove upper radiator support, then the cooling fans and belt tensioner.
8. Disconnect overflow hose from radiator.
9. Remove throttle body coolant hoses and idler pulley.
10. Remove water pump as outlined under "Water Pump, Replace."
11. Remove crankshaft damper as outlined under "Crankshaft Damper, Replace."
12. Raise and support vehicle, then remove starter.
13. Remove righthand torque converter cover, then loosen oil pan attaching bolts.
14. Remove front cover bolts, then the front cover and gasket.
15. Remove front oil seal.
16. Reverse procedure to install, noting the following:

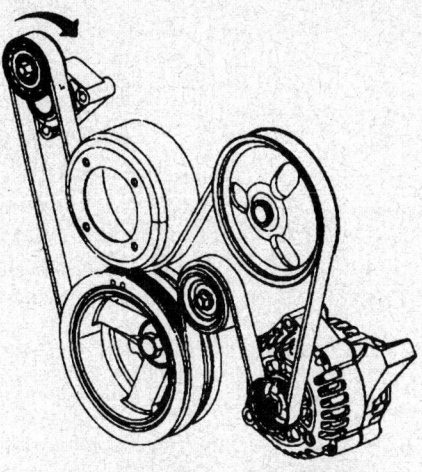

Fig. 5   Accessory drive belt routing (Part 1 of 2)

a. Install front cover and gasket to engine, then hand tighten bolts.
b. Install front cover alignment tool No. J41480, or equivalent and **torque** to 18 ft. lbs.
c. Install seal alignment tool No. J41476, or equivalent and finger tighten.
d. **Torque** front cover bolts to 18 ft. lbs.
e. Place a suitable straightedge across engine block and front cover oil pan sealing surfaces.
f. Avoid contact with portion of gasket that extends into oil pan surface. Insert a suitable feeler gauge between front cover and straightedge.
g. Ensure cover is flush with oil pan surface or .020 inch maximum below flush. If measurements are not as specified, repeat alignment procedure.
h. Install new crankshaft oil seal using installer tool No. J41478, or equivalent.

MAIN BEARINGS

When replacing crankshaft bearings, it is essential that correct tolerances are achieved. If bearing clearance is not within specification, crankshaft position sensor signals may be affected. When replacing main bearings, the M8 bearing cap side bolts must be replaced. Refer to "Engine Rebuilding Specifications" for correct bearing clearance and to **Fig. 4,** for main bearing cap tightening sequence.

When replacing main bearings, proceed as follows:
1. Hand tighten M10 main bearing cap bolts, then tap caps into place using a suitable plastic hammer.
2. Install new M8 bearing cap side bolts.
3. **Torque** inner main bearing cap M10 bolts to 15 ft. lbs., in sequence, **Fig. 4.**
4. Tap crankshaft backward and then forward to align thrust bearings using a suitable plastic hammer.
5. Tighten M10 inner main bearing cap bolts an additional 80° in sequence.

6. **Torque** outer main bearing cap M10 bolts to 15 ft. lbs., in sequence, **Fig. 4.**
7. Tighten M10 outer main bearing cap bolts an additional 53° in sequence.
8. **Torque** M8 bearing cap side bolts to 18 ft. lbs.
9. Tighten cap side bolt, then proceed to opposite side.

REAR COVER
REPLACE

1. Place alignment marks on flywheel and crankshaft for installation reference.
2. Remove flywheel.
3. Remove rear cover attaching bolts, then the cover and gasket.
4. Remove oil seal from cover.
5. Reverse procedure to install, noting the following:
   a. Install cover and gasket to engine, then hand tighten bolts.
   b. Install cover alignment tool No. J41480, or equivalent, and **torque** to 18 ft. lbs.
   c. Rotate crankshaft until two opposing flywheel bolt holes are parallel to oil pan surface.
   d. Install seal alignment tool No. J41476, or equivalent and finger tighten.
   e. **Torque** rear cover bolts to 18 ft. lbs.
   f. Place a suitable straightedge across engine block and rear cover oil pan sealing surfaces.
   g. Avoid contact with portion of gasket that extends into oil pan surface. Insert a suitable feeler gauge between cover and straightedge.
   h. Ensure cover is flush with oil pan surface or .010 inch maximum below flush. If measurements are not as specified, repeat alignment procedure.
   i. Install new crankshaft oil seal using installer tool No. J41479, or equivalent.

CRANKSHAFT SEAL
REPLACE

Refer to "Front Cover, Replace" for front crankshaft seal replacement.

CRANKSHAFT REAR OIL SEAL
REPLACE

Refer to "Rear Cover, Replace" for rear crankshaft seal replacement.

OIL PAN
REPLACE

1. Support engine using engine support tool Nos. J41044, J36462-A, J42451 and J28467-B, or equivalent.
2. Raise and support vehicle.
3. Remove oil filter, then drain engine oil into suitable container.
4. Remove righthand and lefthand engine mount to cradle bolts, then the lower shock bolts.

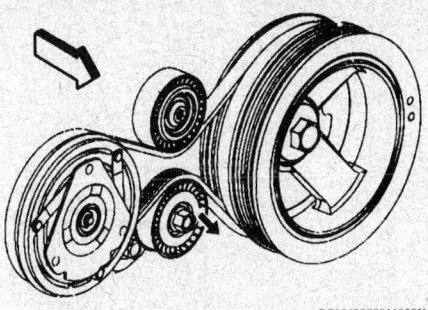

GC1069800911020X

Fig. 5   Accessory drive belt routing (Part 2 of 2)

5. Remove intermediate steering shaft bolt, then support engine cradle.
6. Disconnect and remove oil level sensor.
7. Remove starter, then the righthand and lefthand torque converter covers.
8. Loosen six cradle bolts. Lower cradle and raise engine as required.
9. Remove oil pan attaching bolts, then the oil pan.
10. Reverse procedure to install, noting the following:
    a. Apply a .200 inch bead of GM sealant part No. 12378190, or equivalent where front and rear covers meet engine block.
    b. Install gasket to oil pan. Ensure gasket is properly aligned.
    c. Install oil pan bolts through gasket, then oil pan to engine block. Tighten bolts hand tight.
    d. Ensure oil pan is flush with rear of engine block using a suitable straight edge.
    e. Ensure gap between straight edge and oil pan does not exceed .020 inch using a suitable feeler gauge. If measurement is not within specification, remove oil pan and repeat alignment procedure.
    f. **Torque** oil pan to front cover and block bolts to 18 ft. lbs.
    g. **Torque** oil pan to rear cover bolts to 108 inch lbs.

SERPENTINE DRIVE BELT

1. Rotate drive belt tensioner in clockwise direction.
2. Remove belt, then clean drive belt surfaces.
3. Reverse procedure to install. Refer to **Fig. 5,** for drive belt routing.

COOLING SYSTEM BLEED

1. Fill radiator to below fill neck.
2. Fill coolant recovery bottle to FULL HOT mark.
3. Install coolant recovery reservoir cap.
4. Operate engine with radiator cap off until operating temperature is reached.
5. While engine is at idle, add coolant to radiator until coolant level reaches bottom of fill neck.

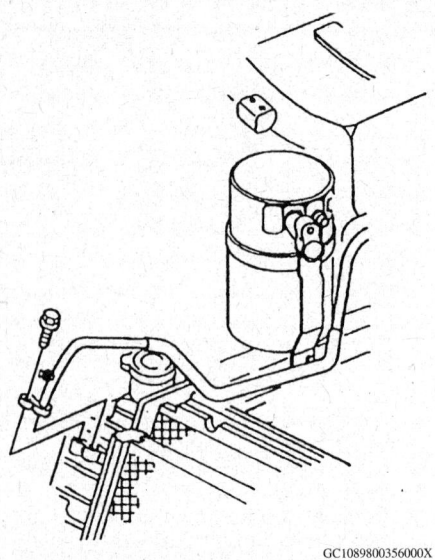

GC10898003560000X

Fig. 6   Evaporator tube removal

6. Install radiator cap and inspect system for leaks.

WATER PUMP
REPLACE

1. Raise and support vehicle.
2. Disconnect cooling fan electrical connectors, then drain coolant into suitable container.
3. Lower vehicle.
4. Disconnect IAT and MAF sensor electrical connectors.
5. Remove air intake duct, then the radiator hose from thermostat housing.
6. Remove water pump inlet hose, then the air cleaner assembly.
7. Remove radiator inlet hose, then the electric cooling fans.
8. Remove accessory drive belts.
9. Remove tensioner from water pump, then the overflow hose from radiator.

10. Remove water pump pulley.
11. Remove water pump attaching bolts, then the water pump.
12. Reverse procedure to install.

RADIATOR
REPLACE

1. Recover refrigerant as outlined under "Air Conditioning" chapter.
2. Drain cooling system into suitable container, then remove radiator hoses.
3. Remove upper evaporator tube bracket bolt, **Fig. 6.**
4. Remove evaporator tube from condenser.
5. Remove upper and lower oil cooler lines from radiator, if equipped.
6. Remove condenser tube from condenser, **Fig. 7.**
7. Remove overflow hose from radiator.
8. Remove air intake duct and air cleaner assembly, then disconnect cooling fan electrical connectors.
9. Remove electric cooling fans, then the coolant level indicator module if equipped.
10. Remove radiator and condenser.
11. Reverse procedure to install.

FUEL PUMP
REPLACE

1. Drain fuel tank into suitable container, then remove fuel tank filler pocket.
2. Raise and support vehicle, then remove filler pipe shield.
3. Remove exhaust system and shields from converter to muffler.
4. Remove rear axle as outlined under "Rear Axle, Replace" in the "Rear Axle & Suspension" section.
5. Clean all fuel and EVAP lines, then disconnect and cap ends.
6. Disconnect fuel tank vent hose from rear brake hose bracket, then remove rear line clip.

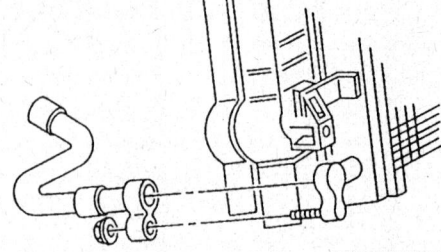

GC10898003570000X

Fig. 7   Condenser tube removal

7. Disconnect fuel electrical harness from fuel tank flange, then the sender and pressure sensor electrical connectors.
8. Support fuel tank, then remove left-hand fuel tank strap bolt from under body bracket.
9. Remove EVAP canister vent solenoid and bracket.
10. Remove righthand fuel tank strap, then the fuel tank.
11. Remove fuel sender retaining nuts, then the retaining ring, sender assembly and seal.
12. Reverse procedure to install noting the following:
    a. Clean all sealing surfaces and install new seal.
    b. Inspect fuel system for leaks.

FUEL FILTER
REPLACE

1. Raise and support vehicle.
2. Clean fuel filter connections.
3. Disconnect fuel filter quick connect fitting using quick disconnect tool No. J37088-A, or equivalent.
4. Disconnect threaded fuel filter line.
5. Cap fuel lines to prevent fuel system contamination.
6. Remove fuel filter from bracket.
7. Reverse procedure to install. Inspect and replace fuel filter O-ring if required.

TIGHTENING SPECIFICATIONS

Year	Component	Torque/Ft. Lbs.
2001–02	A/C Compressor Bolts	37
	A/C Compressor Bracket Bolts	37
	Air Injection Tube To Exhaust Manifold Bolts	15①
	Alternator Bracket	37
	Belt Tensioner Bolts	37
	Camshaft Retainer Bolts	18
	Camshaft Sensor Bolt	18
	Camshaft Sprocket Bolt	18
	Catalytic Converter Nut	18
	Connecting Rod Bolts	15①
	Coolant Temperature Gauge Sensor	15
	Crankshaft Balancer Bolt	②
	Crankshaft Bearing Cap Bolt	③
	Crankshaft Position Sensor	18
	Cylinder Head Bolts	④
	EGR Pipe To Cylinder Head	37
	EGR Valve	18
	Engine Mount Stud To Engine Block	37
	Engine Mount Through Bolts	70
	Engine Mount Through Bolt Nuts	59
	Engine Mount To Engine Block Bolts	37
	Exhaust Manifold	18
	Flywheel Bolts	⑤
	Front Cover	18
	Fuel Sender	58⑥
	Fuel Tank Straps	24
	Ignition Coil	106⑥
	Intake Manifold	⑦
	Lifter Guide Bolts	106⑥
	Oil Filter	22
	Oil Level Sensor	26
	Oil Pan	⑧
	Oil Pan Drain Plug	18
	Oil Pressure Sensor	13
	Oil Pump To Engine Block	18
	Oil Pump Screen To Pump	106⑥
	Oxygen Sensor	31
	Power Steering Pump	18
	Rear Cover Bolts	18
	Rocker Arms	22
	Spark Plugs	12
	Starter Motor	37
	Thermostat Housing	11
	Throttle Body	106⑥
	Valve Cover	106⑥
	Water Pump	18
	Water Pump Pulley	89⑥

① — Tighten additional 60.°
② — Refer to "Crankshaft Damper, Replace."
③ — Refer to "Main Bearings."
④ — Refer to "Cylinder Head, Replace."
⑤ — Tighten in three steps; 1st step, 15 ft. lbs., 2nd step, 37 ft. lbs., 3rd step 74 ft. lbs.
⑥ — Inch lbs.
⑦ — Refer to "Intake Manifold, Replace."
⑧ — Refer to "Oil Pan, Replace."

Rear Axle & Suspension

NOTE: On Air Bag Equipped Models, Refer To "Air Bag System Precautions" Located In The Front Of This Manual For System Disarming & Arming Procedures.

NOTE: Refer To "Computer Relearn Procedures" Located In The Front Of This Manual When Battery Power To The Computer Has Been Interrupted.

INDEX

REAR AXLE

REPLACE

1. Raise and support vehicle, then remove rear wheels.
2. Remove driveshaft, then the stabilizer shaft.
3. Support axle using a suitable jack.
4. Remove rear shock absorbers, then the track bar.
5. Disconnect brake hose from rear brake hose junction block.
6. Remove coil springs as outlined under "Coil Spring, Replace."
7. Remove parking brake cables from axle housing.
8. Disconnect wheel speed sensors if equipped.
9. Remove torque arm, then the lower control arms.
10. Lower axle from vehicle.
11. Reverse procedure to install. Bleed brake system as outlined under "Hydraulic Brake Systems."

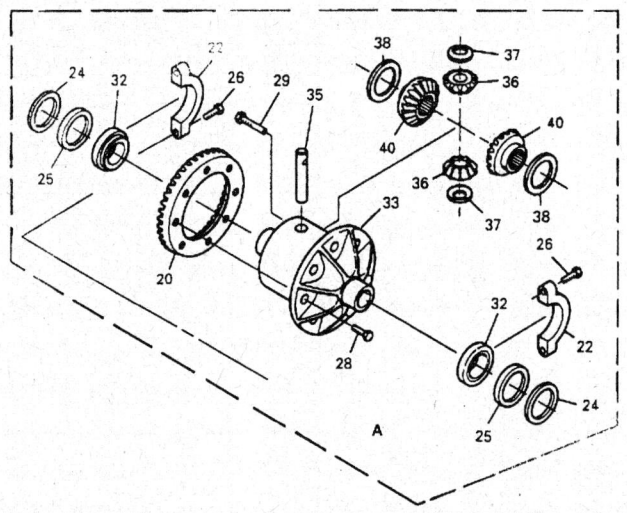

Fig. 1 Pinion gear shaft & lock bolt removal

GC2039600116000X

REAR AXLE SHAFT

REPLACE

If the vehicle is equipped with acceleration slip regulation (ASR) traction control, care must be taken not to damage rear wheel speed sensor reluctor wheel. The sensing wheel is located on the axle shaft and must be replaced if damage occurs.

1. Raise and support vehicle.
2. Clean axle housing cover and disconnect parking brake guide.
3. Remove cover bolts and pry cover loose.
4. Drain lubricant, clean old gasket from both sealing surfaces.
5. Remove rear wheels and brake assembly.
6. **On models less traction control,** install exciter ring protector kit tool No. J39446, or equivalent, to speed sensor reluctor wheel and remove.
7. **On all models,** remove differential pinion gear shaft lock bolt (29) from case (33) and then the pinion gear shaft (35), **Fig. 1.**

8. Remove axle shaft lock by pushing flanged end of axle shaft into housing.
9. Slide axle shaft from housing. Take care in removal as splines on end of shaft may damage seal.
10. Reverse procedure to install, noting the following:
    a. Ensure axle shaft splines mesh with splines on side gears.
    b. When installing axle shaft lock, ensure it seats inside counterbore of side gear.
    c. Install Loctite 242, or equivalent, when installing pinion gear shaft bolt and **torque** to 27 ft. lbs.

PROPELLER SHAFT

REPLACE

1. Raise and support vehicle, then mark relationship of propeller shaft assembly to pinion gear yoke.
2. Remove center support bearing and washers from torque arm assembly.
3. **On two-piece propeller shafts,** remove bolts from center support bearing.

4. **On all propeller shafts,** remove bolts and retainers, then the propeller shaft.
5. Reverse procedure to install, noting the following:
   a. Lubricate slip yoke with .6 ounces of propeller shaft slip yoke lubricant 1050169, or equivalent.
   b. Align marks on pinion gear yoke and propeller shaft.

SHOCK ABSORBER

REPLACE

1. Fold down seat back frame, then remove quarter trim panel.
2. Pull folding carpet back, then raise and support vehicle.
3. Support rear axle, then remove shock absorber.
4. Reverse procedure to install.

COIL SPRING

REPLACE

1. Raise and support vehicle, then support rear axle with an adjustable lifting

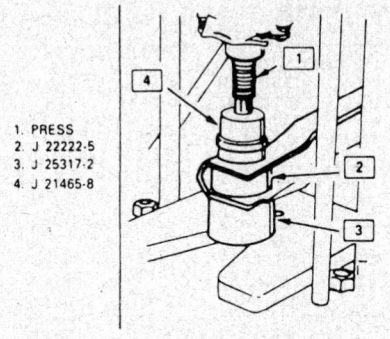

Fig. 2 Control arm bushing removal

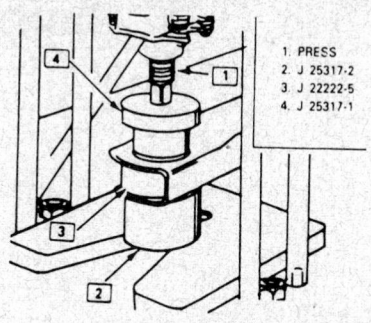

Fig. 3 Control arm bushing installation

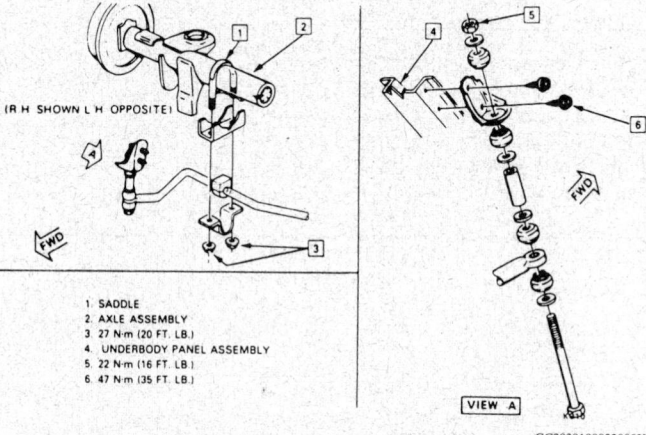

1. SADDLE
2. AXLE ASSEMBLY
3. 27 N·m (20 FT. LB.)
4. UNDERBODY PANEL ASSEMBLY
5. 22 N·m (16 FT. LB.)
6. 47 N·m (35 FT. LB.)

Fig. 4 Stabilizer bar replacement

device. **Do not use twin post type hoist.**
2. Remove shock absorber nuts from rear axle, then lower rear axle.
3. Remove upper insulator assembly, then the rear spring.
4. Reverse procedure to install.

CONTROL ARM
REPLACE
Lower

If both control arms are to be removed, remove one control arm at a time to prevent axle from slipping or rolling.
1. Raise vehicle and support at frame pads. Support nose of axle housing to prevent assembly from twisting when control arm is removed.
2. Remove bolts securing control arm to chassis and rear axle, and the control arm.
3. Reverse procedure to install.

CONTROL ARM BUSHING
REPLACE

1. Raise and support vehicle and remove control arm.
2. Press bushings out of control arm using suitable tools, **Fig. 2.**

3. Reverse procedure to install, ensure bushing is properly seated in control arm, **Fig. 3.** If replacement bushing fits loosely in control arm, or if mounting areas are damaged or deformed, **control arm must be replaced.**

STABILIZER BAR
REPLACE

1. Raise and support vehicle.
2. Remove link bolt nuts, washers, bushings, spacers and link bolts securing stabilizer to chassis, **Fig. 4.**
3. Remove clamps securing stabilizer shaft to rear axle and stabilizer shaft.

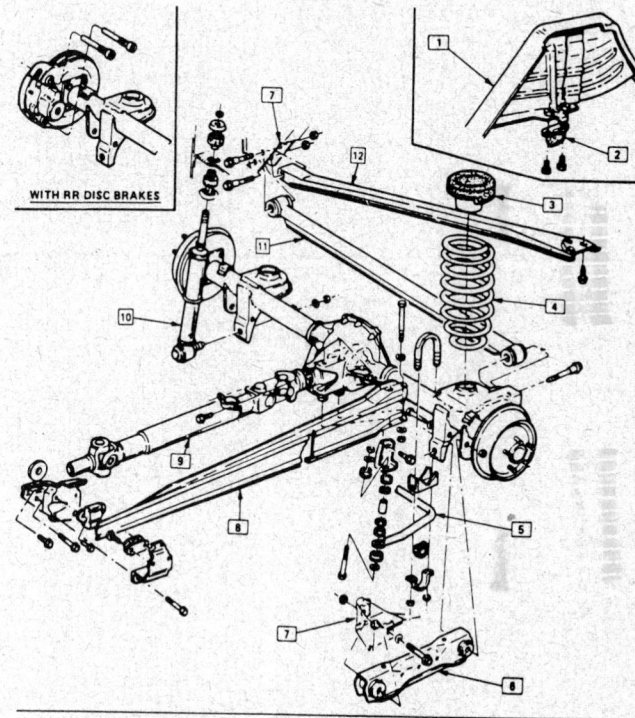

1. RAIL
2. JOUNCE BUMPER
3. SPRING INSULATOR ASSEMBLY
4. COIL SPRING
5. OPTIONAL STABILIZER BAR
6. LOWER CONTROL ARM
7. UNDERBODY
8. TORQUE ARM
9. PROP SHAFT
10. SHOCK ABSORBER
11. TRACK BAR
12. TRACK BAR BRACE

Fig. 5 Track rod replacement

4. Reverse procedure to install.

TRACK ROD
REPLACE

1. Raise vehicle and support rear axle at curb height.
2. Remove track bar mounting bolt and nut from rear axle and from body bracket, then remove track rod, **Fig. 5.**
3. Remove heat shield attaching screws from track bar brace.
4. Remove three track bar to body brace screws.
5. Remove nut and bolt from body bracket, then remove track bar brace.
6. Reverse procedure to install.

TIGHTENING SPECIFICATIONS

Year	Component	Torque/Ft. lbs.
2001–02	Control Arm Bolts	80
	Control Arm Nuts	60
	Differential Pinion Gear Shaft Lock Bolt	27
	Shock Absorber Lower Nut	66
	Shock Absorber Upper Nut	13
	Stabilizer Link	16
	Stabilizer Shaft Bracket Bolts	17
	Stabilizer Shaft Nuts	18
	Torque Arm To Rear Axle Bolts	96
	Torque Arm To Transmission Center Bolt	20
	Torque Arm To Transmission Lower & Upper Bolts	37
	Torque Arm To Transmission Nuts	30
	Wheel Lug Nuts	100
	Yoke Nut	①

① — Tighten until endplay is near 0, then measure preload. If using new bearings, preload should be 15–30 inch lbs. If reinstalling old bearings, ensure preload is 10–15 inch lbs.

Front Suspension & Steering

NOTE: On Air Bag Equipped Models, Refer To "Air Bag System Precautions" Located In The Front Of This Manual For System Disarming & Arming Procedures.

NOTE: Refer To "Computer Relearn Procedures" Located In The Front Of This Manual When Battery Power To The Computer Has Been Interrupted.

INDEX

PRECAUTIONS

Air Bag Systems

Refer to "Air Bag System Precautions" in the front of this manual for system disarming and arming procedures.

Battery Ground Cable

Prior to service, disconnect battery ground cable and isolate as required.

DESCRIPTION

The short/long arm (SLA) front suspension assembly, **Fig. 1,** is designed to allow each wheel to compensate for changes in road surface level without significantly affecting the opposite wheel. Each wheel is independently connected to the frame by a steering knuckle, wheel hub, shock absorber and spring, upper and lower ball studs and upper and lower control arms.

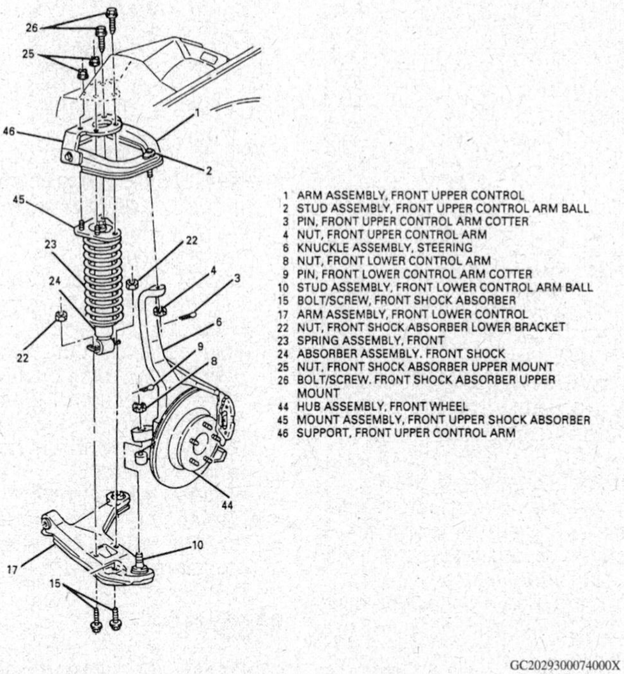

1 ARM ASSEMBLY, FRONT UPPER CONTROL
2 STUD ASSEMBLY, FRONT UPPER CONTROL ARM BALL
3 PIN, FRONT UPPER CONTROL ARM COTTER
4 NUT, FRONT UPPER CONTROL ARM
6 KNUCKLE ASSEMBLY, STEERING
8 NUT, FRONT LOWER CONTROL ARM
9 PIN, FRONT LOWER CONTROL ARM COTTER
10 STUD ASSEMBLY, FRONT LOWER CONTROL ARM BALL
15 BOLT/SCREW, FRONT SHOCK ABSORBER
17 ARM ASSEMBLY, FRONT LOWER CONTROL
22 NUT, FRONT SHOCK ABSORBER LOWER BRACKET
23 SPRING ASSEMBLY, FRONT
24 ABSORBER ASSEMBLY. FRONT SHOCK
25 NUT, FRONT SHOCK ABSORBER UPPER MOUNT
26 BOLT/SCREW. FRONT SHOCK ABSORBER UPPER MOUNT
44 HUB ASSEMBLY, FRONT WHEEL
45 MOUNT ASSEMBLY, FRONT UPPER SHOCK ABSORBER
46 SUPPORT, FRONT UPPER CONTROL ARM

GC2029300074000X

Fig. 1   Exploded view of front suspension

HUB & BEARING
REPLACE

1. Raise and support vehicle, then remove tire and wheel assembly on side to be serviced.
2. Remove brake caliper assembly and brake disc.
3. Disconnect wheel speed sensor electrical connector and secure aside.
4. Remove bolts and screws from hub assembly, then the hub assembly.
5. Reverse procedure to install, **torque** retaining bolts to 63 ft. lbs.

BALL JOINT INSPECTION

Lower

1. Raise and support vehicle by positioning floor stands under both lower control arms, then wipe grease fitting free of dirt and grease.
2. Position dial indicator against wheel rim.
3. While reading dial indicator, pry between lower control arm and steering knuckle. Vertical movement should not exceed .047 inch, if so, replace ball joint.

Upper

1. Raise front end of vehicle and position floor stands under both lower control arms as near to ball joints as possible.
2. Position a dial indicator against wheel rim, **Fig. 2.** Push in on bottom of tire while pulling out at top, then reverse procedure.
3. Deflection on dial indicator should not exceed .125 inch. If deflection exceeds

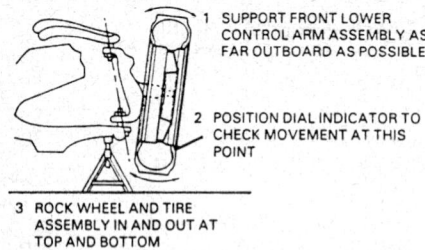

Fig. 2 Upper ball joint inspection

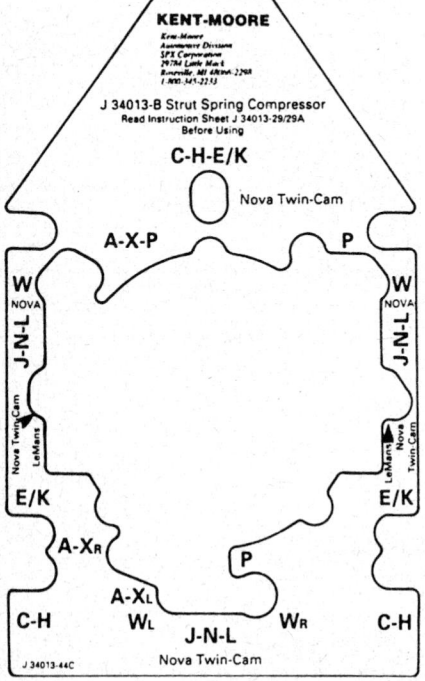

Fig. 4 Modular shock absorber assembly compressor mounting hole locations

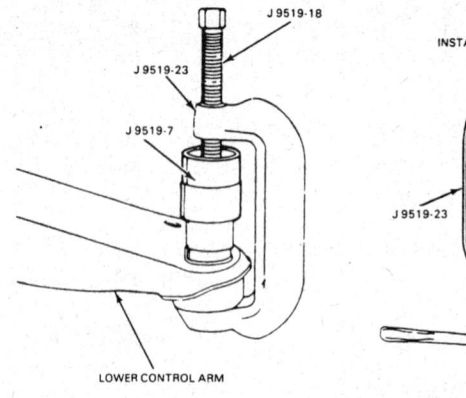

Fig. 3 Lower ball joint replacement

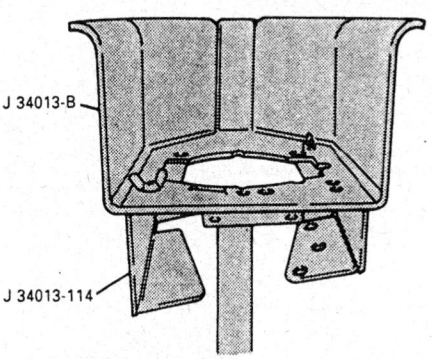

Fig. 5 Modular shock absorber assembly compressor adapter. Driver side

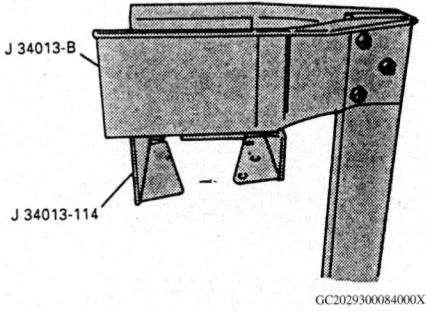

Fig. 6 Modular shock absorber assembly compressor adapter. Passenger side

---

specification, replace ball joint.

4. If ball joint is disconnected from steering knuckle, inspect for looseness or see if ball joint can be twisted in its socket using your fingers.

5. If either of the above conditions exist, replace ball joint.

BALL JOINT

REPLACE

Lower

1. Raise vehicle and support at frame, and remove wheel and tire.

2. Position a suitable jack under lower control arm spring seat, and raise jack to compress coil spring. **Jack must remain in place during ball joint replacement to hold spring and lower control arm in position.**

3. Remove cotter pin and nut securing ball joint stud to steering knuckle, then disconnect joint from knuckle using a suitable tool.

4. Lift knuckle assembly from ball stud,

guiding control arm out of splash shield, then support knuckle aside to allow clearance for joint removal.

5. Remove grease fitting, then press ball joint assembly out of lower control arm using a suitable tool, **Fig. 3.**

6. Press replacement joint into arm by reversing removal tools, fit spindle over ball stud, install washer, if equipped, and retaining nut.

7. Tighten retaining nut.

8. Tighten nut up to an additional 1/16 turn to align hole in ball stud with nut, then install cotter pin.

Upper

1. Raise and support vehicle, then remove wheel.

2. Place a floor jack under shock absorber mounting location on lower control. **Jack must remain in place during ball joint replacement to hold spring and lower control arm in position.**

3. Loosen ball joint from steering knuckle, then remove cotter pin and nut.

4. Support steering knuckle with floor stands, then disconnect ball joint from upper control arm using ball joint/tie rod separator tool No. J39549, or equivalent.

5. With upper control arm in raised position, drill out four rivets approximately 1/4 inch deep using a 1/8 inch drill bit.

6. Drill off rivet heads using a 1/2 inch drill bit, then punch out rivets using a small punch and remove ball joint.

7. Position new ball joint and install bolts and nuts supplied with new ball joint.

8. Remove support from steering knuckle, then connect ball joint to steering knuckle.

9. Tighten nut enough to align slot with stud hole, then tighten nut and install cotter pin.

STRUT SERVICE

1. If servicing driver's side strut, remove brake master cylinder nuts, then move master cylinder aside.

2. Remove upper shock absorber mounting nuts and bolts, then raise and support vehicle.

3. Remove tire and wheel assembly, then disconnect stabilizer shaft link.

4. Remove lower shock absorber mounting nuts and bolts, then separate lower ball joint from steering knuckle.

5. Mark lower mount location relative to upper mount location, then remove shock absorber and spring assembly.

6. Proceed as follows to disassemble shock absorber assembly:

a. Install modular shock assembly compressor adapter tool No. J34013-114, or equivalent, onto strut spring compressor tool No. J34013-B, or equivalent, using wing nuts to secure tool to mounting holes C-H in lower lefthand corner and P in upper righthand corner for driver side shock absorber assembly, **Figs. 4 and 5,** or to holes A-X-P in upper lefthand corner and C-H in lower righthand corner for

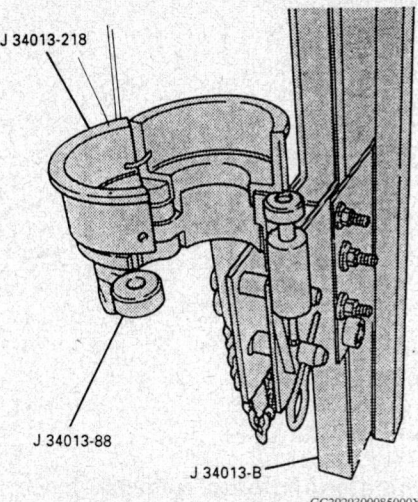

Fig. 7 Strut compressor adapter & modular shock support to strut spring compressor mounting

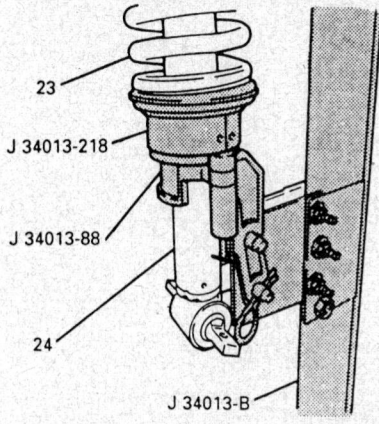

23 SPRING ASSEMBLY, FRONT
24 ABSORBER ASSEMBLY, FRONT SHOCK

GC2029300088000X

Fig. 10 Shock absorber assembly to strut spring compressor installation

passenger side shock absorber assembly, **Fig. 6.**

b. Install strut compressor adapter tool No. J34013-88, or equivalent, and modular shock support tool No. J34013-218, or equivalent, onto strut spring compressor, **Fig. 7.** Ensure strut compressor adapter and modular shock support are aligned so that they can open and close together. If tools are not properly aligned, they will not open.

c. Install shock absorber assembly to top of modular shock assembly compressor adapter, **Figs. 8 and 9.** Ensure top of shock absorber assembly is flat against modular shock assembly compressor adapter. Shock absorber assembly will not be aligned properly if it does not lay flat against tool.

d. Install shock absorber assembly

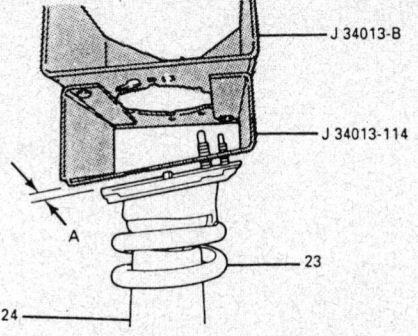

A MATCHING ANGLE BETWEEN SHOCK ABSORBER ASSEMBLY AND J 34013-114
23 SPRING ASSEMBLY, FRONT
24 ABSORBER ASSEMBLY, FRONT SHOCK

GC2029300086000X

Fig. 8 Upper driver side shock absorber assembly to strut spring compressor installation

into strut compressor adapter and modular shock support, **Fig. 10,** then close strut compressor adapter and modular shock support and install locking pin. **Ensure mounting ears of shock absorber assembly are facing downward toward rear of strut spring compressor or shock absorber assembly will not align properly.**

e. Turn screw on strut spring compressor counterclockwise to raise shock absorber assembly up to modular shock assembly compressor adapter. Ensure studs go through guide holes in modular shock assembly compressor adapter and top of shock absorber assembly is flat against tool.

f. Compress front spring assembly approximately ½ inch or three or four complete turns of screw on modular shock assembly compressor adapter. **Do not over compress front spring assembly. Severe overloading may cause tool failure, possibly resulting in personal injury.**

g. Insert J39642-1 from modular shock nut removal set tool No. J39642, or equivalent, on shock absorber nut, then insert tool No. J39642-2, or equivalent, from modular shock nut removal set tool Nos. J39642 through J39642-1, or equivalents, to hold shock absorber rod in place.

h. Remove shock absorber nut and discard, then turn strut spring compressor clockwise to relieve spring pressure.

7. Proceed as follows to assemble shock absorber assembly:

a. Install shock absorber to strut compressor adapter and modular shock support. **Ensure mounting ears of shock absorber assembly are facing downward toward rear of strut spring compressor or shock absorber assembly will not align properly.**

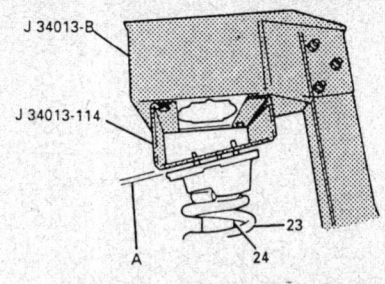

A MATCHING ANGLE BETWEEN SHOCK ABSORBER ASSEMBLY AND J 34013-114
23 SPRING ASSEMBLY, FRONT
24 ABSORBER ASSEMBLY, FRONT SHOCK

GC2029300087000X

Fig. 9 Upper passenger side shock absorber assembly to strut spring compressor installation

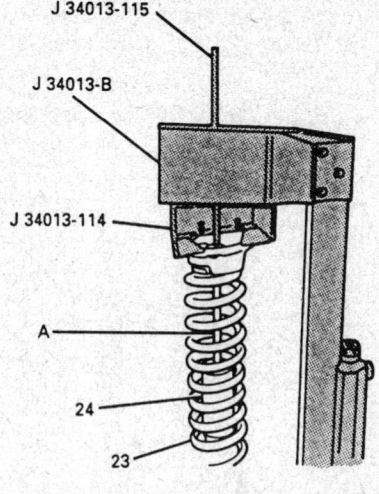

A ROD, FRONT SHOCK ABSORBER
23 SPRING ASSEMBLY, FRONT
24 ABSORBER ASSEMBLY, FRONT SHOCK

GC2029300089000X

Fig. 11 Modular shock assembly alignment rod installation

b. Close strut compressor adapter and modular shock support and install locking pin, then ensure upper and lower spring seats are positioned correctly.

c. Assemble shock absorber assembly to top of modular shock assembly compressor adapter. **Ensure top of shock absorber assembly is flat against modular shock assembly compressor adapter. Shock absorber assembly will not be aligned properly if it does not lay flat against tool.**

d. Turn screw on strut spring compressor counterclockwise to raise shock absorber assembly up to modular shock assembly compressor adapter without compressing spring assembly. Ensure studs on shock absorber assembly go through guide holes in modular shock assembly compressor adapter. **Only turn screw until**

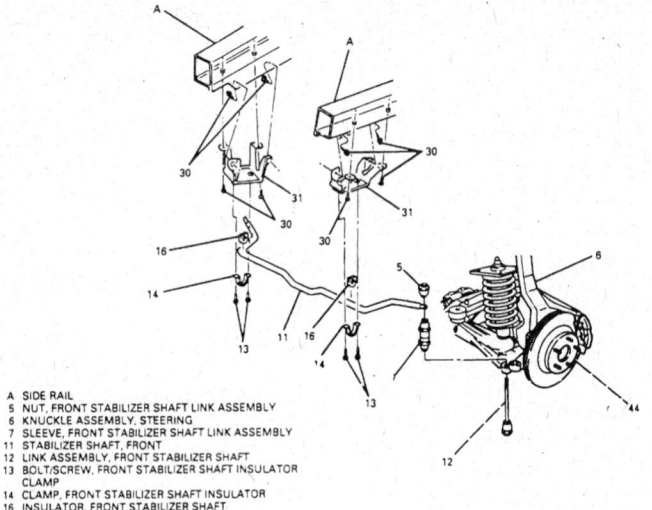

A SIDE RAIL
5 NUT, FRONT STABILIZER SHAFT LINK ASSEMBLY
6 KNUCKLE ASSEMBLY, STEERING
7 SLEEVE, FRONT STABILIZER SHAFT LINK ASSEMBLY
11 STABILIZER SHAFT, FRONT
12 LINK ASSEMBLY, FRONT STABILIZER SHAFT
13 BOLT/SCREW, FRONT STABILIZER SHAFT INSULATOR CLAMP
14 CLAMP, FRONT STABILIZER SHAFT INSULATOR
16 INSULATOR, FRONT STABILIZER SHAFT
30 BOLT/SCREW, FRONT STABILIZER SHAFT BRACKET
31 BRACKET ASSEMBLY, FRONT STABILIZER SHAFT
44 HUB ASSEMBLY, FRONT WHEEL

GC2029500206000X

Fig. 12 Stabilizer shaft replacement

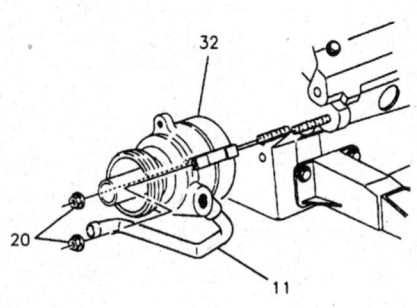

11 HOSE, POWER STEERING FLUID RESERVOIR
20 NUT, POWER STEERING PUMP
32 PUMP, POWER STEERING

GC6049600174000X

Fig. 14 Power steering pump replacement. 3800 engine

shock absorber assembly is held in strut spring compressor by itself. Do not load spring assembly.

e. Place modular shock assembly alignment rod J34013-115 down through top of strut spring compressor, through top of shock absorber assembly and onto shock absorber rod, **Fig. 11. Ensure shock assembly alignment rod is straight with shock absorber assembly. If shock assembly alignment rod is angled, repeat preceding steps until tool is straight.**

f. Turn operating screw clockwise to compress spring assembly until threaded portion of shock absorber rod is through top of shock absorber assembly. **Do not over compress front spring assembly.**

Severe overloading may cause tool failure, possibly resulting in personal injury.

g. Remove modular shock assembly alignment rod, then insert a new shock absorber nut on shock absorber rod. **Always replace shock absorber nut. Do not turn shock absorber rod when tightening nut or shock absorber assembly could be damaged. Retain shock absorber rod in a stationary position when tightening nut.**

h. Place tool No. J39642-1, or equivalent, from modular shock nut removal set tool No. J39642, or equivalent, on shock absorber nut, then insert J39642-2 from modular shock nut removal set J–39642 through J39642-1 to hold shock absorber rod in place and tighten nut.

i. Remove shock absorber assembly from strut spring compressor.

8. Reverse procedure to install.

STABILIZER BAR
REPLACE

1. Raise and support vehicle.
2. Remove nut from link bolt located at each side, then remove bolt, grommets and bushings, **Fig. 12.**
3. Remove stabilizer shaft to body bolts, then remove stabilizer bar.
4. Reverse procedure to install.

POWER STEERING GEAR
REPLACE

1. Raise and support vehicle, then remove wheels.
2. Disconnect inlet and outlet hoses from steering gear, then the steering linkage outer tie rods from steering knuckles, **Fig. 13.**
3. Disconnect steering gear coupling

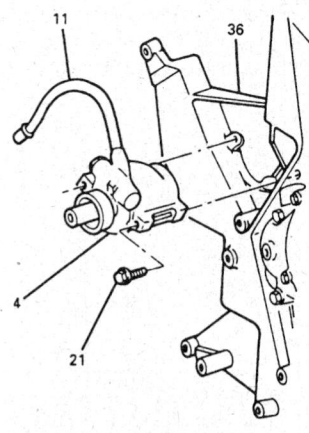

1 GEAR ASSEMBLY, POWER STEERING
8 KNUCKLE ASSEMBLY, STEERING
26 NUT, STEERING GEAR
27 BOLT/SCREW, STEERING GEAR, 85 N·m (63 LB. FT.)
34 CROSSMEMBER ASSEMBLY, FRONT

GC6049300136000X

Fig. 13 Power steering gear installation

4 PUMP ASSEMBLY, POWER STEERING
11 HOSE, POWER STEERING FLUID RESERVOIR
21 BOLT/SCREW, POWER STEERING PUMP, 25 N·m (18 LB. FT.)
36 BRACKET ASSEMBLY, GENERATOR AND AIR CONDITIONER COMPRESSOR AND POWER STEERING PUMP AND DRIVE BELT TENSIONER

GC6049300140000X

Fig. 15 Power steering pump replacement. 5.7L engine

shaft from steering gear, then remove steering gear.

4. Reverse procedure to install, noting the following:
   a. Adjust steering gear so that it aligns as straight as possible with steering gear coupling shaft.
   b. Refill and bleed power steering system.

POWER STEERING PUMP
REPLACE

1. **On models equipped with 5.7L engine,** raise and support vehicle, then drain engine coolant into suitable container.
2. **On all models,** remove serpentine belt, then lower vehicle and remove front air intake duct.
3. **On models equipped with 5.7L engine,** remove alternator, radiator outlet hose and heater inlet/outlet hoses from water pump. Also, remove throttle

body heater return from heater outlet hose and pump bolts.

4. **On models equipped with 3800 engine,** remove pulley from pump and

mounting nuts.

5. **On all models,** remove pump mounting bolts, **Figs. 14 and 15,** then disconnect inlet and reservoir hoses from

pump and remove pump.

6. Reverse procedure to install. Refill and bleed power steering system.

TIGHTENING SPECIFICATIONS

Year	Component	Torque/Ft. Lbs.
2001–02	Lower Ball Joint Nut	81
	Lower Shock Absorber Nuts	48
	Power Steering Gear Mounting Bolts	63
	Power Steering Pump Bolts (3800 Engine)	23
	Power Steering Pump Bolts (5.7L Engine)	18
	Power Steering Pump Support To Pump Nuts & Bolts	37
	Stabilizer Bracket To Frame Bolts	41
	Stabilizer Clamp To Stabilizer Bracket Bolts	41
	Stabilizer Link Nut	17
	Upper Ball Joint Nut	39
	Upper Shock Absorber Mount To Strut Tower Bolts	37
	Upper Shock Absorber Mount To Strut Tower Nuts	32
	Wheel Lug Nuts	100

Wheel Alignment

INDEX

PRELIMINARY INSPECTION

Prior to inspecting or adjusting front suspension alignment, inspect suspension components for damage or excessive wear, and replace as needed. Ensure tire pressures and wheel bearings are properly adjusted, then raise and release front bumper several times to allow vehicle to assume normal ride height.

FRONT WHEEL ALIGNMENT

Caster

1. Jounce front bumper three times to allow vehicle to return to normal ride height, then raise and support vehicle.
2. Loosen front lower control arm nuts, then install camber/caster adjuster tool No. J38658, or equivalent, to slot holes in lower control arm and front crossmember, **Fig. 1.**
3. Adjust caster to specifications by rotating turnbuckle on camber/caster adjuster. Clockwise increases caster, counterclockwise decreases caster.
4. Remove camber/caster adjuster, then **torque** front lower control arm nuts to 96 ft. lbs.

Camber

1. Jounce front bumper three times to allow vehicle to return to normal ride height, then raise and support vehicle.
2. Loosen front lower control arm nuts, then install camber/caster adjuster tool No. J38658, or equivalent, to slot holes in lower control arm and front crossmember, **Fig. 2.**
3. Adjust camber to specifications by rotating turnbuckle on camber/caster adjuster. Clockwise increases caster, counterclockwise decreases caster.
4. Remove camber/caster adjuster, then **torque** front lower control arm nuts to 96 ft. lbs.

Toe-In

Toe adjustments are made separately at each individual wheel.
1. Ensure steering wheel is set in a straight ahead position within ± 3.5.°

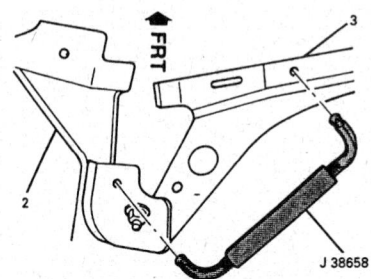

2 CROSSMEMBER ASSEMBLY, FRONT
3 ARM ASSEMBLY, FRONT LOWER CONTROL

GC2049300043000X

Fig. 1   Front caster adjustment tool installation

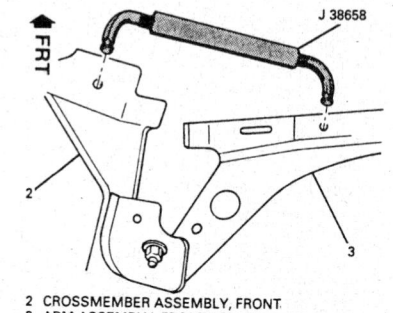

2 CROSSMEMBER ASSEMBLY, FRONT
3 ARM ASSEMBLY, FRONT LOWER CONTROL

GC2049300045000X

Fig. 2   Front camber adjustment tool installation

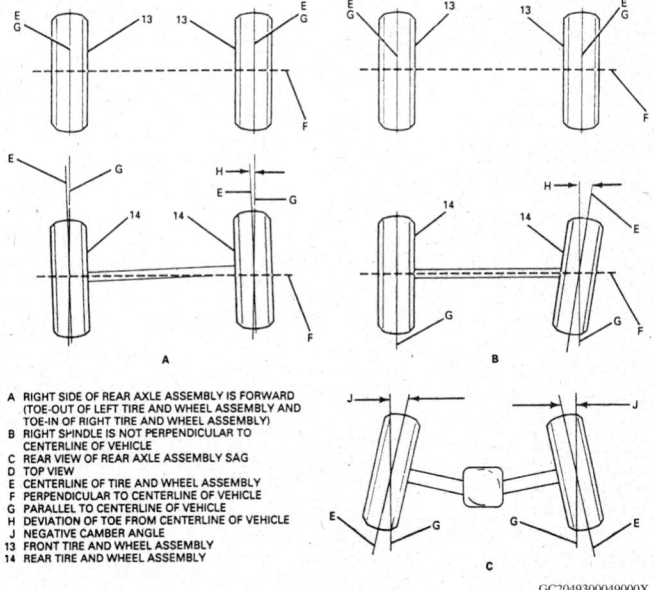

A RIGHT SIDE OF REAR AXLE ASSEMBLY IS FORWARD (TOE-OUT OF LEFT TIRE AND WHEEL ASSEMBLY AND TOE-IN OF RIGHT TIRE AND WHEEL ASSEMBLY)
B RIGHT SHINDLE IS NOT PERPENDICULAR TO CENTERLINE OF VEHICLE
C REAR VIEW OF REAR AXLE ASSEMBLY SAG
D TOP VIEW
E CENTERLINE OF TIRE AND WHEEL ASSEMBLY
F PERPENDICULAR TO CENTERLINE OF VEHICLE
G PARALLEL TO CENTERLINE OF VEHICLE
H DEVIATION OF TOE FROM CENTERLINE OF VEHICLE
J NEGATIVE CAMBER ANGLE
13 FRONT TIRE AND WHEEL ASSEMBLY
14 REAR TIRE AND WHEEL ASSEMBLY

GC2049300049000X

Fig. 3   Rear wheel alignment inspection

2. Loosen nut on inner tie rod, then adjust toe to specifications. Lefthand and righthand toe adjustment should be equal within ± .2.°
3. Ensure steering gear boot is not twisted, then **torque** inner tie rod nut to 35 ft. lbs.

REAR WHEEL ALIGNMENT

After front wheel alignment has been inspected or adjusted, rear wheel alignment angles should be inspected if vehicle still does not track properly or if excessive rear tire wear is present. Rear wheels should be parallel to and the same distance from the vehicle centerline, **Fig. 3.**

Rear wheel alignment is not adjustable. If alignment angles are not within specification, inspect for bent or damaged suspension arms, axle housing or frame.

THRUST ANGLE

If the thrust angle is not within specifications, inspect upper and lower control arms for damage. If control arms are not damaged, inspect frame dimensions.

CATERA

INDEX OF SERVICE OPERATIONS

Specifications

GENERAL ENGINE SPECIFICATIONS

Engine	Fuel System	Bore × Stroke, Inches	Comp. Ratio	Net HP @ RPM	Maximum Torque, Ft. Lbs. @ RPM	Minimum Oil Pressure, psi①
3.0L	SMPI	3.4 × 3.4	10.0	200 @ 6000	192 @ 3600	22

SMPI — Sequential Multi-Port Fuel Injection

① — At idle.

TUNE UP SPECIFICATIONS

Engine	Spark Plug Gap, Inch	Ignition Timing		Idle Speed, RPM	Fuel Pressure, psi	Valve Clearance, Inch
		Firing Order	°BTDC			
3.0L	.035–.043	1-2-3-4-5-6	①	③	40–48	②

BTDC — Before Top Dead Center
① — Not adjustable. Refer to **Fig. A,** for spark plug wire harness routing.

② — Zero lash valve train. Not adjustable.
③ — Refer to Vehicle Emission Control

Information (VECI) label in engine compartment.

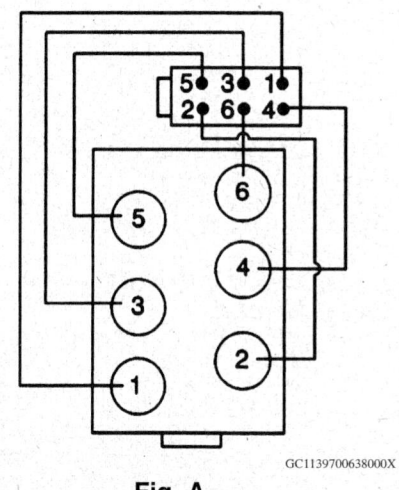

GC1139700638000X

Fig. A

FRONT WHEEL ALIGNMENT SPECIFICATIONS

Year	Caster, Degrees①	Camber, Degrees		Toe, Degrees		Ball Joint Inspection
		Lefthand & Righthand	Max. Cross Camber	Individual	Total	
2001	+4.00 to +6.00	+1.10 to -.10	—	—	+.26 to -.06	②

① — Not adjustable.

② — Refer to "Front Suspension & Steering" section for inspection procedure.

REAR WHEEL ALIGNMENT SPECIFICATIONS

Year	Camber, Degrees	Toe, Degrees	
		Individual	Total
2001	-1.35 to -2.15	+.15 to -.15	+.26 to -.06

VEHICLE RIDE HEIGHT SPECIFICATIONS

Model	Year	Body Style	Manufacturer's Original Tire Size	Measurement Points & Specifications ① ③					
				Front			Rear		
				Dim.	Specification		Dim.	Specification	
					Inches	mm		Inches	mm
Catera	All	All	②	C	6.87	174	D	6.50	165

A Dim. — Measurement From Front Wheel Center to Check Point On Rocker Panel

B Dim. — Measurement From Rear Wheel Center to Check Point On Rocker Panel

C Dim. — Ground to Rocker Panel, Front

D Dim. — Ground to Rocker Panel, Rear

Dim. — Dimension

① — ±.39 in (10 mm) front to rear & side to side.

② — See door sticker or inside of glove box for manufacturer's original tire size specifications. If tires on vehicle do not match manufacturer's original tire size & measurement is not within limits, it will be required to refer to the "Non-Standard Tire & Wheel Size Adjustment To Ride Height Specification & Tire Size Adjustment Charts" in the front of this manual for approximate changes in ride height specifications.

③ — Measurement is with fuel, radiator coolant and engine oil full, spare tire, jack, hand tools and mats in designated positions and tires properly inflated.

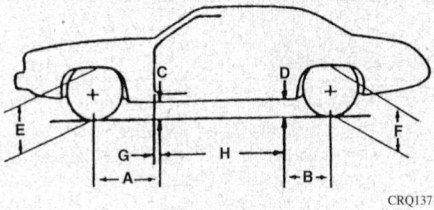

Fig. A

FLUID CAPACITIES & COOLING SYSTEM DATA

Year	Coolant Capacity, Qts.	Coolant Type	Coolant Recovery Reservoir Cap Pressure, Lbs.	Thermo. Opening Temp., °F	Fuel Tank Capacity, Gals.	Engine Oil Refill, Qts. ①	Trans. Oil Refill, Qts.	Rear Axle Oil, Qts.
2001	10	Dex-Cool	14	194	18	5.30	7	1.74

① — With oil filter change.

LUBRICANT DATA

Year	Engine	Transmission	Rear Axle	Power Steering	Brake System
2001	API 10W-30	Dexron III ATF	SAE 80W-90 GL-5	Dexron III ATF	DOT 3

Electrical

NOTE: On Air Bag Equipped Models, Refer To "Air Bag System Precautions" Located In The Front Of This Manual For System Disarming & Arming Procedures.

NOTE: Refer To "Computer Relearn Procedures" Located In The Front Of This Manual When Battery Power To The Computer Has Been Interrupted.

INDEX

PRECAUTIONS

Air Bag Systems

Refer to "Air Bag System Precautions" in the front of this manual for system disarming and arming procedures.

Battery Ground Cable

Prior to service, disconnect battery ground cable and isolate as required.

FUSE PANEL & FLASHER LOCATION

The fuse panel is located below the lefthand side of the instrument panel, near the lower lefthand portion of the steering column. The turn signal flasher is mounted on the relay box, which is below the instrument panel and to the righthand of the steering column.

FUEL PUMP RELAY LOCATION

The fuel pump relay is located at the lefthand front of the engine compartment, in the Engine Control Module (ECM) housing.

RELAY CENTER LOCATION

The relay centers are located behind the lefthand side of the instrument panel, **Fig. 1.**

STARTER
REPLACE

1. Raise and support vehicle.
2. Remove terminal nuts and disconnect electrical leads at starter.
3. Remove starter.
4. Reverse procedure to install, noting the following:
   a. **Torque** starter mounting bolts to 44 ft. lbs.
   b. When lowering engine, guide mount into position and ensure locator tab engages cradle slot.

ALTERNATOR
REPLACE

1. Remove pre-volume chamber.
2. Remove serpentine drive belt from alternator pulley as outlined under "Serpentine Drive Belt" in "3.0L Engine" section.
3. Raise and support vehicle.
4. Remove terminal nuts and disconnect leads at alternator. **Identify leads for installation reference.**
5. Remove alternator air cooling duct and upper nut, **Fig. 2.**
6. Remove lower mounting bolt and nut.
7. Separate alternator from engine and slide upper bolt out through bracket.
8. Lower vehicle and remove alternator.
9. Reverse procedure to install. **Torque** alternator mounting bolts to 30 ft. lbs.

COIL PACK
REPLACE

1. Remove wiper arms, then the lefthand and righthand air inlet grilles.
2. Remove wiper motor as outlined under "Wiper Motor, Replace."

3. Disconnect power brake booster vacuum line at intake plenum and spark plug wiring harness at ignition coil.
4. Disconnect coil electrical connector and remove mounting bolts.
5. Remove coil.
6. Reverse procedure to install. **Torque** coil mounting bolts to 72 inch lbs.

IGNITION LOCK
REPLACE

1. Remove Supplemental Inflatable Restraint (SIR) coil.
2. Insert suitable pointed tool into lock cylinder release pin hole and remove cylinder, **Fig. 3.**
3. Reverse procedure to install. Prior to installation, reset wheel locking device as follows:
   a. Locate locking lever in lock cylinder bore.
   b. Carefully push lever down until click is heard, **Fig. 4.**

IGNITION SWITCH
REPLACE

1. Remove Supplemental Inflatable Restraint (SIR) coil and ignition switch setscrew.
2. Turn ignition to On position and depress connector locking tab using suitable flat-bladed screwdriver.
3. Disconnect electrical connector and remove switch.
4. Reverse procedure to install.

NEUTRAL SAFETY SWITCH
REPLACE

The **Transmission Control Selector**

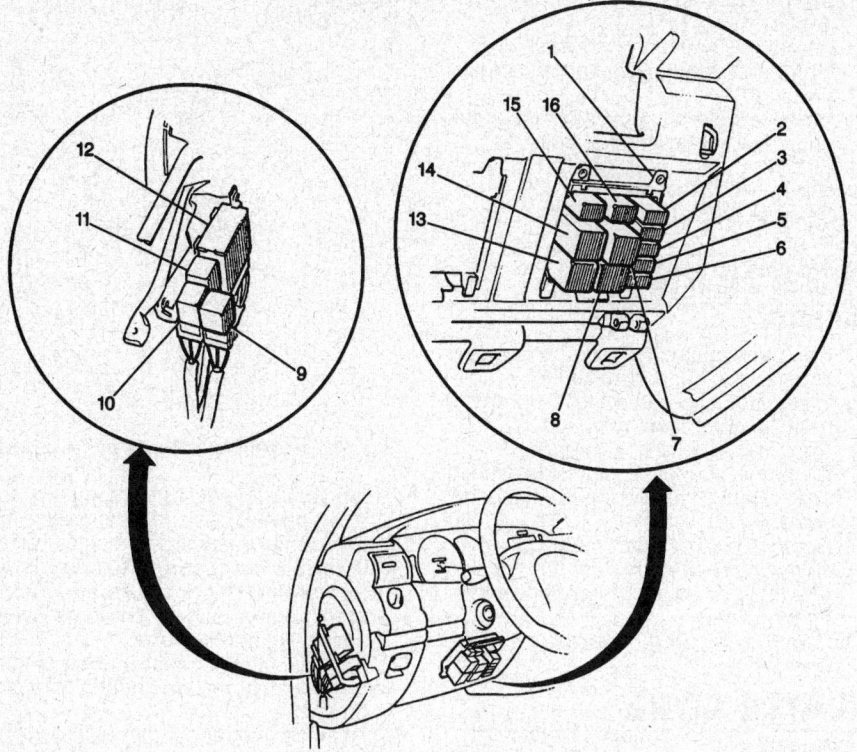

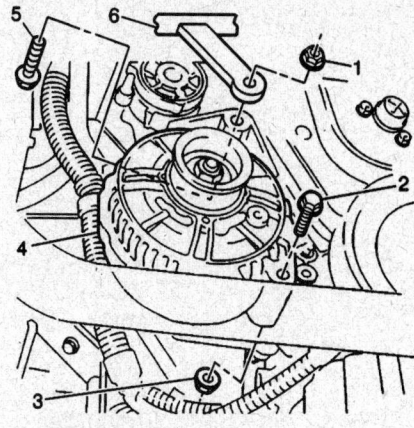

(1) Generator Upper Nut
(2) Generator Lower Bolt
(3) Generator Lower Nut
(4) Generator
(5) Generator Upper Bolt
(6) AIR Injection Crossover Pipe

GC1129700068000X

Fig. 2 Alternator & mounting hardware

(1) Relay Center
(2) Park Lamp Relay
(3) Low Beam Relay
(4) Not Used
(5) Not Used
(6) LH Headlamp (High Beam) Relay
(7) Turn Signal Lamp Flasher
(8) Horn Relay
(9) Passenger Seat Heater Relay
(10) Driver Seat Heater Relay
(11) Power Steering Control Relay
(12) Multifunction Relay Module
(13) RH Headlamp (High Beam) Relay
(14) Heated Outside Rear View Mirror and Rear Window Defogger Relay
(15) Daytime Running Lamp Relay
(16) Rear Suspension Leveling Air Compressor Relay

GC9049700156000X

Fig. 1 Relay center location

Switch incorporates the functions of a neutral safety and back-up lamp switch.
1. Apply parking brake and place selector lever in Neutral position.
2. Raise and support vehicle, then separate muffler from catalytic converter.
3. Support transmission with suitable jack and remove transmission crossmember to body bolts.
4. Lower transmission enough to access switch and remove switch cover.
5. Disconnect switch wire harness at bracket using suitable pry tool.
6. Remove control selector shaft nut and remove lever from shaft.
7. Remove mounting bolts and switch.
8. Reverse procedure to install, noting the following:
   a. Install bolts loosely.
   b. Place transmission in Neutral position.
   c. Align switch shaft and housing slots.
   d. Ensure alignment is proper during installation by inserting ³⁄₃₂ inch drill bit.
   e. **Torque** switch bolts to 96–108 inch lbs.
   f. **Torque** crossmember to body bolts to 33 ft. lbs.
   g. **Torque** muffler to catalytic converter bolts to 30 ft. lbs.

HEADLAMP SWITCH
REPLACE

1. Disengage switch from instrument panel by carefully prying on lefthand side using suitable cloth to protect trim.
2. Remove switch from instrument panel.
3. Reverse procedure to install.

STOP LIGHT SWITCH
REPLACE

1. Remove lefthand instrument panel sound insulator.
2. Remove lefthand front floor air outlet duct and disconnect electrical connector at switch.
3. Compress both locking tabs using suitable angled pliers and remove switch.
4. Reverse procedure to install. **Do not push actuating pin into switch. Pin will adjust itself when brake pedal is released.**

TURN SIGNAL SWITCH
REPLACE

1. Remove upper steering column cover caps and mounting screws .
2. Carefully thread tilt lever out of tilt mechanism. It may be required to use suitable non-marring tool.
3. Remove lock cylinder protective cover and mounting screws from lower steering column cover.
4. Remove lower steering column cover, depress tabs and disconnect turn signal switch electrical connector.
5. Remove switch.
6. Reverse procedure to install. Coat tilt lever threads with GM locking compound P/N 12345382, or equivalent, prior to installation.

STEERING WHEEL
REPLACE

1. Remove air bag module mounting screws from steering wheel rear.
2. Disconnect air bag module electrical connector and carefully remove module.
3. Mark relationship between steering wheel and column for alignment during installation.
4. Disengage steering wheel nut locking tab, then remove nut and tab.
5. Remove steering wheel using puller tool No. J1859-A and puller legs tool No. J36541-A, or equivalents. **Do not use hammer on steering shaft.**
6. Reverse procedure to install, noting the following:
   a. **Torque** steering wheel nut to 21 ft. lbs.
   b. **Torque** air bag module screws to 72 inch lbs.

INSTRUMENT CLUSTER
REPLACE

1. Remove center air deflector.
2. Remove righthand instrument cluster screw and turn steering wheel as required to access upper steering column cover screws.
3. Remove upper column cover plugs and mounting, then lift cover away from column.

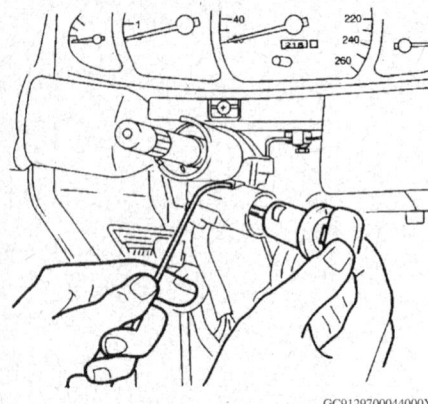

Fig. 3   Ignition lock cylinder removal

4. Remove mounting screw and upper column cover collar.
5. Disengage righthand side of cluster and disconnect cluster electrical connector.
6. Slide cluster toward righthand side until lefthand side clears vent housing and gently move cluster out of instrument panel.
7. Reverse procedure to install.

RADIO
REPLACE

1. Apply parking brake.
2. Move gear selector lever to full rearward position and remove instrument panel center bezel.
3. Remove radio mounting screws and separate radio from HVAC control head bracket.
4. Disconnect antenna lead and electrical harness at radio, then remove radio.
5. Reverse procedure to install.

WIPER MOTOR
REPLACE

1. Remove wiper transmission as outlined under "Wiper Transmission, Replace."
2. Disconnect wiper transmission upper link at wiper motor crank arm and remove wiper transmission nut from motor.
3. Disconnect wiper motor crank arm at wiper motor, then remove motor bracket bolts, **Fig. 5.**
4. Remove wiper motor from transmission.
5. Reverse procedure to install.

WIPER TRANSMISSION
REPLACE

1. Remove air inlet grilles and disconnect brake booster hose.

2. Disconnect wiper motor harness connector.
3. Remove mounting screws, wiper motor and transmission as an assembly.
4. Remove wiper transmission upper link and wiper motor bracket bolts, **Fig. 5.**
5. Separate wiper motor from transmission.
6. Reverse procedure to install.

BLOWER MOTOR
REPLACE

1. Remove righthand side passenger compartment sound insulator.
2. Disengage clip and remove righthand front floor air outlet.
3. Remove glove compartment.
4. Disconnect supply duct at side air vent and remove blower motor housing screws.
5. Remove blower motor housing.
6. Remove blower motor to housing mounting screws and separate motor from housing.
7. Reverse procedure to install.

HEATER CORE
REPLACE

1. Drain engine coolant into suitable container.
2. Disconnect heater hoses at heater core pipes. **Exercise caution when pulling on quick connect fittings.**
3. Remove steering column as outlined in "Steering Columns" chapter.
4. Remove front assist handles, windshield pillar moldings and righthand access panel.
5. Remove righthand air deflector and glove compartment.
6. Remove righthand air ducts, inflatable restraint module trim cover and fasteners.
7. Disconnect inflatable restraint module orange harness connector and remove module.
8. Remove center console and center air duct.
9. Remove radio as outlined under "Radio, Replace."
10. Disconnect and remove climate control head.
11. Remove center air deflector, lefthand access panel and lefthand air deflector.
12. Remove headlamp switch as outlined under "Headlamp Switch, Replace."
13. Remove lefthand vent bracket and remove instrument cluster as outlined under "Instrument Cluster, Replace."
14. Remove mounting screws, fuse and relay panel.
15. Remove steering column support bracket nuts and instrument panel carrier bolts.
16. Remove headlamp automatic control

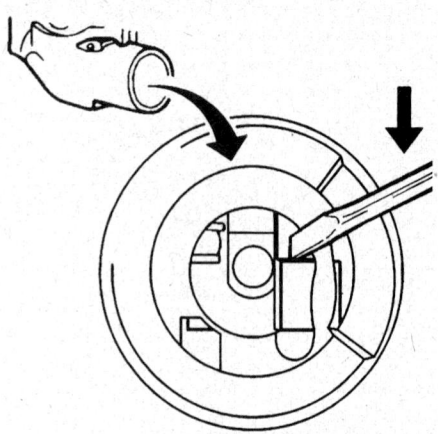

Fig. 4   Steering wheel lock reset

ambient light sensor, disconnect carrier wiring harness and disengage clips.
17. Pull carrier rearward to access heater core. **It is not required to completely remove carrier or to remove instrument panel wiring harness when servicing heater core.**
18. Remove blower motor and housing as an assembly, then the heater core pipe bracket.
19. Remove inlet and outlet pipes and instrument panel support brace bolts.
20. Remove instrument panel support brace, support bracket and heater core mounting screw.
21. Remove heater core and plug ports.
22. Remove cavity rubber seal.
23. Reverse procedure to install, noting the following:
    a. **Torque** passenger air bag module mounting bolts to 84–96 inch lbs.
    b. When installing steering column using new shear bolt.
    c. **Torque** rear support bracket bolt, forward support strap nut and coupler to shaft clamp bolt to 16 ft. lbs. Shear bolt head should snap off at approximately 15 ft. lbs.
    d. When connecting heater hoses, ensure quick disconnects are fully seated and retaining sleeves are in locked position.

EVAPORATOR CORE
REPLACE

1. Discharge and recover air conditioning system as outlined in "Air Conditioning" chapter.
2. Remove mounting screws and Thermal Expansion Valve (TXV).
3. Remove steering column as outlined in "Steering Columns" chapter.
4. Remove brake pedal and bracket as an assembly.
5. Plug evaporator fittings and remove evaporator core, **Fig. 6.**
6. Reverse procedure to install. Install new O-rings lubricated with 525 viscosity mineral oil.

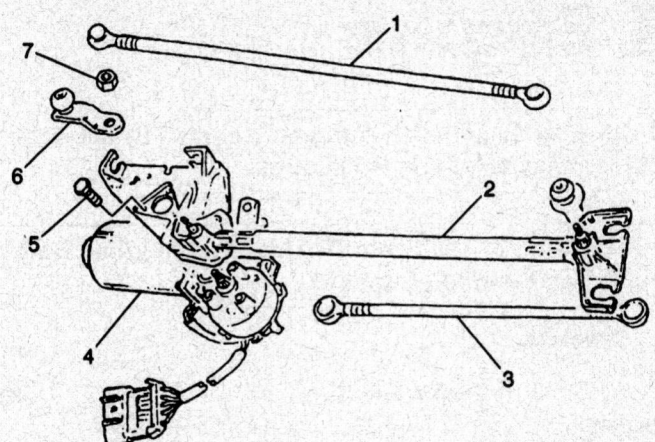

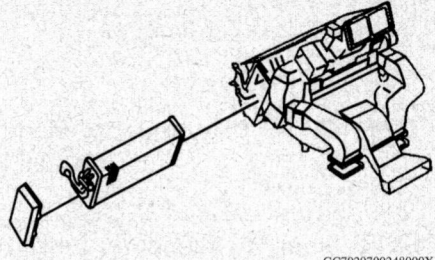

GC7029700248000X

Fig. 6 Evaporator core replacement

(1) Windshield Wiper Transmission Link (Upper)
(2) Windshield Wiper Transmission
(3) Windshield Wiper Transmission Link (Lower)
(4) Windshield Wiper Motor

(5) Windshield Wiper Motor Bracket Bolt
(6) Windshield Wiper Motor Crank Arm
(7) Windshield Wiper Transmission Nut

GC9029700443000X

Fig. 5 Wiper motor & transmission replacement

3.0L Engine

NOTE: On Air Bag Equipped Models, Refer To "Air Bag System Precautions" Located In The Front Of This Manual For System Disarming & Arming Procedures.

NOTE: Refer To "Computer Relearn Procedures" Located In The Front Of This Manual When Battery Power To The Computer Has Been Interrupted.

INDEX

PRECAUTIONS

Air Bag Systems

Refer to "Air Bag System Precautions" in the front of this manual for system disarming and arming procedures.

Battery Ground Cable

Prior to service, disconnect battery ground cable and isolate as required.

Fuel System Pressure Relief

In order to avoid personal injury and possible vehicle damage, fuel system pressure must be relieved prior to servicing any component of the fuel system.
1. Loosen fuel filler cap to release tank pressure.
2. Connect fuel pressure gauge tool No. J34730-1A with adapter hose tool No. J42242, or equivalents, to fuel pressure service port on fuel crossover pipe, **Fig. 1.** Wrap shop towel around fitting to prevent spillage during connection.
3. Place end of bleed hose into suitable gasoline container and open valve to bleed system pressure.
4. Drain residual fuel from gauge tool into suitable container.

COMPRESSION PRESSURE

Inspection

1. Run engine until normal operating temperature is reached.
2. Shut engine off, disable fuel and ignition systems.
3. Remove spark plugs.
4. Disconnect air ducts at throttle body and block throttle plates open.
5. Install compression tester tool No. J38722, or equivalent, in spark plug hole.
6. Crank engine through at least four compression strokes for test cylinder, noting gauge readings at each stroke.
7. Remove gauge and repeat test for each remaining cylinder. **Minimum pressure for any one cylinder is 100 psi. Compression is acceptable if lowest cylinder reading for all cylinders is within 70% of highest.**
8. Remove throttle plates block and connect air ducts.
9. Install spark plugs and tighten.
10. Enable fuel and ignition systems.

ENGINE MOUNT
REPLACE

Removal

1. Raise and support vehicle, then remove engine mount lower nut.
2. Lower vehicle and install engine support fixture tool No. J28467-A, or equivalent.
3. Raise and support vehicle, then remove engine mount upper nut.
4. Remove engine mount.

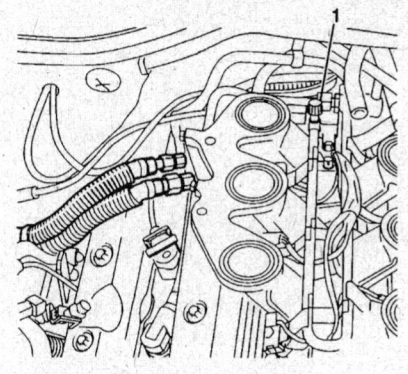

(1) Fuel Pressure Service Connection

GC1069700824000X

Fig. 1 Fuel pressure service port

Installation

1. Raise and support vehicle.
2. Install engine mount. Tighten upper mounting nut.
3. Lower vehicle.
4. Lower engine and remove support fixture tool. **Ensure engine mount guide pin engages in crossmember guide hole (1), Fig. 2.**
5. Raise and support vehicle.
6. Tighten engine mount lower nut.

ENGINE
REPLACE

1. Drain engine coolant and oil into suitable containers. Remove wiper arms.
2. Remove lefthand and righthand air inlet grilles, then the hood. Mark hood position for installation.
3. Remove battery and recover air conditioning system as outlined in "Air Conditioning" chapter.
4. Disconnect black wiring harness connector and body ground wire at battery ground cable end. Identify harnesses and wires for installation reference.
5. Disconnect four power supply wires at battery positive cable end and identify for installation reference.
6. Siphon power steering fluid from reservoir, disconnect power steering suction hose and remove clamp.
7. Disconnect power steering discharge hose at pump and remove threaded brake booster fitting from intake manifold plenum.
8. Disconnect vacuum lines at power brake booster hose. Identify lines for installation reference.
9. Disconnect intake plenum switchover valve vacuum and electrical connections, then remove switchover valve mounting bolts.
10. Identify relays and connections for installation.
11. Remove switchover valve, then the engine control module (ECM) and relays.
12. Disconnect wiring harness at electrical center.
13. Disconnect blue and white wiring harness connectors, then disengage accelerator and cruise control cable retaining clips.
14. Disconnect accelerator and cruise control cables at throttle body.
15. Relieve fuel system pressure as outlined under "Precautions."
16. Disconnect and remove fuel supply and return hoses using suitable backup tool to prevent fuel rail damage.
17. Disconnect coolant return hose at throttle body and vacuum hose at ventilation chamber purge valve.
18. Disconnect vacuum hose at hot water control valve and coolant reservoir hose at coolant intake pipe.
19. Disconnect heater hoses at heater core pipes.
20. Disconnect Mass Air Flow (MAF) and Intake Air Temperature (IAT) sensor electrical connectors.
21. Disconnect resonance chamber air intake hose at air cleaner housing and MAF sensor, then the Idle Air Control (IAC) inlet hose.
22. Disconnect intake plenum air inlet hoses.
23. Disconnect switchover valve electrical connector and all remaining vacuum connections. Identify connections for installation reference.
24. Remove mounting nuts and resonance chamber.
25. Remove radiator as outlined under "Radiator, Replace."
26. Disconnect air conditioning compressor/condenser hose bracket at body and position aside.
27. Disconnect air conditioning compressor hose quick connect fittings at compressor/condenser hose and at evaporator line extension.
28. Install engine support fixture tool No. J28467-A, or equivalent.
29. Raise and support vehicle.
30. Remove splash shield and disconnect air conditioning compressor electrical connector.
31. Drain transmission fluid into suitable container.
32. Disconnect transmission shift lever rod and remove propeller shaft coupling bolts.
33. Separate propeller shaft coupling from drive flange using suitable prying tool.
34. Remove transmission oil pan and bellhousing access plugs.
35. Remove flexplate to torque converter bolts. Mark relationship between flexplate and converter for installation reference.
36. Disconnect oil cooler inlet and outlet pipes at center pipes.
37. Disconnect oxygen sensor electrical connectors and remove catalytic converters.
38. Remove transmission housing to engine oil pan bolts and install transmission support.
39. Remove mounting nuts, bolts and crossmember.
40. Lower transmission to access transmission housing to engine block bolts and disconnect ventilation hose at transmission.
41. Disconnect transmission control selector switch, adapter case, main case

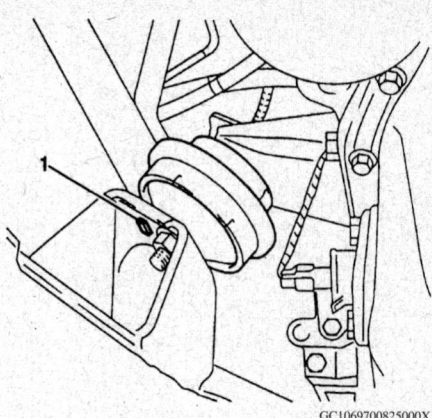

GC1069700825000X

Fig. 2 Engine mount guide pin

and speed sensor electrical connectors.
42. With front of engine supported, remove transmission housing to engine block bolts.
43. Remove transmission.
44. Lower vehicle and connect engine lift chains to three support lift shackles.
45. When weight of engine is supported by engine lift, remove support fixture tool.
46. Remove mount nuts and engine.
47. Reverse procedure to install, noting the following:
    a. Tighten fuel line connections using suitable back-up tool to prevent fuel rail damage.
    b. Adjust shift lever rod by placing selector lever in Park position and loosening adjustment bolt to allow adjuster to slide freely, **Fig. 3.**
    c. Hold transmission selector lever at rear stop and **torque** adjustment bolt to 72 inch lbs.

INTAKE MANIFOLD
REPLACE

1. Remove clamps and intake plenum air inlet hose from throttle body.
2. Remove brake booster vacuum fitting from intake plenum.
3. Remove mounting bolts and position wiring harness channel out of way.
4. Disconnect switchover valve electrical connections and vacuum hose.
5. Disconnect throttle body control electrical connection.
6. Remove mounting bolts and throttle body from plenum.
7. Remove crankcase vent tube adaptor cover by gently prying up on side.
8. Unclip clamp from righthand side plenum bracket and position heater hoses out of way.
9. Remove caps, mounting bolts then the intake plenum.
10. Relieve fuel system pressure as outlined under "Precautions."
11. Remove fuel supply and return hoses from fuel rail.
12. Disconnect fuel injector electrical harness and fuel pressure regulator vacuum connections.
13. Remove mounting bolts and intake manifold, noting the following:
    a. Mask intake manifold spacer ports.

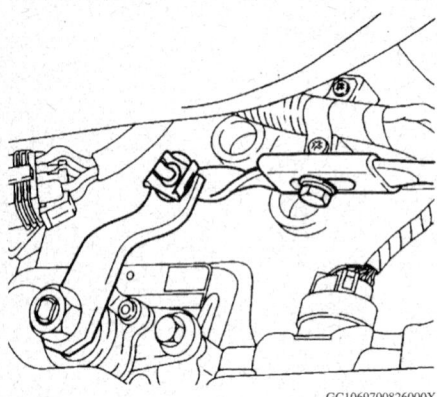

Fig. 3 Shift lever rod adjustment bolt

   b. Clean intake manifold sealing surfaces using suitable nonabrasive tool or solvent.

   c. Ensure machined aluminum surfaces are not damaged.

14. Reverse procedure to install. Tighten intake manifold and plenum bolts.

EXHAUST MANIFOLD

REPLACE

Lefthand

1. Remove engine as outlined under "Engine, Replace."
2. Remove manifold lower and upper heat shields.
3. Remove Secondary Air Injection (AIR) pipe bolts and separate pipe from exhaust manifold to access manifold mounting nuts.
4. Remove coolant pipe/engine lift bracket bolt from cylinder head and dipstick tube by pulling firmly upward.
5. Remove mounting nuts and exhaust manifold.
6. Reverse procedure to install, noting the following:
   a. Tighten mounting bolts and nuts.
   b. Coat AIR pipe and heat shield bolts with GM high temperature anti-seize compound P/N 5613695, or equivalent.

Righthand

1. Remove transmission as outlined under "Engine, Replace."
2. Remove coolant intake pipe.
3. Raise and support vehicle.
4. Remove exhaust manifold lower heat shield.
5. Remove catalytic converter hanger bolt and two lower rear manifold mounting nuts.
6. Lower vehicle and remove lower front manifold mounting nuts.
7. Remove exhaust manifold upper heat shield bolts to access Secondary Air Injection (AIR) pipe. Allow shield to remain in place.
8. Remove AIR pipe bolts and separate pipe from exhaust manifold.

9. Remove mounting nuts and upper manifold.
10. Reverse procedure to install, noting the following:
   a. Tighten mounting bolts and nuts.
   b. Coat AIR pipe and heat shield bolts with GM high temperature anti-seize compound P/N 5613695, or equivalent.

CYLINDER HEAD

REPLACE

Lefthand

1. Remove intake plenum as outlined under "Intake Manifold, Replace."
2. Remove resonance chamber as outlined under "Engine, Replace" and intake manifold as outlined under "Intake Manifold, Replace."
3. Remove intake manifold spacer, coolant bridge and lefthand valve cover.
4. Remove front timing belt cover and timing belt as outlined under "Timing Belt, Replace."
5. **Position crankshaft at 60° Before Top Dead Center (BTDC) to prevent valve and piston interference when cylinder head is installed, Fig. 4.**
6. Remove timing belt tensioner bracket.
7. Remove gears from intake and exhaust camshaft Nos. 3 and 4, then from Nos. 1 and 2 as outlined under "Camshaft, Replace."
8. Remove water pump as outlined under "Water Pump, Replace."
9. Remove timing belt rear cover.
10. Disconnect camshaft sensor electrical connector and remove exhaust camshaft No. 4 as outlined under "Camshaft, Replace."
11. Remove coolant pipe/engine lift bracket from cylinder head, grasp dipstick tube firmly and pull upward to remove.
12. Disconnect upper radiator hose from coolant intake pipe and twist pipe to remove.
13. Separate lefthand exhaust manifold from engine block as outlined under "Exhaust Manifold, Replace." **Because this procedure is performed with engine in vehicle, exhaust manifold cannot be completely removed. It is not required to remove engine to service manifold during this procedure.**
14. Disconnect ignition coil electrical connector and remove cylinder head bolts in reverse order of tightening sequence, **Fig. 5. Discard old cylinder head bolts.**
15. Lift cylinder head off engine, then remove gasket, ignition coil and bracket.
16. Reverse procedure to install, noting the following:
   a. **Ensure crankshaft is still at 60° BTDC to prevent valve and piston interference when cylinder head is installed, Fig. 4.**
   b. Install new cylinder head gasket.
   c. Ensure gasket OBEN/TOP imprint faces front of engine.

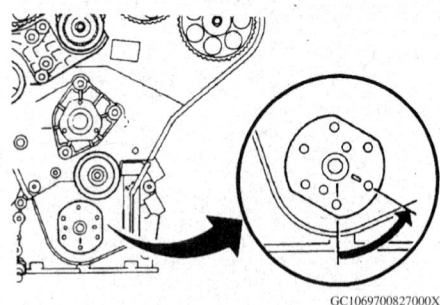

Fig. 4 Crankshaft alignment to 60° BTDC

   d. **Torque** new cylinder head bolts to 18 ft. lbs., in sequence, **Fig. 5.**
   e. Tighten bolts an additional 90° in sequence.
   f. Tighten bolts an additional 90° in sequence.
   g. Tighten bolts an additional 90° in sequence.
   h. Tighten bolts an additional 15° in sequence.
   i. Install new sealing rings on coolant pipe and lubricate with coolant.
   j. Install new valve cover seals and O-rings as outlined under "Valve Cover, Replace."

Righthand

1. Remove resonance chamber as outlined under "Engine, Replace."
2. Remove intake plenum and manifold as outlined under "Intake Manifold, Replace," then the manifold spacer.
3. Remove coolant bridge and righthand valve cover.
4. Remove front timing belt cover and timing belt as outlined under "Timing Belt, Replace."
5. Remove timing belt tensioner bracket.
6. **Position crankshaft at 60° before Top Dead Center (BTDC) to prevent valve and piston interference when cylinder head is installed .**
7. Remove camshaft gears for shaft Nos. 3 and 4, and shaft Nos. 1 and 2 as outlined under "Camshaft, Replace."
8. Remove water pump as outlined under "Water Pump, Replace."
9. Remove rear timing belt cover.
10. Remove exhaust camshaft No. 1 as outlined under "Camshaft, Replace."
11. Remove coolant intake pipe.
12. Separate exhaust manifold from cylinder head as outlined under "Exhaust Manifold, Replace."
13. Remove cylinder head bolts in reverse order of tightening sequence, **Fig. 5. Discard old cylinder head bolts.**
14. Remove cylinder head and gasket from engine block.
15. Reverse procedure to install, noting the following:
   a. **Ensure crankshaft is still at 60° BTDC to prevent valve and piston interference when cylinder head is installed, Fig. 4,**
   b. Install new cylinder head gasket.
   c. Ensure gasket OBEN/TOP imprint faces rear of engine.

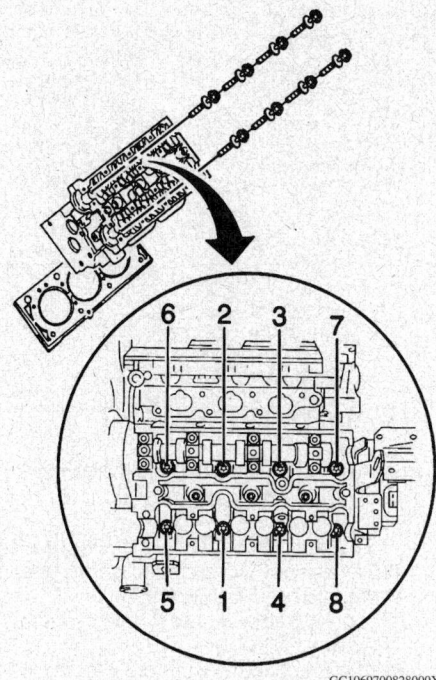

GC1069700828000X

Fig. 5   Cylinder head bolt tightening sequence

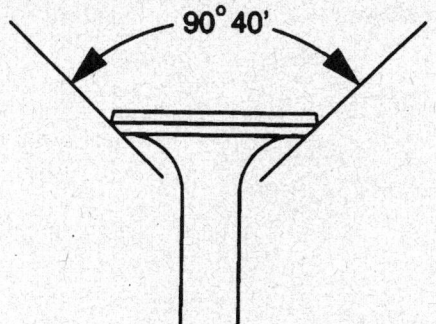

GC1069700843000X

Fig. 6   Valve grinding angle

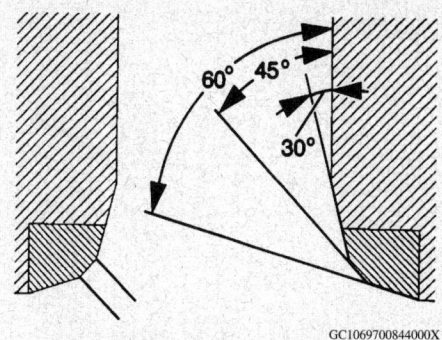

GC1069700844000X

Fig. 7   Valve seat angle

d. **Torque** new cylinder head bolts to 18 ft. lbs., in sequence, **Fig. 5.**
e. Tighten bolts an additional 90° in sequence.
f. Tighten bolts an additional 90° in sequence.
g. Tighten bolts an additional 90° in sequence.
h. Tighten bolts an additional 15° in sequence.
i. Install new valve cover seals and O-rings as outlined under "Valve Cover, Replace."

COMPONENT SERVICE
Cylinder Head
DISASSEMBLE

1. Remove lifters and store in suitable rack. Identify for installation reference.
2. Compress valve springs using valve spring compressor tool No. J8062 and adapter tool No. J41774, or equivalents, and carefully remove stem keys.
3. Remove valve stem caps, springs and seals.
4. Remove valve spring seats and valves from cylinder head. Store valves in suitable rack and identify for installation reference.
5. Clean carbon from combustion chambers and valve train components using suitable brush. **Do not scratch combustion chamber surface.**
6. Clean valve guides.
7. Clean valve stems and heads using suitable buffing wheel.
8. Clean cylinder head bolt holes.

INSPECTION

1. Inspect cylinder head exhaust ports,

combustion chambers and water chamber for cracks. Most cracks occur between exhaust valves or between exhaust valve and spark plug orifice.
2. Inspect valves for burned heads, cracked facing and damaged stems.
3. Ensure valve seats are tight and are not cracked.
4. Place spring on level surface next to square.
5. Rotate spring and measure deviation from square.
6. Replace spring if squareness deviation is .062 inch or less.
7. Measure valve spring tension using valve spring tester tool No. J9666, or equivalent. Replace spring if length is less than 1.338 inches with 56.6 lbs. force.
8. Clamp dial indicator tool No. J8001, or equivalent, on exhaust port side of cylinder head.
9. Position indicator plunger where side to side valve stem movement will be indicated.
10. With valve protruding .39 inch above seat, move valve stem from side to side using light pressure. Record clearance reading.
11. Intake valve clearance should be .0011–.0022 inch and exhaust valve clearance should be .0015–.0026 inch. If not, valve and/or valve guide must be serviced.
12. If valve stem to guide clearance is not as indicated, measure valve stem diameter in three locations.
13. Replace intake valve if stem diameter is less than .2344 inch at narrowest point.
14. Replace exhaust valve if stem diameter is less than .2340 inch at narrowest point, replace valve.
15. Valve guides should be serviced if valve stem diameters are more than minimum specifications.
16. If valve stem to guide clearance is not as indicated and valve stem diameter is satisfactory, use oversize valves and ream valve guides as follows:
a. Clean guide thoroughly.
b. Insert reamer tool No. J42096, or equivalent, from top of cylinder head.
c. Rotate reamer using light hand pressure until it is completely through valve guide.
d. Remove reamer.

e. Clean valve guide and combustion chamber to ensure all metal shavings are removed.
17. If clearances are satisfactory and original valves are to be used, valves and seats can be ground to ensure valve seating is optimal, noting the following:
a. Valves should be ground at 90⅔° angle, **Fig. 6.**
b. Seats should be ground at 90° angle.
c. Intake valve seat width should be .039–.055 inch and exhaust valve seat width should be .055–.070 inch.
d. Control valve seat widths with 30° and 60° stones, **Fig. 7.**

ASSEMBLE

1. Lubricate valve stems with clean engine oil and install valves.
2. Install valve spring seat.
3. Install new valve seal into cylinder head, using seal installer tool No. J41775, or equivalent.
4. Install valve springs and caps.
5. Compress springs using spring compressor tool No. J8062 and adapter tool No. J41774, or equivalents.
6. Install valve stem keys and hold them in place using suitable grease while removing spring compressor and adapter.
7. Ensure keys seat properly in upper groove.
8. Install lifters.

VALVE COVER
REPLACE

1. Remove mounting bolts, throttle body and gasket.
2. Remove crankcase vent tube adapter.
3. Remove mounting bolts and intake plenum.
4. Remove intake manifold as outlined under "Intake Manifold, Replace."
5. **On lefthand side valve cover,** remove oil filler spout by unlocking tab and twisting counter clockwise.
6. **On lefthand side valve cover,** disconnect camshaft position sensor electrical connection and plastic ties.
7. **On both valve covers,** remove spark plug boots from spark plugs and wires from routing retainers.
8. Remove knock sensor wire harness bracket nut and valve cover mounting bolts.

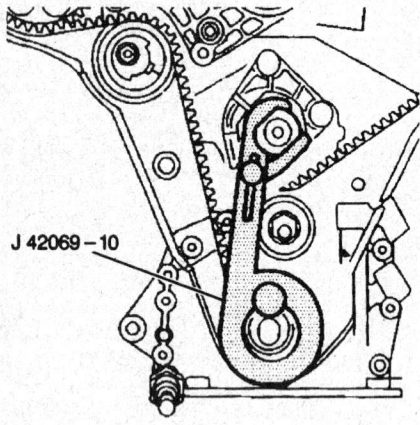

Fig. 8   Crankshaft installation

9. Remove valve cover. **Ensure all eight sealing O-rings are accounted for.**

VALVE GUIDES

Refer to "Component Service" for valve guide service information.

VALVE SEATS

Refer to "Component Service" for valve seat service information.

FRONT COVER

REPLACE

Refer to "Timing Belt, Replace" for timing belt front cover replacement procedures.

TIMING BELT

REPLACE

With the timing belt removed, avoid turning the camshaft or crankshaft. If movement is required, exercise extreme caution to avoid valve damage caused by piston contact.

The steps outlined in this procedure are critical in preventing serious engine damage. Adherence to this sequence is imperative.

Removal

1. Disconnect Mass Air Flow (MAF) and Intake Air Temperature (IAT) sensors' electrical connectors.
2. Remove resonance chamber air intake hose from air cleaner housing and MAF sensor.
3. Remove clamp and Idle Air Control (IAC) inlet hose.
4. Remove intake plenum air inlet hoses, switchover valve electrical connector and remaining vacuum connections.
5. Remove mounting nuts and resonance chamber.
6. Remove intake air plenum as outlined under "Intake Manifold, Replace."
7. Raise and support vehicle, then remove mounting bolts and splash shield.
8. Counterhold mounting bolt from alter-

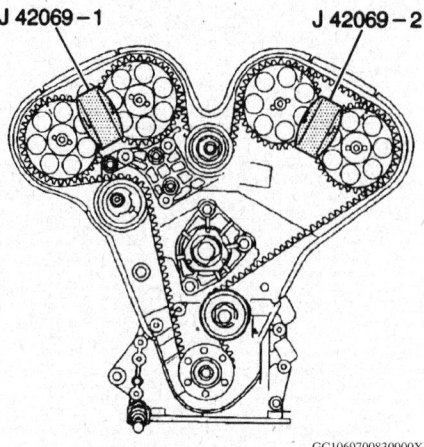

Fig. 9   Locking camshaft gears

nator back side and remove AIR injection crossover pipe bracket nut.
9. Remove AIR crossover pipe bushing nut from lefthand side of engine bracket.
10. Remove clamps and AIR crossover pipe from rubber hose connections.
11. Lower vehicle.
12. Remove diverter hose clamp and connection, then the AIR crossover pipe.
13. Loosen water and power steering pump pulley mounting bolts, then the harmonic balancer bolts. **Do not remove mounting bolts now.**
14. Remove air conditioning compressor hose support strap bolt from AIR injection crossover bracket.
15. Rotate serpentine belt tensioner pulley clockwise using suitable wrench while sliding belt from water pump pulley.
16. Remove serpentine belt from tensioner and engine.
17. Carefully release retaining tabs and remove wiring harness channel cover.
18. Remove wiring harness from channel. Record routing for installation.
19. Remove mounting bolts and water pump pulley, then the power steering pump pulley and serpentine drive belt tensioner.
20. Remove mounting bolts and harmonic balancer.
21. Remove mounting bolts and front timing belt cover. Replace sealing strip if cracked or torn.
22. Rotate crankshaft clockwise to 60° Before Top Dead Center (BTDC), **Fig. 4.**
23. Install timing belt alignment kit tool No. J42069-10, or equivalent, to crankshaft drive gear, **Fig. 8.**
24. Carefully turn crankshaft clockwise using crank hub Torx socket tool No. J42098, or equivalent, until locking tool lever firmly contacts water pump pulley flange.
25. Secure locking tool's moveable lever to water pump pulley flange.
26. **Ensure crankshaft alignment is not 180° off.**
27. **Camshaft gears alignment marks must align with corresponding notches on timing belt rear cover.**
28. Lock camshaft gears using timing belt alignment kit tool No. J42069-1 and

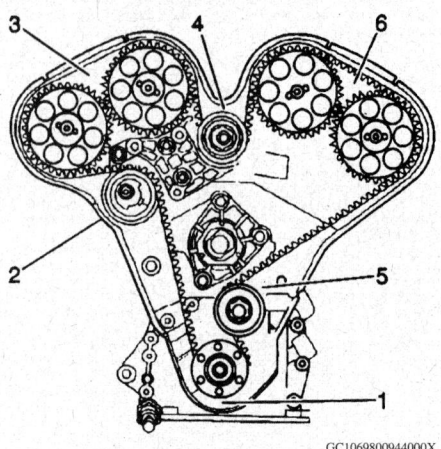

Fig. 10   Timing belt installation sequence

J42069-2, or equivalents, **Fig. 9.** If tools do not fit into camshaft gear teeth, proceed as follows:
  a. Loosen appropriate timing belt idler pulley.
  b. Turn eccentric until tool can be inserted.
29. Loosen timing belt tensioner and remove timing belt. **Do not remove locking tools while belt is removed.**

Installation

Wait until the engine has cooled off before installing a new timing belt.
1. Start installing timing belt at crankshaft drive gear (1), **Fig. 10.**
2. Install timing belt with double dash (TDC) mark aligned with oil pump and belt drive gear marks, **Fig. 11.**
3. Pinch timing belt to prevent splines from jumping using timing belt alignment kit tool No. J42069-30, or equivalent.
4. Route timing belt through timing belt tensioner (2).
5. Slip timing belt through camshaft sprockets one and two simultaneously (3). Ensure any timing belt dash marks align with camshaft gears' marks and rear cover notches.
6. Route timing belt through camshafts 1 and 2 idler pulley (4).
7. Route timing belt through camshafts 3 and 4 idler pulley (5).
8. Slip timing belt through camshaft sprockets 3 and 4 simultaneously (6). Ensure any timing belt dash marks align with camshaft gears' marks and rear cover notches.
9. Measure timing belt deflection between camshaft gear 4, and camshaft gears 3 and 4 idler pulley, **Fig. 12.**
10. Timing belt deflection should not be more than .4 inch. If timing belt deflection is not within specifications, proceed as follows:
  a. Rotate camshafts 3 and 4 timing belt idler pulley eccentric counterclockwise until high point of eccentric is at approximately 12 o'clock position using timing belt alignment

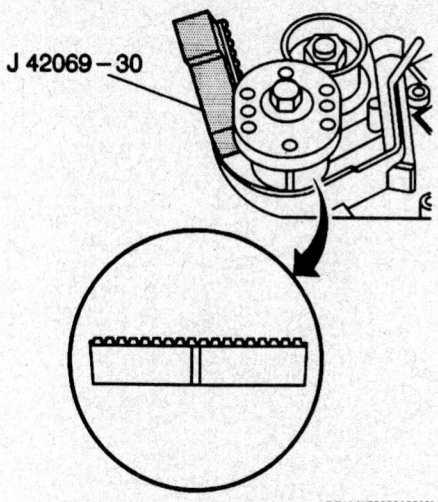

J 42069 – 30

GC1069700831000X

Fig. 11   Timing belt to gear alignment

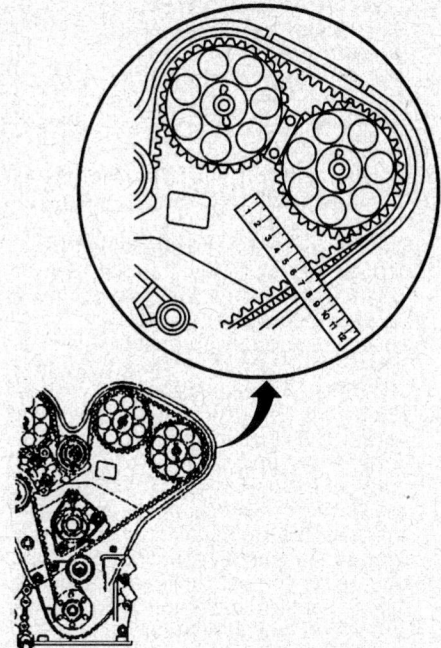

GC1069700832000X

Fig. 12   Measuring timing belt deflection

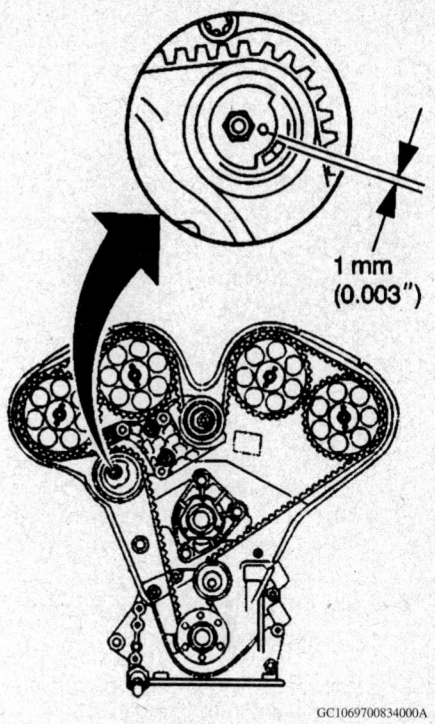

1 mm (0.003")

GC1069700834000A

Fig. 13   Initial timing belt tensioner alignment

kit tool No. No. J42069-40, or equivalent.

b. Tighten pulley lock bolt until snug while holding eccentric using suitable tool.

11. Apply tension to timing belt at camshafts 1 and 2 idler pulley by turning eccentric high point to approximately nine o'clock position.

12. Apply initial tension to timing belt by turning tensioner eccentric counterclockwise to full stop using suitable hex wrench.

13. Turn eccentric back until reference mark is .04 inch over flange, **Fig. 13.**

14. Tighten tensioner locknut until snug. **Do not fully tighten now.**

15. Inspect timing belt alignment marks to ensure they align with sprockets' reference marks, timing belt rear cover and oil pump housing, **Fig. 14.**

16. Remove tools.

17. Rotate engine two revolutions in clockwise direction stopping at 60° BTDC using crank hub Torx socket tool No. J42098, or equivalent.

18. Install crankshaft locking tool No. J42069-10, or equivalent, to crankshaft drive sprocket.

19. Turn crankshaft until crankshaft locking tool lever firmly contacts water pump pulley flange. Secure tool lever to water pump pulley flange.

20. Inspect camshaft sprockets reference marks' alignment with rear timing belt cover notches and reference marks' alignment of crankshaft drive gear and oil pump housing. **Timing belt alignment marks will no longer be aligned with camshaft sprockets marks.**

21. Inspect camshaft sprockets 3 and 4, camshaft sprockets 1 and 2 alignment using gauge tool No. J420969-20, or equivalent. Reference marks on camshaft sprockets must match exactly with gauge marks.

22. If sprocket timing marks are aligned with gauge marks, proceed to next step. If sprocket timing marks are not aligned with gauge marks, refer to

"Timing" procedure.

23. Loosen timing belt tensioner eccentric locknut.

24. Turn eccentric counterclockwise to full stop. Back off eccentric until reference mark is .078–.157 inch above flange reference mark, **Fig. 15.**

25. Tighten timing belt tensioner eccentric locknut.

26. Hold camshaft 1 and 2, and 3 and 4 tensioner eccentrics in place using adjusting wrench tool No. J42069-40, or equivalent. Tighten idler pulley bolts.

27. Ensure camshafts 3 and 4 idler pulley eccentric high point is at approximately 12 o'clock position.

28. Ensure camshafts 1 and 2 idler pulley eccentric high point is at approximately nine o'clock position.

29. Remove gauge and crankshaft locking tools.

30. Rotate engine in clockwise two revolutions to 60° BTDC.

31. Lock crankshaft drive sprocket using crankshaft locking tool No. J42069-10, or equivalent.

32. Turn crankshaft until crankshaft locking tool lever firmly contacts water pump pulley flange. Secure tool lever to water pump pulley flange.

33. Inspect camshaft sprockets reference marks' alignment with rear timing belt cover notches and reference marks' alignment of crankshaft drive gear and oil pump housing. **Timing belt alignment marks will no longer be aligned with camshaft sprockets marks.**

34. Inspect camshaft sprockets 3 and 4, camshaft sprockets 1 and 2 alignment using gauge tool No. J420969-20, or equivalent. Reference marks on camshaft sprockets must match exactly with gauge marks.

35. If sprocket timing marks are aligned with gauge marks, proceed to next step. If sprocket timing marks are not aligned with gauge marks, refer to "Timing" procedure.

36. Remove tools.

37. Install harmonic balancer and tighten mounting bolts.

38. Install timing belt front cover and tighten mounting bolts.

39. Install serpentine drive belt tensioner and tighten mounting bolts.

40. Install power steering pump pulley and tighten mounting bolts snugly.

41. Install water pump pulley and tighten mounting bolts snugly.

42. Route wiring harness into channel and cover.

43. Rotate tensioner clockwise using suitable wrench and install serpentine drive belt. Install over water pump pulley last.

44. Ensure serpentine drive belt is aligned in proper drive pulley grooves.

45. Install air conditioner hose strap bolt and tighten.

46. Tighten water pump and power steering pump pulley mounting bolts.

47. Install AIR diverter hose connections and clamps.

48. Raise and support vehicle.

49. Install AIR crossover pipe into rubber hose connections with clamps.

50. Install AIR crossover pipe bushing nut and tighten.

51. Install AIR crossover pipe support bracket nut to alternator bolt while counterholding alternator bolt.

52. Install splash shield and mounting bolts. Ensure bolts are fully seated and not stripped.

53. Lower vehicle.

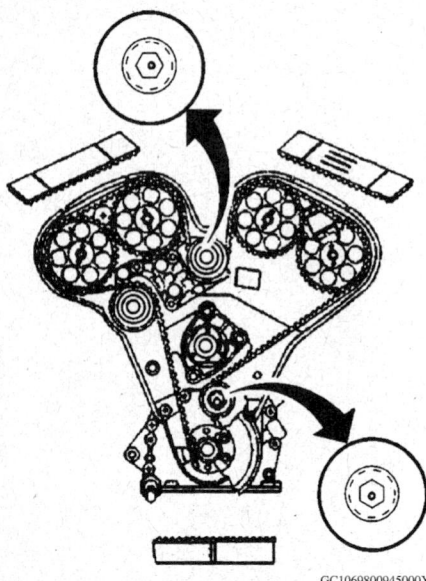

Fig. 14 Timing belt & sprocket alignment marks

54. Install intake plenum, as required.
55. Install pin into rubber mount and resonance chamber.
56. Install switchover valve electrical connector and vacuum hoses.
57. Install intake plenum air inlet hoses, then the IAC inlet hose and clamp.
58. Install resonance chamber air intake hose to air cleaner housing and MAF sensor.
59. Install IAT and MAF sensors' electrical connectors.

Timing

The following procedure is a continuation of the "Timing Belt, Replace" procedure. **Always start adjustment with camshafts 3 and 4. Be ready to make several repeated adjustments and engine revolutions to arrive at the proper timing belt alignment set points.**

INSPECTION

1. Inspect alignment of camshaft sprockets 3 and 4, then camshaft sprockets 1 and 2 using gauge tool No. J420969-20, or equivalent.
2. Camshaft sprockets' reference marks must match exactly with gauge marks.
3. If sprocket timing marks are not aligned with gauge marks, refer to following applicable procedures.

3 & 4 CAMSHAFT SPROCKET MARKS ALIGN TO LEFTHAND OF GAUGE

1. Loosen camshaft sprockets 3 and 4 timing belt idler pulley lock bolt.
2. Turn idler pulley eccentric counterclockwise using adjustment wrench tool No. J42060-40, or equivalent, until camshaft sprocket and gauge marks align, **Fig. 16.**
3. Idler pulley eccentric high point will be at approximately 12 o'clock position.
4. Tighten idler pulley bolt using adjusting

wrench tool No. J42069-40, or equivalent, to hold eccentric in place.
5. Remove tools.
6. Rotate engine two clockwise revolutions stopping at 60° BTDC using crank hub Torx socket tool No. J42098, or equivalent.
7. Lock crankshaft drive sprocket using locking tool No. J42069-10, or equivalent.
8. Turn crankshaft until crankshaft locking tool lever firmly contacts water pump pulley flange. Secure tool lever to water pump pulley flange.
9. Inspect camshaft sprockets 3 and 4 alignment using gauge tool No. J420969-20, or equivalent.
10. Camshaft sprocket reference marks must match exactly with gauge marks.
11. If sprocket timing marks are aligned with gauge marks, inspect adjustment of camshaft sprockets 1 and 2. If sprocket timing marks are not aligned with gauge marks, repeat procedure.
12. After all timing belt timing adjustments have been completed, proceed to "Tensioner Adjustment" procedure.

3 & 4 CAMSHAFT SPROCKET MARKS ALIGN TO RIGHTHAND OF GAUGE

1. Loosen camshaft sprockets 3 and 4 timing belt idler pulley lock bolt.
2. Turn idler pulley eccentric clockwise using adjustment wrench tool No. J42060-40, or equivalent, until camshaft sprocket and gauge tool marks align, **Fig. 17.**
3. Idler pulley eccentric high point will be at approximately 12 o'clock position.
4. Tighten idler pulley bolt using adjusting wrench tool No. J42069-40, or equivalent, to hold eccentric in place.
5. Remove tools.
6. Rotate engine two clockwise revolutions stopping at 60° BTDC using crank hub Torx socket tool No. J42098, or equivalent.
7. Lock crankshaft drive sprocket using locking tool No. J42069-10, or equivalent.
8. Turn crankshaft until crankshaft locking tool lever firmly contacts water pump pulley flange. Secure tool lever to water pump pulley flange.
9. Inspect camshaft sprockets 3 and 4 alignment using gauge tool No. J420969-20, or equivalent.
10. Camshaft sprocket reference marks must match exactly with gauge marks.
11. If sprocket timing marks are aligned with gauge marks, inspect adjustment of camshaft sprockets 1 and 2. If sprocket timing marks are not aligned with gauge marks, repeat procedure.
12. After all timing belt timing adjustments have been completed, proceed to "Tensioner Adjustment" procedure.

1 & 2 CAMSHAFT SPROCKET MARKS ALIGN TO LEFTHAND OF GAUGE

1. Loosen camshaft sprockets 1 and 2 timing belt idler pulley lock bolt.

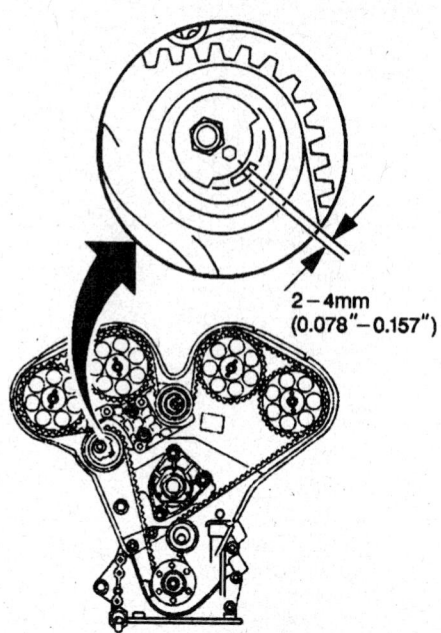

2 – 4mm (0.078" – 0.157")

Fig. 15 Timing belt tensioner alignment

2. Turn idler pulley eccentric counterclockwise using adjustment wrench tool No. J42060-40, or equivalent, until camshaft sprocket and gauge marks align, **Fig. 18.**
3. Idler pulley eccentric high point will be at approximately nine o'clock position.
4. Tighten idler pulley bolt using adjusting wrench tool No. J42069-40, or equivalent, to hold eccentric in place.
5. Remove tools.
6. Rotate engine two clockwise revolutions stopping at 60° BTDC using crank hub Torx socket tool No. J42098, or equivalent.
7. Lock crankshaft drive sprocket using locking tool No. J42069-10, or equivalent.
8. Turn crankshaft until crankshaft locking tool lever firmly contacts water pump pulley flange. Secure tool lever to water pump pulley flange.
9. Inspect camshaft sprockets 3 and 4 alignment using gauge tool No. J420969-20, or equivalent.
10. Camshaft sprocket reference marks must match exactly with gauge marks.
11. If sprocket timing marks are aligned with gauge marks, inspect adjustment of camshaft sprockets 1 and 2. If sprocket timing marks are not aligned with gauge marks, repeat procedure.
12. After all timing belt timing adjustments have been completed, proceed to "Tensioner Adjustment" procedure.

1 & 2 CAMSHAFT SPROCKET MARKS ALIGN TO RIGHTHAND OF GAUGE

1. Loosen camshaft sprockets 3 and 4 timing belt idler pulley lock bolt.
2. Turn idler pulley eccentric clockwise using adjustment wrench tool No. J42060-40, or equivalent, until camshaft sprocket and gauge tool marks

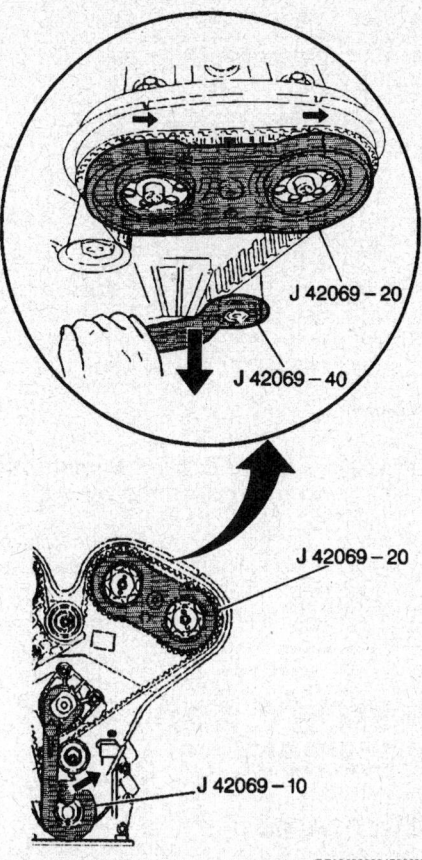

Fig. 16 Camshaft sprockets 3 & 4 mark aligns to lefthand adjustment

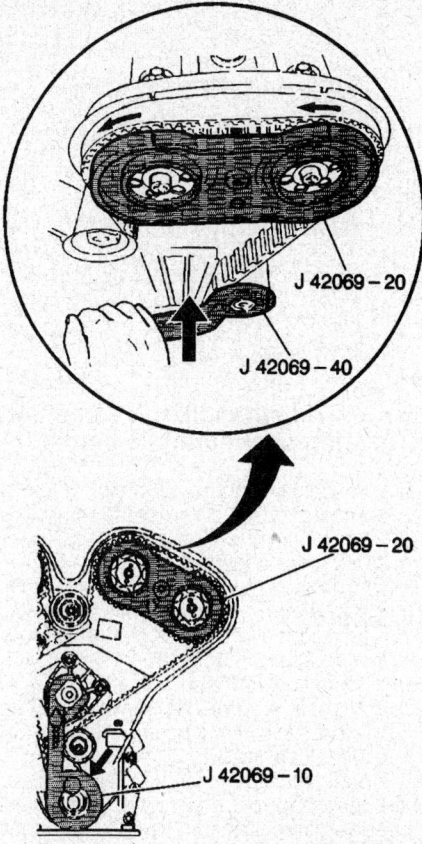

Fig. 17 Camshaft sprockets 3 & 4 aligns to righthand adjustment

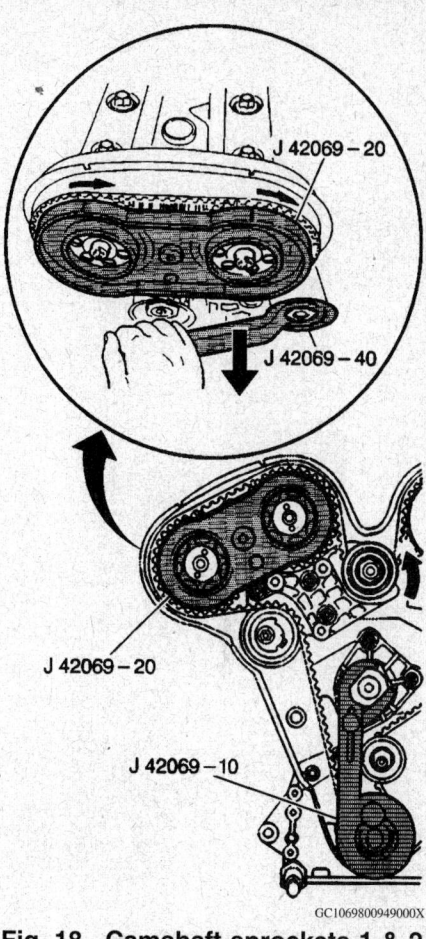

Fig. 18 Camshaft sprockets 1 & 2 aligns to lefthand adjustment

align, **Fig. 19.**

3. Idler pulley eccentric high point will be at approximately nine o'clock position.
4. Tighten idler pulley bolt using adjusting wrench tool No. J42069-40, or equivalent, to hold eccentric in place.
5. Remove tools.
6. Rotate engine two clockwise revolutions stopping at 60° BTDC using crank hub Torx socket tool No. J42098, or equivalent.
7. Lock crankshaft drive sprocket using locking tool No. J42069-10, or equivalent.
8. Turn crankshaft until crankshaft locking tool lever firmly contacts water pump pulley flange. Secure tool lever to water pump pulley flange.
9. Inspect camshaft sprockets 3 and 4 alignment using gauge tool No. J420969-20, or equivalent.
10. Camshaft sprocket reference marks must match exactly with gauge marks.
11. If sprocket timing marks are aligned with gauge marks, inspect adjustment of camshaft sprockets 1 and 2. If sprocket timing marks are not aligned with gauge marks, repeat procedure.
12. After all timing belt timing adjustments have been completed, proceed to "Tensioner Adjustment" procedure.

TENSIONER ADJUSTMENT

This procedure is the completion of installing and/or adjusting the timing belt. **Do**

not perform these steps as a standalone operation.

1. Lock crankshaft at TDC using locking tool No. J42069-10, or equivalent, and loosen timing belt tensioner eccentric locknut.
2. Turn eccentric counterclockwise to full stop. Back off eccentric until reference mark is .078–.157 inch above flange reference mark, **Fig. 15.**
3. Tighten timing belt tensioner eccentric locknut.
4. If not done previously, hold camshaft 3 and 4, and 1 and 2 tensioner eccentrics in place using adjusting wrench tool No. J42069-40, or equivalent and tighten idler pulley bolts.
5. Ensure camshafts 3 and 4 idler pulley eccentric high point is at approximately 12 o'clock position.
6. Ensure camshafts 1 and 2 idler pulley eccentric high point is at approximately nine o'clock position.
7. Remove gauge and crankshaft locking tool.
8. Rotate engine clockwise two revolutions to 60° BTDC.
9. Turn crankshaft until crankshaft locking tool lever firmly contacts water pump pulley flange. Secure tool lever to water pump pulley flange.
10. Inspect camshaft sprockets reference marks' alignment with rear timing belt cover notches and reference marks' alignment of crankshaft drive gear and oil pump housing. **Timing belt align-**

ment marks will no longer be aligned with camshaft sprockets marks.

11. Inspect camshaft sprockets 3 and 4, camshaft sprockets 1 and 2 alignment using gauge tool No. J420969-20, or equivalent. Reference marks on camshaft sprockets must match exactly with gauge marks.
12. If sprocket timing marks are aligned with gauge marks, no further adjustment is required. If sprocket timing marks are not aligned with gauge marks, repeat procedures.

CAMSHAFT
REPLACE
Removal

1. Remove intake plenum as outlined under "Intake Manifold, Replace."
2. Remove resonance chamber as outlined under "Engine, Replace" and appropriate valve cover as outlined under "Valve Cover, Replace."
3. Remove timing belt and front cover as outlined under "Timing Belt, Replace."
4. Turn crankshaft counterclockwise to 60° BTDC, **Fig. 4.**
5. Remove gear bolt using camshaft gear locking tool Nos. J42069-1 and J42069-2, or equivalents, to lock gears in place.

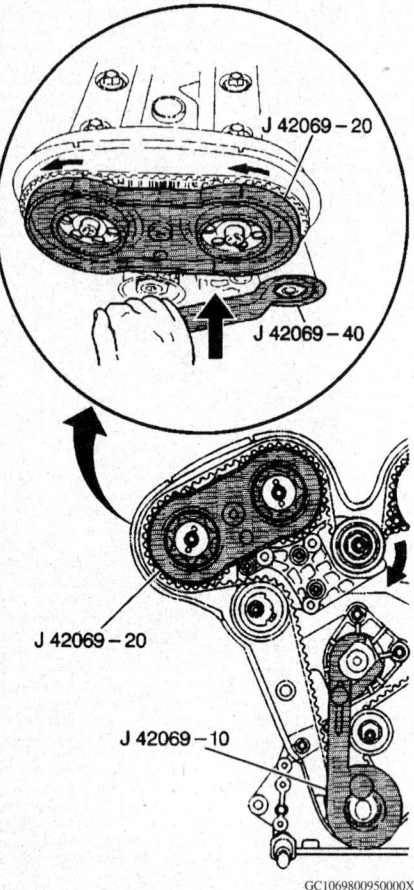

Fig. 19 Camshaft sprockets 1 & 2 aligns to righthand adjustment

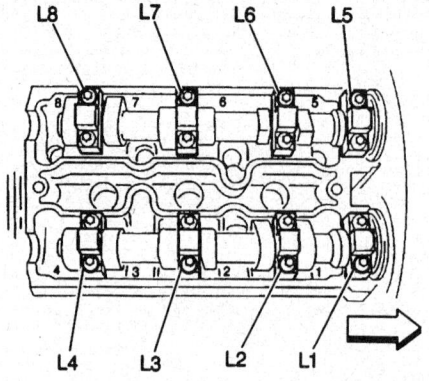

GC1069700840000X

Fig. 20 Righthand bank camshaft bearing cap reference marks

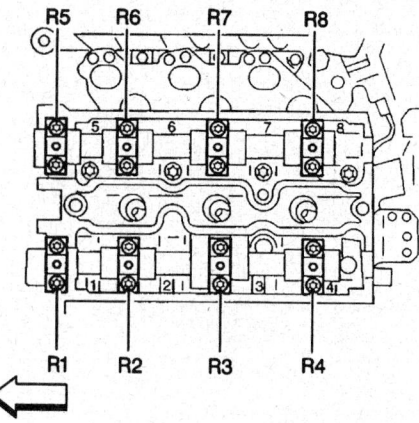

GC1069700841000X

Fig. 21 Lefthand bank camshaft bearing cap reference marks

6. Remove camshaft gear, noting the following:
   a. If righthand intake (No. 2) camshaft is being serviced, ensure camshaft pin points toward 11 o'clock position.
   b. If lefthand intake (No. 3) camshaft is being serviced, ensure camshaft pin points toward seven o'clock position.
   c. If lefthand exhaust (No. 4) camshaft is being serviced, ensure camshaft pin points toward 12 o'clock position and disconnect camshaft sensor electrical connector.
   d. Ensure camshaft is under no pressure from lifters.
7. Starting from center and moving outward in spiral pattern, remove camshaft bearing cap bolts and caps.
8. Remove camshaft with seal and separate seal from shaft.

Installation

1. Lubricate camshaft lobes and lifter contact points with lubricant P/N 12345501, or equivalent.
2. Lubricate bearing surfaces with assembly fluid P/N 1052367, or equivalent.
3. If installing righthand exhaust (No. 1) camshaft, ensure camshaft pin points toward one o'clock position before installing bearing caps.

4. If installing righthand intake (No. 2) camshaft, ensure camshaft pin points toward 11 o'clock position before installing bearing caps.
5. If installing lefthand intake (No. 3) camshaft, ensure camshaft pin points toward seven o'clock position before installing bearing caps.
6. If installing lefthand exhaust (No. 4) camshaft, ensure camshaft pin points toward 12 o'clock position before installing bearing caps.
7. Apply Loctite sealant P/N 573, or equivalent, to bearing cap forward edges prior to installation. **Prevent sealant from entering oil journal.**
8. Position bearing caps over camshafts with reference marks in proper locations, **Figs. 20 and 21. Ensure L coded caps are installed on passenger's side and R coded caps are installed on driver's side.**
9. Tighten camshaft bearing cap bolts in spiral pattern, starting from center bolts and moving outward.
10. If installing lefthand exhaust (No. 4) camshaft, connect camshaft sensor electrical connector.
11. Coat lip of camshaft seal with suitable chassis grease and tap into place using camshaft seal installer tool No. J35268-A, or equivalent. Ensure seal is seated completely and evenly.
12. Ensure camshaft pins are properly positioned, **Fig. 22,** then install camshaft gear using new bolt.
13. Install camshaft gear locking tool Nos. J42069-1 and J42069-2, or equivalents, to prevent gear rotation while tightening bolt.
14. Tighten camshaft gear bolt as follows:
    a. **Torque** camshaft gear bolt to 37 ft. lbs.
    b. Tighten bolt an additional 60°.
    c. Finally, tighten bolt an additional 15°.
15. Turn crankshaft clockwise to Top Dead Center (TDC) position using crank hub socket tool No. J42098, or equivalent.
16. Install and adjust timing belt as outlined under "Timing Belt, Replace."
17. Install timing belt front cover as outlined under "Timing Belt, Replace."
18. Install valve cover as outlined under "Valve Cover, Replace."
19. Install resonance chamber as outlined

under "Engine, Replace" and intake plenum as outlined under "Intake Manifold, Replace."
20. Connect battery ground cable.

PISTON & ROD ASSEMBLY

Removal

1. With engine removed and only crankshaft, pistons and rods remaining in block, turn crankshaft until rod bearing cap bolts are accessible.
2. Remove rod bearing cap bolts, cap and insert.
3. Drive piston and rod assembly from block using suitable wooden block.
4. If piston and connecting rod are to be separated, refer to "Pistons, Pins & Rings."

Installation

1. With piston rings installed and oriented as outlined under "Pistons, Pins & Rings," install guide pin tool No. J41742, or equivalent, in connecting rod end.
2. Install upper rod bearing on rod.
3. Coat piston, rings, cylinder bore and bearing surfaces with Engine Oil Supplement (EOS) P/N 1052368, or equivalent.
4. Compress piston rings using ring compressor tool No. J8037, or equivalent, then gently tap piston into cylinder bore while guiding connecting rod onto crankshaft. **Ensure arrow mark on top of piston faces front of engine.**
5. Remove rod guide pin tool and install connecting rod cap with bearing. **Ensure bumps on connecting rod and cap face rear of engine.**
6. Install new connecting rod cap bolts and tighten bolts alternately as follows:
   a. **Torque** bolts to 26 ft. lbs.
   b. Tighten bolts an additional 45°.
   c. Finally, tighten bolts an additional 15°.

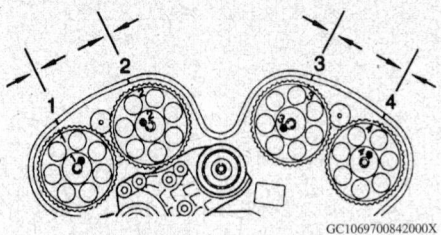

Fig. 22 Camshaft pin orientation

CYLINDER BORE	PISTON SIZE
(8) 85.976 - 85.985 mm (3.3848 - 3.3852 inch)	(8) 85.940 - 85.950 mm (3.3834 - 3.3838 inch)
(99) 85.985 - 85.995 mm (3.3852 - 3.3856 inch)	(99) 85.950 - 85.960 mm (3.3838 - 3.3842 inch)
(00) 85.995 - 86.005 mm (3.3856 - 3.3860 inch)	(00) 85.960 - 85.970 mm (3.3842 - 3.3846 inch)
(01) 86.005 - 86.015 mm (3.3860 - 3.3864 inch)	(01) 85.970 - 85.980 mm (3.3846 - 3.3850 inch)
(02) 86.015 - 86.025 mm (3.3864 - 3.3868 inch)	(02) 85.980 - 85.990 mm (3.3850 - 3.3854 inch)
† (7 + 0.5) 86.465 - 86.475 mm (3.4041 - 3.4045 inch)	† (7 + 0.5) 86.430 - 86.440 mm (3.4027 - 3.4031 inch)

Fig. 23 Piston selection chart

PISTONS, PINS & RINGS

1. If cylinders have been honed, proper size piston must be selected for each bore. Measure cylinder bore after honing and select corresponding piston size, **Fig. 23.**
2. If piston must be separated from connecting rod, note the following:
   a. Heat end of connecting rod to facilitate piston pin replacement.
   b. Press piston pin out of and into piston and connecting rod using press tool No. J24086-C, or equivalent.
   c. When assembling piston and rod, ensure arrow mark on top of piston and bumps on connecting rod face in opposite directions.
   d. Piston arrow mark will face front of engine, while connecting rod bumps will face rear.
3. Measure piston pin bore to piston pin clearance. Maximum clearance is .0003 inch. Replace piston and pin if clearance is more than specifications.
4. After cylinders have been honed, inspect piston ring end gap clearances as follows:
   a. Install compression rings in cylinder bore and measure gap, **Fig. 24.**
   b. Gap should be .0118–.0196 inch.
   c. Install oil control ring in cylinder bore and measure gap.
   d. Gap should be .0157–.0551 inch.
   e. Rings should be replaced if end gap is not as indicated.
5. Inspect piston ring groove clearance, **Fig. 25,** noting the following:
   a. Compression ring groove clearances should be .0008–.0015 inch.
   b. Oil control ring groove clearance should be .0004–.0012 inch.
   c. Replace piston if groove clearance is not as specified.
6. When rings are installed on piston, they must be properly positioned, **Fig. 26.**

MAIN & ROD BEARINGS

Main Bearing Clearance Inspection

1. Select piece of gauging plastic that is full width of crankshaft bearing and place on journal, **Fig. 27.**
2. Measure all five bearing clearances simultaneously. **Do not turn crankshaft** with gauging plastic installed between journal and crankshaft bearing.
3. Install bearing caps and torsional bearing bridge in original positions.
4. Tighten main bearing cap bolts as follows:
   a. **Torque** main bearing cap bolts to 37 ft. lbs.
   b. Tighten bolts an additional 60°.
   c. Finally, tighten bolts an additional 15°.
5. Tighten torsional bearing bridge bolts to specifications, then remove bearing bridge and bearing caps for gauging plastic inspection.
6. Measure gauging plastic at widest point with scale provided in plastic gauge kit.
7. Bearing clearance should be .0006–.0017 inch.
8. Crankshaft main journal diameter should be 2.6763–2.6766 inches (green) or 2.6766–2.6770 inches (brown).
9. If gauging plastic indicates excessive clearance or clearance irregularity exceeding .0010 inch and crankshaft main journal diameter is as indicated, use standard size bearings. **Always replace upper and lower crankshaft bearings as set.**
10. If specified clearance cannot be achieved with standard bearing, grind crankshaft again and use undersize bearing, available in .010 and .020 inch undersizes.

Rod Bearing Clearance Inspection

If the lower half of the connecting rod bearing is worn or damaged, both halves should be replaced. Clearance must be measured at each connecting rod bearing to determine proper sizes, as factory installed bearing sizes may vary between journals.

USING GAUGING PLASTIC

Perform this procedure with pistons and connecting rods installed in engine block. Refer to "Piston & Rod Assembly" for installation procedure.
1. Select piece of gauging plastic that is full width of crankshaft rod bearing and place on journal, **Fig. 28.**
2. Install rod bearing cap in original position. **Do not turn crankshaft while gauging plastic is between journal and bearing.**
3. Tighten bearing cap bolts as outlined under "Piston & Rod Assembly," then remove bearing caps.
4. Measure gauging plastic at widest point using scale provided in plastic gauge kit.
5. Connecting rod bearing clearance should be .0005–.0024 inch.
6. Connecting rod journal diameter should be 1.927–1.928 inches.
7. If gauging plastic indicates excessive clearance or clearance irregularity exceeding .0010 inch and connecting rod journal diameter is satisfactory, use standard size bearing. **Always replace upper and lower bearings as set.**
8. If proper clearance cannot be achieved using standard size bearings, grind crankshaft again and use undersize bearings, available in .010 and .020 inch undersizes.

USING MICROMETER

1. Install connecting rod bearings into rod and cap.
2. Install cap and tighten bolts as outlined under "Piston & Rod Assembly."
3. Measure inside diameter of connecting rod bearings in at least two places 90° apart.
4. Remove bearings and measure connecting rod inside diameter if diameter varies more than .0012 inch.
5. Replace rod if variance is still more than .0012 inch.
6. If diameter does not vary more than .0012 inch, connecting rod is satisfactory.
7. Subtract rod bearing journal diameter from rod bearing inside diameter to obtain bearing clearance.
8. If bearing clearance is not as indicated, replace bearings with new, standard size bearings and measure clearance once again.
9. If clearance is still not as indicated, grind crankshaft again and use undersize bearings.

CRANKSHAFT REAR OIL SEAL

REPLACE

1. Remove transmission as outlined under "Engine, Replace."
2. Hold crankshaft in position and remove flexplate bolts using crank hub socket tool No. J42098, or equivalent.
3. Remove flexplate and center punch rear oil seal steel ring.
4. Carefully drill small, shallow pilot hole into steel ring and thread in self-tapping screw.

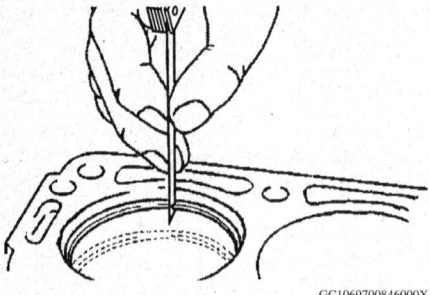

Fig. 24 Piston ring end gap measurement

5. Pull on screw using suitable pliers and extract oil seal from block..
6. Reverse procedure to install, noting the following:
   a. Coat lip of seal with suitable chassis grease prior to installation.
   b. Install seal using rear main oil seal installer tool No. J42067, or equivalent.

OIL PAN

REPLACE

Lower

1. Raise and support vehicle, then remove mounting bolts and splash shield.
2. Drain engine oil into suitable container.
3. Disconnect oil level sensor and remove electrical connector C-clip from upper oil pan.
4. Remove mounting bolts and lower oil pan from upper.
5. Pull oil level sensor electrical connector from upper oil pan.
6. Remove mounting bolts and oil level sensor.
7. Reverse procedure to install, noting the following:
   a. Install new oil pan gasket and oil level sensor O-ring.
   b. Tighten oil pan bolts.

Upper

1. Remove lower oil pan.
2. Remove engine mount lower nuts from frame bracket. **Record alignment tab orientation for installation.**
3. Remove air condition compressor hose strap bolt from upper oil pan front.
4. Remove four transmission mounting bolts from upper oil pan.
5. Remove all but four corner upper oil pan mounting bolts.
6. Mark propeller shaft for installation alignment, then remove mounting bolts and slide shaft rearward. Secure propeller shaft in place.
7. Remove catalytic converter mounting bolts from hanger bracket and nuts from exhaust manifold.
8. Lower catalytic converter and secure using suitable mechanic wire.
9. Remove two idler arm mounting bolts from frame and lower relay rod out of way.
10. Lower vehicle.

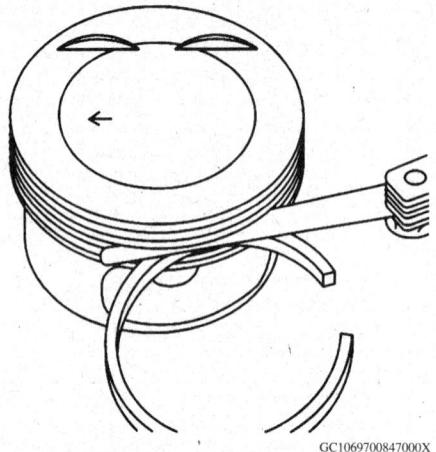

Fig. 25 Piston ring groove clearance measurement

11. Support and raise engine using support fixture tool No. J28467-A, engine support fixture adapter tool No. J28467-450 and lift bracket tools No. J36857, or equivalents. **Do not damage surrounding components.**
12. Raise and support vehicle.
13. Remove remaining upper oil pan mounting bolts.
14. Remove mounting bolts and oil intake pipe.
15. Remove upper oil pan toward vehicle front. **Do not damage aluminum mating surfaces.**
16. Remove rubber seal and RTV sealant.
17. Thoroughly clean oil pan housing and engine block.
18. Reverse procedure to install, noting the following:
    a. Apply bead of silicone sealing compound No. 12346286, or equivalent, in upper oil pan groove bottom.
    b. **Keep bead at least .4 inch from bolt holes.**
    c. **Oil pan must be installed within 10 minutes of applying sealant.**
    d. Install new seal.

OIL PUMP

REPLACE

1. Drain engine coolant into suitable container.
2. Remove resonance chamber as outlined under "Engine, Replace" and timing belt as outlined under "Timing Belt, Replace."
3. Remove rear timing belt cover, install crank hub holding tool No. J42065, or equivalent.
4. Remove crankshaft drive gear bolt using crank hub socket tool No. J42098, or equivalent.
5. Remove crankshaft drive gear and lower alternator bolt.
6. Raise and support vehicle, then remove splash shield and drain engine oil into suitable container.
7. Remove oil pan as outlined under "Oil Pan, Replace."
8. Remove engine mount lower nuts from frame bracket.

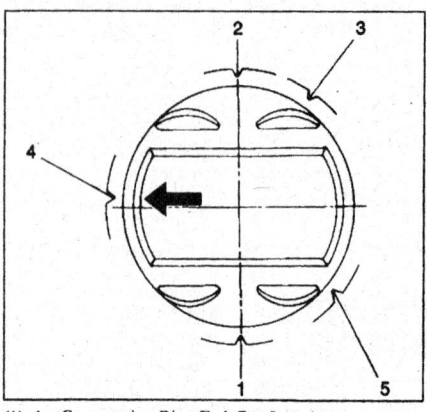

(1) 1st Compression Ring End Gap Location
(2) 2nd Compression Ring End Gap Location
(3) Oil Control Ring Upper Ring End Gap Location
(4) Oil Control Ring Spacer End Gap Location
(5) Oil Control Ring Lower Ring End Gap Location

Fig. 26 Piston ring orientation

9. Remove oil intake pipe and air conditioning compressor hose support strap bolt.
10. Remove oil pan housing bolts leaving four corner bolts in place.
11. Make corresponding marks on propeller shaft and transmission output flange.
12. Remove propeller shaft to transmission flange bolts, slide shaft rearward and secure away from transmission.
13. Remove catalytic converter hanger bolts and lower vehicle.
14. Raise engine slightly and support using support fixture tool No. J28467-A, or equivalent.
15. Raise and support vehicle.
16. Remove remaining mounting bolts, oil pan housing and gasket.
17. Remove mounting bolts and pump.
18. Remove oil pump front main oil seal.
19. Reverse procedure to install, noting the following:
    a. Install front main oil seal using oil seal installer tool No. J35268-A, or equivalent.
    b. Apply sealant P/N 12345997, or equivalent, to engine block and oil pump joints.
    c. Install crank hub holding tool No. J42065, or equivalent.
    d. Install new crankshaft drive gear bolt and **torque** to 184 ft. lbs.
    e. Finally, tighten gear bolt an additional 15°.
    f. Adjust timing belt as outlined under "Timing Belt, Replace."

OIL PUMP SERVICE

1. Remove oil pump pressure regulating valve plug, seal, valve and spring.
2. Remove oil pump pressure relief valve plug, seal, spring and valve.
3. Remove mounting bolts and oil pump cover, then inner and outer gears.
4. Measure oil pump inner and outer gear to housing clearance using suitable feeler gauge and straightedge, **Fig. 29.** Maximum clearance is .003 inch for inner gear and .004 inch for outer gear.

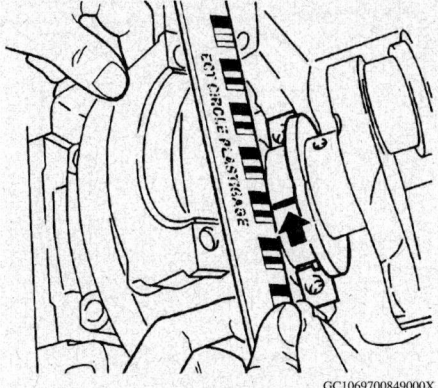

Fig. 27 Main journal gauging plastic installation

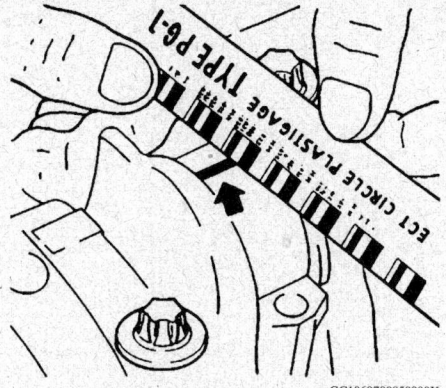

Fig. 28 Rod bearing gauging plastic installation

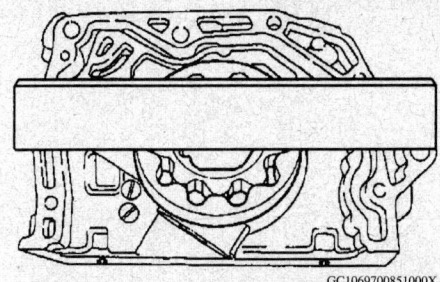

Fig. 29 Oil pump gear to housing clearance measurement

5. Inspect oil pressure regulating and relief valves and springs for excessive wear and damage. Replace if required.
6. Install inner and outer gears with marks facing cover, **Fig. 30.**
7. Install cover and tighten bolts.
8. Install pressure relief and regulating valves, springs, seals and plugs.

OIL COOLER
REPLACE

1. Remove intake plenum and manifold as outlined under "Intake Manifold, Replace."
2. Drain engine coolant and oil into suitable containers.
3. Disconnect coolant temperature sensor and sender electrical connectors.
4. Disconnect throttle body and heater inlet hoses at coolant bridge.
5. Remove mounting bolts and upper seals.
6. Remove engine coolant bridge and lower seals.
7. Loosen lefthand exhaust manifold upper heat shield bolts.
8. Disconnect oil feed and return lines at oil cooler.
9. Raise and support vehicle.
10. Remove lefthand catalytic converter and exhaust pipe.
11. Remove oil filter, crank sensor and engine oil cooler line clamp.
12. Disconnect and remove oil feed and return lines at engine block
13. Lower vehicle.
14. Remove oil cooler inlet and outlet nuts, cover and cooler.
15. Reverse procedure to install, noting the following:
    a. Apply .08 inch bead of silicone sealer P/N 12345997, or equivalent, to oil cooler cover groove in place of original seal.
    b. Install new seals on oil cooler oil feed and return line fittings.
    c. Tighten fittings, mounting bolts and nuts.

BELT TENSION DATA

The serpentine drive belt tensioner features wear indicator marks, **Fig. 31.** These should be used to determine if belt tension is sufficient.

SERPENTINE DRIVE BELT
Belt Replacement

1. Raise and support vehicle.
2. Remove splash shield, air conditioning compressor hose strap bolt and Secondary Air Injection (AIR) crossover pipe bracket nut. Use suitable back-up wrench on alternator bolt.
3. Remove AIR crossover pipe bushing nut from bracket and crossover pipe from rubber hose connections. Move pipe aside to gain working clearance.
4. Turn tensioner pulley clockwise, to release serpentine belt tension, then slide belt off pulleys.
5. Reverse procedure to install, noting the following:
    a. Route belt properly, **Fig. 32.**
    b. Turn tensioner clockwise to easy installation.
    c. Install belt over water pump pulley last.

Tensioner Replacement

1. Remove serpentine drive belt as outlined under "Belt Replacement" and remove tensioner bolts.
2. Remove tensioner.
3. Reverse procedure to install.

COOLING SYSTEM BLEED

The cooling system will bleed automatically during engine warm-up. If reservoir is not full, it may be required to add coolant after the engine has cooled.

THERMOSTAT
REPLACE

1. Drain engine coolant into suitable container.
2. Remove intake plenum as outlined under "Intake Manifold, Replace."

3. Remove intake manifold bolts as outlined under "Intake Manifold, Replace."
4. Lift and support manifold while removing seals.
5. Disconnect radiator inlet hose at thermostat outlet pipe and remove pipe.
6. Remove mounting bolts, housing and thermostat.
7. Remove seal ring.
8. Reverse procedure to install, noting the following:
    a. Install new thermostat seal ring.
    b. Install new intake manifold seal.

WATER PUMP
REPLACE

1. Drain engine coolant into suitable container.
2. Remove resonance chamber as outlined under "Engine, Replace."
3. Remove timing belt front cover as outlined under "Timing Belt, Replace."
4. Remove mounting bolts and water pump.
5. Reverse procedure to install.

RADIATOR
REPLACE

1. Remove battery.
2. Remove upper radiator covers and drain engine coolant into suitable container.
3. Remove resonance chamber as outlined under "Engine, Replace."
4. Disconnect primary cooling fan and cooling fan control switch electrical connectors.
5. Disconnect air bleed hose and transmission oil cooler pipes at radiator. Remove pipe seals.
6. Disconnect coolant hose at secondary auxiliary coolant pump and remove Secondary Air Injection (AIR) cutoff valve bracket bolts from fan housing.
7. Remove condenser to radiator bracket bolts, then disconnect radiator inlet and outlet hoses.
8. Disconnect secondary auxiliary coolant pump electrical connector.
9. Lift radiator and primary fan assembly away from radiator support using rocking motion.
10. Remove upper retainers, primary fan and cooling fan control switches from radiator.
11. Reverse procedure to install. Tighten

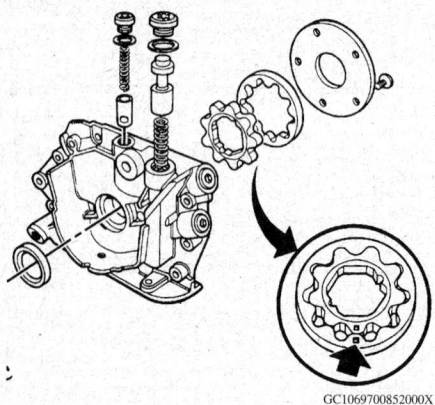

Fig. 30 Oil pump gear orientation

cooling fan control switches, primary fan bolts and oil cooler pipe fittings.

FUEL PUMP

REPLACE

The fuel pump is located inside the modular fuel sender. Refer to "Electrical" section for fuel pump relay location.

1. Relieve fuel system pressure as outlined under "Precautions."
2. Drain fuel tank into suitable container using suitable hand operated pump.
3. Raise and support vehicle.
4. Remove rear bumper fascia and rear frame support.
5. Disconnect fuel feed line at fuel filter and fuel return line near filter.
6. Disconnect fuel tank breather and vent hoses, and fuel sender electrical connector.
7. Support fuel tank supported.
8. Remove tank mounting strap front bolts and both straps.
9. Lower fuel tank and disconnect Evapo-

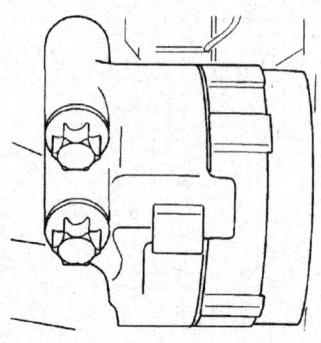

Serpentine Drive Belt Tension Sufficient

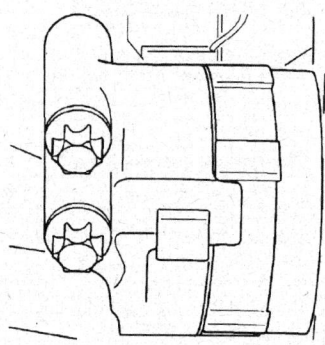

Serpentine Drive Belt Tension Insufficient (Replace Belt)

GC1069700854000X

Fig. 31 Serpentine drive belt tensioner wear indicator

rative Emission (EVAP) tank pressure sensor connector.

10. Remove spring loaded clamp at fuel tank boot, sending unit and wiring harness from tank using fuel tank sender wrench tool No. J42219, or equivalent.
11. Remove seal from sending unit cover

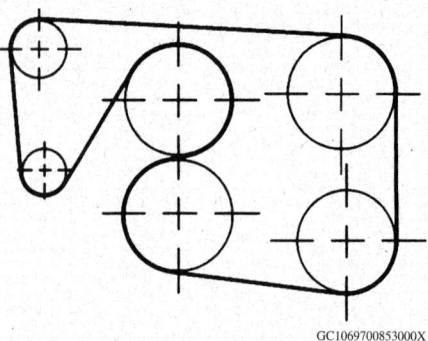

GC1069700853000X

Fig. 32 Serpentine drive belt routing

and drain fuel from sender reservoir into suitable container.
12. Remove fuel level sensor from sender and disconnect fuel feed hose at fuel pump.
13. Disconnect fuel pump electrical connectors.
14. Remove damper ring and fuel pump.
15. Remove fuel pump bracket and strainer.
16. Reverse procedure to install, noting the following:
    a. Install new fuel pump strainer and sending unit lip seal.
    b. Apply thin film of oil to inner diameter of lip seal prior to installation.
    c. Tighten fuel tank sender nut and fuel tank straps.

FUEL FILTER

REPLACE

1. Relieve fuel system pressure as outlined under "Precautions."
2. Grasp filter firmly and remove fuel line fitting bolts.
3. Loosen fuel filter mounting strap and remove filter.
4. Reverse procedure to install.

TIGHTENING SPECIFICATIONS

Year	Component	Torque/Ft. Lbs.
2001	Accelerator & Cruise Control Cable Bracket	72②
	Accessory Bracket	30
	Air Conditioning Compressor Bracket	30
	Air Conditioning Compressor Hose Support Strap	72②
	AIR Injection Crossover Pipe Bushing	108②
	AIR Injection Crossover Pipe Support Bracket	30
	AIR Injection Pipe	15
	Alternator	30
	Camshaft Bearing Cap	72②
	Camshaft Gear	③
	Catalytic Converter	15
	Connecting Rod Caps	⑤
	Coolant Bridge	22
	Cooling Fan Control Switches	16
	Crank Sensor	72②
	Crankshaft Drive Gear	⑥
	Cylinder Head	①
	Cylinder Head Cover	72②
	Engine Mount Lower Nut	41
	Engine Mount Upper Nut	30
	Exhaust Manifold	15
	Exhaust Manifold Heat Shield	72②
	Flexplate To Torque Converter	22
	Fuel Tank Sender	37
	Fuel Tank Straps	26
	Harmonic Balancer	15
	Intake Manifold	15
	Intake Manifold Spacer	15
	Intake Plenum	72②
	Intake Plenum Switchover Valve	72②
	Main Bearing Caps	④
	Oil Cooler Cover	22
	Oil Cooler Inlet & Outlet	15
	Oil Feed & Return Lines	22
	Oil Filter	11
	Oil Intake Pipe	72②
	Oil Pan	72②
	Oil Pan Baffle	72②
	Oil Pan Drain Plug	41
	Oil Pan Housing	11
	Oil Pump Cover	72②
	Oil Pump Housing	53②
	Power Steering Pump Pulley	15

Continued

TIGHTENING
SPECIFICATIONS—Continued

Year	Component	Torque/Ft. Lbs.
2001	Primary Cooling Fan To Radiator	35②
	Propeller Shaft Coupling	70
	Resonance Chamber	27②
	Serpentine Drive Belt Tensioner	30
	Spark Plug	19
	Thermostat Housing	15
	Thermostat Outlet Pipe	15
	Timing Belt Cover	72②
	Timing Belt Idler Pulley	30
	Timing Belt Tensioner	15
	Timing Belt Tensioner Bracket	30
	Torsional Bearing Bridge	15
	Transmission Crossmember To Body	33
	Transmission Crossmember To Mount	15
	Transmission Housing To Engine Block	44
	Transmission Housing To Engine Oil Pan	15
	Transmission Oil Cooler Pipes To Radiator	18
	Valve Cover	72②
	Water Pump	18
	Water Pump Pulley	72②

AIR — Secondary Air Injection
① — Refer to "Cylinder Head, Replace" for tightening procedure & specifications.
② — Inch lbs.
③ — Refer to "Camshaft, Replace" for tightening procedure & specifications.
④ — Refer to "Main & Rod Bearings" for tightening procedure & specifications.
⑤ — Refer to "Piston & Rod Assembly" for tightening procedure & specifications.
⑥ — Refer to "Oil Pump, Replace" for tightening procedure & specifications.

Rear Axle & Suspension

NOTE: On Air Bag Equipped Models, Refer To "Air Bag System Precautions" Located In The Front Of This Manual For System Disarming & Arming Procedures.

NOTE: Refer To "Computer Relearn Procedures" Located In The Front Of This Manual When Battery Power To The Computer Has Been Interrupted.

INDEX

DESCRIPTION

The rear axle and suspension assembly is fully independent and is isolated from the vehicle body by rubber bushings at all mounting points, **Fig. 1.** The differential is supported by cradle, which is also the mounting point for stabilizer shaft. Sealed tie rod ends and wheel bearings eliminate the need for periodic lubrication.

The two drive axle assemblies are essentially inner and outer Constant Velocity (CV) joints joined by shaft. The CV joints do not require periodic lubrication and, although the outer joint can be serviced independently of the axle, the inner joint and axle shaft are non-serviceable items.

REAR AXLE SHAFT

REPLACE

1. Place gear selector lever in Neutral position, then raise and support vehicle.
2. Remove wheel and install hub flange holding adapter tool No. J42066, or equivalent, on flange using wheel bolts.
3. Hold flange holding adapter tool using suitable ratchet and remove flange bolts.
4. Separate drive axle outer end from wheel bearing hub inner flange.
5. Separate drive axle from differential using drive axle separator tool No. J42071, or equivalent, and suitable hammer. **Ensure beveled side of tool is against differential and not against drive axle.**
6. Reverse procedure to install, noting the following:
   a. Lubricate drive axle spline and seal surfaces with suitable differential lubricant.
   b. Drive axle into differential bore using suitable rubber mallet. **Do not use more force than required to seat axle fully in bore.**

DIFFERENTIAL CARRIER

REPLACE

1. Raise and support vehicle.
2. Support differential using suitable transmission jack.
3. Disconnect anti-lock brake system electrical connectors and remove drive axles as outlined under "Rear Axle Shaft, Replace."
4. Remove propeller shaft as outlined under "Propeller Shaft, Replace" and coupling.
5. Remove differential support bracket bolts from bracket and bushing bolts from differential.
6. Remove differential carrier.
7. Reverse procedure to install.

PROPELLER SHAFT

REPLACE

1. Place gear selector lever in Neutral position, then raise and support vehicle.
2. Remove heat shields and bolts securing propeller shaft bearing bracket to underbody.
3. Remove front propeller shaft coupling nuts and bolts, **Fig. 2.**
4. Pry front half of shaft rearward until it clears coupling.
5. Remove rear propeller shaft coupling nuts and bolts, then move rear half of shaft forward slightly.
6. Remove shaft by sliding it between exhaust system components and underbody surface.
7. Reverse procedure to install.

HUB & BEARING

REPLACE

Removal

1. Raise and support vehicle, then remove wheel.
2. Remove driveshaft bolts using holding

tool No. J42066, or equivalent, and suitable breaker bar.
3. Separate driveshaft from rear wheel hub flange and suspend in upward direction. **Do not allow shaft to hang freely.**
4. Disengage clip and separate brake pipe from lower control arm.
5. Remove disc brake pads and caliper. Suspend caliper aside. **Do not open hydraulic system.**
6. Loosen setscrew and slide rotor off hub.
7. Back out three of four brake backing plate bolts approximately .47 inch using socket tool No. J42072, or equivalent.
8. Install spacer tool No. J42094-2 and holding fixture tool No. J42094-1, or equivalents, on rear wheel hub flange and remove hub nut.
9. Remove flange from hub using flange removal tools, **Fig. 3.**
10. Press out hub using hub removal tools, **Fig. 4.**
11. If original bearing is to be used again, inspect seal carefully. **Damage may have occur during hub removal.**
12. Remove wheel bearing retaining ring, **Fig. 5.**
13. Remove wheel bearing using wheel bearing removal tools, **Fig. 6.**

Installation

1. Fully seat bearing using bearing installation tools, **Fig. 7.**
2. Install wheel bearing retaining ring, **Fig. 5,** then assemble hub installation tools, **Fig. 8.**
3. Ensure installer tool is on wheel bearing inner ring.
4. Ensure threaded driver tool is properly centered inside wheel bearing to prevent hub from binding as it is drawn into bearing.
5. Adjust threaded spacer pins as required.

6. Draw hub into bearing by holding threaded driver and turning arbor clockwise.
7. Remove tool assembly.
8. Install flange on hub using flange installation tools, **Fig. 9. Ensure splines are properly aligned.**
9. Remove arbor, driver and thrust bearing tools, leaving holding fixture and spacer in place.
10. Install rear wheel hub nut and tighten. Remove holding fixture and spacer tools.
11. Install retaining washer and stake to hub.
12. Tighten brake backing plate bolts.
13. Install brake rotor and tighten set-screw.
14. Install caliper and secure brake pipe to lower control arm with clip.
15. Connect driveshaft to rear wheel hub flange and install bolts.
16. Tighten driveshaft bolts.
17. Install wheel and lower vehicle.

REAR SUSPENSION
REPLACE

The following procedure is for removal of the differential and axle cradle as a unit. If required, the differential can be replaced independently as outlined under "Differential Carrier, Replace."

1. Raise and support vehicle, allowing working clearance around rear axle support flange bolts.
2. Remove rear wheels and disconnect wheel speed sensor electrical connectors.
3. Remove propeller shaft disc joint bolts from rear differential flange and disconnect exhaust system at rubber body mounts.
4. Disengage clips and separate brake pipes from lower control arms.
5. Release parking brake cables from actuator brackets.
6. Remove disc brake pads and caliper mounting bolts, separate caliper from rotor and suspend aside to prevent damage to brake pipe. **Do not open hydraulic system.**
7. Scribe mark around perimeter of axle cradle mount for installation.
8. Support cradle and each lower control arm.
9. Remove shock absorber lower mounting bolts and cradle mounting bolts. Pivot cradle to allow for spring removal.
10. Remove springs.
11. Lower vehicle while supporting axle cradle.
12. Remove axle support flange, bushing bolts and axle cradle.
13. Reverse procedure to install, noting the following:
    a. Tighten mounting bolts.
    b. Inspect and adjust wheel alignment as outlined in "Wheel Alignment" section.

SHOCK ABSORBER
REPLACE

1. Move rear seat backrest forward to ac-

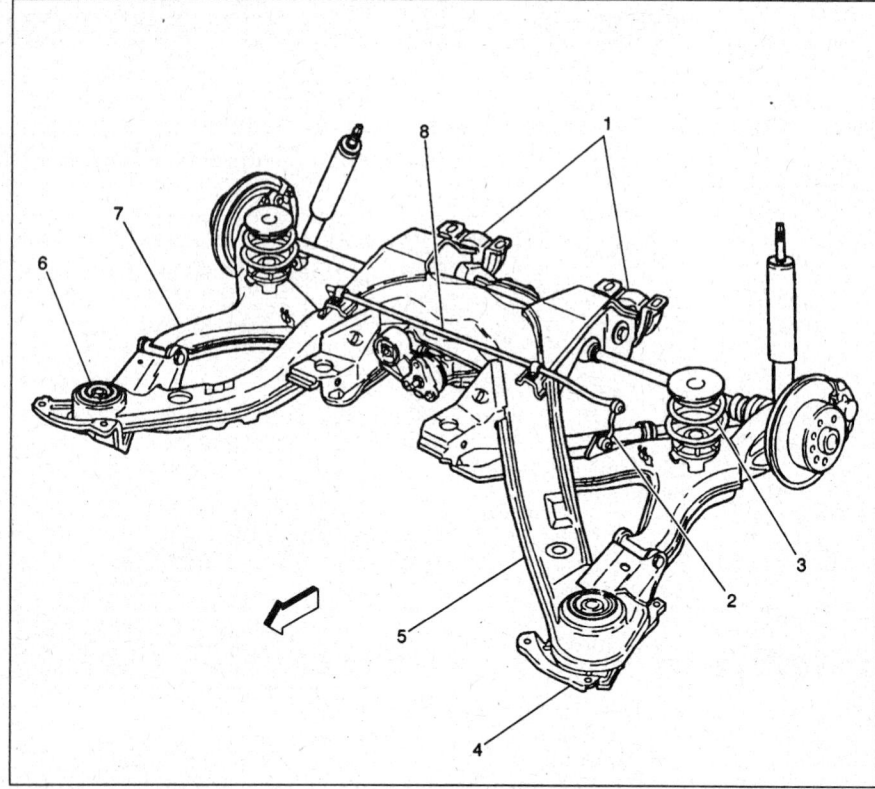

(1) Rear Axle Cradle Mount
(2) Stabilizer Shaft Link
(3) Spring
(4) Rear Axle Support Bushing Flange
(5) Rear Axle Cradle
(6) Rear Axle Support Bushing
(7) Rear Lower Control Arm
(8) Stabilizer Shaft

GC2039700121000X

Fig. 1 Rear axle & suspension assembly

cess upper shock absorber mount and remove protective cap from tower.
2. Remove upper shock absorber mounting nut, washer and grommet.
3. Raise and support vehicle.
4. Disconnect Automatic Level Control (ALC) air line.
5. Remove lower mounting bolt and shock absorber.
6. Reverse procedure to install.

COIL SPRING
REPLACE

1. Raise and support vehicle, then disengage clips and separate brake pipes from lower control arms. **Do not open hydraulic system.**
2. Remove stabilizer shaft link bolts and disconnect link at lower control arms.
3. Disengage exhaust system rubber insulators from hangers to gain working clearance. **Support exhaust system to prevent damage.**
4. Disconnect rear wheel speed sensor electrical connectors.
5. Support lower control arms.
6. Remove shock absorber lower mount bolt and control arm supports.
7. Support differential.
8. Remove rear axle cradle to vehicle body mounting bolts and lower differential until springs can be removed.
9. Remove spring and seat, then separate seat from spring.
10. Reverse procedure to install.

CONTROL ARM
REPLACE

Lower

1. Raise and support vehicle, allowing rear axle support flange bolts to remain accessible.
2. Remove wheel and driveshaft bolts while holding rear wheel hub using holding tool No. J42066, or equivalent.
3. Separate driveshaft from rear wheel hub flange and support in upward position. **Do not suspend from spring.**
4. Disengage clip and separate brake pipe from lower control arm.
5. Remove brake pads and caliper.
6. Suspend caliper to prevent brake pipe damage. **Do not open brake hydraulic system.**
7. Loosen setscrew and slide rotor off hub.
8. Release parking brake cable from actuator bracket.
9. Remove hub, flange and bearing as outlined under "Hub & Bearing, Replace."
10. Remove parking brake shoes and related hardware.
11. Remove rear backing plate bolts using socket tool No. J42072, or equivalent, and separate parking brake anchor from rear brake backing plate.
12. Remove backing plate from control arm and disengage exhaust system

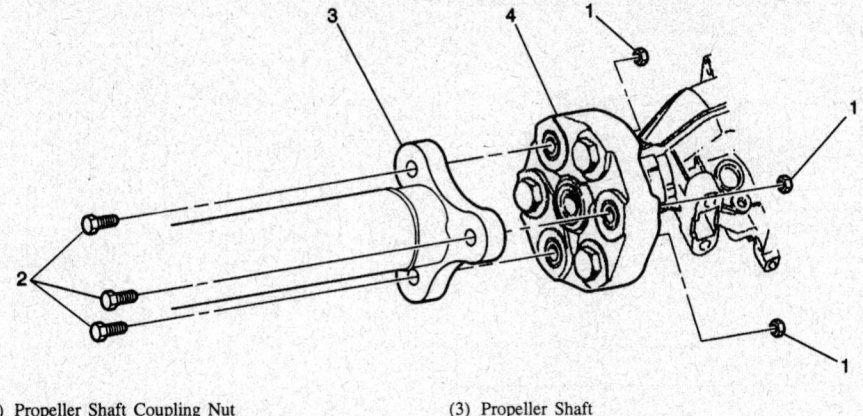

(1) Propeller Shaft Coupling Nut
(2) Propeller Shaft Coupling Bolt
(3) Propeller Shaft
(4) Propeller Shaft Coupling

GC2039700122000X

Fig. 2 Propeller shaft coupling

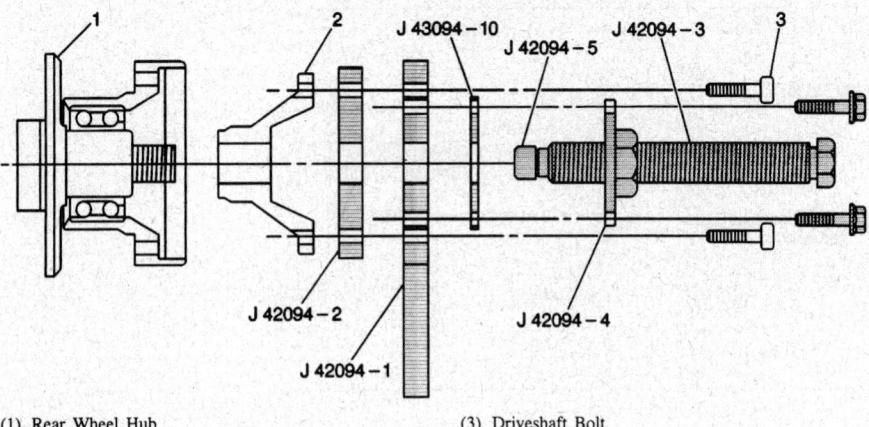

(1) Rear Wheel Hub
(2) Rear Wheel Hub Flange
(3) Driveshaft Bolt

GC2039700123000X

Fig. 3 Hub flange removal tools

hangers from rubber body mounts. **Support exhaust system components to prevent damage.**

13. Remove rear outer tie rod nut and outer tie rod from control arm using tie rod puller tool No. J6627-A, or equivalent.
14. Disconnect stabilizer shaft link at control arm and support cradle at differential.
15. Scribe marks around perimeter of cradle mounts for installation and remove cradle to vehicle body mounting bolts.
16. Support lower control arm.
17. Remove lower shock absorber mounting bolt and lower rear cradle to allow for spring removal.
18. Remove rear spring with differential and control arms supported.
19. Lower control arm to access outboard control arm bolt, then remove inboard and outboard control arm bolts.
20. Remove control arm.
21. Reverse procedure to install, noting following:
    a. Tighten mounting bolts and nuts.
    b. **Torque** steering linkage installer tool No. J42089, or equivalent, to 22 ft. lbs., to seat outer tie rod ball stud taper.
    c. **Install new self-locking tie rod nut.**
    d. Tighten brake backing plate and

driveshaft bolts as outlined under "Hub & Bearing, Replace."
    e. Adjust parking brake, as required.
    f. Adjust wheel alignment as outlined in "Wheel Alignment" section.

CONTROL ARM BUSHING
REPLACE
Removal

1. Remove lower control arm as outlined under "Control Arm, Replace."
2. Cut off inboard bushing collar, **Fig. 10.**
3. Cut off outboard control arm rubber collar.
4. Press out bushing using bushing receiver tool No. J21474-5 and lower control arm bushing replacement tool No. J42200, or equivalents.

INSTALLATION

1. Coat new bushings with suitable lubricant and position inboard bushing with collar toward rear differential.
2. Press in new bushing using special tools, **Fig. 11.**
3. Lubricate outboard bushing with silicone spray and press into place, **Fig. 11.**

4. Install lower control arm as outlined under "Control Arm, Replace."

TIE ROD
REPLACE
Inner

1. Raise and support vehicle.
2. Remove inner tie rod bolt from axle cradle.
3. Separate inner tie rod from cradle.
4. Loosen adjuster nut and remove tie rod from adjuster. **Record number of turns required to remove tie rod.**
5. Reverse procedure to install, noting the following:
    a. Thread inner tie rod into adjuster using same number of turns recorded during removal.
    b. Tighten adjuster nut and inner tie rod bolt.
    c. Adjust wheel alignment as outlined in "Wheel Alignment" section.

Outer

1. Raise and support vehicle.
2. Remove outer tie rod nut from rear lower control arm.
3. Separate outer tie rod from lower control arm using tie rod puller tool No. J6627-A, or equivalent.
4. Loosen adjuster nut and remove tie rod from adjuster. **Record number of turns required to remove tie rod.**
5. Reverse procedure to install, noting the following:
    a. Thread inner tie rod into adjuster using same number of turns recorded during removal.
    b. Tighten adjuster nut and outer tie rod nut.
    c. **Torque** steering linkage installer tool No. J42089, or equivalent, to 22 ft. lbs., to seat ball stud taper. **Install new self-locking tie rod nut.**
    d. Adjust wheel alignment as outlined in "Wheel Alignment" section.

STABILIZER SHAFT
REPLACE

1. Raise and support vehicle, then support rear axle cradle at differential.
2. Scribe mark around perimeter of cradle for installation and remove cradle to vehicle body mounting bolts.
3. Lower cradle slightly and remove cradle mount protective shields.
4. Remove stabilizer shaft link bolts from lower control arm and separate link from control arm.
5. Lower cradle and remove bolts from stabilizer shaft mounting brackets.
6. Remove stabilizer shaft.
7. Reverse procedure to install, noting the following:
    a. Tighten mounting bolts.
    b. Adjust wheel alignment as outlined in "Wheel Alignment" section.

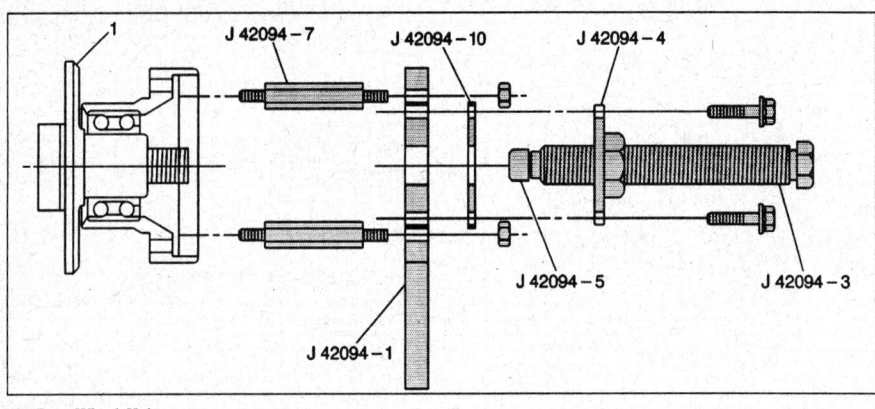

(1) Rear Wheel Hub

GC2039700124000X

Fig. 4 Hub removal tools

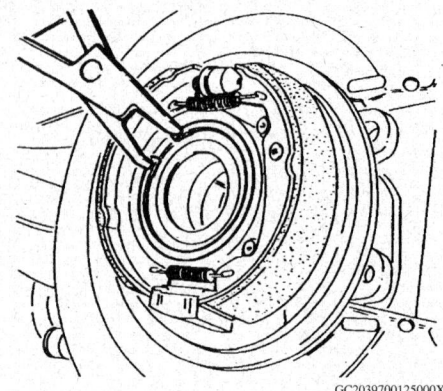

GC2039700125000X

Fig. 5 Wheel bearing retaining ring replacement

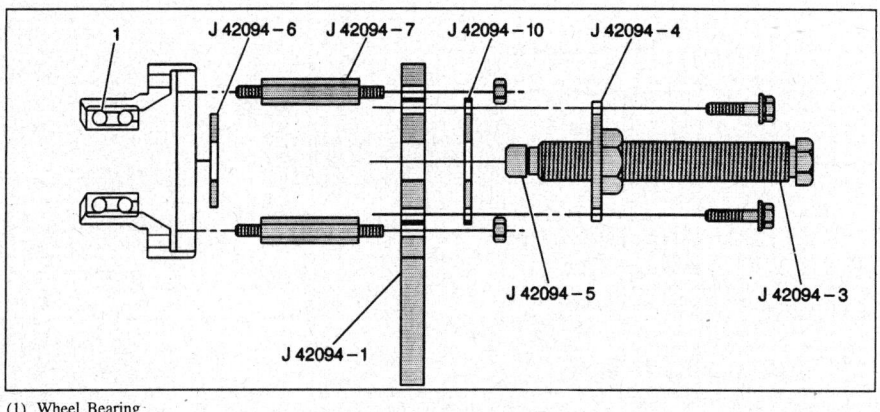

(1) Wheel Bearing

GC2039700126000X

Fig. 6 Wheel bearing removal tools

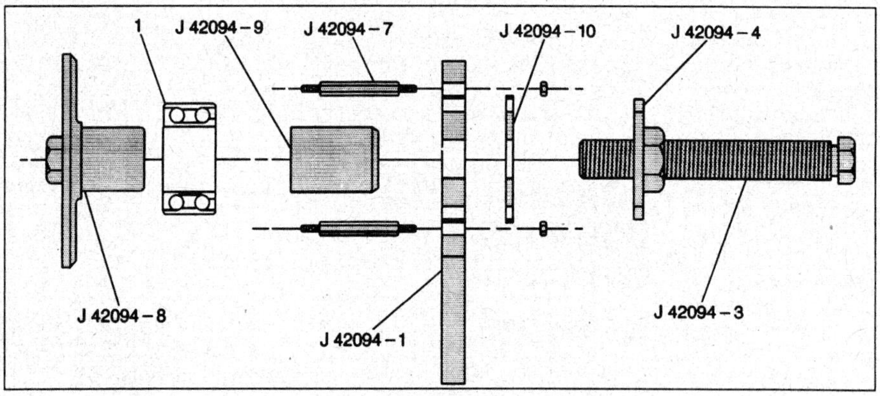

(1) Wheel Bearing

GC2039700127000X

Fig. 7 Wheel bearing installation tools

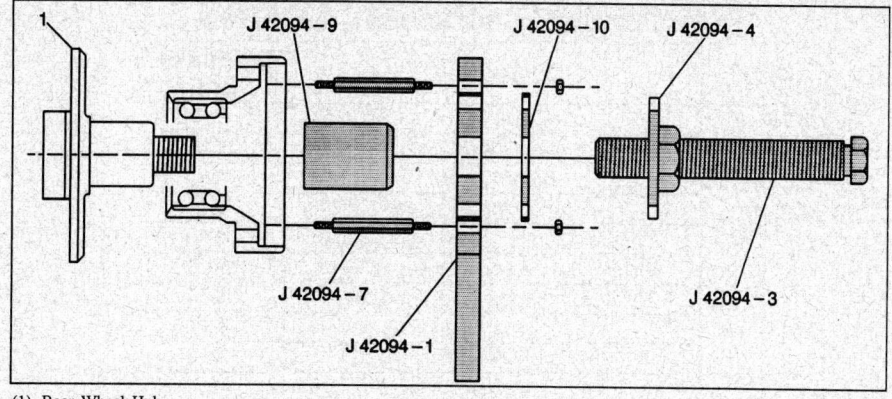

(1) Rear Wheel Hub

GC2039700J28000X

Fig. 8   Hub installation tools

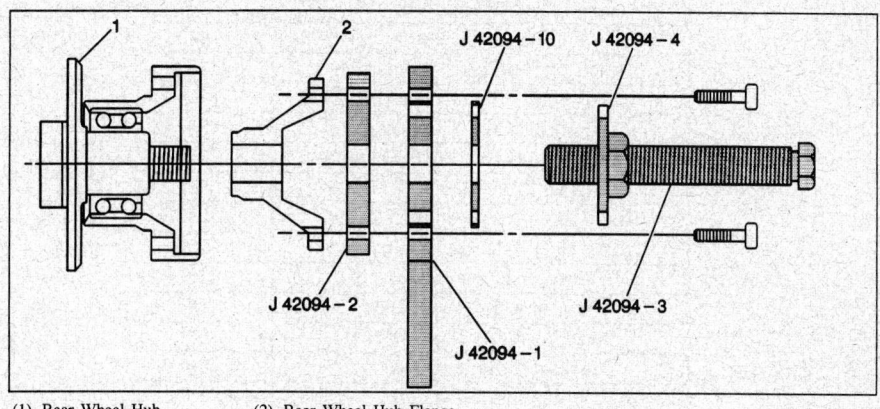

(1) Rear Wheel Hub   (2) Rear Wheel Hub Flange

GC2039700J29000X

Fig. 9   Hub flange installation tools

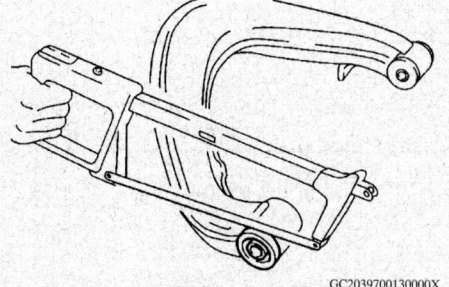

GC2039700130000X

Fig. 10   Control arm bushing collar removal

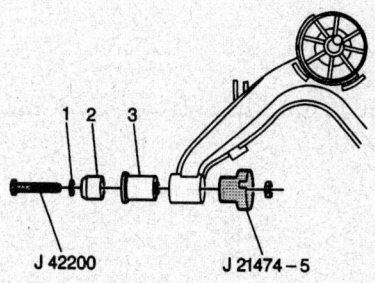

(1) Washer
(2) 30 mm Socket
(3) Bushing

GC2039700131000X

Fig. 11   Control arm bushing installation

TIGHTENING SPECIFICATIONS

Year	Component	Torque/Ft. Lbs.
2001	Axle Nut	221
	Brake Backing Plate	37③
	Brake Caliper	59
	Brake Rotor Setscrew	35④
	Differential Bushing To Differential	74
	Differential Support Bracket, Lower	66①
	Differential Support Bracket, Upper	74
	Drive Axle	37②
	Driveshaft Bolts	37⑤
	Driveshaft Nut	221
	Hub Nut	221
	Inner Tie Rod	66
	Lower Control Arm	74
	Outer Tie Rod	44
	Propeller Shaft Bearing Insulator	16
	Propeller Shaft Center Bearing Bracket	15
	Propeller Shaft Couplings	70
	Propeller Shaft Disc Joint To Differential	70
	Rear Axle Cradle Mount To Body	48
	Rear Axle Cradle Mount To Cradle	74
	Rear Axle Filler Plug	15
	Rear Axle Support Bushing	92
	Rear Axle Support Flange	48
	Shock Absorber Lower Mount	81
	Shock Absorber Upper Mount	15
	Stabilizer Shaft Link	15
	Stabilizer Shaft Mounting Bracket	16
	Tie Rod Adjuster	11
	Wheel To Hub	81

① — Tighten an additional 38°.
② — Tighten an additional 67°.
③ — Tighten an additional 40°.
④ — Inch lbs.
⑤ — Tighten an additional 70°.

Front Suspension & Steering

NOTE: On Air Bag Equipped Models, Refer To "Air Bag System Precautions" Located In The Front Of This Manual For System Disarming & Arming Procedures.

NOTE: Refer To "Computer Relearn Procedures" Located In The Front Of This Manual When Battery Power To The Computer Has Been Interrupted.

INDEX

PRECAUTIONS

Air Bag Systems

Refer to "Air Bag System Precautions" in the front of this manual for system disarming and arming procedures.

Battery Ground Cable

Prior to service, disconnect battery ground cable and isolate as required.

DESCRIPTION

The front suspension features McPherson struts with hydraulic bushings in the lower control arms and gas preloaded dampers. The speed sensitive steering system utilizes recirculating ball type steering gear.

HUB, BEARING & SEAL

REPLACE

1. Raise and support vehicle, then remove front wheel.
2. Remove brake pad wear indicator wire and brake hose from strut bracket.
3. Remove caliper bracket from steering knuckle. Suspend caliper aside to prevent brake pipe damage. **Do not open brake hydraulic system.**
4. Loosen set screw and remove brake rotor, dust cap and wheel hub nut.
5. Remove wheel hub, bearing and seal assembly.
6. Reverse procedure to install, noting the following:
   a. Press outer bearing ring into wheel hub using suitable socket, as required.
   b. Remove old locking compound by

threading M12 × 1.5 tap through caliper bolt holes.
   c. Install new caliper bolts coated in Threadlocker 272, or equivalent.

BALL JOINT INSPECTION

The following procedure applies only to the lower control arm ball stud. Before inspecting the ball stud, ensure the corresponding wheel bearing is in satisfactory condition.
1. Raise and support vehicle.
2. Grasp wheel at top and bottom.
3. Move wheel in and out while observing steering knuckle and lower control arm.
4. If steering knuckle moves up and down independently of control arm, proceed as follows:
   a. Inspect steering knuckle pinch bolt area for ball stud slot movement or distortion. Repair as required.
   b. If pinch bolt area is satisfactory but ball stud movement is observed, replace ball stud.
5. If no vertical movement is observed between steering knuckle and control arm while moving wheel, ball stud and slot are satisfactory.

BALL STUD

REPLACE

1. Raise and support vehicle, then remove front wheel.
2. Remove control arm as outlined under "Control Arm, Replace."
3. Drill out ball stud to lower control arm rivet heads and remove stud.
4. Reverse procedure to install. Install ball stud to control arm bolts from upper side of lower control arm.

COIL SPRING

REPLACE

The coil spring is a component of the strut assembly. Refer to "Strut, Replace" if the entire assembly is to be replaced, or to "Coil Spring & Strut Service" if the spring must be replaced independently.

STRUT

REPLACE

1. Raise and support vehicle, then remove front wheel.
2. Disconnect wheel speed sensor and brake wear indicator electrical connectors, then disengage brake flex hose from clip at strut.
3. Remove caliper bolts and separate caliper from knuckle. Support caliper aside to prevent brake hose damage. **Do not open brake hydraulic system.**
4. Remove stabilizer shaft link nut and separate link from strut.
5. Remove strut lower mounting bolts, then the lower vehicle, upper support plate cap and nut.
6. Remove upper support plate and strut.
7. Reverse procedure to install, noting the following:
   a. Tighten upper support and stabilizer shaft link nuts.
   b. Install new strut to steering knuckle mounting bolts from front of vehicle toward rear.
   c. Tighten bolts only until snug. Final tightening after wheel alignment procedures have been performed.
   d. Install and tighten caliper as outlined under "Hub, Bearing & Seal, Replace."
   e. Adjust wheel alignment as outlined in "Wheel Alignment" section.

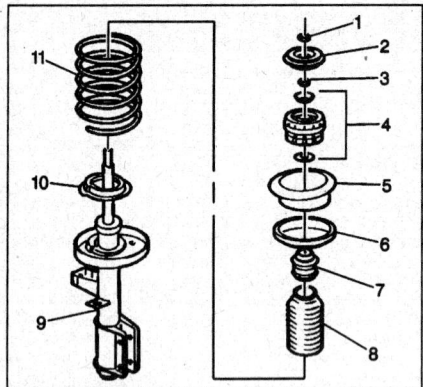

(1) Upper Support Plate Nut
(2) Upper Support Plate
(3) Upper Bearing Support Nut
(4) Bearing and Bearing Plate Assembly
(5) Upper Spring Support Plate
(6) Upper Insulator
(7) Strut Bumper
(8) Strut Cover
(9) Strut
(10) Lower Insulator
(11) Spring

GC2029700219000X

Fig. 1 Coil spring & strut components

f. Tighten strut to steering knuckle bolts.

COIL SPRING & STRUT SERVICE

1. Place strut in strut spring compressor tool No. J34013-A, or equivalent, with adapter tool No. J34013-88, or equivalent.
2. Prevent strut piston from rotating and remove upper bearing support nut.
3. Compress strut spring, then remove bearing and plate.
4. Release spring and remove upper support plate, insulator, strut bumper and cover, **Fig. 1.**
5. Separate spring from strut and remove lower insulator.
6. Reverse procedure to assemble. **Do not allow coil spring protective coating to be chipped or scratched. Premature spring failure may result.**

CONTROL ARM
REPLACE
Lower
REMOVAL

1. Raise and support vehicle, then remove front tire and wheel assembly.
2. Separate brake pad wear indicator sleeve from strut and remove wheel speed sensor.
3. Separate brake hose from strut bracket and remove caliper from steering knuckle. Suspend caliper to prevent brake hose damage. **Do not open brake hydraulic system.**
4. Remove outer tie rod ball stud nut, then separate tie rod from knuckle

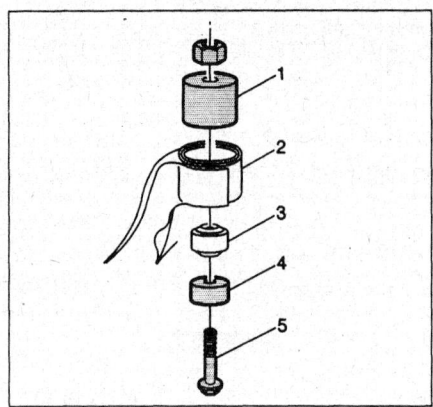

(1) J 42092-1, Receiver
(2) Lower Control Arm
(3) Bushing
(4) J 42092-2, Bushing Remover/Installer Tool
(5) J 42200, Rear Lower Control Arm Bushing Remover/Installer Bolt

GC2029700220000X

Fig. 2 Control arm horizontal bushing replacement

using tie rod separator tool No. J6627-A, or equivalent.
5. Remove stabilizer shaft link nut from shaft and steering knuckle bolts from strut.
6. Remove lower control arm ball stud pinch bolt and separate steering knuckle from ball stud. Allow hub and brake rotor to remain in place.
7. Loosen control arm horizontal and vertical bolts, remove horizontal bolt and turn arm away from support bracket.
8. Remove vertical bolt and control arm.

INSTALLATION

1. Install lower control arm and new vertical bolt.
2. Tighten bolt only until snug. Final tightening will occur after horizontal bolt installation.
3. Position front of control arm in support bracket and install new horizontal bolt from rearward side of vehicle.
4. Ensure control arm is in horizontal position and tighten bolts to specifications.
5. Connect steering knuckle to lower control arm ball stud, using new pinch bolt inserted from rear side of vehicle. Tighten pinch bolt to specifications.
6. Connect steering knuckle to strut using new bolts installed from front of vehicle toward rear. Tighten bolts only until snug.
7. Connect stabilizer shaft link to shaft and tighten mounting nut to specifications.
8. Connect outer tie rod to steering knuckle and position linkage installer tool No. J42089, or equivalent, over tie rod ball stud.
9. **Torque** installer tool to 22 ft. lbs., to seat ball stud taper. Remove tool.
10. Install new self-locking tie rod nut and tighten to specifications.
11. Install caliper on steering knuckle as outlined under "Hub, Bearing & Seal, Replace."

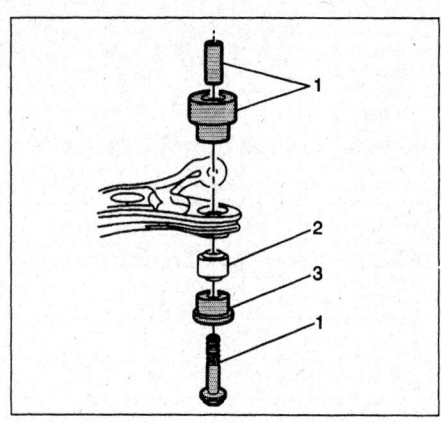

(1) J 21474, Universal Bushing Remover/Installer Kit
(2) Bushing
(3) J 42112-4, Rear Differential Bushing Remover/Installer Tool

GC2029700221000X

Fig. 3 Control arm vertical bushing replacement

12. Attach brake hose to strut bracket, install wheel speed sensor and tighten to specifications.
13. Attach brake pad wear indicator sleeve to strut.
14. Install front wheel and lower vehicle.
15. Adjust wheel alignment as outlined in "Wheel Alignment" section.

CONTROL ARM BUSHING
REPLACE

1. Remove control arm as outlined under "Control Arm, Replace."
2. Press bushing out of control arm using bushing replacement tools turn, **Figs. 2 and 3.**
3. Reverse procedure to install. Ensure bushing is installed flush with control arm.

STEERING KNUCKLE
REPLACE

1. Raise and support vehicle, then remove front wheel.
2. Remove hub as outlined under "Hub, Bearing & Seal, Replace" and brake rotor splash shield.
3. Remove ball stud nut from outer tie rod and separate tie rod from knuckle using tie rod separator tool No. J6627-A, or equivalent.
4. Remove steering knuckle to strut bolts and separate knuckle from strut.
5. Remove lower control arm ball stud pinch bolt and separate knuckle from control arm ball stud.
6. Reverse procedure to install, noting the following:
   a. Install new control arm ball stud pinch bolt and strut to steering knuckle bolts.
   b. Tighten control arm ball stud pinch bolt to specifications.
   c. **Do not tighten strut to steering**

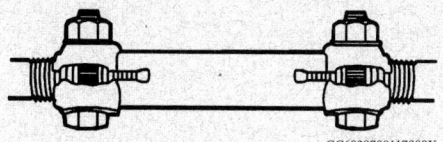

Fig. 4 Tie rod adjuster & clamp orientation

knuckle bolts until wheel alignment is complete.

d. Attach tie rod to knuckle, position linkage using installer tool No. J42089, or equivalent, over tie rod ball stud and **torque** to 22 ft. lbs., to seat taper.
e. Install new self-locking tie rod nut and tighten to specifications.
f. Adjust wheel alignment as outlined in "Wheel Alignment."
g. Tighten strut to steering knuckle bolts as outlined under "Strut, Replace."

STABILIZER BAR
REPLACE

1. Raise and support vehicle.
2. Attach engine support fixture tool No. J28467-A, or equivalent, at engine lift points.
3. Raise and support vehicle, then remove front wheel and tire assemblies.
4. Remove wheel speed sensor and brake wear indicator wires.
5. Remove brake flex hose clips and hose, then the wheel speed sensors.
6. Remove brake caliper and outer tie rods using tie rod/wheel stud puller tool No. J6627-A, or equivalent.
7. Remove lower control arm ball stud pinch bolts and steering knuckles from lower control arm ball studs.
8. Remove stabilizer shaft links from stabilizer shaft and engine mount nuts.
9. Support crossmember frame.
10. Remove mounting bolts and front crossmember frame.
11. Remove insulator bolts and stabilizer shaft.
12. Reverse procedures to install.

STABILIZER BAR BUSHING
REPLACE

Refer to "Stabilizer Bar, Replace" for bar and bushing replacement procedures.

TIE ROD
REPLACE

Never attempt to separate a steering linkage joint by driving a wedge between components.

Inner

1. Raise and support vehicle.
2. Loosen tie rod clamp bolt at end of tie rod adjuster.
3. Remove tie rod ball stud nut and sepa-

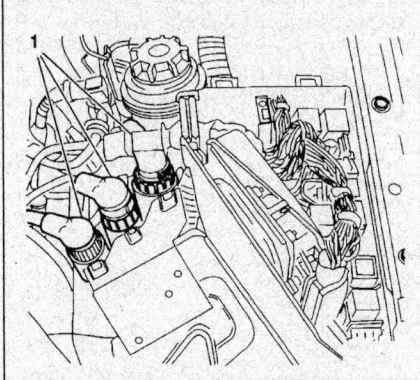

(1) Body Harness Electrical Connector

GC6029700118000X

Fig. 5 Body harness electrical connectors

rate ball stud from relay rod using tie rod separator tool No. J6627-A, or equivalent.
4. Remove tie rod from adjuster, counting number of turns for installation reference.
5. Reverse procedure to install, noting the following:
a. Lubricate tie rod adjuster threads with suitable Extra Pressure (EP) chassis lubricant.
b. To connect tie rod ball stud to relay rod, position linkage tool No. J42089, or equivalent, over ball stud and **torque** tool to 22 ft. lbs. This will seat taper.
c. Install new self-locking tie rod ball stud nut and tighten.
d. With adjuster and clamps positioned, **Fig. 4,** tighten adjuster clamp bolt.
e. Adjust toe as outlined in "Wheel Alignment."

Outer

1. Raise and support vehicle.
2. Loosen tie rod clamp bolt near tie rod end.
3. Remove tie rod ball stud nut and separate tie rod from knuckle using tie rod puller tool No. J6627-A, or equivalent.
4. Remove tie rod from adjuster, noting the following:
a. Outer tie rod has lefthand threads.
b. Count number of turns required to remove tie rod for installation reference.
5. Reverse procedure to install, noting the following:
a. Lubricate tie rod adjuster threads with Extra Pressure (EP) chassis lubricant.
b. Connect tie rod ball stud to steering knuckle, position linkage tool No. J42089, or equivalent, over ball stud and **torque** tool to 22 ft. lbs., to seat taper.
c. Install new self-locking ball stud nut.
d. With adjuster and clamps properly positioned, **Fig. 4,** tighten clamp bolts.

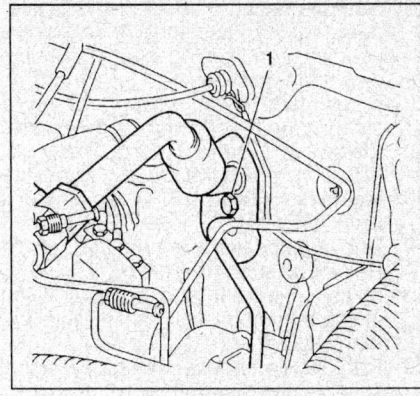

(1) Evaporator Line Extension to Cowl Bolt

GC6029700119000X

Fig. 6 Evaporator line extension bolt

e. Adjust toe as outlined under "Wheel Alignment."

POWER STEERING GEAR
REPLACE

1. Remove windshield wiper assembly.
2. Disconnect three body harness electrical connectors, **Fig. 5,** and remove Engine Control Module (ECM) from electrical box.
3. Drain engine coolant into suitable container and remove upper radiator hose.
4. Discharge and recover air conditioning system as outlined under "Air Conditioning." Remove air conditioning evaporator line extension bolt, **Fig. 6.**
5. Siphon power steering fluid from reservoir, remove reservoir bracket bolt and position reservoir aside.
6. Siphon brake fluid from reservoir and disconnect brake booster vacuum line at intake plenum.
7. Disconnect brake pipes and electrical connector at master cylinder.
8. Make mating marks on steering gear splines and lower steering coupler, then disengage tabs and remove sound insulator.
9. Remove steering coupler mounting bolts. **Do not allow steering wheel to turn when coupler is disconnected.**
10. Place steering wheel in straight ahead position and lock in place. Remove ignition key. **Because substantial steering wheel movement can occur before ignition locking mechanism sets, it is required to lock steering wheel using suitable external locking device.**
11. Carefully spread coupler clamp ears apart until steering shaft can be moved upward and away from steering gear.
12. Remove retaining clip and pin, then disconnect brake pedal from booster link rod.
13. Remove lefthand instrument panel knee bolster, fuse and relay panel screws.
14. Position panels away from upper vacuum booster nuts.

15. Remove vacuum booster and master cylinder as an assembly, then disconnect air conditioning evaporator line extension quick connect fitting.
16. Disconnect power steering hoses at steering gear and position away from Electronic Brake/Traction Control Module (EBTCM)/Brake Pressure Modulator Valve (BPMV). Remove EBTCM/BPMV.
17. Remove upper heat shield bolt.
18. Raise and support vehicle.
19. Make mating marks on pitman arm and steering gear splines, then remove pitman arm nut and washer.
20. Remove arm from steering gear using suitable pitman arm puller.
21. Remove lower heat shield nuts and lower steering gear bolts, nuts and washers.
22. Lower vehicle, remove heat shield and disconnect power steering fluid flow control valve actuator electrical connector.
23. Remove upper steering gear bolt and shims. Record shim positions for installation.
24. Remove steering gear.
25. Reverse procedure to install, noting the following:
    a. Prior to installation, turn stub shaft from stop to stop and count number of turns, then turn shaft back ½ that number of turns.
    b. Align stub shaft mark with steering gear case V mark to center gear.
    c. Upper steering gear bolt should be installed and tightened until snug. **Final tightening should not occur until remaining bolts are installed.**
    d. When connecting air conditioning evaporator line extension fittings, install new O-rings lubricated in 525 viscosity mineral oil.

POWER STEERING PUMP

REPLACE

1. Siphon power steering fluid from reservoir.
2. Loosen power steering pump pulley bolts and remove serpentine drive belt as outlined in "3.0L Engine" section.
3. Remove mounting bolts and pulley, then disconnect gear inlet hose at pump.
4. Remove fluid reservoir inlet hose clamp and hose from power steering pump.

5. Raise and support vehicle.
6. Remove Secondary Air Injection (AIR) crossover pipe support bracket.
7. Remove mounting bolts and power steering pump.
8. Reverse procedure to install.

POWER STEERING SYSTEM BLEED

Refer to **Fig. 7,** for power steering system bleed procedures. If the power steering system has been serviced, the system must be bled to obtain an accurate fluid level reading and to ensure proper system operation.

Before bleeding: Inspect steering system. Check, and correct as needed:

 Hoses must not touch any other part of vehicle.
- Steering system noise could be caused by hose touching frame, body, or engine.

 All hose connections must be tight.
- Loose connections might not leak but could allow air into system.

When to bleed:
After any component replacement
After disconnecting fluid line
In case of steering system noise

Why bleed?
To prevent pump damage
To ensure proper system operation
To stop steering system noise

How to bleed:

❶  Switch ignition off.

❷ Raise front wheels off ground.

❸ Turn steering wheel full left.

❹ Fill fluid reservoir to "FULL COLD" level. Leave cap off.

❺ 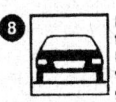 With assistant checking fluid level and condition, turn steering wheel lock-to-lock at least 20 times. Engine remains off.
- On systems with long return lines or fluid coolers, turn steering wheel lock-to-lock at least 40 times.
- Trapped air may cause fluid to overflow. Thoroughly clean any spilled fluid to allow for leak check.
- Keep fluid level at "FULL COLD."

❻ While turning wheel, check fluid constantly.
- No bubbles are allowed.
- For any sign of bubbles, recheck connections. Repeat step 5.

❼ Start engine. With engine idling, maintain fluid level. Reinstall cap.

❽ Return wheels to center. Lower front wheels to ground.

❾ Keep engine running for two minutes.

❿ Turn steering wheel in both directions.

Verify:
- ☑ Smooth power assist
- ☑ Noiseless operation
- ☑ Proper fluid level
- ☑ No system leaks
- ☑ Proper fluid condition
- No bubbles, no foam, no discoloration

⓫ If all proper conditions apply, procedure is complete.

⓬ If any problem remains, see "Special Conditions."

Special Conditions:

Fluid
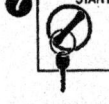
- Foam or bubbles in fluid
  Fluid must be completely free of bubbles. In step 5, be alert to periodic bubbles that could indicate a loose connection or leaky O-ring seal in either the return hose or pressure hose.
- Discolored fluid
  (milky, opaque, or light tan color)

Switch ignition off. Wait two minutes. Recheck hose connections. Repeat steps 7-10. If condition still exists, replace and check a possible cause:
- ☑ Return hose clamps
- ☑ Return hose O-ring
- ☑ Pressure hose O-rings
- ☑ Gear cylinder line O-rings

Fill system and repeat bleed procedure for each possible cause. Repeat steps 7-10 to verify whether noise has been eliminated.

Noise

- Pump whine or groan

With engine running, recheck hoses for possible contact with frame body or engine. If no contact is found, follow either method below to cool down fluid and repressurize system.

Method 1: Normal Cool Down	Method 2: Partial Fluid Replacement
Switch engine off. Wait for system to cool. Install reservoir cap.	Switch engine off. Use a suction device to remove fluid from reservoir. Refill with cool, clean fluid. Install reservoir cap.

After either method of cooling, start engine and allow engine to come up to operating temperature. If noise persists, remove and replace power steering pump. Repeat bleed procedure following pump replacement.

GC6029700120000X

Fig. 7 Power steering system bleed

TIGHTENING SPECIFICATIONS

Year	Component	Torque/Ft. Lbs.
2001	Air Conditioning Evaporator Line Extension	15
	Ball Stud To Lower Control Arm	26
	Brake Caliper	70②
	Brake Pipes To Master Cylinder	12
	Brake Rotor Setscrew	35①
	Brake Rotor Splash Shield	35①
	Brake Vacuum Booster	15
	Heat Shield, Lower Nuts	11
	Heat Shield, Upper Bolt	72①
	Hub (Wheel Bearing)	236
	Lower Control Arm	103
	Lower Control Arm Ball Stud Pinch Bolt	74
	Pitman Arm	118
	Power Steering Fluid Reservoir Clamp	60①
	Power Steering Gear Hoses	21
	Power Steering Pump	15
	Power Steering Pump Pulley	15
	Stabilizer Shaft Insulator	15②
	Stabilizer Shaft Link To Shaft	48
	Steering Gear	30
	Strut Bearing	52
	Strut To Steering Knuckle	66③
	Strut Upper Support	41
	Tie Rod Adjuster Clamp	11
	Tie Rod Ball Studs	44
	Wheel Speed Sensor	72①
	Wheel Lug Nut	80

① — Inch lbs.
② — Tighten an additional 37.°
③ — Tighten an additional 52.°

Wheel Alignment

INDEX

PRELIMINARY INSPECTION

1. Ensure all tires are of recommended size and are inflated to proper pressure.
2. Inspect all tires for damage and uneven tread wear.
3. Ensure wheel bearings, control arm ball studs and bushings, relay rods and tie rod ends are in satisfactory condition. Looseness must be corrected before wheels can be aligned.
4. Inspect wheel and tire radial and lateral runout, as follows:
   a. With wheel and tire assembly off vehicle, runout should be approximately .050 inch.
   b. When on vehicle, runout should be approximately .060 inch.
5. If wheel and tire assembly runout specifications cannot be met, separate tire from wheel and measure wheel runout. Wheel runout should be approximately .030 inch.
6. Inspect vehicle ride height as outlined under "Vehicle Ride Height" in "Specifications" section. If corrections are required, complete them prior to setting wheel alignment.
7. Ensure steering gear is not loose at frame mounting.
8. Inspect stabilizer shafts for loose or missing components.
9. Ensure struts and shocks are not leaking or excessively worn and strut upper mounts are in satisfactory condition.
10. Inspect all remaining suspension and steering components for damage and repair or replace prior to setting wheel alignment.
11. Ensure fuel tank is full or compensating ballast is added for proper weight distribution.
12. Ensure vehicle is on level surface and all loads that are normally carried inside vehicle are present.
13. Jounce front and rear of vehicle three times before beginning wheel alignment procedures.

FRONT WHEEL ALIGNMENT

Caster must be satisfactory prior to adjusting camber. Likewise, camber settings must be satisfactory prior to adjusting toe.

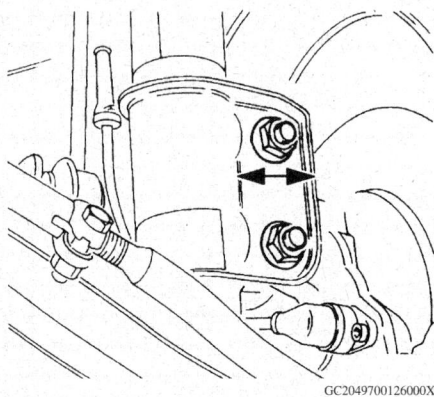

Fig. 1   Front camber adjustment

Adjust rear toe before adjusting front camber or toe.

Caster

Caster angles can be measured but cannot be adjusted. If angles are improper, service suspension components as required.

Camber

1. Raise and support vehicle, then remove front wheel.
2. Separate brake caliper from knuckle. Suspend caliper aside to prevent brake hose damage. **Do not open brake hydraulic system.**
3. Remove strut lower mounting bolts, insert new bolts from front toward rear of vehicle and **torque** to 15 ft. lbs.
4. Inspect brake caliper mounting hole threads in steering knuckle and remove any residual locking compound.
5. Install caliper using new mounting bolts. Coat bolts with suitable thread locking compound.
6. **Torque** mounting bolts to 70 ft. lbs., then tighten an additional 37°.
7. Install wheel and **torque** bolts to 80 ft. lbs.
8. Set camber turn, **Fig. 1.**
9. **Torque** strut lower mounting bolts to 66 ft. lbs., then tighten an additional 52°.

Toe

Toe adjustments are made separately for each wheel.

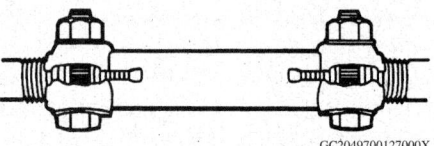

Fig. 2   Front tie rod adjuster & clamp orientation

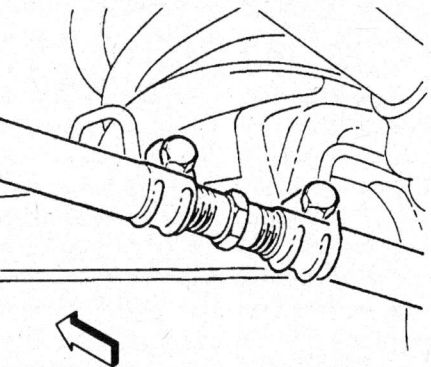

Fig. 3   Rear tie rod adjuster & clamps

1. Set steering wheel in straight ahead position.
2. Turn inner and outer tie rod sockets to limit of control arm ball stud travel.
3. Loosen clamp bolts at each end of tie rod adjuster and turn adjuster until proper toe setting is achieved.
4. Position tie rod adjuster and clamps, **Fig. 2.**
5. **Torque** clamp bolts to 11 ft. lbs.
6. Ensure same number of threads are exposed on either side of adjuster and outer tie rod ends are at righthand angles to steering knuckles.

REAR WHEEL ALIGNMENT

Adjust rear toe before performing procedures outlined under "Front Wheel Alignment."

Toe

1. Loosen both tie rod adjuster clamps, **Fig. 3.**
2. Turn threaded sleeve until proper toe is achieved.
3. **Torque** tie rod adjuster clamp bolts to 11 ft. lbs.

CAVALIER & SUNFIRE

INDEX OF SERVICE OPERATIONS

Specifications

GENERAL ENGINE SPECIFICATIONS

Year	Engine Liter	Engine VIN Code②	Fuel System	Bore/ Stroke	Comp-ression Ratio	Net H.P. @ RPM③	Maximum Torque Ft. Lbs. @ RPM	Normal Oil Pressure psi
2001	2.2L	4	SFI	3.50 × 3.46	8.85	115 @ 5000	135 @ 3600	56④
	2.4L	T	SFI	3.54 × 3.70	9.50	150 @ 5600	155 @ 4400	①
2002	2.2L DOHC	F	SFI	3.38 x 3.72	10.00	140 @ 5600	150 @ 4000	50–80⑤
	2.2L OHV	4	SFI	3.50 × 3.46	8.85	115 @ 5000	135 @ 3600	56④
	2.4L	T	SFI	3.54 × 3.70	9.50	150 @ 5600	155 @ 4400	①
2003–05	2.2L DOHC	F	SFI	3.38 x 3.72	10.00	140 @ 5600	150 @ 4000	50–80⑤

SFI — Sequential fuel injection
① — 10 @ 900 RPM; 30 @ 3000 RPM.
② — The eighth digit denotes engine code.

③ — Ratings are net as installed in vehicle.
④ — At 3000 RPM.

⑤ — Oil pressure @ 1000 RPM.

TUNE UP SPECIFICATIONS

Year & Engine	Spark Plug Gap	Firing Order Fig.	Ignition Timing BTDC	Timing Mark Fig.	Curb Idle Speed	Fast Idle Speed	Fuel Pump Pressure	Valve Lash
2001								
2.2L	.040	②	⑦	⑥	④	④	41–47③	①
2.4L	.050	⑤	⑦	⑥	④	④	52–58③	①
2002								
2.2L DOHC	.042	②	⑦	⑥	④	④	50–60	①
2.2L OHV	.040	②	⑦	⑥	④	④	41–47③	①
2.4L	.050	⑤	⑦	⑥	④	④	52–58③	①
2003–05								
2.2L DOHC	.042	②	⑦	⑥	④	④	50–60	①

BTDC — Before Top Dead Center
① — Equipped w/hydraulic valve lifters. No adjustment is required.
② — Cylinder numbering from front of engine to rear of engine, 1,2,3,4. Firing order 1-3-4-2. Coil connections are stamped on coil assemblies.
③ — Relieve fuel system pressure as outlined in "Fuel System Pressure Relief" in "Precautions" in appropriate engine section. Then, connect suitable fuel pressure gauge between fuel line and fuel rail. Connect battery ground cable. Turn ignition On and record fuel pressure reading.

④ — Idle speeds are controlled by Idle Air Control (IAC) valve.
⑤ — Cylinder numbering from front of engine to rear of engine, 1, 2, 3, 4. Firing order 1-3-4-2. Refer to **Fig. A,** for spark plug wire connection at coil unit.
⑥ — Equipped w/crankshaft sensor.
⑦ — No adjustment.

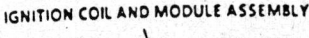

IGNITION COIL AND MODULE ASSEMBLY

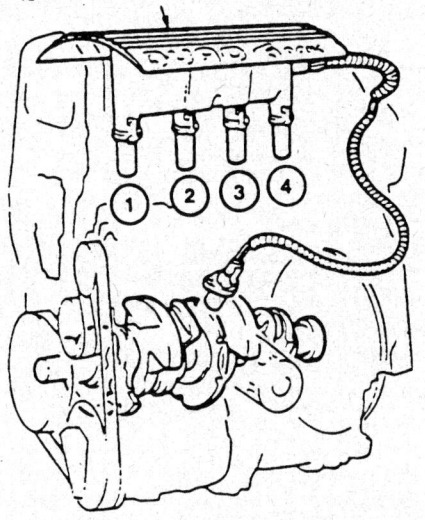

Firing order 1-3-4-2

GC1139500573000X

Fig. A

FRONT WHEEL ALIGNMENT SPECIFICATIONS

Year	Caster Angle, Degrees		Camber Angle, Degrees		Total Toe, Degrees	Ball Joint Wear
	Limits	Desired	Limits	Desired		
2001–05	+3.3 to +5.3①	4.3①	–1 to +1	0	0	②

① — Non-adjustable. For inspection purposes only.

② — Refer to "Front Suspension & Steering" section for ball joint specifications and inspection procedure.

REAR WHEEL ALIGNMENT SPECIFICATIONS

Year	Camber Angle, Degrees①		Thrust Angle, Degrees①		Total Toe, Degrees①	
	Limits	Desired	Limits	Desired	Limits	Desired
2001–05	–1.15 to +.35	–.4	–.25 to +.25	0	–.1 to +.5	+.2

① — Non-adjustable. For inspection purposes only.

VEHICLE RIDE HEIGHT SPECIFICATIONS

Model	Year	Body Style	Manufacturer's Original Tire Size	Front Dim.	Front Spec. Inches	Front Spec. mm	Rear Dim.	Rear Spec. Inches	Rear Spec. mm
Cavalier	2001–05	All	②	A	32.15	816.0	B	22.00	558
				C	9.17	233.0	D	9.45	240
Sunfire	2001–05	All	②	A	32.15	816.6	B	22.00	558
				C	9.19	233.0	D	9.44	240

A Dim. — Measurement From Front Wheel Center to Check Point On Rocker Panel

B Dim. — Measurement From Rear Wheel Center to Check Point On Rocker Panel

C Dim. — Ground to Rocker Panel, Front

D Dim. — Ground to Rocker Panel, Rear

Dim. — Dimension

① — ±..39 in (10 mm) front to rear & side to side.

② — See door sticker or inside of glove box for manufacturer's original tire size specifications.

③ — Measurement is with fuel, radiator coolant and engine oil full, spare tire, jack, hand tools and mats in designated positions and tires properly inflated.

FLUID CAPACITIES & COOLING SYSTEM DATA

Year	Engine	Coolant Capacity, Qts.	Coolant Type	Radiator Cap Relief Pressure, Lbs.	Thermo. Opening Temp.	Fuel Tank Gals.	Engine Oil Refill Qts.②	Transaxle Oil Manual Pts.	Transaxle Oil Automatic Qts.①
2001	2.2L	10.1	Dex-Cool	15	180	14.3	4.0	3.6	④
	2.4L	10.1	Dex-Cool	15	180	14.3	4.0	3.6	④
2002	2.2L DOHC	10.2	Dex-Cool	15	180	14.1	4.0	1.8	③
	2.2L OHV	8.6	Dex-Cool	15	185	14.1	5.0	3.6	④
	2.4L	10.2	Dex-Cool	15	180	14.1	4.5	3.6	④
2003–05	2.2L DOHC	10.0	Dex-Cool	15	195	14.1	4.0	1.8	③

① — Approximate. Make final inspection w/dipstick.

② — When changing engine oil filter additional oil may be required.

③ — Oil pan removal, 6.9 qts.; overhaul, 9.5 qts., dry 12.9 qts.

④ — 3T40 automatic. trans.: oil pan only, 4 qts., after overhaul 7 qts. 4T40E automatic. trans.: oil pan only, 6.9 qts., after overhaul 9.5 qts.

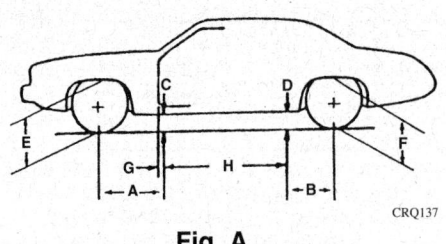

Fig. A

LUBRICANT DATA

Year	Lubricant Type			
	Transaxle		Power Steering	Brake System
	Manual	Automatic		
2001–05	①	DEXRON III	②	DOT-3

① — Manual transmission fluid GM P/N 12345349, or equivalent.

② — Power steering fluid GM P/N 1052884, or equivalent.

Electrical

NOTE: On Air Bag Equipped Models, Refer To "Air Bag System Precautions" Located In The Front Of This Manual For System Disarming & Arming Procedures.

NOTE: Refer To "Computer Relearn Procedures" Located In The Front Of This Manual When Battery Power To The Computer Has Been Interrupted.

NOTE: On Models Equipped With 2.2L DOHC Engine, Refer To "Alero, Grand Am & Malibu" Chapter For Procedures.

INDEX

PRECAUTIONS

Air Bag Systems

Refer to "Air Bag System Precautions" in the front of this manual for system disarming and arming procedures.

Battery Ground Cable

Prior to service, disconnect battery ground cable and isolate as required.

FUSE PANEL & FLASHER LOCATION

The instrument panel fuse panel is located behind the lefthand side of the instrument panel. The underhood fuse panel is located in the engine compartment on the lefthand side.

The turn signal/hazard flasher module is located under the instrument panel on the righthand side of steering column.

FUEL PUMP RELAY LOCATION

The fuel pump relay is located in the front lefthand corner of the engine compartment, in the engine compartment fuse block.

RELAY CENTER LOCATION

The relay center is located in the fuse panels, see "Fuse Panel & Flasher Location" for appropriate locations.

STARTER
REPLACE

2.2L Engine

1. Remove wiring harness bracket nut from starter bolt.
2. Raise and support vehicle using suitable lift.
3. Remove flywheel inspection shield.
4. Remove electrical connectors.
5. Remove starter bolts, then the starter.
6. Reverse procedure to install, noting the following:
   a. **On models equipped with 2.2L OHV engines, torque** starter bolts to 37 ft. lbs.
   b. **On models equipped with 2.2L DOHC engines, torque** starter bolts to 30 ft. lbs.

2.4L Engine

1. Remove air inlet duct to throttle body.
2. Remove top starter bolt.
3. Raise and support vehicle.
4. Remove lower starter bolt and position starter aside.
5. Disconnect electrical wiring and remove starter.
6. Reverse procedure to install.

ALTERNATOR
REPLACE

1. Disconnect alternator electrical connectors.
2. Rotate tensioner counterclockwise with suitable wrench and slide belt from alternator pulley.
3. Release tensioner and remove belt as outlined in "2.2L DOHC" or "2.2L OHV" engine section.
4. Remove alternator through bolts, then the alternator.
5. Reverse procedure to install, noting the following:
   a. **On models equipped with 2.2L OHV engine, torque** upper alternator mounting bolt to 22 ft. lbs. and lower mounting bolt to 37 ft. lbs.
   b. **On models equipped with 2.2L DOHC engine, torque** alternator bolts to 15 ft. lbs. and electrical connector bolts to 13 ft. lbs.
   c. **On models equipped with 2.4L engine, torque** alternator mounting bolts to 37 ft. lbs.

COIL PACK
REPLACE

2.2L DOHC

1. Remove accelerator and cruise control cables from brackets, then the brackets as required.
2. Remove ignition control module (ICM).
3. Remove ignition coil housing attaching bolts.
4. Remove ignition coils and ICM assembly.
5. Reverse procedure to install, **torque** ignition coil retaining bolts to 89 inch lbs.

2.2L OHV

1. Remove air cleaner outlet from air cleaner.
2. Remove ICM electrical connectors, then the spark plug wires.
3. Remove ignition coil attaching bolts.
4. Remove ignition coils and ICM assembly.
5. Reverse procedure to install, **torque** ignition coil bolts to 35 inch lbs.

IGNITION LOCK
REPLACE

Less Ignition Key

1. Remove steering column upper and lower trim covers.
2. Drill out lock button on back of steering column housing.
3. Remove lock cylinder by pulling out from column housing.
4. Disconnect ignition switch electrical connector.
5. Remove metal shavings from lock cylinder steering column housing.
6. Reverse procedure to install.

With Ignition Key

1. **On models equipped with tilt column,** remove tilt lever.
2. **On all models,** remove steering column upper and lower trim covers.
3. Turn lock cylinder to Run.
4. Push against locking button on rear side of bearing and housing, then remove lock cylinder by pulling it out of column.
5. Disconnect lock cylinder electrical connector.
6. Reverse procedure to install, noting the following:
   a. Turn lock cylinder to Run position and depress locking button.
   b. Gently push cylinder into place while rotating key approximately 5° counterclockwise.
   c. Inspect for proper operation.

IGNITION SWITCH
REPLACE

1. Remove steering column trim covers.
2. Remove ignition lock less ignition key as follows:
   a. Remove steering column upper and lower trim covers.
   b. Drill out lock button on back of steering column housing.
   c. Remove lock cylinder by pulling out from column housing.
   d. Disconnect ignition switch electrical connector.
   e. Remove ignition switch retaining screws, then remove switch from lock cylinder.
   f. Remove metal shavings from lock cylinder and steering column housing.
   g. Reverse procedure to install.
3. Remove ignition lock with ignition key as follows:
   a. **On models equipped with tilt column,** remove tilt lever.
   b. **On all models,** remove steering column upper and lower trim covers.
   c. Turn lock cylinder to Run.
   d. Push against locking button on rear side of bearing and housing, then remove lock cylinder by pulling it out of column.
   e. Disconnect lock cylinder electrical connector.
4. Remove Torx head screws, then the ignition switch from steering column.
5. Reverse procedure to install. **Torque** screws to 36 inch lbs.

CLUTCH START SWITCH
REPLACE

1. Remove driver's instrument panel knee bolster.
2. Disconnect clutch start switch electrical connector.
3. Remove clutch start switch from pedal bracket.
4. Reverse procedure to install. Ensure starter cranks only when clutch pedal is fully depressed.

NEUTRAL SAFETY SWITCH

REPLACE

On models equipped with automatic transmission, the neutral start and back-up lamp switches are combined into one unit and must be replaced as an assembly.

1. Disconnect shift linkage.
2. Disconnect electrical connector from switch.
3. Remove mounting bolts and switch.
4. If same switch is to be installed again, proceed as follows:
   a. Place shift shaft in Neutral position.
   b. Align flats of shift shaft with switch and install switch.
   c. Loosely install mounting bolts.
   d. Insert gauge pin or $\frac{3}{32}$ inch drill bit in service adjustment hole and rotate switch until pin drops to depth of $\frac{9}{64}$ inch.
   e. **Torque** mounting bolts to 15 ft. lbs.
5. If new switch is to be installed, proceed as follows:
   a. Place shift shaft in Neutral position.
   b. Align flats of shift shaft with switch and install switch.
   c. If bolt holes do not align with mounting boss on transaxle, ensure shift shaft is in Neutral position and do not rotate switch. Switch is pinned in Neutral position. If switch has been rotated and pin has broken, replace as required.
   d. **Torque** mounting bolts to 15 ft. lbs.
6. Ensure engine will start only in Park or Neutral positions.

HEADLAMP SWITCH

REPLACE

Refer to "Multi-Function Switch, Replace" for replacement procedure.

STOP LIGHT SWITCH

REPLACE

1. Remove driver's side sound insulator.
2. Disconnect and remove electrical connectors.
3. Disconnect brake switch by grasping switch and turning it one quarter turn counterclockwise while pulling toward rear of vehicle.
4. Reverse procedure to install, then adjust switch as follows:
   a. Ensure brake pedal is fully released.
   b. Ensure stoplamp plunger is fully depressed against brake pedal shanks.
   c. Hold brake pedal forward and ensure stoplamp switch and cruise control switch are fully seated into brake pedal bracket.
   d. Pull brake pedal to rear, against internal stop.
   e. Stoplamp switch and cruise control switch will be adjusted.
   f. Inspect stoplamps for proper operation.

MULTI-FUNCTION SWITCH

REPLACE

1. Remove steering wheel center pad and mounting screws.
2. Disable driver's air bag module as outlined in "Air Bag System Precautions" in front of this manual.
3. Remove covers and two driver's air bag module mounting bolts from steering wheel rear.
4. Disconnect driver's air bag module electrical connector.
5. Remove air bag module.
6. Disconnect horn electrical connector.
7. Remove steering wheel nut.
8. Remove steering wheel using steering wheel puller No. J1859A, or equivalent.
9. Disconnect electrical connectors from steering wheel.
10. Remove steering wheel from column.
11. Remove steering column shrouds.
12. Remove two Torx head screws from multi-function switch.
13. Disconnect electrical connectors.
14. Remove multi-function switch from steering column.
15. Reverse procedure to install. **Torque** screws to 36 inch lbs.

TURN SIGNAL SWITCH

REPLACE

Refer to "Multi-Function Switch, Replace" for turn signal switch replacement procedure.

DIMMER SWITCH

REPLACE

Cavalier

1. Remove instrument panel accessory trim plate to access fog lamp switch.
2. Release retainers on fog lamp/dimmer switch housing using suitable flat bladed tool.
3. Remove fog lamp/dimmer switch housing from instrument panel.
4. Release retainers on dimmer switch using a flat bladed tool.
5. Remove dimmer lamp switch from fog lamp/dimmer switch housing.
6. Reverse procedure to install.

Sunfire

1. Remove fog lamp/dimmer switch trim plate from instrument panel using suitable flat bladed tool.
2. Disconnect electrical connectors from fog lamp/dimmer switch.
3. Release retainer tabs on dimmer lamp switch using suitable flat bladed tool on reverse side.
4. Remove dimmer lamp switch from trim plate.
5. Reverse procedure to install.

STEERING WHEEL

REPLACE

1. Remove steering wheel center pad and mounting screws as required.
2. Disable driver's air bag module as outlined in "Air Bag System Precautions" in front of this manual.
3. Remove covers and two driver's air bag module mounting bolts from steering wheel rear.
4. Disconnect driver's air bag module electrical connector.
5. Remove air bag module.
6. Disconnect horn electrical connector.
7. Remove steering wheel nut.
8. Remove steering wheel using steering wheel puller No. J1859A, or equivalent.
9. Disconnect electrical connectors from steering wheel.
10. Remove steering wheel from column.
11. Reverse procedure to install, **torque** steering wheel nut to 30 ft. lbs.

INSTRUMENT CLUSTER

REPLACE

1. Remove instrument panel trim plate.
2. Remove screws from top of cluster.
3. Pull cluster rearward.
4. Remove cluster assembly.
5. Reverse procedure to install.

WIPER MOTOR

REPLACE

1. Remove wiper arm assemblies.
2. Disconnect the washer tubing from air inlet screen.
3. Remove air inlet grille panel push-in retainers from panel using door trim pad and garnish clip remover tool No. J38778, or equivalent.
4. Remove air inlet grille panel from vehicle.
5. Remove electrical connector from wiper motor.
6. Remove screws and wiper drive system module from vehicle.
7. Remove wiper transmission from wiper motor crank arm using wiper transmission separator tool No. J39232, or equivalent.
8. Remove screws, then the wiper motor from frame.
9. Reverse procedure to install, **torque** mounting screws to 88 inch lbs.

WIPER SWITCH

REPLACE

1. Remove steering column trim covers.
2. Remove multi-function switch as outlined in "Multi-Function Switch, Replace."
3. Remove retaining screws, then the wiper switch from column.
4. Disconnect electrical connector.
5. Reverse procedure to install, **torque** attaching screws to 36 inch lbs.

WIPER TRANSMISSION
REPLACE

1. Remove wiper arm assemblies.
2. Disconnect the washer tubing from the air inlet screen.
3. Remove air inlet grille panel push-in retainers from panel using door trim pad and garnish clip remover tool No. J38778, or equivalent.
4. Remove air inlet grille panel from vehicle.
5. Remove wiper drive module.
6. Disconnect electrical connector from wiper motor.
7. Remove wiper transmission from wiper motor crank arm using wiper transmission separator tool No. J39232, or equivalent.
8. Remove cap from wiper transmission.
9. Remove screws and wiper transmission from tube frame.
10. Reverse procedure to install, noting the following:
    a. **Torque** wiper transmission screws to 79 inch lbs.
    b. **Torque** wiper drive system module screws to 88 inch lbs.

BLOWER MOTOR
REPLACE

1. Disconnect blower motor electrical connectors.
2. Remove sound insulator panels as required.
3. Remove mounting screws, then the blower motor assembly.
4. Reverse procedure to install, **torque** attaching screws to 44 inch lbs.

HEATER CORE
REPLACE

1. Drain cooling system into suitable container.
2. Recover refrigerant as outlined in "Air Conditioning" chapter.
3. Remove evaporator lines to evaporator.
4. Raise and support vehicle.
5. Disconnect heater hoses from heater core.
6. Lower vehicle.
7. Remove evaporator case drain tube.
8. Remove instrument panel carrier as outlined in "Dash Panel Service" chapter.
9. Disconnect wiring harness from cross beam.
10. Remove attaching bolts to righthand and lefthand HVAC module.
11. Remove two cross vehicle beam bolts.
12. Remove cross beam.
13. Remove floor console.
14. Reposition floor carpet aside in order to access floor outlet duct connections.
15. Remove floor outlet ducts from heater outlet cover, then the floor outlet ducts.
16. Disconnect wiring harness from HVAC module.
17. Disconnect electrical connections to blower motor and resistor.
18. Remove HVAC module assembly.
19. Remove heater core case cover attaching screws and cover.
20. Remove heater core bracket screws and brackets.
21. Remove heater core from HVAC module assembly.
22. Reverse procedure to install, noting the following:
    a. **Torque** bracket and cover screws to 9 inch lbs.
    b. **Torque** HVAC module mounting bracket bolts and screws to 18 inch lbs.
    c. **Torque** cross vehicle beam bolts and studs to 89 inch lbs.
    d. **Torque** righthand and lefthand side HVAC module support bolts to 18 inch lbs.
    e. **Torque** evaporator tube to evaporator fittings to 18 ft. lbs.

EVAPORATOR CORE
REPLACE

1. Remove HVAC module as outlined in "Heater Core, Replace."
2. Remove heater core as outlined in "Heater Core, Replace."
3. Remove attaching screws and evaporator core brackets.
4. Remove evaporator core assembly.
5. Reverse procedure to install, **torque** evaporator core bracket screws to 9 inch lbs.

2.2L DOHC Engine

NOTE: Refer To "2.2L Engine" In "Alero, Grand Am & Malibu" Chapter For Procedures Not Covered In This Section.

NOTE: On Air Bag Equipped Models, Refer To "Air Bag System Precautions" Located In The Front Of This Manual For System Disarming & Arming Procedures.

NOTE: Refer To "Computer Relearn Procedures" Located In The Front Of This Manual When Battery Power To The Computer Has Been Interrupted.

INDEX

PRECAUTIONS

Air Bag Systems

Refer to "Air Bag System Precautions" in the front of this manual for system disarming and arming procedures.

Battery Ground Cable

Prior to service, disconnect battery ground cable and isolate as required.

Fuel System Pressure Relief

1. Disconnect battery ground cable, isolate as required.
2. Install fuel pressure gauge tool No. J34730-1A, or equivalent.
3. Install bleed hose into suitable container, then open valve to bleed system pressure.
4. Disconnect fuel pressure gauge from fuel pressure connection.

COMPRESSION PRESSURE

Refer to "2.2L Engine" in "Alero, Grand Am & Malibu" chapter for procedure.

ENGINE MOUNT
REPLACE

Refer to "2.2L Engine" in "Alero, Grand Am & Malibu" chapter for engine mount replacement procedure.

ENGINE
REPLACE

Refer to "2.2L Engine" in "Alero, Grand Am & Malibu" chapter for engine replacement procedure.

INTAKE MANIFOLD
REPLACE

Refer to "2.2L Engine" in "Alero, Grand Am & Malibu" chapter for intake manifold replacement procedure.

RADIATOR
REPLACE

1. Drain cooling system into suitable container.
2. Remove hood latch assembly.
3. Remove righthand and lefthand headlamp assemblies.
4. Remove radiator upper mount attaching bolts, then the mounts.
5. Raise vehicle using suitable lift.
6. Remove cooling fan mounting bolts, disconnect electrical connectors, then the cooling fan.
7. Remove radiator outlet hose clamp from radiator using tool No. J38185, or equivalent, then the radiator outlet hose.
8. Remove lower transmission oil cooler line, then lower vehicle.
9. Remove hood latch support bracket and forward sensors with harness.
10. Remove upper transmission oil cooler line from radiator.
11. Remove surge tank hose and clamp from radiator.
12. Remove condenser from radiator.
13. Remove radiator assembly.
14. Reverse procedure to install.

TIGHTENING SPECIFICATIONS

Year	Component	Torque, Ft. Lbs.
2002–05	Accelerator & Cruise Control Cable	89②
	Air Cleaner Clamps	44②
	Air Cleaner Outlet Resonator Mounting Bolt	89②
	Alternator	15
	Engine Mount Strut	74①
	Engine To Transmission Bolts	55
	Power Steering Pump	19
	Radiator Drain Cock	18②
	Righthand Engine Mount Bolts	44①
	Righthand Engine Mount To Body Nuts	55
	Torque Converter Bolts	46
	Upper Air Cleaner Cover Screws	27②

① — Plus 90°.
② — Inch lbs.

2.2L OHV Engine

NOTE: On Air Bag Equipped Models, Refer To "Air Bag System Precautions" Located In The Front Of This Manual For System Disarming & Arming Procedures.

NOTE: Refer To "Computer Relearn Procedures" Located In The Front Of This Manual When Battery Power To The Computer Has Been Interrupted.

INDEX

PRECAUTIONS

Air Bag Systems

Refer to "Air Bag System Precautions" in the front of this manual for system disarming and arming procedures.

Battery Ground Cable

Prior to service, disconnect battery ground cable and isolate as required.

Fuel System Pressure Relief

1. Raise and support vehicle using a suitable lift.
2. Disconnect fuel pump electrical connector.
3. Start engine and run until remaining fuel is consumed.
4. Engage starter for approximately three seconds to ensure relief of any remaining pressure.
5. Disconnect and isolate battery ground cable to avoid possible fuel discharge if any attempt is made to start engine.

COMPRESSION PRESSURE

When inspecting cylinder compression, the throttle should be open, all spark plugs removed and the battery at or near full charge. The lowest reading cylinder should not be less than 70% of the highest and no cylinder reading should be less than 100 psi. Turn ignition key until engine cranks through four compression cycles. Normal compression builds up quickly and evenly to specifications on each cylinder.

ENGINE MOUNT
REPLACE

1. Install engine support fixture tool No. J-28467-360, or equivalent.
2. Raise engine at front lift hook in order to remove weight from engine mount.
3. Remove coolant recovery tank mounting bolt.
4. Position coolant recovery tank aside with hoses attached.
5. Remove engine mount to drive belt tensioner bracket.
6. Remove two nuts on top of engine mount, **Fig. 1.**
7. Remove engine mount to body nuts.
8. Remove engine mount bracket and engine mount.
9. Reverse procedure to install.

ENGINE MOUNT STRUT & STRUT BRACKET
REPLACE

1. Raise and support vehicle using suitable lift.
2. Remove righthand splash shield.
3. Remove engine mount strut bolts and engine mount strut, **Fig. 2.**
4. Remove air conditioning compressor with lines attached and position aside.
5. Remove transmission brace from engine.
6. Remove engine mount strut bracket bolts and strut bracket.
7. Reverse procedure to install.

ENGINE
REPLACE

Automatic Transaxle

1. Recover air conditioning refrigerant as outlined in "Air Conditioning" chapter.
2. Drain and recover coolant in suitable container.
3. Mark positions of hinge to hood locations to ease installation and remove hood.
4. Remove air cleaner assembly.
5. Disconnect brake booster vacuum line at intake manifold.
6. Disconnect accelerator control cable.
7. Disconnect speed control cable and position it aside.
8. Remove fuel injector rail cover.
9. Remove accelerator and speed control cables from cable bracket. **Discard accelerator cable.**
10. Disconnect all required electrical connectors from engine components.
11. Remove cruise control module.
12. Disconnect refrigerant lines from accumulator. Discard O-rings.
13. Mark running direction and remove engine accessory drive belt.
14. Remove coolant surge tank.

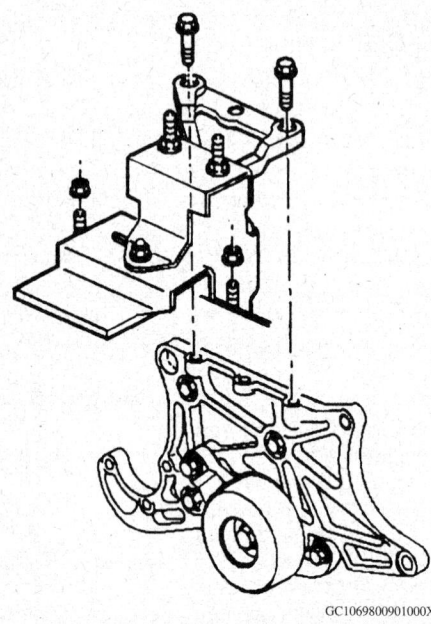

Fig. 1 Engine mount removal

15. Remove upper and lower radiator hoses.
16. Remove fuel feed lines from engine.
17. Raise and support vehicle.
18. Remove coolant pipe.
19. Remove righthand front wheel and tire.
20. Remove righthand front splash shield.
21. Remove engine mount strut as outlined in "Engine Mount Strut & Strut Bracket, Replace."
22. Remove flexplate inspection cover.
23. Remove exhaust pipe and hanger from exhaust manifold.
24. Remove wiring harness bracket nut from starter bolt.
25. Raise and support vehicle using suitable lift.
26. Remove flywheel inspection shield.
27. Remove electrical connectors.
28. Remove starter bolts, then the starter.
29. Remove and support air conditioning compressor with hoses intact.
30. Remove air conditioning compressor bracket.
31. Drain engine oil into suitable container.
32. Remove torque convertor to flexplate bolts.
33. Remove transaxle to engine support brace.
34. Remove transaxle to engine lower bolts.
35. Lower vehicle.
36. Support transaxle using suitable jack.
37. Install suitable engine lifting device to engine lifting eyes.
38. Install engine support fixture tool No. J-28467-360, or equivalent.
39. Raise engine at front lift hook in order to remove weight from engine mount.
40. Remove coolant recovery tank mounting bolt.
41. Position coolant recovery tank aside with hoses attached.
42. Remove engine mount to drive belt tensioner bracket.
43. Remove two nuts on top of engine

mount, **Fig. 1.**
44. Remove engine mount to body nuts.
45. Remove engine mount bracket and engine mount.
46. Remove remaining transaxle to engine bolts.
47. Separate engine from transaxle, carefully lift engine up and out.
48. Reverse procedure to install, noting the following:
    a. Install new accelerator cable.
    b. Install new evaporator O-rings lubricated in clean 525 viscosity refrigerant oil.
    c. Ensure oil pan drain plug is intact with its gasket in place and fill crankcase.
    d. Close radiator petcock and fill cooling system.
    e. Start engine and inspect for any fluid leaks.

Manual Transaxle

1. Drain and recover coolant into suitable container.
2. Remove air cleaner outlet duct.
3. Remove upper radiator hose at coolant outlet.
4. Disconnect brake booster vacuum hose.
5. Disconnect IAC electrical connection.
6. Disconnect alternator electrical connector.
7. Disconnect TPS, MAP, EVAP, EGR, ECT, TCC and O2 sensor electrical connectors.
8. Disconnect injector harness electrical connectors.
9. Disconnect engine ground electrical connections.
10. Rotate tensioner clockwise with suitable wrench and slide belt from alternator pulley.
11. Release tensioner and remove belt, **Figs. 3 and 4.**
12. Remove transmission shift control cable from range select lever and bracket.
13. Remove coolant surge tank and hose.
14. Disconnect vacuum line near master cylinder.
15. Install engine support fixture tool No. J-28467-360, or equivalent.
16. Disconnect lower radiator hose from coolant pump.
17. Raise and support vehicle, then remove front wheels.
18. Remove splash shields.
19. Remove exhaust pipe at exhaust manifold and catalytic converter.
20. Raise and support vehicle using suitable lift.
21. Remove righthand splash shield.
22. Remove engine mount strut bolts and engine mount strut, **Fig. 2.**
23. Remove air conditioning compressor with lines attached and position aside.
24. Remove transmission brace from engine.
25. Remove engine mount strut bracket bolts and strut bracket.
26. Remove wheel speed sensor wire harness from control arms.
27. Separate ball joints from steering

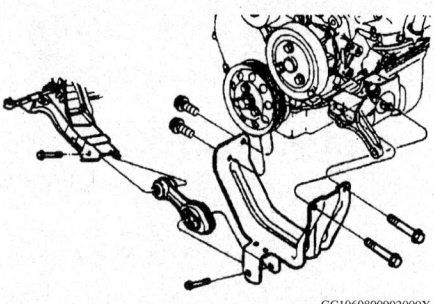

Fig. 2 Engine mount strut & strut bracket removal

knuckles as outlined in "Ball Joint, Replace" in "Front Suspension & Steering" section.
28. Separate tie rod ends from struts.
29. Remove brake lines from suspension support below rack and pinion unit.
30. Disconnect electronic ignition module, VSS, cooling fan, starter, air conditioning compressor, oil pressure sensor, oil level sensor and ground wire electrical connections.
31. Disconnect power steering lines from rack and pinion.
32. Remove flexible coupling joint from rack and pinion.
33. Remove accelerator and cruise control cables from accelerator control bracket.
34. Remove suspension support.
35. Disconnect heater hoses from firewall.
36. Remove drive axles from transaxle and position aside.
37. Disconnect fuel lines and transaxle cooler lines, capping line ends to prevent damage.
38. Remove transmission mount.
39. Install engine support fixture tool No. J-28467-360, or equivalent.
40. Raise engine at front lift hook in order to remove weight from engine mount.
41. Remove coolant recovery tank mounting bolt.
42. Position coolant recovery tank aside with hoses attached.
43. Remove engine mount to drive belt tensioner bracket.
44. Remove two nuts on top of engine mount, **Fig. 1.**
45. Remove engine mount to body nuts.
46. Remove engine mount bracket and engine mount.
47. Lower vehicle until engine rests lightly on suitable support.
48. Remove engine support fixture.
49. Raise and support vehicle using suitable lift.
50. Remove engine and transmission.
51. Place on bench and remove transmission.
52. Reverse procedure to install, noting the following:
    a. Close radiator petcock and fill cooling system.
    b. Ensure all fluids are up to proper levels.
    c. Start engine and inspect for any fluid leaks.

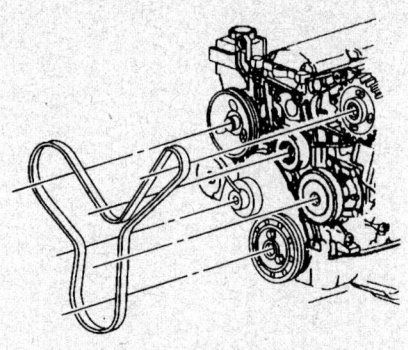

GC1069800906000A

Fig. 3 Serpentine drive belt routing. Less A/C

INTAKE MANIFOLD
REPLACE

1. Remove air cleaner inlet duct.
2. Remove resonator and resonator bracket.
3. Remove accelerator and cruise control cables from accelerator control bracket.
4. Disconnect vacuum hoses at throttle body.
5. Disconnect MAP, TPS and IAC electrical connectors.
6. Remove throttle bracket mounting bolts and bracket, **Fig. 5**.
7. Remove throttle body mounting bolts and throttle body.
8. Remove fuel feed.
9. Remove fuel inlet pipe mounting bolts.
10. Remove mounting nuts, bolts and intake manifold.
11. Reverse procedure to install, noting the following:
    a. Clean mating surface of intake manifold and cylinder head.
    b. Inspect manifold for damage and replace as required.

EXHAUST MANIFOLD
REPLACE

1. Disconnect lead and remove oxygen sensor.
2. Rotate tensioner clockwise with suitable wrench and slide belt from alternator pulley.
3. Release tensioner and remove belt, **Figs. 3 and 4**.
4. Remove alternator mounting bolts and position it aside.
5. Remove alternator rear brace.
6. Drain coolant into suitable container and remove radiator inlet pipe.
7. Raise and support vehicle using suitable container.
8. Disconnect exhaust pipe from exhaust manifold and lower vehicle.
9. Remove oil fill tube, exhaust manifold mounting bolts and exhaust manifold.
10. Reverse procedure to install.

CYLINDER HEAD
REPLACE

1. Drain engine coolant into suitable container and remove radiator inlet pipe.

2. Rotate tensioner clockwise with suitable wrench and slide belt from alternator pulley.
3. Release tensioner and remove belt, **Figs. 3 and 4.**
4. Remove air cleaner outlet duct.
5. Install engine support fixture tool No. J-28467-360, or equivalent.
6. Raise engine at front lift hook in order to remove weight from engine mount.
7. Remove coolant recovery tank mounting bolt.
8. Position coolant recovery tank aside with hoses attached.
9. Remove engine mount to drive belt tensioner bracket.
10. Remove two nuts on top of engine mount, **Fig. 1.**
11. Remove engine mount to body nuts.
12. Remove engine mount bracket and engine mount.
13. Remove intake manifold as outlined in "Intake Manifold, Replace."
14. Disconnect lead and remove oxygen sensor.
15. Remove alternator mounting bolts and position it aside.
16. Remove alternator rear brace.
17. Raise and support vehicle.
18. Disconnect exhaust pipe from exhaust manifold and lower vehicle.
19. Remove oil fill tube, exhaust manifold mounting bolts and exhaust manifold.
20. Disconnect ECT sensor electrical connector.
21. Remove valve cover, **Fig. 6.**
22. Remove rocker arms and pushrods. Keep in order for proper installation.
23. Remove alternator rear brace and alternator.
24. Remove power steering pump and position aside with lines intact.
25. Remove radiator inlet pipe.
26. Remove ignition coil.
27. Remove accessory bracket.
28. Reference mark each spark plug wire and remove from spark plugs.
29. Install engine support fixture tool No. J-28467-360, or equivalent.
30. Remove cylinder head bolts and cylinder head using reverse tightening sequence, **Fig. 7.**
31. Reverse procedure to install, noting the following:
    a. Clean cylinder head to engine block and valve cover mating surfaces.
    b. Tighten cylinder head bolts in sequence, **Fig. 7.**
    c. **Torque** long cylinder head bolts Nos. 1, 4, 5, 8 and 9 to 46 ft. lbs.
    d. **Torque** short bolts Nos. 2, 3, 6, 7 and 10 to 43 ft. lbs.
    e. Finally, tighten cylinder head bolts an additional 90° in sequence.

VALVE CLEARANCE SPECIFICATIONS

This engine is equipped with hydraulic lifters. Clearance is zero.

VALVE ADJUSTMENT

Valve lash is obtained through the use of hydraulic valve lifters. No adjustment is required.

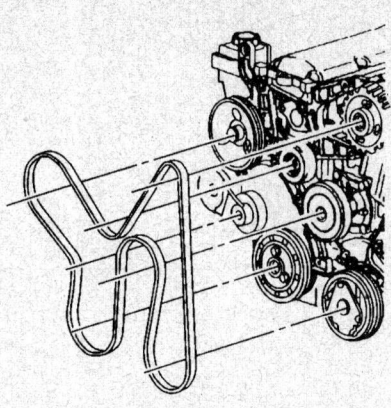

GC1069800907000A

Fig. 4 Serpentine drive belt routing. With A/C

VALVE GUIDES

Valve guides are an integral component of the cylinder head and are not removable. If valve stem clearance becomes excessive, the valve guide should be reamed to the next oversize and the appropriate oversize valves installed. Valves are available in several different oversizes.

HYDRAULIC LIFTERS
REPLACE

1. Remove cylinder head as outlined in "Cylinder Head, Replace."
2. Remove anti-rotation brackets and valve lifters. Keep lifters in order.
3. Inspect lifters for any signs of damage or wear, replacing as required.
4. Reverse procedure to install.

CRANKSHAFT DAMPER
REPLACE

Removal

1. Remove serpentine belt, then raise and support vehicle using suitable lift.
2. Remove righthand front wheel and tire assembly, then inner fender splash shield.
3. Remove three crankshaft pulley mounting bolts, **Fig. 8.**
4. Remove hub bolt and crankshaft pulley.
5. Install crankshaft pulley puller tool No. J-24420-B, or equivalent on hub.
6. Turn puller screw and remove hub.

Installation

1. Coat front cover seal contact area with engine oil.
2. Apply RTV sealer No. 1052917, or equivalent, to keyway in pulley hub.
3. Place crankshaft pulley hub into position over key on crankshaft.
4. Install crankshaft pulley installer tool No. J-29113, or equivalent, into crankshaft so minimum of ¼ inch of thread is engaged.
5. Pull pulley hub into position and remove tool from crankshaft.

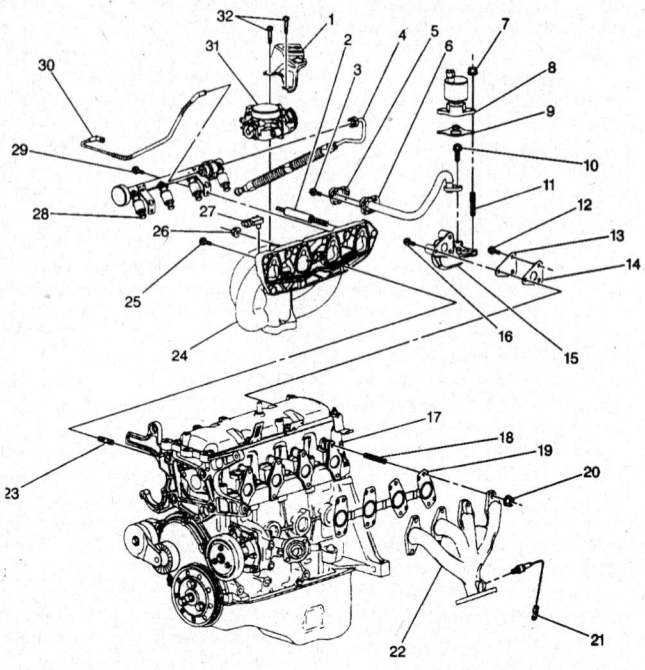

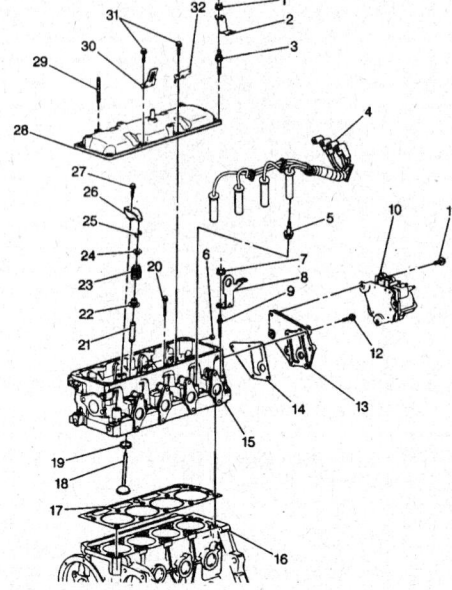

(1) Throttle Cable Bracket	(17) Engine Block
(2) Bolt, Intake Manifold Fuel Rail Bracket	(18) Stud, Exhaust Manifold
(3) Bolt, EGR Pipe	(19) Gasket, Exhaust Manifold
(4) Fuel Line	(20) Nut Exhaust Manifold
(5) Retainer, EGR Pipe	(21) Oxygen Sensor
(6) EGR Pipe	(22) Exhaust Manifold
(7) Nut, EGR Valve	(23) Stud, Intake Manifold
(8) EGR Valve	(24) Intake Manifold
(9) Gasket, EGR Valve	(25) Bolt, Intake Manifold
(10) Bolt, EGR Pipe	(26) Nut, Intake Manifold
(11) Stud, EGR Valve	(27) MAP Sensor
(12) Bolt, EGR Adapter	(28) Fuel Rail And Fuel Injectors
(13) EGR Port Cover (EXPORT ONLY)	(29) Bolt, Fuel Rail
(14) Gasket, EGR Adapter	(30) Vacuum Harness
(15) EGR Adapter	(31) Throttle Body
(16) Bolt, EGR Adapter	(32) Bolts, Throttle Body

GC1069800904000X

Fig. 5 Exploded view of intake and exhaust manifold components

(1) Nut, Secondary Ignition Harness Bracket	(18) Valve
(2) Secondary Ignition Harness Bracket	(19) Valve Seat
(3) Bolt, Valve Rocker Arm Cover	(20) Bolt, Cylinder Head
(4) Secondary Ignition Harness	(21) Valve Guide
(5) Spark Plug	(22) Valve Guide Seal
(6) Oil Passage Plug	(23) Valve Spring
(7) Nut, Engine Lift Hook	(24) Valve Spring Retainer
(8) Engine Lift Hook	(25) Valve Spring Keepers
(9) Bolt, Cylinder Head	(26) Valve Rocker Arm
(10) Ignition Module And Coil Assembly	(27) Bolt, Rocker Arm
(11) Bolt, Ignition Coil Bracket	(28) Valve Rocker Arm Cover
(12) Bolt, Rear Cylinder Head Cover	(29) Stud, Fuel Rail Bracket
(13) Rear Cylinder Head Cover	(30) Bracket, Secondary Ignition Harness
(14) Gasket, Rear Cylinder Head Cover	(31) Bolts, Secondary Ignition and Fuel Injector Harness Brackets
(15) Cylinder Head	(32) Bracket, Fuel Injector Harness
(16) Cylinder Block	
(17) Gasket, Cylinder Head	

GC1069800905000X

Fig. 6 Exploded view of cylinder head components

TIMING CHAIN

REPLACE

1. Remove crankcase front cover as outlined in "Front Cover, Replace."
2. Align marks on crankshaft sprocket and camshaft sprocket, **Fig. 9.**
3. **Before removing chain and sprockets,** measure distance between hole in bracket and unworn tensioner shoe surface. If this distance is more than .314 inch, replace both sprockets, tensioner and timing chain.
4. Remove timing chain tensioner bolts.
5. Remove camshaft sprocket and timing chain.
6. Remove mounting bolt and tensioner.
7. Remove crankshaft sprocket using puller tool No. J-22888-20, or equivalent.
8. Reverse procedure to install, noting the following:
   a. Install crankshaft sprocket fully seated against crankshaft using sprocket installer tool No. J-5590, or equivalent.
   b. Compress tensioner spring and install cotter pin or nail into hole A, **Fig. 10.**
   c. Align marks on camshaft and crankshaft sprockets with tabs on tensioner.
   d. Align dowel in camshaft with dowel

FRONT COVER

REPLACE

1. Remove serpentine belt and belt tensioner.
2. Install engine support fixture tool No. J-28467-360, or equivalent.
3. Install engine support fixture tool No. J-28467-360, or equivalent.
4. Raise engine at front lift hook in order to remove weight from engine mount.
5. Remove coolant recovery tank mounting bolt.
6. Position coolant recovery tank aside with hoses attached.
7. Remove engine mount to drive belt tensioner bracket.
8. Remove two nuts on top of engine mount, **Fig. 1.**
9. Remove engine mount to body nuts.
10. Remove engine mount bracket and engine mount.
11. Remove alternator rear brace.
12. Disconnect alternator electrical connectors.
13. Rotate tensioner clockwise with suitable wrench and slide belt from alternator pulley.
14. Release tensioner and remove belt, **Figs. 3 and 4.**
15. Remove alternator through bolts, then the alternator.
16. Mark running direction and remove serpentine belt.
17. Remove power steering fluid lines.
18. Remove power steering pump mounting bolts.
19. Remove pump and transfer pulley, if required.
20. Raise and support vehicle.
21. Remove oil pan as outlined in "Oil Pan, Replace."
22. Remove crankshaft pulley and hub.
23. Remove mounting bolts and front cover.
24. Reverse procedure to install.

6. Install crankshaft pulley and mounting bolts.
7. Install inner slash shield, then wheel and tire assembly.
8. Lower vehicle and install serpentine belt.

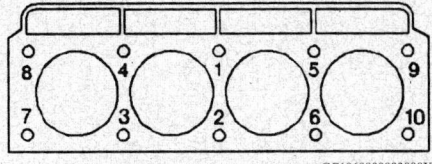

GC1069800903000X

Fig. 7 Cylinder head bolt tightening sequence

hole camshaft sprocket.
e. Draw camshaft sprocket onto camshaft using mounting bolt.

CAMSHAFT

REPLACE

1. Remove crankcase front cover as outlined in "Front Cover, Replace."
2. Align marks on crankshaft sprocket and camshaft sprocket, **Fig. 9.**
3. Before removing chain and sprockets, measure distance between hole in bracket and unworn tensioner shoe surface. If this distance is more than .314 inch, replace both sprockets, tensioner and timing chain.
4. Remove timing chain tensioner bolts.
5. Remove camshaft sprocket and timing chain.
6. Remove mounting bolt and tensioner.
7. Remove crankshaft sprocket using puller tool No. J-22888-20, or equivalent.
8. Drain engine oil into suitable container and remove oil filter.
9. Rotate tensioner clockwise with suitable wrench and slide belt from alternator pulley.
10. Release tensioner and remove belt, **Figs. 3 and 4.**
11. Disconnect alternator electrical connectors.
12. Remove alternator through bolts, then the alternator.
13. Mark running direction and remove serpentine belt.
14. Remove power steering fluid lines.
15. Remove power steering pump mounting bolts.
16. Remove pump and transfer pulley, if required.
17. Remove drive belt tensioner.
18. Remove water pump pulley.
19. Remove crankshaft pulley and hub.
20. Remove cylinder head as outlined in "Cylinder Head, Replace."
21. Remove valve lifters.
22. Remove camshaft sprocket, timing chain and tensioner.
23. Remove oil pump drive.
24. Remove thrust plate.
25. Remove CMP sensor.
26. Carefully remove camshaft. **Avoid damaging camshaft bearings.**
27. Inspect camshaft for galling, gouges, overheating and wear. If any of these conditions exist, replace camshaft.
28. Reverse procedure to install, noting the following:
    a. **Coat camshaft lobes and bearings with camshaft lube No. 1051396, or equivalent.**
    b. **Install camshaft with extreme**

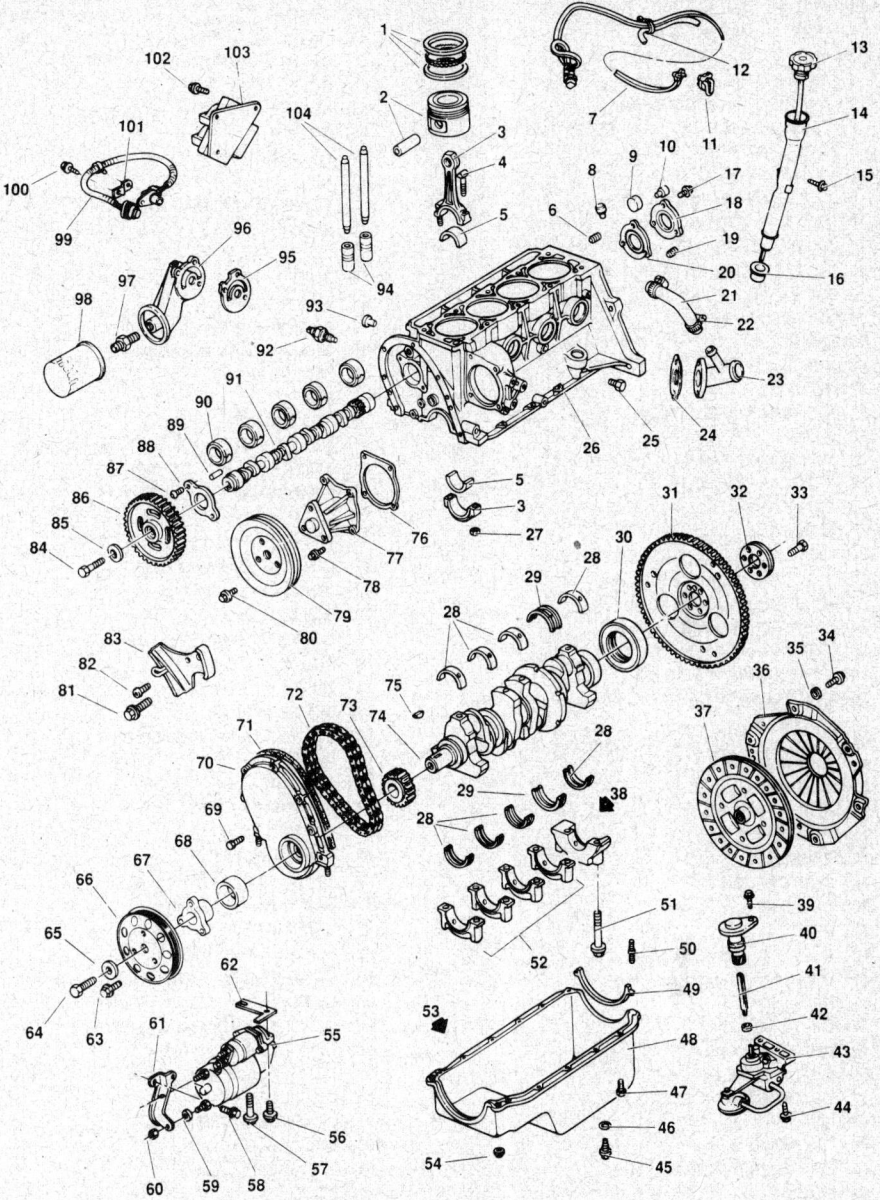

GC106910036800AX

Fig. 8 Exploded view of cylinder block (Part 1 of 2)

care to avoid personal injury and gouging of camshaft bearings.
c. Tighten thrust plate.
d. Lifters must be installed in original bores.
e. **If new camshaft is installed, replace all valve lifters. Some lifters may be oversized. Ensure marking near lifter bore.**
f. Valve mechanism components must be installed in original positions and with same mating surfaces as removed.
g. Replace oil filter.
h. Ensure oil pan drain plug and gasket are intact.

PISTON & ROD ASSEMBLY

Assemble piston to rod with arrow on piston facing toward front of engine, **Fig. 11.**

Measure connecting rod side clearance, Clearance should be .0039–.0149 inch.

PISTONS, PINS & RINGS

Pistons are available in standard size and oversizes of .0015 inch, .002 inch and .004 inch. Piston pins are available in standard size only.

CRANKSHAFT REAR OIL SEAL

REPLACE

1. **On models equipped with automatic transaxle,** remove transaxle as outlined in **MOTOR's "Domestic Transmission Manual, In-Vehicle Service."**
2. **On models equipped with manual**

1. PISTON RINGS
2. PISTON AND PIN
3. CONNECTING ROD
4. CONNECTING ROD BOLT
5. CONNECTING ROD BEARING
6. CYLINDER BLOCK OIL GALLERY HOLE PLUG
7. COOLANT HEATER CORD
8. CYLINDER HEAD DOWEL PIN
9. COOLANT JACKET PLUG
10. CLUTCH HOUSING PIN
11. COOLANT HEATER
12. ADJUSTABLE RETAINER
13. OIL LEVEL RETAINER
14. OIL FILL TUBE
15. BOLT
16. OIL FILL TUBE SEAL
17. BOLT
18. CAMSHAFT REAR COVER
19. PLUG
20. CAMSHAFT REAR COVER GASKET
21. COOLANT INLET HOSE
22. CLAMP
23. COOLANT INLET
24. COOLANT INLET GASKET
25. COOLANT DRAIN PLUG
26. CYLINDER BLOCK
27. CONNECTING ROD NUT
28. CRANKSHAFT BEARING
29. CRANKSHAFT BEARING
30. CRANKSHAFT REAR OIL SEAL
31. FLYWHEEL
32. FLYWHEEL RETAINER (AUTOMATIC TRANSAXLE)
33. BOLT
34. BOLT
35. WASHER
36. PRESSURE PLATE
37. CLUTCH DISC
38. SEALANT
39. BOLT
40. OIL PUMP DRIVE ASSEMBLY
41. OIL PUMP DRIVE SHAFT
42. RETAINER
43. OIL PUMP
44. BOLT
45. OIL DRAIN PLUG
46. OIL DRAIN PLUG GASKET
47. BOLT
48. OIL PAN
49. OIL PAN REAR SEAL
50. STUD
51. BOLT
52. MAIN BEARING CAP

53. SEALER
54. NUT
55. STARTER MOTOR
56. BOLT
57. BOLT
58. BOLT
59. WASHER
60. NUT
61. STARTER MOTOR BRACKET
62. SHIM
63. BOLT
64. BOLT
65. WASHER
66. CRANKSHAFT PULLEY
67. CRANKSHAFT PULLEY HUB
68. SEAL
69. BOLT
70. CRANKCASE
71. CRANKCASE FRONT COVER OIL SEAL
72. TIMING CHAIN
73. CRANKSHAFT SPROCKET
74. CRANKSHAFT
75. KEY
76. COOLANT PUMP GASKET
77. COOLANT PUMP
78. BOLT
79. COOLANT PUMP PULLEY
80. BOLT
81. BOLT
82. BOLT
83. TIMING CHAIN TENSIONER
84. BOLT
85. WASHER
86. CAMSHAFT SPROCKET
87. SCREW
88. THRUST PLATE
89. PIN CAMSHAFT BEARING
90. CAMSHAFT BEARING
91. CAMSHAFT
92. FUEL PUMP SWITCH
93. OIL FILTER BY-PASS VALVE
94. LIFTER
95. OIL FILTER ADAPTER GASKET
96. OIL FILTER ADAPTER
97. OIL FILTER CONNECTOR
98. OIL FILTER
99. CRANKSHAFT SENSOR
100. BOLT
101. RETAINER
102. BOLT
103. COIL
104. PUSHROD

GC106910036800BX

Fig. 8 Exploded view of cylinder block (Part 2 of 2)

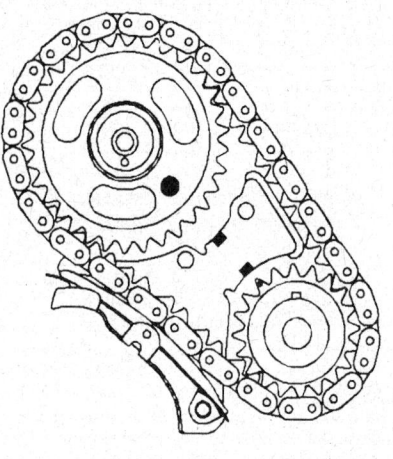

GC1069701047000X

Fig. 9 Timing chain & sprockets

13. Remove air conditioning compressor with lines attached and position aside.
14. Remove transmission brace from engine.
15. Remove engine mount strut bracket bolts and strut bracket.
16. Remove oil level sensor.
17. Remove mounting bolts, nuts and oil pan.
18. Reverse procedure to install, noting the following:
    a. Clean all crankcase, front cover and pan sealing surfaces. Ensure all old RTV has been removed from blind mounting holes.
    b. Apply 1/16 inch diameter bead of Loctite 5900 RTV sealer, or equivalent, on oil pan to block sealing flanges. **Do not apply sealer to rear seal mounting surface.**
    c. Install new oil pan rear seal and apply Loctite 5900 RTV sealer, or equivalent, to ends down to ears.

OIL PUMP

REPLACE

Removal

1. Remove oil pan as outlined in "Oil Pan, Replace."
2. Remove pump to rear main bearing cap bolt, pump, extension shaft and retainer.

Installation

1. Heat retainer in hot water, but not so hot it would crack during installation.
2. Install retainer to extension shaft.
3. Install extension to oil pump.
4. Install oil pan.
5. Start engine and ensure oil pressure is as specified.

OIL PUMP SERVICE

Disassemble

1. Drain oil from pump and remove driveshaft, **Fig. 13.**

transaxle, remove transaxle, pressure plate and clutch disc as outlined in **MOTOR's "Domestic Transmission Manual, In-Vehicle Service."**

3. **On all models,** remove flywheel mounting bolts and flywheel.
4. Pry seal out by insert suitable screwdriver through dust lip, **Fig. 12.**
5. Reverse procedure to install, noting the following:
    a. Lubricate seal bore to seal surface with suitable clean engine oil.
    b. Align seal installation tool No. J-34686, or equivalent, dowel pin with crankshaft dowel pin hole and attach tool to crankshaft.
    c. Tighten tool T-handle to push seal into bore. Continue to tighten until tool is flush against block.

OIL PAN

REPLACE

1. Raise and support vehicle using suitable lift.
2. Drain engine oil into suitable container.
3. Remove righthand front tire and wheel.
4. Remove righthand front splash shield.
5. Remove starter bracket at block.
6. Remove wiring harness bracket nut from starter bolt.
7. Remove flywheel inspection shield.
8. Remove electrical connectors.
9. Remove starter bolts, then the starter.
10. Remove flywheel inspection cover.
11. Remove righthand splash shield.
12. Remove engine mount strut bolts and engine mount strut, **Fig. 2.**

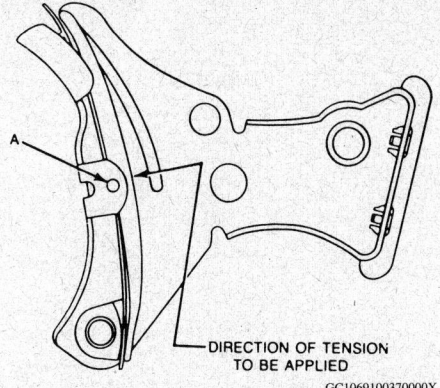

DIRECTION OF TENSION
TO BE APPLIED

GC1069100370000X

Fig. 10 Timing chain tensioner

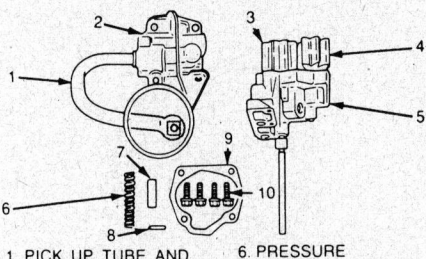

GC1099100051000X

Fig. 13 Exploded view of oil pump

1. PICK UP TUBE AND SCREEN.
2. PUMP COVER.
3. DRIVE GEAR AND SHAFT.
4. IDLER GEAR.
5. PUMP BODY.
6. PRESSURE REGULATOR SPRING
7. PRESSURE REGULATOR VALVE.
8. RETAINING PIN.
9. GASKET.
10. ATTACHING BOLTS.

2. Remove pump cover, **Do not remove pickup tube from cover unless loose or broken.**
3. Remove pump gears and pressure regulator valve. **Pressure regulator valve spring is under pressure.**
4. Remove plug, spring and valve. If valve is stuck, soak pump housing in carburetor cleaning solvent.

Inspection

Thoroughly clean all oil pump components and inspect them for excessive wear or damage.

1. Inspect oil pump clearances using straightedge and feeler gauge, **Figs. 14 through 17.**
2. Install gears and measure lash in several places, within .004–.008 inch.
3. Measure depth and diameter of oil pump gear pocket. Depth should be 1.195–1.198 inches. Diameter, 1.503–1.506 inches.
4. Measure gear side clearance to .001–.004.
5. Measure gear end clearance to .002–.006. When determining pump serviceability based on end clearance, consider depth of wear pattern in pump cover and/or cover plate.

Assemble

1. Lubricate all internal components with engine oil during assembly.

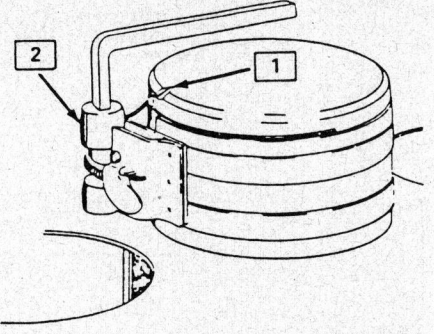

GC1069100371000X

Fig. 11 Piston installation

2. Install pump gears. **To avoid engine damage, all pump cavities must be packed with petroleum jelly before installing gears to ensure priming.**
3. Install oil pump cover and gasket.
4. Install pressure regulator valve, spring and retaining pin.
5. When oil pump is overhauled, clear oil pan of oil and sludge, replace oil filter and fill crankcase with clean oil.

BELT TENSION DATA

The serpentine belt is automatically adjusted by a spring tensioner. No adjustment is required.

SERPENTINE DRIVE BELT

Belt, Replace

1. Rotate tensioner clockwise with suitable wrench and slide belt from alternator pulley.
2. Release tensioner and remove belt.
3. Reverse procedure to install, **Figs. 3 and 4.**

Tensioner, Replace

1. Rotate tensioner clockwise with suitable wrench and slide belt from alternator pulley.
2. Release tensioner and remove belt, **Figs. 3 and 4.**
3. Remove alternator and position it aside.
4. Raise and support vehicle.
5. Remove oil filter.
6. Remove idler pulley.
7. Remove mounting bolt and position air conditioning compressor aside with lines attached.
8. Remove mounting bolts and tensioner.
9. Reverse procedure to install.

COOLING SYSTEM BLEED

1. **On models equipped with bleeder valve,** open valve.
2. **On all models,** fill surge tank or radiator to 1 inch below filler neck.
3. Close bleeder valve.
4. Block drive wheels and apply parking brake.

GC1069701048000X

Fig. 12 Crankshaft rear seal removal

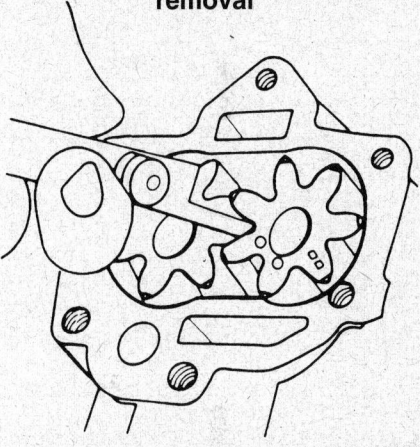

GC1099100052000X

Fig. 14 Oil pump gear lash measurement

5. **On models equipped with automatic transaxle,** place shifter in Park position.
6. **On models equipped with manual transaxle,** place shifter in Neutral position.
7. **On all models,** start engine and turn HVAC controls to HEATER and FULL HOT.
8. Allow engine to run until upper radiator hose is hot.
9. Turn engine off and inspect level of coolant in surge tank or radiator.
10. Allow engine to cool and add coolant, as required.

THERMOSTAT
REPLACE

1. Remove air intake duct.
2. With engine cool, drain engine coolant into suitable container below thermostat level. **Never open cooling system with engine hot.**
3. Disconnect radiator hose or outlet pipe from thermostat housing.
4. Remove mounting nuts, housing, gasket and thermostat.
5. Reverse procedure to install, noting the following:

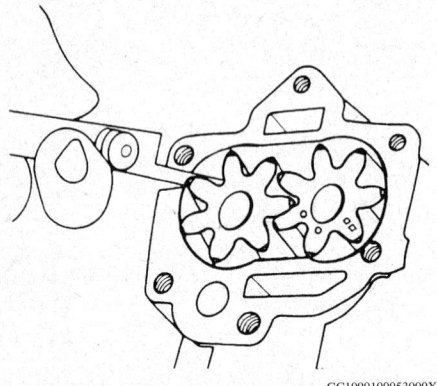

Fig. 15 Gear side clearance measurement

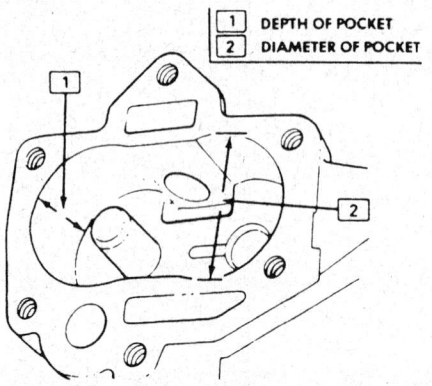

1 DEPTH OF POCKET
2 DIAMETER OF POCKET

Fig. 16 Oil pump gear pocket measurement

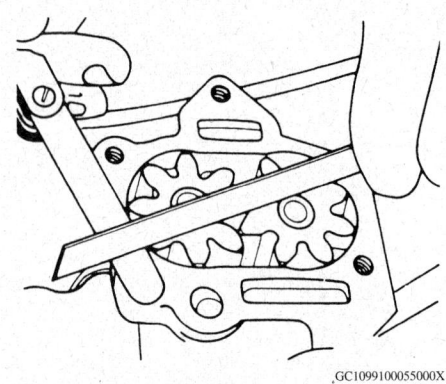

Fig. 17 Oil pump end clearance measurement

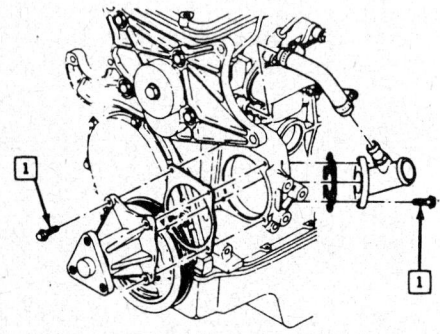

1. BOLT – 25 N·m (18 LBS. FT.)

Fig. 18 Water pump installation

a. Ensure thermostat gasket area is thoroughly clean.
b. Install thermostat with new gasket.
c. Fill and bleed cooling system as required.

WATER PUMP
REPLACE

1. Drain cooling system into suitable container.
2. Loosen water pump pulley mounting bolts.
3. Rotate tensioner clockwise with suitable wrench and slide belt from alternator pulley.
4. Release tensioner and remove belt, **Figs. 3 and 4.**
5. Remove alternator and mounting bracket attaching bolts, then the alternator.
6. Remove mounting bolts and water pump pulley, **Fig. 18.**
7. Remove mounting bolts and water pump.
8. Reverse procedure to install.

RADIATOR
REPLACE

1. Drain and recover engine coolant into

suitable container.
2. Remove hood latch support from mounting plate.
3. Remove both headlamp assemblies.
4. Remove radiator upper mounts.
5. Raise and support vehicle using suitable lift.
6. Disconnect forward discriminating sensor electrical connector.
7. Remove cooling fan.
8. Remove lower radiator hose from radiator.
9. Remove lower transaxle oil cooler line from radiator and lower vehicle.
10. Remove hood latch support bracket and forward discriminating sensor with electrical harness.
11. Disconnect upper transaxle oil cooler line from radiator.
12. Remove upper radiator hose and overflow hose from radiator.
13. Remove condenser from radiator, if equipped.
14. Remove radiator.
15. Reverse procedure to install.

FUEL PUMP
REPLACE

1. Drain fuel tank into suitable container.
2. Raise and support vehicle using suitable lift.
3. Disconnect tank meter harness from body harness connector.
4. Remove ground wire mounting screw from underbody and disconnect hoses from fuel meter.
5. Disconnect hoses at tank from filler and vent pipes.
6. Support fuel tank with jack and disconnect fuel tank mounting straps.
7. Remove tank.
8. Remove fuel tank sending unit and pump by turning cam lock ring counterclockwise. **Sending unit might pop up from its position. Reservoir bucket may be full of fuel.** Tip sending unit slightly to avoid float damage.

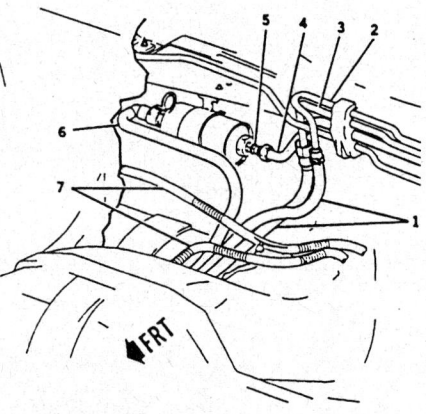

1. HOSE-PART OF FUEL SENDER
2. FUEL VAPOR PIPE
3. FUEL RETURN PIPE
4. FUEL FEED PIPE
5. FUEL FEED PIPE NUT
6. HOSE-PART OF FUEL SENDER
7. ABS AND FUEL SENDER HARNESS

Fig. 19 Fuel filter replacement

9. Lift assembly from fuel tank.
10. Reverse procedure to install.

FUEL FILTER
REPLACE

1. Raise and support vehicle using suitable lift.
2. Remove filter fitting using suitable back-up wrench. If nylon fuel lines become kinked and cannot be straightened, they must be replaced.
3. Twist quick-connect fitting ¼ turn in each direction to loosen dirt within fitting.
4. Clean quick-connect fitting at ends of filter using compressed air.
5. Disconnect quick-connect fittings by squeezing plastic tabs of male end connector and pulling apart.
6. Remove fuel filter, **Fig. 19.**
7. Reverse procedure to install.

TIGHTENING SPECIFICATIONS

Year	Component	Torque/Ft. Lbs.
2001–02	Accelerator Cable Mounting Bracket	90①
	Accessory Bracket	37
	Accessory Drive Belt Idler Pulley	37
	Camshaft Position Sensor To Block	90①
	Camshaft Rear Cover	108①
	Camshaft Sprocket	96
	Camshaft Thrust Plate	108①
	Clutch Cover & Pressure Plate	15④
	Connecting Rod Cap	38
	Crankcase Front Cover	96①
	Crankshaft Main Bearing Cap	70
	Crankshaft Pulley Hub To Crankshaft	77
	Crankshaft Pulley To Hub	37
	Crankshaft Sensor	72①
	Cylinder Head Bolts	③
	Direct Ignition System Coil	18
	EGR Pipe To Adapter	18
	EGR Pipe To Manifold	90①
	EGR Valve Adapter	96①
	EGR Valve Adapter To Cylinder Head Bolts	90①
	EGR Valve To Adapter	19
	Engine Lift Bracket	37
	Engine Mount Cage	33
	Engine Mount To Accessory Bracket	44②
	Engine Mount To Body	55
	Engine Mount Strut	74②
	Engine Mount Strut Bracket (Front)	49
	Engine Mount Strut Bracket (Rear)	44
	Exhaust Manifold	10
	Flexplate Or Flywheel Bolt	55
	Fuel Filter Fitting	20
	Intake Manifold Bolts	17
	Intake Manifold Nuts	17
	Intake Manifold Studs	108①
	Knock Sensor	26
	Large Oil Gallery Plug (Rear Of Engine Block)	24
	Lifter Guide	96①
	Oil Fill Tube	37
	Oil Filter	13
	Oil Filter Adapter	26
	Oil Gallery Plugs (Side Of Block Above Oil Filter)	15
	Oil Pan	90①
	Oil Pump Cover	90①
	Oil Pump Drive	18
	Oil Pump Mounting	32
	Oil Pressure Sensor Switch	108①
	Oxygen Sensor	31
	Rocker Arm	19
	Rocker Arm Cover	90①
	Serpentine Drive Belt Tensioner	37

Continued

TIGHTENING
SPECIFICATIONS—Continued

Year	Component	Torque/Ft. Lbs.
2001–02	Small Oil Gallery Plug (Rear Of Engine Block)	11
	Spark Plugs	13
	Thermostat Housing	10
	Throttle Body To Intake Manifold	90①
	Timing Chain Tensioner	18
	Water Jacket Drain Plug	11
	Water Outlet Pipe	19
	Water Pump	18
	Water Pump Inlet	18
	Water Pump Pulley Bolts	22

① — Inch lbs.
② — Tighten an additional 90°.
③ — Refer to "Cylinder Head, Replace" for tightening sequence and procedure.
④ — Tighten an additional 45°.

2.4L Engine

NOTE: On Air Bag Equipped Models, Refer To "Air Bag System Precautions" Located In The Front Of This Manual For System Disarming & Arming Procedures.

NOTE: Refer To "Computer Relearn Procedures" Located In The Front Of This Manual When Battery Power To The Computer Has Been Interrupted.

NOTE: Refer To "2.4L Engine" in "Alero, Grand Am & Malibu" Chapter For Procedures Not Covered In This Section.

INDEX

PRECAUTIONS

Air Bag Systems

Refer to "Air Bag System Precautions" in the front of this manual for system disarming and arming procedures.

Battery Ground Cable

Prior to service, disconnect battery ground cable and isolate as required.

Fuel System Pressure Relief

1. Raise and support vehicle using suitable lift.
2. Disconnect fuel pump electrical connector.
3. Start engine and run until remaining fuel is consumed.
4. Engage starter for approximately three seconds to ensure relief of any remaining pressure.
5. Disconnect and isolate battery ground cable to avoid possible fuel discharge if any attempt is made to start engine.

COMPRESSION PRESSURE

When inspecting cylinder compression, the throttle should be open, all spark plugs removed and the battery at or near full charge. The lowest reading cylinder should not be less than 70% of the highest and no cylinder reading should be less than 100 psi. Turn ignition key until engine cranks through four compression cycles. Normal compression builds up quickly and evenly to specifications on each cylinder.

ENGINE MOUNT
REPLACE

1. Remove coolant recovery tank mounting bolt and position tank aside.
2. Install engine support tool No. J-28467-360, or equivalent, and raise engine off mount.
3. Remove body to mount mounting nuts, engine bracket to mount bolts and mount.
4. Reverse procedure to install.

ENGINE MOUNT STRUT
REPLACE

1. Raise and support vehicle using a suitable lift.
2. Remove righthand front splash shield.
3. Remove engine mount strut bolts and engine mount strut.
4. Reverse procedure to install.

ENGINE
REPLACE

1. Drain engine coolant into suitable container.

2. **On models equipped with air conditioning,** recover air conditioning refrigerant as outlined in "Air Conditioning" chapter, recover refrigerant and disconnect compressor/condenser hose assembly at compressor.
3. **On all models,** remove lefthand sound insulator and disconnect clutch pushrod from pedal.
4. Disconnect heater hose at thermostat housing and upper radiator hose.
5. Remove air cleaner and coolant fan.
6. Disconnect all vacuum hoses and electrical connectors.
7. Disconnect throttle cable and bracket.
8. Remove power steering rear bracket and power brake vacuum tube as an assembly.
9. Disconnect and position aside power steering pump.
10. Disconnect fuel lines.
11. **On models equipped with automatic transaxle,** disconnect shift cables.
12. **On models equipped with manual transaxle,** disconnect clutch actuator line.
13. **On all models,** remove exhaust manifold and heat shields.
14. Disconnect lower radiator hose, install engine support tool No. J-28467-360, or equivalent, and remove engine mount.
15. Raise and support vehicle, then re-move both front tire and wheel assemblies.
16. Remove righthand side splash shield and radiator air deflector.
17. Remove engine and transaxle mount.
18. Separate ball joints from steering knuckles as outlined in "Front Suspension & Steering" section.
19. Remove suspension supports, crossmember and stabilizer shaft as an assembly.
20. Disconnect air conditioning lines from oil pan.
21. Remove air flywheel housing cover.
22. Position suitable support beneath engine and carefully lower vehicle.
23. Mark threads on support fixture hooks so setting can be duplicated when installing engine.
24. Remove engine support J hooks, then slowly raise vehicle away from engine and transaxle.
25. Reverse procedure to install.

RADIATOR
REPLACE

Refer to "Radiator, Replace" in the "2.2L OHV Engine" section.

TIGHTENING SPECIFICATIONS

Year	Component	Torque/Ft. Lbs.
2001–02	Engine Mount Bracket To Block	44①
	Engine Mount, Front Bolts	49
	Engine Mount, Lower Bolts	96
	Engine Mount To Body, Nuts	55
	Engine Mount Strut, Bolts	74①

① — Tighten an additional 90°.

Rear Axle & Suspension

INDEX

DESCRIPTION

The rear suspension is a semi-independent type consisting of an axle assembly with trailing arms and twisting cross beam, coil springs and coil-over shock absorbers. A stabilizer bar is available and is attached to the inside of the axle beam and to the lower end of the control arms. A single unit hub and bearing assembly is bolted to each end of the axle assembly. The hub and bearing assembly is a sealed, non-serviceable unit and must be replaced as an assembly.

REAR AXLE

REPLACE

1. Raise and support vehicle using suitable lift.
2. Remove rear wheels and tires.
3. Remove brake drums. **Do not hammer on drums.**
4. Remove brake fluid pipe retainer bolts from axle, **Fig. 1.**
5. Disconnect brake pipe at brake hose.
6. Disconnect wheel speed sensor harnesses at sensors.
7. Remove wheel speed sensor harness from retainers on axle.
8. Disconnect parking brake cables from equalizers.
9. Remove parking brake cables from axle.
10. Support rear suspension with suitable jack.
11. Remove shock absorber lower mounting bolts, **Fig. 2.**
12. Remove mounting bolts, washers and nuts from axle.
13. Carefully lower rear axle.
14. Remove control arm to underbody bracket bolts, lower rear axle and remove.
15. Remove hub to rear axle mounting bolts, hubs, bearings and backing plates from rear axle, **Fig. 3.**
16. Reverse procedure to install. Bleed brake system.

HUB & BEARING

REPLACE

1. Raise and support vehicle using suitable lift, then remove wheel and tire assembly.
2. Remove brake drum. **Do not hammer brake drum.**
3. Disconnect wheel speed sensor electrical connector.

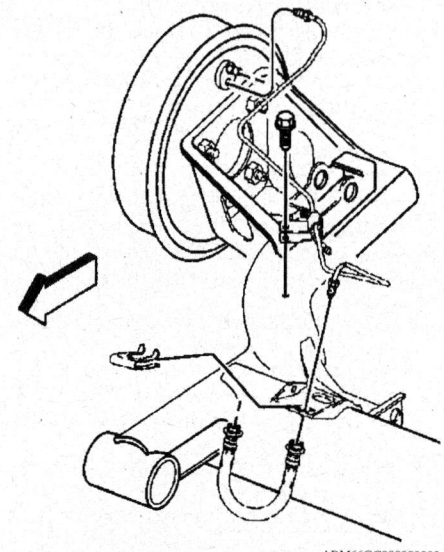

Fig. 1   Brake pipe retainer removal

4. Remove mounting bolts and hub/bearing, **Fig. 4. Upper rear hub mounting bolt may not clear brake shoe when removing hub and bearing. Partially remove hub and bearing prior to removing this bolt.**
5. Reverse procedure to install. **Do not drop hub/bearing assembly.**

SHOCK ABSORBER

REPLACE

1. Raise rear of vehicle and support rear axle using suitable jack.
2. Remove lower mounting bolt, disconnect shock absorber from mounting bracket, **Fig. 5.**
3. Reverse procedure to install.

CONTROL ARM BUSHING

REPLACE

Remove and install one control arm bushing at a time.
1. Raise and support vehicle using suitable jack.
2. Support rear axle with suitable jack.
3. Remove wheels and tires.
4. If replacing righthand bushings, disconnect brake fluid lines at body.
5. If replacing lefthand bushings, discon-

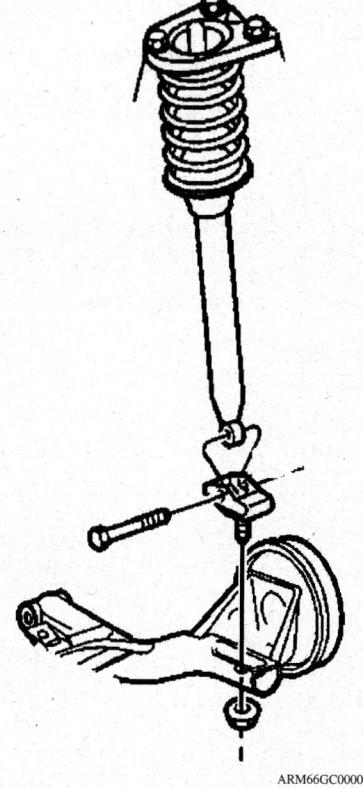

Fig. 2   Lower shock absorber bolt removal

nect brake fluid line bracket from body and parking brake cable from guide hook on body.
6. Remove control arm to body nut, bolt and washer, then rotate control arm downward. **Do not allow axle to hang by brake hose.**
7. Reverse procedure to complete installation, noting the following:
   a. Arrow on installer must align with arrow on receiver, **Fig. 6.**
   b. Apply high pressure lubricant No. J-23444-A, or equivalent, as required.
   c. When bushing reaches its proper position end flange will sit flush against control arm face.
   d. Ensure bushing washer and nut are installed on outboard side.
   e. **Control arm mounting bolt must be tightened after vehicle is lowered to floor and is in its standing height position.**

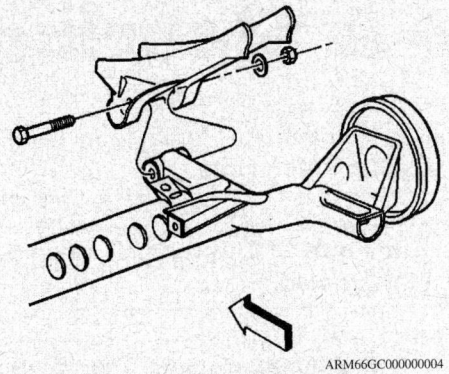

ARM66GC000000004

Fig. 3 Rear axle assembly removal

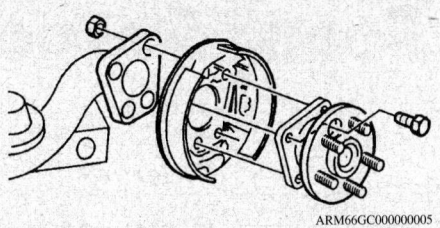

ARM66GC000000005

Fig. 4 Hub & bearing removal

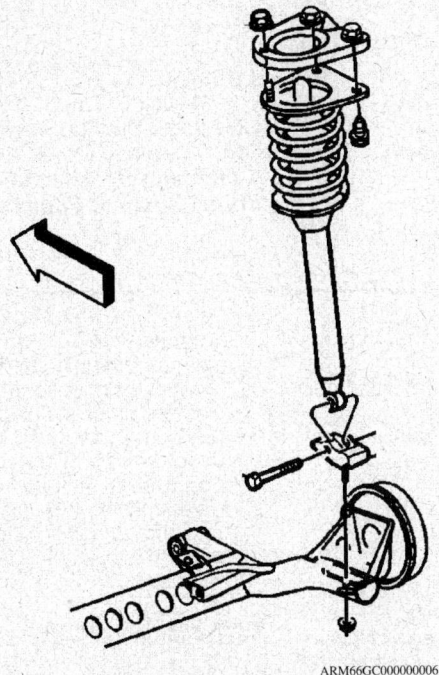

ARM66GC000000006

Fig. 5 Shock absorber removal

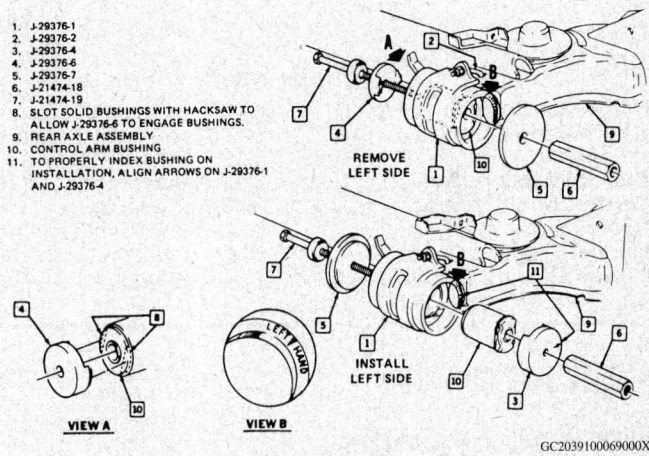

1. J-29376-1
2. J-29376-2
3. J-29376-4
4. J-29376-6
5. J-29376-7
6. J-21474-18
7. J-21474-19
8. SLOT SOLID BUSHINGS WITH HACKSAW TO ALLOW J-29376-6 TO ENGAGE BUSHINGS.
9. REAR AXLE ASSEMBLY
10. CONTROL ARM BUSHING
11. TO PROPERLY INDEX BUSHING ON INSTALLATION, ALIGN ARROWS ON J-29376-1 AND J-29376-4

GC2039100069000X

Fig. 6 Control arm bushing replacement

TIGHTENING SPECIFICATIONS

Year	Component	Torque/Ft. Lbs.
2001–05	Brake Pipe Retainer Bolts To Rear Axle	50①
	Brake Pipe To Bracket Hose	20
	Control Arm Nuts	52
	Hub & Bearing Axle Bolts	44
	Rear Axle Mounting Bolts	88
	Shock Absorber Lower Mounting Bolt	52
	Shock Absorber Upper Mounting Nut	18

① — Inch lbs.

Front Suspension & Steering

NOTE: On Air Bag Equipped Models, Refer To "Air Bag System Precautions" Located In The Front Of This Manual For System Disarming & Arming Procedures.

NOTE: Refer To "Computer Relearn Procedures" Located In The Front Of This Manual When Battery Power To The Computer Has Been Interrupted.

NOTE: Prior To Performing Any Service Operations Listed In This Section, Consult The "Technical Service Bulletins" Section For Related Information.

INDEX

PRECAUTIONS
Air Bag Systems

Refer to "Air Bag System Precautions" in the front of this manual for system disarming and arming procedures.

Battery Ground Cable

Prior to service, disconnect battery ground cable and isolate as required.

DESCRIPTION

The front suspension on these models is a combination strut and spring design. The control arms pivot from the crossmember, **Fig. 1.** The upper end of the strut is isolated by a rubber mount incorporating a non-serviceable bearing for wheel turning. On base models the lower control arm pivots have conventional rubber bushings. Upgraded models have a cross axis bearing rather than bushings. The tie rods connect to the steering arm on the strut, below the spring seat. The lower end of the steering knuckle pivots on a ball stud which is retained to the lower control arm by rivets and is secured to the steering knuckle with a nut and cotter pin. The sealed wheel bearings are integral with the hub and are serviced as an assembly.

WHEEL BEARING
REPLACE

1. Raise and support vehicle using suitable lift.
2. Remove tire and wheel assemblies.
3. Remove drive axle nut, **Fig. 2.**
4. Remove brake caliper and rotor assembly.
5. Remove hub and bearing assembly, **Fig. 3.**
6. Reverse procedure to install.

BALL JOINT INSPECTION

1. Raise and support vehicle so suspension is allowed to hang free.
2. Grasp wheel and tire assembly at top and bottom, then rock top of wheel and tire assembly inward and outward.
3. While rocking wheel and tire assembly, observe movement between steering knuckle and control arm. If any horizontal movement is present, replace ball joint.
4. If ball joint is disconnected from steering knuckle, use hand to try to twist ball joint in its socket. If ball joint can be twisted in its socket, replace ball joint.

BALL JOINT
REPLACE
Removal

1. Raise and support vehicle using suitable lift, then remove wheel and tire.
2. Remove stabilizer link nut from stabilizer link bolt.
3. Remove wiring harness from lower control arm.
4. Remove ball joint cotter pin.
5. Remove ball joint stud mounting nut.
6. Remove ball joint from steering knuckle using ball joint separator tool No. J43828, or equivalent.

7. Remove lower control arm front and rear mounting bolts, **Fig. 4.**
8. Remove lower control arm from vehicle and place in a suitable vice, **Fig. 4.**
9. Drill out three rivets retaining ball joint to lower control arm. Install a 1/8 inch bit in order to make a pilot hole through rivets. Complete drilling rivets using suitable 1/2 drill bit, **Fig. 4.**
10. Remove ball joint from control arm, **Fig. 4.**

Installation

1. Install ball joint into control arm, **Fig. 5.**
2. Install three ball joint bolts and nuts, tighten ball joint bolts, **Fig. 5.**
3. Install lower control arm to front suspension support, **Fig. 6.**
4. Install lower control arm front and rear mounting bolts, **Fig. 6.**
5. Install lower ball joint stud to steering knuckle, **Fig. 7.**
6. Install ball joint stud through steering knuckle.
7. Install and tighten ball joint nut.
8. Install wiring harness to lower control arm and install cotter pin.
9. Install stabilizer link to lower control arm.
10. Install tire and wheel assemblies.
11. Inspect front wheel alignment.

STRUT
REPLACE

1. Remove strut assembly attaching nuts and bolts to body, **Fig. 8.**
2. Raise and support vehicle using suitable lift, install suitable jackstand under crossmember, then lower vehicle for weight to rest slightly on jackstand.

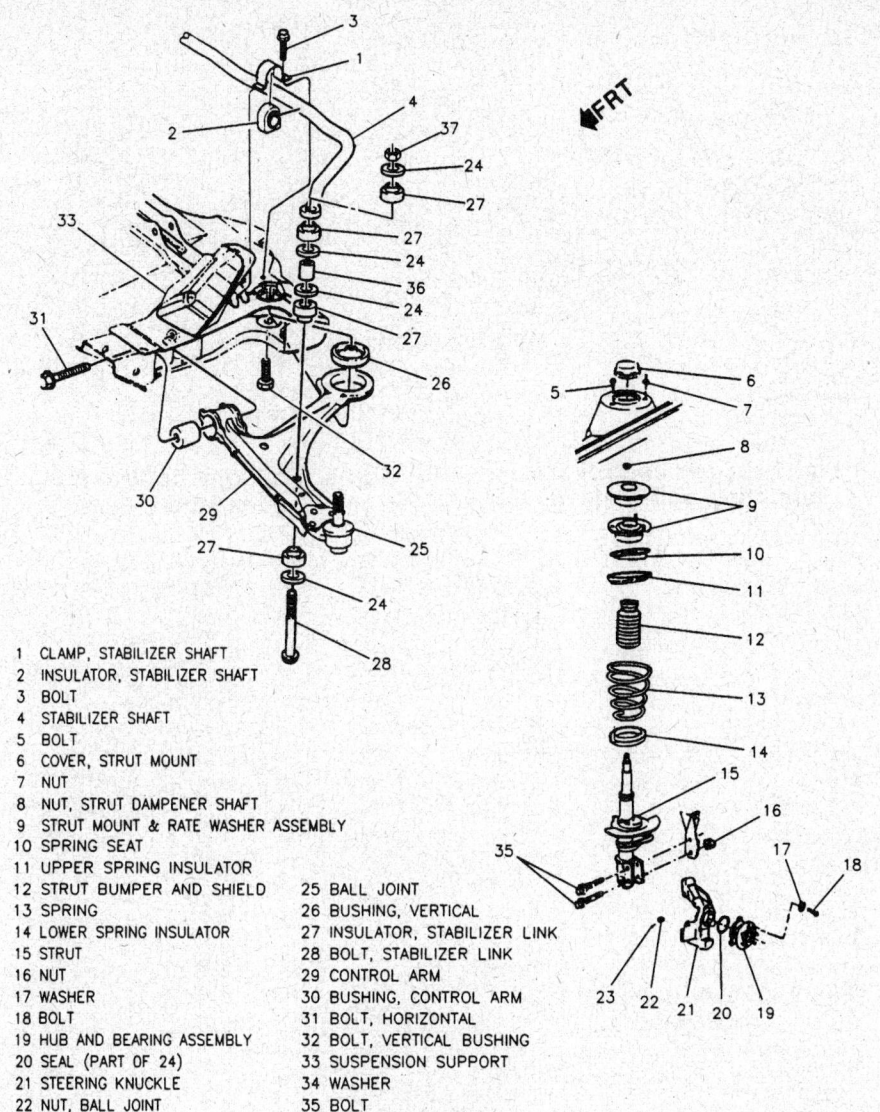

Fig. 1 Exploded view of front suspension

1 CLAMP, STABILIZER SHAFT
2 INSULATOR, STABILIZER SHAFT
3 BOLT
4 STABILIZER SHAFT
5 BOLT
6 COVER, STRUT MOUNT
7 NUT
8 NUT, STRUT DAMPENER SHAFT
9 STRUT MOUNT & RATE WASHER ASSEMBLY
10 SPRING SEAT
11 UPPER SPRING INSULATOR
12 STRUT BUMPER AND SHIELD
13 SPRING
14 LOWER SPRING INSULATOR
15 STRUT
16 NUT
17 WASHER
18 BOLT
19 HUB AND BEARING ASSEMBLY
20 SEAL (PART OF 24)
21 STEERING KNUCKLE
22 NUT, BALL JOINT
23 COTTER PIN
24 WASHER
25 BALL JOINT
26 BUSHING, VERTICAL
27 INSULATOR, STABILIZER LINK
28 BOLT, STABILIZER LINK
29 CONTROL ARM
30 BUSHING, CONTROL ARM
31 BOLT, HORIZONTAL
32 BOLT, VERTICAL BUSHING
33 SUSPENSION SUPPORT
34 WASHER
35 BOLT
36 SPACER, STABILIZER LINK
37 NUT, STABILIZER LINK

GC2029600214000A

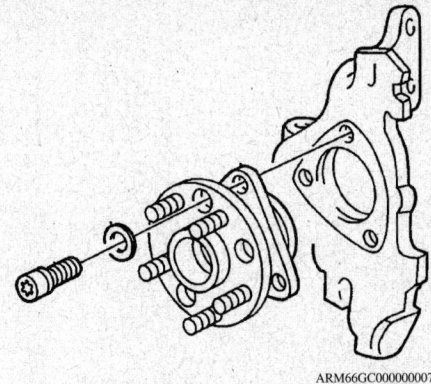

ARM66GC000000007

Fig. 2 Drive axle nut removal

spect inner tie rod shaft for bending or damaged threads.
6. Disconnect ABS wiring harness connector.
7. Remove hub and bearing assembly as outlined in "Wheel Bearing, Replace."
8. Remove steering knuckle to strut bolts and nuts, **Fig. 13.**
9. Remove lower ball joint from steering knuckle.
10. Remove steering knuckle assembly.
11. Reverse procedure to install.

STABILIZER BAR
REPLACE
2001

1. Raise and support vehicle using suitable lift, allowing control arms to hang freely.
2. Remove front wheels and tires.
3. Remove stabilizer shaft links.
4. Support front suspension support with suitable jack.
5. Remove suspension support rear, center and front mounting bolts in order.
6. Lower front suspension support to ease shaft removal.
7. Disconnect stabilizer bar at control arms and control arm supports, **Fig. 14.**
8. Remove stabilizer bar with insulators.
9. Reverse procedure to install.

2002-05

1. Raise and support vehicle using suitable lift.
2. Remove front tire and wheel assemblies.
3. Reposition intermediate steering shaft seal in order to gain access to lower pinch bolt, then remove lower pinch bolt.
4. Remove stabilizer link nut from stabilizer link bolt, then the stabilizer link bolt, insulator and spacer.
5. Support front suspension crossmember using suitable jack stand.
6. Remove suspension crossmember attaching bolts, then lower crossmember six inches using support jack stands.
7. Remove stabilizer shaft insulator brackets and retaining bolts.

3. Remove tire and wheel assembly.
4. Remove brake line bracket.
5. Scribe strut flange using suitable sharp tool.
6. Remove steering knuckle attaching nuts and bolts to strut assembly, **Fig. 9.**
7. Remove strut assembly.
8. Reverse procedure to install. Inspect alignment.

CONTROL ARM
REPLACE

1. Raise and support vehicle using suitable lift.
2. Remove tire and wheel assemblies.
3. Remove stabilizer shaft link bolt, insulator and spacer.
4. On righthand lower control arm, remove engine mount strut bolts, then the engine mount, **Fig. 10.**
5. On lefthand lower control arm, remove

front suspension support brace bolts, then the brace, **Fig. 11.**
6. Remove ball joint from steering knuckle as outlined in "Ball Joint, Replace."
7. Remove wiring harness.
8. Remove lower control arm mounting bolts.
9. Remove lower control arm from suspension crossmember, **Fig. 12.**
10. Reverse procedure to install.

STEERING KNUCKLE
REPLACE

1. Raise and support vehicle using suitable lift.
2. Remove tire and wheel assemblies.
3. Remove attaching nut from outer tie rod ball stud, loosen jam nut.
4. Remove outer tie rod ball stud from steering knuckle using J 24319-B, or equivalent.
5. Remove tie rod end from shaft, then in-

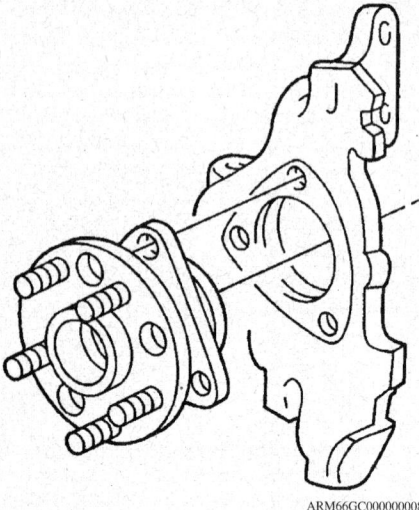

Fig. 3 Hub & bearing assembly removal

ARM66GC000000008

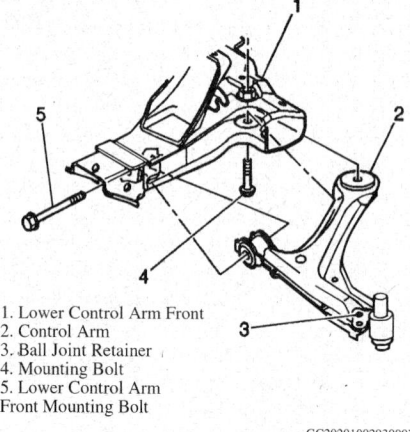

1. Lower Control Arm Front
2. Control Arm
3. Ball Joint Retainer
4. Mounting Bolt
5. Lower Control Arm Front Mounting Bolt

GC2020100293000X

Fig. 4 Lower control arm mounting bolt removal

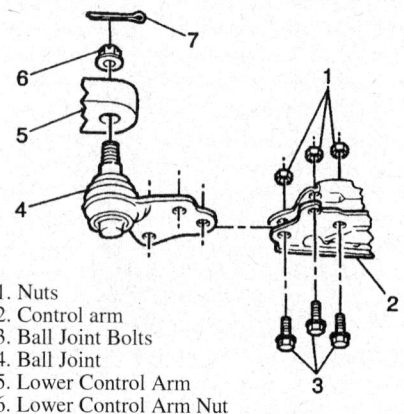

1. Nuts
2. Control arm
3. Ball Joint Bolts
4. Ball Joint
5. Lower Control Arm
6. Lower Control Arm Nut

GC2020100294000X

Fig. 5 Ball joint control arm installation

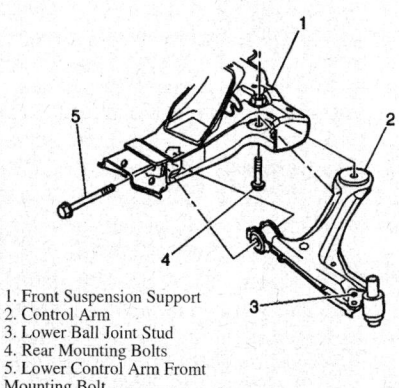

1. Front Suspension Support
2. Control Arm
3. Lower Ball Joint Stud
4. Rear Mounting Bolts
5. Lower Control Arm Fromt Mounting Bolt

GC2020100295000X

Fig. 6 Lower control arm to front suspension installation

8. Remove stabilizer shaft assembly.
9. Reverse procedure to install.

POWER STEERING GEAR

REPLACE

Automatic Transaxle

1. Raise and support vehicle.
2. Remove front tires and wheels.
3. Remove righthand and lefthand splash shields.
4. Remove engine strut from lower engine mount and frame.
5. Remove front exhaust pipe.
6. Disconnect ABS wiring harness from wheel speed sensor and body.
7. Remove steering column lower pinch bolt at steering gear.
8. Separate ball joint from knuckle using ball joint separator tool No. J-43828, or equivalent.
9. Disconnect tie rods from knuckles using universal steering linkage puller tool No. J-24319-01, or equivalent.

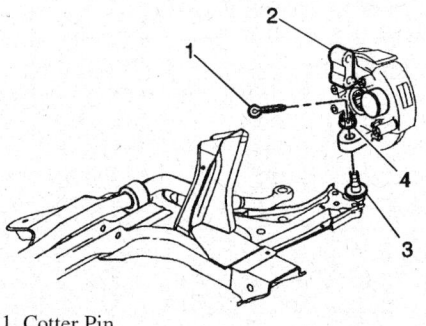

1. Cotter Pin
2. Steering Knuckle
3. Lower Ball Joint Stud
4. Lower Ball Joint Stud Nut

GC2020100296000X

Fig. 7 Lower ball joint stud installation

10. Remove brake fluid lines from frame retainers.
11. Disconnect power steering hoses from steering gear.
12. Remove front suspension support brace.
13. Lower vehicle until front suspension support brace rests on jack stands.
14. Remove front suspension support mounting bolts.
15. Raise vehicle up from front suspension support.
16. Remove steering gear to suspension support mounting bolts and gear.
17. Reverse procedure to install.

Manual Transaxle

1. Raise and support vehicle.
2. Remove front tires and wheels.
3. Remove power steering hoses from steering gear.
4. Disconnect tie rods from knuckles using universal steering linkage puller tool No. J-24319-01, or equivalent.
5. Remove brake fluid lines from frame retainers.
6. Remove steering column lower pinch bolt at steering gear.
7. Support front suspension support with suitable jack stand.

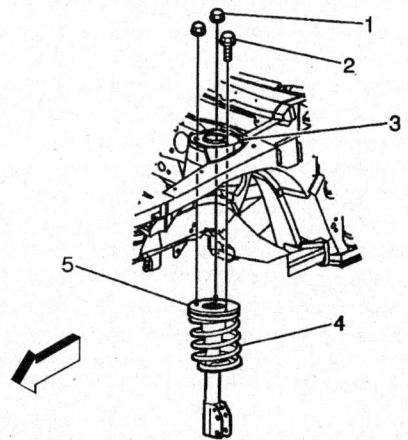

1. Attaching Nuts
2. Attaching Bolts
3. Body
4. Strut Spring
5. Strut Assembly

GC2020100297000X

Fig. 8 Strut assembly removal

8. Remove front suspension crossmember mounting bolts.
9. Lower suspension enough to access steering gear mounting bolts.
10. Remove mounting bolts and steering gear.
11. Reverse procedure to install.

POWER STEERING PUMP

REPLACE

1. **On models equipped with 2.2L engine,** remove EVAP purge valve.
2. **On all models,** remove power steering fluid lines.
3. Remove power steering pump mounting bolts.
4. Remove pump and transfer pulley, if required.
5. Reverse procedure to install.

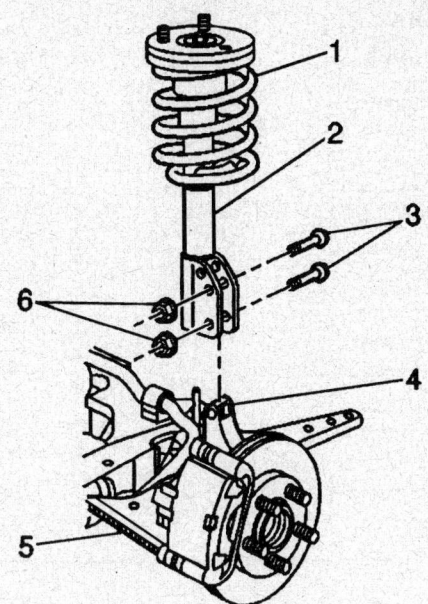

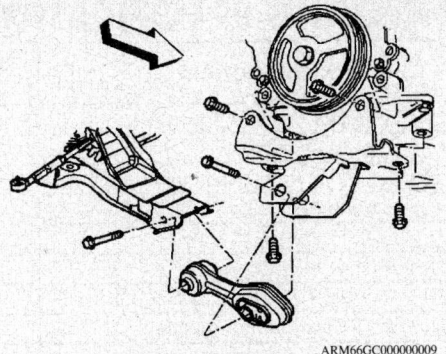

Fig. 10 Righthand lower control arm removal

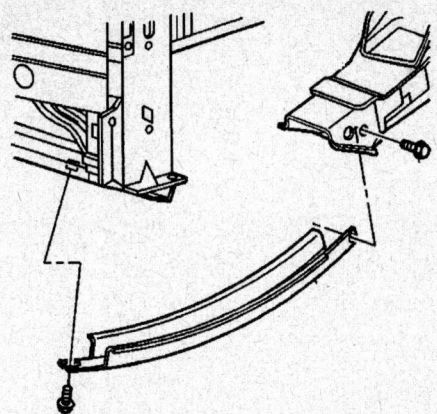

Fig. 11 Lefthand lower control arm & support brace removal

1. Strut Assebly
2. Strut Shaft
3. Strut Attaching Bolts
4. Steering Knuckle
5. Brake Line
6. Strut Attaching Nuts

GC2020100298000X

Fig. 9 Strut to steering knuckle removal

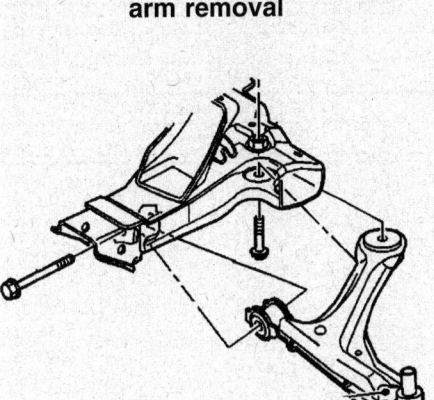

Fig. 12 Lower control arm to front suspension crossmember

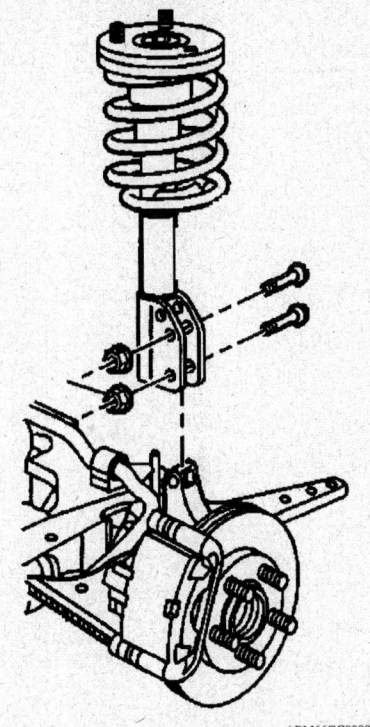

Fig. 13 Steering knuckle to strut removal

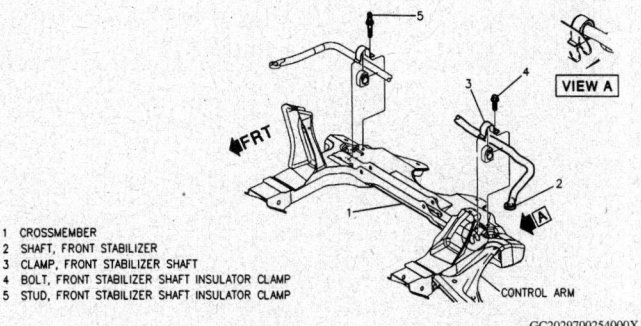

1 CROSSMEMBER
2 SHAFT, FRONT STABILIZER
3 CLAMP, FRONT STABILIZER SHAFT
4 BOLT, FRONT STABILIZER SHAFT INSULATOR CLAMP
5 STUD, FRONT STABILIZER SHAFT INSULATOR CLAMP

GC2029700254000X

Fig. 14 Stabilizer bar removal. 2001

TIGHTENING SPECIFICATIONS

Year	Component	Torque/Ft. Lbs.
2001–05	Ball Joint To Knuckle	41–50
	Caliper	38
	Control Arm To Crossmember, Front	79
	Control Arm To Crossmember, Rear	125
	Hub & Bearing	70
	Hub Nut	185
	Stabilizer Shaft To Control Arm	13
	Stabilizer To Support	49
	Steering Column Pinch Bolt	16
	Steering Knuckle To Strut	133
	Strut To Body	18
	Strut Piston	34
	Tie Rod Jam Nuts	50
	Tie Rod Stud Nuts	33
	Wheel Lugnuts	100

Wheel Alignment

INDEX

PRELIMINARY INSPECTION

1. Ensure all tires are of recommended size and are inflated to proper pressure.
2. Inspect all tires for damage and uneven tread wear.
3. Ensure wheel bearings, control arm ball studs and bushings, relay rods and tie rod ends are in satisfactory condition. Looseness must be corrected before wheels can be aligned.
4. Inspect wheel and tire radial and lateral runout, as follows:
   a. With wheel and tire assembly off vehicle, runout should be approximately .050 inch.
   b. When on vehicle, runout should be approximately .060 inch.
5. If wheel and tire assembly runout specifications cannot be met, separate tire from wheel and measure wheel runout. Wheel runout should be approximately .030 inch.
6. Inspect vehicle ride height as outlined in "Vehicle Ride Height" in "Specifications." If corrections are required, complete them prior to setting wheel alignment.
7. Ensure steering gear is not loose at frame mounting.
8. Inspect stabilizer shafts for loose or missing components.
9. Ensure struts and shocks are not leaking or excessively worn and strut upper mounts are in satisfactory condition.
10. Inspect all remaining suspension and steering components for damage and repair or replace prior to setting wheel alignment.
11. Ensure fuel tank is full or compensating ballast is added for proper weight distribution.
12. Ensure vehicle is on level surface and all loads that are normally carried inside vehicle are present.
13. Jounce front and rear of vehicle three times before beginning wheel alignment procedures.

FRONT WHEEL ALIGNMENT

Caster

Caster is not adjustable. If caster angle is not within specifications, inspect for suspension support misalignment or front suspension damage.

Camber

Toe setting is the only adjustment normally required. However, in special circumstances, such as damage because of road hazard or collision, camber may be adjusted by modifying the strut. Proceed as follows:

1. Mount strut bottom in suitable vise.
2. Enlarge bottom holes in outer flanges with round file until holes in outer flanges match slots in inner flanges, **Fig. 1.**
3. Connect strut to steering knuckle and install bolts hand tight.
4. Grasp top of tire firmly and move tire inboard or outboard until proper camber reading is obtained. Tighten mounting bolts enough to secure camber setting.
5. Remove wheel and tire. **Torque** strut to steering knuckle mounting bolt to 133 ft. lbs.

Toe

Toe-out is controlled by tie rod position. Adjustment is made by loosening the clamp bolts or jam nuts at the steering knuckle end of the tie rods and rotating the rods to obtain proper toe setting, **Fig. 2.** After proper toe setting is obtained, **torque** mounting nuts and bolts to 50 ft. lbs.

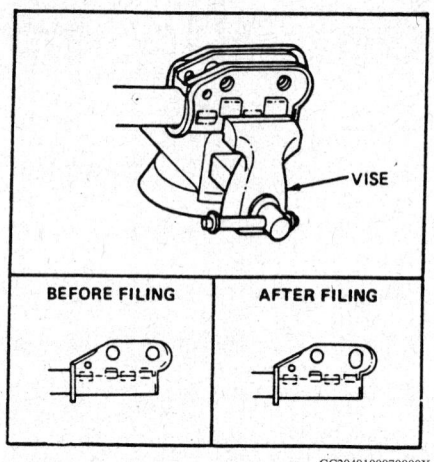

Fig. 1 Strut bracket modification for camber adjustment

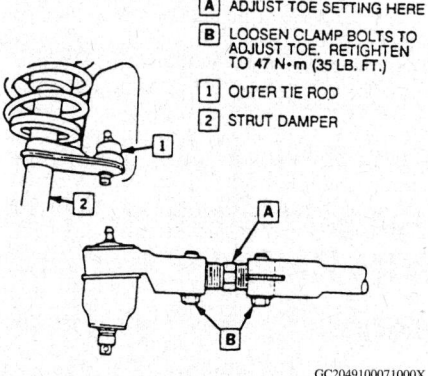

Fig. 2 Typical toe adjustment

CENTURY, GRAND PRIX, IMPALA, INTRIGUE, LACROSSE, LUMINA, MONTE CARLO & REGAL

NOTE: Refer To Rear Of This Manual For Vehicle Manufacturer's Special Service Tool Suppliers.

INDEX OF SERVICE OPERATIONS

Specifications

GENERAL ENGINE SPECIFICATIONS

Year	Engine		Fuel System	Bore & Stroke	Compression Ratio	Net H.P. @ RPM[3]	Maximum Torque Ft. Lbs. @ RPM	Normal Oil Pressure, psi
	Displacement	VIN Code[2]						
2001	3.1L	M	SFI	3.50 × 3.31	9.5	160 @ 5200	185 @ 4000	15[5]
	3.4L	E	SFI	3.62 × 3.31	9.5	180 @ 5200	205 @ 4000	15[5]
	3.5L	H	SFI	3.52 × 3.62	9.3	215 @ 5600	234 @ 4400	[6]
	3.8L[1]	1	SFI	3.80 × 3.40	8.5	240 @ 5200	280 @ 3200	60[4]
	3.8L	K	SFI	3.80 × 3.40	9.4	200 @ 5200	220 @ 4000	60[4]
2002	3.1L	J	SFI	3.50 × 3.31	9.6	175 @ 5200	195 @ 4000	15[5]
	3.4L	E	SFI	3.62 × 3.31	9.5	180 @ 5200	205 @ 4000	15[5]
	3.5L	H	SFI	3.52 × 3.62	9.3	215 @ 5600	234 @ 4400	[6]
	3.8L[1]	1	SFI	3.80 × 3.40	8.5	240 @ 5200	280 @ 3200	60[4]
	3.8L	K	SFI	3.80 × 3.40	9.4	200 @ 5200	220 @ 4000	60[4]
2003–04	3.1L	J	SFI	3.50 × 3.31	9.6	175 @ 5200	195 @ 4000	15[5]
	3.4L	E	SFI	3.62 × 3.31	9.5	180 @ 5200	205 @ 4000	15[5]
	3.8L[1]	1	SFI	3.80 × 3.40	8.5	240 @ 5200	280 @ 3200	60[4]
	3.8L	K	SFI	3.80 × 3.40	9.4	200 @ 5200	220 @ 4000	60[4]
2005	3.1L	J	SFI	3.50 × 3.31	9.6	175 @ 5200	195 @ 4000	60[7]
	3.4L	E	SFI	3.62 × 3.31	9.6	180 @ 5200	205 @ 4000	60[7]
	3.6L	7	SFI	3.70 x 3.37	10.2	240 @ 6000	230 @ 3200	[8]
	3.8L[1]	1	SFI	3.80 × 3.40	8.5	240 @ 5200	280 @ 3600	60[4]
	3.8L	K	SFI	3.80 × 3.40	9.4	200 @ 5200	225 @ 4000	60[4]

SFI — Sequential-Port Fuel Injection

① — Supercharged engine.

② — The eighth digit of the VIN denotes engine code.

③ — Ratings are net as installed in vehicle.

④ — At 1850 RPM, engine at operating temperature using 10W-30 engine oil.

⑤ — Minimum @ 1100 RPM, engine at operating temperature.

⑥ — 35 psi @ 600 RPM, 80 psi @ 3600 RPM.

⑦ — At 1850 RPM, engine at operating temperature using 5W-30 engine oil.

⑧ — Minimum at idle speed, 10 psi; minimum at 2000 RPM, 20 psi.

TUNE UP SPECIFICATIONS

| Year, Engine & VIN Code① | Spark Plug Gap, Inch | Ignition Timing | | | Curb Idle Speed② | Fast Idle Speed | Fuel Pump Pressure, Psi | Valve Clearance, Inch |
		Firing Order Fig.③	°BTDC	Mark Fig.				
2001								
3.1L	.060	⑩	④	⑤	⑥	⑥	41–47⑦	⑪
3.4L	.060	⑩	④	⑤	⑥	⑤	41–47⑦	⑪
3.5L	.050	⑨	④	⑤	⑥	⑥	48–55⑦	⑪
3.8L (K)	.060	⑧	④	⑤	⑥	⑥	48–55⑦	⑪
3.8L (1)	.060	⑧	④	⑤	⑥	⑥	48–55⑦	⑪
2002								
3.1L	.060	⑩	④	⑤	⑥	⑥	52–59⑦	⑪
3.4L	.060	⑩	④	⑤	⑥	⑤	41–47⑦	⑪
3.5L	.050	⑨	④	⑤	⑥	⑥	48–55⑦	⑪
3.8L (K)	.060	⑧	④	⑤	⑥	⑥	53–59⑦	⑪
3.8L (1)	.060	⑧	④	⑤	⑥	⑥	48–54⑦	⑪
2003–04								
3.1L	.060	⑩	④	⑤	⑥	⑥	52–59⑦	⑪
3.4L	.060	⑩	④	⑤	⑥	⑤	41–47⑦	⑪
3.8L (K)	.060	⑧	④	⑤	⑥	⑥	53–59⑦	⑪
3.8L (1)	.060	⑧	④	⑤	⑥	⑥	48–54⑦	⑪
2005								
3.1L	.060	⑩	④	⑤	⑥	⑥	52–59⑦	⑪
3.4L	.060	⑩	④	⑤	⑥	⑥	52–59⑦	⑪
3.6L	.043	⑨	④	⑤	⑥	⑥	55–60⑦	⑪
3.8L (K)	.060	⑧	④	⑤	⑥	⑥	53–59⑦	⑪
3.8L (1)	.060	⑧	④	⑤	⑥	⑥	53–59⑦	⑪

BTDC — Before Top Dead Center

① — The eighth digit of Vehicle Identification Number (VIN) denotes engine code.

② — Idle speed is adjusted in Drive. When adjusting idle speed, set parking brake & block drive wheels. Where two idle speeds are listed, the higher speed is w/the idle or A/C solenoid energized.

③ — Note ignition wire locations before disconnecting from ignition coil.

④ — Computer controlled, no adjustment.

⑤ — Equipped w/crankshaft position sensor.

⑥ — Idle speed is controlled by an idle air control (IAC) valve or idle speed control (ISC) motor.

⑦ — Loosen fuel tank filler cap to relieve fuel vapor pressure. With shop towel wrapped around fuel pressure valve to prevent fuel spillage, connect a suitable fuel pressure gauge to fuel pressure valve. Inspect fuel pressure w/ignition switch On, engine not running.

⑧ — Cylinder numbering as viewed from front of vehicle, front bank, 1, 3, 5; rear bank, 2, 4, 6. Firing order 1-6-5-4-3-2. Refer to **Fig. B**, for spark plug wire connections at coil unit.

⑨ — Cylinder numbering lefthand to righthand as viewed from front of vehicle: front bank, 2, 4, 6; rear bank, 1, 3, 5. Firing order: 1-2-3-4-5-6.

⑩ — Cylinder numbering lefthand to righthand as viewed from front of vehicle: front bank, 2, 4, 6; rear bank, 1, 3, 5. Firing order: 1-2-3-4-5-6. Refer to **Fig. A**, for spark plug wire connections at coil unit.

⑪ — Equipped w/hydraulic valve lash adjusters. There is no provision for valve lash adjustment. If valve lash exists, inspect for excessive pushrod & rocker arm wear & for an inoperative lifter.

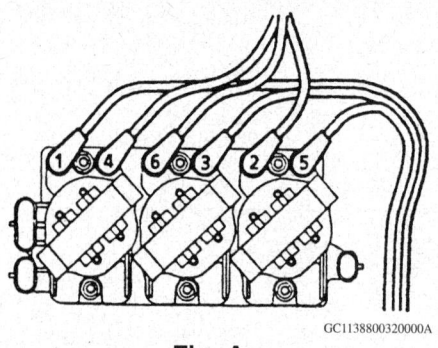

GC1138800320000A

Fig. A

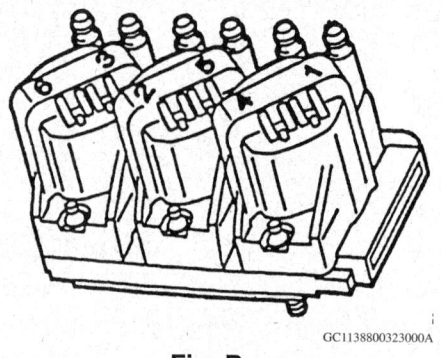

GC1138800323000A

Fig. B

FRONT WHEEL ALIGNMENT SPECIFICATIONS

Year	Model	Caster Angle, Degrees①		Camber Angle, Degrees		Toe-In, Degrees	Steering Angle, Degrees		Ball Joint Wear
		Limits	Desired	Limits	Desired		Limits	Desired	
2001	Century, Grand Prix, Intrigue, Lumina & Regal	+2.5 to +3.5	+3.0	−1.40 to −.40	−.90	−.1 to +.3	−3.5 to +3.5	0	.125 Inch②③④
	Impala	+2.7 to +3.7	+3.2	−1.28 to −.28	−.78	−.1 to +.3	−3.5 to +3.5	0	.125 Inch②③④
	Monte Carlo	+2.7 to +3.7	+3.2	−1.35 to −.35	−.85	−.1 to +.3	−3.5 to +3.5	0	.125 Inch②③④
2002	Century, Grand Prix, Intrigue & Regal	+2.5 to +3.5	+3.0	−1.40 to −.40	−.90	−.1 to +.3	−3.5 to +3.5	0	.125 Inch②③④
	Impala	+2.7 to +3.7	+3.2	−1.28 to −.28	−.78	−.1 to +.3	−3.5 to +3.5	0	.125 Inch②③④
	Monte Carlo	+2.7 to +3.7	+3.2	−1.35 to −.35	−.85	−.1 to +.3	−3.5 to +3.5	0	.125 Inch②③④
2003	Century, Grand Prix & Regal	+2.5 to +3.5	+3.0	−1.40 to −.40	−.90	−.1 to +.3	−3.5 to +3.5	0	.125 Inch②③④
	Impala	+2.7 to +3.7	+3.2	−1.28 to −.28	−.78	−.1 to +.3	−3.5 to +3.5	0	.125 Inch②③④
	Monte Carlo	+2.7 to +3.7	+3.2	−1.35 to −.35	−.85	−.1 to +.3	−3.5 to +3.5	0	.125 Inch②③④
2004	Century	+2.49 to +3.49	+2.99	−1.32 to −.32	−.82	−.1 to +.3	−3.5 to +3.5	0	.125 Inch③④
	Grand Prix	+3.57 to +2.57	+3.07	−1.44 to −.44	−.94	−.1 to +.3	−3.5 to +3.5	0	.125 Inch③④
	Impala	+2.7 to +3.7	+3.2	−1.28 to −.28	−.78	−.1 to +.3	−3.5 to +3.5	0	.125 Inch③④
	Monte Carlo	+2.7 to +3.7	+3.2	−1.35 to −.35	−.85	−.1 to +.3	−3.5 to +3.5	0	.125 Inch③④
	Regal	+2.54 to +3.54	+3.04	−1.40 to −.40	−.90	−.1 to +.3	−3.5 to +3.5	0	.125 Inch③④
2005	Century	+2.25 to +3.75	+3.00	−1.65 to −.15	−.90	−.1 to +.3	−3.5 to +3.5	0	.125 Inch③④
	Grand Prix (GT1, GT2)	+2.05 to +3.55	+2.80	−1.55 to −.05	−.80	−.1 to +.3	−3.5 to +3.5	0	.125 Inch③④
	Grand Prix (GTP)	+2.10 to +3.60	+2.85	−1.75 to −.25	−1.00	−.1 to +.3	−3.5 to +3.5	0	.125 Inch③④
	Impala	+2.25 to +3.75	+3.00	−1.50 to 0	−.75	−.1 to +.3	−3.5 to +3.5	0	.125 Inch③④
	LaCrosse	+2.25 to +3.75	+3.00	−1.55 to −.05	−.80	−.1 to +.3	−3.5 to +3.5	0	.125 Inch③④
	Monte Carlo	+2.25 to +3.75	+3.00	−1.65 to −.10	−.85	−.1 to +.3	−3.5 to +3.5	0	.125 Inch③④

① — Not Adjustable.

② — Support vehicle by wheels to insure weight loading is on ball joints. Wear in ball joints is indicated by .5 inch diameter nipple which retracts into joint cover as joint wears. If nipple is flush with or below joint cover, **Fig. A**, replace ball joint.

③ — Radial play, position suitable dial indicator against wheel rim. Pry between steering knuckle & lower control arm while noting dial indicator reading. If vertical reading exceeds specification, replace ball joint. If seal is torn or cut, if looseness is discovered when ball joint is disconnected from knuckle, or if stud can be twisted in its socket

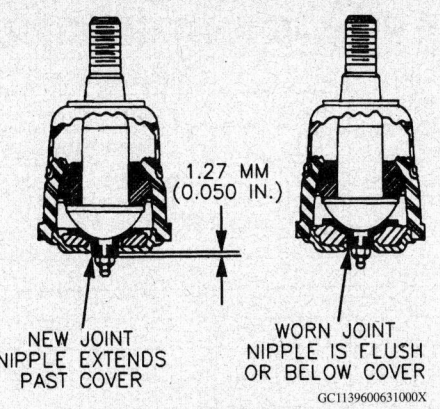

1.27 MM (0.050 IN.)

NEW JOINT NIPPLE EXTENDS PAST COVER

WORN JOINT NIPPLE IS FLUSH OR BELOW COVER

GC1139600631000X

Fig. A

with finger pressure, that ball joint should be replaced.

④ — Axial play, position suitable dial indicator against lowest outboard point on wheel rim. Push inward at top of tire while pulling outward at bottom of tire, while noting dial indicator reading. Reverse push & pull motion, while noting dial indicator reading. If horizontal reading exceeds specification, replace ball joint. If seal is torn or cut, if looseness is discovered when ball joint is disconnected from knuckle, or if stud can be twisted in its socket with finger pressure, ball joint should be replaced.

REAR WHEEL ALIGNMENT SPECIFICATIONS

Year	Model	Camber Angle, Degrees		Total Toe, Degrees	Thrust Angle, Degrees	
		Limits	Desired		Limits	Desired
2001	Century	−1.40 to −.40	−.90	0	−.15 to +.15	0
	Impala	−.50 to −.50	0	+.10	−.15 to +.15	0
	Intrigue	−1.10 to −.10	−.60	+.10	−.15 to +.15	0
	Lumina	−.65 to +.35	−.15	+.10	−.15 to +.15	0
	Monte Carlo	−.70 to +.70	0	+.10	−.15 to +.15	0
	Regal	−1.10 to −.10	−.60	+.10	−.15 to +.15	0
2002	Century	−1.40 to −.40	−.90	0	−.15 to +.15	0
	Impala	−.50 to −.50	0	+.10	−.15 to +.15	0
	Intrigue	−1.10 to −.10	−.60	+.10	−.15 to +.15	0
	Monte Carlo	−.70 to +.70	0	+.10	−.15 to +.15	0
	Regal	−1.10 to −.10	−.60	+.10	−.15 to +.15	0
2003	Century & Regal	−1.10 to −.10	−.60	+.10	−.15 to +.15	0
	Grand Prix	−1.40 to −.40	−.90	+.06	—	—
	Impala	−1.00 to .00	−.50	+.10	−.15 to +.15	0
	Monte Carlo	−1.20 to +.20	−.70	+.10	−.15 to +.15	0
2004	Century	−.96 to +.04	−.46	+.10	−.15 to +.15	0
	Grand Prix	−1.40 to −.40	−.90	+.06	—	—
	Impala	−1.00 to .00	−.50	+.10	−.15 to +.15	0
	Monte Carlo	−1.20 to +.20	−.70	+.10	−.15 to +.15	0
	Regal	−1.10 to −.10	−.60	+.10	−.15 to +.15	0
2005	Century	−1.30 to −.30	−.80	+.10	−.20 to +.20	0
	Grand Prix (GT1, GT2)	−1.45 to −.45	−.95	+.10	−.20 to +.20	0
	Grand Prix (GTP)	−1.65 to −.465	−1.15	+.10	−.20 to +.20	0
	Impala	−1.15 to −.15	−.65	+.10	−.20 to +.20	0
	Impala (Police)	−1.30 to −.30	−.80	+.10	−.20 to +.20	0
	LaCrosse	−1.30 to −.30	−.80	+.10	−.20 to +.20	0
	Monte Carlo	−1.35 to −.35	−.80	+.10	−.20 to +.20	0

VEHICLE RIDE HEIGHT SPECIFICATIONS

Model	Year	Body Style	Manufac-turer's Original Tire Size	Measurement Points & Specifications②③					
				Front			Rear		
				Dim.	Specification		Dim.	Specification	
					Inches	MM		Inches	MM
Century	2001–02	All	①	J	8.4	213	K	8.4	213
	2003–05	All	①	J	8.6	218	K	8.8	223
Grand Prix	2001–05	All	①	J	8.4	213	K	8.4	213
Impala	2001–02	All	①	J	8.4	213	K	8.4	213
	2003–05	Civilian	①	J	9.4	240	K	9.4	240
		9C1 Police	①	J	10.1	256	K	9.6	244
		9C3 Police	①	J	9.8	248	K	9.5	242
		9C6 Taxi	①	J	9.8	248	K	9.5	242
Intrigue	2001–02	All	①	J	8.4	213	K	8.4	213
LaCrossse	2005	④	①	J	9.4	235	K	9.1	235
		⑤	①	J	9.3	235	K	9.3	235
Lumina	2001	All	①	J	8.4	213	K	8.4	213
Monte Carlo	2001–02	All	①	J	8.4	213	K	8.4	213
	2003–05	All	①	J	9.2	234	K	9.1	233
Regal	2001–02	All	①	J	8.4	213	K	8.4	213
	2003–04	All	①	J	8.8	223	K	8.9	225

A Dim. — Measurement From Front Wheel Center to Inspection Point On Rocker Panel

B Dim. — Measurement From Rear Wheel Center to Inspection Point On Rocker Panel

C Dim. — Ground to Rocker Panel, Front

D Dim. — Ground to Rocker Panel, Rear

Dim. — Dimension

① — See door sticker or inside of glove box for manufacturer's original tire size specifications. If tires on vehicle do not match manufactur-er's original tire size & measure-ment is not within limits, refer to the "Non-Standard Tire & Wheel Size Adjustment To Ride Height Specification & Tire Size Adjust-ment Charts" in the front of this manual for approximate changes in ride height specifications.

② — Measurement is with fuel, radiator coolant & engine oil full, spare tire, jack, hand tools & mats in desig-nated positions & tires properly inflated.

③ — Refer to **Fig. A,** for measurement points.

④ — Soft ride suspension.

⑤ — Ride & handling suspension.

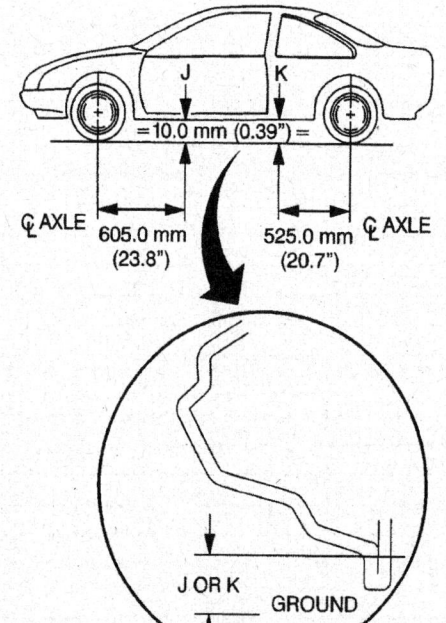

= 10.0 mm (0.39") =

₵ AXLE 605.0 mm (23.8")   525.0 mm (20.7") ₵ AXLE

J OR K   GROUND

ARM040000000169

Fig. A

FLUID CAPACITIES & COOLING SYSTEM DATA

Year	Model	Engine	Coolant Capacity, Qts.	Coolant Type	Radiator Cap Relief Pressure, psi	Thermostat Opening Temp. °F	Fuel Tank Gals.	Engine Oil Refill Qts.①	Transaxle Qts.②	
									Drain & Refill	Total Capacity
2001–02	Century	3.1L	11.6	GM DEX-COOL	15	195	17.0	4.5	7.4	10.0
	Grand Prix	3.1L	11.0	GM DEX-COOL	15	195	17.5	4.5	7.4	10.0
		3.8L	10.2	GM DEX-COOL	15	195	17.0	4.5	7.4	10.0
	Impala & Monte Carlo	3.4L	11.3	GM DEX-COOL	15	195	17.0	4.5	7.4	10.0
		3.8L	11.7	GM DEX-COOL	15	195	17.0	4.5	7.4	10.0
	Intrigue	3.5L	9.8	GM DEX-COOL	15	195	17.0	6.0	7.4	10.0
	Lumina	3.1L	11.6	GM DEX-COOL	15	195	16.5	4.5	7.4	10.0
	Regal	3.8L	12.3	GM DEX-COOL	15	195	17.0	4.5	7.4	10.0
2003–04	Century	3.1L	11.6	GM DEX-COOL	15	195	17.0	4.5	7.4	10.0
	Grand Prix	3.1L	11.0	GM DEX-COOL	15	195	17.5	4.3	7.4	10.0
		3.8L	11.2	GM DEX-COOL	15	195	17.5	4.3	7.4	10.0
	Impala & Monte Carlo	3.4L	11.3	GM DEX-COOL	15	195	17.0	4.3	7.4	10.0
		3.8L	11.7	GM DEX-COOL	15	195	17.0	4.3	7.4	10.0
	Regal	3.8L	12.3	GM DEX-COOL	15	195	17.0	4.5	7.4	10.0
2005	Century	3.1L	11.7	GM DEX-COOL	15	195	17.0	4.0	7.4	10.0
	Grand Prix	3.8L	—	GM DEX-COOL	15	195	17.0	4.5	7.4	10.0
	Impala & Monte Carlo	3.4L	11.3	GM DEX-COOL	15	195	17.0	4.0	7.4	10.0
		3.8L	11.7	GM DEX-COOL	15	195	17.0	4.5	7.4	10.0
	LaCrosse	3.6L	11.0	GM DEX-COOL	15	195	17.5	5.5	7.4	10.0
		3.8L	11.7	GM DEX-COOL	15	195	17.5	4.5	7.4	10.0

① — Additional oil may be required to bring oil level to full mark when changing oil filter.

② — Capacity approximate. Make final inspection w/dipstick & add fluid as required.

LUBRICANT DATA

Year	Lubricant Type		
	Transaxle	Power Steering	Brake System
2001–2005	①	②	DOT 3

① — Dexron III ATF meeting GM "H Revision" specification.

② — Power steering fluid GM P/N 89020661, or equivalent.

Electrical

NOTE: On Air Bag Equipped Models, Refer To "Air Bag System Precautions" Located In The Front Of This Manual For System Disarming & Arming Procedures.

NOTE: Refer To "Computer Relearn Procedures" Located In The Front Of This Manual When Battery Power To The Computer Has Been Interrupted.

NOTE: Prior To Performing Any Service Operations Listed In This Section, Consult The "Technical Service Bulletins" Section For Related Information.

INDEX

PRECAUTIONS

Air Bag Systems

Refer to "Air Bag System Precautions" in the front of this manual for system disarming and arming procedures.

Radio Theft Deterrent System

Anti-theft radios have a coded theft deterrent circuit. **The security code number must be obtained before disconnecting the battery, removing the radio fuse or the radio.**

After service procedure has been performed, connect the radio power supply and turn it On. When "LOC" is displayed, enter security code to activate the radio.

Battery Ground Cable

Prior to service, disconnect battery ground cable and isolate as required.

FUSE PANEL & FLASHER LOCATION

Century & Grand Prix

The fuse panel is located behind the instrument panel, under the glove compartment. The underhood accessory wiring junction block is located on the righthand side of the engine compartment, mounted on the strut tower. The hazard and turn signal flasher module is located behind the lefthand side of the instrument panel, mounted on the multi-purpose bracket, near the Body Control Module (BCM).

Impala

The lefthand instrument panel junction block is located behind the lefthand side of the instrument panel, behind an access panel. The righthand instrument panel junction block is located behind the righthand side of the instrument panel, behind an access panel. The rear junction block is located in the luggage compartment, behind the righthand rear wheelhouse. The

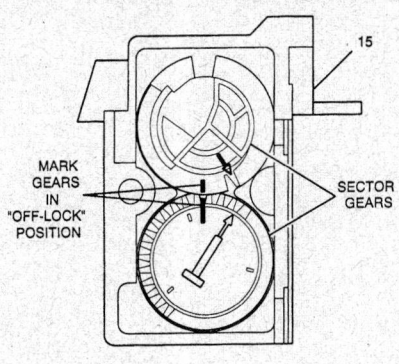

Fig. 1 Lock module sector gear alignment. Century, Grand Prix, LaCrosse & Regal

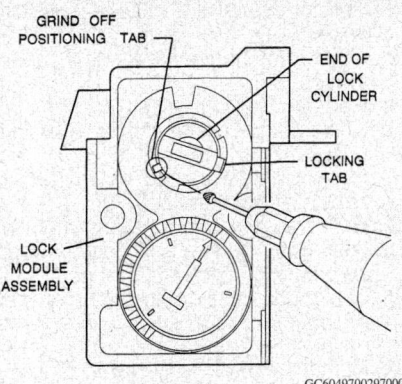

Fig. 2 Lock module positioning tab removal. Century, Grand Prix, LaCrosse & Regal

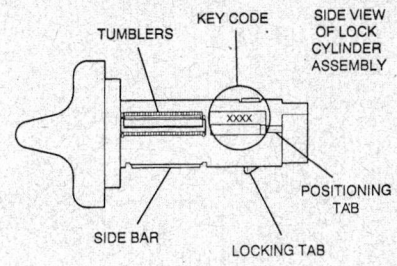

Fig. 3 Lock cylinder removal. Century, Grand Prix, LaCrosse & Regal

underhood junction blocks are located on the righthand side of the engine compartment, forward of the strut tower. The hazard and turn signal flasher is part of the hazard switch assembly, The hazard switch assembly is located behind the righthand side of the instrument panel, in the instrument panel fuse block.

Intrigue

The fuse panel is located behind the instrument panel, under the glove compartment. The underhood accessory wiring junction block is located on the righthand side of the engine compartment, mounted on the strut tower. The hazard and turn signal function is controlled by the hazard switch assembly. The hazard switch assembly is located at the top of the steering column.

LaCrosse

The fuse panel is located on the righthand side of the instrument panel, behind the access panel. The underhood fuse block is located on the righthand side of the engine compartment, mounted on the strut tower. The hazard and turn signals are controlled by the Body Control Module (BCM). The BCM is located behind the lefthand side of the instrument panel, left of the steering column.

Lumina

The instrument panel fuse block is located behind the righthand side of the instrument panel, righthand side of the glove compartment. The No. 1 engine compartment junction block is located on the righthand side of the engine compartment. The No. 2 engine compartment junction block is located on the front lefthand side of the engine compartment. The hazard and turn signal flasher is located behind the lefthand side of the instrument panel, mounted on the bulkhead.

Monte Carlo

The lefthand instrument panel fuse block is located behind the lefthand side instrument panel cluster trim plate, lefthand side of the steering column. The righthand instrument panel fuse block is located behind the fuse block access opening cover, righthand of the glove compartment. The underhood wiring junction block is located on the righthand side of the engine compartment, mounted on the strut tower. The hazard and turn signal flasher is part of the hazard switch assembly, The hazard switch assembly is located behind the righthand side of the instrument panel, in the instrument panel fuse block.

Regal

The fuse panel is located behind the instrument panel, under the glove compartment. The underhood accessory wiring junction block is located on the righthand side of the engine compartment, mounted on the strut tower. The hazard and turn signal flasher is located behind the lefthand side of the instrument panel, mounted on the multi-purpose bracket, near the Body Control Module (BCM).

FUEL PUMP RELAY LOCATION

The fuel pump relay is located in the underhood junction block, on the righthand side of the engine compartment.

STARTER
REPLACE
3.1L Engine

1. Remove air cleaner assembly.
2. Raise and support vehicle.
3. Remove torque converter cover mounting bolts, then the cover.
4. Remove starter motor mounting bolts, lower starter and disconnect starter wiring.
5. Remove starter motor and shims (if used).

6. Reverse procedure to install, noting the following:
   a. Install all shims removed in their original locations.
   b. **Torque** starter motor mounting bolts to 32 ft. lbs.

3.4L Engine

1. Raise and support vehicle.
2. Remove front lower air deflector panel.
3. Remove torque converter covers from transaxle.
4. Remove retaining nuts, then disconnect starter motor electrical connectors from solenoid.
5. Remove starter motor mounting bolts, then the starter motor.
6. Reverse procedure to install. **Torque** starter motor mounting bolts to 32 ft. lbs.

3.5L Engine

1. Raise and support vehicle.
2. Disconnect starter motor electrical connectors.
3. Remove torque converter cover.
4. Remove starter motor bolts and shims, then the starter motor.
5. Reverse procedure to install. **Torque** starter motor mounting bolts to 32 ft. lbs.

3.6L Engine

1. Raise and support vehicle.
2. Disconnect starter motor electrical connectors.
3. Remove starter motor bolts, then the starter motor.
4. Reverse procedure to install. **Torque** starter motor mounting bolts to 37 ft. lbs.

3.8L Engine

1. Raise and support vehicle.
2. Remove torque converter cover mounting bolts, then the cover.
3. Remove starter motor mounting bolts.
4. Disconnect starter motor wiring.
5. Remove starter motor.
6. Reverse procedure to install. **Torque** starter motor mounting bolts to 32 ft. lbs.

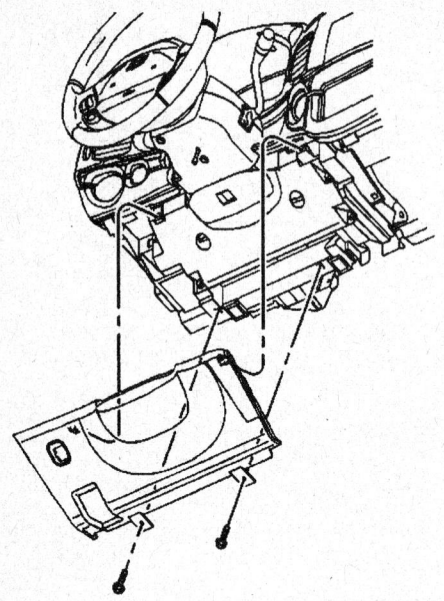

Fig. 4 Steering column filler removal

ARM66GC000000301

ALTERNATOR

REPLACE

3.1L Engine

1. Remove serpentine belt at alternator assembly.
2. Remove cross car brace mounting bolts, then brace.
3. Remove coolant overflow hose from radiator filler neck.
4. Remove coolant reservoir to strut tower mounting bolts, then position reservoir aside.
5. Remove bolts from alternator assembly.
6. Remove power steering gear clip and nut.
7. Remove alternator stud, then disconnect alternator wiring.
8. Loosen alternator front and rear braces from upper intake manifold.
9. Remove alternator assembly.
10. Reverse procedure to install.

3.4L Engine

1. Remove engine compartment cross vehicle brace.
2. Remove serpentine belt.
3. Remove coolant recovery reservoir mounting bolts, then position reservoir aside.
4. Remove alternator mounting bolts, then disconnect alternator electrical connector.
5. Remove retaining nut, then disconnect battery lead.
6. Remove alternator.
7. Reverse procedure to install.

3.5L Engine

1. Drain coolant into suitable container, then remove righthand diagonal brace.

2. Position washer solvent reservoir aside.
3. Lift or rotate tensioner using a suitable breaker bar.
4. Remove serpentine belt.
5. Remove thermostat and radiator outlet hose.
6. Remove battery hold down retainer, battery and battery tray.
7. Remove engine mount strut mounting bolts from radiator and engine mounted brackets, then strut mount.
8. Disconnect cooling fan wiring harness connectors from engine wiring harness.
9. Remove cooling fan shroud mounting bolts, then cooling fan shroud and cooling fan assembly.
10. Remove outboard alternator bolt, then loosen inboard alternator bolt.
11. Remove idler pulley bolt and idler pulley.
12. Disconnect alternator electrical terminals and connectors.
13. Remove inboard alternator bolt, then alternator.
14. Reverse procedure to install noting the following:
    a. **Torque** idler pulley and alternator bolts to 37 ft. lbs.
    b. Route drive belt.

3.6L Engine

1. Remove drive belt from alternator.
2. Raise and support vehicle.
3. Disconnect electrical connector from alternator.
4. Reposition protective boot from alternator output BAT terminal for access.
5. Remove alternator output BAT terminal nut and disconnect battery positive lead from alternator.
6. Remove alternator lower bolts.
7. Lower vehicle and remove alternator upper bolt.
8. Remove alternator from engine.
9. Reverse procedure to install. **Torque** alternator bolts 37 ft. lbs.

3.8L Engine

1. Remove serpentine drive belt tension by rotating drive belt tensioner counterclockwise using a suitable breaker bar.
2. Remove serpentine drive belt from accessory pulleys.
3. Disconnect alternator electrical connectors.
4. Remove alternator retaining bolts, then alternator.
5. Reverse procedure to install.

COIL PACK

REPLACE

1. Disconnect ignition control module electrical connectors.
2. Remove spark plug wires from ignition coils.
3. Remove mounting screws and ignition coils.
4. Reverse procedure to install.

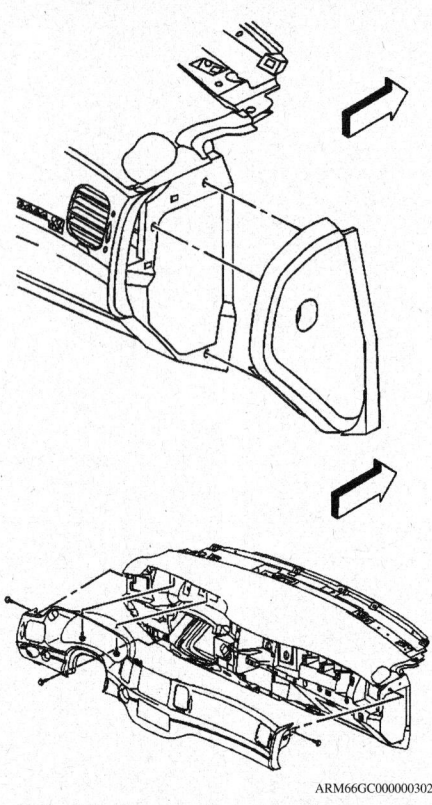

Fig. 5 Fuse/relay panel access cover & instrument cluster trim plate removal

ARM66GC000000302

IGNITION LOCK

REPLACE

Century, Grand Prix, LaCrosse & Regal

LESS IGNITION KEY

1. Remove steering wheel as outlined under "Steering Wheel, Replace."
2. Remove insulator panel from under lefthand side of instrument panel.
3. Remove trim panel from under steering column.
4. Push top of intermediate shaft seal downward, then remove upper intermediate shaft bolt.
5. **On models equipped with column shift,** remove transaxle shift cable from ball stud on steering column, then transaxle shift cable casing from steering column bracket.
6. **On models equipped with floor shift,** remove park lock cable.
7. **On all models,** remove lower and upper steering column bolts.
8. Disconnect steering column electrical connector, then steering column from vehicle.
9. Remove and discard shaft lock retaining ring from top of column using lock plate compressor tool No. J 23653-SIR, or equivalent.
10. Remove shaft lock shield assembly and turn signal cancel cam assembly.
11. Separate key alarm switch from lock module assembly by prying gently with

small bladed screwdriver.

12. Remove ignition key and alarm switch assembly mounting screws, allowing switch to hang free.
13. Remove lock module assembly mounting screws, then lock module assembly from column.
14. Mark lock module sector gears at "OFF-LOCK" position for installation reference, **Fig. 1.**
15. Remove sector gears from lock module assembly.
16. Remove positioning tab on end of lock cylinder with a ⅛ inch burring tool, **Fig. 2.**
17. Push on locking tab and remove lock cylinder from module assembly, **Fig. 3.**
18. Reverse procedure to install, noting the following:
    a. Record key code from old lock cylinder, then discard.
    b. Align marks on sector gears.
    c. Ensure lock module assembly is in "OFF-LOCK" position.
    d. Insert new key in lock cylinder and ensure key is in "OFF-LOCK" position.
    e. Align locking tab and positioning tab with lock module slots, then push lock cylinder into lock module.
    f. Rotate lock cylinder to "ACC" position and inspect alignment arrows on sector gears. Arrows should be pointing towards each other.
    g. Rotate lock cylinder to "LOCK" position.
    h. Align scribe mark on steering wheel and shaft.
    i. **Torque** steering shaft nut to 30 ft. lbs.

WITH IGNITION KEY

1. Remove steering wheel as outlined under "Steering Wheel, Replace."
2. Remove insulator panel from under lefthand side of instrument panel.
3. Remove trim panel from under steering column.
4. Push top of intermediate shaft seal downward, then remove upper intermediate shaft bolt.
5. **On models equipped with column shift,** remove transaxle shift cable from ball stud on steering column, then transaxle shift cable casing from steering column bracket.
6. **On models equipped with floor shift,** remove park lock cable from lock module assembly.
7. **On all models,** remove lower and upper steering column bolts.
8. Disconnect steering column electrical connector, then steering column from vehicle.
9. Mount steering column in a suitable vise, then remove upper and lower steering column shrouds.
10. Hold ignition key in START position.
11. Push lock cylinder retaining pin with a 1/16 inch Allen wrench.
12. Release key to RUN position, then pull lock cylinder set from lock module.
13. Reverse procedure to install.

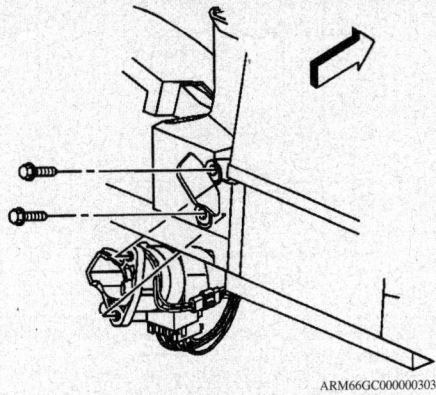

ARM66GC000000303

Fig. 6 Ignition switch bolts & switch removal

Impala & Monte Carlo

1. Remove knee bolster and bracket from under steering column.
2. Remove steering column filler panel retaining screws, **Fig. 4.**
3. Carefully lower filler panel, then disconnect trunk release switch electrical connector and remove panel.
4. Apply parking brake.
5. Remove ignition switch cylinder bezel from cylinder using suitable flat-bladed tool.
6. **On models equipped with column shift,** place gear selector lever in D 1 position.
7. **On all models,** remove lefthand and righthand fuse/relay instrument panel access covers, **Fig. 5.**
8. Starting at righthand end of trim panel, remove instrument cluster trim plate bezel mounting screws, then pull cluster trim plate bezel away from instrument panel trim pad, **Fig. 5.**
9. Remove ignition switch retaining bolts, then lower switch away from instrument panel.
10. Disconnect electrical connector from hazard and traction control switches.
11. Remove ignition switch retaining bolts, then lower switch away form instrument carrier, **Fig. 6.**
12. Insert key into ignition lock cylinder, then turn key to RUN position.
13. Depress detent on bottom of ignition switch housing to release ignition lock cylinder from housing.
14. If ignition switch lock cylinder is seized or will not rotate, proceed as follows:
    a. Protect surrounding area with suitable material such as shop towels or clean fender cover.
    b. Locate release button on ignition lock cylinder plastic switch housing, then center punch a location mark on rib approximately ⅜ inch reward, toward key entry end, from cylinder release button.
    c. Carefully drill pilot hole through plastic housing using an ⅛ inch drill bit, then a larger hole with a 9/32 inch bit at pilot location and slightly into surface of lock cylinder, **Fig. 7.**
    d. Remove lock cylinder from switch

housing, using compressed air blow out ignition switch assembly.
    e. Depress retainer to release transaxle park/lock cable, then remove lock cable by pulling outward.
    f. **The passlock electrical connector cannot be removed until lock cylinder is removed.**
    g. Depress detent on bottom of ignition switch to release and remove ignition lock cylinder with key.
15. Reverse procedure to install.

Intrigue

1. Remove radio as outlined under "Radio, Replace."
2. Insert key and turn ignition On.
3. Depress and hold lock cylinder retaining tab with a small flat-bladed tool.
4. Pull lock cylinder from ignition switch.
5. Reverse procedure to install.

Lumina

1. Remove steering column as outlined in "Steering Columns" chapter.
2. Remove and discard two lower spring retainers.
3. Remove lower bearing spring and lower bearing seat.
4. Remove nut retainer and jam nut, then steering wheel.
5. Remove cancel cam assembly, then hazard knob screw and hazard warning knob.
6. Position turn signal switch so turn signal switch screws and housing screw can be removed through opening in switch.
7. Remove housing screw and column housing cover, then turn signal switch screws.
8. Remove wiring protector from opening in instrument panel bracket on jacket assembly and separate from wires.
9. Disconnect pivot/pulse switch connector then remove pivot screw and pivot/pulse switch assembly.
10. Disconnect turn signal switch connector from ignition and dimmer switch assembly connector.
11. Disconnect 17-way secondary lock from turn signal connector.
12. Disconnect wires on buzzer switch from turn signal connector using terminal remover tool No. J-35689-A, or equivalent. Wrap wire ends with tape.
13. Remove turn signal switch assembly from column.
14. Remove and discard two lower spring retainers.
15. Remove lower bearing spring and seat.
16. Remove adapter screws, then adapter and bearing assembly.
17. **On models equipped with tilt column,** proceed as follows:
    a. Insert Phillips head screwdriver into square opening in spring retainer, push down and turn counterclockwise to release retainer and wheel tilt spring.
    b. Remove spring retainer, tilt spring and tilt spring guide.
    c. Remove two pivot pins using pivot

pin remover tool No. J-21854-01, or equivalent.

18. **On all models,** place lock cylinder in Run position.
19. **On models equipped with tilt column,** pull tilt lever to release steering column housing, then remove steering shaft assembly and steering column housing as a complete unit.
20. **On models less tilt column,** proceed as follows:
    a. Place opening in retaining ring over flat on steering shaft.
    b. Remove retaining ring using a suitable screwdriver.
    c. Remove thrust washer, upper bearing spring and washer.
    d. Remove steering shaft from lower end of jacket and bowl assembly.
    e. Remove housing screws and steering column housing.
    f. Remove housing spacer bearing using a suitable drift. Discard bearing.
21. **On all models,** place lock cylinder in Off-Lock position and remove key.
22. Remove buzzer switch by lifting switch tab with screwdriver and pulling gently on wires.
23. Remove lock retaining screw and lock cylinder.
24. Reverse procedure to install, noting the following:
    a. **Torque** lock retaining screw to 22 inch lbs.
    b. **Torque** steering column housing screws to 88 inch lbs.
    c. **Torque** turn signal switch and column housing cover screws to 35 inch lbs.
    d. **Torque** jam nut to 30 ft. lbs.
    e. Install new lower spring retainers, compressing spring until retainers are positioned 1.14 inches from lower end of steering shaft.

IGNITION SWITCH

REPLACE

Century, Grand Prix, LaCrosse & Regal

1. Remove steering wheel as outlined under "Steering Wheel, Replace."
2. Remove upper and lower steering column shrouds.
3. Remove turn signal and multi-function wire harness retaining straps from steering column and wire harness assembly.
4. Slide turn signal and multi-function switch assembly connectors out of bulkhead connector.
5. Rotate key alarm connector 90°, then pull key alarm connector out of lock module assembly, **Fig. 8.**
6. Remove two ignition and key alarm switch assembly retaining screws, then the ignition and key alarm switch assembly from steering column, **Fig. 9.**

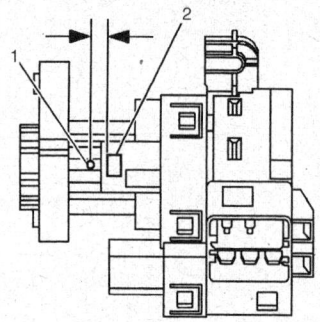

1- CENTER PUNCH LOCATION APPROXIMATELY 3/8 INCH REWARD
2- INGNITION LOCK CYLINDER RELEASE BUTTON

ARM66GC000000304

Fig. 7 Ignition switch lock & switch removal

7. Reverse procedure to install, noting the following:
    a. Align scribe mark.
    b. **Torque** steering shaft nut to 30 ft. lbs.

Impala & Monte Carlo

Refer to "Ignition Lock, Replace" for ignition switch replacement procedure.

Intrigue

1. Remove instrument panel center trim plate.
2. Remove radio as outlined under "Radio, Replace."
3. Remove heater and A/C control assembly retaining screws, then pull assembly away from instrument panel and disconnect electrical connectors.
4. Remove heater and A/C control assembly from instrument panel.
5. Remove push-in retainers from instrument panel insulators, then insulators from under instrument panel, **Fig. 10.**
6. Remove steering column filler panel from under steering column.
7. Remove knee bolster bracket.
8. Turn ignition switch lock cylinder to ACC position and pull park lock cable from ignition switch.
9. Turn ignition switch lock cylinder to ON position.
10. Insert a small flat-bladed tool through access hole on righthand side of ignition switch.
11. Depress locking tab and pull ignition lock cylinder from ignition switch.
12. Disconnect ignition switch electrical connector.
13. Pull ignition switch away from instrument panel.
14. Remove ignition switch to bracket mounting screws, then the bracket from ignition switch.
15. Reverse procedure to install.

Lumina

REMOVAL

1. Place shift lever in Park position and lock cylinder in Off-Lock.
2. Remove steering column from vehicle as outlined in "Steering Columns" chapter.
3. Disconnect turn signal switch connector from ignition and dimmer switch assembly connector.
4. Disconnect pivot and pulse switch connector from ignition and dimmer switch connector.
5. Remove bowl shield screw, bowl shield nut and bowl shield.
6. Remove dimmer switch nut, then upper mounting stud.
7. Remove dimmer switch, then dimmer switch actuator rod.
8. Remove lower mounting stud, then the ignition switch from ignition switch actuator rod.

INSTALLATION

Lock cylinder set must be in the Off-Lock position when installing ignition switch to ensure proper switch slider positioning.

1. Place ignition switch slider in far left-hand position and move back one detent to right, then insert a 3/32 inch drill bit in adjustment hole on ignition switch to hold switch slider in proper position during installation.
2. Install ignition switch to switch rod.
3. Install ignition switch to steering column jacket assembly with lower mounting stud. **Torque** to 35 inch lbs.
4. Remove adjustment tool from ignition switch.
5. Install dimmer switch actuator rod through hole in instrument panel bracket and into hole in dimmer switch rod cap.
6. Install dimmer switch assembly on lower mounting stud with dimmer switch nut and upper mounting stud, but do not tighten.
7. To adjust dimmer switch, insert a 3/32 inch drill bit and push switch against actuator rod to remove all slack.
8. **Torque** dimmer switch nut and upper mounting stud to 35 inch lbs., then remove adjustment tool from dimmer switch.
9. Install bowl shield to column bowl and upper mounting stud, then install shield screw. **Torque** to 35 inch lbs.
10. Install bowl shield nut. **Torque** to 35 inch lbs.
11. Connect turn signal switch connector to ignition and dimmer switch assembly connector and snap in place.
12. Connect pivot and pulse switch connector to ignition and dimmer switch connector.
13. Install steering column and connect battery ground cable.

PARK/NEUTRAL POSITION (PNP) SWITCH

REPLACE

1. Apply parking brake and block drive wheels.
2. Place selector lever in Neutral position.
3. Remove throttle body air inlet duct.
4. Remove automatic transaxle range selector cable from switch assembly.
5. Disconnect switch electrical connectors.
6. Remove range selector lever from switch assembly.
7. Remove switch assembly retaining screws, then the switch from transaxle.
8. Reverse procedure to install, noting the following:
   a. **Do not rotate a new switch assembly. New switch is pinned to Neutral position. If bolts do not align with mounting boss on transaxle, ensure transaxle shaft is in Neutral position.**
   b. Align flats of shift shaft to flats of switch.
   c. **Torque** switch mounting bolts to 18 ft. lbs.

HEADLAMP SWITCH

REPLACE

Century, Grand Prix, LaCrosse & Regal

1. Remove push-in retainers from left-hand side instrument panel sound insulator, then the insulator from under instrument panel.
2. Remove steering column opening filler panel from under steering column.
3. Remove knee bolster bracket from under lefthand side of instrument panel.
4. Remove steering column support to instrument panel retaining bolts, then lower steering column.
5. Pull bottom edge of instrument cluster trim plate away from instrument panel to release retainer clips.
6. Disconnect fog lamp switch electrical connector, then remove instrument cluster trim plate from instrument panel.
7. Pull headlamp switch away from instrument panel and disconnect electrical connector.
8. Reverse procedure to install.

Impala

1. Remove instrument cluster trim plate as outlined under "Ignition Switch, Replace."
2. Remove headlamp switch housing retaining screws, then switch housing from instrument panel.
3. Disconnect electrical connector from headlamp switch housing and fog lamp switch.

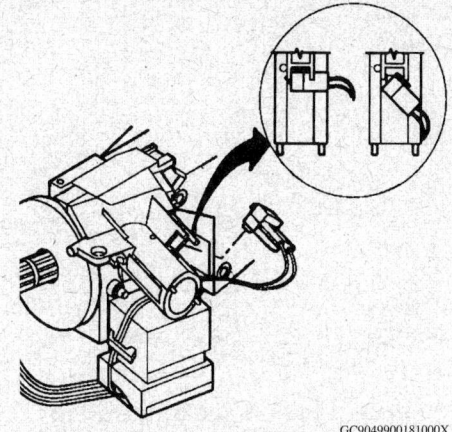

Fig. 8 Key alarm connector. Century, Grand Prix, LaCrosse & Regal

GC9049900181000X

4. Remove headlamp switch from instrument panel using a suitable flat-bladed tool.
5. Reverse procedure to install.

Intrigue

1. Remove push-in retainers from left-hand instrument panel sound insulator.
2. Remove sound insulator from instrument panel.
3. Remove steering column filler panel from under steering column.
4. Remove switch bank retaining screws, then switch bank from instrument panel.
5. Reverse procedure to install.

Lumina

1. Move shift lever to L1 position.
2. Tilt steering column to its lowest position.
3. Unsnap instrument panel cluster trim plate by pulling panel rearward.
4. Remove instrument cluster trim plate from instrument panel.
5. Depress headlamp switch locking tabs, then pull switch away from instrument panel and disconnect electrical connector.
6. Reverse procedure to install.

Monte Carlo

1. Remove instrument cluster trim plate as outlined under "Ignition Switch, Replace."
2. Remove headlamp switch housing retaining screws, then switch housing from instrument panel.
3. Disconnect electrical connector from headlamp switch housing and fog lamp switch.
4. Remove headlamp switch from instrument panel using a suitable flat-bladed tool.
5. Reverse procedure to install.

STOP LIGHT SWITCH

REPLACE

1. Remove push-in retainers from left-hand instrument panel sound insulator.
2. Remove sound insulator from under lefthand side of instrument panel.
3. Remove brake lamp switch to brake pedal bracket retaining screws.
4. Remove brake lamp switch.
5. Reverse procedure to install, adjust brake and cruise control switches as follows:
   a. Push brake pedal as far forward as possible to set brake push rod into booster.
   b. Pull brake pedal rearward, against internal stop. Brake lamp and cruise control switches are now adjusted.
   c. Ensure brake lamps operate properly.

MULTI-FUNCTION SWITCH

REPLACE

1. Remove steering wheel as outlined under "Steering Wheel, Replace."
2. Remove upper and lower steering column trim covers.
3. Remove wire harness straps from wiring harness and upper tilt head assembly.
4. Remove multi-function switch assembly retaining screws, then the switch assembly from steering column.
5. Reverse procedure to install, noting the following:
   a. **Torque** multi-function switch retaining screws to 62 inch lbs.
   b. Align scribe mark.
   c. **Torque** steering shaft nut to 30 ft. lbs.

TURN SIGNAL SWITCH

REPLACE

Refer to "Multi-Function Switch, Replace" for turn signal switch replacement.

STEERING WHEEL

REPLACE

1. Turn ignition Off.
2. Remove air bag module as outlined in "Passive Restraint Systems" chapter.
3. Scribe alignment mark on steering wheel hub inline with slash mark on steering shaft.
4. Loosen steering wheel nut, then position nut flush with end of shaft.
5. Loosen steering wheel using suitable puller. **When removing a steering wheel with accessory controls in hub, use caution to avoid damaging electronic circuits. Steering wheel puller bolts should be turned in no more than four to six threads to avoid contact with electrical circuits.**
6. Remove steering shaft nut and steering wheel.

7. Reverse procedure to install, noting the following:
   a. Align scribe marks.
   b. **Torque** steering shaft nut to 30 ft. lbs.

INSTRUMENT CLUSTER
REPLACE

Century, Grand Prix, LaCrosse & Regal

1. Remove push-in retainers from lefthand side instrument panel sound insulator, then insulator from under instrument panel.
2. Remove steering column opening filler panel from under steering column.
3. Remove knee bolster bracket from under lefthand side of instrument panel.
4. Remove steering column support to instrument panel retaining bolts, then lower steering column.
5. Pull bottom edge of instrument cluster trim plate away from instrument panel to release retainer clips.
6. Disconnect fog lamp switch electrical connector, then remove instrument cluster trim plate from instrument panel.
7. Remove instrument cluster retaining screws.
8. Pull instrument cluster towards rear and upwards to disengage retaining clips.
9. Disconnect cluster electrical connectors and remove cluster from instrument panel.
10. Reverse procedure to install.

Impala & Monte Carlo

1. Remove instrument cluster trim plate bezel as outlined under "Ignition Switch, Replace."
2. Remove instrument cluster mounting bolts.
3. Gently pull cluster away from instrument panel and disconnect electrical connector.
4. Remove cluster from instrument panel.
5. Reverse procedure to install.

Intrigue

1. Remove push-in retainers from lefthand instrument panel sound insulator.
2. Remove sound insulator from instrument panel.
3. Remove steering column filler panel from under steering column.
4. Remove trip odometer and reset switch from instrument cluster trim plate.
5. Remove instrument cluster trim plate mounting screws, then instrument cluster trim plate.
6. Remove instrument cluster retaining screws.

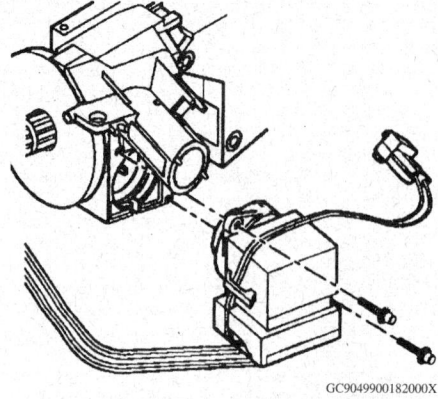

GC9049900182000X

Fig. 9 Ignition & alarm switch removal. Century, Grand Prix, LaCrosse & Regal

7. Pull cluster rearward and disconnect electrical connectors.
8. Remove cluster from instrument panel.
9. Reverse procedure to install.

Lumina

1. Move shift lever to L1 position.
2. Tilt steering column to lowest position.
3. Unsnap instrument panel cluster trim plate by pulling panel rearward.
4. Remove instrument cluster trim plate from instrument panel.
5. Remove instrument cluster retaining screws.
6. Pull cluster away from instrument panel and disconnect electrical connectors.
7. Reverse procedure to install.

RADIO
REPLACE

Century & Regal

1. Remove push-in retainers from lefthand side instrument panel sound insulator, then insulator from under instrument panel.
2. Remove steering column opening filler panel from under steering column.
3. Remove instrument panel accessory trim panel mounting screws.
4. Pull accessory trim plate rearward and release two retaining tabs.
5. Remove accessory trim plate from instrument panel.
6. Remove radio retaining screws.
7. Pull radio away from instrument panel, then disconnect electrical connectors and antenna lead-in cable.
8. Reverse procedure to install.

Grand Prix

1. Remove push-in retainers from lefthand side instrument panel sound insulator, then insulator from under instrument panel.
2. Remove steering column opening filler panel from under steering column.

3. Remove knee bolster bracket from under lefthand side of instrument panel.
4. Remove steering column support to instrument panel retaining bolts, then lower steering column.
5. Pull bottom edge of instrument cluster trim plate away from instrument panel to release retainer clips.
6. Disconnect fog lamp switch electrical connector, then remove instrument cluster trim plate from instrument panel.
7. Remove radio retaining screws.
8. Pull radio away from instrument panel and disconnect electrical connectors and antenna lead-in cable.
9. Remove radio from instrument panel.
10. Reverse procedure to install.

Impala

1. Remove instrument cluster trim plate bezel as outlined under "Ignition Switch, Replace."
2. Remove radio retaining screws.
3. Pull radio away from instrument panel, then disconnect electrical connectors and antenna lead-in cable.
4. Reverse procedure to install.

Intrigue

1. Remove traction control switch from center console trim plate.
2. Open front floor console compartment and remove console trim plate mounting screws.
3. Pull up on trim plate to release retaining clips, then remove console trim plate from console.
4. Remove instrument panel accessory trim plate, then radio mounting screws.
5. Disconnect electrical connectors and antenna lead-in cable, then remove radio.
6. Reverse procedure to install.

Lumina

1. Move shift lever to L1 position.
2. Tilt steering column to lowest position.
3. Unsnap instrument panel cluster trim plate by pulling panel rearward.
4. Remove instrument cluster trim plate from instrument panel.
5. Remove radio retaining screws.
6. Pull radio away from instrument panel and disconnect electrical connectors and antenna lead-in cable.
7. Remove radio from instrument panel.
8. Reverse procedure to install.

Monte Carlo

1. Remove instrument cluster trim plate bezel as outlined under "Ignition Switch, Replace."
2. Remove radio retaining screws.
3. Pull radio away from instrument panel, then disconnect electrical connectors and antenna.
4. Reverse procedure to install.

WIPER MOTOR
REPLACE

1. Remove wiper module as outlined under "Wiper Module, Replace."
2. Remove wiper motor crank arm from wiper transmission using wiper transmission separator tool No. J 39232, or equivalent.
3. Remove wiper motor crank arm to wiper motor retaining nut.
4. Remove wiper motor bracket mounting screws, then wiper motor assembly from tube frame.
5. Reverse procedure to install.

WIPER SWITCH
REPLACE

Refer to "Multi-Function Switch, Replace" for wiper switch replacement procedure.

WIPER TRANSMISSION
REPLACE

Removal

1. Remove wiper module as outlined under "Wiper Module, Replace."
2. Remove two transmission socket screws, then the socket from link ball.
3. Remove righthand and lefthand side bellcrank mounting screws, then the transmission from module.

Installation

1. Connect new transmission to module.
2. Ensure wiper motor is in inner wipe position.
3. Align holes in module and bellcrank, then install transmission socket screws.
4. Ensure body seal is in proper place on righthand side of module and install wiper module.
5. Install passenger side wiper arm and blade. Measure from tip of blade to bottom edge of glass. Ensure distance is approximately 9 ⅛ inches, then tighten nut. Install protective cap and connect washer hose.
6. Install driver side wiper arm and blade. Measure from tip of blade to bottom edge of glass. Ensure distance is approximately two inches, then tighten nut. Install protective cap and connect washer hose.
7. Operate wiper at high and low speeds with wet and tacky windshield. Ensure blades park properly and there is no interference between blades.

WIPER MODULE
REPLACE

The windshield wiper module consists of both the wiper motor and the wiper transmission.

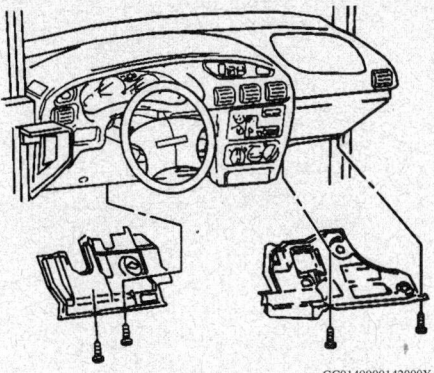

GC9149900142000X

Fig. 10 I/P insulator panel removal. Intrigue

1. Turn ignition to Accessory, then set wiper switch to Pulse/Delay.
2. Wait until wiper arms are in inner wipe position and are not moving, then turn ignition Off.
3. Remove hose from nozzle on wiper arm driveshaft.
4. Remove covers from wiper arm retaining nuts.
5. Remove wiper arm retaining nuts, then wiper arms from wiper transmission driveshaft.
6. Remove inlet shroud mounting bolts, then inlet shroud from vehicle.
7. Disconnect wiper motor electrical connectors.
8. Remove wiper module assembly mounting bolts, then wiper module assembly from vehicle.
9. Reverse procedure to install.

BLOWER MOTOR
REPLACE

1. Remove righthand sound insulator panel from under instrument panel.
2. **On models equipped with convenience center,** remove rear retaining screws from electrical convenience center, then loosen front screw and slide convenience center out.
3. **On all models,** disconnect electrical connector at motor and remove harness from clip.
4. Disconnect blower motor cooling hose.
5. Remove blower motor mounting screws and blower motor.
6. Reverse procedure to install.

CABIN AIR FILTER
REPLACE

1. Operate windshield wipers until blades are in up position, then turn ignition Off.
2. Open hood.
3. Lift righthand side of rear hood seal from flange in area of righthand air inlet grille.
4. Disengage righthand air inlet grille retaining clips using a suitable door trim panel clip remover, then remove grille.

5. Remove cabin air filter element, **Fig. 11.**
6. Reverse procedure to install.

HEATER CORE
REPLACE

1. **On models equipped with 3.1L and 3.4L engines,** remove air cleaner and duct assembly.
2. **On models equipped with 3.5L and 3.8L engines,** remove fuel injector sight shield as follows:
   a. Remove oil filler cap.
   b. Remove fuel injector sight shield to fuel injector rail brace stud retaining nut.
   c. Lift fuel injector sight shield up at front and slide tab out of engine bracket.
   d. Install oil filler cap.
3. **On all models,** drain cooling system, then disconnect heater hoses from heater core.
4. **On models equipped with center console,** proceed as follows:
   a. Position transaxle shift lever in Low position.
   b. Remove floor console storage compartment rubber mat, then floor console front mounting bolts.
   c. Remove floor console rear mounting bracket bolts located behind transaxle shift lever.
   d. Remove floor console lefthand and righthand mounting bolts.
   e. Disconnect console electrical connectors.
   f. Pull console rearward and remove from vehicle.
5. **On all models,** remove push-in retainers from instrument panel insulators, then insulators from under instrument panel.
6. Position heater core outlet cover downward and rearward.
7. Remove heater core outlet cover retaining screws, then disconnect outlet cover from floor duct assembly.
8. Remove heater core cover mounting screws, then cover.
9. Remove and discard seals from heater core cover and heater core.
10. Remove heater core line clamp retaining screw, heater core retaining clamp and heater core pipe retainer clamp screw.
11. Remove heater core from HVAC lower case.
12. Remove and discard heater core lower, center, upper and side seals from HVAC case.
13. Reverse procedure to install, noting the following:
    a. Install all new seals.
    b. **Torque** heater core line clamp screw to 13 inch lbs.
    c. **Torque** heater core mounting clip screw to 13 inch lbs.
    d. **Torque** heater core cover screws to 13 inch lbs.

EVAPORATOR CORE

REPLACE

Century, Intrigue, LaCrosse, Lumina & Regal

1. Recover refrigerant as outlined in "Air Conditioning" chapter.
2. Remove air cleaner and duct assembly.
3. Drain engine coolant.
4. Remove instrument panel as outlined in "Dash Panel Service" chapter.
5. Remove passenger side air bag module as outlined in "Passive Restraints Systems" chapter.
6. Unclip fuse block and position aside.
7. Remove brake pedal bracket and reinforcement.
8. Remove BCM bracket mounting bolts, then position bracket aside.
9. Release instrument panel wiring harness retaining clips, then position harness aside.
10. Remove HVAC module center support bracket mounting bolts, then support bracket.
11. Remove HVAC module upper support bracket mounting bolts, then HVAC module from cross vehicle beam support.
12. Remove support braces from top of engine compartment.
13. Disconnect refrigerant lines from evaporator block fitting.
14. Disconnect heater hoses at heater core.
15. Remove HVAC module to dash panel retaining nuts.
16. Tag their locations, then disconnect HVAC module electrical connectors and vacuum hoses.

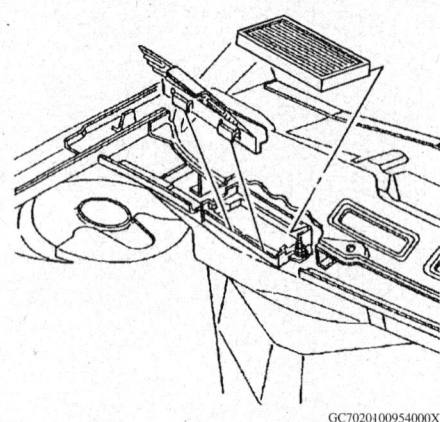

Fig. 11   Cabin air filter replacement

17. Remove HVAC module to cross vehicle support beam mounting bolts and nuts, then HVAC module.
18. Remove all HVAC module outer seals, then air inlet housing.
19. Unclip and remove heater/defrost valve vacuum actuator from HVAC module.
20. Remove HVAC module case upper screws, then separate module case.
21. Remove module seal and evaporator core from lower case.
22. Remove and discard all evaporator core seals and water core filter.
23. Reverse procedure to install, noting the following:
    a. Replace all seals.
    b. **Torque** HVAC case screws to 13 inch lbs.
    c. Charge A/C system refrigerant.

Impala & Monte Carlo

1. Recover A/C refrigerant as outlined in "Air Conditioning" chapter.
2. Drain cooling system.
3. Remove lefthand fender diagonal brace.
4. Remove cross vehicle brace.
5. Disconnect A/C lines from evaporator block fitting, then heater hoses from heater core.
6. Remove instrument panel as outlined in "Dash Panel Service" chapter.
7. Remove cross vehicle beam.
8. Disconnect vacuum hoses and electrical connectors from HVAC module.
9. Disconnect instrument panel wiring harness from HVAC module retainers.
10. Remove evaporator drain elbow.
11. Remove HVAC module to dash panel retaining nuts.
12. Pull HVAC module rearward and disengage from mounting studs.
13. Position dash insulator pad away from HVAC module air inlet opening.
14. Roll HVAC module downward and rearward, then remove heater outlet cover from rear floor air outlet duct.
15. Remove outer HVAC module seals.
16. Remove air inlet housing and heater/defroster valve vacuum actuator from HVAC module.
17. Remove HVAC module case upper screws.
18. Separate module upper case from and lower case.
19. Remove seal from module lower case.
20. Remove evaporator core from case.
21. Reverse procedure to install.

3.1L Engine

NOTE: On Air Bag Equipped Models, Refer To "Air Bag System Precautions" Located In The Front Of This Manual For System Disarming & Arming Procedures.

NOTE: Refer To "Computer Relearn Procedures" Located In The Front Of This Manual When Battery Power To The Computer Has Been Interrupted.

NOTE: Prior To Performing Any Service Operations Listed In This Section, Consult The "Technical Service Bulletins" Section For Related Information.

INDEX

PRECAUTIONS

Air Bag Systems

Refer to "Air Bag System Precautions" in the front of this manual for system disarming and arming procedures.

Battery Ground Cable

Prior to service, disconnect battery ground cable and isolate as required.

Fuel System Pressure Relief

To reduce the risk of fire and personal injury, relieve the fuel system pressure before servicing fuel system components.
1. Loosen fuel tank filler cap to relieve tank pressure.
2. Connect fuel pressure gauge tool No.

J-34730-1, or equivalent, to fuel pressure valve. Wrap a shop towel around fitting while connecting gauge to avoid spillage.
3. Install bleed hose into a suitable container and open valve to bleed system pressure.

COMPRESSION PRESSURE

When inspecting compression, lowest cylinder must be within 70% of the highest cylinder with a minimum pressure of 100 psi. Perform compression test with engine at normal operating temperature, spark plugs removed and throttle wide open.

ENGINE MOUNT

REPLACE

Engine Mount

1. Remove throttle body air inlet duct,

then engine mount struts.
2. Raise and support vehicle, then remove righthand front wheel and tire assembly.
3. Remove catalytic converter pipe from rear exhaust manifold.
4. Remove righthand engine splash shield, then engine mount lower nuts.
5. Place a block of wood under oil pan, then raise engine with suitable floor jack stand.
6. Remove engine mount bracket to oil pan bolts, then engine mount and engine mount bracket.
7. Remove engine upper mount nuts, then engine mount from engine mount bracket.
8. Reverse procedure to install.

Engine Strut

1. Remove bolt from engine mount strut bracket, then bolt from bracket.
2. Remove strut assembly.
3. Reverse procedure to install.

Transaxle Mount

1. Support transaxle using a suitable jack.
2. Remove crossmember to mount mounting nuts, **Fig. 1.**
3. Remove bracket to transaxle mounting bolts.
4. Remove mount and bracket assembly.
5. Separate mount from bracket.
6. Reverse procedure to install.

ENGINE
REPLACE

1. Drain engine coolant into a suitable container.
2. Drain engine oil into a suitable container.
3. Relieve fuel system pressure as outlined under "Precautions."
4. Scribe alignment marks, then remove hood.
5. Remove air flow tube from air cleaner and throttle valve, then the air cleaner assembly.
6. Remove transaxle filler tube assembly.
7. Disconnect required electrical wiring, then the throttle and TV cables.
8. Remove engine mount strut bracket.
9. Disconnect fuel lines.
10. Remove AIR pump belt, then serpentine drive belt cover and belt.
11. Disconnect radiator hoses at engine.
12. Remove A/C compressor bolts from front bracket.
13. Remove power steering pump and position aside.
14. Disconnect heater hoses from engine.
15. Disconnect brake booster vacuum supply line.
16. Disconnect EGR from exhaust.
17. Raise and support vehicle.
18. Remove starter motor assembly.
19. Remove A/C compressor bolts at rear bracket, then position compressor aside.
20. Remove flywheel cover, then disconnect starter and position aside.
21. Remove torque converter bolts, then transaxle mount bracket.
22. Remove engine front mount retaining nuts.
23. Disconnect exhaust pipe at crossover, then lower vehicle.
24. Remove coolant recovery bottle.
25. Disconnect accelerator control cable bracket and move assemblies aside.
26. Disconnect crossover pipe at lefthand manifold.
27. Remove serpentine belt, then alternator.
28. Remove power steering pump assembly.
29. Remove plastic cover from front shock tower, then remove automatic transaxle modulator pipe assembly.
30. **On Century and Grand Prix models,** pull engine assembly forward and support in this position.
31. **On all models,** disconnect crossover pipe at righthand manifold.
32. Disconnect bulkhead connector.
33. **On Century and Grand Prix models,**

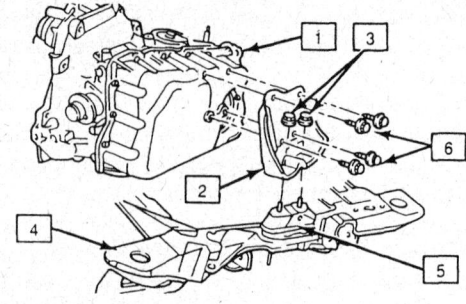

	COVER ASSEMBLY, TRANSAXLE SIDE
1	COVER ASSEMBLY, TRANSAXLE SIDE
2	BRACKET, TRANSAXLE MOUNT TRANSAXLE SIDE
3	NUT, TRANSAXLE MOUNT TRANSAXLE SIDE BRACKET
4	FRAME ASSEMBLY, DRIVETRAIN AND FRONT SUSPENSION
5	MOUNT ASSEMBLY, TRANSAXLE
6	BOLT/SCREW, TRANSAXLE MOUNT TRANSAXLE SIDE BRACKET

GC1069400816000X

Fig. 1 Transaxle mount

remove engine support and allow engine to roll to normal position.
34. **On all models,** remove engine to transaxle mounting bolts, attach lifting device to engine and support transaxle.
35. Remove engine assembly.
36. Reverse procedure to install.

INTAKE MANIFOLD
REPLACE

Upper

1. Disconnect vacuum hose from throttle body air inlet duct, then wiring harness from intake air temperature sensor.
2. Remove throttle body air inlet duct, then drain engine coolant into a suitable container.
3. Remove accelerator control and cruise control cables with bracket from throttle body.
4. Disconnect wiring harness connectors from throttle body, then front spark plug wires.
5. Disconnect wiring harness attachment clips from camshaft position sensor, front spark plug wire harness and engine wiring harness.
6. Disconnect thermostat bypass pipe coolant hoses from throttle body.
7. Remove ignition coil bracket with coils, purge solenoid and vacuum canister solenoid.
8. Disconnect vacuum hose at MAP sensor and upper intake manifold, then remove MAP sensor and bracket.
9. Disconnect emission control vacuum harness, then upper intake manifold to vacuum booster vacuum hose.
10. Disconnect automatic transaxle vacuum modulator hose.
11. Disconnect heater/air conditioning vacuum source hose and fuel pressure regulator vacuum hose.
12. Remove front and rear alternator braces, then alternator bracket.
13. Remove EGR valve, then upper intake manifold bolts and studs.

14. Remove upper intake manifold and gaskets.
15. Reverse procedure to install.

Lower

1. Relieve fuel system pressure as outlined under "Precautions."
2. Remove upper intake manifold as outlined under "Intake Manifold, Replace."
3. Remove both valve covers, then disconnect ECT wiring harness.
4. Remove fuel pipe clip bolt, then fuel pipe clip.
5. Disconnect fuel feed and fuel return pipes from fuel injector rail.
6. Remove fuel injector rail, then power steering pump from front engine cover and set aside.
7. Disconnect heater inlet pipe with heater hose from lower intake manifold and position aside.
8. Disconnect radiator inlet hose from engine, then thermostat bypass hose from thermostat bypass pipe and lower intake manifold pipe.
9. Remove lower intake manifold bolts, then the lower intake manifold. Discard bolts.
10. Remove pushrods, then the lower intake manifold gaskets and seals.
11. Reverse procedure to install, noting the following:
    a. Place new intake manifold gaskets in position.
    b. Apply .31–.39 inch drops of RTV sealant P/N 12346141, or equivalent, to four corners of manifold to block joints (1), **Fig. 2.**
    c. Connect sealant drops with sealant beads .31–.39 inch wide and .12–.20 inch thick , **Fig. 2.**
    d. Install rocker arms and pushrods.
    e. **Do not use old manifold mounting bolts. Always install new ones.**
    f. **Vertical bolts must be tightened before diagonal bolts or an oil leak could occur.**
    g. **Torque** bolts in sequence, **Fig. 3,**

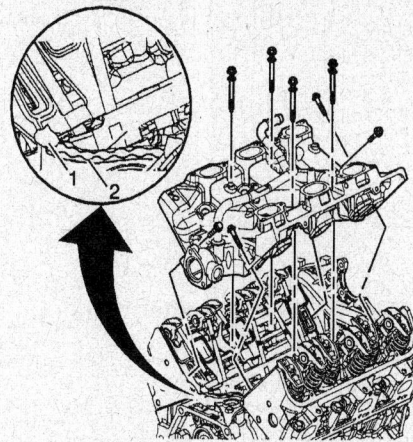

1. Corner sealant
2. Manifold to block sealant

ARM0400000000164

Fig. 2 Lower intake manifold replacement

to 62 inch lbs.
h. **Torque** bolts 1, 2, 3 and 4 in sequence to 115 inch lbs.
i. **Torque** bolts 5, 6, 7 and 8 in sequence to 18 ft. lbs.

EXHAUST MANIFOLD
REPLACE
Lefthand

1. Remove throttle body air inlet duct, then drain engine coolant into a suitable container.
2. Remove righthand engine mount strut bracket, then disconnect radiator inlet hose from engine.
3. Remove automatic transaxle vacuum modulator pipe, then thermostat bypass pipe.
4. Remove exhaust crossover pipe heat shield, then exhaust crossover bolts to exhaust manifold.
5. Remove exhaust manifold heat shied bolts, then heat shield.
6. Remove exhaust manifold nuts, then exhaust manifold and gasket.
7. Reverse procedure to install.

Righthand

1. Remove throttle body air inlet duct, then drain engine coolant into a suitable container.
2. Remove righthand engine mount strut bracket, then disconnect radiator inlet hose from engine.
3. Remove automatic transaxle vacuum modulator pipe, then the thermostat bypass pipe.
4. Remove exhaust crossover pipe heat shield, then exhaust crossover bolts to exhaust manifold.
5. Remove exhaust manifold heat shield bolts, then the heat shield.
6. Disconnect heated oxygen sensor wiring harness connector, then raise and support vehicle.
7. Remove EGR tube from exhaust man-

ifold, then exhaust manifold upper heat shield bolts and upper heat shield.
8. Remove exhaust lower heat shield bolts and lower heat shield, then exhaust manifold nuts and exhaust manifold.
9. Reverse procedure to install.

CYLINDER HEAD
REPLACE
Lefthand

1. Drain engine coolant into a suitable container.
2. Drain engine oil.
3. Remove upper and lower intake manifolds as outlined under "Intake Manifold, Replace."
4. Remove valve cover as outlined under "Valve Cover, Replace."
5. Remove exhaust crossover, then oil lever indicator bracket.
6. Remove lefthand exhaust manifold as outlined under "Exhaust Manifold, Replace."
7. Disconnect plug wires at lefthand head, then remove pushrods. Intake pushrods are marked orange and are 5.68 inches long. Exhaust pushrods are marked blue and are six inches long.
8. Remove cylinder head mounting bolts, then the cylinder head.
9. Reverse procedure to install, noting following:
   a. Clean gasket surfaces on head, cylinder block and intake manifold, cylinder block bolt threads and cylinder head bolts.
   b. Coat cylinder head bolt threads with suitable sealant.
   c. **Torque** cylinder head bolts to 44 ft. lbs., using tightening sequence, **Fig. 4,** then rotate an additional 95.°

Righthand

1. Raise and support vehicle, then drain engine coolant into a suitable container.
2. Drain engine oil, then lower the vehicle.
3. Remove upper and lower intake manifolds as outlined under "Intake Manifold, Replace."
4. Disconnect plug wires at righthand head, then remove pushrods. Intake pushrods are marked orange and are 5.68 inches long. Exhaust pushrods are marked blue and are six inches long.
5. Remove exhaust crossover pipe, then the righthand head spark plug wires and plugs.
6. Remove cylinder head mounting bolts, then the cylinder head.
7. Reverse procedure to install, noting the following:
   a. Clean gasket surfaces on head, cylinder block and intake manifold, cylinder block bolt threads and cylinder head bolts.

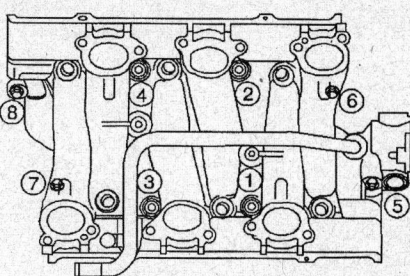

ARM0400000000165

Fig. 3 Lower intake manifold bolt tightening sequence

   b. Coat cylinder head bolt threads with suitable sealant.
   c. **Torque** cylinder head bolts to 44 ft. lbs., then rotate an additional 95° in sequence, **Fig. 4.**

VALVE COVER
REPLACE
Lefthand

1. Remove lefthand side spark plug wires, then automatic transaxle vacuum modulator pipe.
2. Remove PCV valve, then lefthand valve cover bolts.
3. Remove lefthand valve cover and gasket.
4. Reverse procedure to install, noting the following:
   a. Clean sealing surfaces on cylinder head and cover.
   b. Install new gasket and ensure gasket is seated properly in rocker cover groove.
   c. Apply suitable sealer into cylinder head notch.

Righthand

1. Remove serpentine drive belt, then the alternator braces.
2. Remove alternator, then the righthand head spark plug wires.
3. Remove ignition coil bracket with coils, then the purge solenoid and vacuum canister solenoid.
4. Remove vacuum hose from grommet in valve cover.
5. Remove valve cover bolts, then the valve cover and gasket.
6. Reverse procedure to install, noting the following:
   a. Clean sealing surfaces on cylinder head and cover.
   b. Install new gasket and ensure gasket is seated properly in rocker cover groove.
   c. Apply suitable sealer into cylinder head notch.

VALVE ARRANGEMENT
Front To Rear

Cowl side.................................E-I-E-I-I-E
Radiator side...........................E-I-I-E-I-E

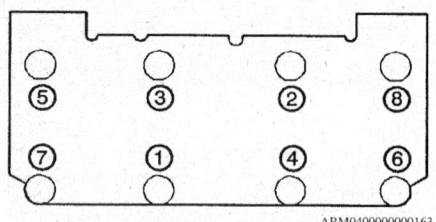

ARM0400000000163

Fig. 4 Cylinder head bolt tightening sequence

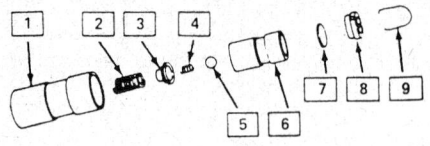

1—LIFTER BODY
2—PLUNGER SPRING
3—BALL CHECK RETAINER
4—BALL CHECK SPRING
5—BALL CHECK
6—PLUNGER
7—OIL METERING VALVE
8—PUSH ROD SEAT
9—RETAINER RING

GC1069100448000X

Fig. 5 Exploded view of valve lifter

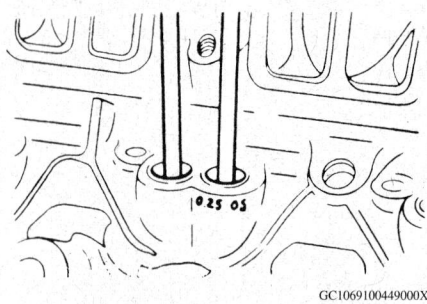

GC1069100449000X

Fig. 6 Oversize lifter marking

VALVE LIFTERS

Roller type valve lifters, **Fig. 5,** are used in this engine. They must be replaced whenever the camshaft is replaced.

Valve lifters should be kept in order so they will be installed in their original positions. Some engines will have both standard and .010 inch oversize valve lifters.

Where oversize lifters are used, crankcase will be marked ".25 OS" with white paint on lifter boss, **Fig. 6.**

If lifters are removed, they must be installed in their original locations. If replacement is required, use lifters with a narrow flat ground along the lower ¾ of the lifter. These flats provide additional oil to the cam lobe and lifter surfaces.

CAMSHAFT LOBE LIFT SPECIFICATIONS

Intake .... .2500
Exhaust.. .2550

VALVE CLEARANCE SPECIFICATIONS

This engine is equipped with hydraulic lifters. Valve lash should always be zero. If valve lash exists, inspect pushrod and rocker arm for excessive wear and inspect for inoperative lifters.

VALVE ADJUSTMENT

There is no valve adjustment for these engines.

ROCKER ARMS
REPLACE

1. Remove valve covers as outlined under "Valve Cover, Replace."
2. Remove rocker arms, identifying components so they can be installed in same location.
3. Remove rocker arm pivot balls and rocker arms, then the pushrods. **Exhaust pushrods are longer than intakes. Exhaust pushrods have blue marks. Intake pushrods are marked with orange.**
4. Reverse procedure to install.

PUSH RODS

1. Remove valve covers as outlined under "Valve Cover, Replace."
2. Remove rocker arms, identifying components so they can be installed in same location.

3. Remove rocker arm pivot balls and rocker arms, then the pushrods. **Exhaust pushrods are longer than intakes. Exhaust pushrods have blue marks. Intake pushrods are marked with orange.**
4. Reverse procedure to install, noting the following:
   a. Ensure pushrods seat in lifters.
   b. Coat bearing surfaces of rocker arms and pivot balls with Molykote, or equivalent lubricant.

HYDRAULIC LIFTERS
REPLACE

1. Remove upper and lower intake manifolds as outlined under "Intake Manifold, Replace."
2. Remove valve rocker arms and pushrods as outlined under "Rocker Arms, Replace" and "Pushrods."
   a. Remove valve covers as outlined under "Valve Cover, Replace."
   b. Remove rocker arms, identifying components so they can be installed in same locations.
   c. Remove rocker arm pivot balls and rocker arms, then the pushrods. **Intake and exhaust pushrods are different lengths. Intake pushrods are marked orange. Exhaust pushrods are marked blue.**
3. Remove intake manifold oil splash shield.
4. Remove lifter guide bolts and lifter guides, then the lifters. **Keep lifters in order for installation reference.**
5. Reverse procedure to install, noting the following:
   a. Clean all gasket surfaces and valve train components.
   b. Coat lifters with pre-lube P/N 1052365, or equivalent.
   c. Install lifters in their original position.
   d. Ensure pushrods seat in lifter.
   e. Coat bearing surfaces of rocker arms and pivot balls with Molykote, or equivalent, lubricant.

FRONT COVER
REPLACE

1. Drain engine coolant into a suitable container.

2. Remove serpentine drive belt cover, then the drive belt.
3. Remove serpentine drive belt tensioner, then alternator.
4. Remove power steering pump and position aside.
5. Remove cross vehicle brace mounting bolts, then the brace.
6. Remove coolant overflow hose from radiator neck.
7. Remove coolant reservoir retaining nuts, then reservoir from strut tower.
8. Raise and support vehicle, then drain engine oil into a suitable container.
9. Remove inner splash shield, then the flywheel cover.
10. Remove starter; then the crankshaft balancer using torsional dampner remover tool No. J-24420, or equivalent.
11. Remove serpentine drive belt idler pulley.
12. Remove lower timing cover mounting bolts, then lower vehicle.
13. Remove throttle body air inlet duct, then the lefthand engine mount strut.
14. Remove spark plug wires from lefthand bank.
15. Disconnect radiator hose at water pump and heater coolant hose from cooling system fill pipe.
16. Disconnect bypass, overflow and canister purge hoses.
17. Remove thermostat bypass pipe from front cover.
18. Remove water pump pulley mounting bolts, then the pump pulley.
19. Remove lower crankshaft position sensor wiring harness bracket from engine front cover.
20. Remove upper timing cover mounting bolts, then the timing cover.
21. Reverse procedure to install, noting the following:
   a. Clean sealing surfaces on front cover and cylinder block.
   b. Install new gasket.
   c. Apply sealant as illustrated, **Fig. 7.**

FRONT COVER SEAL
REPLACE

1. Remove inner splash shield.
2. Remove crankshaft balancer, using torsional dampner remover tool No. J-24420, or equivalent.
3. Pry out seal using a suitable flat-bladed tool. **Do not damage crankshaft.**
4. Reverse procedure to install, noting the following:

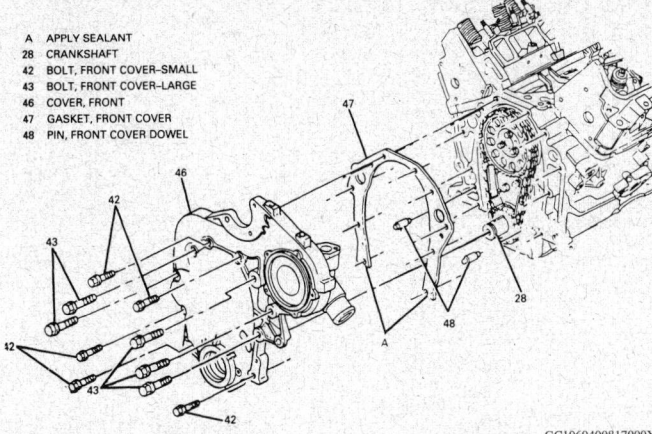

A	APPLY SEALANT
28	CRANKSHAFT
42	BOLT, FRONT COVER–SMALL
43	BOLT, FRONT COVER–LARGE
46	COVER, FRONT
47	GASKET, FRONT COVER
48	PIN, FRONT COVER DOWEL

GC1069400817000X

Fig. 7 Front cover installation

a. Lubricate new seal with clean engine oil and insert in front cover with lip facing engine.
b. Drive seal into place with front cover alignment and oil seal installer tool No. J-35468, or equivalent.

TIMING CHAIN
REPLACE
Removal

1. Remove front cover as outlined under "Front Cover, Replace."
2. Rotate crankshaft until timing marks are aligned, **Fig. 8.**
3. Remove camshaft sprocket retaining bolt, then the sprocket and timing chain.
4. Remove timing chain dampner bolts, then the dampner.
5. Remove crankshaft sprocket using sprocket removal tool No. J-5825-A, or equivalent.

Installation

1. Install new crankshaft sprocket until sprocket is fully seated on flange of crankshaft, using sprocket installer tool No. J-38612, or equivalent.
2. Coat camshaft and crankshaft sprockets with engine oil.
3. Hold camshaft sprocket with chain hanging down and align marks on camshaft and crankshaft sprockets with cast timing marks on engine block, **Fig. 9.**
4. Install front cover as outlined under "Front Cover, Replace."

CAMSHAFT
REPLACE

1. Remove engine as outlined under "Engine, Replace."
2. Remove valve lifters as outlined under "Hydraulic Lifters, Replace."
3. Remove timing chain and sprocket as outlined under "Timing Chain, Replace."
4. Remove camshaft thrust plate mounting bolts, then the thrust plate.

5. Install a suitable large screwdriver into camshaft bolt hole. **Do not damage threads.**
6. Carefully rotate, then pull camshaft from engine.
7. Reverse procedure to install, noting the following:
   a. If installing new camshaft, coat camshaft lobes with GM E.O.S. P/N 1052367, or equivalent.
   b. Lubricate camshaft journals with engine oil.

PISTON & ROD ASSEMBLY

When installing piston and rod assemblies into cylinder block, ensure arrow on top of piston faces toward front of engine, **Fig. 10.**

MAIN & ROD BEARINGS

Engine bearings are of the precision insert type. They are available for service use in standard and various undersizes, **Fig. 11.**

To determine proper replacement insert size, bearing clearance must be measured as follows:

1. Measure crankshaft journal diameter in several places, approximately 90° apart, then average the measurements.
2. Measure taper and runout, which should be .0002 inch (maximum).
3. Install bearing inserts and tighten rod and main bearing cap bolts to specifications, then measure I.D. with an inside micrometer. Measure connecting rod I.D. in same direction as length of rod.
4. Select a suitable set of inserts to provide specified clearance limits. **Do not mix inserts of different nominal size in same bearing bore.** If clearance limits cannot be met, crankshaft journal must be reconditioned and undersized bearing inserts installed.

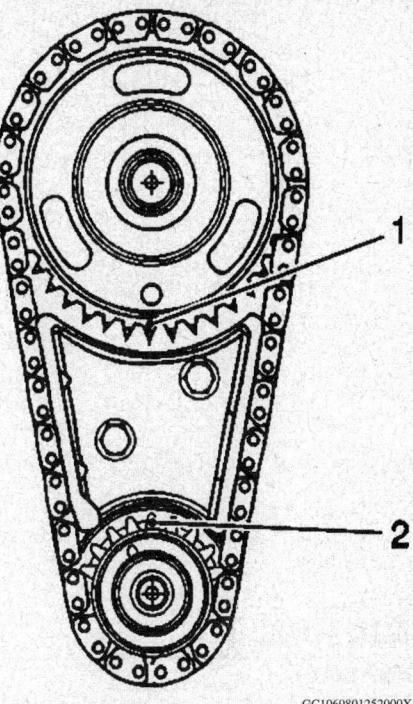

GC1069801252000X

Fig. 8 Timing mark alignment

CRANKSHAFT REAR OIL SEAL
REPLACE
Removal

1. Support engine with engine support fixture tool No. J-28467, or equivalent, and an extra support leg.
2. Remove transaxle as outlined in **MOTOR's "Domestic Transmission, In-Vehicle Service"** manual.
3. Remove flywheel.
4. Remove seal by inserting a suitable tool through dust lip at an angle, **Fig. 12,** then pry seal out by moving tool handle toward end of crankshaft pilot, repeating around circumference of seal as required. **Avoid damage to crankshaft outer surface.**

Installation

1. Inspect seal bore for nicks or burrs and repair as required.
2. Inspect crankshaft for burrs or nicks on surface which contacts seal, repairing or replacing crankshaft as required.
3. Apply engine oil to inner and outer diameters of new seal, then slide seal over mandrel until back of seal bottoms squarely against collar of rear main bearing seal installer tool No. J-34686, or equivalent, **Fig. 13.**
4. Align tool dowel pin with crankshaft dowel pin by hand, then **torque** mounting screws to 45 inch lbs., **Fig. 13.**
5. Turn tool "T" handle so collar pushes seal into bore, turning handle until collar is tight against case.
6. Loosen "T" handle until it comes to a stop, then remove mounting screws.

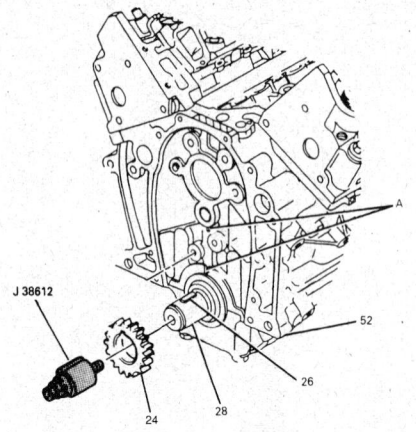

A   TIMING ALIGNMENT MARKS
24 SPROCKET, CRANKSHAFT
26 KEY, CRANKSHAFT
28 CRANKSHAFT
52 BLOCK, ENGINE

GC1069400818000X

Fig. 9 Timing chain installation

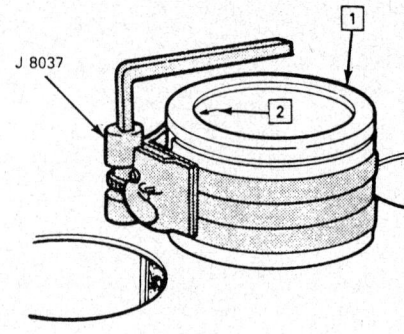

1 PISTON
2 ARROW TOWARDS FRONT OF ENGINE

GC1069100455000X

Fig. 10 Piston marking

7. Ensure seal is seated squarely in bore.
8. Install flywheel, then the transaxle assembly.

OIL PAN
REPLACE

1. Remove engine mount struts from engine.
2. Remove A/C compressor mounting bolts and set compressor aside.
3. Install engine support fixture tool No. J 28467-A, engine support fixture adapter tool No. J 28467-90 and engine support adapter leg tool No. J 36462, or equivalents.
4. Raise and support vehicle, then disconnect three way catalytic converter pipe from rear exhaust manifold.
5. Drain engine oil, then remove oil level sensor harness connector.
6. Remove starter as outlined under "Starter, Replace" in "Electrical" section.
7. Remove transaxle brace from oil pan.
8. Remove transaxle mount lower nuts, then the engine mount lower nuts.
9. Raise engine to gain access to oil pan.
10. Remove engine mount bracket with engine mount from oil pan.
11. Remove rear oil pan side bolts, then the front oil pan side bolts.
12. Remove oil pan retaining bolts, then the oil pan and gasket.
13. Reverse procedure to install, noting the following:
    a. Clean oil pan flanges, oil pan rail, front cover, rear main bearing cap and threaded holes.
    b. Install a new gasket.
    c. Install any shims removed in their original location.

OIL PUMP
REPLACE

1. Remove oil pan as outlined under "Oil Pan, Replace."
2. Remove crankshaft oil deflector retaining nuts, then the oil deflector.
3. Remove oil pump mounting bolt, then the oil pump and drive rod.
4. Reverse procedure to install.

OIL PUMP SERVICE
Disassemble

1. Drain oil from pump.
2. Remove pump cover and pump gears, **Fig. 14.**
3. Remove pressure regulator valve. If valve is stuck, soak pump housing in carburetor cleaning solvent.
4. Carefully remove pressure regulator valve spring retaining pin. **Spring may be under pressure.**
5. Clean sludge, oil and/or varnish from all components.

Inspection

1. Inspect pump housing and cover for cracks or damaged threads, replacing as required. **Do not attempt to repair pump housing.** Replace spring as required.
2. Inspect idler gear shaft. If loose in housing, replace pump.
3. Inspect pressure regulator valve for scoring or sticking. Burrs may be removed with a fine oil stone.
4. Inspect pressure regulator valve spring for loss of tension or bending.
5. Inspect suction pipe and screen assembly for looseness, if permanently pressed into pump body. If pipe is loose or has been removed, pump body cover must be replaced. Inspect for broken wire mesh or screen.
6. Inspect gears for chipping, galling or wear.
7. Measure gear lash in several positions, **Fig. 15,** which should be .0037–.0077 inch.
8. Measure pump housing gear pocket depth, **Fig. 16,** which should be as follows:
    a. **On models equipped with aluminum pump body,** pump depth should be 1.195–1.198 inches.
    b. **On models equipped with cast pump body,** pump depth should be 1.202–1.204 inches.
9. **On all models,** measure pump housing gear pocket diameter, **Fig. 16,** which should be 1.503–1.505 inches.
10. Measure pump gear diameters,

Fig. 17, which should be 1.498–1.500 inches.
11. Measure pump gear side clearance, **Fig. 18,** which should be .001–.003 inch.
12. Measure oil pump end clearance, **Fig. 19,** as follows:
    a. **On models equipped with aluminum pump body,** end clearance should be .0016–.0067 inch.
    b. **On models equipped with cast pump body,** end clearance should be .002–.005 inch.

Assemble

1. Lubricate all internal components with engine oil.
2. Install pump gears.
3. Prime engine oil galleries by removing engine oil pump drive unit and rotating oil pump, using drill motor, appropriate socket and extension.
4. Install cover and gasket. **Use only original equipment gaskets as gasket thickness is critical to proper pump operation.**
5. Install pin. Ensure pin is properly secured.
6. Install cover bolts.

BELT TENSION DATA

Belt tension is maintained automatically by a spring tensioned idler pulley. Adjustment of serpentine belt is not required.

If belt slippage is indicated and belt tensioner indicator is within normal operating range, measure belt tension as follows:

1. Run engine for ten minutes, then shut off and measure belt tension between any two pulleys using V-belt tension gauge tool No. J 23600-B, or equivalent.
2. Run engine for 30 seconds and repeat measurement.
3. Repeat preceding step, then average all three belt tension measurements, which should be 30–50 lbs.
4. Replace serpentine drive belt if tension is not as specified.

SERPENTINE DRIVE BELT

Replacement

1. Lift or rotate tensioner using a ½ inch breaker bar.
2. Remove serpentine belt.
3. Reverse procedure to install, routing drive belt as illustrated, **Fig. 20.**

Adjustment

There is no provision for serpentine belt adjustment. Refer to "Belt Tension Data" for belt tension measurement procedures and to determine whether belt requires replacement.

COOLING SYSTEM BLEED

1. Open vent valves located on thermostat housing and throttle body return pipe above water pump, **Fig. 21.** Turn both vents screws two to three turns.
2. Fill cooling system to base of radiator neck.
3. Close both vent valves. **Do not overtighten vent valves.**
4. Install radiator cap.
5. Add sufficient coolant to recovery tank.
6. Start engine and observe low coolant warning lamp.
7. If lamp remains illuminated, repeat bleed procedure.

THERMOSTAT

REPLACE

1. Drain engine coolant into a suitable container.
2. Disconnect radiator hose from thermostat housing.
3. Remove thermostat housing bolts, thermostat housing and thermostat.
4. Reverse procedure to install.

WATER PUMP

REPLACE

1. Drain engine coolant into a suitable container.
2. Remove serpentine drive belt, then disconnect radiator and heater hose.
3. Remove water pump mounting bolts, then the water pump, **Fig. 22.**
4. Reverse procedure to install.

RADIATOR

REPLACE

1. Remove battery, then drain cooling system into a suitable container.
2. Remove air cleaner assembly, then drain engine coolant into a suitable container.
3. Remove engine strut upper brace bolts from upper tie bar and rotate strut and brace rearward.
4. Disconnect upper radiator mounting panel bolts and clamps.
5. Disconnect cooling fan electrical connector.

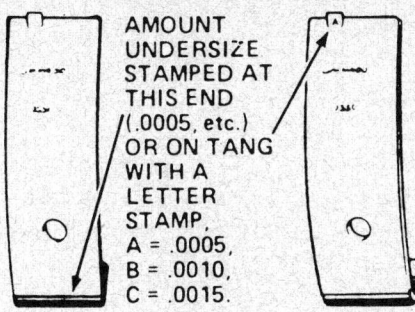

AMOUNT UNDERSIZE STAMPED AT THIS END (.0005, etc.) OR ON TANG WITH A LETTER STAMP. A = .0005, B = .0010, C = .0015.

GC1069100458000X

Fig. 11 Main bearing insert markings

6. Remove cooling fan mounting bolts and fan, then upper radiator bracket.
7. Remove upper and lower radiator hoses at radiator.
8. Disconnect low coolant sensor wiring.
9. Disconnect oil cooler lines, then remove radiator.
10. Reverse procedure to install.

FUEL PUMP

REPLACE

1. Relieve fuel system pressure as outlined under "Precautions."
2. Remove spare tire cover, jack, spare tire and trunk liner.
3. Remove seven fuel pump access panel retaining nuts, then fuel pump access panel.
4. Disconnect fuel tank pressure sensor electrical connector, then clean fuel pipes and fuel pump assembly to prevent fuel contamination.
5. Disconnect quick connect fittings at fuel pump assembly, then remove fuel pump retaining snap ring.
6. Remove modular fuel pump assembly.
7. Reverse procedure to install.

FUEL FILTER

REPLACE

1. Relieve fuel system pressure as outlined under "Precautions."
2. Raise and support vehicle.
3. Remove bracket mounting screw and filter bracket, **Fig. 23.**
4. Grasp filter and fuel line fitting. Twist quick-connect fitting ¼ turn in each direction to loosen any dirt within fitting.
5. Blow out dirt from quick-connect fitting.
6. Remove feed pipe nut from fuel filter, then drain any remaining fuel into a suitable container.
7. Remove fuel filter.
8. Reverse procedure to install.

TECHNICAL SERVICE BULLETINS

Banging, Clunking From Rear Of Vehicle

2004

On these models, there may be noises coming from the rear of the vehicle, most noticeable when stopping or during parking lot maneuvers. Drivers may also report the noise occurs when the fuel tank is between ½ full and full. This may be caused by fuel sloshing in the tank.

To correct this condition, install a revised fuel tank P/N 15141578. The PCM will require flashing with a new service calibration due to revised evaporative characteristics. Contact General Motors for further information.

Composite Rocker Cover Engine Oil Leaks

On some of these models, there may be a rocker cover oil leak, possibly be caused by the rocker cover material composition.

To correct this condition, install revised aluminum rocker covers (lefthand, P/N 24504669; righthand, P/N 24504670).

Intake Manifold Inspection After Engine Replacement

In cases where an engine has been replaced due to internal damage, use extra care when transferring the intake manifold to the new engine or long block. Internal damage may result in potential discharge of internal engine component debris in the intake manifold through bent, broken, or missing intake valves. After removing the intake manifold from the engine, carefully inspect all of the cylinder head intake ports to determine if the valve heads are intact and not bent. Usually when the valve heads are missing or sufficiently bent, internal engine component debris will appear in the cylinder head intake ports. If this debris is present in any of the ports, install a new intake manifold.

Ticking Noise During Cold Engine Operation

Some of these engines may exhibit a ticking noise during the first one or two minutes of engine operation or until the engine reaches operating temperature. This condition may be caused by excessive piston to bore clearance in the No. 1 and No. 4 cylinders.

To correct this condition, replace pistons with P/N 12564009. This condition is a customer satisfaction issue only. If pistons are not replaced, it will not affect the durability or life of the engine.

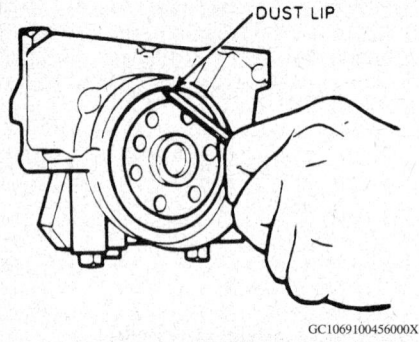

Fig. 12 Rear main seal removal

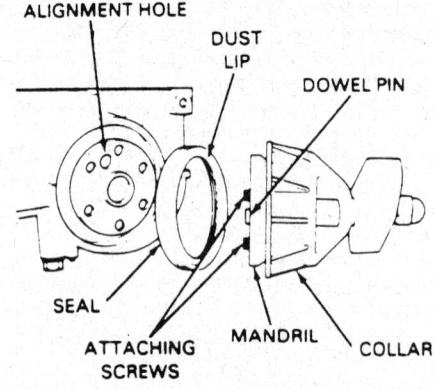

Fig. 13 Rear main seal installation

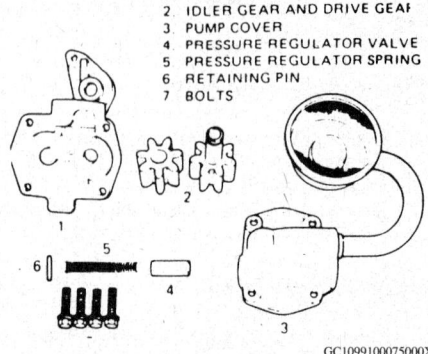

1 PUMP BODY
2 IDLER GEAR AND DRIVE GEAR
3 PUMP COVER
4 PRESSURE REGULATOR VALVE
5 PRESSURE REGULATOR SPRING
6 RETAINING PIN
7 BOLTS

Fig. 14 Exploded view of oil pump

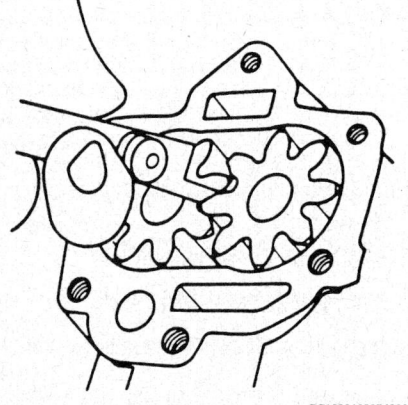

Fig. 15 Oil pump gear lash measurement

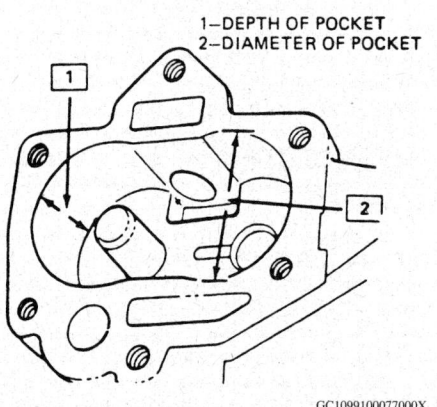

1—DEPTH OF POCKET
2—DIAMETER OF POCKET

Fig. 16 Oil pump gear pocket measurement

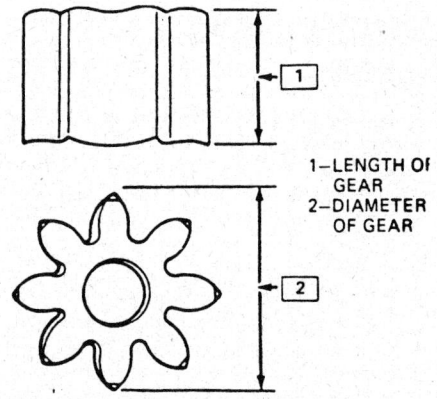

1—LENGTH OF GEAR
2—DIAMETER OF GEAR

Fig. 17 Oil pump gear measurement

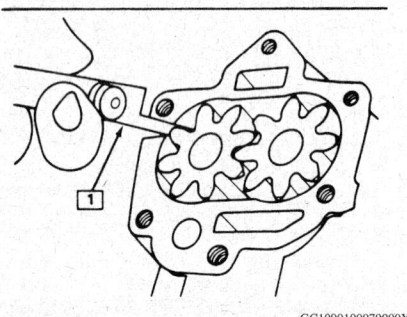

1 CHECK CLEARANCE BETWEEN GEAR TEETH AND SIDE WALL

Fig. 18 Gear side clearance measurement

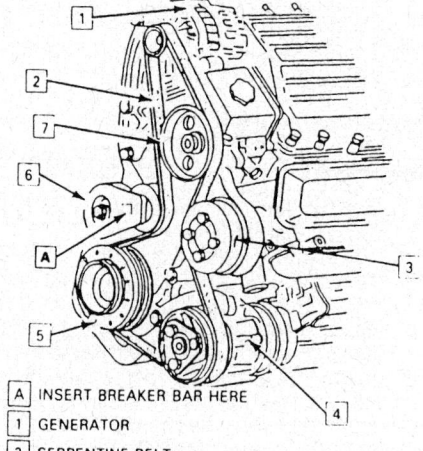

A INSERT BREAKER BAR HERE
1 GENERATOR
2 SERPENTINE BELT
3 WATER PUMP
4 AIR CONDITIONING COMPRESSOR
5 CRANKSHAFT
6 BELT TENSIONER
7 POWER STEERING PUMP

Fig. 20 Serpentine drive belt routing

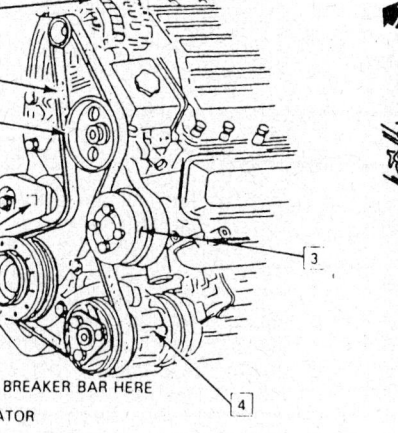

1 WATER OUTLET
2 THERMOSTAT
3 INLET
4 BLEEDER
5 BOLT/SCREW 25 N•m (18 LB. FT.)

Fig. 21 Cooling system bleed vent

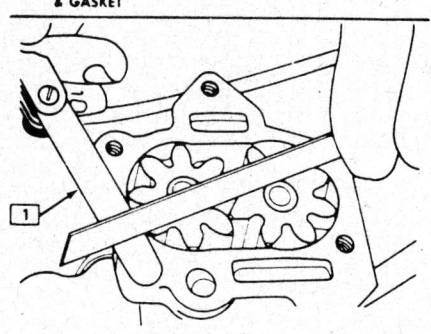

1 CHECK CLEARANCE BETWEEN STRAIGHT EDGE & GASKET

Fig. 19 Oil pump end clearance measurement

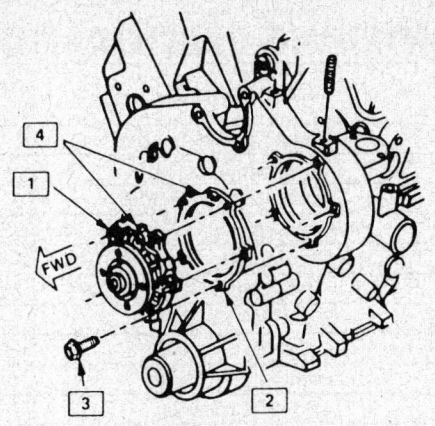

1. WATER PUMP
2. GASKET
3. 10 N·m (89 LB. IN.)
4. LOCATOR – MUST BE VERTICAL

GC1089100171000X

Fig. 22 Water pump mounting

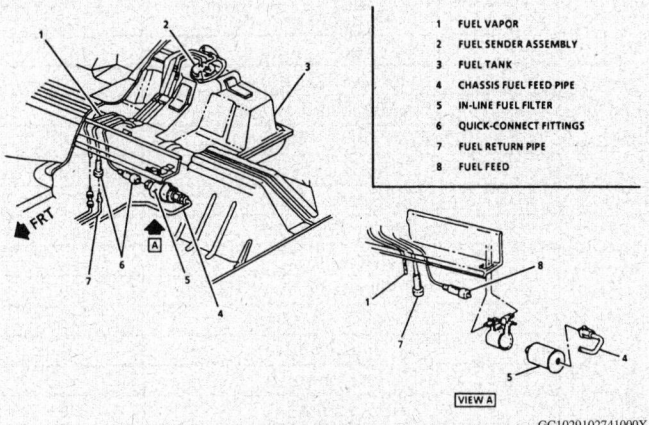

1	FUEL VAPOR
2	FUEL SENDER ASSEMBLY
3	FUEL TANK
4	CHASSIS FUEL FEED PIPE
5	IN-LINE FUEL FILTER
6	QUICK-CONNECT FITTINGS
7	FUEL RETURN PIPE
8	FUEL FEED

GC1029102741000X

Fig. 23 Fuel filter replacement

TIGHTENING SPECIFICATIONS

Year	Component	Torque/Ft. Lbs.
2001–04	Camshaft Position Sensor	89③
	Camshaft Sprocket	103
	Camshaft Thrust Plate	89③
	Connecting Rod Bearing	18⑤
	Coolant Drain Plug	14
	Coolant Temperature Sensor	17
	Crankshaft Balancer	76
	Cylinder Head	②
	Drive Belt Idler Pulley	37
	Drive Belt Shield	89③
	Drive Belt Tensioner	37
	Engine Mount Bracket	43
	Engine Mount	35
	Engine Mount Strut Bracket To Engine	35
	Engine Mount Strut Bracket To Radiator	21
	Exhaust Manifold Heat Shield	96③
	Exhaust Manifold Nut	12
	Exhaust Manifold Stud	12
	Flywheel	52
	Front Cover (Large)	41
	Front Cover (Small)	20
	Intake Manifold (Lower)	⑥
	Intake Manifold (Upper)	18
	Intake Manifold Stud (Upper)	18
	Main Bearing Cap	37④
	Oil Cooler Connector	50
	Oil Filter	10
	Oil Filter Adapter	29
	Oil Dipstick Retainer	18
	Oil Level Sensor	96③
	Oil Pan (Lower)	18
	Oil Pan (Side)	35
	Oil Pan Drain Plug	18
	Oil Pump	30
	Oil Pump Cover	96③
	Oil Pump Drive Assembly	27
	Rocker Arm	14①
	Serpentine Drive Belt Tensioner	40
	Spark Plugs	15
	Timing Chain Dampner	15
	Valve Cover	89③
	Valve Lifter Guide	89③
	Water Pump	96③
	Water Pump Pulley	18

Continued

TIGHTENING
SPECIFICATIONS—Continued

Year	Component	Torque/Ft. Lbs.
2005	Camshaft Position Sensor	89③
	Camshaft Sprocket	103
	Camshaft Thrust Plate	89③
	Connecting Rod Bearing	15⑦
	Coolant Drain Plug	14
	Coolant Temperature Sensor	17
	Crankshaft Balancer	52⑧
	Cylinder Head	②
	Drive Belt Idler Pulley	37
	Drive Belt Shield	89③
	Drive Belt Tensioner	37
	Engine Mount Bracket	43
	Engine Mount	35
	Engine Mount Strut Bracket To Engine	35
	Engine Mount Strut Bracket To Radiator	21
	Exhaust Manifold Heat Shield	96③
	Exhaust Manifold Nut	12
	Exhaust Manifold Stud	13
	Flywheel	52
	Front Cover (Large & Medium)	41
	Front Cover (Small)	20
	Intake Manifold (Lower)	⑥
	Intake Manifold (Upper)	18
	Intake Manifold Stud (Upper)	18
	Main Bearing Cap	37④
	Oil Filter	10
	Oil Filter Adapter	29
	Oil Dipstick Retainer	18
	Oil Pan (Lower)	18
	Oil Pan (Side)	37
	Oil Pan Drain Plug	18
	Oil Pump	30
	Oil Pump Cover	96③
	Oil Pump Drive Clamp Bolt	27
	Rocker Arm	14①
	Serpentine Drive Belt Tensioner	37
	Spark Plugs	15
	Timing Chain Dampner	15
	Valve Cover	89③
	Valve Lifter Guide	89③
	Water Pump	96③
	Water Pump Pulley	18

① — Rotate an additional 30°.
② — Refer to "Cylinder Head, Replace" for tightening procedure.
③ — Inch lbs.
④ — Rotate an additional 77°.
⑤ — Rotate an additional 100°.
⑥ — Refer to "Intake Manifold, Replace" for tightening procedure.
⑦ — Rotate an additional 75°.
⑧ — Rotate an additional 72°.

3.4L Engine

NOTE: On Air Bag Equipped Models, Refer To "Air Bag System Precautions" Located In The Front Of This Manual For System Disarming & Arming Procedures.

NOTE: Refer To "Computer Relearn Procedures" Located In The Front Of This Manual When Battery Power To The Computer Has Been Interrupted.

INDEX

PRECAUTIONS

Air Bag Systems

Refer to "Air Bag System Precautions" in the front of this manual for system disarming and arming procedures.

Battery Ground Cable

Prior to service, disconnect battery ground cable and isolate as required.

Fuel System Pressure Relief

To reduce the risk of fire and personal injury, it is required to relieve the fuel system pressure before servicing fuel system components.
1. Loosen fuel tank filler cap to relieve tank pressure.
2. Remove fuel injection sight shield.
3. Connect fuel pressure gauge tool No. J-34730-1, or equivalent, to fuel pressure valve. Wrap a shop towel around fitting while connecting gauge to avoid spillage.
4. Install bleed hose into a suitable container and open valve to bleed system pressure.

COMPRESSION PRESSURE

When inspecting compression, lowest cylinder must be within 70 percent of the highest cylinder with a minimum pressure of 100 psi. Perform compression test with engine at normal operating temperature, spark plugs removed and throttle wide open.

ENGINE MOUNT
REPLACE

Front

1. Disconnect air inlet duct from throttle body.
2. Remove lefthand and righthand engine mount struts.
3. Raise and support vehicle.
4. Disconnect catalytic converter pipe from righthand exhaust manifold.
5. Remove righthand front wheel and tire assembly.
6. Remove righthand side engine splash shield.
7. Remove engine mount to subframe nuts.
8. Lower vehicle, then install engine lifting tool No. J 28467-B, or equivalent.
9. Raise engine until mount is clear of subframe.
10. Raise and support vehicle.

11. Remove engine mount mounting bolts, **Fig. 1.**
12. Reverse procedure to install.

Lefthand

1. Remove engine mount strut from engine mount strut bracket.
2. Remove engine exhaust crossover pipe.
3. Remove thermostat housing as outlined under "Thermostat, Replace."
4. Remove engine mount strut bracket mounting bolts.
5. Remove engine mount strut bracket.
6. Reverse procedure to install.

Righthand
LOWER

1. Remove righthand lower engine mount strut bracket mounting bolts, **Fig. 2.**
2. Remove engine mount retaining nut, then the engine mount.
3. Reverse procedure to install.

UPPER

1. Remove righthand engine mount strut from upper engine strut mount bracket.
2. Remove fuel injector sight shield.
3. Remove EVAP emissions canister purge valve.
4. Remove righthand upper engine mount strut bracket bolts, then the

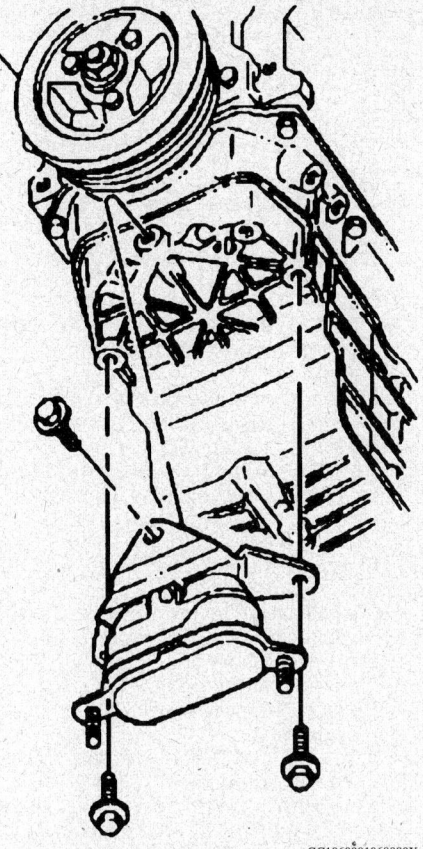

Fig. 1 Front engine mount

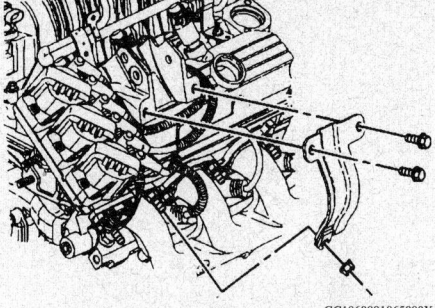

Fig. 2 Righthand lower engine mount removal

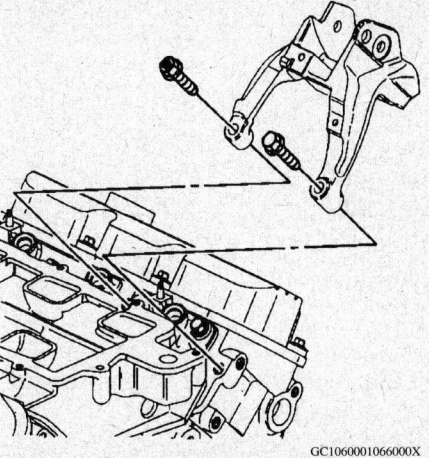

Fig. 3 Righthand upper engine mount bracket removal

bracket, **Fig. 3.**

5. **On models equipped with oil cooler,** remove oil cooler pipe bracket bolt from righthand engine mount strut bracket.
6. **On all models,** remove A/C compressor mounting bolts and position aside.
7. Remove vertical bolt from righthand engine mount strut bracket, **Fig. 4.**
8. Remove righthand engine mount bracket.
9. Reverse procedure to install.

ENGINE
REPLACE

1. Relieve fuel system pressure as outlined under "Precautions."
2. Remove hood assembly, then cross vehicle brace from engine compartment.
3. Remove throttle body air inlet duct and mass air flow sensor from air cleaner assembly.
4. Remove engine mount struts, then accessory drive belt.
5. Disconnect brake booster hose from upper intake manifold.
6. Disconnect and mark the following electrical connectors:
   a. Heated oxygen sensor.
   b. AIR check valve solenoid.
   c. EGR valve.
   d. EVAP valve.
   e. TP sensor.
   f. IAC valve.

   g. Alternator.
   h. Ignition coil.
   i. Harness grounds.
   j. Body wiring harness to engine wiring harness.
7. Raise and support vehicle.
8. Remove lower radiator air baffle, then righthand side engine splash shield.
9. Drain engine cooling system and oil.
10. Remove oil filter, then disconnect following electrical connectors:
    a. Vehicle speed sensor.
    b. Oil level sensor.
    c. Oil pressure switch.
    d. Engine block heater.
    e. Knock sensor.
    f. Heated oxygen sensor.
    g. Crankshaft position sensor.
    h. A/C compressor.
    i. Wiring harness grounds.
11. Remove catalytic converter from righthand exhaust manifold.
12. Remove engine mount lower retaining nuts.
13. Remove torque converter cover, then the starter motor.
14. Remove air conditioning compressor mounting bolts, then position and secure compressor aside.
15. Remove torque converter mounting bolts.
16. Remove transaxle brace, then lower transaxle to engine bolt and stud.
17. Disconnect lower radiator outlet hose from engine.
18. Lower vehicle, then disconnect accelerator and cruise control cables from throttle body and cable bracket.
19. Disconnect upper intake manifold and EVAP vacuum hoses.
20. Disconnect fuel feed and return hoses.
21. Disconnect AIR check valve hose.
22. Remove power steering pump and position aside.
23. Disconnect heater inlet and outlet hoses from engine.
24. Disconnect upper radiator hose from engine.
25. Support transaxle assembly with suitable floor stands.
26. Attach a suitable lifting device to engine.
27. Remove upper engine to transaxle bolts.
28. Remove engine assembly from vehicle.
29. Reverse procedure to install.

INTAKE MANIFOLD
REPLACE

Upper

1. Disconnect vacuum hose from throttle body air inlet duct.
2. Disconnect IAT sensor electrical connector, then the air inlet duct from throttle body.
3. Drain engine coolant into suitable container.
4. Disconnect accelerator and cruise control cables from throttle body.
5. Disconnect TP sensor and IAC valve electrical connectors.
6. Disconnect wiring harness attachment clips for CMP sensor and lefthand side spark plug wires.
7. Disconnect thermostat bypass hose from throttle body, then remove rear alternator brace.
8. Disconnect vacuum lines from upper intake manifold.
9. Remove MAP sensor, EGR valve, spark plug wires and ignition control module.
10. Remove upper intake manifold mounting bolts, then the intake manifold.
11. Reverse procedure to install.

Lower

1. Relieve fuel system pressure as outlined under "Precautions."
2. Remove upper intake manifold.
3. Remove righthand and lefthand valve covers as outlined under "Valve Cover, Replace."
4. Disconnect ECT sensor electrical connector.
5. Disconnect fuel injector and MAP sensor electrical connectors.
6. Remove fuel pipe clip bolt, then fuel pipe clip.
7. Disconnect fuel feed and return pipes from fuel rail.
8. Remove fuel injector rail.
9. Remove power steering pump from front engine cover and position aside.

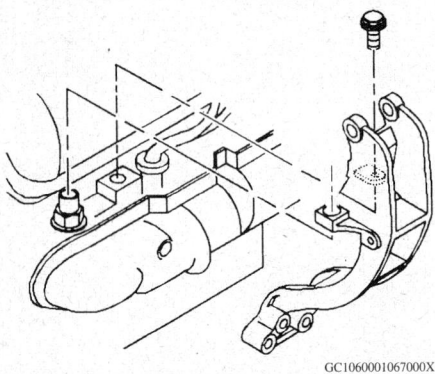

GC1060001067000X

Fig. 4   Righthand engine mount strut bracket

10. Disconnect heater inlet pipe with heater hose from lower intake manifold and position aside.
11. Disconnect upper radiator hose from engine, then the thermostat bypass hose from bypass pipe and lower intake manifold pipe.
12. Remove lower intake manifold mounting bolts, then the lower manifold and gaskets.
13. Reverse procedure to install, noting the following:
    a. Place new intake manifold gaskets in position.
    b. Apply .31–.39 inch drops of RTV sealant P/N 12346141, or equivalent, to four corners of manifold to block joints, **Fig. 5.**
    c. Connect sealant drops with sealant beads .31–.39 inch wide and .12–.20 inch thick, **Fig. 5.**
    d. Install rocker arms and pushrods.
    e. **Do not use old manifold mounting bolts. Always install new ones.**
    f. **Vertical bolts must be tightened before diagonal bolts or an oil leak could occur.**
    g. **Torque** bolts in sequence, **Fig. 6,** to 62 inch lbs.
    h. **Torque** bolts 1, 2, 3 and 4 in sequence to 115 inch lbs.
    i. **Torque** bolts 5, 6, 7 and 8 in sequence to 18 ft. lbs.

EXHAUST MANIFOLD
REPLACE
Righthand

1. Disconnect throttle body air inlet duct.
2. Remove righthand engine mount strut bracket, then the AIR pipe.
3. Remove thermostat bypass pipe.
4. Remove exhaust crossover pipe heat shield, then the crossover pipe.
5. Remove exhaust manifold heat shield mounting bolts, then the heat shield.
6. Remove exhaust manifold retaining nuts and exhaust manifold.
7. Reverse procedure to install.

Lefthand

1. Disconnect throttle body air inlet duct.
2. Remove AIR check valve.

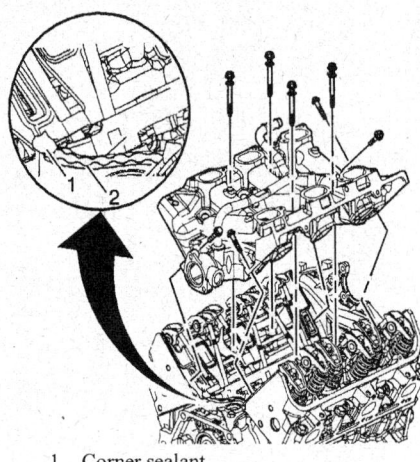

1. Corner sealant
2. Manifold to block sealant

ARM0400000000167

Fig. 5   Lower intake manifold replacement

3. Remove exhaust crossover pipe heat shield, then the crossover pipe.
4. Disconnect oxygen sensor electrical connector.
5. Raise and support vehicle, then remove catalytic converter from exhaust manifold.
6. Remove EGR valve from lower intake manifold.
7. Remove exhaust manifold head shield mounting bolts, then the heat shield.
8. Remove exhaust manifold retaining nuts, then the exhaust manifold and gasket.
9. Reverse procedure to install.

CYLINDER HEAD
REPLACE
Righthand

1. Raise and support vehicle, then drain engine coolant and oil.
2. Lower vehicle, then remove lower intake manifold as outlined under "Intake Manifold, Replace."
3. Remove righthand valve cover as outlined under "Valve Cover, Replace."
4. Remove exhaust crossover pipe, then the righthand engine mount strut bracket.
5. Remove oil dipstick tube.
6. Remove spark plugs, then the righthand exhaust manifold as outlined under "Exhaust Manifold, Replace."
7. Remove cylinder head mounting bolts, then the cylinder head and gasket.
8. Reverse procedure to install, noting the following:
    a. Clean cylinder head and gasket mating surfaces.
    b. **Torque** cylinder head bolts to 44 ft. lbs., then rotate an additional 95° in sequence, **Fig. 7.**

Lefthand

1. Raise and support vehicle, then drain engine coolant and oil.

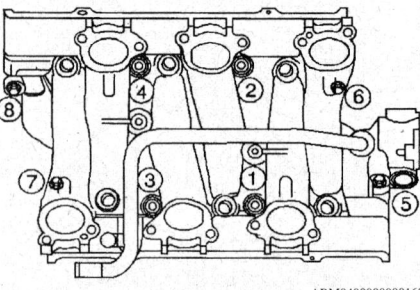

ARM0400000000168

Fig. 6   Lower intake manifold bolt tightening sequence

2. Lower vehicle, then remove lower intake manifold as outlined under "Intake Manifold, Replace."
3. Remove lefthand valve cover as outlined under "Valve Cover, Replace."
4. Remove exhaust crossover pipe.
5. Remove fuel line bracket.
6. Disconnect spark plug wires, then remove spark plugs.
7. Remove exhaust manifold as outlined under "Exhaust Manifold, Replace."
8. Remove cylinder head mounting bolts, then the cylinder head.
9. Reverse procedure to install, noting the following:
    a. Clean cylinder head and gasket mating surfaces.
    b. **Torque** cylinder head bolts to 44 ft. lbs., then rotate an additional 95° in sequence, **Fig. 7.**

VALVE COVER
REPLACE
Lefthand

1. Rotate tensioner clockwise using a box end wrench.
2. Remove serpentine belt.
3. Remove coolant recovery reservoir mounting bolts, then position reservoir aside.
4. Remove alternator mounting bolts, then disconnect alternator electrical connector.
5. Remove retaining nut, then disconnect battery lead.
6. Remove alternator and the alternator bracket.
7. Disconnect righthand spark plug wires, then the EVAP vacuum hoses from EVAP valve.
8. Remove EVAP and AIR check valves.
9. Remove ignition coils and bracket.
10. Remove vacuum hose from valve cover grommet.
11. Remove valve cover mounting bolts, then the valve cover.
12. Reverse procedure to install.

Righthand

1. Drain engine coolant into suitable container.
2. Disconnect spark plug wires, then remove engine mount strut from engine.
3. Remove AIR check valve.
4. Remove thermostat bypass hose and pipe.

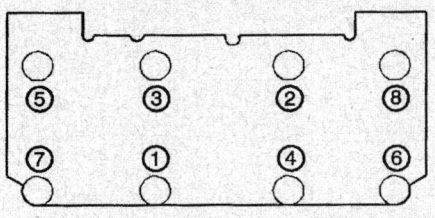

Fig. 7   Cylinder head bolt tightening sequence

5. Remove PCV valve.
6. Remove valve cover mounting bolts, then the valve cover.
7. Reverse procedure to install.

VALVE LIFTERS
Replace

1. Remove both valve covers as outlined under "Valve Cover, Replace."
2. Remove lower intake manifold as outlined under "Intake Manifold, Replace."
3. Remove rocker arm retaining bolts.
4. Remove rocker arms and push rods. Keep valve train components in order.
5. Remove lifter guide bolts, lifter guides and valve lifters.
6. Reverse procedure to install. Ensure valve train components are installed in their original position.

CAMSHAFT LOBE LIFT SPECIFICATIONS

Intake	2727 inch
Exhaust	2727 inch

ROCKER ARMS
REPLACE

1. Remove both valve covers as outlined under "Valve Cover, Replace."
2. Remove rocker arm retaining bolts.
3. Remove rocker arms and push rods. Keep valve train components in order.
4. Reverse procedure to install. Ensure valve train components are installed in their original position.

CRANKSHAFT DAMPER
REPLACE

1. Rotate belt tensioner clockwise using a box end wrench, then remove serpentine belt.
2. Raise and support vehicle.
3. Remove righthand tire and wheel assembly, then the engine splash shield.
4. Support frame with a suitable jack, then remove righthand side frame bolts and lower frame to access crankshaft balancer bolt.
5. Remove front lower air deflector panel.
6. Remove torque converter covers from transaxle.
7. Remove retaining nuts, then disconnect starter motor electrical connectors from solenoid.

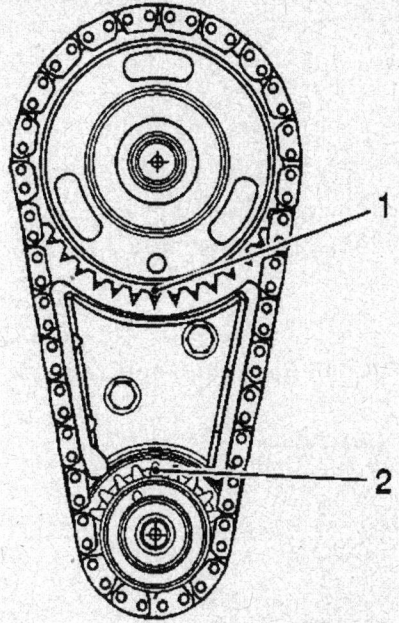

Fig. 8   Timing chain alignment marks

8. Remove starter motor mounting bolts, then the starter motor.
9. Attach flywheel holding tool No. J-37096, or equivalent, to flywheel.
10. Remove crankshaft pulley bolt and pulley.
11. Remove crankshaft damper/balancer using crankshaft damper removal tool No. J-24430, or equivalent.
12. Reverse procedure to install, noting the following:
    a. Coat front cover oil seal with engine oil.
    b. Install suitable sealant to keyway of damper before installation.
    c. Install damper using crankshaft damper installer tool No. J-29113, or equivalent.

FRONT COVER
REPLACE

1. Raise and support vehicle, then drain engine coolant and oil.
2. Remove crankshaft balancer as outlined under "Crankshaft Dampner, Replace."
3. Remove drive belt tensioner mounting bolt, then the drive belt tensioner.
4. Remove power steering pump with lines and position aside.
5. Disconnect thermostat bypass pipe from front cover, then the radiator outlet hose from water pump.
6. Remove water pump pulley mounting bolts, then the pulley.
7. Disconnect CKP sensor wiring harness bracket from front cover.
8. Remove front cover mounting bolts, then the front cover and gasket.
9. Remove drive belt shield, CKP sensor and water pump from front cover.
10. Reverse procedure to install.

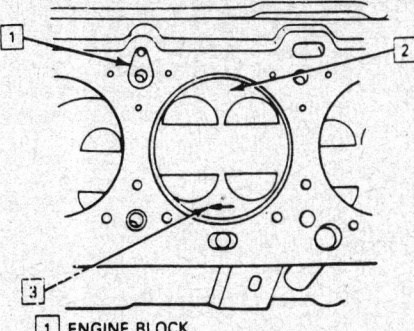

1	ENGINE BLOCK
2	PISTON
3	ARROW FACES TOWARDS FRONT OF ENGINE

Fig. 9   Piston marking

FRONT COVER SEAL
REPLACE

1. Remove crankshaft pulley and dampner as outlined under "Crankshaft Dampner, Replace."
2. Pry out seal using a suitable pry tool.
3. Reverse procedure to install, noting the following:
    a. Lubricate seal with oil.
    b. Install seal using seal installer tool No. J-34995, or equivalent.

TIMING CHAIN
REPLACE

1. Remove engine front cover as outlined under "Front Cover, Replace."
2. Rotate crankshaft until timing marks are aligned, **Fig. 8.**
3. Remove camshaft sprocket bolt.
4. Remove camshaft sprocket with timing chain.
5. Reverse procedure to install. Coat crankshaft and camshaft sprockets with oil before installing front cover.

CAMSHAFT
REPLACE

1. Remove timing chain as outlined under "Timing Chain, Replace."
2. Remove camshaft thrust plate mounting bolts, then the thrust plate.
3. Insert a large screwdriver into camshaft bolt hole.
4. Carefully rotate and pull camshaft out of camshaft bearings.
5. Reverse procedure to install, noting the following:
    a. Coat camshaft journals with clean engine oil.
    b. Coat camshaft lobes with pre-lube P/N 1052365, or equivalent.

PISTON & ROD ASSEMBLY

When installing piston and rod assemblies into cylinder block, ensure arrow on top of piston faces toward the front of the engine, **Fig. 9.**

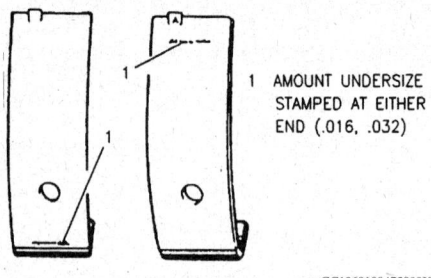

1 AMOUNT UNDERSIZE
STAMPED AT EITHER
END (.016, .032)

GC1069100475000X

Fig. 10 Bearing marking

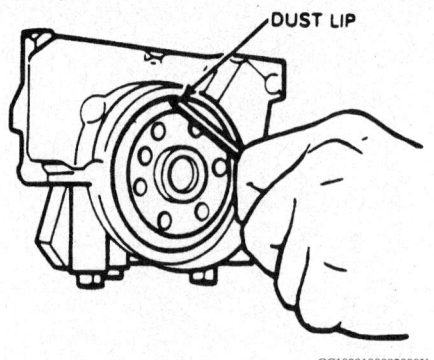

GC1099100082000X

Fig. 11 Rear main seal removal

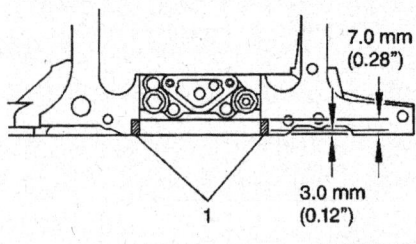

GC1060001143000X

Fig. 12 Oil pan sealant application

MAIN & ROD BEARINGS

Connecting rod and main bearing are of the precision insert type. They are available for service use in standard and two undersizes of .016 and .032 inch. Bearing undersize amount is stamped at either end of the bearing, **Fig. 10.**

CRANKSHAFT REAR OIL SEAL

REPLACE

1. Remove transaxle as outlined in **MOTOR's "Domestic Transmission, In-Vehicle Service"** manual.
2. Remove flywheel.
3. Remove oil seal using a suitable pry tool, **Fig. 11.**
4. Reverse procedure to install. Use seal installer tool No. J-34686, or equivalent.

OIL PAN

REPLACE

1. Remove engine mount struts from engine.
2. Remove A/C compressor mounting bolts, then position compressor aside.
3. Install engine support fixture tool No. J 28467-360, or equivalent.
4. Raise and support vehicle.
5. Remove catalytic converter from exhaust manifold.
6. Drain engine oil, then disconnect oil level sensor electrical connector.
7. Remove starter motor, then the transaxle brace from oil pan.
8. Remove transaxle lower mount retaining nuts.
9. Remove engine mount lower retaining nuts.
10. Raise engine slightly, then remove engine mount bracket and engine mount from oil pan.
11. Remove righthand and lefthand side oil pan mounting bolts.
12. Remove oil pan to engine block mounting bolts, then the oil pan.
13. Reverse procedure to install. Apply suitable sealant to main bearing cap and engine block, **Fig. 12.**

OIL PUMP

REPLACE

1. Remove oil pan as outlined under "Oil Pan, Replace."

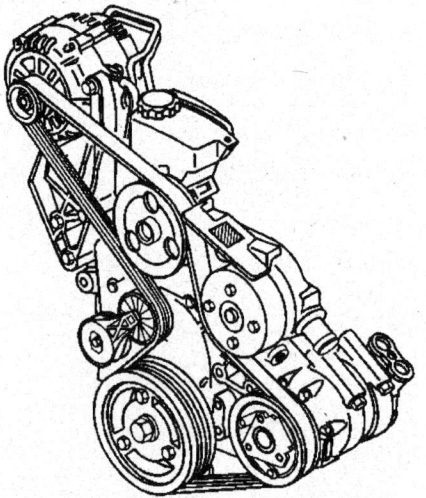

GC1060001144000X

Fig. 13 Serpentine drive belt routing

2. Remove oil pump to crankshaft rear bearing cap mounting bolt, then the oil pump.
3. Reverse procedure to install.

BELT TENSION DATA

Belt tension is maintained automatically by a spring tensioned idler pulley. No adjustment of serpentine belt is required.

If belt slippage is indicated and belt tensioner indicator is within normal operating range, measure belt tension as follows:

1. Run engine for ten minutes, then shut off and measure belt tension between any two pulleys using V-belt tension gauge tool No. J 23600-B, or equivalent.
2. Run engine for 30 seconds and repeat measurement.
3. Repeat preceding step, then average all three belt tension measurements, which should be 35–55 lbs.
4. Replace drive belt if tension is not as specified.

SERPENTINE DRIVE BELT

Belt Replacement

1. Rotate tensioner clockwise using a box end wrench.
2. Remove serpentine belt.
3. Reverse procedure to install, routing belt as illustrated, **Fig. 13.**

Tensioner Replacement

1. Remove serpentine drive belt as outlined in this section.
2. Remove tensioner bolt, then the tensioner.
3. Reverse procedure to install.

COOLING SYSTEM BLEED

1. Open air bleed vents on thermostat housing and heater water inlet pipe.
2. Fill system with water and coolant until level of coolant has reached base of radiator neck.
3. Close bleed vents and add clean water if required to bring coolant level to base of radiator neck.

THERMOSTAT

REPLACE

1. Remove throttle body air inlet duct.
2. Partially drain cooling system into suitable container.
3. Remove radiator hose from thermostat housing.
4. Remove exhaust crossover pipe.
5. Remove thermostat housing bolts, then the thermostat housing.
6. Remove thermostat.
7. Reverse procedure to install.

WATER PUMP

REPLACE

1. Remove air cleaner assembly.
2. Drain engine coolant into a suitable container.
3. Rotate belt tensioner clockwise using a box end wrench, then remove serpentine belt.
4. Remove water pump pulley.
5. Remove water pump bolts, then the water pump and gasket, **Fig. 14.**
6. Reverse procedure to install.

RADIATOR

REPLACE

1. Remove air cleaner assembly, then drain engine coolant into a suitable container.

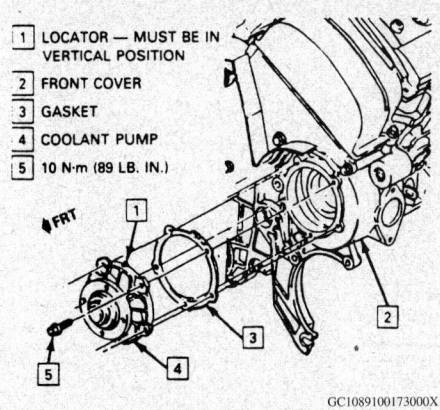

1. LOCATOR — MUST BE IN VERTICAL POSITION
2. FRONT COVER
3. GASKET
4. COOLANT PUMP
5. 10 N·m (89 LB. IN.)

GC1089100173000X

Fig. 14 Water pump assembly

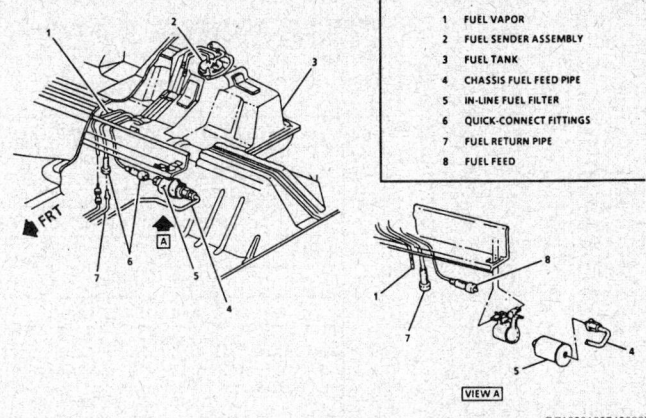

1. FUEL VAPOR
2. FUEL SENDER ASSEMBLY
3. FUEL TANK
4. CHASSIS FUEL FEED PIPE
5. IN-LINE FUEL FILTER
6. QUICK-CONNECT FITTINGS
7. FUEL RETURN PIPE
8. FUEL FEED

VIEW A

GC1029102742000X

Fig. 15 Fuel filter replacement

2. Remove engine strut upper brace bolts from upper tie bar and rotate strut and brace rearward.
3. Disconnect upper radiator mounting panel bolts and clamps.
4. Disconnect cooling fan electrical connector.
5. Remove cooling fan mounting bolts and fan, then the upper radiator bracket.
6. Remove upper and lower radiator hoses at radiator.
7. Disconnect low coolant sensor wiring.
8. Disconnect oil cooler lines, then remove radiator.
9. Reverse procedure to install.

FUEL PUMP
REPLACE

1. Relieve fuel system pressure as outlined under "Precautions."
2. Remove fuel pump/sender assembly access cover from luggage compartment.
3. Remove fuel pump/sender assembly mounting bolts.
4. Pull assembly upward and disconnect electrical connector.
5. Remove pump/sender assembly from fuel tank.
6. Reverse procedure to install.

FUEL FILTER
REPLACE

1. Relieve fuel system pressure as outlined under "Precautions."
2. Raise and support vehicle.
3. Remove bracket mounting screw and filter bracket, **Fig. 15.**
4. Grasp filter and fuel line fitting. Twist quick-connect fitting ¼ turn in each direction to loosen any dirt within fitting.
5. Blow out dirt from quick-connect fitting.
6. Remove feed pipe nut from fuel filter, then drain any remaining fuel into a suitable container.
7. Remove fuel filter.
8. Reverse procedure to install.

TECHNICAL SERVICE BULLETINS

Banging, Clunking From Rear Of Vehicle

2004

On these models, there may be noises coming from the rear of the vehicle, most noticeable when stopping or during parking lot maneuvers. Drivers may also report the noise occurs when the fuel tank is between ½ full and full. This may be caused by fuel sloshing in the tank.

To correct this condition, install a revised fuel tank P/N 15141578. The PCM will require flashing with a new service calibration due to revised evaporative characteristics. Contact General Motors for further information.

Intake Manifold Inspection After Engine Replacement

In cases where an engine is being replaced due to internal damage, use extra care when transferring the intake manifold to the new engine or long block. Internal damage may result in potential discharge of internal engine component debris in the intake manifold through bent, broken, or missing intake valves. After removing the intake manifold from the engine, carefully inspect all of the cylinder head intake ports to determine if the valve heads are intact and not bent. Usually when the valve heads are missing or sufficiently bent, internal engine component debris will appear in the cylinder head intake ports. If this debris is present in any of the ports, install a new intake manifold.

TIGHTENING SPECIFICATIONS

Year	Component	Torque/Ft. Lbs.
2001–05	Accelerator Control Cable Bracket	89
	Alternator Brace Bracket	37
	Camshaft Position Sensor	89①
	Camshaft Sprocket	103
	Camshaft Thrust Plate	89①
	Connecting Rod Cap	15②
	Coolant Drain Plug	14
	Crankshaft Balancer	76
	Crankshaft Main Bearing Cap	37④
	Crankshaft Oil Deflector	18
	Crankshaft Position Sensor Bolt	89①
	Crankshaft Position Sensor Stud	98①
	Crankshaft Position Sensor Wiring Bracket	20
	Cylinder Head	③
	Drive Belt Tensioner	37
	EGR Valve To EGR Valve Pipe	18
	EGR Valve Adapter Pipe	18
	Engine Flywheel	52
	Engine Mount Bracket	43
	Engine Mount Lower Nut	32
	Engine Mount Strut & Lift Bracket (Lefthand Side)	52
	Engine Mount Strut & Lift Bracket (Righthand Side)	37
	Engine Mount Strut Bolt/Nut	35
	Engine Mount Strut Bracket Bolt (Upper Radiator Support)	21
	Engine Mount Strut Bracket Bolt (Vehicle Righthand Side)	37
	Engine Mont Upper Nut	35
	Engine Oil Pressure Indicator Switch	12
	Exhaust Crossover Heat Shield	89①
	Exhaust Crossover	18
	Exhaust Manifold Heat Shield	89①
	Exhaust Manifold Nut	12
	Exhaust Manifold Pipe Stud	13
	Front Cover (Large & Medium Bolts)	41
	Front Cover (Small Bolts)	20
	Fuel Injector Rail Nut	89①
	Fuel Pipe Clip Bolt	71①
	Fuel Return Pipe To Fuel Injector Rail Nut	13
	Heated Oxygen Sensor	31
	Ignition Coil Bracket	18
	Intake Manifold Coolant Pipe Bolt	89①
	Intake Manifold, Lower	⑥
	Intake Manifold, Upper	18
	Main Bearing Cap	37④
	MAP Sensor	44①
	Oil Cooler Connector	37
	Oil Cooler Hose Fitting	14
	Oil Filter	22
	Oil Filter Bypass Hole Plug	14
	Oil Gallery Plug ¼ Inch	14
	Oil Gallery Plug ⅜ Inch	24
	Oil Dipstick Tube	18

Continued

TIGHTENING
SPECIFICATIONS—Continued

Year	Component	Torque/Ft. Lbs.
2001–05	Oil Level Sensor	89①
	Oil Pan	18
	Oil Pan Drain Plug	18
	Oil Pump Cover	89①
	Oil Pump Drive Clamp Bolt	27
	Oil Pump Mounting Bolt	30
	Spark Plug (2001)	20
	Spark Plug (2002)	⑦
	Spark Plug (2003–05)	⑧
	Thermostat Bypass Pipe To Cylinder Head Nut	18
	Thermostat Bypass Pipe To Front Cover	106①
	Thermostat Bypass Pipe To Throttle Body	18
	Throttle Body Bolt/Nut	18
	Timing Chain Dampner	15
	Transaxle To Engine	55
	Valve Lifter Guide	89①
	Valve Rocker Arm	14⑤
	Valve Rocker Arm Cover	89①
	Water Outlet	18
	Water Pump	98①
	Water Pump Pulley	18

① — Inch lbs.
② — Rotate an additional 75°.
③ — Refer to "Cylinder Head, Replace."
④ — Rotate an additional 77°.
⑤ — Rotate an additional 30°.
⑥ — Refer to "Intake Manifold, Replace" for tightening procedure.
⑦ — New cylinder head, 15 ft. lbs. Existing cylinder head, 11 ft. lbs.
⑧ — Initial installation, 15 ft. lbs. Later installation, 13 ft. lbs.

3.5L Engine

NOTE: On Air Bag Equipped Models, Refer To "Air Bag System Precautions" Located In The Front Of This Manual For System Disarming & Arming Procedures.

NOTE: Refer To "Computer Relearn Procedures" Located In The Front Of This Manual When Battery Power To The Computer Has Been Interrupted.

INDEX

PRECAUTIONS

Air Bag Systems

Refer to "Air Bag System Precautions" in the front of this manual for system disarming and arming procedures.

Battery Ground Cable

Prior to service, disconnect battery ground cable and isolate as required.

Fuel System Pressure Relief

To reduce the risk of fire and personal injury, relieve the fuel system pressure before servicing fuel system components.

1. Loosen fuel tank filler cap to relieve tank pressure.
2. Connect fuel pressure gauge tool No. J-34730-1, or equivalent, to fuel pressure valve. Wrap a shop towel around fitting while connecting gauge to avoid spillage.
3. Install bleed hose into a suitable container and open valve to bleed system pressure.

COMPRESSION PRESSURE

When inspecting compression, lowest cylinder must be within 70 percent of the highest cylinder with a minimum pressure of 140 psi. Perform compression test with engine at normal operating temperature, spark plugs removed and throttle wide open.

ENGINE MOUNT

REPLACE

1. Remove bolt and nut from engine mount strut at engine bracket.
2. Remove bolt and nut from engine mount strut at radiator support bracket.
3. Remove engine mount strut, then bracket from radiator support.
4. Install engine support fixture No. J 28467-B using adapter set Nos. J 36462-A and J 28467-90A, or equivalents.
5. Raise and support vehicle, then remove lower engine mount nuts.
6. Lower vehicle, then raise engine to gain access to engine mount.
7. Raise and support vehicle, then remove upper engine mount nuts.
8. Remove engine mount from bracket.
9. Reverse procedure to install.

ENGINE

REPLACE

The throttle cable must be replaced when removing or replacing the engine.

1. Remove fuel injector sight shield and throttle body air inlet duct.
2. Remove engine mount strut as outlined under "Engine Mount, Replace."
3. Relieve fuel system pressure as outlined under "Precautions," then disconnect fuel lines from fuel rail and position aside.
4. Disconnect fuel vapor line, then remove throttle and cruise control cables with mounting brackets from throttle body.
5. Disconnect automatic range selector from park/neutral position switch and vacuum booster hose from engine.
6. Disconnect air conditioning vacuum hose from engine, then the wiring harness connectors from engine and transmissions.
7. Drain coolant into suitable container, then disconnect radiator inlet hose from engine.
8. Disconnect transaxle cooler lines from radiator, surge tank inlet hose and heater hoses from engine.
9. Raise and support vehicle, then drain engine oil.
10. Remove lower radiator air deflector, then disconnect AIR pipe from AIR inlet valve.
11. Remove battery cables from retainers,

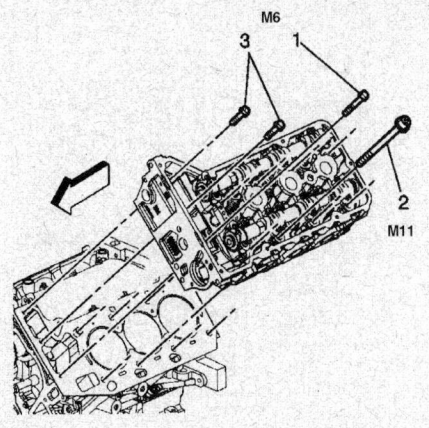

Fig. 1 Cylinder head bolt removal

then disconnect radiator outlet hose from engine.

12. Remove air conditioning compressor and secure to frame.
13. Remove torque converter cover.
14. Disconnect starter motor electrical connectors and remove starter motor.
15. Reference mark flywheel to torque converter location, then remove flywheel to torque converter mounting bolts.
16. Remove catalytic converter pipe from rear exhaust manifold, then the lower engine to transaxle bolts.
17. Remove front wheel and tire assemblies, then the inner fender splash shield.
18. Disconnect fog lamp electrical connectors, then remove wheel speed sensor harness conduits from lower control arm retainers.
19. Remove tie rod ends and lower ball joints from steering knuckles.
20. Disconnect drive axles from transaxle and secure to vehicle.
21. Remove pinch bolt at intermediate shaft, then disconnect intermediate shaft from steering gear.
22. Place universal engine support table No. J 39580, or equivalent, under engine/transaxle/frame.
23. Lower the vehicle to universal engine support table to support engine/transaxle/frame.
24. Secure vehicle to hoist, then remove frame to body bolts.
25. Raise and support vehicle, then remove universal engine support table with engine/transaxle/frame from under vehicle.
26. Remove engine mount bracket to engine bolts, then the transaxle brace.
27. Remove serpentine drive belt and power steering pump from engine and position aside.
28. Remove alternator and upper engine to transaxle bolts.
29. Remove engine from transaxle/frame.
30. Reverse procedure to install. **Ensure intermediate shaft is fully seated prior to installing pinch bolt.**

INTAKE MANIFOLD
REPLACE

1. Disconnect throttle body air inlet duct, then partially drain coolant into suitable container.
2. Remove fuel injector sight shield, then disconnect throttle and cruise control cables from throttle body.
3. Relieve fuel system pressure as outlined under "Precautions."
4. Disconnect fuel lines and coolant hoses from throttle body.
5. Disconnect fuel vapor line from EVAP canister purge solenoid.
6. Disconnect vacuum hose from brake booster and A/C vacuum hose from intake manifold.
7. Disconnect surge tank inlet pipe retainer from fuel rail.
8. Disconnect electrical connectors from the following:
   a. Fuel injectors.
   b. Throttle position sensor.
   c. IAC valve.
   d. EVAP canister purge solenoid.
   e. MAP sensor.
9. Remove engine wiring harness and channel from valve cover and position aside.
10. Disconnect fuel pressure regulator vacuum line from regulator and throttle body.
11. Remove PCV valve and feed tubes from valve cover and intake manifold.
12. Remove EGR valve outlet pipe and water crossover from intake manifold.
13. Disconnect fuel rail snap lock retainers by pushing toward valve cover and lifting.
14. Remove fuel rail and injectors as an assembly.
15. Remove intake manifold bolts, then the intake manifold.
16. Reverse procedure to install.

EXHAUST MANIFOLD
REPLACE
Lefthand

1. Remove engine as outlined under "Engine, Replace."
2. Remove lefthand exhaust manifold crossover pipe from righthand exhaust manifold.
3. Disconnect EGR valve pipe from exhaust crossover pipe.
4. Remove lefthand exhaust manifold retaining bolts, then the exhaust manifold.
5. Remove oxygen sensor and replace as required.
6. Replace exhaust manifold studs.
7. Reverse procedure to install.

Righthand

1. Remove fuel injector sight shield, then the engine mount strut and bracket.
2. Drain coolant into suitable container, then remove engine cooling fans.
3. Remove radiator inlet and outlet hoses.

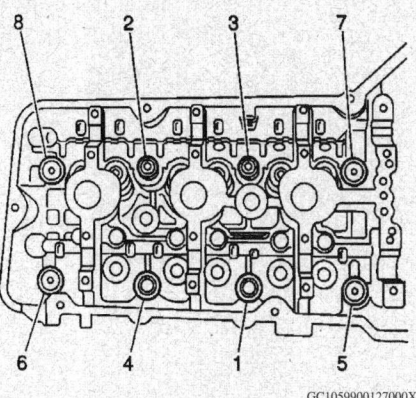

Fig. 2 Cylinder head bolt tightening sequence

4. Remove transaxle cooler lines from radiator.
5. Remove radiator from vehicle.
6. Position washer solvent reservoir aside.
7. Lift or rotate belt tensioner using a suitable breaker bar, then remove serpentine belt.
8. Remove thermostat and radiator outlet hose.
9. Remove battery hold down retainer, battery and battery tray.
10. Remove engine mount strut mounting bolts from radiator and engine mounted brackets, then strut mount.
11. Disconnect cooling fan wiring harness to engine wiring harness connectors.
12. Remove cooling fan shroud mounting bolts, then the cooling fan shroud and cooling fan assembly.
13. Remove outboard alternator bolt, then loosen inboard alternator bolt.
14. Remove idler pulley bolt and idler pulley.
15. Disconnect alternator electrical terminals and connectors.
16. Remove inboard alternator bolt, then the alternator.
17. Remove exhaust manifold heat shield and oil dipstick tube.
18. Disconnect vacuum tube from AIR control valve.
19. Disconnect feed pipe nut from exhaust manifold.
20. Remove AIR control from engine mount strut bracket.
21. Loosen exhaust manifold retaining bolts.
22. Remove exhaust manifold crossover pipe flange retaining studs.
23. Remove exhaust manifold bolts, then the exhaust manifold.
24. Reverse procedure to install.

CYLINDER HEAD
REPLACE

1. Remove intake manifold as outlined under "Intake Manifold, Replace."
2. Remove water outlet housing and engine mount strut bracket from righthand cylinder head.
3. Remove water crossover pipe.

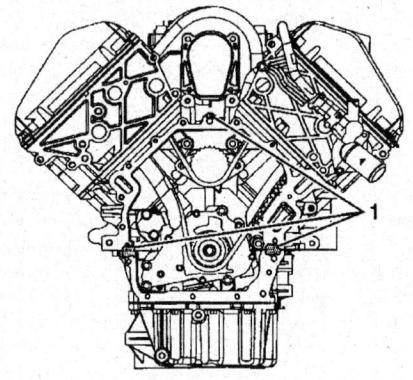

GC1059900128000X

Fig. 3 Front cover RTV application points

4. Remove exhaust manifold as outlined under "Exhaust Manifold, Replace."
5. Remove camshaft covers, then install camshaft holding fixture No. J 42038, or equivalent.
6. Remove primary camshaft drive chain, then the camshafts.
7. Remove rocker arms and lifters.
8. Remove ECT sensor from lefthand cylinder head.
9. Remove and discard M6 and M11 bolts, **Fig. 1. Do not use cylinder head bolts again. Always install new ones.**
10. Remove cylinder head.
11. Reverse procedure to install, noting the following:
    a. Ensure cylinder head locating pins are secured in cylinder block.
    b. Install new M6 and M11 bolts as outlined, **Fig. 1.**
    c. Tighten M11 bolts in three steps in sequence, **Fig. 2.** First step, **torque** bolts to 30 ft. lbs.; second step, rotate an additional 100°; third step, rotate an additional 100°.
    d. **Torque** long M8 bolt to 106 inch lbs.
    e. **Torque** two short M8 bolts to 106 inch lbs.

VALVE COVER
REPLACE
Lefthand

1. Remove fuel injector sight shield and bracket.
2. Disconnect PCV feed tube from lefthand valve cover.
3. Disconnect Inlet hose from coolant over flow tank.
4. Remove coolant over flow tank retaining nuts, then position tank aside.
5. Release clips from power steering lines, then position lines aside.
6. Remove engine wiring harness channel bolt from lefthand valve cover, then position harness aside.
7. Remove engine wiring harness from retainers at lefthand rear camshaft cover.
8. Disconnect oxygen sensor, then remove lefthand coil assembly from valve cover.

9. Remove lefthand valve cover retaining bolts, then lift evenly off of cylinder head.
10. Reverse procedure to install.

Righthand

1. Remove fuel injector sight shield.
2. Remove oil tube bolt, then adjust tube for access.
3. Disconnect PCV valve and feed tube from righthand valve cover.
4. Remove coil assembly from righthand valve cover.
5. Remove engine harness channel bolt from righthand valve cover, then position harness aside.
6. Remove engine harness from retainers on righthand valve cover and position aside.
7. Remove righthand valve cover retaining bolts, then lift cover off evenly.
8. Reverse procedure to install.

VALVE ARRANGEMENT

On the lefthand side of engine, exhaust valves are on the lefthand side, intake valves on the righthand side. On the righthand side of engine, intake valves are on the lefthand side, exhaust valves on the righthand side.

CAMSHAFT LOBE LIFT SPECIFICATIONS

Exhaust.....................................394 inch
Intake ....413 inch

VALVE ADJUSTMENT

There is no valve adjustment for these engines.

FRONT COVER
REPLACE

1. Drain coolant into suitable container, then remove righthand diagonal brace.
2. Remove battery and battery tray.
3. Remove engine coolant and washer solvent reservoirs.
4. Reposition underhood accessory wiring junction block for access, then remove serpentine drive belt.
5. Remove power steering pump pulley and serpentine drive belt idler pulley.
6. Remove water pump pulley retaining bolts, then the pump pulley.
7. Remove water pump and housing as an assembly.
8. Support engine cradle, then remove righthand side cradle bolts.
9. Lower engine cradle, then remove crankshaft balancer.
10. Remove coolant drain plug from front cover and drain coolant from engine block into suitable container.
11. Remove ten perimeter bolts from front cover.
12. Remove front cover and gasket from engine. **Use plastic scraper when removing remaining gasket material to avoid sealing surface damage.**
13. Reverse procedure to install. Apply

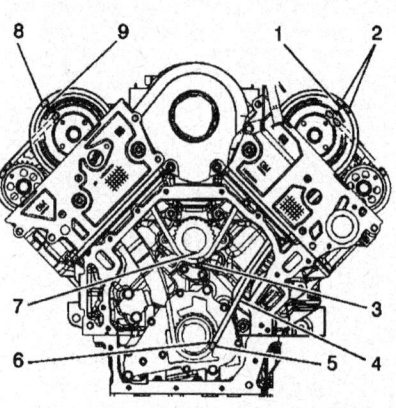

GC1059900129000X

Fig. 4 Primary timing chain alignment

short beads of RTV to engine block in locations outlined, **Fig. 3.**

FRONT COVER SEAL
REPLACE

1. Remove crankshaft balancer.
2. Carefully pry out seal using suitable flat blade screwdriver.
3. Install new seal using installer tool No. J 42041, or equivalent.
4. Seal should protrude .039–.078 inch from front cover.
5. Install crankshaft balancer.

TIMING CHAIN
REPLACE
Primary
REMOVAL

1. Remove valve covers as outlined under "Valve Cover, Replace."
2. Install camshaft holding fixture No. J 42038, or equivalent.
3. Remove front cover as outlined under "Front Cover, Replace."
4. Remove front engine lift bracket and camshaft position sensor.
5. Remove lefthand cylinder exhaust camshaft sprocket bolt.
6. Remove four chain guide access plugs in cylinder heads.
7. Loosen both primary tensioner bolts, then remove lower tensioner bolt and allow tensioner to swing downward and expand.
8. Remove upper tensioner bolt, then the tensioner.
9. Remove primary timing chain tensioner shoe attaching bolt, then the tensioner shoe by pushing guide downward slightly and pulling up through cylinder head.
10. Remove primary timing chain from lefthand camshaft sprocket and allow chain to fall into oil pump area of cylinder block.
11. Remove primary timing chain.

INSTALLATION

1. Install primary timing chain.
2. Set base engine timing by rotating crankshaft until cylinder No. 1 is at Top Dead Center as indicated by crankshaft sprocket timing mark (6) in position, **Fig. 4.**
3. Rotate balance shaft until timing mark (7) is in position, **Fig. 4.**
4. Ensure painted marks on timing chain face toward front of engine.
5. Center timing mark on righthand camshaft sprocket between pair of painted marks on primary timing chain, then wrap chain around sprocket.
6. Fabricate hook tool out of wire, then pull primary timing chain up through lefthand cylinder head to camshaft sprocket.
7. While pulling primary timing chain up, align painted marks with timing marks on balance shaft sprocket and crankshaft sprocket, **Fig. 4.**
8. Wrap primary timing chain around lefthand camshaft sprocket and align painted link with timing mark on sprocket, **Fig. 4.**
9. Install primary timing chain tensioner shoe and retaining bolt through access hole in cylinder head. Ensure all sprocket timing marks are aligned with painted marks on timing chain.
10. Collapse primary timing chain tensioner as follows:
    a. Rotate ratchet release lever counterclockwise and hold.
    b. Collapse tensioner shoe and hold.
    c. Release ratchet lever and slowly release pressure on shoe.
    d. As ratchet lever moves to first click, hold shoe inward and insert pin through hole in release lever.
    e. Locked ratchet mechanism should hold shoe in collapsed position.
11. Install primary timing chain tensioner.
12. Ensure all timing marks are aligned, then release pin holding tensioner to eliminate any slack in primary timing chain.
13. Install four chain guide plugs and front engine lift bracket.
14. Install camshaft position sensor, then remove camshaft holding fixture tool No. J 42038.
15. Install valve covers and front cover.

Secondary

LEFTHAND

REMOVAL

1. Remove lefthand valve cover as outlined under "Valve Cover, Replace."
2. Install camshaft holding fixture No. J 42038, or equivalent.
3. Remove camshaft position sensor.
4. Remove camshaft sprocket bolts, then install sprocket holding fixture No. J 42042, or equivalent.
5. Evenly slide secondary drive chain and camshaft sprockets off camshafts on to sprocket holding fixture.

INSTALLATION

1. Install secondary timing chain, aligning

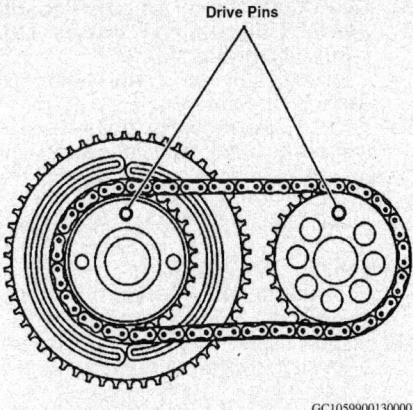

Drive Pins

GC1059900130000X

Fig. 5 Secondary sprocket drive pin alignment

drive pins as outlined, **Fig. 5.**
2. Slide camshaft sprockets off sprocket holding fixture and onto camshafts, then align drive pins in camshafts.
3. Remove sprocket holding fixture, then install intake camshaft sprocket retaining bolts.
4. Remove camshaft holding fixture, then install camshaft position sensor.
5. Install valve cover.

RIGHTHAND

REMOVAL

1. Partially drain coolant into suitable container, then remove thermostat housing.
2. Remove righthand valve cover as outlined under "Valve Cover, Replace."
3. Install camshaft holding fixture tool No. J 42038 or equivalent onto righthand camshafts.
4. Remove camshaft sprocket bolts, then install sprocket holding fixture No. J 42042 or equivalent.
5. Evenly slide secondary drive chain and sprockets onto sprocket holding fixture.

INSTALLATION

1. Install secondary timing chain, aligning drive pins as outlined, **Fig. 5.**
2. Slide camshaft sprockets off sprocket holding fixture and onto camshafts, then align drive pins in camshafts.
3. Remove sprocket holding fixture, then install intake camshaft sprocket retaining bolts.
4. Remove camshaft holding fixture, then install valve cover.
5. Install thermostat housing. Refill coolant system.

CAMSHAFT

REPLACE

Removal

1. Remove valve cover as outlined under "Valve Cover, Replace."
2. **On righthand cylinder head,** partially drain coolant into suitable container, then remove thermostat housing.

3. **On lefthand cylinder head,** remove CMP sensor.
4. **On all models,** remove camshaft sprockets as outlined under "Timing Chain, Replace."
5. Remove camshaft bearing caps. Identification markings and positions are as follows:
    a. Letter "I" indicates intake camshaft and letter "E" indicates exhaust camshaft.
    b. Number indicates journal position from front of engine.
    c. Raised feature goes toward outboard side of engine.
    d. Cap closest to front of engine is the thrust cap and cannot be installed in any other position.
6. Remove camshafts.

Installation

1. Apply liberal amount of clean engine oil to rocker arms, then position on lifter and valve tip.
2. Camshafts for righthand and lefthand cylinder heads are different lengths and identified as follows:
    a. Righthand cylinder head camshafts are longer than lefthand cylinder head camshafts.
    b. Intake camshaft identification rings are between first and second sets of lobes.
    c. Exhaust camshaft identification rings are between second and third sets of lobes.
3. Apply liberal amount of clean engine oil to camshaft journals and camshaft carriers, then install camshafts.
4. Place camshafts in position with notch for camshaft sprocket drive pins at top of rotation.
5. Install camshaft bearing thrust caps in first journal of each camshaft. Thrust caps are wider and have machined undercuts not present on other caps.
6. Tighten bearing caps to specifications.
7. Rotate camshaft so rear flat on camshaft is facing cylinder head.
8. Install camshaft holding fixture tool No. J 42038 or equivalent.
9. Compress secondary timing chain tensioner and lock into position by inserting wire pin into access hole on side of tensioner.
10. Slowly release pressure on tensioner shoes.
11. Install camshaft sprockets as outlined under "Timing Chain, Replace."
12. Remove wire pin from tensioner and allow tensioner shoes to expand.
13. **On lefthand cylinder head,** install camshaft position sensor.
14. **On righthand cylinder head,** install thermostat housing, then fill coolant system.
15. **On all models,** install valve covers.

PISTON & ROD ASSEMBLY

When installing piston and rod assemblies into cylinder block, ensure arrow on top of piston faces toward front of engine.

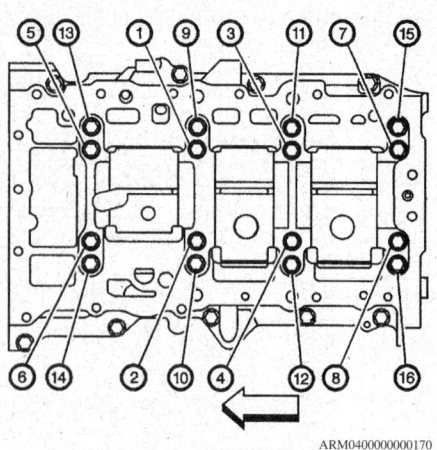

Fig. 6   Main bearing bolt tightening sequence

1. **Torque** connecting rod bolts to 22 ft. lbs.
2. Loosen bolts completely.
3. **Torque** bolts to 18 ft. lbs.
4. Rotate bolts an additional 110.°

MAIN & ROD BEARINGS

Engine bearings are of the precision insert type. Undersized bearings are not available. Crankshaft or connecting rod replacement is required if bearing clearances exceed specifications. Use the following procedure to tighten main bearing cap bolts.

1. **Torque** main bearing bolts to 15 ft. lbs., in sequence, **Fig. 6.**
2. Rotate main bearing bolts an additional 70°.
3. **Torque** perimeter bolts to 22 ft. lbs., in sequence, **Fig. 7.**

CRANKSHAFT REAR OIL SEAL

REPLACE

Removal

1. Remove transaxle as outlined in **MOTOR's "Domestic Transmission, In-Vehicle Service"** manual.
2. Install crankshaft rear oil seal removal tool No. J 42841 or equivalent.
3. Install eight 1 inch self tapping screws into seal using guide holes in removal tool.
4. Tighten center screw on removal tool to pull seal off end of crankshaft.

Installation

1. Place small amount of gasket maker P/N 1052942, or equivalent, at crankcase split line across end of upper/lower crankcase seal.
2. Coat outer diameter of cylinder block rear crankshaft seal area with clean engine oil.
3. Coat outer rubber surface of rear crankshaft seal with clean engine oil.

Do not put any oil on green coating of seal. This coating is a sealant that cannot be contaminated.

4. Loosen center bolt of seal installer No. J 42842 or equivalent.
5. Thread three mounting bolts of seal installer into crankshaft flange and tighten until seal installer is firmly mounted on crankshaft.
6. Install seal by tightening center bolt of seal installer until installer bottoms against crankcase.
7. Loosen center bolt, then remove installer tool.
8. Inspect seal to ensure installation depth is equal around seal circumference.
9. Install transaxle as outlined in **MOTOR's "Domestic Transmission, In-Vehicle Service"** manual.

OIL PAN

REPLACE

1. Raise and support vehicle, then drain engine oil into a suitable container.
2. Remove oil filter cap, then discard oil filter element.
3. Disconnect oil level sensor electrical connector, then remove transaxle brace.
4. Remove oil pan retaining bolts, then the oil pan.
5. Transfer oil level switch to new oil pan.
6. Reverse procedure to install, noting the following:
   a. Ensure rear edge of oil pan is flush with rear of cylinder block face.
   b. Press forward portion of oil pan against transaxle brace when tightening.
   c. **Torque** oil pan mounting bolts to 18 ft. lbs., in sequence, **Fig. 8.**

OIL PUMP

REPLACE

1. Remove front cover as outlined under "Front Cover, Replace."
2. Remove valve covers as outlined under "Valve Cover, Replace."
3. Install camshaft holding fixture tool No. J 42038 or equivalent.
4. Remove camshaft drive chain tensioner.
5. Remove primary timing chain from drive sprocket.
6. Remove four large oil pump housing bolts, then slide pump housing with drive sprocket off of crankshaft.
7. Reverse procedure to install, noting the following:
   a. Align crankshaft sprocket splines with oil pump gerotor when installing drive sprocket into oil pump.
   b. Ensure crankshaft sprocket is aligned with drive pin in crankshaft.
   c. Crankshaft sprocket should protrude from oil pump and face of sprocket should be behind machined step in crankshaft.

OIL PUMP SERVICE

The internal components of the oil pump are not serviceable. The oil pump is replaced as an assembly only.

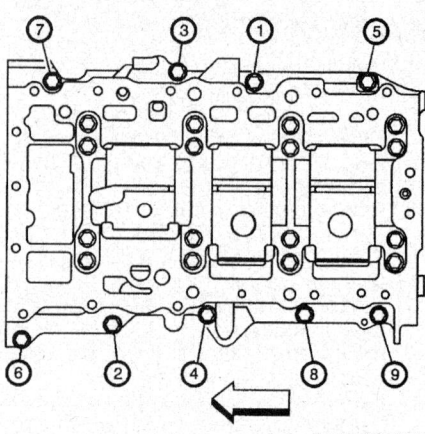

Fig. 7   Perimeter bolt tightening sequence

BELT TENSION DATA

Belt tension is maintained automatically by a spring tensioned idler pulley. Adjustment of serpentine belt is not required.

If belt slippage is indicated and belt tensioner indicator is within normal operating range, measure belt tension as follows:

1. Run engine for ten minutes, then shut off and measure belt tension between any two pulleys using V-belt tension gauge tool No. J 23600-B, or equivalent.
2. Run engine for 30 seconds and repeat measurement.
3. Repeat preceding step, then average all three belt tension measurements, which should be 30–50 lbs.
4. Replace belt if tension is not as specified.

SERPENTINE DRIVE BELT

Replacement

1. Lift or rotate tensioner using a ½ inch breaker bar.
2. Remove serpentine belt.
3. Reverse procedure to install, routing drive belt as illustrated, **Fig. 9.**

Adjustment

There is no provision for serpentine belt adjustment. Refer to "Belt Tension Data" for belt tension measurement procedures and to determine whether belt requires replacement.

COOLING SYSTEM BLEED

1. Open radiator bleed valve.
2. Fill cooling system until coolant starts to come out of bleed valve.
3. Close bleed valve, then slowly add coolant until level reaches FULL COLD mark.
4. Run engine to operating temperature while adding coolant to FULL mark. Shut engine off and wait 2 minutes.

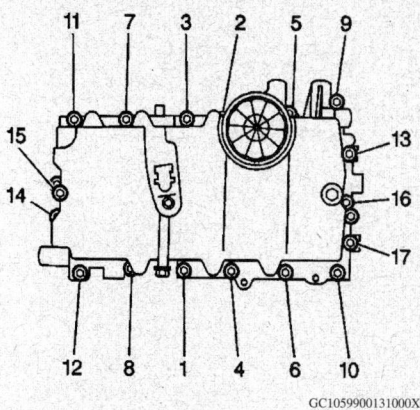

Fig. 8 Oil pan bolt tightening sequence

5. Inspect level and add coolant as required to restore level to FULL COLD mark.
6. Inspect coolant level after engine completes three thermal cycles and add coolant as required.

THERMOSTAT

REPLACE

1. Partially drain coolant into suitable container, then remove hoses from water outlet housing.
2. Remove water housing outlet bolts, then the water outlet housing.
3. Replace thermostat and housing as an assembly.
4. Reverse procedure to install.

WATER PUMP

REPLACE

1. Partially drain coolant into a suitable container, then loosen water pump pulley bolts.
2. Remove drive belt, idler pulley bolt and idler pulley.
3. Remove water pump pulley bolts and pump pulley.
4. Remove water pump bolts, then the water pump.
5. Reverse procedure to install.

RADIATOR

REPLACE

1. Drain coolant into suitable container, then remove engine mount strut.
2. Remove engine mount strut bracket from upper radiator support, then disconnect cooling fan electrical connector.
3. Disconnect hoses from radiator, then remove cooling fan shroud, motors and fans from radiator.
4. Disconnect transaxle cooler lines from radiator, then remove radiator mounting brackets.
5. Remove radiator and mounts.
6. Reverse procedure to install.

FUEL PUMP

REPLACE

1. Relieve fuel system pressure as outlined under "Precautions."
2. Remove spare tire cover, jack, spare tire and trunk liner.
3. Remove seven fuel pump access panel retaining nuts, then fuel pump access panel.
4. Disconnect fuel tank pressure sensor electrical connector, then clean fuel pipes and fuel pump assembly to prevent fuel contamination.
5. Disconnect quick connect fittings at fuel pump assembly, then remove fuel pump retaining snap ring.
6. Remove modular fuel pump assembly.
7. Reverse procedure to install.

FUEL FILTER

REPLACE

1. Relieve fuel system pressure as outlined under "Precautions."
2. Raise and support vehicle.
3. Remove bracket mounting screw and filter bracket.
4. Grasp filter and fuel line fitting. Twist quick-connect fitting ¼ turn in each direction to loosen any dirt within fitting.
5. Blow out dirt from quick-connect fitting.
6. Remove feed pipe nut from fuel filter,

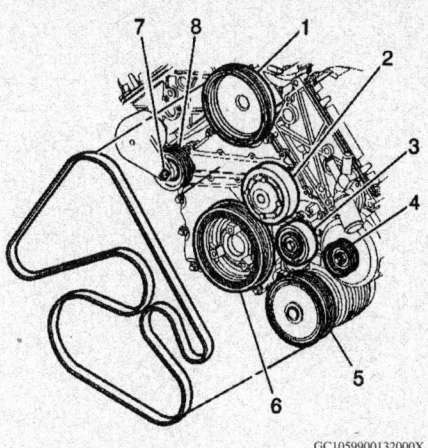

Fig. 9 Serpentine belt routing

then drain any remaining fuel into a suitable container.
7. Remove fuel filter.
8. Reverse procedure to install.

TECHNICAL SERVICE BULLETINS

Intake Manifold Inspection After Engine Replacement

In cases where an engine is being replaced due to internal damage, use extra care when transferring the intake manifold to the new engine or long block. Internal damage may result in potential discharge of internal engine component debris in the intake manifold through bent, broken, or missing intake valves. After removing the intake manifold from the engine, carefully inspect all of the cylinder head intake ports to determine if the valve heads are intact and not bent. Usually when the valve heads are missing or sufficiently bent, internal engine component debris will appear in the cylinder head intake ports. If this debris is present in any of the ports, install a new intake manifold.

TIGHTENING SPECIFICATIONS

Year	Component	Torque/Ft. Lbs.
2001–02	Accelerator Cable Bracket	84③
	Camshaft Bearing Caps	71①
	Camshaft Position Sensor	84③
	Camshaft Sprocket	18②
	Connecting Rod	⑥
	Coolant Drain Plug (Engine Block)	10
	Coolant Drain Plug (Front Cover)	89③
	Coolant Temperature Sensor	15
	Cylinder Head	⑤
	Cylinder Head Water Jacket Hole Plug	59

TIGHTENING
SPECIFICATIONS—Continued

Year	Component	Torque/Ft. Lbs.
2001–02	Drive Belt Idler Pulley	37
	Drive Belt Tensioner	37
	EGR to Crossover Pipe	44
	Engine Mount Nuts	35
	Engine Mount Strut Bolt	35
	Engine Mount Strut Bracket Bolt	21
	Engine To Transaxle	55
	Exhaust Manifold	18
	Exhaust Manifold Crossover Stud	18
	Exhaust Manifold Stud	53③
	EVAP Canister Purge Solenoid	72⑦
	Flywheel	11⑦
	Front Cover	11
	Front Cover Coolant Drain Plug	96③
	Front Lift Bracket Hex Bolt	37
	Front Lift Bracket Torx Bolt	18
	Idler Pulley	37
	Intake Manifold	62③
	Main Bearing Cap	④
	Lower Crankcase	④
	Oil Gallery Plug (Cylinder Head)	41
	Oil Gallery Plug (Lower Crankcase)	48
	Oil Level Sensor	84③
	Oil Pan	18⑧
	Oil Pan Drain Plug	15
	Oil Pump Cover	97③
	Oil Pump To Cylinder Block	18
	Oxygen Sensor	30
	Power Steering Pump To Cylinder Block	18
	Radiator Bracket	18
	Throttle Body	108③
	Timing Chain Guide Access Plug	44③
	Timing Chain Guide	22
	Timing Chain Tensioner (Primary)	18
	Timing Chain Tensioner (Secondary)	106③
	Timing Chain Tensioner Shoe Bolt	22
	Torque Converter Cover	80③
	Transaxle Brace	18
	Valve Cover	80③
	Water Crossover To Cylinder Head	18
	Water Pump	11
	Water Pump Pulley	108③
	Water Outlet Housing	84③

① — Rotate an additional 22°.
② — Rotate an additional 45°.
③ — Inch lbs.
④ — Refer to "Main & Rod Bearings" for tightening procedure.
⑤ — Refer to "Cylinder Head, Replace" for tightening procedure.
⑥ — Refer to "Piston & Rod Assembly" for tightening procedure.
⑦ — Rotate an additional 50°.
⑧ — Refer to "Oil Pan, Replace" for tightening procedure.

3.6L Engine

NOTE: Refer To "3.6L Engine" Located In The "CTS" Chapter For Procedures Not Covered In This Section.

NOTE: On Air Bag Equipped Models, Refer To "Air Bag System Precautions" Located In The Front Of This Manual For System Disarming & Arming Procedures.

NOTE: Refer To "Computer Relearn Procedures" Located In The Front Of This Manual When Battery Power To The Computer Has Been Interrupted.

INDEX

PRECAUTIONS

Air Bag Systems

Refer to "Air Bag System Precautions" in the front of this manual for system disarming and arming procedures.

Battery Ground Cable

Prior to service, disconnect battery ground cable and isolate as required.

Fuel System Pressure Relief

To reduce the risk of fire and personal injury, relieve the fuel system pressure before servicing fuel system components.
1. Turn ignition Off.
2. Remove fuel pump fuse and fuel pump relay.
3. Loosen fuel filler cap to relieve fuel tank vapor pressure.
4. Attempt to start engine and allow engine to run until it stops.
5. Loosen fuel tank filler cap to relieve tank pressure.
6. Connect fuel pressure gauge tool No. J-34730-1, or equivalent, to fuel pressure valve. Wrap a shop towel around fitting while connecting gauge to avoid spillage.
7. Install bleed hose into a suitable container and open valve to bleed system pressure.

COMPRESSION PRESSURE

1. Ensure battery is at full charge.

2. Start and run engine until it reaches normal operating temperature.
3. Turn engine Off, then remove Powertrain Control Module (PCM) and ignition fuse from instrument panel fuse block.
4. Remove spark plugs from all cylinders.
5. Remove air duct from throttle body, then block throttle plate in open position.
6. Thread compression gauge into spark plug hole.
7. Crank engine through at least four compression strokes.
8. Record readings on gauge at each stroke.
9. Repeat test on each cylinder.
10. Lowest reading should not be less than 70 percent of the highest reading. No cylinder reading should be less than 140 psi.

ENGINE MOUNT

REPLACE

1. Remove throttle body air inlet duct.
2. Remove engine mount struts as outlined under "Engine Mount Strut, Replace."
3. Raise and support vehicle.
4. Remove three-way catalytic converter pipe from engine right side exhaust manifold.
5. Remove right front wheel and tire, then the right engine splash shield.
6. Remove engine mount lower nuts.
7. Place a suitable adjustable jack stand with a block of wood under engine.
8. Remove engine mount bracket to oil pan bolts.
9. Remove engine mount bracket to engine bolts.
10. Remove engine mount and engine mount bracket.

11. Reverse procedure to install.

ENGINE MOUNT STRUT

REPLACE

1. Remove bolt and nut from engine mount strut at engine mount strut bracket on engine.
2. Remove bolt and nut from engine mount strut at engine mount strut bracket on upper radiator support.
3. Remove engine mount strut.
4. Reverse procedure to install.

ENGINE

REPLACE

1. Remove fuel injector sight shield and throttle body air inlet duct.
2. Remove engine mount strut as outlined under "Engine Mount, Replace."
3. Relieve fuel system pressure as outlined under "Precautions," then disconnect fuel lines from fuel rail and position aside.
4. Disconnect cooling fan electrical connectors.
5. Remove cooling fan wiring harnesses from fan shroud. Secure wiring harnesses to the vehicle.
6. Drain cooling system.
7. Remove throttle and cruise control cables with mounting brackets from throttle body.
8. Disconnect surge tank outlet hose from surge tank.
9. Position and secure surge hose to engine.
10. Disconnect surge tank inlet (vent) hose from water outlet housing and radiator. Position and secure surge tank inlet (vent) hose to vehicle.
11. Disconnect heater hoses from heater core.

12. Disconnect purge line from purge solenoid.
13. Disconnect fuel pipe from fuel rail.
14. Plug fuel pipe and cap fuel rail to prevent fuel loss and/or contamination.
15. Evacuate A/C refrigerant as oultined in "Air Conditioning" chapter.
16. Remove wiper module.
17. Disconnect air conditioning suction hose from evaporator and remove suction hose bracket from shock tower. Position and secure suction hose to engine. **Do not disconnect the suction hose from the A/C compressor.**
18. Disconnect air conditioning pressure switch electrical connector and remove liquid line from compressor. **Do not disconnect liquid line from condenser.**
19. Remove radiator support brackets.
20. Disconnect brake booster check valve and vacuum hose from brake booster. Position and secure brake booster hose to engine.
21. Disconnect brake fluid level switch electrical connector from master cylinder.
22. Disconnect mass air flow sensor electrical connector.
23. Unlock and disconnect instrument panel electrical connector from engine located at rear of left bank cylinder head. Position and secure instrument panel harness to vehicle.
24. Disconnect engine module wiring harness connectors from underhood electrical center.
25. Disconnect wiring harness from Transmission Control Module (TCM).
26. Remove ground bolt and wire from longitudinal rail.
27. Disconnect engine harness electrical connector at longitudinal rail. Position and secure ground wire, engine harness and TCM harness to vehicle.
28. Remove master cylinder nuts, then reposition and secure master cylinder to engine. **Do not disconnect the brake pipes from the master cylinder.**
29. Raise and support vehicle.
30. Remove muffler assembly.
31. Remove propeller shaft, then the air deflector.
32. Remove washer bottle bracket. **Do not remove water bottle.**
33. Disconnect radiator side air baffles from radiator.
34. Disconnect left front brake pipe retainer with brake pipe from longitudinal rail.
35. Remove right front brake pipe from brake pipe bundle retainer.
36. Disconnect rear brake pipes (two center pipes) from Brake Modulator Valve (BPVM). Cap and/or plug brake pipes and BPMV to prevent brake fluid loss.
37. Remove front tire and wheel assemblies.
38. Remove intermediate steering shaft.
39. Remove lower engine mount nuts.
40. Disconnect shift linkage from transaxle.
41. Disconnect low oil level sensor electrical connector. Secure low oil level sensor electrical connector and harness to engine mount bracket.
42. Remove headlamp leveling sensors.
43. Secure shock modules to lower control arms with a suitable strap in order to prevent damage to front brake hoses.
44. Remove right and left shock module upper mounting bolts.
45. Raise vehicle enough to place a suitable lift table under engine, transmission, front frame and front suspension assembly.
46. Raise lift table and lower vehicle to support frame, engine and transmission.
47. Remove transmission brace to underbody bolts and front frame bolts.
48. Lower table and remove engine, transmission, front frame and suspension assembly from vehicle.
49. Separate front frame and suspension assembly from engine.
50. Reverse procedure to install.

RADIATOR

REPLACE

1. Remove air cleaner assembly.
2. Drain cooling system.
3. Remove right and left engine mount struts.
4. Remove inlet hose from radiator, then the PCM harness clip from fan shroud.
5. Remove transmission oil cooler lines from retainer clip at bottom of cooling fan shroud.
6. Remove fan shroud clip from condenser tubes.
7. Remove fan shroud to condenser hold down bracket bolt.
8. Remove air deflectors from top of radiator.
9. Remove cooling fan shroud bolts, then the coolant reservoir hose from radiator overflow neck.
10. Remove radiator upper support brackets, then the fan shroud attaching bolts.
11. Disconnect engine cooling fan motors electrical connectors.
12. Remove cooling fan motors electrical harness from fan shroud clips.
13. Remove cooling fan shroud.
14. Remove outlet hose from radiator.
15. Disconnect transaxle oil cooler pipes from radiator.
16. Tilt top of radiator rearward.
17. Remove condenser hold down bracket from radiator.
18. Lift condenser from mounting tabs on radiator.
19. Position condenser aside, then remove radiator.
20. Reverse procedure to install.

FUEL PUMP

REPLACE

1. Relieve fuel system pressure as outlined under "Precautions."
2. Raise and support vehicle.
3. Remove fuel tank filler hose from fuel tank.
4. Disconnect fuel feed and fuel return pipe from tank.
5. Disconnect EVAP pipes located at fuel filter area.
6. Support exhaust system, then remove rubber exhaust pipe hangers and allow exhaust system to drop slightly.
7. Separate two halves of EVAP fresh air hose at splice.
8. Remove fuel tank shield push pins, then fuel tank shield.
9. Support fuel tank with a suitable adjustable jack.
10. Remove fuel tank strap bolts.
11. Lower fuel tank and disconnect fuel sender assembly electrical connectors.
12. Remove fuel tank.
13. Note routing of pipe assemblies and retaining clips for installation reference.
14. Disconnect and remove fuel feed, fuel return and EVAP pipe assemblies from fuel tank.
15. Remove EVAP canister from fuel tank and insulator pads from fuel tank. Note location of insulator pads for installation reference.
16. Disconnect fuel sender module electrical connectors.
17. Disconnect fuel pipes from fuel sender.
18. Remove fuel sender lock ring with lock ring removal tool No. J 45722, or equivalent, and a long breaker-bar.
19. Remove fuel sender from fuel tank.
20. Remove and discard fuel sender seal.
21. Remove fuel level sensor from fuel sender module.
22. Reverse procedure to install.

TIGHTENING SPECIFICATIONS

Year	Component	Torque Ft. Lbs.
2005	A/C Compressor Bracket Front Bolt	37
	A/C Compressor Bracket Rear Bolt	17
	A/C Compressor Hose Assembly	80①
	Alternator Bolt	37
	Catalytic Converter To Exhaust Manifold	10
	Coolant Outlet Bolt	89①
	Drive Belt Idler Pulley Bolt	37
	Drive Belt Tensioner Bolt	37
	ECM Bolt	89①
	Engine Mount Bracket To Cylinder Block (M8 Bolt)	28
	Engine Mount Bracket To Cylinder Block (M11 Bolt)	45
	Engine Mount To Bracket	59
	Heater Inlet/Outlet Pipe Assembly Bolt	89①
	Power Steering Pump Bracket To Engine Bolt	37
	Power Steering Pump Reservoir Lower Bolt	18

① — Inch lbs.

3.8L Engine

NOTE: For Procedures Not Found In This Section, Refer To The "3.8L Engine" Section In the "Bonneville, LeSabre & Park Avenue" Chapter.

NOTE: On Air Bag Equipped Models, Refer To "Air Bag System Precautions" Located In The Front Of This Manual For System Disarming & Arming Procedures.

NOTE: Refer To "Computer Relearn Procedures" Located In The Front Of This Manual When Battery Power To The Computer Has Been Interrupted.

NOTE: Prior To Performing Any Service Operations Listed In This Section, Consult The "Technical Service Bulletins" Section For Related Information.

INDEX

PRECAUTIONS

Air Bag Systems

Refer to "Air Bag System Precautions" in the front of this manual for system disarming and arming procedures.

Battery Ground Cable

Prior to service, disconnect battery ground cable and isolate as required.

Fuel System Pressure Relief

To reduce the risk of fire and personal injury, it is required to relieve the fuel system pressure before servicing fuel system components.

1. Loosen fuel tank filler cap to relieve tank pressure.
2. Connect fuel pressure gauge tool No. J-34730-1, or equivalent, to fuel pressure valve. Wrap a shop towel around fitting while connecting gauge to avoid spillage.
3. Install bleed hose into a suitable container, then open valve to bleed system pressure.

COMPRESSION PRESSURE

When inspecting compression, lowest cylinder must be within 70 percent of the highest cylinder with a minimum pressure of 100 psi. Perform compression test with engine at normal operating temperature, spark plugs removed and throttle wide open.

ENGINE MOUNT
REPLACE
Engine Block Mounts

1. Remove engine mount struts, then install engine support fixture tool No. J 28467-A, engine support fixture adapter tool No. J28467-90 and engine support adapter leg tool No. J 36462, or equivalents.
2. Raise and support vehicle, then remove righthand front wheel and tire assembly.
3. Remove righthand engine splash shield, then engine mount lower retaining nuts from frame.
4. Raise and support engine, then remove A/C compressor and position aside.
5. Remove front engine mount bracket bolts, then the rear engine mount bracket from engine.
6. Remove engine mount with engine mount bracket from engine, then the engine mount upper retaining nuts.
7. Remove engine mount from engine mount bracket.
8. Reverse procedure to install.

Transaxle Mount

1. Remove engine torque strut from engine.
2. Raise and support vehicle.
3. Remove lefthand tire and wheel assembly and lower splash shield.
4. Support transaxle using a suitable jack.
5. Remove mount nuts then mount.
6. Reverse procedure to install.

ENGINE
REPLACE

1. Mark and remove hood assembly.
2. Remove air cleaner assembly.
3. Relieve fuel system pressure as outlined under "Precautions."
4. Remove fuel lines from rail and mounting bracket.
5. Remove coolant bottle and inner fender electrical cover.
6. Remove fuel injector sight cover.
7. Remove throttle cables, bracket and vacuum line from throttle body.
8. Remove heat shield from exhaust crossover pipe then crossover pipe.
9. Remove engine torque strut from engine.
10. Remove engine cooling fan.
11. Remove vacuum line from transaxle module.
12. Remove serpentine drive belt.
13. Remove power steering pump and alternator from engine.
14. Disconnect all required electrical connectors.
15. Remove upper and lower radiator and heater hoses from engine.
16. Remove transaxle to engine bolts and ground wire harness with bolt.
17. Raise and support vehicle.
18. Remove righthand tire and wheel assembly and inner splash shield.
19. Remove flywheel cover, then scribe torque converter to flywheel for installation.
20. Remove flywheel to converter bolts.
21. Disconnect wire harness clamps from frame near radiator.
22. Remove A/C compressor and position aside.
23. Remove starter motor.
24. Remove transaxle to engine bolt through wheelwell using suitable extension.
25. Disconnect engine mount to frame nuts.
26. Remove oil filter.
27. Disconnect front exhaust pipe from manifold.
28. Disconnect oil cooler piper from hose connections.
29. Lower vehicle.
30. Install lifting device and remove engine assembly.
31. Reverse procedure to install, noting the following:
    a. Align engine with transaxle dowel pins.
    b. **Torque** torque strut bolts to 41 ft. lbs.

   c. **Torque** flywheel to converter bolts to 46 ft. lbs.

FUEL PUMP
REPLACE

Refer to "Fuel Pump, Replace" in the "3.1L Engine" section.

FUEL FILTER
REPLACE

1. Relieve fuel system pressure as outlined under "Precautions."
2. Raise and support vehicle.
3. Remove bracket retaining screw, then the filter bracket, **Fig. 1.**
4. Grasp filter and fuel line fitting. Twist quick-connect fitting ¼ turn in each direction to loosen any dirt within fitting.
5. Clean any debris away from quick-connect fitting.
6. Remove feed pipe nut from fuel filter, then drain any remaining fuel into a suitable container.
7. Remove fuel filter.
8. Reverse procedure to install.

TECHNICAL SERVICE BULLETINS

Banging, Clunking From Rear Of Vehicle
2004

On these models, there may be noises coming from the rear of the vehicle, most noticeable when stopping or during parking lot maneuvers. Drivers may also report the noise occurs when the fuel tank is between ½ full and full. This may be caused by fuel sloshing in the tank.

To correct this condition, install a revised fuel tank P/N 15141578. The PCM will require flashing with a new service calibration due to revised evaporative characteristics. Contact General Motors for further information.

Intake Manifold Inspection After Engine Replacement

In cases where an engine is being replaced due to internal damage, use extra care when transferring the intake manifold to the new engine or long block. Internal damage may result in potential discharge of internal engine component debris in the intake manifold through bent, broken, or missing intake valves. After removing the intake manifold from the engine, carefully inspect all of the cylinder head intake ports to determine if the valve heads are intact and not bent. Usually when the valve heads are missing or sufficiently bent, internal engine component debris will appear in the cylinder head intake ports. If this debris is present in any of the ports, install a new intake manifold.

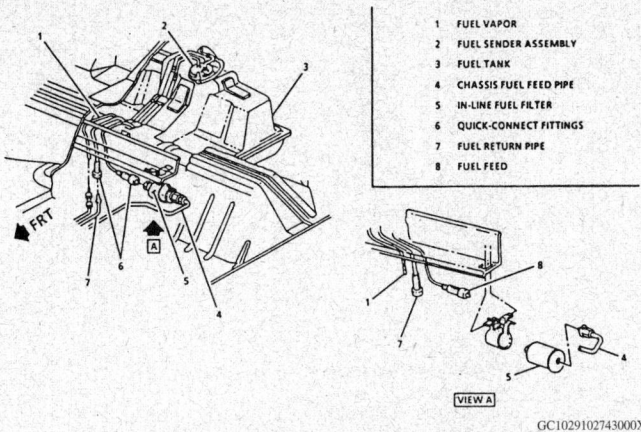

1. FUEL VAPOR
2. FUEL SENDER ASSEMBLY
3. FUEL TANK
4. CHASSIS FUEL FEED PIPE
5. IN-LINE FUEL FILTER
6. QUICK-CONNECT FITTINGS
7. FUEL RETURN PIPE
8. FUEL FEED

GC1029102743000X

Fig. 1 Fuel filter replacement

Rear Axle & Suspension

NOTE: On Air Bag Equipped Models, Refer To "Air Bag System Precautions" Located In The Front Of This Manual For System Disarming & Arming Procedures.

NOTE: Refer To "Computer Relearn Procedures" Located In The Front Of This Manual When Battery Power To The Computer Has Been Interrupted.

INDEX

DESCRIPTION

These vehicles use a tri-link independent rear suspension system with a transverse leaf spring and tubular struts with large lateral links attached to the body crossmember. The three mounting points are the crossmember, strut tower and trailing arm. The crossmember is stamped steel and the composite fiberglass mono leaf spring is transversely mounted to the under side of the crossmember, with its padded ends free riding on the cast knuckle assembly.

HUB & BEARING
REPLACE

The rear hub and bearing assembly is not serviceable. If the hub and/or bearing is damaged, the complete assembly must be replaced.

1. Raise and support vehicle, then remove tire and wheel assembly.

2. Remove brake caliper with hose attached and suspend out of way.
3. Remove brake rotor.
4. Disconnect anti-lock brake system electrical harness connector.
5. Remove hub and bearing to knuckle bolts.
6. Remove parking brake lever bracket, then the parking brake actuator.
7. Remove hub and bearing assembly.
8. Reverse procedure to install.

STRUT
REPLACE

1. Remove three strut to body mount retaining nuts.
2. Raise and support vehicle, then remove rear wheel and tire assembly.
3. Disconnect stabilizer shaft link from strut.
4. Scribe matching marks on strut and knuckle.
5. Remove strut to knuckle bolts, then the strut from vehicle.

6. Reverse procedure to install. Inspect rear wheel alignment as outlined in "Wheel Alignment" section.

STRUT SERVICE

1. Position strut assembly into strut spring compressor tool No. J 34013-B, or equivalent.
2. Compress spring assembly approximately ½ inch.
3. Hold shaft with Torx T45 bit, then remove and discard shaft nut.
4. Release spring tension and remove upper mount plate, spring, baffle and lower mount plate.
5. Reverse procedure to assemble.

COIL SPRING
REPLACE

Refer to "Strut Service" for coil spring replacement procedure.

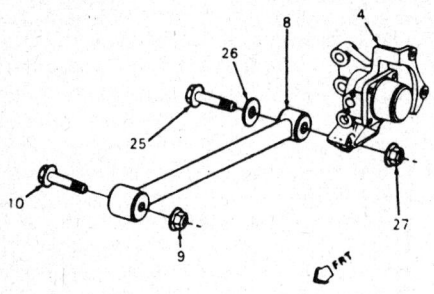

4   KNUCKLE ASSEMBLY
8   TRAILING LINK
9   65 N•m (48 lbs ft.)
10 BOLT
25 BOLT
26 WASHER
27 NUT   260 N•m (192 lbs ft.)

GC2039100085000X

Fig. 1   Trailing arm removal

1   BODY
99   NUT   25 N•m (18 lbs ft.)
101 NUT
102 BRACKET-STABILIZER SHAFT
103 BOLT   25 N•m (18 lbs ft.)
104 BOLT-STABILIZER SHAFT LINK
105 BOLT   50 N•m (57 lbs ft.)
106 LINK—STABILIZER SHAFT
107 INSULATOR
108 STABILIZER SHAFT

GC2039100083000X

Fig. 2   Stabilizer shaft assembly replacement

KNUCKLE
REPLACE

Century, Grand Prix, Impala, Intrigue, LaCrosse, Monte Carlo & Regal

1. Raise and support vehicle.
2. Remove wheel and tire assembly.
3. Scribe matching marks on strut and knuckle assembly, for installation reference.
4. Disconnect rear spindle rods from knuckle.
5. Remove brake caliper and bracket, then the brake rotor.
6. Disconnect ABS electrical connector.
7. Remove wheel hub and bearing.
8. Disconnect trailing arm from knuckle.
9. Remove rear suspension strut to knuckle mounting bolts.
10. Remove knuckle assembly.
11. Reverse procedure to install.

Lumina

1. Raise and support vehicle, then remove wheel and tire assemblies.
2. Place scribe marks on strut and knuckle to ensure installation in same position.
3. Remove rear wheel spindle rods from knuckle, then the caliper and rotor (brake hose bracket and drum if equipped).
4. Disconnect ABS connector, then remove rear wheel hub.
5. Disconnect trailing arm from knuckle.
6. Remove strut to knuckle retaining nuts, then the knuckle assembly.
7. Reverse procedure to install.

TRAILING ARM
REPLACE

1. Raise and support vehicle.

2. Disconnect ABS electrical harness connector.
3. Remove trailing arm to knuckle mounting nut and bolt, then trailing rod (link) to body mounting nut and bolt, **Fig. 1.**
4. Remove trailing arm.
5. Reverse procedure to install.

STABILIZER BAR
REPLACE

1. Raise and support vehicle, then remove rear wheel and tire assemblies.
2. Remove righthand and lefthand stabilizer shaft link bolts, then open brackets to remove insulator.
3. Remove righthand and lefthand strut to knuckle to stabilizer shaft nuts, **Fig. 2. Do not remove strut to knuckle bolts.**
4. Remove insulator brackets from bolts and from stabilizer shaft, then the stabilizer shaft.
5. Reverse procedure to install.

LATERAL LINK
REPLACE
Front

1. Raise and support vehicle, then remove tire and wheel assembly.
2. Remove rod to knuckle bolt, then the exhaust pipe heat shield.
3. Lower fuel tank to gain access.
4. Remove lateral link to knuckle mounting bolt.
5. Remove lateral link to suspension crossmember mounting nut and bolt, then the lateral link.
6. Reverse procedure to install.

Rear

1. Raise and support vehicle, then remove tire and wheel assembly.

2. Remove transverse spring as outlined under "Coil Spring, Replace."
3. Remove lower auxiliary spring bracket from rod.
4. Remove rear lateral link mounting nut from crossmember.
5. Push bolt forward enough to provide clearance for link removal, then remove rear lateral link.
6. Reverse procedure to install.

TECHNICAL SERVICE BULLETINS

Rear Strut Thumping Or Squeaking

On some of these models, the rear struts may have a muted thumping noise, oil canning or squeak, especially at low speed over irregular road surfaces.

This condition may be caused by the strut jounce bumper system. To correct this condition, replace both rear strut jounce bumper assemblies with revised units service kit P/N 22063945.

Banging, Clunking From Rear Of Vehicle
2004

On these models, there may be noises coming from the rear of the vehicle, most noticeable when stopping or during parking lot maneuvers. Drivers may also report the noise occurs when the fuel tank is between ½ full and full. This may be caused by fuel sloshing in the tank.

To correct this condition, install a revised fuel tank P/N 15141578. The PCM will require flashing with a new service calibration due to revised evaporative characteristics. Contact General Motors for further information.

TIGHTENING SPECIFICATIONS

Year	Component	Torque/Ft. Lbs.
CENTURY, IMPALA, GRAND PRIX, LACROSSE, MONTE CARLO & REGAL		
2001–05	Brake Hose Bracket Bolt	20
	Brake Hose To Brake Caliper Bolt	40
	Caliper Bolts	32
	Caliper Bracket Bolts	85
	Spindle Rods To Knuckle Nut	110
	Spindle Rods To Rear Suspension Support Nut	103
	Stabilizer Shaft Insulator Bracket Nuts	35
	Stabilizer Shaft Link Nuts	38
	Strut Mount To Body Nuts	33
	Strut Shaft Nut	55
	Strut To Knuckle Nuts	90
	Suspension Support Mounting Bolt	81
	Trailing Arm Bolt To Body Bracket Bolt	37
	Trailing Arm To Knuckle Bolt	52①
	Wheel Hub To Knuckle Bolts	55
	Wheel Lug Nuts	100
INTRIGUE		
2001–02	Brake Hose Bolt	40
	Caliper Bolts	32
	Caliper Bracket Bolts	85
	Spindle Rod To Knuckle Nut	110
	Stabilizer Shaft Insulator Bracket Bolts	35
	Stabilizer Shaft Link Nuts	26
	Strut Mount To Body Nuts	30
	Strut Shaft Nut	55
	Strut To Knuckle Nuts	90
	Suspension Support Mounting Bolts	81
	Trailing Arm Bracket To Body Nut	40
	Trailing Arm To Knuckle Bolt	52①
	Wheel Hub To Knuckle Bolts	55
	Wheel Spindle Rod To Rear Suspension Support Nut	103
	Wheel Lug Nuts	100
LUMINA		
2001	Caliper Bolts	63
	Caliper Bracket Bolts	137
	Spindle Rod Front & Rear To Knuckle Bolt	177
	Spindle Rod Front & Rear To Suspension Support Nut	111
	Stabilizer Shaft Link Bolt	52
	Stabilizer Shaft Link To Body Bracket	40
	Strut Mount To Body Nut	37
	Strut To Knuckle Nut	82
	Suspension Strut Nut	55
	Suspension Support Mounting Bolt	85
	Trailing Arm To Body Nut & Bolt	70
	Trailing Arm To Knuckle Nut & Bolt (16 × 2 × 90)	66②
	Trailing Arm To Knuckle Nut & Bolt (16 × 2 × 105)	52①
	Wheel Hub Bolt	52
	Wheel Lug Nuts	100

① — Rotate an additional 65°.
② — Rotate an additional 75°.

Front Suspension & Steering

NOTE: On Air Bag Equipped Models, Refer To "Air Bag System Precautions" Located In The Front Of This Manual For System Disarming & Arming Procedures.

NOTE: Refer To "Computer Relearn Procedures" Located In The Front Of This Manual When Battery Power To The Computer Has Been Interrupted.

NOTE: Prior To Performing Any Service Operations Listed In This Section, Consult The "Technical Service Bulletins" Section For Related Information.

INDEX

PRECAUTIONS

Air Bag Systems

Refer to "Air Bag System Precautions" in the front of this manual for system disarming and arming procedures.

DESCRIPTION

The front suspension system on these vehicles is of the McPherson strut design. This design incorporates McPherson struts with coil springs and a one piece configuration with lower control arms. The use of tapered top coil springs on top of the struts provides a well controlled ride and allows a lower hood profile.

HUB & BEARING

REPLACE

Century, Grand Prix, Impala, Intrigue, LaCrosse, Monte Carlo & Regal

1. Raise and support vehicle, then remove tire and wheel assembly.
2. Disconnect ABS wheel speed sensor electrical connector.
3. Remove wheel speed sensor electrical connector from bracket.
4. Remove brake caliper and position aside using suitable wire hanger.
5. Remove caliper bracket and brake rotor.
6. Remove driveshaft nut and discard.
7. Attach front hub spindle remover tool No. J 28733-B, or equivalent, to wheel hub and bearing assembly.
8. Push driveshaft out of wheel hub and bearing assembly.
9. Remove hub and bearing assembly mounting bolts, then the hub and bearing assembly from steering knuckle. Discard mounting bolts.
10. Reverse procedure to install. **Use new bearing assembly to knuckle mounting bolts.**

Lumina

1. Raise and support vehicle, then remove wheel and tire assembly.

2. Loosen drive axle shaft nut one turn.
3. Remove brake caliper and position aside, **Fig. 1.**
4. Remove brake caliper mounting bracket bolts, then caliper mounting bracket.
5. Remove brake rotor, then drive axle shaft retaining nut. Discard nut.
6. Loosen front wheel driveshaft bearing to knuckle mounting bolts.
7. Push axle splines back out of bearing assembly using front hub spindle removal tool No. J 28733-A, or equivalent.
8. Remove driveshaft bearing to knuckle mounting bolts.
9. Remove ABS sensor mounting bolts, then the ABS sensor. Position sensor aside.
10. Remove driveshaft bearing assembly from knuckle.
11. Reverse procedure to install.

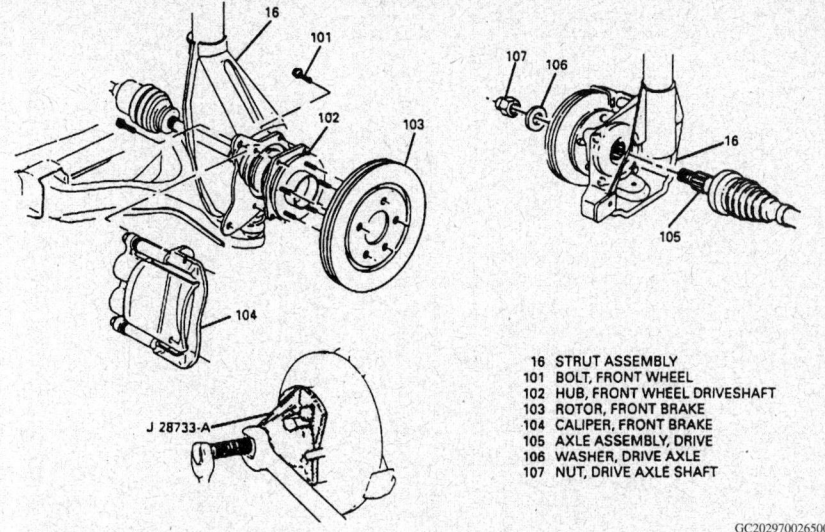

16 STRUT ASSEMBLY
101 BOLT, FRONT WHEEL
102 HUB, FRONT WHEEL DRIVESHAFT
103 ROTOR, FRONT BRAKE
104 CALIPER, FRONT BRAKE
105 AXLE ASSEMBLY, DRIVE
106 WASHER, DRIVE AXLE
107 NUT, DRIVE AXLE SHAFT

GC2029700265000X

Fig. 1 Front wheel driveshaft bearing replacement. Lumina

BALL JOINT INSPECTION

With vehicle raised and supported to allow front suspension to hang freely, grasp wheel at top and bottom and attempt to move bottom of wheel inward and outward. **Ball joints must be replaced if looseness is observed between knuckle and control arm.**

BALL JOINT
REPLACE
Century, Grand Prix, Impala, Intrigue, LaCrosse, Monte Carlo & Regal

1. Raise and support vehicle.
2. Remove control arm as outlined under "Control Arm, Replace."
3. Drill out three retaining rivets holding ball joint to control arm, then remove ball joint from control arm.
4. Reverse procedure to install.

Lumina

1. Raise and support vehicle, then remove wheel and tire assembly.
2. Remove ball joint heat shield mounting bolts, then heat shield.
3. Remove lower ball joint cotter pin and retaining nut.
4. Loosen stabilizer shaft bushing bolts. **Do not remove bolts.**
5. Separate ball joint from lower control arm using tie rod puller/ball joint remover tool No. J 35917, or equivalent.
6. Drill out four rivets retaining ball joint to steering knuckle. Use a 1/8 inch drill bit to make a pilot hole, then use a 1/2 inch drill bit to finish drilling rivets.
7. Reverse procedure to install.

STRUT
REPLACE
Century, Grand Prix, Impala, Intrigue, LaCrosse, Monte Carlo & Regal

1. Remove three strut to body nuts, **Fig. 2.**
2. Raise and support vehicle, then remove tire and wheel assembly.
3. Remove strut to knuckle mounting bolts. **After removing bolts, retain knuckle in its original position. Failure to retain knuckle could cause ball joint or drive axle damage.**
4. Remove strut assembly from vehicle.
5. Reverse procedure to install.

Lumina

1. Scribe alignment marks on cover plate, then loosen cover plate retaining nuts, **Fig. 3.**
2. Raise and support vehicle.
3. Remove tire and wheel assembly.
4. Remove brake caliper and position aside. **Do not disconnect brake hose.**
5. Remove brake rotor, then hub and bearing as outlined under "Hub & Bearing, Replace."
6. Separate axle from transaxle, then remove tie rod to knuckle mounting nut.
7. Separate tie rod from steering knuckle using tie rod puller/ball joint removal tool No. J-35917, or equivalent.
8. Remove lower ball joint to knuckle retaining nut.
9. Separate lower ball joint from lower control arm using tie rod puller/ball joint removal tool.
10. Remove cover plate retaining nuts, then the strut and knuckle assembly.
11. Reverse procedure to install.

STRUT SERVICE
Century, Grand Prix, Impala, Intrigue, LaCrosse, Monte Carlo & Regal
DISASSEMBLE

Springs are under high tension. Do not remove strut shaft nut without using a suitable spring compressing tool.

1. Mount strut and knuckle assembly into strut spring compressor tool No. J-34013-A and strut compressor adapter tool No. J-34013-88, or equivalents, then compress spring with compressor forcing screw just enough to release tension from upper spring insulator.
2. Remove strut shaft nut using suitable Torx bit and strut rod nut remover/installer tool No. J-35669, or equivalents.
3. Relieve all spring tension, then remove spring and strut components.

ASSEMBLE

1. Install spring seat and bearing.
2. Install lower spring insulator. Lower spring coil end must be visible between step and first retention tab of insulator.
3. Install front suspension spring.
4. Install dust shield to lower spring seat.
5. Install jounce bumper.
6. Install upper spring insulator. Upper spring coil end must be between step and location mark on insulator.
7. Install jounce bumper retainer to strut mount using strut mount plate wrench tool No. J-35670, or equivalent.
8. Install strut mount and upper strut mount bushing.
9. Compress strut assembly using strut spring compressor and strut compressor adapter tools No. J-34013-A and J-34013-38, or equivalents.

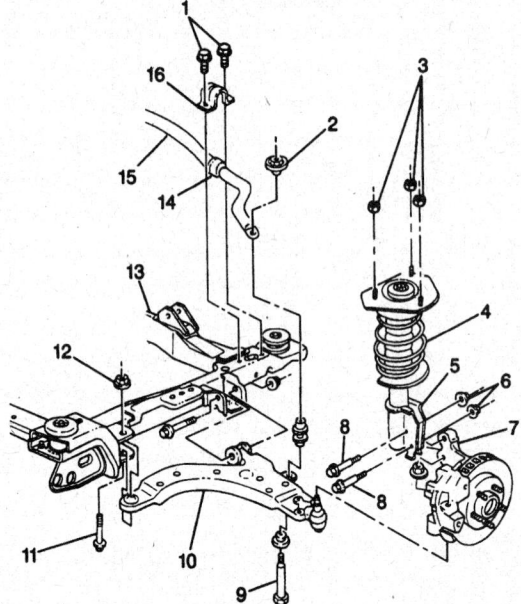

(1) Front Stabilizer Shaft Insulator Clamp Bolt/screw
(2) Front Stabilizer Shaft Link Nut
(3) Front Suspension Strut Mount Nut
(4) Front Suspension Spring
(5) Front Suspension Strut
(6) Strut To Knuckle Nut
(7) Front Steering Knuckle
(8) Strut To Knuckle Bolt/screw
(9) Front Stabilizer Shaft Link]
(10) Front Lower Control Arm
(11) Front Lower Control Arm Bolt/screw
(12) Front Lower Cotrol Arm Nut
(13) Frame
(14) Front Stabilizer Shaft Insulator
(15) Front Stabilizer Shaft
(16) Front Stabilizer Shaft Clamp

GC2029700266000X

Fig. 2 Front suspension. Century, Grand Prix, Impala, Intrigue, LaCrosse, Monte Carlo & Regal

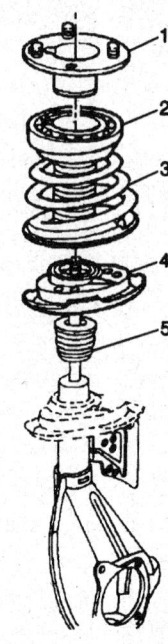

(1) Front Suspension Strut Mount Retainer
(2) Front Spring Upper Insulator
(3) Front Spring
(4) Front Spring Seat
(5) Front Suspension Strut Bumper

GC2029700267000X

Fig. 3 Exploded view of strut assembly. Lumina

10. Align strut cartridge shaft with strut extension rod tool No. J-35668, or equivalent.
11. Install strut shaft nut using strut rod nut remover/installer tool No. J-35669, or equivalent, and a suitable Torx bit.

Lumina

Do not service strut unless weight of vehicle is on suspension.

REMOVAL

1. Scribe alignment marks on cover plate.
2. Remove cover plate retaining nuts, then the cover plate.
3. Remove strut shaft using Torx T50 bit and strut rod remover/installer tool No. J-35669, or equivalents.
4. Remove strut mount bushing by prying with suitable tool.
5. Remove jounce bumper retainer using strut mount plate wrench tool No. J-35670, or equivalent.
6. Attach strut extension rod tool No. J-35668, or equivalent, to strut shaft and extend shaft.
7. Remove tool and, using strut cap nut wrench tool No. J-35671, or equivalent, unscrew closure nut.
8. Remove strut cartridge.
9. Remove oil from strut tube using suitable suction device.

INSTALLATION

1. Install self contained replacement cartridge, using strut cap nut wrench tool No. J-35671, or equivalent.
2. Install jounce bumper, then using strut mount plate wrench tool No. J-35670, or equivalent, jounce bumper retainer.
3. Install strut mount bushing. If required, use strut extension rod tool No. J-35668, or equivalent after bushing is partially installed and position strut shaft as required. Lubricate bushing with a soap solution to ease installation.
4. Install strut shaft nut using Torx T50 bit and strut rod remover/installer tool No. J-35669, or equivalents.
5. Install strut mount cover, aligning scribe marks.

CONTROL ARM
REPLACE

Century, Grand Prix, Impala, Intrigue, LaCrosse, Monte Carlo & Regal

1. Raise and support vehicle, then remove wheel and tire assembly.
2. Remove steering gear outer tie rod from steering knuckle, then stabilizer shaft to lower control arm insulator bracket bolts.
3. Disconnect ABS speed sensor, then remove control arm mounting bolts.
4. Remove cotter pin, then loosen nut from ball joint, **Fig. 2.**

5. Separate front lower control arm ball joint from steering knuckle using ball joint separator tool No. J 41820, or equivalent.
6. Remove control arm from frame.
7. Reverse procedure to install, noting the following:
   a. Lower control arm to frame bolts must be installed as outlined, **Fig. 4.**
   b. **Torque** lower ball joint nut 40 ft. lbs. Rotate to align next slot in nut with cotter pin hole in stud. **Do not rotate more than 60° to align with hole and do not loosen nut at any time during installation.**

Lumina

1. Raise and support vehicle, then remove wheel and tire assembly.
2. Remove engine splash shields.
3. Remove stabilizer shaft to lower control arm insulator bracket bolts.
4. Remove lower ball joint cotter pin and nut, then separate ball joint from lower control arm using tie rod puller/ball joint remover tool No. J-35917, or equivalent.
5. Remove lower control arm to frame mounting nuts and bolts, then lower control arm assembly.
6. Reverse procedure to install, noting the following:
   a. Lower control arm to frame bolts must be installed as outlined, **Fig. 5.**
   b. **Torque** lower ball joint nut 15 ft. lbs., then rotate an additional 90°. Rotate to align next slot in nut with

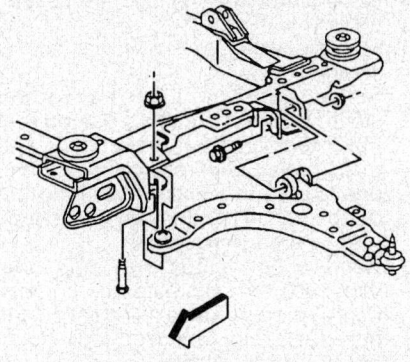

GC2029800225000X

Fig. 4 Lower control arm installation. Century, Grand Prix, Impala, Intrigue, LaCrosse, Monte Carlo & Regal

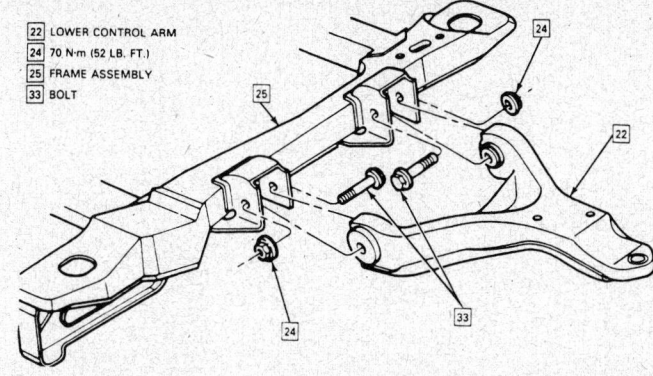

22	LOWER CONTROL ARM
24	70 N·m (52 LB. FT.)
25	FRAME ASSEMBLY
33	BOLT

GC2029100174000X

Fig. 5 Lower control arm installation. Lumina

cotter pin hole in stud. **Do not rotate more than 60° to align with hole and do not loosen nut at any time during installation.**

STEERING KNUCKLE
REPLACE

Century, Grand Prix, Impala, Intrigue, LaCrosse, Monte Carlo & Regal

1. Raise and support vehicle, then remove wheel and tire assembly.
2. Remove front wheel driveshaft bearing as outlined in "Front Wheel Drive Axles" chapter.
3. Remove hub and bearing assembly as outlined under "Hub & Bearing, Replace."
4. Remove lower control arm ball joint cotter pin and retaining nut.
5. Separate ball joint from control arm, using ball joint stud separator tool No. J 41820, or equivalent.
6. Separate outer tie rod end from steering knuckle using universal steering linkage puller tool No. J 24319-B, or equivalent.
7. Scribe matching marks on strut and steering knuckle for installation reference.
8. Remove strut to knuckle mounting bolts, then the steering knuckle from vehicle.
9. Reverse procedure to install.

Lumina

1. Scribe alignment marks on cover plate, then loosen cover plate retaining nuts, **Fig. 3.**
2. Raise and support vehicle.
3. Remove tire and wheel assembly.
4. Remove brake caliper and position aside. **Do not disconnect brake hose.**
5. Remove brake rotor, then hub and

bearing as outlined under "Hub & Bearing, Replace."
6. Separate axle from transaxle, then remove tie rod to knuckle mounting nut.
7. Separate tie rod from steering knuckle using tie rod puller/ball joint removal tool No. J-35917, or equivalent.
8. Remove lower ball joint to knuckle retaining nut.
9. Separate lower ball joint from lower control arm using tie rod puller/ball joint removal tool.
10. Remove cover plate retaining nuts, then strut and knuckle assembly.
11. Reverse procedure to install.

STABILIZER BAR
REPLACE

Century, Grand Prix, Impala, Intrigue, LaCrosse, Monte Carlo & Regal
REMOVAL

1. Raise and support vehicle, then remove tire and wheel assembly.
2. Move steering shaft dust seal to access lower intermediate shaft pinch bolt, then remove pinch bolt.
3. Loosen all insulator clamp mounting nuts and bolts, **Fig. 6.**
4. Place a suitable jackstand under center of rear frame crossmember.
5. Loosen two front frame to body mounting bolts four turns.
6. Remove two rear frame to body mounting bolts, then lower rear of frame enough to remove stabilizer shaft. Discard frame to body bolts.
7. Remove insulators and clamps from frame.
8. Remove stabilizer bar links from control arms.
9. Pull stabilizer shaft rearward, swing shaft downward and remove from lefthand side of vehicle.

INSTALLATION

1. Install stabilizer shaft from lefthand side of vehicle.
2. Loosely install stabilizer shaft link to

control arm. **Do not tighten stabilizer link retaining nut at this time. Weight of vehicle must be supported by control arms so that trim height is obtained before tightening link nut.**
3. Install insulator clamps onto frame, then raise frame into position while guiding steering shaft onto steering gear.
4. Install new frame to body mounting bolts and remove jackstand.
5. Install intermediate shaft pinch bolt.
6. Install dust seal onto steering gear.
7. Support vehicle weight with control arms and tighten stabilizer link nut to specifications.
8. Install tire and wheel assembly.

Lumina

1. Raise and support vehicle, then remove wheel and tire assembly.
2. Move steering shaft dust shield to access pinch bolt.
3. Remove pinch bolt from lower intermediate steering shaft.
4. Loosen all insulator clamp mounting nuts and bolts, **Fig. 7.**
5. Place a suitable jack under center of rear frame crossmember.
6. Loosen two front frame to body bolts four turns.
7. Remove two rear frame to body bolts.
8. Lower rear of frame just enough to gain access for stabilizer shaft removal.
9. Remove insulators and clamps from frame and control arms.
10. Pull stabilizer shaft rearward, swing down and remove from lefthand side of vehicle.
11. Reverse procedure to install.

TIE ROD END
REPLACE

Inner
REMOVAL

1. Remove steering gear as outlined under "Power Steering Gear, Replace."
2. Loosen outer tie rod end to inner tie rod jam nut.
3. Turn outer tie rod counterclockwise to

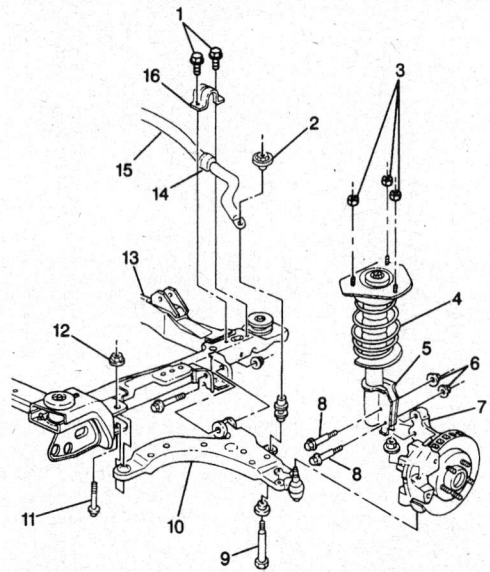

(1) Front Stabilizer Shaft Insulator Clamp Bolt/Screw
(2) Front Stabilizer Shaft Link Nut
(3) Front Suspension Strut Mount Nut
(4) Front Suspension Spring
(5) Front Suspension Strut
(6) Strut-to-Knuckle Nut
(7) Front Steering Knuckle
(8) Strut-to-Knuckle Bolt/Screw
(9) Front Stabilizer Shaft Link
(10) Front Lower Control Arm
(11) Front Lower Control Arm Bolt/Screw
(12) Front Lower Control Arm Nut
(13) Frame
(14) Front Stabilizer Shaft Insulator
(15) Front Stabilizer Shaft
(16) Front Stabilizer Shaft Clamp

GC2029800226000X

Fig. 6 Stabilizer shaft & insulators replacement. Century, Grand Prix, Impala, Intrigue, LaCrosse, Monte Carlo & Regal

remove from inner tie rod end using a suitable pipe wrench to hold inner tie rod.

4. Loosen rack and pinion boot inner and outer clamps, then remove boot and breather tube.
5. Slide shock dampner boot back on rack, then place a pipe wrench on rack next to inner tie rod housing.
6. Place a suitable wrench on flats of inner tie rod housing, then turn outer tie rod counterclockwise to remove from inner tie rod end.

INSTALLATION

1. Apply Loctite 262 or equivalent to inner tie rod threads.
2. Place a suitable pipe wrench on rack next to inner tie rod housing, then **torque** tie rod to 74 ft. lbs.
3. Place tie rod assembly in a suitable vise, then stake both sides of female inner tie rod assembly housing to male rack.
4. Insert a .25 MM gage between male rack and female inner tie rod housing in order to inspect both stakes. Feeler gauge must not pass between rack and housing stake.
5. Slide shock dampner over inner tie rod housing until front lip of dampner bottoms against inner tie rod housing.
6. Install rack and pinion boot and breather tube using new boot clamps.
7. Install outer tie rod end to inner tie rod, then loosely install jam nut.
8. Install steering gear as outlined under "Power Steering Gear, Replace."
9. Set front wheel toe as outlined under "Front Wheel Alignment" in "Wheel Alignment" section.
10. **Torque** jam nut to 50 ft. lbs.

Outer

1. Raise and support vehicle, then remove tire and wheel assembly.
2. Remove and discard hex torque prevailing nut, then loosen jam nut, **Fig. 8.**
3. Separate tie rod end from steering knuckle using universal steering linkage puller tool No. J 24319-01, or equivalent.
4. Loosen outer tie rod end to inner tie rod jam nut.
5. Turn outer tie rod counterclockwise to remove from inner tie rod end using a suitable pipe wrench to hold inner tie rod.
6. Reverse procedure to install. **Torque** jam nut to 50 ft. lbs.

POWER STEERING GEAR
REPLACE
Century, Grand Prix, Impala, Intrigue, LaCrosse, Monte Carlo & Regal

1. Set steering wheel to 12 o'clock position with wheels straight ahead, then turn ignition switch to LOCK position.
2. Raise and support vehicle, then re-

move lefthand wheel and tire assembly.
3. Remove steering shaft lower bolt at steering gear.
4. Separate steering shaft from power steering gear. **Failure to disconnect intermediate shaft from rack and pinion shaft stub may result in damage to steering gear and/or intermediate shaft. This damage can cause loss of steering control.**
5. Remove hex torque prevailing nuts, then separate both outer tie rod ends from steering knuckle using tie rod end puller/ball joint remover tool No. J 35917, or equivalent.
6. Support frame with suitable jackstands.
7. Remove frame bolts, then lower rear of frame. **Do not lower frame too far as damage to engine components near cowl may result.**
8. Remove pipe retaining clip from steering gear.
9. Place a suitable drain pan under steering rack fluid pipes, then remove inlet pipes and outlet line from steering gear.
10. Remove steering gear mounting bolts and nuts.
11. Remove power steering gear through wheel opening.
12. Reverse procedure to install. Bleed power steering system as outlined under "Power Steering System Bleed."

Lumina

1. Raise and support vehicle. **Provide additional support at rear of vehicle.**
2. Remove front wheel and tire assemblies.
3. Remove intermediate shaft lower pinch bolt at steering gear, **Fig. 9.**
4. Remove intermediate shaft from stub shaft. **Failure to disconnect intermediate shaft from rack and pinion shaft stub may result in damage to steering gear and/or intermediate shaft. This damage can cause loss of steering control.**
5. Disconnect tie rod ends from knuckle and strut assembly using tie rod puller/ball joint remover tool No. J-35917, or equivalent.
6. Support body with suitable stands, then remove rear frame mounting bolts and lower rear frame no more than five inches. **Do not lower rear of frame too far. Damage to engine components near cowl may result.**
7. Remove heat shield, then pipe retaining clip from steering gear.
8. Place a suitable drain pan under engine, then disconnect inlet pipes and outlet line from power steering gear.
9. Remove remaining brackets and clips.
10. Remove rack and pinion mounting nuts and bolts, then rack and pinion assembly through lefthand wheel opening.
11. Reverse procedure to install. Bleed power steering system as outlined under, "Power Steering System Bleed."

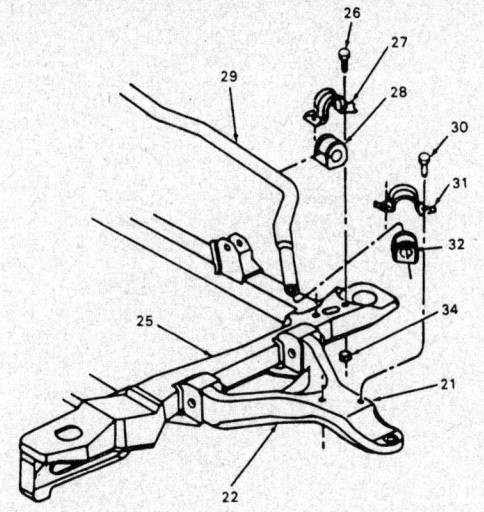

21 WELD NUTS
22 LOWER CONTROL ARM
25 FRAME
26 CLAMP BOLT
27 CLAMP
28 INSULATOR
29 STABILIZER SHAFT
30 BOLT 47 N•m (35 lbs. ft.)
31 CLAMP
32 INSULATOR
34 NUT 47 N•m (35 lbs. ft.)

GC2029100171000X

Fig. 7 Stabilizer shaft & insulators replacement. Lumina

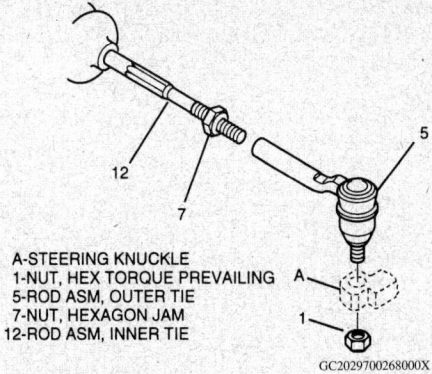

A-STEERING KNUCKLE
1-NUT, HEX TORQUE PREVAILING
5-ROD ASM, OUTER TIE
7-NUT, HEXAGON JAM
12-ROD ASM, INNER TIE

GC2029700268000X

Fig. 8 Tie rod end replacement

POWER STEERING PUMP

REPLACE

Century, Grand Prix, LaCrosse & Regal

1. **On models equipped with 3.1L engine,** place a suitable drain pan under engine, then remove coolant recovery reservoir and position aside.
2. **On all models,** remove accessory drive belt from pump.
3. **On models equipped with 3.1L engine,** disconnect ignition control wiring harness near pump and position aside.
4. **On all models,** place a suitable drain pan under engine, then disconnect inlet and outlet hoses from pump.
5. Remove pump assembly mounting bolts, then pump.
6. Transfer pulley to new pump, if required.
7. Reverse procedure to install. Bleed power steering system as outlined under "Power Steering System Bleed."

Impala

3.4L ENGINE

1. Place a suitable drain pan under vehicle, then remove coolant recovery reservoir.
2. Remove accessory drive belt from power steering pump pulley.
3. Remove ignition wiring harness from retainer near power steering pump.
4. Disconnect power steering pressure and return hoses.
5. Remove power steering pump mounting bolts, then steering pump from engine mounting.
6. Reverse procedure to install.

3.8L ENGINE

1. Remove accessory drive belt.
2. Raise and support vehicle, then remove tire and wheel assembly.
3. Place a suitable drain pan under vehicle, then disconnect pressure and return lines from power steering pump.
4. Remove power steering pump mounting bolts, then steering pump assembly.
5. Remove fluid reservoir from pump, then pulley.
6. Transfer pulley and reservoir to new pump, if required.
7. Reverse procedure to install. Bleed power steering system as outlined under "Power Steering System Bleed."

Intrigue

1. Place a suitable drain pan under vehicle, then remove coolant surge tank.
2. Remove fuel injector sight shield.
3. Remove accessory drive belt, then accessory wiring junction block, position junction block aside.
4. Remove power steering pump pulley, using power steering pump pulley remover tool No. J 25034-C, or equivalent.
5. Remove pressure and return lines from pump.
6. Remove pump mounting bolts, then steering pump and reservoir assembly.
7. Remove reservoir from pump.
8. Reverse procedure to install. Bleed power steering system as outlined under "Power Steering System, Replace."

Lumina

1. Place a suitable drain pan under engine, then remove coolant recovery reservoir and position aside.

2. Remove accessory drive belt from pump.
3. Disconnect ignition control wiring harness near pump and position aside.
4. place a suitable drain pan under engine, then disconnect inlet and outlet hoses from pump.
5. Remove pump assembly mounting bolts, then pump.
6. Transfer pulley to new pump, if required.
7. Reverse procedure to install. Bleed power steering system as outlined under "Power Steering System Bleed."

Monte Carlo

1. Place a suitable drain pan under vehicle, then remove coolant recovery reservoir.
2. Remove accessory drive belt from power steering pump pulley.
3. Remove ignition wiring harness from retainer near power steering pump.
4. Disconnect power steering pressure and return hoses.
5. Remove power steering pump mounting bolts, then steering pump from engine mounting.
6. Reverse procedure to install.

POWER STEERING SYSTEM BLEED

1. Turn wheels all way to the left.
2. Add power steering to Cold mark on fluid level indicator.
3. Start engine and run at fast idle, then add fluid, if required to bring level to Cold mark.
4. Bleed system by turning wheels from side to side without hitting stops. Keep fluid level at Cold mark.
5. Return wheels to center position and continue running engine for two to three minutes.
6. Road test vehicle to ensure steering functions normally and is free of noise.
7. Inspect fluid level and ensure level is at Hot mark after system has stabilized at its normal operating temperature.

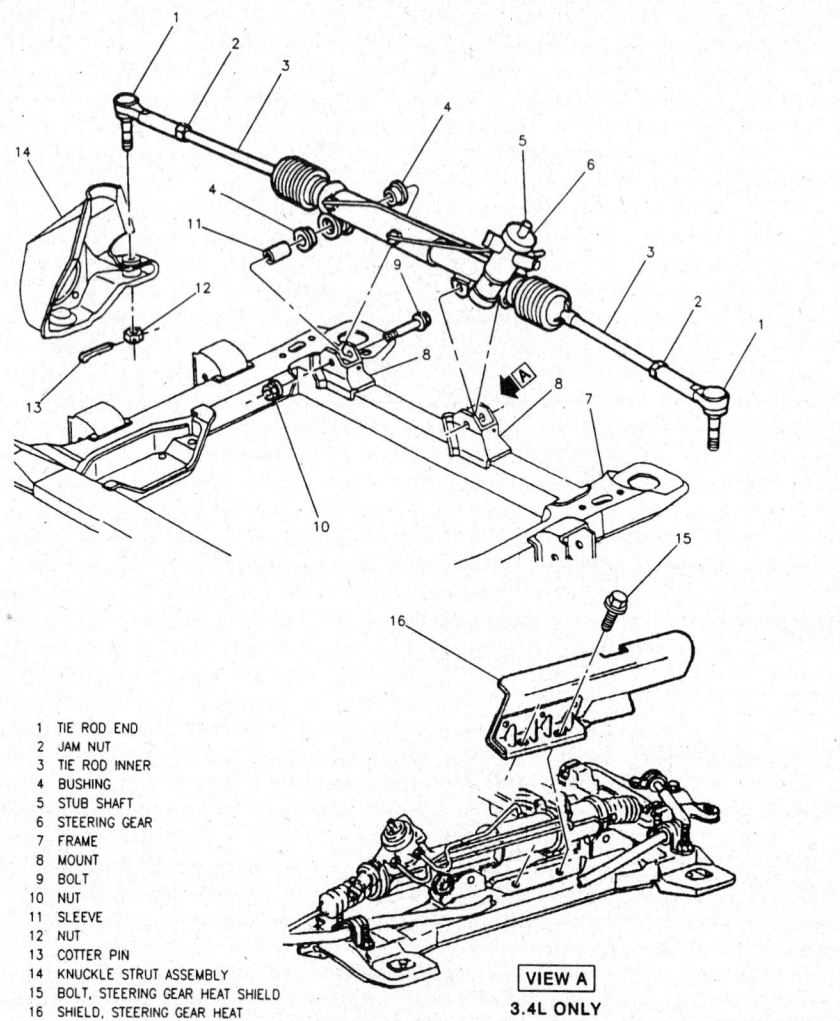

1 TIE ROD END
2 JAM NUT
3 TIE ROD INNER
4 BUSHING
5 STUB SHAFT
6 STEERING GEAR
7 FRAME
8 MOUNT
9 BOLT
10 NUT
11 SLEEVE
12 NUT
13 COTTER PIN
14 KNUCKLE STRUT ASSEMBLY
15 BOLT, STEERING GEAR HEAT SHIELD
16 SHIELD, STEERING GEAR HEAT

VIEW A
3.4L ONLY

GC2029700269000X

Fig. 9 Power steering gear replacement. Lumina

TIGHTENING SPECIFICATIONS

Year	Component	Torque/Ft. Lbs.
CENTURY, LACROSSE & REGAL		
2001–05	Ball Joint To Control Arm Nuts	50
	Ball Joint To Knuckle Nut	22①
	Frame To Body Bolts	122
	Hub & Bearing Bolts	96
	Inner Tie Rod	74
	Lower Control Arm Nuts	92
	O-Ring Union Fitting	55
	Outer Tie Rod End Nut	34
	Rack Bearing Preload Lock Nut	50
	Stabilizer Shaft Bracket Bolt	38
	Stabilizer Shaft Link Nut	17
	Steering Cooler Pipe/Hose Mounting Bolt	89①
	Steering Gear Cylinder Line Fittings	13
	Steering Gear Mounting Bolts	59
	Steering Gear Pipe Fittings	20
	Steering Pump Flow Control Valve Union Fitting	55
	Steering Pump Mounting Bolts	25
	Strut Mount Nut	63
	Strut To Body Mount Nuts	24
	Strut To Knuckle Bolts	90
	Tie Rod End Jam Nut	50
	Wheel Lug Nuts	100
GRAND PRIX, IMPALA & MONTE CARLO		
2001–05	Ball Joint To Control Arm Nuts	50
	Ball Joint To Knuckle Nut	22①
	Hub & Bearing Bolts	96
	Inner Tie Rod	74
	Lower Control Arm Nuts	92
	O-Ring Union Fitting	55
	Outer Tie Rod End Nut	34
	Rack Bearing Preload Lock Nut	50
	Stabilizer Shaft Bracket Bolt	22
	Stabilizer Shaft Link Nut	44
	Steering Cooler Pipe/Hose Mounting Bolt	89①
	Steering Cooler Retainer Nuts	11
	Steering Gear Cylinder Line Fittings	13
	Steering Gear Mounting Bolts	59
	Steering Gear Valve End Fittings	20
	Steering Pipe Fittings	20
	Steering Pump Flow Control Valve	55
	Steering Pump Mounting Bolts	25
	Strut Shaft Nut	63
	Strut To Knuckle Bolts	90
	Strut Upper Mounting Nuts	24
	Tie Rod End Jam Nut	50
	Wheel Lug Nuts	100

Continued

TIGHTENING
SPECIFICATIONS—Continued

Year	Component	Torque/Ft. Lbs.
INTRIGUE		
2001–02	Ball Joint To Control Arm Nuts	50
	Ball Joint To Knuckle Nut	22①
	Frame To Body Bolts	122
	Hub & Bearing Bolts	96
	Inner Tie Rod	74
	Lower Control Arm Nuts	92
	Rack Bearing Preload Lock Nut (Magnasteer)	50
	Rack Bearing Preload Lock Nut (Quiet Valve)	55
	Stabilizer Shaft Bracket Bolt	38
	Stabilizer Shaft Link Nut	17
	Steering Cooler Pipe Bolt	84①
	Steering Gear Cylinder Line Fittings	13
	Steering Gear Mounting Bolts	59
	Steering Gear Valve End Fittings	20
	Steering Pump Flow Control Valve	55
	Steering Pump Mounting Bolts	25
	Strut Mount Nut	63
	Strut To Body Mount Nuts	24
	Strut To Knuckle Bolts	90
	Tie Rod End Jam Nut	50
	Tie Rod End Nut	22②
	Wheel Lug Nuts	100
LUMINA		
2001	Ball Joint Heat Shield Bolts	62②
	Ball Joint Nuts	63
	Drive Axle Nuts	159
	Hub & Bearing To Knuckle Bolts	52
	Insulator Bracket To Frame Nuts	27
	Insulator Clamp To Frame Nuts	35
	Insulator Clamp To Lower Control Arm Bolts	35
	Intermediate Steering Shaft Pinch Bolts	35
	Lower Control Arm To Frame Bolts	52
	Steering Gear Mounting Bolts	59
	Stabilizer Shaft Bushing Clamp Bolts	35
	Steering Pump Mounting Bolts	25
	Steering Cooler Pipe Bolt	84①
	Steering Gear Cylinder Line Fittings	13
	Steering Gear Valve End Fittings	20
	Strut Closure Nuts	82
	Strut Mount Cover Plate Nuts	24
	Strut Piston Shaft Nuts	59
	Tie Rod End Nut	22②
	Tie Rod End Jam Nut	50
	Inner Tie Rod	74
	Wheel Lug Nuts	100

① — Inch lbs.

② — Rotate an additional 115°.

Wheel Alignment

INDEX

PRECAUTIONS

When adjusting wheel alignment, always adjust both front and rear alignment. Begin with rear wheel camber, then proceed to rear wheel toe, tracking and final adjustment of front wheel camber and toe.

PRELIMINARY INSPECTION

1. Ensure tires are inflated to proper pressure and inspect for uneven wear.
2. Inspect front wheel bearings and related suspension components for damage and replace as required to eliminate improper alignment due to faulty components.
3. Inspect ball joints and tie rods.
4. Inspect vehicle trim heights.
5. Inspect steering gear for looseness at frame.
6. Inspect struts for improper operation.
7. Inspect for loose control arms.
8. Inspect for loose or missing stabilizer shaft attachments.

FRONT WHEEL ALIGNMENT

Camber

CENTURY, GRAND PRIX, IMPALA, INTRIGUE, LACROSSE, MONTE CARLO & REGAL

1. Remove strut assembly as outlined in "Front Suspension & Steering" section.
2. Place strut assembly in a suitable vise.
3. File lower strut to knuckle mounting hole oblong as outlined, **Fig. 1.**
4. Install strut assembly and adjust camber as required.
5. **Torque** strut to knuckle bolts to 90 ft. lbs.

LUMINA

1. Open hood and remove three strut cover plate nuts and cover plate.
2. Lift front of vehicle until strut stud clears strut tower and top cover of strut. **Do not overextend drive axle or lift by suspension.**
3. To mark holes use strut alignment template tool No. J-36892, or equivalent, then file three existing mounting holes. File inboard or outboard of existing hole depending or camber requirement. **Do not file more than .2 inch in either direction. Paint exposed metal with red oxide primer and matching body color.**
4. Lower front of vehicle and guide strut studs into slotted holes.
5. Install three strut cover plate nuts.
6. Set camber to specifications by moving strut, then **torque** strut cover plate nuts to 24 ft. lbs.

Toe

1. Remove power steering gear seal clamps.
2. With steering wheel in straight ahead position, loosen jam nuts on tie rods.
3. Rotate inner tie rod to obtain proper toe angle, then ensure number of threads showing on each tie rod is approximately equal.
4. Ensure tie rod ends are square, then **torque** jam nuts to 50 ft. lbs.
5. Ensure seals are not twisted, then install seal clamps.

REAR WHEEL ALIGNMENT

Camber

1. Remove strut assembly as outlined in "Rear Suspension" section.

2. Place strut assembly in a suitable vise.
3. File upper strut to knuckle mounting hole oblong, **Fig. 2.**
4. Install strut assembly and adjust camber as required.
5. **Torque** strut to knuckle bolts to 88 ft. lbs.

Toe

CENTURY, GRAND PRIX, IMPALA, INTRIGUE, LACROSSE, MONTE CARLO & REGAL

1. Loosen hex nuts at rear wheel spindle rod.
2. Adjust toe to specifications.
3. **Torque** hex nuts to 50 ft. lbs.

LUMINA

1. lubricate tie rod threads, then install rear toe adjusting tool No. J-38118, or equivalent.
2. Hand tighten turnbuckle portion of tool in direction of adjustment. Equal amounts of threads should be showing on both sides of turnbuckle.
3. Loosen rear rod nut at crossmember a minimum of four turns.
4. Rotate turnbuckle portion of tool to reach proper toe specification.
5. **Torque** rear rod to crossmember nut to 111 ft. lbs.
6. Remove tool.

VEHICLE RIDE HEIGHT

Refer to "Vehicle Ride Height Specifications" in the "Specifications" section for vehicle ride height measurement points and specifications.

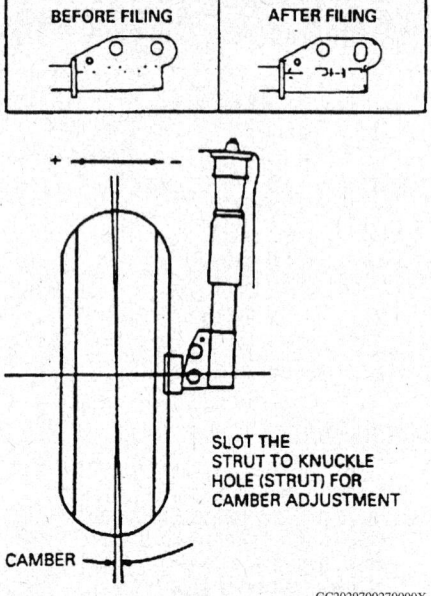

Fig. 1   Front camber adjustment. Century, Grand Prix, Impala, Intrigue, LaCrosse, Monte Carlo & Regal

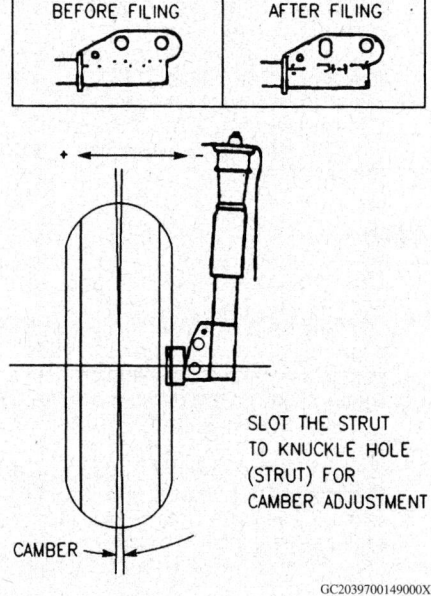

Fig. 2   Rear camber adjustment

CORVETTE

NOTE: Refer To The Rear Of This Manual For Vehicle Manufacturer's Special Tool Suppliers.

INDEX OF SERVICE OPERATIONS

CORVETTE

Specifications

GENERAL ENGINE SPECIFICATIONS

Year	Engine		Fuel System	Bore & Stroke	Compression Ratio	Net Brake H.P. @ RPM②	Maximum Torque	Normal Oil Pressure psi
	Liter	VIN Code①						
2001–04	5.7L	G	SFI	3.90 x 3.62	10.1	345 @ 5200	④	③
	5.7L	S	SFI	3.90 x 3.62	10.5	405 @ 6000	400 @ 4800	③
2005	6.0L	U	SFI	4.00 x 3.62	10.9	400 @ 6000	400 @ 4400	③

SFI — Sequential Fuel Injection
VIN — Vehicle Identification Number
① — The eighth digit of the VIN denotes engine code.
② — Ratings are net, as installed in vehicle.

③ — Engine hot, minimum oil pressure @ 1000 RPM, 6 psi.; @ 2000 RPM, 18 psi.; @ 4000 RPM, 24 psi.

④ — Manual transmission, 375 ft. lbs., @ 4400 RPM; automatic transmission, 360 ft. lbs., @ 4000 RPM.

TUNE UP SPECIFICATIONS

Year	Engine	Spark Plug Gap	Ignition Timing BTDC				Curb Idle Speed③		Fast Idle Speed		Fuel Pump Pressure psi	Valve Clearance Inch
			Firing Order	Man. Trans.	Auto. Trans.	Mark Fig.	Man. Trans.	Auto. Trans.	Man. Trans.	Auto. Trans.		
2001–04	5.7L	.060	1-8-7-2-6-5-4-3	①	①	—	④	④	④	④	55–61⑤	②
2005	6.0L	.04	1-8-7-2-6-5-4-3	①	①	—	④	④	④	④	55–61⑤	②

BTDC — Before Top Dead Center
VIN — Vehicle Identification Number
① — Computer controlled. No adjustment.
② — Equipped w/hydraulic lifters. No adjustment is required.

③ — When inspecting idle speed, set parking brake & block drive wheels.
④ — Idle speed is controlled by an idle speed control motor.
⑤ — With shop towel wrapped around

fuel pressure fitting to prevent fuel spillage, connect a suitable fuel pressure gauge. Inspect fuel pressure with ignition On, but engine not running.

FRONT WHEEL ALIGNMENT SPECIFICATIONS

Year	Models	Caster Angle, Degrees		Camber Angle, Degrees		Toe Per Wheel, Degrees		Steering Wheel Angle, Degrees	Ball Joint Wear	
		Limits	Desired	Limits	Desired	Limits	Desired		Upper	Lower
2001–04	FE1 & FE3	+7.9 to +6.9	7.4	.3 to -.7	-.2	.28 to -.12	.08	1.0 to -1.0	①	①
	FE4 (Z06)	+7.4 to +6.4	6.9	.3 to -.7	-.2	.14 to -.06	.08	1.0 to -1.0	①	①
2005	All	8.5 to 7.3	7.9	.15 to -1.05	-.45	.30 to -.10	.10	-3.5 to 3.5	①	①

① — Refer to "Front Suspension & Steering" for proper wear.

REAR WHEEL ALIGNMENT SPECIFICATIONS

Year	Models	Camber Angle, Degrees		Toe Per Wheel, Degrees		Thrust Angle, Degrees	
		Limits	Desired	Limits	Desired	Limits	Desired
2001–04	FE1 & FE3	-.68 to .32	-.18	-.22 to +.18	-.02	-.1 to +.1	0
	FE4 (Z06)	-1.18 to -.18	-.68	-.22 to +.18	-.02	-.1 to +.1	0
2005	All	-.95 to .05	-.45	-.2 to +.2	0	-.2 to +.1	0

VEHICLE RIDE HEIGHT SPECIFICATIONS

Model	Year	Body Style	Manu-facturer's Original Tire Size	Measurement Points & Specifications①③					
				Front			Rear		
				Dim.	Spec.		Dim.	Spec.	
					Inches	mm		Inches	mm
Corvette	All	All	(c)②	C	5.9	150	D	5.31	135

A Dim. — Measurement From Front Wheel Center to Check Point On Rocker Panel

B Dim. — Measurement From Rear Wheel Center to Check Point On Rocker Panel

C Dim. — Ground to Rocker Panel, Front

D Dim. — Ground to Rocker Panel, Rear

Dim. — Dimension

① — ± .39 in (10 mm) front to rear & side to side.

② — See door sticker or inside of glove box for manufacturers original tire size specifications. If tires on

vehicle do not match manufacturers original tire size & measurement is

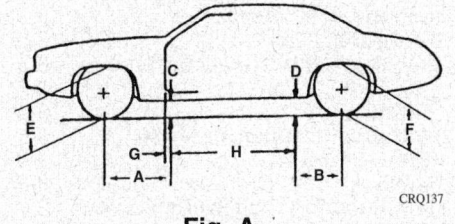

Fig. A

CRQ137

not within limits, it will be required to refer to the "Non-Standard Tire & Wheel Size Adjustment To Ride Height Specification & Tire Size Adjustment Charts" in the front of this manual for approximate changes in ride height specifica-tions.

③ — Measurement is with fuel, radiator coolant and engine oil full, spare tire, jack, hand tools and mats in designated positions and tires prop-erly inflated.

FLUID CAPACITIES & COOLING SYSTEM DATA

Year	Model Or Engine (VIN)①	Coolant Capa-city, Qts.	Coolant Type	Radiator Cap Relief Pres-sure, psi	Therm-o. Open-ing Temp. °F	Fuel Tank, Gals.	Engine Oil, Qts.②		Transmission Oil			Rear Axle Pts.
							Less Filter Change	With Filter Change	Man Trans. Pts.	Auto. Trans. Qts.③		
										Drain & Refill	Total Capa-city	
2001–04	5.7L (G)	⑤	Dex-Cool	15	187	18.5	6.0④	6.5④	8.2	5	10.8	3.4
	5.7L (S)	⑤	Dex-Cool	15	187	18.5	6.0④	6.5④	3.9	—	—	3.4
2005	6.0L (U)	12.6	Dex-Cool	18	195	18.0	5.5	—	4.1	—	—	3.6

VIN — Vehicle Identification Number

① — The eighth digit of the VIN denotes engine code.

② — After refilling, inspect oil level again.

③ — Approximate. Make final inspection w/dipstick.

④ — Recommended engine oil SG SAE 5W-30 synthetic engine oil meeting GM specification GM4718M.

⑤ — On models w/A/T, 11.5 qts.; w/M/T, 11.8 qts.

⑥ — On models w/A/T, 12.3 qts.; w/M/T, 12.6 qts.

LUBRICANT DATA

Year	Lubricant Type				
	Transmission		Rear Axle	Power Steering System	Brake System
	Automatic	Manual			
All	Dexron III	Dexron III	①	②	DOT 3 Brake Fluid

① — 75W-90 synthetic axle lubricant P/N 12378261, or an equivalent meeting GM specification 9986115.

When completely draining & filling add 4 ounces of lubricant additive P/N 1052358, or equivalent.

② — Power steering fluid P/N 89021184 or equivalents.

Electrical

NOTE: On Air Bag Equipped Models, Refer To "Air Bag System Precautions" Located In The Front Of This Manual For System Disarming & Arming Procedures.

NOTE: Refer To "Computer Relearn Procedures" Located In The Front Of This Manual When Battery Power To The Computer Has Been Interrupted.

NOTE: Prior To Performing Any Service Operations Listed In This Section, Consult The "Technical Service Bulletins" Section For Related Information.

INDEX

PRECAUTIONS

Air Bag Systems

Refer to "Air Bag System Precautions" in the front of this manual for system disarming and arming procedures.

Battery Ground Cable

Prior to service, disconnect battery ground cable and isolate as required.

FUSE PANEL & FLASHER LOCATION

The fuse panel is located behind the far righthand corner of the instrument panel. The turn signal and hazard flasher is incorporated into the hazard warning switch, which is located behind the center air vent.

FUEL PUMP RELAY LOCATION

The fuel pump relay is located in the underhood electrical center.

RELAY CENTER LOCATION

The relay center, or underhood electrical

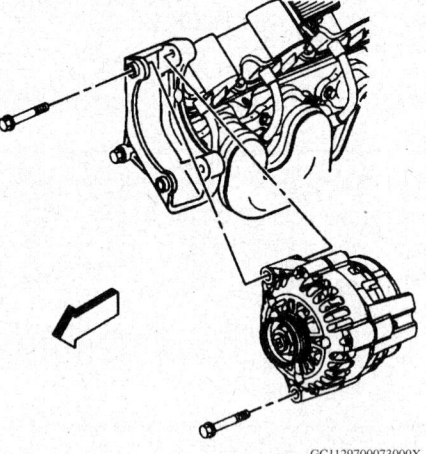

GC1129700073000X

Fig. 1 Alternator removal

center, is located on the righthand side of the engine compartment, in front of the battery.

STARTER

REPLACE

1. Raise and support vehicle.
2. Disconnect HO2S electrical connectors.
3. Remove takedown pipe flange nuts.

4. Remove intermediate pipe to rear pipe mounting bolts.
5. Remove takedown pipe bracket front exhaust hanger bolts.
6. Remove rear intermediate exhaust pipes rear exhaust hanger bolts.
7. Remove intermediate pipe.
8. Remove intermediate pipe rear HO2S.
9. Record starter motor wiring orientation, then remove nuts and disconnect electrical connections.
10. Remove starter motor mounting bolts while supporting starter motor.
11. Remove starter motor.
12. Reverse procedure to install, noting the following:
    a. **Torque** starter motor mounting bolts to 37 ft. lbs.
    b. **Torque** S-terminal mounting nut to 35 inch lbs.
    c. **Torque** battery cable mounting nuts to 71 inch lbs.

ALTERNATOR

REPLACE

1. Disconnect regulator electrical connector and battery to alternator terminal.
2. Release accessory drive belt tensioner.
3. Remove accessory drive belt from alternator pulley.
4. Remove alternator mounting bolts, **Fig. 1**.

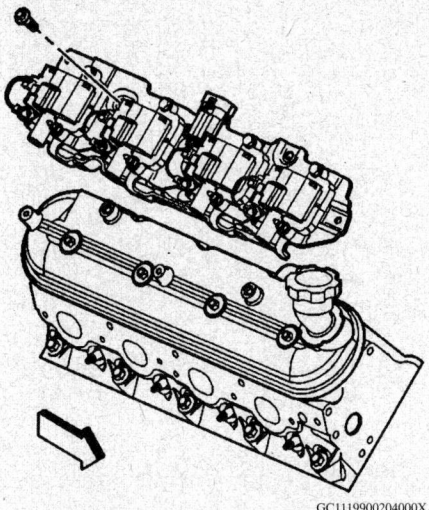

Fig. 2 Coil pack removal

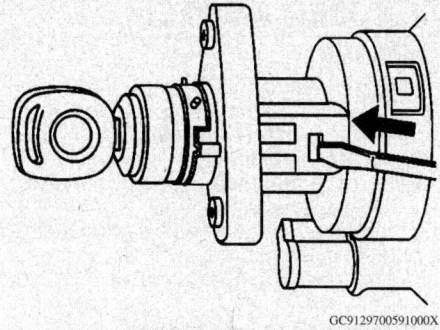

Fig. 3 Ignition lock cylinder removal

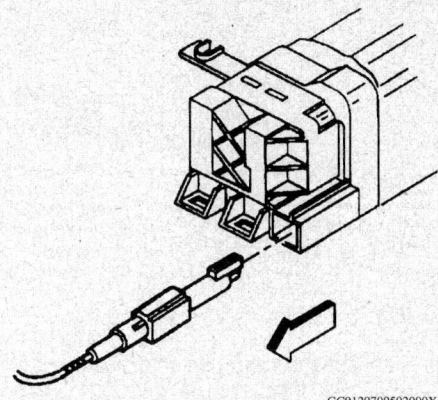

Fig. 4 Park lock cable removal

5. Remove alternator.
6. Reverse procedure to install, noting the following:
   a. **Torque** alternator mounting bolts to 37 ft. lbs.
   b. **Torque** battery terminal nut to 10 ft. lbs.

COIL PACK
REPLACE

1. Remove fuel rail cover.
2. Disconnect ignition coil harness electrical connector.
3. Disconnect spark plug wires at ignition coils.
4. Remove ignition coil mounting bolts, **Fig. 2.**
5. Remove ignition coils.
6. Reverse procedure to install. **Torque** coil mounting bolts to 106 inch lbs.

IGNITION LOCK
REPLACE
2001-04

1. Apply parking brake and remove console.
2. Remove instrument panel accessory trim plate.
3. Remove driver's knee bolster trim panel.
4. Record routing of ignition switch lock cylinder wire wraps around switch bezel.
5. Remove ignition switch lock cylinder electrical connector from mounting tab.
6. Disconnect lock cylinder electrical connector.
7. Insert key and turn to run position.
8. Depress and hold ignition lock cylinder mounting tab located on righthand lower side of switch, using suitable flat-bladed screwdriver, **Fig. 3.**
9. Pull to remove ignition lock cylinder.
10. Remove ignition switch bezel. Carefully pull to unsnap it.
11. Reverse procedure to install, noting the following:

a. Wrap ignition switch wire around base of switch bezel as in original fashion.
b. Align bezel slots to cylinder pins and push to secure in place.
c. Press cylinder into place and listen for retaining tab to produce definite click.

IGNITION SWITCH
REPLACE
2001-04

1. Remove ignition lock cylinder as outlined in "Ignition Lock, Replace."
2. Remove hazard warning switch wiring harness from ignition switch retainer.
3. Disconnect ignition switch electrical connectors.
4. **On models equipped with automatic transmission,** disconnect park lock cable from ignition switch using suitable screwdriver to depress retaining tab, **Fig. 4.**
5. **On all models,** remove ignition switch mounting bolts.
6. Remove ignition switch.
7. Reverse procedure to install. **Torque** ignition switch mounting bolts to 49 inch lbs.

2005

1. Lower steering column to its lowest position.
2. Pull outward on lower edge of trim panel, to release lower clips.
3. Disconnect electrical connectors, then remove instrument panel cluster trim plate.
4. Release switch from trim plate using a flat bladed tool.
5. Reverse procedure to install.

CLUTCH START SWITCH
REPLACE

1. Disconnect clutch start switch electrical connector.
2. Insert feeler gauge between switch and clutch pedal bracket to release switch tab.
3. Remove clutch start switch by lifting slightly then pulling.
4. Reverse procedure to install.

NEUTRAL SAFETY SWITCH
REPLACE

1. Raise and support vehicle.
2. Disconnect HO2S connectors.
3. Remove exhaust takedown pipe flange nuts.
4. Remove intermediate pipe to rear pipe mounting bolts.
5. Remove takedown pipe bracket front exhaust hanger bolts.
6. Remove rear intermediate exhaust pipe rear exhaust hanger bolts.
7. Remove intermediate pipe.
8. Remove intermediate pipe rear HO2S.
9. Shift transmission to Neutral position.
10. Remove transmission shift control cable bracket to transmission nuts.
11. Disconnect transmission shift control cable from transmission range selector lever. **Rod end guide tubes cannot endure much abuse.**
12. Position transmission shift cable and bracket aside.
13. Disconnect neutral safety switch electrical connectors.
14. Remove mounting nut and range selector shift lever using suitable wrench on manual shaft flats to prevent rotation.
15. Ensure transmission is still in neutral.
16. Remove neutral safety switch mounting bolts.
17. Slide switch off manual shaft.
18. Reverse procedure to install, noting the following:
   a. Install switch alignment tool No. J 41364-A, or equivalent, to neutral safety switch.
   b. Align two lower slots on switch with two lower tabs on tool.
   c. Turn tool until its upper pin aligns with slot on top of switch.
   d. Ensure transmission is still in neutral.
   e. Ensure switch hub flats align with those on shaft, then install switch and tool onto manual shaft until switch mounting bracket meets transmission case mounting bosses.
   f. **Torque** switch mounting bolts to 20 ft. lbs.
   g. Remove alignment tool.

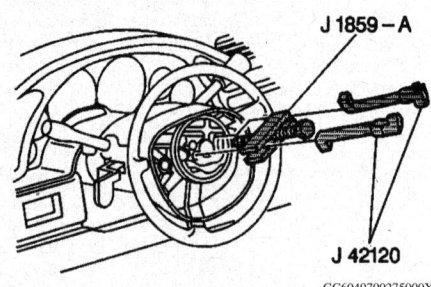

Fig. 5 Steering wheel removal

GC6049700275000X

   h. **Torque** range selector lever nut to 15 ft. lbs.

HEADLAMP SWITCH
REPLACE

Refer to "Multi-Function Switch, Replace" for headlamp switch replacement procedure.

STOP LIGHT SWITCH
REPLACE

1. Remove instrument panel lower trim panel.
2. Disconnect stop lamp switch electrical connectors.
3. Remove stop lamp switch.
4. Reverse procedure to install, noting the following:
   a. While keeping brake pedal depressed, insert switch into retainer until switch body has seated.
   b. Listen for clicks as threaded portion of switch travels through retainer.
   c. Slowly pull brake pedal fully rearward until clicks have stopped. Switch will move in retainer and self-adjust.

MULTI-FUNCTION SWITCH
REPLACE

1. Release tilt wheel lever locking tab using suitable small screwdriver and slide lever straight out of steering column.
2. Remove steering wheel as outlined in "Steering Wheel, Replace."
3. Remove driver's side knee bolster trim panel.
4. Remove upper and lower steering column covers.
5. Disconnect multi-function turn signal switch electrical connectors.
6. Release upper and lower retaining clips.
7. Slide multi-function turn signal switch away from steering column lock module.
8. Reverse procedure to install.

TURN SIGNAL SWITCH
REPLACE

Refer to "Multi-Function Switch, Replace" for procedure.

DIMMER SWITCH
REPLACE

1. Remove instrument panel cluster.
2. Disconnect electrical connectors at instrument panel dimmer switch and driver information center switch.
3. Remove mounting screws and instrument panel cluster bezel.
4. Remove mounting screws and instrument panel dimmer switch.
5. Reverse procedure to install.

STEERING WHEEL
REPLACE
Removal

1. Remove driver's air bag module as outlined in "Passive Restraint Systems."
2. Disconnect steering column horn wiring harness.
3. Disconnect steering column ground wire.
4. Remove and discard steering wheel set nut.
5. Install steering wheel puller and legs tool Nos. J 1859-A and J 42120, or equivalents, **Fig. 5.**
6. Tighten puller center screw against steering column shaft until wheel slides off shaft.

Installation

1. Install steering wheel onto column.
2. Install new steering wheel set nut.
3. **Torque** steering wheel set nut to 30 ft. lbs.
4. Connect horn electrical connector.
5. Install air bag as outlined in "Passive Restraint Systems."

INSTRUMENT CLUSTER
REPLACE
2001-04

1. Remove instrument panel upper trim pad.
2. **On models equipped with Head Up Display (HUD),** carefully lift HUD electrical harness from between cluster and display, then disconnect electrical connector.
3. **On all models,** remove Instrument Panel Cluster (IPC) to steering column bracket mounting screws.
4. Lift rear of IPC slightly to release locator tab, then lift IPC to access and disconnect electrical connectors.
5. Remove IPC.
6. Reverse procedure to install, ensuring cluster retaining tab is properly positioned to steering column bracket.

2005

1. Lower steering column to its lowest position.
2. Pull outward on lower edge of trim panel, to release lower clips.

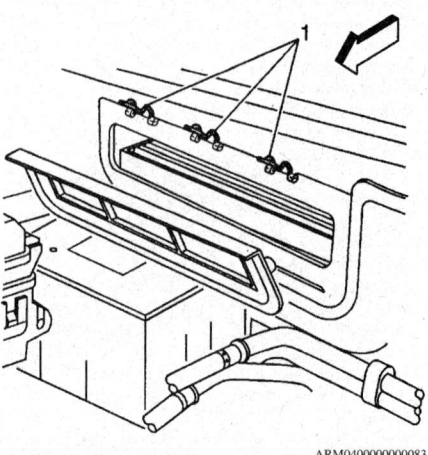

ARM0400000000083

Fig. 6 Cabin air filter removal

3. Disconnect electrical connectors, then remove instrument panel cluster trim plate.
4. Remove retaining bolt, then the instrument panel cluster.
5. Reverse procedure to install.

RADIO
REPLACE

1. Remove front floor kick-up panel.
2. Remove instrument panel electrical center cover.
3. Remove instrument panel electrical center RDO/CD Mini-Fuse No. 5 fuse.
4. Remove console.
5. Remove instrument panel accessory trim plate.
6. Remove screws mounting radio control to instrument panel center support bracket.
7. Remove radio control from center support bracket enough to access rear electrical connectors.
8. Disconnect electrical, audio and coaxial connectors.
9. Remove radio control.
10. Reverse procedure to install.

WIPER MOTOR
REPLACE

1. Remove wiper arm assemblies.
2. Remove air inlet screen.
3. Remove wiper motor module.
4. Disconnect wiper transmission linkage from crank arm using linkage separator tool No. J 39232, or equivalent.
5. Remove three wiper motor to wiper motor module mounting screws.
6. Remove wiper motor.
7. Reverse procedure to install, noting the following:
   a. Install motor into module.
   b. Connect linkage to crank arm using linkage installer tool No. J 39529, or equivalent.

WIPER SWITCH
REPLACE

1. Remove tilt wheel lever as outlined in "Steering Columns" chapter.

2. Remove driver's side knee bolster trim panel.
3. Remove upper and lower steering column covers.
4. Disconnect wiring harness electrical connector.
5. Release upper and lower mounting clips, then slide wiper washer switch from steering column lock module.
6. Reverse procedure to install.

WIPER TRANSMISSION
REPLACE

1. Remove wiper arm assemblies.
2. Remove air inlet screen.
3. Remove wiper motor module.
4. Remove mounting bolts and righthand wiper transmission from linkage.
5. Disconnect wiper transmission linkage from module using linkage separator tool No. J 39232, or equivalent.
6. Remove mounting bolts and lefthand wiper transmission from linkage.
7. Reverse procedure to install. Connect linkage to crank arm using linkage installer tool No. J 39529, or equivalent.

BLOWER MOTOR
REPLACE

1. Remove front floor kick-up panel.
2. Remove passenger floor hush panel.
3. Disconnect blower motor electrical connectors.
4. Remove cooling tube.
5. Remove blower motor to evaporator and heater core module mounting screws.
6. Remove blower motor and fan.
7. Reverse procedure to install.

CABIN AIR FILTER
REPLACE

1. Disengage passenger compartment air filter housing cover retainer clips, **Fig. 6.**
2. Remove passenger compartment air filter housing cover, then the filter.
3. Reverse procedure to install.

HEATER CORE
REPLACE

1. Evacuate air conditioning system refrigerant as outlined in "Air Conditioning" chapter.
2. Drain coolant into suitable container.
3. Remove battery and heat shield.
4. Remove intake manifold.
5. Remove heater pipe to dash panel bracket nut.
6. Position heater pipe bracket aside.

7. Remove heater pipe to core mounting bolt.
8. Cap or plug heater pipe and core to prevent contamination and spillage.
9. Remove accumulator hose to evaporator mounting bolt.
10. Disconnect evaporator accumulator hose and tube-rear. Cap or plug air conditioning lines.
11. Remove evaporator and HVAC module drain tube from module.
12. Remove floor console.
13. Remove instrument panel accessory trim plate.
14. Remove glove compartment.
15. Remove righthand hush panel.
16. Remove driver's side knee bolster trim panel.
17. Remove lefthand hush panel.
18. Remove instrument panel upper trim pad.
19. Remove instrument cluster to steering column bracket mounting screws.
20. Position cluster to allow room for HVAC module removal.
21. Remove lefthand side window defroster lower outlet duct.
22. **On models equipped with Automatic Temperature Control (ATC),** remove inside air temperature sensor aspirator duct and muffler.
23. **On all models,** disconnect Daytime Running Lamp (DRL) sensor electrical connector from lefthand side of windshield defroster duct.
24. Disconnect temperature valve actuator electrical connector.
25. Remove instrument panel center support bracket.
26. Remove ignition switch housing bracket.
27. Remove mounting screws and lefthand floor air outlet duct.
28. Remove lefthand rear floor air outlet duct by rotating it 90° clockwise.
29. Remove righthand side window defroster lower outlet.
30. Remove passenger's air bag module bracket and knee bolster bracket.
31. **On models equipped with ATC,** disconnect sunload sensor electrical connector from righthand side of windshield defroster duct.
32. **On all models,** remove mounting screws and righthand floor air outlet duct.
33. Pull front floor carpet away from righthand side of floor tunnel.
34. Remove righthand rear floor air outlet duct by rotating 90° counterclockwise.
35. Remove blower motor.
36. Disconnect instrument panel vacuum harness from HVAC module harness.
37. Disconnect vacuum electric solenoid electrical connector.

38. Remove mounting screws and windshield defroster duct.
39. Position air conditioning refrigerant lines to ease removal of HVAC module retaining and sealing nuts from dash panel, as required.
40. Remove instrument panel upper support beam HVAC module mounting screws.
41. Carefully remove HVAC module.
42. Remove and discard seals at module air inlet, drain and plumbing seals.
43. Remove mounting screws and heater core outlet cover.
44. Remove mounting screws and heater core cover.
45. Remove and discard heater core cover cavity, whistle and permagum seals.
46. Remove and discard heater core outer seal.
47. Remove heater core retaining clamp screw, clamp and pipe retainer clamp screw.
48. Remove heater core.
49. Remove and discard heater core lower, center, upper and side seals at HVAC module lower case.
50. Release retaining tab using suitable flat-bladed screwdriver and open up heater core pipe retainer clamp, then remove pipes clamp.
51. Reverse procedure to install, noting the following:
    a. Install new gaskets, O-rings and seals.
    b. **Torque** heater core cover and outlet mounting screws to 14 inch lbs.
    c. Ensure cutouts on dash mat are properly aligned so air inlet, drain and plumbing seals are seated directly against dash panel, not dash mat.
    d. Ensure dash panel drain opening aligns with HVAC module drain.
    e. Coat new refrigerant line O-rings with suitable 525 viscosity refrigerant oil.

EVAPORATOR CORE
REPLACE

1. Remove HVAC module as outlined in "Heater Core, Replace."
2. Release vacuum harness retainers on HVAC case below air inlet housing.
3. Remove upper heater evaporator module screws.
4. Separate upper and lower heater evaporator module halves.
5. Remove and discard seal.
6. Remove evaporator core.
7. Remove and discard lower, side and upper evaporator core seals.
8. Remove and discard water core filter.
9. Reverse procedure to install.

5.7L Engine

NOTE: On Air Bag Equipped Models, Refer To "Air Bag System Precautions" Located In The Front Of This Manual For System Disarming & Arming Procedures.

NOTE: Refer To "Computer Relearn Procedures" Located In The Front Of This Manual When Battery Power To The Computer Has Been Interrupted.

NOTE: Prior To Performing Any Service Operations Listed In This Section, Consult The "Technical Service Bulletins" Section For Related Information.

INDEX

PRECAUTIONS

Fuel System Pressure Relief

Failure to relieve system pressure prior to disconnecting fuel system components may cause fire or personal injury.
1. Disconnect and isolate battery ground cable.
2. Remove fuel tank filler cap to release fuel tank pressure.
3. Remove lefthand fuel rail cover.
4. Prior to disconnecting fuel line, position shop towel over fitting.
5. Connect pressure gauge tool No. J 34730-1A, or equivalent, to pressure tap on fuel rail.
6. Position bleed hose into suitable container.
7. Slowly relieve fuel system pressure.

Battery Ground Cable

Prior to service, disconnect battery ground cable and isolate as required.

COMPRESSION PRESSURE

When measuring compression, lowest cylinder must be within 70% of the highest cylinder with a minimum pressure of 100 psi. Compression test results will fall into one of the following categories:
1. Normally, compression builds up quickly and evenly to specifications on each cylinder.
2. If piston rings are faulty, compression will be low on first stroke, then build up on following strokes but will not reach specifications. Improvement is considerable with addition of approximately three squirts oil.
3. If valves are faulty, compression will be low on first stroke and will not tend to build up on following strokes. It will not improve much with addition of oil.
4. Ensure battery is fully charged.
5. Bring engine to operating temperature.
6. Disconnect electrical connector at crankshaft ignition timing sensor.
7. Disable fuel injection system.
8. Remove spark plugs.
9. Ensure throttle is wide open.
10. Install compression gauge tool No. J 38722, or equivalent.
11. Crank engine through four complete compression strokes, then record results for each cylinder.

ENGINE MOUNT
REPLACE
1. Remove alternator from accessory mount bracket.
2. Remove windshield washer reservoir.
3. Disconnect coolant switch electrical connector and position wiring aside.
4. Disconnect headlamp electrical connector and position wiring aside.
5. Support engine using engine support tool Nos. J 41803 and J 28467-B, or equivalent.
6. Raise and support vehicle.
7. Remove front wheels.
8. Remove tie rod end nuts.
9. Remove tie rod ends from steering knuckles using separator tool No. J 42188, or equivalent.
10. Remove stabilizer bar bolts and straps.
11. Disconnect stabilizer from cradle.
12. Remove power steering cooler bolts.
13. Disconnect power steering cooler from cradle and position it upward.

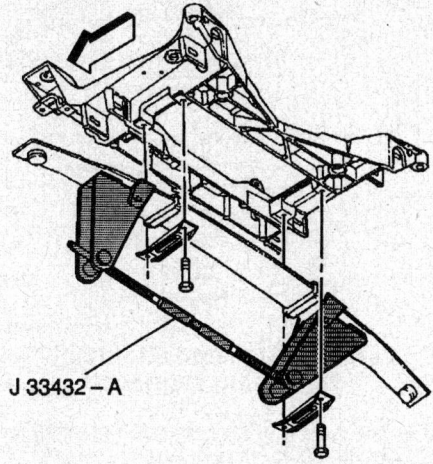

J 33432 – A

GC1069700891000A

Fig. 1 Transverse leaf spring compression

14. Remove power steering gear from cradle and position it upward.
15. Compress spring using transverse leaf spring compressor tool No. J 33432-A, or equivalent, **Fig. 1.**
16. Remove shock absorber lower mounting bolts.
17. Loosen, but do not remove, lower ball joint nuts.
18. Separate lower ball joints using separator tool No. J 42188, or equivalent.
19. Remove tool and ball joint nuts.
20. Disconnect crossmember electrical connectors.
21. Disconnect cradle electrical harnesses.
22. Remove brake pressure valve modulator valve bracket bolts, then position valve and bracket away from crossmember.
23. Remove motor mount to cradle nuts, **Fig. 2.**
24. Support cradle using suitable transmission jack, or equivalent.
25. Remove mounting nuts and cradle.
26. Remove upper engine mount nut, **Fig. 3.**
27. Remove engine mount.
28. Remove engine block bolts and motor mount bracket.
29. Reverse procedure to install.

ENGINE
REPLACE

1. Raise and support vehicle.
2. Drain coolant into suitable container.
3. Lower vehicle.
4. Recover air conditioning refrigerant charge.
5. Disconnect electrical connectors at IAT and MAF sensors.
6. Disconnect air intake duct fuel pressure regulator purge tube.
7. Position air intake duct and air cleaner forward.
8. Remove radiator as outlined in "Radiator, Replace."
9. Remove EBTCM/BPMV and bracket, then position brake pipes aside, cap and plug lines.

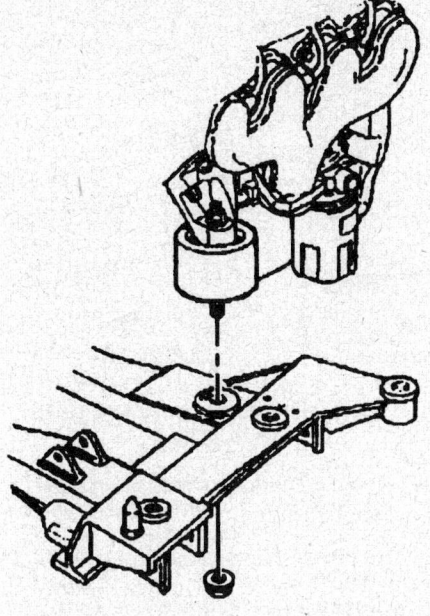

GC1069700889000X

Fig. 2 Engine mount to cradle removal

10. Remove serpentine belt as outlined in "Serpentine Drive Belt."
11. Remove lefthand fuel line from connector at front of firewall. Cap and plug fittings and openings.
12. Remove engine appearance covers.
13. Disconnect fuel lines at fuel rail. Cap and plug fittings and openings.
14. Disconnect radiator hoses and heater hoses at water pump.
15. Disconnect the following electrical connectors:
    a. Fuel injectors.
    b. Ignition coil main connectors.
    c. EVAP solenoid.
    d. Electric throttle motor.
    e. Throttle position sensor.
    f. ECT sensor.
    g. Air conditioning compressor.
    h. Alternator.
16. Remove alternator rear bracket bolts and bracket.
17. Remove alternator mounting bolts then the alternator as outlined in "Alternator, Replace" in "Electrical" section.
18. Disconnect brake booster vacuum hose.
19. Remove steering intermediate shaft to steering gear bolt.
20. Disconnect steering intermediate shaft from steering gear and position it to lefthand onto frame rail.
21. Disconnect lefthand exhaust manifold AIR hose.
22. Raise and support vehicle, then remove front tires and wheels.
23. Disconnect and unclip intermediate exhaust pipes' HO2S electrical connectors.
24. Remove intermediate exhaust pipes.
25. Remove mounting bolts and closeout panel.
26. Disconnect starter electrical connectors and wiring.
27. Remove starter mounting bolts, then

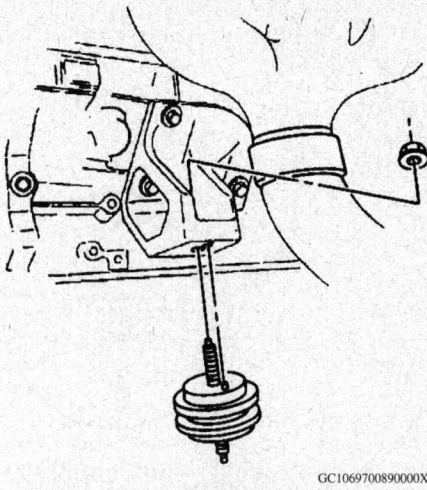

GC1069700890000X

Fig. 3 Upper engine mount removal

the starter as outlined in "Starter, Replace" in "Electrical" section.
28. Disconnect righthand and rear engine block wiring harness clips.
29. Disconnect oil level, CKP and righthand HO2S sensors electrical connectors.
30. Remove mounting bolt and air conditioning compressor hose.
31. Disconnect engine oil temperature and lefthand HO2S sensors electrical connectors.
32. Remove mounting bolts and straps, then disconnect front stabilizer bar from cradle.
33. Disconnect electric cooling fans' electrical connectors and harness.
34. Slide up and remove electric cooling fans.
35. Loosen nuts and remove tie rod ends from steering knuckles using ball joint separator tool No. J 42188, or equivalent.
36. Disconnect ABS electrical, EVO and RTD connectors clips from cradle.
37. Remove lower shock absorber mounting bolts.
38. Compress and remove front transverse spring using transverse spring compressor tool No. J33432-A, or equivalent, **Fig. 1.**
39. **On models equipped with automatic transmission,** proceed as follows:
    a. Disconnect fluid cooler lines at bellhousing junction.
    b. Disconnect cooler pipe clamps from front and rear of engine oil pan.
    c. Disconnect cooler pipes from radiator.
    d. Remove two plugs in driveline support.
    e. Install M10 1.5 × 2.166 inches, or longer bolt, in each plug location, **Fig. 4,** and **torque** to 26 ft. lbs.
    f. Remove bellhousing lower inspection cover.
    g. Position transmission flexplate hub collar downward to access and loosen mounting bolt.
    h. Unclip wiring harness from engine and position it to driveline.

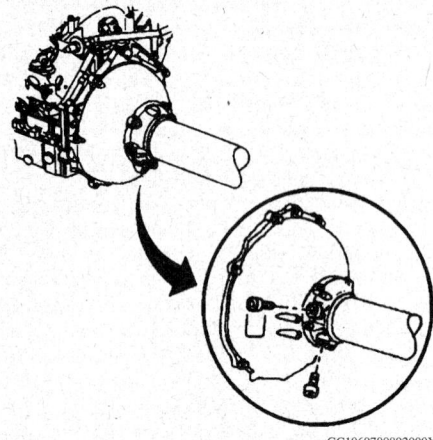

Fig. 4 Propeller shaft support bolt installation

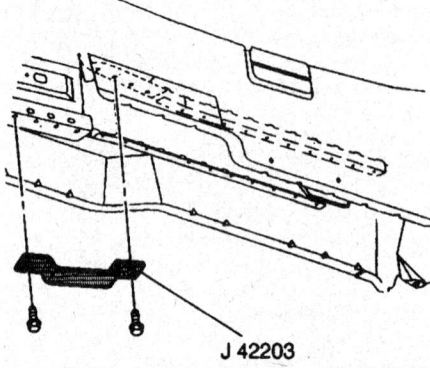

J 42203

GC1069700893000X

Fig. 5 Driveline support tool installation

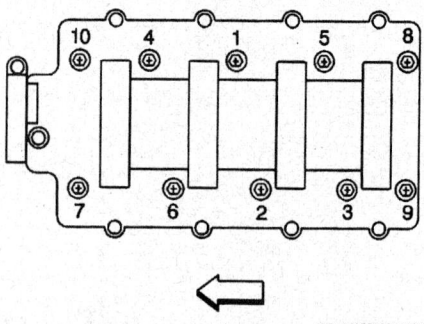

GC1069700894000A

Fig. 6 Intake manifold bolt tightening sequence

40. **On models equipped with manual transmission,** proceed as follows:
    a. Unclip hydraulic clutch actuator hose from bellhousing clip.
    b. Depress white circular release ring on actuator hose using hydraulic clutch line separator tool No. J 36221, or equivalent, while pulling lightly on master cylinder hose. This will separate two portions.
    c. Plug both open hydraulic hose ends.
    d. Remove driveline support bellhousing bolts.
41. **On all models,** install driveline support tool No. J 42203, or equivalent, to closeout panel flange, **Fig. 5. Do not support engine weight with driveline line support tool.**
42. Slowly lower vehicle on to engine support table tools Nos. J 39580 and No. J 39580-500, or equivalents.
43. Remove front and rear cradle nuts by hand.
44. Partially raise vehicle.
45. Remove and position AIR tube bracket bolt to access and remove lefthand rear ground strap at cylinder head.
46. Disconnect following electrical connectors:
    a. Engine oil pressure sensor.
    b. Camshaft position sensor.
    c. MAP sensor.
    d. Knock sensor.
    e. Ground on rear of lefthand head.
    f. All remaining electrical connections.
47. Remove front driveline support bolts.
48. Pry engine loose from driveline using suitable flat-bladed screwdriver, between edge of driveline support and bellhousing.
49. Slowly and carefully pull engine away from driveshaft.
50. Slowly raise vehicle as soon as input shaft clears bellhousing.
51. Slide engine and cradle forward to clear driveshaft spline.
52. **Ensure wiring harnesses are free and clear,** then carefully raise vehicle completely off engine and cradle.
53. Remove power steering pump using pulley removal tool No. J 25034-B, or equivalent.

54. Remove mounting bolts, then position power steering pump and reservoir aside.
55. Remove air conditioning belt, mounting bolts, nut, stud and air conditioning compressor.
56. Remove exhaust manifolds' mounting bolts and AIR tube.
57. Install engine lifting brackets tool No. J 41798, or equivalent.
58. Install suitable lifting device to lifting brackets.
59. Mark locations, disconnect wires and remove spark plugs.
60. Remove cradle mount nuts and engine.
61. Reverse procedure to install, noting the following:
    a. **Only use hand tools to install new engine cradle nuts.**
    b. **On models equipped with automatic transmission,** tighten flexplate hub collar bolt by hand after bellhousing to driveline support bolts have been tightened.
    c. After running engine to operating temperature and allowing to cool to room temperature.

INTAKE MANIFOLD
REPLACE

1. Raise and support vehicle.
2. Drain cooling system into suitable container and lower vehicle.
3. Disconnect IAT and MAF sensors electrical connectors.
4. Disconnect air intake duct fuel regulator purge line.
5. Remove air intake duct and air cleaner.
6. Remove fuel rail covers.
7. Disconnect fuel rail lines. Cap and plug open fittings.
8. Remove vacuum and PCV hoses.
9. Remove throttle body coolant outlet hose.
10. Disconnect fuel injector and knock sensor electrical connectors.
11. Disconnect remaining intake manifold electrical connectors.
12. Remove intake manifold bolts and fuel rail stop bracket.
13. Remove lefthand and righthand valve covers' PCV valve pipe.

14. Remove throttle body coolant air bleed hose.
15. Remove throttle body heater outlet hose.
16. Remove intake manifold and gaskets.
17. Remove manifold to cylinder head gaskets from intake manifold.
18. Reverse procedure to install, noting the following:
    a. Install new intake manifold to cylinder head gaskets.
    b. Apply threadlocker P/N 12345383, or equivalent, to intake manifold bolt threads.
    c. **Torque** intake manifold bolts to 44 inch lbs., in sequence, **Fig. 6.**
    d. Final **torque** bolts to 89 inch lbs., in sequence.
    e. Lubricate MAP sensor grommet with suitable clean engine oil before installing.
    f. Install new fuel injector O-rings lubricated with suitable clean engine oil.

EXHAUST MANIFOLD
REPLACE
Lefthand Side

1. Raise and support vehicle.
2. Remove lefthand intermediate exhaust pipe flange nuts from exhaust manifold studs.
3. Disconnect HO2S electrical connector and remove HO2S.
4. Lower vehicle and remove lefthand fuel rail cover.
5. Remove accessory drive belt as outlined in "Serpentine Drive Belt."
6. Remove alternator as outlined in "Alternator, Replace" in "Electrical" section.
7. Remove Secondary Air Injection (SAI) hoses.
8. Remove SAI pipe, bolts and gasket, then position aside.
9. Remove spark plug wires.
10. Remove spark plugs.
11. Remove No. 5 coil bolts and position aside.
12. Remove exhaust manifold and mounting bolts.
13. Reverse procedure to install, noting the following:
    a. Install new exhaust manifold gasket.

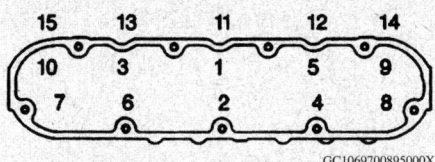

Fig. 7 Cylinder head bolt tightening sequence

  b. Apply threadlocker P/N 12345493, or equivalent, to exhaust manifold bolt threads.

  c. **Torque** exhaust manifold bolts to 11 ft. lbs., beginning with center two bolts, then alternate from side to side and work toward outside bolts.

  d. Final **Torque** to 18 ft. lbs., in sequence.

  e. Bend over exposed edge of exhaust manifold gasket at rear of lefthand cylinder head using suitable flat punch.

  f. Install AIR pipe and gasket and **torque** to 15 ft. lbs.

Righthand Side

1. Raise and support vehicle.
2. Remove intermediate exhaust pipe nuts from exhaust manifold studs.
3. Remove HO2S.
4. Lower vehicle.
5. Remove righthand exhaust manifold AIR pipe, bolts and gasket.
6. Remove spark plug wires from spark plugs.
7. Remove engine oil dipstick.
8. Remove mounting bolt and dipstick tube.
9. Remove exhaust manifold and mounting bolts.
10. Reverse procedure to install, noting the following:
    a. Install new exhaust manifold gasket.
    b. Apply threadlocker P/N 12345493, or equivalent, to exhaust manifold bolt threads.
    c. **Torque** exhaust manifold bolts to 11 ft. lbs., beginning with center two bolts, then alternate from side to side and work toward outside bolts.
    d. Final **torque** to 18 ft. lbs., in sequence.
    e. Bend over exposed edge of exhaust manifold gasket at front of righthand cylinder head using suitable flat punch.
    f. Install AIR pipe and gasket and **torque** to 15 ft. lbs.

CYLINDER HEAD
REPLACE

This procedure has been revised by a Technical Service Bulletin.

Lefthand Side
REMOVAL

1. Remove valve cover, rocker arms, pedestal and pushrods.

2. Remove lefthand exhaust manifold as outlined in "Exhaust Manifold, Replace."
3. Remove intake manifold as outlined in "Intake Manifold, Replace."
4. Remove vapor vent pipe.
5. Remove power steering pump pulley using pulley puller tool No. J 25034-B, or equivalent.
6. Remove power steering pump mounting bolts.
7. Remove power steering reservoir bracket bolts, then position pump and reservoir aside.
8. Remove mounting bolts and lower accessory mounting bracket.
9. Remove cylinder head rear ground wire bolt.
10. Remove spark plugs.
11. Remove and discard cylinder head bolts.
12. Remove cylinder head.

INSTALLATION

1. Clean cylinder head bolt holes using compressed air.
2. Inspect cylinder head locating pins for proper installation.
3. Install new lefthand cylinder head gasket onto locating pins. When properly installed, tab on lefthand cylinder head gasket will be located lefthand side of center or closer to front of engine.
4. Ensure THIS SIDE UP and engine displacement are visible.
5. Install cylinder head onto locating pins and gasket.
6. Install M11 cylinder head bolts.
7. Apply threadlocker P/N 12345382, or equivalent, to threads of M8 cylinder head bolts.
8. Install M8 cylinder head bolts.
9. Tighten cylinder head bolts as follows:
    a. **Torque** M11 cylinder head bolts 1–10 to 22 ft. lbs., in sequence, **Fig. 7.**
    b. Tighten M11 cylinder head bolts 1–10 an additional 90° in sequence.
    c. Final tighten M11 cylinder head bolts 1–8 an additional 90° in sequence.
    d. Final tighten M11 medium length cylinder head bolts 9 and 10 at front and rear of each head an additional 50° in sequence.
    e. **Torque** M8 inner cylinder head bolts 11–15 to 22 ft. lbs., beginning with center bolt 11, then alternating side to side while working outward.
10. Install spark plugs into cylinder head.
11. Install ground wire bolt into rear of cylinder head.
12. Install accessory mounting bracket.
13. Install lower accessory mounting bracket bolts.
14. Install power steering reservoir bracket bolts.
15. Install power steering pump mounting bolts.
16. Install power steering pump pulley.
17. Install vapor vent pipe.
18. Install intake manifold as outlined in "Intake Manifold, Replace."
19. Install lefthand exhaust manifold to cylinder head as outlined in "Exhaust

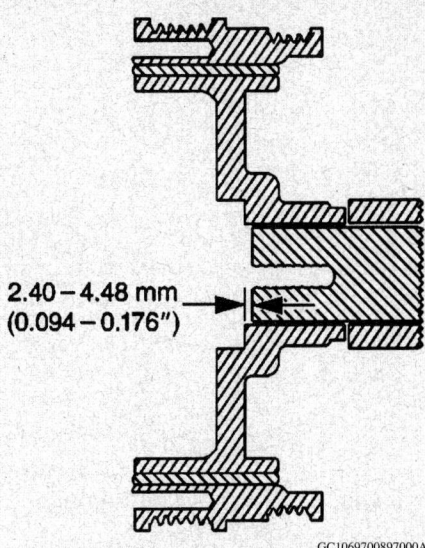

2.40 – 4.48 mm (0.094 – 0.176")

Fig. 8 Damper installed measurement

Manifold, Replace."
20. Install valve rocker arms, pedestal and pushrods.

Righthand Side
REMOVAL

1. Remove valve rocker arms, pedestal and pushrods.
2. Remove righthand exhaust manifold as outlined in "Exhaust Manifold, Replace."
3. Remove intake manifold as outlined in "Intake Manifold, Replace."
4. Remove vapor vent pipe.
5. Remove spark plugs.
6. Remove and discard cylinder head bolts.
7. Remove cylinder head.

INSTALLATION

1. Clean cylinder head bolt holes using compressed air.
2. Inspect cylinder head locating pins for proper installation.
3. Install new righthand cylinder head gasket onto locating pins. When properly installed, tab on righthand cylinder head gasket will be located lefthand side of center or closer to front of engine.
4. Ensure THIS SIDE UP and engine displacement are visible.
5. Install cylinder head onto locating pins and gasket.
6. Install M11 cylinder head bolts.
7. Apply threadlocker P/N 12345382, or equivalent, to threads of M8 cylinder head bolts.
8. Install M8 cylinder head bolts.
9. Tighten cylinder head bolts as follows:
    a. **Torque** M11 cylinder head bolts 1–10 to 22 ft. lbs., in sequence, **Fig. 7.**
    b. Tighten M11 cylinder head bolts 1–10 an additional 90° in sequence.
    c. Final tighten M11 cylinder head

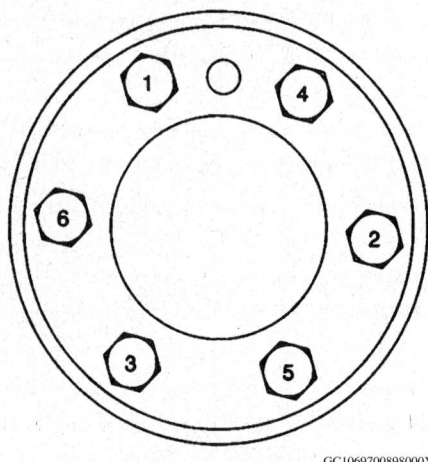

Fig. 9 Flywheel tightening sequence

bolts 1–8 an additional 90° in sequence.

d. Final tighten M11 medium length cylinder head bolts 9 and 10 at front and rear of each head an additional 50° in sequence.

e. **Torque** M8 inner cylinder head bolts 11–15 to 22 ft. lbs., beginning with center bolt 11, then alternating side to side while working outward.

10. Install spark plugs into cylinder head.
11. Install vapor vent pipe.
12. Install intake manifold as outlined in "Intake Manifold, Replace."
13. Install righthand exhaust manifold to cylinder head as outlined in "Exhaust Manifold, Replace."
14. Install valve rocker arms, pedestal and pushrods.

VALVE COVER
REPLACE
Lefthand Side

1. Remove lefthand fuel rail cover.
2. Disconnect fuel rail lines.
3. Disconnect electrical connectors at alternator and coolant temperature sensors.
4. Disconnect check valve secondary AIR hose.
5. Remove lefthand valve cover PCV valve pipe.
6. Disconnect ignition coils' spark plug wires.
7. Disconnect ignition coil main harness electrical connector.
8. Disconnect EVAP purge solenoid valve hoses.
9. Remove intake manifold EVAP purge solenoid.
10. Remove crankcase vent vacuum tube.
11. Remove valve rocker arm cover bolts and cover.
12. Remove and discard lefthand cover crankcase vent valve grommet.
13. Remove ignition coil wire harness.
14. Remove ignition coils and bolts.
15. Remove cover gasket and bolt grommets.

16. Discard gasket. Bolt grommets may be used again if not damaged.
17. Reverse procedure to install, noting the following:
    a. Install new cover gasket and PCV valve grommet.
    b. **Torque** valve cover mounting bolts to 106 inch lbs.
    c. **Torque** ignition coil mounting bolts to 106 inch lbs.

Righthand Side

1. Remove righthand fuel rail cover.
2. Remove exhaust manifold secondary AIR hose.
3. Disconnect check valve AIR hose.
4. Remove valve cover breather pipes PCV hoses.
5. Remove ignition coils' spark plug wires.
6. Disconnect ignition coil main harness electrical connector.
7. Remove ignition coil, bracket and bolts.
8. Remove valve rocker arm cover bolts and cover.
9. Remove oil fill cap and tube, if required. Discard tube.
10. Remove gasket and bolt grommets.
11. Discard gasket. Bolt grommets may be used again if not damaged.
12. Remove ignition coil bolts, wire harness and coils.
13. Reverse procedure to install, noting the following:
    a. Install new cover gasket.
    b. Install new oil fill tube, as required.
    c. **Torque** valve cover mounting bolts to 106 inch lbs.
    d. **Torque** ignition coil mounting bolts to 106 inch lbs.

VALVE ARRANGEMENT
Front To Rear
All ....I-E-I-E-I-E-I-E

VALVE CLEARANCE SPECIFICATIONS

This engine is equipped with hydraulic valve lash adjusters. No adjustment is required.

VALVE ADJUSTMENT

This engine is equipped with hydraulic valve lash adjusters. No adjustment is required.

ROCKER ARMS
Removal

It is required to keep components in original order if they will be installed again.
1. Remove valve rocker arm bolts and arms.
2. Remove valve rocker arm pedestals.

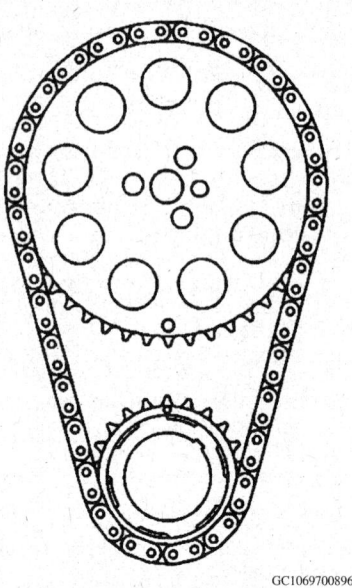

Fig. 10 Camshaft & crankshaft sprocket alignment

Installation

When using valve train components over again, always install them into original location and position. Valve lash is net build. No valve adjustment is required.

1. Lubricate valve rocker arms with suitable clean engine oil.
2. Lubricate flange of valve rocker arm bolts with suitable clean engine oil.
3. Lubricate flange or washer surface of bolt that will contact valve rocker arm.
4. Install valve rocker arm pedestals.
5. Install rocker arms and bolts. Ensure pushrods seat properly to valve lifter sockets and in ends of rocker arms.
6. Turn crankshaft until number one piston is at top dead center of compression stroke. Cylinders 1, 3, 5 and 7 are lefthand in bank. Cylinders 2, 4, 6 and 8 are in righthand bank. In this position sprocket marks on crankshaft and camshaft will be aligned.
7. With engine in number one firing position, proceed as follows:
    a. **Torque** exhaust valve rocker arm bolts 1, 2, 7 and 8 to 22 ft. lbs.
    b. **Torque** intake valve rocker arm bolts 1, 3, 4 and 5 to 22 ft. lbs.
8. Rotate crankshaft 360° and proceed as follows:
    a. **Torque** exhaust valve rocker arm bolts 3, 4, 5 and 6 to 22 ft. lbs.
    b. **Torque** intake valve rocker arm bolts 2, 6, 7 and 8 to 22 ft. lbs.

PUSH RODS
Removal

It is required to keep components in original order if they will be installed again.
1. Remove valve rocker arm bolts, arms and pedestals as outlined in "Rocker Arms."
2. Remove pushrods.

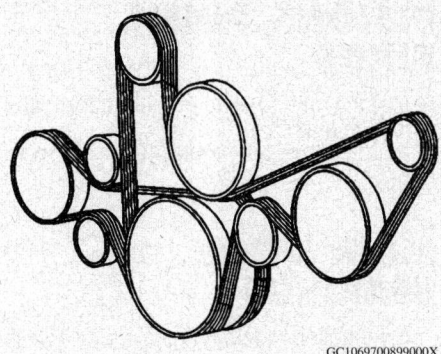

Fig. 11 Serpentine drive belt routing

Installation

When using valve train components over again, always install them into original location and position. Valve lash is net build. No valve adjustment is required.

1. Lubricate valve rocker arms and pushrods with suitable clean engine oil.
2. Lubricate flange of valve rocker arm bolts with suitable clean engine oil.
3. Lubricate flange or washer surface of bolt that will contact valve rocker arm.
4. Install valve rocker arm pedestal.
5. Install rocker arms and bolts.
6. Install pushrods. Ensure pushrods seat properly to valve lifter sockets and in ends of rocker arms.
7. Turn crankshaft until number one piston is at top dead center of compression stroke. Cylinders 1, 3, 5 and 7 are lefthand in bank. Cylinders 2, 4, 6 and 8 are in righthand bank. In this position sprocket marks on crankshaft and camshaft will be aligned.
8. With engine in number one firing position, proceed as follows:
   a. **Torque** exhaust valve rocker arm bolts 1, 2, 7 and 8 to 22 ft. lbs.
   b. **Torque** intake valve rocker arm bolts 1, 3, 4 and 5 to 22 ft. lbs.
9. Rotate crankshaft 360° and proceed as follows:
   a. **Torque** exhaust valve rocker arm bolts 3, 4, 5 and 6 to 22 ft. lbs.
   b. **Torque** intake valve rocker arm bolts 2, 6, 7 and 8 to 22 ft. lbs.

HYDRAULIC LIFTERS
REPLACE

1. Remove cylinder head as outlined in "Cylinder Head, Replace."
2. Remove valve lifter guide bolts.
3. Remove valve lifters and guide. If lifters stick in bores use valve lifter removal tool No. J 3049-A, or equivalent, to remove them.
4. Remove guide valve lifters.
5. Organize or mark components so that they can be installed in original positions.
6. Reverse procedure to install, noting the following:
   a. Lubricate valve lifters and bores with suitable clean engine oil.
   b. Align lifters' and bores' flat sides.

CRANKSHAFT DAMPER
REPLACE

1. Release accessory drive belt tensioner and remove drive belt as outlined in "Serpentine Drive Belt."
2. Remove electronic brake control module from its bracket and position aside. Cap and plug open lines.
3. Remove power steering gear as outlined in "Power Steering Gear, Replace" in "Front Suspension & Steering."
4. Remove starter motor as outlined in "Starter, Replace" in "Electrical" section.
5. Remove power steering cooler mounting bolts and cooler from front crossmember, then position aside.
6. Release tensioner and remove air conditioning drive belt.
7. Install flywheel holding tool No. J 42386, or equivalent, and flywheel mounting bolts. **Torque** mounting bolts to 37 ft. lbs.
8. Remove crankshaft damper bolt.
9. Mark crankshaft damper and end of crankshaft. Record damper installed position on crankshaft for installation. Also record location of any weights, which must return to original positions.
10. Remove crankshaft damper using crankshaft end protector and damper removal tool Nos. J 41816 and J 41816-2, or equivalents.
11. Reverse procedure to install, noting the following:
    a. Install damper using crankshaft balancer and sprocket installer tool No. J 41665, or equivalent.
    b. **Torque** used crankshaft damper bolt to 240 ft. lbs.
    c. Remove bolt and measure for properly installed damper, **Fig. 8.**
    d. **Torque** new crankshaft damper bolt to 37 ft. lbs.
    e. Tighten bolt an additional 140°.

FRONT COVER
REPLACE
Removal

1. Drain coolant into suitable container.
2. Disconnect air intake duct fuel regulator purge line.
3. Remove air intake duct and air cleaner.
4. Remove crankshaft damper as outlined in "Crankshaft Damper, Replace."
5. Remove water pump radiator and heater hoses.
6. Remove water pump mounting bolts, pump and gaskets.
7. Remove front cover bolts.
8. Remove front cover and gasket. **Avoid sliding front cover or gasket across oil pan gasket.**
9. Remove and discard crankshaft oil seal.

Installation

1. Apply .20 inch bead of GM silicone

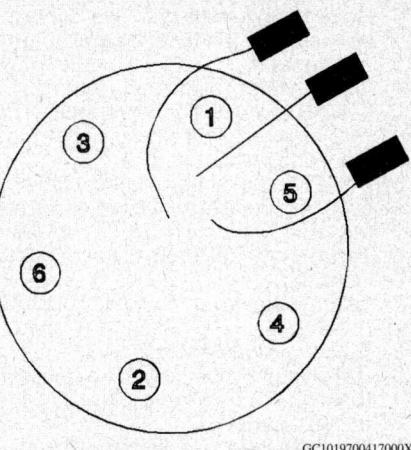

Fig. 12 Fuel sender bolt tightening sequence

gasket P/N 12378190, or equivalent, to corner where oil pan meets engine block.
2. Install new gasket, front cover and mounting bolts to engine block. Tighten bolts hand tight.
3. Align cover alignment tool No. J 41476, or equivalent, on front of crankshaft.
4. Install crankshaft damper bolt and hand tighten.
5. Hand tighten oil pan to cover bolts so cover properly positions itself at pan rail.
6. **Torque** front cover bolts to 18 ft. lbs.
7. Remove alignment tool.
8. Install crankshaft oil seal using oil seal installer tool No. J 41478, or equivalent. **Do not lubricate oil seal sealing surface.**
9. Install water pump, gaskets and mounting bolts.
10. Install radiator and heater hoses to water pump.
11. Fill cooling system.
12. Install crankshaft damper as outlined in "Crankshaft Damper, Replace."
13. Install air intake duct and air cleaner.
14. Connect fuel regulator purge line to air intake duct.

REAR COVER
REPLACE
Removal

1. Mark crankshaft end and flywheel for installation, then remove flywheel.
2. Remove engine rear cover mounting bolts and cover. Discard gasket.
3. Remove and discard crankshaft rear cover oil seal.

Installation

1. Apply .20 inch bead of GM silicone gasket P/N 12378190, or equivalent, to corner were oil pan meets engine block.
2. Install rear cover, gasket and bolts onto engine, hand tighten bolts.

3. Rotate crankshaft until two opposing flywheel bolt holes are parallel to oil pan surface.
4. Install cover alignment tool No. J 41476, or equivalent, and bolts onto rear of crankshaft. Hand tighten tool mounting bolts.
5. Hand tighten oil pan to cover bolts so cover properly positions itself at pan rail.
6. **Torque** oil pan to cover bolts to 106 inch lbs.
7. **Torque** rear cover mounting bolts to 18 ft. lbs.
8. Remove alignment tool.
9. Install crankshaft rear oil seal using rear oil seal installer tool No. J 41479, or equivalent.
10. Install flywheel as follows:
    a. Align alignment mark made during removal and install mounting bolts hand tight.
    b. **Torque** flywheel mounting bolts to 15 ft. lbs., in sequence, **Fig. 9.**
    c. **Torque** flywheel mounting bolts to 37 ft. lbs., in sequence.
    d. **Torque** flywheel mounting bolts to 74 ft. lbs., in sequence.

TIMING CHAIN
REPLACE
Removal

1. Remove oil pump as outlined in "Oil Pump, Replace."
2. Rotate crankshaft until crankshaft and camshaft sprocket timing marks are aligned.
3. Remove camshaft sprocket bolts.
4. Remove camshaft sprocket and timing chain.
5. Remove crankshaft sprocket using puller tool Nos. J 8433, J 21427-01, J 41816-2 and J 41558, or equivalents.
6. Remove crankshaft sprocket key, if required.

Installation

1. Install key into crankshaft keyway.
2. Install crankshaft sprocket onto front of crankshaft, aligning key with keyway.
3. Install crankshaft sprocket using sprocket installation tool No. J 41665, or equivalent. Ensure sprocket fully seats against crankshaft flange.
4. Rotate crankshaft sprocket until alignment mark is in 12 o'clock position.
5. Install camshaft sprocket and timing chain.
6. Properly locate camshaft sprocket locating pin with camshaft sprocket alignment hole.
7. Sprocket teeth and timing chain must mesh properly.
8. Camshaft and crankshaft sprocket alignment marks must be aligned properly, **Fig. 10.** Locate camshaft sprocket alignment mark in 6 o'clock position.
9. Install camshaft sprocket bolts.
10. Install oil pump as outlined in "Oil Pump, Replace."

CAMSHAFT
REPLACE

1. Remove valve lifters as outlined in "Hydraulic Lifters, Replace."
2. Remove radiator as outlined in "Radiator, Replace."
3. Remove timing chain and sprockets as outlined in "Timing Chain, Replace."
4. Remove camshaft sensor bolt and sensor.
5. Remove camshaft retainer plate bolts and retainer.
6. Install three M8 1.25 × 3.937 inches bolts in camshaft front bolt holes.
7. Carefully rotate and pull camshaft out of engine block using bolts as handle.
8. Remove camshaft bolts.
9. Reverse procedure to install, noting the following:
   a. Ensure camshaft journals are lubricated with suitable clean engine oil before installation.
   b. Install camshaft retainer plate with sealing gasket facing engine block.
   c. Lubricate camshaft sensor O-ring with suitable clean engine oil.

PISTON & ROD ASSEMBLY

1. Insert piston onto piston pin press tool No. J 24086-C, or equivalent. Record location of alignment mark on top of piston.
2. Apply mild heat to pin end of connecting rod using torch. This will ease piston and pin assembly.
3. Position connecting rod so bolt flange flat area faces engine block front.
4. Press pin into connecting rod using piston pin press tool.
5. Measure piston, pin and connecting rod for proper assembly as follows:
   a. Place piston and connecting rod with flat top of piston on flat surface.
   b. Slide connecting rod and pin to one side and hold firmly against inside of piston.
   c. Measure pin for proper installation. Properly installed piston pin should protrude .05 inch from piston side.
6. Install piston ring assembly onto piston as follows:
   a. Install oil control ring spacer in groove. Ends of oil control ring spacer should not overlap.
   b. Install upper and lower control rings. Oil control rings do not have dimple or orientation mark and may be installed in either direction.
   c. Stagger three oil control ring end gaps minimum of 90°.
   d. Install upper and lower compression rings. Upper compression ring does not have dimple or orientation mark and may be installed in either direction.
   e. Stagger compression ring end gaps minimum of 1 inch.

PISTONS, PINS & RINGS

Pistons are available in standard and .010 inch oversize.
Piston rings are available in standard and .010 inch oversize.

MAIN & ROD BEARINGS

Connecting rod bearings are available in standard size only.
Main bearings are available in standard size only.

CRANKSHAFT SEAL
REPLACE

Refer to "Front Cover, Replace" for crankshaft front seal replacement.

CRANKSHAFT REAR OIL SEAL
REPLACE

Refer to "Rear Cover, Replace" for crankshaft rear seal replacement.

OIL PAN
REPLACE

1. Drain engine oil into suitable container and remove oil filter.
2. Remove engine cradle as outlined in "Engine Mount, Replace."
3. **On models equipped with automatic transmission,** remove fluid cooler line front and rear mounting clamp bolts.
4. **On all models,** remove engine flywheel housing to oil pan bolts.
5. Remove engine flywheel housing cover bolts.
6. Remove lefthand and righthand closeout cover bolts and covers.
7. Disconnect electrical connector and remove engine oil level sensor.
8. Disconnect engine oil temperature sensor electrical connector.
9. Remove oil pan mounting bolts and oil pan.
10. Remove and discard oil pan gasket and pan rivets.
11. Remove oil pan baffle bolt and baffle.
12. Reverse procedure to install, noting the following:
    a. Ensure block and oil pan rears are flush or even. **Rear of pan must never protrude beyond block and bellhousing plane.**
    b. Apply .20 inch wide by .80 inch long beads of GM silicone gasket sealer P/N 12378190, or equivalent, to front and rear cover gasket surfaces where covers attach to oil pan mating surface.
    c. Install mounting bolts through oil pan and gasket before installation.

OIL PUMP
REPLACE

1. Remove engine front cover as outlined in "Front Cover, Replace."
2. Remove oil pan as outlined in "Oil Pan, Replace."
3. Remove oil pump screen bolt and nuts.
4. Remove oil pump screen.
5. Remove and discard O-ring seal.
6. Remove remaining crankshaft oil deflector nuts.
7. Remove crankshaft oil deflector.
8. Remove oil pump bolts.
9. Reverse procedure to install, noting the following:
   a. Ensure pump and oil gallery passages are clean and free of obstructions.
   b. Align crankshaft sprocket's and oil pump's splined surfaces.
   c. Install oil pump onto crankshaft sprocket until pump housing contacts engine block face.

SERPENTINE DRIVE BELT

Belt Routing

Refer to **Fig. 11,** for serpentine drive belt routing.

Belt Replacement

1. Reduce tension by rotating tensioner away from belts using suitable hex-head socket.
2. Remove accessory drive belts.
3. Clean accessory drive belt surfaces.
4. Install accessory drive belts. Record running direction or arrow markings.
5. Tighten accessory drive belt tensioners to increase tension on accessory drive belts.
6. Ensure accessory drive belts are aligned in proper pulley grooves.

COOLING SYSTEM BLEED

1. Park vehicle on level surface.
2. Fill cooling system.
3. Start engine and let idle for one minute.
4. Install radiator surge tank cap.
5. Cycle RPM from idle to 3000 RPM in 30 second intervals until engine coolant reaches 210°F.
6. Shut off engine and carefully remove radiator surge tank cap.
7. Start engine and idle for one minute.
8. Fill surge tank to ½ inch above COLD FULL mark.
9. Install radiator surge tank cap and cycle RPM as stated.
10. Shut off engine and remove radiator surge tank cap.
11. Fill surge tank to ½ inch above cold full line.

12. Rinse any excess coolant piston from engine and compartment.

THERMOSTAT
REPLACE

1. Drain cooling system into suitable container.
2. Remove radiator outlet hose clamp at thermostat housing using clamp pliers tool No. J 38185, or equivalent.
3. Disconnect thermostat housing radiator outlet hose.
4. Record position of thermostat before removing.
5. Remove mounting bolts and thermostat housing.
6. Remove and discard gasket.
7. Reverse procedure to install.

WATER PUMP
REPLACE

1. Drain cooling system into suitable container.
2. Disconnect IAT and MAF sensor electrical connectors.
3. Remove air intake duct fuel regulator purge line.
4. Remove air intake duct cleaner.
5. Remove drive belts as outlined in "Serpentine Drive Belt."
6. Remove radiator inlet and outlet hose clamps, then the water pump hoses using clamp pliers tool No. J 38185, or equivalent.
7. Remove heater hose clamps and water pump hoses.
8. Remove water pump pulley bolts and pulley.
9. Remove mounting bolts and water pump.
10. Reverse procedure to install, noting the following:
    a. **Torque** water pump mounting bolts to 11 ft. lbs., then to 22 ft. lbs.
    b. **Torque** water pump pulley bolts to 90 inch lbs., then to 18 ft. lbs.

RADIATOR
REPLACE

1. Disconnect Intake Air Temperature (IAT) and Mass Air Flow (MAF) sensor connectors.
2. Remove air intake duct/cleaner.
3. Remove mounting bolts and radiator upper support. Record upper radiator support position in relation to fan shroud for installation.
4. Raise and support vehicle, then drain coolant into suitable container.
5. Remove fan shroud electrical connectors and harness.
6. Remove fan shroud.
7. Remove radiator hoses.
8. **On models equipped with automatic transmission,** remove radiator cooler lines.
9. **On all models,** remove condenser and position forward. **Disconnecting condenser air conditioning lines is not required.**
10. Lower and remove radiator.
11. Reverse procedure to install. Tighten mounting bolts.

FUEL PUMP
REPLACE

1. Raise and support vehicle.
2. Remove lefthand rear wheel and tire.
3. Clean fuel line connections before disconnecting.
4. Drain lefthand fuel tank into suitable container, then mark and disconnect fuel lines.
5. Cap fuel lines.
6. Disconnect fuel sender electrical connector.
7. Remove fuel tank strap and shield.
8. Support fuel tank.
9. Remove mounting bolts and fuel sender.
10. Record positioning of fuel pump strainer before discarding.
11. Reverse procedure to install, noting the following:
    a. Install new fuel pump strainer, ensuring it is properly positioned as noted during removal.
    b. Align sender cover and tank marks.
    c. Look through tank opening to ensure long side of strainer is visible. It should be approximately one inch from tank opening. Rotate sender counterclockwise approximately 90°, as required.
    d. Hand tighten new breakaway head sender mounting bolts, then tighten using suitable wrench until upper heads break off in sequence, **Fig. 12.**

FUEL FILTER
REPLACE

1. Raise and support vehicle.
2. Clean fuel filter connections before disconnecting.
3. **On models equipped with automatic transmission,** proceed as follows:
   a. Disconnect stabilizer bar from rear cradle.
   b. Remove exhaust intermediate pipe to muffler bolts.
   c. Lower lefthand muffler.
4. **On all models,** remove fuel filter bracket nut from mounting stud.
5. Disconnect fuel filter quick-connect fittings and cap fuel lines.
6. Disconnect filter mounting stud ground strap.
7. Remove fuel filter and bracket, then filter from bracket.
8. Reverse procedure to install. Ensure mounting bracket anti-rotation tab is securely seated into tunnel reinforcement hole.

TIGHTENING SPECIFICATIONS

Year	Component	Torque/Ft. Lbs.
2001–04	Air Conditioning Compressor Bracket	37
	Air Conditioning Idler Pulley	37
	Air Conditioning Tensioner	18
	AIR Pipe To Exhaust Manifold	15
	AIR Righthand Side Pipe Bracket To Cylinder Head	15
	Alternator & Power Steering Pump Bracket	37
	Alternator Rear Bracket	37
	Camshaft Retainer	18
	Camshaft Sensor	18
	Camshaft Sprocket	26
	Connecting Rod Bolts	15⑩
	Coolant Temperature Gauge Sensor	15
	Crankshaft Bearing Cap Bolts	15③
	Crankshaft Bearing Cap Side Bolts	18
	Crankshaft Bearing Cap Studs	④
	Crankshaft Damper	②
	Crankshaft Oil Deflector	18
	Crankshaft Position Sensor	18
	Cylinder Head Bolts	⑤
	Cylinder Head Coolant Plug	15
	Cylinder Head Core Hole Plug	15
	Drive Belt Idler Pulley	37
	Drive Belt Tensioner	37
	Engine Block Coolant Drain Plugs	44
	Engine Block Heater	30
	Engine Block Oil Gallery Plugs	44
	Engine Flywheel Hub Collar Bolt (Automatic Transmission)	96
	Engine Front Cover	18
	Engine Mount Bracket To Engine Block	37
	Engine Rear Cover	18
	Engine Service Lift Bracket (M8 Bolts)	18
	Engine Service Lift Bracket (M10 Bolts)	37
	Engine Valley Cover	18
	Exhaust Manifold	⑦
	Flywheel	⑥
	Fuel Injection Fuel Rail	90①
	Ignition Coil	106①
	Ignition Coil Wire Harness Connector	106①

Continued

TIGHTENING SPECIFICATIONS—Continued

Year	Component	Torque/Ft. Lbs.
2001–04	Intake Manifold Bolts	⑧
	Knock Sensors	15
	Oil Dipstick Tube	12
	Oil Filter	22
	Oil Filter Fitting	40
	Oil Level Sensor	115①
	Oil Pan Baffle	106①
	Oil Pan Cover	106①
	Oil Pan Drain Plug	18
	Oil Pan M8 Bolts (Oil Pan To Engine Block & Oil Pan To Front Cover)	18
	Oil Pan M6 Bolts (Oil Pan To Rear Cover)	106①
	Oil Pressure Sensor	15
	Oil Pump Cover	106①
	Oil Pump Relief Valve Plug	106①
	Oil Pump Screen	18
	Oil Pump Screen To Oil Pump	106①
	Oil Pump To Engine Block	18
	Oil Temperature Sensor	15
	Oil Transfer Cover Bolts	106①
	Oxygen Sensor	30
	Power Steering Pump	18
	Power Steering Pump & Alternator Bracket	37
	Power Steering Reservoir Bracket	37
	Spark Plugs	⑪
	Starter Motor	37
	Throttle Body	106①
	Valve Lifter Guide	106①
	Valve Rocker Arm	22
	Valve Rocker Arm Cover	106①
	Vapor Vent Pipe	106①
	Water Inlet Housing	11
	Water Pump	⑨
	Water Pump Cover	11
	Water Pump Pulley	⑨

① — Inch lbs.

② — Refer to "Crankshaft Damper, Replace."

③ — Then tighten an additional 80°.

④ — Then tighten an additional 53°.

⑤ — Refer to "Cylinder Head, Replace."

⑥ — Refer to "Rear Cover, Replace."

⑦ — Refer to "Exhaust Manifold, Replace."

⑧ — Refer to "Intake Manifold, Replace."

⑨ — Refer to "Water Pump, Replace."

⑩ — First design (single dimple/mark on bolt head), then tighten an additional 60°; Second design (two dimples/marks on bolt head), then tighten an additional 75°.

⑪ — New cylinder head, 15 ft. lbs.; Used cylinder head, 11 ft. lbs.

6.0L Engine

NOTE: On Air Bag Equipped Models, Refer To "Air Bag System Precautions" Located In The Front Of This Manual For System Disarming & Arming Procedures.

NOTE: Refer To "Computer Relearn Procedures" Located In The Front Of This Manual When Battery Power To The Computer Has Been Interrupted.

NOTE: Prior To Performing Any Service Operations Listed In This Section, Consult The "Technical Service Bulletins" Section For Related Information.

INDEX

PRECAUTIONS

Fuel System Pressure Relief

1. Disconnect and isolate battery ground cable.
2. Remove fuel tank filler cap to release fuel tank pressure.
3. Remove lefthand fuel rail cover.
4. Prior to disconnecting fuel line, position shop towel over fitting.
5. Connect pressure gauge tool No. J 34730-1A, or equivalent, to pressure tap on fuel rail.
6. Position bleed hose into suitable container.
7. Slowly relieve fuel system pressure.

Battery Ground Cable

Prior to service, disconnect battery ground cable and isolate as required.

COMPRESSION PRESSURE

When measuring compression, lowest cylinder must be within 70% of the highest cylinder with a minimum pressure of 100 psi. Compression test results will fall into one of the following categories:

1. Normally, compression builds up quickly and evenly to specifications on each cylinder.
2. If piston rings are faulty, compression will be low on first stroke, then build up on following strokes but will not reach specifications. Improvement is considerable with addition of approximately three squirts oil.
3. If valves are faulty, compression will be low on first stroke and will not tend to build up on following strokes. It will not improve much with addition of oil.
4. Ensure battery is fully charged.
5. Bring engine to operating temperature.
6. Disconnect electrical connector at crankshaft ignition timing sensor.
7. Disable fuel injection system.
8. Remove spark plugs.
9. Ensure throttle is wide open.
10. Install compression gauge tool No. J 38722, or equivalent.
11. Crank engine through four complete compression strokes, then record results for each cylinder.

ENGINE MOUNT
REPLACE

1. Remove front suspension crossmember.
2. Remove engine mount to bracket nut, then the mount, **Fig. 1.**
3. Remove engine mount heat shield from mount.
4. Reverse procedure to install.

ENGINE
REPLACE

1. Recover air conditioning refrigerant as

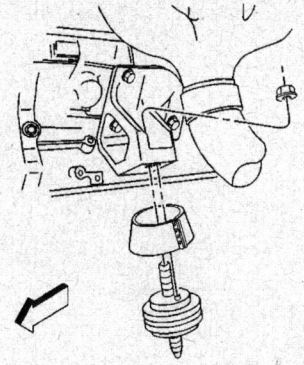

1. Remove the front suspension crossmember.
2. Remove the engine mount-to-engine mount bracket nut.
3. Remove the engine mount.
4. Remove the engine mount heat shield from the engine mount, if necessary.

ARM0400000000082

Fig. 1 Engine mount removal

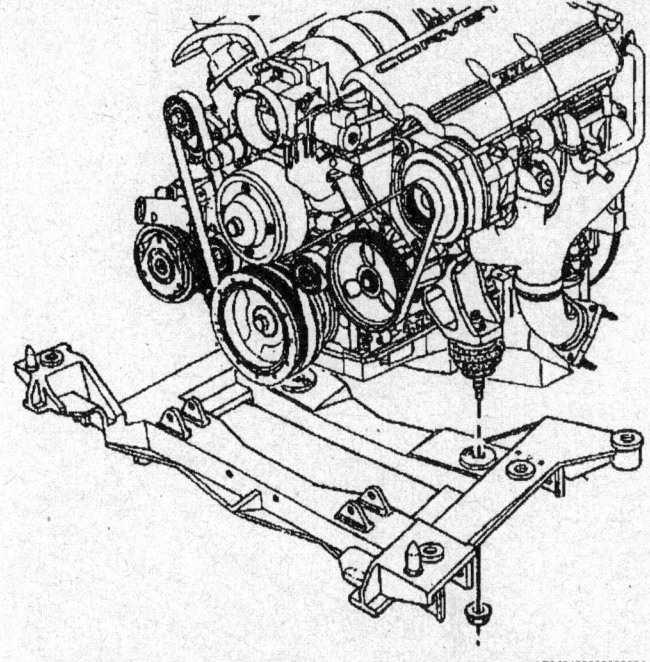

ARM0400000000084

Fig. 2 Engine mount nuts removal

outlined in "Air Conditioning" chapter.
2. Drain engine coolant into a suitable container.
3. Remove radiator as outlined under "Radiator, Replace."
4. Remove BPMV and bracket, then position brake pipes aside, cap and plug lines.
5. Remove serpentine belt as outlined under "Serpentine Drive Belt."
6. Remove righthand side fuel injection rail cover, then relieve fuel system pressure as outlined under "Fuel System Pressure Relief."
7. Disconnect evaporative emission canister purge hose at fuel line.
8. Remove fuel feed hose, then the radiator hoses from water pump.
9. Remove heater hoses from water pump, then disconnect the following connectors:
   a. Fuel injectors.
   b. Ignition coil main harness connectors.
   c. EVAP solenoid and a/c compressor.
   d. Electric throttle motor and throttle position sensor.
   e. Engine coolant temperature sensor.
10. Remove alternator as outlined under "Alternator, Replace."
11. Remove power brake booster vacuum hose, then the intermediate steering shaft to steering gear bolt.
12. Remove intermediate steering shaft from steering gear, then position it to lefthand side frame rail.
13. Raise and support vehicle, then remove front tires and wheels.
14. Install adjustable jack stands under front and rear of intermediate pipe.
15. Loosen exhaust muffler band clamps, then separate lefthand side and righthand side mufflers from intermediate pipe.
16. Remove exhaust pipe hanger lower bolts, then the exhaust manifold nuts and seal.
17. Lower jack stands, then remove intermediate pipe.
18. Remove oxygen sensors from catalytic convertor, then the mounting nuts and gasket from exhaust manifold.
19. Remove catalytic convertor from vehicle
20. Remove driveline tunnel close-out panel bolts, then the close-out panel.
21. Remove starter as outlined under "Starter, Replace."
22. Disconnect electrical connectors from crankshaft position sensor, oil level sensor and righthand side heated oxygen sensor.
23. Remove A/C compressor and condenser hose bolt at compressor, then separate hoses from A/C compressor.
24. Disconnect electrical connectors from oil temperature sensor and lefthand side heated oxygen sensor.
25. Remove ground strap bolt, then Remove ground straps from engine block.
26. Disconnect wheel speed sensor electrical connectors.
27. **On models equipped with real time damping system,** disconnect electrical connectors from shock absorber damper and position sensor pigtail.
28. **On all models,** unclip transmission wire harness, then disconnect electronic variable orifice control connector clips from crossmember.
29. Remove transmission harness clip bolts from engine block, then transmission wire harness from engine wire harness.
30. Remove stabilizer shaft link nuts from stabilizer shaft, then the stabilizer shaft insulator clamps from front crossmember.
31. Remove stabilizer shaft from vehicle.
32. Loosen steering knuckle nut from lower control arm ball stud, then separate steering knuckle and lower control arm ball stud using tool No. J 42188 or equivalent.
33. Disconnect antilock brake system electrical connector clips from crossmember.
34. Remove front transverse leaf spring as outlined under "Transverse Leaf Spring, Replace."
35. **On models equipped with automatic transmission,** proceed as follows:
   a. disconnect automatic transmission fluid cooler pipe clip from front of engine oil pan.
   b. Disconnect front automatic transmission fluid cooler pipes from rear pipes.
   c. Disconnect automatic transmission cooler pipe clip at righthand side transmission cover.
   d. Remove driveline support hole plug bolts.
   e. Install a M10.0 - 1.5 x 55 mm bolt or longer in each plug location, tighten M10 bearing support bolts to 26 ft. lbs.
   f. Remove flywheel housing plug, then orientate prop shaft hub clamp for access to bolt.
   g. Position clamp bolt facing downward, then loosen prop shaft hub clamp bolt.
   h. Remove bolts attaching transmission wire harness bracket to flywheel housing, then the transmission wire harness from mounting location, rearward toward driveline support.
36. **On models equipped with manual transmission,** proceed as follows:
   a. Unclip clutch actuator hose from clutch actuator hose clip.

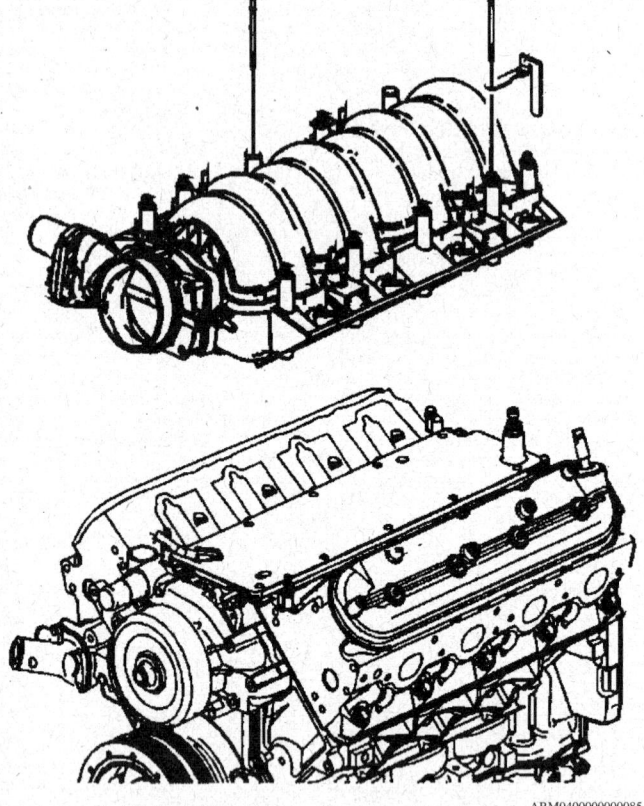

Fig. 3 Intake manifold removal

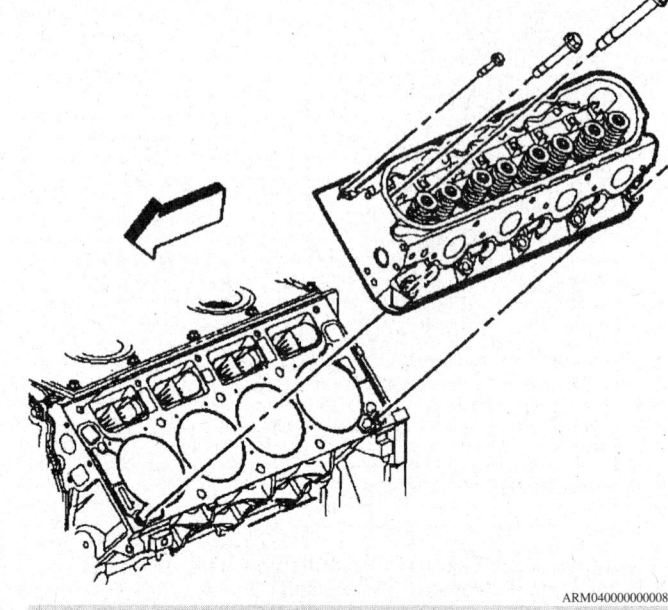

Fig. 4 Cylinder head removal

b. Depress white circular release ring on actuator hose and simultaneously pull lightly on master cylinder hose to disconnect using tool No. J 36221.

c. Protect both ends from dirt and damage.

37. **On all models,** install tool No. J 42203 or equivalent to close-out panel flange, then slowly lower vehicle onto tool Nos. J 39580 and J 39580-500 or equivalents.

38. Support engine and crossmember on Tool Nos. J 39580 and J 39580-500 or equivalents.

39. Remove front and rear crossmember nuts.

40. Remove AIR pipe bracket bolt at rear of cylinder head, then AIR pipe with check valve and gasket.

41. Remove ground strap bolt, then the ground strap from lefthand side rear cylinder head.

42. Disconnect electrical connectors from engine oil pressure sensor, manifold absolute pressure sensor and camshaft position sensor.

43. Disconnect electrical connectors for knock sensors, then the vacuum hose from MAP sensor.

44. Remove driveline support bolts, then insert a flat-bladed screwdriver between edge of driveline support and flywheel housing and separate.

45. Slowly pull engine away from propeller

shaft, and as soon as propeller input shaft clears flywheel housing, slowly raise vehicle.

46. Slide engine and crossmember forward to clear propeller shaft spline.

47. Raise vehicle completely off of engine and crossmember, remove power steering pump pulley hub cap if required.

48. Remove power steering pump pulley using tool No. J 25034-C.

49. Remove power steering pump bolts, then the power steering pump brace.

50. Remove power steering pump with reservoir from engine, then reposition them to crossmember.

51. Remove A/C compressor bracket, then the alternator bracket bolts.

52. Remove alternator bracket and power steering pump bracket.

53. Install tool No. J 41798 or equivalent to engine, then remove spark plugs.

54. Remove engine mount nuts, then using engine hoist and J 41798 or equivalent slowly raise engine, **Fig. 2.**

55. Remove engine from the crossmember.

56. Reverse procedure to install.

INTAKE MANIFOLD
REPLACE

1. Remove engine sight cover, then drain coolant into a suitable container.

2. Disconnect electrical connector from

fuel injectors and throttle body, then the fuel feed to fuel injectors.

3. Remove vacuum hose from brake booster, then disconnect electrical connector from manifold absolute pressure sensor.

4. Remove MAP sensor, then the grommet from sensor as required.

5. Remove EVAP clip, bolt, bracket, valve, and tubes.

6. Remove bolts, fuel rail stop bracket and intake manifold **Fig. 3.**

7. Remove intake manifold gaskets and discard. **Do not reuse gasket.**

8. Reverse procedure to install.

EXHAUST MANIFOLD
REPLACE
Lefthand Side

1. Remove engine sight cover, then raise and support vehicle.

2. Disconnect bank 1 oxygen sensor electrical connector and remove sensor. Lower vehicle.

3. Remove spark plug from engine, then the alternator as outlined under "Alternator, Replace."

4. Remove mounting nuts and gasket from exhaust manifold, then the catalytic convertor from vehicle.

5. Remove exhaust manifold. **It maybe required to remove heat shield from exhaust manifold to gain enough clearance to remove exhaust manifold.**

6. Reverse procedure to install noting the following:

a. Install new exhaust manifold gasket.

b. Apply threadlock GM P/N

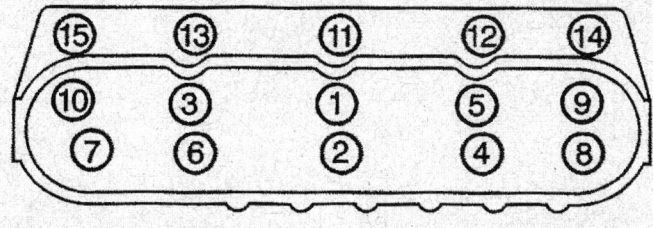

Fig. 5 Cylinder head bolt tightening sequence

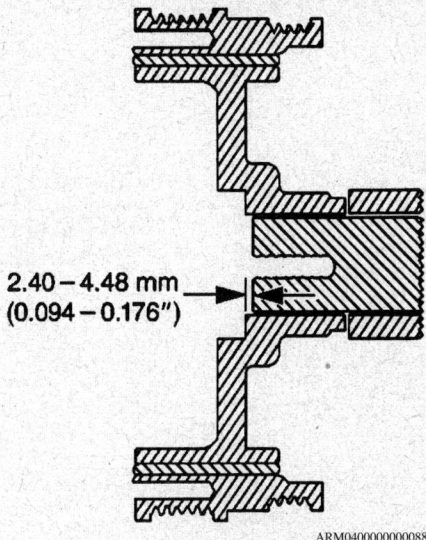

2.40 – 4.48 mm
(0.094 – 0.176″)

Fig. 6 Damper installed measurement

12345493 or equivalent to exhaust manifold bolt threads.

c. **Torque** exhaust manifold bolts to 11 ft. lbs., beginning with two center bolts, alternating from side-to-side working toward outside bolts.

d. Finally **torque** exhaust manifold bolts to 18 ft. lbs., beginning with two center bolts, alternating from side-to-side working toward outside bolts.

Righthand Side

1. Remove engine sight cover, then spark plug from engine.
2. Raise vehicle, then disconnect bank 2 oxygen sensor electrical connector and remove sensor. Lower vehicle.
3. Remove oil dipstick, then the oil dipstick tube bolt and tube.
4. Remove mounting nuts and gasket from exhaust manifold, then the catalytic convertor from vehicle.
5. Remove exhaust manifold. **It maybe required to remove heat shield from exhaust manifold to gain enough clearance to remove exhaust manifold.**
6. Reverse procedure to install noting the following:
   a. Install new exhaust manifold gasket.
   b. Apply threadlock GM P/N 12345493 or equivalent to exhaust manifold bolt threads.
   c. **Torque** exhaust manifold bolts to 11 ft. lbs., beginning with two center bolts, alternating from side-to-side working toward outside bolts.
   d. Finally **torque** exhaust manifold bolts to 18 ft. lbs., beginning with two center bolts, alternating from side-to-side working toward outside bolts.

CYLINDER HEAD
REPLACE

Lefthand Side
REMOVAL

1. Remove Valve rocker arms as outlined under "Rocker Arms."
2. Remove push rods as outlined under "Push Rods."
3. Drain engine coolant into a suitable container, then disconnect electrical connector from intake air temperature sensor.

4. Remove air intake duct, then disconnect air control valve electrical connector.
5. Disconnect electrical connector from throttle position sensor, then the crankcase ventilation hose from throttle body.
6. Remove throttle body attaching bolts, then throttle body.
7. Remove coolant air bleed hose, then the coolant air bleed pipe mounting bolts and coolant air bleed pipe and O-rings.
8. Remove alternator as outlined under "Alternator, Replace."
9. Remove power steering pump as outlined under "Power Steering Pump, Replace."
10. Remove alternator bracket bolts, then the bracket and power steering reservoir bracket.
11. Remove exhaust manifold as outlined under "Exhaust Manifold, Replace."
12. Remove engine wiring harness ground bolt from rear of lefthand side cylinder head, then move engine wire harness ground strap away from cylinder head.
13. Remove cylinder head bolts and cylinder head, **Fig. 4. Do not reuse cylinder head bolts.**
14. Remove cylinder head gasket and discard gasket.

INSTALLATION

1. Clean engine block cylinder head bolt holes using tool No. J42385-107 or equivalent.
2. Spray cleaner GM P/N 12346139, GM P/N 12377981 or equivalent into hole.
3. Clean cylinder head bolt holes with compressed air, then install cylinder head locating pins.
4. Inspect locating pins for proper installation and displacement markings on gasket for proper usage.
5. Install new cylinder head gasket onto locating pins, then the cylinder head onto locating pins and gasket.
6. Install new cylinder head bolts, then tighten as follows:
   a. **Torque** M11 cylinder head bolts 1–10 to 22 ft. lbs., in sequence, **Fig. 5.**
   b. Tighten M11 cylinder head bolts 1–10 a second pass additional 90° in sequence.
   c. Tighten M11 cylinder head bolts 1–10 a final pass to 70° in sequence.
   d. Tighten M8 cylinder head bolts 11–15 to 22 ft. lbs., beginning with cen-

ter bolt 11, alternating side to side while working outward.
7. Install engine wiring harness ground strap to rear of lefthand side cylinder head.
8. Install exhaust manifold as outlined under "Exhaust Manifold, Replace."
9. Install power steering reservoir bracket, then the alternator bracket and bolts.
10. Install alternator as outlined under "Alternator, Replace."
11. Install coolant air bleed pipe and O-rings, then the coolant air bleed hose.
12. Install throttle body, then connect crankcase ventilation hose and electrical connector to throttle body.
13. Connect air control valve and intake air temperature sensor electrical connectors.
14. Install push rods as outlined under "Push Rods."
15. Install valve rocker arms as outlined under "Rocker Arms."
16. Refill cooling system.

Righthand Side
REMOVAL

1. Remove Valve rocker arms as outlined under "Rocker Arms."
2. Remove push rods as outlined under "Push Rods."
3. Drain engine coolant into a suitable container, then disconnect electrical connector from intake air temperature sensor.
4. Remove air intake duct, then disconnect air control valve electrical connector.
5. Disconnect electrical connector from throttle position sensor, then the crankcase ventilation hose from throttle body.
6. Remove throttle body attaching bolts, then throttle body.
7. Remove coolant air bleed hose, then the coolant air bleed pipe mounting

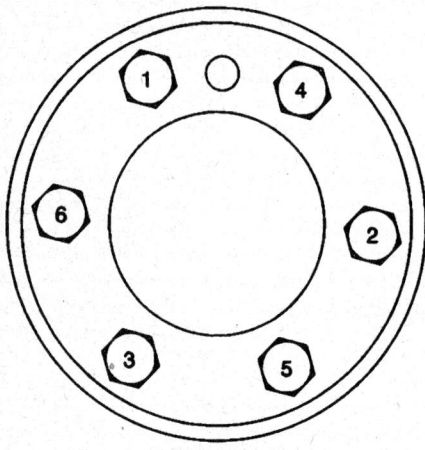

Fig. 7   Flywheel tightening sequence

ARM0400000000089

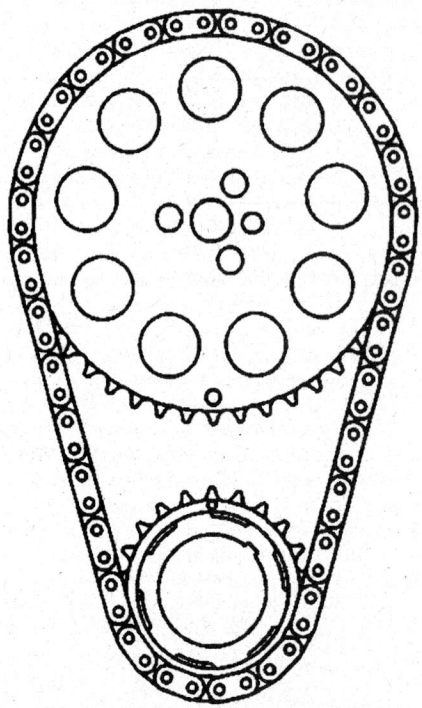

Fig. 8   Camshaft & crankshaft sprocket alignment

ARM0400000000090

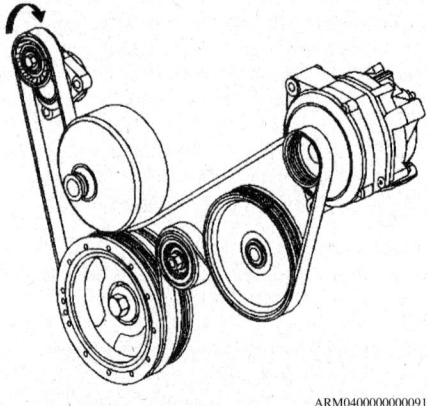

ARM0400000000091

Fig. 9   Accessory drive belt routing

bolts and coolant air bleed pipe and O-rings.
8. Remove alternator as outlined under "Alternator, Replace."
9. Remove power steering pump as outlined under "Power Steering Pump, Replace."
10. Remove alternator bracket bolts, then the bracket and power steering reservoir bracket.
11. Drain engine coolant into a suitable container, then disconnect electrical connector from intake air temperature sensor.
12. Remove air intake duct, then disconnect air control valve electrical connector.
13. Disconnect electrical connector from throttle position sensor, then the crankcase ventilation hose from throttle body.
14. Remove throttle body attaching bolts, then throttle body.
15. Remove coolant air bleed hose, then the coolant air bleed pipe mounting bolts and coolant air bleed pipe and O-rings.
16. Remove exhaust manifold as outlined under "Exhaust Manifold, Replace."
17. Remove oil dipstick tube bolt, then the oil dipstick tube bolt and reposition tube.
18. Remove wiring harness from clip at rear of cylinder head.
19. Remove cylinder head bolts and cylinder head. **Do not reuse cylinder head bolts.**
20. Remove cylinder head gasket and discard gasket.

INSTALLATION

1. Clean engine block cylinder head bolt holes using tool No. J 42385-107 or equivalent.
2. Spray cleaner GM P/N 12346139, GM P/N 12377981 or equivalent into hole.
3. Clean cylinder head bolt holes with compressed air, then install cylinder head locating pins.
4. Inspect locating pins for proper instal-

lation and displacement markings on gasket for proper usage.
5. Install new cylinder head gasket onto locating pins, then the cylinder head onto locating pins and gasket.
6. Install new cylinder head bolts, then tighten as follows:
   a. **Torque** M11 cylinder head bolts 1–10 to 22 ft. lbs., in sequence, **Fig. 5.**
   b. Tighten M11 cylinder head bolts 1–10 a second pass additional 90° in sequence.
   c. Tighten M11 cylinder head bolts 1–10 a final pass to 70° in sequence.
   d. Tighten M8 cylinder head bolts 11–15 to 22 ft. lbs., beginning with center bolt 11, alternating side to side while working outward.
7. Install engine wiring harness ground strap to rear of lefthand cylinder head.
8. Install wiring harness to clip at rear of cylinder head.
9. Install oil dipstick tube bolt.
10. Install exhaust manifold as outlined under "Exhaust Manifold, Replace."
11. Install coolant air bleed pipe and O-rings, then the coolant air bleed hose.
12. Install throttle body, then connect crankcase ventilation hose and electrical connector to throttle body.
13. Connect air control valve and intake air temperature sensor electrical connectors.
14. Install push rods as outlined under "Push Rods."
15. Install valve rocker arms as outlined under "Rocker Arms."

16. Refill cooling system.

VALVE COVER
REPLACE
Lefthand Side

1. Remove lefthand engine sight cover, then disconnect alternator electrical connector.
2. Remove engine wiring harness alternator lead nut and lead.
3. Remove fuel rail cover, then disconnect ignition coil harness connector and spark plug wire at ignition coil.
4. Remove ignition coil mounting bolts and coils.
5. Loosen valve rocker arm cover bolts, then the valve rocker cover.
6. Remove gasket from rocker cover and discard old gasket.
7. Reverse procedure to install.

Righthand Side

1. Remove lefthand side engine sight cover.
2. Disconnect engine vacuum pipe from EVAP canister purge solenoid valve to intake manifold EVAP pipe.
3. Disconnect engine purge pipe from EVAP canister purge valve, then disconnect electrical connector.
4. Remove EVAP canister purge valve from purge bracket.
5. Remove retaining clips, then the EVAP pipes.
6. Remove EVAP pipe from intake air temperature sensor at air intake duct valve cover then the hose from throttle body to engine valley cover.
7. Remove fuel rail cover, then disconnect ignition coil connector and spark plug wire at ignition coil.
8. Remove mounting bolts, then the ignition coil.
9. Remove retaining bolt, then the valve rocker arm cover.
10. Remove gasket from rocker cover and discard old gasket.
11. Reverse procedure to install.

VALVE ARRANGEMENT

Front To Rear

All ....I-E-I-E-I-E-I-E

VALVE CLEARANCE SPECIFICATIONS

This engine is equipped with hydraulic valve lash adjusters. No adjustment is required.

VALVE ADJUSTMENT

This engine is equipped with hydraulic valve lash adjusters. No adjustment is required.

ROCKER ARMS

Removal

Place components in a rack so that they can be installed in same location from which they were removed.
1. Remove valve rocker arm cover as outlined under "Valve Cover, Replace."
2. Remove valve rocker arm bolts, then the valve rocker arms.
3. Remove valve rocker arm pivot support, then the pushrods.
4. Clean and inspect valve rocker arms and pushrods.

Installation

When using valve train components over again, always install them into original location and position. Valve lash is net build. No valve adjustment is required.
1. Lubricate valve rocker arms with suitable clean engine oil.
2. Lubricate flange of valve rocker arm bolts with clean engine oil.
3. Install valve rocker arm pivot support. **Ensure pushrods seat properly to valve lifter socket.**
4. Install pushrods, then ensure pushrods seat properly to ends of rocker arms. **Do not tighten rocker arm bolts at this time.**
5. Install rocker arms and bolts.
6. Turn crankshaft until number one piston is at top dead center of compression stroke. Cylinders 1, 3, 5 and 7 are lefthand in bank. Cylinders 2, 4, 6 and 8 are in righthand bank. In this position sprocket marks on crankshaft and camshaft will be aligned.
7. With engine in number one firing position, proceed as follows:
   a. **Torque** exhaust valve rocker arm bolts 1, 2, 7 and 8 to 22 ft. lbs.
   b. **Torque** intake valve rocker arm bolts 1, 3, 4 and 5 to 22 ft. lbs.
8. Rotate crankshaft 360° and proceed as follows:
   a. **Torque** exhaust valve rocker arm bolts 3, 4, 5 and 6 to 22 ft. lbs.
   b. **Torque** intake valve rocker arm bolts 2, 6, 7 and 8 to 22 ft. lbs.
9. Install valve rocker arm cover as outlined under "Valve Cover, Replace."

PUSH RODS

Refer to "Rocker Arms" for push rod removal procedure.

HYDRAULIC LIFTERS

REPLACE

1. Remove cylinder head as outlined under "Cylinder Head, Replace."
2. Remove guide bolts, then the guides with lifters.
3. Note installed position of guides, notched area of guide is to align with locating tab on block.
4. Remove valve lifters from guide.
5. Organize or mark components so they can be installed in original positions.
6. Reverse procedure to install, noting the following:
   a. Lubricate valve lifters and bores with suitable clean engine oil.
   b. Align lifters' and bores' flat sides.

CRANKSHAFT DAMPER

REPLACE

1. Release accessory drive belt tensioner and remove drive belt as outlined in "Serpentine Drive Belt."
2. Remove power steering gear as outlined in "Power Steering Gear, Replace"
3. Remove starter motor as outlined in "Starter, Replace."
4. Remove power steering cooler mounting bolts and cooler from front crossmember, then position aside.
5. Release tensioner and remove air conditioning drive belt.
6. Install flywheel holding tool No. J 42386, or equivalent, and flywheel mounting bolts. **Torque** mounting bolts to 37 ft. lbs.
7. Remove crankshaft damper bolt.
8. Mark crankshaft damper and end of crankshaft. Record damper installed position on crankshaft for installation. Also record location of any weights, which must return to original positions.
9. Remove crankshaft damper using crankshaft end protector and damper removal tool Nos. J 41816 and J 41816-2, or equivalents.
10. Reverse procedure to install, noting the following:
    a. Install damper using crankshaft balancer and sprocket installer tool No. J 41665, or equivalent.
    b. **Torque** used crankshaft damper bolt to 240 ft. lbs.
    c. Remove bolt and measure for properly installed damper, **Fig. 6.**
    d. **Torque** new crankshaft damper bolt to 37 ft. lbs.
    e. Tighten bolt an additional 140°.

FRONT COVER

REPLACE

Removal

1. Remove crankshaft damper as outlined under "Crankshaft Damper, Replace."
2. Remove water pump as outlined under "Water Pump, Replace."
3. Remove front cover bolts, then the front cover and gasket. Discard front cover gasket and oil seal.

Installation

1. Apply .20 inch bead of GM silicone gasket P/N 12378190, or equivalent, to corner where oil pan meets engine block.
2. Install new gasket, front cover and mounting bolts to engine block. Tighten bolts hand tight.
3. Align cover alignment tool No. J 41476, or equivalent, on front of crankshaft.
4. Install crankshaft damper bolt and hand tighten.
5. Hand tighten oil pan to cover bolts so cover properly positions itself at pan rail.
6. **Torque** front cover bolts to 18 ft. lbs.
7. Remove alignment tool.
8. Install crankshaft oil seal using oil seal installer tool No. J 41478, or equivalent. **Do not lubricate oil seal sealing surface.**
9. Install water pump as outlined under "Water Pump, Replace."
10. Remove crankshaft damper as outlined under "Crankshaft Damper, Replace."

REAR COVER

REPLACE

Removal

1. Mark crankshaft end and flywheel for installation, then remove flywheel.
2. Remove engine rear cover mounting bolts and cover. Discard gasket.
3. Remove and discard crankshaft rear cover oil seal.

Installation

1. Apply .20 inch bead of GM silicone gasket P/N 12378190, or equivalent, to corner were oil pan meets engine block.
2. Install rear cover, gasket and bolts onto engine, hand tighten bolts.
3. Rotate crankshaft until two opposing flywheel bolt holes are parallel to oil pan surface.
4. Install cover alignment tool No. J 41476, or equivalent, and bolts onto rear of crankshaft. Hand tighten tool mounting bolts.
5. Hand tighten oil pan to cover bolts so cover properly positions itself at pan rail.
6. **Torque** oil pan to cover bolts to 106 inch lbs.
7. **Torque** rear cover mounting bolts to 18 ft. lbs.
8. Remove alignment tool.
9. Install crankshaft rear oil seal using rear oil seal installer tool No. J 41479, or equivalent.
10. Install flywheel as follows:

CORVETTE

a. Align alignment mark made during removal and install mounting bolts hand tight.
b. **Torque** flywheel mounting bolts to 15 ft. lbs., in sequence, **Fig. 7.**
c. **Torque** flywheel mounting bolts to 37 ft. lbs., in sequence.
d. **Torque** flywheel mounting bolts to 74 ft. lbs., in sequence.

TIMING CHAIN
REPLACE
Removal

1. Remove oil pump as outlined in "Oil Pump, Replace."
2. Rotate crankshaft until crankshaft and camshaft sprocket timing marks are aligned.
3. Remove camshaft sprocket bolts.
4. Remove camshaft sprocket and timing chain.
5. Remove crankshaft sprocket using puller tool Nos. J 8433, J 41816-2 and J 41558, or equivalents.
6. Remove crankshaft sprocket key, if required.

Installation

1. Install key into crankshaft keyway.
2. Install crankshaft sprocket onto front of crankshaft, aligning key with keyway.
3. Install crankshaft sprocket using sprocket installation tool No. J 41665, or equivalent. Ensure sprocket fully seats against crankshaft flange.
4. Rotate crankshaft sprocket until alignment mark is in 12 o'clock position.
5. Install camshaft sprocket and timing chain.
6. Properly locate camshaft sprocket locating pin with camshaft sprocket alignment hole.
7. Sprocket teeth and timing chain must mesh properly.
8. Camshaft and crankshaft sprocket alignment marks must be aligned properly, **Fig. 8.** Locate camshaft sprocket alignment mark in 6 o'clock position.
9. Install camshaft sprocket bolts.
10. Install oil pump as outlined in "Oil Pump, Replace."

CAMSHAFT
REPLACE
Removal

1. Remove engine assembly as outlined under "Engine, Replace."
2. Remove crankshaft damper as outlined under "Crankshaft Damper, Replace."
3. Remove oil dipstick tube.
4. Remove exhaust manifolds as outlined under "Exhaust Manifold, Replace."
5. Remove water pump as outlined under "Water Pump, Replace."
6. Remove intake manifold as outlined under "Intake Manifold, Replace."

7. Remove engine valley cover, then the coolant air bleed pipe.
8. Remove lefthand side and righthand side valve rocker arm covers as outlined under "Valve Cover, Replace."
9. Remove valve rocker arms and push rods as outlined under "Rocker Arms."
10. Remove lefthand side and righthand side cylinder heads as outlined under "Cylinder Head, Replace."
11. Remove valve lifters as outlined under "Hydraulic Lifters."
12. Remove oil pan to front cover bolts, the front cover bolts.
13. Remove front cover and gasket, then discard old gasket.
14. Rotate engine in order to align timing marks, **Fig. 8.**
15. Remove camshaft sprocket bolts, then the timing chain from camshaft sprocket. Allow timing chain to rest on crankshaft sprocket.
16. Remove camshaft retainer bolts and retainer.
17. Install three M8 - 1.25 x 4.0 inch bolts in camshaft front bolt holes.
18. Carefully rotate and pull camshaft out of engine block using bolts handle.
19. Remove bolts from front of camshaft.

Installation

If camshaft replacement is required, valve lifters must also be replaced.
1. Lubricate camshaft journals and bearings with clean engine oil.
2. Install three M8 - 1.25 x 4.0 inch bolts into camshaft front bolt holes.
3. Carefully install camshaft into engine block using bolts handle. Remove three bolts from front of camshaft.
4. Install camshaft retainer and bolts.
5. Align camshaft sprocket alignment mark in 6 o'clock position, then install camshaft sprocket and timing chain.
6. Install camshaft sprocket bolts.
7. Apply a .2 inch bead of sealant GM P/N 12378190, or equivalent .8 inch long to oil pan to engine block junction.
8. Install front cover and a new gasket, then the cover bolts until snug.
9. Install oil pan to front cover bolts until snug.
10. Install tool No. J 41476 or equivalent and crankshaft balancer bolt to front cover.
11. Align tapered legs of J 41476 or equivalent with machined alignment surfaces on the front cover.
12. Install crankshaft balancer bolt until snug, then tighten oil pan and front cover bolts to 18 ft. lbs. Remove tool.
13. Install a new crankshaft front oil seal, then install valve lifters as outlined under "Hydraulic Lifters."
14. Install righthand side and lefthand side cylinder heads, as outlined under "Cylinder Head, Replace."
15. Install valve rocker arms and push rods as outlined under "Rocker Arms."
16. Install righthand side and lefthand side valve rocker arm covers as outlined under "Valve Cover, Replace."
17. Install coolant air bleed pipe.
18. Install intake manifold as outlined under "Intake Manifold, Replace."

19. Install water pump as outlined under "Water Pump, Replace."
20. Install lefthand side and righthand side exhaust manifolds as outlined under "Exhaust Manifold, Replace."
21. Install oil dipstick tube.
22. Install crankshaft damper as outlined under "Crankshaft Damper, Replace."
23. Install engine assembly as outlined under "Engine, Replace."

PISTON & ROD ASSEMBLY

1. Install retaining clip, clip should be seated in groove of pin bore.
2. Install piston pin to piston and connecting rod.
3. Install retaining clip, clip should be seated in groove of pin bore.
4. Identify compression and oil control rings for proper installation, upper compression ring can be identified by a paint mark located 180° from end gap.
5. Lower compression ring can be identified by a paint mark located 90° from end gap, then install upper and lower with orientation marks facing top of piston.
6. Install piston rings onto piston using piston ring pliers, then position oil control ring end gaps a minimum 1 inch from each other.
7. Position compression ring end gaps 180° opposite each other.
8. Install connecting rod bearings to rod and cap.

PISTONS, PINS & RINGS

Pistons are available in standard and .010 inch oversize.
Piston rings are available in standard and .010 inch oversize.

MAIN & ROD BEARINGS

Connecting rod bearings are available in standard size only.
Main bearings are available in standard size only.

CRANKSHAFT SEAL
REPLACE

Refer to "Front Cover, Replace" for crankshaft front seal replacement.

CRANKSHAFT REAR OIL SEAL
REPLACE

Refer to "Rear Cover, Replace" for crankshaft rear seal replacement.

OIL PAN
REPLACE

1. Drain engine oil into a suitable container, then remove oil filter.

2. Remove lefthand side and righthand side rear transmission covers.
3. Remove starter motor assembly as outlined under "Starter, Replace."
4. Disconnect electrical connectors from engine oil level and engine oil temperature sensors.
5. Remove transmission lines from rear and front of oil pan.
6. Remove oil pan mounting bolts, then the oil pan from engine block.
7. Remove oil pan gasket from engine block.
8. Reverse procedure to install.

OIL PUMP

REPLACE

1. Remove engine front cover as outlined in "Front Cover, Replace."
2. Remove oil pan as outlined in "Oil Pan, Replace."
3. Remove oil pump screen bolt and nuts.
4. Remove oil pump screen.
5. Remove and discard O-ring seal.
6. Remove remaining crankshaft oil deflector nuts.
7. Remove crankshaft oil deflector.
8. Remove oil pump bolts.
9. Reverse procedure to install, noting the following:
   a. Ensure pump and oil gallery passages are clean and free of obstructions.
   b. Align crankshaft sprocket's and oil pump's splined surfaces.
   c. Install oil pump onto crankshaft sprocket until pump housing contacts engine block face.

SERPENTINE DRIVE BELT

Belt Routing

Refer to **Fig. 9,** for serpentine drive belt routing.

Belt Replacement

1. Reduce tension by rotating tensioner away from belts using suitable hex-head socket.
2. Remove accessory drive belts.
3. Clean accessory drive belt surfaces.
4. Install accessory drive belts. Record running direction or arrow markings.
5. Tighten accessory drive belt tensioners to increase tension on accessory drive belts.
6. Ensure accessory drive belts are aligned in proper pulley grooves.

COOLING SYSTEM BLEED

1. Fill cooling system.
2. Start engine and let idle for approximately four minutes.
3. Slowly fill coolant mixture until level stabilizes at base of surge tank fill neck.
4. Run engine between 2000–2500 RPM for approximately two minutes.

5. Allow engine to idle and add approximately 1.1 quarts of coolant to surge tank.
6. Install coolant pressure cap, then shut engine Off.
7. Allow engine to cool, then top off coolant as required.
8. Inspect concentration of engine coolant using tool No. J 26568 or equivalent.
9. Rinse any excess coolant from engine and compartment. Inspect cooling system for leaks.

THERMOSTAT

REPLACE

1. Drain engine coolant into a suitable container.
2. Remove outlet hose from water pump inlet, then the bolts and water pump inlet.
3. Remove bolts, then thermostat housing. **O-ring seal is integral to thermostat housing.**
4. Reverse procedure to install.

WATER PUMP

REPLACE

1. Drain engine coolant into a suitable container.
2. Remove air cleaner intake duct.
3. Reduce tension by rotating tensioner away from belts using suitable hex-head socket.
4. Remove accessory drive belts.
5. Remove inlet and outlet hoses from water pump.
6. Remove heater inlet and surge tank outlet hoses from water pump.
7. Remove retaining bolts, then the water pump and gasket.
8. Reverse procedure to install noting the following:
   a. **Torque** water pump mounting bolts a first pass to 11 ft. lbs.
   b. **Torque** water pump mounting bolts a final pass to 22 ft. lbs.

RADIATOR

REPLACE

1. Recover air conditioning refrigerant as outlined in "Air Conditioning" chapter.
2. Drain engine coolant into a suitable container.
3. Remove splash shield from vehicle, then disconnect electrical connector from mass air flow/intake air temperature sensor.
4. Remove connection for IAT sensor, then air intake duct, MAF/IAT sensor and air cleaner assembly.
5. Disconnect surge tank inlet hose assembly from radiator support tabs, then remove bolts and radiator support.
6. Disconnect A/C compressor hose assembly from A/C condenser fitting, then remove and discard seal washer.
7. Cap or tape A/C compressor hose assembly.
8. Raise and support vehicle, then disconnect front evaporator inlet line from

A/C condenser, then remove and discard seal washer.
9. Cap or tape A/C compressor hose assembly, then lower vehicle.
10. Remove lefthand side and righthand side radiator air baffle upper retainer pins.
11. Gently tilt air baffle forward for additional clearance.
12. Raise A/C condenser along radiator to release A/C condenser tabs from radiator slots and remove from vehicle.
13. Disengage tension on radiator inlet hose clamp at radiator using tool No. J 38185 or equivalent.
14. Disconnect radiator inlet hose from radiator, then the engine wiring harness from cooling fan shroud.
15. Disconnect surge tank outlet hose from retaining clips on cooling fan shroud and position aside.
16. Raise and support vehicle, then remove tire and wheel assemblies.
17. Remove nuts and insulator clamps, then the stabilizer shaft from vehicle.
18. Disconnect cooling fan electrical connector.
19. **On models equipped with transmission fluid cooler,** disconnect transmission oil cooler lines from radiator, using tool Nos. J 41623-B, DT 47624 and DT-47731 or equivalents.
20. **On models equipped with engine oil cooler,** disconnect engine oil cooler pipes from radiator using tool No. DT-47731 or equivalent.
21. Remove retaining bolts, then the cooling fan and shroud.
22. Disconnect surge tank hoses from radiator, then radiator outlet hose.
23. Remove radiator from vehicle.
24. Reverse procedure to install.

FUEL PUMP

REPLACE

Lefthand Side

1. Relieve fuel system pressure as outlined under "Fuel System Pressure Relief."
2. Remove fuel tank filler pipe cap, then drain fuel through fuel tank filler pipe using a hand or air operated fuel pump device and J 45004 or equivalent.
3. Remove lefthand rear wheel and tire, then the lefthand side rear wheelhouse panel.
4. Install adjustable jack stands under front and rear of intermediate pipe, then loosen exhaust muffler band clamps.
5. Separate lefthand side and righthand side mufflers from intermediate pipe, then remove exhaust pipe hanger lower bolts exhaust manifold nuts and exhaust seals.
6. Lower jack stands, then remove intermediate pipe from jack stands.
7. Remove mufflers from hangers, then mufflers from vehicle.
8. Remove oxygen sensors from catalytic convertors, then the catalytic convertors from vehicle.

9. Remove driveline tunnel closeout panel bolts and panel.
10. **On models equipped with automatic transmission,** proceed as follows:
    a. Remove rear bellhousing access plug, then matchmark transmission flexplate to transmission torque converter through access hole in rear bellhousing.
    b. Remove starter motor as outlined under "Starter, Replace."
    c. Remove access plug from driveline support assembly, then matchmark transmission flexplate to transmission torque converter through access hole.
    d. Turn engine flywheel through starter motor opening until one of flexplate to torque converter bolts lines up with access hole.
    e. Install tool No. J 42386-A to flywheel, then remove flexplate to torque converter bolts.
    f. Remove two plastic plugs from front of driveline support assembly.
    g. Install two bolts, M10 - 1.5 X 55 mm or longer in place of plastic plugs. **Long bolts are used to maintain propeller input shaft front bearing in original position during removal and installation.**
    h. Tighten propeller input shaft front bearing positioning bolts to 26 ft. lbs.
    i. Remove engine flywheel housing access plug, then loosen propeller shaft hub clamp bolt.
    j. Remove nuts retaining transmission shift cable bracket to transmission.
    k. Disconnect transmission shift control cable from transmission shift lever, Unsnap to release cable.
    l. Reposition transmission shift cable and bracket.
11. **On models equipped with manual transmission,**
    a. Remove instrument panel accessory trim plate, then the center console trim plate.
    b. Remove bolts, nuts and floor console. Disconnect electrical connector.
    c. Pry off shift control knob button, then the shift control knob retainer and remove retainer.
    d. Unscrew shift control knob, release shift boot retaining tabs from instrument panel accessory trim plate.
    e. Lift boot away from trim plate and remove boot.
    f. Remove shift control closeout boot, then place shiftier into neutral.
    g. Press down to engage shift control neutral lock pin, then remove transmission shift rod clamp bolt and shift control mounting bolts.
    h. Raise shift control to release locator from shiftier bracket on side of driveline support assembly.
    i. Release shift control from transmission shift rod clamp and remove shift control assembly.
    j. Remove lefthand side I/P lower insulator panel, then the clutch master cylinder pushrod retainer.
    k. Disconnect clutch master cylinder pushrod from clutch pedal,
    l. Raise and support vehicle, then remove clutch actuator cylinder hose from hose retaining clip at rear of engine.
    m. Depress white circular release ring on actuator cylinder hose and simultaneously pull lightly on master cylinder hose to disconnect using tool No. J 36221 or equivalent.
12. **On all models,** using tool No. J 33432-A or equivalent compress transverse spring.
13. Disconnect shock absorber from lower control arm, then loosen but do not remove upper ball joint stud nut.
14. Separate the upper joint stud from suspension knuckle using tool No. J 42188 or equivalent, then remove upper ball joint stud nut from suspension knuckle.
15. Remove nut from wheel drive shaft on suspension knuckle.
16. Loosen but do not remove lower ball joint stud nut, then separate lower ball joint stud from suspension knuckle using tool No. J 42188 or equivalent.
17. Remove two and lower ball joint stud nut from suspension knuckle.
18. Remove stabilizer shaft link from lower control arm.
19. Mark position of, then remove cam bolts, washers, and nuts retaining control arm to crossmember.
20. Remove lower control arms from vehicle.
21. Remove transverse spring bolts and retainers, discard old transverse spring bolts.
22. Remove transverse spring from vehicle.
23. Install tool No. J 42055 or equivalent to a transmission jack, then position and firmly secure tool with transmission jack to transmission.
24. Disconnect wiring harness and brake pipe clip retainers from rear suspension crossmember.
25. Remove transaxle mount to rear crossmember nuts, then position a transmission jack under rear suspension crossmember and firmly secure crossmember to jack.
26. Remove rear suspension crossmember retaining nuts using only hand tools.
27. With aid of an assistant, slowly lower rear suspension crossmember away from vehicle frame rails and remove the crossmember.
28. Remove transaxle mount with bracket, then using a pry bar release wheel drive shafts from differential.
29. Tie off wheel drive shafts to underbody to support shafts out of way. Lefthand side muffler assembly pipe toward rear offers a good location.
30. Release retainer securing wiring harness to L-shaped brackets along driveline support assembly, then slide harness up out of brackets and position out of way.
31. Slowly lower driveline approximately two inches, while simultaneously adjusting angle of tilt to access electrical connectors.
32. Disconnect vehicle speed sensor electrical connector, then wiring harness retainer from stud at differential rear cover.
33. Disconnect wiring harness retainer clip from top of differential then the transmission harness 20-way connector
34. Disconnect park/neutral position switch electrical connectors, then remove bolt retaining transmission wiring harness to lefthand side side of transmission case.
35. Slowly lower driveline, observe relationship between top rear of differential and lowest part of rear compartment panel floor.
36. Differential should not be lowered more than approximately even with specified body point of reference. Engine positive crankcase ventilation pipes which route along rear of engine intake manifold.
37. Release wiring harness from harness retainer along top of transmission, ensure wiring harness is free from driveline being removed.
38. Disconnect transmission oil cooler rear pipes from junction fittings at engine flywheel housing, then cap pipes and plug junction fittings to prevent contamination.
39. Place a jack under rear of engine oil pan for support and prevent contact with composite dash panel using a block of wood to protect engine oil pan.
40. Remove five driveline support assembly to engine flywheel housing bolts.
41. Bend wiring harness bracket away from driveline and toward driveline tunnel wall to make a clear removal path for driveline.
42. Have an assistant insert a flat bladed tool between edge of driveline support assembly and engine flywheel housing, then begin to pry driveline loose from engine.
43. Have assistant guide front of driveline during removal, then slowly lower driveline completely out of vehicle.
44. Disconnect fuel fill hose and recirc line from fill pipe, then the fuel pump jumper harness connector.
45. Disconnect fuel feed pipe at rear of lefthand side fuel tank, then cap fuel pipes to prevent fuel system contamination.
46. Loosen fuel tank strap to drop tank approximately one inch.
47. Disengage crossover tube connector position assurance retainer, then rotate crossover tube collar counterclockwise to disengage.
48. Disconnect crossover tube from lefthand side fuel tank by pulling straight out.
49. Disconnect evaporative emission crossover pipe quick connect fitting at lefthand side fuel tank. Cap EVAP pipe to prevent system contamination.
50. Remove fuel tank strap mounting bolts, then the fuel tank strap from the vehicle.
51. Remove fuel tank, then place tank on a

suitable work surface.

52. Disconnect fuel pump jumper harness from fuel pump module, then the jet line insert connector from crossover tube to fuel tank opening.
53. Disconnect fuel feed line from welded clip on side of fuel tank. **Fuel pump module is spring loaded and will spring upward when locking ring is removed.**
54. Remove fuel pump module locking ring using tool No. J 39765-A or equivalent.
55. Remove fuel pump module from fuel tank with jet lines connected, then disconnect jet line quick-connect connectors from fuel pump module inner port.
56. Remove jet line from module retainer cup, then the fuel pump module O-ring from fuel tank opening.
57. Remove jet line insert through crossover tube to fuel tank opening.
58. Reverse procedure to install.

Righthand Side

1. Relieve fuel system pressure as outlined under "Fuel System Pressure Relief."
2. Remove fuel tank filler pipe cap, then drain fuel through fuel tank filler pipe using a hand or air operated fuel pump device and J 45004 or equivalent.
3. Raise and support vehicle, then remove righthand side rear tire.
4. Remove righthand side rear wheel-house panel, then the evaporative emission canister access cover.
5. Disconnect fill limit vent valve hose at EVAP canister, then the fuel pump module harness connector.
6. Remove crossover tube from clamp located above transmission.
7. Disengage crossover tube connector position assurance retainer by pulling tab outward and rotate.
8. Rotate crossover tube collar counter-clockwise and disengage.
9. Disconnect crossover tube from right-hand side fuel tank by pulling the tube straight out of fuel tank connection.
10. Disconnect EVAP crossover pipe quick connect fitting at righthand side fuel tank. Cap EVAP pipe to prevent system contamination.
11. Remove fuel tank strap from vehicle, then the fuel tank.
12. Place fuel tank on a suitable work surface, then disconnect evaporative emission purge line from fuel pump module.
13. Disconnect fuel pump module harness connector, then the fuel tank pressure sensor harness connector.
14. Pry fuel tank pressure sensor out of fuel tank with a screwdriver.
15. Disconnect jet line insert connector from crossover tube to fuel tank opening.
16. Remove fuel pump module locking ring using tool No. J 39765-A or equivalent.
17. Remove fuel pump module from fuel tank with jet lines connected. Do not damage fuel sender float arm.
18. Disconnect jet line quick-connect connectors from fuel pump module, noting location of lines for installation.
19. Remove fuel pump module O-ring from fuel tank opening.
20. Remove jet line insert through crossover tube to fuel tank opening.
21. Reverse procedure to install.

FUEL FILTER
REPLACE

1. Raise and support vehicle.
2. Clean fuel filter connections before disconnecting.
3. **On models equipped with automatic transmission,** proceed as follows:
   a. Disconnect stabilizer bar from rear cradle.
   b. Remove exhaust intermediate pipe to muffler bolts.
   c. Lower lefthand muffler.
4. **On all models,** remove fuel filter bracket nut from mounting stud.
5. Disconnect fuel filter quick-connect fittings and cap fuel lines.
6. Disconnect filter mounting stud ground strap.
7. Remove fuel filter and bracket, then filter from bracket.
8. Reverse procedure to install. Ensure mounting bracket anti-rotation tab is securely seated into tunnel reinforcement hole.

TIGHTENING SPECIFICATIONS

Year	Component	Torque/Ft. Lbs.
2005	Alternator	37
	Camshaft Position Sensor	106①
	Camshaft Retainer	18
	Camshaft Sprocket	18
	Clutch Pressure Plate	52
	Connecting Rod	②
	Coolant Temperature Sensor	15
	Crankshaft Damper	③
	Crankshaft Bearing Cap	④
	Crankshaft Bearing Cap Side	18
	Crankshaft Position Sensor	18
	Cylinder Head Bolts	⑤
	Cylinder Head Coolant Plug	15
	Drive Belt Pulley	37
	Drive Belt Tensioner	37
	Engine Block Coolant Heater	30
	Engine Block Oil Gallery/Coolant Plugs	44
	Engine Front Cover	18
	Engine Mount	48
	Engine Mount Bracket	37
	Engine Rear Cover	18
	Exhaust Manifold	⑦
	Flywheel	⑥
	Fuel Rail	89①
	Ignition Coil	89①
	Intake Manifold	⑧
	Knock Sensor	15
	Oil Filter	22
	Oil Filter Fitting	40
	Oil Dipstick Tube Bolt	18
	Oil Level Sensor	15
	Oil Pan Closeout Cover	80①
	Oil Pan Cover Bolts	106①
	Oil Pan Drain Plug	18
	Oil Pan M6 Bolts Oil Pan to Rear Cover	106①
	Oil Pan M8 Bolts Oil Pan to Engine Block and Oil Pan to Front Cover	18

Continued

TIGHTENING
SPECIFICATIONS—Continued

Year	Component	Torque/Ft. Lbs.
2005	Oil Pressure Sensor	15
	Oil Pump Cover	106①
	Oil Pump Regulator Valve Plug	106①
	Oil Pump Screen	18
	Oil Pump Screen to Oil Pump	106①
	Oil Pump to Engine Block	18
	Power Steering Pump	18
	Power Steering Reservoir Bracket to Engine	37
	Spark Plugs	⑩
	Starter Motor	37
	Throttle Body	89①
	Timing Chain Guide	18
	Valley Cover	18
	Valve Lifter Guide	89①
	Valve Rocker Arm	22
	Valve Rocker Arm Cover	106①
	Water Inlet Housing	11
	Water Pump	⑨
	Water Pump Cover	11
	Water Pump Pulley	⑨

① — Inch lbs.

② — First pass tighten to 15 ft. lbs., final pass an additional 75°.

③ — Refer to "Crankshaft Damper, Replace."

④ — First pass tighten to 15 ft. lbs., final pass on inner bolts an additional 80° and outer bolts an additional 51°.

⑤ — Refer to "Cylinder Head, Replace."

⑥ — Refer to "Rear Cover, Replace."

⑦ — Refer to "Exhaust Manifold, Replace."

⑧ — Refer to "Intake Manifold, Replace."

⑨ — Refer to "Water Pump, Replace."

⑩ — New cylinder head, 15 ft. lbs.; used cylinder head 11 ft. lbs.

Rear Axle & Suspension

NOTE: On Air Bag Equipped Models, Refer To "Air Bag System Precautions" Located In The Front Of This Manual For System Disarming & Arming Procedures.

NOTE: Refer To "Computer Relearn Procedures" Located In The Front Of This Manual When Battery Power To The Computer Has Been Interrupted.

INDEX

REAR AXLE
REPLACE

Refer to **MOTOR's "Domestic Transmission, In-Vehicle Service"** manual, for rear axle replacement.

REAR WHEEL SHAFT
REPLACE

1. Apply parking brake and shift transmission into park or neutral.
2. Raise and support vehicle and remove rear wheel and tire.
3. Prevent wheel hub and bearing turning by insert suitable drift or punch into brake rotor cooling fins and against brake caliper.
4. Remove spindle nut mounting rear wheel driveshaft to hub.
5. Remove drift or punch.
6. Release parking brake.
7. Remove rear transverse spring as outlined in "Transverse Leaf Spring, Replace."
8. Separate outer tie rod end from knuckle and position tie rod toward rear of vehicle. **Do not loosen outer tie rod jam nut.**
9. Disconnect wheel speed sensor electrical connector.
10. Disconnect parking brake cable from parking brake lever at rear hub.
11. Remove parking brake cable from bracket and position toward vehicle rear.
12. Install rear hub spindle remover tool No. J 42129, or equivalent, onto wheel hub and secure with lugnuts.
13. Begin to disengage driveshaft from wheel hub and bearing. This will give additional clearance to lower ball joint nut.
14. Separate lower ball joint from suspension knuckle.
15. Disengage driveshaft completely from wheel hub and bearing.
16. Support driveshaft, suspension knuckle and upper control arm, then position knuckle toward front.

17. Remove driveshaft using axle shaft remover, extension and slide hammer tool Nos. J 42128, J 29794 & J 2619-01, or equivalents.
18. Remove rear hub spindle remover tool.
19. Reverse procedure to install.

PROPELLER SHAFT
REPLACE

Refer to **MOTOR's "Domestic Transmission, In-Vehicle Service"** manual, for propeller shaft replacement.

HUB & BEARING
REPLACE

1. Raise and support vehicle, then remove tire and wheel.
2. Disconnect wheel speed sensor electrical connector.
3. Disconnect ESC rear position sensor link.
4. **On models equipped with Real Time Damping (RTD) suspension,** disconnect RTD position sensor link.
5. **On all models,** remove brake caliper and disc rotor.
6. Remove shock absorber solenoid electrical connector.
7. Separate outer tie rod end from suspension knuckle.
8. Remove spindle nut retainer, nut and washer.
9. Separate suspension knuckle from upper control arm.
10. Separate suspension knuckle from lower control arm ball joint stud.
11. Remove suspension knuckle.
12. Remove wheel hub mounting bolts.
13. Remove hub and bearing from suspension knuckle.
14. Reverse procedure to install, noting the following:
    a. **Front and rear hub and bearing are not interchangeable. Ensure proper replacement component is being installed.**

b. Tighten mounting bolts, nuts and screws.

SPINDLE KNUCKLE
REPLACE

1. Raise and support vehicle, then remove tire and wheel assembly.
2. Disconnect wheel speed sensor electrical connector.
3. Disconnect the ESC position sensor link.
4. **On models equipped with Real Time Damping (RTD) suspension,** disconnect RTD position sensor link.
5. **On all models,** disconnect shock absorber electrical connector.
6. Remove brake caliper and disc rotor.
7. Separate outer tie rod end from suspension knuckle.
8. Remove spindle nut retainer, nut and washer.
9. Separate suspension knuckle from upper control arm.
10. Separate suspension knuckle from lower control arm ball joint stud.
11. Remove suspension knuckle.
12. Reverse procedure to install.

REAR WHEEL SPINDLE
REPLACE

Refer to "Hub & Bearing, Replace" for rear wheel spindle replacement.

SHOCK ABSORBER
REPLACE

1. Raise and support vehicle, then remove tire and wheel.
2. Disconnect shock absorber solenoid electrical connector.
3. Remove lower shock absorber to lower control arm mounting bolt.
4. Remove upper mounting bolts.
5. Remove shock absorber from lower control arm and shock tower.
6. Remove upper insulator retainer and insulator.
7. Reverse procedure to install.

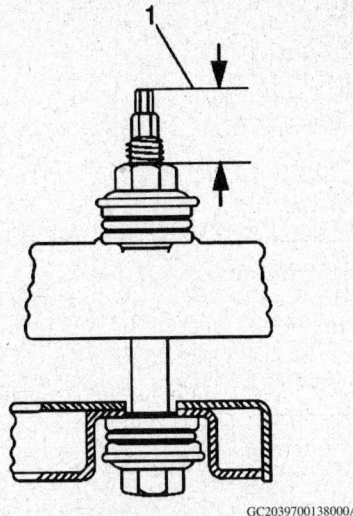

Fig. 1 Spring stud height measurement

TRANSVERSE LEAF SPRING
REPLACE

1. Raise and support vehicle, then remove both rear tires and wheels.
2. Measure transverse spring stud height, **Fig. 1.**
3. Install transverse leaf spring compressor and adapters, tool Nos. J 33432-A and J 33432-97, or equivalents, **Fig. 2.**
4. Compress spring.
5. Remove spring to control arm mounting nuts, bolts and insulators.
6. Remove spring to crossmember retainer bolts, retainer, spring spacers and insulators.
7. Remove transverse leaf spring.
8. Reverse procedure to install, noting the following:
   a. Set spring stud height to that noted during removal.
   b. Ensure spring stud bolt has minimum of two threads showing above nut.
   c. Tighten mounting bolts, nuts and screws.

CONTROL ARM
REPLACE
Lower

1. Raise and support vehicle, then re-

move tire and wheel.
2. Remove transverse leaf spring as outlined under "Transverse Leaf Spring, Replace."
3. Support lower control arm using suitable jack stand and remove shock absorber to lower control arm mounting bolt.
4. Loosen lower ball joint stud nut.
5. Separate lower ball joint stud from suspension knuckle using separator tool No. J 42188, or equivalent.
6. Remove separator tool and lower ball joint stud nut from suspension knuckle.
7. Remove stabilizer bar link from lower control arm.
8. Mark position of control arm to crossmember cam bolts, washers and nuts, then remove.
9. Remove jack stand and control arm.
10. Reverse procedure to install, noting the following:
   a. Use hex-head wrench to hold ball joint stud in place when installing stud nut, as required.
   b. **Torque** stud nut to 15 ft. lbs., to seat stud.
   c. Turn nut an additional 3½ flats.
   d. Inspect stud nut for minimum final **torque** of 41 ft. lbs.

Upper

1. Raise and support vehicle, then remove tire and wheel.
2. Disconnect electronic suspension control sensor link.
3. Support lower control arm using suitable jack stand.
4. **On models equipped with Real Time Damping (RTD) suspension,** disconnect RTD position sensor link at upper control arm.
5. **On all models,** loosen upper ball joint stud nut, but do not remove it.
6. Separate upper ball joint stud from upper control arm using separator tool No. J 42188, or equivalent.
7. Remove separator tool and stud nut.
8. Remove mounting bolts and upper control arm.
9. Reverse procedure to install, noting the following:
   a. Use hex-head wrench to hold ball joint stud in place when installing stud nut, as required.
   b. **Torque** stud nut to 15 ft. lbs., to seat stud.
   c. Tighten nut an additional 250° and inspect stud nut for minimum final **torque** of 41 ft. lbs.

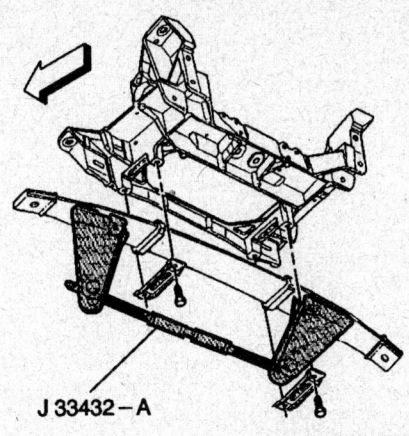

Fig. 2 Transverse leaf spring compressor

TIE ROD
REPLACE

1. Raise and support vehicle, then remove tire and wheel.
2. Loosen outer tie rod end stud nut, but do not remove it.
3. Separate tie rod end from suspension knuckle using ball joint separator tool No. J 42188, or equivalent.
4. Remove rear suspension adjustment link to crossmember mounting nut.
5. Remove rear suspension adjustment link.
6. Reverse procedure to install. Tighten outer tie rod end stud nut as follows:
   a. **Torque** to 15 ft. lbs.
   b. Tighten an additional 160°.
   c. **Torque** to 33 ft. lbs.

STABILIZER SHAFT
REPLACE

1. Raise and support vehicle, then remove tires and wheels.
2. Remove stabilizer bar link mounting nuts from lower control arms.
3. Remove stabilizer bar to crossmember bracket mounting bolts and bracket.
4. Remove stabilizer bar.
5. Remove stabilizer bar link mounting nuts and shaft links.
6. Reverse procedure to install.

TIGHTENING SPECIFICATIONS

Year	Component	Torque/Ft. Lbs.
2001–05	Clutch Actuator Cylinder	106①
	Driveline Support To Engine Flywheel Housing	37
	Driveline Tunnel Closeout Panel	80①
	EBTCM Lefthand Mounting Bracket	37
	Flexplate To Propeller Shaft Rear Bearing	37
	Input Shaft To Front Propeller Shaft Coupler	41
	Lower Control Arm Ball Joint	②
	Lower Control Arm Cam, Front	107
	Lower Control Arm Cam, Rear	70
	Outer Tie Rod	④
	Outer Tie Rod End Jam	44
	Propeller Input Shaft Front Bearing	26
	Propeller Shaft Hub Clamp	96
	Rear Bearing To Driveline Support Tube	48
	Rear Bearing To Rear Propeller Shaft Coupler	52
	Rear Crossmember	81③
	Rear Drive Axle Spindle	118
	Rear Exhaust Hanger	37
	Rear Shock Absorber, Lower	162
	Rear Shock Absorber, Upper	22
	Rear Spring Anchor Plate	46
	Shift Control	22
	Shift Control Closeout Boot	106①
	Stabilizer Bar Insulator, Lower	70
	Stabilizer Bar Insulator, Upper	49
	Stabilizer Bar Link	53
	Tie Rod	50
	Upper Control Arm	81
	Upper Control Arm Ball Joint	②
	Wheel Hub	96

① — Inch lbs.
② — Refer to "Control Arm, Replace" for tightening specifications and procedure.
③ — Always install new nuts and tighten them using hand tools only.
④ — Refer to "Tie Rod, Replace" for tightening specifications and procedures.

Front Suspension & Steering

NOTE: On Air Bag Equipped Models, Refer To "Air Bag System Precautions" Located In The Front Of This Manual For System Disarming & Arming Procedures.

NOTE: Refer To "Computer Relearn Procedures" Located In The Front Of This Manual When Battery Power To The Computer Has Been Interrupted.

INDEX

HUB & BEARING
REPLACE

1. Raise and support vehicle, then remove tire and wheel.
2. Remove brake caliper and rotor.
3. Remove stabilizer shaft link from lower control arm.
4. Disconnect wheel speed sensor electrical connector.
5. Support lower control arm using suitable jack stand.
6. Disconnect steering linkage outer tie rod from steering knuckle using separator tool No. J 42188, or equivalent.
7. Loosen upper and lower ball joint stud nuts.
8. Separate steering knuckle from upper and lower control arm using ball joint separator tool No. J 42188, or equivalent.
9. Remove upper and lower ball joint stud nuts.
10. Remove steering knuckle from upper and lower control arms.
11. Remove wheel hub mounting bolts.
12. Remove hub and bearing from steering knuckle.
13. Reverse procedure to install, noting the following:
    a. **Front and rear hub and bearing are not interchangeable. Ensure proper replacement component is being installed.**
    b. Tighten mounting bolts, nuts and screws.

BALL JOINT INSPECTION

1. Raise and support front of vehicle, then position jack stands under lower control arms.
2. Shake tire and wheel assembly while inspecting for stud end movement at knuckle bosses.
3. Shake tire and wheel assembly while

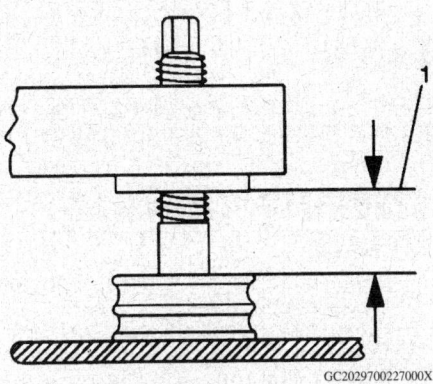

GC2029700227000X

Fig. 1   Transverse spring adjuster gap

inspecting for loose prevailing torque nuts at knuckle bosses.
4. Visually inspect for damaged or worn ball studs and knuckles.
5. Replace ball joint if looseness is indicated.

BALL JOINT
REPLACE

Upper

1. Remove steering knuckle as outlined in "Steering Knuckle, Replace."
2. Remove ball joint from knuckle using ball joint remover kit tool Nos. J 9519-E and J 21474-5, or equivalents.
3. Install new ball joint into knuckle using ball joint removal tool kit No. J 9519-E and installer tool No. J 28685, or equivalents.
4. **Torque** ball stud nut to 15 ft. lbs., tighten an additional 250° and inspect nut for final **torque** of 41 ft. lbs.
5. Install knuckle onto vehicle.

Lower

1. Remove lower control arm as outlined in "Transverse Leaf Spring, Replace."
2. Remove ball joint from control arm using ball joint tool Nos. J 9519-98 and J 9519-E, or equivalents.
3. Install new ball joint into control arm using ball joint tool Nos. J 9519-99 and J 9519-E, or equivalents.
4. **Torque** ball stud nut to 15 ft. lbs., tighten an additional 210° and inspect nut for final **torque** of 52 ft. lbs.
5. Install lower control arm onto vehicle.

SHOCK ABSORBER
REPLACE

Removal

1. Raise and support vehicle, then remove tire and wheel.
2. Remove shock absorber upper mounting nut, insulator retainer and insulator.
3. Remove shock absorber lower mounting nuts.
4. **On models equipped with heavy duty shock option (FE3),** proceed as follows:
    a. Compress shock absorber from bottom upward using suitable pry bar.
    b. Install shock support tool No. J 43822, or equivalent, onto shock to keep it compressed.
5. **On all models,** remove shock absorber from lower control arm and shock tower.
6. Remove shock support tool.
7. Remove insulator and retainer.

Installation

1. **On models less heavy duty shock option (FE3),** proceed as follows:

a. Install retainer and insulator to new shock absorber.
b. Install absorber to upper tower.
c. Install upper insulator, retainer and nut.
d. Install absorber lower mounting bolts and nuts.

2. **On models equipped with heavy duty shock option (FE3),** proceed as follows:
   a. Install shock support tool No. J 43822, or equivalent, onto new shock absorber.
   b. Install absorber onto vehicle.
   c. Install upper insulator, retainer and nut.
   d. Remove shock support tool.
   e. Compress transverse spring using spring compressor tool No. J 33432-A, or equivalent.
   f. Raise lower control arm, then install absorber lower mounting bolts and nuts.
   g. Tighten mounting bolts and nuts.
   h. Remove spring compressor tool.

3. **On all models,** install tire and wheel, then lower vehicle.

TRANSVERSE LEAF SPRING
REPLACE

1. Raise and support vehicle, then remove tires and wheels.
2. Measure and record front spring adjuster bolt gap, **Fig. 1.**
3. Install transverse spring compressor tool No. J 33432-A and adapters, or equivalents.
4. Compress transverse spring.
5. Remove lower shock absorber mounting bolts from one lower control arm.
6. Disconnect stabilizer bar link from lower control arm.
7. Loosen lower ball joint nut on control arm, but do not remove it.
8. Separate lower ball joint from steering knuckle using ball joint separator tool No. J 42188, or equivalent.
9. Remove separator tool, ball joint nut and ball joint from steering knuckle. Discard ball joint stud nut.
10. Support lower control arms using suitable jack stands.
11. Mark position of cam bolts for reference.
12. Remove cam bolts from lower control arm.
13. Remove lower control arm.
14. Remove transverse spring retainers.
15. Remove and discard transverse spring bolts.
16. Remove transverse leaf spring.
17. Remove compressor tool.
18. Reverse procedure to install, noting the following:
    a. Install spring adjuster bolts to height measured.
    b. Install cam bolts to position marked.

c. Align front wheels.

CONTROL ARM
REPLACE

Upper

1. Raise and support vehicle, then remove tire and wheel.
2. Support lower control arm using suitable jack stand.
3. **On models equipped with Real Time Damping (RTD) suspension,** disconnect RTD sensor link.
4. **On all models,** loosen ball joint stud nut, but do not remove it.
5. Separate upper ball joint stud from upper control arm using ball joint separator tool No. J 42188, or equivalent.
6. Remove tool, nut and ball joint.
7. Remove upper control arm mounting bolts and shims. Record number and position of shims.
8. Remove upper control arm.
9. Reverse procedure to install. **Torque** ball stud nut to 15 ft. lbs., tighten an additional 250° and inspect nut for final **torque** of 41 ft. lbs.

Lower

Refer to "Transverse Leaf Spring, Replace" for lower control arm replacement procedure.

STEERING KNUCKLE
REPLACE

1. Raise and support vehicle, then remove tire and wheel.
2. Remove brake caliper and rotor.
3. Disconnect stabilizer shaft link from lower control arm.
4. Disconnect wheel speed sensor electrical connector.
5. Support lower control arm using suitable jack stand.
6. Separate outer tie rod ball stud from steering knuckle using ball joint separator tool No. J 42188, or equivalent.
7. Separate upper ball joint stud from upper control arm using separator tool.
8. Separate lower ball joint stud from steering knuckle using separator tool.
9. Remove steering knuckle.
10. Reverse procedure to install.

STABILIZER BAR
REPLACE

1. Raise and support vehicle, then remove tire and wheel.
2. Remove stabilizer bar link nuts and link from stabilizer bar and lower control arm.
3. Remove stabilizer bar insulator clamps from front crossmember.
4. Remove stabilizer bar.
5. Reverse procedure to install.

POWER STEERING GEAR
REPLACE
2001-04

Refer to "Engine Mount, Replace" in "5.7L Engine" section for power steering gear replacement procedure.

2005

1. Raise and support vehicle, then remove tire and wheel.
2. Disconnect tie rod ends from steering knuckles.
3. Turn steering wheel far to lefthand side to gain access, then remove upper coupling bolt.
4. Insert tool No. J 42640 or equivalent into steering column access hole to maintain orientation.
5. Remove lower coupling shield, then the lower coupling retaining bolt.
6. Remove stabilizer shaft as outlined under "Stabilizer Bar, Replace."
7. Remove power steering pressure and return hoses from power steering gear.
8. Remove power steering line holddowns from crossmember, then the brake pressure modulator valve bracket.
9. Remove two front crossmember mounting nuts, then using hand tools loosen two rear crossmember mounting nuts .394 inch.
10. Disconnect height sensor arm to control arm then support front of crossmember.
11. Compress coil spring tool allow crossmember lower enough to remove gear using tool No. J 33432-A or equivalent.
12. Remove lower shock mounting bolts, then the brake pipe bracket for lefthand side front brake caliper from crossmember.
13. Remove plastic brake pipe hold down for righthand side front brake pipe.
14. Remove power steering gear mounting bolts and nuts.
15. Move steering gear around brake lines, then remove from vehicle through lefthand side wheelhouse opening.
16. Reverse procedure to install.

POWER STEERING PUMP
REPLACE

1. Remove EBTCM/BPMV and bracket. Position brake pipes aside as required. Cap and plug open lines.
2. Drain power steering fluid into suitable container.
3. Remove power steering fluid reservoir.
4. Remove accessory drive belt.
5. Remove power steering pump pulley

using pulley removal tool No. J 25034-B, or equivalent.

6. Disconnect power steering gear inlet hose.

7. Remove power steering pump mounting bolts.

8. Remove power steering pump and bracket.

9. Reverse procedure to install.

TIGHTENING SPECIFICATIONS

Year	Component	Torque/Ft. Lbs.
2000–05	Crossmember	81①
	Lower Control Arm	125
	Lower Control Arm Ball Stud	②
	Power Steering Pump	18
	Power Steering Reservoir Bracket	37
	Power Steering Line End Fittings	20
	Shock Absorber, Lower	21
	Shock Absorber, Upper	19
	Steering Link Outer Tie Rod End Stud	③
	Stabilizer Bar Insulator Clamp	43
	Stabilizer Bar Link	53
	Transverse Leaf Spring	46①
	Upper Control Arm	48
	Upper Control Arm Ball Stud	②
	Wheel Hub Bearing	96

① — Always install new bolts and nuts. Do not use old bolts and nuts.

② — Refer "Ball Joint, Replace" for tightening specifications and procedure.

③ — **Torque** outer tie rod end nut to 15 ft. lbs., to seat outer tie rod stud. Turn the nut an additional 160°. Inspect outer tie rod end nut for a minimum **torque** of 33 ft. lbs.

Wheel Alignment

INDEX

Prior to inspecting or adjusting front suspension alignment, inspect suspension components and wheel bearings for damage or excessive wear and replace as required. Ensure tire pressure is properly adjusted, then raise and release front bumper several times to allow vehicle to assume normal ride height. The following items should be inspected prior to performing wheel alignment procedures:

1. Inspect tires for proper inflation pressure.
2. Inspect hubs and bearings for excessive wear.
3. Inspect ball joints and tie rod ends for looseness and wear.
4. Inspect for bent wheel rims, wheel runout and faulty tires (belt shifts).
5. Inspect suspension and steering components for looseness and wear.
6. Inspect for excessive cargo loads.
7. Measure vehicle trim height.

FRONT WHEEL ALIGNMENT

Caster

1. Loosen lower control arm cam bolt nuts.
2. Rotate cam bolts to caster specification setting.
3. Maintain caster setting while **torquing** cam bolt nuts to 125 ft. lbs.
4. Inspect caster and camber settings after tightening. Adjust as required.

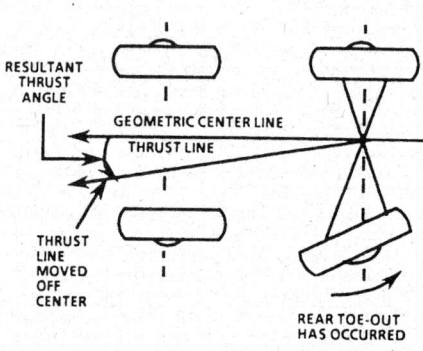

Fig. 1   Vehicle thrust angle

Camber

1. Loosen lower control arm cam bolt nuts.
2. Rotate cam bolts to required camber specification setting.
3. Maintain camber setting while **torquing** cam bolt nuts to 125 ft. lbs.
4. Inspect caster and camber settings after tightening. Adjust as required.
5. To obtain additional negative camber beyond cam adjustment capability, remove shims from upper control arms.

Toe-In

1. Loosen jam nut on tie rod.
2. Rotate inner tie rod to toe specification setting.
3. **Torque** jam nut on tie rod end to 50 ft. lbs.

4. Inspect toe setting after tightening. Adjust as required.

REAR WHEEL ALIGNMENT

Camber

1. Loosen lower control arm cam bolt nuts.
2. Rotate cam bolts to required camber specification setting.
3. Maintain camber setting while **torquing** front cam bolt nut to 107 ft. lbs., and rear cam bolt nut to 70 ft. lbs.
4. Inspect caster and camber settings after tightening. Adjust as required.

Toe-In

1. Loosen rear suspension adjustment link locknut.
2. Rotate inner tie rod to toe specification setting.
3. **Torque** rear suspension adjustment link lock nut to 44 ft. lbs.
4. Inspect toe setting after tightening. Adjust as required.

THRUST ANGLE

The vehicle is steered by the front wheels. The path the rear wheels follow is the thrust angle, **Fig. 1**. Thrust angle should be aligned with the vehicle centerline.

CTS

INDEX OF SERVICE OPERATIONS

Specifications

GENERAL ENGINE SPECIFICATIONS

Year	Engine		Fuel Injection System	Bore & Stroke	Compression Ratio	Net H.P. @ RPM	Maximum Torque Ft. Lbs. @ RPM	Normal Oil Pressure Pounds
	Liter	VIN Code①						
2003	3.2L	N	SMFI	3.45 x 3.47	10.0:1	220 @ 6000	220 @ 3400	21.7
2004	3.2L	N	SMFI	3.45 x 3.47	10.0:1	220 @ 6000	220 @ 3400	21.7
	3.6L	7	SMFI	3.70 x 3.37	10.2:1	255 @ 6500	252 @ 2800	②
	5.7L	S	SMFI	3.90 x 3.62	10.5:1	400 @ 6000	395 @ 4800	②
2005	3.6L	7	SMFI	3.70 x 3.37	10.2:1	255 @ 6500	252 @ 2800	②
	5.7L	S	SMFI	3.90 x 3.62	10.5:1	400 @ 6000	395 @ 4800	②

① — The eight digit denotes engine code.

② — Engine hot, minimum oil pressure 6 psi @ 1000 RPM; 18 psi @ 2000 RPM; 24 psi @ 4000 RPM.

TUNE UP SPECIFICATIONS

Year & Engine, VIN①	Spark Plug Gap	Ignition Timing			Curb Idle Speed	Fast Idle Speed	Fuel Pump Pressure, psi	Valve Lash
		Firing Order Fig.	Degrees BTDC	Mark Fig.				
2003								
3.2L/N	.053	②	③	—	③	③	49–55	④
2004								
3.2L/N	.053	②	③	—	③	③	49–55	④
3.6L/7	.043	②	③	—	③	③	55–60	④
5.7L/S	.040	1-8-7-2-6-5-4-3	③	—	③	③	55–62	④
2005								
3.6L/7	.043	②	③	—	③	③	55–60	④
5.7L/S	.040	1-8-7-2-6-5-4-3	③	—	③	③	55–62	④

① — The eight digit denotes engine code.

② — Cylinder numbering from front to rear; righthand bank, 1, 3, 5; lefthand bank, 2, 4, 6. Firing order, 1-2-3-4-5-6.

③ — Computer controlled, not adjustable.

④ — Equipped w/hydraulic lash adjusters.

FRONT WHEEL ALIGNMENT SPECIFICATIONS

Year	Caster Angle, Degrees		Camber Angle, Degrees		Total Toe, Degrees		Ball Joint Inspection
	Limits	Desired	Limits	Desired	Limits	Desired	
2003–04	+4.6 to +5.6②	+5.1②	–1 to 0②	–.5②	0 to +.4	+.2	①
2005	+4.5 to +5.7③	+5.1③	–1.1 to +1③	–.5③	0 to +.4	+.2	①

① — Refer to Front Suspension & Steering section for ball joint inspection procedure.

② — Cross caster or camber (LH-RH) 0 (+/-.5°).

③ — Cross caster or camber (LH-RH) 0 (+/-.6°).

REAR WHEEL ALIGNMENT SPECIFICATIONS

Year	Model	Camber Angle, Degrees		Total Toe, Degrees		Thrust Angle, Degrees	
		Limits	Desired	Limits	Desired	Limits	Desired
2003–04	①	–1.4 to –.6③	–1.0③	+.08 to +.40	+.24	–.15 to +.15	0
	②	–1.8 to –1.0③	–1.4③	+.08 to +.40	+.24	–.15 to +.15	0
2005	①	–1.5 to –.5	–.5	0 to +.40	+.20	–.20 to +.20	0
	④	–1.5 to –.5	–.5	0 to +.40	+.20	–.20 to +.20	0

① — Soft ride suspension FE1.
② — Sport suspension FE3.

③ — Cross camber (LH-RH) 0 (+/-.75°).

④ — Optional suspensions FE2, FE3 & FE4.

VEHICLE RIDE HEIGHT SPECIFICATIONS

Model	Year	Body Style	Manufacturer's Original Tire Size	Measurement Points & Specifications					
				Front			Rear		
				Dim.	Specification		Dim.	Specification	
					Inches	mm		Inches	mm
All	2003–05	All	①	Z②	1.7–2.5	43.6–63.6	D③	2.0–2.7	49.7–69.7
FE2	2005	All	①	②	1.7–2.5	43.6–63.6	③	2.4	59.7
FE3	2005	All	①	②	1.7–2.5	43.6–63.6	③	2.3	59.5
FE4	2005	All	①	②	1.7–2.5	33.2–53.2	③	1.9	48.7

① — See door sticker or inside of glove compartment for manufacturers original tire size specifications. If tires on vehicle do not match original tire size and measurement is not within limits, it will be required you refer to the Non-Standard Tire & Wheel Size Adjustment To Ride Height Specification & Tire Size Adjustment Charts.

② — Refer to **Fig. 1,** for measurement location.

③ — Refer to **Fig. 2,** for measurement location.

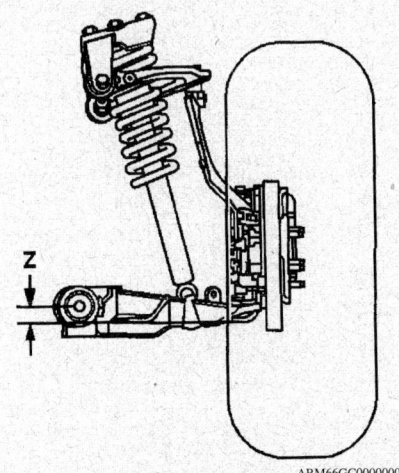

ARM66GC000000013

Fig. 1   Front suspension measurement

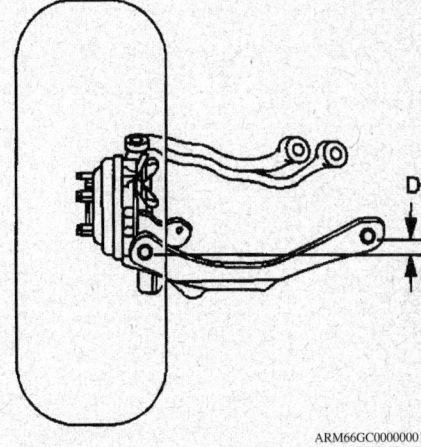

ARM66GC000000014

Fig. 2   Rear suspension measurement

CTS

FLUID CAPACITIES & COOLING SYSTEM DATA

Year	Engine/Liter	Coolant Capacity, Qts.	Coolant Type	Radiator Cap Relief Pressure, Lbs.	Thermo-stat Opening Temp., F°	Fuel Tank Gals	Engine Oil Refill, Qts.	Transmission Oil		Rear Axle Oil, Pts.
								Manual, Pts.	Auto-matic, Qts.	
2003	3.2L	10.4	Dex-Cool	—	194	17.5	5.0	2.6	9.0	2.74
2004	3.2L	10.4	Dex-Cool	—	194	17.5	5.0	2.6	9.0	2.74
	3.6L	10.4	Dex-Cool	—	194	17.5	6.0	2.6	9.0	2.74
	5.7L	13.2	Dex-Cool	—	194	17.5	6.0	①	9.0	2.74
2005	3.6L	10.4	Dex-Cool	—	194	17.5	6.0	2.6	9.0	2.74
	5.7L	13.2	Dex-Cool	—	194	17.5	6.0	①	9.0	2.74

① — CTS, 3.8 pts. CTS-V, 7.4 pts.

LUBRICANT DATA

Year	Model	Lubricant Type		
		Automatic Transaxle	Power Steering	Brake System
2003–05	All	Dexron III	①	DOT 3

① — Power steering fluid GM part No. 1052884, or equivalent.

Electrical

NOTE: On Air Bag Equipped Models, Refer To "Air Bag System Precautions" Located In The Front Of This Manual For System Disarming & Arming Procedures.

NOTE: Refer To "Computer Relearn Procedures" Located In The Front Of This Manual When Battery Power To The Computer Has Been Interrupted.

INDEX

PRECAUTIONS

Air Bag Systems

Refer to "Air Bag System Precautions" in the front of this manual for system disarming and arming procedures.

Battery Ground Cable

Prior to service, disconnect battery ground cable and isolate as required.

Fuel Pressure Relief

1. Turn ignition in "Off" position.
2. Disconnect battery ground cable and isolate as required.
3. Loosen fuel filler cap to relieve fuel tank vapor pressure.
4. Remove cap to fuel pressure service connection.
5. Install tool Nos. J34730-1A and J42242, or equivalents, to fuel pressure service connection.
6. Place bleed hose into suitable container, then open bleed valve to relieve fuel system.
7. Place a suitable shop towel under connections to protect fuel spillage.
8. Remove tool Nos. J34730-1A and J42242, or equivalents, from service connections.
9. Install cap to fuel pressure service connection.

FUSE PANEL & FLASHER LOCATION

The lethand side rear passenger compartment fuse block is located under the lefthand side of the rear seat. The righthand side rear passenger compartment fuse block is located under the righthand side of the rear seat. The steering column fuse block is located behind the driver knee bolster, at the base of the steering column. The underhood fuse block is located on the righthand side front corner of the engine compartment.

The turn signal/hazard lamp control flasher module is located behind the lefthand side of the instrument panel.

FUEL PUMP RELAY LOCATION

The fuel pump relay is located in the fuse block under the righthand side of the rear seat.

RELAY CENTER LOCATION

Relays are located in the rear and underhood fuse blocks, refer to "Fuse Panel & Flasher Location."

STARTER

REPLACE

3.2L Engine

1. Raise and support vehicle using suitable lift.
2. Disconnect HO2S electrical connector at sensor.
3. Remove exhaust pipe to lefthand and righthand catalytic converter attaching nuts.
4. Lower exhaust and allow to rest on floor panel brace.
5. Remove lefthand and righthand converter seal and gasket.
6. Remove converter to hanger and then the converter to exhaust manifold attaching nuts.
7. Remove righthand catalytic converter.
8. Remove starter heat shield bolt and nut, then the starter heat shield.
9. Remove starter solenoid S terminal and disconnect lead from starter.
10. Remove starter terminal nut, then the battery positive from starter.
11. Remove starter mounting bolts, then the starter assembly.
12. Reverse procedure to install, noting the following:
    a. **Torque** starter motor bolts to 30 ft. lbs.
    b. **Torque** battery positive cable to 10 ft. lbs.
    c. **Torque** starter S terminal nut to 44 inch lbs.

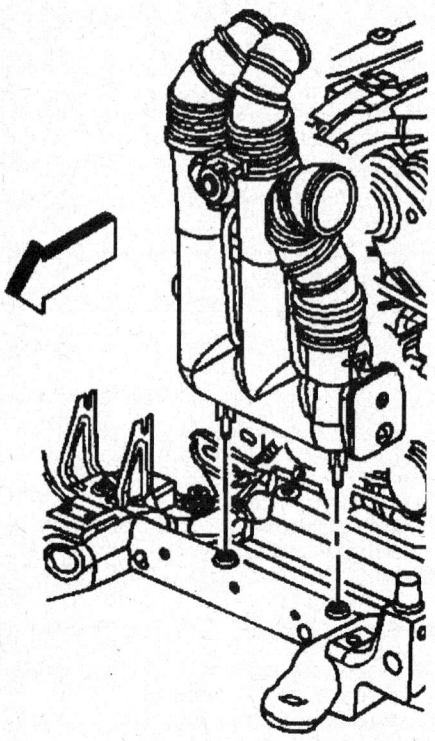

Fig. 1 Air resonator removal. 3.2L engine

d. **Torque** starter heat shield nuts to 71 inch lbs.
e. **Torque** exhaust manifold pipe nuts to 18 ft. lbs.
f. **Torque** converter hanger nuts to 18 ft. lbs.
g. **Torque** catalytic converter nuts to 11 ft. lbs.

3.6L Engine

1. Raise and support vehicle.
2. Disconnect starter solenoid electrical connector.
3. Remove starter terminal nut, then the positive battery cable from starter.
4. Remove starter motor mounting bolts, then the starter.
5. Reverse procedure to install, noting the following:
   a. **Torque** starter motor mounting bolts to 37 ft. lbs.
   b. **Torque** starter terminal nut to 115 inch lbs.

5.7L Engine

1. Raise and support vehicle.
2. Support exhaust system with suitable jack.
3. Disconnect exhaust system from lefthand and righthand catalytic converters.
4. Disconnect oxygen sensor electrical connector.
5. Remove righthand catalytic converter to exhaust manifold retaining nuts.
6. Remove catalytic converter. Discard seal.

---

7. Remove positive battery cable retaining nut.
8. Remove starter motor mounting bolts, then the starter.
9. Reverse procedure to install. **Torque** starter motor mounting bolts to 37 ft. lbs.

ALTERNATOR
REPLACE
3.2L Engine

1. Disconnect air intake duct hose from Mass Air Flow (MAF) and Intake Air Temperature (IAT) sensor.
2. Remove intake air resonator to cooling fan attaching bolts.
3. Disconnect air intake duct hoses from throttle body then lift intake air resonator from frame, **Fig. 1.**
4. Rotate drivebelt tensioner clockwise to release tension.
5. Slide drive belt from water pump pulley, allowing tensioner to return and then remove drive belt from accessory pulleys.
6. Loosen drive belt tensioner bolts, then remove tensioner bolts and tensioner from engine.
7. Remove alternator mounting bolts.
8. Disconnect electrical connector wiring harness, then the battery positive cable.
9. Remove alternator assembly.
10. Reverse procedure to install, noting the following:
    a. **Torque** battery terminal nut to 111 inch lbs.
    b. **Torque** alternator mounting nuts to 26 ft. lbs.
    c. Route drive belt as outlined in "Serpentine Drive Belt" in "3.2L Engine" section.
    d. **Torque** drive belt tension bolts to 26 ft. lbs.

3.6L Engine

1. Remove drive belt as outlined in "Serpentine Drive Belt" in "3.6L Engine" section.
2. Install suitable engine support tool.
3. Raise and support vehicle.
4. Disconnect alternator electrical connector.
5. Position alternator output BAT terminal boot aside, then remove terminal nut and disconnect battery positive lead from alternator.
6. Disconnect electronic brake control module electrical connector.
7. Remove engine mount lower retaining nuts.
8. Remove lower alternator mounting bolts.
9. Lower vehicle.
10. Raise engine using suitable engine support tool.
11. Remove upper alternator mounting bolts, then the alternator.
12. Reverse procedure to install, noting the following:

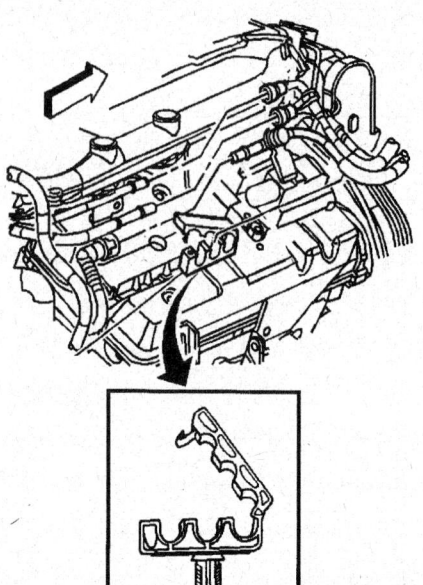

ARM66GC000000018

Fig. 2 Quick connect fitting removal (lefthand). 3.2L engine

a. **Torque** alternator mounting bolts to 37 ft. lbs.
b. **Torque** "BAT" terminal nut to 89 inch lbs.

5.7L Engine

1. Remove air cleaner assembly.
2. Drain coolant into suitable container.
3. Disconnect surge tank hose.
4. Remove fan shroud to radiator mounting bolts.
5. Disconnect upper radiator hose at radiator.
6. Remove A/C line retaining clip retaining screw.
7. Disconnect fan motor electrical connector.
8. Pull upward to remove fan assembly.
9. Remove accessory drive belt.
10. Remove alternator mounting bolts.
11. Remove alternator from mounting bracket.
12. Disconnect alternator electrical connectors.
13. Reverse procedure to install. **Torque** alternator mounting bolts to 37 ft. lbs.

COIL PACK
REPLACE
3.2L Engine
LEFTHAND

1. Relieve fuel pressure as outlined in "Precautions."
2. Disconnect return hose/pipe and feed hose/pipe quick connect fittings from fuel rail, **Fig. 2.**
3. Disconnect EVAP quick connect fitting, then open retainer at engine control module (ECM) bracket to remove chassis hose/pipes, **Fig. 3.**

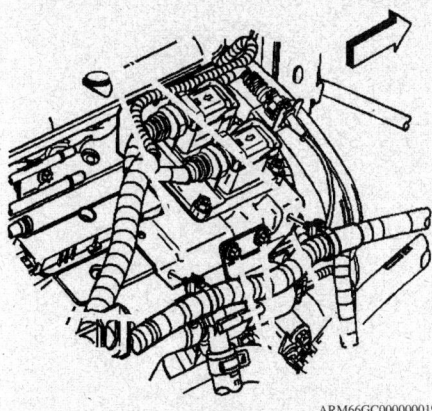

ARM66GC000000019

Fig. 3 EVAP & retainer connect fitting removal (lefthand). 3.2L engine

4. Disconnect electrical wiring harness at ECM bracket.
5. Remove coolant pump attaching bolts to ECM bracket.
6. Remove ECM ground wire at ECM, **Fig. 4.**
7. Disconnect ECM connectors from ECM.
8. Remove coolant inlet pipe to ECM bracket attaching bolt.
9. Remove ECM bracket bolts from intake plenum and cylinder head.
10. Remove ECM bracket from engine with ECM attached.
11. Disconnect electrical connectors from righthand knock sensor.
12. Disconnect electrical connectors from coil pack.
13. Remove coil pack attaching bolts, then install tool No. J43301, or equivalent, into coil pack and pull coil pack evenly from camshaft cover, **Fig. 5.**
14. Reverse procedure to install, noting the following:
    a. **Torque** coil pack bolts to 71 inch lbs.
    b. **Torque** ECM bracket to cylinder head bolt to 15 ft. lbs.
    c. **Torque** ECM bracket to intake plenum bolts to 71 ft. lbs.
    d. **Torque** coolant pipe support bolt to 15 ft. lbs.
    e. **Torque** ECM screw to 40 inch lbs.
    f. **Torque** coolant pump to ECM bracket to 89 inch lbs.

RIGHTHAND

1. Remove oil filler spout.
2. Disconnect vacuum brake booster hose and wiring harness from remote power steering fluid reservoir.
3. Disconnect vacuum brake booster hose from vacuum.
4. Remove remote power steering fluid reservoir mounting bolts Nos. 1 and 3, **Fig. 6.**
5. Disconnect coil pack electrical connector.
6. Remove coil pack attaching bolts, install tool No. J43301, or equivalent, into coil pack and remove coil pack pulling evenly off from camshaft cover, **Fig. 5.**

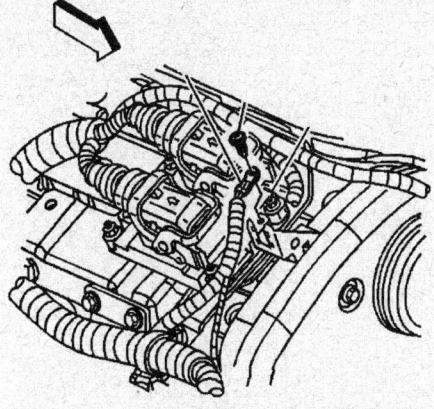

ARM66GC000000020

Fig. 4 ECM wire removal (lefthand). 3.2L engine

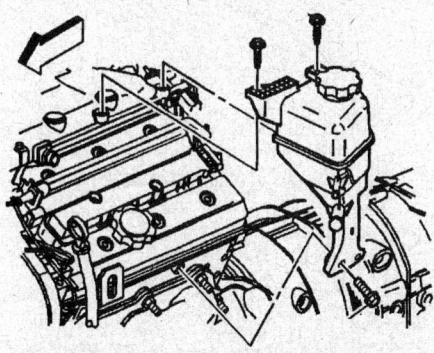

ARM66GC000000027

Fig. 6 Power steering reservoir mounting bolt Nos. 1 & 3 (righthand). 3.2L engine

7. Reverse procedure to install, noting the following:
   a. **Torque** coil pack bolts to 71 inch lbs.
   b. **Torque** intake plenum mounting bolts to 80 inch lbs.
   c. **Torque** cylinder head mounting bolts to 18 ft. lbs.

3.6L Engine

1. Remove engine cover.
2. Disconnect air cleaner duct from throttle body.
3. **On cylinders 1, 2 and 3,** reposition intake manifold as follows:
   a. Disconnect PCV hose from camshaft cover.
   b. Remove intake manifold attaching bolts.
   c. Remove intake manifold brace bolts, then the brace.
   d. Reposition upper and lower intake manifolds to gain access to ignition coils.
4. **On all cylinders,** disconnect ignition coil electrical connector.
5. Remove ignition coil retaining bolts, then the coil.
6. Reverse procedure to install.

5.7L Engine

1. Remove fuel injector sight shield.

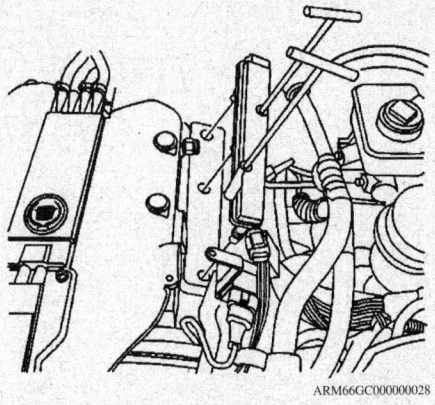

ARM66GC000000028

Fig. 5 Coil pack removal. 3.2L engine

2. Disconnect coil assembly electrical connector.
3. Disconnect spark plug wire at ignition coils.
4. Remove ignition coil bracket mounting bolts.
5. Remove ignition coil assembly.
6. Reverse procedure to install. Torque ignition coil bracket mounting bolts to 106 inch lbs.

IGNITION LOCK
REPLACE

1. Ensure ignition switch is in the START position.
2. Press in release button using suitable awl tool.
3. Place ignition switch in the run position, then remove ignition lock cylinder.
4. Reverse procedure to install.

IGNITION SWITCH
REPLACE

1. Remove upper and lower steering column trim covers.
2. Remove ignition lock cylinder as outlined in "Ignition Lock, Replace."
3. Disconnect electrical connector from theft deterrent control module.
4. Remove theft deterrent control module.
5. Rotate key alarm 90°, then remove key alarm connector from ignition lock cylinder, **Fig. 7.**
6. Disconnect electrical connector from ignition switch.
7. Remove wires located within ignition switch clip.
8. Remove ignition switch assembly, **Fig. 8.**
9. Reverse procedure to install.

CLUTCH START SWITCH
REPLACE

1. Remove driver's side lower instrument panel.
2. Disconnect clutch pedal position switch electrical connector.
3. Remove retaining plate from clutch pedal position switch, then the switch from cylinder push rod.
4. Reverse procedure to install.

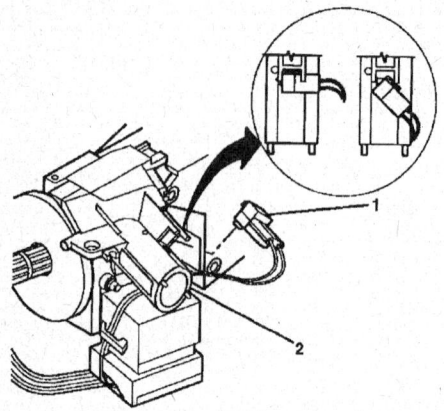

Fig. 7 Key alarm connector

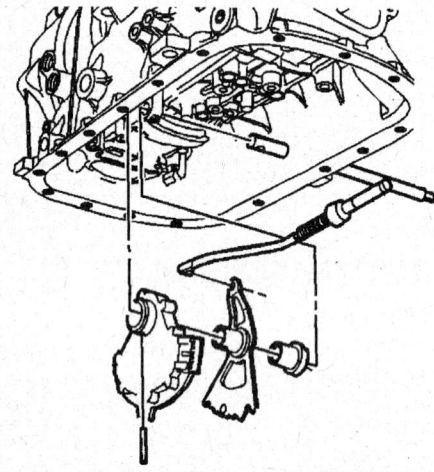

Fig. 10 Manual shift shaft
assembly

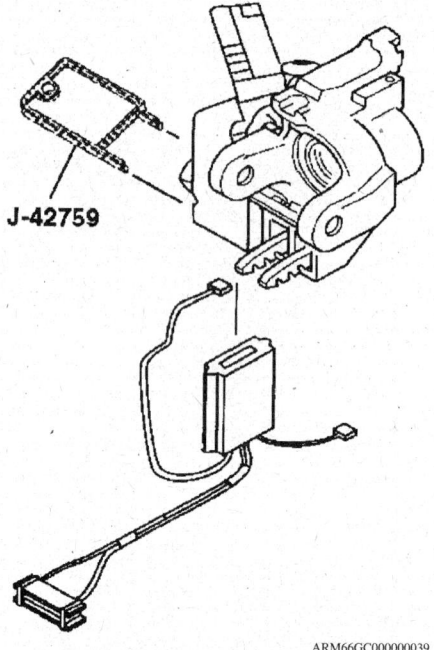

J-42759

Fig. 8 Ignition switch

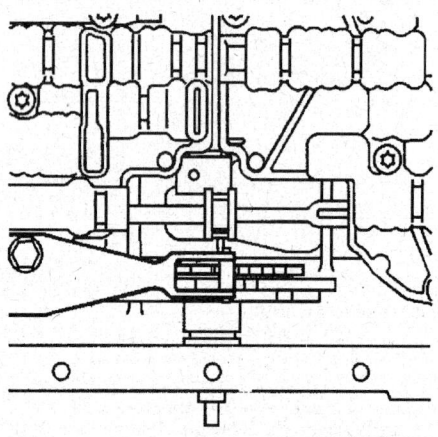

Fig. 11 Spacer installation

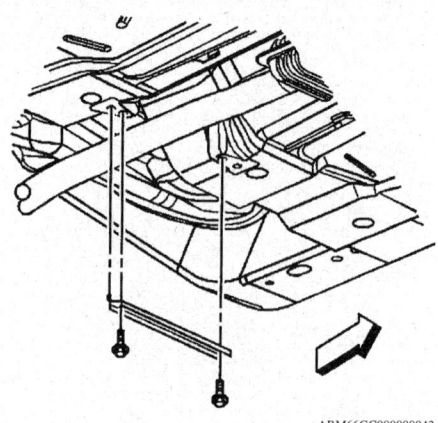

Fig. 9 Floor panel removal

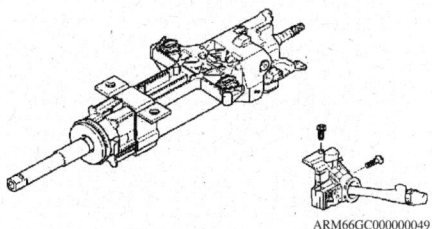

Fig. 12 Multi-function switch
assembly

NEUTRAL SAFETY SWITCH

REPLACE

1. Raise and support vehicle.
2. Remove transmission manual shift shaft attaching nut.
3. Disconnect transmission manual shift shaft shift linkage.
4. Remove floor panel tunnel brace to floor panel attaching bolts, then the tunnel brace from floor panel, **Fig. 9.**
5. Remove exhaust pipe to catalytic converter nuts.
6. Disconnect propeller shaft coupler from transmission flange.
7. Push front propeller shaft toward rear of vehicle to release coupler from transmission flange.
8. Secure front propeller shaft to shift control lever using suitable wire.
9. Remove and discard shaft seal and cup plug using suitable screwdriver.
10. Remove transmission oil pan and filter as outlined in **MOTOR's "Domestic Transmission, In-Vehicle Service"** manual.
11. Disconnect electrical connector from manual shift shaft position switch.
12. Remove manual shift shaft position

switch retaining pin.
13. Remove manual shaft spring and bolts.
14. Support transmission using a suitable transmission jack.
15. Lower transmission jack to access manual shift shaft.
16. Remove manual shaft shaft position assembly from transmission, **Fig. 10.**
17. Reverse procedure to install, noting the following:
    a. Install a 0.8 mm spacer between lever and spring, **Fig. 11.**
    b. **Torque** detent spring bolts to 97 inch lbs.
    c. **Torque** manual shift shaft nut to 11 ft. lbs.
    d. **Torque** catalytic converter nuts to 11 ft. lbs.
    e. **Torque** floor panel tunnel brace bolts to 18 ft. lbs.
    f. **Torque** propeller shaft bolts to 63 ft. lbs.
    g. **Torque** support bearing nuts to 37 ft. lbs.

HEADLAMP SWITCH

REPLACE

Refer to "Multi-Function Switch, Replace" for headlamp switch replacement procedure.

MULTI-FUNCTION SWITCH

REPLACE

1. Remove upper and lower steering column trim covers.
2. Place tilt column in CENTER position.
3. Disconnect multi-function switch assembly electrical connectors, then remove assembly mounting screws, **Fig. 12.**
4. Remove multi-function switch assembly.
5. Reverse procedure to install, noting the following:
    a. **Torque** multi-function switch top of column screw to 27 inch lbs.
    b. **Torque** multi-function switch front face screw to 62 inch lbs.

TURN SIGNAL SWITCH

REPLACE

Refer to "Multi-Function Switch, Replace" for turn signal switch replacement procedure.

STEERING WHEEL

REPLACE

1. Remove driver's air bag module from steering wheel as outlined in "Passive Restraint Systems" chapter.

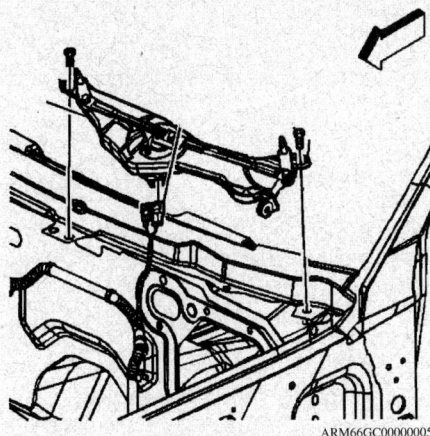

Fig. 13 Wiper motor module

2. Disconnect steering column electrical connector.
3. Remove steering wheel retaining nut.
4. Remove steering wheel using steering wheel puller tool Nos. J42578 and J1859A, or equivalent.
5. Reverse procedure to install. **Torque** steering wheel nut to 30 ft. lbs.

INSTRUMENT CLUSTER
REPLACE

1. Tilt steering wheel to lowest position.
2. Remove instrument panel cluster trim panel using suitable flat bladed tool.
3. Remove instrument panel to cluster attaching screws.
4. Install suitable flat bladed tool between cluster and instrument panel, release cluster retainers, then remove cluster and disconnect electrical connectors.
5. Reverse procedure to install. **Torque** screws to 18 inch lbs.

RADIO
REPLACE

1. Remove center instrument panel air vents.
2. Remove screw behind ashtray.
3. Remove HVAC control module trim plate.
4. Disconnect HVAC control module and ash tray electrical connectors.
5. Remove HVAC control module.
6. Remove radio to instrument panel attaching screws.
7. Disconnect electrical connectors, then remove radio.
8. Reverse procedure to install, noting the following:
   a. **Torque** ashtray attaching screw to 18 inch lbs.
   b. **Torque** HVAC control module screws to 18 inch lbs.
   c. **Torque** radio assembly screws to 80 inch lbs.

WIPER MOTOR
REPLACE

1. Remove wiper motor fuses from underhood fuse block.
2. Remove wiper arm assemblies.

3. Remove air inlet grille attaching screws, then the inlet grille.
4. Remove wiper motor module mounting bolts.
5. Disconnect module electrical connector, then remove module, **Fig. 13.**
6. Remove drive links from wiper motor crank arm.
7. Remove wiper motor to wiper motor module retaining screws.
8. Remove wiper motor.
9. Reverse procedure to install. **Torque** attaching bolts and screws to 89 inch lbs.

WIPER SWITCH
REPLACE

Refer to "Multi-Function Switch, Replace" for wiper switch replacement procedure.

WIPER TRANSMISSION
REPLACE

1. Remove drive links from wiper crank arm and wiper transmission shafts as outlined in "Wiper Motor, Replace."
2. Remove transmission links from module.
3. Reverse procedure to install.

BLOWER MOTOR
REPLACE

1. Remove righthand side lower instrument panel trim panel.
2. Release locking tabs, then disconnect instrument panel trim panel electrical connector.
3. Release glove compartment door tabs.
4. Lower door and remove glove compartment door attaching screws.
5. Remove instrument panel compartment screws, then the compartment.
6. Disconnect blower motor electrical connector.
7. Disconnect blower motor processor electrical connector.
8. Remove blower motor attaching screws, then the blower motor.
9. Reverse procedure to install, noting the following:
   a. **Torque** lower instrument panel and glove compartment screws to 18 inch lbs.
   b. **Torque** blower motor screws to 13 inch lbs.
   c. **Torque** air inlet housing bolts to 53 inch lbs.

CABIN AIR FILTER
REPLACE

1. Remove air inlet grille as outlined in "Wiper Motor, Replace."
2. Remove access cover by releasing tabs on either side.
3. Lift filter cover, then remove cabin air filter, **Fig. 14.**
4. Reverse procedure to install.

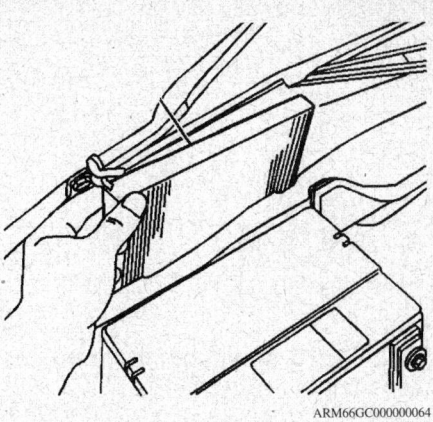

Fig. 14 Cabin air filter removal

HEATER CORE
REPLACE

1. Recover refrigerant as outlined in "Air Conditioning" chapter.
2. Remove battery, then drain engine coolant into suitable container.
3. Disconnect heater inlet and heater outlet hoses.
4. Disconnect both A/C lines at cowl panel.
5. Install probe tool No. J45689, or equivalent, into two small openings of plastic quick joint, then remove quick joint clamps, **Fig. 15.**
6. Disconnect both A/C lines.
7. Remove gearshift trim cover and disconnect electrical connector.
8. Remove console lethand side and righthand trim panels.
9. Remove six mounting screws, then the console.
10. Remove upper A/C vents.
11. Remove mounting screws and radio, then disconnect electrical connectors and antenna lead.
12. Remove glove compartment.
13. Tilt steering column to lowest position.
14. Remove cluster trim cover by prying upward using a suitable small flat bladed tool.
15. Remove cluster mounting screws.
16. Pry cluster upward at top to release retainers, then pull out and disconnect electrical connectors.
17. Pry upward on defroster grille using suitable flat bladed tool to release retainers.
18. Disconnect sunload sensor connector, then remove defroster grille.
19. Remove lefthand insulator panel mounting screws. Disconnect courtesy lamp electrical connector.
20. Remove righthand insulator panel mounting screws and pull downward to release retainers. Disconnect courtesy lamp electrical connector.
21. Remove driver side airbag module as outlined in "Passive Restraint Systems" chapter.
22. Remove steering wheel as outlined in "Steering Wheel, Replace."
23. Remove steering column tilt lever.
24. Remove lower column trim cover mounting screws, then tilt downward and slide back to release retainers.

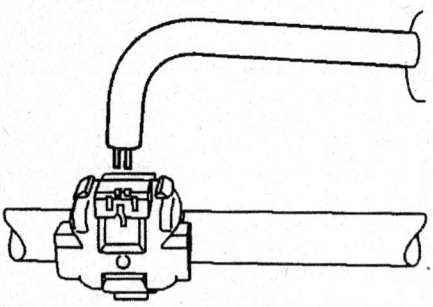

Fig. 15 Quick joint clamp removal

25. Remove upper column trim cover mounting screws, then the trim cover.
26. Remove mounting nuts, then lower steering column.
27. Remove lower retainer support bracket mounting bolts.
28. Remove mounting screws from side of instrument panel to carrier.
29. Remove mounting screws from lower center trim panel.
30. Remove instrument panel mounting screws from behind glove compartment.
31. Remove mounting screws and instrument panel.
32. Remove air inlet assemblies.

33. Disconnect HVAC module electrical connector, HVAC module drain tube at floor and release lefthand duct from HVAC module.
34. Disconnect lefthand rear heater duct from HVAC module.
35. Release tab to righthand rear duct from HVAC module.
36. Disconnect righthand rear heater ducts from HVAC module.
37. Remove lower lefthand HVAC module mounting nut.
38. Remove upper lefthand HVAC module nut.
39. Remove HVAC module from vehicle.
40. Remove heater hose bracket screw, then the heater hose bracket.
41. Remove heater core from HVAC module.
42. Reverse procedure to install, noting the following:
    a. **Torque** heater hose bracket screws to 9 inch lbs.
    b. **Torque** HVAC mounting nuts to 80 inch lbs.

EVAPORATOR CORE
REPLACE

1. Remove HVAC module as outlined in "Heater Core, Replace."
2. Remove TXV insulation, **Fig. 16**.

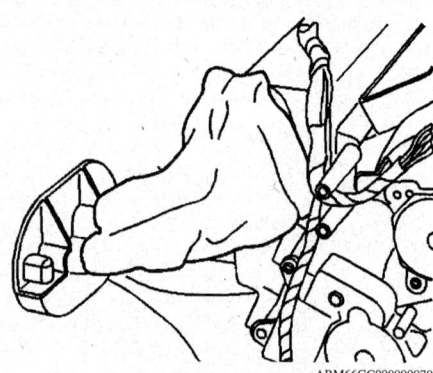

Fig. 16 TXV insulation

3. Remove HVAC line clamp screw, then the line clamp.
4. Remove TXV to evaporator bolts.
5. Remove TXV line bracket, then the TXV from evaporator core.
6. Separate lines from A/C, then remove TXV.
7. Remove case attaching screws, clips then disconnect thermistor electrical connector.
8. Separate HVAC module, then remove thermistor from evaporator core.
9. Remove evaporator core assembly.
10. Reverse procedure to install.

3.2L Engine

NOTE: On Air Bag Equipped Models, Refer To "Air Bag System Precautions" Located In The Front Of This Manual For System Disarming & Arming Procedures.

NOTE: Refer To "Computer Relearn Procedures" Located In The Front Of This Manual When Battery Power To The Computer Has Been Interrupted.

NOTE: Prior To Performing Any Service Operations Listed In This Section, Consult The "Technical Service Bulletins" Section For Related Information.

INDEX

PRECAUTIONS

Air Bag Systems

Refer to "Air Bag System Precautions" in the front of this manual for system disarming and arming procedures.

Battery Ground Cable

Prior to service, disconnect battery ground cable and isolate as required.

Fuel Pressure Relief

1. Turn ignition in "Off" position.
2. Disconnect battery ground cable and isolate as required.
3. Loosen fuel filler cap to relieve fuel tank vapor pressure.
4. Remove cap to fuel pressure service connection.
5. Install tool Nos. J34730-1A and J42242, or equivalents, to fuel pressure service connection.
6. Place bleed hose into suitable container, then open bleed valve to relieve fuel system.
7. Place a suitable shop towel under connections to protect fuel spillage.
8. Remove tool Nos. J34730-1A and J42242, or equivalents, from service connections.
9. Install cap to fuel pressure service connection.

COMPRESSION PRESSURE

The minimum compression in any one cylinder should not be less than 70 percent of the highest cylinder. No cylinder should read less than 690 kPa (100 psi).

ENGINE MOUNT
REPLACE

1. Raise and support vehicle.
2. Remove starter as outlined in "Starter, Replace" in "Electrical" section.
3. Disconnect HO2S at sensor, then remove HO2S.
4. Remove catalytic converter attaching nuts, position exhaust system rearward to allow rear of catalytic converters to clear exhaust pipe flange.
5. Rest exhaust system on floor panel tunnel brace.
6. Remove catalytic converter seal, then the catalytic converter gasket.
7. Remove catalytic converter to catalytic converter hanger bracket attaching nuts.
8. Remove catalytic converter to exhaust manifold attaching nuts, then the catalytic converter and seal.
9. Install a suitable adjustable jack with a block of wood under engine oil pan.
10. Remove upper engine mount retaining nut.
11. Remove engine mount bracket retaining bolts, then the engine mount bracket.

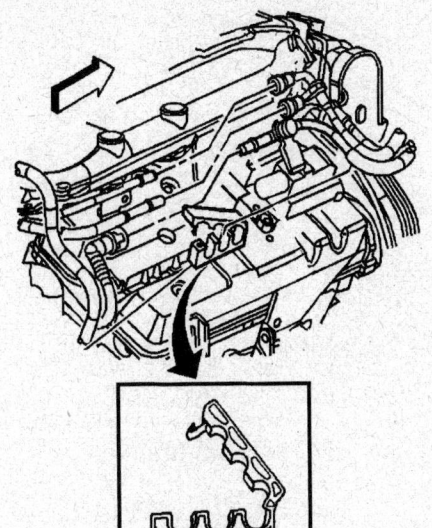

ARM66GC000000080

Fig. 1 Quick connect fitting removal

12. Remove lower engine mount retaining nut, then the engine mount.
13. Reverse procedure to install.

ENGINE
REPLACE

1. Open and support hood.
2. Mark upper hood hinge location using suitable grease pencil, remove hood.
3. Remove front clips to air inlet panel and battery tray/cowl assembly.
4. Remove front air inlet panel.
5. Remove battery ground cable to side rail attaching bolt and disconnect body electrical harness from battery ground cable.
6. Remove underhood fuse block cover.
7. Remove battery positive cable from underhood fuse block.
8. Disconnect engine wiring harness from underhood fuse block and righthand shock tower, then secure to engine.
9. Disconnect electrical connectors from transmission control module, then secure harness to engine.
10. Remove Mass Air Flow (MAF)/Intake Air Temperature (IAT) sensor.
11. Remove air cleaner assembly.
12. Remove intake air resonator to cooling fan assembly attaching bolt.
13. Disconnect air intake duct hoses from throttle body and lift intake air resonator from front frame.
14. Disconnect electrical connectors, vacuum hoses, upper radiator hose and surge tank inlet hose.
15. Remove air intake resonator assembly.
16. Disconnect coolant bypass solenoid electrical connector, then remove bolt securing engine wiring harness ground lead to righthand body rail.

17. Drain cooling system into suitable container.
18. Remove surge tank inlet hose, inlet radiator hose and outlet radiator hose using suitable hose clamp pliers.
19. Remove coolant bypass outlet hose from coolant inlet pipe using suitable hose clamp pliers.
20. Disconnect quick connect fittings to return hose and feed hose from fuel rail, plug ports to prevent fuel loss and contamination, Fig. 1.
21. Disconnect EVAP quick connect fitting, the open retainer at ECM bracket to release chassis hose.
22. Remove outlet heater hose from coolant pump using suitable clamp pliers.
23. Remove inlet hose from heater core.
24. Remove surge tank outlet hose from tank and then secure hose to engine.
25. Disconnect electrical connector from air conditioning refrigerant pressure sensor.
26. Disconnect engine wiring harness from lefthand side body rail connectors.
27. Remove power steering hose nut from air conditioning compressor stud.
28. Disconnect engine wiring harness to A/C pressure hose and secure to engine.
29. Remove drive belt as outlined in "Serpentine Drive Belt."
30. Remove power steering pump mounting bolts, then position pump aside.
31. Disconnect vacuum brake booster and wiring harness from power steering fluid reservoir.
32. Disconnect vacuum brake booster hose from vacuum source.
33. Remove power steering fluid reservoir mounting bolts, then position reservoir aside.
34. Disconnect A/C compressor electrical connector.
35. Remove A/C compressor mounting bolts and place compressor aside.
36. Raise and support vehicle.
37. Remove bolts securing floor panel tunnel brace to floor panel, then the floor panel tunnel brace from floor panel.
38. Remove nuts securing exhaust pipe to catalytic converter, and suitable support exhaust system.
39. Pry front exhaust hanger free from rear suspension hanger rod, then lower exhaust system.
40. Remove catalytic converter seal. Do not reuse seal.
41. Disconnect oxygen sensor retainers from catalytic converter hanger bracket.
42. Remove bolts securing catalytic converter hanger bracket to transmission, then the catalytic converter hanger bracket from catalytic converters.
43. Disconnect Electronic Brake Control Module (EBCM) electrical connector.
44. Disconnect Anti-Lock Brake System (ABS) electrical connectors from speed sensors.
45. Remove ABS wiring harness retainers from lower control arms, engine frame and cooling fan.
46. Remove transmission fluid cooler pipes.

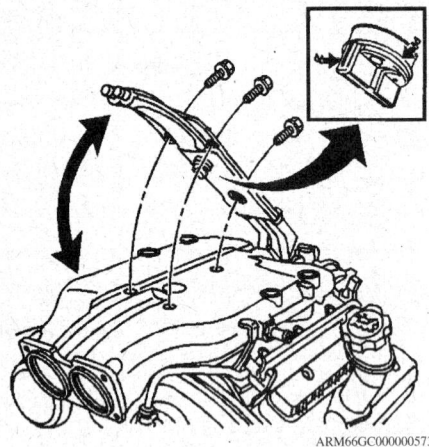

Fig. 2   Crankshaft vent bolt

47. Drain engine oil into suitable container.
48. Remove engine mount retaining nut.
49. Remove transmission shift shaft nut, then disconnect linkage from transmission.
50. Remove propeller shaft as outlined in "Neutral Safety Switch, Replace" in "Electrical" section.
51. **On models equipped with manual transmission,** remove retaining pin from transmission and disconnect shift reaction and control arm.
52. **On all models,** remove transmission inner mounting nuts, then lower vehicle using a jack to support rear of transmission.
53. Remove transmission outer support mounting nuts, then the transmission support from vehicle.
54. Install engine lift chain to lift brackets, carefully raise engine assembly using suitable lifting devise.
55. Reverse procedure to install, noting the following:
    a. With engine ignition in Off position, crank engine several times listening for unusual noises/binding components.
    b. Inspect oil pressure gauge and confirm engine has acceptable oil pressure.
    c. Idle engine at 1000 RPM until engine reaches normal operating temperature.
    d. Inspect for oil, coolant and exhaust leaks.
    e. Perform idle relearn procedure as outlined in "Computer Relearn Procedures" in the front of this manual.

INTAKE PLENUM
REPLACE

1. Remove intake plenum clamps and hoses from throttle body, then disconnect fuel pressure regulator.
2. Remove throttle body to intake plenum attaching bolts, then the throttle body from intake plenum.
3. Remove throttle body O-rings.
4. Remove crankcase adapter to intake plenum attaching bolts, then lift adapter from intake plenum and place aside, **Fig. 2.**

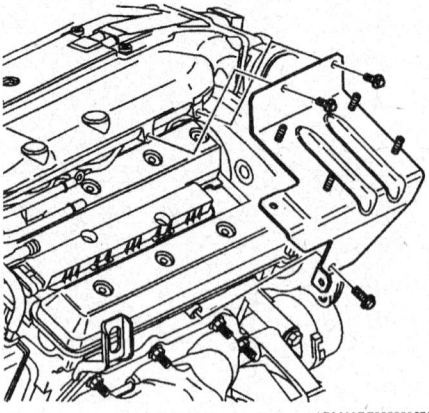

Fig. 3   ECM bracket

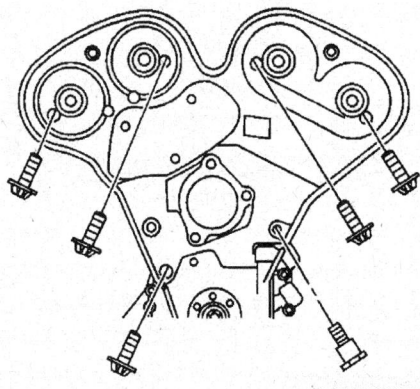

Fig. 5   Rear timing belt cover bolt removal

5. Disconnect crankcase vent air hose retainer from fuel pipe.
6. Remove power steering fluid reservoir mounting bolts.
7. Disconnect electrical connector and vacuum hose from valve at rear of plenum.
8. Remove throttle body to heater hose attaching bolt, then disconnect vacuum brake booster hose.
9. Remove ECM bracket to intake plenum attaching bolts, then the bracket, **Fig. 3.**
10. Remove intake plenum bolts, then the intake plenum from intake manifold.
11. Reverse procedure to install, noting the following:
    a. Lightly coat plenum O-rings with suitable engine oil.
    b. Apply suitable engine oil to crankcase vent seal.

INTAKE MANIFOLD
REPLACE

1. Remove intake plenum as outlined in "Intake Plenum, Replace."
2. Remove and disconnect quick connect fittings from return hose/pipe, then plug outlet ports to prevent fuel loss and contamination.
3. Disconnect fuel injector electrical harness connector from engine wiring harness.

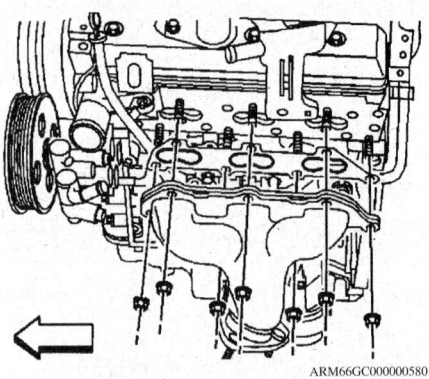

Fig. 4   Exhaust manifold

4. Disconnect fuel pressure regulator, then the fuel rail assembly.
5. Remove intake manifold bolts, then the intake manifold and seals.
6. Remove intake manifold flange bolts, then the intake manifold flange from cylinder heads.
7. Reverse procedure to install.

EXHAUST MANIFOLD
REPLACE
Lefthand

1. Remove air cleaner and intake air resonator.
2. Disconnect HO2S sensor from wiring harness.
3. Remove lefthand catalytic converter.
4. Remove lefthand exhaust manifold retaining nuts, then the exhaust manifold, **Fig. 4.**
5. Reverse procedure to install.

Righthand

1. Remove drive belt tensioner.
2. Disconnect engine wiring harness to ECM bracket.
3. Remove coolant pump to ECM bracket bolts, then the coolant pump.
4. Disconnect HO2S sensor from wiring harness connector.
5. Remove righthand exhaust manifold nuts, then the exhaust manifold.
6. Reverse procedure to install.

CYLINDER HEAD
REPLACE

1. Drain coolant into suitable container.
2. Remove intake manifold flange as outlined in "Intake Manifold, Replace."
3. Disconnect electrical connector from engine coolant temperature (ECT) sensor, then the throttle body heater hose from fitting.
4. Remove following from cylinder heads with heater hose still attached: water crossover fittings, upper and lower seals, water crossover.
5. Remove camshafts as outlined in "Camshaft, Replace."
6. Remove timing belt tensioner as outlined in "Timing Belt, Replace."
7. Remove rear timing belt cover to cylinder head attaching bolts, **Fig. 5.**

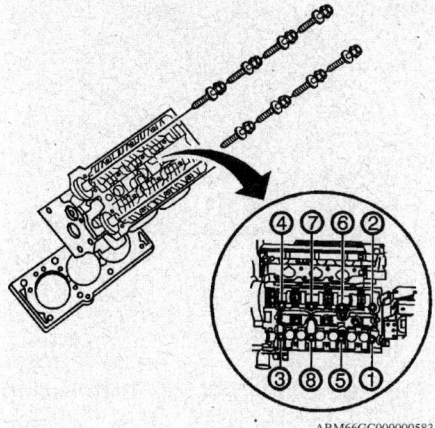

Fig. 6   Cylinder head bolt removal
sequence

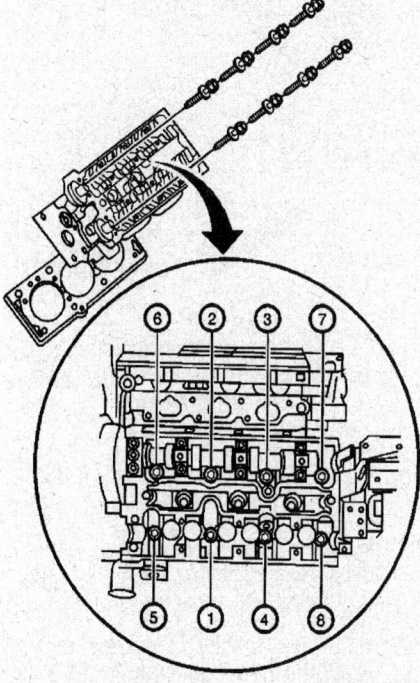

Fig. 9   Cylinder head bolt
tightening sequence

8. Remove cylinder head bolts in sequence, **Fig. 6.** Discard bolts.
9. Remove cylinder head and gasket.
10. Reverse procedure to install, noting the following:
   a. Remove gaskets material from cylinder head and cylinder block.
   b. Install new righthand gasket, **Fig. 7.**
   c. Install new lefthand gasket, **Fig. 8.**
   d. Tighten new cylinder head bolts in five steps using sequence, **Fig. 9.** First step, **torque** bolts to 18 ft. lbs.; second step, tighten bolts an additional 30°; third step, tighten bolts an additional 30°; fourth step, tighten bolts an additional 30°; fifth step, tighten bolts an additional 15°.

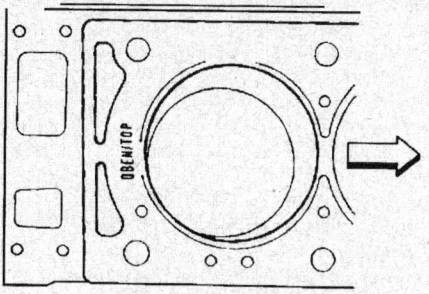

Fig. 7   Righthand cylinder head
gasket installation

VALVE COVER
REPLACE

1. Remove intake manifold as outlined in "Intake Manifold, Replace."
2. Remove ignition coil as outlined in "Ignition Coil, Replace" in "Electrical" section.
3. Remove knock sensor wire harness bolt and bracket, then disconnect front throttle body heater inlet hose bracket.
4. Disconnect HO2S from rear of throttle body heater inlet hose, then remove throttle body heater inlet hose to engine bracket attaching bolt.
5. Remove camshaft cover attaching bolts, then the camshaft cover.
6. Reverse procedure to install.

VALVE ADJUSTMENT

This engine is equipped with hydraulic valve lash adjusters. No adjustment is required.

FRONT COVER
REPLACE

1. Remove intake air resonator as outlined in "Engine, Replace."
2. Remove intake plenum as outlined in "Intake Plenum, Replace."
3. Remove drive belt tensioner.
4. Remove water pump pulley attaching bolts, then the water pump pulley.
5. Remove power steering pump attaching bolts, then the power steering pump from bracket.
6. Remove timing belt cover attaching bolts, then the cover.
7. Reverse procedure to install.

TIMING BELT
REPLACE

Removal

1. Remove timing belt cover as outlined in "Front Cover, Replace."
2. Remove intake air resonator as outlined in "Engine, Replace."
3. Remove the drive belt as outlined in "Alternator, Replace" in "Electrical" section.

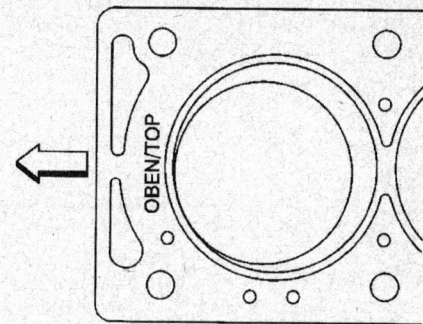

Fig. 8   Lefthand cylinder head
gasket installation

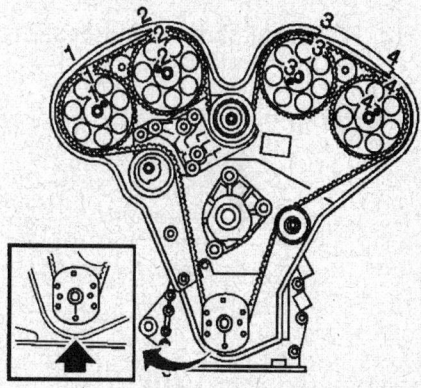

Fig. 10   No. 1 cylinder TDC
rotation & alignment

4. Remove crankshaft balancer bolts, then the crankshaft balancer from crankshaft sprocket.
5. Rotate crankshaft clockwise using crank hub tool No. J42098, or equivalent to top dead center (TDC) on compression stroke, **Fig. 10.** Reference marks on camshaft gears should be aligned with notches on rear timing belt cover, crankshaft sprocket and oil pump housing.
6. Rotate crankshaft counterclockwise using crank hub tool No. J42098, or equivalent, to 60° before TDC to index mark on oil pump cover, **Fig. 11.**
7. Install timing belt alignment tool No. J42069-10, or equivalent, to crankshaft sprocket, **Fig. 12,** rotate crankshaft clockwise using crank hub tool No. J42098, or equivalent, until lever of tool No. J42069-10, or equivalent, contacts water pump pulley flange. No. 1 cylinder is at TDC.
8. Ensure that reference marks on camshaft gears should be aligned with notches on rear timing belt cover. If not aligned, engine is 180° off.
9. Install tool Nos. J42069-1 and J42069-2, or equivalents, to camshaft gears, **Fig. 13.**
10. Loosen timing belt tensioner nut, upper idler pulley bolt, then remove lower idler pulley bolt and pulley with spacer.

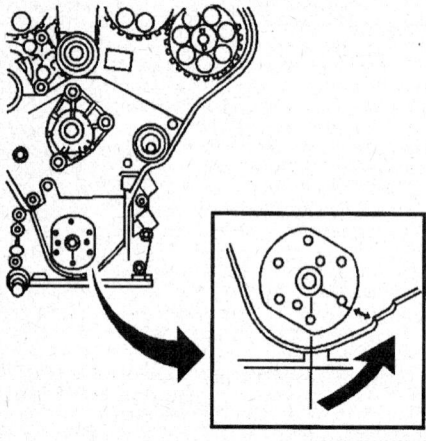

Fig. 11 Crankshaft 60° indication mark

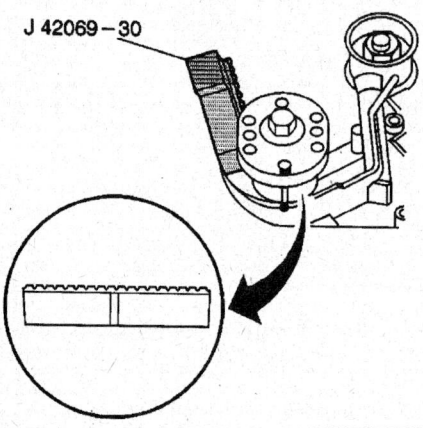

Fig. 14 Timing belt starting installation starting point

11. Remove timing belt alignment tool No. J42069-10, or equivalent, then the timing belt.

Installation

Arrows are printed on timing belt indicating required direction of travel and installation. Ensure that arrows are installed in correct clockwise direction. Inspect timing belt for wear or damage and replace as required.

1. Install timing belt starting at crankshaft sprocket, aligning double dash TDC mark on timing belt with marks on oil pump housing and on crankshaft sprocket, **Fig. 14.** Secure tool No. J42069-30, or equivalent, in between oil pump housing and timing belt to prevent belt from moving.
2. Install timing belt through numbered sequence, **Fig. 15,** slide timing belt over camshaft gears simultaneously, ensuring that dash marks on timing belt align with marks on camshaft gears and notches on rear timing belt cover.
3. Rotate crankshaft counterclockwise to 3° BTDC using crank hub tool No. J42098, or equivalent, allowing timing belt to slide on tool No. J42069-30, or

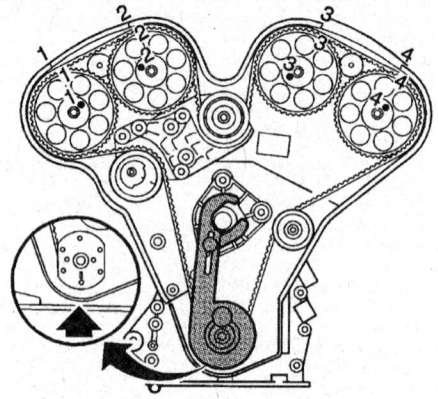

Fig. 12 Timing belt alignment tool installation

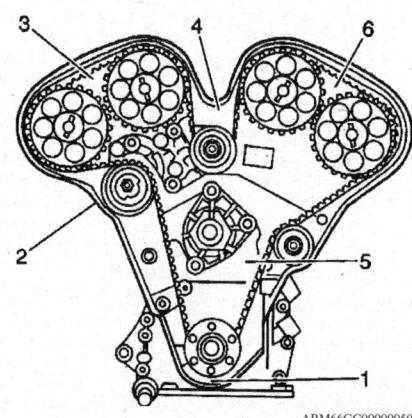

Fig. 15 Timing belt installation

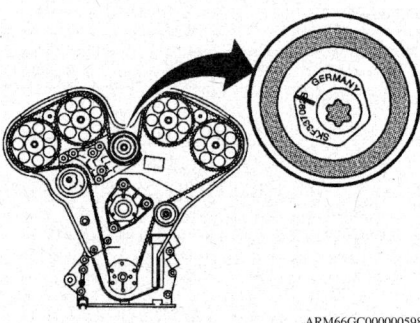

Fig. 17 Idler pulley bolt tightening

equivalent, **Fig. 16.**
4. Install lower idler pulley and spacer, then tighten.
5. Rotate crankshaft back to TDC using crank hub tool No. J42098, or equivalent.
6. Tighten idler pulley locking bolt, while holding eccentric using tool No. J42069-40, or equivalent, **Fig. 17.**
7. Rotate tensioner eccentric counterclockwise to full stop, turn eccentric back until reference mark is .03 inch over flange, **Fig. 18.**
8. Tighten timing belt tensioner locking nut, lock nut will be tightened after final adjustments.
9. Inspect and ensure that alignment marks on timing belt and reference

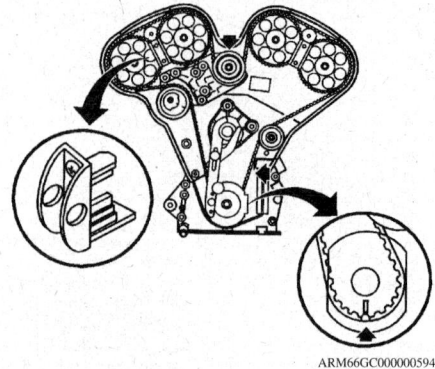

Fig. 13 Camshaft tool installation

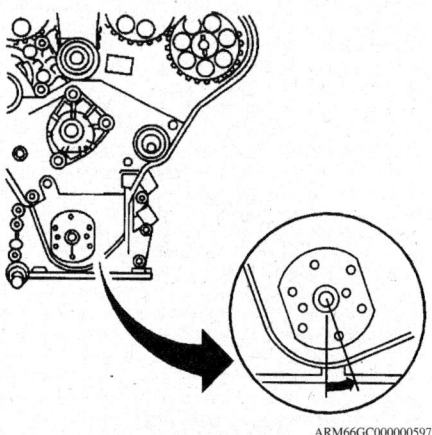

Fig. 16 Crankshaft counterclockwise timing belt installation

points, **Fig. 19.**
10. Remove tool Nos. J42069-30, J42069-1 and J42069-2, or equivalents.
11. Rotate crankshaft clockwise two revolutions using tool No. J42098, or equivalent, until No. 1 cylinder is 60° BTDC, **Fig. 11.**
12. Install timing belt alignment tool No. J42069-10, or equivalent, to crankshaft sprocket, **Fig. 12,** secure lever of tool to water pump pulley flange.
13. Inspect alignment of reference marks on camshaft gears with notches on rear timing belt cover and crankshaft sprocket and oil pump housing. **Alignment marks on timing belt will no longer align with marks on camshaft gears after one or more engine revolutions.**
14. Inspect alignment of camshaft gears 1 and 2, then 3 and 4 using tool No. J42069-20, **Fig. 20.**
15. Loosen timing belt eccentric locking nut, then turn eccentric counterclockwise to full stop, then back to .118–.157 inch for new belt and reference mark alignment with datum line for used belt, **Fig. 21.** Tighten belt tensioner locking nut.
16. Secure upper idler pulley using tool No. J42069-40, or equivalent, **Fig. 22,** and tighten.
17. Remove tool No. J42069-20, or equivalent, from camshaft gears.

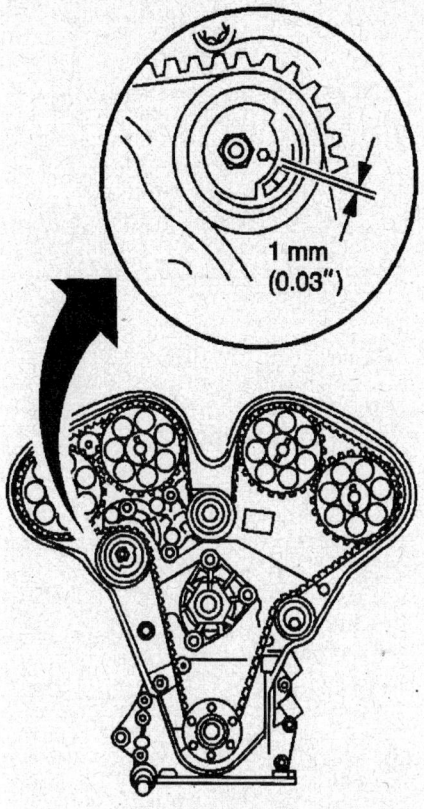

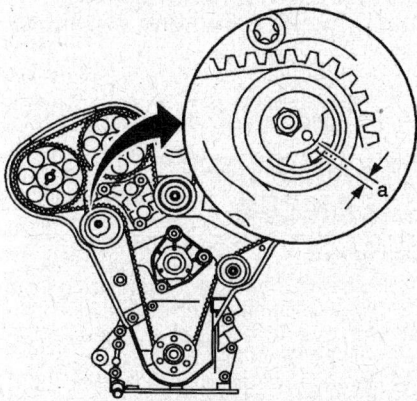

Fig. 18 Initial timing belt tension

Fig. 21 Timing belt tension adjustment

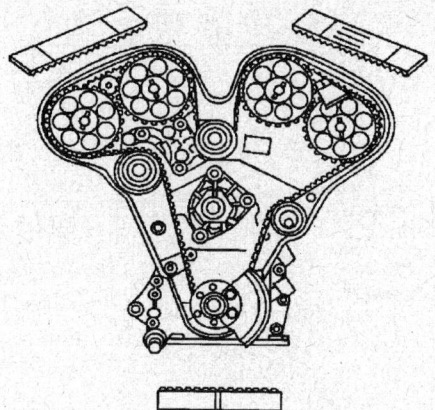

Fig. 19 Alignment marks & reference points

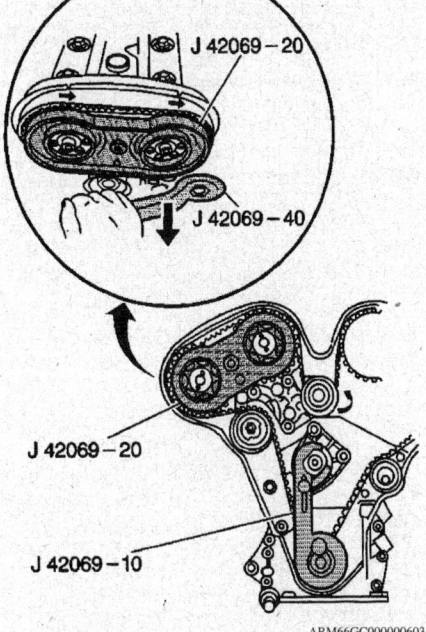

Fig. 22 Upper idler pulley

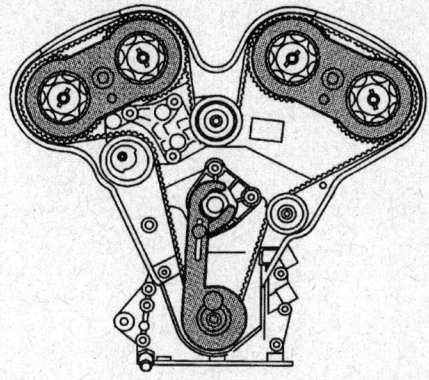

Fig. 20 Camshaft gear alignment inspections

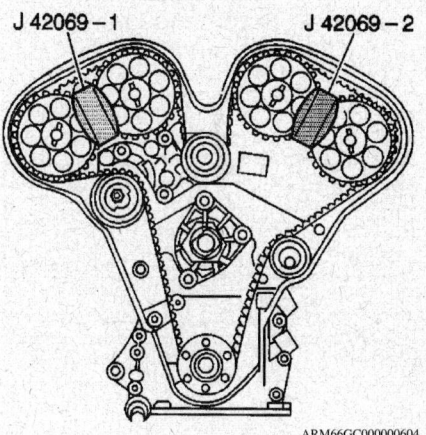

Fig. 23 Camshaft drive sprocket bolt removal

18. Remove tool No. J42069-10, or equivalent from engine.
19. Rotate crankshaft in clockwise direction two revolutions using tool No. J42098, or equivalent, reaching 60° BTDC.
20. Install timing belt alignment tool No. J42069-10, or equivalent.
21. Rotate crankshaft in clockwise direction using tool No. J42098, or equivalent, until lever contacts water pump pulley flange. Secure lever tool to water pump pulley flange.
22. Inspect alignment of reference marks on camshaft gears with notches on rear timing belt cover. Alignment marks

will no longer align with marks on camshaft gears after one or more revolutions.
23. Install tool No. J42069-20, or equivalent, to inspect alignment of camshaft gears.
24. Remove crankshaft balancer bolts, then the crankshaft balancer from crankshaft sprocket.
25. Remove the drive belt as outlined in "Alternator, Replace" in "Electrical" section.
26. Remove intake air resonator as outlined in "Engine, Replace."
27. Remove timing belt cover as outlined in "Front Cover, Replace."

CAMSHAFT
REPLACE

1. Remove camshaft cover(s) as outlined in "Valve Cover, Replace."

2. Remove timing belt as outlined in "Timing Belt, Replace."
3. Install tool Nos. J42069-1 and J42069-2, or equivalents, then remove camshaft drive sprocket bolts, **Fig. 23.** Discard bolts.
4. Remove tool Nos. J42069-1 and J42069-2, or equivalents, then the camshaft sprockets.
5. Alternately loosen camshaft bearing bolts in numbered sequence, **Figs. 24 and 25.**
6. Remove camshaft bearing caps, then the camshafts, **Figs. 26 and 27.**
7. Reverse procedure to install, noting the following:
   a. Intake camshaft is stamped with a "G" next to bearing 1.
   b. Exhaust camshaft is stamped with a "J" next to bearing 1.
   c. Lubricate camshaft bearing and lobe surfaces using suitable engine oil.
   d. Apply small amount of GM part No. 1052942, or equivalent, to forward edge of front bearing caps.
   e. Install camshaft bearing caps by identification mark.
   f. Tighten camshaft bearing cap bolts in sequence, **Figs. 28 and 29.**

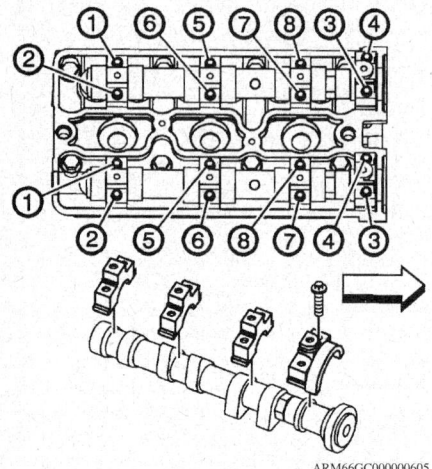

Fig. 24 Righthand camshaft bearing cap removal

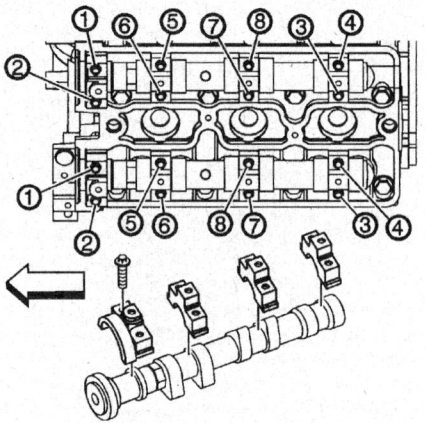

Fig. 25 Lefthand camshaft bearing cap removal

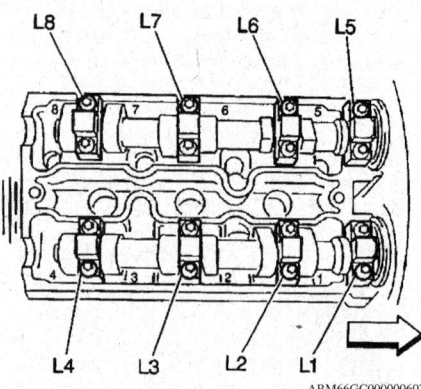

Fig. 26 Lefthand bearing cap identification

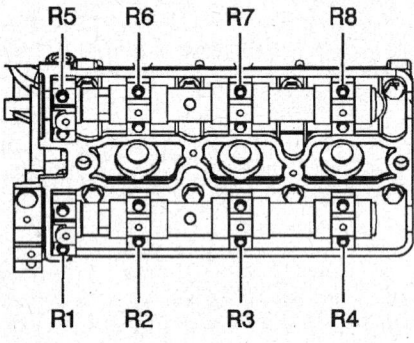

Fig. 27 Righthand bearing cap identification

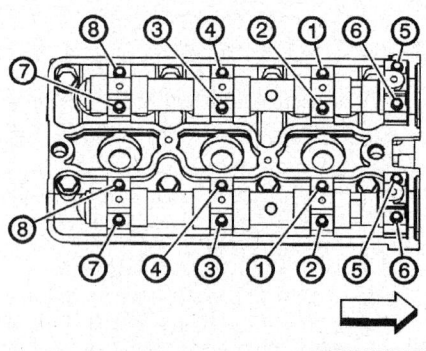

Fig. 28 Righthand camshaft bearing cap tightening sequence

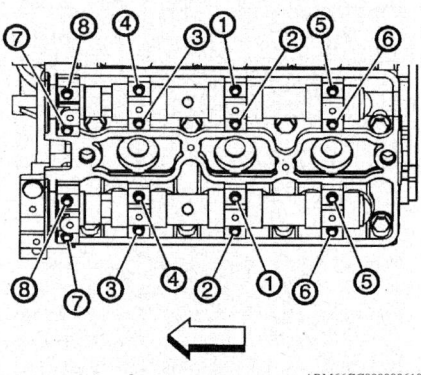

Fig. 29 Lefthand camshaft bearing cap tightening sequence

PISTON & ROD ASSEMBLY

When installing piston and rod assemblies into cylinder block, ensure that arrow on top of piston faces toward front of engine. Ensure flat area on bottom of piston aligns with small dimple above connecting rod crankshaft bearing bore.

PISTONS, PINS & RINGS

Pistons and rings are available in standard size and oversize. Pistons and their pins are serviced as an assembly.

MAIN & ROD BEARINGS

Main and rod bearings are available in standard size only. Tighten main bearing cap bolts in three steps: First step, **torque** bolts to ft. lbs.; second step, tighten bolts an additional 60°; third step, tighten bolts an additional 15°.

CRANKSHAFT FRONT OIL SEAL

REPLACE

1. Remove timing belt as outlined in "Tim-

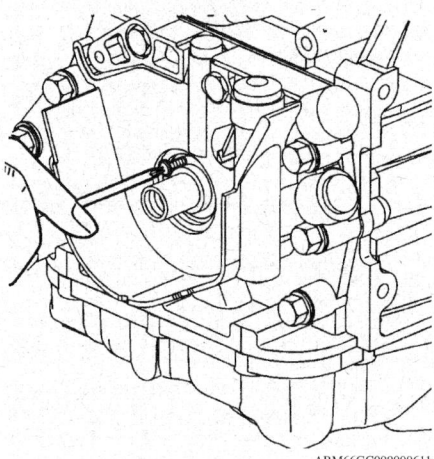

Fig. 30 Crankshaft front oil seal removal

ing Belt, Replace."
2. Install tool No. J42065, or equivalent, to crankshaft gear.
3. Counterhold crankshaft gear using tool No. J42065, or equivalent, remove crankshaft gear bolt using tool No. J42098, or equivalent. Discard crankshaft gear bolt.
4. Remove crankshaft gear, then the oil pump collar.
5. Drill a small pilot hole into steel ring of crankshaft front oil seal, **Fig. 30,** screw a self-tapping screw, then using suit-

able pliers, remove crankshaft front oil seal.
6. Reverse procedure to install.

CRANKSHAFT BALANCER

REPLACE

1. Remove intake air resonator as outlined in "Engine, Replace."
2. Remove drive belt as outlined in "Serpentine Drive Belt."
3. Remove crankshaft balancer bolts, then the crankshaft balancer, **Fig. 31.**
4. Reverse procedure to install.

CRANKSHAFT REAR OIL SEAL

REPLACE

1. Remove transmission as outlined in **MOTOR's "Domestic Transmission, In-Vehicle Service"** manual.
2. Counterhold crankshaft using tool No. J42098 and remove flywheel bolts. Discard flywheel bolts as required.
3. Remove engine flywheel and retainer from crankshaft.
4. Center punch steel ring of rear main oil seal, then drill small pilot hole into steel ring of rear main oil seal.
5. Screw a self-tapping screw into seal, then using suitable pliers, remove seal, **Fig. 32.**
6. Reverse procedure to install.

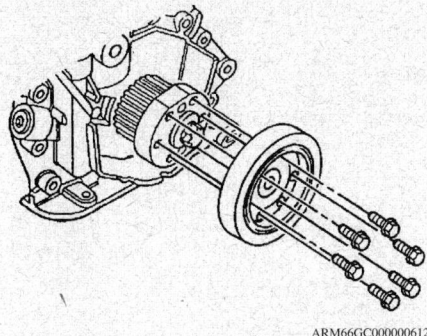

Fig. 31 Crankshaft balancer removal

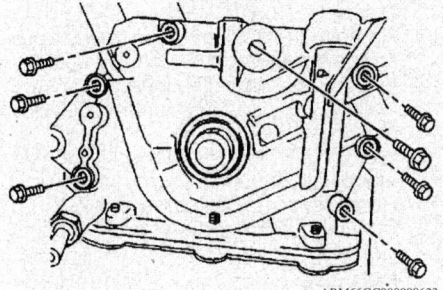

Fig. 34 Oil pump removal

OIL PAN
REPLACE

1. Drain engine oil into suitable container.
2. Install suitable engine lifting device.
3. Remove front tire and wheel assemblies.
4. Remove front air deflector.
5. Disconnect electrical wiring harness, secure harness to frame.
6. Disconnect rearward retainer and anti-lock brake wiring harness from lower control arms.
7. Remove brake lines and brake line bracket from frame.
8. Support radiator and condenser assembly using suitable wire to front absorber bracket bolt.
9. Remove washer bottle bracket, then loosen brake pressure modulator valve nuts to separate brake pressure valve from bracket.
10. Loosen stabilizer shaft mounting bolts, then remove lower stabilizer shaft link retaining nut and link from lower control arm.
11. Remove power steering pressure hose retaining nut from air conditioning compressor.
12. Remove power steering gear mounting bolts, support gear using suitable wire.
13. Remove outer tie rod retaining nut, then separate outer tie rod from steering knuckle using tool No. J24319-B, or equivalent.
14. Remove lower shock bolts, then disconnect lower ball joint from steering knuckle as outlined in "Control Arm, Replace" in "Front Suspension & Steering" section.
15. Remove engine mount lower retaining nuts.

Fig. 32 Crankshaft rear oil seal removal

16. Install tool No. J39580, or equivalent, then lower engine to frame support table and remove frame bolts.
17. Raise engine from frame.
18. Remove transmission fluid cooler pipes brace to engine, then the three lower transmission mounting bolts.
19. Remove oil pan bolts, then pry oil pan from engine block using suitable flat bladed tool.
20. Reverse procedure to install, noting the following:
    a. Apply a suitable bead of silicone sealing compound GM part No. 12346286, or equivalent, to oil pan surface.
    b. Tighten oil pan to engine block bolts in sequence, **Fig. 33**.

OIL PUMP
REPLACE

1. Remove oil pan as outlined in "Oil Pan, Replace."
2. Remove oil pump pipe screen brace bolts, screen bolts, then the oil pump pipe screen from engine.
3. Remove crankshaft drive gear as outlined in "Crankshaft Front Oil Seal, Replace."
4. Remove engine oil pressure switch.
5. Remove alternator and position aside.
6. Remove oil pump bolts, pump and gasket, **Fig. 34**.
7. Reverse procedure to install, noting the following:
    a. Clean and inspect oil pump gasket surfaces.
    b. Install oil pump bolts in numbered sequence, **Fig. 35**.

SERPENTINE DRIVE BELT
Replace

1. Rotate drivebelt tensioner clockwise to release tension.
2. Slide drive belt from water pump pulley, allowing tensioner to return.
3. Remove drive belt from accessory pulleys.
4. Reverse procedure to install. Refer to **Fig. 36**, for serpentine drive belt routing.

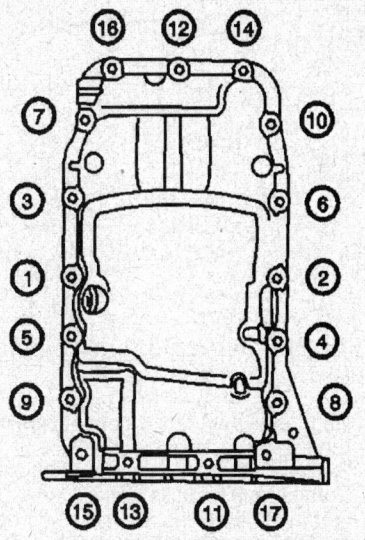

Fig. 33 Oil pan bolt tightening sequence

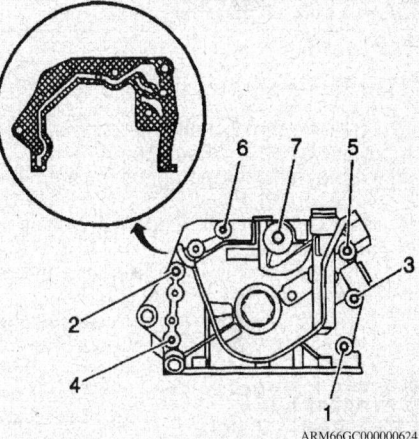

Fig. 35 Oil pump bolt installation

COOLING SYSTEM BLEED

1. Place transmission in Park or Neutral position.
2. Engage park brake.
3. Run engine until thermostat opens.
4. Stop engine.
5. Fill system using only clean drinkable water.
6. Repeat procedure if required, until fluid is nearly colorless.
7. Fill coolant reservoir to FULL HOT mark.

THERMOSTAT
REPLACE

1. Drain cooling system into suitable container. Position J38185 to clamp in order to remove O-ring seals from coolant outlet pipe. Discard O-rings.
2. Remove radiator inlet hose from coolant outlet pipe.
3. Remove bolts securing oil dipstick tube, coolant outlet pipe, engine front

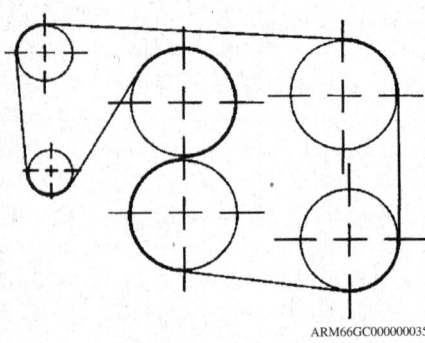

Fig. 36 Serpentine drive belt routing

lift bracket and coolant outlet pipe from the thermostat housing.
4. Remove intake manifold as outlined in "Intake Manifold, Replace."
5. Remove thermostat housing bolts, then the thermostat housing.
6. Remove thermostat.
7. Reverse procedure to install.

WATER PUMP
REPLACE

1. Drain cooling system into suitable container.
2. Remove timing belt cover as outlined in "Front Cover, Replace."
3. Remove water pump bolts, then the water pump, **Fig. 37.**
4. Reverse procedure to install, noting the following:
   a. Clean and inspect surfaces as required.
   b. Apply seal ring silicone grease GM part No. 12345579, or equivalent.

RADIATOR
REPLACE

1. Drain engine coolant into suitable container.
2. Remove condenser seal, radiator attaching bolts, then the support brackets.
3. Disconnect surge tank hose, then remove fan shroud attaching bolts.
4. Disconnect upper radiator hose to radiator using tool No. J38185, or equivalent.

5. Remove coolant bypass valve, placing aside, then release solenoid from fan shroud.
6. Remove air cleaner assembly.
7. Rotate, then remove A/C retaining clip and disconnect fan motor electrical connectors.
8. Remove coolant bypass hose from radiator using suitable pliers.
9. Remove fan shroud attaching bolts, then the fan assembly.
10. Remove upper condenser attaching bolts, raise and support vehicle using suitable lift.
11. Disconnect lower transaxle oil cooler line and lower radiator hose from radiator using suitable pliers.
12. Remove lower condenser bolts, then the radiator seal push pins.
13. Lower vehicle, then remove radiator assembly.
14. Reverse procedure to install.

FUEL PUMP
REPLACE

1. Drain fuel tank into suitable container.
2. Raise and support vehicle.
3. Remove catalytic converter attaching nuts, support exhaust system.
4. Remove exhaust system from front and rear hanger rods.
5. Remove floor panel brace, then the exhaust system.
6. Disconnect propeller shaft coupler from transmission flange.
7. Push front propeller shaft toward rear of vehicle to release coupler from transmission flange.
8. Secure front propeller shaft to shift control lever using suitable wire.
9. Disconnect filler hose and vent tube from fuel tank.
10. Disconnect fuel feed, fuel return and fuel EVAP hoses, then the fuel tank electrical connector.
11. Disconnect EVAP hoses and retainer from underside of vehicle.
12. Support shock absorber using a suitable jack, then the remove lower shock absorber bolts.
13. Install a suitable jack under rear tie bar, to support front of rear frame, remove two rear frame attaching bolts.

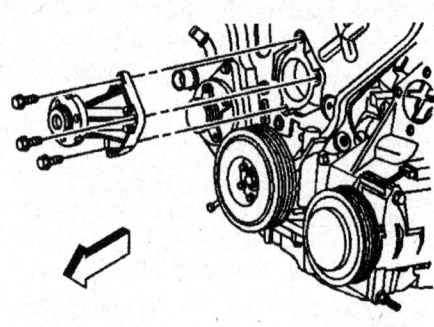

Fig. 37 Water pump removal

14. Lower jack until there is two inches of clearance between front surface and chassis.
15. Remove fuel tank strap bolts, then pull straps downward and position aside.
16. Lower tank and disconnect pressure and return hose from primary fuel tank module.
17. Disconnect primary fuel tank module electrical connector.
18. Remove fuel tank from vehicle.
19. Turn cam lock counterclockwise using lock ring tool No. J45747, or equivalent.
20. Remove primary fuel tank module from tank.
21. Reverse procedure to install.

FUEL FILTER
REPLACE

1. Disconnect fuel filter bracket release tabs.
2. Twist quick-connect fitting ¼ turn in each direction to loosen dirt within fitting.
3. Clean quick-connect fitting at ends of filter.
4. Disconnect quick-connect fittings by squeezing plastic tabs of male end connector and pulling apart.
5. Disconnect threaded fitting at fuel filter outlet.
6. Remove fuel filter.
7. Reverse procedure to install, noting the following:
   a. Turn ignition On for two seconds, then Off for ten seconds.
   b. Turn ignition On and inspect for fuel leakage.

TIGHTENING SPECIFICATIONS

Year	Component	Torque Ft. Lbs.
2003–04	Accessory Mounting Bracket Bolt	26
	A/C Compressor Mounting Bolt	15
	A/C Condenser Mounting Bolt	58①
	A/C Line Clip To Fan Shroud Screw	40①
	Afterboil Coolant Pump Bolt	89①
	Alternator Mounting Bolt	26
	Auxiliary Cooling Fan Mounting Bolt	58①
	Battery Cable To Battery Bolt	13
	Battery Ground To Side Rail Bolt	27
	Battery Positive To Underhood Fuse Block Nut	11
	Blow-By Plate To Cylinder Block Bolt	71①
	Bumper Nut	18
	Camshaft Bearing Cap Bolt	71①
	Camshaft Cover Bolt	71
	Camshaft Position Sensor Bolt	71
	Camshaft Sprocket Bolt	②
	Catalytic Converter Hanger Bracket Bolt	37
	Catalytic Converter Hanger Bracket Nut	18
	Catalytic Converter Nut	11
	Center Bearing Heat Shield Bolt	71①
	Coil Ground To Lefthand Cylinder Head Bolt	37
	Connecting Rod	③
	Coolant Bypass Inlet Hose/Pipe Bolt	80①
	Coolant Bypass Valve Bolt	58①
	Coolant Heater	44
	Coolant Heater Ground Lead Bolt	80①
	Coolant Inlet Pipe Bolt	15
	Coolant Inlet Pipe Support Bolt	15
	Coolant Jacket Plug	48
	Coolant Jacket Support Plug	48
	Crankcase Vent Housing Bolt	71①
	Crankcase Ventilation Tube Adapter Bolt	71①
	Crankshaft Balancer Bolt	15
	Crankshaft Bearing Bridge Adjusting Sleeve	15
	Crankshaft Bearing Bridge Bolt	15
	Crankshaft Bearing Cap	④
	Crankshaft Drive Gear Bolt	⑤
	Crankshaft Position Sensor Bolt	71①
	Crankshaft Reluctor Ring Screw	11
	Cylinder Head Bolts	⑥
	Drive Belt Tensioner Bolt	26
	ECM Bracket To Cylinder Head Bolt	15
	ECM Bracket To Intake Plenum Bolt	71①
	ECM To Bracket Nut	71①
	Electric Cooling Fan Blade Retaining Nut	62①
	Electric Cooling Fan Motor Mounting Screw	44①
	Electric Cooling Fan To Plenum Mounting Bolt	58①
	Electric Cooling Fan To Radiator Mounting Bolt	58①
	Engine Coolant Temperature Sensor	13
	Engine Ground Lead To Lefthand Cylinder Head Bolt	22
	Engine Mount Bracket Bolt	44

Continued

TIGHTENING
SPECIFICATIONS—Continued

Year	Component	Torque Ft. Lbs.
2003–04	Engine Mount Nut	59
	Engine Rear Lift Bracket Bolt	15
	Engine Wiring Harness Ground Lead Bolt	80①
	Engine Wiring Harness Retainer To Oil Pan Bolt	37
	EVAP Canister Purge Valve Bracket Bolt	71①
	Exhaust Manifold Nut	15
	Exhaust Manifold Pipe Nut	18
	Exhaust Manifold Stud	22
	Floor Panel Tunnel Brace Bolt	18
	Front Air Inlet Panel	53①
	Fuel Rail Bolt	71①
	Ignition Coil Cassette Bolt	71①
	Intake Manifold Bolt	15
	Intake Manifold Flange Bolt	15
	Intake Plenum Bolt	15
	Intake Plenum Tuning Solenoid Bolt	71①
	Intake Plenum Tuning Valve Bolt	71①
	Knock Sensor Bolt	15
	Knock Sensor Wire Harness Bracket Bolt	71①
	Oil Baffle Bolt	71①
	Oil Cooler Cover Bolt	15
	Oil Cooler Feed & Return Lines To Engine Block	22
	Oil Cooler Inlet & Outlet Nut	22
	Oil Cooler Pipe Fitting To Oil Cooler	22
	Oil Filter Adapter Bolt	15
	Oil Filter Adapter Female Screw	18
	Oil Filter Adapter Plug	18
	Oil Filter Cartridge Housing Drain Plug	89①
	Oil Filter Cartridge Plastic Cap To Adapter	18
	Oil Intake Pipe Bolt	71①
	Oil Intake Pipe Brace Bolt	71①
	Oil Dipstick Tube Bolt	15
	Oil Pan Bolt	11
	Oil Pan Drain Plug	89①
	Oil Pressure Sender	26
	Oil Pump Bolt	15
	Oil Pump Cover Bolt	71①
	Power Steering Hose Retaining Nut	71①
	Power Steering Pump Mounting Bolt	26
	Radiator Support Bracket Bolt	80①
	Remote Power Steering Fluid Reservoir To Cylinder Head Mounting Bolt	18
	Remote Power Steering Fluid Reservoir To Intake Plenum Mounting Bolt	80①
	Spark Plug	18
	Surge Tank Outlet Pipe To Vent Housing Bolt	80①
	Thermostat Housing Bolt	15
	Threaded Block Heater	44
	Throttle Body Bolt	71①
	Throttle Body Heater Inlet Hose/Pipe Bolt	80①
	Throttle Body Inlet Heater Hose Fitting	15
	Timing Belt Front Cover Bolt	71①
	Timing Belt Idler Pulley Bolt	30
	Timing Belt Rear Cover Bolt	71①

Continued

TIGHTENING
SPECIFICATIONS—Continued

Year	Component	Torque Ft. Lbs.
2003–04	Timing Belt Rear Cover Threaded Pin	89①
	Timing Belt Tensioner Bracket Bolt	30
	Timing Belt Tensioner Pulley Nut	15
	Torque Converter Bolt	46
	Transmission Fluid Cooler Pipes Retaining Bolt	18
	Transmission Manual Shift Shaft Nut	80①
	Transmission Mounting Bolt (M10)	37
	Transmission Mounting Bolt (M12)	55
	Transmission Mount Nut	44
	Transmission Support Mounting Bolt	44
	Vacuum Brake Booster Fitting	18
	Water Crossover Bolt	22
	Water Crossover Fitting	15
	Water Crossover Pipe Plug	44①
	Water Pump Bolt	18
	Water Pump Pulley Bolt	71①

① — Inch lbs.
② — First pass, 37 ft. lbs.; second pass, 60°; third pass, 15°.
③ — First pass, 26 ft. lbs.; second pass, 45°; third pass, 15°.
④ — First pass, 37 ft. lbs.; second pass, 60°; third pass, 15°.
⑤ — First pass, 184 ft. lbs.; second pass, 45°; third pass, 15°.
⑥ — Refer to "Cylinder Head, Replace" for tightening sequence.

3.6L Engine

NOTE: On Air Bag Equipped Models, Refer To "Air Bag System Precautions" Located In The Front Of This Manual For System Disarming & Arming Procedures.

NOTE: Refer To "Computer Relearn Procedures" Located In The Front Of This Manual When Battery Power To The Computer Has Been Interrupted.

NOTE: Prior To Performing Any Service Operations Listed In This Section, Consult The "Technical Service Bulletins" Section For Related Information.

NOTE: For Procedures Not Found In This Section, Refer To "3.2L Engine" Section.

INDEX

PRECAUTIONS

Air Bag Systems

Refer to "Air Bag System Precautions" in the front of this manual for system disarming and arming procedures.

Battery Ground Cable

Prior to service, disconnect battery ground cable and isolate as required.

Fuel Pressure Relief

1. Turn ignition in "Off" position.
2. Disconnect battery ground cable and isolate as required.
3. Loosen fuel filler cap to relieve fuel tank vapor pressure.
4. Remove cap to fuel pressure service connection.
5. Install tool Nos. J34730-1A and J42242, or equivalents, to fuel pressure service connection.
6. Place bleed hose into suitable container, then open bleed valve to relieve fuel system.
7. Place a suitable shop towel under connections to protect fuel spillage.
8. Remove tool Nos. J34730-1A and J42242, or equivalents, from service connections.
9. Install cap to fuel pressure service connection.

COMPRESSION PRESSURE

The minimum compression in any one cylinder should not be less than 70 percent of the highest cylinder. No cylinder should read less than 965 kPa (140 psi).

ENGINE MOUNT

REPLACE

1. Raise and support vehicle.
2. Place a suitable adjustable jack stand with a block of wood under engine oil pan.
3. Remove upper engine mount retaining nut.
4. Remove lefthand engine mount bracket retaining nut, then the bracket.
5. Remove lower engine mount retaining nut, then the engine mount.
6. Reverse procedure to install.

ENGINE

REPLACE

1. Turn front wheels to straight ahead position.
2. Turn ignition lock cylinder to Lock position and remove key.
3. Lock steering column by inserting steering column anti-rotation pin tool No. J 42640, or equivalent, through access hole in lower steering column trim cover.
4. Relieve fuel system pressure as outlined in "Precautions."
5. Raise and support vehicle.
6. Mark relationship of center intermediate shaft to lower intermediate shaft for installation reference.
7. Remove center intermediate shaft to lower intermediate shaft retaining bolt.
8. Remove lower intermediate shaft to power steering gear retaining bolt.
9. Mark relationship of lower intermediate shaft to power steering gear for installation reference.

10. Disconnect lower intermediate shaft from power steering gear.
11. Remove lower intermediate shaft from center intermediate shaft.
12. Remove battery and fuel injector sight shield.
13. Remove air cleaner duct, then disconnect cooling fan electrical connectors.
14. Remove cooling fan wiring harness from shroud, then secure harnesses aside.
15. Drain cooling system.
16. Disconnect outlet hose from surge tank. Secure hose aside.
17. Disconnect surge tank inlet hose from water outlet housing and radiator. Secure hose aside.
18. Disconnect hoses from heater core.
19. Disconnect purge line from purge solenoid.
20. Recover A/C system refrigerant as outlined in "Air Condition" chapter.
21. Remove wiper module assembly as outlined in electrical section.
22. Disconnect suction hose from evaporator and remove suction hose bracket from shock tower. Secure suction hose to engine.
23. Disconnect A/C pressure switch electrical connector, then remove liquid line.
24. Remove radiator support brackets.
25. Disconnect brake booster check valve, then brake booster vacuum hose. Secure booster hose to engine.
26. Disconnect brake fluid level switch electrical connector.
27. Disconnect Mass Air Flow (MAF) sensor electrical connector.
28. Disconnect instrument cluster electrical connector from rear of lefthand cylinder head. Secure electrical harness aside.
29. Disconnect engine module wiring harness connectors from underhood electrical center.
30. Disconnect Transmission Control Module (TCM) electrical connector.
31. Remove ground wire to rail retaining bolt, then position ground wire aside.
32. Disconnect engine harness electrical connector. Harness connector is located on engine compartment longitudinal rail. Position TCM harness aside.
33. Secure ground wire, engine harness and TCM harness to engine.
34. Remove master cylinder retaining nuts, then secure master cylinder to engine.
35. Raise and support engine.
36. Remove exhaust system and propeller shaft.
37. Remove air deflector and washer bottle bracket.
38. Disconnect side air baffles from radiator.
39. Remove lefthand front brake pipe retainer and brake pipe rail.
40. Remove righthand front brake pipe from pipe retainer.
41. Disconnect rear brake pipes from BPVM valve.
42. Remove front tire and wheel assemblies.
43. Remove intermediate steering shaft from steering gear.

44. Remove lower engine mount retaining nut.
45. Disconnect transmission shift linkage from transmission.
46. Disconnect low oil level sensor electrical connector, then secure sensor harness and connector to engine.
47. Remove headlamp leveling sensors.
48. Secure shock modules to lower control arms with a suitable strap in order to prevent damage to front brake hoses.
49. Remove righthand side and lethand side shock modules upper mounting bolts.
50. Place a suitable lift platform in engine and transmission assembly.
51. Remove transmission brace to underbody attaching bolts.
52. Remove front frame bolts.
53. Lower lift platform and remove engine transmission assembly from vehicle.
54. Separate transmission assembly from engine.
55. Reverse procedure to install.
56.

INTAKE MANIFOLD
REPLACE

Upper

1. Remove fuel injector sight shield from top of engine.
2. Remove air inlet duct, then disconnect brake booster vacuum hose from intake manifold.
3. Disconnect electrical connector and purge line from purge solenoid valve, **Fig. 1.**
4. Remove wiring harness retainer from front of intake manifold.
5. Disconnect throttle body electrical connector.
6. Remove upper intake manifold brake bolts, then the brace.
7. Disconnect PCV hose from righthand camshaft cover.
8. Disconnect barometric pressure sensor and intake manifold runner control solenoid electrical connectors.
9. Remove injector harness bracket attaching bolt, then the lefthand ignition coil wiring harness from bracket.
10. Remove upper intake manifold attaching bolts, then the manifold with throttle body from engine.
11. Reverse procedure to install.

Lower

1. Remove upper intake manifold as outlined under "Upper."
2. Remove lower intake manifold attaching bolts.
3. Position intake manifold to gain access to fuel pipe connector.
4. Remove fuel feed pipe retainer, then disconnect fuel feed pipe from fuel rail.
5. Remove lower intake manifold.
6. Reverse procedure to install.

EXHAUST MANIFOLD
REPLACE

Lefthand

1. Remove heat shield attaching bolts, then the heat shield.
2. Remove exhaust manifold upper and lower insulators from oil dipstick tube.
3. Remove lefthand catalytic converter.
4. Remove lefthand exhaust manifold retaining nuts, then the exhaust manifold.
5. Reverse procedure to install.

Righthand

1. Remove exhaust manifold heat shield attaching bolts, then the heat shield.
2. Remove Engine Coolant Temperature (ECT) sensor.
3. Remove exhaust manifold to cylinder head attaching bolts, then the exhaust manifold.
4. Reverse procedure to install.

CYLINDER HEAD
REPLACE

Lefthand

1. Remove lefthand secondary timing chain as outlined under "Timing Chain, Replace."
2. Remove oil dipstick.
3. Remove heat shield from coolant temperature sensor and disconnect sensor electrical connector.
4. Remove wiring harness ground from cylinder head.
5. Disconnect wiring harness electrical connector from side of cylinder head.
6. Remove wiring harness connector bracket from cylinder head.
7. Remove power steering pump mounting bolts. **Do not disconnect power steering pipes or hoses.**
8. Remove surge tank hose from cylinder head bracket.
9. Remove wiring harness bracket from rear of cylinder head.
10. Remove lefthand catalytic converter.
11. Remove oil dipstick and oil filter adapter upper bolt.
12. Remove exhaust manifold attaching bolts, then the exhaust manifold.
13. Remove cylinder head attaching bolts, then the cylinder head. **Discard cylinder head M11 bolts.**
14. Reverse procedure to install, noting the following:
    a. Install new M11 bolts.
    b. **Torque** M11 bolts to 33 ft. lbs., then tighten an additional 120°.
    c. **Torque** M8 bolts to 10 ft. lbs., then tighten an additional 60°.

Righthand

1. Remove righthand secondary timing chain as outlined under "Timing Chain, Replace."
2. Remove coolant inlet pipe.

3. Remove wiring harness ground from cylinder head.
4. Disconnect wiring harness electrical connector from side of cylinder head.
5. Remove wiring harness conduit upper bolt from cylinder head, then position conduit aside.
6. Remove battery cable from cylinder head.
7. Remove righthand catalytic converter.
8. Remove exhaust manifold attaching bolts, then the exhaust manifold.
9. Remove cylinder head attaching bolts, then the cylinder head. **Discard cylinder head M11 bolts.**
10. Reverse procedure to install, noting the following:
   a. Install new M11 bolts.
   b. **Torque** M11 bolts to 33 ft. lbs., then tighten an additional 120°.
   c. **Torque** M8 bolts to 10 ft. lbs., then tighten an additional 60°.

VALVE COVER
REPLACE

1. Remove intake manifold as outlined under "Intake Manifold, Replace."
2. Remove wiring harness from side of camshaft cover.
3. Remove wiring harness conduit retainers from camshaft cover by rotating counterclockwise.
4. Remove wiring harness from front of camshaft cover. Position harness aside.
5. Remove ignition coil as outlined under "Ignition Coil, Replace" in "Electrical" section.
6. Remove camshaft cover attaching bolts, then the camshaft cover, **Fig. 2.**
7. Reverse procedure to install.

VALVE ADJUSTMENT

This engine is equipped with hydraulic valve lash adjusters. No adjustment is required.

CRANKSHAFT BALANCER
REPLACE

1. Remove drive belts as outlined under "Serpentine Drive Belt."
2. Raise and support vehicle.
3. Remove crankshaft balancer retaining bolt.
4. Remove crankshaft balancer using harmonic balancer pulling tool No. J 24420-C, or equivalent.
5. Reverse procedure to install.

FRONT COVER
REPLACE

1. Remove fuel injector sight shield.
2. Remove upper and lower intake manifolds as outlined under "Intake Manifold, Replace."
3. Remove camshaft covers as outlined under "Valve Cover, Replace."
4. Drain engine coolant and disconnect purge vent hose from water outlet.

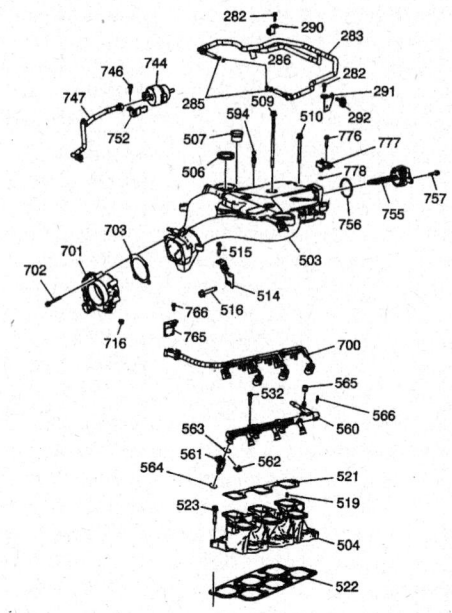

(282) PCV Hose Bolt
(282) PCV Hose Bolt
(283) Dirty PCV Hose
(285) PCV Hose O-Ring Outer/Larger
(286) PCV Hose O-Ring Inner/Smaller
(290) PCV Hose Right Bracket
(291) PCV Hose Left Bracket
(292) PCV Hose Clip
(503) Upper Intake Manifold
(504) Lower Intake Manifold
(506) Expansion Plug
(507) Sight Plug
(509) Upper Intake Manifold Bolt - Long
(510) Upper Intake Manifold Bolt - Short
(514) Intake Manifold Brace
(515) Intake Manifold Brace Small Bolt
(516) Intake Manifold Brace Large Bolt
(519) Lower Intake Manifold to Upper Intake Manifold
(521) Upper Intake Manifold Gasket
(522) Lower Intake Manifold Gasket
(523) Lower Intake Manifold Bolt
(532) Fuel Rail Bolt
(560) Fuel Rail
(561) Fuel Injector

(562) Fuel Injector Retainer
(563) Fuel Injector Upper Seal
(564) Fuel Injector Lower Seal
(565) Fuel Pressure Service Valve Cap
(566) Fuel Pressure Service Valve
(594) Fuel Injector Sight Shield Cover Ball Stud
(700) Fuel Injector Wiring Harness
(701) Throttle Body
(702) Throttle Body Bolt
(703) Throttle Body Gasket
(716) Throttle Body Engine Wiring Harness Clip
(744) EVAP Purge Solenoid
(746) EVAP Purge Solenoid Bolt
(747) EVAP Purge Solenoid Tube
(752) EVAP Purge Solenoid Bracket
(755) Intake Manifold Tuning Valve
(756) Intake Manifold Tuning Valve O-Ring
(757) Intake Manifold Tuning Valve Bolt
(765) Fuel Injector Wiring Harness Bracket
(766) Fuel Injector Wiring Harness Bracket Bolt
(776) BARO Sensor Bolt
(777) BARO Sensor
(778) BARO Sensor O-Ring

ARM0300000000251

Fig. 1 Exploded view of intake manifold

5. Remove water outlet with radiator hose and position aside.
6. Remove accessory drive belts as outlined under "Serpentine Drive Belt."
7. Remove idler pulley and drive belt tensioners.
8. Remove alternator and alternator bracket.
9. Remove power steering fluid reservoir and position aside.
10. Remove power steering pump pulley.
11. Remove power steering pump upper front bolt, then loosen two remaining bolts.
12. Remove crankshaft balancer as outlined under "Crankshaft Balancer, Replace."
13. Remove camshafts as outlined under "Camshaft, Replace."

14. Remove camshaft position actuator solenoid valves, **Fig. 3.**
15. Remove front cover attaching bolts, then the cover.
16. Reverse procedure to install.

TIMING CHAIN
REPLACE
Primary Drive Chain
REMOVAL

1. Remove spark plugs.
2. Remove front cover as outlined under "Front Cover, Replace."
3. Remove righthand side secondary

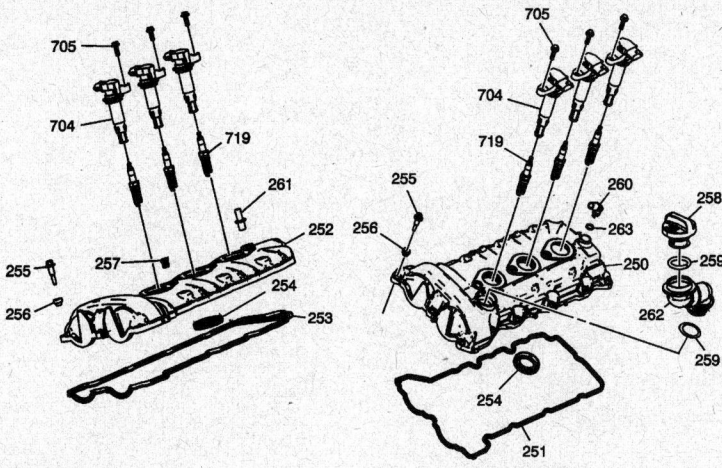

(250) Left Camshaft Cover
(251) Left Camshaft Cover Gasket
(252) Right Camshaft Cover
(253) Right Camshaft Cover Gasket
(254) Camshaft Cover Spark Plug Port Seal
(254) Camshaft Cover Spark Plug Port Seal
(255) Camshaft Cover Bolt
(255) Camshaft Cover Bolt
(256) Camshaft Cover Bolt Insulator
(256) Camshaft Cover Bolt Insulator
(257) Ignition Coil Bolt Thread Insert
(258) Oil Fill Cap

(259) Oil Fill O-Ring
(259) Oil Fill O-Ring
(260) Left Camshaft Cover PCV Fitting
(261) Right Camshaft Cover PCV Fitting Orifice
(262) Oil Fill Tube
(263) Left Camshaft Cover PCV Fitting O-Ring
(704) Ignition Coil
(704) Ignition Coil
(705) Ignition Coil Bolt
(705) Ignition Coil Bolt
(719) Spark Plug
(719) Spark Plug

ARM0300000000252

Fig. 2 Exploded view of camshaft covers

camshaft drive chain tensioner attaching bolts, then the drive chain tensioner, **Fig. 4.**
4. Remove righthand side secondary timing chain shoe, then the righthand side secondary drive chain.
5. Remove primary camshaft drive chain tensioner.
6. Remove primary camshaft drive chain upper guide, then the primary chain.

INSTALLATION

1. Hold righthand camshafts in place by installing camshaft holding tool No. EN 46105, or equivalent, onto camshafts.
2. Wrap primary camshaft drive chain around large sprockets of each camshaft intermediate chain idler and crankshaft sprocket.
3. Align lethand side camshaft intermediate drive chain idler timing mark with bright plated camshaft drive chain link, **Fig. 5.**
4. Align righthand side camshaft intermediate drive chain idler timing mark with bright plated camshaft drive chain link, **Fig. 5.**
5. Align crankshaft sprocket timing mark with bright plated camshaft drive chain link, **Fig. 5.**
6. Compress primary drive chain tensioner plunger into tensioner body using tensioner tool No. J 45027, or equivalent.
7. Install tensioner retraction pins tool No. EN 46112, or equivalent, into tensioner body to hold plunger in place.
8. Install a new primary camshaft drive

chain tensioner gasket to primary camshaft drive chain tensioner.
9. Install primary camshaft drive chain tensioner bolts through primary camshaft drive chain tensioner and gasket.
10. Install drive tensioner, then tighten bolts loosely.
11. Ensure tensioner gasket is in place, then tighten tensioner bolts to specification.
12. Remove tensioner retraction pins and release tensioner plunger.
13. Place righthand side secondary camshaft drive chain around righthand side camshaft intermediate drive chain idler outer sprocket, align bright plated camshaft drive link with alignment access hole in camshaft drive chain idler inner sprocket, **Fig. 6.**
14. Wrap secondary camshaft drive chain around both righthand side actuator drive sprockets, ensure there are seven darkened links between bright plated camshaft drive chain links for camshaft position actuator sprockets, **Fig. 7.**
15. Align righthand side exhaust camshaft position actuator sprocket alignment triangle mark with bright plated camshaft drive chain link, **Fig. 8.**
16. Align righthand side intake camshaft position actuator sprocket alignment triangle mark with bright plated camshaft drive chain link, **Fig. 9.**
17. Install chain guide.
18. Compress righthand side secondary camshaft drive chain tensioner plunger into tensioner body using tensioner

tool No. J 45027, or equivalent.
19. Install tensioner retraction pins tool No. EN 46112, or equivalent, into tensioner body to hold plunger in place.
20. Install a new righthand side secondary camshaft drive chain tensioner gasket to drive chain tensioner.
21. Install righthand side secondary camshaft drive chain tensioner bolts through drive chain tensioner and gasket.
22. Install drive tensioner, then tighten bolts loosely.
23. Ensure tensioner gasket is in place, then tighten tensioner bolts to specification.
24. Remove tensioner retraction pins and release tensioner plunger.
25. Ensure all timing marks are aligned, **Fig. 10.**
26. Install front cover as outlined under "Front Cover, Replace."
27. Install spark plugs.

Right Secondary Drive Chain

REMOVAL

1. Remove spark plugs.
2. Remove front cover as outlined under "Front Cover, Replace."
3. Remove righthand side secondary camshaft drive chain tensioner attaching bolts, then the drive chain tensioner, **Fig. 4.**
4. Remove righthand side secondary timing chain shoe, then the righthand side secondary drive chain.

INSTALLATION

1. Hold righthand camshafts in place by installing camshaft holding tool No. EN 46105, or equivalent, onto camshafts.
2. Place righthand side secondary camshaft drive chain around righthand side camshaft intermediate drive chain idler outer sprocket, align bright plated camshaft drive link with alignment access hole in camshaft drive chain idler inner sprocket, **Fig. 6.**
3. Wrap secondary camshaft drive chain around both righthand side actuator drive sprockets, ensure there are seven darkened links between bright plated camshaft drive chain links for camshaft position actuator sprockets, **Fig. 7.**
4. Align righthand side exhaust camshaft position actuator sprocket alignment triangle mark with bright plated camshaft drive chain link, **Fig. 8.**
5. Align righthand side intake camshaft position actuator sprocket alignment triangle mark with bright plated camshaft drive chain link, **Fig. 9.**
6. Compress righthand side secondary camshaft drive chain tensioner plunger into tensioner body using tensioner tool No. J 45027, or equivalent.
7. Install tensioner retraction pins tool No. EN 46112, or equivalent, into tensioner body to hold plunger in place.
8. Install a new righthand side secondary camshaft drive chain tensioner gasket

to drive chain tensioner.

9. Install righthand side secondary cam-shaft drive chain tensioner bolts through drive chain tensioner and gasket.
10. Install drive tensioner, then tighten bolts loosely.
11. Ensure tensioner gasket is in place, then tighten tensioner bolts to specification.
12. Remove tensioner retraction pins and release tensioner plunger.
13. Ensure all timing marks are aligned, **Fig. 10.**
14. Install front cover as outlined under "Front Cover, Replace."
15. Install spark plugs.

Left Secondary Drive Chain

REMOVAL

1. Remove primary drive chain as outlined under "Primary Drive Chain."
2. Remove lethand side secondary cam-shaft drive chain tensioner and chain guide.
3. Remove lethand side secondary cam-shaft drive chain idler.
4. Remove lethand side secondary cam-shaft drive chain.

INSTALLATION

1. Hold lefthand camshafts in place by installing camshaft holding tool No. EN 46105, or equivalent, onto camshafts.
2. Ensure crankshaft is in "Stage 1" timing drive assembly position, **Fig. 11.**
3. Place lethand side secondary cam-shaft drive chain around inner sprocket of camshaft intermediate drive chain idler with bright plated drive chain link aligned to access hole in idler outer sprocket, **Fig. 12.**
4. Wrap secondary camshaft drive chain around both lethand side actuator drive sprockets.
5. Ensure there are seven darkened links between bright plated camshaft drive chain links for camshaft position actuator sprockets, **Fig. 13.**
6. Align lethand side exhaust camshaft position actuator sprocket alignment circle mark with bright plated camshaft drive chain link, **Fig. 14.**
7. Align lethand side intake camshaft position actuator sprocket alignment circle mark with bright plated camshaft drive chain link, **Fig. 15.**
8. Install chain guide.
9. Compress lethand side secondary camshaft drive chain tensioner plunger into tensioner body using tensioner tool No. J 45027, or equivalent.
10. Install tensioner retraction pins tool No. EN 46112, or equivalent, into tensioner body to hold plunger in place.
11. Install a new lethand side secondary camshaft drive chain tensioner gasket to drive tensioner.
12. Install lethand side secondary cam-shaft drive chain tensioner bolts through drive chain tensioner and gasket.

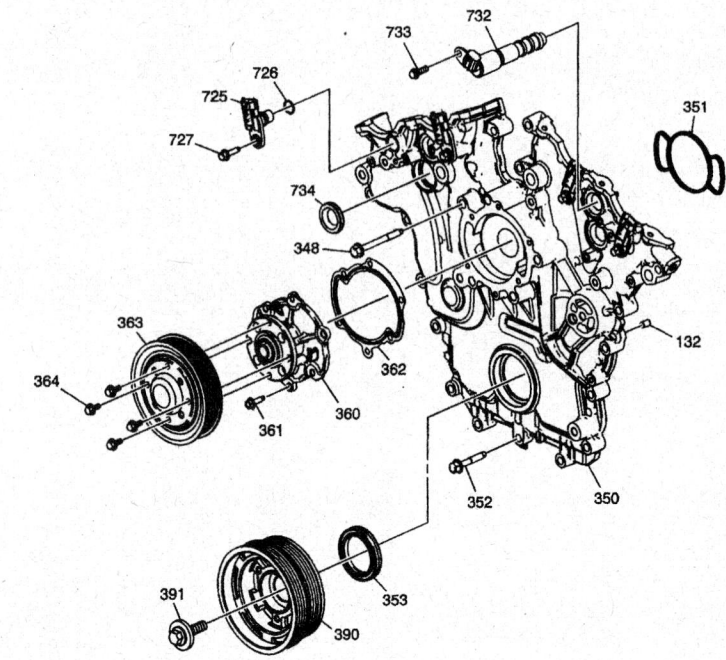

(132) Engine Front Cover Locating Pin
(348) Engine Front Cover Bolt - M10
(350) Engine Front Cover
(351) Engine Front Cover Gasket
(352) Engine Front Cover Bolt - M8
(353) Engine Front Cover Seal
(360) Water Pump Assembly
(361) Water Pump Bolt
(362) Water Pump Gasket
(363) Water Pump Pulley
(364) Water Pump Pulley Bolt
(390) Crankshaft Balancer
(391) Crankshaft Balancer Bolt
(725) Camshaft Position Sensor
(726) Camshaft Position Sensor O-Ring
(727) Camshaft Position Sensor Bolt
(732) Camshaft Position Actuator Solenoid Valve
(733) Camshaft Position Actuator Solenoid Valve Bolt
(734) Camshaft Position Actuator Solenoid Valve Seal

ARM0300000000253

Fig. 3   Exploded view of front cover

13. Install drive tensioner, then tighten bolts loosely.
14. Ensure tensioner gasket is in place, then tighten tensioner bolts to specification.
15. Remove tensioner retraction pins and release tensioner plunger.
16. Install righthand side camshaft secondary and primary timing chains.
17. Ensure all timing marks are aligned, **Fig. 10.**
18. Install front cover as outlined under "Front Cover, Replace."

CAMSHAFT

REPLACE

1. Remove camshaft cover as outlined under "Valve Cover, Replace."
2. Remove camshaft position actuator solenoid.
3. Remove crankshaft balancer as outlined under "Crankshaft Balancer, Replace."
4. Rotate crankshaft until camshafts are in a neutral (low tension) position. Camshaft flats will be parallel with camshaft cover rail.
5. Hold camshafts in place with a suitable open end wrench, then loosen camshaft position actuator (sprocket) bolts.

6. Install timing chain retention tool No. EN 46108, or equivalent, over lethand side secondary timing chain.
7. Mark timing chain and actuators (sprockets) for installation reference.
8. Remove camshaft actuator (sprocket) attaching bolts.
9. Prior to removing camshafts, observe markings on camshaft bearing caps as follows:
   a. Each bearing cap is marked in order to identify its location.
   b. Raised feature on cap must always be oriented toward center of cylinder head.
   c. Stamped letter "I" indicates intake camshaft and stamped letter "E" indicates exhaust camshaft.
   d. Stamped number indicates journal position from front of engine.
10. Remove camshafts from cylinder head.
11. Reverse procedure to install, noting the following:
   a. Apply a liberal amount of lubricant GM part No. 12345501, or equivalent, to camshaft journals and lethand side cylinder head camshaft carriers.
   b. Position camshaft lobes in a neutral position with flats on back of camshafts up and parallel with cylinder

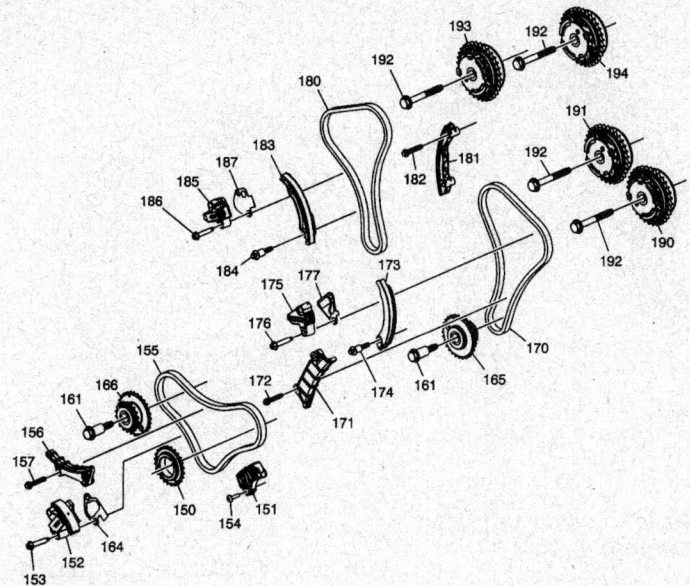

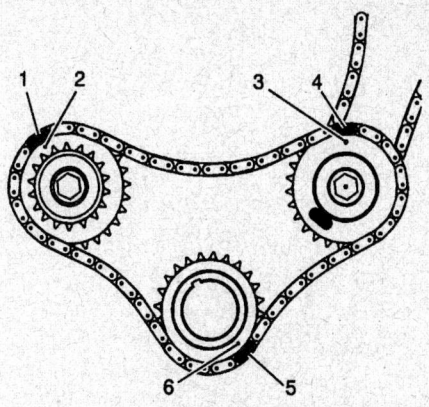

Fig. 5 Primary timing chain alignment marks

(150) Crankshaft Sprocket
(151) Lower Primary Timing Chain Guide
(152) Primary Timing Chain Tensioner
(153) Primary Timing Chain Tensioner Bolt
(154) Lower Primary Timing Chain Guide Bolt
(155) Primary Timing Chain
(156) Upper Primary Timing Chain Guide
(157) Upper Primary Timing Chain Guide Bolt
(161) Camshaft Intermediate Drive Shaft Sprocket Bolt
(164) Primary Timing Chain Tensioner Gasket
(165) Left Camshaft Intermediate Drive Shaft Sprocket
(166) Right Camshaft Intermediate Drive Shaft Sprocket
(170) Left Secondary Timing Chain
(171) Left Secondary Timing Chain Guide
(172) Left Secondary Timing Chain Guide Bolt
(173) Left Secondary Timing Chain Shoe
(174) Left Secondary Timing Chain Shoe Bolt
(175) Left Secondary Timing Chain Tensioner

(176) Left Secondary Timing Chain Tensioner Bolt
(177) Left Secondary Timing Chain Tensioner Gasket
(180) Right Secondary Timing Chain
(181) Right Secondary Timing Chain Guide
(182) Right Secondary Timing Chain Guide Bolt
(183) Right Secondary Timing Chain Shoe
(184) Right Secondary Timing Chain Shoe Bolt
(185) Right Secondary Timing Chain Tensioner
(186) Right Secondary Timing Chain Tensioner Bolt
(187) Right Secondary Timing Chain Tensioner Gasket
(190) Left Exhaust Camshaft Position Actuator
(191) Left Intake Camshaft Position Actuator
(192) Camshaft Position Actuator Bolt
(192) Camshaft Position Actuator Bolt
(192) Camshaft Position Actuator Bolt
(192) Camshaft Position Actuator Bolt
(193) Right Exhaust Camshaft Position Actuator
(194) Right Intake Camshaft Position Actuator

ARM0300000000254

Fig. 4 Primary & secondary timing chains

head camshaft cover rail.
c. Apply a liberal amount of lubricant GM part No. 12345501, or equivalent, to camshaft bearing caps.
d. **Torque** camshaft bearing cap bolts to 89 inch lbs., using sequence, **Fig. 16.**
e. Loosen center intake camshaft bearing cap bolts (1 and 2) and center exhaust camshaft bearing cap bolts (3 and 4), then **torque** camshaft bearing cap bolts 1, 2, 3 and 4 to 89 inch lbs.

PISTON & ROD ASSEMBLY

When installing piston and rod assemblies into cylinder block, ensure dot on top of piston faces toward front of engine.

Tighten connecting rod bolts in four steps as follows: First step, **torque** bolts to 22 ft. lbs.; second step, loosen bolts; third step, **torque** bolts to 18 ft. lbs.; fourth step, tighten bolts an additional 110°.

PISTONS, PINS & RINGS

Pistons and rings are available in standard size and oversize. Pistons and their pins are serviced as an assembly.

MAIN & ROD BEARINGS

Main and rod bearings are available in standard size only. Tighten main bearing cap bolts as follows: **Torque** inboard bolts to 15 ft. lbs., then tighten an additional 80°; **torque** outboard bolts to 11 ft. lbs., then tighten an additional 110°; **torque** short inner and long outer bolts to 22 ft. lbs.

CRANKSHAFT FRONT OIL SEAL
REPLACE

1. Remove crankshaft balancer as outlined under "Crankshaft Balancer, Replace."

2. Remove seal using a suitable flat-bladed tool.
3. Reverse procedure to install.

CRANKSHAFT REAR OIL SEAL
REPLACE

1. Remove transmission as outlined in **MOTOR's "Domestic Transmission, In-Vehicle Service"** manual.
2. Remove flywheel bolts, then the flywheel from crankshaft
3. Remove oil pan as outlined under "Oil Pan, Replace."
4. Remove crankshaft rear oil seal housing bolts.
5. Pry oil seal housing from cylinder block using pry points located at edge of housing.
6. Remove oil seal from housing.
7. Reverse procedure to install.

OIL PAN
REPLACE

1. Remove front cover as outlined under "Front Cover Replace."
2. Remove power steering hose retainer from A/C compressor bracket.
3. Disconnect intermediate steering shaft from steering gear.
4. Remove engine mount lower nuts.
5. Remove A/C compressor bracket bolts and position compressor and bracket aside.
6. Drain engine oil.
7. Remove transmission oil cooler pipe retainer from engine righthand side.
8. Install suitable engine support fixture, then raise engine enough to access oil pan.
9. Remove oil pan bolts, then pry oil pan from engine block using suitable flat bladed tool.
10. Reverse procedure to install, noting the following:
    a. Apply a suitable bead of silicone sealing compound GM part No. 12346286, or equivalent, to oil pan surface.
    b. Tighten oil pan to engine block bolts to specification.

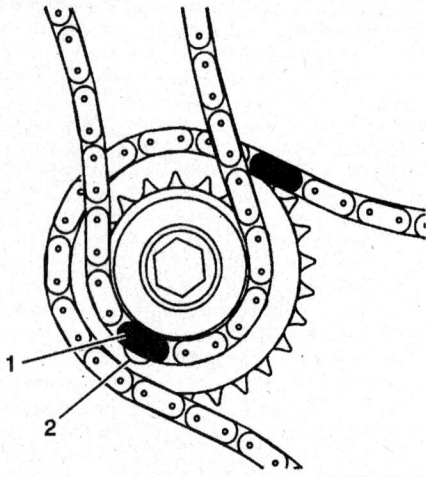

Fig. 6 Righthand camshaft drive chain & intermediate idler sprocket alignment

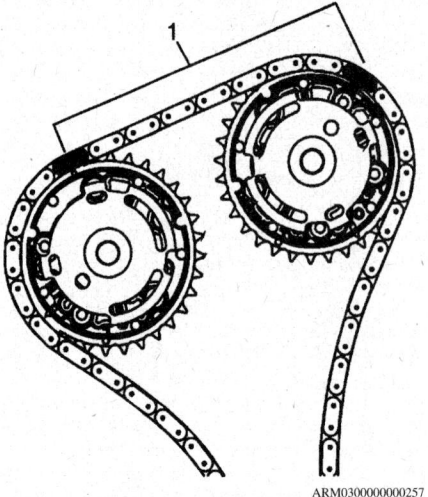

Fig. 7 Righthand camshaft drive chain installation

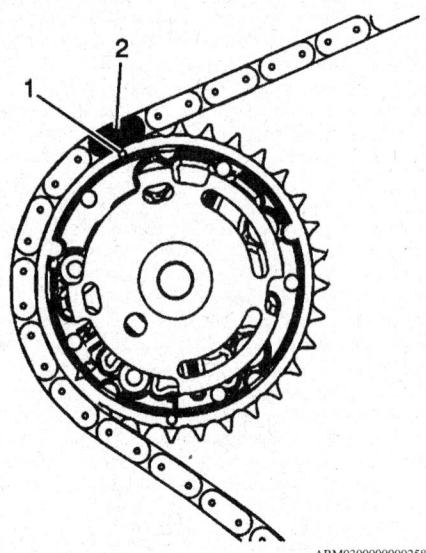

Fig. 8 Righthand camshaft drive chain & exhaust camshaft sprocket alignment

OIL PUMP

REPLACE

1. Remove primary timing chain as outlined under "Timing Chain, Replace."
2. Remove crankshaft sprocket.
3. Remove oil pump bolts and the oil pump, **Fig. 17.**
4. Reverse procedure to install.

OIL PUMP SERVICE

There are no serviceable components inside the oil pump. If pump is not working properly, it must be replaced.

SERPENTINE DRIVE BELT

REPLACE

Alternator & Water Pump

1. Rotate drive belt tensioner clockwise to release drive belt tension.
2. Slide drive belt off of water pump pulley.
3. Slowly release drive belt tensioner and remove drive belt from accessory drive pulleys.
4. Reverse procedure to install.

Air Conditioning & Power Steering

1. Remove alternator and water pump drive belt as outlined under "Alternator & Water Pump."
2. Rotate drive belt tensioner clockwise to release drive belt tension.
3. Remove drive belt from power steering pulley.
4. Slowly release drive belt tensioner and remove drive belt from accessory drive pulleys.

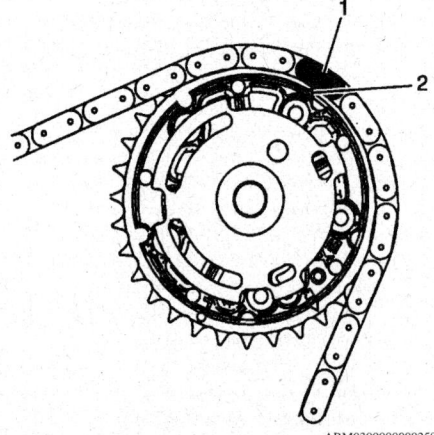

Fig. 9 Righthand camshaft drive chain & intake camshaft sprocket alignment

5. Reverse procedure to install.

COOLING SYSTEM BLEED

1. Place transmission in Park or Neutral position.
2. Engage park brake.
3. Run engine until thermostat opens.
4. Stop engine.
5. Fill system using only clean drinkable water.
6. Repeat procedure if required, until fluid is nearly colorless.
7. Fill coolant reservoir to FULL HOT mark.

THERMOSTAT

REPLACE

1. Remove lower intake manifold as outlined under "Intake Manifold, Replace."
2. Disconnect surge tank hose from thermostat.

3. Remove coolant pipe/thermostat housing bolt.
4. Remove coolant pipe upper bolt, then the coolant inlet pipe from thermostat.
5. Remove thermostat housing bolts, then the thermostat housing.
6. Remove thermostat and discard seal.
7. Reverse procedure to install.

WATER PUMP

REPLACE

1. Drain cooling system into suitable container.
2. Remove alternator drive belt as outlined under "Serpentine Drive Belt."
3. Hold water pump pulley with pulley holding tool No. EN 46104, or equivalent.
4. Remove water pump pulley bolts, then the pulley.
5. Remove water pump attaching bolts, then the pump. Discard water pump seal.
6. Reverse procedure to install.

RADIATOR

REPLACE

Refer to "Radiator, Replace" in the "3.2L Engine" section.

FUEL PUMP

REPLACE

Refer to "Fuel Pump, Replace" in the "3.2L Engine" section.

FUEL FILTER

REPLACE

Refer to "Fuel Filter, Replace" in the "3.2L Engine" section.

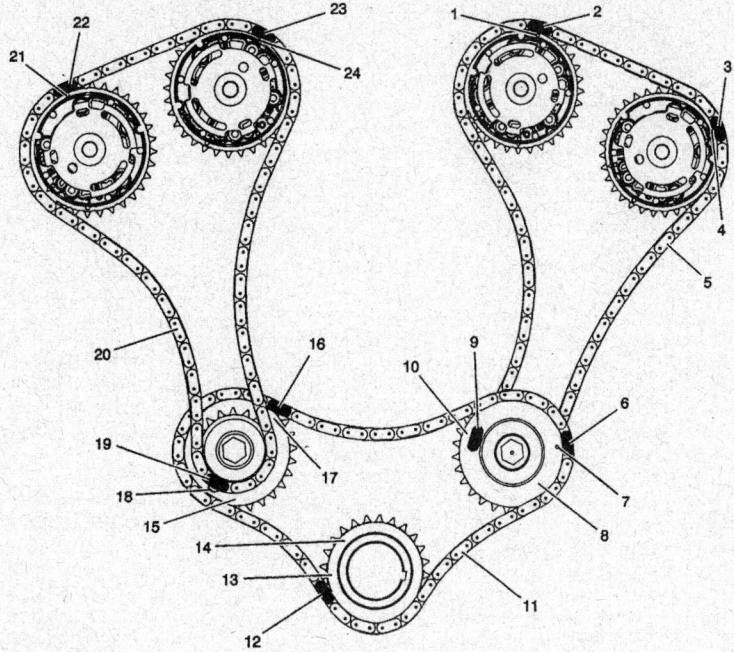

(1) Left Intake Camshaft Position Actuator (CMP) Timing Mark

(2) Left Intake Secondary Camshaft Timing Drive Chain Bright Plated Link

(3) Left Exhaust Secondary Camshaft Timing Drive Chain Bright Plated Link

(4) Left Exhaust Camshaft Position Actuator (CMP) Timing Mark

(5) Left Secondary Camshaft Timing Drive Chain

(6) Primary Camshaft Drive Chain Bright Plated Link for the Left Primary Camshaft Intermediate Drive Chain Sprocket

(7) Left Primary Camshaft Intermediate Drive Chain Sprocket Timing Mark for the Primary Camshaft Drive Chain

(8) Left Primary Camshaft Intermediate Drive Chain Sprocket

(9) Left Secondary Camshaft Timing Drive Chain Bright Plated Link for the Left Primary Camshaft Intermediate Drive Chain Sprocket

(10) Left Primary Camshaft Intermediate Drive Chain Sprocket Timing Window

(11) Primary Camshaft Drive Chain

(12) Primary Camshaft Drive Chain Bright Plated Link for the Crankshaft Sprocket

(13) Crankshaft Sprocket Timing Mark

(14) Crankshaft Sprocket

(15) Right Primary Camshaft Intermediate Drive Chain Sprocket

(16) Primary Camshaft Drive Chain Bright Plated Link for the Right Primary Camshaft Intermediate Drive Chain Sprocket

(17) Right Primary Camshaft Intermediate Drive Chain Sprocket Timing Mark for the Primary Camshaft Drive Chain

(18) Right Primary Camshaft Intermediate Drive Chain Sprocket Timing Mark/Window for the Right Secondary Camshaft Timing Drive Chain

(19) Right Secondary Camshaft Timing Drive Chain Bright Plated Link for the Right Primary Camshaft Intermediate Drive Chain Sprocket

(20) Right Secondary Camshaft Timing Drive Chain

(21) Right Exhaust Camshaft Position Actuator (CMP) Timing Mark

(22) Right Exhaust Secondary Camshaft Timing Drive Chain Bright Plated Link

(23) Right Intake Camshaft Position Actuator (CMP) Timing Mark

(24) Right Intake Camshaft Position Actuator (CMP) Timing Mark

ARM0300000000261

Fig. 10   Timing chain alignment

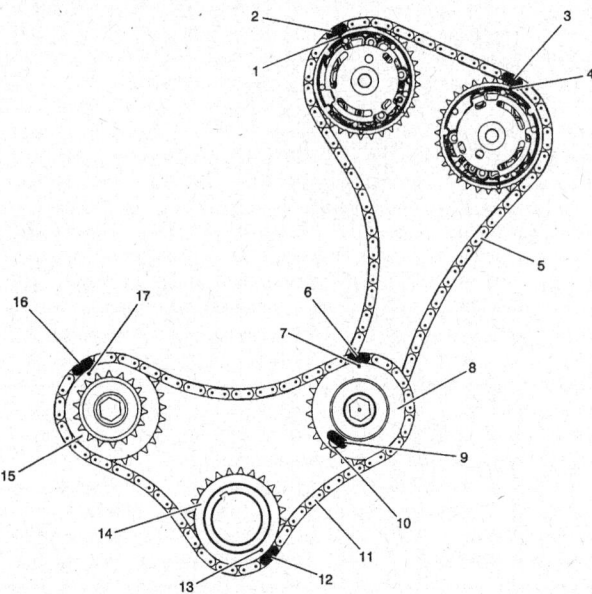

(1) Left Intake Camshaft Position Actuator (CMP) Timing Mark
(2) Left Intake Secondary Camshaft Timing Drive Chain Bright Plated Link
(3) Left Exhaust Secondary Camshaft Timing Drive Chain Bright Plated Link
(4) Left Exhaust Camshaft Position Actuator (CMP) Timing Mark
(5) Left Secondary Camshaft Timing Drive Chain
(6) Primary Camshaft Drive Chain Bright Plated Link for the Left Primary Camshaft Intermediate Drive Chain Sprocket
(7) Left Primary Camshaft Intermediate Drive Chain Sprocket Timing Mark for the Primary Camshaft Drive Chain
(8) Left Primary Camshaft Intermediate Drive Chain Sprocket
(9) Left Secondary Camshaft Timing Drive Chain Bright Plated Link for the Left Primary Camshaft Intermediate Drive Chain Sprocket
(10) Left Primary Camshaft Intermediate Drive Chain Sprocket Timing Window for the Left Secondary Camshaft Timing Drive Chain Bright Plated Link
(11) Primary Camshaft Drive Chain
(12) Primary Camshaft Drive Chain Bright Plated Link for the Crankshaft Sprocket
(13) Crankshaft Sprocket Timing Mark
(14) Crankshaft Sprocket
(15) Right Primary Camshaft Intermediate Drive Chain Sprocket
(16) Primary Camshaft Drive Chain Bright Plated Link for the Right Primary Camshaft Intermediate Drive Chain Sprocket
(17) Right Primary Camshaft Intermediate Drive Chain Sprocket Timing Mark

ARM0300000000260

Fig. 11   Camshaft timing drive chain alignment (stage 1)

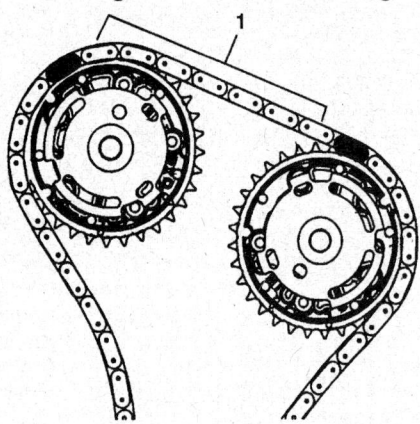

ARM0300000000263

Fig. 13   Lefthand camshaft drive chain installation

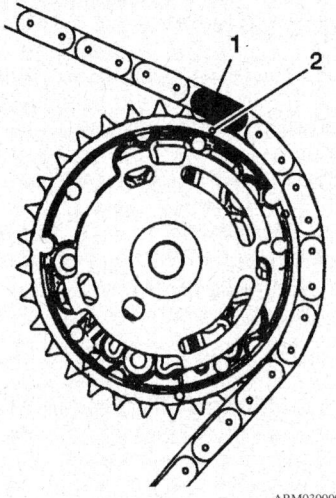

ARM0300000000264

Fig. 14   Lefthand camshaft drive chain & exhaust camshaft sprocket alignment

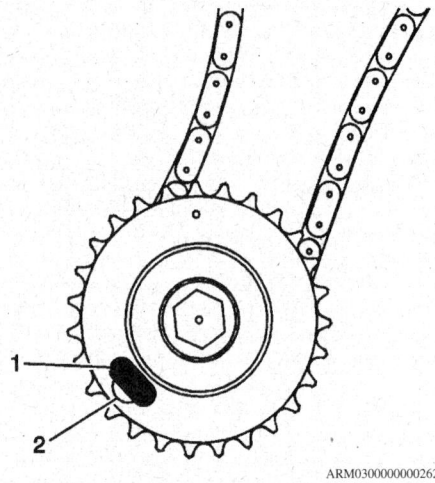

ARM0300000000262

Fig. 12   Lefthand camshaft drive chain idler sprocket alignment

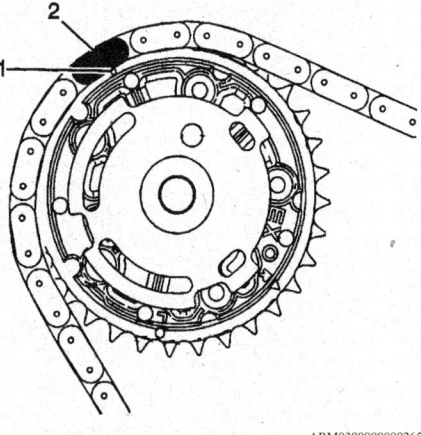

ARM0300000000265

Fig. 15   Lefthand camshaft drive chain & intake camshaft sprocket alignment

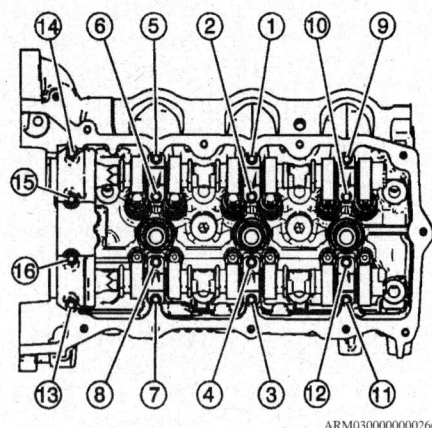

ARM0300000000266

Fig. 16   Camshaft bearing cap bolt tightening sequence

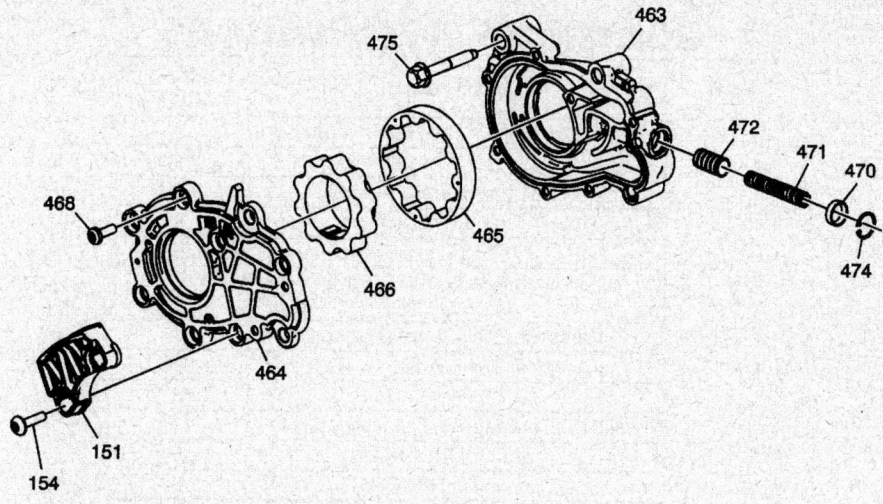

(151) Lower Primary Timing Chain Guide
(154) Lower Primary Timing Chain Guide Bolt
(463) Oil Pump Housing
(464) Oil Pump Cover
(465) Oil Pump Driven Gear
(466) Oil Pump Drive Gear
(468) Oil Pump Cover Bolt
(470) Oil Pressure Relief Valve Bore Plug
(471) Oil Pressure Relief Valve Spring
(472) Oil Pressure Relief Valve
(474) Oil Pressure Relief Valve Bore Plug Retainer Clip
(475) Oil Pump Bolt

ARM0300000000267

Fig. 17   Exploded view of oil pump

TIGHTENING SPECIFICATIONS

Year	Component	Torque Ft. Lbs.
2004–05	A/C Compressor Bracket Front Bolt	37
	A/C Compressor Bracket Rear Bolt	17
	A/C Compressor Hose Assembly	80①
	Alternator Bolt	37
	Camshaft Cap Bolts	89①
	Camshaft Intermediate Drive Idler Sprocket Bolt	48
	Camshaft Position Actuator Bolt	48
	Camshaft Position Sensor Bolt	89①
	Camshaft (Valve) Cover	89①
	Catalytic Converter To Exhaust Manifold	10
	Close Out Cover Bolt	89①
	Connecting Rod Bolts	②
	Coolant Manifold Pipe	89①
	Coolant Outlet Bolt	89①
	Crankshaft Balancer Bolt	③
	Crankshaft Main Bearing (Inner) Bolts	④
	Crankshaft Main Bearing (Outer) Bolts	⑤
	Crankshaft Main Bearing (Side) Bolts	22
	Crankshaft Position Sensor	89①
	Cylinder Head Bolt (M8 Bolt)	⑥
	Cylinder Head Bolt (M11 Bolt)	⑦
	Drive Belt Idler Pulley Bolt	37
	Drive Belt Tensioner Bolt	37
	ECM Bolt	89①
	ECT Sensor	18
	Engine Mount Bracket To Cylinder Block (M8 Bolt)	28
	Engine Mount Bracket To Cylinder Block (M11 Bolt)	45
	Engine Mount To Bracket	59
	EVAP Purge Valve Bolt	89①
	Exhaust Manifold Bolt	15
	Exhaust Manifold Heat Shield Bolt	89①
	Flywheel Bolts	⑧
	Front Cover Bolts	17
	Fuel Rail Bolt	89①
	Ground Cable Bolt	37
	Heater Inlet/Outlet Pipe Assembly Bolt	89①
	Ignition Coil Bolt	89①
	Intake Manifold (Upper) To Cylinder Head Bolts	17
	Intake Manifold (Upper) To Intake Manifold (Lower) Bolts	17
	Knock Sensor Bolt	17
	Main Bearing (Inner) Bolts	④
	Main Bearing (Outer) Bolts	⑤
	Main Bearing (Side) Bolts	22
	MAP Sensor Bolt	89①
	Oil Dipstick Tube Bolt	89①
	Oil Drain Plug	18
	Oil Filter Cap	18
	Oil Filter Housing Adapter To Cylinder Block	17
	Oil Filter Housing Adapter To Cylinder Head	48
	Oil Gallery Plug	23
	Oil Level Sensor	89①

Continued

TIGHTENING
SPECIFICATIONS—Continued

Year	Component	Torque Ft. Lbs.
2004–06	Oil Pan To Cylinder Block Bolts	17
	Oil Pressure Sender	15
	Oil Pump Bolt	17
	Oxygen Sensor	30
	Power Steering Pump Bracket To Engine Bolt	37
	Power Steering Pump Reservoir Lower Bolt	18
	Power Steering Pump Reservoir Upper Bolt	80①
	Power Steering Pump To Bracket Bolt	16
	Primary Camshaft Drive Chain Guide Bolt	17
	Primary Camshaft Drive Chain Tensioner Bolt	17
	Secondary Camshaft Drive Chain Guide Bolt	17
	Secondary Camshaft Drive Chain Tensioner Bolt	17
	Starter Motor Bolts	37
	Suction Screen Bolt	89①
	Thermostat Housing Bolt	89①
	Throttle Body Bolt	89①
	Torque Converter Bolts	47
	Transmission Mount To Transmission Bolt	45
	Transmission To Engine Bolts	37
	Water Pump Bolts	89①
	Water Pump Pulley Bolts	106①

① — Inch lbs.
② — Refer to "Piston & Rod Assembly" for tightening procedure.
③ — First pass, 74 ft. lbs.; final pass, 150°.
④ — First pass, 15 ft. lbs.; final pass, 80°.
⑤ — First pass, 10 ft. lbs.; final pass, 110°.
⑥ — First pass, 10 ft. lbs.; final pass, 60°.
⑦ — First pass, 33 ft. lbs.; final pass, 120°.
⑧ — First pass, 22 ft. lbs.; final pass, 45°.

5.7L Engine

NOTE: On Air Bag Equipped Models, Refer to "Air Bag System Precautions" Located In The Front Of This Manual For System Disarming & Arming Procedures.

NOTE: Refer To "Computer Relearn Procedures" Located In The Front Of This Manual When Battery Power To The Computer Has Been Interrupted.

NOTE: Prior To Performing Any Service Operations Listed In This Section, Consult The "Technical Service Bulletins" Section For Related Information.

NOTE: For Procedures Not Found In This Section, Refer To The "5.7L Engine" In The "Corvette" Chapter.

INDEX

PRECAUTIONS

Air Bag Systems

Refer to "Air Bag System Precautions" in the front of this manual for system disarming and arming procedures.

Battery Ground Cable

Prior to service, disconnect battery ground cable and isolate as required.

Fuel Pressure Relief

1. Turn ignition in "Off" position.
2. Disconnect battery ground cable and isolate as required.
3. Loosen fuel filler cap to relieve fuel tank vapor pressure.
4. Remove cap to fuel pressure service connection.
5. Install tool Nos. J34730-1A and J42242, or equivalents, to fuel pressure service connection.
6. Place bleed hose into suitable container, then open bleed valve to relieve fuel system.
7. Place a suitable shop towel under connections to protect fuel spillage.
8. Remove tool Nos. J34730-1A and

J42242, or equivalents, from service connections.
9. Install cap to fuel pressure service connection.

COMPRESSION PRESSURE

The minimum compression in any one cylinder should not be less than 70 percent of the highest cylinder. No cylinder should read less than 690 kPa (100 psi).

ENGINE MOUNT

REPLACE

Lefthand

1. Raise and support vehicle.
2. Place suitable adjustable jack stand with a block of wood under engine oil pan.
3. Remove engine mount bracket to engine retaining bolts.
4. Remove engine mount bracket to frame mounting bolts.
5. Remove lower engine mount bracket retaining nuts.
6. Remove lefthand engine mount bracket to frame bolt, then the bracket.

7. Remove engine mount from engine mount bracket.
8. Reverse procedure to install.

Righthand

1. Raise and support vehicle.
2. Remove starter motor as outlined under "Starter Motor, Replace" in the "Electrical" section.
3. Place suitable adjustable jack stand with a block of wood under engine oil pan.
4. Remove righthand engine mount upper retaining nut.
5. Remove righthand engine mount bracket mounting bolts, then the bracket.
6. Remove engine mount retaining nut, then the mount.
7. Reverse procedure to install.

ENGINE

REPLACE

1. Turn front wheels to straight ahead position.
2. Turn ignition lock cylinder to Lock position and remove key.
3. Lock steering column by inserting steering column anti-rotation pin tool

No. J-42640, or equivalent, through access hole in lower steering column trim cover.
4. Remove shifter assembly mounting bolts.
5. Raise and support vehicle.
6. Disconnect exhaust system from catalytic converters, then remove exhaust. Do not reuse catalytic converter seals.
7. Remove propeller shaft.
8. Support transmission with suitable jack and block of wood.
9. Remove transmission lower mount retaining nuts, inner and outer transmission mounting bolts, then remove transmission support from vehicle.
10. Lower transmission assembly for access to top of transmission.
11. Remove shift control rods from shift control assembly using a suitable flat bladed tool, then remove shift control assembly.
12. Lower vehicle.
13. Remove underhood cross vehicle brace.
14. Remove fuel injector sight shield and air cleaner assembly.
15. Disconnect throttle body heater outlet hose from throttle body and secure to radiator.
16. Recover A/C refrigerant as outlined in "Air Conditioning" chapter.
17. Disconnect A/C suction hose from evaporator, then remove from shock tower retainer and secure to engine.
18. Disconnect A/C liquid line and remove from vehicle.
19. Disconnect brake booster vacuum hose from brake booster and secure to engine.
20. Remove electrical connector from brake fluid level switch.
21. Remove master cylinder retaining nuts.
22. Disconnect master cylinder brake lines from shock tower retainers, then secure master cylinder to engine.
23. Disconnect electrical connectors from C105 and C107 at lefthand shock tower.
24. Disconnect body fuel line from engine fuel line at righthand side rear of engine.
25. Disconnect engine to chassis EVAP pipe at righthand side rear of engine.
26. Disconnect electrical connector to C102 at front of dash.
27. Remove underhood fuse block electrical connector.
28. Remove battery ground cable retaining bolt from inner fender and secure to engine.
29. Disconnect battery positive cable from fuse block and secure to engine.
30. Disconnect electrical connectors from throttle actuator control (TAC) module, then remove (TAC) module.
31. Disconnect ground strap from righthand frame rail.
32. Drain coolant into suitable container.
33. Remove fan shroud to radiator attaching bolts.
34. Disconnect upper radiator hose at radiator.
35. Disconnect cooling fan motor electrical connector, then remove cooling fan.

36. Remove condenser seal.
37. Remove radiator support bracket mounting bolts, then the brackets.
38. Remove upper condenser mounting bolts.
39. Disconnect surge tank hose from radiator.
40. Raise and support vehicle, then remove air deflector.
41. Disconnect lower radiator hose from radiator.
42. Disconnect lower transmission oil cooler line from radiator.
43. Remove lower condenser mounting bolts.
44. Separate side seals from radiator.
45. Disconnect A/C discharge hose mounting bolt, then remove hose.
46. Remove condenser tube mounting bolt, then tube.
47. Lower vehicle and remove radiator and condenser.
48. Remove power steering oil cooler retaining nuts from frame, then secure to engine.
49. Raise and support vehicle.
50. Remove front tire and wheel assemblies.
51. Remove righthand front wheel well liner, then remove windshield washer reservoir to frame brace.
52. Remove upper intermediate shaft to center intermediate shaft attaching bolt, then separate shafts.
53. Lower vehicle.
54. Disconnect heater hoses from engine.
55. Disconnect rear brake lines from brake pressure modulator valve.
56. Secure brake lines away from wire harness
57. Raise and support vehicle.
58. Disconnect electrical connectors to back-up lamp switch, reverse lockout solenoid, gear select/skip shift solenoid, VSS and transmission fluid temperature sensor.
59. Remove transmission as outlined in **MOTOR's "Domestic Transmission, In-Vehicle Service"** manual.
60. Remove brake bundle retainer clips from righthand and lefthand frame rails, then remove rear brake lines from retainer clip on righthand frame rail.
61. Remove PCM wire harness attaching screws, then remove PCM. Secure wire harness to engine.
62. Lower vehicle.
63. Remove righthand and lefthand shock module mounting bolts, then secure modules to frame.
64. Raise engine enough to install suitable lift under engine, front frame and front suspension.
65. Support rear of vehicle.
66. Raise lift to remove weight of engine from front frame.
67. Remove front frame mounting bolts.
68. Raise vehicle on suitable lift to clear engine assembly.
69. Reverse procedure to install.

INTAKE MANIFOLD
REPLACE

1. Drain coolant into suitable container.

2. Remove fuel injector sight shield.
3. Remove air cleaner outlet duct.
4. Disconnect air control valve electrical connector.
5. Disconnect TPS electrical connector.
6. Disconnect crankcase ventilation hose from throttle body.
7. Disconnect coolant hose from throttle body.
8. Remove throttle body mounting bolts, then the throttle body. Do not reuse gasket.
9. Disconnect fuel rail quick-connect fitting from fuel line.
10. Disconnect EVAP line from purge valve.
11. Disconnect fuel injector electrical connectors, noting their locations for installation reference.
12. Remove fuel rail mounting bolts, then the fuel rail, noting location of fuel rail ground strap.
13. Disconnect EVAP canister purge tube from purge solenoid valve, then from fuel line.
14. Disconnect TPS electrical connector.
15. Remove coolant air bleed hose.
16. Disconnect electrical connectors from EVAP canister purge valve and electronic throttle control.
17. Remove EVAP canister valve from bracket.
18. Disconnect power brake booster vacuum hose from booster.
19. Remove TPS harness retainer from PCV tube.
20. Remove PCV tube from righthand valve cover.
21. Remove intake manifold bolts, then fuel rail stop bracket.
22. Disconnect MAP sensor electrical connector and vacuum hose.
23. Remove intake manifold. Do not reuse gasket.
24. Reverse procedure to install, noting the following:
   a. Apply thread lock No. 12345382, or equivalent, to threads of intake manifold mounting bolts.
   b. **Torque** intake manifold bolts to 44 inch lbs., in sequence, **Fig. 1.**
   c. **Torque** intake manifold bolts to 89 inch lbs., in sequence.

EXHAUST MANIFOLD
REPLACE
Lefthand

1. Turn front wheels to straight ahead position.
2. Lock steering column by inserting steering column anit-rotation pin tool No. J-42640, or equivalent, through access hole in lower steering column trim cover.
3. Remove fuel injector sight shield.
4. Disconnect ignition wires at ignition coils.
5. Disconnect ignition coil bank electrical connector.
6. Remove ignition coil assembly mounting bolts, then ignition coil assembly.
7. Remove spark plugs.
8. Raise and support vehicle.

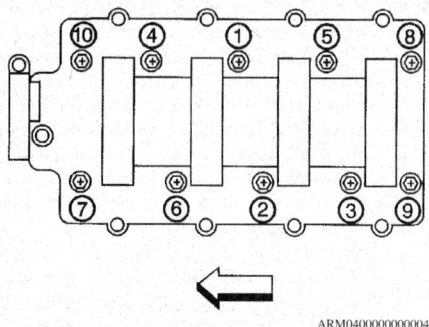

Fig. 1 Intake manifold bolt tightening sequence

9. Support exhaust system with suitable jack, then disconnect exhaust pipes from lefthand and righthand catalytic converters.
10. Disconnect oxygen sensor electrical connector.
11. Remove lefthand catalytic converter to exhaust manifold attaching nuts.
12. Remove catalytic converter from exhaust manifold.
13. Remove transmission as outlined in **MOTOR's "Domestic Transmission, In-Vehicle Service"** manual.
14. Remove center steering shaft to lower steering shaft attaching bolt, then separate shafts.
15. Remove exhaust manifold mounting bolts, then the manifold. Do not reuse gasket.
16. Reverse procedure to install, noting the following:
    a. **Torque** exhaust manifold bolts to 12 ft. lbs., beginning with center two bolts, then alternate from side to side and work toward outside bolts.
    b. Final **Torque** to 18 ft. lbs., in sequence.
    c. Bend over exposed edge of exhaust manifold gasket at rear of lefthand cylinder head using suitable flat punch.

Righthand

1. Remove fuel injector sight shield.
2. Remove ignition wires at ignition coils.
3. Remove ignition coil bank electrical connector.
4. Remove ignition coil assembly mounting bolts, then the ignition coil assembly.
5. Remove spark plugs.
6. Remove oil level dip stick tube.
7. Raise and support vehicle.
8. Support exhaust system using suitable jack, then disconnect lefthand and righthand exhaust pipes from catalytic converters.
9. Disconnect oxygen sensor electrical connector.
10. Remove righthand catalytic converter to exhaust manifold attaching nuts.
11. Remove transmission and clutch housing as outlined in **MOTOR's "Domestic Transmission, In-Vehicle Service"** manual.

12. Remove starter motor, then lower vehicle.
13. Remove exhaust manifold mounting bolts.
14. Raise and support vehicle.
15. Remove exhaust manifold. Do not reuse gasket.
16. Reverse procedure to install, noting the following:
    a. **Torque** exhaust manifold bolts to 12 ft. lbs., beginning with center two bolts, then alternate from side to side and work toward outside bolts.
    b. Final **Torque** to 18 ft. lbs., in sequence.
    c. Bend over exposed edge of exhaust manifold gasket at rear of lefthand cylinder head using suitable flat punch.

CYLINDER HEAD
REPLACE
Lefthand

1. Remove fuel injector sight shield and air cleaner assembly.
2. Disconnect spark plug wires from ignition coils.
3. Disconnect ignition coil wire harness electrical connector.
4. Disconnect EVAP canister purge tube connections from intake manifold, EVAP canister purge solenoid valve, fuel supply line then at rear of righthand cylinder head.
5. Disconnect EVAP purge valve electrical connector, then remove valve from bracket.
6. Remove ignition coil bracket mounting bolts, then the bracket.
7. Remove valve cover mounting bolts, then valve cover.
8. Remove rocker arm mounting bolts, rocker arms and pushrods.
9. Remove intake manifold as outlined under "Intake Manifold, Replace."
10. Raise and support vehicle.
11. Remove front air deflector.
12. Remove drive belt as outlined under "Serpentine Drive Belt."
13. Remove power steering pulley.
14. Remove power steering pump and bracket.
15. Remove exhaust manifold as outlined under "Exhaust Manifold, Replace."
16. Remove engine wire harness ground mounting bolt from rear of lefthand cylinder head, then secure ground away from cylinder head.
17. Remove cylinder head mounting bolts, then cylinder head. **Discard cylinder head M11 bolts.**
18. Reverse procedure to install, noting the following:
    a. **Torque** new M11 cylinder head bolts 1–10 to 22 ft. lbs., in sequence, **Fig. 2.**
    b. Tighten M11 cylinder head bolts 1–10 an additional 90° in sequence.
    c. Final tighten M11 cylinder head bolts 1–10 an additional 70° in sequence.

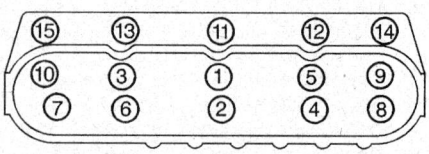

ARM0400000000005

Fig. 2 Cylinder head bolt tightening sequence

d. **Torque** M8 inner cylinder head bolts 11–15 to 22 ft. lbs., beginning with center bolt 11, then alternating side to side while working outward.

Righthand

1. Remove fuel injector sight shield and air cleaner assembly.
2. Remove PCV hose from throttle body and valve cover.
3. Disconnect spark plug wires from ignition coils.
4. Disconnect ignition coil wire harness electrical connector.
5. Remove ignition coil bracket mounting bolts, then the bracket.
6. Remove valve cover mounting bolts, then valve cover.
7. Remove rocker arm mounting bolts, rocker arms and pushrods.
8. Remove intake manifold as outlined under "Intake Manifold, Replace."
9. Remove exhaust manifold as outlined under "Exhaust Manifold, Replace."
10. Remove oil level dip stick tube.
11. Remove battery ground cable from righthand cylinder head.
12. Remove cylinder head mounting bolts, then cylinder head. **Discard cylinder head M11 bolts.**
13. Reverse procedure to install, noting the following:
    a. **Torque** M11 cylinder head bolts 1–10 to 22 ft. lbs., in sequence, **Fig. 2.**
    b. Tighten M11 cylinder head bolts 1–10 an additional 90° in sequence.
    c. Final tighten M11 cylinder head bolts 1–10 an additional 70° in sequence.
    d. Torque M8 inner cylinder head bolts 11–15 to 22 ft. lbs., beginning with center bolt 11, then alternating side to side while working outward.

VALVE COVER
REPLACE
Lefthand

1. Remove fuel injector sight shield.
2. Disconnect spark plug wires from ignition coils.
3. Disconnect ignition coil wire harness electrical connector.
4. Disconnect EVAP canister purge tube connections from intake manifold, purge solenoid valve, fuel supply line, then at rear of righthand cylinder head.

5. Disconnect EVAP canister purge valve electrical connector, then remove valve from bracket.
6. Remove ignition coil bracket mounting bolts, then the bracket.
7. Remove valve cover mounting bolts, then valve cover. Do not reuse gasket.
8. Reverse procedure to install. **Torque** valve cover mounting bolts to 106 inch lbs.

Righthand

1. Remove fuel injector sight shield.
2. Remove PCV hose from throttle body and valve cover.
3. Disconnect spark plug wires from ignition coils.
4. Disconnect ignition coil wire harness electrical connector.
5. Remove ignition coil bracket mounting bolts, then the bracket.
6. Remove valve cover mounting bolts, then valve cover. Discard gasket.
7. Reverse procedure to install. **Torque** valve cover mounting bolts to 106 inch lbs.

VALVE ADJUSTMENT

This engine is equipped with hydraulic valve lash adjusters. No adjustment is required.

CRANKSHAFT BALANCER

REPLACE

1. Drain coolant into suitable container.
2. Recover A/C system refrigerant as outlined in "Air Conditioning" chapter.
3. Remove radiator as outlined under "Radiator, Replace."
4. Disconnect A/C discharge hose from condenser, then remove condenser.
5. Remove starter motor as outlined under "Starter Motor, Replace" in the "Electrical" section.
6. Remove crankshaft balancer bolt, noting the following:
   a. Crankshaft balancer weights must be installed in same location on new balancer as the old balancer.
   b. Crankshaft balancer must be installed in original position on crankshaft.
7. Remove crankshaft balancer using balancer removal tool No. J-41816, or equivalent.
8. Reverse procedure to install.

FRONT COVER

REPLACE

1. Remove crankshaft balancer as outlined under "Crankshaft Balancer, Replace."
2. Remove water pump as outlined under "Water Pump, Replace."
3. Remove fan shroud to radiator mounting bolts.
4. Disconnect upper radiator hose at radiator.
5. Remove A/C line retaining clip mounting screw.

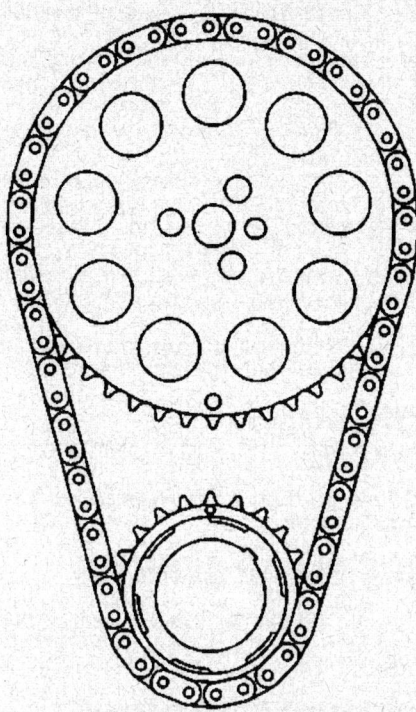

ARM0400000000006

Fig. 3 Camshaft & crankshaft sprocket alignment

6. Disconnect fan motor electrical connectors.
7. Pull upward to remove electric cooling fan.
8. Remove A/C drive belt tensioner bolt, then the tensioner.
9. Remove drive belt idler pulley.
10. Remove alternator as outlined under "Alternator, Replace" in the "Electrical" section, then remove alternator bracket.
11. Remove oil pan to front cover mounting bolts.
12. Remove front cover mounting bolts.
13. Remove front cover. Discard gasket.
14. Reverse procedure to install.

TIMING CHAIN

REPLACE

Refer to "Timing Chain, Replace" in "Corvette" chapter.

CAMSHAFT

REPLACE

1. Remove engine as outlined under "Engine, Replace."
2. Remove intake manifold as outlined under "Intake Manifold, Replace."
3. Remove lefthand and righthand cylinder heads as outlined under "Cylinder Head, Replace."
4. Remove camshaft sensor.
5. Remove engine front cover as outlined under "Front Cover, Replace."
6. Remove valve lifter guide mounting bolts.
7. Remove lifters and guides.

8. Rotate engine to align timing marks, **Fig. 3.**
9. Remove camshaft sprocket mounting bolts.
10. Remove timing chain from camshaft sprocket allowing it to rest on crankshaft sprocket.
11. Remove camshaft retainer bolts, then the retainer.
12. Install three M8 1.25 x 100mm bolts in camshaft front bolt holes.
13. Carefully rotate and pull camshaft out of engine using bolts as handle.
14. Reverse procedure to install, noting the following:
    a. Lubricate camshaft journals with clean engine oil before installation.
    b. Install camshaft retainer plate with sealing gasket facing engine block.
    c. Lubricate camshaft sensor O-ring with clean engine oil.

PISTON & ROD ASSEMBLY

1. Install retaining clip into groove inside of pin bore.
2. Install piston pin to piston and connecting rod.
3. Install retaining clip into groove inside of pin bore.

PISTONS, PINS & RINGS

Pistons and rings are available in standard size and oversize. Pistons and their pins are serviced as an assembly.

MAIN & ROD BEARINGS

Main and rod bearings are available in standard size only. Tighten main bearing cap bolts as follows: **Torque** inboard bolts to 15 ft. lbs., then tighten an additional 80°; **torque** outboard bolts to 15 ft. lbs., then tighten an additional 51°; **torque** short inner and long outer bolts to 18 ft. lbs.

CRANKSHAFT SEAL

REPLACE

1. Remove crankshaft balancer as outlined under "Crankshaft Balancer, Replace."
2. Pry crankshaft oil seal from front cover using suitable flat bladed tool.
3. Reverse procedure to install.
4.

CRANKSHAFT REAR OIL SEAL

REPLACE

1. Remove transmission as outlined in **MOTOR's "Domestic Transmission, In-Vehicle Service"** manual.
2. Mark end of crankshaft and flywheel.
3. Remove flywheel mounting bolts, then the flywheel noting the position and location of flywheel balance weights.

4. Pry crankshaft rear oil seal from housing using suitable flat bladed tool.
5. Reverse procedure to install.

OIL PAN
REPLACE

1. Install suitable engine support fixture.
2. Raise and support vehicle.
3. Drain engine oil into suitable container.
4. Remove lefthand closeout cover.
5. Remove starter motor as outlined under "Starter Motor, Replace" in "Electrical" section.
6. Remove righthand transmission closeout cover.
7. Remove two bottom transmission housing to oil pan mounting bolts.
8. Disconnect oil temperature sensor electrical connector.
9. Remove front wheels and air deflector.
10. Disconnect engine harness to frame wire harness retainers.
11. Disconnect righthand and lefthand rearward wire harness retainers.
12. Disconnect ABS wire harness from lower control arms.
13. Disconnect brake lines from frame.
14. Support radiator and A/C condenser using suitable mechanics wire, or equivalent to front inner energy absorber bracket.
15. Remove washer bottle bracket retaining nuts, then the bracket.
16. Loosen brake pressure modulator retaining nuts, then separate brake pressure modulator from bracket.
17. Mark position of stabilizer shaft to ease installation , then loosen stabilizer shaft mounting bolts.
18. Remove stabilizer shaft link retaining nut, then remove link from control arm.
19. Remove power steering hose to A/C compressor retaining nut and position steering hose aside.
20. Remove power steering gear mounting bolts.
21. Support power steering gear to bolt bracket on oil pan using suitable mechanics wire, or equivalent.
22. Remove outer tie rod retaining nut, then separate outer tie rod from steering knuckle using tie rod pulling tool No. J24319-B or equivalent.
23. Remove lower shock mounting bolts.
24. Remove engine mount lower retaining nuts.
25. Install suitable engine support stand, or equivalent, then lower vehicle.
26. Remove frame mounting bolts.
27. Carefully raise body from frame with aid of an assistant.
28. Remove power steering and A/C line retainers from front of oil pan and position aside.
29. Reposition power steering gear to gain access to oil pan.
30. Remove oil level sensor from oil pan.
31. Remove oil pan mounting bolts, then the oil pan.
32. Reverse position to install, noting the following:
    a. Apply a bead of sealer part number 12378190, or equivalent along engine block and on tabs of front and rear cover gaskets.
    b. **Torque** oil pan to engine block and front cover mounting bolts to 18 ft. lbs.
    c. **Torque** oil pan to rear cover mounting bolts to 106 inch lbs.

OIL PUMP
REPLACE

Refer to "Oil Pump, Replace" in "Corvette" chapter.

OIL PUMP SERVICE

There are no serviceable components inside the oil pump. If pump is not working properly, it must be replaced.

SERPENTINE DRIVE BELT

Accessory

1. Rotate drive belt tensioner clockwise to release drive belt tension.
2. Slide drive belt off of water pump pulley.
3. Slowly release drive belt tensioner and remove drive belt from accessory drive pulleys.
4. Reverse procedure to install.

Air Conditioning

1. Remove accessory drive belt as outlined under "Serpentine Drive Belt."
2. Disconnect surge tank hose.
3. Remove fan shroud to radiator mounting bolts.
4. Disconnect upper radiator hose at radiator.
5. Remove air cleaner assembly.
6. Remove A/C line retaining clip mounting screw.
7. Disconnect fan motor electrical connectors.
8. Pull upward on fan assembly to remove from vehicle.
9. Rotate A/C drive belt tensioner clockwise to release tension from belt.
10. Remove A/C drive belt from pulleys.
11. Slowly release drive belt tensioner.
12. Reverse procedure to install.

COOLING SYSTEM BLEED

1. Start engine and let idle for two minutes intermittently raising idle to 3000 RPM.
2. Inspect surge tank for consistent flow.
3. Allow engine to cool.
4. Remove surge tank cap and fill to FULL COLD level.

THERMOSTAT
REPLACE

Thermostat is serviced as an assembly with the thermostat housing.
1. Drain cooling system into suitable container.
2. Disconnect surge tank hose.
3. Remove fan shroud to radiator mounting bolts.
4. Disconnect upper radiator hose.
5. Remove A/C line retaining clip attaching screw.
6. Disconnect fan motor electrical connector.
7. Pull upward to remove fan assembly from vehicle.
8. Remove outlet hose from water pump.
9. Remove thermostat housing mounting bolts, then the thermostat.
10. Reverse procedure to install. **Torque** thermostat housing bolts to 11 ft. lbs.

WATER PUMP
REPLACE

Refer to "Water Pump, Replace" in "Corvette" chapter.

RADIATOR

Refer to "Radiator, Replace" in "Corvette" chapter.

FUEL PUMP
REPLACE

Refer to "Fuel Pump, Replace" in "3.2L Engine" section.

FUEL FILTER
REPLACE

1. Remove fuel injector sight shield.
2. Raise and support vehicle.
3. Disconnect fuel filter inlet quick-connect fittings.
4. Disconnect fuel filter outlet threaded fitting.
5. Remove fuel pipe O-ring, then fuel filter.
6. Reverse procedure to install.

TIGHTENING SPECIFICATIONS

Year	Component	Torque/Ft. Lbs.
2004–05	Air Conditioning Compressor Bracket	37
	Air Conditioning Idler Pulley	37
	Air Conditioning Tensioner	18
	AIR Pipe To Exhaust Manifold	15
	AIR Righthand Side Pipe Bracket To Cylinder Head	15
	Alternator & Power Steering Pump Bracket	37
	Alternator Rear Bracket	37
	Camshaft Retainer	18
	Camshaft Sensor	18
	Camshaft Sprocket	26
	Connecting Rod Bolts	15⑩
	Coolant Temperature Gauge Sensor	15
	Crankshaft Bearing Cap Bolts	15③
	Crankshaft Bearing Cap Side Bolts	18
	Crankshaft Bearing Cap Studs	④
	Crankshaft Damper	②
	Crankshaft Oil Deflector	18
	Crankshaft Position Sensor	18
	Cylinder Head Bolts	⑤
	Cylinder Head Coolant Plug	15
	Cylinder Head Core Hole Plug	15
	Drive Belt Idler Pulley	37
	Drive Belt Tensioner	37
	Engine Block Coolant Drain Plugs	44
	Engine Block Heater	30
	Engine Block Oil Galley Plugs	44
	Engine Flywheel Hub Collar Bolt (Automatic Transmission)	96
	Engine Front Cover	18
	Engine Mount Bracket To Engine Block	44
	Engine Rear Cover	18
	Engine Service Lift Bracket (M8 Bolts)	18
	Engine Service Lift Bracket (M10 Bolts)	37
	Engine Valley Cover	18
	Exhaust Manifold	⑦
	Flywheel	⑥
	Fuel Injection Fuel Rail	90①
	Ignition Coil	106①
	Ignition Coil Wire Harness Connector	106①
	Intake Manifold Bolts	⑧
	Knock Sensors	15
	Oil Filter	22
	Oil Filter Fitting	40
	Oil Dipstick Tube	37
	Oil Level Sensor	115①
	Oil Pan Baffle	106①
	Oil Pan Cover	106①
	Oil Pan Drain Plug	18
	Oil Pan M8 Bolts (Oil Pan To Engine Block & Oil Pan To Front Cover)	18
	Oil Pan M6 Bolts (Oil Pan To Rear Cover)	106①
	Oil Pressure Sensor	15
	Oil Pump Cover	106①
	Oil Pump Relief Valve Plug	106①
	Oil Pump Screen	18
	Oil Pump Screen To Oil Pump	106①

Continued

TIGHTENING
SPECIFICATIONS—Continued

Year	Component	Torque/Ft. Lbs.
2004–05	Oil Pump To Engine Block	18
	Oil Temperature Sensor	15
	Oil Transfer Cover Bolts	106①
	Oxygen Sensor	30
	Power Steering Pump	18
	Power Steering Pump & Alternator Bracket	37
	Power Steering Reservoir Bracket	37
	Spark Plugs	⑪
	Starter Motor	37
	Throttle Body	106①
	Valve Lifter Guide	106①
	Valve Rocker Arm	22
	Valve Rocker Arm Cover	106①
	Vapor Vent Pipe	106①
	Water Inlet Housing	11
	Water Pump	⑨
	Water Pump Cover	11
	Water Pump Pulley	⑨

① — Inch lbs.
② — Refer to "Crankshaft Damper, Replace."
③ — Then tighten an additional 80°.
④ — Then tighten an additional 53°.
⑤ — Refer to "Cylinder Head, Replace."
⑥ — Refer to "Rear Cover, Replace."
⑦ — Refer to "Exhaust Manifold, Replace."
⑧ — Refer to "Intake Manifold, Replace."
⑨ — Refer to "Water Pump, Replace."
⑩ — First design (single dimple/mark on head bolt), then tighten an additional 60°; Second design (two dimples/marks on bolt head), then tighten an additional 75°.
⑪ — New cylinder head, 15 ft. lbs.; Used cylinder head, 11 ft. lbs.

Rear Suspension

NOTE: On Air Bag Equipped Models, Refer To "Air Bag System Precautions" Located In The Front Of This Manual For System Disarming & Arming Procedures.

NOTE: Refer To "Computer Relearn Procedures" Located In The Front Of This Manual When Battery Power To The Computer Has Been Interrupted.

NOTE: Prior To Performing Any Service Operations Listed In This Section, Consult The "Technical Service Bulletins" Section For Related Information.

INDEX

PRECAUTIONS

Air Bag Systems

Refer to "Air Bag System Precautions" in the front of this manual for system disarming and arming procedures.

Battery Ground Cable

Prior to service, disconnect battery ground cable and isolate as required.

HUB & BEARING
REPLACE

1. Raise and support vehicle.
2. Remove tire and wheel assembly.
3. Remove rear brake caliper and caliper mounting bracket as an assembly.
4. Remove brake rotor mounting screw, then the brake rotor.
5. Remove and discard drive shaft nut.
6. Disconnect ABS connector from backing plate.
7. Remove parking brake cable mounting bolts, then the parking brake cable from knuckle, **Fig. 1**.
8. Remove hub and bearing using tool No. J42129, or equivalent, **Fig. 2**.
9. Reverse procedure to install. Install new wheel drive shaft nut.

SHOCK ABSORBER
REPLACE

1. Remove sill plate retainers, then the sill plate, **Fig. 3**.
2. Remove rear compartment floor trim panel and side trim retainers, then the trim panels, **Fig. 4**.

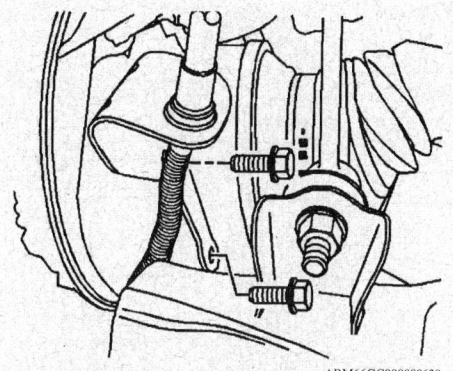

ARM66GC000000629

Fig. 1 Parking brake cable removal

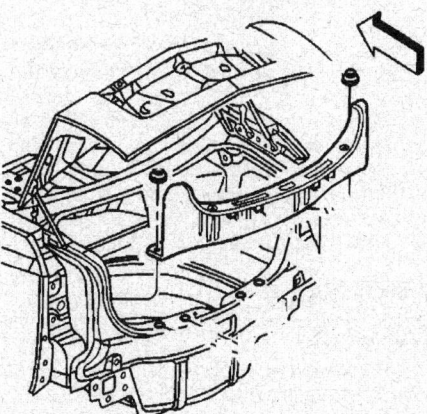

ARM66GC000000631

Fig. 3 Sill plate removal

3. Remove seat upper retaining nuts from rear of back seat, then the rear seat cushion.
4. Remove shock upper mounting nuts.

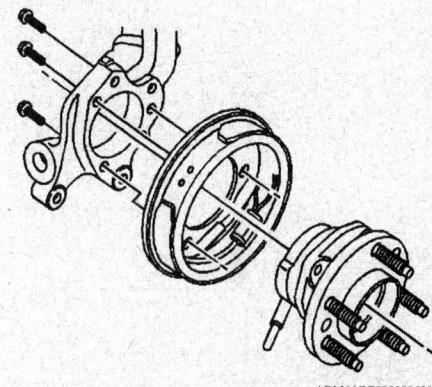

ARM66GC000000630

Fig. 2 Hub & bearing removal

5. Raise and support vehicle.
6. Remove lower shock bolt, then the shock absorber, **Fig. 5**.
7. Reverse procedure to install.

COIL SPRING
REPLACE

1. Raise and support vehicle.
2. Remove tire and wheel assemblies.
3. Remove brake pipe bracket nuts and bracket from mounts, **Fig. 6**.
4. Support lower control arm using suitable jack.
5. Remove lower shock bolt, then lower control arm and jack.
6. Support engine cradle using suitable jack.
7. Remove engine cradle bolts and washers.
8. Lower engine cradle and remove coil spring from vehicle.
9. Reverse procedure to install.

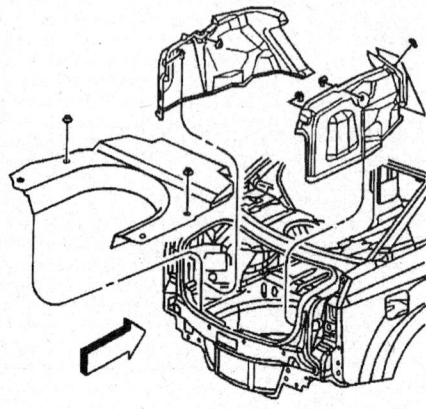

Fig. 4 Floor & side trim panel removal

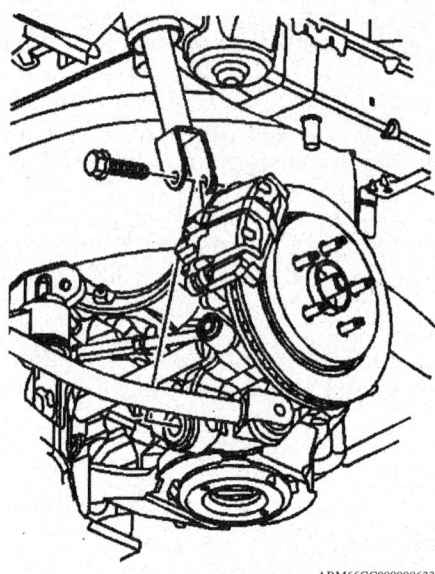

Fig. 5 Lower shock bolt removal

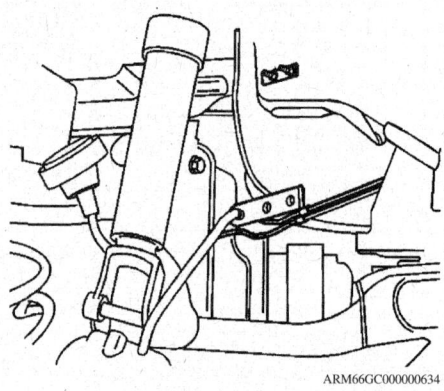

Fig. 6 Brake pipe bracket removal

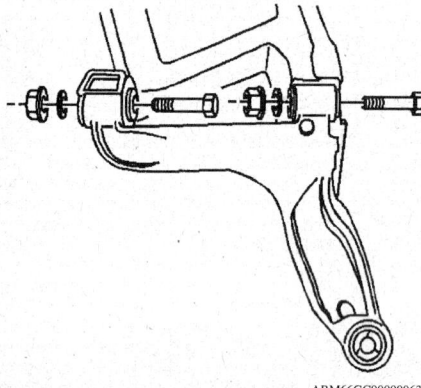

Fig. 7 Upper control arm removal

CONTROL ARM
REPLACE

Upper

1. Raise and support vehicle.
2. Remove tire and wheel assemblies.
3. Remove shock absorber as outlined under "Shock Absorber, Replace."
4. Remove brake rotor as outlined under "Hub & Bearing, Replace."
5. Remove upper control arm nuts and bolts, **Fig. 7.**
6. Remove upper ball joint nut, then separate ball joint from knuckle using tool No. J43631, or equivalent, **Fig. 8.**
7. Remove upper control arm assembly.
8. Reverse procedure to install.

Lower

1. Raise and support vehicle.
2. Remove tire and wheel assemblies.
3. Remove stabilizer shaft link nut, then disconnect link from lower control arm, **Fig. 9.**
4. Remove rear drive shaft nut.
5. Remove shock lower mounting bolt.
6. Remove lower control arm to knuckle bolt.

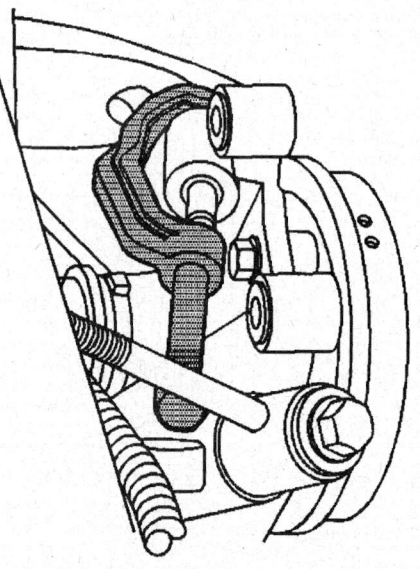

Fig. 8 Upper ball joint removal

7. Remove lower control arm frame attaching nut and bolt.
8. Separate lower control arm from knuckle, then lower jack and remove rear coil spring and lower control arm.
9. Reverse procedure to install.

KNUCKLE
REPLACE

1. Raise and support vehicle.
2. Remove tire and wheel assemblies.
3. Remove brake caliper and caliper mounting bracket as an assembly from suspension knuckle, support caliper assembly with suitable wire.
4. Remove driveshaft nut, then disconnect ABS electrical connector.

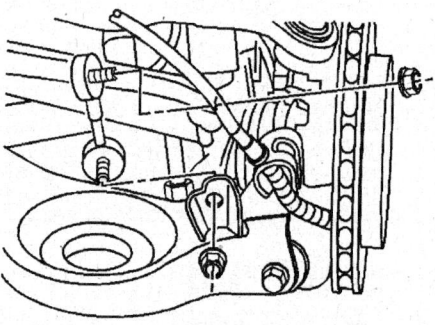

Fig. 9 Stabilizer shaft link removal

5. Remove parking brake cable bracket from knuckle.
6. Remove upper ball joint mounting nut, then the ball stud from knuckle as outlined under "Lower Control Arm, Replace."
7. Remove lower control arm and trailing arm to knuckle bolts, **Fig. 10.**
8. Remove adjustment link to knuckle mounting bolt, **Fig. 11.**
9. Separate drive shaft from hub as outlined under "Hub & Bearing, Replace."
10. Remove knuckle.
11. Reverse procedure to install.

STABILIZER SHAFT
REPLACE

1. Raise and support vehicle.
2. Remove tire and wheel assemblies.
3. Remove stabilizer links from shafts, **Fig. 12.**
4. Remove stabilizer shaft attaching bolts and brackets, then the shaft from vehicle, **Fig. 13.**
5. Reverse procedure to install.

ADJUSTMENT LINK
REPLACE

1. Raise and support vehicle.
2. Remove tire and wheel assemblies.
3. Remove adjustment link to knuckle bolt, then the link, **Fig. 14.**
4. Reverse procedure to install.

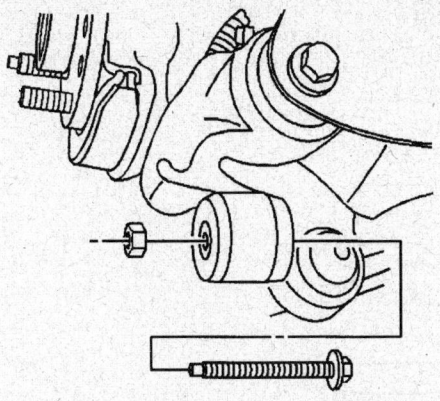

ARM66GC000000640

Fig. 10   Trailing arm removal

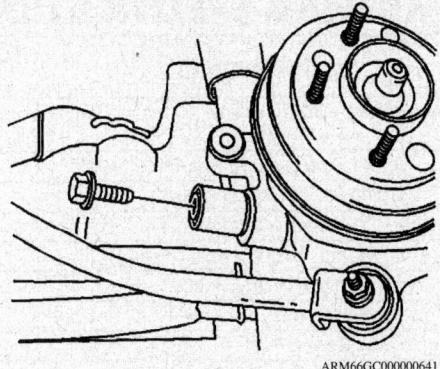

ARM66GC000000641

Fig. 11   Adjustment link removal

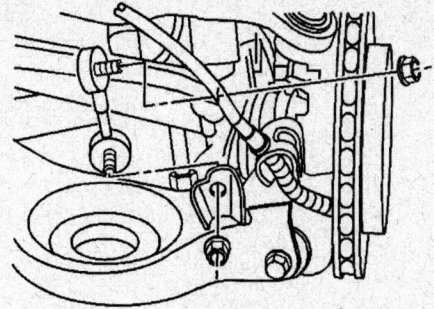

ARM66GC000000642

Fig. 12   Stabilizer shaft link removal

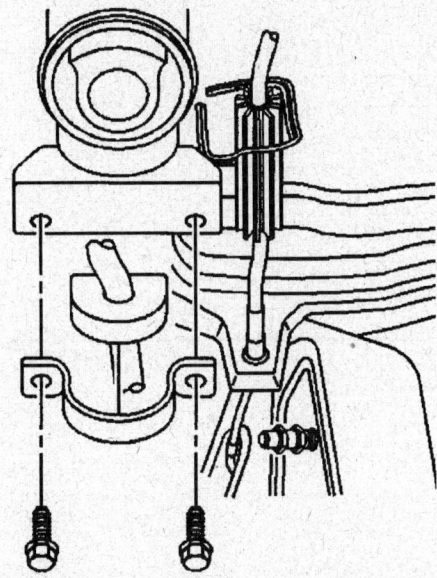

ARM66GC000000643

Fig. 13   Stabilizer shaft removal

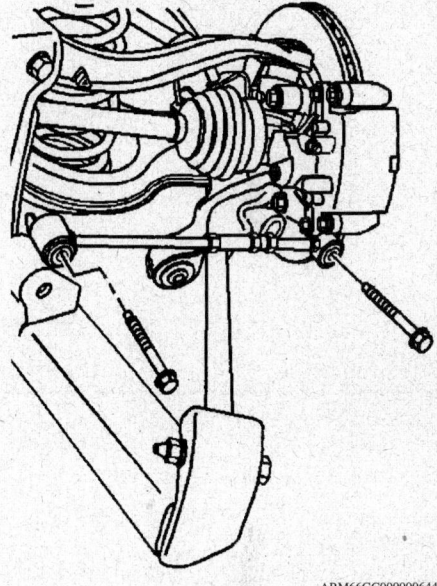

ARM66GC000000644

Fig. 14   Adjustment link removal

TIGHTENING SPECIFICATIONS

Year	Component	Torque Ft. Lbs.
2003–05	Adjustment Link To Frame Retaining Nut & Bolt	129
	Brake Pipe Bracket Retaining Nuts	89①
	Differential To Frame Mounting Bolts	129
	Drive Shaft Nut	118
	Frame To Body Bolts (Front)	195
	Frame To Body Bolts (Rear)	141
	Lower Control Arm To Frame Retaining Nut	111
	Lower Control Arm To Knuckle Bolts	129
	Parking Brake Cable Bracket Bolts	44
	Shock Absorber To Body Retaining Nuts	18
	Shock Absorber To Knuckle Retaining Bolt	111
	Stabilizer Shaft Bracket Bolts	44
	Stabilizer Shaft Link Nuts	37
	Trailing Link To Frame Retaining Nut	66
	Trailing Link To Knuckle Retaining Bolt	129
	Upper Control Arm Ball Stud To Retaining Nut	②
	Upper Control Arm To Frame Retaining Bolt	129
	Wheel Bearing & Hub Assembly Retaining Bolts	92

① — Inch lbs.
② — Torque to 15 ft. lbs., plus additional 210° rotation.

Front Suspension & Steering

NOTE: On Air Bag Equipped Models, Refer To "Air Bag System Precautions" Located In The Front Of This Manual For System Disarming & Arming Procedures.

NOTE: Refer To "Computer Relearn Procedures" Located In The Front Of This Manual When Battery Power To The Computer Has Been Interrupted.

NOTE: Prior To Performing Any Service Operations Listed In This Section, Consult The "Technical Service Bulletins" Section For Related Information.

INDEX

PRECAUTIONS

Air Bag Systems

Refer to "Air Bag System Precautions" in the front of this manual for system disarming and arming procedures.

Battery Ground Cable

Prior to service, disconnect battery ground cable and isolate as required.

HUB & BEARING

REPLACE

1. Raise and support vehicle.
2. Remove tire and wheel assembly.
3. Remove brake caliper and caliper mounting bracket as an assembly.
4. Disconnect ABS electrical connector, then remove connector from splash shield, **Fig. 1.**
5. Remove hub and bearing mounting bolts, then the hub and bearing, **Fig. 2.**
6. Reverse procedure to install.

BALL JOINT INSPECTION

Refer to **Figs. 3 and 4,** for ball joint and bearing inspections.
1. Inspect any aftermarket devices which could affect operation of suspension systems.
2. Inspect system components for damage or conditions which could cause symptoms.
3. Inspect proper tire size and inflation pressure.

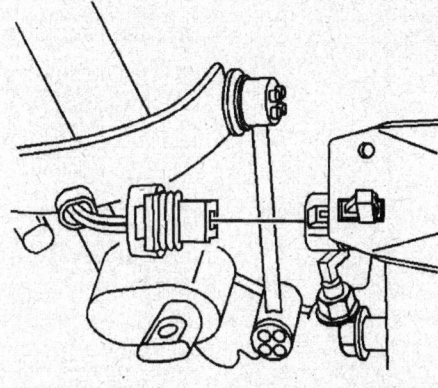

ARM66GC000000626

Fig. 1   ABS connector removal

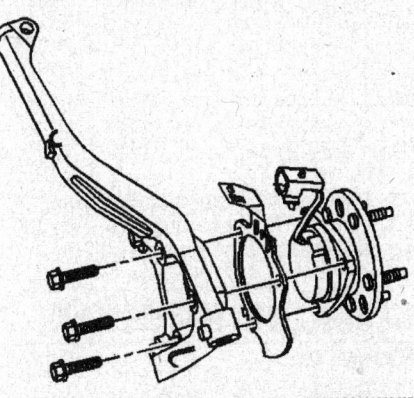

ARM66GC000000627

Fig. 2   Hub & bearing removal

BALL JOINT

REPLACE

Refer to "Control Arm, Replace" for ball joint replacement procedure.

COIL SPRING

REPLACE

Refer to "Strut Service" for coil spring replacement.

STRUT

REPLACE

1. Raise and support vehicle.
2. Remove tire and wheel assemblies.
3. Remove upper control arm to steering knuckle bolt and nut, **Fig. 5.**
4. Remove strut lower mounting bolts, **Fig. 6.**
5. Lower vehicle, then remove air conditioning line and bracket, position and secure line and bracket aside.
6. Remove strut upper bolts, then the strut assembly, **Fig. 7.**
7. Reverse procedure to install.

STRUT SERVICE

1. Install strut in suitable spring compression tool. Mark upper control arm and insulator for assembly alignment.
2. Compress spring, then remove upper retaining nut and strut absorber.
3. Loosen compressor screw, then remove upper control arm bracket and coil spring.
4. Reverse procedure to assemble.

CONTROL ARM

REPLACE

1. Raise and support vehicle.
2. Remove tire and wheel assemblies.
3. Remove stabilizer shaft link lower retaining nut, then the link from lower control arm, **Fig. 8.**
4. Remove strut lower bolts.

Step	Action	Values	Yes	No
1	Did you review the General Description and perform the necessary inspections?	--	Go to Step 2	Symptoms
2	1. Raise and support the vehicle. 2. Clean the ball joint and inspect the seal for damage. Is the ball joint seal damaged?	--	Go to Step 6	Go to Step 3
3	Check the wheel bearing for looseness. Did you find and correct the condition?	--	Go to Step 7	Go to Step 4
4	**Important** Remove tension from the ball joints. Check the ball joint for horizontal looseness using the following procedure: 1. Position the J 8001 Dial Indicator against the lowest outboard point of the wheel rim. 2. Rock the wheel in and out while reading the dial indicator. Does the dial indicator measure greater than the specified value?	3.18 mm (0.125 in)	Go to Step 6	Go to Step 5

ARM66GC000000646

Fig. 3 Ball joint inspection (Part 1 of 2)

Step	Action	Values	Yes	No
5	**Important** Remove tension from the ball joints. Check the ball joint for vertical looseness using the following procedure: 1. Install the J 8001 . 2. Move the ball joint up and down while reading the dial indicator. Does the dial indicator measure greater than the specified value?	3.18 mm (0.125 in)	Go to Step 6	Go to Step 7
6	Replace the ball joint. Did you complete the repair?	--	Go to Step 7	--
7	Operate the system in order to verify the repair. Did you correct the condition?	--	System OK	Go to Step 2

ARM66GC000000647

Fig. 3 Ball joint inspection (Part 2 of 2)

Step	Action	Values	Yes	No
1	Did you review the General Description and perform the necessary inspections?	--		Symptoms
2	Road test the vehicle in order to verify the customer's complaint. Does the vehicle operate normally?	--	System OK	Go to Step 3
3	1. Raise and support the vehicle. 2. Inspect for tire or wheel damage. Did you find and correct the condition?	--	Go to Step 7	Go to Step 4
4	1. Install the J 39570 Chassis Ear. 2. Road test the vehicle to verify the location of the wheel bearing noise. Did you locate the source of the wheel bearing noise?	--	Go to Step 6	Go to Step 5

ARM66GC000000648

Fig. 4 Wheel bearing inspection (Part 1 of 2)

Step	Action	Values	Yes	No
5	**Important** Support the vehicle by the lower control arms or the rear axle to prevent movement during wheel bearing/hub inspection. 1. Mount and secure the J 8001 Dial Indicator. 2. Ensure that the dial indicator contacts the vertical surface of the wheel as close as possible to the top wheel stud. 3. Push and pull on the top of the tire in order to inspect the total travel indicated by the dial indicator. Is the measurement greater then the specified value?	0.27 mm (0.005 in)	Go to Step 6	System OK
6	Replace the wheel bearing. Did you complete the repair?	--	Go to Step 7	--
7	Road test the vehicle to verify the repair. Does the vehicle operate normally?	--	System OK	Go to Step 3

ARM66GC000000649

Fig. 4 Wheel bearing inspection (Part 2 of 2)

5. Remove outer tie rod to steering knuckle nut, then separate tie rod end from knuckle using tool No. J24319-B, or equivalent, **Fig. 9.**
6. Remove upper control arm to steering knuckle bolt, then separate upper control arm from knuckle.
7. Remove lower ball joint nut and discard, **Fig. 10.**
8. Remove lower ball joint from steering knuckle using tool No. J43631, or equivalent.

9. Remove ABS electrical harness.
10. Remove lower control arm, **Fig. 11.**
11. Reverse procedure to install.

STEERING KNUCKLE
REPLACE

1. Raise and support vehicle.
2. Remove tire and wheel assemblies.
3. Remove hub and bearing as outlined under "Hub & Bearing, Replace."
4. Separate steering knuckle from control arm as outlined under "Control Arm, Replace."
5. Remove steering knuckle from lower ball joint stud.
6. Reverse procedure to install.

STABILIZER BAR
REPLACE

1. Raise and support vehicle.
2. Remove tire and wheel assemblies.
3. Disconnect ABS wiring harness.
4. Remove stabilizer shaft link to shaft nuts, **Fig. 12.**

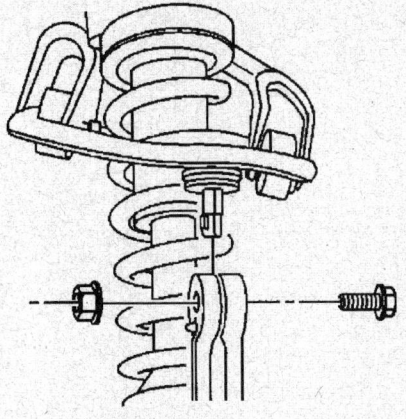

Fig. 5 Upper control arm to strut bolt removal

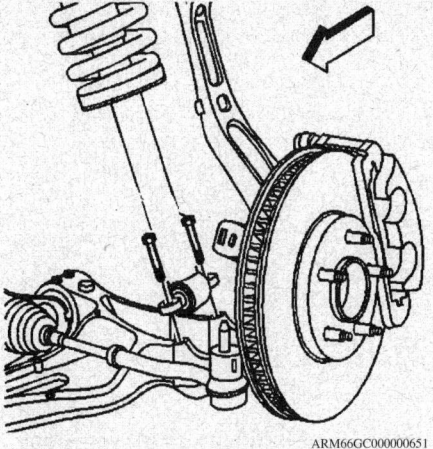

Fig. 6 Lower strut bolt removal

Fig. 7 Upper strut bolt removal

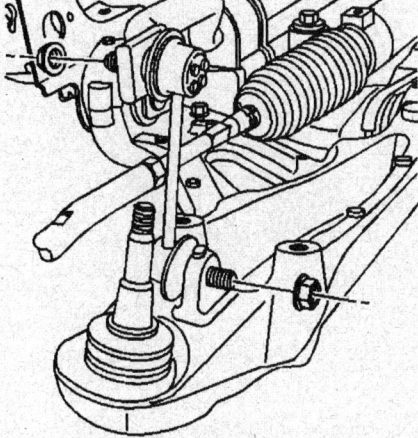

Fig. 8 Stabilizer shaft link removal

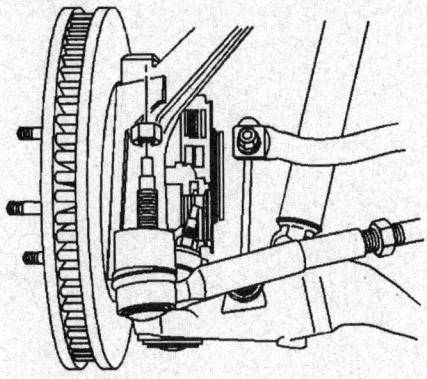

Fig. 9 Outer tie rod removal

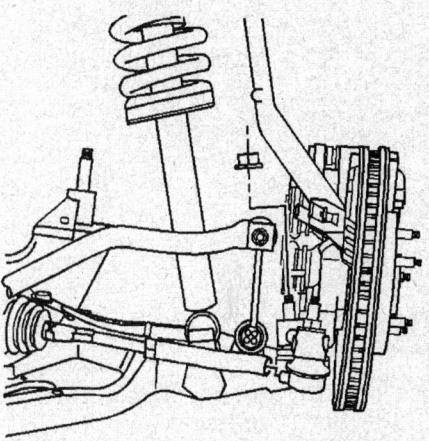

Fig. 10 Lower ball joint removal

5. Remove stabilizer shaft bolts and brackets, then the stabilizer shaft, **Fig. 13.**
6. Reverse procedure to install.

TIE ROD

REPLACE

Inner

Refer to the "Power Steering" chapter for inner tie rod end replacement.

Outer

1. Raise and support vehicle.
2. Remove tire and wheel assembly.
3. Loosen tie rod end jam nut.
4. Remove tie rod end ball joint to steering knuckle retaining nut.
5. Separate tie rod end ball joint from steering knuckle using ball joint separator tool No. J24319-B, or equivalent.
6. Remove tie rod end from steering gear.
7. Reverse procedure to install. Adjust front end alignment as outlined in "Wheel Alignment" section.

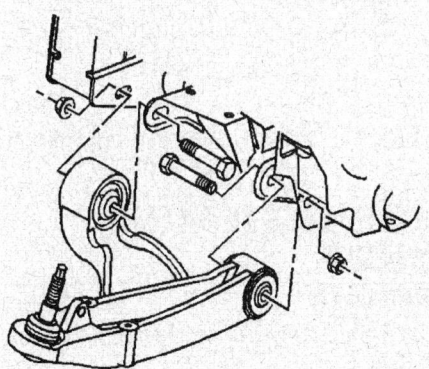

Fig. 11 Lower control arm removal

POWER STEERING GEAR

REPLACE

1. Install steering column anti-rotation pin No. J42640, or equivalent, to steering column, **Fig. 14.**
2. Raise and support vehicle.
3. Remove tire and wheel assemblies.
4. Remove front lower air deflector.
5. Remove intermediate shaft lower pinch bolt, then disconnect intermedi-

ate shaft from power steering gear, **Fig. 15.**
6. Remove outer tie rod as outlined under "Tie Rod End, Replace."
7. Disconnect variable effort steering electrical connector from steering gear.
8. Remove stabilizer bar a outlined under "Stabilizer Bar, Replace."
9. Disconnect and remove power steering gear pressure and return hoses from gear.
10. Remove power steering pressure hose retaining bolt from gear.
11. Remove power steering gear mounting bolts.
12. Remove gear through lefthand wheel opening.
13. Reverse procedure to install, noting the following:
   a. Bleed power steering system as outlined in "Power Steering" chapter.

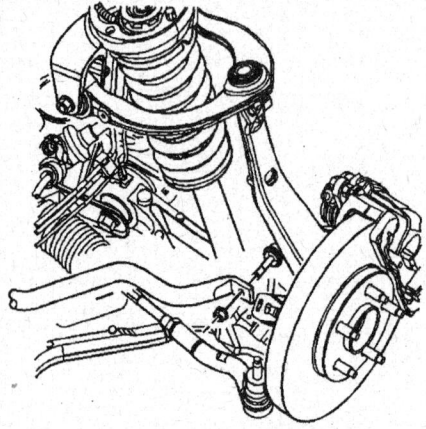

Fig. 12 Stabilizer shaft link attaching bolt removal

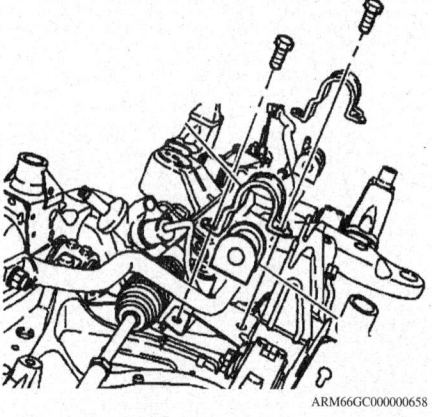

Fig. 13 Stabilizer shaft removal

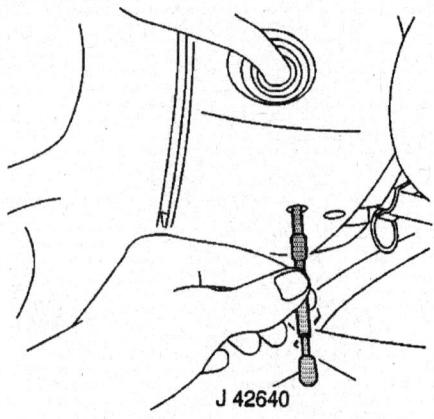

Fig. 14 Steering column anti-rotation pin installation

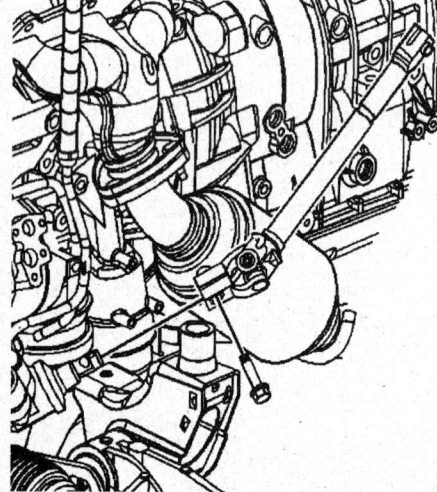

Fig. 15 Intermediate shaft removal

b. Adjust front toe outlined in "Wheel Alignment" section.

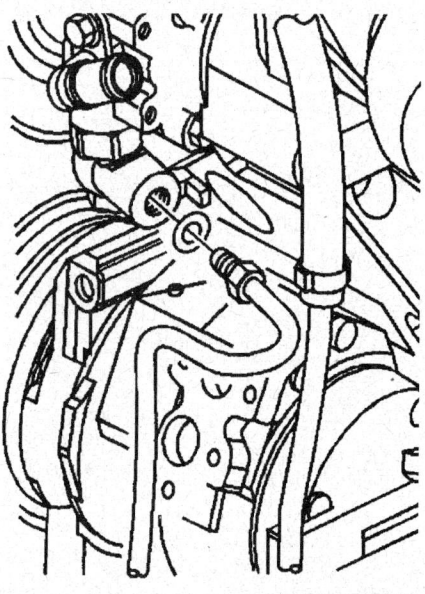

Fig. 16 Power steering reservoir hose removal

POWER STEERING PUMP
REPLACE

1. Remove air cleaner assembly, then the

Fig. 17 Power steering pump removal

drive belt as outlined under "Alternator, Replace" in "Electrical" section.
2. Remove power steering pulley pump using tool No. J25034-C, or equivalent.
3. Disconnect power steering reservoir outlet hose from pump, then the power steering pressure hose from pump, **Fig. 16**.
4. Remove power steering pump bolts, then the pump, **Fig. 17**.
5. Reverse procedure to install. Bleed power steering system as outlined in "Power Steering" chapter.

TIGHTENING SPECIFICATIONS

Year	Components	Torque Ft. Lbs.
2003–05	A/C Line Bracket To Shock Tower Stud Retaining Nut	80①
	Intermediate Steering Shaft Pinch Bolt	35
	Lower Ball Joint To Knuckle Nut	②
	Lower Control Arm To Cradle Nut	100
	Lower Strut Module To Lower Control Arm Bolts	18
	Outer Tie Rod To Knuckle Retaining Nut	55
	Power Steering Cooler Screws	48①
	Power Steering Cooler To Frame	80①
	Power Steering Lines To Power Steering Gear	22
	Power Steering Pressure Line To Power Steering Pump	30
	Power Steering Pressure Hose To Frame	80①
	Power Steering Pressure Hose To Power Steering Gear Retainer Bolt	80①
	Power Steering Pump Mounting Bolts	26
	Power Steering Reservoir Lower Bolt	18
	Power Steering Reservoir Upper Bolt	80①
	Power Steering Return & Pressure Hose Nuts	71①
	Stabilizer Shaft Bracket Bolt	44
	Stabilizer Shaft Link Nut	37
	Steering Gear Mounting Bolts	70
	Tie Rod To Knuckle Nut	52
	Upper Strut Module To Body Bolts	83
	Upper Control Arm To Steering Knuckle Bolt	44
	Wheel Bearing/Hub To Knuckle Bolts	100

① — Inch lbs.
② — Torque to 15 ft. lbs., then additional 210° rotation.

Wheel Alignment

INDEX

PRELIMINARY INSPECTION

1. Inspect tires for proper inflation and irregular tire wear.
2. Inspect runout of wheels and tires.
3. Inspect wheel bearings for backlash and excessive play.
4. Inspect ball joints and tie rod ends for looseness or wear.
5. Inspect control arms and stabilizer shaft for looseness or wear.
6. Inspect steering gear for looseness at frame.
7. Inspect shock absorbers for wear, leaks, and any noticeable noises.
8. Inspect vehicle trim height.
9. Inspect steering wheel for excessive drag or poor return due to stiff or rusted linkage or suspension components.
10. Inspect the fuel level.

FRONT WHEEL ALIGNMENT

Caster

1. Jounce vehicle three times, then allow vehicle to return to normal ride height.
2. Ensure trim height is as specified in "Specifications."
3. Identify caster and camber angles, **Figs. 1 and 2.**
4. Install caster and camber adjusting tool No. J45845, or equivalent, to lower control arm and frame, **Fig. 3.**
5. Loosen control arm adjustment nuts, then adjust caster and camber as required.
6. **Torque** lower control arm adjustment bolts to 100 ft. lbs., and verify alignment is within specifications as outlined under "Specifications."

Camber

Refer to "Caster" in this section for alignment procedure.

Toe

1. Loosen outer tie rod nut, **Fig. 4.**
2. Rotate inner tie rod to set required toe adjustment within "Specifications."
3. **Torque** outer tie rod nut to 55 ft. lbs.
4. Inspect toe setting after tightening.

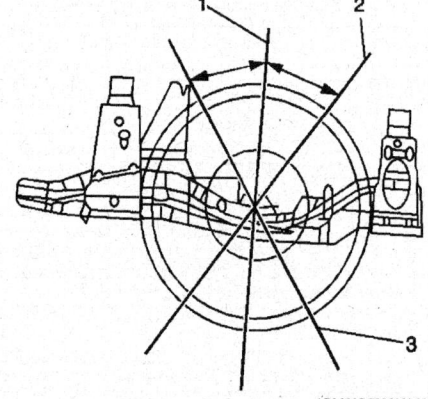

ARM66GC000000664

Fig. 1   Caster angle locations

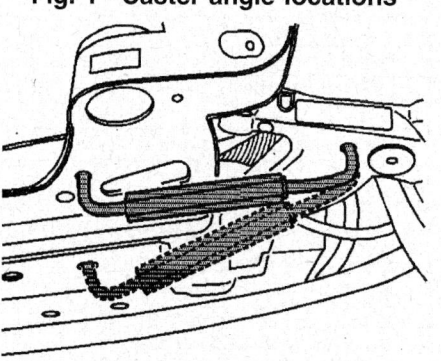

ARM66GC000000667

Fig. 3   Caster/camber tool installation

REAR WHEEL ALIGNMENT

Camber

1. Install caster and camber adjusting tool No. J45845, or equivalent to lower control arm and frame.
2. Loosen lower control arm to frame bolt, then adjust angle as required.
3. **Torque** bolt to 111 ft. lbs., and verify alignment is within specifications as outlined under "Specifications."

Toe

1. Loosen adjustment link nuts, **Fig. 5.**
2. Rotate turnbuckle to adjust toe as required.
3. **Torque** adjustment nuts to 55 ft. lbs., then inspect toe, verify alignment is

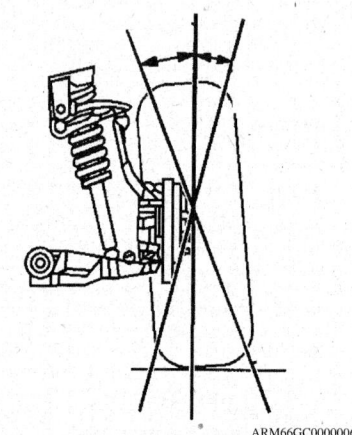

ARM66GC000000665

Fig. 2   Camber angle locations

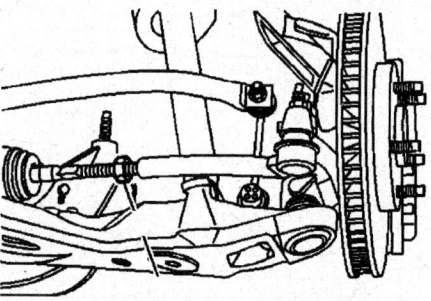

ARM66GC000000668

Fig. 4   Tie rod nut adjustment

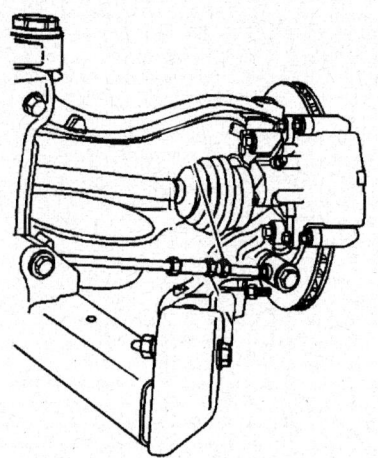

ARM66GC000000669

Fig. 5   Adjustment link nut locations

within specifications as outlined under "Specifications."

DEVILLE, ELDORADO, SEVILLE & STS

NOTE: Refer To Rear Of This Manual For Vehicle Manufacturer's Special Service Tool Suppliers.

INDEX OF SERVICE OPERATIONS

Specifications

GENERAL ENGINE SPECIFICATIONS

Year	Engine		Fuel Injection System	Bore & Stroke	Compression Ratio	Net H.P. @ RPM③	Maximum Torque Ft. Lbs. @ RPM	Normal Oil Pressure Pounds①
	Liter	VIN Code②						
2001–04	4.6L	Y	TPFI	3.66 × 3.31	10.0	275 @ 5600	300 @ 4400	35
	4.6L	9	TPFI	3.66 × 3.31	10.0	300 @ 6000	295 @ 4400	35
2005	3.6L	7	SMFI	3.70 x 3.37	10.2	255 @ 6500	252 @ 2800	20
	4.6L	A	TPFI	3.66 × 3.31	10.0	300 @ 6000	295 @ 4400	35
	4.6L	Y	TPFI	3.66 × 3.31	10.0	275 @ 5600	300 @ 4400	35
	4.6L	9	TPFI	3.66 × 3.31	10.0	300 @ 6000	295 @ 4400	35

TPFI — Tuned Port Fuel Injection
① — At 2000 RPM.

② — The eighth digit denotes engine code.

③ — Ratings are net as installed in vehicle.

TUNE UP SPECIFICATIONS

Year & Engine, VIN①	Spark Plug Gap	Ignition Timing			Curb Idle Speed③	Fast Idle Speed	Fuel Pump Pressure, psi	Valve Lash
		Firing Order Fig.④	Degrees BTDC	Mark Fig.				
2001–04								
4.6L/Y	.050	②	⑤	⑨	⑥	⑥	41–47⑦	⑧
4.6L/9	.050	②	⑤	⑨	⑥	⑥	41–47⑦	⑧
2005								
3.6L/7	.043	⑩	⑤	⑨	—	⑨	55–60	⑧
4.6L/A	.050	②	⑤	⑨	⑥	⑥	41–47⑦	⑧
4.6L/Y	.050	②	⑤	⑨	⑥	⑥	41–47⑦	⑧
4.6L/9	.050	②	⑤	⑨	⑥	⑥	41–47⑦	⑧

BTDC — Before top dead center

① — The eighth digit denotes engine code.

② — Cylinder numbering from lefthand to righthand as viewed from front of vehicle, front bank, 2, 4, 6, 8; rear bank, 1, 3, 5, 7. Firing order 1-2-7-3-4-5-6-8. Refer to **Fig. A**, for spark plug wire connections at coil unit.

③ — On auto. trans. models, idle speed is adjusted in Drive. When adjusting idle speed, set parking brake & block drive wheels.

④ — Before disconnecting wires from distributor cap or coil pack, determine location of No. 1 wire, as position may have been altered from that illustrated at end of this chart.

⑤ — Computer controlled. No adjustment.

⑥ — Idle speed is controlled by an idle speed control (ISC) motor or an idle air control (IAC) valve.

⑦ — With shop towel wrapped around fuel pressure valve to prevent fuel spillage, connect a suitable fuel pressure gauge to fuel pressure valve. Measure fuel pressure w/ignition switch in the On position, engine not running.

⑧ — Equipped w/non adjustable hydraulic valve lifters.

⑨ — Equipped w/crankshaft position sensor.

⑩ — Cylinder numbering from front to rear; righthand bank, 1, 3, 5; lefthand bank, 2, 4, 6. Firing order, 1-2-3-4-5-6.

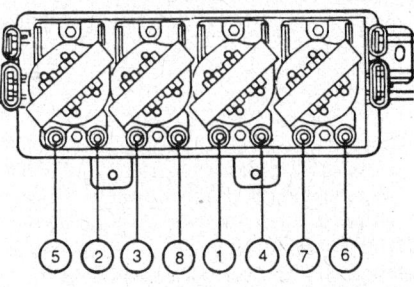

GC1139100136000X

Fig. A

FRONT WHEEL ALIGNMENT SPECIFICATIONS

Year	Model	Caster Angle, Degrees		Camber Angle, Degrees		Total Toe, Degrees①		Ball Joint Inspection
		Limits	Desired	Limits	Desired	Limits	Desired	
2001–02	DeVille	+4.5 to +5.5⑤	+5.0⑤	–.7 to +.3⑤	–.2⑤	0 to +.4	+.2	②
	Eldorado	+1.3 to +3.3④	+2.3④	–.5 to +.5③	0③	0 to +.4	+.2	②
	Seville	+4.5 to +5.5⑤	+5.0⑤	–.7 to +.3⑤	–.2⑤	0 to +.4	+.2	②
2003–04	DeVille	+4.5 to +5.5⑤	+5.0⑤	–.7 to +.3⑤	–.2⑤	0 to +.4	+.2	②
	Seville	+4.5 to +5.5⑤	+5.0⑤	–.7 to +.3⑤	–.2⑤	0 to +.4	+.2	②
2005	DeVille	+4.5 to +5.5⑤	+5.0⑤	–.7 to +.3⑤	–.2⑤	0 to +.4	+.2	②
	STS	+4.9 to +6.1⑥	+5.5⑥	–1.1 to +.1⑥	–.5	0 to +.4	+.2	②
	STS (RWD)	5.25 to 6.45	+5.8	–1.1 to +.1⑥	–.5	0 to +.4	+.2	②

① — Toe-In (+). Toe-Out (–).

② — Refer to "Ball Joint Inspection" in "Front Suspension & Steering."

③ — Cross caster or camber (lefthand to right), 0° (+/-.75°).

④ — Cross caster or camber (lefthand to right), 0° (+/-1°).

⑤ — Cross caster or camber within .5°.

⑥ — Cross caster or camber within .6°.

REAR WHEEL ALIGNMENT SPECIFICATIONS

Year	Model	Camber Angle, Degrees		Total Toe, Degrees①		Thrust Angle, Degrees	
		Limits	Desired	Limits	Desired	Limits	Desired
2001–02	DeVille	–.8 to +.2	–.3	0 to +.4	+.2	–.1 to +.1	0
	Eldorado	–.5 to +.5②	0②	0 to +.4	+.2	—	—
	Seville	–.8 to +.2	–.3	0 to +.4	+.2	–.1 to +.1	0
2003–04	DeVille	–.8 to +.2	–.3	0 to +.4	+.2	–.1 to +.1	0
	Seville	–.8 to +.2	–.3	0 to +.4	+.2	–.1 to +.1	0
2005	DeVille	–.8 to +.2	–.3	0 to +.4	+.2	–.1 to +.1	0
	STS	–1.4 to –.4	–.90	0 to +.4	+.2	–.2 to +.2	0

① — Toe-In (+). Toe-Out (–).

② — Cross camber (lefthand to right) 0° (+/-.75°).

VEHICLE RIDE HEIGHT SPECIFICATIONS

Model	Year	Body Style	Manufacturer's Original Tire Size	Front Dim.	Front Spec. Inches	Front Spec. mm	Rear Dim.	Rear Spec. Inches	Rear Spec. mm
DeVille	2001–05	All	③	H	1.57	40.00	H	3.39	86.00
Eldorado	2001–02	All	③	H	1.96	49.00	I	1.15	29.00
Seville	2001–04	SLS④	③	Z	1.20–2.00	30.48–50.80	D	3.00–3.80	76.20–96.52
		SLS⑤	③	Z	.78–1.60	19.81–40.64	D	2.60–3.40	66.04–86.36
		STS	③	Z	.78–1.60	19.81–40.64	D	2.60–3.40	66.04–86.36
STS	2005	All	③	Z	1.54	39	D	2.52	64

A Dim. — Measurement From Front Wheel Center to Check Point On Rocker Panel

B Dim. — Measurement From Rear Wheel Center to Check Point On Rocker Panel

C Dim. — Ground to Rocker Panel, Front

D Dim. — Lowest Point On Ball Joint Housing Minus Grease Fitting To Centerline Of Rear Bushing

H Dim. — Distance Between Lower Ball Joint Cover to Center of Lower Arm Bushing Bolt

I Dim. — Distance Between Center of Lower Arm Inner & Outer Bushing Bolts

Z Dim. — Distance Between Pivot Bolt Center Line Down To Lower Corner Of Lower Ball Joint, **Fig. C.**

Dim. — Dimension

① — ±..39 in (10 MM) front to rear & side to side.

② — Measurement is with fuel, radiator coolant and engine oil full, spare tire, jack, hand tools & mats in designated positions and tires properly inflated.

③ — See door sticker or inside of glove box for manufacturer's original tire

size specifications. If tires on vehicle do not match manufacturer's original tire size & measurement is not within limits, refer to the "Non-Standard Tire & Wheel Size Adjustment To Ride Height Specification & Tire Size Adjustment Charts" in the front of this manual for approximate changes in ride height specifications.

④ — Soft Ride Suspension System & Chassis Continuous Valve Real Time Damping.

⑤ — Sport Suspension System.

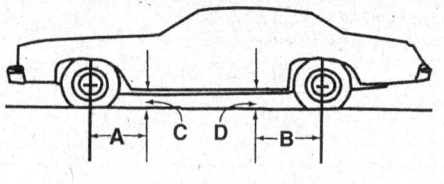

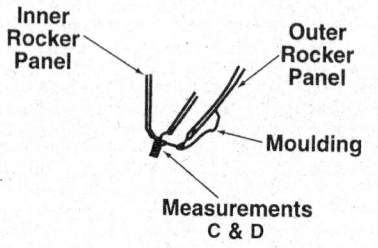

Fig. A Seville

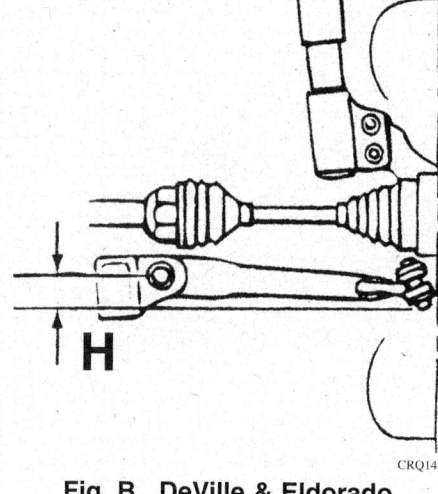

Fig. B DeVille & Eldorado

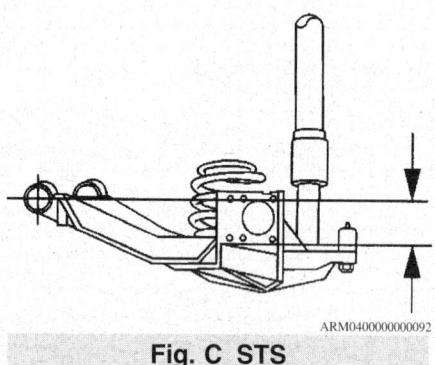

Fig. C STS

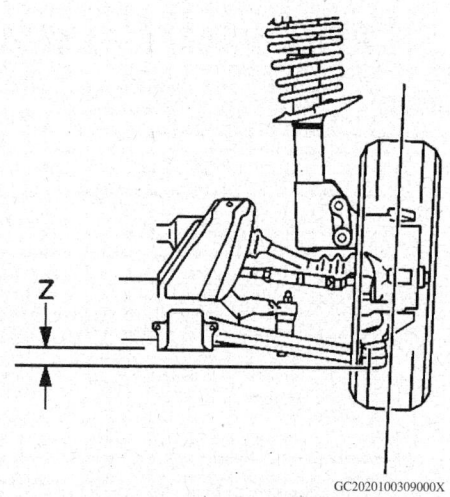

Fig. D Dimension "Z"

FLUID CAPACITIES & COOLING SYSTEM DATA

Model/ Year	Engine/ Liter	Coolant Capacity, Qts.	Coolant Type	Radiator Cap Relief Pressure, Lbs.	Thermostat Opening Temp., °F	Fuel Tank Gals	Engine Oil Refill Qts. ①	ATF Qts.②
DEVILLE								
2001–05	4.6L	12.5	Dex-Cool	18	197	19	7.5	③
ELDORADO								
2001–02	4.6L	12.5	Dex-Cool	18	197	19	7.5	③
SEVILLE								
2001–04	4.6L	12.5	Dex-Cool	18	197	19	7.5	③
STS								
2005	3.6L	13	Dex-Cool	18	194	17.5	6	③
	4.6L	13	Dex-Cool	18	185	17.5	8	③

① — Includes filter.

② — Approximate. Make final inspection w/dipstick.

③ — Drain & refill 11 qts.; after overhaul 12.6 qts.; dry refill 15 qts.

LUBRICANT DATA

Year	Model	Lubricant Type		
		Automatic Transaxle	Power Steering	Brake System
2001–05	All	Dexron III	GM Power Steering Fluid①	DOT 3

① — GM part Nos. 1052884, 89021184
or equivalents.

Electrical

NOTE: On Air Bag Equipped Models, Refer To "Air Bag System Precautions" Located In The Front Of This Manual For System Disarming & Arming Procedures.

NOTE: Refer To "Computer Relearn Procedures" Located In The Front Of This Manual When Battery Power To The Computer Has Been Interrupted.

INDEX

PRECAUTIONS

Air Bag Systems

Refer to "Air Bag System Precautions" in the front of this manual for system disarming and arming procedures.

Battery Ground Cable

Prior to service, disconnect battery ground cable and isolate as required.

FUSE PANEL & FLASHER LOCATION

DeVille & Seville

The engine compartment fuse/relay center is located at the righthand rear of the engine compartment near the power steering pump.

The rear fuse block is located in the lefthand rear of passenger compartment under the rear seat.

The hazard/turn flasher is located at the lefthand side of the instrument panel behind the knee bolster.

Eldorado

The engine compartment fuse/relay center is located on the lefthand front side of the engine compartment, near the strut tower. The lefthand and righthand Maxifuse blocks are located on the front lefthand side of the engine compartment, near the fuse/relay center.

The rear compartment fuse block is located in the front lefthand side of the luggage compartment.

The hazard flasher is located under the lefthand side of the instrument panel near the kick panel. The turn flasher module is located under the lefthand side of the instrument panel near the knee bolster.

STS

The engine compartment fuse/relay center is located on the righthand side of the engine compartment.

The rear fuse block is located in the righthand rear of passenger compartment under the rear seat.

The hazard/turn flasher is located behind the lefthand side of the instrument panel, behind the instrument panel close-out insulator.

FUEL PUMP RELAY LOCATION

DeVille

The fuel pump relay is located in the rear fuse block, under the lefthand side of the rear seat.

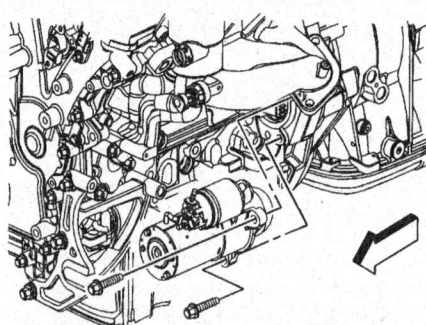

ARM0400000000093

Fig. 1 Starter motor replacement. 3.6L engine

Eldorado

The fuel pump relay is located on the front lefthand side of the engine compartment, in the engine compartment fuse/relay center.

Seville

The fuel pump relay is located in the rear fuse block, under the lefthand side of the rear seat.

STS

The fuel pump relay is located in the rear fuse block, under the righthand side of rear seat.

RELAY CENTER LOCATION

DeVille

The rear compartment relay center is located in the lefthand rear of passenger compartment under the lefthand side of the rear seat.

Eldorado

The engine compartment relay center is located on the front lefthand side of the engine compartment, near the strut tower.

The rear compartment relay center Nos. 1–4 are located behind the lefthand side of the rear seat.

Seville

The rear compartment relay center is located under the side of the rear seat.

STS

The rear compartment relay center is located under the righthand side of the rear seat.

STARTER
REPLACE

3.6L Engine

1. Disconnect starter "S" terminal wire and battery cable, **Fig. 1.**
2. Remove mounting bolts and starter.
3. Remove solenoid and battery cable terminal nuts.
4. Reverse procedure to install, noting the following:
   a. **Torque** starter mounting bolts to 37 ft. lbs.
   b. **Torque** battery cable lead to 115 inch lbs.

4.6L Engine

1. Remove intake manifold as outlined in "Intake Manifold, Replace" in "4.6L Engine" section.
2. Disconnect starter "S" terminal wire and battery cable, **Fig. 2.**
3. Remove mounting bolts and starter.
4. Remove solenoid and battery cable terminal nuts.
5. Reverse procedure to install, noting the following:
   a. **Torque** starter mounting bolts to 22 ft. lbs.
   b. **Torque** battery cable lead to 89 inch lbs.
   c. **Torque** S terminal nuts to 35 inch lbs.

ALTERNATOR
REPLACE

3.6L Engine

1. Remove drive belt as outlined in "Serpentine Belt" in "3.6L Engine" section.
2. Raise and support vehicle.
3. Disconnect alternator electrical connector.
4. Position alternator output BAT terminal boot aside, then remove terminal nut and disconnect battery positive lead from alternator.
5. Remove lower alternator mounting bolts.
6. Lower vehicle.
7. Remove upper alternator mounting bolts, then the alternator.
8. Reverse procedure to install, noting the following:
   a. **Torque** alternator mounting bolts to 37 ft. lbs.
   b. **Torque** BAT terminal nut to 89 inch lbs.

4.6L Engine

2001-04

1. Remove drive belt as outlined in "Serpentine Belt" in "4.6L Engine" section.
2. Disconnect electrical connector from alternator, then position protective

boot away from alternator output BAT terminal for access.

3. Remove alternator output BAT terminal nut, then disconnect positive lead.
4. Loosen lower alternator bolt, then remove bolts and alternator from vehicle.
5. Reverse procedure to install.

2005

DEVILLE

1. Remove drive belt as outlined in "Serpentine Belt" in "4.6L Engine" section.
2. Remove radiator belt as outlined in "Radiator, Replace" in "4.6L Engine" section.
3. Disconnect electrical connector from alternator, then position protective boot away from alternator output BAT terminal for access.
4. Remove alternator output BAT terminal nut, then disconnect positive lead.
5. Loosen lower alternator bolt, then remove bolts and alternator from vehicle.
6. Reverse procedure to install.

STS

All Wheel Drive

1. Remove drive belt as outlined in "Serpentine Belt" in "4.6L Engine" section.
2. Remove upper alternator mounting bolts, then raise and support vehicle.
3. Remove front air deflector.
4. Remove front wheels and right side wheelhouse liner.
5. Remove right and left side stabilizer shaft links as outlined under "Stabilizer Bar, Replace" in "Front Suspension & Steering" section.
6. Rotate stabilizer shaft downward to gain access to alternator.
7. Lift alternator off of mounting bracket to for access to connector and alternator output BAT terminal nut.
8. Disconnect electrical connector from alternator, then position protective boot away from alternator output battery terminal for access.
9. Remove alternator output battery terminal nut, then disconnect battery positive lead.
10. Remove alternator from vehicle
11. Reverse procedure to install.

Two Wheel Drive

1. Remove drive belt as outlined in "Serpentine Belt" in "4.6L Engine" section.
2. Remove upper alternator mounting bolts, then raise and support vehicle.
3. Remove front air deflector.
4. Cut tie strap securing wiring harness to alternator, then remove lower mounting bolt.
5. Lift alternator off of mounting bracket to for access to connector and alternator output BAT terminal nut.
6. Disconnect electrical connector from alternator, then position protective boot away from alternator output battery terminal for access.
7. Remove alternator output battery terminal nut, then disconnect battery positive lead.
8. Remove alternator from vehicle
9. Reverse procedure to install.

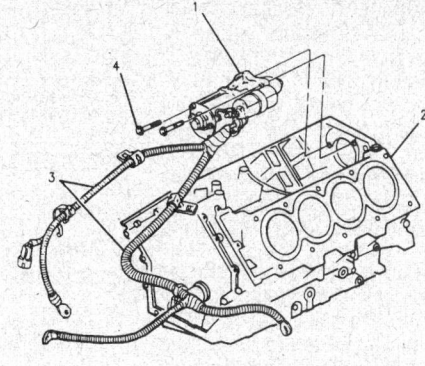

1 STARTER MOTOR ASSEMBLY
2 ENGINE BLOCK ASSEMBLY
3 STARTER SOLENOID
  CABLE ASSEMBLY
4 BOLT, 30 N•m (22 LB. FT.)

GC11296000079000X

Fig. 2 Starter motor replacement. 4.6L engine

COIL PACK
REPLACE

3.6L Engine

1. Remove engine cover.
2. Disconnect air cleaner duct from throttle body.
3. **On cylinders 1, 2 and 3,** reposition intake manifold as follows:
   a. Disconnect PCV hose from camshaft cover.
   b. Remove intake manifold attaching bolts.
   c. Remove intake manifold brace bolts, then the brace.
   d. Reposition upper and lower intake manifolds to gain access to ignition coils.
4. **On all cylinders,** disconnect ignition coil electrical connector.
5. Remove ignition coil retaining bolts, then the coil.
6. Reverse procedure to install.

4.6L Engine

2001–04
LEFTHAND

1. Remove mounting bolts and engine sight shield.
2. Disconnect ignition control module electrical connector.
3. Remove engine oil dipstick as required.
4. Remove ignition assembly mounting bolts in sequence, **Fig. 3.**
5. Remove ignition assembly.
6. Remove mounting screws and ignition control module.
7. Reverse procedure to install, noting the following:
   a. **Torque** ignition control module mounting screws to seven inch lbs.
   b. **Torque** ignition assembly mounting bolts to 80 inch lbs., in reverse of removal sequence, **Fig. 3.**
   c. **Torque** engine sight shield mounting bolts to 70 inch lbs.

RIGHTHAND

1. Remove mounting bolts and engine

sight shield, then disconnect ignition control module electrical connector.
2. **On models equipped with Secondary Air Injection (AIR),** proceed as follows:
   a. Disconnect AIR vent solenoid.
   b. Remove AIR pipe to exhaust manifold mounting bolts.
   c. Tag their positions, then disconnect AIR vacuum hoses.
   d. Remove AIR assembly.
3. **On all models,** remove ignition assembly bolts in sequence, **Fig. 3.**
4. Remove ignition assembly.
5. Remove mounting screws and ignition control module.
6. Reverse procedure to install, noting the following:
   a. **Torque** ignition control module mounting screws to 7 inch lbs.
   b. **Torque** ignition assembly mounting bolts to 80 inch lbs., in reverse of removal sequence, **Fig. 3.**
   c. **Torque** engine sight shield mounting bolts to 70 inch lbs.

2005

1. Remove mounting bolts and engine sight shield.
2. Remove ignition coil cover from cam cover by lifting straight up.
3. Disconnect electrical connector ignition coil, then remove ignition coil retaining bolt.
4. **On DeVille models,** if removal of all coils are required, disconnect main coil electrical connector at cam cover.
5. **On all models,** remove ignition coil assembly from vehicle.
6. Reverse procedure to install.

IGNITION LOCK
REPLACE

DeVille

1. Remove lefthand knee bolster.
2. Turn ignition Off.
3. Remove air bag module as outlined in "Passive Restraint Systems" chapter.
4. Remove horn contact by pushing slightly and twisting counterclockwise.

5. Disconnect Connector Position Assurance (CPA) and coil assembly electrical connector from air bag module.
6. Remove steering column shaft nut.
7. Remove steering wheel using puller tool No. J-1859-A and legs tool No. J-42578, or equivalents. **Do not thread puller bolts too far into steering wheel.**
8. Remove steering column upper shroud.
9. Remove one screw from upper shroud to access lock cylinder access hole.
10. Turn ignition to Start, then push down on ignition lock cylinder retaining pin through access hole using suitable bent tip awl.
11. Release lock cylinder to Run position and remove it by pulling away from steering column.
12. Reverse procedure to install.

Eldorado

1. Remove lefthand closeout insulator panel as required.
2. Remove air bag module as outlined in "Passive Restraint Systems" chapter.
3. Remove horn contact by pushing slightly and twisting counterclockwise.
4. Disconnect Connector Position Assurance (CPA) and coil assembly electrical connector from air bag module.
5. Remove steering column shaft nut.
6. Remove steering wheel using puller tool No. J-1859-A and legs tool No. J-42578, or equivalents. **Do not thread puller bolts too far into steering wheel.**
7. Remove turn signal switch as outlined in "Turn Signal Switch, Replace."
8. Remove key from lock, then the buzzer switch.
9. Place key in Lock position and remove lock mounting screw, **Fig. 4.**
10. Disconnect electrical connector and retaining clip from housing cover.
11. Remove lock cylinder.
12. Reverse procedure to install, noting the following:
   a. **Torque** lock mounting screw to 25 inch lbs.
   b. **Ensure forward edge of insulator is properly installed onto retainer studs at front of dash. Improper installation may result in brake or accelerator pedal binding.**

Seville

1. Apply parking brake.
2. Remove radio as outlined in "Radio, Replace."
3. Remove HVAC control head.
4. Turn ignition to Run position.
5. Looking through radio opening, depress lock cylinder retaining tab located on righthand lower side of ignition switch using suitable flat-headed tool.
6. Remove ignition cylinder.
7. Reverse procedure to install, noting the following:
   a. Insert ignition key into lock cylinder, then turn to Run.
   b. Install lock cylinder into instrument

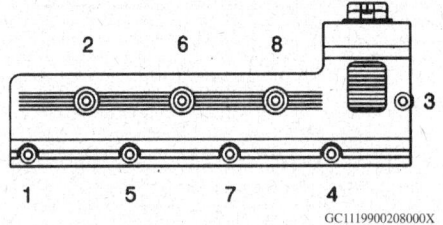

Fig. 3 Ignition control module assembly bolt removal sequence

panel opening.
   c. Cylinder release button will produce an audible click when fully engaged.
   d. Pull lightly on lock cylinder to ensure secure engagement.

STS

Refer to "Turn Signal Switch, Replace," for replacement procedure.

IGNITION SWITCH
REPLACE

DeVille

1. Remove lefthand knee bolster.
2. Remove steering column as outlined in "Steering Columns" chapter.
3. Remove ignition lock cylinder.
4. Remove upper and lower trim covers.
5. Disconnect coded key controller electrical connector.
6. Slide coded key controller from lock module assembly.
7. Disconnect electrical connector from bottom of ignition and key alarm switch assembly.
8. Remove lead inside clip on side of ignition and key alarm switch assembly.
9. Remove ignition and key alarm switch assembly mounting screws, then the switch assembly.
10. Reverse procedure to install. **Torque** ignition and key alarm switch assembly mounting screws to 13 inch lbs.

Eldorado

1. Remove steering column as outlined in "Steering Columns" chapter.
2. Disconnect headlamp dimmer switch electrical connector.
3. Remove dimmer switch mounting nut and bolt.
4. Disconnect rod from dimmer switch.
5. Remove dimmer switch.
6. Remove ignition switch mounting stud.
7. Remove ignition switch, then disconnect electrical connector.
8. Reverse procedure to install, noting the following:
   a. Ensure all wiring and electrical connectors are properly routed to avoid pinching.
   b. **Torque** headlamp dimmer and ignition switch mounting stud to 35 inch lbs.
   c. **Torque** dimmer switch mounting nut and bolt to 35 inch lbs.

Seville

1. Apply parking brake and ensure ignition switch is in Off or Lock position.
2. Remove radio as outlined in "Radio, Replace."
3. Remove HVAC control head and knee bolster.
4. Lock steering column using lockpin tool No. J-42640, or equivalent, in underside of column.
5. Disconnect electrical connectors as required.
6. Remove lamp socket from ignition switch.
7. Disconnect park lock cable from ignition switch.
8. Turn ignition to Run.
9. Depress park lock cable release button located on bottom of ignition switch at 6 o'clock position, then pull cable in order to disconnect from ignition switch.
10. Remove ignition lock cylinder as outlined in "Ignition Lock, Replace."
11. Remove ignition switch mounting screws located at access hole in steering column opening and through radio opening, then the switch.
12. Reverse procedure to install. **Torque** ignition switch mounting screws to 18 inch lbs.

STS

1. Pull outward on center trim to release clip retainers, then remove trim.
2. Pull outward on cluster trim to release clips, then disconnect electrical connector and aspirator tube.
3. Release tabs securing switch to trim panel, then remove ignition switch.
4. Reverse procedure to install.

HEADLAMP SWITCH
REPLACE

DeVille

1. Remove lefthand instrument panel end cap.
2. Remove switch by pushing on rear.
3. Disconnect electrical connector.
4. Reverse procedure to install.

Eldorado

1. Insert suitable flat-bladed tool between instrument panel and top of headlamp switch assembly, **Fig. 5,** and depress two tabs securing top of switch to instrument panel.
2. Depress two lower tabs to remove switch.
3. Disconnect electrical connector.
4. Reverse procedure to install, noting the following:
   a. Ensure electrical connector is securely connected.
   b. Push in on switch with even pressure at all four corners and ensure all tabs engage instrument panel.

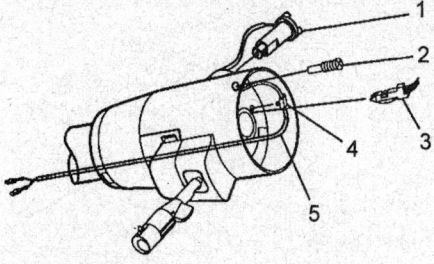

1. Lock cylinder
2. Cylinder retaining screw
3. Warning buzzer switch
4. Retaining clip
5. Wires

GC9120101371000X

Fig. 4 Lock cylinder set replacement. Eldorado

Seville

1. Remove lefthand instrument panel end cap.
2. Remove switch by pushing on rear.
3. Disconnect electrical connector.
4. Reverse procedure to install.

STS

Refer to "Turn Signal Switch, Replace," for replacement procedure.

MULTI-FUNCTION SWITCH

REPLACE

DeVille, Eldorado & Seville

1. Remove steering wheel as outlined under "Steering Wheel, Replace."
2. Remove steering column shrouds, trim covers and wiring tie straps as required.
3. Install pressing tool No. J 23653-SIR, or equivalent, to upper steering shaft and depress shaft lock.
4. Remove bearing retainer from upper steering shaft, then the pressing tool from steering shaft.
5. Note orientation of steering column wiring harness routing in lower harness shield for proper installation.
6. Remove shaft lock, turn signal cancel cam assembly and upper bearing spring.
7. Remove tilt lever handle.
8. Remove multi-function switch mounting screws.
9. Disconnect electrical connectors, then remove multi-function switch.
10. Reverse procedure to install. **Torque** multi-function switch mounting screws to 62 inch lbs.

STS

1. Disarm air bag system as outlined in "Passive Restraint Systems" chapter.
2. Remove steering wheel as outlined under "Steering Wheel Replace."

3. Remove screws, disconnect electrical connector and pull out left closeout insulator panel from instrument panel.
4. Release clips and remove left knee bolster trim pane.
5. Remove retaining screws from lower steering column trim cover, then disconnect closeout shroud from lower trim cover.
6. Disconnect electrical connector for power tilt and telescopic switch and remove from lower trim cover.
7. Remove retaining screw from upper steering column trim cover, then Lift upper trim cover to gain access to lock cylinder access hole.
8. Using a bent tip awl, insert tip into access hole, then turn ignition lock cylinder to START position.
9. Using bent tip awl push down on ignition lock cylinder retaining pin.
10. Release ignition lock cylinder to RUN position, then remove lock cylinder.
11. Remove upper trim cover, then the closeout shroud from upper trim cover.
12. Remove retaining screws from multifunction switch, then disconnect electrical connector.
13. Remove multifunction switch.
14. Reverse procedure to install.

DIMMER SWITCH

REPLACE

DeVille, Eldorado & Seville

1. **On models equipped with floor shift,** place transaxle selector in Park and turn ignition to Run.
2. **On all models,** remove lefthand hush panel, steering column lower cover, toe plate insulator and steering column lower mounting screws.
3. Remove upper steering column bracket to instrument panel mounting nuts and lower column. Prior to lowering column disconnect shift indicator cable and electrical connectors, as required. **Do not force column down.**
4. Remove mounting nut, screw and dimmer switch. Tape actuator rod to steering column.

STS

1. Pull outward on center trim to release clip retainers, then remove trim.
2. Pull outward on cluster trim to release clips, then disconnect electrical connector and aspirator tube.
3. Release tabs, then disconnect electrical connector and remove dimmer switch.
4. Reverse procedure to install.

STEERING WHEEL

REPLACE

1. Turn ignition Off.
2. Remove air bag module as outlined in "Passive Restraint Systems" chapter.
3. Remove horn contact by pushing slightly and twisting counterclockwise.

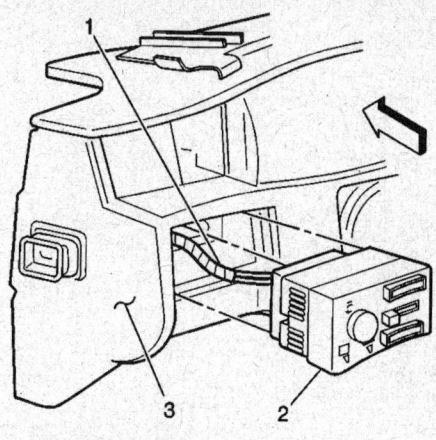

1. Wiring harness
2. Headlamp switch
3. Instrument panel

GC9040104901000X

Fig. 5 Headlamp switch replacement. Eldorado

4. Disconnect Connector Position Assurance (CPA) and coil assembly electrical connector from air bag module.
5. Remove steering column shaft nut.
6. Remove steering wheel using puller tool No. J-1859-A and legs tool No. J-42578, or equivalents. **Do not thread puller bolts too far into steering wheel.**
7. Reverse procedure to install.

INSTRUMENT CLUSTER

REPLACE

DeVille

1. Remove instrument panel upper trim pad.
2. Remove instrument cluster trim panel.
3. Remove cluster to instrument panel retainer mounting screws.
4. Disconnect cluster electrical connectors.
5. Remove cluster assembly from retainer.
6. Reverse procedure to install. **Torque** cluster mounting screws to 18 inch lbs.

Eldorado

1. Remove RLY IGN 1, IGN O-BODY and CLUSTER fuses from rear compartment fuse block.
2. Remove HAZARD and MIRROR fuses from front fuse block.
3. Remove instrument panel upper trim pad.
4. Disconnect electrical connectors from top of instrument cluster.
5. Remove cluster to instrument panel mounting screws.
6. Slide cluster upward and remove from vehicle. **Do not allow cluster to sit on its face any more than 15 minutes or damage to the fluid-filled air core gauges may result.**
7. Reverse procedure to install, noting the following:
   a. Ensure all electrical connectors

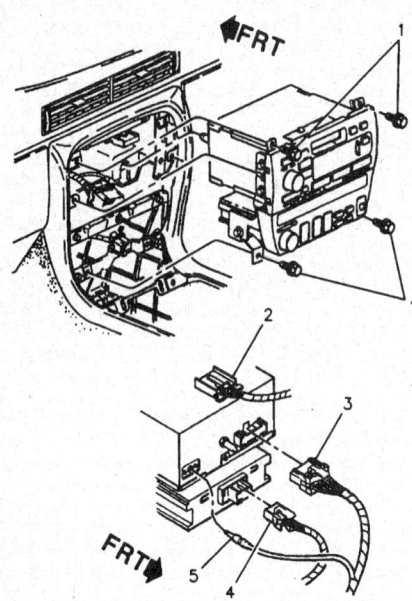

1 SCREW (4)
2 DIC HARNESS
3 RADIO HARNESS
4 HVAC HARNESS
5 ANTENNA COAX

GC9039600042000X

Fig. 6 Radio replacement (console shift). Eldorado

and wiring are properly routed to avoid pinching.
b. Position cluster locating pins into instrument panel guide holes.
c. **Torque** cluster mounting screws to 18 inch lbs.

Seville

Refer to "DeVille" for instrument cluster replacement procedure.

STS

1. Pull outward on center trim to release clip retainers, then remove trim.
2. Pull outward on cluster trim to release clips, then disconnect electrical connector and aspirator tube.
3. Remove screws, then disconnect electrical connector and instrument panel cluster.
4. Reverse procedure to install.

RADIO
REPLACE
Console Shift
DEVILLE & SEVILLE
LESS NAVIGATION SYSTEM

1. Remove instrument panel center trim plate, then the HVAC control head.
2. Push and hold release tabs on lefthand and righthand sides of radio.
3. Remove radio.

---

4. Disconnect antenna lead and electrical connectors.
5. Remove mounting brackets and studs. They will need to be transferred if a new radio will be installed.
6. Reverse procedure to install.

NAVIGATION SYSTEM

1. Remove rear shelf trim panel.
2. Remove rear shelf carrier panel.
3. Remove radio to radio/navigation processor bracket nuts.
4. Disconnect electrical connectors and antenna lead-in from radio.
5. Remove radio from mounting bracket.
6. Reverse procedure to install. **Torque** radio mounting nuts to 44 inch lbs.

ELDORADO

1. Remove shifter trim plate and ashtray.
2. Disconnect Driver Information System switch.
3. Disconnect electrical connectors.
4. Remove screws from radio and HVAC control assembly.
5. Disconnect electrical harness, **Fig. 6**.
6. Remove brackets, **Fig. 7**.
7. Remove plastic loading pin and clip stud from rear of radio.
8. Remove radio.
9. Reverse procedure to install.

STS

1. Pull outward on center trim to release clip retainers, then remove trim from instrument panel.
2. Remove bolts, then disconnect electrical connectors.
3. Remove radio from vehicle.
4. Reverse procedure to install.

Column Shift

1. Remove radio trim plate.
2. Push in on locking tabs on side of radio and pull out, **Fig. 8**.
3. Remove electrical harness.
4. Remove both brackets, **Fig. 9**.
5. Remove plastic loading pin and clip stud from rear of radio. They will need to be transferred if a new radio will be installed.
6. Remove radio.
7. Reverse procedure to install.

WIPER MOTOR
REPLACE
DeVille

1. Remove wipers arms and air inlet grille panel.
2. Remove windshield frame reinforcement bolts and nuts, then the reinforcement.
3. Rotate wiper motor crank arm to opposite of park position by pushing or pulling on transmission linkage.
4. Disconnect wiper motor electrical connector, then push harness and grommet through hole in plenum.
5. Remove wiper transmission mounting bolts, then the transmission.
6. Remove drive link from wiper motor

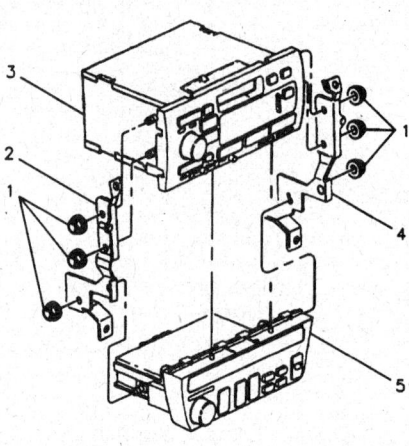

1 NUT (6)
2 LEFT RADIO BRACKET
3 RADIO
4 RIGHT RADIO BRACKET
5 HVAC CONTROLLER

GC9039600044000X

Fig. 7 Radio bracket replacement (console shift). Eldorado

crank arm using separator tool No. J-39232, or equivalent.
7. Remove wiper motor mounting screws, then the motor.
8. Reverse procedure to install, noting the following:
   a. **Torque** motor mounting screws to 71 inch lbs.
   b. Install drive link onto motor crank arm using installer tool No. J-39529, or equivalent.
   c. **Torque** wiper transmission mounting screws to 71 inch lbs.
   d. **Torque** windshield frame reinforcement bolts and nuts to 80 inch lbs.
   e. **Torque** wiper arm nuts to 24 ft. lbs.

Eldorado

1. Remove wipers arms and air inlet grille panel.
2. Remove windshield frame reinforcement bolts and nuts, then the reinforcement.
3. Rotate wiper motor crank arm to opposite of park position by pushing or pulling on transmission linkage.
4. Disconnect wiper motor electrical connector, then push harness and grommet through hole in plenum.
5. Remove wiper transmission mounting bolts, then the transmission.
6. Remove drive link from wiper motor crank arm using separator tool No. J-39232, or equivalent.
7. Remove wiper motor mounting screws, then the motor.
8. Reverse procedure to install, noting the following:
   a. **Torque** motor mounting screws to 71 inch lbs.
   b. Install drive link onto motor crank arm using installer tool No. J-39529, or equivalent.
   c. **Torque** wiper transmission mounting screws to 71 inch lbs.

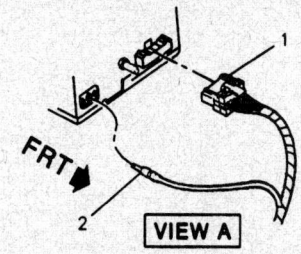

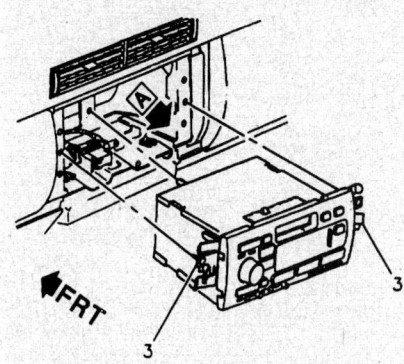

1 HARNESS
2 ANTENNA COAX
3 ALIGNMENT BULLETS AND
   LOCKING TABS

GC9039600043000X

Fig. 8 Radio replacement. Column shift

d. **Torque** windshield frame reinforcement bolts and nuts to 80 inch lbs.
e. **Torque** wiper arm nuts to 24 ft. lbs.

Seville

1. Disconnect wiper motor electrical connector.
2. Remove motor mounting screws.
3. Move wiper arms six to eight inches up windshield from park position.
4. Pull wiper motor away from firewall.
5. Disconnect transmission drive link from motor crank arm using removal tool No. J-39232, or equivalent.
6. Reverse procedure to install, noting the following:
   a. Ensure wiper arms are still six to eight inches up windshield from park position.
   b. Connect transmission drive link to motor crank arm using installer tool No. J-39529, or equivalent.
   c. Mount wiper motor onto firewall. **Torque** screws to 80 inch lbs.

STS

1. Remove wiper motor mini 10 A and 30 A fuses located in underhood fuse block.
2. Open hood assembly. Driver side wiper aligns with an orange line at tip of wiper blade located at center lower windshield.
3. Passenger side wiper aligns with an orange dot at tip of wiper blade located on right lower side of windshield.

4. Remove covers from wiper arm nuts, then the nut from wiper arm drive spindle.
5. Remove upper hood assist rods from assist rod ball studs at driver side wiper arm.
6. Tilt hood rearward to air inlet grille panel, then support hood assembly.
7. Remove wiper arm from wiper arm drive spindle, then the air inlet grille.
8. Remove wiper motor module mounting bolts, then disconnect wiper motor electrical connector.
9. Remove wiper motor module from vehicle.
10. Remove drive links from wiper motor crank arm to wiper motor using tool No. J-39232 or equivalent.
11. Remove screws, then the wiper motor from wiper motor module.
12. Reverse procedure to install.

WIPER SWITCH
REPLACE

DeVille & Seville

1. Remove steering wheel as outlined under "Steering Wheel, Replace."
2. Remove knee bolster and steering column nuts.
3. Lower steering column, then remove tilt lever, steering column shrouds and wire harness assembly.
4. **On models equipped with power tilt and telescope,** disconnect and remove interface module and harness. Record harness placement for installation.
5. **On all models,** depress tabs, then disconnect and remove switch.
6. Reverse procedure to install, noting the following:
   a. **Torque** steering column upper trim cover mounting screw to 13 inch lbs.
   b. **Torque** steering column lower trim cover mounting screws to 31 inch lbs.

Eldorado

1. Remove steering wheel as outlined under "Steering Wheel, Replace."
2. Slide connector cover toward front of vehicle, then unplug electrical connector.
3. Push lever in and rotate clockwise ¼ turn, then pull out switch.
4. Reverse procedure to install.

STS

1. Remove steering wheel as outlined under "Steering Wheel Replace."
2. Remove screws, disconnect electrical connector and pull out elf closeout insulator panel from instrument panel.
3. Release clips and remove left knee bolster trim pane.
4. Remove retaining screws from lower steering column trim cover, then disconnect closeout shroud from lower trim cover.
5. Disconnect electrical connector for

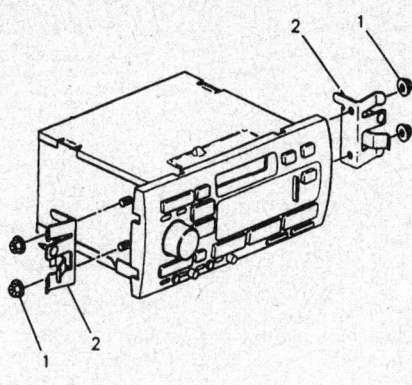

1 NUT (4)
2 LEFT AND RIGHT BRACKET

GC9039600045000X

Fig. 9 Radio bracket replacement. Column shift

power tilt and telescopic switch and remove from lower trim cover.
6. Remove retaining screw from upper steering column trim cover, then lift upper trim cover to gain access to lock cylinder access hole.
7. Using a bent tip awl, insert tip into access hole, then turn ignition lock cylinder to START position.
8. Using bent tip awl push down on ignition lock cylinder retaining pin.
9. Release ignition lock cylinder to RUN position, then remove lock cylinder.
10. Remove upper trim cover, then the closeout shroud from upper trim cover.
11. Remove steering column wiring harness tie straps, then disconnect electrical connectors from windshield wiper switch.
12. Depress locking tab on windshield wiper and washer switch, then remove switch from steering column.
13. Reverse procedure to install.

WIPER TRANSMISSION
REPLACE

DeVille & STS

1. Remove wipers arms and air inlet grille panel.
2. Remove windshield frame reinforcement bolts and nuts, then the reinforcement.
3. Rotate wiper motor crank arm to opposite of park position by pushing or pulling on transmission linkage.
4. Disconnect wiper motor electrical connector, then push harness and grommet through hole in plenum.
5. Remove wiper transmission mounting bolts, then the transmission.
6. Reverse procedure to install.

Eldorado & Seville

1. Remove wiper arm nut caps, then the nuts.

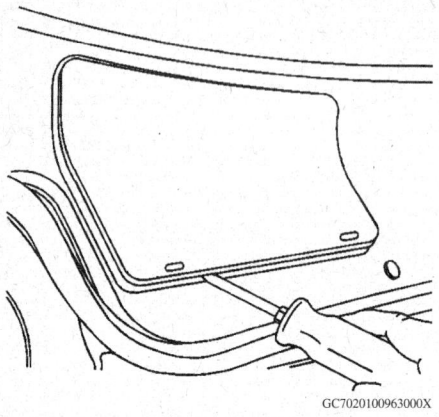

Fig. 10 Cabin air filter access door removal. DeVille

2. Remove wiper arms using puller tool No. J-39822, or equivalent.
3. Remove shroud air inlet grille panel.
4. Remove drive link from wiper motor crank arm using separator tool No. J-39232, or equivalent.
5. Remove mounting screws and wiper transmission.
6. Reverse procedure to install, noting the following:
   a. Connect transmission drive link socket to motor crank arm ball using installer tool No. J-39529, or equivalent.
   b. **Torque** wiper arm mounting nuts to 24 ft. lbs.

BLOWER MOTOR
REPLACE

DeVille

1. Remove righthand side sound insulator panel.
2. Remove glove compartment as required.
3. Pull back carpet, then remove Dash Integration Module and position aside.
4. Remove mounting screws, then disconnect blower motor electrical connector.
5. Remove blower motor.
6. Reverse procedure to install.

Eldorado

1. Remove righthand cam cover as outlined in "Valve Cover, Replace" in "4.6L Engine" section.
2. Remove inertial plate screws, then the inertial plate from blower motor.
3. Disconnect blower motor electrical connector.
4. Remove blower motor mounting screws, then the motor.
5. Reverse procedure to install, noting the following:
   a. **Torque** motor mounting screws to 35 inch lbs.
   b. **Torque** inertial plate screws to 35 inch lbs.

Seville

1. Remove righthand side sound insulator panel.
2. Remove glove compartment as required.
3. Pull back carpet, then remove Dash Integration Module and position aside.
4. Remove mounting screws, then disconnect blower motor electrical connector.
5. Remove blower motor.
6. Reverse procedure to install.

STS

1. Remove righthand side sound insulator panel.
2. Remove glove compartment.
3. Remove screws, then disconnect electrical connectors.
4. Remove blower motor from vehicle.
5. Reverse procedure to install.

CABIN AIR FILTER
REPLACE

DeVille

1. Open hood.
2. Remove cabin air filter access cover from righthand side of cowl panel, **Fig. 10**.
3. Remove cabin air filter element from filter housing. Flex righthand side of filter housing to aid in filter removal, **Fig. 11**.
4. Install new cabin air filter into filter housing. Flex righthand side of filter housing to aid in filter installation, **Fig. 11**.
5. Install cabin air filter access cover.

Seville

1. Remove two mounting screws from rear edge of lefthand sound insulator.
2. Push in on snap tabs to release insulator.
3. Disconnect lefthand sound insulator electrical connectors, then remove insulator.
4. Twist shift cable grommet and position away from cabin air filter access door. Cutting tie strap and peeling back foam insulation may be required to position grommet away from filter door.
5. Remove cabin air filter access cover from HVAC module, **Fig. 12**.
6. Remove tape, then pull out first filter element using filter tab, **Fig. 13**.
7. Remove tape, then pull out second element.
8. Remove tape, then pull out third element.
9. Lubricate new filter guides with suitable silicone spray to ease installation.
10. Install first new filter into case. Raise filter using a long thin-blade screwdriver and filter tab until it is parallel with HVAC module. Ensure leading edge of filter engages filter case holding rib.
11. Engage new second filter in tab of first filter. Slide second filter into remaining

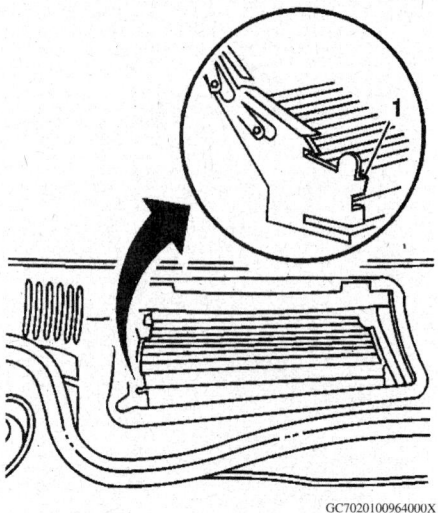

Fig. 11 Cabin air filter replacement. DeVille

channels of first filter. Using filter tab, raise filter until it is parallel with HVAC module. Ensure leading edge of filter engages filter case holding rib.
12. Engage third new cabin air filter in tab of second filter. Slide third filter into remaining channels of second filter.
13. Fold tab of second filter down.
14. Fold tab of third filter up and over second filter.
15. Install air conditioning and heater module filter cover. Ensure cover is properly seated.
16. Position shift cable grommet, **Fig. 14**.
17. Position lefthand sound insulator to instrument panel, then connect electrical connectors.
18. Install lefthand sound insulator fasteners in proper locations. **Torque** fasteners to 18 inch lbs.

STS

1. Remove air inlet grille panel, then with two hands release tabs on each side of access cover.
2. Lift up filter access cover, then remove filter from filter housing.
3. Reverse procedure to install.

HEATER CORE
REPLACE

DeVille

1. Drain coolant into suitable container.
2. Disconnect heater hoses from heater core using clamp tool No. J-37097-A, or equivalent.
3. Remove instrument panel as outlined in "Dash Panel Service" chapter.
4. Remove heat shield.
5. Remove heater core cover retainers and straps, then the cover.
6. Remove heater core. Discard case side seals.
7. Reverse procedure to install, noting the following:
   a. Install heater core with new case side seals.

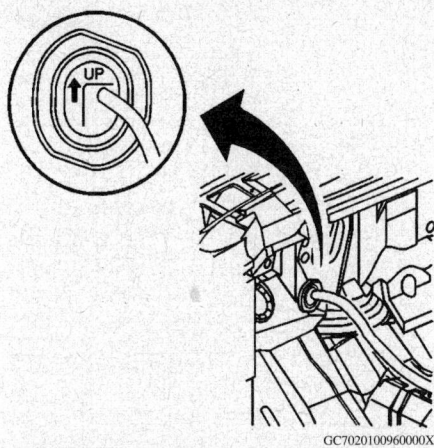

Fig. 12 Cabin air filter access cover location. Seville

b. Ensure all electrical connectors and wiring are properly routed to avoid pinching.
c. Fill coolant to proper level and inspect for leakage.

Eldorado

1. Drain coolant into suitable container.
2. Remove mounting screws, glove compartment and righthand lower sound insulator.
3. Remove bracket mounting screws and position Engine Control Module (ECM) aside to access rear programmer mounting screw.
4. Disconnect electrical and vacuum connectors, then remove mounting screws and processor, **Fig. 15.**
5. Disconnect electrical connectors, then remove ECM and mounting bracket.
6. Disconnect lefthand and righthand air mix actuators.
7. Remove heater core cover, then disconnect heater core hoses using clamp tool No. J-37097-A, or equivalent.
8. Remove heater core mounting screws, then the core.
9. Reverse procedure to install. Prior to installing glove compartment, adjust air mix door link rods as follows:
   a. Set temperature control for 90° F.
   b. If ambient temperature is above 90° F, disconnect inside air temperature sensor.
   c. Allow 45 seconds for processor arm to travel to maximum heat position.
   d. Move temperature door to full hot position.
   e. Pull driver's temperature door link toward processor until door hits its stop.
   f. Push threaded portion of link into driver's temperature door crank slot.

g. Pull passenger's door link from temperature door retainer, then snap door link into retainer.

Seville

1. Drain coolant into suitable container.
2. Disconnect heater hoses from heater core using clamp tool No. J-37097-A, or equivalent.
3. Remove instrument panel as outlined in "Dash Panel Service" chapter.
4. Remove heat shield.
5. Remove heater core cover retainers and straps, then the cover.
6. Remove heater core. Discard case side seals.
7. Reverse procedure to install, noting the following:
   a. Install heater core with new case side seals.
   b. Ensure all electrical connectors and wiring are properly routed to avoid pinching.
   c. Fill coolant to proper level and inspect for leakage.

STS

1. Recover air conditioning refrigerant as outlined in "Air Conditioning" chapter.
2. Disconnect both battery cables, then remove heat shield and battery.
3. Drain coolant into suitable container.
4. Using tool No. J–38185 or equivalent, disconnect heater inlet and outlet hoses.
5. Disconnect both A/C lines at cowl using tool No. J–45689 or equivalent.
6. Remove instrument panel as outlined in "Dash Panel Service" chapter.
7. Remove air inlet assembly, then disconnect HVAC module electrical connector.
8. Disconnect HVAC module drain tube from floor, then press tab and release left rear duct from HVAC module.
9. Disconnect left rear heater duct from HVAC module, then press tab and release right rear duct from the HVAC module.
10. Disconnect right rear heater ducts from HVAC module, then remove lower left HVAC module mounting nut.
11. Remove upper left HVAC module mounting nut, then the HVAC module from vehicle.
12. Remove heater hose bracket, then slide heater core out of HVAC module.
13. Reverse procedure to install.

EVAPORATOR CORE
REPLACE
DeVille

1. Recover refrigerant as outlined in "Air Conditioning" chapter.

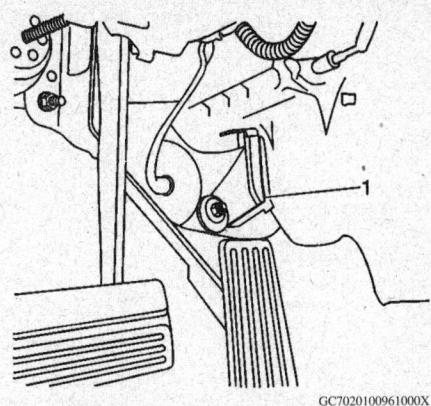

Fig. 13 Cabin air filter replacement. Seville

2. Disconnect evaporator lines.
3. Disconnect heater hoses using clamp tool No. J-37097-A, or equivalent.
4. Remove center console assembly.
5. Remove instrument panel as outlined in "Dash Panel Service" chapter.
6. Remove evaporator drain, defroster and heater duct assembly.
7. Remove heater and evaporator module.
8. Remove heater and evaporator tube seal, then the upper evaporator case.
9. Remove evaporator core and case seals.
10. Reverse procedure to install, noting the following:
    a. **Torque** HVAC module mounting nuts to 80 inch lbs.
    b. **Torque** evaporator nut to 18 ft. lbs.

Eldorado

1. Recover refrigerant as outlined in "Air Conditioning" chapter.
2. Lower engine and transaxle assembly as required. Refer to "Engine, Replace" in "4.6L Engine" section.
3. Disconnect accumulator tube and evaporator tube from evaporator core.
4. Remove blower motor.
5. Remove evaporator core rubber barrier cover and evaporator core cover.
6. Remove evaporator core.
7. Reverse procedure to install, noting the following:
   a. **Torque** evaporator core cover screws to 44 inch lbs.
   b. **Torque** evaporator core rubber barrier cover screws to 44 inch lbs.
   c. Ensure all electrical connectors and wiring are properly routed to avoid pinching.
   d. Charge air conditioning system, then inspect fittings for leakage using halogen leak detector tool No. J-39400-A, or equivalent.

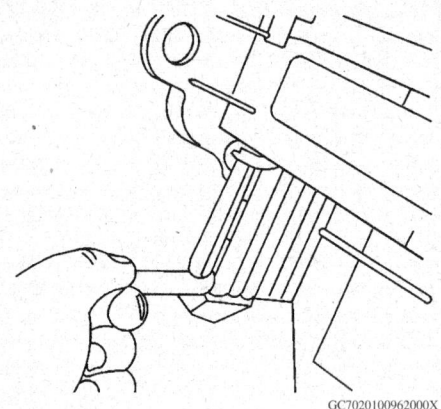

Fig. 14 Positioning shift cable grommet. Seville

Seville

1. Recover refrigerant as outlined in "Air Conditioning" chapter.
2. Disconnect evaporator lines.
3. Disconnect heater hoses using clamp tool No. J-37097-A, or equivalent.
4. Remove center console assembly.
5. Remove instrument panel as outlined in "Dash Panel Service" chapter.
6. Remove evaporator drain, defroster and heater duct assembly.
7. Remove heater and evaporator module.
8. Remove heater and evaporator tube seal, then the upper evaporator case.
9. Remove evaporator core and case seals.
10. Reverse procedure to install, noting the following:
    a. **Torque** HVAC module mounting nuts to 80 inch lbs.
    b. **Torque** evaporator nut to 18 ft. lbs.

STS

1. Recover air conditioning refrigerant as outlined in "Air Conditioning" chapter.
2. Disconnect both battery cables, then remove heat shield and battery.
3. Drain coolant into suitable container.
4. Using tool No. J-38185 or equivalent, disconnect heater inlet and outlet hoses.
5. Disconnect both A/C lines at cowl using tool No. J-45689 or equivalent.
6. Remove instrument panel as outlined in "Dash Panel Service" chapter.
7. Remove air inlet assembly, then disconnect HVAC module electrical connector.
8. Disconnect HVAC module drain tube from floor, then press tab and release left rear duct from HVAC module.
9. Disconnect left rear heater duct from HVAC module, then press tab and release right rear duct from the HVAC module.
10. Disconnect right rear heater ducts from HVAC module, then remove lower left HVAC module mounting nut.
11. Remove upper left HVAC module mounting nut, then the HVAC module from vehicle.
12. Remove insulation from thermal expansion valve, then the HVAC line clamp screw and clamp.
13. Remove TXV to evaporator bolts then the TXV line bracket.
14. Remove TXV from evaporator core, then separate TXV from A/C lines by pulling straight out.
15. Remove screws and clips that hold case together.
16. Disconnect thermistor electrical connector, then separate HVAC module.
17. Remove thermistor from evaporator core, then the evaporator core.
18. Reverse procedure to install.

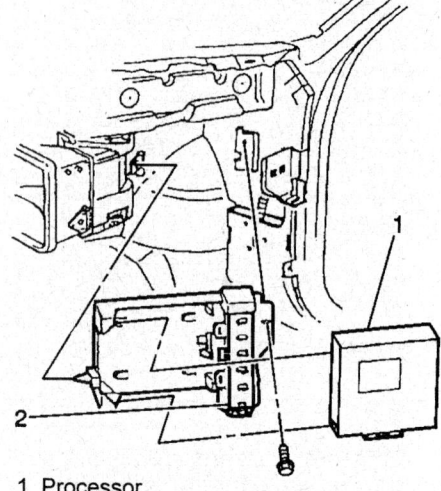

1. Processor
2. Mounting bracket

Fig. 15 Processor removal. Eldorado

TECHNICAL SERVICE BULLETINS

Analog Instrument Cluster Erratic Or Inoperative Operation

2001 DEVILLE & SEVILLE

On these models equipped with cluster kilo and miles mechanical display, DeVille through VIN 1U219979 and Seville through VIN 1U219978, there may be occurrences of fuel gauges sticking on empty, temperature gauges remaining on cold or erratic Driver Information Center (DIC) operation.

This may be caused by the cluster software.

To correct this condition, install a replacement cluster assembly part No. 25696232 (88890684 REMAN).

3.6L Engine

NOTE: On Air Bag Equipped Models, Refer To "Air Bag System Precautions" Located In The Front Of This Manual For System Disarming & Arming Procedures.

NOTE: Refer To "Computer Relearn Procedures" Located In The Front Of This Manual When Battery Power To The Computer Has Been Interrupted.

NOTE: Prior To Performing Any Service Operations Listed In This Section, Consult The "Technical Service Bulletins" Section For Related Information.

NOTE: For Procedures Not Found In This Section, Refer To "3.6L Engine" in "CTS chapter."

INDEX

PRECAUTIONS

Air Bag Systems

Refer to "Air Bag System Precautions" in the front of this manual for system disarming and arming procedures.

Battery Ground Cable

Prior to service, disconnect battery ground cable and isolate as required.

Fuel Pressure Relief

Refer to "3.6L Engine" in "CTS" chapter for procedure.

COMPRESSION PRESSURE

Refer to "3.6L Engine" in "CTS" chapter for procedure.

ENGINE MOUNT

REPLACE

Lefthand Side

1. Raise and support vehicle, then install suitable jack with a block of wood under oil pan for support.
2. Remove lower engine mount retaining nut, then raise engine using jack until weight is relieved from mount.
3. Remove upper mount retaining nut, then the engine mount from vehicle.
4. Reverse procedure to install. **Torque** engine mount nuts to 59 ft. lbs.

Righthand Side

ALL WHEEL DRIVE

1. Raise and support vehicle.
2. Remove righthand exhaust manifold as outlined under "Exhaust Manifold Replace."
3. Install suitable jack with a block of wood under oil pan for support.
4. Remove right engine mount upper retaining nut, **ensure not to distort or bend engine mount heat shield.**
5. Remove right engine mount bracket mounting bolts, then engine mount bracket from vehicle.
6. Remove retaining nut, then the engine mount from vehicle.
7. Reverse procedure to install, noting the following:
   a. **Torque** engine mount nuts to 59 ft. lbs.
   b. **Torque** engine mount bracket mounting bolts to 44 ft. lbs.

TWO WHEEL DRIVE

1. Raise and support vehicle, then install suitable jack with a block of wood under oil pan for support.
2. Remove lower engine mount retaining nut, then raise engine using jack until weight is relieved from mount.
3. Remove upper mount retaining nut, then the engine mount from vehicle.
4. Reverse procedure to install. **Torque** engine mount nuts to 59 ft. lbs.

ENGINE

REPLACE

1. Turn front wheels to straight ahead position.
2. Turn ignition lock cylinder to Lock position and remove key.
3. Lock steering column by inserting steering column anti-rotation pin tool No. J 42640, or equivalent, through access hole in lower steering column trim cover.
4. Recover air conditioning refrigerant as outlined in "Air Conditioning" chapter.
5. Relieve fuel system pressure as outlined in "Precautions."
6. Remove fuel injector sight shield, then the PCV hose from air cleaner duct resonator.

7. Loosen air cleaner duct clamps, then remove air cleaner duct.

8. Disconnect cooling fan electrical connectors, then remove cooling fan wiring harnesses from fan shroud.

9. Secure wiring harnesses to vehicle, then drain cooling system into a suitable container. **Do not disconnect surge hoses from engine or radiator.**

10. Disconnect surge tank outlet hose from surge tank, then position and secure surge hose to engine.

11. Disconnect surge tank inlet hose from water outlet housing and radiator, then position and secure surge tank inlet hose to vehicle.

12. Remove cowl panel, then the inlet heater hose from heater core.

13. Disconnect purge line from purge solenoid, then fuel pipe from fuel rail.

14. Plug fuel pipe and cap fuel rail to prevent fuel loss or contamination.

15. Remove wiper module, as outlined under "Wiper Motor Replace," in "Electrical" section

16. Disconnect air conditioning suction hose from evaporator, then remove suction hose bracket from shock tower. **Do not disconnect suction hose from A/C compressor or liquid line from condenser.**

17. Position and secure suction hose to engine, then disconnect air conditioning pressure switch electrical connector and remove liquid line.

18. Remove bolts, then the radiator support brackets.

19. Disconnect brake booster check valve and vacuum hose from brake booster and secure hose to engine.

20. Disconnect brake fluid level switch electrical connector from master cylinder.

21. Disconnect electrical connector from mass air flow sensor.

22. Unlock and disconnect I/P electrical connector from engine located at rear of left bank two cylinder head. Position and secure I/P harness to vehicle.

23. Disconnect engine module wiring harness connectors from underhood electrical center, then the wiring harness from transmission control module.

24. Remove ground bolt and wire from longitudinal rail, then disconnect engine harness electrical connector at longitudinal rail.

25. Position and secure ground wire, engine harness and TCM harness to engine.

26. Remove master cylinder nuts, **Do not disconnect brake pipes from master cylinder.** Secure master cylinder to engine.

27. Raise and support vehicle, then remove heated oxygen sensors from exhaust pipes.

28. Remove bolts, then the floor panel tunnel brace from floor panel.

29. Support exhaust system with a suitable jack, then remove nuts securing exhaust pipes to exhaust manifolds.

30. Pry front exhaust hangers free from rear suspension hanger rods, then tail pipe hangers free from tail pipe hanger rods.

31. With aid of an assistant, lower exhaust system, then remove exhaust manifold seals.

32. Using a suitable jack, support propeller shaft close to support bearing.

33. Reference mark location of propeller shaft consent velocity joint to transfer case flange.

34. Remove retainers, then push front propeller shaft toward rear and out of vehicle.

35. Remove air deflector, then the washer bottle bracket. Do not remove water bottle.

36. Disconnect side air baffles from radiator, then the left front brake pipe retainer along with brake pipe from longitudinal rail.

37. Remove right front brake pipe from brake pipe bundle retainer, then disconnect rear brake pipes from brake pressure modulator valve.

38. Plug brake pipes and brake modulator valve to minimize brake fluid loss.

39. Remove front tire and wheel assemblies, then place match marks.

40. Remove center intermediate shaft to lower intermediate shaft retaining bolt, then the lower intermediate shaft to power steering gear retaining bolt.

41. Remove lower intermediate shaft from center intermediate shaft.

42. Remove lower engine mount nuts, then disconnect transmission shift linkage from transmission.

43. Disconnect electrical connector to low oil level sensor, then remove headlamp leveling sensors.

44. Secure shock modules to lower control arms with a suitable strap to prevent damage to front brake hoses.

45. Remove shock to yoke retaining nut, then the shock to yoke retaining bolt by pulling up slightly on lower control arm.

46. Remove yoke to lower control arm retaining nut, using tool No. J–24319-B or equivalent, separate yoke from the lower control arm.

47. Remove yoke from vehicle.

48. **On models equipped with magnaride or headlamp sensors,** disconnect sensor link from the upper control arm.

49. **On all models,** insert a hex head tool to hold upper control arm to steering knuckle.

50. Remove upper control arm to steering knuckle nut, then separate upper control arm from steering knuckle.

51. Lower vehicle, then remove shock module from vehicle.

52. Raise vehicle enough to position a suitable powertrain or engine lift table below frame, engine and transmission.

53. Remove bolts which secure transmission brace to underbody, then the front frame bolts.

54. With aid of an assistant lower table or raise vehicle to remove engine, transmission, front frame and front suspension assembly from vehicle. **Ensure that all hoses, wires, pipes and shock modules clear vehicle during removal process.**

55. Reverse procedure to install.

INTAKE MANIFOLD
REPLACE

Refer to "3.6L Engine" in "CTS" chapter for procedure.

EXHAUST MANIFOLD
REPLACE

Refer to "3.6L Engine" in "CTS" chapter for procedure.

CYLINDER HEAD
REPLACE

Refer to "3.6L Engine" in "CTS" chapter for procedure.

VALVE COVER
REPLACE

Refer to "3.6L Engine" in "CTS" chapter for procedure.

VALVE ADJUSTMENT

This engine is equipped with hydraulic valve lash adjusters. No adjustment is required.

CRANKSHAFT BALANCER
REPLACE

Refer to "3.6L Engine" in "CTS" chapter for procedure.

FRONT COVER
REPLACE

Refer to "3.6L Engine" in "CTS" chapter for procedure.

TIMING CHAIN
REPLACE

Refer to "3.6L Engine" in "CTS" chapter for procedure.

CAMSHAFT
REPLACE

Refer to "3.6L Engine" in "CTS" chapter for procedure.

PISTON & ROD ASSEMBLY

Refer to "3.6L Engine" in "CTS" chapter for procedure.

PISTONS, PINS & RINGS

Refer to "3.6L Engine" in "CTS" chapter for procedure.

MAIN & ROD BEARINGS

Refer to "3.6L Engine" in "CTS" chapter for procedure.

CRANKSHAFT FRONT OIL SEAL

REPLACE

Refer to "3.6L Engine" in "CTS" chapter for procedure.

CRANKSHAFT REAR OIL SEAL

REPLACE

Refer to "3.6L Engine" in "CTS" chapter for procedure.

OIL PAN

REPLACE

Refer to "3.6L Engine" in "CTS" chapter for procedure.

OIL PUMP

REPLACE

Refer to "3.6L Engine" in "CTS" chapter for procedure.

OIL PUMP SERVICE

There are no serviceable components inside the oil pump. If pump is not working properly, it must be replaced.

SERPENTINE DRIVE BELT

REPLACE

Refer to "3.6L Engine" in "CTS" chapter for procedure.

COOLING SYSTEM BLEED

Refer to "3.6L Engine" in "CTS" chapter for procedure.

THERMOSTAT

REPLACE

Refer to "3.6L Engine" in "CTS" chapter for procedure.

WATER PUMP

REPLACE

Refer to "3.6L Engine" in "CTS" chapter for procedure.

RADIATOR

REPLACE

Refer to "3.6L Engine" in "CTS" chapter for procedure.

FUEL PUMP

REPLACE

Refer to "3.6L Engine" in "CTS" chapter for procedure.

FUEL FILTER

REPLACE

Refer to "3.6L Engine" in "CTS" chapter for procedure.

TIGHTENING SPECIFICATIONS

Year	Component	Torque Ft. Lbs.
2005	A/C Compressor Bracket Front Bolt	37
	A/C Compressor Bracket Rear Bolt	17
	A/C Compressor Hose Assembly	80①
	Alternator Bolt	37
	Camshaft Cap Bolts	89①
	Camshaft Intermediate Drive Idler Sprocket Bolt	48
	Camshaft Position Actuator Bolt	48
	Camshaft Position Sensor Bolt	89①
	Camshaft (Valve) Cover	89①
	Catalytic Converter To Exhaust Manifold	10
	Close Out Cover Bolt	89①
	Connecting Rod Bolts	②
	Coolant Manifold Pipe	89①
	Coolant Outlet Bolt	89①
	Crankshaft Balancer Bolt	③
	Crankshaft Main Bearing (Inner) Bolts	④
	Crankshaft Main Bearing (Outer) Bolts	⑤
	Crankshaft Main Bearing (Side) Bolts	22
	Crankshaft Position Sensor	89①
	Cylinder Head Bolt (M8 Bolt)	⑥
	Cylinder Head Bolt (M11 Bolt)	⑦
	Drive Belt Idler Pulley Bolt	37
	Drive Belt Tensioner Bolt	37
	ECM Bolt	89①
	ECT Sensor	18
	Engine Mount Bracket To Cylinder Block (M8 Bolt)	28

Continued

TIGHTENING
SPECIFICATIONS—Continued

Year	Component	Torque Ft. Lbs.
2005	Engine Mount Bracket To Cylinder Block (M11 Bolt)	45
	Engine Mount To Bracket	59
	EVAP Purge Valve Bolt	89①
	Exhaust Manifold Bolt	15
	Exhaust Manifold Heat Shield Bolt	89①
	Front Cover Bolts	17
	Flywheel Bolts	⑧
	Fuel Rail Bolt	89①
	Ground Cable Bolt	37
	Heater Inlet/Outlet Pipe Assembly Bolt	89①
	Ignition Coil Bolt	89①
	Intake Manifold (Upper) To Cylinder Head Bolts	17
	Intake Manifold (Upper) To Intake Manifold (Lower) Bolts	17
	Knock Sensor Bolt	17
	Main Bearing (Inner) Bolts	④
	Main Bearing (Outer) Bolts	⑤
	Main Bearing (Side) Bolts	22
	MAP Sensor Bolt	89①
	Oil Drain Plug	18
	Oil Filter Cap	18
	Oil Filter Housing Adapter To Cylinder Block	17
	Oil Filter Housing Adapter To Cylinder Head	48
	Oil Gallery Plug	23
	Oil Dipstick Tube Bolt	89①
	Oil Level Sensor	89①
	Oil Pan To Cylinder Block Bolts	17
	Oil Pressure Sender	15
	Oil Pump Bolt	17
	Oxygen Sensor	30
	Power Steering Pump Bracket To Engine Bolt	37
	Power Steering Pump Reservoir Lower Bolt	18
	Power Steering Pump Reservoir Upper Bolt	80①
	Power Steering Pump To Bracket Bolt	16
	Primary Camshaft Drive Chain Guide Bolt	17
	Primary Camshaft Drive Chain Tensioner Bolt	17
	Secondary Camshaft Drive Chain Guide Bolt	17
	Secondary Camshaft Drive Chain Tensioner Bolt	17
	Starter Motor Bolts	37
	Suction Screen Bolt	89①
	Thermostat Housing Bolt	89①
	Throttle Body Bolt	89①
	Torque Converter Bolts	47
	Transmission Mount To Transmission Bolt	45
	Transmission To Engine Bolts	37
	Water Pump Bolts	89①
	Water Pump Pulley Bolts	106①

① — Inch lbs.

② — Refer to "Piston & Rod Assembly" for tightening procedure.

③ — First pass, 74 ft. lbs.; final pass, 150°.

④ — First pass, 15 ft. lbs.; final pass, 80°.

⑤ — First pass, 10 ft. lbs.; final pass, 110°.

⑥ — First pass, 10 ft. lbs.; final pass, 60°.

⑦ — First pass, 33 ft. lbs.; final pass, 120°.

⑧ — First pass, 22 ft. lbs.; final pass, 45°.

4.6L Engine

NOTE: On Air Bag Equipped Models, Refer To "Air Bag System Precautions" Located In The Front Of This Manual For System Disarming & Arming Procedures.

NOTE: Refer To "Computer Relearn Procedures" Located In The Front Of This Manual When Battery Power To The Computer Has Been Interrupted.

NOTE: Prior To Performing Any Service Operations Listed In This Section, Consult The "Technical Service Bulletins" Section For Related Information.

INDEX

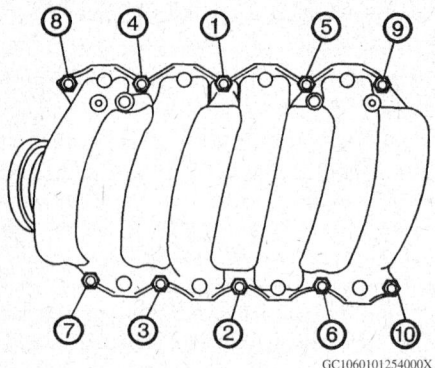

Fig. 1 Intake manifold bolt & nut tightening sequence

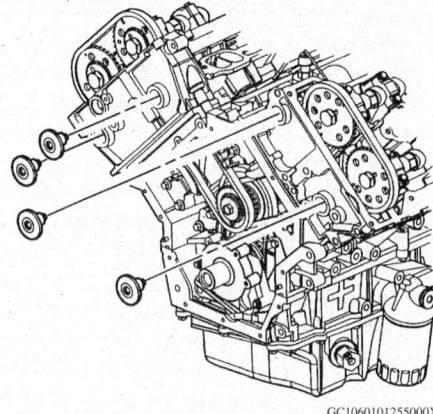

Fig. 2 Chain guide access plug replacement

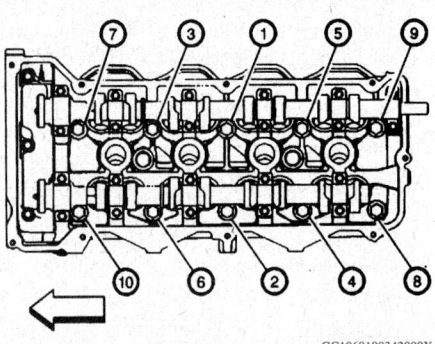

Fig. 3 Cylinder head bolt tightening sequence. Lefthand

PRECAUTIONS

Air Bag Systems

Refer to "Air Bag System Precautions" in the front of this manual for system disarming and arming procedures.

Battery Ground Cable

Prior to service, disconnect battery ground cable and isolate as required.

Fuel System Pressure Relief

A small amount of fuel may be released when servicing fuel connections even after pressure is released. Cover all fuel connections with shop towel before servicing.
1. Disconnect and isolate battery ground cable.
2. Remove intake manifold top cover.
3. Loosen fuel tank filler cap.
4. Install fuel pressure gauge tool No. J-34730-1A, or equivalent, to fuel pressure connection. Wrap shop towel around fitting while connecting gauge.
5. Install bleed hose into approved container, then open valve on gauge to relieve system pressure.

RELEARN PROCEDURES

Computer

Refer to "Computer Relearn Procedure" located in the front of this manual for computer relearn procedures.

Throttle Position (TP) Sensor

The TP Sensor Learn Procedure should be performed whenever the TP sensor, throttle body or ECM/PCM is replaced.
1. Ensure nothing is touching or obstructing accelerator or brake pedals.
2. Turn ignition On.
3. Wait 60 seconds.
4. Turn ignition Off.
5. Wait 15 seconds.

Idle Air Control (IAC)

If the IAC disconnected or interrupted, proceed as follows:
1. Start and idle engine for 15 seconds.
2. Turn ignition Off.
3. Wait 15 seconds.
4. Start engine and inspect for proper idling function.

COMPRESSION PRESSURE

Perform compression test with engine at normal operating temperature, spark plugs removed and throttle wide open. Disable the ignition and fuel systems. Lowest cylinder must be within 70% of highest cylinder with a minimum pressure of 140 psi.

ENGINE MOUNT

REPLACE

DeVille, Seville & STS

FRONT

1. **On Seville models,** remove radiator cooling fans.
2. **On all models,** install engine lift bracket tool No. J-42504 and engine support fixture tool No. J-28467-A, or equivalents.
3. Raise and support vehicle.
4. Remove mount bracket to engine block mounting nuts.
5. Remove mount to frame mounting nut.
6. Lower vehicle.
7. Remove bracket to engine upper mounting bolts.
8. Raise engine, then remove mount and bracket.
9. Reverse procedure to install, noting the following:
   a. **Torque** front engine mount to bracket nut to 44 ft. lbs.
   b. **Torque** front engine mount nut to 59 ft. lbs.

RIGHTHAND

1. Raise and support vehicle, then support engine with suitable jack.

2. Remove mount to bracket mounting nut.
3. Lower engine slightly.
4. Remove mounting nut, bolts and mount.
5. Reverse procedure to install.

Eldorado

FRONT

REMOVAL

1. Raise and support vehicle.
2. Remove front mount to frame nuts.
3. Install powertrain dolly tool No. J-39580, or equivalent.
4. Remove engine frame if required.
5. Remove mount bracket to cylinder head upper bolts.
6. Remove mount bracket to engine block bolts.
7. Remove brace to transaxle bolts.
8. Remove transaxle support brace.
9. Remove engine front mount and bracket.

INSTALLATION

1. Position mount bracket to engine.
2. Loosely install upper mount bracket to cylinder head bolts.
3. Install transaxle support brace.
4. Loosely install transaxle support brace and two lower front mount bracket nuts.
5. Tighten nuts and bolts in the following sequence:
   a. **Torque** lower engine mount bracket nuts to 30 ft. lbs.
   b. **Torque** transaxle support brace bolt to 37 ft. lbs.
   c. **Torque** upper engine mount brace bolts to 37 ft. lbs.
   d. **Torque** front engine mount nuts to 37 ft. lbs.

MOUNT STRUT

1. Remove core support sight shield.
2. Remove mount strut to engine bolts, then the mount strut.
3. Reverse procedure to install. Tighten bolts and nuts in following sequence:
   a. Install mount strut to radiator tie bar bolts. **Torque** to 18 ft. lbs.
   b. **Torque** engine mount strut bolts to 58 ft. lbs.

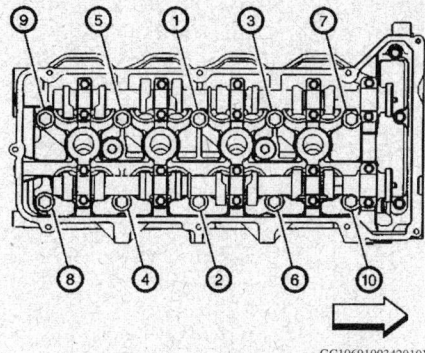

GC1069100342010X

Fig. 4   Cylinder head bolt tightening sequence. Righthand

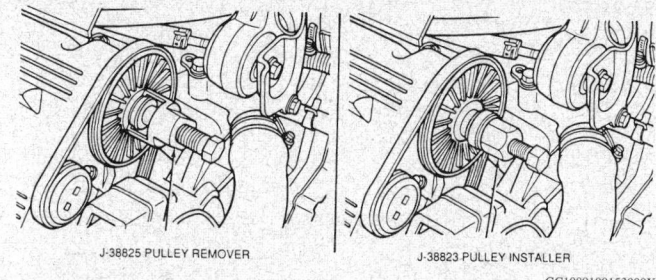

J-38825 PULLEY REMOVER   J-38823 PULLEY INSTALLER

GC1089100153000X

Fig. 5   Water pump pulley replacement. Eldorado

LEFTHAND STRUT BRACKET

1. Partially drain coolant into suitable container.
2. Remove engine mount strut.
3. Remove secondary AIR pipe mounting bolt from mount strut bracket
4. Disconnect surge tank inlet hose from coolant outlet fitting.
5. Remove coolant outlet fitting.
6. Remove mount strut bracket to water crossover bolts.
7. Reverse procedure to install.

RIGHTHAND STRUT BRACKET

1. Remove engine mount strut.
2. Mark running direction, then remove serpentine belt.
3. Remove power steering return hose to righthand mount strut bracket bolt, then position hose aside.
4. Remove battery ground cable to engine mounting bolt.
5. Remove alternator to mount strut bracket upper mounting bolt.
6. Remove mount strut bracket to cylinder head bolts, then the bracket.
7. Reverse procedure to install.

ENGINE
REPLACE

DeVille, Eldorado & Seville

1. Drain coolant into suitable container.
2. Disconnect both battery cables.
3. Recover air conditioning refrigerant as outlined in "Air Conditioning" chapter.
4. Remove upper filler panel.
5. Disconnect electrical connectors from PCM.
6. Remove air cleaner assembly.
7. Drain engine oil into suitable container.
8. Remove intake manifold sight shield.
9. Remove lower radiator hose using clamp tool No. J-37097-A, or equivalent.
10. Remove upper radiator hose from thermostat housing using clamp tool No. J-38185, or equivalent.
11. Disconnect upper and lower transaxle fluid cooler lines from radiator.

12. Disconnect surge tank inlet hose from engine.
13. Disconnect surge tank outlet hose from heater pipe.
14. **Always replace accelerator cable with a new one whenever engine is removed from vehicle. Position cruise control cable aside during engine removal or installation. Do not pry on, lean against or kink cruise control cable.**
15. Disconnect accelerator and cruise control cables from TBI unit.
16. Disconnect heater hoses from engine.
17. Disconnect two brake fluid lines from master cylinder. Cap open lines and ports to prevent entry of dirt and debris.
18. Remove bracket and shift cable from manual shift lever, then position aside.
19. Disconnect vacuum hose from brake booster.
20. Disconnect hose from EVAP purge valve.
21. Disconnect secondary AIR relay from relay bracket and secure to top of engine.
22. Disconnect fuel inlet and return fittings at fuel rail.
23. Disconnect engine ground wire from body frame rail.
24. Disconnect main engine harness.
25. Disconnect wiring harness from underhood fuse block.
26. Remove strut tower bolts.
27. Raise and support vehicle.
28. Remove front tires and wheels.
29. Disconnect dampening sensor links from lower control arms.
30. Disconnect wheel speed and road sensing suspension sensor electrical connectors.
31. Disconnect two brake lines from both front subframe brackets and at rear of engine subframe. Cap open lines to prevent system contamination.
32. Remove air deflector.
33. Remove front fascia extensions.
34. Remove and discard engine oil cooler quick-connect fittings from oil filter adapter with oil lines still attached, then position lines aside. **Quick-connect fittings must be replaced whenever they are removed from adapter.**
35. Remove dust cover from quick-connect joint.
36. Remove internal spring clip from engine oil cooler fittings.
37. Remove engine oil cooler lines from cooler fittings.
38. Disconnect secondary AIR inlet hose

from secondary AIR pump.
39. Disconnect air conditioning suction and discharge hoses from compressor. Cap open lines and fittings to prevent system contamination.
40. Ensure front wheels are in straight-ahead position.
41. Lock steering column using lockpin tool No. J-42640, or equivalent, in underside of column.
42. Remove steering intermediate shaft pinch bolt.
43. Disconnect steering gear from intermediate shaft.
44. Disconnect wheel speed and brake wear sensors at strut towers.
45. Disconnect downstream heated oxygen sensor electrical connector.
46. Remove front exhaust pipe.
47. Remove engine oil pan to transaxle case brace.
48. Remove flexplate inspection cover.
49. Mark flexplate to torque converter orientation, then remove mounting bolts.
50. Lower vehicle.
51. Position powertrain support dolly tool No. J-39580, or equivalent, under engine assembly. Four suitable jack stands may be substituted if a dolly is not available.
52. Remove engine mount to engine mount bracket nuts.
53. Secure front hoist pads to vehicle.
54. Remove subframe mount bolts.
55. Slowly raise vehicle. **Ensure powertrain assembly and subframe assembly clear all wiring, hoses and fluid lines.**
56. Attach suitable lifting crane to engine.
57. Remove heater pipes.
58. Disconnect coil pack ground wire from cylinder head.
59. Remove crossover pipe from cylinder head.
60. Remove power steering pump.
61. Remove front and rear transaxle brace bolt and nuts, then braces.
62. Remove front engine mount to engine subframe nut.
63. Remove transaxle to engine mounting bolts.
64. Raise engine from subframe and transaxle assembly.
65. Reverse procedure to install.

STS

1. Install tool No. J–42640 to steering column, then disconnect both battery cables.
2. Open hood, then remove bolts and cross vehicle brace from vehicle.

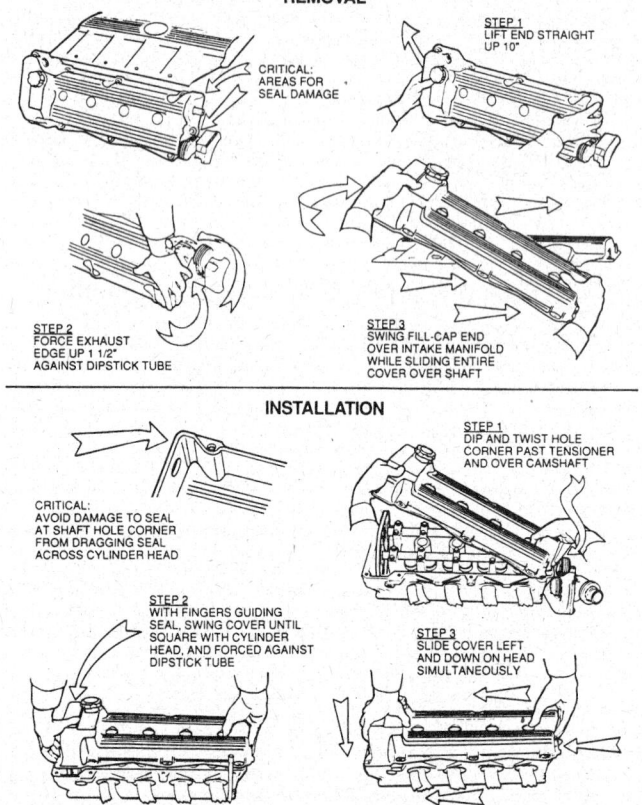

Fig. 6 Valve cover replacement. Eldorado

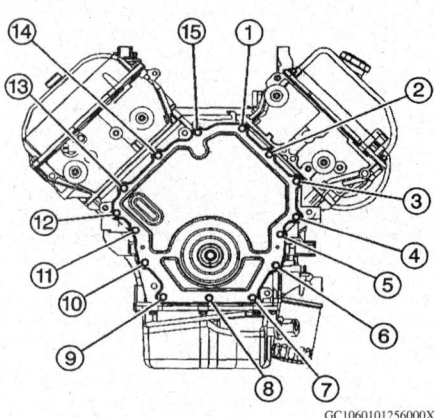

Fig. 7 Front cover bolt tightening sequence. DeVille, Seville & Eldorado

3. Remove fuel injector sight shield, then disconnect PCV tube from air cleaner duct.
4. Loosen air duct clamp at throttle body, then the air duct clamp at MAF/IAT sensor.
5. Remove air cleaner duct from vehicle.
6. Disconnect surge tank inlet hose and position hose to engine.
7. Recover air conditioning refrigerant as outlined in "Air Conditioning" chapter.
8. Disconnect air conditioning suction hose fitting at top of left shock tower.
9. Remove suction hose from retaining feature, then position line to engine.
10. Disconnect air conditioning liquid line from condenser, then remove air conditioning liquid line from retaining feature on fan shroud.
11. Disconnect vacuum line from brake booster, then position brake booster line to engine.
12. Disconnect electrical connector on brake fluid level switch from master cylinder, then remove master cylinder mounting nuts.
13. Position master cylinder to engine using mechanics wire, do not disconnect brake lines.
14. Relieve fuel system pressure as outlined in "Precautions."
15. Remove fuel line retainer, located on bracket attached to heater lines on front of dash.
16. Disconnect engine wiring harness connector at front of dash, then remove underhood electrical center cover.

17. Remove cable retainer from stud on right shock tower, then cable from electrical center and position cables to engine.
18. Disconnect chassis electrical connector at top of right shock tower, then the electrical connector for transmission control module and position to engine.
19. Disconnect engine wiring harness connector from inside of underhood electrical center, then at right frame rail.
20. Loosen fan nut from crank adapter shaft using tool No. J–41240-5A or equivalent, then raise and support vehicle.
21. Remove fan from crank adapter shaft, then the front tire and wheel assemblies.
22. Remove push-in retainers, then the splash shields and both wheelhouse liners from vehicle.
23. Working through right wheelhouse, remove windshield washer reservoir brace from front frame.
24. Place a suitable drain pan under vehicle, disconnect transmission oil cooler lines through left wheelhouse.
25. Remove bolt, then separate center intermediate shaft from lower intermediate shaft.
26. Drain cooling system into a suitable container.
27. Remove bolt securing power steering cooler lines to radiator assembly, then lower vehicle.

28. Remove radiator outlet and inlet hoses, then the surge tank inlet hose from radiator.
29. Remove radiator support brackets, then disconnect upper air baffle retaining pins from radiator.
30. Remove radiator, condenser, and transmission oil cooler as an assembly.
31. Raise vehicle, then remove bolts from mounting bracket on power steering oil cooler. Position oil cooler to engine.
32. **On models equipped with transfer case,** remove transfer case as outlined in **MOTOR's "Domestic Transmission, In-Vehicle Service."**
33. **On all models,** remove transmission as outlined under **MOTOR's "Domestic Transmission, In-Vehicle Service."**
34. Remove brake bundle clips from right and left frame rails. Do not remove clips from brake lines.
35. Disconnect fuel line from fuel filter, then the evaporative emission hose connection at rear of fuel filter.
36. Disconnect rear brake lines from bracket above rear axle assembly.
37. Remove fuel and brake line bundle retainers from frame rail along length of vehicle. Do not remove retainers from lines.
38. Remove fuel filter bracket for access path for fuel and brake line bundle assembly.
39. Remove fuel and brake line bundle bracket from right side wheelhouse, then lower vehicle.
40. Disconnect heater outlet hose from pipe and position hose to engine, then inlet hose from water housing and position hose to vehicle.
41. Disconnect electrical connectors from top of both shock modules, then remove upper mounting bolts.
42. Secure shock modules to front frame, then raise vehicle enough to place a suitable lift table under engine, front frame, and front suspension assembly.
43. **To avoid any vehicle damage, serious personal injury or death when major components are removed**

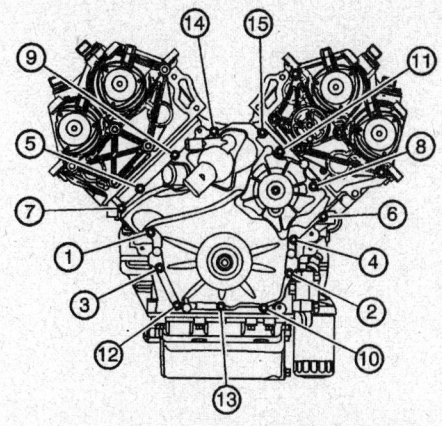

ARM0400000000094

Fig. 8   Front cover bolt tightening sequence. STS

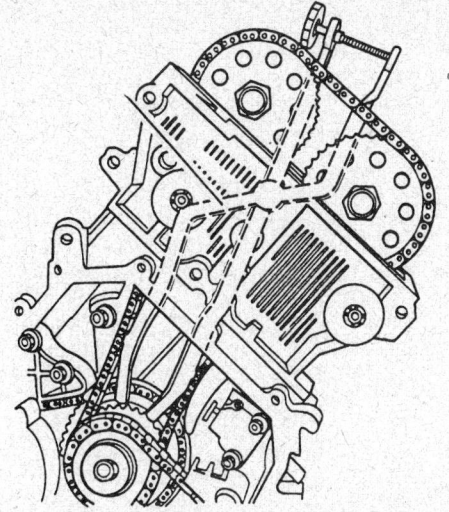

GC1069100343000X

Fig. 9   Drive chain tensioning

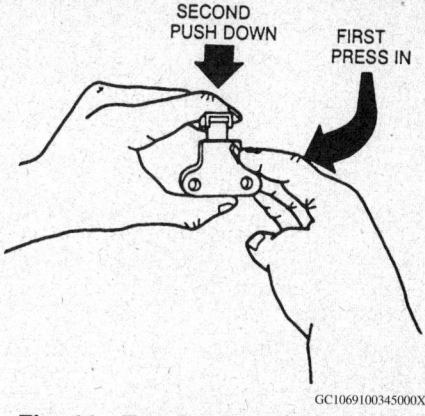

GC1069100345000X

Fig. 10   Tensioner release lever rotation

from vehicle and vehicle is supported by a hoist, support vehicle with jack stands at opposite end from which components are being removed.

44. Support rear of vehicle with suitable jack stands, then raise lift table and or lower vehicle to preload weight of assembly.
45. Remove front frame bolts.
46. With aid of an assistant lower, table and/or raise vehicle to remove engine, front frame, fuel/brake bundle and front suspension assembly from vehicle.
47. Ensure that all hoses, wires, pipes and shock modules clear vehicle during removal process.
48. Install engine support fixture J–28467-86 and J–28467-87 or equivalents to right and left cylinder heads.
49. Using a suitable engine lift, remove engine from front frame assembly.
50. Reverse procedure to install.

INTAKE MANIFOLD
REPLACE
DeVille, Eldorado & Seville

1. Drain coolant into suitable container.
2. Remove intake manifold sight shield.
3. Relieve fuel system pressure as outlined in "Precautions."
4. Remove air intake duct from TBI unit.
5. Remove transaxle vent hose and transaxle shift cable at bracket.
6. Disconnect TP sensor and IAC valve electrical connectors.
7. Disconnect accelerator cable and cruise control cable at TBI unit.
8. Tag their locations, then disconnect front bank spark plug wires or coil units and position aside.
9. Disconnect TBI unit coolant hoses at TBI unit and surge tank pipe.
10. Disconnect EGR pipe and crankcase ventilation pipe at TBI unit spacer.
11. Disconnect vacuum lines, PCV hoses and electrical connectors as required.

12. Disconnect brake booster vacuum hose at intake manifold vacuum fitting.
13. Remove fuel rail ground wire at rear cylinder head.
14. Twist fuel rail fuel line female quick-connector fittings ¼ turn in each direction to loosen any dirt within fitting. Blow dirt out of fitting using compressed air.
15. Disconnect fuel line quick-connect fittings using separator tool No. J-37088-A, or equivalent.
16. Disconnect fuel rail bracket at EGR valve.
17. Disconnect PCV hose at intake manifold.
18. Disconnect injector harness main electrical connector.
19. Remove intake manifold mounting bolts and studs, then manifold. Carrier gaskets are attached to manifold through a snap-lock feature and will remain attached when removing manifold.
20. If installing a new manifold, proceed as follows:
    a. Remove fuel rail.
    b. Remove carrier gaskets from manifold.
    c. Remove TBI unit.
    d. Remove MAP sensor.
21. Reverse procedure to install, noting the following:
    a. Clean all gasket and O-ring sealing surfaces.
    b. After engine has cooled, tighten manifold mounting bolts and nuts in sequence, **Fig. 1.**
    c. Ensure all electrical connectors and wiring are properly routed to avoid pinching.
    d. Turn ignition On for two seconds, then Off for 10 seconds.
    e. Turn ignition On and inspect for fuel leakage.

STS

1. Remove bolts and cross vehicle brace from engine compartment.
2. Remove fuel injector sight shield, then

disconnect PCV fresh air tube from left camshaft cover and air cleaner outlet duct.
3. Remove retaining clip, then disconnect PCV dirty air tube from PCV orificed tube.
4. Remove PCV dirty air tube from intake manifold.
5. Remove nuts, then the remove sight shield bracket.
6. Disconnect electrical connectors from left side and right side fuel injector, then the evaporative emissions purge valve line and connector.
7. Remove EVAP line from retaining feature at rear of right cylinder head, then position line aside.
8. Relieve fuel system pressure as outlined in "Precautions."
9. Disconnect fuel line from fuel rail, then remove fuel line from retainer at rear of right cylinder head.
10. Remove fasteners attaching fuel rail to intake manifold, then lift entire fuel rail and injector assembly from intake manifold.
11. Loosen plenum duct clamp at front of intake manifold, then the bolts attaching intake manifold to cylinder heads.
12. Remove intake manifold by using an upward lifting motion at rear of manifold assembly.
13. Reverse procedure to install noting the following:
    a. Ensure new gaskets are installed.
    b. Clean all passages and grooves.
    c. **Torque,** intake manifold bolts in sequence **Fig. 1,** to 89 inch lbs.

EXHAUST MANIFOLD
REPLACE
DeVille, Eldorado & Seville
LEFTHAND

1. Disconnect AIR pipe from manifold as required.
2. Remove engine mount as outlined in "Engine Mount, Replace."
3. Remove manifold outlet flange mounting bolts.

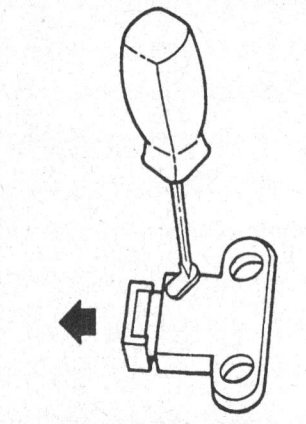

1 RELEASE TO FIRST CLICK
2 INSTALL LOCK PIN

GC1069100346000X

Fig. 11 Tensioner in collapsed position

4. Disconnect oxygen sensor electrical connector.
5. Remove manifold mounting bolts.
6. Remove exhaust manifold and oxygen sensor.
7. Reverse procedure to install. Coat oxygen sensor threads with high temperature anti-seize compound.

RIGHTHAND

1. Disconnect both battery cables, then rear oxygen sensor electrical connector and harness clip.
2. Lock steering column in straight-ahead position using lockpin tool No. J-42640, or equivalent in underside of column.
3. Raise and support vehicle.
4. Disconnect exhaust pipe from catalytic converter.
5. Disconnect AIR pipe from manifold as required.
6. Disconnect suspension position sensor at both lower control arms.
7. Remove heat shields from power steering gear, VSS and transaxle.
8. Remove steering intermediate shaft pinch bolt.
9. Disconnect intermediate shaft from steering gear.
10. Remove righthand engine mount to mount bracket nut.
11. Remove lefthand transaxle mount to mount bracket nut.
12. Support engine cradle rear crossmember with suitable screw jack and remove cradle to body mounting bolts.
13. Lower rear of engine cradle.
14. Remove pipe to exhaust manifold and crossover exhaust pipe mounting bolts.
15. Remove righthand side cylinder head to transaxle brace.
16. Remove mounting nuts and exhaust manifold.
17. Reverse procedure to install. Coat oxygen sensor threads with high temperature anti-seize compound.

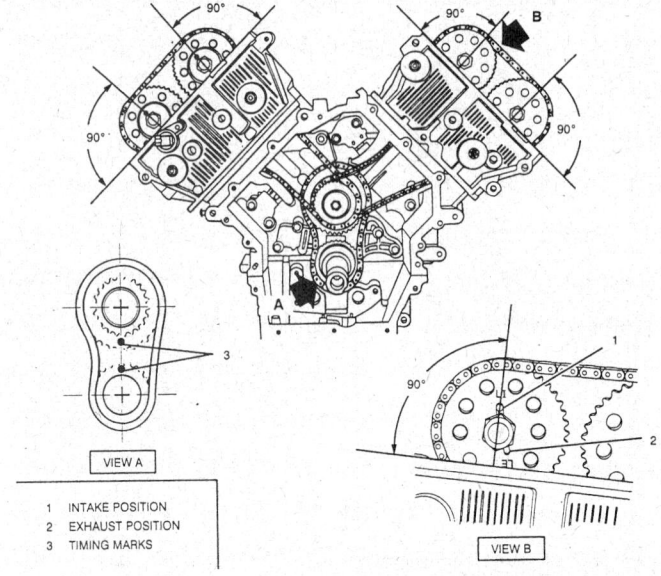

VIEW A

1 INTAKE POSITION
2 EXHAUST POSITION
3 TIMING MARKS

VIEW B

GC1069100347000X

Fig. 12 Camshaft timing procedure

STS

1. Disconnect heated oxygen sensor connector, then raise and support vehicle.
2. Remove bolts, then the exhaust manifold heat shield from engine.
3. Remove manifold bolts and nuts, then discard bolts.
4. Remove the exhaust manifold studs, then the exhaust manifold and gasket from engine. **Do not reuse gasket.**
5. Reverse procedure to install.

CYLINDER HEAD
REPLACE

DeVille, Eldorado & Seville

1. Remove exhaust manifolds as outlined in "Exhaust Manifold, Replace."
2. Remove intake manifold as outlined in "Intake Manifold, Replace."
3. Remove valve covers as outlined in "Valve Cover, Replace."
4. Remove crankshaft dampener as outlined in "Crankshaft Dampener, Replace."
5. Remove front cover as outlined in "Front Cover, Replace."
6. Remove timing chain tensioner from cylinder head.
7. Remove camshaft sprockets. **Timing chains should remain in chain case.**
8. Remove timing chain guide mounting screws through access plugs at cylinder head front, **Fig. 2.**
9. Remove water crossover and exhaust manifold as outlined in "Exhaust Manifold, Replace."
10. Remove cylinder head mounting bolts. Discard M11 bolts. M6 bolts can be used again.

11. Remove cylinder head and gasket. **When camshafts remain in cylinder head some valves will be open at all times. Do not rest cylinder head on a flat surface with head face down.**
12. Reverse procedure to install, noting the following:
   a. Install new M11 bolts. M6 bolts can be used again.
   b. **Torque** M11 bolts to 30 ft. lbs., in numbered sequence, **Figs. 3 and 4.**
   c. Tighten M11 cylinder head bolts an additional 70° in sequence.
   d. Tighten M11 bolts an additional 60° in sequence.
   e. Finally, tighten M11 bolts an additional 60° in sequence.
   f. **Torque** M6 bolts to 106 inch lbs.

STS

1. Remove exhaust manifolds as outlined in "Exhaust Manifold, Replace."
2. Drain engine coolant into a suitable container, then remove fuel injector sight shield.
3. Disconnect positive crankcase ventilation tube from air cleaner duct, then loosen air duct clamp at throttle body.
4. Loosen air duct clamp at mass air flow/ intake air temperature sensor.
5. Remove air cleaner duct from vehicle, then disconnect electrical connector from throttle body assembly.
6. Remove throttle body and throttle body gasket from water housing. Discard throttle body gasket.
7. Remove manifold absolute pressure sensor, then disconnect EVAP canister purge solenoid valve hose and electrical connector.
8. Remove heater inlet and outlet hoses, then radiator inlet hose, bypass and surge tank inlet hose.
9. Loosen intake manifold duct clamp,

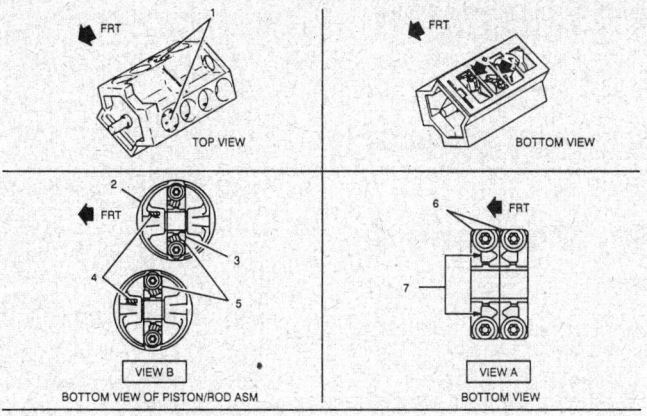

1 PISTON ARROW TOWARD CHAIN CASE ON BOTH SIDES
2 PISTON
3 ROD CAP
4 LOCATER LUGS INDICATE PISTON FRONT TOWARDS ENGINE FRONT
5 BEARING CAP ARROWS POINT TOWARD EACH OTHER ON PAIRED RODS
6 ROD CAPS
7 BEARING CAP ARROWS POINT TOWARD EACH OTHER ON PAIRED RODS

GC1069100349000X

Fig. 13 Piston & rod assembly. DeVille, Eldorado & Seville

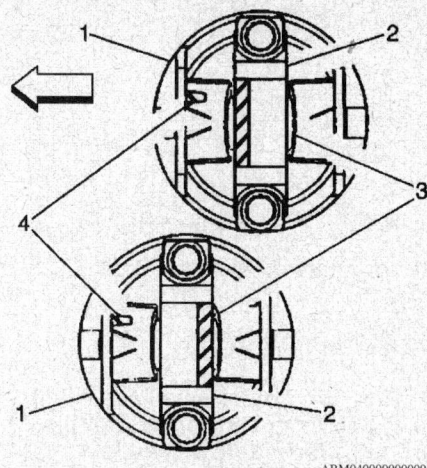

ARM0400000000095

Fig. 14 Piston & rod assembly. STS

then remove bolts securing water outlet housing to cylinder heads.
10. Remove water outlet housing from vehicle, then the intake manifold as outlined under "Intake Manifold Replace."
11. Remove secondary camshaft drive chain as outlined under "Timing Chain Replace."
12. Remove camshafts as outlined under "Camshaft Replace."
13. Remove M6 external drive bolts from front portion of cylinder head.
14. Remove and discard M11 internal drive cylinder head bolts. **Do not reuse M11 cylinder head bolts.**
15. Remove cylinder head, then ensure that no dowel guide pins are stuck in cylinder head.
16. Remove any remaining bolt thread sealant material from threaded cylinder block holes.
17. Remove cylinder head gasket.
18. Reverse procedure to install noting the following:
    a. Install new M11 bolts. M6 bolts can be used again.
    b. **Torque** M11 bolts to 22 ft. lbs., in numbered sequence, **Figs. 3 and 4.**
    c. Tighten M11 cylinder head bolts an additional 60° in sequence.
    d. Tighten M11 bolts an additional 60° in sequence.
    e. Finally, tighten M11 bolts an additional 60° in sequence.
    f. **Torque** M6 bolts to 106 inch lbs.

VALVE COVER
REPLACE
DeVille & Seville
LEFTHAND

1. Remove intake manifold sight shield and upper filler panel.

2. Partially drain coolant into suitable container.
3. Remove radiator hose from water crossover and position aside.
4. Disconnect PCV fresh air tube.
5. Tag their locations, then remove ignition coils and spark plug boots.
6. Remove engine coolant heater wire and position aside.
7. Disconnect alternator cooler outlet hose from pipe and position pipe aside.
8. Remove shield and water pump drive belt.
9. Remove water pump belt tensioner and dust cap from end of camshaft.
10. Remove water pump drive pulley using pulley removal tool No. J-38825, or equivalent.
11. Remove camshaft seal and discard.
12. Remove valve cover mounting bolts.
13. Lift valve cover drive end and remove reward to clear water pump driveshaft.
14. Reverse procedure install, noting the following:
    a. Install a new camshaft seal. Apply sealer part No. 1052080, or equivalent, to retainer bolt threads.
    b. Install water pump pulley using pulley installer tool No. J-38823, or equivalent.

RIGHTHAND

1. Remove intake manifold sight shield.
2. Disconnect PCV valve and oxygen sensor wire.
3. Disconnect AIR vent solenoid vacuum tubes and electrical connector, then remove AIR bracket and tube.
4. Tag their locations, then disconnect and remove ignition coils and spark plug boots.
5. Remove valve cover mounting bolts, then the cover.
6. Reverse procedure to install.

Eldorado
LEFTHAND

1. Disconnect and isolate both battery cables.
2. Partially drain coolant into suitable container.
3. Disconnect upper radiator hose at water crossover using clamp tool No. J-38185, or equivalent.
4. Tag their locations, then disconnect spark plug wires and ignition coil units.
5. Remove righthand cooling fan as required.
6. Disconnect PCV fresh air tube from valve cover.
7. Remove lefthand and righthand torque struts.
8. Remove water pump drive belt shield.
9. Disconnect water pump drive belt.
10. Remove plastic dust cap from end of intake camshaft.
11. Remove water pump pulley, **Fig. 5.**
12. Remove camshaft seal mounting bolts.
13. Remove and discard camshaft seal.
14. Disconnect battery cable retainer at front of valve cover and remove valve cover mounting screws.
15. Remove valve cover mounting bolts, then the cover, **Fig. 6.**
16. Reverse procedure to install, noting the following:
    a. Install a new camshaft seal. Apply sealer part No. 1052080, or equivalent, to retainer bolt threads.
    b. Install water pump pulley using pulley installer tool No. J-38823, or equivalent.

RIGHTHAND

1. Disconnect and isolate both battery cables.
2. Remove tower-to-tower brace, then raise and support vehicle.
3. Disconnect rear exhaust manifold at converter, then position convertor

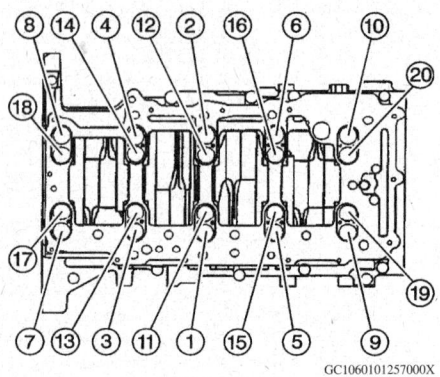

Fig. 15 Lower crankcase bolt tightening sequence. DeVille, Eldorado & Seville

aside and lower vehicle.
4. Disconnect ignition coil electrical connectors.
5. Tag their locations, then remove mounting bolts, ignition coils and righthand bank spark plug wires.
6. Disconnect PCV valve and remove purge canister solenoid from rear of cover.
7. Remove wiring harness and valve cover mounting screws.
8. Support front of engine cradle and remove front cradle mounting screws.
9. Remove lefthand and righthand torque struts.
10. Lower engine cradle to provide clearance at rear of engine compartment.
11. Remove valve cover mounting bolts, then the cover.
12. Reverse procedure to install.

STS

1. Open hood, then remove bolts and cross vehicle brace from vehicle.
2. Remove fuel injector sight shield, then disconnect PCV fresh air tube from valve cover.
3. Remove ignition coil cover from Valve cover by lifting straight up.
4. Disconnect electrical connector from ignition module.
5. Remove retaining bolts and studs, then the ignition module assembly.
6. Remove bolt connecting the ground strap to valve cover.
7. Remove bolt securing oil level indicator tube to left cylinder head, then reposition tube away from valve cover.
8. Remove valve cover bolts, lift camshaft drive end of valve cover up to clear cover.
9. Reverse procedure install, noting the following:
   a. Install a new cover gasket.
   b. Apply sealer part No. 12345739, or equivalent, to split line of left cylinder head and left camshaft position actuator housing.

VALVE CLEARANCE SPECIFICATIONS

This engine is equipped with hydraulic lifters. Valve adjustment is not required.

VALVE ADJUSTMENT

This engine is equipped with hydraulic lifters. Valve adjustment is not required.

CRANKSHAFT DAMPER
REPLACE

DeVille, Eldorado & Seville

1. Mark running direction, then remove serpentine belt.
2. Raise and support vehicle.
3. Remove righthand front wheel and splash shields.
4. Remove brace between engine oil pan and transaxle case.
5. Remove flexplate inspection cover.
6. Install flexplate holder tool No. J-44214, or equivalent.
7. Remove balancer mounting bolt.
8. Support engine cradle with suitable screw jack.
9. Remove engine mount to mount bracket nut.
10. Lower the engine assembly to allow clearance for puller tool below body rail.
11. Install pilot into end of crankshaft.
12. Remove crankshaft dampener using puller tool No. J-41816, or equivalent.
13. Reverse procedure to install, noting the following:
   a. Install crankshaft balancer using installer tool No. J-41998-B, or equivalent.
   b. Clean all dirt and debris from balancer bolt threads, then apply clean engine oil.
   c. **Torque** balancer bolt to 37 ft. lbs., then tighten an additional 120°.

STS

1. Mark running direction, then remove serpentine belt.
2. Disconnect positive crankcase ventilation tube from air cleaner duct, then loosen air duct clamp at throttle body.
3. Loosen air duct clamp at mass air flow/intake air temperature sensor.
4. Remove air cleaner duct from vehicle, then loosen fan nut from crank adapter shaft using tool No. J-41240-5A or equivalent.
5. Raise and support vehicle, disconnect engine wiring harness from engine frame and reposition aside.
6. Remove fan nut, then disconnect fan from crank adapter shaft.
7. Remove fan from vehicle, then with aid of an assistant tap engine ignition until fan bracket to crankshaft balancer bolts are accessible.
8. Remove fan bracket to crankshaft balancer bolts, then the fan bracket to engine block bolts.
9. Remove fan bracket from vehicle.
10. Remove starter motor as outlined under "Starter Replace."
11. Install too No. EN46326 or equivalent, then remove crankshaft balancer bolt.
12. Place tool No. J-38416-2 or equiva-

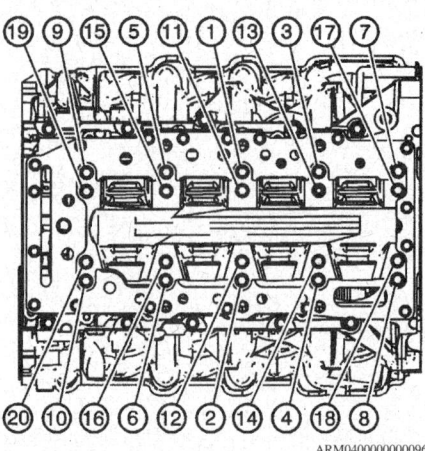

Fig. 16 Lower crankcase bolt tightening sequence. STS

lent, into end of crankshaft, then install tool No. J-24420-C or equivalent on crankshaft balancer.
13. Remove crankshaft damper from vehicle.
14. Reverse procedure to install, noting the following:
   a. Install crankshaft balancer using installer tool No. J-41998-B, or equivalent.
   b. Clean all dirt and debris from balancer bolt threads, then apply clean engine oil.
   c. **Torque** balancer bolt to 37 ft. lbs., then tighten an additional 120°.

FRONT COVER
REPLACE

DeVille & Seville

1. Remove serpentine drive belt.
2. Remove crankshaft dampener as outlined in "Crankshaft Dampener, Replace."
3. Remove belt tensioner, then belt idler pulley.
4. Raise and support vehicle, then support engine assembly using suitable jack.
5. Remove engine mount to mount bracket and bracket to engine mounting nuts.
6. Remove front cover mounting bolts, then the cover. **Do not discard gasket unless it is damaged.**
7. Reverse procedure to install, noting the following:
   a. Apply a small amount of sealant part No. 12345739, or equivalent, at split line of upper and lower crankcases.
   b. Place gasket evenly over dowel pins.
   c. Tighten front cover bolts in sequence, Fig. 7.

Eldorado

1. Remove serpentine drive belt.

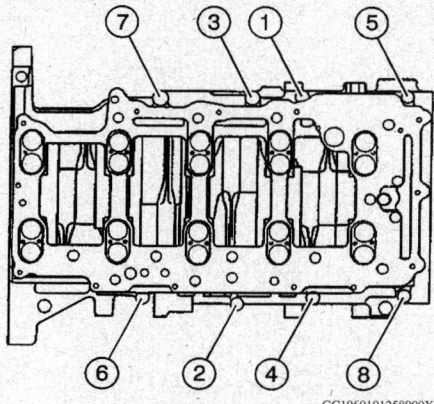

Fig. 17 Crankcase perimeter bolt tightening sequence

2. Remove crankshaft dampener as outlined in "Crankshaft Dampener, Replace."
3. Remove belt tensioner, then belt idler pulley.
4. Raise and support vehicle, then support engine assembly using suitable jack.
5. Remove engine mount to mount bracket and bracket to engine mounting nuts.
6. Remove front cover mounting bolts, then the cover. **Do not discard gasket unless it is damaged.**
7. Reverse procedure to install, noting the following:
   a. Apply a small amount of sealant part No. 12345739, or equivalent, at split line of upper and lower crankcases.
   b. Place gasket evenly over dowel pins.
   c. Tighten front cover bolts in sequence, **Fig. 7.**

STS

1. Drain engine coolant into a suitable container.
2. Disconnect positive crankcase ventilation tube from air cleaner duct, then loosen air duct clamp at throttle body.
3. Loosen air duct clamp at mass air flow/intake air temperature sensor.
4. Remove air cleaner duct from vehicle, then the heater hose from thermostat housing.
5. Disconnect electrical connector then remove afterboil coolant pump.
6. Mark running direction, then remove serpentine belt.
7. Remove bolt, then the drive belt idler pulley and water pump pulley.
8. Raise and support vehicle, then remove crankshaft damper as outlined in "Crankshaft Damper Replace."
9. Remove cover bolts, then the engine front cover. Discard engine front cover gasket.
10. Reverse procedure to install, noting the following:
    a. Apply a small amount of sealant part No. 12345739, or equivalent, at split line of upper and lower

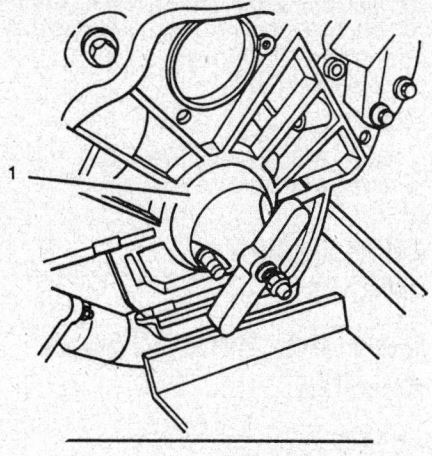

1 J 38817

GC1099100047000X

Fig. 18 Rear main seal installation. Lip type seal

crankcases.
   b. Place gasket evenly over dowel pins.
   c. Tighten front cover bolts in sequence to 11 ft. lbs., **Fig. 8.**

FRONT COVER SEAL
REPLACE

1. Remove crankshaft dampener as outlined in "Crankshaft Dampener, Replace."
2. Pry out seal using suitable screwdriver. **Do not score seal or crankshaft cover bore.**
3. Reverse procedure to install, noting the following:
   a. Lubricate seal lips with suitable engine oil.
   b. Position seal to front cover with garter spring side toward engine.
   c. Push seal into front cover using front cover seal installer tool No. J-38818 and balancer installer tool No. J-39344, or equivalent, until tool bottoms on cover.

TIMING CHAIN
REPLACE
Primary

DEVILLE, ELDORADO & SEVILLE

1. Remove engine as outlined in "Engine, Replace," then mount on suitable stand.
2. Mark running direction, then remove serpentine belt.
3. Remove idler pulley and belt tensioner.
4. Remove front cover as outlined in "Front Cover, Replace."
5. Remove oil pump assembly as outlined in "Oil Pump, Replace."
6. Remove valve covers as outlined in "Valve Cover, Replace."
7. Remove timing chain tensioners and camshaft sprockets.

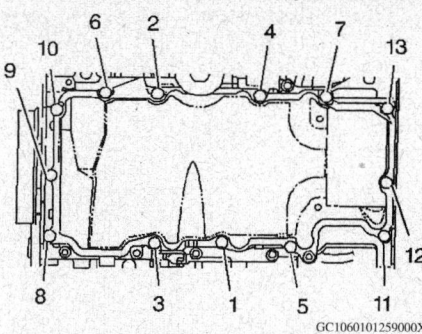

GC1060101259000X

Fig. 19 Oil pan bolt tightening sequence

8. Remove secondary drive chains from intermediate shaft sprocket.
9. Remove one intermediate shaft sprocket bolt, then slide gears and primary drive chain off crankshaft and intermediate shaft.
10. Reverse procedure to install. Time camshafts as outlined in "Camshaft, Replace."

STS

1. Remove oil pump assembly as outlined in "Oil Pump, Replace."
2. Align primary timing marks using tool No. J-39946 or equivalent.
3. Remove camshaft position actuator housing. DO NOT remove actuator solenoids from housing.
4. Install tool No. EN46328 on camshafts, then create two reference marks to identify chain link adjacent to each actuator timing mark.
5. Install an engine front cover bolt into front of engine, then Wrap mechanics wire tightly around both secondary camshaft drive chain shoe and front cover bolt.
6. Loosen and remove the right secondary timing chain tensioner bolts and tensioner
7. Remove bolts attaching secondary camshaft drive chain tensioner to engine block.
8. Remove secondary camshaft drive chain tensioner, allowing tensioner to expand as you remove it.
9. Use an open-end wrench on hex cast into camshaft in camshaft from rotating when removing camshaft oil control valve.
10. Loosen, then remove camshaft position oil control valves.
11. Slide exhaust camshaft position actuator off camshaft, then remove secondary timing chain from camshaft actuator teeth.
12. Align primary timing marks using tool No. J-39946 or equivalent.
13. Remove bolts attaching primary camshaft drive chain tensioner to engine block.
14. Remove primary camshaft drive chain tensioner, allowing tensioner to expand as you remove it.
15. Remove oil outlet tube, then the primary camshaft drive chain guide bolts and guide.
16. Remove camshaft intermediate

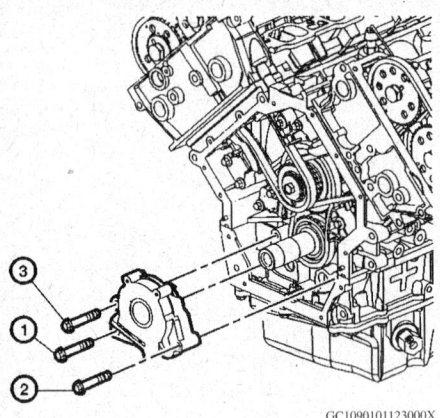

GC1090101123000X

Fig. 20 Oil pump replacement

sprocket retaining bolt, then the primary camshaft drive chain, crankshaft sprocket and camshaft intermediate sprocket.
17. Reverse procedure to install.

Secondary

DEVILLE, ELDORADO & SEVILLE

1. Remove front cover as outlined in "Front Cover, Replace."
2. Remove lefthand valve cover as outlined in "Valve Cover, Replace."
3. Align timing marks.
4. Remove lefthand secondary chain tensioner.
5. Remove lefthand chain guide as outlined in "Cylinder Head, Replace."
6. Remove lefthand cam sprocket bolts and sprockets.
7. Remove lefthand secondary drive chain, **Fig. 9.**
8. Remove righthand secondary drive chain as outlined for lefthand removal in previous steps. Substitute righthand for lefthand.
9. Reverse procedure to install. Time camshafts as outlined in "Camshaft, Replace."

STS

Refer to "Timing Chain Replace, "Primary" for replacement procedure.

Tensioner, Replace

DEVILLE, ELDORADO & SEVILLE

REMOVAL

1. Remove front cover as outlined in "Front Cover, Replace."
2. Remove mounting bolts and tensioner.

INSTALLATION

1. Rotate ratchet release lever counter clockwise and hold, **Fig. 10.**
2. Collapse tensioner shoe and hold.
3. Release ratchet lever and slowly release pressure on shoe.
4. As ratchet lever moves to first click hold tensioner shoe inward and insert pin through release lever hole, **Fig. 11.**

5. Install tensioner and bolts.
6. Remove retaining pin allowing tensioner shoe to extend.
7. Install front cover.

STS

Refer to "Timing Chain Replace, "Primary" for replacement procedure.

CAMSHAFT
REPLACE
DeVille, Eldorado & Seville
REMOVAL

1. Remove valve cover as outlined in "Valve Cover, Replace."
2. Secure cam sprocket to timing chain by installing four tie wraps per sprocket through sprocket holes.
3. Install cam chain holder tool No. J-38822, or equivalent, behind camshaft sprockets, positioned between chain tensioner and chain guide, **Fig. 9.**
4. Apply tension to tool by tightening tension adjusting screw.
5. Remove camshaft sprocket bolts. **Record cam drive pins location in camshafts end for installation.**
6. Work sprockets off cams using play in chain.
7. Loosen cam bearing cap bolts a few turns at a time until all valve spring pressure has been released.
8. Remove bolts, bearing caps and camshaft.

INSTALLATION

1. Apply camshaft prelube part No. 1052365, or equivalent, to face of each cam lobe.
2. Install camshaft and position cam bearing caps to cylinder head noting the following:
   a. Arrow on top of bearing cap points towards front of engine.
   b. "E" mark on top of bearing cap indicates cap for exhaust cam.
   c. "I" mark on top of bearing cap indicates cap for intake cam.
   d. "No. 1" mark on top of bearing cap should be towards front of engine.
3. Loosely install cam bearing cap bolts.
4. Alternately tighten each bearing cap bolt a few turns at a time against valve spring pressure until all bolts are snug.
5. Tighten bearing cap bolts.
6. Rotate camshaft until drive pins are in position to engage cam sprockets over cams and install mounting bolts.
7. Remove chain holder tool and tie wraps.
8. Install cam cover.

STS

1. Remove both left and right camshaft position actuators as outlined in "Timing Chain Replace."
2. **Bearing caps must remain with their**

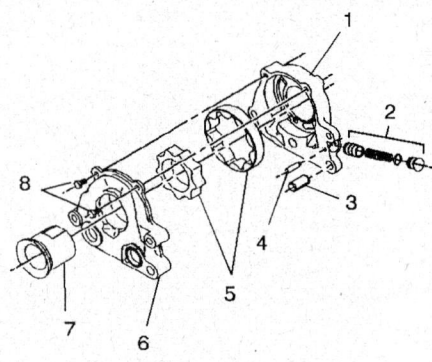

1. Housing rear section
2. Pressure relief valve assembly
3. Locating dowel
4. Valve cap retainer pin
5. Rotors
6. Housing front section
7. Drive spacer
8. Screws

GC1090101124000X

Fig. 21 Exploded view of oil pump

original cylinder head and in their original location. Do not mix bearing caps.
3. Remove camshaft bearing cap bolts, then the camshaft bearing caps. Store bearing caps in a clean shop towel.
4. Remove camshaft, place in a secure location.
5. Reverse procedure noting the following:
   a. Clean camshaft journals with a clean lint-free cloth.
   b. Apply a liberal amount of lubricant GM P/N 12345001 or equivalent to camshaft bearing journals.
   c. **Torque,** camshaft bearing cap bolts to 44 inch lbs.
   d. **Torque,** camshaft bearing cap bolts final pass an additional 30°.

Camshaft Timing

Setting camshaft timing is required whenever the camshaft drive system has been disturbed, such that the relationship between any chain and sprocket has been lost. Even when only one sprocket is involved, the following procedure should be observed since one crankshaft rotation will not provide conditions where proper timing can be confirmed.

1. Remove valve covers as outlined in "Valve Cover, Replace."
2. Remove front cover as outlined in "Front Cover, Replace."
3. Remove or retract three chain tensioners. **Tensioners may be in installed positions but must be fully retracted as outlined in "Timing Chain, Replace."**
4. Remove oil pump assembly as outlined in "Oil Pump, Replace."
5. Primary and secondary chain guides should be installed if previously removed.
6. Rotate crankshaft until sprocket drive key is at approximately 1 o'clock position using crankshaft rotation socket tool No. J-39946, or equivalent.
7. Install crankshaft and intermediate

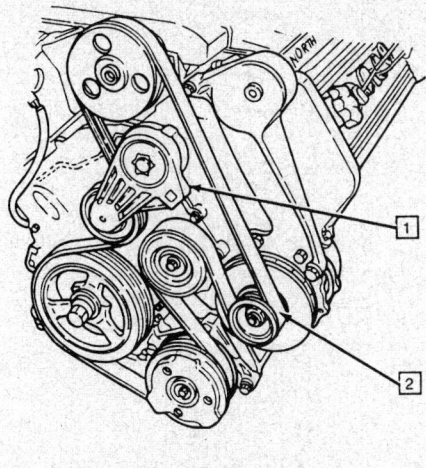

DRIVE BELT TENSIONER
2 **SERPENTINE DRIVE BELT**

GC1069100351000X

Fig. 22 Serpentine drive belt routing. Except STS

shaft sprockets to primary drive chain with timing marks aligned, **Fig. 12.**

8. Install crank and intermediate shaft sprockets over their respective shafts.
9. Rotate crankshaft so crankshaft key engages sprocket without changing timing mark position using crankshaft rotation socket tool.
10. Tighten intermediate sprocket mounting bolt.
11. Install primary chain tensioner and release tensioner shoe. Tighten tensioner mounting bolts.
12. Lock crankshaft in position using flexplate holder tool No. J-39411, or equivalent.
13. Route lefthand cylinder head secondary drive chain over intermediate shaft inner row teeth.
14. **Righthand exhaust camshaft sprocket (marked RE) must contain camshaft position sensor pickup.**
15. Route secondary drive chain over chain guide and install exhaust camshaft sprocket to chain so that camshaft drive pin engages lefthand head exhaust sprocket notch (marked LE). There should be no slack in lower section of chain and camshaft drive pin must be perpendicular to cylinder head face, **Fig. 12.**
16. Install intake camshaft sprocket into chain so notch on lefthand head intake sprocket (marked LI) engages cam drive pin while pin remains perpendicular to cylinder head face.
17. A hex is cast into camshafts behind cylinders Nos. 1 and 2 so an open end wrench can be used to provide minor positioning of camshafts.
18. Loosely install exhaust and intake cam sprocket bolts.
19. Install chain tensioner and release tension on shoe. Tighten tensioner mounting bolts.
20. Tighten camshaft sprocket bolts.
21. **Righthand exhaust camshaft sprocket (marked RE) must contain**

camshaft position sensor pickup.

22. Route righthand cylinder head secondary drive chain over intermediate shaft outer row of teeth, then repeat procedure for righthand cams.

PISTON & ROD ASSEMBLY

Refer to **Figs. 13 and 14** for proper piston and rod assembly installation.

Coat piston and rod assemblies with prelube lubricant part No. 1052367, or equivalent, before installation.

The arrow marks on the piston crowns must face the front of the engine.

The locating mark cast into the underside of the piston should point toward the front of the engine. The connecting rod cap locating notch should point toward the rear of the engine on odd-numbered cylinders and toward the front of the engine on even-numbered cylinders.

PISTONS, PINS & RINGS

This procedure has been revised by a Technical Service Bulletin.

When removing and installing piston rings install oil ring expander with ends facing toward piston top. Installing expander with ends facing away from piston top could prevent oil rings from rotating during engine operation.

MAIN & ROD BEARINGS

Shell type main bearings of steel backed aluminum are used at all positions. The upper halves are interchangeable, as are the lower halves except for the No. 3 thrust bearings.

If bearing clearance is more than .003 inch and new bearings do not reduce clearance to .0005–.002 inch, a new crankshaft will be required. Undersized bearing are not available and crankshaft grinding is not allowed.

1. **Torque** lower crankcase bolt Nos. 1–20 in sequence to 15 ft. lbs., **Figs. 15 and 16.**
2. Rotate bolt Nos. 1–20 an additional 65°.
3. **Torque** upper-to-lower crankcase perimeter bolts to 22 ft. lbs., in sequence, **Fig. 17.**
4. Maximum crankshaft endplay is .0197 inch.
5. Coat bearings with prelube lubricant part No. 1052367, or equivalent.
6. Ensure crankshaft journals are covered completely with lubricant.

CRANKSHAFT REAR OIL SEAL
REPLACE
Lip Type Seal
REMOVAL

1. Remove transaxle assembly. Refer to

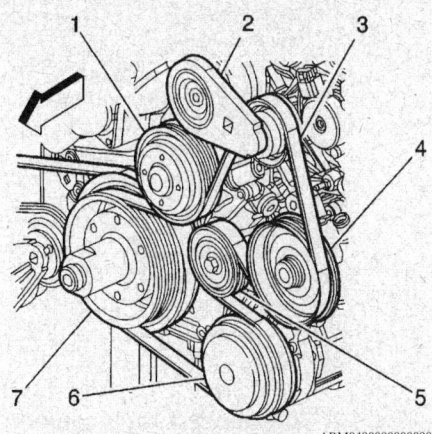

ARM0400000000098

Fig. 23 Serpentine drive belt routing. STS

MOTOR's "Domestic Transmission, In-Vehicle Service" manual.
2. Remove mounting bolts and flexplate.
3. Drill a ⅛ inch hole into rear main seal metal body.
4. Remove seal using suitable slide hammer.

INSTALLATION

1. Place small amount of suitable RTV sealant at crankcase split line across end of upper/lower crankcase seal.
2. Lubricate new oil seal with suitable engine oil, then slide seal over arbor of seal installer tool No. J-38817, or equivalent.
3. Thread seal installer tool into crankshaft flange, then install seal by turning handle until tool bottoms against crankcase, **Fig. 18.**
4. Install flexplate, then tighten bolts.

Cartridge Type Seal
REMOVAL

1. Remove transaxle assembly. Refer to **MOTOR's "Domestic Transmission, In-Vehicle Service"** manual.
2. Remove mounting bolts and flexplate.
3. Install eight one inch self-tapping screws using guide holes in crankshaft rear oil seal removal tool No. J-42841, or equivalent, and variable speed drill motor with socket adapter.
4. Remove tool mounting bolts, then install tool center screw.
5. Remove seal by tightening tool.

INSTALLATION

1. Clean any debris from crankshaft rear oil seal drain.
2. Coat outer diameter of cylinder block with suitable clean engine oil.
3. Oil seal has a pre-applied green sealant coating. **Do not allow engine oil on area where oil seal is to be pressed on crankshaft or on inner diameter of oil seal.**
4. Loosen crankshaft rear oil seal installer tool No. J-42842, or equivalent's center bolt until center hub protrudes approximately one inch, then install on

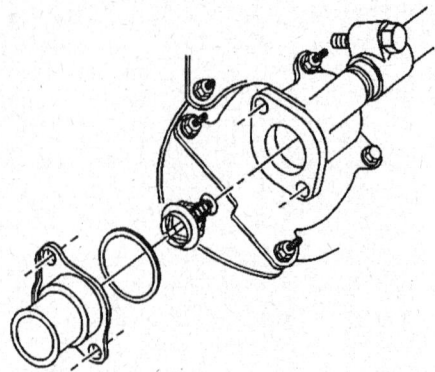

GC1080100687000X

Fig. 24 Thermostat replacement

to crankshaft by threading mounting bolts to crankshaft flange.

5. Install rear oil seal by tightening rear oil seal installer tool until it bottoms against crankcase. Remove tool.
6. Ensure installation depth of crankshaft rear oil seal is equal around circumference.
7. Install flexplate, then tighten bolts.

OIL PAN
REPLACE
DeVille, Eldorado & Seville

1. Drain engine oil into suitable container.
2. Remove exhaust crossover pipe if required. Discard flange gaskets.
3. Remove oil pan mounting bolts, then the pan. **Do not remove gasket from pan groove unless replacement is required. It can be used again if it is not damaged.**
4. Reverse procedure to install. Tighten oil pan bolts in sequence, **Fig. 19.**

STS

1. Install engine support fixture, then raise and support vehicle and remove front wheels.
2. Remove front air deflector, then disconnect electrical harness retainers securing engine harness to frame.
3. Disconnect left and right rearward frame retainer, then the antilock brake wiring harness from the lower control arms.
4. Loosen brake line bracket nut, then disconnect brake lines from frame.
5. Using mechanics wire, support radiator and AC condenser assembly to front inner energy absorber bracket bolt.
6. Remove nuts, then the washer bottle bracket.
7. Loosen brake pressure modulator valve nuts, then separate BPMV from bracket assembly.
8. **Mark stabilizer shaft to ensure cor-**

rect position when reinstalling, then loosen stabilizer shaft mounting bolts.

9. Remove lower stabilizer shaft link retaining nut, then the stabilizer shaft link from lower control arm.
10. Remove power steering pressure hose retaining nut from air conditioning compressor, then position power steering pressure hose aside.
11. Remove power steering gear mounting bolts, then support power steering gear to bolt bracket installed in oil pan.
12. Remove outer tie rod retaining nut, then lower shock bolts. **Brake calipers do not need to be removed from knuckle assembly.**
13. Disconnect lower ball joint from steering knuckle and position knuckle assembly away from lower control arms.
14. Remove engine mounts lower retaining nuts, then lower vehicle to frame support table.
15. Remove frame mounting bolts, with aid of an assistant raise body from frame.
16. Ensure when raising body that brake pipes, steering knuckle assembly and wheel speed sensor electrical harness are clear from frame.
17. Remove lower control arm to cradle nuts and bolts, then the lower control arm by lowering lower control arm at frame and moving ball stud upwards.
18. With aid of an assistant, remove frame from support fixture.
19. **On models equipped with differential carrier,** remove differential carrier as outlined in **MOTOR's "Domestic Transmission, In-Vehicle Service."**
20. **On all models,** disconnect electrical connector, then remove engine oil level sensor from oil pan.
21. Remove retaining bolts, then the oil pan.
22. Reverse procedure to install. Tighten oil pan bolts in sequence, **Fig. 19.**

OIL PUMP
REPLACE
Removal

1. Remove front cover as outlined in "Front Cover, Replace."
2. Remove mounting bolts, pump and drive spacer, **Fig. 20.**

Installation

1. Ensure all gasket and sealing surfaces are clean and free of damage.
2. Install oil pump drive spacer into oil pump from rear so that drive flat engages pump rotor.
3. Position pump over crankshaft and loosely install bolts.
4. Apply upward pressure while tightening mounting bolts.
5. **Torque** pump mounting bolts to 89 inch lbs., in sequence, **Fig. 20.**
6. Tighten bolts an additional 35°.

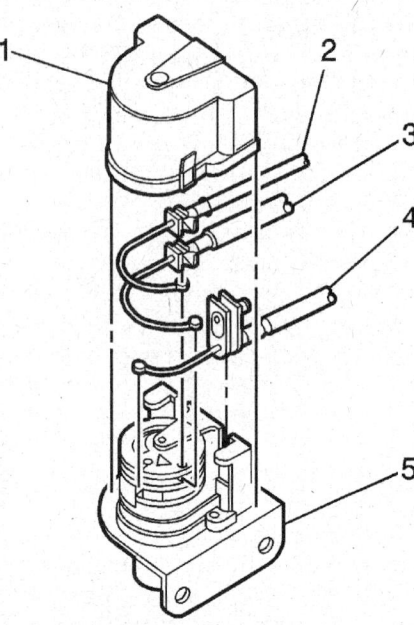

1. Throttle Relaxer Cover
2. Accelerator Cable
3. Accelerator Cable
4. Cruise Control Cable
5. Mounting Bracket

ARM0400000000099

Fig. 25 Water pump bolt removal. STS

7. Install front cover assembly as outlined in "Front Cover, Replace."

OIL PUMP SERVICE
Disassembly

1. Remove pump housing drive spacer, **Fig. 21.**
2. Remove screws holding pump housing sections together.
3. Mark mating surfaces for installation, then remove inner and outer rotors.
4. Remove pressure relief valve cap retainer pin.
5. Remove retainer cap. **Avoid damaging O-ring.**
6. Slide valve spring and piston from bore.

Inspection

Internal components of oil pump are not serviceable. Replace entire pump assembly if wear or damage is noted.

1. Inspect pump housing sections for nicks, burrs, chips or debris that may cause a leak or binding condition in rotor pocket.
2. Inspect drive or driven rotors for nicks or burrs.
3. Inspect pump cover and interior surface for excessive wear or score marks.

Assembly

1. Install inner and outer rotors to pump cover. **Align marks made during pump disassembly.**
2. Install pressure relief valve seat, spring and pilot.
3. Assemble housing and cover over locating dowel.
4. Align housing and cover using suitable drill bit in pump mounting hole on opposite side.

SERPENTINE DRIVE BELT

1. Mark running direction.
2. Rotate drive belt tensioner mechanism upward and away from drive belt using suitable ½ inch breaker bar.
3. Remove serpentine drive belt.
4. Reverse procedure to install. Refer to **Figs. 22 and 23** for serpentine drive belt routing.

COOLING SYSTEM BLEED

1. Fill radiator with proper antifreeze solution.
2. Install radiator cap.
3. Start and idle engine.
4. Place HVAC controls in any air conditioning mode except Max and temperature at highest setting.
5. Idle engine until lower radiator to water pump hose is hot.
6. Turn ignition Off.
7. Allow engine to cool to ambient temperature.
8. Ensure coolant in surge tank is at proper level.

THERMOSTAT
REPLACE

1. Drain coolant into suitable container.
2. Remove engine cover and air cleaner as required.
3. Disconnect radiator hose at thermostat housing using clamp tool No. J-38185, or equivalent.
4. Remove mounting bolts and thermostat housing, **Fig. 24.**
5. Remove thermostat and O-ring.
6. Reverse procedure to install, noting the following:
   a. Ensure all sealing surfaces are free of dirt and debris.
   b. Tighten mounting bolts.
   c. Fill and bleed cooling system as outlined in "Cooling System Bleed."

WATER PUMP
REPLACE
DeVille, Eldorado & Seville

1. Drain coolant into suitable container.
2. Remove air cleaner.

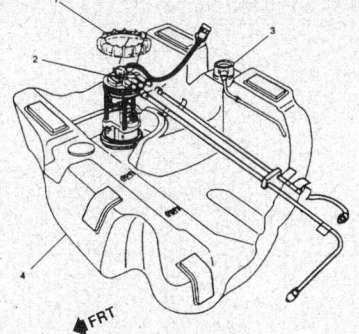

GC1029503759000X

Fig. 26 Modular fuel sending unit/fuel pump removal. Eldorado

1 FUEL SENDER RETAINER (LOCKING NUT)
2 MODULAR FUEL SENDER ASSEMBLY
3 TANK VENT VALVE
4 FUEL TANK

3. Remove engine cover and front end filler panel as required.
4. **On models equipped with AIR,** remove check valve.
5. **On all models,** remove water pump belt shield.
6. Mark running direction, then remove water pump drive belt.
7. Disconnect radiator outlet hose from thermostat housing using clamp tool No. J-38185, or equivalent.
8. Remove water pump cover bolts, then the cover.
9. Disconnect heater return hose.
10. Rotate pump clockwise to remove from housing using coolant pump remover/installer tool No. J-38816-1A, or equivalent.
11. Remove support plate from water housing crossover.
12. Remove water pump assembly.
13. Remove seal from water crossover.
14. Reverse procedure to install, noting the following:
    a. Install new seal into recessed portion of water crossover. **Ensure notched locking ear is in 7 o'clock position.**
    b. Index water pump locking ears with water crossover tangs.
    c. **Torque** remover/installer tool No. J-38816-A, or equivalent, counterclockwise to 74 ft. lbs.
    d. Fill and bleed cooling system as outlined in "Cooling System Bleed."

STS

1. Drain engine coolant into a suitable container.
2. Disconnect positive crankcase ventilation tube from air cleaner duct, then loosen air duct clamp at throttle body.
3. Loosen air duct clamp at mass air flow/intake air temperature sensor.
4. Remove air cleaner duct from vehicle, then disengage surge tank inlet hose from retainers on cooling fan shroud and position aside.
5. Remove cooling fan shroud to radiator upper and left lower retaining bolts.
6. Disconnect electrical connectors from cooling fan, then raise and support vehicle.
7. Remove front air deflector, then the cooling fan shroud to radiator right lower retaining bolt.

8. Disconnect and position engine wiring harness from engine frame.
9. Remove power steering line to cooling fan shroud retaining bolts, then the transmission oil cooler lines to cooling fan shroud retaining bolts.
10. Lower vehicle and remove cooling fan assembly.
11. Remove drive belts, then the drive belt tensioner and bolt from engine.
12. Remove water pump pulley from water pump, then the water pump bolts, **Fig. 25.**
13. Remove water pump and seal. Do not reuse seal.
14. Reverse procedure to install.

RADIATOR
REPLACE
DeVille

1. Drain coolant into suitable container.
2. Remove radiator outlet hose using clamp tool No. J-38185, or equivalent.
3. Remove cooling fans as outlined in "Engine Cooling Fans" chapter.
4. Disconnect lower transaxle fluid cooler line.
5. Disconnect lower engine oil cooler line.
6. Remove alternator cooler inlet hose.
7. Remove mounting bolts and lift condenser up slightly to release radiator lower mounting feet.
8. Lift up on air conditioning condenser to release lower mounting feet. **Do not damage radiator and condenser lower attachment points.**
9. Remove radiator by lifting up and out.
10. Reverse procedure to install, noting the following:
    a. Position radiator alignment dowels to align with insulators.
    b. Tighten mounting bolts.
    c. Fill and bleed cooling system as outlined in "Cooling System Bleed."

Eldorado

1. Drain coolant into suitable container.
2. Remove SRS forward discriminating sensor mounting bolts, then position aside as required.
3. Remove air cleaner.

4. Remove cooling fans as outlined in "Engine Cooling Fans" chapter.
5. Disconnect radiator inlet and outlet hoses using clamp tool No. J-38185, or equivalent.
6. Disconnect engine oil cooler lines.
7. Disconnect transaxle fluid cooler lines.
8. Remove upper radiator support mounting screws.
9. Remove radiator by lifting up and out.
10. Reverse procedure to install. Fill and bleed cooling system as outlined in "Cooling System Bleed."

Seville

Refer to "DeVille" for radiator replacement procedures.

STS

1. Drain engine coolant into a suitable container.
2. Disconnect positive crankcase ventilation tube from air cleaner duct, then loosen air duct clamp at throttle body.
3. Loosen air duct clamp at mass air flow/intake air temperature sensor.
4. Remove air cleaner duct from vehicle, then disengage surge tank inlet hose from retainers on cooling fan shroud and position aside.
5. Remove cooling fan shroud to radiator upper and left lower retaining bolts.
6. Disconnect electrical connectors from cooling fan, then raise and support vehicle.
7. Remove front air deflector, then the cooling fan shroud to radiator right lower retaining bolt.
8. Disconnect and position engine wiring harness from engine frame.
9. Remove power steering line to cooling fan shroud retaining bolts, then the transmission oil cooler lines to cooling fan shroud retaining bolts.
10. Lower vehicle and remove cooling fan assembly.
11. Remove upper and lower condenser mounting bolts, then disconnect side air baffle lower retaining pins from radiator.
12. **Position condenser away to access transmission oil cooler mounting bolts,** then remove transmission oil cooler mounting bolts.
13. Disengage tension on hose clamp, then remove radiator outlet and inlet hoses from radiator.
14. Disengage tension on hose clamp, then remove surge tank inlet hose from radiator.
15. Remove radiator support brackets, then disconnect upper air baffle retaining pins from radiator.
16. Remove radiator from vehicle.
17. Reverse procedure to install.

FUEL PUMP

REPLACE

The fuel pump is combined with the tank level sending unit and is not serviced separately.

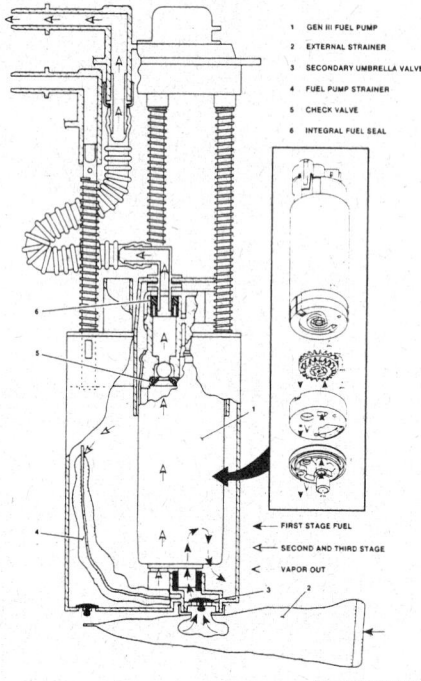

GC1029503760000X

Fig. 27 Fuel pump removal. Eldorado

DeVille

1. Adjust tank fuel level to ¾ full by draining fuel into suitable container.
2. Remove spare tire cover, jack, spare tire and rear compartment floor trim.
3. Remove fuel sender access panel.
4. Disconnect quick-connect fittings at fuel sender.
5. Disconnect electrical connections at modular fuel sender and fuel tank pressure sensor.
6. Remove fuel sender mounting ring using fuel sender locknut wrench tool No. J-39765, or equivalent.
7. Remove fuel sending unit by pulling straight up while pumping fuel from reservoir.
8. Reverse procedure to install. Install new fuel sender O-ring.

Eldorado

1. Drain fuel from tank into suitable container.
2. Raise and support vehicle, then remove fuel tank.
3. Remove locking nut using fuel sender locknut wrench tool No. J-39765, or equivalent, **Fig. 26.**
4. Remove modular fuel tank sending unit/fuel pump.
5. Remove fuel pump from modular fuel sending unit, **Fig. 27.**
6. Reverse procedure to install.

Seville

Refer to "DeVille" for fuel pump replacement procedure.

STS

1. Remove fuel filler cap, then install tool No. J–42960-2 or equivalent into fuel fill pipe hold door open.
2. Lubricate fuel drain hose with J-36850 or equivalent to aid in hose insertion and removal. **Do not use an unapproved lubricant.**
3. Insert J-45004 or equivalent into fuel tank until hose reaches bottom of fuel tank.
4. Use an air operated pump device to drain fuel into an approved gasoline container. Up to 7 gallons of residual fuel may remain in secondary side of fuel tank.
5. Simultaneously twist and pull to remove from fuel tank.
6. Relieve fuel system pressure as outlined in "Precautions."
7. Raise and support vehicle, then disconnect oxygen sensor electrical connectors.
8. Remove oxygen sensor from exhaust pipe, then the floor panel tunnel brace from floor panel.
9. Suitably support exhaust system, then remove nuts securing exhaust pipes to exhaust manifolds.
10. Pry front exhaust hangers and tail pipe hangers free from rear suspension hanger rods.
11. With aid of an assistant, lower exhaust system and remove.
12. Remove propeller shaft. Refer to **MOTOR's "Domestic Transmission, In-Vehicle Service"** manual.
13. Disconnect filler hose from fuel tank, then the filler vent tube from evaporative emission hose.
14. Disconnect fuel tank electrical connector, then the hoses from EVAP canister.
15. Pull outward on retainer tab to disengage retainer from chassis, then disconnect electrical connector from EVAP canister.
16. Raise lower control arms using a suitable screw jack to remove load from lower shock bolts.
17. Remove lower shock bolts, then the screw jack.
18. Support front of rear frame using screw jack, then remove front bolts from rear frame.
19. Lower screw jack until there is approximately inch between front mounting surface of rear frame and chassis.
20. Remove fuel tank strap bolts, then position fuel tank straps downward around rear frame.
21. Carefully bend fuel tank straps enough to allow fuel tank to be removed.
22. With aid of an assistant, lower fuel tank from vehicle.
23. Disconnect electrical connector from module, then rotate cam lock ring counter-clockwise using tool No. J-45747 or equivalent.
24. Remove cam lock ring from fuel tank, then lift fuel tank module from fuel tank to access transfer tube.
25. Pull locking mechanism away from module, then remove transfer tube from module.
26. Remove secondary or primary fuel

tank module from fuel tank, then the module seal.

27. Reverse procedure to install.

FUEL FILTER

REPLACE

1. Disconnect fuel filter bracket release tabs.

2. Twist quick-connect fitting ¼ turn in each direction to loosen dirt within fitting.
3. Clean quick-connect fitting at ends of filter.
4. Disconnect quick-connect fittings by squeezing plastic tabs of male end connector and pulling apart.
5. Disconnect threaded fitting at fuel filter outlet.

6. Remove fuel filter.
7. Reverse procedure to install, noting the following:
   a. **Torque** threaded fitting to 22 ft. lbs.
   b. Turn ignition On for two seconds, then Off for 10 seconds.
   c. Turn ignition On and inspect for fuel leakage.

TIGHTENING SPECIFICATIONS

Year	Component	Torque/Ft. Lbs.
DEVILLE, ELDORADO & SEVILLE		
2001–05	Alternator Upper	37
	Belt Tensioner	37
	Camshaft Cover	89①
	Camshaft Bearing Cap	44⑨
	Camshaft Drive Chain Tensioner	18
	Camshaft Seal Retainer To Cover	27①
	Camshaft Sprocket	89
	Catalytic Converter To Exhaust Inlet Pipe	18
	Cooling Fan	53①
	Crankshaft Balancer	37④
	Cylinder Head	③
	Engine Frame To Body (DeVille & Seville)	141
	Engine Frame To Body (Eldorado)	72
	Engine Mount Bracket	⑧
	Engine Mount To Frame	⑧
	Engine Mount Front	⑧
	Engine Mount Righthand	⑧
	Engine To Transaxle	55
	Exhaust Manifold To Cylinder Head	18
	Flexplate	11⑤
	Flexplate Inspection Cover	80①
	Front Cover	89①
	Fuel Filter	22
	Ignition Module	80①
	Intake Manifold	⑦
	Intake Manifold Cover	27①
	Lefthand Strut Bracket To Water Crossover	17
	Main Bearing Cap Bolts	⑥
	Oil Filter Adapter	12
	Oil Pan	89①
	Oil Pan Drain Plug	15
	Oil Pump	②
	Oil Pump To Suction Pipe	89①
	O2 Sensor	30
	Power Steering Return Hose	115①
	Righthand Strut Bracket	37
	Secondary AIR Pipe	80①
	TBI Unit	106①
	Thermostat Housing	89①
	Torque Strut Bracket To Cylinder Head	⑧
	Torque Strut Bracket To Water Manifold	18
	Transaxle Brace	35
	Water Pump	74
	Water Pump Cover	89①

Continued

TIGHTENING
SPECIFICATIONS—Continued

Year	Component	Torque/Ft. Lbs.
STS		
2005	Alternator	37
	Belt Tensioner	37
	Camshaft Cover	89①
	Camshaft Bearing Cap	106①
	Camshaft Drive shaft	89①
	Camshaft Sprocket	44
	Catalytic Converter To Exhaust Manifold	37
	Cooling Fan	44①
	Crankshaft Balancer	37⑩
	Cylinder Head	③
	Engine Mount Bracket	43
	Engine Mount	43
	Exhaust Manifold	18
	Front Cover	11
	Fuel Filter	22
	Ignition Module	89①
	Intake Manifold	⑦
	Main Bearing Cap Bolts	⑥
	Oil Filter	18
	Oil pan	18
	Oil Pan Drain Plug	18
	Oil Pump	②
	Oil Pump To Suction Pipe	89①
	O2 Sensor	31
	Power Steering Pump	18
	Thermostat Housing	89①
	Throttle Body Bolts	89①
	Water Outlet Housing	18
	Water Pump	89①
	Water Pump Pulley	89①

① — Inch pounds.
② — Refer to "Oil Pump, Replace" for tightening specifications & sequence.
③ — Refer to "Cylinder Head, Replace" for tightening specifications & sequence.
④ — Tighten an additional 120°.
⑤ — Tighten an additional 50°.
⑥ — Refer to "Main & Rod Bearings" for tightening specifications & sequence.
⑦ — Refer to "Intake Manifold, Replace" for tightening specifications & sequence.
⑧ — Refer to "Engine Mount, Replace" for tightening specifications & sequence.
⑨ — Tighten an additional 30°.
⑩ — Tighten an additional 150°.

Rear Suspension

NOTE: On Air Bag Equipped Models, Refer To "Air Bag System Precautions" Located In The Front Of This Manual For System Disarming & Arming Procedures.

NOTE: Refer To "Computer Relearn Procedures" Located In The Front Of This Manual When Battery Power To The Computer Has Been Interrupted.

NOTE: Prior To Performing Any Service Operations Listed In This Section, Consult The "Technical Service Bulletins" Section For Related Information.

INDEX

PRECAUTIONS

Air Bag Systems

Refer to "Air Bag System Precautions" in the front of this manual for system disarming and arming procedures.

Battery Ground Cable

Prior to service, disconnect battery ground cable and isolate as required.

HUB & BEARING
REPLACE

DeVille, Eldorado & Seville

SOFT RIDE & SPORT SUSPENSION

1. Raise and support vehicle.
2. Remove tire and wheel.
3. Remove brake caliper mounting bolts, then position caliper aside using suitable wire or rope. **Do not disconnecting fluid line from caliper.**

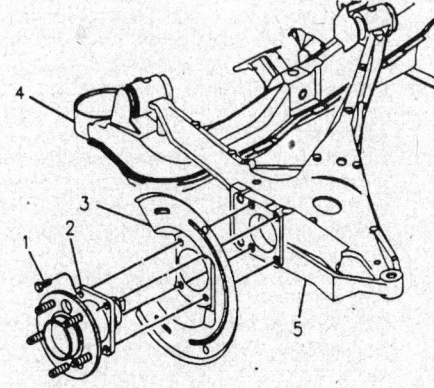

1 BOLT
2 HUB & BEARING
3 BRAKE SHIELD
4 REAR SUSPENSION SUPPORT ASSEMBLY
5 CONTROL ARM

GC2039500108000X

Fig. 1 Hub & bearing replacement. DeVille & Seville w/soft ride & sport suspension

4. Remove brake rotor and ABS sensor wire connector.
5. Remove hub and bearing mounting bolts, then the hub and bearing, Fig. 1.
6. Remove brake shield from control arm.
7. Reverse procedure to install.

HEAVY DUTY FRONT & REAR SUSPENSION

1. Raise and support vehicle, then remove tire and wheel assembly.
2. Remove brake caliper mounting bolts, then position caliper aside using suitable wire or rope. **Do not suspend caliper by brake line.**
3. Remove brake rotor.
4. Disconnect ABS sensor electrical connector.
5. Disconnect parking brake cable from lower control arm.
6. Remove wheel speed sensor.
7. Remove hub and bearing mounting bolts, Fig. 2.
8. Remove and discard wheel speed sensor reluctor ring. **Do not use reluctor ring again after it has been removed.**
9. Remove bearing nut and washer from hub.
10. Remove brake shield.
11. Remove bearing from hub.
12. Reverse procedure to install, noting the following:

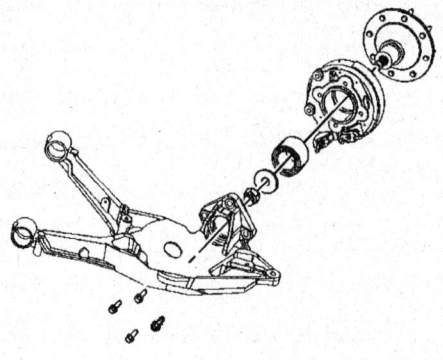

GC2030100166000X

Fig. 2 Hub & bearing replacement. DeVille w/heavy duty front & rear suspension

a. Install a new ABS wheel speed sensor reluctor ring using reluctor installer tool No. J-44253, or equivalent. Turn installer to thread reluctor until it just touches ring.
b. Install a new ABS sensor using installer tool No. J-44252, or equivalent.
c. Measure wheel speed sensor signal AC voltage using suitable multimeter. Voltage should be greater than 100 mV while wheel is revolving.

STS

1. Raise and support vehicle.
2. Remove tire and wheel.
3. Remove brake caliper mounting bolts, then position caliper aside using suitable wire or rope. **Do not disconnecting fluid line from caliper.**
4. Disconnect wheel speed sensor electrical connector, then remove wheel drive shaft retaining nut and discard.
5. Remove upper control arm to knuckle retaining nut, then using tool No. J-43631 or equivalent separate upper control arm from knuckle.
6. **Avoid tool contact to outer constant velocity boot seal,** then remove wheel bearing/hub retaining bolts, **Fig. 3.**
7. Using tool No. J-45859 or equivalent, separate wheel driveshaft from wheel bearing/hub.
8. Remove wheel bearing/hub from vehicle.
9. Reverse procedure to install noting the following:
   a. **Torque,** bearing/hub retaining bolts to 92 ft. lbs.
   b. **Torque,** upper ball joint nut to 15 ft. lbs. plus additional 210°.
   c. **Torque,** new wheel drive shaft retaining nut to 118 ft. lbs.

REAR SUSPENSION
REPLACE
DeVille

1. Raise and support vehicle, then remove rear tires and wheels.

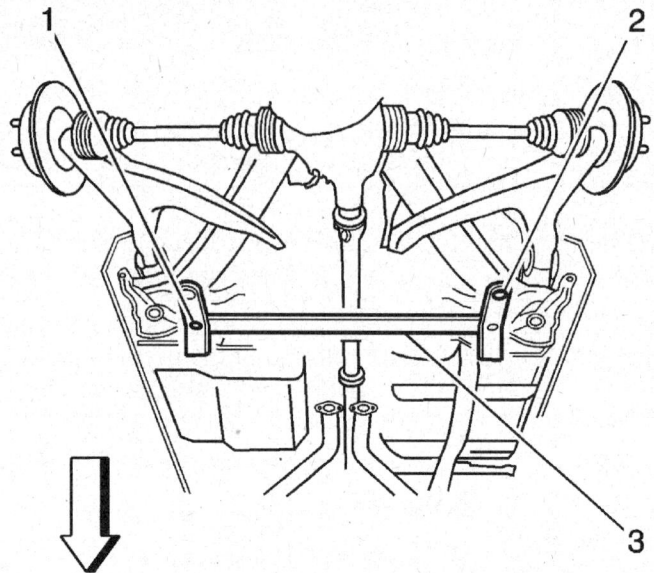

1. Body Datum Holes
2. Location Pins
3. Rear Cross-member Centering Tool

ARM0400000000100

Fig. 3 Hub & bearing replacement. STS

2. Disconnect exhaust system components as required to provide clearance.
3. Remove rear springs as outlined in "Coil Spring, Replace."
4. Remove brake calipers from control arms. Disconnecting hydraulic lines at calipers is not required. **Support calipers from frame using suitable wire or rope. Do not allow calipers to hang by brake lines.**
5. Disconnect parking brake cables at calipers and rear suspension support assembly.
6. Disconnect rear suspension support assembly electrical connectors from electrical harness, then the Electronic Level Control (ELC) electrical connector and vent hose.
7. Disconnect ELC air tube from compressor.
8. **On DeVille models equipped with heavy duty front and rear suspension,** remove center support brackets.
9. **On all models,** support rear suspension using suitable jack, **Fig. 4.**
10. Remove support bracket to body bolts from each side.
11. Remove front and rear anchor bolts and lower rear suspension support assembly.
12. Reverse procedure to install.

Eldorado

1. Raise and support vehicle, then remove rear tires and wheels.
2. Remove lefthand caliper assembly mounting bolts, then position aside using suitable wire or rope. **Do not allow caliper to hang by brake line.**
3. Remove suspension components at-

tached to suspension assembly as required.
4. Remove intermediate parking brake cable from equalizer, then position cable clear of suspension support.
5. Remove rear brake crossover pipe and lefthand rear brake hose from bracket. Plug open fittings to prevent entry of dirt and debris.
6. Disconnect rear chassis wiring harness from main body harness.
7. Support rear suspension using suitable jack stands.
8. Remove suspension support forward arm bolts, upper mounting bolts and lower insulators.
9. Lower jack stands while observing position of brake calipers, brake hoses and fluid lines.
10. Reverse procedure to install, noting the following:
    a. Slowly raise suspension support into vehicle. Align the support with vehicle body as it is raised.
    b. Install both forward arm bolts in proper direction with nuts installed on righthand side of arm. Cupshaped washer is used on lefthand forward arm bolt installation only.
    c. Tighten righthand side support forward arm nut.
    d. Tighten lefthand side support forward arm nut.
    e. Tighten upper mounting bolts.
    f. Bleed brakes as outlined in "Brake System Bleed" in "Hydraulic Brake Systems" chapter.

Seville

Refer to "DeVille" for rear suspension replacement procedure.

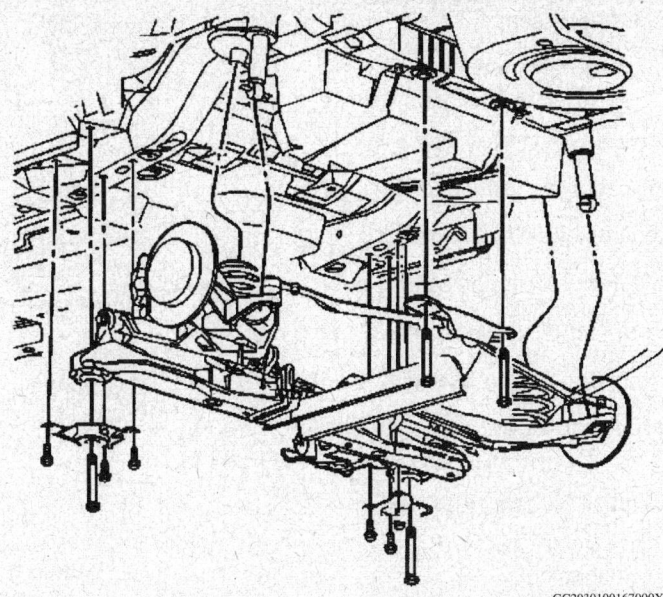

Fig. 4 Rear suspension assembly replacement.
DeVille & Seville

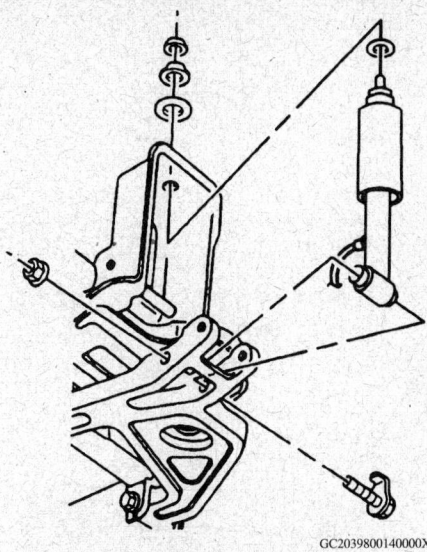

Fig. 5 Shock absorber
replacement. Eldorado

SHOCK ABSORBER
REPLACE
Except STS

1. Raise and support vehicle, then remove tire and wheel assembly.
2. Disconnect shock absorber electrical connector from rear suspension support.
3. Relieve spring load by supporting lower control arm using suitable screw type jack.
4. Remove lower shock absorber bolt(s), **Figs. 5 and 6.**
5. Disconnect electrical connector from top of shock absorber.
6. **On Eldorado models,** remove upper mounting nut, retainer and insulator using tool No. J-35669, or equivalent.
7. **On DeVille and Seville models,** remove upper mounting dust cap, nuts and reinforcement, **Fig. 7.**
8. **On all models,** reverse procedure to install.

STS

1. Remove trim panel, then move sound insulator away from shock tower.
2. Disconnect electrical connector, then remove upper shock mounting nuts.
3. Raise and support vehicle, then disconnect automatic level control from shock.
4. Remove lower shock mounting bolt, then the shock from vehicle, **Fig. 8.**
5. Reverse procedure to install.

COIL SPRING
REPLACE
DeVille
REMOVAL

1. Raise and support vehicle, then remove tire and wheel assembly.
2. Support control arm using suitable jack.
3. Disconnect electronic level control air tube from shock.
4. Remove shock to control arm mounting bolts.
5. Remove cotter pin and hex nut.
6. Separate adjustment link from knuckle using universal steering linkage puller tool No. J-24319-B, or equivalent.
7. **On DeVille models equipped with heavy duty front and rear suspension,** install coil spring compressor tool No. J-4425, or equivalent.
8. **On all models,** lower control arm until it bottoms on support assembly.
9. Pry under lower spring insulator using suitable pry bar and remove spring with insulator, **Fig. 9.**
10. Remove upper insulator by pulling downward.

INSTALLATION

1. **On DeVille models equipped with heavy duty front and rear suspension,** install coil spring into compressor tool No. J-4425, or equivalent.

2. **On all models,** install upper spring insulator in body.
3. Install lower spring insulator in control arm.
4. Install spring, ensuring insulator is seated in control arm.
5. Raise lower control arm and install shock to control arm mounting bolts.
6. Install adjustment link to control arm.
7. **On DeVille models equipped with soft ride and sports suspension, torque** adjustment link nut to 22 ft. lbs., then tighten an additional 180°.
8. **On DeVille models equipped with heavy duty front and rear suspension, torque** adjustment link nut to 22 ft. lbs., then tighten an additional 200°.
9. **On Seville models, torque** adjustment link nut to 55 ft. lbs.
10. **On all models,** connect electronic level control air tube to shock absorber.
11. Install tire and wheel, then tighten lug nuts.

Eldorado

Refer to "Lower Control Arm, Replace" for coil spring replacement procedures.

Seville

Refer to "DeVille" for coil spring replacement procedure.

STS

Refer to "Lower Control Arm, Replace" for coil spring replacement procedures.

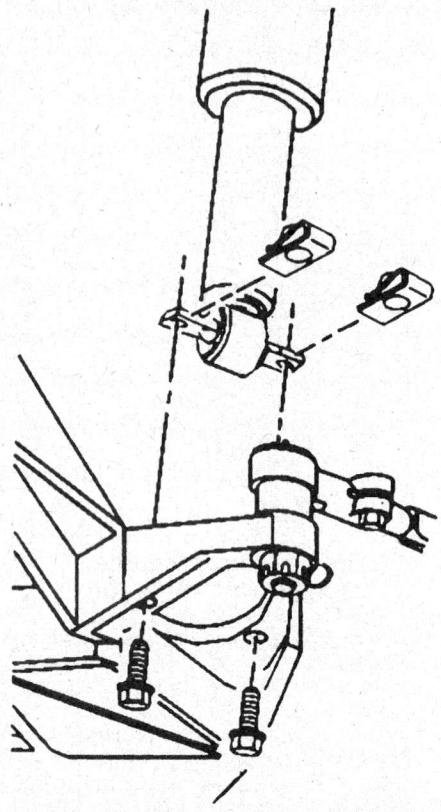

Fig. 6 Shock absorber lower mount replacement. DeVille & Seville

CONTROL ARM
REPLACE
DeVille

1. Remove rear suspension support assembly as outlined in "Rear Suspension, Replace."
2. If lefthand control arm is being replaced, disconnect Electronic Level Control (ELC) height sensor link.
3. Remove stabilizer link bolt and nut, then disconnect ABS electrical connector.
4. Remove hub and bearing, if required, as outlined in "Hub & Bearing, Replace."
5. **On DeVille models equipped with heavy duty front and rear suspension,** remove center support bracket bolts.
6. **On all models,** remove control arm to rear suspension support mounting bolt and nut.
7. Reverse procedure to install, noting the following:
   a. Tighten control arm nuts with vehicle weight resting on rear wheels.
   b. Install tires and wheels, then tighten lug nuts.

Eldorado
LOWER

1. Raise and support vehicle, then re-

---

move tire and wheel assembly.
2. Support inboard end of lower control arm using suitable transmission jack. Position brackets on jack to securely hold control arm.
3. Remove stabilizer link lower attachment.
4. Remove shock absorber lower attachment.
5. Remove inboard lower control arm nuts and bolts.
6. Relieve coil spring pressure by slowly lowering transmission jack.
7. Remove coil spring by pulling lower control arm down.
8. Remove outboard mounting bolt and lower control arm.
9. Reverse procedure to install.

UPPER

1. Raise and support vehicle, then remove tire and wheel assembly.
2. Disconnect electronic level control height sensor connector.
3. Disconnect Road Sensing Suspension (RSS) position sensor and bracket from shock tower.
4. Remove inner and outer upper control arm bolts.
5. Remove upper control arm by lifting up and over shock tower.
6. Reverse procedure to install.

Seville

Refer to "DeVille" for control arm replacement procedure.

STS
LOWER

1. Raise and support vehicle, then remove tire and wheel assembly.
2. Remove stabilizer shaft link lower retaining nut, then disconnect stabilizer shaft link from lower control arm.
3. Disconnect automatic level control sensor link from upper control arm, then the automatic level control sensor link from upper control arm.
4. Support and raise lower control arm using a suitable jack, then remove shock absorber lower mounting bolt.
5. Lower control arm, then remove support.
6. Support rear frame with a suitable jack, then remove frame bolts from side that coil spring is to replaced.
7. Lower frame enough, then remove coil spring without going past guide pins.
8. Remove lower control arm to knuckle bolt, then the lower control arm to frame bolt and nut.
9. Remove lower control arm from vehicle.
10. Reverse procedure to install.

UPPER

1. Raise and support vehicle, then remove tire and wheel assembly.
2. Remove upper control arm to knuckle retaining nut, **Do not free ball stud by using a pickle fork or a wedge-type tool.**
3. Disconnect upper control arm from

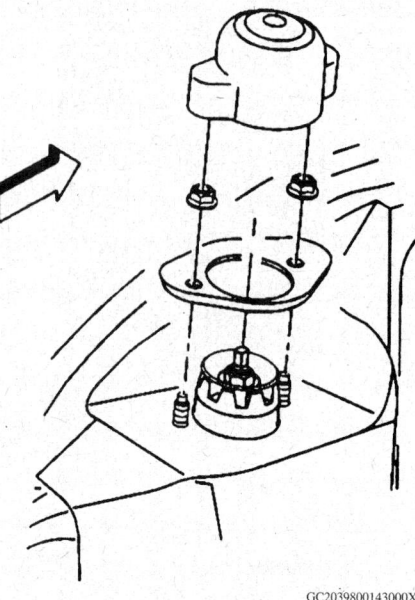

Fig. 7 Shock absorber upper mount replacement. DeVille & Seville

knuckle using tool No. J–43631 or equivalent.
4. Remove upper control arm to frame mounting nuts and discard, then the upper control arm from vehicle.
5. Reverse procedure to install noting the following:
   a. Tighten upper control arm to knuckle nut to 15 ft. lbs. plus an additional 210°.
   b. Tighten new upper control arm to frame bolts and nuts to 111 ft. lbs.

CONTROL ARM BUSHING
REPLACE
DeVille

1. Remove control arm as outlined in "Control Arm, Replace."
2. Drive bushing from control arm using bushing replacement tools, **Fig. 10.**
3. Remove bushing replacement tools.
4. Reverse procedure to install. Start new bushing into control arm with flat on bushing positioned vertically and rearward.

Seville

Refer to "DeVille" for control arm bushing replacement procedure.

STABILIZER SHAFT
REPLACE
DeVille

1. Raise and support vehicle, then remove tires and wheels.
2. Remove stabilizer shaft link assembly bolt, nut, retainer and insulators from control arm, **Fig. 11.**

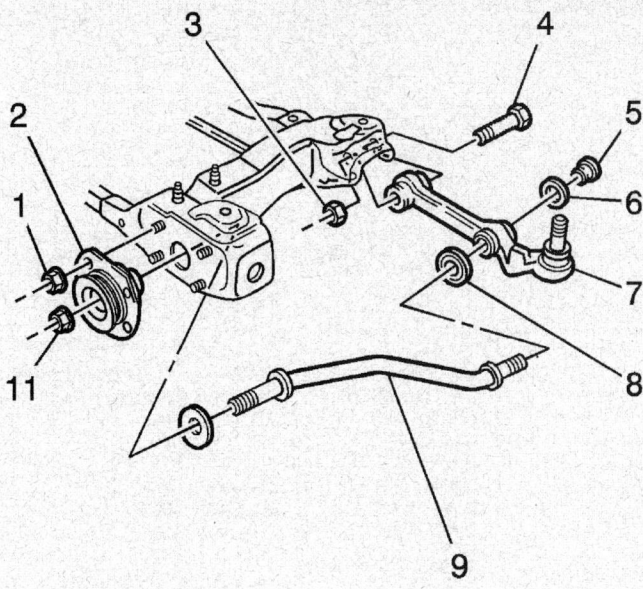

1. Lug Nuts
2. Hub
3. Mounting Nut
4. Mounting Bolt
5. Mounting Nut
6. Washer
7. Control Arm
8. Retainer
9. Control Arm Rod

ARM0400000000101

Fig. 8 Shock absorber replacement. STS

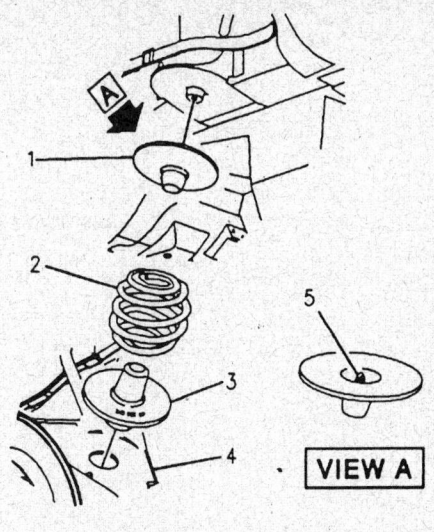

1 JOUNCE BUMPER
2 SPRING
3 LOWER SPRING INSULATOR
4 CONTROL ARM
5 RETAINER

GC2039500111000X

Fig. 9 Coil spring replacement. DeVille & Seville

3. Remove clamp bolt, then bend open end of clamp upward.
4. Remove stabilizer shaft and insulators.
5. Reverse procedure to install, noting the following:
   a. Install stabilizer shaft insulator to shaft with slit facing forward.
   b. Ensure stabilizer shaft is centered before tightening clamp bolt.

Seville

Refer to "DeVille" for stabilizer shaft replacement procedure.

STS

Refer to "DeVille" for stabilizer shaft replacement procedure.

ADJUSTMENT LINK
REPLACE
DeVille

1. Raise and support vehicle.

2. Remove adjustment link nut.
3. Separate adjustment link from control arm using universal steering linkage puller tool No. J-24319-B, or equivalent.
4. Support exhaust and rear support assembly using suitable block of wood.
5. Remove exhaust hangers and rear support mounting bolts.
6. Lower support assembly and exhaust together.
7. Remove cam nut and bolt, then the adjustment link from rear support.
8. Reverse procedure to install. Inspect and adjust rear toe as outlined in "Wheel Alignment" section.

Seville
INNER

1. Raise and support vehicle, then remove tire and wheel assembly.
2. Loosen pinch bolt.
3. Support exhaust and rear suspension support with suitable wood block at least seven inches long.
4. Remove exhaust hangers and rear suspension support mounting bolts.

5. Lower support and exhaust together.
6. Remove cam bolt and nut, then the adjustment link.
7. Remove inner link from outer link. **Note number of turns for installation.**
8. Reverse procedure to install. Inspect and adjust rear toe as outlined in "Wheel Alignment" section.

OUTER

1. Raise and support vehicle, then remove tire and wheel assembly.
2. Loosen pinch bolt.
3. Remove cotter pin and clotted hex nut.
4. Separate adjustment link from knuckle using universal steering linkage puller tool No. J-24319-B, or equivalent. **Do not drive wedge between joint and attached part.**
5. Remove outer link from inner link. **Note number of turns for installation.**
6. Reverse procedure to install. Inspect and adjust rear toe as outlined in "Wheel Alignment" section.

STS

1. Raise and support vehicle, then remove tire and wheel assembly.
2. Remove mounting bolt and nut, then the adjustment link from vehicle.
3. Reverse procedure to install.

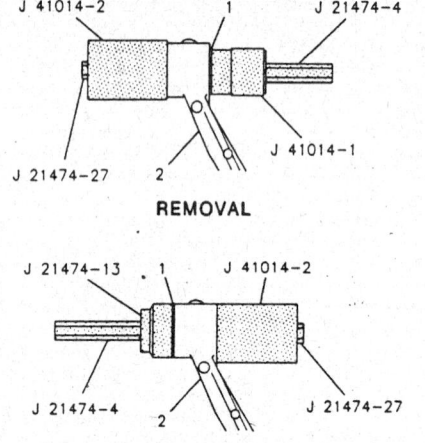

Fig. 10 Control arm bushing replacement tool installation. DeVille & Seville

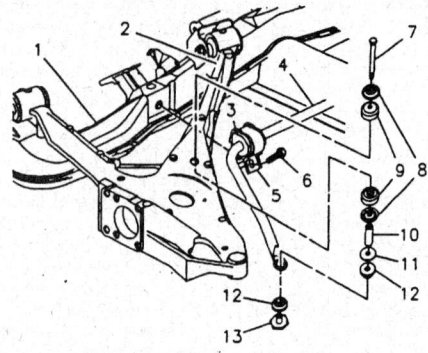

1	REAR SUSPENSION SUPPORT ASSEMBLY	7	BOLT, 13 N·m (115 LB. IN.)
2	CONTROL ARM	8	RETAINER, UPPER
3	INSULATOR, STABILIZER SHAFT	9	INSULATOR, UPPER
		10	SLEEVE
4	SHAFT, STABILIZER	11	RETAINER, LOWER
5	CLAMP, STABILIZER SHAFT	12	INSULATOR, LOWER
6	BOLT, 33 N·m (24 LB. IN.)	13	NUT

Fig. 11 Stabilizer shaft replacement. DeVille & Seville

TIGHTENING SPECIFICATIONS

Year	Component	Torque Ft. Lbs.
DEVILLE w/SOFT RIDE & SPORT SUSPENSION		
2001–05	Adjustment Link Cam	59
	Adjustment Link To Control Arm	②
	Control Arm	78
	ELC Height Sensor	60①
	Hub & Bearing	50
	Rear Insulator To Body	57
	Rear Suspension Support Assembly To Body Rear	141
	Shock Absorber To Control Arm	18
	Shock Absorber Upper	18
	Stabilizer Link	11
	Stabilizer Shaft Clamp	24
	Stabilizer Shaft Link	11
	Wheel Lug Nuts	80
DEVILLE w/HEAVY DUTY FRONT & REAR SUSPENSION		
2001–05	Adjustment Link Cam	77
	Adjustment Link To Control Arm	②
	Control Arm	110
	Front Insulator To Body	63
	Front Support Assembly To Body	138
	Hub & Bearing	87
	Rear Insulator To Body	57
	Rear Support Assembly To Body	153
	Shock Absorber To Control Arm	27
	Shock Absorber Upper	21
	Stabilizer Link	11
	Stabilizer Shaft Bracket	38
	Suspension Support Insulator Bracket	94
	Wheel Bearing	147
	Wheel Lug Nuts	80

Continued

TIGHTENING
SPECIFICATIONS—Continued

Year	Component	Torque Ft. Lbs.
ELDORADO		
2001–02	Caliper	83
	Crossmember Forward Arm, (Righthand Side)	46
	Crossmember Forward Arm, (Lefthand Side)	75
	Crossmember Upper	75
	Hub	53
	Lower Control Arm Inner	75
	Lower Control Arm Outer	80
	Parking Brake Cable Bracket	32
	Shock Absorber, Lower	75
	Shock Absorber, Upper	55
	Stabilizer Bracket	44
	Stabilizer Link Lower	38
	Stabilizer Link Lower	44
	Stabilizer Link Upper	44
	Toe Link, Inner	42
	Toe Link, Outer	55
	Upper Control Arm Inner	42
	Upper Control Arm Outer	44
	Wheel Lug Nuts	100
SEVILLE		
2001–04	Adjustment Link Cam	55
	Adjustment Link To Control Arm	②
	Body Bracket Front	63
	Control Arm	78
	ELC Height Sensor	60①
	Hub & Bearing	50
	Rear Body Mount	38
	Rear Suspension Support Assembly To Body Rear	141
	Shock Absorber To Control Arm	18
	Shock Absorber Upper	18
	Stabilizer Link	108①
	Stabilizer Shaft Clamp	24
	Wheel Lug Nuts	100
STS		
2005	Adjustment Link To Frame	125
	Adjustment Link To Knuckle	118
	Hub & Bearing	92
	Lower Control Arm To Frame	100
	Lower Control Arm To Knuckle	118
	Shock Absorber Upper	18
	Shock Absorber Lower	111
	Stabilizer Shaft Bracket Bolt	44
	Stabilizer Shaft Link Nuts	49
	Upper Control Arm Ball Stud To Knuckle	③
	Upper Control Arm To Frame	89
	Wheel Driveshaft To Wheel Bearing	118
	Wheel Lug Nuts	100

① — Inch lbs.
② — Refer to "Coil Spring, Replace" for tightening specifications.
③ — Refer to "Control Arm, Replace" for tightening specifications.

NOTE: On Air Bag Equipped Models, Refer To "Air Bag System Precautions" Located In The Front Of This Manual For System Disarming & Arming Procedures.

NOTE: Refer To "Computer Relearn Procedures" Located In The Front Of This Manual When Battery Power To The Computer Has Been Interrupted.

NOTE: Prior To Performing Any Service Operations Listed In This Section, Consult The "Technical Service Bulletins" Section For Related Information.

INDEX

PRECAUTIONS

Air Bag Systems

Refer to "Air Bag System Precautions" in the front of this manual for system disarming and arming procedures.

Battery Ground Cable

Prior to service, disconnect battery ground cable and isolate as required.

HUB & BEARING
REPLACE

Except STS

1. Raise and support vehicle, then remove tire and wheel assembly.
2. Remove hub nut and washer using suitable punch to keep rotor stationary. Discard hub nut.
3. Remove caliper, support and rotor.
4. Separate drive axle from hub using drive axle separator tool No. J-28733-B, or equivalent, **Fig. 1.**
5. Remove hub and bearing mounting bolts.

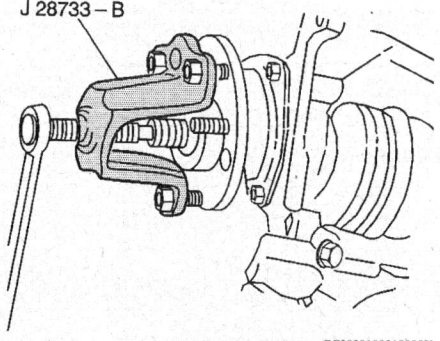

J 28733 – B

GC2020100310000X

Fig. 1 Drive axle separation. Except STS

6. Disconnect speed sensor connector.
7. Remove hub and bearing assembly.
8. Reverse procedure to install, noting the following:
   a. Clean rust and dirt from knuckle bore, chamber and mounting face allow proper seating of bearing and knuckle.
   b. Apply a light coating of grease to steering knuckle bore.
   c. **Do not use old hub nut. Always install a new one.**
   d. Draw hub and bearing onto axle with hub nut.

STS

1. Raise and support vehicle, then remove tire and wheel assembly.
2. Remove wheel driveshaft retaining nut and discard.
3. Remove brake caliper and caliper mounting bracket as an assembly from suspension knuckle and support. Ensure that there is no tension on hydraulic brake flexible hose.
4. Matchmark position of brake rotor to wheel studs, then remove brake rotor.
5. Disconnect ABS electrical connector, then remove connector from splash shield.
6. **On models equipped with AWD,** proceed as follows:
   a. **Avoid tool contact to outer constant velocity boot seal,** then remove wheel bearing/hub mounting bolts.
   b. Using tool No. J–45859 or equivalent, disengage wheel driveshaft from wheel bearing/hub, **Fig. 2.**
7. **On all models,** remove wheel bearing/hub from vehicle.
8. Reverse procedure to install.

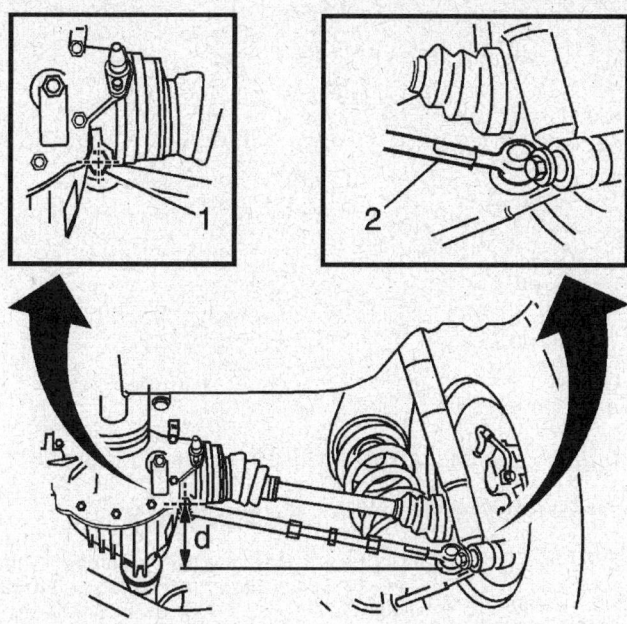

1. Center Line Of Inner Adjustment Link Pivot Bolt
2. Bottom Of Outer Adjustment Link

ARM0400000000102

Fig. 2 Wheel driveshaft separation. STS w/AWD

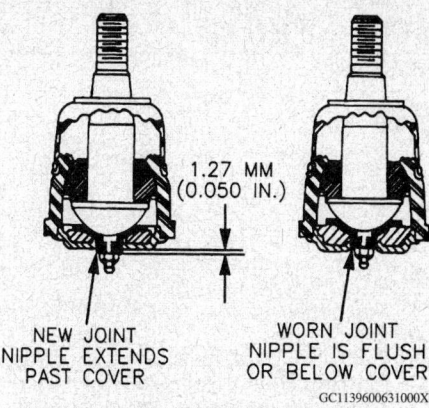

GC1139600631000X

Fig. 3 Ball joint vertical wear inspection

BALL JOINT INSPECTION

Replace ball joints if any looseness is detected in the joint or ball joint seal is cut. Complete the following steps in order to inspect ball joint.
1. Raise and support front of vehicle.
2. Support lower control arm with suitable jack stand as far outboard as possible near lower ball joint.
3. Wipe ball joint clean. Inspect seals for tears or cuts.
4. Mount dial indicator kit tool No. J-8001, or equivalent, against lowest outboard point on wheel rim.
5. Grasp tire at top and bottom and rock it in and out.
6. Dial indicator reading should not exceed .125 inch. If reading is too high, inspect lower ball joint for vertical looseness as follows:
   a. Wear in ball joints is indicated by a .50 inch diameter nipple which retracts into joint cover as joint wears.
   b. Replace ball joint if nipple is flush with or below joint cover, **Fig. 3.**
7. Replace ball joint if ball stud is disconnected from knuckle and looseness is detected or ball stud twists in its socket while using hand pressure.
8. Inspect for ball stud tightness in knuckle boss. Shake wheel and feel for movement of stud end or nut at knuckle boss.
9. Replace all worn or damaged ball joints and knuckles.

BALL JOINT
REPLACE
DeVille

1. Raise and support vehicle with control arms hanging free. Remove tire and wheel.
2. Disconnect stabilizer link to control arm bolt.
3. Remove cotter pin and loosen nut from ball stud.
4. Separate ball joint from knuckle using separator tool No. J-35315, or equivalent.
5. Remove mounting bolts and control arm.
6. Reverse procedure to install, noting the following:
   a. **On models equipped with soft ride & sport suspension, torque** ball joint mounting nut to 88 inch lbs., then tighten an additional 150°.
   b. **On models equipped with heavy duty front and rear suspension suspension, torque** ball joint nut to 22 ft. lbs., then tighten an additional 190°.
   c. Ball joint mounting nut to 88 inch lbs., then tighten an additional 180–300°, or three to five flats.
   d. **On all models, continue rotating for cotter pin installation if required, but do not exceed 60° additional rotation. Do not back off ball joint nut for cotter pin alignment.**

Eldorado

1. Remove control arm bushing bolt and brake reaction rod nut, retainer and insulator, **Fig. 4.**
2. Support transaxle lefthand side with suitable screw jack and wood block.
3. Remove two transaxle mount nuts, then raise transaxle to access control arm mounting bolt.
4. Remove mounting bolts and control arm.
5. Reverse procedure to install noting the following:
   a. Install control arm bushing bolt and nut, retainer and insulator. Do not tighten bolt, **Fig. 5.**
   b. **Torque** ball joint mounting nut to 88 inch lbs., then tighten an additional 150°.
   c. **Continue rotating for cotter pin installation if required, but do not exceed 60° additional rotation. Do not back off ball joint nut for cotter pin alignment.**

Seville

1. Raise and support vehicle with control arms hanging free. Remove tire and wheel.
2. Disconnect stabilizer link to control arm bolt.
3. Remove cotter pin and loosen nut from ball stud.
4. Separate ball joint from knuckle using separator tool No. J-35315, or equivalent.
5. Remove mounting bolts and control arm.
6. Reverse procedure to install, noting the following:
   a. **Torque** ball joint mounting nut to 88 inch lbs., then tighten an additional 180–300°, or three to five flats.
   b. **On all models, continue rotating for cotter pin installation if required, but do not exceed 60° additional rotation. Do not back off ball joint nut for cotter pin alignment.**

COIL SPRING
REPLACE
STS

1. Raise and support vehicle, then remove tire and wheel.
2. Remove shock yoke retainers, then using tool No. J–24319-B or equivalent separate yoke from lower control arm.
3. Remove yoke from vehicle.
4. Disconnect sensor links from upper control arm.
5. **Ball stud must not rotate during disassembly or assembly.** Hold upper control arm to steering knuckle and remove retaining nut.
6. Separate upper control arm from steering knuckle, then lower vehicle.
7. Disconnect electrical connector from sensor, then remove mounting bolts and shock module from vehicle.
8. Install shock module into spring compressor, then mark upper control arm assembly and insulator for proper installation.
9. Turn spring compressor forcing screw until coil spring is compressed, then remove magnaride sensor nut.
10. Remove upper retaining nut, then the shock absorber from shock.
11. Loosen compressor forcing screw until upper mounting plate and coil spring may be removed.
12. Remove upper control arm bracket assembly, insulator and coil spring from spring compressor.
13. Reverse procedure to install.

STRUT
REPLACE
DeVille

1. Remove strut to body mounting bolts.
2. Raise and support vehicle with suspension hanging free.
3. Remove tire and wheel assembly.
4. Disconnect ABS front wheel speed sensor electrical connector.
5. Remove speed sensor bracket from strut.
6. Remove brake line bracket from left-hand strut.
7. Remove strut to knuckle bolts. **Knuckle must be retained after strut to knuckle bolts have been removed.**
8. Remove strut.
9. Reverse procedure to install.

Eldorado

Do not overextend driveshaft tri-pot joints when replacing suspension components.
1. Remove nuts securing top of strut assembly to body, **Fig. 6.**
2. Raise and support vehicle, then remove tire and wheel.
3. Scribe inboard surface of strut along upper knuckle radius, **Fig. 7.**
4. Scribe knuckle along lower curve of strut.

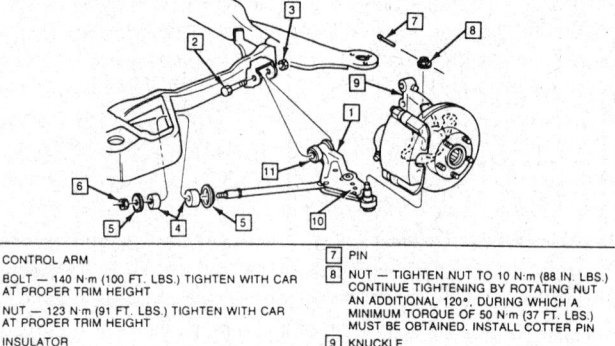

1	CONTROL ARM
2	BOLT — 140 N·m (100 FT. LBS.) TIGHTEN WITH CAR AT PROPER TRIM HEIGHT
3	NUT — 123 N·m (91 FT. LBS.) TIGHTEN WITH CAR AT PROPER TRIM HEIGHT
4	INSULATOR
5	RETAINER
6	NUT — 70 N·m (52 FT. LBS.)
7	PIN
8	NUT — TIGHTEN NUT TO 10 N·m (88 IN. LBS.) CONTINUE TIGHTENING BY ROTATING NUT AN ADDITIONAL 120°. DURING WHICH A MINIMUM TORQUE OF 50 N·m (37 FT. LBS.) MUST BE OBTAINED. INSTALL COTTER PIN
9	KNUCKLE
10	BALL JOINT ATTACHMENT RIVETS
11	BUSHING

GC2029100129000X

Fig. 4 Lower control arm replacement. Eldorado

5. Scribe mark along strut/knuckle interface.
6. Disconnect brake line bracket from strut.
7. Remove strut to stabilizer link mounting bolt and stabilizer link.
8. Remove strut to steering knuckle mounting, then support knuckle using suitable wire or rope.
9. Remove strut.
10. Reverse procedure to install, noting the following:
    a. Align scribe marks made during removal.
    b. Tighten mounting bolts and nuts.
    c. Inspect and adjust alignment as required.

Seville

1. Remove strut to body mounting bolts.
2. Raise and support vehicle with suspension hanging free.
3. Remove tire and wheel assembly.
4. Disconnect ABS front wheel speed sensor electrical connector.
5. Remove speed sensor bracket from strut.
6. Remove brake line bracket from left-hand strut.
7. Remove strut to knuckle bolts. **Knuckle must be retained after strut to knuckle bolts have been removed.**
8. Remove strut.
9. Reverse procedure to install.

STRUT SERVICE
Disassembly

1. Compress spring slightly using strut compressor tool No. J-34013, **Fig. 8.**
2. Remove dampener shaft top nut. Prevent shaft from turning by using a T-50 Torx bit.
3. Guide dampener shaft out of assembly using rod tool No. J-34013-38, or equivalent.
4. Loosen compressor screw while guiding dampener shaft out of assembly.
5. Continually loosening compressor screw till strut dampener and spring can be removed. **Do not chip or crack spring coating.**

Assembly

1. Install strut dampener in strut compressor tool No. J-34013 with clamp tool No. J-34013-20, or equivalents, **Fig. 9.**
2. Install spring over strut in proper position.
3. Move assembly upright in strut compressor and install upper lockpin. **Flat on upper spring seat must face out from centerline of vehicle. If mounted in strut compressor, spring seat faces same direction as steering knuckle mounting flange.**
4. Guide dampener shaft onto strut using installer rod tool No. J-34013-38, or equivalent.
5. Center dampener shaft by turning compressor tool screw clockwise while guiding rod.
6. Continue turning compressor screw until dampener shaft threads are visible through top of strut assembly.
7. Install washer and nut. Remove clamp tool.
8. Hold dampener shaft with socket, then tighten dampener shaft nut.

SHOCK ABSORBER
REPLACE
STS

Refer to "Coil Spring Replace," for replacement procedure.

CONTROL ARM
REPLACE

Do not overextend driveshaft tri-pot joints when replacing suspension components.

DeVille

1. Raise and support vehicle with control arms hanging free. Remove tire and wheel.
2. Disconnect stabilizer link to control arm bolt.
3. Remove cotter pin and loosen nut from ball stud.

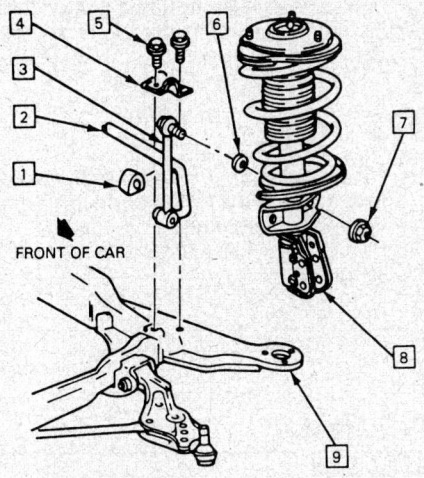

1	INSULATOR – INSTALL WITH SLIT TO REAR OF CAR
2	STABILIZER SHAFT
3	STABILIZER LINK
4	BRACKET
5	BOLT – 47 N·m (35 lbs. ft.)
6	WASHER
7	NUT – 65 N·m (48 lbs. ft.)
8	SPRING & STRUT ASSEMBLY
9	FRAME

GC2029100128000X

Fig. 5 Stabilizer shaft replacement. Eldorado

4. Separate ball joint from knuckle using separator tool No. J-35315, or equivalent.
5. Remove mounting bolts and control arm.
6. Reverse procedure to install, noting the following:
   a. **On models equipped with soft ride & sport suspension, torque** ball joint mounting nut to 88 inch lbs., then tighten an additional 150°.
   b. **On models equipped with heavy duty front and rear suspension suspension, torque** ball joint nut to 22 ft. lbs., then tighten an additional 190°.
   c. **On all models, continue rotating for cotter pin installation if required, but do not exceed 60° additional rotation. Do not back off ball joint nut for cotter pin alignment.**

Eldorado

1. Remove control arm bushing bolt and brake reaction rod nut, retainer and insulator, **Fig. 4.**
2. Support transaxle lefthand side with suitable screw jack and wood block.
3. Remove two transaxle mount nuts, then raise transaxle to access control arm mounting bolt.
4. Remove mounting bolts and control arm.
5. Reverse procedure to install noting the following:
   a. Install control arm bushing bolt and

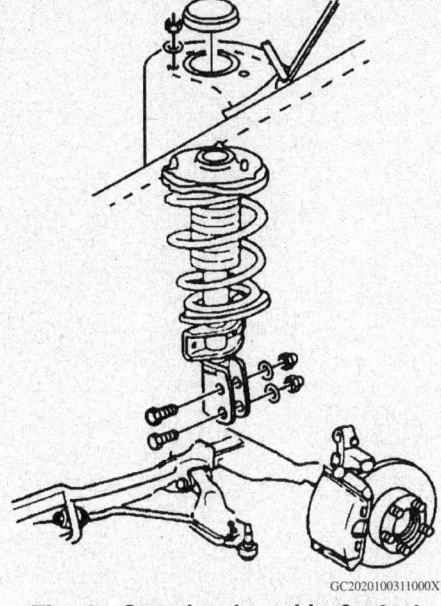

GC2020100311000X

Fig. 6 Steering knuckle & strut replacement. Eldorado

nut, retainer and insulator. Do not tighten bolt.
   b. **Torque** ball joint mounting nut to 88 inch lbs., then tighten an additional 150°.
   c. **On all models, continue rotating for cotter pin installation if required, but do not exceed 60° additional rotation. Do not back off ball joint nut for cotter pin alignment.**

Seville

1. Raise and support vehicle with control arms hanging free. Remove tire and wheel.
2. Disconnect stabilizer link to control arm bolt.
3. Remove cotter pin and loosen nut from ball stud.
4. Separate ball joint from knuckle using separator tool No. J-35315, or equivalent.
5. Remove mounting bolts and control arm.
6. Reverse procedure to install, noting the following:
   a. **Torque** ball joint mounting nut to 88 inch lbs., then tighten an additional 180–300°, or three to five flats.
   b. **On all models, continue rotating for cotter pin installation if required, but do not exceed 60° additional rotation. Do not back off ball joint nut for cotter pin alignment.**

STS

1. Raise and support vehicle, then remove tire and wheel.
2. Remove shock yoke retainers, then using tool No. J-24319-B or equivalent separate yoke from lower control arm.
3. Remove yoke from vehicle.
4. Remove stabilizer shaft link lower re-

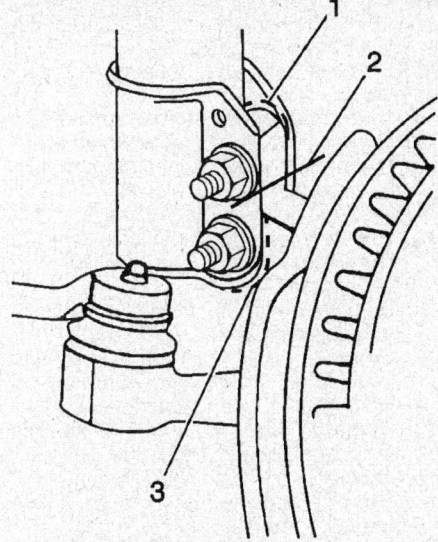

1. Upper knuckle radius
2. Strut/knuckle interface
3. Lower curve of strut

GC2020100312000X

Fig. 7 Steering knuckle & strut alignment marking. Eldorado

taining nut, then the stabilizer shaft link from lower control arm.
5. Remove ABS wire harness from lower control arm, then the lower control arm to steering knuckle nut.
6. Using tool No. J-43631 or equivalent, separate lower control arm from steering knuckle.
7. Loosen power steering gear retaining bolts and raise power steering gear.
8. Remove lower control arm to cradle nuts and bolts, then the lower control arm by lowering it at frame and moving ball stud upwards.
9. Reverse procedure to install noting the following:
   a. **Torque** lower control arm ball stud retaining nut to 15 ft. lbs.
   b. Tighten additional 180° at second pass.
   c. Install ABS wire harness to lower control arm.

CONTROL ARM BUSHING
REPLACE

On these models the control arm bushings are incorporated into the lower control arm and are not serviced separately.

STEERING KNUCKLE
REPLACE

Except STS

1. Raise and support vehicle, then remove tire and wheel assembly.
2. Remove hub nut and washer using suitable punch to keep rotor stationary. Discard hub nut.
3. Remove caliper, support and rotor.

4. Separate drive axle from hub using drive axle separator tool No. J-28733-B, or equivalent, **Fig. 1.**
5. Remove hub and bearing mounting bolts.
6. Disconnect speed sensor connector.
7. Remove hub and bearing assembly.
8. Disconnect wheel speed sensor electrical connector.
9. Remove tie rod mounting nut.
10. Separate tie rod from knuckle using tie rod separator tool No. J-24319-B, or equivalent.
11. Remove cotter pin and lower ball joint mounting nut.
12. Separate ball joint from steering knuckle using ball joint separator tool No. J-43828, or equivalent.
13. Remove strut to steering knuckle mounting bolts, then the steering knuckle.
14. Reverse procedure to install, noting the following:
    a. Refer to "Control Arm, Replace" for ball joint nut tightening specifications.
    b. Tighten outer tie rod to knuckle mounting nut.

STS

1. Raise and support vehicle, then remove tire and wheel.
2. Remove wheel bearing/hub as outlined under "Hub & Bearing Replace."
3. Remove outer tie rod to steering knuckle retaining nut, then using tool No. J–24319-B or equivalent disconnect tie rod from steering knuckle.
4. Remove brake hose bracket to steering knuckle retaining bolts, then upper control arm ball stud to steering knuckle retaining nut.
5. Separate upper control arm ball stud from steering knuckle, then remove lower control arm ball stud to steering knuckle retaining nut.
6. Using tool No. J–43631 or equivalent, separate lower control arm ball stud from steering knuckle.
7. Remove steering knuckle from vehicle.
8. Reverse procedure to install.

STABILIZER BAR

REPLACE

DeVille

1. Raise and support vehicle with control arms hanging free. Remove front tires and wheels.
2. Remove lefthand and righthand stabilizer link bolts.
3. Remove lefthand and righthand stabilizer bar brackets.
4. Remove lefthand tie rod end from knuckle using linkage puller tool No. J-24319-B, or equivalent.
5. Separate ball joint from steering knuckle using ball joint separator tool No. J-36226, or equivalent.
6. Turn righthand steering knuckle to lefthand, then guide stabilizer shaft out righthand side in an upward direction.

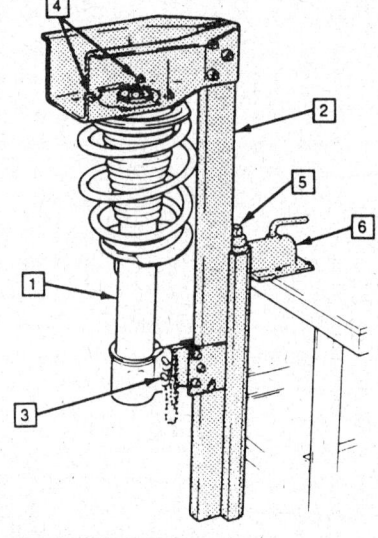

1	STRUT ASSEMBLY
2	STRUT COMPRESSOR J-34013
3	INSTALL LOCKING PINS THROUGH STRUT ASSEMBLY
4	TIGHTEN NUTS TILL FLUSH WITH STRUT COMPRESSOR
5	COMPRESSOR FORCING SCREW
6	HOLDING FIXTURE J3289-20

GC2029100135000X

Fig. 8 Strut spring compression

7. Remove stabilizer shaft out of bottom center.
8. Reverse procedure to install.

Eldorado

1. Raise and support vehicle. **Ensure vehicle weight rests on frame, not on lower control arms.**
2. Remove righthand front tire and wheel.
3. **On models equipped with road sensing suspension,** disconnect position sensor from lower control arm.
4. **On all models,** remove lefthand and righthand mounting bolts, brackets and insulators, **Fig. 5.**
5. Remove lefthand and righthand stabilizer links.
6. Disconnect exhaust pipe from rear manifold, raise pipe to gain clearance, then remove stabilizer shaft.
7. Reverse procedure to install.

Seville

1. Raise and support vehicle with control arms hanging free. Remove front tires and wheels.
2. Remove lefthand and righthand stabilizer link bolts.
3. Remove lefthand and righthand stabilizer bar brackets.
4. Remove lefthand tie rod end from knuckle using linkage puller tool No. J-24319-B, or equivalent.
5. Separate ball joint from steering knuckle using ball joint separator tool No. J-36226, or equivalent.
6. Turn righthand steering knuckle to lefthand, then guide stabilizer shaft out hand, then guide stabilizer shaft out

righthand side in an upward direction.
7. Remove stabilizer shaft out of bottom center.
8. Reverse procedure to install.

STS

1. Raise and support vehicle, **hold shaft link studs with hex tool to prevent damage to link seal.**
2. Remove stabilizer shaft link upper and lower retaining nuts.
3. Remove stabilizer shaft link from the vehicle.
4. Reverse procedure to install.

TIE ROD

REPLACE

Inner

1. Remove steering gear as outlined in "Power Steering Gear, Replace."
2. Remove outer tie rod jam nut.
3. Remove inner tie rod assembly jam nut and end clamp.
4. Remove boot clamp using suitable side cutters.
5. Mark breather tube location on steering gear for installation.
6. Remove rack and pinion boot, then the breather tube.
7. Loosen inner tie rod assembly shock dampener and slide back on rack.
8. Hold rack in suitable vise.
9. Turn inner tie rod housing counterclockwise and remove using one wrench on rack assembly flats and another on inner tire rod housing flats.
10. Reverse procedure to install. Gap between rack and housing stakes should be .01 inch.

Outer

1. Remove cotter pin and hex slotted nut.
2. Loosen jam nut.
3. Remove outer tie rod from steering knuckle using universal steering linkage puller tool No. J-24319-01, or equivalent.
4. Remove outer from inner tie rod.
5. Reverse procedure to install.

POWER STEERING GEAR

REPLACE

DeVille

REMOVAL

1. Ensure front wheels are in straight-ahead position.
2. Lock steering column using lockpin tool No. J-42640, or equivalent, in underside of steering column.
3. Disconnect intermediate shaft lower coupling.
4. Disconnect Magnasteer electrical connector and remove heat shield.

5. Separate outer tie rod ends from steering knuckles using separator tool No. J-24319-B, or equivalent.
6. Remove righthand transaxle mount. **Frame must be properly supported before partially lowering and should not be lowered any further than required to access steering gear.**
7. Position suitable drain pan below steering gear fluid pipe fittings.
8. Disconnect steering gear pressure and return pipes.
9. Remove steering gear mounting bolts.
10. Position suitable floor jack below rear side of frame.
11. Remove rear mounting bolts from frame.
12. Lower the rear portion of frame.
13. Remove steering gear assembly from vehicle.

INSTALLATION

1. Install steering gear onto frame.
2. Raise rear portion of frame and install mounting bolts.
3. Install transaxle mount nuts.
4. Install steering gear mounting bolts.
5. Install power steering pressure and return hoses.
6. Connect Magnasteer electrical connector and install heat shield.
7. Connect outer tie rod ends to knuckles.
8. Connect intermediate shaft to steering gear.
9. Install tires and wheels, then tighten lug nuts.
10. Fill and bleed power steering fluid system as outlined in "Power Steering System Bleed" in "Power Steering" chapter.

Eldorado

1. Ensure front wheels are in straight-ahead position, then lock steering wheel.
2. Disconnect intermediate shaft lower coupling.
3. Raise and support vehicle, then remove lefthand front tire and wheel assembly.
4. Disconnect RSS position sensor and links.
5. Disconnect both tie rod ends from knuckles.
6. Disconnect exhaust pipe at converter.
7. Support frame with suitable jack stands.
8. Loosen body mount bolts No. 2 and No. 3, then slightly lower rear of frame. **Do not lower any more than required to access steering gear.**
9. Remove heat shield and plastic line retainer.
10. Disconnect steering gear pressure and return lines.
11. Disconnect Magnasteer electrical connector.
12. Remove mounting bolts and steering gear by sliding out to side.
13. Reverse procedure to install.

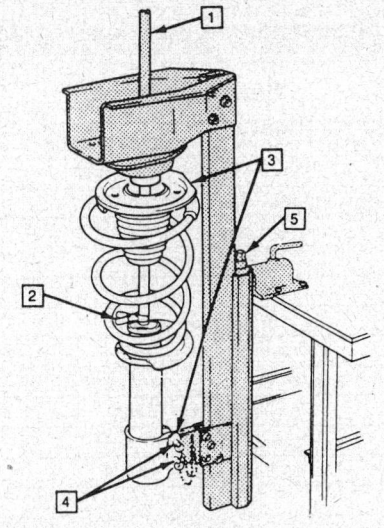

1	ROD J-34013-38 INSTALLED
2	CLAMP J-34013-20 INSTALLED
3	FLAT ON SPRING SEAT MUST FACE SAME DIRECTION AS STEERING KNUCKLE FLANGE
4	BOTH LOCKING PINS INSTALLED
5	COMPRESSOR FORCING SCREW

GC2029100136000X

Fig. 9 Strut assembly

Seville

Refer to "DeVille" for power steering gear replacement procedure.

STS

1. Ensure front wheels are in straight-ahead position.
2. Lock steering column using lockpin tool No. J-42640, or equivalent, in underside of steering column.
3. Remove front tires and wheels, then the front air deflector.
4. Remove intermediate shaft lower pinch bolt, then disconnect intermediate shaft from power steering gear.
5. Disconnect electrical connector variable effort steering, then remove outer tie rod retaining nuts.
6. Using tool No. J-24319-B or equivalent, separate outer tie rod from steering knuckles.
7. Place a drain pan under vehicle, then remove power steering hoses to power steering gear retaining bolt.
8. Disconnect power steering hoses from power steering gear, then the left brake line from brake hose. Plug brake line.
9. Position brake line to side.
10. **On all wheel drive models,** support bottom of front differential housing, loosen right engine mount nut and raise differential housing to clear steering rack bolt.
11. **On all models,** remove power steering gear mounting bolts, then the left rearward lower control arm to frame mounting nut and bolt.
12. Remove power steering gear through left wheel opening.
13. Reverse procedure to install.

POWER STEERING PUMP

REPLACE

DeVille, Eldorado & Seville

1. Mark running direction, then remove serpentine belt.
2. Drain power steering fluid from reservoir into suitable container.
3. Position suitable drain pan below steering pump fluid pipe fittings.
4. Disconnect steering pump fluid lines.
5. Remove mounting bolt and power steering pump assembly.
6. If replacement pump arrived without pulley and reservoir, proceed as follows:
   a. Place pump assembly in suitable soft jawed vise.
   b. Remove power steering pump and reservoir from bracket.
   c. Remove pump pulley using pulley removal tool No. J-25034-C, or equivalent.
   d. Remove pump mounting bracket bolts, then the bracket.
   e. Remove retaining clips from reservoir using clip removal tool No. J-42649, or equivalent.
   f. Remove reservoir from pump. Discard O-rings.
7. Reverse procedure to install, noting the following:
   a. Lubricate new O-ring seals with fresh power steering fluid, then install O-rings onto reservoir.
   b. Ensure retaining clip is fully seated on reservoir assembly so reservoir assembly and pump housing are securely installed.
   c. Install power steering pump pulley using pulley installation tool No. J-25033-C, or equivalent.

STS

1. Remove front air deflector, then the front compartment sight shields.
2. Remove PCV hose, MAF/IAT sensor from air cleaner duct resonator and air cleaner duct.
3. Rotate drive belt tensioner clockwise to release drive belt tension, then remove drive belts.
4. Using tool No. J-25034-C or equivalent, remove power steering pump pulley from power steering pump.
5. Place a drain pan under vehicle, then remove bolts and remove air cleaner.
6. Disconnect power steering reservoir outlet hose and power steering pressure hose from power steering pump.
7. Remove power steering bracket to engine mounting bolts.
8. Remove power steering pump with bracket from vehicle.
9. Remove power steering pump bracket from power steering pump.
10. Reverse procedure to install.

TIGHTENING SPECIFICATIONS

Year	Component	Torque/Ft. Lbs.
DEVILLE w/SOFT RIDE & SPORT SUSPENSION		
2001–05	Ball Joint To Control Arm Nut	①
	Brake Line & Speed Sensor Bracket	13
	Caliper Pin	②
	Control Arm	116
	Drive Axle Nut	118
	Hub & Bearing	96
	Power Steering Gear	70
	Power Steering Gear Hose	22
	Power Steering Pump	37
	Stabilizer Shaft Bracket	24
	Stabilizer Shaft Link	13
	Strut Mount	55
	Strut To Body	30
	Strut To Knuckle	108
	Tie Rod End To Knuckle	22③⑤
	Wheel Lug Nuts	100
DEVILLE w/HEAVY DUTY SUSPENSION		
2001–05	Ball Joint To Control Arm	①
	Brake Line & Speed Sensor Bracket	13
	Caliper Pin	②
	Control Arm	108
	Drive Axle	159
	Hub & Bearing	112
	Power Steering Gear	70
	Power Steering Gear Hose	22
	Power Steering Pump	37
	Stabilizer Shaft Bracket	49
	Stabilizer Shaft Link	17
	Strut Mount	55
	Strut To Body	49
	Strut To Knuckle	131
	Tie Rod End To Knuckle	22③⑥
	Wheel Lug Nuts	100
ELDORADO		
2001–02	Adjuster Plug	50
	Ball Joint To Control Arm	50
	Ball Joint To Knuckle	37
	Brake Reaction Rod To Frame	58
	Caliper Pin	63
	Caliper Mounting Bracket	137
	Control Arm Bushing	100
	Cylinder Line Fittings	20
	Hub & Bearing To Knuckle	70
	Hub To Drive Axle	110
	Inner Tie Rod Housing To Rack	74
	Intermediate Shaft Pinch Bolts	35
	Outer Tie Rod Jam Nut	50
	Power Steering Line Fittings	20
	Stabilizer Bracket To Frame	33
	Stabilizer Link	41
	Strut Mount To Body	18
	Strut To Knuckle	108
	Strut To Strut Top Mount	④
	Tie Rod End To Knuckle	55

Continued

TIGHTENING
SPECIFICATIONS—Continued

Year	Component	Torque/Ft. Lbs.
ELDORADO		
2001–02	Tie Rod Pinch Bolts	41
	Wheel Lug Nuts	100
SEVILLE		
2001–04	Adjuster Plug Nut	55
	Ball Joint	①
	Brake Line & Speed Sensor Bracket	13
	Caliper Bracket	137
	Caliper Pin	63
	Control Arm	117
	Drive Axle	118
	Hub & Bearing	96
	Inner Tie Rod	74
	Power Steering Gear	89
	Power Steering Gear Hose	20
	Power Steering Pump	37
	Stabilizer Bracket	24
	Stabilizer Shaft Link	13
	Strut Mount	55
	Strut Tower	33
	Strut To Knuckle	108
	Tie Rod End To Knuckle	35
	Wheel Lug Nuts	100
STS		
2005	Hub & Bearing	100
	Lower Control Arm Ball Stud	①
	Lower Control Arm To Cradle	96
	Power Steering Gear To Cradle	133
	Shock Absorber Nut	18
	Shock Module To Body	83
	Shock To Yoke Nut	66
	Shock Yoke To Lower Control Arm	133
	Stabilizer Shaft Bracket	81
	Stabilizer Shaft Link	95
	Tie Rod End To Knuckle	22⑤
	Wheel Lug Nuts	100

① — Refer to "Control Arm, Replace" for tightening specifications & procedure.
② — With standard brakes, 63 ft. lbs.; w/J55 heavy duty brakes, 83 ft. lbs.
③ — Do not counter-rotate nut for cotter pin insertion.
④ — Torque old design (flanged) nut to 75 ft. lbs., & new design (non-flanged) nut to 55 ft. lbs.
⑤ — Tighten an additional 180°.
⑥ — Tighten an additional 200°. If required, tighten another 60° to allow cotter pin installation.

Wheel Alignment

INDEX

PRELIMINARY INSPECTION

1. Inspect all tires for proper inflation pressures and approximately equal tread wear.
2. Inspect hub and bearing assemblies for excessive wear, correcting as required.
3. Inspect ball joints and tie rod ends. If they are excessively loose, correct before making adjustment.
4. Measure runout of wheels and tires.
5. Inspect vehicle trim height, correcting as required before adjusting alignment.
6. Inspect for proper operation of Electronic Level Control system.
7. Inspect strut dampeners for proper operation.
8. Inspect control arms for loose bushings.
9. Inspect stabilizer bar for loose or missing components.

FRONT WHEEL ALIGNMENT

1. Install alignment equipment following manufacturers instructions.
2. Jounce front and rear bumpers three times to normalize suspension prior to measuring angles.
3. Measure alignment angles and record the readings.
4. If adjustments are required, they must be made in order:
   a. Caster.
   b. Camber.
   c. Toe.

DeVille & Seville

CASTER

1. Remove top strut nuts and washers.
2. Raise and support front of vehicle to separate strut from inner wheel housing.
3. Drill two ⅜ inch holes at front and rear of oval strut mounting hole on lefthand and righthand strut towers, **Fig. 1.**

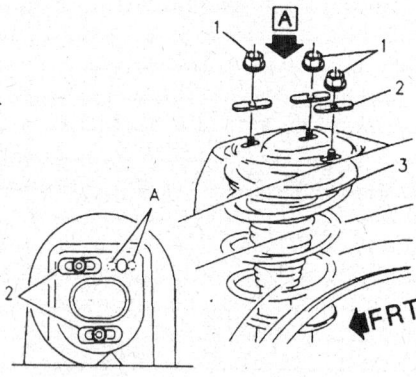

```
A  DRILL 13/32 IN. HOLES
1  NUT, 47 N•m (35 LB. FT.)
2  WASHERS
3  STRUT
```
GC2049500108000X

Fig. 1 Front caster adjustment. DeVille & Seville

4. File excess metal to create slotted holes. **Paint exposed metal with rust resistant paint or primer.**
5. Lower front of vehicle.
6. Install strut mounting nuts. **Do not tighten just yet.**
7. Adjust caster by moving top of strut forward or rearward. A .040 inch position change at tower is approximately .1° change in caster.
8. When caster is within specifications, **torque** strut mounting nuts to 30 ft. lbs.

CAMBER

1. Raise and support vehicle, then remove both front tires and wheels.
2. Tap out upper and lower strut to knuckle bolts, then separate strut from knuckle.
3. Grind lower bolt hole on struts inner metal plate to match outside plates diameter.

4. File excess metal to make slotted holes, then paint exposed metal with rust resistant paint or primer.
5. Replace strut to knuckle and install bolts. **Do not tighten just yet.**
6. Set camber to specifications using camber adjustment tool No. J-39601, or equivalent,
7. **On models equipped with soft or sports suspension, torque** strut to knuckle mounting nuts to 108 ft. lbs.
8. **On models equipped with heavy duty suspension, torque** strut to knuckle mounting nuts to 131 ft. lbs.

TOE

1. Loosen locknuts on tie rod ends. **Ensure boots are not twisted or damaged during adjustment.**
2. Rotate inner tie rod to adjust toe to specifications.
3. **Torque** locknuts to 47 ft. lbs.

Eldorado

CASTER

1. Support vehicle by wheels, then loosen top strut mounting nuts and washers.
2. Set caster to specification by moving strut forward or rearward, as required. Adjustment sensitivity is approximately .1° per millimeter moved.
3. Tighten top strut mounting nuts and washers.

CAMBER

1. Loosen both strut to knuckle bolts just enough to allow movement.
2. Adjust camber by rotating adjustment bolt with adjustment tool No. J-39601, or equivalent, **Fig. 2.**
3. Tighten strut to knuckle nuts.
4. **Torque** camber adjustment bolt to 84 inch lbs.

TOE

1. Loosen inner tie rod locknuts, **Fig. 3.**
2. Adjust toe by turning inner tie rods.
3. Adjust boots so they are not twisted.
4. **Torque** locknuts to 46 ft. lbs.

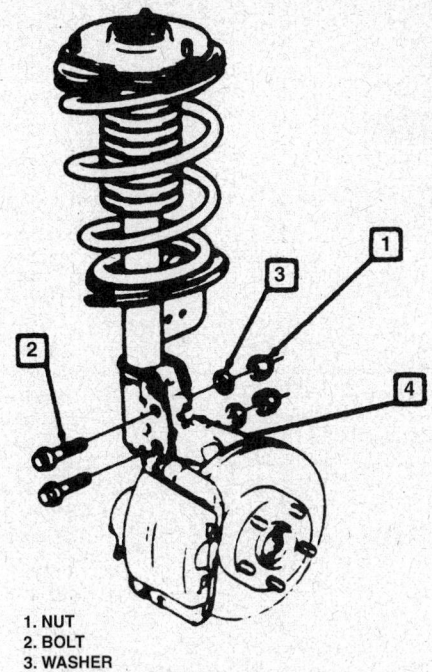

1. NUT
2. BOLT
3. WASHER
4. CAMBER ADJUSTMENT BOLT

GC2049100064000X

Fig. 2 Front wheel camber adjustment. Eldorado

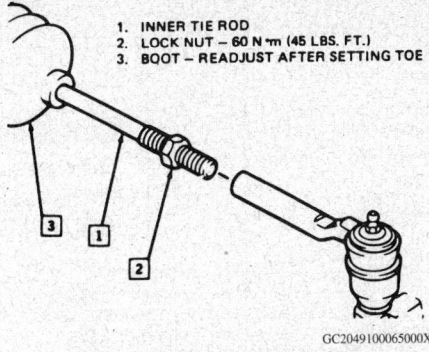

1. INNER TIE ROD
2. LOCK NUT – 60 N·m (45 LBS. FT.)
3. BOOT – READJUST AFTER SETTING TOE

GC2049100065000X

Fig. 3 Front wheel toe adjustment. Eldorado

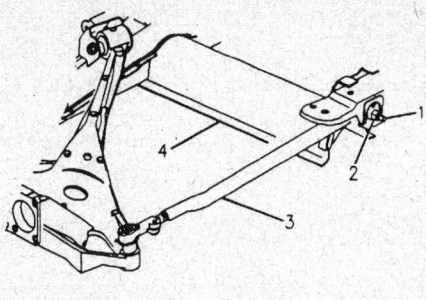

1 CAM BOLT
2 NUT, 75 N·m (55 LB. FT.)
3 INNER ADJUSTMENT LINK
4 REAR SUSPENSION SUPPORT ASSEMBLY

GC2049500110000X

Fig. 4 Rear toe adjustment. DeVille & Seville

STS

CAMBER

1. Install tool No. J–45845 or equivalent, to lower control arm and frame, then loosen lower control arm to frame bolt.
2. Adjust camber angle by turning turnbuckle on tool No. J–45845 or equivalent, until specifications have been met. **Torque** bolt to 96 ft. lbs.
3. Ensure camber is still within specifications.

TOE

1. Loosen jam nut on outer tie rod.
2. Rotate inner tie rod to set toe to specification.
3. **Torque** jam nut to outer tie rod to 40 ft. lbs.
4. **Torque** locknuts to 30 ft. lbs.

REAR WHEEL ALIGNMENT

DeVille & Seville

Adjust lefthand and righthand toe separately.
1. Loosen inner adjustment link cam nut, **Fig. 4.**
2. Rotate cam bolt using suitable 18 MM wrench or socket and adjust toe to specifications.
3. **Torque** cam nut to 55 ft. lbs.

Eldorado

Before inspecting rear trim height or measuring rear alignment angles, the following procedure should be performed to ensure the rear air adjustable struts are filled with residual pressure only.
1. Place weight of at least 300 lbs., in vehicle trunk.
2. Turn ignition On, then wait for vehicle leveling lamp to light.
3. Turn ignition Off and remove weight from trunk.
4. Wait at least 30 seconds for ELC system to exhaust.
5. Roll vehicle forward or backward several complete tire rotations to eliminate effects of tire rotation change.
6. Jounce front and rear bumpers three times to normalize suspension prior to measuring angles.

CAMBER

1. Loosen front and rear inside control arm mounting bolts.
2. Move control arm to change camber and adjust to specifications.
3. **Torque** control arm mounting bolts to 66 ft. lbs.

TOE

1. Loosen inner toe link bolts.
2. Insert suitable screwdriver or pry bar between inside rear toe link mounting bolt and rear crossmember assembly.
3. Move toe link to adjust toe and adjust to specifications.
4. **Torque** toe link mounting bolts to 66 ft. lbs.

STS

The caster and camber adjustments are made by loosening the lower control arm adjustment bolts and repositioning the lower control arm.

CAMBER & CASTER

1. For an accurate reading, do not push or pull on tires during alignment process.
2. Determine caster angle, **Fig. 5.**
3. Determine the camber angle, **Fig. 6.**
4. Install tool No. J–45845 to lower control arm and frame.
5. Loosen lower control arm adjustment nuts.
6. Adjust caster and camber angle by re-positioning lower control arm until specifications have been met.
7. When adjustments are complete, hold lower control arm in position to ensure specifications do not change while tightening lower control arm adjustment bolts.
8. **Torque** lower control arm adjustment bolts to 96 ft. lbs.

TOE

Complete the left and right rear toe adjustments separately.
1. Loosen adjustment link jam nuts, then rotate turnbuckle.
2. Hold turnbuckle when tightening jam nuts.
3. **Torque** jam nuts to 30 ft. lbs.

VEHICLE RIDE HEIGHT

Refer to **Fig. 7,** for ride height measurements and to "Vehicle Ride Height Specifications" in "Specifications" section. When inspecting ride height measurements, note the following:
1. Fuel tank should be full.
2. Tires should be at proper pressure.
3. Front seat should be in rearmost position.
4. Luggage compartment should be empty except for spare tire and jack.
5. Vehicle should be on level ground.
6. If fuel tank is not full, add weight to trunk to compensate for amount fuel vehicle is below the full level.
7. Prior to inspecting ride height, lift front bumper upward approximately 1 ½ inches and release three times.
8. Inspect front ride height.
9. Push front bumper downward approximately 1 ½ inches and release three times.
10. Inspect front ride height.
11. Average out both readings to determine vehicle ride height.
12. Inspect rear ride height in same manner, lifting and pushing rear bumper.

Cause	Correction
Important	
	• Inspect for the proper gear oil levels prior to performing system diagnosis.
	• Operate the vehicle turning in tight circles in both left and right directions. A chatter type concern may indicate an incorrect type gear oil, lack of the friction modifier additive, or worn friction discs and/or plates.
Worn or loose rear axle mount and/or bracket	Repair or replace as required.
Worn axle shaft constant velocity joints	Replace the constant velocity joints as required.
Worn wheel bearings	Replace the wheel bearings as required.
Incorrect gear oil	Drain and fill to the proper level with the correct gear oil and friction modifier additive. Adding friction modifier to the existing fluid without draining will not correct this condition.
Worn clutch plates	Replace the friction discs and plates as required.

ARM0400000000103

Fig. 5 Rear caster angle. STS

(1) Ratio
(2) GM Part Number
(3) Getrag Part Number
(4) Serial Number

Available Axle Ratios

Axle Ratio	Drive/Engine	Flange Size
3:23	RWD/4.6L V8	105 mm
3:23	AWD/4.6L V8	96 mm
3:73	RWD/3.6L V6	105 mm
3:91	AWD/3.6L V6	96 mm

ARM0400000000104

Fig. 6 Rear camber angle. STS

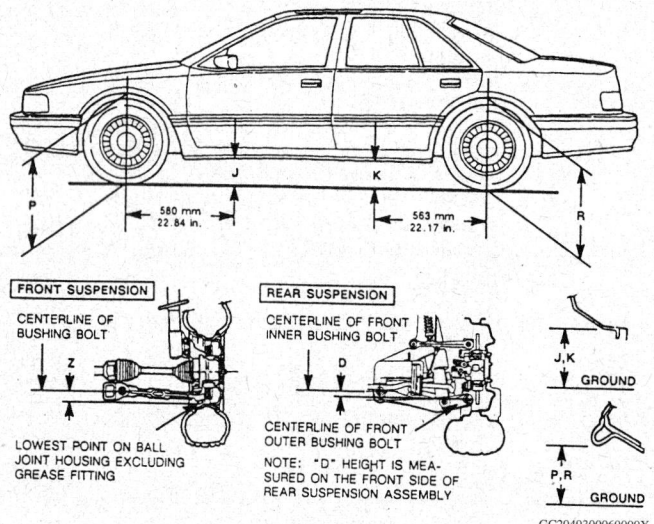

GC2049300069000X

Fig. 7 Ride height measurement locations

METRO

NOTE: Refer To The Rear Of This Manual For Vehicle Manufacturer's Special Tool Suppliers.

INDEX OF SERVICE OPERATIONS

Specifications

GENERAL ENGINE SPECIFICATIONS

Year	Engine Liter	Fuel System	Bore & Stroke Inches	Comp. Ratio	Net. H.P. @ RPM	Maximum Torque, Ft. Lbs. @ RPM	Normal Oil Pressure, psi
2001	1.0L	TBI	2.91 x 3.54	9.5	55 @ 5700	58 @ 3300	47–61
	1.3L	SFI	2.91 x 3.54	9.5	79 @ 6000	75 @ 3000	47–61

TBI — Throttle Body Injection

SFI — Sequential Multi-Port Fuel Injection

TUNE UP SPECIFICATIONS

Engine	Spark Plug Gap	Ignition Timing, BTDC				Curb Idle Speed, RPM		Fast Idle Speed, RPM		Fuel Pump Pressure, psi	Valve Lash
		Firing Order Fig.	Man. Trans.	Auto. Trans.	Mark Fig.	Man. Trans.	Auto. Trans.	Man. Trans.	Auto. Trans.		
1.0L	.041	A	5①	5①	C	850	850	②	②	23–31	③
1.3L	.041	B	5①	5①	C	750–875	750–875	②	②	28–35	③

BTDC — Before Top Dead Center

① — When inspecting ignition timing connect jumper wire between diagnostic connector terminals 4 & 5.

Diagnostic connector is located next to lefthand strut tower.

② — Controlled by an idle speed control motor.

③ — Equipped w/hydraulic valve lash adjusters.

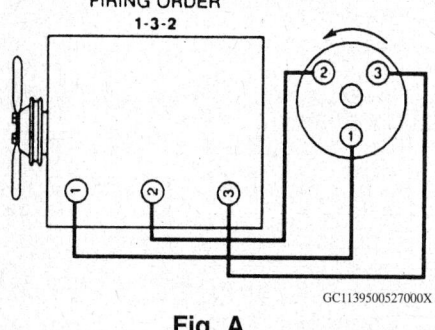

FIRING ORDER 1-3-2

GC1139500527000X

Fig. A

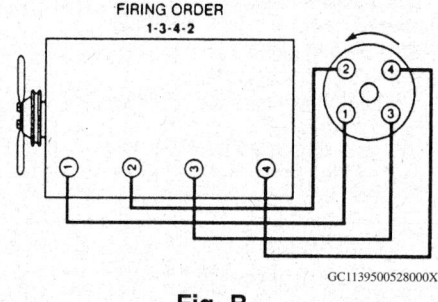

FIRING ORDER 1-3-4-2

GC1139500528000X

Fig. B

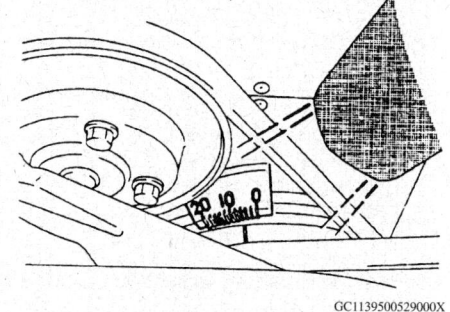

GC1139500529000X

Fig. C

FRONT WHEEL ALIGNMENT SPECIFICATIONS

Year	Caster Angle, Degrees		Camber Angles, Degrees		Total Toe, Degrees	Turning Angle, Degrees		Ball Joint Wear
	Limits	Desired	Limits	Desired		Inner Wheel	Outer Wheel	
2001	+1 to +5	+3	−.5 to +1.5	+.5	0 to +.32	38	32	①

① — Refer to "Ball Joint Inspection," in the "Front Suspension & Steering" section, for proper inspection of ball joints.

REAR WHEEL ALIGNMENT SPECIFICATIONS

| Year | Camber Angles, Degrees | | | | Total Toe, Degree |
| | Limits | | Desired | | |
	Left	Right	Left	Right	
2001	−.01 to +1	−.01 to +1	0	0	+.3 to +.6

VEHICLE RIDE HEIGHT SPECIFICATIONS

Year	Manu-facturer's Original Tire Size	Measurement Points & Specifications①③						
		Front			Rear			
		Dim.	Specification		Dim.	Specification		
			Inches	mm		Inches	mm	
2001	②	A	17.75	450	B	17.75	450
		C	8.25	210	D	8.81	225

A Dim. — Measurement From Front Wheel Center to Check Point On Rocker Panel

B Dim. — Measurement From Rear Wheel Center to Check Point On Rocker Panel

C Dim. — Ground to Rocker Panel, Front

D Dim. — Ground to Rocker Panel, Rear

Dim. — Dimension

① — ±.39 in (10 mm) front to rear & side to side.

② — See door sticker or inside of glove box for manufacturer's original tire size specifications. If tires on vehicle do not match manufactur-er's original tire size & measure-ment is not within limits, refer to the Non-standard Tire & Wheel Size Adjustment To Ride Height Specification & Tire Size Adjust-ment Charts.

③ — Measurement is with fuel, radiator coolant and engine oil full, spare tire, jack, hand tools and mats in designated positions and tires properly inflated.

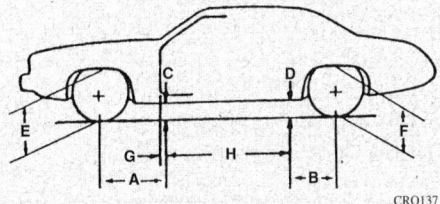

Fig. A

CRQ137

FLUID CAPACITIES & COOLING SYSTEM DATA

| Year | Engine | Coolant Capacity, Qts. | Coolant Type | Radiator Cap Relief Pressure, psi | Thermo-stat Open Temp. °F | Fuel Tank Gals. | Engine Oil Qts. | Transaxle | |
								Man. Pts.	Auto. Qts.①
2001	1.0L	4.13	Ethylene Glycol	15.7	190	10.6	3.5②	5	③
	1.3L	5.00	Ethylene Glycol	15.7	190	10.6	3.5②	5	③

① — Make final inspection w/dipstick.

② — Additional oil may be required to bring oil level to full mark when changing oil filter.

③ — Oil pan only, 1.6 qts.; after over-haul less torque converter, 3.7 qts.; after overhaul with new torque converter, 5.2 qts.

LUBRICANT DATA

| Year | Lubricant Type, Transaxle | | Power Steering | Brake System |
	Manual	Automatic		
2001	75W-90 GL-4①	Dexron III	Dexron III	DOT 3

① — Synthetic type gear lubricant.

Electrical

NOTE: On Air Bag Equipped Models, Refer To "Air Bag System Precautions" Located In The Front Of This Manual For System Disarming & Arming Procedures.

NOTE: Refer To "Computer Relearn Procedures" Located In The Front Of This Manual When Battery Power To The Computer Has Been Interrupted.

INDEX

PRECAUTIONS

Air Bag Systems

Refer to "Air Bag System Precautions" in the front of this manual for system disarming and arming procedures.

Battery Ground Cable

Prior to service, disconnect battery ground cable and isolate as required.

FUSE PANEL & FLASHER LOCATION

The main fuse panel (alternator and ignition switch fuses and main fuse for junction fuse panel) is located in the engine compartment on the lefthand fender apron. The junction fuse panel (fuses for other components) is located under the lefthand side of the instrument panel. The air bag fuse panel, if equipped, is located behind the lefthand side of the instrument panel on the junction block support bracket.

The turn signal and hazard flasher is located under the lefthand side of the instrument panel near the fuse panel.

FUEL PUMP RELAY LOCATION

The fuel pump relay is located in the engine compartment relay center at the front lefthand side of the engine compartment next to battery, **Figs. 1 and 2.**

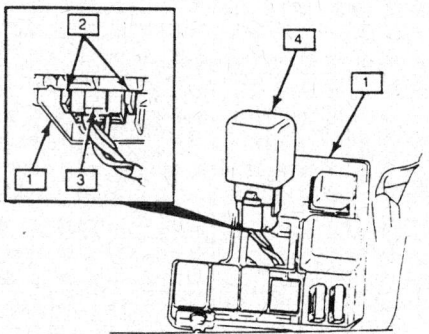

1	MAIN FUSE BOX
2	LOCK TABS
3	FUEL PUMP RELAY ELECTRICAL CONNECTOR
4	FUEL PUMP RELAY

GC1029102746000X

Fig. 1 Fuel pump relay location. 1.0L engine

RELAY CENTER LOCATION

The relay center is located at the lefthand side of the engine compartment, near the battery.

STARTER
REPLACE

1. Disconnect solenoid lead and battery cable.
2. Remove mounting bolts and starter.

3. Reverse procedure to install. **Torque** starter mounting bolts to 17 ft. lbs.

ALTERNATOR
REPLACE

1. Remove air cleaner assembly.
2. Remove rubber insulator and mounting nut, then the battery terminal wire from alternator.
3. Remove alternator upper mounting bolt, then the drive belt.
4. Remove lower alternator mounting bolts, then the alternator.
5. Reverse procedure to install, noting the following:
   a. Adjust drive belt tension so with 22 lbs., of pressure exerted at center of belt, there is .24–.31 inch of deflection.
   b. **Torque** alternator mounting bolts to 17 ft. lbs.
   c. **Torque** battery terminal nut to 71 inch lbs.

DISTRIBUTOR
REPLACE

1. Disconnect electrical connectors and vacuum lines.
2. Remove distributor cap and mark rotor position on housing.
3. Mark distributor position on engine.
4. Remove flange bolts and distributor.
5. Reverse procedure to install. Ensure alignment marks match.

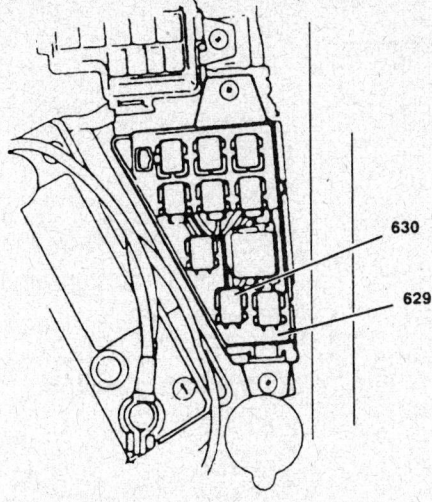

629   **RELAY BOX**

630   **FUEL PUMP RELAY**

GC1029503761000X

Fig. 2   Fuel pump relay location. 1.3L engine

IGNITION COIL
REPLACE

1. Disconnect ignition coil spark plug wires and electrical connector.
2. Remove mounting bolts and ignition coil.
3. Reverse procedure to install, **torque** ignition coil mounting bolts to 96 inch lbs.

IGNITION SWITCH
REPLACE
Removal

1. Remove turn signal/dimmer switch as outlined in "Turn Signal Switch, Replace."
2. Disconnect ignition switch and key warning electrical connectors.
3. Lift up floor mat at steering shaft and remove steering column coupling cover.
4. Remove upper steering shaft coupling bolt, then connect ignition switch and key warning electrical connectors.
5. Remove mounting nuts and steering column.
6. Loosen and remove steering lock mounting bolts using suitable center punch, **Fig. 3.**
7. Place ignition switch in ACC or ON position and remove from steering column.

Installation

1. Position oblong hole on steering shaft at center of hole in steering column, **Fig. 4.**
2. Place ignition switch in ACC or ON position.
3. Position ignition switch to steering col-

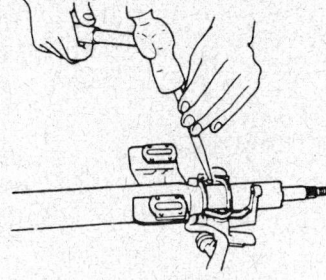

| 1 | CENTER PUNCH (WITH SHARP POINT) |
| 2 | IGNITION SWITCH MOUNTING BOLTS |

GC9129100029000X

Fig. 3   Ignition switch removal

umn and place switch in LOCK position.
4. Align ignition switch hub with oblong hole on steering shaft and rotate steering shaft to ensure it locks.
5. Install replacement ignition switch mounting bolts. Tighten bolts until bolt head breaks off, **Fig. 5.**
6. Place ignition switch in ON or ACC and inspect for smooth steering shaft rotation. Also inspect steering shaft lock for proper operation.
7. Align ignition switch hub to steering shaft oblong hole, rotate shaft to ensure steering shaft is locked, **Fig. 6.**
8. Position steering column mounting brackets to mounting studs. **Torque** mounting nuts to 10 ft. lbs.
9. Install steering shaft coupling bolt and **torque** to 18 ft. lbs.
10. Install steering shaft coupling cover.
11. Install turn signal/dimmer switch as outlined in "Turn Signal Switch, Replace."

CLUTCH START SWITCH
ADJUST

1. Disconnect electrical connector at clutch start switch.
2. Loosen switch locknut and back off switch adjustment.
3. Connect suitable ohmmeter between switch terminals.
4. Position clutch pedal at approximately .6–1.2 inches from floor and hold.
5. Rotate switch into bracket until ohmmeter just indicates continuity and tighten locknut. **Torque** locknut to 10 ft. lbs.
6. Connect switch electrical connector.

NEUTRAL SAFETY SWITCH
REPLACE

1. Remove mounting bolt and neutral safety switch.
2. Place shift lever in Neutral position.
3. Position neutral safety switch using suitable screwdriver, **Fig. 7.** Switch should click at this position.
4. Install neutral safety switch to manual shift shaft and loosely install mounting bolt.
5. Rotate switch slightly until click is

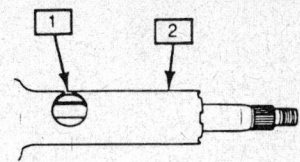

| 1 | STEERING SHAFT |
| 2 | STEERING COLUMN |

GC9129100030000X

Fig. 4   Steering shaft & column alignment

heard and **torque** mounting bolt to 10–16 ft. lbs., **Fig. 8.**
6. Connect electrical connector to switch and inspect switch for proper operation.

HEADLAMP SWITCH
REPLACE

1. Remove steering column trim panel.
2. Lower steering column.
3. Remove instrument cluster bezel screws and pull bezel out.
4. Remove headlamp switch from bezel.
5. Remove cluster to instrument panel mounting screws.
6. Pull cluster rearward to reach and disconnect headlamp switch connector.
7. Remove headlamp switch.
8. Reverse procedure to install.

STOP LIGHT SWITCH
REPLACE

Pull up brake pedal and adjust switch position so that clearance between end of thread and brake pedal contact plate A is .02–.04 inch, **Fig. 9.** Tighten locknut.

TURN SIGNAL SWITCH
REPLACE

1. Remove steering wheel, refer to "Steering Wheel, Replace."
2. Remove steering column covers, **Fig. 10.**
3. Disconnect turn signal/dimmer switch electrical connector.
4. Remove turn signal/dimmer switch mounting screws and switch, **Fig. 10.**
5. Reverse procedure to install.

DIMMER SWITCH
REPLACE

Replace dimmer switch as an assembly with turn signal switch as outlined in "Turn Signal Switch, Replace."

STEERING WHEEL
REPLACE

1. Remove driver's side air bag module as outlined in "Passive Restraint Systems" chapter.
2. Remove steering wheel nut, then

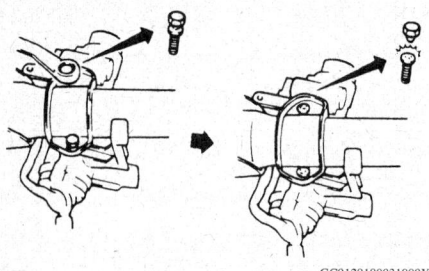

Fig. 5 Ignition switch mounting bolt installation

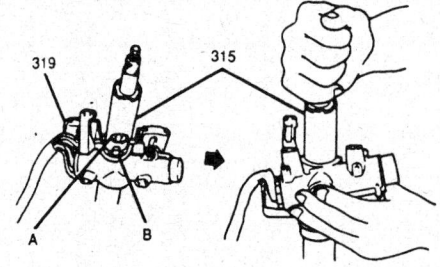

A COLUMN AND SHAFT HOLES
B IGNITION SWITCH HUB
315 STEERING COLUMN
319 IGNITION SWITCH

Fig. 6 Ignition switch hub to steering shaft alignment

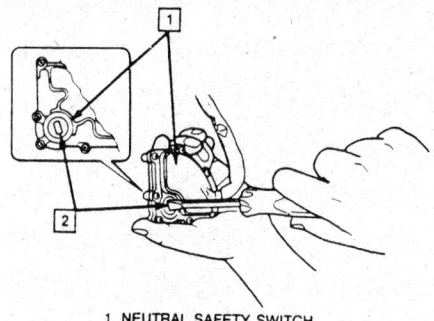

1. NEUTRAL SAFETY SWITCH
2. NEUTRAL SAFETY SWITCH JOINT

Fig. 7 Neutral safety switch position

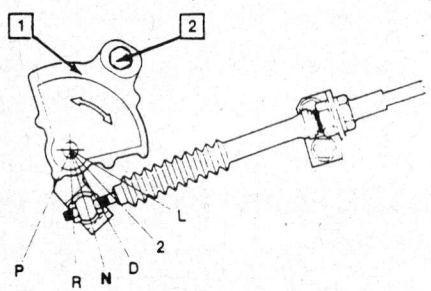

1. NEUTRAL SAFETY SWITCH
2. BOLT

Fig. 8 Neutral safety switch to manual lever installation

place alignment marks on steering shaft and wheel for use during installation.
3. Remove steering wheel using suitable puller tool.
4. Reverse procedure to install. When installing steering wheel, align marks made during removal. **Torque** steering wheel nut to 24 ft. lbs.

INSTRUMENT CLUSTER
REPLACE

1. Remove cluster lower cover mounting screws and covers.
2. Remove mounting screws and gauge cluster bezel.
3. Depress speedometer plastic tabs to disconnect cable.
4. Remove cluster mounting screw.
5. Disconnect cluster electrical connectors and remove cluster.
6. Reverse procedure to install.

RADIO
REPLACE

1. Through glove compartment, disconnect radio and antenna electrical connector.
2. Pull ashtray outward, push downward and pull ashtray rearward to remove.
3. Remove mounting screws and instrument panel center trim bezel.
4. Through instrument panel ashtray cutout, remove cross recess screw below rear of radio.
5. Remove mounting screws, then pull radio and mounting brackets rearward.

6. Remove mounting bracket to radio mounting screws, if required, and radio.
7. Reverse procedure to install.

WIPER MOTOR
REPLACE
Front

1. Disconnect wiper motor electrical connector.
2. Remove wiper motor mounting screws, then wiper linkage to motor mounting nut and washer, **Fig. 11.**
3. Remove wiper motor.
4. Reverse procedure to install.

Rear

1. Disconnect hatchback inner door trim panel clips and remove panel.
2. Disconnect wiper motor electrical connector.
3. Remove wiper motor ground screw, **Fig. 12.**
4. Remove wiper motor mounting nuts.
5. Disconnect wiper linkage and remove wiper motor.
6. Reverse procedure to install. **Torque** wiper motor mounting bolts 15 ft. lbs.

WIPER SWITCH
REPLACE
Front

1. Remove steering column trim panel.
2. Lower steering column.
3. Remove instrument cluster bezel screws and pull bezel out.
4. Remove wiper switch from bezel.
5. Remove cluster to instrument panel mounting screws.
6. Pull cluster rearward to reach and disconnect wiper switch connector.
7. Remove wiper switch.
8. Reverse procedure to install.

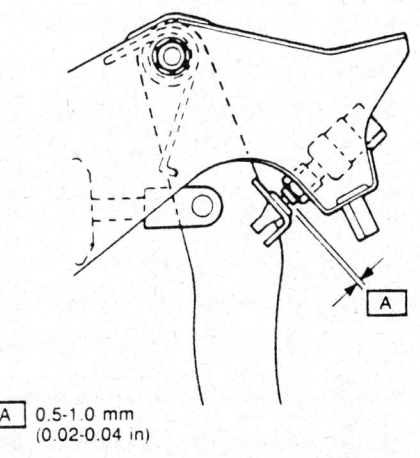

A 0.5-1.0 mm (0.02-0.04 in)

Fig. 9 Stop lamp switch adjustment

Rear

1. Remove lower steering column trim cover.
2. Remove both steering column mounting nuts and lower steering column.
3. Remove instrument panel cluster trim bezel.
4. Remove rear wiper switch from bezel.
5. Reverse procedure to install.

WIPER TRANSMISSION
REPLACE
Front

1. Inspect wiper arms, for proper installation location.
2. Remove wiper arm cover and mounting nut.
3. Disconnect plastic mounting clips and remove cowl vent grill.
4. Remove wiper transmission to cowl mounting nuts.
5. Disconnect wiper motor electrical connector, remove motor mounting bolts and pull motor rearward from bulkhead.
6. Pry wiper transmission from motor crank arm. **Do not disconnect crank arm from motor.**
7. Remove wiper motor and transmission.

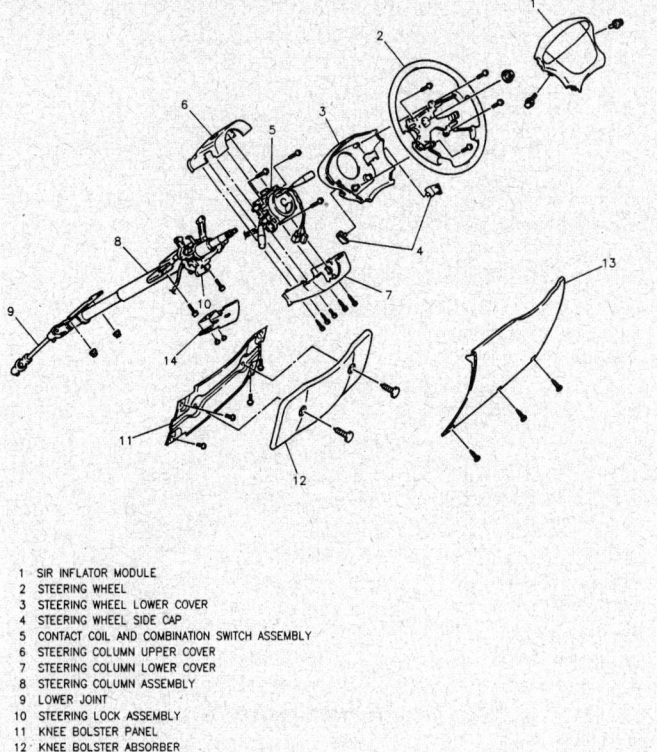

1. SIR INFLATOR MODULE
2. STEERING WHEEL
3. STEERING WHEEL LOWER COVER
4. STEERING WHEEL SIDE CAP
5. CONTACT COIL AND COMBINATION SWITCH ASSEMBLY
6. STEERING COLUMN UPPER COVER
7. STEERING COLUMN LOWER COVER
8. STEERING COLUMN ASSEMBLY
9. LOWER JOINT
10. STEERING LOCK ASSEMBLY
11. KNEE BOLSTER PANEL
12. KNEE BOLSTER ABSORBER
13. STEERING COLUMN HOLE COVER
14. KNEE PROTECTOR

GC9049100119000X

Fig. 10 Turn signal/dimmer switch removal

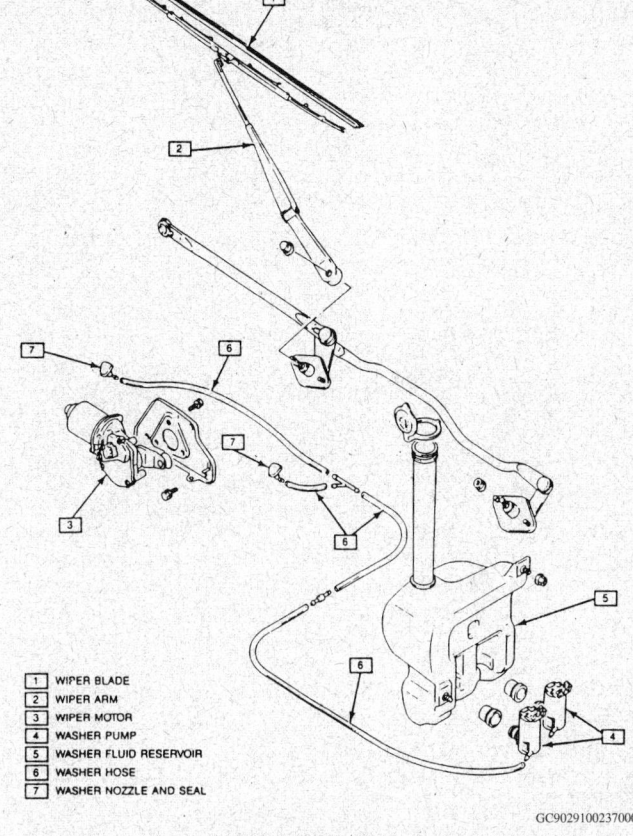

1. WIPER BLADE
2. WIPER ARM
3. WIPER MOTOR
4. WASHER PUMP
5. WASHER FLUID RESERVOIR
6. WASHER HOSE
7. WASHER NOZZLE AND SEAL

GC9029100237000X

Fig. 11 Front windshield wiper/washer motor & linkage assembly

8. Reverse procedure to install. **Torque** transmission mounting nuts to 11 ft. lbs.

Rear

1. Inspect wiper arms, for proper installation location.
2. Lift wiper arm nut plastic cover and remove arm mounting nut.
3. Remove wiper arm from transmission.
4. Remove hatchback door inner trim panel.
5. Disconnect wiper motor electrical connector.
6. Remove motor ground lead mounting screw.
7. Remove mounting nuts and separate motor from door.
8. Pry transmission from motor crank arm and wiper arm base, then slide transmission rearward to remove.
9. Remove wiper arm base from door. **Do not disconnect crank arm from motor.**
10. Reverse procedure to install. **Torque** wiper arm nut to 15 ft. lbs.

BLOWER MOTOR

REPLACE

1. Depress glove compartment stopper and pull rearward.
2. Remove glove compartment to instrument panel mounting screws, then the glove compartment.
3. Disconnect electrical connectors, then remove mounting screws and ECM.

4. Disconnect blower motor and blower resistor electrical connectors.
5. Disconnect fresh air control cable from blower motor.
6. Remove mounting bolts and blower motor housing, **Fig. 13.**
7. Remove air hose and mounting screws, then separate blower motor from housing, **Fig. 14.**
8. Reverse procedure to install.

HEATER CORE

REPLACE

1. Remove instrument panel as outlined in "Dash Panel Service" chapter
2. Drain coolant into suitable container.
3. Remove heater core clamps and hoses, through engine compartment.
4. Remove blower case to heater case air duct.
5. Remove heater case mounting nuts and bolts, **Fig. 15,** then heater case.
6. Remove heater case clip and mounting screws, then separate case halves, **Fig. 16.**
7. Remove heater core from case.
8. Reverse procedure to install. **Torque** heater case mounting nuts and bolts to 90 inch lbs.

EVAPORATOR CORE

REPLACE

1. Evacuate and recover refrigerant as outlined in "Air Conditioning" chapter.

2. Depress glove compartment stopper and pull rearward.
3. Remove glove compartment to instrument panel mounting screws, then the glove compartment.
4. Disconnect electrical connectors, then remove mounting screws and ECM.
5. Disconnect blower motor and blower resistor electrical connectors.
6. Disconnect fresh air control cable from blower motor.
7. Remove mounting bolts and blower motor housing, **Fig. 13.**
8. Remove air hose and mounting screws, then separate blower motor from housing, **Fig. 14.**
9. Disconnect air conditioning amplifier and evaporator thermistor electrical connectors.
10. Disconnect and cap evaporator case refrigerant inlet and outlet pipes.
11. Remove evaporator case drain hose.
12. Remove mounting bolts, nut and evaporator case.
13. Depress lower locking tabs and slide air conditioning amplifier upward to remove.
14. Disengage evaporator case clips, to separate case halves.
15. Remove evaporator core from case.
16. Reverse procedure to install, noting the following:
    a. **Torque** evaporator case bolts to 90 inch lbs.
    b. **Torque** inlet pipe nut to 26 ft. lbs.
    c. **Torque** outlet pipe nut to 33 ft. lbs.

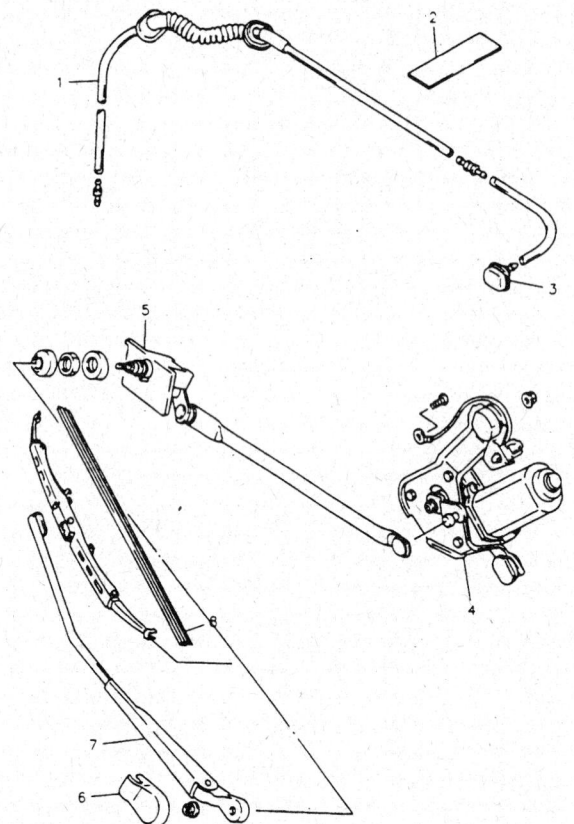

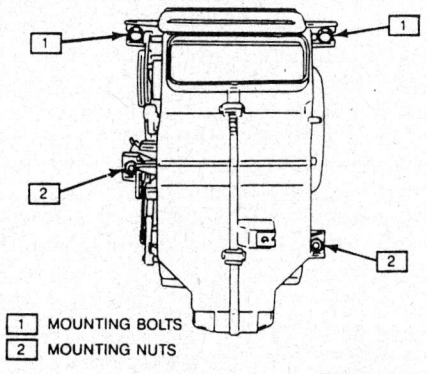

1 REAR WASHER HOSE
2 REAR WASHER HOSE COVER
3 REAR WASHER NOZZLE
4 REAR WIPER MOTOR
5 REAR WIPER LINKAGE
6 REAR WIPER NUT COVER
7 REAR WIPER ARM
8 REAR WIPER BLADE

GC9029500248000X

Fig. 12   Rear windshield wiper motor & linkage assembly

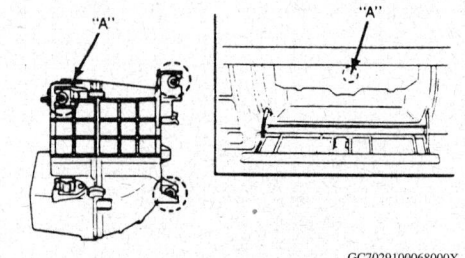

GC7029100068000X

Fig. 13   Blower motor case mounting screw locations

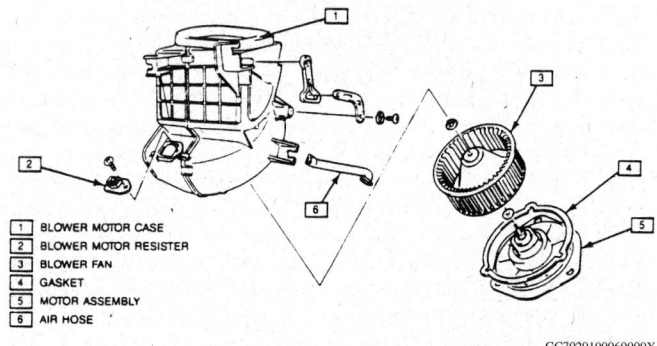

1	BLOWER MOTOR CASE
2	BLOWER MOTOR RESISTER
3	BLOWER FAN
4	GASKET
5	MOTOR ASSEMBLY
6	AIR HOSE

GC7029100069000X

Fig. 14   Blower motor & case

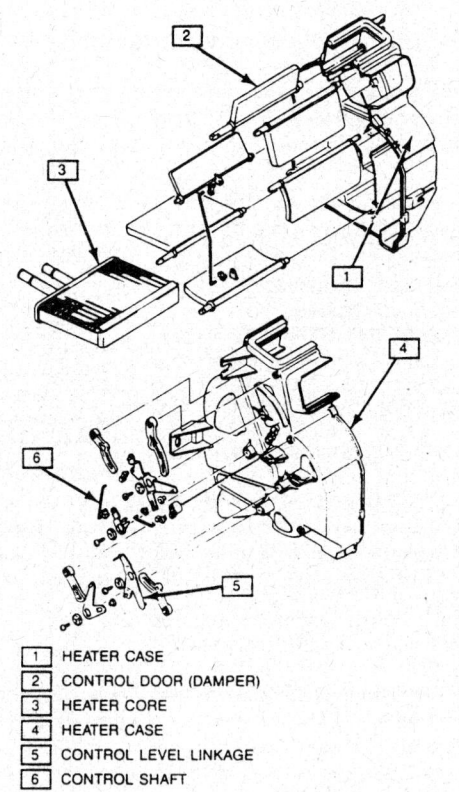

1	MOUNTING BOLTS
2	MOUNTING NUTS

GC7029100071000X

Fig. 15   Heater case mounting bolt & nut locations

1	HEATER CASE
2	CONTROL DOOR (DAMPER)
3	HEATER CORE
4	HEATER CASE
5	CONTROL LEVEL LINKAGE
6	CONTROL SHAFT

GC7029100072000X

Fig. 16   Exploded view of heater case

1.0L Engine

NOTE: On Air Bag Equipped Models, Refer To "Air Bag System Precautions" Located In The Front Of This Manual For System Disarming & Arming Procedures.

NOTE: Refer To "Computer Relearn Procedures" Located In The Front Of This Manual When Battery Power To The Computer Has Been Interrupted.

INDEX

PRECAUTIONS

Air Bag Systems

Refer to "Air Bag System Precautions" in the front of this manual for system disarming and arming procedures.

Battery Ground Cable

Prior to service, disconnect battery ground cable and isolate as required.

Fuel System Pressure Relief

1. Loosen fuel filler cap to relieve fuel tank pressure
2. Remove fuel pump relay from relay box located at lefthand front of engine compartment, next to battery.
3. Crank engine and allow to stall. Crank engine for several seconds more to ensure relief of any remaining fuel.
4. Remove battery ground cable.

COMPRESSION PRESSURE

1. Turn ignition switch to Lock position.
2. Remove spark plugs.
3. Disconnect distributor electrical connector and remove FI fuse from fuse and relay box.
4. Install spark plug port adapter tool No. J-22794, or equivalent, and suitable compression gauge into spark plug hole.

5. **On models equipped with manual transaxle,** depress clutch and accelerator to floor.
6. **On all models,** crank engine and take four pressure readings, recording highest reading obtained.
7. Compression should increase quickly and evenly. Compression pressure at 250 RPM is 199 psi standard and 156 psi minimum. Maximum allowable pressure difference between any two cylinders at 250 RPM is 14 psi.
8. Repeat compression test procedure for remaining cylinders.
9. After completion, install FI fuse, spark plugs and distributor electrical connector.

ENGINE MOUNT
REPLACE

Front

1. Remove engine mount nut, then raise and support vehicle.
2. Support engine using suitable engine support fixture.
3. Remove engine mount and frame bracket, then mount from bracket.
4. Reverse procedure to install.

Rear

1. Remove engine mount nut, then raise and support vehicle.
2. Remove nut mounting mount to body bracket.
3. Support engine using suitable engine support fixture.
4. Remove frame bracket and mount.

5. Reverse procedure to install.

ENGINE
REPLACE

1. Remove cables, battery and battery tray.
2. Drain cooling system into suitable container.
3. Remove hood.
4. Remove air cleaner.
5. Remove radiator with cooling fan.
6. Disconnect coolant temperature gauge sensor, throttle position sensor and EGR solenoid electrical connectors.
7. Disconnect EGR bypass valve.
8. Disconnect idle speed control solenoid valve, oxygen sensor, fuel injector, MAP sensor and power steering pressure switch electrical connectors.
9. Disconnect intake manifold ground wires.
10. Disconnect oil pressure switch, alternator and air conditioning compressor electrical connectors.
11. Disconnect starter solenoid electrical connector.
12. Disconnect back-up lamp switch.
13. Disconnect direct clutch and second brake solenoids.
14. Release main engine harness from clamps.
15. Disconnect the following vacuum hoses:
    a. Intake manifold front and rear canister purge.
    b. Canister pipe.
    c. Intake manifold pressure sensor.
    d. Intake manifold brake booster.

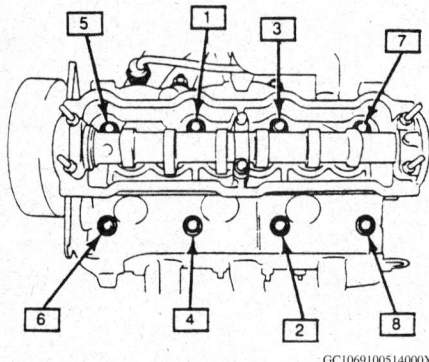

Fig. 1 Cylinder head bolt tightening sequence

GC1069100514000X

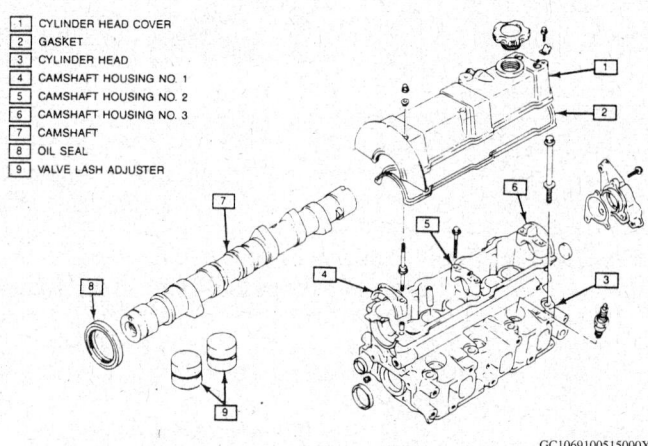

1	CYLINDER HEAD COVER
2	GASKET
3	CYLINDER HEAD
4	CAMSHAFT HOUSING NO. 1
5	CAMSHAFT HOUSING NO. 2
6	CAMSHAFT HOUSING NO. 3
7	CAMSHAFT
8	OIL SEAL
9	VALVE LASH ADJUSTER

GC1069100515000X

Fig. 2 Camshaft & hydraulic valve lash adjusters

e. Throttle body idle speed control.
16. Disconnect the following cables:
   a. Throttle body accelerator.
   b. Transaxle clutch.
   c. Transaxle shift select and throttle valve.
   d. Transaxle speedometer.
17. Remove inlet and outlet hoses.
18. Remove throttle body fuel return and feed hoses.
19. Install universal support fixture tool No. J-28467-A with engine support adapters tool No. J-28467-89, or equivalents.
20. Raise and support vehicle.
21. Disconnect exhaust system from exhaust manifold.
22. Remove front pipe/catalytic converter.
23. **On models equipped with manual transaxle,** remove gearshift control shaft and extension rod.
24. **On all models,** drain engine oil and transaxle fluid into suitable container.
25. Remove lefthand and righthand drive axles from transaxle as outlined in "Front Wheel Drive Axle," chapter. **It is not required to remove driveshafts from steering knuckles.**
26. Remove air conditioning compressor from bracket and position aside. **Do not disconnect air conditioning hoses from compressor.**
27. Disconnect power steering pump hoses.
28. **On models equipped with automatic transaxle,** remove torque rod.
29. **On all models,** lower vehicle.
30. Remove tool Nos. J-28467-A and J-28467-89, or equivalents, and install suitable engine lifting device.
31. Remove lefthand transaxle mount, righthand side engine mount and rear engine mount.
32. Remove engine with transaxle.
33. Reverse procedure to install.

INTAKE MANIFOLD
REPLACE

1. Drain cooling system into suitable container remove air cleaner.
2. Disconnect coolant temperature sender, engine and coolant temperature sensor electrical connectors.
3. Disconnect EGR vacuum switching valve electrical connector.
4. Disconnect idle speed control valve,

throttle position switch and fuel injector electrical connectors.
5. Disconnect intake manifold ground wires,
6. Disconnect throttle body fuel hoses.
7. Disconnect intake manifold coolant and MAP sensor hoses.
8. Disconnect evaporative emission hoses from intake manifold and tube.
9. Disconnect intake manifold power brake unit vacuum hose.
10. Disconnect PCV valve hose from cylinder head cover.
11. Disconnect throttle body accelerator cable.
12. Disconnect all other electrical connectors and hoses to permit intake manifold and throttle body removal.
13. Remove intake manifold to cylinder head mounting nuts and bolts, then the intake manifold and throttle body as an assembly.
14. Reverse procedure to Install.

EXHAUST MANIFOLD
REPLACE

1. Disconnect oxygen sensor electrical connector and release wiring harness from clamps.
2. Disconnect exhaust pipe from exhaust manifold.
3. Remove mounting bolts, nuts and exhaust manifold.
4. Reverse procedure to install.

CYLINDER HEAD
REPLACE

1. Drain cooling system into suitable container and remove air cleaner.
2. Disconnect distributor cap coil wire.
3. Disconnect distributor electrical connector.
4. Disconnect coolant temperature sender, engine coolant temperature sensor and engine cooling fan switch electrical connectors.
5. Disconnect EGR vacuum switching valve electrical connector.
6. Disconnect idle speed control valve, throttle position switch and fuel injector electrical connectors.

7. Disconnect oxygen sensor electrical connector and wiring harness from clamps.
8. Disconnect intake manifold ground wires.
9. Disconnect intake manifold heater and thermostat housing radiator hoses.
10. Disconnect throttle body fuel hoses.
11. Disconnect intake manifold MAP sensor hose.
12. Disconnect evaporative emission hoses from intake manifold and tube.
13. Disconnect intake manifold power brake unit vacuum hose.
14. Disconnect throttle body accelerator cable.
15. Raise and support vehicle, then disconnect exhaust pipe from exhaust manifold.
16. Lower vehicle and remove cylinder head cover.
17. Remove mounting bolts and cylinder head.
18. Reverse procedure to install. Tighten cylinder head bolts in several passes in sequence, **Fig. 1.**

VALVE ARRANGEMENT
Front To Rear

1.0L ....I-E-I-E-I-E

VALVE ADJUSTMENT

These engines are equipped with hydraulic valve lash adjusters and no adjustment is required.

VALVE GUIDES

Valves and valve guides are available in standard size only. The valve guide can be driven from cylinder bore using valve guide replacement tool No. J-37968-1, or equivalent. The valve guide should be driven from the combustion chamber side of the cylinder head out through the valve spring side.

The cylinder head valve guide bore should be reamed with an .433 inch reamer prior to valve guide installation. Heat cylinder head to 176–212°F, then drive valve guide into cylinder head bore using valve guide replacement tool No. J-37968-1 and valve guide installer tool No. J-37968-2, or

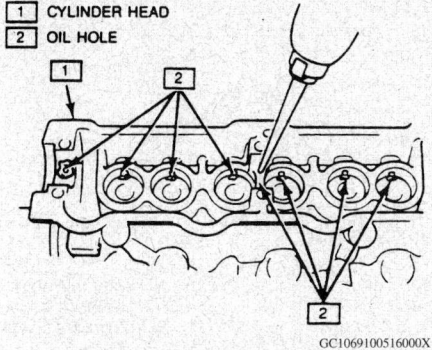

1 CYLINDER HEAD
2 OIL HOLE

GC1069100516000X

Fig. 3 Applying engine oil to camshaft oil holes

equivalents. Valve guide should be driven in until tool contacts cylinder head. Valve guide protrusion should be .45 inch from cylinder head surface. After installation, ream valve guide with .217 inch reamer.

HYDRAULIC VALVE LASH ADJUSTER SERVICE

Hydraulic valve lash adjusters should not be disassembled.
1. Remove camshaft as outlined in "Camshaft, Replace."
2. Remove hydraulic valve lash adjusters, **Fig. 2**.
3. Inspect hydraulic valve lash adjusters for wear and damage and replace as required.
4. Measure outside diameter of hydraulic valve lash adjuster. Outside diameter should be 1.2188–1.2194 inches.
5. Measure hydraulic valve lash adjuster bore in cylinder head. Bore diameter should be 1.2205–1.2214 inches.
6. To determine hydraulic valve lash adjuster to cylinder head bore clearance, subtract adjuster outside diameter from cylinder head adjuster bore diameter. Adjuster to bore clearance should be .0010–.0025 inch. If clearance is more than .0059 inch, replace adjuster or cylinder head, as required.
7. Place valve lash adjuster in clean engine oil prior to installation. Also pour engine oil through camshaft journal oil holes, until oil is emitted from hydraulic valve lash adjuster oil holes, **Fig. 3**.
8. Apply engine oil to valve lash adjuster, position adjuster in cylinder head bore and install camshaft.

TIMING BELT
REPLACE
Removal

1. Raise and support vehicle.
2. Remove fender apron extension from righthand side.
3. Remove drive belt and water pump pulley.
4. Remove mounting bolts and crankshaft pulley.
5. Remove outer timing belt cover, **Fig. 4**.

6. Align camshaft and crankshaft timing marks, **Fig. 5**.
7. Remove timing belt tensioner, tensioner plate, spring and damper.
8. Remove timing belt.

Inspection

Inspect timing belt for wear and cracks and replace as required. Inspect timing belt tensioner for smoothness of rotation and replace as required.

Installation

1. Position lug on tensioner plate to hole in tensioner, **Fig. 6**.
2. Position tensioner and tensioner plate to engine, then install and hand tighten mounting bolt. Ensure tensioner and tensioner plate move in same direction, **Fig. 7**. If movement is not as indicated, remove tensioner and insert tensioner plate lug into tensioner.
3. Ensure camshaft and crankshaft timing marks are aligned, **Fig. 5**.
4. With tensioner plate pushed upward, install timing belt over camshaft and crankshaft pulleys. **Arrow on timing belt should face toward direction of crankshaft rotation. When installing timing belt, keep drive side of belt free of slack.**
5. Install tensioner spring and damper, then hand tighten tensioner stud.
6. Rotate crankshaft two revolutions clockwise direction to remove slack from belt. **Ensure slack is removed from drive belt, and camshaft and crankshaft timing marks are aligned.**
7. Tighten tensioner stud and bolt.
8. Install timing belt outer cover and crankshaft pulley. **Ensure seal is between oil pump housing and water pump.**
9. Install water pump pulley and drive belt.
10. Install righthand side fender apron extension and lower vehicle.

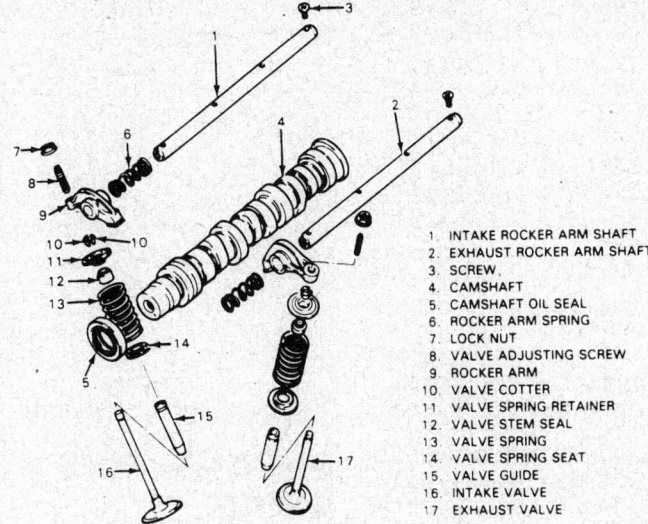

1. INTAKE ROCKER ARM SHAFT
2. EXHAUST ROCKER ARM SHAFT
3. SCREW
4. CAMSHAFT
5. CAMSHAFT OIL SEAL
6. ROCKER ARM SPRING
7. LOCK NUT
8. VALVE ADJUSTING SCREW
9. ROCKER ARM
10. VALVE COTTER
11. VALVE SPRING RETAINER
12. VALVE STEM SEAL
13. VALVE SPRING
14. VALVE SPRING SEAT
15. VALVE GUIDE
16. INTAKE VALVE
17. EXHAUST VALVE

GC1069100517000X

Fig. 4 Timing belt & cover

CAMSHAFT
REPLACE

This procedure has been revised by a Technical Service Bulletin.

Removal

1. Remove air cleaner and cylinder head cover.
2. Remove distributor.
3. Remove timing belt as outlined in "Timing Belt, Replace."
4. Position crankshaft sprocket key, **Fig. 8**.
5. **On models equipped with spoked camshaft timing gear,** position gear so camshaft timing gear pulley pin engages with slot No. 1 on camshaft timing gear, **Fig. 9**.
6. **On all models,** hold camshaft in position by inserting rod into .39 inch hole in camshaft and remove camshaft sprocket mounting bolt, **Fig. 10**. Place shop cloth under rod to prevent damage to cylinder head surface.
7. Remove camshaft housings to cylinder head mounting bolts and studs, **Fig. 2**.
8. Remove camshaft. **Hydraulic valve lash adjusters should also be removed and placed in engine oil until installation.**

Installation

1. Pour engine oil into camshaft journal oil holes until oil is emitted from hydraulic valve lash adjuster holes, **Fig. 3**.
2. Lubricate valve lash adjusters with engine oil and install on cylinder head.
3. Lubricate camshaft with engine oil and position on cylinder head with sprocket pin hole positioned, **Fig. 11**.
4. **On models equipped with spoked**

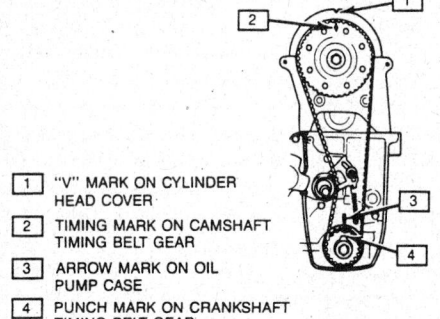

1. "V" MARK ON CYLINDER HEAD COVER
2. TIMING MARK ON CAMSHAFT TIMING BELT GEAR
3. ARROW MARK ON OIL PUMP CASE
4. PUNCH MARK ON CRANKSHAFT TIMING BELT GEAR

GC1069100518000X

Fig. 5 Camshaft & crankshaft sprocket timing mark alignment

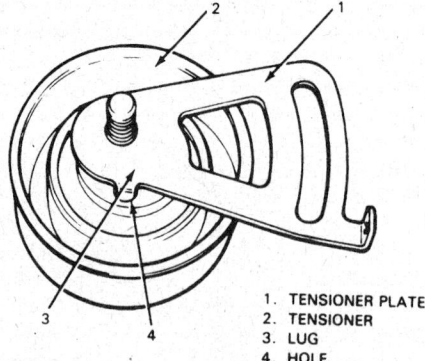

1. TENSIONER PLATE
2. TENSIONER
3. LUG
4. HOLE

GC1069100519000X

Fig. 6 Tensioner

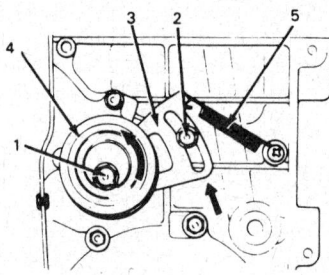

1. TENSIONER BOLT
2. TENSIONER STUD
3. TENSIONER PLATE
4. TENSIONER
5. SPRING

GC1069100520000X

Fig. 7 Tensioner plate movement inspect

(as opposed to solid) camshaft timing gears, install gear so pulley pin engages with slot No. 1 on camshaft timing gear.

5. **On all models,** lubricate camshaft journal bores in camshaft housing with engine oil.
6. Apply sealant to cylinder head mating surface of camshaft housings No. 1 and No. 3, **Fig. 12.**
7. Position camshaft housings over camshaft and onto cylinder head mating surface. **Arrow on camshaft housing should face camshaft sprocket side of cylinder head.** Camshaft housings are numbered from one to three. Housings are positioned on cylinder head in numerical order, starting with No. 1 at camshaft sprocket side of cylinder head, **Fig. 13.**
8. Apply engine oil to camshaft housing mounting bolts and studs, then loosely install bolts and studs. Tighten bolts and studs in sequence, **Fig. 14.**
9. Apply engine oil to camshaft oil seal lip and install seal. Seal surface should be flush with housing surface.
10. Hold camshaft in position by inserting rod into .39 inch hole in camshaft, then install and tighten camshaft sprocket mounting bolt, **Fig. 10.** Place shop cloth under rod.
11. Install cylinder head cover.
12. Install timing belt as outlined in "Timing Belt, Replace."
13. Install ignition distributor and air cleaner.
14. Adjust ignition timing.

PISTON & ROD ASSEMBLY

Refer to **Fig. 15,** when assembling piston and connecting rod. When installing piston and connecting rod, arrow on piston head should face front of engine and oil hole in connecting rod should face intake manifold. When installing connecting rod cap, arrow on cap should face front of engine.

Measure rod bearing side clearance using suitable feeler gauge. Connecting rod bearing side clearance should be .0039 to .0078 inch.

PISTONS, PINS & RINGS

Pistons and rings are available in standard size and oversizes of .010 and .020 inch. Piston pins are supplied with pistons in matched sets.

MAIN & ROD BEARINGS

Main and rod bearings are available in standard size and under size of .010 inch. Crankshaft thrust bearings are available in standard size and under size of .005 inch.

CRANKSHAFT REAR OIL SEAL

REPLACE

1. Remove transaxle as outlined in **MOTOR's "Domestic Transmission, In Vehicle Service"** manual.
2. **On models with equipped manual transaxle,** remove pressure plate and clutch disc.
3. **On all models,** remove flywheel.
4. Remove seal retainer and seal from retainer.
5. Reverse procedure to install.

OIL PAN

REPLACE

1. Raise and support vehicle.
2. Drain oil pan into suitable container.
3. Remove flywheel dust cover.
4. Disconnect exhaust pipe at manifold.
5. Remove oil pan bolts and pan, **Fig. 16.**
6. Remove oil pump screen.
7. Reverse procedure to install. Apply continuous bead of silicon type sealer to oil pan flange inside bolt holes. When tightening oil pan mounting bolts, start at center and working outward.

OIL PUMP

REPLACE

Removal

1. Remove timing belt as outlined in "Timing Belt, Replace."

2. Raise and support vehicle.
3. Drain oil pan into suitable container.
4. Remove flywheel dust cover.
5. Disconnect exhaust pipe at manifold.
6. Remove oil pan bolts and pan, **Fig. 16.**
7. Remove oil pump screen.
8. Remove crankshaft timing belt sprocket.
9. Remove alternator mounting bracket, if required.
10. **On models equipped with air conditioning,** remove compressor mounting bracket.
11. **On all models,** remove alternator adjusting bolt and upper cover bolt, if required.
12. Remove oil pump bolts and pump, **Fig. 17.**

Installation

1. Install oil pump pins and gasket on engine block.
2. Install oil seal guide tool No. J-34853, or equivalent, onto crankshaft to prevent damage to oil seal lip, **Fig. 18.** Apply engine oil to special tool.
3. Install oil pump onto crankshaft and engine block, then the mounting bolts, **Fig. 19.** No. 1 bolts are shorter then No. 2 bolts.
4. After installing oil pump, ensure oil seal lip is not twisted and remove tool.
5. Install rubber seal between oil pump and water pump, **Fig. 20.**
6. Trim oil pump seal edges flush with oil pan mating surface, as required.
7. Install timing belt guide, key and crankshaft timing sprocket. Timing belt guide must be installed so curved side faces oil pump.
8. Install timing belt and tensioner components.
9. Adjust water pump belt tension.
10. Fill crankcase.
11. Run engine to ensure oil pressure is correct.

OIL PUMP SERVICE

1. Remove dipstick tube from oil pump.
2. Remove gear/rotor plate screws and gear plate.
3. Remove outer and inner gears/rotors.

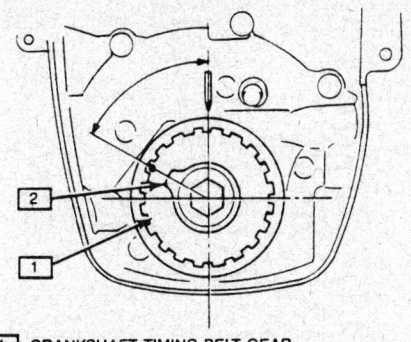

1 CRANKSHAFT TIMING BELT GEAR
2 KEY

GC1069100521000X

Fig. 8 Positioning crankshaft sprocket key

4. Inspect oil seal lip for damage and replace, as required.
5. Inspect outer and inner gears/rotors, gear/rotor plate and oil pump case for excessive wear or damage.
6. Inspect radial clearance between outer gear/rotor and crescent, **Fig. 21.** If clearance is more than .0122 inch, replace outer gear/rotor.
7. Measure side clearance which should not exceed .0059 inch using straight-edge and feeler gauge, **Fig. 22.**
8. Wash, clean and dry all oil pump components.
9. Apply light coat of engine oil to inner and outer gears/rotors, oil seal lip portion and inside surfaces of oil pump case and plate.
10. Install outer and inner gears/rotors in pump case.
11. Install gear/rotor plate and tighten screws. Ensure gears turn smoothly by hand.
12. Install O-ring in pump case and dipstick tube.

BELT TENSION DATA

Belt	Belt Deflection Inch①
AIR CONDITIONING COMPRESSOR	
All	.28–.35
ALTERNATOR & WATER PUMP	
New	.20–.27
Used	.24–.31

① — With thumb pressure applied.

COOLING SYSTEM BLEED

These engines do not require a specific bleed procedure. After filling cooling system, run engine to operating temperature with radiator/pressure cap off. Air will then be automatically bled through cap opening.

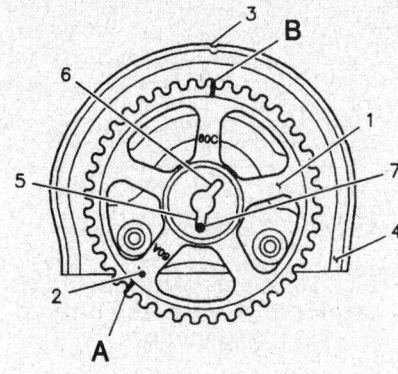

1	CAMSHAFT TIMING PULLEY	5	SLOT NO. 1
2	TIMING MARK	6	SLOT NO. 2
3	"V" MARK	7	PULLEY PIN
4	BELT INSIDE COVER		

GC1069500820000X

Fig. 9 Camshaft timing gear (spoked type)

THERMOSTAT
REPLACE

1. Drain cooling system into suitable container.
2. Remove radiator inlet hose at thermostat housing.
3. Remove thermostat housing and thermostat.
4. Clean both gasket surfaces thoroughly.
5. Reverse procedure to install.

WATER PUMP
REPLACE

1. Drain cooling system into suitable container.
2. Remove drive belt, water pump pulley, crankshaft pulley, timing belt outside cover, timing belt and timing belt tensioner.
3. Remove water pump mounting bolts and nuts and water pump.
4. Install water pump on engine block.
5. Install rubber seals between water pump and oil pump and between water pump and cylinder head, **Fig. 23.**
6. Install timing belt tensioner, timing belt, timing belt outside cover, crankshaft pulley, water pump pulley and drive belt.
7. Tighten drive belt so it deflects .25–.35 inch on span between water pump pulley and crankshaft pulley.
8. Install valve cover and air cleaner.
9. Fill cooling system.

RADIATOR
REPLACE

1. Drain cooling system into suitable container.

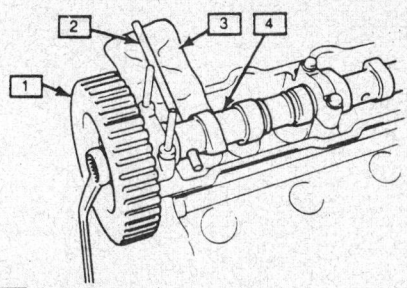

1 CAMSHAFT TIMING BELT GEAR
2 ROD
3 SHOP CLOTH
4 CAMSHAFT

GC1069100522000X

Fig. 10 Camshaft sprocket bolt removal & installation

2. Remove radiator upper, lower and overflow hoses.
3. Disconnect cooling fan electrical connector.
4. **On models equipped with automatic transaxle,** disconnect transaxle cooling lines from bottom of radiator.
5. **On all models,** remove mounting bolts and radiator/fan assembly.
6. Reverse procedure to install.

FUEL PUMP
REPLACE

1. Remove rear seat cushion, disconnect fuel pump and sending unit electrical connections, then push harness through floor pan grommet.
2. Drain fuel tank into suitable container.
3. Raise and support vehicle.
4. Remove muffler and exhaust pipe.
5. Remove fuel filler neck hose, fuel breather hose and EVAP canister air inlet hose.
6. Remove parking brake cable and position aside.
7. Remove EVAP canister vapor hose, fuel feed and return hoses at fuel tank and pump.
8. Remove mounting bolts and lower fuel tank.
9. Disconnect fuel sender electrical connections and vapor hoses, then fuel feed and return lines.
10. Remove fuel sender.
11. Separate fuel pump from fuel sender, as required.
12. Reverse procedure to install.

FUEL FILTER
REPLACE

The fuel filter is a component of the fuel sender located in the fuel tank. The fuel sender must be removed in order to replace fuel sender subassembly that contains fuel filter as outlined in "Fuel Pump, Replace."

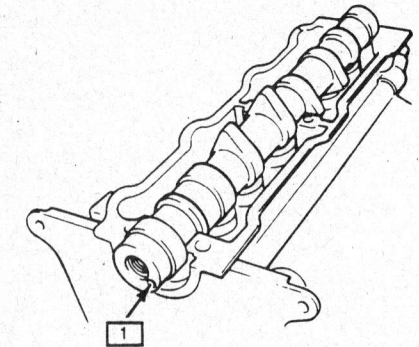

1 | TIMING BELT GEAR PIN HOLE

GC1069100523000X

Fig. 11 Position camshaft sprocket pin hole

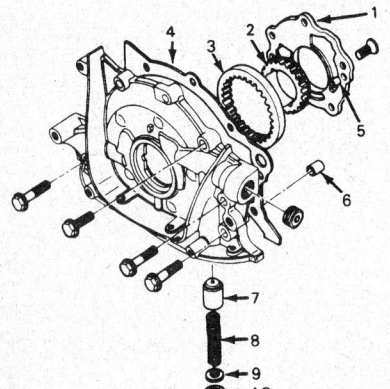

GC1069100526000X

Fig. 14 Camshaft housing bolt tightening sequence

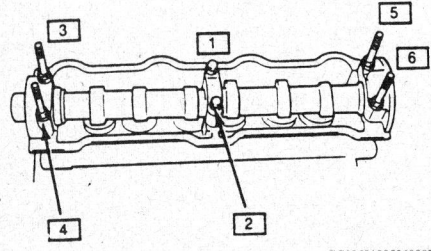

1 | APPLY SEALANT

GC1069100524000X

Fig. 12 Camshaft housing to cylinder head surface sealant application

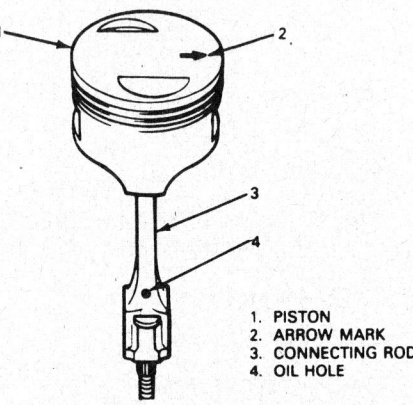

1. PISTON
2. ARROW MARK
3. CONNECTING ROD
4. OIL HOLE

GC1069100527000X

Fig. 15 Piston & connecting rod assembly

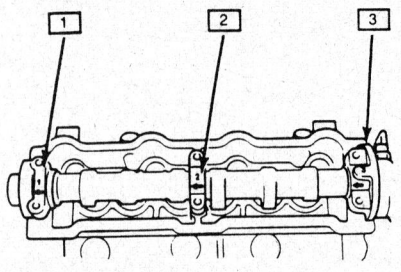

1 | NO. 1 HOUSING
2 | NO. 2 HOUSING
3 | NO. 3 HOUSING

GC1069100525000X

Fig. 13 Camshaft housing locations

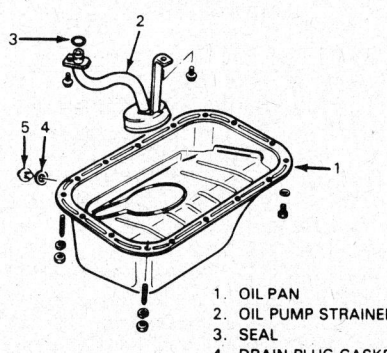

1. OIL PAN
2. OIL PUMP STRAINER
3. SEAL
4. DRAIN PLUG GASKET
5. DRAIN PLUG

GC1099100086000X

Fig. 16 Oil pan & pick-up tube

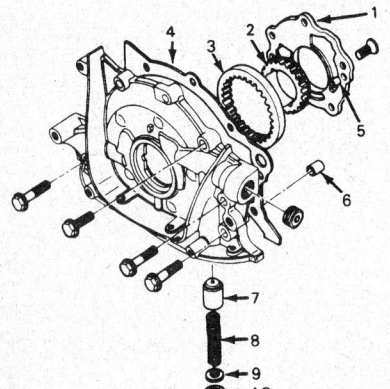

1. GEAR PLATE
2. INNER GEAR
3. OUTER GEAR
4. GASKET
5. PIN
6. PIN
7. RELIEF VALVE
8. SPRING
9. RETAINER
10. RETAINER RING

GC1099100087000X

Fig. 17 Rotor type (Trochoid) oil pump

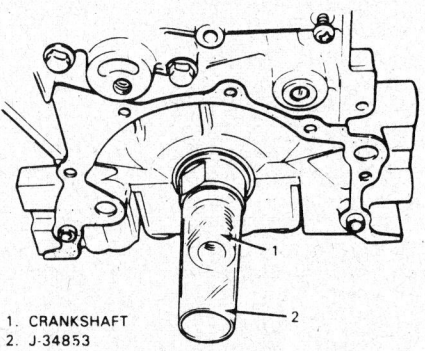

1. CRANKSHAFT
2. J-34853

GC1099100088000X

Fig. 18 Crankshaft oil seal guide tool installation

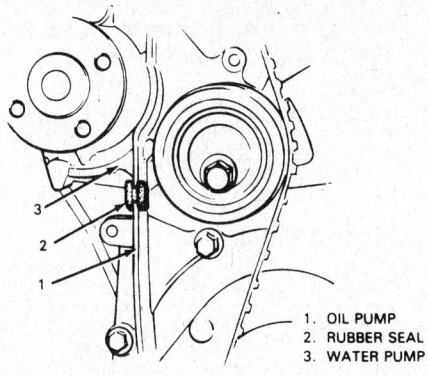

1. OIL PUMP
2. RUBBER SEAL
3. WATER PUMP

GC1099100090000X

Fig. 20 Rubber seal installation

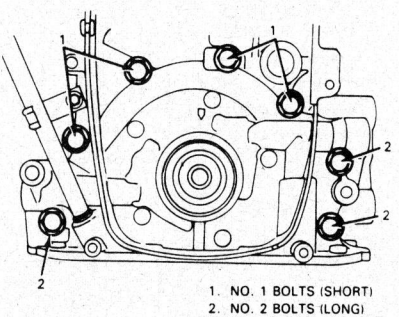

1. NO. 1 BOLTS (SHORT)
2. NO. 2 BOLTS (LONG)

GC1099100089000X

Fig. 19 Oil pump bolt location

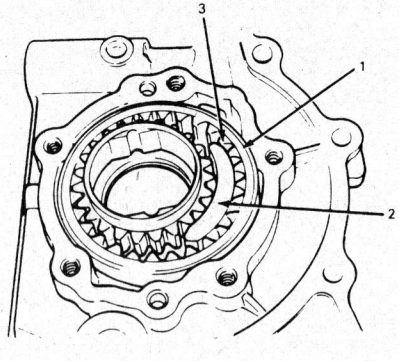

1. OUTER GAUGE
2. CRESCENT
3. CLEARANCE

GC1099100091000X

Fig. 21 Oil pump gear radial clearance inspect. Rotor type similar

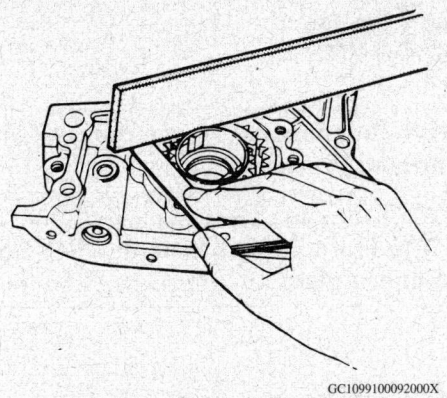

GC1099100092000X

Fig. 22 Oil pump gear side clearance inspect. Rotor type similar

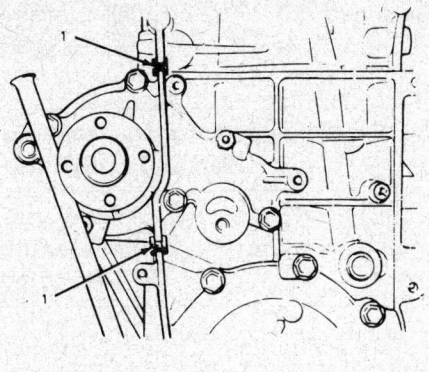

1. RUBBER SEAL

GC1099100093000X

Fig. 23 Rubber seal installation

TIGHTENING SPECIFICATIONS

Tightening specifications are for clean and lightly lubricated threads only. Dry or dirty threads produce increased friction which prevents accurate measurement of tightness.

Year	Component	Torque/Ft. Lbs.
2001	Alternator Mounting	17
	Camshaft Housing To Cylinder Head	97①
	Camshaft Sprocket	44
	Connecting Rod Cap Bolts	26
	Crankshaft Pulley	12
	Crankshaft Sprocket	94
	Cylinder Head	54
	Cylinder Head Cover	97①
	Exhaust Manifold To Cylinder Head	17
	Flywheel To Crankshaft	55
	Ignition Distributor To Cylinder Head	120①
	Intake Manifold To Cylinder Head	17
	Main Bearing Cap Bolts	40
	Oil Pan Drain Plug	26
	Oil Pan To Engine	97①
	Oil Pressure Switch	120①
	Oil Pump Pickup Tube	97①
	Oil Pump Rotor Plate	97①
	Oil Pump To Engine	97①
	Spark Plug	21
	Starter	17
	Timing Belt Cover	97①
	Timing Belt Tensioner Bolt	20
	Timing Belt Tensioner Stud	97①
	Water Pump To Engine	120①

① — Inch lbs.

1.3L Engine

NOTE: On Air Bag Equipped Models, Refer To "Air Bag System Precautions" Located In The Front Of This Manual For System Disarming & Arming Procedures.

NOTE: Refer To "Computer Relearn Procedures" Located In The Front Of This Manual When Battery Power To The Computer Has Been Interrupted.

INDEX

PRECAUTIONS

Air Bag Systems

Refer to "Air Bag System Precautions" in the front of this manual for system disarming and arming procedures.

Battery Ground Cable

Prior to service, disconnect battery ground cable and isolate as required.

Fuel System Pressure Relief

1. Loosen fuel filler cap to relieve fuel tank pressure.
2. Remove fuel pump relay from relay box located at lefthand front of engine compartment, next to battery.
3. Crank engine and allow to stall. Crank engine for several seconds more to ensure relief of any remaining fuel.
4. Remove battery ground cable.

COMPRESSION PRESSURE

1. Turn ignition switch to Lock position.
2. Clean debris from spark plug holes, as required, and remove spark plugs.
3. Disconnect ignition coils electrical connectors.
4. Install spark plug port adapter tool No. J-22794, or equivalent, and suitable compression gauge into spark plug hole.
5. **On models equipped with manual transaxle,** depress clutch and accelerator to floor.
6. **On all models,** crank engine and take four pressure readings, recording highest reading obtained.
7. Compression should increase quickly and evenly. Compression pressure at 250 RPM is 199 psi standard and 156 psi minimum. Maximum allowable pressure difference between any two cylinders at 250 RPM is 14 psi.
8. Repeat compression test procedure for remaining cylinders.
9. After completion, install FI fuse, spark plugs and distributor electrical connector.

ENGINE MOUNT
REPLACE
Lefthand

1. Remove engine mount nut, then raise and support vehicle.
2. Support engine using suitable engine support fixture.
3. Remove engine mount and frame bracket, then mount from bracket.
4. Reverse procedure to install.

Righthand

1. Remove engine mount nut, then raise and support vehicle.
2. Support engine using suitable engine support fixture.
3. Remove engine mount and frame bracket, then mount from bracket.
4. Reverse procedure to install.

Rear

1. Remove engine mount nut, then raise and support vehicle.
2. Remove nut mounting mount to body bracket.
3. Support engine using suitable engine support fixture.
4. Remove frame bracket and mount.
5. Reverse procedure to install.

Torque Rod

1. Remove engine mount nut, then raise and support vehicle.
2. Remove nut mounting mount to body bracket.
3. Support engine using suitable engine support fixture.
4. Remove frame bracket and mount.
5. Reverse procedure to install.

ENGINE
REPLACE

1. Remove both battery cables, battery and battery tray.
2. Drain cooling system into suitable container.
3. Remove hood.
4. Remove air cleaner.
5. Remove radiator with cooling fan.
6. Disconnect coolant temperature gauge sensor, throttle position sensor and EGR solenoid electrical connectors.

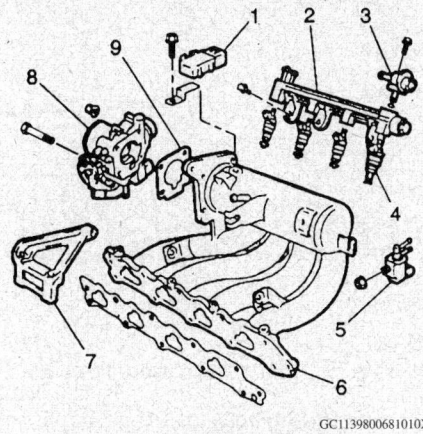

1. MAP SENSOR
2. FUEL RAIL
3. FUEL PRESSURE REGULATOR
4. FUEL INJECTOR
5. EVAP CANISTER PURGE VALVE
6. INTAKE MANIFOLD
7. BRACKET
8. THROTTLE BODY
9. THROTTLE BODY GASKET

GC1139800681010X

Fig. 1 Intake manifold replacement (Part 1 of 2)

7. Disconnect EGR bypass valve.
8. Disconnect idle speed control solenoid valve, oxygen sensor, fuel injector, MAP sensor and power steering pressure switch electrical connectors.
9. Disconnect intake manifold ground wires.
10. Disconnect oil pressure switch, alternator and air conditioning compressor connectors.
11. Disconnect starter solenoid connectors.
12. Disconnect backup lamp switch.
13. Disconnect direct clutch and second brake solenoids.
14. Release main engine harness from clamps.
15. Disconnect following vacuum hoses:
    a. Intake manifold front and rear canister purge.
    b. Canister pipe.
    c. Intake manifold pressure sensor.
    d. Intake manifold brake booster.
    e. Throttle body idle speed control.
16. Disconnect the following cables:
    a. Throttle body accelerator.
    b. Transaxle clutch.
    c. Transaxle shift select and throttle valve.
    d. Transaxle speedometer.
17. Remove inlet and outlet hoses.
18. Remove throttle body fuel return and feed hoses.
19. Install universal support fixture tool No. J-28467-A with engine support adapters tool No. J-28467-89, or equivalents.
20. Raise and support vehicle.
21. Disconnect exhaust system from exhaust manifold.
22. Remove front pipe/catalytic converter.
23. **On models equipped with manual transaxle,** remove gearshift control shaft and extension rod.
24. **On all models,** drain engine oil and transaxle fluid into suitable container.
25. Remove lefthand and righthand drive axles from transaxle as outlined in "Front Wheel Drive Axle" chapter. **It is not required to remove driveshafts from steering knuckles.**
26. Remove air conditioning compressor from compressor bracket. **Do not disconnect air conditioning hoses**

1. MAP SENSOR
2. FUEL RAIL
3. FUEL PRESSURE REGULATOR
4. FUEL INJECTOR
5. EVAP CANISTER PURGE VALVE
6. INTAKE MANIFOLD
7. BRACKET
8. THROTTLE BODY
9. THROTTLE BODY GASKET

GC1139800681020X

Fig. 1 Intake manifold replacement (Part 2 of 2)

from compressor.
27. Disconnect power steering pump hoses.
28. **On models equipped with automatic transaxle,** remove torque rod.
29. **On all models,** lower vehicle.
30. Remove tool Nos. J-28467-A and J-28467-89, or equivalents, and install suitable engine lifting device.
31. Remove lefthand transaxle mount, righthand side engine mount and rear engine mount.
32. Remove engine with transaxle.
33. Reverse procedure to install.

INTAKE MANIFOLD
REPLACE

1. Drain cooling system into suitable container.
2. Remove air cleaner.
3. Disconnect intake manifold ground wires.
4. Disconnect fuel injector, MAP sensor, TP sensor, IAC valve and EVAP canister purge valve electrical connectors, **Fig. 1.**
5. Disconnect wiring harness from retaining clamps.
6. Remove throttle body coolant hoses.
7. Remove intake manifold canister purge and brake booster hoses.
8. Remove throttle body accelerator cable.
9. Remove intake manifold mounting nuts and bolts.
10. Remove intake manifold with throttle body and wire clamps from cylinder head still attached.
11. Reverse procedure to install. Adjust accelerator cable freeplay as follows:
    a. Measure accelerator pedal free play with throttle closed, **Fig. 2.**
    b. If freeplay is not .08–.27 inch, loosen accelerator control cable locknut and turn accelerator control cable adjusting nut.
    c. Depress accelerator pedal to floor.
    d. Measure distance between throttle lever and throttle stop.
    e. If measure is not .02–.07 inch, adjust height of pedal stopper bolt.
    f. Operate accelerator control cable from inside of vehicle to ensure throttle movement is smooth and not binding.

EXHAUST MANIFOLD
REPLACE

1. Raise and support vehicle.
2. Disconnect catalytic converter from manifold and lower vehicle.
3. Disconnect oxygen sensor electrical connector and release wiring harness from clamps.
4. Remove heat shield and engine hanger.

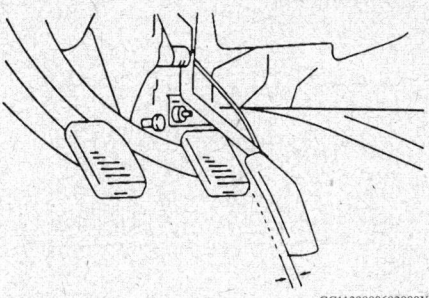

GC1139800682000X

Fig. 2 Accelerator pedal freeplay

5. Disconnect exhaust pipe from exhaust manifold.
6. Remove mounting bolts and nuts, then the exhaust manifold.
7. Reverse procedure to install. Install new gasket.

CYLINDER HEAD
REPLACE

1. Remove intake manifold as outlined in "Intake Manifold, Replace."
2. Raise and support vehicle.
3. Disconnect catalytic converter from manifold and lower vehicle.
4. Disconnect oxygen sensor electrical connector and release wiring harness from clamps.
5. Remove heat shield and engine hanger.
6. Disconnect exhaust pipe from exhaust manifold.
7. Remove mounting bolts and nuts, then the exhaust manifold.
8. Remove timing belt and belt tensioner as outlined in "Timing Belt, Replace."
9. Remove valve cover.
10. Loosen all valve lash adjusting screw locknuts.
11. Turn back valve lash adjusting screw until all valve are closed.
12. Remove head bolts in sequence, **Fig. 3.**
13. Remove cylinder head and discard gasket.
14. Reverse procedure to install, noting the following:
    a. Install cylinder head bolts loosely to secure cylinder head.
    b. **Torque** cylinder head bolts evenly and in small increments to 49 ft. lbs., in sequence, **Fig. 4.**
    c. Refill cooling system.

VALVE ARRANGEMENT
Front To Rear

1.3L.....................................I-E-I-E-I-E-I-E

VALVE ADJUSTMENT

1. Intake valve lash is .005–.007 inch, cold and .007–.009 hot; Exhaust valve lash is .009–.011 cold and .011–.013 hot.
2. Set No. 1 cylinder to top dead center on compression stroke.
3. Ensure camshaft is in proper phase.
4. Adjust valves 1, 2, 8 and 6, **Fig. 5.**
5. Rotate crankshaft 360.°
6. Adjust valves 3, 4, 7 and 5, **Fig. 5.**

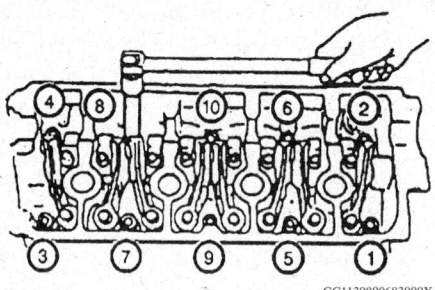

Fig. 3   Cylinder head loosening sequence

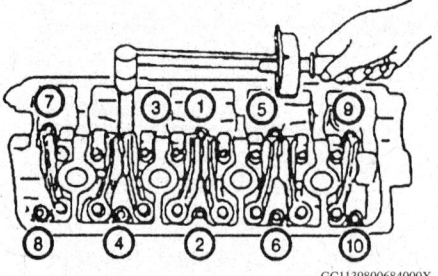

Fig. 4   Cylinder head tightening sequence

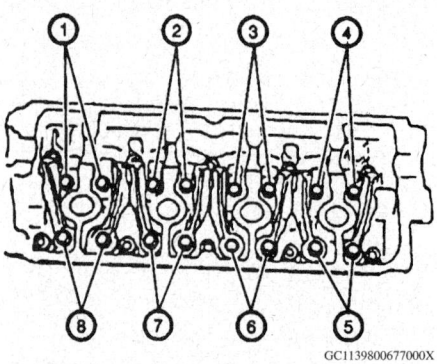

Fig. 5   Valve lash adjustment

VALVE GUIDES

Valves and valve guides are available in standard size only. The valve guide can be driven from cylinder bore using valve guide replacement tool No. J-34834, or equivalent. The valve guide should be driven from the combustion chamber side of the cylinder head out through the valve spring side.

The cylinder head valve guide bore should be reamed with .472 inch reamer tool No. 34831, or equivalent, prior to valve guide installation. Drive valve guide into heated cylinder head bore using valve guide replacement tool No. J-34834, or equivalent. Valve guide should be driven in until tool contacts cylinder head. Valve guide protrusion should be .55 inch from cylinder head surface. After installation, ream valve guide with .277 inch reamer tool No. J-34832, or equivalent.

TIMING BELT

REPLACE

Removal

1. Raise and support vehicle.
2. Remove crankshaft timing pulley.
3. Remove timing belt cover, **Fig. 6.**
4. Align upper and lower timing marks, **Figs. 7 and 8,** by turning crankshaft.
5. Remove tensioner and timing belt.

Inspection

1. Inspect radial clearance between outer gear/rotor and crescent, timing belt for wear and cracks and replace.
2. Inspect radial clearance between outer gear/rotor and crescent, timing belt tensioner for smoothness of rotation.
3. Replace as required.

Installation

1. Position lug on tensioner plate to hole in tensioner, **Fig. 9.**
2. Position tensioner and tensioner plate to engine, then install and hand tighten mounting bolt. Ensure tensioner and tensioner plate move in same direction, **Fig. 10.** If movement is not as indicated, remove tensioner and reinsert tensioner plate lug into tensioner.
3. Ensure camshaft and crankshaft timing marks are aligned.
4. Remove cylinder head cover and com-

pletely loosen all valve adjusting screws on intake and exhaust rocker arms. This will permit free rotation of camshaft and prevent damage to valves during timing belt adjustment.
5. With tensioner plate pushed upward, install timing belt over camshaft and crankshaft pulleys. **Arrow on timing belt should face toward direction of crankshaft rotation. When installing timing belt, keep drive side of belt free of slack.**
6. Install tensioner spring and damper, then hand tighten tensioner stud.
7. Rotate crankshaft two revolutions clockwise direction to remove slack from belt. **Ensure slack is removed from drive belt, and camshaft and crankshaft timing marks are aligned.**
8. Tighten tensioner stud and bolt.
9. Install timing belt outer cover and crankshaft pulley. **Ensure seal is between oil pump housing and water pump.**
10. Adjust valve lash, install cylinder head cover and lower vehicle.

CAMSHAFT

REPLACE

Removal

1. Remove valve cover as outlined in "Valve Cover, Replace."
2. Remove timing belt and timing belt tensioner as outlined in "Timing Belt, Replace."
3. Remove mounting bolt and camshaft timing sprocket.
4. Disconnect cam sensor electrical connector.
5. Disconnect spark plug wires and ignition coil electrical connectors.
6. Remove ignition coils.
7. Remove cam sensor.
8. Loosen all valve adjusting screw lock nuts, back off adjusting screws to allow rocker arms to move freely.
9. Gradually remove camshaft housing bolts in sequence, **Fig. 11.**

Installation

1. Apply clean engine oil to camshaft, journals and oil seal.
2. Install camshaft to cylinder head.
3. Apply clean engine oil to housing bolts

and **torque** bolts to 96 inch lbs., in sequence, **Fig. 12.**
4. Install camshaft timing sprocket to camshaft.
5. Ensure pin on camshaft fits slot on sprocket.
6. **Torque** camshaft timing sprocket to 43 ft. lbs.
7. Perform valve lash adjustment as outlined in "Valve Adjustment."
8. Connect cam sensor connector, spark plug wires and ignition coil assemblies.
9. Install timing belt as outlined in "Timing Belt, Replace."
10. Install valve cover.

PISTON & ROD ASSEMBLY

Refer to **Fig. 13,** when assembling piston and connecting rod. When installing piston and connecting rod, arrow on piston head should face front of engine and oil hole in connecting rod should face intake manifold. When installing connecting rod cap, arrow on cap should face front of engine.

Measure rod bearing side clearance using feeler gauge. Connecting rod bearing side clearance should be .0039 to .0078 inch.

PISTONS, PINS & RINGS

Pistons and rings are available in standard size and oversizes of .0098 and .0197 inch. Piston pins are supplied with pistons in matched sets.

MAIN & ROD BEARINGS

Main and rod bearings are available in standard size and under size of .010 inch.

CRANKSHAFT REAR OIL SEAL

REPLACE

1. Remove transaxle as outlined in **MOTOR's "Domestic Transmission, In Vehicle Service."**
2. **On models equipped with manual transaxle,** remove pressure plate and clutch disc.

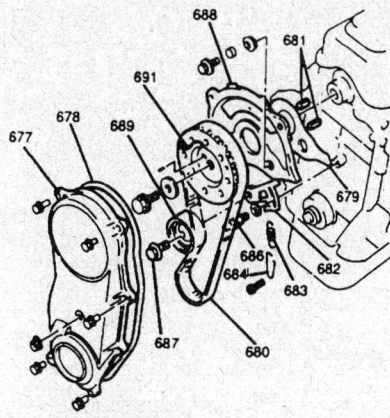

677 TIMING BELT COVER
678 OUTER TIMING BELT COVER GASKET
679 TIMING BELT INNER SEAL
680 TIMING BELT
681 SEAL
682 TENSIONER PLATE
683 TENSIONER SPRING
684 SPRING DAMPER
686 TENSIONER STUD
687 TENSIONER BOLT
688 TIMING BELT INNER COVER
689 TIMING BELT TENSIONER
691 CAMSHAFT TIMING GEAR SPROCKET

GC1069500587000X

Fig. 6   Timing belt assembly

3. **On all models,** mark flywheel to engine position and remove flywheel.
4. Remove oil pan as outlined in "Oil Pan, Replace."
5. Remove seal retainer and seal from retainer.
6. Reverse procedure to install, ensuring to install new seal.

OIL PAN
REPLACE

1. Raise and support vehicle.
2. Drain engine oil into suitable container.
3. Remove front pipe/catalytic converter from exhaust manifold and resonator/center pipe.
4. Remove crankshaft position sensor.
5. Remove mounting bolts and nuts and engine oil pan.
6. Reverse procedure to install, noting the following:
   a. Apply continuous bead of silicone P/N 12346240, or equivalent, to engine oil pan mating surface.
   b. **Torque** engine oil pan nuts and bolts to 96 inch lbs.
   c. **Torque** engine oil drain plug to 26 ft. lbs.
   d. Install new front pipe/catalytic converter seal.

OIL PUMP
REPLACE
Removal

1. Remove timing belt as outlined in "Timing Belt, Replace."
2. Raise and support vehicle.

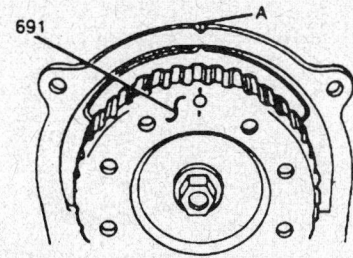

A   "V" MARK
691   CAMSHAFT TIMING GEAR SPROCKET

GC1069500588000X

Fig. 7   Camshaft timing mark

3. Drain engine oil into suitable container.
4. Remove front pipe/catalytic converter from exhaust manifold and resonator/center pipe.
5. Remove crankshaft position sensor.
6. Remove mounting bolts and nuts and engine oil pan.
7. Remove crankshaft timing belt sprocket.
8. Remove alternator mounting bracket, as required.
9. Remove air conditioning compressor mounting bracket, if equipped.
10. Remove alternator adjusting bolt and upper cover bolt, as required.
11. Remove oil pump bolts and pump, **Fig. 14.**

Installation

1. Install oil pump pins and gasket on engine block.
2. Install oil seal guide tool No. J-34853, or equivalent, onto crankshaft to prevent damage to oil seal lip, **Fig. 15.** Apply engine oil to special tool.
3. Install oil pump onto crankshaft and engine block.
4. Install mounting bolts and tighten. No. 1 bolts are shorter than No. 2 bolts, **Fig. 16.**
5. Ensure oil seal lip is not twisted and remove tool.
6. Install rubber seal between oil pump and water pump, **Fig. 17.**
7. Trim oil pump seal edges flush with oil pan mating surface, as required.
8. Install timing belt guide, key and crankshaft timing sprocket. Timing belt guide must be installed so curved side faces oil pump.
9. Install timing belt and tensioner components.
10. Adjust water pump belt tension.
11. Fill crankcase.
12. Run engine and ensure oil pressure is correct.

OIL PUMP SERVICE

1. Drain oil into suitable container and remove dipstick tube from oil pump.
2. Remove rotor plate.
3. Remove outer and inner rotors.
4. Inspect oil seal lip for damage. Replace as required
5. Inspect outer and inner rotors, rotor plate and oil pump case for excessive wear or damage.

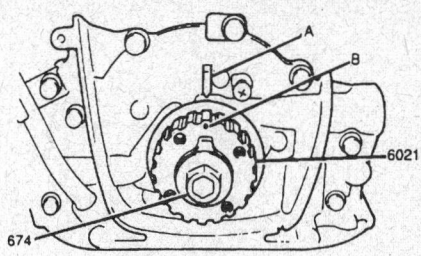

A   ARROW MARK ON OIL PUMP CASE
B   PUNCH MARK ON CRANKSHAFT TIMING GEAR
674   CRANKSHAFT PULLEY TIMING GEAR BOLT
6021   CRANKSHAFT TIMING GEAR

GC1069500601000X

Fig. 8   Crankshaft timing mark

6. Inspect radial clearance between outer gear/rotor and crescent, radial clearance between outer rotor and crescent, **Fig. 18.** If clearance is more than .0122 inch, replace outer rotor.
7. Measure side clearance which should not exceed .0059 inch sing straightedge and feeler gauge, **Fig. 19.**
8. Wash, clean and dry all oil pump components.
9. Apply light coat of engine oil to inner and outer rotors, oil seal lip portion and inside surfaces of oil pump case and plate.
10. Install outer and inner rotors in pump case.
11. Install rotor plate and tighten screws. Ensure gears turn smoothly by hand.
12. Install O-ring in pump case and dipstick tube.

BELT TENSION DATA

Belt	Belt Deflection Inch①
Air Conditioning Compressor & Power Steering Pump	.28–.35
Water Pump & Alternator	.25–.32

① — With 22 lbs. pressure applied.

COOLING SYSTEM BLEED

These engines do not require a specific bleed procedure. After filling cooling system, run engine to operating temperature with radiator pressure cap off. Air will then be automatically bled through cap opening.

THERMOSTAT
REPLACE

1. Drain cooling system into suitable container.
2. Remove radiator inlet hose at thermostat housing.
3. Remove thermostat housing and thermostat.
4. Clean both gasket surfaces thoroughly.
5. Reverse procedure to install, ensuring to use new gasket.

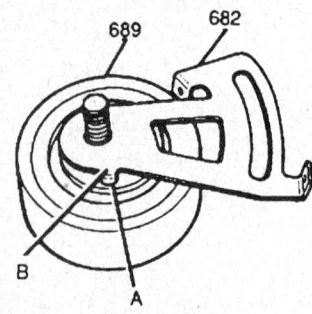

A TIMING BELT TENSIONER HOLE
B TENSIONER PLATE LUG
682 TENSIONER PLATE
689 TIMING BELT TENSIONER

GC1069500590000X

Fig. 9 Timing belt tensioner

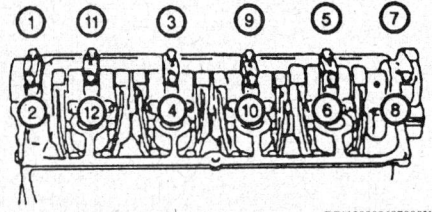

GC1139800687000X

Fig. 12 Camshaft housing bolts tightening sequence

WATER PUMP
REPLACE

Removal

1. Drain cooling system into suitable container.
2. Remove air cleaner.
3. **On models equipped with air conditioning,** remove compressor suction pipe bracket.
4. **On all models,** loosen, but do not remove, water pump bolts.
5. Raise and properly support vehicle.
6. Remove righthand lower splash shield.
7. **On models equipped with air conditioning,** remove compressor drive belt.
8. **On all models,** remove lower alternator cover plate, loosen alternator adjusting bolt and remove water pump/alternator drive belt.
9. Remove crankshaft pulley and water pump pulley.
10. Remove timing belt as outlined in "Timing Belt, Replace."
11. Remove dipstick tube.
12. Remove upper alternator adjusting bracket.
13. Remove rubber seals, **Fig. 20.**
14. Remove water pump mounting bolts,

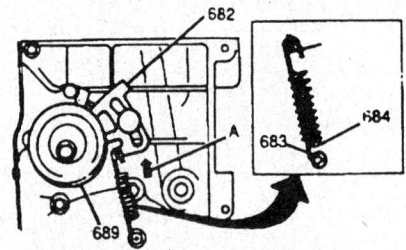

A DIRECTION OF TENSIONER MOVEMENT
682 TENSIONER PLATE
683 TENSIONER SPRING
684 SPRING DAMPER
689 TIMING BELT TENSIONER

GC1069500591000X

Fig. 10 Tensioner adjustment

nuts and water pump.

Installation

1. Install water pump on engine block, ensuring to use new gasket.
2. Install rubber seals between water pump and oil pump and between water pump and cylinder head,
3. Install upper alternator adjusting bracket to water pump.
4. Install dipstick tube.
5. Install timing belt.
6. Install and hand tighten water pump pulley.
7. Install crankshaft pulley.
8. Install water pump/alternator drive belt and lower alternator cover plate.
9. **On models equipped with air conditioning,** install compressor drive belt.
10. **On all models,** install righthand lower splash shield.
11. Lower vehicle.
12. **On models equipped with air conditioning,** install compressor suction pipe bracket.
13. **On all models,** tighten upper alternator adjustment bolt.
14. Tighten water pump/alternator drive belt.
15. Fill cooling system.

RADIATOR
REPLACE

1. Drain cooling system into suitable container.
2. Remove radiator upper, lower and overflow hoses.
3. Disconnect cooling fan electrical connector.
4. **On models with automatic transaxle,** disconnect transaxle cooling lines from bottom of radiator.
5. **On all models,** remove mounting bolts and radiator/fan.
6. Reverse procedure to install.

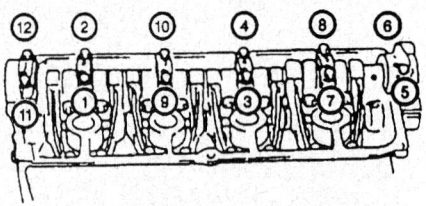

GC1139800686000X

Fig. 11 Camshaft housing bolt removal sequence

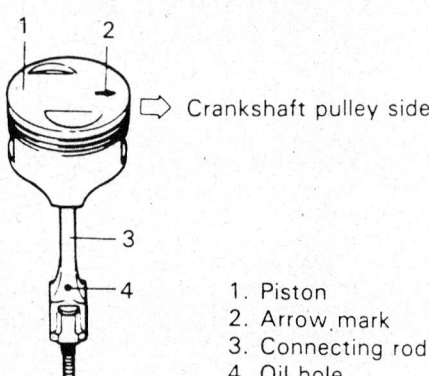

1. Piston
2. Arrow mark
3. Connecting rod
4. Oil hole

GC1069500595000X

Fig. 13 Piston & connecting rod assembly

FUEL PUMP
REPLACE

1. Remove rear seat cushion, disconnect fuel pump and sending unit electrical connections, then push harness through floor pan grommet.
2. Drain fuel tank into suitable container, then raise and support vehicle.
3. Remove muffler and exhaust pipe.
4. Remove fuel filler neck hose, fuel breather hose and EVAP canister air inlet hose.
5. Remove parking brake cable and position aside.
6. Remove EVAP canister vapor hose and fuel feed and return hoses at fuel tank and pump.
7. Remove mounting bolts and lower fuel tank.
8. Disconnect fuel sender electrical connections and vapor hoses, then the fuel feed and return lines.
9. Remove fuel sender.
10. Separate fuel pump from fuel sender, as required.
11. Reverse procedure to install.

FUEL FILTER
REPLACE

The fuel filter is a component of the fuel sender located in the fuel tank. The fuel sender must be removed in order to replace fuel sender subassembly that contains fuel filter as outlined in "Fuel Pump, Replace."

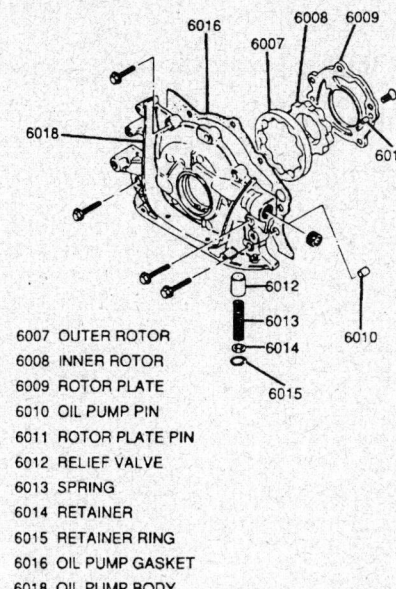

6007 OUTER ROTOR
6008 INNER ROTOR
6009 ROTOR PLATE
6010 OIL PUMP PIN
6011 ROTOR PLATE PIN
6012 RELIEF VALVE
6013 SPRING
6014 RETAINER
6015 RETAINER RING
6016 OIL PUMP GASKET
6018 OIL PUMP BODY

GC1099500107000X

Fig. 14 Rotor type oil pump

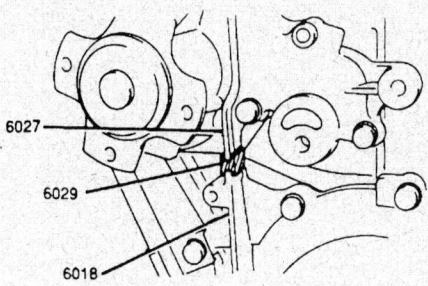

6018 OIL PUMP BODY
6027 COOLANT PUMP
6029 RUBBER SEAL

GC1099500110000X

Fig. 17 Seal installation

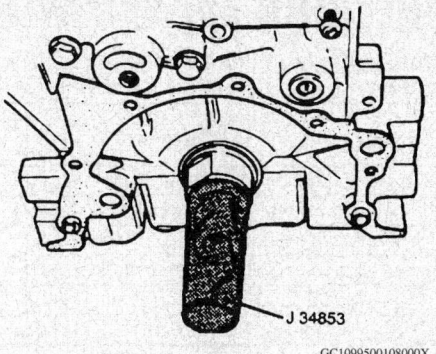

J 34853

GC1099500108000X

**Fig. 15 Crankshaft oil seal guide
tool**

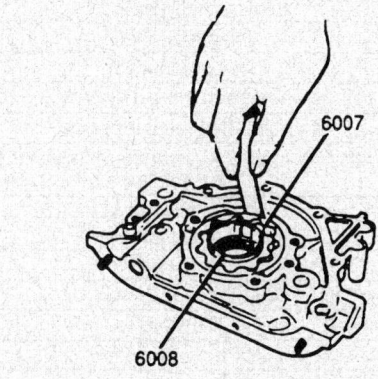

6007 OUTER ROTOR
6008 INNER ROTOR

GC1099500111000X

**Fig. 18 Rotor radial clearance
inspection**

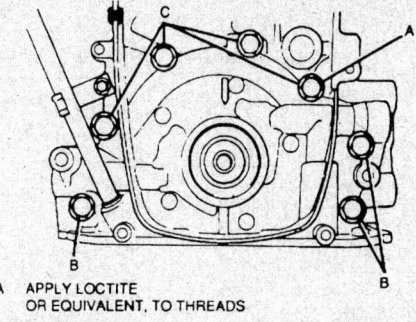

A   APPLY LOCTITE
     OR EQUIVALENT, TO THREADS
B   SHORT BOLTS
C   LONG BOLTS

GC1099500109000X

Fig. 16 Oil pump bolt location

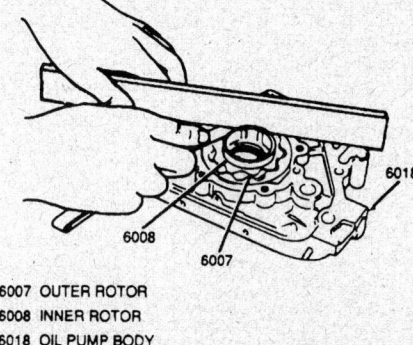

6007 OUTER ROTOR
6008 INNER ROTOR
6018 OIL PUMP BODY

GC1099500112000X

**Fig. 19 Rotor side clearance
inspection**

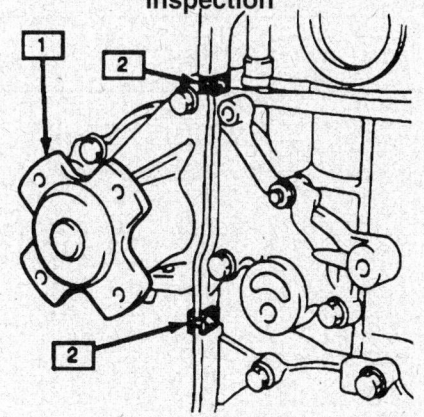

1 COOLANT PUMP
2 RUBBER SEALS

GC1089500243000X

Fig. 20 Water pump rubber seals

TIGHTENING SPECIFICATIONS

Tightening specifications are for clean and lightly lubricated threads only. Dry or dirty threads produce increased friction which prevents accurate measurement of tightness.

Year	Component	Torque/Ft. Lbs.
2001	Air Cleaner To Cylinder Head	89①
	Camshaft Timing Sprocket	43
	Connecting Bracket To Rear Mount	41
	Connecting Rod Bearing Cap	26
	Coolant Pump Pulley	97①
	Coolant Return Pipe	15
	Crankshaft Timing Pulley	12
	Crankshaft Timing Sprocket	94
	Cylinder Head To Engine Block	49
	Engine Oil Drain Plug	26
	Engine Oil Pan	97①
	Exhaust Manifold	17
	Flywheel (Automatic Transaxle)	69
	Flywheel (Manual Transaxle)	57
	Front Pipe/Catalytic Converter (To Exhaust Manifold)	37
	Front Pipe/Catalytic Converter (To Resonator/Center Pipe)	26
	Main Bearing Cap	40
	Oil Pressure Switch	10
	Oil Pump	97①
	Oil Pump Strainer	97①
	Rear Main Seal Housing	97①
	Rocker Arm Shaft	97①
	Timing Belt Cover	97①
	Timing Belt Tensioner	18
	Timing Belt Tensioner	97①
	Torque Rod Bracket	41

① — Inch lbs.

Rear Axle & Suspension

NOTE: On Air Bag Equipped Models, Refer To "Air Bag System Precautions" Located In The Front Of This Manual For System Disarming & Arming Procedures.

NOTE: Refer To "Computer Relearn Procedures" Located In The Front Of This Manual When Battery Power To The Computer Has Been Interrupted.

INDEX

PRECAUTIONS

Air Bag Systems

Refer to "Air Bag System Precautions" in the front of this manual for system disarming and arming procedures.

Battery Ground Cable

Prior to service, disconnect battery ground cable and isolate as required.

HUB & BEARING

REPLACE

1. Raise and support rear of vehicle, then remove wheel.
2. Remove wheel bearing dust cap from brake drum.
3. Unstake wheel bearing nut using suitable chisel, then remove wheel bearing nut and washer .
4. Loosen parking brake cable adjusting nuts, then remove plug from backing plate and back off drum brake adjustment.
5. Remove brake drum using suitable puller, .
6. Remove wheel bearings from brake drum using suitable brass drift.
7. Reverse procedure to install, noting the following:
   a. Fill Hub cavity (A) with lithium wheel bearing grease, **Fig. 1.**
   b. Install wheel bearings and spacer using bearing and hub installer tool Nos. J-7079-2 and J-34842, or equivalents, with sealed side facing outward, **Fig. 1.**
   c. Install brake drum on spindle.
   d. Tighten wheel bearing nut to specifications, then stake nut in position.
   e. After completing installation, adjust drum brake and parking brake.
   f. Bleed and inspect brake system for proper operation.

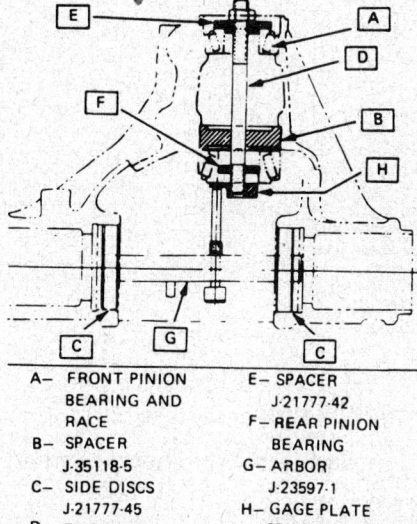

A— FRONT PINION BEARING AND RACE
B— SPACER J-35118-5
C— SIDE DISCS J-21777-45
D— THRU BOLT J-21777-43
E— SPACER J-21777-42
F— REAR PINION BEARING
G— ARBOR J-23597-1
H— GAGE PLATE 35118-2

GC3039100227000X

Fig. 1   Wheel bearing installation

STRUT

REPLACE

1. **On two-door models,** open hatchback for access to upper strut mounting.
2. **On four-door models,** open trunk for access to upper strut mounting.
3. **On all models,** raise and support rear of vehicle, then remove wheel.
4. Support suspension using suitable jack.
5. Remove strut upper support nuts and push downward on strut, **Fig. 2.**
6. Remove strut lower mounting bolt, **Fig. 3.**
7. Separate strut from rear suspension knuckle by compressing strut. **If strut is difficult to remove, open slit on knuckle just enough to allow strut removal.**

8. Reverse procedure to install. When installing strut, align projection on strut with slit on rear suspension knuckle, **Fig. 4.**

COIL SPRING

REPLACE

1. Raise and support rear of vehicle, then remove wheel.
2. Place alignment marks on control rod and control rod washer (A), **Fig. 5,** for setting toe during installation.
3. Remove control rod to body mounting bolt and separate control rod from bracket.
4. Remove nut from rear suspension knuckle stud and disconnect control rod from wheel side of control rod.
5. Loosen, but do not remove suspension arm rear mounting nut.
6. Loosen rear suspension knuckle lower mounting nut.
7. Position suitable jack under suspension arm and remove knuckle lower mounting nut.
8. Raise lower arm slightly to allow removal of rear suspension knuckle lower mounting bolt.
9. Disengage rear suspension knuckle from suspension arm, lower suspension arm and remove coil spring, **Fig. 6.**
10. Remove remaining suspension arm mounting bolts and nuts and remove suspension arm, as required.
11. Reverse procedure to install. When installing spring, position spring end to stepped portion of suspension arm, **Fig. 7.** When installing control rod to body bracket, align marks made on washer and control rod during removal. **Do not tighten control rod or suspension arm mounting nuts and bolts until after vehicle has been lowered.**

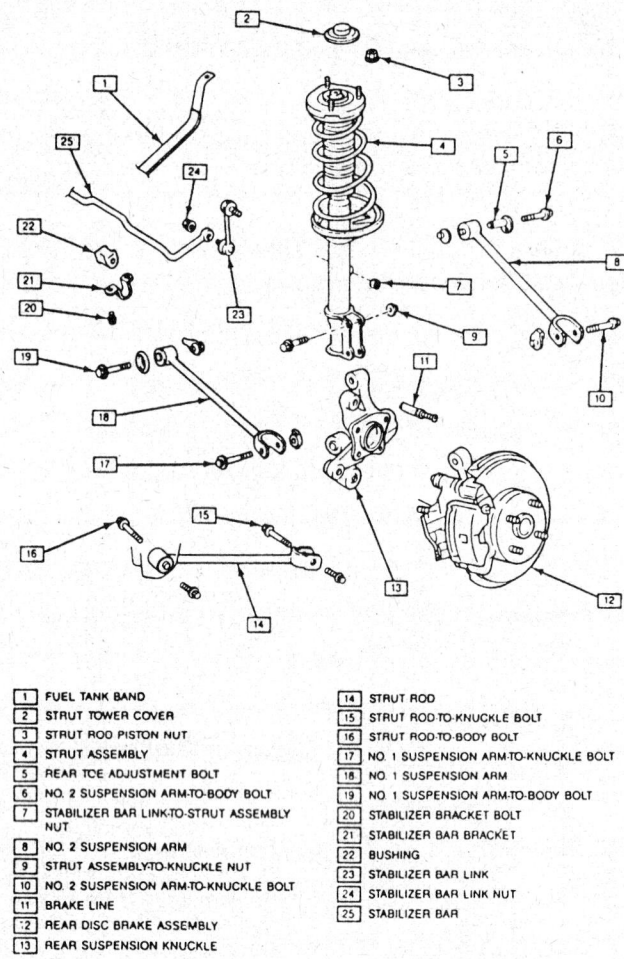

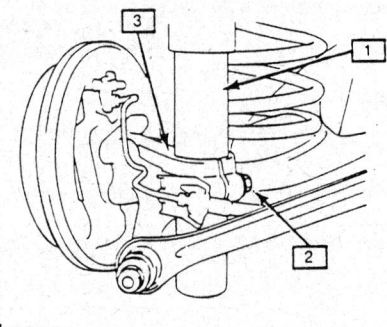

1	STRUT
2	MOUNT BOLT
3	KNUCKLE

GC2039100087000X

Fig. 3 Strut lower mounting bolt

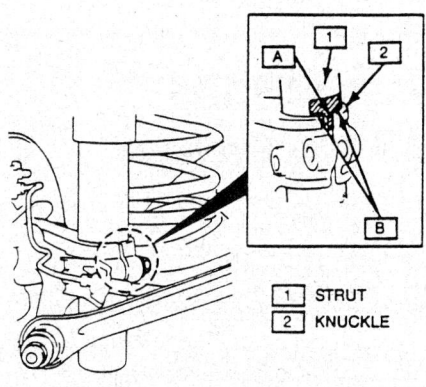

| 1 | STRUT |
| 2 | KNUCKLE |

GC2039100088000X

Fig. 4 Strut to rear suspension knuckle position

1	FUEL TANK BAND	14	STRUT ROD
2	STRUT TOWER COVER	15	STRUT ROD-TO-KNUCKLE BOLT
3	STRUT ROD PISTON NUT	16	STRUT ROD-TO-BODY BOLT
4	STRUT ASSEMBLY	17	NO. 1 SUSPENSION ARM-TO-KNUCKLE BOLT
5	REAR TOE ADJUSTMENT BOLT	18	NO. 1 SUSPENSION ARM
6	NO. 2 SUSPENSION ARM-TO-BODY BOLT	19	NO. 1 SUSPENSION ARM-TO-BODY BOLT
7	STABILIZER BAR LINK-TO-STRUT ASSEMBLY NUT	20	STABILIZER BRACKET BOLT
8	NO. 2 SUSPENSION ARM	21	STABILIZER BAR BRACKET
9	STRUT ASSEMBLY-TO-KNUCKLE NUT	22	BUSHING
10	NO. 2 SUSPENSION ARM-TO-KNUCKLE BOLT	23	STABILIZER BAR LINK
11	BRAKE LINE	24	STABILIZER BAR LINK NUT
12	REAR DISC BRAKE ASSEMBLY	25	STABILIZER BAR
13	REAR SUSPENSION KNUCKLE		

GC2039100086000X

Fig. 2 Strut upper mounting nuts

CONTROL ARM
REPLACE

1. Raise and support rear of vehicle, then remove wheel.
2. Remove E-ring and detach brake hose from control rod.
3. Place alignment marks on control rod and control rod washer at body bracket for setting toe during installation, **Fig. 5.**
4. Remove control rod to rear suspension knuckle mounting nut, **Fig. 8.**
5. Remove bracket mounting bolt and control rod.
6. Reverse procedure to install, noting the following:
   a. Position control rod to vehicle, **Fig. 9.**
   b. When installing control rod to body bracket, align marks made on washer and control rod during removal.
   c. **Do not tighten control rod mounting nuts and bolts until after vehicle has been lowered.**

KNUCKLE
REPLACE

1. Raise and support rear of vehicle, then remove wheel.
2. Remove brake drum and disconnect brake hose from rear suspension knuckle bracket.
3. Disconnect brake line from wheel cylinder. Cap brake line and wheel cylinder fitting bore.
4. Remove mounting bolts and brake backing plate.
5. Position suitable jack under suspension arm.
6. Place alignment marks on control rod and control rod washer at body bracket for setting toe during installation.
7. Remove control rod to body bracket mounting nut and washer.
8. Remove knuckle stud nut and control rod.
9. Remove strut to rear suspension knuckle mounting bolt.

10. Remove strut to suspension arm mounting bolt and separate rear suspension knuckle from suspension arm and strut. **If strut is difficult to remove, open slit on knuckle just enough to allow strut removal.**
11. Reverse procedure to install, noting the following:
    a. When installing control rod to body bracket, align marks made on washer and control rod during removal.
    b. Do not tighten control rod or suspension arm mounting nuts and bolts until after vehicle has been lowered.
    c. Prior to installation, apply sealer to mating surface of brake backing plate and rear suspension knuckle.
    d. When installing brake drum, tighten wheel bearing nut to specification and stake nut in place using suitable chisel.
    e. After completing installation, adjust and bleed brake system, then inspect for proper brake operation before moving vehicle.

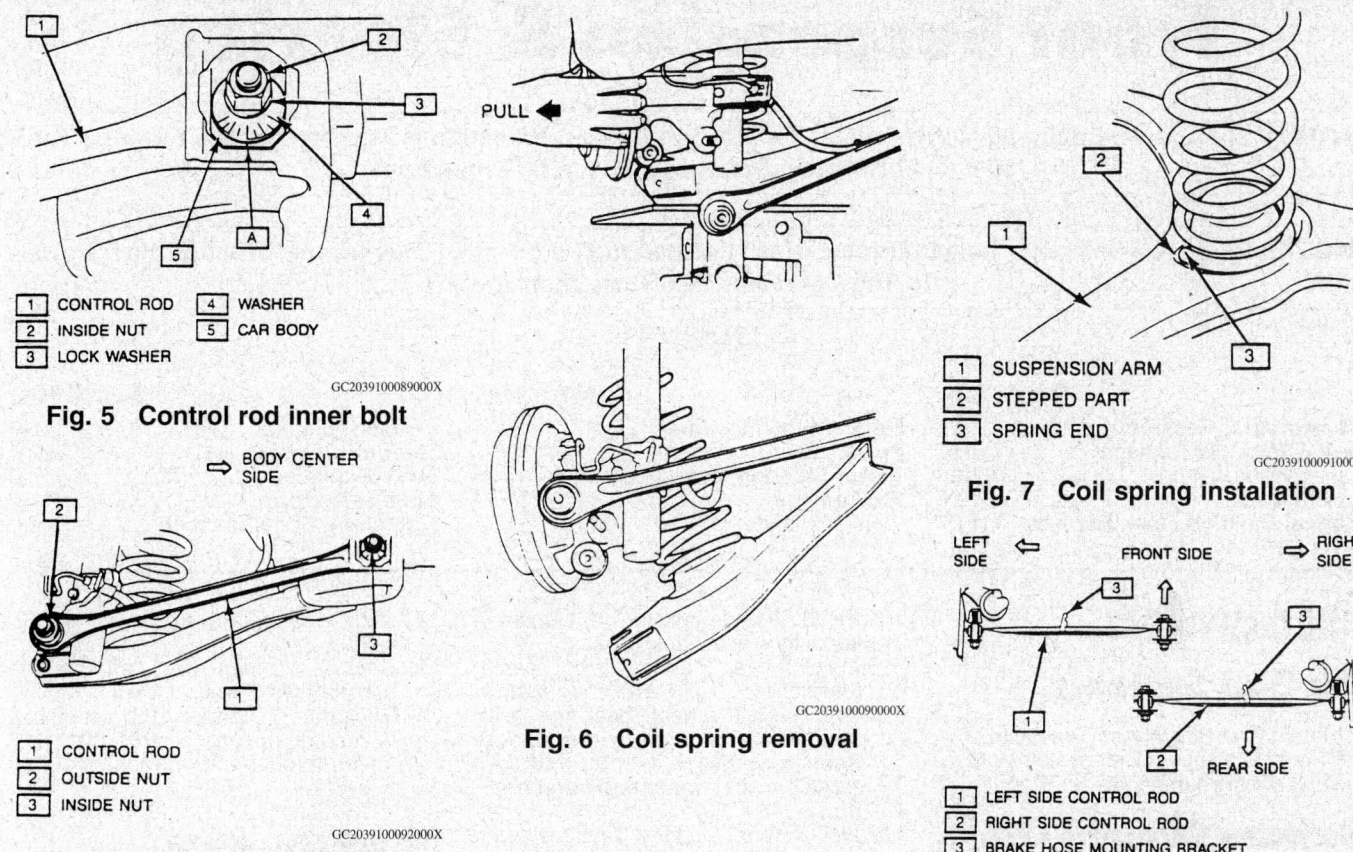

Fig. 5   Control rod inner bolt

1	CONTROL ROD	4	WASHER
2	INSIDE NUT	5	CAR BODY
3	LOCK WASHER		

GC2039100089000X

1	CONTROL ROD
2	OUTSIDE NUT
3	INSIDE NUT

GC2039100092000X

Fig. 8   Control arm installation

GC2039100090000X

Fig. 6   Coil spring removal

1	SUSPENSION ARM
2	STEPPED PART
3	SPRING END

GC2039100091000X

Fig. 7   Coil spring installation

1	LEFT SIDE CONTROL ROD
2	RIGHT SIDE CONTROL ROD
3	BRAKE HOSE MOUNTING BRACKET

GC2039100093000X

Fig. 9   Control arm installation

TIGHTENING SPECIFICATIONS

Year	Component	Torque/Ft. Lbs.
2001	Brake Backing Plate	17
	Brake Line Bracket	17
	Brake Line Fitting To Wheel Cylinder	12
	Control Rod	59
	Rear Suspension Knuckle Arm Lower	27
	Spindle Nut	②
	Stabilizer Bar	19
	Stabilizer Link To Bar	38
	Stabilizer Link To Control Arm	19
	Strut Lower	44
	Strut Support	24
	Strut Upper	37
	Suspension Arm Front Mounting	33
	Suspension Arm To Knuckle	37
	Suspension Arm Rear	27
	Wheel Bearing	74①
	Wheel Lug Nuts	44

① — Tighten nut and stake in position.
② — Revised by Technical Service Bulletin: models less ABS, 74 ft. lbs.; models w/ABS, 120 ft. lbs.

Front Suspension & Steering

NOTE: On Air Bag Equipped Models, Refer To "Air Bag System Precautions" Located In The Front Of This Manual For System Disarming & Arming Procedures.

NOTE: Refer To "Computer Relearn Procedures" Located In The Front Of This Manual When Battery Power To The Computer Has Been Interrupted.

INDEX

PRECAUTIONS

Air Bag Systems

Refer to "Air Bag System Precautions" in the front of this manual for system disarming and arming procedures.

Battery Ground Cable

Prior to service, disconnect battery ground cable and isolate as required.

HUB & BEARING

REPLACE

When inspecting wheel bearings, raise and support front of vehicle, then rotate wheel to inspect bearing for smoothness of rotation and noise. Also inspect wheel bearing endplay with a dial indicator. Wheel bearing endplay should not exceed .016 inch.

Removal

1. Raise and support vehicle, then remove front wheel.
2. Unstake and remove hub mounting nut.
3. Remove mounting bolts and caliper with brake line attached. Suspend caliper from chassis with suitable wire.
4. Measure dimension A for assembly, **Fig. 1.** Pull hub out of knuckle.
5. Disconnect tie rod end from knuckle with tie rod end remover tool No. J-21687-02, or equivalent.
6. Remove strut to knuckle bolts and ball joint stud pinch bolt, **Fig. 2.**
7. Remove knuckle.
8. Remove outer and inner bearing from knuckle using suitable drift.

Installation

1. Apply suitable grease to balls and oil seal lips of wheel bearings. Fill area A,

Fig. 3, to approximately 40 percent of capacity with suitable grease.
2. Install wheel bearings using bearing installer tool No. J-34856, or equivalent. **Install wheel bearings with sealed side facing outward. Ensure spacer is spacer is snug and centered between inner and outer bearings.**
3. Install wheel bearing seal (5) using seal installer tool No. J-34881, or equivalent, **Fig. 3.**
4. Install spacer on hub with bevel side first, **Fig. 4.**
5. Ensure wheel bearing spacer bore is aligned with bearing bores. If not, move spacer until aligned.
6. Tap hub lightly into knuckle using suitable plastic hammer. Ensure alignment is maintained.
7. Drive hub until dimension A is obtained using wheel hub installer tool No. J-34856 and handle tool No. J-7079-2, or equivalents.
8. Install brake caliper.
9. Tighten caliper bolts.
10. Tighten driveshaft castle.
11. Stake nut in position.
12. Install wheel and lower vehicle.

STRUT

REPLACE

1. Raise and support vehicle allowing front suspension to hang free.
2. Remove front wheel.
3. Remove E-clip from brake hose and disengage hose from strut bracket, **Fig. 5.**
4. Support lower control arm and knuckle, then remove strut to knuckle bolts.
5. Remove upper strut mount nuts and strut.
6. Reverse procedure to install.

STRUT SERVICE

1. Mount strut in suitable spring compressor.

2. Compress spring approximately ½ inch.
3. Remove nut from strut shaft, then the components, **Fig. 6.**
4. Reverse procedure to assemble. Compress spring so strut shaft protrudes through cap by approximately one inch.

CONTROL ARM

REPLACE

1. Raise and support vehicle, then remove wheel.
2. Remove ball joint stud to steering knuckle pinch bolt.
3. Remove control arm bracket nut and bracket bolts.
4. Remove control arm and bracket.
5. If control arm bushing is to be replaced, proceed as follows:
   a. Remove control arm.
   b. Press rear bushing from control arm.
   c. Cut flange off front bushing and press front bushing from control arm, **Fig. 7.**
   d. Apply soap and water to outer surface of front bushing, then press front bushing into control arm until centered.
   e. Position rear bushing to control arm and drive bushing into control arm, **Figs. 8 and 9.**
6. Reverse procedure to install.

POWER STEERING GEAR

REPLACE

1. Remove forward section of driver's side floor carpeting.
2. Remove steering shaft joint plastic cover, **Fig. 10.**
3. Loosen upper steering shaft joint bolt, **Fig. 11. Do not remove.**
4. Remove lower steering shaft joint bolt to separate shaft from pinion.
5. Raise and support vehicle.

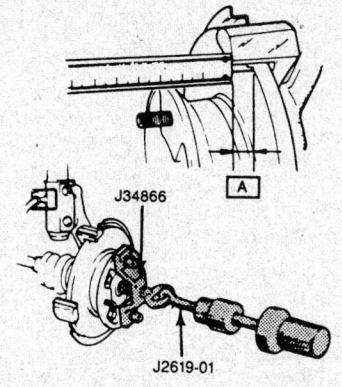

A NOTE DIMENSION "A" AS SHOWN BEFORE HUB REMOVAL AS AN AID IN INSTALLATION.

GC3039100228000X

Fig. 1   Hub installation inspection

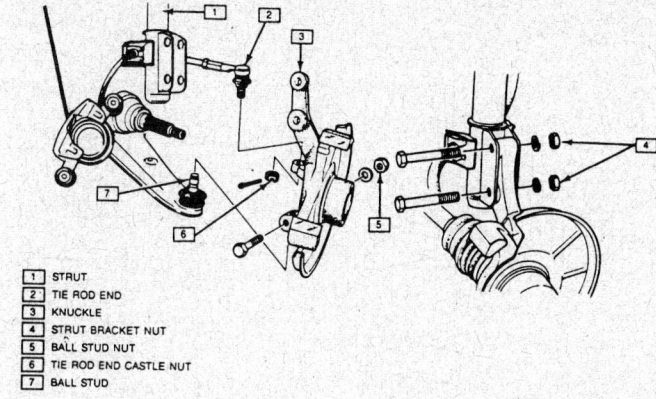

1	STRUT
2	TIE ROD END
3	KNUCKLE
4	STRUT BRACKET NUT
5	BALL STUD NUT
6	TIE ROD END CASTLE NUT
7	BALL STUD

GC2029100177000X

Fig. 2   Steering knuckle removal

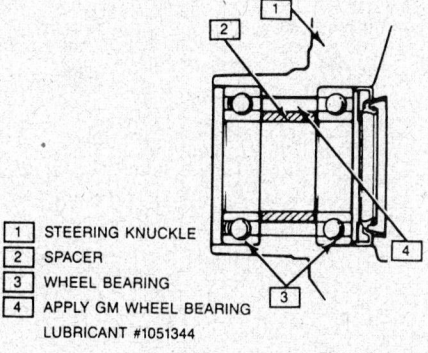

1	STEERING KNUCKLE
2	SPACER
3	WHEEL BEARING
4	APPLY GM WHEEL BEARING LUBRICANT #1051344

GC2029100178000X

Fig. 3   Steering knuckle hub bearings & seal

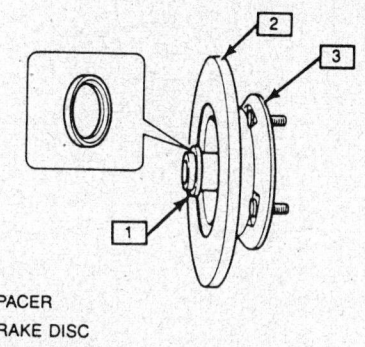

1	SPACER
2	BRAKE DISC
3	WHEEL HUB

GC2029100179000X

Fig. 4   Wheel hub spacer installation

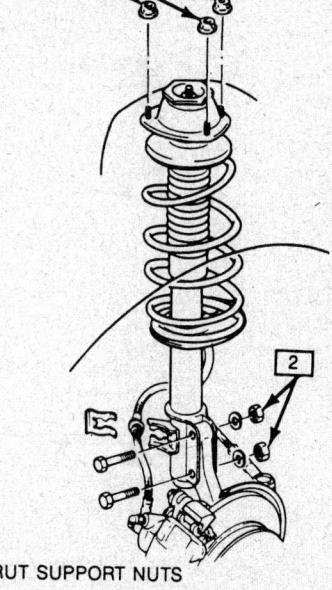

| 1 | STRUT SUPPORT NUTS |
| 2 | STRUT BRACKET BOLTS |

GC2029100184000X

Fig. 5   Strut mounting nut bolt locations

6. Remove both front wheels.
7. Remove cotter pin and castle nut from each tie rod end nut, **Fig. 12.**
8. Separate tie rod ends from lefthand and righthand steering knuckles using tie rod end remover tool No. J-21687-02, or equivalent, **Fig. 13.**
9. Remove front exhaust pipe assembly.
10. Remove shift linkage and extension rod from manual transaxle, if equipped.
11. Remove engine rear torque rod bracket from automatic transaxle, if equipped.
12. Remove steering gear outlet pipe, inlet pipe and cylinder pipe assemblies, **Fig. 14.**
13. Remove four mounting bolts from gear mounting brackets, **Fig. 15.**
14. Remove steering gear from vehicle as follows:
    a. Slide steering gear slightly to driver's side.
    b. Rotate steering gear counterclockwise so that pinion gear is between transaxle case and frame rail.
    c. Slide steering gear to passenger side until lefthand outer tie rod clears through frame opening.
    d. Lower steering gear on a 45 degree angle.
    e. Remove steering gear.
15. Reverse procedure to install.

MANUAL STEERING GEAR
REPLACE

1. Slide driver's seat rearward.
2. Pull back front of floor mat on driver's side and remove steering shaft joint cover.
3. Loosen steering shaft upper joint bolt without removing, **Fig. 16.**
4. Remove steering shaft lower joint bolt and disconnect lower joint from pinion.
5. Raise and properly support vehicle.
6. Remove front wheel and tire assemblies.
7. Remove cotter pins and castle nuts from tie rod ends.
8. Disconnect tie rods from knuckles using tie rod end remover tool No. J-21687-02, or equivalent.
9. Remove steering gear housing mounting bolts, brackets and steering gear, **Fig. 17.**
10. Reverse procedure to install.

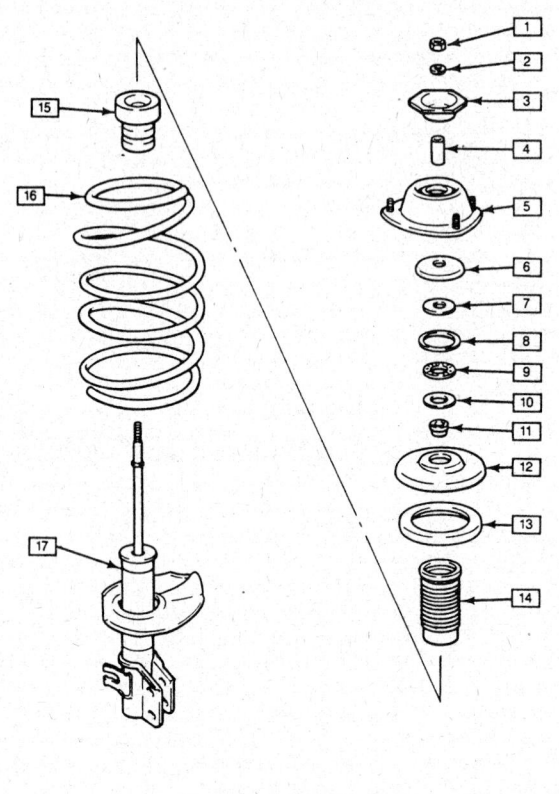

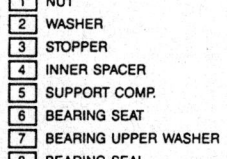

1	NUT
2	WASHER
3	STOPPER
4	INNER SPACER
5	SUPPORT COMP.
6	BEARING SEAT
7	BEARING UPPER WASHER
8	BEARING SEAL
9	BEARING
10	BEARING LOWER WASHER
11	BEARING SPACER
12	COIL SPRING UPPER SEAT
13	COIL SPRING SEAT
14	STRUT COVER
15	BUMP STOPPER
16	COIL SPRING
17	STRUT

GC2029100185000X

Fig. 6   Exploded view of strut

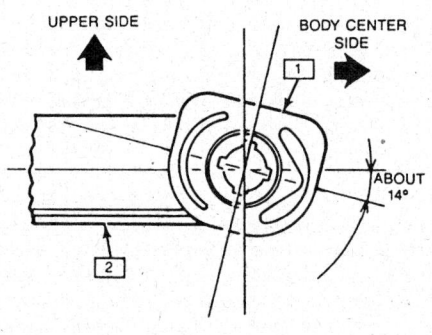

1	FRONT BUSHING
2	SUSPENSION ARM

GC2029100181000X

Fig. 7   Cutting flange from control arm front bushing

1	REAR BUSHING
2	SUSPENSION ARM

GC2029100182000X

Fig. 8   Rear bushing to control arm installation

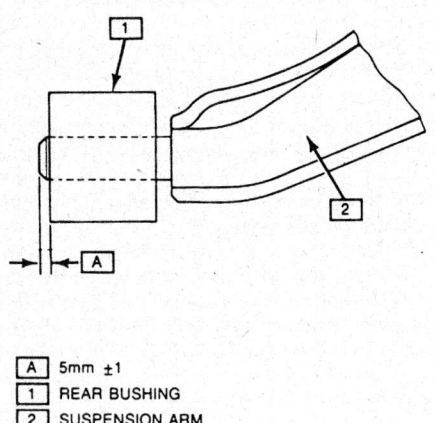

A	5mm ±1
1	REAR BUSHING
2	SUSPENSION ARM

GC2029100183000X

Fig. 9   Rear bushing positioning

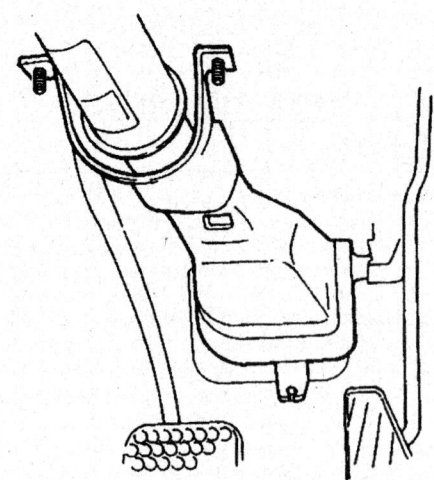

GC6020100471000X

Fig. 10   Steering shaft joint cover removal

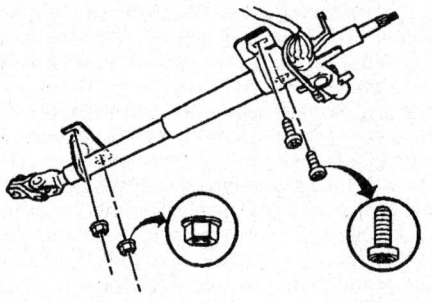

GC6020100472000X

Fig. 11   Upper steering shaft joint bolt

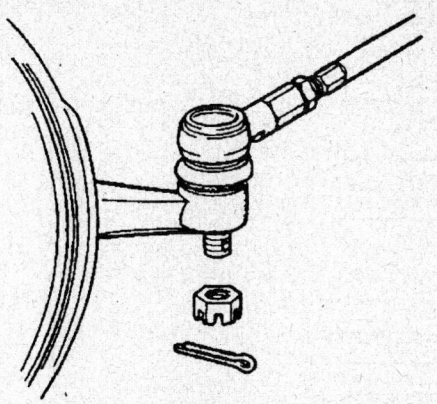

Fig. 12 Cotter pin & castle nut removal

GC6020100473000X

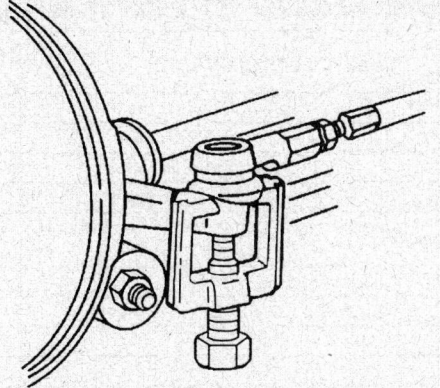

Fig. 13 Tie rod end remover tool No. J-21687-02 installation

GC6020100474000X

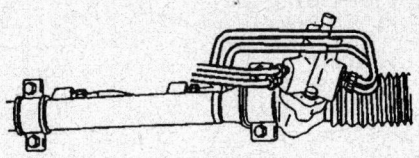

GC6020100475000X

Fig. 14 Steering gear component removal

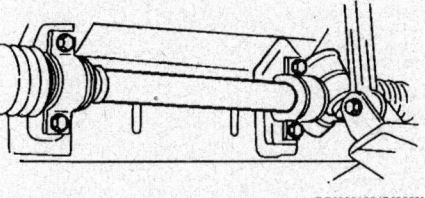

GC6020100476000X

Fig. 15 Gear mounting bracket bolt removal

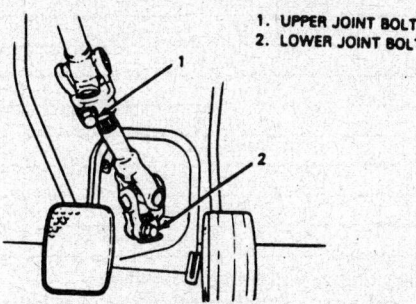

1. UPPER JOINT BOLT
2. LOWER JOINT BOLT

GC2029100186000X

Fig. 16 Steering shaft upper & lower joint bolts

1. CAR BODY
2. STEERING GEAR CASE
3. CASE MOUNT BOLT
4. PINION SIDE BRACKET
5. RACK SIDE BRACKET

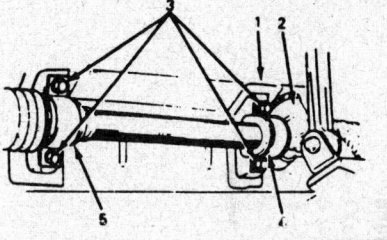

GC6039100051000X

Fig. 17 Steering gear mounting bolts & brackets

TIGHTENING SPECIFICATIONS

Year	Component	Torque/Ft. Lbs.
2001	Ball Joint Stud	44
	Brake Caliper To Knuckle	22
	Control Arm Front Bracket	66
	Control Arm Rear Bracket	32
	Cylinder Pipe Assembly Nuts To Steering Shaft	20
	Cylinder Pipe Assembly Nuts To Pump	13
	Front Control Arm Bracket	92
	Hub Bearing	129①
	Inlet & Outlet Pipes	29
	Stabilizer Bar Link	20
	Stabilizer Bar Mounting	20
	Steering Gear Mounting Bracket	18
	Steering Shaft Coupling	18
	Steering Shaft Joint Bolts	18
	Strut Bracket	59
	Strut Nut	37
	Strut Upper Mounting	21
	Tie Rod Ball	51
	Tie Rod End Castle	32
	Tie Rod End Locknut	32
	Wheel Lug Nuts	44

① — After tightening, stake nut in position.

Wheel Alignment

INDEX

DESCRIPTION

Wheel alignment, is the angular relationship between the wheels, suspension mounting components and ground. The angle of the knuckle away from the vertical, pointing in or out of wheels, tilt of the wheels from vertical (when viewed from front of vehicle) and tilt of suspension members from vertical (when viewed from side of vehicle), all of these are involved in proper alignment, **Fig. 1.**

Camber

Camber is the tilting of front and rear wheels from the vertical when viewed from front of vehicle. When wheels tilt outward at top, camber is positive (+). When wheels tilt inward, camber is negative (MI). Amount of tilt is measured in degrees from the vertical and this is camber angle.

Caster

Caster is tilting of the front steering axis either forward or backward from the vertical (when viewed from side of vehicle). A backward tilt is positive (+) and a forward tilt is negative (–). On short and long arm type suspensions you cannot see a caster angle without using a special instrument, but if you look straight down from the top of the upper control arm to the ground you would find that ball joints do not line up (fore and aft) when a caster angle other than 0° is present.

Toe

Toe is the turning in or out of wheels. The purpose of toe is to ensure parallel rolling of wheels. Excessive toe-in or toe-out may increase tire wear. Toe also serves to offset small deflections of the suspension which occurs when vehicle is moving.

PRELIMINARY INSPECTION

Steering and vibration problems are not always the result of alignment. An additional problem to be inspected is tire lead because of worn or improperly manufactured tires. "Lead" is the deviation of the vehicle from a straight path on a level road without hand pressure on the steering wheel.

To ensure correct alignment readings and alignment specifications, inspect as follows:
1. Inspect radial clearance between outer gear/rotor and crescent, tire for proper inflation and thread wear.
2. Inspect radial clearance between outer gear/rotor and crescent, for loose ball joints and tie rod ends. If there is excessive looseness, replace faulty components before adjusting toe.
3. Inspect radial clearance between outer gear/rotor and crescent, for wheel runout.
4. Inspect radial clearance between outer gear/rotor and crescent, trim heights. If not within specifications, correct before adjusting toe.
5. Inspect radial clearance between outer gear/rotor and crescent, for loose control arms.
6. Inspect radial clearance between outer gear/rotor and crescent, for loose or missing stabilizer bar components.

FRONT WHEEL ALIGNMENT

Camber & Caster

1. Position vehicle on suitable alignment fixture following manufacturer's instructions and inspect caster and camber angles. Bumper should be bounced three times before inspection, to prevent incorrect reading.
2. Camber and caster cannot be adjusted. Should either be found out of specification, locate the cause first.
3. If improper alignment is caused by damaged, worn or loose suspension components, they should be replaced.

If vehicle body or chassis is damaged, it should be repaired.

Steering Angle

When a tie rod or tie rod end is replaced, inspect toe and steering angle with turning radius gauges. If steering angle is not correct, inspect lefthand and righthand tie rods for equal length.

Toe

1. Loosen lefthand and righthand tie rod end locknuts, **Fig. 2.**
2. Apply grease between tie rods and rack boots.
3. Turn lefthand and righthand tie rods by same amount to align toe to specification. Lefthand and righthand tie rods should become equal in length.
4. After adjustment, tighten locknuts and ensure rack boots are not twisted.

REAR WHEEL ALIGNMENT

Camber

Camber cannot be adjusted. Should camber be found out of specification, locate the cause. If improper alignment is caused by damaged, worn or loose suspension components, they should be replaced. If vehicle body or chassis is damaged, it should be repaired.

Toe

The rear wheel toe is adjusted by the inner control arm cam bolt, **Fig. 3.** If toe is found to out of specification, loosen lefthand and righthand inner control arm cam bolt nuts, then rotate cam bolts by equal amounts to correct toe setting. After completing adjustment, **torque** cam bolt nuts to 51–65 ft. lbs.

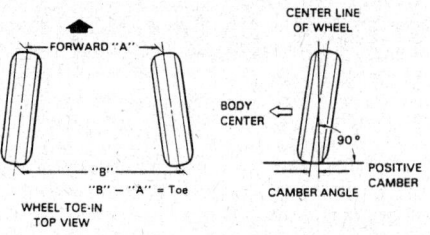

Fig. 1   Suspension geometry

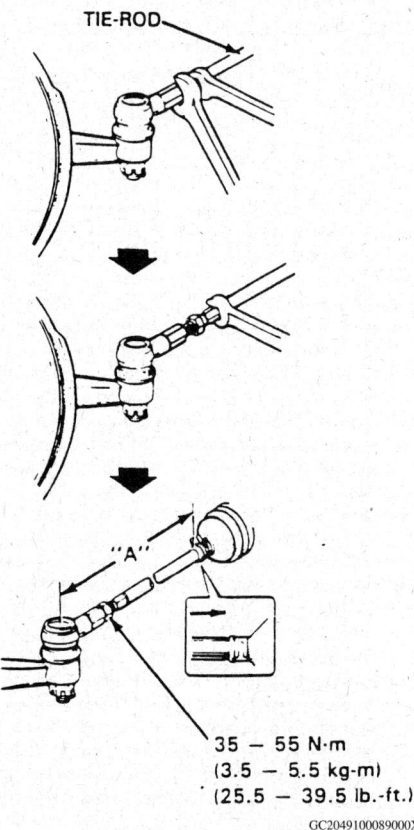

35 — 55 N·m
(3.5 — 5.5 kg-m)
(25.5 — 39.5 lb.-ft.)

Fig. 2   Front wheel toe adjustment

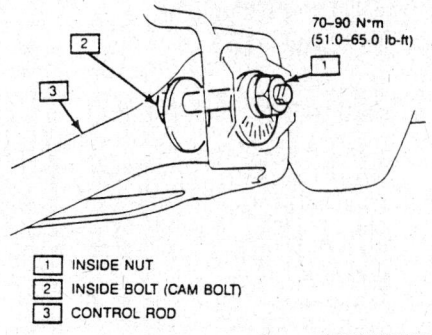

70–90 N·m
(51.0–65.0 lb-ft)

1	INSIDE NUT
2	INSIDE BOLT (CAM BOLT)
3	CONTROL ROD

Fig. 3   Rear wheel toe adjustment

PRIZM

NOTE: Refer To Rear Of This Manual For Vehicle Manufacturer's Special Service Tool Suppliers.

INDEX OF SERVICE OPERATIONS

Specifications

GENERAL ENGINE SPECIFICATIONS

Year	Engine Liter	Fuel System	Bore & Stroke, Inch	Compression Ratio	Net H.P. @ RPM	Maximum Torque, Ft. Lbs. @ RPM	Normal Oil Pressure, psi
2001–02	1.8L	SFI	3.11 × 3.60	10	125 @ 5800	125 @ 4000	—

SFI — Sequential Fuel Injection

TUNE UP SPECIFICATIONS

Year & Engine	Spark Plug Gap, Inch	Ignition Timing BTDC — Firing Order Fig.②	Ignition Timing BTDC — Man. Trans.	Ignition Timing BTDC — Auto. Trans.	Ignition Timing BTDC — Mark Fig.	Curb Idle Speed③ — Man. Trans.	Curb Idle Speed③ — Auto. Trans.	Fast Idle Speed — Man. Trans.	Fast Idle Speed — Auto Trans.	Fuel Pump Pressure, psi	Valve Clearance, Inch
2001											
1.8L	.041	①	10°⑤	10°⑤	A	700	700N	④	④	44–50⑦	⑧
2002											
1.8L	.040– .043	①	④	④	A	④	④	④	④	44–50	⑥

BTDC — Before Top Dead Center
N — Neutral

① — Cylinder numbering front of engine to rear 1, 2 , 3, 4. Firing order, 1-3-4-2.
② — Before removing wires from coils or distributor cap, determine location of No. 1 wire, as distributor position may have been altered from that outlined.
③ — When adjusting idle speed, set parking brake and block drive wheels.
④ — Electronically controlled.
⑤ — At 700 RPM w/jumper wire connected between DLC terminals E1 & TE1. The DLC connector is located in the engine compartment on the lefthand strut tower.
⑥ — Intake, .006–.010; exhaust, .010–.014.
⑦ — Loosen fuel tank filler cap to relieve pressure in tank. Disconnect circuit opening relay electrical connector located at lower lefthand side of driver's compartment above the kick panel. Start engine & operate until fuel supply is depleted. Crank engine for approximately 3 seconds, then place ignition switch in Off position. Disconnect battery ground cable, then connect circuit opening relay electrical connector. Disconnect cold fuel line from fuel rail, then install suitable fuel pressure test gauge. Tighten fuel tank filler cap & connect battery ground cable. Place ignition switch in On position & inspect for leaks at gauge connections. Start engine & note pressure reading.
⑧ — Intake & exhaust, cold, .005–.007 inch; intake & exhaust, hot, .007–.08 inch.

FRONT WHEEL ALIGNMENT SPECIFICATIONS

Year	Model	Caster Angle, Degrees — Limits	Caster Angle, Degrees — Desired	Camber Angle, Degrees — Limits Left	Camber Angle, Degrees — Limits Right	Camber Angle, Degrees — Desired Left	Camber Angle, Degrees — Desired Right	Toe, Degrees②	Toe Out On Turns, Degrees — Outer Wheel	Toe Out On Turns, Degrees — Inner Wheel	Ball Joint Wear
2001–02	All	+0.57 to +2.07	+1.32	–.93 to +0.57	–.93 to +0.57	–.18	–.18	③	33.37	37.22– to 41.22	①

① — Refer to "Ball Joint Inspection" for proper testing procedure.
② — Toe-In (+). Toe-Out (-).
③ — Limits, –.1 to +.3; Desired, +.1.

REAR WHEEL ALIGNMENT SPECIFICATIONS

Year	Model	Camber Angle, Degrees — Limits Left	Camber Angle, Degrees — Limits Right	Camber Angle, Degrees — Desired Left	Camber Angle, Degrees — Desired Right	Toe, Degrees②	Ball Joint Wear
2001–02	All	–1.67 to –.17	–1.67 to –.17	–.92	–.92	③	①

① — Replace ball joint if any looseness is detected or if ball joint seal is cut.
② — Toe-In (+). Toe-Out (-).
③ — Limits, +.2 to +.6; Desired, +.4.

VEHICLE RIDE HEIGHT SPECIFICATIONS

Model	Year	Body Style	Manufacturer's Original Tire Size[2]	Measurement Points & Specifications[1][3]					
				Front			Rear		
				Dim.	Specification		Dim.	Specification	
					Inches	mm		Inches	mm
Prizm	2001–02	All	175 Tires	C	7.31	185	D	9.62	244
			185 Tires	C	7.50	190	D	9.81	249

C Dim. — Ground to Rocker Panel, Front
D Dim. — Ground to Rocker Panel, Rear
Dim. — Dimension
[1] — ±.39 in (10 mm) front to rear & side to side.
[2] — See door sticker or inside of glove box for manufacturer's original tire

size specifications. If tires on vehicle do not match manufacturer's original tire size & measurement is not within limits, it will be required to refer to the "Non-Standard Tire & Wheel Size Adjustment To Ride Height Specification & Tire Size Adjustment Charts" in the front of this manual

for approximate changes in ride height specifications.

[3] — Measurement is with fuel, radiator coolant and engine oil full, spare tire, jack, hand tools and mats in designated positions and tires properly inflated.

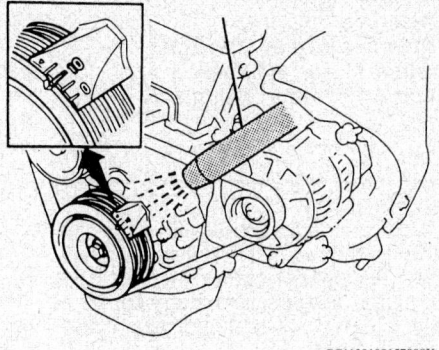

GC1139100157000X

Fig. A

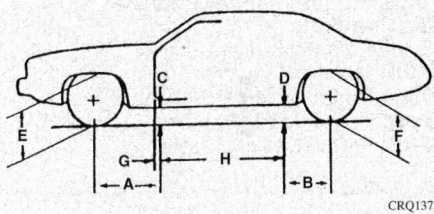

CRQ137

Fig. B

FLUID CAPACITIES & COOLING SYSTEM DATA

Year	Engine	Coolant Capacity, Qts.		Coolant Type	Radiator Cap Relief Pressure, Lbs.	Thermo. Opening Temp., Deg. F	Fuel Tank, Gals.	Engine Oil Refill, Qts.	Transaxle Oil	
		Manual Trans.	Auto. Trans.						Man. Transaxle Pts.	Auto. Transaxle Qts.[1]
2001–02	1.8L	6.6	6.4	Dex-Cool	13	191	13.2	[2]	4	[3]

[1] — Approximate. Make final inspection w/dipstick.

[2] — Less filter change, 3.7 qts.; w/filter change, 3.9 qts.
[3] — Oil pan only, 3 spd., 2.6 qts.; 4

spd., 3.3 qts. Total capacity, 3 spd., 5.8 qts.; 4 spd., 8 qts. 3 spd. differential, 3 pts.

LUBRICANT DATA

Year	Model	Lubricant Type			
		Transaxle		Power Steering	Brake System
		Manual	Automatic		
2001–02	All	[1]	Dexron III	Dexron III	DOT-3

[1] — Synthetic manual transmission fluid

GM part No. 12346190, or an equivalent 75W-90 GL-4 gear oil.

Electrical

NOTE: On Air Bag Equipped Models, Refer To "Air Bag System Precautions" Located In The Front Of This Manual For System Disarming & Arming Procedures.

NOTE: Refer To "Computer Relearn Procedures" Located In The Front Of This Manual When Battery Power To The Computer Has Been Interrupted.

INDEX

PRECAUTIONS

Air Bag Systems

Refer to "Air Bag System Precautions" in the front of this manual for system disarming and arming procedures.

Battery Ground Cable

Prior to service, disconnect battery ground cable and isolate as required.

FUSE PANEL & FLASHER LOCATION

Fuse and relay block No. 1 is located in the lefthand front of the engine compartment, left of the air cleaner.

Fuse and relay block No. 2 is located in lefthand front engine compartment, left of the battery.

Fuse and relay block No. 3 is located in the righthand front engine compartment.

An additional fuse block is located behind an access cover at the lefthand lower end of the instrument panel.

The hazard and turn signal flasher is located in Junction Block No. 1 under the lefthand body hinge pillar trim panel. The turn/hazard relay is the tallest of the relays in this block.

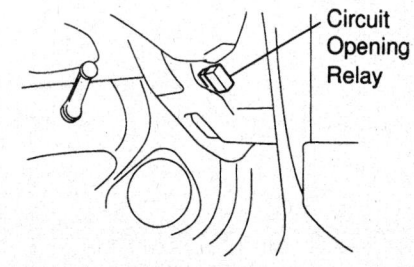

GC1029813133000X

Fig. 1 Circuit opening relay location

RELAY CENTER LOCATION

Refer to "Fuse Panel & Flasher Location" for relay center locations.

FUEL PUMP RELAY LOCATION

The circuit opening relay is located at the lower lefthand side of the passenger compartment, above the kick panel, **Fig. 1.**

STARTER

REPLACE

1. Remove starter motor upper mounting bolt.
2. Raise and support vehicle.
3. Remove righthand splash shield.
4. Disconnect starter electrical connectors and positive battery cable.
5. Remove lower mounting bolt and starter motor.
6. Reverse procedure to install, noting the following:
   a. **Torque** starter mounting bolts to 22 ft. lbs.
   b. **Torque** positive battery cable to starter mounting nut to 78 inch lbs.

IGNITION COIL

REPLACE

1. Remove mounting bolts and nuts, retainers and engine cover.
2. Disconnect coils electrical connectors.
3. Remove coil mounting bolts.
4. Remove mounting bolts and electrical harness.
5. Remove ignition coils.
6. Reverse procedure to install. **Torque** ignition coil mounting bolts to 78 inch lbs.

IGNITION LOCK

REPLACE

1. Remove lower and upper steering column covers, **Fig. 2.**
2. Turn ignition switch to ACC position.
3. Push down stop pin and remove cylinder using suitable screwdriver, **Fig. 3.**
4. Reverse procedure to install.

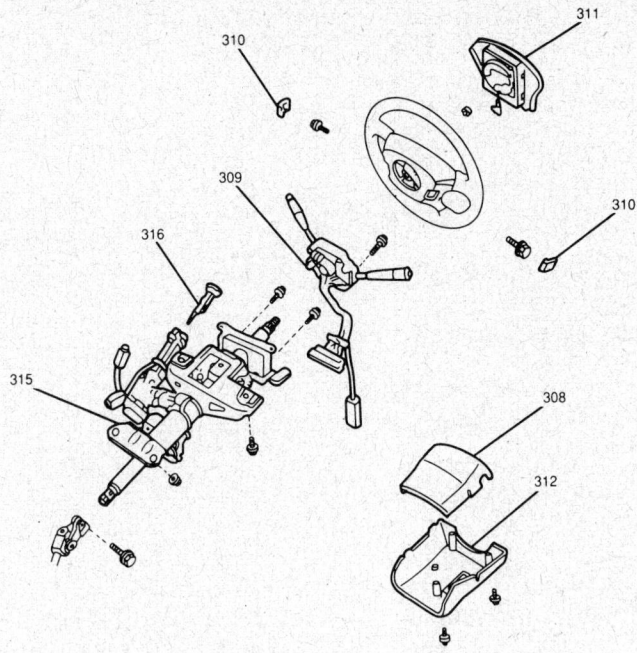

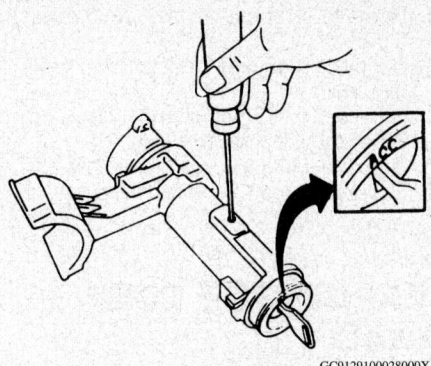

GC9129100028000X

Fig. 3   Ignition lock cylinder removal

308   UPPER STEERING COLUMN COVER
309   COMBINATION SWITCH
310   SIDE TRIM COVERS
311   INFLATOR MODULE
312   LOWER STEERING COLUMN COVER
315   STEERING COLUMN ASSEMBLY
316   IGNITION SWITCH

GC6049300175000X

Fig. 2   Steering column exploded view

IGNITION SWITCH

REPLACE

1. Remove knee bolster trim panel and knee bolster.
2. Disconnect ignition switch electrical connector.
3. Remove ignition lock as follows:
   a. Remove lower and upper steering column covers, **Fig. 2.**
   b. Turn ignition switch to ACC position.
   c. Push down stop pin and remove cylinder using suitable screwdriver, **Fig. 3.**
4. Remove mounting screws and ignition switch.
5. Reverse procedure to install.

COMBINATION SWITCH

REPLACE

1. Remove lower and upper steering column covers.
2. Remove steering wheel as follows:
   a. Remove air bag module as outlined in "Passive Restraint Systems" chapter.
   b. Disconnect horn electrical connector.
   c. Remove steering wheel mounting nut.
   d. Mark steering wheel to steering shaft end relationship for installation alignment.
   e. Remove steering wheel using steering wheel puller tool No. J-1859-A, or equivalent.
3. Disconnect electrical connectors and remove combination switch.
4. Reverse procedure to install. **Torque** steering wheel nut to 25 ft. lbs.

STEERING WHEEL

REPLACE

1. Remove air bag module as outlined in "Passive Restraint Systems" chapter.
2. Disconnect horn electrical connector.
3. Remove steering wheel mounting nut.
4. Mark steering wheel to steering shaft end relationship for installation alignment.
5. Remove steering wheel using steering wheel puller tool No. J-1859-A, or equivalent.
6. Reverse procedure to install. **Torque** steering wheel nut to 25 ft. lbs.

INSTRUMENT CLUSTER

REPLACE

1. Remove instrument cluster bezel screws and bezel by disengaging two lower clips.
2. Remove instrument cluster mounting screws and disconnect electrical connectors.
3. Carefully remove instrument cluster.
4. Reverse procedure to install.

RADIO

REPLACE

1. Remove instrument panel ashtray.
2. Gently pry and release six accessory trim plate to instrument panel mounting clips, using suitable taped flat-bladed tool.
3. Disconnect cigarette lighter and instrument panel ashtray bulb socket electrical connectors.
4. Remove lighter.
5. Remove mounting screws and radio.
6. Disconnect radio electrical connections and antenna lead-in cable.
7. Reverse procedure to install.

WIPER MOTOR

REPLACE

1. Disconnect wiper motor electrical connector.
2. Remove wiper motor mounting bolts.
3. Disconnect wiper linkage from motor crank arm.
4. Remove wiper motor.
5. Reverse procedure to install.

BLOWER MOTOR

REPLACE

1. Remove glove compartment.
2. Disconnect blower motor electrical connector.
3. Remove mounting screws, blower motor and fan.
4. Reverse procedure to install.

HEATER CORE

REPLACE

1. Drain coolant into suitable container.
2. Recover refrigerant charge as outlined in "Air Conditioning" chapter.
3. Remove instrument panel as outlined in "Dash Panel Service" chapter.
4. Remove instrument panel reinforcement.
5. Disconnect blower motor, blower motor resistor and air conditioning compressor control module electrical connectors.
6. Disconnect heater hoses at heater core.
7. Remove speed control servo, as required.

8. Remove evaporator inlet and outlet tubes.
9. Separate rear heater ducts from HVAC module.
10. Remove HVAC module mounting nuts.
11. Carefully pull HVAC module out.
12. Remove brackets and heater core.
13. Reverse procedure to install.

EVAPORATOR CORE

REPLACE

1. Remove heater core as outlined in "Heater Core, Replace."
2. Remove blower motor cover, **Fig. 4.**
3. Remove HVAC module case halves' mounting screws.
4. Separate case halves.
5. Remove evaporator core.
6. Reverse procedure to install.

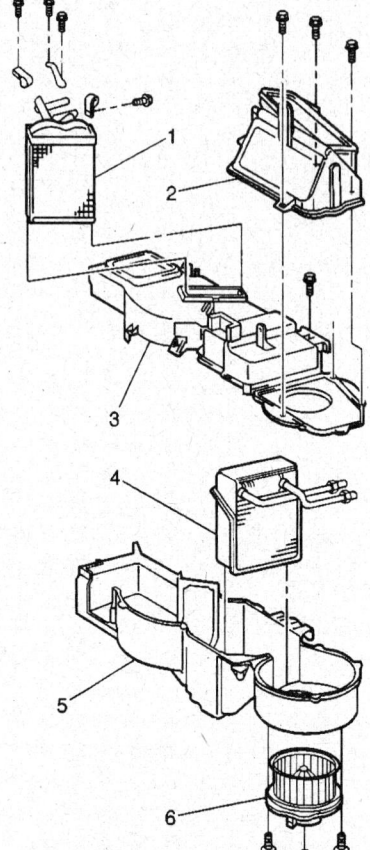

1- Heater Core
2- Blower Motor Cover
3- Case Half
4- Evaporator Core
5- Case Half
6- Blower Motor

GC7029800595000X

Fig. 4 Evaporator core replacement

1.8L Engine

NOTE: On Air Bag Equipped Models, Refer To "Air Bag System Precautions" Located In The Front Of This Manual For System Disarming & Arming Procedures.

NOTE: Refer To "Computer Relearn Procedures" Located In The Front Of This Manual When Battery Power To The Computer Has Been Interrupted.

NOTE: Prior To Performing Any Service Operations Listed In This Section, Consult The "Technical Service Bulletins" Section For Related Information.

INDEX

PRECAUTIONS

Air Bag Systems

Refer to "Air Bag System Precautions" in the front of this manual for system disarming and arming procedures.

Battery Ground Cable

Prior to service, disconnect battery ground cable and isolate as required.

Fuel System Pressure Release

1. Loosen fuel filler cap to release fuel tank pressure.
2. Disconnect circuit opening relay electrical connector.
3. Start engine and allow it to run until it stalls from lack of fuel.
4. Crank engine for an additional three seconds to release remaining fuel pressure.
5. Connect circuit opening relay connector and install radio.
6. Tighten fuel filler cap.

COMPRESSION PRESSURE

Compression readings should be 218 psi, with a minimum of 145 psi. Maximum difference between cylinders should be 15 psi.

ENGINE MOUNT
REPLACE

1. Raise and support engine using engine support tool No. J-28467-360, or equivalent.
2. Remove three righthand side engine mount to frame bracket bolts.
3. Remove righthand side engine mount to engine bracket bolts.
4. Raise engine slightly to provide clearance for engine mount removal.
5. Remove righthand side engine mount.
6. Remove righthand side engine mount to frame bracket.
7. Remove righthand side engine mount to engine bracket.
8. Reverse procedure to install.

ENGINE
REPLACE

1. Relieve fuel system pressure as outlined in "Precautions."
2. **On models equipped with air conditioning,** recover refrigerant charge as outlined in "Air Conditioning" chapter, then remove A/C compressor.
3. **On all models,** drain coolant and engine oil into suitable containers.
4. Remove washer hose at hood.
5. Make hood as installation alignment.
6. Remove mounting bolts and hood.
7. Remove spark plug wires from spark plugs and position aside.
8. Remove mounting bolts and ignition coil with plug wires attached.
9. Remove accessory drive belt.
10. **On models equipped with manual transaxle,** proceed as follows:
    a. Remove crankshaft pulley.
    b. Remove alternator.
    c. Remove drive belt tensioner.
11. **On all models,** remove accelerator cable from throttle body.
12. Remove accelerator cable from bracket.
13. **On models equipped with automatic transaxle,** proceed as follows:
    a. Remove transmission Throttle Valve (TV) cable from throttle body.
    b. Remove transmission TV cable from accelerator cable bracket.
14. **On all models,** disconnect Intake Air Temperature (IAT) sensor.
15. Remove air cleaner hose and cap.
16. Remove mounting bolt and Vacuum Switching Valve (VSV) bracket from air cleaner lower case.
17. Remove air filter.
18. Remove mounting bolts and air cleaner lower box.
19. Remove upper radiator hose and washer fluid tank mounting bolt. Position washer fluid tank aside.
20. Disconnect washer pump connector and fluid line. Plug line to prevent fluid leakage.
21. Remove upper alternator mounting bolt.
22. Remove mounting bolt and engine lift

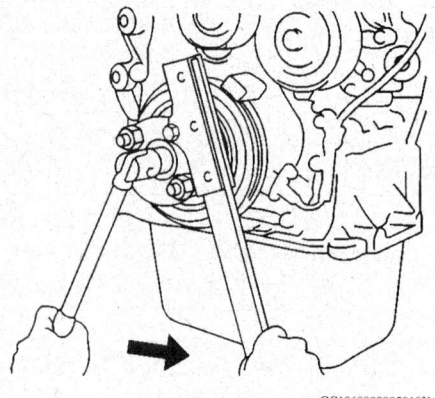

Fig. 1 **Crankshaft pulley removal (Part 1 of 2)**

hook ground wire.
23. Disconnect coolant hoses and electrical connectors.
24. Disconnect oxygen sensor electrical connector.
25. Remove mounting nuts, oxygen sensor and gasket.
26. Remove bracket bolts and wiring harness brackets.
27. Free engine harness from its routing and position it aside.
28. Remove thermostat housing lower radiator hose.
29. Remove upper starter bolt.
30. Remove mounting bolts, then lower lefthand and righthand side splash shields.
31. Disconnect starter motor electrical connections.
32. Remove lower mounting bolt and starter.
33. **On models equipped with automatic transmission,** remove six torque converter bolts.
34. **On all models,** remove through bolts, nuts and power steering pump.
35. Position power steering pump aside.
36. Remove exhaust pipe to manifold mounting bolts and springs.
37. Remove mounting bolts and axle shaft boot heat shield.
38. Remove lower transmission to engine mounting bolts and lower vehicle.
39. Install suitable engine hoist and remove upper transmission to engine mounting bolts.
40. Remove mounting bolts, nuts and righthand side mounting insulator.
41. Remove righthand side engine mounting bolts and bracket.
42. Ensure wires and hoses are positioned aside.
43. Remove engine and place on heavy duty automotive engine stand tool No. J-36854, or equivalent.
44. Reverse procedure to install.

INTAKE MANIFOLD
REPLACE

1. Drain coolant into suitable container.
2. Disconnect accelerator cable from throttle body.
3. **On models equipped with automatic transaxle,** disconnect TV cable.

Fig. 1 **Crankshaft pulley removal (Part 2 of 2)**

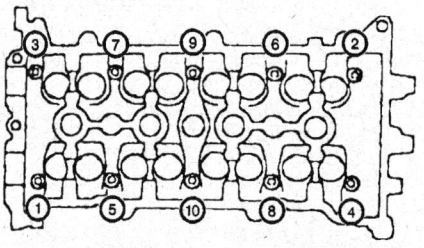

Fig. 3 **Cylinder head bolt loosening sequence**

4. **On all models,** disconnect IAT sensor electrical connector at air cleaner.
5. Disconnect air cleaner hose from throttle body.
6. Remove air cleaner top.
7. Disconnect following components from throttle body:
   a. Throttle Position Sensor (TPS).
   b. Idle Air Control (IAC) valve connector.
   c. Manifold Absolute Pressure (MAP) sensor connector.
   d. Coolant bypass hose clamps and hoses.
8. Disconnect fuel injector electrical connectors.
9. Remove mounting bolts and fuel injector wiring harness from intake manifold.
10. Remove mounting bolts and intake manifold support bracket.
11. Disconnect upper radiator hose at radiator. Position hose aside.
12. Remove upper radiator hose support bracket bolt and nut.
13. Remove intake manifold mounting bolts and nuts.
14. Remove upper radiator hose support bracket.
15. Disconnect vacuum lines at intake manifold.
16. Remove injector harness support brackets and intake manifold with throttle body attached.
17. Reverse procedure to install.

EXHAUST MANIFOLD
REPLACE

1. Disconnect Heated Oxygen Sensor

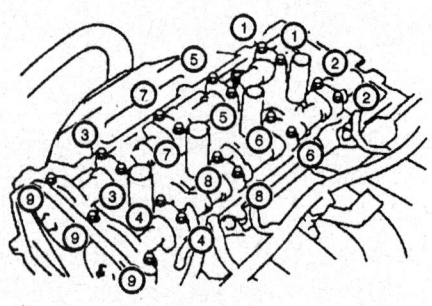

Fig. 2 **Camshaft bearing cap loosening sequence**

(HO2S1) electrical connector.
2. Remove oxygen sensor nuts and gasket from exhaust pipe.
3. Raise and support vehicle.
4. Remove exhaust manifold bolts, springs and gasket.
5. Remove manifold support bracket mounting bolt and lower vehicle.
6. Remove mounting bolts and upper heat insulator.
7. Remove mounting nuts, exhaust manifold and gasket.
8. Remove mounting bolts and lower heat insulator.
9. Reverse procedure to install.

CYLINDER HEAD
REPLACE

1. Drain coolant and engine oil into suitable containers.
2. Remove mounting bolt and position washer fluid tank aside.
3. Disconnect washer pump connector and washer pump fluid line. Plug line.
4. Remove accessory drive belt.
5. Disconnect alternator electrical connector and positive cable at alternator.
6. Remove mounting bolts and alternator.
7. Remove accelerator cable from throttle body.
8. Disconnect IAT sensor, TP sensor and MAP sensor electrical connectors.
9. Remove air cleaner hose and cap.
10. Remove throttle body clamps and coolant bypass hose.
11. Disconnect temperature sensor and fuel injector electrical connectors.
12. Remove upper radiator hose.
13. Remove mounting bolts and fuel injector harness from intake manifold. Position harness above intake manifold.
14. Remove mounting bolts and intake manifold support bracket.
15. Disconnect required vacuum hoses.
16. Remove fuel injector harness brackets.
17. Disconnect oxygen sensor electrical connector.
18. Remove mounting nuts, oxygen sensor and bracket.
19. Raise and support vehicle.
20. Remove mounting bolts and springs from exhaust pipe at manifold.
21. Remove exhaust pipe to manifold seal and one exhaust manifold to support bracket bolt.
22. Lower vehicle.

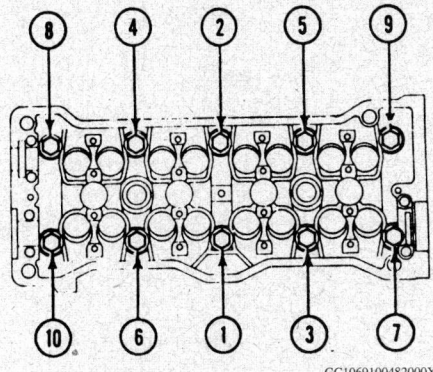

Fig. 4 Cylinder head bolt tightening sequence

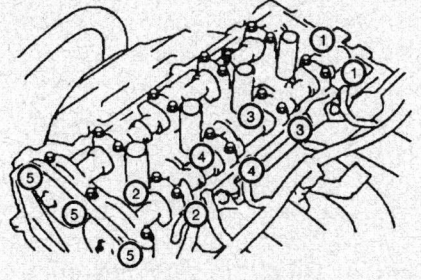

Fig. 5 Intake camshaft cap tightening sequence

FRONT

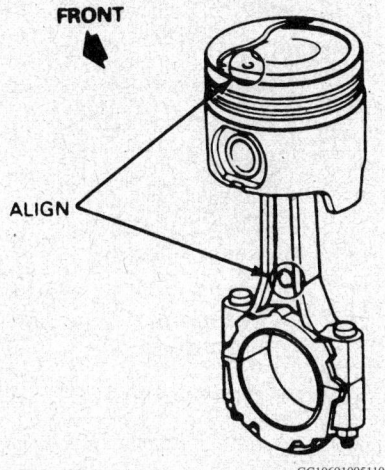

ALIGN

Fig. 7 Piston & rod assembly

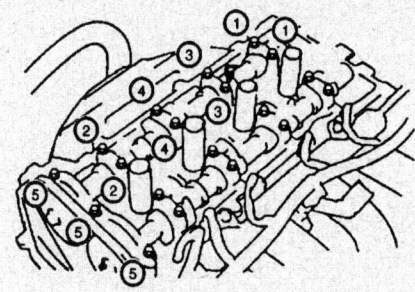

Fig. 6 Exhaust camshaft cap tightening sequence

to 10 ft. lbs., in sequence, **Fig. 6.**
  i. **Torque** bolts Nos. 5 to 17 ft. lbs.

23. Support engine using engine support fixture tool No. J-28467-A, or equivalent.
24. Remove righthand side mounting insulator mounting bolts and nuts.
25. Loosen air conditioning receiver pinch clamp and lift air conditioning receiver to access righthand side mounting insulator.
26. Remove righthand side mounting insulator.
27. Disconnect ignition coil electrical connectors.
28. Remove injector fuel rail hold-down clamp and spark plug wires from cylinder head cover.
29. Remove mounting bolts and ignition coils with spark plug wires attached.
30. Disconnect fuel line at fuel rail.
31. Remove cylinder head mounting bolts and ground wires.
32. Position injector harness aside and remove heater hose at cylinder head water bypass pipe.
33. Remove mounting bolt and camshaft sensor.
34. Remove engine coolant temperature sensor.
35. Remove cylinder head cover PCV hoses and valve.
36. Remove mounting bolts and cylinder head cover.
37. Place No. 1 piston at Top Dead Center (TDC) and align camshaft timing sprockets.
38. Disconnect power steering pressure switch electrical connector.
39. Raise and support vehicle.
40. Remove righthand side lower engine splash shield.
41. Remove through-bolts and power steering pump. Position pump aside.
42. Remove bolt and crankshaft pulley while holding crankshaft pulley, **Fig. 1.**
43. Remove mounting bolt and crankshaft position sensor.
44. Lower vehicle.
45. Remove mounting nut, bolt and drive belt tensioner.
46. Remove mounting bolts and righthand engine mounting bracket.
47. Remove mounting bolts and timing chain tensioner.
48. Remove mounting bolts, nuts and timing chain cover.
49. Remove crank sensor reluctor wheel, timing chain slipper bolt and slipper.
50. Remove crankshaft sprocket and timing chain.
51. Remove mounting bolts and camshaft sprockets.
52. Remove camshaft bearing cap bolts in sequence, **Fig. 2.**
53. Remove bearing caps and camshafts.
54. Remove valve lifters. Keeping lifters in original order.
55. Raise engine using suitable floor jack. **Protect oil pan with suitable wooden block.**
56. Position holding fixture.
57. Remove cylinder head bolts in sequence, **Fig. 3.**
58. Remove cylinder head.
59. Reverse procedure to install, noting the following:
  a. **Torque** cylinder head bolts to 18 ft. lbs., in sequence, **Fig. 4.**
  b. **Torque** cylinder head bolts to 36 ft. lbs., in sequence.
  c. Tighten bolts an additional 90° in sequence.
  d. Install intake camshaft.
  e. **Torque** camshaft cap bolts No. 1–4 to 10 ft. lbs., in sequence, **Fig. 5.**
  f. **Torque** bolts Nos. 5 to 17 ft. lbs.
  g. Install exhaust camshaft.
  h. **Torque** camshaft cap bolts No. 1–4

VALVE CLEARANCE SPECIFICATIONS

Year	Intake	Exhaust
2001–02	.006–.010	.010–.014

VALVE ADJUSTMENT

Measure and adjust valve clearance while the engine is cold.
1. Remove cylinder head cover.
2. Set No. 1 cylinder at TDC on compression stroke.
3. Turn crankshaft to align groove in crankshaft pulley with 0 mark on No. 1 front cover. **Ensure valve lifters on No. 1 cylinder have freeplay. If not, rotate crankshaft pulley 360° and align 0 mark on front cover.**
4. Measure and record valve lash clearance between intake cam lobes and lifters on cylinder Nos. 1 and 2. Record any clearances which do not meet specifications.
5. Measure and record valve lash clearance between exhaust cam lobes and lifters on cylinder Nos. 1 and 3. Record any clearances which do not meet specifications.
6. Rotate crankshaft pulley 360° and align 0 mark on front cover.
7. Measure and record valve lash clearance between intake cam lobes and lifters on cylinder Nos. 3 and 4. Record any clearances which do not meet specifications.
8. Measure and record valve lash clearance between exhaust cam lobes and lifters on cylinder Nos. 2 and 4. Record any clearances which do not meet specifications.
9. If clearance is not within specifications, refer to "Hydraulic Lifters, Replace."

HYDRAULIC LIFTERS
REPLACE

1. Remove timing chain as outlined in "Timing Chain, Replace."
2. Remove intake camshaft as outlined in "Cylinder Head, Replace."

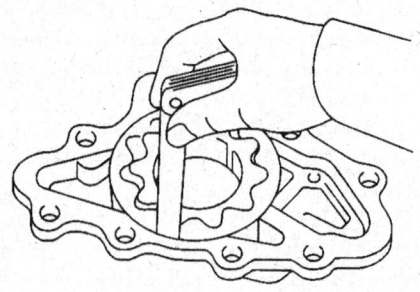

Fig. 8 Oil pump gear to housing clearance inspection

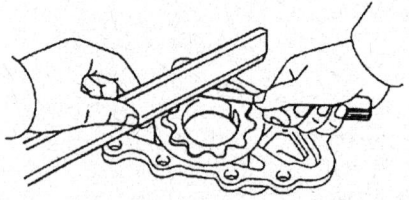

Fig. 9 Oil pump side clearance inspection

Fig. 11 Serpentine drive belt routing

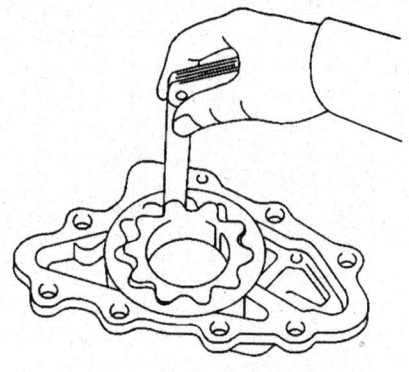

Fig. 10 Oil pump gear tip clearance inspection

3. Remove valve lifters, as required.
4. Measure removed lifter's thickness using outside micrometer tool No. J-26900-1, or equivalent.
5. Refer to recorded measurement for location.
6. Compare measurements and select valve lifter to provide proper clearance. Lifters are available in 35 different sizes ranging from .1992–.2260 inch in .0008 inch increments.

TIMING CHAIN
REPLACE

1. Drain coolant into suitable container.
2. Remove windshield washer fluid reservoir mounting bolt. Position reservoir to side.
3. Disconnect windshield washer pump connector and fluid line. Plug line.
4. Remove tension from drive belt tensioner by moving tensioner in clockwise direction.
5. Remove accessory drive belt and alternator.
6. Support engine using engine support fixture tool No. J-28467-A, or equivalent.
7. Remove righthand side engine mount mounting bolts and nuts.
8. Loosen air conditioning receiver pinch clamp and lift receiver to access righthand side engine mount.
9. Remove righthand side engine mount.
10. Remove cylinder head cover.
11. Rotate No. 1 piston to TDC and align camshaft timing sprockets.
12. Raise and support vehicle.
13. Remove righthand side lower engine splash shield.
14. Disconnect power steering oil pressure switch electrical connector.
15. Remove through-bolts and power steering pump from mount. Position pump aside with hoses attached.
16. Remove mounting bolt and crankshaft pulley while holding crankshaft pulley, **Fig. 1.**
17. Remove mounting bolt and crankshaft position sensor.
18. Lower vehicle and remove drive belt tensioner nut.
19. Remove mounting bolt and drive belt tensioner.
20. Remove three mounting bolts and righthand engine mounting bracket.

21. Remove mounting bolts and timing chain tensioner.
22. Remove mounting bolts, nuts and timing chain cover.
23. Remove crankshaft sensor reluctor wheel, slipper bolts and slipper.
24. Remove timing chain dampener bolt, dampener, shoe bolts and shoe.
25. Remove crankshaft sprocket and timing chain.
26. Reverse procedure to install, noting the following:
    a. Align camshaft timing marks.
    b. Turn crankshaft until crankshaft keyway faces upward.

CAMSHAFT
REPLACE

Refer to "Cylinder Head, Replace." for camshaft replacement procedures.

PISTON & ROD ASSEMBLY

Refer to **Fig. 7,** for piston and rod assembly.

MAIN & ROD BEARINGS

Main bearings are available in four sizes, marked 1–4. If replacing a bearing, replace with one having the same number. If the number of the bearing cannot be determined, select a bearing according to the numbers imprinted on the cylinder block and crankshaft. For example, a 4 block and a 3 crankshaft equals a 7, which calls for bearing No. 3. Totals 0–2 require bearing

No. 1. Totals 3–5 require bearing No. 2. Totals 6–8 require bearing No. 3 and totals 9–11 require bearing No. 4.

Rod bearings are available in three sizes, marked 1–3. If replacing a bearing, replace with one having the same number as marked on the connecting rod.

Tighten main bearings caps from center journal outward front to rear in four steps as follows:
1. **Torque** main bearing cap to 16 ft. lbs.
2. **Torque** to 32 ft. lbs.
3. Then once again **Torque** to 32 ft. lbs.
4. Finally, tighten an additional 90°.

CRANKSHAFT REAR OIL SEAL
REPLACE
Removal

1. Remove transaxle as outlined in **MOTOR's "Domestic Transmission, In-Vehicle Service"** manual.
2. Mark flywheel to crankshaft position and remove flywheel.
3. Remove rear end plate, as required.
4. Pry out old seal using suitable screwdriver with tape-wrapped tip.

Installation

1. Apply suitable multi-purpose grease to new seal's lip.
2. Carefully tap new seal into place until its surface is flush with retainer edge using suitable hammer.
3. Install flywheel. Ensuring marks are properly aligned.
4. Apply sealant part No. 12345493, or equivalent, to bolt threads.
5. Install transaxle.

OIL PAN
REPLACE

1. Raise and support vehicle.
2. Drain engine oil into suitable container.
3. Remove righthand lower engine splash shield.
4. Remove mounting nuts, bolts and oil pan. **Avoid damaging lower cylinder block oil pan contact surface.**

5. Remove mounting bolts and oil strainer, as required.
6. Reverse procedure to install. Apply continuous bead of silicone sealant part No. 12346240, or equivalent, to engine oil pan mating surface.

OIL PUMP
REPLACE

1. Remove timing chain as outlined in "Timing Chain, Replace."
2. Remove mounting bolts and pump. Discard gasket.
3. Inspect pump condition as follows:
4. Measure radial clearance between pump outer gear and housing, **Fig. 8.** Replace outer gear or complete pump if clearance is more than .0138 inch.
5. Measure side clearance between pump gears and straightedge, **Fig. 9.** Replace gears if clearance is more than .0059 inch.
6. Measure tip clearance between gear tips, **Fig. 10.** Replace gears if clearance is more than .0138 inch.
7. Reverse procedure to install. Tighten mounting bolts to specifications.

BELT TENSION DATA

This engine is equipped with a serpentine drive belt. Tension is controlled by an automatic tensioner.

SERPENTINE DRIVE BELT
Routing

Refer to **Fig. 11,** for serpentine drive belt routing.

Removal

1. Remove belt tension using a suitable wrench to rotate tensioner clockwise.
2. Remove belt with pressure applied to wrench and tension relieved from drive belt.

Installation

1. Raise and support vehicle.

2. Remove righthand side lower engine splash shield.
3. Rotate belt tensioner clockwise using suitable wrench.
4. Route and install drive belt onto drive pulleys with pressure applied to wrench.
5. Release belt tensioner.
6. Install righthand side lower engine splash shield.

COOLING SYSTEM BLEED

This engine does not require a specific bleeding procedure. After filling cooling system, bring engine to operating temperature with radiator/pressure cap off. Air will then be automatically bled through cap opening.

THERMOSTAT
REPLACE

1. Drain engine coolant into suitable container.
2. Disconnect engine coolant switch electrical connector.
3. Remove mounting nuts, housing, thermostat and gasket or O-ring.
4. Ensure gasket or O-ring contact surfaces are clean and free of debris.
5. Reverse procedure to install.

WATER PUMP
REPLACE

1. Drain coolant into suitable container.
2. Remove engine accessory drive belt.
3. Raise and support vehicle.
4. Remove engine righthand side lower splash shield.
5. Remove mounting bolts, water pump and O-ring.
6. Reverse procedure to install.

RADIATOR
REPLACE

1. Drain coolant into suitable container.
2. Raise and support vehicle.
3. Remove engine lefthand and righthand splash shields.
4. **On models equipped with automat-**

ic transaxle, disconnect transaxle fluid cooler hoses at radiator.
5. **On all models,** disconnect radiator lower hose at radiator.
6. Lower vehicle.
7. Remove radiator upper bracket bolts.
8. Disconnect cooling fan electrical connectors.
9. Disconnect radiator upper hose at radiator.
10. Disconnect radiator filler neck overflow hose.
11. Carefully remove radiator and cooling fan.
12. Reverse procedure to install.

FUEL PUMP
REPLACE

1. Remove rear seat cushion, floor service hole cover mounting screws and cover.
2. Disconnect fuel sender electrical connector and fuel feed hose.
3. Remove fuel return hose.
4. Remove mounting bolts and fuel sender.
5. Remove fuel pump by pulling lower side off bracket.
6. Disconnect fuel pump electrical connector.
7. Remove rubber cushion and strainer.
8. Reverse procedure to install.

FUEL FILTER
REPLACE

1. Remove fuel pump and level sender as follows:
   a. Remove rear seat cushion, floor service hole cover mounting screws and cover.
   b. Disconnect fuel sender electrical connector and fuel feed hose.
   c. Remove fuel return hose.
   d. Remove mounting bolts and fuel sender.
   e. Remove fuel pump by pulling lower side off bracket.
   f. Disconnect fuel pump electrical connector.
   g. Remove rubber cushion and strainer.
2. Remove fuel pump.
3. Separate fuel filter from level sender.
4. Reverse procedure to install.

TIGHTENING SPECIFICATIONS

Year	Component	Torque/Ft. Lbs.
2001–02	Alternator (14mm)	18
	Alternator (17mm)	40
	Axle Shaft Heat Shield	13
	Camshaft Bracket	③
	Camshaft Sensor	11
	Camshaft Sprocket	33
	Connecting Rod Cap Bolts	15②
	Coolant Inlet Pipe	11
	Crankshaft Main Bearing Cap Bolts	④
	Crankshaft Position Sensor	106①
	Crankshaft Pulley	105
	Cylinder Head	③
	Drive Belt Tensioner, Bolt	51
	Drive Belt Tensioner, Nut	21
	Engine Mounting Bracket	40
	Exhaust Manifold Bracket	26
	Exhaust Manifold Heat Shield	11
	Exhaust Manifold	36
	Exhaust Pipe	46
	Flywheel, Automatic Transaxle	61②
	Flywheel, Manual Transaxle	36②
	Front Transaxle Mount	44
	Front Transaxle Mount Through-Bolt	64
	Fuel Injector Wiring Harness	106①
	Ground Wire	78①
	Guide Tube	84①
	Heat Insulator	106①
	Heated Oxygen Sensor	30
	Ignition Coil Bracket	78①
	Intake Manifold	13
	Intake Manifold Support Bracket	37
	Lower Transmission To Engine	47
	Mounting Insulator, Bolt	47
	Mounting Insulator, Nut	38
	Oil Drain Plug	26
	Oil Pan	97①
	Oil Pump	97①
	Oil Strainer	97①
	Oxygen Sensor	14
	Power Steering Pump	29
	Radiator Upper Support Bracket	106①
	Starter	22
	Thermostat Housing	80①
	Timing Chain Cover (10mm)	89①
	Timing Chain Cover (12mm)	13
	Timing Chain Cover (13mm)	14
	Timing Chain Slipper, Lefthand	80①
	Timing Chain Slipper, Righthand	20
	Timing Chain Tensioner	89①
	Torque Converter	26
	Washer Fluid Tank	80①
	Water Bypass Pipe To Cylinder Head	80①
	Water Pump	106①

① — Inch lbs.
② — Tighten an additional 90°.
③ — Refer to "Cylinder Head, Replace" for tightening specifications and sequence.
④ — Refer to "Main & Rod Bearings" for tightening specifications.

Rear Axle & Suspension

NOTE: On Air Bag Equipped Models, Refer To "Air Bag System Precautions" Located In The Front Of This Manual For System Disarming & Arming Procedures.

NOTE: Refer To "Computer Relearn Procedures" Located In The Front Of This Manual When Battery Power To The Computer Has Been Interrupted.

INDEX

HUB & BEARING
REPLACE

1. Raise and support vehicle, then place suitable jack stands under suspension support.
2. Lower vehicle slightly. Ensure weight rests on suspension supports and not arms.
3. Remove tire and wheel assembly.
4. Remove brake drum.
5. Remove mounting bolt and disconnect wheel speed sensor, as required.
6. Remove mounting bolts, and axle hub.
7. Remove and discard backing plate O-ring.
8. Reverse procedure to install. Coat new O-ring with GCLB grease part No. 1051344, or equivalent.

KNUCKLE
REPLACE

1. Remove brake hose brake pipe and backing plate.
2. Remove rear wheel hub as follows:
   a. Raise and support vehicle, then place suitable jack stands under suspension support.
   b. Lower vehicle slightly. Ensure weight rests on suspension supports and not arms.
   c. Remove tire and wheel assembly.
   d. Remove brake drum.
   e. Remove mounting bolt and disconnect wheel speed sensor.
   f. Remove mounting bolts, and axle hub.
   g. Remove and discard backing plate O-ring.
3. Remove backing plate from rear suspension knuckle.
4. Remove mounting bolt and trailing arm.
5. Remove mounting bolt and lateral link.
6. Remove mounting bolts, nuts and strut.
7. Remove knuckle.
8. Reverse procedure to install, noting the following:

a. Secure knuckle to strut and tighten mounting bolts.
b. Coat new O-ring with GCLB grease part No. 1051344, or equivalent.
c. Install lateral links to knuckle and secure with bolt and nut. **Do not fully tighten now.**
d. Lower vehicle to ground.
e. Install trailing arm to knuckle. Tighten lateral link mounting bolts to specifications.

STRUT
REPLACE

1. Remove rear lower seat cushion and rear seatback side cushion.
2. Raise and support vehicle, then place suitable jack stands under suspension support.
3. Lower vehicle slightly. Ensure weight rests on jack stands and not suspension arms.
4. Remove rear wheels.
5. Disconnect ABS speed sensor wiring harness clamp from strut.
6. Remove brake hose brake pipe.
7. Remove bracket clip and brake hose,
8. Prevent master cylinder reservoir from draining by connecting brake pipe to brake hose.
9. Disconnect wheel speed sensor wire harness from strut.
10. Remove stabilizer shaft joint from strut.
11. Remove rear suspension knuckle strut mounting bolts and nuts.
12. Remove suspension support jack stands and lower vehicle.
13. Remove strut support mounting nuts.
14. Remove strut.
15. Reverse procedure to install.

COIL SPRING
REPLACE

1. Remove strut as outlined in "Strut, Replace."
2. Mount strut compressor tool No. J-34013 into holding fixture tool No. J-3289-20, or equivalents.

3. Mount strut into compressor tool using strut compressor adapter tool No. J-34013-88, or equivalent.
4. Carefully compress coil spring. **Do not compress too far.**
5. Remove strut rod piston nut.
6. Carefully release compressed spring and remove it from strut.
7. Reverse procedure to install.

STABILIZER BAR
REPLACE

1. Raise and support rear of vehicle, then remove rear wheels.
2. Scribe alignment marks between stabilizer shaft bushings, clamps, shaft and body.
3. Remove brake hose from strut.
4. Remove both stabilizer bar links and bushings.
5. Remove lefthand and righthand stabilizer shaft joints.
6. Remove lefthand and righthand stabilizer shaft bushing retainers.
7. Remove stabilizer shaft bushings.
8. Support fuel tank, then remove rear fuel tank bands mounting bolts and allow bands to hang.
9. Support suspension crossmember using suitable jack.
10. Remove six suspension crossmember to body mounting bolts.
11. Lower suspension crossmember.
12. Disconnect EVAP canister hoses.
13. Disconnect fuel filler neck and vapor hoses from fuel tank.
14. Remove stabilizer shaft by aiming it toward lefthand side of vehicle.
15. Reverse procedure to install.

LATERAL LINK & TRAILING ARM
REPLACE

1. Raise and support vehicle.
2. Remove rear tires and wheels.
3. Remove mounting bolts, nuts and trailing arm.
4. Reverse procedure to install. Adjust wheel alignment as required.

TIGHTENING SPECIFICATIONS

Year	Component	Torque/Ft. Lbs.
2001–02	Axle Hub To Knuckle	59
	Brake Pipe Fittings	11
	Crossmember To Body, Inner	14
	Crossmember To Body, Outer	55
	Fuel Tank Band	29
	Lateral Link	89
	Resonator/Intermediate Pipe To Converter	32
	Resonator/Intermediate Pipe To Muffler	14
	Stabilizer Bar Joint To Shaft	33
	Stabilizer Bar Joint To Strut	33
	Stabilizer Shaft Bushing	14
	Strut	29
	Strut To Knuckle	105
	Trailing Arm	67
	Wheel Speed Sensor	69①

① — Inch lbs.

Front Suspension & Steering

NOTE: On Air Bag Equipped Models, Refer To "Air Bag System Precautions" Located In The Front Of This Manual For System Disarming & Arming Procedures.

NOTE: Refer To "Computer Relearn Procedures" Located In The Front Of This Manual When Battery Power To The Computer Has Been Interrupted.

INDEX

PRECAUTIONS

Air Bag Systems

Refer to "Air Bag System Precautions" in the front of this manual for system disarming and arming procedures.

Battery Ground Cable

Prior to service, disconnect battery ground cable and isolate as required.

DESCRIPTION

The front suspension is a McPherson strut design, **Fig. 1.** The upper end of the strut is anchored to the body by a strut support. The strut and strut support are isolated by a rubber mount. The lower end of the strut is connected to the upper end of the steering knuckle. The lower end of the knuckle is attached to the ball joint, which is attached to the suspension control arm assembly. Movement of the steering wheel is transmitted to the tie rod end and then to the knuckle, turning the wheel and tire assembly.

WHEEL HUB

REPLACE

1. Remove knuckle as outlined in "Steering Knuckle, Replace."
2. Mount knuckle in suitable soft-jawed vise.
3. Record installation direction and remove dust deflector using suitable screwdriver.
4. Remove inner grease seal using seal remover tool No. J-26941 and slide hammer tool No. J-23907, or equivalents, **Fig. 2.**
5. Remove inner bearing snap ring and disc brake dust shield.

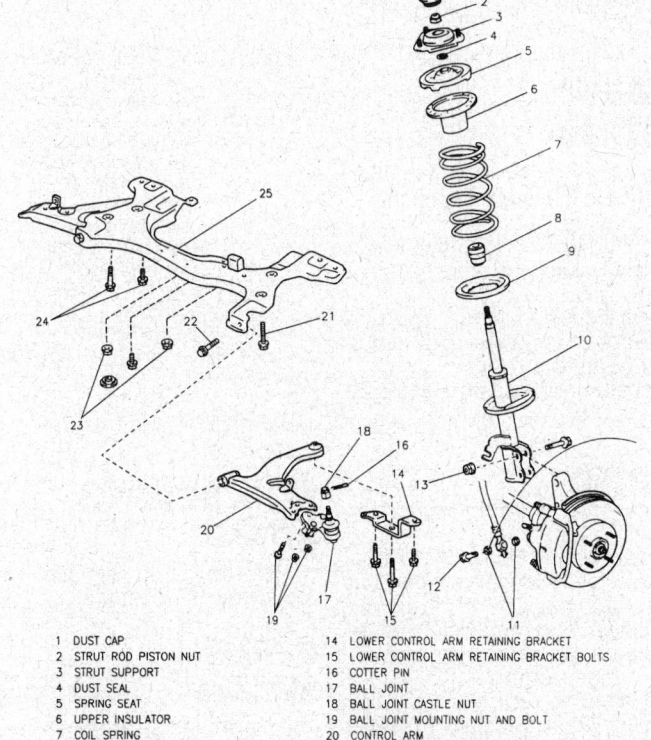

1	DUST CAP	14	LOWER CONTROL ARM RETAINING BRACKET
2	STRUT ROD PISTON NUT	15	LOWER CONTROL ARM RETAINING BRACKET BOLTS
3	STRUT SUPPORT	16	COTTER PIN
4	DUST SEAL	17	BALL JOINT
5	SPRING SEAT	18	BALL JOINT CASTLE NUT
6	UPPER INSULATOR	19	BALL JOINT MOUNTING NUT AND BOLT
7	COIL SPRING	20	CONTROL ARM
8	SPRING BUMPER	21	CROSSMEMBER MOUNTING BOLTS
9	LOWER INSULATOR	22	CROSSMEMBER-TO-CONTROL ARM BOLT
10	STRUT	23	CROSSMEMBER MOUNTING NUTS
11	BRAKE LINE GASKETS	24	CROSSMEMBER MOUNTING BOLTS
12	BRAKE LINE-TO-CALIPER BOLT	25	SUSPENSION CROSSMEMBER
13	STRUT MOUNTING NUT AND BOLT		

GC2029700255000X

Fig. 1   Disassembled view of front suspension

6. Push out hub using hub remover tool Nos. J-25287 and J-35378, or equivalents.

7. Remove outer bearing race using hub remover tools.

8. Remove outer grease seal using suitable seal remover tool and slide hammer.
9. Remove bearing using bearing remover tool No. J-22912-01, or equivalent, and suitable press.
10. Remove wheel bearing using driver handle tool No. J-8092 and side bearing installer tool No. J-21784, or equivalents.
11. Remove inner race and receiver cup.
12. Reverse procedure to install, noting the following:
    a. Install hub bearing using bearing installation tool Nos. J-8092 and J-35411, or equivalents.
    b. Apply GCLB grease part No. 1051344, or equivalent, to outer grease seal lip.
    c. Install outer grease seal using seal installation tool No. J-35737-01, or equivalent.
    d. Install hub using installation tool Nos. J-8092 and J-35399, or equivalents.
    e. Install inner grease seal using bearing installer tool No. J-35737-01, or equivalent.
    f. Ensure dust deflector ring faces in its proper direction and install using ring installation tool No. J-35379, or equivalent.

BALL JOINT INSPECTION

1. Remove steering knuckle w/hub, then clamp knuckle into suitable soft-jawed vise.
2. Flip ball stud back & forth five times, then install castle nut onto ball joint stud.
3. Rotate nut continuously for one turn every 2–4 seconds, then note torque reading on fifth turn.
4. Replace ball joint if reading is not 9–26 inch lbs.

BALL JOINT
REPLACE

1. Raise and support vehicle. Place suitable jack stands under suspension crossmember.
2. Lower vehicle slightly so weight of vehicle rests on suspension crossmember and not control arms.
3. Remove steering knuckle with axle hub as outlined in "Steering Knuckle, Replace."
4. Clamp steering knuckle with axle hub in suitable soft-jawed vise.
5. **On models equipped with ABS,** remove dust deflector.
6. **On all models,** remove cotter pin and nut.
7. Remove ball joint using separator tool No. J-24319-B, or equivalent.
8. Reverse procedure to install, noting the following:
    a. Install new self-locking nut and cotter pin.
    b. Adjust wheel alignment, as required.

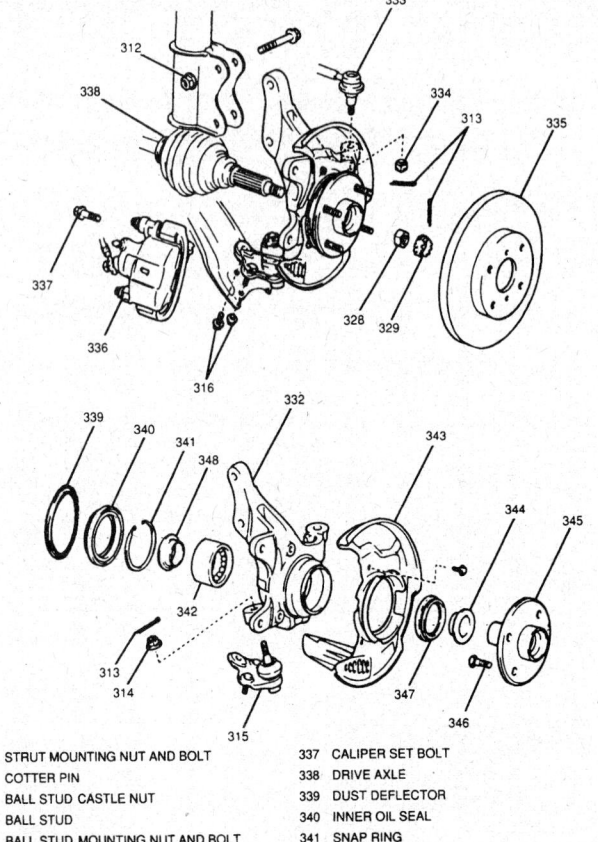

312	STRUT MOUNTING NUT AND BOLT	337	CALIPER SET BOLT
313	COTTER PIN	338	DRIVE AXLE
314	BALL STUD CASTLE NUT	339	DUST DEFLECTOR
315	BALL STUD	340	INNER OIL SEAL
316	BALL STUD MOUNTING NUT AND BOLT	341	SNAP RING
328	DRIVE AXLE NUT	342	HUB BEARING
329	LOCK CAP	343	DUST COVER
332	STEERING KNUCKLE	344	BEARING INNER RACE (OUTSIDE)
333	TIE ROD END	345	AXLE HUB
334	TIE ROD END NUT	346	WHEEL STUD
335	BRAKE ROTOR	347	OUTER OIL SEAL
336	BRAKE CALIPER	348	BEARING INNER RACE (INSIDE)

GC3039700336000X

Fig. 2 Disassembled view of hub & bearing

COIL SPRING
REPLACE

Refer to "Strut, Replace" for coil spring replacement procedure.

STRUT
REPLACE

1. Raise and support vehicle. Place suitable jack stands under suspension crossmember.
2. Lower vehicle slightly so weight of vehicle rests on suspension crossmember and not control arms.
3. Remove brake hose from disc brake caliper.
4. Remove brake hose clip.
5. Remove brake hose from bracket.
6. Loosen bolts and nuts mounting strut to steering knuckle.
7. Lower vehicle slightly.
8. Remove strut mounting nuts at top of shock tower.
9. Remove strut.

10. Reverse procedure to install, noting the following:
    a. Avoid cracking or scratching spring coating.
    b. Coat threads lower side nuts with suitable clean engine oil.
    c. Install strut lower bolts and nuts. **Do not tighten now.**
    d. Install strut to tower nuts.
    e. Tighten strut lower bolts and nuts.

COIL SPRING & STRUT SERVICE

1. Remove strut as outlined in "Strut, Replace."
2. Compress spring slightly using strut holding/spring compression tool No. J-34013-B, or equivalent. **Ensure spring seat is secure and will not turn.**
3. Mount compression tool into holding fixture tool No. J-3289-20, or equivalent.

4. Mount strut into holding fixture using adapter tool No. J-34013-88, or equivalent.
5. Remove strut rod dust cap and piston nut.
6. Remove strut support, dust seal, spring seat, upper insulator, coil spring, bumper and lower insulator.
7. Reverse procedure to install.

CONTROL ARM
REPLACE

On models equipped with automatic transaxle, it may be required to remove the crossmember, transaxle support, both control arms and stabilizer shaft together as a complete unit.

Removal

1. Install engine support fixture tool No. J-28467-360, or equivalent.
2. Raise and support vehicle.
3. Remove lower control arm mounting nuts and bolts.
4. Disconnect stabilizer bar links, as required.
5. Remove mounting bolts, nuts and suspension crossmember with control arms attached.
6. Remove mounting bolts, nuts and control arm.

Installation

1. Install control arm. **Do not tighten mounting bolts now.**
2. Install stabilizer shaft and links to control arms. **Do not tighten mounting bolts now.**
3. Install control arm bracket to crossmember. Tighten mounting bolts.
4. Install stabilizer shaft insulator clamps. Tighten mounting nuts. **Do not tighten mounting bolts now.**
5. Tighten control arm to knuckle mounting bolts.
6. Install suspension support brace and tighten mounting bolts.
7. Install tires and wheels, then lower vehicle.
8. Raise vehicle on drive-on lift or suitable alignment rack.
9. Settle suspension by jouncing vehicle up and down few times.
10. Tighten bolt Nos. 9, 1, 3, 11 and 8 in sequence, **Fig. 3.**
11. Tighten stabilizer shaft link stud nut.

CONTROL ARM BUSHING
REPLACE

The control arm bushings are not serviceable separately. If the bushing are excessively worn or damaged, replace the control arm assembly.

STEERING KNUCKLE
REPLACE

1. Raise and support vehicle, then remove tire and wheel.

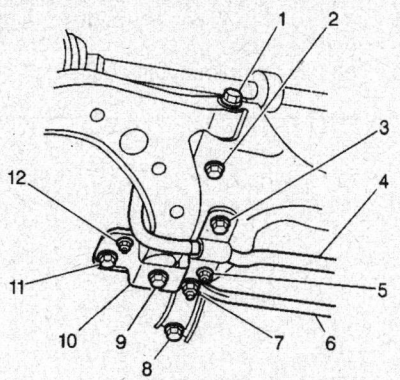

GC2029700256000X

Fig. 3 Front crossmember & control arm tightening sequence

2. **On models equipped with ABS,** remove sensor from knuckle and position aside.
3. **On all models,** remove front brake hose from strut and position aside.
4. Remove control arm to knuckle bolt and nuts.
5. Remove drive axle cotter pin and driveshaft nut retainer.
6. Remove driveshaft nut with assistant holding brake pedal.
7. Remove caliper housing and bracket. Suspend them with suitable wire or rope.
8. Carefully remove brake rotor. Avoid damaging speed sensor rotor, boot and inner oil seal.
9. Loosen nuts on lower side of strut. Do not remove bolts.
10. Remove outer tie rod cotter pin and nut, then separate tie rod end using separator tool No. J-24319-B, or equivalent.
11. Remove strut lower nuts and bolts.
12. Remove knuckle with hub.
13. Remove ball joint cotter pin and nut, then separate ball joint end from knuckle using separator tool No. J-24319-B, or equivalent.
14. Remove hub, bearing and seal.
15. Reverse procedure to install, noting the following:
    a. Coat strut lower side nut threads with suitable clean engine oil.
    b. Install strut lower bolts and nuts. **Do not tighten now.**
    c. Tighten driveshaft nut while assistant holds brake pedal.
    d. Tighten strut lower bolts and nuts.

STABILIZER BAR
REPLACE

1. Raise and support vehicle.
2. Remove mounting nuts and stabilizer links.
3. Remove mounting nuts and suspension support brace.
4. Remove stabilizer shaft mounting bolts and stabilizer bar links.
5. Remove clamp bolts, nuts, studs and stabilizer bar.

6. Reverse procedure to install.

TIE ROD END
REPLACE

Refer to "Power Steering Gear, Replace" for tie rod end replacement procedure.

POWER STEERING GEAR
REPLACE

1. Ensure front wheels are in straight-ahead position and remove ignition key.
2. Remove steering column upper column cover from firewall.
3. Remove steering shaft lower coupling bolt.
4. Remove outlet pipe heat shield.
5. Remove lefthand steering gear inlet and outlet pipe clip bolt.
6. Remove righthand steering gear outlet pipe clip bolt.
7. Remove lefthand steering gear inlet and outlet pipe clip.
8. Place suitable drain pan under vehicle to catch power steering fluid.
9. Disconnect steering gear inlet pipe.
10. Disconnect O2S electrical connector, then remove sensor and gasket.
11. Install engine support fixture tool No. J-28467-360, or equivalent.
12. Raise and support vehicle.
13. Remove front tires and wheels.
14. Remove engine lefthand and righthand lower splash shields.
15. Remove driveshaft exhaust heat shield.
16. Remove outer tie rod cotter pin, nut and outer tie rods using separator tool No. J-24319-B, or equivalent.
17. Remove front suspension brace.
18. Remove suspension crossmember, transaxle support, control arms and stabilizer shaft as unit.
19. Remove transaxle rear mount through-bolt and mount.
20. Remove transaxle rear mount bracket.
21. Disconnect exhaust pipe at manifold.
22. Remove steering gear exhaust heat shield.
23. Remove steering gear clamps.
24. Carefully route steering gear to vehicle's righthand side, then lower and remove it through lefthand side.
25. Remove steering gear insulators.
26. Reverse procedure to install, noting the following:
    a. Install new steering gear insulators, as required.
    b. Install new exhaust donut.
    c. Bleed power steering fluid system.
    d. Adjust wheel alignment, as required.

POWER STEERING PUMP
REPLACE

1. Siphon as much power steering fluid from reservoir as possible.
2. Remove pump drive belt.

3. Remove pump gear inlet hose fitting and inlet pipe.
4. Remove fluid reservoir hose.
5. Raise and support vehicle.
6. Remove righthand front tire and wheel.
7. Remove engine righthand lower splash shield.
8. Remove pump mounting bolts.
9. Carefully remove power steering pump.
10. Reverse procedure to install. Bleed power steering fluid system.

TIGHTENING SPECIFICATIONS

Year	Component	Torque/Ft. Lbs.
2001–02	ABS Hose	22①
	ABS Speed Sensor	71①
	ABS Wire Harness	48①
	Axle Nut	166
	Ball Joint To Control Arm	105
	Ball Joint To Steering Knuckle	91
	Brake Caliper To Steering Knuckle	65
	Control Arm Retainer Bracket, Inner	129
	Control Arm Retainer Bracket, Outer Bolt	109
	Control Arm Retainer Bracket, Outer Nut	14
	Control Arm Retainer Bracket, Rear	91
	Control Arm To Crossmember, Front	158
	Crossmember Front Outer	167
	Drive Axle Nut	166
	Engine Crossmember To Suspension	45
	Front Suspension Crossmember	42
	Front Transaxle Mount	47
	Stabilizer Shaft Link Nut	33
	Stabilizer Shaft Mount Bracket Front Bolt	167
	Stabilizer Shaft Mount Bracket Nut	14
	Stabilizer Shaft Mount Bracket Stud	109
	Strut	29
	Strut Rod Piston	34
	Suspension Support Brace	51
	Tie Rod End	36
	Wheel Lug	76

① — Inch lbs.

Wheel Alignment

INDEX

PRECAUTIONS

Air Bag Systems

Refer to "Air Bag System Precautions" in the front of this manual for system disarming and arming procedures.

PRELIMINARY INSPECTION

Steering and vibration problems are not always the result of improper alignment. They may also be caused by wheel and tire imbalance or other factors. To ensure proper alignment readings, the following inspections should be done and corrections made before inspecting caster, camber or toe:

1. Inspect tires for proper inflation pressures and even tread wear.
2. Inspect wheel bearings for looseness.
3. Inspect ball joints and tie rod ends for excessive looseness.
4. Inspect steering gear operation and mounting.
5. Inspect operation of struts.
6. Inspect control arms.
7. Inspect hub and bearing for excessive wear.

FRONT WHEEL ALIGNMENT

Caster

Caster cannot be adjusted. Should caster be out of specification, locate cause first. If components are damaged, bent, loose, dented or worn, they should be replaced. To prevent an improper caster reading, jounce the bumper three times before inspecting.

Camber

1. Estimate amount camber must be adjusted.

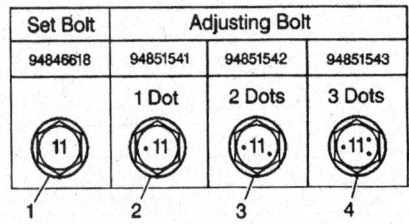

Set Bolt	Adjusting Bolt		
94846618	94851541	94851542	94851543
	1 Dot	2 Dots	3 Dots
11	.11	.11.	.11:
1	2	3	4

GC2029800257000X

Fig. 1   Front camber adjustment bolts

GC2049100085000X

Fig. 2   Front toe adjustment

2. Select proper combination of bolts, **Fig. 1.**
3. To obtain .25° camber, install bolt No. 1 in upper position and bolt No. 2 in lower position.
4. To obtain .50° camber, install bolt No. 1 in upper position and bolt No. 3 in lower position.
5. To obtain .75° camber, install bolt No. 1 in upper position and bolt No. 4 in lower position.
6. To obtain 1.00° camber, install bolt No. 2 in upper position and bolt No. 4 in lower position.
7. To obtain 1.25° camber, install bolt No. 3 in upper position and bolt No. 4 in lower position.
8. To obtain 1.50° camber, install bolt No. 4 in upper position and bolt No. 4 in lower position.

9. Install bolts, inspect alignment and adjust as required.

Toe-In

Toe-in is adjusted by changing tie rod length.
1. Loosen boot clamps and slide from boot.
2. Loosen lefthand and righthand tie rod end locknuts.
3. Turn lefthand and righthand tie rods to align toe-in to specifications.
4. Lefthand and righthand tie rods must be equal length, **Fig. 2.**
5. Install boot clamps and tighten nuts.
6. Ensure rack boots are not twisted.
7. Tighten strut to knuckle nut.
8. **Torque** tie rod locking nut to 41 ft. lbs.

REAR WHEEL ALIGNMENT

Toe

1. Loosen lefthand and righthand lateral link or tie rod locknuts.
2. Adjust total rear toe by turning adjusting tubes. One revolution of adjusting tube will adjust rear to approximately 1.2°.
3. **Torque** lateral link or tie rod locknuts to 41 ft. lbs.

Camber & Caster

Rear caster and camber cannot be adjusted. Should camber be out of specification, locate cause first. If components are damaged, bent loose, dented or worn, they should be replaced. To prevent an improper camber reading, jounce the bumper three times before inspecting. If a tie rod or tie rod end is replaced, inspect toe and steering angle with turning radius gauges. If steering angle is not proper, inspect lefthand and righthand tie rods for equal length. If tie rod length is changed to correct steering, inspect toe once again.

VIBE

INDEX OF SERVICE OPERATIONS

Specifications

GENERAL ENGINE SPECIFICATIONS

Year	Engine Liter	Fuel System	Bore & Stroke, Inch	Compression Ratio	Net H.P. @ RPM	Maximum Torque, Ft. Lbs. @ RPM	Normal Oil Pressure, psi
2003–05	1.8L①	SFI	3.11 × 3.60	10.0	123 @ 6000	118 @ 4400	43–78 @ 3000
	1.8L②	SFI	3.11 × 3.60	10.0	130 @ 6000	125 @ 4400	43–78 @ 3000
	1.8L HO	SFI	3.23 x 3.35	11.5	170 @ 7600	127 @ 4400	43–78 @ 3000

SFI — Sequential Fuel Injection ① — All wheel drive (AWD). ② — Two wheel drive (2WD).

TUNE UP SPECIFICATIONS

Engine	Spark Plug Gap, Inch	Ignition Timing BTDC			Curb Idle Speed		Fast Idle Speed		Fuel Pump Pressure, psi	Valve Clearance, Inch
		Firing Order Fig.	Man. Trans.	Auto. Trans.	Mark Fig.	Man. Trans.	Auto. Trans.	Man. Trans.	Auto Trans.		
1.8L	.043	1-3-4-2	10–18①	10–18①	A	700	750N	②	②	44–50	③
1.8L HO	.043	1-3-4-2	8–12①	8–12①	A	800	750N	②	②	44–50	④

BTDC — Before Top Dead Center
N — Neutral
① — With check connector terminals T & E shorted.

② — Electronically controlled.
③ — Intake, .006–.010; exhaust, .010–.014.

④ — Intake, .006–.010; exhaust, .014–.018.

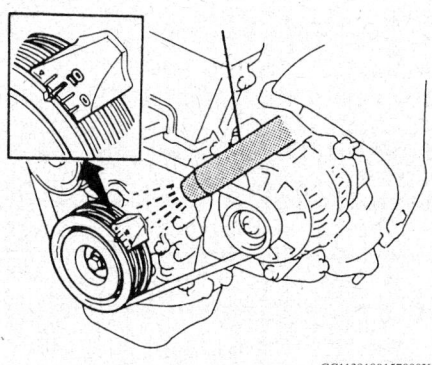

GC1139100157000X

Fig. A

FRONT WHEEL ALIGNMENT SPECIFICATIONS

Year	Model	Caster Angle, Degrees		Camber Angle, Degrees				Toe-In, Inch	Toe Out On Turns, Degrees		Ball Joint Wear
		Limits	Desired	Limits		Desired			Outer Wheel	Inner Wheel	
				Left	Right	Left	Right				
2003–05	AWD	+2.02 to +3.52	+2.77	−1.23 to +.27	−1.23 to +.27	−.48	−.48	−.02 to +.02	—	—	①
	FWD	+2.03 to +3.53	+2.78	−1.32 to +.18	−1.32 to +.18	−.57	−.57	−.20 to +.02	—	—	①

① — Refer to "Ball Joint Inspection" for proper resting procedure.

REAR WHEEL ALIGNMENT SPECIFICATIONS

| Year | Model | Camber Angle, Degrees | | | | Toe-In, Inch | Ball Joint Wear |
| | | Limits | | Desired | | | |
		Left	Right	Left	Right		
2003–05	AWD	−1.48 to +.02	−1.48 to +.02	−.73	−.73	+.20	①
	FWD	−1.95 to −.95	−1.95 to −.95	−1.45	−1.45	+.26	①

① — Replace ball joint if any looseness is detected or if ball joint seal is cut.

VEHICLE RIDE HEIGHT SPECIFICATIONS

Model	Year	Body Style	Manufac-turer's Original Tire Size②	Measurement Points & Specifications①③					
				Front			Rear		
				Dim.	Specification		Dim.	Specification	
					Inches	mm		Inches	mm
AWD	2003–05	All	205	Z	2.2	57	D	1.5	38
FWD	2003–05	All	215	Z	2.0	51	D	1.6	41

Z Dim. — Center line of control arm pivot bolt to the lower edge of steering knuckle ball joint, Front

D Dim. — 2WD, center line of the rear wheel to the center line of the rear axle pivot bolt; 4WD, center line of the rear wheel to the lower control arm pivot bolt, Rear

Dim. — Dimension
① — ± .40 in (10 MM) front to rear & side to side.
② — See door sticker or inside of glove box for manufacturer's original tire size specifications. If tires on vehicle do not match manufacturer's original tire size & measurement is not within limits, refer to the "Non-Standard Tire & Wheel

Size Adjustment To Ride Height Specification & Tire Size Adjustment Charts" in the front of this manual for approximate changes in ride height specifications.
③ — Measurement is with fuel, radiator coolant and engine oil full, spare tire, jack, hand tools & mats in designated positions & tires properly inflated.

FLUID CAPACITIES & COOLING SYSTEM DATA

| Year | Engine | Coolant Capacity, Qts. | | Coolant Type | Radiator Cap Relief Pressure, Lbs. | Thermo. Opening Temp., Deg. F | Fuel Tank, Gals. | Engine Oil Refill, Qts. | Transaxle Oil | |
		Manual Trans.	Auto. Trans.						Man. Trans-axle Qts.	Auto. Transaxle Qts.①
2003–04	1.8L	6.9	6.9	Dex-Cool	16.0	183	④	3.9	②	③
	1.8L HO	7.1	7.1	Dex-Cool	16.0	183	13	4.8	②	3.3
2005	1.8L	6.9	6.9	⑤	13.0	183	④	3.9	②	③
	1.8L HO	7.1	7.1	⑤	13.0	183	13	4.8	②	3.3

① — Approximate. Make final inspection w/dipstick.

② — 5-speed transaxle, 2.0 qts.; 6-speed transaxle, 2.4 qts.

③ — AWD drive, 3.3 qts.; 2WD, 3.0 qts.

④ — AWD, 12 gals.; 2WD, 13 gals.

⑤ — Use a 50/50 mixture of distilled water & GM coolant P/N 1238560,

or equivalent conforming to GM Specification 1825M. An approved recycled coolant conforming to GM Specification 1825M may also be used.

LUBRICANT DATA

| Year | Model | Lubricant Type | | | |
| | | Transaxle | | Power Steering | Brake System |
		Manual	Automatic		
2003–04	All	75W-90 GL-4 or GL-5	ATF Type T-IV	①	DOT-3
2005	All	②	ATF Type T-IV	①	DOT-3

① — Dexron III Revision "H."

② — Synthetic Manual Transmission

Fluid GM P/N 12346190, or an equivalent SAE 75W-90 GL-4 gear oil.

Electrical

NOTE: On Air Bag Equipped Models, Refer To "Air Bag System Precautions" Located In The Front Of This Manual For System Disarming & Arming Procedures.

NOTE: Refer To "Computer Relearn Procedures" Located In The Front Of This Manual When Battery Power To The Computer Has Been Interrupted.

INDEX

PRECAUTIONS

Air Bag Systems

Refer to "Air Bag System Precautions" in the front of this manual for system disarming and arming procedures.

Battery Ground Cable

Prior to service, disconnect battery ground cable and isolate as required.

FUSE PANEL & FLASHER LOCATION

The instrument panel fuse block is located behind the lefthand side of the instrument panel, lefthand side of the steering column. The lefthand instrument panel junction block is located behind the lefthand side of the instrument panel, above the instrument panel fuse block. The righthand instrument panel junction block is located behind the righthand side of the instrument panel, above the instrument panel storage compartment. The underhood fuse block is located on the lefthand side of the engine compartment. The flasher relay is located behind the lefthand side of the instrument panel, in the instrument panel fuse block.

RELAY CENTER LOCATION

Refer to "Fuse Panel & Flasher Location" for relay center location.

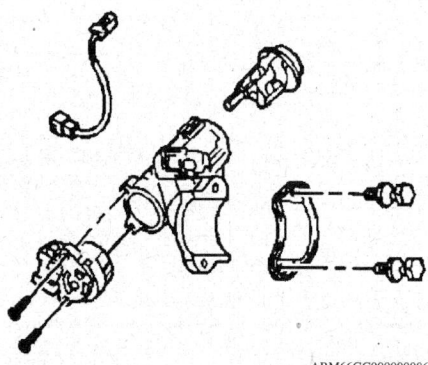

ARM66GC000000086

Fig. 1 Ignition lock replacement

FUEL PUMP RELAY LOCATION

The circuit opening/fuel pump relay is located behind the lefthand side of the instrument panel, in the instrument panel fuse block. The EFI relay is located on the lefthand side of the engine compartment, in the underhood fuse block.

STARTER
REPLACE

1. Disconnect starter motor electrical connectors and positive battery cable.
2. Remove starter motor upper and lower mounting bolts, then the starter motor from vehicle.
3. Reverse procedure to install, noting the following:
   a. **Torque** starter mounting bolts to 27 ft. lbs.
   b. **Torque** positive battery cable to starter mounting nut to 84 inch lbs.

ALTERNATOR
REPLACE

1. Rotate drive belt tensioner clockwise and remove drive belt.
2. Disconnect wire harness clamp from retaining clip.
3. Remove wire terminal cap and retaining nut.
4. Disconnect alternator connector.
5. Remove alternator mounting bolts, then the alternator.
6. Reverse procedure to install, noting the following:
   a. **Torque** upper mounting bolt to 18 ft. lbs.
   b. **On models equipped wth HO engine, torque** lower mounting bolts to 43 ft. lbs.
   c. **On models less HO engine, torque** lower mounting bolts to 40 ft. lbs.

IGNITION COIL
REPLACE

1. Remove retainers, then the engine cover.
2. Disconnect electrical connectors from ignition coils.
3. Remove bolts from ignition coils, then the electrical harness.
4. Remove electrical harness package, then the ignition coils from cylinder head.
5. Reverse procedure to install. **Torque** coil mounting bolts to 80 inch lbs.

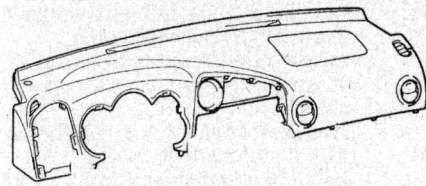

Fig. 2 Upper trim panel replacement. Vibe

IGNITION LOCK
REPLACE

1. Remove lower and upper steering column covers.
2. Insert key into ignition lock cylinder, then turn key to Accessory.
3. Push down stop pin, then remove cylinder using a suitable screwdriver, **Fig. 1.**
4. Reverse procedure to install.

IGNITION SWITCH
REPLACE

1. Remove lower and upper steering column covers.
2. Disconnect ignition switch electrical connector.
3. Remove screws, then the ignition switch.
4. Reverse procedure to install.

HEADLAMP SWITCH
REPLACE

Refer to "Combination Switch, Replace" for headlamp switch replacement.

COMBINATION SWITCH
REPLACE

1. Remove lower and upper steering column covers.
2. Disconnect turn signal/headlamp switch electrical connector.
3. Remove turn signal/headlamp switch from steering column by depressing tab.
4. Reverse procedure to install.

TURN SIGNAL SWITCH
REPLACE

Refer to "Combination Switch, Replace" for turn signal switch replacement.

STEERING WHEEL
REPLACE

1. Remove air bag module as outlined in "Passive Restraint Systems" chapter.
2. Disconnect horn electrical connector, then remove cruise control switch.
3. Remove steering wheel mounting nut.
4. Place match marks on steering wheel and on steering shaft.
5. Remove steering using steering wheel puller tool No. J 1859-A or equivalent.
6. Reverse procedure to install. **Torque** steering wheel nut to 37 ft. lbs.

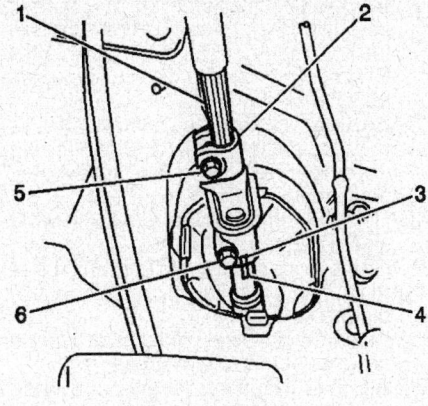

1. Steering Column Shaft
2. Upper Coupling
3. Lower Coupling
4. Lower Shaft
5 & 6. Pinch Bolts

Fig. 3 Steering column removal. Vibe

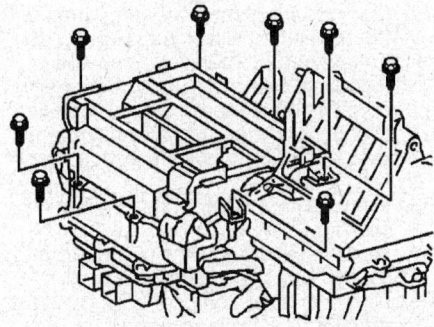

Fig. 5 Evaporator core replacement

INSTRUMENT CLUSTER
REPLACE

1. Remove instrument cluster bezel screws, then the bezel by disengaging two lower clips.
2. Remove instrument cluster mounting screws, then disconnect electrical connectors.
3. Carefully remove instrument cluster.
4. Reverse procedure to install.

RADIO
REPLACE

1. Remove instrument panel accessory center trim plate.
2. Remove screws, then the clamp from radio receiver bracket.
3. Pull radio from instrument panel, then disconnect electrical connector and antenna lead in cable.
4. Reverse procedure to install.

WIPER MOTOR
REPLACE

1. Remove plastic nut cover from wiper

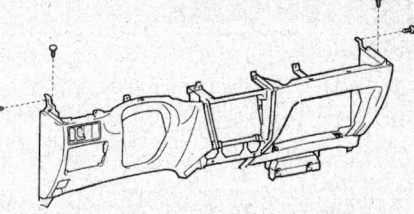

Fig. 4 Lower trim panel replacement. Vibe

arm, then the retaining nut and wiper arm.
2. Remove air inlet grille panel, then disconnect wiper motor electrical connector.
3. Remove wiper motor assembly bolts, then the wiper motor assembly.
4. Disengage meshing of inner rod from crank arm pivot using a flat bladed tool, then remove wiper transmission from wiper motor.
5. Reverse procedure to install.

WIPER SWITCH
REPLACE

1. Remove lower and upper steering column covers.
2. Disconnect turn signal/headlamp switch electrical connector.
3. Remove wiper/washer switch from steering column by depressing tab.
4. Reverse procedure to install.

BLOWER MOTOR
REPLACE

1. Remove two retainers from PCM close out panel below instrument panel compartment door.
2. Swing PCM close out panel down, then open instrument panel compartment door.
3. Push in on both sides of instrument panel compartment door in order to release safety catches and remove door.
4. Remove PCM bracket retainers, then pull PCM with brackets outward and swing both down away from under instrument panel.
5. Disconnect blower motor electrical connector, then remove blower motor cooling tube.
6. Remove bolts, then blower motor and fan (1) from vehicle.
7. Reverse procedure to install.

CABIN AIR FILTER
REPLACE

1. Open instrument panel compartment.
2. Remove screw from righthand side of compartment door.
3. Push in on each side of compartment door and lower door.
4. Push down on tabs and open filter door.
5. Remove filter from vehicle.
6. Reverse procedure to install.

HEATER CORE
REPLACE

1. Drain coolant into suitable container.
2. Recover refrigerant charge as outlined in "Air Conditioning" chapter.
3. Disconnect heater hoses at heater core.
4. Remove evaporator inlet and outlet tubes from evaporator.
5. Remove center instrument panel trim plate using a suitable taped flat bladed tool.
6. Disconnect A/C, hazard warning, rear defogger and passenger's side seat belt indicator electrical connectors.
7. Remove mounting screws and disconnect bracket clamp to pull radio out.
8. Disconnect radio electrical connector and antenna lead.
9. **On models equipped with manual transaxle,** remove gearshift knob.
10. **On all models,** remove center A/C control knob and screw.
11. Remove front floor console trim plate using a suitable taped flat bladed tool.
12. Disconnect two cigarette lighters and accessory power receptacle electrical connectors.
13. Disconnect HVAC control electrical connector, then the mode, temperature and A/C cables.
14. Remove HVAC control.
15. Remove driver's air bag module as outlined in "Passive Restraint Systems" chapter.
16. Remove steering wheel as outlined under "Steering Wheel, Replace."
17. Remove three attaching screws, then the steering column lower and upper trim covers.
18. Disconnect electrical connectors, then remove turn signal/headlamp and wiper/washer switches.
19. Disconnect electrical connector and remove clockspring.
20. Remove passenger's air bag module as outlined in "Passive Restraint Systems" chapter.
21. Remove cluster trim plate using a suitable flat bladed tool.
22. **Ensure ignition is turned Off,** remove mounting screw and release two lower retainers, then disconnect electrical connector.
23. Remove lefthand and righthand windshield garnish moldings.
24. Remove lefthand instrument panel trim plate using a suitable taped flat bladed tool.
25. Disconnect power mirror and dimmer switch electrical connectors.
26. Remove mounting screws and upper instrument panel by pulling rearward, **Fig. 2.**
27. **On models equipped with automatic transaxle,** proceed as follows:
    a. Insert and turn ignition key to Accessory.
    b. Disconnect park lock cable by pushing release button.
    c. Remove ignition key and lock steering column in original position.
28. **On all models,** position insulator pad away from steering column.
29. Mark steering shaft coupling and shaft for installation alignment, **Fig. 3.**
30. Loosen upper coupling pinch bolt.
31. Remove lower pinch bolt and position coupling on to steering column shaft.
32. Disconnect steering column connectors and release wire harness retainers.
33. Remove mounting bolts and steering column.
34. Remove lefthand and righthand door sill and kick panel trim plates.
35. Remove front floor console compartment door.
36. Remove mounting screws, then pull front floor console rearward and up.
37. Open door and remove glove compartment mounting screw.
38. Release upper tabs and remove glove compartment by pulling it out.
39. **On models equipped with automatic transaxle,** remove manual selector as follows:
    a. Disconnect cable from gearshift by pushing retainer clip in.
    b. Disconnect park lock cable from bracket using a suitable flat bladed tool.
    c. Disconnect shift cable from gearshift lever and plate.
    d. Disconnect electrical connectors and wire harness clip.
    e. Remove four mounting nuts and manual selector.
40. **On all models,** gently pry hood release handle from knee bolster trim.
41. Disconnect cable and remove hood release handle.
42. Remove eight mounting bolts and four retainers, then the wire harness clamps.
43. Remove lower instrument panel by pulling it rearward, **Fig. 4.**
44. Remove instrument panel reinforcement.
45. Disconnect blower motor electrical connector.
46. Separate rear heater ducts from HVAC module.
47. Remove HVAC module mounting nuts.
48. Carefully pull HVAC module out.
49. Remove brackets and heater core.
50. Reverse procedure to install.

EVAPORATOR CORE
REPLACE

1. Remove heater core as outlined under "Heater Core, Replace."
2. Remove blower motor cover, **Fig. 5.**
3. Remove HVAC module case halves' mounting screws.
4. Separate case halves.
5. Remove evaporator core.
6. Reverse procedure to install.

1.8L Engine

NOTE: On Air Bag Equipped Models, Refer To "Air Bag System Precautions" Located In The Front Of This Manual For System Disarming & Arming Procedures.

NOTE: Refer To "Computer Relearn Procedures" Located In The Front Of This Manual When Battery Power To The Computer Has Been Interrupted.

INDEX

PRECAUTIONS

Air Bag Systems

Refer to "Air Bag System Precautions" in the front of this manual for system disarming and arming procedures.

Battery Ground Cable

Prior to service, disconnect battery ground cable and isolate as required.

Fuel System Pressure Relief

1. Loosen fuel filler cap to relieve fuel tank pressure.
2. Remove instrument panel compartment door.
3. Reach through compartment opening and remove fuel pump (circuit opening) relay from instrument panel fuse block, **Fig. 1.**
4. Start engine and allow it to run until it stalls from lack of fuel.
5. Crank engine for an additional three seconds to relieve remaining fuel pressure, then turn ignition Off.
6. Install relay, then install instrument panel compartment door.
7. Tighten fuel filler cap.

COMPRESSION PRESSURE

Compression readings should be 218

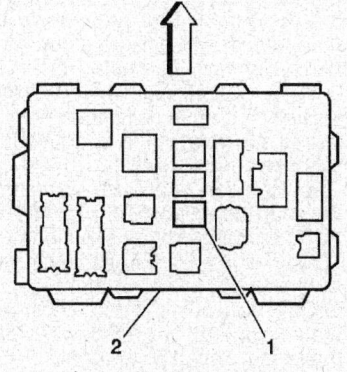

1. Circuit opening relay
2. I/P fuse block

ARM0400000000175

Fig. 1 Fuel pump (circuit opening) relay location

psi, with a minimum of 145 psi. Maximum difference between cylinders should be 15 psi.

ENGINE MOUNT
REPLACE

1. Raise and support engine using engine support tool No. J 28467-B, or equivalent.
2. Remove three righthand side engine mount to frame bracket bolts.
3. Remove righthand side engine mount to engine bracket bolts.
4. Raise engine slightly to provide clearance for engine mount removal.
5. Remove righthand side engine mount.

6. Remove righthand side engine mount to frame bracket.
7. Remove righthand side engine mount to engine bracket.
8. Reverse procedure to install.

ENGINE
REPLACE
Except HO Engine

1. From inside vehicle, disconnect ECM connectors and cowl wire electrical connectors from connector mounting bracket.
2. Pull engine harness wire from passenger compartment.
3. Remove engine cover, then relieve fuel pressure as outlined under "Precautions."
4. Raise and support vehicle, then drain coolant into a suitable container and remove engine undercovers.
5. Drain engine oil into a suitable container, then lower vehicle, release tensioner and remove accessory drive belt.
6. **On models equipped with air conditioning,** recover A/C refrigerant as outlined in "Air Conditioning" chapter.
7. **On models equipped with manual transaxle,** remove crankshaft pulley retaining bolt using tool No. J 8614-01 or equivalent, then the bolt, nut and drive belt tensioner.
8. **On all models,** remove accelerator cable and cable bracket from throttle body.

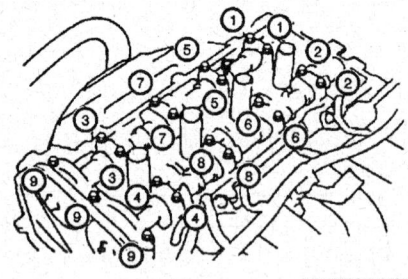

Fig. 2 Camshaft bearing cap bolt loosening sequence. Except HO engine

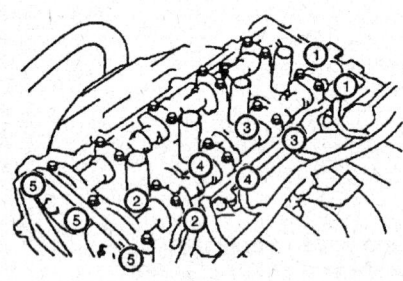

Fig. 5 Camshaft bearing cap bolt tightening sequence. Except HO engine

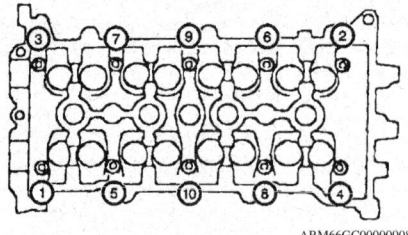

Fig. 3 Cylinder head bolt loosening sequence

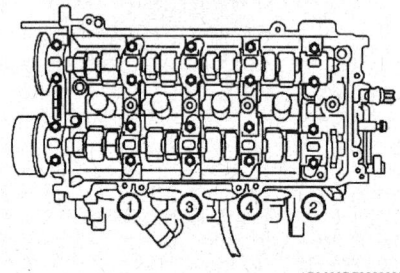

Fig. 6 Camshaft bearing cap bolt loosening sequence. HO engine

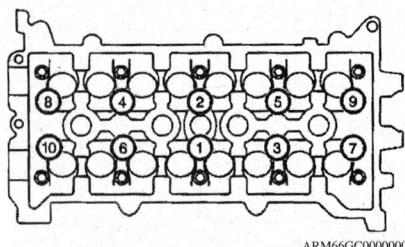

Fig. 4 Cylinder head tightening sequence. Except HO engine

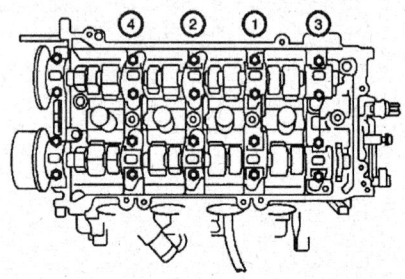

Fig. 7 Camshaft bearing cap bolt tightening sequence. HO engine

9. Disconnect IAT and MAF sensor electrical connectors, then the vacuum hoses from air cleaner.
10. Disconnect air intake hoses from throttle body, then unclip and remove air cleaner cap.
11. Remove air filter, disconnect wire harness retaining clip from air cleaner lower case.
12. Remove bolt, then the vacuum switching valve bracket.
13. Remove retaining bolts, then air cleaner lower box.
14. Disconnect cruise control actuator electrical connector, then remove fuel line hose clamp.
15. Disconnect fuel hose from fuel line, then the heater hose from water bypass pipe.
16. Disconnect heater hose from water hose union on the cylinder head, then the brake booster vacuum hose from brake booster.
17. Remove radiator inlet and outlet hoses from radiator.
18. Disconnect electrical connectors, then remove retaining bolts and alternator from vehicle.
19. Disconnect transmission oil cooler lines, then the fan motor electrical connector and fan motor electrical harness clamps from fan shroud.
20. Remove radiator mounting bolts, then the radiator fan with motor and radiator.
21. Remove engine relay box cover, then disconnect engine compartment relay box connectors.
22. Disconnect ground cables from front lefthand side of engine compartment, then the wire harness clamps.
23. Remove clutch actuator cylinder fluid line, then the clutch actuator cylinder

from transaxle.
24. **On models equipped with manual transaxle,** unclip cable from mounting bracket and disconnect transaxle control cables from transaxle.
25. **On models equipped with automatic transaxle,** proceed as follows:
    a. Unclip cable from mounting bracket and remove shift cable nut.
    b. Unclip wire harness then remove shift cable mounting bracket bolt and disconnect oil cooler hoses.
26. **On all models,** remove driveshaft as outlined under "Driveshaft, Replace" in "Front Wheel Drive Axles" chapter.
27. **On models equipped with AWD,** remove propeller shaft as outlined under "Propeller Shaft, Replace" in "Rear Axle & Suspension" section.
28. **On all models,** disconnect power steering lines and drain power steering fluid into a suitable container.
29. Remove oxygen sensors, then the floor panel brace.
30. Remove bolts, then springs and front exhaust pipe from vehicle.
31. Disconnect front stabilizer link assembly from strut.
32. Support front suspension crossmember.
33. Remove lower control arm from ball joint, then the cotter pin and nut from ball joint stud.
34. Remove ball joint from knuckle.
35. Set engine lift, then remove lefthand side mounting insulator bolt and nut.
36. Remove bolts and nuts from righthand side engine mount, then crossmember bolts.
37. Lower engine and transaxle assembly.
38. Reverse procedure to install.

HO Engine

1. From inside vehicle, disconnect ECM connectors and cowl wire electrical

connectors from connector mounting bracket.
2. Pull engine harness wire from passenger compartment.
3. Lock steering column, then ensure front wheels are in straight ahead position.
4. Move silencer pad away from steering column, then place match marks on steering shaft coupling and on shaft.
5. Remove upper bolt, then the lower bolt from couplings and move coupling onto steering column shaft.
6. Remove coupling from steering column shaft.
7. Remove engine cover, then relieve fuel pressure as outlined under "Precautions."
8. Drain coolant into a suitable container, then disconnect accelerator cable.
9. Remove air cleaner cover, then the air filter, air cleaner case bolts and air cleaner.
10. Remove fuel tube clamp, then disconnect fuel tube from fuel pipe using tool No. J 43178, or equivalent.
11. Disconnect heater hose from water by pass pipe, then heater hose from water hose union on cylinder head.
12. Disconnect brake booster vacuum hose from brake booster.
13. Disconnect radiator inlet and outlet hoses.
14. Mark running direction, then release tensioner and remove accessory drive belt.
15. Disconnect electrical connectors, then remove retaining bolts and alternator from vehicle.
16. Disconnect ATF cooler lines, then the fan motor electrical connector and fan motor electrical harness clamps from fan shroud.

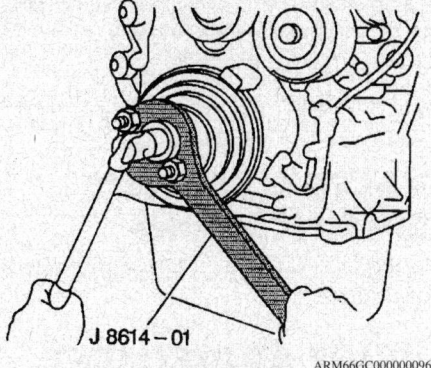

Fig. 8 Crankshaft pulley bolt removal

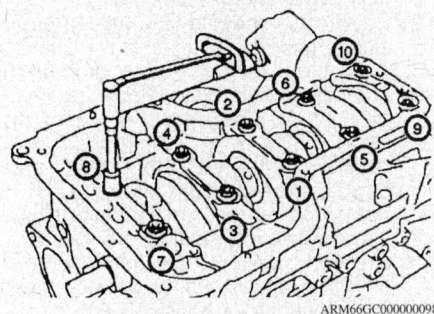

Fig. 11 Main bearing cap tightening sequence

17. Remove radiator mounting bolts, then the radiator fan with motor and radiator.
18. Remove clutch slave cylinder bolts, then the cylinder line bolt and cylinder line bracket bolt.
19. Remove engine relay box cover, then disconnect engine compartment relay box connector.
20. Disconnect wire harness clamps, then the ground cables from transaxle and engine.
21. **On models equipped with manual transaxle,** proceed as follows:
    a. Remove clutch actuator cylinder fluid line.
    b. Remove clutch actuator cylinder from transaxle.
    c. Unclip cable from mounting bracket and disconnect transaxle control cables from transaxle.
22. **On models equipped with automatic transaxle,** unclip cable from mounting bracket and remove shift cable nut.
23. **On all models,** raise and support vehicle, then remove lefthand and righthand engine splash shields.
24. Drain engine oil into a suitable container.
25. Place reference mark on pinion flange yoke and differential pinion flange.
26. Remove retaining bolts and nuts, then the mid shaft bearing support bolts.
27. Remove sliding yoke and two piece propeller shaft assembly from transaxle.
28. Disconnect power steering lines and drain power steering fluid into a suitable container.
29. Remove oxygen sensors, then the

Fig. 9 Timing mark alignment

floor panel brace.
30. Remove bolts, then springs and front exhaust pipe from vehicle.
31. Remove righthand and lefthand driveshaft locknut, then separate lefthand and righthand tie rod ends.
32. Disconnect front stabilizer link assembly from strut.
33. Support front suspension crossmember.
34. Remove lower control arm from ball joint, then the cotter pin and nut from ball joint stud.
35. Remove ball joint from knuckle.
36. Set engine lift, then remove lefthand side mounting insulator bolt and nut.
37. Remove bolts and nuts from righthand side engine mount, then crossmember bolts.
38. Lower engine and transaxle assembly.
39. Reverse procedure to install.

INTAKE MANIFOLD
REPLACE

1. Remove engine cover attaching nuts and retainers, then the cover.
2. Remove air inlet duct from throttle body assembly.
3. Remove PCV breather hose.
4. Disconnect TP sensor electrical connectors.
5. Rotate throttle lever, then disconnect accelerator cable and throttle valve cable.
6. Disconnect IAC valve electrical connector.
7. Drain cooling system, then remove coolant hoses from throttle body.
8. Remove accelerator control cable and throttle body brackets.
9. Remove manifold support bracket attaching bolts.
10. Remove throttle body bolts and position the throttle body aside.
11. Disconnect ECT and CMP sensor connectors.
12. Disconnect camshaft position actuator and rocker arm control solenoid valve connectors.
13. Disconnect oil pressure switch and ground connectors.
14. Release clamps and remove engine harness wire protector from intake manifold.
15. Disconnect EVAP and brake booster vacuum hoses.
16. Remove oil dipstick guide.
17. Remove intake manifold attaching

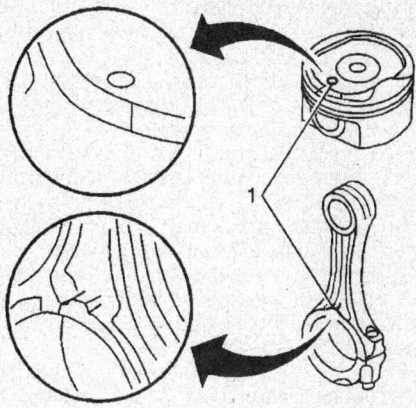

Fig. 10 Piston & rod assembly

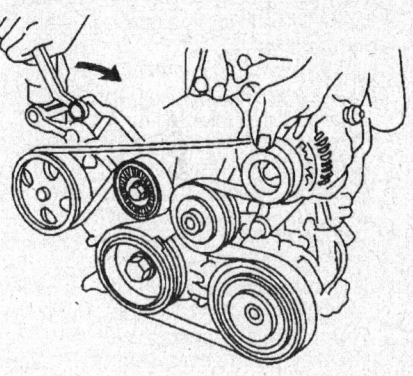

Fig. 12 Serpentine drive belt routing

bolts and nuts, then the intake manifold, gasket and insulator.
18. Reverse procedure to install.

EXHAUST MANIFOLD
REPLACE

1. **On models equipped with AWD,** disconnect Secondary AIR pump hose clamp and remove AIR pipe retaining bolt.
2. **On all models,** raise and support vehicle.
3. Remove HO2S.
4. Remove exhaust pipe hanger.
5. Remove front exhaust pipe to manifold flange attaching bolts, then the exhaust pipe and flange gasket.
6. Remove exhaust manifold brace to manifold attaching bolt.
7. Lower vehicle and remove upper heat insulator attaching bolts, then the heat insulator.
8. Remove exhaust manifold attaching bolts and nuts.
9. Remove exhaust manifold and gasket.
10. Reverse procedure to install.

CYLINDER HEAD
REPLACE

Except High Output (HO) Engine

1. Relieve fuel pressure as outlined

under "Precautions."

2. Drain engine coolant, then engine oil into suitable containers.
3. Mark drive belt running direction.
4. Release drive belt tensioner and remove accessory drive belt.
5. Remove alternator as outlined under "Alternator, Replace" in "Electrical" section.
6. Remove intake manifold as outlined under "Intake Manifold, Replace."
7. Disconnect fuel injector connectors, then remove radiator inlet hose.
8. Remove bolts, then the fuel injector harness.
9. Remove exhaust manifold as outlined under "Exhaust Manifold, Replace."
10. Install engine support fixture tool No. J 28467-A, or equivalent.
11. Remove righthand side engine mount, then disconnect ignition coil electrical connectors.
12. Disconnect fuel line at fuel rail, then remove fuel injector fuel rail hold down clamp and ignition coils.
13. Remove fuel rail and ground wires from cylinder head.
14. Position injector harness aside, then remove heater hose at cylinder head.
15. Remove water bypass pipe from cylinder head.
16. Remove camshaft and engine coolant temperature sensors.
17. Remove PCV hoses and valve from cylinder head cover, then the cylinder head cover.
18. Set number 1 piston to top dead center, then align camshaft timing sprockets.
19. Disconnect power steering oil pressure switch connector.
20. Remove both engine splash shields, then the power steering through bolts and nut.
21. Remove power steering pump and position aside.
22. Remove crankshaft pulley retaining bolt using tool No. J 8614-01 or equivalent.
23. Remove CKP sensor, then the drive belt tensioner.
24. Remove righthand side engine mounting bracket, then the timing chain tensioner.
25. Remove timing chain cover, then the CKP sensor reluctor.
26. Remove timing chain slipper, then the crankshaft sprocket and timing chain.
27. Remove camshaft sprockets.
28. Remove camshaft bearing cap bolts in sequence, **Fig. 2,** then the camshafts and lifters. Keep lifters in order to ensure installation in original locations.
29. Raise engine, then reposition holding fixture.
30. Disconnect EVAP hose for on-board refueling vapor recovery, then the brake booster vacuum hose.
31. Remove oil dipstick guide bolt, then the intake manifold bolts and nuts.
32. Remove intake manifold, gasket and intake manifold insulator.
33. Remove upper heat insulator, then exhaust manifold nuts and bolts.
34. Remove exhaust manifold, gasket and lower heat insulator.

35. Remove cylinder head bolts and washers in sequence, **Fig. 3.**
36. Remove cylinder head, then the gasket.
37. Reverse procedure to install, noting the following:
    a. **Torque** cylinder head bolts in three steps in sequence, **Fig. 4.** First step, to 18 ft. lbs.; second step, to 36 ft. lbs.; third step, rotate bolts an additional 90°.
    b. **Torque** camshaft bearing cap bolts to 10 ft. lbs., then **torque** front bearing cap bolts to 17 ft. lbs., in sequence, **Fig. 5.**

High Output (HO) Engine

1. Remove engine undercovers, then drain engine oil into a suitable container.
2. Remove engine sight shield, then the air cleaner assembly.
3. Disconnect accelerator cable, then relieve fuel pressure as outlined under "Precautions."
4. Release tensioner and remove accessory drive belt.
5. Remove alternator as outlined under "Alternator, Replace" in "Electrical" section.
6. Remove timing chain dampner bolts, then the dampner.
7. Remove timing chain shoe bolts, then the shoe.
8. Remove crankshaft sprocket with timing chain.
9. Remove exhaust pipe, then the exhaust manifold bracket nut and bolts.
10. Remove ignition coils as outlined under "Ignition Coil, Replace" in "Electrical" section.
11. Remove spark plugs, then disconnect PCV hoses from cylinder head cover and throttle body.
12. Remove intake manifold as outlined under "Intake Manifold, Replace."
13. Disconnect coupling for fuel feed hose from fuel feed pipe of fuel rail using tool No. J 43178, or equivalent.
14. Disconnect electrical connectors to four fuel injectors.
15. Remove retainers from fuel supply pipe bracket, then the fuel rail and spacers from engine.
16. Remove fuel injectors with O-rings and grommets from cylinder head.
17. Remove both intake and exhaust camshaft bearing cap bolts in sequence, **Fig. 6.**
18. Remove bolt, then gasket and oil control valve filter.
19. Disconnect upper radiator hose, then the heater hose from water hose union.
20. Remove cylinder head bolts in sequence, **Fig. 3.**
21. Remove water bypass to cylinder block bolt.
22. Remove cylinder head from engine.
23. Reverse procedure to install, noting the following:
    a. **Torque** cylinder head bolts to 26 ft. lbs., in sequence, **Fig. 4.**

    b. Mark front of cylinder head bolts with paint, then rotate an additional 180° using torque angle meter tool No. J 36660-A, or equivalent.
    c. **Torque** camshaft bearing cap bolts to 14 ft. lbs., in sequence, **Fig. 7.**

VALVE CLEARANCE SPECIFICATIONS

Refer to "Tune Up Specification Chart" in this chapter.

VALVE ADJUSTMENT

Measure and adjust valve clearance while the engine is cold.
1. Remove cylinder head cover.
2. Set No. 1 cylinder at TDC on compression stroke.
3. Turn crankshaft to align groove in crankshaft pulley with 0 mark on No. 1 front cover. **Ensure valve lifters on No. 1 cylinder have freeplay. If not, rotate crankshaft pulley 360° and align 0 mark on front cover.**
4. Measure and record valve lash clearance between intake cam lobes and lifters on cylinder Nos. 1 and 2. Record any clearances which do not meet specifications.
5. Measure and record valve lash clearance between exhaust cam lobes and lifters on cylinder Nos. 1 and 3. Record any clearances which do not meet specifications.
6. Rotate crankshaft pulley 360° and align 0 mark on front cover.
7. Measure and record valve lash clearance between intake cam lobes and lifters on cylinder Nos. 3 and 4. Record any clearances which do not meet specifications.
8. Measure and record valve lash clearance between exhaust cam lobes and lifters on cylinder Nos. 2 and 4. Record any clearances which do not meet specifications.
9. If clearance is not within specifications, refer to "Hydraulic Lifters, Replace."

HYDRAULIC LIFTERS
REPLACE

1. Remove timing chain as outlined under "Timing Chain, Replace."
2. Remove intake camshaft as outlined under "Cylinder Head, Replace."
3. Remove valve lifters as required.
4. Reverse procedure to install.

TIMING CHAIN
REPLACE

1. Release tensioner and remove accessory drive belt.
2. Remove alternator as outlined under "Alternator, Replace" in "Electrical" section.
3. Drain engine coolant into a suitable container.
4. Install a suitable engine support fixture to engine.

5. **On models equipped with air conditioning,** loosen A/C receiver pinch clamps and lift receiver for access.
6. **On all models,** remove righthand side engine mount, then the cylinder head cover as outlined under "Cylinder Head, Replace."
7. Rotate No. 1 piston to TDC and align camshaft timing sprockets.
8. Disconnect power steering oil pressure switch connector.
9. Raise and support vehicle, then remove engine splash shields.
10. Remove power steering pump through bolts and nut, then move pump aside from mounting surface.
11. Remove crankshaft pulley retaining bolt using tool No. J 8614-01 or equivalent, **Fig. 8.**
12. Remove crankshaft pulley.
13. Remove CKP sensor, then lower the vehicle.
14. Remove drive belt tensioner mounting bolt and nut, then the tensioner.
15. Remove timing chain tensioner bolt, then the tensioner.
16. Remove timing chain cover bolt, then the nut and timing chain cover.
17. Remove crankshaft sensor reluctor.
18. Remove timing chain dampner bolt, then the dampner.
19. Remove timing chain shoe bolt and shoe.
20. Remove crankshaft sprocket and timing chain.
21. Reverse procedure to install, noting the following:
    a. Align camshaft timing marks, **Fig. 9.**
    b. Turn crankshaft until crankshaft keyway faces upward.

CAMSHAFT
REPLACE

Refer to "Cylinder Head, Replace" for replacement procedure.

PISTON & ROD ASSEMBLY

Refer to **Fig. 10,** for piston and rod assembly.

The connecting rod bearings are available in standard and various undersizes. If replacing a bearing, replace with one having the same number as marked on the connecting rod.

Torque connecting rod bearing cap bolts to 22 ft. lbs., then rotate an additional 90°.

MAIN & ROD BEARINGS

Main bearings are available in standard and various undersizes. If using a standard bearing, replace it with one having the same number. If the number of the bearing cannot be determined, select the proper bearing by determining the numbers imprinted on the cylinder block 1–5.

Torque main bearing cap bolts to 32 ft. lbs., in sequence, **Fig. 11,** then rotate an additional 90°.

CRANKSHAFT REAR OIL SEAL
REPLACE
Removal

1. Remove transaxle as outlined in **MOTOR's "Domestic Transmission, In-Vehicle Service"** manual.
2. Mark flywheel to crankshaft position and remove flywheel.
3. Remove rear end plate.
4. Pry out old seal using suitable screwdriver with tape-wrapped tip.

Installation

1. Apply suitable multi-purpose grease to lip of new seal.
2. Carefully tap new seal into place until its surface is flush with retainer edge.
3. Install flywheel, ensure marks are properly aligned.
4. Apply sealant P/N 12345493, or equivalent, to bolt threads.
5. Install transaxle.

OIL PAN
REPLACE

1. Raise and support vehicle.
2. Drain engine oil into a suitable container.
3. Remove lefthand side engine splash shield.
4. **On models equipped with manual transaxle,** remove flywheel inspection cover.
5. **On all models,** remove oil pan mounting bolts, nuts and oil pan.
6. Reverse procedure to install. Apply continuous bead of silicone sealant P/N 12346240, or equivalent to engine oil pan mating surface.

OIL PUMP
REPLACE

1. Remove timing chain as outlined under "Timing Chain, Replace."
2. Remove mounting bolts and pump. Discard gasket.
3. Reverse procedure to install.

BELT TENSION DATA

This engine is equipped with a serpentine drive belt. Tension is controlled by an automatic tensioner.

SERPENTINE DRIVE BELT
Routing

Refer to **Fig. 12,** for serpentine drive belt routing.

Removal

1. Rotate belt tensioner clockwise using a suitable wrench.
2. Continue to apply pressure to tensioner, then remove belt.

Installation

1. Raise and support vehicle.
2. Remove righthand side lower engine splash shield.
3. Rotate belt tensioner clockwise using suitable wrench.
4. Route and install drive belt onto drive pulleys with pressure applied to tensioner.
5. Release belt tensioner.
6. Install righthand side lower engine splash shield.

COOLING SYSTEM BLEED

This engine does not require a specific bleeding procedure. After filling cooling system, bring engine to operating temperature with radiator/pressure cap off. Air will then be automatically bled through cap opening.

THERMOSTAT
REPLACE

1. Drain engine coolant into a suitable container.
2. Remove alternator as outlined under "Alternator, Replace" in "Electrical" section.
3. Remove thermostat housing mounting nuts, then the housing, thermostat and O-ring.
4. Reverse procedure to install. Ensure O-ring contact surfaces are clean and free of debris.

WATER PUMP
REPLACE

1. Drain coolant into suitable container.
2. Remove serpentine drive belt.
3. Raise and support vehicle.
4. Remove engine splash shields.
5. Remove alternator as outlined under "Alternator, Replace" in "Electrical" section.
6. **On models less HO engine,** remove water pump pulley.
7. **On all models,** remove mounting bolts, water pump and O-ring.
8. Reverse procedure to install.

RADIATOR
REPLACE

1. Drain engine coolant into a suitable container.
2. Remove radiator inlet hose, then the outlet hose.
3. **On models equipped with automatic transaxle,** disconnect ATF cooler hoses at radiator.
4. **On all models,** disconnect fan motor electrical connectors, then the electrical harness clamps from shroud.
5. Remove radiator mounting bolts, then the radiator and cooling fan.
6. Reverse procedure to install.

FUEL PUMP
REPLACE

1. Remove rear seat cushion, then the lefthand side door opening sill plate.
2. Fold back carpet, then remove floor service hole cover mounting screws and cover.
3. Disconnect fuel sender and fuel tank pressure sensor electrical connectors.
4. Remove fuel feed and return hoses, then disconnect fuel tank vapor line.
5. Remove mounting bolts and fuel sender.
6. Remove bottom cap, then the lower cushion from fuel sender.
7. Remove fuel pressure regulator.
8. Disconnect fuel level sensor connector and remove sensor.
9. Disconnect fuel pump electrical connector.
10. Remove fuel pump from fuel filter, then the retaining ring from fuel pump.
11. Reverse procedure to install.

FUEL FILTER
REPLACE

1. Remove fuel sender assembly as outlined under "Fuel Pump, Replace."
2. Remove fuel filter and pump assembly.
3. Separate fuel filter from fuel pump.
4. Reverse procedure to install.

TIGHTENING SPECIFICATIONS

Year	Component	Torque/Ft. Lbs.
EXCEPT HIGH OUTPUT (HO) ENGINE		
2003–05	Air Cleaner	62①
	Alternator	17
	Camshaft Bearing	②
	Camshaft Sprocket	40
	Connecting Rod Cap Bolts	22④
	Crankshaft Main Bearing Cap Bolts	③
	Crankshaft Position Sensor	80①
	Crankshaft Pulley	87
	Cylinder Head	②
	Drive Belt Tensioner, Bolt	74
	Drive Belt Tensioner, Nut	21
	Engine Crossmember To Body	29
	Engine Mount Lefthand Side	60
	Engine Mount Righthand Side	38
	Engine Mount Insulator Righthand Side	38
	Exhaust Manifold Bracket	26
	Exhaust Manifold Heat Shield	15
	Exhaust Manifold	37
	Exhaust Pipe	32
	Flywheel, Automatic Transaxle	65
	Flywheel, Manual Transaxle	36④
	Front Engine Mount	38
	Fuel Injector Wiring Harness	106①
	Heat Insulator	106①
	Heated Oxygen Sensor	32
	Ignition Coil Bracket	10
	Intake Manifold Upper	25
	Intake Manifold Lower	34
	Intake Manifold Support Bracket	18
	Lower Transmission To Engine	47
	Oil Drain Plug	26
	Oil Pan	80①
	Oil Pump	97①
	Oil Strainer	80①
	Power Steering Pump	27
	Radiator Upper Support Bracket	14
	Starter	27
	Thermostat Housing	84①
	Timing Chain Cover (10 MM)	89①
	Timing Chain Cover (12 MM)	14
	Timing Chain Tensioner	89①
	Torque Converter	26
	Water Bypass Pipe To Cylinder Head Bolt	75①
	Water Bypass Pipe To Cylinder Head Nut	84①
	Water Pump	80①

TIGHTENING
SPECIFICATIONS—Continued

Year	Component	Torque/Ft. Lbs.
HIGH OUTPUT (HO) ENGINE		
2003–05	A/C Compressor Hose	89①
	A/C Mounting Bolts	18
	Air Cleaner Mounting	89①
	Alternator	17
	Axle Shaft Heat Shield	13
	Camshaft Bearing Cap	②
	Camshaft Sensor	11
	Camshaft Sprocket	40
	Connecting Rod Cap Bolts	22④
	Coolant Inlet Pipe	11
	Crankshaft Main Bearing Cap Bolts	③
	Crankshaft Position Sensor	106①
	Crankshaft Pulley	105
	Cylinder Head	②
	Drive Belt Tensioner, Bolt	51
	Drive Belt Tensioner, Nut	21
	Engine Mounting Bracket	40
	Engine Ground Wire	11
	Exhaust Manifold Bracket	26
	Exhaust Manifold Heat Shield	11
	Exhaust Manifold	36
	Exhaust Pipe	46
	Flywheel, Auto Transaxle	61
	Flywheel, Manual Transaxle	36④
	Fuel Injector Wiring Harness	106①
	Heat Insulator	106①
	Heated Oxygen Sensor	30
	Ignition Coil Bracket	10
	Intake Manifold	13
	Intake Manifold Support Bracket	37
	Lower Transmission To Engine	47
	Mounting Insulator, Bolt	47
	Mounting Insulator, Nut	38
	Oil Drain Plug	26
	Oil Pan	97①
	Oil Pump	97①
	Oil Strainer	97①
	Oxygen Sensor	31
	Power Steering Pump	27
	Radiator Upper Support Bracket	14
	Starter	27
	Thermostat Housing	84①
	Timing Chain Cover (10 MM)	89①
	Timing Chain Cover (12 MM)	14
	Timing Chain Dampner	14
	Timing Chain Shoe	89①
	Timing Chain Tensioner	89①
	Torque Converter	26
	Washer Fluid Tank	80①
	Water Bypass Pipe To Cylinder Head	80①
	Water Pump	80①

① — Inch lbs.
② — Refer to "Cylinder Head, Replace" for tightening specifications and sequence.
③ — Refer to "Main & Rod Bearings" for tightening specifications.
④ — Rotate an additional 90°.

Rear Axle & Suspension

NOTE: On Air Bag Equipped Models, Refer To "Air Bag System Precautions" Located In The Front Of This Manual For System Disarming & Arming Procedures.

NOTE: Refer To "Computer Relearn Procedures" Located In The Front Of This Manual When Battery Power To The Computer Has Been Interrupted.

INDEX

REAR AXLE SHAFT
REPLACE

1. Raise and support vehicle.
2. Remove tire and wheel assembly.
3. Remove cotter pin and lock cap.
4. Apply parking brake, then remove and discard drive shaft nut.
5. Release parking brake.
6. Remove suspension knuckle as outlined under "Knuckle, Replace."
7. Remove rear wheel driveshaft from vehicle using slide hammer tool No. J 2619-01 and axle shaft remover tool No. J 45341, or equivalents.
8. Reverse procedure to install.

DIFFERENTIAL CARRIER
REPLACE

1. Raise and support vehicle.
2. Place drain pan under differential carrier.
3. Remove differential carrier drain plug and drain differential carrier.
4. Remove propeller shaft as outlined under "Propeller Shaft, Replace."
5. Remove rear tire and wheel assemblies.
6. Remove lefthand and righthand knuckles as outlined under "Knuckle, Replace."
7. Remove lefthand and righthand drive shafts from vehicle as outlined under "Rear Axle Shaft, Replace."
8. Remove catalytic converter.
9. Place a suitable jack under differential assembly.
10. Remove rear differential support bracket bolts.
11. Remove lower differential support bolts.
12. Carefully lower differential assembly with differential support from vehicle.
13. Remove bolts and nuts from differential, then the differential support from differential carrier.

14. Reverse procedure to install.

PROPELLER SHAFT
REPLACE

1. Raise and support vehicle.
2. Place a reference mark on pinion flange yoke and differential pinion flange.
3. Remove pinion flange yoke to differential pinion flange attaching bolts and nuts.
4. Remove mid shaft bearing support bolts.
5. Remove sliding yoke and two piece propeller shaft assembly from transaxle.
6. Reverse procedure to install.

HUB & BEARING
REPLACE
AWD

1. Remove rear knuckle as outlined under "Knuckle, Replace."
2. Remove dust deflector.
3. Remove retaining bolts, then the wheel bearing and hub assembly.
4. Reverse procedure to install.

2WD

1. Release parking brake, then raise and support vehicle.
2. Remove tire and wheel assembly.
3. **On models equipped with rear disc brakes,** remove brake caliper and pads as an assembly from suspension knuckle. Support assembly with heavy mechanic's wire, then remove brake rotor.
4. **On models equipped with rear drum brakes,** remove rear brake drum.
5. **On all models,** disconnect rear wheel speed sensor.

6. Remove retaining bolts, then the wheel bearing and hub assembly.
7. Reverse procedure to install.

SHOCK ABSORBER
REPLACE

1. Unlock rear compartment front side panel by turning knob, then lift up and remove rear compartment from vehicle.
2. Remove tool storage access panel, then the bolt and panel.
3. Remove spare tire retainer, then the rear storage compartment.
4. Remove shock absorber fastener access panel.
5. **On 2WD models,** remove shock absorber retaining nuts.
6. **On all models,** raise and support vehicle.
7. **On 2WD models,** proceed as follows:
   a. Support rear axle and lower control arm.
   b. Remove nut, then the stabilizer shaft link stud from lower control arm.
8. **On all models,** remove all retaining nuts and bolt.
9. Remove shock absorber with coil spring.
10. Reverse procedure to install.

COIL SPRING
REPLACE

1. Remove shock absorber with coil spring as outlined under "Shock Absorber, Replace."
2. Compress coil spring using spring compressor tool No. J 45400, or equivalent.
3. Disassemble components using a suitable wrench.
4. Carefully release compressed spring and remove it from shock absorber.
5. Reverse procedure to install.

CONTROL ARM
REPLACE

Lower

1. Raise and support vehicle, then remove rear tire and wheel assembly.
2. Remove bolts, then separate parking brake cable from lower control arm.
3. Remove nut, then the stabilizer shaft link stud from lower control arm.
4. Support lower control arm with a suitable jack.
5. Place match marks on cams and on lower control arm, then remove cam and bolt.
6. Remove nut and bolt, then separate shock absorber from lower control arm.
7. Remove bolts and nuts, then the lower control arm from vehicle.
8. Reverse procedure to install.

Upper

1. Raise and support vehicle, then remove rear tire and wheel assemblies.
2. Remove heated oxygen sensor, then bolts retaining front pipe to catalytic converter.
3. Remove three-way catalytic converter to muffler/tail pipe assembly bolt and clamp.
4. Remove hangers from rear of three-way catalytic converter, then the converter from vehicle.
5. Place match mark on pinion flange yoke and differential pinion flange.
6. Remove mid shaft bearing support bolts, then sliding yoke and two piece propeller shaft assembly from transaxle.
7. Remove rear wheel speed sensor and pigtail.
8. Remove brake drum, then the brake shoes and brake hardware.
9. Place a suitable container below backing plate, then remove brake pipe from back of wheel cylinder.
10. Remove bleeder valve, then the wheel cylinder.
11. Remove lefthand, then the righthand rear park brake cables from equalizers.
12. Remove bolts and nuts, then separate rear shocks from lower control arms.
13. Remove bolts and nuts, then separate rear lower control arms from body.
14. Place match marks on camber adjust cams and on upper control arm.
15. Remove nut and bolt then separate upper control arm from knuckle.
16. Remove nut from cam bolt, then the rear cam from cam bolt.
17. Remove cam bolt and upper control arm from crossmember.
18. Reverse procedure to install.

KNUCKLE
REPLACE

1. Apply parking brake, then raise and support vehicle.
2. Remove tire and wheel assembly.
3. Remove nut, then separate stabilizer shaft link stud from knuckle.
4. Remove and discard cotter pin from wheel drive shaft nut.
5. Remove and discard wheel drive shaft nut, then release parking brake.
6. Remove rear wheel speed sensor and pigtail.
7. Remove brake drum, then the brake shoes and brake hardware.
8. Place a suitable container below backing plate, then remove brake pipe from back of wheel cylinder.
9. Remove bleeder valve, then the wheel cylinder.
10. Place match marks on camber adjust cams, then remove cam.
11. Remove nut and bolt, then separate lower control arm from knuckle.
12. Remove nut and bolt, then separate upper control arm from knuckle.
13. Support wheel drive shaft with a suitable jack.
14. Remove the knuckle from the wheel drive shaft, then the wheel bearing and hub assembly and drum brake backing plate from knuckle.
15. Reverse procedure to install.

STABILIZER BAR
REPLACE

1. Raise and support vehicle, then remove rear tire and wheel assemblies.
2. Remove heated oxygen sensor, then the bolts retaining front pipe to catalytic converter.
3. Remove three-way catalytic converter to muffler/tail pipe assembly bolt and clamp.
4. Remove hangers from rear of three-way catalytic converter, then the converter from vehicle.
5. Place match mark on pinion flange yoke and differential pinion flange.
6. Remove mid shaft bearing support bolts, then sliding yoke and two piece propeller shaft assembly from transaxle.
7. Remove rear wheel speed sensor and pigtail.
8. Remove brake drum, then the brake shoes and brake hardware.
9. Place a suitable container below backing plate, then remove brake pipe from back of wheel cylinder.
10. Remove bleeder valve, then the wheel cylinder.
11. Remove lefthand, then the righthand rear park brake cables from equalizers.
12. Remove bolts and nuts, then separate rear shocks from lower control arms.
13. Remove bolts and nuts, then separate rear lower control arms from body.
14. Place a jack under differential support.
15. Remove bolts, then nuts and separate rear suspension crossmember and rear drive module from body.
16. Lower rear drive module, then remove stabilizer link from knuckle and shaft.
17. Place match marks on stabilizer shaft insulators and on stabilizer shaft.
18. Remove stabilizer shaft insulators, then the stabilizer shaft from rear suspension crossmember.
19. Reverse procedure to install.

TIGHTENING SPECIFICATIONS

Year	Component	Torque/Ft. Lbs.
2003–05	Axle Hub To Knuckle (2WD)	45
	Axle Hub To Knuckle (AWD)	41
	Axle Shaft Nut	159
	Brake Pipe Fittings	11
	Crossmember To Body	77
	Differential Carrier Drain Plug	29
	Differential Carrier Fill Plug	29
	Differential Carrier To Differential Support	76
	Differential Carrier To Rear Differential Support	123
	Differential Support To Rear Suspension Crossmember	87
	Driveshaft Nut	159
	Lower Control Arm To Body Front Bolt (AWD)	48
	Lower Control Arm To Crossmember (AWD)	55
	Lower Control Arm To Knuckle (AWD)	55
	Mid Shaft Bearing Support Bolts	27
	Parking Brake Cable Bracket	48①
	Propeller Shaft Flange To Pinion Flange	54
	Rear Axle To Body (2WD)	63
	Rear Differential Support To Rear Suspension Crossmember	101
	Rear Wheel Drive Shaft Spindle Nut	159
	Shock Absorber Piston Rod Nut	41
	Shock Absorber To Lower Control Arm (AWD)	103
	Shock Absorber To Rear Axle (2WD)	59
	Spring Mount	59
	Stabilizer Shaft Insulator Bracket (AWD)	13
	Stabilizer Shaft Link Nut	33
	Stabilizer Shaft To Rear Axle (2WD)	144
	Upper Control Arm To Crossmember (AWD)	55
	Upper Control Arm To Knuckle (AWD)	55
	Wheel Lug Nuts	76

① — Inch lbs.

Front Suspension & Steering

NOTE: On Air Bag Equipped Models, Refer To "Air Bag System Precautions" Located In The Front Of This Manual For System Disarming & Arming Procedures.

NOTE: Refer To "Computer Relearn Procedures" Located In The Front Of This Manual When Battery Power To The Computer Has Been Interrupted.

INDEX

PRECAUTIONS

Air Bag Systems

Refer to "Air Bag System Precautions" in the front of this manual for system disarming and arming procedures.

Battery Ground Cable

Prior to service, disconnect battery ground cable and isolate as required.

WHEEL HUB
REPLACE

1. Remove steering knuckle as outlined under "Steering Knuckle, Replace."
2. Remove wheel bearing retainer using snap ring pliers, **Fig. 1.**
3. Place a bearing driver collar on inside end of hub.
4. Remove hub from wheel bearing using a press. Press from inside end of hub toward outside of hub.
5. Remove brake shield from knuckle, then using a press and a split plate remove bearing outside inner race from hub.
6. Place a bearing driver collar on bearing outside outer race.
7. Remove bearing from knuckle using suitable press. Press from outside of knuckle toward inside of knuckle.
8. Reverse procedure to install.

BALL JOINT INSPECTION

1. Remove steering knuckle w/hub, then clamp knuckle into suitable soft-jawed vise.
2. Flip ball stud back & forth five times, then install castle nut onto ball joint stud.
3. Rotate nut continuously for one turn every 3–5 seconds, then note torque reading on fifth turn.

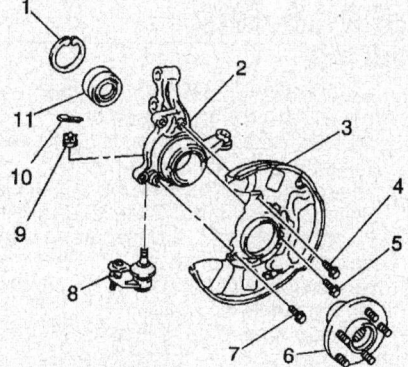

1. Bearing retainer
2. Steering knuckle
3. Brake shield
4. Bolt
5. Bolt
6. Axle hub
7. Bolt
8. Ball stub
9. Ball stud castle nut
10. Cotter pin
11. Hub bearing

ARM66GC000000100

Fig. 1 Exploded view of hub & bearing assembly

4. Replace ball joint if reading is not 9–26 inch lbs.

BALL JOINT
REPLACE

1. Raise and support vehicle, then support front suspension crossmember.
2. Remove retainers, then the lower control arm from ball joint.
3. Remove cotter pin, then the nut from ball joint stud.
4. Remove ball joint from knuckle using a suitable ball joint remover.

5. Reverse procedure to install, noting the following:
   a. Install new self-locking nut and cotter pin.
   b. Adjust wheel alignment.

COIL SPRING
REPLACE

Refer to "Strut Service" for coil spring replacement procedure.

STRUT
REPLACE

1. Raise and support vehicle, then remove front tire and wheel assembly.
2. Remove nut and stud from bracket and separate link from strut using a wrench hold front stabilizer shaft link stud.
3. Remove wheel speed sensor from steering knuckle, then position sensor aside.
4. Remove front brake hose bolt and hose from bracket on strut, then position hose and bolt aside.
5. Loosen nuts on lower side of strut assembly, do not remove bolts.
6. Partially lower vehicle, then remove nuts and bolts from top of strut.
7. Remove nuts and bolts from lower side of strut.
8. Remove strut assembly from vehicle.
9. Reverse procedure to install.

STRUT SERVICE

1. Remove strut as outlined under "Strut, Replace."
2. Compress spring slightly using strut holding/spring compression tool No. J 45400, or equivalent.
3. Remove strut mount cover, then the strut mount nuts.
4. Remove seal, then the spring seat and strut shield.
5. Remove spring, then the strut bumper and spring lower insulator.

6. Remove the absorber portion of the strut.
7. Reverse procedure to install.

CONTROL ARM
REPLACE

1. Install engine support fixture.
2. Raise and support vehicle, then remove tire and wheel assembly.
3. Remove nuts from studs, then separate links from front struts.
4. Remove engine splash shields.
5. Remove lower control arm mounting nuts and bolts.
6. Use wire to suspend steering gear.
7. Remove mounting bolts, nuts and support crossmember with a jack.
8. Lower jack and crossmember.
9. Remove mounting bolts, nuts and control arm.
10. Reverse procedure to install.

STEERING KNUCKLE
REPLACE

1. Raise and support vehicle, then remove tire and wheel assembly.
2. Remove wheel speed sensor from steering knuckle, then position sensor aside.
3. Remove drive shaft nut from drive axle with an assistant holding brake pedal.
4. Remove nuts and bolt from lower control arm.
5. Remove caliper housing and bracket. Suspend them with suitable wire or rope.
6. Carefully remove brake rotor. Avoid damaging speed sensor rotor, boot and inner oil seal.
7. Loosen nuts on lower side of strut. Do not remove bolts.
8. Remove outer tie rod cotter pin and nut, then separate tie rod end using separator tool No. J 6627-A, or equivalent.
9. Remove strut lower nuts and bolts.
10. Remove steering knuckle from strut.
11. Remove front wheel bearing and disc brake shield as outlined under "Wheel Hub, Replace."
12. Remove steering knuckle cotter pin and ball stud nut.

13. Remove ball joint from steering knuckle using tool No. J 24319-B or equivalent.
14. Reverse procedure to install.

STABILIZER BAR
REPLACE

1. Install engine support fixture.
2. Raise and support vehicle, then remove tire and wheel assembly.
3. Remove nuts from studs, then separate links from front struts.
4. Remove engine splash shields.
5. Remove lower control arm mounting nuts and bolts.
6. Use wire to suspend steering gear.
7. Remove mounting bolts, nuts and support crossmember with a jack.
8. Lower jack and crossmember.
9. Remove nuts, then the stabilizer shaft links from stabilizer shaft.
10. Remove stabilizer shaft clamps, then the stabilizer shaft insulators.
11. Remove stabilizer shaft from crossmember.
12. Reverse procedure to install.

TIE ROD END
REPLACE

1. Raise and support vehicle, then remove tire and wheel assembly.
2. Remove cotter pin from outer tie rod nut, then the outer tie rod nut.
3. Separate outer tie rod from knuckle using tool No. J 6627-A or equivalent.
4. Place match marks on inner tie rod, lock nut and outer tie rod.
5. Loosen lock nut, then remove outer tie rod from inner tie rod.
6. Reverse procedure to install.

POWER STEERING GEAR
REPLACE

1. Ensure front wheels are in a straight ahead position and remove ignition key.
2. Move silencer pad away from steering column.
3. Place match marks on steering shaft coupling and on intermediate shaft.
4. Loosen upper coupling bolt, then remove lower coupling bolt.

5. Remove steering column hole cover from bulkhead.
6. Install a suitable engine support fixture tool, then raise and support vehicle.
7. Remove front tire and wheel assemblies, then the engine splash shields.
8. Remove tie rod ends as outlined under "Tie Rod End, Replace."
9. Place a drain pan under vehicle, then remove pressure and return pipes from steering gear.
10. Remove bolt and pipe bracket from steering gear.
11. Remove nuts from studs, then separate link from front struts.
12. Remove front suspension brace.
13. Remove suspension crossmember, transaxle support, control arms and stabilizer shaft as unit.
14. Remove engine rear mount insulator, then the bracket from crossmember.
15. Place match marks on intermediate shaft and steering gear.
16. Remove retaining bolt and intermediate shaft.
17. Remove retaining bolts, then the steering gear from crossmember.
18. Reverse procedure to install.

POWER STEERING PUMP
REPLACE

1. Siphon as much power steering fluid from reservoir as possible.
2. Raise and support vehicle, then remove tire and wheel assemblies.
3. Remove engine splash shields, then release tensioner and remove drive belt.
4. Loosen hose clamp on power steering pump inlet hose and remove hose from pump.
5. Remove bolt from power steering pump outlet pipe bracket, then the outlet pipe fitting from pump.
6. Disconnect power steering pressure switch connector.
7. Remove nuts and bolt from power steering pump front bracket, then power steering pump.
8. Remove rear bracket from pump.
9. **On AWD models,** remove heat shield from pump.
10. **On all models,** reverse procedure to install.

TIGHTENING SPECIFICATIONS

Year	Component	Torque/Ft. Lbs.
2003–05	Brake Hose Clamp	21
	Brake Shield	73①
	Control Arm To Lower Ball Joint	66
	Crossmember Center	38
	Crossmember Front Corner	83
	Crossmember Rear Corner	116
	Driveshaft Nut	159
	Lower Ball Joint To Steering Knuckle	76
	Lower Control Arm To Crossmember	101
	Outer Tie Rod	36
	Power Steering Gear (2WD)	43
	Power Steering Gear (4WD)	94
	Stabilizer Shaft Insulator Clamp	14
	Stabilizer Shaft Link Nut	55
	Steering Column Intermediate Shaft	26
	Steering Shaft Coupling	26
	Strut Mount To Absorber Shaft Nut	35
	Strut To Strut Tower	29
	Strut To Steering Knuckle	162
	Trans Support Bolts	38
	Wheel Lug Nuts	76

① — Inch lbs.

Wheel Alignment

INDEX

PRECAUTIONS

Air Bag Systems

Refer to "Air Bag System Precautions" in the front of this manual for system disarming and arming procedures.

PRELIMINARY INSPECTION

Steering and vibration problems are not always the result of improper alignment. They may also be caused by wheel and tire imbalance or other factors. To ensure proper alignment readings, the following inspections should be done and corrections made before inspecting caster, camber or toe:

1. Inspect tires for proper inflation pressures and even tread wear.
2. Inspect wheel bearings for looseness.
3. Inspect ball joints and tie rod ends for excessive looseness.
4. Inspect steering gear operation and mounting.
5. Inspect operation of struts.
6. Inspect control arms.
7. Inspect hub and bearing assemblies for excessive wear.

FRONT WHEEL ALIGNMENT

Caster

Caster cannot be adjusted. Should caster be out of specification, locate the cause first. If components are damaged, bent, loose, dented or worn, they should be replaced. To prevent an improper caster reading, jounce the bumper three times before inspection.

Camber

1. Estimate amount camber must be adjusted.
2. Select proper combination of bolts, **Fig. 1.**
3. To obtain .25° camber, install bolt No. 1 in upper position and bolt No. 2 in lower position.
4. To obtain .50° camber, install bolt No. 1 in upper position and bolt No. 3 in lower position.

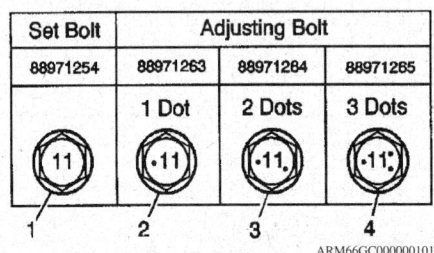

Set Bolt	Adjusting Bolt		
88971254	88971263	88971284	88971265
	1 Dot	2 Dots	3 Dots
(11)	(.11)	(.11.)	(.11:)
1	2	3	4

ARM66GC000000101

Fig. 1   Front camber adjustment bolts

5. To obtain .75° camber, install bolt No. 1 in upper position and bolt No. 4 in lower position.
6. To obtain 1.00° camber, install bolt No. 2 in upper position and bolt No. 4 in lower position.
7. To obtain 1.25° camber, install bolt No. 3 in upper position and bolt No. 4 in lower position.
8. To obtain 1.50° camber, install bolt No. 4 in upper position and bolt No. 4 in lower position.
9. Install bolts, inspect alignment and adjust as required.

Toe-In

1. Ensure steering wheel is in straight ahead position.
2. Remove clamp from steering gear boot.
3. Rotate inner tie rod to adjust toe to specifications, **Fig. 2.**
4. Ensure number of threads visible on righthand inner tie rod is same as number of threads on lefthand inner tie rod.
5. Tighten nut to the outer tie rod.
6. **Torque** tie rod locking nut to 55 ft. lbs.
7. Measure alignment and adjust toe if required.
8. Ensure boots are not twisted, then install clamps to steering gear boots.

REAR WHEEL ALIGNMENT

Camber & Toe Adjustment

AWD

1. Loosen nut on upper control arm cam bolt.

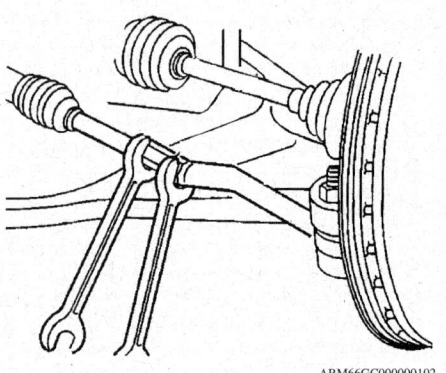

ARM66GC000000102

Fig. 2   Front toe adjustment

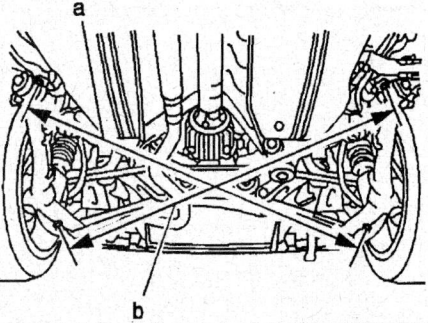

ARM66GC000000103

Fig. 3   Rear camber & toe adjustment

2. Loosen nut on lower control arm cam bolt.
3. Rotate cam bolts to adjust camber and toe to specification.
4. Measure distance from lower lefthand control arm bracket to righthand rear crossmember bolt.
5. Measure distance from lower righthand control arm bracket to lefthand rear crossmember bolt, **Fig. 3.**
6. Ensure difference between measurements "a" and "b" is within specifications.
7. Tighten nuts on control arm cam bolts, then **torque** to 55 ft. lbs.
8. Inspect alignment, then adjust rear camber and toe if required.

SATURN

NOTE: Refer To The Rear Of This Manual For Vehicle Manufacturer's Special Tool Suppliers.

INDEX OF SERVICE OPERATIONS

Specifications

GENERAL ENGINE SPECIFICATIONS

Engine/Liter (VIN)①	Fuel Injection System	Bore & Stoke	Compression Ratio	Net H.P. @ RPM	Maximum Torque, Ft. Lbs. @ RPM	Normal Oil Pressure, psi
2001–02						
1.9L SOHC (8)	SPFI	3.23 × 3.54	9.3	100 @ 5000	114 @ 2400	36.0②
1.9L DOHC (7)	SPFI	3.23 × 3.54	9.5	124 @ 5600	122 @ 4800	36.0②
2.2L DOHC (F)	SPFI	3.39 × 3.72	9.5	135 @ 5200	142 @ 4400	65.0③
3.0L DOHC (R)	SPFI	3.39 × 3.34	10.0	182 @ 6000	190 @ 3600	21.7④
2003–04						
2.0L (P)	SPFI	3.39 × 3.39	9.5	205 @ 5,600	200 @ 4,400	50–80③
2.2L DOHC (F)	SPFI	3.39 × 3.72	10.0	135 @ 5200	142 @ 4400	65.0③
3.0L DOHC (R)	SPFI	3.39 × 3.34	10.0	182 @ 6000	190 @ 3600	21.7④
2005						
2.0L (P)	SPFI	3.39 × 3.39	9.5	205 @ 5,600	200 @ 4,400	50–80③
2.2L DOHC (F)	SPFI	3.39 × 3.72	10.0	140 @ 5,800	145 @ 4,400	50–80③
3.0L DOHC (R)	SPFI	3.39 × 3.34	10.0	182 @ 5,600	190 @ 3,600	16④

MPFI — Multi-Point Fuel Injection
SPFI — Sequential-Point Fuel Injection
DOHC — Dual Overhead Cam
SOHC — Single Overhead Cam

① — Eighth digit of Vehicle Identification Number (VIN) denotes engine code.
② — At 2000 RPM.

③ — At 1000 RPM.
④ — At idle.

TUNE UP SPECIFICATIONS

Year & Engine/ Liter (VIN) ①	Spark Plug Gap	Ignition Timing BTDC				Curb Idle Speed ②		Fast Idle Speed ②		Fuel Pump Pressure, psi.	Valve Lash, Inch
		Firing Order	Man. Trans.	Auto. Trans.	Mark Fig.	Man. Trans.	Auto. Trans.	Man. Trans.	Auto. Trans.		
2001–02											
1.9L (8) SOHC MFI	.040	④	⑤	⑤	⑥	700–800⑦	600–700D⑦⑪	⑦	⑦	40–55⑨	③
1.9L (7) DOHC MFI	.040	④	⑤	⑤	⑥	800–900⑦⑧	700–800D⑦⑪	⑦	⑦	65–94⑨	③
2.2L (F) DOHC SPFI	.045	④	⑤	⑤	⑥	850–875⑦	750–775N⑦	⑦	⑦	50–60⑨	③
3.0L (R) DOHC SPFI	.039	⑩	—	⑤	⑥	—	750–775N⑦	—	⑦	39–49⑨	③
2003–04											
2.2L (F) DOHC SPFI	.042	④	⑤	⑤	⑥	850–875⑦	750–775N⑦	⑦	⑦	50–80⑨	③
3.0L (R) DOHC SPFI	.039	⑩	—	⑤	⑥	—	750–775N⑦	—	⑦	39–49⑨	③
2005											
2.0L (P) DOHC SPFI	.039	⑫	⑤	⑤	⑥	⑦	⑦	⑦	⑦	50–60⑨	③
2.2L (F) DOHC SPFI	.042	④	⑤	⑤	⑥	850–875⑦	750–775N⑦	⑦	⑦	50–80⑨	③
3.0L (R) DOHC SPFI	.040	⑩	—	⑤	⑥	—	750–775N⑦	—	⑦	39–49⑨	③

BTDC — Before Top Dead Center
D — Drive
N — Neutral

① — Eighth digit of Vehicle Identification Number (VIN) denotes engine code.
② — When adjusting idle speed, set parking brake & block drive wheels. Where two idle speeds are listed, higher speed is w/idle or A/C solenoid energized.
③ — Equipped w/hydraulic valve lifters.

④ — Cylinder numbering from front of engine to rear 1, 2, 3, 4. Firing order 1-3-4-2. Refer to **Fig. A** for spark plug wire connections at coil unit.
⑤ — Equipped w/Distributorless Ignition System (DIS). No adjustment.
⑥ — Equipped w/crankshaft position sensor.
⑦ — Idle speed is controlled by Idle Air Control (IAC) valve or Idle Speed Control (ISC).
⑧ — With A/C on, 825–925 RPM.

⑨ — Wrap shop towel around fuel pressure test port to prevent fuel spillage. Connect suitable fuel pressure gauge to fuel pressure test port. Energize fuel pump using a suitably programmed scan tool & inspect fuel pressure.
⑩ — 1-2-3-4-5-6.
⑪ — With A/C on, 725–825 RPM.
⑫ — Cylinder numbering from front of engine to rear 1, 2, 3, 4. Firing order 1-3-4-2.

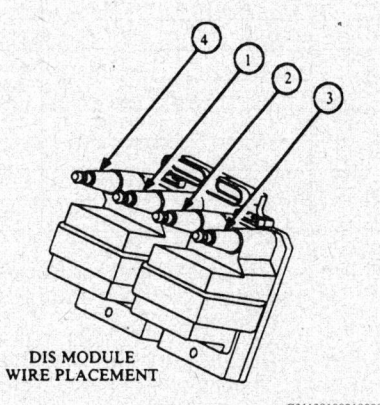

DIS MODULE WIRE PLACEMENT

G31139100019000X

Fig. A

FRONT WHEEL ALIGNMENT SPECIFICATIONS

Model	Caster Angle, Degrees[1]		Camber Angle, Degrees[1]		Total Toe, Degrees[2]		Ball Joint Wear
	Limits	Desired	Limits	Desired	Limits	Desired	
ION (2003–05) [5]	+2.50 to +4[4]	+3.25[4]	−1.75 to −.25	−1.0	−.10 to +.30	+.20	[3]
ION (2003–05) [6]	+2.85 to +4.35	+3.60[4]	−1.65 to −.15	−.90	−.10 to +.30	+.20	[3]
L-Series	+3.2 to +4.2[4]	+3.7[4]	−1.75 to −.50	−1.0	+.04 to +.36	+.20	[3]
S-Series	+1.1 to +2.3	+1.7	−1.20 to +.20	−.5	0 to +.40	+.20	[3]

[1] — Cross camber, 0° (±1°).

[2] — Toe-In (+). Toe-Out (−).

[3] — Refer to "Ball Joint Inspection" in "Front Suspension & Steering" section.

[4] — Caster is not adjustable.

[5] — FE1 & FE2 suspension.

[6] — FE3 & Tuner suspension.

REAR WHEEL ALIGNMENT SPECIFICATIONS

Model	Year	Camber Angle, Degrees		Total Toe, Degrees[1]	
		Limits	Desired	Limits	Desired
ION	2003–04	−2.15 to −.65	−1.4	0 to +.50	+.20
	2005[2]	−1.90 to −.40	−1.15	−.30 to +.30	0
	2005[3]	−1.15 to −.05	−.80	−.05 to +.55	+.25
L-Series	2001–05	−1.50 to −.50	−1.0	+.13 to +.47	+.30
S-Series	2001–02	−1.4 to 0	−.7	0 to +.50	+.20

[1] — Toe-In (+). Toe-Out (−).

[2] — FE1 & FE2 suspension.

[3] — FE3 & Tuner suspension.

VEHICLE RIDE HEIGHT SPECIFICATIONS

Model	Year	Body Style	Manufacturer's Original Tire Size	Measurement Points & Specifications[1][2]					
				Front			Rear		
				Dim.	Specification		Dim.	Specification	
					Inches	MM		Inches	MM
ION	2003–05	2 Door[4]	[3]	J	8.90	225	K	9.20	234
				Z	.40	10	D	8.90	225
		2 Door[5]	[3]	J	8.90	225	K	9.20	234
				Z	.90	22	D	8.40	214
		2 Door[6]	[3]	J	8.50	215	K	8.80	224
				Z	1.10	28	D	9.00	230
		4 Door[4]	[3]	J	8.90	225	K	9.20	234
				Z	.40	10	D	8.90	225
		4 Door[5]	[3]	J	8.90	225	K	9.20	234
				Z	.90	22	D	8.40	214
L-Series	2001–05	All	[3]	E	15.56	395	F	15.21	386.4
S-Series	2001–02	Coupe	[3]	A	5.90	150	B	5.40	138
				C	7.80–9.10	200–232	D	7.90–9.40	201–233
		Sedan	[3]	A	4.60	117	B	4.10	105
				C	7.80–9.00	200–233	D	8.00–9.30	201–233
		Wagon	[3]	A	4.60	117	B	4.10	105
				C	7.80–9.10	200–232	D	8.10–9.50	202–234

A Dim. — Measurement From Front Wheel Opening to Inspection Point On Rocker Panel Flange

B Dim. — Measurement From Rear Wheel Opening to Inspection Point On Rocker Panel Flange

C Dim. — Distance from Front Rocker Flange Panel to Ground

D Dim. — Distance from Rear Rocker Panel Flange to Ground (S-Series)

D Dim. — Distance from Bottom Edge Upper Spring Seat to Notch In Lower Spring Seat (ION)

E Dim. — Measure from Bottom Center of Front Bumper

F Dim. — Measure from Bottom Center of Rear Bumper

J Dim. — Measure from Front Inboard Pinch-Weld Flange to Ground

K Dim. — Measure from Rear Inboard Pinch-Weld Flange to Ground

Z Dim. — Measure from Cradle to Bottom of Front Ball Joint

Dim. Dimension

① — Measurement is with fuel, radiator coolant & engine oil full, spare tire, jack, hand tools & mats in designated positions & tires properly inflated.

② — L-Series, ± .98 inch (25 MM); ION, ± .39 inch (10 MM); S-Series, ±.62 inch (16 MM).

③ — See door sticker or inside of glove box for manufacturer's original tire size specifications. If tires on vehicle do not match manufacturer's original tire size & measurement is not within limits, refer to the "Non-Standard Tire & Wheel Size Adjustment To Ride Height Specifi-

cation & Tire Size Adjustment Charts" in the front of this manual for approximate changes in ride height specifications.

④ — FE1 Soft Ride Suspension System.

⑤ — FE2 Handling Suspension System.

⑥ — FE3 Sport Suspension System.

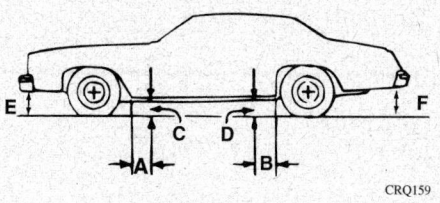

Fig. A

CRQ159

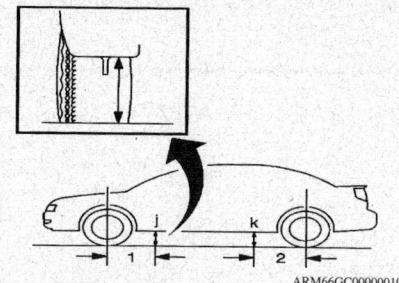

Fig. B   Dimensions J & K

ARM66GC000000104

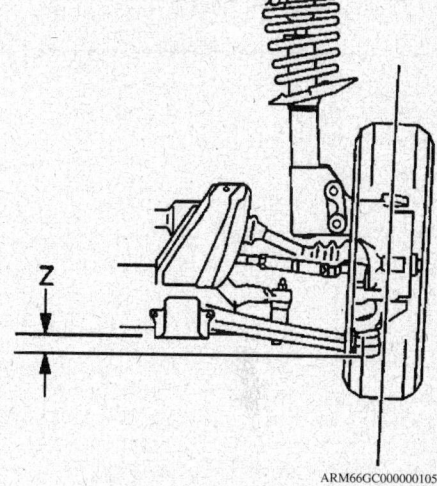

Fig. C   Dimension Z

ARM66GC000000105

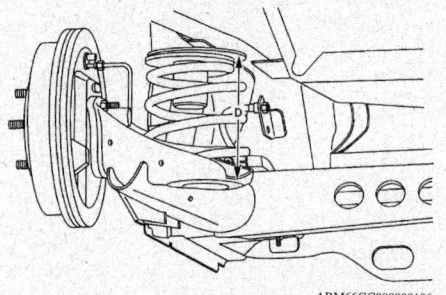

Fig. D   Dimension D. ION

ARM66GC000000106

FLUID CAPACITIES & COOLING SYSTEM DATA

Engine/ Liter ①	Cooling Capacity, Qts.	Coolant Type	Radiator Cap Relief Pressure, Lbs.	Thermo. Opening Temp. Deg. F	Fuel Tank Gals.	Engine Oil Refill Qts.③	Transaxle Oil	
							Manual Transaxle Pts.	Auto. Transaxle Qts.②
2001								
1.9L	7.2	DEX-COOL	13–17	186	12.1	4.0	5.2	④
2.2L	7.4	DEX-COOL	13–17	194	12.1	5.0	4.0	⑤
3.0L	7.8	DEX-COOL	20–21	188–196	12.1	5.0	—	⑤
2002								
1.9L	7.2	DEX-COOL	13–17	186	12.1	4.0	5.2	④
2.2L	9.0	DEX-COOL	13–17	194	15.7	5.0	4.0	⑤
3.0L	10.2	DEX-COOL	20–21	188–196	15.7	5.0	—	⑤
2003–04								
2.0L	7.9	DEX-COOL	13–17	194	13.5	6.0⑥	3.6	6.9
2.2L	9.0	DEX-COOL	13–17	194	15.7	5.0	4.0	⑤
3.0L	10.2	DEX-COOL	20–21	188–196	15.7	5.0	—	⑤
2005								
2.0L	7.9	DEX-COOL	13–17	194	13.5	6.0⑥	3.6	6.9
2.2L	9.0	DEX-COOL	13–17	194	13.5	5.0	4.0	⑤
3.0L	10.2	DEX-COOL	20–21	188–196	15.7	5.0	—	⑤

① — Eighth digit of Vehicle Identification Number (VIN) denotes engine code.

② — Approximate, make final inspection w/dipstick.

③ — Additional oil may be required to bring oil level to full mark when changing oil filter.

④ — Drain & refill, 4 qts.; drain & refill w/new filter, 4.2 qts.; total capacity, 7.4 qts.

⑤ — Bottom pan removal, 6.9 qts.; complete overhaul, 9.5 qts.; total capacity, 12.9 qts.

⑥ — Intercooler system, 2.0 qts.

LUBRICANT DATA

Year	Lubricant Type		Power Steering	Brake System	Hydraulic Clutch
	Transaxle				
	Manual	Automatic			
2001–05	①	①	②	DOT 3	DOT 3

① — Dexron III ATF meeting GM "H Revision" specification.

② — Must meet GM specification 9985010.

Electrical

NOTE: On Air Bag Equipped Models, Refer To "Air Bag System Precautions" Located In The Front Of This Manual For System Disarming & Arming Procedures.

NOTE: Refer To "Computer Relearn Procedures" Located In The Front Of This Manual When Battery Power To The Computer Has Been Interrupted.

INDEX

PRECAUTIONS

Air Bag Systems

Refer to "Air Bag System Precautions" in the front of this manual for system disarming and arming procedures.

Battery Ground Cable

Prior to service, disconnect battery ground cable and isolate as required.

FUSE PANEL & FLASHER LOCATION

ION

The underhood junction block is located at the lefthand front of the engine compartment. The instrument panel junction block and the flasher module are located behind the center instrument panel.

L-Series

The underhood fuse block is located on the rear lefthand side of the engine compartment. The lefthand instrument panel fuse block is located behind the lefthand side kick panel. The righthand instrument panel fuse block is located behind the righthand side kick panel.

The hazard switch, located in the center of the instrument panel, controls turn signal and hazard lamp flashing.

S-Series

The underhood junction block is located at the lefthand front of the engine compartment at the fender apron. The instrument panel junction block and the flasher module are located behind the center instrument panel, in front of the console.

FUEL PUMP RELAY LOCATION

ION

The fuel pump relay is located in the instrument panel fuse block, behind the center of the instrument panel.

L-Series

The fuel pump relay is located behind the lefthand side kick panel, on the lefthand instrument panel fuse block.

SATURN

S-Series

The fuel pump relay is located in the instrument panel fuse block, behind the center of the instrument panel.

RELAY CENTER LOCATION

ION

Relays are in the located in both the underhood junction block and the instrument panel junction block. Refer to "Fuse Panel & Flasher Location" for junction block locations.

L-Series

Relays are located in three fuse panels. Refer to "Fuse Panel & Flasher Location" for fuse block locations.

S-Series

Relays are in the located in both the underhood junction block and the instrument panel junction Block. Refer to "Fuse Panel & Flasher Location" for junction block locations.

STARTER
REPLACE

1.9L Engine

1. Raise and support vehicle.
2. Disconnect electrical connectors and position aside.
3. Remove starter mounting bolts.
4. Pull starter rearward and toward lefthand side.
5. Remove starter motor.
6. Reverse procedure to install, noting the following:
   a. Starter must be guided into flywheel housing and rotated until starter flange lower bolt hole and engine mounting hole align.
   b. **Torque** starter mounting bolts to 27 ft. lbs.
   c. **Torque** starter solenoid terminal nut to 44 inch lbs.
   d. **Torque** positive terminal nut to 96 inch lbs.

2.0L Engine

1. Raise and support vehicle.
2. Remove intercooler pump outer bracket bolts, then the bracket.
3. Disconnect electrical connectors and position aside.
4. Remove mounting bolts and starter.
5. Reverse procedure to install, noting the following:
   a. Ensure wiring and electrical connectors are properly routed to prevent pinching.
   b. **Torque** starter mounting bolts to 37 ft. lbs.
   c. **Torque** intercooler pump outer bracket bolts to 15 ft. lbs.

2.2L Engine

1. Raise and support vehicle.
2. Disconnect electrical connectors and position aside.
3. Remove mounting bolts and starter.
4. Reverse procedure to install. **Torque** starter mounting bolts to 30 ft. lbs.

3.0L Engine

1. Raise and support vehicle.
2. Remove righthand front wheel and disconnect starter electrical connectors.
3. Loosen electrical harness bracket to engine block fastener.
4. Remove lower starter mounting bolt. Lower vehicle.
5. Remove upper starter mounting bolt.
6. Move starter to righthand side to clear engine block, then to the left and out of flywheel housing.
7. Reverse procedure to install. **Torque** starter mounting bolts to 30 ft. lbs.

ALTERNATOR
REPLACE

1.9L Engine

1. Remove drive belt.
2. Raise and support vehicle, then remove righthand wheel.
3. Remove righthand wheelwell and alternator splash shields, then disconnect field wires.
4. Prevent B+ output stud from rotating using alternator output stud wrench tool No. SA-9401-C, or equivalent, and disconnect fusible link wire.
5. Remove lower and upper mounting bolts, then the alternator through wheelwell opening.
6. Reverse procedure to install, noting the following:
   a. **Torque** mounting bolts to 24 ft. lbs.
   b. Ensure fusible link wire is between 10 and 11 o'clock position.
   c. **Torque** positive terminal and alternator splash shield nuts to 96 inch lbs.

2.0L Engine

1. Remove supercharger as outlined under "Supercharger, Replace" in "2.0L Engine" section.
2. Disconnect alternator electrical connectors.
3. Remove alternator mounting bolts, then the alternator from vehicle.
4. Reverse procedure to install, noting the following:
   a. **Torque** alternator mounting bolts to 18 ft. lbs.
   b. **Torque** alternator terminal nut to 15 ft. lbs.

2.2L Engine

1. Remove throttle body air duct and accessory drive belt.
2. Disconnect alternator electrical connectors.

3. Remove mounting bolts and alternator.
4. Reverse procedure to install. **Torque** alternator mounting bolts to 16 ft. lbs.

3.0L Engine

1. Turn steering wheel toward righthand side.
2. Mark running direction, then remove accessory drive belt and belt tensioner.
3. Remove upper alternator to engine block bolts.
4. Raise and support vehicle.
5. Remove lower alternator bolt, then lower the vehicle.
6. Separate alternator from engine block.
7. Disconnect electrical connectors and remove alternator.
8. Reverse procedure to install. **Torque** alternator mounting bolts to 30 ft. lbs.

COIL PACK
REPLACE

1.9L Engine

1. Turn ignition Off.
2. Mark spark plug wire positions for installation.
3. Remove spark plug wires from coil towers.
4. Remove ignition coil from ignition module by rotating coil upward.
5. Reverse procedure to install, noting the following:
   a. Ensure electrical connectors align before seating.
   b. **Torque** mounting bolts to 71 inch lbs.

2.2L Engine

1. Turn ignition Off.
2. Remove accelerator cable from bracket, then the cable bracket.
3. Disconnect ignition module electrical connector.
4. Remove mounting screws and electronic ignition module.
5. Remove mounting bolts and coil pack.
6. Reverse procedure to install, noting the following:
   a. **Torque** coil pack bolts to 84 inch lbs.
   b. **Torque** ignition module mounting screws to 13 inch lbs.

3.0L Engine

1. Turn ignition Off.
2. Remove upper intake manifold runner as outlined under "Intake Manifold, Replace" in "3.0L Engine" section.
3. Disconnect electrical connector, then remove ignition coil and gasket.
4. Reverse procedure to install.

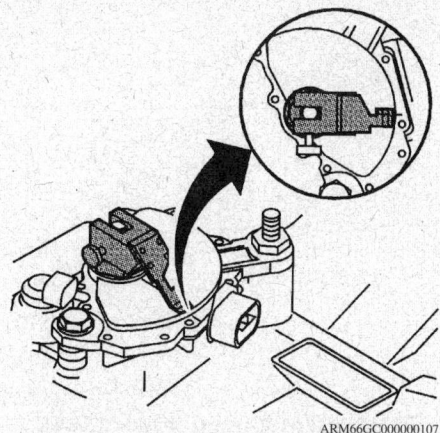

Fig. 1 Transaxle range switch alignment. ION w/AF23-5 transaxle

ARM66GC000000107

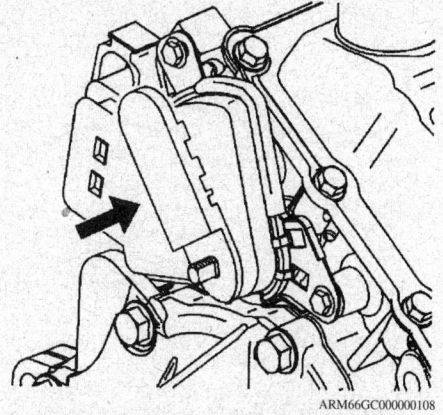

Fig. 2 Transaxle range switch alignment. ION w/VT25-E transaxle

ARM66GC000000108

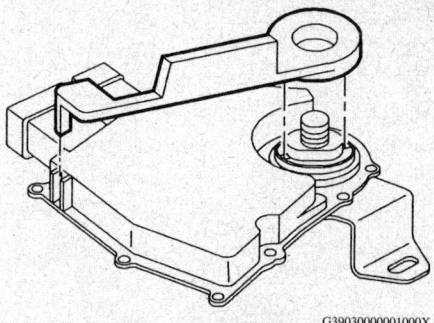

G39030000001000X

Fig. 3 Transaxle range switch alignment. L-Series

IGNITION COIL

REPLACE

2.0L Engine

1. Disconnect ignition coil electrical connector.
2. Remove coil mounting bolt, then the coil from vehicle.
3. Reverse procedure to install. **Torque** coil mounting bolt to 89 inch lbs.

IGNITION LOCK

REPLACE

1. Remove ignition lock bezel.
2. Remove upper steering column shroud panel.
3. Insert ignition key in switch.
4. **On S-Series,** turn key to Accessory.
5. **On L-Series and ION models,** turn key to Start, then back to Run.
6. **On all models,** depress locking button at top and remove lock cylinder.
7. Reverse procedure to install.

IGNITION SWITCH

REPLACE

ION

1. Remove steering column upper and lower shrouds.
2. Disconnect ignition switch electrical connector.
3. Turn ignition to Run.
4. Remove ignition switch mounting screws, then the ignition switch from steering column.
5. Reverse procedure to install. **Torque** switch mounting screws to 17 inch lbs.

L-Series

1. Remove ignition lock cylinder bezel from steering column shroud.
2. Remove steering column upper and lower shrouds.
3. Remove ignition switch to steering column mounting screws.
4. Disconnect electrical connector and remove switch.

5. Reverse procedure to install. **Torque** switch mounting screws to 13 inch lbs.

S-Series

1. Remove steering wheel as outlined under "Steering Wheel, Replace."
2. Remove lefthand side lower filler panel mounting screws.
3. Loosen DLC to filler panel mounting screws and lower filler panel.
4. Disconnect hood release cable and remove filler panel.
5. Remove air bag module Connector Position Assurance (CPA) retainer.
6. Disconnect connectors and remove lever control switch.
7. **On models equipped with automatic transaxle,** disconnect park lock cable from ignition module.
8. **On all models,** disconnect pass lock sensor and ignition switch electrical connectors from ignition module.
9. Make small notch in shear bolt head using suitable chisel and hammer.
10. Tap chisel to rotate and loosen bolt.
11. Remove shear bolts.
12. Remove ignition module.
13. Reverse procedure to install.

CLUTCH START SWITCH

REPLACE

1. Disconnect clutch switch electrical connector.
2. Remove mounting bolt and switch.
3. Reverse procedure to install. **Torque** clutch switch mounting bolt to 96 inch lbs.

TRANSAXLE RANGE SWITCH

REPLACE

ION

AF23-5 TRANSAXLE

REMOVAL

1. Apply parking brake and place control lever in Neutral position.
2. Disconnect shift cable from transaxle

control using removal tool No. J-36346, or equivalent.
3. Disconnect PNP switch electrical connector, then remove control nut and lever.
4. Bend lock washer tabs down on manual shaft nut using a small screwdriver.
5. Remove manual shaft nut, lock washer and flat washer.
6. Remove PNP switch bolt, stud, lock washer and switch from transaxle.

INSTALLATION

1. Install PNP switch to manual valve lever and transaxle, then the bolt and lock washers. Hand tighten only.
2. Install flat washer, lock tab washer and nut to manual shaft. **Torque** to 62 inch lbs.
3. Insert transaxle range switch alignment tool No. J-45404, or equivalent over manual shaft, **Fig. 1.**
4. Rotate switch as needed to align neutral base line to pointer, then remove tool.
5. **Torque** switch mounting bolts to 18 ft. lbs.
6. Lock manual switch shaft nut by bending lock washer tabs, then connect switch electrical connector.
7. Install control lever nut, then **torque** to 12 ft. lbs.
8. Connect shift cable to transaxle control lever and ensure vehicle starts only in Park or Neutral.

VT25-3 TRANSAXLE

REMOVAL

1. Apply parking brake, then place control lever in Neutral position.
2. Disconnect transaxle control module connectors, noting proper orientation.
3. Remove bolt, then disconnect large engine control module connector and engine wiring harness retainer near ECM.
4. Disconnect EVAP purge solenoid connector, then lay aside.
5. Remove control cable assembly from PNP switch lever using tool No. J-36346, or equivalent.
6. Disconnect PNP switch lever nut and lever.
7. Remove retaining bolt and ensure manual shaft is fully seated into transaxle, then the PNP switch from vehicle.

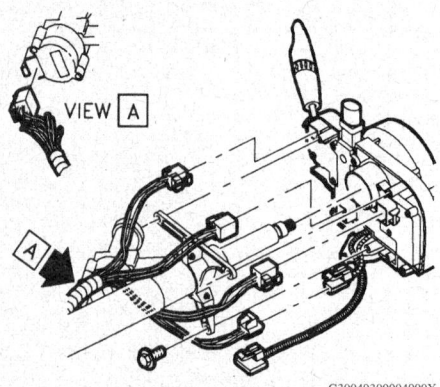

G39049300004000X

Fig. 4 Multi-function switch replacement. S-Series

INSTALLATION

1. Place transaxle manual shift shaft in NEUTRAL position.
2. Align flats on manual shift shaft with flats on PNP switch, loosely install switch bolts.
3. Insert transaxle range switch alignment tool No. J-44810, or equivalent over manual shaft, **Fig. 2.**
4. Rotate switch until alignment tool drops into position.
5. **Torque** switch mounting bolts to 97 inch lbs.
6. **Torque** switch lever mounting nut to 12 ft. lbs.
7. Connect switch electrical connectors.
8. Install control cable assembly and ensure vehicle starts only in Park or Neutral.
9. Connect EVAP purge solenoid connector, then install engine wiring harness retainer and ECM connectors.
10. Connect transaxle control module connectors in proper orientation.

L-Series

REMOVAL

1. Apply parking brake and place control lever in Neutral position.
2. Remove shift control cable from transaxle range switch lever.
3. Disconnect transaxle range switch electrical connectors.
4. Remove range switch lever nut and lever.
5. Remove mounting bolts and transaxle range.

INSTALLATION

1. Ensure transaxle manual shaft is in Neutral position.
2. Align transaxle shift shaft and transaxle range switch flats, then install switch.
3. Loosely install switch mounting bolts.
4. Insert transaxle range switch alignment tool No. J-41545, or equivalent over manual shaft, **Fig. 3.**
5. Rotate switch until alignment tool drops into position.
6. **Torque** switch mounting bolts to 15 ft. lbs.
7. **Torque** switch lever mounting nut to 26 ft. lbs.

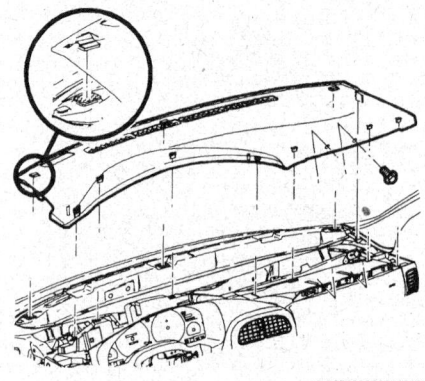

GC9090000051000X

Fig. 5 Upper trim panel replacement. S-Series

8. Connect switch electrical connectors.
9. Install control cable and ensure vehicle starts only in Park or Neutral.

S-Series

REMOVAL

1. Turn ignition Off.
2. Remove air cleaner and duct.
3. Disconnect transaxle range switch harness connectors.
4. Disconnect shifter cable from control lever.
5. Place control lever in full clockwise position.
6. Remove control lever to manual shift shaft mounting nut while holding control lever in place.
7. Remove mounting bolts and switch.

INSTALLATION

1. Install switch and mounting bolts. **Do not tighten bolts just yet.**
2. Install control lever onto manual shaft.
3. **Torque** mounting nut to 108 inch lbs. while holding control lever.
4. Ensure control lever is in Park position by moving lever to full clockwise position until it clicks and cannot be moved any further.
5. Release control cable adjustment lock tab using suitable screwdriver.
6. Connect control cable to control lever.
7. Move control cable housing back and forth in adjuster. Record endplay.
8. Center control cable in middle of endplay and depress control cable lock tab.
9. Place transaxle in Drive position.
10. Connect suitable ohmmeter between transaxle range switch connector terminals.
11. Rotate transaxle range switch toward engine until ohmmeter indicates continuity.
12. **Torque** switch to case mounting bolts to 10 ft. lbs. Ensure continuity still exists between terminals.
13. Connect switch electrical connectors.
14. Install air cleaner and duct.
15. While moving shifter lever to all gear positions, ensure each position reads properly using suitably programmed scan tool.

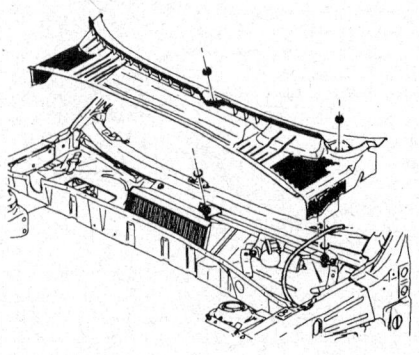

G39029900001100X

Fig. 6 Windshield cowl screen replacement. L-Series

MULTI-FUNCTION SWITCH

REPLACE

ION & L-Series

1. Remove steering column upper and lower shrouds.
2. Disconnect multi-function switch electrical connector.
3. Remove retaining screws, then the multi-function switch from steering column.
4. Reverse procedure to install.

S-Series

1. Remove steering wheel as outlined under "Steering Wheel, Replace."
2. Remove Supplemental Inflatable Restraint (SIR) coil assembly as outlined in "Passive Restraints Systems" chapter.
3. Remove Connector Position Assurance (CPA) device and disconnect electrical connectors from multi-function switch, **Fig. 4.**
4. Remove multi-function switch.
5. Reverse procedure to install.

STEERING WHEEL

REPLACE

This procedure has been revised by a Technical Service Bulletin.

1. Remove driver's air bag module as outlined in "Passive Restraint Systems" chapter.
2. Disconnect horn and cruise control switch electrical connectors.
3. Remove and discard steering wheel mounting nut.
4. Remove steering wheel using suitable steering wheel puller tool.
5. Feed electrical wiring through steering wheel and remove steering wheel.
6. Insert yellow tab into SIR coil or use tape to prevent SIR coil rotation.
7. Reverse procedure to install, noting the following:
   a. **On ION and L Series, torque** new steering wheel mounting nut to 31 ft. lbs.

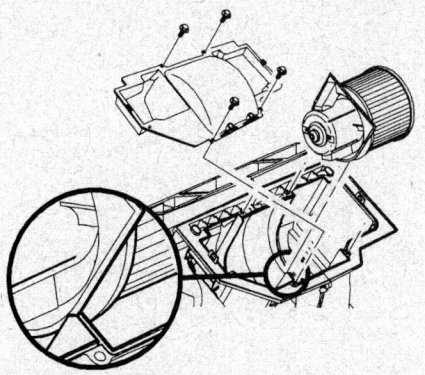

Fig. 7 Blower motor replacement. L-Series

G37029900003400X

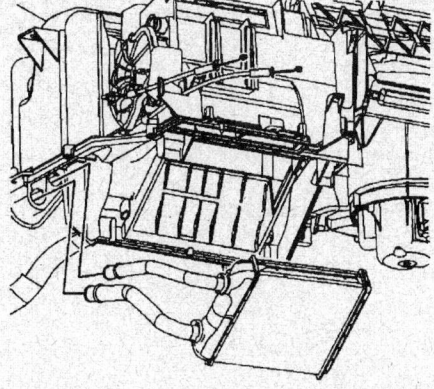

Fig. 8 Heater core replacement. ION

ARM66GC000000109

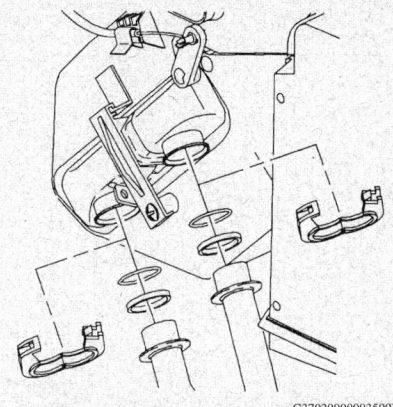

Fig. 9 Heater core pipe replacement. L-Series

G37029900003500X

b. **On S Series, torque** new steering wheel mounting nut to 26 ft. lbs.
c. **On all models, torque** air bag module mounting bolts to 96 inch lbs.

INSTRUMENT CLUSTER
REPLACE
ION

1. Remove accessory trim panel, then disconnect electrical connectors.
2. Remove screw retaining cluster trim plate to center trim panel.
3. Lift up on cluster trim plate to release retaining fasteners, then remove cluster trim plate.
4. Remove cluster screws, then pull cluster out and disconnect electrical connector.
5. Remove cluster from the vehicle.
6. Reverse procedure to install.

L-Series

1. Remove steering wheel as outlined under "Steering Wheel, Replace."
2. Remove hush panel from under lefthand side of instrument panel.
3. Remove knee bolster panel from under steering column.
4. Remove upper and lower steering column covers.
5. Lower the steering column to its lowest position.
6. Remove mounting screws and instrument cluster trim plate.
7. Remove mounting screws and instrument cluster.
8. Reverse procedure to install.

S-Series

1. Remove instrument panel upper trim pad mounting screws, **Fig. 5.**
2. Disconnect trim panel retaining clips by grasping edges of trim panel and lifting up.
3. Disconnect hook and loop fasteners at rear of upper trim panel by reaching under trim panel and lifting straight up.
4. Raise upper trim panel enough to clear VIN plate.

5. Loosen steering column filler panel mounting bolts. **Do not remove weatherstrips.**
6. Remove lefthand side endcap to instrument panel mounting screws.
7. Disconnect retaining clips and remove instrument panel endcap.
8. Remove upper and lower steering column covers.
9. Lower steering column to its lowest position.
10. Disconnect retaining clips and pull instrument panel bezel outward.
11. Disconnect dimmer/traction control switch electrical connector.
12. Remove instrument panel bezel.
13. Remove mounting screws and pull cluster away from instrument panel.
14. Disconnect electrical connectors and remove cluster.
15. Reverse procedure to install.

RADIO
REPLACE
ION

1. Remove accessory trim panel, then disconnect electrical connectors.
2. Remove retaining screws from radio and pull the radio out.
3. Disconnect radio electrical connectors and remove radio.
4. Reverse procedure to install.

L-Series & S-Series

1. Remove control cover push pin fasteners, then pull radio, and heater and air conditioning control cover rearward.
2. Disconnect single traction control, fog lamp and rear defroster electrical connectors.
3. Remove radio mounting screws.
4. Depress both radio side spring clips and pull out slightly.
5. Disconnect antenna and electrical connectors.
6. **On models equipped with base radio,** remove storage tray by pulling out toward front of radio.
7. **On all models,** remove radio.
8. Reverse procedure to install.

WIPER MOTOR
REPLACE
ION

1. Remove wiper arm finish cap and mounting screw.
2. Remove wiper arm from pivot using tool No. J-39637, or equivalent.
3. Remove cowl trim panel.
4. Disconnect electrical connector from wiper motor.
5. Remove retainers, then the wiper motor assembly.
6. Reverse procedure to install.

L-Series

1. Remove wiper arm finish cap.
2. Scribe wiper arm positions on windshield with felt marker for installation alignment.
3. Remove mounting nuts and wiper arms.
4. Remove weatherstrip from rear of hood.
5. Remove mounting nuts and cowl screen, **Fig. 6.**
6. Disconnect wiper motor electrical connector.
7. Remove mounting bolts and wiper motor.
8. Separate wiper motor from transmission.
9. Reverse procedure to install. **Torque** wiper motor mounting bolts to 44 inch lbs. and wiper arm mounting nuts to 21 ft. lbs.

S-Series

1. Remove wiper arm finish cap and mounting screw.
2. Lift and remove wiper arm from pivot.
3. Remove cowl trim panel.
4. Remove instrument panel top cover.
5. Remove mounting screws and position defroster duct aside to allow access to wiper module mounting screws.
6. Place wiper motor arm in 12 o'clock position.

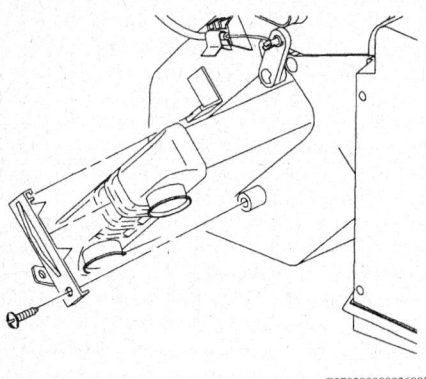

Fig. 10 Heater core replacement. L-Series

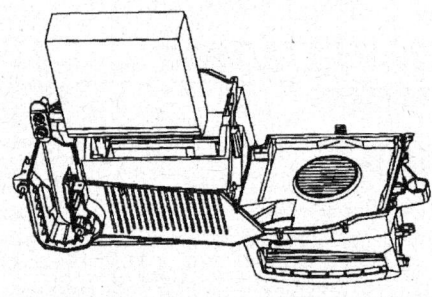

Fig. 13 Evaporator core replacement. ION

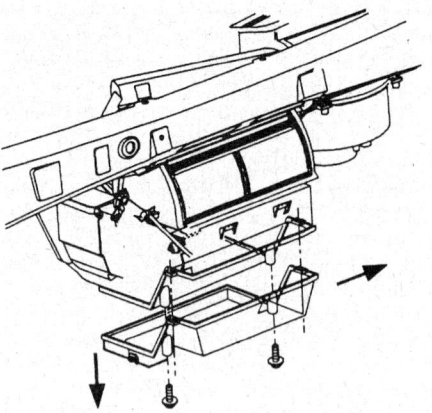

Fig. 11 Lower heater duct replacement. S-Series

4. Reverse procedure to install.

S-Series

Refer to "Multi-Function Switch, Replace" for wiper switch replacement procedure.

WIPER TRANSMISSION
REPLACE

Refer to "Wiper Motor, Replace" for wiper transmission replacement procedure.

BLOWER MOTOR
REPLACE
ION

1. Disconnect blower motor electrical connector.
2. Remove blower motor and cup from lower case by cutting through case between circular ribs around motor with a sharp utility knife.
3. Remove blower motor nuts, then release motor retaining tab and remove motor from cup.
4. Reverse procedure to install.

L-Series

1. Turn ignition On, then select Outside Air on control head.
2. Remove cowl screen as outlined under "Wiper Motor, Replace."
3. Release and remove filter by rotating locking tabs outward.
4. Remove mounting bolts and filter housing.
5. Remove mounting screws and blower motor housing, **Fig. 7.**
6. Disconnect electrical connector and remove blower motor.
7. Reverse procedure to install. **Torque** blower motor housing screws to 9 inch lbs. and filter housing bolts to 31 inch lbs.

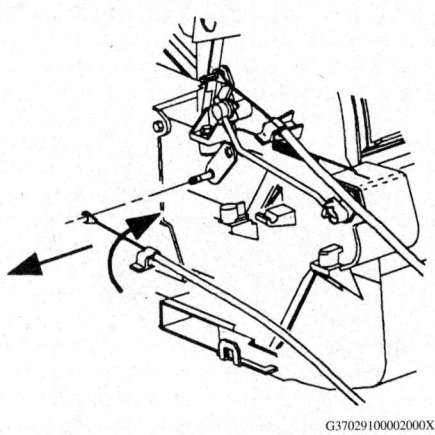

Fig. 12 Temperature cable replacement. S-Series

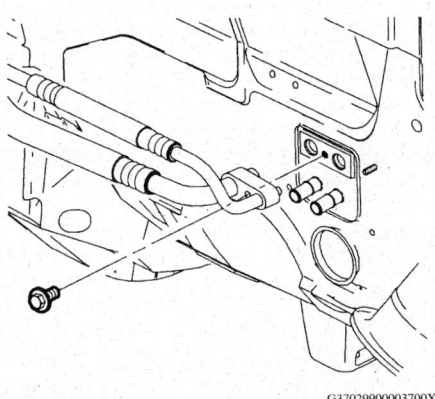

Fig. 14 Suction/liquid line replacement. L-Series

S-Series

1. Remove righthand instrument panel lower sound insulator.
2. Disconnect blower motor electrical connector.
3. Remove mounting screws and blower motor.
4. Reverse procedure to install.

HEATER CORE
REPLACE
ION

1. Park vehicle on a level surface, then remove surge tank cap.
2. Raise and support vehicle, then place a drain pan under water pump drain port.
3. Loosen water pump drain bolt and drain coolant from water pump.
4. Lower vehicle, then reposition heater outlet and inlet hose clamps at heater core using tool No. SA9111E, or equivalent.
5. Remove heater outlet and inlet hoses from heater core.
6. Apply parking brake.
7. **On models equipped with automatic transaxle,** shift transaxle into Neutral and remove console shift lever bezel.

7. Remove wiper module mounting bolts and nuts.
8. Partially remove wiper module and disconnect electrical connectors.
9. Remove wiper module and place in suitable vise.
10. Remove links from motor arm.
11. Remove mounting bolts and motor.
12. Reverse procedure to install, noting the following:
   a. **Torque** wiper motor mounting bolts to 96 inch lbs.
   b. Install outboard module bolt first, then inboard bolt.
   c. **Torque** mounting bolts to 13 ft. lbs.
   d. **Torque** mounting nuts to 72 inch lbs.

WIPER SWITCH
REPLACE
ION

1. Remove steering column upper and lower shrouds.
2. Disconnect wiper switch electrical connector.
3. Remove retaining screws, then the wiper switch from steering column.
4. Reverse procedure to install.

L-Series

1. Remove steering wheel as outlined under "Steering Wheel, Replace."
2. Remove ignition switch bezel, then the upper and lower steering column covers.
3. Remove wiper/washer switch.

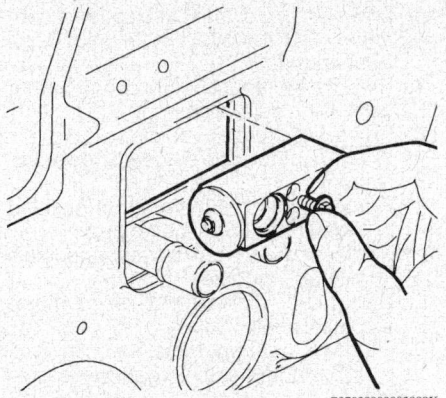

Fig. 15   TXV replacement.
L-Series

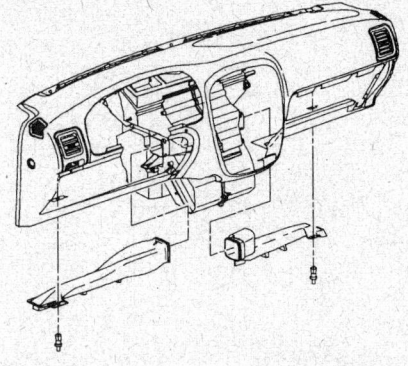

Fig. 16   Heater duct replacement.
L-Series

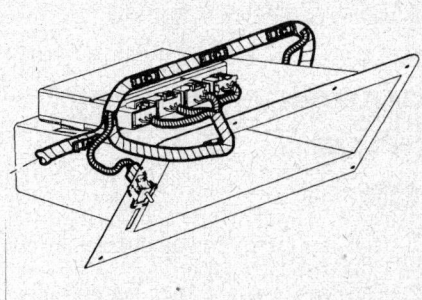

Fig. 17   BCM replacement.
L-Series

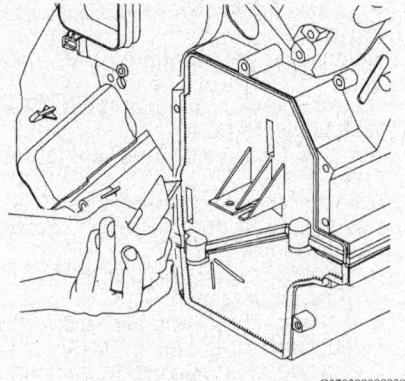

Fig. 18   Evaporator core
replacement. L-Series

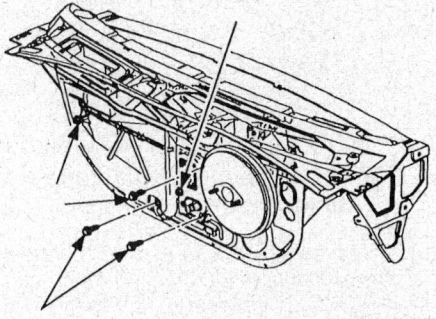

Fig. 19   HVAC module
replacement. S-Series

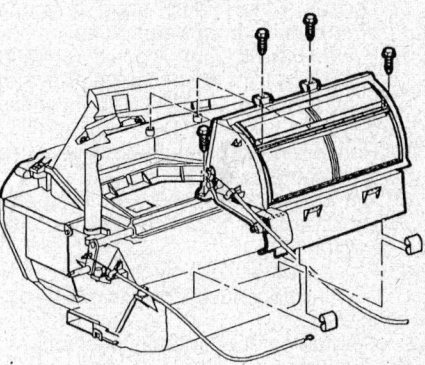

Fig. 20   Mode valve replacement.
S-Series

8. **On models equipped with manual transaxle,** unsnap shift boot from front console cupholder.
9. **On all models,** lift front console cupholder to disengage retainers, then disconnect cigar lighter electrical connector.
10. Remove front console cupholder.
11. **On models equipped with manual transaxle,** slide shift boot through front console cupholder.
12. **On all models,** turn retainer counterclockwise and remove lefthand and righthand extension retainers.
13. Remove lefthand and righthand console extensions by pulling rearward to disengage.
14. Remove console center extension screws, then pull out on console center extension to disengage retainers and remove extension.
15. Remove wiring harness rosebud from righthand side center support bracket.
16. Pull back carpet at bottom of righthand side center support bracket and remove lower nuts.
17. Remove center support bracket nuts and remove the bracket.
18. Disconnect harness connectors from body control module, then remove nuts and BCM from vehicle.
19. Remove accelerator control pedal

from front of dash and position out of the way.
20. Raise center floor outlet duct while pushing floor ducts down to disengage ducts.
21. Rotate center floor outlet duct forward in vehicle, then pull down to disengage duct from HVAC module.
22. Remove heater core cover retainers, then pull heater core cover down enough to clear locating pins from HVAC module.
23. Slide heater core cover rearward until drain tube clears front of dash.
24. Slide heater core cover down, rearward and to righthand side to remove.
25. Remove heater core, **Fig. 8.**
26. Reverse procedure to install.

L-Series

1. Drain engine coolant into suitable container.
2. Remove heater inlet and return hoses.
3. Place heater return hose end in suitable container, apply low air pressure to inlet hose and blow coolant out of heater core.
4. Remove righthand console extension.
5. Remove heater core pipe to heater core clamps and pipe from core end tank, **Fig. 9.**
6. Remove core mounting screw and strap.
7. Pull center console forward edge outward for access.

8. Pull heater core out of module into passenger foot area, **Fig. 10.**
9. Reverse procedure to install.

S-Series

1. Drain coolant into suitable container.
2. Raise and support vehicle.
3. Move heater hose clamps upward. Lower vehicle.
4. Remove heater core hoses and blow coolant from heater core using suitable air hose.
5. Disconnect lower instrument panel center trim panels from under instrument panel and rotate trim panels outward to disconnect from front of console.
6. Remove instrument panel lower closeout panel by pulling outward at top edge and rotating downward.
7. Remove mounting screws, drop lower heater duct straight down and slide out sideways, **Fig. 11.**
8. Release temperature cable hold down clip from lower heater core cover by lifting upward on plastic tab while pushing down on top of cable, **Fig. 12.**
9. Slide cable off hook and remove temperature cable.
10. Remove mounting screws and heater core side cover.
11. Remove mounting screws and lower heater core cover.
12. Remove lower heater core retainer

mounting screw.
13. Remove heater core.
14. Reverse procedure to install.

EVAPORATOR CORE
REPLACE
ION

1. Recover refrigerant as outlined in "Air Conditioning" chapter.
2. Park vehicle on a level surface, then remove surge tank cap.
3. Raise and support vehicle, then place a drain pan under water pump drain port.
4. Loosen water pump drain bolt and drain coolant from water pump.
5. Lower vehicle, then reposition heater outlet and inlet hose clamps at heater core using tool No. SA9111E, or equivalent.
6. Remove heater outlet and inlet hoses from heater core.
7. Remove condenser tube and evaporator hose from TXV, then discard seal washers.
8. Raise center floor outlet duct while pushing floor ducts down to disengage ducts.
9. Rotate center floor outlet duct forward in vehicle, then pull down to disengage duct from HVAC module.
10. Disconnect blower motor electrical connectors
11. Remove instrument panel as outlined in "Dash Panel Service" chapter.
12. Disconnect recirculation actuator electrical connector.
13. Remove HVAC module from vehicle.
14. Remove heater core cover retainers, then the cover and heater core.
15. Unsnap and open passenger compartment filter door.
16. Remove lower HVAC case screws and case.
17. Remove evaporator core, **Fig. 13.**
18. Reverse procedure to install.

L-Series

1. Remove blower motor as outlined under "Blower Motor, Replace."
2. Recover refrigerant as outlined in "Air Conditioning" chapter.
3. Remove mounting bolts and suction/liquid line from Thermo Expansion Valve (TXV), **Fig. 14.** Cap suction/liquid line hose.
4. Remove TXV mounting bolts.
5. Install suction/liquid line bolt hand tight.
6. Remove TXV from evaporator by gently pulling forward using bolt as handle, **Fig. 15.**
7. Open glove box door and remove lamp by pulling on plunger.
8. Disconnect glove box lamp electrical connector.
9. Remove righthand side instrument panel lower dash insulator retainers.

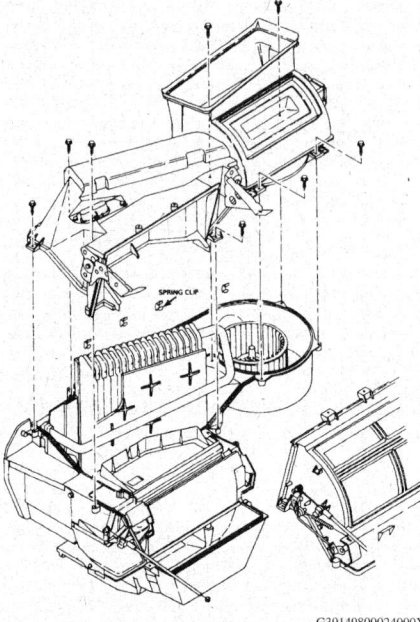

Fig. 21 Upper air inlet case replacement. S-Series

G39149800024000X

10. Pull insulator rearward to disconnect from forward insulator retainers.
11. Remove retainer and righthand side heater duct, **Fig. 16.**
12. Remove glove box door and bin fasteners.
13. Slowly tilt glove box bin downward to expose BCM, **Fig. 17.**
14. Slide BCM out of mounting slots and remove glove box bin.
15. Remove hush panel support from front of dash.
16. Cut evaporator access door through module wall following inside of raised bead as guide using suitable sharp utility knife, **Fig. 18. Several passes may be required.**
17. Slide evaporator core out through access door opening. Cap pipes.
18. Reverse procedure to install, noting the following:
    a. Add 2.4 ounces of PAG oil to new evaporator.
    b. **Torque** TXV and suction/liquid mounting bolts to 62 inch lbs.
    c. Lubricate O-rings using clean mineral oil.
    d. Apply provided sealant to service door at tongue and groove locations.

S-Series

1. Recover refrigerant as outlined in "Air Conditioning" chapter.
2. Remove air cleaner housing cover and air intake tube.
3. Remove suction hose and liquid line from expansion valve.
4. Remove expansion valve from evaporator.
5. Install protective covers over air conditioning lines.

6. Drain cooling system into suitable container and remove heater inlet hose from engine.
7. Blow remaining coolant from heater core using suitable air hose.
8. Raise and support vehicle.
9. Remove heater core hoses. Lower vehicle.
10. Remove instrument panel as outlined in "Dash Panel Service" chapter.
11. Remove wiring harnesses and clips from HVAC module.
12. Disconnect blower and recirc motor electrical connectors.
13. Remove fuel vapor line and clip from HVAC module stud to gain access to nut.
14. Remove HVAC module to cowl mounting nuts and screws, **Fig. 19.**
15. Remove HVAC module.
16. Remove and discard cowl panel seals.
17. Remove mode valve screws and clips, **Fig. 20.**
18. Remove mode valve from HVAC module.
19. Remove upper air inlet case from lower case, **Fig. 21.**
20. Remove evaporator tube clamp and screw.
21. Lift evaporator from lower case.
22. Reverse procedure to install, noting the following:
    a. Add 2.25 ounces of fresh PAG oil to new evaporator.
    b. **Torque** HVAC module mounting nuts and screws to 44 inch lbs.
    c. **Torque** steering column mounting bolts to 26 ft. lbs.
    d. **Torque** suction hose and liquid line to 19 ft. lbs.

CABIN AIR FILTER
REPLACE
ION

1. Open instrument panel compartment door.
2. Tilt instrument panel compartment door down, then squeeze in on each side of bin until door stops can be removed from tracks.
3. Lower instrument panel compartment completely.
4. Open cabin air filter door through opening in rear of I/P compartment, raising tab until door can be opened downward.
5. slide filter out of passenger compartment filter housing.
6. Reverse procedure to install.

L-Series

1. Open hood, then open filter access door in cowl leaf screen using a screwdriver.
2. Remove any debris in filter area.
3. Rotate locking tabs outward to release filter assembly.
4. Remove filter by pulling straight out.
5. Reverse procedure to install.

1.9L Engine

NOTE: On Air Bag Equipped Models, Refer To "Air Bag System Precautions" Located In The Front Of This Manual For System Disarming & Arming Procedures.

NOTE: Refer To "Computer Relearn Procedures" Located In The Front Of This Manual When Battery Power To The Computer Has Been Interrupted.

NOTE: Prior To Performing Any Service Operations Listed In This Section, Consult The "Technical Service Bulletins" Section For Related Information.

INDEX

PRECAUTIONS

Air Bag Systems

Refer to "Air Bag System Precautions" in the front of this manual for system disarming and arming procedures.

Battery Ground Cable

Prior to service, disconnect battery ground cable and isolate as required.

Fuel System Pressure Relief

1. Connect fuel gauge bar kit tool No. SA-9127-E and adapter tool No. SA-9403-E, or equivalents to fuel pressure test port, **Fig. 1.**
2. Place end of bleed hose into suitable container and open valve to bleed system pressure.
3. Remove gauge and replace cap.

COMPRESSION PRESSURE

1. Start engine and allow to reach normal operating temperature.
2. Turn ignition Off and disconnect ignition module harness electrical plug.
3. Ensure battery is fully charged.
4. Remove spark plugs.
5. Install compression gauge tool No. SA-9127-E, or equivalent in spark plug hole.
6. Prop throttle wide open.
7. Measure compression while cranking engine, noting the following:
   a. Cylinder should puff or compression gauge needle should bounce at least 10 times.
   b. **Do not crank engine for more than 15 seconds.**
8. Repeat preceding steps for each cylinder.
9. Normal compression pressure is 185–205 psi. Minimum pressure is 180 psi.

ENGINE MOUNT

REPLACE

1. Remove engine mount to mid-rail bracket mounting nuts, **Fig. 2.**
2. Unload mount by raising engine using suitable floor jack under oil pan with suitable wood block between pan and jack.
3. Remove three engine to front cover mounting nuts and engine mount, **Fig. 3.**
4. Reverse procedure to install.

ENGINE

REPLACE

1. Remove coolant bottle cap and drain coolant into suitable container.
2. Remove air cleaner.
3. Disconnect the following engine electrical connectors:
   a. Coolant temperature sensors.
   b. Oxygen sensor and clip, at front transaxle mount bracket.
   c. Idle air control valve.
   d. Ignition coil.
   e. Throttle position sensor.
   f. Manifold absolute pressure sensor.
   g. EGR solenoid.
   h. Cylinder head rear grounds rear at transaxle.
   i. Injectors.
4. Disconnect brake booster hose at booster or intake manifold.
5. Disconnect the following transaxle connectors:
   a. Neutral safety/selector switch.
   b. Valve body actuator.
   c. Turbine speed sensor.

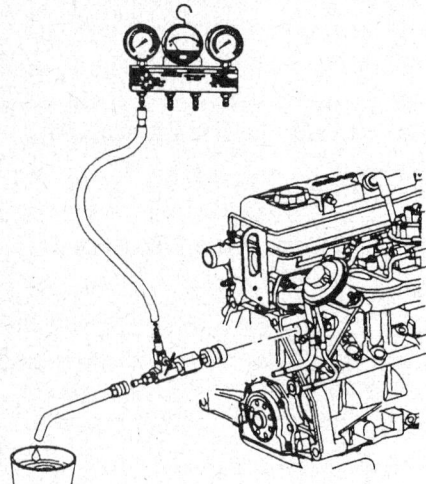

Fig. 1   Fuel pressure bleed

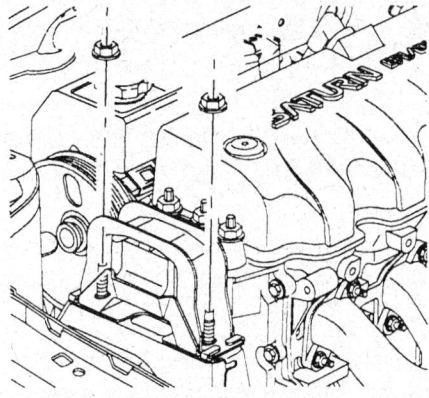

Fig. 2   Engine mount to mid-rail bracket replacement

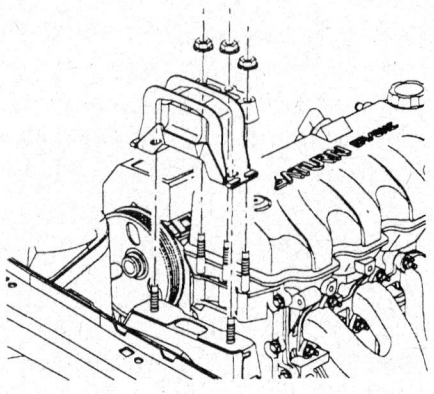

Fig. 3   Engine to front cover mount replacement

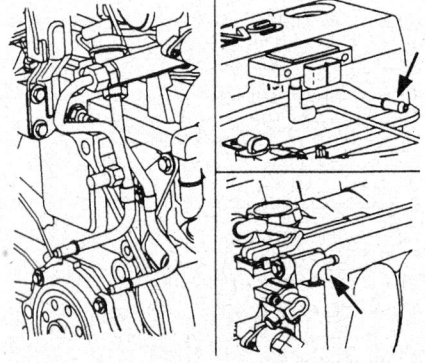

Fig. 4   Fuel line removal

d. Temperature sensor.
e. **On models equipped with manual transaxle,** disconnect back-up lamp switch.
6. **On all models,** disconnect accelerator cables.
7. Bleed residual fuel pressure into suitable container using gauge bar tool No. SA-9127-E, or equivalent.
8. **Place cloth around fuel line fittings,** then disconnect fuel lines using fuel line tool No. SA-9157-E, or equivalent, **Fig. 4.**
9. **Cap or suspend open fuel lines.**
10. Disconnect upper radiator and de-aeration hoses at engine.
11. Disconnect air conditioning compressor and position aside.
12. Pinch tabs to disconnect and plug cooler lines at transaxle. Wrap transaxle cooler line fittings with suitable cloth.
13. **On models equipped with automatic transaxle,** disconnect shifter cable, **Fig. 5.**
14. **On models equipped with manual transaxle,** proceed as follows:
    a. Remove hydraulic dampner to clutch housing stud nuts.
    b. Slide dampner and bracket from studs.
    c. Disconnect connector and remove by rotating clutch actuator ¼ turn counterclockwise while pushing toward housing.
    d. Position clutch hydraulic system aside.
15. **On all models,** secure radiator, condenser and fan module to front crossbar using suitable wire.
16. Raise and support vehicle.
17. Remove front wheel assemblies, then the front and side shields from cradle.
18. Remove bracket mounting bolts and position caliper aside.
19. Disconnect lower radiator and heater inlet and return hoses at engine.
20. Disconnect steering shaft and power steering pressure switch electrical connector, as required.
21. Remove front exhaust pipe, catalytic converter and powertrain stiffener

bracket. **Do not remove torque restrictor bracket to transaxle.**
22. Remove automatic transaxle flywheel cover and torque converter to flexplate mounting bolts.
23. Remove alternator and starter shields.
24. Disconnect the following electrical connectors:
    a. Starter feed.
    b. Alternator feed.
    c. Oil pressure sensor.
    d. Knock sensor.
    e. Crankshaft position sensor.
    f. EVO solenoid, if equipped.
    g. Vehicle speed sensor.
    h. Canister purge solenoid.
    i. PCM/EC and oxygen sensor.
    j. ABS wheel sensor grounds.
25. Disconnect brake lines from rear of cradle and remove electrical harness from engine. Lay electrical harness on underhood junction block and battery cover.
26. Lower vehicle.
27. Place suitable 1 × 1 × 2 inch wood block between torque strut and cradle, **Fig. 6.**
28. Remove upper engine torque axis mount to front cover nuts and mount to mid-rail bracket nuts.
29. Support cradle using suitable powertrain support dolly and two 4 × 4 × 36 inch wood pieces.
30. Remove cradle to body mounting bolts and lower cradle. Ensure two large rear cradle spacers are attached.

31. Install suitable engine lifting equipment.
32. Remove spark plug wire ends at ignition module.
33. Remove power steering pump with bracket and attach in upright position to steering gear or cradle using suitable wire.
34. Remove transaxle housing mounting bolts.
35. Remove front engine mount and disconnect motion restrictor, as required.
36. Place ½ × 1 × 3 inch wood block under axle shaft.
37. Remove starter bracket.
38. **On models equipped with DOHC engine,** remove intake manifold bracket.
39. **On all models,** remove three axle shaft bracket bolts and allow bracket to rotate rearward. It may be required to lift engine slightly to allow clearance between starter bracket and driveshaft bracket.
40. Place suitable 4 × 4 × 6 inch wood block under transaxle housing.
41. Remove engine strut bracket and torque strut. Engine may have to be lifted slightly to allow engine strut removal, **Fig. 7.**
42. Remove transaxle housing mounting bolts.
43. Lift engine and install on engine stand.
44. Reverse procedure to install.

INTAKE MANIFOLD
REPLACE

SOHC Engine

1. Drain engine coolant into suitable container.
2. Remove air cleaner and disconnect fresh air hose at cam cover.
3. Remove PCV hose.
4. Remove fuel line bracket bolt; then disconnect fuel supply and return line by depressing retaining tabs. Discard retainer.
5. Disconnect throttle cable from throttle body and remove bracket mounting nuts.
6. Disconnect the following electrical connectors:
    a. Fuel injectors.

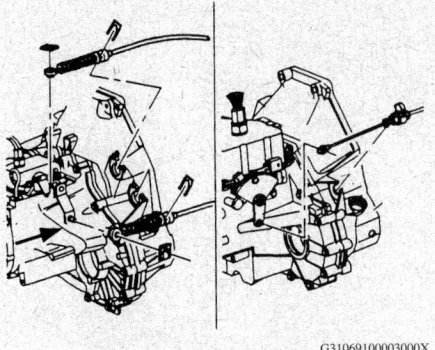

Fig. 5 Transaxle shifter cable replacement

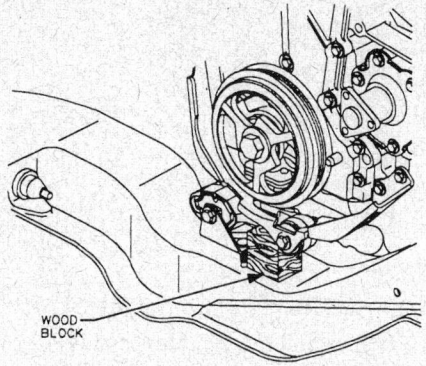

Fig. 6 Torque strut & cradle support

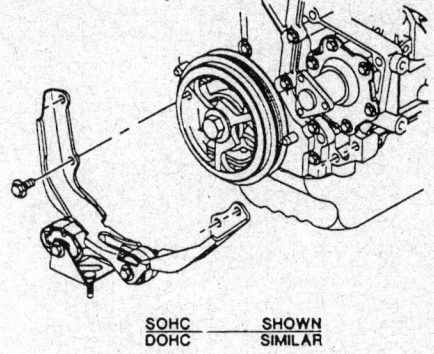

Fig. 7 Engine strut bracket & torque strut replacement

b. Idle air control (IAC).
c. Throttle position sensor (TPS).
d. EGR valve.
e. Manifold absolute pressure sensor.

7. Remove wires with tubes and position harness onto fuel relay.
8. Disconnect and label vacuum hoses.
9. Disconnect heater hose, then remove cylinder head coolant outlet de-aeration line fitting and clamps. Position aside.
10. Remove intake manifold support bracket to block mounting bolt and accessory drive belt.
11. Remove mounting bolts and position power steering pump aside.
12. Remove mounting nuts, intake manifold and gasket.
13. Reverse procedure to install. **Torque** intake manifold mounting nuts to 22 ft. lbs. in sequence, **Fig. 8.**

DOHC Engine

1. Drain engine coolant into suitable container.
2. Remove air inlet tube/resonator, disconnect fresh air hose at cam cover and lift resonator upward to disconnect from engine.
3. Remove PCV hose.
4. Remove fuel line bracket bolt; then disconnect fuel supply and return lines by depressing plastic retaining tabs of line fitting. Discard retainer.
5. Disconnect throttle cable from throttle body and remove bracket mounting nuts.
6. Disconnect the following electrical connectors:
   a. Fuel injectors.
   b. Idle air control (IAC).
   c. Throttle position sensor (TPS).
   d. Manifold absolute pressure sensor.
   e. EGR valve.
7. Disconnect heater and de-aeration hoses at intake manifold outlet.
8. Disconnect EGR solenoid vacuum hose.
9. Position electrical harness over brake master cylinder.
10. Remove intake manifold support bracket to block mounting bolt.
11. Remove accessory drive belt.
12. Remove mounting bolts and position power steering pump aside.

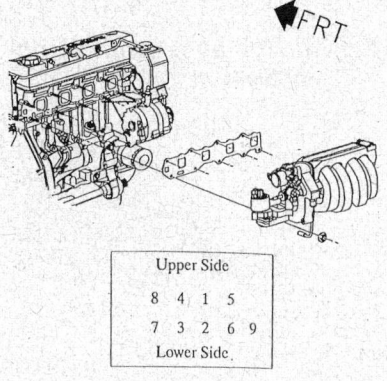

Upper Side				
8	4	1	5	
7	3	2	6	9
Lower Side				

Fig. 8 Intake manifold bolt tightening sequence. SOHC engine

13. Remove upper intake manifold mounting nuts.
14. Raise and support vehicle.
15. Remove lower power steering bracket.
16. Remove intake manifold bracket mounting bolt.
17. Disconnect canister purge relay and brake booster vacuum hose.
18. Remove lower intake manifold mounting stud.
19. Lower vehicle and remove manifold.
20. Reverse procedure to install. **Torque** intake manifold mounting nuts to 22 ft. lbs. in sequence, **Fig. 9.**

EXHAUST MANIFOLD
REPLACE

1. Raise and support vehicle.
2. Remove exhaust pipe to manifold mounting nuts.
3. Lower exhaust pipe and discard gasket. Lower vehicle.
4. Remove air conditioning compressor and rear compressor bracket.
5. Remove front exhaust pipe to engine stiffening bracket mounting bolts.
6. Disconnect electrical connector and remove oxygen sensor.
7. Remove mounting nuts, exhaust manifold and gasket.
8. Reverse procedure to install, noting the following:

a. Install new gasket.
b. **On models equipped with DOHC engines, torque** exhaust manifold mounting nuts to 23 ft. lbs. in sequence, **Fig. 10.**
c. **On models equipped with SOHC engines, torque** exhaust manifold mounting nuts to 16 ft. lbs. in sequence, **Fig. 10.**

CYLINDER HEAD
REPLACE

SOHC Engine
REMOVAL

1. Remove coolant bottle cap.
2. Drain coolant into suitable container.
3. Remove air cleaner and air inlet duct, then disconnect PCV and fresh air hose.
4. Disconnect accelerator cable from throttle lever and bracket from intake manifold.
5. Disconnect the following electrical connectors:
   a. Coolant temperature and PCM.
   b. Injectors.
   c. Idle air control valve.
   d. Manifold air pressure sensor.
   e. Throttle position sensor/switch.
   f. Spark plug wires.
   g. Oxygen sensor.
   h. Air conditioning compressor.
6. Position electrical harness on underhood junction block.
7. Disconnect and label canister purge valve hose and brake booster hose.
8. Disconnect PCV hose at camshaft cover, fuel regulator vacuum hose and throttle body connector.
9. Disconnect upper radiator hose at cylinder head, heater hose at intake manifold and de-aeration hose at throttle body or intake manifold.
10. Remove fuel line clamp to intake manifold base mounting bolt.
11. Disconnect fuel supply and return lines at throttle body.
12. Remove lower intake manifold support bracket stud.
13. Disconnect lower splash shield, then place suitable 1 × 1 × 2 inch wood block between torque strut and cradle.

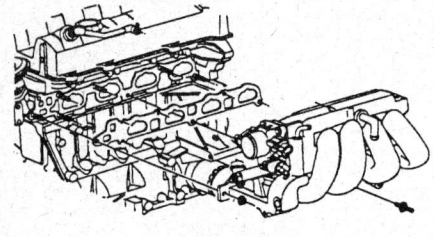

Upper Side

5 2 3

7 4 1 6

Lower Side

G31059100002000X

Fig. 9   Intake manifold bolt tightening sequence. DOHC engine

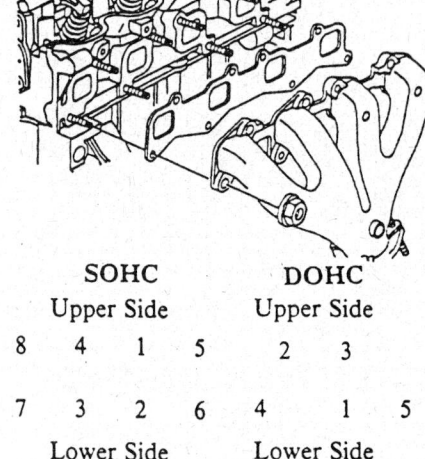

SOHC				DOHC		
Upper Side				Upper Side		
8	4	1	5	2	3	
7	3	2	6	4	1	5
Lower Side				Lower Side		

G31079100001000X

Fig. 10   Exhaust manifold bolt tightening sequence

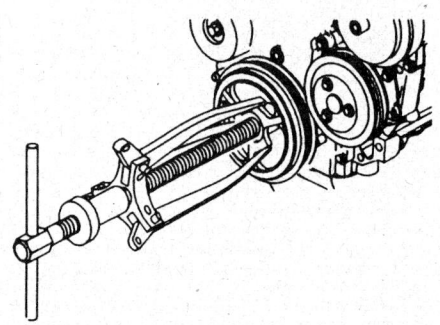

G31069100007000X

Fig. 12   Crankshaft dampner removal

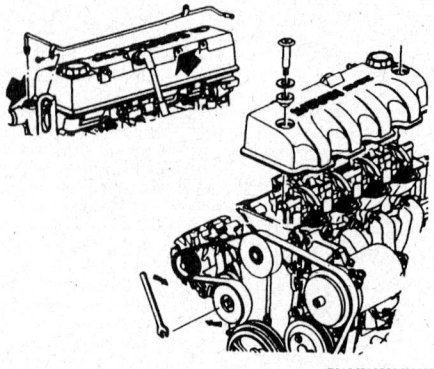

G31069100006000X

Fig. 11   Valve cover replacement. SOHC engine

14. Remove three righthand upper engine torque axis mount to front cover mounting nuts, allowing engine to rest on wood block.
15. Mark running direction, then remove accessory drive belt.
16. Disconnect de-aeration line at cylinder head water outlet and support bracket, then remove rocker cover, **Fig. 11.**
17. Remove air conditioning compressor front bracket to cylinder head and rear bracket mounting bolts. Position compressor aside. **A/C refrigerant recovery is not required.**
18. Remove bracket mounting bolts and position power steering pump aside.
19. Raise and support vehicle, then drain engine oil into suitable container.
20. Remove righthand wheel and splash shield.
21. Remove drive belt tensioner.
22. Remove crankshaft pulley bolt.
23. Remove front crankshaft dampner using suitable universal three-jaw puller while holding dampner, **Fig. 12. Do not pry against cover.**
24. Hold front crankshaft timing sprocket using crankshaft gear retaining tool No. SA-9104-E, or equivalent, with flat side toward crankshaft sprocket.
25. Remove front oil pan and front cover mounting bolts.
26. Cut RTV seal from front cover using RTV cutter tool No. SA-9123-E, or equivalent.
27. Remove cover using front cover pry tangs.
28. Remove and discard oil gallery transfer seals.
29. **Position crankshaft 90° off TDC so pistons will not contact valves during assembly.**
30. Rotate crankshaft clockwise as viewed from crankshaft accessory belt end. Ensure crankshaft sprocket and keyway timing marks align with main bearing cap split line.
31. Remove timing chain, tensioner, guides, camshaft sprocket and chained, using suitable ⅞ inch wrench

to hold camshaft when removing sprocket, **Fig. 13.**
32. Loosen and remove head bolts uniformly and in sequence, **Fig. 14.**
33. Remove cylinder head from block dowels.

INSTALLATION

1. **Torque** cylinder head bolts to 48 ft. lbs. in sequence, **Fig. 15.**
2. Remove bolts and apply light coating of suitable engine oil to threads.
3. First, **torque** cylinder head bolts to 22 ft. lbs. in sequence.
4. Second, **torque** bolts to 33 ft. lbs. in sequence.
5. Finally, rotate bolts an additional 90° in sequence.
6. Ensure crankshaft is 90° past TDC, **Fig. 16.**
7. Position camshaft to No. 1 TDC by loosely installing sprocket and rotating clockwise until timing pin can be installed, **Fig. 17.**
8. Rotate crankshaft counterclockwise until cylinder No. 1 is at TDC and crankshaft sprocket timing mark will align with cylinder block timing mark, **Fig. 18.**
9. One silver link plate aligns with camshaft sprocket pip marks.
10. Another paired link plates aligns with

crankshaft sprocket tooth at 6 o'clock position. Crankshaft sprocket pip mark must be aligned with block timing mark.
11. Place timing chain over camshaft sprocket and under crankshaft sprocket. Camshaft sprocket FRT letters must face forward, **Fig. 19.**
12. **Keep excess chain slack to chain tensioner side of cylinder block when installing timing chain.**
13. Install camshaft sprocket timing pin using suitable ³⁄₁₆ inch drill bit, **Fig. 17.**
14. Install camshaft washer and bolt. Tighten mounting bolt while holding cam.
15. Install fixed chain guide and inspect clearance between block and head.
16. Ensure guide is installed with "FRONT" facing away from cylinder block and chain is tight against guide.
17. Install pivoting chain guide.
18. Inspect clearance between block and head.
19. Ensure guide pivots freely.
20. Retract tensioner plunger and hold ratchet using suitable ⅛ inch drill bit.
21. Install tensioner, then remove drill bit and allow plunger to extend.
22. Ensure timing marks are properly aligned.
23. Remove camshaft timing pins.
24. Install crankshaft timing gear retaining tool No. SA-9104-E, or equivalent.
25. Install front cover, then **torque** perimeter mounting bolts to 22 ft. lbs. in sequence, **Fig. 20.**
26. Pump 6–12 drops of oil through front oil seal drainback hole to ensure hole is not plugged.

DOHC Engine

REMOVAL

1. Remove coolant bottle cap.
2. Drain coolant into suitable container.
3. Remove air cleaner cover and air inlet duct.
4. Lift resonator upward to disconnect button from engine support bracket.
5. Disconnect cam cover air hose at cam cover.
6. Disconnect accelerator cable from throttle body and intake manifold bracket.

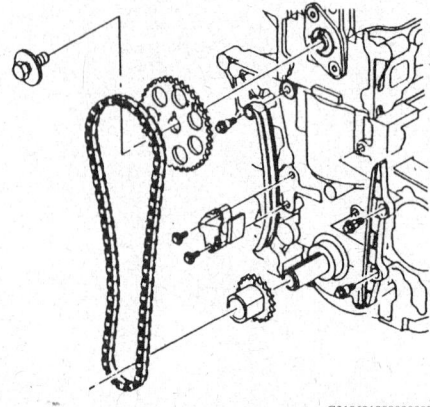

G31069100008000X

Fig. 13 Timing chain replacement. SOHC engine

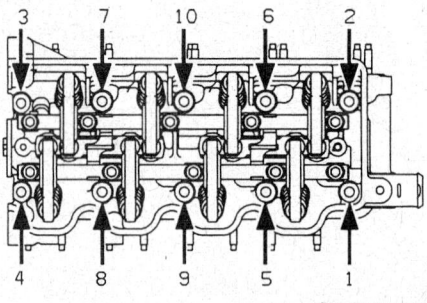

G31069100009000X

Fig. 14 Cylinder head bolt loosening sequence

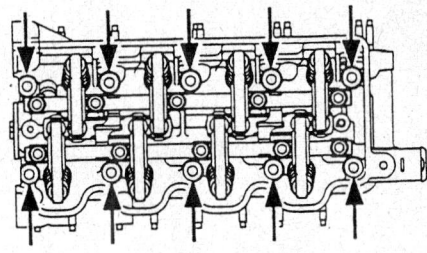

Intake Side

8 4 1 5 9

7 3 2 6 10

Exhaust Side

G31069100010000X

Fig. 15 Cylinder head bolt tightening sequence

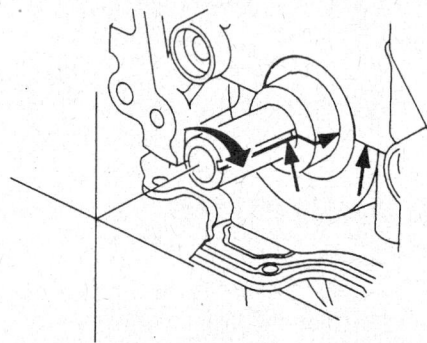

G31069100011000X

Fig. 16 Crankshaft at 90° past TDC

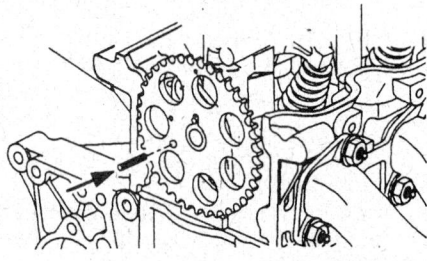

G31069100012000X

Fig. 17 Camshaft at No. 1 TDC. SOHC engine

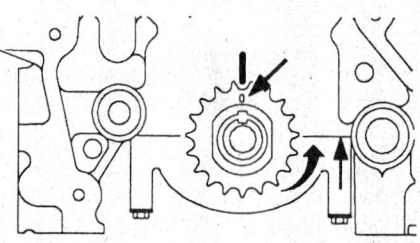

G31069100013000X

Fig. 18 Crankshaft sprocket & block timing mark alignment

7. Disconnect the following electrical connectors:
   a. Coolant temperature gauge and PCM.
   b. Injectors.
   c. Idle air control valve.
   d. Throttle position sensor/switch.
   e. Manifold air pressure sensor.
   f. Oxygen sensor.
   g. Spark plug wires.
   h. Air conditioning compressor.
   i. EGR solenoid.
8. Lay electrical harness onto underhood junction block and battery cover.
9. Disconnect and label the following vacuum hoses:
   a. Canister purge valve.
   b. PCV valve at cam cover.
   c. EGR valve.
   d. Fuel regulator, if equipped.
   e. Throttle body connector.
   f. Brake vacuum booster.
10. Disconnect the following hose clamps using clamp tool No. SA-911-E, or equivalent:
    a. Upper radiator hose at cylinder head outlet.
    b. De-aeration hose at intake manifold.
    c. Heater hose at intake manifold or front of firewall.
11. Bleed fuel pressure into suitable container using gauge bar kit tool No. SA-9127-E, or equivalent.
12. Remove fuel line clamp to intake manifold base mounting bolt.

13. Disconnect fuel supply and return line to fuel rail.
14. Disconnect fuel line at regulator.
15. Remove upper intake manifold support bracket mounting bolt.
16. Disconnect lower splash shield and place 1 × 1 × 2 inch wood block between torque strut and cradle.
17. Remove three righthand upper engine torque axis mount to front cover mounting nuts, allowing engine to rest on wood block.
18. Mark running direction, then remove accessory drive belt and tensioner. **Do not remove water pump pulley.**
19. Remove accessory drive belt idler pulley.
20. Remove camshaft cover.
21. Remove bracket mounting bolts and position power steering pump aside.
22. Remove front and rear bracket mounting bolts, then position air conditioning compressor aside. **A/C refrigerant recovery is not required.**
23. Raise and support vehicle, then drain engine oil into suitable container.
24. Remove righthand wheel and splash shield.
25. Remove intake manifold bracket to intake manifold mounting bolts.
26. Remove front dampner mounting bolt while holding dampner with suitable strap wrench or ¾ inch square × 12 inch long piece of wood wedged between dampner spoke and lower rear side of front cover.
27. Remove front crankshaft dampner using universal three-jaw puller while holding dampner, **Fig. 12. Do not pry against cover.**
28. Disconnect exhaust pipe from exhaust manifold.
29. Hold sprocket using crankshaft gear retaining tool No. SA-9104-E, or equiv-

alent, with flat side toward sprocket.
30. Remove front oil pan bolts and cut seal from front cover using RTV cutter tool No. SA-9123-E, or equivalent.
31. Remove mounting bolts and pry front cover from cylinder block using suitable screwdriver.
32. **Position crankshaft 90° off TDC so pistons will not contact valves during installation.**
33. Rotate crankshaft clockwise viewed from crankshaft accessory belt end.
34. Ensure sprocket and keyway timing marks align with main bearing cap split line, **Fig. 21.**
35. Remove timing chain tensioner, guides, camshaft sprockets and chain.
36. Remove sprocket mounting bolts using suitable ⅞ inch wrench to hold camshaft. **Do not place fingers or tools between camshaft sprocket and chain during removal or installation.**
37. Loosen and remove cylinder head bolts in sequence, **Fig. 14.**
38. Remove cylinder head from engine block dowels.

INSTALLATION

1. **Torque** cylinder head bolts to 48 ft. lbs. in sequence, **Fig. 15.**
2. Remove bolts and apply light coating of suitable engine oil to threads.
3. First, **torque** cylinder head bolts to 22 ft. lbs. in sequence.
4. Second, **torque** head bolts to 37 ft. lbs. in sequence.

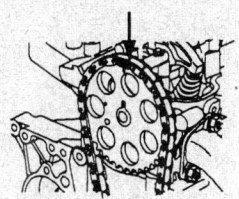
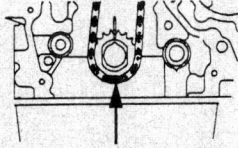

Fig. 19 Timing chain alignment. SOHC engine

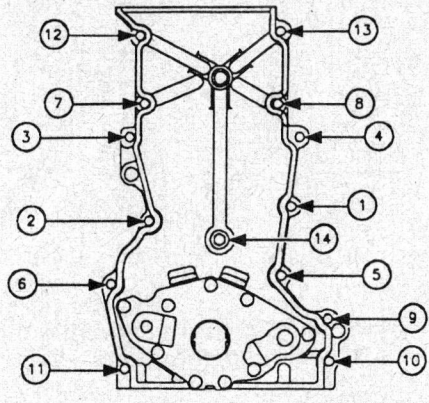

Fig. 20 Front cover bolt tightening sequence. SOHC engine

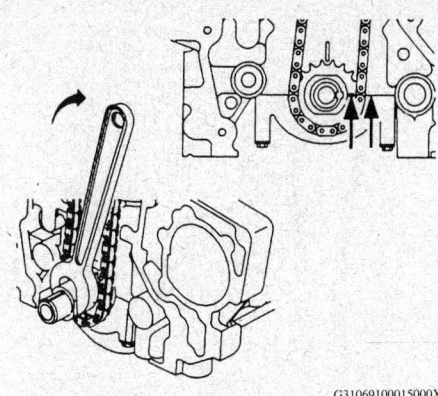

Fig. 21 Crankshaft sprocket & keyway alignment. DOHC engine

5. Finally, rotate bolts an additional 90° in sequence.
6. Ensure crankshaft is 90° past TDC, **Fig. 16.**
7. Install camshaft timing gears mounting bolts and washer. **Sprocket FRT label must face forward away from cylinder head.**
8. Tighten mounting bolts while holding camshaft.
9. **Do not tighten camshaft mounting bolts against 3/16 inch timing pins.**
10. Position camshaft at cylinder No. 1 TDC by rotating camshaft and sprocket until timing pins can be installed.
11. Rotate crankshaft counterclockwise until cylinder No. 1 is at TDC and crankshaft sprocket and cylinder block timing marks aligns, **Fig. 18.**
12. Align two separated silver link plates with camshaft sprocket pip marks.
13. Align another two paired link plates with crankshaft sprocket tooth at 6 o'clock position. Crankshaft sprocket pip mark must be aligned with block timing mark.
14. Place timing chain over camshaft sprockets and under crankshaft sprocket.
15. **Keep excess chain slack to chain tensioner side (movable guide) of cylinder block.**
16. Position silver colored link plates over pip mark on cam sprocket.
17. Position crankshaft sprocket tooth to pointed downward at 6 o'clock position between two silver colored links. Crankshaft sprocket pip mark should be aligned with block timing mark.
18. Align timing pin holes, crankshaft sprocket pip mark with block mark, colored links with camshaft and crankshaft, **Fig. 22.**
19. Install fixed guide. Ensure chain is tight against guide.
20. Install pivoting chain guide. Inspect clearance between head and block. Tighten bolt and ensure guide moves freely.
21. Retract tensioner plunger and hold ratchet lever using suitable 1/8 inch drill. Install tensioner.
22. Remove drill and allow plunger to extend.
23. Ensure timing marks align.

24. Remove camshaft timing pins.
25. Install crankshaft retaining tool No. SA-9140-E, or equivalent.
26. Install front cover, then **torque** perimeter mounting bolts to 22 ft. lbs. in sequence, **Fig. 23.**
27. Pump 6–12 drops of oil into oil seal drainback hole and ensure hole is not plugged.

VALVE COVER
REPLACE

Refer to procedure in "Cylinder Head, Replace."

CAMSHAFT LOBE LIFT SPECIFICATIONS

Engine	Intake	Exhaust
SOHC	.2531–.2556	.2531–.2556
DOHC	.3528–.3559	.3409–.3441

VALVE ADJUSTMENT

This engine is equipped with hydraulic lifters and no adjustment is required.

VALVE GUIDES

Valve guides are an integral part of the cylinder head and are pressed in. If valve stem clearance becomes excessive, the valve guides must be reamed to the oversize and the oversize valves installed. Valves are available in .010 inch oversize.

FRONT COVER
REPLACE

1. Disconnect lower splash shield, then place suitable 1 x 1 x 2 inch long wood block between torque strut and cradle.
2. Remove three righthand upper engine torque axis mount to front cover mounting nuts, allowing engine to rest on wood block.
3. Remove accessory drive belt, idler pulley, tensioner, crankshaft dampner and power steering pump.
4. Remove front cover mounting bolts.

5. Remove front cover by prying at upper and lower corners using suitable screwdriver.
6. Reverse procedure to install. Tighten mounting bolts in sequence, **Figs. 20 through 23.**

TIMING CHAIN
REPLACE

Refer to "Cylinder Head, Replace" for timing chain replacement procedure. If required, timing chain may be inspected as follows:

1. Inspect chain for wear and damaged links.
2. Measure chain inner diameter, **Fig. 24.**
3. **On models equipped with DOHC engine,** standard I.D. is 22.83–22.95 inches. Service limit is 23.15 inches.
4. **On models equipped with SOHC engine,** standard I.D. is 16.50–16.61 inches. Service limit is 16.77 inches.
5. **On all models,** inspect chain guides for wear and cracks.
6. Measure chain track wear, **Fig. 25.** Standard is zero inches. Service limit is .0984 inch.
7. Inspect timing sprocket teeth on crankshaft, camshaft and key for wear.
8. Inspect camshaft thrust plate and sprocket thrust surface for cracks and wear.
9. Inspect tensioner operation, release plunger lock and ensure piston moves freely.
10. Ensure oil feed hole is open, submerge tensioner in oil or solvent, depress plunger and inspect flow from tensioner body. Inspect cylinder block port for blockage.
11. Install timing chain and guides installed.
12. Measure plunger travel, **Fig. 26,** which should be as follows:
    a. **On models equipped with DOHC engine,** standard is .045–.388 inch. Service limit is .8626 inch.
    b. **On models equipped with SOHC engine,** standard is .0696–.4380 inch. Service limit is .8626 inch.

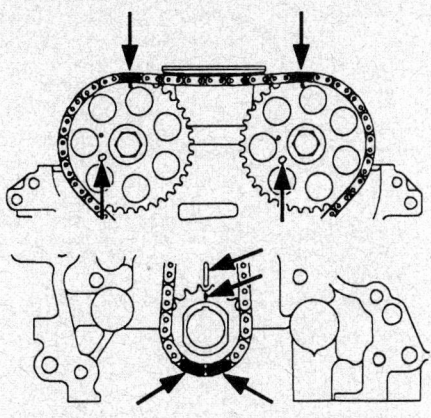

Fig. 22 Crankshaft alignment. DOHC engine

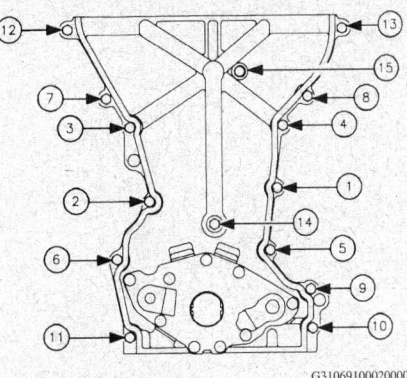

Fig. 23 Front cover bolt tightening sequence. DOHC engine

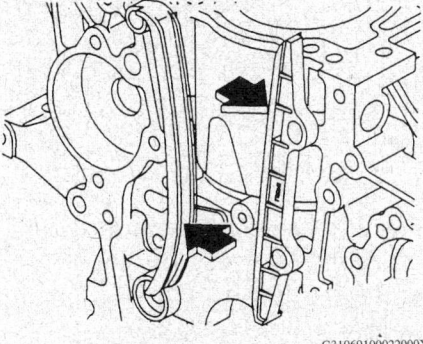

Fig. 25 Timing chain guide track wear measurement

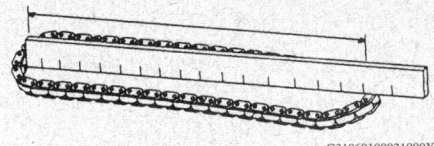

Fig. 24 Timing chain length inspection

CAMSHAFT
REPLACE

SOHC Engine

1. Remove battery cover and battery.
2. Remove valve covers, timing chain, gears and guides as outlined under "Cylinder Head, Replace."
3. Remove rocker arms and lifter assemblies.
4. Push camshaft plug inward using suitable driver.
5. Remove camshaft using suitable magnet through rear of cylinder head, **Fig. 27.**
6. Reverse procedure to install, noting the following:
   a. Apply Loctite 242, or equivalent sealant, to new cylinder head plug.
   b. Install plug using suitable bushing driver.

DOHC Engine

1. Remove spark plug wires, accessory drive belt, EGR valve solenoid mounting screw, PCV fresh air hose and cam cover.
2. Position cylinder No. 1 to TDC by aligning dampner mark with front cover arrow mark, **Fig. 28.**
3. Remove camshaft timing sprocket mounting bolts and washer preventing camshaft from rotating using suitable ⅞ inch open end wrench.
4. Install front support fixture, aligning two holes in each camshaft sprocket, sprocket adapter and front support fixture.
5. Install, but do not tighten, fixture mounting nuts, **Fig. 29.**
6. Install suitable camshaft sprocket adapter to each camshaft, but do not tighten pilot bolts, **Fig. 30.**
7. Remove upper timing chain guide and front camshaft bearing caps.
8. **Torque** sprocket pilot bolts to 18 ft. lbs. while holding camshaft using suitable ⅞ inch wrench.
9. Move camshaft sprocket off end of each camshaft onto sprocket adapter, **Fig. 31.**

10. Install four ⅜ inch nuts and bolts with blocks through camshaft sprocket, sprocket adapter and front support fixture.
11. Install steel blocks against rearward side of camshaft sprocket.
12. **Torque** nuts and bolts to 18 ft. lbs.
13. Install two 6 MM front support fixture hex bolts to front cover and **torque** bolts to 84 inch lbs.
14. Remove camshaft sprocket pilot bolt while holding camshaft using suitable ⅞ inch wrench.
15. Move cam rearward enough to ensure camshaft end is no longer inside sprocket pilot.
16. Loosen and remove camshaft bearing cap mounting bolts in several passes. **Keep lifters in order if removed. Store with camshaft contact facing downward.**
17. Reverse procedure to install.

PISTON & ROD ASSEMBLY

Assemble connecting rod to the piston with the bearing tang slots oriented toward the exhaust manifold, **Fig. 32.**

On models equipped with DOHC engine, align two eyebrow cuts in piston top toward intake side of engine.

On models equipped with SOHC engine, align paint dot or pip mark on piston top toward front of engine. If mark is not visible, align piston pin retaining ring pry slots toward intake side of engine.

On all models, if pistons are already installed, ensure pin boss with rectangular shaped casting is pointing toward rear of engine, **Fig. 33.**

PISTONS, PINS & RINGS

Pistons are available in .005 inch and .0157 inch oversizes.

To inspect piston fit in bore, measure piston diameter at righthand side angle to piston pin hole center line 20 inch from bottom of piston using suitable micrometer. Piston diameter plus piston clearance minus .002 inch allowance for finish honing will give piston size to be bored to.

MAIN & ROD BEARINGS

Main and thrust bearings are available in .0005 and .001 inch undersizes to adjust for proper main journal clearance.

When installing main bearing caps, ensure arrow points toward the front of the engine.

Torque cap bolts to 37 ft. lbs. in sequence in several steps, **Fig. 34.**

CRANKSHAFT REAR OIL SEAL
REPLACE

This procedure has been revised by a Technical Service Bulletin.

On 2001 models equipped with one-piece stamped steel seal, replace one-piece design with two-piece cast aluminum carrier seal part No. 21006927. Install seal using four new .787 inch long bolts part No. 11513762.

1. Remove transaxle, flywheel and cover.
2. If only oil seal requires replacement, proceed as follows:
   a. Insert suitable screwdriver into pry tangs of seal carrier and remove seal.
   b. Apply engine oil to seal lip and inside diameter of seal carrier.
   c. Install seal using seal installer tool No. SA-9121-E equivalent.
3. If seal and carrier require replacement, proceed as follows:
   a. Remove oil pan as outlined under "Oil Pan, Replace."
   b. Remove seal carrier.
   c. Remove seal from carrier using suitable screwdriver and hammer.

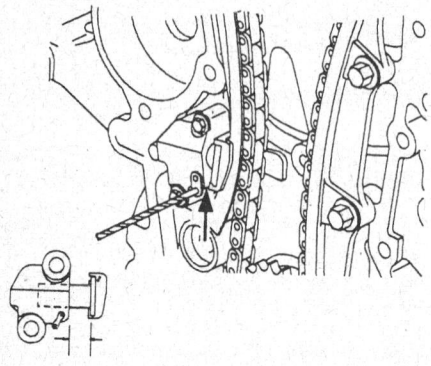

Fig. 26 Timing chain tensioner measurement

G31069100023000X

Fig. 27 Camshaft removal. SOHC engine

G31069800035000X

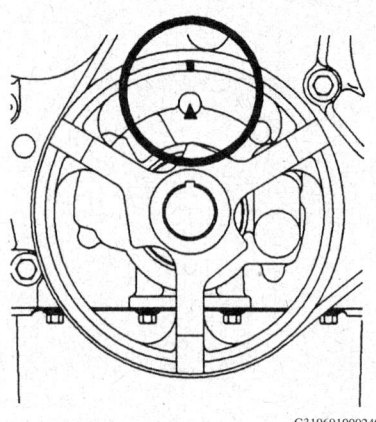

Fig. 28 Cylinder No. 1 at TDC. DOHC engine

G31069100024000X

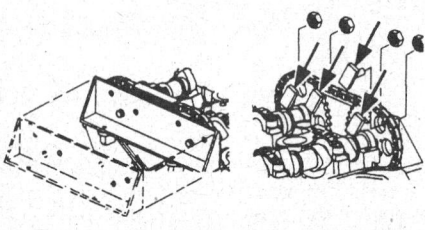

Fig. 29 Camshaft front support fixture. DOHC engine

G31069100025000X

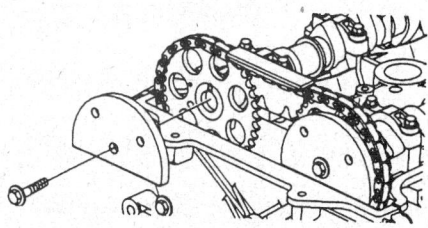

Fig. 30 Camshaft support fixture installation. DOHC engine

G31069100026000X

Fig. 31 Camshaft replacement. DOHC engine

G31069100027000X

d. Apply engine oil to seal lip and inside of carrier.
e. Seal carrier with .080 inch diameter bead of suitable RTV.
f. Install seal carrier.
g. Install seal using seal installer tool No. SA-9121-E, or equivalent.
4. Install transaxle and flywheel.

OIL PAN
REPLACE

1. Drain engine oil into suitable container.
2. Remove front exhaust pipe.
3. Remove engine stiffening bracket and flywheel cover.
4. Remove righthand side tire, splash shield and vibration dampner.
5. Loosen, but do not remove, four front engine mount mounting bolts approximately ½ inch.
6. Remove oil pan mounting bolts.
7. Pry front engine mount away from cylinder block to allow oil pan removal.
8. Drive sharp edge of RTV removal tool No. SA-9123-E, or equivalent, between pan and block.
9. Shear the seal seam with RTV removal tool.
10. Remove oil pan by tapping sideways with a suitable rubber mallet.
11. Reverse procedure to install. Apply .160 inch bead of RTV sealant to inside edge of oil pan groove.

OIL PUMP
REPLACE

1. Raise and support vehicle.
2. Drain engine oil into suitable container.

3. Remove righthand front wheel assembly and splash shield.
4. Place 1 × 1 × 2 inch wood block between torque strut and cradle.
5. Remove drive belt.
6. Remove crankshaft pulley bolt.
7. Remove front crankshaft dampner using universal three-jaw puller while holding dampner, **Fig. 12. Do not pry against cover.**
8. Remove idler pulley.
9. Remove power steering pump and position aside.
10. Remove belt tensioner.
11. Remove valve cover as outlined under "Valve Cover, Replace."
12. Remove three righthand upper engine torque axis mount to front cover mounting nuts, allowing engine to rest on wood block.
13. Hold front crankshaft timing sprocket using crankshaft timing gear tool No. SA-9104-E, or equivalent, with flat side toward crankshaft sprocket.
14. Remove front oil pan and front cover mounting bolts.
15. Cut RTV seal from front cover using RTV cutter tool No. SA-9123-E, or equivalent.
16. Remove oil gallery transfer seals using front cover pry tangs. Discard seals.
17. Reverse procedure to install.

OIL PUMP SERVICE
Disassemble

1. Remove cover plate mounting bolts.
2. Remove drive and driven rotors.

3. Remove and discard relief valve using tool No. SA-9103-E, or equivalent.

Inspection

1. Measure clearance between driven rotor and pump body, **Fig. 35.** Replace pump rotor set if clearance is more than .006–.011 inch.
2. Inspect clearance between both rotor tips, **Fig. 36.** Maximum clearance is .006 inch.
3. Measure clearance between side of gear rotor assembly and cover plate, **Fig. 37.** Standard clearance is .0016–.0049 inch. Maximum is .0050 inch.

Assemble

1. Remove front cover oil seal using suitable screwdriver or punch.
2. Install new oil seal using seal installer tool No. SA-9140-E, or equivalent, and suitable press.
3. If relief valve was removed, proceed as follows:
   a. Coat new relief valve with suitable engine oil.
   b. Install relief valve using driver tool No. SA-9103-E, or equivalent, and suitable hammer.
4. Pack oil pump with suitable petroleum jelly.
5. Install drive and driven rotors to pump body with chamfer toward front oil seal.
6. Install pump body cover and new bolts.

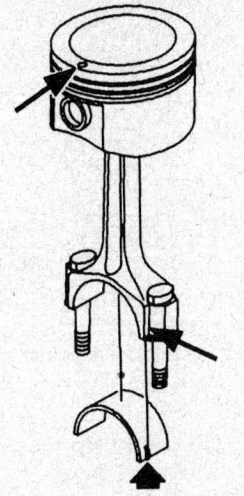

G31069100028000X

Fig. 32 Piston & rod assembly

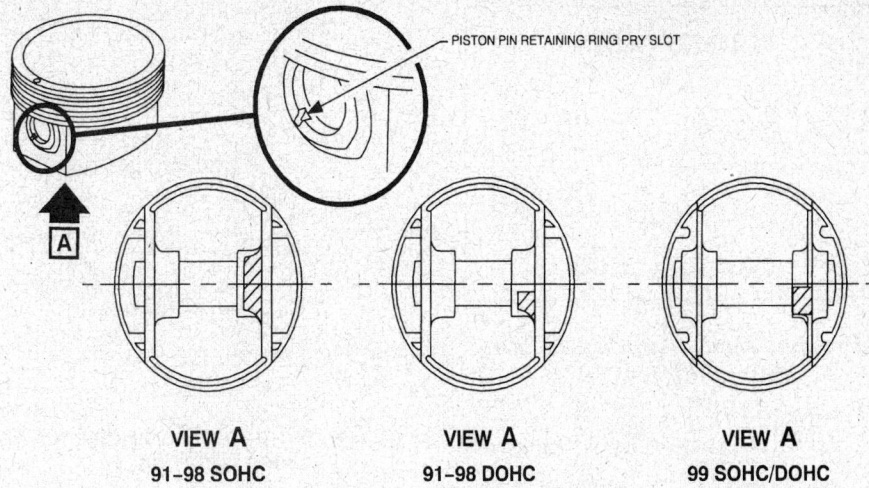

VIEW **A**	VIEW **A**	VIEW **A**
91–98 SOHC	91–98 DOHC	99 SOHC/DOHC

PISTON PIN RETAINING RING PRY SLOT

⧄ CASTING FEATURE LOCATED TOWARD BACK OF ENGINE
G31060000080000X

Fig. 33 Piston boss configuration

BELT TENSION DATA

Belt	Tension, Lbs.	
	New	Used
Accessory	50–65	45

SERPENTINE DRIVE BELT

Belt Routing

Refer to **Figs. 38 and 39** for serpentine belt routing.

Tensioner, Replacement

Do not disassemble tensioner. Internal components are not serviceable.

1. Disconnect lower splash shield and place suitable 1 × 1 × 2 inch wood block between torque strut and cradle.
2. Remove three righthand upper engine torque axis mount to front cover mounting nuts, allowing engine to rest on wood block.
3. Remove belt as outlined under "Belt, Replacement."
4. Remove power steering pump with bracket.
5. Remove tensioner upper and lower mounting bolts, **Fig. 40.**
6. Move engine slightly toward driver's fender using suitable pry bar between steel engine mount and rail, as required.
7. Remove tensioner.
8. Reverse procedure to install.

Belt Replacement

REMOVAL

1. Depress tensioner arm using suitable wrench, **Fig. 41.**
2. Remove belt from idler and accessory pulleys.

INSTALLATION

1. Route belt over pulleys, except front cover idler or air conditioning compressor.
2. Depress tensioner arm using suitable wrench.
3. Install belt to idler pulley and air conditioning compressor.

COOLING SYSTEM BLEED

These engines do not require a special bleed procedure. After filling cooling system, run engine and allow to reach normal operating temperature with pressure cap off. Air will then automatically bleed through cap opening.

THERMOSTAT

REPLACE

Removal

Do not remove pressure cap while engine is running or when engine is still warm.

1. Remove engine drain plug at righthand front of engine and open petcock at lower part of radiator to drain coolant into suitable container. Ensure coolant level is below thermostat housing.
2. Disconnect lower radiator hose at thermostat housing using Snap On hose removal tool No. HCP10, or equivalent.
3. Remove water inlet housing mounting bolts.
4. Remove water inlet and thermostat as an assembly. Discard O-ring.
5. Remove thermostat element using service tool provided with replacement part, noting the following:
   a. If oil is found in coolant, flush entire system before replacing thermostat.

b. New component will not function properly if it comes in contact with oil.
6. Ensure no damage or seat deterioration is found within water inlet housing. **Do not damage machined aluminum surfaces.**

Installation

1. Install new thermostat using service tool provided, ensuring tangs are properly seated in legs and piston is properly positioned in water inlet housing.
2. Install new water inlet housing O-ring.
3. Install water inlet housing and thermostat.
4. Close radiator and engine drain plugs.
5. Install lower radiator hose. Ensure vehicle is on level surface.
6. Fill coolant system.
7. Start engine and run for several minutes.
8. Fill cooling system surge tank to full cold line.
9. Install pressure cap and inspect for leaks.

WATER PUMP

REPLACE

1. Drain coolant into suitable container.
2. Remove accessory drive belt.
3. Raise and support vehicle.
4. Remove righthand wheel assembly, then inner wheelwell splash shield.
5. Remove mounting bolts and position air conditioning compressor aside.
6. Place a one inch wood block between crankshaft and water pump pulley.
7. Remove mounting bolts and allow pulley to hang on pump hub.
8. Remove mounting bolts, water pump and gasket.
9. Reverse procedure to install. Install new gasket.

RADIATOR

REPLACE

1. Drain coolant into suitable container.

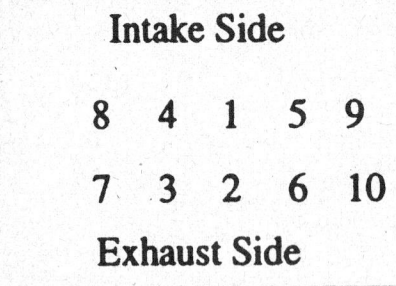

Intake Side

8	4	1	5	9
7	3	2	6	10

Exhaust Side

G31069700076000X

Fig. 34 Main bearing cap bolt tightening sequence

2. Remove air intake duct.
3. Remove upper radiator clamp and hose.
4. **On models equipped with automatic transaxle,** remove upper transaxle oil cooler line.
5. **On all models,** remove electric cooling fan.
6. Disconnect lower radiator hose.
7. Raise and support vehicle.
8. Remove lower splash shield.
9. **On models equipped with automatic transaxle,** remove transaxle lower oil cooler line.
10. **On all models,** remove lower condenser bracket to radiator bolts and support condenser with suitable wire.
11. Lower vehicle, then remove upper radiator mounting nuts and brackets.
12. **On models equipped with air conditioning,** remove upper radiator seal.
13. **On all models,** remove radiator.
14. Reverse procedure to install.

FUEL PUMP
REPLACE

When removing fuel system lines and hoses, wrap a suitable shop towel around fitting and have an suitable container available to catch any fuel that may spill.
1. If fuel pump is operational, drain fuel tank into suitable container as follows:
   a. Remove air cleaner inlet hose from throttle body.
   b. Disconnect fuel feed line at fuel rail and install fuel adapter fitting tool No. SA-3097-38, or equivalent.
   c. Connect one end of suitable fuel line to adapter and other end to suitable fuel handling cart.
   d. Connect suitably programmed scan tool to Data Link Connector (DLC) and turn ignition On.
   e. Turn fuel pump on using scan tool and pump fuel into suitable container.
2. If fuel pump is inoperative, siphon fuel using siphon hose tool No. SA-980-E, or equivalent, **Fig. 42.**
3. Remove fuel filler cap and rubber closeout grommet.
4. Remove filler pipe mounting screw.
5. Raise and support vehicle.

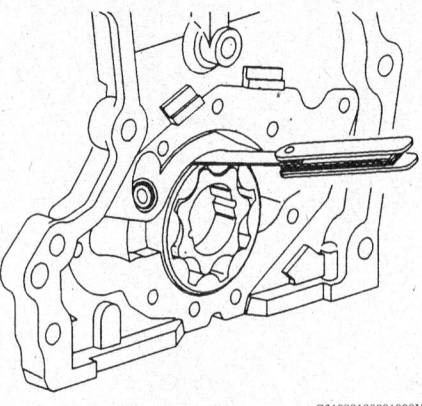

G31099100001000X

Fig. 35 Oil pump body clearance measurement

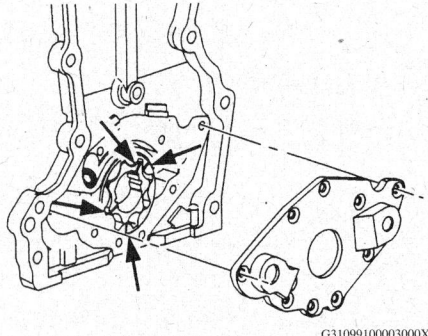

G31099100003000X

Fig. 37 Oil pump end to end clearance measurement

6. Remove wheelwell inner cover.
7. Disconnect wiring harness from EVAP vent solenoid.
8. Remove filler pipe lower mounting screw.
9. Disconnect EVAP canister vent pipe at ⅝ inch quick connect to canister hose.
10. Remove fuel filler pipe from fuel tank. Ensure fuel fill check valve is not dislodged from filler pipe.
11. Disconnect fuel feed line from fuel pressure regulator.
12. Disconnect fuel vapor line from quick connect fitting.
13. Remove filter bracket from under brake lines.
14. Support fuel tank with suitable lifting device and remove strap mounting bolts.
15. Lower tank enough to access, then disconnect fuel pump and tank pressure sensor electrical connectors.
16. Lower fuel tank.
17. Disconnect fuel feed and return lines from pressure regulator.
18. Disconnect fuel pump vapor line from fuel tank vent pipe.
19. Remove fuel pump retaining ring using lock ring removal tool No. SA-9156-E, or equivalent.
20. Lift pump slightly to disconnect tabs and rotate 90° clockwise until lines are

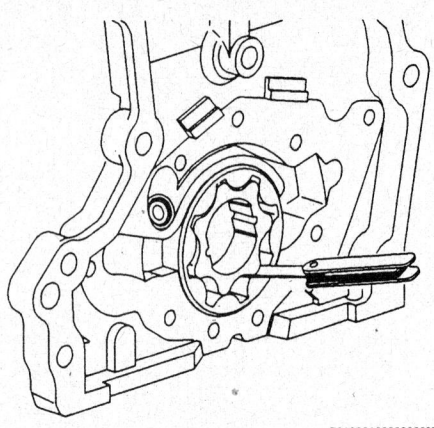

G31099100002000X

Fig. 36 Oil pump tip clearance measurement

facing 1 o'clock position.
21. Lift pump until bottom is close to tank opening.
22. Tilt pump 45° toward righthand side of tank and lift out.
23. Reverse procedure to install, noting the following:
   a. Install new fuel pump green seal. **Do not use black seal.**
   b. White locator button located on lefthand side of fuel tank should be flush with lefthand side rail when installation is complete.
   c. Replace plastic fuel line retainers on lines which were disconnected.

FUEL FILTER
REPLACE

The fuel filter/regulator assembly is located on the underbody near the front lefthand side of the fuel tank.
1. Raise and support vehicle.
2. Remove fuel filter bracket mounting screws.
3. Unlatch fuel line bundle retaining clip at lefthand side of fuel tank.
4. Disconnect EVAP purge line at 90° quick-connect.
5. Slide outlet of filter from support on fuel tank bracket and remove fuel feed line at 90° quick-connect.
6. Pivot filter down while moving leg of bracket from under brake lines.
7. Disconnect fuel feed and return lines, then remove filter/regulator and bracket.
8. Reverse procedure to install, noting the following:
   a. Install new plastic fuel line retainers.
   b. Ensure fuel feed and purge lines are routed on top of emergency brake cable.
   c. Ensure emergency brake cable is secured firmly to underbody to support lines.
   d. Operate fuel pump and inspect system for leaks.

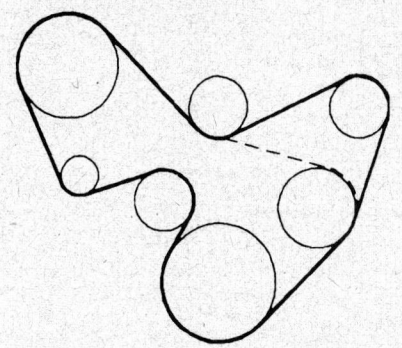

G31069600034000X

Fig. 38 Serpentine belt routing. DOHC engine

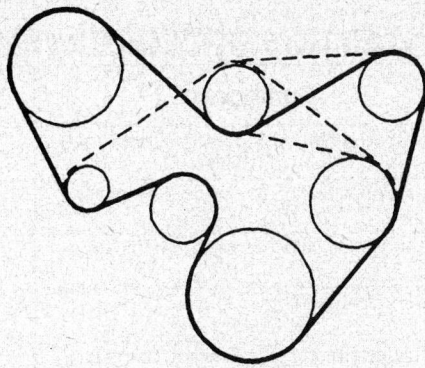

G31069100029000X

Fig. 39 Serpentine belt routing. SOHC engine

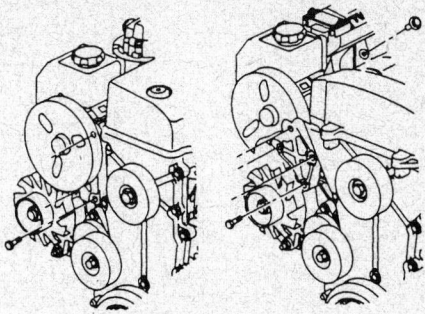

G31069100030000X

Fig. 40 Belt tensioner replacement

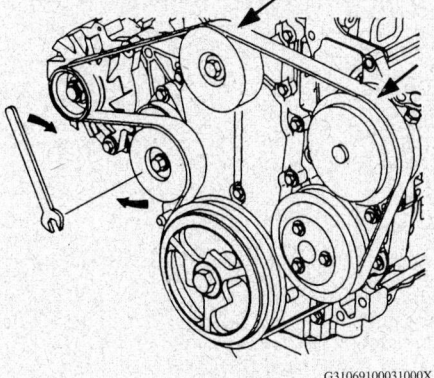

G31069100031000X

Fig. 41 Belt tensioner arm replacement

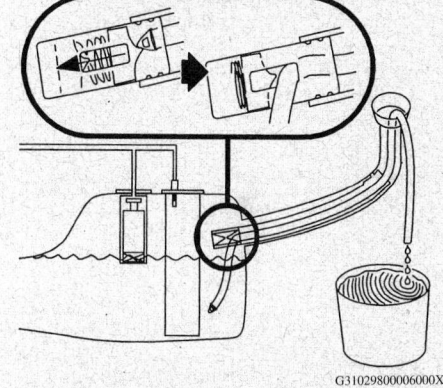

G31029800006000X

Fig. 42 Fuel tank siphoning

TIGHTENING SPECIFICATIONS

Year	Component	Torque/Ft. Lbs.
2001–02	Air Conditioning Compressor Front Bracket To Block	35
	Air Conditioning Compressor Front/Rear Bracket To Head	23
	Air Conditioning Compressor To Front Bracket	40
	Air Conditioning Compressor To Rear Bracket	22
	Accelerator Cable Bracket To Intake Manifold	19
	Air Cleaner Duct Clamp	15①
	Air Cleaner/Resonator	96①
	Air Cleaner/Resonator Clamp	18①
	Alternator Positive Terminal	84①
	Alternator To Block	24
	Axle Shaft Intermediate Bracket To Block	41
	Battery Cable	13
	Belt Idler Pulley To Front Cover	20
	Belt Tensioner To Block	22
	Block Oil Gallery Plug	22
	Camshaft Bearing Cap To Head (DOHC)	10
	Camshaft Cover To Head (DOHC)	96①
	Camshaft Sprocket To Camshaft	75
	Camshaft Thrust Plate To Head (SOHC)	19
	Canister Band Clamp	31①
	Canister Purge Solenoid To Block	22
	Clutch Pressure Plate To Flywheel	19
	Connecting Rod	19⑥
	Coolant Drain Plug	22
	Coolant Temperature Sensor	72①
	Cradle To Body	151
	Crankshaft Bearing Cap To Block	④
	Crankshaft Dampner To Crankshaft	159
	Crankshaft Position Sensor	84①
	Crankshaft Rear Oil Seal Carrier To Block	96①
	Cylinder Head	③
	De-aeration Line Fitting To Head	96①
	De-aeration Line Nut To Head (SOHC)	84①
	EGR Solenoid Bracket (DOHC)	84①
	EGR Solenoid Bracket (SOHC)	19
	EGR Valve	19
	Engine Block Heater To Block	18
	Engine Lift Bracket To Block	22
	Engine Mount To Front Cover	37
	Engine Mount To Mid-Rail Bracket	37
	Engine Support Bracket	23
	ESC Knock Sensor	11
	Exhaust Manifold Studs To Front Pipe	10
	Exhaust Manifold Studs To Head	108①
	Exhaust Manifold To Head	②
	Exhaust Pipe To Converter	35
	Flexplate To Converter	52
	Flexplate To Crankshaft	44
	Flywheel/Flexplate Cover	84①
	Flywheel To Crankshaft	59
	Front Cover To Block (Center)	84①

Continued

TIGHTENING
SPECIFICATIONS—Continued

Year	Component	Torque/Ft. Lbs.
2001–02	Front Cover To Block (Perimeter)	③
	Front Engine Mount To Block	52
	Fuel Canister Bracket To Frame Rail	22
	Fuel Filter Bracket	72①
	Fuel Line Support Bracket	22
	Fuel Line Support Clip	108①
	Fuel Rail To Intake Manifold	84①
	Fuel Tank Fill Hose	35①
	Fuel Tank Fill Pipe Bracket	72①
	Fuel Tank Straps	35
	Fuel/Vapor Line To Body	27①
	Heater Outlet To Intake Manifold	19
	Heater Return Nipple	37
	Idle Air Control Sensor	28
	Idle Air Control Valve	28①
	Ignition Module To Transaxle Case	72①
	Intake Manifold	⑤
	Intake Manifold Bracket To Block (Lefthand)	22
	Intake Manifold Bracket To Block (Righthand) (DOHC)	41
	Intake Manifold Bracket To Manifold (DOHC)	22
	Intake Manifold Bracket To Manifold (SOHC)	21
	Intake Manifold Stud To Fuel Line Clamp (SOHC)	60①
	Intake Manifold Stud To Head	108①
	Intake Manifold Stud To Head (Power Steering Bracket) (DOHC)	22
	Intake Manifold Stud To Head (Power Steering Bracket) (SOHC)	16
	MAP Sensor	44①
	Motion Restrictor Bracket	40
	Motion Restrictor To Side Of Block	22
	Oil Baffle Plate To Block	41
	Oil Drain Plug	26
	Oil Pan To Block	84①
	Oil Pickup Tube (DOHC)	11
	Oil Pipe Bracket To Baffle Plate	11
	Oil Pipe Bracket To Block (DOHC)	11
	Oil Pipe Bracket To Block (SOHC)	41
	Oil Pressure Sensor	26
	Oil Pump Cover	96①
	Oxygen Sensor	33
	Power Steering Hoses	20
	Power Steering Pump Bracket	28
	Power Steering Pump To Bracket	22
	Power Steering Return Hose Clamp	18①
	Radiator Upper Bracket	96①
	Rear Engine Mount To Block	35
	Rocker Arm Cover To Head (SOHC)	22
	Rocker Arm Shaft To Head	19
	Spark Plug	20
	Starter Motor	27
	Starter Motor Bracket To Axle Shaft	22
	Starter Positive Terminal	96①

Continued

1.9L ENGINE

TIGHTENING SPECIFICATIONS—Continued

Year	Component	Torque/Ft. Lbs.
2001–02	Starter Solenoid Terminal	35①
	Steering Joint To Gear	35
	Stiffening Bracket	40
	Strut To Knuckle	148
	Thermostat Housing To Block	22
	Throttle Body To Air Intake Manifold	23
	Throttle Position Sensor	18①
	Timing Chain Guides	19
	Timing Chain Tensioner	14
	Transaxle Case To Block (Lower)	96
	Transaxle Case To Block (Upper)	66
	Transaxle Lower Mount To Cradle	41
	Transaxle Lower Mount To Transaxle	23
	Transaxle Rear Mount	36
	Valve Cover (DOHC)	96①
	Valve Cover (SOHC)	22
	Vapor Canister To Body	22
	Vehicle Speed Sensor	19①
	Water Pump	22
	Water Pump Pulley	18

DOHC — Dual Over Head Cam
SOHC — Single Over Head Cam
① — Inch lbs.
② — Refer to "Exhaust Manifold, Replace" for tightening
specifications & sequence.
③ — Refer to "Cylinder Head, Replace" for tightening specifications & sequence.
④ — Refer to "Main & Rod Bearings" for tightening specifications & sequence.
⑤ — Refer to "Intake Manifold, Replace" for tightening specifications & sequence.
⑥ — Rotate an additional 75°.

2.0L Engine

NOTE: On Air Bag Equipped Models, Refer To "Air Bag System Precautions" Located In The Front Of This Manual For System Disarming & Arming Procedures.

NOTE: Refer To "Computer Relearn Procedures" Located In The Front Of This Manual When Battery Power To The Computer Has Been Interrupted.

INDEX

PRECAUTIONS

Air Bag Systems

Refer to "Air Bag System Precautions" in the front of this manual for system disarming and arming procedures.

Battery Ground Cable

Prior to service, disconnect battery ground cable and isolate as required.

Fuel System Pressure Relief

1. Loosen fuel filler cap to relieve fuel tank vapor pressure.
2. Remove fuel pressure service port cap.
3. Remove engine identification cover nuts, then the cover.
4. Connect pressure test kit tool No. SA-9127-E, or equivalent to fuel pressure service port connection. Wrap a shop towel around port during connection to prevent spillage.
5. Place end of bleed hose in suitable container and open valve to bleed system pressure.
6. Remove gauge after pressure has dissipated, then replace cap.
7. Install engine identification cover.
8. Tighten fuel filler cap.

COMPRESSION PRESSURE

1. Start and run engine until it reaches normal operating temperature.
2. Turn ignition Off, then disconnect ignition module electrical connectors.
3. Ensure battery is fully charged.
4. Remove ignition coils and spark plugs.
5. Install suitable compression gauge tool in spark plug hole.
6. Ensure throttle is wide open.
7. Crank engine through four compression strokes for each cylinder.
8. Lowest reading cylinder should be within 70% of highest.
9. No cylinder should read less than 100 psi.

ENGINE MOUNT

REPLACE

Removal

1. Support engine with a suitable floor jack and a wooden block under oil pan.
2. Remove engine mount to intermediate bracket bolts.
3. Remove engine mount to mid-rail nuts, then the mount from vehicle.

Installation

1. Place engine mount onto mid-rail and start nuts by hand.
2. **Torque** mid-rail nuts to 74 ft. lbs.
3. Start engine mount to intermediate bracket bolts by hand. **Do not pry engine mount to align holes.**
4. **Torque** engine mount to intermediate bracket bolts, starting with center bolt, to 37 ft. lbs.
5. Remove jack and wooden block.

ENGINE

REPLACE

1. Ensure front wheels are in straight ahead position.
2. Remove air outlet duct.
3. Secure cooling module to upper body structure.
4. Drain coolant into an approved container.
5. Drain engine oil.
6. Relieve fuel system pressure as outlined under "Fuel System Pressure Relief."
7. Disconnect fuel line from fuel rail.
8. Remove radiator inlet hose.
9. Remove surge tank to cylinder head pipe.
10. Remove radiator outlet hose.
11. Remove heater inlet and outlet hoses.
12. Disconnect the following electrical connectors:
    a. MAP sensor.
    b. Electronic Temperature Control (ETC).
    c. MAP sensor.
    d. BARO sensor.
    e. CKP sensor.
    f. Oil pressure sensor.
    g. EVAP purge solenoid.
    h. Ignition coils.

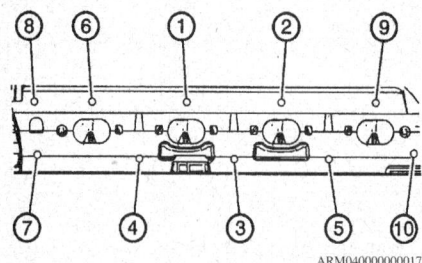

Fig. 1 Exhaust manifold nut tightening sequence

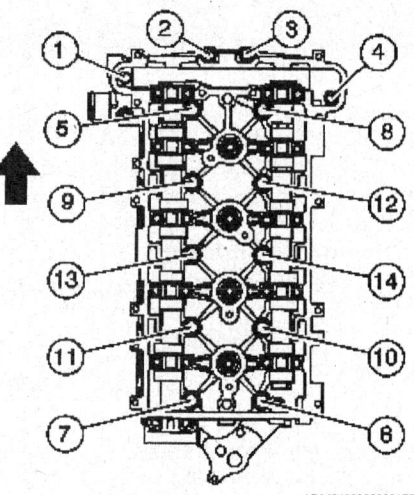

Fig. 2 Cylinder head bolt loosening sequence

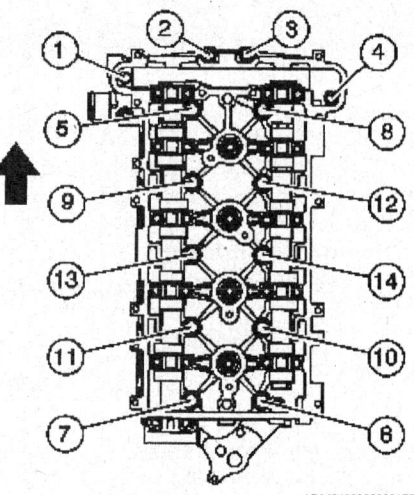

Fig. 3 Cylinder head bolt tightening sequence

i. O2 sensor.
j. VSS.
k. ECT sensor.
l. Boost solenoid.
m. Back-up lamp switch.
13. Remove righthand front fender liner.
14. Mark serpentine belt running direction.
15. Slowly rotate belt tensioner counter-clockwise to relieve tension, then remove serpentine belt.
16. Raise and support vehicle.
17. Recover refrigerant as outlined in "Air Conditioning" chapter.
18. Disconnect A/C suction discharge hose assembly from compressor.
19. Remove A/C compressor mounting bolts, then position compressor aside.
20. Disconnect electrical connectors from starter and alternator.
21. Disconnect front exhaust pipe from exhaust manifold.
22. Disconnect shift cable from transaxle.
23. Support powertrain assembly between frame and powertrain using suitable wooden blocks.
24. Remove engine mount as outlined under "Engine Mount, Replace."
25. Remove transaxle lefthand mount.
26. Disconnect stabilizer links from stabilizer bar.
27. Disconnect outer tie rod ends from steering knuckles.
28. Remove lefthand front tire and wheel assembly.
29. Remove and discard intermediate shaft to steering gear pinch bolt. **Do not attempt to rotate steering shaft. This might lead to air bag module deployment.**
30. Disconnect intermediate shaft from steering gear.
31. Disconnect lower control arms from steering knuckles. **Do not separate ball joint with a pickle fork or a wedge type tool.**
32. Remove wheel driveshaft nut. Insert a drift or a flat bladed tool into caliper and rotor to prevent rotor from turning.
33. Carefully loosen wheel driveshaft splines from wheel bearing/hub assembly using a wooden block and hammer. Temporarily install nut to protect threads.
34. Disconnect outer tie rod assembly from steering knuckle. **Do not loosen tie rod adjustment jamb nut.**
35. Loosen outer tie rod to inner tie rod jam nut.

36. Remove and discard tie rod to steering knuckle nut.
37. Separate outer tie rod from steering knuckle using tool No. SA91100C, or equivalent.
38. Mark frame to body position using paint or a felt tip marker.
39. Lower vehicle to approximately three feet off ground in order to position a lift table under frame.
40. Position wooden blocks as required between lift table and frame to support assembly.
41. Slowly remove front frame bolts.
42. Partially remove rear frame bolts until 1½ inches of bolt shank is exposed.
43. Slowly lower table to floor.
44. Attach a suitable crane or hoist to engine lift hooks.
45. Remove starter mounting bolts, then the starter.
46. Remove transaxle to engine bolts, then separate engine from transaxle.
47. **On models equipped with manual transaxle,** remove clutch pressure plate and disk.
48. **On all models,** reverse procedure to install.

INTAKE MANIFOLD
REPLACE

1. Remove supercharger as outlined under "Supercharger, Replace."
2. Disconnect alternator electrical connectors.
3. Remove alternator mounting bolts, then the alternator from vehicle.
4. Drain coolant into an approved container.
5. Disconnect charged air cooling system inlet and outlet hoses.
6. Remove charged air coolant pump.
7. Remove cooling fan assembly.
8. Remove AC compressor mounting bolts, then position compressor aside.
9. Remove oil level dipstick tube bolt.

10. Remove intake manifold mounting nuts and bolts, then the manifold from vehicle.
11. Reverse procedure to install.

EXHAUST MANIFOLD
REPLACE

1. Remove exhaust manifold heat shield.
2. Disconnect oxygen sensor electrical connector.
3. Remove oxygen sensor using wrench tool No. J 39194-C, or equivalent.
4. Raise and safely support vehicle.
5. Remove exhaust pipe to manifold nuts. **Do not bend exhaust flex decoupler more than 3° in any direction.**
6. Pull down and back on exhaust pipe to disengage pipe from manifold.
7. Lower the vehicle.
8. Remove exhaust manifold to cylinder head nuts, then the manifold and gasket from vehicle. Discard nuts and gasket.
9. Reverse procedure to install, noting the following:
   a. Clean all sealing surfaces as required.
   b. Place new gasket and manifold in position.
   c. **Torque** new exhaust manifold mounting nuts to 115 inch lbs. in sequence, **Fig. 1.**

CYLINDER HEAD
REPLACE

1. Remove supercharger as outlined under "Supercharger, Replace."
2. Remove intake manifold as outlined under "Intake Manifold, Replace."
3. Remove exhaust manifold as outlined under "Exhaust Manifold, Replace."
4. Remove timing chain as outlined under "Timing Chain, Replace."
5. Loosen cylinder head bolts in sequence, **Fig. 2,** then remove and discard bolts.
6. Remove cylinder head, then discard gasket.
7. Reverse procedure to install, noting the following:

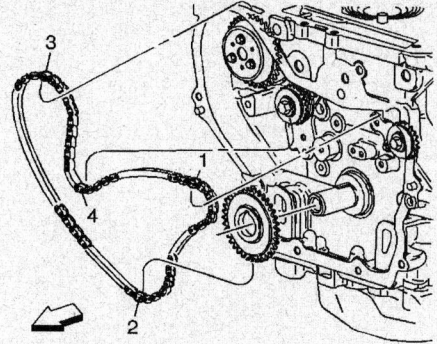

1. Uniquely colored link
2. First matching colored link
3. Balancer shaft chain
4. Last matching colored link

ARM0400000000179

Fig. 4 Balance shaft chain mark alignment

a. Clean all gasket and sealing surfaces.
b. **Torque** cylinder head bolts to 22 ft. lbs. in sequence, **Fig. 3.**
c. Rotate bolts an additional 155° in sequence, **Fig. 3.**
d. Install new cylinder head front bolts and **torque** to 26 ft. lbs.

VALVE ADJUSTMENT

This engine is equipped with hydraulic lifters and no adjustment is required.

FRONT COVER
REPLACE

1. Remove serpentine belt as outlined under "Serpentine Drive Belt."
2. Prevent crankshaft rotation with holder tool No. J 38122-A, or equivalent.
3. Remove and discard crankshaft balancer bolt.
4. Remove crankshaft balancer.
5. Remove belt tensioner mounting bolts, then the tensioner.
6. Remove idler pulley mounting bolts, then the idler pulley.
7. Remove front cover to water pump bolt.
8. Remove remaining front cover bolts, then the front cover.
9. Remove front engine mount as outlined under "Engine Mount, Replace."
10. Remove front engine mount bracket.
11. Discard front cover gasket.
12. Reverse procedure to install.

TIMING CHAIN
REPLACE
Removal

1. Disconnect ignition coil electrical connectors.

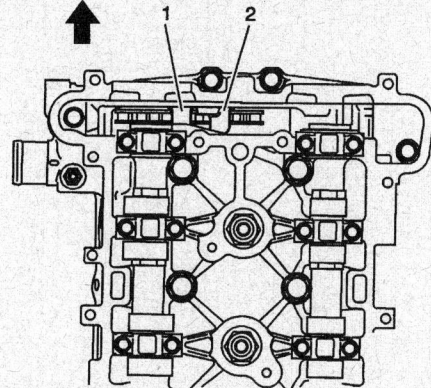

1. Boss
2. Boss

ARM0400000000180

Fig. 5 Timing chain routing around block bosses

2. Remove coil mounting bolts, then the coils from vehicle.
3. Remove ground strap and stud.
4. Disconnect PCV hose from camshaft cover.
5. Disconnect fuel feed pipe from fuel rail.
6. Remove camshaft cover mounting bolts, then the cover.
7. Raise and safely support vehicle.
8. Remove engine front cover as outlined under "Front Cover, Replace."
9. Lower the vehicle.
10. Remove spark plugs.
11. Use a 24 MM open end wrench on camshaft flats to rotate or hold camshafts. **Rotate in a clockwise direction only.**
12. Place No. 1 piston at approximately 60° before TDC by rotating intake camshaft sprocket until diamond shaped hole on sprocket reaches 12 o'clock position.
13. Remove timing chain tensioner.
14. Remove fixed timing chain guide access plug, then the guide.
15. Remove upper timing chain guide.
16. Remove and discard exhaust camshaft sprocket bolt.
17. Remove exhaust camshaft sprocket.
18. Remove timing chain tensioner guide.
19. Remove and discard intake camshaft sprocket bolt.
20. Remove intake camshaft sprocket.
21. Remove timing chain through top of cylinder head.
22. Remove crankshaft sprocket.
23. Remove oil nozzle and bolt.
24. Remove balance shaft drive chain tensioner.
25. Remove adjustable balance shaft chain guide.
26. Remove small balance shaft drive chain guide.
27. Remove upper balance shaft drive chain guide.
28. Remove balance shaft drive chain. **This may be more easily removed by gathering all chain slack be-**

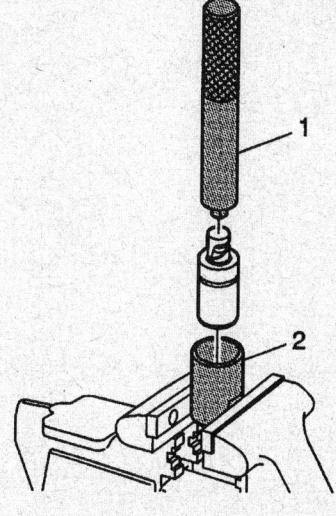

1. J 45027-1
2. J45027-2

ARM0400000000181

Fig. 6 Timing chain tensioner compression

tween crankshaft and water pump sprockets.

Installation

1. Install upper balance shaft chain guide.
2. Align uniquely colored link with timing mark on intake side balance shaft sprocket, **Fig. 4.**
3. Work clockwise around chain and align first matching colored link with crankshaft drive sprocket timing mark.
4. Place chain on water pump drive sprocket.
5. Align last matching colored link with exhaust side balance shaft drive sprocket timing mark.
6. Install small balance shaft chain guide.
7. Install adjustable balance shaft drive chain guide.
8. Rotate tensioner plunger 90° in its bore and compress plunger until a paper clip can be inserted through plunger body hole and into hole in plunger.
9. Install timing chain tensioner.
10. Remove paper clip from tensioner.
11. Install oil nozzle and bolt.
12. Install crankshaft sprocket with timing mark at 5 o'clock position.
13. Lower new timing chain through opening in top of cylinder head, ensure chain goes around both sides of cylinder block bosses, **Fig. 5.**
14. Install intake camshaft sprocket with "INT" diamond at 2 o'clock position.
15. Install a new intake camshaft sprocket bolt hand tight.
16. Route timing chain around crankshaft sprocket with matching colored link aligning with timing mark.

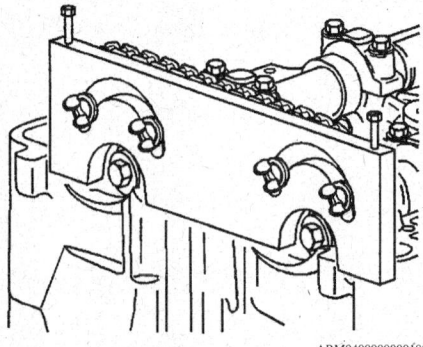

Fig. 7   Holding tool No. J 43655

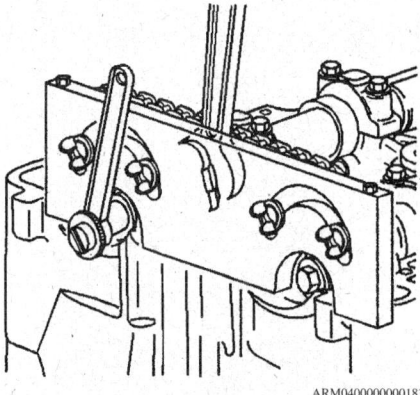

ARM0400000000183

Fig. 8   Camshaft sprocket bolt removal

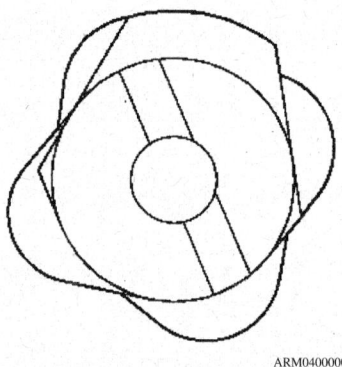

ARM0400000000184

Fig. 9   Camshaft sprocket alignment notches

17. Route timing chain around intake camshaft sprocket with uniquely colored link aligned with "INT" diamond.
18. Install timing chain tensioner guide through opening in the top of cylinder head.
19. Install exhaust camshaft sprocket with timing chain matching colored link at "EXH" triangle aligned at 10 o'clock position.
20. Use 24 MM wrench to rotate camshaft slightly until exhaust sprocket aligns with camshaft.
21. Install new exhaust camshaft sprocket bolt hand tight.
22. Install fixed timing chain guide.
23. Apply Saturn sealant compound part No. 21485277, or equivalent to threads, then install timing chain guide bolt access hole plug.
24. Install timing chain upper guide.
25. Inspect timing chain tensioner body bore for dirt, debris and damage. Clean out dirt or debris with a lint-free cloth.
26. Measure timing chain tensioner assembly from end to end. A new tensioner under compression should measure 2.83 inches. In the active state it should measure 3.35 inches.
27. If tensioner is not in compressed state, proceed as follows:
    a. Pull piston assembly out of tensioner body.
    b. Install tool No. J 45027-2, or equivalent, into a suitable vise, **Fig. 6.**
    c. Install notch end of piston assembly into J 45027-2.
    d. Turn ratchet cylinder into piston using J 45027-1.
28. Install compressed piston assembly back into tensioner body until it stops at bottom of bore.
29. Tensioner should measure approximately 2.83 inches from end to end. Repeat compression procedure if tensioner does not measure as specified.
30. Install timing chain tensioner.
31. Use a suitable tool with a rubber ended tip. Route tool down through camshaft drive chain to rest on timing chain, then give a sharp downward diagonal jolt to release tensioner.
32. Hold camshaft using a 24 MM wrench.
33. Install camshaft cover.
34. Install ground strap to camshaft cover.
35. Install spark plugs and ignition coils.

36. Connect fuel feed pipe to fuel rail.
37. Install fuel pipe bracket.
38. Connect PCV hose to cam cover.
39. Install a new engine front cover gasket.
40. Install front engine mount bracket and engine mount.
41. Install engine front cover and water pump.
42. Install idler pulley.
43. Install serpentine belt tensioner.
44. Install crankshaft balancer with a new bolt.
45. Install serpentine belt.
46. Install fender liner, then the tire and wheel.

CAMSHAFT
REPLACE
Intake
REMOVAL

1. Disconnect ignition coil electrical connectors.
2. Remove coil mounting bolts, then the coils from vehicle.
3. Remove ground strap and stud.
4. Disconnect PCV hose from camshaft cover.
5. Disconnect fuel feed pipe from fuel rail.
6. Remove camshaft cover mounting bolts, then the cover.
7. Remove timing chain upper guide mounting bolts, then the upper guide.
8. Install sprocket holding tool No. J 43655, or equivalent, **Fig. 7.**
9. Remove and discard both intake and exhaust camshaft sprocket bolts, **Fig. 8.**
10. Move camshaft sprockets forward.
11. Mark intake camshaft bearing caps to ensure installation in original locations.
12. Remove each bearing cap bolt one turn at a time until spring tension disappears.
13. Remove bearing caps, then the intake camshaft.
14. Remove camshaft roller followers, then the lash adjusters.

INSTALLATION
1. Lubricate valve tips.

2. Install lash adjusters, then the roller followers.
3. Ensure alignment notches are aligned with camshaft sprocket, **Fig. 9.**
4. Install intake camshaft and camshaft bearing caps. Tighten cap bolts in three steps until they are seated, then **torque** to 89 inch lbs.
5. Apply a 0.197 inch bead of Permatex Anaerobic Gasket Maker part No. 51813, or equivalent, to rear camshaft bearing cap.
6. Install rear bearing cap bolts.
7. Install sprockets onto camshafts. **Do not use old bolts.**
8. Remove sprocket holding tool, **Fig. 7.**
9. **Torque** sprocket bolts to 63 ft. lbs., then rotate an additional 30°.
10. Install timing chain upper guide. **Torque** bolts to 89 inch lbs.
11. Install camshaft cover. **Torque** bolts to 89 inch lbs.
12. Install ground strap to camshaft cover. **Torque** stud to 89 inch lbs.
13. Install ignition coils. **Torque** bolts to 89 inch lbs., then connect electrical connectors.
14. Install fuel feed pipe to fuel rail. **Torque** to 10 ft. lbs.
15. Install fuel pipe bracket. **Torque** bolts to 89 inch lbs.
16. Connect PCV hose to camshaft cover.

Exhaust
REMOVAL

1. Disconnect ignition coil electrical connectors.
2. Remove coil mounting bolts, then the coils from vehicle.
3. Remove ground strap and stud.
4. Disconnect PCV hose from camshaft cover.
5. Disconnect fuel feed pipe from fuel rail.
6. Remove camshaft cover mounting bolts, then the cover.
7. Remove timing chain upper guide mounting bolts, then the upper guide.
8. Install sprocket holding tool No. J 43655, or equivalent, **Fig. 7.**
9. Remove and discard both intake and exhaust camshaft sprocket bolts, **Fig. 8.**
10. Move camshaft sprockets forward.

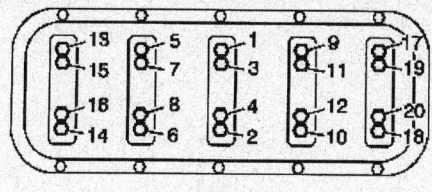

Fig. 10 Lower crankcase inner bolt tightening sequence

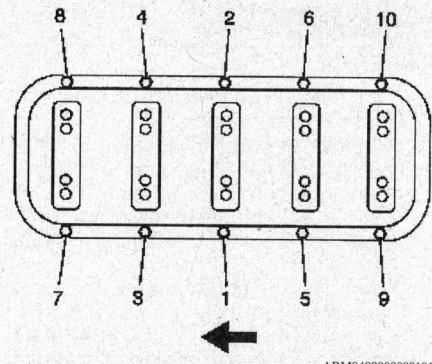

Fig. 11 Lower crankcase outer bolt tightening sequence

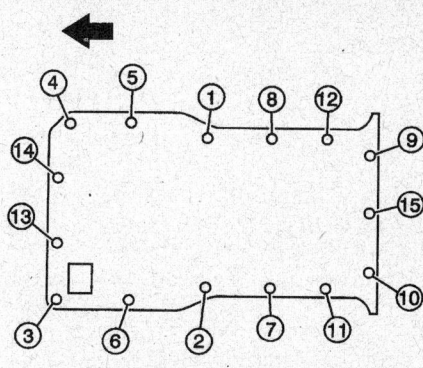

Fig. 12 Oil pan bolt tightening sequence

11. Mark exhaust camshaft bearing caps to ensure installation in original locations.
12. Remove each bearing cap bolt one turn at a time until spring tension disappears.
13. Remove bearing caps, then the exhaust camshaft.
14. Remove camshaft roller followers, then the lash adjusters.

INSTALLATION

1. Lubricate valve tips.
2. Install lash adjusters, then the roller followers.
3. Ensure alignment notches are aligned with camshaft sprocket, **Fig. 9.**
4. Install exhaust camshaft and camshaft bearing caps. Tighten cap bolts in three steps until they are seated, then **torque** to 89 inch lbs.
5. Apply a 0.197 inch bead of Permatex Anaerobic Gasket Maker part No. 51813, or equivalent, to rear camshaft bearing cap.
6. Install rear bearing cap bolts. **Torque** bolts to 18 ft. lbs.
7. Install sprockets onto camshafts. Tighten new camshaft sprocket bolts hand tight. **Do not use old bolts.**
8. Remove sprocket holding tool, **Fig. 7.**
9. **Torque** sprocket bolts to 63 ft. lbs., then rotate an additional 30°.
10. Install timing chain upper guide.
11. Install camshaft cover.
12. Install ground strap to camshaft cover.
13. Install ignition coils, then connect electrical connectors.
14. Install fuel feed pipe to fuel rail.
15. Install fuel pipe bracket.
16. Connect PCV hose to camshaft cover.

PISTON & ROD ASSEMBLY

Install the piston onto the connecting rod with the arrow pointed toward the front of the engine.

PISTONS, PINS & RINGS

Replace any pistons that show signs of damage or excessive wear. Piston pin bores and pins must be free of varnish or scuffing. Use an outside micrometer to measure the piston contact areas and piston pin bore. Subtract the measurement of the piston pin bore from the piston pin.

MAIN & ROD BEARINGS

1. Install crankshaft bearing caps using suitable brass, lead, leather, or equivalent soft faced mallet. **Do not use lower crankcase bolts to pull bearing caps into seats.**
2. **Torque** lower crankcase inner bolts to 15 ft. lbs. in sequence, **Fig. 10.**
3. **Torque** lower crankcase outer bolts to 18 ft. lbs., then rotate bolts an additional 70° in sequence, **Fig. 11.**

CRANKSHAFT REAR OIL SEAL

REPLACE

1. Remove transaxle as outlined in **MOTOR's "Domestic Transmission In-Vehicle Service"** manual.
2. Remove flywheel and cover.
3. Insert suitable screwdriver into pry tangs of seal carrier and remove seal.
4. Apply suitable clean engine oil to seal lip and inside diameter of seal carrier.
5. Install seal using seal installer tool No. J 42067, or equivalent.
6. Install transaxle and flywheel.

OIL PAN

REPLACE

1. Raise and support vehicle.
2. Drain engine oil into suitable container and remove front exhaust pipe.
3. Remove righthand front wheel, splash shield and vibration dampner.
4. Remove mounting bolts and oil pan.
5. Reverse procedure to install, noting the following:
   a. Apply a 0.08 inch bead of RTV part No. 21019581, or equivalent, around perimeter of oil pan and oil suction port opening. **Do not apply an excessive amount of RTV.**
   b. **Torque** oil pan attaching bolts to 18 ft. lbs. in sequence, **Fig. 12.**

OIL PUMP

REPLACE

1. Remove air cleaner, then raise and support vehicle.
2. Drain engine oil into suitable container, then remove righthand front wheel and splash shield.
3. Mark accessory drive belt running direction, then remove drive belt.
4. Remove crankshaft pulley using pulley holding tool No. J 38122, or equivalent.
5. Remove belt tensioner as outlined under "Serpentine Drive Belt."
6. Install engine support fixture tool No. SA 9150-E, or equivalent.
7. Remove engine mount as outlined under "Engine Mount, Replace."
8. Remove front cover bolts, then the bolts under water pump cover.
9. Remove front cover and gasket.
10. Reverse procedure to install.

OIL PUMP SERVICE

Disassemble

1. Remove pressure relief valve.
2. Remove cover plate mounting bolts.
3. Mark drive and driven rotors for assembly reference.
4. Remove drive and driven rotors.

Assemble

1. Remove front cover oil seal using suitable screwdriver or punch.
2. Install new oil seal using oil seal installer tool No. J 35268-A, or equivalent, and suitable press.
3. Install pressure relief valve, valve spring and oil pump pressure relief valve plug.
4. Lubricate drive and driven rotors with clean engine oil, then align marks on drive and driven rotors.
5. Install drive and driven rotors into pump body.
6. Fill oil pump with petroleum jelly to prime oil pump.

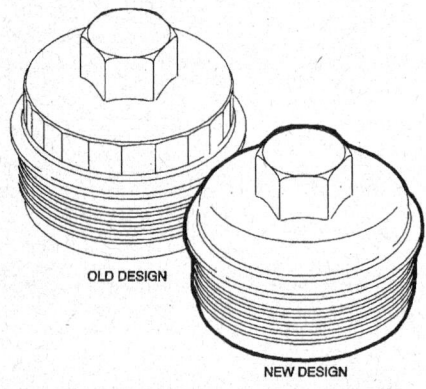

OLD DESIGN

NEW DESIGN

ARM0400000000194

Fig. 13 Oil filter cap identification

7. Install oil pump gear cover plate screws.

SERPENTINE DRIVE BELT

Belt, Replace

1. Remove righthand front fender liner.
2. Mark serpentine belt running direction.
3. Slowly rotate belt tensioner counterclockwise to relieve tension, then remove serpentine belt.
4. Reverse procedure to install.

Tensioner, Replace

1. Remove serpentine belt as outlined under "Belt, Replace" in this section.
2. Remove belt tensioner bolts, then the tensioner.
3. Reverse procedure to install.

COOLING SYSTEM BLEED

1. Remove surge tank cap.
2. Raise and support vehicle.
3. Place a suitable drain pan below righthand side of radiator lower mount.
4. Open petcock and drain coolant into container.
5. After all coolant has drained, close petcock hand tight.
6. Lower the vehicle, then disconnect radiator upper hose from righthand side of radiator.
7. Slowly add a 50/50 mixture of Dex-Cool antifreeze and deionized water to engine through upper hose.
8. Connect upper hose to radiator.
9. Slowly add antifreeze and water mixture to surge tank to just above Cold Fill line.
10. Install surge tank cap, then start engine.
11. Run engine at 2000–2500 RPM for three minutes.
12. Idle engine for 30 seconds, then turn ignition Off.
13. Inspect coolant level and add if required.

THERMOSTAT
REPLACE

1. Drain engine coolant into suitable container.
2. Remove thermostat housing to water pump feed pipe mounting bolts, then the feed pipe.
3. Note orientation, then remove thermostat and retaining sleeve. Discard O-ring.
4. Reverse procedure to install, noting the following:
   a. Install new thermostat and retaining sleeve with dimple placed into housing slot.
   b. Lubricate new O-ring with soapy water or coolant before installation into water pump.
   c. Fill and bleed cooling system as outlined under "Cooling System Bleed."

RADIATOR
REPLACE

1. Remove surge tank cap.
2. Raise and support vehicle.
3. Place a suitable drain pan below righthand side of radiator lower mount.
4. Open petcock and drain coolant into container.
5. Place drain pan below water pump drain plug.
6. Open drain plug and drain coolant into container.
7. After all coolant has drained, close petcock hand tight.
8. Install water pump drain plug, then **torque** to 16 ft. lbs.
9. Lower the vehicle, then remove air cleaner outlet resonator.
10. Disconnect radiator inlet and outlet hoses from radiator.
11. **On models equipped with automatic or VTi transaxle,** proceed as follows:
    a. Clean transaxle upper oil cooler line connection point, then disconnect line from radiator.
    b. Remove lefthand front wheelhouse liner.
    c. Remove engine lefthand splash shield.
    d. Clean transaxle lower oil cooler line connection point, then disconnect line from radiator.
12. **On all models,** remove cooling fan assembly from radiator by pushing up on fan shroud and unsnapping retainers.
13. Position cooling fan assembly away from radiator, then support fan assembly as required.
14. Remove air dam push-in retainer, then the air dam.
15. Remove A/C condenser mounting bolts.
16. Slide condenser down to disengage upper mounting tabs from radiator.
17. Position condenser away from radiator, then support condenser as required.
18. Remove radiator righthand and lefthand side baffles.
19. Remove engine righthand splash shield to radiator mount push-in retainer.

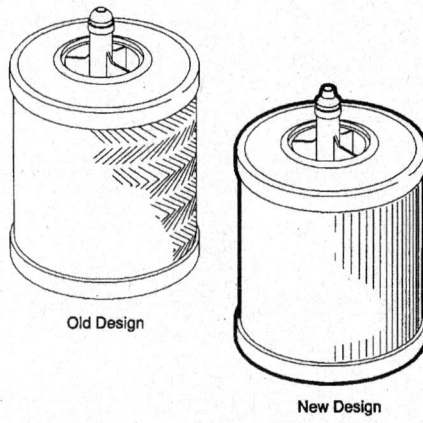

Old Design

New Design

ARM0400000000195

Fig. 14 Oil filter element identification

20. **On models equipped with manual transaxle,** remove engine lefthand splash shield to radiator mount push-in retainer.
21. **On all models,** remove radiator lower mounts, brackets and bolts.
22. Tilt A/C condenser forward, then the cooling fan rearward.
23. Remove radiator from vehicle.
24. Remove upper air baffle from radiator.
25. Reverse procedure to install, noting the following:
    a. Ensure radiator upper mounts are intact in vehicle.
    b. Ensure radiator upper mount pins align with upper mounts.
    c. Tighten all fasteners to specifications.
    d. Fill and bleed cooling system as outlined under "Cooling System Bleed" in this section.

FUEL PUMP
REPLACE

Whenever fuel line fittings are loosened or removed, wrap a shop cloth around the fitting and have a suitable container available to collect any fuel spillage.

1. Connect suitably programmed scan tool to Diagnostic Link Connector (DLC) and turn ignition On.
2. Raise and support vehicle, keeping scan tool outside of vehicle and accessible.
3. Disconnect fuel feed line at outlet to filter.
4. Install $\frac{3}{8} \times \frac{1}{4}$ inch adapter onto flow/pressure adapter tool No. SA-9127E-7, or equivalent, and insert adapter into fuel feed line.
5. Connect one end of suitable drain hose to other end of adapter. Connect other end of drain hose to suitable fuel handling cart.
6. Turn fuel pump on using scan tool and pump fuel into suitable container.
7. If fuel pump is inoperative, proceed as follows:
   a. Insert siphon hose guide/funnel into fuel filler pipe.
   b. Insert siphon hose J 43290, or

equivalent, into guide funnel and fuel filler pipe. Some resistance may be encountered when tip of siphon hose reaches inlet check valve. Repeated probing may be required to slide hose tip through check valve.

c. Begin siphon process and collect fuel in suitable container.

8. Ensure fuel tank is less than quarter full.
9. Remove exhaust system intermediate pipe and rear heat shield mounting bolts.
10. Remove fuel filler pipe lower bracket mounting screw and disconnect EVAP canister vent hose.
11. Loosen fuel filler pipe hose clamp closest to fuel tank and remove tank ground strap mounting screw near fuel filter.
12. Disconnect fuel feed line after fuel filter.
13. Disconnect fuel return and EVAP canister purge lines between tank and chassis fuel bundle.
14. Disconnect fuel tank electrical connectors.
15. Loosen, but do not remove, front tank strap bolt.
16. Remove rear tank mounting strap bolts with assistance.
17. Remove tank by lowering at the rear, then sliding downward and rearward.
18. Disconnect fuel lines from fuel pump module cover. **Do not attempt to remove retainer using 12 inch or shorter ratchet or breaker bar.**
19. Remove fuel pump module retainer ring using lock ring service tool No. J 43827, or equivalent.
20. To prevent bending of sending unit float arm, remove sending unit first by pulling retaining clip toward float arm and lifting upward.
21. Carefully lift fuel pump straight up from fuel tank. Clips must be disconnected at same time to disconnect fuel pump

from housing.

22. Discard fuel pump module to tank seal and remove fuel feed line from bottom of fuel pump cover using removal tool No. J 44078, or equivalent.
23. Disconnect fuel pump electrical connector from fuel pump cover.
24. Inspect fuel tank for metal chips or debris. Remove contaminants and replace inline fuel filter before installing new pump.
25. Reverse procedure to install, noting the following:
    a. Replace plastic fuel line retainers.
    b. Install new module to tank seal lubricated with suitable clean engine oil.

FUEL FILTER
REPLACE

1. Raise and support vehicle.
2. Remove fuel filter bracket screw, then disconnect fuel lines from inlet and outlet sides of fuel filter.
3. Slide fuel filter out of bracket.
4. Reverse procedure, noting the following:
   a. Turn ignition On for two seconds, then Off for 10 seconds.
   b. Turn ignition On.
   c. Inspect fuel system for leaks.

SUPERCHARGER
REPLACE

1. Remove serpentine belt as outlined under "Serpentine Drive Belt."
2. Remove EVAP tube and EVAP valve.
3. Remove air cleaner outlet duct.
4. Disconnect EVAP purge line.
5. Disconnect TBI unit control harness electrical connector.
6. Remove TBI unit attaching bolts, then the unit from supercharger. Discard gasket.
7. Remove supercharger inlet pressure (SCIP) sensor.

8. Disconnect vacuum brake booster hose.
9. Remove intercooler fill neck bracket bolts.
10. Remove supercharger.
11. Reverse procedure to install, noting the following:
    a. Inspect supercharger mounting gasket and install a new one if required.
    b. Install TBI unit with a new gasket.
    c. Tighten all fasteners to specifications.

TECHNICAL SERVICE BULLETINS

Oil Filter Cap Assembly & Element Design Update
2003-04 ION

On these models, equipped with 2.0L or 2.2L engines, the oil filter caps and elements have been updated.

Inspect the vehicle for the new design filter cap, **Fig. 13.** If a vehicle is equipped with the new cap part No. 12580254 (PF2259G), the new design filter element part No. 12579143 (PF456G) must be used, **Fig. 14.**

The new design oil filter cap can be identified by a rounded contour on the outer edges, as opposed to the flat edges on the older style. The new design cap can be used to service all previous model year vehicles. The new style oil filter element must be used to service vehicles equipped with the new style filter cap.

Do not install the older filter element part No. 22685727 with the newer filter cap. This could result in severe engine damage.

TIGHTENING SPECIFICATIONS

Year	Component	Torque/Ft. Lbs.
2004–05	A/C Compressor To Block	15
	A/C Condenser Mounting Bolts	88①
	Alternator Bracket Bolt	31
	Alternator Connector Nut	15
	Alternator To Block	15
	ATF Cooler Lines To Radiator	15
	Axle Shaft Nut	81
	Balance Shaft Bearing Carrier To Block Bolt	89①
	Balance Shaft Chain Guide Bolts	89①
	Balance Shaft Sprocket Bolt	37
	BARO Sensor & Coolant Return Line Assembly	71①
	Boost Solenoid Bracket Nut	89①
	Camshaft Bearing Cap Bolts	⑩
	Camshaft Cover To Ground Cable Bolt & Stud	89①
	Camshaft Cover To Head	89①
	CMP Sensor Bolt	71①
	CMP Sensor Housing Stud	16
	Camshaft Sprocket Bolt	63②
	Chain Guide Access Hole Plug	59
	Connecting Rod	18③
	Crankshaft Bearing Lower Crankcase To Block Bolts	④
	CKP Sensor Bolt	89①
	Crankshaft Pulley	74⑤
	Cylinder Head	⑥
	Cylinder Head Oil Gallery Plug	26
	Dipstick Guide to Intake Manifold Bolt	89①
	Driveshaft Nut	81
	Electronic ICM Cover Bolt	71①
	ECT Sensor	16
	Engine Lift Bracket	18
	Engine Mount Intermediate Bracket Bolts	74
	Engine Mount To Intermediate Bracket Bolts	37
	Engine Mount To Mid-Rail Nuts	74
	Exhaust Manifold Heat Shield Bolt	15
	Exhaust Manifold Pipe Flange Nuts	37
	Exhaust Manifold Pipe Flange Studs	12
	Exhaust Manifold To Cylinder Head Nut	115①
	Exhaust Manifold To Cylinder Head Stud	89①
	Exhaust Takedown Pipe Nuts	22
	Flywheel (Manual Transaxle)	39⑦
	Frame Bolt, Rear	148
	Frame To Body	74⑧
	Front Cover To Block	18
	Fuel Feed Line	10
	Fuel Feed Line & Injector Harness Bracket	89①
	Fuel Rail Bracket	89①
	Fuel Supply Line Fitting	10
	Fuel Tank Strap	18
	Idler Pulley	16
	Ignition Coil Bolt	71①
	Intake Camshaft Rear Cap	18
	Intake Manifold To Cylinder Head Nut	106①
	Intake Manifold To Cylinder Head Stud	89①

Continued

2.0L ENGINE

TIGHTENING
SPECIFICATIONS—Continued

Year	Component	Torque/ Ft. Lbs.
2004–05	Intercooler Fill Neck Bracket Bolts	89①
	Knock Sensor	18
	Lift Bracket Bolt, Rear	16
	Main Bearings	④
	MAF Sensor Screws	18①
	Oil Bypass Tube	16
	Oil Cooler	16
	Oil Filter Housing Cover	18
	Oil Gallery Plug	26
	Oil Gallery Plug, Rear	44
	Oil Level Indicator Tube Bolt	89①
	Oil Pan	⑨
	Oil Pan Drain Plug	18
	Oil Pressure Sensor	13
	Oil Pump Gerotor Cover Bolt	53①
	Oil Pump Pressure Relief Valve Plug	30
	Oxygen Sensor	31
	Power Steering Pump Blockout Plate Bolts	18
	Radiator Lower Mounting Bolts	18
	Serpentine Belt Tensioner Bolts	33
	Spark Plugs	15
	Starter Motor	30
	Starter Terminal Nut	13
	SCIP Sensor	89①
	Supercharger Bolts	18
	Thermostat Housing To Block	89①
	Throttle Body	89①
	Timing Chain Guides	89①
	Timing Chain Nozzle	89①
	Timing Chain Tensioner	55
	Torque Converter Bolts	46
	Transaxle To Engine Bolts	55
	Transaxle Mount, Front	37
	Transaxle Mount Through Bolt	74
	Transaxle Mount Bracket To Transmission Bolts, Rear	44
	Transaxle Mount Through Bolt, Rear	74
	Transaxle Mount to Frame Bolts, Rear	44
	Transaxle Mount To Mid-Rail Bolts, Side	25
	Transaxle To Engine Bolts	55
	Transaxle Mount Bolts, Side	33
	Transaxle Mount To Mid-Rail Bolts	20
	Vent Tube To Cylinder Head	11
	Water Pipe Support Bracket Bolt	89①
	Water Pump	18
	Water Pump Access Cover	62①
	Water Pump/Balance Shaft Chain Tensioner	89①
	Water Pump Feed Pipe Bolt	18①
	Water Pump Sprocket	89①
	Wheel Lug Nuts	100

① — Inch lbs.
② — Rotate an additional 30°.
③ — Rotate an additional 100°.
④ — Refer to "Main & Rod Bearings" for tightening specifications & sequence.

⑤ — Rotate an additional 75°.
⑥ — Refer to "Cylinder Head, Replace" for tightening specifications & sequence.
⑦ — Rotate an additional 25°.

⑧ — Rotate an additional 180°.
⑨ — Refer to "Oil Pan, Replace" for tightening specifications & sequence.

⑩ — Torque to 89 inch lbs. in three steps.

2.2L Engine

NOTE: On Air Bag Equipped Models, Refer To "Air Bag System Precautions" Located In The Front Of This Manual For System Disarming & Arming Procedures.

NOTE: Refer To "Computer Relearn Procedures" Located In The Front Of This Manual When Battery Power To The Computer Has Been Interrupted.

INDEX

PRECAUTIONS

Air Bag Systems

Refer to "Air Bag System Precautions" in the front of this manual for system disarming and arming procedures.

Battery Ground Cable

Prior to service, disconnect battery ground cable and isolate as required.

Fuel System Pressure Relief

1. Connect gauge bar tool No. 53476, or equivalent, to fuel gauge pressure adapter tool No. 309725, or equivalent, using flexible hose from pressure test kit tool No. SA-9127-E, or equivalent.
2. Ensure needle valve on pressure kit is closed and connect pressure adapter to fuel line test port, **Fig. 1.**
3. Place end of bleed hose in suitable container and open valve to bleed system pressure.
4. Remove gauge and replace cap.

COMPRESSION PRESSURE

1. Start and run engine until it reaches normal operating temperature.
2. Turn engine off, disconnect ignition module wiring and remove spark plugs.
3. Install suitable compression gauge tool in spark plug hole.
4. Ensure battery is charged and throttle is fully open.
5. Crank engine through four compression strokes for each cylinder.
6. Lowest reading cylinder should be within 70% of highest.
7. No cylinder should read less than 100 psi.
8. Place shop towel over spark plug holes and crank engine a few seconds without compression gauge or spark plugs installed.
9. Repeat compression measuring steps on all cylinders.

ENGINE MOUNT

REPLACE

1. Remove air cleaner.
2. Install engine support fixture tool No. SA-9150-E, or equivalent.

3. Remove engine mount to bracket fasteners.
4. Remove engine mount to body mounting bolts, **Fig. 2.**
5. Remove engine mount.
6. Reverse procedure to install.

ENGINE

REPLACE

L-Series

AUTOMATIC TRANSAXLE

1. Remove battery and disconnect fuse block main wire feed.
2. Disconnect lefthand fenderwell main ground and intake air temperature electrical connector.
3. Remove air cleaner lid and inlet duct.
4. Remove air box and disconnect purge hose from throttle body and position aside.
5. Disconnect EVAP purge solenoid and rear oxygen sensor electrical connectors, then the main master cylinder wiring harness.
6. Remove cowl cover and PCM boot from cowl.

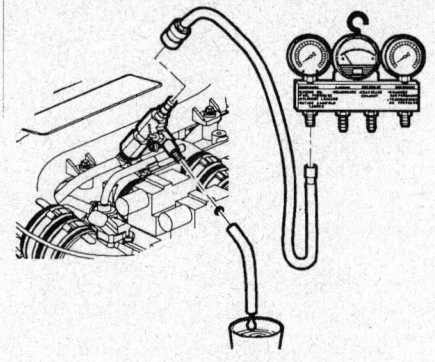

G31029900155000X

Fig. 1   Fuel pressure bleed

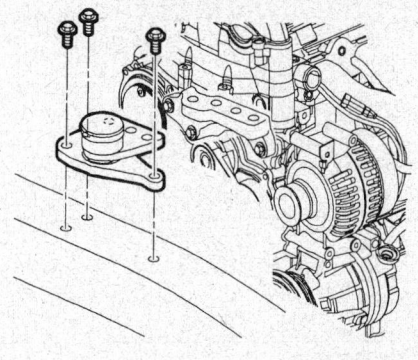

G31069900036000X

Fig. 2   Engine mount replacement

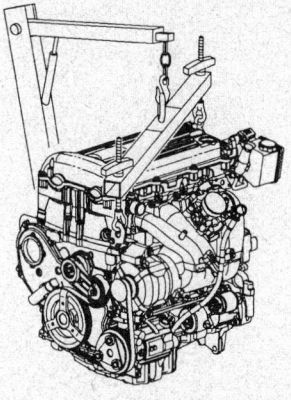

G31069900037000X

Fig. 3   Engine lift hoist attachment

7. Disconnect PCM electrical connector and secure to engine.
8. Remove fuse block lid and disconnect engine harness main connector from bottom of fuse block.
9. Remove battery and fuse block trays.
10. Disconnect cruise control and throttle cables.
11. Disconnect brake assist vacuum line from throttle body and position aside.
12. Remove coolant reservoir cap.
13. Disconnect fuel lines and EVAP purge hose at EVAP purge solenoid.
14. Raise and support vehicle.
15. Drain engine coolant into suitable container.
16. Disconnect heater hoses at lower cowl and remove starter.
17. Remove torque converter bolts.
18. Remove exhaust system from catalytic converter forward.
19. Disconnect transaxle nose bracket, remove mounting bolts and secure air conditioning compressor to frame rail. **Do not disconnect air conditioning lines.**
20. Disconnect lower engine to transaxle bell housing bolts. **Do not remove upper bolts just yet.**
21. Lower vehicle and remove main hose to coolant reservoir from engine inlet adapter.
22. Remove engine lower and upper radiator hoses.
23. Drain power steering fluid into suitable container by removing smaller hose from under reservoir.
24. Disconnect metal power steering line.
25. Support engine using suitable engine lift hoist to engine lift hooks, **Fig. 3.**
26. Support transaxle weight using suitable floor jack or jack stand.
27. Remove righthand front engine mount from wheel housing and engine mount bracket from engine.
28. Remove upper bell housing bolts and remove engine.
29. Reverse procedure to install.

MANUAL TRANSAXLE

1. Remove steering gear to intermediate shaft pinch bolt.
2. Remove battery and disconnect fuse block main wire feed.
3. Disconnect lefthand fenderwell main ground and intake air temperature electrical connector.

4. Remove air cleaner lid and inlet duct.
5. Remove air box, disconnect purge hose from throttle body and position aside.
6. Disconnect EVAP purge solenoid, rear oxygen sensor and transaxle back-up lamp switch electrical connectors, then the master cylinder main harness connector.
7. Remove dash cover front and PCM boot.
8. Disconnect PCM electrical connector and secure to engine.
9. Remove fuse block lid and disconnect engine harness main connector from bottom of fuse block.
10. Remove battery and fuse block trays.
11. Disconnect cruise control and throttle cables.
12. Disconnect brake assist vacuum line from throttle body and lay aside.
13. Loosen control rod to lever pinch bolt. **Control shaft lever retaining pin has spring loaded locking feature securing pin in place.**
14. Remove control shaft lever to shaft retaining pin.
15. Remove control shaft lever to transaxle and frame brackets retaining clips.
16. Remove control shaft lever by pulling straight up from pivot pins.
17. Drain coolant into suitable container.
18. Remove dash front heater hoses, then the radiator upper and lower hoses.
19. Disconnect fuel lines and secure radiator to upper radiator support.
20. Raise and support vehicle, then remove righthand front wheel and tire assembly.
21. Remove righthand front splash shield and lefthand front wheel liner push pin from frame.
22. Install suitable wood blocks between transaxle case and frame, and between crank pulley and frame.
23. Lower vehicle.
24. Disconnect righthand engine and lefthand transaxle mounts by removing mount to engine/transaxle bolts. Mount brackets will remain on engine and transaxle.
25. Disconnect rear oxygen sensor harness from frame at two attachment points.
26. Remove exhaust manifold pipe from catalytic converter forward.

27. Remove A/C line to frame attachment clip at front of frame. **Do not disconnect A/C lines.**
28. Remove A/C compressor from engine and secure to cooling module.
29. Remove tie rod to steering knuckle bolts and separate tie rod from steering knuckle using tool No. SA-91100-C, or equivalent. Discard tie rod bolts.
30. Remove stabilizer bar links from strut.
31. Remove lower ball stud bolt and separate ball from steering knuckle using suitable tool. **Do not separate ball studs using pickle fork or wedge type separator tool.**
32. Remove suspension support assemblies and suspension support cage nuts from body. Discard cage nuts.
33. Support powertrain and frame with powertrain lifting table and service tool No. J 43628, or equivalent, **Fig. 4.**
34. Remove remaining frame to body mounting bolts.
35. Carefully lower powertrain and frame.
36. Remove remaining cage nuts and discard.
37. Attach engine lift hoist to engine lift hooks, **Fig. 3.**
38. Place suitable 1¾ × 2 × 4 inch and 1¼ × 2 × 4 inch long wood blocks under transaxle housing support. **Engine must be moved approximately four inches forward in cradle to disconnect input shaft.**
39. Remove transaxle bell housing mounting bolts.
40. Carefully lift engine from cradle and mount on suitable engine stand or transportation pallet.
41. Reverse procedure to install.

ION

1. Position tires in straight ahead, then remove key from ignition.
2. Disconnect IAT sensor harness connector, then loosen air cleaner assembly fresh air duct to resonator clamp.
3. Remove push pin from air outlet resonator/duct assembly to support bracket.
4. Loosen resonator to throttle body clamp, then disconnect air cleaner assembly fresh air duct from resonator

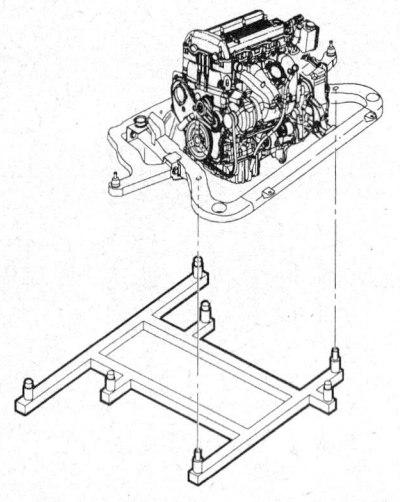

Fig. 4 Frame alignment tool

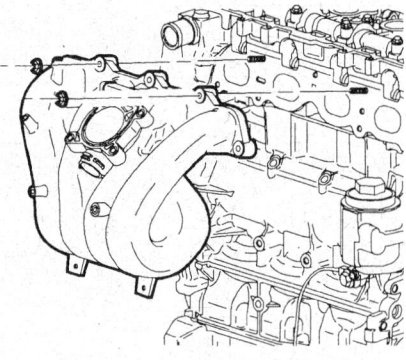

Fig. 5 Intake manifold replacement

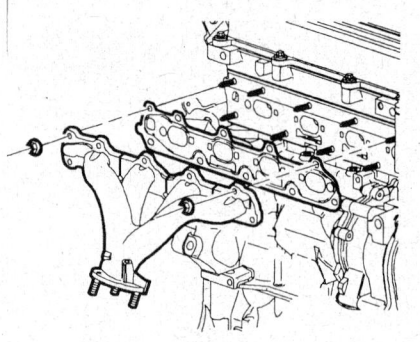

Fig. 6 Exhaust manifold replacement

and remove from throttle body.

5. Secure cooling module to upper body structure then disconnect accelerator cable from throttle body.
6. Relieve fuel system pressure as outlined under "Precautions."
7. Disconnect fuel lines from fuel rail, then drain coolant into a suitable container.
8. Remove radiator inlet and outlet hoses from radiator, then the surge tank to cylinder head hose.
9. Remove inlet and outlet heater hoses.
10. Disconnect the following harness connectors:
    a. IAC motor and throttle position sensor.
    b. Manifold absolute pressure, crankshaft and oil pressure sensors.
    c. Purge solenoid, ignition coil and module assembly.
    d. Oxygen and vehicle speed sensors.
    e. Engine temperature sensor and back-up lamp switch.
11. Raise and support vehicle, then remove front wheels.
12. Remove righthand side fender liner, then release tensioner and remove drive belt.
13. Remove A/C compressor bolts and set compressor aside.
14. Disconnect electrical connectors from stater and alternator, then drain engine oil into a suitable container.
15. Disconnect front exhaust pipe from exhaust manifold.
16. Disconnect transaxle electrical connectors, then the shift cable from transaxle.
17. Support powertrain assembly between frame and powertrain, using blocks of wood.
18. Remove engine mount to intermediate bracket bolts, then the engine mount to mid-rail nuts and engine mount from engine compartment.
19. Remove transaxle mount to transaxle bolts, then transaxle mount to mid rail bolts.
20. Remove transaxle mount from vehicle.

21. Remove tie rod to steering knuckle bolts and separate tie rod from steering knuckle using tool No. SA-91100-C, or equivalent. Discard tie rod bolts.
22. Remove stabilizer bar links from strut.
23. Remove intermediate shaft to steering gear pinch bolt, then discard bolt and disconnect intermediate shaft from steering gear.
24. Remove ball stud to steering knuckle pinch bolt and nut, then separate ball stud from steering knuckle.
25. Remove wheel drive shaft nut, then separate front wheel drive axle from front wheel hub using a hammer and a block of wood.
26. Match mark frame to body position.
27. Lower vehicle to about 3 feet off ground in order to position lift table under frame.
28. Slowly remove front frame bolts, then partially unscrew rear bolts until 1.5 inches of bolt shank is exposed.
29. Slowly lower table to floor, then attach engine lift hoist to engine lift hooks.
30. Remove starter, then the torque converter to flywheel bolts.
31. Remove transaxle to engine bolts, then separate engine from transaxle.
32. Reverse procedure to install.

INTAKE MANIFOLD
REPLACE

Intake manifold is made of a composite plastic and can be damaged if removed when engine is hot. Do not remove the manifold from a hot engine. Allow engine to cool to ambient temperature.

1. Remove air inlet tube and air cleaner.
2. Disconnect fuel lines using fuel line disconnection tools Nos. J-37088-1A and J-37088-2A, or equivalents.
3. Disconnect throttle position sensor, IAC and MAP sensor electrical connectors.
4. Disconnect throttle and cruise control cables.
5. Disconnect fuel pressure regulator hose from throttle body and fuel rail.
6. Remove mounting bolts and throttle body.
7. Remove fuel rail.
8. Remove mounting bolts, nuts and intake manifold, **Fig. 5.**

9. Remove intake manifold gasket.
10. If intake manifold needs to be replaced, transfer throttle body and gasket.
11. Reverse procedure to install.

EXHAUST MANIFOLD
REPLACE

1. Remove oxygen sensor from exhaust manifold.
2. Remove exhaust manifold heat shield.
3. Remove mounting nuts and exhaust manifold, **Fig. 6.**
4. Reverse procedure to install, noting the following:
   a. Install new exhaust manifold studs.
   b. Coat oxygen sensor threads with anti seize compound, Saturn No. 21485279, or equivalent.

CYLINDER HEAD
REPLACE
Removal

1. Remove exhaust and intake manifolds as outlined under "Exhaust Manifold, Replace" and "Intake Manifold, Replace."
2. Remove mounting bolt and crankshaft pulley using crankshaft pulley holder tool No. J 38122, or equivalent, **Fig. 7.**
3. Remove camshaft cover grounding strap, ignition module and coil.
4. Remove camshaft cover, **Fig. 8.**
5. Remove accessory drive belt tensioner as outlined under "Tensioner, Replacement."
6. Remove mounting bolts and engine front cover.
7. Remove upper timing chain guide. **Timing chain tensioner must be removed to unload chain tension before timing chain is removed.**
8. Remove timing chain tensioner plunger. **Do not allow any tension on timing chain when loosening camshaft sprocket bolt.**
9. Remove exhaust cam sprocket using suitable 7/8 open end wrench to hold camshaft while loosening camshaft sprocket bolt. Discard bolt.

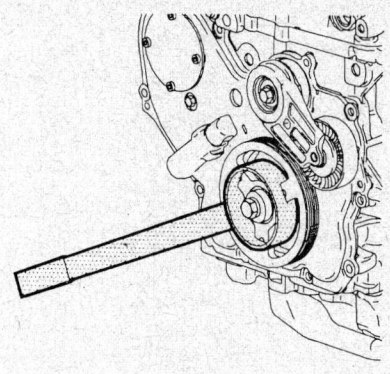

G31069900039000X

Fig. 7 Crankshaft pulley replacement

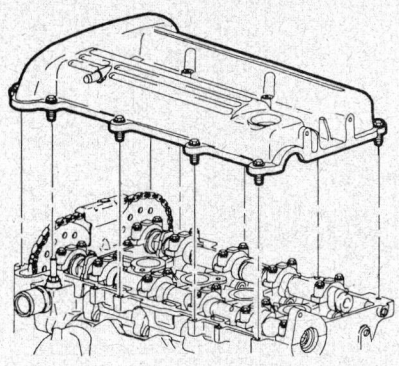

G31069900040000X

Fig. 8 Camshaft cover replacement

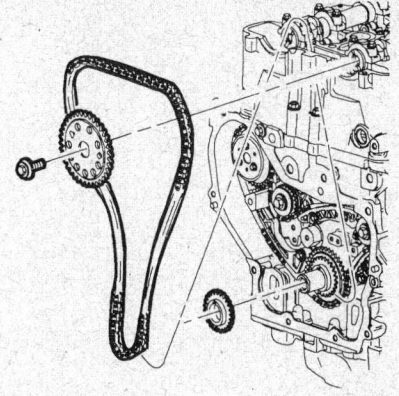

G31069900041000X

Fig. 9 Intake camshaft sprocket timing chain replacement

10. Remove adjustable timing chain guide and fixed timing chain guide bolt access plug.
11. Remove fixed timing guide.
12. Remove intake cam sprocket timing chain through top of cylinder head, **Fig. 9.**
13. Remove crankshaft sprocket and oiling nozzle.
14. Remove each cap one turn at a time until there is no spring tension on camshaft.
15. Mark bearing caps for installation. Keep roller finger followers and hydraulic element adjusters in order so they can be installed in original positions.
16. Remove mounting bolts, intake camshaft bearing caps and camshaft, **Fig. 10.**
17. Remove intake camshaft roller finger followers and hydraulic element adjusters.
18. Remove exhaust camshaft bearing cap bolts, bearing caps and camshaft, **Fig. 11.**
19. Remove balance shaft drive chain tensioner and adjustable balance shaft chain guide.
20. Remove small balance shaft drive chain guide and upper balance shaft chain guide.
21. Remove balance shaft drive chain and crankshaft drive sprocket.
22. Remove bearing carrier bolts and balance shafts, **Fig. 12.**
23. Keep each balance shaft separate. **Do not remove front balance shaft bearing bolts.**
24. Remove thermostat and water feed pipe mounting bolts.
25. Remove thermostat housing and water feed pipe from water pump cover. Ensure bolt through front of engine block is removed.
26. Remove mounting bolts and water pump.
27. Remove cylinder head to block bolts in sequence, **Fig. 13.**
28. Remove cylinder head and gasket.

Installation

1. Install new gasket and cylinder head. **Do not use any sealing material.**

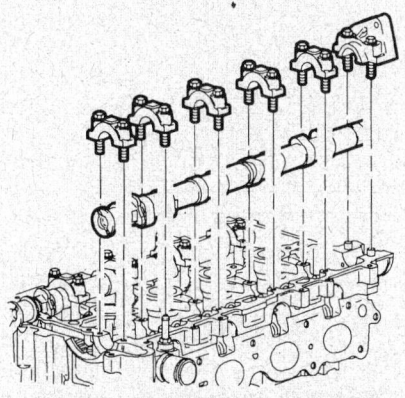

G31069900042000X

Fig. 10 Intake camshaft & bearing caps replacement

2. Lightly apply clean engine oil to threads and bottom side of flange of head bolt. Allow oil to drain before installation.
3. **Torque** cylinder head bolts to 22 ft. lbs. in sequence, **Fig. 14.**
4. Rotate cylinder head bolts additional 155° in sequence.
5. **Torque** front cylinder head bolts to 18 ft. lbs., **Fig. 15.**
6. Lubricate and install hydraulic element lash adjusters into cylinder head bores.
7. Lubricate valve tips with suitable engine oil supplement, then position roller followers on tip of valve stem and lash adjuster. Ensure roller followers are lubricated.
8. Set intake and exhaust camshaft on top of roller followers in camshaft bearing journals. Lubricate with engine oil supplement.
9. Install camshaft bearing caps and hand start camshaft cap bolts.
10. Timing chain sprocket alignment notch should be oriented to 11 o'clock position, **Fig. 16.**
11. Tighten camshaft bearing cap bolts in increments of three turns until seated.
12. Apply ¹³⁄₆₄ inch bead of Loctite Anerobic Gasket Maker 578, or equivalent, to rear intake camshaft bearing cap.
13. Place piston No. 1 to top dead center and install balance shaft drive chain sprocket on crankshaft.

14. Install balance shafts in bores.
15. Install water pump, feed tube and thermostat housing.
16. Position chain so copper colored and chrome links are visible, **Fig. 17.**
17. Align copper colored link with intake side balance shaft sprocket timing mark.
18. Working clockwise around chain, align first chrome link with crankshaft drive sprocket timing mark (approximately 5 o'clock position).
19. Align last chrome link with exhaust side balance shaft drive sprocket timing mark and install balance shaft chain guides.
20. Turn tensioner plunger 30° in bore and compress plunger until paper clip can be inserted through hole in plunger body and tensioner plunger.
21. Install timing chain tensioner. Remove paper clip from balance shaft drive chain tensioner.
22. Install timing chain drive sprocket to crankshaft with timing mark in 5 o'clock position.
23. Assemble intake camshaft sprocket to timing chain. Align timing mark with copper colored link.
24. Lower timing chain through opening in cylinder head.
25. Route timing chain around crankshaft sprocket and align second link with timing mark on crankshaft sprocket (approximately 5 o'clock position).
26. Install intake camshaft sprocket onto intake camshaft. Hand tighten new sprocket mounting bolt. Sprocket to camshaft offset notch alignment is not required now.
27. Install adjustable timing chain guide through opening in cylinder head.
28. Install exhaust camshaft sprocket onto exhaust camshaft. Hand tighten new sprocket mounting bolt. Align sprocket timing mark with silver link.
29. Ensure colored links and timing marks are aligned.
30. Install fixed and upper timing chain guides.
31. Tighten intake and exhaust camshafts' hex using suitable ⅞ inch wrench, **Fig. 18.**
32. Install new sealing washer and timing chain tensioner.

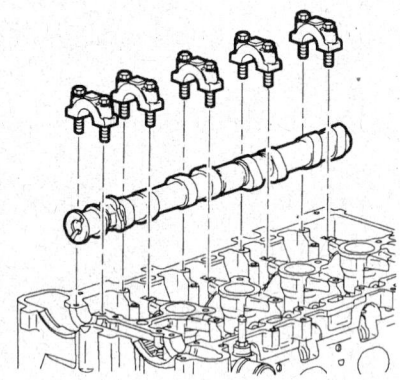

Fig. 11 Exhaust camshaft & bearing caps replacement

33. Install timing chain oiling nozzle.
34. Apply Loctite 242 thread locker compound, or equivalent, and install timing chain guide bolt access hole plug.
35. Install engine front cover and new gasket.
36. Install accessory drive belt tensioner, camshaft cover and gasket.
37. Install crankshaft pulley.
38. Install intake and exhaust manifolds.

VALVE ADJUSTMENT

This engine is equipped with hydraulic lifters and no adjustment is required.

VALVE GUIDES

Valve guides are an integral part of the cylinder head and are pressed in. If valve stem clearance becomes excessive, the valve guides must be hand reamed to the oversize using valve guide reamer tool J 42096, or equivalent. Service valves are available in standard and .003 inch oversize.

FRONT COVER
REPLACE

1. Remove air cleaner, then raise and support vehicle.
2. Drain engine oil into suitable container, then remove righthand front wheel and splash shield.
3. Remove engine accessory drive belt as outlined under "Serpentine Drive Belt."
4. Install crankshaft holder tool J 38122, or equivalent, onto crankshaft pulley.
5. Remove crankshaft pulley and discard bolt.
6. Remove belt tensioner as outlined under "Serpentine Drive Belt."
7. Remove righthand engine mount as outlined under "Engine Mount, Replace.".
8. Remove front cover and gasket.
9. Reverse procedure to install.

TIMING CHAIN
REPLACE

Refer to "Cylinder Head, Replace" for timing chain replacement.

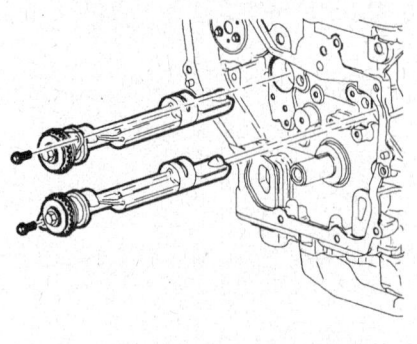

Fig. 12 Balance shaft replacement

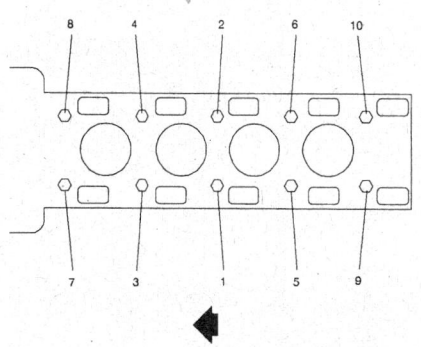

Fig. 14 Cylinder head bolt tightening sequence

CAMSHAFT
REPLACE

1. Remove ignition coil, accessory drive belt, PCV fresh air hose and cam cover.
2. Position cylinder No. 1 piston at Top Dead Center (TDC) with intake and exhaust valves closed. **No. 1 piston must be at TDC when removing or installing camshafts.**
3. Remove upper timing chain guide and timing chain tensioner.
4. Install camshaft sprocket holding tool No. J 43655, or equivalent, onto cylinder head, **Fig. 19. Torque** holding tool to 108 inch lbs.
5. Remove camshaft timing sprockets mounting bolts and washers while holding each camshaft in place using suitable 7/8 inch open end wrench.
6. Remove remaining camshaft bearing cap bolts in several passes.
7. Slide camshaft sprockets away from camshafts.
8. Carefully pull camshafts straight up to avoid damaging cylinder head thrust surface, **Fig. 20.**
9. Reverse procedure to install.

PISTON & ROD ASSEMBLY

Install the piston onto the connecting rod with the arrow pointed toward the front of the engine.

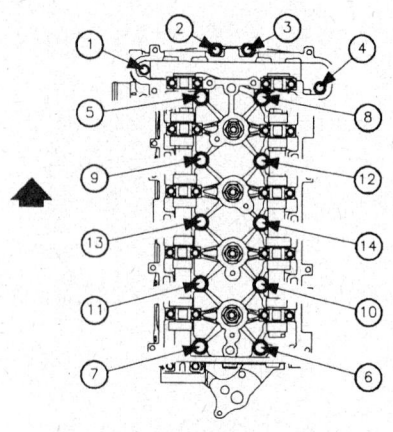

Fig. 13 Cylinder head bolt loosening sequence

PISTONS, PINS & RINGS

Replace any pistons that show signs of damage or excessive wear. Piston pin bores and pins must be free of varnish or scuffing. Use an outside micrometer to measure the piston contact areas and piston pin bore. Subtract the measurement of the piston pin bore from the piston pin.

MAIN & ROD BEARINGS

1. Install crankshaft bearing caps using suitable brass, lead, leather, or equivalent soft faced mallet. **Do not use lower crankcase bolts to pull bearing caps into seats.**
2. **Torque** lower crankcase inner bolts to 15 ft. lbs. in sequence, **Fig. 21.**
3. **Torque** lower crankcase outer bolts to 18 ft. lbs., then rotate bolts an additional 70° in sequence, **Fig. 22.**

CRANKSHAFT REAR OIL SEAL
REPLACE

1. Remove transaxle as outlined in **MOTOR's "Domestic Transmission In-Vehicle Service"** manual.
2. Remove flywheel and cover.
3. Insert suitable screwdriver into pry tangs of seal carrier and remove seal.
4. Apply suitable clean engine oil to seal lip and inside diameter of seal carrier.
5. Install seal using seal installer tool No. J 42067, or equivalent.
6. Install transaxle and flywheel.

OIL PAN
REPLACE

1. Raise and support vehicle.
2. Drain engine oil into suitable container and remove front exhaust pipe.
3. Remove righthand front wheel, splash shield and vibration dampner.
4. Remove mounting bolts and oil pan.

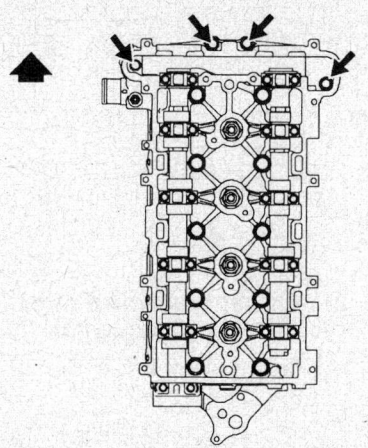

G31069900047000X

Fig. 15 Front cylinder head bolt locations

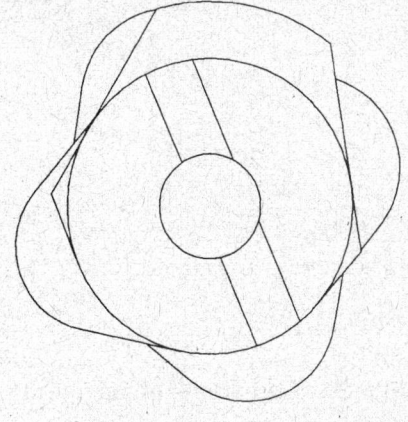

G31069900048000X

Fig. 16 Timing chain sprocket notch alignment

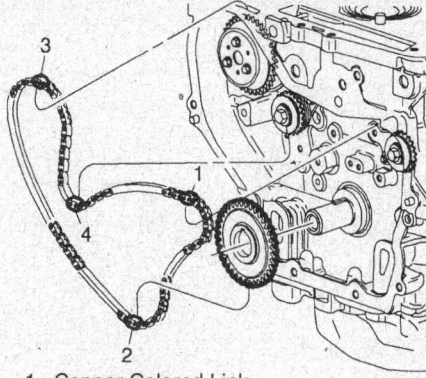

1- Copper Colored Link
2- First Chrome Link
3- Last Chrome Link

G31069900049000X

Fig. 17 Balance shaft drive chain installation

5. Reverse procedure to install, noting the following:
   a. Apply a 0.08 inch bead of RTV part No. 21019581, or equivalent, around perimeter of oil pan and oil suction port opening. **Do not apply an excessive amount of RTV.**
   b. **Torque** oil pan attaching bolts to 18 ft. lbs. in sequence, **Fig. 23.**

OIL PUMP

REPLACE

1. Remove air cleaner, then raise and support vehicle.
2. Drain engine oil into suitable container, then remove righthand front wheel and splash shield.
3. Mark running direction, then remove accessory drive belt.
4. Remove crankshaft pulley using pulley holding tool No. J 38122, or equivalent.
5. Remove belt tensioner as outlined under "Serpentine Drive Belt."
6. Install engine support fixture tool No. SA 9150-E, or equivalent.
7. Remove engine mount as outlined under "Engine Mount, Replace."
8. Remove front cover bolts, then the bolts under water pump cover.
9. Remove front cover and gasket.
10. Reverse procedure to install.

OIL PUMP SERVICE

Disassemble

1. Remove cover plate mounting bolts.
2. Mark drive and driven rotors for assembly reference.
3. Remove drive and driven rotors, then the pressure relief valve.

Inspection

1. Measure clearance between driven rotor and pump body, **Fig. 24,** which should not exceed .012 inch.
2. Inspect clearance between both tips, **Fig. 25,** which should not exceed .006 inch.

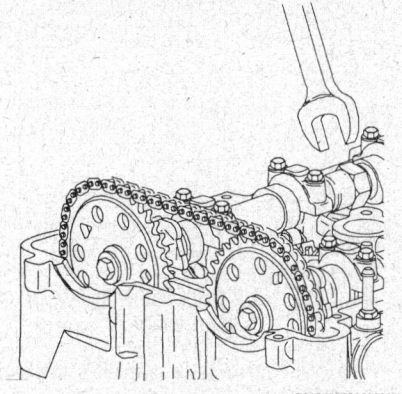

G31069900050000X

Fig. 18 Camshaft sprocket bolts installation

3. Measure clearance between side of drive and driven rotors, and oil pump cover plate, **Fig. 26,** which should not exceed .003 inch.

Assemble

1. Remove front cover oil seal using suitable screwdriver or punch.
2. Install new oil seal using oil seal installer tool No. J 35268-A, or equivalent, and suitable press.
3. Install pressure relief valve, valve spring and oil pump pressure relief valve plug.
4. Lubricate drive and driven rotors with clean engine oil, then align marks on drive and driven rotors.
5. Install drive and driven rotors into pump body.
6. Fill oil pump with petroleum jelly to prime oil pump.
7. Install oil pump gear cover plate screws.

SERPENTINE DRIVE BELT

Belt Routing

Refer to **Fig. 27** for serpentine belt routing.

Tensioner, Replace

Do not disassemble tensioner. Internal components are not serviceable.

1. Depress tensioner arm and remove accessory drive belt.
2. Remove mounting bolts and tensioner, **Fig. 28.**
3. Reverse procedure to install.

Belt, Replace

REMOVAL

1. Mark belt running direction.
2. Depress tensioner arm using suitable ⅜ inch drive breaker bar, **Fig. 27.**
3. Remove belt from idler or air conditioning compressor pulley and accessory pulleys.

INSTALLATION

1. Route belt around pulleys, except for idler pulley.
2. Depress tensioner arm using ⅜ inch drive breaker bar.
3. Ensure belt is properly aligned on pulleys and slip belt over idler pulley.

COOLING SYSTEM BLEED

1. Remove surge tank cap.
2. Raise and support vehicle.
3. Place a suitable drain pan below righthand side of radiator lower mount.
4. Open petcock and drain coolant into container.
5. **On models equipped with water pump drain plug,** place drain pan below drain plug, **Fig. 29,** then open plug and drain coolant into container.
6. **On all models,** after all coolant has drained, close petcock hand tight.
7. **On models equipped with water pump drain plug,** install drain plug, then **torque** to 16 ft. lbs.
8. **On all models,** lower the vehicle, then disconnect radiator upper hose from righthand side of radiator.

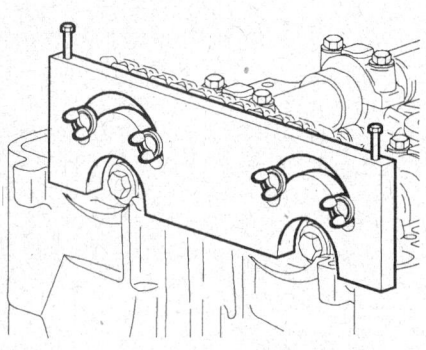

Fig. 19 Camshaft sprocket holding tool installation

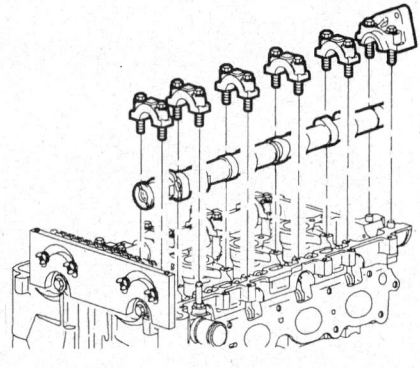

Fig. 20 Camshaft replacement

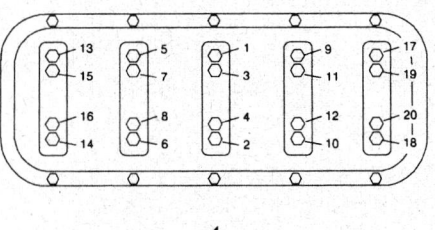

Fig. 21 Lower crankcase inner bolt tightening sequence

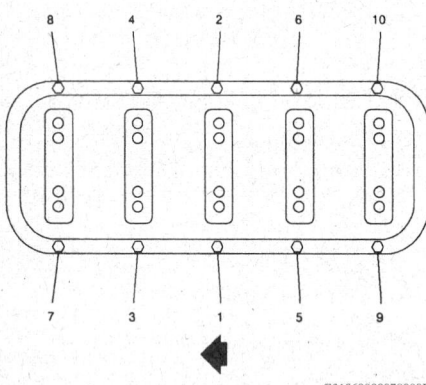

Fig. 22 Lower crankcase outer bolt tightening sequence

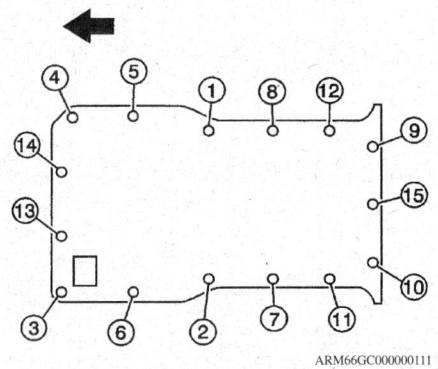

Fig. 23 Oil pan bolt tightening sequence

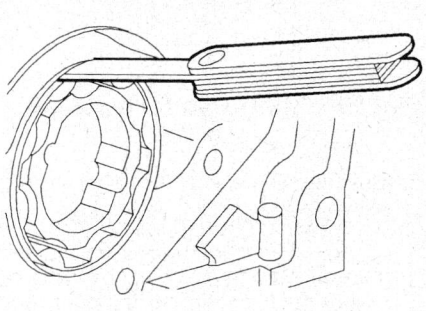

Fig. 24 Oil pump body clearance measurement

9. Slowly add a 50/50 mixture of Dex-Cool antifreeze and deionized water to engine through upper hose.
10. Connect upper hose to radiator.
11. Slowly add antifreeze and water mixture to surge tank to just above Cold Fill line.
12. Install surge tank cap, then start engine.
13. Run engine at 2000–2500 RPM for three minutes.
14. Idle engine for 30 seconds, then turn ignition Off.
15. Inspect coolant level and add if required.

THERMOSTAT

REPLACE

1. Drain engine coolant into suitable container.
2. Disconnect lower radiator hose at thermostat housing using Snap-On hose removal tool HCP10, or equivalent. Twist water feed pipe and remove from water pump.
3. Remove thermostat, water feed and housing mounting bolts.
4. Remove thermostat housing and element.
5. Inspect thermostat components for damage and seat deterioration.
6. **Thermostat will not function properly if contacted by oil. If oil is found in cooling system, it must be**
flushed and thermostat's cartridge replaced.
7. Reverse procedure to install. Install new O-ring.

WATER PUMP

REPLACE

1. Remove air inlet tube and air cleaner.
2. Drain coolant into suitable container and remove exhaust manifold heat shield.
3. Remove thermostat and water feed mounting bolts.
4. Remove water pump sprocket access plate from front cover and install water pump sprocket holding tool J 43651, or equivalent.
5. Remove water pump mounting bolts accessed from front of engine block, then the water pump.
6. Reverse procedure to install.

RADIATOR

REPLACE

1. Remove battery and drain coolant into suitable container.
2. Disconnect cooling fans electrical connectors and slide electrical connectors out of retainers.
3. Remove pusher fan electrical harness from fan shroud retaining tabs.
4. Remove wiring harness from clamp on fan shroud.
5. **On models equipped with automatic transaxle,** disconnect upper transaxle cooler lines from radiator end tank. Cap line.
6. **On all models,** disconnect upper radiator hose from radiator.
7. Remove mounting bolts and fan shroud.
8. Remove forward wiring harness from retaining clips and lower radiator hose from radiator.
9. **On models equipped with automatic transaxle,** remove lower transaxle cooler line. Cap line.
10. **On all models,** remove mounting bolts, upper bracket and rubber mounts.
11. Secure condenser away from upper rail using suitable tie strap.
12. Raise and support vehicle.
13. Remove condenser mounting bolts.
14. Pull condenser and pusher fan down slightly to disconnect radiator tabs.
15. Lower vehicle.
16. Remove radiator.
17. Remove upper radiator to condenser gaskets.
18. Reverse procedure to install.

FUEL PUMP

REPLACE

This procedure has been revised by a Technical Service Bulletin.

Whenever fuel line fittings are loosened or removed, wrap a shop cloth around the fitting and have a suitable container available to collect any fuel spillage.

1. Connect suitably programmed scan tool to Diagnostic Link Connector (DLC) and turn ignition On.
2. Raise and support vehicle, keeping scan tool outside of vehicle and accessible.

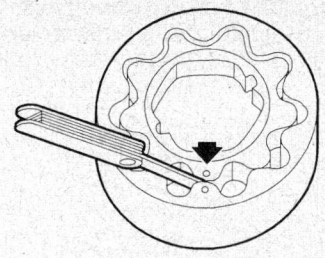

Fig. 25 Oil pump tip clearance measurement

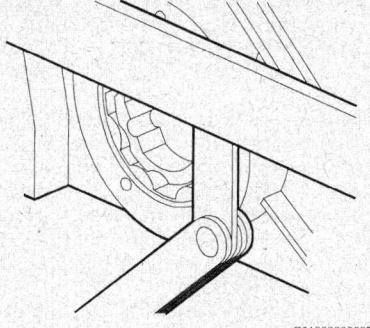

Fig. 26 Oil pump end to end clearance measurement

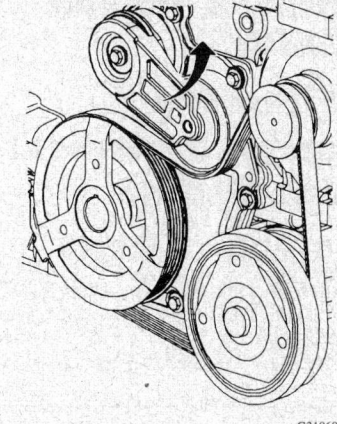

Fig. 27 Serpentine belt routing

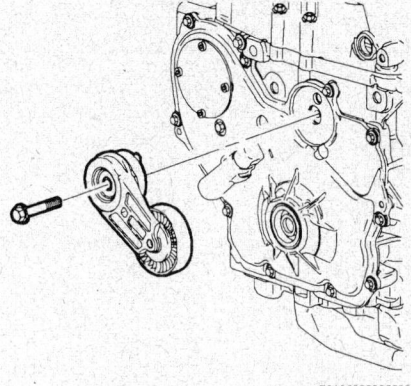

Fig. 28 Belt tensioner replacement

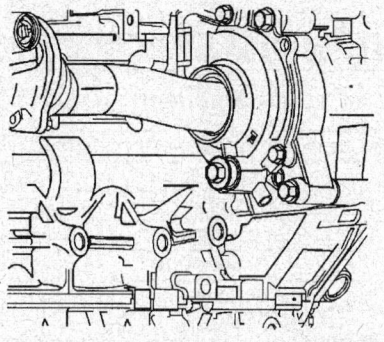

Fig. 29 Water pump drain plug

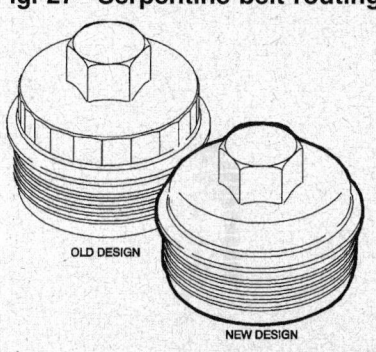

Fig. 30 Oil filter cap identification

3. Disconnect fuel feed line at outlet to filter.
4. Install ⅜ × ¼ inch adapter onto flow/pressure adapter tool No. SA-9127E-7, or equivalent, and insert adapter into fuel feed line.
5. Connect one end of suitable drain hose to other end of adapter. Connect other end of drain hose to suitable fuel handling cart.
6. Turn fuel pump on using scan tool and pump fuel into suitable container.
7. If fuel pump is inoperative, proceed as follows:
   a. Insert siphon hose guide/funnel into fuel filler pipe.
   b. Insert siphon hose J 43290, or equivalent, into guide funnel and fuel filler pipe. Some resistance may be encountered when tip of siphon hose reaches inlet check valve. Repeated probing may be required to slide hose tip through check valve.
   c. Begin siphon process and collect fuel in suitable container.
8. Ensure fuel tank is less than quarter full.
9. Remove exhaust system intermediate pipe and rear heat shield mounting bolts.
10. Remove fuel filler pipe lower bracket mounting screw and disconnect EVAP canister vent hose.
11. Loosen fuel filler pipe hose clamp closest to fuel tank and remove tank ground strap mounting screw near fuel filter.
12. Disconnect fuel feed line after fuel filter.

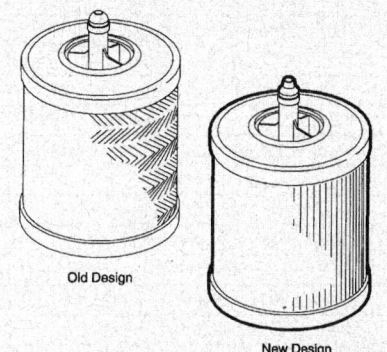

Fig. 31 Oil filter element identification

13. Disconnect fuel return and EVAP canister purge lines between tank and chassis fuel bundle.
14. Disconnect fuel tank electrical connectors.
15. Loosen, but do not remove, front tank strap bolt.
16. Remove rear tank mounting strap bolts with assistance.
17. Remove tank by lowering at the rear, then sliding downward and rearward.
18. Disconnect fuel lines from fuel pump module cover. **Do not attempt to remove retainer using 12 inch or shorter ratchet or breaker bar.**
19. Remove fuel pump module retainer ring using lock ring service tool No. J 43827, or equivalent.
20. To prevent bending of sending unit float arm, remove sending unit first by

pulling retaining clip toward float arm and lifting upward.
21. Carefully lift fuel pump straight up from fuel tank. Clips must be disconnected at same time to disconnect fuel pump from housing.
22. Discard fuel pump module to tank seal and remove fuel feed line from bottom of fuel pump cover using removal tool No. J 44078, or equivalent.
23. Disconnect fuel pump electrical connector from fuel pump cover.
24. Inspect fuel tank for metal chips or debris. Remove contaminants and replace inline fuel filter before installing new pump.
25. Reverse procedure to install, noting the following:
   a. Replace plastic fuel line retainers.
   b. Install new module to tank seal lubricated with suitable clean engine oil.

FUEL FILTER
REPLACE

1. Raise and support vehicle.
2. Remove fuel filter bracket screw, then disconnect fuel lines from inlet and outlet sides of fuel filter.
3. Slide fuel filter out of bracket.
4. Reverse procedure, noting the following:
   a. Turn ignition On for two seconds, then Off for 10 seconds.
   b. Turn ignition On.
   c. Inspect fuel system for leaks.

TECHNICAL SERVICE BULLETINS

Oil Filter Cap Assembly & Element Design Update

2000-2004 L-SERIES

On these models, equipped with 2.2L engines, the oil filter caps and elements have been updated.

Inspect the vehicle for the new design filter cap, **Fig. 30.** If a vehicle is equipped with the new cap part No. 12580254 (PF2259G), the new design filter element part No. 12579143 (PF456G) must be used, **Fig. 31.**

The new design oil filter cap can be identified by a rounded contour on the outer edges, as opposed to the flat edges on the older style. The new design cap can be used to service all previous model year vehicles. The new style oil filter element must be used to service vehicles equipped with the new style filter cap.

Do not install the older filter element part No. 22685727 with the newer filter cap. This could result in severe engine damage.

TIGHTENING SPECIFICATIONS

Year	Component	Torque/Ft. Lbs.
2001–04	Air Conditioning Compressor To Block	18
	Alternator To Block	18
	Battery Hold-Down Bracket	15
	Battery Terminal	13
	Battery Tray	11
	Belt Tensioner To Block	37
	Block Oil Gallery Plug	26
	Camshaft Bearing Cap	89①
	Cam Cover To Head	89①
	Camshaft Sprocket	63②
	Chain Guide Plug	59
	Connecting Rod	18⑨
	Crankshaft Pulley	74⑧
	Crankshaft Position Sensor	96①
	Crankshaft Rear Oil Seal Carrier To Block	96①
	Cylinder Head	③
	Drive Belt Tensioner	33
	EGR Pipe To Cylinder Head	96①
	EGR Valve	18
	Engine Lift Bracket, Front	18
	Engine Lift Bracket, Rear	18
	Engine Mount Bracket	66
	Engine Mount To Body	41
	Exhaust Manifold To Cylinder Head, Stud	18
	Exhaust Manifold To Cylinder Head, Nut	13
	Exhaust Manifold Pipe Flange	12
	Flexplate (Automatic Transaxle)	39 ⑥
	Flywheel (Manual Transaxle)	39 ⑥
	Frame To Body	75④
	Front Cover To Block	18
	Fuel Fill Neck To Fuel Tank Clamp	44①
	Fuel Filter Bracket	35①
	Fuel Line Bracket	89①
	Fuel Line Support Clip	89①
	Fuel Rail Bracket	96①
	Fuel Tank Strap	15
	Fuel Tank Ground Strap	40①
	Fuel Pressure Regulator	44①
	Heater Shield To Exhaust Manifold	96①
	Idle Air Control Motor	27①
	Ignition Coil	89①

Continued

TIGHTENING
SPECIFICATIONS—Continued

Year	Component	Torque/Ft. Lbs.
2001–04	Intake Camshaft Rear Cap	18
	Intake Manifold To Cylinder Head, Bolt	96①
	Intake Manifold To Cylinder Head, Nut	96①
	Intake Manifold To Cylinder Head, Stud	53
	Knock Sensor	18
	Main Bearings	⑤
	Oil Drain Plug	18
	Oil Pan	⑦
	Oil Pump Pressure Relief Valve Plug	30
	Oil Pump Cover	53①
	Oxygen Sensor	22
	Power Steering Pump	18
	Radiator Upper Bracket	53①
	Spark Plug	15
	Starter Motor	37
	Thermostat Housing To Block	96①
	Throttle Body	96①
	Throttle Position Sensor	18①
	Timing Chain Guides	96①
	Timing Chain Nozzle	96①
	Timing Chain Tensioner	55
	Transaxle Mount	41
	Transaxle Range Switch	18
	Transaxle Range Switch Lever	26
	Vent Tube To Cylinder Head	11
	Water Pump	18
	Water Pump Access Cover	96①
	Water Pump Drain Plug	15
	Water Pump/Balance Shaft Chain Tensioner	96①
	Water Pump Sprocket	89①

① — Inch lbs.
② — Rotate an additional 30°.
③ — Refer to "Cylinder Head, Replace" for tightening specifications & sequence.
④ — Rotate an additional 45°.
⑤ — Refer to "Main & Rod Bearings" for tightening specifications & sequence.
⑥ — Rotate an additional 25°.
⑦ — Refer to "Oil Pan, Replace" for tightening specifications & sequence.
⑧ — Rotate an additional 75°.
⑨ — Rotate an additional 70°.

3.0L Engine

NOTE: On Air Bag Equipped Models, Refer To "Air Bag System Precautions" Located In The Front Of This Manual For System Disarming & Arming Procedures.

NOTE: Refer To "Computer Relearn Procedures" Located In The Front Of This Manual When Battery Power To The Computer Has Been Interrupted.

INDEX

PRECAUTIONS

Air Bag Systems

Refer to "Air Bag System Precautions" in the front of this manual for system disarming and arming procedures.

Battery Ground Cable

Prior to service, disconnect battery ground cable and isolate as required.

Fuel System Pressure Relief

WITH SCAN TOOL

Start vehicle and locate SPECIAL TESTS, select ECM, then select fuel delivery. Select FUEL PUMP, then command fuel pump off.

LESS SCAN TOOL

Remove Schrader valve cap and install fuel pressure gauge tool No. SA-9127-E, or equivalent. Open valve on pressure gauge and drain fuel into suitable container.

COMPRESSION PRESSURE

1. Start and run engine until it reaches normal operating temperature. Turn engine off.
2. Remove ignition modules and spark plugs.
3. Connect compression gauge tool No. SA-9127-E, or equivalent, into spark plug hole.
4. Open throttle fully.
5. Crank engine at not less than 250 RPM.
6. Measure compression while cranking engine. Prior to reading compression gauge needle should bounce at least 10 times.
7. Repeat previous steps for each cylinder.
8. Minimum compression on any one cylinder should not be less than 70% of highest cylinder. No cylinder should read less than 100 psi.
9. Place shop towel over spark plug holes and crank engine over a few seconds without compression gauge or spark plugs installed.
10. Repeat compression measuring steps on each cylinder.

ENGINE MOUNT

REPLACE

1. Disconnect MAF sensor and remove air box.
2. Remove EVAP purge assembly and position aside.
3. Loosen hose clamp at throttle body, then slide off MAF hose to throttle body hose and unclamp air cleaner lid.
4. Remove air box mount bolt and box.
5. Install engine support fixture and adapter tools Nos. SA-9150E and J 43405, or equivalents.
6. Remove engine mount and bracket.
7. Reverse procedure to install.

ENGINE

REPLACE

1. Disconnect MAF sensor, then remove air cleaner and battery.
2. Remove positive main feed cable at fuse block.
3. Disconnect main TCM connector under cowl cover and position aside.
4. Disconnect inline TCM connector near brake master cylinder.
5. Disconnect air conditioning pressure connector.
6. Disconnect black engine harness connector from under fuse block and lower weather pack connector inside fuse block.
7. Remove fuse block and position aside.
8. Secure engine harness to top of engine.
9. Remove battery tray.
10. Disconnect EVAP purge connector.
11. Disconnect righthand front speed sensor and secure to engine.
12. Disconnect front oxygen sensor.
13. Disconnect transaxle ground, main connector, shift control and rear ECM connectors.
14. Remove brake booster vacuum hose.
15. Disconnect fuel lines and position aside.
16. Disconnect EVAP purge hose at EVAP purge solenoid.
17. Remove starter and torque converter mounting bolts.
18. Remove exhaust system from catalytic convertor forward.
19. Disconnect transaxle nose bracket.
20. Remove air conditioning compressor and position aside.

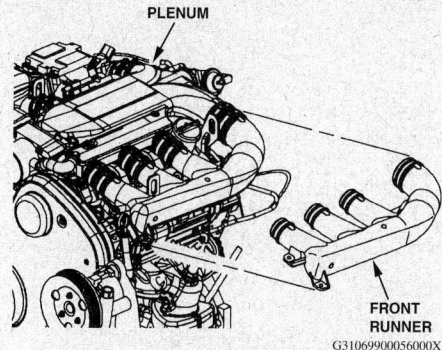

Fig. 1 Upper intake manifold front runner & plenum replacement

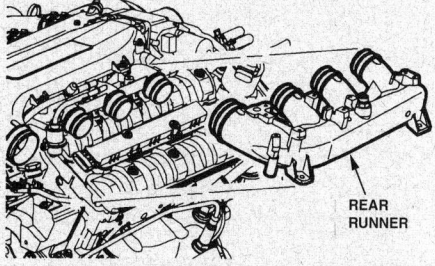

Fig. 2 Upper intake manifold rear runner replacement

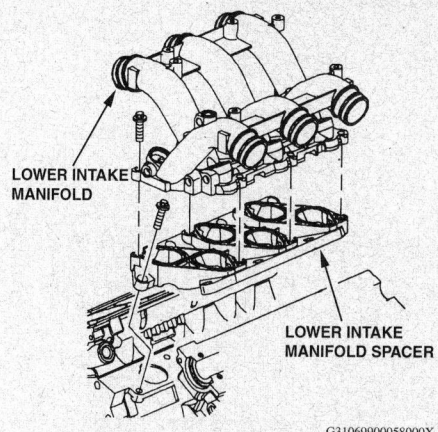

Fig. 3 Lower intake manifold & spacer replacement

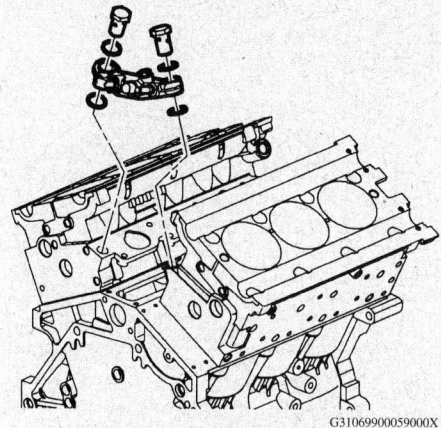

Fig. 4 Coolant bridge replacement

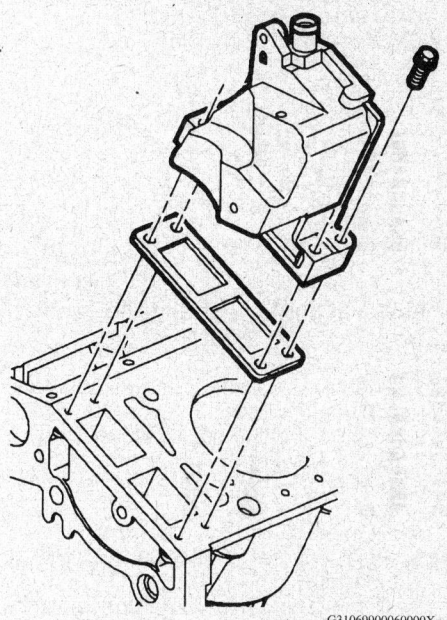

Fig. 5 Engine ventilation chamber replacement

21. Drain engine coolant into suitable container and disconnect heater hoses at cowl.
22. Remove lower engine to transaxle bell housing bolts. **Do not remove upper bolts just yet.**
23. Remove main coolant reservoir hose from engine inlet adapter.
24. Remove upper and lower radiator hoses from engine.
25. Remove small hose under power steering fluid reservoir and drain fluid into suitable container.
26. Disconnect metal power steering line.
27. Remove power steering reservoir and secure to engine.
28. Support engine using suitable engine lift hoist.
29. Remove righthand front engine mount and bracket.
30. Remove upper bell housing bolts.
31. Remove engine.
32. Reverse procedure to install. Ensure engine aligns with dowel pins on transaxle.

INTAKE MANIFOLD
REPLACE
Upper

1. Remove front runner rubber boot hose clamps using hose clamp pliers tool No. J 43914, or equivalent.

2. Remove front runner, **Fig. 1.**
3. Remove ECM.
4. Remove rear runner rubber boot hose clams using hose clamp pliers tool No. J 43914, or equivalent.
5. Disconnect brake vacuum hose.
6. Disconnect intake plenum switch over valve vacuum hose from switch over valve. Mark hose routing for installation.
7. Disconnect throttle body vent hose. Mark hose routing for installation.
8. Remove rear runner, **Fig. 2.**
9. Disconnect throttle body electrical connectors.
10. Remove electrical connector and vacuum hoses from plenum switch over valve solenoid.
11. Remove fuel pressure regulator vacuum and throttle body heater hoses.
12. Remove plenum.
13. Mask off ports to lower intake.
14. Remove upper intake manifold.
15. Reverse procedure to install.

Lower

1. Remove upper intake as outlined under "Intake Manifold Replace," "Upper."
2. Remove fuel supply and return hoses from fuel rail using fuel line separator tool No. SA-9805-E, or equivalent.
3. Disconnect and remove fuel injector harness.
4. Remove fuel rail.
5. Remove lower intake manifold, **Fig. 3.**
6. Remove lower intake manifold spacer.
7. Mask off ports to lower intake manifold spacer.
8. Remove sealing rings.
9. Clean manifold sealing surfaces with nonabrasive cleaner.
10. Reverse procedure to install. Apply Loctite 242, or equivalent, to lower intake manifold spacer and lower intake manifold mounting bolts.

EXHAUST MANIFOLD
REPLACE

1. Remove front oxygen sensor using oxygen sensor socket tool No. J 39194-C, or equivalent.
2. Remove front exhaust manifold and gasket.
3. Remove rear oxygen sensor using oxygen sensor socket tool.
4. Disconnect EGR pipe.

5. Remove rear exhaust manifold and gasket.
6. Reverse procedure to install.

CYLINDER HEAD
REPLACE

1. Remove air cleaner.
2. Remove upper and lower intake manifolds as outlined under "Intake Manifold, Replace."
3. Remove coolant intake and heater hoses.
4. Remove coolant bridge and seals, **Fig. 4.**
5. Remove engine ventilation chamber, **Fig. 5.**
6. Drain coolant into suitable container.
7. Remove upper radiator hose.
8. Remove exhaust manifold heat shield.
9. Remove exhaust pipe to exhaust manifold mounting nuts.
10. Remove front exhaust pipes from exhaust manifolds.

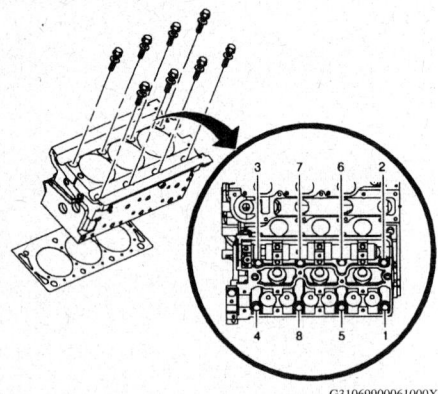

Fig. 6 Cylinder head bolt loosening sequence

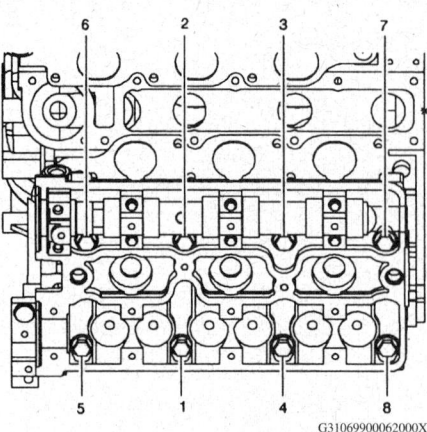

Fig. 7 Cylinder head bolt tightening sequence

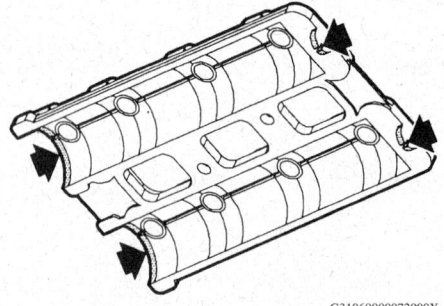

Fig. 8 Valve cover sealant application points

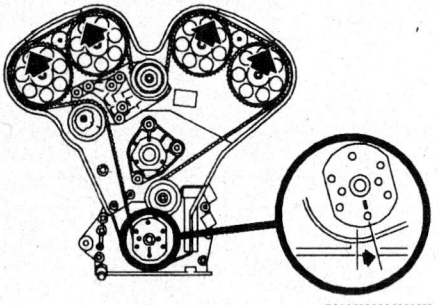

Fig. 9 Crankshaft aligned at 60° BTDC

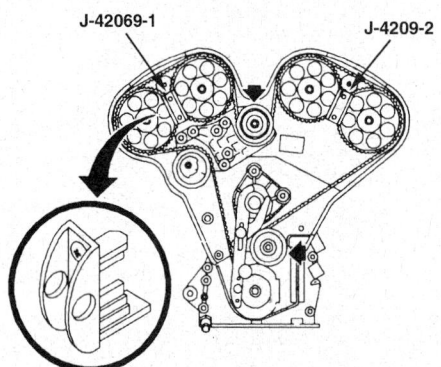

Fig. 10 Camshaft gear locking tool installation

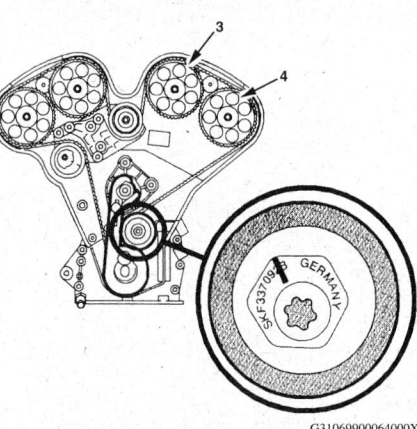

Fig. 11 Camshaft Nos. 3 & 4 idler pulley replacement

11. Support powertrain using suitable floor jack under oil pan.
12. Remove front transaxle mount bolt.
13. Raise powertrain using floor jack to gain access to coolant extension housing.
14. Remove oil dipstick tube.
15. Twist and remove coolant extension housing.
16. Remove grounds from front lift bracket.
17. Disconnect oxygen sensor connector.
18. Remove EGR to exhaust manifold pipe.
19. Remove camshaft cover.
20. Remove front timing belt cover as outlined under "Front Cover, Replace."
21. Remove timing belt as outlined under "Timing Belt, Replace."
22. Remove timing belt tensioner bracket.
23. Remove rear timing belt cover as outlined under "Front Cover, Replace."
24. Disconnect camshaft sensor connector.
25. Remove exhaust camshaft as outlined under "Camshaft, Replace."
26. Loosen and remove cylinder head bolts in several steps in sequence, **Fig. 6.**
27. Remove cylinder head and gasket.
28. Remove exhaust manifold.
29. Clean and inspect cylinder head and sealing surfaces.
30. Reverse procedure to install, noting the following:
    a. Ensure new cylinder head gasket part number imprint is facing toward top of engine.
    b. **Torque** cylinder head bolts to 18 ft.

lbs. in sequence, **Fig. 7.**
    c. Rotate cylinder head bolts an additional 90° in sequence.
    d. Rotate head bolts an additional 90° in sequence.
    e. Rotate bolts an additional 90° in sequence.
    f. Finally, rotate cylinder head bolts an additional 15° in sequence.
    g. Replace sealing rings on coolant pipe and lubricate with coolant.

VALVE COVER
REPLACE

1. Remove upper and lower intake manifolds as outlined under "Intake Manifold, Replace."
2. Remove ignition coils and lift bracket.
3. Remove rear cover knock sensor wire harness and disconnect CMP sensor.
4. Remove cover and O-ring seals. Ensure O-rings are accounted for.
5. Clean cover and sealing surfaces.
6. Reverse procedure to install. Apply thin coat of Loctite 5900, or equivalent to front and rear of cover, **Fig. 8.**

CAMSHAFT LOBE LIFT SPECIFICATIONS

Exhaust cam lobe lift is .3409–.3441 inch. Minimum service limit is .339 inch.

VALVE ADJUSTMENT

This engine is equipped with hydraulic lifters. No adjustment is required.

FRONT COVER
REPLACE

1. Remove air cleaner.
2. Raise and support vehicle, then remove righthand front wheel and splash shield.
3. Lower vehicle, then loosen, but do not remove, water pump pulley bolts.
4. Install engine support fixture and adapters tools Nos. SA-9150-E and J 43405, or equivalents.
5. Remove serpentine belt as outlined under "Serpentine Drive Belt."
6. Remove water pump and power steering pulleys.
7. Remove serpentine belt tensioner and crankshaft balancer.
8. Disconnect air conditioning pressure connector to allow additional slack in harness, remove wiring harness channel from front cover and position away from front of engine.
9. Remove timing belt front cover.
10. Inspect outer edge sealing strip on front timing cover for cracks or tears and replace as required.
11. Remove timing belt as outlined under "Timing Belt, Replace."
12. To prevent valve to piston contact, rotate crankshaft counterclockwise to 60° BTDC, **Fig. 9.**

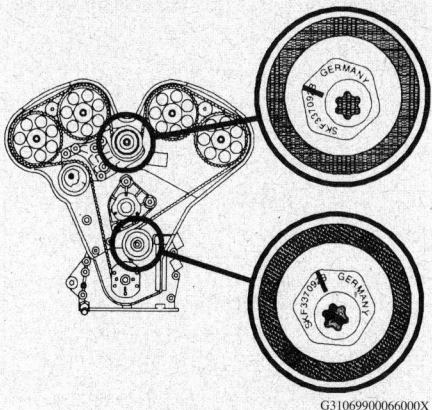

Fig. 12 Upper & lower idler
pulleys alignment

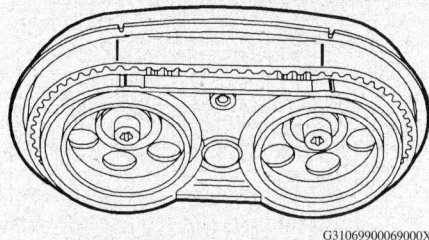

Fig. 15 Timing belt alignment
retarded .0394 inch

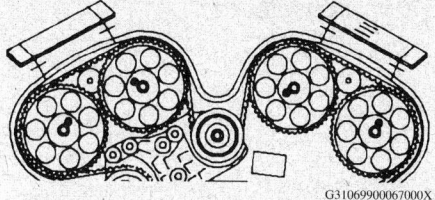

Fig. 13 Timing belt alignment

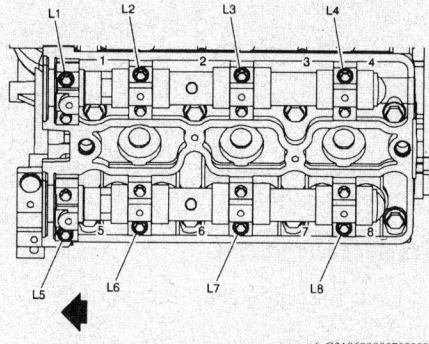

Fig. 16 Rear cylinder head
bearing cap locations

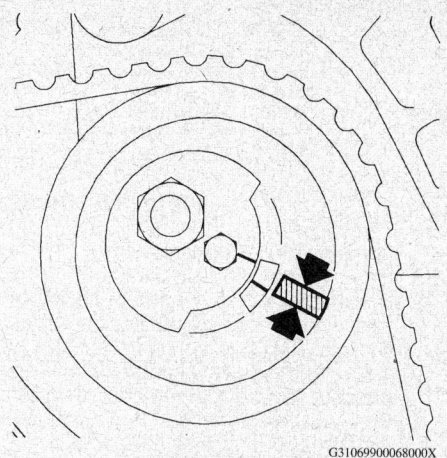

Fig. 14 Timing belt tensioner
alignment

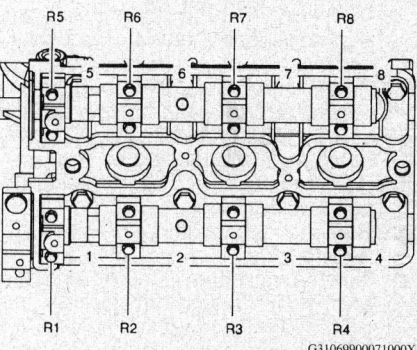

Fig. 17 Front cylinder head
bearing cap locations

13. Remove camshaft gears using cam-shaft lock tools Nos. J 42069-1 and J 42069-2, or equivalents, when initially loosening camshaft bolts, **Fig. 10.**
14. Remove timing belt tensioner bracket.
15. Remove timing belt idler pulley for camshaft Nos. 3 and 4, **Fig. 11.**
16. Remove mounting bolts, threaded pin and rear timing belt cover.
17. Reverse procedure to install, noting the following:
    a. Install threaded pin with Loctite 242, or equivalent.
    b. Tighten timing belt idler pulley until snug. After final timing belt adjustments are made, tighten to specifications.
    c. Adjust timing belt as outlined under "Timing Belt, Replace."
    d. Install new camshaft gear bolts.

TIMING BELT

REPLACE

Removal

1. Remove timing belt front cover as outlined under "Front Cover, Replace."
2. Rotate crankshaft using crank hub Torx socket tool No. J 42098, or equivalent, until cylinder No. 1 is at 60° BTDC, **Fig. 9.**
3. Install crankshaft locking tool No. J 42069-10, or equivalent.
4. Rotate crankshaft clockwise using crank hub Torx socket tool No. J 42098, or equivalent, until cylinder No. 1 is at TDC and tighten lever arm to water pump pulley flange.
5. **Ensure alignment of crankshaft is not 180° off. Alignment marks must**

align with corresponding notches on rear timing belt cover.
6. Install camshaft gear locking tools Nos. J 42069-1 and J 42069-2, or equivalents, **Fig. 10.**
7. Remove upper and lower idler pulleys.
8. Remove timing belt tensioner.
9. Remove timing belt.
10. **Do not rotate crankshaft if camshaft locking tools are not in place.**
11. **Do not rotate camshafts unless crankshaft is at 60° BTDC.**

Installation

1. Remove crankshaft locking tool.
2. Mark furthest point from Torx head bolt on upper and lower idler pulleys, **Fig. 12.**
3. Idler pulleys provide adjustment by rotating eccentric circle around mounting bolt.
4. Install lower idler pulley allowing pulley to rotate with slight resistance using idler pulley wrench tool No. J 42069-40, or equivalent.
5. Align marks on timing belt with marks on camshaft sprockets Nos. 3 and 4, **Fig. 13.**
6. Route timing belt around lower idler pulley and crankshaft sprocket. Ensure timing belt and crankshaft sprocket marks align.
7. Lock timing belt to crankshaft sprocket using plastic wedge tool No. J 42069-30, or equivalent.
8. Route belt around timing belt tensioner, then around Nos. 1 and 2 camshaft sprockets. Ensure timing belt and sprockets' marks align.
9. Install upper idler pulley using idler pulley wrench tool No. J 42069-40, or equivalent. Allow pulley to rotate.
10. Install crankshaft locking tool No. J 42069-10, or equivalent, and tighten lever arm to water pump pulley flange.
11. Adjust timing belt tensioner alignment

mark ⅛ inch above mark on spring loaded idler, **Fig. 14.**
12. Adjust mark on upper idler pulley to 10 o'clock position to align Nos. 1 and 2 timing marks close to settings. Snug the pulley, but do not fully tighten.
13. Adjust mark on lower idler pulley to 11 o'clock position to align Nos. 3 and 4 timing marks close to settings. Snug the pulley, but do not fully tighten.
14. Remove camshaft locking tools and install inspecting gauge tool No. J 42069-20, or equivalent.
15. Pull timing belt between tensioner and crankshaft sprocket to remove slack between camshaft Nos. 3 and 4 and lower idler pulley. Ensure timing marks on camshaft Nos. 3 and 4 are .0394 inch on retard side, **Fig. 15.** If timing marks are not .0394 inch on retard side, turn lower idler clockwise and repeat procedure.
16. Remove crankshaft locking tool.
17. Rotate crankshaft 1¾ turns clockwise and install crankshaft locking tool at TDC.
18. Tighten lever arm to water pump pulley flange.
19. If TDC is passed, do not rotate counterclockwise, rotate crankshaft an additional two turns.
20. Rotate lower idler pulley counterclockwise until timing marks on camshaft sprocket Nos. 3 and 4 align with marks on inspecting gauge tool.
21. Hold idler pulley using idler pulley

CYLINDER BORE	PISTON SIZE
(8) 85.976 - 85.985 mm (3.3848 - 3.3852 inch)	(8) 85.940 - 85.950 mm (3.3834 - 3.3838 inch)
(99) 85.985 - 85.995 mm (3.3852 - 3.3856 inch)	(99) 85.950 - 85.960 mm (3.3838 - 3.3842 inch)
(00) 85.995 - 86.005 mm (3.3856 - 3.3860 inch)	(00) 85.960 - 85.970 mm (3.3842 - 3.3846 inch)
(01) 86.005 - 86.015 mm (3.3860 - 3.3864 inch)	(01) 85.970 - 85.980 mm (3.3846 - 3.3850 inch)
(02) 86.015 - 86.025 mm (3.3864 - 3.3868 inch)	(02) 85.980 - 85.990 mm (3.3850 - 3.3854 inch)
† (7 + 0.5) 86.465 - 86.475 mm (3.4041 - 3.4045 inch)	† (7 + 0.5) 86.430 - 86.440 mm (3.4027 - 3.4031 inch)

GC1069700845000X

Fig. 18 Piston selection chart

wrench tool and tighten.

22. Remove crankshaft locking tool.
23. Rotate crankshaft 1¾ turns clockwise and install crankshaft locking tool. Stop at TDC and tighten lever arm to water pump pulley flange. If TDC is passed, do not rotate counterclockwise, rotate crankshaft an additional two turns.
24. Inspect alignment marks on camshaft Nos. 3 and 4, realign if required.
25. Install inspecting gauge tool on camshaft Nos. 1 and 2, then install camshaft locking tool on camshaft Nos. 2 and 4.
26. Rotate upper idler pulley counterclockwise until timing marks on camshaft sprocket Nos. 1 and 2 align with marks on inspecting gauge tool.
27. Hold idler pulley and tighten using idler pulley wrench tool.
28. Remove camshaft and crankshaft locking tools.
29. Rotate crankshaft 1¾ turns clockwise and install crankshaft locking tool. Stop at TDC and tighten lever arm to water pump pulley flange. If TDC is passed, do not rotate counterclockwise, rotate crankshaft an additional two turns.
30. Inspect both pairs of camshaft timing marks using inspecting gauge tool. Adjust as required.
31. Adjust timing belt tensioner mark ⅛ inch above alignment mark on spring loaded idler, **Fig. 14.**
32. Remove crankshaft locking tool and inspecting gauge tool.
33. Install timing belt front cover.

CAMSHAFT

REPLACE

Removal

1. Remove upper and lower intake manifold as outlined under "Intake Manifold, Replace."
2. Remove air cleaner.
3. Remove timing belt cover as outlined under "Front Cover, Replace."
4. Remove timing belt as outlined under "Timing Belt, Replace."
5. Rotate crankshaft counterclockwise to 60° BTDC to prevent valve to piston contact, **Fig. 9.**
6. Remove gear bolt and gear using camshaft locking tools Nos. J 42069-1 and J 42069-2, or equivalents.
7. Ensure camshaft is not under load from lifters.
8. Remove bearing cap bolts, starting in center and moving outward in spiral direction, in stages of ½–1 turn.

9. Code marks on bearing caps are as follows:
   a. Rear cylinder head cylinders Nos. 1, 3 and 5 bearing caps are marked with L followed by a number.
   b. Front cylinder head cylinders Nos. 2, 4 and 6 bearing caps are marked with R followed by a number.
10. Remove camshaft with seal, then clean bearing and sealing surfaces.

Installation

1. Lubricate camshaft bearing surfaces with oil.
2. Install camshafts as follows:
   a. **When installing rear exhaust camshaft,** ensure pin points toward 1 o'clock position.
   b. **When installing rear intake camshaft,** ensure pin points toward 11 o'clock position.
   c. **When installing front exhaust camshaft,** ensure pin points toward 12 o'clock position.
   d. **When installing front intake camshaft,** ensure pin points toward 7 o'clock position.
3. Apply sealant Loctite 573, or equivalent, to forward edge of front bearing cap, ensure sealant does not enter oil journal.
4. Install bearing caps in appropriate positions, **Figs. 16 and 17.**
5. Tighten bearing caps, starting in center and moving outward in spiral direction.
6. Coat lip of camshaft seal with engine oil and tap into place using camshaft front seal installer tool No. J 35268-A, or equivalent, ensure seal is fully seated.
7. Install camshaft gear with new bolts and camshaft locking tool.
8. Install new camshaft gear mounting bolts.
9. Install and adjust timing belt.
10. Install valve cover.
11. Install upper and lower intake manifold.
12. Install air cleaner.

PISTON & ROD ASSEMBLY

Ensure arrow on piston head faces toward front of engine and bump on connecting rod face toward rear of engine.

Tighten connecting rod cap bolts in three steps: first step, **torque** bolts to 26 ft. lbs.; second step, rotate an additional 45°; third step, rotate an additional 15°.

PISTONS, PINS & RINGS

1. If cylinders have been honed, proper

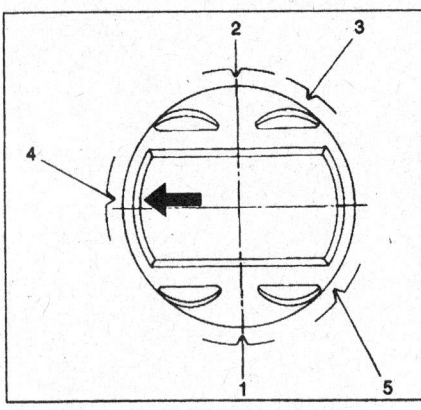

(1) 1st Compression Ring End Gap Location
(2) 2nd Compression Ring End Gap Location
(3) Oil Control Ring Upper Ring End Gap Location
(4) Oil Control Ring Spacer End Gap Location
(5) Oil Control Ring Lower Ring End Gap Location

GC1069700848000X

Fig. 19 Piston ring orientation

size piston must be selected for each bore from chart, **Fig. 18.**
2. If piston must be separated from connecting rod.
3. Remove and install piston pin clips using piston pin clip replacement tool No. J 43654, or equivalent.
4. Remove or install piston from connecting rod using piston pin remover/ installer tool No. SA-9101-E, or equivalent.
5. Ensure arrow on top of piston and bump on connecting rod face in opposite directions when assembling piston and rod. Arrow on piston will face front of engine block, bump on connecting rod will face rear of engine block.
6. Measure piston pin bore to piston pin clearance. Replace piston and piston pin if clearance is not .0001–.0003 inch.
7. Hone cylinders.
8. Install 1st and 2nd compression rings in cylinder bore. Gap should be .0118–.0196 inch.
9. Install oil control ring in cylinder bore. Gap should be .0157–.0551 inch.
10. Replace rings if end gap clearance is more than specified.
11. First and 2nd compression ring groove clearance should be .0008–.0015 inch.
12. Oil control ring groove clearance should be .0004–.0012 inch.
13. Replace piston if ring groove clearance is more than specified.
14. Refer to **Fig. 19** for piston ring orientation.

MAIN & ROD BEARINGS

The crankshaft main bearing caps are numbered 1, 2 and 3 from the front of the engine. The rear bearing cap is not numbered and contains the thrust bearings. The Nos. 2 and 3 bearing shells do not have oil grooves on the cap sides.

There is a 0 or a 1 stamped on the cylinder block oil pan mating flange near the end of each main bearing cap. This is the Determining Number. The Determining Number

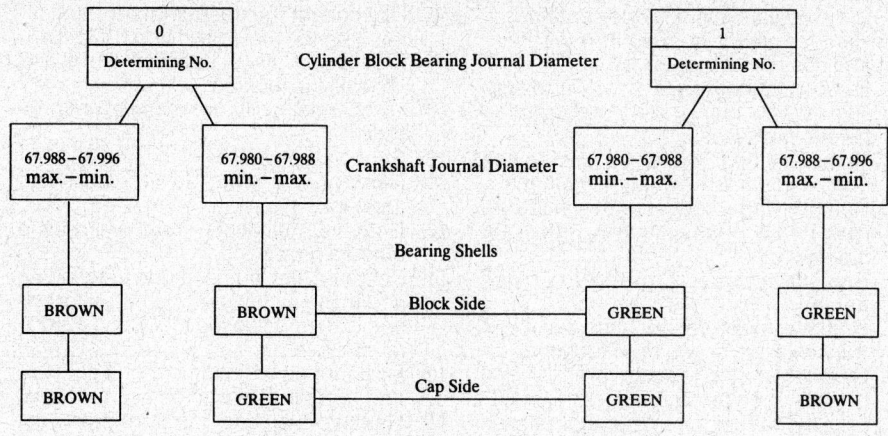

Note: Brown Bearing Thickness 1.989–1.995 mm. Green Bearing Thickness 1.995–2.001 mm.
G31069900079000X

Fig. 20 Main bearing selective fits chart

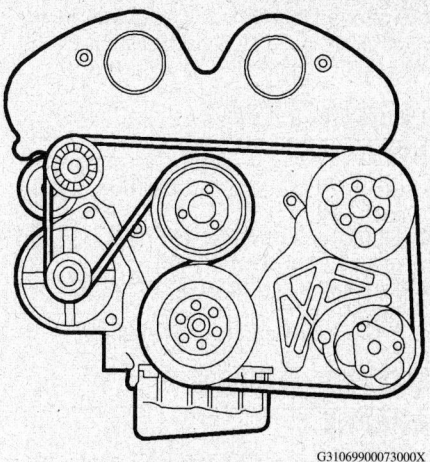

G31069900073000X

Fig. 21 Serpentine drive belt routing

corresponds to each crankshaft main bearing size and color to be installed. The main journal diameter for a determining Number 0 is 2.8368–2.8371 inches. The main journal diameter for a determining Number 1 is 2.8371–2.8373 inches.

To select the proper main bearing, measure crankshaft main bearing journal diameter and refer to main bearing selective fits chart, **Fig. 20.**

Tighten main bearing cap bolts in three steps: first step, **torque** bolts to 37 ft. lbs.; second step, rotate bolts an additional 60°; third step, rotate bolts an additional 15°.

CRANKSHAFT REAR OIL SEAL
REPLACE

1. Remove transaxle as outlined in **MOTOR's "Domestic Transmission In-Vehicle Service"** manual.
2. Counterhold crankshaft using crank hub Torx socket tool No. J 42098, or equivalent, and remove flexplate.
3. Center punch steel ring in rear oil seal, then drill small, shallow pilot hole in steel ring.
4. Screw self tapping screw into steel ring and remove rear oil seal using suitable pliers.
5. Reverse procedure to install, noting the following:
   a. Coat lip of rear oil seal with suitable clean engine oil.
   b. Install rear oil seal using rear main oil seal installer tool No. J 42067, or equivalent.

OIL PAN
REPLACE

1. Raise and support vehicle.
2. Remove nose cone bracket bolts from oil pan.
3. Remove lower transaxle flange to oil pan bolts.
4. Remove oil pan using RTV cutter tool No. SA-9123-E, or equivalent, to break pan loose from engine block.

5. Reverse procedure to install using Loctite 5900, or equivalent, .118 inch from inside edge of oil pan.

OIL PUMP
REPLACE

1. Drain coolant into suitable container.
2. Remove air cleaner.
3. Remove timing belt front and rear covers as outlined under "Front Cover, Replace."
4. Remove timing belt as outlined under "Timing Belt, Replace."
5. Remove and position air conditioning compressor and power steering pump aside.
6. Pivot alternator aside.
7. Remove oil pan as outlined under "Oil Pan, Replace."
8. Remove oil pump pickup tube.
9. Hold crankshaft drive gear using crank hub holding tool No. J 42065, or equivalent.
10. Remove drive gear using crank hub Torx socket tool No. J 42098, or equivalent.
11. Remove oil pan housing bolts and oil pump.
12. Remove front main oil seal and collar from oil pump.
13. Reverse procedure to install, noting the following:
    a. Coat pump side of new oil pump gasket with anaerobic sealant Loctite 518, or equivalent.
    b. Install oil pump and align using guide pins. Apply thread sealant Loctite 242, or equivalent, to bolts.
    c. Coat lip of front main oil seal with suitable clean engine oil, then install using front main seal installer tool No. J 35268-A, or equivalent. Ensure seal is fully and evenly seated.
    d. Install new crankshaft drive gear bolt.
    e. Tighten oil pump after alternator and drive belt idler pulley for camshafts Nos. 3 and 4 have been tightened.

f. Fill and bleed cooling system as required.

BELT TENSION DATA

1. Allow engine to run for approximately 10 minutes with accessories turned on to ensure engine is warmed up.
2. Rotate tensioner arm clockwise until belt becomes loose and slowly apply tension back on belt.
3. Marking on tensioner arm must fall within two marks on tensioner body. Replace drive belt if tensioner marks fall outside operating range.
4. Record belt tension at mid span using calibrated belt tension gauge tool No. SA-9181-NE, or equivalent. This inspection can be performed with engine removed. If engine is in vehicle, upper engine mount must be removed.
5. Repeat previous steps three times. Determine average belt tension.
6. New belt tension should be 50–65 lbs. Used belt tension should be at least 45 lbs.

SERPENTINE DRIVE BELT

Belt Routing

Refer to **Fig. 21** for serpentine belt routing.

Belt Replacement

1. Remove righthand front engine mount as outlined under "Engine Mount, Replace."
2. Remove belt by rotating tensioner pulley clockwise and sliding drive belt off tensioner.
3. Reverse procedure to install.

COOLING SYSTEM BLEED

Run engine until thermostat opens, then cycle engine speed from idle to 3000 RPM in 30 second intervals. Add coolant as required to bring level to cold line on reservoir after engine has cooled.

THERMOSTAT
REPLACE

1. Remove thermostat housing extension bolt.
2. Remove extension by pulling it out from thermostat housing.
3. Remove thermostat housing and thermostat.
4. Reverse procedure to install.

WATER PUMP
REPLACE

1. Remove air cleaner inlet duct from throttle body, then raise and support vehicle.
2. Remove lefthand front wheel and splash shield.
3. Loosen but do not remove water pump and power steering pump pulley bolts.
4. Remove accessory drive belt as outlined under "Serpentine Drive Belt."
5. Remove water pump and power steering pump pulleys, then the drive belt tensioner.
6. Remove front timing belt cover as outlined under "Front Cover, Replace."
7. Remove water pump and O-ring.
8. Reverse procedure to install.

RADIATOR
REPLACE

1. Slide fan control module up and off bracket, then position aside.
2. Remove battery.

3. Drain coolant into suitable container.
4. Remove power steering fluid reservoir and position to rear of vehicle.
5. Disconnect both cooling fans and auxiliary water pump, then remove fan shroud harnesses.
6. Remove upper transaxle cooler line and unsnap front end tank retainer.
7. Remove upper radiator hose and auxiliary water pump outlet and inlet hoses.
8. Remove fan shroud and forward wiring harness.
9. Remove lower radiator hose and lower transaxle cooler line from radiator.
10. Remove upper radiator bracket and mounts, then the upper hose.
11. Support condenser from upper rail and remove condenser block bolt from radiator end tank.
12. Remove condenser bolts, then disconnect radiator tabs by pulling condenser and pusher fan down.
13. Remove radiator leaving condenser and pusher fan, then the upper and lower radiator to condenser gaskets.
14. Reverse procedure to install.

FUEL PUMP
REPLACE

1. Drain fuel tank into suitable container using suitable hand operated pump.
2. Remove exhaust system intermediate pipe with muffler and heat shield.
3. Remove fuel filler pipe lower bracket and disconnect filler pipe hose from tank.
4. Disconnect EVAP canister vent hose and quick connect at recirc line.
5. Remove fuel tank grounding strap.

6. Disconnect fuel feed line after fuel filter, then the fuel return and EVAP canister purge lines between tank and chassis fuel bundle.
7. Disconnect fuel tank electrical connections.
8. Support fuel tank.
9. Remove rear mounting strap bolts and fuel tank.
10. Remove fuel lines from fuel pump module cover.
11. Remove fuel pump module retaining ring using suitable ½ inch breaker bar and lock ring service tool No. J 43827, or equivalent.
12. Disconnect fuel pump housing clips and remove fuel pump from fuel tank.
13. Remove fuel feed line from bottom of fuel pump using fuel clamp pliers tool No. J 44078, or equivalent.
14. Disconnect fuel pump connector from fuel pump cover.
15. Reverse procedure to install, noting the following:
    a. Install new fuel pump seal.
    b. Install pump cover lock ring with bumps facing away from tank using lock ring service tool.
    c. Install new retainers into female portion of quick connect fitting on fuel and EVAP canister purge lines.

FUEL FILTER
REPLACE

1. Disconnect fuel feed lines.
2. Remove fuel filter.
3. Reverse procedure to install. Install new fuel line retainers into fuel line fittings' female portion.

TIGHTENING SPECIFICATIONS

Year	Component	Torque/Ft. Lbs.
2001–04	Accelerator Pedal Bracket	89①
	Accelerator Pedal Position Sensor	53①
	Accessory Bracket, Air Conditioning & Power Steering	30
	Accessory Drive Belt Tensioner	30
	Air Conditioning Compressor Bracket	30
	Air Conditioning Compressor Hose Support Strap	71①
	Alternator	30
	Battery Hold Down Bracket	15
	Battery Terminal	13
	Battery Tray	11
	Bell Housing	48
	Belt Tensioner	30
	Camshaft Bearing	71①
	Camshaft Cover	71①
	Camshaft Gear	37⑤
	Camshaft Position Sensor	71①
	Catalytic Converter	15
	Catalytic Converter Hanger	15
	Connecting Rod Cap	⑦
	Coolant Bridge	22
	Crankshaft Balancer	15
	Crankshaft Main Bearing	②
	Crankshaft Torsional Bearing Bridge	15
	Crankshaft Drive Gear	184⑥
	Crankshaft Position Sensor	71①
	Crankshaft Reluctor Ring	11
	Crankshaft Sensor	71①
	Cylinder Head	④
	Drive Belt Tensioner	30
	Engine Control Module	71①
	Engine Coolant Temperature Sensor	13
	Engine Mount	41
	Engine Mount Bracket	41
	Engine Oil Cooler Cover	22
	Engine Oil Cooler Inlet & Outlet	15
	Engine Rear Cover	71①
	Engine Rear Cover Threaded Pin	89①
	Engine Ventilation Chamber	71①
	Exhaust Gas Recirculation Pipe	19
	Exhaust Gas Recirculation Valve	15
	Exhaust Manifold	15
	Flexplate	65
	Front Timing Belt Cover	48③
	Fuel Fill Neck To Fuel Tank Clamp	71①
	Fuel Fill Pipe To Body, Lower	114①
	Fuel Fill Pipe To Body, Upper	35①
	Fuel Filter Bracket	35①
	Fuel Line Stone Chip Guard	106①
	Fuel Rail	71①
	Fuel Tank Mounting Strap	15
	Fuel Tank Pressure Sensor	18①
	Heated Oxygen Sensor	37
	Ignition Coil	71①
	Ignition Module	71①
	Intake Manifold	15

Continued

TIGHTENING
SPECIFICATIONS—Continued

Year	Component	Torque/Ft. Lbs.
2001–04	Intake Manifold Spacer	15
	Intake Plenum	71①
	Intake Plenum Switchover Valve	71①
	Intake Runner	71①
	Knock Sensors	15
	Main Bearing	②
	Manifold Absolute Pressure Sensor	44①
	Battery Ground To Chassis	114①
	Oil Cooler Inlet & Outlet	15
	Oil Filter Cap	19
	Oil Filter Cartridge Housing Drain Plug	89①
	Oil Filter Cartridge Housing To Engine Block	33
	Oil Intake Pipe	71①
	Oil Pan Baffle	71①
	Oil Pan	11
	Oil Pan Drain Plug	19
	Oil Pressure Switch	30
	Oil Pump	80①
	Oxygen Sensors, Exhaust Manifold	37
	Oxygen Sensors, Lower Exhaust Pipe	33
	Power Steering Pump Pulley	15
	Rear Timing Belt Cover Threaded Pin	89①
	Rear Timing Cover	71①
	Resonance Chamber	27①
	Spark Plug	19
	Starter	30
	Thermostat Housing	15
	Throttle Boot	71①
	Timing Belt Idler Pulley	30
	Timing Belt Tensioner Bracket	30
	Timing Belt Tensioner	15
	Torque Convertor Bolts	48
	Transaxle Cooler Line, Lower	36①
	Transaxle Cooler Line, Upper	18
	Transaxle Range Switch	18
	Transaxle Range Switch Lever	26
	Water Pump	19
	Water Pump Pulley	71①
	Wheel Bolt	92
	Wiring Channel	71①

① — Inch lbs.
② — Refer to "Main & Rod Bearings" for tightening specifications & sequence.
③ — Rotate an additional 30°, then an additional 15°.
④ — Refer to "Cylinder Head, Replace" for tightening specifications & sequence.
⑤ — Rotate an additional 60°, then an additional 15°.
⑥ — Rotate an additional 45°, then an additional 15°.
⑦ — Refer to "Piston & Rod Assembly" for tightening specifications & sequence.

Rear Axle & Suspension

NOTE: On Air Bag Equipped Models, Refer To "Air Bag System Precautions" Located In The Front Of This Manual For System Disarming & Arming Procedures.

NOTE: Refer To "Computer Relearn Procedures" Located In The Front Of This Manual When Battery Power To The Computer Has Been Interrupted.

NOTE: Prior To Performing Any Service Operations Listed In This Section, Consult The "Technical Service Bulletins" Section For Related Information.

INDEX

PRECAUTIONS

Air Bag Systems

Refer to "Air Bag System Precautions" in the front of this manual for system disarming and arming procedures.

Battery Ground Cable

Prior to service, disconnect battery ground cable and isolate as required.

HUB & BEARING

REPLACE

ION

1. Raise and support vehicle.
2. Remove tire and wheel assembly.
3. Remove brake drum.
4. Remove plug from drum brake actuator access hole in backing plate.
5. Install a support for brake backing plate through actuator access hole.
6. Disconnect wheel speed sensor electrical connector.
7. Remove wheel bearing and hub assembly mounting nuts.
8. Remove wheel hub and bearing assembly from rear axle assembly and brake backing plate.
9. Reverse procedure to install.

L-Series & S-Series

1. Raise and support vehicle, then remove wheel assembly.
2. **On models equipped with ABS,** disconnect wheel speed sensor harness.
3. **On all models,** remove brake drum and hub to knuckle mounting bolts.
4. Remove hub.
5. Reverse procedure to install.

STRUT

REPLACE

L-Series

1. Raise and support vehicle, then remove wheel assembly.
2. Remove inner wheel liner and shock to knuckle bolt. Discard bolt.
3. Remove upper carrier to body bolts.
4. Loosen lower carrier to body bolts until carrier slides out.
5. Reverse procedure to install.

S-Series

1. Remove rear window trim finish panel.
2. Raise and support vehicle, then remove wheel assembly.
3. Loosen but do not remove knuckle to strut mounting nuts.
4. Support knuckle using suitable floor jack and remove upper strut mounting nuts.

5. Disconnect ABS electrical harness from strut.
6. Remove strut to knuckle nuts and strut.
7. Reverse procedure to install.

STRUT SERVICE

L-Series & S-Series

1. Position strut in strut spring compressor tool No. SA-9155-S, or equivalent, mounted in suitable holding device.
2. Fasten strut to tool using one strut to knuckle bolt and nut in lower strut mounting hole.
3. Compress spring until upper spring supports are completely unladen.
4. Remove strut shaft nut while holding strut shaft in position using suitable Torx wrench.
5. Release spring compressor and tilt strut outward, then remove upper spring support and spring.
6. Remove dust shield and strut from compressor tool.
7. Inspect rubber spring support and dust shield for cracks or deterioration. Replace as required.
8. Inspect spring for signs of damage.
9. Extend and retract strut shaft. Replace strut if movement is not smooth or resistance is not even.
10. Reverse procedure to assemble, noting the following:
    a. Compress spring only enough to install upper washer and shaft nut.

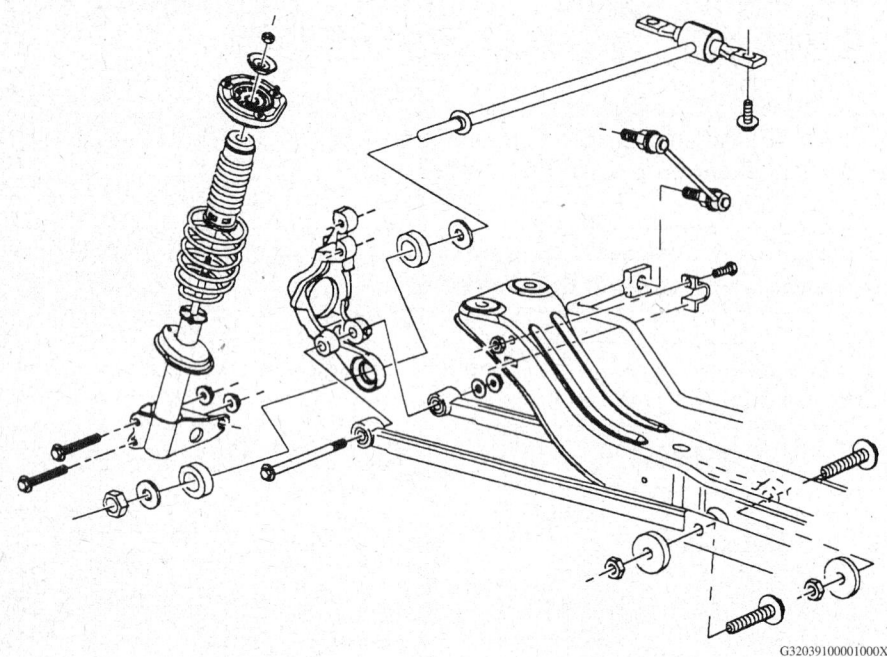

Fig. 1 Exploded view of rear suspension

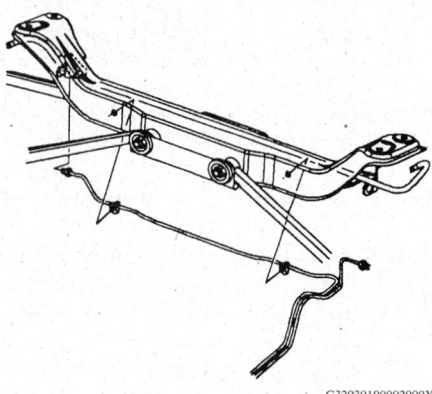

G32039100002000X

Fig. 2 Brake line replacement

3. Remove mounting bolts and hub.
4. Loosen but do not remove lateral link and strut to knuckle mounting bolts.
5. Remove trailing arm to knuckle mounting nut and arm to body mounting bolts, then slide arm from knuckle.
6. Remove mounting bolts and link.
7. Reverse procedure to install.

TRAILING ARM
REPLACE
S-Series

1. Raise and support vehicle, then remove wheel assemblies.
2. Remove trailing arm to knuckle mounting nut, **Fig. 1.**
3. Remove trailing arm to body mounting bolts and slide arm from knuckle.
4. Reverse procedure to install.

SUSPENSION SUPPORT
REPLACE
L-Series

1. Raise and support vehicle, then remove wheel assemblies.
2. Remove rear exhaust system from resonator back, then heat shield from rear suspension support.
3. Remove upper and lower control arm to rear axle control arm mounting bolts and nuts.
4. Remove both stabilizer bar links from rear axle control arms.
5. Support rear suspension using suitable jack stand.
6. Remove four rear suspension support to body bolts. Discard bolts.
7. Remove rear suspension support.
8. Reverse procedure to install.

STABILIZER BAR
REPLACE
L-Series

1. Raise and support vehicle, then remove wheel assemblies.
2. Remove heat shield from rear suspension.

Do not compress spring beyond this point.
  b. Ensure spring is properly seated in spring supports.

SHOCK ABSORBER
REPLACE
ION

1. Raise and support vehicle, then remove tire and wheel assembly.
2. Support rear axle with a suitable jack stand near shock absorber.
3. Remove upper and lower shock bolts, then the shock absorber from vehicle.
4. Reverse procedure to install.

COIL SPRING
REPLACE
ION

1. Raise and support vehicle.
2. Support rear axle with suitable jack stands near each rear shock absorber.
3. Remove U-clips from rear brake hose brackets at rear axle.
4. Remove lower shock bolts, slowly lower rear axle to relieve tension from rear springs.
5. Remove spring, then the upper spring seat/jounce bumper from spring while leaving lower spring seat on axle.
6. Reverse procedure to install.

L-Series & S-Series

Refer to "Strut Service" for coil spring replacement procedure.

CONTROL ARM BUSHING
REPLACE
ION

1. Raise and support vehicle, then remove rear wheels.
2. Place two screw type jack stands under both ends of rear axle.
3. Remove U-clips from rear brake hose brackets at rear axle, then the lower shock bolts.
4. Lower the jacks and remove coil springs. **Avoid kinking brake pipes while lowering axle.**
5. Temporarily install lower shock bolts to support axle.
6. Remove bushing bracket to body bolts from both ends of rear axle.
7. Raise rear of axle until bushing brackets pivot away from body.
8. Remove axle bushing through bolts, then the bushing brackets.
9. Note depth and orientation of old bushing before removal.
10. Insert tool No. J 44570-3 through tool No. J 44570-1 and axle bushing.
11. Install washer and nut by hand, tightening until tool is snug.
12. Drive bushing from axle sleeve.
13. Disassemble tool, then remove bushing.
14. Reverse procedure to install.

KNUCKLE
REPLACE
S-Series

1. Raise and support vehicle.
2. Remove wheel assembly and brake drum.

3. Remove lefthand and righthand rear stabilizer bar links to rear axle control arm bolts.
4. Remove mounting bolts and stabilizer bar.
5. Reverse procedure to install.

S-Series

1. Raise and support vehicle, then remove wheel assembly.
2. Position suitable drain container at lefthand rear brake line, then disconnect and plug lefthand brake line.
3. Remove lefthand and righthand stabilizer bar link to knuckle mounting nuts, then bar to crossmember nuts.
4. Loosen but do not remove lateral link to knuckle mounting bolts.
5. Remove trailing arm to knuckle and arm to body mounting nuts.
6. Slide trailing arm from knuckle.
7. Remove mounting bolt and swing lateral link downward.
8. Disconnect brake lines from crossmember, **Fig. 2.**
9. Remove stabilizer bar.
10. Reverse procedure to install.

LATERAL LINK
REPLACE
S-Series

1. Remove fuel tank as outlined under "Fuel Pump, Replace" in "1.9L Engine" section.
2. Raise and support vehicle, then remove wheel assembly.
3. Remove lateral link to knuckle and lateral link to crossmember mounting bolts, **Fig. 1.**
4. Remove rear lateral link.
5. Remove rear brake line mounting nut.
6. Support crossmember using suitable jack stand.
7. Remove crossmember to body mounting bolts.
8. Lower crossmember and remove inboard lateral link to crossmember mounting bolt.
9. Remove mounting bolt and front lateral link.
10. Reverse procedure to install, noting the following:
    a. Do not tighten lateral link mounting bolts until crossmember is aligned and tightened.
    b. Ensure wheel alignment is within specification.

TIGHTENING SPECIFICATIONS

Year	Component	Torque/Ft. Lbs.
ION		
2003–05	Bearing Hub	37
	Bracket To Body	66
	Brake Hose Fittings	14
	Lower Shock	81
	Through Bushing	66②
	Upper Shock	66
	Wheel Lug Nut	100
L-SERIES		
2001–04	Heat Shield To Rear Suspension Support	72①
	Rear Axle Control Bracket	65②
	Rear Brake Drum To Hub	35①
	Rear Brake Hose Bracket To Control Arm	72①
	Rear Caliper To Back Plate	59
	Rear Hub To Knuckle	35③
	Stabilizer Bar Clamp	41
	Stabilizer To Control Arm	41
	Strut Carrier To Body	41
	Strut To Knuckle	110③
	Suspension Control Arm To Knuckle	66④
	Suspension Control Arm To Suspension Support	90④
	Suspension Support To Body	66⑤
S-SERIES		
2001–02	ABS Electrical Harness	53①
	Brake Line	14
	Crossmember To Body	89
	Front Lateral Link To Crossmember	89
	Front Lateral Link To Knuckle	122
	Hub To Knuckle	63
	Lateral Link To Knuckle	122
	Rear Caliper To Knuckle	63
	Rear Lateral Link To Crossmember	89
	Stabilizer Bar Link To Bracket	30
	Stabilizer Bar To Crossmember	41
	Strut Shaft	37
	Strut To Knuckle	126
	Strut Upper Support	21
	Trailing Arm To Body	89
	Trailing Arm To Knuckle	74
	Wheel Lug Nuts	103

① — Inch lbs.
② — Rotate an additional 60°.
③ — Rotate an additional 30°.
④ — Rotate an additional 60–75°.
⑤ — Rotate an additional 90–115°.

Front Suspension & Steering

NOTE: On Air Bag Equipped Models, Refer To "Air Bag System Precautions" Located In The Front Of This Manual For System Disarming & Arming Procedures.

NOTE: Refer To "Computer Relearn Procedures" Located In The Front Of This Manual When Battery Power To The Computer Has Been Interrupted.

NOTE: Prior To Performing Any Service Operations Listed In This Section, Consult The "Technical Service Bulletins" Section For Related Information.

INDEX

PRECAUTIONS

Air Bag Systems

Refer to "Air Bag System Precautions" in the front of this manual for system disarming and arming procedures.

Battery Ground Cable

Prior to service, disconnect battery ground cable and isolate as required.

WHEEL HUB & STEERING KNUCKLE
REPLACE

L-Series & S-Series

1. Depress brake pedal and loosen axle to hub nut.
2. Raise and support vehicle, then remove wheel assembly.
3. Remove caliper to knuckle mounting bolts. Suspend caliper with mechanics wire.
4. Loosen but do not remove knuckle to strut mounting bolts.

5. If rotor is difficult to remove, use two M8 × 1.25 self tapping bolts, **Fig. 1.**
6. Remove axle nut and washer, then discard lower control arm ball stud cotter pin.
7. Loosen castle nut until level with top of ball stud.
8. Remove and discard tie rod cotter pin.
9. Remove tie rod and castle nut.
10. Separate lower control arm from knuckle using lower control arm ball stud separator tool No. SA-9132-S, or equivalent. **Do not use pickle fork or wedge type tool to separate.**
11. Remove lower ball joint castle nut, **Fig. 2.**
12. Separate tie rod end from steering knuckle using tie rod separator tool No. SA-91100-C, or equivalent.
13. **On models equipped with Anti-Lock Brakes (ABS),** disconnect wheel speed sensor electrical connector.
14. **On all models,** support or suspend drive axle.
15. Remove strut to knuckle mounting bolts, then knuckle and hub. If it is difficult to separate axle from hub, tap end of drive axle shaft using suitable wood block wood and hammer. **Do not hammer end of axle.**
16. Reverse procedure to install.

ION

1. Raise and support vehicle, then remove wheel and tire assembly.
2. Remove wheel drive shaft nut, insert a flat bladed tool into caliper and rotor to prevent rotor from turning.
3. Remove and support front brake caliper and bracket as an assembly, then the front brake rotor.
4. **On models equipped with ABS,** disconnect electrical connector from wheel speed sensor, then release wheel speed sensor jumper connector from bracket on strut.
5. **On all models,** remove wheel bearing mounting bolts from behind steering knuckle.
6. Remove wheel bearing/hub assembly and spacer from steering knuckle and wheel drive shaft.
7. Remove outer tie rod to knuckle nut, then using tool No. SA91100C or equivalent, separate tie rod from steering knuckle.
8. Remove lower control arm ball stud to steering knuckle pinch bolt and nut.
9. Lower control arm to separate ball stud

from steering knuckle.
10. Remove strut to steering knuckle nuts and bolts, then the steering knuckle from vehicle.
11. Reverse procedure to install.

HUB & BEARING SERVICE

L-Series & S-Series

1. Remove steering knuckle as outlined under "Wheel Hub & Steering Knuckle, Replace."
2. Remove splash shields and ABS wheel speed sensor.
3. Install wheel bearing/hub removal tool No. SA-9159-S, or equivalent, **Fig. 3.**
4. Place assembly in suitable soft jawed vise.
5. Hold hub drive using suitable wrench. Tighten driver screw to remove hub.
6. Remove inner bearing race using inner race puller, **Fig. 4.**
7. Remove steering knuckle from vise, then the retainer and bridge.
8. Remove bridge snap ring using suitable snap ring pliers.
9. Press out bearing using knuckle support tube and small driver, **Fig. 5.**
10. Reverse procedure to assemble.

BALL JOINT INSPECTION

1. Raise and support front of vehicle.
2. Grasp tire at top and bottom, then move bottom of tire in and out.
3. While moving bottom of tire in and out, observe ball joint for any side to side movement.
4. If any side to side movement is noticed, replace lower control arm.

BALL JOINT

REPLACE

L-Series & S-Series

LOWER

The ball joint and the lower control arm are serviced as an assembly. Refer to "Control Arm, Replace" for replacement procedure.

ION

LOWER

1. Raise and support vehicle, then remove wheel and tire.
2. Remove ball stud to steering knuckle pinch bolt and nut, then separate ball stud from steering knuckle.
3. Remove rear frame bolt, then the control arm to frame bolts.
4. Remove control arm from frame, then place lower control arm in a vice.
5. Drill a pilot hole through rivets using a ⅛ inch drill bit.
6. Complete drilling rivets using a 31/64 inch drill bit.

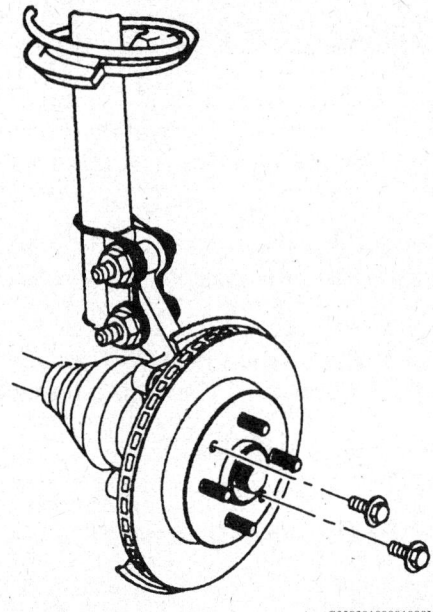

G32029100001000X

Fig. 1   Brake rotor replacement

7. Remove ball joint from lower control arm.
8. Reverse procedure to install, following instructions in ball joint kit.

COIL SPRING

REPLACE

Refer to "Strut Service" for coil spring replacement procedure.

STRUT

REPLACE

L-Series & S-Series

REMOVAL

1. Raise and support vehicle, then remove wheel assembly.
2. **On models equipped with ABS,** disconnect wheel speed sensor electrical connector bracket.
3. **On all models,** loosen, but do not remove steering knuckle to strut housing mounting bolts.
4. Support lower control arm using suitable floor jack.
5. Remove and discard upper strut mounting nuts.
6. Slowly raise vehicle and lower strut.
7. Remove knuckle to housing mounting bolts, **Fig. 2.** Place cloth over CV joint seal.
8. Remove strut.

INSTALLATION

1. Install new upper strut mounting nuts.
2. Install strut to steering knuckle mounting bolts. **Do not use old nuts. Always install new ones.**
3. **On models equipped with ABS,** install sensor electrical connector bracket.

ION

1. Raise and support vehicle, then remove front wheels.
2. Disconnect stabilizer link from strut.
3. Remove strut to steering knuckle nuts, then reposition wheel speed sensor harness and bracket.
4. Remove strut to steering knuckle bolts, then the upper strut cap to body nut.
5. **Place a shop towel over CV joint to prevent joint boot damage.**
6. Remove strut from vehicle.
7. Reverse procedure to install.

STRUT SERVICE

Disassemble

1. Compress spring to unload upper strut mount using spring compressor tool No. SA-9155-C, or equivalent, and suitable holding fixture.
2. While holding strut shaft, remove strut shaft nut.
3. Release spring compressor and tilt strut outward.
4. Remove upper strut assembly, inspect for damage. Replace as required.
5. Remove strut spring and dust shield; inspect for damage and replace as required.
6. Remove strut from holding fixture.

Assemble

1. Place strut in compressor tool and attach with strut to knuckle bolt through lower mounting hole.
2. Extend strut shaft to travel limit.
3. Install dust shield, spring isolator and mount, ensure spring is properly seated in seat and isolator.
4. Compress spring and install strut shaft mounting nut.

CONTROL ARM

REPLACE

L-Series & S-Series

LOWER

1. Raise and support vehicle, then remove wheel assembly.
2. Remove and discard lower control arm ball stud cotter pin.
3. Loosen lower control ball stud castle nut until level with top of ball stud.
4. Separate lower control arm from knuckle using lower control arm ball stud separator tool No. SA-9132-S, or equivalent. **Do not use pickle fork or a wedge type tool.**
5. Remove lower control arm ball stud castle nut.
6. Remove inner front fender splash shield.
7. Remove lower control arm to cradle mounting nut and bolt, **Fig. 2.**
8. Remove lower control arm to tension strut mounting nut, then arm.
9. Reverse procedure to install.

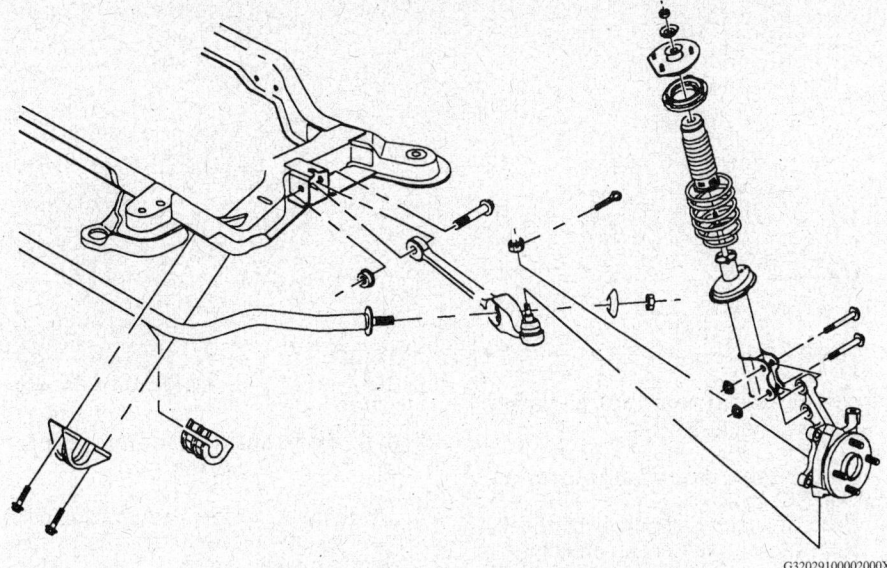

Fig. 2 Exploded view of front suspension

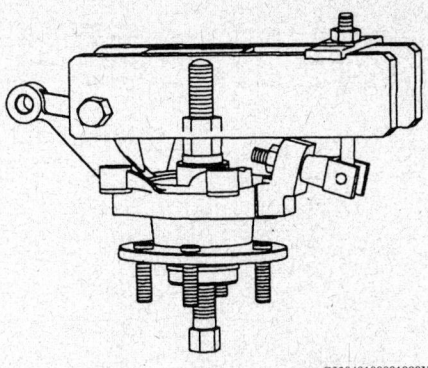

G32049100001000X

Fig. 3 Wheel bearing/hub removal. L-Series & S-Series

ION
LOWER

1. Raise and support vehicle, then remove wheel and tire.
2. Remove ball stud to steering knuckle pinch bolt and nut, then separate ball stud from steering knuckle.
3. Remove rear frame bolt, then the control arm to frame bolts.
4. Remove control arm from frame.
5. Reverse procedure to install.

CONTROL ARM BUSHING
REPLACE
ION

1. Raise and support vehicle, then remove wheel and tire.
2. Remove ball stud to steering knuckle pinch bolt and nut, then separate ball stud from steering knuckle.
3. Remove rear frame bolt, then the control arm to frame bolts.
4. Remove control arm from frame.
5. Wrap control arm with a shop towel, then place it in a vise.
6. **Note depth and orientation of old bushing before removal,** then install tool No. J-41211, or equivalent, onto control arm bushing.
7. Hold hex end of threaded shaft while turning large nut to pull bushing through control arm.
8. Disassemble tools, then remove bushing.
9. Reverse procedure to install noting the following:
   a. Place new bushing onto tapered side of control arm.
   b. Pull new bushing through opposite direction of control arm using tool No. J-41211.
   c. Install control arm.

d. Tighten all fasteners to specifications.

STABILIZER BAR
REPLACE

1. Raise and support vehicle.
2. Remove rear transaxle mount through bolt and heat shield.
3. Remove rear transaxle mount to frame bolts, then the rear transaxle mount.
4. Remove front wheels, then the steering gear to intermediate shaft pinch bolt and discard.
5. Disconnect intermediate shaft from steering gear.
6. Remove both steering gear outer tie rod to knuckle nuts and discard nuts.
7. Separate outer tie rods from steering knuckles using tool No. SA91100C, or equivalent.
8. Remove steering gear bolts, then the steering gear from frame and vehicle through lefthand wheel opening.
9. Disconnect stabilizer link from stabilizer shaft.
10. Remove stabilizer bar mounting clamp bolts and clamps from both sides of vehicle.
11. Remove bushings from stabilizer bar, then lift and rotate stabilizer bar up and to right.
12. Remove stabilizer bar from righthand side of vehicle.
13. Reverse procedure to install.

TENSION STRUT
REPLACE

1. Raise and support vehicle, then remove wheel assembly.
2. Remove and discard lower control arm ball stud cotter pin.
3. Loosen but do not remove lefthand lower control arm ball stud castle nut.
4. **On lefthand side of vehicle,** proceed as follows:
   a. Separate lower control arm from steering knuckle using lower con-

trol arm ball stud separator tool No. SA-9132-S, or equivalent. **Do not use pickle fork or a wedge type tool.**
   b. Remove lower control arm ball joint castle nut.
   c. Remove lefthand front inner fender splash shield.
   d. Remove lower control arm to cradle mounting nut and bolt.
5. **On righthand side of vehicle,** turn wheel lefthand for access, then remove tension strut to lower control arm mounting nut and washer.
6. **On both sides of vehicle,** remove tension strut to cradle bracket mounting bolts.
7. Remove tension strut and lefthand control arm.
8. Remove control arm to tension strut mounting nut and washer, then separate.
9. Reverse procedure to install.

TIE ROD
REPLACE
Inner

1. Raise and support vehicle, then remove wheel assemblies.
2. Remove outer tie rod to inner tie rod locknut.
3. Remove steering gear.
4. Remove outer tie rod from inner tie rod.
5. Remove outer tie rod locknut.
6. Remove steering gear boot.
7. Slide shock dampner toward steering gear and remove from inner tie rod.
8. Remove inner tie rod, noting the following:
   a. **Hold steering gear rack using suitable wrench on rack teeth.**
   b. **Protect teeth with suitable shop cloth.**
   c. When removing righthand inner tie rod it may be required to remove lefthand side boot to access teeth.
9. Reverse procedure to install, noting the following:
   a. Apply Loctite No. 262, or equivalent, evenly to inner tie rod threads.
   b. Install inner tie rod using tool No. SA-9209-C, or equivalent.

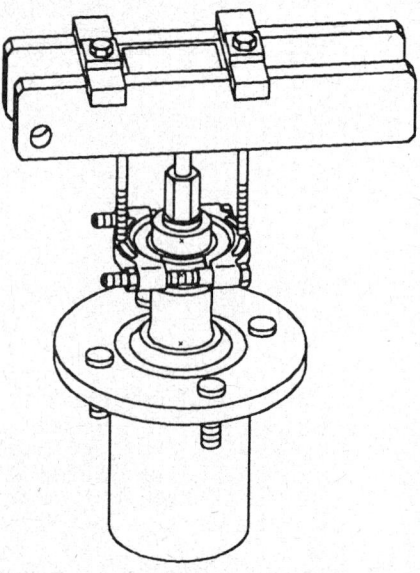

Fig. 4 Inner bearing race removal. L-Series & S-Series

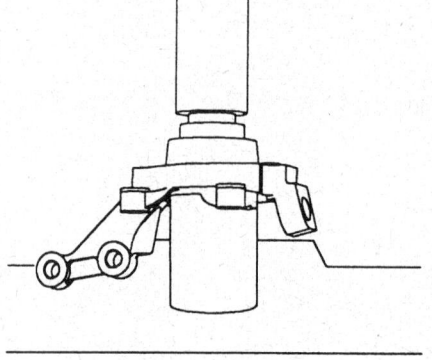

Fig. 5 Bearing removal. L-Series & S-Series

Fig. 6 Belt spring tension relief. S-Series

Outer

1. Raise and support vehicle, then remove front wheels.
2. Loosen outer tie rod to inner tie rod jam nut, then remove tie rod to steering knuckle nut and discard.
3. Separate outer tie rod from steering knuckle using tool No. SA91100C or equivalent.
4. Remove outer tie rod from inner tie rod, record number of turns used in removal for installation reference.
5. Remove outer to inner tie rod jam nut and discard.
6. Reverse procedure to install.

POWER STEERING GEAR

REPLACE

ION

1. Turn steering wheel to straight ahead position, then lock steering column in place.
2. Raise and support vehicle, then remove front wheels.
3. Remove steering gear to intermediate shaft pinch bolt and discard.
4. Disconnect intermediate shaft from steering gear.
5. Remove both steering gear outer tie rod to knuckle nuts and discard nuts.
6. Separate outer tie rods from steering knuckles using tool No. SA91100C or equivalent.
7. Remove steering gear mounting bolts, then the steering gear through lefthand wheel opening.
8. Reverse procedure to install.

L-Series

Rotating steering wheel while it is dis-

connected from the steering gear may damage SIR coil.

1. Remove pinch bolt and disconnect intermediate shaft from steering gear.
2. **On models equipped with 3.0L engine,** remove rear exhaust manifold heat shield.
3. **On all models,** remove rear transaxle mount through bolt and transaxle mount to frame bolt.
4. Place suitable drain container under steering gear pressure and return hoses.
5. Remove power steering gear hoses and allow fluid to drain.
6. Raise and support vehicle, then remove wheel assemblies.
7. Remove righthand front lower splash shield.
8. **On models equipped with 3.0L engine,** remove exhaust manifold pipe and remaining transaxle mount to frame bolts.
9. **On all models,** remove and discard tie rod end torque prevailing nuts.
10. Separate tie rod end from steering knuckle using tie rod end separator tool No. SA-91100-C, or equivalent.
11. Remove steering gear to frame mounting bolts and steering gear heat shield.
12. Remove stabilizer bar links from strut and front suspension supports.
13. Loosen remaining mounting bolts until there is enough clearance to remove gear through lefthand side wheel opening.
14. Remove steering gear.
15. Reverse procedure to install.

S-Series

1. Raise and support vehicle.
2. Remove and discard tie rod end cotter pins.
3. Remove tie rod end to knuckle castle nuts.
4. Remove tie rod end from steering knuckle using tie rod separator tool No. SA-91100-C, or equivalent. **Do not separate joint using pickle fork or a wedge type tool.**
5. Remove lefthand inner fender splash shield.
6. Loosen intermediate shaft cover from steering gear.
7. Raise slightly and remove pinch bolt.

8. Disconnect power steering pressure switch, then place suitable drain container under pressure and return hoses.
9. Disconnect pressure and return hoses and allow system to drain.
10. Remove mounting bolts and steering gear through lefthand fenderwell.
11. Reverse procedure to install, noting the following:
    a. Install new steering gear mounting nuts.
    b. Apply Loctite 242, or equivalent, to pinch bolt.

POWER STEERING PUMP

REPLACE

ION

1. Remove power steering pump reservoir fill cap.
2. Place suitable container under power steering hoses at steering gear.
3. Remove steering gear power hoses and allow to drain. **Do not rotate steering wheel.**
4. Remove pressure and return hoses at power steering pump, then pump to cylinder head bolts.
5. Remove pump.
6. Reverse procedure to install.

L-Series

2.2L ENGINE

1. Remove power steering pump reservoir fill cap.
2. Place suitable container under power steering hoses at steering gear.
3. Remove steering gear power hoses and allow to drain. **Do not rotate steering wheel.**
4. Remove pressure and return hoses at power steering pump, then pump to cylinder head bolts.
5. Remove pump.
6. Reverse procedure to install.

3.0L ENGINE

1. Remove air cleaner and power steering pulley bolts.

2. Remove accessory drive belt and power steering pump pulley.
3. Place suitable container under power steering pump.
4. Remove power steering pump pressure and return hoses, allow to drain.
5. Remove bracket mounting bolts and power steering pump.
6. Reverse procedure to install.

S-Series

1. Remove power steering pump reservoir fill cap.
2. Raise and support vehicle.
3. Place drain container under steering gear hoses.
4. Remove steering gear hoses and allow system to drain. **Do not rotate steering wheel.**
5. Mark running direction, then relieve spring tension from accessory drive belt using suitable box end wrench and remove belt, **Fig. 6.**
6. **On models equipped with DOHC engine,** remove pump to intake manifold and pump to engine block brackets.
7. **On all models,** remove pump to engine block mounting bolts.
8. Raise pump and disconnect EVO electrical connector.
9. Remove pump and hose assembly, then the hoses.
10. Reverse procedure to install.

MANUAL STEERING GEAR

REPLACE

1. Raise and support vehicle, then remove front wheel assemblies.
2. Remove and discard tie rod end cotter pins.
3. Remove tie rod end from steering knuckle using tie rod separator tool No. SA-91100-C, or equivalent. **Do not separate joint using pickle fork or a wedge type tool.**
4. Remove lefthand inner fender splash shield.
5. Loosen intermediate shaft cover from steering gear.
6. Raise slightly and remove pinch bolt.
7. Remove mounting bolts and steering gear cradle through lefthand fenderwell.
8. Reverse procedure to install, noting the following:
   a. Install new steering gear mounting nuts.
   b. Apply Loctite 242, or equivalent, to pinch bolt.

TECHNICAL SERVICE BULLETINS

Steering Wheel Shake Or Vibration

2001 S-SERIES

On some of these models, built before VIN YY697119, there may be a steering wheel shake or vibration at highway speeds, possibly caused by vehicle sensitivity to out-of-balance tire and wheel assemblies.

To correct this condition, ensure tire and wheel assemblies are balanced within .1 ounce or less, and replace front lower control arm rear bushings as follows:

1. Remove righthand frame lower splash shield.
2. Remove ball stud bolt and nut.
3. Separate ball stud from steering knuckle using suitable pry bar. **Do not damage ABS speed sensor ring.**
4. Remove mounting bolts and lower control arm. Discard bolts.
5. Press out rear control arm bushings using bushing removal tools Nos. KM-907-21, KM-907-22 and KM-671, or equivalents.
6. Install new, updated bushings part No. 22671497 with notched cutout areas aligned with front lower control arm weld flanges using bushing installer tools Nos. KM-907-23, KM-907-24 and KM-671, or equivalents.
7. Ensure bushing is fully pressed and seated in control arm.
8. Install control arm using new bolts part No. 11096192. Hand tighten.
9. Install ball stud to steering knuckle using new bolt part No. 90496191 and nut part No. 90538057. **Torque** to 75 ft. lbs.
10. Place suitable support stand under ball joint area.
11. Load control arm until there is gap between hoist contact pad and vehicle frame.
12. **Torque** front lower control arm bolts to 65 ft. lbs., then rotate an additional 75°.
13. Remove support stand and install lower splash shield.
14. Vehicle front end wheel alignment is not required.

TIGHTENING SPECIFICATIONS

Year	Component	Torque/ Ft. Lbs.
ION		
2003–05	Ball Joint To Control Arm	50
	Ball Joint To Steering Knuckle	④
	Control Arm To Front Frame	41
	Control Arm To Rear Frame	74②
	Intermediate Shaft Pinch	25
	Outer Tie Rod	15②
	Stabilizer Shaft Clamp	37
	Stabilizer Link To Strut	48
	Stabilizer Shaft Link To Bar	63
	Steering Gear	81
	Strut To Steering Knuckle	89
	Strut Cap To Body	81
	Strut Shaft	52
	Transaxle Mount To Frame	37
	Transaxle Through Bolt	74
	Wheel Bearing/Hub To Knuckle	85
	Wheel Driveshaft Nut	81
	Wheel Lug Nuts	100

Continued

TIGHTENING
SPECIFICATIONS—Continued

Year	Component	Torque/ Ft. Lbs.
L-SERIES		
2001–05	ABS Sensor Bracket To Knuckle	72
	Caliper Bracket To Knuckle	70
	Control Arm To Frame	65
	Frame To Body	66
	Inner Tie Rod To Steering Gear	70
	Intermediate Shaft To Steering Column	20
	Intermediate Shaft To Steering Gear	20
	Power Steering High Pressure Line	20
	Power Steering Pump Pulley	15
	Power Steering Pump To Bracket	15
	Power Steering Pump To Engine	18
	Stabilizer Bar To Link	50
	Steering Wheel Nut	26
	Strut Shaft To Body	40
	Strut Shaft To Mount	40
	Strut To Steering Knuckle	①
	Wheel Lug Nut (2001–02)	100
	Wheel Lug Nut (2003–05)	③
S-SERIES		
2001–02	ABS Electrical Connector Bracket	72
	Axle To Hub Nut	148
	Ball Joint Stud Castle Nut	55
	Brake Dust Shield	18
	Caliper Bracket To Knuckle	81
	Control Arm To Cradle, Bolt	92
	Control Arm To Cradle, Nut	74
	Control Arm To Tension Strut	106
	Hub To Driveshaft Nut	148
	Inner Tie Rod	70
	Intermediate Shaft To Steering Gear Pinch Bolt	35
	Power Steering Pressure & Return Line Fittings	20
	Power Steering Pump Bracket	28
	Pump To Engine Block	28
	Pump To Intake Manifold Bracket (DOHC)	22
	Steering Gear Cradle	37
	Strut Shaft Nut	37
	Strut To Body	21
	Strut To Steering Knuckle	126
	Tension Strut Bracket To Cradle	103
	Tie Rod End To Steering Knuckle	33
	Upper Strut Mount	21
	Wheel Lug Nuts	100

DOHC — Dual Overhead Cam.
① — Torque strut to knuckle mounting bolts, first to 37 ft. lbs., then to 73 ft. lbs., On 2001–02 models, rotate an additional 30–45°. On 2003–05 models, rotate an additional 30–40°.
② — Rotate an additional 180°.
③ — First step, 46 ft. lbs.; second step, 92 ft. lbs.
④ — First step, torque to 37 ft. lbs.; second step, loosen nut ¾ turn; third step, torque to 37 ft. lbs.; fourth step, rotate an additional 30°.

Wheel Alignment

INDEX

PRELIMINARY INSPECTION

1. Inspect tires for proper inflation, wear pattern or out of round condition.
2. Inspect suspension and steering components for wear and damage.
3. Inspect strut bushings for wear or damage.
4. Inspect vehicle ride height as outlined under "Vehicle Ride Height."
5. Road test vehicle.
6. Wheel alignment should be performed in the following order:
   a. Rear camber.
   b. Rear toe.
   c. Righthand front camber and caster.
   d. Lefthand front camber and caster.
   e. Front toe.

FRONT WHEEL ALIGNMENT

Rear wheel alignment must be set to specifications before front alignment adjustment.

L-Series

CASTER

Front wheel caster is non adjustable on these vehicles. These angles can be measured but are set by design of the front suspension.

CAMBER

1. Raise and support vehicle, then remove wheel assemblies.
2. Remove strut to knuckle mounting bolts and discard.
3. Remove material from strut bracket lower hole using suitable file or grinder, **Fig. 1.**
4. To increase negative camber, remove from outside hole. To increase positive camber, remove from inside hole.
5. **Torque** strut to knuckle mounting bolts, first to 37 ft. lbs., then to 73 ft. lbs.
6. **On 2001–02 models,** rotate bolts an additional 30–45°.
7. **On 2003–05 models,** rotate bolts an additional 30–40°.
8. **On 2001–02 models, torque** wheel lug nuts to 100 ft. lbs.

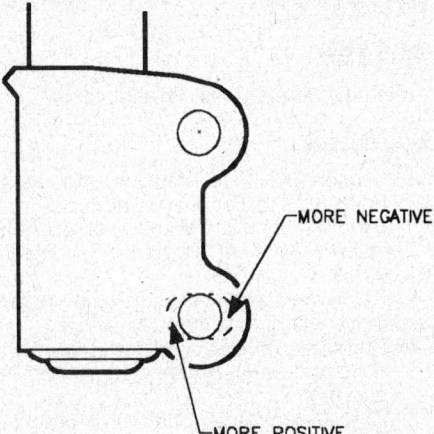

Fig. 1 Front & rear camber adjustment

9. **On 2003–05 models, torque** wheel lug nuts, first to 46 ft. lbs., then to 92 ft. lbs.
10. **On all models,** lower the vehicle, then inspect camber angle. Adjust as required.

TOE-IN

1. Lock steering wheel in straight ahead position.
2. Loosen both inner tie rod jam nuts and inner tie rod seal to boot surface. **Ensure tie rods rotate freely from boot seal surface. Do not allow boot to rotate.**
3. Use a suitable wrench on tie rod flats to adjust toe angle to specifications.
4. **Torque** inner tie rod end jam nuts to 44 ft. lbs.
5. Inspect toe angle and adjust if required.

ION

CASTER

Front wheel caster is non adjustable on these vehicles. These angles can be measured but are set by design of the front suspension.

CAMBER

1. Loosen both strut to knuckle nuts just enough to allow for movement.

2. Disconnect strut from knuckle.
3. File lower hole out to groove of stamped ring around hole.
4. Connect strut to knuckle.
5. Adjust camber by moving top of wheel in or out.

TOE-IN

1. Lock steering wheel in straight ahead position.
2. Loosen tie rod jam nut.
3. Adjust toe by turning adjuster.
4. **Torque** tie rod jam nut to 50 ft. lbs.

S-Series

CASTER

1. Lock steering wheel in straight ahead position.
2. Remove and discard upper strut mount mounting nuts.
3. Slide strut forward or rearward to adjust caster. Movement of approximately .157 inch will change caster by approximately ½°.
4. Body attachment holes may need to be filed or ground into oval slots to allow enough front to rear strut movement to adjust caster to specifications. **Do not exceed .354 inch in slot width.**
5. **Torque** new upper strut mount mounting nuts to 21 ft. lbs.
6. Inspect caster angle.

CAMBER

1. Lock steering wheel in straight ahead position.
2. Loosen strut to knuckle mounting bolts, then pull or push to adjust.
3. If more than 1½° of camber is required, inspect for bent suspension components.
4. Raise and support vehicle, then remove wheel assembly.
5. Remove strut to knuckle mounting bolts and separate knuckle from strut bracket.
6. Remove material from strut bracket lower hole using suitable file or grinder, **Fig. 1.**
7. To increase negative camber, remove from outside hole. To increase positive camber, remove from inside hole.
8. **Torque** strut to knuckle mounting bolts to 126 ft. lbs.
9. **Torque** wheel lug nuts to 100 ft. lbs.

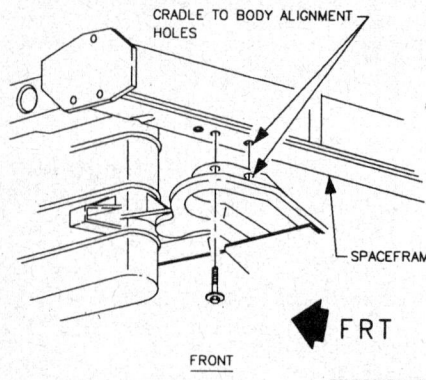

Fig. 2 Cradle alignment. S-Series

10. Inspect camber setting and lower vehicle.

TOE-IN

Refer to "L-Series" for adjustment procedures.

CRADLE

Inspect cradle to body alignment at two alignment holes using ⁵⁄₁₆ inch rod, **Fig. 2.** If cradle to body alignment is improper, loosen cradle mounting bolts and align cradle to body.

REAR WHEEL ALIGNMENT
L-Series

Rear wheel alignment involves setting the toe angle. Rear wheel camber is not adjustable.

TOE-IN

1. Remove and discard rear axle control arm bolts.
2. Install new bolts. **Do not tighten just yet.** Leave inside forward bolt out.
3. Move rear axle control arm in direction of required toe correction using rear toe adjusting tool No. KM-900, or equivalent.
4. Snug rear axle control arm bolts. **Do not tighten just yet.**
5. Inspect toe. Adjust as required.
6. **Torque** rear axle control arm bolts to 65 ft. lbs., then rotate an additional 30–45°.
7. Repeat procedure for other rear wheel.

S-Series
CASTER

Rear wheel caster is not adjustable.

CAMBER

1. Loosen strut to knuckle mounting bolts, then pull or push to adjust.
2. If more than 1½° of camber is desired, inspect for bent suspension components.
3. Raise and support vehicle, then remove wheel assembly.
4. Remove strut to knuckle mounting bolts and separate knuckle from strut bracket.
5. Remove material from strut bracket lower hole using suitable file or grinder, **Fig. 1.**
6. To increase negative camber, remove from outside hole, to increase positive camber, remove from inside hole.

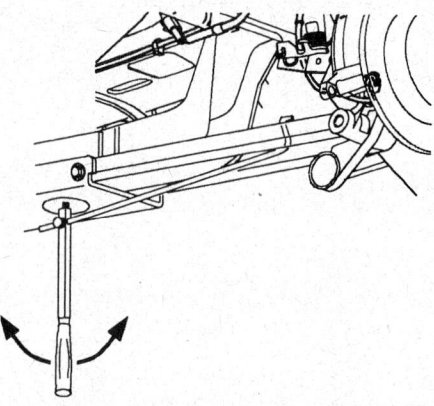

Fig. 3 Rear toe adjustment. S-Series

7. **Torque** strut to knuckle mounting bolts to 126 ft. lbs.
8. **Torque** wheel lug nuts to 100 ft. lbs.
9. Inspect camber setting and lower vehicle.

TOE-IN

1. Loosen rearmost lateral link to crossmember mounting bolts.
2. Move lateral link to adjust using rear toe adjusting tool No. SA-9158-C, or equivalent, **Fig. 3.**
3. **Torque** lateral link to 89 ft. lbs.
4. Inspect toe.
5. Repeat procedure for other wheel.

XLR

NOTE: Refer To The Rear Of This Manual For Manufacturer's Special Service Tool Supplies.

INDEX OF SERVICE OPERATIONS

Specifications

GENERAL ENGINE SPECIFICATIONS

Engine Liter/VIN Code①	Fuel System	Bore & Stroke	Compression Ratio	Net H.P. @ RPM②	Maximum Torque Ft. Lbs. @ RPM	Normal Oil Pressure, psi
4.6L/A	SFI	3.66 X 3.31	10.5	320 @ 6400	310 @ 4400	③

① — Eighth digit of VIN denotes engine code.

② — Ratings are net-as installed in vehicle.

③ — 5 psi @ idle speed, 35 psi @ 2000 RPM.

TUNE UP SPECIFICATIONS

| Engine Liter/VIN Code① | Spark Plug Gap | Ignition Timing | | Idle Speed | Fuel Pump Pressure, psi④ | Valve Clearance, Inch |
		Firing Order	Wire Connections Fig.			
4.6L/A	.050	②	—	⑤	55–62	③

① — Eighth digit of VIN denotes engine code.

② — Cylinder numbering from lefthand side to righthand side as viewed from front of vehicle, front bank 2, 4, 6, 8; rear bank 1, 3, 5, 7. Firing order, 1-2-7-3-4-5-6-8.

③ — Equipped w/hydraulic valve lifters; no adjustment required.

④ — With shop towel wrapped around fuel pressure gauge & fuel pressure test port to prevent spillage, connect fuel pressure gauge to fuel pressure test port. Inspect fuel pressure w/ignition key in On position and engine not running.

⑤ — Idle speed is controlled by a throttle actuator motor.

FRONT WHEEL ALIGNMENT SPECIFICATIONS

| Year | Model | Caster Angle, Degrees | | Camber Angle, Degrees | | Total Toe, Degree | Steering Angle, Degrees | Ball Joint Wear |
		Limits	Desired	Limits	Desired			
2004–05	All	+7.5 to +8.5	+8	-1.0 to 0	-.5	-.10 to +.3	-1 to +1	①

① — Refer to "Ball Joint Inspection" in "Front Suspension & Steering" section.

REAR WHEEL ALIGNMENT SPECIFICATIONS

| Year | Model | Camber Angle, Degrees | | Total Toe, Degrees | Thrust Angle, Degrees |
		Limits	Desired		
2004–05	All	-1.0 to 0	-.5	-.2 to +.2	-.1 to +.1

VEHICLE RIDE HEIGHT SPECIFICATIONS

Model	Year	Body Style	Manufacturer's Original Tire Size	Measurement Points & Specifications①					
				Front			Rear		
				Dim.	Specification		Dim.	Specification	
					Inches	mm		Inches	mm
XLR	2004–05	All	②	Z	1.48–1.98	37.6–50.4	D	4.0–4.5	101.6–114.4

Dim. — Dimension.

D Dim. — Rear suspension measurement from front outboard control arm bolt center line to bottom of control arm ball joint, **Fig. A**.

Z Dim. — Front suspension measurement from front pivot bolt center line to lowest point of ball joint, **Fig. B**.

① — Measurement is with fuel, radiator coolant and engine oil full, spare tire, jack, hand tools and mats in designated positions and tires properly inflated.

② — See door sticker or inside of glove compartment for manufacturers original tire size specifications.

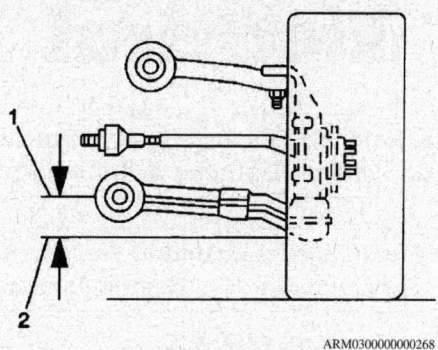

ARM0300000000268

Fig. A   Rear "D" dimension trim height inspection

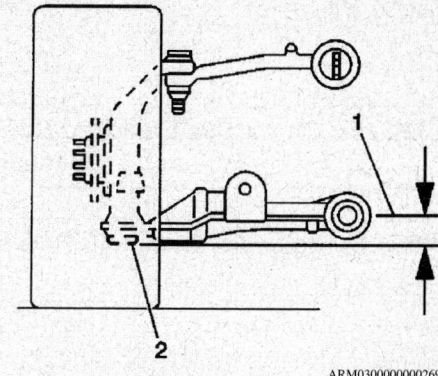

ARM0300000000269

Fig. B   Front "Z" dimension trim height inspection

FLUID CAPACITIES & COOLING SYSTEM DATA

Model	Engine Liter/VIN Code①	Coolant Capacity, Qts.	Coolant Type	Radiator Cap Relief Pressure, Lbs.	Thermo Opening Temp.	Fuel Tank, Gallons	Engine Oil Refill, Qts. ③	Auto Transaxle, Qts.
XLR	4.6L/A	14.8	DEX-COOL②	15	188	18.5	8.0	9.5

① — Eighth digit of VIN denotes engine code.
② — DEX-COOL, or equivalent, silicant-free antifreeze conforming to GM specification No. 6277M.
③ — With filter change.

LUBRICANT DATA

Year	Model	Lubricant Type			
		Automatic Transaxle	Power Steering System	Rear Differential	Brake System
2004–05	All	Dexron III	GM Part No. 89021184	75W-90 Synthetic GM Part No. 12378261	DOT 3

Electrical

NOTE: On Air Bag Equipped Models, Refer To "Air Bag System Precautions" Located In The Front Of This Manual For System Disarming & Arming Procedures.

NOTE: Refer To "Computer Relearn Procedures" Located In The Front Of This Manual When Battery Power To The Computer Has Been Interrupted.

INDEX

PRECAUTIONS

Air Bag Systems

Refer to "Air Bag System Precautions" in the front of this manual for system disarming and arming procedures.

Battery Ground Cable

Prior to service, disconnect battery ground cable and isolate as required.

FUSE PANEL & FLASHER LOCATION

The instrument panel fuse block is located in the righthand footwell, mounted on the toe board, behind the carpet. The underhood fuse block is located on the righthand side of the engine compartment. The turn signal and hazard flasher operation is controlled by the Body Control Module (BCM), the BCM is located in the righthand footwell, mounted on the toe board, behind the carpet.

FUEL PUMP RELAY LOCATION

Fuel pump operation is controlled by the fuel pump control module. The module is mounted on a brace in the lefthand side rear quarter panel, on the side of the fuel filler neck.

RELAY CENTER LOCATION

The instrument panel righthand relay

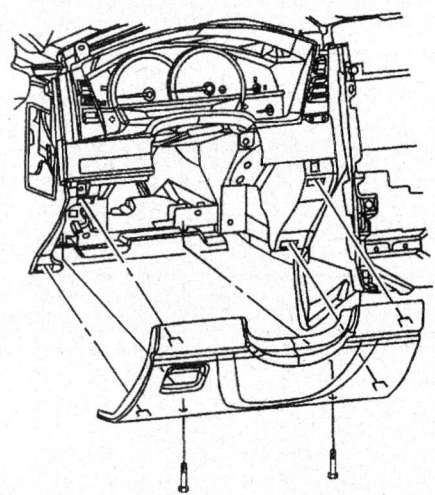

ARM0300000000292

Fig. 1   Driver knee bolster removal

block is located in the righthand footwell, mounted on the toe board, behind the carpet.

STARTER
REPLACE

1. Remove intake manifold as outlined under "Intake Manifold, Replace" in "4.6L Engine" section.
2. Disconnect starter solenoid "S" and battery terminals electrical connectors.
3. Remove mounting bolts and starter.
4. Reverse procedure to install, noting the following:
   a. **Torque** starter mounting bolts to 22 ft. lbs.

b. **Torque** "S" terminal nut to 35 inch lbs.
c. **Torque** battery terminal nut to 89 inch lbs.

ALTERNATOR
REPLACE

1. Rotate drive belt tensioner and remove drive belt.
2. Raise and support vehicle, then drain cooling system.
3. Remove tire and wheel assemblies.
4. Loosen, do not remove, outer tie rod end stud nut from outer tie rod end ball stud.
5. Loosen outer tie rod end stud to steering knuckle connection using tie rod remover tool No. J 42188, or equivalent.
6. Remove outer tie rod end stud nut and separate tie rod from steering knuckle.
7. Loosen jam nut on inner tie rod assembly, then remove outer tie rod end from inner tie rod assembly.
8. Disconnect Electronic Suspension Control (ESC) sensor links.
9. Remove stabilizer shaft link nuts from stabilizer shaft.
10. Remove stabilizer shaft insulator clamps from front crossmember, then the stabilizer shaft from vehicle
11. Turn steering wheel far enough to lefthand side to gain access to intermediate shaft bolts, then place ignition in locked position.
12. Remove upper to lower intermediate shaft bolts, then the lower coupling shield.
13. Remove lower coupling pinch bolt, then the lower coupling from steering gear.
14. Slide lower intermediate shaft from

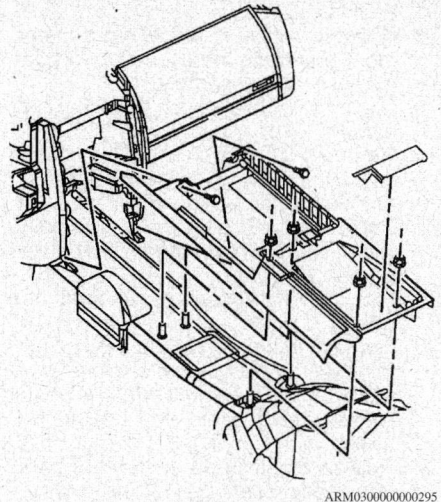

Fig. 2 Console removal

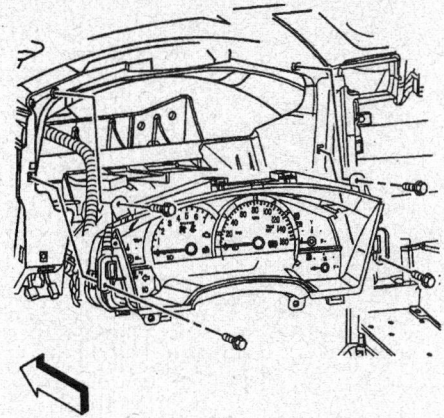

Fig. 3 Instrument cluster removal

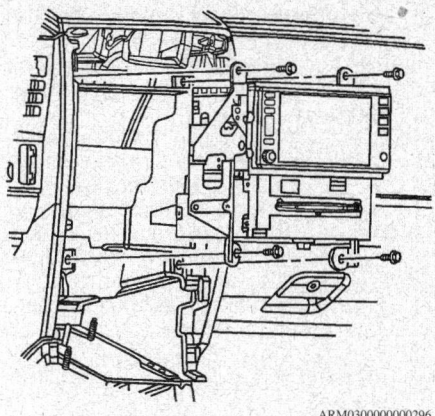

Fig. 4 Radio removal

upper intermediate shaft and remove lower intermediate shaft from vehicle.
15. Remove bolts from Electronic Brake Control Module/Brake Pressure Modulator Valve (EBCM/BPMV) bracket.
16. Support and reposition EBCM/BPMV and bracket away from crossmember.
17. Remove power steering gear mounting bolts.
18. Remove power steering fluid cooler from crossmember.
19. Lift power steering gear off of crossmember and support.
20. Remove transverse spring from vehicle.
21. Remove lower shock absorber bolts from lower control arms.
22. Remove lower control arm bolts from crossmember.
23. Place a transmission jack under crossmember, then remove engine mount lower nuts.
24. Disconnect wheel speed sensor wiring harness from crossmember.
25. Disconnect electrical harness and brake pipe from clips on crossmember.
26. Remove crossmember mounting nuts, then lower crossmember from vehicle.
27. Remove bolt from alternator coolant hose assembly on alternator.
28. Disconnect alternator coolant hose assembly from alternator stud.
29. Slide boot back along cable, then remove starter cable nut.
30. Remove starter cable terminal from stud.
31. Remove upper alternator mounting bolt.
32. Remove idler pulley thru-bolt and nut.
33. Remove idler pulley assembly, then the alternator.
34. Reverse procedure to install.

IGNITION COILS

REPLACE

1. Remove fuel injector sight shield from top of engine.
2. Disconnect ignition coil wiring harness connector.
3. Remove ignition coil retaining bolt, then the coil.

4. Reverse procedure to install.

IGNITION LOCK

REPLACE

1. Remove steering wheel as outlined under "Steering Wheel, Replace."
2. Pry fuel door and rear compartment lid release switch from knee bolster, then disconnect switch electrical connectors.
3. Remove driver knee bolster trim panel lower retaining screws, **Fig. 1.**
4. Grasp knee bolster trim panel at side edges, then remove trim panel by pulling firmly to release locking tabs.
5. Remove lower steering column trim cover retaining screws.
6. Disconnect closeout shroud from steering column lower trim cover.
7. Disconnect steering column power tilt and telescopic switch electrical connectors.
8. Remove lower trim cover from steering column.
9. Remove steering column upper trim cover retaining screw.
10. Lift upper trim cover to gain access to the lock cylinder access hole.
11. Insert tip of a suitable bent tip awl into ignition lock cylinder access hole.
12. Turn ignition lock cylinder to the START position, then push bent tip awl down on lock cylinder retaining pin.
13. Turn ignition lock cylinder to the RUN position and remove from steering column.
14. Reverse procedure to install.

IGNITION SWITCH

REPLACE

1. Pry fuel door and rear compartment lid release switch from knee bolster, then disconnect switch electrical connectors.
2. Remove driver knee bolster trim panel lower retaining screws, **Fig. 1.**
3. Grasp knee bolster trim panel at side edges, then remove trim panel by pulling firmly to release locking tabs.
4. Carefully pry instrument panel courtesy lamp assembly from lefthand side

lower closeout panel using a suitable flat-bladed tool.
5. Insert instrument panel courtesy lamp assembly up through opening in closeout panel.
6. Release notch in righthand side forward edge of closeout panel from tab on accelerator pedal bracket, then remove closeout panel.
7. Remove retaining screws from bottom of Driver Information Center (DIC) switch pad.
8. Pull outward on DIC switch pad to disengage retaining clip, then disconnect switch pad electrical connectors.
9. Remove DIC switch retaining screws, then the switch.
10. Disconnect ignition switch electrical connector, then remove ignition switch from DIC pod.
11. Reverse procedure to install.

NEUTRAL SAFETY SWITCH

REPLACE

On these models, the transmission range function is controlled by the transmission manual shift shaft switch. The switch, which is mounted on the side of the transmission case, inputs the Park/Neutral position to the Transmission Control Module (TCM). The TCM will then input this signal to the Powertrain Control Module (PCM). The PCM based on this signal will allow the engine to start.

STOP LIGHT SWITCH

REPLACE

Brake lamp operation is controlled by the Body Control Module (BCM). The BCM uses an input signal from the brake pedal position sensor to determine when the brake lamps should operate. Use the following procedure to replace the brake pedal position sensor.

1. Carefully pry instrument panel courtesy lamp assembly from lefthand side lower closeout panel using a suitable flat-bladed tool.
2. Remove push-on retaining nut from steering column bracket stud.
3. Release lefthand side lower closeout

panel to instrument panel lower support beam push-in retainers.

4. Insert instrument panel courtesy lamp assembly up through opening in close-out panel.

5. Release notch in righthand side forward edge of closeout panel from tab on accelerator pedal bracket, then lower and remove closeout panel.

6. Disengage but do not remove Connector Position Assurance (CPA) from brake pedal position sensor connector.

7. Disconnect brake pedal position sensor electrical connector.

8. Remove brake pedal position sensor retaining screw, then the sensor from bracket.

9. Reverse procedure to install.

MULTI-FUNCTION SWITCH
REPLACE

1. Remove steering wheel as outlined under "Steering Wheel, Replace."

2. Pry fuel door and rear compartment lid release switch from knee bolster, then disconnect switch electrical connectors.

3. Remove driver knee bolster trim panel lower retaining screws, **Fig. 1.**

4. Grasp knee bolster trim panel at side edges, then remove trim panel by pulling firmly to release locking tabs.

5. Remove lower steering column trim cover retaining screws.

6. Disconnect closeout shroud from steering column lower trim cover.

7. Disconnect steering column power tilt and telescopic switch electrical connectors.

8. Remove lower trim cover from steering column.

9. Remove steering column upper trim cover retaining screw.

10. Remove lock cylinder from steering column as outlined under "Ignition Lock, Replace."

11. Remove upper trim cover from steering column.

12. Remove multi-function switch retaining screws.

13. Disconnect multi-function switch electrical connectors, then remove switch from steering column.

14. Reverse procedure to install.

STEERING WHEEL
REPLACE

1. Remove air bag module from steering wheel.

2. Disconnect horn electrical connector.

3. Insert steering column lock pin tool No. J 42640, or equivalent, into steering column.

4. Remove and discard steering wheel retaining nut.

5. Remove steering wheel from steering column using steering wheel puller tool No. J 1859-A, or equivalent.

6. Reverse procedure to install. **Torque** new steering wheel retaining nut to 30 ft. lbs.

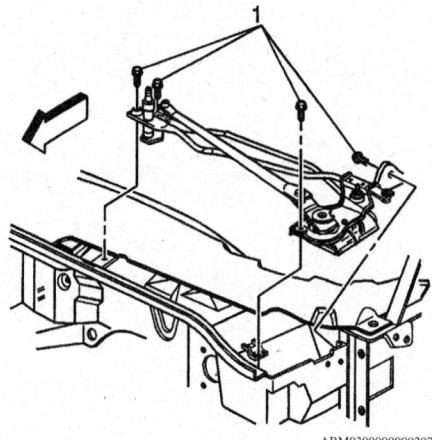

Fig. 5   Wiper drive system module removal

ARM0300000000297

INSTRUMENT CLUSTER
REPLACE

1. Remove shifter knob, then open center console door.

2. Remove hinge cover from console bin, then pull at rear of cover to disengage retainer.

3. Remove console cupholder, ashtray and trim plate.

4. Remove console retaining nuts, **Fig. 2.**

5. Remove front of console to instrument panel carrier retaining bolts.

6. Lift rear of console slightly and pull rearward to release front of console from under instrument panel carrier.

7. Disconnect accessory plug electrical connector.

8. Remove accessory plug retainer from housing, then the housing from console.

9. Disengage lamp from retainer using a suitable flat-bladed tool.

10. Push lamp through hole in console bin, then remove console from vehicle.

11. Pry fuel door and rear compartment lid release switch from knee bolster, then disconnect switch electrical connectors.

12. Remove driver knee bolster trim panel lower retaining screws, **Fig. 1.**

13. Grasp knee bolster trim panel at side edges, then remove trim panel by pulling firmly to release locking tabs.

14. Carefully pry instrument panel courtesy lamp assembly from lefthand side lower closeout panel using a suitable flat-bladed tool.

15. Insert instrument panel courtesy lamp assembly up through opening in closeout panel.

16. Release notch in righthand side forward edge of closeout panel from tab on accelerator pedal bracket, then remove closeout panel.

17. Remove retaining screws from bottom of Driver Information Center (DIC) switch pad.

18. Pull outward on DIC switch pad to disengage retaining clip, then disconnect switch pad electrical connectors.

19. Remove DIC switch retaining screws, then the switch.

20. Remove retaining screw from instrument panel dimmer/Head-Up Display (HUD) switch assembly.

21. Disconnect HUD switch electrical connector.

22. Remove HUD switch to bezel retaining screws, then the switch from bezel.

23. Manually open folding top.

24. Pull windshield side garnish molding with its retainers from windshield frame.

25. Remove instrument panel side trim panels.

26. Remove instrument panel trim pad retaining screws. Screws are located at each end of instrument panel, in center of instrument panel and behind DIC switch.

27. Pull up carefully on instrument panel trim pad to disengage retaining clips.

28. Disconnect sunload/twilight sensor from trim pad, then remove trim pad from vehicle.

29. Carefully lift HUD electrical harness from between instrument panel cluster and HUD.

30. Disconnect HUD electrical connector from cluster.

31. Remove cluster to steering column bracket retaining screws, **Fig. 3.**

32. Raise rear of cluster slightly, then disconnect cluster electrical connector.

33. Remove cluster from vehicle.

34. Reverse procedure to install.

RADIO
REPLACE

1. Remove cover from instrument panel electrical center.

2. Remove RDO/CD MiniFuse from electrical center.

3. Remove center console trim plate.

4. Pull top edge of instrument panel accessory trim plate rearward to disengage retaining clips.

5. Disconnect hazard flasher switch electrical connector.

6. Remove hazard flasher switch from trim plate.

7. Remove radio control to instrument panel center support bracket retaining screws, **Fig. 4.**

8. Pull radio rearward and disconnect electrical/audio and coaxial cable connectors from radio.

9. Remove radio from instrument panel.

10. Reverse procedure to install.

WIPER MOTOR
REPLACE

1. Turn ignition switch to ACCY position and wiper switch to DELAY position.

2. Turn ignition switch OFF when wiper arms are in mid-wipe position.

3. Place a piece of masking tape onto windshield at tip of each wiper blade for installation reference.

4. Disconnect washer hose from air inlet grille panel.

5. Remove wiper arm nut cover, then the wiper arm nut.

6. Grasp wiper arm at hinged joint, then

remove arm from shaft by applying a rocking motion toward windshield to loosen arm.

7. Remove air inlet grille panel push-in retainers.
8. Disconnect washer hose connector.
9. Remove air inlet grille panel to fender retainers, then the grille panel from the vehicle.
10. Separate wiper transmission from wiper motor crank arm using wiper linkage separator tool No. J 39232, or equivalent.
11. Remove wiper drive system module mounting screws, then the wiper drive system module from plenum, **Fig. 5.**
12. Disconnect wiper motor electrical connector.
13. Remove wiper drive system module from vehicle.
14. Remove the wiper motor mounting screws, then the wiper motor from wiper motor module.
15. Reverse procedure to install.

WIPER SWITCH
REPLACE

1. Remove steering wheel as outlined under "Steering Wheel, Replace."
2. Pry fuel door and rear compartment lid release switch from knee bolster, then disconnect switch electrical connectors.
3. Remove driver knee bolster trim panel lower retaining screws, **Fig. 1.**
4. Grasp knee bolster trim panel at side edges, then remove trim panel by pulling firmly to release locking tabs.
5. Remove lower steering column trim cover retaining screws.
6. Disconnect closeout shroud from steering column lower trim cover.
7. Disconnect steering column power tilt and telescopic switch electrical connectors.
8. Remove lower trim cover from steering column.
9. Disconnect windshield wiper and washer switch assembly.
10. Press on switch locking tabs, then pull switch assembly out of switch mounting bracket.
11. Reverse procedure to install.

BLOWER MOTOR
REPLACE

1. Carefully pry instrument panel courtesy lamp assembly from righthand side lower closeout panel.
2. Remove righthand side lower closeout panel to instrument panel lower support beam push-in retainers.
3. Lower righthand side lower closeout panel slightly, then carefully maneuver lefthand side of closeout panel from above driveline tunnel.
4. Insert courtesy lamp assembly up through closeout panel opening.
5. Remove closeout panel from instrument panel.
6. Disconnect blower motor electrical connector.
7. Remove blower motor retaining

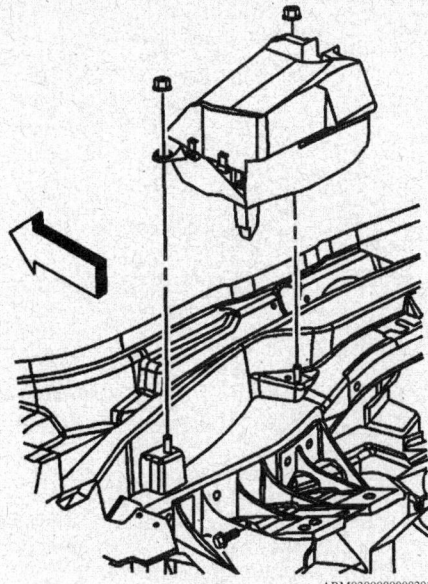

Fig. 6 Head-Up Display (HUD) unit removal

screws, then the blower motor from HVAC module.
8. Reverse procedure to install.

CABIN AIR FILTER
REPLACE

Under normal operating conditions the cabin air filter should be replaced every 12 months or 15,000 miles. In dusty areas change the cabin air filter more often.
1. Open hood.
2. Lift up cabin air filter access cover located on air inlet panel.
3. Remove cabin air filter element from housing.
4. Install new cabin air filter into filter housing.
5. Close cabin air filter access cover.
6. Close hood.

HEATER CORE
REPLACE

1. Recover air conditioning refrigerant as outlined in "Air Conditioning" chapter.
2. Drain cooling system.
3. Remove intake manifold as outlined under "Intake Manifold, Replace" in "Engine" section.
4. Disconnect front evaporator inlet line from the body retaining clip.
5. Disconnect refrigerant pressure sensor electrical connector.
6. Disconnect and remove A/C tube connectors from evaporator rear line assembly. Cap lines to prevent contamination.
7. Disconnect front evaporator inlet line from the evaporator rear line assembly. Remove and discard O-rings.
8. Disconnect A/C compressor line from evaporator rear line assembly. Remove and discard O-rings.
9. Remove heater pipe bracket retaining nut from cowl stud.

10. Remove TXV block fitting nut and disconnect evaporator rear line assembly from TXV.
11. Disconnect evaporator rear line assembly from retainer bracket.
12. Remove rear evaporator line assembly from the vehicle. Remove and discard seal washers.
13. Release and reposition heater inlet and outlet hose clamps.
14. Separate heater hoses from heater pipes. Cap or plug open heater hoses.
15. Remove heater pipe assembly to heater core retaining bolt. **Do not apply excessive force on the heater core pipes during hose removal.**
16. Disconnect heater pipe assembly from the heater pipe bracket retainer.
17. Disconnect heater pipe assembly from heater core.
18. Remove heater pipe assembly from vehicle. Remove and discard sealing washers. Cap or plug heater core.
19. Remove evaporator drain tube from HVAC module.
20. Remove shifter knob, then open center console door.
21. Remove hinge cover from console bin, then pull at rear of cover to disengage retainer.
22. Remove console cupholder, ashtray and trim plate.
23. Remove console retaining nuts, **Fig. 2.**
24. Remove front of console to instrument panel carrier retaining bolts.
25. Lift rear of console slightly and pull rearward to release front of console from under instrument panel carrier.
26. Disconnect accessory plug electrical connector.
27. Remove accessory plug retainer from housing, then the housing from console.
28. Disengage lamp from retainer using a suitable flat-bladed tool.
29. Push lamp through hole in console bin, then remove console from vehicle.
30. Remove radio as outlined under "Radio, Replace."
31. Carefully pry instrument panel courtesy lamp assembly from righthand side lower closeout panel.
32. Remove righthand side lower closeout panel to instrument panel lower support beam push-in retainers.
33. Lower righthand side lower closeout panel slightly, then carefully maneuver lefthand side of closeout panel from above driveline tunnel.
34. Insert courtesy lamp assembly up through closeout panel opening.
35. Remove righthand closeout panel from instrument panel.
36. Pry fuel door and rear compartment lid release switch from knee bolster, then disconnect switch electrical connectors.
37. Remove driver knee bolster trim panel lower retaining screws, **Fig. 1.**
38. Grasp knee bolster trim panel at side edges, then remove trim panel by pulling firmly to release locking tabs.
39. Carefully pry instrument panel courtesy lamp assembly from lefthand side lower closeout panel using a suitable

40. Insert instrument panel courtesy lamp assembly up through opening in close-out panel.
41. Release notch in righthand side forward edge of closeout panel from tab on accelerator pedal bracket, then remove lefthand closeout panel.
42. Open door on instrument panel compartment, then disconnect door dampener.
43. Disconnect instrument panel compartment lamp switch electrical connector.
44. With compartment open, depress both rear corners of compartment and swing compartment down towards floor.
45. Starting at outboard side, release compartment hinge from pin at bottom of door.
46. Slowly pull compartment far enough out of instrument panel to disconnect wiring harness connector from inflatable restraint module switch.
47. Remove instrument panel compartment.
48. Mark location of driver knee bolster bracket for installation reference.
49. Remove driver knee bolster bracket to steering column bracket retaining screws, then the driver knee bolster bracket from instrument panel.
50. Remove retaining screw from bottom of lefthand side trim panel.
51. Pull lefthand side trim panel outward to disengage retaining clips, then disconnect electrical connectors.
52. Remove fastener attaching top of upper trim panel and windshield side garnish molding to hinge pillar.
53. Unsnap hinge pillar upper trim from hinge pillar.
54. Remove lower hinge pillar trim.
55. Manually open folding top.
56. Pull windshield side garnish molding with its retainers from windshield frame.
57. Remove instrument panel trim pad retaining screws. Screws are located at each end of instrument panel, in center of instrument panel and behind DIC switch.
58. Pull up carefully on instrument panel trim pad to disengage retaining clips.
59. Disconnect sunload/twilight sensor from trim pad, then remove trim pad from vehicle.
60. Carefully lift HUD electrical harness from between instrument panel cluster and HUD.
61. Disconnect HUD electrical connector from cluster.
62. Remove cluster to steering column bracket retaining screws.
63. Raise rear of cluster slightly, then dis-

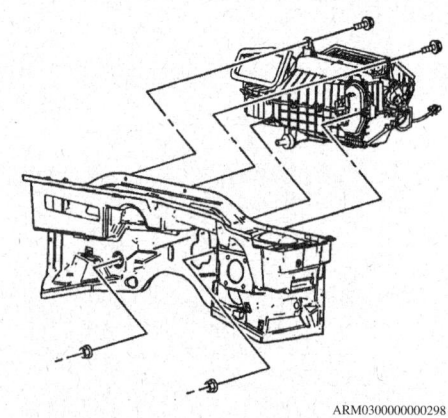

ARM0300000000298

Fig. 7   HVAC module removal

connect cluster electrical connector.
64. Remove cluster from vehicle.
65. Remove speaker retaining screws from speakers, then lift the speaker out from instrument panel carrier.
66. Disconnect speaker wire harness.
67. Remove GPS antenna to instrument panel carrier plastic rivet retainers, then the GPS antenna with antenna lead from carrier.
68. Remove remote control door lock receiver retaining screws, then the receiver from carrier.
69. Remove steering wheel as outlined under "Steering Wheel, Replace."
70. Remove instrument panel carrier retaining bolts and nuts.
71. Remove carrier retaining bolts from lower beam behind compartment door.
72. Remove compartment striker from carrier.
73. Remove instrument panel carrier from mounting, then slowly route all wiring from carrier.
74. Remove instrument panel carrier from vehicle.
75. Remove retainers from upper defogger duct on lefthand side window, then the upper defogger outlet duct.
76. Disconnect Head Up Display (HUD) electrical connector.
77. Remove HUD retaining nuts, then the screw that secures HUD to steering column bracket, **Fig. 6.**
78. Remove lower defogger outlet duct retainer, then the outlet duct from defroster duct.
79. Remove floor air outlet duct to lower instrument panel beam retainer.
80. Disconnect floor air outlet duct from rear floor air outlet duct.
81. Remove upper outlet duct to righthand side window defogger retainers, then the upper outlet duct from defogger.
82. Disconnect defogger lower outlet duct

from knee bolster bracket and defroster duct.
83. Remove righthand side knee bolster bracket to passenger SIR bracket attaching bolts, then the knee bolster bracket.
84. Remove sealing nuts from the cowl, then the upper instrument pane cross vehicle beam retaining bolts.
85. Loosen front lefthand recirculation housing retaining screw.
86. Disconnect recirculation actuator electrical connector and HVAC module wiring harness from recirculation housing.
87. Remove remaining recirculation housing retaining screws, then the housing from HVAC module.
88. Carefully remove HVAC module from vehicle, **Fig. 7.**
89. Remove and discard HVAC module assembly foam seal.
90. Disconnect discharge temperature management (DTM) sensor electrical connectors.
91. Disconnect HVAC module wiring harness retainer pin from HVAC module.
92. Disconnect wiring harness from heater core cover wire harness retainer and position harness aside.
93. Remove heater cover retaining screws, then heater cover from HVAC module.
94. Remove heater core from HVAC module.
95. Reverse procedure to install.

EVAPORATOR CORE
REPLACE

1. Recover air conditioning refrigerant as outlined in "Air Conditioning" chapter.
2. Remove HVAC module as outlined under "Heater Core, Replace."
3. Remove and discard HVAC module assembly foam seal.
4. Remove TXV mounting bolts, then the TXV from the evaporator core. Remove and discard sealing washers.
5. Disconnect Discharge Temperature Management (DTM) sensor electrical connectors.
6. Disconnect HVAC module wiring harness retainer pin from HVAC module.
7. Disconnect wiring harness from heater core cover wire harness retainers and position harness aside.
8. Remove heater cover screws, then the heater cover from HVAC module.
9. Remove HVAC module case retaining screws and separate HVAC module upper case from lower case.
10. Remove evaporator core from HVAC module.
11. Reverse procedure to install.

Engine

NOTE: On Air Bag Equipped Models, Refer To "Air Bag System Precautions" Located In The Front Of This Manual For System Disarming & Arming Procedures.

NOTE: Refer To "Computer Relearn Procedures" Located In The Front Of This Manual When Battery Power To The Computer Has Been Interrupted.

NOTE: Refer To "4.6L Engine" Section In The "DeVille, Eldorado, Seville & 2005 STS" Chapter For Procedures Not Covered In This Section.

INDEX

PRECAUTIONS

Air Bag Systems

Refer to "Air Bag System Precautions" in the front of this manual for system disarming and arming procedures.

Battery Ground Cable

Prior to service, disconnect battery ground cable and isolate as required.

Fuel Pressure Relief

1. Turn ignition off and remove fuel pump relay.
2. Loosen fuel filler cap.
3. Remove mounting nuts and fuel injector sight shield.
4. Connect suitable fuel pressure gauge to fuel pressure connection located on fuel rail assembly. Wrap connection with a suitable shop towel to prevent fuel leakage.
5. Install suitable bleed hose to gauge and into a suitable container, then open pressure valve to bleed system pressure.

COMPRESSION PRESSURE

Refer To "4.6L Engine" Section In The "DeVille, Eldorado, Seville & 2005 STS" Chapter.

ENGINE MOUNT
REPLACE

1. Rotate drive belt tensioner and remove drive belt.
2. Raise and support vehicle, then drain cooling system.
3. Remove tire and wheel assemblies.
4. Loosen, do not remove, outer tie rod end stud nut from outer tie rod end ball stud.
5. Loosen outer tie rod end stud to steering knuckle connection using tie rod remover tool No. J 42188, or equivalent.
6. Remove outer tie rod end stud nut and separate tie rod from steering knuckle.
7. Loosen jam nut on inner tie rod assembly, then remove outer tie rod end from inner tie rod assembly.
8. Disconnect Electronic Suspension Control (ESC) sensor links.
9. Remove stabilizer shaft link nuts from stabilizer shaft.
10. Remove stabilizer shaft insulator clamps from front crossmember, then the stabilizer shaft from vehicle.
11. Turn steering wheel far enough to lefthand side to gain access to intermediate shaft bolts, then place ignition in locked position.
12. Remove upper to lower intermediate shaft bolts, then the lower coupling shield.
13. Remove lower coupling pinch bolt, then the lower coupling from steering gear.
14. Slide lower intermediate shaft from upper intermediate shaft and remove lower intermediate shaft from vehicle.
15. Remove bolts from Electronic Brake Control Module/Brake Pressure Modulator Valve (EBCM/BPMV) bracket.
16. Support and reposition EBCM/BPMV and bracket away from crossmember.
17. Remove power steering gear mounting bolts.
18. Remove power steering fluid cooler from crossmember.
19. Lift power steering gear off of crossmember and support.
20. Remove transverse spring from vehicle
21. Remove lower shock absorber bolts from lower control arms.
22. Remove lower control arm bolts from crossmember.
23. Place a transmission jack under crossmember, then remove engine mount lower nuts.
24. Disconnect wheel speed sensor wiring harness from crossmember.
25. Disconnect electrical harness and brake pipe from clips on crossmember.
26. Remove crossmember mounting nuts, then lower crossmember from vehicle.
27. Remove engine mount to engine mount bracket nut, **Fig. 1.**
28. Remove engine mount from engine mount bracket.
29. Remove engine mount heat shield from engine mount.
30. Reverse procedure to install.

ENGINE
REPLACE

1. Relieve fuel system pressure as outlined under "Precautions."
2. Disconnect Electronic Suspension Control (ESC) control module electrical connectors. ESC control module is located in luggage compartment.
3. Recover A/C system refrigerant as outlined in "Air Conditioning" chapter.
4. Remove fuel injector sight shield.

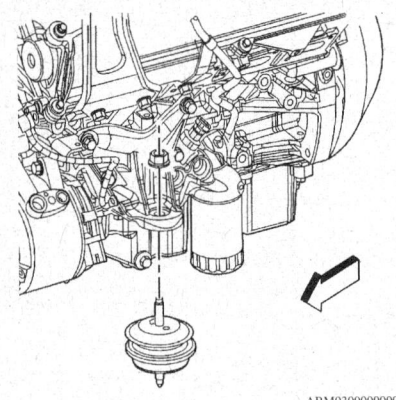

ARM0300000000299

Fig. 1 Engine mount removal

5. Disconnect EVAP emission canister purge pipe from chassis purge pipe. Cap open pipes to prevent contamination.
6. Disconnect fuel inlet quick-connect fitting at fuel line.
7. Remove air cleaner assembly.
8. Remove radiator as outlined under "Radiator, Replace."
9. Remove surge tank.
10. Remove air conditioning condenser.
11. Disconnect vacuum brake booster hose from brake booster.
12. Disconnect electrical connector from brake fluid level sensor.
13. Remove brake master cylinder nuts from brake booster studs, then pull master cylinder forward. Secure master cylinder to engine.
14. Remove bolts from intermediate steering shaft, then disconnect steering shaft from steering gear. Tie-wrap steering shaft to engine.
15. Remove battery, then the battery tray.
16. Remove engine ground strap nut and terminal from stud on frame.
17. Disconnect A/C electrical connector from pressure sensor.
18. Remove hydraulic junction block from wheelhouse, then disconnect wiring harness connector from junction block. Secure wiring harness to engine.
19. Raise and support vehicle, then remove front wheels and tires.
20. Remove righthand side front wheelhouse panel.
21. Disconnect and secure Engine Control Module (ECM) electrical harness, engine electrical harness.
22. Disconnect A/C lines from front of dash connections.
23. Disconnect heater hoses from heater pipes.
24. Disconnect wheel speed sensor electrical connectors.
25. Disconnect road sensing suspension position sensor links from front lower control arms.
26. Support righthand lower control arm with a straight jack.
27. Remove righthand shock absorber lower mounting bolts.
28. Disconnect upper righthand ball joint from suspension knuckle.
29. Remove straight jack from under control arm.
30. Support lefthand lower control arm with a straight jack.
31. Remove lefthand shock absorber lower mounting bolts.
32. Disconnect upper lefthand ball joint from suspension knuckle.
33. Remove straight jack from under control arm.
34. Disconnect rear wheel speed sensor electrical connectors.
35. Disconnect road sensing suspension position sensor links from the rear lower control arms.
36. Support rear lefthand lower control arm with a straight jack.
37. Remove rear lefthand shock absorber lower mounting bolt.
38. Disconnect lefthand upper ball joint from suspension knuckle.
39. Remove straight jack from control arm.
40. Support rear righthand lower control arm with a straight jack.
41. Remove rear righthand shock absorber lower mounting bolt.
42. Disconnect righthand upper ball joint from suspension knuckle.
43. Remove straight jack from control arm.
44. Remove righthand and lefthand muffler assemblies.
45. Remove bolts from driveline tunnel closeout panel, then the closeout panel from under vehicle.
46. Remove retaining transmission shift cable bracket to transmission retaining nuts.
47. Disconnect transmission shift control cable from transmission shift lever. Position shift cable and bracket aside.
48. Position a suitable powertrain table under front cradle.
49. Position a suitable powertrain table under rear cradle.
50. Slowly lower vehicle on to powertrain tables.
51. Remove front and rear crossmember nuts.
52. Carefully raise vehicle to clear supported powertrain assembly.
53. Remove lefthand side exhaust manifold assembly, then the lefthand side engine mount bracket.
54. Remove drive belt tensioner.
55. Remove bolt securing starter/alternator harness clip to front of engine.
56. Remove bolts and nut securing engine wiring harness to lefthand side of engine.
57. Remove righthand side exhaust manifold assembly, then the righthand side engine mount bracket.
58. Disconnect engine oil level sensor electrical connector.
59. Remove power steering reservoir bracket.
60. Remove A/C compressor and bracket.
61. Remove transmission cooler lines, then the Engine Coolant Temperature (ECT) sensor.
62. Remove wiring harness to engine attaching bolts and nut.
63. Disconnect throttle body assembly electrical connector.
64. Remove throttle body attaching bolts, then the throttle body and gasket. Discard gasket.
65. Remove lefthand side and righthand

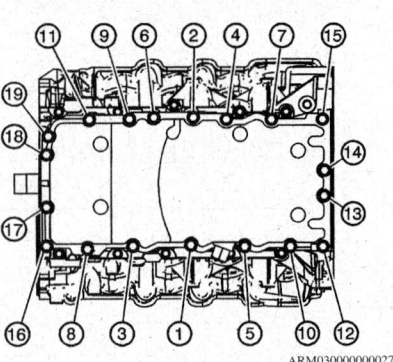

ARM0300000000274

Fig. 2 Oil pan bolt tightening sequence

side ignition module assemblies.
66. Remove starter motor from engine.
67. Disconnect lefthand and righthand knock sensor electrical connectors.
68. Disconnect crank sensor electrical connector.
69. Remove driveline support bolts.
70. Insert a suitable flat-headed screwdriver between driveline support and flywheel housing, then separate driveline assembly from engine.
71. Slowly pull driveline support assembly away from engine.
72. Install engine lift brackets tool Nos. J 28467-86 and J 28467-87, or equivalent to engine.
73. Install engine hoist tool No. J 41798, or equivalent, to lift brackets.
74. Remove flywheel housing bolts, then separate flywheel housing from engine.
75. Remove engine from lift table.
76. Reverse procedure to install.

OIL PAN
REPLACE

1. Rotate drive belt tensioner and remove drive belt.
2. Raise and support vehicle, then drain cooling system.
3. Remove tire and wheel assemblies.
4. Loosen, do not remove, outer tie rod end stud nut from outer tie rod end ball stud.
5. Loosen outer tie rod end stud to steering knuckle connection using tie rod remover tool No. J 42188, or equivalent.
6. Remove outer tie rod end stud nut and separate tie rod from steering knuckle.
7. Loosen jam nut on inner tie rod assembly, then remove outer tie rod end from inner tie rod assembly.
8. Disconnect Electronic Suspension Control (ESC) sensor links.
9. Remove stabilizer shaft link nuts from stabilizer shaft.
10. Remove stabilizer shaft insulator clamps from front crossmember, then the stabilizer shaft from vehicle.
11. Turn steering wheel far enough to lefthand side to gain access to intermediate shaft bolts, then place ignition in locked position.
12. Remove upper to lower intermediate shaft bolts, then the lower coupling shield.
13. Remove lower coupling pinch bolt,

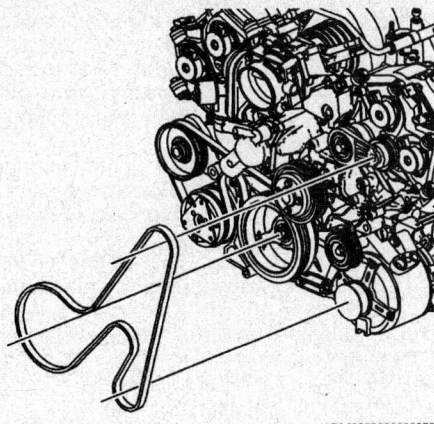

ARM0300000000272

Fig. 3 Drive belt routing

then the lower coupling from steering gear.

14. Slide lower intermediate shaft from upper intermediate shaft and remove lower intermediate shaft from vehicle.
15. Remove bolts from Electronic Brake Control Module/Brake Pressure Modulator Valve (EBCM/BPMV) bracket.
16. Support and reposition EBCM/BPMV and bracket away from crossmember.
17. Remove power steering gear mounting bolts.
18. Remove power steering fluid cooler from crossmember.
19. Lift power steering gear off of crossmember and support.
20. Remove transverse spring from vehicle.
21. Remove lower shock absorber bolts from lower control arms.
22. Remove lower control arm bolts from crossmember.
23. Place a transmission jack under crossmember, then remove engine mount lower nuts.
24. Disconnect wheel speed sensor wiring harness from crossmember.
25. Disconnect electrical harness and brake pipe from clips on crossmember.
26. Remove crossmember mounting nuts, then lower crossmember from vehicle.
27. Drain engine oil, then remove oil filter and allow to drain.
28. Remove transmission fluid cooler lines.
29. Disconnect engine oil level sensor electrical connector.
30. Remove oil level sensor.
31. Remove oil pan bolts, then the oil pan.
32. Reverse procedure to install. Using sequence, **Fig. 2, torque** oil pan bolts to 18 ft. lbs.

SERPENTINE DRIVE BELT

Routing

Refer to **Figs. 3 and 4,** for drive belt and accessory drive belt routings.

Drive Belt, Replace

1. Install a suitable 1/2 inch drive breaker

bar into belt drive tensioner.
2. Push down on breaker bar to release tension.
3. Remove drive belt from the tensioner pulley.
4. Slowly return tensioner to original position.
5. Raise and support vehicle, then remove belt.
6. Reverse procedure to install.

Accessory Drive Belt, Replace

1. Remove drive belt as outlined under "Drive Belt, Replace."
2. Place a drain pan under the vehicle.
3. Remove capstick from power steering fluid reservoir.
4. Remove power steering fluid reservoir from bracket.
5. Install a suitable wrench on accessory drive belt tensioner, then rotate tensioner to release tension.
6. With the tension applied, remove belt from power steering pulley.
7. Reverse procedure to install.

RADIATOR
REPLACE

1. Recover refrigerant from A/C system as outlined in "Air Conditioning" chapter.
2. Drain cooling system.
3. Remove condenser, then disconnect radiator inlet hose from radiator and engine.
4. Lift upward on cooling fan and shroud assembly to disengage tabs from radiator slots, then remove cooling fan and shroud assembly from radiator.
5. Disconnect surge tank inlet hose, then the upper transmission oil cooler line from radiator.
6. Raise and support vehicle.
7. Disconnect radiator outlet hose and lower transmission oil cooler line from radiator.
8. Disconnect alternator cooling hose from radiator.
9. Lower vehicle, then remove radiator from vehicle.
10. Reverse procedure to install.

FUEL PUMP
REPLACE
Lefthand

1. Relieve fuel system pressure as outlined under "Precautions."
2. Drain fuel tank.
3. Raise and support vehicle.
4. Remove rear tire and wheel assemblies.
5. Remove lefthand rear wheelhouse liner panel.
6. Loosen lefthand side and righthand side exhaust muffler clamps, then slide mufflers from hangers.
7. Remove intermediate exhaust pipe.
8. Remove driveline tunnel closeout panel bolts, then the closeout panel.

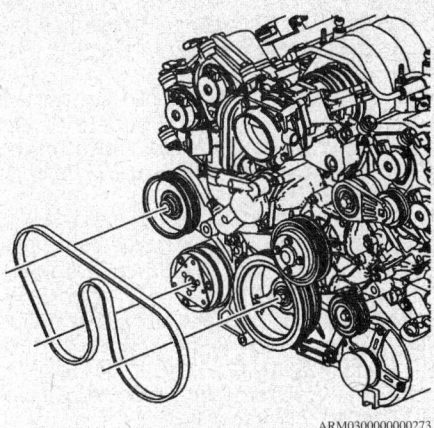

ARM0300000000273

Fig. 4 Accessory drive belt routing

9. Disconnect fuel fill hose and recirculation line from fill pipe.
10. Disconnect fuel pump jumper harness connector.
11. Disconnect fuel feed pipe from rear of lefthand side fuel tank. Cap fuel pipes to prevent contamination.
12. Loosen fuel tank strap and lower tank approximately one inch.
13. Disengage crossover tube CPA retainer by pulling tab outward and rotate, **Fig. 5.**
14. Disengage crossover tube collar by rotating counterclockwise.
15. Disconnect crossover tube from lefthand side fuel tank by pulling straight out.
16. Disconnect EVAP crossover pipe quick connect fitting from lefthand side fuel tank. Cap EVAP pipe to prevent system contamination.
17. Remove fuel tank strap mounting bolts, then the fuel tank from vehicle.
18. Disconnect fuel pump jumper harness from fuel pump module.
19. Disconnect jet line insert connector from fuel tank opening crossover tube.
20. Disconnect fuel feed line from welded clip on side of fuel tank.
21. Remove fuel pump module locking ring using lock ring removal tool No. J39765-A, or equivalent. **Fuel pump module is spring loaded and will spring upward when the locking ring is removed.**
22. Carefully remove fuel pump module from fuel tank, with the jet lines connected. **Ensure not to damage fuel sender float arm.**
23. Disconnect jet line quick-connect connectors from fuel pump module inner port.
24. Remove jet line from module retainer cup.
25. Remove fuel pump module O-ring from fuel tank opening.
26. Remove jet line insert through crossover tube to fuel tank opening.
27. Reverse procedure to install.

Righthand

1. Relieve fuel system pressure as outlined under "Precautions."
2. Drain fuel tank.

3. Raise and support vehicle, then remove righthand side rear tire and wheel assembly.

4. Remove righthand side rear wheelhouse liner panel.

5. Remove EVAP canister access cover.

6. Disconnect FLVV hose at EVAP Canister.

7. Disconnect fuel pump module harness connector, then remove crossover tube from clamp located above transmission.

8. Disengage crossover tube CPA retainer by pulling the tab outward and rotate, **Fig. 5.**

9. Disengage crossover tube collar by rotating counterclockwise.

10. Disconnect crossover tube from fuel tank by pulling tube straight out of fuel tank connection.

11. Disconnect EVAP crossover pipe quick connect fitting at righthand side fuel tank. Cap EVAP pipe to prevent system contamination.

12. Remove fuel tank strap mounting bolts, then the fuel tank strap and fuel tank from vehicle.

13. Disconnect EVAP purge line from fuel pump module.

14. Disconnect fuel pump module harness

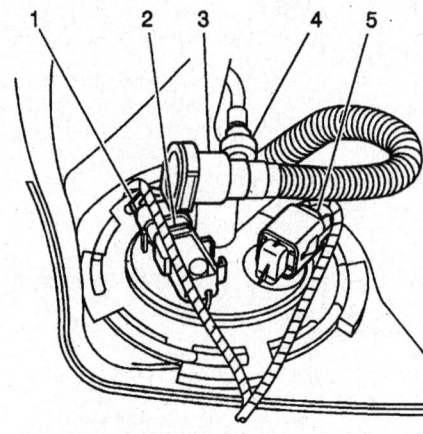

1 Sensor harness connnector
2 FTP sensor
3 Fuel pump harness
4 EVAP purge line
5 Fuel pump module harness connector

ARM0300000000270

Fig. 5 Fuel pump module

and Fuel Tank Pressure (FTP) sensor connectors.

15. Remove FTP sensor.

16. Remove fuel pump module locking ring using lock ring removal tool No. J39765-A, or equivalent. **Fuel pump module is spring loaded and will spring upward when the locking ring is removed.**

17. Carefully remove fuel pump module from fuel tank, with the jet lines connected. **Ensure not to damage fuel sender float arm.**

18. Disconnect jet line quick-connect connectors from fuel pump module inner port.

19. Remove jet line from module retainer cup.

20. Remove fuel pump module O-ring from fuel tank opening.

21. Remove jet line insert through crossover tube to fuel tank opening.

22. Reverse procedure to install.

FUEL FILTER
REPLACE

The fuel filter is contained within the fuel sender assembly, inside the lefthand side fuel tank. Refer to "Fuel Pump, Replace" for fuel filter replacement.

TIGHTENING SPECIFICATIONS

Year	Component	Torque, Ft. Lbs.
2004–05	A/C Compressor, Mounting Bolt	37
	A/C Compressor & Power Steering Bracket Bolt	37
	A/C Drive Belt Tensioner	18
	Alternator	37
	Alternator Coolant Inlet Hose Fitting	18
	Alternator Coolant Line Bolt	19
	Alternator Rear Brace Bolt	37
	Alternator Stud	106①
	Bell Housing Bolt	37
	Block Coolant Drain Hole Plug	15
	Camshaft Position Sensor	89①
	Crossmember	81
	Cylinder Head Coolant Plug	60
	Drive Belt Idler Bolt	37
	Drive Belt Idler Nut	37
	Drive Belt Tensioner Bolt	37
	ECT Sensor	15
	Engine Mount Bracket Bolt	43
	Engine Mount Nut	43
	Flywheel To Torque Converter	②
	Fuel Injector Sight Shield	89①
	Intermediate Shaft Pinch Bolt	25
	Lower Control Arm Cam Bolt	125
	Oil Filter Bypass Hole Plug	22
	Oil Filter Fitting	21
	Oil Filter Mounting Bolt	18
	Oil Dipstick Tube Bolt	37
	Oil Level Sensor	15
	Oil Pan	18
	Oil Pan Drain Plug	18
	Oil Pressure Switch	15
	Oxygen Sensor	31
	Power Steering Pump	18
	Power Steering Pump Reservoir Bracket Nut	89①
	Steering Rack	74
	Throttle Body	89①
	Tie Rod	33
	Wheel Lug Nuts	100

① — Inch lbs.
② — First pass, 11 ft. lbs.; second pass, tighten an additional 50°.

Rear Axle & Suspension

NOTE: On Air Bag Equipped Models, Refer To "Air Bag System Precautions" Located In The Front Of This Manual For System Disarming & Arming Procedures.

NOTE: Refer To "Computer Relearn Procedures" Located In The Front Of This Manual When Battery Power To The Computer Has Been Interrupted.

INDEX

DESCRIPTION

The rear suspension uses a single lightweight fiberglass transverse spring mounted to the crossmember and lower control arms. The rear suspension uses the following lightweight aluminum components; rear suspension knuckles, upper control arms, lower control arms, rear suspension toe links, crossmember and drive shaft support tube. The shock absorbers are attached to the frame and the lower control arm. Shock absorbers reduce crash-through at full jounce and rebound. The electronically controlled shock absorbers are gas charged to reduce aeration (foaming) of the shock fluid.

REAR AXLE SHAFT

REPLACE

Removal

1. Shift transmission into PARK, then apply parking brake.
2. Raise and support vehicle.
3. Remove tire and wheel assembly.
4. Insert a drift or punch into brake rotor cooling fins and against brake caliper to prevent wheel hub and bearing from turning.
5. Remove spindle nut retaining rear wheel drive shaft to hub.
6. Remove drift or punch, then release parking brake.
7. Loosen, do not remove, outer tie rod end stud nut from outer tie rod end ball stud.
8. Install ball joint separator tool No. J 42188, or equivalent, between suspension knuckle and outer tie rod end stud, then tighten bolt on separator tool until knuckle and outer tie rod end stud separate.
9. Separate outer tie rod end from knuckle and reposition tie rod toward rear of vehicle.
10. Disconnect wheel speed sensor electrical connector.
11. Disconnect parking brake cable from parking brake lever.
12. Remove parking brake cable from bracket and reposition toward rear of vehicle.
13. Install rear hub spindle remover tool No. J 42129, or equivalent, onto wheel hub and secure with wheel nuts, **Fig. 1.**
14. Begin to separate drive shaft from wheel hub and bearing to provide additional clearance to lower ball joint nut.
15. Loosen, but do not remove upper ball joint stud nut. **Do not allow ball joint to rotate.** Use a suitable Torx wrench inserted into top of ball stud while removing ball stud nut, **Fig. 2.**
16. Separate lower ball joint from suspension knuckle.
17. Separate drive shaft completely from wheel hub and bearing.
18. Support drive shaft, suspension knuckle and upper control arm. Reposition knuckle toward front of vehicle.
19. Assemble axle shaft remover tool No. J 42128, extension tool No. J 29794 and slide hammer tool No. J 2619-O1, or equivalents, onto rear beveled surface of drive shaft inner joint housing, **Fig. 3.**
20. Separate drive shaft from rear axle differential, then remove tool assembly.
21. Remove drive shaft from vehicle, then the spindle remover tool from wheel hub.

Installation

1. Support drive shaft until it is completely installed.
2. Position drive shaft to rear axle differential output shaft. **Do not damage rear axle differential output shaft seal.**
3. Carefully align and guide drive shaft onto differential output shaft.
4. Engage drive shaft fully onto differential output shaft using light force.
5. Align and guide drive shaft into wheel hub and bearing, but do not seat fully.
6. Install lower ball joint to suspension knuckle.
7. Install parking brake cable into bracket.
8. Connect parking brake cable to parking brake lever.
9. Connect wheel speed sensor electrical connector.
10. Install outer tie rod end on to suspension knuckle.
11. Apply parking brake, then insert a drift or punch into the brake rotor cooling fins and against the caliper to prevent the wheel hub and bearing from turning.
12. Begin to install drive shaft retaining nut onto drive shaft by hand.
13. Slowly tighten nut to draw drive shaft into wheel hub and bearing.
14. Tighten drive axle spindle nut to specifications, then remove drift or punch and release parking brake.
15. Install tire and wheel assembly, then lower vehicle.

DIFFERENTIAL CARRIER

REPLACE

1. Raise and support vehicle.
2. Remove rear tire and wheel assemblies.
3. Install adjustable jack stands under the front and rear of exhaust intermediate pipe.
4. Loosen exhaust muffler band clamps, then separate lefthand side and righthand side tailpipe/muffler assemblies from intermediate pipe.
5. Remove exhaust intermediate pipe from vehicle.
6. Slide lefthand side and righthand side muffler assemblies from hangers, then remove mufflers from vehicle.

7. Disconnect rear park brake cables from actuator levers.
8. Disconnect rear wheel speed sensor electrical connectors.
9. Disconnect rear position sensor electrical connectors.
10. Disconnect suspension rear position sensor servo arms from lower control arms.
11. Remove rear brake calipers from caliper brackets. Support righthand caliper to lower control arm and lefthand caliper to body with heavy mechanic's wire, or equivalent. **Ensure there is no tension on hydraulic brake flexible hose.**
12. **On righthand side,** proceed as follows:
    a. Disconnect righthand rear brake pipe at union on lefthand side of transmission. Plug openings in brake pipe to prevent fluid loss and contamination.
    b. Insert a drift or punch into brake rotor cooling fins and against brake caliper to prevent wheel hub and bearing from turning.
    c. Remove spindle nut retaining rear wheel drive shaft to hub.
    d. Remove drift or punch, then release parking brake.
    e. Support lower control arm with a straight jack.
    f. Install ball joint separator tool No. J 42188, or equivalent, between suspension knuckle and outer tie rod end stud, then tighten bolt on separator tool until knuckle and outer tie rod end stud separate.
    g. Separate outer tie rod end from knuckle and reposition tie rod toward rear of vehicle.
    h. Remove shock absorber lower mounting bolt.
    i. Disconnect upper ball joint from suspension knuckle, **Fig. 2,** then remove straight jack from control arm.
13. **On lefthand side,** proceed as follows:
    a. Disconnect lefthand rear brake pipe at union on lefthand side of transmission. Plug openings in brake pipe to prevent fluid loss and contamination.
    b. Insert a drift or punch into brake rotor cooling fins and against brake caliper to prevent wheel hub and bearing from turning.
    c. Remove spindle nut retaining rear wheel drive shaft to hub.
    d. Remove drift or punch, then release parking brake.
    e. Support lower control arm with a straight jack.
    f. Install ball joint separator tool No. J 42188, or equivalent, between suspension knuckle and outer tie rod end stud, then tighten bolt on separator tool until knuckle and outer tie rod end stud separate.
    g. Separate outer tie rod end from knuckle and reposition tie rod toward rear of vehicle.
    h. Remove shock absorber lower mounting bolt.
    i. Disconnect upper ball joint from

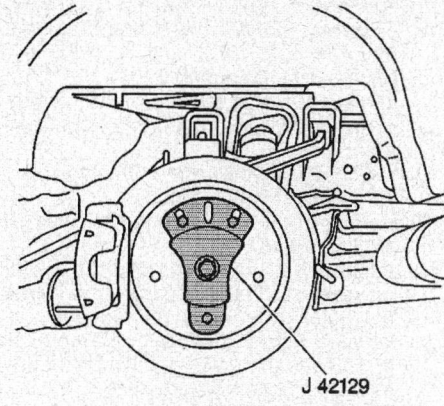

Fig. 1 Spindle remover tool installation

suspension knuckle, **Fig. 2,** then remove straight jack from control arm.
14. Remove exhaust pipe lower hanger bolts to gain access to dampener bolts.
15. Remove the two vibration dampener bolts, then the dampener.
16. Install transmission support tool No. J 42055, or equivalent, to a suitable transmission jack.
17. Position and secure tool and transmission jack to transmission.
18. Disconnect wiring harness, wiring ground and brake pipe clip retainers from rear suspension crossmember.
19. Position righthand side wiring harness through cradle and position aside.
20. Remove transaxle mount to side crossmember nuts.
21. Position a transmission jack under rear suspension crossmember and firmly secure crossmember to jack.
22. Remove rear suspension crossmember retaining nuts. **Using hand tools only.**
23. Slowly lower rear suspension crossmember away from vehicle frame rails and remove crossmember.
24. Remove rear wheel drive shafts from rear differential as outlined under "Rear Axle Shaft, Replace."
25. Remove differential to transmission bolts and nuts.
26. Place a suitable jack under rear differential.
27. Slowly slide differential from the transmission. **Use care when separating differential from transmission to prevent damage to transmission output shaft seal in differential plate.**
28. Reverse procedure to install.

HUB & BEARING
REPLACE

1. Shift transmission into PARK, then apply parking brake.
2. Raise and support vehicle.
3. Remove tire and wheel assembly.
4. Disconnect wheel speed sensor harness connector.
5. Disconnect Electronic Suspension Control (ESC) rear position sensor link.

6. Remove brake caliper and rotor as outlined in "Disc Brakes" chapter.
7. Disconnect shock absorber ESC harness connector.
8. Loosen, do not remove, outer tie rod end stud nut from outer tie rod end ball stud.
9. Install ball joint separator tool No. J 42188, or equivalent, between suspension knuckle and outer tie rod end stud, then tighten bolt on separator tool until knuckle and outer tie rod end stud separate.
10. Separate outer tie rod end from suspension knuckle.
11. Insert a drift or punch into brake rotor cooling fins and against brake caliper to prevent wheel hub and bearing from turning.
12. Remove spindle nut retaining rear wheel drive shaft to hub.
13. Remove drift or punch, then release parking brake.
14. Separate upper control arm from the suspension knuckle, **Fig. 2.**
15. Separate suspension knuckle from lower control arm ball joint stud.
16. Remove suspension knuckle from vehicle.
17. Remove wheel hub mounting bolts, then the hub and bearing assembly from suspension knuckle.
18. Reverse procedure to install.

SHOCK ABSORBER
REPLACE

1. Raise and support vehicle.
2. Remove tire and wheel assembly.
3. Disconnect rear shock electronic suspension control (ESC) harness connector, **Fig. 4.**
4. Disconnect harness pigtail from upper shock tower clip.
5. Remove lower shock absorber to lower control arm retaining bolt.
6. Remove upper shock absorber mounting bolts.
7. Loosen, do not remove, outer tie rod end stud nut from outer tie rod end ball stud.
8. Install ball joint separator tool No. J 42188, or equivalent, between suspension knuckle and outer tie rod end stud, then tighten bolt on separator tool until knuckle and outer tie rod end stud separate.
9. Separate outer tie rod end from suspension knuckle.
10. Remove shock absorber from vehicle. **Use caution when routing the ESC pigtail and connector through upper shock tower.**
11. Remove upper insulator retainer and insulator from shock absorber.
12. Reverse procedure to install.

BALL JOINT
REPLACE

Refer to "Control Arm, Replace" for ball joint replacement.

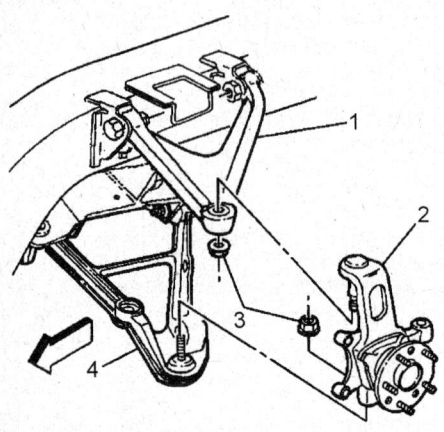

1 Upper control arm
2 SUspension knuckle
3 Ball stud nuts
4 Lower control arm

ARM0300000000271

Fig. 2 Suspension knuckle & control arms

TRANSVERSE SPRING
REPLACE

1. Raise and support vehicle.
2. Remove tire and wheel assemblies.
3. Measure rear spring adjuster bolt gap, **Fig. 5.** This measurement should be used in installation procedure to setup vehicle trim height.
4. Remove one lower control arm as outlined under "Control Arms, Replace."
5. Compress transverse spring using spring compressor tool No. J 33432-A, or equivalent. Do not scratch transverse spring.
6. Remove transverse spring bolts and retainers. Discard old transverse spring bolts.
7. Remove transverse spring from vehicle.
8. Remove transverse spring compressor from transverse spring.
9. Reverse procedure to install.

CONTROL ARM
REPLACE
Lower

1. Raise and support vehicle.
2. Remove tire and wheel assembly.
3. Compress transverse spring using transverse spring compressor tool No. J 33432-A, or equivalent.
4. Place a suitable jack stand under lower control arm.
5. Disconnect shock absorber from lower control arm.
6. Loosen, but do not remove upper ball joint stud nut. **Do not allow ball joint to rotate.** Use a suitable Torx wrench inserted into top of ball stud while removing ball stud nut.
7. Remove upper ball joint stud nut from suspension knuckle.
8. Separate upper ball joint stud from

suspension knuckle using ball joint separator tool No. J 42188, or equivalent.
9. Insert a drift or punch into brake rotor cooling fins and against brake caliper to prevent wheel hub and bearing from turning.
10. Remove spindle nut retaining rear wheel drive shaft to hub.
11. Remove drift or punch, then release parking brake.
12. Loosen, but do not remove the lower ball joint stud nut. Separate the lower ball joint stud from the suspension knuckle using J 42188 . Remove J 42188 and the lower ball joint stud nut from the suspension knuckle.
13. Remove stabilizer shaft link from lower control arm.
14. Mark position of lower control arm cam bolts, then remove cam bolts, washers and nuts. retaining control arm to the crossmember.
15. Remove jack stand, then the lower control arm from vehicle.
16. Reverse procedure to install.

Upper

1. Raise and support vehicle.
2. Remove tire and wheel assembly.
3. Disconnect wheel speed sensor electrical connector.
4. Disconnect Electronic Suspension Control (ESC) sensor link.
5. Separate suspension knuckle from upper control arm using ball joint separator tool No. J 42188, or equivalent.
6. Support lower control arm with a suitable jack stand.
7. Loosen upper ball joint stud nut, but do not remove the nut.
8. Remove ball joint stud nut from ball joint stud.
9. Remove upper control arm to frame attaching bolts.
10. Remove upper control arm from vehicle.
11. Reverse procedure to install.

TIE ROD
REPLACE
Inner

1. Raise and support vehicle.
2. Remove tire and wheel assembly.
3. Loosen, do not remove, outer tie rod end stud nut from outer tie rod end ball stud.
4. Install ball joint separator tool No. J 42188, or equivalent, between suspension knuckle and outer tie rod end stud, then tighten bolt on separator tool until knuckle and outer tie rod end stud separate.
5. Separate outer tie rod end from suspension knuckle.
6. Remove nut retaining rear suspension adjustment link (inner tie rod) to crossmember.
7. Remove rear suspension adjustment link (inner tie rod) from vehicle.
8. Reverse procedure to install.

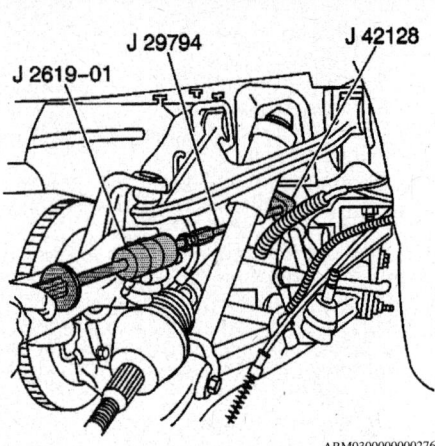

ARM0300000000276

Fig. 3 Axle shaft removal

Outer

1. Raise and support vehicle.
2. Remove tire and wheel assembly.
3. Loosen, do not remove, outer tie rod end stud nut from outer tie rod end ball stud.
4. Install ball joint separator tool No. J 42188, or equivalent, between suspension knuckle and outer tie rod end stud, then tighten bolt on separator tool until knuckle and outer tie rod end stud separate.
5. Separate outer tie rod end from suspension knuckle.
6. Loosen jam nut on rear suspension adjustment link.
7. Remove outer tie rod end from rear suspension adjustment link.
8. Reverse procedure to install.

REAR CROSSMEMBER
REPLACE

1. Raise and support vehicle.
2. Remove tire and wheel assemblies.
3. Disconnect wheel speed sensors harness connectors.
4. Remove stabilizer shaft as outlined under "Stabilizer Shaft, Replace."
5. Disconnect rear suspension adjustment link (inner tie rod end) studs from rear crossmember.
6. Disconnect lower control arms from crossmember as outlined under "Control Arms, Replace."
7. Support rear drive shafts and rear suspension knuckles.
8. Remove transverse spring as outlined under "Transverse Spring, Replace."
9. Remove transmission mount lower nuts.
10. Disconnect all electrical harness and connectors from crossmember.
11. Disconnect brake pipes from crossmember.
12. Support transmission with a suitable transmission jack.
13. Remove rear crossmember mounting nuts. **Using hand tools only.**
14. Remove crossmember from vehicle. Discard crossmember mounting nuts.
15. Reverse procedure to install.

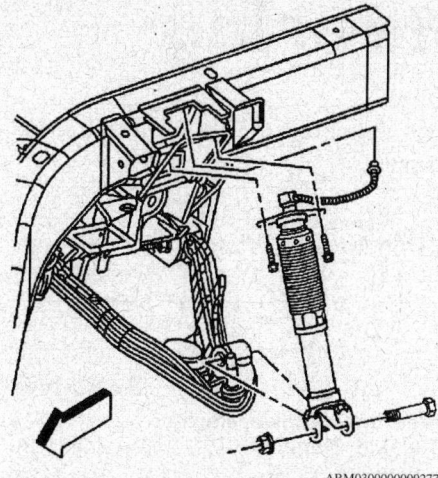

Fig. 4   Shock absorber removal

SUSPENSION KNUCKLE
REPLACE

Refer to "Hub & Bearing, Replace" for rear wheel suspension knuckle replacement.

STABILIZER SHAFT
REPLACE

1. Raise and support vehicle.
2. Remove tire and wheel assemblies.
3. Remove stabilizer shaft link nuts from stabilizer shaft.
4. Remove stabilizer shaft clamps, bolts and nuts retaining shaft to crossmember.
5. Remove stabilizer shaft from vehicle.
6. Reverse procedure to install.

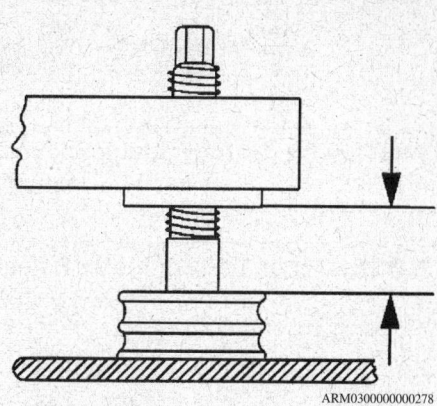

Fig. 5   Spring adjuster bolt gap measurement

TIGHTENING SPECIFICATIONS

Year	Component	Torque/Ft. Lbs.
2004–05	Crossmember Mounting Nuts	81
	Lower Control Arm Ball Joint Stud Nut	①
	Lower Control Arm Front Cam Bolt Nut	107
	Lower Control Arm Rear Cam Bolt Nut	70
	Outer Tie Rod End Stud Nut	②
	Rear Suspension Adjustment Link To Crossmember Nut	44
	Shock Absorber Lower Mounting Bolt	162
	Shock Absorber Upper Mounting Bolts	22
	Stabilizer Shaft Insulator Clamp Bolt	49
	Stabilizer Shaft Insulator Clamp Nut	70
	Stabilizer Shaft Link Nuts	53
	Transverse Spring Mounting Bracket Bolts	46
	Upper Control Arm Ball Joint Stud Nut	③
	Wheel Hub Mounting Bolts	96
	Wheel Lug Nuts	100

① — First step, 15 ft. lbs.; second step, 3½ flats; third step, 52 ft. lbs.

② — First step, 15 ft. lbs.; second step, an additional 160°; third step, 33 ft. lbs.

③ — First step, 15 ft. lbs.; second step, an additional 250°; third step, 41 ft. lbs.

Front Suspension & Steering

NOTE: On Air Bag Equipped Models, Refer To "Air Bag System Precautions" Located In The Front Of This Manual For System Disarming & Arming Procedures.

NOTE: Refer To "Computer Relearn Procedures" Located In The Front Of This Manual When Battery Power To The Computer Has Been Interrupted.

INDEX

HUB & BEARING
REPLACE

1. Raise and support vehicle.
2. Remove tire and wheel assembly.
3. Disconnect wheel speed sensor harness connector.
4. Remove brake caliper and rotor as outlined in "Disc Brakes" chapter.
5. Remove stabilizer shaft link from lower control arm.
6. Support lower control arm using a suitable jackstand.
7. Remove outer tie rod end ball stud to steering knuckle retaining nut.
8. Separate outer tie rod ball stud from steering knuckle using ball joint separator tool No. J 42188, or equivalent.
9. Remove lower ball joint stud to steering knuckle retaining nut.
10. Separate lower ball joint stud from steering knuckle using ball joint separator tool No. J 42188, or equivalent.
11. Remove wheel hub mounting bolts, then the hub and bearing assembly from steering knuckle.
12. Reverse procedure to install.

BALL JOINT INSPECTION

1. Raise and support vehicle.
2. Support lower control arm with a jack stand, as far outboard as possible, near lower ball joint.
3. Wipe ball joints clean, then inspect seal for cuts and tears. If ball joint seal is cut or torn, replace ball joint.
4. Position dial indicator tool No. J 8001, or equivalent, against lowest outboard point on wheel rim.
5. Rock wheel in and out while reading dial indicator. Dial indicator reading should be no more than .125 inch. If reading is too high, proceed to next step.

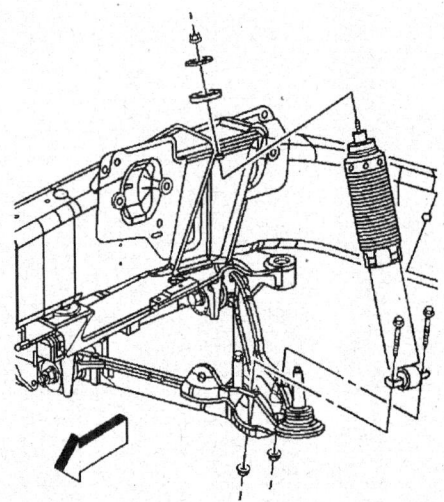

Fig. 1 Shock absorber removal

6. Inspect lower ball joints for wear and for vertical looseness as follows:
   a. Position of housing into which grease fitting is threaded indicates wear. This round housing projects .050 inch beyond surface of lower ball joint cover on a new ball joint.
   b. Under normal wear, surface of lower ball joint housing retreats inward very slowly.
   c. Remove any dirt from housing, if housing is flush with or inside of cover, replace lower control arm.
7. Position dial indicator tool No. J 8001, or equivalent, against spindle.
8. Pry between lower control arm and outer bearing race with a suitable pry bar while reading dial indicator. If dial indicator reading is more than .125 inch, replace lower control arm.
9. Inspect upper ball joint for wear.
10. Disconnect upper ball joint from steering knuckle as outlined under "Ball Joint, Replace." If there is any looseness or stud can be twisted with your fingers, replace upper ball joint.

BALL JOINT
REPLACE

Lower

The ball joint is part of the lower control arm and cannot be serviced separately. Refer to "Control Arm, Replace" for replacement procedure.

Upper

The upper ball joint is part of the steering knuckle and cannot be serviced separately. Refer to "Steering Knuckle, Replace" for replacement procedure.

SHOCK ABSORBER
REPLACE

1. Disconnect shock Electronic Suspension Control (ESC) harness connector.
2. Raise and support vehicle.
3. Remove tire and wheel assembly.
4. Remove upper mounting nut, insulator retainer and insulator. **Use hand tools only.**
5. Remove shock absorber lower mounting bolts and nuts, **Fig. 1.**
6. Compress shock absorber from bottom upward using a suitable pry bar.
7. With shock in compressed position, install shock support tool No. J 43822, or equivalent.
8. Remove shock absorber from vehicle, then the support tool from shock.
9. Remove insulator and insulator retainer from shock absorber.
10. Reverse procedure to install.

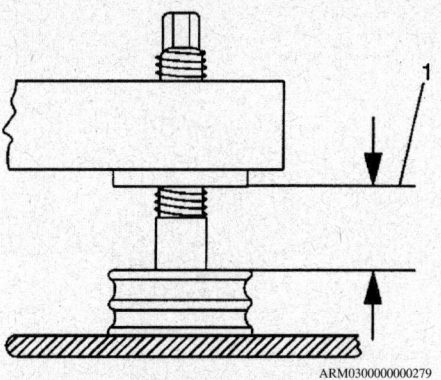

Fig. 2 Transverse spring adjuster bolt gap measurement

ARM0300000000279

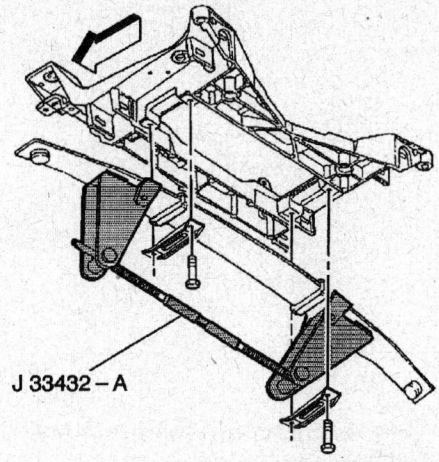

J 33432 – A

ARM0300000000280

Fig. 3 Transverse spring removal

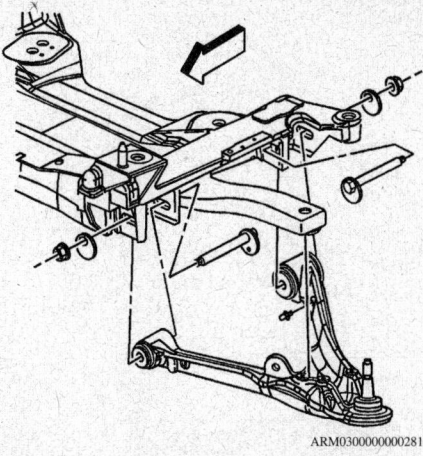

ARM0300000000281

Fig. 4 Lower control arm removal

TRANSVERSE SPRING
REPLACE

1. Raise and support vehicle.
2. Remove tire and wheel assemblies.
3. If transverse spring is to be replaced, measure front spring adjuster bolt gap, **Fig. 2.** This measurement will be used during installation to setup vehicle trim height.
4. Compress transverse spring with spring compressor tool No. J 33432-A, or equivalent, **Fig. 3.**
5. Remove lower shock absorber mounting bolts from lower control arm.
6. Disconnect stabilizer shaft link from lower control arm.
7. Loosen lower ball joint stud nut on lower control arm. **Do not remove the nut.**
8. Separate lower ball joint from steering knuckle using ball joint separator tool No. J 42188, or equivalent.
9. Remove lower ball joint stud nut and discard.
10. Support lower control arms with jackstands.
11. Mark position of cam bolts for installation reference.
12. Remove cam bolts from lower control arm.
13. Remove lower control arm.
14. Remove transverse spring bolts and retainers, then the transverse spring and spring compressor from vehicle. Discard transverse spring bolts transverse spring compressor from transverse spring.
15. Reverse procedure to install.

CONTROL ARM
REPLACE

Lower

1. Raise and support vehicle.
2. Remove tire and wheel assembly.
3. Remove transverse spring as outlined under "Transverse Spring, Replace."
4. Disconnect wheel speed sensor electrical connector.
5. Remove shock absorber from lower control arm.
6. Remove stabilizer shaft link from lower control arm.

7. Loosen ball joint stud nut. **Do not remove nut.**
8. Separate lower ball joint stud from steering knuckle using ball joint separator tool No. J 42188, or equivalent.
9. Remove ball joint stud nut, then the ball joint stud from steering knuckle.
10. Mark position of cam bolts for installation reference.
11. Remove cam bolts, washers and nuts attaching control arm to crossmember, **Fig. 4.**
12. Remove lower control arm from vehicle.
13. Reverse procedure to install.

Upper

1. Raise and support vehicle.
2. Remove tire and wheel assembly.
3. Disconnect Electronic Suspension Control (ESC) sensor links.
4. Support lower control arm with a jackstand.
5. Loosen ball joint stud nut. **Do not remove nut.**
6. Separate upper ball joint stud from upper control arm using ball joint separator tool No. J 42188, or equivalent.
7. Remove ball joint stud nut from ball joint stud.
8. Remove upper control arm bolts and shims, **Fig. 5.** Upper control arm shims will have an effect on camber and caster, be sure to use an equal thickness of shims on both sides of each individual upper control arm bushing. Note number and position of shims for installation reference.
9. Remove upper control arm from vehicle.
10. Reverse procedure to install.

STEERING KNUCKLE
REPLACE

1. Raise and support vehicle.
2. Remove brake caliper and rotor as outlined in "Disc Brakes" chapter.
3. Remove stabilizer shaft link from lower control arm.
4. Disconnect wheel speed sensor electrical connector.

5. Support lower control arm with a suitable jackstand.
6. Remove outer tie rod end to steering knuckle retaining nut.
7. Separate outer tie rod ball stud from steering knuckle using ball joint separator tool No. J 42188, or equivalent.
8. Loosen ball joint stud nut. **Do not remove nut.**
9. Separate upper ball joint stud from upper control arm using ball joint separator tool No. J 42188, or equivalent.
10. Remove ball joint stud nut from ball joint stud.
11. Loosen ball joint stud nut. **Do not remove nut.**
12. Separate lower ball joint stud from steering knuckle using ball joint separator tool No. J 42188, or equivalent.
13. Remove lower ball joint stud nut, then the ball joint stud from steering knuckle.
14. Remove steering knuckle from vehicle.
15. Reverse procedure to install.

STABILIZER BAR
REPLACE

1. Raise and support vehicle.
2. Remove tire and wheel assemblies.
3. Remove stabilizer shaft link nuts from stabilizer shaft, **Fig. 6.**
4. Remove stabilizer shaft insulator clamps from front crossmember.
5. Remove stabilizer shaft from vehicle.
6. Reverse procedure to install.

CROSSMEMBER
REPLACE

1. Attach engine support fixture tool No. J 28467-B, or equivalent, to engine.
2. Raise and support vehicle.
3. Remove tire and wheel assemblies.
4. Remove steering linkage outer tie rod end stud nuts as outlined under "Tie Rod End, Replace."
5. Disconnect Electronic suspension control (ESC) sensor links.
6. Remove stabilizer shaft from vehicle as outlined under "Stabilizer Bar, Replace."

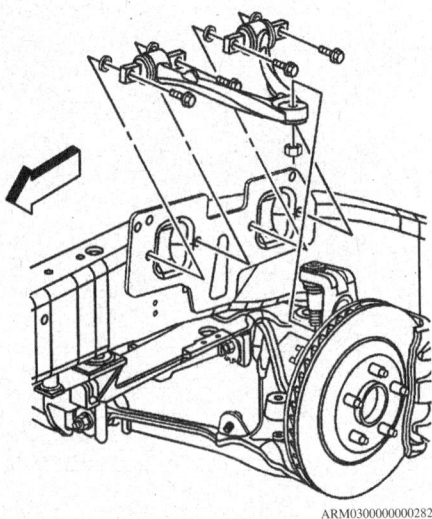

ARM0300000000282

Fig. 5 Upper control arm removal

7. Disconnect intermediate shaft lower coupling from steering gear.
8. Remove bolts from Electronic Brake Control Module/Brake Pressure Modulator Valve (EBCM/BPMV) bracket. Support and position EBCM/BPMV and bracket away from crossmember.
9. Remove power steering gear mounting bolts, then the power steering fluid cooler from crossmember.
10. Lift power steering gear off of crossmember and support.
11. Remove transverse spring as outlined under "Transverse Spring, Replace."
12. Remove lower shock absorber to lower control arms attaching bolts.
13. Remove lower control arm to crossmember mounting bolts.
14. Place a suitable transmission jack under crossmember.
15. Remove engine mount lower retaining nuts.
16. Disconnect wheel speed sensor wiring harness from crossmember.
17. Disconnect electrical harness from clips on crossmember.
18. Disconnect brake pipe from clips on crossmember.
19. Remove crossmember mounting nuts, then lower crossmember out of vehicle, **Fig. 7.**
20. Reverse procedure to install.

TIE ROD
REPLACE

Inner

1. Raise and support vehicle.
2. Remove tire and wheel assembly.
3. Remove rack and pinion boot. **Do not change rack bearing preload adjustment before removing inner tie rod from steering rack. This could cause damage to pinion or steering rack or both.**

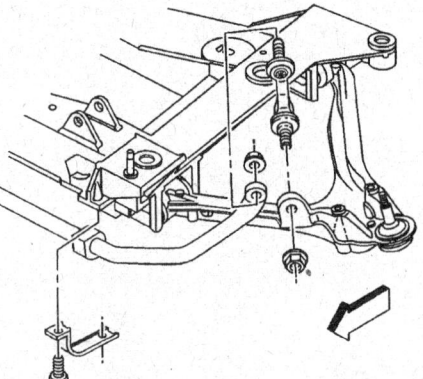

ARM0300000000284

Fig. 6 Stabilizer shaft removal

4. Remove shock dampener from inner tie rod.
5. Slide shock dampener back onto rack. **Do not hold steering rack while removing inner tie rod.**
6. Place a wrench on flats of inner tie rod housing, then rotate inner tie rod housing counterclockwise until inner tie rod separates from rack.
7. Remove inner tie rod from rack assembly.
8. Reverse procedure to install, noting the following:
   a. Remove old Loctite from threads of rack and inner tie rod.
   b. Apply Loctite 262, or equivalent, to inner tie rod threads.

Outer

1. Raise and suitable support vehicle.
2. Remove tire and wheel assemblies.
3. Loosen, but do not remove outer tie rod end stud nut from outer tie rod end ball stud.
4. Loosen outer tie rod end stud to steering knuckle connection using ball joint separator tool No. J 42188.
5. Remove outer tie rod end stud nut in order to separate tie rod from steering knuckle.
6. Loosen jam nut on inner tie rod assembly.
7. Remove outer tie rod end from inner tie rod assembly.
8. Reverse procedure to install.

POWER STEERING GEAR
REPLACE

1. Remove Brake Pressure Modulator Valve (BPMV) bracket.
2. Raise and support vehicle.
3. Remove tires and wheels.
4. Disconnect tie rod ends from steering knuckles.
5. Remove lower shock mounting bolts.
6. Disconnect intermediate shaft from power steering gear.
7. Remove stabilizer shaft as outlined under "Stabilizer Bar, Replace."

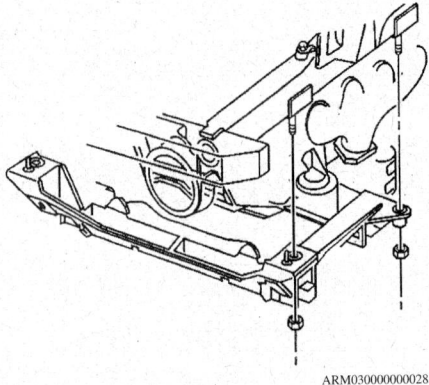

ARM0300000000285

Fig. 7 Crossmember removal

8. Remove power steering pressure and return hoses.
9. Remove brake pipes from crossmember.
10. Remove power steering gear mounting bolts and nuts. **Use hand tools only.**
11. Remove four crossmember mounting nuts, then the power steering gear from vehicle through lefthand side wheelhouse opening.
12. Reverse procedure to install. Bleed power steering.

POWER STEERING PUMP
REPLACE

1. Remove power steering fluid reservoir.
2. Remove power steering pump pulley.
3. Remove power steering reservoir outlet pipe/hose.
4. Remove power steering pressure hose.
5. Remove power steering pump mounting bolts, then the power steering pump.
6. Reverse procedure to install.

POWER STEERING SYSTEM BLEED

1. Ensure hoses do not touch any other part of vehicle.
2. Verify all hose connections are tight. Loose connections may not leak, but could allow air into steering system.
3. Maintain fluid level throughout bleed procedure.
4. Fill pump reservoir with fluid to FULL COLD level.
5. Attach power steering bleeder adapter tool No. J 43485, or equivalent, into pump reservoir filler neck.
6. Apply a vacuum of 20 in Hg maximum, then wait five minutes.
7. Typical vacuum drop is 2-3 in Hg.
8. Install pump reservoir cap.
9. Start engine and allow engine to idle, then turn off engine and verify fluid level.

TIGHTENING SPECIFICATIONS

Year	Component	Torque Ft. Lbs.
2004–05	Adjuster Plug Lock Nut	50
	Crossmember Mounting Nuts	81
	Cylinder Line End Fittings	20
	Cylinder Line Valve End Fittings	13③
	Inner Tie Rod	74
	Lower Control Arm Ball Joint Stud Nut	①
	Lower Control Arm Mounting Bolt Nuts	125
	Outer Tie Rod End Stud Nut To Knuckle	④
	Power Steering Cooler To Crossmember Mounting Bolts	97③
	Power Steering Gear Mounting Bolts & Nuts	74
	Power Steering Hose Fittings	20
	Power Steering Pump Mounting Bolts	18
	Power Steering Reservoir Bracket Bolts	84③
	Shock Absorber Lower Mounting Nuts	21
	Shock Absorber Upper Mounting Nut	19
	Stabilizer Shaft Insulator Clamp Bolts	43
	Stabilizer Shaft Link Nuts	53
	Transverse Spring Retainer Bolts	46
	Upper Control Arm Ball Joint Stud Nut	②
	Upper Control Arm Mounting Bolts	48
	Wheel Hub/Bearing Mounting Bolts	96
	Wheel Lug Nuts	100

① — First step, 15 ft. lbs.; second step, an additional 210°; third step, 41 ft. lbs.

② — First step, 15 ft. lbs.; second step, an additional 250°; third step, 41 ft. lbs.

③ — Inch lbs.

④ — First step, 15 ft. lbs.; second step, an additional 160°; third step, 33 ft. lbs.

Wheel Alignment

INDEX

PRELIMINARY INSPECTION

Inspect tires for proper inflation.

Inspect tie rods for lateral end motion relative to the steering knuckle and tie rod end seals for any visible signs of damage. Replace tie rod end if either of these conditions exist.

Inspect runout of wheels and tires.

Inspect trim height. If out of specifications, correct before alignment. Inspect shocks, rack and pinion and control arms for looseness and proper operation. Replace any damaged steering/suspension components.

If any excess weight is normally carried in the trunk of vehicle, alignment is recommended with load in place.

Ensure vehicle is level.

FRONT WHEEL ALIGNMENT

Caster & Camber

1. Loosen lower control arm cam bolt nuts.
2. Rotate cam bolts to specification setting. Refer to "Front Wheel Alignment Specifications" in "Specifications" section.
3. Maintain caster or camber setting while tightening cam bolt nuts. **Torque** cam bolt nuts to 125 ft. lbs.
4. Inspect toe setting after changing camber or caster.

Toe

1. Loosen jam nut on tie rod.
2. Rotate inner tie rod to specification. Refer to "Front Wheel Alignment Specifications" in "Specifications" section.
3. **Torque** jam nut on tie rod 50 ft. lbs.

REAR WHEEL ALIGNMENT

Camber

1. Loosen lower control arm cam bolt nuts.
2. Rotate cam bolts to specification. Refer to "Rear Wheel Alignment Specifications" in "Specifications" section.
3. Maintain camber setting and **torque** lower control arm front bolt nut to 107 ft. lbs.
4. **Torque** lower control arm rear bolt nut to 71 ft. lbs.
5. Inspect toe setting after changing camber.

Toe

1. Loosen rear suspension adjustment link lock nut, **Fig. 1.**
2. Rotate the inner tie rod to specification. Refer to "Rear Wheel Alignment Specifications" in "Specifications" section.
3. **Torque** rear suspension adjustment link lock nut to 44 ft. lbs.

VEHICLE RIDE HEIGHT

Measurement

FRONT

1. With vehicle on a flat surface, lift upward on rear bumper approximately 1.5 inches.
2. Allow vehicle to settle into position, then repeat jouncing operation two more times for a total of three times.
3. Measure distance between lowest point of ball joint and center of front side of the lower control arm mounting bolt, **Fig. 2.**
4. Refer to "Vehicle Ride Height Specifications" in "Specifications" section for correct vehicle ride height.

REAR

1. Manually push rear of vehicle down approximately 1.5 inches, then let vehicle settle.
2. Repeat jouncing operation two more times for a total of three times.
3. Raise and support vehicle.
4. Measure distance between lowest point of the ball joint and center of front side of lower control arm mounting bolt, **Fig. 3.**
5. Refer to "Vehicle Ride Height Specifications" in "Specifications" section for correct vehicle ride height.

Adjustment

FRONT

1. Adjust trim height using trim height adjustment tool J 42743, or equivalent, to turn spring adjuster bolt, **Fig. 4.**
2. Lower transverse spring back onto lower control arm and remove trim height adjustment tool.

REAR

1. Remove retainers on top of transverse spring bolts, **Fig. 5.**
2. Adjust trim height by turning spring bolt, **Fig. 6.**
3. Measure trim height again.
4. Measure rear spring stud heights, maximum difference between lefthand and righthand sides should be .196 inches.
5. Install retainers to bolts and lower vehicle.

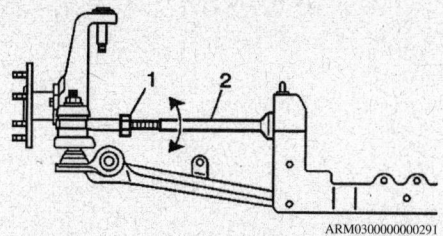

Fig. 1   Rear toe adjustment

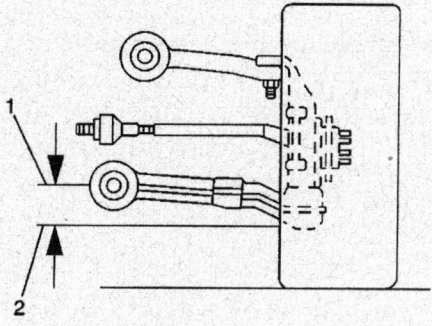

**Fig. 3   Rear vehicle ride height
measurement**

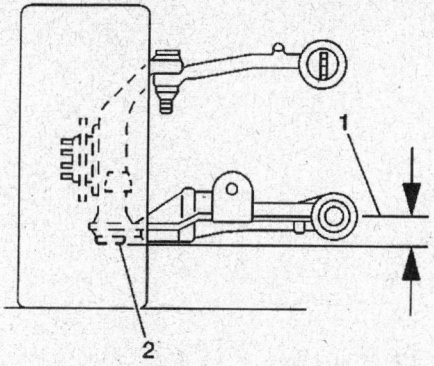

**Fig. 2   Front vehicle ride height
measurement**

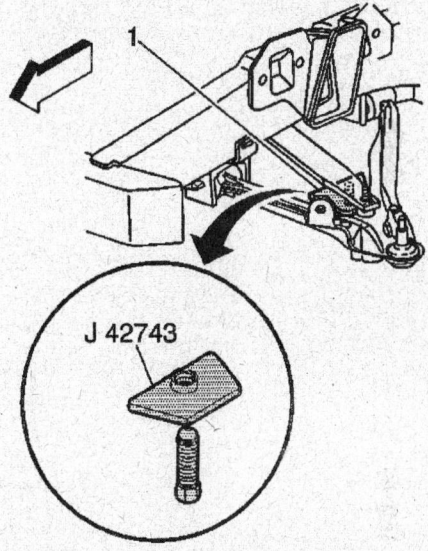

**Fig. 4   Front trim height
adjustment**

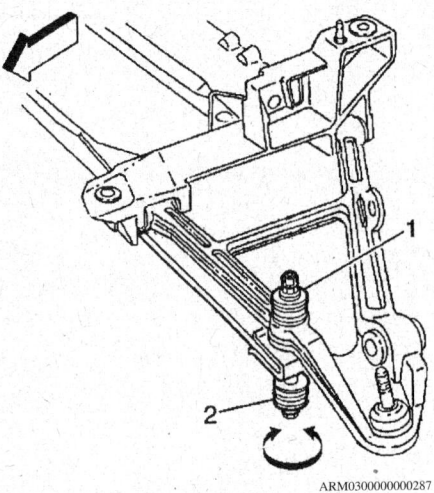

ARM030000000287

Fig. 5   Transverse spring bolt retainers

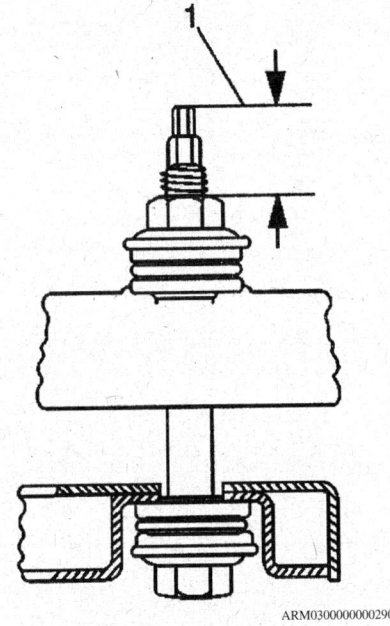

ARM030000000290

Fig. 6   Rear trim height adjustment

G6 & MALIBU MAXX

INDEX OF SERVICE OPERATIONS

Specifications

GENERAL ENGINE SPECIFICATIONS

Engine Liter	Fuel Injection System	Bore & Stroke	Compression Ratio	Net H.P. @ RPM②	Maximum Torque Ft. Lbs. @ RPM	Normal Oil Pressure psi
3.5L	SFI	3.70 x 3.31	9.8:1	200 @ 5400	220 @ 3200	60①

SFI — Sequential Fuel Injection

① — 1850 RPM w/engine at operating temperature.

② — Ratings are as installed in vehicle.

TUNE UP SPECIFICATIONS

Engine	Spark Plug Gap, Inch	Ignition Timing, ° BTDC			Curb Idle Speed RPM③		Fast Idle Speed RPM		Fuel Pump Pressure, psi	Valve Lash
		Firing Order	Man. Trans.	Auto. Trans.	Mark Fig.	Man. Trans.	Auto. Trans.	Man. Trans.	Auto. Trans.	
3.5L	.060	1-2-3-4-5-6	—	①	⑤	—	④	—	④	50–60	②

BTDC — Before Top Dead Center

① — Ignition timing is controlled by Powertrain Control Module (PCM).

② — Vehicle is equipped w/hydraulic valve lifters. No adjustment is required.

③ — P: Park. When adjusting idle speed, set parking brake & block drive wheels.

④ — Idle speed is controlled by an idle air control (IAC) valve or an idle speed control (ISC) motor.

⑤ — Equipped with crankshaft position sensor.

FRONT WHEEL ALIGNMENT SPECIFICATIONS

Model	Caster Angle, Degrees		Camber Angle, Degrees		Total Toe, Degrees	Ball Joint Wear
	Limits	Desired	Limits	Desired		
G6	+2.35 to +3.85	+3.10	②	③	-.20 to +.20	①
Malibu Maxx	+2.25 to +3.75	+3.00	④	⑤	-.20 to +.20	①

① — Refer to "Front Suspension & Steering" section for ball joint inspection procedure.

② — Lefthand wheel, -1.85 to -.35; righthand wheel, -1.35 to +.15.

③ — Lefthand wheel, -1.10; righthand wheel, -.60.

④ — Lefthand wheel, -1.75 to -.25; righthand wheel, -1.25 to +.25.

⑤ — Lefthand wheel, -1.00; righthand wheel, -.50.

REAR WHEEL ALIGNMENT SPECIFICATIONS

Year	Camber Angle, Degrees		Total Toe, Degrees	Thrust Angle, Degrees
	Limits	Desired		
2004–05	-1.3 to -.3	-.8	.0 to +.4	-.30 to +.30

VEHICLE RIDE HEIGHT SPECIFICATIONS

Model	Year	Body Style	Manu-facturer's Original Tire Size	Measurement Points & Specifications					
				Front			Rear		
				Dim.	Specification		Dim.	Specification	
					Inches	mm		Inches	mm
G6	2005	All	①	C	9.30	235	D	9.45	240
Malibu Maxx	2004–05	All	①	C	9.30	235	D	9.60	245

C Dim. — Ground to Rocker Panel, Front

D Dim. — Ground to Rocker Panel, Rear
Dim. — Dimension

① — See door sticker or inside of glove box for manufacturers original tire size specifications.

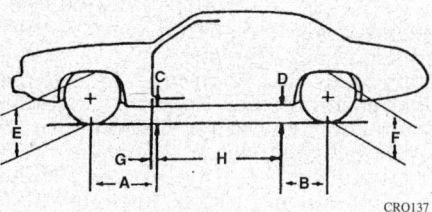

CRQ137

Fig. A

FLUID CAPACITIES & COOLING SYSTEM DATA

Year	Engine	Coolant Capacity, Qts.	Coolant Type	Surge Tank Cap Relief Pressure, psi	Thermo. Opening Temp. Deg. F	Fuel Tank Gals.	Engine Oil Refill Qts.	Transaxle Oil	
								5 Speed Manual Transaxle Pts.	Auto. Transaxle Qts.①
G6	3.5L	9.6	Dex-Cool	15	195	16.3	4.5	—	②
Malibu Maxx	3.5L	10.0	Dex-Cool	15	195	16.5	4.0	—	②

① — Approximate. Make final inspection w/dipstick.

② — Oil pan removal, 6.9 qts.; overhaul, 9.5 qts.; dry 12.9 qts.

LUBRICANT DATA

Year	Model	Lubricant Type				
		Transaxle		Clutch Hydraulic System	Power Steering System	Brake System
		Automatic	Manual			
2004–05	All	Dexron III	Dexron III	DOT 3	①	DOT 3

① — Power Steering Fluid, GM P/N 1052884 (pint), 1050017 (quart) or equivalent.

Electrical

NOTE: On Air Bag Equipped Models, Refer To "Air Bag System Precautions" Located In The Front Of This Manual For System Disarming & Arming Procedures.

NOTE: Refer To "Computer Relearn Procedures" Located In The Front Of This Manual When Battery Power To The Computer Has Been Interrupted.

INDEX

PRECAUTIONS

Air Bag Systems

Refer to "Air Bag System Precautions" in the front of this manual for system disarming and arming procedures.

Battery Ground Cable

Prior to service, disconnect battery ground cable and isolate as required.

FUSE PANEL & FLASHER LOCATION

The rear fuse block is located on the rear lefthand side of the passenger compartment, behind the wheelwell. The underhood fuse block is located on the lefthand side of the engine compartment. The turn signal and hazard flasher module is an internal component of the hazard switch located behind the center of the instrument panel.

FUEL PUMP RELAY LOCATION

The fuel pump relay is located on the rear lefthand side of the passenger compartment, in the rear fuse block.

RELAY CENTER LOCATION

Relays are located in all the fuse and junction blocks, refer to "Fuse Panel & Flasher Location" for relay center locations.

STARTER
REPLACE
Removal

1. Raise and support vehicle.
2. Remove flywheel inspection cover.
3. Remove starter electrical connectors.
4. Remove mounting bolts and starter.

Installation

1. Tighten solenoid BAT terminal nut next to cap while starter is still on bench.
2. Connect solenoid electrical terminal.
3. **Torque** solenoid battery terminal inside nut to 13 ft. lbs.
4. Install electrical connectors to starter.
5. **Torque** solenoid battery terminal outside nut to 89 inch lbs.
6. **Torque** solenoid S terminal outside nut to 27 inch lbs.
7. Install starter onto engine and **torque** mounting bolts to 32 ft. lbs.
8. Install inspection cover and **torque** bolts to 84 inch lbs.

ALTERNATOR
REPLACE

1. Remove air cleaner assembly.
2. Remove engine mount strut from front of engine and radiator support.
3. Rotate drive belt tensioner using tool No. J 37059 or equivalent, then remove serpentine drive belt.
4. Remove alternator mounting bolts and nuts.
5. Disconnect electrical connectors and remove alternator.

6. Reverse procedure to install. **Torque** mounting bolts to 37 ft. lbs., and nuts to 22 ft. lbs.

COIL PACK
REPLACE

1. Note position of spark plug wires for installation reference, then disconnect wires from ignition coil and module assembly.
2. Remove ignition coil and module assembly mounting screws, then separate assembly from bracket.
3. Reverse procedure to install. **Torque** mounting screws to 40 inch lbs.

IGNITION LOCK
REPLACE

1. Remove outer trim cover from lefthand side of instrument panel.
2. Remove lower trim panels from lower lefthand closeout panel.
3. Remove lower lefthand closeout panel from lefthand knee bolster.
4. Turn ignition switch to the RUN position.
5. Depress lock cylinder retaining tab, then remove lock cylinder.
6. Reverse procedure to install.

IGNITION SWITCH
REPLACE

1. Tilt steering column upper trim cover upward and remove nuts from instrument panel seal.
2. Remove steering column upper trim cover.

3. Remove steering column lower trim cover attaching screws.
4. Lower steering column rake lever and lower steering column, then fully telescope column toward driver and remove lower trim cover from column.
5. Remove instrument panel cluster trim plate bezel attaching screws, then the bezel from cluster.
6. Remove fog lamp and adjustable pedal switch.
7. Remove instrument panel dimmer switch, then the lefthand center instrument panel trim panel.
8. Remove righthand instrument panel trim panel.
9. Remove righthand closeout panel and glove compartment from instrument panel.
10. Remove instrument panel center trim bezel.
11. Remove outer trim cover from lefthand side of instrument panel.
12. Remove lower trim panels from lower lefthand closeout panel.
13. Remove lower lefthand closeout panel from lefthand knee bolster.
14. Remove knee bolster from under lefthand side of instrument panel.
15. Disconnect ignition switch and theft deterrent control module harness connectors.
16. Turn ignition switch to the RUN position.
17. Disconnect park lock cable from ignition switch.
18. Remove ignition switch to instrument panel attaching screws.
19. Remove ignition switch from instrument panel.
20. Reverse procedure to install.

NEUTRAL SAFETY SWITCH
REPLACE
Removal

1. Apply parking brake and place shift lever in Neutral.
2. Remove shift control cable from switch lever.
3. Disconnect switch electrical connectors.
4. Remove switch lever nut and lever.
5. Remove switch attaching bolts and the switch.

Installation

1. Place shift shaft in Neutral position and align flats on shaft with flats on switch.
2. Loosely install switch with marks properly aligned.
3. Insert Park/Neutral Switch Aligner tool No. J 41545 as outlined and rotate switch until tool drops into position
4. **Torque** switch bolts to 15 ft. lbs., and remove alignment tool.

HEADLAMP SWITCH
REPLACE

Refer to "Multi-Function Switch, Replace" for replacement procedure.

STOP LIGHT SWITCH
REPLACE

1. Remove closeout panel from under lefthand side of instrument panel.
2. Remove steering column stub shaft bolt, then position steering column stub shaft aside.
3. Disconnect brake pedal position sensor electrical connector.
4. Remove brake pedal position sensor retaining bolt, then the sensor.
5. Reverse procedure to install.

MULTI-FUNCTION SWITCH
REPLACE

1. Tilt steering column upper trim cover upward and remove nuts from instrument panel seal.
2. Remove steering column upper trim cover.
3. Remove steering column lower trim cover attaching screws.
4. Lower steering column rake lever and lower steering column, then fully telescope column toward driver and remove lower trim cover from column.
5. Remove mounting screw and switch.
6. Reverse procedure to install.

TURN SIGNAL SWITCH
REPLACE

Refer to "Multi-Function Switch, Replace" for replacement procedure.

STEERING WHEEL
REPLACE

1. Remove mounting screws for horn pad or air bag module.
2. **On models equipped with radio controls,** remove wire protector plate connector.
3. **On all models,** remove horn pad or air bag module and horn lead, then the steering wheel retainer and nut.
4. Remove steering wheel using puller tool No. J 1859-A and legs tool No. J 42120 or equivalent.
5. Reverse procedure to install, noting the following:
   a. **Torque** steering wheel nut to 27–30 ft. lbs.
   b. **Torque** air bag module screws to 89 inch lbs.

INSTRUMENT CLUSTER
REPLACE

1. Tilt steering column upper trim cover upward and remove nuts from instrument panel seal.
2. Remove steering column upper trim cover.
3. Remove steering column lower trim cover attaching screws.
4. Lower steering column rake lever and lower steering column, then fully telescope column toward driver and remove lower trim cover from column.
5. Remove instrument panel cluster trim plate bezel attaching screws, then the bezel from cluster.
6. Remove instrument cluster to instrument panel mounting screws.
7. Disconnect cluster electrical connectors and remove instrument cluster.
8. Reverse procedure to install.

RADIO
REPLACE

1. Remove fog lamp, dimmer and adjustable pedal switches from lower lefthand trim panel.
2. Remove trim panels from under lefthand and righthand sides of instrument panel.
3. Remove closeout panel from under righthand side of instrument panel.
4. Remove instrument panel compartment from front of center console.
5. Remove knee bolster from under lefthand side of instrument panel.
6. Remove instrument panel center trim bezel.
7. Remove hazard warning switch.
8. Remove heater-A/C control head from center of instrument panel.
9. Remove radio retaining screws, then the radio.
10. Reverse procedure to install.

WIPER MOTOR
REPLACE

1. Remove wiper arm and blade.
2. Remove cowl cover.
3. Disconnect drive link from crank arm using wiper transmission separator tool No. J 39232 or equivalent.
4. Disconnect wiper motor electrical connectors.
5. Remove mounting screws and wiper motor.
6. Reverse procedure to install, noting the following:
   a. **Torque** motor mounting screws to 84 inch lbs.
   b. Connect drive link to crank arm using wiper transmission installer tool No. J 39529 or equivalent.

WIPER SWITCH
REPLACE

Refer to "Multi-Function Switch, Replace" for replacement procedure.

WIPER TRANSMISSION
REPLACE

1. Remove wiper arm and blades.
2. Remove cowl cover and disconnect wiper motor connector.
3. Remove mounting screws and wiper drive system module.
4. Remove wiper motor as outlined under "Wiper Motor, Replace."
5. Remove caps, wiper motor grommets and transmission.
6. Reverse procedure to install. **Torque** mounting screws to 72 inch lbs.

BLOWER MOTOR
REPLACE

The blower motor and fan are located in the lower righthand corner of the Heating, Ventilation and Air Conditioning (HVAC) module. The fan and motor are serviced only as a complete assembly.

1. Remove righthand closeout panel and insulator.
2. Disconnect blower motor electrical connectors.
3. Remove mounting screws, blower motor and fan.
4. Reverse procedure to install. **Torque** blower motor mounting screws to 45 inch lbs.

HEATER CORE
REPLACE

1. Drain coolant.
2. Remove inlet and outlet heater hoses from heater core.
3. Recover A/C system refrigerant.
4. Remove suction hose from thermostatic expansion valve.
5. Remove and discard sealing washers.
6. Disconnect the HVAC module to front of dash plate bolts.
7. Remove righthand and lefthand console trim panels.
8. Remove front console screw covers from behind console.
9. Remove front console screws, then position front seats to full forward position.
10. Remove rear console bolts, then place shifter in drive.
11. Remove lefthand closeout panel and both instrument panel outer trim panels.
12. Disconnect instrument panel to body wire harness and antenna connectors.
13. Disconnect instrument panel to wire harness righthand connectors.
14. Remove knee bolster from under lefthand side of instrument panel.
15. Remove accelerator pedal, then disconnect steering column to instrument panel wire harness connector.
16. Remove crush bracket to front of dash plate nuts.
17. Remove upper steering column shroud from lower shroud.
18. Remove stalk switches and SIR coil connectors.
19. Position steering wheel in full forward telescoping position, then place front seat in full rearward position.
20. Remove steering column mounting bolts.
21. Remove brake pedal assembly.
22. Remove Body Control Module (BCM).
23. Remove center support bracket floor bolts, then the shifter assembly.
24. Remove both windshield pillar garnish moldings.
25. Remove instrument panel upper trim panel.
26. Remove lefthand and righthand instrument panel to body bolts.
27. Remove righthand and lefthand floor heater ducts from center floor heater duct.
28. Remove instrument panel.
29. Remove and discard HVAC module drain seal and dash seal.
30. Remove lower center floor air outlet duct.
31. Remove upper center floor air outlet duct screws, then the upper center floor air outlet duct.
32. Drill out heater core cover heat stakes.
33. Remove heater core cover screws, then the cover.
34. Remove heater core from module.
35. Reverse procedure to install.

EVAPORATOR CORE
REPLACE

1. Recover air conditioning refrigerant as outlined in "Air Conditioning" chapter.
2. Drain coolant into suitable container.
3. Remove HVAC assembly as outlined under "Heater Core, Replace."
4. Remove thermal expansion valve screw, then the thermal expansion valve.
5. Remove and discard sealing washers.
6. Remove evaporator core.
7. Reverse procedure to install. Use new sealing washers.

3.5L Engine

NOTE: For Procedures Not Found In This Section, Refer To The "3.5L Engine" Section In the "Alero, Grand Am & Malibu" Chapter.

NOTE: On Air Bag Equipped Models, Refer To "Air Bag System Precautions" Located In The Front Of This Manual For System Disarming & Arming Procedures.

NOTE: Refer To "Computer Relearn Procedures" Located In The Front Of This Manual When Battery Power To The Computer Has Been Interrupted.

INDEX

PRECAUTIONS

Air Bag Systems

Refer to "Air Bag System Precautions" in the front of this manual for system disarming and arming procedures.

Battery Ground Cable

Prior to service, disconnect battery ground cable and isolate as required.

Fuel System Pressure Relief

Failure to relieve system pressure prior to disconnecting fuel system components may cause fire or personal injury.
1. Loosen fuel tank filler cap to relieve tank pressure.
2. Raise and support vehicle.
3. Disconnect fuel pump electrical connector.
4. Lower vehicle.
5. Start and operate engine until fuel supply is consumed.
6. Crank engine for approximately three seconds to relieve remaining pressure.
7. Disconnect and isolate battery ground cable, then connect fuel pump electrical connector.

COMPRESSION PRESSURE

When inspecting cylinder compression, the throttle should be open, the spark plugs removed and the battery at or near full charge. The lowest reading cylinder should not be less than 70% of the highest and no cylinder reading should be less than 100 psi. Crank engine until it runs through four compression cycles. Normal compression builds up quickly and evenly to specified compression on each cylinder.

ENGINE MOUNT
REPLACE

1. Raise and support vehicle.
2. Remove righthand tire and wheel assembly.
3. Remove splash shield from under engine.
4. Remove engine mount to engine mount bracket nuts.
5. Remove engine mount to frame nuts.
6. Raise engine with a suitable jackstand.
7. Remove motor mount from vehicle.
8. Reverse procedure to install.

ENGINE MOUNT STRUT
REPLACE

1. Remove air cleaner assembly.
2. Remove engine mount strut to engine attaching bolts.
3. Rotate engine mount strut to a vertical position.
4. Remove engine mount strut to body attaching bolts, then the strut from vehicle.
5. Reverse procedure to install.

ENGINE
REPLACE

1. Relieve fuel system pressure as outlined under "Precautions."
2. Drain coolant into suitable container.
3. Drain engine oil.
4. Remove engine air cleaner assembly.
5. Mark engine hinge locations for installation reference, then remove hood.
6. Remove serpentine belt.
7. Remove engine mount strut as outlined under "Engine Mount Strut, Replace."
8. Disconnect the following electrical connectors:
   a. Knock sensor.
   b. Camshaft Position (CMP) sensor.
   c. Crankshaft Position (CKP) sensor.
   d. Oxygen sensor.
   e. Manifold Absolute Pressure (MAP) sensor.
   f. EGR valve.
   g. Evaporative (EVAP) emission canister purge solenoid.
   h. Electronic throttle control.
   i. Ignition coil.
   j. Body wiring harness to engine harness.
9. Raise and support vehicle.
10. Remove exhaust crossover pipe retaining nuts, then the pipe.
11. Remove engine wiring harness grounds from transaxle.
12. Remove engine mount lower nuts.
13. Remove torque converter covers and starter motor.
14. Remove A/C compressor from mount. **Do not discharge A/C system refrigerant.**
15. Remove torque converter attaching bolts.
16. Remove transaxle support brace.
17. Remove lower transaxle to engine attaching bolts.
18. Remove radiator outlet hose from engine.
19. Lower vehicle and support transaxle with a suitable lifting device.
20. Remove heater inlet and outlet hoses from engine.
21. Remove vacuum and brake booster hoses from upper intake manifold.
22. Remove fuel lines from fuel rail.
23. Remove radiator inlet hose from engine.

24. Install a suitable engine lifting device to engine.
25. Remove upper transaxle to engine attaching bolts.
26. Remove engine from vehicle.
27. Reverse procedure to install.

RADIATOR

REPLACE

1. Drain engine coolant.
2. Remove lefthand headlamp assembly attaching bolts.
3. Lift headlamp assembly to unseat tabs on bottom edge of fender.
4. Disconnect headlamp assembly electrical connector and remove assembly from vehicle.
5. Remove righthand headlamp assembly attaching bolts.
6. Lift headlamp assembly to unseat tabs on bottom edge of fender.
7. Disconnect headlamp assembly electrical connector and remove assembly from vehicle.
8. Loop a suitable rope around upper two tabs of condenser, then tie rope around upper engine compartment tie bar.
9. Remove upper radiator support bracket bolts and support brackets.
10. Remove surge tank outlet hose from radiator.
11. Remove radiator inlet hose from radiator.
12. Raise and support vehicle.
13. Remove lower radiator air deflector retainers and the deflector.

14. Remove front fender liner retainers and fender liner.
15. Remove righthand and lefthand radiator air deflector retainers and deflectors.
16. Remove radiator outlet hose from radiator.
17. Place a suitable drain pan under transaxle cooler lines, then remove cooler lines from transaxle.
18. Remove lower radiator support bracket bolts and support brackets.
19. Remove radiator lower mounts.
20. Remove and discard condenser mounting bolts from radiator.
21. Push upward on radiator and downward on condenser to unsnap condenser mounting tabs from radiator clips.
22. Remove and discard condenser mounting nuts from radiator.
23. Remove radiator air side seals.
24. Remove radiator, cooling fan shroud and transaxle cooler line assembly.
25. Remove transaxle cooler lines from radiator.
26. Pry upward on fan shroud tabs, then remove cooling fan and shroud assembly from radiator.
27. Reverse procedure to install.

FUEL PUMP

REPLACE

1. Relieve fuel system pressure as outlined under "Precautions."
2. Drain fuel tank.
3. Raise and support vehicle.

4. Disconnect fuel pump module electrical harness connector from vehicle underbody wiring harness.
5. Disconnect EVAP vent valve solenoid harness electrical connector from vehicle underbody wiring harness.
6. Remove ABS wiring harness from retainer on EVAP canister.
7. Disconnect fuel feed and purge lines from fuel and brake line bundle on righthand side of vehicle.
8. Cap or plug fuel tank feed and vapor lines to prevent fuel loss or contamination.
9. Disconnect fuel filler pipe jumper hose from fuel tank.
10. Disconnect vapor recirculation line that runs parallel to fuel filler pipe jumper hose.
11. Remove exhaust pipe and muffler insulators from underbody hangers, then support exhaust system with suitable jackstand.
12. Support fuel tank with a suitable jackstand.
13. Remove lefthand and righthand fuel tank strap bolts.
14. Carefully lower righthand side of tank until is clear of frame rail, then remove tank toward righthand side of vehicle.
15. Remove fuel pump module assembly from fuel tank using fuel sender lock ring wrench tool No. J 45722 or equivalent.
16. Reverse procedure to install.

TIGHTENING SPECIFICATIONS

Year	Component	Torque/Ft. Lbs.
2004–05	Camshaft Position Sensor Bolt	89①
	Camshaft Sprocket Bolt	103
	Camshaft Thrust Plate	89①
	Connecting Rod Bearing Cap Bolt	②
	Coolant Drain Plug	14
	Coolant Temperature Sensor	17
	Crankshaft Balancer Bolt	③
	Crankshaft Main Bearing Cap Bolt	④
	Cylinder Head Bolts	⑤
	Drive Belt Tensioner Bolt	37
	EGR Valve Assembly Bolt	22
	EGR Valve Pipe Bolt (Exhaust Manifold)	89①
	EGR Valve Pipe Bolt (EGR)	18
	Engine Mount Strut To A/C Bracket Bolt	37
	Engine Mount Strut To Alternator Bracket	37
	Engine Mount Strut To Lift Bracket Bolt	52
	Engine Mount Strut To Support Bracket Bolt	18
	Engine Oil Pressure Switch	12
	Engine Wiring Harness Bracket	115①
	EVAP Purge Valve Bolt	12

TIGHTENING
SPECIFICATIONS—Continued

Year	Component	Torque/Ft. Lbs.
2004–05	Exhaust Manifold Heat Shield Bolt	89①
	Exhaust Manifold Nut	12
	Flywheel Bolt	52
	Front Cover (Large & Medium Bolts)	41
	Front Cover (Small Bolts)	20
	Fuel Feed Pipe To Injector Rail Bolt	89①
	Fuel Injector Rail Bolt	89①
	Heater Inlet Pipe Nut	18
	Ignition Coil Bracket Bolt	18
	Intake Manifold Coolant Pipe Bolt	89①
	Intake Manifold (Lower)	⑥
	Intake Manifold (Upper)	18
	Knock Sensor	18
	Main Bearing Cap Bolt	④
	MAP Sensor	89①
	Oil Filter Adapter Bolt	18
	Oil Filter	22
	Oil Filter Bypass Hole Plug	14
	Oil Filter Fitting	29
	Oil Dipstick Tube Bolt	18
	Oil Pan Bolt	18
	Oil Pan Drain Plug	18
	Oil Pan Side Bolt	37
	Oil Pump Cover Bolt	89①
	Oil Pump Drive Clamp Bolt	27
	Oil Pump Mounting Bolt	30
	Oxygen Sensor	31
	PCV Tube Clip Bolt	89①
	Rocker Arm Bolt	24
	Spark Plug	15
	Thermostat Bypass Pipe To Front Cover	89①
	Thermostat Bypass Pipe To Throttle Body	89①
	Throttle Body Bolt	89①
	Timing Chain Dampener Bolt	15
	Valve Lifter Guide Bolt	89①
	Valve Rocker Arm Bolt	24
	Valve Cover Bolts	89①
	Water Outlet Bolt	18
	Water Pump Bolt	89①
	Water Pump Pulley Bolt	18

① — Inch lbs.
② — 18 ft. lbs., plus an additional 110.°
③ — 52 ft. lbs., plus an additional 70.°
④ — 37 ft. lbs., plus an additional 77.°
⑤ — Refer to "Cylinder Head, Replace" in "Alero, Grand Am & Malibu" chapter for tightening procedure.
⑥ — Refer to "Intake Manifold, Replace" in "Alero, Grand Am & Malibu" chapter for tightening procedure.

Rear Axle & Suspension

INDEX

DESCRIPTION

The rear suspension used on these vehicles is an independent link type. Coil springs are mounted between the body and lower control arms. The coil springs are controlled by shock absorbers attached to the knuckles and body.

HUB & BEARING
REPLACE

1. Raise and support vehicle.
2. Remove tire and wheel assembly.
3. Remove brake rotor as outlined in "Disc Brakes" chapter.
4. Disconnect wheel speed sensor electrical connector.
5. Remove stabilizer from wheel bearing and hub assembly, then loosen stabilizer shaft insulator bolts enough to position stabilizer shaft aside.
6. Remove wheel bearing and hub assembly retaining nuts, then the assembly from knuckle.
7. Reverse procedure to install.

SUPPORT ASSEMBLY
REPLACE

1. Raise and support vehicle.
2. Remove rear wheels and tires.
3. Remove exhaust system.
4. Remove lower control arms as outlined under "Control Arms, Replace."
5. Remove upper control arm to support assembly attaching bolts and nuts.
6. Remove toe links as outlined under "Toe Links, Replace."
7. Remove stabilizer shaft to knuckle attaching bolts.
8. Remove vehicle wiring harness from support assembly retaining clips.
9. Place a suitable jack stand under support assembly.
10. Remove support assembly to body attaching bolts.
11. Remove support assembly from vehicle.
12. Reverse procedure to install.

SHOCK ABSORBER
REPLACE

1. Raise and support vehicle.
2. Remove tire and wheel assembly.
3. Place a suitable jack stand under knuckle assembly, then raise jack to relieve spring tension.
4. Remove lower shock absorber to knuckle attaching bolt.
5. Remove upper shock absorber to support assembly attaching bolt, then the shock absorber from vehicle.
6. Reverse procedure to install.

COIL SPRING
REPLACE

1. Raise and support vehicle.
2. Remove tire and wheel assembly.
3. Remove rear splash shield to inner fender fasteners, then the splash shield from inner fender.
4. Compress coil spring with spring compressor tool No. OTC 204-167 or equivalent.
5. Place a suitable adjustable jack stand under lower control arm.
6. Remove lower control arm to knuckle attaching bolt and nut.
7. Lower control arm with coil spring attached.
8. Remove coil spring from lower control arm.
9. Reverse procedure to install.

CONTROL ARM
REPLACE

Lower

1. Raise and support vehicle.
2. Remove wheel and tire assembly.
3. Remove coil spring as outlined under "Coil Spring, Replace."
4. Remove lower control arm to support assembly attaching bolt and nut.
5. Remove lower control arm from vehicle.
6. Reverse procedure to install.

Upper

1. Raise and support vehicle.
2. Remove wheel and tire assembly.
3. Disconnect ABS harness connector and position aside. Note position of harness for installation reference.
4. Remove upper control arm to support assembly attaching bolt.
5. Remove upper control arm to knuckle bolt and nut.
6. Remove upper control arm from vehicle through wheelwell opening.
7. Reverse procedure to install.

KNUCKLE
REPLACE

1. Raise and support vehicle.
2. Remove tire and wheel assembly.
3. Remove rear wheel bearing as outlined under "Wheel Bearing & Hub, Replace."
4. Place a suitable jack stand under steering knuckle, then raise knuckle to relieve tension from shock absorber.
5. Remove lower shock absorber to steering knuckle attaching bolt.
6. Remove coil spring as outlined under "Coil Spring, Replace."
7. Remove toe link as outlined under "Toe Link, Replace."
8. Remove upper control arm to knuckle attaching bolt and nut.
9. Remove trailing arm to knuckle bolts.
10. Remove stabilizer shaft link to knuckle attaching bolt, then the knuckle from vehicle.
11. Reverse procedure to install.

TRAILING ARM
REPLACE

1. Raise and support vehicle.
2. Remove wheel and tire assembly.
3. Remove trailing arm bracket to body attaching bolts.
4. Remove trailing arm to knuckle through bolt.
5. Disconnect parking brake cable from trailing arm.
6. Remove trailing arm to bracket bolt and nut.
7. Remove trailing arm from bracket.
8. Reverse procedure to install.

STABILIZER SHAFT
REPLACE

1. Raise and support vehicle, then remove tire and wheel assemblies.
2. Remove link bolts.
3. Remove mounting nuts and insulator brackets.
4. Remove stabilizer shaft.
5. Reverse procedure to install.

TOE LINK
REPLACE

1. Raise and support vehicle.
2. Remove tire and wheel assembly.
3. Remove toe link to steering knuckle attaching bolt.

4. Remove toe link to support assembly attaching bolt and nut, then the toe link from vehicle.

5. Reverse procedure to install.

TIGHTENING SPECIFICATIONS

Year	Component	Torque/Ft. Lbs.
2004–05	Lower Control Arm To Knuckle	②
	Lower Control Arm To Support Assembly	81
	Shock Absorber To Body	66
	Shock Absorber To Knuckle	133
	Stabilizer Shaft Insulator Bracket	26
	Stabilizer Shaft Link To Knuckle	37
	Support Assembly To Body	③
	Toe Link To Steering Knuckle	133
	Trailing Arm To Body	③
	Trailing Arm To Bracket Through Bolt	②
	Trailing Arm To Knuckle	133
	Upper Control Arm To Knuckle	①
	Upper Control Arm To Support Assembly	②
	Wheel Bearing & Hub Assembly	47
	Wheel Lug Nut	100

① — **Torque** to 81 ft. lbs, then tighten an additional 70°.
② — **Torque** to 44 ft. lbs, then tighten an additional 60°.
③ — **Torque** to 66 ft. lbs, then tighten an additional 30°.

Front Suspension & Steering

INDEX

PRECAUTIONS

Air Bag Systems

Refer to "Air Bag System Precautions" in the front of this manual for system disarming and arming procedures.

Battery Ground Cable

Prior to service, disconnect battery ground cable and isolate as required.

DESCRIPTION

The front suspension on these vehicles, **Fig. 1,** is of the strut and spring design. The lower control arms pivot from the lower side rails through rubber bushings. The upper end of the strut is isolated by a rubber mount incorporating a bearing for wheel turning. The tie rods connect to the steering arm on the strut, below the spring seat. The lower end of the steering knuckle pivots on a ball stud which is retained to the lower control arm by rivets and is secured to the steering knuckle with a nut and cotter pin. The sealed wheel bearings are integral with the hub and are serviced as an assembly.

WHEEL BEARING
REPLACE

1. Raise and support vehicle.
2. Remove tire and wheel assembly.
3. Insert suitable drift punch into caliper and rotor to prevent turning, then remove axle shaft nut.
4. Remove brake rotor as outlined in "Disc Brakes."
5. Disconnect wheel speed sensor electrical connector.
6. Remove wheel speed sensor connector from bracket.
7. Remove hub and bearing assembly attaching bolts.
8. Remove hub and bearing assembly from drive shaft using hub and bearing removal tool No. J 42129 or equivalent.
9. Reverse procedure to install.

BALL JOINT INSPECTION

Ball joints must be replaced if any looseness is detected in the joint or the seal is cut.

To inspect the ball joints, raise the front of the vehicle allowing the suspension to hang free. Grasp the tire at the top and bottom and move the top of tire with an in-and-out motion. Look for any horizontal movement of the steering knuckle relative to the front lower control arm.

If the ball stud is disconnected from the steering knuckle and any looseness is detected or if the ball stud can be twisted in its socket using hand pressure, replace the ball joint.

Ball stud tightness in the steering knuckle boss should also be inspected when inspecting the ball joint. This may be done by shaking the wheel and feeling for movement of the stud end or castellated nut at the knuckle boss. Inspecting the torque at the castellated nut is an alternative method of inspecting for wear. A loose nut can indicate a bent stud or an opened-up hole in the knuckle boss. Worn or damaged ball joints and knuckles must be replaced.

BALL JOINT
REPLACE

To replace the lower ball joint on these vehicles, the lower control arm must be replaced. Refer to "Control Arm, Replace" for procedure.

COIL SPRING
REPLACE

Refer to "Strut Service" for coil spring replacement.

STRUT
REPLACE

1. Raise and support vehicle.
2. Remove wheel and tire assembly.
3. Disconnect stabilizer link from strut.
4. Remove strut to steering knuckle nuts.
5. Position wheel speed sensor harness aside.
6. Remove strut to steering knuckle attaching bolts.

7. Remove upper strut cap to body retaining nuts.
8. Remove strut assembly from vehicle.
9. Reverse procedure to install. Adjust front end alignment as required, refer to "Wheel Alignment" section.

STRUT SERVICE
Disassemble

1. Position strut compressor tool No. J 34013-B in holding fixture J 3289-20 with adapter tool No. J 34013-88 or equivalents.
2. Compress strut to approximately half of its height. **Do not bottom spring or damper rod.**
3. Remove nut from strut dampener shaft and position alignment rod tool No. J 34013-27 or equivalent, on dampener shaft. Position dampener shaft down through bearing cap while compressing coil spring using guide rod tool.
4. Remove strut components, **Fig. 2.**

Assemble

1. Install bearing cap.
2. Mount strut to strut compressor tool using bottom locking pin only.
3. Extend dampener shaft and install dampener rod clamp tool No. J 34013-20 or equivalent.
4. Install spring over dampener.
5. Swing strut assembly up and install upper locking pin.
6. Install upper insulator, dust shield, bumper and upper spring seat. Flat on upper spring seat should face in same direction as centerline of strut knuckle, **Fig. 3.**
7. Compress strut using guide rod tool until dampener shaft threads are visible. Remove guide rod tool and install mounting nut.
8. While holding dampener shaft in position with suitable wrench, tighten mounting nut.
9. Remove dampener rod clamp tool.

CONTROL ARM
REPLACE

1. Raise and support vehicle.
2. Remove wheel and tire assembly.

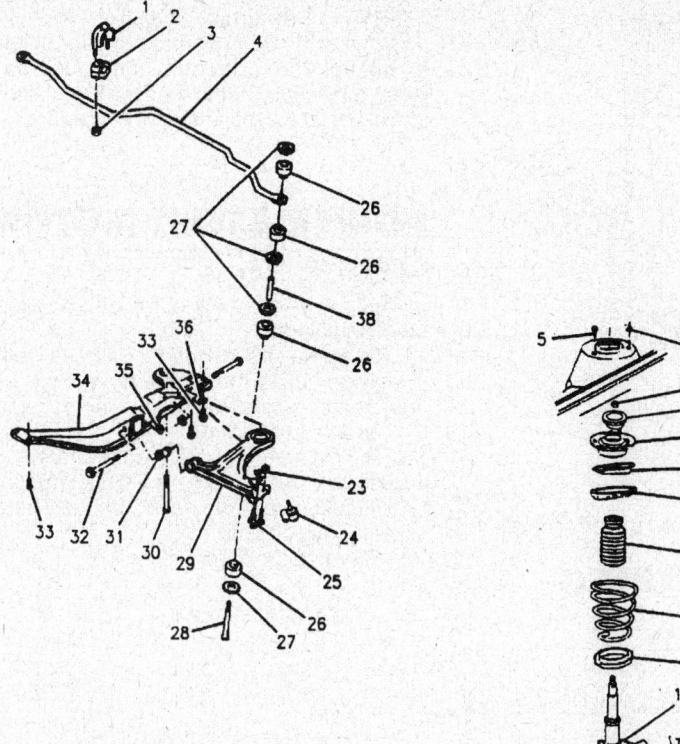

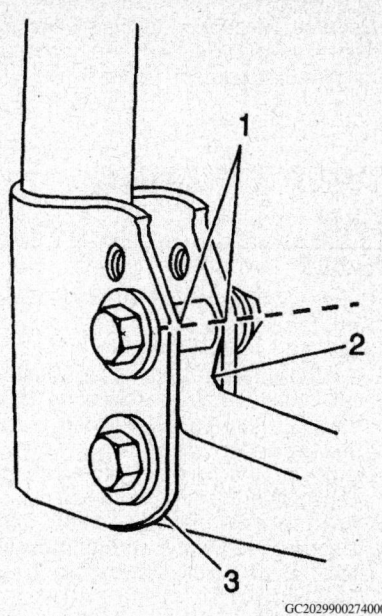

GC2029900274000X

Fig. 2 Exploded view of strut

1 CLAMP, STABILIZER SHAFT
2 INSULATOR, STABILIZER SHAFT
3 NUT
4 STABILIZER SHAFT
5 BOLT
6 NUT
7 NUT, STRUT DAMPENER SHAFT
8 RATE WASHER
9 STRUT MOUNT
10 UPPER SPRING SEAT
11 UPPER SPRING INSULATOR
12 DUST TUBE ASSEMBLY
13 SPRING
14 LOWER SPRING INSULATOR
15 STRUT
16 NUT
17 WASHER
18 BOLT
19 HUB AND BEARING ASSEMBLY

20 STEERING KNUCKLE
21 NUT, BALL JOINT
22 COTTER PIN
23 NUT
24 BALL JOINT
25 BOLT
26 INSULATOR, STABILIZER LINK
27 WASHER, STABILIZER LINK
28 BOLT, STABILIZER LINK
29 CONTROL ARM
30 BOLT
31 BUSHING, CONTROL ARM

32 BOLT
33 BOLT
34 SUSPENSION SUPPORT
35 NUT
36 WASHER
37 BOLT
38 SPACER, STABILIZER LINK

GC2029700271000X

Fig. 1 Exploded view of front suspension

3. **On lefthand control arm,** remove transaxle mount.
4. **On righthand control arm,** remove engine mount.
5. **On lefthand and righthand control arms,** remove front control arm bushing to frame attaching bolt and nut.
6. Remove rear control arm bushing to frame attaching bolts and nuts.
7. Remove control arm ball stud to steering knuckle pinch bolt.
8. Separate ball stud from steering knuckle, then remove knuckle from vehicle.
9. Reverse procedure to install.

STEERING KNUCKLE
REPLACE

1. Raise and support vehicle.
2. Remove wheel and tire assembly.

3. Remove wheel bearing and hub assembly as outlined under "Wheel Hub & Bearing, Replace."
4. Remove outer tie rod to steering knuckle retaining nut, then separate steering knuckle from tie rod.
5. Remove strut to steering knuckle attaching bolts and nuts.
6. Remove steering knuckle from vehicle.
7. Reverse procedure to install. Adjust front end alignment as required, refer to "Wheel Alignment" section.

STABILIZER BAR
REPLACE

1. Raise and support vehicle.
2. Remove tire and wheel assemblies.
3. Disconnect stabilizer links from stabilizer shaft.

4. Place a suitable jack stand under rear of frame assembly.
5. Remove frame support to body attaching bolts.
6. Remove rear frame assembly mounting bolts.
7. Lower rear of cradle to access stabilizer shaft.
8. Remove stabilizer bar clamps and insulators.
9. Remove stabilizer shaft through frame and body opening.
10. Reverse procedure to install.

TIE ROD END
REPLACE
Inner

1. Raise and support vehicle.
2. Remove tire and wheel assembly.
3. Remove outer tie rod as outlined under "Outer."
4. Remove steering gear as outlined under "Power Steering Gear, Replace."
5. Remove steering gear boot.
6. Slide shock damper toward steering gear, then remove inner tie rod from steering gear using two suitable wrenches.
7. Reverse procedure to install. Adjust front end alignment as required, refer to "Wheel Alignment" section.

Outer

1. Raise and support vehicle.
2. Remove tire and wheel assembly.
3. Loosen outer tie rod end jam nut.
4. Remove outer tie rod end to steering knuckle retaining nut.
5. Separate tie rod end from knuckle with tie rod separator tool No. J 24319-B or equivalent.
6. Remove outer tie rod end from inner tie rod end.

7. Reverse procedure to install. Adjust front end alignment as required, refer to "Wheel Alignment" section.

POWER STEERING GEAR

REPLACE

1. Place steering wheel in straight forward position.
2. Raise and support vehicle.
3. Remove wheel and tire assemblies.
4. Disconnect outer tie rod ends from steering knuckles as outlined under "Tie Rod End, Replace."
5. Remove and discard intermediate shaft to steering gear pinch bolt.
6. Separate intermediate shaft from steering gear. **Do not rotate intermediate shaft after separating from steering gear.**
7. Remove steering gear to frame mounting bolts, then remove steering gear through lefthand side wheelwell.
8. Reverse procedure to install. Adjust front end alignment as required, refer to "Wheel Alignment" section.

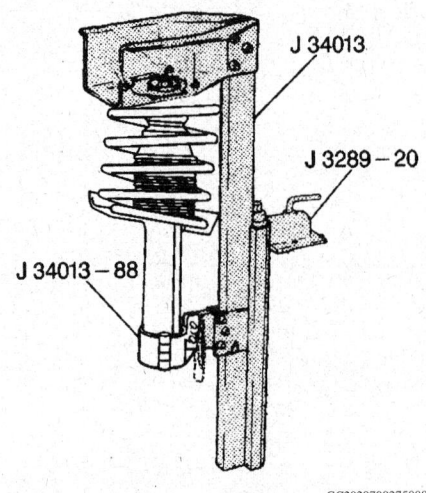

J 34013

J 3289 – 20

J 34013 – 88

GC2029700275000X

Fig. 3 Strut replacement

POWER STEERING PUMP

REPLACE

These models use a power assist motor, Power Steering Control Module (PSCM), Powertrain Control Module (PCM) and the Body Control Module (BCM) to control the power steering function. Refer to "Power Steering Assist Motor, Replace" for motor replacement procedure.

POWER ASSIST MOTOR

REPLACE

The power assist motor is located on the steering column.

1. Disconnect sensor wire harness from power assist motor assembly.
2. Remove wire strap clip using suitable needle nose pliers.
3. Remove power assist motor mounting screws with a suitable TORX wrench.
4. Remove power assist motor from steering column.
5. Reverse procedure to install.

TIGHTENING SPECIFICATIONS

Year	Component	Torque/Ft. Lbs.
2004–05	Ball Stud Pinch Bolt	32
	Control Arm Bushing To Frame	37
	Drive Shaft Nut	159
	Frame Support Bracket To Body	①
	Hub & Bearing Assembly	85
	Intermediate Shaft To Steering Gear Pinch Bolt	36
	Lower Control Arm To Bushing	32
	Outer Tie Rod End To Steering Knuckle	②
	Power Steering Gear To Frame	③
	Rear Frame To Body	①
	Stabilizer Link Nut	48
	Stabilizer Shaft Clamp	18
	Steering Knuckle To Strut	89
	Upper Strut Cap To Body	18
	Upper Strut Shaft	52
	Wheel Lug Nut	100

① — **Torque** to 74 ft. lbs., then tighten an additional 90°.
② — **Torque** to 15 ft. lbs., then tighten an additional 180°.
③ — **Torque** to 52 ft. lbs., then tighten an additional 90°.

Wheel Alignment

INDEX

PRELIMINARY INSPECTION

Ensure tires are properly inflated.

Before measuring and setting front wheel alignment, rest front wheels on turn plates.

Before setting rear toe, rest rear wheels on slider plates or turn plates.

Before setting any alignment angle, jounce the vehicle three times at each end to establish trim height.

Special adapters are available for using magnetic hub gauge at rear wheels. Depending on type of equipment used, these may not be required. After removing hub cap and bearing cap, hub gauge will snap into place on brake drum. Magnetic mounting toe gauges may also be installed in the same manner.

Always perform wheel alignment on level alignment rack. Before doing alignment, proceed as follows:
1. Inspect for worn suspension components.
2. Inspect standing curb height.
3. Remove heavy weights from trunk.
4. Inspect wheel bearings for excessive freeplay.
5. Ensure gas tank is full.
6. Place front seats in full rear position.
7. Inspect rear toe adjustment.
8. Always road test vehicle after adjusting alignment, noting the following:
   a. If vehicle still pulls, switch front tires.
   b. If vehicle pulls in same direction, inspect alignment and rear tracking.
   c. If vehicle pulls in opposite direction, rotate tires and road test.

FRONT WHEEL ALIGNMENT

Caster

Caster angle is not adjustable. If caster angle is not within specifications, **Fig. 1**, inspect suspension support for improper alignment and suspension components for damage.

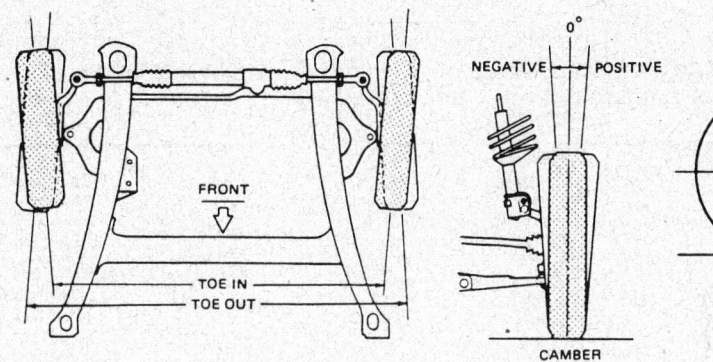

Fig. 1   Caster, camber & toe angles

GC2049100100000X

Camber

Toe setting is the only adjustment normally required. In special circumstances such as damage because of road hazard or collision, the camber angle may be adjusted by modifying the strut, **Fig. 1**.
1. **With strut on vehicle,** disconnect strut from steering knuckle.
2. **With strut off vehicle,** secure strut bottom in suitable vise.
3. **On all models,** enlarge bottom holes in outer flanges with suitable round file, until holes in outer flanges match slots in inner flanges, **Fig. 2**.
4. Install or connect strut to steering knuckle and install bolts hand tight.
5. Grasp top of tire firmly and move tire inboard or outboard until proper camber reading is obtained. Tighten mounting bolts enough to retain camber setting.
6. Remove wheel and tire assembly, then tighten strut to steering knuckle mounting bolts.

Toe

The toe is controlled by tie rod position, **Fig. 1**.
1. Ensure front wheels are in straight-ahead position.
2. Loosen jam nut, **Fig. 3**.
3. Turn adjuster to obtain proper toe setting.
4. **Torque** jam nut to 50 ft. lbs.

REAR WHEEL ALIGNMENT

After front wheel alignment has been inspected or adjusted, rear wheel alignment angles should be inspected if vehicle still does not track properly or if excessive rear tire wear is present. Rear wheels should be parallel to and the same distance from the vehicle centerline.

Rear wheel alignment is not adjustable. If alignment angles are not within specification, inspect for bent or damaged suspension arms, components or underbody.

THRUST ANGLE

The vehicle is steered by the front wheels. The path the rear wheels follow is the thrust angle, **Fig. 4**. In an ideal setting, the thrust angle would be aligned with the vehicle centerline.

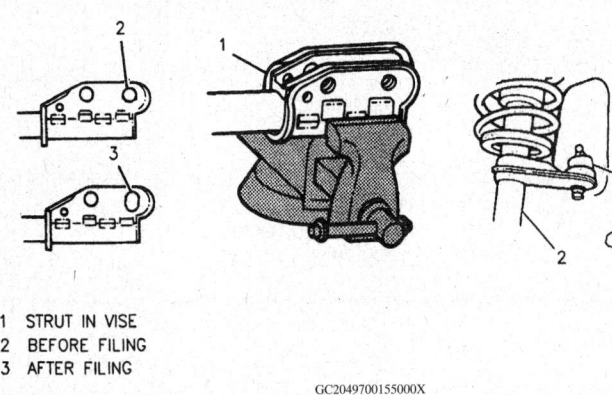

1 STRUT IN VISE
2 BEFORE FILING
3 AFTER FILING

GC2049700155000X

Fig. 2 Strut bracket modification for camber adjustment

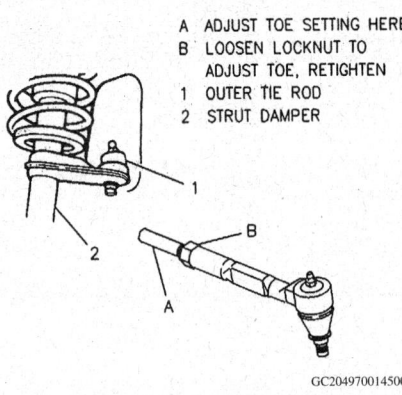

A ADJUST TOE SETTING HERE
B LOOSEN LOCKNUT TO ADJUST TOE, RETIGHTEN
1 OUTER TIE ROD
2 STRUT DAMPER

GC2049700145000X

Fig. 3 Toe adjustment

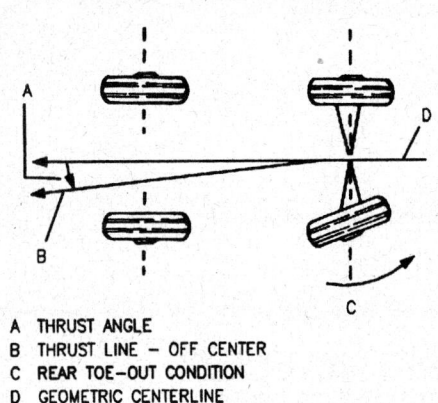

A THRUST ANGLE
B THRUST LINE – OFF CENTER
C REAR TOE–OUT CONDITION
D GEOMETRIC CENTERLINE

GC2049700156000X

Fig. 4 Thrust angle

AVEO

INDEX OF SERVICE OPERATIONS

Specifications

GENERAL ENGINE SPECIFICATIONS

Engine Liter	Fuel Injection System	Bore & Stroke	Compression Ratio	Net H.P. @ RPM②	Maximum Torque Ft. Lbs. @ RPM	Normal Oil Pressure psi
1.6L	SFI	3.11 x 3	9.5:1	103 @ 6000	107 @ 3600	35①

SFI — Sequential Fuel Injection   ① — At idle speed.   ② — Ratings are as installed in vehicle.

TUNE UP SPECIFICATIONS

Engine	Spark Plug Gap, Inch	Ignition Timing, ° BTDC①				Curb Idle Speed RPM		Fast Idle Speed RPM		Fuel Pump Pressure, psi	Valve Lash
		Firing Order	Man. Trans.	Auto. Trans.	Mark Fig.	Man. Trans.	Auto. Trans.	Man. Trans.	Auto Trans.		
1.6L	.041	1-3-4-2	4	4	③	④	④	④	④	55–62	②

BTDC — Before Top Dead Center

① — Ignition timing is controlled by Powertrain Control Module (PCM).

② — Vehicle is equipped w/hydraulic valve lifters. No adjustment is required.

③ — Equipped with crankshaft position sensor.

④ — Idle speed is controlled by an idle air control (IAC) valve or an idle speed control (ISC) motor.

FRONT WHEEL ALIGNMENT SPECIFICATIONS

Year	Caster Angle, Degrees		Camber Angle, Degrees		Total Toe, Degrees	Ball Joint Wear
	Limits	Desired	Limits	Desired		
2004–05	+1.75 to +3.25	+2.5	-1.15 to +0.35	-0.75	-0.10 to +0.24	①

① — Refer to "Front Suspension & Steering" section for ball joint inspection procedure.

REAR WHEEL ALIGNMENT SPECIFICATIONS

Year	Camber Angle, Degrees		Total Toe, Degrees	Thrust Angle, Degrees
	Limits	Desired		
2004–05	-2.0 to -1.0	-1.5	-0.08 to +0.58	—

FLUID CAPACITIES & COOLING SYSTEM DATA

Year	Engine	Coolant Capacity, Qts.	Coolant Type	Surge Tank Cap Relief Pressure, psi	Thermo. Opening Temp. Deg. F	Fuel Tank Gals.	Engine Oil Refill Qts.	Transaxle Oil	
								5 Speed Manual Transaxle Pts.	Auto. Transaxle Qts.①
2004–05	1.6L	7.4	Ethylene Glycol	15	195	16.3	4	4	6.2

① — Approximate. Make final inspection w/dipstick.

LUBRICANT DATA

Year	Model	Lubricant Type				
		Transaxle		Clutch Hydraulic System	Power Steering System	Brake System
		Automatic	Manual			
2004–05	All	①	②	DOT 3 Or DOT 4	Dexron III	DOT 3 Or DOT 4

① — ESSO JWS 3309 or T-IV automatic transmission fluid (GM Part No. 88900925).

② — Manual transaxle fluid Part No. B0400075, or equivalent.

Electrical

NOTE: On Air Bag Equipped Models, Refer To "Air Bag System Precautions" Located In The Front Of This Manual For System Disarming & Arming Procedures.

NOTE: Refer To "Computer Relearn Procedures" Located In The Front Of This Manual When Battery Power To The Computer Has Been Interrupted.

INDEX

PRECAUTIONS

Air Bag Systems

Refer to "Air Bag System Precautions" in the front of this manual for system disarming and arming procedures.

Battery Ground Cable

Prior to service, disconnect battery ground cable and isolate as required.

FUSE PANEL & FLASHER LOCATION

The instrument panel fuse block is located behind the lefthand side of the instrument panel, left of the steering column. The underhood fuse block is located on the front lefthand side of the engine compartment. The turn signal/hazard flasher is located behind the lefthand side of the instrument panel, next to the instrument panel fuse block.

FUEL PUMP RELAY LOCATION

The fuel pump relay is located on the front lefthand side of the engine compartment, in the underhood fuse block.

RELAY CENTER LOCATION

Relays are located in the instrument panel and underhood fuse blocks.

STARTER
REPLACE

1. Raise and support vehicle.
2. Disconnect electrical connectors from starter solenoid.
3. Remove starter motor mounting bolts, then the starter.
4. Reverse procedure to install.

ALTERNATOR
REPLACE

1. Disconnect intake air temperature (IAT) sensor electrical connector from air intake tube.
2. Remove breather tube clamp and all other clamps, then the air intake tube.
3. Disconnect battery harness connector from alternator.
4. Remove alternator shackle bracket bolt.
5. Loosen alternator adjustment bolt and remove drive belt.
6. Remove alternator lower mounting bolts, then the alternator.
7. Reverse procedure to install.

COIL PACK
REPLACE

1. Disconnect electronic ignition (EI) system ignition coil connector.
2. Remove ignition wire. Note position of wire for installation reference.

3. Remove ignition coil retaining nuts, then the ignition coil.
4. Reverse procedure to install.

IGNITION LOCK
REPLACE

1. Remove lower and upper steering column covers.
2. Turn switch to ACC position.
3. Press down on detent spring with a suitable allen wrench, then pull lock cylinder out of switch.
4. Reverse procedure to install.

IGNITION SWITCH
REPLACE

1. Remove lower and upper steering column covers.
2. Remove ignition switch retaining screw.
3. Disconnect switch electrical connector, then remove switch from steering column.
4. Reverse procedure to install.

NEUTRAL SAFETY SWITCH
REPLACE
Removal

1. Disconnect Park/Neutral Position (PNP) switch electrical connector.
2. Remove E-ring and disconnect shift control cable from PNP switch lever.
3. Remove retaining nut, then the washer and control lever.
4. Unstake lock washer and remove nut.

Installation

1. Install PNP switch onto manual valve lever shaft.
2. Temporarily install two adjusting bolts.
3. Install new lock washer and nuts, **torque** nuts to 106 inch lbs.
4. Temporarily install control lever.
5. Turn lever counterclockwise until it stops, then turn it clockwise two notches.
6. Remove control lever and align groove with neutral basic line.
7. Install two bolts and **torque** to 48 inch lbs.
8. Install control lever, washer and nut. **Torque** nut to 106 inch lbs.

HEADLAMP SWITCH
REPLACE

Refer to "Multi-Function Switch, Replace" for switch replacement procedure.

STOP LIGHT SWITCH
REPLACE

1. Remove lefthand trim panel attaching screws, then the trim panel from under lefthand side of instrument panel.
2. Turn stop lamp switch and connector

assembly, then pull switch from brake pedal bracket.
3. Disconnect stop lamp switch connector and remove switch.
4. Reverse procedure to install.

MULTI-FUNCTION SWITCH
REPLACE

1. Remove lower and upper steering column covers.
2. Remove switch by pushing in on tabs on either side of switch housing.
3. Disconnect switch electrical connectors, then remove switch from steering column.
4. Reverse procedure to install.

TURN SIGNAL SWITCH
REPLACE

Refer to "Multi-Function Switch, Replace" for switch replacement procedure.

STEERING WHEEL
REPLACE

1. Remove air bag module.
2. Remove steering wheel retaining nut and clip.
3. Remove steering wheel using steering wheel puller tool KM-210-A or J 1859-A with J 36541-A. Unclip contact ring from steering wheel.
4. Reverse procedure to install.

INSTRUMENT CLUSTER
REPLACE

1. Remove instrument cluster trim panel retaining screws, then the trim panel.
2. Remove instrument cluster retaining screws.
3. Disconnect cluster electrical connectors, then remove cluster.
4. Reverse procedure to install.

WIPER MOTOR
REPLACE
Front

1. Place wiper arms in upright position.
2. Remove nuts and wiper arms.
3. Remove lefthand side air inlet grille retaining screws, then the grille.
4. Remove wiper arm linkage to motor drive shaft retaining nut.
5. Pry wiper arm linkage off motor drive shaft.
6. Disconnect wiper motor electrical connectors.
7. Remove wiper motor attaching bolts, then the motor.
8. Reverse procedure to install.

Rear

1. Remove rear window wiper arm, then open hatchback door.

2. Remove lower garnish molding retaining clips, then the lower garnish molding.
3. Remove rear wiper motor retaining bolts.
4. Disconnect wiper motor electrical connector, then remove motor from hatchback door.
5. Reverse procedure to install.

WIPER SWITCH
REPLACE

1. Remove lower and upper steering column covers.
2. Remove switch by pushing in on tabs on either side of switch housing.
3. Disconnect switch electrical connectors, then remove switch from steering column.
4. Reverse procedure to install.

BLOWER MOTOR
REPLACE

The blower motor is located behind the righthand side of the instrument panel, in the heater/air distribution case.
1. Disconnect blower motor electrical connector.
2. Remove blower cooling hose.
3. Remove motor to heater/air distribution case attaching screws.
4. Remove motor and seal from heater/air distribution case by gently pulling the motor straight down and out.
5. Reverse procedure to install.

HEATER CORE
REPLACE

1. Remove instrument panel as outlined in "Dash Panel Service."
2. Drain cooling system.
3. Recover A/C refrigerant as outlined in "Air Conditioning" chapter.
4. Remove two heater hoses from core lines at cowl.
5. Turn condensation drain hose and pull hose off.
6. Remove A/C suction hose and liquid evaporator pipe connector block retaining nuts at cowl.
7. From engine side of cowl, remove heater/air distribution case assembly to cowl attaching screws.
8. Remove heater/air distribution case assembly from vehicle.
9. Remove linkage screw from lower heater core cover post.
10. Remove linkage lever. Note position of all levers for installation reference.
11. Remove heater core cover attaching screws.
12. Slowly separate lower heater core cover from assembly. Retain sealant.
13. Remove screw and bracket clamp that secure heater core lines to case.
14. Remove heater core body to case spring clamp, then the heater core from case.
15. Reverse procedure to install.

EVAPORATOR CORE

REPLACE

1. Remove instrument panel as outlined in "Dash Panel Service."
2. Drain cooling system.
3. Recover A/C refrigerant as outlined in "Air Conditioning" chapter.

4. Remove two heater hoses from core lines at cowl.
5. Turn condensation drain hose and pull hose off.
6. Remove A/C suction hose and liquid evaporator pipe connector block retaining nuts at cowl.
7. From engine side of cowl, remove heater/air distribution case assembly

to cowl attaching screws.
8. Remove heater/air distribution case assembly from vehicle.
9. Remove evaporator case cover attaching screws, then the cover.
10. Slide evaporator flange support plate upward, then remove evaporator core from case.
11. Reverse procedure to install.

1.6L Engine

NOTE: On Air Bag Equipped Models, Refer To "Air Bag System Precautions" Located In The Front Of This Manual For System Disarming & Arming Procedures.

NOTE: Refer To "Computer Relearn Procedures" Located In The Front Of This Manual When Battery Power To The Computer Has Been Interrupted.

INDEX

PRECAUTIONS

Air Bag Systems

Refer to "Air Bag System Precautions" in the front of this manual for system disarming and arming procedures.

Battery Ground Cable

Prior to service, disconnect battery ground cable and isolate as required.

Fuel System Pressure Relief

1. Remove fuel cap.
2. Remove fuel pump fuse EF10 from underhood fuse box.
3. Start engine and allow engine to stall.
4. Crank engine for an additional 10 seconds.

COMPRESSION PRESSURE

1. Start and run engine until it reaches normal operating temperature.
2. Turn engine off and remove spark plugs.
3. Ensure battery is fully charged and

place approximately 3 squirts of oil from a plunger-type oiler into each spark plug port.
4. Insert engine compression gage into each spark plug port.
5. With throttle wide open crank test each cylinder with 4-5 compression strokes.
6. Lowest reading should not be less than 70 percent of highest reading.
7. Compression gage reading should not be less than 100 psi for any cylinder.

ENGINE MOUNT

REPLACE

1. Remove upper radiator cover.
2. Raise and support vehicle, then remove right front splash shield.
3. Support engine assembly using the Universal Engine Support Fixture J 28467-B, or equivalent.
4. Remove engine mount bracket retaining bolts.
5. Remove engine mount retaining nuts.
6. Lower engine and remove engine mount.
7. Reverse procedure to install.

ENGINE

REPLACE

1. Drain engine oil, then remove battery and battery tray.

2. Recover A/C refrigerant as outlined in "Air Conditioning" chapter.
3. Relieve fuel system pressure as outlined under "Precautions."
4. Drain engine coolant.
5. Remove radiator and engine cooling fans as outlined under "Radiator, Replace."
6. Disconnect upper radiator hose from thermostat housing.
7. Disconnect power steering return hose from the power steering pump.
8. Remove union nut from power steering pressure hose, then disconnect power steering pressure hose from power steering pump.
9. Disconnect Intake Air Temperature (IAT) sensor connector.
10. Disconnect breather tube from valve cover and air intake tube from throttle body.
11. Remove air cleaner assembly.
12. Remove spark plug cover attaching bolts, then the cover.
13. Disconnect Idle Air Control (IAC) valve and Throttle Position Sensor (TPS) connectors.
14. **On models equipped with air conditioning,** disconnect A/C pressure transducer connector.
15. **On all models,** disconnect Camshaft Position (CMP) sensor connector.
16. Disconnect throttle cable from throttle body and from intake manifold bracket.

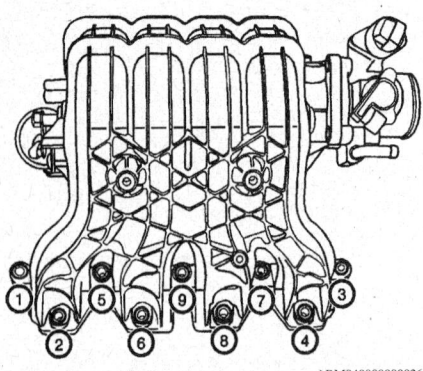

Fig. 1 Intake manifold bolt removal sequence

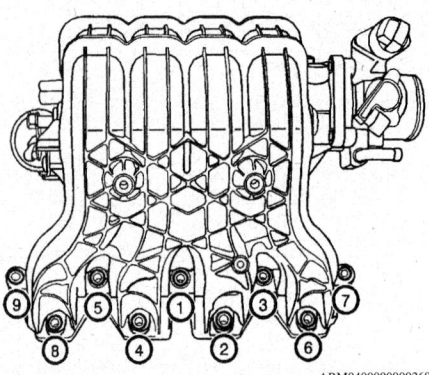

Fig. 2 Intake manifold bolt tightening sequence

17. Disconnect Manifold Absolute Pressure (MAP) sensor connector.
18. Disconnect ignition wires from the spark plugs.
19. Disconnect surge tank coolant hose at throttle body.
20. Disconnect fuel injector connectors.
21. Disconnect EGR valve, ignition coil, oxygen sensor and Crankshaft Position Sensor (CPS) connectors.
22. Disconnect all necessary vacuum lines.
23. Disconnect brake booster vacuum hose at intake manifold.
24. Disconnect fuel feed line from fuel rail.
25. Remove battery tray support.
26. Disconnect lower radiator hose from coolant pipe.
27. **On models equipped with air conditioning,** remove bolt from A/C compressor pipe and hose assembly, then the pipe and hose assembly from compressor.
28. **On all models,** raise and support vehicle, then remove front tire and wheel assemblies.
29. Remove front splash shield and engine undercover.
30. **On models equipped with automatic transaxle,** disconnect automatic A/T oil cooler inlet/outlet pipe, shift cable and all electrical connectors from transaxle.
31. **On models equipped with air conditioning,** disconnect A/C compressor coil connector.
32. **On all models,** disconnect rear heated oxygen sensor connector.
33. Remove lower flange nuts from exhaust manifold studs. Retain gasket.
34. Remove front muffler pipe retaining nuts, then the front exhaust pipe as a unit. Retain gasket.
35. Remove damping block connection attaching bolt and nut.
36. Remove rear mounting bracket attaching bolts, then the bracket.
37. **On models equipped with automatic transaxle,** remove drive axles as outlined "Front Wheel Drive Axles" chapter.
38. **On all models,** disconnect oil pressure switch electrical connector.
39. Remove battery harness connector nut from alternator, then the connector from alternator voltage regulator.
40. Disconnect EVAP emission canister purge solenoid electrical connector.
41. Remove intake manifold support bracket attaching bolts, then the support bracket.
42. Disconnect Engine Coolant Temperature (ECT) sensor connector.
43. Remove lower starter mounting bolt, then the solenoid nuts to disconnect electrical cable.
44. Remove lower engine wire harness.
45. Remove rubber from oil pan, torque converter service cover and bolts.
46. Install suitable engine lifting device.
47. Remove retaining bolts from engine mount bracket, then the bracket from engine block.
48. Remove upper transaxle mounting bracket attaching bolts.
49. Lift up vehicle slowly to separate engine and transaxle assembly from vehicle.
50. Separate engine block from transaxle.
51. Reverse procedure to install.

INTAKE MANIFOLD
REPLACE

1. Drain engine coolant.
2. Relieve fuel system pressure as outlined under "Precautions."
3. Disconnect Intake Air Temperature (IAT) sensor connector, then the air intake tube from throttle body.
4. Disconnect Idle Air Control (IAC) valve and Throttle Position Sensor (TPS) connectors.
5. Remove alternator adjusting bolt and alternator drive belt.
6. Disconnect Engine Coolant Temperature (ECT) sensor connector.
7. Disconnect heater inlet hose from cylinder head and surge tank coolant hose from throttle body.
8. Disconnect all necessary vacuum hoses, including the vacuum hose at fuel pressure regulator and brake booster.
9. Disconnect throttle body cable from throttle body and intake manifold.
10. Remove fuel injector rail and fuel injectors as an assembly.
11. Remove alternator adjusting bracket bolt, then the adjusting bracket from intake manifold.
12. Remove intake manifold support bracket attaching bolts, then the support bracket.
13. Remove intake manifold retaining nuts/bolts in sequence, **Fig. 1.**
14. Remove intake manifold and gasket.
15. Reverse procedure to install, noting the following:
    a. Clean sealing surfaces of intake manifold and cylinder head.
    b. Using sequence, **Fig. 2, torque** intake manifold retaining bolts to 18 ft lbs.

EXHAUST MANIFOLD
REPLACE

1. Disconnect pre-converter oxygen sensor connector.
2. Remove exhaust manifold heat shield attaching bolts, then the heat shield.
3. Remove auxiliary catalytic converter nuts from exhaust manifold.
4. Remove exhaust manifold retaining nuts in sequence, **Fig. 3.**
5. Remove exhaust manifold and gasket.
6. Reverse procedure to install. Using sequence, **Fig. 4, torque** manifold retaining nuts to 18 ft. lbs.

CYLINDER HEAD
REPLACE

1. Drain engine coolant.
2. Relieve fuel system pressure as outlined under "Precautions."
3. Remove valve cover as outlined under "Valve Cover, Replace."
4. Disconnect the intake air temperature (IAT) sensor connector. Disconnect the air intake tube from the throttle body
5. Remove the air filter housing bolts. Remove the air filter housing.
6. Disconnect A/C Pressure Transducer (ACP), idle air control (IAC) valve and Throttle Position (TP) sensor connectors.
7. Disconnect throttle cable from throttle body and intake manifold.
8. Disconnect engine coolant inlet/outlet hose from throttle body.
9. Disconnect Manifold Absolute Pressure (MAP) sensor connector.
10. Disconnect brake booster vacuum hose.
11. Disconnect Variable Geometry Induction Solenoid (VGIS) connector, then the VGIS vacuum tank hose.
12. Remove engine cover bolts and cover.
13. Disconnect Camshaft Position (CMP) sensor connector, then the ignition wires from spark plugs.
14. Disconnect fuel injector harness connectors.
15. Disconnect fuel line.
16. Remove bracket nut from power steering pressure pipe, then the power steering pressure pipe.
17. Remove alternator adjusting nut and the accessory drive belt.

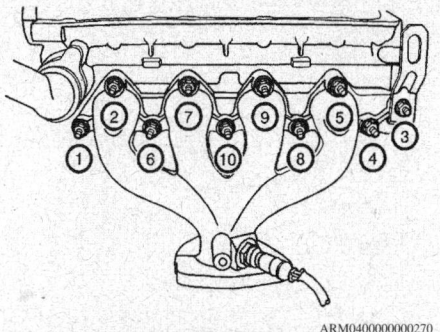

Fig. 3 Exhaust manifold bolt removal sequence

VALVE COVER
REPLACE

1. Remove engine cover bolts and cover.
2. Disconnect breather tube and crankcase ventilation tube from valve cover.
3. Disconnect all necessary vacuum lines.
4. Disconnect ignition wires from spark plugs.
5. Remove valve cover attaching bolts and the valve cover.
6. Reverse procedure to install.

TIMING BELT
REPLACE

Removal

1. Disconnect Intake Air Temperature (IAT) sensor connector.
2. Disconnect air intake tube from throttle body and breather tube from valve cover.
3. Remove air filter housing.
4. Raise and support vehicle, then remove right front wheel and splash shield.
5. Remove accessory drive belt.
6. Remove crankshaft pulley bolt and crankshaft pulley.
7. Remove upper front timing belt cover attaching bolts and the cover.
8. Remove lower front timing belt cover attaching bolts and the cover.
9. Remove power steering pump mounting bolts.
10. Install crankshaft pulley bolt, then use crankshaft pulley bolt to rotate crankshaft clockwise until timing mark on crankshaft gear is aligned with notch at bottom of rear timing belt cover, **Fig. 7.**
11. Slightly loosen coolant pump retaining bolts, then rotate coolant pump counterclockwise to release timing belt tension.
12. Remove timing belt.

Installation

1. Align timing mark on crankshaft gear to notch on bottom of rear timing belt cover, **Fig. 7.**
2. Align timing marks on camshaft gears and install timing belt.
3. Rotate coolant pump clockwise using until adjust arm pointer of timing belt automatic tensioner is aligned to notch in timing belt automatic tensioner bracket.
4. Tighten coolant pump retaining bolts.
5. Rotate crankshaft two full turns clockwise using crankshaft pulley bolt.
6. Loosen coolant pump retaining bolts and rotate coolant pump until adjust arm pointer of timing belt automatic tensioner is aligned with pointer on timing belt automatic tensioner bracket.
7. Tighten coolant pump retaining bolts.
8. Install upper and lower front timing belt covers.

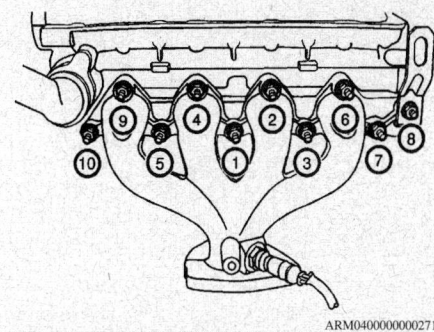

Fig. 4 Exhaust manifold bolt tightening sequence

9. Install crankshaft pulley, then tighten crankshaft pulley bolt in three steps. First step, **torque** bolt to 70 ft. lbs.; second step, tighten bolt an addtional 30°; third step, tighten an additional 15.°
10. Install accessory drive belt, then the right front splash shield and right front wheel.
11. Install air filter housing.
12. Connect air intake tube to throttle body and breather tube to throttle body.
13. Connect IAT sensor connector.

CAMSHAFT
REPLACE

1. Remove the valve cover and gasket.
2. While holding intake camshaft firmly in place, remove intake camshaft gear retaining bolt, then the gear.
3. While holding exhaust camshaft firmly in place, remove exhaust camshaft gear retaining bolt, then the gear.
4. Remove camshaft cap bolts gradually and in sequence, **Fig. 8.**
5. Remove intake camshaft caps, then the intake camshaft. Note position of caps for installation reference.
6. Remove exhaust camshaft caps, then the exhaust camshaft. Note position of caps for installation reference.
7. Reverse procedure to install, noting the following:
   a. Lubricate camshaft journals and caps with clean engine oil.
   b. Reverse loosening sequence, **Fig. 8, torque** camshaft cap bolts to 12 ft. lbs.

MAIN & ROD BEARINGS

Tighten crankshaft bearing cap bolts in two steps: First step, **torque** bolts to 37 ft. lbs.; second step, tighten bolts an addional 45.°

Tighten connecting rod bearing cap bolts in two steps: First step, **torque** bolts to 18 ft. lbs.; second step, tighten bolts an additional 30°; third step, tighten bolts an additional 15.°

18. Disconnect EGR valve and the ignition coil connector.
19. Disconnect front Heated Oxygen Sensor (HO2S) connector.
20. Raise and support vehicle, then remove right front wheel.
21. Remove engine undercover bolt and nuts, then the engine undercover.
22. Remove canister purge solenoid valve at intake manifold support bracket.
23. Remove bracket bolts from upper intake manifold support and lower intake manifold support.
24. Disconnect Engine Coolant Temperature (ECT) sensor connector.
25. Remove exhaust manifold heat shield bolts and the heat shield.
26. Remove catalytic converter.
27. Disconnect upper radiator hose from thermostat housing.
28. Remove timing belt as outlined under "Timing Belt, Replace."
29. While holding intake camshaft firmly in place, remove intake camshaft gear bolt and intake camshaft gear.
30. While holding exhaust camshaft firmly in place, remove exhaust camshaft gear bolt and exhaust camshaft gear.
31. Remove timing belt automatic tensioner mounting bolts, then the tensioner.
32. Remove Camshaft Position (CMP) sensor and timing belt idler pulley.
33. Remove rear timing belt cover.
34. Disconnect heater outlet hose from coolant pipe.
35. Loosen cylinder head bolts gradually and in sequence, **Fig. 5.**
36. Remove cylinder head with intake manifold and exhaust manifold attached.
37. Reverse procedure to install, tighten cylinder head bolts as follows:
   a. Refer to sequence, **Fig. 6,** then tighten cylinder head bolts in five steps.
   b. **First step, torque** bolts to 18 ft. lbs.
   c. **Second step,** tighten bolts an additional 60.°
   d. **Third step,** tighten bolts an additional 60.°
   e. **Fourth step,** tighten bolts an additional 60.°
   f. **Fifth step,** tighten bolts an additional 10.°

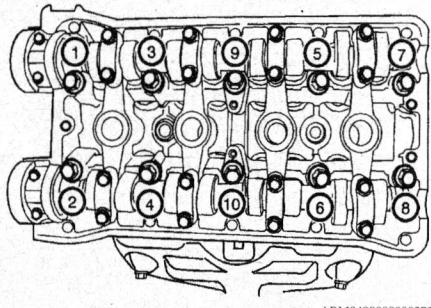

Fig. 5 Cylinder head bolt removal sequence

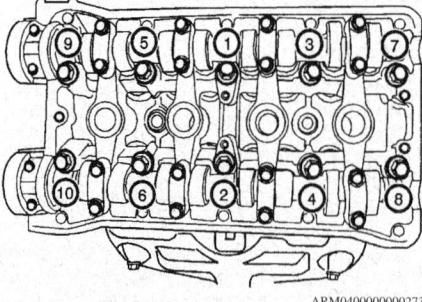

Fig. 6 Cylinder head bolt tightening sequence

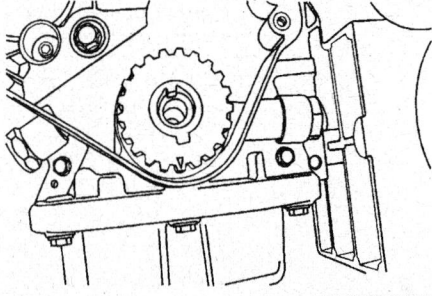

Fig. 7 Crankshaft gear alignment

OIL PAN
REPLACE

1. Raise and support vehicle, then remove right front wheel.
2. Remove right front splash shield and drain engine oil.
3. Disconnect Heated Oxygen Sensor (HO2S) connector.
4. Remove catalytic lower flange nuts from exhaust manifold.
5. Remove front pipe to manifold retaining nuts, then the catalytic converter and exhaust pipe as a unit.
6. Remove oil pan to transaxle housing attaching bolts.
7. Remove oil pan retaining bolts, then the oil pan and gasket from engine block.
8. Reverse procedure to install.

OIL PUMP
REPLACE

1. Remove timing belt as outlined under "Timing Belt, Replace."
2. Remove Crankshaft Position (CKP) sensor bolt, then the CKP sensor.
3. Remove oil pan as outlined under "Oil Pan, Replace."
4. Remove oil pump pickup tube and support bracket.
5. Remove pump retaining bolts, then carefully separate oil pump and gasket from engine block and oil pan.
6. Reverse procedure to install.

COOLING SYSTEM BLEED

1. Add suitable coolant to surge tank.
2. Fill tank slowly so upper reservoir hose remains above water line, this will allow air inside cooling system to escape.
3. Start and run engine until thermostat opens.

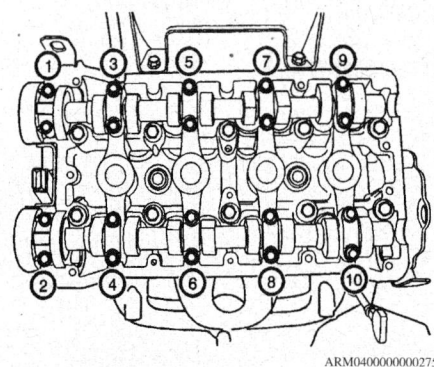

Fig. 8 Camshaft cap bolt removal sequence

4. Turn engine off and check coolant level.

THERMOSTAT
REPLACE

1. Drain engine coolant.
2. Disconnect upper radiator hose from thermostat housing.
3. Disconnect throttle body coolant inlet hose from thermostat housing.
4. Remove thermostat housing attaching bolts, then the housing, thermostat and gasket.
5. Reverse procedure to install.

WATER PUMP
REPLACE

1. Drain engine coolant.
2. Remove timing belt as outlined under "Timing Belt, Replace."
3. While holding intake camshaft firmly in place, remove intake camshaft gear bolt and intake camshaft gear.
4. While holding exhaust camshaft firmly in place, remove exhaust camshaft gear bolt and exhaust camshaft gear.

5. Remove timing belt automatic tensioner mounting bolts, then the tensioner.
6. Remove Camshaft Position (CMP) sensor and timing belt idler pulley.
7. Remove rear timing belt cover.
8. Remove water pump mounting bolts, then the water pump.
9. Remove seal ring from pump.
10. Reverse procedure to install.

RADIATOR
REPLACE

1. Drain engine coolant.
2. Remove electric cooling fans.
3. Remove upper radiator hose clamp.
4. Disconnect upper and lower radiator hoses from radiator.
5. Disconnect surge tank hose from radiator.
6. Remove left and right upper radiator retaining brackets.
7. Remove radiator from vehicle.
8. Reverse procedure to install.

FUEL PUMP
REPLACE

1. Relieve fuel system pressure as outlined under "Precautions."
2. Remove rear seat.
3. Remove fuel pump access cover.
4. Disconnect electrical connector at fuel pump assembly.
5. Disconnect fuel line.
6. Remove fuel pump assembly clip, then the fuel pump assembly from tank.
7. Remove and discard gasket.
8. Reverse procedure to install.

FUEL FILTER
REPLACE

The fuel filter is located in the fuel sender assembly. Refer to "Fuel Pump, Replace" for replacement procedure.

TIGHTENING SPECIFICATIONS

Year	Component	Torque, Ft. Lbs
2004–05	A/C Compressor	20
	A/C Compressor Bracket	37
	Alternator Adjusting	15
	Auxiliary Catalytic Converter	30
	Camshaft Cap	12
	Camshaft Gear	49
	Camshaft Pressure Plate	89①
	Connecting Rod Bearing Caps	②
	Coolant Temperature Sensor	15
	Crankshaft Bearing Cap	②
	Crankshaft Position Sensor	89①
	Crankshaft Pulley	③
	Cylinder Head	④
	EGR Valve Adapter	18
	Engine Mounting Bracket	48
	Engine Mount Bracket To Engine Mount	44
	Exhaust Manifold	18
	Flywheel	⑤
	Fuel Rail	18
	Intake Manifold	18
	Intake Manifold Support Bracket	30
	Oil Pan	89①
	Oil Pressure Switch	30
	Oil Pump Rear Cover	53①
	Power Steering Pump	18
	Spark Plugs	18
	Thremostat Housing	15
	Throttle Cable Bracket	71①
	Timing Belt Automatic Tensioner	18
	Timing Belt Idler Pulley	30①
	Timing Belt Cover (Lower)	89①
	Timing Belt Cover (Rear)	89①
	Timing Belt Cover (Upper)	89①
	Torque Converter	48
	Transaxle Bell Housing	55
	Transaxle Brace	30
	Valve Cover	89①

① — Inch lbs.
② — Refer to "Main & Rod Bearings" for tightening procedure.
③ — Tigthten in three steps: 1st step, torque to 70 ft. lbs; 2nd step, an additional 30°; 3rd step, an additional 15°.
④ — Refer to "Cylinder Head, Replace" for tightening procedure.
⑤ — Tigthten in three steps: 1st step, torque to 26 ft. lbs; 2nd step, an additional 30°; 3rd step, an additional 15°.

Rear Axle & Suspension

INDEX

REAR AXLE

REPLACE

1. Raise and support vehicle, then remove rear wheel and tire assemblies.
2. Disconnect parking brake and antilock brake sensor line.
3. Disconnect brake pipes from brake hoses at rear axle brackets. Cap brake hose openings to prevent contamination.
4. Remove brake hose from rear axle brackets.
5. Place suitable jack stands under arms of rear axle, then raise rear axle arms slightly.
6. Remove shock absorbers as outlined under "Shock Absorber, Replace."
7. Lower support jacks and remove rear springs, **Fig. 1.**
8. Remove left and right rear axle mounting bolts, then the right rear axle mounting bracket bolts.
9. Remove rear axle.
10. Reverse procedure to install.

HUB & BEARING

REPLACE

The hub and bearing assembly are part of the brake drum assembly.
1. Release parking brake, then apply brake pedal at least 10 times.
2. Raise and support vehicle, then remove wheel and tire assembly.
3. Remove lock ring and caulking nut from spindle, **Fig. 1.**
4. Pull drum straight off of spindle.
5. Reverse procedure to install.

SHOCK ABSORBER

REPLACE

1. Remove shock absorber upper mounting bolts, **Fig. 1.**
2. Raise and support vehicle, then place suitable jack stands under rear axle.
3. Remove shock absorber to axle bolt, then the shock absorber.
4. Reverse procedure to install.

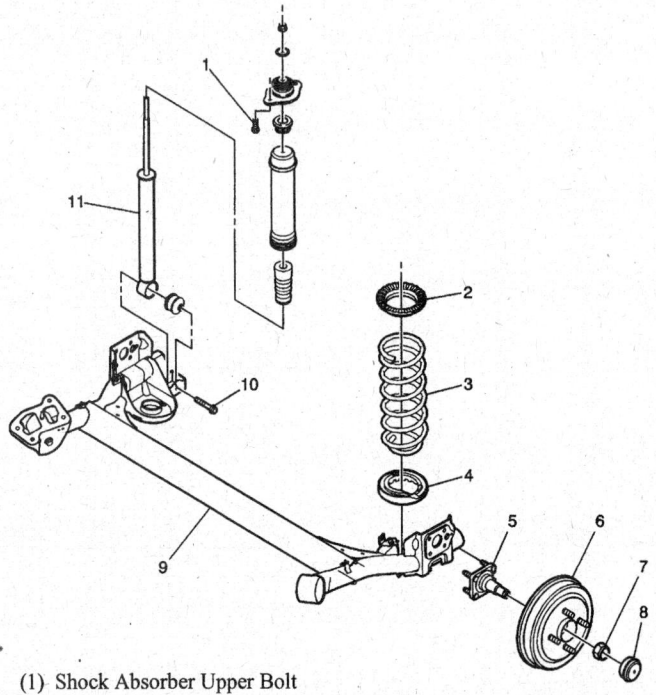

(1) Shock Absorber Upper Bolt
(2) Spring Upper Insulator
(3) Coil Spring
(4) Spring Lower Insulator
(5) Wheel Bearing Spindle
(6) Brake Drum
(7) Caulking Nut
(8) Spindle Cap
(9) Rear Axle
(10) Shock Absorber Lower Bolt
(11) Shock Absorber

ARM0400000000276

Fig. 1 Exploded view of rear suspension

COIL SPRING

REPLACE

1. Raise and support vehicle, then place suitable jack stands under rear axle.
2. Remove tire and wheel assembly.
3. Remove left and right shock absorber to axle mounting bolts.
4. Lower rear axle and remove coil springs.
5. Reverse procedure to install.

TIGHTENING SPECIFICATIONS

Year	Component	Torque, Ft. Lbs.
2004–05	Rear Axle to Body Bracket Bolt	85
	Rear Axle Mounting Bracket Bolts	52
	Shock Absorber Bolt (Lower)	53
	Shock Absorber Bolt (Upper)	37
	Wheel Hub & Bearing	30
	Wheel Lug Nut	88

Front Suspension & Steering

INDEX

PRECAUTIONS

Air Bag Systems

Refer to "Air Bag System Precautions" in the front of this manual for system disarming and arming procedures.

Battery Ground Cable

Prior to service, disconnect battery ground cable and isolate as required.

DESCRIPTION

The front suspension on this vehicle is a combination knuckle/strut and spring design. The control arms pivot from the body and the lower control arm pivots use rubber bushings. The upper end of the strut is isolated by a rubber mount and contains a bearing to allow the wheel to turn. The lower end of the steering knuckle pivots on a ball joint bolted to the control arm. The ball joint is fastened to the steering knuckle with a nut, and to the lower control arm with rivets.

WHEEL BEARING

REPLACE

1. Remove drive axle from wheel hub as outlined in "Front Drive Axle" section.
2. Remove inner retaining ring from hub, **Fig. 1.**
3. Remove wheel hub from steering knuckle using bearing puller tool No. J 36661-2, or equivalent.
4. Remove disc brake splash shield, then the outer snap ring from knuckle.
5. Remove wheel bearing from steering knuckle using puller tool No. J 36661-2, or equivalent.
6. Reverse procedure to install.

BALL JOINT INSPECTION

1. Raise front of vehicle and allow front suspension to hang free.
2. Grasp tire at top and bottom, then move top of tire in an in-and-out motion.
3. Inspect for any horizontal movement of knuckle relative to control arm.
4. Ball joints must be replaced under any of the following conditions:
   a. Joint is loose or ball seal is cut.
   b. Ball stud is disconnected from knuckle. ball stud is loose at the knuckle. The ball stud can be twisted in its socket with finger pressure.

BALL JOINT

REPLACE

1. Raise and support vehicle.
2. Place suitable jackstands under frame of vehicle, then lower vehicle slightly so weight of vehicle rests on jackstands and not on control arms.
3. Remove tire and wheel assembly.
4. Remove control arm as outlined under "Control Arm, Replace."
5. Remove ball joint to control arm mounting nuts, then the ball joint from control arm.
6. Reverse procedure to install.

COIL SPRING

REPLACE

Refer to "Strut Service" for coil spring replacement.

STRUT

REPLACE

1. Loosen top strut to body retaining nut, **Fig. 1.**

2. Raise and support vehicle.
3. Place jackstands under frame of vehicle.
4. Lower vehicle slightly so weight of vehicle rests on jackstands. **Control arms should not rest on jackstands.**
5. Remove tire and wheel assemblies.
6. Remove brake caliper from knuckle/strut assembly and support caliper. **Do not hang caliper from hydraulic brake hose.**
7. Disconnect ABS speed sensor electrical connector.
8. Remove ball joint to knuckle strut nut.
9. Separate steering knuckle assembly from ball joint using ball joint remover tool No. KM-507-C, or equivalent.
10. Remove outer tie rod from the steering knuckle assembly.
11. Push drive axle shaft from front wheel hub and support drive axle.
12. Lower vehicle to gain access to strut to body nuts and washers, then remove strut assembly to body nuts.
13. Remove strut assembly from vehicle.
14. Reverse procedure to install.

STRUT SERVICE

Disassemble

1. Position strut assembly to spring compressor tool No. KM-329-A, or equivalent.
2. Compress front spring, then while holding threaded piston rod with a suitable open end wrench, remove piston rod nut, **Fig. 1.**
3. Mark position of front spring seat to strut assembly to knuckle bracket for assembly reference.
4. Remove strut mount, strut bearing, spring upper seat, spring upper insulator, hallow bumper, coil spring and strut.

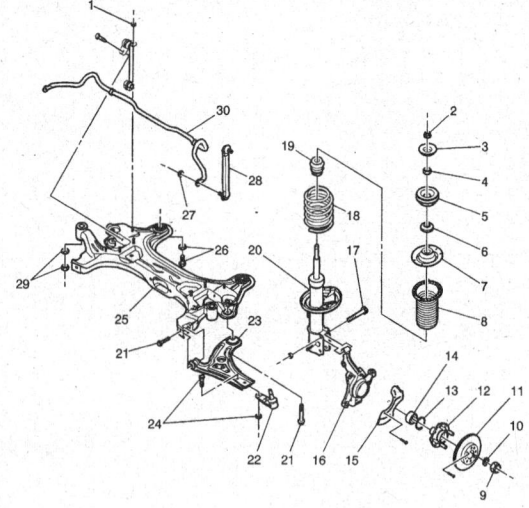

(1) Stabilizer Bar Nut
(2) Strut Upper Nut
(3) Washer
(4) Piston Rod Nut
(5) Strut Mount
(6) Bearing
(7) Spring Upper Seat
(8) Spring Upper Insulator
(9) Caulking Nut
(10) Washer
(11) Brake Disc
(12) Wheel Hub
(13) Retaining Ring
(14) Wheel Bearing
(15) Cover Seat

(16) Steering Knuckle
(17) Thrust Bracket Bolt
(18) Coil Spring
(19) Hallow Bumper
(20) Thrust
(21) Control Arm Connecting Bolt
(22) Ball Joint
(23) Control Arm
(24) Ball Joint Connecting Bolt
(25) Crossmember
(26) Crossmember Bolt - Front Direction
(27) Stabilizer Link Nut
(28) Stabilizer Link
(29) Crossmember Nut
(30) Stabilizer Bar

ARM0400000000278

Fig. 1   Exploded view of front suspension assembly

(1) Bulk Head Retaining Ring
(2) Tie Rod End
(3) Tie Rod End Lock Nut
(4) Rack and Pinion Boot
(5) Tie Rod
(6) Bearing
(7) Pinion Valve
(8) Pinion Shaft Seal
(9) Bushing
(10) Rack Bearing

(11) Adjust Spring
(12) Adjust Plug
(13) Retaining Ring
(14) Pinion Bearing
(15) Grommet
(16) Rack Inner Seal
(17) Cylinder Liner Cut
(18) Cylinder Liner Cut
(19) Steering Rack Gear
(20) Bush and Cylinder Bulk Head

ARM0400000000279

Fig. 2   Exploded view of steering gear

Assemble

1. Install lower spring insulator and spring.
2. Compress spring using spring compressor tool No. KM-329-A, or equivalent.
3. Install strut mount, strut bearing spring upper seat, spring upper insulator, hallow bumper, coil spring and strut.
4. Use an open end wrench to hold threaded piston rod, then install rod nut.

CONTROL ARM
REPLACE

1. Raise and support vehicle.
2. Place jackstands under frame of vehicle.
3. Lower vehicle slightly so weight of vehicle rests on jackstands and not on control arms.
4. Remove wheel and tire assembly.
5. Disconnect stabilizer shaft from control arm by removing control arm-link bolt assembly.
6. Remove retaining clip and ball joint to knuckle/strut nut from ball joint.
7. Disconnect ball joint from steering knuckle using joint remover tool No. KM-507-C, or equivalent.

8. Remove control arm front mounting bolt.
9. Remove control arm rear mounting bolts and bracket.
10. Remove control arm from vehicle.
11. Reverse procedure to install.

STEERING KNUCKLE
REPLACE

1. Remove front wheels.
2. Remove caulking nut, then the tie rod end from knuckle.
3. Remove control arm ball joint and the brake caliper.
4. Remove brake disk and ABS wheel speed sensor.
5. Remove backing plate, then the front strut bolts.
6. Remove knuckle assembly.
7. Reverse procedure to install.

TIE ROD END
REPLACE

Inner

Refer to "Power Steering" chapter from inner tie rod replacement.

Outer

1. Raise and support vehicle.
2. Loosen tie rod end jam nut, **Fig. 2.**
3. Remove tie rod end to steering knuckle nut, then separate tie rod end ball joint from steering knuckle.
4. Remove tie rod end from steering gear. For installation reference, count number of times tie rod end has to be turned to remove from steering gear.
5. Reverse procedure to install.

POWER STEERING GEAR
REPLACE

1. Position tires straight ahead.
2. Raise and support vehicle.
3. Remove intermediate shaft, then the front tires.
4. Drain power steering fluid from rack and pinion.
5. Disconnect steering gear inlet and outlet pipe fittings.
6. Remove outer tie rod hex nuts.
7. Remove ball joint hex nuts and disconnect stabilizer shaft from knuckle.
8. Remove cross member to underbody attaching nuts and bolts.
9. Remove steering gear bracket assembly retaining nuts, then steering gear.
10. Reverse procedure to install.

POWER STEERING PUMP

REPLACE

1. Remove air cleaner housing.
2. Rotate drive belt auto-tensioner and remove pump drive belt from pulley.
3. Remove power steering pump pulley bolt and the pulley.
4. Drain power steering fluid by disconnecting pressure and supply lines from pump.
5. Remove pump assembly retaining bolts and the pump.
6. Reverse procedure to install.

TIGHTENING SPECIFICATIONS

Year	Component	Torque, Ft. Lbs.
2004–05	Adjuster Plug	108①
	Adjuster Plug Locknut	52
	Backing Plate Screws	35①
	Ball Joint Hex Nut	33
	Ball Joint To Control Arm Nuts	47
	Ball Joint To Knuckle Nut	41
	Control Arm Front Mounting Bolt	81
	Control Arm Rear Mounting Bolts	81
	Crossmember Assembly To Body Nut	111
	Drive Axle To Hub Caulking Nut	221
	Engine Mounting Reaction Rod Bolts	44
	Knuckle Assembly To Front Strut Bolts	74
	Outer Tie Rod Hex Nut	33
	Outer Tie Rod Nuts	40
	Pinion Locknut	22
	Piston Rod Nut	44
	Power Steering Pipe Fittings	16
	Power Steering Pump Pulley Bolts	18
	Power Steering Pump Retaining Bolts	18
	Stabilizer Shaft To Knuckle Bolts	33
	Stabilizer Shaft To Link Nut	37
	Steering Gear Inlet & Outlet Fittings	21
	Steering Gear Retaining Bracket Nuts	37
	Strut Assembly To Body	44
	Tie Rod End Ball Joint Nut	33
	U-Clamp Bolt	18
	Wheel Lug Nut	88

① — Inch lbs.

Wheel Alignment

INDEX

PRELIMINARY INSPECTION

1. Inspect tires for proper inflation pressures and normal tread wear.
2. Inspect wheel bearings for looseness.
3. Inspect for loose ball joints and tie rod ends.
4. Inspect runout of wheels and tires.
5. Inspect vehicle trim heights.
6. Inspect for loose rack and pinion mounting.
7. Inspect for loose control arms.

FRONT WHEEL ALIGNMENT

Caster

Front caster is not adjustable. If the front caster measurements are not within specifications, locate and replace or repair any damaged, loose, bent, dented, or worn suspension part.

Camber

Front camber is not adjustable. If the front camber measurements are not within specifications, locate and replace or repair any damaged, loose, bent, dented, or worn suspension part.

Toe

1. Raise and support vehicle.
2. Loosen right and left rod lock bolts. **In this adjustment, the right and left tie rods must be equal in length.**
3. Turn right and left tie rod adjusters to align toe to specifications.
4. **Torque** tie rod lock bolts 47 ft. lbs.

REAR WHEEL ALIGNMENT

Camber

Rear camber is not adjustable. If the rear front camber measurements are not within specifications, locate and replace or repair any damaged, loose, bent, dented, or worn suspension part.

Toe

Rear toe is not adjustable. If the toe measurement is not within specification, inspect the rear axle assembly and the hub and bearing assembly for possible damage.

GTO

INDEX OF SERVICE OPERATIONS

Specifications

GENERAL ENGINE SPECIFICATIONS

Year	Engine		Fuel System	Bore & Stroke	Comp-ression Ratio	Net Brake H.P. @ RPM②	Maximum Torque, Ft. Lbs @ RPM	Normal Oil Pressure psi
	Liter	VIN Code①						
2004	5.7L	G	SFI	3.897 x 3.898	10:1	350 @ 5200	365 @ 4000	③

SFI — Sequential Fuel Injection
VIN — Vehicle Identification Number
① — The eighth digit of the VIN denotes engine code.

② — Ratings are net, as installed in vehicle.
③ — 6 psi @ 1000 RPM; 18 psi @ 2000 RPM; 24 psi @ 4000 RPM.

TUNE UP SPECIFICATIONS

Year	Engine	Spark Plug Gap	Ignition Timing BTDC				Curb Idle Speed③		Fast Idle Speed		Fuel Pump Pres-sure psi	Valve Clear-ance Inch
			Firing Order	Man. Trans.	Auto. Trans.	Mark Fig.	Man. Trans.	Auto. Trans.	Man. Trans.	Auto. Trans.		
2004	5.7L	.060	1-8-7-2-6-5-4-3	①	①	—	④	④	④	④	55–61⑤	②

BTDC — Before Top Dead Center
VIN — Vehicle Identification Number
① — Computer controlled. No adjust-ment.
② — Equipped w/hydraulic lifters. No adjustment is required.

③ — When inspecting idle speed, set parking brake & block drive wheels.
④ — Idle speed is controlled by an idle speed control motor.
⑤ — With shop towel wrapped around

fuel pressure fitting to prevent fuel spillage, connect a suitable fuel pressure gauge. Inspect fuel pres-sure with ignition On, but engine not running.

FRONT WHEEL ALIGNMENT SPECIFICATIONS

Year	Caster Angle, Degrees		Camber Angle, Degrees		Toe Per Wheel, Degrees		Steering Wheel Angle, Degrees		Ball Joint Wear
	Limits	Desired	Limits	Desired	Limits	Desired	Limits	Desired	
2004	+6.50 to +9.00	+7.75	-.7 to +.3	-.2	0 to +.34	.17	-3.5 to +3.5	0	—

REAR WHEEL ALIGNMENT SPECIFICATIONS

Year	Camber Angle, Degrees		Toe Per Wheel, Degrees		Thrust Angle, Degrees	
	Limits	Desired	Limits	Desired	Limits	Desired
2004	-.41 to -1.68	-1.05	-.06 to -.74	+.4	-.17 to +.17	0

VEHICLE RIDE HEIGHT SPECIFICATIONS

Model	Year	Body Style	Manufacturer's Original Tire Size	Front Dim.	Front Spec. Inches	Front Spec. mm	Rear Dim.	Rear Spec. Inches	Rear Spec. mm
GTO	2004	Coupe	①	Z	.8–1.6	21–41	D	1.6–2.4	41–61

Dim. — Dimension

D Dim. — Measurement Of Vertical Distance From The Bottom Of The Outer Adjustment Link (2) To The Center Line Of The Inner Adjustment Link Pivot Bolt (1), **Fig. A.**

Z Dim. — Measurement Of Vertical Distance From The Bottom Of The Control Arm (2), Below

The Ball Joint, To The Center Line Of The Control Arm Pivot Bolt (1), **Fig. B.**

① — See door sticker or inside of glove box for manufacturers original tire size specifications. If tires on vehicle do not match manufacturers original tire size & measurement is not within limits, it will be required

to refer to the "Non-Standard Tire & Wheel Size Adjustment To Ride Height Specification & Tire Size Adjustment Charts" in the front of this manual for approximate changes in ride height specifications.

② — Measurement is with fuel, radiator coolant and engine oil full, spare tire, jack, hand tools and mats in designated positions and tires properly inflated.

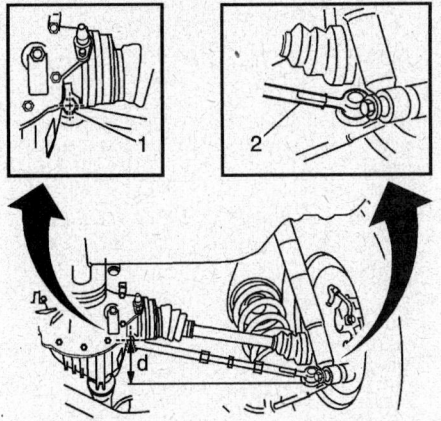

1. Center Line Of Inner Adjustment Link Pivot Bolt
2. Bottom Of Outer Adjustment Link

ARM0400000001022

Fig. A

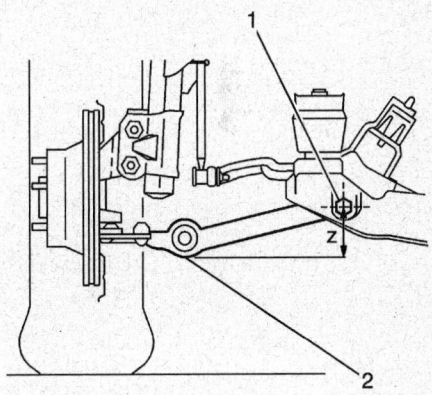

1. Center Line Of Control Arm Pivot Bolt
2. Bottom Of Control Arm

ARM0400000001021

Fig. B

FLUID CAPACITIES & COOLING SYSTEM DATA

Year	Engine (VIN)①	Coolant Capacity, Qts.	Coolant Type	Radiator Cap Relief Pressure, psi	Thermo. Opening Temp. °F	Fuel Tank, Gals.	Engine Oil, Qts.② Less Filter Change	Engine Oil, Qts.② With Filter Change	Man Trans. Pts.	Auto. Trans. Qts.③ Drain & Refill	Auto. Trans. Qts.③ Total Capacity	Rear Axle Pts.
2004	5.7 (G)	15.1	DEX-COOL	15	176–183	18.6	5.4	6.0	4.6	5.2	11.4	3.38④

VIN — Vehicle Identification Number

① — The eighth digit of the VIN denotes engine code.

② — After refilling, inspect oil level again.

③ — Approximate. Make final inspection w/dipstick.

④ — Plus 1.0 oz GM part No. 89021958 Limited Slip Differential Friction Modifier 7098.

LUBRICANT DATA

Year	Lubricant Type				
	Transmission		Rear Axle	Power Steering System	Brake System
	Automatic	Manual			
2004	Dexron III	Dexron III	①	Dexron III	DOT 4

① — 75W-140W GL-5 final drive lubricant GM part No. 89021809 & Limited Slip Differential Friction Modifier 7098, GM part No. 89021958.

Electrical

NOTE: On Air Bag Equipped Models, Refer To "Air Bag System Precautions" Located In The Front Of This Manual For System Disarming & Arming Procedures.

NOTE: Refer To "Computer Relearn Procedures" Located In The Front Of This Manual When Battery Power To The Computer Has Been Interrupted.

INDEX

PRECAUTIONS

Air Bag Systems

Refer to "Air Bag System Precautions" in the front of this manual for system disarming and arming procedures.

Battery Ground Cable

Prior to service, disconnect battery ground cable and isolate as required.

FUSE PANEL LOCATION

The instrument panel fuse block in on the under the lefthand side of the instrument panel.

The underhood fuse block is on the righthand side of the engine compartment, mounted to the strut tower.

FUEL PUMP RELAY LOCATION

The fuel pump relay is located in the underhood fuse block.

STARTER

REPLACE

1. Raise and suitably support vehicle.
2. Remove lefthand catalytic converter.
3. Remove mounting bolts and lower starter motor.
4. Remove mounting nuts, then the wiring harness starter lead and washer.
5. Remove mounting nut and positive cable nut at starter solenoid.
6. Remove starter motor.
7. Reverse procedure to install, noting the following:
   a. **Torque** positive battery cable nut at starter solenoid to 89 inch lbs.
   b. Ensure starter lead is wrapped with heat protective tape.
   c. Ensure starter lead does not contact positive cable and/or connection.
   d. **Torquel** wiring harness starter lead nut to 18 inch lbs.
   e. **Torque** starter motor mounting to 37 ft. lbs.

ALTERNATOR

REPLACE

1. Disconnect intake Air Temperature (IAT) and Mass Air Flow (MAF) sensor wiring harness connectors.
2. Loosen air intake duct to throttle body and MAF sensor to air cleaner upper body clamps.
3. Remove duct with IAT and MAF sensors installed.
4. Install suitable breaker bar with hex-head socket to drive belt tensioner bolt.
5. Relieve tension on belt by rotating drive belt tensioner clockwise.
6. Remove belt from pulleys and drive belt tensioner.
7. Slowly release tension on drive belt tensioner, then remove breaker bar and socket from drive belt tensioner bolt.
8. Place suitable drain pan below vehicle to catch power steering fluid.
9. Loosen hose clamp and remove power steering fluid reservoir outlet hose.
10. Loosen hose clamp and remove reservoir inlet hose.
11. Disconnect tab using suitable, flat-blade tool and remove power steering fluid reservoir.
12. Remove power steering gear inlet pipe and flare nut from pump.
13. Remove and discard high pressure port O-ring.
14. Loosen clamp and remove reservoir outlet hose from power steering pump.
15. Remove two mounting bolts and power steering pump.
16. Pull positive terminal cap back, then remove nut and positive cable from stud.
17. Disconnect alternator electrical connector.
18. Remove alternator rear bracket mounting bolt.
19. Remove front mounting bolts and alternator.
20. Reverse procedure to install, noting the following:
    a. **Torque** alternator front and bracket rear mounting bolts to 37 ft. lbs.
    b. **Torque** positive cable nut to 11 ft. lbs.
    c. **Torque** power steering pump mounting bolts to 21 ft. lbs.
    d. Lubricate new high pressure port O-ring with DEXRON-III, or equivalent Automatic Transmission Fluid (ATF).
    e. **Torque** high pressure port flare nut to 22 ft. lbs.
    f. **Torque** air cleaner lower housing duct clamp to 89 inch lbs.
    g. **Torque** air cleaner upper housing

mounting screws to 44 inch lbs.
  h. **Torque** intake air duct clamp to 18 inch lbs.

COIL PACK

REPLACE

1. Disconnect ignition coils harness connectors.
2. Disconnect spark plug wire at ignition coils.
3. Remove mounting bolts and ignition coil.
4. Reverse procedure to install. **Torque** ignition coil mounting bolts to 106 inch lbs.

IGNITION LOCK

REPLACE

Removal

1. Disconnect three retaining clips by grabbing knee bolster panel upper and pulling it outwards.
2. Swing knee bolster panel open.
3. Disconnect knee bolster panel from instrument panel by holding each side of knee bolster panel, pulling lefthand side rearwards just enough disconnect clip.
4. Move knee bolster panel to outboard side of vehicle to disconnect retainer's pin, then remove panel.
5. Disconnect steering column position locking lever and tilt column to lowest position.
6. Remove steering column lower cover mounting screw.
7. Position steering wheel to access covers rear portion.
8. Push rear portion of lower cover in to disconnect two upper cover tabs.
9. Raise, disconnect tab and remove upper cover.
10. Push theft deterrent reader outer ring into lower cover.
11. Remove reader ignition lock illumination socket and electrical connector.
12. Slide lower cover rearward, disconnect tab and remove cover.
13. Tilt column to lowest and telescope to longest positions.
14. Disconnect theft deterrent reader connector.
15. Remove ignition lock illumination socket and bulb.
16. Remove reader from ignition lock cylinder.
17. Insert key into ignition lock cylinder and turn it to ON position.
18. Ensure steering column is not locked.
19. Insert Allen key, or equivalent .098 in diameter drift, into locking pin hole, **Fig. 1.**
20. Release ignition lock cylinder by pressing spring loaded barrel locking latch.
21. Remove ignition lock cylinder from housing by rotating key slightly.

Installation

1. Ensure steering column is not locked.

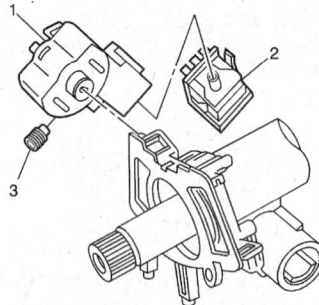

1. Ignition Switch
2. Ignition Lock Cylinder Solenoid
3. Set Screw

ARM0400000000993

Fig. 1   Exploded view of ignition switch

If steering column is locked, proceed as follows:
  a. Place suitable, flat-bladed tool on steering column lock tab.
  b. Rotate steering wheel slightly and push lock tab down.
2. Insert key into ignition lock cylinder.
3. Turn key to ON position.
4. Rotate key slightly and align keyed tip of ignition lock cylinder with keyed hole in ignition switch.
5. Install cylinder. Ensure latch locks into housing.
6. Remove key. Ensure ignition lock cylinder spring moves lock cylinder toward righthand side of vehicle.
7. Align theft deterrent reader and ignition lock cylinder flat edges.
8. Align reader indexing lug with ignition lock cylinder groove.
9. Install reader by gently pushing on reader between flat edge and indexing lug.
10. Install bulb and illumination socket to reader.
11. Connect reader connector.
12. Install steering column trim covers and knee bolster.

IGNITION SWITCH

REPLACE

1. Remove ignition lock cylinder as outlined under "Ignition Lock, Replace."
2. Insert suitable, small flat-bladed tool into ignition switch connector housing clip opening.
3. Disconnect clip by pushing.
4. Disconnect ignition switch connector.
5. Remove ignition switch mounting bolt.
6. Disconnect ignition switch from roll pin.
7. Remove ignition switch.
8. Remove ignition switch washers.
9. **On models equipped with automatic transmission,** remove ignition lock cylinder solenoid from ignition switch.
10. **On all models,** reverse procedure to install. **Torque** ignition switch mounting bolt to 10.6 inch lbs.

CLUTCH START SWITCH

REPLACE

1. Remove lefthand closeout panel to HVAC retainer.

2. Remove two lefthand closeout panel to instrument panel retainers.
3. Lower lefthand closeout panel and withdraw retaining lug from pedal bracket.
4. Remove step well lamp by rotating socket and removing from closeout panel.
5. Remove closeout panel
6. Disconnect clutch pedal position switch harness electrical connector.
7. Rotate clutch pedal position switch counterclockwise quarter turn.
8. Remove switch from pedal bracket.
9. Reverse procedure to install.

NEUTRAL SAFETY SWITCH

REPLACE

The switches are incorporated into the wiring harness and cannot be serviced separately.

1. Place transmission selector lever in PARK position.
2. Raise and suitably support vehicle.
3. Remove selector lever shift linkage adjusting bolt and washers.
4. Slide trunnion, sleeve and insulator from selector linkage end.
5. Position linkage aside.
6. Remove four selector lever mounting nuts.
7. Lower vehicle.
8. Remove floor console tray insert by lifting upwards to disconnect it from console.
9. Remove console trim plate to floor console mounting screw.
10. Pull console trim plate up and disconnect six mounting tabs.
11. Disconnect power window switch and traction control switch connectors.
12. Depress six retaining tabs and remove power window switch
13. Remove traction control switch Refer to Traction Control Switch Replacement in Antilock Brakes System.
14. Disconnect three tabs and traction control switch connector.
15. Remove selector lamp holder.
16. Remove lower housing, upper cover, gearshift lever, knob and boot from shift lever.
17. Separate lower housing from upper cover by releasing four locking tabs.
18. Remove traction control switch.
19. Remove cup holder by disconnecting retaining tab.
20. Slightly selector lever raise and disconnect Traction Control (T/C) switch connector.
21. Rotate selector lever indicator lamp counterclockwise and remove lamp assembly.
22. Remove selector lever.
23. Shift selector lever to D position using manual override lever.
24. Remove mounting screw and selector knob.
25. Disconnect selector rear wiring harness connector.
26. Disconnect selector lever housing from base by depressing four tabs

27. Lift shift lever housing and remove insulator from base.
28. Disconnect shift lock solenoid wiring harness connector.
29. Remove mounting screws and solenoid.
30. Record micro switch wiring harness routing for installation alignment.
31. Remove mounting screws, then the park lock micro switch and wiring harness from floor shift control base plate.
32. Reverse procedure to install, noting the following:
    a. **Torque** park lock micro switch mounting screws to 4 inch lbs.
    b. **Torque** solenoid mounting screws to 18 inch lbs.
    c. **Torque** selector lever mounting nuts to 11 ft. lbs.
    d. **Torque** shift linkage adjusting bolt mounting nuts to 18 ft. lbs.
    e. **Torque** selector knob mounting screw to 18 inch lbs.
    f. **Torque** console trim plate mounting screw to 18 inch lbs.

HEADLAMP SWITCH
REPLACE

1. Release steering column adjustment lever, move column to its lowers position and lock into place with adjustment lever.
2. Remove two instrument cluster trim panel to instrument panel mounting screws.
3. Tilt cluster trim panel top away from instrument panel and disconnect retaining clips on each side.
4. Unhook each retaining lug.
5. Disconnect fuel filler door release switch wiring connector.
6. Remove cluster trim panel.
7. Remove three instrument panel outer cover to instrument panel mounting screws.
8. Remove instrument panel as outlined in "Dash Panel Service" chapter.
9. Disconnect passenger's air bag module connector.
10. Remove mounting nuts, bolts and passenger's air bag module.
11. Remove mounting screw, and separate driver side inner duct from outer duct.
12. Remove inner duct from HVAC module outlet.
13. Remove driver side inner and outer ducts.
14. Squeeze retaining clips on each side from rear and push headlamp switch part way from cavity.
15. Hold retaining clips using suitable, plastic flat-bladed tool and slowly removing switch from cavity.
16. Disconnect wiring connector and remove switch.
17. Reverse procedure to install, noting the following:
    a. **Torque** passenger's air bag module mounting nuts to 33 ft. lbs.
    b. **Torque** passenger's air bag module mounting bolts to 84 inch lbs.
    c. **Torque** driver side outer duct mounting screws to 18 inch lbs.

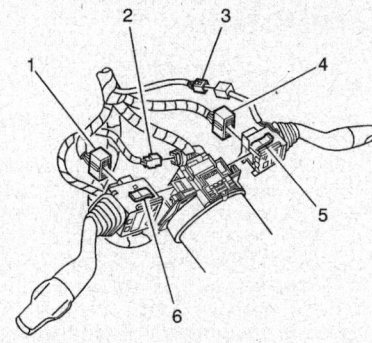

1. Turn Signal Switch Connector
2. Crusie Control Switch Connector
3. Wiper Switch Connector
4. Wiper Switch Connector
5. Tab
6. Tab

ARM0400000000996

Fig. 2   Multi-function switch replacement

d. **Torque** instrument panel outer cover mounting to 18 inch lbs.
e. **Torque** instrument cluster trim panel mounting screws 18 inch lbs.

STOP LIGHT SWITCH
REPLACE

1. Disconnect three retaining clips by grabbing knee bolster panel upper and pulling it outwards.
2. Swing knee bolster panel open.
3. Disconnect knee bolster panel from instrument panel by holding each side of knee bolster panel, pulling lefthand side rearwards just enough disconnect clip.
4. Move knee bolster panel to outboard side of vehicle to disconnect retainer's pin, then remove panel.
5. Disconnect stop lamp switch electrical connector.
6. Remove stop lamp switch from brake pedal bracket.
7. Reverse procedure to install. Adjust switch as follows:
    a. With brake pedal fully released, ensure that stop lamp plunger is fully depressed against brake pedal shanks.
    b. Disconnect switch wiring harness connector.
    c. Ensure gap between switch and support bracket is .20–.23 inch.
    d. Adjust gap by rotating switch clockwise or counterclockwise to decrease or increase gap distance.

MULTI-FUNCTION SWITCH
REPLACE

1. Remove lighting fusible link from engine compartment fuse block.
2. Disconnect steering column position locking lever and tilt column to lowest position.
3. Remove steering column lower cover mounting screw.

4. Position steering wheel to access covers rear portion.
5. Push rear portion of lower cover in to disconnect two upper cover tabs.
6. Raise, disconnect tab and remove upper cover.
7. Push theft deterrent reader outer ring into lower cover.
8. Remove reader ignition lock illumination socket and electrical connector.
9. Slide lower cover rearward, disconnect tab and remove cover.
10. Press two tabs and remove switch, **Fig. 2**.
11. Disconnect cruise control and turn signal switch connectors.
12. Reverse procedure to install.

TURN SIGNAL SWITCH
REPLACE

Refer to "Multi-Function Switch, Replace" for turn signal switch replacement procedure.

DIMMER SWITCH
REPLACE

Refer to "Multi-Function Switch, Replace" for dimmer switch replacement procedure.

STEERING WHEEL
REPLACE

1. Lock steering column and ensure front wheels are in straight ahead position.
2. Disconnect steering column position locking lever and tilt column to lowest position.
3. Remove steering column lower cover mounting screw.
4. Position steering wheel to access covers rear portion.
5. Push rear portion of lower cover in to disconnect two upper cover tabs.
6. Raise, disconnect tab and remove upper cover.
7. Push theft deterrent reader outer ring into lower cover.
8. Remove reader ignition lock illumination socket and electrical connector.
9. Slide lower cover rearward, disconnect tab and remove cover.
10. Rotate steering wheel 90° exposing two of four steering wheel hub access holes.
11. Relieve tension on two spring loaded retaining clips using inflatable restraint steering wheel module removal tool No. EL-46844, or equivalent. Driver's air bag I module will move slightly away from steering wheel.
12. Rotate steering wheel 180° and repeat previous step on remaining clips.
13. Disconnect steering wheel module connectors and remove driver's air bag module.
14. Remove steering wheel mounting bolt.
15. Mark steering wheel and shaft for installation alignment.
16. Remove steering wheel using steering wheel puller tool No. J-1859-A, or equivalent.

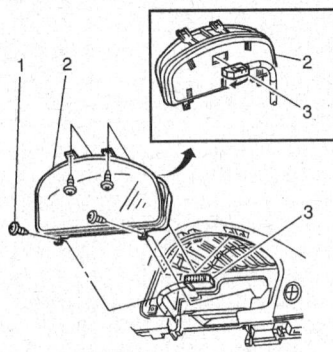

1. Mounting Screws
2. Instrument Cluster
3. Connector

ARM0400000000994

Fig. 3 Instrument cluster replacement

17. Reverse procedure to install, noting the following:
    a. Ensure SIR coil green indexing tab is aligned coil casing window.
    b. Apply Loctite 242, or equivalent, to steering wheel bolt.
    c. **Torque** steering wheel mounting bolt to 33 ft. lbs.

INSTRUMENT CLUSTER
REPLACE

1. Release steering column adjustment lever, move column to its lowers position and lock into place with adjustment lever.
2. Remove two instrument cluster trim panel to instrument panel mounting screws, **Fig. 3.**
3. Tilt cluster trim panel top away from instrument panel and disconnect retaining clips on each side.
4. Unhook each retaining lug.
5. Disconnect fuel filler door release switch wiring connector.
6. Remove cluster trim panel.
7. Remove four screws instrument cluster mounting screws.
8. Pull top of cluster from its cavity.
9. Open cluster wiring connector locking tab using suitable, flat-bladed tool.
10. Remove instrument cluster.
11. Reverse procedure to install, noting the following:
    a. **Torque** instrument cluster mounting screws to 18 inch lbs
    b. **Torque** instrument cluster trim panel mounting screws 18 inch lbs.

RADIO
REPLACE
Removal

1. Insert radio removal tools No. BO-46862, or equivalent, into access holes and push service tool in to engage barbs of retaining spring clips.
2. Apply outward pressure on tools to release spring clips and pull radio out of cradle.
3. Remove tools.

Installation

1. **Do not apply pressure to radio buttons or display.**
2. Slide radio into cradle, then using finger pressure over removal tool holes, push radio in until spring clips engage.
3. If new radio head has been installed, enter new security code, as follows:
    a. Turn ignition switch to ON position.
    b. Switch radio to ON if turned OFF.
    c. Display shows CODE 1_ _ _ _.
    d. Use preset buttons to enter PIN code. Example: If PIN code belonging to radio is 3651. Press preset button 3. Display shows 3 _ _ _ Press preset button 6. Display shows 3 6 _ _ Press preset button 5. Display shows 3 6 5 _ Press preset button 3 6 5 1
    e. If wrong PIN code has been entered display will show CODE ERROR WAIT.
    f. After waiting time CODE 2 _ _ _ will be shown on display indicating that this is second attempt.
    g. Correct code should now be entered.
    h. After three attempts delay time will be 1 hour.
    i. Display will show LOCK OUT 1 HOUR.
    j. After delay time another three attempts at entering code will be possible.

WIPER MOTOR
REPLACE

There is a specific wiper arm for each side. The arms are identified by the letters LHD D for the drivers side and LHD P for the passengers side, located on the underside of the arm.

1. Raise hood and pry cap from front wiper arm.
2. Remove wiper arm to drive spindle nut.
3. Remove wiper arm from drive spindle. **Do not to allow wiper arm to contact rear edge of hood.**
4. Remove six air inlet grille panels retainers.
5. Pull left and righthand air inlet grille panels forward to disconnect them from windshield retainer.
6. Remove left and righthand air inlet grille panels by lifting them upwards while maneuvering them from hood hinge.
7. Squeeze locking tab and disconnect main wiper motor harness connector, **Fig. 4.**
8. Remove four wiper transmission mounting bolts.
9. Remove wiper motor ground strap mounting bolt. Ground strap bolt is secured to strap by spacer and cannot be separated.
10. Remove wiper transmission.
11. Remove wiper transmission to wiper motor pivot mounting nut.
12. Remove three wiper motor to transmission bracket mounting bolts.
13. Remove wiper motor.

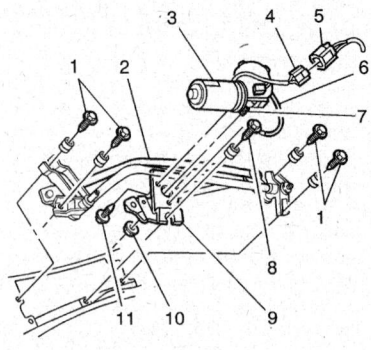

1. Mounting Bolts
2. Wiper Transmission
3. Wiper Motor
4. Main Wiper Motor Connector
5. Wiring Harness
6. Ground Strap
7. Wuper Motor Pivot
8. Mounting Bolt
9. Transmission Bracket
10. Mounting Nut
11. Mounting Bolts

ARM0400000000995

Fig. 4 Wiper motor replacement

14. Reverse procedure to install, noting the following:
    a. **Torque** wiper motor mounting bolts to 71 inch lbs.
    b. **Torque** wiper motor pivot mounting nut to 13 ft. lbs.
    c. **Torque** wiper motor ground strap bolt to 44 inch lbs.
    d. **Torque** wiper transmission mounting bolts 44 inch lbs.
    e. Ensure wiper motor linkages are in parked position.
    f. Install arms so blade tip is 1.18–1.57 inches above air inlet screen edge.
    g. **Torque** wiper arm nut to 16 ft. lbs.

WIPER SWITCH
REPLACE

1. Disconnect steering column position locking lever and tilt column to lowest position.
2. Remove steering column lower cover mounting screw.
3. Position steering wheel to access covers rear portion.
4. Push rear portion of lower cover in to disconnect two upper cover tabs.
5. Raise, disconnect tab and remove upper cover.
6. Push theft deterrent reader outer ring into lower cover.
7. Remove reader ignition lock illumination socket and electrical connector.
8. Slide lower cover rearward, disconnect tab and remove cover.
9. Disconnect wiper control switch harness connector by depressing retaining tab and pulling connectors apart, **Fig. 2.**
10. Press two tabs and lift wiring harness connector retaining tabs up on each side switch, then pull connector from switch.
11. Remove wiper switch assembly.
12. Reverse procedure to install.

WIPER TRANSMISSION

REPLACE

Refer to "Wiper Motor, Replace" for wiper transmission replacement procedure

BLOWER MOTOR

REPLACE

1. Carefully pull righthand closeout panel downwards to disconnect two retaining clips.
2. Remove righthand closeout panel from hinge pillar panel, disconnecting two lugs.
3. Lower closeout panel and remove step well lamp by rotating socket and removing from closeout panel .
4. Remove closeout panel.
5. Disconnect blower motor electrical connector.
6. Remove three mounting screws and blower motor.
7. Reverse procedure to install. **Torque** blower motor mounting screws and 15 inch lbs.

HEATER CORE

REPLACE

1. Recover refrigerant as outlined in "Air Conditioning" chapter.
2. Drain cooling system into suitable container.
3. Remove instrument panel as outlined in "Dash Panel Service" chapter.
4. Disconnect passenger's air bag module connector.
5. Remove mounting nuts, bolts and passenger's air bag module.
6. Remove righthand side duct from HVAC unit.
7. Remove lefthand inner brace to lower radio bracket mounting bolt.
8. Remove HVAC unit to lower radio bracket mounting bolt.
9. Remove instrument panel righthand end bracket to lower radio bracket mounting bolt.
10. Remove instrument panel righthand end bracket to lower radio bracket mounting screw .
11. Remove lower radio bracket mounting screws and disconnect electrical connector.
12. Remove lower radio bracket.
13. Carefully pull righthand closeout panel downwards and disconnect two retaining clips.
14. Remove righthand closeout panel from hinge pillar panel and disconnect two retaining lugs.
15. Lower righthand closeout panel and remove step well lamp by rotating socket .
16. Remove righthand closeout panel.
17. Remove mounting screw, disconnect rear retaining tab and gently remove Body Control Module (BCM) from mounting bracket.
18. Disconnect four BCM wiring harness connectors.
19. Remove righthand end bracket to lower radio bracket mounting screw.
20. Remove righthand end bracket to lower radio bracket mounting bolt.
21. Remove righthand end bracket mounting bolts.
22. Remove righthand end bracket to passenger air bag module mounting bolts.
23. Disconnect wiring harness and remove righthand end bracket.
24. Remove center support brace to lower radio bracket mounting screw and bolts.
25. Remove four mounting bolts and drivers knee bolster bracket.
26. Remove two mounting bolts and drivers inner bracket.
27. Remove bolt and center support brace.
28. Remove radio antenna lead from three HVAC unit retaining clips.
29. Mark heater hoses for install alignment.
30. Remove heater hoses from core pipes.
31. Disconnect water valve vacuum and vacuum supply hoses from check valve.
32. Recover refrigerant as outlined in "Air Conditioning" chapter.
33. Remove mounting bolt, then Thermal Expansion Valve (TXV) tube plate, inlet and outlet tubes. Remove and discard O-rings.
34. Remove mounting bolts and TXV. Remove and discard O-rings.
35. Cap or tape open evaporator inlet and outlet tubes.
36. Cap evaporator inlet and outlet tube.
37. Remove fuel line retaining bracket and nut from HVAC mounting stud.
38. Remove mounting stud and screws, then the HVAC unit.
39. Remove two heater core pipe clamp.
40. Remove mounting screws and heater core retaining strap.
41. Remove mounting screws and heater pipe bracket.
42. Remove heater core. **Do not damage foam seal on top and sides of heater core.**
43. Remove mounting screw, clamps and heater pipe. Remove and discard O-rings.
44. Reverse procedure to install, noting the following:
    a. Install O-rings on heater pipes.
    b. **Torque** heater pipes clamps and screws to 15 inch lbs.
    c. **Torque** heater pipe bracket mounting screws to 14 inch lbs.
    d. **Torque** heater core retaining strap mounting screws to 14 inch lbs.
    e. **Torque** heater core pipe clamps to 14 inch lbs.
    f. **Torque** HVAC module inside mounting nuts to 53 inch lbs.
    g. **Torque** HVAC module engine compartment mounting nuts to 89 inch lbs.
    h. **Torque** fuel line bracket nut to 89 inch lbs.
    i. **Torque** TXV mounting bolts to 40 inch lbs.
    j. Install new O-rings.
    k. **Torque** evaporator tube plate mounting bolt to 93 inch lbs.
    l. **Torque** center support brace mounting bolts to 80 inch lbs.
    m. **Torque** drivers knee bolster bracket mounting bolts to 80 inch lbs.
    n. **Torque** BCM mounting screws to 18 inch lbs.
    o. **Torque** righthand end bracket mounting bolts to 80 inch lbs.
    p. **Torque** lower radio bracket mounting screws to 18 inch lbs.
    q. **Torque** instrument panel right end bracket mounting 18 inch lbs.
    r. **Torque** lower radio bracket mounting bolt to 80 inch lbs.
    s. **Torque** HVAC unit mounting bolt to 80 inch lbs.

EVAPORATOR CORE

REPLACE

1. Remove HVAC module as outlined under "Heater Core, Replace."
2. Remove mounting screws and TXV joint bracket.
3. Remove heater core as outlined under "Heater Core, Replace."
4. Disconnect recirculation/intake actuator vacuum line.
5. Remove front HVAC module case vacuum lines and retainers.
6. Remove vacuum line and actuator rod from lever, then the mounting screws and defroster actuator.
7. Remove front HVAC module case to upper and lower cases' mounting screws.
8. Separate front HVAC module case from upper and lower cases.
9. Remove upper to lower HVAC module mounting screws and clips.
10. Separate upper from lower HVAC module case.
11. Remove evaporator core.
12. Remove mounting screw and evaporator core pipes. Remove and discard O-rings.
13. Reverse procedure to install, noting the following:
    a. Install new O-rings.
    b. **Torque** evaporator core pipes mounting screw to 44 inch lbs.
    c. **Torque** case mounting screws and 14 inch lbs.
    d. **Torque** defroster actuator mounting screws to 14 inch lbs.
    e. **Torque** TXV joint bracket mounting screws to 14 inch lbs.

5.7L Engine

NOTE: For Procedures Not Found In This Section, Refer To The "5.7L Engine" Section In The "Corvette" Chapter.

NOTE: On Air Bag Equipped Models, Refer To "Air Bag System Precautions" Located In The Front Of This Manual For System Disarming & Arming Procedures.

NOTE: Refer To "Computer Relearn Procedures" Located In The Front Of This Manual When Battery Power To The Computer Has Been Interrupted.

INDEX

PRECAUTIONS

Fuel System Pressure Relief

Failure to relieve system pressure prior to disconnecting fuel system components may cause fire or personal injury.
1. Turn ignition switch to OFF position.
2. Disconnect and isolate negative battery cable.
3. Relieve fuel tank vapor pressure by loosening fuel filler cap.
4. Remove lefthand fuel rail cover.
5. Connect fuel pressure gauge tool No. J34730-1A, or equivalent, to fuel pressure connection.
6. Wrap shop towel around fitting while connecting gauge.
7. Install gauge bleed hose into suitable container.
8. Open gauge valve and bleed system pressure.
9. Drain remaining gauge fuel into suitable container.

Battery Ground Cable

Prior to service, disconnect battery ground cable and isolate as required.

ENGINE MOUNT

REPLACE

Lefthand

1. Remove lefthand exhaust manifold as outlined under "Exhaust Manifold, Replace."
2. Remove mounting nuts and lefthand engine mount.
3. Reverse procedure to install.

Righthand

1. Remove righthand exhaust manifold as outlined under "Exhaust Manifold, Replace."
2. Remove mounting nuts and righthand engine mount.
3. Reverse procedure to install.

ENGINE

REPLACE

1. Recover air conditioning refrigerant as outlined in "Air Conditioning" chapter.
2. Open hood.
3. Apply suitable tape to hood corners and adjacent surfaces.
4. Cut end and remove secondary latch rivet, then remove secondary latch and spring.
5. Loosen nut and remove hood latch striker bolt ensuring washer, hood pop-up spring and hood pop-up spring retainer remain on bolt.
6. **On models equipped with hood scoops,** proceed as follows:
   a. Remove hood air extractor by gently squeezing to unhook tabs.
   b. Starting at rear of hood and working toward front, remove 13 hood insulator retainers.
   c. Slide insulator from slots in hood inner panel and remove.
   d. Remove plug, retainer and scoop.
7. **On models equipped less hood scoops,** starting at rear of hood and working toward front, remove hood insulator retainers.
8. **On all models,** place suitable container under washer solvent container.
9. Reach between front bumper fascia and washer solvent container, then disconnect washer solvent hose from pump.
10. Allow washer solvent to drain from container.
11. Remove washer hose from behind fuse panel and disconnect hose adjacent to hood strut.
12. Separate and remove washer hoses from washer nozzles.
13. Squeeze retaining tabs on washer nozzle base and push nozzle out through top of hood. Remove nozzle.
14. Remove hood adjustable bumper by rotating it counterclockwise.
15. Mark upper hood hinge location to hood for installation alignment.
16. Provide alternate hood support.
17. Remove assit rod clip using suitable, small flat-bladed tool.
18. Remove assist rod to fender mounting bolts.
19. Disconnect and remove assist rod from hood strut pin.
20. Have assistant hold hood, then remove upper hood hinge mounting bolts and hood.
21. Remove four mounting nuts and front suspension support brace.
22. Remove fuel rail covers.
23. Disconnect air intake sensor connector.

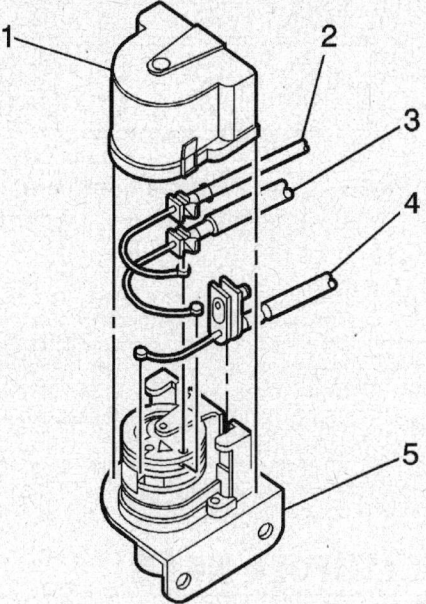

1. Throttle Relaxer Cover
2. Accelerator Cable
3. Accelerator Cable
4. Cruise Control Cable
5. Mounting Bracket

ARM0400000000999

Fig. 1   Throttle relaxer replacement

24. Loosen hose clamps and remove intake duct.
25. Disconnect and isolate negative battery cable.
26. Relieve fuel tank vapor pressure by loosening fuel filler cap.
27. Remove lefthand fuel rail cover.
28. Connect fuel pressure gauge tool No. J34730-1A, or equivalent, to fuel pressure connection.
29. Wrap shop towel around fitting while connecting gauge.
30. Install gauge bleed hose into suitable container.
31. Open gauge valve and bleed system pressure.
32. Remove radiator as outlined under "Radiator, Replace."
33. Remove radiator and heater hoses from water pump.
34. Remove air conditioning compressor and condenser hose nut.
35. Separate compressor and condenser hose from compressor. Cap hoses and inlets.
36. Remove ground lead screw from engine block and lefthand engine mount.
37. Remove nut securing battery harness ground terminals to antilock brake system (ABS)/traction control system (TCS) control module bracket stud.
38. Disconnect positive lead terminal from battery. Lay harness on engine.
39. Disconnect air conditioning wiring harness connector.
40. Disconnect wiring harness retaining

clips from engine compartment.
41. Disconnect theft deterrent horn connector.
42. Disconnect radiator hose from surge tank inlet fitting.
43. Disconnect surge tank vapor and overflow hoses.
44. Pivot surge tank to remove from rear anchor plate.
45. Pull tank inward toward engine and remove it from anchor plate on inner fender.
46. Disconnect coolant level switch electrical connector.
47. Remove Powertrain Control Module (PCM) harness connector cover.
48. Loosen and remove PCM connectors.
49. Disconnect PCM wiring harness retaining clip.
50. Remove engine wiring harness retaining clip from power steering pipe bracket.
51. Remove throttle relaxer cover and disconnect connector, **Fig. 1**.
52. Remove both fuel rail covers.
53. Disconnect throttle and cruise control cables form relaxer.
54. Remove mounting nuts and throttle relaxer.
55. Cut wiring harness straps and discard.
56. Disconnect powertrain to main wiring harness connector.
57. Remove harness to dash panel grommet, then feed harness and connectors out into engine bay
58. Place powertrain wiring harness on top of engine.
59. Lift throttle cable at throttle body mounting bracket and remove it from cam lever. Set throttle cable aside.
60. Relieve vapor pressure by loosening fuel filler cap.
61. Disconnect engine compartment fuel feed pipe at fuel rail, **Fig. 2**.
62. Disconnect engine compartment EVAP pipe at EVAP canister purge solenoid.
63. Disconnect engine compartment fuel feed pipe at chassis fuel feed pipe.
64. Disconnect engine compartment EVAP pipe at chassis EVAP pipe.
65. Cap fuel pipes.
66. Disconnect line from purge valve.
67. Loosen power steering reservoir return hose clamp.
68. Place suitable container under reservoir, then remove hose and drain reservoir fluid.
69. Remove power steering pump outlet fitting high pressure line flare nut and O-ring.
70. Disconnect brake booster vacuum hose and heater control, vacuum hose from rear of intake manifold.
71. Remove four mounting bolts and undertray from crossmember.
72. Remove two power steering high pressure line brackets to oil pan mounting bolts.
73. Remove exhaust manifolds as outlined under "Exhaust Manifold, Replace."
74. Remove transmission as outlined in

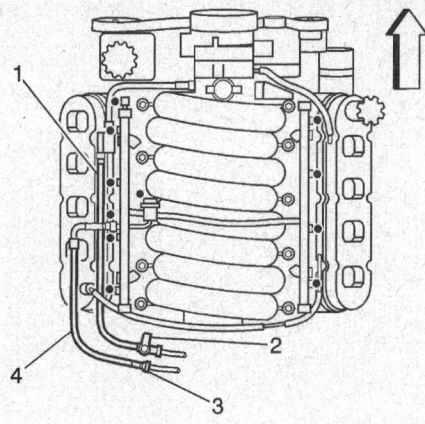

1. Engine Compartment EVAP Pipe
2. Chassis EVAP Pipe
3. Chassis Fuel Feed Pipe
4. Engine Compartment Fuel Feed Pipe

ARM0400000001000

Fig. 2   Fuel line replacement

MOTOR's "Domestic Transmission Manual, In-Vehicle Service."
75. Remove left and righthand engine mount to engine bracket nuts.
76. Attach suitable lifting chain and hooks to two engine lifting brackets.
77. Slightly raise engine to clear engine mount stud. using suitable lifting crane.
78. Slowly lift and remove engine.
79. Reverse procedure to install.

EXHAUST MANIFOLD
REPLACE

Lefthand

1. Remove fuel rail covers.
2. Support engine using universal engine support fixture tools Nos. J-41803 and J-28467-B, or equivalent.
3. Remove four mounting nuts and front suspension support brace.
4. Lift locking lever, then remove Mass Air Flow (MAF) and Intake Air Temperature (IAT) sensors' electrical connectors.
5. Loosen two clamps and remove intake duct.
6. Relieve fuel tank vapor pressure by loosening fuel filler cap.
7. Remove lefthand fuel rail cover.
8. Connect fuel pressure gauge tool No. J34730-1A, or equivalent, to fuel pressure connection.
9. Wrap shop towel around fitting while connecting gauge.
10. Install gauge bleed hose into suitable container.
11. Open gauge valve and bleed system pressure.

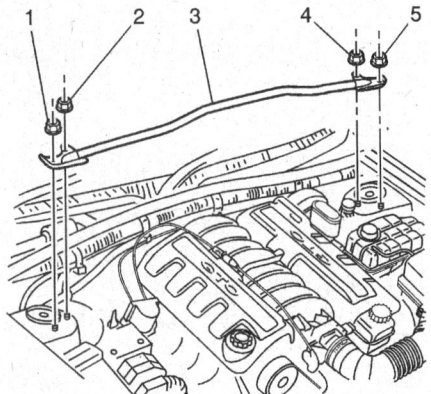

1. Mounting Nut
2. Mounting Nut
3. Front Suspension Support Brace
4. Mounting Nut
5. Mounting Nut

ARM0400000000992

Fig. 3 Front suspension support brace tightening sequence

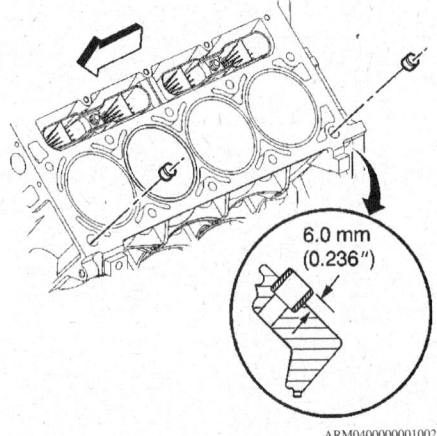

ARM0400000001002

Fig. 4 Cylinder head gasket installation

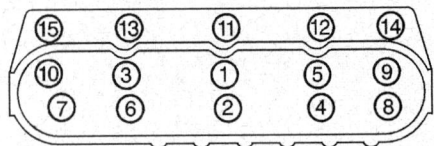

ARM0400000001003

Fig. 5 Cylinder head tightening sequence

12. Partially drain cooling system into suitable container.
13. Remove coolant temperature sensor.
14. Raise and support vehicle.
15. **Do not damage oxygen sensors.**
16. Remove lefthand exhaust manifold to exhaust pipe flange nuts.
17. Lower vehicle.
18. Disconnect spark plug wire at each spark plug by twisting each ½ turn and pulling only on boot.
19. Loosen each spark plug 1–2 turns. Remove dirt from spark plugs. using suitable brush or compressed air.
20. Remove spark plugs one at a time and place each plug in tray marked with corresponding cylinder numbers.
21. Remove exhaust manifold mounting bolts, working from outside to center.
22. Remove exhaust manifold and gasket.
23. Remove mounting bolts and heat shield.
24. Reverse procedure to install, noting the following:
    a. Apply .2 inch wide band of suitable threadlocker to exhaust manifold mounting bolts' threads.
    b. **Torque** exhaust manifold mounting bolts from center to outsides to 11 ft. lbs.
    c. **Torque** exhaust manifold mounting bolts from center to outsides to 18 ft. lbs.
    d. Bend over exposed edge of exhaust manifold gasket at rear of cylinder head.
    e. **Torque** front suspension support brace mounting nuts to 22 ft. lbs. in sequence, **Fig. 3.**

Righthand

1. Remove fuel rail covers.
2. Support engine using universal engine support fixture tools Nos. J-41803 and J-28467-B, or equivalent.
3. Remove four mounting nuts and front suspension support brace.
4. Lift locking lever, then remove Mass Air Flow (MAF) and Intake Air Temperature (IAT) sensors' electrical connectors.
5. Loosen two clamps and remove intake duct.
6. Relieve fuel tank vapor pressure by loosening fuel filler cap.
7. Remove lefthand fuel rail cover.
8. Connect fuel pressure gauge tool No. J34730-1A , or equivalent, to fuel pressure connection.
9. Wrap shop towel around fitting while connecting gauge.
10. Install gauge bleed hose into suitable container.
11. Open gauge valve and bleed system pressure.
12. Partially drain cooling system into suitable container.
13. Remove oil level indicator from tube
14. Remove oil level indicator tube bolt from righthand cylinder head and oil pan. Plug opening of oil level indicator tube.
15. Raise and support vehicle.
16. **Do not damage oxygen sensors.**
17. Remove righthand exhaust manifold to exhaust pipe flange nuts.
18. Lower vehicle.
19. Disconnect spark plug wire at each spark plug by twisting each ½ turn and pulling only on boot.
20. Loosen each spark plug 1–2 turns. Remove dirt from spark plugs. using suitable brush or compressed air.
21. Remove spark plugs one at a time and place each plug in tray marked with corresponding cylinder numbers.
22. Remove exhaust manifold mounting bolts, working from outside to center.
23. Remove exhaust manifold and gasket.
24. Remove mounting bolts and heat shield.
25. Reverse procedure to install, noting the following:
    a. Apply .2 inch wide band of suitable threadlocker to exhaust manifold mounting bolts' threads.
    b. **Torque** exhaust manifold mounting bolts from center to outsides to 11

ft. lbs.
    c. **Torque** exhaust manifold mounting bolts from center to outsides to 18 ft. lbs.
    d. Bend over exposed edge of exhaust manifold gasket at rear of cylinder head.
    e. **Torque** front suspension support brace mounting nuts to 22 ft. lbs. in sequence, **Fig. 3.**

CYLINDER HEAD
REPLACE
Lefthand

1. Remove valve cover as outlined under "Valve Cover, Replace."
2. Remove mounting bolts, rocker arms pivot support. and pushrods. **Place rocker arms, pushrods and pivot support in suitable rack so they can be installed in original position.**
3. Remove coolant air bleed hose from throttle body, then the studs, coolant air bleed pipe and gaskets.
4. Remove two mounting bolts and power steering pump.
5. Remove lefthand exhaust manifold as outlined under "Exhaust Manifold Replace."
6. Remove mounting bolts and position engine wiring harness ground aside.
7. Remove and discard cylinder head bolts. **Cylinder head bolts are not reusable.**
8. Remove cylinder head and place it on two suitable wood blocks.
9. Remove and discard head gasket.
10. Reverse procedure to install, noting the following.
    a. **Do not use any type of sealant on cylinder head gasket.**
    b. Install head gasket in proper direction and position onto locating pins, **Fig. 4.** When properly installed, tab on gasket will be located left of center, or closer to front of engine and words This Side Up and engine displacement visible.
    c. Install new cylinder head bolts.
    d. **Torque** M11 cylinder head bolts 1–10 to 22 ft. lbs. in sequence, **Fig. 5.**
    e. Tighten M11 cylinder head bolts 1–10 an additional 90° in sequence.
    f. Tighten M11 cylinder head bolts 1–8 an additional 90° in sequence.
    g. Tighten M11 cylinder head bolts 9–10) and additional 50° in sequence.

h. **Torque** M8 cylinder head bolts 11—15 to 22 ft. lbs., begin with center bolt 11 and alternating side-to-side, work outward.

i. Lubricate rocker arms and push-rods, then rocker arm bolts and flange with suitable, clean engine oil.

j. Ensure pushrods seat properly to rocker arms ends.

k. After rocker arms and bolts are install, rotate crankshaft until piston No. 1 is at Top Dead Center (TDC) of compression stroke. In this position, cylinder No. 1 rocker arms will be off lobe lift and crankshaft sprocket key will be at 1:30 position.

l. **Torque** exhaust valve rocker arm bolts Nos. 1, 2, 7 and 8 to 22 ft. lbs.

m. **Torque** intake valve rocker arm bolts Nos. 1, 3, 4 and 5 to 22 ft. lbs.

n. Rotate crankshaft 360°.

o. **Torque** exhaust valve rocker arm bolts Nos. 3, 4, 5 and 6 to 22 ft. lbs.

p. **Torque** intake valve rocker arm bolts Nos. 2, 6, 7 and 8 to 22 ft. lbs.

Righthand

1. Drain coolant into suitable container.
2. Disconnect clamp and separate inlet heater hose from heater pipe.
3. Disconnect clamp and separate heater inlet hose from water pump.
4. Remove clips and separate heater inlet hoses from water valve ports.
5. Remove inlet heater hoses.
6. Remove valve cover as outlined under "Valve Cover, Replace."
7. Remove mounting bolts, rocker arms pivot support. and pushrods. **Place rocker arms, pushrods and pivot support in suitable rack so they can be installed in original position.**
8. Remove coolant air bleed hose from throttle body, then the studs, coolant air bleed pipe and gaskets.
9. Remove righthand exhaust manifold as outlined under "Exhaust Manifold Replace."
10. Remove engine wiring harness clip bolt.
11. Remove and discard cylinder head bolts. **Cylinder head bolts are not reusable.**
12. Remove cylinder head and place it on two suitable wood blocks.
13. Remove and discard head gasket.
14. Reverse procedure to install, noting the following:
    a. **Do not use any type of sealant on cylinder head gasket.**
    b. Install head gasket in proper direction and position onto locating pins, **Fig. 4.** When properly installed, tab on gasket will be located left of center, or closer to front of engine and words This Side Up and engine displacement visible.
    c. Install new cylinder head bolts.
    d. **Torque** M11 cylinder head bolts 1–10 to 3 22 ft. lbs. in sequence, **Fig. 5.**
    e. Tighten M11 cylinder head bolts 1–10 an additional 90° in

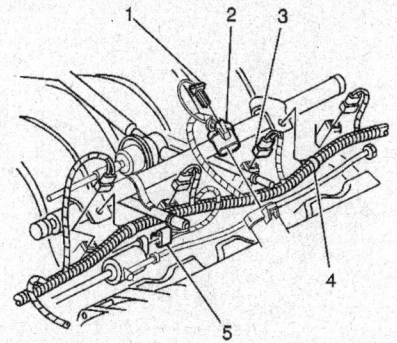

1. CPA Clip
2. Ignition Coil Wire Harness Main Electrical Connector
3, 4 & 5. Harness Clips

ARM0400000001001

Fig. 6   Valve cover replacement. Lefthand

sequence.

f. Tighten M11 cylinder head bolts 1–8 an additional 90° in sequence.

g. Tighten M11 cylinder head bolts 9–10) and additional 50° in sequence.

h. **Torque** M8 cylinder head bolts 11–15 to 22 ft. lbs., begin with center bolt 11 and alternating side-to-side, work outward.

i. Lubricate rocker arms and push-rods, then rocker arm bolts and flange with suitable, clean engine oil.

j. Ensure pushrods seat properly to rocker arms ends.

k. After rocker arms and bolts are install, rotate crankshaft until piston No. 1 is at Top Dead Center (TDC) of compression stroke. In this position, cylinder No. 1 rocker arms will be off lobe lift and crankshaft sprocket key will be at 1:30 position.

l. **Torque** exhaust valve rocker arm bolts Nos. 1, 2, 7 and 8 to 22 ft. lbs.

m. **Torque** intake valve rocker arm bolts Nos. 1, 3, 4 and 5 to 22 ft. lbs.

n. Rotate crankshaft 360°.

o. **Torque** exhaust valve rocker arm bolts Nos. 3, 4, 5 and 6 to 22 ft. lbs.

p. **Torque** intake valve rocker arm bolts Nos. 2, 6, 7 and 8 to 22 ft. lbs.

VALVE COVER

REPLACE

Lefthand

1. Remove four mounting nuts and front suspension support brace.
2. Remove both fuel rail covers.
3. Disconnect air intake sensor connector.
4. Loosen clamps and remove intake duct.
5. Turn ignition switch to OFF position.
6. Disconnect and isolate negative battery cable.
7. Relieve fuel tank vapor pressure by loosening fuel filler cap.
8. Connect fuel pressure gauge tool No.

J34730-1A, or equivalent, to fuel pressure connection.
9. Wrap shop towel around fitting while connecting gauge.
10. Install gauge bleed hose into suitable container.
11. Open gauge valve and bleed system pressure.
12. Relieve vapor pressure by loosening fuel filler cap.
13. Disconnect engine compartment fuel feed pipe at fuel rail, **Fig. 2.**
14. Disconnect engine compartment EVAP pipe at EVAP canister purge solenoid.
15. Disconnect engine compartment fuel feed pipe at chassis fuel feed pipe.
16. Disconnect engine compartment EVAP pipe at chassis EVAP pipe.
17. Cap fuel pipes.
18. Disconnect line from purge valve.
19. Disconnect spark plug wires from ignition coils.
20. Remove Connector Position Assurance (CPA) Clip, **Fig. 6.**
21. Disconnect ignition coil wire harness main electrical connector.
22. Remove mounting bolts and screw, then the ignition coil bracket.
23. Remove mounting bolts and valve cover. Remove and discard gasket.
24. Reverse procedure to install, noting the following:
    a. Install new valve cover gasket.
    b. Install new valve cover bolt grommets.
    c. Apply suitable threadlock to ignition coil bracket studs' threads.
    d. **Torque** front suspension support brace mounting nuts to 22 ft. lbs. in sequence, **Fig. 3.**

Righthand

1. Remove four mounting nuts and front suspension support brace.
2. Remove both fuel rail covers.
3. Disconnect air intake sensor connector.
4. Loosen clamps and remove intake duct.
5. Remove spark plug wires from ignition coils.
6. Remove Connector Position Assurance (CPA) clip.
7. Disconnect ignition coil wire harness main electrical connector.
8. Remove mounting bolts and screw, then the ignition coil bracket.
9. Disconnect spark plug wires from ignition coils.
10. Remove Connector Position Assurance (CPA) Clip, **Fig. 7.**
11. Disconnect ignition coil wire harness main electrical connector.
12. Remove mounting bolts and screw, then the ignition coil bracket.
13. Remove mounting bolts and valve cover. Remove and discard gasket.
14. Reverse procedure to install, noting the following:
    a. Install new valve cover gasket.
    b. Install new valve cover bolt grommets.
    c. Apply suitable threadlock to ignition coil bracket studs' threads.

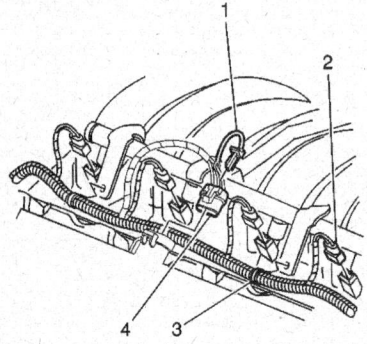

1. CPA Clip
2. Connector
3. Clip
4. Ignition Coil Wire Harness Main Electrical Connector

ARM0400000001004

Fig. 7 Valve cover replacement. Righthand

d. **Torque** front suspension support brace mounting nuts to 22 ft. lbs. in sequence, **Fig. 3.**

SERPENTINE DRIVE BELT

Belt Routing

Refer to **Fig. 8** for serpentine drive belt routing.

Belt Replacement

REMOVAL

1. Install suitable breaker bar with hex-head socket to drive belt tensioner bolt.
2. Relieve tension on belt by rotating drive belt tensioner clockwise.
3. Remove belt from pulleys and drive belt tensioner.
4. Slowly release tension on drive belt tensioner. Remove breaker bar and socket from drive belt tensioner bolt.

INSTALLATION

1. Route drive belt around all pulleys, except water pump and belt tensioner.
2. Install suitable breaker bar with hex-head socket to belt tensioner bolt.
3. Relieve tension on tension by rotating belt tensioner clockwise.
4. Install drive belt under water pump pulley and onto belt tensioner.
5. Slowly release tension.
6. Remove breaker bar and socket from belt tensioner bolt.
7. Inspect drive belt for proper alignment.

COOLING SYSTEM BLEED

1. Slowly fill cooling system through upper radiator hose with suitable coolant mixture until coolant comes out coolant air bleed hose.
2. Fill radiator suitable coolant through surge tank opening to full line.
3. Install coolant pressure cap.

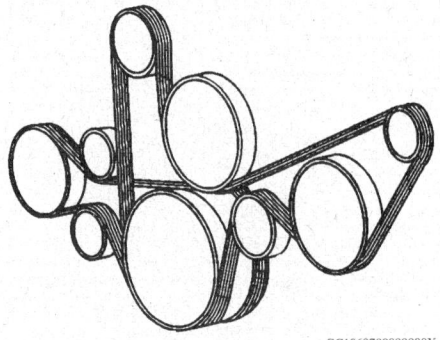

GC1069700899000X

Fig. 8 Serpentine drive belt routing

4. Start engine and run at 2000–2500 RPM until engine reaches normal operating temperature.
5. Allow engine to idle for three minutes.
6. Shut off and allow engine to cool.
7. Adjust coolant level as required.

THERMOSTAT

REPLACE

The water pump inlet and thermostat are replaced as an assembly. The thermostat is not serviceable separately.
1. Drain cooling system into suitable container.
2. Position clamp and remove outlet hose from water pump inlet.
3. Remove mounting bolts and water pump inlet.
4. Remove thermostat housing. O-ring seal is integral to thermostat housing.
5. Reverse procedure to install.

WATER PUMP

REPLACE

1. Lift locking lever and disconnect Mass Air Flow (MAF) sensor electrical connector.
2. Lift locking lever on Intake Air Temperature (IAT) sensor electrical connector.
3. Loosen two clamps and remove intake duct.
4. Install suitable breaker bar with hex-head socket to drive belt tensioner bolt.
5. Relieve tension on belt by rotating drive belt tensioner clockwise.
6. Remove belt from pulleys and drive belt tensioner.
7. Slowly release tension on drive belt tensioner. Remove breaker bar and socket from drive belt tensioner bolt.
8. Drain cooling system into suitable container.
9. Disconnect two heater hoses, then the water pump inlet and outlet hoses.
10. Remove two mounting bolts and drive belt tensioner.
11. Remove six mounting bolts and water pump.
12. Remove and discard gaskets.
13. Reverse procedure to install, noting the following:
    a. **Torque** water pump mounting bolts to 11 ft. lbs.
    b. **Torque** mounting bolts to 18 ft. lbs.

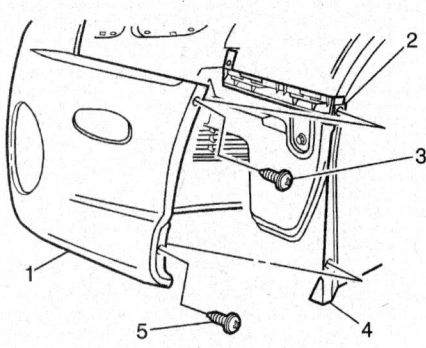

1. Fascia
2. Fassuca Support
3. Mounting Screw
4. Wheelhouse Liner
5. Mounting screw

ARM0400000000997

Fig. 9 Fascia replacement (Part 1 of 2)

RADIATOR

REPLACE

1. Lift locking levers, then disconnect Mass Air Flow (MAF) and Intake Air Temperature (IAT) sensors' electrical connectors.
2. Loosen two clamps and remove intake duct.
3. Drain cooling system into suitable container.
4. Remove vapor hose from radiator fan shroud clips and radiator clamp, then position it aside.
5. Remove vapor hose to surge tank clamp at radiator and position it aside.
6. Remove five upper shroud to radiator retainers.
7. Lift shroud on righthand side and release lefthand side locating tab.
8. Loosen and remove radiator outlet hose from radiator and thermostat housing.
9. Remove coolant vapor hose from fan shroud retaining clip.
10. Disconnect left and righthand cooling fan motor electrical connector.
11. Push shroud locking tab down, then lift fan and should assembly up. **Do not lift fan and shroud by fan rings.**
12. Disconnect intermediate fan motor electrical connector and remove motor wire harness from fan shroud retaining clips.
13. Remove four mounting screws, then the fan motor and wiring.
14. Remove outlet hose radiator and thermostat housing.
15. Remove inlet hose from radiator and radiator inlet pipe.
16. Release refrigerant pipe-to-receiver drier retaining clip on lefthand side of radiator.
17. Remove fascia to wheelhouse liner mounting screws on each side, **Fig. 9.**
18. Remove fascia to support mounting screws.
19. Unclip fascia from support by grabbing upper end and pulling it away.
20. Disconnect fog lamp and sidemarker

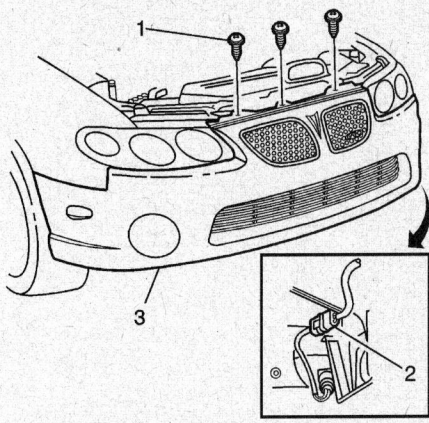

1. Mounting Screw
2. Fog Lamp Connector
3. Fascia

ARM0400000000998

Fig. 9 Fascia replacement (Part 2 of 2)

lamp harness connector from lefthand side.
21. Remove three fascia to front upper panel mounting screws, then the fascia.
22. Press down on 1st locking tab while lifting on condenser.
23. Press down on 2nd locking tab lift, then slightly pull condenser assembly forward to clear radiator mounting lugs.
24. Disconnect transmission cooler lines.
25. Remove two radiator upper mounting brackets.
26. Lift radiator upwards and move it rearwards on lefthand side, then across to lefthand side to allow righthand side to clear mounting brackets.
27. Reverse procedure to install.

FUEL PUMP
REPLACE

1. Remove fuel filler cap.
2. Hold flapper door open using fuel flapper door holder tool No. J 42960-2, or equivalent.
3. Insert fuel tank drain hose tool No. J 42960-1, or equivalent, into fuel tank until hose reaches bottom of fuel tank.
4. Siphon as much fuel as possible from fuel tank using suitable air operated pump.
5. Remove seven retainers and luggage compartment center trim panel carpet.
6. Remove two luggage compartment support brace to panel frame mounting nuts, **Fig. 10**.
7. Remove two luggage compartment support brace to underbody side rail brackets mounting nuts.

8. Remove mounting bolts, then lean support brace forward off studs and remove it.
9. Disconnect body wiring harness to fuel tank harness electrical connector.
10. Unscrew fuel filler cap from behind fuel filler door and cover end of fuel filler neck with suitable material.
11. Remove three fuel filler neck to filler pocket mounting nuts.
12. Raise and support vehicle.
13. Disconnect fuel feed line quick connect fittings and place line aside.
14. Remove fuel tank vent line quick connect fitting.
15. Remove lower fuel tank mounting strap mounting nuts.
16. Lower vehicle and remove two fuel tank upper mounting strap nuts from within luggage compartment, then the mounting straps.
17. Remove fuel tank and filler neck.
18. Disconnect fuel tank pressure sensor and fuel pump connectors, then the EVAP vapor hose quick connector from modular fuel pump and sender cover.
19. Remove modular fuel pump and sender ground terminal to fuel tank flange stud nut.
20. Remove fuel tank wiring harness.
21. Remove cover retainer lock ring by turning in counterclockwise direction using fuel sender lock ring wrench No. J 45722, or equivalent, and suitable half-inch breaker bar.
22. Partially lift modular fuel pump and sender away from fuel tank. **Do not damage fuel level sender.**
23. Disconnect fuel tank EVAP vapor line quick connector from underside of modular fuel pump and sender cover.
24. Insert hand into fuel tank opening and disconnect fuel feed line quick connector.
25. Remove modular fuel pump and sender.
26. Seal fuel tank opening using suitable plug and place suitable cover over plug.
27. Remove and discard modular fuel pump and sender to fuel tank seal.
28. Reverse procedure to install, noting the following:
    a. Only use custom sized O-rings. **Do not use off-the-shelf O-rings.**
    b. Stand assembly upright on flat surface.
    c. Ensure distance between middle of fuel sender float and flat surface is .276–.551 inch.

FUEL FILTER
REPLACE

1. Remove modular fuel sender from fuel

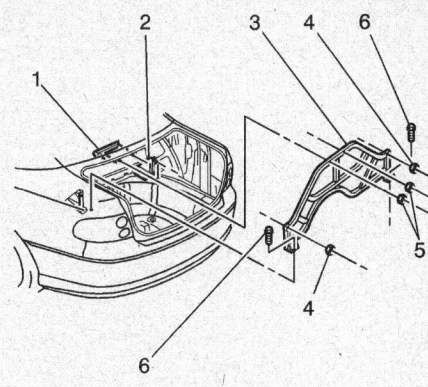

1. Rear Compartment Panel Frame
2. Underbody Side Rail Brackets
3. Rear Compartment Support Brace
4. Mounting Nuts
5. Mounting Nuts
6. Mounting Bolts

ARM0400000001005

Fig. 10 luggage compartment support brace replacement

tank as outlined under "Fuel Pump, Replace."
2. Removal of fuel level sender and fuel pump harness connectors from underneath modular fuel pump and sender cover using suitable flat blade screwdriver.
3. Press in tang and remove fuel pump connector.
4. Remove modular fuel pump and sender cover from reservoir.
5. Remove fuel pressure regulator.
6. Pry open both tangs securing fuel outlet connector to bottom of motor and filter.
7. Remove fuel outlet pipe from motor and filter.
8. Push motor and filter down spring shafts and remove shaft circlip (only one shaft is fitted with circlip).
9. Support fuel filter and pump by clamping protruding end of modular fuel pump in suitable soft jawed vice. **Do not over tighten vice.**
10. Insert suitable pair of medium sized flat-bladed screwdrivers through each service holes in fuel filter.
11. Firmly slide blade between fuel pump end cap and internal fuel filter clips holding fuel pump.
12. Push screwdrivers in far enough that internal fuel filter clips are deflected just free of each of fuel pump end cap retainer shoulders.
13. Hold screwdrivers in place with one hand and move fuel filter in an upward direction to separate it from fuel pump.
14. Remove fuel pump.
15. Remove black ground wiring bridge from fuel filter.
16. Reverse procedure to install.

TIGHTENING SPECIFICATIONS

Year	Component	Torque/Ft. Lbs.
2004	Air Conditioning Compressor & Condenser Hose	22
	Assist Rod	79①
	Coolant Air Bleed	106①
	Coolant Temperature Sensor	15
	Cylinder Head	④
	Engine Mount	59
	Exhaust Manifold	②
	Exhaust Manifold Heat Shield	80①
	Exhaust Manifold To Exhaust Pipe	18
	Fan Motor	62①
	Fascia, Side & Wheel Housing	18①
	Fascia, Upper	26①
	Front Suspension Support Brace	②
	Fuel Filler Neck	44①
	Fuel Tank Flange Stud	62①
	Fuel Tank Mounting Strap, Lower	30
	Fuel Tank Mounting Strap, Upper	15
	Engine Wiring Harness Ground	37
	Hood Hinge, Upper	13
	Hood Latch Striker	18
	Hood Strut Pin	13
	Ignition Coil Bracket	106①
	Oil Level Indicator Tube	18
	PCM Connector	80①
	Power Steering Pump	21
	Luggage Compartment Support Brace	15
	Rocker Arms	④
	Spark Plug	③
	Undertray	22
	Valve Cover	106①
	Water Pump	⑤
	Water Pump Inlet	10

① — Inch lbs.
② — Refer to "Engine Mount, Replace" for tightening specifications and sequence.
③ — Tighten spark plug on a NEW cylinder head to 15 ft. lbs.; on subsequent installations to 11 ft. lbs.
④ — Refer to "Cylinder Head, Replace" for tightening specifications and sequence.
⑤ — Refer to "Water Pump, Replace" for tightening specifications and sequence.

Rear Axle & Suspension

NOTE: On Air Bag Equipped Models, Refer To "Air Bag System Precautions" Located In The Front Of This Manual For System Disarming & Arming Procedures.

NOTE: Refer To "Computer Relearn Procedures" Located In The Front Of This Manual When Battery Power To The Computer Has Been Interrupted.

NOTE: Refer To The Rear Of This Manual For Vehicle Manufacturer's Special Tool Suppliers.

INDEX

PRECAUTIONS

Air Bag Systems

Refer to "Air Bag System Precautions" in the front of this manual for system disarming and arming procedures.

Battery Ground Cable

Prior to service, disconnect battery ground cable and isolate as required.

DESCRIPTION

The differential is a four-pinion type limited slip differential final drive assembly mounted to and independent rear suspension. The differential is mounted directly to the crossmember which is rubber mounted to the underbody. The differential case and drive pinon are mounted in opposed taper roller bearing in the carrier. Differential case side bearing preload adjustment is provided by screw adjusters in the sides of the case. Pinon bearing pre-load is provided by a collapsible spacer. Torque is transferred from the propeller shaft to the differential via the pinon flange which is splined to the hypoid pinon. The torque is then transferred from the pinon through the ring gear, differential case, differential pinon cross shafts, differential pinons, side gears, and then via splines to the inner axle shafts and the drive shafts.

The hub is retained to the wheel drive shaft flange by a nut. The hub rotates inside a sealed wheel bearing. The wheel bearing is pressed into the lower control arm.

The forward end of the lower control arm attaches to the rear suspension support with semi-rigid bushings. The adjustment link connects between the rear suspension support and the lower control arms. The inner adjustment link has a bushing. The outer adjustment link has a ball joint. The adjustment link assembly controls rear wheel camber and toe angles during suspension travel. The adjustment link also provides a means of adjusting the rear wheel toe.

The stabilizer shaft connects between the left lower control arm and the righthand lower control arm through the stabilizer shaft links. Insulators and clamps retain the stabilizer shaft to the rear suspension support. The stabilizer shaft controls the amount of independent movement of the suspension when the vehicle turns.

REAR AXLE SHAFT
REPLACE

1. Raise and support vehicle
2. Position suitable container under axle.
3. Remove inner axle using suitable slide hammer and puller plate.
4. Reverse procedure to install, noting the following:
   a. Lubricate seal lip with suitable Lithium grease.
   b. Ensure axle shaft splines or retainer ring do not damage axle seal when installing axle.
   c. Lightly hit end of axle with suitable, soft faced hammer until retainer clip snaps into place.

REAR WHEEL SHAFT
REPLACE

1. Shift transmission into PARK or NEUTRAL position.
2. Raise and support vehicle.
3. **Support drive shaft until removed.**
4. Mark inner constant velocity joint and inner axle for installation alignment.

5. Remove mounting bolts and inner constant velocity joint retaining plates.
6. Remove mounting bolts and outer constant velocity join retaining plates.
7. Remove drive shaft.
8. Reverse procedure to install, noting the following:
   a. **Torque** inner mount and retainer plates bolts to 37 ft. lbs.
   b. Tighten bolts an additional 68°.
   c. **Torque** outer constant velocity joint mounting bolts to 37 ft. lbs,
   d. Tighten bolts an additional 68°.

DIFFERENTIAL CARRIER
REPLACE

1. Remove propeller shaft as outlined under "Propeller Shaft, Replace."
2. Pull park brake lever boot to side and loosen park brake cable adjustment nut.
3. Raise and support vehicle.
4. Remove rear cable grommet from clip and wrap cloth or tape around cable near equalizer.
5. Pull rear cable forward and up to release cable from equalizer using suitable pliers on wrapped portion of cable.
6. Pull insulation for cable rearward to release cable from bracket.
7. Wrap cloth or tape around cable near rear clevis.
8. Pull cable rearward to release clevis from park brake actuating lever using suitable pliers on wrapped portion of cable.
9. Pull insulation for cable forward to release cable from control arm retainer.
10. Remove rear parking brake cable.
11. Disconnect brake line from hose at rear suspension control arm bracket

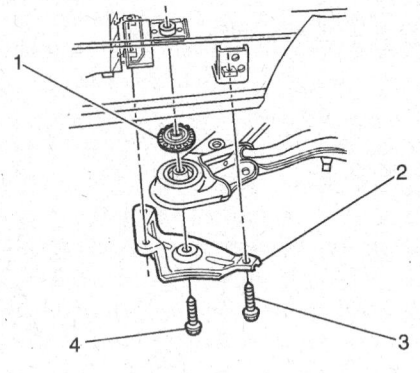

1. Isolating Rubber
2. Braces
3. Underbody Bolts
4. Mounting Bolt

ARM0400000001007

Fig. 1 Brace replacement

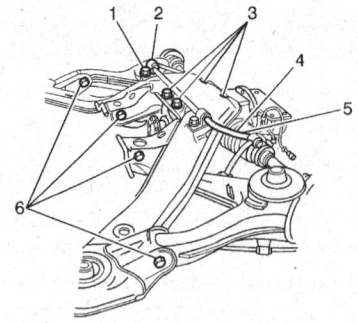

1. Stabilizer Shaft Mounting Bracket Bolts
2. Stabilizer Shaft Mounting Bracket
3. Differential Carrier To Rear Suspension Support Mounting Bolts
4. Stabilizer Shaft
5. Stabilizer Link Mounting Nuts
6. Control Arm To Rear Suspension Support Mounting Bolts & Nuts

ARM0400000001008

Fig. 2 Rear suspension support replacement

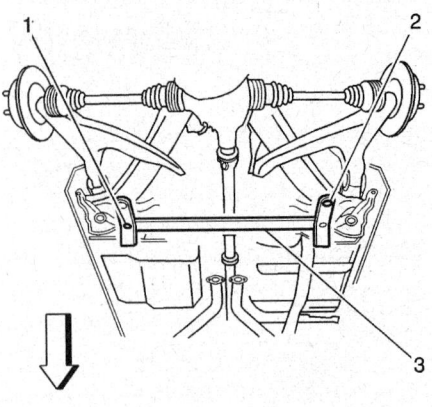

1. Body Datum Holes
2. Location Pins
3. Rear Cross-member Centering Tool

ARM0400000001009

Fig. 3 Rear suspension support centering

and remove brake hose retaining clip. Plug open ends of both pipes and hoses.
12. Pull differential carrier breather hose out of vehicle underbody rear suspension support hole.
13. Remove ABS sensor lead connectors from underbody retaining clips and disconnect them from body harness connectors.
14. Mark rear mount to vehicle under body location for installation alignment.
15. Support differential carrier with suitable floor jack.
16. Remove and discard four rear mount to vehicle underbody mountings bolts.
17. Lower differential carrier and rear suspension at least 2.36 inches.
18. Remove rear springs as outlined under, "Coil Spring, Replace."
19. Raise differential carrier and rear suspension support on floor jack until rear mount contacts vehicle underbody.
20. Remove three brace to underbody bolts from each side, **Fig. 1.**
21. Remove and discard rear suspension support to underbody mounting bolt on each side.
22. Remove braces.
23. With assistant supporting front end of rear suspension support, lower assembly and remove.
24. Remove differential carrier and rear suspension support from jack, then support rear control arms, drive shafts and differential carrier off ground.
25. Remove mounting bolts and stabilizer shaft mounting bracket, **Fig. 2.**
26. Remove and discard differential carrier to rear suspension support mounting bolts.
27. Remove rear suspension control arm to rear suspension support mounting bolts and nuts. Discard nuts.
28. Disconnect control arms from rear suspension support
29. Loosen stabilizer link mounting nuts at each end and on each side, then swing stabilizer shaft back from rear suspension support.

30. Lift up and remove rear suspension support.
31. Mark inner constant velocity joints to axle shafts for installation alignment.
32. Remove inner drive shaft constant velocity joint bolts and retainer plates.
33. Support drive shafts so they do not hang.
34. Remove rear differential mount bolts from differential cover.
35. Remove differential carrier mounting bolts from crossmember.
36. Remove differential carrier.
37. Reverse procedure to install, noting the following:
    a. **Torque** new cross-member to differential carrier mounting bolts to 66 ft. lbs.
    b. Tighten bolts an additional 68°.
    c. **Torque** inner constant velocity joints to axle shaft bolts to 37 ft. lbs.
    d. Tighten bolts an additional 68°.
    e. Install new, self locking rear control arms mounting nuts.
    f. Install new differential carrier to rear suspension support mounting bolts.
    g. Install new rear mount to vehicle underbody mounting bolts.
    h. Fit rear cross-member centering tool No. CH-46839, or equivalent, into .74 inch diameter body datum holes forward of rear suspension support, **Fig. 3.**
    i. With an assistant, position rear suspension support until rear cross-member centering tool location pins engage alignment holes on rear suspension support.
    j. **Torque** brace to underbody bolts to 92 ft. lbs.
    k. Tighten bolts an additional 40°.
    l. **Torque** rear differential mount mounting bolts to 26 ft. lbs.
    m. Tighten bolts an additional 60°
    n. With vehicle at curb weight, bounce rear vehicle several times to settle suspension.
    o. Tighten rear control arm mounting nuts, rear stabilizer shaft link nuts and lower rear shock absorber mounting bolts.

PROPELLER SHAFT
REPLACE

1. Raise and support vehicle rear, then remove rear tire and wheel assemblies.
2. Remove two support hangers clips and rubber hangers.
3. Loosen two ring clamp nuts and remove both rear pipes by sliding them out of muffler pipe slip joints.
4. Support catalytic converter and muffler with suitable jackstand.
5. Remove flange bolts and separate catalytic converter and muffler. Remove gasket from flange joint.
6. Remove four clips and four rubber hangers from left and righthand left muffler support hangers.
7. Remove mufflers.
8. Mark propeller shaft to pinion gear flange for installation alignment.
9. Support propeller shaft near support bearing with suitable stand.
10. Remove pinon flange coupling bolts.
11. Mark center bearing bracket position in four places for installation alignment.
12. Remove center bearing support bolts.
13. Slide propeller shaft forward to disconnect differential pinon support pin.
14. Remove sliding yoke and two-piece propeller shaft from transmission.
15. Reverse procedure to install, noting the following:
    a. Lubricate sliding yoke with suitable transmission lubricant.
    b. Lubricate pinion support pin with molybdenum disulfide grease, or equivalent.

U-JOINT
REPLACE
Removal

1. Remove propeller shaft as outlined under "Propeller Shaft, Replace."

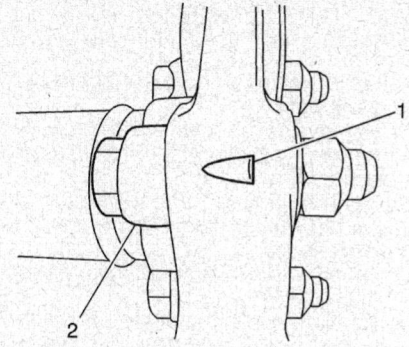

1. Couping Arrow
2. Propeller Shaft Flange

ARM0400000001010

Fig. 4   Coupling alignment

2. Remove and discard propeller shaft sliding yoke bolts, nuts and washers.
3. Remove and discard propeller shaft coupling bolts.

Installation

1. Align coupling triangle point to face propeller shaft flange, **Fig. 4.**
2. Install new propeller shaft coupling to propeller shaft bolts, nuts and washers.
3. **Torque** bolts to 13 ft. lbs.
4. Tighten bolts an additional 55°.
5. Install new propeller shaft yoke to propeller coupling bolts, nuts and washers.
6. **Torque** bolts to 13 ft. lbs.
7. Tighten bolts an additional 55°.
8. Install propeller shaft as outlined under "Propeller Shaft Replace."

HUB & BEARING
REPLACE

Removal

1. Remove rear suspension lower control arm as outlined under "Control Arm, Replace."
2. Align holes wheel hub remover and installer tool No. J-42094-2, or equivalent, with holes in rear wheel drive shaft flange, **Fig. 5.**
3. Align holes in wheel hub remover and installer tool J-42094-1-B, or equivalent, marked B with holes in tool No. J-42094-2 and holes in flange.
4. Retain tools to flange using outer constant velocity joint mounting bolts.
5. Unstake hub nut retainer.
6. Hold wheel hub remover and installer tool No. J-42094-1-B, or equivalent, in suitable vise.
7. Remove and discard retainer and hub nut.
8. Remove tool from vise, but leave tools on assembly.
9. Lubricate tool No. J-42094-3 threads with Extreme Press Lubricant ¼ Ounce Tub No. J 23444-A, or equivalent.

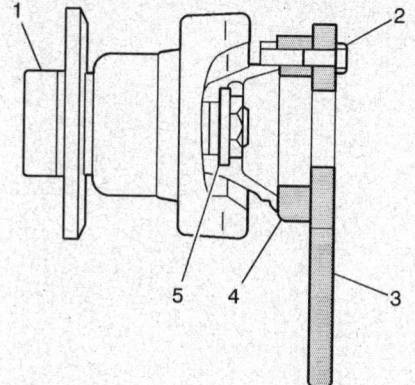

1. Rear Wheel Drive Shaft Flange
2. Outer Constant Velocity Joint Bolts
3. Tool No. J-42094-1-B
4. Tool No. J-42094-2
5. Hub Nut Retainer

ARM0400000001011

Fig. 5   Wheel & hub replacement (Part 1 of 2)

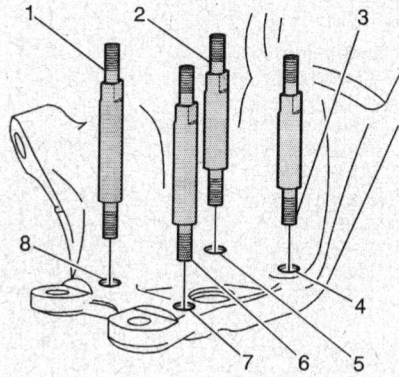

1. Support Tool No. J-42094-7-A
2. Support Tool No. J-42094-7-AUS-2
3. Support Tool No. J-42094-7-AUS-1
4. Thread
5. Thread
6. Support Tool No. J-42094-7-A
7. Thread
8. Thread

ARM0400000001013

Fig. 6   Control arm w/supports

10. Install tool J-42094-3 to J-42094-4-A.
11. Lubricate ball end of tool No. J-42094-5-B with extreme press lubricant.
12. Install tool No. J-42094-5-B to end of tool No. J-42094-3.
13. Install tool No. J-42094-4-A and three mounting bolts tool No. J-42094-1-B.
14. Adjust position of tool No. J-42094-3 in tool No. J-42094-4-A to allow tool No. J-42094-4-A to be in full contact with tool No. J-42094-1-B.
15. Ensure tool No. J-42094-1-B is secure in suitable vise.
16. Have an assistant hold and support control arm.
17. Remove rear wheel drive shaft flange from hub by turning tool No. J-42094-3.
18. Remove tools.
19. Remove two Torx mounting bolts and washers from brake backing plate shield. Ensure park brake adjuster anchor bracket remains on shield.

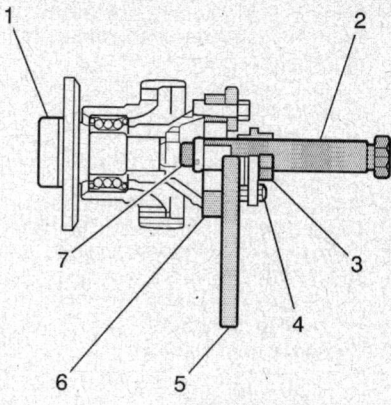

1. Rear Wheel Drive Shaft Flange
2. Tool No. J-42094-3
3. Tool No. J-42094-4-A
4. Bolt
5. Tool No. J-42094-1-B
6. Three Bolts
7. Tool No. J-42094-5-B

ARM0400000001012

Fig. 5   Wheel & hub replacement (Part 2 of 2)

20. Remove two park brake adjuster anchor bracket mounting bolts.
21. Clean control arm threads from inboard to outboard side using suitable M10 X 1.25 bottoming tap and suitable lubricant, **Fig. 6.**
22. Install two support tools No. J-42094-7-A, or equivalent, in two shallowest control arm to shield bolt holes, near caliper mounting holes.
23. Install support tool No. J-42094-7-AUS-2 in deepest control arm to shield bolt hole.
24. Install support tool No. J-42094-7-AUS-1 in remaining control arm to shield bolt hole.
25. Ensure four supports are in correct positions.
26. Attach tool No. J-42094-1-B to supports and install four mounting nuts to retain tool, **Fig. 7.**
27. Install tool No. J-42094-3 to tool No. J-42094-4-A.
28. Lubricate tool No. J-42094-5-B ball end with extreme press lubricant.
29. Install tool No. J-42094-5-B to tool No. J-42094-3 end.
30. Install tools Nos. J-42094-5-B and J-42094-3 through center hole in tool No. J-42094-1-B.
31. Install tool No. J-42094-4-A and three mounting bolts to tool No. J-42094-1-B.
32. Adjust position of tool No. J-42094-3 in tool No. J-42094-4-A to allow tool No. J-42094-4-A to be in full contact with tool No. J-42094-1-B.
33. Ensure handle of tool No. J-42094-1-B is secure in vise.
34. Have assistant hold and support control arm assembly.
35. Press out ear wheel hub by turn tool No. J-42094-3.
36. Remove hub and bearing outside inner race from control arm.
37. Turn tool No. J-42094-3 away from

38. Remove shield and park brake anchor bracket from control arm.
39. If hub is not to be replaced, remove bearing outside inner race from using split plate bearing puller tool No. J 22912-01, or equivalent, and suitable press.
40. Remove control arm wheel bearing retainer using suitable snap ring pliers.
41. Install tool No. J-42094-6 to end of tool No. J-42094-5-B.
42. Press out control arm bearing by turning tool No. J-42094-3.
43. Discard wheel bearing.

Installation

1. Ensure control arm bearing bore is clean and free of foreign matter.
2. Apply wheel bearing lubricant No. 1051344, or equivalent lithium lubricant, to control arm bearing bore and outside of outer races of new wheel bearing.
3. Remove mounting bolts and tools Nos. J-42094-4-A and J-42094-3.
4. Apply wheel bearing lubricant No. 1051344, or equivalent lithium lubricant, to outside of outer race of tool No. J-42094-10 ball bearing.
5. Install tool No. J-42094-10 to flanged end of tool No. J-42094-4-A.
6. Install tools Nos. J-42094-10 and J-42094-4-A to tool No. J-42094-1-B. **Do not install tool No. J-42094-4-A to tool No. J-42094-1-B bolts**
7. Install tool No. J-42094-3 to tool No. J-42094-1-B
8. Install new wheel bearing to tool No. J-42094-8-A.
9. Position wheel bearing on control arm bearing bore.
10. Engage minimum of eight threads tool No. J-42094-3 with tool No. J-42094-8-A.
11. Hold tool No. J-42094-3 using suitable breaker bar.
12. Rotate tool No. J-42094-4-A to press wheel bearing into control arm. Ensure wheel bearing is seated properly in control arm.
13. Remove tool No. J-42094-8-A from bearing.
14. Install control arm bearing retainer using suitable snap ring pliers.
15. Remove tools from control arm.
16. Install rear disc brake backing plate shield and park brake anchor bracket.
17. Install two Torx bolts and washers to shield. Align cut edge of washers with surface of hub. Tighten bolts.
18. Apply Loctite No. 242, or equivalent, to anchor bracket bolt threads.
19. Install and tighten anchor bracket bolts.
20. Support outside end of hub on suitable hydraulic press using suitable bearing driver collar and press plates. Ensure hub weight is on outside end and not on wheel studs.
21. Position control arm and wheel bearing on hub.
22. Have assistant hold and support control arm.
23. Place tool No. J-42094-9-A on bearing

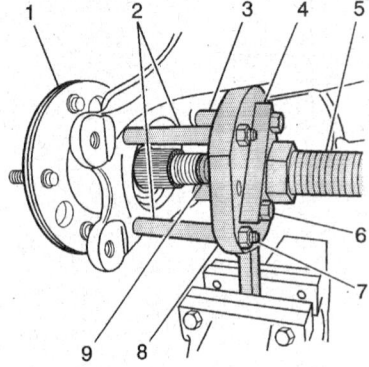

1. Hub
2. Support
3. Support
4. Tool No. J-42094-4-A
5. Tool No. J-42094-3
6. Bolts
7. Tool No. J-42094-1-B
8. Tool No. J-42094-1-B
9. Tool No. J-42094-5-B

ARM0400000001014

Fig. 7 Wheel bearing press out

inside inner race.
24. Place suitable steel pipe on tool No. J-42094-9-A.
25. Press hub to wheel bearing.
26. Remove steel pipe and tool No. J-42094-9-A.
27. Position tool No. J-42094-2 on rear wheel drive shaft flange and tool No. J-42094-1-B on tool No. J-42094-2.
28. Retain tools Nos. J-42094-2 and J-42094-1-B to flange using outer constant velocity joint bolts.
29. Apply wheel bearing lubricant No. 1051344, or equivalent lithium lubricant, to flange splines and threads on inside end of hub.
30. Align flange and hub splines.
31. Position flange on inside end of hub with outside end of hub on collar and press plates.
32. Place tool No. J-42094-9-A on flange and suitable steel pipe on tool No. J-42094-9-A.
33. Press flange to hub and bearing.
34. Remove steel pipe tool No. J-42094-9-A.
35. Remove control arm from press with tools Nos. J-42094-2 and J-42094-1-B on flange.
36. Hold tool No. J-42094-1-B using suitable vise.
37. Install and tighten new hub nut to inside end of hub.
38. Remove tool No. J-42094-1-B and control arm from vise.
39. Remove bolts from tool No. J-42094-1-B.
40. Remove tools Nos. J-42094-2 and J-42094-1-B from control arm.
41. Install and stake new hub nut retainer.
42. Install rear suspension lower control arm as outlined under "Control Arm Replace."

SHOCK ABSORBER
REPLACE

1. Raise and support vehicle
2. Remove shock absorber lower mount-

ing bolt and washer.
3. Separate shock absorber from control arm.
4. Lower vehicle to access luggage compartment.
5. Remove seven retainers and rear center trim panel carpet from luggage compartment.
6. **If removing righthand shock absorber,** loosen clamp and remove filler neck hose.
7. **On all models,** remove shock absorber cap.
8. Remove upper mounting nut, washer, upper mounting upper bushing and shock absorber.
9. If required, remove upper mounting lower bushing and washer.
10. Reverse procedure to install. With weight of vehicle on tire and wheel assemblies, bounce rear of vehicle several times to stabilize rear suspension, then tighten shock absorber to control arm mounting bolt.

COIL SPRING
REPLACE

1. Raise and support vehicle, then remove tire and wheel assembly.
2. Keep hub from turning by installing rear hub holding tool No. J 42066, or equivalent, and two wheel nuts onto two studs.
3. Support wheel drive shaft by tieing suitable wire upper shock mount and to wheel drive shaft. **Do not allow wheel drive shaft to hang freely.**
4. Remove mounting bolts and outer constant velocity joint to drive shaft flange retaining plates, Fig. 8.
5. Separate wheel drive shaft from drive shaft flange.
6. Loosen stabilizer shaft to shaft link nut.
7. Remove stabilizer shaft to shaft link mounting nut and bolt.
8. Loosen outer adjustment link to control arm mounting nut.
9. Position top of nut with top of outer adjustment link stud.
10. Separate stud from control arm using tie rod puller tool No. J 6627-A, or equivalent.
11. Remove and discard stud nut.
12. Position adjustment link away from control arm
13. Support control arm with suitable jack and block of wood. Raise jack slightly to reduce spring load on control arm.
14. Remove mounting bolt and washer, then separate shock absorber from control arm.
15. Lower jack and control arm.
16. Push down gently on control arm, then remove spring and two insulators. **Do not pull on brake hose.**
17. Remove insulators.
18. Reverse procedure to install from spring, noting the following:
    a. Weight of vehicle must be on tire and wheel assemblies before tightening suspension mounting bolts and nuts.
    b. Install new outer adjustment link stud nut.
    c. **Torque** outer constant velocity joint

to drive shaft flange retainer bolts to 37 ft. lbs.

d. Tighten bolts an additional 68°.

CONTROL ARM
REPLACE

1. Raise and support vehicle on suitable alignment rack. Ensure lift pads are positioned to minimize interference with control arms and rear suspension support.
2. Remove rear tire and wheel assemblies.
3. Remove two support hangers clips and rubber hangers.
4. Loosen two ring clamp nuts and remove both rear pipes by sliding them out of muffler pipe slip joints.
5. Support catalytic converter and muffler with suitable jackstand.
6. Remove flange bolts and separate catalytic converter and muffler. Remove gasket from flange joint.
7. Remove four clips and four rubber hangers from left and righthand left muffler support hangers.
8. Remove mufflers.
9. Loosen two rear suspension support braces to body six mounting bolts.
10. Loosen two rear suspension support to body mounting bolts.
11. Loosen stabilizer shaft to shaft link mounting nut.
12. Remove stabilizer shaft link to lower control arm mounting nut and bolt.
13. Loosen outer adjustment link to control arm mounting nut.
14. Position top of nut with top of outer adjustment link stud.
15. Separate outer adjustment link stud from control arm using tie rod puller tool No. J 6627-A, or equivalent.
16. Remove and discard outer adjustment link stud nut.
17. Position adjustment link assembly away from control arm.
18. Remove brake hose clip, then pull brake pipe and hose forward from bracket.
19. Lift brake pipe up through slot in bracket and separate brake pipe and hose from control arm.
20. Loosen brake pipe flare nut.
21. Remove backing plate bracket clip and brake pipe from brake hose. Plug brake hose.
22. Remove brake pipe from backing plate bracket. Plug brake pipe.
23. Remove two mounting bolts and brake caliper.
24. Pull park brake lever boot to side and loosen park brake cable adjustment nut.
25. Raise and support vehicle.
26. Remove rear cable grommet from clip and wrap cloth or tape around cable near equalizer.
27. Pull rear cable forward and up to release cable from equalizer using suitable pliers on wrapped portion of cable.
28. Pull insulation for cable rearward to release cable from bracket.

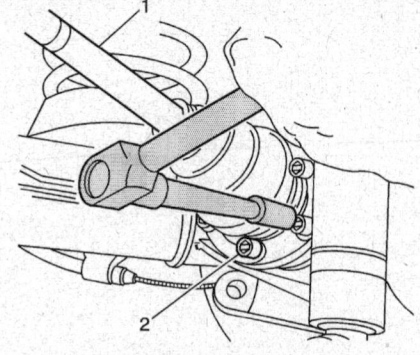

1. Wheel Drive Shaft
2. Retaining Plate Mounting Bolt

ARM0400000001006

Fig. 8 Outer constant velocity joint to drive shaft flange retaining plate replacement

29. Wrap cloth or tape around cable near rear clevis.
30. Pull cable rearward to release clevis from park brake actuating lever using suitable pliers on wrapped portion of cable.
31. Pull insulation for cable forward to release cable from control arm retainer.
32. Remove rear parking brake cable.
33. For required access, it my be necessary to remove propeller shaft as outlined under "Propeller Shaft, Replace"
34. Mark brake rotor to wheel stud and to hub for installation alignment.
35. Remove brake rotor from hub. If rotor does not slide off hub easily, proceed as follows:
   a. Select block of wood longer than wheel studs.
   b. Place wood on tor between wheel studs.
   c. Tap wood with suitable hammer to loosen rotor from hub.
36. Remove spring as outlined under "Coil Spring, Replace."
37. Pull differential carrier breather hose out of hole.
38. Separate two wheel speed sensor wires from clips and disconnect connectors from body harness.
39. Mark differential carrier mount on body for installation alignment.
40. Support differential carrier mount using suitable jack.
41. Remove and discard four mount to body bolts.
42. Remove and discard two rear suspension support to body bolts.
43. Loosen six brace bolts to access control arm.
44. Lower jack with mount and rear suspension support to access control arm.
45. Remove and discard two control arm to rear suspension support mounting nuts.
46. Remove two mounting bolts and control arm.
47. If control arm is to be replaced, remove following parts.
   a. Park brake components.
   b. Brake backing plate.

c. Wheel bearing.
d. Hub.
e. Wheel drive shaft flange.
48. Reverse procedure to install, noting the following:
   a. Weight of vehicle must be on tire and wheel assemblies before tightening mounting bolts and nuts.
   b. Install two new control arm to rear suspension support mounting nuts.
   c. If hub was not replace, thoroughly clean corrosion from hub flange mating surface using wheel hub resurfacing kit tool No. J 42450-A, or equivalent.
   d. If brake rotor was not replaced, thoroughly clean corrosion from rotor mating surface using rotor resurfacing kit tool No. J 41013, or equivalent.
   e. If hub or wheel drive shaft flange were replaced, measure assembled lateral runout of rotor to ensure optimum performance.
   f. Bounce rear of vehicle several times in order to stabilize suspension.
   g. Tighten control arm to rear suspension support mounting nuts and bolts.
   h. Tighten stabilizer shaft link mounting nuts and bolts.
   i. Tighten shock absorber to control arm mounting bolt
   j. Tighten outer adjustment link to control arm mounting nut.

STABILIZER SHAFT
REPLACE

1. Raise and support vehicle on suitable alignment rack. Ensure lift pads are positioned to minimize interference with control arms and rear suspension support.
2. Remove rear tire and wheel assemblies.
3. Remove two support hangers clips and rubber hangers.
4. Loosen two ring clamp nuts and remove both rear pipes by sliding them out of muffler pipe slip joints.
5. Support catalytic converter and muffler with suitable jackstand.
6. Remove flange bolts and separate catalytic converter and muffler. Remove gasket from flange joint.
7. Remove four clips and four rubber hangers from left and righthand left muffler support hangers.
8. Remove mufflers.
9. Loosen two rear suspension support braces to body six mounting bolts.
10. Loosen two rear suspension support to body mounting bolts.
11. Mark differential carrier mount on body for installation alignment.
12. Support differential carrier mount using suitable jack.
13. Remove and discard four mount to body bolts,
14. Lower jack with mount and rear suspension support to access stabilizer shaft insulator brackets to rear suspension support bolts **Do not allow**

propeller shaft or wheel drive shafts
to touch exhaust system.

15. Remove mounting bolts and nuts, then
the stabilizer shaft links from control
arms.
16. Remove stabilizer shaft insulator
brackets to rear suspension support
mounting bolts.
17. Remove two brackets from rear suspension support using suitable, flat-
bladed tool as lever.
18. Remove stabilizer shaft.
19. If required, remove the following:
   a. Two stabilizer shaft link nuts.
   b. Two stabilizer shaft link bolts.
   c. Two stabilizer shaft links.
   d. Two stabilizer shaft insulator
   brackets.
   e. Two stabilizer shaft insulators
20. Reverse procedure to install, noting
the following:
   a. Weight of vehicle must be on tire
   and wheel assemblies before tightening mounting bolts and nuts.
   b. Fit rear cross-member centering
   tool No. CH-46839, or equivalent,
   into .74 inch diameter body datum
   holes forward of rear suspension
   support, **Fig. 3.**
   c. With an assistant, position rear suspension support until rear crossmember centering tool location
   pins engage alignment holes on
   rear suspension support.
   d. **Torque** brace to underbody bolts to
   92 ft. lbs.
   e. Tighten bolts an additional 40°.
   f. **Torque** rear differential mount
   mounting bolts to 26 ft. lbs.
   g. Tighten bolts an additional 60°
   h. With vehicle at curb weight, bounce
   rear vehicle several times to settle
   suspension.
   i. Tighten stabilizer shaft link mounting bolts and nuts.

ADJUSTMENT LINK
REPLACE

1. Raise and support vehicle.
2. Measure and record distance between
two center adjuster lock nuts.
3. Mark two center adjuster lock nuts position to installation alignment.
4. Loosen outer adjustment link to control
arm nut.
5. Position top of nut with top of outer adjustment link stud.
6. Separate stud from control arm using
tie rod puller tool No. J 6627-A, or
equivalent.
7. Remove and discard nut.
8. Remove inner adjustment link to rear
suspension support mounting bolt and
nut Discard nut.
9. Remove inner adjustment link from
rear suspension support.
10. Hold center adjuster in suitable soft
jaws vise, **Fig. 9.**
11. **These components have lefthand
threads: inner adjustment link,
inner lock nut and corresponding
end of center adjuster.**

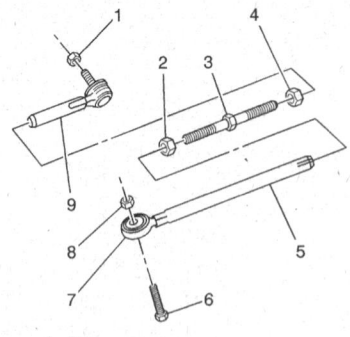

1. Nut
2. Inner Lock Nut
3. Center Adjuster
4. Nut
5. Inner Adjustment Link
6. Bolt
7. Inner Adjustment Link
8. Nut
9. Outer Adjustment Link

ARM0400000001015

Fig. 9 Adjustment link assembly

12. Loosen inner lock nut and remove
inner adjustment link from center adjuster. **Count turns required for removal of inner adjustment link.**
13. Loosen outer lock nut and remove
outer adjustment link from center adjuster. **Count turns required for removal of outer adjustment link.**
14. Reverse procedure to install, noting
the following:
   a. Weight of vehicle must be on tire
   and wheel assemblies before tightening suspension bolts and nuts.
   b. Protruding side of bushing must be
   toward front of vehicle.
   c. Install new inner adjustment link to
   rear suspension support mounting
   nut and bolt.
   d. Install outer adjustment link and
   new nut to control arm.
   e. With weight of vehicle on tire and
   wheel assemblies, bounce rear of
   vehicle several times in order to
   stabilize rear suspension.
   f. Measure wheel alignment.
   g. Tighten inner adjustment link to
   rear suspension support and outer
   adjustment link to control arm
   mounting nuts and bolts.

Inner

1. Raise and support vehicle.
2. Mark position of inner lock nut on center adjuster for installation alignment.
3. Remove inner adjustment link to rear
suspension support mounting nut and
bolt. Discard nut.
4. Remove inner adjustment link from
rear suspension support.
5. Following components have lefthand
threads: inner adjustment link, inner
lock nut and corresponding end of center adjuster.
6. Loosen inner lock nut.
7. Remove inner adjustment link from
center adjuster. **Count turns necessary for removal of inner adjustment link.**
8. Reverse procedure to install, noting

the following:
   a. Weight of vehicle must be on tire
   and wheel assemblies before tightening suspension bolts and nuts.
   b. Protruding side of bushing must be
   toward front of vehicle.
   c. Install new inner adjustment link to
   rear suspension support nut.
   d. With weight of vehicle on tire and
   wheel assemblies, bounce rear of
   vehicle several times in order to
   stabilize rear suspension.
   e. Measure wheel alignment.
   f. Adjust rear toe to specification and
   tighten inner lock nut.

Outer

1. Raise and support vehicle.
2. Mark outer lock nut on center adjuster
for installation alignment.
3. Loosen outer adjustment link to control
arm nut.
4. Position top of nut with top of outer adjustment link stud.
5. Separate stud from control arm using
tie rod puller tool No. J 6627-A, or
equivalent.
6. Remove and discard nut.
7. Loosen outer lock nut.
8. Remove outer adjustment link from adjuster. **Count turns necessary for removal of outer adjustment link.**
9. Reverse procedure to install, noting
the following:
   a. Weight of vehicle must be on tire
   and wheel assemblies before tightening mounting nuts.
   b. Install outer adjustment link and
   new mounting nut to control arm.
   c. With weight of vehicle on tire and
   wheel assemblies, bounce rear of
   vehicle several times in order to
   stabilize rear suspension.
   d. Measure wheel alignment.
   e. Adjust rear toe to specification and
   tighten outer lock nut

TECHNICAL SERVICE BULLETINS
Knocking Noise From Rear,

On some of these models built prior to
VIN 4L246712 there may be a knocking
noise from the rear suspension during hard
or aggressive acceleration.
This condition may be caused by rear
cross member.
To correct this condition, proceed as follows:
1. Install two rubber insulators above rear
cross member to correct a knocking
noise during hard or aggressive acceleration.
2. **Torque** new mounting bolt to 92 ft. lbs.
3. Tighten mounting bolt an additional
30–40°.
4. **Torque** brace mounting bolts to 48 ft.
lbs.

TIGHTENING SPECIFICATIONS

Year	Component	Torque/Ft. Lbs.
2004	Adjustment Link	46
	Brace To Underbody	②
	Brake Caliper	63
	Brake Line	11
	Brake Pike To Hose	12
	Brake Shield To Lower Control Arm, Lower	65
	Brake Shield To Lower Control Arm, Upper	85
	Catalytic Converter To Muffler Flange	33
	Constant Velocity Joint	③
	Cross-Member To Differential Carrier	②
	Differential Carrier	66
	Differential Mount	②
	Differential Rear Mount To Differential Cover	70
	Hub Nut	221
	Inner Adjustment Link To Rear Suspension Support	46
	Inner Constant Velocity Joints To Axle Shaft	②
	Muffler Pipe Slip	32
	Outer Adjustment Link To Control Arm	46
	Outer Constant Velocity Joint Retainer	①
	Park Brake Anchor Bracket	65
	Propeller Shaft Center Bearing	21
	Propeller Shaft Coupling	④
	Propeller Shaft Pinon Flange	85
	Rear Control Arm	74
	Rear Differential Mount	②
	Rear Control Arm	72
	Rear Suspension Brace To Body	52
	Rear Suspension Support Insulator Bracket	52
	Rear Suspension Support To Body	③
	Shield Torx Bolts	55
	Shock Absorber, Upper	10
	Shock Absorber To Control Arm	85
	Stabilizer Mounting Bracket	16
	Stabilizer Shaft Link	72
	Wheel Drive Shaft To Axle Stub Shaft	37⑤

① — Refer to "Coil Spring, Replace" for tightening specifications and sequence.
② — Refer to "Differential Carrier, Replace" for tightening specifications and sequence.
③ — Refer to "Rear Wheel Shaft, Replace" for tightening specifications and sequence.
④ — Refer to "U-Joint, Replace" for tightening specifications and sequence.
⑤ — Final tighten an additional 67°.

Front Suspension & Steering

NOTE: On Air Bag Equipped Models, Refer To "Air Bag System Precautions" Located In The Front Of This Manual For System Disarming & Arming Procedures.

NOTE: Refer To "Computer Relearn Procedures" Located In The Front Of This Manual When Battery Power To The Computer Has Been Interrupted.

NOTE: Refer To The Rear Of This Manual For Vehicle Manufacturer's Special Tool Suppliers.

INDEX

PRECAUTIONS

Air Bag Systems

Refer to "Air Bag System Precautions" in the front of this manual for system disarming and arming procedures.

Battery Ground Cable

Prior to service, disconnect battery ground cable and isolate as required.

DESCRIPTION

The steering knuckle is suspended between a lower control arm, a lower control arm rod and a strut assembly. The lower control arm attaches to the steering knuckle at the outermost point of the control arm. The attachment is through a ball and socket type joint. The ball joint allows the steering knuckle to maintain the perpendicular relationship to the road surface. The innermost end of the control arm is attached to the front frame with a semi-rigid bushing. The lower control arm is allowed to pivot at the vehicle frame in a vertical fashion. The rod is attached to the lower control arm with a semi-rigid bushing. The front of the lower control arm rod is attached to the front frame with a fluid filled insulator bushing. The upper portion of the steering knuckle is attached to a strut assembly. The strut assembly is attached to the vehicle body with an upper bearing. The steering knuckle moves up and down independent of the vehicle body structure.

This up and down motion of the steering knuckle as the vehicle travels over bumps is absorbed predominantly by the coil spring. This spring is retained under tension over the strut assembly. The strut has an absorber in order to dampen out the oscillations of the coil spring.

The front suspension has a stabilizer shaft. The stabilizer shaft connects between the left and the righthand strut through the stabilizer shaft links. Insulators and clamps retain the stabilizer shaft to the front frame.

The power steering system is a closed loop system. The system consists of the following components: power steering fluid reservoir, power steering pump, power steering gear, and power steering pipes and hoses.

The power steering fluid flows from the fluid reservoir through a hose to the power steering pump. The engine drive belt rotates the pump pulley. The pulley turns the pump drive shaft. The shaft turns the pump rotor. The vanes in the rotor pressurize the power steering fluid. The engine speed sensing type flow control valve controls the fluid pressure. This valve reduces the fluid pressure as the engine speed increases. The fluid flows, under pressure, from the pump, through the pipe and the hose, to the steering gear.

The steering gear is a rack and pinion type steering system. The steering gear has a control valve which directs the fluid to either side of the rack piston. The piston uses hydraulic pressure to move the rack to the left and to the right. The rack moves the tie rods. The tie rods move the steering knuckles. The steering knuckles rotate on ball joints and strut bearings and turn the front wheels and tires.

The power steering fluid flows from the steering gear, through the pipe and the hose, to the reservoir. If the hydraulic assist fails, the driver maintains manual steering control. Under this condition, however, the driver must use more steering effort.

COIL SPRING

REPLACE

Refer to "Strut, Replace" and "Strut Service" for coil spring replacement procedure

STRUT

REPLACE

Removal

1. Raise and support vehicle, then remove front tire and wheel assembly.
2. Remove upper nut, washer and insulator, then the retainer. Hold stabilizer shaft link upper stud using suitable wrench.
3. Separate wheel speed sensor harness and insulator from strut bracket.
4. Turn brake hose to strut bracket sleeve and align flats with strut bracket opening.
5. Separate brake hose from strut bracket.
6. Support control arm using suitable jack and block of wood below ball joint.
7. Remove and discard two mounting nuts, washers and bolts.
8. Lift locking tab and disconnect wheel speed sensor connector from knuckle.
9. Separate knuckle from strut.

10. Remove cap and strut nut while holding end of strut rod shaft using suitable wrench.
11. Remove and discard strut nut.
12. Remove strut bumper stop.
13. Lower strut, then remove stabilizer shaft link from bracket.
14. Remove strut.
15. Reverse procedure to install.

Installation

1. Tighten strut mount nut.
2. Install top of stabilizer shaft link to strut bracket.
3. Install strut to tower.
4. Install strut bumper stop.
5. Install new strut nut. **Do not tighten strut nut now.**
6. Install two new strut to knuckle bolts, washers and nuts. Tighten nuts.
7. Tighten strut to tower mounting nut holding strut rod shaft with suitable wrench.
8. Install strut nut cap.
9. Remove jack and block of wood.
10. Align brake hose sleeve flats with strut bracket opening and install brake hose. Turn sleeve to retain brake hose to strut bracket.
11. Connect wheel speed sensor connector. ensure locking tab is secure.
12. Install wheel speed sensor harness and insulator to strut bracket.
13. Install retainer, upper insulator and upper washer.
14. Install and tighten upper nut while holding stabilizer shaft link upper stud with suitable wrench. **Do not use power tools on upper nut .**
15. Install front tire and wheel assembly, then lower vehicle onto an alignment rack to place weight of vehicle onto tires.
16. Push down on front bumper three times to stabilize suspension.
17. Measure wheel alignment.
18. Rotate camber adjustment screw to adjust front camber.
19. **Torque** two strut to knuckle nuts to 74 ft. lbs.
20. Final tighten nuts an additional 90°.

STRUT SERVICE

Disassemble

1. Compress spring using strut spring compressor tool No. J 45400, or equivalent.
2. **Do not grip strut rod with any tools below hex shaped portion.**
3. Hold end of strut rod shaft using suitable wrench.
4. Remove nut, strut mount and washers.
5. Mark strut bearing on upper spring seat orientation for assembly alignment.
6. Remove strut bearing from upper spring seat.
7. Remove and discard strut shield strap.
8. Remove upper spring seat, spring upper insulator and strut bumper,
9. Release compression and remove spring.

10. Remove and discard strut shield clamp.
11. Remove strut dust shield and filter.

Assemble

1. Hold strut rod and housing, then pull rod to maximum length. **Do not grip strut rod with any tools below hex shaped portion.**
2. Install strut dust shield. Ensure filter remains seated inside boot portion of strut dust shield.
3. Position strut dust shield on strut housing tube. Ensure distance between bottom of strut dust shield and bottom of lower spring seat is 1.182–1.379 inches.
4. Install new strut dust shield to strut housing tube clamp.
5. Install spring to strut housing.
6. Install straight projecting lower end of spring to lower spring seat.
7. Compress spring using strut spring compressor tool No. J 45400, or equivalent.
8. Install strut bumper.
9. Install upper insulator with step straight projecting upper end of spring.
10. Install upper spring seat. Ensure double notch in upper flange of is on inboard side of strut.
11. Pull strut rod to maximum length.
12. If strut rod nut is on strut rod, remove it.
13. Install strut bearing to upper spring seat in same orientation as in removal procedure. Ensure narrow outer section faces towards upper spring seat collar.
14. Install lower washer. Ensure dish shape side of lower washer faces downward.
15. Install strut mount. Ensure lower washer does not bind with lower edge of mount.
16. Install upper washer. Ensure dish shape side of upper washer faces upward.
17. Install and tighten strut mount nut while holding strut rod shaft end with suitable wrench.
18. Install strut dust shield to upper spring seat. Fit upper end of strut dust shield over lower flange of spring seat collar.
19. Install new strut dust shield to upper spring seat strap.
20. Remove strut from strut spring compressor tool.

CONTROL ARM
REPLACE
Removal

1. Raise and support vehicle, then remove front tire and wheel assembly.
2. Turn steering wheel to access control arm ball joint stud.
3. Remove and discard control arm ball joint stud to knuckle nut.
4. Separate control arm ball joint stud from knuckle using ball joint separator tool No. J 42188, or equivalent.
5. Push control arm away from knuckle using suitable block of wood.

6. Remove and discard control arm rod to control arm mounting nut. Remove washer.
7. Remove and discard control arm to front frame nut.
8. Remove mounting bolt and control arm from front frame.
9. Remove control arm from rod. **Do not remove retainer.**

Installation

1. Ensure control arm rod retainer is on properly.
2. Install control arm to rod, then the control arm and mounting bolt to front frame.
3. Install new control arm to front frame mounting nut. **Do not tighten nut now.**
4. Install washer and new nut to rod. **Do not tighten nut now.**
5. Support control arm with suitable jack and block of wood below ball joint.
6. Install control arm ball joint stud to knuckle.
7. Raise jack to seat control arm ball joint stud.
8. Install and tighten new control arm ball joint stud nut.
9. Remove jack and block of wood.
10. Lower vehicle.
11. With weight of vehicle on tire and wheel assemblies, push down on front bumper three times to stabilize suspension.
12. Tighten control arm to front frame mounting.
13. Tighten control arm rod to control arm mounting nut.

STEERING KNUCKLE
REPLACE
REMOVAL

1. Raise and support vehicle, then remove front tire and wheel assembly.
2. Remove mounting bolts, caliper and bracket from brake rotor, then support assembly with heavy mechanic's wire, or equivalent. **Do not disconnect hydraulic brake flexible hose from caliper.** Ensure there is no tension on brake hose
3. If match marks are not evident, mark brake rotor, wheel stud and hub for installation alignment.
4. Remove brake rotor, **Fig. 1.** If brake rotor does not slide off of hub easily, proceed as follows:
   a. Select block of wood longer than wheel studs.
   b. Place wood on rotor between wheel studs.
   c. Tap wood with suitable hammer to loosen rotor from hub.
5. If removing lefthand front brake shield, turn steering wheel to left. If removing righthand front brake shield, turn steering wheel to right.
6. Lift locking tab and disconnect wheel speed sensor connector from knuckle.
7. If required for access, remove and discard strut to knuckle mounting nuts and bolts.

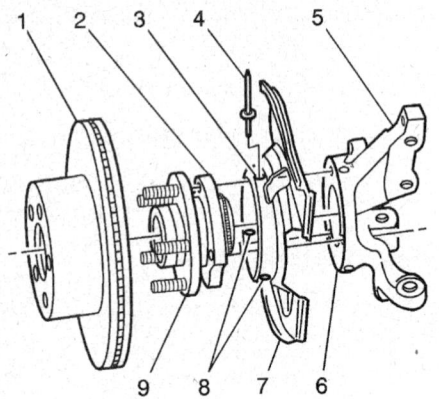

1. Rotor
2. Hub
3. Brake Shield
4. Rivets
5. Knuckle
6. Knuckle
7. Brake Shield
8. Rivets
9. Hub

ARM0400000001017

Fig. 1 Steering knuckle replacement

8. Remove three Allen bolts and hub from knuckle If required, tap Allen bolts to loosen hub from knuckle.
9. Remove three rivet heads and brake shield. Drill out rivet remains.
10. Remove cotter pin and outer tie rod nut.
11. Separate outer tie rod from knuckle using Pitman arm puller removal tool No. OTC 7314A, or equivalent.
12. Remove and discard two mounting nuts, washers and bolts.
13. If replacing knuckle, remove camber adjusting screw.
14. Remove steering knuckle from strut.
15. Remove and discard control arm ball joint stud to knuckle mounting nut.
16. Separate control arm ball joint stud from knuckle using ball joint separator tool No. J 42188, or equivalent.
17. Remove knuckle.

INSTALLATION

The weight of the vehicle must be on the tire and wheel assemblies before tightening the mounting bolts and nuts.
1. Install steering knuckle to control arm ball joint stud.
2. Align knuckle and strut bolt holes.
3. Do not use knuckle Allen bolts more than three times. If in doubt, replace 3 Allen bolts.
4. Install two knuckle to strut mounting bolts, two washes and two new nuts. **Do not tighten bolts or nuts now.**
5. Support control arm using suitable jack and block of wood below ball joint.
6. Raise jack and seat knuckle on control arm ball joint stud.
7. Install and tighten control arm ball joint stud nut.
8. Remove jack and wood.
9. Ensure plastic spacer is on ball stud for outer tie rod end.
10. Install outer tie rod to knuckle.

11. Install and tighten ball stud for outer tie rod nut.
12. Align cotter pin slot by tightening nut up to $\frac{1}{6}$ additional turn or maximum **torque** of 63 ft. lbs. **Do not loosen nut to insert cotter pin.**
13. install cotter pin.
14. If camber adjusting screw was removed, install adjusting screw to knuckle.
15. Install brake shield to knuckle. Ensure brake shield position is correct to provide clearance for brake caliper.
16. Install pop-rivets
17. Align sensor connection on hub.
18. Install hub.
19. Lower vehicle.
20. Push down on front bumper three times to stabilize suspension.
21. Measure wheel alignment. Rotate amber adjusting screw i to adjust front camber.
22. **Torque** strut to knuckle mounting nuts to 62 ft. lbs.
23. **Torque** mounting nuts to 74 ft. lbs.
24. Final tighten nuts an additional 90°.
25. **Torque** caliper mounting bolts to 63 ft. lbs.
26. Final tighten bolts an additional 45°.

STABILIZER BAR
REPLACE

1. Remove mounting nuts, insulator brackets and insulator, **Fig. 2.**
2. Remove nuts and stabilizer shaft from links. Hold link lower studs using suitable wrench.
3. Remove stabilizer shaft.
4. Reverse procedure to install, noting the following:
   a. Ensure insulators slots face forward.
   b. Ensure insulator curved portions seat in front frame curved mating surfaces.

STABILIZER LINK
REPLACE

1. Raise and support vehicle, then remove front tire and wheel assembly
2. Hold stabilizer shaft link upper stud using suitable wrench.
3. Remove upper nut, washer and insulator.
4. Remove retainer.
5. Hold link lower stud using suitable wrench.
6. Remove mounting nut and stabilizer shaft from link lower stud.
7. Remove link, then lower insulator and washer.
8. Reverse procedure to install.

TIE ROD END
REPLACE
Outer
REMOVAL

1. Raise and support vehicle, then remove front tire and wheel assembly.

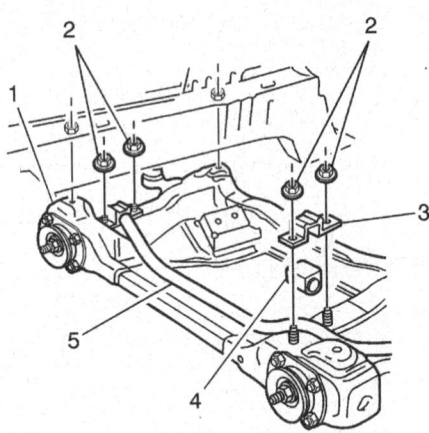

1. Front Frame
2. Nuts
3. Insulator Brackets
4. Insulators
5. Stabilizer Shaft

ARM0400000001018

Fig. 2 Stabilizer bar replacement

2. Remove cotter pin and outer tie rod nut.
3. Separate outer tie rod from knuckle using Pitman arm puller removal tool No. OTC 7314A, or equivalent.
4. Mark inner tie rod, lock nut and outer tie rod for installation alignment.
5. Loosen lock nut and remove outer tie rod from inner tie rod.

INSTALLATION

1. Install outer to inner tie rod.
2. Align outer tie rod with match marks. **Do not tighten lock nut.**
3. Ensure plastic spacer is on ball stud for outer tie rod end.
4. Install outer tie rod to steering knuckle.
5. Install outer tie rod nut to ball stud for outer tie rod. Tighten nut.
6. Align cotter pin slot by tightening outer tie rod nut up to $\frac{1}{6}$ additional turn or **torque** of 63 ft. lbs, maximum. **Do not loosen nut to insert cotter pin.**
7. Install cotter pin into hole in tie rod stud.
8. Install front tire and wheel assembly.
9. Adjust front toe.
10. Tighten lock nut against outer tie rod.
11. Ensure steering gear boot is not twisted.

POWER STEERING GEAR
REPLACE

1. Lock steering column and ensure front wheels are in straight ahead position.
2. Raise and support vehicle, then remove front tire and wheel assemblies.
3. Place suitable drain pan under vehicle to collect power steering system fluid.
4. Remove pressure and return pipes from steering gear. Remove and discard two O-rings.
5. Remove and discard steering shaft coupling to steering gear pinion nut.
6. Remove bolt and separate coupling from pinion.

7. Raise and support vehicle, then remove front tire and wheel assembly.
8. Remove cotter pin and outer tie rod nut
9. Separate outer tie rod from knuckle using Pitman arm puller removal tool No. OTC 7314A, or equivalent.
10. Mark inner tie rod, lock nut and outer tie rod for installation alignment.
11. Loosen lock nut and remove outer tie rod from inner tie rod.
12. Remove mounting nuts and bolts, then the steering gear.
13. Reverse procedure to install, noting the following:
    a. **Torque** steering gear mounting nuts to 44 ft. lbs.
    b. Tighten mounting nuts and additional 45°.
    c. Lubricate two new steering gear O-rings with suitable ATF.
    d. Install new coupling bolt.

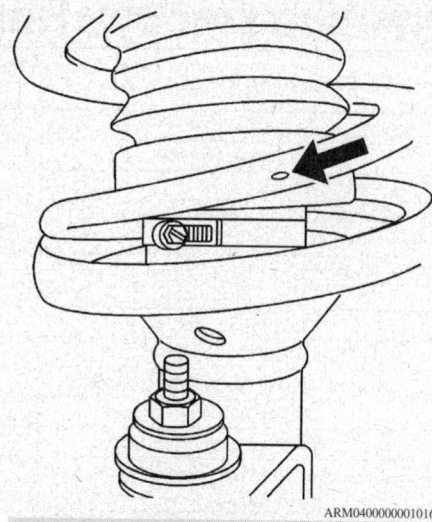

ARM0400000001016

Fig. 3   Coil spring rub mark

POWER STEERING PUMP

REPLACE

1. Disconnect Intake Air Temperature (IAT) sensor and Mass Air Flow (MAF) sensor connectors.
2. Loosen air intake duct to throttle body and MAF sensor to air cleaner upper body clamps,
3. Position intake air duct away from power steering pump IAT and MAF sensors still attached.
4. Install suitable breaker bar with hex-head socket to drive belt tensioner bolt.
5. Relieve tension on belt by rotating drive belt tensioner clockwise.
6. Remove belt from pulleys and drive belt tensioner.
7. Slowly release tension on drive belt tensioner. Remove breaker bar and socket from drive belt tensioner bolt.
8. Place suitable drain pan below vehicle.
9. Loosen clamps, then remove power steering fluid reservoir outlet and inlet hoses.
10. Release bracket tab using suitable, flat-blade tool and remove reservoir.
11. Remove power steering gear inlet pipe and flare nut from pump.
12. Remove and discard O-ring from high pressure port.
13. Loosen hose clamp and remove reservoir outlet hose from pump.
14. Remove two mounting bolts and power steering pump.
15. Reverse procedure to install. Lubricate new high pressure port O-ring with suitable Automatic Transmission Fluid (ATF).

POWER STEERING SYSTEM BLEED

1. Ensure hoses do not touch any other part of vehicle.
2. Ensure all hose connections are tight. Loose connections may not leak, but could allow air into steering system.
3. Remove power steering fluid reservoir cap. Ensure fluid level is correct. Add fluid as required.
4. Attach power steering bleeder adapter tool No. J 43485 to Mity Vac tool No. J 35555, or equivalents.
5. Place adapter on or in reservoir filler neck.
6. Apply vacuum of 20 inches Hg, maximum.
7. Wait five minutes. Typical vacuum drop is 2–3 inches Hg.
8. If vacuum does not remain steady, inspect for power steering fluid leaks.
9. Remove tools and install reservoir cap.
10. Start and idle engine.
11. Turn engine off.
12. Ensure fluid level is correct and adjust as required.
13. Start and idle engine.
14. Turn steering wheel 180–360° in both directions five times. **Do not turn steering wheel to lock.**
15. Turn ignition switch to OFF position .
16. Remove reservoir cap and ensure fluid level is correct. Adjust fluid level as required.
17. Attach power steering bleeder adapter Mity Vac tools.
18. Place adapter on or in pump reservoir filler neck.
19. Apply vacuum of 20 inches Hg, maximum.
20. Wait five minutes.
21. Remove tools.
22. Ensure fluid level is correct and adjust as required.
23. Install reservoir cap.

TECHNICAL SERVICE BULLETINS

Knock Noise From Front Suspension

On some of these models there may be a knock noise from the front suspension when driving at low speeds over bumps/uneven road surfaces.

This condition may be caused by the lower coil of the spring touching on the side lip of the spring seat, **Fig. 3**. The spring coils contacting the body sheet metal within the wheelhouse area may also cause this condition.

To correct this condition, proceed as follows:

1. Inspect tightness of all front suspension nuts and bolts.
2. Inspect body sheet metal around inside of strut tower for signs of spring coil rubbing.
3. Inspect second lower coil on inboard side of spring for signs of chipped or marked paint, **Fig. 3**.
4. If marks are found, remove spring from strut assembly and install it upside down (with thin coil end resting on spring seat).
5. Carefully install upper bearing (yellow plastic housing). Ensure it is located correctly in upper spring seat.
6. While strut is removed, cycle control arm up and down.
7. If noise is heard from lower control arm rod front insulator bushing, install strut and proceed next step. If no noise is heard, proceed as follows:
   a. Install new strut-to-steering knuckle mounting bolts and nuts.
   b. Tighten nuts while applying pressure to top of brake rotor to ensure camber adjustment bolt is against strut tube, eliminating need to perform front end alignment.
   c. **Torque** nuts to 62 ft. lbs.
   d. **Torque** nuts 74 ft. lbs.
   e. Tighten nuts an additional 90°.
8. Remove front lower control arm rod nut.
9. Install new nut, but do not fully tighten.
10. Bounce front of vehicle up and down several times to stabilize suspension.
11. **Torque** control arm rod nuts to 109 ft. lbs.

TIGHTENING SPECIFICATIONS

Year	Component	Torque/Ft. Lbs.
2004	Brake Caliper	②
	Brake Hose Fitting	26
	Control Arm Ball Joint Stud To Knuckle	44
	Control Arm Rod Insulator Bushing To Front Frame	17
	Control Arm Rod To Control Arm Insulator Bushing	109
	Control Arm Rod To Control Arm	76
	Control Arm To Front Frame	72
	Front Suspension Support Brace To Body	22
	Hub To Knuckle	80
	Inner Tie Rod To Outer Tie Rod End	37
	Outer Tie Rod End Ball Stud To Steering Knuckle	50
	Power Steering Cooler To Body	58①
	Power Steering Cooler To Cooler Bracket	58①
	Power Steering Fluid Reservoir Bracket	37
	Power Steering Gear Inlet Pipe To Engine Bracket	18
	Power Steering Gear Inlet Pipe To Frame	58①
	Power Steering Gear Inlet Pipe To Power Steering Gear	27
	Power Steering Gear Inlet Pipe To Power Steering Pump	22
	Power Steering Gear Outlet Pipe To Power Steering Gear	27
	Power Steering Gear Outlet Pipe Clip To Front Frame	58①
	Power Steering Gear Outlet Pipe Clip To Lefthand Frame	58①
	Power Steering Pump To Cylinder Head	21
	Stabilizer Shaft Insulator Bracket To Front Frame	20
	Stabilizer Shaft Link Lower Stud To Stabilizer Shaft	37
	Stabilizer Shaft Link Upper Stud To Strut Bracket	12
	Steering Coupling To Steering Gear Pinion	21
	Steering Gear Housing To Front Frame	③
	Strut Rod Shaft To Strut Mount	58
	Strut To Body	41
	Strut To Knuckle	②

① — Inch lbs.
② — Refer to "Hub & Bearing, Replace" for tightening specifications and sequence.
③ — Refer to "Power Steering Gear, Replace" for tightening specifications and sequence.

Wheel Alignment

NOTE: On Air Bag Equipped Models, Refer To "Air Bag System Precautions" Located In The Front Of This Manual For System Disarming & Arming Procedures.

NOTE: Refer To "Computer Relearn Procedures" Located In The Front Of This Manual When Battery Power To The Computer Has Been Interrupted.

NOTE: Refer To The Rear Of This Manual For Vehicle Manufacturer's Special Tool Suppliers.

INDEX

PRELIMINARY INSPECTION

1. Inspect tires for proper inflation and irregular tire wear.
2. Inspect runout of wheels and tires
3. Inspect wheel bearings for backlash and excessive play.
4. Inspect ball joints and tie rod ends for looseness or wear.
5. Inspect control arms and stabilizer shaft for looseness or wear.
6. Inspect steering gear for looseness at frame.
7. Inspect struts/shock absorbers for wear, leaks and any noticeable noises.
8. Inspect vehicle trim height.
9. Inspect steering wheel excessive drag or poor return because of stiff or rusted linkage or suspension components.
10. Inspect fuel level. The fuel tank should be full or vehicle should have compensating load added.
11. Give consideration to excess loads, such as tool boxes, sample cases, etc. If normally carried in vehicle, these items should remain in vehicle during alignment adjustments.
12. Give consideration also to condition of equipment being used for alignment.
13. Install alignment equipment according to manufacturer's instructions.
14. Jounce front and rear bumpers three times prior to checking wheel alignment.
15. Measure and record alignment angles.
16. When performing adjustments to vehicles requiring four-wheel alignment, set rear wheel alignment angles first to obtain proper front alignment angles.

FRONT WHEEL ALIGNMENT

Caster

1. Raise and support vehicle, then re-

move front tire and wheel assembly.
2. Remove and discard front lower control arm rod to front lower control arm rod insulator bushing nut.
3. Remove four insulator bushing to front frame mounting nuts.
4. Remove insulator bushing.
5. At factory, one washer is on front of lefthand control arm rod.
6. On side of vehicle with higher caster reading, install one washer to front of control arm rod. **Do not add more than one washer to control arm rod.**
7. Install insulator bushing over front of rod and to frame studs.
8. Install four insulator bushing to frame mounting nuts and **Torque** to 17 ft, lbs.
9. Install new rod to insulator bushing mounting nut. **Do not tighten nut now.**
10. Install front tire and wheel assembly, then lower vehicle.
11. With weight of vehicle on tire and wheel assemblies, push down on front bumper three times to stabilize suspension.
12. **Torque** rod to insulator bushing mounting nut to 109 ft. lbs.
13. Measure and adjust wheel alignment, as required.

Camber

1. Raise and support vehicle on suitable alignment rack.
2. If required, remove front tire and wheel assembly.
3. Remove and discard two strut to knuckle mounting nuts.
4. Remove two washers, then remove and discard two strut to knuckle mounting bolts.
5. Install two new strut to knuckle bolts. **Do not fully tighten bolts now.** Install two washers to bolts.
6. Install two new strut to knuckle mounting nuts to bolts. **Do not fully tighten nuts and bolts now.**

7. If front tire and wheel assembly were removed, install them, then lower vehicle onto alignment rack to place weight of vehicle onto tires.
8. Push down on front bumper three times to stabilize suspension.
9. Measure alignment.
10. **Camber adjustment screw has thread sealant in form of micro-encapsulation.**
11. Rotate camber adjustment screw to adjust front camber to specification.
12. **Torque** strut to knuckle mounting nuts to 63 ft. lbs.
13. **Torque** mounting nuts to 74 ft. lbs.
14. Final tighten nuts an additional 90°.

Toe

1. Ensure steering wheel and gear are in straight ahead position.
2. Measure wheel alignment.
3. Loosen steering gear boot clamp and outer tie rod end lock nut.
4. Rotate inner tie rod to adjust front toe to specification. **Do not twisted boots when rotating inner tie rods.**
5. Ensure number of threads on righthand inner tie rod is same as number on lefthand inner tie rod.
6. **Torque** lock nut to 37 ft. lbs.
7. Ensure boot is not twisted. Install boot clamp .

REAR WHEEL ALIGNMENT

Toe

The following components have lefthand threads: The inner adjustment link, inner lock nut , and the corresponding end of adjuster.

1. Measure wheel alignment.
2. Loosen two rear adjustment link lock nuts.

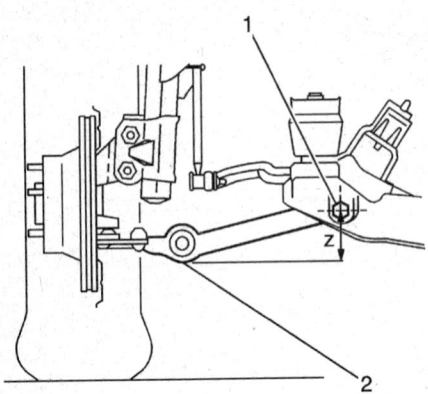

1. Center Line Of Control Arm Pivot Bolt
2. Bottom Of Control Arm

ARM0400000001023

Fig. 1 Front ride height measurement

3. Rotate center adjuster to adjust rear toe to specification.
4. Increasing length of adjustment link will increase rear wheel toe.
5. Hold ball joint position using suitable wrench on hexagonal crimped section of outer adjustment link.
6. **Torque** lock nuts to 37 ft. lbs.

VEHICLE RIDE HEIGHT

1. Set tire pressure to specifications on tire placard.
2. Ensure tires match tire size specifications on tire placard.

3. Ensure wheels match wheel size specifications on tire placard.
4. Ensure fuel tank is full. Add additional weight in order to simulate a full tank, if required.
5. Ensure luggage compartment is empty except for spare tire and weight simulating full fuel tank.
6. Ensure vehicle is on level surface, such as alignment rack.
7. Close hood, doors and luggage compartment lid.
8. Ensure vehicle is not damaged from collision.

Front

1. Lift front bumper of vehicle up approximately 1.5 inches using hands.
2. Gently remove hands and to allow vehicle to settle.
3. Push front bumper of vehicle down approximately 1.5 inches using hands.
4. Gently remove hands to allow vehicle to settle.
5. Measure Z height dimension for lefthand righthand sides of vehicle on front lower control arms.
6. Measure vertical distance from bottom of control arm, below ball joint, to center line of control arm pivot bolt, **Fig. 1**.
7. If measurement is not within .4 inch of specification, replace front springs.

Rear

1. Lift rear bumper of vehicle up approximately 1.5 inches by hand.
2. Gently hands to allow vehicle to settle.

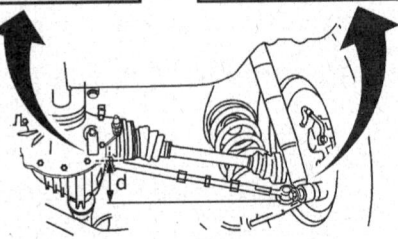

1. Center Line Of Inner Adjustment Link Pivot Bolt
2. Bottom Of Outer Adjustment Link

ARM0400000001024

Fig. 2 Rear ride height measurement

3. Push rear bumper of vehicle down approximately 1.5 inches using hands
4. Gently remove hands to allow vehicle to settle.
5. Measure D height dimension for left and righthand side of vehicle on rear suspension adjustment link, **Fig. 2**.
6. Measure vertical distance from bottom of outer adjustment link to center line of inner adjustment link pivot bolt.
7. If measurement is not within .4 inch of specification, replace rear springs.

AIR CONDITIONING

TABLE OF CONTENTS

System Testing

NOTE: On Air Bag Equipped Models, Refer To "Air Bag System Precautions" Located In The Front Of This Manual For System Disarming & Arming Procedures.

NOTE: Refer To "Computer Relearn Procedures" Located In The Front Of This Manual When Battery Power To The Computer Has Been Interrupted.

INDEX

PRECAUTIONS

Air Bag Systems

Refer to "Air Bag System Precautions" in the front of this manual for system disarming and arming procedures.

Battery Ground Cable

Prior to service, disconnect battery ground cable and isolate as required.

System

R-134a refrigerant is a non toxic, nonflammable, clear and odorless liquefied gas.

R-134a refrigerant is not compatible with R-12 refrigerant. Even small amounts of R-12 in a R-134a system will cause lubricant contamination, compressor failure or improper A/C performance. Never add R-12 to a R-134a system.

Avoid breathing R-134a refrigerant and lubricant vapor or mist. Exposure may irritate eyes, nose and throat. Use only approved service equipment to discharge R-134a systems. Do not heat refrigerant containers with open flame, if container warming is required, place bottom of container in a pail of warm water. R-134a refrigerant will displace oxygen, work only in a well ventilated area to prevent suffocation.

Always wear goggles and wrap clean cloth around fittings, valves and connections when performing work that involves opening the refrigerant system. Keep work area well ventilated and do not steam clean or weld on or near any of the air conditioning lines or components. If liquid coolant does touch the eyes, bathe eyes quickly in cold water, then apply a bland disinfectant oil. See an eye doctor.

Before removing and replacing any of the air conditioning refrigeration lines or components, the refrigerant must be completely removed. The refrigerant system may be evacuated and charged using an air conditioning service charging station or a manifold and gauge set with a 30 lb., drum of R-134a. **Never charge the air conditioning system through the high pressure side of the system.**

For efficient operation of the air conditioning system, be careful not to contaminate the system with foreign materials, such as dirt, air or moisture. Contamination of the air conditioning system will change the chemical stability of the R-134a refrigerant, in turn changing the viscosity of the refrigerant oil. They will also effect pressure, temperature and create corrosion and abnormal wear of moving components.

TROUBLESHOOTING

Refer to **Figs. 1 through 4,** for symptom troubleshooting charts.

PERFORMANCE TEST

Remove leaves and debris from front of the condenser core, mounted at the front of the radiator. All obstructions must be removed, as they will reduce heat transfer and impair the efficiency of the system. Ensure space between the condenser and the radiator is free of foreign matter.

Ensure the evaporator drain is open. The evaporator cools and dehumidifies the air before it enters the passenger compartment. As the core cools the air, moisture condenses on it and is drained through the evaporator water drain tube.

The system should be operated for at least 15 minutes to allow sufficient time for all components to become completely stabilized. Determine if the system is fully charged by the use of test gauges and sight glass if one is installed on system. Head pressure will read from 180–220 psi or higher, depending upon ambient temperature and the type of unit being tested. The sight glass should be free of bubbles. Low

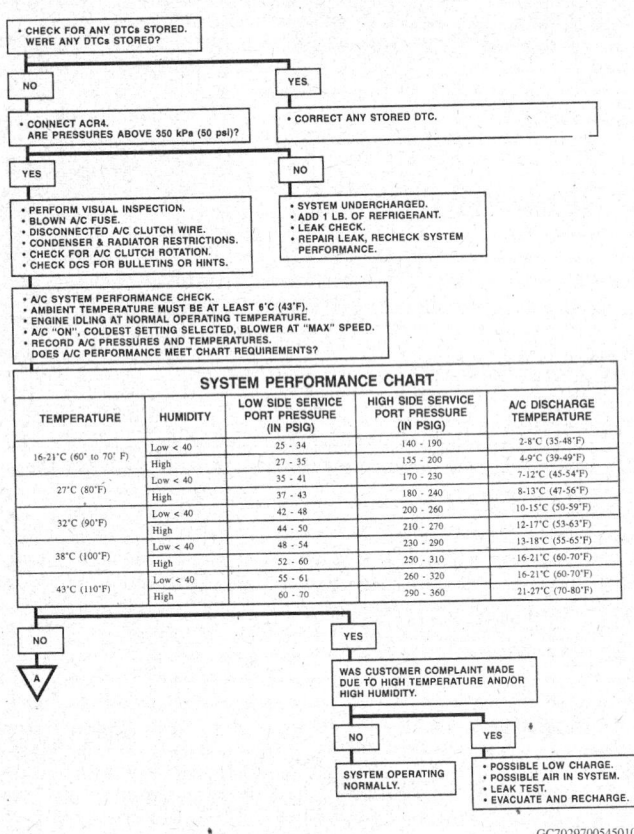

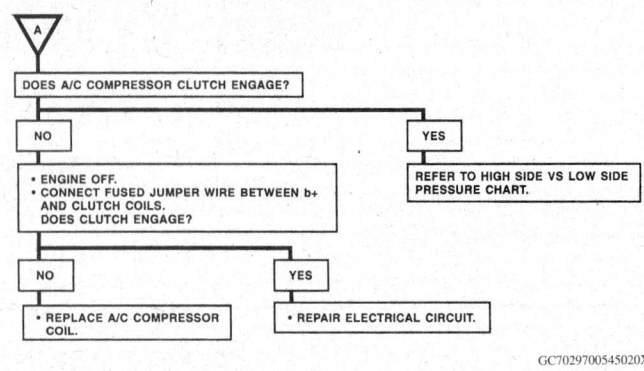

Fig. 1 Insufficient A/C cooling troubleshooting (Part 2 of 2)

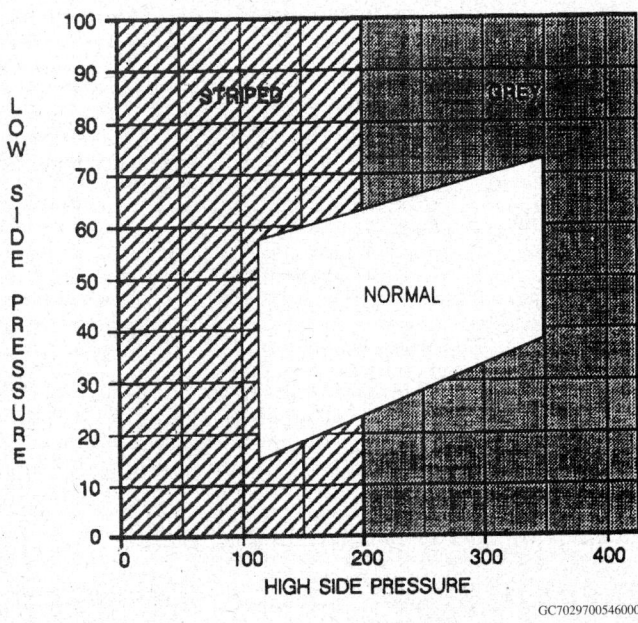

Fig. 2 High side vs. low side pressure chart

Fig. 1 Insufficient A/C cooling troubleshooting (Part 1 of 2)

side pressures should read approximately 15–30 psi, depending on the ambient temperature and the unit being tested. The type of control and component installation used on a particular system will directly influence the pressure readings on the high and low sides, **Fig. 5.**

The high side pressure will be affected by the ambient or outside air temperature. Refer to **Fig. 6,** for approximate high side pressure readings at various ambient temperatures.

Relative Temperature Of High & Low Sides

The high side of the system should be uniformly hot to the touch throughout. A difference in temperature will indicate a partial blockage of liquid or gas at this point.

The low side of the system should be uniformly cool to the touch with no excessive sweating of the suction line or low side service valve. Excessive sweating or frosting of the low side service valve usually indicates an expansion valve is allowing an excessive amount of refrigerant into the evaporator.

LEAK TEST

Before beginning any leak test, attach a manifold gauge set and note pressure. If little or no pressure is indicated, a partial charge must be installed. Inspect all con-

nections, compressor head gasket, oil filler plug and compressor shaft seal for leaks.

Electronic Leak Detectors

Current versions of electronic leak detectors have three settings, one for R-12, one for R-134a and one for gross. The gross setting is for isolating very large leaks already found in one of the other two settings. Refer to operating instructions for the unit being used and observe these general procedures.

1. Move detector probe one inch per second in areas of suspected leaks.
2. Position probe below test point, as refrigerant gas is heavier than air.
3. Inspect service access gauge port valve fittings, particularly when valve caps are missing, as dirt accumulations can destroy sealing area of valve core when manifold gauge set is attached. Replace missing valve caps after cleaning valve core area. **Valve caps should only be finger tightened. Using pliers to tighten valve**

caps may distort sealing surface of valve.
4. Inspect for leaks in manifold gauge set and hoses, as well as rest of system.

Flame-Type (Halide) Leak Detectors

1. Adjust detector flame as low as possible to obtain maximum sensitivity. Ensure copper element is cherry red and not burned away, flame will be almost colorless.
2. Slowly move detector along areas of suspected leaks. A slight leak will cause flame to change to a bright yellow-green color. A significant leak will be indicated by a brilliant blue flame. Position flame under areas being tested as refrigerant gas is heavier than air. **Presence of dust in pickup hose may cause a change in color of flame. If not recognized, a false diagnosis could be made. Store leak detector in a clean place and ensure hose is free of dust before leak testing.**
3. Inspect manifold gauge set and hoses

Gray Area Diagnosis and Service	
Check the following if pressures intersect in the gray area:	
NOTE V5 clutch cycling can occur when discharge pressure exceeds 400 psi.	
1. Improper condenser operation. This can result from :	• Extremely high ambient humidity. • Insufficient air flow across condenser. • Damaged or dirty condenser fins. • Faulty fan relay.
2. High side refrigerant restriction.	• Feel liquid line before expansion tube (orifice). If line feels cold, it indicates restriction in high side. • Visually check for frost spot to locate restriction and repair as necessary.
3. Refrigerant system overcharged (High discharge and high suction pressures).	• The clutch may cycle on/off and cause the compressor to be noisy.
4. Expansion tube (orifice) blocked (Low suction pressures).	
5. Air in system (High discharge and high suction pressures). Items 4, 5 and 6 in the striped area can be corrected by the same procedure.	• Discharge refrigerant system slowly using the low pressure fitting to prevent oil loss. • Check expansion (orifice) tube for blockage. Clean or replace as required. • Evacuate system to a vacuum. Improper evacuation of system prior to recharge will cause air to remain in system. • Recharge system with proper amount of refrigerant. • Leak check system.

GC7029700547000X

Fig. 3   Gray area diagnosis & service

for leaks, as well as rest of system.

4. Use a small fan to ventilate areas where leak detector indicates refrigerant constantly. These areas are contaminated with refrigerant and must be ventilated before leak can be pinpointed.

Fluid Leak Detectors

Apply leak detector solution around joints to be tested. A cluster of bubbles will form immediately if there is a leak. A white foam that forms after a short while will indicate an extremely small leak. In some confined areas such as sections of the evaporator and condenser, use of an electronic leak detector is recommended.

Fluorescent Leak Detectors

The high density black light tool No. J-2848-E, tracer dye injector tool No. J-41436 and tracer dye tool No. J-41447, or equivalents, were developed to detect refrigerant leaks on R-134a systems. **Do not use any other tracer dye in these systems.** Another type dye may cause premature compressor failure. **Use only a ¼ ounce charge of dye, larger amounts may effect system performance.** After adding tracer dye, clean service valves and all affected surfaces of the dye with GM engine degreaser part No. 1050436, or equivalent, to prevent any false leak diagnosis.

DISCHARGING SYSTEM
Refrigerant Recovery

The refrigerant system must be discharged using an air conditioning refrigerant recovery and recycling system. After completing any required repairs the refrigerant system can be evacuated and charged using an air conditioning service charging station. Service fitting caps are color coded for easy reference. Red cap indicates high side port. Blue cap indicates low side port.

Failure to inspect for residual oil from previous recovery can result in adding

extra oil to the current vehicle being serviced. This will result in reduced performance and possible compressor damage.

1. Start vehicle and run with A/C On for two minutes, then attach manifold gauge set to A/C system, **Fig. 7.** Attach recovery station inlet hose to center fitting of manifold gauge set.
2. Open both valves of manifold gauge set. Ensure refrigerant tank vapor valve and liquid valve are open.
3. Turn main power switch On.
4. Depress compressor start switch. Amber Compressor On light will come on and compressor will start. Compressor will shutoff automatically when recovery is complete.
5. Wait two minutes and inspect for pressure rise. If pressure rise occurs, depress compressor start switch to repeat recovery procedure.
6. To drain receiver dehydrator of A/C system oil, open receiver dehydrator pressurizing valve for 15 seconds to allow compressor discharge pressure back into receiver dehydrator.
7. Open oil drain valve slowly and drain receiver dehydrator. When oil stops draining, close oil drain valve.
8. **Do not allow receiver dehydrator to completely depressurize.**

Refrigerant Recycling

1. Turn main power switch On.
2. Open both valves on recovery tank.
3. Turn Recycle Start switch On. Amber Recycle On light will come on and refrigerant pump will start.
4. Refrigerant will be seen going through Moisture Indicator at start up. If there is a sufficient supply of refrigerant, bubbles will clear after a few seconds. When bubbles clear from Moisture In-

Striped Area Diagnosis and Service	
Check the following if pressures intersect in the striped area:	
1. Compressor may be internally damaged.	• If suction and discharge pressure are equal and do not change when the A/C mode is turned on and off, the compressor may be internally damaged. • Excess heat at the clutch surfaces or a free wheeling clutch driver are signs of internal compressor damage. • When replacing the compressor, follow component replacement procedures to maintain correct oil charge in the system.
2. Missing expansion tube (orifice).	• Feel liquid line after expansion tube. If line is warm, discharge system and inspect for proper installation of expansion tube. If expansion tube or o-ring is missing replace expansion tube. • If expansion tube is present, remove, clean, or replace tube as necessary and install in system. • Evacuate and charge system.
3. Compressor at minimum stroke.	• If compressor discharge pressures remains only 10-30 psi above suction pressure, compressor may be at minimum stroke. • Run engine at approximately 3000 RPM for three minutes until pressures become normal. During this period, cycle mode lever from vent to A/C every 20 seconds. If no change, perform control valve low load test (step 4).
4. Compressor control valve set improperly. Run low load test to verify. Perform low load test as follows. This procedure is designed to create a low cooling load causing the V5 compressor to go toward minimum stroke which is absolutely necessary for evaluation of control valve set point.	• Start engine and run at fast idle speed. • Open hood, close windows and doors. • Set A/C controls to LOW blower and MAX cooling. • Record and evaluate test results: 　1. If suction pressure is 25-35 psi, control valve is functioning properly. 　2. If suction pressure is outside limits of 25-35 psi, replace control valve.
5. Refrigerant system undercharged.	• This condition may exist when the suction pressure is below 35 psi during the high load test (step 3). • The suction line before the accumulator will be warm if charge is low. • Add 1 lb. of refrigerant and recheck. Pressures should come into white area. If so, find source of refrigerant leak and repair. • Evacuate and charge system with correct amount of refrigerant.
6. Expansion tube (orifice) blocked.	• Refer to step 5 in the gray area for diagnosis.

GC7029700548000X

Fig. 4   Striped area diagnosis & service

dicator, refrigerant pump is operating at maximum efficiency.

5. Allow station to operate until dot in center of Moisture Indicator turns green. Moisture Indicator Dot should change to a shade indicated on reference decal. Always run recycling system a minimum of 30 minutes. If Moisture Indicator starts out yellow, it could take as long as two hours to turn green, depending on moisture content of refrigerant.
6. Turn Off station when recycling is complete.

Refrigerant Recovery & Recycling Operating Hints

1. When using recovery station in conjunction with a charging station, attach center port hose of manifold gauge set to inlet port of recovery station, then follow normal operating procedures for recovery/recycling station.
2. When using recovery station in conjunction with an automatic charging station, attach exhaust hose to inlet of recovery station.
3. **On automatic A/C service stations,** a hole has been added at rear of cabinet for access to exhaust hose.
4. **On older type stations,** open front doors of cabinet to reach exhaust hose.
5. **On all stations,** after attaching exhaust hose to recovery station, depress main power switch on automatic charging station. Depress exhaust switch. Then follow normal operating procedures for recovery station.

Evaporator Pressure Gauge Reading	Evaporator Temperature F°	High Pressure Gauge Reading	Ambient Temperature
0	-21°	45	20°
0.6	-20°	55	30°
2.4	-15°	72	40°
4.5	-10°	86	50°
6.8	-5°	105	60°
9.2	0°	126	70°
11.8	5°	140	75°
14.7	10°	160	80°
17.1	15°	185	90°
21.1	20°	195	95°
22.5	22°	220	100°
23.9	24°	240	105°
25.4	26°	260	110°
26.9	28°	275	115°
28.5	30°	290	120°
37.0	40°	305	125°
46.7	50°	325	130°
57.7	60°		
70.1	70°		
84.1	80°		
99.6	90°		
116.9	100°		
136.0	110°		
157.1	120°		
179.0	130°		

GC7029100025000X

Fig. 5 Pressure-temperature relationship. Conditions equivalent to 30 mph or 1750 engine RPM

6. Air is automatically vented from recovery tank during recycling. This feature eliminates need to purge hoses before recovering refrigerant.
7. Operating engine with A/C Off during recovery may reduce recovery time.
8. To help prevent escape of refrigerant to atmosphere, recovery station can be attached to a Dial A Charge cylinder top vent port when filling cylinder.
9. Always inspect recovery station for residual oil from previous recovery.

SYSTEM EVACUATION

Charging Station

A vacuum pump is built into the charging station. Complete moisture removal from the system is possible only with a vacuum pump constructed for the purpose.

The system must be completely discharged before it can be evacuated. Damage to the vacuum pump may result if pressurized refrigerant is allowed to enter.

1. Connect hose to vacuum pump, if system was discharged through charging station.
2. Open low side gauge hand valve of charging station.
3. Turn vacuum pump on according to instructions for specific station being used.
4. Evacuate system with vacuum pump until low pressure gauge reads at least 28 inches of vacuum. Continue evacuating system for an additional 15 minutes for routine system servicing or

Ambient Temp., °F	High Side Pressure
80	150–170
90	175–195
95	185–205
100	210–230
105	230–250
110	250–270

Fig. 6 High side pressure specifications

20–30 minutes, if any components have been replaced.
5. Close low side gauge hand valve, then turn vacuum pump off.
6. Verify ability of system to hold vacuum. Watch low side gauge to see that gauge does not rise at a rate faster than 1 inch vacuum every 4–5 minutes. If low side gauge rises at too rapid a rate, install partial charge and leak test.
7. If system holds vacuum, charge system with refrigerant.

Vacuum Pump

The specification for A/C system pumpdown is 28–29½ inches vacuum. This reading can be attained at or near sea level only. For each 1000 feet of altitude, the reading will be 1 inch vacuum lower. As an example, at 5000 feet elevation, only 23–24 ½ inch of vacuum can be obtained. **The system must be completely discharged before it can be evacuated. Damage to vacuum pump may result if pressurized refrigerant is allowed to enter pump.**

1. With manifold gauge set connected to system, remove cap from vacuum hose connector. Install manifold gauge set center hose to vacuum pump connector. Open low side gauge manifold hand valve only.
2. Ensure low side gauge is calibrated correctly. It should be reading zero. If not, adjust calibration.
3. Evacuate system with vacuum pump until low pressure gauge reads at least 28 inches of vacuum.
4. Continue evacuating system for an additional 15 minutes for routine system servicing or 20–30 minutes, if components have been replaced.
5. When system evacuation is complete, close low side gauge manifold hand valve, then turn vacuum pump off.
6. Verify ability of system to hold vacuum. Watch low side gauge to see that gauge does not rise at a rate faster than 1 inch vacuum every 4–5 minutes. If low side gauge rises at too rapid a rate, install partial charge and leak test.
7. Correct leaks as required and evacuate system.
8. If system holds vacuum, charge system with refrigerant.

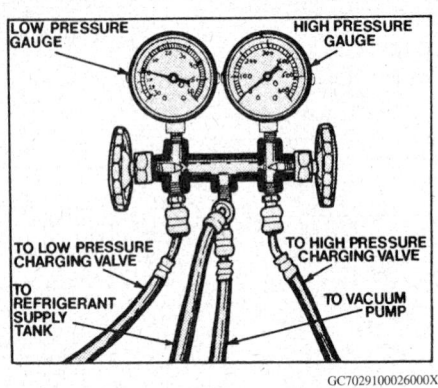

GC7029100026000X

Fig. 7 Manifold gauge set hose connections

CHARGING SYSTEM

Charging Station

Use of the following procedures will prevent charging station from being accidentally exposed to high-side vehicle system pressure.

Use instructions provided with charging station noting the following:

1. Do not connect high pressure line to A/C system.
2. Always keep high pressure valve closed on charging station.
3. Perform all evacuation and charging through low-side pressure service fitting.

Disposable Cans Or Refrigerant Drum

CHARGING SYSTEM

Never use disposable cans to charge into the high pressure side of the system (compressor discharge port) or into a system that is at high temperature, high system pressures could be transferred into the charging can causing it to explode.

1. Start and run engine until normal operating temperature is reached and allow to warm up (choke off, normal idle). Set A/C control lever to OFF.
2. **On all models except Cadillac equipped with display diagnosis,** when 1 lb., of refrigerant has entered system, engage compressor by setting A/C lever to NORM and blower switch to HI to draw in remainder of charge.
3. **On Cadillac models equipped with display diagnosis,** when 1 lb., of refrigerant has entered system, engage compressor by setting climate control panel to AUTO and blower switch to HI to draw in remainder of charge. If system switches to ECON when AUTO is pressed, low refrigerant is indicated, and compressor will not operate. To obtain compressor operation, clear diagnostic trouble codes and select AUTO again.

4. **On all models,** cooling condenser with a large fan will speed up charging procedure by maintaining condenser temperature below charging cylinder temperature.
5. Close refrigerant supply valve and run engine for 30 seconds to clear lines and gauges.
6. With engine running, remove charging low side hose adapter from accumulator service fitting. Unscrew rapidly to avoid excessive refrigerant loss. **Do not remove a gauge line from its adapter when line is connected to A/C system. To disconnect line, always remove line adapter from service fitting. Do not remove charging hose at gauge set while attached to** accumulator, as system will be discharged due to depressed Schraeder valve.

7. Replace protective cap on accumulator fitting and turn engine off.
8. Inspect system for leaks.
9. Start engine and inspect for proper system pressures.

System Service

NOTE: On Air Bag Equipped Models, Refer To "Air Bag System Precautions" Located In The Front Of This Manual For System Disarming & Arming Procedures.

NOTE: Refer To "Computer Relearn Procedures" Located In The Front Of This Manual When Battery Power To The Computer Has Been Interrupted.

NOTE: Prior To Performing Any Service Operations Listed In This Section, Consult The "Technical Service Bulletins" Section For Related Information.

INDEX

OIL CHARGE

When replacing certain components of an air conditioning system, an oil charge must be added to the system. Refer to "Oil Charge Data Table" for oil charge specifications.

If the refrigerant charge is abruptly lost due to a large refrigerant leak, approximately three ounces of refrigerant oil will be carried out of the system with the refrigerant. Upon replacement of a component which caused a large refrigerant leak, add three ounces of oil to the system plus the amount required for any component replaced as outlined in "Oil Charge Data Table." If possible, add oil directly to the replacement component.

OIL CHARGE DATA TABLE

Except Saturn

Model	Year	Compressor Model	Oil Charge (Fl. Oz.) When Replacing Component				
			Compressor	Evaporator	Conden- ser	Accumulator	Receiver & Dehydrator
BUICK							
Century	2001	V-5	2.00⑪	3.00⑪	1.00⑪	2.0⑪	—
	2002–05	V-5	2.00⑪	3.00⑪	1.00⑪	⑩	—
LaCrosse	2005	7CVC	2.00⑪	3.00⑪	2.00⑪	⑩	—
LeSabre	2001–05	V-5	2.00⑪	3.00⑪	1.00⑪	2.0⑩	—
Park Avenue	2001–05	V-5	2.00⑪	3.00⑪	1.00⑪	⑩	—
Regal	2001	V-5	2.00⑪	3.00⑪	1.00⑪	2.0⑪	—
	2002–04	V-5	2.00⑪	3.00⑪	1.00⑪	⑪	—
CADILLAC							
Catera	2001	V-5	2.00⑪	3.00⑪	1.00⑪	—	1.00⑪
CTS	2003–05	Denso	1.18	1.35	1.35	—	—
DeVille	2001	HD6	2.80⑪	1.00⑪	1.00⑪	4.0⑪	—
	2002–05	Mitsubushi ASTT	2.70	1.00	1.00	4.0⑩	—
Edorado	2001	HD6	2.00⑪	3.00⑪	1.00⑪	2.0⑪	—
	2002	HD6	2.00⑪	3.00⑪	1.00⑪	2.0⑩	—

Continued

OIL CHARGE DATA TABLE—Continued

Except Saturn

Model	Year	Compressor Model	Oil Charge (Fl. Oz.) When Replacing Component				
			Compressor	Evaporator	Conden- ser	Accumu- lator	Receiver & Dehydrator
CADILLAC							
Seville	2001	HD6	2.80⑪	1.00⑪	1.00⑪	4.0	—
	2002–04	Mitsubushi ASTT	2.70	1.00	1.00	4.0⑩	—
STS	2005	Denso	4.73	1.35	1.35	—	—
XLR	2004–05	Delphi CVC	5.00	1.50	2.00	—	2.00 —
CHEVROLET/GEO							
Aveo	2005	V-5	③	—	—	⑤	—
Camaro	2001–02	V-5 & V-7	2.00⑪	3.00⑪	1.00⑪	2.0⑩	—
Cavalier	2001	V-5	2.80⑪	2.00⑪	1.00⑪	3.0⑪	—
	2002②	V-5	2.00⑪	2.00⑪	1.00⑪	⑩	—
	2002⑨	CVC6	2.50⑪	1.00⑪	1.00⑪	⑤	—
	2003–05	CVC6	2.50⑪	1.00⑪	1.00⑪	1.5⑤	—
Corvette	2001	V-7	2.00⑪	3.00⑪	1.00⑪	2.0⑩	—
	2002–04	V-7	2.00⑪	2.00⑪	2.00⑪	2.0⑩	—
	2005	CVC	5.00	1.5	2.0	—	—
Impala	2001	V-5	③	3.00	1.00	④	—
	2002–03	V-5	2.00	3.00	1.00	2.0⑩	—
	2004–05	CVC7	2.50⑪	3.00	2.00	—	1.00⑫
Lumina	2001	V-5	③	3.00	1.00	④	—
Malibu	2001	V-5	2.00⑪	3.00⑪	1.00⑪	3.5⑪	—
	2002–03	V-5	2.00⑪	3.00⑪	1.00⑪	⑩	—
	2004–05	CVC7	2.50⑪	1.50⑪	1.00⑪	—	—
Metro	2001	⑦	3.20	—	1.00	—	.30
Monte Carlo	2001	V-5	③	3.00	1.00	④	—
	2002–03	V-5	2.00	3.00	1.00	2.0⑩	—
	2004–05	CVC7	2.50⑪	3.00	2.00	—	1.00⑫
Prizm	2001–02	V-5	2.00①	2.00	2.00	2.0	—
OLDSMOBILE							
Alero	2001	V-5	2.00⑪	3.00⑪	1.00⑪	3.5⑪	—
	2002–03⑨	CVC7	2.50⑪	2.00⑪	1.00⑪	1.5⑥	—
	2002–04⑧	V-5	2.00⑪	3.00⑪	1.00⑪	2.0⑩	—
Aurora	2001–03	Mitsubushi ASTT	2.70⑪	3.00⑪	1.00⑪	2.0⑪	—
Intrigue	2001	V-7	2.00⑪	3.00⑪	1.00⑪	2.0⑪	—
	2002	V-7	2.00⑪	3.00⑪	1.00⑪	2.0⑩	—
PONTIAC							
Bonnevile Less 5.7L Engine	2001–05	V-5	2.00	3.00	1.00	2.0⑩	—
Bonneville w/5.7L Engine	2005	Mitsubushi	2.7	1.0	1.0	4.0	—
Firebird	2001–02	V-5 & V-7	2.00⑪	3.00⑪	1.00⑪	2.0⑩	—
Grand Am	2001	V-5	2.00⑪	3.00⑪	1.00⑪	3.5⑪	—
	2002–05⑨	CVC7	2.50⑪	2.00⑪	1.00⑪	1.5⑥	—
	2002–05⑧	V-5	2.00⑪	3.00⑪	1.00⑪	2.0⑩	—
Grand Prix	2001–03	V-5	2.00⑪	3.00⑪	1.00⑪	2.0⑪	—
	2004–05	CVC7	2.50⑪	3.00	2.00	—	1.00⑫
GTO	2004–05	V-7	2.00⑪	2.0⑪	2.0⑪	2.0	—
G6	2005	CVC7	2.50⑪	1.5⑪	1.0⑪	—	—
Sunfire	2001	V-5	2.80⑪	2.00⑪	1.00⑪	3.0⑪	—
	2002②	V-5	2.00⑪	2.00⑪	1.00⑪	⑩	—
	2003–05⑨	CVC6	2.50⑪	1.00⑪	1.00⑪	1.50⑫	—
Vibe	2003–05	CVC6	2.50⑪	2.00⑪	2.00⑪	—	2.00⑪

① — Plus amount drained from old compressor.

② — 2.2L OHV & 2.4L engines.

③ — Drain oil from old compressor and measure, then drain new compressor. If more than 1 ounce is drained from old compressor, add equal amount to new compressor. If less than 1 ounce is drained from compressor, add 2 ounces.

④ — Drain oil from accumulator and measure. Add equal amount of oil to new accumulator, plus 1 ounce.

If no oil is drained, add 2 ounces to new accumulator.

⑤ — Drain oil from accumulator and measure. Add equal amount of oil to new accumulator, plus specified amount.

⑥ — Drain oil from accumulator and measure. Add equal amount of oil to new accumulator, plus 1.5 ounces. If no oil is drained, add 1.5 ounces to new accumulator.

⑦ — Sanden swash type.

⑧ — 3.4L engine.

⑨ — 2.2L DOHC engine.

⑩ — Drain oil from accumulator and measure. Add equal amount of oil to new accumulator, plus 2 ounces. If no oil is drained, add 2 ounces to new accumulator.

⑪ — If more than specified amount of PAG oil was drained from component, add equal amount of new oil to component.

⑫ — Add PAG oil equal to amount drained from old accumulator or receiver dehydrator, plus specified amount.

Saturn

| Model | Year | Oil Charge (Fl. Oz.) When Replacing Component | | | |
		Compressor	Evaporator	Condenser	Accumulator
ION	2003–05	2.5②	.75②	.75②	—
L-Series	2000–05	①	2.40	1.30	.4
S-Series	2001–02	①	1.14	.75	1.0

① — Drain oil from old compressor. Drain oil from replacement compressor. Add equal amount of new compressor oil as drained from removed compressor. New replacement compressors are charged with 2.21 ounces of oil.

② — If more than specified amount of PAG oil was drained from component, add equal amount of new oil to component.

OIL LEVEL CHECK

Air conditioning oil levels can only be inspected with system discharged and compressor removed from vehicle. Replacement compressor may be shipped with new refrigerant oil. Drain the new oil into a suitable container and retain for later use.

1. Operate system for several minutes to stabilize system. Turn engine Off.
2. Discharge A/C system using a suitable refrigerant recovery/recycling station.
3. Remove compressor from vehicle.
4. Drain and measure refrigerant oil from old compressor through suction and discharge ports, and drain plug.
5. If no compressor oil leaks were noted and more than one ounce of oil is drained, add drained amount using new refrigerant oil.
6. If less than one ounce of oil is drained from compressor, add two ounces of new refrigerant oil.
7. When replacing other A/C components, add specified amount of new refrigerant oil to component as detailed in "Oil Charge Data Table."
8. Install compressor.
9. Evacuate and recharge system, perform leak test.
10. Ensure A/C system is operating properly.

Specifications

INDEX

A/C SPECIFICATIONS

Except Saturn

Model	Year	Refrigerant Capacity, Lbs.	Refrigerant Type	Refrigeration Oil			Compressor Clutch Air Gap, Inch
				Viscosity	Total System Capacity, Ounces	Compressor Oil Level	
BUICK							
Century	2001	2.20	R-134a	⑤	9.00	①	.015
	2002–05	2.20	R-134a	⑧	9.00	①	.015
LaCrosse	2005	2.30	R-134a	⑧	⑩	①	.016
LeSabre	2001–05	2.20	R-134a	⑤	9.00	①	.015
Park Avenue	2001–05	2.20	R-134a	②	9.00	①	.015
Regal	2001	2.20	R-134a	⑤	9.00	①	.015
	2002–04	2.20	R-134a	⑧	9.00	①	.015
CADILLAC							
Catera	2001	2.10	R-134a	⑤	9.00	①	.015–.020
CTS	2003–05	1.30	R-134a	⑧	4.75	①	—
Deville	2001	2.20	R-134a	⑤	8.80	①	—
	2002–05	2.20	R-134a	⑤	8.70	①	—
Eldorado	2001	2.20	R-134a	⑤	9.00	①	.020–.030
	2002	2.20	R-134a	②	9.00	①	.020–.030
Seville	2001	2.20	R-134a	⑤	8.80	①	—
	2002–04	2.20	R-134a	⑤	8.70	①	—
STS	2005	1.38	R-134a	⑧	4.73	①	—
XLR	2004–05	1.40	R-134a	⑧	5.00	①	— —
CHEVROLET/GEO							
Aveo	2005	—	R-134a	⑧	—	—	.015–.025
Camaro	2001–02	1.50	R-134a	②	9.00	①	④
Cavalier	2001	1.50	R-134a	⑤	9.00	①	.015–.020
	2002⑨	1.35	R-134a	②	9.00	①	.015–.020
	2002⑦	1.35	R-134a	⑧	5.00	①	.015–.020
	2003–05	1.50	R-134a	⑧	5.00	①	.012–.024
Corvette	2001	1.50	R-134a	②	9.00	①	.015
	2002–04	1.75	R-134a	⑧	9.00	①	.015
	2005	1.40	R-134a	⑧	5.0	①	.011–.024
Impala	2001	2.20	R-134a	②	9.00	①	.015–.020
	2003	2.20	R-134a	⑧	9.00	①	.015–.020
	2004–05	2.30	R-134a	⑧	8.00	①	.012–.024
Lumina	2001	2.20	R-134a	②	9.00	①	.015–.020
Malibu	2001	1.35	R-134a	⑤	9.50	①	.016–.020
	2002	1.35	R-134a	②	9.00	①	.015–.020
	2003	1.35	R-134a	⑧	9.00	①	.015–.020
	2004–05	1.10	R-134a	⑧	5.00	①	.012–.024
Metro	2001	1.32	R-134a	②	3.40	①	.014–.025

Continued

A/C SPECIFICATIONS—Continued

Except Saturn

Model	Year	Refrigerant Capacity, Lbs.	Refrigerant Type	Refrigeration Oil			Compressor Clutch Air Gap, Inch
				Viscosity	Total System Capacity, Ounces	Compressor Oil Level	
CHEVROLET/GEO							
Monte Carlo	2001–02	2.20	R-134a	②	9.00	①	.015–.020
	2003	2.20	R-134a	⑧	9.00	①	.015–.020
	2004–05	2.30	R-134a	⑧	8.00	①	.012–.024
Prizm	2001–02	1.65	R-134a	②	8.00	①	.014–.025
OLDSMOBILE							
Alero	2001	1.35	R-134a	②	9.00	①	.016–.020
	2002–03⑥	1.35	R-134a	②	9.00	①	.016–.020
	2002–04⑦	1.35	R-134a	⑧	5.00	①	.012–.024
Aurora	2001–03	2.20	R-134a	②	9.00	①	—
Intrigue	2001	2.20	R-134a	⑤	9.00	①	.015
	2002	2.20	R-134a	②	9.00	①	.015
PONTIAC							
Bonneville Less 5.7L Engine	2001–05	2.20	R-134a	⑤	9.00	①	.015–.020
Bonneville w/5.7L Engine	2005	2.20	R134a	⑧	8.70	①	.015–.020
Firebird	2001–02	1.50	R-134a	②	9.00	①	④
Grand Am	2001	1.35	R-134a	②	9.00	①	.016–.020
	2002–04⑥	1.35	R-134a	②	9.00	①	.016–.020
	2002–05⑦	1.35	R-134a	⑧	5.00	①	.016–.020
Grand Prix	2001	2.20	R-134a	⑤	9.00	①	.015
	2002–03	2.20	R-134a	②	9.00	①	.015
	2004–05	2.30	R-134a	⑧	8.00	①	.012–.024
GTO	2004–05	1.75	R-134a	⑧	9.00	①	.015
G6	2005	1.10	R-134a	⑧	5.00	①	.012–.024
Sunfire	2001	1.50	R-134a	⑤	9.00	①	.015–.020
	2002⑨	1.35	R-134a	②	9.00	①	.015–.020
	2002⑦	1.35	R-134a	⑧	5.00	①	.015–.020
	2003–05	1.50	R-134a	⑧	5.00	①	.012–.024
Vibe	2003–05	1.41	R-134a	⑧	8.00	①	.012–.024

① — Oil Level cannot be inspected. Refer to total capacity in ounces.
② — GM PAG refrigerant oil No. 12345923, or equivalent.
③ — Models equipped with L26, 8.0 ounces; equipped with LY7, 6.6 ounces.
④ — Models w/3.8L engine & V-5 compressor, .015–.020 inch. Models w/5.7L engine & V-7 compressor, .015 inch.
⑤ — GM PAG refrigerant oil No. 12356151, or equivalent.
⑥ — 3.4L engine.
⑦ — 2.2L DOHC engine.
⑧ — GM PAG refrigerant oil No. 12378526, or equivalent.
⑨ — 2.2L OHV & 2.4L engines.

AIR CONDITIONING

Saturn

Model	Refrigerant Type	Refrigerant Capacity, Lbs.	Refrigerant Oil		Compressor Clutch Air Gap, Inch
			Total System Capacity, Ounces	Compressor Oil Level	
2001–02					
L Series	R-134a	1.88	7.50	①	.012–.024
S Series	R-134a	1.50	5.07	①	.018–.030
2003–05					
ION	R-134a	.90	5.00	①	.012–.024
L Series	R-134a	2.09	7.43	①	.012–.024

① — Oil level cannot be inspected. If compressor replacement is required, measure amount removed from old compressor, then add equal amount to new compressor. Saturn service compressors are charged with 5.07 ounces for 1.9L engine & 7.5 ounces for 2.2L & 3.0L engines.

CHARGING VALVE LOCATION

Except Saturn

The high pressure charging valve is located on the high pressure line, and the low pressure charging valve is located either on the accumulator or low pressure line.

Saturn

ION & L-SERIES

The high pressure charging valve is located either on the high pressure line, and the low pressure charging valve is located either on the accumulator or low pressure line.

S-SERIES

Refer to **Fig. 1,** for charging valve locations.

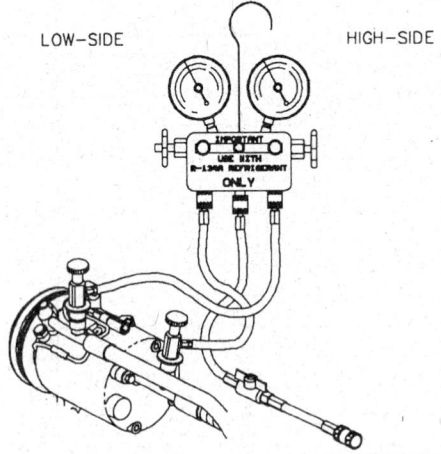

LOW–SIDE   HIGH–SIDE

G37029500028000X

Fig. 1   Service valve locations. Saturn S-Series

BELT TENSION

Except Metro, Prizm & Saturn

Belt tension is controlled automatically by the belt tensioner.

Metro & Prizm

Engine	Belt Deflection, Inch①
METRO	
1.0L	.28–.35
1.3L	.28–.35
PRIZM	
1.6L	.20–.32
1.8L	.20–.32

① — Belt deflection measured in inches, using 22 lbs. of force.

Saturn

Model	Tension, Lbs.	
	New	Used
ION	①	①

Model	Tension, Lbs.	
	New	Used
L-Series	①	①
S-Series	50–65	45

① — Belt tension is controlled automatically by the belt tensioner.

COOLING FANS

TABLE OF CONTENTS

Variable Speed Fans, General Motors

INDEX

DESCRIPTION

The fan drive clutch, **Fig. 1,** is a fluid coupling containing silicone oil. Fan speed is regulated by the torque carrying capacity of the silicone oil. The more silicone oil in the coupling, the greater the fan speed. The less silicone oil, the slower the fan speed.

Two types of fan drive clutches are in use. On one type of drive clutch, a bi-metallic strip and control piston on the front of the fluid coupling regulates the amount of silicone oil entering the coupling, **Fig. 2.** The bi-metallic strip flexes outward with an increase in surrounding temperature and allows a piston to move outward. The piston opens a valve regulating the flow of silicone oil into the coupling from a reserve chamber. The silicone oil is returned to the reserve chamber through a bleed hole when the valve is closed.

On the other type of fan drive clutch, a heat-sensitive, bi-metal spring connected to an opening plate brings about a similar result, **Fig. 3.** Both units cause the fan speed to increase with a rise in temperature and to decrease as the temperature goes down.

In some cases a flex-fan is used instead of a fan drive clutch. Flexible blades vary the volume of air being drawn through the radiator, automatically increasing the pitch at low engine speeds.

COMPONENT DIAGNOSIS & TESTING
Fan Drive Clutch Test

Do not operate the engine until the fan has been inspected for possible cracks and separations.

FAN DRIVE CLUTCH

GC1089100032000X

Fig. 1   Typical variable speed cooling fan

Run the engine at a fast idle speed (1000 RPM) until normal operating temperature is reached. This process can be expedited by blocking off the front of the radiator with a suitable piece of cardboard. Regardless of temperature, the unit must be operated for at least five minutes before being tested.

Stop the engine and, using a glove or a cloth, immediately inspect the effort required to turn the fan. If considerable effort is required, it can be assumed that the coupling is operating satisfactorily. If very little effort is required to turn the fan, it is an indication that the coupling is not operating properly and should be replaced.

If the clutch fan is the coiled bi-metal spring type, it may be tested while the vehicle is being driven. To inspect, disconnect the bi-metal spring, **Fig. 4,** and rotate the spring 90° counterclockwise. This disables the temperature controlled free wheeling

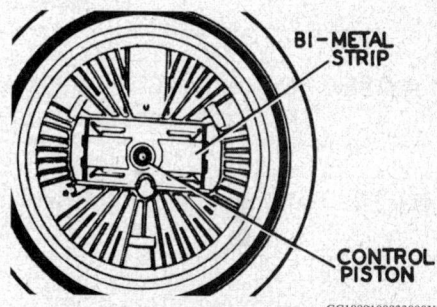

BI-METAL STRIP

CONTROL PISTON

GC1089100033000X

Fig. 2   Variable speed fan w/flat bi-metal thermostatic spring

feature and the clutch performs like a conventional fan. If this cures the overheating condition, replace the fan clutch.

COMPONENT SERVICE

To prevent silicone fluid from draining into fan drive bearing, do not store or place drive unit on bench with rear of shaft pointing downward.

The removal procedure for either type of fan clutch assembly is similar for all vehicles. The unit must be unfastened from the water pump, then it may be lifted from the vehicle.

The type of unit outlined in **Fig. 2,** may be partially disassembled for inspection and cleaning as follows:
1. Remove bolts holding assembly together and separate fan from drive clutch.
2. Remove metal strip on front of fan clutch by pushing one end toward fan clutch body to clear retaining bracket.
3. Push strip aside until its opposite end springs out of place, then remove small control piston.
4. Inspect piston for free movement in

Fig. 3 Variable-speed fan w/coiled bi-metal thermostatic spring

BI-METAL SPRING

GC1089100034000X

coupling device. If piston sticks, clean it with emery cloth. If bi-metal strip is damaged, replace entire unit. **These strips are not interchangeable.**

5. When reassembling, install control piston so that projection on end will contact metal strip, then install metal strip.
6. After reassembly, clean clutch drive with a solvent soaked cloth. Avoid dipping clutch assembly in any type of liquid.
7. Install assembly in vehicle.

The coil spring type of fan clutch cannot be disassembled, serviced or repaired. If it does not function properly, it must be replaced with a new unit.

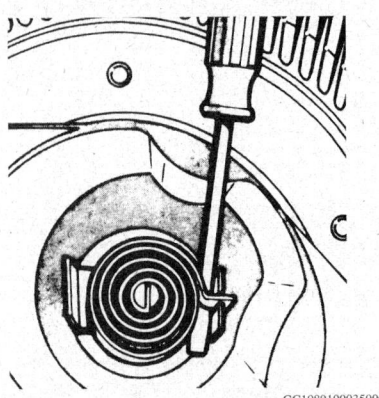

GC1089100035000X

Fig. 4 Bi-metal spring disengagement

Electric Cooling Fans, General Motors

NOTE: On Air Bag Equipped Models, Refer To Air Bag System Precautions Located In The Front Of This Manual For System Disarming & Arming Procedures.

NOTE: "Wire Color Code & Electrical Symbol Identification" Located In The Front Of This Manual Can Be Used As An Aid When Using Wiring Circuits Found In This Section.

NOTE: Refer To "Computer Relearn Procedures" Located In The Front Of This Manual When Battery Power To The Computer Has Been Interrupted.

INDEX

PRECAUTIONS

Air Bag Systems

Refer to "Air Bag System Precautions" in the front of this manual for system disarming and arming procedures.

Battery Ground Cable

Prior to service, disconnect battery ground cable and isolate as required.

DESCRIPTION

Alero & Grand Am

The electric cooling fans are controlled by the Body Control Module (BCM) which enables the fans through the PCM. The PCM enables the ground path for the three cooling fan relays. The relays are used to control the high current flow to power the cooling fan motors.

When minimum cooling is required, the BCM will command the PCM to energize the No. 1 cooling fan relay and since both fans are connected in series through the Mode Control relay, both fans will run at low speed. When maximum cooling is required, the BCM will command the PCM to energize all three cooling fan relays. Power is supplied to the left fan through the No. 1 cooling fan relay and is grounded through the Mode Control relay. The right fan is powered directly through the No. 2 cooling fan relay, causing both fans to run at high speed.

Aurora

The electric cooling fans are used to cool engine coolant flowing through the radiator. They are also used to cool the refrigerant flowing through the A/C condenser.

The electric cooling fans are controlled by the PCM. The PCM controls the ground path for the three cooling fan relays. The relays are used to control the high current flow to power the cooling fan motors. Both fans operate together. When minimum cooling is required, the PCM energizes the low speed cooling fan relay No. 1, and both fans operate at low speed since the fans are connected in series thorough the series/parallel cooling fan relay No. 2. The series/parallel coolant fan relay is a dual position switch and while de-energized,

supplies a ground path for the low speed fan circuit. When maximum cooling is required, the PCM energizes all three cooling fan relays. The left hand coolant fan is still power through the low speed cooling fan relay No. 1, but is now grounded through the series/parallel cooling fan relay No. 2 and operates at high speed. The right hand coolant fan is powered directly through the high speed cooling fan relay No. 3 and also operates at high speed.

The low speed cooling fans are controlled by the PCM based on inputs from the A/C system, Engine Coolant Temperature (ECT) sensor and Vehicle Speed Sensor (VSS). The PCM will command low speed fans to turn On when ECT sensor is above 223°F. The PCM will turn the fans Off when the temperature drops about 5°F. The minimum On time for low speed fans is 50 seconds.

The PCM will command high speed fans to turn On at idle when a certain DTC is set, the ECT is above 234°F or the A/C head pressure is above 240 psi. If the high speed fans were turned On by the ECT, the PCM will switch the fans back to low speed when the temperature drops about 5°F. Minimum On time for high speed fans is 30 seconds.

Aveo

The cooling fans are actuated by the engine control module (ECM) using a low speed cooling fan relay and a high speed cooling fan relay. On A/C equipped vehicles a series/parallel cooling fan relay is used. The ECM will turn the cooling fans ON at low speed when coolant temperature reaches (109°F) and high speed at (207°F). The ECM will change the cooling fan from high speed to low speed at (201°F) and turn the cooling fans OFF at (194°F).

The ECM will turn the cooling fans ON at low speed when the A/C system is ON. The ECM will change to high speed when the coolant temperature reaches (207°F) or high side A/C pressure reaches (273 psi). The cooling fans will return to low speed when the coolant temperature reaches (210°F) or high side A/C pressure reaches (210 psi).

Bonneville & LeSabre

The PCM controls the operation of the cooling fans. This is accomplished by providing a ground path for the cooling fan relay coils within the PCM. The relay contacts will close and complete the circuit between the fusible link at the battery junction block and the fan motors. Whenever the fans are commanded on both fans will be running.

Power for the fan motors is supplied through the Cooling Fan fuse in the right-hand Maxi fuse block. The cooling fan relays are energized when current from the Cooling Fan fuse flows through the relay coils to ground through the PCM.

Low speed fan operation will be commanded on anytime engine coolant temperature exceeds 221°F, A/C is requested and ambient temperature is more than 48°F, or A/C pressure is greater than 190 psi.

Before the PCM operates the fans at high speed, it will delay control of the series/parallel and high speed fan relays for six seconds. This six second delay ensures the cooling fan electrical load will not exceed the capacity of the system.

Camaro & Firebird

Power for the fan motors is supplied through a 40 amp Maxifuse located in the underhood fuse block. The cooling fan relays receive power from a 25 amp fuse located in the underhood fuse block.

During low fan speed operation the PCM supplies a ground path for the No. 1 engine cooling fan relay. This closes the cooling fan relay contacts, allowing current to flow from the 40 amp Maxifuse, through the relays contacts and to left engine cooling fan. The ground path for the left cooling fan is through the No. 3 cooling fan relay and right cooling fan. The result is a series circuit with both fans running at low. The PCM will complete the ground circuit for low speed cooling fan operation anytime engine coolant temperature exceeds 221°F, A/C is requested and ambient temperature is more than 50°F, or A/C pressure is more than 190 psi.

During high speed operation, the PCM supplies a ground path for the No. 1 engine cooling fan relay. After a six second delay, the PCM supplies a ground path for the No. 2 and No. 3 cooling fan relays. The six second delay ensures the cooling fan electrical load will not exceed the capacity of the system. During high speed operation, both coolant fans are supplied current from the 40 amp maxifuse and each cooling fan has its own ground path. The PCM will complete the ground circuit for high speed cooling fan operation anytime engine coolant

COOLING FANS

temperature exceeds 235°F or A/C refrigerant pressure is more than 275 psi.

Catera

This system consists of one engine coolant fan, two auxiliary coolant fans, two temperature switches, an A/C refrigerant pressure switch, seven fan control relays and a coolant fan resistor.

Battery voltage is supplied to the auxiliary water pump whenever the ignition switch is in the On position. When coolant temperature reaches 212°F (100°C), the primary cooling fan temperature switch stage 1 will close, enabling the Engine Control Module (ECM) relay K48 and the fan control relay K26 to energize. When the ECM relay K48 energizes, battery voltage is applied to the ECM cooling blower. When fan control K26 energizes, battery voltage is applied to the No. 1 and No. 2 auxiliary cooling fans, causing the fans to operate at half speed. The fan control relay K26 will also supply battery voltage to the engine coolant fan through the engine coolant fan resistor. The resistor will cause the engine coolant fan to operate at half speed. The fan control relay K26 will supply battery voltage to the timing control pump through the normally closed contacts of the auxiliary water pump relay K22. This allows the timing control pump to operate. The primary cooling fan temperature switch stage No. 1 contacts will open when the coolant temperature reaches 203°F (95°C). This will turn off all three coolant fans, the ECM blower and the timing control pump, unless the A/C is on.

If the ignition switch is in the OFF position and the coolant temperature is above 212°F (100°C), both auxiliary fans, engine coolant fan and timing control pump will remain on until coolant temperature drops below 203°F (95°C).

Cavalier & Sunfire

Cooling fan operation is controlled by the PCM through the fan relay. The PCM uses signals from the engine coolant temperature sensor, intake air temperature sensor, A/C refrigerant pressure sensor and vehicle speed sensor to determine when and how long the fan should operate. The PCM turns the cooling fan on by providing a ground path for the cooling fan control circuit which activates the coolant fan relay.

The relay will be commanded on anytime engine coolant temperature exceeds 223°F, A/C clutch is requested, vehicle speed is less than 38 mph or any Diagnostic Trouble Code (DTC) that causes the MIL lamp to illuminate.

Century & Regal

The engine coolant fan motors receive power from maxifuses located in the underhood electrical center.

During low speed fan operation, the PCM supplies a ground path for the No. 1 Cool Fan relay. This energizes the relay coil, closes the fan relay contacts and supplies current to the primary cooling fan. The

ground path for the primary is through the No. 2 Cool Fan relay and secondary fan motor. This results in a series circuit with both fans running at low speed.

To operate the fans at high speed, the PCM first supplies a ground path for the No. 1 Cool Fan relay, then after a three second delay the PCM supplies a ground circuit for the No. 2 and No. 3 Cool Fan relays. This results in a parallel circuit with both fan running at high speed.

Corvette

2001-2004

The PCM controls low speed operation by providing a ground path for the Cool Fan 1 relay. This closes the relay switch and allows current to flow from the battery, through the switch to the lefthand cooling fan. The ground circuit for the lefthand fan motor runs through the Cool Fan 3 relay to the righthand cooling fan. This creates a series circuit with both fans running at low speed.

The PCM controls high speed fan operation by providing a ground path for Cool Fan 1, Cool Fan 2 and Cool Fan 3 relays. Providing separate ground paths for the relays creates a parallel circuit, which allows both fans to run at high speed.

2005

The engine cooling fan is a variable speed fan. The ECM controls the fan speed by sending a pulse width modulated signal to the cooling fan control module. The cooling fan control module varies the voltage drop across the engine cooling fan motor in relation to the pulse width modulated signal.

Cooling fan speed is effected by many different conditions and can be adjusted from 10% to 90% duty cycle (PWM), 90% is considered high speed fan. When multiple cooling fan speed requests are received the ECM uses the highest cooling fan speed of all the requests.

The ECM commands the cooling fan ON under the following conditions: Cooling fan duty cycle starts when engine coolant temperature reaches approximately (204°F) and reaches high speed at temperatures above (235°F). Cooling fan duty cycle starts when A/C pressure reaches approximately (160 psi) and reaches high speed at A/C pressures of above (360 psi). At engine oil temperature above approximately (302°F) the cooling fan duty cycle will be commanded to high speed. At transmission oil temperature above approximately (270°F) the cooling fan duty cycle will be commanded to high speed. After the vehicle is shut OFF if the engine coolant temperature at key-off is greater then (235°F) or the A/C pressure above is greater than (249 psi) the cooling fan duty cycle is set to 50%, low speed. If the coolant temperature drops below (230°F) and the A/C PRESSURE DROPS BELOW (241 psi) then fan will shut OFF. The fans will automatically shut OFF after 2 minutes regardless of coolant temperature.

CTS

The engine cooling fan system consists of, two electrical cooling fans and three fan relays. The relays are arranged in a series/parallel that allows the Engine Control Module (ECM) to operate both fans together at low or high speeds. The fans and relays receive battery positive power from the underhood fuse block. The ground path is provided at ground circuit G104.

During low speed operation, the ECM supplies the ground path to the low speed fan cooling relay control circuit. This energizes the low speed fan relay coil, closes the relay contacts, and supplies positive battery voltage to the lefthand or (low) speed cooling fan motor. The ground path for the lefthand cooling fan is through the cooling fan S/P relay and the righthand cooling fan. The result is a series circuit with both fans running at low speed.

During high speed operation the ECM supplies the ground path for the high speed fan relay control circuit. After a three second delay, the ECM supplies a ground path to the high speed fan relay control circuit. This energizes the cooling fan S/P relay coil, closes the relay contacts and provides a ground path for the lefthand cooling fan. At the same time the high speed fan relay coil is energized closing the relay contacts and provides positive voltage from the high fan fuse in the cooling fan voltage supply circuit to the right cooling fan. During this high speed fan operation both engine cooling fan have there own ground path. the results is a parallel circuit with both fans running at high speed.

The ECM commands the low speed fans On under the following conditions: Engine coolant temperature exceeds approximately (202°F). A/C refrigerant pressure exceeds (210 psi). After the vehicle is shut Off and the ignition key is in the Off position, and coolant temperature is (214°F), the low speed fans will run for a minimum of 60 seconds. After coolant temperature drops below 214°F the fans will shut Off. The fan will automatically shut Off after three minutes regardless of coolant temperature. If engine coolant temperature exceeds approximately (220°F) or the A/C refrigerant pressure exceeds 265 psi. The ECM will record a DTC and the engine MIL light will come on and a code will be recorded into the ECM memory.

DeVille, Eldorado & Seville

The PCM will command low speed fan operation when engine temperature is in excess of 229°F, transaxle fluid temperature is greater than 302°F, when A/C is requested, or after the vehicle is shutoff and coolant temperature is more than 304°F and system voltage is more than 12 volts the fans will stay on for approximately three minutes.

The PCM will command high fan speed operation when engine coolant temperature is in excess of 234°F, transaxle fluid temperature is greater than 304°F, or when certain DTCs are set.

To operate the fans at low speed the PCM provides a ground path for the Cooling Fan No. 1 relay. This allows current to flow through both cooling fans in a series circuit to ground.

To operate the fans at high speed the PCM provides a ground path for all three cooling fan relays. This changes the circuit to parallel and operates both fans at high speed.

Grand Prix

The cooling fan motors receive power from maxifuses located in the underhood accessory wiring junction block.

During low speed fan operation, the PCM supplies a ground path for the Cool Fan 1 relay. This energizes the relay coil, closes the relay contacts and supplies current to the lefthand cooling fan motor. The ground path for the lefthand cooling fan motor is through the Cool Fan relay and righthand coolant fan motor. This results in a series circuit with both fans running at low speed.

To operate the fans at high speed, the PCM first supplies a ground path for the Cool Fan 1 relay. After a 3–5 second delay, the PCM supplies a ground path for the Cool Fan and Cool Fan 2 relays. The result is a parallel circuit with both fans running at high speed.

GTO

The cooling system includes two dual speed engine cooling fans motors, both of which drive fans with five asymmetrical blades to reduce air noise. The fans remove heat from both engine coolant flowing through the radiator and the refrigerant flowing through the air conditioning condenser. The fan and motor assemblies are mounted on a common shroud, which in turn is mounted onto the engine side of the radiator. The A/C condenser is mounted to the front of the radiator.

There are two relays used to control fan operation. The engine cooling fan relay one for low speed operation and the engine cooling fan relay two for high speed operation. The engine cooling fan relay one is energized by the body control module (BCM) in response to a request from the powertrain control module (PCM). The engine cooling fan relay two is energized by the PCM. After the PCM requests a change in the state of engine cooling fan one, the BCM will send a serial data response message back to the PCM confirming it received the message. Serial data communication between the PCM and BCM is via the powertrain interface module (PIM). The PCM determines when to enable and disable both engine cooling fan relays based on inputs from the A/C request signal, the engine coolant temperature (ECT) sensor and the vehicle speed sensor (VSS).

The engine cooling fan relay one will be turned ON and both fans driven at low speed when the A/C request indicates yes and either: Vehicle speed is less than (19 mph). A/C refrigerant pressure is greater than (218 psi). ECT is greater than (227°F). If an ECT fault is detected and a DTC is set. When and ECT sensor failure in conjunction with an intake air temperature (IAT) sensor failure is detected by the PCM. When the ignition switch is turned from ON and OFF and the ECT is above (235°F), the BCM continues to energize the engine cooling fan relay for 4 minutes. The low speed cooling fan run-on time has a minimum default value of 30 seconds.

The engine cooling fan relay two is controlled by the PCM. The PCM will turn on the engine cooling high speed relay fan if the engine cooling fan relay one has been on for two seconds and the following conditions are satisfied: There is a BCM to PIM message response fault which will cause a PIM DTC to set. An ECT sensor fault is detected and a DTC is set. The ECT is greater than (235°F). The A/C refrigerant pressure is greater than (348 psi). The engine cooling fan relay two will be turned off when any of the following conditions have been met: The ECT is less than (227.3°F). An A/C request is not indicated. An A/C request is indicated and the A/C refrigerant pressure is less than (276 psi).

G6

The engine cooling fan consists of two electrical cooling fans and three relays. The relays are arranged in a series/parallel configuration that allows the powertrain control module (PCM) to operate both fan together at low or high speeds. The cooling fans and fan relays receive battery positive voltage from the underhood fuse block. The ground path is provided at G106.

During low speed operating the PCM supplies the ground path for the cooling fan one relay through the low speed cooling fan relay control circuit. After a three second delay, the PCM supplies a ground path for the cooling fan two relay and the cooling fan S/P relay through the high speed cooling fan relay control circuit. This energizes the cooling fan two relay coil, closes the relay contacts, and provides a ground path for the left cooling fan. At the same time the cooling fan S/P relay coil is energized closing the relay contact and provides batter positive voltage from the cooling fan two fuse on the cooling fan motor supply voltage circuit to the right cooling fan. During high speed fan operation, both engine cooling fans have their own ground path. The result is a parallel circuit with both fans running at high speed.

The PCM commands Low Speed Fans on under the following conditions: Engine coolant temperature exceeds approximately (223°F). When A/C is requested and the ambient temperature is more than (122°F). A/C refrigerant pressure exceeds (190 psi). After the vehicle is shut off if the engine coolant temperature at key-off is more than (284°F) and system voltage is more than 12 volts. The fans will stay on for approximately three minutes.

The PCM commands High Speed Fans on under the following conditions: Engine coolant temperature exceeds approximately (233°F). A/C refrigerant pressure exceeds (240 psi). When certain DTCs set.

Impala & Monte Carlo

This coolant fan system is equipped with two electric cooling fans and three fan relays which are controlled by the PCM. The relays are wired in a series/parallel arrangement that allows the PCM to operate both fans together at low or high speed.

The PCM controls low fan speed operation by grounding the control circuit for Cool Fan No. 1 relay. The relay supplies current to the No. 1 fan motor. The ground path for the No. 1 fan motor is through the Cool Fan No. 2 relay and the No. 2 fan motor. This results in a series circuit which operates both fans at low speed. The PCM operates the cooling fans at low speed whenever engine coolant temperature exceeds 223°F, A/C operation is requested and ambient temperature is greater than 50°F, A/C refrigerant pressure is greater than 190 psi, or the engine is shutoff and coolant temperature is more than 284.°

To control high speed fan operation, the PCM grounds the control circuit for the Cool Fan No. 1 relay. Then after a three second delay, the PCM grounds the control circuit for Cool Fan No. 2 and No. 3 relays. When the Cool Fan No. 2 relay is energized, both the fans have their own ground path creating a parallel circuit. This parallel circuit causes both fans to operate at high speed. The PCM operates the cooling fans at high speed whenever engine coolant temperature exceeds 230°F, A/C refrigerant pressure exceeds 240 psi.

Intrigue

This coolant fan system is equipped with two electric cooling fans and three fan relays which are controlled by the PCM. The relays are wired in a series/parallel arrangement that allows the PCM to operate both fans together at low or high speed.

The PCM controls low fan speed operation by grounding the control circuit for fan relay No. 1. The relay supplies current to the No. 1 fan motor. The ground path for the No. 1 fan motor is through the No. 2 fan relay and the No. 2 fan motor. This results in a series circuit which operates both fans at low speed. The PCM operates the cooling fans at low speed whenever engine coolant temperature exceeds 229°F, A/C operation is requested, or the engine is shutoff and coolant temperature is more than 304°F and system voltage is more than 12 volts. The PCM will shutoff the fans whenever coolant temperature drops below 216°F.

To control high speed fan operation, the PCM grounds the control circuit for the No. 1 fan relay. Then after a three second delay, the PCM grounds the control circuit for the No. 2 and No. 3 fan relays. When the No. 2 fan relay is energized, both the fans have their own ground path creating a parallel circuit. This parallel circuit causes both fans to operate at high speed. The PCM operates the cooling fans at high speed whenever engine coolant temperature exceeds

COOLING FANS

234°F, A/C refrigerant pressure exceeds 240 psi, or certain Diagnostic Trouble Codes (DTC)s are set:

LaCrosse

The engine cooling fan system consists of two electrical cooling fans and three fan relays. The relays are arranged in a series/parallel configuration that allows the powertrain control module (PCM) to operate both fans together at low or high speeds. The cooling fans and fan relays receive battery positive voltage from the underhood fuse block. The ground path is provided at G100.

During low speed operation, the PCM supplies the ground path for the low speed fan relay through the low speed cooling fan relay control circuit. This energizes the fan 1 relay coil, closes the relay contacts, and supplies battery positive voltage from the fan 1 fuse through the cooling fan motor supply voltage circuit to the left cooling fan. The ground path for the left cooling fan is through the fan 2 relay and the right cooling fan. The result is a series circuit with both fans running at low speed.

During high speed operation the PCM supplies the ground path for the fan 1 relay through the low speed cooling fan relay control circuit. After a 3-second delay, the PCM supplies a ground path for the fan 2 relay and the fan 3 relay through the high speed cooling fan relay control circuit. This energizes the fan 2 relay coil, closes the relay contacts, and provides a ground path for the left cooling fan. At the same time the fan 3 relay coil is energized closing the relay contacts and provides battery positive voltage from the fan 2 fuse on the cooling fan motor supply voltage circuit to the right cooling fan. During high speed fan operation, both engine cooling fans have there own ground path. The result is a parallel circuit with both fans running at high speed.

Lumina

Power for the cooling fan motors is supplied through a fusible link at the battery junction block. The cooling fans are energized when current flows from the PCM fuse in the No. 1 underhood electrical center and the Fan fuse in the No. 2 underhood electrical center through the relay coils to ground through the PCM.

During low speed fan operation, the PCM supplies a ground path for the No. 1 engine cooling fan relay. This closes the fan relay contacts and allows current to flow to the left engine coolant fan. The ground path for the left cooling fan is the No. 3 cooling fan relay. This results in a series circuit with both cooling fans running at low speed.

During high speed fan operation, the PCM supplies a ground path for the No. 1, No. 2 and No. 3 engine cooling fan relays. With all three relays closed, each fan is supplied current from the battery junction block and has its own ground path.

Malibu

2001-03

Power for the fan motors is supplied by fuses and relays in the Underhood Electrical Center (U/H BEC). The cooling fan relays are energized when current from the No. 1 and No. 2 Cool Fan fuses flows through the relay coils to ground through the PCM. The No. 1 fan control relay circuit is grounded for low speed fan operation. The No. 1 fan control relay, mode control relay and No. 2 fan control relay are all grounded for high speed fan operation.

During low speed fan operation, the PCM supplies a ground path for the No. 1 fan control relay. This closes the fan control relay contacts, allowing current to flow from the U/H BEC through the relay contacts and to the left cooling fan motor. The ground path for the lefthand cooling fan motor is through the No. 2 fan control relay and righthand cooling fan motor. This results in a series circuit with both fans running at low speed.

During high speed fan operation, the PCM supplies a ground path for the No. 1 fan control relay. The PCM also supplies a ground path for the No. 2 fan control relay and the mode control relay. The No. 1 cooling fan relay is grounded through the Mode Control relay. The right fan is powered directly through the No. 2 cooling fan relay, causing both fans to run at high speed.

2004-05

The engine cooling fan system consists of two electrical cooling fans and three relays. The relays are arranged in a series/parallel configuration that allows the Powertrain Control Module (PCM) to operate both fans together at low or high speeds. The cooling fans and fan relays receive battery positive voltage from the underhood fuse block.

During low speed operation, the PCM supplies the ground path for the low speed fan relay through the low speed cooling fan relay control circuit. This energizes the cooling fan No. 1 relay coil, closes the relay contacts and supplies battery positive voltage from the cool fan No. 1 fuse through the cooling fan motor supply voltage circuit to the left cooling fan. The ground path for the left cooling fan is through the cooling fan s/p relay and the right cooling fan. The result is a series circuit with both fans running at low speed.

During high speed operation the PCM supplies the ground path for the cooling fan No. 1 relay through the low speed cooling fan relay control circuit. After a 3-second delay, the PCM supplies a ground path for the cooling fan No. 2 relay and the cooling fan s/p relay through the high speed cooling fan relay control circuit. This energizes the cooling fan No. 2 relay coil, closes the relay contacts and provides a ground path for the left cooling fan. At the same time the cooling fan s/p relay coil is energized closing the relay contacts and provides battery

positive voltage from the cool fan No. 2 fuse on the cooling fan motor supply voltage circuit to the right cooling fan. During high speed fan operation, both engine cooling fans have there own ground path. The result is a parallel circuit with both fans running at high speed.

Metro

RADIATOR FAN

When ignition switch is in On position, system voltage is applied through ignition fuse to radiator fan switch. Fan switch closes when engine coolant temperature reaches 208°F. With fan switch closed, voltage is applied to radiator fan motor. Since the fan motor is permanently grounded, fan operates as soon as voltage is applied. When temperature falls below 199°F, fan switch opens and voltage to fan motor is interrupted.

A/C CONDENSER FAN

When ignition switch is in On position, system voltage is applied to dual pressure switch through heater fuse on vehicles equipped with automatic transaxle, or ignition fuse on vehicles equipped with manual transaxle. With dual pressure switch closed, voltage is applied to A/C clutch relay. A/C clutch relay is energized when A/C amplifier grounds coil of relay. With A/C clutch relay energized, voltage is applied through A/C fuse and closed contacts of A/C clutch relay to coil of A/C condenser fan relay. Since A/C condenser fan relay is permanently grounded, relay energizes, contacts close, and voltage is applied to condenser fan. Since condenser fan is permanently grounded, an operates as soon voltage is applied.

Park Avenue

Power for the cooling fan motors is supplied by the Cool Fan No. 1 and Cool Fan No. 2 Maxi fuses.

During low speed fan operation, the PCM supplies a ground path for the No. 1 Cool Fan relay through the low speed fan control circuit. This energizes the relay coil, closes the relay contacts and supplies current to the primary cooling fan. The ground path for the primary cooling fan is through the No. 2 Cool Fan (series/parallel) relay and secondary cooling fan motor. This results in a series circuit with both fans running at low speed.

To operate the cooling fans at high speed, the PCM first supplies a ground path for No. 1 Cool Fan relay. After a three second delay the PCM supplies a ground path for the No. 2 and No. 3 Cool Fan relays. During high speed operation, both the primary and secondary cooling fans are supplied current through their respective maxifuse and each fan has its own ground.

Prizm

When the ignition switch is in either the Run or Start positions, system voltage is applied to the coils of the main engine relay and to fan relay 1. Because the main relay is grounded at G108, the relay is energized, its contacts close, and battery voltage is applied through the relay and the radiator fan fusible link to the contacts of fan relay 1.

When engine coolant temperature is below 194°F, the cooling fan temperature switch provides a ground for relay 1, the relay energizes and its contacts are pulled open.

Whenever engine coolant temperature reaches or exceeds 194°F, the cooling fan temperature switch opens, fan relay 1 is de-energized, its contacts close, and system voltage is applied through the relay to the cooling fan motor. Since the fan motor is grounded at G108, it start to operate as soon as voltage is applied.

When engine coolant temperature drops below 194°F, the cooling fan temperature switch closes to ground, fan relay 1 is energized the relay contacts are pulled open and system voltage is no longer applied to the fan motor.

STS

The engine cooling fan system consists of two puller type electrical cooling fans and three fan relays. The relays are arranged in a series parallel (S/P) configuration that allows the engine control module (ECM) to operate both fans together at low or high speeds. The cooling fans and fan relays receive battery positive voltage from the underhood fuse block. The ground path is provided at G104.

During low speed operation, the ECM supplies the ground path for the low speed fan relay through the low speed cooling fan relay control circuit. This energizes the low speed fan relay, closes the relay contacts, and supplies battery positive voltage from the low fan fuse through the cooling fan motor supply voltage circuit to the left cooling fan. The ground path for the left cooling fan is through the cooling fan S/P relay and the right cooling fan. The result is a series circuit with both fans running at low speed.

During high speed operation the ECM supplies the ground path for the low speed fan relay through the low speed cooling fan relay control circuit After a three second delay, the ECM supplies a ground path for the high speed fan relay and the cooling fan S/P relay through the high speed cooling fan relay control circuit. This energizes the cooling fan S/P relay coil, closes the relay contacts, and provides a ground path for left cooling fan. At the same time , the high speed fan relay is energized closing the relay contacts, and provides battery positive voltage from the high fan fuse on the cooling fan motor supply voltage circuit, to the right cooling fan. During high speed fan operation, both engine cooling fans have their own ground path. The result is a parallel circuit with both fans running at high speed.

The ECM commands the low speed cooling fans ON under the following conditions: Engine coolant temperature exceeds approximately (202°F). A/C refrigerant pressure exceeds (210 psi). After the vehicle is shut OFF, if the engine coolant temperature at key-off is greater then (214°F), the fans will shut OFF. The fans will automatically shut OFF after three minutes, regardless of coolant temperature.

The ECM commands the fans ON under the following conditions: Engine coolant temperature exceeds approximately (202°F). A/C refrigerant pressure exceeds approximately (265 psi). When certain DTCs set. At idle and very low vehicle speeds the cooling fans are only allowed to increase in speed, if required. This ensures isle stability by preventing the fans from cycling between high and low speed.

Vibe

The engine cooling fan system of one electrical cooling fan, two fan relays and a fan resistor. The No. 1 relay controls power to the fan motor. The No. 2 relay control the ground path to the fan motor. The gauge fuse supplies ignition voltage to the coils of both the fan motor and the No. 1 fan relay. The Powertrain Control Module (PCM) controls the ground for the coils of both relays. The PCM controls low and high speed fan operation by energizing and de-energizing the No. 2 fan relay which changes the ground path of the fan motor.

During low sped operation when the A/C is operating and engine coolant temperature is below (181°F), The PCM supplies the ground path for the No. 1 fan relay through the fan 1 relay control circuit. This energizes the relay, closes the fan 1 relay contacts, and supplies battery voltage from the RDI fuse through the cooling fan motor supply voltage circuit to the fan motor. The fan motor ground path is through the closed contacts of the de-energized No. 2 fan relay, and the fan resistor to ground circuit No. G103.

During high speed fan operation when the engine coolant temperature reaches (199°F) or the A/C system pressure exceeds (220 psi), the PCM supplies the ground path for fan relay No. 1 through cooling fan 1 relay control circuit. this energizes the relay, closes the No. 1 fan relay contacts, and supplies battery voltage from the RDI fuse through the cooling fan motor supply voltage circuit to the fan motor. The PCM also supplies the ground path for fan relay No. 2. This energizes the relay, switches the fan 2 relay contacts and supplies a ground for the fan motor directly to ground circuit No. G103. The result is a series circuit with the fan running at high speed.

The A/C refrigerant pressure switch is in parallel with the PCM controlled ground for the coil of the No. 2 fan relay. If the A/C system pressure exceeds (220 psi), the pressure switch closes the ground circuit to the coil of the No. 1 fan relay, initiating high speed fan operation. The PCM commands low speed fan operation when all of the following conditions occur: The A/C system is operating. The A/C pressure is below (178 psi). The engine coolant temperature is below (181° F). The PCM commands high speed fan operation when all of the following conditions occur: The engine coolant temperature reaches (199° F). The A/C system pressure exceeds (220 psi).

XLR

The engine cooling fan is a variable speed fan. The ECM controls the fan speed by sending a pulse width modulated signal to the cooling fan control module. The cooling fan control module varies the voltage drop across the engine cooling fan motor in relation to the pulse width modulated signal. Cooling fan speed is effected by many different conditions and can be adjusted from 10% to 90% duty cycle (PWM), 90% is considered high speed fan. When multiple cooling fan speed requests are received the ECM uses the highest cooling fan speed of all the requests.

TROUBLESHOOTING

Except Metro

1. Inspect for open fuses.
2. Inspect for open fusible links.
3. Inspect for corrosion on cooling fan and cooling fan relay connectors.
4. Inspect for clean and tight grounds.

Metro

PRELIMINARY CHECK

1. Inspect A/C fuse for open.
2. Inspect IG fuse for open.
3. Inspect fusible link "B"for open.
4. Inspect radiator fan fuse for open.
5. Inspect engine coolant level.
6. Inspect A/C system for proper refrigerant charge.
7. Inspect grounds G101, G104, and G201 are clean and tight.

SYSTEM CHECK

1. Run engine until engine coolant temperature reaches 208°F. Cooling fan should run.
2. Turn A/C switch to On position. A/C compressor clutch should engage and a/c condenser fan motor should run.
3. Turn A/C switch to Off position. A/C compressor clutch should disengage and A/C condenser fan motor should stop.

SYSTEM DIAGNOSIS & TESTING

Wiring Diagrams

ALERO & GRAND AM

Refer to **Fig. 1,** for wiring diagram.

AURORA

Refer to **Fig. 2,** for wiring diagrams.

BONNEVILLE & LESABRE

Refer to **Fig. 3,** for wiring diagram.

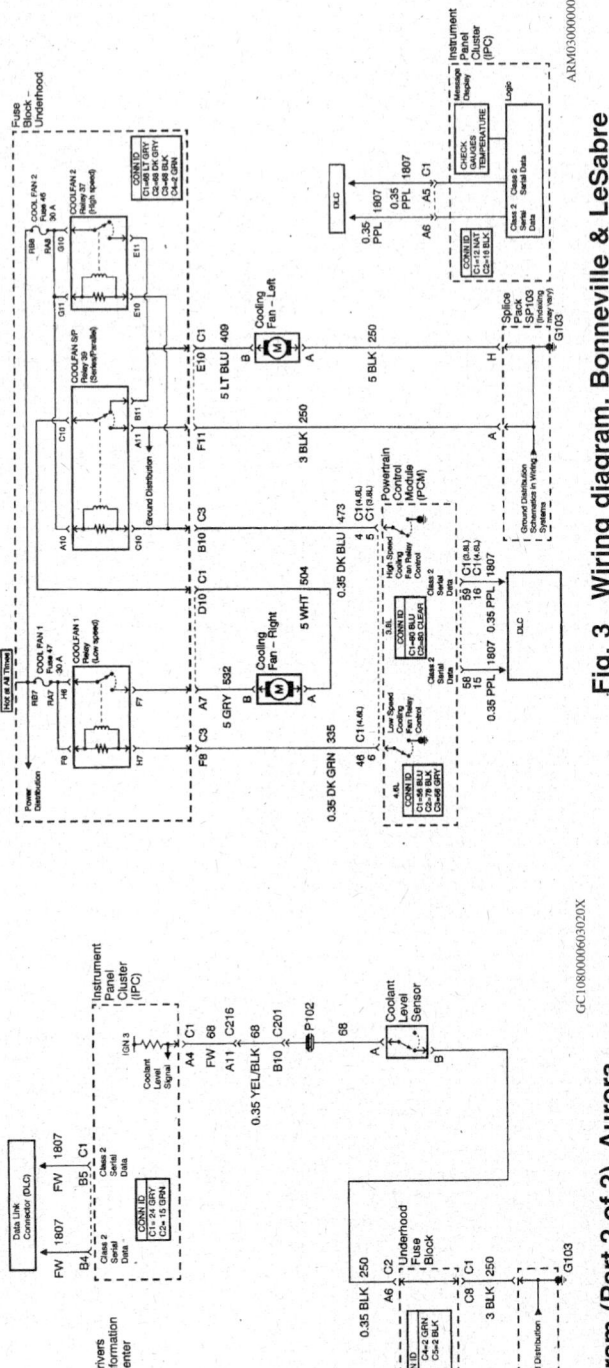

Fig. 2 Wiring diagram (Part 1 of 2). Aurora

Fig. 3 Wiring diagram. Bonneville & LeSabre

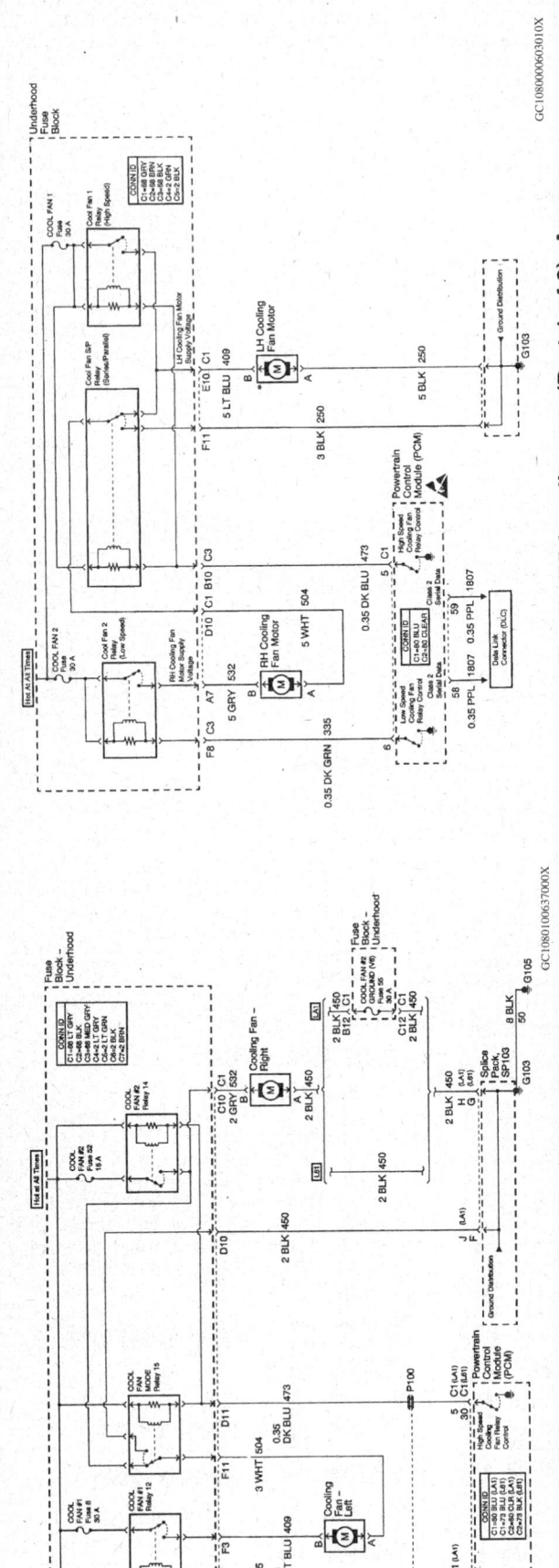

Fig. 1 Wiring diagram. Alero & Grand Am

Fig. 2 Wiring diagram (Part 2 of 2). Aurora

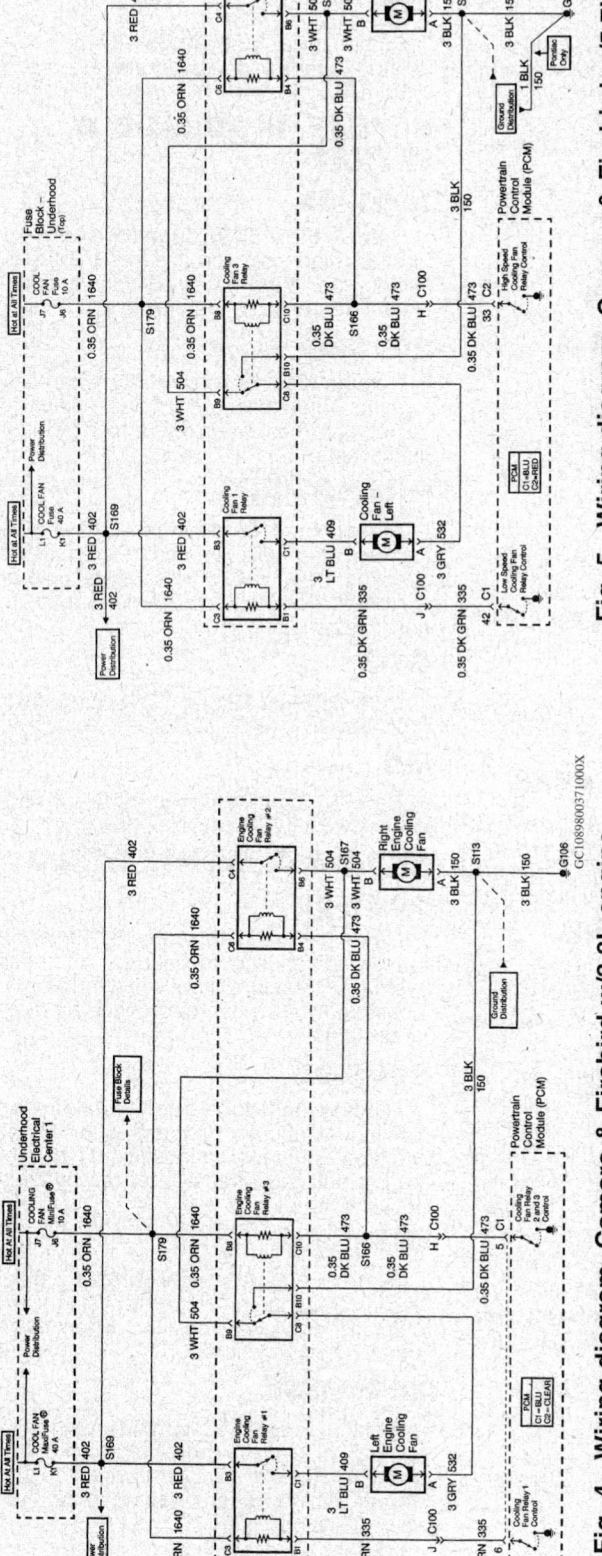

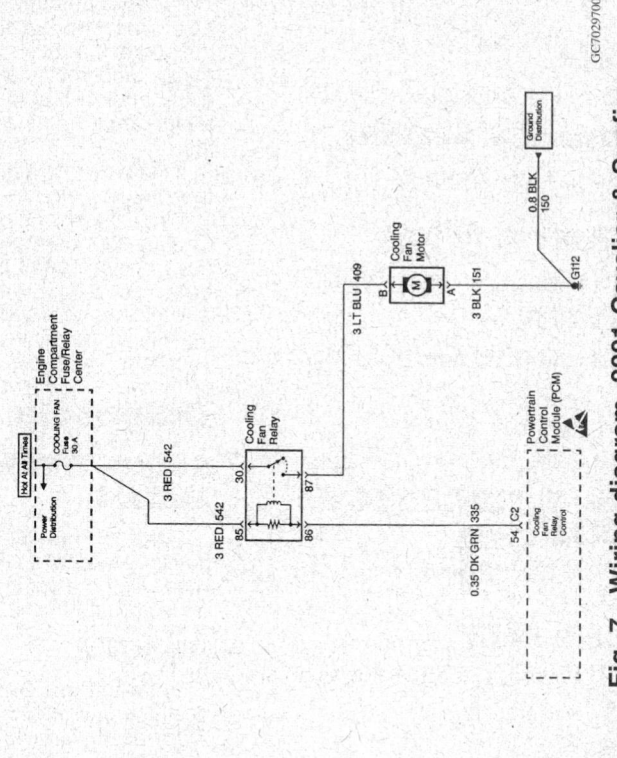

Fig. 5 Wiring diagram. Camaro & Firebird w/5.7L engine

Fig. 7 Wiring diagram. 2001 Cavalier & Sunfire

Fig. 4 Wiring diagram. Camaro & Firebird w/3.8L engine

Fig. 6 Wiring diagram. Catera

COOLING FANS

CAMARO & FIREBIRD

Refer to **Figs. 4 and 5,** for wiring diagrams.

CATERA

Refer to **Fig. 6,** for wiring diagram.

CAVALIER & SUNFIRE

Refer to **Figs. 7 and 8,** for wiring diagrams.

CENTURY & REGAL

Refer to **Fig. 9,** for wiring diagram.

CORVETTE

Refer to **Figs. 10 and 11,** for wiring diagrams.

CTS

Refer to **Fig. 12,** for wiring diagram.

DEVILLE, ELDORADO & SEVILLE

Refer to **Figs. 13 and 14,** for wiring diagrams.

GRAND PRIX

Refer to **Figs. 15 and 16,** for wiring diagrams.

GTO

Refer to **Fig. 17,** for wiring diagram.

G6

Refer to **Fig. 18,** for wiring diagram.

IMPALA & MONTE CARLO

Refer to **Fig. 19,** for wiring diagram.

INTRIGUE

Refer to **Fig. 20,** for wiring diagram.

LACROSSE

Refer to **Fig. 21,** for wiring diagram.

LUMINA

Refer to **Fig. 22,** for wiring diagram.

MALIBU

Refer to **Figs. 23 and 24,** for wiring diagrams.

METRO

Refer to **Fig. 25,** for wiring diagram.

PARK AVENUE

Refer to **Fig. 26,** for wiring diagram.

PRIZM

Refer to **Fig. 27,** for wiring diagram.

STS

Refer to **Fig. 28,** for wiring diagram.

VIBE

Refer to **Fig. 29,** for wiring diagram.

XLR

Refer to **Fig. 30,** for wiring diagram.

Diagnostic Aids

If the temperature light or gauge indicated overheating, but no boil over is detected, the gauge or light should be inspected. The gauge accuracy can also be inspected using a scan tool to compare the coolant temperature reading with the gauge reading.

If the engine is actually overheating, and the gauge indicates overheating, but the cooling fan is not operating, the Engine Coolant Temperature (ETC) sensor may have shifted out of calibration and should be replaced.

If the engine is overheating and the cooling fan is operating, the cooling system should be inspected.

Diagnostic Tests

ALERO, GRAND AM & MALIBU

Refer to **Figs. 31 through 33,** for diagnostic procedure. Refer to "Diagnostic Aids" as previously outlined when referenced by diagnostic tests.

AURORA

Refer to **Figs. 34 through 36,** for diagnostic procedures. Refer to "Diagnostic Aids" as previously outlined when referenced by diagnostic tests.

AVEO

Refer to **Figs. 37 and 38,** for diagnostic procedures.

BONNEVILLE & LESABRE

Refer to **Figs. 39 through 41,** when performing diagnostic procedures. Refer to "Diagnostic Aids" as previously outlined when referenced by diagnostic tests.

CAMARO & FIREBIRD

Refer to **Figs. 42 through 44,** for diagnostic procedures. Refer to "Diagnostic Aids" as previously outlined when referenced by diagnostic tests.

CAVALIER & SUNFIRE

Refer to **Figs. 45 and 46,** for diagnostic procedures. Refer to "Diagnostic Aids" when referenced by diagnostic tests.

CENTURY & REGAL

2001

Refer to **Figs. 47 through 49,** when performing diagnostic procedures on these systems. Refer to "Diagnostic Aids" when referenced by diagnostic tests.

2002-05

Refer to **Figs. 50 through 52,** when performing diagnostic procedures on these systems. Refer to "Diagnostic Aids" when referenced by diagnostic tests.

CORVETTE

2001-04

Refer to **Figs. 53 through 55,** for diag-

nostic procedures. Refer to "Diagnostic Aids" as previously outlined when referenced by diagnostic tests.

2005

Refer to **Figs. 56 through 58,** for diagnostic procedures.

CTS

Refer to **Figs. 59 through 62,** when performing diagnostic procedures on these systems.

DEVILLE, ELDORADO & SEVILLE

2001-02

Refer to **Figs. 63 through 65,** when performing diagnostic procedures. Refer to "Diagnostic Aids" as previously outlined when referenced by diagnostic tests.

2003-05

Refer to **Figs. 66 through 68,** when performing diagnostic procedures. Refer to "Diagnostic Aids" when referenced by diagnostic tests.

GRAND PRIX

Refer to **Figs. 69 through 71,** when performing diagnostic procedures on these systems. Refer to "Diagnostic Aids" as previously outlined when referenced by diagnostic tests.

GTO

Refer to **Figs. 72 and 73,** for diagnostic procedures.

G6

Refer to **Figs. 74 through 76,** for diagnostic procedures.

IMPALA & MONTE CARLO

2001-02

Refer to **Figs. 77 through 79,** when performing diagnostic procedures on these systems. Refer to "Diagnostic Aids" as previously outlined when referenced by diagnostic tests.

2003-05

Refer to **Figs. 80 through 82,** when performing diagnostic procedures on these systems. Refer to "Diagnostic Aids" as previously outlined when referenced by diagnostic tests.

INTRIGUE

Refer to **Figs. 83 through 85,** for diagnostic procedures. Refer to "Diagnostic Aids" as previously outlined when referenced by diagnostic tests.

LACROSSE

Refer to **Figs. 86 through 91,** when performing diagnostic procedures on these systems. Refer to "Diagnostic Aids" as previously outlined when referenced by diagnostic tests.

LUMINA

Refer to **Figs. 92 through 95,** when performing diagnostic procedures on these systems. Refer to "Diagnostic Aids" as previously outlined when referenced by diagnostic tests.

MALIBU

2001-03

Refer to **Figs. 96 through 98,** when performing diagnostic procedures on these systems. Refer to "Diagnostic Aids" when referenced by diagnostic tests.

2004-05

Refer to **Figs. 99 through 101,** when performing diagnostic procedures on these systems. Refer to "Diagnostic Aids" when referenced by diagnostic tests.

METRO

Refer to **Fig. 102,** when performing diagnostic procedures. Refer to "Diagnostic Aids" as previously outlined when referenced by diagnostic tests.

PARK AVENUE

2001

Refer to **Figs. 103 through 105,** when performing diagnostic procedures.

2002-05

Refer to **Figs. 106 through 108,** when performing diagnostic procedures.

PRIZM

Refer to **Figs. 109 through 112,** when performing diagnostic procedures. Refer to "Diagnostic Aids" as previously outlined when referenced by diagnostic tests.

STS

Refer to **Figs. 113 through 115,** for diagnostic procedures.

VIBE

Refer to **Figs. 116 through 121,** for diagnostic procedures.

XLR

Refer to **Figs. 122 through 124,** for diagnostic procedures.

COMPONENT REPLACEMENT

Cooling Fan Assembly

ALERO & GRAND AM

2001-02

1. Remove A/C line bracket retaining bolt, then position A/C line aside.
2. Remove air deflector shield.
3. Remove electrical harness from retainers, then disconnect electrical connector.
4. Remove fan upper retaining bolts.
5. Raise and support vehicle.
6. Remove lower closeout panel.
7. Remove fan lower retaining bolts, then the fan and shroud assembly from vehicle.

8. Disconnect fan electrical connector.
9. Remove fan from shroud.
10. Reverse procedure to install.

2003-05

1. Remove battery and battery tray.
2. Recover A/C refrigerant as outlined in "Air Conditioning" chapter.
3. Drain cooling system into suitable container.
4. Remove radiator inlet hose from radiator.
5. Remove surge tank/radiator outlet hose from surge tank.
6. Remove radiator vent hose from radiator.
7. Remove upper transaxle cooler line.
8. Disconnect refrigerant pressure sensor electrical connector.
9. Remove condenser inlet fitting from discharge hose. Discard sealing washer.
10. Disconnect cooling fan electrical connectors.
11. Remove surge tank/radiator outlet hose retaining bolt from intake manifold.
12. Raise and support vehicle.
13. Remove lower closeout panel.
14. Remove surge tank/radiator outlet hose from radiator.
15. Remove transaxle lower cooler line.
16. Disconnect evaporator hose from condenser. Discard sealing washer.
17. Remove lower radiator support mounting panel.
18. Remove radiator, fan and condenser from vehicle as an assembly.
19. Remove cooling fan shroud from radiator.
20. Reverse procedure to install.

AURORA

1. Remove headlamp fascia panel support bracket retainers, then the bracket, **Fig. 125.**
2. Remove radiator support brackets.
3. Remove air cleaner assembly.
4. Position Powertrain Control Module (PCM) aside.
5. Remove upper tie bar retaining bolts, then tie bar from vehicle.
6. Raise and support vehicle.
7. **On models equipped with 4.0L engine,** drain engine coolant into a suitable container, then remove radiator hose and position hose aside.
8. **On models equipped with 3.5L engine,** remove lower under body air deflector retainers, then the air deflector, **Fig. 126.**
9. **On all models,** disconnect cooling fan electrical connectors.
10. Remove wiring harness to fan shroud retaining clips, then position harness aside.
11. Disconnect transaxle cooler line bolt and clip from fan shroud.
12. Remove upper transaxle oil cooler line quick connect joint using cooler line removal tool No. J-41623–B, or equivalent.
13. Remove two fan shroud mounting bolts, then the cooling fan assembly, **Fig. 127.**
14. Remove fan blade retaining nut from

fan motor shaft, then fan blade from motor, **Fig. 128.**
15. Remove fan motor to shroud retaining bolts, then the fan motor, **Fig. 128.**
16. Reverse procedure to install, noting the following:
    a. **Torque** fan motor to shroud bolts and fan blade retaining nut to 53 inch lbs.
    b. **Bolt retaining condenser to radiator end tank is a special length and must be installed in same location or radiator end tank damage will occur.**
    c. **Torque** cooling fan/shroud mounting bolts to 53 inch lbs.
    d. **Torque** upper tie bar mounting bolts to 89 inch lbs.
    e. **Torque** headlamp panel support bolts to 80 inch lbs.
    f. Push transaxle cooler line quick connect fitting, together until a "click" is heard.

AVEO

1. Disconnect cooling fan electrical connector.
2. Remove cooling fan mounting bolts, then the cooling fan.
3. Reverse procedure to install.

BONNEVILLE

3.8L ENGINE

1. Remove headlamp/fascia panel support brackets and bolts.
2. Remove upper tie bar bolts, then the upper tie bar from vehicle.
3. Disconnect wiring harness electrical connector from motor and fan bracket.
4. Remove transaxle oil cooler pipe bracket bolt from fan shroud.
5. Remove two fan mounting bolts, then lift fan assembly off lower holding tabs and remove from vehicle.
6. Reverse procedure to install.

4.6L ENGINE

1. Remove headlamp/fascia support bracket mounting bolts, then the support bracket.
2. Remove radiator support bracket.
3. Remove air cleaner assembly.
4. Drain coolant into suitable container.
5. Remove engine oil cooler bracket from fan shroud.
6. Remove transaxle oil cooler bracket from fan shroud.
7. Remove upper transaxle oil cooler pipe from radiator.
8. Disconnect cooling fan motor wiring harness electrical connectors.
9. Remove radiator outlet hose from radiator.
10. Remove two cooling fan mounting bolts.
11. Remove lower transaxle oil cooler line from radiator.
12. Remove fan assembly from vehicle.
13. Reverse procedure to install.

CAMARO & FIREBIRD

1. **On models equipped with 5.7L engine,** disconnect Intake Air Temperature (IAT) and Mass Air Flow (MAF)

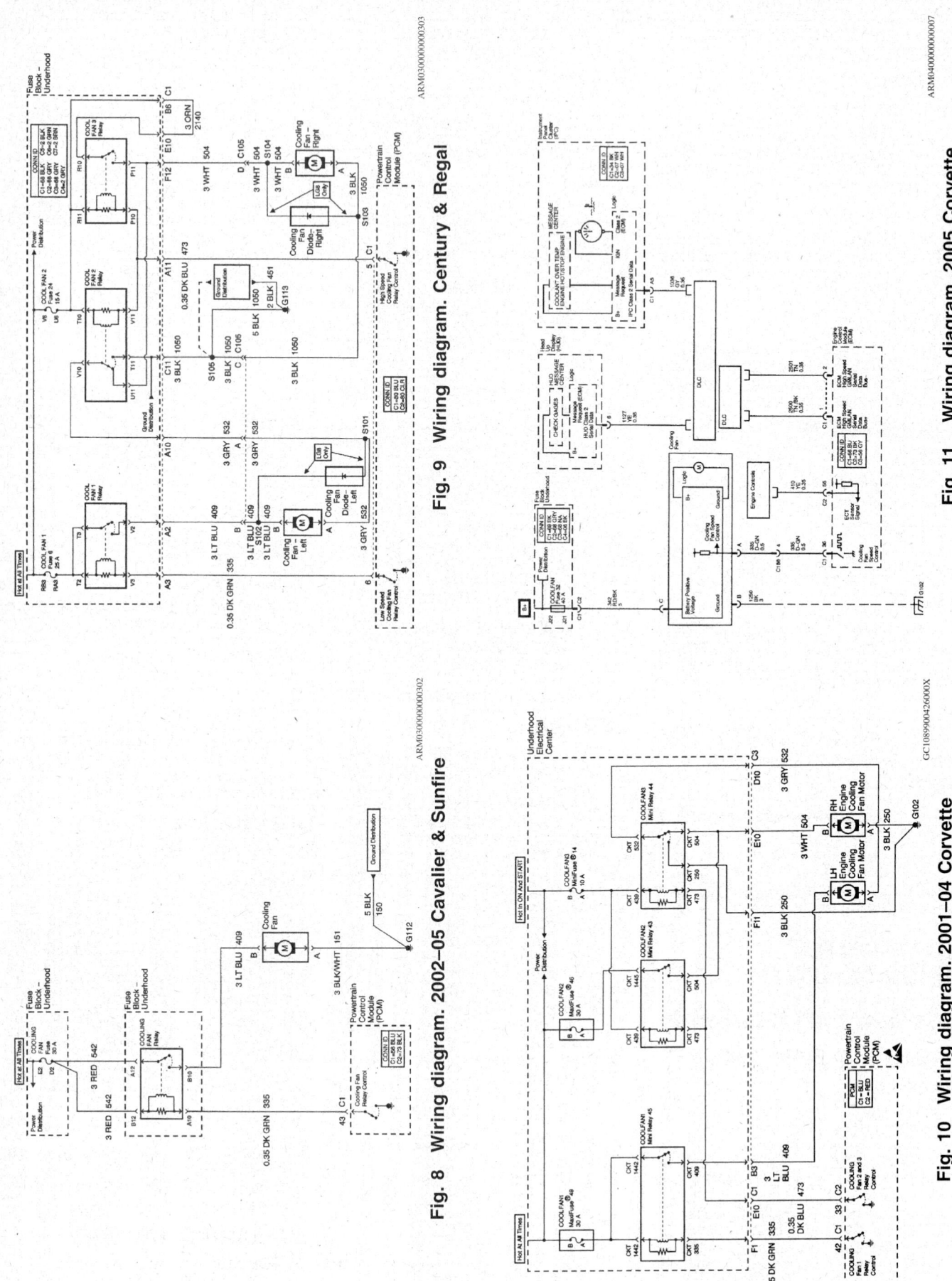

Fig. 9 Wiring diagram. Century & Regal

Fig. 11 Wiring diagram. 2005 Corvette

Fig. 8 Wiring diagram. 2002–05 Cavalier & Sunfire

Fig. 10 Wiring diagram. 2001–04 Corvette

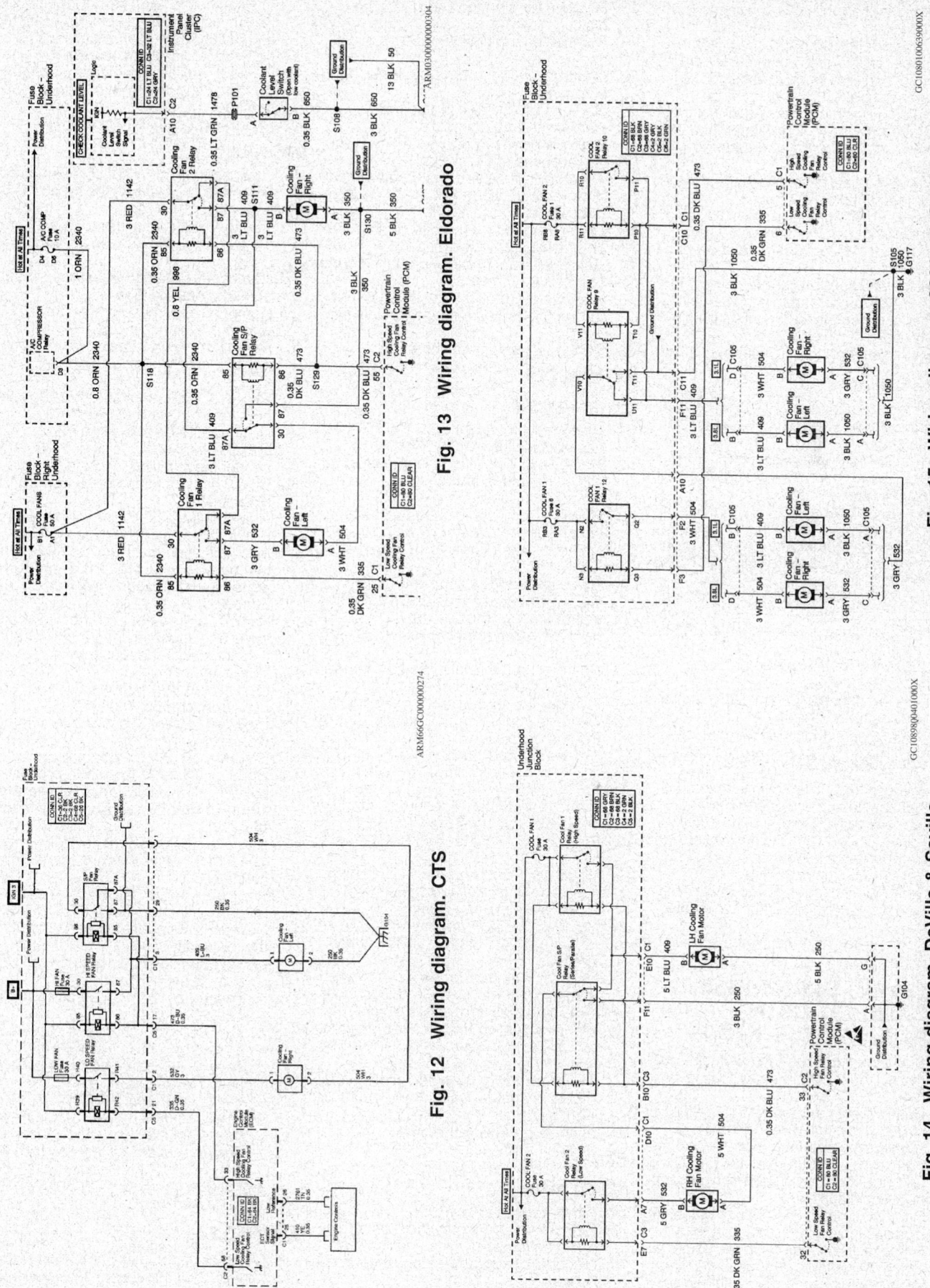

Fig. 13 Wiring diagram. Eldorado

Fig. 12 Wiring diagram. CTS

Fig. 15 Wiring diagram. 2001–03 Grand Prix

Fig. 14 Wiring diagram. DeVille & Seville

sensors, then remove air cleaner outlet duct.
2. **On models equipped with 3.8L engines,** disconnect intake Air Temperature (IAT) sensor connector and remove intake air duct resonator.
3. **On all models,** release retaining strap latches, then lift air cleaner housing cover off and remove air cleaner element.
4. Remove radiator support bolts and the radiator support.
5. Remove wiring harness from rosebud clips located on fan shroud.
6. Disconnect cooling fan electrical connectors.
7. Raise and support vehicle.
8. Remove fan shroud.
9. Remove cooling fan brackets from fan shroud
10. Reverse procedure to install.

CATERA

1. Remove secondary air cutoff bracket bolts, then bracket from cooling fan housing.
2. Remove resonance chamber.
3. Release upper radiator covers self locking tabs.
4. Remove upper radiator covers attaching screws, then covers.
5. Disconnect primary fan motor and primary fan cooling switch electrical connectors.
6. Remove auxiliary water pump from primary fan housing.
7. Remove upper transmission oil cooler fittings.
8. Loosen lower transmission cooler fittings.
9. Remove fan housing bolts, then fan housing from vehicle.
10. Reverse procedure to install.

CAVALIER & SUNFIRE

1. Remove hood close out filler retainers, then the hood close out filler panel.
2. Remove upper radiator mount bolts.
3. Remove hood latch support bolts, then the hood latch support.
4. Raise and support vehicle.
5. Remove cooling fan mounting bolt, then disconnect fan electrical connector.
6. Remove cooling fan assembly.
7. Reverse procedure to install.

CENTURY, GRAND PRIX, IMPALA, INTRIGUE, MONTE CARLO & REGAL

1. Disconnect cooling fan electrical connector, then partially drain cooling system.
2. Remove engine mount strut to engine strut bracket attaching bolt and nut.
3. Remove engine mount strut to upper radiator support bracket attaching bolt and nut, then the engine mount strut from vehicle.
4. Remove front fender upper diagonal brace to inner fender attaching bolt.
5. Remove front fender upper diagonal brace to radiator support bolts, then the diagonal brace from engine compartment.

6. Remove air cleaner and duct assembly.
7. Remove radiator inlet hose from radiator.
8. Remove PCM harness from fan shroud clip.
9. Remove cooling fan shroud bolts.
10. Raise and support vehicle.
11. Remove push pin retainer from lower lefthand side of fan shroud.
12. Remove transmission oil cooler lines from retainer clip at bottom of cooling fan shroud.
13. Lower vehicle and remove cooling fan shroud clip from top of radiator.
14. Remove fan shroud upper support brackets.
15. Remove fan motor heat shields, then the cooling fan shroud and fan assembly.
16. Reverse procedure to install.

CORVETTE

2001-2004

1. Disconnect Mass Air Flow (MAF) sensor electrical connector.
2. Remove engine wiring harness from clip on radiator support.
3. Remove air cleaner intake duct.
4. Remove radiator support attaching bolts, then the radiator support.
5. Remove radiator inlet hose from radiator.
6. Raise and support vehicle.
7. Disconnect cooling fan electrical connectors, then remove forward lamp harness from retaining clips on fan shroud.
8. Remove radiator outlet hose from the radiator, then lower vehicle.
9. Remove fan shroud and fan assembly.
10. Remove cooling fan blade nut, then the cooling fan.
11. Reverse procedure to install.

2005

1. Remove radiator support mounting bolts, then the support.
2. Disconnect engine wiring harness from cooling fan shroud.
3. Disconnect surge tank outlet hose from retaining clips and position aside.
4. Raise and support vehicle.
5. Remove stabilizer from vehicle.
6. Disconnect cooling fan electrical connectors.
7. **On vehicles equipped with transmission fluid cooler,** disconnect lower oil cooler line from radiator.
8. **On vehicles equipped with engine oil cooler,** disconnect upper and lower oil cooler pipes.
9. **On all models,** remove cooling fan shroud mounting bolts, then the cooling fan.
10. Reverse procedure to install.

CTS

AUXILIARY

1. Raise and support vehicle.
2. Remove air deflector push-in retainers, then the air deflector, **Fig. 129.**
3. Disconnect auxiliary fan electrical connector.
4. Place a suitable container under trans-

mission fluid cooler lines, then remove transmission fluid cooler lines using fitting disconnect tool No. J44827, or equivalent, position cooler lines aside.
5. Remove auxiliary cooling fan assembly mounting bolts, then the fan assembly.
6. Reverse procedure to install.

PRIMARY

1. Drain coolant into a suitable container.
2. Disconnect radiator to surge tank hose.
3. Remove radiator to fan shroud, then the fan shroud to air plenum attaching bolts.
4. Remove remaining fan shroud to radiator attaching bolts.
5. Remove upper radiator hose from radiator.
6. Remove coolant bypass valve retaining bolt, then position bypass valve aside.
7. Remove coolant bypass valve solenoid from fan shroud, **Fig. 130.**
8. Disconnect Mass Air Flow (MAF) sensor and Intake Air Temperature (IAT) sensor electrical connectors.
9. Disconnect air intake hose from MAF/IAT sensors.
10. Remove MAF/IAT sensor retaining screws from air cleaner assembly, then MAF/IAT sensors. **Handle MAF sensor carefully to prevent damage to sensor and screen located on air inlet end.**
11. Remove air cleaner assembly to shock tower and upper tie bar mounting bolts, then the air cleaner assembly.
12. Remove electrical connector from fan motor, then the harness clip and harness from shroud.
13. Remove coolant bypass hose from radiator.
14. Remove fan shroud attaching bolts.
15. Carefully lift fan and shroud assembly upward. **Do not damage radiator when removing fan shroud assembly.**
16. Remove fan blade retaining nut from fan motor, then the fan blade from motor.
17. Remove cooling fan motor retaining bolts, then the fan motor, **Fig. 131.**
18. Reverse procedure to install, noting the following:
    a. **Torque** cooling fan motor to shroud bolts to 44 inch lbs.
    b. **Torque** cooling fan blade to motor nut to 62 inch lbs.
    c. **Torque** fan shroud to plenum mounting bolts to 58 inch lbs.
    d. **Torque** A/C retaining clip mounting bolt to 9 inch lbs.
    e. Install MAF/IAT sensors using a small amount of a suitable soap based solution to aid in installation.
    f. **Torque** sensor screws to 20 inch lbs.
    g. **Torque** air cleaner mounting bolts to 80 inch lbs.

DEVILLE

1. Remove upper filler panel push-in retainers, then the upper filler panel from engine compartment.

2. Raise and support vehicle.
3. Remove front air deflector push-in retainers, then the front air deflector from engine compartment.
4. Lower vehicle.
5. Remove hood latch support fasteners, then place a suitable fender cover on front bumper fascia and rest hood latch support on front bumper.
6. Pull upper radiator hose away from upper tie bar and temporarily position hose away from tie bar.
7. Remove upper radiator hose support to upper tie bar fastener, then the upper radiator hose support from upper tie bar.
8. Remove upper radiator brackets to upper tie bar fasteners, then the brackets from upper tie bar.
9. Hold windshield solvent filler tube to side and remove righthand upper tie bar fasteners.
10. Remove lefthand upper tie bar fasteners, then the upper tie bar from vehicle.
11. Remove engine oil cooler pipe retaining clip and bolt from fan shroud.
12. Raise and support vehicle.
13. Drain cooling system.
14. Disconnect fan electrical connectors.
15. Remove fan to lower cradle attaching screws.
16. Lower vehicle.
17. Disconnect radiator hose.
18. Disconnect upper engine oil cooler pipe from radiator.
19. Remove upper transaxle oil cooler pipe retaining bolt from fan shroud.
20. Slide plastic cap off upper transaxle oil cooler pipe quick connect fitting, then disconnect upper transaxle oil cooler pipe from radiator.
21. Disconnect wiring harness electrical connectors from cooling fan motors.
22. Remove clips attaching harness to fan shroud, then disconnect A/C discharge hose retainers.
23. Remove cooling fan mounting bolts.
24. Position cooling fan assembly towards lefthand side of vehicle, then pull upward on righthand side of fan assembly.
25. Position fan assembly towards righthand side of vehicle.
26. Pull upward on fan assembly and remove from vehicle.
27. Reverse procedure to install.

ELDORADO

1. Open hood, then rotate filler panel to front fender flange fasteners a quarter of a turn.
2. Lift and remove filler panel from front fender flange.
3. Remove radiator support sight shield.
4. Remove primary hood latch retaining bolts, then disconnect hood latch release cable from latch.
5. Remove primary hood latch from radiator center support.
6. Disconnect ambient temperature sensor electrical connector.
7. Loosen power steering cooler pipe bolt at center support.
8. Remove radiator center support attaching bolts and nuts, then the center

support from vehicle.
9. Remove left and right diagonal brace to radiator support attaching bolts, then the braces from vehicle.
10. Remove air cleaner.
11. Remove inflatable restraint front end discriminating sensor.
12. Remove engine mount strut to core support bolt.
13. Disconnect upper transmission line from radiator.
14. Remove cooling fan attaching bolts, then the radiator upper support.
15. Disconnect cooling fan electrical connectors and remove cooling fans.
16. Reverse procedure to install.

GTO

1. Release locking lever on MAF sensor, then disconnect MAF electrical connector.
2. Release locking lever on IAT sensor, then disconnect IAT electrical connector.
3. Remove intake duct.
4. Drain cooling system into suitable container.
5. Disconnect vapor hose from retaining clips on fan shroud and radiator, then position aside.
6. Disconnect vapor hose retaining clip to surge tank at radiator and position aside.
7. Remove upper shroud retainers, then remove shroud by lifting up on righthand side then release the locating tab on the lefthand side.
8. Remove radiator outlet hose.
9. Disconnect lefthand and righthand fan motor electrical connectors.
10. Depress fan shroud locking tab, then lift assembly upwards.
11. Disconnect intermediate fan motor electrical connector.
12. Reverse procedure to install.

G6

1. Drain coolant into suitable container.
2. Remove lefthand and righthand headlamp assemblies.
3. Remove upper transmission oil cooler pipe from radiator.
4. Secure condenser to upper tie bar.
5. Remove upper radiator support bracket mounting bolts, then the support bracket.
6. Raise and support vehicle.
7. Remove lower radiator air deflector.
8. Remove front righthand inner fender shield.
9. Remove righthand and lefthand radiator air deflectors.
10. Remove radiator outlet hose from radiator.
11. Remove fan wire harness retainers.
12. Remove lower radiator support bracket mounting bolts, then the support bracket.
13. Place suitable drain pan under transmission oil cooler pipes, then remove cooler pipes from transmission.
14. Remove transmission oil cooler pipe retaining clip from fan shroud.
15. Remove lower transmission oil cooler pipe from radiator.

16. Remove transmission oil cooler pipes.
17. Remove cooling fan assembly.
18. Reverse procedure to install.

LACROSSE

3.6L ENGINE

1. Remove cooling fan attaching nut, then the cooling fan.
2. Remove cooling fan motor rivets.
3. Remove cooling fan motor assembly.
4. Reverse procedure to install.

3.8L ENGINE

1. Disconnect battery ground cable and isolate as required.
2. Remove lefthand and righthand engine mounts as outlined in "3.8L Engine" section of "Century, Grand Prix, Impala, Intrigue, LaCrosse, Lumina, Monte Carlo & Regal" chapter.
3. Remove air cleaner assembly.
4. Remove PCM harness retainer from shroud.
5. Remove transmission oil cooler lines from lower fan shroud clip and reposition coil outside cooler lines.
6. Remove fan shroud clip from condenser tubes.
7. Remove radiator upper bracket bolts and brackets.
8. Remove cooling fan shroud bolts.
9. Remove bolt that connects fan shroud to the condenser hold down bracket.
10. Disconnect engine cooling fan motors electrical connectors.
11. Remove cooling fan electrical harness from fan shroud clips.
12. Remove cooling fan shroud.
13. Remove engine cooling fan blade nut, then the blade.
14. Remove engine cooling fan motor bolts, then the fan motor assembly.
15. Reverse procedure to install.

LESABRE & PARK AVENUE

1. Drain cooling system.
2. Remove air cleaner assembly.
3. Remove lefthand and righthand headlamp assembly to bracket retaining screws, then pull headlamp assemblies forward to disengage rear retaining pins.
4. Remove headlamp assemblies from vehicle and disconnect electrical connectors.
5. Remove upper radiator seal.
6. Remove battery ground to transmission oil cooler line clip and position cable aside.
7. Remove oil fill cap from sight shield. then the engine oil dipstick.
8. Disconnect upper transmission oil cooler line.
9. Disconnect upper radiator hose from radiator.
10. Disconnect cooling fan motor wiring harness connectors.
11. Remove cooling fan to radiator mounting bolts.
12. Remove coolant overflow hose from fan assembly.
13. Release cooling fan lower mounting tabs, then raise lefthand side of fans and remove fans from vehicle.

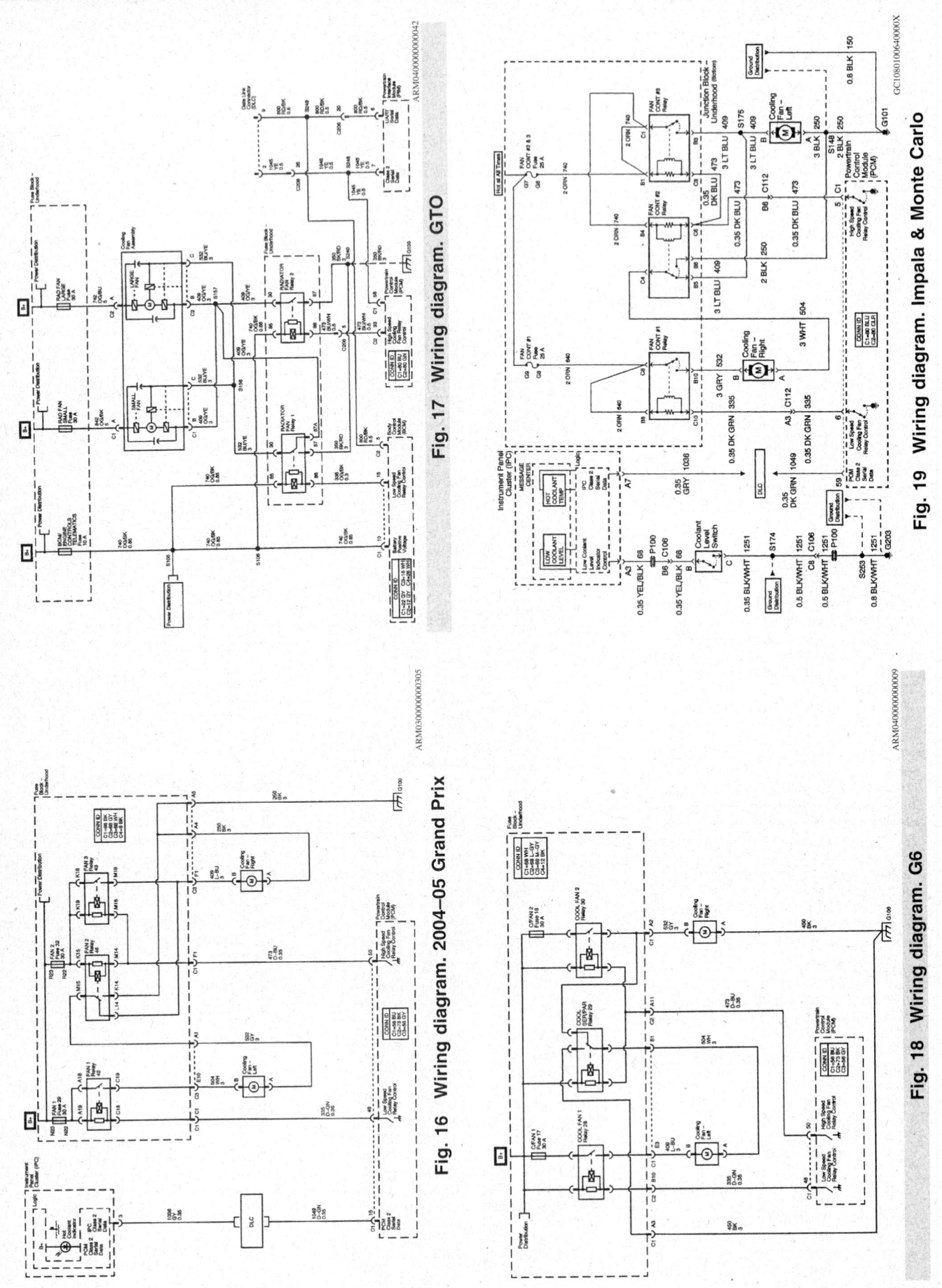

Fig. 17   Wiring diagram. GTO

Fig. 19   Wiring diagram. Impala & Monte Carlo

Fig. 16   Wiring diagram. 2004–05 Grand Prix

Fig. 18   Wiring diagram. G6

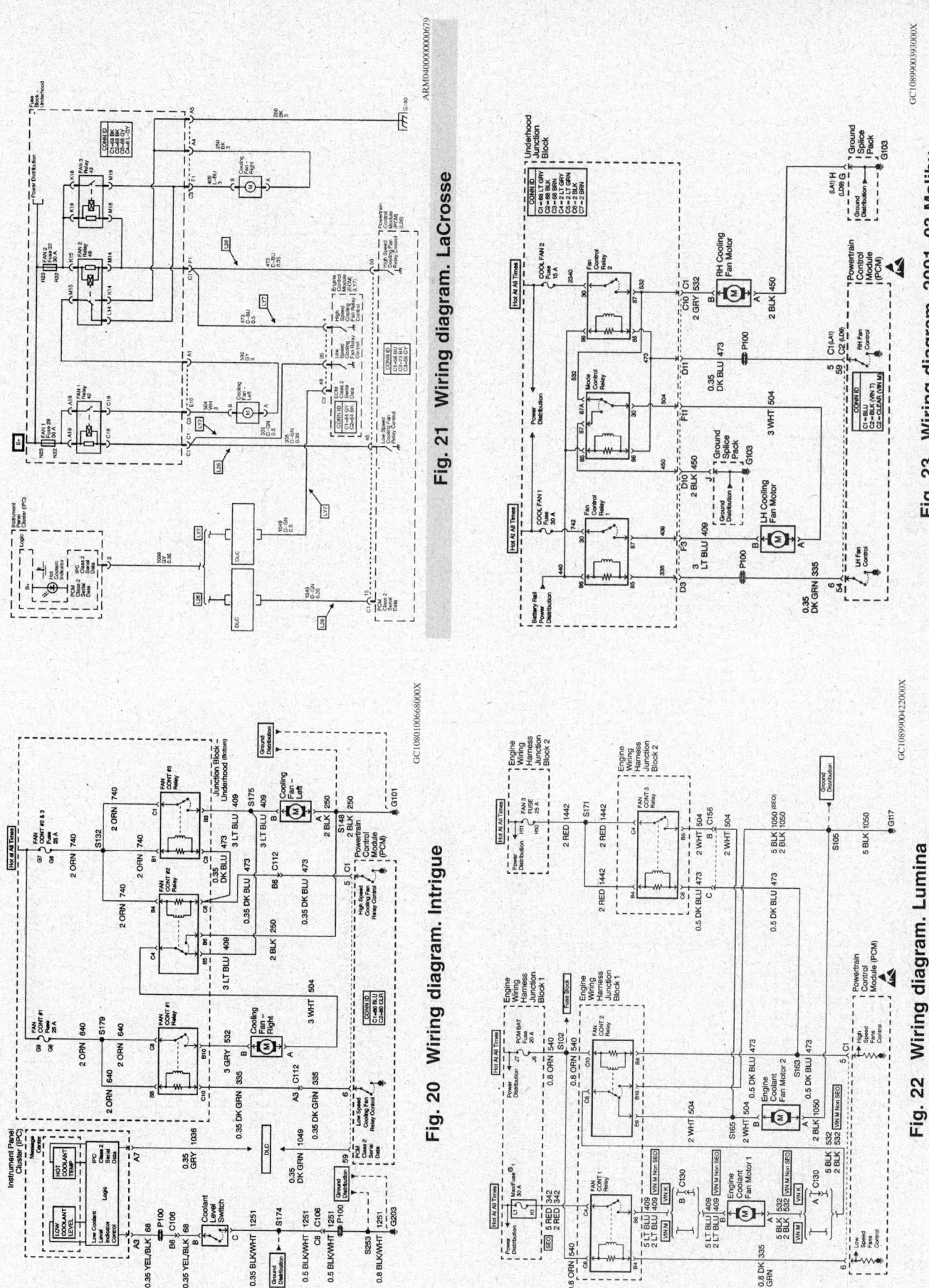

Fig. 20 Wiring diagram. Intrigue

Fig. 21 Wiring diagram. LaCrosse

Fig. 22 Wiring diagram. Lumina

Fig. 23 Wiring diagram. 2001–03 Malibu

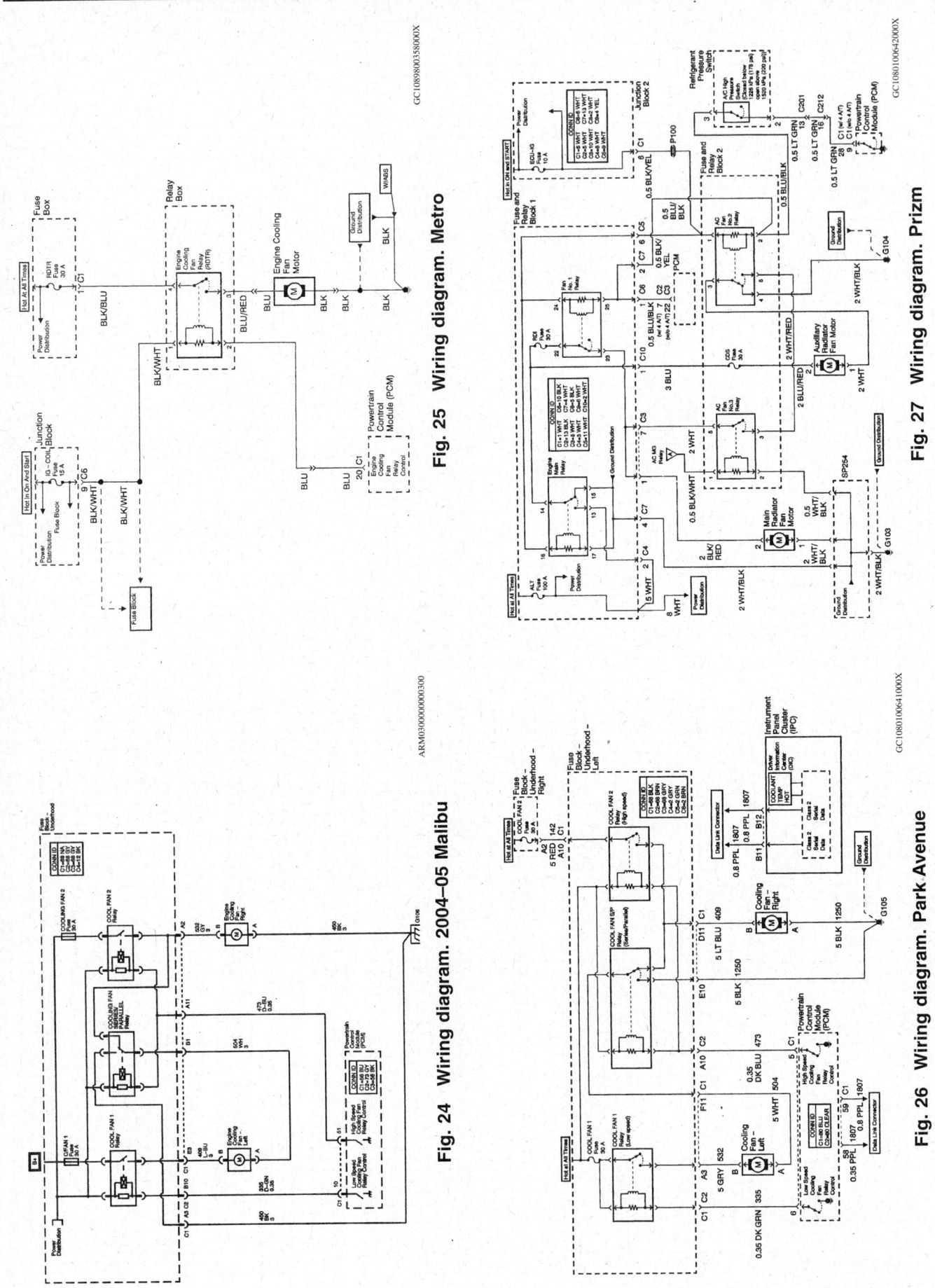

Fig. 25 Wiring diagram. Metro

Fig. 27 Wiring diagram. Prizm

Fig. 24 Wiring diagram. 2004–05 Malibu

Fig. 26 Wiring diagram. Park Avenue

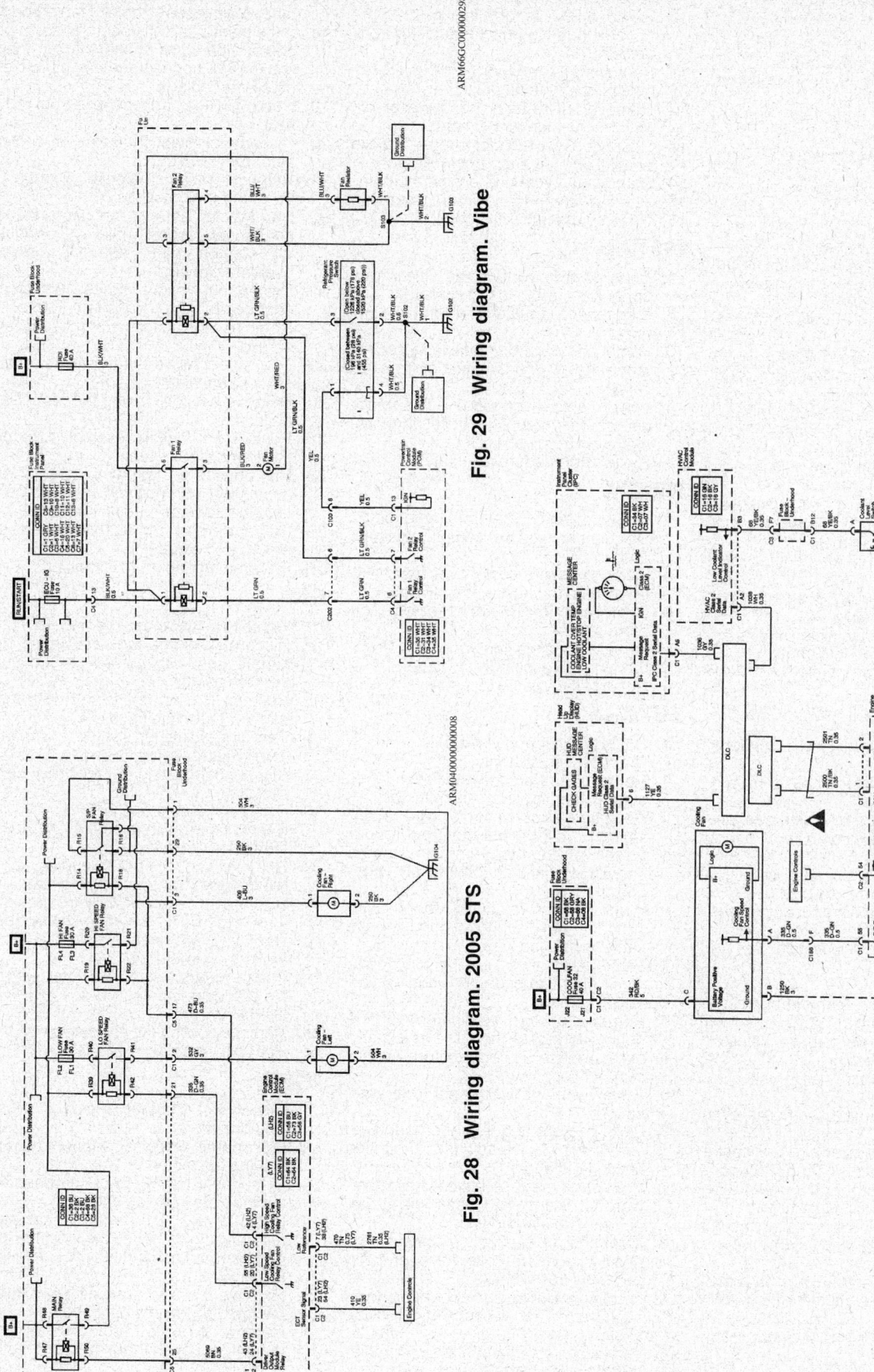

Fig. 29 Wiring diagram. Vibe

Fig. 28 Wiring diagram. 2005 STS

Fig. 30 Wiring diagram. XLR

14. Reverse procedure to install.

LUMINA

1. Remove air cleaner assembly.
2. Disconnect wiring harness from fan motors and fan frames.
3. Remove fan mounting bolts and fan assembly.
4. Reverse procedure to install

MALIBU

2001-03

1. Remove and battery tray.
2. Recover A/C system refrigerant as outlined in "Air Conditioning" chapter.
3. Drain cooling system.
4. Remove radiator inlet hose from radiator.
5. Remove surge tank radiator outlet hose from surge tank, then the radiator vent hose from radiator.
6. Remove upper transaxle cooler line.
7. Disconnect refrigerant pressure sensor electrical connector.
8. Remove condenser inlet fitting from discharge hose.
9. Remove and discard sealing washer. Cap open A/C discharge hose to prevent system contamination.
10. Disconnect cooling fan electrical connectors.
11. Remove surge tank outlet hose bolt from intake manifold.
12. Raise and support vehicle.
13. Remove lower closeout panel.
14. Remove surge tank outlet hose from radiator.
15. Remove lower transaxle cooler line from radiator.
16. Remove evaporator hose to condenser attaching bolt.
17. Remove evaporator hose from condenser.
18. Remove and discard sealing washer.
19. Remove lower radiator support mounting panel.
20. Remove radiator, fan and condenser as an assembly from vehicle.
21. Remove fan attaching nuts from fans, then the fans and fan motors.
22. Reverse procedure to install.

2004-05

1. Remove right and lefthand headlamp assembly mounting bolts, then lift headlamp assembly to unseat tabs on bottom edge of fender.
2. Disconnect headlamp assembly electrical connectors.
3. Remove headlamp assemblies from vehicle.
4. Unclip upper transmission oil cooler pipe from fan shroud. **Do not disconnect transmission oil cooler pipe from transmission or radiator.**
5. Loop a rope around each of upper two tabs on condenser and tie rope around upper tie bar.
6. Remove upper radiator support bracket bolts, then the brackets from vehicle.
7. Pry upward on fan shroud tabs at radiator clips.
8. Raise and support vehicle.
9. Remove lower radiator air deflector retainers, then the air deflector.
10. Remove front fender liner push-in retainers, then the front fender liner from vehicle.
11. Remove right radiator air deflector retainers, then the air deflector.
12. Remove left radiator air deflector retainers, then the air deflector.
13. Remove lower radiator support bracket bolts and the support brackets.
14. Remove fan wire harness connectors.
15. Remove fan and fan shroud assembly.
16. Reverse procedure to install.

METRO

1. Drain cooling system and disconnect upper radiator hose from radiator.
2. Disconnect fan motor electrical connector.
3. Raise and support vehicle, then remove one lower mounting bolt from fan shroud.
4. Lower vehicle and remove two upper cooling fan mounting bolts, then remove fan from vehicle.
5. Reverse procedure to install.

PRIZM

1. Drain engine coolant from radiator.
2. Disconnect oxygen sensor electrical connector.
3. Remove engine coolant recovery reservoir cap and hoses, then the tank.
4. Remove upper radiator hose from radiator.
5. Remove cooling fan mounting bolts, then the fan assembly.
6. Reverse procedure to install.

SEVILLE

1. Raise and support vehicle.
2. Drain cooling system.
3. Remove front air deflector push-in retainers, then the front air deflector.
4. Remove engine oil cooler pipe retaining bolt and retainer from fan shroud.
5. Lower vehicle, then remove fasteners securing hood latch to hood latch support.
6. Remove hood latch from hood latch support, then disconnect hood release cable from hood latch.
7. Disconnect lower engine oil cooler pipe from radiator and position aside.
8. Lower vehicle.
9. Remove push-in retainers securing upper filler panel, then disconnect ambient outside air temperature sensor electrical connector.
10. Remove upper filler panel from vehicle.
11. Remove right and lefthand headlamp assembly to headlamp mounting bracket fasteners.
12. Pull headlamp assemblies straight forward to disengage locator pin at outboard edge of headlamp.
13. Disconnect headlamp electrical connectors, then remove headlamp assemblies from vehicle.
14. Disconnect lower and upper engine oil cooler pipe from radiator and position aside.
15. Remove inlet radiator hose from radiator and place aside over engine.
16. Remove air cleaner assembly.

17. Remove upper transaxle oil cooler pipe retaining bolt from the fan shroud.
18. Slide plastic cap off upper transaxle oil cooler pipe quick connect fitting, then disconnect upper transaxle oil cooler pipe from radiator.
19. Remove outlet radiator hose from radiator.
20. Disconnect lower transaxle oil cooler pipe from radiator.
21. Remove radiator bracket mounting bolts and the brackets.
22. Remove fan shroud, then lift radiator/condenser assembly from lower radiator support pads and tilt top of assembly forward.
23. Disconnect wiring harness electrical connectors from cooling fan motors.
24. Remove clips attaching harness to fan shroud.
25. Disconnect A/C discharge hose to fan shroud retaining clip.
26. Remove electric cooling fan mounting bolts.
27. Position cooling fan assembly towards righthand side of vehicle.
28. Pull upward on righthand side of fan assembly, then position fan assembly towards lefthand side of vehicle.
29. Pull upward on fan assembly and remove from vehicle.
30. Reverse procedure to install.

STS

1. Remove air cleaner assembly.
2. Disconnect surge tank inlet hose retainers from cooling fan shroud and position aside.
3. Remove cooling fan shroud to upper radiator mounting bolts.
4. Remove cooling fan shroud to lefthand lower radiator mounting bolts.
5. Disconnect cooling fan electrical connectors.
6. Raise and support vehicle.
7. Remove air deflector mounting bolts, then the air deflector.
8. Remove cooling fan shroud to righthand lower radiator mounting bolts.
9. Disconnect engine wiring harness from engine frame and position aside.
10. Remove power steering line to cooling fan shroud retainers.
11. Remove transmission oil cooler lines to fan shroud retainers.
12. Lower vehicle.
13. Remove cooling fan assembly.
14. Reverse procedure to install.

VIBE

1. Disconnect coolant reservoir hose from radiator.
2. Disconnect electrical connector from cooling fan motor.
3. Disconnect two electrical harness retaining clips from fan shroud.
4. Remove two fan shroud to radiator mounting bolts, then the cooling fan and shroud assembly from vehicle, **Fig. 132.**
5. Remove fan blade retaining nut, then the fan blade from motor shaft.
6. Remove two fan motor to shroud mounting bolts, then the fan motor from shroud.
7. Reverse procedure to install.

Step	Action	Yes	No
1	Install a scan tool. Does the scan tool power up?	Go to Step 2	Diagnose Data Link Communications
2	1. Turn ON the ignition, with the engine OFF. 2. Attempt to establish communication with the following control modules: • Instrument Cluster • Powertrain Control Module. Does the scan tool communicate with the control modules?	Go to Step 3	Diagnose Data Link Communications
3	Select the powertrain control module display DTCs function on the scan tool. Does the scan tool display any DTCs?	Go to Step 4	Diagnose Engine Cooling
4	Does the scan tool display any DTCs which begin with a "U"?	Diagnose Data Link Communications	Diagnose Trouble Code (DTC)

GC1080100643000X

Fig. 31 Diagnostic system check. Alero, Grand Am & Malibu

Step	Action	Yes	No
	DEFINITION: One or both engine cooling fan motors run continuously in high or low speed modes.		
1	Did you perform the Engine Cooling Diagnostic System Check?	Go to Step 2	Go To Diagnostic System Check -
2	Turn ON the ignition, with the engine OFF. Are one or both cooling fans running all the time?	Go to Step 3	Test for Intermittent and Poor Connections
3	Are both cooling fans running continuously?	Go to Step 5	Go to Step 4
4	Remove the cooling fan S/P relay. Did the eng cool RH fan turn OFF?	Go to Step 6	Go to Step 7
5	Repair the short in the eng cool LH fan supply voltage circuit. Did you complete the repair?	Go to Step 8	—
6	Repair the short in the eng cool LH fan low circuit. Did you complete the repair?	Go to Step 8	—
7	Repair the short in the eng cool RH fan supply voltage circuit. Did you complete the repair?	Go to Step 8	—
8	Operate the system in order to verify the repair. Did you correct the condition?	System OK	Go to Step 2

GC1080100644000X

Fig. 32 Cooling fan always on. Alero, Grand Am & Malibu

Step	Action	Yes	No
	DEFINITION: One or both engine cooling fan motors do not operate properly in high or low speed modes.		
1	Did you perform the Engine Cooling Diagnostic System Check?	Go to Step 2	Go to Diagnostic System Check -
2	1. Install a scan tool. 2. Turn ON the ignition, with the engine OFF. 3. With a scan tool, command the Fans Low Speed ON and OFF. Do the low speed engine cooling fans turn ON and OFF with each command?	Go to Step 3	Go to Step 4
3	Important: Before the PCM changes the speed of the cooling fans, a 3-second delay will occur. With a scan tool, command the Fans High Speed ON and OFF. Do the high speed engine cooling fans turn ON and OFF with each command?	Test Intermittent and Poor Connections	Go to Step 13
4	1. Turn the ignition OFF. 2. Disconnect the cooling fan 1 relay. 3. Turn the ignition ON, with the engine OFF. 4. Probe the battery positive voltage circuit of the cooling fan 1 relay switch side with a test lamp connected to a good ground. Does the test lamp illuminate?	Go to Step 5	Go to Step 20
5	Connect a 20 A fused jumper between the battery positive voltage circuit of the cooling fan 1 relay and the cooling fan motor supply voltage circuit of the cooling fan 1 relay. Do both cooling fans operate in low speed?	Go to Step 15	Go to Step 6
6	1. Leave the fused jumper wire in place of the cooling fan 1 relay. 2. Remove the cooling fan S/P relay. 3. Connect a 20 A fused jumper between the eng cool LH fan low circuit of the cooling fan S/P relay and the eng cool RH fan supply voltage circuit of the cooling fan S/P relay. Do both cooling fans operate in low speed?	Go to Step 16	Go to Step 7
7	1. Leave the fused jumper wire in place of the cooling fan 1 relay. 2. Connect a 20 A fused jumper between the battery positive voltage circuit of the cooling fan S/P relay and the cooling fan motor supply voltage circuit of the cooling fan S/P relay. Does the eng cool RH fan operate in high speed?	Go to Step 11	Go to Step 8
8	1. Leave the fused jumper wire in place of the cooling fan 1 relay. 2. Install the cooling fan S/P relay. 3. Disconnect the eng cool RH fan electrical connector. Does the eng cool LH fan operate in high speed?	Go to Step 24	Go to Step 9
9	1. Leave the fused jumper wire in place of the cooling fan 1 relay. 2. Connect a 20 Amp fused jumper wire from the cooling fan motor supply voltage circuit of the eng cool RH fan electrical connector to the cooling fan motor ground circuit of the eng cool RH fan electrical connector. Does the eng cool LH fan operate in high speed?	Go to Step 18	Go to Step 10

GC1080100645010X

Fig. 33 Cooling fan inoperative (Part 1 of 3). Alero, Grand Am & Malibu

XLR

1. Remove air cleaner assembly.
2. Disconnect MAF sensor wire from radiator support retainer clip.
3. Disconnect surge tank inlet hose from radiator support tabs.
4. Remove radiator support bolts, then the radiator support.
5. Disconnect engine wiring harness from cooling fan shroud.
6. Disconnect surge tank outlet hose from retaining clips on cooling fan shroud.
7. Raise and support vehicle.
8. Remove tire and wheel assemblies.
9. Remove stabilizer shaft link nuts from stabilizer shaft.
10. Remove stabilizer shaft insulator clamps from front crossmember, then the stabilizer shaft from vehicle.
11. Disconnect cooling fan electrical connector.
12. Disconnect lower transmission oil cooler line from radiator.
13. Lift up on cooling fan and shroud to disengage retaining tabs from radiator.
14. Remove cooling fan and shroud.
15. Reverse procedure to install.

Step	Action	Yes	No
10	1. Leave the fused jumper wire in place of the cooling fan 1 relay. 2. Connect a 20 Amp fused jumper wire from the cooling fan motor supply voltage circuit of the eng cool RH fan electrical connector to a good ground. Does the eng cool LH fan operate in high speed?	Go to Step 23	Go to Step 24
11	1. Leave the fused jumper wire in place of the cooling fan 1 relay. 2. Install the cooling fan S/P relay. 3. Disconnect the eng cool LH fan electrical connector. 4. Connect a 20 Amp fused jumper wire from battery positive voltage circuit of the eng cool LH fan electrical connector to the cooling fan motor ground circuit of the eng cool LH fan electrical connector. Does the eng cool RH fan operate in high speed?	Go to Step 19	Go to Step 12
12	1. Leave the fused jumper wire in place of the cooling fan 1 relay. 2. Connect a 20 Amp fused jumper wire from battery positive voltage to the eng cool LH fan low circuit of the of the eng cool LH fan electrical connector. Does the eng cool RH fan operate in high speed?	Go to Step 21	Go to Step 25
13	Is the eng cool RH fan operating properly in high speed?	Go to Step 14	Go to Step 17
14	1. Remove the cooling fan S/P relay. 2. Connect a 20 A fused jumper between the eng cool LH fan low circuit of the cooling fan S/P relay and the ground circuit of the cooling fan S/P relay. Does the eng cool LH fan operate properly in high speed?	Go to Step 16	Go to Step 22
15	Inspect for poor connections at the cooling fan 1 relay. Did you find and correct the condition?	Go to Step 31	Go to Step 26
16	Inspect for poor connections at the cooling fan S/P relay. Did you find and correct the condition?	Go to Step 31	Go to Step 27
17	Inspect for poor connections at the cooling fan 2 relay. Did you find and correct the condition?	Go to Step 31	Go to Step 28
18	Inspect for poor connections at the harness connector of the eng cool RH fan. Did you find and correct the condition?	Go to Step 31	Go to Step 29
19	Inspect for poor connections at the harness connector of the eng cool LH fan. Did you find and correct the condition?	Go to Step 31	Go to Step 30
20	Repair the battery positive voltage circuit of the cooling fan 1 relay switch side. Did you complete the repair?	Go to Step 31	—
21	Repair the eng cool LH fan supply voltage circuit. Did you complete the repair?	Go to Step 31	—
22	Repair the eng cool LH fan ground circuit. Did you complete the repair?	Go to Step 31	—

GC1080100645020X

Fig. 33 Cooling fan inoperative (Part 2 of 3). Alero, Grand Am & Malibu

Step	Action	Yes	No
23	Repair the eng cool RH fan ground circuit. Did you complete the repair?	Go to *Step 31*	—
24	Repair the eng cool RH fan supply voltage circuit. Did you complete the repair?	Go to *Step 31*	—
25	Repair the eng cool LH fan low circuit. Did you complete the repair?	Go to *Step 31*	—
26	Replace the cooling fan 1 relay. Did you complete the repair?	Go to *Step 31*	—
27	Replace the cooling fan S/P relay. Did you complete the repair?	Go to *Step 31*	—
28	Replace the cooling fan 2 relay. Did you complete the repair?	Go to *Step 31*	—
29	Replace the eng cool RH fan. Did you complete the repair?	Go to *Step 31*	—
30	Replace the eng cool LH fan. Did you complete the repair?	Go to *Step 31*	—
31	Operate the system in order to verify the repair. Did you correct the condition?	System OK	Go to *Step 2*

GC1080100645030X

Fig. 33 Cooling fan inoperative (Part 3 of 3). Alero, Grand Am & Malibu

Step	Action	Yes	No
	DEFINITION: One or both engine cooling fan motors do not operate properly in high or low speed modes. SCHEMATIC REFERENCE: <u>Cooling Fan Motors and Relays</u>		
1	Has the Engine Cooling Diagnostic System Check been performed?	Go to Step 2	Go to A Diagnostic System Check - Engine Cooling
2	1. Install a scan tool. 2. Turn ON the ignition, with the engine OFF. 3. With a scan tool, command the Low Speed Fan Relay ON and OFF. Do the low speed engine cooling fans turn ON and OFF with each command?	Go to Step 3	Go to Step 4
3	Important: The cooling fans will remain in low speed operation for 3 seconds before the PCM grounds the high speed fan relay control to turn on the high speed fans. With a scan tool, command the S/P High Speed Fan Relay ON and OFF. Do the high speed engine cooling fans turn ON and OFF with each command?	Go to Testing for Intermittent and Poor Connections	Go to Step 11
4	1. Remove the Cool Fan 2 relay. 2. Connect a 20 A fused jumper between the battery positive voltage circuit of the Cool Fan 2 relay and the cooling fan motor supply voltage circuit of the Cool Fan 2 relay. Do both cooling fans operate in low speed?	Go to Step 13	Go to Step 5
5	1. Leave the fused jumper wire in place of the Cool Fan 2 relay. 2. Remove the Cool Fan S/P relay 3. Connect a 20 A fused jumper between the right cooling fan low circuit of the Cool Fan S/P relay and the left cooling fan motor supply voltage circuit of the Cool Fan S/P relay. Do both cooling fans operate in low speed?	Go to Step 14	Go to Step 6

GC1080000605010X

Fig. 35 Cooling fan inoperative (Part 1 of 6). Aurora

Test Description

The number(s) below refer to the step number(s) on the diagnostic table.

2. Lack of communication may be due to a partial malfunction of the class 2 serial data circuit or due to a total malfunction of the class 2 serial data circuit. The specified procedure will determine the particular condition.

3. The symptom list in Symptoms will determine the correct diagnostic procedure to use.

4. The presence of DTCs which begin with "U" indicate some other module is not communicating. The specified procedure will compile all the available information before tests are performed.

Step	Action	Yes	No
1	1. Install a scan tool. 2. Turn ON the ignition, with the engine OFF. Does the scan tool power up?	Go to Step 2	Go to Scan Tool Does Not Power Up
2	1. Turn ON the ignition, with the engine OFF. 2. Attempt to establish communication with the following: o Instrument Panel Cluster (IPC) o Dash Integration Module (DIM) o Powertrain Control Module (PCM) Does the scan tool communicate with the IPC, DIM and PCM?	Go to Step 3	Go to Scan Tool Does Not Communicate with Class 2 Device
3	Select the IPC, DIM and the PCM display DTC function on the scan tool. Does the scan tool display any DTCs?	Go to Step 4	Go to Symptoms - Engine Cooling
4	Does the scan tool display any DTCs which begin with a U?	Go to Scan Tool Does Not Communicate with Class 2 Device	Go to Step 5
5	Does the scan tool display DTC P1258, P0480, or P0481?	Go to Diagnostic Trouble Code (DTC) List	Go to Step 6
6	Does the scan tool display DTC B1000, B1004, B1007, or B1009?	Go to Diagnostic Trouble Code (DTC) List	Go to Step 7
7	Does the scan tool display DTC B1327, B1513, or B1514?	Go to Diagnostic Trouble Code (DTC)	Go to Control Module References

GC1080000604010X

Fig. 34 Diagnostic system check. Aurora

Step	Action	Yes	No
6	1. Leave the fused jumper wire in place of the Cool Fan 2 relay. 2. Connect a 20 A fused jumper between the battery positive voltage circuit of the Cool Fan S/P relay and the cooling fan motor supply voltage circuit of the Cool Fan S/P relay. Does the left cooling fan motor operate in high speed?	Go to Step 9	Go to Step 7
7	1. Leave the fused jumper wire in place of the Cool Fan 2 relay. 2. Install the Cool Fan S/P relay. 3. Disconnect the left cooling fan motor electrical connector. 4. Connect a 20 Amp fused jumper wire from the cooling fan motor supply voltage circuit of the left cooling fan motor electrical connector to the cooling fan motor ground circuit of the left cooling fan motor electrical connector. Does the right cooling fan motor operate in high speed?	Go to Step 16	Go to Step 8
8	1. Leave the fused jumper wire in place of the Cool Fan 2 relay. 2. Connect a 20 Amp fused jumper wire from the cooling fan motor supply voltage circuit of the left cooling fan motor electrical connector to a good ground. Does the right cooling fan motor operate in high speed?	Go to Step 20	Go to Step 21

GC1080000605020X

Fig. 35 Cooling fan inoperative (Part 2 of 6). Aurora

Step	Action	Yes	No
9	1. Leave the fused jumper wire in the Cool Fan 2 relay. 2. Install the Cool Fan S/P relay. 3. Disconnect the right cooling fan motor electrical connector. 4. Connect a 20 Amp fused jumper wire from battery positive voltage circuit of the right cooling fan motor electrical connector to the cooling fan motor ground circuit of the right cooling fan motor electrical connector. Does the left cooling fan motor operate in high speed?	Go to Step 17	Go to Step 10
10	1. Leave the fused jumper wire in place of the Cool Fan 2 relay. 2. Connect a 20 Amp fused jumper wire from battery positive voltage to the right cooling fan motor low circuit of the of the right cooling fan motor electrical connector. Does the left cooling fan motor operate in high speed?	Go to Step 18	Go to Step 22
11	Is the left cooling fan motor operating properly in high speed?	Go to Step 12	Go to Step 15

GC1080000605030X

Fig. 35   Cooling fan inoperative (Part 3 of 6). Aurora

Step	Action	Yes	No
17	Inspect for poor connections at the harness connector of the right cooling fan motor. Did you find and correct the condition?	Go to Step 28	Go to Step 27
18	Repair the right cooling fan motor supply voltage circuit. Did you complete the repair?	Go to Step 28	--
19	Repair the right cooling fan motor ground circuit. Did you complete the repair?	Go to Step 28	--
20	Repair the left cooling fan motor ground circuit. Did you complete the repair?	Go to Step 28	--
21	Repair the left cooling fan motor supply voltage circuit. Did you complete the repair?	Go to Step 28	--
22	Repair the right cooling fan motor low circuit. Did you complete the repair?	Go to Step 28	--
23	Replace the Cool Fan 2 relay. Is the repair complete?	Go to Step 28	--
24	Replace the Cool Fan S/P relay. Is the repair complete?	Go to Step 28	--
25	Replace the Cool Fan 1 relay. Is the repair complete?	Go to Step 28	--

GC1080000605050X

Fig. 35   Cooling fan inoperative (Part 5 of 6). Aurora

Step	Action	Yes	No
12	1. Remove the Cool Fan S/P relay 2. Connect a 20 A fused jumper between the right cooling fan low circuit of the Cool Fan S/P relay and the ground circuit of the Cool Fan S/P relay. Does the right cooling fan operate properly in high speed?	Go to Step 14	Go to Step 19
13	Inspect for poor connections at the Cool Fan 2 relay. Did you find and correct the condition?	Go to Step 28	Go to Step 23
14	Inspect for poor connections at the Cool Fan S/P relay. Did you find and correct the condition?	Go to Step 28	Go to Step 24
15	Inspect for poor connections at the Cool Fan 1 relay. Did you find and correct the condition?	Go to Step 28 v	Go to Step 25
16	Inspect for poor connections at the harness connector of the left cooling fan motor. Did you find and correct the condition?	Go to Step 28	Go to Step 26

GC1080000605040X

Fig. 35   Cooling fan inoperative (Part 4 of 6). Aurora

Step	Action	Yes	No
26	Replace the left cooling fan motor. Is the repair complete?	Go to Step 28	--
27	Replace the right cooling fan motor. Is the repair complete?	Go to Step 28	--
28	Operate the system in order to verify the repair. Did you correct the condition?	System OK	Go to Step 3

GC1080000605060X

Fig. 35   Cooling fan inoperative (Part 6 of 6). Aurora

Step	Action	Yes	No
	DEFINITION: One or both engine cooling fan motors run continuously in high or low speed modes. SCHEMATIC REFERENCE: Cooling Fan Motors and Relays		
1	Did you perform the Engine Cooling Diagnostic System Check?	Go to Step 2	Go to A Diagnostic System Check - Engine Cooling
2	Turn ON the ignition, with the engine OFF. Are one or both cooling fans running all the time?	Go to Step 3	Go to Testing for Intermittent and Poor Connections
3	Are both cooling fans running continuously?	Go to Step 5	Go to Step 4
4	Remove the Cool Fan S/P relay. Did the left cooling fan turn OFF?	Go to Step 6	Go to Step 7
5	Repair the short in the right cooling fan motor supply voltage circuit. you complete the repair?	Go to Step 8	--
6	Repair the short in the right cooling fan motor low circuit. Did you complete the repair?	Go to Step 8	--
7	Repair the short in the left cooling fan motor supply voltage circuit. Did you complete the repair?	Go to Step 8	--
8	Operate the system in order to verify the repair. Did you correct the condition?	System OK	Go to Step 2

GC1080000606000X

Fig. 36   Cooling fan always on. Aurora

Step	Action	Yes	No
1	Install a scan tool. Does the scan tool power up?	Go to Step 2	Diagnose Data Link Communications
2	1. Turn On the ignition, with the engine OFF. 2. Attempt to establish communication with the engine control module (ECM). Does the scan tool communicate with ECM?	Go to Step 3	Diagnose Data Link Communications
3	Select the ECM. Display DTCs function on the scan tool. Does the scan tool display any DTCs?	Go to Diagnostic Trouble Code (DTC) List	Go to Symptoms

ARM0400000000034

Fig. 37 Diagnostic system check. Aveo

Step	Action	Yes	No
6	1. Turn the ignition OFF. 2. Disconnect the engine control module (ECM) connector. 3. Connect a fused jumper between the ECM low cooling fan relay control circuit and ground. 4. Turn the ignition ON. Does the cooling fan run at low speed?	Go to Step 21	Go to Step 7
7	1. Turn the ignition OFF. 2. Connect a fused jumper between the ECM low cooling fan relay control circuit and ground. 3. Disconnect the cooling fan connector. 4. Connect a test light between the cooling fan connector terminal 2 and ground. 5. Turn the ignition ON. Is the test light ON?	Go to Step 8	Go to Step 9
8	1. Turn the ignition OFF. 2. Connect a test light between the cooling fan connector terminal 1 and battery positive. Is the test light ON?	Go to Step 18	Go to Step 17
9	1. Turn the ignition OFF. 2. Remove the jumper from the ECM low cooling fan control circuit. 3. Using a test light, connect to ground, probe the low speed relay connector terminal 86. 4. Turn the ignition ON. Is the test light ON?	Go to Step 10	Go to Step 13

ARM0400000000036

Fig. 38 Cooling fan circuit diagnosis (Part 2 of 4). Aveo

Step	Action	Yes	No
10	1. Turn the ignition OFF. 2. Connect a test light between the cooling fan relay LOW connector terminal 30 and ground. Is the test light ON?	Go to Step 11	Go to Step 14
11	Connect a test light between the cooling fan relay LOW connector terminal 87 and battery positive. Is the test light ON?	Go to Step 12	Go to Step 16
12	1. Connect a fused jumper between the ECM low cooling fan relay control circuit and ground. 2. Connect a test light between the cooling fan relay LOW connector terminal 85 and battery positive. Is the test light ON?	Go to Step 19	Go to Step 15
13	Repair the open wire between the cooling fan relay LOW connector terminal 85 and the ignition voltage supply. Is the repair complete?	System OK	--
14	Repair the open wire between the cooling fan relay LOW connector terminal 30 and the fuse EF3. Is the repair complete?	System OK	--
15	Repair the open wire between the cooling fan relay LOW connector terminal 86 and the ECM low cooling fan relay control circuit. Is the repair complete?	System OK	--
16	Inspect for an open wire between the cooling fan relay LOW connector terminal 87 and the cooling fan connector terminal 2. Is the problem found?	Go to Step 20	Go to Step 17

ARM0400000000037

Fig. 38 Cooling fan circuit diagnosis (Part 3 of 4). Aveo

Step	Action	Yes	No
1	Did you perform the Diagnostic Starting Point - Engine Cooling?	Go to Step 2	Go to Diagnostic Starting Point
2	1. Inspect the I/P fuse block fuse F18 for the 1.4L/1.5L application, or underhood fuse EF2 for the 1.2L. 2. Replace the fuse as needed. Is the fuse OK?	Go to Step 3	Go to Diagnostic Aids
3	1. Inspect the engine fuse block fuse EF3. 2. Replace the fuse as needed. Is the fuse OK?	Go to Step 4	Go to Diagnostic Aids
4	1. Turn the ignition OFF. 2. Connect the scan tool to the data link connector (DLC). 3. Start the engine. 4. The cooling fan should run at low speed when the coolant temperature reaches 93°C (199°F). Does the cooling fan run at low speed?	Go to Step 5	Go to Step 6
5	1. Turn the ignition OFF. 2. Connect a scan tool to the DLC. 3. Start the engine. 4. The cooling fan should run at high speed when the coolant temperature reaches 97°C (207°F). Does the cooling fan run at high speed?	System OK	Go to Step 22

ARM0400000000035

Fig. 38 Cooling fan circuit diagnosis (Part 1 of 4). Aveo

Step	Action	Yes	No
17	Inspect for an open wire between the cooling fan connector terminal 1 and ground. Is the problem found?	Go to Step 20	Go to Step 18
18	Replace the cooling fan. Is the repair complete?	System OK	--
19	Replace the cooling fan relay LOW. Is the repair complete?	System OK	--
20	Repair the wire as needed. Is the repair complete?	System OK	--
21	Replace the ECM. Is the repair complete?	System OK	--
22	1. Turn the ignition OFF. 2. Disconnect the ECM connector. 3. Connect a fused jumper between the ECM low cooling fan relay control circuit and ground. 4. Connect a fused jumper between the ECM high cooling fan relay control circuit and ground. 5. Turn the ignition ON. Does the cooling fan run at high speed?	Go to Step 21	Go to Step 23
23	1. Turn the ignition OFF. 2. Disconnect the cooling fan relay HI. 3. Connect a test light between the cooling fan relay high connector terminal 85 and ground. 4. Turn the ignition ON. Is the test light ON?	Go to Step 24	Go to Step 28

ARM0400000000038

Fig. 38 Cooling fan circuit diagnosis (Part 4 of 4). Aveo

Step	Action	Yes	No
1	Install a scan tool. Does the scan tool power up?	Go to Step 2	Diagnose Data Link Communications
2	1. Turn ON the ignition, with the engine OFF. 2. Attempt to establish communication with the following control modules: • Instrument Cluster • Powertrain Control Module — Does the scan tool communicate with the control modules?	Go to Step 3	Diagnose Data Link Communications
3	Select the powertrain control module display DTCs function on the scan tool. Does the scan tool display any DTCs?	Go to Step 4	Diagnose Symptoms - Engine Cooling
4	Does the scan tool display any DTCs which begin with a "U"?	Diagnose Data Link Communications	Diagnose Trouble Code

GC1080100646000X

Fig. 39   Diagnostic system check. Bonneville & LeSabre

Schematic Reference: Engine Cooling Schematics

Step	Action	Yes	No
1	Did you perform the Engine Cooling Diagnostic System Check?	Go to Step 2	Go to Diagnostic System Check -
2	Important: The cooling fan 1 relay and cooling fan 2 relay are improperly identified in the underhood fuse block. 1. Install a scan tool. 2. Turn ON the ignition, with the engine OFF. 3. With a scan tool, command the Fans Low Speed ON and OFF. Do the low speed engine cooling fans turn ON and OFF with each command?	Go to Step 3	Go to Step 4
3	Important: Before the PCM changes the speed of the cooling fans, a 3-second delay will occur. With a scan tool, command the Fans High Speed ON and OFF. Do the high speed engine cooling fans turn ON and OFF with each command?	Test Intermittent and Poor Connections	Go to Step 11
4	Important: Following this step, do NOT remove the 20-A fused jumper wire that is connected during this step. While performing the following steps, use a second 20-A fused jumper wire. 1. Disconnect the cooling fan 1 relay. 2. Connect a 20-A fused jumper between the battery positive voltage circuit of the cooling fan 1 relay and the cooling fan motor supply voltage circuit of the cooling fan 1 relay. Do both cooling fans operate in low speed?	Go to Step 13	Go to Step 5

GC1080100648010X

Fig. 41   Cooling fan inoperative (Part 1 of 3). Bonneville & LeSabre

Step	Action	Yes	No
17	Inspect for poor connections at the harness connector of the right cooling fan. Did you find and correct the condition?	Go to Step 28	Go to Step 27
18	Repair the right cooling fan motor supply voltage circuit. Did you complete the repair?	Go to Step 28	—
19	Repair the left cooling fan ground circuit. Did you complete the repair?	Go to Step 28	—
20	Repair the right cooling fan ground circuit. Did you complete the repair?	Go to Step 28	—
21	Repair the left cooling fan motor supply voltage circuit. Did you complete the repair?	Go to Step 28	—
22	Repair the cooling fan low reference circuit. Did you complete the repair?	Go to Step 28	—
23	Replace the cooling fan 1 relay. Did you complete the repair?	Go to Step 28	—
24	Replace the cooling fan S/P relay. Did you complete the repair?	Go to Step 28	—
25	Replace the cooling fan 2 relay. Did you complete the repair?	Go to Step 28	—
26	Replace the left cooling fan. Did you complete the repair?	Go to Step 28	—
27	Replace the right cooling fan. Did you complete the repair?	Go to Step 28	—
28	Operate the system in order to verify the repair. Did you correct the condition?	System OK	Go to Step 3

GC1080100648030X

Fig. 41   Cooling fan inoperative (Part 3 of 3). Bonneville & LeSabre

Step	Action	Yes	No
	DEFINITION: One or both engine cooling fan motors run continuously in high or low speed.		
1	Did you perform the Engine Cooling Diagnostic System Check?	Go to Step 2	Go To Diagnostic System Check -
2	Important: The cooling fan 1 relay and cooling fan 2 relay are improperly identified in the underhood fuse block. Turn ON the ignition, with the engine OFF. Are one or both cooling fans ON?	Go to Step 3	Test Intermittent and Poor Connections
3	Are both cooling fans running continuously?	Go to Step 5	Go to Step 4
4	Remove the cooling fan S/P relay. Did the left cooling fan turn OFF?	Go to Step 6	Go to Step 7
5	Repair the short to voltage in the right cooling fan motor supply voltage circuit. Did you complete the repair?	Go to Step 8	—
6	Repair the short to voltage in the cooling fan low reference circuit. Did you complete the repair?	Go to Step 8	—
7	Repair the short to voltage in the left cooling fan motor supply voltage circuit. Did you complete the repair?	Go to Step 8	—
8	Operate the system in order to verify the repair. Did you correct the condition?	System OK	Go to Step 2

GC1080100647000X

Fig. 40   Cooling fan always on. Bonneville & LeSabre

Step	Action	Yes	No
5	1. Disconnect the cooling fan S/P relay. 2. Connect the second 20-A fused jumper between the right cooling fan ground circuit of the cooling fan S/P relay and the left cooling fan motor supply voltage circuit of the cooling fan S/P relay. Do both cooling fans operate in low speed?	Go to Step 14	Go to Step 6
6	Connect a 20-A fused jumper between the battery positive voltage circuit of the cooling fan S/P relay and the cooling fan motor supply voltage circuit of the cooling fan S/P relay. Does the left cooling fan operate in high speed?	Go to Step 9	Go to Step 7
7	1. Install the cooling fan S/P relay. 2. Disconnect the left cooling fan electrical connector. 3. Connect the second 20-Amp fused jumper wire from the cooling fan motor supply voltage circuit of the left cooling fan electrical connector to the ground circuit of the left cooling fan electrical connector. Does the right cooling fan operate in high speed?	Go to Step 16	Go to Step 8
8	Connect a 20-Amp fused jumper wire from the cooling fan motor supply voltage circuit of the left cooling fan electrical connector to a good ground. Does the right cooling fan operate in high speed?	Go to Step 20	Go to Step 21
9	1. Install the cooling fan S/P relay. 2. Disconnect the right cooling fan electrical connector. 3. Connect the second 20-Amp fused jumper wire from the cooling fan motor supply voltage circuit of the right cooling fan electrical connector to the cooling fan low reference circuit of the right cooling fan electrical connector. Does the left cooling fan operate in high speed?	Go to Step 17	Go to Step 10
10	Connect the second 20-Amp fused jumper wire from battery positive voltage to the cooling fan low reference circuit of the of the right cooling fan electrical connector. Does the left cooling fan operate in high speed?	Go to Step 18	Go to Step 22
11	Is the left cooling fan operating properly in high speed?	Go to Step 12	Go to Step 15
12	1. Disconnect the cooling fan S/P relay. 2. Connect the second 20-A fused jumper between the cooling fan low reference circuit of the cooling fan S/P relay and the ground circuit of the cooling fan S/P relay. Does the right cooling fan operate properly in high speed?	Go to Step 14	Go to Step 19
13	Inspect for poor connections at the cooling fan 1 relay. Did you find and correct the condition?	Go to Step 28	Go to Step 23
14	Inspect for poor connections at the cooling fan S/P relay. Did you find and correct the condition?	Go to Step 28	Go to Step 24
15	Inspect for poor connections at the cooling fan 2 relay. Did you find and correct the condition?	Go to Step 28	Go to Step 25
16	Inspect for poor connections at the harness connector of the left cooling fan. Did you find and correct the condition?	Go to Step 28	Go to Step 26

GC1080100648020X

Fig. 41   Cooling fan inoperative (Part 2 of 3). Bonneville & LeSabre

Step	Action	Yes	No
1	Install a scan tool. Does the scan tool power up?	Go to Step 2	Diagnose Data Link Communications
2	1. Turn ON the ignition, with the engine OFF. 2. Attempt to establish communication with the following control modules: • Instrument Cluster • Powertrain Control Module — Does the scan tool communicate with the control modules?	Go to Step 3	Diagnose Data Link Communications
3	Select the powertrain control module display DTCs function on the scan tool. Does the scan tool display any DTCs?	Go to Step 4	Diagnose Engine Cooling
4	Does the scan tool display any DTCs which begin with a "U"?	Go to Scan Tool Does Not Communicate with Class 2 Device	Diagnose Trouble Code

GC1080100650000X

Fig. 42   Diagnostic system check. Camaro & Firebird

Step	Action	Yes	No
	DEFINITION: One or both engine cooling fan motors run continuously in high or low speed.		
1	Did you perform the Engine Cooling Diagnostic System Check?	Go to Step 2	Go To Diagnostic System Check -
2	Turn ON the ignition, with the engine OFF. Are one or both cooling fans ON?	Go to Step 3	Test for Intermittent and Poor Connections
3	Are both cooling fans running continuously?	Go to Step 5	Go to Step 4
4	Remove the cooling fan 3 relay. Did the right cooling fan turn OFF?	Go to Step 6	Go to Step 7
5	Repair the short to voltage in the left cooling fan motor supply voltage circuit. Did you complete the repair?	Go to Step 8	—
6	Repair the short to voltage in the left cooling fan low reference circuit. Did you complete the repair?	Go to Step 8	—
7	Repair the short to voltage in the right cooling fan motor supply voltage circuit. Did you complete the repair?	Go to Step 8	—
8	Operate the system in order to verify the repair. Did you correct the condition?	System OK	Go to Step 2

GC1080100651000X

Fig. 43   Cooling fan always on. Camaro & Firebird

Step	Action	Yes	No
	DEFINITION: One or both engine cooling fan motors do not operate properly in high or low speed modes.		
1	Did you perform the Engine Cooling Diagnostic System Check?	Go to Step 2	Go to Diagnostic System Check -
2	1. Install a scan tool. 2. Turn ON the ignition, with the engine OFF. 3. With a scan tool, command the Fans Low Speed ON and OFF. Do the low speed engine cooling fans turn ON and OFF with each command?	Go to Step 3	Go to Step 4
3	Important: Before the PCM changes the speed of the cooling fans, a 3-second delay will occur. With a scan tool, command the Fans High Speed ON and OFF. Do the high speed engine cooling fans turn ON and OFF with each command?	Test for Intermittent and Poor Connections	Go to Step 11
4	Important: Following this step, do NOT remove the 20-A fused jumper wire that is connected during this step. While performing the following steps, use a second 20-A fused jumper wire. 1. Remove the cooling fan 1 relay. 2. Connect a 20-A fused jumper between the battery positive voltage circuit of the cooling fan 1 relay and the cooling fan motor supply voltage circuit of the cooling fan 1 relay. Do both cooling fans operate in low speed?	Go to Step 13	Go to Step 5

GC1080100652010X

Fig. 44   Cooling fan inoperative (Part 1 of 3). Camaro & Firebird

Step	Action	Yes	No
5	1. Disconnect the cooling fan 3 relay 2. Connect the second 20-A fused jumper between the left cooling fan ground circuit of the cooling fan 3 relay and the right cooling fan motor supply voltage circuit of the cooling fan 3 relay. Do both cooling fans operate in low speed?	Go to Step 14	Go to Step 6
6	Connect the second 20-A fused jumper between the battery positive voltage circuit of the cooling fan 3 relay and the cooling fan motor supply voltage circuit of the cooling fan 3 relay. Does the right cooling fan operate in high speed?	Go to Step 9	Go to Step 7
7	1. Install the cooling fan 3 relay. 2. Disconnect the right cooling fan electrical connector. 3. Connect the second 20-Amp fused jumper wire from the cooling fan motor supply voltage circuit of the right cooling fan electrical connector to the circuit of the right cooling fan electrical connector. Does the left cooling fan operate in high speed?	Go to Step 16	Go to Step 8
8	Connect the second 20-Amp fused jumper wire from the cooling fan motor supply voltage circuit of the right cooling fan electrical connector to a good ground. Does the left cooling fan operate in high speed?	Go to Step 20	Go to Step 21
9	1. Install the cooling fan 3 relay. 2. Disconnect the left cooling fan electrical connector. 3. Connect the second 20-Amp fused jumper wire from the cooling fan motor supply voltage circuit of the left cooling fan electrical connector to the cooling fan low reference circuit of the left cooling fan electrical connector. Does the right cooling fan operate in high speed?	Go to Step 17	Go to Step 10
10	Connect the second 20-Amp fused jumper wire from battery positive voltage to the low reference circuit of the of the left cooling fan electrical connector. Does the right cooling fan operate in high speed?	Go to Step 18	Go to Step 22
11	Is the right cooling fan operating properly in high speed?	Go to Step 12	Go to Step 15
12	1. Disconnect the cooling fan 3 relay 2. Connect the second 20-A fused jumper between the left cooling fan low reference circuit of the cooling fan 3 relay and the ground circuit of the cooling fan 3 relay. Does the left cooling fan operate properly in high speed?	Go to Step 14	Go to Step 19
13	Inspect for poor connections at the cooling fan 1 relay. Did you find and correct the condition?	Go to Step 28	Go to Step 23
14	Inspect for poor connections at the cooling fan 3 relay. Did you find and correct the condition?	Go to Step 28	Go to Step 24
15	Inspect for poor connections at the cooling fan 3 relay. Did you find and correct the condition?	Go to Step 28	Go to Step 25
16	Inspect for poor connections at the harness connector of the right cooling fan. Did you find and correct the condition?	Go to Step 28	Go to Step 26

GC1080100652020X

Fig. 44   Cooling fan inoperative (Part 2 of 3). Camaro & Firebird

Step	Action	Yes	No
17	Inspect for poor connections at the harness connector of the left cooling fan. Did you find and correct the condition?	Go to Step 28	Go to Step 27
18	Repair the left cooling fan motor supply voltage circuit. Did you complete the repair?	Go to Step 28	—
19	Repair the left cooling fan low reference circuit. Did you complete the repair?	Go to Step 28	—
20	Repair the right cooling fan ground circuit. Did you complete the repair?	Go to Step 28	—
21	Repair the right cooling fan motor supply voltage circuit. Did you complete the repair?	Go to Step 28	—
22	Repair the left cooling fan low reference circuit. Did you complete the repair?	Go to Step 28	—
23	Replace the cooling fan 1 relay. Did you complete the repair?	Go to Step 28	—
24	Replace the cooling fan 3 relay. Did you complete the repair?	Go to Step 28	—
25	Replace the cooling fan 3 relay. Did you complete the repair?	Go to Step 28	—
26	Replace the right cooling fan. Did you complete the repair?	Go to Step 28	—
27	Replace the left cooling fan. Did you complete the repair?	Go to Step 28	—
28	Operate the system in order to verify the repair. Did you correct the condition?	System OK	Go to Step 3

GC1080100652030X

Fig. 44   Cooling fan inoperative (Part 3 of 3). Camaro & Firebird

Step	Action	Yes	No
	DEFINITION: The engine cooling fan motor runs continuously.		
1	Did you perform the Engine Cooling Diagnostic System Check?	Go to Step 2	Go To Diagnostic System Check
2	Turn ON the ignition, with the engine OFF. Is the engine cooling fan running all the time?	Go to Step 3	Test for Intermittent and Poor Connections
3	Remove the cooling fan relay. Did the cooling fan turn OFF?	Go to Step 5	Go to Step 4
4	Repair the short to power in the cooling fan motor supply voltage circuit. Did you complete the repair?	Go to Step 7	--
5	Inspect for poor connections at the cooling fan relay. Did you find and correct the condition?	Go to Step 7	Go to Step 6
6	Replace the cooling fan relay. Did you complete the repair?	Go to Step 7	
7	Operate the system in order to verify the repair. Did you correct the condition?	System OK	Go to Step 2

ARM0300000000307

Fig. 45 Cooling fan always on diagnosis. Cavalier & Sunfire

Step	Action	Yes	No
6	Probe the harness connector of the cooling fan motor with a test lamp connected between the cooling fan motor supply voltage circuit and the ground circuit of the cooling fan motor. Does the test lamp illuminate?	Go to Step 11	Go to Step 9
7	Repair the battery positive circuit of the cooling fan relay. Did you complete the repair?	Go to Step 14	--
8	Repair the supply voltage circuit of the cooling fan motor. Did you complete the repair?	Go to Step 14	--
9	Repair the ground circuit of the cooling fan motor. Did you complete the repair?	Go to Step 14	--
10	Inspect for poor connections at the cooling fan relay. Did you find and correct the condition?	Go to Step 14	Go to Step 12
11	Inspect for poor connections at the harness connector of the cooling fan motor. Did you find and correct the condition?	Go to Step 14	Go to Step 13
12	Replace the cooling fan relay. Did you complete the repair?	Go to Step 14	--
13	Replace the cooling fan motor. Did you complete the repair?	Go to Step 14	--
14	Operate the system in order to verify the repair. Did you correct the condition?	System OK	Go to Step 2

ARM0300000000309

Fig. 46 Cooling fan inoperative (Part 2 of 2). Cavalier & Sunfire

Step	Action	Yes	No
	DEFINITION: The engine cooling fan motor does not operate.		
1	Did you perform A Diagnostic System Check-Engine Cooling?	Go to Step 2	Go to Diagnostic System Check
2	1. Install a scan tool. 2. Turn ON the ignition, with the engine OFF. 3. With a scan tool, command the cooling fan ON and OFF. Does the engine cooling fan turn ON and OFF with each command?	Test for Intermittent and Poor Connections	Go to Step 3
3	1. Turn OFF the ignition. 2. Remove the cooling fan relay. 3. Probe the battery positive voltage circuit of the cooling fan relay switch side with a test lamp that is connected to a good ground. Does the test lamp illuminate?	Go to Step 4	Go to Step 7
4	Connect a 20 A fused jumper wire between the battery positive voltage circuit of the cooling fan relay and the cooling fan motor supply voltage circuit of the cooling fan relay. Does the cooling fan operate?	Go to Step 10	Go to Step 5
5	1. Disconnect the cooling fan connector. 2. Probe the cooling fan motor supply voltage circuit at the harness connector with a test lamp that is connected to a good ground. Does the test lamp illuminate?	Go to Step 6	Go to Step 8

ARM0300000000308

Fig. 46 Cooling fan inoperative (Part 1 of 2). Cavalier & Sunfire

Step	Action	Yes	No
1	Install a scan tool. Does the scan tool power up?	Go to Step 2	Diagnose Data Link Communications
2	1. Turn ON the ignition, with the engine OFF. 2. Attempt to establish communication with the following control modules: • Instrument Cluster • Powertrain Control Module Does the scan tool communicate with the control modules?	Go to Step 3	Diagnose Data Link Communications
3	Select the powertrain control module display DTCs function on the scan tool. Does the scan tool display any DTCs?	Go to Step 4	Diagnose Engine Cooling
4	Does the scan tool display any DTCs which begin with a "U"?	Go to Scan Tool Does Not Communicate with Class 2 Device	Diagnose Trouble Code

GC1080100653000X

Fig. 47 Diagnostic system check. 2001 Century & Regal

Step	Action	Yes	No
	DEFINITION: One or both engine cooling motors run continuously in high or low speed.		
1	Did you perform the Engine Cooling Diagnostic System Check?	Go to Step 2	Go To Diagnostic System Check
2	Turn ON the ignition, with the engine OFF. Are one or both cooling fans ON?	Go to Step 3	Test for Intermittent and Poor Connections
3	Are both cooling fans running continuously?	Go to Step 5	Go to Step 4
4	Remove the cooling fan 2 relay. Did the right cooling fan turn OFF?	Go to Step 6	Go to Step 7
5	Repair the short to voltage in the left cooling fan supply voltage circuit. Did you complete the repair?	Go to Step 8	--
6	Repair the short to voltage in the left cooling fan low reference circuit. Did you complete the repair?	Go to Step 8	--
7	Repair the short to voltage in the right cooling fan supply voltage circuit. Did you complete the repair?	Go to Step 8	--
8	Operate the system in order to verify the repair. Did you correct the condition?	System OK	Go to Step 2

GC1080100654000X

Fig. 48 Cooling fan always on. 2001 Century & Regal

Step	Action	Yes	No
	DEFINITION: One or both engine cooling fan motors do not operate properly in high or low speed modes.		
1	Did you perform the Engine Cooling Diagnostic System Check?	Go to Step 2	Go to Diagnostic System Check
2	1. Install a scan tool. 2. Turn ON the ignition, with the engine OFF. 3. With a scan tool, command the Fans Low Speed ON and OFF. Do the low speed engine cooling fans turn ON and OFF with each command?	Go to Step 3	Go to Step 4
3	Important: Before the PCM changes the speed of the cooling fans, a 3-second delay will occur. With a scan tool, command the Fans High Speed ON and OFF. Do the high speed engine cooling fans turn ON and OFF with each command?	Test for Intermittent and Poor Connections	Go to Step 11
4	Important: Following this step, do NOT remove the 20-A fused jumper wire that is connected during this step. While performing the following steps, use a second 20-A fused jumper wire. 1. Remove the cooling fan 1 relay. 2. Connect a 20-A fused jumper between the battery positive voltage circuit of the cooling fan 1 relay and the cooling fan motor supply voltage circuit of the cooling fan 1 relay. Do both cooling fans operate in low speed?	Go to Step 13	Go to Step 5

GC1080100655010X

Fig. 49 Cooling fan inoperative (Part 1 of 3). 2001 Century & Regal

Step	Action	Yes	No
5	1. Disconnect the cooling fan 2 relay. 2. Connect a second 20-A fused jumper between the left cooling fan low reference circuit of the cooling fan 2 relay and the right cooling fan supply voltage circuit of the cooling fan 2 relay. Do both cooling fans operate in low speed?	Go to Step 14	Go to Step 6
6	Connect the second 20-A fused jumper between the battery positive voltage circuit of the cooling fan 2 relay and the cooling fan motor supply voltage circuit of the cooling fan 2 relay. Does the right cooling fan operate in high speed?	Go to Step 9	Go to Step 7
7	1. Install the cooling fan 2 relay. 2. Disconnect the right cooling fan electrical connector. 3. Connect the second 20-Amp fused jumper wire from the cooling fan motor supply voltage circuit of the right cooling fan electrical connector to the cooling fan ground circuit of the right cooling fan electrical connector. Does the left cooling fan operate in high speed?	Go to Step 16	Go to Step 8
8	Connect the second 20-Amp fused jumper wire from the cooling fan motor supply voltage circuit of the right cooling fan electrical connector to a good ground. Does the left cooling fan operate in high speed?	Go to Step 20	Go to Step 21
9	1. Install the cooling fan 2 relay. 2. Disconnect the left cooling fan electrical connector. 3. Connect the second 20-Amp fused jumper wire from the cooling fan motor supply voltage circuit of the left cooling fan electrical connector to the cooling fan ground circuit of the left cooling fan electrical connector. Does the right cooling fan operate in high speed?	Go to Step 17	Go to Step 10
10	Connect the second 20-Amp fused jumper wire from battery positive voltage to the left cooling fan low circuit of the of the left cooling fan electrical connector. Does the right cooling fan operate in high speed?	Go to Step 18	Go to Step 22
11	Does the right cooling fan operate in high speed?	Go to Step 12	Go to Step 15
12	1. Disconnect the cooling fan 2 relay. 2. Connect a 20-A fused jumper between the left cooling fan low reference circuit of the cooling fan 2 relay and the ground circuit of the cooling fan 2 relay. Does the left cooling fan operate properly in high speed?	Go to Step 14	Go to Step 19
13	Inspect for poor connections at the cooling fan 1 relay. Did you find and correct the condition?	Go to Step 28	Go to Step 23
14	Inspect for poor connections at the cooling fan 2 relay. Did you find and correct the condition?	Go to Step 28	Go to Step 24
15	Inspect for poor connections at the cooling fan 3 relay. Did you find and correct the condition?	Go to Step 28	Go to Step 25
16	Inspect for poor connections at the harness connector of the right cooling fan. Did you find and correct the condition?	Go to Step 28	Go to Step 26

GC1080100655020X

Fig. 49 Cooling fan inoperative (Part 2 of 3). 2001 Century & Regal

Step	Action	Yes	No
17	Inspect for poor connections at the harness connector of the left cooling fan. Did you find and correct the condition?	Go to Step 28	Go to Step 27
18	Repair the left cooling fan motor supply voltage circuit. Did you complete the repair?	Go to Step 28	—
19	Repair the left cooling fan ground circuit. Did you complete the repair?	Go to Step 28	—
20	Repair the right cooling fan ground circuit. Did you complete the repair?	Go to Step 28	—
21	Repair the right cooling fan motor supply voltage circuit. Did you complete the repair?	Go to Step 28	—
22	Repair the left cooling fan low reference circuit. Did you complete the repair?	Go to Step 28	—
23	Replace the cooling fan 1 relay. Did you complete the replacement?	Go to Step 28	—
24	Replace the cooling fan 2 relay. Did you complete the replacement?	Go to Step 28	—
25	Replace the cooling fan 3 relay. Did you complete the replacement?	Go to Step 28	—
26	Replace the right cooling fan. Did you complete the replacement?	Go to Step 28	—
27	Replace the left cooling fan. Did you complete the replacement?	Go to Step 28	—
28	Operate the system in order to verify the repair. Did you correct the condition?	System OK	Go to Step 3

GC1080100655030X

Fig. 49 Cooling fan inoperative (Part 3 of 3). 2001 Century & Regal

Step	Action	Yes	No
1	Install a scan tool. Does the scan tool power up?	Go to Step 2	Diagnose Data Link Communications
2	1. Turn ON the ignition, with the engine OFF. 2. Attempt to establish communication with the following control modules: • Instrument Cluster • Powertrain Control Module Does the scan tool communicate with the control modules?	Go to Step 3	Diagnose Data Link Communications
3	Select the powertrain control module display DTCs function on the scan tool. Does the scan tool display any DTCs?	Go to Step 4	Diagnose engine cooling
4	Does the scan tool display any DTCs which begin with a "U"?	Diagnose Data Link Communications	Diagnose Diagnostic Trouble Code (DTC)

ARM0300000000318

Fig. 50 Diagnostic system check. 2002–05 Century & Regal

Step	Action	Yes	No
	DEFINITION: One or both engine cooling fan motors run continuously in high or low speed modes.		
1	Did you perform the Engine Cooling Diagnostic System Check?	Go to Step 2	Go to Diagnostic System Check
2	Turn ON the ignition, with the engine OFF. Are one or both cooling fans ON?	Go to Step 3	Test for Intermittent and Poor Connections
3	Are both cooling fans running continuously?	Go to Step 5	Go to Step 4
4	Remove the cooling fan 2 relay. Did the right cooling fan turn OFF?	Go to Step 8	Go to Step 6
5	Remove the cooling fan 1 relay. Did the cooling fans turn OFF?	Go to Step 10	Go to Step 7
6	Remove the cooling fan 3 relay. Did the right cooling fan turn OFF?	Go to Step 11	Go to Step 9

ARM0300000000310

Fig. 51 Cooling fan always on (Part 1 of 2). 2002–05 Century & Regal

Step	Action	Yes	No
7	Repair the short to voltage in the left cooling fan motor supply voltage circuit. Did you complete the repair?	Go to Step 14	--
8	Repair the short to voltage in the left cooling fan low reference circuit. Did you complete the repair?	Go to Step 14	--
9	Repair the short to voltage in the right cooling fan motor supply voltage circuit. Did you complete the repair?	Go to Step 14	--
10	Inspect for poor connections at the cooling fan 1 relay. Did you find and correct the condition?	Go to Step 14	Go to Step 12
11	Inspect for poor connections at the cooling fan 3 relay. Did you find and correct the condition?	Go to Step 14	Go to Step 13
12	Replace the cooling fan 1 relay. Did you complete the replacement?	Go to Step 14	--
13	Replace the cooling fan 3 relay. Did you complete the replacement?	Go to Step 14	--
14	Operate the system in order to verify the repair. Did you correct the condition?	System OK	Go to Step 2

ARM0300000000311

Fig. 51 Cooling fan always on (Part 2 of 2). 2002–05 Century & Regal

	Action	Yes	No
1	Did you perform the Engine Cooling Diagnostic System Check?	Go to Step 2	Go to Diagnostic System Check
2	1. Install a scan tool. 2. Turn ON the ignition, with the engine OFF. 3. With a scan tool, command the Fans Low Speed ON and OFF. Do the low speed engine cooling fans turn ON and OFF with each command?	Go to Step 3	Go to Step 4
3	Important: A 3-second delay occurs before the PCM changes the cooling fan speed. With a scan tool, command the Fans High Speed ON and OFF. Do the high speed engine cooling fans turn ON and OFF with each command?	Test for Intermittent and Poor Connections	Go to Step 12
4	Important: Do NOT remove the 20-A fused jumper wire connected during this step. Use a second 20-A fused jumper wire while performing the following steps. 1. Remove the cooling fan 1 relay. 2. Connect a 20-A fused jumper between the battery positive switch side voltage circuit and the cooling fan motor supply voltage circuit of the cooling fan 1 relay. Do both cooling fans operate in low speed?	Go to Step 22	Go to Step 5

ARM0300000000312

Fig. 52 Cooling fan inoperative (Part 1 of 6). 2002–05 Century & Regal

	Action	Yes	No
5	1. Disconnect the cooling fan 2 relay 2. Connect the second 20-A fused jumper between the cooling fan low reference circuit and the cooling fan motor supply voltage circuit of the cooling fan 2 relay. Do both cooling fans operate in low speed?	Go to Step 23	Go to Step 6
6	Connect the second 20-A fused jumper between the battery positive voltage circuit and the cooling fan motor supply voltage circuit of the cooling fan 2 relay. Does the right cooling fan operate in high speed?	Go to Step 9	Go to Step 7
7	1. Install the cooling fan 2 relay. 2. Disconnect the right cooling fan electrical connector. 3. Connect the second 20-Amp fused jumper wire from the cooling fan motor supply voltage circuit to the ground circuit of the right cooling fan electrical connector. Does the left cooling fan operate in high speed?	Go to Step 25	Go to Step 8
8	Connect the second 20-Amp fused jumper wire from the cooling fan motor supply voltage circuit of the right cooling fan electrical connector to a good ground. Does the left cooling fan operate in high speed?	Go to Step 29	Go to Step 30
9	1. Install the cooling fan 2 relay. 2. Disconnect the left cooling fan electrical connector. 3. Connect the second 20-Amp fused jumper wire from the cooling fan motor supply voltage circuit to the cooling fan low reference circuit of the left cooling fan electrical connector. Does the right cooling fan operate in high speed?	Go to Step 26	Go to Step 10
10	Connect the second 20-Amp fused jumper wire from the coil side battery positive voltage circuit to the cooling fan low reference circuit of the of the left cooling fan electrical connector. Does the right cooling fan operate in high speed?	Go to Step 11	Go to Step 31

ARM0300000000313

Fig. 52 Cooling fan inoperative (Part 2 of 6). 2002–05 Century & Regal

Step	Action	Yes	No
11	Probe the battery positive voltage circuit on the switch side of the cooling fan 1 relay with a test lamp that is connected to a good ground. Does the test lamp illuminate?	Go to Step 27	Go to Step 32
12	Is the right cooling fan operating properly in high speed?	Go to Step 19	Go to Step 13
13	1. Turn off the ignition. 2. Disconnect the cooling fan 3 relay. 3. Turn ON the ignition, with the engine OFF. 4. Connect a test lamp between the high speed cooling fan relay control circuit and the battery positive voltage circuit on the coil side of the cooling fan 3 relay. 5. With a scan tool command the High Speed Fans ON and OFF. Does the test lamp turn ON and OFF with each command?	Go to Step 15	Go to Step 14
14	Probe the battery positive voltage circuit on the coil side of cooling fan 3 relay with a test lamp that is connected to a good ground. Does the test lamp illuminate?	Go to Step 34	Go to Step 33
15	Install a 20 amp fused jumper between the battery positive voltage circuit on the switch side of the cooling fan 3 relay and the cooling fan motor supply voltage circuit. Does the right cooling fan operate in high speed?	Go to Step 24	Go to Step 16
16	Probe the battery positive voltage circuit on the switch side of the cooling fan 3 relay with a test lamp connected to a good ground. Does the test lamp illuminate?	Go to Step 17	Go to Step 33
17	With the 20 amp fused jumper still installed. 1. Disconnect the right cooling fan electrical connector. 2. Connect a test lamp from the cooling fan motor supply voltage circuit to the ground circuit of the right cooling fan electrical connector. Does the test lamp illuminate?	Go to Step 25	Go to Step 18

ARM0300000000314

**Fig. 52 Cooling fan inoperative (Part 3 of 6).
2002–05 Century & Regal**

Step	Action	Yes	No
18	Probe the cooling fan motor supply voltage circuit of the right cooling fan electrical connector with a test lamp that is connected to a good ground. Does the test lamp illuminate?	Go to Step 29	Go to Step 30
19	1. Turn OFF the ignition. 2. Disconnect the cooling fan 2 relay 3. Turn ON the ignition, with the engine OFF. 4. Connect a 20-A fused jumper between the cooling fan low reference circuit and the ground circuit of the cooling fan 2 relay. 5. With a scan tool command the Fans High Speed ON and OFF. Does the left cooling fan operate in high speed?	Go to Step 20	Go to Step 28
20	1. Connect a test lamp between the high speed cooling fan relay control circuit of the cooling fan 2 relay and the battery positive voltage circuit of the cooling fan 2 relay. 2. With a scan tool command the Fans High Speed ON and OFF. Does the test lamp turn ON and OFF with each command?	Go to Step 23	Go to Step 21
21	Probe the battery positive voltage circuit of the cooling fan 2 relay with a test lamp that is connected to a good ground. Does the test lamp illuminate?	Go to Step 34	Go to Step 33
22	Inspect for poor connections at the cooling fan 1 relay. Did you find and correct the condition?	Go to Step 40	Go to Step 35
23	Inspect for poor connections at the cooling fan 2 relay. Did you find and correct the condition?	Go to Step 40	Go to Step 36
24	Inspect for poor connections at the cooling fan 3 relay. Did you find and correct the condition?	Go to Step 40	Go to Step 37

ARM0300000000315

**Fig. 52 Cooling fan inoperative (Part 4 of 6).
2002–05 Century & Regal**

Step	Action	Yes	No
25	Inspect for poor connections at the harness connector of the right cooling fan. Did you find and correct the condition?	Go to Step 40	Go to Step 38
26	Inspect for poor connections at the harness connector of the left cooling fan. Did you find and correct the condition?	Go to Step 40	Go to Step 39
27	Repair the left cooling fan motor supply voltage circuit for an open. Is the repair complete?	Go to Step 40	--
28	Repair the left cooling fan ground circuit for an open. Is the repair complete?	Go to Step 40	--
29	Repair the right cooling fan ground circuit for an open. Is the repair complete?	Go to Step 40	--
30	Repair the right cooling fan motor supply voltage circuit for an open. Is the repair complete?	Go to Step 40	--
31	Repair the left cooling fan low reference circuit for a short to ground or an open. Is the repair complete?	Go to Step 40	--
32	Repair the cooling fan 1 relay battery positive voltage circuit for an open. Is the repair complete?	Go to Step 40	--

ARM0300000000316

**Fig. 52 Cooling fan inoperative (Part 5 of 6).
2002–05 Century & Regal**

Step	Action	Yes	No
33	Repair the battery positive voltage circuit for the cooling fan 2 and 3 relay for an open. Is the repair complete?	Go to Step 40	--
34	Repair the high speed cooling fan relay control circuit for an open. Is the repair complete?	Go to Step 40	--
35	Replace the cooling fan 1 relay. Is the repair complete?	Go to Step 40	--
36	Replace the cooling fan 2 relay. Is the repair complete?	Go to Step 40	--
37	Replace the cooling fan 3 relay. Is the repair complete?	Go to Step 40	--
38	Replace the right cooling fan. Is the repair complete?	Go to Step 40	--
39	Replace the left cooling fan. Is the repair complete?	Go to Step 40	--
40	Operate the system in order to verify the repair. Did you correct the condition?	System OK	Go to Step 3

ARM0300000000317

**Fig. 52 Cooling fan inoperative (Part 6 of 6).
2002–05 Century & Regal**

Test Description

The number(s) below refer to the step number(s) on the diagnostic table.

2. Lack of communication may be due to a partial malfunction of the class 2 serial data circuit or due to a total malfunction of the class 2 serial data circuit. The specified procedure will determine the particular condition.

3. Determine if the Instrument Cluster or Powertrain Control Modules have set DTC's which may affect Engine Cooling operation are present.

4. The presence of DTCs which begin with "U" indicate some other module is not communicating. The specified procedure will compile all the available information before tests are performed.

Step	Action	Yes	No
1	Install a scan tool. Does the scan tool power up?	Go to Step 2	Diagnose Data Link Communications
2	1. Turn ON the ignition, with the engine OFF. 2. Attempt to establish communication with the following control modules: o Instrument Cluster o Powertrain Control Module Does the scan tool communicate with the control modules?	Go to Step 3	Diagnose Data Link Communications
3	Select the powertrain control module display DTCs function on the scan tool. Does the scan tool display any DTCs?	Go to Step 4	Diagnose Engine Cooling
4	Does the scan tool display any DTCs which begin with a "U"?	Diagnose Data Link Communications	Go to Diagnostic Trouble Code (DTC) List

GC1080100656000X

Fig. 53 Diagnostic system check. 2001–04 Corvette

Step	Action	Yes	No
DEFINITION: One or both engine cooling fan motors do not operate properly in high or low speed modes.			
1	Did you perform the Engine Cooling Diagnostic System Check?	Go to Step 2	Go to Diagnostic System Check
2	1. Install a scan tool. 2. Turn ON the ignition, with the engine OFF. 3. With a scan tool, command the Fan Relay 1 ON and OFF. Do the low speed engine cooling fans turn ON and OFF with each command?	Go to Step 3	Go to Step 4
3	With a scan tool, command the Fan Relays 1, 2 & 3 ON and OFF. Do the high speed engine cooling fans turn ON and OFF with each command?	Test Intermittent and Poor Connections	Go to Step 11
4	**Important** Do NOT remove the 20-A fused jumper wire connected during this step. Use a second 20-A fused jumper wire while performing the following steps: 1. Disconnect the cool fan 1 relay. 2. Connect the first 20-A fused jumper between the battery positive voltage circuit of the cool fan 1 relay and the cooling fan motor supply voltage circuit of the cool fan 1 relay. Do both cooling fans operate in low speed?	Go to Step 13	Go to Step 5
5	1. Disconnect the cool fan 3 relay. 2. Connect the second 20-A fused jumper between the left cooling fan circuit of the cool fan 3 relay and the right cooling fan motor supply voltage circuit of the cool fan 3 relay. Do both cooling fans operate in low speed?	Go to Step 14	Go to Step 6

GC1080100658010X

Fig. 55 Cooling fan inoperative (Part 1 of 4). 2001–04 Corvette

Step	Action	Yes	No
DEFINITION: One or both engine cooling fan motors run continuously in high or low speed.			
1	Did you perform the Engine Cooling Diagnostic System Check?	Go to Step 2	Go To Diagnostic System Check
2	Turn ON the ignition, with the engine OFF. Are one or both cooling fans ON?	Go to Step 3	Test for Intermittent and Poor Connections
3	Are both cooling fans running continuously?	Go to Step 5	Go to Step 4
4	Remove the cool fan 3 relay. Did the right cooling fan turn OFF?	Go to Step 6	Go to Step 7
5	Repair the short to voltage in the left cooling fan motor supply voltage circuit. Did you complete the repair?	Go to Step 8	--
6	Repair the short to voltage in the left cooling fan low reference circuit. Did you complete the repair?	Go to Step 8	--
7	Repair the short to voltage in the right cooling fan motor supply voltage circuit. Did you complete the repair?	Go to Step 8	--
8	Operate the system in order to verify the repair. Did you correct the condition?	System OK	Go to Step 2

GC1080100657000X

Fig. 54 Cooling fan always on. 2001–04 Corvette

Step	Action	Yes	No
6	Connect the second 20-A fused jumper from the battery positive voltage to the cooling fan motor supply voltage circuit of the cool fan 3 relay. Does the right cooling fan operate in high speed?	Go to Step 9	Go to Step 7
7	1. Install the cool fan 3 relay. 2. Disconnect the right cooling fan electrical connector. 3. Connect the second 20-Amp fused jumper wire from the cooling fan motor supply voltage circuit of the right electrical connector to the cooling fan ground circuit of the right electrical connector. Does the left cooling fan operate in high speed?	Go to Step 16	Go to Step 8
8	Connect the second 20-Amp fused jumper wire from the cooling fan supply voltage circuit of the right cooling fan electrical connector to a good ground. Does the left cooling fan motor operate in high speed?	Go to Step 20	Go to Step 21
9	1. Install the cool fan 3 relay. 2. Disconnect the left cooling fan electrical connector. 3. Connect the second 20-Amp fused jumper from the cooling fan motor supply voltage circuit of the left cooling fan electrical connector to the low reference circuit of the left cooling fan electrical connector. Does the right cooling fan motor operate in high speed?	Go to Step 17	Go to Step 10
10	Connect the second 20-Amp fused jumper wire from battery positive voltage to the left cooling fan low reference circuit of the left cooling fan electrical connector. Does the right cooling fan operate in high speed?	Go to Step 18	Go to Step 22
11	Does the right cooling fan operate in high speed?	Go to Step 12	Go to Step 15
12	1. Disconnect the cool fan 3 relay. 2. Connect a 20-A fused jumper between the left cooling fan low reference circuit of the cool fan 3 relay and the ground circuit of the cool fan 3 relay. Does the left cooling fan operate properly in high speed?	Go to Step 14	Go to Step 19
13	Inspect for poor connections at the cool fan 1 relay. Did you find and correct the condition?	Go to Step 28	Go to Step 23
14	Inspect for poor connections at the cool fan 3 relay. Did you find and correct the condition?	Go to Step 28	Go to Step 24
15	Inspect for poor connections at the cool fan 2 relay. Did you find and correct the condition?	Go to Step 28	Go to Step 25

GC1080100658020X

Fig. 55 Cooling fan inoperative (Part 2 of 4). 2001–04 Corvette

		Yes	No
16	Inspect for poor connections at the harness connector of the right cooling fan. Did you find and correct the condition?	Go to Step 28	Go to Step 26
17	Inspect for poor connections at the harness connector of the left cooling fan. Did you find and correct the condition?	Go to Step 28	Go to Step 27
18	Repair the left cooling fan motor supply voltage circuit. Did you complete the repair?	Go to Step 28	--
19	Repair the left cooling fan ground circuit. Did you complete the repair?	Go to Step 28	--
20	Repair the right cooling fan ground circuit. Did you complete the repair?	Go to Step 28	--
21	Repair the right cooling fan motor supply voltage circuit. Did you complete the repair?	Go to Step 28	--
22	Repair the left cooling fan low reference circuit. Did you complete the repair?	Go to Step 28	--
23	Replace the cool fan 1 relay. Is the repair complete?	Go to Step 28	--
24	Replace the cool fan 3 relay. Is the repair complete?	Go to Step 28	--

GC1080100658030X

Fig. 55   Cooling fan inoperative (Part 3 of 4). 2001–04 Corvette

Step	Action			Yes	No
1	Perform the following preliminary inspections: • Ensure that the battery is fully charged. • Ensure that the battery cables are clean and tight. • Inspect for any open fuses. • Inspect the easily accessible systems or the visible system components for obvious damage or conditions that could cause the symptom. • Ensure that the grounds are clean, tight, and in the correct location. • Inspect for aftermarket devices that could affect the operation of the system. • Search for applicable service bulletins. Did you find and correct the condition?			System OK	Go to Step 2

ARM0400000000010

Fig. 56   Diagnostic system check (Part 1 of 2). 2005 Corvette

Step	Action	Values	Yes	No
	DEFINITION: Engine cooling fan operates all the time when the vehicle is started or not started.			
1	Did you perform the Diagnostic System Check - Vehicle?	--	Go to Step 2	Go to Diagnostic System Check
2	**Important** The vehicle must be allowed to cool down. The HVAC control system must be in the OFF position and the coolant temperature must stay below 91° (195°F) for this diagnostic. 1. Start the vehicle. 2. Turn OFF the HVAC system. Is the cooling fan ON?	--	Go to Step 3	Go to Diagnostic Aids
3	1. Turn OFF the ignition. 2. Disconnect the fan control module connector. 3. Probe the cooling fan speed control circuit of the fan control module with a test lamp that is connected to voltage. Does the test lamp illuminate?	--	Go to Step 7	Go to Step 4

ARM0400000000012

Fig. 57   Cooling fan always on (Part 1 of 2). 2005 Corvette

		Yes	No
25	Replace the cool fan 2 relay. Is the repair complete?	Go to Step 28	--
26	Replace the right cooling fan. Is the repair complete?	Go to Step 28	--
27	Replace the left cooling fan. Is the repair complete?	Go to Step 28	--
28	Operate the system in order to verify the repair. Did you correct the condition?	System OK	Go to Step 3

GC1080100658040X

Fig. 55   Cooling fan inoperative (Part 4 of 4). 2001–04 Corvette

2	Install a scan tool. Does the scan tool power up?	Go to Step 3	Diagnose Scan Tool Does Not Power Up
3	Turn ON the ignition, with the engine OFF. Is the NO FOB DETECTED message displayed on the driver information center (DIC)?	Go to Key Fob Not Detected in Keyless Entry	Go to Step 4
4	1. Turn ON the ignition, with the engine OFF. 2. Attempt to establish communication with all of the control modules on the vehicle. Does the scan tool communicate with all of the expected vehicle control modules?	Go to Step 5	Diagnose Data Link References
5	Attempt to start the engine. Does the engine crank?	Go to Step 6	Go to Symptoms
6	Attempt to start the engine. Does the engine start and idle?	Go to Step 7	Go to Engine Cranks but Does Not Run

ARM0400000000011

Fig. 56   Diagnostic system check (Part 2 of 2). 2005 Corvette

			Yes	No
4	Inspect the battery positive voltage circuit of the cooling fan motor for a short to voltage. Did you find and correct the condition?	-	Go to Step 9	Go to Step 5
5	Inspect for poor connections at the fan control module. Did you find and correct the condition?	-	Go to Step 9	Go to Step 6
6	Replace the fan control module. Did you complete the replacement?	-	Go to Step 9	--
7	Inspect for poor connections at the engine control module (ECM). Did you find and correct the condition?	-	Go to Step 9	Go to Step 8
8	Replace the ECM. Did you complete the replacement?	-	Go to Step 9	--
9	Operate the system in order to verify the repair. Did you correct the condition?	-	System OK	Go to Step 2

ARM0400000000013

Fig. 57   Cooling fan always on (Part 2 of 2). 2005 Corvette

Step	Action	Values	Yes	No
1	Did you perform the Diagnostic System Check - Vehicle?	--	Go to Step 2	Go to Diagnostic System Check
2	1. Install a scan tool. 2. Turn ON the ignition, with the engine OFF. 3. With a scan tool, command the cooling fan ON and OFF. Does the cooling fan turn ON and OFF with each command?		Go to Diagnostic Aids	Go to Step 3

ARM0400000000014

Fig. 58   Cooling fan inoperative (Part 1 of 3). 2005 Corvette

Step	Action		Yes	No
3	1. Turn OFF the ignition. 2. Disconnect the fan control module connector. 3. Probe the battery positive voltage circuit of the fan control module with a test lamp that is connected to a good ground. Does the test lamp illuminate?	--	Go to Step 4	Go to Step 10
4	Inspect the ground circuit of the fan control module for an open. Did you complete the repair	--	Go to Step 16	Go to Step 5
5	1. Install a scan tool. 2. Turn ON the ignition, with the engine OFF. 3. Command the cooling fan ON to 90 percent. 4. Measure the voltage on the cooling fan speed control circuit at the fan control module. Is the voltage near the specified value?	0.45 V	Go to Step 6	Go to Step 9
6	**Important** When using jumpers in this step, if the wire gage of the jumpers you use is smaller than the production wire gage supplied to the cooling fan, the wires may get hot. Connect the jumper wires long enough to verify that the cooling fan motor operates, then remove the jumpers. 1. Jumper the fan control module ground circuit and the cooling fan motor ground circuit together at the fan control module connector. 2. Jumper the fan control module battery voltage circuit and the cooling fan motor battery voltage circuit together at the fan control module connector. Does the cooling fan operate?		Go to Step 7	Go to Step 11

ARM0400000000015

Fig. 58   Cooling fan inoperative (Part 2 of 3). 2005 Corvette

Step	Action	Yes	No
7	Inspect for poor connections at the fan control module. Did you find and correct the condition?	Go to Step 16	Go to Step 8
8	Replace the fan control module. Did you complete the replacement?	Go to Step 16	--
9	Inspect the cooling fan speed control circuit for the following: • An open • A short to ground • A short to voltage Did you find and correct the condition?	Go to Step 16	Go to Step 14
10	Repair the battery positive voltage circuit of the fan control module for an open or short to ground. Did you complete the repair?	Go to Step 16	--

ARM0400000000016

Fig. 58   Cooling fan inoperative (Part 3 of 3). 2005 Corvette

Step	Action	Yes	No
1	Did you perform the Engine Cooling System Check?	Go to Step 2	Check Engine Cooling
2	Turn ON the ignition, with the engine OFF. Are one or both cooling fans ON?	Go to Step 3	Test for Intermittent and Poor Connections
3	Are both cooling fans running continuously?	Go to Step 5	Go to Step 4
4	Remove the s/p fan relay. Did the right cooling fan turn OFF?	Go to Step 6	Go to Step 7
5	Repair the short to voltage in the left cooling fan motor supply voltage circuit. Did you complete the repair?	Go to Step 8	--
6	Repair the short to voltage in the left cooling fan low reference circuit. Did you complete the repair?	Go to Step 8	--
7	Repair the short to voltage in the right cooling fan motor supply voltage circuit. Did you complete the repair?	Go to Step 8	--
8	Operate the system in order to verify the repair. Did you correct the condition?	System OK	Go to Step 2

ARM66GC000000275

Fig. 59   Primary cooling fan always on. CTS

Step	Action	Yes	No
1	Did you perform the Engine Cooling System Check?	Go to Step 2	Check - Engine Cooling
2	1. Install a scan tool. 2. Turn ON the ignition, with the engine OFF. 3. With a scan tool, command the Fans Low Speed ON and OFF. Do the low speed engine cooling fans turn ON and OFF with each command?	Go to Step 3	Go to Step 4
3	**Important:** A 3-second delay occurs before the PCM changes the cooling fan speed. With a scan tool, command the Fans High Speed ON and OFF. Do the high speed engine cooling fans turn ON and OFF with each command?	Test for Intermittent and Poor Connections	Go to Step 11
4	**Important** Do NOT remove the 20-A fused jumper wire connected during this step. Use a second 20-A fused jumper wire while performing the following steps. 1. Disconnect the low speed fan relay. 2. Connect the first 20-A fused jumper between the battery positive voltage circuit of the low speed fan relay and the cooling fan motor supply voltage circuit of the low speed fan relay. Do both cooling fans operate in low speed?	Go to Step 13	Go to Step 5
5	1. Disconnect the s/p fan relay. 2. Connect the second 20-A fused jumper between the left cooling fan motor low reference circuit of the s/p fan relay and the right cooling fan motor supply voltage circuit of the s/p fan relay. Do both cooling fans operate in low speed?	Go to Step 14	Go to Step 6
6	Reconnect the second 20-A fused jumper between the battery positive voltage circuit of the s/p fan relay and the cooling fan motor supply voltage circuit of the s/p fan relay. Does the right cooling fan operate in high speed?	Go to Step 9	Go to Step 7

ARM66GC000000276

Fig. 60   Primary cooling fan inoperative (Part 1 of 3). CTS

Step	Action	Yes	No
7	1. Install the s/p fan relay. 2. Disconnect the right cooling fan electrical connector. 3. Reconnect the second 20-Amp fused jumper wire from the cooling fan motor supply voltage circuit of the right cooling fan electrical connector to the cooling fan motor ground circuit of the right cooling fan electrical connector. Does the left cooling fan operate in high speed?	Go to Step 16	Go to Step 8
8	Reconnect the second 20-Amp fused jumper wire from the cooling fan motor supply voltage circuit of the right cooling fan electrical connector to a good ground. Does the left cooling fan operate in high speed?	Go to Step 20	Go to Step 21
9	1. Install the s/p fan relay. 2. Disconnect the left cooling fan electrical connector. 3. Reconnect the second 20-Amp fused jumper wire from cooling fan motor supply voltage circuit of the left cooling fan electrical connector to the cooling fan low reference circuit of the left cooling fan electrical connector. Does the right cooling fan operate in high speed?	Go to Step 17	Go to Step 10
10	Reconnect the second 20-Amp fused jumper wire from battery positive voltage to the left cooling fan low reference circuit of the of the left cooling fan electrical connector. Does the right cooling fan operate in high speed?	Go to Step 18	Go to Step 22
11	Does the right cooling fan operate in high speed?	Go to Step 12	Go to Step 15
12	1. Disconnect the s/p fan relay. 2. Connect a 20-A fused jumper between the left cooling fan low reference circuit of the s/p fan relay and the ground circuit of the s/p fan relay. Does the left cooling fan operate properly in high speed?	Go to Step 14	Go to Step 19
13	Inspect for poor connections at the low speed fan relay. Did you find and correct the condition?	Go to Step 28	Go to Step 23
14	Inspect for poor connections at the s/p fan relay. Did you find and correct the condition?	Go to Step 28	Go to Step 24

ARM66GC000000277

Fig. 60 Primary cooling fan inoperative (Part 2 of 3). CTS

Step	Action	Yes	No
15	Inspect for poor connections at the high speed fan relay Did you find and correct the condition?	Go to Step 28	Go to Step 25
16	Inspect for poor connections at the harness connector of the right cooling fan. Did you find and correct the condition?	Go to Step 28	Go to Step 26
17	Inspect for poor connections at the harness connector of the left cooling fan Did you find and correct the condition?	Go to Step 28	Go to Step 27
18	Repair the left cooling fan motor supply voltage circuit. Did you complete the repair?	Go to Step 28	--
19	Repair the left cooling fan motor ground circuit. Did you complete the repair?	Go to Step 28	--
20	Repair the right cooling fan motor ground circuit. Did you complete the repair?	Go to Step 28	--
21	Repair the right cooling fan motor supply voltage circuit. Systems. Did you complete the repair?	Go to Step 28	--
22	Repair the left cooling fan low reference circuit. Did you complete the repair?	Go to Step 28	--
23	Replace the low speed fan relay. Did you complete the replacement?	Go to Step 28	--
24	Replace the s/p fan relay. Did you complete the replacement?	Go to Step 28	--
25	Replace the high speed fan relay. Did you complete the replacement?	Go to Step 28	--
26	Replace the right cooling fan. Did you complete the replacement?	Go to Step 28	--
27	Replace the left cooling fan. Did you complete the replacement?	Go to Step 28	--
28	Operate the system in order to verify the repair. Did you correct the condition?	System OK	Go to Step 3

ARM66GC000000278

Fig. 60 Primary cooling fan inoperative (Part 3 of 3). CTS

Step	Action	Yes	No
1	Did you perform the Engine Cooling System Check?	Go to Step 2	Check Engine Cooling
2	Is the auxiliary cooling fan always ON?	Go to Step 3	Test for Intermittent and Poor Connections
3	Disconnect the auxiliary cooling fan relay. Does the auxiliary cooling fan turn OFF?	Go to Step 5	Go to Step 4
4	Repair the short to voltage in the auxiliary cooling fan motor supply voltage circuit. Did you complete the repair?	Go to Step 10	--
5	Probe the control circuit of the auxiliary fan relay with a test lamp connected to battery positive voltage. Does the test lamp illuminate?	Go to Step 7	Go to Step 6
6	Inspect for poor connections at the auxiliary cooling fan relay Did you find and correct the condition?	Go to Step 10	Go to Step 8
7	Inspect for poor connections at the harness connector of the Engine Control Module (ECM). Did you find and correct the condition?	Go to Step 10	Go to Step 9
8	Replace the auxiliary cooling fan relay. Did you complete the replacement?	Go to Step 10	--
9	**Important:** Perform the programming procedure for the ECM. Replace the ECM. Did you complete the repair?	Go to Step 10	--
10	Operate the system in order to verify the repair. Did you correct the condition?	System OK	Go to Step 3

ARM66GC000000279

Fig. 61 Auxiliary cooling fan always on. CTS

Step	Action	Yes	No
1	Did you perform the Engine Cooling System Check?	Go to Step 2	Check - Engine Cooling
2	1. Install a scan tool. 2. Turn ON the ignition, with the engine OFF. 3. With a scan tool, command the auxiliary cooling fan ON and OFF. Does the auxiliary cooling fan turn ON and OFF with each command?	Test for Intermittent and Poor Connections	Go to Step 3
3	1. Disconnect the auxiliary fan relay. 2. Probe the control circuit of the auxiliary fan relay with a test lamp connected to battery positive voltage. Does the test lamp illuminate?	Go to Step 4	Go to Step 6
4	Probe the battery positive voltage circuit of the auxiliary fan relay with a test lamp that is connected to a good ground. Does the test lamp illuminate?	Go to Step 5	Go to Step 7
5	Connect a 20-A fused jumper between the battery positive voltage circuit of the auxiliary fan relay and the auxiliary cooling fan motor supply voltage circuit of the auxiliary fan relay. Does the auxiliary cooling fan operate?	Go to Step 12	Go to Step 8
6	Test the control circuit of the auxiliary fan relay for an open or high resistance. Did you find and correct the condition?	Go to Step 17	Go to Step 11
7	Test the battery positive voltage circuit of the auxiliary fan relay for a short to ground or an open. Did you find and correct the condition?	Go to Step 17	Go to Step 10
8	Test the auxiliary cooling fan motor supply voltage circuit of the auxiliary cooling fan for an open or high resistance. Did you find and correct the condition?	Go to Step 17	Go to Step 9
9	Test the auxiliary cooling fan motor ground circuit for an open or high resistance. Did you find and correct the condition?	Go to Step 17	Go to Step

ARM66GC000000280

Fig. 62 Auxiliary cooling fan inoperative (Part 1 of 2). CTS

Step	Action	Yes	No
10	Repair the auxiliary cooling fan motor supply voltage circuit for a short to ground. Did you complete the repair?	Go to Step 17	--
11	Inspect for poor connections Engine Control module (ECM). Did you find and correct the condition?	Go to Step 17	Go to Step 14
12	Inspect for poor connections at the auxiliary fan relay. Did you find and correct the condition?	Go to Step 17	Go to Step 15
13	Inspect for poor connections at the harness connector of the auxiliary cooling fan. Did you find and correct the condition?	Go to Step 17	Go to Step 16
14	Important: Perform the programming procedure for the ECM. Replace the ECM. Did you complete the repair?	Go to Step 17	--
15	Replace the auxiliary fan relay. Did you complete the replacement?	Go to Step 17	--
16	Replace the auxiliary cooling fan. Did you complete the replacement?	Go to Step 17	--
17	Operate the system in order to verify the repair. Did you correct the condition?	System OK	Go to Step 2

ARM66GC000000281

Fig. 62 Auxiliary cooling fan inoperative (Part 2 of 2). CTS

Test Description

The number(s) below refer to the step number(s) on the diagnostic table.

2. Lack of communication may be due to a partial malfunction of the class 2 serial data circuit or due to a total malfunction of the class 2 serial data circuit. The specified procedure will determine the particular condition.

3. Determine if the Instrument Cluster or Powertrain Control Modules have set DTC's which may affect Engine Cooling operation are present.

4. The presence of DTCs which begin with a "U" indicate some other module is not communicating. The specified procedure will compile all the available information before tests are performed.

Step	Action	Yes	No
1	Install a scan tool. Does the scan tool power up?	Go to Step 2	Diagnose Link Communications
2	1. Turn ON the ignition, with the engine OFF. 2. Attempt to establish communication with the following control modules: • Instrument Cluster • Powertrain Control Module. Does the scan tool communicate with the control modules?	Go to Step 3	Diagnose Data Link Communications
3	Select the powertrain control module display DTCs function on the scan tool. Does the scan tool display any DTCs?	Go to Step 4	Diagnose Engine Cooling
4	Does the scan tool display any DTCs which begin with a "U"?	Diagnose Data Link Communications	Diagnose Trouble Code

GC1080100659000X

Fig. 63 Diagnostic system check. 2001–02 DeVille, Eldorado & Seville

Step	Action	Yes	No
	DEFINITION: One or both engine cooling fan motors run continuously in high or low speed.		
1	Did you perform the Engine Cooling Diagnostic System Check?	Go to Step 2	Engine Cooling
2	Turn ON the ignition, with the engine OFF. Are one or both cooling fans ON?	Go to Step 3	Test for Intermittent and Poor Connections
3	Are both cooling fans running continuously?	Go to Step 5	Go to Step 4
4	Remove the cooling fan S/P relay. Did the right cooling fan turn OFF?	Go to Step 6	Go to Step 7
5	Repair the short to voltage in the left cooling fan motor supply voltage circuit. Did you complete the repair?	Go to Step 8	--
6	Repair the short to voltage in the left cooling fan low reference circuit. Did you complete the repair?	Go to Step 8	--
7	Repair the short to voltage in the right cooling fan motor supply voltage circuit. Did you complete the repair?	Go to Step 8	--
8	Operate the system in order to verify the repair. Did you correct the condition?	System OK	Go to Step 2

GC1080100660000X

Fig. 64 Cooling fan always on. 2001–02 DeVille, Eldorado & Seville

Step	Action	Yes	No
	DEFINITION: One or both engine cooling fan motors do not operate properly in high or low speed modes.		
1	Did you perform the Engine Cooling Diagnostic System Check?	Go to Step 2	Diagnose Engine Cooling
2	1. Install a scan tool. 2. Turn ON the ignition, with the engine OFF. 3. With a scan tool, command the Fans Low Speed ON and OFF. Do the low speed engine cooling fans turn ON and OFF with each command?	Go to Step 3	Go to Step 4
3	Important: Before the PCM changes the speed of the cooling fans, a 3-second delay will occur. With a scan tool, command the Fans High Speed ON and OFF. Do the high speed engine cooling fans turn ON and OFF with each command?	Test for Intermittent and Poor Connections	Go to Step 11
4	Important: Following this step, do NOT remove the 20-A fused jumper wire that is connected during this step. While performing the following steps, use a second 20-A fused jumper wire. 1. Remove the cooling fan 1 relay. 2. Connect a 20-A fused jumper between the battery positive voltage circuit of the cooling fan 1 relay and the cooling fan motor supply voltage circuit of the cooling fan 1 relay. Do both cooling fans operate in low speed?	Go to Step 13	Go to Step 5
5	1. Remove the cooling fan S/P relay. 2. Connect the second 20-A fused jumper between the left cooling fan low reference circuit of the cooling fan S/P relay and the right cooling fan supply voltage circuit of the cooling fan S/P relay. Do both cooling fans operate in low speed?	Go to Step 14	Go to Step 6
6	Connect the second 20-A fused jumper between the battery positive voltage circuit of the cooling fan S/P relay and the cooling fan motor supply voltage circuit of the cooling fan S/P relay. Does the right cooling fan operate in high speed?	Go to Step 9	Go to Step 7
7	1. Install the cooling fan S/P relay. 2. Disconnect the right cooling fan electrical connector. 3. Connect the second 20-Amp fused jumper wire from the cooling fan motor supply voltage circuit of the right cooling fan electrical connector to the ground circuit of the right cooling fan electrical connector. Does the left cooling fan operate in high speed?	Go to Step 16	Go to Step 8
8	Connect the second 20-Amp fused jumper wire from the cooling fan motor supply voltage circuit of the right cooling fan electrical connector to a good ground. Does the left cooling fan operate in high speed?	Go to Step 20	Go to Step 21
9	1. Install the cooling fan S/P relay. 2. Disconnect the left cooling fan electrical connector. 3. Connect the second 20-Amp fused jumper wire from the cooling fan motor supply voltage circuit of the left cooling fan electrical connector to the cooling fan low reference circuit of the left cooling fan electrical connector. Does the right cooling fan operate in high speed?	Go to Step 17	Go to Step 10
10	1. Leave the fused jumper wire in place of the cooling fan 1 relay. 2. Connect a 20 Amp fused jumper wire from battery positive voltage to the left cooling fan low circuit of the of the left cooling fan electrical connector. Does the right cooling fan operate in high speed?	Go to Step 18	Go to Step 22
11	Is the right cooling fan operating properly in high speed?	Go to Step 12	Go to Step 15

GC1080100661010X

Fig. 65 Cooling fan inoperative (Part 1 of 2). 2001–02 DeVille, Eldorado & Seville

Step	Action	Yes	No
12	1. Disconnect the cooling fan S/P relay 2. Connect the second 20-A fused jumper between the left cooling fan low reference circuit of the cooling fan S/P relay and the ground circuit of the cooling fan S/P relay. Does the left cooling fan operate properly in high speed?	Go to Step 14	Go to Step 19
13	Inspect for poor connections at the cooling fan 1 relay. Did you find and correct the condition?	Go to Step 28	Go to Step 23
14	Inspect for poor connections at the cooling fan S/P relay. Did you find and correct the condition?	Go to Step 28	Go to Step 24
15	Inspect for poor connections at the cooling fan 2 relay. Did you find and correct the condition?	Go to Step 28	Go to Step 25
16	Inspect for poor connections at the harness connector of the right cooling fan. Did you find and correct the condition?	Go to Step 28	Go to Step 26
17	Inspect for poor connections at the harness connector of the left cooling fan. Did you find and correct the condition?	Go to Step 28	Go to Step 27
18	Repair the left cooling fan motor supply voltage circuit. Did you complete the repair?	Go to Step 28	—
19	Repair the left cooling fan ground circuit. Did you complete the repair?	Go to Step 28	—
20	Repair the right cooling fan ground circuit. Did you complete the repair?	Go to Step 28	—
21	Repair the right cooling fan motor supply voltage circuit. Did you complete the repair?	Go to Step 28	—
22	Repair the left cooling fan low reference circuit. Did you complete the repair?	Go to Step 28	—
23	Replace the cooling fan 1 relay. Is the repair complete?	Go to Step 28	—
24	Replace the cooling fan S/P relay. Is the repair complete?	Go to Step 28	—
25	Replace the cooling fan 2 relay. Is the repair complete?	Go to Step 28	—
26	Replace the right cooling fan. Is the repair complete?	Go to Step 28	—
27	Replace the left cooling fan. Is the repair complete?	Go to Step 28	—
28	Operate the system in order to verify the repair. Did you correct the condition?	System OK	Go to Step 3

GC1080100661020X

Fig. 65 Cooling fan inoperative (Part 2 of 2). 2001–02 DeVille, Eldorado & Seville

Step	Action	Yes	No
1	Install a scan tool. Does the scan tool power up?	Go to Step 2	Diagnose Data Link Communications
2	1. Turn ON the ignition, with the engine OFF. 2. Attempt to establish communication with the following control modules: o Instrument Cluster o Powertrain Control Module Does the scan tool communicate with the control modules?	Go to Step 3	Diagnose Data Link Communications
3	Select the powertrain control module display DTCs function on the scan tool. Does the scan tool display any DTCs?	Go to Step 4	Diagnose engine cooling
4	Does the scan tool display any DTCs which begin with a "U"?	Diagnose Data Link Communications	Diagnose Diagnostic Trouble Code (DTC)

ARM0300000000319

Fig. 66 Diagnostic system check. 2003–05 DeVille & Seville

Step	Action	Yes	No
7	Repair the short to voltage in the right cooling fan motor supply voltage circuit. Did you complete the repair?	Go to Step 14	--
8	Repair the short to voltage in the right cooling fan low reference circuit. Did you complete the repair?	Go to Step 14	--
9	Repair the short to voltage in the left cooling fan motor supply voltage circuit. Did you complete the repair?	Go to Step 14	--
10	Inspect for poor connections at the cooling fan 1 relay. Did you find and correct the condition?	Go to Step 14	Go to Step 12
11	Inspect for poor connections at the cooling fan 2 relay. Did you find and correct the condition?	Go to Step 14	Go to Step 13
12	Replace the cooling fan 1 relay. Did you complete the replacement?	Go to Step 14	--
13	Replace the cooling fan 2 relay. Did you complete the replacement?	Go to Step 14	--
14	Operate the system in order to verify the repair. Did you correct the condition?	System OK	Go to Step 2

ARM0300000000321

Fig. 67 Cooling fan always on (Part 2 of 2). 2003–05 DeVille & Seville

Step	Action	Yes	No
	DEFINITION: One or both engine cooling fan motors run continuously in high or low speed modes.		
1	Did you perform the Engine Cooling Diagnostic System Check?	Go to Step 2	Go To Diagnostic System Check
2	**Important** The cooling fan fuses and cooling fan relays 1 and 2 are labeled incorrectly on the underhood sticker. Turn ON the ignition, with the engine OFF. Are one or both cooling fans ON?	Go to Step 3	Test for Intermittent and Poor Connections
3	Are both cooling fans running continuously?	Go to Step 5	Go to Step 4
4	Remove the cooling fan S/P relay. Did the left cooling fan turn OFF?	Go to Step 8	Go to Step 6
5	Remove the cooling fan 1 relay. Did the cooling fans turn OFF?	Go to Step 10	Go to Step 7
6	Remove the cooling fan 2 relay. Did the left cooling fan turn OFF?	Go to Step 11	Go to Step 9

ARM0300000000320

Fig. 67 Cooling fan always on (Part 1 of 2). 2003–05 DeVille & Seville

1	Did you perform the Engine Cooling Diagnostic System Check?	Go to Step 2	Go to Diagnostic System Check
2	**Important** The cooling fan fuses and cooling fan relays 1 and 2 are labeled incorrectly on the underhood sticker. 1. Install a scan tool. 2. Turn ON the ignition, with the engine OFF. 3. With a scan tool, command the Fans Low Speed ON and OFF. Do the low speed engine cooling fans turn ON and OFF with each command?	Go to Step 3	Go to Step 4
3	**Important:** A 3-second delay occurs before the PCM changes the cooling fan speed. With a scan tool, command the Fans High Speed ON and OFF. Do the high speed engine cooling fans turn ON and OFF with each command?	Test for Intermittent and Poor Connections	Go to Step 12
4	**Important** Do NOT remove the 20-A fused jumper wire connected during this step. Use a second 20-A fused jumper wire while performing the following steps. 1. Remove the cooling fan 1 relay. 2. Connect a 20-A fused jumper between the battery positive switch side voltage circuit and the cooling fan motor supply voltage circuit of the cooling fan 1 relay. Do both cooling fans operate in low speed?	Go to Step 22	Go to Step 5

ARM0300000000642

Fig. 68   Cooling fan inoperative (Part 1 of 6). 2003–05 DeVille & Seville

5	1. Disconnect the cooling fan S/P relay 2. Connect the second 20-A fused jumper between the cooling fan low reference circuit and the cooling fan motor supply voltage circuit of the cooling fan S/P relay. Do both cooling fans operate in low speed?	Go to Step 23	Go to Step 6
6	Connect the second 20-A fused jumper between the battery positive voltage circuit and the cooling fan motor supply voltage circuit of the cooling fan S/P relay. Does the left cooling fan operate in high speed?	Go to Step 9	Go to Step 7
7	1. Install the cooling fan S/P relay. 2. Disconnect the left cooling fan electrical connector. 3. Connect the second 20-Amp fused jumper wire from the cooling fan motor supply voltage circuit to the ground circuit of the left cooling fan electrical connector. Does the right cooling fan operate in high speed?	Go to Step 25	Go to Step 8
8	Connect the second 20-Amp fused jumper wire from the cooling fan motor supply voltage circuit of the left cooling fan electrical connector to a good ground. Does the right cooling fan operate in high speed?	Go to Step 29	Go to Step 30
9	1. Install the cooling fan S/P relay. 2. Disconnect the right cooling fan electrical connector. 3. Connect the second 20-Amp fused jumper wire from the cooling fan motor supply voltage circuit to the cooling fan low reference circuit of the right cooling fan electrical connector. Does the left cooling fan operate in high speed?	Go to Step 26	Go to Step 10
10	Connect the second 20-Amp fused jumper wire from the coil side battery positive voltage circuit to the cooling fan low reference circuit of the of the right cooling fan electrical connector. Does the left cooling fan operate in high speed?	Go to Step 11	Go to Step 31

ARM0300000000643

Fig. 68   Cooling fan inoperative (Part 2 of 6). 2003–05 DeVille & Seville

11	Probe the battery positive voltage circuit on the switch side of the cooling fan 1 relay with a test lamp that is connected to a good ground. Does the test lamp illuminate?	Go to Step 27	Go to Step 32
12	Is the left cooling fan operating properly in high speed?	Go to Step 19	Go to Step 13
13	1. Turn off the ignition. 2. Disconnect the cooling fan 2 relay. 3. Turn ON the ignition, with the engine OFF. 4. Connect a test lamp between the high speed cooling fan relay control circuit and the battery positive voltage circuit on the coil side of the cooling fan 2 relay. 5. With a scan tool command the High Speed Fans ON and OFF. Does the test lamp turn ON and OFF with each command?	Go to Step 15	Go to Step 14
14	Probe the battery positive voltage circuit on the coil side of the cooling fan 2 relay with a test lamp that is connected to a good ground. Does the test lamp illuminate?	Go to Step 34	Go to Step 33
15	Install a 20 amp fused jumper between the battery positive voltage circuit on the switch side of the cooling fan 2 relay and the cooling fan motor supply voltage circuit. Does the left cooling fan operate in high speed?	Go to Step 24	Go to Step 16
16	Probe the battery positive voltage circuit on the switch side of the cooling fan 2 relay with a test lamp connected to a good ground. Does the test lamp illuminate?	Go to Step 17	Go to Step 33
17	1. With the 20 amp fused jumper still installed. 2. Disconnect the left cooling fan electrical connector. 3. Connect a test lamp from the cooling fan motor supply voltage circuit to the ground circuit of the left cooling fan electrical connector. Does the test lamp illuminate	Go to Step 25	Go to Step 18

ARM0300000000644

Fig. 68   Cooling fan inoperative (Part 3 of 6). 2003–05 DeVille & Seville

18	Probe the cooling fan motor supply voltage circuit of the left cooling fan electrical connector with a test lamp that is connected to a good ground. Does the test lamp illuminate?	Go to Step 29	Go to Step 30
19	1. Turn OFF the ignition. 2. Disconnect the cooling fan S/P relay 3. Turn ON the ignition, with the engine OFF. 4. Connect a 20-A fused jumper between the cooling fan low reference circuit and the ground circuit of the cooling fan S/P relay. 5. With a scan tool command the Fans High Speed ON and OFF. Does the right cooling fan operate in high speed?	Go to Step 20	Go to Step 28
20	1. Connect a test lamp between the high speed cooling fan relay control circuit of the cooling fan S/P relay and the battery positive voltage circuit of the cooling fan S/P relay. 2. With a scan tool command the Fans High Speed ON and OFF. Does the test lamp turn ON and OFF with each command?	Go to Step 23	Go to Step 21
21	Probe the battery positive voltage circuit of the cooling fan S/P relay with a test lamp that is connected to a good ground. Does the test lamp illuminate?	Go to Step 34	Go to Step 33
22	Inspect for poor connections at the cooling fan 1 relay. Did you find and correct the condition?	Go to Step 40	Go to Step 35
23	Inspect for poor connections at the cooling fan S/P relay. Did you find and correct the condition?	Go to Step 40	Go to Step 36
24	Inspect for poor connections at the cooling fan 2 relay. Did you find and correct the condition?	Go to Step 40	Go to Step 37

ARM0300000000645

Fig. 68   Cooling fan inoperative (Part 4 of 6). 2003–05 DeVille & Seville

		Yes	No
25	Inspect for poor connections at the harness connector of the left cooling fan. Did you find and correct the condition?	Go to Step 40	Go to Step 38
26	Inspect for poor connections at the harness connector of the right cooling fan. Did you find and correct the condition?	Go to Step 40	Go to Step 39
27	Repair the right cooling fan motor supply voltage circuit for an open. Is the repair complete?	Go to Step 40	--
28	Repair the right cooling fan ground circuit for an open. Is the repair complete?	Go to Step 40	--
29	Repair the left cooling fan ground circuit for an open. Is the repair complete?	Go to Step 40	--
30	Repair the left cooling fan motor supply voltage circuit for an open. Is the repair complete?	Go to Step 40	--
31	Repair the right cooling fan low reference circuit for a short to ground or an open. Is the repair complete?	Go to Step 40	--
32	Repair the cooling fan 1 relay battery positive voltage circuit for an open. Is the repair complete?	Go to Step 40	--

ARM0300000000646

Fig. 68   Cooling fan inoperative (Part 5 of 6). 2003–05 DeVille & Seville

		Yes	No
33	Repair the battery positive voltage circuit for the cooling fan S/P and 2 relay for an open. Is the repair complete?	Go to Step 40	--
34	Repair the high speed cooling fan relay control circuit for an open. Is the repair complete?	Go to Step 40	--
35	Replace the cooling fan 1 relay. Is the repair complete?	Go to Step 40	--
36	Replace the cooling fan S/P relay. Is the repair complete?	Go to Step 40	--
37	Replace the cooling fan 2 relay. Is the repair complete?	Go to Step 40	--
38	Replace the left cooling fan. Is the repair complete?	Go to Step 40	--
39	Replace the right cooling fan. Is the repair complete?	Go to Step 40	--
40	Operate the system in order to verify the repair. Did you correct the condition?	System OK	Go to Step 3

ARM0300000000647

Fig. 68   Cooling fan inoperative (Part 6 of 6). 2003–05 DeVille & Seville

Test Description

The number(s) below refer to the step number(s) on the diagnostic table.

2. Lack of communication may be due to a partial malfunction of the class 2 serial data circuit or due to a total malfunction of the class 2 serial data circuit. The specified procedure will determine the particular condition.

3. Determine if the Instrument Cluster or Powertrain Control Modules have set DTCs which may affect Engine Cooling operation are present.

4. The presence of DTCs which begin with "U" indicate some other module is not communicating. The specified procedure will compile all the available information before tests are performed.

Step	Action	Yes	No
1	Install a scan tool. Does the scan tool power up?	Go to Step 2	Diagnose Data Link Communications
2	1. Turn ON the ignition, with the engine OFF. 2. Attempt to establish communication with the powertrain control module. Does the scan tool communicate with the powertrain control module?	Go to Step 3	Data Link Communications
3	Select the powertrain control module display DTCs function on the scan tool. Does the scan tool display any DTCs?	Go to Step 4	Engine Cooling
4	Does the scan tool display any DTCs which begin with a "U"?	Data Link Communications	Diagnostic Trouble Code

GC1080100662000X

Fig. 69   Diagnostic system check. Grand Prix

Step	Action	Yes	No
	DEFINITION: One or both engine cooling fan motors run continuously in high or low speed.		
1	Did you perform the Engine Cooling Diagnostic System Check?	Go to Step 2	Diagnose System Check - Engine Cooling
2	Turn ON the ignition, with the engine OFF. Are one or both cooling fans ON?	Go to Step 3	Test for Intermittent and Poor Connections
3	Are both cooling fans running continuously?	Go to Step 5	Go to Step 4
4	Remove the cool fan relay. Did the left cooling fan turn OFF?	Go to Step 6	Go to Step 7
5	Repair the short to voltage in the right cooling fan supply voltage circuit. Did you complete the repair?	Go to Step 8	—
6	Repair the short to voltage in the right cooling fan low reference circuit. Did you complete the repair?	Go to Step 8	—
7	Repair the short to voltage in the left cooling fan supply voltage circuit. Did you complete the repair?	Go to Step 8	—
8	Operate the system in order to verify the repair. Did you correct the condition?	System OK	Go to Step 2

GC1080100663000X

Fig. 70   Cooling fan always on. Grand Prix

Step	Action	Yes	No
	DEFINITION: One or both engine cooling fan motors do not operate properly in high or low speed modes.		
1	Did you perform the Engine Cooling Diagnostic System Check?	Go to Step 2	Diagnose Engine Cooling
2	1. Install a scan tool. 2. Turn ON the ignition, with the engine OFF. 3. With a scan tool, command the Fans Low Speed ON and OFF. Do the low speed engine cooling fans turn ON and OFF with each command?	Go to Step 3	Go to Step 4
3	Important: Before the PCM changes the speed of the cooling fans, a 3-second delay occurs. With a scan tool, command the Fans High Speed ON and OFF. Do the high speed engine cooling fans turn ON and OFF with each command?	Test for Intermittent and Poor Connections	Go to Step 11
4	Important: Following this step, do not remove the 20-A fused jumper wire that is connected during this step. While performing the following steps, use a second 20-A fused jumper wire. 1. Disconnect the cool fan 1 relay. 2. Connect a 20-A fused jumper between the battery positive voltage circuit of the cool fan 1 relay and the cooling fan motor supply voltage circuit of the cool fan 1 relay. Do both cooling fans operate in low speed?	Go to Step 13	Go to Step 5
5	1. Disconnect the cool fan relay. 2. Connect the second 20-A fused jumper between the right cooling fan low reference circuit of the cool fan relay and the left cooling fan motor supply voltage circuit of the cool fan relay. Do both cooling fans operate in low speed?	Go to Step 14	Go to Step 6
6	Connect the second 20-A fused jumper between the battery positive voltage circuit of the cool fan relay and the cooling fan motor supply voltage circuit of the cool fan relay. Does the left cooling fan operate in high speed?	Go to Step 9	Go to Step 7
7	1. Install the cool fan relay. 2. Disconnect the left cooling fan electrical connector. 3. Connect the second 20-Amp fused jumper wire from the cooling fan motor supply voltage circuit of the left cooling fan electrical connector to the cooling fan ground circuit of the left cooling fan electrical connector. Does the right cooling fan operate in high speed?	Go to Step 16	Go to Step 8
8	Connect the second 20-Amp fused jumper wire from the cooling fan motor supply voltage circuit of the left cooling fan electrical connector to a good ground. Does the right cooling fan operate in high speed?	Go to Step 20	Go to Step 21
9	1. Install the cool fan relay. 2. Disconnect the right cooling fan electrical connector. 3. Connect the second 20-Amp fused jumper wire from the motor supply voltage circuit of the right cooling fan electrical connector to the low reference circuit of the right cooling fan electrical connector. Does the left cooling fan operate in high speed?	Go to Step 17	Go to Step 10
10	Connect the second 20-Amp fused jumper wire from battery positive voltage to the right cooling fan low reference circuit of the right cooling fan electrical connector. Does the left cooling fan operate in high speed?	Go to Step 18	Go to Step 22
11	Is the left cooling fan operating properly in high speed?	Go to Step 12	Go to Step 15

GC1080100664010X

Fig. 71 Cooling fan inoperative (Part 1 of 2). Grand Prix

Step	Action	Yes	No
12	1. Disconnect the cool fan relay. 2. Connect the second 20-A fused jumper between the right cooling fan low reference circuit of the cool fan relay and the ground circuit of the cool fan relay. Does the right cooling fan operate properly in high speed?	Go to Step 14	Go to Step 19
13	Inspect for poor connections at the cool fan 1 relay. Did you find and correct the condition?	Go to Step 28	Go to Step 23
14	Inspect for poor connections at the cool fan relay. Did you find and correct the condition?	Go to Step 28	Go to Step 24
15	Inspect for poor connections at the cool fan 2 relay. Did you find and correct the condition?	Go to Step 28	Go to Step 25
16	Inspect for poor connections at the harness connector of the left cooling fan. Did you find and correct the condition?	Go to Step 28	Go to Step 26
17	Inspect for poor connections at the harness connector of the right cooling fan. Did you find and correct the condition?	Go to Step 28	Go to Step 27
18	Repair the right cooling fan supply voltage circuit. Did you complete the repair?	Go to Step 28	—
19	Repair the right cooling fan ground circuit. Did you complete the repair?	Go to Step 28	—
20	Repair the left cooling fan ground circuit. Did you complete the repair?	Go to Step 28	—
21	Repair the left cooling fan supply voltage circuit. Did you complete the repair?	Go to Step 28	—
22	Repair the right cooling fan low reference circuit. Did you complete the repair?	Go to Step 28	—
23	Replace the cool fan 1 relay. Is the repair complete?	Go to Step 28	—
24	Replace the cool fan relay. Is the repair complete?	Go to Step 28	—
25	Replace the cool fan 2 relay. Is the repair complete?	Go to Step 28	—
26	Replace the left cooling fan. Is the repair complete?	Go to Step 28	—
27	Replace the right cooling fan. Is the repair complete?	Go to Step 28	—
28	Operate the system in order to verify the repair. Did you correct the condition?	System OK	Go to Step 3

GC1080100664020X

Fig. 71 Cooling fan inoperative (Part 2 of 2). Grand Prix

Step	Action	Yes	No
1	Install a scan tool. Does the scan tool power up?	Go to Step 2	Diagnose Data Link Communications
2	1. Turn ON the ignition, with the engine OFF. 2. Attempt to establish communication with the following modules: o Powertrain control module (PCM) o Powertrain interface module (PIM) o Body control module (BCM) o Instrument panel cluster (IPC) Does the scan tool communicate with all of the modules?	Go to Step 3	Diagnose Data Link Communications

ARM0400000000039

Fig. 72 Diagnostic system check. GTO

Step	Action	Yes	No
1	Did you review the Cooling System Description and Operation and perform the necessary inspections?	Go to Step 2	Go to Symptoms
2	1. Connect a scan tool. 2. Use the scan tool to command the low speed fan ON. Do the cooling fans operate at low speed?	Test for Intermittent Conditions and Poor Connections	Go to Step 3
3	1. Disconnect the low speed fan motor. 2. Connect a test lamp from the fan motor supply voltage circuit to the fan motor low speed ground circuit. 3. Use the scan tool to command the low speed fan ON. Does the test lamp illuminate?	Go to Step 10	Go to Step 4
4	1. Remove the fan 1 relay. 2. Install a 30-amp fused jumper between the low speed fan motor ground circuit and the fan 1 relay ground circuit, between cavities 30 and 87, of the cooling fan 1 relay connector. Do the cooling fans operate at low speed?	Go to Step 5	Go to Step 7

ARM0400000000040

Fig. 73 Cooling fan inoperative (Part 1 of 2). GTO

		Yes	No
5	Test the fan 1 relay coil supply voltage circuit for an open. Did you find and correct the condition?	Go to Step 13	Go to Step 6
6	Test the fan 1 relay coil control circuit for an open. Did you find and correct the condition?	Go to Step 13	Go to Step 9
7	Test the fan motor low speed ground circuit for an open between the fan motors and the fan 1 relay. Did you find and correct the condition?	Go to Step 13	Go to Step 8
8	Repair the open in the fan motor low speed ground circuit between the fan 1 relay and S240. Did you find and correct the condition?	Go to Step 13	--
9	Inspect for a poor connection at the harness connector of the fan 1 relay. Did you find and correct the condition?	Go to Step 13	Go to Step 11

ARM0400000000041

Fig. 73 Cooling fan inoperative (Part 2 of 2). GTO

		Yes	No
2	Install a scan tool. Does the scan tool power up?	Go to Step 3	Diagnose Scan Tool Does Not Power Up
3	1. Turn ON the ignition, with the engine OFF. 2. Attempt to establish communication with all of the control modules on the vehicle. Does the scan tool communicate with all of the expected vehicle control modules?	Go to Step 4	Diagnose Data Link References
4	**Important** • To ensure that retained accessory power (RAP) mode is inactive, if equipped, open the driver door during the following step. • The engine may start during the following step. Turn OFF the engine as soon as you have observed the crank power mode. 1. Access the Power Mode parameter on the scan tool. 2. Rotate the ignition switch, operate the ignition mode switch, through all positions while observing the Power Mode parameter. Does the Power Mode parameter reading on the scan tool match the ignition switch position for all switch positions?	Go to Step 5	Go to Power Mode Mismatch
5	Attempt to start the engine. Does the engine crank?	Go to Step 6	Go to Symptoms

ARM0400000000026

Fig. 74 Diagnostic system check (Part 2 of 3). G6

Step	Action	Yes	No
1	Perform the following preliminary inspections: • Ensure that the battery is fully charged. • Ensure that the battery cables are clean and tight. • Inspect for any open fuses. • Inspect the easily accessible systems or the visible system components for obvious damage or conditions that could cause the symptom. • Ensure that the grounds are clean, tight, and in the correct location. • Inspect for aftermarket devices that could affect the operation of the system. • Search for applicable service bulletins. Did you find and correct the condition?	System OK	Go to Step 2

ARM0400000000025

Fig. 74 Diagnostic system check (Part 1 of 3). G6

			Go to Engine Cranks but Does Not Run
6	Attempt to start the engine. Does the engine start and idle?	Go to Step 7	

7	**Important**
	
	Do NOT clear any DTCs unless instructed by a diagnostic procedure.
	
	1. Diagnose the DTCs in the order that the DTCs appear on the scan tool or mis-diagnosis may occur.
	2. If multiple powertrain DTCs are stored, diagnose the DTCs in the following order:
	  A. Component level DTCs, such as sensor DTCs, solenoid DTCs, and relay DTCs.
	  B. System level DTCs, such as misfire DTCs, evaporative emission (EVAP) system DTCs, and fuel trim DTCs.
	
	Advance to the List All DTCs screen on the scan tool.
	
	Does the scan tool display any DTCs?
		Go to Diagnostic Trouble Code (DTC) List	Go to Step 8

8	Is the customers concern with inspection/maintenance (I/M) testing?	Perform Inspection/Maintenance (I/M) System Check	Go to Symptoms

ARM0400000000027

Fig. 74 Diagnostic system check (Part 3 of 3). G6

1	Did you perform the Diagnostic System Check - Vehicle?	Go to Step 2	Go to Diagnostic System Check
2	Turn ON the ignition, with the engine OFF. Are one or both cooling fans ON?	Go to Step 3	Test for Intermittent Conditions and Poor Connections
3	Are both cooling fans running continuously?	Go to Step 4	Go to Step 6
4	Are both fans running continuously in high speed?	Go to Step 5	Go to Step 7
5	Test the low reference circuit of the A/C refrigerant pressure sensor for an open.	Go to Step 18	Go to Step 14
6	Remove the cooling fan s/p relay. Did the right cooling fan turn OFF?	Go to Step 10	Go to Step 8
7	Remove the cooling fan 1 relay. Did the cooling fans turn OFF?	Go to Step 12	Go to Step 9
8	Remove the cooling fan 2 relay. Did the right cooling fan turn OFF?	Go to Step 13	Go to Step 11
9	Repair the short to voltage in the left cooling fan motor supply voltage circuit. Did you complete the repair?	Go to Step 18	--
10	Repair the short to voltage in the left cooling fan motor low reference circuit. Did you complete the repair?	Go to Step 18	--

ARM0400000000028

Fig. 75 Cooling fan always on (Part 1 of 2). G6

Step	Action	Yes	No
11	Repair the short to voltage in the right cooling fan motor supply voltage circuit. Did you complete the repair?	Go to Step 18	--
12	Inspect for poor connections at the cool fan 1 relay. Did you find and correct the condition?	Go to Step 18	Go to Step 15
13	Inspect for poor connections at the cool fan 2 relay. Did you find and correct the condition?	Go to Step 18	Go to Step 16
14	Inspect for poor connections at the A/C refrigerant pressure sensor. Did you find and correct the condition?	Go to Step 18	Go to Step 17
15	Replace the cool fan 1 relay. Did you complete the replacement?	Go to Step 18	--
16	Replace the cool fan 2 relay. Did you complete the replacement?	Go to Step 18	--
17	Replace the A/C refrigerant pressure sensor. Did you complete the replacement?	Go to Step 18	--
18	Operate the system in order to verify the repair. Did you correct the condition?	System OK	Go to Step 2

ARM0400000000029

Fig. 75 Cooling fan always on (Part 2 of 2). G6

Step	Action	Yes	No
1	Did you perform the Diagnostic System Check - Vehicle?	Go to Step 2	Go to Diagnostic System Check
2	1. Install a scan tool. 2. Turn ON the ignition, with the engine OFF. 3. With a scan tool, command the Fan Control Relay 1 ON and OFF. Do the low speed engine cooling fans turn ON and OFF with each command?	Go to Step 3	Go to Step 4
3	Important: A 3 second delay occurs before the powertrain control module (PCM) changes the cooling fan speed. With a scan tool, command the Fan Control Relay 2 and 3 ON and OFF. Do the high speed engine cooling fans turn ON and OFF with each command?	Test for Intermittent Conditions and Poor Connections	Go to Step 6

ARM0400000000030

Fig. 76 Cooling fan inoperative (Part 1 of 4). G6

Step	Action	Yes	No
8	1. Install the S/P fan relay. 2. Disconnect the left cooling fan electrical connector. 3. With a test lamp connected to a good ground, probe the cooling fan motor supply voltage circuit at the left cooling fan motor connector. Does the test lamp illuminate?	Go to Step 12	Go to Step 13
9	1. Install the S/P fan relay. 2. Disconnect the right cooling fan motor connector. 3. With a test lamp connected to a good ground, probe the cooling fan motor supply voltage circuit at the right cooling fan connector. Does the test lamp illuminate?	Go to Step 11	Go to Step 10
10	Inspect the cooling fan motor supply voltage circuit for an open or high resistance. Did you find and correct the condition?	Go to Step 25	Go to Step 15
11	Inspect the ground circuit of the right cooling fan for an open or high resistance. Did you find and correct the condition?	Go to Step 25	Go to Step 18
12	Inspect the cooling fan low reference circuit for an open or high resistance. Did you find and correct the condition?	Go to Step 25	Go to Step 17

ARM0400000000032

Fig. 76 Cooling fan inoperative (Part 3 of 4). G6

Step	Action	Yes	No
4	Important: Do NOT remove the jumper wire that you will be connecting until your testing is completed. If the cool fan 1 fuse opens when you connect the jumper wire, repair the cooling fan motor supply voltage circuit of the left cooling fan motor for a short to ground. 1. Disconnect the cool fan 1 relay. 2. Connect a jumper wire between the battery positive voltage circuit and the cooling fan motor supply voltage circuit of the cool fan 1 relay. Do both cooling fans operate in low speed?	Go to Step 14	Go to Step 5
5	1. Disconnect the S/P fan relay. 2. With a test lamp connected to a good ground, probe the cooling fan low reference circuit at the S/P fan relay. Does the test lamp illuminate?	Go to Step 9	Go to Step 8
6	Does the left cooling fan operate at high speed?	Go to Step 16	Go to Step 7
7	Inspect the ground circuit of the S/P fan relay for an open or high resistance. Did you find and correct the condition?	Go to Step 25	Go to Step 15

ARM0400000000031

Fig. 76 Cooling fan inoperative (Part 2 of 4). G6

Step	Action	Yes	No
13	Inspect the cooling fan motor supply voltage circuit of the left cooling fan for an open or high resistance. Did you find and correct the condition?	Go to Step 25	Go to Step 19
14	Inspect for poor connections at the cool fan 1 relay. Did you find and correct the condition?	Go to Step 25	Go to Step 20
15	Inspect for poor connections at the S/P fan relay. Did you find and correct the condition?	Go to Step 25	Go to Step 21
16	Inspect for poor connections at the cool fan 2 relay. Did you find and correct the condition?	Go to Step 25	Go to Step 22
17	Inspect for poor connections at the harness connector of the left cooling fan. Did you find and correct the condition?	Go to Step 25	Go to Step 23
18	Inspect for poor connections at the harness connector of the right cooling fan. Did you find and correct the condition?	Go to Step 25	Go to Step 24

ARM0400000000033

Fig. 76 Cooling fan inoperative (Part 4 of 4). G6

Test Description

The number(s) below refer to the step number(s) on the diagnostic table.

2. Lack of communication may be due to a partial malfunction of the class 2 serial data circuit or due to a total malfunction of the class 2 serial data circuit. The specified procedure will determine the particular condition.

3. Determine if the Instrument Cluster or Powertrain Control Modules have set DTCs which may affect Engine Cooling operation are present.

4. The presence of DTCs which begin with "U" indicate some other module is not communicating. The specified procedure will compile all the available information before tests are performed.

Step	Action	Yes	No
1	Install a scan tool. Does the scan tool power up?	Go to Step 2	Diagnose Data Link
2	1. Turn ON the ignition, with the engine OFF. 2. Attempt to establish communication with the following control modules: ○ Instrument Cluster ○ Powertrain Control Module Does the scan tool communicate with the control modules?	Go to Step 3	Diagnose Data Link Communications
3	Select the powertrain control module display DTCs function on the scan tool. Does the scan tool display any DTCs?	Go to Step 4	Diagnose Go to Symptoms - Engine Cooling
4	Does the scan tool display any DTCs which begin with a "U"?	Diagnose Device in Data Link Communications	Diagnose Trouble Code (DTC) List

GC1080100665000X

Fig. 77   Diagnostic system check. 2001–02 Impala & Monte Carlo

Step	Action	Yes	No
1	Did you perform the Engine Cooling Diagnostic System Check?	Go to Step 2	Diagnose Engine Cooling
2	1. Install a scan tool. 2. Turn ON the ignition, with the engine OFF. 3. With a scan tool, command the Fans Low Speed ON and OFF. Do the low speed engine cooling fans turn ON and OFF with each command?	Go to Step 3	Go to Step 4
3	**Important** Before the PCM changes the speed of the cooling fan, a 3-second delay occurs. With a scan tool, command the Fans High Speed ON and OFF. Do the high speed engine cooling fans turn ON and OFF with each command?	Test for Intermittent and Poor Connections	Go to Step 11
4	**Important** Do NOT remove the 20-A fused jumper wire connected during this step. Use a second 20-A fused jumper wire while performing the following steps. 1. Disconnect the cooling fan 1 relay. 2. Connect a 20-A fused jumper between the battery positive voltage circuit of the cooling fan 1 relay and the cooling fan motor supply voltage circuit of the cooling fan 1 relay. Do both cooling fans operate in low speed?	Go to Step 13	Go to Step 5
5	1. Disconnect the cooling fan 2 relay. 2. Connect the second 20-A fused jumper between the right cooling fan low reference circuit of the cooling fan 2 relay and the left cooling fan motor supply voltage circuit of the cooling fan 2 relay. Do both cooling fans operate in low speed?	Go to Step 14	Go to Step 6

GC1080100667010X

Fig. 79   Cooling fan inoperative (Part 1 of 4). 2001–02 Impala & Monte Carlo

Step	Action	Yes	No
1	Did you perform the Engine Cooling Diagnostic System Check?	Go to Step 2	Diagnose Engine Cooling
2	Turn ON the ignition, with the engine OFF. Are one or both cooling fans ON?	Go to Step 3	Test for Intermittent and Poor Connections
3	Are both cooling fans running continuously?	Go to Step 5	Go to Step 4
4	Remove the cooling fan 2 relay. Did the left cooling fan turn OFF?	Go to Step 6	Go to Step 7
5	Repair the short to voltage in the right cooling fan motor supply voltage circuit. Did you complete the repair?	Go to Step 8	--
6	Repair the short to voltage in the right cooling fan low reference circuit. Did you complete the repair?	Go to Step 8	--
7	Repair the short to voltage in the left cooling fan motor supply voltage circuit. Did you complete the repair?	Go to Step 8	--
8	Operate the system in order to verify the repair. Did you correct the condition?	System OK	Go to Step 2

GC1080100666000X

Fig. 78   Cooling fan always on. 2001–02 Impala & Monte Carlo

Step	Action	Yes	No
6	Connect the second 20-A fused jumper between the battery positive voltage circuit of the cooling fan 2 relay and the cooling fan motor supply voltage circuit of the cooling fan 2 relay. Does the left cooling fan operate in high speed?	Go to Step 9	Go to Step 7
7	1. Install the cooling fan 2 relay. 2. Disconnect the left cooling fan electrical connector. 3. Connect the second 20-amp fused jumper wire from the cooling fan motor supply voltage circuit of the left cooling fan electrical connector to the cooling fan ground circuit of the left cooling fan electrical connector. Does the right cooling fan operate in high speed?	Go to Step 16	Go to Step 8
8	Connect the second 20-amp fused jumper wire from the cooling fan motor supply voltage circuit of the left cooling fan electrical connector to a good ground. Does the right cooling fan operate in high speed?	Go to Step 20	Go to Step 21
9	1. Install the cooling fan 2 relay. 2. Disconnect the right cooling fan electrical connector. 3. Connect the second 20-amp fused jumper wire from the cooling fan motor supply voltage circuit of the right cooling fan electrical connector to the cooling fan low reference circuit of the right cooling fan electrical connector. Does the left cooling fan operate in high speed?	Go to Step 17	Go to Step 10
10	Connect the second 20-amp fused jumper wire from battery positive voltage to the right cooling fan low reference circuit of the of the right cooling fan electrical connector. Does the left cooling fan operate in high speed?	Go to Step 18	Go to Step 22
11	Does the left cooling fan operate properly in high speed?	Go to Step 12	Go to Step 15
12	1. Disconnect the cooling fan 2 relay. 2. Connect the second 20-A fused jumper between the right cooling fan low reference circuit of the cooling fan 2 relay and the ground circuit of the cooling fan 2 relay. Does the right cooling fan operate properly in high speed?	Go to Step 14	Go to Step 19
13	Inspect for poor connections at the cooling fan 1 relay. Did you find and correct the condition?	Go to Step 28	Go to Step 23
14	Inspect for poor connections at the cooling fan 2 relay. Did you find and correct the condition?	Go to Step 28	Go to Step 24

GC1080100667020X

Fig. 79   Cooling fan inoperative (Part 2 of 4). 2001–02 Impala & Monte Carlo

Step	Action	Yes	No
15	Inspect for poor connections at the cooling fan 3 relay. / Did you find and correct the condition?	Go to Step 28	Go to Step 25
16	Inspect for poor connections at the harness connector of the left cooling fan. / Did you find and correct the condition?	Go to Step 28	Go to Step 26
17	Inspect for poor connections at the harness connector of the right cooling fan. / Did you find and correct the condition?	Go to Step 28	Go to Step 27
18	Repair the right cooling fan motor supply voltage circuit. / Did you complete the repair?	Go to Step 28	--
19	Repair the right cooling fan ground circuit. / Did you complete the repair?	Go to Step 28	--
20	Repair the left cooling fan ground circuit. / Did you complete the repair?	Go to Step 28	--
21	Repair the left cooling fan motor supply voltage circuit. / Did you complete the repair?	Go to Step 28	--
22	Repair the right cooling fan low reference circuit. / Did you complete the repair?	Go to Step 28	--
23	Replace the cooling fan 1 relay. / Did you complete the repair?	Go to Step 28	--
24	Replace the cooling fan 2 relay. / Did you complete the repair?	Go to Step 28	--

GC1080100667030X

Fig. 79   Cooling fan inoperative (Part 3 of 4). 2001–02 Impala & Monte Carlo

Step	Action	Yes	No
25	Replace the cooling fan 3 relay. / Did you complete the repair?	Go to Step 28	--
26	Replace the left cooling fan. / Did you complete the repair?	Go to Step 28	--
27	Replace the right cooling fan. / Did you complete the repair?	Go to Step 28	--
28	Operate the system in order to verify the repair. / Did you correct the condition?	System OK	Go to Step 3

GC1080100667040X

Fig. 79   Cooling fan inoperative (Part 4 of 4). 2001–02 Impala & Monte Carlo

Step	Action	Yes	No
	DEFINITION: One or both engine cooling fan motors run continuously in high or low speed modes.		
1	Did you perform the Engine Cooling Diagnostic System Check?	Go to Step 2	Go To Diagnostic System Check
2	Turn ON the ignition, with the engine OFF. Are one or both cooling fans ON?	Go to Step 3	Test for Intermittent and Poor Connections
3	Are both cooling fans running continuously?	Go to Step 5	Go to Step 4
4	Remove the FAN CONT #2 relay. Did the left cooling fan turn OFF?	Go to Step 8	Go to Step 6
5	Remove the FAN CONT #1 relay. Did the cooling fans turn OFF?	Go to Step 10	Go to Step 7
6	Remove the FAN CONT #3 relay. Did the left cooling fan turn OFF?	Go to Step 11	Go to Step 9
7	Repair the short to voltage in the right cooling fan motor supply voltage circuit. / Did you complete the repair?	Go to Step 14	--

ARM0300000000649

Fig. 81   Cooling fan always on (Part 1 of 2). 2003–05 Impala & Monte Carlo

Step	Action	Yes	No
1	Install a scan tool. / Does the scan tool power up?	Go to Step 2	Diagnose Data Link Communications
2	1. Turn ON the ignition, with the engine OFF. 2. Attempt to establish communication with the following control modules: o Instrument Cluster o Powertrain Control Module / Does the scan tool communicate with the control modules?	Go to Step 3	Diagnose Data Link Communications
3	Select the powertrain control module display DTCs function on the scan tool. / Does the scan tool display any DTCs?	Go to Step 4	Diagnose engine cooling
4	Does the scan tool display any DTCs which begin with a "U"?	Diagnose Data Link Communications	Diagnose Diagnostic Trouble Code (DTC)

ARM0300000000648

Fig. 80   Diagnostic system check. 2003–05 Impala & Monte Carlo

Step	Action	Yes	No
8	Repair the short to voltage in the right cooling fan low reference circuit. / Did you complete the repair?	Go to Step 14	--
9	Repair the short to voltage in the left cooling fan motor supply voltage circuit. / Did you complete the repair?	Go to Step 14	--
10	Inspect for poor connections at the FAN CONT #1 relay. / Did you find and correct the condition?	Go to Step 14	Go to Step 12
11	Inspect for poor connections at the FAN CONT #3 relay. / Did you find and correct the condition?	Go to Step 14	Go to Step 13
12	Replace the FAN CONT #1 relay. / Did you complete the replacement?	Go to Step 14	--
13	Replace the FAN CONT #3 relay. / Did you complete the replacement?	Go to Step 14	--
14	Operate the system in order to verify the repair. / Did you correct the condition?	System OK	Go to Step 2

ARM0300000000650

Fig. 81   Cooling fan always on (Part 2 of 2). 2003–05 Impala & Monte Carlo

#	Step		
1	Did you perform the Engine Cooling Diagnostic System Check?	Go to Step 2	Go to Diagnostic System Check
2	1. Install a scan tool. 2. Turn ON the ignition, with the engine OFF. 3. With a scan tool, command the Fans Low Speed ON and OFF. Do the low speed engine cooling fans turn ON and OFF with each command?	Go to Step 3	Go to Step 4
3	**Important:** A 3-second delay occurs before the PCM changes the cooling fan speed. With a scan tool, command the Fans High Speed ON and OFF. Do the high speed engine cooling fans turn ON and OFF with each command?	Test for Intermittent and Poor Connections	Go to Step 12
4	**Important** Do NOT remove the 20-A fused jumper wire connected during this step. Use a second 20-A fused jumper wire while performing the following steps. 1. Remove the FAN CONT #1 relay. 2. Connect a 20-A fused jumper between the battery positive switch side voltage circuit and the cooling fan motor supply voltage circuit of the FAN CONT #1 relay. Do both cooling fans operate in low speed?	Go to Step 22	Go to Step 5
5	1. Disconnect the FAN CONT #2 relay 2. Connect the second 20-A fused jumper between the cooling fan low reference circuit and the cooling fan motor supply voltage circuit of the FAN CONT #2 relay. Do both cooling fans operate in low speed?	Go to Step 23	Go to Step 6

ARM0300000000651

**Fig. 82 Cooling fan inoperative (Part 1 of 7).
2003–05 Impala & Monte Carlo**

#	Step		
6	Connect the second 20-ampere fused jumper between the battery positive voltage circuit and the cooling fan motor supply voltage circuit of the FAN CONT #2 relay. Does the left cooling fan operate in high speed?	Go to Step 9	Go to Step 7
7	1. Install the FAN CONT #2 relay. 2. Disconnect the left cooling fan electrical connector. 3. Connect the second 20-ampere fused jumper wire from the cooling fan motor supply voltage circuit to the ground circuit of the left cooling fan electrical connector. Does the right cooling fan operate in high speed?	Go to Step 25	Go to Step 8
8	Connect the second 20-ampere fused jumper wire from the cooling fan motor supply voltage circuit of the left cooling fan electrical connector to a good ground. Does the right cooling fan operate in high speed?	Go to Step 29	Go to Step 30
9	1. Install the FAN CONT #2 relay. 2. Disconnect the right cooling fan electrical connector. 3. Connect the second 20-ampere fused jumper wire from the cooling fan motor supply voltage circuit to the cooling fan low reference circuit of the right cooling fan electrical connector. Does the left cooling fan operate in high speed?	Go to Step 26	Go to Step 10
10	Connect the second 20-ampere fused jumper wire from the coil side battery positive voltage circuit to the cooling fan low reference circuit of the of the right cooling fan electrical connector. Does the left cooling fan operate in high speed?	Go to Step 11	Go to Step 31

ARM0300000000652

**Fig. 82 Cooling fan inoperative (Part 2 of 7).
2003–05 Impala & Monte Carlo**

#	Step		
11	Probe the battery positive voltage circuit on the switch side of the FAN CONT #1 relay with a test lamp that is connected to a good ground. Does the test lamp illuminate?	Go to Step 27	Go to Step 32
12	Is the left cooling fan operating properly in high speed?	Go to Step 19	Go to Step 13
13	1. Turn off the ignition. 2. Disconnect the FAN CONT #3 relay. 3. Turn ON the ignition, with the engine OFF. 4. Connect a test lamp between the high speed cooling fan relay control circuit and the battery positive voltage circuit on the coil side of the FAN CONT #3 relay. 5. With a scan tool command the High Speed Fans ON and OFF. Does the test lamp turn ON and OFF with each command?	Go to Step 15	Go to Step 14
14	Probe the battery positive voltage circuit on the coil side of the FAN CONT #3 relay with a test lamp that is connected to a good ground. Does the test lamp illuminate?	Go to Step 34	Go to Step 33
15	Install a 20 amp fused jumper between the battery positive voltage circuit on the switch side of the FAN CONT #3 relay and the cooling fan motor supply voltage circuit. Does the left cooling fan operate in high speed?	Go to Step 24	Go to Step 16
16	Probe the battery positive voltage circuit on the switch side of the FAN CONT #3 relay with a test lamp connected to a good ground. Does the test lamp illuminate?	Go to Step 17	Go to Step 33

ARM0300000000653

**Fig. 82 Cooling fan inoperative (Part 3 of 7).
2003–05 Impala & Monte Carlo**

#	Step		
17	1. With the 20 amp fused jumper still installed. 2. Disconnect the left cooling fan electrical connector. 3. Connect a test lamp from the cooling fan motor supply voltage circuit to the ground circuit of the left cooling fan electrical connector. Does the test lamp illuminate?	Go to Step 25	Go to Step 18
18	Probe the cooling fan motor supply voltage circuit of the left cooling fan electrical connector with a test lamp that is connected to a good ground. Does the test lamp illuminate?	Go to Step 29	Go to Step 30
19	1. Turn OFF the ignition. 2. Disconnect the FAN CONT #2 relay 3. Turn ON the ignition, with the engine OFF. 4. Connect a 20-A fused jumper between the cooling fan low reference circuit and the ground circuit of the FAN CONT #2 relay. 5. With a scan tool command the Fans High Speed ON and OFF. Does the right cooling fan operate in high speed?	Go to Step 20	Go to Step 28
20	1. Connect a test lamp between the high speed cooling fan relay control circuit of the FAN CONT #2 relay and the battery positive voltage circuit of the FAN CONT #2 relay. 2. With a scan tool command the Fans High Speed ON and OFF. Does the test lamp turn ON and OFF with each command?	Go to Step 23	Go to Step 21
21	Probe the battery positive voltage circuit of the FAN CONT #2 relay with a test lamp that is connected to a good ground. Does the test lamp illuminate?	Go to Step 34	Go to Step 33
22	Inspect for poor connections at the FAN CONT #1 relay. Did you find and correct the condition?	Go to Step 40	Go to Step 35

ARM0300000000654

**Fig. 82 Cooling fan inoperative (Part 4 of 7).
2003–05 Impala & Monte Carlo**

	Action	Yes	No
23	Inspect for poor connections at the FAN CONT #2 relay. Did you find and correct the condition?	Go to Step 40	Go to Step 36
24	Inspect for poor connections at the FAN CONT #3 relay. Did you find and correct the condition?	Go to Step 40	Go to Step 37
25	Inspect for poor connections at the harness connector of the left cooling fan. Did you find and correct the condition?	Go to Step 40	Go to Step 38
26	Inspect for poor connections at the harness connector of the right cooling fan. Did you find and correct the condition?	Go to Step 40	Go to Step 39
27	Repair the right cooling fan motor supply voltage circuit for an open. Is the repair complete?	Go to Step 40	--
28	Repair the right cooling fan ground circuit for an open. Is the repair complete?	Go to Step 40	--

ARM0300000000655

Fig. 82 Cooling fan inoperative (Part 5 of 7). 2003–05 Impala & Monte Carlo

	Action	Yes	No
29	Repair the left cooling fan ground circuit for an open. Is the repair complete?	Go to Step 40	
30	Repair the left cooling fan motor supply voltage circuit for an open. Is the repair complete?	Go to Step 40	
31	Repair the right cooling fan low reference circuit for a short to ground or an open. Is the repair complete?	Go to Step 40	
32	Repair the FAN CONT #1 relay battery positive voltage circuit for an open. Is the repair complete?	Go to Step 40	
33	Repair the battery positive voltage circuit for the FAN CONT #2 and #3 relay for an open. Is the repair complete?	Go to Step 40	

ARM0300000000656

Fig. 82 Cooling fan inoperative (Part 6 of 7). 2003–05 Impala & Monte Carlo

	Action	Yes	No
34	Repair the high speed cooling fan relay control circuit for an open. Is the repair complete?	Go to Step 40	--
35	Replace the FAN CONT #1 relay. Is the repair complete?	Go to Step 40	--
36	Replace the FAN CONT #2 relay. Is the repair complete?	Go to Step 40	--
37	Replace the FAN CONT #3 relay. Is the repair complete?	Go to Step 40	--
38	Replace the left cooling fan. Is the repair complete?	Go to Step 40	--
39	Replace the right cooling fan. Is the repair complete?	Go to Step 40	--
40	Operate the system in order to verify the repair. Did you correct the condition?	System OK	Go to Step 3

ARM0300000000657

Fig. 82 Cooling fan inoperative (Part 7 of 7). 2003–05 Impala & Monte Carlo

Step	Action	Yes	No
1	Install a scan tool. Does the scan tool power up?	Go to Step 2	Diagnose Data Link Communications
2	1. Turn ON the ignition, with the engine OFF. 2. Attempt to establish communication with the following control modules: • Instrument Cluster • Powertrain Control Module. Does the scan tool communicate with the control modules?	Go to Step 3	Diagnose Data Link Communications
3	Select the powertrain control module display DTCs function on the scan tool. Does the scan tool display any DTCs?	Go to Step 4	Diagnose Engine Cooling
4	Does the scan tool display any DTCs which begin with a "U"?	Diagnose Data Link Communications	Diagnose Trouble Code

GC1080100669000X

Fig. 83 Diagnostic system check. Intrigue

Step	Action	Yes	No
	DEFINITION: One or both engine cooling fan motors run continuously in high or low speed.		
1	Did you perform the Engine Cooling Diagnostic System Check?	Go to Step 2	Diagnose Engine Cooling
2	Turn ON the ignition, with the engine OFF. Are one or both cooling fans ON?	Go to Step 3	Test For Intermittent and Poor Connections
3	Are both cooling fans running continuously?	Go to Step 5	Go to Step 4
4	Remove the cooling fan S/P relay. Did the left cooling fan turn OFF?	Go to Step 6	Go to Step 7
5	Repair the short to voltage in the right cooling fan motor supply voltage circuit. Did you complete the repair?	Go to Step 8	—
6	Repair the short to voltage in the right cooling fan low reference circuit. Did you complete the repair?	Go to Step 8	—
7	Repair the short to voltage in the left cooling fan motor supply voltage circuit. Did you complete the repair?	Go to Step 8	—
8	Operate the system in order to verify the repair. Did you correct the condition?	System OK	Go to Step 2

GC1080100670000X

Fig. 84 Cooling fan always on. Intrigue

Fig. 85 Cooling fan inoperative (Part 1 of 2). Intrigue

Step	Action	Yes	No
	DEFINITION: One or both engine cooling fan motors do not operate properly in high or low speed modes.		
1	Did you perform the Engine Cooling Diagnostic System Check?	Go to *Step 2*	*Diagnose Engine Cooling*
2	1. Install a scan tool. 2. Turn ON the ignition, with the engine OFF. 3. With a scan tool, command the Fans Low Speed ON and OFF. Do the low speed engine cooling fans turn ON and OFF with each command?	Go to *Step 3*	Go to *Step 4*
3	**Important:** A 3-second delay occurs before the PCM changes the cooling fan speed. With a scan tool, command the Fans High Speed ON and OFF. Do the high speed engine cooling fans turn ON and OFF with each command?	*Test for Intermittent and Poor Connections*	Go to *Step 11*
4	**Important:** Do NOT remove the 20-A fused jumper wire connected during this step. Use a second 20-A fused jumper wire while performing the following steps. 1. Remove the cooling fan 1 relay. 2. Connect a 20-A fused jumper between the battery positive voltage circuit of the cooling fan 1 relay and the cooling fan motor supply voltage circuit of the cooling fan 1 relay. Do both cooling fans operate in low speed?	Go to *Step 13*	Go to *Step 5*
5	1. Disconnect the cooling fan S/P relay. 2. Connect the second 20-A fused jumper between the right cooling fan low reference circuit of the cooling fan S/P relay and the left cooling fan motor supply voltage circuit of the cooling fan S/P relay. Do both cooling fans operate in low speed?	Go to *Step 14*	Go to *Step 6*
6	Connect the second 20-A fused jumper between the battery positive voltage circuit of the cooling fan S/P relay and the cooling fan motor supply voltage circuit of the cooling fan S/P relay. Does the left cooling fan operate in high speed?	Go to *Step 9*	Go to *Step 7*
7	1. Install the cooling fan S/P relay. 2. Disconnect the left cooling fan electrical connector. 3. Connect the second 20-Amp fused jumper wire from the cooling fan motor supply voltage circuit of the left cooling fan electrical connector to the cooling fan ground circuit of the left cooling fan electrical connector. Does the right cooling fan operate in high speed?	Go to *Step 16*	Go to *Step 8*
8	Connect the second 20-Amp fused jumper wire from the cooling fan motor supply voltage circuit of the left cooling fan electrical connector to a good ground. Does the right cooling fan operate in high speed?	Go to *Step 20*	Go to *Step 21*
9	1. Install the right cooling fan S/P relay. 2. Disconnect the right cooling fan electrical connector. 3. Connect the second 20-Amp fused jumper wire from the motor supply voltage circuit of the right cooling fan electrical connector to the low reference circuit of the right cooling fan electrical connector. Does the left cooling fan operate in high speed?	Go to *Step 17*	Go to *Step 10*
10	Connect the second 20-Amp fused jumper wire from battery positive voltage to the right cooling fan low reference circuit of the of the right cooling fan electrical connector. Does the right cooling fan operate in high speed?	Go to *Step 18*	Go to *Step 22*
11	Is the left cooling fan operating properly in high speed?	Go to *Step 12*	Go to *Step 15*

GC1080100671010X

Fig. 85 Cooling fan inoperative (Part 2 of 2). Intrigue

Step	Action	Yes	No
12	1. Disconnect the cooling fan S/P relay. 2. Connect the second 20-A fused jumper between the right cooling fan low reference circuit of the cooling fan S/P relay and the ground circuit of the cooling fan S/P relay. Does the right cooling fan operate properly in high speed?	Go to *Step 14*	Go to *Step 19*
13	Inspect for poor connections at the cooling fan 1 relay. Did you find and correct the condition?	Go to *Step 28*	Go to *Step 23*
14	Inspect for poor connections at the cooling fan S/P relay. Did you find and correct the condition?	Go to *Step 28*	Go to *Step 24*
15	Inspect for poor connections at the cooling fan 2 relay. Did you find and correct the condition?	Go to *Step 28*	Go to *Step 25*
16	Inspect for poor connections at the harness connector of the left cooling fan. Did you find and correct the condition?	Go to *Step 28*	Go to *Step 26*
17	Inspect for poor connections at the harness connector of the right cooling fan. Did you find and correct the condition?	Go to *Step 28*	Go to *Step 27*
18	Repair the right cooling fan motor supply voltage circuit. Did you complete the repair?	Go to *Step 28*	—
19	Repair the right cooling fan ground circuit. Did you complete the repair?	Go to *Step 28*	—
20	Repair the left cooling fan ground circuit. Did you complete the repair?	Go to *Step 28*	—
21	Repair the left cooling fan motor supply voltage circuit. Did you complete the repair?	Go to *Step 28*	—
22	Repair the right cooling fan low reference circuit. Did you complete the repair?	Go to *Step 28*	—
23	Replace the cooling fan 1 relay. Is the repair complete?	Go to *Step 28*	—
24	Replace the cooling fan S/P relay. Is the repair complete?	Go to *Step 28*	—
25	Replace the cooling fan 2 relay. Is the repair complete?	Go to *Step 28*	—
26	Replace the left cooling fan. Is the repair complete?	Go to *Step 28*	—
27	Replace the right cooling fan. Is the repair complete?	Go to *Step 28*	—
28	Operate the system in order to verify the repair. Did you correct the condition?	System OK	Go to *Step 3*

GC1080100671020X

Fig. 86 Engine coolant temperature indicator always on. LaCrosse

Step	Action	Yes	No
1	Did you perform the Diagnostic System Check - Vehicle?	Go to Step 2	Go to Diagnostic System Check
2	Start the engine. Does the hot coolant indicator illuminate?	Go to Step 3	Test for Intermittent Conditions and Poor Connections
3	1. Install a scan tool. 2. With a scan tool, observe the engine coolant temperature (ECT) sensor parameter in the Powertrain Control Module data list. Does the scan tool indicate that the coolant temperature is within the temperature range shown on the temperature gauge?		Go to Step 4
4	Replace the IPC. Did you complete the replacement?	Go to Step 5	--
5	Operate the system in order to verify the repair. Did you correct the condition?	System OK	Go to Step 2

ARM0400000000680

Fig. 87 Cooling fan always on (Part 1 of 2). LaCrosse

Step	Action	Yes	No
1	Did you perform the Diagnostic System Check - Vehicle?	Go to Step 2	Go to Diagnostic System Check
2	Turn ON the ignition, with the engine OFF. Are one or both cooling fans ON?	Go to Step 3	Test for Intermittent Conditions and Poor Connections
3	Are both cooling fans running continuously?	Go to Step 5	Go to Step 4
4	Remove the fan 2 relay. Did the right cooling fan turn OFF?	Go to Step 8	Go to Step 6
5	Remove the fan 1 relay. Did the cooling fans turn OFF?	Go to Step 10	Go to Step 7
6	Remove the fan 3 relay. Did the right cooling fan turn OFF?	Go to Step 11	Go to Step 9
7	Repair the short to voltage in the left cooling fan motor supply voltage circuit. Did you complete the repair?	Go to Step 14	--
8	Repair the short to voltage in the left cooling fan low reference circuit. Did you complete the repair?	Go to Step 14	--
9	Repair the short to voltage in the right cooling fan motor supply voltage circuit. Did you complete the repair?	Go to Step 14	--

ARM0400000000681

10	Inspect for poor connections at the fan 1 relay. Did you find and correct the condition?	Go to Step 14	Go to Step 12
11	Inspect for poor connections at the fan 3 relay. Did you find and correct the condition?	Go to Step 14	Go to Step 13
12	Replace the fan 1 relay. Did you complete the replacement?	Go to Step 14	--
13	Replace the fan 3 relay. Did you complete the replacement?	Go to Step 14	--
14	Operate the system in order to verify the repair. Did you correct the condition?	System OK	Go to Step 2

ARM0400000000682

Fig. 87   Cooling fan always on (Part 2 of 2). LaCrosse

5	1. Disconnect the fan 2 relay. 2. Connect the second 20-amp fused jumper between the cooling fan low reference circuit and the cooling fan motor supply voltage circuit of the fan 2 relay. Do both cooling fans operate in low speed?	Go to Step 23	Go to Step 6
6	Connect the second 20-amp fused jumper between the battery positive voltage circuit and the cooling fan motor supply voltage circuit of the fan 2 relay. Does the right cooling fan operate in high speed?	Go to Step 9	Go to Step 7
7	1. Install the fan 2 relay. 2. Disconnect the right cooling fan electrical connector. 3. Connect the second 20-amp fused jumper wire from the cooling fan motor supply voltage circuit to the ground circuit of the right cooling fan electrical connector. Does the left cooling fan operate in high speed?	Go to Step 25	Go to Step 8
8	Connect the second 20-amp fused jumper wire from the cooling fan motor supply voltage circuit of the right cooling fan electrical connector to a good ground. Does the left cooling fan operate in high speed?	Go to Step 29	Go to Step 30
9	1. Install the fan 2 relay. 2. Disconnect the left cooling fan electrical connector. 3. Connect the second 20-amp fused jumper wire from the cooling fan motor supply voltage circuit to the cooling fan low reference circuit of the left cooling fan electrical connector. Does the right cooling fan operate in high speed?	Go to Step 26	Go to Step 10
10	Connect the second 20-amp fused jumper wire from the coil side battery positive voltage circuit to the cooling fan low reference circuit of the cooling fan electrical connector. **Does the right cooling fan operate in high speed?**	Go to Step 11	Go to Step 31

ARM0400000000684

Fig. 88   Cooling fan inoperative (Part 2 of 6). LaCrosse

Step	Action	Yes	No
	DEFINITION: One or both engine cooling fan motors do not operate properly in high or low speed modes.		
1	Did you perform the Diagnostic System Check - Vehicle?	Go to Step 2	Go to Diagnostic System Check
2	1. Install a scan tool. 2. Turn ON the ignition, with the engine OFF. 3. With a scan tool, command the Fans Low Speed ON and OFF. Do the low speed engine cooling fans turn ON and OFF with each command?	Go to Step 3	Go to Step 4
3	**Important:** A 3-second delay occurs before the powertrain control module (PCM) changes the cooling fan speed. With a scan tool, command the Fans High Speed ON and OFF. Do the high speed engine cooling fans turn ON and OFF with each command?	Test for Intermittent Conditions and Poor Connections	Go to Step 12
4	**Important** Do NOT remove the 20-amp fused jumper wire connected during this step. Use a second 20-amp fused jumper wire while performing the following steps. 1. Remove the fan 1 relay. 2. Connect a 20-amp fused jumper between the battery positive switch side voltage circuit and the fan motor supply voltage circuit of the cooling fan 1 relay. Do both cooling fans operate in low speed?	Go to Step 22	Go to Step 5

ARM0400000000683

Fig. 88   Cooling fan inoperative (Part 1 of 6). LaCrosse

11	Probe the battery positive voltage circuit on the switch side of the fan 1 relay with a test lamp that is connected to a good ground. Does the test lamp illuminate?	Go to Step 27	Go to Step 32
12	Is the right cooling fan operating properly in high speed?	Go to Step 19	Go to Step 13
13	1. Turn OFF the ignition. 2. Disconnect the fan 3 relay. 3. Turn ON the ignition, with the engine OFF. 4. Connect a test lamp between the high speed cooling fan relay control circuit and the battery positive voltage circuit on the coil side of the fan 3 relay. 5. With a scan tool command the High Speed Fans ON and OFF. Does the test lamp turn ON and OFF with each command?	Go to Step 15	Go to Step 14
14	Probe the battery positive voltage circuit on the coil side of the fan 3 relay with a test lamp that is connected to a good ground. Does the test lamp illuminate?	Go to Step 34	Go to Step 33
15	Install a 20-amp fused jumper between the battery positive voltage circuit on the switch side of the fan 3 relay and the cooling fan motor supply voltage circuit. Does the right cooling fan operate in high speed?	Go to Step 24	Go to Step 16
16	Probe the battery positive voltage circuit on the switch side of the fan 3 relay with a test lamp connected to a good ground. Does the test lamp illuminate?	Go to Step 17	Go to Step 33
17	1. With the 20-amp fused jumper still installed. 2. Disconnect the right cooling fan electrical connector. 3. Connect a test lamp from the cooling fan motor supply voltage circuit to the ground circuit of the right cooling fan electrical connector. Does the test lamp illuminate?	Go to Step 25	Go to Step 18

ARM0400000000685

Fig. 88   Cooling fan inoperative (Part 3 of 6). LaCrosse

18	Probe the cooling fan motor supply voltage circuit of the right cooling fan electrical connector with a test lamp that is connected to a good ground.		
	Does the test lamp illuminate?	Go to Step 29	Go to Step 30
19	1. Turn OFF the ignition. 2. Disconnect the fan 2 relay. 3. Turn ON the ignition, with the engine OFF. 4. Connect a 20-amp fused jumper between the cooling fan low reference circuit and the ground circuit of the fan 2 relay. 5. With a scan tool command the Fans High Speed ON and OFF.		
	Does the left cooling fan operate in high speed?	Go to Step 20	Go to Step 28
20	1. Connect a test lamp between the high speed cooling fan relay control circuit of the fan 2 relay and the battery positive voltage circuit of the fan 2 relay. 2. With a scan tool command the Fans High Speed ON and OFF.		
	Does the test lamp turn ON and OFF with each command?	Go to Step 23	Go to Step 21
21	Probe the battery positive voltage circuit of the fan 2 relay with a test lamp that is connected to a good ground.		
	Does the test lamp illuminate?	Go to Step 34	Go to Step 33
22	Inspect for poor connections at the fan 1 relay.		
	Did you find and correct the condition?	Go to Step 40	Go to Step 35
23	Inspect for poor connections at the fan 2 relay.		
	Did you find and correct the condition?	Go to Step 40	Go to Step 36
24	Inspect for poor connections at the fan 3 relay. Wiring Systems.		
	Did you find and correct the condition?	Go to Step 40	Go to Step 37

ARM0400000000686

Fig. 88   Cooling fan inoperative (Part 4 of 6). LaCrosse

25	Inspect for poor connections at the harness connector of the right cooling fan.		
	Did you find and correct the condition?	Go to Step 40	Go to Step 38
26	Inspect for poor connections at the harness connector of the left cooling fan.		
	Did you find and correct the condition?	Go to Step 40	Go to Step 39
27	Repair the left cooling fan motor supply voltage circuit for an open.		
	Is the repair complete?	Go to Step 40	--
28	Repair the left cooling fan ground circuit for an open.		
	Is the repair complete?	Go to Step 40	--
29	Repair the right cooling fan ground circuit for an open.		
	Is the repair complete?	Go to Step 40	--
30	Repair the right cooling fan motor supply voltage circuit for an open.		
	Is the repair complete?	Go to Step 40	--
31	Repair the left cooling fan low reference circuit for a short to ground or an open.		
	Is the repair complete?	Go to Step 40	--
32	Repair the fan 1 relay battery positive voltage circuit for an open.		
	Is the repair complete?	Go to Step 40	--
33	Repair the battery positive voltage circuit for the fan 2 relay and fan 3 relay for an open.		
	Is the repair complete?	Go to Step 40	--

ARM0400000000687

Fig. 88   Cooling fan inoperative (Part 5 of 6). LaCrosse

34	Repair the high speed cooling fan relay control circuit for an open.		
	Is the repair complete?	Go to Step 40	--
35	Replace the fan 1 relay.		
	Is the repair complete?	Go to Step 40	--
36	Replace the fan 2 relay.		
	Is the repair complete?	Go to Step 40	--
37	Replace the fan 3 relay.		
	Is the repair complete?	Go to Step 40	--
38	Replace the right cooling fan.		
	Is the repair complete?	Go to Step 40	--
39	Replace the left cooling fan.		
	Is the repair complete?	Go to Step 40	--
40	Operate the system in order to verify the repair.		
	Did you correct the condition?	System OK	Go to Step 3

ARM0400000000688

Fig. 88   Cooling fan inoperative (Part 6 of 6). LaCrosse

Step	Action	Yes	No
1	Did you perform the necessary inspections?	Go to Step 2	Go to Symptoms
2	Test the engine coolant heater power supply cord for an open or short to ground. Did you find a condition?	Go to Step 3	Go to Step 4
3	Replace the engine coolant heater power supply cord. Did you complete the repair?	Go to Step 6	--
4	Inspect for poor connections at the harness connector of the engine coolant heater. Did you find and correct the condition?	Go to Step 6	Go to Step 5
5	Replace the engine coolant heater. Refer to Coolant Heater Replacement. Did you complete the repair?	Go to Step 6	--
6	Operate the system in order to verify the repair. Did you correct the condition?	System OK	Go to Step 2

ARM0400000000689

Fig. 89   Coolant heater inoperative. LaCrosse

Step	Action	Yes	No
	DEFINITION: Either of the following conditions indicate a probable engine overheat condition.		
	• The engine temperature gage is in the red (overheat) zone and/or the engine temperature indicator is ON. • Hot engine coolant overflows from the coolant recovery reservoir and/or radiator cap onto the ground while the engine is running.		
1	1. Inspect and fill the cooling system, as necessary. 2. Inspect the cooling system for leaks, as necessary. 3. Repair the cooling system leaks, as necessary. Has the inspection/repair been performed?	Go to Step 2	--
2	1. Start the engine and allow the engine to run at approximately 1,200 RPM. 2. Use the scan tool in order to verify the overheat condition. Does the Scan Tool verify the engine overheat condition?	Go to Step 3	Go to in Instrument Panel, Gauges and Console
3	1. Verify that the cooling fans are operating properly. 2. Repair the cooling fan system, as necessary. Does the engine still overheat?	Go to Step 4	System OK
4	Perform the following inspections: • Inspect the radiator and the A/C condenser cooling fins for debris or any other obstruction. • Inspect the drive belt system and the drive belt tensioner for proper operation in order to ensure that the coolant pump is rotating properly. • Inspect for loose, damaged and/or missing air deflector(s). • Inspect for a pinched or kinked cooling system hose. • Repair the systems as necessary. Does the engine still overheat?	Go to Step 5	System OK
5	Inspect the thermostat for proper operation. Is the thermostat operating properly?	Go to Step 7	Go to Step 6
6	Replace the thermostat. Does the engine still overheat?	Go to Step 7	System OK

ARM0400000000690

Fig. 90 Engine overheating (Part 1 of 2). LaCrosse

Step	Action	Yes	No
7	**Important** Excessive coolant freeze point protection MAY cause the coolant to boil at low temperatures. 1. Inspect for the proper coolant concentration (mixture). Correct the coolant concentration as necessary. 2. Remove the radiator cap. 3. Start the engine and inspect for a constant flow of air bubbles in the engine coolant. Is there a constant flow of air bubbles in the engine coolant?	Go to Step 8	Go to Step 9
8	The probable cause of the engine overheat is combustion chamber gasses leaking into the cooling system. This condition is usually caused by the following: • A worn or damaged cylinder head gasket • A worn or damaged cylinder head • A worn and/or damaged engine block Verify this condition by inspecting the spark plug electrodes and porcelain surrounding the spark plug electrode for signs of coolant. Replace and/or repair the engine internal component(s), as necessary, in order to repair the engine internal coolant leak. Does the engine still overheat?	Go to Step 1	System OK
9	The engine overheat may be caused by a cooling system blockage. Flush the cooling system. Does the engine still overheat?	Go to Step 10	System OK
10	**Important** It is unlikely that the water pump is the cause of the overheat condition. If NONE of the cooling system passages are restricted, replace the coolant pump. Does the engine still overheat?	Go to Step 1	System OK

ARM0400000000691

Fig. 90 Engine overheating (Part 2 of 2). LaCrosse

Step	Action	Yes	No
1	1. Ensure that the cooling system is full. 2. Allow the engine to cool. 3. Start the engine. 4. Turn the air conditioning system OFF. 5. Inspect the engine cooling fans. Is the electric cooling fan on?	Go to Step 2	Go to Step 3
2	1. Diagnose and repair the cooling fan system. 2. Verify the customer complaint. Does the engine still fail to reach normal operating temperature?	Go to Step 3	System OK
3	Install the scan tool to the data link connector (DLC). Compare the scan tool coolant temperature reading to the instrument panel (I/P) cluster coolant temperature. Is the I/P cluster coolant temperature close to the reading on the scan tool?	Go to Step 5	Go to Step 4
4	1. Diagnose and repair the coolant temperature gage system. 2. Verify the customer complaint. Does the engine still fail to reach normal operating temperature?	Go to Step 5	System OK
5	Inspect the thermostat for proper operation. Is the thermostat operating properly?	Go to Step 1	Go to Step 6
6	1. Replace the thermostat. 2. Verify the customer complaint. Does the engine still fail to reach normal operating temperature?	Go to Step 1	System OK

ARM0400000000692

Fig. 91 Engine fails to reach normal operating temperature. LaCrosse

Step	Action	Value(s)	Yes	No
1	Did you perform the Powertrain On-Board Diagnostic (OBD) System Check?	—	Go to Step 2	Go to A Powertrain On Board Diagnostic (OBD) System Check
2	Are any DTCs set?	—	Go to applicable DTCs	Go to Step 3
3	1. Install a scan tool. 2. Engine coolant temperature must be below the specified value for all the fan diagnoses. 3. Turn ON the Ignition, with the engine and A/C OFF. Are the cooling fans OFF?	100°C (212°F)	Go to Step 4	Go to Cooling Fan table #1
4	With a scan tool, command Low Speed Fans ON. Are both cooling fans ON?	—	Go to Step 5	Go to Cooling Fan table #2
5	**Important:** Allow a 3–5 second delay before determining if the fans have switched from low to high speed. With a scan tool, command High Speed Fans ON. Do both cooling fans switch to high speed?	—	Go to Step 6	Go to Cooling Fan table #3
6	1. Exit outputs screen on the scan tool. 2. Idle the engine leaving the A/C OFF. Are the cooling fans ON?	—	Go to Step 8	Go to Step 7
7	Turn ON the A/C. Are the cooling fans ON?	—	System OK	Go to Step 9
8	Does the scan tool display A/C request as YES?	—	Go to Cooling Insufficient, A/C System	Go to Step 10
9	Does the scan tool display A/C request as YES?	—	Go to A/C Compressor Control Circuit Diagnosis	Go to Cooling Insufficient, A/C System
10	**Important:** The replacement PCM must be programmed. Replace the PCM. Is the action complete?	—	System OK	—

GC1080000591000X

Fig. 92 Cooling fan functional check. Lumina

Step	Action	Values	Yes	No
1	Did you perform the Cooling Fan Functional Check?	—	Go to Step 2	Go to Cooling Fan Functional Check
2	Disconnect Cool Fan 1 Relay. Are both fans OFF?	—	Go to Step 8	Go to Step 3
3	Disconnect Cool Fan 3 Relay. Are both fans OFF?	—	Go to Step 4	Go to Step 10
4	1. Disconnect the right fan. 2. Probe terminal B of the right fan connector using a test lamp that is connected to a known good ground. Does the test lamp illuminate?	—	Go to Step 11	Go to Step 5
5	Probe terminal A of the right fan connector using a test lamp that is connected to a known good ground. Does the test lamp illuminate?	—	Go to Step 12	Go to Step 6
6	Probe the High Speed Fans control circuit (473) at the Cool Fan 3 Relay connector in the Underhood Accessory Wiring Junction Block using a test lamp that is connected to battery positive voltage. Does the test lamp illuminate?	—	Go to Step 7	Go to Step 13
7	1. Turn OFF the ignition. 2. Leave the test lamp installed. 3. Disconnect the PCM. 4. Turn ON the ignition, with the engine OFF. Is the test lamp still illuminated?	—	Go to Step 14	Go to Step 16
8	Probe the Low Speed Fans Control circuit (335) at the Cool Fan 1 Relay connector using the test lamp that is connected to battery positive voltage. Does the test lamp illuminate?	—	Go to Step 9	Go to Step 13
9	1. Turn OFF the ignition. 2. Leave the test lamp installed. 3. Disconnect the PCM. 4. Turn ON the ignition, with the engine OFF. Is the test lamp still illuminated?	—	Go to Step 14	Go to Step 16
10	Repair the LH fan feed circuit (409) for a short to voltage. Did you find and correct the condition?	—	Go to Cooling Fan Functional Check	Go to Step 15
11	Repair the RH fan feed circuit (532) for a short to voltage. Is the action complete?	—	Go to Cooling Fan Functional Check	—
12	Repair the short to voltage in the Cool Fan 2 Relay feed circuit (740). Is the action complete?	—	Go to Cooling Fan Functional Check	—
13	Replace the Cool Fan 1 Relay. Is the action complete?	—	Go to Cooling Fan Functional Check	—
14	Repair the High Speed Fans Control circuit (473) or the Low Speed Fans Control circuit (335) for a short to ground. Is the action complete?	—	Go to Cooling Fan Functional Check	—
15	Replace the Cool Fan 2 Relay. Is the action complete?	—	Go to Cooling Fan Functional Check	—
16	**Important:** Program the replacement PCM. Replace the PCM. Is the action complete?	—	Go to Cooling Fan Functional Check	—

GC1080000592000X

Fig. 93   Cooling fan table 1. Lumina

Step	Action	Values	Yes	No
14	Inspect the PCM connections. Repair faulty connections as necessary. Did you find a problem and correct the problem?	—	Go to Cooling Fan Functional Check	Go to Step 27
15	Repair the Low Speed Fans Control circuit (335) for an open or shorted to battery positive voltage. Is the action complete?	—	Go to Cooling Fan Functional Check	—
16	Inspect the fan motor ground circuit for a open or the left fan motor connections and repair as necessary. Did you find and correct the condition?	—	Go to Cooling Fan Functional Check	Go to Step 17
17	Replace the left fan motor. Is the action complete?	—	Go to Cooling Fan Functional Check	—
18	Repair the RH fan feed circuit (504) for an open. Is the action complete?	—	Go to Cooling Fan Functional Check	—
19	Replace the fan which was not operating. Is the action complete?	—	Go to Cooling Fan Functional Check	—
20	Replace Cool Fan 3 Relay. Is the action complete?	—	Go to Cooling Fan Functional Check	—
21	Repair the Cool Fan 2 Relay feed circuit (740) for a short to ground. Did you find and correct the condition?	—	Go to Cooling Fan Functional Check	Go to Step 26
22	Repair the open or the grounded circuit for the circuit that did not light. Is the action complete?	—	Go to Cooling Fan Functional Check	—
23	Replace Cool Fan 1 Relay. Is the action complete?	—	Go to Cooling Fan Functional Check	—
24	Repair the LH fan feed circuit (409) for a open. Is the action complete?	—	Go to Cooling Fan Functional Check	—
25	Repair the Cool Fan 2 Relay feed circuit (504) for a open. Is the action complete?	—	Go to Cooling Fan Functional Check	—
26	Replace Cool Fan 2 Relay. Is the action complete?	—	Go to Cooling Fan Functional Check	—
27	**Important:** Program the replacement PCM. Replace the PCM. Is the action complete?	—	Go to Cooling Fan Functional Check	—

GC1080000593020X

Fig. 94   Cooling fan table 2 (Part 2 of 2). Lumina

Step	Action	Values	Yes	No
1	Did you perform the Cooling Fan Functional Check?	—	Go to Step 2	Go to Cooling Fan Functional Check
2	Did either fan turn ON when Cool Fan 1 Relay was commanded ON?	—	Go to Step 3	Go to Step 5
3	1. Install a scan tool. 2. With a scan tool, command Low Speed Fans ON. Did the other fan turn OFF?	—	Go to Step 19	Go to Step 4
4	Disconnect Cool Fan 2 Relay. Did the fan turn ON?	—	Go to Step 20	Go to Step 21
5	1. With a scan tool, command Low Speed Fans ON. 2. Disconnect Cool Fan 1 Relay. 3. Probe Low Speed Fans Control circuit (335) at the Cool Fan 1 Relay connector using a test lamp that is connected to battery positive voltage. Does the test lamp illuminate?	—	Go to Step 6	Go to Step 13
6	Probe both feed circuits (640) at the Cool Fan 1 Relay Connector locations using a test lamp that is connected to ground. Does test lamp illuminate for both circuits?	—	Go to Step 7	Go to Step 22
7	**Important:** Leave jumper in place for remainder of this table. Connect a fused jumper wire between the switch feed circuit (740) and the RH fan feed circuit (409) at the Cool Fan 1 Relay Connector locations. Do both fans turn ON?	—	Go to Step 23	Go to Step 8
8	1. Disconnect the right fan. 2. Probe fan harness connector terminal B with a test lamp that is connected to a known good ground. Does the test lamp illuminate?	—	Go to Step 9	Go to Step 24
9	Connect a second fused jumper wire between the right fan harness connector terminals. Is the left fan ON?	—	Go to Step 16	Go to Step 10
10	1. Reconnect the right fan. 2. Disconnect Cool Fan 2 Relay. 3. Probe the switch feed circuit (504) at Cool Fan 2 Relay connector using a test lamp that is connected to a known good ground. Does the test lamp illuminate?	—	Go to Step 11	Go to Step 25
11	Using the second jumper wire, jumper the switch feed circuit (504) and the LH fan feed circuit (409) together at Cool Fan 2 Relay connector. Do the fans come ON?	—	Go to Step 26	Go to Step 12
12	1. Reconnect Cool Fan 2 Relay. 2. Disconnect the left fan. 3. Probe left fan harness connector terminal B with a test lamp that is connected to a known good ground. Is the right fan ON?	—	Go to Step 16	Go to Step 18
13	1. Keep test lamp connected. 2. Turn OFF the ignition. 3. Disconnect the PCM. 4. Probe the Low Speed Fans Control circuit at the PCM connector, with a fused jumper wire that is connected to a known good ground. Is the test lamp ON?	—	Go to Step 20	Go to Step 21

GC1080000593010X

Fig. 94   Cooling fan table 2 (Part 1 of 2). Lumina

Step	Action	Values	Yes	No
1	Did you perform the Cooling Fan Functional Check?	—	Go to Step 2	Go to Cooling Fan Functional Check
2	1. With a scan tool, command Low Speed Fans ON. 2. Command High Speed Fans ON. Did both fans operate with no change?	—	Go to Step 8	Go to Step 3
3	Did the left fan stop operating?	—	Go to Step 9	Go to Step 4
4	1. Disconnect Cool Fan 3 Relay. 2. Probe the High Speed Fans Control circuit (473) at Cool Fan 3 Relay connector using a test lamp that is connected to battery positive voltage. 3. Command High Speed Fans ON using a scan tool. Does the test lamp illuminate after several seconds?	—	Go to Step 5	Go to Step 12
5	Probe the coil feed circuit (740) at Cool Fan Relay connector using a test lamp that is connected to a known good ground. Does the test lamp illuminate?	—	Go to Step 6	Go to Step 13
6	Probe the switch feed circuit (740) at the Cool Fan 3 Relay connector using a test lamp that is connected to a good ground. Does the test lamp illuminate?	—	Go to Step 7	Go to Step 14
7	Jumper the switch feed circuit (740) and the LH fan feed circuit (409) together at the Cool Fan 3 Relay connector. Is the left fan ON?	—	Go to Step 15	Go to Step 16
8	1. Turn OFF the ignition. 2. Disconnect the PCM. 3. Disconnect Cool Fan 1 Relay. 4. Jumper the switch feed circuit (640) and the RH fan feed circuit (532) together at the Cool Fan 1 Relay connector. 5. Turn ON the ignition. 6. Probe the PCM harness connector for the High Speed Fans Control circuit with a fused jumper that is connected to a known good ground. Do the fans switch from low to high speed?	—	Go to Step 22	Go to Step 17
9	1. Disconnect Cool Fan 3 Relay. 2. Probe the High Speed Fans Control Cirucit (473) at the Cool Fan 3 Relay connector using a test lamp that is connected to battery positive voltage. 3. Command High Speed Fans ON using a scan tool. Does the test lamp illuminate?	—	Go to Step 10	Go to Step 18
10	Probe the ground circuit (250) at the Cool Fan 2 Relay connector using a test lamp that is connected to battery positive voltage. Does the test lamp illuminate?	—	Go to Step 11	Go to Step 19
11	Probe the coil feed circuit (740) at the Cool Fan 2 Relay connector using a test lamp that is connected to a known good ground. Does the test lamp illuminate?	—	Go to Step 20	Go to Step 21
12	Repair the High Speed Fans Control circuit (473) for an open between Cool Fan 3 Relay and the splice. Is the action complete?	—	Go to Cooling Fan Functional Check	—
13	Repair the open in the Cool Fan 3 Relay coil feed circuit (740). Is the action complete?	—	Go to Cooling Fan Functional Check	—

GC1080000594010X

Fig. 95   Cooling fan table 3 (Part 1 of 2). Lumina

Step	Action	Values	Yes	No
14	Repair the open in the Cool Fan 3 Relay switch feed circuit (740). Is the action complete?	—	Go to Cooling Fan Functional Check	—
15	Replace Cool Fan 3 Relay. Is the action complete?	—	Go to Cooling Fan Functional Check	—
16	Repair the open in the LH fan feed circuit (409) between Cool Fan 3 Relay and the splice. Is the action complete?	—	Go to Cooling Fan Functional Check	—
17	Repair the High Speed Fans Control circuit (473) for an open or for a short to battery positive voltage. Is the action complete?	—	Go to Cooling Fan Functional Check	—
18	Repair the open in the High Speed Fans Control circuit (473) between Cool Fan 2 Relay and the splice. Is the action complete?	—	Go to Cooling Fan Functional Check	—
19	Repair the open in the ground circuit (250). Is the action complete?	—	Go to Cooling Fan Functional Check	—
20	Replace the Cool Fan 2 relay. Is the action complete?	—	Go to Cooling Fan Functional Check	—
21	Repair the open in Cool fan 2 Relay coil feed circuit (740). Is the action complete?	—	Go to Cooling Fan Functional Check	—
22	1. Inspect the PCM connections. 2. Repair faulty connections as necessary. Did you find and correct the condition?	—	Go to Cooling Fan Functional Check	Go to Step 23
23	**Important:** Program the replacement PCM. Replace the PCM. Is the action complete?	—	Go to Cooling Fan Functional Check	—

GC1080000594020X

Fig. 95   Cooling fan table 3 (Part 2 of 2). Lumina

Step	Action	Yes	No
	DEFINITION: One or both engine cooling fan motors run continuously in high or low speed.		
1	Did you perform the Engine Cooling Diagnostic System Check?	Go to Step 2	Go To Diagnostic System Check
2	Turn ON the ignition, with the engine OFF. Are one or both cooling fans ON?	Go to Step 3	Test for Intermittent and Poor Connections
3	Are both cooling fans running continuously?	Go to Step 5	Go to Step 4
4	Remove the cooling fan S/P relay. Did the right cooling fan turn OFF?	Go to Step 6	Go to Step 7
5	Repair the short to voltage in the left cooling fan supply voltage circuit. Did you complete the repair?	Go to Step 8	--
6	Repair the short to voltage in the left cooling fan low reference circuit. Did you complete the repair?	Go to Step 8	--
7	Repair the short to voltage in the right cooling fan supply voltage circuit. Did you complete the repair?	Go to Step 8	--
8	Operate the system in order to verify the repair. Did you correct the condition?	System OK	Go to Step 2

ARM0300000000668

Fig. 97   Cooling fan always on. 2001–03 Malibu

Step	Action	Yes	No
1	Install a scan tool. Does the scan tool power up?	Go to Step 2	Diagnose Data Link Communications
2	1. Turn ON the ignition, with the engine OFF. 2. Attempt to establish communication with the following control modules: ○ Instrument Cluster ○ Powertrain Control Module Does the scan tool communicate with the control modules?	Go to Step 3	Diagnose Data Link Communications
3	Select the powertrain control module display DTCs function on the scan tool. Does the scan tool display any DTCs?	Go to Step 4	Diagnose engine cooling
4	Does the scan tool display any DTCs which begin with a "U"?	Diagnose Data Link Communications	Diagnose Diagnostic Trouble Code (DTC)

ARM0300000000667

Fig. 96   Diagnostic system check. 2001–03 Malibu

Step	Action	Yes	No
	DEFINITION: One or both engine cooling fan motors do not operate properly in high or low speed.		
1	Did you perform the Engine Cooling Diagnostic System Check?	Go to Step 2	Go to Diagnostic System Check
2	1. Install a scan tool. 2. Turn ON the ignition, with the engine OFF. 3. With a scan tool, command the Fans Low Speed ON and OFF. Do the low speed engine cooling fans turn ON and OFF with each command?	Go to Step 3	Go to Step 4
3	**Important:** A 3-second delay occurs before the PCM changes the cooling fan speed. With a scan tool, command the Fans High Speed ON and OFF. Do the high speed engine cooling fans turn ON and OFF with each command?	Test for Intermittent and Poor Connections	Go to Step 13
4	Test the fused battery positive voltage circuit of the cooling fan 1 relay for an open or short to ground. Did you find and correct the condition?	Go to Step 30	Go to Step 5
5	Test the cooling fan motor supply voltage circuit for a short to ground. Did you find and correct the condition?	Go to Step 30	Go to Step 6

ARM0300000000669

**Fig. 98   Cooling fan inoperative (Part 1 of 5).
 2001–03 Malibu**

6	1. Disconnect the cooling fan 1 relay. 2. Connect the first 20-A fused jumper between the battery positive voltage circuit of the cooling fan 1 relay and the cooling fan motor supply voltage circuit of the cooling fan 1 relay. Do both cooling fans operate in low speed?	Go to Step 15	Go to Step 7
7	1. Disconnect the cooling fan S/P relay 2. Connect the second 20-A fused jumper between the left cooling fan low reference circuit of the cooling fan S/P relay and the right cooling fan supply voltage circuit of the cooling fan S/P relay. Do both cooling fans operate in low speed?	Go to Step 16	Go to Step 8
8	Connect the second 20-A fused jumper between the battery positive voltage circuit of the cooling fan S/P relay and the cooling fan motor supply voltage circuit of the cooling fan S/P relay. Does the right cooling fan operate in high speed?	Go to Step 11	Go to Step 9
9	1. Install the cooling fan S/P relay. 2. Disconnect the right cooling fan electrical connector. 3. Connect the second 20-Amp fused jumper wire from the cooling fan motor supply voltage circuit of the right cooling fan electrical connector to the cooling fan motor ground circuit of the right cooling fan electrical connector. Does the left cooling fan operate in high speed?	Go to Step 18	Go to Step 10
10	Connect the second 20-Amp fused jumper wire from the cooling fan motor supply voltage circuit of the right cooling fan electrical connector to a good ground. Does the left cooling fan operate in high speed?	Go to Step 22	Go to Step 23

ARM0300000000670

Fig. 98 Cooling fan inoperative (Part 2 of 5). 2001–03 Malibu

11	1. Install the cooling fan S/P relay. 2. Disconnect the left cooling fan electrical connector. 3. Connect the second 20-Amp fused jumper wire from the cooling fan motor supply voltage circuit of the left cooling fan electrical connector to the cooling fan low reference circuit of the left cooling fan electrical connector. Does the right cooling fan operate in high speed?	Go to Step 19	Go to Step 12
12	Connect the second 20-Amp fused jumper wire from battery positive voltage to the left cooling fan low reference circuit of the of the left cooling fan electrical connector. Does the right cooling fan operate in high speed?	Go to Step 20	Go to Step 24
13	Is the right cooling fan operating properly in high speed?	Go to Step 14	Go to Step 17
14	1. Disconnect the cooling fan S/P relay 2. Connect the second 20-A fused jumper between the left cooling fan low reference circuit of the cooling fan S/P relay and the ground circuit of the cooling fan S/P relay. Does the left cooling fan operate properly in high speed?	Go to Step 16	Go to Step 21
15	Inspect for poor connections at the cooling fan 1 relay. Did you find and correct the condition?	Go to Step 30	Go to Step 25
16	Inspect for poor connections at the cooling fan S/P relay. Did you find and correct the condition?	Go to Step 30	Go to Step 26

ARM0300000000671

Fig. 98 Cooling fan inoperative (Part 3 of 5). 2001–03 Malibu

17	Inspect for poor connections at the cooling fan 2 relay. Did you find and correct the condition?	Go to Step 30	Go to Step 27
18	Inspect for poor connections at the harness connector of the right cooling fan. Did you find and correct the condition?	Go to Step 30	Go to Step 28
19	Inspect for poor connections at the harness connector of the left cooling fan. Did you find and correct the condition?	Go to Step 30	Go to Step 29
20	Repair the left cooling fan supply voltage circuit. Did you complete the repair?	Go to Step 30	--
21	Repair the left cooling fan ground circuit. Did you complete the repair?	Go to Step 30	--
22	Repair the right cooling fan ground circuit. Did you complete the repair?	Go to Step 30	--

ARM0300000000672

Fig. 98 Cooling fan inoperative (Part 4 of 5). 2000–03 Malibu

23	**Important** Do NOT remove the 20-A fused jumper wire connected during this step. Use a second 20-A fused jumper while performing the following steps. Repair the right cooling fan supply voltage circuit. Did you complete the repair?	Go to Step 30	--
24	Repair the left cooling fan low reference circuit. Did you complete the repair?	Go to Step 30	--
25	Replace the cooling fan 1 relay. Did you complete the repair?	Go to Step 30	--
26	Replace the cooling fan S/P relay. Did you complete the repair?	Go to Step 30	--
27	Replace the cooling fan 2 relay. Did you complete the repair?	Go to Step 30	--
28	Replace the right cooling fan. Did you complete the repair?	Go to Step 30	--
29	Replace the left cooling fan. Did you complete the repair?	Go to Step 30	--
30	Operate the system in order to verify the repair. Did you correct the condition?	System OK	Go to Step 3

ARM0300000000673

Fig. 98 Cooling fan inoperative (Part 5 of 5). 2001–03 Malibu

Step	Action	Yes	No
1	Perform the following preliminary inspections: 1. Ensure that the battery is fully charged. 2. Ensure that the battery cables are clean and tight. 3. Inspect for any open fuses. 4. Inspect the easily accessible systems or the visible system components for obvious damage or conditions that could cause the symptom. 5. Ensure that the grounds are clean, tight, and in the correct location. 6. Inspect for aftermarket devices that could affect the operation of the system. 7. Search for applicable service bulletins. Did you find and correct the condition?	System OK	Go to Step 2

ARM0300000000674

Fig. 99   Diagnostic system check (Part 1 of 3). 2004–05 Malibu

Step	Action	Yes	No
2	**Important** CANdi module J-45289 must be used with the Tech2. Install a scan tool. Does the scan tool power up?	Go to Step 3	Diagnose Scan Tool Does Not Power Up
3	1. Turn ON the ignition, with the engine OFF. 2. Select the Vehicle DTC Information on the scan tool. Does the scan tool display No Comm. for any control module?	Diagnose Data Link Communications	Go to Step 4
4	Attempt to start the engine. Does the engine crank over?	Go to Step 5	Diagnose Engine Electrical
5	Attempt to start the engine. Does the engine start and idle?	Go to Step 6	Diagnose Engine Cranks but Does Not Run

ARM0300000000675

Fig. 99   Diagnostic system check (Part 2 of 3). 2004–05 Malibu

Step	Action	Yes	No

6	**Important**
	
	Do NOT clear the DTCs unless instructed by a diagnostic procedure.
	
	1. Diagnose the DTCs in the order that the DTCs appear on the scan tool or mis-diagnosis may occur.
	2. If multiple powertrain DTCs are stored, diagnose the DTCs in the following order:
	  A. Component level DTCs, such as sensor DTCs, solenoid DTCs, and relay DTCs.
	  B. System level DTCs, for example, misfire DTCs, EVAP system DTCs, and fuel trim DTCs.
	
	Advance to the List All DTCs screen on the scan tool.
	
	Does the scan tool display any DTCs?
		Go to Step 7	System OK

7	If there are any powertrain DTCs, select Captured Info in order to store the powertrain DTC information with a scan tool. Did you complete the action?	Diagnose Trouble Code (DTC)	--

ARM0300000000676

Fig. 99   Diagnostic system check (Part 3 of 3). 2004–05 Malibu

Step	Action	Yes	No
	DEFINITION: The engine cooling fan motor runs continuously in high or low speed.		
1	Did you perform the Vehicle Diagnostic System Check?	Go to Step 2	Go to Diagnostic System Check
2	Turn the ignition ON, with the engine OFF. Are one or both cooling fans ON?	Go to Step 3	Test for Intermittent and Poor Connections
3	Are both cooling fans running continuously?	Go to Step 4	Go to Step 6
4	Are both fans running continuously in high speed?	Go to Step 5	Go to Step 7
5	Test the low reference circuit of the A/C refrigerant pressure sensor for an open.	Go to Step 18	Go to Step 14
6	Remove the cooling fan s/p relay. Did the right cooling fan turn OFF?	Go to Step 10	Go to Step 8
7	Remove the cooling fan 1 relay. Did the cooling fans turn OFF?	Go to Step 12	Go to Step 9
8	Remove the cooling fan 2 relay. Did the right cooling fan turn OFF?	Go to Step 13	Go to Step 11
9	Repair the short to voltage in the left cooling fan motor supply voltage circuit. Did you complete the repair?	Go to Step 18	--

ARM0300000000677

Fig. 100   Coolant fan always on (Part 1 of 2). 2004–05 Malibu

10	Repair the short to voltage in the left cooling fan motor low reference circuit. Did you complete the repair?	Go to Step 18	--
11	Repair the short to voltage in the right cooling fan motor supply voltage circuit. Did you complete the repair?	Go to Step 18	--
12	Inspect for poor connections at the cool fan 1 relay. Did you find and correct the condition?	Go to Step 18	Go to Step 15
13	Inspect for poor connections at the cool fan 2 relay. Did you find and correct the condition?	Go to Step 18	Go to Step 16
14	Inspect for poor connections at the A/C refrigerant pressure sensor. Did you find and correct the condition?	Go to Step 18	Go to Step 17
15	Replace the cool fan 1 relay. Did you complete the replacement?	Go to Step 18	--
16	Replace the cool fan 2 relay. Did you complete the replacement?	Go to Step 18	--
17	Replace the A/C refrigerant pressure sensor. Did you complete the replacement?	Go to Step 18	--
18	Operate the system in order to verify the repair. Did you correct the condition?	System OK	Go to Step 2

ARM0300000000678

Fig. 100 Coolant fan always on (Part 2 of 2). 2004–05 Malibu

1	Did you perform the Diagnostic System Check-Vehicle?	Go to Step 2	Go to Diagnostic System Check
2	1. Install a scan tool. 2. Turn ON the ignition, with the engine OFF. 3. With a scan tool, command the Fan Control Relay 1 ON and OFF. Do the low speed engine cooling fans turn ON and OFF with each command?	Go to Step 3	Go to Step 4
3	**Important:** A 3-second delay occurs before the PCM changes the cooling fan speed. With a scan tool, command the Fan Control Relay 2 and 3 ON and OFF. Do the high speed engine cooling fans turn ON and OFF with each command?	Test for Intermittent and Poor Connections	Go to Step 6
4	**Important** Do NOT remove the jumper wire that you will be connecting until your testing is completed. If the cool fan 1 fuse opens when you connect the jumper wire, repair the cooling fan motor supply voltage circuit of the left cooling fan motor for a short to ground. 1. Disconnect the cool fan 1 relay. 2. Connect a jumper wire between the battery positive voltage circuit and the cooling fan motor supply voltage circuit of the cool fan 1 relay. Do both cooling fans operate in low speed?	Go to Step 14	Go to Step 5

ARM0300000000679

Fig. 101 Coolant fan inoperative (Part 1 of 4). 2004–05 Malibu

5	1. Disconnect the S/P fan relay. 2. With a test lamp connected to a good ground, probe the cooling fan low reference circuit at the S/P fan relay. Does the test lamp illuminate?	Go to Step 9	Go to Step 8
6	Does the left cooling fan operate at high speed?	Go to Step 16	Go to Step 7
7	Inspect the ground circuit of the S/P fan relay for an open or high resistance. Did you find and correct the condition?	Go to Step 25	Go to Step 15
8	1. Install the S/P fan relay. 2. Disconnect the left cooling fan electrical connector. 3. With a test lamp connected to a good ground, probe the cooling fan motor supply voltage circuit at the left cooling fan motor connector. Does the test lamp illuminate?	Go to Step 12	Go to Step 13
9	1. Install the S/P fan relay. 2. Disconnect the right cooling fan motor connector. 3. With a test lamp connected to a good ground, probe the cooling fan motor supply voltage circuit at the right cooling fan connector. Does the test lamp illuminate?	Go to Step 11	Go to Step 10
10	Inspect the cooling fan motor supply voltage circuit for an open or high resistance. Did you find and correct the condition?	Go to Step 25	Go to Step 15

ARM0300000000680

Fig. 101 Coolant fan inoperative (Part 2 of 4). 2004–05 Malibu

11	Inspect the ground circuit of the right cooling fan for an open or high resistance. Did you find and correct the condition?	Go to Step 25	Go to Step 18
12	Inspect the cooling fan low reference circuit for an open or high resistance. Did you find and correct the condition?	Go to Step 25	Go to Step 17
13	Inspect the cooling fan motor supply voltage circuit of the left cooling fan for an open or high resistance. Did you find and correct the condition?	Go to Step 25	Go to Step 19
14	Inspect for poor connections at the cool fan 1 relay. Did you find and correct the condition?	Go to Step 25	Go to Step 20
15	Inspect for poor connections at the S/P fan relay. Did you find and correct the condition?	Go to Step 25	Go to Step 21
16	Inspect for poor connections at the cool fan 2 relay. Did you find and correct the condition?	Go to Step 25	Go to Step 22

ARM0300000000681

Fig. 101 Coolant fan inoperative (Part 3 of 4). 2004–05 Malibu

	Action		Yes	No
17	Inspect for poor connections at the harness connector of the left cooling fan.			
	Did you find and correct the condition?		Go to Step 25	Go to Step 23
18	Inspect for poor connections at the harness connector of the right cooling fan.			
	Did you find and correct the condition?		Go to Step 25	Go to Step 24
19	Repair the battery positive voltage circuit for an open or high resistance.			
	Did you complete the repair?		Go to Step 25	--
20	Replace the cool fan 1 relay.			
	Did you complete the replacement?		Go to Step 25	--
21	Replace the S/P fan relay.			
	Did you complete the replacement?		Go to Step 25	--
22	Replace the cool fan 2 relay.			
	Did you complete the replacement?		Go to Step 25	--
23	Replace the left cooling fan.			
	Did you complete the replacement?		Go to Step 25	--
24	Replace the right cooling fan.			
	Did you complete the replacement?		Go to Step 25	--
25	Operate the system in order to verify the repair.			
	Did you correct the condition?		System OK	Go to Step 3

ARM0300000000682

Fig. 101   Coolant fan inoperative (Part 4 of 4). 2004–05 Malibu

Step	Action	Value(s)	Yes	No
1	Did you perform the Powertrain On-Board Diagnostic System Check?	—	Go to Step 2	Go to Powertrain OBD System Check
2	1. Start engine and obtain operating temperature. 2. Turn OFF all the accessories. 3. Install a scan tool. 4. Observe the ECT sensor parameter on the scan tool. Does the cooling fan turn ON when ECT reaches above the specified value?	97.5°C (208°F)	Go to Step 3	Go to Step 8

GC1089800359010X

Fig. 102   Cooling fan diagnosis (Part 1 of 3). Metro

Step	Action	Value(s)	Yes	No
15	Repair the open in the ignition feed circuit between the cooling fan relay terminal 1 and the junction block. Is the action complete?	—	Go to Step 20	
16	Repair the open in the battery feed circuit between the cooling fan relay terminal 4 and the fuse box. Is the action complete?	—	Go to Step 20	
17	Replace the cooling fan relay. Is the action complete?	—	Go to Step 20	
18	Replace the PCM. Is the action complete?	—	Go to Step 20	
19	Replace the cooling fan motor. Is the action complete?	—	Go to Step 20	
20	1. Clear the scan tool information and road test the vehicle within the Freeze Frame conditions that set the DTC. 2. Review the scan tool data and check for DTCs. The repair is complete if no DTCs are stored. Are any DTCs displayed on the scan tool?	—	Go to the Applicable DTC Table	System OK

GC1089800359030X

Fig. 102   Cooling fan diagnosis (Part 3 of 3). Metro

Step	Action	Yes	No
1	Install a scan tool. Does the scan tool power up?	Go to Step 2	Diagnose Data Link Communications
2	1. Turn ON the ignition, with the engine OFF. 2. Attempt to establish communication with the following control modules: • Instrument Cluster • Powertrain Control Module. Does the scan tool communicate with the control modules?	Go to Step 3	Diagnose Data Link Communications
3	Select the powertrain control module display DTCs function on the scan tool. Does the scan tool display any DTCs?	Go to Step 4	Diagnose Go to Symptoms - Engine Cooling
4	Does the scan tool display any DTCs which begin with a "U"?	Diagnose Data Link Communications	Diagnose Trouble Code

GC1080100672000X

Fig. 103   Diagnostic system check. 2001 Park Avenue

Step	Action	Yes	No
	DEFINITION: One or both engine cooling fan motors run continuously in high or low speed.		
1	Did you perform the Engine Cooling Diagnostic System Check?	Go to Step 2	Diagnose Engine Cooling
2	Important: The cooling fan 1 relay and cooling fan 2 relay are improperly identified in the underhood fuse block. Turn ON the ignition, with the engine OFF. Are one or both cooling fans ON?	Go to Step 3	Test for Intermittent and Poor Connections
3	Are both cooling fans running continuously?	Go to Step 5	Go to Step 4
4	Remove the cooling fan S/P relay. Did the right cooling fan turn OFF?	Go to Step 6	Go to Step 7
5	Repair the short to voltage in the left cooling fan motor supply voltage circuit. Did you complete the repair?	Go to Step 8	--
6	Repair the short to voltage in the left cooling fan low reference circuit. Did you complete the repair?	Go to Step 8	--
7	Repair the short to voltage in the right cooling fan motor supply voltage circuit. Did you complete the repair?	Go to Step 8	--
8	Operate the system in order to verify the repair. Did you correct the condition?	System OK	Go to Step 2

GC1080100673000X

Fig. 104   Cooling fan always on. 2001 Park Avenue

Step	Action	Value(s)	Yes	No
3	Does the cooling fan turn OFF when the ECT drops below the specified value?	92.5°C (199°F)	"Inspect ECT and ECT wiring."	Go to Step 4
4	1. Check that the ECT is below the specified value. 2. Disconnect the cooling fan relay. Is the cooling fan OFF?	92.5°C (199°F)	Go to Step 5	Go to Step 6
5	Probe the cooling fan relay connector cavity 2 with a test lamp connected to B+. Did the test lamp illuminate?	—	Go to Step 7	Go to Step 17
6	Repair the short to voltage in the power feed circuit between the cooling fan relay and the cooling fan motor. Is the action complete?	—	Go to Step 20	—
7	1. Check for a short to ground in the cooling fan relay control circuit between the PCM and the cooling fan relay. 2. Repair as necessary. Was a repair necessary?	—	Go to Step 20	Go to Step 18
8	1. Start the engine. 2. Check that the ECT is above the specified value. 3. Disconnect the cooling fan relay. 4. Probe the cooling fan relay connector cavity 2 with a test lamp connected to B+. Did the test lamp illuminate?	97.5°C (208°F)	Go to Step 9	Go to Step 15
9	Probe the cooling fan relay connector cavity 1 with a test lamp to ground. Did the test lamp illuminate?	—	Go to Step 10	Go to Step 15
10	Probe the cooling fan relay connector cavity 4 with a test lamp to ground. Did the test lamp illuminate?	—	Go to Step 11	Go to Step 16
11	Connect a fused jumper wire between the cooling fan relay connector cavities 3 and 4. Is the cooling fan motor ON?	—	Go to Step 17	Go to Step 13
12	1. Check for an open in the cooling fan relay control circuit between the PCM and the cooling fan relay. 2. Repair as necessary. Was a repair necessary?	—	Go to Step 20	Go to Step 18
13	1. Check for an open in the power feed circuit between the cooling fan relay and the cooling fan motor. 2. Repair as necessary. Was a repair necessary?	—	Go to Step 20	Go to Step 14
14	1. Check for an open or a faulty connection in the ground circuit between the cooling fan motor and ground. 2. Repair as necessary. Was a repair necessary?	—	Go to Step 20	Go to Step 19

GC1089800359020X

Fig. 102   Cooling fan diagnosis (Part 2 of 3). Metro

Step	Action	Yes	No
	DEFINITION: One or both engine cooling fan motors do not operate properly in high or low speed modes.		
1	Did you perform the Engine Cooling Diagnostic System Check?	Go to *Step 2*	*Engine Cooling*
2	**Important:** The cooling fan 1 relay and cooling fan 2 relay are improperly identified in the underhood fuse block. Refer to *Engine Cooling Schematics* for proper identification. 1. Install a scan tool. 2. Turn ON the ignition, with the engine OFF. 3. With a scan tool, command the Fans Low Speed ON and OFF. Do the low speed engine cooling fans turn ON and OFF with each command?	Go to *Step 3*	Go to *Step 4*
3	**Important:** The cooling fans will remain in low speed operation for 3 seconds before the PCM grounds the high speed fan relay control to turn on the high speed fans. With a scan tool, command the Fans High Speed ON and OFF. Do the high speed engine cooling fans turn ON and OFF with each command?	*Test for Intermittent and Poor Connections*	Go to *Step 13*
4	1. Turn the ignition OFF. 2. Disconnect the cooling fan 1 relay. 3. Turn the ignition ON, with the engine OFF. 4. Probe the battery positive voltage circuit of the cool fan 1 relay switch side with a test lamp connected to a good ground. Does the test lamp illuminate?	Go to *Step 5*	Go to *Step 20*
5	**Important:** Following this step, do not remove the 20-A fused jumper wire that is connected during this step. While performing the following steps, use a second 20-A fused jumper wire. Connect a 20-A fused jumper between the battery positive voltage circuit of the cooling fan 1 relay and the cooling fan motor supply voltage circuit of the cooling fan 1 relay. Do both cooling fans operate in low speed?	Go to *Step 15*	Go to *Step 6*
6	1. Disconnect the cooling fan S/P relay. 2. Connect the second 20-A fused jumper between the cooling fan low reference circuit of the cooling fan S/P relay and the right cooling fan motor supply voltage circuit of the cooling fan S/P relay. Do both cooling fans operate in low speed?	Go to *Step 16*	Go to *Step 7*
7	Connect the second 20-A fused jumper between the battery positive voltage circuit of the cooling fan S/P relay and the cooling fan motor supply voltage circuit of the cooling fan S/P relay. Does the right cooling fan operate in high speed?	Go to *Step 11*	Go to *Step 8*
8	1. Turn the ignition OFF. 2. Install the cooling fan S/P relay. 3. Disconnect the right cooling fan electrical connector. 4. Turn the ignition ON, with the engine OFF. Does the left cooling fan operate in high speed?	Go to *Step 24*	Go to *Step 9*
9	Connect the second 20-A fused jumper wire from the cooling fan motor supply voltage circuit of the right cooling fan electrical connector to the ground circuit of the right cooling fan electrical connector. Does the left cooling fan operate in high speed?	Go to *Step 18*	Go to *Step 10*

GC1080100674010X

Fig. 105   Cooling fan inoperative (Part 1 of 3). 2001 Park Avenue

Step	Action	Yes	No
10	Connect the second 20-A fused jumper wire from the cooling fan motor supply voltage circuit of the right cooling fan electrical connector to a good ground. Does the left cooling fan operate in high speed?	Go to *Step 23*	Go to *Step 24*
11	1. Install the cooling fan S/P relay. 2. Disconnect the left cooling fan electrical connector. 3. Connect the second 20-A fused jumper wire from the cooling fan motor supply voltage circuit of the left cooling fan electrical connector to the cooling fan low reference circuit of the left cooling fan electrical connector. Does the right cooling fan operate in high speed?	Go to *Step 19*	Go to *Step 12*
12	Connect the second 20-A fused jumper wire from battery positive voltage to the cooling fan low reference circuit of the of the left cooling fan electrical connector. Does the right cooling fan operate in high speed?	Go to *Step 21*	Go to *Step 25*
13	Is the right cooling fan operating properly in high speed?	Go to *Step 14*	Go to *Step 17*
14	1. Disconnect the cooling fan S/P relay. 2. Connect the second 20-A fused jumper between the cooling fan low reference circuit of the cooling fan S/P relay and the ground circuit of the cooling fan S/P relay. Does the left cooling fan operate in high speed?	Go to *Step 16*	Go to *Step 22*
15	Inspect for poor connections at the cooling fan 1 relay. Did you find and correct the condition?	Go to *Step 31*	Go to *Step 26*
16	Inspect for poor connections at the cooling fan S/P relay. Did you find and correct the condition?	Go to *Step 31*	Go to *Step 27*
17	Inspect for poor connections at the cooling fan 2 relay. Did you find and correct the condition?	Go to *Step 31*	Go to *Step 28*
18	Inspect for poor connections at the harness connector of the right cooling fan. Did you find and correct the condition?	Go to *Step 31*	Go to *Step 29*
19	Inspect for poor connections at the harness connector of the left cooling fan. Did you find and correct the condition?	Go to *Step 31*	Go to *Step 30*
20	Repair the battery positive voltage circuit of the cool fan 1 relay switch side. Did you complete the repair?	Go to *Step 31*	—
21	Repair the left cooling fan motor supply voltage circuit. Did you complete the repair?	Go to *Step 31*	—
22	Repair the left cooling fan ground circuit. Did you complete the repair?	Go to *Step 31*	—
23	Repair the right cooling fan motor ground circuit. Did you complete the repair?	Go to *Step 31*	—

GC1080100674020X

Fig. 105   Cooling fan inoperative (Part 2 of 3). 2001 Park Avenue

Step	Action	Yes	No
24	Repair the right cooling fan motor supply voltage circuit. Did you complete the repair?	Go to *Step 31*	—
25	Repair the left cooling fan low reference circuit. Did you complete the repair?	Go to *Step 31*	—
26	Replace the cooling fan 1 relay. Did you complete the repair?	Go to *Step 31*	—
27	Replace the cooling fan S/P relay. Did you complete the repair?	Go to *Step 31*	—
28	Replace the cooling fan 2 relay. Did you complete the repair?	Go to *Step 31*	—
29	Replace the right cooling fan. Did you complete the repair?	Go to *Step 31*	—
30	Replace the left cooling fan. Did you complete the repair?	Go to *Step 31*	—
31	Operate the system in order to verify the repair. Did you correct the condition?	System OK	Go to *Step 2*

GC1080100674030X

Fig. 105   Cooling fan inoperative (Part 3 of 3). 2001 Park Avenue

Step	Action	Yes	No
1	Install a scan tool. Does the scan tool power up?	Go to Step 2	Diagnose Data Link Communications
2	1. Turn ON the ignition, with the engine OFF. 2. Attempt to establish communication with the following control modules: • Instrument Cluster • Powertrain Control Module Does the scan tool communicate with the control modules?	Go to Step 3	Diagnose Data Link Communications
3	Select the powertrain control module display DTCs function on the scan tool. Does the scan tool display any DTCs?	Go to Step 4	Diagnose engine cooling
4	Does the scan tool display any DTCs which begin with a "U"?	Diagnose Data Link Communications	Diagnose Diagnostic Trouble Code (DTC)

ARM0300000000658

Fig. 106   Diagnostic system check. 2002–05 Park Avenue

Step	Action	Yes	No
	DEFINITION: One or both engine cooling fan motors run continuously in high or low speed.		
1	Did you perform the Engine Cooling Diagnostic System Check?	Go to Step 2	Go To Diagnostic System Check
2	**Important** The cooling fan fuses and cooling fan relays 1 and 2 are labeled incorrectly on the underhood sticker. Turn ON the ignition, with the engine OFF. Are one or both cooling fans ON?	Go to Step 3	Test for Intermittent and Poor Connections
3	Are both cooling fans running continuously?	Go to Step 5	Go to Step 4
4	Remove the cool fan S/P relay. Did the right cooling fan turn OFF?	Go to Step 8	Go to Step 6
5	Remove the cool fan 1 relay. Did the cooling fans turn OFF?	Go to Step 10	Go to Step 7
6	Remove the cool fan 2 relay. Did the right cooling fan turn OFF?	Go to Step 11	Go to Step 9
7	Repair the short to voltage in the left cooling fan motor supply voltage circuit. Did you complete the repair?	Go to Step 14	--

ARM0300000000659

Fig. 107   Cooling fan always on (Part 1 of 2). 2002–05 Park Avenue

Step	Action	Yes	No
8	Repair the short to voltage in the left cooling fan low reference circuit. Did you complete the repair?	Go to Step 14	--
9	Repair the short to voltage in the right cooling fan motor supply voltage circuit. Did you complete the repair?	Go to Step 14	--
10	Inspect for poor connections at the cool fan 1 relay. Did you find and correct the condition?	Go to Step 14	Go to Step 12
11	Inspect for poor connections at the cool fan 2 relay. Did you find and correct the condition?	Go to Step 14	Go to Step 13
12	Replace the cool fan 1 relay. Did you complete the replacement?	Go to Step 14	--
13	Replace the cool fan 2 relay. Did you complete the replacement?	Go to Step 14	--
14	Operate the system in order to verify the repair. Did you correct the condition?	System OK	Go to Step 2

ARM0300000000660

Fig. 107   Cooling fan always on (Part 2 of 2). 2002–05 Park Avenue

Step	Action	Yes	No
1	Did you perform the Engine Cooling Diagnostic System Check?	Go to Step 2	Go to Diagnostic System Check
2	**Important** The cooling fan fuses and cooling fan relays 1 and 2 are labeled incorrectly on the underhood sticker. 1. Install a scan tool. 2. Turn ON the ignition, with the engine OFF. 3. With a scan tool, command the Fans Low Speed ON and OFF. Do the low speed engine cooling fans turn ON and OFF with each command?	Go to Step 3	Go to Step 4
3	**Important:** A 3-second delay occurs before the PCM changes the cooling fan speed. With a scan tool, command the Fans High Speed ON and OFF. Do the high speed engine cooling fans turn ON and OFF with each command?	Test for Intermittent and Poor Connections	Go to Step 12
4	**Important** Do NOT remove the 20-A fused jumper wire connected during this step. Use a second 20-A fused jumper wire while performing the following steps. 1. Remove the cooling fan 1 relay. 2. Connect a 20-A fused jumper between the battery positive switch side voltage circuit and the cooling fan motor supply voltage circuit of the cooling fan 1 relay. Do both cooling fans operate in low speed?	Go to Step 22	Go to Step 5

ARM0300000000661

Fig. 108   Cooling fan inoperative (Part 1 of 6). 2002–05 Park Avenue

Step	Action	Yes	No
5	1. Disconnect the cooling fan S/P relay 2. Connect the second 20-A fused jumper between the cooling fan low reference circuit and the cooling fan motor supply voltage circuit of the cooling fan S/P relay. Do both cooling fans operate in low speed?	Go to Step 23	Go to Step 6
6	Connect the second 20-A fused jumper between the battery positive voltage circuit and the cooling fan motor supply voltage circuit of the cooling fan S/P relay. Does the right cooling fan operate in high speed?	Go to Step 9	Go to Step 7
7	1. Install the cooling fan S/P relay. 2. Disconnect the right cooling fan electrical connector. 3. Connect the second 20-Amp fused jumper wire from the cooling fan motor supply voltage circuit to the ground circuit of the right cooling fan electrical connector. Does the left cooling fan operate in high speed?	Go to Step 25	Go to Step 8
8	Connect the second 20-Amp fused jumper wire from the cooling fan motor supply voltage circuit of the right cooling fan electrical connector to a good ground. Does the left cooling fan operate in high speed?	Go to Step 29	Go to Step 30
9	1. Install the cooling fan S/P relay. 2. Disconnect the left cooling fan electrical connector. 3. Connect the second 20-Amp fused jumper wire from the cooling fan motor supply voltage circuit to the cooling fan low reference circuit of the left cooling fan electrical connector. Does the right cooling fan operate in high speed?	Go to Step 26	Go to Step 10
10	Connect the second 20-Amp fused jumper wire from the coil side battery positive voltage circuit to the cooling fan low reference circuit of the of the left cooling fan electrical connector. Does the right cooling fan operate in high speed?	Go to Step 11	Go to Step 31

ARM0300000000662

Fig. 108   Cooling fan inoperative (Part 2 of 6). 2002–05 Park Avenue

Step		Yes	No
11	Probe the battery positive voltage circuit on the switch side of the cooling fan 1 relay with a test lamp that is connected to a good ground. Does the test lamp illuminate?	Go to Step 27	Go to Step 32
12	Is the right cooling fan operating properly in high speed?	Go to Step 19	Go to Step 13
13	1. Turn off the ignition. 2. Disconnect the cooling fan 2 relay. 3. Turn ON the ignition, with the engine OFF. 4. Connect a test lamp between the high speed cooling fan relay control circuit and the battery positive voltage circuit on the coil side of the cooling fan 2 relay. 5. With a scan tool command the High Speed Fans ON and OFF. Does the test lamp turn ON and OFF with each command?	Go to Step 15	Go to Step 14
14	Probe the battery positive voltage circuit on the coil side of the cooling fan 2 relay with a test lamp that is connected to a good ground. Does the test lamp illuminate?	Go to Step 34	Go to Step 33
15	Install a 20 amp fused jumper between the battery positive voltage circuit on the switch side of the cooling fan 2 relay and the cooling fan motor supply voltage circuit. Does the right cooling fan operate in high speed?	Go to Step 24	Go to Step 16
16	Probe the battery positive voltage circuit on the switch side of the cooling fan 2 relay with a test lamp connected to a good ground. Does the test lamp illuminate?	Go to Step 17	Go to Step 33
17	1. With the 20 amp fused jumper still installed. 2. Disconnect the right cooling fan electrical connector. 3. Connect a test lamp from the cooling fan motor supply voltage circuit to the ground circuit of the right cooling fan electrical connector. Does the test lamp illuminate?	Go to Step 25	Go to Step 18

ARM0300000000663

**Fig. 108   Cooling fan inoperative (Part 3 of 6).
2002–05 Park Avenue**

Step		Yes	No
18	Probe the cooling fan motor supply voltage circuit of the right cooling fan electrical connector with a test lamp that is connected to a good ground. Does the test lamp illuminate?	Go to Step 29	Go to Step 30
19	1. Turn OFF the ignition. 2. Disconnect the cooling fan S/P relay 3. Turn ON the ignition, with the engine OFF. 4. Connect a 20-A fused jumper between the cooling fan low reference circuit and the ground circuit of the cooling fan S/P relay. 5. With a scan tool command the Fans High Speed ON and OFF. Does the left cooling fan operate in high speed?	Go to Step 20	Go to Step 28
20	1. Connect a test lamp between the high speed cooling fan relay control circuit of the cooling fan S/P relay and the battery positive voltage circuit of the cooling fan S/P relay. 2. With a scan tool command the Fans High Speed ON and OFF. Does the test lamp turn ON and OFF with each command?	Go to Step 23	Go to Step 21
21	Probe the battery positive voltage circuit of the cooling fan S/P relay with a test lamp that is connected to a good ground. Does the test lamp illuminate?	Go to Step 34	Go to Step 33
22	Inspect for poor connections at the cooling fan 1 relay. Did you find and correct the condition?	Go to Step 40	Go to Step 35

ARM0300000000664

**Fig. 108   Cooling fan inoperative (Part 4 of 6).
2002–05 Park Avenue**

Step		Yes	No
23	Inspect for poor connections at the cooling fan S/P relay. Did you find and correct the condition?	Go to Step 40	Go to Step 36
24	Inspect for poor connections at the cooling fan S/P relay. Did you find and correct the condition?	Go to Step 40	Go to Step 37
25	Inspect for poor connections at the harness connector of the right cooling fan. Did you find and correct the condition?	Go to Step 40	Go to Step 38
26	Inspect for poor connections at the harness connector of the left cooling fan. Did you find and correct the condition?	Go to Step 40	Go to Step 39
27	Repair the left cooling fan motor supply voltage circuit for an open. Is the repair complete?	Go to Step 40	--
28	Repair the left cooling fan ground circuit for an open. Is the repair complete?	Go to Step 40	--
29	Repair the right cooling fan ground circuit for an open. Is the repair complete?	Go to Step 40	--
30	Repair the right cooling fan motor supply voltage circuit for an open. Is the repair complete?	Go to Step 40	--

ARM0300000000665

**Fig. 108   Cooling fan inoperative (Part 5 of 6).
2002–05 Park Avenue**

Step		Yes	No
31	Repair the left cooling fan low reference circuit for a short to ground or an open. Is the repair complete?	Go to Step 40	--
32	Repair the cooling fan 1 relay battery positive voltage circuit for an open. Is the repair complete?	Go to Step 40	--
33	Repair the battery positive voltage circuit for the cooling fan S/P and 2 relay for an open. Is the repair complete?	Go to Step 40	--
34	Repair the high speed cooling fan relay control circuit for an open. Is the repair complete?	Go to Step 40	--
35	Replace the cooling fan 1 relay. Is the repair complete?	Go to Step 40	--
36	Replace the cooling fan S/P relay. Is the repair complete?	Go to Step 40	--
37	Replace the cooling fan 2 relay. Is the repair complete?	Go to Step 40	--
38	Replace the right cooling fan. Is the repair complete?	Go to Step 40	--
39	Replace the left cooling fan. Is the repair complete?	Go to Step 40	--
40	Operate the system in order to verify the repair. Did you correct the condition?	System OK	Go to Step 3

ARM0300000000666

**Fig. 108   Cooling fan inoperative (Part 6 of 6).
2002–05 Park Avenue**

Reference Table

Symptom	Causes
Main fan always ON	• Faulty fan 1 relay • Open in the fan 1 relay coil ground circuit • Short to voltage in the main fan motor supply voltage circuit
Auxiliary fan always ON	• Faulty fan 2 relay • Short to ground in the auxiliary fan motor ground circuit
Both fans always ON	• Faulty fan 3 relay • Faulty A/C MG relay • Open in the fan 2 relay coil ground circuit • Short to voltage in the fan 3 relay coil supply voltage circuit • Engine coolant temperature (ECT) sensor or powertrain control module (PCM) malfunction

Step	Action	Yes	No
	The main fan motor is mounted on the left side of the radiator/condenser assembly. The auxiliary fan motor is mounted on the right side of the radiator/condenser assembly. The fans run at low speed in series configuration when the A/C is operating and the engine coolant temperature (ECT) is below 83°C (181°F). The fans run at high speed in parallel configuration when the ECT is above 93°C (199°F). An open in the ground circuit of the A/C fan 1 and 2 relays will cause both fans to operate at high speed when the ECT is below 93°C (199°F). This table assumes that the main fan motor and/or the auxiliary fan motor runs continuously with the ignition switch in the RUN position and the ECT below 93°C (199°F).		
1	Did you review the *Cooling System* and perform the necessary inspections?	Go to *Step 2*	*Engine Cooling*
2	1. Ensure that the ECT is below 93°C (199°F) 2. Depress the A/C switch to the OFF position. 3. Turn the blower switch to the OFF position. 4. Turn the ignition switch to the RUN position. Is only the main fan motor running continuously?	Go to *Step 5*	Go to *Step 3*
3	Is only the auxiliary fan motor running continuously?	Go to *Step 9*	Go to *Step 4*
4	Are both fan motors running continuously?	Go to *Step 12*	Go to *Step 1*
5	Remove the fan 1 relay from fuse and relay block 1. Does the main fan motor run?	Go to *Step 6*	Go to *Step 7*
6	Repair the short to voltage in the main fan motor supply voltage circuit. Did you find and correct the condition?	Go to *Step 18*	—
7	Test the fan 1 relay control circuit for an open. Did you find and correct the condition?	Go to *Step 18*	Go to *Step 8*
8	Replace the fan 1 relay. Did you complete the replacement?	Go to *Step 18*	—
9	Remove the fan 2 relay from fuse and relay block 2. Does the auxiliary fan motor run?	Go to *Step 10*	Go to *Step 11*
10	Repair the short to ground in the circuit between the auxiliary fan motor and fuse and relay block 2. Did you find and correct the condition?	Go to *Step 18*	
11	Replace the fan 2 relay. Did you complete the replacement?	Go to *Step 18*	—

GC1080100675010X

Fig. 109 Cooling fan always on (Part 1 of 2). Prizm

Problem	Causes
Both fans inoperative	• Open in the supply voltage circuit to the fan 1 and the engine main relays in fuse and relay block 1 • High resistance or poor connection in fuse and relay block 1 • Faulty engine main relay • Short to ground in the fan 1 or the fan 2 coil ground circuit • Engine coolant temperature (ECT) sensor or powertrain control module (PCM) malfunction
Main fan inoperative	• Faulty main fan motor • Faulty fan 1 relay • Open in the main fan circuit
Auxiliary fan inoperative	• Faulty auxiliary fan motor • Faulty fan 2 relay • Open in the auxiliary fan circuit
Both fans inoperative in low speed	• Faulty fan 2 relay • Faulty fan 1 relay • Open in the series portion of fan circuit

GC1080100676010X

Fig. 110 Main cooling fan inoperative (Part 1 of 2). Prizm

Step	Action	Yes	No
12	Remove the fan 3 relay from fuse and relay block 2. Do both fan motors run?	Go to *Step 13*	Go to *Step 15*
13	Test the fan 2 relay control circuit (including the A/C refrigerant pressure switch) for an open. Did you find and correct the condition?	Go to *Step 18*	Go to *Step 14*
14	1. Inspect the ECT sensor for incorrect performance or for an incorrect input to the PCM. 2. If the ECT sensor is operating correctly, replace the PCM. Did you find and correct the condition?	Go to *Step 18*	—
15	1. Test the A/C MG relay for continuity between terminals 3 and 5. 2. Test the fan 3 relay for continuity between terminals 3 and 5. Does continuity exist in either relay?	Go to *Step 16*	Go to *Step 17*
16	Replace the faulty relay. Did you complete the replacement?	Go to *Step 18*	—
17	Repair the short to voltage in the fan 3 relay coil supply voltage circuit. Did you find and correct the condition?	Go to *Step 18*	—
18	Operate the system in order to verify the repair. Did you correct the condition?	System OK	Go to *Step 3*

GC1080100675020X

Fig. 109 Cooling fan always on (Part 2 of 2). Prizm

Step	Action	Yes	No
	The main fan motor is mounted on the left side of the radiator/condenser assembly. The fans run at low speed in series configuration when the A/C is operating and the engine coolant temperature (ECT) is below 83°C (181°F). The fans run at high speed in parallel configuration when the ECT is above 93°C (199°F). A short to ground in the coil ground circuit of the fan 1 and 2 relays will cause both fans to be inoperative once the ECT reaches 93°C (199°F). This table assumes that the auxiliary fan motor is functioning normally.		
1	Did you review the *Cooling System* and perform the necessary inspections?	Go to *Step 2*	*Diagnose Engine Cooling*
2	Run the engine until operating temperature is reached and the thermostat opens. Do the cooling fans operate?	*Test for Intermittent and Poor Connections*	Go to *Step 3*
3	Exchange the fan 1 relay with a known good relay (the fan 3 relay, the A/C MG relay, or the horn relay). Did you find and correct the condition?	Go to *Step 14*	Go to *Step 4*
4	1. Stop the engine. 2. Disconnect the main fan motor connector. 3. Connect a test lamp across the main fan motor connector. 4. Start the engine. Does the test lamp illuminate?	Go to *Step 12*	Go to *Step 5*
5	Test the main fan motor ground circuit for an open. Did you find and correct the condition?	Go to *Step 14*	Go to *Step 6*
6	Test the main fan motor supply voltage circuit for an open. Did you find and correct the condition?	Go to *Step 14*	Go to *Step 7*
7	Test the supply voltage circuit to fuse and relay block 1 for an open. This circuit supplies voltage to the coils of the fan 1 relay and the engine main relay. Did you find and correct the condition?	Go to *Step 14*	Go to *Step 8*
8	Test the fan 1 relay switch supply voltage circuit for an open. Did you find and correct the condition?	Go to *Step 14*	Go to *Step 9*
9	Test the engine main relay switch supply voltage circuit for an open. Did you find and correct the condition?	Go to *Step 14*	Go to *Step 10*
10	Test the engine main relay control circuit for an open. Did you find and correct the condition?	Go to *Step 14*	Go to *Step 11*
11	1. Remove fuse and relay block 1 from the inner fender. 2. Inspect the connectors in fuse and relay block 1 for poor connections and high resistance. Did you find and correct the condition?	Go to *Step 14*	
12	Inspect for a poor connection at the harness connector of the main fan motor. Did you find and correct the condition?	Go to *Step 14*	Go to *Step 13*
13	Replace the main fan motor. Did you complete the replacement?	Go to *Step 14*	—
14	Operate the system in order to verify the repair. Did you correct the condition?	System OK	Go to *Step 3*

GC1080100676020X

Fig. 110 Main cooling fan inoperative (Part 2 of 2). Prizm

Step	Action	Yes	No
	The auxiliary fan motor is mounted on the right side of the radiator/condenser assembly. The fans run at low speed in series configuration when the A/C is operating and the engine coolant temperature (ECT) is below 83°C (181°F). The fans run at high speed in parallel configuration when the ECT is above 93°C (199°F). A short to ground in the ground circuit of the fan 1 and 2 relays will cause both fans to be inoperative once the ECT reaches 93°C (199°F). This table assumes that the main fan motor is functioning normally.		
1	Did you review the *Cooling System* and perform the necessary inspections?	Go to *Step 2*	Diagnose *Engine Cooling*
2	Run the engine until operating temperature is reached and the thermostat opens. Do the cooling fans operate?	Test for *Intermittent and Poor Connections*	Go to *Step 3*
3	1. Stop the engine. 2. Disconnect the auxiliary fan motor connector. 3. Connect a test lamp across the auxiliary fan motor connector. 4. Start the engine. Does the test lamp illuminate?	Go to *Step 7*	Go to *Step 4*
4	Test auxiliary fan motor supply voltage circuit for an open. Did you find and correct the condition?	Go to *Step 9*	Go to *Step 5*
5	1. Remove the fan 2 relay from fuse and relay block 2. 2. Test the circuit between the auxiliary fan motor and the fan 2 relay for an open. 3. Test the fan 2 relay ground circuit for an open. Did you find and correct the condition?	Go to *Step 9*	Go to *Step 6*
6	Replace the fan 2 relay. Did you complete the replacement?	Go to *Step 9*	—
7	Inspect for a poor connection at the harness connector of the auxiliary fan motor. Did you find and correct the condition?	Go to *Step 9*	Go to *Step 8*
8	Replace the auxiliary fan motor. Did you complete the replacement?	Go to *Step 9*	—
9	Operate the system in order to verify the repair. Did you correct the condition?	System OK	Go to *Step 3*

GC1080100677000X

Fig. 111   Auxiliary cooling fan inoperative. Prizm

Step	Action	Yes	No
	The main fan motor is mounted on the left side of the radiator/condenser assembly. The auxiliary fan motor is mounted on the right side of the radiator/condenser assembly. The fans run at low speed in series configuration when the A/C is operating and the engine coolant temperature (ECT) is below 83°C (181°F). The fans run at high speed in parallel configuration when the ECT is above 93°C (199°F). A short to ground in the ground circuit of the fan 1 and 2 relays will cause both fans to be inoperative once the ECT reaches 93°C (199°F). This table assumes that the parallel portion of the circuit and the A/C system are functioning normally. Therefore, the malfunction is in the series portion of the circuit.		
1	Did you review the *Cooling System* and perform the necessary inspections?	Go to *Step 2*	*Engine Cooling*
2	1. Connect a scan tool. The engine must be below operating temperature. 2. Move the blower speed switch to any position except OFF. 3. Depress the A/C switch to the ON position. 4. Use the scan tool to command the A/C compressor clutch (MG) relay ON. When the MG relay is energized the cooling fans will also turn on at low speed. Do the cooling fans operate at low speed?	Test for *Intermittent and Poor Connections*	Go to *Step 3*
3	Exchange the fan 3 relay with a known good relay (the fan 1 relay, the A/C MG relay or the horn relay). Do the cooling fans operate at low speed?	Go to *Step 8*	Go to *Step 4*
4	Test the fan 3 relay coil supply voltage circuit for an open. Did you find and correct the condition?	Go to *Step 9*	Go to *Step 5*
5	Test the fan 3 relay coil ground circuit for an open. Did you find and correct the condition?	Go to *Step 9*	Go to *Step 6*
6	Test the circuit between the fan 3 relay and the fan 2 relay for an open. Did you find and correct the condition?	Go to *Step 9*	Go to *Step 7*
7	Test the fan 3 relay switch supply voltage circuit for an open. Did you find and correct the condition?	Go to *Step 9*	Go to *Step 8*
8	Replace the fan 3 relay. Did you complete the replacement?	Go to *Step 9*	—
9	Operate the system in order to verify the repair. Did you correct the condition?	System OK	Go to *Step 3*

GC1080100678000X

Fig. 112   Cooling fan inoperative at low speed. Prizm

Step	Action	Yes	No
1	Perform the following preliminary inspections: • Ensure that the battery is fully charged. • Ensure that the battery cables are clean and tight. • Inspect for any open fuses. • Inspect the easily accessible systems or the visible system components for obvious damage or conditions that could cause the symptom. • Ensure that the grounds are clean, tight, and in the correct location. • Inspect for aftermarket devices that could affect the operation of the system. • Search for applicable service bulletins. Did you find and correct the condition?	System OK	Go to Step 2

ARM0400000000017

Fig. 113   Diagnostic system check (Part 1 of 2). 2005 STS

Step	Action	Yes	No
2	Install a scan tool. Does the scan tool power up?	Go to Step 3	Diagnose Scan Tool Does Not Power Up
3	Turn ON the ignition, with the engine OFF. Is the NO FOB DETECTED message displayed on the driver information center (DIC)?	Go to Key Fob Not Detected in Keyless Entry	Go to Step 4
4	1. Turn ON the ignition, with the engine OFF. 2. Attempt to establish communication with all of the control modules on the vehicle. Does the scan tool communicate with all of the expected vehicle control modules?	Go to Step 5	Go to Data Link References
5	Attempt to start the engine. Does the engine crank?	Go to Step 6	Go to Symptoms
6	Attempt to start the engine. Does the engine start and idle?	Go to Step 7	Go to Engine Cranks but Does Not Run

ARM0400000000018

Fig. 113   Diagnostic system check (Part 2 of 2). 2005 STS

Step	Action	Yes	No
	DEFINITION: One or both engine cooling fan motors run continuously in high or low speed.		
1	Did you perform the Diagnostic System Check - Vehicle?	Go to Step 2	Go to Diagnostic System Check
2	Turn ON the ignition, with the engine OFF. Are both cooling fans operating at low speed?	Go to Step 4	Go to Step 3
3	Is the left cooling fan operating at high speed?	Go to Step 5	Test for Intermittent Conditions and Poor Connections
4	Remove the low speed fan relay. Did the fans turn OFF?	Go to Step 8	Go to Step 6
5	Remove the high speed fan relay. Did the left cooling fan turn OFF?	Go to Step 9	Go to Step 7
6	Repair the cooling fan motor supply voltage circuit of the right cooling fan for a short to voltage. Did you complete the repair?	Go to Step 12	--
7	Repair the cooling fan motor supply voltage circuit of the left cooling fan for a short to voltage. Did you complete the repair?	Go to Step 12	--

ARM0400000000019

Fig. 114 Cooling fan always on (Part 1 of 2). 2005 STS

Step	Action	Yes	No
8	Inspect for poor connections at the low speed fan relay. Did you find and correct the condition?	Go to Step 12	Go to Step 10
9	Inspect for poor connections at the high speed fan relay. Did you find and correct the condition?	Go to Step 12	Go to Step 11
10	Replace the low speed fan relay. Did you complete the replacement?	Go to Step 12	--
11	Replace the high speed fan relay. Did you complete the replacement?	Go to Step 12	--
12	Operate the system in order to verify the repair. Did you correct the condition?	System OK	Go to Step 2

ARM0400000000020

Fig. 114 Cooling fan always on (Part 2 of 2). 2005 STS

Step	Action	Yes	No
1	Did you perform the Diagnostic System Check - Vehicle?	Go to Step 2	Go to Diagnostic System Check
2	1. Install a scan tool. 2. Turn ON the ignition, with the engine OFF. 3. With a scan tool, command the Fans Low Speed ON and OFF. Do the low speed engine cooling fans turn ON and OFF with each command?	Go to Step 3	Go to Step 4
3	Important A 3-second delay occurs before the powertrain control module (PCM) changes the cooling fan speed. With a scan tool, command the Fans High Speed ON and OFF. Do the high speed engine cooling fans turn ON and OFF with each command?	Test for Intermittent Conditions and Poor Connections	Go to Step 6

ARM0400000000021

Fig. 115 Cooling fan inoperative (Part 1 of 4). 2005 STS

Step	Action	Yes	No
4	Important Do NOT remove the jumper wire that you will be connecting until your testing is completed. If the low speed fan fuse opens when you connect the jumper wire, repair the cooling fan motor supply voltage circuit of the right cooling fan motor for a short to ground. 1. Disconnect the low speed fan relay. 2. Connect a jumper wire between the battery positive voltage circuit and the cooling fan motor supply voltage circuit of the low speed fan relay. Do both cooling fans operate in low speed?	Go to Step 14	Go to Step 5
5	1. Disconnect the S/P fan relay. 2. With a test lamp connected to a good ground, probe the cooling fan low reference circuit at the S/P fan relay. Does the test lamp illuminate?	Go to Step 9	Go to Step 8
6	Does the right cooling fan operate at high speed?	Go to Step 16	Go to Step 7
7	Inspect the ground circuit of the S/P fan relay for an open or high resistance. Did you find and correct the condition?	Go to Step 25	Go to Step 15

ARM0400000000022

Fig. 115 Cooling fan inoperative (Part 2 of 4). 2005 STS

Step	Action	Yes	No
8	1. Install the S/P fan relay. 2. Disconnect the right cooling fan electrical connector. 3. With a test lamp connected to a good ground, probe the cooling fan motor supply voltage circuit at the right cooling fan motor connector. Does the test lamp illuminate?	Go to Step 12	Go to Step 13
9	1. Install the S/P fan relay. 2. Disconnect the left cooling fan motor connector. 3. With a test lamp connected to a good ground, probe the cooling fan motor supply voltage circuit at the left cooling fan connector. Does the test lamp illuminate?	Go to Step 11	Go to Step 10
10	Inspect the cooling fan motor supply voltage circuit for an open or high resistance. Did you find and correct the condition?	Go to Step 25	Go to Step 15
11	Inspect the ground circuit of the left cooling fan for an open or high resistance. Did you find and correct the condition?	Go to Step 25	Go to Step 18
12	Inspect the cooling fan low reference circuit for an open or high resistance. Did you find and correct the condition?	Go to Step 25	Go to Step 17

ARM0400000000023

Fig. 115 Cooling fan inoperative (Part 3 of 4). 2005 STS

Step	Action	Yes	No
13	Inspect the cooling fan motor supply voltage circuit of the right cooling fan for an open or high resistance. Did you find and correct the condition?	Go to Step 25	Go to Step 19
14	Inspect for poor connections at the low speed fan relay. Did you find and correct the condition?	Go to Step 25	Go to Step 20
15	Inspect for poor connections at the S/P fan relay. Did you find and correct the condition?	Go to Step 25	Go to Step 21
16	Inspect for poor connections at the high speed fan relay. Did you find and correct the condition?	Go to Step 25	Go to Step 22
17	Inspect for poor connections at the harness connector of the right cooling fan. Did you find and correct the condition?	Go to Step 25	Go to Step 23
18	Inspect for poor connections at the harness connector of the left cooling fan. Did you find and correct the condition?	Go to Step 25	Go to Step 24

ARM0400000000024

Fig. 115 Cooling fan inoperative (Part 4 of 4). 2005 STS

Step	Action	Yes	No
1	Did you review the Cooling System Description and Operation and perform the necessary inspections?	Go to Step 2	Check Engine Cooling
2	1. Ensure that the ECT is below 93°C (199°F). 2. Depress the A/C switch to the OFF position. 3. Turn the blower switch to the OFF position. 4. Turn the ignition switch to the RUN position. Is the fan motor running continuously?	Go to Step 3	Test for Intermittent and Poor Connections
3	Remove the fan 1 relay from the underhood fuse block. Is the fan motor running continuously?	Go to Step 4	Go to Step 5
4	Repair the short to voltage in the fan motor supply voltage circuit. Did you find and correct the condition?	Go to Step 6	--
5	Replace the fan 1 relay. Did you complete the replacement?	Go to Step 6	--
6	Operate the system in order to verify the repair. Did you correct the condition?	System OK	Go to Step 3

ARM66GC000000289

Fig. 116 Cooling fan always On. Vibe

Step	Action	Yes	No
7	Inspect for a poor connection at the harness connector of the Powertrain Control Module (PCM). Did you find and correct the condition?	Go to Step 12	Go to Step 11
8	Repair the short to ground in the fan motor ground circuit. Did you complete the repair?	Go to Step 12	--
9	Replace the fan 2 relay. Did you complete the replacement?	Go to Step 12	--
10	Replace the refrigerant pressure switch Did you complete the replacement?	Go to Step 12	--
11	Replace the PCM. Did you complete the replacement?	Go to Step 12	--
12	Operate the system in order to verify the repair. Did you correct the condition?	System OK	Go to Step 3

ARM66GC000000291

Fig. 117 Cooling fan inoperative low speed operates in high speed (Part 2 of 2). Vibe

Step	Action	Yes	No
1	Did you review the Cooling System Description and Operation and perform the necessary inspections?	Go to Step 2	Check Engine Cooling
2	1. Connect a scan tool. The engine must be below operating temperature. 2. Use the scan tool to command the A/C compressor clutch relay ON. When the relay is energized the cooling fan will also run at low speed. Does the cooling fan operate at high speed?	Test for Intermittent and Poor Connections	Go to Step 3
3	1. Remove the fan 2 relay. 2. Use the scan tool to command the cooling fan ON. Does the cooling fan operate at high speed?	Go to Step 8	Go to Step 4
4	Test the fan 2 relay. The relay should be normally open between terminals 3 and 5 and normally closed between terminals 3 and 4. Did the relay test OK?	Go to Step 5	Go to Step 9
5	Test the fan 2 relay coil control circuits for a short to ground. Did you find and correct the condition?	Go to Step 12	Go to Step 6
6	Test the refrigerant pressure switch for a closed condition. The switch should be normally open between terminals 2 and 3. Did the switch test OK?	Go to Step 7	Go to Step 10

ARM66GC000000290

Fig. 117 Cooling fan inoperative low speed operates in high speed (Part 1 of 2). Vibe

Step	Action	Yes	No
1	Did you review the Cooling System Description and Operation and perform the necessary inspections?	Go to Step 2	Check Engine Cooling
2	Run the engine until operating temperature is reached and the thermostat opens. Does the cooling fan operate at high speed?	Test for Intermittent and Poor Connections	Go to Step 3
3	Test the fan 2 relay coil supply voltage circuit for an open. Did you find and correct the condition?	Go to Step 11	Go to Step 4
4	Test the fan 2 relay coil control circuits for an open or for a short to B+. Did you find and correct the condition?	Go to Step 11	Go to Step 5
5	1. Remove the fan 2 relay. 2. Install a 30 amp fused jumper between the fan motor control circuit and the high speed fan circuit (between cavities 3 and 5) of the fan 2 relay connector. Does the cooling fan operate at high speed?	Go to Step 7	Go to Step 6
6	Test for an open in the fan 2 relay high speed ground circuit. Did you find and correct the condition?	Go to Step 11	Go to Step 8

ARM66GC000000292

Fig. 118 Cooling fan inoperative in high speed (Part 1 of 2). Vibe

Step	Action	Yes	No
7	Inspect for a poor connection at the harness connector of the fan 2 relay. Did you find and correct the condition?	Go to Step 11	Go to Step 9
8	Inspect for a poor connection at the harness connector of the Powertrain Control Module (PCM). Did you find and correct the condition?	Go to Step 11	Go to Step 10
9	Replace the fan 2 relay. Did you complete the replacement?	Go to Step 11	--
10	Replace the PCM. Did you complete the replacement?	Go to Step 11	--
11	Operate the system in order to verify the repair. Did you correct the condition?	System OK	Go to Step 3

ARM66GC000000293

Fig. 118 Cooling fan inoperative in high speed (Part 2 of 2). Vibe

Step	Action	Yes	No
1	Did you review the Cooling System Description and Operation	Go to Step 2	Check Engine Cooling
2	Run the engine until operating temperature is reached and the thermostat opens. Does the cooling fan operate?	Test for Intermittent and Poor Connections	Go to Step 3
3	1. Stop the engine. 2. Disconnect the fan motor connector. 3. Connect a test lamp across the fan motor connector. 4. Start the engine. Does the test lamp illuminate?	Go to Step 11	Go to Step 4
4	1. Connect the fan motor. 2. Exchange the fan 1 relay with a known good relay (the horn relay). Does the cooling fan operate?	Go to Step 10	Go to Step 5
5	Test the fan 1 relay and the fan 2 relay supply voltage circuits for an open or a short to ground. Did you find and correct the condition?	Go to Step 16	Go to Step 6
6	Test the fan 1 relay coil control circuit for an open or a short to B+. Did you find and correct the condition?	Go to Step 16	Go to Step 7
7	Test the fan 2 relay coil control circuit for a short to B+. Did you find and correct the condition?	Go to Step 16	Go to Step 8
8	Test the fan motor supply voltage circuit for an open or a short to ground. Did you find and correct the condition?	Go to Step 16	Go to Step

ARM66GC000000295

Fig. 120 Cooling fan inoperative (Part 1 of 2). Vibe

Step	Action	Yes	No
1	Did you review the Cooling System Description and Operation	Go to Step 2	Check Engine Cooling
2	1. Connect a scan tool. The engine must be below operating temperature. 2. Use the scan tool to command the A/C compressor clutch relay ON. When the relay is energized the cooling fan will also run at low speed. Does the cooling fan operate at low speed?	Test for Intermittent and Poor Connections	Go to Step 3
3	1. Remove the fan 2 relay. 2. Install a 30 amp fused jumper between the fan motor control circuit and the low speed fan circuit (between cavities 3 and 4) of the cooling fan 2 relay connector. 3. Use the scan tool to command the A/C compressor clutch relay ON. When the relay is energized the cooling fan will also run at low speed. Does the cooling fan operate at low speed?	Go to Step 6	Go to Step 4
4	Test the low speed fan motor ground circuit for an open, or a short to B+, between the fan 2 relay terminal 4 and S103. Did you find and correct the condition?	Go to Step 9	Go to Step 5
5	Inspect for a poor connection at the harness connector of the fan resistor. Did you find and correct the condition?	Go to Step 9	Go to Step 8
6	Inspect for a poor connection at the harness connector of the fan 2 relay. Did you find and correct the condition?	Go to Step 9	Go to Step 7
7	Replace the fan 2 relay. Did you complete the replacement?	Go to Step 9	--
8	Replace the fan resistor. Did you complete the replacement?	Go to Step 9	--
9	Operate the system in order to verify the repair. Did you correct the condition?	System OK	Go to Step

ARM66GC000000294

Fig. 119 Cooling fan inoperative in low speed. Vibe

Step	Action	Yes	No
9	Test the fan motor ground circuit for an open or a short to ground Did you find and correct the condition?	Go to Step 16	Go to Step 12
10	Inspect for a poor connection at the harness connector of the fan 1 relay. Did you find and correct the condition?	Go to Step 16	Go to Step 13
11	Inspect for a poor connection at the harness connector of the fan motor. Did you find and correct the condition?	Go to Step 16	Go to Step 14
12	Inspect for a poor connection at the harness connector of the powertrain control module (PCM). Did you find and correct the condition?	Go to Step 16	Go to Step 15
13	Replace the fan 1 relay. Did you complete the replacement?	Go to Step 16	--
14	Replace the fan motor. Did you complete the replacement?	Go to Step 16	--
15	Replace the PCM. Did you complete the replacement?	Go to Step 16	--
16	Operate the system in order to verify the repair. Did you correct the condition?	System OK	Go to Step

ARM66GC000000296

Fig. 120 Cooling fan inoperative (Part 2 of 2). Vibe

Symptom	Causes
Fan motor inoperative in both speeds	• Open or short to ground in the fan 1 relay supply voltage circuits. • Open or short to B+ in the fan 1 relay coil control circuit. • Open or short to ground in the fan motor supply voltage circuit. • Short to ground in the fan 2 coil supply voltage circuit. • Open or short to B+ in the fan motor ground circuit. • Short to B+ in the fan 2 coil control circuit.
Fan motor inoperative in high speed only	• Open in the fan 2 relay supply voltage circuit. • Open in the fan 2 relay coil control circuit. • Open in the fan 2 relay high speed ground circuit.
Fan motor low speed operates at high speed	• Short to ground in the fan motor ground circuit. • Short to ground in the fan resistor circuit.
Fan motor inoperative in low speed only	Open or short to B+ in the fan resistor circuit.

ARM66GC000000297

Fig. 121   Cooling fan symptom table. Vibe

Step	Action	Yes	No
2	Install a scan tool. Does the scan tool power up?	Go to Step 3	Diagnose Scan Tool Does Not Power Up
3	1. Turn ON the ignition, with the engine OFF. 2. Select Vehicle Control Systems, Computer/Integrating Systems and then Vehicle DTC Information on the scan tool. Does the scan tool display No Comm. for any control module?	Diagnose Data Link Communications	Go to Step 4
4	Attempt to start the engine. Does the engine crank over?	Go to Step 5	Diagnose Engine Electrical
5	Attempt to start the engine. Does the engine start and idle?	Go to Step 6	Diagnose Engine Cranks but Does Not Run

ARM0300000000684

Fig. 122   Diagnostic system check (Part 2 of 3). XLR

Step	Action	Yes	No

6	**Important**
	Do NOT clear the DTCs unless instructed by a diagnostic procedure.
	
	1. Diagnose the DTCs in the order that the DTCs appear on the scan tool or mis-diagnosis may occur.
	2. If multiple powertrain DTCs are stored, diagnose the DTCs in the following order:
	  A. Component level DTCs, such as sensor DTCs, solenoid DTCs, and relay DTCs.
	  B. System level DTCs, for example, misfire DTCs, EVAP system DTCs, and fuel trim DTCs.
	
	Advance to the List All DTCs screen on the scan tool.
	
	Does the scan tool display any DTCs?
		Go to Step 7	System
			OK

7	If there are any powertrain DTCs, select Captured Info in order to store the powertrain DTC information with a scan tool. Did you complete the action?	Diagnose Trouble Code (DTC)	--

ARM0300000000685

Fig. 122   Diagnostic system check (Part 3 of 3). XLR

Step	Action	Yes	No
1	Perform the following preliminary inspections: 1. Ensure that the battery is fully charged. 2. Ensure that the battery cables are clean and tight. 3. Inspect for any open fuses. 4. Inspect the easily accessible systems or the visible system components for obvious damage or conditions that could cause the symptom. 5. Ensure that the grounds are clean, tight, and in the correct location. 6. Inspect for aftermarket devices that could affect the operation of the system. 7. Search for applicable service bulletins. Did you find and correct the condition?	System OK	Go to Step 2

ARM0300000000683

Fig. 122   Diagnostic system check (Part 1 of 3). XLR

Step	Action	Yes	No
	Connector End View Reference: Cooling System Connector End Views		
1	Did you perform the Vehicle Diagnostic System Check?	Go to Step 2	Go to Diagnostic System Check
2	Turn ON the ignition with the engine OFF. Turn OFF the HVAC controls. Does the engine cooling fan operate?	Go to Step 3	Go to Diagnostic Aids
3	Turn OFF the ignition. Does the cooling fan still operate?	Go to Step 4	Go to Step 5
4	Replace the cooling fan speed control processor. Did you complete the replacement?	Go to Step 6	--
5	**Important** Perform the set up procedure for the ECM. Replace the ECM. Did you complete the replacement?	Go to Step 6	--
6	Operate the system in order to verify the repair. Did you correct the condition?	System OK	Go to Step 2

ARM0300000000686

Fig. 123   Cooling fan always on. XLR

	Step	Value	Yes	No
1	Did you perform the Vehicle Diagnostic System Check?	--	Go to Step 2	Go to Diagnostic System Check
2	1. Install a scan tool. 2. Turn ON the ignition, with the engine OFF. 3. With a scan tool, command the cooling fan ON and OFF. Does the cooling fan turn ON and OFF with each command?	--	Go to Diagnostic Aids	Go to Step 3
3	1. Turn OFF the ignition. 2. Disconnect the cooling fan. 3. Probe the battery positive voltage circuit of the cooling fan assembly with a test lamp that is connected to a good ground. Does the test lamp illuminate?	--	Go to Step 4	Go to Step 7
4	Inspect the ground circuit of the cooling fan assembly for an open. Did you complete the repair	--	Go to Step 12	Go to Step 5
5	1. Install a scan tool. 2. Turn ON the ignition, with the engine OFF. 3. Command the cooling fan ON to 90%. 4. Measure the voltage on the cooling fan speed control circuit. Is the specified voltage present?	4-5 V	Go to Step 8	Go to Step 6
6	Inspect the cooling fan speed control circuit for an open short to ground or short to voltage. Did you find and correct the condition?	--	Go to Step 12	Go to Step 10

ARM0300000000687

Fig. 124   Cooling fan inoperative (Part 1 of 2). XLR

	Step	Value	Yes	No
7	Repair the battery positive voltage circuit of the cooling fan assembly for an open or short to ground. Did you complete the repair	--	Go to Step 12	--
8	Inspect for poor connections at the cooling fan assembly. Did you find and correct the condition?	--	Go to Step 12	Go to Step 9
9	Replace the cooling fan assembly. Did you complete the replacement?	--	Go to Step 12	--
10	Inspect for poor connections at the ECM. Did you find and correct the condition?	--	Go to Step 12	Go to Step 11
11	**Important** Perform the setup procedure for the ECM. Replace the ECM. Did you complete the replacement?	--	Go to Step 12	--
12	Operate the system in order to verify the repair. Did you correct the condition?		System OK	Go to Step 2

ARM0300000000688

Fig. 124   Cooling fan inoperative (Part 2 of 2). XLR

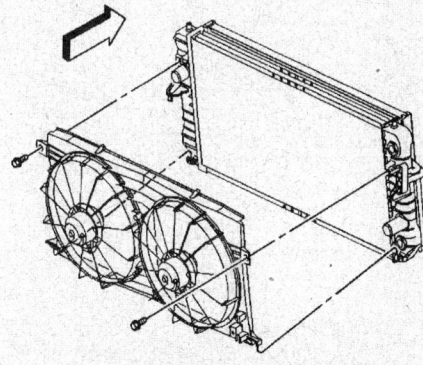

ARM66GC000000272

Fig. 127   Cooling fan assembly removal. Aurora

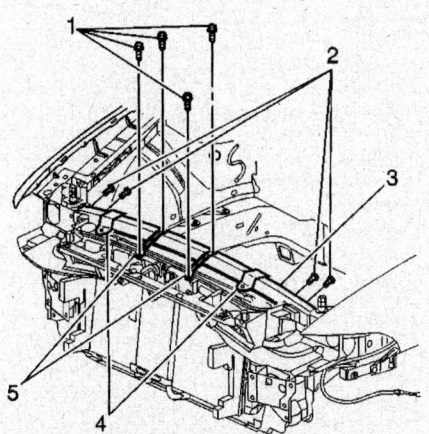

1- SUPPORT BRACKET RETAINERS
2- UPPER TIE BAR RETAINERS
3- UPPER TIE BAR
4- RADIATOR SUPPORT BRACKETS
5- HEADLAMP FASCIA PANEL SUPPORT BRACKETS

ARM66GC000000269

Fig. 125   Upper body tie bar removal. Aurora

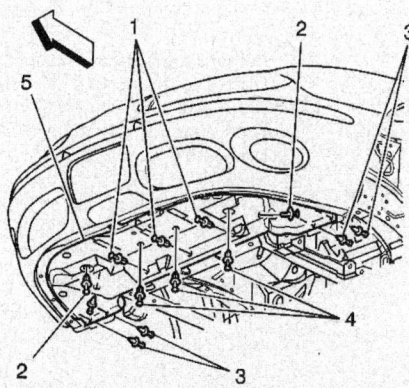

No. 1, 2, 3 & 4 AIR DEFLECTOR RETAINERS
No. 5 FRONT AIR DEFLECTOR

ARM66GC000000270

Fig. 126   Air deflector removal. Aurora w/3.5L engine

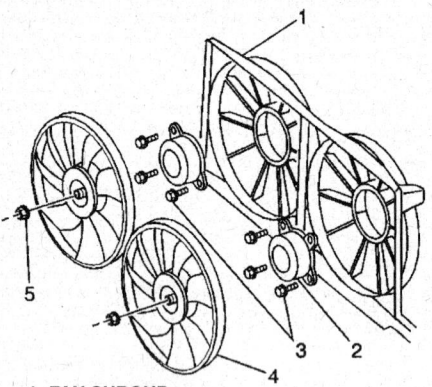

1- FAN SHROUD
2- COOLING FAN MOTOR
3- MOTOR RETAINING BOLTS
4- COOLING FAN BLADE
5- COOLING FAN BLADE RETAINING NUT

ARM66GC000000273

Fig. 128   Cooling fan blade & motor removal. Aurora

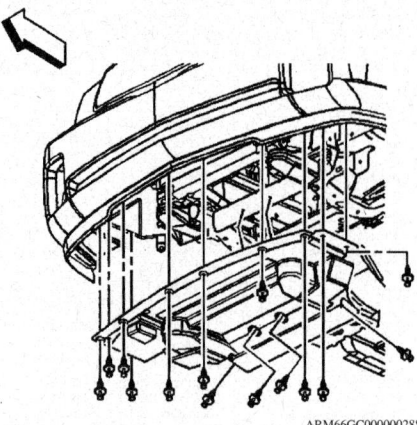

ARM66GC000000288

Fig. 129   Air deflector removal. CTS

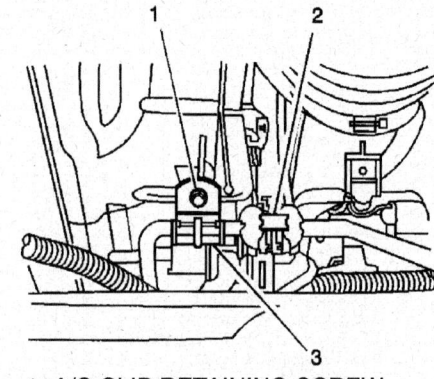

1- A/C CLIP RETAINING SCREW
2- COOLANT BYPASS VALVE
3- A/C LINE RETAINING CLIP

ARM66GC000000282

Fig. 130   Coolant bypass valve removal. CTS

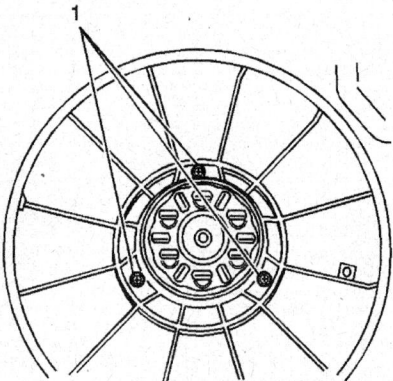

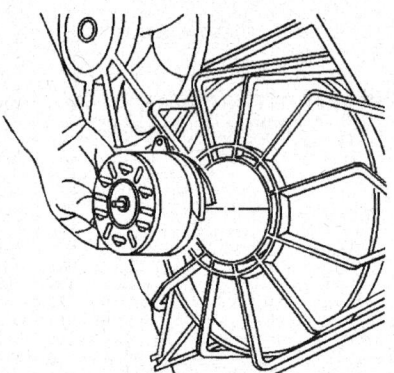

1- FAN MOTOR RETAINING BOLTS

ARM66GC000000287

Fig. 131   Cooling fan motor removal. CTS

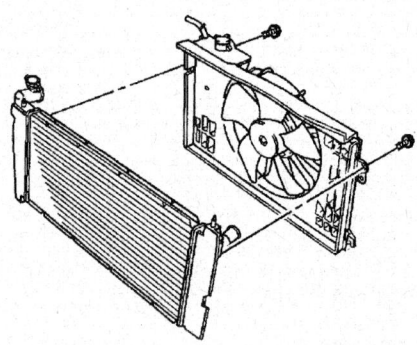

1. Disconnect the reservoir hose from the radiator.
2. Disconnect the fan motor electrical connector.
3. Disconnect two fan motor electrical harness clamps from the fan shroud.
4. Remove two fan shroud bolts.
5. Remove the fan shroud and motor assembly.
6. Remove the fan retaining nut.
7. Remove two radiator fan mount bolts.
8. Remove the radiator fan motor.

ARM66GC000000299

Fig. 132   Cooling fan assembly removal. Vibe

Saturn

NOTE: On Air Bag Equipped Models, Refer To "Air Bag System Precautions" Located In The Front Of This Manual For System Disarming & Arming Procedures.

NOTE: "Electrical Symbol & Wire Color Code Identification" Located In The Front Of This Manual Can Be Used As An Aid When Using Wiring Circuits Found In This Section.

NOTE: Refer To "Computer Relearn Procedures" Located In The Front Of This Manual When Battery Power To The Computer Has Been Interrupted.

INDEX

DESCRIPTION

Ion

On these models a cooling fan control module is used by the Powertrain Control Module (PCM) to control engine cooling fan operation. The engine cooling fan is turned On or Off by the Engine Control Module (ECM) dependent upon engine coolant temperature or A/C pressure. Under high ambient conditions, the cooling fan and heater water pump may run for several minutes after the ignition is turn to the Off position.

S Series

On models equipped with A/C, the cooling fan has five unequally spaced blades to provide air flow through the radiator and condenser. the fan is driven by an electric motor which is attached to the radiator support. The fan motor is activated by a coolant temperature switch.

On models less A/C, the cooling fan has four unequally spaced blades that have curled tips to provide minimum noise. A fan shroud is used to prevent recirculation of air around the fan.

L Series

On these models a cooling fan control module is used by the Powertrain Control Module (PCM) to control engine cooling fan operation. These models have two cooling fan motors, the pusher fan mounted on the A/C or front side of the condenser/radiator assembly, pushes air through the front of the radiator/condenser assembly aiding in refrigerant and coolant heat disbursement, while the puller fan mounted to the radiator side of the condenser/radiator assembly further assist in engine coolant and ambient heat disbursement, these fans are turned On or Off by the Engine Control Module (ECM) dependent upon engine coolant temperature or A/C pressure. Under high ambient conditions, the cooling fans and heater water pump may run for several minutes after the ignition is turn to the Off position.

SYSTEM DIAGNOSIS & TESTING

Wiring Diagrams

Refer to **Figs. 1 through 3,** for electric cooling fan wiring diagrams.

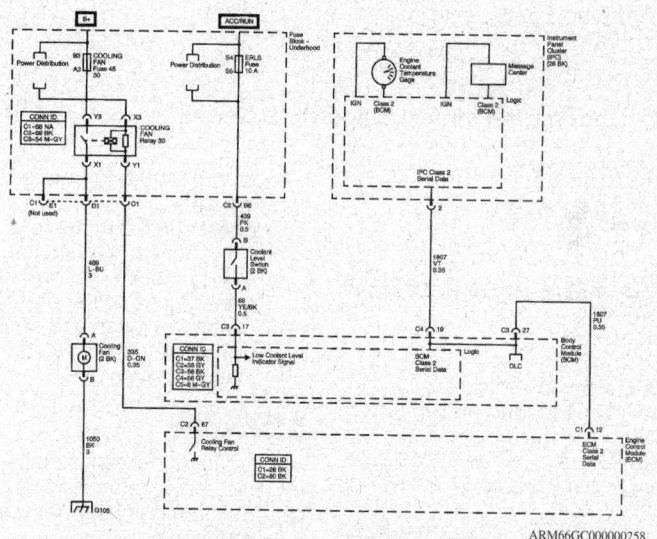

ARM66GC000000258

Fig. 1 Cooling fan wiring diagram. ION

Diagnostic Tests

ION

Refer to **Figs. 4 and 5,** for diagnostic procedures.

L SERIES

Refer to **Fig. 6,** for diagnostic procedures.

S SERIES

Refer to **Figs. 7 and 8,** for diagnostic procedures.

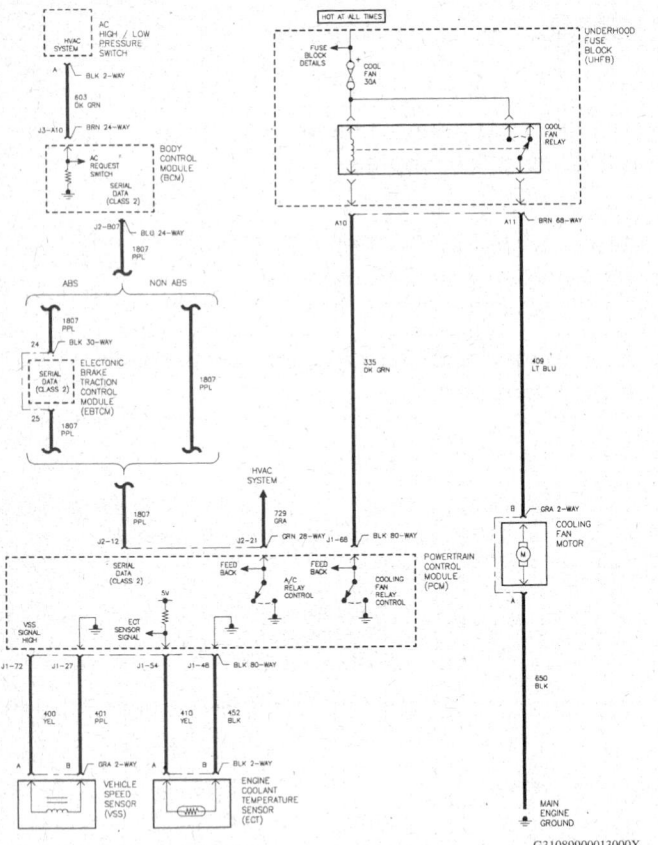

Fig. 2 Cooling fan wiring diagram. S Series

Fig. 3 Cooling fan wiring diagram (Part 1 of 2). L Series

COMPONENT REPLACEMENT

Cooling Fan Assembly

ION

1. Raise and support vehicle.
2. Disconnect cooling fan electrical connector.
3. Release wire harness retaining clips, then remove wire harness from shroud and position aside.
4. From under vehicle, push upward on fan shroud to unsnap cooling fan shroud assembly from radiator.
5. Position cooling fan shroud assembly away from radiator.
6. Remove air dam push-in retainers, then the right and lefthand splash shield to radiator push-in retainers, **Fig. 9.**
7. Remove air dam and splash shield.
8. Remove lower radiator mounting bolts and mount, then support radiator and condenser assemblies, **Fig. 10.**
9. Tilt radiator/condenser assemblies forward, then lower cooling fan and shroud assembly out of vehicle, **Fig. 11.**
10. Scribe an index mark on cooling fan blade and fan motor end shaft for installation reference.
11. Remove cooling fan blade retaining clip, then the fan blade, **Fig. 12.**
12. Remove cooling fan motor mounting bolts, then the fan motor from shroud, **Fig. 13.**
    a. **Torque** fan motor to shroud mounting bolts to 70 inch lbs.
    b. Align index scribe marks on fan blade and motor end shaft, then install fan blade and retaining clip.
    c. **Torque** lower radiator mount bolts to 18 ft. lbs.

S SERIES

1. Remove intake air ducts and disconnect temperature sensor connector.
2. Disconnect wiring harness from cooling fan motor.
3. Loosen and remove top hold-down bolts from cooling fan assembly.
4. **On models equipped with automatic transaxle and A/C,** it may be required to loosen top transaxle oil cooler line for clearance.
5. **On all models,** lift cooling fan off of lower mounting brackets. Move assembly to left and rotate counterclockwise while lifting upward past upper radiator hose.
6. Remove cooling fan assembly from vehicle.
7. While holding fan, remove fan blade to motor nut (lefthand thread). Pull fan blade off of motor shaft.
8. Remove screws securing fan motor to shroud.
9. Remove motor from fan shroud.
10. Reverse procedure to install. **Torque** motor nut to 27–44 inch lbs.

Pusher Fan Assembly

L SERIES

1. Disconnect pusher fan electrical connector.
2. Release tabs, then remove pusher fan harness from puller fan shroud retainers and move harness clear of radiator end tank.
3. Raise and support vehicle, then remove pusher fan to condenser retaining bolts, **Fig. 14.**
4. Pull lower fan shroud forward, then downward to remove fan.
5. If fan is being replaced, release four finger guard to fan retaining clips, then remove finger guard, **Fig. 15.**
6. Reverse procedure to install. **Torque** lower fan to shroud bolts to 35 inch lbs.

Puller Fan Assembly

L SERIES

2.2L ENGINE

1. Disconnect battery ground and positive cables. **It is not required to disconnect fan control module electrical connector.**
2. Disconnect both cooling fan electrical connectors, then slide connectors out of retainers.
3. Remove pusher fan electrical harness from fan shroud retainer tabs, then wiring harness from clamp on fan shroud.
4. Remove battery hold-down and fan

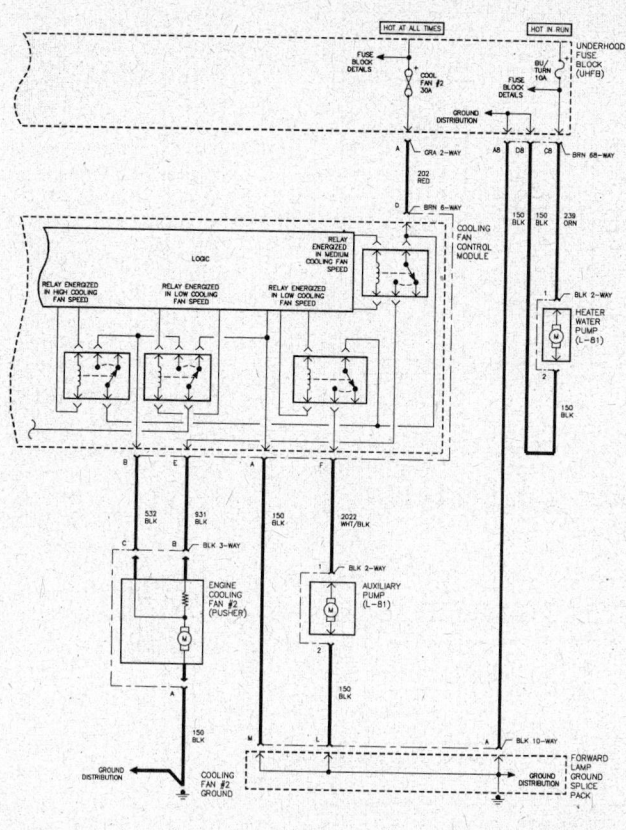

Fig. 3   Cooling fan wiring diagram (Part 2 of 2). L Series

G31089900014020X

Step	Action	Yes	No
1	Did you perform the Engine Cooling System Check?	Go to Step 2	Check Engine Cooling
2	Turn ON the ignition, with the engine OFF. Is the engine cooling fan running all the time?	Go to Step 3	Test for Intermittent and Poor Connections
3	Remove the cooling fan relay. Did the cooling fan turn OFF?	Go to Step 5	Go to Step 4
4	Repair the short to B+ in the cooling fan motor supply voltage circuit. Did you complete the repair?	Go to Step 7	—
5	Inspect for poor connections at the cooling fan relay. Did you find and correct the condition?	Go to Step 7	Go to Step 6
6	Replace the cooling fan relay. Did you complete the repair?	Go to Step 7	
7	Operate the system in order to verify the repair. Did you correct the condition?	System OK	Go to Step 2

ARM66GC000000261

Fig. 4   Cooling fan always on. ION

control module bracket, **Fig. 16.**

5. Remove battery insulating cover, then battery.
6. Remove fan shroud to radiator bolts, then fan and shroud assembly, **Fig. 17.**
7. Reverse procedure to install. **Torque** lower fan to shroud bolts to 35 inch lbs.

3.0L ENGINE

1. Disconnect battery ground. **It is not required to disconnect fan control module electrical connector.**
2. Remove fan control module by sliding up and off bracket. Lay module and wiring aside.
3. Remove battery insulator cover, then battery hold-down and fan control module bracket.

4. Remove battery, then drain engine coolant into a suitable container.
5. Remove power steering fluid reservoir to fan shroud bolts, position reservoir rearward in vehicle.
6. Disconnect both cooling fan electrical connectors, then slide connectors out of retainers.
7. Remove pusher fan electrical harness from fan shroud retainer tabs.
8. Disconnect auxiliary water pump electrical connector, then remove harness from clip.
9. Remove upper transaxle cooler line from radiator, then unsnap from retainer at radiator end.
10. Remove auxiliary water pump outlet hose from radiator, then remove upper radiator hose.
11. Raise and support vehicle, then remove auxiliary water pump inlet hose from radiator.
12. Lower vehicle, then remove fan shroud to radiator bolts.
13. Remove fan and shroud assembly from vehicle.
14. Reverse procedure to install.

Step	Action	Yes	No
1	Did you perform System Check-Engine Cooling?	Go to *Step 2*	*Check Engine Cooling*
2	1. Install a scan tool. 2. Turn ON the ignition, with the engine OFF. 3. With a scan tool, command the cooling fan ON and OFF. Does the engine cooling fan turn ON and OFF with each command?	*Test for Intermittent and Poor Connections*	Go to *Step 3*
3	1. Turn OFF the ignition. 2. Remove the cooling fan relay. 3. Probe the battery positive voltage circuit of the cooling fan relay switch side with a test lamp that is connected to a good ground. Does the test lamp illuminate?	Go to *Step 4*	Go to *Step 7*
4	Connect a 20 A fused jumper wire between the battery positive voltage circuit of the cooling fan relay and the cooling fan motor supply voltage circuit of the cooling fan relay. Does the cooling fan operate?	Go to *Step 10*	Go to *Step 5*
5	1. Disconnect the cooling fan connector. 2. Probe the cooling fan motor supply voltage circuit at the harness connector with a test lamp that is connected to a good ground. Does the test lamp illuminate?	Go to *Step 6*	Go to *Step 8*

ARM66GC000000262

Fig. 5   Cooling fan inoperative (Part 1 of 2). ION

Step	Action	Yes	No
6	Probe the harness connector of the cooling fan motor with a test lamp connected between the cooling fan motor supply voltage circuit and the ground circuit of the cooling fan motor. Does the test lamp illuminate?	Go to *Step 11*	Go to *Step 9*
7	Repair the battery positive circuit of the cooling fan relay. Did you complete the repair?	Go to *Step 14*	—
8	Repair the supply voltage circuit of the cooling fan motor. Did you complete the repair?	Go to *Step 14*	—
9	Repair the ground circuit of the cooling fan motor. Did you complete the repair?	Go to *Step 14*	—
10	Inspect for poor connections at the cooling fan relay. Did you find and correct the condition?	Go to *Step 14*	Go to *Step 12*
11	Inspect for poor connections at the harness connector of the cooling fan motor. Did you find and correct the condition?	Go to *Step 14*	Go to *Step 13*
12	Replace the cooling fan relay. Did you complete the repair?	Go to *Step 14*	—
13	Replace the cooling fan motor. Did you complete the repair?	Go to *Step 14*	—
14	Operate the system in order to verify the repair. Did you correct the condition?	System OK	Go to *Step 2*

ARM66GC000000263

Fig. 5   Cooling fan inoperative (Part 2 of 2). ION

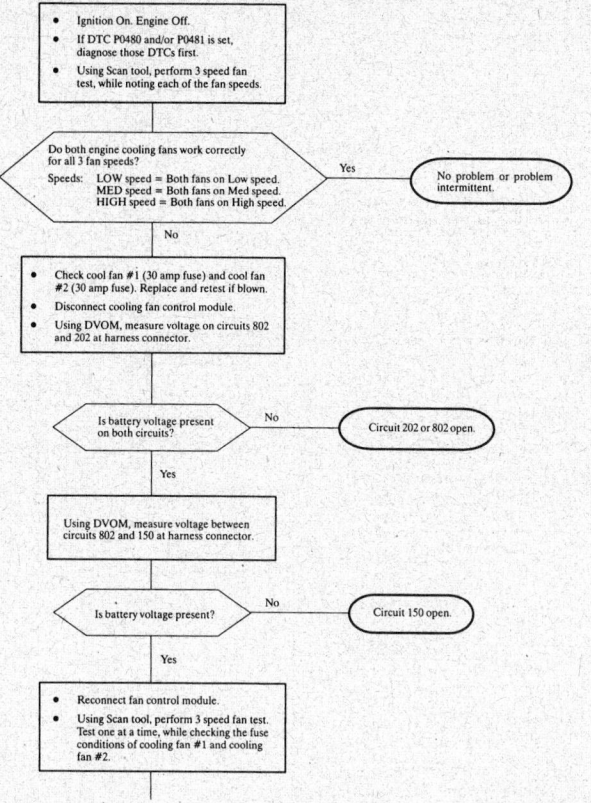

Fig. 6   Cooling fan inoperative (Part 1 of 2). L Series

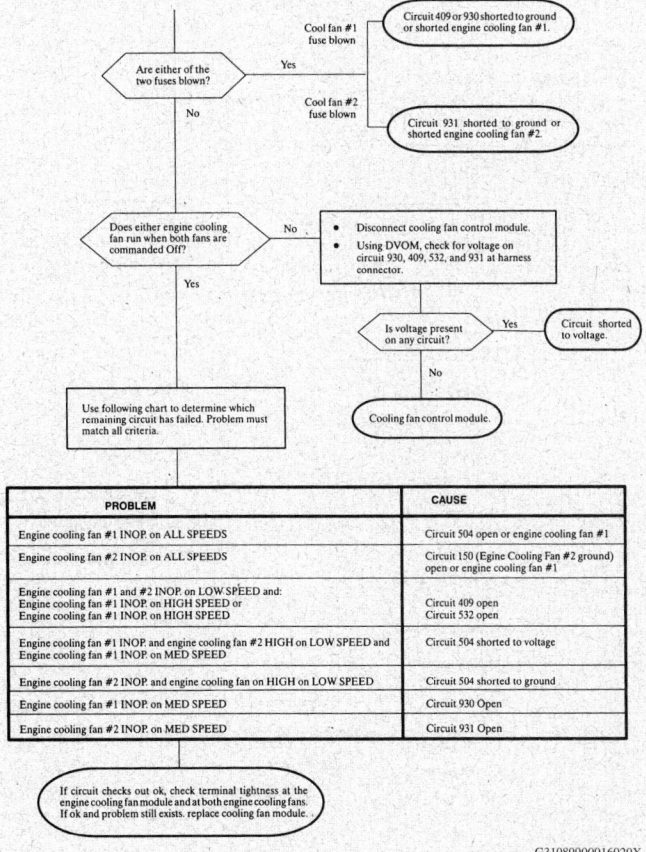

Fig. 6   Cooling fan inoperative (Part 2 of 2). L Series

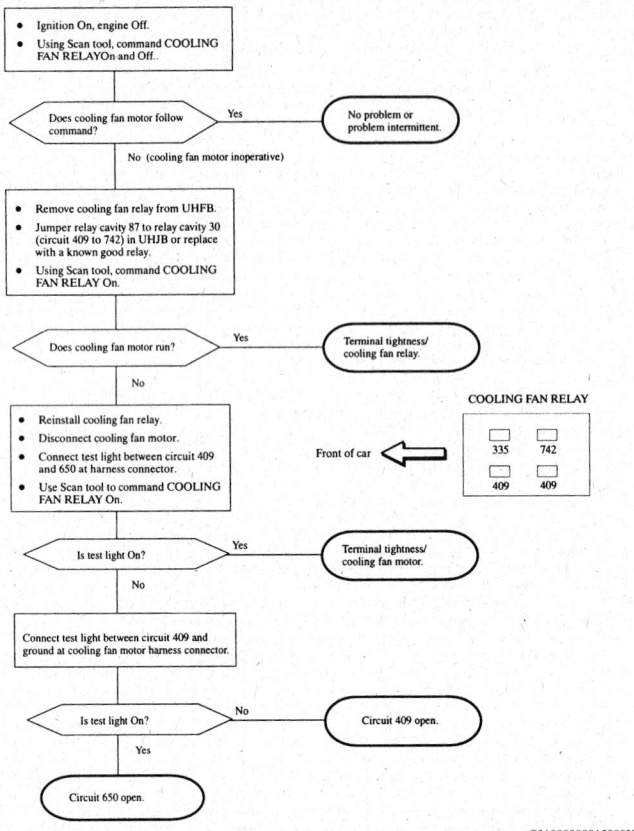

Fig. 7   Cooling fan inoperative. S Series

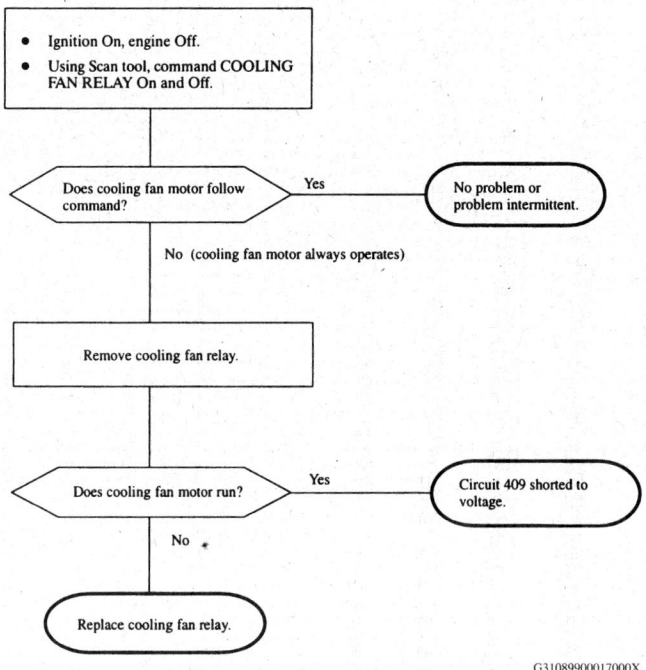

Fig. 8   Cooling fan constant operation diagnosis. S Series

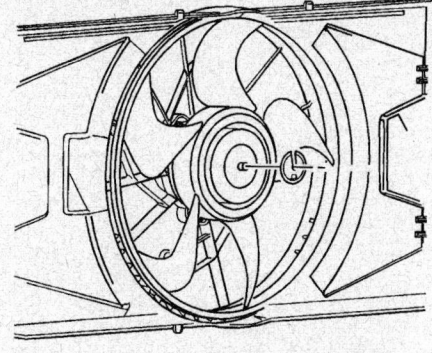

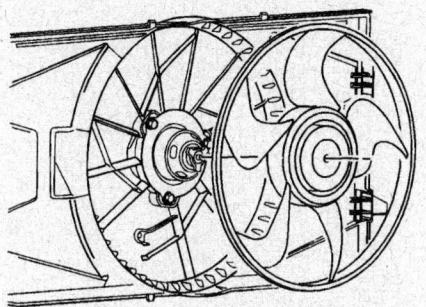

Fig. 9   Air dam & splash shield removal. ION

Fig. 10   Lower radiator mount assembly removal. ION

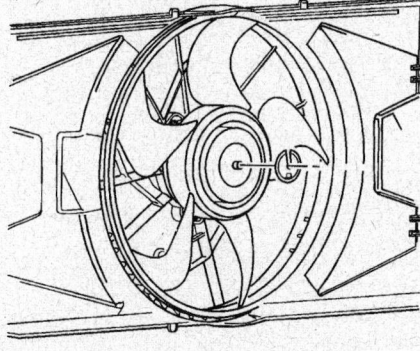

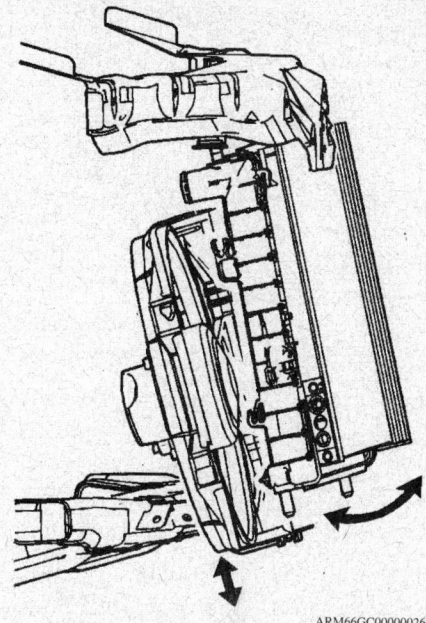

Fig. 11   Cooling fan & shroud assembly removal. ION

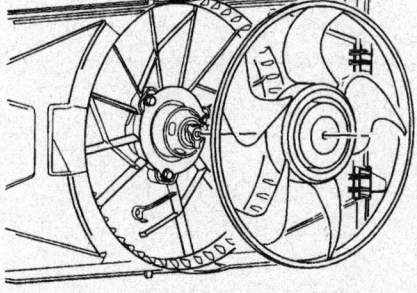

Fig. 12   Cooling fan blade removal. ION

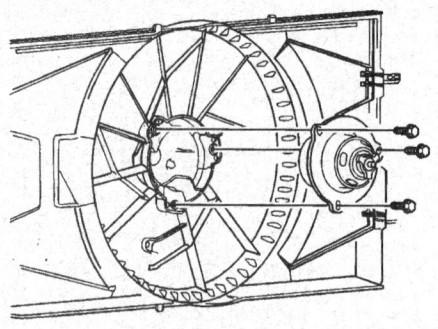

ARM66GC000000268

Fig. 13   Cooling fan motor removal. ION

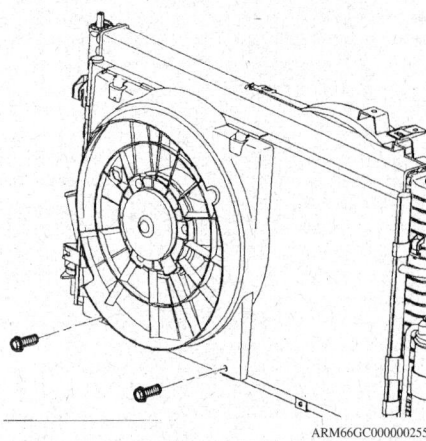

ARM66GC000000255

Fig. 14   Pusher fan removal. L Series

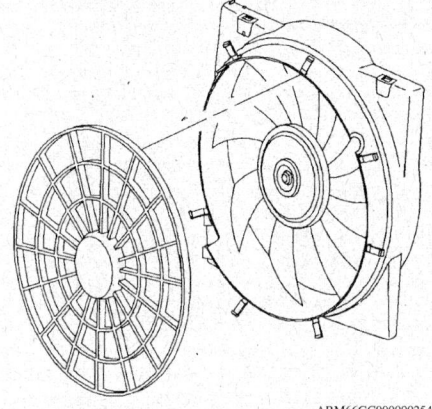

ARM66GC000000254

Fig. 15   Pusher fan finger guard removal. L Series

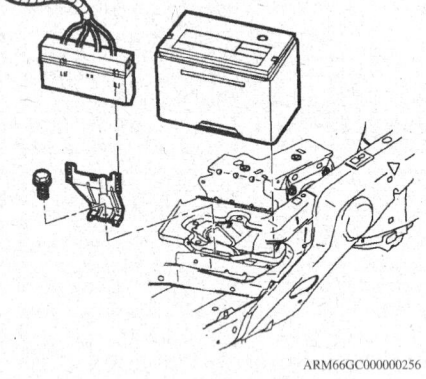

ARM66GC000000256

Fig. 16   Battery hold-down & fan control module bracket removal. L Series w/2.2L engine

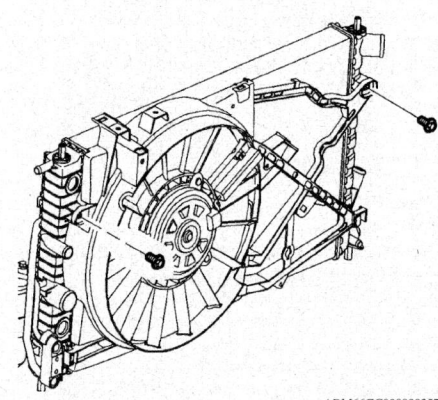

ARM66GC000000257

Fig. 17   Fan & shroud assembly removal. L Series w/2.2L engine

STARTER MOTORS

TABLE OF CONTENTS

Application Chart

Year	Engine	VIN①	Manufacturer	Model
ALERO & GRAND AM				
2001–05	2.2L	F	AC-Delco	PG-260D
	2.4L	T	AC-Delco	PG-260D
	3.4L	E	AC-Delco	PG-260D
AURORA				
2001–03	3.5L	H	Denso	PG-260M
	4.0L	C	AC-Delco	PG-260L
AVEO				
2005	1.6L	6	—	—
BONNEVILLE & LESABRE				
2001–05	3.8L	K	AC-Delco	PG-260L
	3.8L	1	AC-Delco	PG-260L
2004–05	4,6L	Y	AC-Delco	PG-260G
CAMARO & FIREBIRD				
2001–02	3.8L	K	AC-Delco	PG-260 F2
	5.7L	G	AC-Delco	PG-260M
CATERA				
2001	3.0L	R	Mitsubishi	—
CAVALIER & SUNFIRE				
2001–02	2.2L	4	AC-Delco	PG-260D
	2.4L	T	AC-Delco	PG-260L
2003–05	2.2L	4	AC-Delco	PG-260D
CENTURY, GRAND PRIX & REGAL				
2001	3.1L	J	AC-Delco	PG 260D
	3.8L	K	AC-Delco	PG260G
	3.8L	1	AC-Delco	PG-260M
2002–05	3.1L	J	AC-Delco	PG 260D
	3.8L	K	AC-Delco	PG260G
	3.8L	1	AC-Delco	PG-260L
CORVETTE				
2001–02	5.7L	G	AC-Delco	PG260M
2003–04	5.7L	G	AC-Delco	PG-260L
2005	6.0L	U	—	PG
CTS				
2003–05	3.2L	N	Bosch	—
	3.6L	7	AC-Delco	PG260G
DEVILLE, ELDORADO & SEVILLE				
2000–05	4.6L	9	AC-Delco	PG-260L
	4.6L	Y	AC-Delco	PG-260L
GTO				
2005	5.7L	G	Mitsubishi	—
G6				
2005	3.5L	8	AC-Delco	PG-260D

Continued

STARTER MOTORS

Year	Engine	VIN①	Manufacturer	Model
IMPALA				
2001–02	3.4L	E	AC-Delco	PG260D
	3.8L	K	AC-Delco	PG260 F2
2003–05	3.4L	E	AC-Delco	PG260D
	3.8L	K	AC-Delco	PG260G
INTRIGUE				
2001–02	3.5L	H	Denso	PG260M
LACROSSE				
2005	3.6L	7	—	PG
	3.8L	K/1	—	PG
MALIBU				
2001–03	3.1L	J	AC-Delco	PG-260D
2004–05	2.2L	F	AC-Delco	PG-260D
	3.5L	8	AC-Delco	PG-260D
METRO				
2001	1.0L	6	—	30005925
	1.3L	2	—	30005563
MONTE CARLO				
2001–02	3.4L	E	AC-Delco	PG260D
	3.8L	K	AC-Delco	PG260 F2
2003–05	3.4L	E	AC-Delco	PG260D
	3.8L	K	AC-Delco	PG260G
	3.8L	1	AC-Delco	PG260G
PARK AVENUE				
2001	3.8L	K	AC-Delco	PG-260 F2
	3.8L	1	AC-Delco	PG-260M
2002–05	3.8L	K	AC-Delco	PG-260G
	3.8L	1	AC-Delco	PG-260L
PRIZM				
2001–02	1.8L	8	Denso	—
STS				
2005	4.6L	A	—	PG
VIBE				
2003–04	1.8L	8/L	Denso	—
XLR				
2004–05	4.6L	A	AC-Delco	PG-260L
SATURN L-SERIES				
2001–05	2.2L	F	AC-Delco	PG-260D
	3.0L	R	Mitsubishi	—
SATURN S-SERIES				
2001–02	1.9L	7/8	AC-Delco	—
SATURN ION				
2003–05	2.2L	F	AC-Delco	PG-260D

① — The eighth digit of VIN denotes engine code.

AC-Delco, Bosch & Denso Starters

NOTE: On Air Bag Equipped Models, Refer To "Air Bag System Precautions" Located In The Front Of This Manual For System Disarming & Arming Procedures.

NOTE: Refer To "Computer Relearn Procedures" Located In The Front Of This Manual When Battery Power To The Computer Has Been Interrupted.

INDEX

PRECAUTIONS

Air Bag Systems

Refer to "Air Bag System Precautions" in the front of this manual for system disarming and arming procedures.

Battery Ground Cable

Prior to service, disconnect battery ground cable and isolate as required.

DESCRIPTION

These starter motors are a non-repairable starter motor. They have pole pieces that are arranged around the armature. Both solenoid windings are energized. The pull-in winding circuit is completed to the ground through the starter motor. The windings work together magnetically to pull and hold in the plunger moves the shift lever. This action causes the starter drive assembly to rotate on the armature shaft spline as it engages with the flywheel ring gear on the engine. Moving at the same time, the plunger also closes the solenoid switch contacts in the starter solenoid. Full battery voltage is applied directly to the starter motor and it cranks the engine.

TROUBLESHOOTING

AC-Delco

Refer to **Figs 1 through 4,** for troubleshooting procedures.

Step	Action	Yes	No
1	Did you perform the Battery Inspection/Test?	Go to *Step 2*	Battery Inspection/Test
2	1. Install a scan tool 2. Turn ON the ignition, with the engine OFF. Does the scan tool power up?	Go to *Step 3*	Go to Scan Tool Does Not Power Up
3	Attempt to establish communication with the following components: • Body Control Module (BCM) • Instrument Panel Cluster (IPC) • Powertrain Control Module (PCM) • Vehicle Theft Deterrent Module (VTD) Does the scan tool communicate with the BCM, IPC, PCM and VTD?	Go to *Step 4*	Scan Tool Does Not Communicate with Class 2 Device
4	Select the BCM, IPC, PCM and VTD display DTC function on the scan tool. Does the scan tool display any DTCs?	Go to *Step 5*	Go to *Symptoms*
5	Does the scan tool display any DTCs which begin with a U?	Scan Tool Does Not Communicate with Class 2 Device	Go to *Step 6*
6	Does the scan tool display any DTCs in the PCM which begin with a P?	Diagnostic Trouble Code (DTC) List/Type	Go to *Step 7*
7	Does the scan tool display any DTCs in the VTD which begin with B?	Diagnostic Trouble Code (DTC) List/Type	Go to *Step 8*
8	Does the scan tool display any DTCs in the BCM which begin with B?	Diagnostic Trouble Code (DTC) List/Type	Go to *Step 9*
9	Does the scan tool display any DTCs in the IPC which begin with B?	Diagnostic Trouble Code (DTC) List/Type	System OK

GC1120100173000X

Fig. 1 System check. AC-Delco

Bosch

Refer to **Figs. 5 through 9,** for troubleshooting procedures.

Denso

Refer to **Figs. 10 through 12,** for troubleshooting procedures.

DIAGNOSIS & TESTING

Refer to **MOTOR's "Domestic Engine Performance & Driveability Manual"** for diagnosis and testing procedures.

Step	Action	Yes	No
1	Did you perform the Diagnostic System Check for starting and charging?	Go to Step 2	System Check
2	Turn the ignition to the START position. Does the engine crank?	Go to Intermittent and Poor Connections	Go to Step 3
3	1. Install a scan tool. 2. With a scan tool, observe the Crank Request parameter in the PCM data list. 3. Turn the ignition switch to the START position. Does the scan tool display Yes?	Go to Step 5	Go to Step 4
4	1. With a scan tool, observe the Crank parameter in the IPC data list. 2. Turn the ignition switch to the START position. Does the scan tool display Yes?	Go to Step 12	Go to Step 13
5	Turn the ignition to the START position. Does the CRANK relay click?	Go to Step 8	Go to Step 6

GC1120100170010X

Fig. 2 Starter solenoid does not click (Part 1 of 3). AC-Delco

Step	Action	Yes	No
19	Inspect for poor connection at the PCM harness connector. Did you find and correct the condition?	Go to Step 29	Go to Step 26
20	Inspect for poor connections at the ignition switch harness connector. Did you find and correct the condition?	Go to Step 29	Go to Step 27
21	Inspect for poor connections at the starter solenoid. Did you find and correct the condition?	Go to Step 29	Go to Step 28
22	Repair the open or high resistance in the battery positive voltage circuit of the CRANK relay switch. Did you complete the repair?	Go to Step 29	—
23	Repair the high resistance or short to ground in the supply voltage circuit of the starter solenoid. Did you complete the repair?	Go to Step 29	—
24	Replace the PNP switch. Did you complete the replacement?	Go to Step 29	—
25	Replace the crank relay. Did you complete the replacement?	Go to Step 29	—
26	**Important:** Perform the set up procedures for the PCM. Replace the PCM. Did you complete the replacement?	Go to Step 29	—
27	Replace the Ignition Switch. Did you complete the replacement?	Go to Step 29	—
28	Replace the Starter Motor. Did you complete the replacement?	Go to Step 29	—
29	Operate the system for which the symptom occurred. Did you correct the condition?	System OK	Go to Step 2

GC1120100170030X

Fig. 2 Starter solenoid does not click (Part 3 of 3). AC-Delco

Step	Action	Yes	No
6	1. Turn OFF the ignition. 2. Disconnect the CRANK relay. 3. Turn ON the ignition, with the Engine OFF. 4. Connect a test lamp between the battery positive voltage circuit of the CRANK relay coil and a good ground. Does the test lamp illuminate?	Go to Step 7	Go to Step 14
7	1. Connect a test lamp between the battery positive voltage circuit of the CRANK relay coil and the control circuit of the CRANK relay. 2. Turn the ignition to the START position. Does the test lamp illuminate?	Go to Step 18	Go to Step 15
8	1. Turn OFF the ignition. 2. Disconnect the CRANK relay. 3. Connect a test lamp between the battery positive voltage circuit of the CRANK relay switch circuit and a good ground. Does the test lamp illuminate?	Go to Step 9	Go to Step 22
9	Connect a 30 amp fused jumper between the battery positive voltage circuit of the START relay switch circuit and the supply voltage circuit of the starter solenoid. Does the engine crank?	Go to Step 18	Go to Step 10
10	1. Disconnect the park neutral position (PNP) switch. 2. Connect a 30 amp fused jumper between the starter solenoid supply voltage circuits of the PNP switch harness connector. Does the engine crank?	Go to Step 17	Go to Step 11
11	Does the fuse in either jumper open?	Go to Step 23	Go to Step 16
12	Test the crank request signal circuit of the PCM for an open or high resistance. Did you find and correct the condition?	Go to Step 29	Go to Step 19
13	Test the crank signal circuit of the IPC for an open or high resistance. Did you find and correct the condition?	Go to Step 29	Go to Step 20
14	Test the battery positive voltage circuit of the CRANK relay coil for an open or high resistance. Did you find and correct the condition?	Go to Step 29	Go to Step 20
15	Test the control circuit of the CRANK relay for an open, high resistance or short to battery voltage. Did you find and correct the condition?	Go to Step 29	Go to Step 19
16	Test the supply voltage circuit of the starter solenoid for an open or high resistance. Did you find and correct the condition?	Go to Step 29	Go to Step 21
17	1. Inspect the PNP switch for proper operation. 2. Inspect for poor connection at the PNP switch harness connector. Did you find and correct the condition?	Go to Step 29	Go to Step 24
18	Inspect for poor connections at the CRANK relay. Did you find and correct the condition?	Go to Step 29	Go to Step 25

GC1120100170020X

Fig. 2 Starter solenoid does not click (Part 2 of 3). AC-Delco

Step	Action	Yes	No
1	Did you review the engine electrical operation and perform the necessary inspections?	Go to Step 2	Go to Symptoms
2	Start the engine. Does the starter operate normally?	Test Intermittent and Poor Connections	Go to Step 3
3	Start the engine while listening to the starter motor turn. Is there a loud "whoop" (it may sound like a siren if the engine is revved while the starter is engaged) after the engine starts, but while the starter is still held in the engaged position?	Go to Step 6	Go to Step 4
4	Do you hear a "rumble", a "growl", or, in some cases, a "knock" as the starter is coasting down to a stop after starting the engine?	Go to Step 7	Go to Step 5
5	When the engine is cranked, do you hear a high-pitched whine after the engine cranks and starts normally? (This is often diagnosed as a starter drive gear hang-in or a weak solenoid.)	Go to Step 8	Go to Step 7
6	Inspect the flywheel ring gear for the following: • Chipped gear teeth • Missing gear teeth • milled teeth. Does the flywheel have damaged teeth or is bent?	Go to Step 9	Go to Step 10
7	1. Remove the starter motor. 2. Inspect the starter motor bushings and clutch gear. Does the clutch gear have chipped or milled teeth or worn bushings?	Go to Step 10	Go to Step 9
8	Shim the starter motor away from the flywheel by adding shims one at a time, between the starter motor and the engine block. Flywheel runout may make this noise appear to be intermittent. Did you complete the repair?	Go to Step 11	—
9	Replace the flywheel. Did you complete the replacement?	Go to Step 11	—
10	Replace the starter motor. Has the noise stopped?	Go to Step 11	—
11	Operate the system in order to verify the repair. Did you correct the condition?	System OK	Go to Step 2

GC1120100172000X

Fig. 4 Starter motor noise. AC-Delco

Step	Action	Yes	No
1	Did you perform the Diagnostic System Check for starting and charging?	Go to Step 2	System Check
2	Turn the ignition to the START position. Did the starter solenoid click?	Go to Step 3	Go to Starter Solenoid Does Not Click
3	Inspect the engine and belt drive system for mechanical binding (seized engine, seized generator). Does the engine move freely?	Go to Step 4	Go to Engine Overhaul
4	Test the battery positive cable between the battery and the starter solenoid for high resistance. Did you find and correct the condition?	Go to Step 8	Go to Step 5
5	Test the ground circuit between the battery and the starter motor for a high resistance. Did you find and correct the condition?	Go to Step 8	Go to Step 6
6	Inspect for poor connections at the starter. Did you find and correct the condition?	Go to Step 8	Go to Step 7
7	Replace the Starter. Did you complete the replacement?	Go to Step 8	—
8	Operate the system for which the symptom occurred. Did you correct the condition?	System OK	Go to Step 2

GC1120100171000X

Fig. 3 Starter solenoid clicks, engine does not crank. AC-Delco

Step	Action	Yes	No
1	Did you perform the Battery Inspection/Test?	Go to Step 2	Battery Inspection
2	1. Install a scan tool. 2. Turn ON the ignition, with the engine OFF. Does the scan tool power up?	Go to Step 3	Scan Tool Does Not Power Up
3	**Important** The engine may start during the following step. Turn OFF the engine as soon as you have observed the Crank power mode. 1. Access the Class 2 Power Mode in the Diagnostic Circuit Check on the scan tool. 2. Rotate the ignition switch through all positions while observing the Class 2 Power Mode parameter. Does the ignition switch parameter reading match the ignition switch position for all switch positions?	Go to Step 4	Power Mode Mismatch
4	1. Turn ON the ignition, with the engine OFF. 2. Attempt to communicate with each of the following modules on the class 2 serial data circuit: o Amplifier (AMP) o Climate Control Panel (CCP) o Dash Integration Module (DIM) o Instrument Panel Cluster (IPC) o Onstar (ONS) o Radio (IRC) o Rear Integration Module (RIM) o Remote Function Actuator (RFA) o Powertrain Control Module (PCM) o Supplemental Inflatable Restraint (SIR) Does the scan tool communicate with all modules on the class 2 serial data circuit?	Go to Step 5	Scan Tool Does Not Power Up

ARM66GC000000670

Fig. 5 System check (Part 1 of 2). Bosch

Step	Action	Yes	No
5	1. Select the Display DTCs function for each module. If using a Tech 2, use the Class 2 DTC Check feature in order to determine which modules have DTCs set. 2. Record all of the displayed DTCs, the DTC status, and the module which set the DTC. Does the scan tool display any DTCs?	Go to Step 6	Symptoms
6	Does the scan tool display any DTCs which begin with a "U"?	Scan Tool Does Not Communicate with Class 2 Device	Go to Step 7
7	Does the scan tool display DTC B1000, B1004, B1007, B1009, B1013 or B1014?	Diagnostic Trouble Code (DTC)	Diagnostic Trouble Code

ARM66GC000000671

Fig. 5 System check (Part 2 of 2). Bosch

Step	Action	Yes	No
7	1. Turn ON the ignition, with the engine OFF. 2. Verify that the transmission is in Park or Neutral. 3. With a scan tool, observe the IMS Range parameter in the Transmission data list. Does the scan tool display Park or Neutral?	Go to Step 24	Diagnostic System Check
8	1. Turn OFF the ignition. 2. Disconnect the ECM. 3. Connect a test lamp between the Start Command circuit of the EMC and a good ground. 4. Turn the ignition to the Start position. Does the test lamp illuminate?	Go to Step 24	Go to Step 17
9	1. Turn OFF the ignition. 2. Disconnect the Run/Crank Relay. 3. Connect a test lamp between the battery positive voltage circuit of the Run/Crank Relay coil circuit and a good ground. 4. Turn On the ignition, with the engine OFF. Does the test lamp illuminate?	Go to Step 10	Go to Step 25
10	1. Turn OFF the ignition. 2. Connect a test lamp between the ignition 1 voltage circuit of the Run/Crank Relay coil and the ground circuit of the Run/Crank Relay coil. 3. Turn On the ignition, with the engine OFF. Does the test lamp illuminate?	Go to Step 11	Go to Step 26
11	1. Connect a 10 amp fused jumper between the battery positive voltage circuit of the Run/Crank Relay switch and the Starter Relay Ignition 1 circuit of the Run Crank Relay switch. 2. Turn the ignition switch to the START position. Does the starter solenoid click?	Go to Step 20	Go to Step 12

ARM66GC000000673

Fig. 6 Starter solenoid does not click (Part 2 of 5). Bosch w/automatic transmission

Step	Action	Yes	No
1	Did you perform the Diagnostic System Check for Engine Electrical?	Go to Step 2	Diagnostic System Check
2	Turn the ignition to the START position. Does the starter solenoid click?	Test for Intermittent and Poor Connections	Go to Step 3
3	1. Install a scan tool. 2. With a scan tool, observe the Starter Relay Command parameter in the ECM data list. 3. Turn the ignition switch to the START position. Does the scan tool display On?	Go to Step 4	Go to Step 5
4	Turn the ignition back and forth from the OFF to ON position a few times. Does the Starter Relay click each time the ignition is turned to the ON position?	Go to Step 15	Go to Step 9
5	1. Turn ON the ignition, with the engine OFF. 2. With a scan tool, observe the Crank Request parameter in the ECM data list. 3. Turn the ignition switch to the START position. Does the scan tool display Yes?	Go to Step 6	Go to Step 8
6	1. Turn ON the ignition, with the engine OFF. 2. With a scan tool, observe the Start Disabled parameter in the VTD data list. Does the scan tool display Yes?	Diagnostic System Check	Go to Step 7

ARM66GC000000672

Fig. 6 Starter solenoid does not click (Part 1 of 5). Bosch w/automatic transmission

12	**Important** Leave the fused jumper in place. 1. Disconnect the Starter Relay. 2. Connect a test lamp between the ignition 1 voltage circuit of the Starter Relay coil and a good ground. Does the test lamp illuminate?	Go to Step 13	Go to Step 27
13	1. Connect a test lamp between the ignition 1 voltage circuit of the Starter Relay coil and the control circuit of the Starter Relay coil. 2. Turn the ignition to the Start position. Does the test lamp illuminate?	Go to Step 21	Go to Step 14
14	1. Turn OFF the ignition. 2. Disconnect the ECM. 3. Install the Starter Relay. 4. Connect a test lamp between the control circuit of the Starter Relay and a good ground. Does the test lamp illuminate?	Go to Step 24	Go to Step 28
15	**Important** The engine may crank when the fused jumper is put into place. Connect a 30 amp fused jumper between the battery positive voltage circuit of the Starter relay switch circuit and the supply voltage circuit of the starter solenoid. Does the engine crank?	Go to Step 21	Go to Step 16
16	Does the fuse in the jumper open?	Go to Step 18	Go to Step 19
17	Test the Start Command circuit of the ECM for a high resistance or open. Did you find and correct the condition?	Go to Step 34	Go to Step 23
18	Test the supply voltage circuit of the starter solenoid for a short to ground. Did you find and correct the condition?	Go to Step 34	Go to Step 22

ARM66GC000000674

Fig. 6 Starter solenoid does not click (Part 3 of 5). Bosch w/automatic transmission

19	Test the supply voltage circuit of the starter solenoid for a high resistance or open. Did you find and correct the condition?	Go to Step 34	Go to Step 22
20	Inspect for poor connection at the Run/Crank Relay. Did you find and correct the condition?	Go to Step 34	Go to Step 29
21	Inspect for poor connection at the Starter Relay. Did you find and correct the condition?	Go to Step 34	Go to Step 30
22	Inspect for poor connection at the starter solenoid. Did you find and correct the condition?	Go to Step 34	Go to Step 31
23	Inspect for poor connection at the ignition switch. Did you find and correct the condition?	Go to Step 34	Go to Step 32
24	Inspect for poor connection at the ECM. Did you find and correct the condition?	Go to Step 34	Go to Step 33
25	Repair the high resistance or open in the ignition 1 voltage circuit of the Run/Crank Relay coil. Did you complete the repair?	Go to Step 34	--
26	Repair the high resistance or open in the ground circuit of the Run/Crank Relay coil. Did you complete the repair?	Go to Step 34	--

ARM66GC000000675

Fig. 6 Starter solenoid does not click (Part 4 of 5). Bosch w/automatic transmission

27	Repair the high resistance or open in the ignition 1 voltage circuit of the Starter relay coil. Did you complete the repair?	Go to Step 34	--
28	Repair the high resistance or open in the control circuit of the Starter relay. Did you complete the repair?	Go to Step 34	--
29	Replace the Run/Crank relay. Did you complete the replacement?	Go to Step 34	--
30	Replace the Starter relay. Did you complete the replacement?	Go to Step 34	--
31	Replace the starter. Did you complete the replacement?	Go to Step 34	--
32	Replace the ignition switch. Did you complete the replacement?	Go to Step 34	--
33	**Important:** Perform the set up procedures for the ECM. Replace the ECM. Did you complete the replacement?	Go to Step 34	--
34	Operate the system for which the symptom occurred. Did you correct the condition?	System OK	Go to Step 2

ARM66GC000000676

Fig. 6 Starter solenoid does not click (Part 5 of 5). Bosch w/automatic transmission

Step	Action	Yes	No
1	Did you perform the Diagnostic System Check for Engine Electrical?	Go to Step 2	Diagnostic System Check
2	1. Depress the clutch pedal. 2. Turn the ignition to the START position. Does the starter solenoid click?	Test for Intermittent and Poor Connections	Go to Step 3
3	1. Install a scan tool. 2. Depress the clutch pedal. 3. With a scan tool, observe the Starter Relay Command parameter in the ECM data list. 4. Turn the ignition switch to the START position. Does the scan tool display On?	Go to Step 4	Go to Step 5
4	1. Depress the clutch pedal. 2. Turn the ignition back and forth from the OFF to ON position a few times. Does the Starter Relay click each time the ignition is turned to the ON position?	Go to Step 17	Go to Step 9
5	1. With a scan tool, observe the Crank Request parameter in the ECM data list. 2. Turn the ignition switch to the START position. Does the scan tool display Yes?	Go to Step 6	Go to Step 8
6	1. Turn ON the ignition, with the engine OFF. 2. With a scan tool, observe the Start Disabled parameter in the VTD data list. Does the scan tool display Yes?	Diagnostic System Check	Go to Step 7

ARM66GC000000677

Fig. 7 Starter solenoid does not click (Part 1 of 6). Bosch w/manual transmission

AC-DELCO, BOSCH & DENSO STARTERS

Step	Action		
7	1. Turn ON the ignition, with the engine OFF. 2. Depress the clutch pedal. 3. With a scan tool, observe the Clutch Start Switch parameter in the ECM data list. Does the scan tool display On?	Go to Step 31	Go to Step 16
8	1. Turn OFF the ignition. 2. Disconnect the ECM. 3. Connect a test lamp between the Start Command circuit of the ECM and a good ground. 4. Turn the ignition to the Start position. Does the test lamp illuminate?	Go to Step 31	Go to Step 21
9	1. Turn OFF the ignition. 2. Disconnect the Run/Crank Relay. 3. Connect a test lamp between the battery positive voltage circuit of the Run/Crank Relay coil circuit and a good ground. 4. Turn On the ignition, with the engine OFF. Does the test lamp illuminate?	Go to Step 10	Go to Step 33
10	1. Turn OFF the ignition. 2. Connect a test lamp between the ignition 1 voltage circuit of the Run/Crank Relay coil and the ground circuit of the Run/Crank Relay coil. 3. Turn On the ignition, with the engine OFF. Does the test lamp illuminate?	Go to Step 11	Go to Step 34
11	1. Connect a 10 amp fused jumper between the battery positive voltage circuit of the Run/Crank Relay switch and the Ignition 1 voltage circuit of the clutch switch. 2. Depress the clutch pedal. 3. Turn the ignition switch to the START position. Does the starter solenoid click?	Go to Step 26	Go to Step 12
12	**Important** Leave the fused jumper in place. 1. Disconnect the Starter Relay. 2. Connect a test lamp between the ignition 1 voltage circuit of the Starter Relay coil and a good ground. 3. Depress the clutch pedal. Does the test lamp illuminate?	Go to Step 13	Go to Step 15

ARM66GC000000678

Fig. 7   Starter solenoid does not click (Part 2 of 6). Bosch w/manual transmission

Step	Action		
13	1. Connect a test lamp between the ignition 1 voltage circuit of the Starter Relay coil and the control circuit of the Starter Relay coil. 2. Depress the clutch pedal. 3. Turn the ignition to the Start position. Does the test lamp illuminate?	Go to Step 27	Go to Step 14
14	1. Turn OFF the ignition. 2. Disconnect the ECM. 3. Install the Starter Relay. 4. Connect a test lamp between the control circuit of the Starter Relay and a good ground. 5. Depress the clutch pedal. Does the test lamp illuminate?	Go to Step 31	Go to Step 35
15	1. Turn OFF the ignition. 2. Disconnect the clutch switch. 3. Connect a test lamp between the ignition 1 voltage circuit of the clutch switch and a good ground. Does the test lamp illuminate?	Go to Step 22	Go to Step 32
16	1. Turn OFF the ignition. 2. Disconnect the clutch switch. 3. With a scan tool, observe the Clutch Start Switch parameter in the ECM data list. 4. Turn ON the ignition, with the engine OFF. Does the scan tool display On?	Go to Step 28	Go to Step 23
17	1. Place the transmission in neutral. 2. Apply the parking brake. **Important** The engine may crank when the fused jumper is put into place. 3. Connect a 30 amp fused jumper between the battery positive voltage circuit of the Starter relay switch circuit and the supply voltage circuit of the starter solenoid. Does the engine crank?	Go to Step 27	Go to Step 20
20	Does the fuse in the jumper open?	Go to Step 24	Go to Step 25
21	Test the Start Command circuit of the ECM for a high resistance or open. Did you find and correct the condition?	Go to Step 42	Go to Step 30

ARM66GC000000679

Fig. 7   Starter solenoid does not click (Part 3 of 6). Bosch w/manual transmission

Step	Action		
22	Test the Starter Relay coil supply voltage circuit for a high resistance or open. Did you find and correct the condition?	Go to Step 42	Go to Step 28
23	Test the clutch pedal position switch signal for a short to battery voltage. Did you find and correct the condition?	Go to Step 42	Go to Step 31
24	Test the supply voltage circuit of the starter solenoid for a short to ground. Did you find and correct the condition?	Go to Step 42	Go to Step 29
25	Test the supply voltage circuit of the starter solenoid for a high resistance or open. Did you find and correct the condition?	Go to Step 42	Go to Step 29
26	Inspect for poor connection at the Run/Crank Relay. Did you find and correct the condition?	Go to Step 42	Go to Step 36
27	Inspect for poor connection at the Starter Relay. Did you find and correct the condition?	Go to Step 42	Go to Step 37
28	Inspect for poor connection at the clutch switch. Did you find and correct the condition?	Go to Step 42	Go to Step 38
29	Inspect for poor connection at the starter solenoid. Did you find and correct the condition?	Go to Step 42	Go to Step 39

ARM66GC000000680

Fig. 7   Starter solenoid does not click (Part 4 of 6). Bosch w/manual transmission

Step	Action		
30	Inspect for poor connection at the ignition switch. Did you find and correct the condition?	Go to Step 42	Go to Step 40
31	Inspect for poor connection at the ECM. Did you find and correct the condition?	Go to Step 42	Go to Step 41
32	Repair the high resistance or open in the ignition 1 voltage circuit of the clutch switch. Did you complete the repair?	Go to Step 42	--
33	Repair the high resistance or open in the ignition 1 voltage circuit of the Run/Crank Relay coil. Did you complete the repair?	Go to Step 42	--
34	Repair the high resistance or open in the ground circuit of the Run/Crank Relay coil. Did you complete the repair?	Go to Step 42	--
35	Repair the high resistance or open in the control circuit of the Starter relay. Did you complete the repair?	Go to Step 42	--
36	Replace the Run/Crank relay. Did you complete the replacement?	Go to Step 42	--
37	Replace the Starter relay. Did you complete the replacement?	Go to Step 42	--
38	Replace the clutch switch. Did you complete the replacement?	Go to Step 42	--
39	Replace the starter. Did you complete the replacement?	Go to Step 42	--

ARM66GC000000681

Fig. 7   Starter solenoid does not click (Part 5 of 6). Bosch w/manual transmission

Step	Action	Yes	No
40	Replace the ignition switch. / Did you complete the replacement?	Go to Step 42	--
41	**Important:** Perform the set up procedures for the ECM. / Replace the ECM. / Did you complete the replacement?	Go to Step 42	--
42	Operate the system for which the symptom occurred. / Did you correct the condition?	System OK	Go to Step 2

ARM66GC000000682

Fig. 7 Starter solenoid does not click (Part 6 of 6). Bosch w/manual transmission

Step	Action	Yes	No
1	Did you perform the Diagnostic System Check for Engine Electrical?	Go to Step 2	Diagnostic System Check
2	Start the engine. / Does the starter operate normally?	Test for Intermittent and Poor Connections	Go to Step 3
3	Start the engine while listening to the starter motor turn. / Is there a loud "whoop", it may sound like a siren if the engine is revved while the starter is engaged, after the engine starts, but while the starter is still held in the engaged position?	Go to Step 6	Go to Step 4
4	Do you hear a "rumble", a "growl", or, in some cases, a "knock" as the starter is coasting down to a stop after starting the engine?	Go to Step 7	Go to Step 5
5	**Important** / This is often diagnosed as a starter drive gear hang-in or a weak solenoid. / When the engine is cranked, do you hear a high-pitched whine after the engine cranks and starts normally?	Go to Step 8	Go to Step 7

ARM66GC000000684

Fig. 9 Starter motor noise diagnosis (Part 1 of 2). Bosch

Step	Action	Yes	No
6	Inspect the flywheel ring gear for the following: • Chipped gear teeth • Missing gear teeth • Milled teeth / Is the flywheel bent, or does it have damaged teeth?	Go to Step 9	Go to Step 10
7	1. Remove the starter motor. 2. Inspect the starter motor bushings and clutch gear. / Does the clutch gear have chipped or milled teeth or worn bushings?	Go to Step 10	Go to Step 9
8	Shim the starter motor away from the flywheel by adding shims between the starter motor and the engine block one at a time. / Flywheel runout may make this noise appear to be intermittent. / Did you complete the repair?	Go to Step 11	--
9	Replace the flywheel. / Did you complete the replacement?	Go to Step 11	--
10	Replace the starter motor. / Did you complete the replacement?	Go to Step 11	--
11	Operate the system in order to verify the repair. / Did you correct the condition?	System OK	Go to Step 3

ARM66GC000000685

Fig. 9 Starter motor noise diagnosis (Part 2 of 2). Bosch

Step	Action	Yes	No
1	Did you perform the Diagnostic System Check for Engine Electrical?	Go to Step 2	Diagnostic System Check -
2	Turn the ignition to the START position. / Did the starter solenoid click?	Go to Step 3	Go to Starter Solenoid Does Not Click
3	Inspect the engine and belt drive system for mechanical binding, seized engine, seized generator. / Does the engine move freely?	Go to Step 4	Engine Will Not Crank - Crankshaft Will Not Rotate
4	Test the battery positive cable between the battery and the starter solenoid for high resistance. / Did you find and correct the condition?	Go to Step 8	Go to Step 5
5	Test the ground circuit between the battery and the starter motor for a high resistance. / Did you find and correct the condition?	Go to Step 8	Go to Step 6
6	Inspect for poor connections at the starter. / Did you find and correct the condition?	Go to Step 8	Go to Step 7
7	Replace the starter. / Did you complete the replacement?	Go to Step 8	--
8	Operate the system for which the symptom occurred. / Did you correct the condition?	System OK	Go to Step 2

ARM66GC000000683

Fig. 8 Starter solenoid clicks, engine does not crank. Bosch

Step	Action	Yes	No
1	Did you review following description and operations and perform the necessary inspections? • Starting System Description and Operation	Go to Step 2	Symptoms
2	Turn the ignition to the START position. / Does the starter solenoid click?	Test for Intermittent and Poor Connections	Go to Step 3
3	Is the security indicator flashing?	Diagnostic Starting Point	Go to Step 4
4	1. Install a scan tool. 2. With a scan tool, observe the Starter Switch parameter in the Engine Data list. 3. Turn the ignition switch to the START position. / Does the scan tool display Cranking?	Go to Step 5	Go to Step 17
5	Does the vehicle have Theft Deterrent?	Go to Step 6	Go to Step 8
6	Turn the ignition to the START position. / Does the Starter Cut Relay click?	Go to Step 7	Go to Step 9
7	Turn the ignition to the START position. / Does the ST Relay click?	Go to Step 15	Go to Step 11
8	Turn the ignition to the START position. / Does the ST Relay click?	Go to Step 15	Go to Step 12
9	1. Turn OFF the ignition. 2. Disconnect the Starter Cut Relay. 3. Connect a test lamp between the crank voltage circuit of the Starter Cut Relay coil and ground. 4. Turn the ignition to the START position. / Does the test lamp illuminate?	Go to Step 10	Go to Step 32

ARM66GC000000686

Fig. 10 Starter solenoid does not click (Part 1 of 6). Denso

Step	Action	Yes	No
10	1. Connect a test lamp between the crank voltage circuit of the Starter Cut Relay coil and the control circuit of the Starter Cut Relay coil. 2. Turn the ignition to the START position. Does the test lamp illuminate?	Go to Step 25	Go to Step 22
11	1. Turn OFF the ignition. 2. Disconnect the ST Relay. 3. Connect a test lamp between the crank voltage circuit of the ST Relay coil and ground. 4. Turn the ignition to the START position. Does the test lamp illuminate?	Go to Step 13	Go to Step 14
12	1. Turn OFF the ignition. 2. Disconnect the ST Relay. 3. Connect a test lamp between the crank voltage circuit of the ST Relay coil and a good ground. 4. Turn the ignition to the START position. Does the test lamp illuminate?	Go to Step 13	Go to Step 33
13	1. Connect a test lamp between the crank voltage circuit of the ST Relay coil and the ground circuit of the ST Relay coil. 2. Turn the ignition to the START position. Does the test lamp illuminate?	Go to Step 26	Go to Step 34
14	1. Leaving the test lamp in place. 2. Turn OFF the ignition. 3. Disconnect the Starter Cut Relay. 4. Connect a 3 Amp fused jumper between the ignition voltage circuits of the Starter Cut Relay switch. 5. Turn the ignition to the START position. Does the test lamp illuminate?	Go to Step 25	Go to Step 35
15	1. Turn OFF the ignition. 2. Disconnect the ST Relay. 3. Connect a test lamp between the battery positive voltage circuit of the ST Relay switch and a good ground. Does the test lamp illuminate?	Go to Step 16	Go to Step 36
16	**Important** The engine may crank during this procedure. Connect a 30 amp fused jumper between the battery positive voltage circuit of the ST Relay switch and the starter solenoid crank voltage circuit. Does the engine crank?	Go to Step 26	Go to Step 23

ARM66GC000000687

Fig. 10 Starter solenoid does not click (Part 2 of 6). Denso

Step	Action	Yes	No
17	Does the vehicle have an automatic transmission?	Go to Step 18	Go to Step 20
18	1. Turn OFF the ignition. 2. Disconnect the Park/Neutral Position (PNP) switch. 3. Connect a 10 Amp fused jumper between the crank voltage circuit and the starter solenoid crank voltage circuit of the PNP switch. 4. Turn the ignition to the START position. Does the engine crank?	Go to Step 27	Go to Step 19
19	1. Connect a test lamp between the crank voltage circuit of the PNP switch and ground. 2. Turn the ignition to the START position. Does the test lamp illuminate?	Go to Step 37	Go to Step 24
20	1. Turn OFF the ignition. 2. Disconnect the Clutch Pedal Position (CPP) switch. 3. Connect a 10 Amp fused jumper between the crank voltage circuit and the starter solenoid crank voltage circuit of the CPP switch. 4. Turn the ignition to the START position. Does the engine crank?	Go to Step 28	Go to Step 21
21	1. Connect a test lamp between the crank voltage circuit of the CPP switch and a good ground. 2. Turn the ignition to the START position. Does the test lamp illuminate?	Go to Step 38	Go to Step 24
22	Test the control circuit of the Starter Cut Relay coil for a high resistance or an open. Did you find and correct the condition?	Go to Step 46	Go to Step 31
23	Test the starter solenoid crank voltage circuit for a high resistance or an open. Did you find and correct the condition?	Go to Step 46	Go to Step 30
24	Test the crank voltage circuit of the PNP or CPP switch a high resistance or an open. Did you find and correct the condition?	Go to Step 46	Go to Step 29

ARM66GC000000688

Fig. 10 Starter solenoid does not click (Part 3 of 6). Denso

Step	Action	Yes	No
25	Inspect for a poor connection at the Starter Cut Relay. Did you find and correct the condition?	Go to Step 46	Go to Step 39
26	Inspect for a poor connection at the ST Relay. Did you find and correct the condition?	Go to Step 46	Go to Step 40
27	Inspect for a poor connection at the PNP switch. Did you find and correct the condition?	Go to Step 46	Go to Step 41
28	Inspect for a poor connection at the CPP switch. Did you find and correct the condition?	Go to Step 46	Go to Step 42
29	Inspect for a poor connection at the ignition switch. Did you find and correct the condition?	Go to Step 46	Go to Step 43
30	Inspect for a poor connection at the starter solenoid. Did you find and correct the condition?	Go to Step 46	Go to Step 44
31	Inspect for a poor connection at the Theft Deterrent Module. Did you find and correct the condition?	Go to Step 46	Go to Step 45
32	Repair the high resistance or open in the crank voltage circuit of the Start Cut Relay between the Start Cut Relay and S111 for manual transmissions or SP108 for automatic transmissions. Did you complete the repair?	Go to Step 46	--
33	Repair the high resistance or open in the crank voltage circuit of the ST relay between the ST relay and S111 for manual transmissions or SP108 for automatic transmissions. Did you complete the repair?	Go to Step 46	--

ARM66GC000000689

Fig. 10 Starter solenoid does not click (Part 4 of 6). Denso

Step	Action	Yes	No
34	Repair the high resistance or open in the ground circuit of the ST Relay coil. Did you complete the repair?	Go to Step 46	--
35	Repair the high resistance or open in the crank voltage circuit of the ST Relay coil between the ST Relay and Starter Cut Relay. Did you complete the repair?	Go to Step 46	--
36	Repair the high resistance or open in the battery positive voltage circuit of the ST Relay switch. Did you complete the repair?	Go to Step 46	--
37	Repair the high resistance or open in the starter solenoid crank voltage circuit between the PNP switch and S111. Did you complete the repair?	Go to Step 46	--
38	Repair the high resistance or open in the starter solenoid crank voltage circuit between the CPP switch and SP108. Did you complete the repair?	Go to Step 46	--
39	Replace the Starter Cut Relay. Did you complete the replacement?	Go to Step 46	--
40	Replace the ST Relay. Did you complete the replacement?	Go to Step 46	--
41	Replace the PNP switch. Did you complete the replacement?	Go to Step 46	--
42	Replace the CPP switch. Did you complete the replacement?	Go to Step 46	--

ARM66GC000000690

Fig. 10 Starter solenoid does not click (Part 5 of 6). Denso

Step	Action	Yes	No
43	Replace the ignition switch.		
	Did you complete the replacement?	Go to Step 46	--
44	Replace the starter.		
	Did you complete the replacement?	Go to Step 46	--
45	Replace the Theft Deterrent Module.		
	Did you complete the replacement?	Go to Step 46	--
46	Operate the system for which the symptom occurred.		
	Did you correct the condition?	System OK	Go to Step 4

ARM66GC000000691

Fig. 10   Starter solenoid does not click (Part 6 of 6). Denso

Step	Action	Yes	No
1	Did you review the Diagnostic Starting Point for Engine Electrical and perform the necessary inspections?	Go to Step 2	Diagnostic Starting Point -
2	Start the engine. Does the starter operate normally?	Test for Intermittent and Poor Connections	Go to Step 3
3	Start the engine while listening to the starter motor turn. Is there a loud "whoop?" It may sound like a siren if the engine is revved while the starter is engaged, after the engine starts, but while the starter is still held in the engaged position.	Go to Step 6	Go to Step 4
4	Do you hear a "rumble", a "growl", or, in some cases, a "knock" as the starter is coasting down to a stop after starting the engine?	Go to Step 7	Go to Step 5
5	When the engine is cranked, do you hear a high-pitched whine after the engine cranks and starts normally? This is often diagnosed as a starter drive gear hang-in or a weak solenoid.	Go to Step 8	Go to Step 7
6	Inspect the flywheel ring gear for the following: • Chipped gear teeth • Missing gear teeth • Milled teeth Is the flywheel bent, or does it have damaged teeth?	Go to Step 9	Go to Step 10

ARM66GC000000693

Fig. 12   Starter motor diagnosis (Part 1 of 2). Denso

Step	Action	Yes	No
1	Did you review the following description and operations and perform the necessary inspections? • Starting System Description and Operation	Go to Step 2	Symptoms
2	Turn the ignition to the START position. Did the starter solenoid click?	Go to Step 3	Starter Solenoid Does Not Click
3	Inspect the engine and belt drive system for mechanical binding, seized engine, seized generator. Does the engine move freely?	Go to Step 4	Symptoms
4	Test the battery positive cable between the battery and the starter solenoid for high resistance. Did you find and correct the condition?	Go to Step 8	Go to Step 5
5	Test the ground circuit between the battery and the starter motor for a high resistance. Did you find and correct the condition?	Go to Step 8	Go to Step 6
6	Inspect for poor connections at the starter. Did you find and correct the condition?	Go to Step 8	Go to Step 7
7	Replace the Starter. Did you complete the replacement?	Go to Step 8	--
8	Operate the system for which the symptom occurred. Did you correct the condition?	System OK	Go to Step 3

ARM66GC000000692

Fig. 11   Starter solenoid clicks, engine does not crank. Denso

Step	Action	Yes	No
7	1. Remove the starter motor. 2. Inspect the starter motor bushings and clutch gear. Does the clutch gear have chipped or milled teeth or worn bushings?	Go to Step 10	Go to Step 9
8	Shim the starter motor away from the flywheel by adding shims between the starter motor and the engine block one at a time. Flywheel runout may make this noise appear to be intermittent. Did you complete the repair?	Go to Step 11	--
9	Replace the flywheel. Did you complete the replacement?	Go to Step 11	--
10	Replace the starter motor. Did you complete the replacement?	Go to Step 11	--
11	Operate the system in order to verify the repair. Did you correct the condition?	System OK	Go to Step 3

ARM66GC000000694

Fig. 12   Starter motor diagnosis (Part 2 of 2). Denso

STARTER SPECIFICATIONS

Starter Identification No.	Free Speed Test			Solenoid	
	Amps	Volts	RPM	Hold-In Windings, Amps	Pull-In Windings, Amps
PG-260D	60–120	10.0	2900–3400	—	—
PG-260 F1	40–90	12.0	3200–4800	6–12	30–45
PG-260 F2	35–85	12.0	2550–4150	6–12	30–45
PG-260G	60–96	11.5	2925–3375	6–12	30–45
PG-260 M	60–96	11.5	2925–3375	6–12	30–45
Bosch	—	—	—	—	—
Denso	90	11.5	—	—	—

Mitsubishi Starters

NOTE: On Air Bag Equipped Models, Refer To "Air Bag System Precautions" Located In The Front Of This Manual For System Disarming & Arming Procedures.

NOTE: Refer To "Computer Relearn Procedures" Located In The Front Of This Manual When Battery Power To The Computer Has Been Interrupted.

INDEX

PRECAUTIONS

Air Bag Systems

Refer to "Air Bag System Precautions" in the front of this manual for system disarming and arming procedures.

Battery Ground Cable

Prior to service, disconnect battery ground cable and isolate as required.

DESCRIPTION

Mitsubishi starters, **Figs. 1 and 2,** are either conventional or reduction gear types. The conventional type used on manual transmissions consists of a frame and field assembly, an armature assembly, an overrunning clutch assembly, a starter solenoid assembly, a commutator end housing, a brush holder and a shift lever. The reduction gear type starters used on automatic transmissions use all of the above components along with a reduction gear and shock absorber assembly.

TROUBLESHOOTING

Slow Or Not Cranking

1. Turn headlamps On.
2. Ensure headlamps are burning with normal intensity.
3. If headlamps are burning dim, inspect battery charge condition, then charge as required.
4. If battery is fully charged, operate starter motor.
5. Note whether headlamps go out, dim considerably, or stay bright without starter activating.
6. Refer to the following diagnostic procedures as applicable.

LAMPS GO OUT

If the lamps go out as the starter switch is closed, it indicates a poor connection between the battery and starter motor.
1. Inspect battery terminals.
2. If corroded, remove, clean and reinstall.
3. Apply corrosion inhibitor to terminals to retard formation of corrosion.

LAMPS DIM

If the lamps dim considerably as the starter switch is closed and the starter operates slowly or not at all, perform the following:
1. Inspect for a discharged battery, recharge or replace as required.
2. If the battery is fully charged, inspect the engine or the starter motor.
3. Inspect the engine for tight bearings, pistons, or other components.
4. Inspect engine timing, adjust as required.
5. Inspect for heavy engine oil. Low temperatures thicken engine oil and add considerable load to starting system.
6. Inspect starter motor for bent armature, loose pole screws, or worn bearings.
7. Inspect for thrown armature windings or commutator bars.

LAMPS STAY BRIGHT, NO CRANKING ACTION

Inspect for an open circuit in the starter, the starter switch or control circuit.
1. Place a heavy jumper lead across solenoid main terminals.
2. Starter should engage and operate.
3. If starter fails to perform as indicated, remove and inspect starter.

Starter Drive Problems

If the starter does not turn over or if it drags, inspect the starter or electrical supply system. If the starter is noisy, if it turns but does not engage the engine, or if the starter will not disengage after the engine is started, inspect for the following:
1. Worn or chipped ring gear or starter pinion.
2. Improper pinion clearance.
3. Bent starter armature shaft. Maximum radial runout is .003 inch.

DRIVE CLUTCH FAILURE

The overrunning clutch is directly activated by a fork and lever. If the overrunning clutch will not turn engine over, inspect for worn out overrunning clutch. Proper meshing of the pinion is controlled by the end clearance between the pinion gear and the starter housing or pinion stop, if used.
1. Inspect and adjust pinion clearance (if applicable).
2. If pinion clearance is not adjustable, remove starter and inspect for excessive wear of solenoid linkage, shift lever mechanism, or improper assembly of components.
3. Inspect overrunning clutch for signs of overheating.
4. If clutch shows signs of overheating (bluish color), inspect for rust or gum buildup between armature shaft and drive or for burred splines.
5. Clean or deburr splines as required.
6. Overrunning clutches are not serviceable. Replace as required.

DRIVE FAILURE

If a Bendix type drive does not engage, inspect the following:
1. Inspect for a broken drive spring, or for sheared drive spring bolts.
2. If spring is broken, or spring bolts are sheared off, remove drive and replace damaged components.
3. Inspect for screw shaft.
4. If screw shaft threads are gummed or rusty, clean with kerosene or steel wool.
5. Ensure flywheel has adequate ventilation. Inspect breather hole in bottom of

flywheel housing and clean if required.
6. If screw shaft threads are clean and rust free, look for mechanical failure within the drive itself.

Solenoid Switches

The solenoid switch on a cranking motor closes the circuit between the battery and the cranking motor and also shifts the drive pinion into mesh with the engine flywheel ring gear. This is done by means of a linkage between the solenoid switch plunger and the shift lever on the cranking motor.

There are two windings in the solenoid: a pull-in and a hold-in. Both windings are energized when the external control switch is closed. They produce a magnetic field which pulls the plunger in so that the drive pinion is shifted into mesh, and the main contacts in the solenoid switch are closed to connect the battery directly to the cranking motor. Closing the main switch contacts shorts out the pull-in winding since this winding is connected across the main contacts. The magnetism produced by the hold-in winding is sufficient to hold the plunger in, and shorting out the pull-in winding reduces battery drain. When the control switch is opened, it disconnects the hold-in winding from the battery. When the hold-in winding is disconnected from the battery, the shift lever spring withdraws the plunger from the solenoid, opening the solenoid switch contacts and at the same time withdrawing the drive pinion from mesh. Proper operation of the switch depends on maintaining a definite balance between the magnetic strength of the pull-in and hold-in windings.

This balance is determined by the size of the wire and the number of turns specified. An open circuit in the hold-in winding or attempts to crank with a discharged battery will cause the switch to chatter.

DIAGNOSIS & TESTING

Refer to **Figs. 3 through 6,** when performing diagnostic testing procedures on these starter motors.

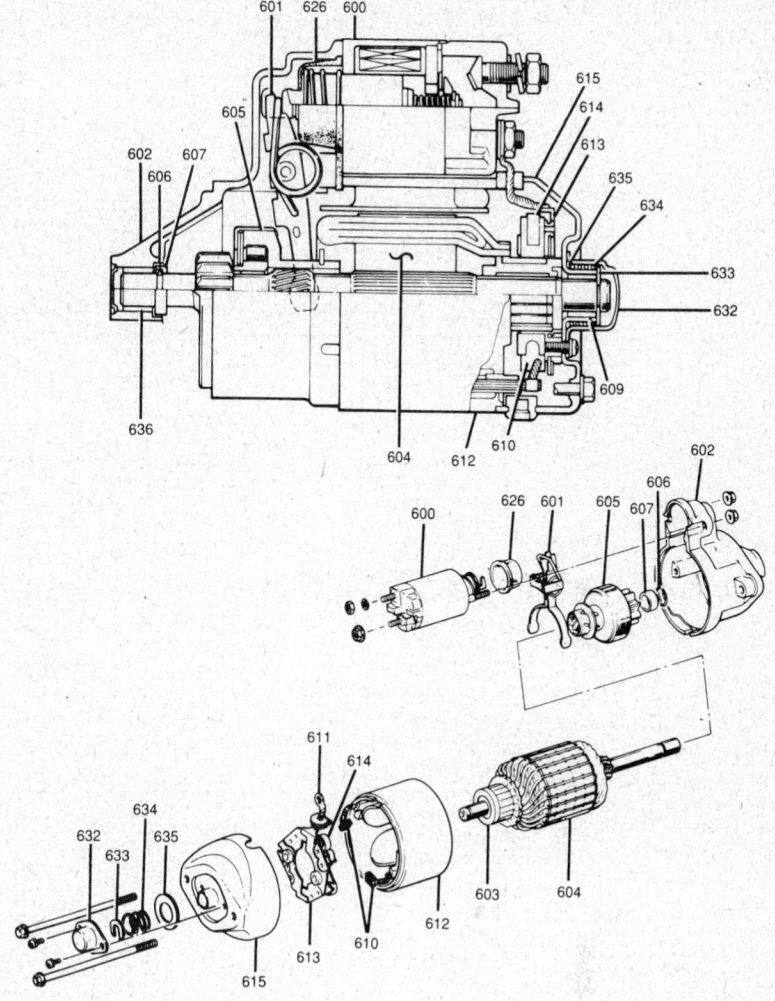

600	SOLENOID	607	ARMATURE STOP RING	615	COMMUTATOR END COVER
601	PINION DRIVE LEVER	609	COMMUTATOR END BUSHING	626	BOOT
602	DRIVE HOUSING	610	BRUSHES	632	COMMUTATOR END CAP
603	COMMUTATOR END	611	FIELD COIL LEAD WIRE	633	ARMATURE PLATE
604	ARMATURE	612	YOKE	634	ARMATURE BRAKE SPRING
605	OVERRUNNING CLUTCH ASSEMBLY	613	BRUSH HOLDER	635	END CAP GASKET
606	ARMATURE RETAINING RING	614	BRUSH SPRINGS	636	DRIVE HOUSING BUSHING

GC1129100033000X

Fig. 1 Exploded view of starter motor. Conventional w/manual transaxle

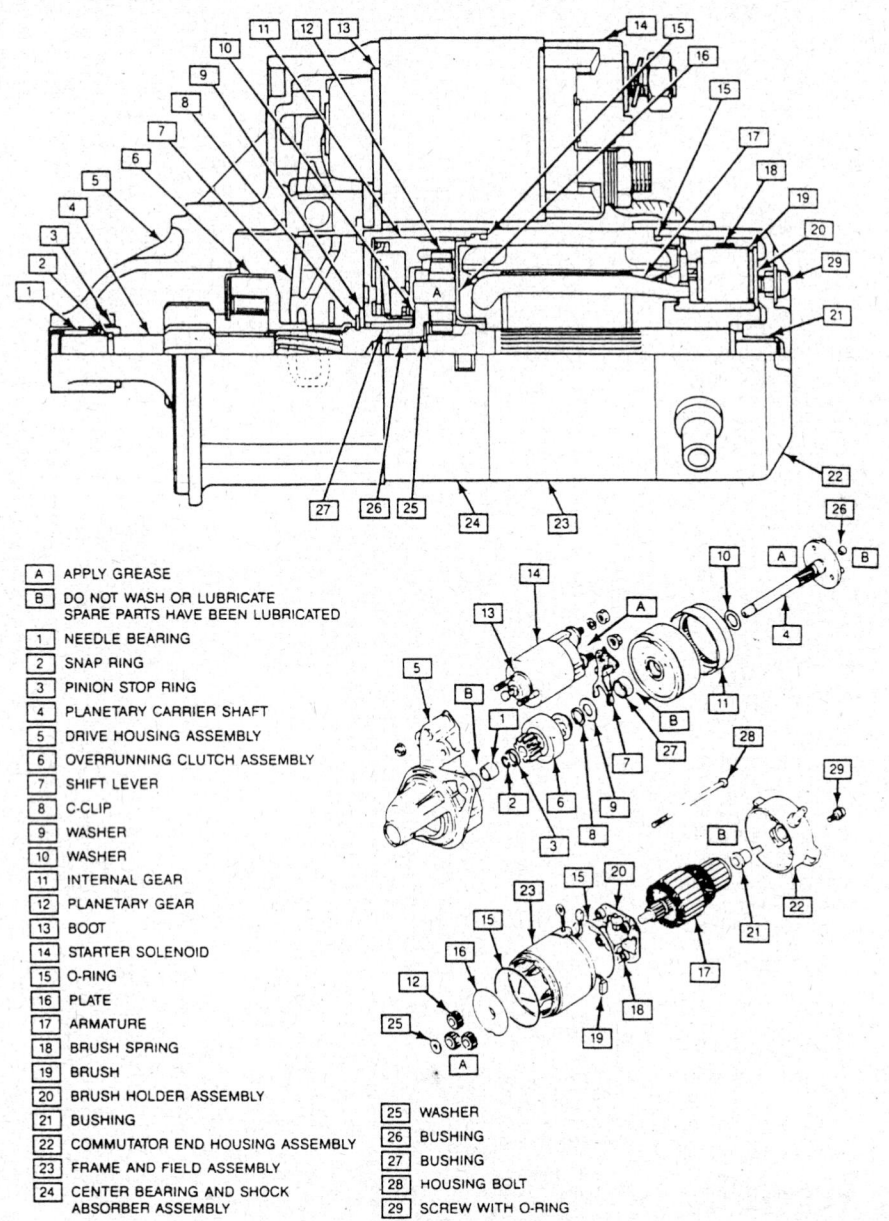

A	APPLY GREASE
B	DO NOT WASH OR LUBRICATE SPARE PARTS HAVE BEEN LUBRICATED
1	NEEDLE BEARING
2	SNAP RING
3	PINION STOP RING
4	PLANETARY CARRIER SHAFT
5	DRIVE HOUSING ASSEMBLY
6	OVERRUNNING CLUTCH ASSEMBLY
7	SHIFT LEVER
8	C-CLIP
9	WASHER
10	WASHER
11	INTERNAL GEAR
12	PLANETARY GEAR
13	BOOT
14	STARTER SOLENOID
15	O-RING
16	PLATE
17	ARMATURE
18	BRUSH SPRING
19	BRUSH
20	BRUSH HOLDER ASSEMBLY
21	BUSHING
22	COMMUTATOR END HOUSING ASSEMBLY
23	FRAME AND FIELD ASSEMBLY
24	CENTER BEARING AND SHOCK ABSORBER ASSEMBLY
25	WASHER
26	BUSHING
27	BUSHING
28	HOUSING BOLT
29	SCREW WITH O-RING

GC1129100034000X

Fig. 2 Exploded view of starter motor. Reduction w/automatic transaxle

Step	Action	Yes	No
1	Turn the ignition to the START position. Does the starter solenoid click?	Test for Intermittent and Poor Connections	Go to Step 2
2	1. Turn OFF the ignition. 2. Disconnect the starter solenoid crank voltage circuit from the starter solenoid. 3. Connect a test lamp between the starter solenoid crank voltage circuit of the starter solenoid and a good ground. 4. Turn the ignition to the START position. Does the test lamp illuminate?	Go to Step 6	Go to Step 3
3	1. Turn OFF the ignition. 2. Disconnect the Automatic Transmission Range switch. **Important:** Use a minimum of 10 gauge wire for the fused jumper. 3. Connect a 20 Amp fused jumper between the crank voltage circuit of the Automatic Transmission Range switch and the starter solenoid crank voltage circuit of the Automatic Transmission Range switch. 4. Turn the ignition to the START position. Does the test lamp illuminate?	Go to Step 7	Go to Step 4

ARM0300000000690

Fig. 3 Starter solenoid does not click (Part 1 of 3). Catera

Step	Action	Yes	No
4	1. Connect a test lamp between the crank voltage circuit of the Automatic Transmission Range switch and a good ground. 2. Turn the ignition to the START position. Does the test lamp illuminate?	Go to Step 10	Go to Step 5
5	Test the crank voltage circuit of the Automatic Transmission Range switch for a high resistance or an open. Did you find and correct the condition?	Go to Step 14	Go to Step 9
6	Inspect for poor connection at starter solenoid. Did you find and correct the condition?	Go to Step 14	Go to Step 11
7	Inspect the Automatic Transmission Range switch for proper operation. Did you find and correct the condition?	Go to Step 14	Go to Step 8
8	Inspect for poor connection at the Automatic Transmission Range switch. Did you find and correct the condition?	Go to Step 14	Go to Step 12
9	Inspect for poor connection at the ignition switch. Did you find and correct the condition?	Go to Step 14	Go to Step 13

ARM0300000000691

Fig. 3 Starter solenoid does not click (Part 2 of 3). Catera

Step	Action	Yes	No
10	Repair the high resistance or open in the starter solenoid crank voltage circuit. Did you complete the repair?	Go to Step 14	--
11	Replace the starter. Did you complete the replacement?	Go to Step 14	--
12	Replace the Automatic Transmission Range switch. Did you complete the replacement?	Go to Step 14	--
13	Replace the ignition switch. Did you complete the replacement?	Go to Step 14	--
14	Operate the system for which the symptom occurred. Did you correct the condition?	System OK	Go to Step 1

ARM0300000000692

Fig. 3 Starter solenoid does not click (Part 3 of 3). Catera

Step	Action	Yes	No
1	Turn the ignition to the START position. Did the starter solenoid click?	Go to Step 2	Diagnose Starter Solenoid Does Not Click
2	Inspect the engine and belt drive system for mechanical binding (seized engine, seized generator). Does the engine move freely?	Go to Step 3	Diagnose Engine Will Not Crank - Crankshaft Will Not Rotate
3	Test the battery positive cable between the battery and the starter solenoid for high resistance. Did you find and correct the condition?	Go to Step 7	Go to Step 4
4	Test the ground circuit between the battery and the starter motor for a high resistance. Did you find and correct the condition?	Go to Step 7	Go to Step 5
5	Inspect for poor connections at the starter. Did you find and correct the condition?	Go to Step 7	Go to Step 6
6	Replace the Starter. Did you complete the replacement?	Go to Step 7	--
7	Operate the system for which the symptom occurred. Did you correct the condition?	System OK	Go to Step 1

ARM0300000000693

Fig. 4 Starter solenoid clicks, engine does not crank. Catera

STARTER MOTORS

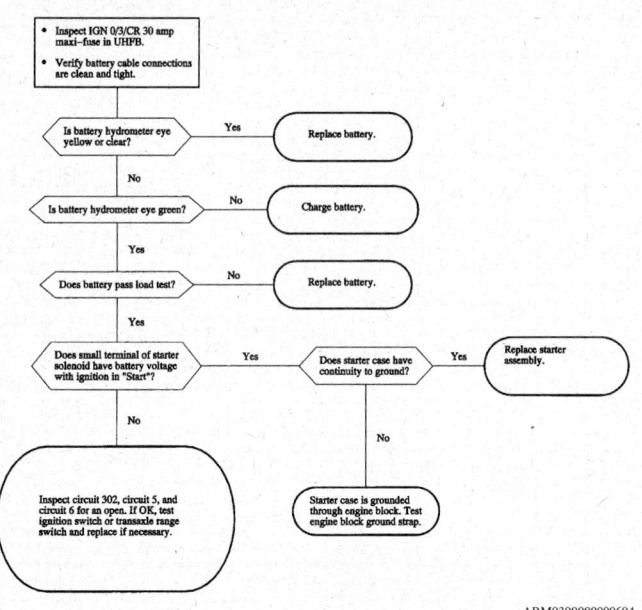

Fig. 5   No click/no crank. Saturn L-Series

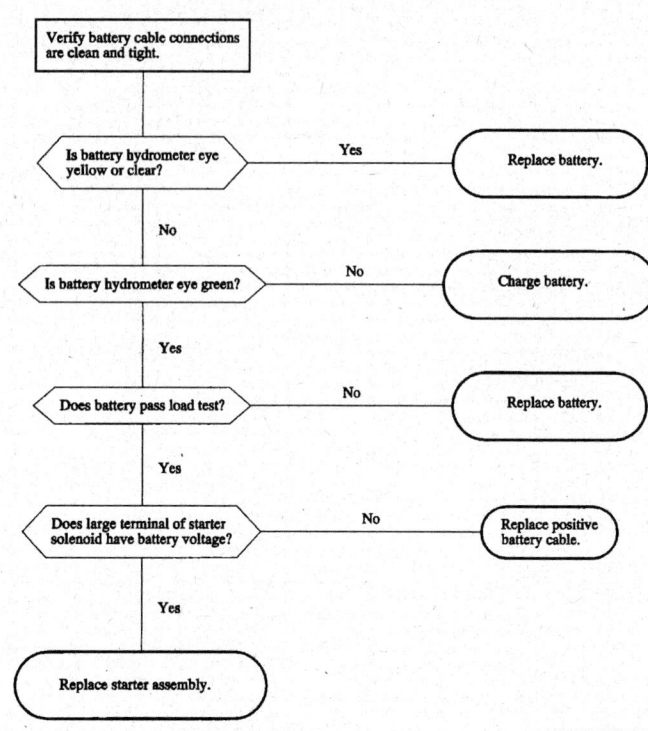

Fig. 6   Click/no crank. Saturn L-Series

STARTER SPECIFICATIONS

| Starter Identification No. | Free Speed Test | | | Solenoid | |
	Amps	Volts	RPM	Hold-In Windings, Amps	Pull-In Windings, Amps
30005925①	75	11.0	—	—	—
30005226②	60	11.0	—	—	—
30005563②	60	11.0	—	—	—
90542967	—	—	—	—	—
94857220	90	11.5	3000	—	—

① — Automatic transaxle.
② — Manual transaxle.

ALTERNATORS

TABLE OF CONTENTS

Application Chart

Model	Year	Manufacturer
BUICK		
Century	2001–05	Delphi
LaCrosse	2005	—
LeSabre	2001–05	Delphi
Park Avenue	2001–05	Delphi
Regal	2001–04	Delphi
CADILLAC		
Catera	2001	Bosch
CTS	2003–05	Denso
Deville	2001–05	Denso
Eldorado	2001–02	Delphi
Seville	2001–04	Denso
XLR	2004–05	Hitachi
STS	2005	Denso
CHEVROLET		
Aveo	2005	Delphi
Camaro	2001–02	Delphi
Cavalier	2001–02	Delphi
	2003–05	Valeo
Corvette	2001–04	Valeo
Corvette	2005	Valeo
Impala	2001–05	Bosch①
	2001–05	Delphi
Lumina	2001	Delphi
Malibu	2001–03	Delphi
	2004–05	Valeo
Metro	2001	Mitsubishi
Monte Carlo	2001–05	Delphi
Prizm	2001–02	Denso
OLDSMOBILE		
Alero	2001	Delphi
	2002–04	Valeo
Aurora	2001–03	Delphi
Intrigue	2001–02	Delphi
PONTIAC		
Bonneville	2001–05	Delphi
Firebird	2001–02	Delphi
Grand Am	2001	Delphi
	2002–05	Valeo
Grand Prix	2001–05	Delphi
GTO	2004–05	Mitsubishi
G6	2005	Valeo

Continued

Model	Year	Manufacturer
PONTIAC		
Sunfire	2001–02	Delphi
SATURN		
ION	2003–05	Valeo
L-Series	2001–05	Valeo
S-Series	2001–02	Delphi

① — Police & taxi options.

Delphi Alternators

NOTE: On Air Bag Equipped Models, Refer To "Air Bag System Precautions" Located In The Front Of This Manual For System Disarming & Arming Procedures.

NOTE: Refer To "Computer Relearn Procedure" Located In The Front Of This Manual When Battery Power To The Computer Has Been Interrupted.

INDEX

APPLICATION CHART

Model	Year	Model
BUICK		
Century	2001	CS130DP
	2002	CS130D
	2003–05	AD230
LeSabre	2001–05	AD230
Park Avenue	2001–05	①
Regal	2001	CS130DP
	2002	CS130D
	2003–04	AD230
CADILLAC		
DeVille	2001–05	SC1
Eldorado	2001–02	CS144 Gen II
Seville	2001–04	SC1
CHEVROLET		
Aveo	2005	CS-121D
Camaro	2001–02	CS130D
Cavalier	2001–02	CS130D
	2003–05	SG-10
Corvette	2001–02	A14V1
Corvette	2003–05	TG15
Impala	2001–02	CS130D
	2003–05	AD230
Lumina	2001	②
Malibu	2001–03	CS130D
	2004–05	TG-11
Monte Carlo	2001–02	CS130D
	2003–05	AD230

Continued

APPLICATION CHART—Continued

Model	Year	Model
OLDSMOBILE		
Alero	2001	CS130D
Aurora	2001–03	AD 237
Intrigue	2001–02	AD 237
PONTIAC		
Bonneville	2001–05	①
Firebird	2001–02	CS130D
Grand Am	2001–02	CS130D
Grand Prix	2001	CS130DP
	2002–05	CS130D
GTO	2004–05	—
Sunfire	2001–02	CS130D
SATURN		
S-Series	20001–02	CS130

① — VIN K engine AD230; VIN 1 engine AD237.
② — Standard application CS130D; optional high output application CS144.

PRECAUTIONS

Air Bag Systems

Refer to "Air Bag System Precautions" in the front of this manual for system disarming and arming procedures.

Battery Ground Cable

Prior to service, disconnect battery ground cable and isolate as required.

Charging System

1. Ensure battery polarity is proper when servicing units. Reversed battery polarity will damage rectifiers and regulators.
2. If booster battery is used for starting, use proper polarity in hookup.
3. When a fast charger is used to charge a vehicle battery, vehicle battery cables should be disconnected unless fast charger is equipped with a special Alternator Protector, in which case vehicle battery cables need not be disconnected. **Fast chargers should never be used to start a vehicle as rectifier damage will result.**
4. Unless this system includes a load relay or field relay, grounding alternator output terminal will damage alternator and/or circuits. This is true even when system is not in operation since no circuit breaker is used and battery is applied to alternator output terminal at all times. Field or load relay acts as a circuit breaker in that it is controlled by ignition switch.
5. Before making any on vehicle tests of alternator or regulator, battery should be inspected and circuit inspected for faulty wiring or insulation. loose or corroded connections and poor ground circuits.
6. Inspect alternator belt tension and condition.

7. Ignition should be Off and battery ground cable disconnected before making any test connections to prevent system damage.
8. Do not reverse connections to alternator.
9. Do not short across or ground any of terminals in charging system.
10. Never disconnect output terminal while alternator is running.
11. Vehicle battery must be fully charged when testing charging system.

GENERAL INFORMATION

Alternators are composed of the same functional components as the conventional DC alternator but they operate differently. The field is called a rotor and is the turning portion of the unit. The generating part, called a stator, is the stationary member, comparable to the armature in a DC alternator. The regulator, similar to those used in a DC system, regulates the alternator-rectifier system output.

The power source of the system is the alternator. Current is transmitted from the field terminal of the regulator through a slip ring to the field coil and back to ground through another slip ring. The strength of the field regulates the output of the alternating current. This alternating current is then transmitted from the alternator to the rectifier where it is converted to direct current.

These alternators employ a three-phase stator winding in which the phase windings are electrically 120° apart. The rotor consists of a field coil encased between interleaved sections producing. When the rotor is energized, a magnetic field with alternate north and south poles is created. By rotating the rotor inside the stator the alternating current is induced in the stator windings. This alternating current is rectified (changed to DC) by silicon diodes and brought out to the output terminal of the alternator.

Diode Rectifiers

Six silicon diode rectifiers are used and act as electrical one-way valves. Three of the diodes have ground polarity and are pressed or screwed into a heat sink which is grounded. The other three diodes (ungrounded) are pressed or screwed into and insulated from the end head; these diodes are connected to the alternator output terminal.

Since the diodes have a high resistance to the flow of current in one direction and a low resistance in the opposite direction, they may be connected in a manner which allows current to flow from the alternator to the battery in the low resistance direction. The high resistance in the opposite direction prevents the flow of current from the battery to the alternator. Because of this feature no circuit breaker is required between the alternator and battery.

DESCRIPTION

CS Alternators

The CS alternator is available in two sizes: CS130 and CS144, **Fig. 1.** The numerals denote the outer diameter of the stator laminations in millimeters and the letters CS stand for charging system.

These alternators use a conventional fan mounted next to the pulley to pull air through the assembly for cooling. An internal fan mounted on the rotor pulls air through the slip ring end frame to cool the rectifier, bridge and regulator. Air is expelled through openings in the frame. No periodic maintenance is required.

LR Alternators

The LR series alternator is available in only one size with an output of 140 amps. The LR series alternator has a liquid cooled end frame. Engine coolant is passed through a tube molded into the end frame

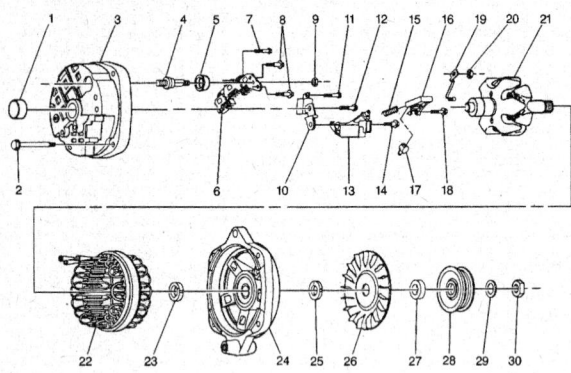

(1) Generator Rotor Slip Ring End Frame Bearing
(2) Generator Through Bolt
(3) Generator Slip Ring End Frame
(4) Generator Battery Terminal Stud
(5) Generator Battery Terminal Sleeve
(6) Generator Rectifier Bridge
(7) Generator Rectifier Bridge Bolt
(8) Generator Rectifier Bridge Bolt (Insulated)
(9) Generator Battery Terminal Nut
(10) Generator Capacitor
(11) Generator Rectifier Bridge Bolt
(12) Generator Capacitor/Rectifier Bolt (Insulated)
(13) Generator Voltage Regulator
(14) Generator Voltage Regulator Attaching Bolt (Insulated)
(15) Generator Brush Spring

(16) Generator Brush Holder
(17) Dust Shield
(18) Generator Brush Holder Bolt
(19) Generator Voltage Regulator Connector Strap
(20) Generator Stator Lead Attaching Nut
(21) Generator Rotor
(22) Generator Stator
(23) Generator Rotor Drive End Bearing Inside Collar
(24) Generator Rotor Drive End Bearing Frame
(25) Generator Rotor Drive End Bearing Outside Collar
(26) Generator Fan
(27) Generator Rotor Drive End Fan Collar
(28) Generator Pulley
(29) Generator Rotor Shaft Drive End Washer
(30) Generator Rotor Shaft Drive End Nut

GC1129700090000X

Fig. 1 Exploded view of CS type alternator

Step	Action	Value (s)	Yes	No
1	Did you perform the Diagnostic System Check for Engine Electrical?	--	Go to Step 2	Go to Diagnostic System Check -
2	Start the engine, observe the charge indicator on the instrument cluster (IPC) or message in the driver information center (DIC). Does the charge indicator illuminate or the DIC display a charging system message?	--	Go to Step 3	Test for Intermittent and Poor Connections
3	**Important** The green POWER lamp of the tester should remain illuminated while the tester is being used. 1. Turn OFF the ignition. 2. Connect the red lead of the J 41450-B Generator Electronic Tester to the generator output terminal. 3. Connect the black lead of the J 41450-B Generator Electronic Tester to the metal generator housing. Does the green POWER lamp on the tester illuminate?	--	Go to Step 6	Go to Step 4
4	Measure the voltage from the output terminal of the generator to the generator metal housing. Does the voltage measure equal to the specified value?	B +	Go to Step 14	Go to Step 5

ARM66GC000000730

Fig. 2 Charging system test (Part 1 of 4). AD & CS alternators

next to the electronic components of the alternator. This cooling supplements the air cooling action of the internal fans and helps prevent overheating of the alternator during periods of high electrical demands.

AD Alternators

The AD alternators are similar to CS type alternators except for their dual cooling fans. The "AD" stands for Air-Cooled Dual internal fan. The "2" is an electric design designator. The "30" or "37" denotes the outside diameter of the stator laminations in millimeters.

SYSTEM OPERATION

AD & CS Alternators

The AD and CS alternators may be used with only two connections. The battery positive BAT terminal must be connected to a battery during operation. The second required connection is through the Powertrain Control Module (PCM) to the indicator lamp. Three other regulator terminals are available for optional use in vehicle systems. The P terminal is connected to the stator and may be connected to a tachometer or other device. The F terminal is connected internally to field positive and may be used as a fault indicator. The S terminal may be connected externally to a voltage, such as battery voltage, to sense voltage to be controlled.

The regulator voltage setting varies with temperature, and limits system voltage by controlling rotor field current. Unlike others regulators, this regulator switches field current on and off at a fixed frequency of about 400 cycles per second. By varying on–off time, proper average field current is obtained to provide proper system voltage. At high speeds, the on time may be 10% and off time 90%. At low speeds with high electrical loads, on–off time may be 90% and 10% respectively.

LR Alternators

The LR series alternator provides the voltage to operate the vehicle's electrical system and to charge the battery through circuit No. 1 (red). When the ignition is turned On, voltage is supplied to the alternator L terminal by the Powertrain Control Module (PCM), turning on the voltage regulator. The voltage regulator controls current to the rotor, which controls alternator output voltage. When the engine starts, the regulator senses alternator rotation by detecting AC voltage at the stator through an internal wire. Once the engine is running, the regulator varies the field current by controlling the pulse width. The alternator F terminal is connected internally to the voltage regulator and externally to the PCM. The PCM monitors the field voltage on the alternator F terminal.

The PCM turns on the CHARGE indicator lamp by sending a message to the instrument cluster whenever a under-voltage, over-voltage or a stopped alternator is detected.

DIAGNOSIS & TESTING

AD & CS Alternators

IN-VEHICLE TEST

Refer to **Fig. 2,** for in-vehicle charging system test on these alternators.

BENCH TESTING

1. Make connections as illustrated, **Fig. 3,** but leave carbon pile disconnected. Ground polarity of alternator and battery must be same. Battery must be fully charged. Use a 30-500 ohm resistor between battery and L terminal.
2. Slowly increase alternator speed and observe voltage.
3. If voltage is uncontrolled and increases above 16 volts, rotor field is shorted, regulator is faulty or both. A shorted rotor field can cause regulator to become faulty. **Battery must be fully charged when making this test.**
4. If voltage is below 16 volts, increase speed and adjust carbon pile obtain maximum amperage output, maintain voltage above 13 volts.
5. If output is within 15 amps of rated output, alternator is satisfactory.
6. If output is not within 15 amps of rated output, alternator is faulty and requires repair.

LR Alternators

Refer to **Fig. 4,** for alternator and charging system diagnosis. The LR series alternator is serviced by replacement only.

Step		Value	Yes	No
5	Measure the voltage from the output terminal of the generator to the battery negative terminal. Does the voltage measure equal to the specified value?	B +	Go to Step 12	Go to Step 11
6	**Caution** Make sure that the load is completely turned off before connecting or disconnecting a carbon pile load tester to the battery. Otherwise, sparking could ignite battery gasses which are extremely flammable and may explode violently. 1. Connect a carbon pile tester to the vehicle. **Important** Be sure all of generator output circuit wires pass through the inductive probe. 2. Connect an inductive ammeter to the output circuit of the generator. 3. Disconnect the generator harness connector. 4. Locate the matching harness connector on the J 41450-B and connect it to the generator. Does the red DIAGNOSTIC lamp on the tester illuminate?	--	Go to Step 7	Go to Step 13
7	1. Start the engine and allow it to idle for 30 seconds. 2. Increase the engine speed to 2500 RPM. Does the red DIAGNOSTIC lamp on the tester illuminate?	--	Go to Step 15	Go to Step 8

ARM66GC000000731

Fig. 2 Charging system test (Part 2 of 4). AD & CS alternators

Step		Value	Yes	No
8	1. Maintain the engine speed at 2500 RPM. **Important** If the generator is not capable of producing the Load Test amps, operate the generator at it's maximum possible output. 2. Turn ON the load of the carbon pile tester and increase the load until the generator output is greater than or equal to the load test value given in Generator Usage . Does the red DIAGNOSTIC lamp on the tester illuminate?	--	Go to Step 15	Go to Step 9
9	1. Maintain the engine speed at 2500 RPM and continue to operate the generator at the load test value. 2. Measure the voltage drop from the output terminal of the generator to the positive terminal on the battery. Does the voltage measure greater than the specified value?	0.5 V	Go to Step 11	Go to Step 10
10	1. Maintain the engine speed at 2500 RPM and continue to operate the generator at the load test value. 2. Measure the voltage drop from the battery negative terminal to the metal housing of the generator. Does the voltage measure greater than the specified value?	0.5 V	Go to Step 12	Go to Step 16
11	Repair the high resistance or an open in the output circuit of the generator. Did you complete the repair?	--	Go to Step 16	--

ARM66GC000000732

Fig. 2 Charging system test (Part 3 of 4). AD & CS alternators

Step		Value	Yes	No
12	Repair the high resistance or open in the ground circuit of the generator. Did you complete the repair?	--	Go to Step 16	--
13	1. Disconnect the J 41450-B tester harness connector from the generator, but leave the alligator clips connected so that the green POWER lamp remains illuminated. 2. Connect a jumper lead, with an in-line 100-ohm resistor between the J 41450-B tester harness connector terminal B and a good ground. Does the red DIAGNOSTIC lamp illuminate?	--	Go to Step 15	Go to Step 14
14	There is a problem with the J 41450-B . Refer to the manufacturers instructions, how to test the J 41450-B for proper operation. Has the J 41450-B tester been replaced?	--	Go to Step 3	--
15	Replace the generator. Did you complete the replacement?	--	Go to Step 16	--
16	Operate the vehicle in order to verify the repair. Did you correct the condition?	--	System OK	Go to Step 2

ARM66GC000000733

Fig. 2 Charging system test (Part 4 of 4). AD & CS alternators

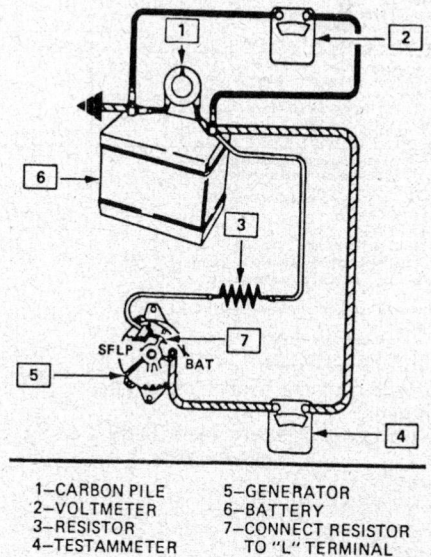

1—CARBON PILE   5—GENERATOR
2—VOLTMETER   6—BATTERY
3—RESISTOR   7—CONNECT RESISTOR
4—TESTAMMETER   TO "L" TERMINAL

GC1129100038000X

Fig. 3 Alternator bench inspection. AD & CS alternators

DEFINITION: Generator on-vehicle test which will test the generator independently from the vehicle wiring.

Step	Action	Value(s)	Yes	No
2	1. Connect the red alligator clip of a *J 41450-B* CS Generator Electronic Tester to the generator output terminal. (The output wire is attached to the generator with a ring terminal and nut.) 2. Connect the black alligator clip of the *J 41450-B* to the metal generator housing. The green POWER lamp of the tester will light and remain lighted while the tester is being used. Does the green POWER lamp on the tester light?	—	Go to *Step 9*	Go to *Step 3*
3	1. Recheck the alligator clip connections that were made in Step 2. 2. Correct the connections if they were reversed. Does the green POWER lamp on the tester light after the correct connections are verified?	—	Go to *Step 9*	Go to *Step 4*
4	Connect a *J 39200* digital multimeter (DMM) from the generator output terminal to the generator metal housing. Is the measured voltage within the specified range?	Above 12 V	Go to *Step 18*	Go to *Step 5*
5	Use a DMM to check the voltage between the battery terminals. Is the measured voltage within the specified range?	Above 12 V	Go to *Step 6*	Go to *Step 8*

GC1129800091010X

Fig. 4   Charging system test (Part 1 of 5). LR series alternator

Step	Action	Value(s)	Yes	No
11	*Caution: Make sure that the load is completely turned off before connecting or disconnecting a carbon pile load tester to the battery. Otherwise, sparking could ignite battery gasses which are extremely flammable and may explode violently.* 1. Prior to connecting a carbon pile load tester, make sure that the load dial of the carbon pile tester is turned completely to the OFF position. 2. Connect the cable leads of the carbon pile tester to the battery of the vehicle. 3. Connect an inductive ammeter to the output lead(s) of the generator. Make sure that all output leads pass through the ammeter inductive clip. The carbon pile tester may have its own inductive ammeter, or use a *J 35590* Current Clamp. 4. Start the engine and allow it to idle briefly. Does the red DIAGNOSTIC lamp on the *J 41450-B* light?	—	Go to *Step 19*	Go to *Step 12*
12	Increase the engine speed to 2500 RPM. Does the red DIAGNOSTIC lamp on the *J 41450-B* light?	—	Go to *Step 19*	Go to *Step 13*
13	1. Maintain the engine speed at 2500 RPM. 2. Turn on the load of the carbon pile tester, and increase the load until the generator output is equal to the load test value given in Generator Usage. As the load is increased, is the generator capable of producing the amount of load test current specified in Generator Usage?	—	Go to *Step 14*	Go to *Step 19*
14	Maintain the engine speed at 2500 RPM and continue to operate the generator at the load test value. Is the red DIAGNOSTIC lamp on the *J 41450-B* lit?	—	Go to *Step 19*	Go to *Step 15*
15	1. Maintain the engine speed at 2500 RPM and continue to operate the generator at the load test value. 2. Connect a DMM from the generator output terminal to the battery positive (+) terminal. Is the measured voltage within the specified range?	Above 0.5 V	Go to *Step 22*	Go to *Step 16*
16	1. Maintain the engine speed at 2500 RPM and continue to operate the generator at the load test value. 2. Connect a DMM from the generator metal housing to the battery negative (–) terminal. Is the measured voltage within the specified range?	Above 0.5 V	Go to *Step 23*	Go to *Step 17*
17	*Caution: Make sure that the load is completely turned off before connecting or disconnecting a carbon pile load tester to the battery. Otherwise, sparking could ignite battery gasses which are extremely flammable and may explode violently.* 1. Disconnect the DMM. 2. Turn OFF the load in the carbon pile tester. 3. Turn the ignition switch to LOCK to stop the engine. 4. Disconnect the carbon pile tester cables from the battery. 5. Disconnect the *J 41450-B* 4-way connector from the generator. 6. Inspect the generator 4-way connector on the vehicle. Does the vehicle have a wire in the L terminal cavity (or B terminal for CS 130D, LR, and AD generators) of the generator 4-way connector?	—	Go to *Step 26*	Go to *Step 24*

GC1129800091030X

Fig. 4   Charging system test (Part 3 of 5). LR series alternator

Step	Action	Value(s)	Yes	No
6	1. Inspect the circuit between the generator output terminal and the battery positive terminal for a loose connection or open circuit condition. Be sure to check for an open fusible link and/or any blown in-line fuses that may be used on the vehicle. 2. If a loose connection or open circuit was located, repair it. If an open fusible link or blown fuse was found, be sure to check the system for possible causes of a circuit overload, such as a direct B+ short to ground. Is the circuit okay between the generator output terminal and the battery positive terminal?	—	Go to *Step 7*	
7	Repair the loose connection or open circuit between the battery negative terminal and the generator housing. Is the repair complete?	—	Go to *Step 26*	
8	1. Inspect the battery. 2. Charge or replace the battery if necessary. Is the battery OK?	—	Go to *Step 26*	
9	1. Leave the *J 41450-B* alligator clips attached as in Step 2, and disconnect the vehicle 4-way generator connector. 2. Locate the matching 4-way connector of the *J 41450-B* and connect it to the generator. Does the red DIAGNOSTIC lamp on the tester light?	—	Go to *Step 11*	Go to *Step 10*
10	Perform the following test of the DIAGNOSTIC lamp of the *J 41450-B*: 1. Disconnect the *J 41450-B* 4-way connector from the generator, but leave the J41450-B alligator clips connected as in step 2. 2. Prepare a jumper wire with an in-line 100 ohm resistor. The watt rating of the resistor is not important. (An inexpensive 100Ω resistor can be purchased at an electronics supply store.) 3. At one end of the prepared jumper wire, attach a Metri-Pack 150 male terminal probe adapter from a *J 35616-A* Connector Test Adapter Kit. 4. Connect the prepared jumper wire to the *J 41450-B* L terminal (which is called the B terminal on CS 130D, LR, and AD generators). The tester connector terminals are the same as the generator connector terminals, so terminal identification on the *J 41450-B* can be accomplished by referring to Starting and Charging Connector End Views. 5. Connect the other end of the jumper to the battery negative terminal. Does the red DIAGNOSTIC lamp on the tester light when the jumper is connected?	—	Go to *Step 19*	Go to *Step 18*

GC1129800091020X

Fig. 4   Charging system test (Part 2 of 5). LR series alternator

Step	Action	Value(s)	Yes	No
18	There is an internal problem in the *J 41450-B*. Replace the *J 41450-B*. Has the *J 41450-B* been replaced?	—	Go to *Step 26*	—
19	*Important:* Before generator repair or replacement, the L terminal circuit (if applicable) must be tested for resistance in order to avoid a repeat failure. Disconnect and examine the generator 4-way connector. Is there a wire in the L cavity (or B cavity for CS 130D, LR, and AD generators) of the generator connector?	—	Go to *Step 20*	Go to *Step 24*
20	1. Be sure the 4-way generator connector is disconnected. 2. Turn the ignition key to the RUN position. 3. Connect a fused jumper wire *J 36169-A* (with a 5 amp fuse) from ground to the vehicle 4-way generator connector terminal L (or B terminal for CS 130D, LR, and AD generators). To connect the jumper to the generator; use a Metri-Pack 150 connector test adapter from *J 35616-A*. Refer to Starting and Charging Connector End Views. Does the fuse blow?	—	Go to *Step 21*	Go to *Step 25*
21	There is a short to B+ voltage when the ignition key is in the RUN position. The short may be a result of a miswired condition. The L terminal circuit must be a resistance circuit either through a charge indicator or the PCM. If direct battery voltage is applied to the generator at the L terminal, the regulator will eventually be destroyed, causing a repeat failure. Repair the short to B+ voltage in the L terminal circuit (or B terminal circuit for CS 130D, LR, and AD generators). Is the short circuit repaired?	—	Go to *Step 25*	—
22	1. Turn off the engine. 2. Disconnect the battery negative terminal. 3. Inspect the circuit between the battery positive terminal and the generator output terminal for a high-resistance connection. Disassemble and clean all connections in this circuit. 4. Assemble the connections 5. Connect the battery negative terminal. Is the repair complete?	—	Go to *Step 26*	—
23	1. Turn off the engine. 2. Inspect the ground circuit for high resistance from the battery negative terminal to the generator housing. Disassemble and clean all connections. 3. Assemble the connections Is the repair complete?	—	Go to *Step 26*	—

GC1129800091040X

Fig. 4   Charging system test (Part 4 of 5). LR series alternator

Step	Action	Value(s)	Yes	No
24	The tester turns the generator on in a different way than the vehicle does, so an additional test is necessary. This Step is applicable only for vehicles that do not use an L terminal connection (or B terminal for CS 130D, LR, and AD generators). 1. Remove the 4-way connector from the generator. 2. Measure the generator internal resistance between the L and I/F terminals (B and C terminals for CS 130D, LR, and AD generators). Use Metri-Pack 150 terminal adapters from a *J 35616-A* Connector Test Adapter Kit. The L and I/F terminals are the two middle terminals on the generator. Is the measured resistance within the specified range?	Below 500 Ω	Go to *Step 26*	Go to *Step 25*
25	Repair or replace the generator. Is the repair complete?	—	Go to *Step 26*	—
26	1. Make sure any components removed during diagnosis are installed in place and that all connectors are connected. 2. Repeat the system check. Is the system check complete?	—	System OK	—

GC1129800091050X

Fig. 4   Charging system test (Part 5 of 5). LR series alternator

ALTERNATOR SPECIFICATIONS

Alternator Model	Rated Hot Output Amps
AD230	105
AD237	125
CS121D	—
CS130	105
CS130D	105
CS130 DIF	105
CS130DP	107
CS144①	124
CS144②	150
LR630	150

① — Except service part identification code KG9.
② — Service part identification code KG9.

Bosch Alternators

NOTE: On Air Bag Equipped Models, Refer To "Air Bag System Precautions" Located In The Front Of This Manual For System Disarming & Arming Procedures.

NOTE: Refer To "Computer Relearn Procedure" Located In The Front Of This Manual When Battery Power To The Computer Has Been Interrupted.

NOTE: "Electrical Symbol & Wire Color Code Identification" Located In The Front Of This Manual May Be Used As An Aid When Using Wiring Circuits Found In This Section.

INDEX

APPLICATION CHART

Model	Year	Rated Hot Output Amps
Catera	2001	120
Impala	2001–05	125

GENERAL INFORMATION

Refer to "Delphi Alternators" for general information.

PRECAUTIONS

Air Bag Systems

Refer to "Air Bag System Precautions" in the front of this manual for system disarming and arming procedures.

Battery Ground Cable

Prior to service, disconnect battery ground cable and isolate as required.

Charging System

1. Ensure battery polarity is proper when servicing units. Reversed battery polarity will damage rectifiers and regulators.
2. If booster battery is used for starting, use proper polarity in hookup.
3. When a fast charger is used to charge a vehicle battery, vehicle battery cables should be disconnected unless fast charger is equipped with a special Alternator Protector, in which case vehicle battery cables need not be disconnected. **Fast chargers should never be used to start a vehicle as rectifier damage will result.**
4. Unless system includes a load relay or field relay, grounding alternator output terminal will damage alternator and/or circuits. This is true even when system is not in operation since no circuit breaker is used and battery is applied to alternator output terminal at all times. Field or load relay acts as a circuit breaker in that it is controlled by ignition switch.
5. Before making any on vehicle tests of alternator or regulator, battery should be inspected and circuit inspected for faulty wiring or insulation. loose or corroded connections and poor ground circuits.
6. Inspect alternator belt tension and condition.
7. Ignition should be Off and battery ground cable disconnected before making any test connections to prevent damage to system.
8. Do not reverse connections to alternator.
9. Do not short across or ground any of terminals in charging system.
10. Never disconnect output terminal while alternator is running.
11. Vehicle battery must be fully charged when testing charging system.

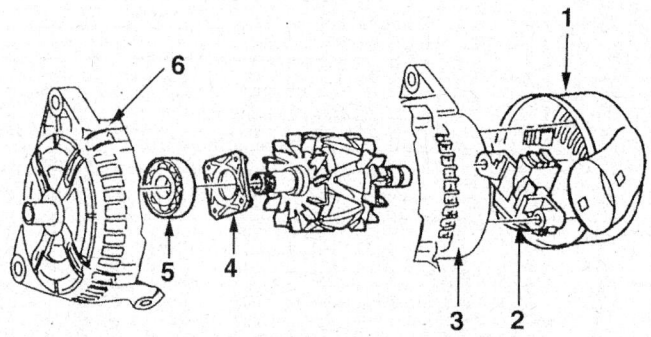

1. REAR CAP
2. REGULATOR
3. REAR COVER
4. FRONT BEARING RETAINER
5. FRONT BEARING
6. FRONT COVER
7. ARMATURE

GC1129800080000X

Fig. 1   Exploded view of Bosch alternator

DESCRIPTION

Catera

The Bosch alternator is a 120 amp output alternator. The main components are the rotor, field coil, regulator and rectifier bridge, **Fig. 1**. The alternator is water cooled. The coolant hose runs directly from the radiator to the alternator housing. No periodic maintenance is required.

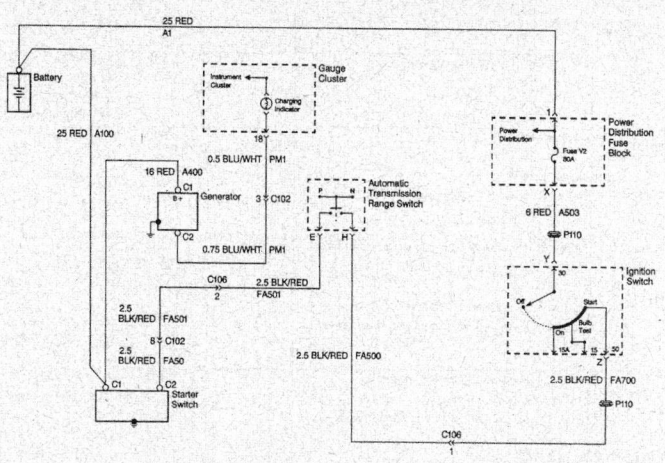

Fig. 2   Charging system wiring diagram. Catera

Step	Action	Value(s)	Yes	No
5	1. Reconnect the generator connector. 2. Turn OFF all the accessories. 3. Run the engine at fast idle. 4. Use the DMM to measure the voltage between the positive and the negative terminals of the battery. Is the measured voltage within the specified value?	12.5–14.5V	Go to Step 7	Go to Step 6
6	Repair or replace the generator. Is the repair or replacement complete?	—	Go to Step 8	—
7	1. Load test the generator. 2. Replace the battery if the generator passed the load test. Is the replacement complete?	—	Go to Step 8	—
8	1. Connect all of the connectors and components that were disconnected. 2. Verify that the generator operates properly. Does the generator operate properly?	—	System OK	Go to Step 1

GC1129800082020X

Fig. 3   Battery is undercharged or overcharged (Part 2 of 2). Catera

Impala

The Bosch alternator is a 125 amp output alternator. The main components are the rotor, field coil, rectifier bridge and a digital regulator.

System Operation

A regulator supplies current to the field coil of the rotor. When the field coil is supplied with voltage, a magnetic field is created. As the rotor turns, this magnetic field creates AC voltage and current in the stator windings. The AC voltage and current is converted to DC by a rectifier bridge which is available to the vehicle's electrical system.

DIAGNOSIS & TESTING

Catera

Refer to wiring diagram, **Fig. 2,** and diagnosis charts, **Figs. 3 through 5,** for charging system diagnosis.

Impala

Refer to wiring diagrams, **Fig. 6,** and to diagnosis tests, **Figs. 7 and 8,** for charging system diagnosis.

Step	Action	Value(s)	Yes	No
1.	1. Disconnect the generator connector C2. 2. Turn the ignition switch to the ON position. 3. Use the DMM to measure the voltage between the generator connector C2 and a known good ground. Is the measured voltage within the specified value?	B+	Go to Step 3	Go to Step 2
2	1. Locate an open or a high resistance in circuit PM1. 2. Repair the open or the high resistance in circuit PM1. Is the repair complete?		Go to Step 8	
3	Disconnect generator connector C1. 2. Use the DMM to measure the voltage between the generator connector C1 and a known good ground. Is the measured voltage within the specified value?	B+	Go to Step 5	Go to Step 4
4	1. Locate an open or a high resistance in circuits A100 and/or A400. 2. Repair the open or the high resistance in circuits A100 and/or A400. Is the repair complete?		Go to Step 5	

GC1129800082010X

Fig. 3   Battery is undercharged or overcharged (Part 1 of 2). Catera

Step	Action	Value(s)	Yes	No
1	1. Disconnect generator connector C2. 2. Turn the ignition switch to the ON position. Is the charging indicator lamp illuminated?	—	Go to Step 3	Go to Step 2
2	Repair or replace the generator. Is the repair or replacement complete?	—	Go to Step 6	
3	Disconnect connector C102. Is the charging indicator lamp illuminated?	—	Go to Step 5	Go to Step 4
4	1. Locate the short to ground in circuit PM1 between the generator connector C2 and connector C102 terminal 3. 2. Repair the short to ground in circuit PM1. Is the repair complete?		Go to Step 6	
5	1. Locate a short to ground in circuit PM1 between the gauge cluster connector terminal 18 and connector C102 terminal 3. 2. Repair the short to ground in circuit PM1 between the gauge cluster connector terminal 18 and connector C102 terminal 3. 3. Replace the gauge cluster if circuit PM1 is OK. Is the repair or replacement complete?		Go to Step 6	
6	1. Connect all connectors and components that were disconnected. 2. Verify that the charging indicator lamp operates properly. Does the charging indicator lamp operate properly?	—	System OK	Go to Step 1

GC1129800083000X

Fig. 4   Charge indicator always on. Catera

Step	Action	Value(s)	Yes	No
1	1. Disconnect generator connector C2. 2. Attach a fused jumper from the generator connector C2 to ground. 3. Turn the ignition switch to the ON position. Is the charging indicator lamp illuminated?	—	Go to Step 2	Go to Step 3
2	Repair or replace the generator. Is the repair or replacement complete?	—	Go to Step 6	
3	1. Disconnect connector C102. 2. Attach a fused jumper between terminal 3 of connector C102 and a known good ground. Is the charging indicator lamp illuminated?	—	Go to Step 4	Go to Step 6
4	1. Locate an open or a high resistance in circuit PM1 between terminal 3 of connector C102 and the generator connector C2. 2. Repair the open or the high resistance in circuit PM1 between terminal 3 of connector C102 and the generator connector C2. Is the repair complete?	—	Go to Step 6	
5	1. Locate an open or a high resistance in circuit PM1 between terminal 3 of connector C102 and terminal 18 of the gauge cluster connector. 2. Repair the open or the high resistance in circuit PM1 between terminal 3 of connector C102 and terminal 18 of the gauge cluster connector. 3. Replace the gauge cluster if circuit PM1 is OK. Is the repair or replacement complete?	—	Go to Step 6	
6	1. Connect all of the connectors and components that were disconnected. 2. Verify that the charging indicator operates properly. Does the charging indicator lamp operate properly?	—	System OK	Go to Step 1

GC1129800084000X

Fig. 5   Charge indicator inoperative. Catera

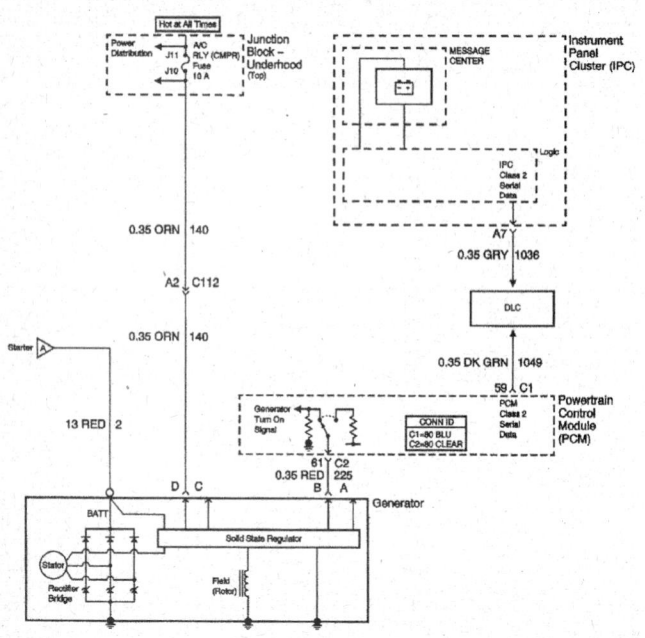

Fig. 6 Charging system wiring diagram. Impala

Step	Action	Value(s)	Yes	No
6	**Caution** Make sure that the load is completely turned off before connecting or disconnecting a carbon pile load tester to the battery. Otherwise, sparking could ignite battery gasses which are extremely flammable and may explode violently. 1 Connect a carbon pile tester to the vehicle. 2 Connect an inductive ammeter to the output circuit of the generator. 3 Start the engine and allow it to idle briefly. Does the red DIAGNOSTIC lamp on the tester light?		Go to Step 15	Go to Step 7
7	Increase the engine speed to 2500 RPM. Does the red DIAGNOSTIC lamp on the tester light?		Go to Step 15	Go to Step 8
8	1 Maintain the engine speed at 2500 RPM. 2 Turn on the load of the carbon pile tester and increase the load until the generator output is equal to the load test value. Is the generator output greater than the load test value?		Go to Step 9	Go to Step 15
9	Maintain the engine speed at 2500 RPM and continue to operate the generator at the load test value. Does the red DIAGNOSTIC lamp on the tester light?		Go to Step 15	Go to Step 10
10	1 Maintain the engine speed at 2500 RPM and continue to operate the generator at the load test value. 2 Measure the voltage from the output terminal of the generator to the positive terminal on the front relay block. Does the voltage measure greater than the specified value?	0.5 V	Go to Step 15	Go to Step 11

GC1120000102020X

Fig. 7 Charging system test (Part 2 of 3). 2001–02 Impala

Step	Action	Value(s)	Yes	No
1	Inspect battery & starting system. Are systems operating properly?		Go to Step 2	Repair or replace components as needed.
2	Connect the J 41450-B to the generator. Does the green POWER lamp on the tester light?		Go to Step 4	Go to Step 3
3	Measure the voltage from the output terminal of the J 41450-B to the metal housing of the generator. Does the voltage measure greater than the specified value?	12 V	Go to Step 12	Go to Step 4
4	1 Disconnect the generator harness connector. 2 Locate the matching harness connector on the J 41450-B and connect it to the generator. Does the red DIAGNOSTIC lamp on the tester light?		Go to Step 6	Go to Step 5
5	**Notice:** The J 41450-B connector terminals are the same as the generator connector terminals. 1 Disconnect the J 41450-B harness connector from the generator. 2 Prepare a jumper wire with an in-line 100Ω resistor. 3 Attach a Metri-Pack 150 male terminal probe adapter from a J 35616-A 4 Connect the jumper wire between the L terminal of the J 41450-B and a good ground. Does the red DIAGNOSTIC lamp on the tester light?		Go to Step 15	Go to Step 13

GC1120000102010X

Fig. 7 Charging system test (Part 1 of 3). 2001–02 Impala

Step	Action	Value(s)	Yes	No
11	1 Maintain the engine speed at 2500 RPM and continue to operate the generator at the load test value. 2 Measure the voltage from the housing of the generator to a good ground. Does the voltage measure greater than the specified value?	0.5 V	Go to Step 15	Go to Step 13
12	There is an internal problem in the J 41450-B. . Replace the J 41450-B Has the J 41450-B been replaced?		Go to Step 2	
13	Test the output circuit of the generator for a high resistance or an open. Did you find and correct the condition?		Go to Step 17	Go to Step 14
14	Test the ground circuit of the generator for a high resistance or an open. Did you find and correct the condition?		Go to Step 17	Go to Step 15
15	Inspect for poor connections at the harness connector of the generator. Did you find and correct the condition?		Go to Step 17	Go to Step 16
16	Replace the generator. Is the repair complete?		Go to Step 17	
17	Operate the system for which the symptom occurred. Does the symptom reoccur?		Go to Step 2	System OK

GC1120000102030X

Fig. 7 Charging system test (Part 3 of 3). 2001–02 Impala

Step	Action	Value(s)	Yes	No
1	Did you perform the Diagnostic System Check for Engine Electrical?	--	Go to Step 2	Go to Diagnostic System Check -
2	**Important** The battery must be above a 70 percent state of charge. Did you perform the Battery Inspection Test?	--	Go to Step 3	Battery Inspection/Test
3	1. Install a scan tool. 2. Start the engine. 3. With a scan tool, command the GEN-L Terminal OFF and ON. 4. Observe the Ignition 1 Signal parameter. Does the voltage change with each command?	--	Go to Step 4	Go to Step 8
4	1. Turn ON the following accessories: o Headlights (high beams) o A/C on Max o Blower fan (on high) o Heated seats (if equipped) 2. With a scan tool, observe the ignition 1 signal parameter in the engine data list. 3. Increase engine speed to 2,500 RPM. Is the voltage within the specified value?	12.0-15.5 V	Go to Step 5	Go to Step 6

ARM66GC000000724

Fig. 8   Charging system test, (Part 1 of 4). 2003–05 Impala

Step	Action	Value(s)	Yes	No
5	1. Turn OFF all accessories. 2. Turn OFF the Ignition. **Caution** **Make sure that the load is completely turned off before connecting or disconnecting a carbon pile load tester to the battery. Otherwise, sparking could ignite battery gasses which are extremely flammable and may explode violently.** 3. Connect a carbon pile tester to the vehicle. **Important** When measuring generator output current, be sure the inductive probe encircles the generator output wire. 4. Connect an inductive ammeter probe to the output circuit of the generator. 5. Start the engine. 6. With a scan tool, command the GEN-L Terminal ON. 7. Increase engine speed to 2,500 RPM. 8. Adjust the carbon pile as necessary in order to obtain the maximum current output. Is the generator output greater than or equal to the load test value as specified in Generator Usage ?	--	Generator OK	Go to Step 7
6	Is the voltage measured greater than 15.5 volts?	--	Go to Step 12	Go to Step 7
7	1. Leave the vehicle accessories ON or maintain load test value. 2. Maintain engine speed at 2,500 RPM. 3. Measure the voltage between the generator output terminal and the generator metal housing Is the voltage measured equal to the specified value?	battery voltage	Go to Step 14	Go to Step 9

ARM66GC000000725

Fig. 8   Charging system test, (Part 2 of 4). 2003–05 Impala

Step	Action	Value(s)	Yes	No
8	1. Turn ON the ignition, with the engine OFF. 2. Disconnect the generator harness connector. 3. Measure the voltage between the generator turn on signal circuit and ground. 4. With a scan tool, command the GEN-L Terminal ON and OFF. Does the voltage measure greater than the first value ON and near the second value OFF?	4.7 V 0 V	Go to Step 14	Go to Step 11
9	1. Maintain the engine speed at 2500 RPM and continue to operate the generator at the load test value. 2. Measure the voltage drop from the battery negative terminal to the metal housing of the generator. Is the voltage measured less than the specified value?	0.5 V	Go to Step 10	Go to Step 15
10	1. Maintain the engine speed at 2500 RPM and continue to operate the generator at the load test value. 2. Measure the voltage drop from the output terminal of the generator to the positive terminal on the battery. Is the voltage measured less than the specified value?	0.5 V	Go to Step 14	Go to Step 16
11	Test the generator turn on signal circuit for a short, or open. Did you find and correct the condition?	--	Go to Step 19	Go to Step 13

ARM66GC000000726

Fig. 8   Charging system test, (Part 3 of 4). 2003–05 Impala

Step	Action	Value(s)	Yes	No
12	Test the generator battery voltage sense circuit, if equipped, for an open or high resistance. Did you find and correct the condition?	--	Go to Step 19	Go to Step 14
13	Inspect for poor connections at the harness connector of the PCM. Did you find and correct the condition?	--	Go to Step 19	Go to Step 17
14	Inspect for poor connections at the generator. Did you find and correct the condition?	--	Go to Step 19	Go to Step 18
15	Repair the high resistance or open in the ground circuit of the generator. Did you complete the repair?	--	Go to Step 19	--
16	Repair the high resistance or open in the generator output circuit. Did you complete the repair?	--	Go to Step 19	--
17	Replace the PCM. Did you complete the replacement?	--	Go to Step 19	--
18	Replace the generator. Did you complete the replacement?	--	Go to Step 19	--
19	Operate the vehicle in order to verify the repair. Did you correct the condition?	--	Generator OK	Go to Step 2

ARM66GC000000727

Fig. 8   Charging system test, (Part 4 of 4). 2003–05 Impala

ALTERNATOR SPECIFICATIONS

Model	Year	Rated Hot Output Amps	Regulated Voltage	Brush Length Minimum, Inch	Commutator Diameter Minimum, Inch
Catera	2001	120	14.7–15.0	.315	1.228
Impala	2001–05	125	—	—	—

Denso & Mitsubishi Alternators

NOTE: On Air Bag Equipped Models, Refer To "Air Bag System Precautions" Located In The Front Of This Manual For System Disarming & Arming Procedures.

NOTE: Refer To "Computer Relearn Procedure" Located In The Front Of This Manual When Battery Power To The Computer Has Been Interrupted.

INDEX

APPLICATION CHART

Model	Year	Manufacturer	Rated Hot Output Amps
CTS	2003–05	Denso	140
DeVille	2001–05	Denso	140
GTO	2004–05	Mitsubishi	140
Metro	2001	Mitsubishi	55
Prizm	2001–02	Denso	80
Seville	2001–04	Denso	140
STS	2005	Denso	155
Vibe	2003–05	Denso	80

GENERAL INFORMATION

Refer to "Delphi Alternators" for general information.

PRECAUTIONS

Air Bag Systems

Refer to "Air Bag System Precautions" in the front of this manual for system disarming and arming procedures.

Battery Ground Cable

Prior to service, disconnect battery ground cable and isolate as required.

Charging System

1. Ensure battery polarity is proper when servicing units. Reversed battery polarity will damage rectifiers and regulators.
2. If booster battery is used for starting, use proper polarity in hookup.
3. When a fast charger is used to charge a vehicle battery, vehicle battery cables should be disconnected unless fast charger is equipped with a special Alternator Protector, in which case vehicle battery cables need not be disconnected. **Fast chargers should never be used to start a vehicle as rectifier damage will result.**
4. Unless system includes a load relay or field relay, grounding alternator output terminal will damage alternator and/or circuits. This is true even when system is not in operation since no circuit breaker is used and battery is applied to alternator output terminal at all times. Field or load relay acts as a circuit breaker in that it is controlled by ignition switch.
5. Before making any on vehicle tests of alternator or regulator, battery should be inspected and circuit inspected for faulty wiring or insulation. loose or corroded connections and poor ground circuits.
6. Inspect alternator belt tension and condition.
7. Ignition should be Off and battery ground cable disconnected before making any test connections to prevent system damage.
8. Do not reverse connections to alternator.
9. Do not short across or ground any of terminals in charging system.
10. Never disconnect output terminal

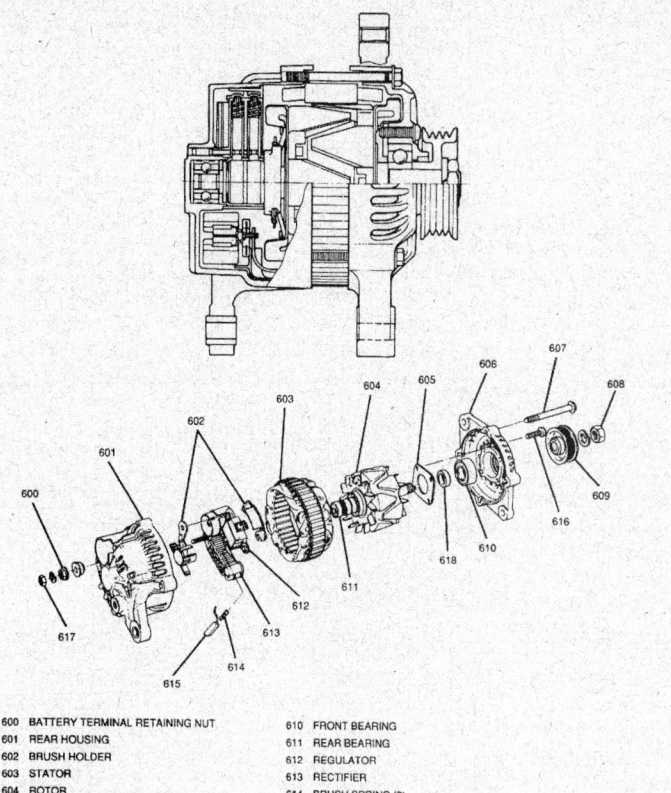

600	BATTERY TERMINAL RETAINING NUT
601	REAR HOUSING
602	BRUSH HOLDER
603	STATOR
604	ROTOR
605	FRONT BEARING RETAINER
606	FRONT HOUSING
607	GENERATOR HOUSING BOLT (4)
608	DRIVE PULLEY RETAINING NUT
609	DRIVE PULLEY
610	FRONT BEARING
611	REAR BEARING
612	REGULATOR
613	RECTIFIER
614	BRUSH SPRING (2)
615	BRUSH (2)
616	FRONT BEARING RETAINING SCREW (4)
617	"BAT" TERMINAL RETAINING NUT
618	FRONT BEARING SPACER

GC1129500063000X

Fig. 1   Exploded view of Mitsubishi alternator

609	ROTOR
614	FRONT BEARING
615	FRONT BEARING RETAINER
616	PULLEY
617	PULLEY NUT
618	BRUSH
619	REAR BEARING
620	BEARING COVER
621	RECTIFIER END FRAME
622	RUBBER INSULATOR
623	IC REGULATOR
634	TERMINAL INSULATOR
635	BRUSH HOLDER
637	BRUSH HOLDER COVER
638	REAR END COVER
639	RECTIFIER HOLDER
640	DRIVE END FRAME

GC1129100036000X

Fig. 2   Exploded view of Denso alternator

while alternator is running.

11. Vehicle battery must be fully charged when testing charging system.

DESCRIPTION

These alternators have IC integral solid state regulators, **Figs. 1 and 2.** All regulator components are enclosed into a solid mold and are attached to the slip ring end frame along with the brush holder assembly. The alternator voltage setting cannot be adjusted.

The alternator rotor bearings contain enough grease to eliminate the need for periodic lubrication. Two brushes carry current through the two slip rings to the field coil mounted on the rotor.

The stator windings are assembled on the inside of a laminated core that form part of the alternator frame. The rectifier bridge contains six diodes which electrically change stator AC voltage into DC voltage.

The neutral diodes serve to convert the voltage fluctuation at the neutral point to direct current for increasing alternator output.

DIAGNOSIS & TESTING

System Test

METRO

1. Connect a voltmeter across battery.
2. Start engine and allow to run at 2,000 RPM, then inspect voltmeter reading, which should be at least 13.5 volts.
3. If voltage reading is not as specified, disconnect battery ground cable.
4. Disconnect alternator B terminal wire.
5. Connect ammeter red lead to alternator B terminal and black lead to disconnected B terminal wire.
6. Connect a voltmeter between alternator B terminal and chassis ground.

7. Connect battery ground cable, then start engine and turn all accessories on.
8. Operate engine at sufficient RPM (approximately 2000 RPM) to obtain maximum alternator current output.
9. Repair or replace alternator if current reading is not within 10 amps of maximum rated output or voltage reading is not 13.5-16 volts.

Regulator Test

METRO & PRIZM

1. Connect a voltmeter and fast charger to battery.
2. Turn ignition On and slowly increase charge rate. Indicator lamp in vehicle will begin to dim when voltage setting is reached.
3. Observe voltmeter. Lamp should dim at 13.5-16.0 volts.
4. If no voltage is present, replace voltage regulator.

Refer to wiring diagrams, **Figs. 3 through 7,** and diagnostic charts **Figs. 8 through 10,** for charging system diagnosis.

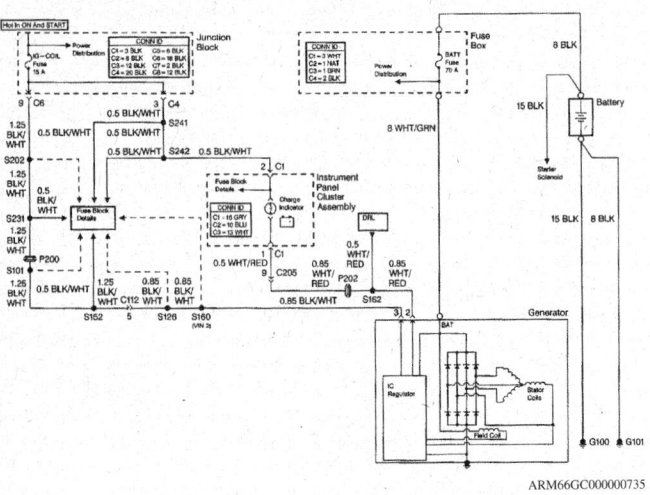

Fig. 3 Wiring diagram. Metro

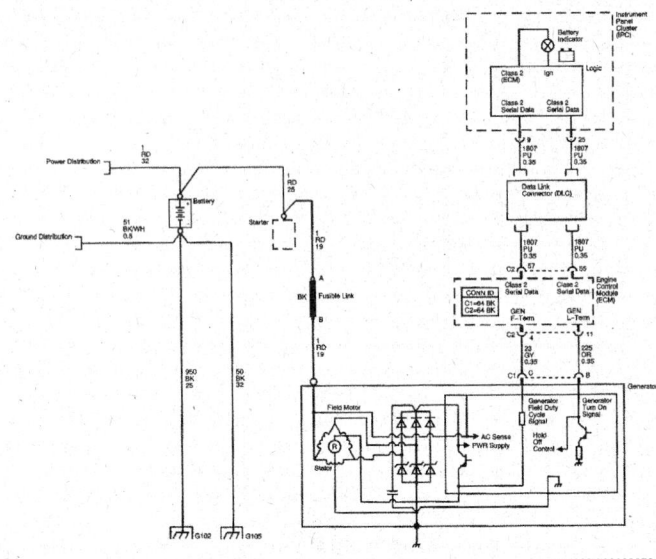

Fig. 4 Wiring diagram. CTS

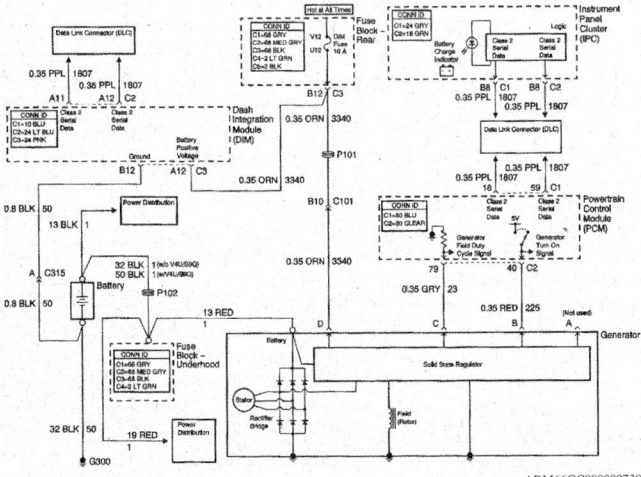

Fig. 5 Wiring diagram. Deville

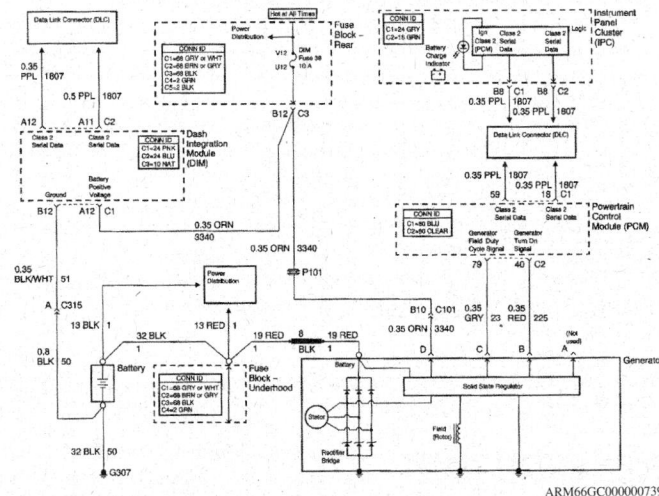

Fig. 6 Wiring diagram. Seville

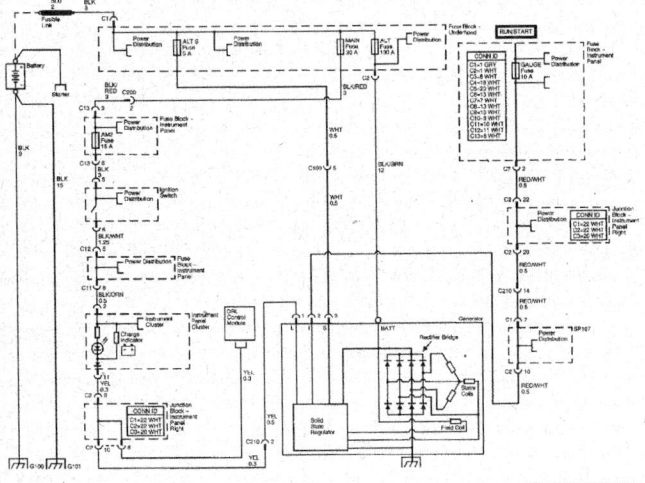

Fig. 7 Wiring diagram. Vibe

Important			
1	The battery must be above a 70 percent state of charge. Did you perform the Battery Inspection Test?	--	Go to Step 2	Go to Battery Inspection/Test
2	1. Install a scan tool. 2. Start the engine. 3. With a scan tool, command the GEN-L Terminal OFF and ON. 4. Observe the Ignition 1 Signal parameter. Does the voltage change with each command?	--	Go to Step 3	Go to Step 7
3	1. Turn ON the following accessories: 　o Headlights -- high beams 　o A/C on Max 　o Blower fan -- ON high 　o Heated seats -- if equipped 2. With a scan tool, observe the ignition 1 signal parameter in the engine data list. 3. Increase engine speed to 2,500 RPM. Is the voltage within the specified value?	12.0-15.5 V	Go to Step 4	Go to Step 5

ARM0300000000696

Fig. 8 Charging system test (Part 1 of 4). CTS, DeVille & Seville

#	Action	Value		
4	1. Turn OFF all accessories. 2. Turn OFF the ignition. **Caution** **Make sure that the load is completely turned off before connecting or disconnecting a carbon pile load tester to the battery. Otherwise, sparking could ignite battery gasses which are extremely flammable and may explode violently.** 3. Connect a carbon pile tester to the vehicle. **Important** When measuring generator output current, be sure the inductive probe encircles the generator output wire. 4. Connect an inductive ammeter probe to the output circuit of the generator. 5. Start the engine. 6. With a scan tool, command the GEN-L Terminal ON. 7. Increase engine speed to 2,500 RPM. 8. Adjust the carbon pile as necessary in order to obtain the maximum current output. Is the generator output greater than or equal to **98 amps**?	--	System OK	Go to Step 8
5	Is the voltage measured greater than 15.5 volts?	--	Go to Step 11	Go to Step 6
6	1. Leave the vehicle accessories ON or maintain load test value. 2. Maintain engine speed at 2,500 RPM. 3. Measure the voltage between the generator output terminal and the generator metal housing. Is the voltage measured equal to the specified value?	B+	Go to Step 13	Go to Step 8

Fig. 8 Charging system test (Part 2 of 4). CTS, DeVille & Seville

ARM0300000000697

#	Action	Value		
7	1. Turn ON the ignition, with the engine OFF. 2. Disconnect the generator harness connector. 3. Measure the voltage between the generator turn ON signal circuit and ground. 4. With a scan tool, command the GEN-L Terminal ON and OFF. Does the voltage measure greater than the first value ON and near the second value OFF?	4.7 V 0 V	Go to Step 13	Go to Step 10
8	1. Maintain the engine speed at 2,500 RPM and continue to operate the generator at the load test value. 2. Measure the voltage drop from the battery negative terminal to the metal housing of the generator. Is the voltage measured less than the specified value?	0.5 V	Go to Step 9	Go to Step 14
9	1. Maintain the engine speed at 2,500 RPM and continue to operate the generator at the load test value. 2. Measure the voltage drop from the output terminal of the generator to the positive terminal on the battery. Is the voltage measured less than the specified value?	0.5 V	Go to Step 13	Go to Step 15
10	Test the generator turn on signal circuit for a short, or open. Did you find and correct the condition?	--	Go to Step 18	Go to Step 12
11	Test the generator battery voltage sense circuit, if equipped, for an open or high resistance. Did you find and correct the condition?	--	Go to Step 18	Go to Step 13

Fig. 8 Charging system test (Part 3 of 4). CTS, DeVille & Seville

ARM0300000000698

#	Action	Value		
12	Inspect for poor connections at the harness connector of the powertrain control module (PCM). Did you find and correct the condition?	-	Go to Step 18	Go to Step 16
13	Inspect for poor connections at the generator. Did you find and correct the condition?	-	Go to Step 18	Go to Step 17
14	Repair the high resistance or open in the ground circuit of the generator. Did you complete the repair?	-	Go to Step 18	--
15	Repair the high resistance or open in the generator output circuit. Did you complete the repair?	-	Go to Step 18	--
16	Replace the PCM. Did you complete the replacement?	-	Go to Step 18	--
17	Replace the generator. Did you complete the replacement?	-	Go to Step 18	--
18	Operate the vehicle in order to verify the repair. Did you correct the condition?	-	System OK	Go to Step 1

Fig. 8 Charging system test (Part 4 of 4). CTS, DeVille & Seville

ARM0300000000699

#	Action	Value		
1	**Important** MC The battery must be above a 70% state of charge. Did you perform the Battery Inspection Test?	--	Go to Step 2	Go to Battery Inspection/Test
2	1. Install a scan tool. 2. Start the engine. 3. Turn ON the following accessories: o Headlights (high beams) o A/C on Max o Blower fan (on high) 4. Increase engine speed to 2,500 RPM. 5. Measure the voltage between the generator output terminal and ground. Is the voltage measured within the specified value?	12.0-15.5 V	Go to Step 3	Go to Step 4
3	1. Turn OFF all accessories. 2. Turn OFF the ignition. **Caution** **Make sure that the load is completely turned off before connecting or disconnecting a carbon pile load tester to the battery. Otherwise, sparking could ignite battery gasses which are extremely flammable and may explode violently.** 3. Connect a carbon pile tester to the vehicle. Follow the manufacturer's instructions. **Important** When measuring generator output current, be sure the inductive probe encircles the generator output wire. 4. Connect an inductive ammeter probe to the output circuit of the generator. 5. Start the engine. 6. Increase engine speed to 2,500 RPM. 7. Adjust the carbon pile as necessary in order to obtain the maximum current output. Is the generator output greater than or equal to the load test value as specified in Generator Usage ?	--	Go to Step 14	Go to Step 5

Fig. 9 Charging system test (Part 1 of 3). Vibe

ARM0300000000700

	Action	Value(s)	Yes	No
4	Is the voltage measured greater than the specified value?	15.5 V	Go to Step **8**	Go to Step **5**
5	1. Turn OFF the accessories. 2. Turn OFF the ignition. 3. Disconnect the generator harness connector. 4. Turn ON the ignition, with the engine OFF. 5. Measure the voltage between the generator turn on signal circuit, terminal 2, of the generator harness connector and ground. Does the voltage measure near the specified value?	B+	Go to Step **6**	Go to Step **10**
6	1. Reconnect the generator harness connector. 2. Start the engine. 3. Turn ON the vehicle accessories. 4. Increase the engine speed at 2500 RPM. 5. Measure the voltage drop between the generator output terminal and the battery positive terminal. Is the voltage above the specified value?	0.5 V	Go to Step **11**	Go to Step **7**
7	1. Maintain the engine speed at 2500 RPM. 2. Measure the voltage drop between the battery negative terminal and the generator metal housing. Is the voltage above the specified value?	0.5 V	Go to Step **12**	Go to Step **9**
8	Test the sense circuit of the generator for a high resistance. Did you find and correct the condition?	--	Go to Step **14**	Go to Step **9**

ARM03000000000701

Fig. 9   Charging system test (Part 2 of 3). Vibe

	Action		Yes	No
9	Inspect for poor connection at the generator. Did you find and correct the condition?	-	Go to Step 14	Go to Step **13**
10	Repair the high resistance or open in the generator turn on signal circuit. Did you complete the repair?	-	Go to Step 14	--
11	Repair the high resistance in the battery positive circuit between the generator output terminal and the battery positive terminal. Did you complete the repair?	-	Go to Step 14	--
12	Repair the high resistance in the ground circuit between the generator housing and the battery negative terminal. Did you complete the repair?	-	Go to Step 14	--
13	Replace the generator. Did you complete the repair?	-	Go to Step 14	--
14	Operate the system in order to verify the repair. Did you correct the condition?	-	System OK	Go to Step 1

ARM03000000000702

Fig. 9   Charging system test (Part 3 of 3). Vibe

Step	Action	Value(s)	Yes	No
	Schematic Reference: Starting and Charging Schematics			
1	Did you review the Battery Description and Operation , the Starting System Description and Operation and the Charging System Description and Operation and perform the necessary inspections?	--	Go to Step 2	Engine Electrical
2	1. Turn OFF all electrical loads. 2. Start the engine. 3. Install a scan tool. 4. With a scan tool view the Battery Voltage parameter in the Powertrain data list. Does the scan tool indicate the voltage is within the specified value?	11.0-15.5 V	Go to Step 3	Test for Intermittent and Poor Connections
3	1. Turn OFF the ignition. 2. Connect a charging system tester to the battery (follow the manufacturer's instructions). 3. Operate the engine at 2500 RPM. 4. Adjust the carbon pile as necessary in order to obtain the maximum current output. Is the generator output within 10 A of the specified value?	89 A	Go to Step 9	Go to Step 4
4	1. Maintain the engine speed at 2500 RPM and continue to operate the generator at the load test value. 2. Measure the voltage drop between the generator output terminal and the battery positive terminal. Is the voltage above the specified value?	0.5 V	Go to Step 6	Go to Step 5

ARM66GC000000740

Fig. 10   Charging system test (Part 1 of 2). Prizm

	Action	Value(s)	Yes	No
5	1. Maintain the engine speed at 2500 RPM and continue to operate the generator at the load test value. 2. Measure the voltage drop between the battery negative terminal and the generator metal housing. Is the voltage above the specified value?	0.5 V	Go to Step 7	Go to Step 8
6	Test the battery positive circuit between the generator output terminal and the battery positive terminal for a high resistance. Did you find and correct the condition?	--	Go to Step 9	Go to Step 7
7	Repair the high resistance in the ground circuit between the generator housing and the battery negative terminal. Did you complete the repair?	--	Go to Step 9	
8	Replace the generator. Did you complete the repair?	--	Go to Step 9	--
9	Operate the system in order to verify the repair. Did you correct the condition?	--	System OK	Go to Step 3

ARM66GC000000741

Fig. 10   Charging system test (Part 2 of 2). Prizm

ALTERNATOR SPECIFICATIONS

Model	Year	Alternator Manufacturer	Rated Hot Output Amps	Regulated Voltage
CTS	2003–05	Denso	140	13.5–15
DeVille	2001–05	Denso	140	13.5–15
Metro	2001	Mitsubishi	55	14.7–15
Prizm	2001–02	Denso	80	13.5–15
Seville	2001–04	Denso	140	13.5–15
Vibe	2003–05	Denso	80	13.5–15

Valeo Alternators

NOTE: On Air Bag Equipped Models, Refer To "Air Bag System Precautions" Located In The Front Of This Manual For System Disarming & Arming Procedures.

NOTE: Refer To "Computer Relearn Procedure" Located In The Front Of This Manual When Battery Power To The Computer Has Been Interrupted.

NOTE: "Electrical Symbol & Wire Color Code Identification" Located In The Front Of This Manual May Be Used As An Aid When Using Wiring Circuits Found In This Section.

INDEX

APPLICATION CHART

Model	Year	Rated Output Amps
Alero	2002	102
Alero	2003–04	105
Cavalier	2003–05	105
Corvette	2001–02	110
Corvette	2003–05	140
Grand Am	2002–05	105
G6	2005	128
ION	2003–05	105
Sunfire	2003–05	105

GENERAL INFORMATION

Refer to "Delphi Alternators" for general information.

PRECAUTIONS

Air Bag Systems

Refer to "Air Bag System Precautions" in the front of this manual for system disarming and arming procedures.

Battery Ground Cable

Prior to service, disconnect battery ground cable and isolate as required.

Charging System

1. Ensure battery polarity is proper when servicing units. Reversed battery polarity will damage rectifiers and regulators.
2. If booster battery is used for starting, use proper polarity in hookup.
3. When a fast charger is used to charge a vehicle battery, vehicle battery cables should be disconnected unless fast charger is equipped with a special Alternator Protector, in which case vehicle battery cables need not be disconnected. **Fast chargers should never be used to start a vehicle as rectifier damage will result.**
4. Unless system includes a load relay or field relay, grounding alternator output terminal will damage alternator and/or circuits. This is true even when system is not in operation since no circuit breaker is used and battery is applied to alternator output terminal at all times. Field or load relay acts as a circuit breaker in that it is controlled by ignition switch.

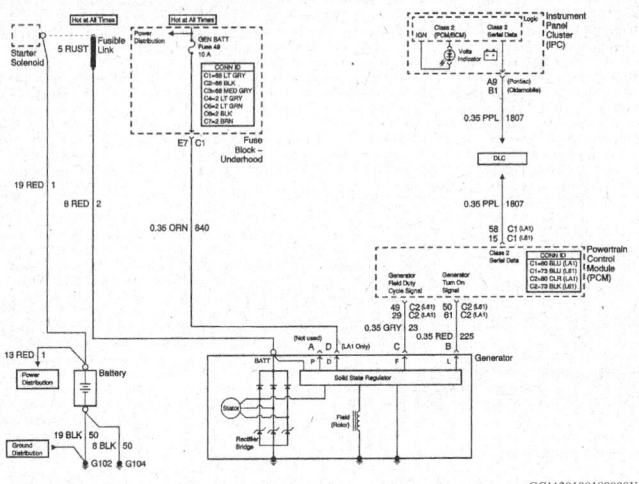

Fig. 1 Wiring diagram. Alero & Grand Am

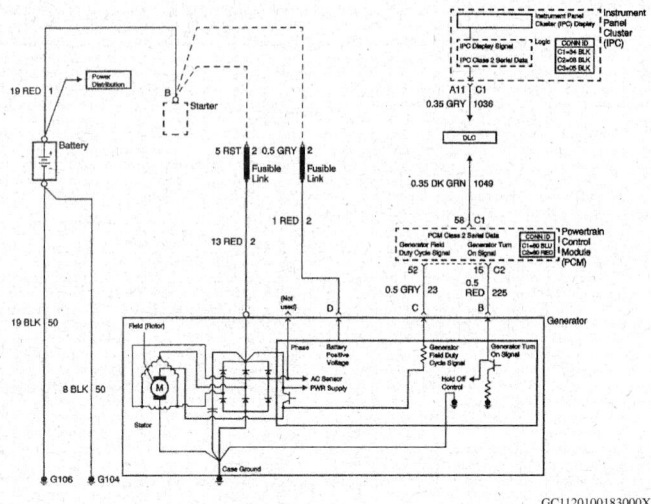

Fig. 2 Wiring diagram. Corvette

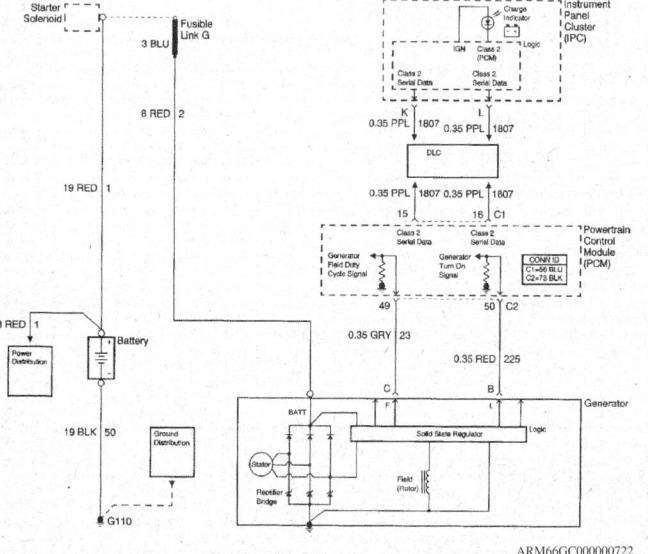

Fig. 3 Wiring diagram. Cavalier & Sunfire

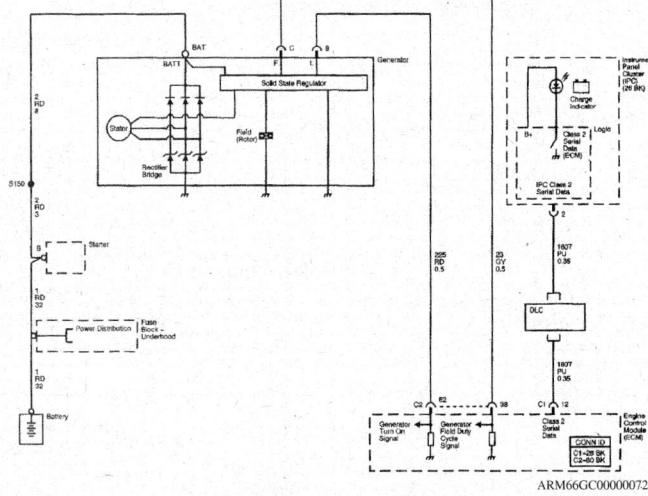

Fig. 4 Wiring diagram. Ion

5. Before making any on vehicle tests of alternator or regulator, battery should be inspected and circuit inspected for faulty wiring or insulation. loose or corroded connections and poor ground circuits.

6. Inspect alternator belt tension and condition.

7. The ignition should be Off and battery ground cable disconnected before making any test connections to prevent damage to system.

8. Do not reverse connections to alternator.

9. Do not short across or ground any terminals in charging system.

10. Never disconnect output terminal while alternator is running.

11. Vehicle battery must be fully charged when testing charging system.

DESCRIPTION

The Valeo alternator is available in one size with a maximum output of 110 amps.

The main components are the rotor, regulator and rectifier bridge. No periodic maintenance is required.

DIAGNOSIS & TESTING

Refer to wiring diagrams, **Figs. 1 through 5,** and diagnosis charts, **Figs. 6 through 9,** for charging system diagnosis.

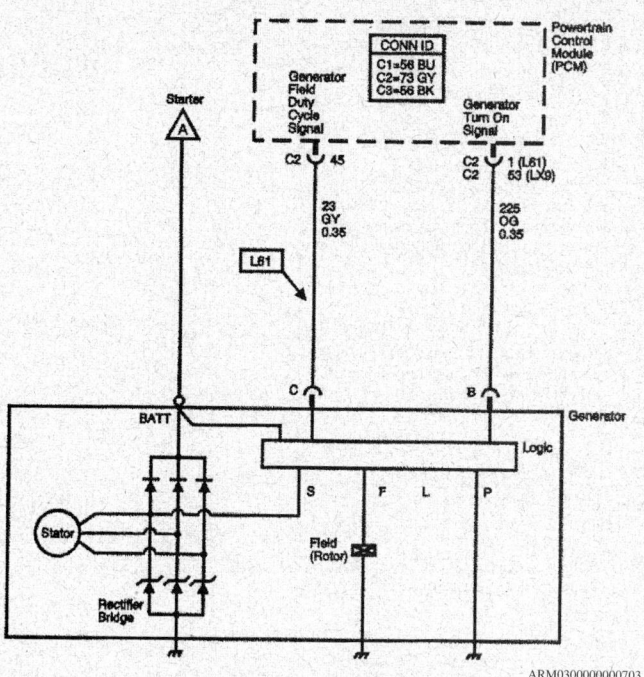

Fig. 5   Wiring diagram. Malibu

ARM0300000000703

Step	Action	Values	Yes	No
1	Did you perform the Diagnostic System Check for Engine Electrical?	--	Go to Step 2	Perform Diagnostic System Check
2	Start the engine, observe the charge indicator on the instrument cluster (IPC) or message in the driver information center (DIC). Does the charge indicator illuminate or the DIC display a charging system message?	--	Go to Step 3	Test for Intermittent and Poor Connections
3	**Important** The green POWER lamp of the tester should remain illuminated while the tester is being used. 1. Turn OFF the ignition. 2. Connect the red lead of the J 41450-B to the generator output terminal. 3. Connect the black lead of the J 41450-B to the metal generator housing. Does the green POWER lamp on the tester illuminate?	--	Go to Step 6	Go to Step 4
4	Measure the voltage from the output terminal of the generator to the generator metal housing. Does the voltage measure equal to the specified value?	B +	Go to Step 14	Go to Step 5
5	Measure the voltage from the output terminal of the generator to the battery negative terminal. Does the voltage measure equal to the specified value?	B +	Go to Step 12	Go to Step 11

GC1120100186010X

Fig. 6   Charging system test (Part 1 of 3). Alero & Grand Am

	Action	Values	Yes	No
	Caution Make sure that the load is completely turned off before connecting or disconnecting a carbon pile load tester to the battery. Otherwise, sparking could ignite battery gasses which are extremely flammable and may explode violently.			
6	1. Connect a carbon pile tester to the vehicle. **Important** Be sure all of generator output circuit wires pass through the inductive probe. 2. Connect an inductive ammeter to the output circuit of the generator. 3. Disconnect the generator harness connector. 4. Locate the matching harness connector on the J 41450-B and connect it to the generator. Does the red DIAGNOSTIC lamp on the tester light?	--	Go to Step 7	Go to Step 13
7	1. Start the engine and allow it to idle for 30 seconds. 2. Increase the engine speed to 2,500 RPM. Does the red DIAGNOSTIC lamp on the tester illuminate?	--	Go to Step 15	Go to Step 8
8	1. Maintain the engine speed at 2,500 RPM. **Important** If the generator is not capable of producing the Load Test amps, operate the generator at it's maximum possible output. 2. Turn ON the load of the carbon pile tester and increase the load until the generator output is greater than or equal to the load test value Does the red DIAGNOSTIC lamp on the tester illuminate?	--	Go to Step 15	Go to Step 9
9	1. Maintain the engine speed at 2,500 RPM and continue to operate the generator at the load test value. 2. Measure the voltage drop from the output terminal of the generator to the positive terminal on the battery. Does the voltage measure greater than the specified value?	0.5 V	Go to Step 11	Go to Step 10

GC1120100186020X

Fig. 6   Charging system test (Part 2 of 3). Alero & Grand Am

	Action	Values	Yes	No
10	1. Maintain the engine speed at 2,500 RPM and continue to operate the generator at the load test value. 2. Measure the voltage drop from the battery negative terminal to the metal housing of the generator. Does the voltage measure greater than the specified value?	0.5 V	Go to Step 12	Go to Step 16
11	Repair the high resistance or an open in the output circuit of the generator. Did you complete the repair?	--	Go to Step 16	--
12	Repair the high resistance or open in the ground circuit of the generator. Did you complete the repair?	--	Go to Step 16	--
13	1. Disconnect the J 41450-B tester harness connector from the generator, but leave the alligator clips connected so that the green POWER lamp remains illuminated. 2. Connect a jumper lead, with an in-line 100-ohm resistor between the J 41450-B tester harness connector terminal B and a good ground. Does the red DIAGNOSTIC lamp illuminate?	--	Go to Step 15	Go to Step 14
14	There is a problem with the J 41450-B . Refer to the manufacturers instructions on how to test the J 41450-B for proper operation. Has the J 41450-B tester been replaced?	--	Go to Step 3	--
15	Replace the generator. Did you complete the replacement?	--	Go to Step 16	--
16	Operate the vehicle in order to verify the repair. Did you correct the condition?	--	System OK	Go to Step 2

GC1120100186030X

Fig. 6   Charging system test (Part 3 of 3). Alero & Grand Am

Step	Action	Value(s)	Yes	No
1	Did you perform the Diagnostic System Check for Starting and Charging?	--	Go to Step 2	Go to Diagnostic System Check
2	1. Turn OFF all electrical loads. 2. Start the engine. 3. Install a scan tool. 4. With a scan tool view the Ignition 1 parameter in the PCM data list. Does the scan tool indicate the voltage is within the specified value?	11.0-15.5 Volts	Go to Step 3	Test for Intermittent and Poor Connections
3	1. Turn OFF the ignition. 2. Connect a charging system tester to the battery (follow the manufactures instructions). 3. Operate the engine at 2500 RPM. 4. Adjust the carbon pile as necessary in order to obtain the maximum current output. Is the generator output within 10 A of the specified value?	85 Amps	Go to Step 9	Go to Step 4
4	1. Maintain the engine speed at 2500 RPM and continue to operate the generator at the load test value. 2. Measure the voltage drop between the generator output terminal and the battery positive terminal. Is the voltage above the specified value?	0.5 V	Go to Step 6	Go to Step 5

ARM66GC000000728

Fig. 7 Charging system test (Part 1 of 2). Corvette

Step	Action	Value(s)	Yes	No
5	1. Maintain the engine speed at 2500 RPM and continue to operate the generator at the load test value. 2. Measure the voltage drop between the battery negative terminal and the generator metal housing. Is the voltage above the specified value?	0.5 V	Go to Step 7	Go to Step 8
6	Test the battery positive circuit between the generator output terminal and the battery positive terminal for a high resistance. Did you find and correct the condition?	--	Go to Step 9	Go to Step 7
7	Repair the high resistance in the ground circuit between the generator housing and the battery negative terminal. Did you complete the repair?	--	Go to Step 9	--
8	Replace the generator. Did you complete the repair?	--	Go to Step 9	--
9	Operate the system in order to verify the repair. Did you correct the condition?	--	System OK	Go to Step 3

ARM66GC000000729

Fig. 7 Charging system test (Part 2 of 2). Corvette

Step	Action	Value(s)	Yes	No
1	Did you perform the Diagnostic System Check for Engine Electrical?	--	Go to Step 2	Go to Diagnostic System Check
2	Start the engine, observe the charge indicator on the instrument panel cluster (IPC) or message in the driver information center (DIC). Does the charge indicator illuminate or the DIC display a charging system message?	--	Go to Step 3	Test for Intermittent and Poor Connections
3	1. Turn OFF the ignition. 2. Connect the red lead of the SA9154Z-A to the battery positive terminal 3. Connect the grey lead of the SA9154Z-A to the output circuit of the generator. 4. Start the engine. 5. Turn On the SA9154Z-A. 6. Turn Off all vehicle accessories Off. 7. Follow the SA9154Z-A prompts. 8. Press CHARGING SYSTEM TEST. Is the voltage displayed within the specified value?	13.0 V - 15.5 V	Go to Step 4	Go to Step 5

ARM66GC000000742

Fig. 8 Charging system test (Part 1 of 2). Ion

Step	Action	Value(s)	Yes	No
4	Is the generator output current greater than or equal to the load test value given in Generator Usage ?	--	Go to Step 6	Go to Step 5
5	Replace the generator. Did you complete the replacement?	--	Go to Step 6	--
6	Operate the vehicle in order to verify the repair. Did you correct the condition?	--	Generator OK	Go to Step 2

ARM66GC000000743

Fig. 8 Charging system test (Part 2 of 2). Ion

Step	Action	Value(s)	Yes	No
1	**Important** The battery must be above a 70 percent state of charge. Did you perform the Battery Inspection Test?	--	Go to Step	Inspect/Test Battery
2	1. Install a scan tool. 2. Start the engine. 3. With a scan tool, command the GEN-L Terminal OFF and ON. 4. Observe the Ignition 1 Signal parameter. Does the voltage change with each command?	--	Go to Step 3	Go to Step 7
3	1. Turn ON the following accessories: o Headlights (high beams) o A/C on Max o Blower fan (on high) o Heated seats (if equipped) 2. With a scan tool, observe the Ignition 1 Signal parameter in the engine data list. 3. Increase engine speed to 2,500 RPM. Is the voltage within the specified value?	12.0-15.5 V	Go to Step 4	Go to Step 5

ARM0300000000704

Fig. 9 Charging system test (Part 1 of 4). Malibu

| 4 | 1. Turn OFF all accessories.
2. Turn OFF the Ignition.

Caution

Make sure that the load is completely turned off before connecting or disconnecting a carbon pile load tester to the battery. Otherwise, sparking could ignite battery gasses which are extremely flammable and may explode violently.

3. Connect a carbon pile tester to the vehicle.

Important

When measuring generator output current, be sure the inductive probe encircles the generator output wire.

4. Connect an inductive ammeter probe to the output circuit of the generator.
5. Start the engine.
6. With a scan tool, command the GEN-L Terminal ON.
7. Increase engine speed to 2,500 RPM.
8. Adjust the carbon pile as necessary in order to obtain the maximum current output.

Is the generator output greater than or equal to the load test value **80 amps**? | | Generator OK | Go to Step **6** |

ARM0300000000705

Fig. 9 Charging system test (Part 2 of 4). Malibu

Step	Description			
5	Is the voltage measured greater than 15.5 volts?	--	Go to Step **11**	Go to Step **6**
6	1. Leave the vehicle accessories ON or maintain load test value. 2. Maintain engine speed at 2,500 RPM. 3. Measure the voltage of the battery. 4. Measure the voltage between the generator output terminal and the generator metal housing Is the voltage measured of the generator within 0.2 volts of the battery voltage?	--	Go to Step **13**	Go to Step **8**
7	1. Turn ON the ignition, with the engine OFF. 2. Disconnect the generator harness connector. 3. Measure the voltage between the generator turn on signal circuit and ground. 4. With a scan tool, command the GEN-L Terminal ON and OFF. Does the voltage measure greater than the first value ON and near the second value OFF?	4.7 V 0 V	Go to Step **13**	Go to Step **10**
8	1. Maintain the engine speed at 2,500 RPM and continue to operate the generator at the load test value. 2. Measure the voltage drop from the battery negative terminal to the metal housing of the generator. Is the voltage measured less than the specified value?	0.5 V	Go to Step **9**	Go to Step **14**
9	1. Maintain the engine speed at 2,500 RPM and continue to operate the generator at the load test value. 2. Measure the voltage drop from the output terminal of the generator to the positive terminal on the battery. Is the voltage measured less than the specified value?	0.2 V	Go to Step **13**	Go to Step **15**

ARM0300000000706

Fig. 9 Charging system test (Part 3 of 4). Malibu

Step	Description			
10	Test the generator turn on signal circuit for a short or an open. Did you find and correct the condition?	-	Go to Step **18**	Go to Step **12**
11	Test the generator battery voltage sense circuit, if equipped, for an open or high resistance. Did you find and correct the condition?	-	Go to Step **18**	Go to Step **13**
12	Inspect for poor connections at the harness connector of the powertrain control module (PCM). Did you find and correct the condition?	-	Go to Step **19**	Go to Step **17**
13	Inspect for poor connections at the generator. Did you find and correct the condition?	-	Go to Step **18**	Go to Step **17**
14	Repair the high resistance or open in the ground circuit of the generator. Did you complete the repair?	-	Go to Step **18**	--
15	Repair the high resistance or open in the generator output circuit. Did you complete the repair?	-	Go to Step **18**	--
16	Replace the PCM. Did you complete the replacement?	-	Go to Step **18**	--
17	Replace the generator. Did you complete the replacement?	-	Go to Step **18**	--
18	Operate the vehicle in order to verify the repair. Did you correct the condition?	-	Generator OK	Go to Step **1**

ARM0300000000707

Fig. 9 Charging system test (Part 4 of 4). Malibu

ALTERNATOR SPECIFICATIONS

Model	Year	Rated Hot Output Amps
Alero & Grand Am	2002	①
	2003–05	105
Cavalier	2003–05	105
Corvette	2001–02	110
Corvette	2003–05	140
Ion	2003–05	105
Sunfire	2003–05	105

① — Models equipped w/2.2L engine 105 amps; models equipped w/3.4L engine 102 amps.

Hitachi Alternators

NOTE: On Air Bag Equipped Models, Refer To "Air Bag System Precautions" Located In The Front Of This Manual For System Disarming & Arming Procedures.

NOTE: Refer To "Computer Relearn Procedure" Located In The Front Of This Manual When Battery Power To The Computer Has Been Interrupted.

NOTE: "Electrical Symbol & Wire Color Code Identification" Located In The Front Of This Manual May Be Used As An Aid When Using Wiring Circuits Found In This Section.

INDEX

APPLICATION CHART

Model	Year	Rated Output Amps
XLR	2004–05	150

PRECAUTIONS

Air Bag Systems

Refer to "Air Bag System Precautions" in the front of this manual for system disarming and arming procedures.

Battery Ground Cable

Prior to service, disconnect battery ground cable and isolate as required.

Charging System

1. Ensure battery polarity is proper when servicing units. Reversed battery polarity will damage rectifiers and regulators.
2. If booster battery is used for starting, use proper polarity in hookup.
3. When a fast charger is used to charge a vehicle battery, vehicle battery cables should be disconnected unless fast charger is equipped with a special Alternator Protector, in which case vehicle battery cables need not be disconnected. **Fast chargers should never be used to start a vehicle as rectifier damage will result.**
4. Unless system includes a load relay or field relay, grounding alternator output terminal will damage alternator and/or circuits. This is true even when system is not in operation since no circuit breaker is used and battery is applied to alternator output terminal at all times. Field or load relay acts as a circuit breaker in that it is controlled by ignition switch.
5. Before making any on vehicle tests of alternator or regulator, battery should be inspected and circuit inspected for faulty wiring or insulation. loose or corroded connections and poor ground circuits.
6. Inspect alternator belt tension and condition.
7. The ignition should be Off and battery ground cable disconnected before making any test connections to prevent damage to system.
8. Do not reverse connections to alternator.
9. Do not short across or ground any terminals in charging system.
10. Never disconnect output terminal while alternator is running.
11. Vehicle battery must be fully charged when testing charging system.

DIAGNOSIS & TESTING

Refer to wiring diagram, **Fig. 1,** and diagnosis chart, **Fig. 2,** for charging system diagnosis.

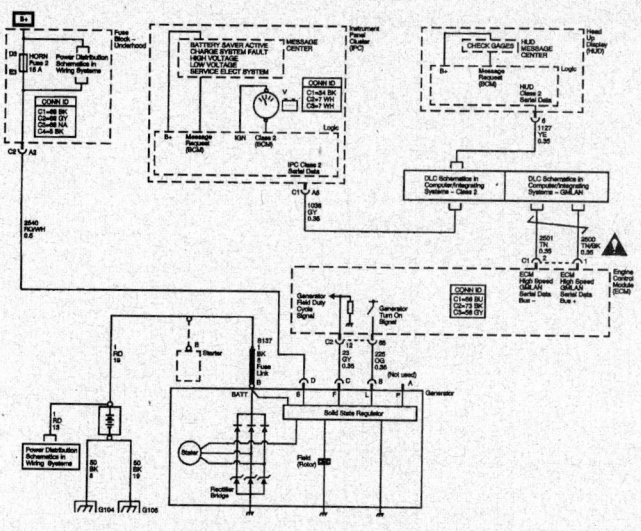

Fig. 1   Wiring diagram. XLR

ARM0300000000708

2	**Important** The battery must be above a 70 percent state of charge. Did you perform the Battery Inspection Test?	--	
		Go to Step 3	Inspect/Test Battery
3	1. Install a scan tool. 2. Start the engine. 3. With a scan tool, command the GEN-L Terminal OFF and ON. 4. Observe the Ignition 1 Signal parameter. Does the voltage change with each command?	--	
		Go to Step 4	Go to Step 8
4	1. Turn ON the following accessories: 　o Headlights (high beams) 　o A/C on Max 　o Blower fan (on high) 　o Heated seats (if equipped) 2. With a scan tool, observe the Ignition 1 Signal parameter in the engine data list. 3. Increase engine speed to 2,500 RPM. Is the voltage within the specified value?	12.0-15.5 V	
		Go to Step 5	Go to Step 6

ARM0300000000709

Fig. 2   Charging system test (Part 1 of 4). XLR

5	1. Turn OFF all accessories. 2. Turn OFF the Ignition. **Caution** **Make sure that the load is completely turned off before connecting or disconnecting a carbon pile load tester to the battery. Otherwise, sparking could ignite battery gasses which are extremely flammable and may explode violently.** 3. Connect a carbon pile tester to the vehicle. **Important** When measuring generator output current, be sure the inductive probe encircles the generator output wire. 4. Connect an inductive ammeter probe to the output circuit of the generator. 5. Start the engine. 6. With a scan tool, command the GEN-L Terminal ON. 7. Increase engine speed to 2,500 RPM. 8. Adjust the carbon pile as necessary in order to obtain the maximum current output. Is the generator output greater than or equal to the load test value as specified in <u>Generator Usage</u>?	Generator OK	Go to Step 7

ARM0300000000710

Fig. 2   Charging system test (Part 2 of 4). XLR

6	Is the voltage measured greater than 15.5 volts?	--	Go to Step 12	Go to Step 7
7	1. Leave the vehicle accessories ON or maintain load test value. 2. Maintain engine speed at 2,500 RPM. 3. Measure the voltage of the battery. 4. Measure the voltage between the generator output terminal and the generator metal housing Is the voltage measured of the generator within 0.2 volts of the battery voltage?	--	Go to Step 14	Go to Step 9
8	1. Turn ON the ignition, with the engine OFF. 2. Disconnect the generator harness connector. 3. Measure the voltage between the generator turn on signal circuit and ground. 4. With a scan tool, command the GEN-L Terminal ON and OFF. Does the voltage measure greater than the first value ON and near the second value OFF?	4.7 V 0 V	Go to Step 14	Go to Step 11
9	1. Maintain the engine speed at 2,500 RPM and continue to operate the generator at the load test value. 2. Measure the voltage drop from the battery negative terminal to the metal housing of the generator. Is the voltage measured less than the specified value?	0.5 V	Go to Step 10	Go to Step 15
10	1. Maintain the engine speed at 2,500 RPM and continue to operate the generator at the load test value. 2. Measure the voltage drop from the output terminal of the generator to the positive terminal on the battery. Is the voltage measured less than the specified value?	0.2 V	Go to Step 14	Go to Step 16

ARM0300000000711

Fig. 2   Charging system test (Part 3 of 4). XLR

11	Test the generator turn on signal circuit for a short or an open.		
	Did you find and correct the condition?	Go to Step 19	Go to Step 13
12	Test the generator battery voltage sense circuit, if equipped, for an open or high resistance.		
	Did you find and correct the condition?	Go to Step 19	Go to Step 14
13	Inspect for poor connections at the harness connector of the powertrain control module (PCM).		
	Did you find and correct the condition?	Go to Step 19	Go to Step 17
14	Inspect for poor connections at the generator.		
	Did you find and correct the condition?	Go to Step 19	Go to Step 18
15	Repair the high resistance or open in the ground circuit of the generator.		
	Did you complete the repair?	Go to Step 19	--
16	Repair the high resistance or open in the generator output circuit.		
	Did you complete the repair?	Go to Step 19	--
17	Replace the PCM.		
	Did you complete the replacement?	Go to Step 19	--
18	Replace the generator.		
	Did you complete the replacement?	Go to Step 19	--
19	Operate the vehicle in order to verify the repair.		
	Did you correct the condition?	Generator OK	Go to Step 2

ARM0300000000712

Fig. 2   Charging system test (Part 4 of 4). XLR

ALTERNATOR SPECIFICATIONS

Model	Year	Rated Hot Output Amps
XLR	2004–05	150

STEERING COLUMNS

NOTE: On Air Bag Equipped Models, Refer To "Air Bag System Precautions" Located In The Front Of This Manual For System Disarming & Arming Procedures.

NOTE: Refer To "Computer Relearn Procedures" Located In The Front Of This Manual When Battery Power To The Computer Has Been Interrupted.

NOTE: Prior To Performing Any Service Operations Listed In This Section, Consult The "Technical Service Bulletins" Section For Related Information.

INDEX

STEERING COLUMN EXPLODED VIEWS

Model	Year	Type		Shifter Position		Page No.	Fig. No.
		Standard	Tilt	Column	Floor		
Alero	2001–04	—	X	—	X	23-14	23
Aurora	2001–03	—	X	—	X	23-14	24
Aveo	2005	—	X	—	X	—	—
Bonneville & LeSabre	2001–05	—	X	X	—	23-20	31
Camaro & Firebird	2001–02	—	X	—	X	23-16	25
Catera	2001	—	X	—	X	23-21	32
Cavalier & Sunfire	2001–05	X	—	—	X	23-22	34
		—	X	—	X	23-23	35
Century	2001–05	—	X	X	—	23-25	37
Corvette		—	X	—	X	23-17	26①
	2001–04	—	X	—	X	23-18	27②
		—	X	—	X	23-18	28③
	2005	—	X	—	X	—	—
CTS	2003–05	—	X	—	X	23-26	38
DeVille & Seville	2001–05	—	X	X	—	23-32	57
		—	X	—	X	23-33	58
Eldorado	2001–02	—	X	X	—	23-32	57
		—	X	—	X	23-33	58
Grand Am	2000–05	—	X	—	X	23-14	23
Grand Prix & Regal	2001–05	—	X	—	X	23-24	36
		—	X	X	—	23-25	37
GTO	2004–05	—	X	—	X	—	—
G6	2005	—	X	—	X	23-36	—
Impala	2001–05	—	X	X	—	23-36	64
		—	X	—	X	23-36	64
Intrigue	2001–02	—	X	—	X	23-24	36
		—	X	X	—	23-25	37
Lacrosse	2005	—	X	X	—	23-25	—
Lumina	2001	—	X	X	—	23-38	68
		—	X	—	X	23-39	69

Continued

STEERING COLUMN EXPLODED VIEWS—Continued

Model	Year	Type		Shifter Position		Page No.	Fig. No.
		Standard	Tilt	Column	Floor		
Malibu	2001–03	—	X	—	X	23-29	51
	2004–05	—	x	—	x	23-31	54
Metro	2001	X	—	—	X	23-40	79
Monte Carlo	2001–05	—	X	—	X	23-36	64
Park Avenue	2001–05	—	X	X	—	23-41	81
Prizm	2001–02	—	X	—	X	23-41	82
STS	2005	—	X	—	X	23-42	—
Vibe	2003–05	—	X	—	X	23-43	84
XLR	2004–05	—	X	—	X	23-45	85

① — Non-telescoping less sensor.   ② — Non-telescoping w/sensor.   ③ — Telescoping.

PRECAUTIONS

Air Bag Systems

Refer to "Air Bag System Precautions" in the front of this manual for system disarming and arming procedures.

Battery Ground Cable

Prior to service, disconnect battery ground cable and isolate as required.

Service

Use only the specified screws, bolts and nuts during the mandatory assembling sequence to ensure proper breakaway action of column under impact. Avoid using excessively long bolts as they may prevent a portion of the steering column from collapsing under impact.

When removing or installing, steering wheel, ignition switch or lock, turn signal switch, adjusting transmission linkage, or installing and adjusting neutral-start or back-up light switch, refer to appropriate chapter.

If a shift tube shows a sheared plastic injection, a new shift tube must be installed. If a steering shaft shows a sheared plastic, but it is not bent, it can be repaired by using a service steering shaft repair kit P/N 7810077. The kit contains instructions and dimensions for all steering columns. On some models, the attaching brackets will shear under impact and must also be replaced.

Steering Column Damage

When the steering column is removed, it is extremely susceptible to damage. Dropping the steering column on its end could collapse the steering shaft or loosen plastic injections that keep the steering column rigid. Leaning on the steering column could cause the jacket to bend or deform. Any of these conditions could impair the steering column's collapsible design. If the steering wheel must be removed, use only the specified steering wheel puller and steering wheel puller bolts. Never hammer on the end of the shaft.

SIR Coil Damage

The front wheels of the vehicle must be in a straight ahead position and the steering column must be in the locked position before disconnecting the steering column or intermediate shaft. Failure to follow these procedures will cause improper alignment of some components during installation and result in damage to the SIR coil.

Steering Column Collision Damage

Vehicles involved in accidents resulting in frame damage, major body or sheet metal damage, or where steering column has been impacted, or where supplemental inflatable restraints systems deployed, may also have a damaged or misaligned steering column. When performing service operations on steering columns, inspect the following components:

1. Ensure steering column bracket capsules are securely seated in bracket slots.
2. Inspected for steering column bracket capsules any looseness when pushed or pulled by hand, **Fig. 1.**
3. Replace bracket or jacket, as required.
4. Inspect for jacket assembly collapse by measuring distance from lower edge of upper jacket, **Fig. 2.** If measured dimensions are not as specified, replace jacket assembly.
5. Visually inspect steering column for sheared plastic, **Fig. 3.**
6. If steering shaft shows sheared plastic, replace steering shaft.
7. Remove inflatable restraint coil and allow to hang freely.
8. Rotate steering wheel and measure steering shaft lower end runout using suitable dial indicator.
9. If runout is more than .063 inch, replace steering shaft.

TROUBLESHOOTING

Refer to **Fig. 4,** for steering column troubleshooting.

STEERING COLUMN

REPLACE

Alero & Grand Am

1. Ensure wheels are in straight ahead position and ignition switch is in LOCK position.
2. Remove steering wheel as outlined in "Electrical" section of "Alero & Grand Am" chassis chapter.
3. Remove tilt lever, as required.
4. Remove upper mounting screws and steering column cover.
5. Remove lower mounting screws and steering column cover.
6. Disconnect headlamp switch and windshield wiper switch.
7. Disconnect cruise control electrical connector.
8. Remove instrument cluster as outlined in "Electrical" section of "Alero & Grand Am" chassis chapter.
9. Cut plastic wire wrap and route SIR coil wiring out of way.
10. Remove lefthand lower sound insulator retaining screws, then the cluster.
11. Position upper intermediate shaft boot out of way and remove upper shaft pinch bolt.
12. Remove lower steering column bracket support bolts.
13. Loosen upper column bolts.
14. Spread lower steering column intermediate shaft joint apart with suitable screwdriver.
15. Remove upper column bolts.
16. Rotate steering column 45° counterclockwise and remove steering column.
17. Reverse procedure to install.

Aurora

1. Ensure wheels are in straight ahead position.
2. Lock steering column by inserting

STEERING COLUMNS

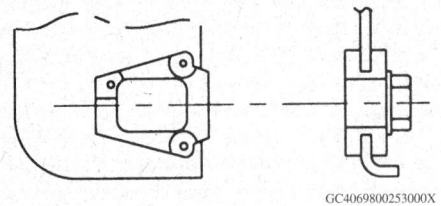

GC4069800253000X

Fig. 1 Inspecting for looseness on steering column bracket assembly

steering column lock pin tool No. J42640, or equivalent, into steering column access hole.
3. If steering column is to be disassemble, remove steering wheel as outlined in "Electrical" section of "Aurora" chassis chapter.
4. Depress hazard button.
5. Remove knee bolster and bracket or reinforcement.
6. Disconnect steering column wiring harness connector from main body wiring harness.
7. Remove steering column shaft from intermediate shaft. Position seal, as required.
8. Remove upper intermediate shaft pinch bolt.
9. Remove upper steering column support mounting nuts. Discard upper steering column support clips.
10. Remove steering column.
11. Reverse procedure to install.

Aveo

1. Remove upper and lower steering column trim covers.
2. Ensure wheels are in straight ahead position and ignition switch is in lock position.
3. Remove turn signal switch by depressing tabs on both sides of switch housing.
4. Remove wiper/washer switch by depressing tabs on both sides of switch housing.
5. Remove lower instrument panel trim cover.
6. Disconnect air bag electrical connections.
7. Remove key interlock solenoid, do not drop key interlock solenoid spring.
8. Remove key reminder switch.
9. Disconnect ignition switch electrical connector.
10. Remove upper steering column shaft pinch bolt.
11. Remove steering column jacket assembly rear bracket retaining nut.
12. Remove steering column jacket assembly front bracket retaining nuts.
13. Remove steering column.
14. Reverse procedure to install.

Bonneville & LeSabre

1. Ensure wheels are in straight ahead position and ignition switch is in LOCK position.
2. Remove steering wheel as outlined in "Electrical" section of "Bonneville, Le-

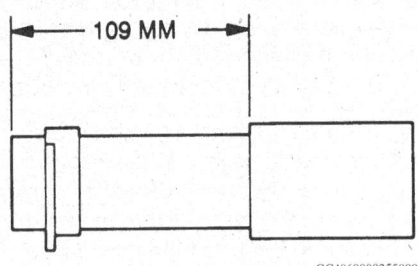

GC4069800255000X

Fig. 2 Jacket assembly collapse measurement

Sabre & Park Avenue" chassis chapter.
3. Remove deflector retaining screws.
4. **On models equipped with column shift,** disconnect shift indicator cable.
5. **On all models,** loosen column support bracket bolts.
6. Remove mounting bolt and steering column support brace, **Fig. 5.**
7. Disconnect steering column wiring harness, then support column and remove support bracket bolts, **Fig. 6.**
8. **On models equipped with column shift,** disconnect shift control cable from actuator and slot in lower column bracket.
9. **On models equipped with console shift,** disconnect park lock cable from ignition switch inhibitor.
10. **On all models,** remove upper intermediate steering shaft pinch bolt.
11. Disconnect steering column shaft from intermediate steering shaft.
12. Remove steering column.
13. Reverse procedure to install.

Camaro & Firebird

1. Ensure wheels are in straight ahead position and ignition switch is in LOCK position.
2. Remove steering wheel as outlined in "Electrical" section of "Camaro & Firebird" chassis chapter.
3. Remove lefthand instrument panel insulator, knee bolster and deflector.
4. Remove intermediate shaft retaining bolt from steering gear coupling shaft, then separate coupler from shaft, **Fig. 7.**
5. Disconnect electrical connectors, then remove steering column support nuts and shims.
6. **On models equipped with automatic transmission,** disconnect park lock cable from ignition switch.
7. **On all models,** remove steering column.
8. Reverse procedure to install.

Catera

If replacement steering column is being installed, do not remove the anti-rotation pin until after the column has been connected to the steering gear. Removing the anti-rotation pin before the column is connected to the steering gear may cause damage to the SIR coil.
1. Ensure wheels are in straight ahead

CHECK FOR SHEARED INJECTED PLASTIC AT THESE LOCATIONS.

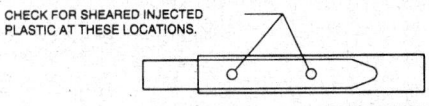

GC4069800254000X

Fig. 3 Inspecting for sheared plastic

position and ignition switch is in LOCK position.
2. Remove steering wheel as outlined in "Electrical" section of "Catera" chassis chapter.
3. Remove SIR coil as outlined in "Passive Restraint Systems" chapter.
4. Remove ignition lock cylinder as outlined in "Electrical" section of "Catera" chassis chapter.
5. Disconnect and remove theft deterrent immobilizer.
6. Remove ignition switch, windshield washer switch and turn signal switch as outlined in "Electrical" section of "Catera" chassis chapter.
7. Remove driver's knee bolster and sound insulator.
8. Remove coupler bolt from steering column shaft connection.
9. Separate coupler enough to allow for shaft removal.
10. Remove forward support strap nut.
11. Rotate forward support strap shear bolt using suitable chisel.
12. Remove rear support bracket bolt.
13. Pull steering column straight back through dash panel.
14. Reverse procedure to install.

Cavalier & Sunfire

1. Ensure wheels are in straight ahead position and ignition switch is in LOCK position.
2. Remove steering wheel as outlined in "Electrical" section of "Cavalier & Sunfire" chassis chapter.
3. Remove lefthand lower sound insulator and side instrument panel covers.
4. Remove instrument panel pad by removing retaining screws located in righthand and lefthand A/C vents, two screws in glove compartment toward lefthand rear and three screws along glove compartment top.
5. Remove tilt lever, then the upper and lower column covers as outlined in "Steering Column Cover."
6. Disconnect cruise control, headlamp switch and windshield wiper switch connectors.
7. Remove ignition switch as outlined in "Electrical" section of "Cavalier & Sunfire" chassis chapter.
8. Disconnect Passlock cylinder connector.
9. **On models equipped with automatic transaxle,** disconnect shift interlock cable from lock cylinder housing.
10. **On all models,** remove upper flexible joint pinch bolt and lefthand side wire harness retaining clip, **Fig. 8.**
11. Remove lower column bracket support bolts.
12. Remove upper column support bolts.
13. Spread lower steering column flexible

Condition	Cause
The lock system does not lock.	• A broken lock bolt spring • A worn lock bolt spring • A damaged sector • A damaged lock cylinder • A burr on the lock bolt • A damaged housing • A damaged rack • Interference between the bowl and the rack coupling • A binding ignition switch • A restricted actuator rod • The sector is installed incorrectly. • The shift lever is not in the PARK position. • The park lock cable is incorrectly adjusted. • The park lock components are damaged.

Condition	Cause
The lock system sticks in START.	• A deformed actuator rod • High Lock Effort Between the Off Lock Positions

Condition	Cause
The key cannot be removed in the OFF-LOCK position.	• The ignition switch is not set correctly. • A damaged lock cylinder • An improperly adjusted linkage • The shift lever is not in the PARK position.

Condition	Cause
The lock cylinder can be removed without depressing the retainer.	A missing lock cylinder retaining screw

Condition	Cause
The lock cylinder effort between OFF and OFF-LOCK is high.	A distorted rack

Condition	Cause
The lock bolt hits the shift lock in the OFF position and the PARK position.	The ignition switch is set incorrectly.

GC6049900276010X

Fig. 4 Steering column troubleshooting chart (Part 1 of 5)

Condition	Causes

A high lock effort exists.	• The lock cylinder is damaged.
	• The ignition switch is damaged.
	• A rack preload spring is broken.
	• A rack preload spring is broken.
	• Burrs exist on the following items:
	  – The sector
	  – The rack
	  – The housing
	  – The support
	  – The actuator rod coupling
	• The sector shaft is bent.
	• A rack is damaged.
	• The housing is extreme misaligned to the cover.
	• A coupling slot in the rack is distorted.
	• An actuator rod is damaged.
	• The ignition switch mounting bracket is bent.
	• An actuator rod is restricted.
	• The key cut is damaged.
	• The key cut is incorrect.
	• The park lock cable is incorrectly adjusted.
	• The park lock components are damaged.

Condition	Causes
Noise is present in the steering column.	• The pinch bolts are loose in the intermediate shaft coupling. • The column is misaligned • The contact ring is not lubricated. • The bearing lacks lubrication. • The column components are loose. • The steering shaft bearings are worn. • The steering shaft bearings are broken. • The shaft lock snap ring is not seated. • The spherical joint is not lubricated. • The dust seal is rubbing the column shaft coupling. • The contact ring is worn. • The contact ring is damaged. • The brushes are worn. • The brushes are damaged. • The lock bolt is bolt. • The lock bolt is improperly lubricated.

GC6049900276020X

Fig. 4 Steering column troubleshooting chart (Part 2 of 5)

joint apart using suitable screwdriver and remove steering column.
14. Reverse procedure to install.

Century, Grand Prix, Intrigue, Lumina, Monte Carlo & Regal

1. Ensure wheels are in straight ahead position and ignition switch is in LOCK position.
2. Remove steering wheel as outlined in "Electrical" section of "Century, Grand Prix, Impala, Intrigue, LaCrosse, Lumina, Monte Carlo & Regal" chassis chapter.
3. Remove lefthand instrument panel insulator.
4. **On Century and Regal models,** remove knee bolster bracket.
5. **On all models,** remove trim panel below steering column.
6. Push top of intermediate shaft seal down, then remove upper intermediate steering shaft pinch bolt, **Fig. 9.**
7. **On models equipped with console shift,** disconnect shift indicator cable and park lock cable from shift cam and automatic transmission control indicator.
8. **On models equipped with column shift,** disconnect transaxle shift cable from ball stud on steering column and transaxle shift cable casing from steering column bracket.
9. **On all models,** remove upper and lower steering column retaining bolts.
10. Disconnect electrical connector and remove steering column.
11. Reverse procedure to install.

Corvette

1. Ensure wheels are in straight ahead position and ignition switch is in LOCK position.
2. Remove driver's air bag module as outlined in "Passive Restraint Systems" chapter.
3. Remove upper intermediate steering shaft pinch bolt.
4. Remove steering wheel and tilt lever.
5. Remove lefthand knee bolster trim panel and knee bolster.
6. Disconnect electrical connectors from column.
7. Remove lower steering column support plate nuts, **Fig. 10.**
8. Remove upper steering column bracket nuts, then the steering column.
9. Reverse procedure to install.

CTS

1. Ensure wheels are in straight ahead position.
2. Lock steering column using tool No. J42640, or equivalent.
3. Raise and support vehicle.
4. Remove upper to lower intermediate shaft retaining bolt, then lower vehicle.
5. Remove driver side lower instrument panel pad.
6. Remove steering column trim covers.
7. Disconnect steering column electrical connectors.
8. Supporting steering column, then remove column to support bracket nuts

steering column, **Fig. 11.**
9. Reverse procedure to install.

DeVille, Eldorado & Seville

1. Ensure wheels are in straight ahead position and ignition switch is in LOCK position.
2. Remove steering wheel as outlined in "Electrical" section of "DeVille, Eldorado, Seville & STS" chassis chapter.
3. Remove knee bolster and steering column reinforcement plate.
4. Disconnect electrical connectors from column.
5. Remove pinch bolt from intermediate shaft, **Fig. 12.**
6. Remove lower support bracket, **Fig. 13.**
7. Remove upper support and column.
8. Reverse procedure to install.

GTO

1. Ensure wheels are in straight ahead position and ignition switch is in LOCK position.
2. Remove lefthand lower instrument panel trim panel and outer trim panel cover.
3. Remove lefthand side ventilation ducts.
4. Remove steering wheel as outlined in "Electrical" section of "GTO" chassis chapter.
5. Remove SIR coil.
6. Remove ignition switch, wiper/washer switch and multifunction switch as outlined in "Electrical" section of "GTO" chassis chapter.

Condition	Causes
High steering shaft effort exists.	• The column is misaligned. • The dust sel is improperly installed. • The dust seal is deformed. • The upper bearing is damaged. • The lower bearing is damaged. • The intermediate steering shaft universal joint is tight. • The shroud is rubbing on the column cover.

Condition	Causes
Lash exists in the steering column.	• The IP-to-column mounting bolts for the upper bracket are loose. • The IP-to-column mounting bolts for the lower bracket are loose. • The weld nuts on the jacket are broken. • The IP upper bracket capsule is sheared. • The shoes in the housing are loose. • The tilt head pivot pins are loose. • The shoe lock pin in the support is loose. • The support screws are loose. • The upper bracket-to-jacket bolts in the column are loose. • The lower bracket-to-jacket bolts in the column are loose. • The lower bracket-to-adapter screws are loose. • The bearing assembly mounting screws are loose. • The IP-to-jacket mounting bolts are loose.

Condition	Causes
The steering wheel is loose.	• Excessive clearance exists between the pivot pin diameters and the holes in the support or in the housing. • The anti-lash spring in the spheres is damaged. • The anti-lash spring in the spheres is missing. • The upper bearing is not seated in the housing. • The inner race seal is missing from the upper bearing. • The support screws are loose. • The bearing preload spring is missing. • The bearing preload spring is broken.

Condition	Causes
The steering wheel is loose in every other tilt position.	• A loose fit exists between the shoe and the shoe pivot pin. • The shoe is not free in the slot.

GC6049900276030X

Fig. 4 Steering column troubleshooting chart (Part 3 of 5)

Condition	Causes
The steering wheel does not lock in any tilt position.	• The shoe seized on the pivot pin. • Burrs are present in the shoe grooves. • Dirt is present in the shoe grooves. • The shoe lock spring is weak. • The shoe lock spring is broken.

Condition	Causes
The steering wheel does not return to the top tilt position.	• The pivot pins are binding. • The wheel tilt spring is broken. • The wheel tilt spring is weak. • The turn signal switch wires are too tight.

Condition	Causes
Noise is present when tilting the column.	• The upper tilt bumpers are worn. • The tilt spring rubs in the housing.

Condition	Causes
The turn signal will not indicate lane change.	• The lane change pressure pad is broken. • The spring hanger is broken. • The lane change spring is broken. • The lane change spring is missing. • The lane change spring is misproportioned. • The base is jammed. • The wires are jammed.

Condition	Causes
The turn signal will not stay in the turn position.	• Foreign material is impeding movement of the yoke. • Loose parts are impeding movement of the yoke. • A detent is broken. • A detent is missing. • A canceling spring is broken. • A canceling spring is missing.

GC6049900276040X

Fig. 4 Steering column troubleshooting chart (Part 4 of 5)

7. Loosen steering column to instrument panel mounting bolts. Do not remove at this time.
8. Raise and support vehicle.
9. Remove steering shaft coupling to steering gear pinion retaining nut. Do not reuse nut.
10. Remove mount bolt from coupling, then separate coupling from pinion.
11. Lower vehicle.
12. Remove lower column retaining nuts.
13. Support column, then remove upper column mounting bolts.
14. Remove steering column.
15. Reverse procedure to install.

G6

1. Ensure wheels are in straight ahead position and ignition switch is in LOCK position.
2. Remove steering wheel as outlined in "Electrical" section of "Malibu Maxx & G6" chassis chapter.
3. Remove SIR coil assembly.
4. Remove multifunction switch as outlined in "Electrical" section of "Malibu Maxx & G6" chassis chapter.
5. Remove steering column knee bolster.
6. Remove steering column shaft to intermediate shaft pinch bolt.
7. Disconnect steering column electrical connectors.
8. Remove adjustable pedal bracket and position aside, leaving brake cable and motor attached.
9. Remove upper steering column mounting bolt.
10. Remove lower steering column mounting bolt.
11. Remove steering column from vehicle.

12. Reverse procedure to install.

ION

1. Ensure steering wheel is in straight ahead position.
2. Remove steering wheel as outlined in "Electrical" section of "Saturn" chassis chapter.
3. Remove instrument panel lower panel.
4. Remove steering column trim covers, **Fig. 14**.
5. Disconnect head lamp, wiper washer and SIR electrical harness from SIR coil module, **Fig. 15**.
6. Remove SIR coil module as outlined in "Passive Restraint Systems" chapter.
7. Disconnect ignition lock cylinder and switch electrical connector.
8. Place matching marks on intermediate shaft to steering column, then remove intermediate shaft pinch bolt, **Fig. 16**.
9. Disconnect Electric Power Steering (EPS) control module electrical harness connectors.
10. Remove steering column pivot bolt, mounting bolts, then the steering column, **Fig. 17**.
11. Remove ignition lock cylinder case, **Fig. 18**.
12. Reverse procedure to install.

LaCrosse

1. Ensure wheels are in straight ahead position, then LOCK steering column by inserting steering column lock pin tool No. J42640, or equivalent, into steering column access hole.
2. Remove steering wheel air bag module.

3. Remove steering wheel as outlined in "Electrical" section of "Century, Grand Prix, Impala, Intrigue, LaCrosse, Lumina, Monte Carlo & Regal" chassis chapter.
4. Remove lefthand instrument panel closeout panel.
5. Remove lefthand knee bolster.
6. Remove intermediate shaft from steering column.
7. Remove shift indicator cable, casing from shift cam and the automatic control indicator adjuster or park lock cable.
8. Disconnect A/T range selector cable from ball stud on steering column.
9. Remove transaxle shift cable casing from steering column bracket.
10. Remove lower and upper steering column mounting bolts.
11. Disconnect steering column electrical connectors.
12. Loosen steering column electrical connector bolt.
13. Separate electrical connector halves.
14. Remove steering column.
15. Reverse procedure to install.

L-Series

1. Ensure steering wheel is in straight ahead position.
2. Remove steering wheel as outlined in "Electrical" section of "Saturn" chassis chapter.
3. Remove HVAC duct and knee bolster.
4. Disconnect the following electrical connectors:
   a. Wiper/washer and headlamp/turn signal switches.
   b. Ignition switch from lefthand side of steering column.
   c. Interlock solenoid to righthand side

Condition	Causes
The turn signal will not cancel.	• The switch mounting screws are loose. • A switch is broken. • The anchor bosses are broken. • A detent is broken. • A return is broken. • A canceling spring is broken. • A detent is missing. • A return is missing. • A canceling spring is missing. • A detent is out-of-position. • A return is out-of-position. • A canceling spring is out-of-position. • A cancelling cam is worn.

Condition	Causes
The turn signal is difficult to operate.	• A turn signal lever screw is loose. • A yoke is broken. Replace the switch. • A yoke is distorted. Replace the switch. • The springs are loose. • The springs are mispositioned. • Interference caused by foreign material exists. • The turn signal switch mounting screws are loose.

Condition	Causes
The electrical system will not function.	• The ignition switch is damaged. • The ignition switch is improperly adjusted. • A loose connection at the ignition switch exists. • A loose connection at the column connectors exists.

Condition	Causes
The switch cannot be set correctly.	• The switch actuator rod is deformed. • The sector is engaged in the wrong rack tooth.

GC6049900276050X

**Fig. 4 Steering column troubleshooting chart
(Part 5 of 5)**

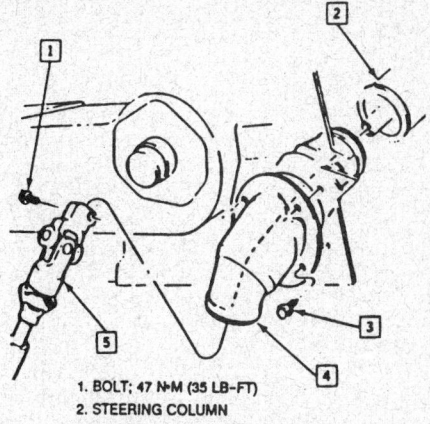

1. BOLT; 47 N•M (35 LB-FT)
2. STEERING COLUMN
3. SCREW (4); 2.4 N•M (21 LB-IN)
4. SEAL ASSEMBLY
5. INTERMEDIATE SHAFT ASSEMBLY

GC6049100044000X

Fig. 5 Intermediate shaft & boot installation. Bonneville & LeSabre

11. Remove steering column.
12. Reverse procedure to install.

of steering column.
  d. Ignition switch to righthand side of steering wheel.
5. Remove wiper/washer and headlamp/turn signal switches.
6. Remove signal switch housing and upper intermediate shaft bolt, then disconnect shaft from steering column.
7. Remove lower and upper steering column support bolts and nuts.
8. Remove steering column.
9. If new column is to be installed, ignition module must be removed as follows:
  a. Place steering column in suitable soft-jawed vise.
  b. Mark ignition module shear bolts center using suitable center punch.
  c. Drill ⅛ inch hole in bolts at each center mark.
  d. Remove bolts using suitable screw extractor and separate ignition module from column.
10. Reverse procedure to install.

Malibu

2001-03

1. Ensure wheels are in straight ahead position and ignition switch is in LOCK position.
2. Remove steering wheel as outlined in "Electrical" section of "Alero, Grand Am & Malibu" chassis chapter.
3. Remove column covers as outlined in "Steering Column Cover."
4. Remove tilt lever, then disconnect cruise control, headlamp and windshield wiper switch connectors.
5. Remove instrument cluster as outlined in "Electrical" section of "Alero, Grand Am & Malibu" chassis chapter.
6. Remove lefthand lower sound insulator.
7. Disconnect SIR coil wiring harness and remove plastic zip tie.

8. Position upper intermediate shaft boot aside and remove shaft coupler pinch bolt.
9. Remove steering column to support bracket retaining bolts, **Fig. 19.**
10. Spread lower steering column intermediate shaft joint apart using suitable screwdriver and remove upper column bolts.
11. Rotate column counterclockwise approximately 45° and remove column.
12. Reverse procedure to install.

2004

Do not bend the steering column energy absorbing straps located on the upper steering column mounting bracket.
1. Ensure wheels are in straight ahead position and ignition switch is in LOCK position.
2. Remove steering wheel and multifunction switch as outlined in "Electrical" section of "Alero, Grand Am & Malibu" chassis chapter.
3. Remove steering column knee bolster retaining screws, then the bolster.
4. Remove clockspring as outlined in "Passive Restraint Systems" chapter.
5. Remove steering column shaft pinch bolt from intermediate steering shaft.
6. Secure rake lever to full up (LOCK) position using suitable tie straps, **Fig. 20. Rack lever must remain in LOCK position during removal and installation.**
7. Disconnect electrical connectors and harness from steering column.
8. Remove accelerator pedal position sensor electrical connector.
9. Remove accelerator pedal mounting nuts from bracket, then the pedal assembly.
10. Remove upper and lower steering column mounting bolt.

Impala

1. Ensure wheels are in straight ahead position and ignition switch is in LOCK position.
2. Remove steering wheel as outlined in "Electrical" section of "Century, Grand Prix, Impala, Intrigue, LaCrosse, Lumina, Monte Carlo & Regal" chassis chapter.
3. Remove lefthand instrument panel insulator.
4. Remove trim panel below steering column.
5. Remove steering column knee bolster.
6. Remove steering column intermediate shaft pinch bolt from coupler.
7. Remove shift indicator cable, casing from shift cam and automatic control indicator adjuster and park lock cable.
8. Disconnect transaxle range selector cable from ball stud on steering column.
9. Remove transaxle shift cable casing from steering column bracket by depressing two tabs.
10. Disconnect steering column electrical connectors.
11. Remove steering column electrical connector retaining bolt, then Separate electrical connectors.
12. Remove lower steering column mounting bolts.
13. Remove upper mounting bolts, then the steering column.
14. Reverse procedure to install.

Metro

1. Ensure wheels are in straight ahead position and ignition switch is in LOCK position.
2. Remove steering wheel as outlined in "Electrical" section of "Metro" chassis chapter.
3. Remove knee bolster, then loosen steering column support bolts and lower column slightly.

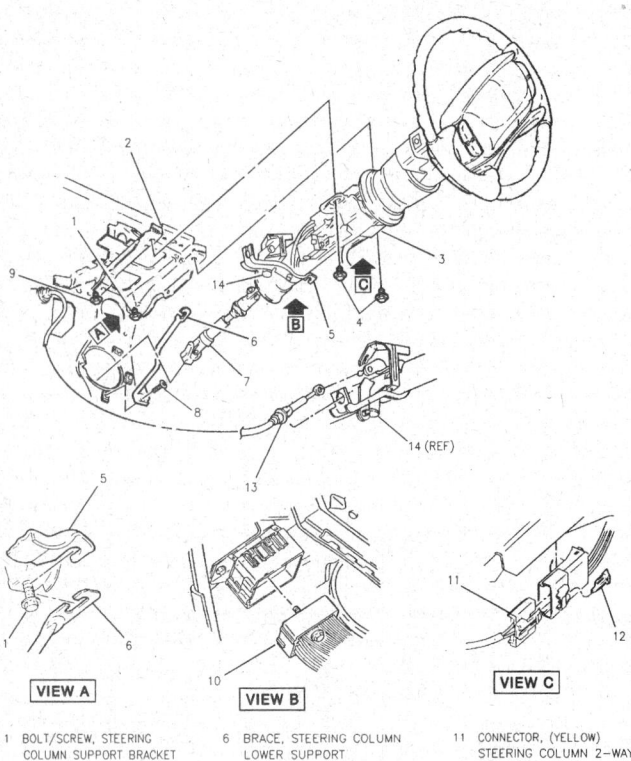

VIEW A · VIEW B · VIEW C

1 BOLT/SCREW, STEERING
   COLUMN SUPPORT BRACKET
   27 Nm (20 LB. FT.)
2 STEERING COLUMN SUPPORT
   BRACKET
3 UPPER SUPPORT BRACKET
4 BOLT/SCREW
   27 Nm (20 LB. FT.)
5 LOWER SUPPORT

6 BRACE, STEERING COLUMN
   LOWER SUPPORT
7 INTERMEDIATE SHAFT
8 BOLT/SCREW
   9.5 Nm (84 LB. IN.)
9 BOLT/SCREW
   27 Nm (20 LB. FT.)
10 CONNECTOR, STEERING
   COLUMN WIRING HARNESS

11 CONNECTOR, (YELLOW)
   STEERING COLUMN 2-WAY
12 RETAINER
13 CABLE, SHIFT CONTROL
   (COLUMN SHIFT)
14 SOLENOID, BRAKE
   TRANSMISSION SHIFT
   INTERLOCK

GC6049100045000A

Fig. 6 Steering column replacement. Bonneville & LeSabre

4. Disconnect SIR coil and combination switch connectors, then remove upper and lower steering column covers, **Fig. 21.**
5. Remove SIR coil and combination switch, then disconnect ignition wiring connectors from junction block.
6. Remove intermediate shaft joint upper pinch bolt.
7. Remove upper and lower steering column mounting nuts and bolts.
8. Lower steering column and disconnect shift interlock cable from ignition switch.
9. Remove steering column.
10. Reverse procedure to install.

Park Avenue

1. Ensure wheels are in straight ahead position and ignition switch is in LOCK position.
2. Remove steering wheel as outlined in "Electrical" section of "Bonneville, LeSabre & Park Avenue" chassis chapter.
3. Depress hazard button, then remove knee bolster and bracket.
4. **On models equipped with column shift,** remove shift lever cable.
5. **On models equipped with console shift,** unlock ignition and remove park lock cable, then lock ignition.
6. **On all models,** disconnect steering column electrical connectors.
7. Remove upper intermediate shaft pinch bolt, **Fig. 22.**
8. Remove steering column shaft from intermediate shaft, loosen do not remove lower steering column support mounting nuts.
9. Support steering column and remove upper steering column support mounting nuts. **Discard upper steering column support clips.**
10. Remove lower support nuts, then the steering column.
11. Reverse procedure to install.

Prizm

1. Ensure wheels are in straight ahead position and ignition switch is in LOCK position.
2. Remove steering wheel as outlined in "Electrical" section of "Prizm" chassis chapter.
3. Unclip lefthand front carpet retainer.
4. Remove hood release lever mounting screws.
5. Remove trim caps and knee bolster to instrument panel mounting bolts.
6. Remove lefthand instrument panel ventilation duct using suitable trim tool.
7. Remove upper and lower steering column trim covers.
8. Disconnect steering column electrical connectors.

A CONNECTOR, RADIO ASSEMBLY ELECTRICAL
   (PONTIAC ONLY)
B CONNECTOR, SIR COIL ASSEMBLY ELECTRICAL
C LEAD, HORN
D BUTTON, STEERING GEAR COUPLING HEAT SHIELD
1 MODULE ASSEMBLY, INFLATABLE RESTRAINT
   STEERING WHEEL
2 WHEEL ASSEMBLY, STEERING
3 BOLT/SCREW, STEERING WHEEL
4 NUT, STEERING COLUMN UPPER SUPPORT
5 LEVER ASSEMBLY, TURN SIGNAL AND HEADLAMP
   DIMMER SWITCH AND CRUISE CONTROL ACTUATOR
   AND WINDSHIELD WIPER AND WINDSHIELD WASHER
6 LEVER ASSEMBLY, STEERING COLUMN TILT WHEEL
   RELEASE
7 BOLT/SCREW, STEERING COLUMN
8 BOLT/SCREW, INTERMEDIATE STEERING SHAFT
9 SHAFT ASSEMBLY, STEERING GEAR COUPLING
10 BOLT/SCREW, INTERMEDIATE STEERING SHAFT

11 CLAMP, STEERING GEAR COUPLING SHIELD
12 BOOT, STEERING GEAR
13 SHIELD, STEERING GEAR COUPLING HEAT
14 COVER ASSEMBLY, STEERING COLUMN DASH PANEL
15 COLUMN ASSEMBLY, STEERING
16 BOLT/SCREW, STEERING COLUMN GUIDE,
17 GUIDE, STEERING COLUMN
18 BOLT/SCREW, HAZARD WARNING SWITCH KNOB
19 BUTTON, HAZARD WARNING SWITCH
20 SPRING, HAZARD WARNING SWITCH KNOB
21 KNOB, HAZARD WARNING SWITCH
22 NUT, STEERING WHEEL
23 SEALER, STEERING COLUMN
31 LEVER ASSEMBLY, TURN SIGNAL AND HEADLAMP
   DIMMER SWITCH AND WINDSHIELD WIPER AND
   WINDSHIELD WASHER

GC6049100052000A

Fig. 7 Steering column replacement. Camaro & Firebird

9. Remove steering column intermediate shaft pinch bolt.
10. Remove steering column mounting bolts and nuts, then the steering column.
11. Reverse procedure to install.

S-Series

1. Remove steering wheel as outlined in "Electrical" section of "Saturn" chassis chapter.
2. Remove steering column lower filler panel screws and loosen Data Link Connector (DLC) screws, then pull filler panel outward and down.
3. Release hood release cable housing retainer.
4. Pull cable and housing downward until cable can pass through cutout in handle, then slide cable out of handle.
5. Remove steering column lower filler panel and multi-function switch as outlined in "Electrical" section of "Saturn" chassis chapter.
6. Disconnect ignition switch electrical connector from steering column upper support bracket, as required.
7. **On models equipped with automatic transmission,** disconnect park lock cable from ignition module.
8. **On all models,** remove intermediate shaft bolt and disconnect shaft from column.
9. Remove upper and lower column mounting bolts and nuts.
10. Disconnect harness clamps and remove steering column.
11. If new column is to be installed, ignition

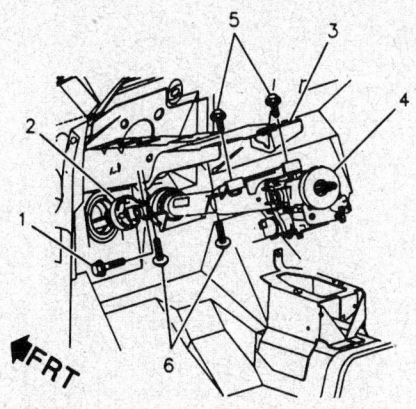

1 UPPER PINCH BOLT
2 FLANGE AND STEERING COUPLING
3 UPPER COLUMN SUPPORT
4 STEERING COLUMN
5 UPPER COLUMN BOLT
6 LOWER COLUMN BOLT

GC6049700227000X

Fig. 8 Steering column replacement. Cavalier & Sunfire

module must be removed as follows:
   a. Place steering column in suitable soft-jawed vise.
   b. Mark ignition module shear bolts center using suitable center punch.
   c. Drill ⅛ inch hole in bolts from each center mark.
   d. Remove bolts using suitable screw extractor and separate ignition module from column.
12. Reverse procedure to install, noting the following:
   a. When installing ignition module, use new shear bolts and tighten until bolt heads break off.
   b. Tighten to specification.

STS

1. Ensure wheels are in straight ahead position and ignition switch is in LOCK position.
2. Lock steering column by inserting steering column lock pin tool No. J42640, or equivalent, into steering column access hole.
3. Raise and support vehicle.
4. Remove upper intermediate shaft to lower intermediate shaft retaining bolt, then lower vehicle.
5. Remove knee bolster.
6. Remove steering wheel as outlined in "Electrical" section of "Deville, Eldorado, Seville & STS" chassis chapter.
7. Disconnect steering column electrical connectors.
8. Support steering column, then remove steering column mounting bolts.
9. Remove steering column.
10. Remove upper intermediate shaft to steering column attaching bolt, then disconnect upper intermediate shaft from steering column.
11. Reverse procedure to install.

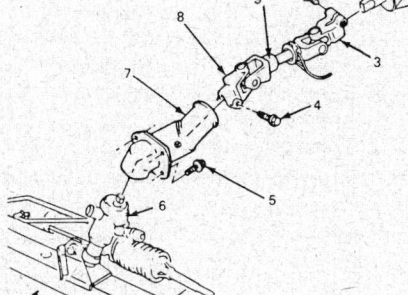

1 STEERING SHAFT-LOWER END
2 STEERING COLUMN ASSEMBLY
3 INTERMEDIATE SHAFT COUPLING-UPPER
4 PINCH BOLT-LOWER COUPLING
5 SCREW
6 STEERING GEAR
7 SEAL-INTERMEDIATE SHAFT
8 INTERMEDIATE SHAFT COUPLING-LOWER
9 INTERMEDIATE SHAFT
10 PINCH BOLT-UPPER COUPLING
11 BRACKET-BRAKE PEDAL
12 BOLT-LOWER STEERING COLUMN
13 BOLT-UPPER STEERING COLUMN

GC6049100057000X

Fig. 9 Steering column replacement. Century, Grand Prix, Intrigue, Lumina, Monte Carlo & Regal

Vibe

1. Ensure wheels are in straight ahead position and ignition switch is in LOCK position.
2. Remove steering wheel and multi-function switch as outlined in "Electrical" section of "Vibe" chassis chapter.
3. Remove steering column trim covers.
4. Remove SIR coil as outlined in "Passive Restraint Systems" chapter.
5. **On models equipped with automatic transmission,** install key into cylinder, turn key to ACC position, release button, then disconnect park lock cable.
6. Lock steering column in original position, then remove ignition key.
7. **On all models,** remove lower pad from steering column.
8. Loosen upper bolt, then remove lower bolt from steering column intermediate shaft coupling.
9. Disconnect coupling at steering column.
10. Disconnect steering column electrical connectors.

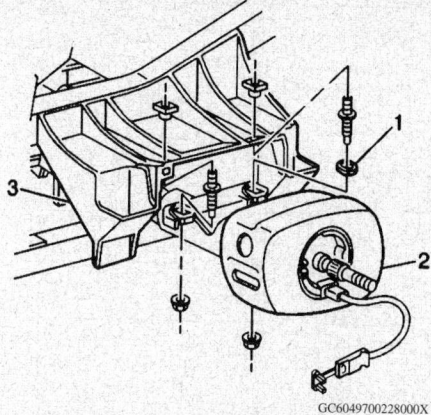

GC6049700228000X

Fig. 10 Steering column replacement. Corvette

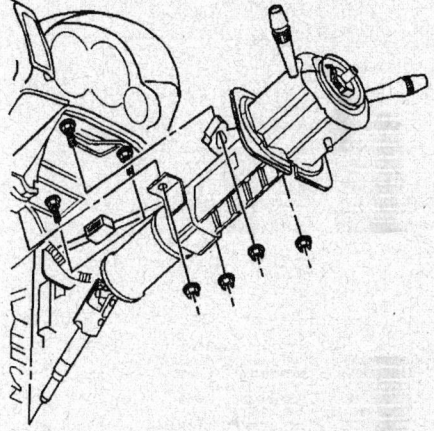

ARM66GC000000699

Fig. 11 Steering column removal. CTS

11. Remove steering column retaining bolts, then the steering column.
12. Reverse procedure to install.

XLR

If steering column connectors are disconnected with the ignition in the ON position, the BCM will enter a fail enable mode and prevent steering column lock operation. The PCM will also inhibit vehicle motion by disabling fuel. To clear the BCM fail enable mode, disconnect BCM fuse #25 for 15 seconds.

1. Turn steering wheel far enough to left-hand side to gain access to upper coupling bolt, then remove upper coupling bolt.
2. Turn steering wheel back to right-hand side until wheels are in a straight ahead position, then lock steering column and install steering column lock pin tool No. J 42640, or equivalent, into steering column.
3. Remove trim panel from driver knee bolster.
4. Remove driver knee bolster bracket.
5. Disconnect electrical connectors from instrument panel wiring harness.

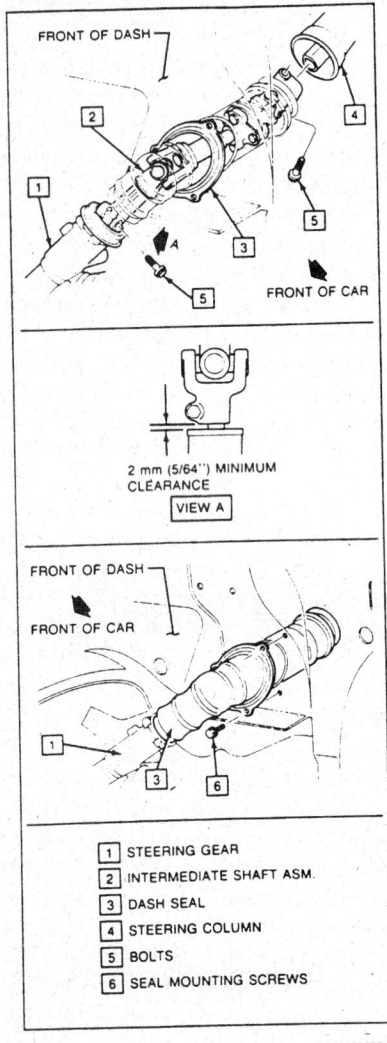

Fig. 12 **Intermediate shaft & boot. DeVille, Eldorado & Seville**

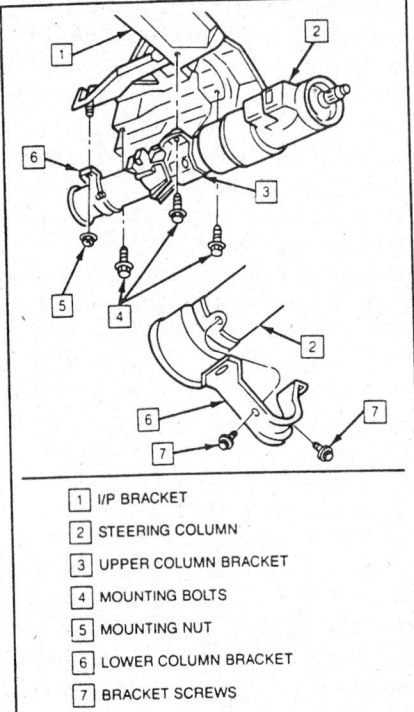

Fig. 13 **Steering column replacement. DeVille, Eldorado & Seville**

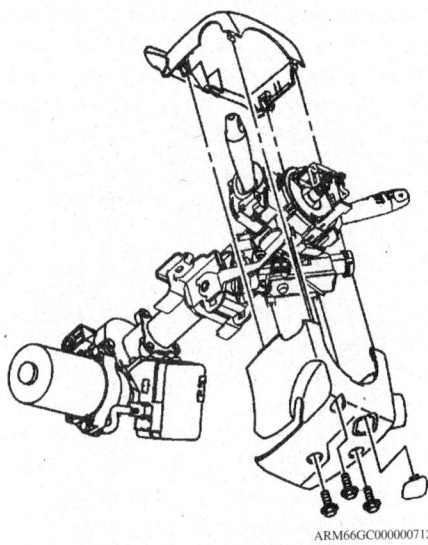

Fig. 14 **Steering column trim cover removal. ION**

Fig. 15 **Electrical harness removal. ION**

6. Disconnect steering column lock module harness from steering column lock module.
7. Remove lower steering column support plate mounting nuts.
8. Remove upper steering column bracket nuts from upper reinforcement assembly.
9. Slide steering column off of intermediate shaft.
10. Remove steering column from vehicle. Rotate steering column clockwise as bottom of steering column reaches reinforcement assembly. This will allow telescoping steering column motor and steering wheel position sensor room to clear instrument panel brace.
11. Reverse procedure to install.

STEERING COLUMN SERVICE

Alero & Grand Am

Refer to **Fig. 23,** for exploded view of this steering column.

TILT SPRING

1. Move tilt column into up position.
2. Pry spring upward until bulge occurs and most of spring tension is removed.
3. Secure spring with locking pliers.
4. Continue prying on spring until tilt spring disengages from post on steering column support and steering column housing.
5. Remove tilt spring guide from tilt spring.
6. Reverse procedure to install.

STEERING COLUMN TILT HEAD

1. Remove steering column as outlined in "Steering Column, Replace."
2. Remove SIR coil.
3. Compress cam orientation plate using lock plate compressor tool No. J23653-SIR and cam orientation plate adapter No. J42137, or equivalents.
4. Remove and dispose of bearing retainer.
5. Remove cam orientation plate.
6. Remove turn signal cam.
7. Remove upper bearing spring, inner race seat and inner race.
8. Remove pivot pins using pivot pin remover tool No. J21854-1, or equivalent.
9. Pull tilt arm to disengage steering wheel lock shoes from dowel pins in steering column support.
10. Remove bearing and housing.
11. Reverse procedure to assemble, noting the following:
   a. Lubricate pivot pins with grease.
   b. Press pivot pins until seated and stake at three locations.

LOWER BEARING, LOWER STEERING SHAFT & COLUMN JACKET

1. Remove steering column as outlined in "Steering Column, Replace."
2. Remove steering shaft seal from sensor retainer.
3. Remove sensor retainer from end of steering shaft.
4. Remove lower spring retainer and steering wheel speed sensor, then the lower bearing spring and seat from steering shaft.
5. Remove adapter and bearing from steering column jacket.
6. Remove upper tilt head components.
7. Remove mounting screws from steering column support.
8. Remove steering shaft from steering column support.
9. Remove steering column support from steering column jacket.
10. Index mark, upper and lower steering shaft and race to ensure proper assembly.
11. Tilt race and upper shaft 90° toward each other.

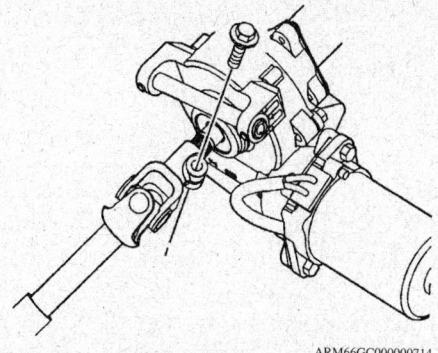

ARM66GC000000714

Fig. 16 Pinch bolt removal. ION

12. Disengage, then remove race and upper shaft.
13. Remove centering sphere from race and upper shaft by rotating centering sphere 90°.
14. Lift centering sphere out of race and upper shaft.
15. Remove joint preload spring from centering sphere.
16. Inspect centering sphere and joint preload spring. Replace components, as required.
17. Reverse procedure to install, noting the following:
    a. Grease centering sphere with lithium grease.
    b. Assemble centering sphere and joint preload spring using centering sphere installer tool No. J41688, or equivalent.
    c. Apply lithium grease to exposed shaft engagement areas.

SIR COIL CENTERING

The SIR coil will become uncentered if the steering column is separated from the steering gear and rotates, or if the centering spring is pushed down and the hub rotates while the coil is removed from the steering column. To center the coil, proceed as follows:
1. Remove clockspring coil as outlined in "Passive Restraint Systems" chapter.
2. Remove coil from steering column.
3. Hold coil with bottom facing upward.
4. Depress spring lock and rotate hub counterclockwise until it stops.
5. Ensure coil ribbon is wound against center hub.
6. Rotate coil hub clockwise approximately 2½ turns.
7. Release spring lock between locking tabs.

Aurora

Refer to **Fig. 24,** for exploded view of steering column.

INTERMEDIATE STEERING SHAFT

1. Ensure wheels are in straight ahead position and ignition switch is in LOCK position.
2. Turn ignition key must to OFF or LOCK position.
3. Lock steering column by inserting steering column lock pin tool No.

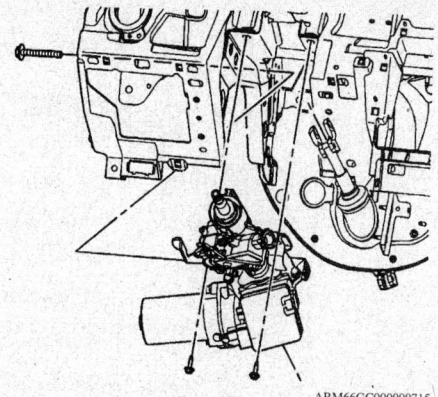

ARM66GC000000715

Fig. 17 Steering column removal. ION

J42640, or equivalent, into steering column access hole.
4. Remove steering gear stub shaft pinch bolt.
5. Remove lefthand instrument panel sound insulator.
6. Remove upper intermediate shaft coupler pinch bolt.
7. Disconnect and remove shaft.
8. Reverse procedure to install.

TURN SIGNAL & MULTI-FUNCTION SWITCH

Refer to the "Electrical" section in the "Aurora" chassis chapter.

STEERING WHEEL

Refer to the "Electrical" section in the "Aurora" chassis chapter.

STEERING COLUMN COVERS

1. Remove steering column as outlined in "Steering Column, Replace."
2. Place bottom of column holding fixture tool No. J41352, or equivalent, into suitable vise.
3. Set steering column in bottom of fixture.
4. Place top piece of tool onto column and secure using suitable screws.
5. Remove mounting screws and unsnap lower close-out shroud.
6. Remove lower shroud.
7. Remove mounting screw and upper shroud with close-out.
8. Remove close-out shroud.
9. Reverse procedure to install. Ensure shift lever seal is seated correctly in shrouds.

TILT SPRING

REMOVAL

1. Remove steering column as outlined in "Steering Column, Replace."
2. Remove upper and lower covers.
3. Tilt column to up position using tilt lever.
4. Pry tilt spring up until bulge occurs and most of tilt spring tension is removed.
5. Secure tilt spring with suitable locking pliers, continue prying until it disengages from steering column support post and tilt head.

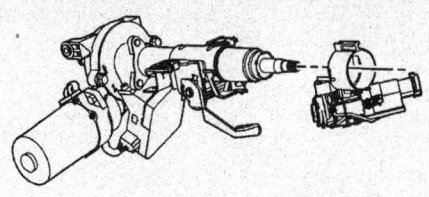

ARM66GC000000716

Fig. 18 Ignition lock cylinder case removal. ION

6. Remove spring guide from tilt spring.

INSTALLATION

1. Lubricate spring guide with suitable synthetic grease.
2. Install spring guide into tilt spring.
3. Install tilt spring to steering column support assembly post and secure.
4. Install upper and lower covers.
5. Install steering column as outlined in "Steering Column, Replace."

TURN SIGNAL CANCEL CAM & UPPER BEARING INNER RACE

1. Remove steering column as outlined in "Steering Column, Replace."
2. Remove upper and lower covers as outlined in "Steering Column Covers."
3. Remove wire harness from wire restraint clip, then the straps.
4. Remove black SIR connector from fused jumper assembly connector.
5. Remove retaining ring using suitable snap ring pliers, then the SIR coil.
6. Remove wave washer.
7. Remove bearing retainer using lock plate compressor tool No. J23653-SIR, or equivalent.
8. Remove shaft lock shield and turn signal cancel cam.
9. Remove upper bearing spring, inner race seat and inner race.
10. Disconnect pivot and pulse switch connector.
11. Depress locking tabs, then pull pivot and pulse switch out of switch mounting bracket.
12. Remove mounting screws and bracket.
13. Reverse procedure to install, noting the following:
    a. **Do not use paints, lubricants or corrosion inhibitors on bolts and nuts or joint surfaces unless specified.**
    b. Lubricate turn signal cancel cam.
    c. Turn signal and multi-function switch electrical contact must rest on turn signal cancel cam.
    d. Center SIR coil as outlined in "SIR Coil, Centering."
    e. **Improper routing of wire harness may damage SIR coil.**

SIR COIL, CENTERING.

NEW

A new inflatable restraint steering wheel module coil is pre-centered. **Do not remove the centering tab until the installation is complete.**
1. Ensure wheels are straight ahead.

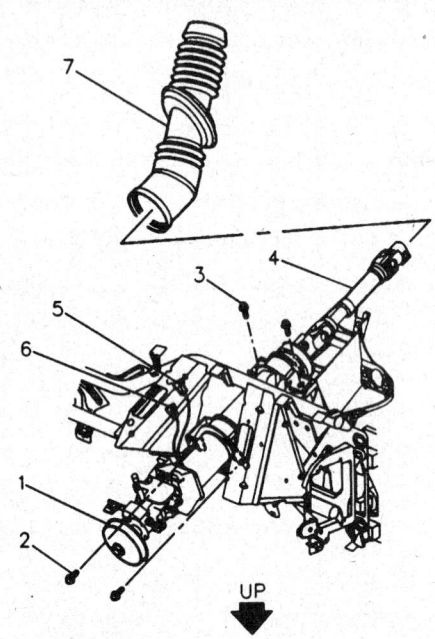

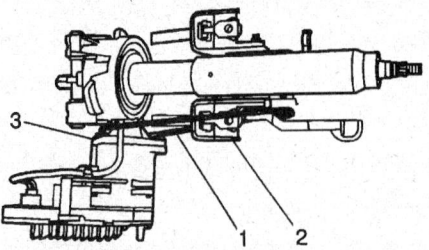

1 Tie straps
2 Rake lever bracket assemby
3 Electria Power Steering (EPS) assist mechanism bracket

ARM0300000000587

Fig. 20 Rake lever in LOCK position. 2004 Malibu

(1) Coil, SIR
(2) Bolt, Steering Column (Lower)
(3) Bolt, Steering Column (Upper)
(4) Intermediate Shaft
(5) Connection, SIR
(6) Connector, Cruise
(7) Intermediate Shaft Boot

GC6049700224000X

Fig. 19 Steering column replacement. 2001–03 Malibu

2. Align steering shaft block tooth to 12 o'clock position.
3. Ensure ignition switch is in LOCK position.
4. Align SIR coil with horn tower sticking through shaft lock shield.
5. Slide SIR coil onto steering shaft.
6. Remove and discard new SIR coil centering tab.

EXISTING

1. Ensure wheels are straight ahead.
2. Align steering shaft block tooth to 12 O.' clock position.
3. Ensure ignition switch is in LOCK position.
4. If SIR coil front has centering window and back has spring service lock, proceed as follows:
   a. Hold SIR coil with face up.
   b. While depressing spring service lock, rotate coil hub clockwise until coil ribbon stops.
   c. Rotate coil hub slowly, counterclockwise, until centering window appears yellow and both arrows line up.
   d. Release spring service lock between locking tab.
   e. Coil is now centered.
   f. Align centered coil with horn tower and slide onto steering column shaft.

5. If SIR coil front has centering window and back has no spring service lock, proceed as follows:
   a. Hold SIR coil with face up.
   b. Rotate coil hub clockwise until coil ribbon stops.
   c. Rotate coil hub slowly, counterclockwise until centering window appears yellow and both arrows line up.
   d. Coil is now centered.
   e. While holding coil hub in center position, align coil with horn tower and slide onto steering column shaft assembly.
6. If SIR coil front has no centering window, but back has spring service lock, proceed as follows:
   a. Hold coil with back side up.
   b. While depressing spring service lock, rotate coil hub counterclockwise until coil ribbon stops.
   c. Still pressing spring service lock, rotate coil hub in opposite direction 2½ revolutions.
   d. Release spring service lock between locking tabs.
   e. Coil is now centered.
   f. Align centered coil with horn tower and slide onto steering column shaft.
7. If inflatable restraint steering wheel module coil front has no centering window and back has no spring service lock, proceed as follows:
   a. Hold coil with face up.
   b. Rotate coil hub clockwise until coil ribbon stops.
   c. Rotate coil hub slowly counterclockwise for 2½ revolutions.
   d. Coil is now centered.
   e. While maintaining coil hub in center position, align centered coil with horn tower and slide onto steering column.

LOWER BEARING, JACKET & STEERING SHAFT

1. Remove switch mounting bracket as outlined in "Turn Signal Cancel Cam & Upper Bearing Inner Race."
2. Remove turn signal and multi-function switch as outlined in "Electrical" section of "Aurora" chassis chapter.

3. Remove tilt spring as outlined in "Tilt Spring."
4. Remove steering column support pivot pins using pivot pin removal tool No. J21854-1, or equivalent.
5. Remove dual triangle sensor.
6. Remove boot seal, steering shaft seal, sensor retainer and steering shaft seal.
7. Remove tilt head mounting screws and cable support bracket.
8. Remove tilt head with lower steering shaft attached.
9. Remove tilt head assembly from steering shaft.
10. Index mark race, upper shaft, and lower steering shaft to ensure proper alignment.
11. Tilt upper shaft assembly 90° and disengage.
12. Reverse procedure to install, noting the following:
    a. Apply suitable lithium grease to race and upper shaft.
    b. Lubricate bracket mounting screws with suitable Loctite.
    c. **Do not use paints, lubricants or corrosion inhibitors on fasteners or joint surfaces unless specified.**
    d. **Replace steering column support assembly if it has been staked three times.**
    e. Lubricate pivot pins with suitable synthetic grease.

SIR Coil

1. Remove driver air bag module.
2. Remove steering wheel as outlined in "Electrical" section of "Aveo" chassis chapter.
3. Remove upper and lower steering column covers.
4. Remove drivers knee bolster.
5. Disconnect driver air bag, horn and connectors from lower steering column.
6. Remove and discard screws.
7. Remove clock spring from steering shaft.
8. Reverse procedure to install.

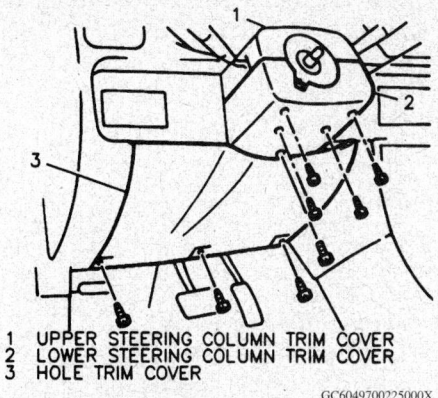

1 UPPER STEERING COLUMN TRIM COVER
2 LOWER STEERING COLUMN TRIM COVER
3 HOLE TRIM COVER

GC6049700225000X

Fig. 21 Steering column cover replacement. Metro

Camaro, Corvette & Firebird

Refer to **Figs. 25 through 28,** for exploded view of these steering columns.

LOCK CYLINDER SET, SHAFT LOCK, SIR COIL, TURN SIGNAL SWITCH & UPPER BEARING SPRING

1. Remove steering wheel as outlined in "Electrical" section of "Corvette" chassis chapter.
2. Remove SIR coil and let hang freely. Remove wave washer.
3. Remove shaft lock retaining ring lock plate using compressor tool No. J23653-SIR, or equivalent
4. Remove shaft lock assembly.
5. Remove turn signal cancel cam and upper bearing spring.
6. Remove upper bearing race seat and inner race.
7. Remove turn signal switch.
8. Remove wire protector and wire harness strap.
9. Attach suitable length of mechanics wire to both coil terminal connectors and gently pull wires through column.
10. Remove key from pass key lock cylinder set, then the buzzer switch.
11. Insert key in pass key lock cylinder and remove lock mounting screw.
12. Disconnect pass key lock cylinder terminal connector from bulkhead connector and remove wire protector.
13. Remove retaining clip from housing cover and gently pull wire harness through column.
14. Reverse procedure to install.

DIMMER SWITCH ACTUATOR ROD, LOCK HOUSING COVER, PIVOT SWITCH & TILT SPRING

1. Remove lock cylinder set, shaft lock, SIR coil, turn signal switch & upper bearing spring as outlined in "Lock Cylinder Set, Shaft Lock, SIR Coil, Turn Signal Switch & Upper Bearing Spring."
2. Remove lock cover housing end cap.

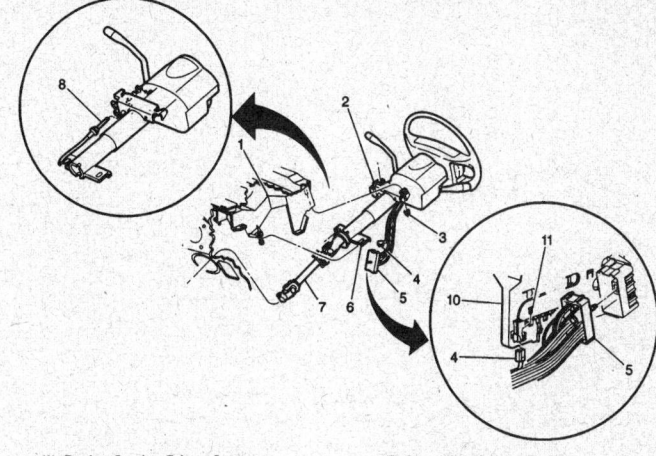

(1) Bracket, Steering Column Support
(2) Support, Steering Column Upper
(3) Nut
(4) Connector, SIR
(5) Connector, Steering Column Wiring Harness
(6) Support, Steering Column Lower
(7) Intermediate Steering Shaft
(8) Shift Lever Cable
(9) Park Lock Cable
(10) Bracket, Multiuse Module
(11) Connector, Position Assurance (CPA)

GC6049700226000X

Fig. 22 Steering column replacement. Park Avenue

3. Remove mounting screws, lock housing cover and tilt lever.
4. Remove base plate and dimmer switch actuator rod, then gently pull pivot switch wiring harness through column housing and gear shift lever bowl.
5. **On models equipped with cruise control,** unplug connector from base plate and remove multi-function switch lever.
6. Pry tilt spring up until bulge occurs and most of tilt spring tension is removed.
7. Secure tilt spring with suitable locking pliers, continue prying until it disengages from steering column support post and tilt head.
8. Remove spring retainer, then the spring guide from tilt spring.
9. **On all models,** remove pin and pivot switch.
10. Reverse procedure to install, noting the following:
   a. Coat spring guide and spring with lithium grease.
   b. Tighten lock housing cover screw in three steps:
   c. First step, tighten to 12 o'clock position.
   d. Second step, tighten to 8 o'clock position.
   e. Third step, tighten to 3 o'clock position.

ACTUATOR SECTOR, BEARINGS, COLUMN HOUSING, LOCK BOLT, LOCK SHOES & SWITCH ACTUATOR RACK

1. Remove lock cylinder set, shaft lock, SIR coil, turn signal switch & upper bearing spring as outlined in "Lock Cylinder Set, Shaft Lock, SIR Coil, Turn Signal Switch & Upper Bearing Spring."
2. Remove dimmer switch actuator rod, lock housing cover, pivot switch & tilt spring as outlined in "Dimmer Switch Actuator Rod, Lock Housing Cover,

Pivot Switch & Tilt Spring."
3. Remove lock housing cover retaining and tilt lever.
4. **On models equipped with cruise control,** unplug connector from base plate and remove multi-function lever.
5. **On all models,** remove retainer, spring and guide.
6. Remove tilt head pivot pins using pivot pin removal tool No. J21854-01, or equivalent, **Fig. 29,** then install tilt lever.
7. Remove column housing by pulling back on tilt lever and pulling housing down and away from column.
8. Remove bearing and mounting screw.
9. Remove lock bolt spring and lock bolt, then the switch actuator rack and rack preload spring.
10. Remove driveshaft and switch actuator sector.
11. Remove release lever pin and shoe release lever.
12. Remove release lever spring and dowel pin.
13. Remove steering wheel lock shoes and lock shoe springs.
14. Reverse procedure to install.

COLUMN HOUSING SUPPORT & SHIFT TUBE

1. Remove driver's side air bag module as outlined in "Passive Restraint Systems" chapter.
2. Remove ignition switch electrical connector.
3. Remove ignition switch mounting bolts, then the switch, **Fig. 30.**
4. Remove dimmer switch from actuator rod and wiring harness strap.
5. Disconnect positive assurance terminal, and dimmer switch connector from bulkhead connector.
6. Reverse procedure to install.

Bonneville & LeSabre

Refer to **Fig. 31,** for exploded view of these steering columns.

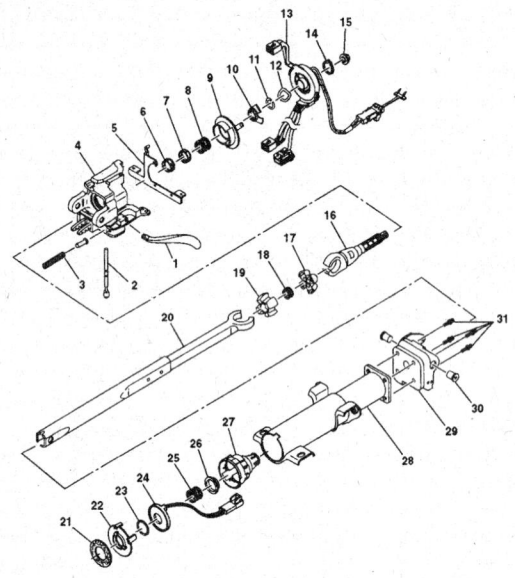

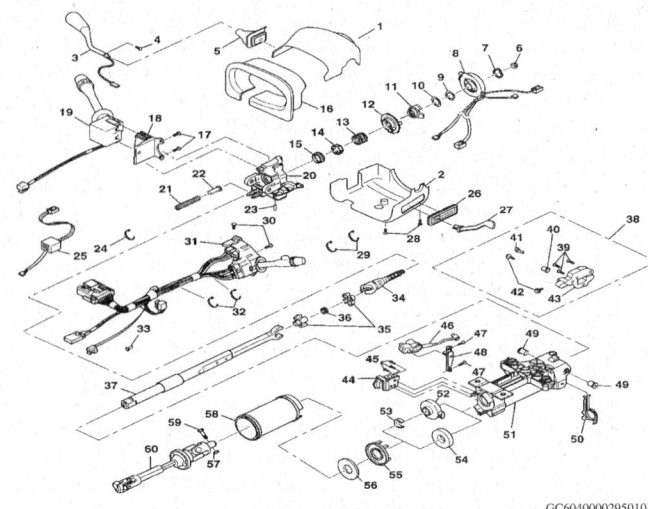

Fig. 24   Exploded view of steering column
(Part 1 of 3). Aurora

(1) Tilt Lever
(2) Anti-Rotation Pin
(3) Tilt Spring and Guide
(4) Bearing and Housing Assembly
(5) Switch Adapter Plate
(6) Upper Bearing Spring
(7) Upper Bearing Inner Race Seat
(8) Upper Bearing Spring
(9) Turn Signal Cancel Cam Assembly
(10) Cam Orientation Plate

(11) Bearing Retainer
(12) Wave Washer
(13) SIR Coil Assembly
(14) Snap Ring
(15) Flanged Prevailing Torque Nut
(16) Race and Upper Shaft Assembly
(17) Centering Sphere
(18) Joint Preload Spring
(19) Centering Sphere
(20) Lower Shaft Assembly

GC6049900252000X

**Fig. 23   Exploded view of tilt steering column. Alero
& Grand Am**

SIR COIL

1. Remove steering wheel as outlined in "Electrical" section of "Bonneville, Le-Sabre & Park Avenue" chassis chapter.
2. Remove steering column as outlined in "Steering Column, Replace."
3. Remove upper and lower steering column shrouds.
4. Remove wire harness straps and wire harness from wire restraint clip.
5. Remove black SIR connector from fused jumper connector.
6. Remove retaining ring using suitable snap ring pliers, then the SIR coil.
7. Remove wave washer.
8. Reverse procedure to assemble.

SIR COIL, CENTERING

Refer to "Passive Restraint Systems" chapter.

LINEAR SHIFT

1. Remove steering wheel as outlined in "Electrical" section of "Bonneville, Le-Sabre & Park Avenue" chassis chapter.
2. Remove steering column as outlined in "Steering Column, Replace."
3. Remove upper and lower steering column shrouds.
4. Remove wire harness straps and wire harness from wire restraint clip.
5. Disconnect shift lever electrical con-

nector, slide shift lever seal up shift lever and remove lever mounting screw.
6. Remove shift lever and electric BTSI actuator from steering column.
7. Lock cylinder should be in Off-Lock position.
8. Remove mounting screws and linear shift from steering column.
9. Reverse procedure to assemble. Tighten to specification.

TILT SPRING

The tilt spring and guide are under pressure and could become projectiles. During disassembly and assembly procedures, secure the tilt spring.
1. Remove upper and lower steering column shrouds.
2. Move steering column to Up position.
3. Pry tilt spring until bulge occurs and most of tilt spring tension is removed.
4. Secure tilt spring and continue to pry until tilt spring disengages from post on steering wheel column and column tilt head.
5. Remove tilt spring guide from tilt spring.
6. Reverse procedure to assemble.

LOCK MODULE

1. Remove steering wheel as outlined in "Electrical" section of "Bonneville, Le-Sabre & Park Avenue" chassis chapter.

2. Remove coded key controller, ignition and key alarm switch.
3. Remove upper tilt head components.
4. Lock cylinder should be in Off-Lock position.
5. Insert suitable small screwdriver into slot on lock module, push against locking tab to remove.
6. Disconnect park lock cable.
7. Remove lock module mounting screws, then the module.
8. Reverse procedure to install noting the following:
   a. Ensure gear shift lever is in park position.
   b. Put ignition switch in Off-Lock position.
   c. Unlock adjuster ring on park lock cable with park lock cable pliers tool No. J41396, or equivalent.
   d. Pull on cable until park lock latch contacts gear shift lever. Release cable.
   e. Lock adjuster ring securely in place on park lock cable with suitable cable pliers.

STEERING COLUMN TILT
HEAD HOUSING

1. Remove steering wheel as outlined in "Electrical" section of "Bonneville, Le-Sabre & Park Avenue" chassis chapter.
2. Remove bearing retainer using bearing removal tool No. J23653-SIR, or equivalent.
3. Remove shaft lock shield and turn signal cancel cam.
4. Remove upper bearing spring and inner race seat.
5. Remove inner race.
6. Reverse procedure to assemble.

LOWER BEARING &
STEERING SHAFT

1. Remove steering wheel as outlined in "Electrical" section of "Bonneville, Le-Sabre & Park Avenue" chassis chapter.
2. Remove upper tilt head components.

(1) Upper Trim Cover
(2) Lower Trim Cover
(3) Shift Lever Assembly
(4) Shift Lever Screw
(5) Shift Lever Seal
(6) Flanged Prevailing Torque Nut
(7) Retaining Ring
(8) Inflatable Restraint Steering Wheel Module Coil
(9) Wave Washer
(10) Bearing Retainer
(11) Cam Orientation Plate
(12) Turn Signal Cancel Cam Assembly
(13) Upper Bearing Spring
(14) Upper Bearing Inner Race Seat
(15) Inner Race
(16) Steering Column Closeout Trim Cover
(17) Pan Head Tapping Screw
(18) Turn Signal Switch Housing
(19) Windshield Wiper and Washer Switch Assembly
(20) Steering Column Tilt Head Assembly
(21) Tilt Spring
(22) Spring Guide
(23) Release Lever Pin
(24) Wire Harness Strap
(25) Fused Jumper Assembly
(26) Tilt Lever Closeout
(27) Tilt Knob

GC6040000295020X

Fig. 24 Exploded view of steering column (Part 2 of 3). Aurora

3. Disconnect electrical connector from pivot and pulse switch.
4. Press on locking tabs of pivot and pulse switch, then pull out pivot and pulse switch from mounting bracket.
5. Remove screws and mounting bracket.
6. Remove turn signal and multi-function switch.
7. Remove tilt spring, linear shift, shift lever and BTSI actuator.
8. Remove steering column support pivot pins using pivot pin removal tool No. J21854-1, or equivalent.
9. Remove dual triangle sensor retainer, then the sensor.
10. Remove boot and steering shaft seals.
11. Remove mounting screws and cable support bracket.
12. Remove tilt head from steering column support with lower steering shaft still attached.
13. Remove tilt head from steering shaft.
14. Index mark race, upper shaft and lower steering shaft to ensure proper alignment.
15. Reverse procedure to assemble.

Catera

Refer to **Fig. 32,** for exploded view of this steering column.

STEERING COLUMN HOUSING

1. Remove mounting screws and signal switch housing.
2. Remove heads from lock housing shear bolts using suitable ¼ inch drill bit.
3. Remove steering column housing lock and shear bolts using suitable locking type pliers.

(28) Pan Head Tapping Screws
(29) Wire Harness Straps
(30) Pan Head Tapping Screws
(31) Turn Signal and Multifunction Switch Assembly
(32) Wire Harness Straps
(33) Axial Position Assurance Connector
(34) Race and Upper Shaft Assembly
(35) Centering Sphere
(36) Joint Preload Spring
(37) Lower Shaft Assembly
(38) Linear Shift Assembly
(39) Flat Head 6-Lobed Soc Tap Screw
(40) Cam Bushing
(41) Ball and Actuator Assembly
(42) Hexagon Flange Head Bolt
(43) Gearshift Lever Assembly Support Bracket
(44) Cable Support Bracket
(45) Flat Head Screw
(46) Automatic Transmission Shift Lock Control
(47) Pan Head Tapping Screw
(47) Pan Head Tapping Screw
(48) Automatic Transmission Shift Lock Control Mounting Bracket Assembly
(49) Pivot Pin
(49) Pivot Pin
(50) Wire Restraint Clip
(51) Steering Column Support Assembly
(52) Dual Triangle Sensor Assembly
(53) Sensor Locator
(54) Boot Seal
(55) Sensor Retainer
(56) Steering Shaft Seal
(57) Bolt Retainer
(58) Boot
(59) Bolt and Retainer Assembly
(60) Intermediate Steering Shaft Assembly

GC6040000295030X

Fig. 24 Exploded view of steering column (Part 3 of 3). Aurora

4. Remove retaining ring using lock plate compressor tool No. J23653-SIR, with compressor plate adapter tool No. J23653-91, or equivalents.
5. Remove spring retainer, upper bearing spring, inner race seat and inner race.
6. Insert No. 2 Phillips head screwdriver into square opening in tilt spring retainer, **Fig. 33,** then depress tilt spring retainer and turn screwdriver to unlock tilt spring retainer.
7. Remove tilt spring retainer and tilt spring by pushing spring out towards front of column.
8. Remove pivot pins using pivot pin remover tool No. J21854-01, or equivalent, and pull tilt lever forward to release tilt shoes from column support.
9. Remove steering column.
10. Reverse procedure to install. Install new retaining ring.

LOWER BEARING, COLUMN JACKET, LOWER STEERING SHAFT & COLUMN JACKET

1. Remove steering column housing as outlined in "Steering Column, Replace."
2. Remove steering shaft from steering column housing support and jacket. **Make alignment marks on upper**

and lower steering shaft prior to disassembly.
3. Remove bearing, support screws and steering column housing.
4. Disconnect upper and lower steering shaft by tilting upper steering shaft 90° from lower steering shaft.
5. Rotate centering sphere 90° and lift centering sphere away from upper steering shaft.
6. Remove shaft preload spring from centering sphere.
7. Reverse procedure to install, noting the following:
   a. Install new centering sphere.
   b. Preload spring using centering sphere installer tool No. J41688, or equivalent, and suitable vise.

Cavalier & Sunfire

Refer to **Figs. 34 and 35,** for exploded views of these steering columns.

COLUMN LOCK CYLINDER SET, SHAFT LOCK, TURN SIGNAL CANCEL CAM & UPPER BEARING

STANDARD COLUMN

1. Remove driver's air bag module as

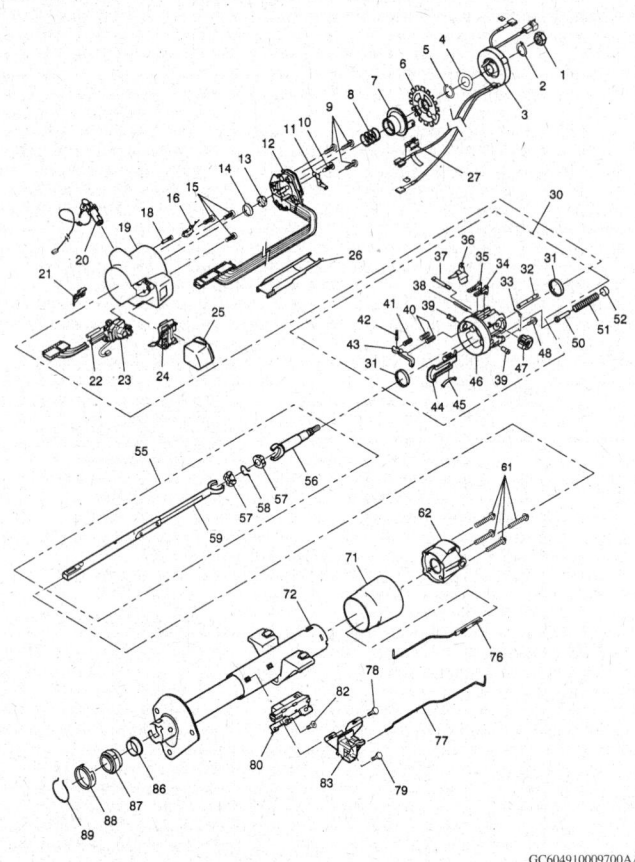

1- NUT, HEX LOCKING (M14x1.5)
2- RING, RETAINING
3- COIL ASM, INFL RESTRAINT
4- WASHER, WAVE
5- RING, RETAINING
6- LOCK, SHAFT
7- CAM ASM, TURN SIG CANCEL
8- SPRING, UPPER BEARING
9- SCREW, BNDG HD CR RECESS
10- SCREW, RD WASH HD (M4.2x1.41)
11- ARM ASM, SIGNAL SWITCH
12- SWITCH ASM, TURN SIGNAL
13- SEAT, UPPER BRG INNER RACE
14- RACE, INNER
15- SCREW, PAN HD SOC TAP
16- SWITCH ASM, BUZZER
18- SCREW, LOCK RETAINING
19- COVER ASM, LOCK HOUSING
20- LOCK CYLINDER SET, STRG COL PASS KEY
21- ACTUATOR, DIMMER SW ROD
22- PIN, SWITCH ACTUATOR PIVOT
23- SWITCH ASM, PIVOT & (PULSE)
24- BASE PLATE, COL HSG CVR END
25- CAP, COL HSG COVER END
26- PROTECTOR, WIRING
27- SHROUD, CONNECTOR
30- HOUSING ASM, STRG COLUMN
31- BEARING ASM
32- BOLT, LOCK
33- SPRING, LOCK BOLT
34- SHOE, STEERING WHEEL LOCK
35- SHOE, STEERING WHEEL LOCK
36- SHIELD, WIRE PROTECTOR
37- SHAFT, DRIVE
38- PIN, DOWEL
39- PIN, PIVOT
40- SPRING, SHOE
41- SPRING, RELEASE LEVER
42- PIN, RELEASE LEVER
43- LEVER, SHOE RELEASE
44- RACK, SWITCH ACTUATOR
45- SPRING, RACK PRELOAD
46- HOUSING, STRG COLUMN
47- SECTOR, SWITCH ACTUATOR
48- SCREW, HEX WASHER HEAD

50- GUIDE, SPRING
51- SPRING, WHEEL TILT
52- RETAINER, SPRING
54- SHAFT ASM, STEERING COLUMN
55- SHAFT ASM, RACE & UPPER
57- SPHERE, CENTERING
58- SPRING, JOINT PRELOAD
59- SHAFT ASM, LOWER STEERING
61- SCREW, SUPPORT
62- SUPPORT ASM, STRG COL HSG
71- SHROUD, STRG COLUMN HOUSING
72- JACKET ASM, STRG COL
76- ACTUATOR ASM, IGNITION SWITCH
77- ROD, DIMMER SWITCH
78- SCREW, WASH HD (#10-24X.25)
79- SCREW, HEX WASH HD TAP
80- SWITCH ASM, IGNITION
82- SCREW, FLT HD (#10-24X.31)
83- SWITCH ASM, DIMMER
86- ADAPTER, LOWER BEARING
87- BEARING ASM
88- RETAINER, BEARING ADAPTER
89- CLIP, LOWER BEARING ADAPTER

Service Kits

201- RACK SERV KIT, COL SECTOR &
     -INCLUDES: 14,31,33,44,47,48
202- SPRING SERV KIT, TILT COLUMN
     -INCLUDES: 13,14,39,50,51,52
203- COIL SERV KIT, INFL RESTRAINT
     -INCLUDES: 3,4,27
204- SPHERE SERV KIT, TILT COLUMN
     -INCLUDES: 57,58
205- GREASE SERV KIT, (SYNTHETIC)

GC604910009700BA

Fig. 25 Exploded view of steering column (Part 2 of 2). Camaro & Firebird

GC604910009700AA

Fig. 25 Exploded view of steering column (Part 1 of 2). Camaro & Firebird

outlined in "Passive Restraint Systems" chapter.

2. Remove steering wheel as outlined in "Electrical" section of "Cavalier & Sunfire" chassis chapter.

3. Remove shaft lock cover and shaft lock retaining ring using plate compressor tool No. J23653-SIR, or equivalent, to depress shaft lock.

4. Remove shaft lock, turn signal canceling cam, upper bearing spring and thrust washer.

5. Move turn signal to righthand turn position.

6. Remove multi-function lever and hazard knob.

7. Remove screw and signal switch arm, then the turn signal switch screws.

8. Remove turn signal switch and allow switch to hang freely.

9. Remove key from lock cylinder set, then the buzzer switch.

10. Install key in lock cylinder and turn to Lock position.

11. Remove mounting screw and lock cylinder set.

12. Reverse procedure to install.

TILT COLUMN

1. Remove steering wheel as outlined in "Electrical" section of "Cavalier & Sunfire" chassis chapter.

2. Remove shaft lock cover and retaining ring using plate compressor J23653-C, or equivalent, to depress shaft lock.

3. Remove shaft lock, turn signal cancel-

ing cam, upper bearing spring, upper bearing inner race seat and inner race.

4. Move turn signal to righthand turn position.

5. Remove multi-function lever and hazard knob.

6. Remove screw and signal switch arm, then the turn signal switch screws.

7. Remove turn signal switch and allow switch to hang freely.

8. Remove key from lock cylinder set, then the buzzer switch.

9. Install key in lock cylinder and turn to Lock position.

10. Remove mounting screw and lock cylinder.

11. Reverse procedure to install.

COLUMN HOUSING, IGNITION SWITCH ACTUATOR, PIVOT SWITCH, STEERING SHAFT, STEERING WHEEL LOCK SHOE, TILT SPRING & TURN SIGNAL SWITCH

STANDARD COLUMN

1. Remove steering wheel as outlined in "Electrical" section of "Cavalier & Sunfire" chassis chapter.

2. Remove steering column as outlined in "Steering Column, Replace."

3. Inspect steering column for damage.

4. Remove steering shaft retaining ring,

then the shaft.

5. Remove steering column support bracket from housing.

6. Remove turn signal switch, mounting screw and nut, then the switch.

7. Remove dimmer switch, dimmer switch rod and switch mounting stud.

8. Remove ignition switch, mounting screws and inhibitor housing.

9. Remove cover screws and lock housing cover with floor shift lever bowl and shift bowl shroud. Pull housing cover from jacket and remove upper bearing retainer.

10. Remove mounting screws, floor shift lever bowl with shift bowl shroud and shroud from bowl.

11. If required, disassemble steering column housing as follows:
    a. Remove switch actuator rack with spring and bolt.
    b. Remove spring and bolt from switch actuator rack.
    c. Remove switch actuator rod from rack.
    d. Remove spring thrust washer from spring and bolt.
    e. Remove switch actuator sector, rack preload spring, switch actuator pivot pin and switch actuator pivot.
    f. Remove bearing retaining bushing using suitable punch.
    g. Remove bearing using suitable punch.

12. Reverse procedure to install. Assemble spring and bolt with switch actuator rack to housing. **First tooth of rack must interact with first and second tooth of sector. With rack fully inserted, block tooth of sector will rest in block tooth of rack.**

TILT COLUMN

1. Remove steering wheel as outlined in "Electrical" section of "Cavalier & Sunfire" chassis chapter.

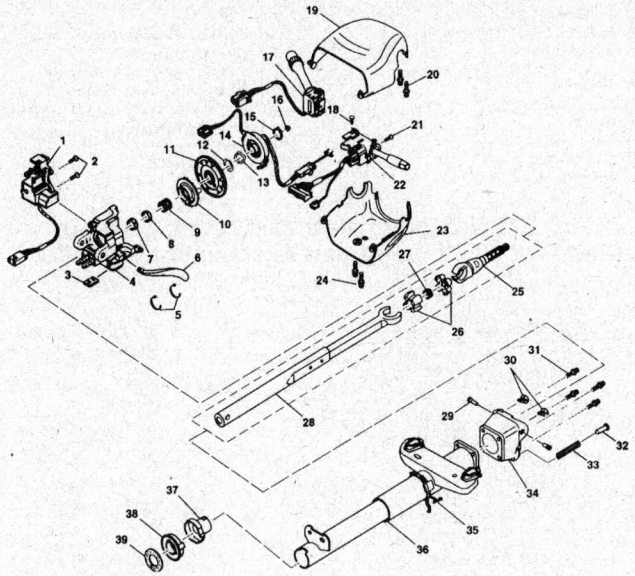

(1) Electric Column Lock
(2) Pan Head Tapping Screws
(3) Wire Harness Spacer
(4) Steering Column Tilt Head Assembly
(5) Wire Harness Straps
(6) Tilt Lever
(7) Inner Race
(8) Upper Bearing Inner Race Seat
(9) Upper Bearing Spring
(10) Turn Signal Cancel Cam Assembly
(11) Shaft Lock Shield Assembly
(12) Bearing Retainer
(13) Wave Washer

(14) SIR Coil Assembly
(15) Retaining Ring
(16) Flanged Prevailing Torque Nut
(17) Pivot and Pulse Switch Assembly
(18) Pan Head Tapping Screws
(19) Upper Shroud
(20) TORX® Head Screw
(21) Pan Head Tapping Screws
(22) Turn Signal and Multifunction Switch Assembly
(23) Lower Shroud
(24) Torx Head Screw
(25) Race and Upper Shaft Assembly

GC6049900278010X

Fig. 26 Exploded view of steering column (Part 1 of 2). Corvette non telescoping less sensor

(26) Centering Sphere
(27) Joint Preload Spring
(28) Lower Steering Shaft Assembly
(29) Pivot Pin
(30) Tilt Bumper
(31) TORX® Head Screw
(32) Spring Guide

(33) Tilt Spring
(34) Steering Column Support Assembly
(35) Wire Harness Strap
(36) Steering Column Jacket Assembly
(37) Adapter and Bearing Assembly
(38) Sensor Retainer
(39) Steering Shaft Seal

GC6049900278020X

Fig. 26 Exploded view of steering column (Part 2 of 2). Corvette non telescoping less sensor

2. Remove steering column as outlined in "Steering Column, Replace."
3. Inspect steering column for damage.
4. Disassemble lock housing cover, column housing cover end cap, pivot and pulse switch, dimmer switch rod actuator and tilt spring.
5. Remove turn signal switch with lock housing cover from steering column.
6. Remove mounting bolts and support bracket from steering column.
7. Remove wiring protectors and gently pull wire harness through column.
8. Remove pivot pins using pivot pin removal tool No. J21854-01, or equivalent, and install tilt lever.
9. Remove steering column housing and pull back on tilt lever, then pull steering column housing down and away from column.
10. Disassemble steering column housing as follows:
    a. Remove bearing , mounting screw, lock bolt spring, lock bolt, switch actuator rack and rack preload spring.
    b. Remove driveshaft and switch actuator sector.
    c. Remove release lever pin using lock shoe and release lever pin remover/installer tool No. J22635, or equivalent.
    d. Remove shoe release lever, release lever spring and dowel pin using lock shoe and release lever pin remover/installer tool No.

J22635, or equivalent.
    e. Remove lock shoes and shoe springs.
11. Assemble steering column housing as follows:
    a. Install shoe springs and lock shoes.
    b. Install dowel pin using lock shoe and release lever pin remover/installer tool No. J22635, or equivalent.
    c. Install release lever spring and shoe release lever.
    d. Install release lever pin using lock shoe and release lever pin remover/installer tool No. J22635, or equivalent.
    e. Install switch actuator sector, driveshaft and rack preload spring.
    f. Install switch actuator rack to actuator sector.
    g. Assemble bearing lubricated with lithium grease to column housing using steering column housing bearing installer tool No. J38639 and driver handle tool No. J8092, or equivalents.
    h. Install lock bolt, lock bolt spring and mounting screw.
12. Remove steering column jacket bushing and shaft.
13. Index mark upper and lower steering shaft to ensure proper alignment.
14. Disassemble steering column shaft as follows:
    a. Disassemble upper shaft from

lower steering shaft. Tilt 90° to each other and disengage.
    b. Disassemble centering sphere from upper shaft. Rotate sphere 90° and slip out.
    c. Remove joint preload spring from centering sphere.
15. Assemble steering column shaft as follows:
    a. Install joint preload spring to centering sphere.
    b. Lubricate centering sphere with lithium grease.
    c. Slip into upper shaft and rotate sphere 90°.
    d. Install upper shaft to lower steering shaft.
    e. Align marks and tilt assemblies 90° to each other.
16. Remove mounting screws and column housing support with dimmer switch rod from steering column jacket. Remove rod from support.
17. Remove lock plate from steering column jacket and housing shroud.
18. Remove dimmer switch mounting nut & screw, then the switch.
19. Remove mounting stud and ignition switch with switch actuator.
20. Remove switch actuator.
21. Remove mounting screws and ignition switch inhibitor housing.
22. Remove ignition switch inhibitor from ignition switch.
23. Reverse procedure to install.

LOCK HOUSING COVER & TILT SPRING

1. Remove steering wheel as outlined in "Electrical" section of "Cavalier & Sunfire" chassis chapter.
2. Remove tilt lever, cover screws and lock housing cover. Let cover hang freely.
3. Remove column housing cover end cap with dimmer switch rod actuator and actuator from end cap.
4. Remove pivot, pivot and pulse switch actuator.
5. Remove spring retainer using suitable cross recess head screwdriver to push retainer down and turn clockwise to release.
6. Remove spring and spring guide.
7. Reverse procedure to install, noting the following:
    a. Coat spring guide and spring with lithium grease.
    b. Tighten lock housing cover screw in three steps:
    c. First step, tighten to 12 o'clock position.
    d. Second step, tighten to 8 o'clock position.

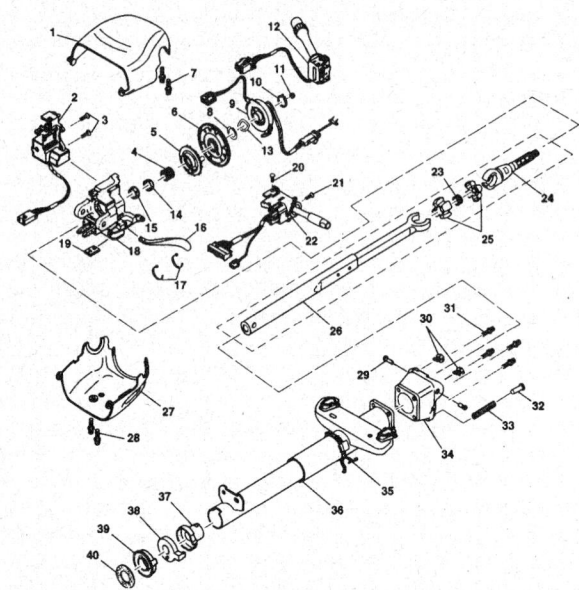

(23) Joint Preload Spring
(24) Race and Upper Shaft Assembly
(25) Centering Sphere
(26) Lower Steering Shaft Assembly
(27) Lower Shroud
(28) TORX® Head Screw
(29) Pivot Pin
(30) Tilt Bumper
(31) TORX® Head Screw
(32) Spring Guide

(33) Tilt Spring
(34) Steering Column Support Assembly
(35) Wire Harness Strap
(36) Steering Column Jacket Assembly
(37) Adapter and Bearing Assembly
(38) High Resolution Steering Wheel Position Sensor Assembly
(39) Sensor Retainer
(40) Steering Shaft Seal

GC6049900277020X

Fig. 27 Exploded view of steering column (Part 2 of 2). Corvette non telescoping w/sensor

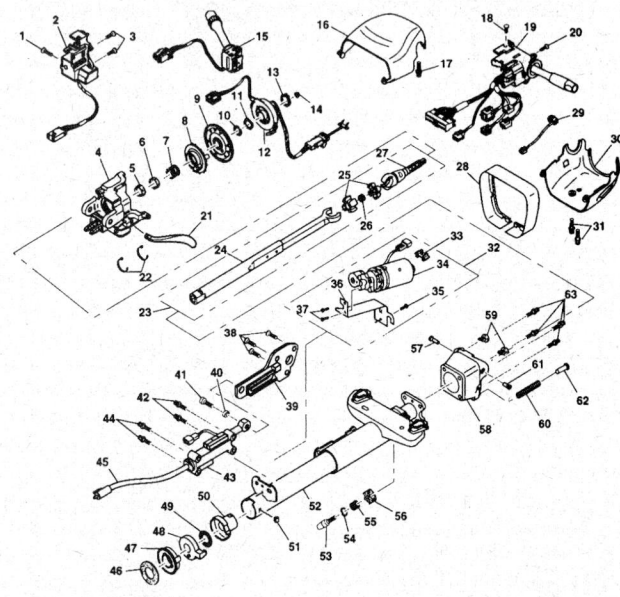

(1) Upper Shroud
(2) Electric Column Lock
(3) Pan Head Tapping Screw
(4) Upper Bearing Spring
(5) Turn Signal Cancel Cam Assembly
(6) Shaft Lock Shield Assembly
(7) Torx Head Screw
(8) Bearing Retainer
(9) SIR Coil Assembly
(10) Retaining Ring
(11) Flanged Prevailing Torque Nut
(12) Pivot and Pulse Switch Assembly
(13) Wave Washer
(14) Upper Bearing Inner Race Seat
(15) Inner Race
(16) Tilt Lever
(17) Wire Harness Straps
(18) Steering Column Tilt Head Assembly
(19) Wire Harness Spacer
(20) Pan Head Tapping Screws
(21) Pan Head Tapping Screws
(22) Turn Signal and Multifunction Switch Assembly

GC6049900277010X

Fig. 27 Exploded view of steering column (Part 1 of 2). Corvette non telescoping w/sensor

e. Third step, tighten to 3 o'clock position.

Century, Grand Prix, Intrigue & Regal

Refer to **Figs. 36 and 37,** for exploded view of steering columns.

UPPER COLUMN

1. Remove steering column as outlined in "Steering Column, Replace."
2. Remove retaining ring and SIR coil.
3. Remove shaft lock retaining ring using lock plate compressor tool No. J23653-SIR, or equivalent, and shaft lock plate.
4. Remove turn signal cancel cam, then the upper bearing spring, race seat and inner race.
5. Reverse procedure to install.

MID COLUMN

1. Remove steering column cover as outlined in "Steering Column, Replace."
2. Remove mounting bolt, ball and actuator.
3. Disconnect park lock cable and remove park lock cable mounting screws.
4. Remove shift lever clevis and park lock cable from support bracket.
5. Disconnect BTSI actuator arm from outer shift cable ball stud and transaxle shift cable from inner ball stud.

6. Remove mounting bolt and cable shift cam.
7. Remove cam bushing and cam mounting screws.
8. Remove gearshift lever support bracket.
9. Reverse procedure to install.

LOWER COLUMN

1. Remove steering guide from steering column jacket and steering column covers as outlined in "Steering Column, Replace."
2. Remove turn signal and multi-function switch.
3. Remove cam mounting bolt, ball and actuator.
4. Disconnect park lock cable and remove park lock cable mounting screws.
5. Remove shift lever clevis.
6. Pry up on tilt spring and spring guide until bulge appears and most spring

(1) Pan Head Tapping Screws
(2) Electric Column Lock
(3) Pan Head Tapping Screws
(4) Steering Column Tilt Head Assembly
(5) Inner Race
(6) Upper Bearing Inner Race Seat
(7) Upper Bearing Spring
(8) Turn Signal Cancel Cam Assembly
(9) Shaft Lock Shield Assembly
(10) Bearing Retainer
(11) Wave Washer
(12) SIR Coil Assembly
(13) Retaining Ring
(14) Flanged Prevailing Torque Nut
(15) Pivot and Pulse Switch Assembly
(16) Upper Shroud
(17) TORX® Head Screw
(18) Pan Head Tapping Screws
(19) Turn Signal and Multifunction Switch Assembly
(20) Pan Head Tapping Screws
(21) Tilt Lever
(22) Wire Harness Strap
(23) Steering Shaft Assembly
(24) Lower Steering Yoke Assembly
(25) Centering Sphere

GC6049900279010X

Fig. 28 Exploded view of steering column (Part 1 of 2). Corvette telescoping

tension is removed.
7. Secure spring with suitable pair of locking pliers and continue to pry until spring disengages from post.
8. Remove spring guide from spring.
9. Remove steering shaft seal and sensor retainer from adapter and bearing.
10. Remove lower spring retainer, bearing spring and seat.
11. Remove adapter and bearing from steering column jacket.
12. Remove pivot pins using pivot pin removal tool No J21854-01, or equivalent.
13. Remove steering column tilt head with steering shaft by installing and pulling tilt arm to disengage steering wheel lock shoes from dowel pins in steering column support.
14. Disconnect upper and lower steering shaft by tilting upper steering shaft 90° from lower steering shaft.
15. Rotate centering sphere 90° and lift

(26) Joint Preload Spring
(27) Race and Upper Shaft Assembly
(28) Steering Column Close Out Shroud
(29) Telescoping Switch Assembly
(30) Lower Shroud
(31) Pan Head Tapping Screw
(32) Telescope Motor and Bracket Assembly
(33) Connector Clip
(34) Telescope Drive Motor Assembly
(35) Pan Head Tapping Screws
(36) Telescope Drive Bracket
(37) Pan Head Tapping Screws
(38) Flat Head 6–Lobed Soc Tap Screw
(39) Telescope Adapter Assembly
(40) Telescope Drive Ball
(41) Telescope Drive Bolt
(42) TORX® Head Screw
(43) Telescope Actuator Assembly
(44) TORX® Head Screw
(45) Cable Assembly

(46) Steering Shaft Seal
(47) Sensor Retainer
(48) Hi Resolution Steering Wheel Position Sensor Assembly
(49) Lower Spring Retainer
(50) Adapter and Bearing Assembly
(51) Switch Housing Blocking Plug
(52) Telebearing and Jacket Assembly
(53) Shoulder Bolt
(54) Retaining Ring
(55) Compression Spring
(56) Anti Rotation Ball
(57) Pivot Pin
(58) Steering Column Support Assembly
(59) Tilt Bumper
(60) Tilt Spring
(61) Pivot Pin
(62) Spring Guide
(63) Support Screw

GC6049900279020X

Fig. 28 Exploded view of steering column (Part 2 of 2). Corvette telescoping

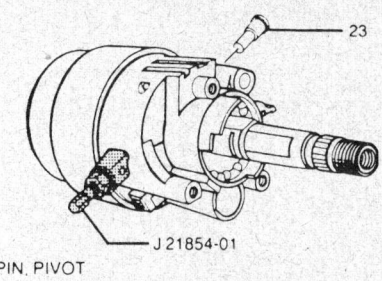

23 PIN, PIVOT

GC6049100092000X

Fig. 29 Pivot pin removal. Camaro, Corvette, DeVille, Firebird & Park Avenue

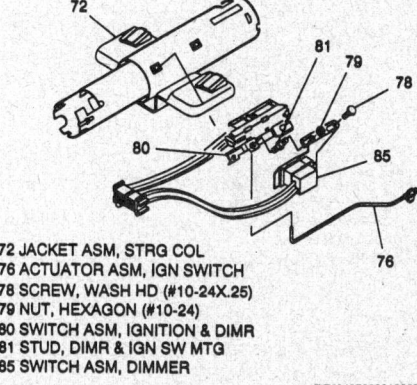

72 JACKET ASM, STRG COL
76 ACTUATOR ASM, IGN SWITCH
78 SCREW, WASH HD (#10-24X.25)
79 NUT, HEXAGON (#10-24)
80 SWITCH ASM, IGNITION & DIMR
81 STUD, DIMR & IGN SW MTG
85 SWITCH ASM, DIMMER

GC6049700231000X

Fig. 30 Ignition & dimmer switch replacement. Camaro, Corvette & Firebird

centering sphere away from upper steering shaft.
16. Remove shaft preload spring from centering sphere.
17. Reverse procedure to install, noting the following:
   a. Install new centering sphere.
   b. Preload spring, using centering sphere installer tool No. J41688, or equivalent, and suitable vise.

SHAFT LOCK SHIELD, TURN SIGNAL CAM, UPPER BEARING SPRING, UPPER BEARING INNER RACE SEAT & INNER RACE

1. Remove steering wheel as outlined in "Electrical" section of "Century, Grand Prix, Impala, Intrigue, LaCrosse, Lumina, Monte Carlo & Regal" chassis chapter.
2. Remove SIR coil and let hang freely.
3. Remove shaft lock by push down using lock plate compressor tool No. J23653-SIR, or equivalent.
4. Remove shaft lock shield.
5. Remove turn signal cancel cam.
6. Remove upper bearing spring, inner race seat, and inner race.
7. Reverse procedure to install.

LOCK MODULE

1. Remove steering wheel as outlined in "Electrical" section of "Century, Grand Prix, Impala, Intrigue, LaCrosse, Lumina, Monte Carlo & Regal" chassis chapter.
2. Remove shaft lock shield, turn signal cam, upper bearing spring, upper bearing inner race seat, and inner race.
3. Put lock cylinder in Off-Lock position and gear shift into Park position.
4. Insert small blade screwdriver into slot in lock module.
5. Push against locking tab on end of cable and remove.
6. Pry retaining clip on alarm switch with suitable small blade screwdriver.
7. Rotate alarm switch ¼ turn and remove.
8. Remove from ignition and key alarm switch mounting screws. Let switch hang freely.

9. **Lock bolt is under slight spring pressure from lock bolt spring. Hold lock bolt in place while removing lock module.**
10. Remove mounting screws and lock module.
11. Remove lock bolt with spring.
12. Remove spring from lock bolt.
13. Remove lock cylinder.
14. Reverse procedure to install.

ELECTRIC PARK LOCK

1. Remove transmission fuse No. 24 in instrument panel fuse panel.
2. Remove filler plug on bottom of lower shroud.
3. Insert suitable small screwdriver into hole and push up on manual override of electric park lock.
4. Turn key to Lock position, and remove.
5. Remove upper and lower steering column covers.
6. Remove mounting screw and black connector.
7. Remove electronic park lock from lock module with suitable small screwdriver.
8. Reverse procedure to install.

TILT SPRING

Tilt spring and spring guide are under pressure. During removal and installation secure spring with suitable locking pliers.
1. Remove lower shroud mounting screws.
2. Tilt shroud down, slide back to disengage locking tabs and remove.
3. Tilt column to up position.
4. Pry spring up until bulge occurs and most of spring tension is removed.
5. Secure spring with locking pliers and continue prying until spring disengages from post on steering column.
6. Remove spring guide from tilt spring.
7. Reverse procedure to install.

LINEAR SHIFT

Linear shift may be removed as an assembly or certain components may be disassembled as required to do repairs. Remove or disassemble only those components required to do repairs.
1. Remove upper and lower covers as outlined in "Steering Column, Replace."

2. Place lock cylinder in Off-Lock position and gear shift in Park position.
3. Insert suitable small blade screwdriver into slot in lock module.
4. Push against locking tab on end of cable to release and remove park lock cable.
5. Pry actuator arm of electrical actuator from outer shift cable ball stud on cable shift cam and mounting pin on jacket.
6. Remove transaxle cable from inner shift cable ball stud on cable shift cam.
7. Shift column to Neutral position to gain access to lower mounting screw.
8. Remove mounting screws and linear shift.
9. Reverse procedure to install.

CTS

Refer to **Fig. 38,** for exploded view of steering column.

INTERMEDIATE STEERING SHAFT

UPPER

1. Ensure wheels are in straight ahead position and ignition in LOCK position with key removed.
2. Lock steering column using tool No. J42640, or equivalent.
3. Raise and support vehicle using suitable lift.
4. Remove upper to lower intermediate

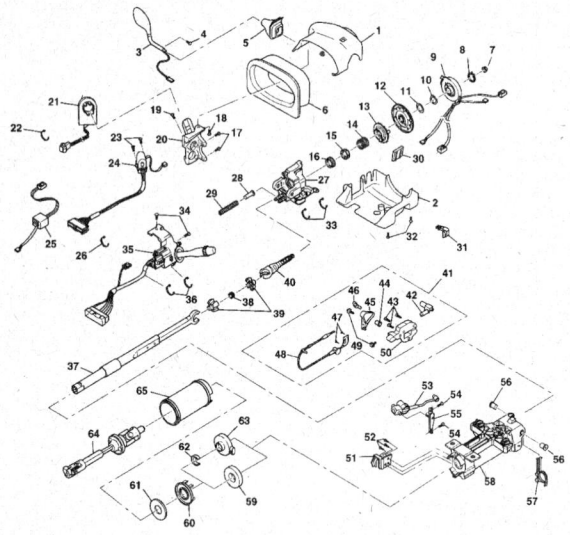

(1) Upper Shroud
(2) Lower Shroud
(3) Automatic Transmission Control Lever Assembly
(4) Shift Lever Screw
(5) Shift Lever Seal
(6) Steering Column Closeout Shroud
(7) Hexagon Locking Nut
(8) Retaining Ring
(9) SIR Coil Assembly
(10) Wave Washer
(11) Bearing Retainer
(12) Shaft Lock Shield Assembly
(13) Turn Signal Cancel Cam Assembly
(14) Upper Bearing Spring
(15) Upper Bearing Inner Race Seat
(16) Inner Race
(17) Pan Head Tapping Screw
(18) TORX® Head Screw
(19) Pan Head Tapping Screw
(20) Lock Module Assembly
(21) Coded Key Controller
(22) Wire Harness Strap
(23) Tapping Screw

(24) Ignition & Key Alarm Switch Assembly
(25) Fused Jumper Assembly
(26) Wire Harness Strap
(27) Tilt Spring
(28) Spring Guide
(29) Steering Column Tilt Head Assembly
(30) Shroud Protector
(31) Tilt Lever Assembly
(32) Pan Head Tapping Screw
(33) Wire Harness Strap
(34) Pan Head Tapping Screw
(35) Turn Signal and Multifunction Switch
(36) Wire Harness Strap
(37) Lower Steering Shaft Assembly
(38) Joint Preload Spring
(39) Centering Sphere
(40) Race and Upper Shaft Assembly
(41) Linear Shift Assembly
(42) Shift Lever Clevis
(43) Flat Head 6-Lobed Socket Tapping Screw
(44) Cam Bushing

(45) Cable Shift Cam Assembly
(46) Ball and Actuator Assembly
(47) Oval Head 6-Lobed Socket Tapping Screw
(48) Park Lock Cable Assembly
(49) Hex Flanged Head Bolt
(50) Gear Shift Lever Assembly Support Bracket
(51) Cable Support Bracket
(52) Flat Head Screw
(53) Electrical BTSI Actuator
(54) Pan Head Tapping Screw
(55) BTSI Mounting Bracket Assembly
(56) Pivot Pin
(57) Wire Restraint Clip
(58) Steering Column Support Assembly
(59) Steering Shaft Seal
(60) Sensor Retainer
(61) Steering Shaft Seal
(62) Sensor Locator
(63) Sensor Steer Sensor Assembly
(64) Intermediate Steering Shaft Assembly
(65) Boot Seal

GC6049900286010X

GC6049900286020X

Fig. 31 Exploded view of steering column (Part 1 of 2). Bonneville & LeSabre

Fig. 31 Exploded view of steering column (Part 2 of 2). Bonneville & LeSabre

shaft attaching bolt, then lower vehicle, **Fig. 39.**
5. Remove steering column as outlined in "Steering Column, Replace."
6. Remove upper intermediate shaft to steering column attaching bolt, then the shaft from steering column.
7. Reverse procedure to install.

LOWER

1. Ensure wheels are in straight ahead position and ignition in LOCK position with key removed.
2. Lock steering column using tool No. J42640, or equivalent.
3. Raise and support vehicle using suitable lift.
4. Remove upper to lower intermediate shaft attaching bolt, then lower vehicle, **Fig. 39.**
5. Remove lower intermediate shaft to power steering gear retaining bolt, then the shaft from steering gear.
6. Remove lower intermediate shaft from upper shaft.
7. Reverse procedure to install.

STEERING COLUMN TRIM COVERS

1. Remove steering wheel as outlined in "Electrical" section of "CTS" chassis chapter.
2. Remove tilt steering column lever.
3. Remove trim plug of lower trim cover.
4. Remove lower trim cover to steering column attaching screws, then the

lower trim cover.
5. Remove upper trim cover screws, then the upper cover.
6. Reverse procedure to install.

IGNITION SWITCH

Refer to "Ignition Switch, Replace" in "Electrical" section of "CTS" chassis chapter for ignition switch replacement procedure.

IGNITION LOCK

Refer to "Ignition Lock, Replace" in "Electrical" section of "CTS" chassis chapter for ignition lock replacement procedure.

IGNITION LOCK CYLINDER CASE

Refer to "Ignition Switch, Replace" in "Electrical" section of "CTS" chassis chapter for ignition switch replacement procedure.

MULTI-FUNCTION SWITCH

Refer to "Multi-Function Switch, Replace" in "Electrical" section of "CTS" chassis chapter for multi-function switch replacement procedure.

TILT LEVER

Pull tilt lever straight out from steering column to remove. Slide lever into position to install.

TILT SPRING

1. Remove steering column trim covers

as outlined in "Steering Column Trim Covers."
2. Ensure tilt lever is in UP position, **Fig. 40.**
3. Remove tilt spring from steering column support using suitable locking pliers, **Fig. 41.**
4. Remove spring guide from tilt spring, **Fig. 42.**
5. Reverse procedure to install.

STEERING COLUMN TILT HEAD

1. Remove steering column as outlined in "Steering Column, Replace."
2. Remove lock cylinder as outlined in "Electrical" section of "CTS" chassis chapter.
3. Remove multi-function switch as outlined in "Electrical" section of "CTS" chassis chapter.
4. Remove tilt spring as outlined in "Tilt Spring."
5. Remove pivot pins from steering column tilt head using tool No. J21854-01, **Fig. 43.**
6. Install tilt lever to steering column tilt head assembly, then pull back lever at same time pull steering column tilt head assembly down and away from steering column.
7. Remove steering column tilt head, steering shaft and steering column jacket assembly, **Fig. 44,** then the tilt lever.
8. Remove lower bearing and sensor, then the steering shaft from steering column assembly, **Fig. 45.**
9. Reverse procedure to install.

TURN SIGNAL CANCEL CAM & UPPER BEARING

1. Remove steering wheel as outlined in "Electrical" section of "CTS" chassis chapter.
2. Remove SIR coil as outlined in "Passive Restraint Systems."
3. Remove bearing retainer using tool Nos. J23653 and J42137, or equivalents, **Fig. 46.**
4. Disassemble and remove cam and race in numbered sequence, **Fig. 47.**
5. Reverse procedure to install.

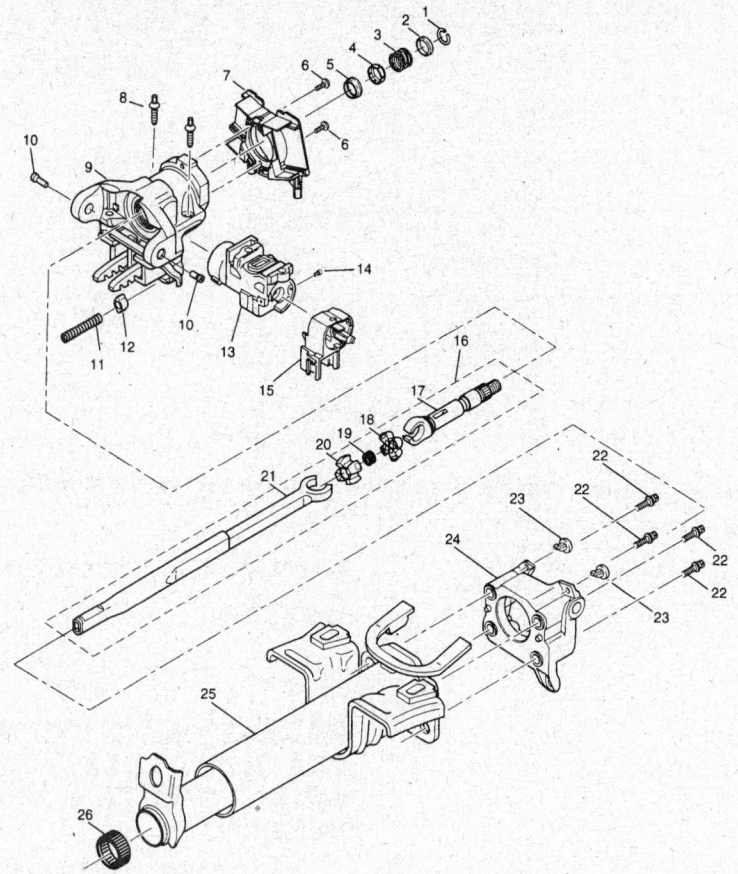

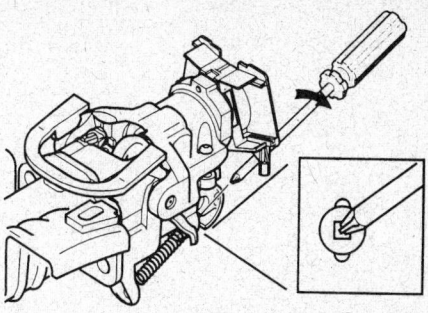

Fig. 33 Tilt spring replacement. Catera

GC6049700243000X

1. Ring, Retaining
2. Retainer, Spring
3. Spring, Upper Bearing
4. Seat, Inner Race
5. Race, Inner
6. Screw, Support
7. Housing, Signal Switch
8. Bolt, Shear
9. Housing, Steering Column
10. Pin, Pivot
11. Spring, Wheel Tilt
12. Retainer, Spring
13. Housing Asm, Lock Ay A/Trns

14. Screw, Set
15. Switch Asm, Ignition
16. Shaft Assembly, Steering
17. Shaft Assembly, Race and Upper
18. Sphere, Centering
19. Spring, Joint Preload
20. Sphere, Centering
21. Shaft Assembly, Lower Steering
22. Screw, Support
23. Bumper
24. Support, Strging Column Housing
25. Jacket Asm, Steering Column
26. Bearing Assembly, Lower Shaft

GC6049700242000X

Fig. 32 Exploded view of steering column. Catera

STEERING COLUMN WIRING HARNESS

1. Remove steering column trim covers as outlined in "Steering Column Trim Covers."
2. Remove wire harness strap, then the theft deterrent control module.
3. Remove lock cylinder as outlined in "Electrical" section of "CTS" chassis chapter.
4. Disconnect connector from theft deterrent control module.
5. Remove theft deterrent control module from ignition lock cylinder case assembly.
6. Rotate key alarm connector 90°, then pull connector from ignition lock cylinder case.
7. Disconnect ignition switch electrical connector, then remove wires in switch clip on side of ignition switch.

8. Disconnect all electrical connectors to wiring harness, **Fig. 48.**
9. Reverse procedure to install.

STEERING WHEEL POSITION SENSOR

1. Remove multi-function switch as outlined in "Electrical" section of "CTS" chassis chapter.
2. Remove tilt spring as outlined in "Tilt Spring."
3. Remove pivot pins using tool No. J21854, or equivalent, from steering column support, **Fig. 49.**
4. **On models equipped with sensor,** remove sensor locator, then the sensor, **Fig. 50.**
5. **On models less sensor,** remove steering shaft seal and sensor retainer, **Fig. 50.**
6. **On all models,** reverse procedure to install.

Malibu

2001-03

Refer to **Fig. 51,** for exploded view of this steering column.

STEERING COLUMN COVERS

1. Remove tilt lever and lower steering column cover mounting screws.
2. Separate column covers by snapping apart.
3. Reverse procedure to install.

SIR COIL

1. Remove steering wheel as outlined in "Electrical" section of "Alero, Grand Am & Malibu" chassis chapter.
2. Remove nut, retaining ring and coil.
3. Remove wave washer.
4. Reverse procedure to install. Center SIR coil as outlined in "SIR Coil, Centering."

SIR COIL, CENTERING

Refer to "Passive Restraint Systems" chapter for SIR centering procedure.

PIVOT PINS, SHAFT LOCK, STEERING COLUMN HOUSING, TILT SPRING & UPPER BEARING

1. Remove steering wheel as outlined in "Electrical" section of "Alero, Grand Am & Malibu" chassis chapter.
2. Remove SIR coil assembly.
3. Remove retaining ring using lock plate compressor tool No. J23653-SIR, or equivalent.
4. Remove turn signal cancel cam orientation plate and turn signal cancel cam.
5. Remove tilt spring, guide and upper bearing spring.
6. Remove upper bearing inner race seat and race.
7. Remove two pivot pins using pivot pin remover tool No. J21854-01, or equivalent.
8. Pull tilt arm to disengage steering wheel lock shoes from dowel pins in steering column support.
9. Remove steering column housing and bearing.
10. Reverse procedure to install.

STEERING COLUMN SHAFT

1. Remove steering wheel as outlined in "Electrical" section of "Alero, Grand Am & Malibu" chassis chapter.

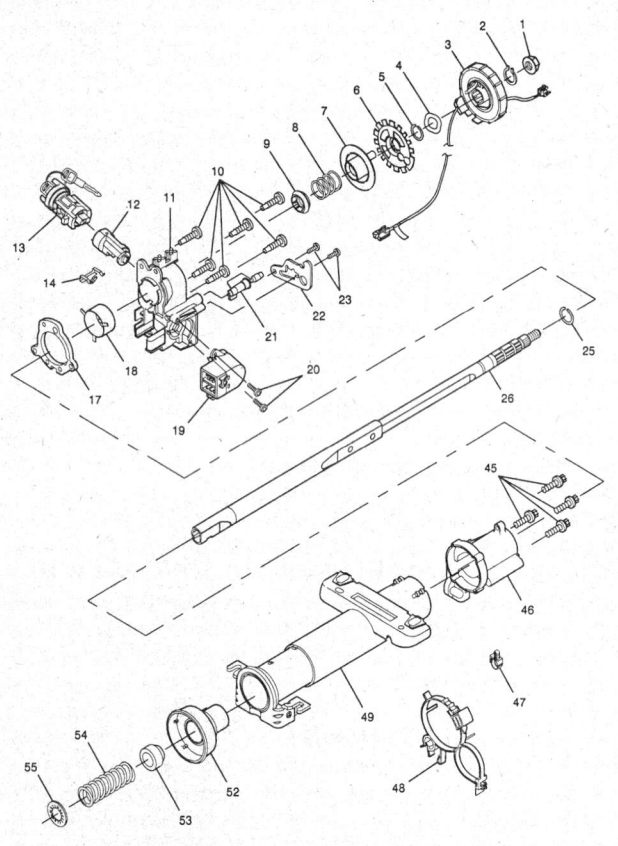

1-NUT, HEX LOCKING (M14x1.5)
2-RING, RETAINING
3-COIL ASM, SIR
4-WASHER, WAVE
5-RING, RETAINING
6-LOCK, SHAFT
7-CAM ASM, T/SIG CANCEL
8-SPRING, UPPER BEARING
9-SPACER, UPPER BEARING
10-SCREW, ADAPTER
11-HOUSING ASM, STRG COLUMN
12-ACTUATOR ASM, IGNITION LOCK
13-LOCK CYL SET, STRG COLUMN
14-SPRING, LOCK PRE-LOAD
17-PLATE, MOUNTING
18-RETAINER, BEARING
19-SWITCH ASM, IGNITION
20-SCREW, TAPPING
21-BOLT ASM, LOCK
22-BRACKET, LOCK BOLT SUPPORT
23-SCREW, TAPPING
25-RING, RETAINING
26-SHAFT ASM, STEERING
45-SCREW, SUPPORT
46-ADAPTER, SUPPORT MOUNTING
47- CLIP, WIRE RESTRAINT

48-STRAP, WIRE
49-JACKET ASM, STRG COL
52-BEARING ASM, ADAPTER &
53-SEAT, LOWER BEARING
54-SPRING, LOWER BEARING
55-RETAINER, LOWER SPRING

Service Kits

201-GREASE SERV KIT, (SYNTHETIC)

GC604950016600BX

Fig. 34 Exploded view of standard steering column (Part 2 of 2). Cavalier & Sunfire

GC604950016600AX

Fig. 34 Exploded view of standard steering column (Part 1 of 2). Cavalier & Sunfire

2. Remove upper tilt head components.
3. Remove steering shaft seal and sensor retainer, then the lower bearing seat, spring and retainer, **Fig. 52.**
4. Remove adapter and bearing from jacket, then the steering shaft from steering column jacket.
5. Remove lower and upper steering shaft.
6. Remove centering sphere from upper shaft by rotating sphere 90° then slide sphere from shaft, **Fig. 53.**
7. Remove shaft preload spring from centering sphere.
8. Reverse procedure to install, noting the following:
   a. Install new centering sphere.
   b. Preload spring, using centering sphere installer tool No. J41688, or equivalent, and suitable vise.
   c. Install lower bearing seat, lower bearing spring and lower spring retainer.
   d. Compressing lower bearing spring to 0.91–0.94 inches between lower bearing seat and retainer.

2004

Refer to **Fig. 54,** for exploded view of this steering column.

SIR COIL

1. Remove steering wheel as outlined in "Electrical" section of "Alero, Grand Am & Malibu" chassis chapter.
2. Remove nut, retaining ring and coil.
3. Remove wave washer.
4. Reverse procedure to install. Center SIR coil as outlined in "SIR Coil, Centering."

SIR COIL, CENTERING

1. Remove steering wheel as outlined in "Electrical" section of "Alero, Grand Am & Malibu" chassis chapter.
2. Ensure wheels are in straight ahead position and ignition switch is in LOCK position.
3. Ensure block tooth and centering mark of steering shaft assembly is in 12 o'clock position, **Fig. 55.**
4. Hold SIR coil by casing with face of coil pointing upward.
5. Rotate coil hub clockwise 2 ½ turns, then rotate coil hub 2 ½ turns counterclockwise.
6. Ensure ribbon cable is present in centering window, **Fig. 56.**
7. Ensure sub stator and rotator arrows are aligned, **Fig. 56.**
8. Slide SIR coil onto steering shaft.

DeVille, Eldorado & Seville

Refer to **Figs. 57 and 58,** for exploded view of these steering column.

PASS KEY LOCK CYLINDER SET, SHAFT LOCK, TURN SIGNAL SWITCH & UPPER BEARING

1. Remove steering wheel as outlined in "Electrical" section of "DeVille, Eldorado, Seville & STS" chassis chapter.
2. Remove retaining ring and coil. Remove wave washer.
3. Remove shaft lock retaining ring using compressor tool No. J23653-C, or equivalent, to push down shaft lock.
4. Remove shaft lock and turn signal canceling cam.
5. Remove upper bearing spring and upper bearing inner race seat.
6. Remove inner race and move turn signal to righthand turn position.
7. Remove multi-function lever and hazard knob.
8. Remove signal switch arm and mounting screws.
9. Disconnect turn signal switch connector from bulkhead connector.
10. Remove wiring protector.
11. Gently pull wire harness through column.
12. **SIR coil will become uncentered if steering column is separated from steering gear and is allowed to rotate; or if centering spring is pushed down, letting hub rotate while coil is removed from steering column.**
13. Remove coil terminal from vehicle harness.
14. Remove yellow connector shroud from black terminal connector.
15. Remove wiring protector.
16. Attach suitable length of mechanics

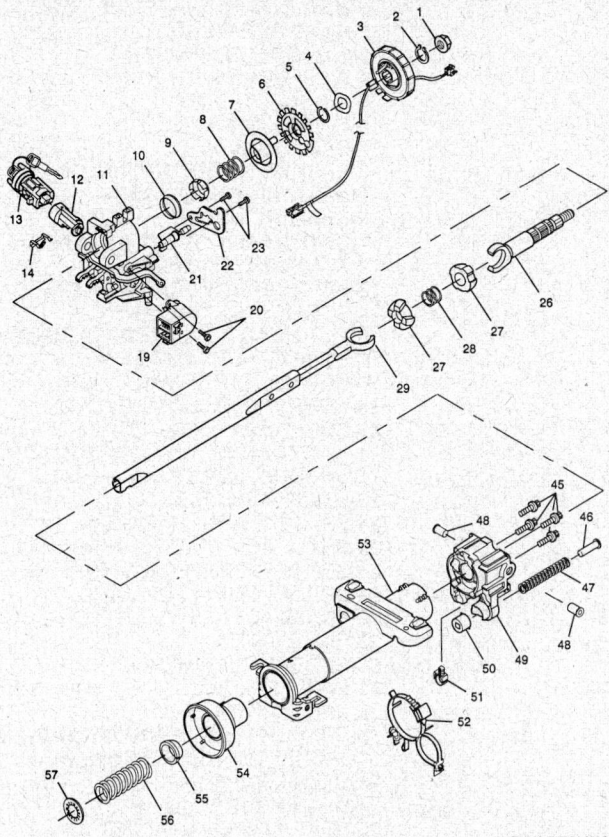

1- NUT, HEX LOCKING (M14x1.5)
2- RING, RETAINING
3- COIL ASM, SIR
4- WASHER, WAVE
5- RING, RETAINING
6- LOCK, SHAFT
7- CAM ASM, T/SIG CANCEL
8- SPRING, UPPER BEARING
9- SEAT, UPPER BEARING INNER RACE
10- RACE, INNER
11- HOUSING ASM, BRG &
12- ACTUATOR ASM, IGNITION LOCK
13- LOCK CYL SET, STRG COLUMN
14- SPRING, LOCK PRE-LOAD
19- SWITCH ASM, IGNITION
20- SCREW, TAPPING
21- BOLT ASM, LOCK
22- BRACKET, LOCK BOLT SUPPORT
23- SCREW, TAPPING
26- SHAFT ASM, RACE & UPPER
27- SPHERE, CENTERING
28- SPRING, JOINT PRELOAD
29- SHAFT ASM, LOWER
45- SCREW, SUPPORT
46- GUIDE, SPRING
47- SPRING, WHEEL TILT
48- PIN, PIVOT
49- SUPPORT ASM, STRG COL
50- RETAINER, SPRING
51- CLIP, WIRE RESTRAINT
52- STRAP, WIRE

53- JACKET ASM, STRG COL
54- BEARING ASM, ADAPTER &
55- SEAT, LOWER BEARING
56- SPRING, LOWER BEARING
57- RETAINER, LOWER SPRING

Service Kits

201- SPRING SERV KIT, TILT COLUMN
   -INCLUDES: 9,10,47
202- SPHERE SERV KIT, TILT COLUMN
   -INCLUDES: 27,28
203- GREASE SERV KIT, (SYNTHETIC)

GC604950016700BX

Fig. 35 Exploded view of tilt steering column (Part 2 of 2). Cavalier & Sunfire

GC604950016700AX

Fig. 35 Exploded view of tilt steering column (Part 1 of 2). Cavalier & Sunfire

wire to coil terminal connector.
17. Gently pull wire through column.
18. Remove key from pass key lock cylinder set, **Fig. 59.**
19. Remove buzzer switch and insert key in pass key in lock cylinder. Ensure key is in Lock position.
20. Remove lock mounting screw.
21. Disconnect pivot switch connector from bulkhead connector and remove 13-way secondary lock.
22. Disconnect terminals of pass key wire harness from switch connector.
23. Remove retaining clip from housing cover and gently pull wire harness through column.
24. Reverse procedure to install, noting the following:
    a. Route wire from pass key lock cylinder, **Fig. 60,** and snap retaining clip into hole in housing.
    b. While holding SIR coil, depress spring lock to rotate hub clockwise until it stops, **Fig. 61.**
    c. Rotate coil hub counterclockwise approximately 2½ turns. Release spring lock between locking tabs in front of arrow, **Fig. 61.**
    d. Align opening in coil with horn tower and locating bump between two tabs on housing cover, **Fig. 62.**

COLUMN HOUSING COVER END CAP, LOCK HOUSING COVER, PIVOT SWITCH, & TILT SPRING

1. Remove upper column as outlined in "Steering Column, Replace."
2. Remove housing end cap.
3. Remove cruise control and multi-function lever connectors from base plate and disconnect.
4. Remove multi-function lever.
5. Remove cover screws and tilt lever.
6. Remove lock housing cover.
7. Remove base plate and dimmer switch rod actuator.
8. Remove pin, pivot and pulse switch actuator, noting the following:
    a. Allow switch to hang freely if removal is not required.
    b. Disconnect pivot switch connector from bulkhead connector.
    c. Gently pull wire harness through column.
9. Remove spring retainer, spring and spring guide.
10. Reverse procedure to install, noting the following:
    a. Coat spring guide and spring with lithium grease.

b. Tighten lock housing cover screw in three steps:
c. First step, tighten to 12 o'clock position.
d. Second step, tighten to 8 o'clock position.
e. Third step, tighten to 3 o'clock position.

BEARING, LOCK BOLT, SHIFT TUBE, STEERING COLUMN HOUSING, STEERING SHAFT & STEERING WHEEL LOCK SHOE

1. Remove steering column as outlined in "Steering Column, Replace."
2. Perform all disassembling steps outlined in "Housing Cover."
3. Remove pivot pins using pivot pin removal tool No. J21854-01, or equivalent. Install tilt lever.
4. Remove steering column housing. Pull back on tilt lever and pull steering column housing down and away from column.
5. Remove the following components to disassemble steering column housing assembly:
    a. Bearing.
    b. Wire abrasion shield.
    c. Mounting screw.
    d. Lock bolt spring.
    e. Lock bolt.
    f. Switch actuator rack and rack preload spring.
    g. Driveshaft.
    h. Switch actuator sector.
    i. Release lever pin using lock shoe and release lever pin tool No. J22635, or equivalent.
    j. Shoe release lever.

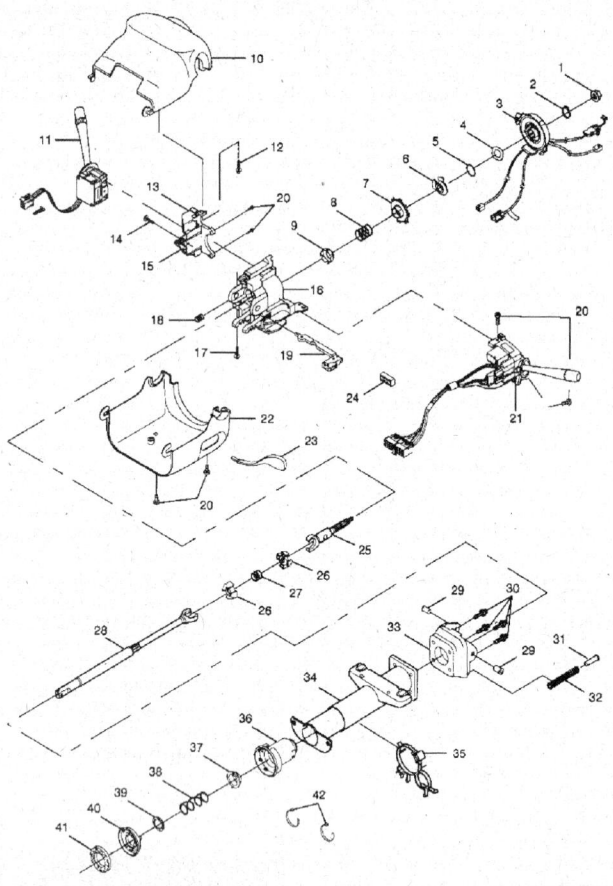

Fig. 36 Exploded view of steering column (Part 1 of 2). Intrigue & Grand Prix w/floor shift

1-NUT, FLANGED PREVAIL TORQUE
2-RING, RETAINING
3-SIR, COIL ASSEMBLY
4-WASHER, WAVE
5-RING, RETAINING
6-SHIELD, SHAFT LOCK
7-CAM, T/S CANCEL
8-SPRING, UPPER BEARING
9-SEAT, UPPER BEARING
10-SHROUD, UPPER
11-SWITCH ASM, PIVOT & PULSE
12-SCREW, TORX HEAD
13-BRACKET, SWITCH MOUNTING
14-SCREW, TORX HEAD
16-TILT HEAD ASM, STRG COLUMN
17-SCREW, TORX HEAD
18-SPRING, TILT LEVER
19-LEVER ASM, SHOE RELEASE
20-SCREW, PAN HEAD TAPPING
21-SWITCH ASM, T/S MULTIFUNCTION
22-SHROUD, LOWER
23-LEVER ASM, TILT
24-SPACER, WIRE HARNESS
25-SHAFT ASM, RACE & UPPER
26-SPHERE, CENTERING
27-SPRING, JOINT PRELOAD
28-SHAFT ASM, LOWER STRG
29-PIN, PIVOT
30-SCREW, TORX HEAD
31-SPRING, GUIDE
32-SPRING, TILT
33-SUPPORT ASM, STRG COLUMN
34-JACKET ASM, STRG COLUMN
35-STRAP, WIRE HARNESS
36-BEARING ASM, ADAPTER &
37-SEAT, LOWER BEARING
38-SPRING, LOWER BEARING
39-RETAINER, LOWER SPRING
40-RETAINER, SENSOR
41-SEAL, STRG SHAFT
42-STRAP, WIRE HARNESS

Fig. 36 Exploded view of steering column (Part 2 of 2). Intrigue & Grand Prix w/floor shift

k. Release lever spring.
l. Dowel pin using lock shoe and release lever pin tool No. J22635, or equivalent.
m. Lock shoes and shoe springs.
6. Remove lower spring retainer.
7. Remove bearing and seal retainer.
8. Remove lower spring retainer.
9. Remove lower bearing spring and lower bearing seat.
10. Remove mounting bolts, adapter and bearing.
11. Remove steering column shaft.
12. Mark upper shaft and lower steering shaft to ensure proper alignment.
13. Disassemble steering column shaft as follows:
   a. Separate upper shaft from lower steering shaft. Tilt 90° to disengage.
   b. Separate centering sphere from upper shaft by rotating sphere 90° and sliding out.
   c. Remove joint preload spring from centering sphere.
14. Remove column housing support with dimmer switch rod from steering column jacket.
15. Remove mounting screws and shift lever gate from support.
16. Remove shift tube retaining ring, thrust washers and lock plate.
17. Remove wave washer and thrust washers, then the gearshift lever bowl with gearshift bowl shroud and shift tube.
18. Remove shroud from bowl.
19. Remove shift lever spring and shift tube from bowl. Use suitable press, as required.
20. Remove PRNDL adjuster mounting nut and screw.
21. Remove PRNDL adjuster bracket and dimmer switch.
22. Remove dimmer and ignition switch mounting stud.
23. Remove ignition switch from ignition switch actuator.
24. Remove cam retainer.
25. Remove dimmer and ignition switch mounting screws and stud.
26. Remove cable clip from upper location of steering column jacket.
27. Remove cable mounting clip from solenoid bracket.
28. Remove ball joint socket from solenoid.
29. Remove ball joint spring.
30. Remove interlock solenoid and solenoid bracket to steering column jacket mounting screw.
31. Remove solenoid bracket to steering column jacket mounting screws.
32. Reverse procedure to install.

G6

Refer to **Fig. 63,** for exploded view of steering column.

Intermediate Steering Shaft

1. Ensure steering column is in full up and LOCK position.
2. Raise and support vehicle.
3. Remove lefthand front wheel.
4. Remove intermediate to steering gear pinch mounting bolt.
5. Disconnect intermediate shaft from steering gear.
6. Lower vehicle.
7. Remove intermediate shaft to steering column pinch bolt. Discard pinch bolt.
8. Remove intermediate shaft from steering column shaft.
9. Remove intermediate shaft seal by pressing tabs on seal, then pull inwards.
10. Remove intermediate shaft from vehicle.
11. Reverse procedure to install.

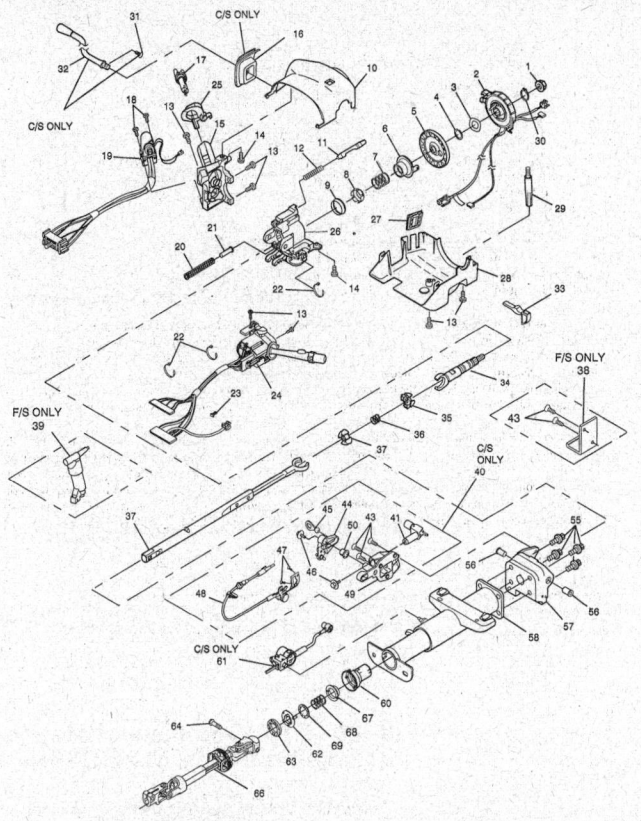

1-NUT, HEXAGON LOCKING (M14x1.5)
2-COIL ASM, SIR
3-WASHER, WAVE
4-RING, RETAINING
5-SHIELD ASM, SHAFT LOCK
6-CAM ASM, T/SIG CANCEL
7-SPRING, UPPER BEARING
8-SEAT, UPPER BEARING INNER RACE
9-RACE, INNER
10-SHROUD, UPPER
11-BOLT ASM, LOCK
12-SPRING, LOCK BOLT
13-SCREW, PAN HD TAPPING
14-SCREW, TORX HEAD
15-ASM, LOCK MODULE
16-SEAL, SHIFT LEVER
17-LOCK CYL SET, STRG COLUMN
18-SCREW, TAPPING
19-SWITCH ASM, IGN & KEY ALARM
20-SPRING, TILT
21-GUIDE, SPRING
22-STRAP, WIRE HARNESS
23-CONNECTOR, AXIAL POSN ASSUR
24-SWITCH ASM, T/S & MULTIFUNCTION
25-RING, TRIM
26- TILT HEAD ASM, STRG COL
27-PROTECTOR, SHROUD
28-SHROUD, LOWER
29-STUD, SHROUD MOUNTING
30-RING, RETAINING
31- SCREW, SHIFT LEVER
32-LEVER ASM, A/TRNS CONTROL
33-LEVER ASM, TILT
34-SHAFT ASM, RACE & UPPER
35-SPHERE, CENTERING
36-SPRING, JOINT PRELOAD
37-SHAFT ASM, LOWER STRG
38-STRAP REINFORCEMENT, STRG
39-ELEC PARK LOCK, STRG COL
40-SHIFT ASM, LINEAR
41-CLEVIS, SHIFT LEVER
43-SCREW, FLAT HD 6-LOBED SOC TAP
44-CAM ASM, CABLE SHIFT
45-ACTUATOR ASM, BALL &
46-BOLT, HEX FLANGE HEAD
47-SCREW, OVAL HD 6-LOBED SOC TAP
48-CABLE ASM, PARK LOCK
49-BRACKET, G/S LEVER ASM SUPPORT
50-BUSHING, CAM
55-SCREW, TORX HEAD
56-PIN, PIVOT

57-SUPPORT ASM, STRG COL
58-JACKET ASM, STRG COL
60-BEARING ASM, ADAPTER &
61-ACTUATOR, ELECTRICAL (BTSI)
62-RETAINER, SENSOR
63-SEAL, STEERING SHAFT
64-BOLT, PINCH
65-SHAFT ASM, INTER STRG
66-SHAFT ASM, INTER STRG
67-SEAT, LOWER BEARING
68-SPRING, LOWER BEARING
69-RETAINER, LOWER SPRING

GC604970024500AX

GC604970024500BX

Fig. 37 Exploded view of steering column (Part 1 of 2). Century, Grand Prix & Regal w/column shift

Fig. 37 Exploded view of steering column (Part 2 of 2). Century, Grand Prix & Regal w/column shift

Steering Column Trim Covers

1. Lift upper steering column trim cover, then remove retaining nuts from instrument panel seal.
2. Remove upper trim cover.
3. Remove lower column trim cover retaining screws, then remove cover.
4. Lower steering column and fully telescope toward driver, then remove lower trim cover.
5. Reverse procedure to install.

GTO

1. Tilt column to the lowest position.
2. Remove lower trim cover retaining screws, then press on back of lower cover to release tabs from upper cover.
3. Raise upper cover, release tab, then remove cover.
4. Push outer ring of theft deterrent reader into lower trim cover.
5. Remove ignition lock illumination socket and electrical connector from theft deterrent reader.
6. Slide lower trim cover rearward, disengage tab, then remover cover.
7. Reverse procedure to install.

LaCrosse

INTERMEDIATE STEERING SHAFT

1. Ensure wheels are in straight ahead position and ignition switch in LOCK position.
2. Raise and support vehicle.
3. Move seal to access lower pinch bolt on intermediate shaft.
4. Remove lower pinch bolt from power steering gear stub shaft.
5. Disconnect intermediate shaft from power steering gear stub shaft, noting shaft to gear alignment for installation reference.
6. Lower vehicle.
7. Reposition seal for access to upper intermediate shaft pinch bolt. then remove pinch bolt.
8. Disconnect intermediate steering shaft from steering column, noting intermediate shaft to steering column alignment for installation reference.
9. Remove intermediate shaft from vehicle.
10. Reverse procedure to install.

ION

The steering column is serviced only as an assembly. If a steering column fault or defect is found, replacement is required.

Impala & Monte Carlo

Refer to **Fig. 64,** for exploded view of this steering column.

INTERMEDIATE STEERING SHAFT

1. Raise and support vehicle.
2. Position intermediate steering shaft seal in order to provide access to lower pinch bolt.
3. Remove intermediate steering shaft lower pinch bolt from power steering gear stub shaft, **Fig. 65.** Front wheels must be maintained in straight ahead position and ignition must be in Lock position before disconnecting steering column or intermediate shaft.
4. Remove intermediate steering shaft from power steering gear stub shaft.
5. Lower vehicle.
6. Remove lefthand instrument panel insulator.
7. Position intermediate steering shaft seal to gain access to upper pinch bolt.
8. Remove intermediate steering shaft from steering column.
9. Disconnect intermediate steering shaft from steering column.
10. Remove intermediate shaft.
11. Reverse procedure to install.

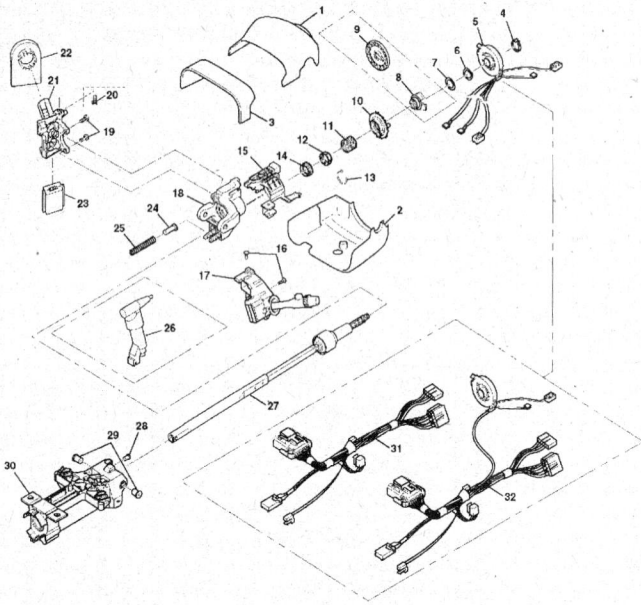

(1) Upper Trim Cover
(2) Lower Trim Cover
(3) Steering Column Closeout Trim Cover
(4) Retaining Ring
(5) Inflatable Restraint Steering Wheel Module Coil

ARM66GC000000697

**Fig. 38 Exploded view of steering column
(Part 1 of 2). CTS**

(6) Wave Washer
(7) Bearing Retainer
(8) Cam Orientation Plate
(9) Shaft Lock Shield Assembly
(10) Turn Signal Cancel Cam Assembly
(11) Upper Bearing Spring
(12) Upper Bearing Inner Race Seat
(13) Wire Harness Strap
(14) Inner Race
(15) Signal Switch Housing
(16) Pan Head Tapping Screws
(17) Turn Signal and Multifunction Switch Assembly
(18) Steering Column Tilt Head Assembly
(19) Pan Head Tapping Screws
(20) TORX® Head Screw
(21) Ignition Lock Cylinder Case
(22) Coded Key Controller
(23) Ignition and Key Alarm Switch Assembly
(24) Spring Guide
(25) Tilt Spring
(26) Theft Deterrent Control Module Electric Park Lock
(27) Steering Shaft Assembly
(28) Tilt Bumper
(29) Pivot Pins
(30) Steering Column Support Assembly
(31) Coil Wire Harness Assembly
(32) Coil Wire Harness Assembly (Export)

ARM66GC000000698

**Fig. 38 Exploded view of steering
column (Part 2 of 2). CTS**

STEERING COLUMN COVER

1. Remove tilt lever.
2. Remove ignition lock cylinder as outlined in "Electrical" section of "Century, Grand Prix, Impala, Intrigue, LaCrosse, Lumina, Monte Carlo & Regal" chassis chapter.
3. Remove mounting screws and steering column trim covers, **Figs. 66 and 67.**
4. Reverse procedure to install.

STEERING WHEEL CONTROL SWITCH

1. Remove driver's air bag module as outlined in "Passive Restraint Systems" chapter.
2. Remove steering wheel controls, wire harness from retainers in steering wheel aluminum insert and plastic back shroud.
3. Remove cruise control switch bezel to steering wheel insert mounting screw.
4. Disconnect electrical connector from back of cruise control switch.
5. Remove steering wheel controls switch and bezel from steering wheel.
6. Reverse procedure to install.

L Series

The steering column is serviced only as an assembly. If a steering column fault or defect is found, replacement is required.

Lumina

Refer to **Figs. 68 and 69,** for exploded view of this steering column.

UPPER COLUMN

1. Remove steering wheel as outlined in "Electrical" section of "Century, Grand Prix, Impala, Intrigue, LaCrosse, Lumina, Monte Carlo & Regal" chassis chapter.
2. Remove SIR retaining ring.
3. Remove wave washer.
4. Push down on shaft lock using lock plate compressor tool No. J23653-SIR, or equivalent, then remove bearing retainer.
5. Remove turn signal canceling cam.
6. Remove upper bearing spring, inner race seat, and inner race.
7. Remove multi-function lever.
8. Push top and bottom edges of housing end cover cap out of slots in housing using fingers.
9. Remove mounting screws, then the pivot and pulse dimmer switch connector from bulkhead connector.
10. Pry on upper and lower wings of switch body using suitable screwdriver, **Fig. 70.**
11. Remove wiring protector and wire harness clamp from tab inside housing, pull wire harness from column.
12. Pry knob from hazard warning switch using suitable small screwdriver.
13. Place turn signal switch to righthand turn position.
14. Remove turn signal switch mounting

screws. Allow switch to hang freely.
15. Remove wiring protector from SIR coil and attach suitable length of mechanics wire to coil terminal terminals to ease assembly.
16. Remove coil and pull wires through column.
17. Remove key from lock cylinder set.
18. Remove buzzer switch.
19. Insert key and move switch to Lock position.
20. Remove steering lock cylinder set mounting screw.
21. Remove terminal of pass key wiring harness from vehicle wire harness.
22. Remove wiring protector.
23. Attach suitable length of mechanics wire to terminal for ease of assembly.
24. Remove steering column lock cylinder set retaining clip, pull lock and wiring harness through steering column.
25. Remove mounting screws, tilt lever, lock housing cover and sleeve, then the wire protector shield.
26. Seat counterbore of tilt spring compressor No. J39246, or equivalent, over end race and upper shaft.
27. Thread and seat standard flanged previously torqued nut on to race and upper shaft assembly, **Fig. 71.**
28. Align square extension on end of tool bolt with square hole in spring retainer and seat.
29. Rotate tool bolt clockwise with wrench until it contacts surface of tool block.
30. Spring retainer must be compressed approximately ¼ inch into steering column housing.
31. Rotate hexagon section on end of tool bolt counterclockwise approximately ¼ turn.
32. Unscrew tool boot until spring and

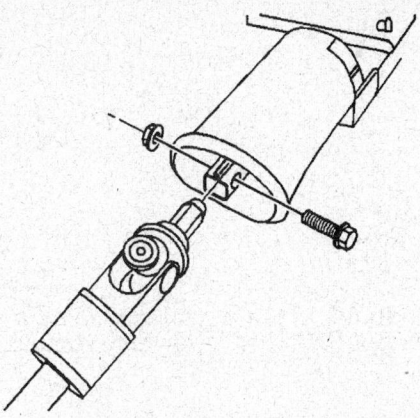

ARM66GC000000700

Fig. 39 Upper to lower intermediate bolt removal. CTS

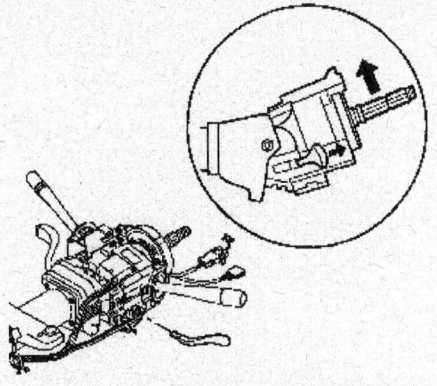

ARM66GC000000701

Fig. 40 Tilt column placement. CTS

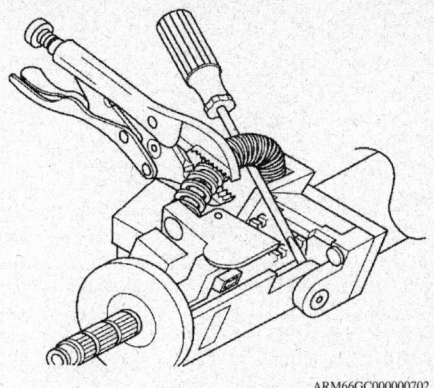

ARM66GC000000702

Fig. 41 Tilt spring removal

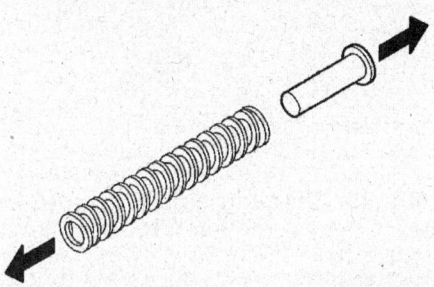

ARM66GC000000703

Fig. 42 Tilt guide spring removal

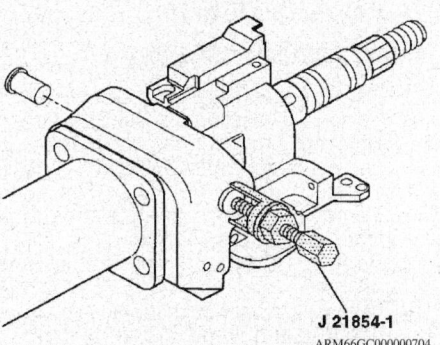

J 21854-1

ARM66GC000000704

Fig. 43 Pivot pin removal. CTS

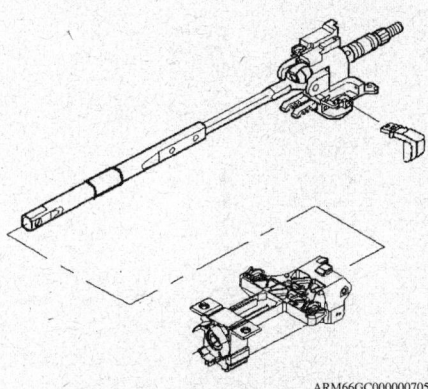

ARM66GC000000705

Fig. 44 Steering column disassembly. CTS

spring retainer are loose and free of tool.

33. Remove spring retainer, tilt spring and spring guide.
34. Reverse procedure to install, noting the following:
    a. Refer to **Fig. 72,** for proper wire routing.
    b. Set steering shaft so block tooth on race and upper shaft is at 12 o'clock position. Wheels should be straight ahead.
    c. Set steering column lock cylinder set to Lock position.
    d. **SIR coil will become uncentered if steering column is allowed to rotate or centering spring is pushed down, letting hub rotate while coil is removed from column. If this occurs, proceed to next step and refer to Fig. 73.**
    e. Position vehicle wheels straight ahead.
    f. Remove coil.
    g. Hold coil assembly with bottom up.
    h. While holding coil, depress spring lock to rotate hub in direction of arrow until it stops.
    i. Coil ribbon should be wound up snug against center hub.
    j. Rotate coil hub in opposite direction approximately 2½ turns.
    k. Release spring lock between locking tabs.
35. If new SIR coil is being installed, assemble pre-centered coil to steering

column. Remove and dispose of centering tab.
36. SIR coil wires must be kept tight with no slack while installing SIR coil assembly.

MID COLUMN

1. Remove steering wheel as outlined in "Electrical" section of "Century, Grand Prix, Impala, Intrigue, LaCrosse, Lumina, Monte Carlo & Regal" chassis chapter.
2. Remove steering column as outlined in "Steering Column, Replace."
3. Remove upper column.
4. Remove pivot pins using pivot pin remover No. J21854-01 or equivalent.
5. Install tilt lever.
6. Pull back on tilt lever and pull steering column housing down and away from column.
7. Remove sensor retainer.
8. Remove steering wheel speed sensor from adapter and bearing.
9. Remove and dispose of lower spring retainer.
10. Remove lower spring.
11. Remove lower bearing seat.
12. Remove adapter and bearing.
13. Remove steering shaft.
14. Disassemble lower steering shaft from race and upper shaft.
15. Tilt lower steering shaft assembly 90° to race and upper shaft and disengage.
16. Remove housing support.
17. Remove shift lever gate from steering

column housing support.
18. Remove shift tube retaining ring and thrust washers.
19. Turn gearshift lever bowl clockwise to 4 o'clock position.
20. Push lock plate with thumb and rotate counterclockwise until loose.
21. Remove wave washer, two thrust washers, and cam retainer.
22. Remove gearshift lever bowl with shift tube.
23. Remove shift lever spring and shift tube from bowl using suitable press.
24. Remove shift bowl protector from gearshift lever bowl.
25. Remove park position switch from stud and bracket.
26. Remove PRNDL adjuster bracket.
27. Remove ignition switch from ignition switch actuator.
28. Remove BTSI cable assembly from interlock solenoid and ignition switch actuator.
29. Ensure BTSI cable remains straight and does not become kinked during removal and installation.

LOWER COLUMN

1. Remove axial position assurance connector and vehicle wire harness connector from interlock solenoid.
2. Remove BTSI cable from interlock solenoid. Ensure BTSI cable does not become kinked during removal. Remove interlock solenoid.

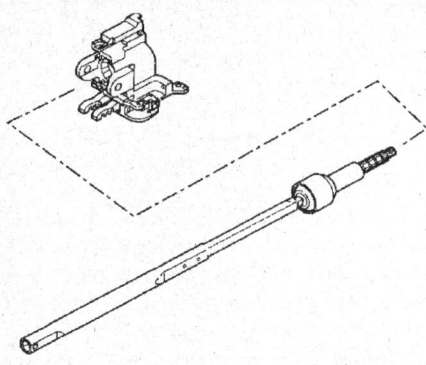

Fig. 45 Steering shaft removal. CTS

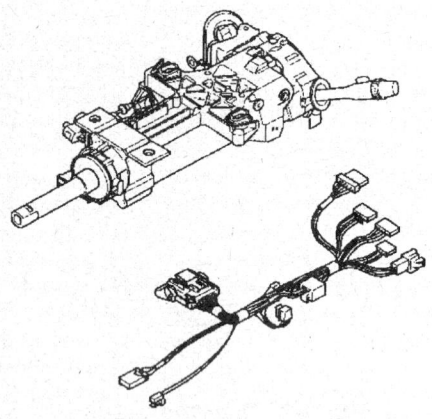

Fig. 48 Electrical connector removal. CTS

STEERING COLUMN HOUSING

1. Remove steering wheel as outlined in "Electrical" section of "Century, Grand Prix, Impala, Intrigue, LaCrosse, Lumina, Monte Carlo & Regal" chassis chapter.
2. Remove steering column as outlined in "Steering Column, Replace."
3. To disassemble steering column housing, remove the following:
   a. Switch actuator rack.
   b. Rack preload spring.
   c. Mounting screw.
   d. Lock bolt spring and shaft lock bolt, **Fig. 74.**
   e. Switch actuator sector.
   f. Drive shaft.
   g. Bearing.
   h. Release lever pin, using lock shoe and release lever pin remover and installer No. J22635, or equivalent.
   i. Shoe release lever, **Fig. 75.**
   j. Release lever spring.
   k. Dowel pin using tool No. J22635, or equivalent.
   l. Steering wheel lock shoes.
   m. Shoe springs.

STEERING SHAFT

1. Tilt race and upper and lower steering shaft 90° to each other and disengage.
2. Rotate centering sphere 90° and slip out.

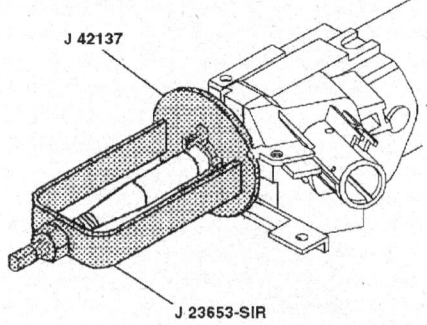

Fig. 46 Bearing retainer removal. CTS

3. Remove joint preload spring from centering sphere, **Fig. 76.**

CENTERING SPHERE

1. Remove steering wheel as outlined in "Electrical" section of "Century, Grand Prix, Impala, Intrigue, LaCrosse, Lumina, Monte Carlo & Regal" chassis chapter.
2. Remove steering column as outlined in "Steering Column, Replace."
3. Remove old centering spring and sphere.
4. Clean and inspect, replace components, as required.
5. Grease sphere with lithium grease. Grease lower half of sphere in upper shaft engagement areas.
6. Grease upper half of sphere in shaft engagement areas opposite to greased areas of lower half of sphere.
7. Place centering sphere installer tool No. J41688, or equivalent, in suitable vise.
8. Place bottom half of centering sphere, spring, top half of centering sphere and driver in installer tool, **Fig. 77.**
9. Compress spring and rotate driver 90° in clockwise direction.
10. Ensure feet of driver slide into grooves in base. Rotate driver until arms lock in place.
11. Once sphere is locked in place, attach race and upper shaft.
12. After race and upper shaft is attached to centering sphere, rotate shaft 90° downward to lock centering sphere in place.
13. Remove centering sphere installer, race and upper shaft from vise.
14. Disassemble tool by separating base, then remove shaft and sphere.
15. Apply lithium grease to exposed shaft engagement area and install lower shaft.

IGNITION SWITCH

REMOVAL

1. Remove steering column as outlined in "Steering Column, Replace."
2. Remove PRNDL adjuster bracket.
3. Remove mounting screws and dimmer switch mounting stud, then the switch from ignition switch actuator.
4. Remove turn signal switch connector from bulkhead connector.

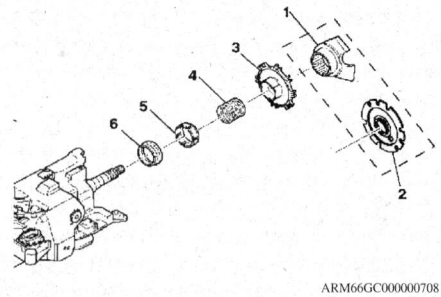

Fig. 47 Turn signal cancel cam & upper bearing inner race removal. CTS

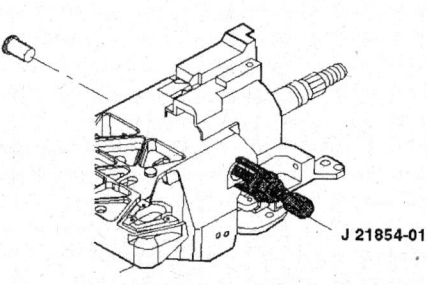

Fig. 49 Steering column pivot pin removal. CTS

5. Remove pivot and pulse dimmer switch connector from bulkhead connector.

INSTALLATION

1. Install ignition switch to steering column jacket with ignition switch in Off-Lock position.
2. New ignition switch will be pinned in Off-Lock position. Remove plastic pin after switch is assembled to column.
3. Move slider switch to extreme right-hand position.
4. Move slider switch one detent to left-hand Off-Lock position.
5. Install 3/32 inch drill bit in hole on switch to limit travel.
6. Install ignition switch to ignition switch actuator.
7. Install dimmer switch mounting stud.
8. Install mounting screw.
9. Remove drill bit from ignition switch.
10. Install remaining components in reverse order of removal.

ADAPTER & BEARING, STEERING WHEEL SPEED SENSOR

1. Remove steering column as outlined in "Steering Column, Replace."
2. Remove sensor retainer and steering shaft seal from retainer.
3. Remove steering wheel speed sensor from adapter and bearing.
4. Remove and dispose of lower spring retainer.
5. Remove lower bearing spring and seat.
6. Remove adapter and bearing.
7. Lubricate inner surface of lower bearing with suitable lithium grease.
8. Install adapter and bearing, lower bearing seat and lower bearing spring.

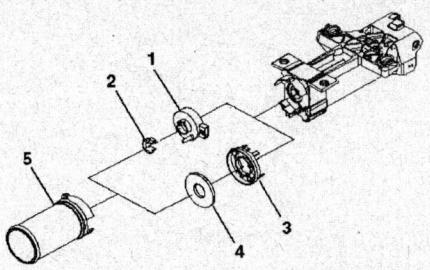

Fig. 50 Steering wheel position sensor removal. CTS

9. Install new lower spring retainer and press retainer onto steering shaft until spring retainer is flush with adapter and bearing, **Fig. 78.**

Metro

Refer to **Fig. 79,** for exploded view of this steering column.

SIR COIL, DIMMER SWITCH & TURN SIGNAL

1. Remove steering wheel as outlined in "Electrical" section of "Metro" chassis chapter.
2. Remove knee bolster, loosen upper steering column mounting bolts and lower column slightly.
3. Remove upper and lower steering column covers, then disconnect coil and combination switch electrical connectors.
4. Loosen switch electrical harness wire bands on lower steering column, then remove coil and combination switch screws.
5. Remove coil and combination switch.
6. Disconnect all wiring connectors from junction block and pull back forward section of driver's side floor carpet.
7. Move aside steering shaft joint cover by hand, then remove steering shaft joint upper pinch bolt and lower column.
8. Disconnect shift interlock cable from ignition switch and remove steering column.
9. Remove ignition switch from steering column.
10. Reverse procedure to install.

STEERING COLUMN LOCK

1. Remove steering wheel as outlined in "Electrical" section of "Metro" chassis chapter.
2. Remove mounting screw and ignition switch.
3. Remove mounting screws and ignition key warning switch.
4. Loosen and remove steering column lock mounting bolts using suitable center punch, **Fig. 80. Do not damage aluminum components.**
5. Turn ignition key to On or ACC position and remove lock from steering column.
6. Reverse procedure to install.

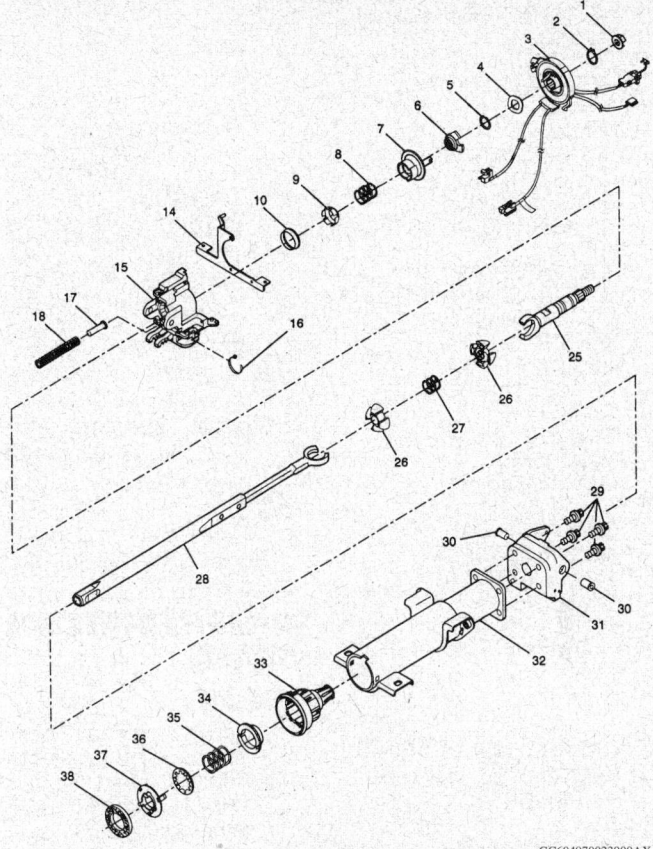

Fig. 51 Exploded view of steering column (Part 1 of 2). 2001–03 Malibu

Park Avenue

Refer to **Fig. 81,** for exploded view of steering column.

STEERING COLUMN COVERS

1. Remove steering wheel as outlined in "Electrical" section of "Bonneville, Le-Sabre & Park Avenue" chassis chapter.
2. Remove tilt lever and lower column cover mounting screws.
3. Tilt lower column cover downward, slide back cover to disengage from locking tabs and remove column cover protector.
4. Remove mounting screws and upper column cover.
5. Reverse procedure to install.

SHAFT LOCK, SIR COIL, TURN SIGNAL CANCEL CAM & UPPER BEARING

1. Remove column covers as outlined in "Steering Column Covers."
2. Remove steering column wiring harness straps and coil retaining ring.
3. Remove coil and wave washer.
4. Remove retaining ring using lock plate compressor tool No. J23653-SIR, or equivalent, and shaft lock.
5. Remove turn signal cancel cam and upper bearing spring.

6. Remove upper bearing inner race seat and race.
7. Reverse procedure to install.

LINEAR SHIFT, PARK LOCK CABLE, SHIFT GATE LEVER & SHIFT LEVER CLEVIS

1. Remove steering column as outlined in "Steering Column, Replace."
2. Tilt column to center position and remove lower column cover mounting screws.
3. Remove lower and upper column cover mounting screws.
4. Remove upper column cover and shift lever.
5. Remove shift lever seal and park lock cable from lock module.
6. Pry actuator arm of electrical actuator from outer shift cable ball stud on cable shift cam and mounting pin on jacket.
7. Remove mounting bolt, ball and actuator.
8. Lifting up on shift gate, rotate shift lever clevis and remove clevis from gearshift lever support bracket.
9. Pry locking ring off of park lock cable and move park lock latch to gain access to lower mounting screw.
10. Remove shift gate mounting screws and park lock cable.
11. Pry transaxle shift cable from inner ball stud on cable shift cam and remove mounting bolt.
12. Remove cam bushing from cable shift cam and mounting screws.

1-NUT, HEXAGON LOCKING (M14x1.5)
2-RING, RETAINING
3-COIL ASM, SIR (2 CONDUCTOR)
3-COIL ASM, SIR (6 CONDUCTOR)
4-WASHER, WAVE
5-RING, RETAINING
6-PLATE, CAM ORIENTATION
7-CAM ASM, T/SIG CANCEL
8-SPRING, UPPER BEARING
9-SEAT, UPPER BEARING INNER RACE
10-RACE, INNER
14-PLATE, SWITCH ADAPTER
15-HOUSING & BEARING ASM, STRG COL
16-STRAP, WIRE HARNESS
17-GUIDE, SPRING
18-SPRING, TILT
25-SHAFT ASM, RACE & UPPER
26-SPHERE, CENTERING
27-SPRING, JOINT PRELOAD
28-SHAFT ASM, LOWER
29-SCREW, TORX HEAD
30-PIN, PIVOT
31-SUPPORT ASM, STRG COL
32-JACKET ASM, STRG COL
33-BEARING ASM, ADAPTER &
34-SEAT, LOWER BEARING
35-SPRING, LOWER BEARING
36-RETAINER, LOWER SPRING
37-RETAINER, SENSOR
38-SEAL, STRG SHAFT

GC604970023900BX

Fig. 51 Exploded view of steering column (Part 2 of 2). 2001–03 Malibu

13. Remove gearshift lever support bracket.
14. Reverse procedure to install.

Prizm

The steering column cannot be serviced, a faulty column can only be replaced.
Refer to **Fig. 82,** for exploded view of steering column.
1. Disconnect combination switch electrical connector.
2. Loosen mounting screws and remove combination switch from steering column.
3. Mark ignition switch housing mounting bolt using suitable center punch.
4. Drill into bolts using suitable .12–.16 inch drill bit.
5. Remove mounting bolts using suitable bolt extractor.
6. Remove ignition switch housing.
7. Remove upper snap ring using suitable snap ring pliers.
8. Remove shaft from steering column tube.
9. Remove snap ring from shaft.
10. Reverse procedure to install. Tighten tapered-head bolts until heads snap off.

S Series

The steering column is serviced only as an assembly. If a steering column fault or defect is found, replacement is required.

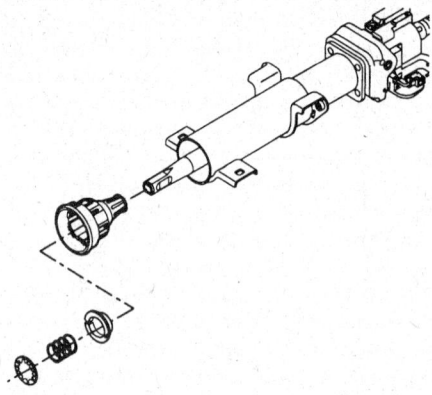

GC6049700240000X

Fig. 52 Steering column shaft. 2001–03 Malibu

STS

Refer to **Fig. 83,** for exploded view of steering column.

INTERMEDIATE STEERING SHAFT

UPPER

1. Remove steering column as outlined under "Steering Column, Replace."
2. Remove upper intermediate shaft to steering column mounting bolt, noting the position of the upper intermediate shaft to steering column for installation reference.
3. Remove upper intermediate shaft from steering column.
4. Reverse procedure to install. **Torque** upper intermediate shaft bolt to 35 ft. lbs.

LOWER

1. Ensure wheels are in straight ahead position and ignition in LOCK position with key removed.
2. Lock steering column by inserting lock pin tool No. J42640, or equivalent.
3. Raise and support vehicle.
4. Remove center intermediate shaft to lower intermediate shaft mounting bolt.
5. Remove lower intermediate shaft to power steering gear mounting bolt.
6. Disconnect lower intermediate shaft from power steering gear.
7. Remove lower intermediate shaft from center intermediate shaft.
8. Reverse procedure to install.

Steering Column Trim Covers

1. Remove steering wheel as outlined in "Electrical" section of "Deville, Eldorado, Seville & STS" chassis chapter.
2. Remove knee bolster.
3. Remove lower steering column trim cover, then disconnect closeout shroud from lower trim cover.

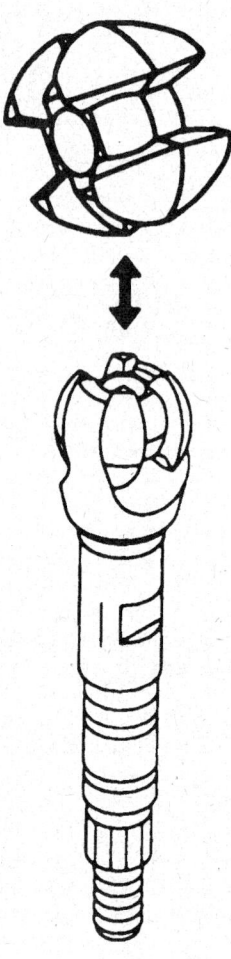

GC6049700241000X

Fig. 53 Lower steering shaft. 2001–03 Malibu

4. Disconnect electrical connectors for power tilt and telescopic switch.
5. Remove telescopic switch electrical connector from lower trim cover.
6. Remove upper steering column trim cover retaining screws.
7. Lift upper trim cover to access lock cylinder access hole.
8. Insert bent tip awl or equivalent, into access hole.
9. Turn ignition lock cylinder to start position.
10. Press down on ignition lock cylinder retaining pin using bent tip awl, or equivalent.
11. Release ignition lock cylinder to run position, then remove lock cylinder.
12. Remove upper trim cover.
13. Remove closeout shroud from upper trim cover.
14. Reverse procedure to install.

Steering Column Tilt Head

1. Ensure wheels are in straight ahead

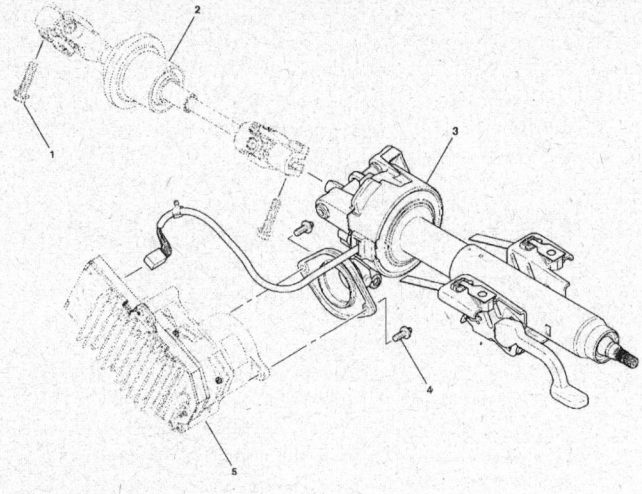

(1) Pinch Bolt
(2) Intermediate Steering Shaft
(3) Steering Column
(4) TORX® Bolts
(5) Motor/ Module Assembly

ARM0300000000586

Fig. 54 Exploded view of steering column. 2004 Malibu

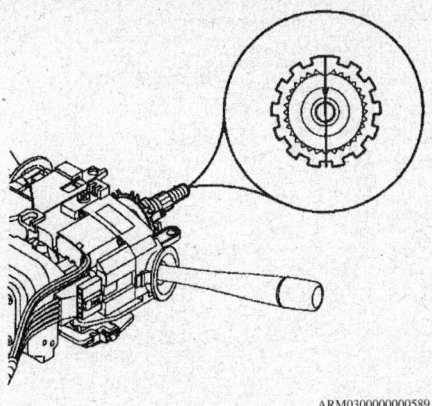

ARM0300000000589

Fig. 55 Steering shaft alignment. 2004 Malibu

IGNITION SWITCH

Refer to "Electrical" section of "Vibe" chassis chapter for ignition switch replacement.

IGNITION LOCK CYLINDER

Refer to "Electrical" section of "Vibe" chassis chapter for ignition lock replacement.

XLR

STEERING COLUMN LOCK CONTROL MODULE

1. Remove shifter knob, then open center console door.
2. Remove hinge cover from console bin, then pull at rear of cover to disengage retainer.
3. Remove console cupholder, ashtray and trim plate.
4. Remove console retaining nuts.
5. Remove front of console to instrument panel carrier retaining bolts.
6. Lift rear of console slightly and pull rearward to release front of console from under instrument panel carrier.
7. Disconnect accessory plug electrical connector.
8. Remove accessory plug retainer from housing, then the housing from console.
9. Disengage lamp from retainer using a suitable flat-bladed tool.
10. Push lamp through hole in console bin, then remove console from vehicle.
11. Remove radio, then carefully pry instrument panel courtesy lamp assembly from righthand side lower closeout panel.
12. Remove righthand side lower closeout panel to instrument panel lower support beam push-in retainers.
13. Lower righthand side lower closeout panel slightly, then carefully maneuver lefthand side of closeout panel from above driveline tunnel.
14. Insert courtesy lamp assembly up through closeout panel opening.
15. Remove righthand closeout panel from instrument panel.
16. Pry fuel door and rear compartment lid release switch from knee bolster, then

---

position and ignition switch is in LOCK position.
2. Remove steering wheel as outlined in "Electrical" section of "Deville, Eldorado, Seville & STS" chassis chapter.
3. Remove SIR coil.
4. Remove bearing retainer using tool No. J23653–SIR, or equivalent.
5. Remove shaft lock shield assembly.
6. Remove turn signal cancel cam assembly.
7. Remove upper bearing spring.
8. Reverse procedure to install.

Steering Column Wire Harness Assembly

1. Remove steering column as outlined under "Steering Column, Replace."
2. Remove upper and lower steering column trim covers.
3. Disconnect all electrical connectors attached to wire harness assembly.
4. Remove bulkhead connector from column shift and tilt motor bracket.
5. Reverse procedure to install.

Steering Wheel Position Sensor

1. Remove steering column as outline under "Steering Column, Replace."
2. Remove from steering shaft: Boot seal, steering shaft seal, sensor retainer and sensor locator.
3. Remove steering wheel position sensor.
4. Reverse procedure to install.

Vibe

Refer to **Fig. 84,** for exploded views of these steering columns.

STEERING SHAFT COUPLING

1. Ensure front wheels are in straight ahead position and ignition switch is in LOCK position.
2. Remove steering column silencer pad.
3. Place matching marks on steering shaft coupling and shaft assemblies.
4. Remove upper and lower bolts from coupling.
5. Raise coupling onto steering column shaft, then remove from steering shaft.
6. Reverse procedure to install.

INTERMEDIATE STEERING SHAFT w/FWD

1. Ensure front wheels are in straight ahead position and ignition switch is in LOCK position.
2. Place matching marks on intermediate steering shaft and steering gear pinion shaft assemblies.
3. Remove intermediate shaft attaching bolt, then the intermediate shaft.
4. Remove steering column silencer pad.
5. Place matching marks on steering shaft coupling and intermediate steering shaft assemblies.
6. Loosen upper and lower bolts from coupling.
7. Raise coupling to steering column shaft, then separate coupling from intermediate shaft.
8. Remove intermediate steering shaft from steering gear pinion shaft.
9. Reverse procedure to install.

STEERING COLUMN TRIM COVERS

1. Remove lower trim cover retaining screws, then the lower and upper trim covers.
2. Reverse procedure to install.

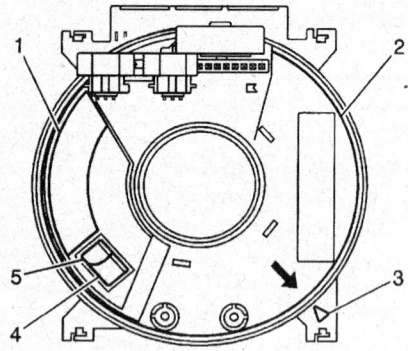

1 SIR coil face
2 Casing
3 Sub-stator alignment arrow
4 Cebtering window
5 Ribbon cable

ARM0300000000590

Fig. 56 SIR coil centering. 2004 Malibu

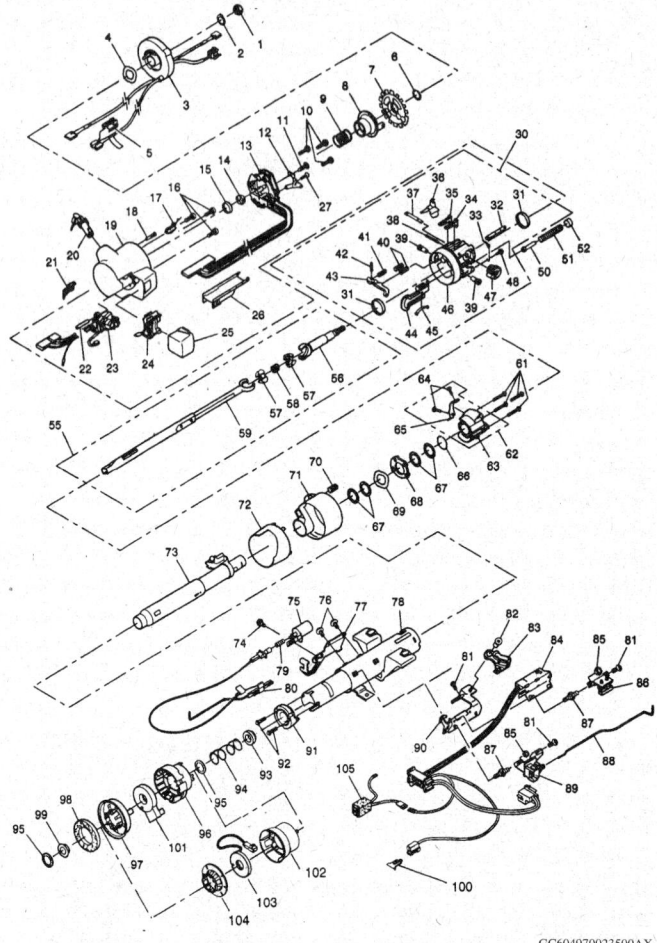

GC604970023500AX

Fig. 57 Exploded view of steering column (Part 1 of 2). DeVille, Eldorado & Seville w/column shift

disconnect switch electrical connectors.

17. Remove driver knee bolster trim panel lower retaining screws.
18. Grasp knee bolster trim panel at side edges, then remove trim panel by pulling firmly to release locking tabs.
19. Carefully pry instrument panel courtesy lamp assembly from lefthand side lower closeout panel using a suitable flat-bladed tool.
20. Insert instrument panel courtesy lamp assembly up through opening in closeout panel.
21. Release notch in righthand side forward edge of closeout panel from tab on accelerator pedal bracket, then remove lefthand closeout panel.
22. Open door on instrument panel compartment, then disconnect door dampener.
23. Disconnect instrument panel compartment lamp switch electrical connector.
24. With compartment open, depress both rear corners of compartment and swing compartment down towards floor.
25. Starting at outboard side, release compartment hinge from pin at bottom of door.
26. Slowly pull compartment far enough out of instrument panel to disconnect wiring harness connector from inflatable restraint module switch.
27. Remove instrument panel compartment
28. Mark location of driver knee bolster bracket for installation reference.
29. Remove driver knee bolster bracket to steering column bracket retaining screws, then the driver knee bolster bracket from instrument panel.
30. Remove retaining screw from bottom of lefthand side trim panel.
31. Pull lefthand side trim panel outward to disengage retaining clips, then disconnect electrical connectors.

32. Remove fastener attaching top of upper trim panel and windshield side garnish molding to hinge pillar.
33. Unsnap hinge pillar upper trim from hinge pillar.
34. Remove lower hinge pillar trim.
35. Manually open folding top.
36. Pull windshield side garnish molding with its retainers from windshield frame.
37. Remove instrument panel trim pad retaining screws. Screws are located at each end of instrument panel, in center of instrument panel and behind DIC switch.
38. Pull up carefully on instrument panel trim pad to disengage retaining clips.
39. Disconnect sunload/twilight sensor from trim pad, then remove trim pad from vehicle.
40. Carefully lift HUD electrical harness from between instrument panel cluster and HUD.
41. Disconnect HUD electrical connector from cluster.
42. Remove cluster to steering column bracket retaining screws.
43. Raise rear of cluster slightly, then disconnect cluster electrical connector.
44. Remove cluster from vehicle.

45. Remove speaker retaining screws from speakers, then lift the speaker out from instrument panel carrier.
46. Disconnect speaker wire harness.
47. Remove GPS antenna to instrument panel carrier plastic rivet retainers, then the GPS antenna with antenna lead from carrier.
48. Remove remote control door lock receiver retaining screws, then the receiver from carrier.
49. Remove steering wheel.
50. Remove instrument panel carrier retaining bolts and nuts.
51. Remove carrier retaining bolts from lower beam behind compartment door.
52. Remove compartment striker from carrier.
53. Remove instrument panel carrier from mounting, then slowly route all wiring from carrier.
54. Remove instrument panel carrier from vehicle.
55. Disconnect lock module electrical connectors at lock module.
56. Pull module outward to release retaining clips, then remove module by sliding upward.
57. Reverse procedure to install.

1 - NUT, HEXAGON LOCKING (M14x1.5)
2 - RING, RETAINING
3 - COIL ASM, SIR
4 - WASHER, WAVE
5 - SHROUD, CONNECTOR
6 - RING, RETAINING
7 - LOCK, SHAFT
8 - CAM ASM, T/SIG CANCEL
9 - SPRING, UPPER BEARING
10 - SCREW, BNDG HD CR RECESS
11 - SCREW, RD WASH HD (M4.2x1.41)
12 - ARM ASM, SIGNAL SWITCH
13 - SWITCH ASM, TURN SIGNAL
14 - SEAT, UPPER BRG INNER RACE
15 - RACE, INNER
16 - SCREW, PAN HD 6 LOBED SOC TAP
17 - SWITCH ASM, BUZZER
18 - SCREW, LOCK RETAINING
19 - COVER ASM, LOCK HOUSING
20 - LOCK CYLINDER SET, STRG COL
21 - ACTUATOR, DIMMER SW ROD
22 - PIN, SWITCH ACTUATOR PIVOT
23 - SWITCH ASM, PIVOT & (PULSE)
24 - BASE PLATE, COL HSG CVR END
25 - CAP, COL HSG COVER END
26 - PROTECTOR, WIRING
27 - SCREW, FLAT HEAD TAPPING
30 - HOUSING ASM, STRG COLUMN
31 - BEARING ASM
32 - BOLT, LOCK
33 - SPRING, LOCK BOLT
34 - SHOE, STEERING WHEEL LOCK
35 - SHOE, STEERING WHEEL LOCK
36 - SHIELD, WIRE PROTECTOR
37 - SHAFT, DRIVE
38 - PIN, DOWEL
39 - PIN, PIVOT
40 - SPRING, SHOE
41 - SPRING, RELEASE LEVER
42 - PIN, RELEASE LEVER
43 - LEVER, SHOE RELEASE
44 - RACK, SWITCH ACTUATOR
45 - SPRING, RACK PRELOAD
46 - HOUSING, STRG COLUMN
47 - SECTOR, SWITCH ACTUATOR
48 - SCREW, HEX WASHER HEAD
50 - GUIDE, SPRING
51 - SPRING, WHEEL TILT
52 - RETAINER, SPRING
55 - SHAFT ASM, STEERING
56 - SHAFT ASM, RACE & UPPER
57 - SPHERE, CENTERING
58 - SPRING, JOINT PRELOAD
59 - SHAFT ASM, LOWER STEERING
61 - SCREW, SUPPORT

62 - SUPPORT ASM, STRG COL HSG
63 - SUPPORT, STRG COL HSG
64 - SCREW, OVL HD CROSS RECESS
65 - GATE, SHIFT LEVER
66 - RING, SHIFT TUBE RETAINING
67 - WASHER, THRUST
68 - PLATE, LOCK
69 - WASHER, WAVE
70 - SPRING, SHIFT LEVER
71 - BOWL ASM, GEARSHIFT LEVER
72 - SHROUD, GEARSHIFT BOWL
73 - TUBE ASM, SHIFT
74 - SCREW, HEX WASH HD (#10-24X.25)
75 - SOLENOID ASM, INTERLOCK
76 - SCREW, WASH HD (#10-24X.25)
77 - BRACKET, SOLENOID
78 - JACKET ASM, STRG COL
79 - SPRING, BALL JOINT
80 - ACTUATOR ASM, IGNITION SWITCH
81 - SCREW, TORX WASHER HEAD
82 - RETAINER, CAM
83 - CAM ASM, CABLE SHIFT
84 - SWITCH ASM, IGNITION
85 - NUT, HEXAGON (#10-24)
86 - ADJUSTER ASM, PRNDL
87 - STUD, DIMR SW MTG
88 - ROD, DIMMER SWITCH
89 - SWITCH ASM, DIMMER
90 - BRACKET ASM, STUD &
91 - BEARING ASM, ADAPTER &
92 - SCREW, HEX WASHER HD TAP
93 - SEAT, LOWER BEARING
94 - SPRING, LOWER BEARING
95 - RETAINER, LOWER SPRING
96 - ADAPTER, STRG SENSOR
97 - RETAINER, SENSOR
98 - SEAL, STEERING SHAFT
99 - BUSHING, SEAL RETAINING
100 - CONNECTOR, AXIAL POSN ASSURANCE
101 - SENSOR ASM, HI RES STRG WHL POSN
102 - RETAINER, BEARING
103 - SENSOR ASM, STRG WHL POSN
104 - DAMPENER ASM, ROTATIONAL
105 - HARNESS ASM, JUMPER

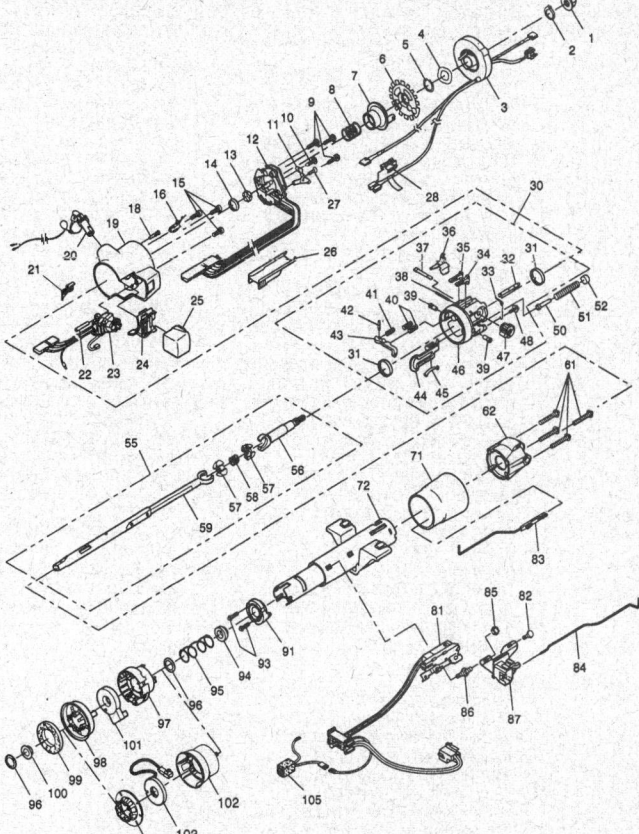

GC604970023500BX

Fig. 57 Exploded view of steering column (Part 2 of 2). DeVille, Eldorado & Seville w/column shift

GC604970023600AX

Fig. 58 Exploded view of steering column (Part 1 of 2). DeVille, Eldorado & Seville w/console shift

TURN SIGNAL CANCEL CAM & STEERING SHAFT UPPER BEARING SPRING

1. Remove steering wheel and SIR coil assembly as outlined in "Electrical" section of "XLR" chassis chapter.
2. Remove bearing retainer using steering column lock plate tool No. J 23653, or equivalent, **Fig. 85.**
3. Remove shaft lock shield assembly.
4. Remove turn signal cancel cam assembly, then the upper bearing spring.
5. Reverse procedure to install.

STEERING WHEEL CONTROL SWITCH ASSEMBLY

1. Remove steering wheel inflatable restraint module.
2. Disconnect steering wheel control switch electrical connectors.
3. Remove steering wheel control switch retaining screws.
4. Remove steering wheel control harness retainer and screw, **Fig. 85.**
5. Carefully pull steering wheel control switch assembly away from steering wheel, then remove wire harness from control switch assembly.
6. Reverse procedure to install.

TILT ACTUATOR ASSEMBLY

1. Remove driver knee bolster, then the lower trim cover from steering column.

2. Disconnect tilt actuator assembly electrical connector, **Fig. 85.**
3. Remove tilt actuator assembly fasteners, then the tilt actuator assembly (2) from steering column.
4. Remove potentiometer housing from tilt actuator assembly.
5. Disconnect tilt cable from tilt actuator assembly.
6. Reverse procedure to install.

TELESCOPE ACTUATOR SWITCH

1. Remove driver knee bolster.
2. Remove lower steering column trim cover retaining screws.
3. Disconnect lower trim cover from closeout shroud.
4. Disconnect telescope actuator switch electrical connector.
5. Remove telescope actuator switch from lower trim cover.
6. Reverse procedure to install.

TELESCOPE ACTUATOR ASSEMBLY

1. Remove driver knee bolster.
2. Disconnect telescope actuator assembly electrical connector.
3. Remove telescope actuator assembly fasteners.
4. Remove telescope actuator assembly from steering column, **Fig. 85.**

5. Remove potentiometer housing from telescope actuator assembly.
6. Disconnect telescope cable from telescope actuator assembly.
7. Reverse procedure to install.

TILT SPRING

1. Remove steering column upper and lower trim covers, **Fig. 85.**
2. Install tilt lever onto steering column tilt head assembly, then use tilt lever to tilt column to UP position.
3. Pry tilt spring upward until a bulge occurs and most tilt spring tension is removed.
4. Secure tilt spring with suitable locking pliers.
5. Continue prying up on tilt spring until tilt spring disengages from post on steering column support assembly and tilt head assembly.
6. Remove tilt spring from steering column support assembly and tilt head assembly.
7. Remove spring guide from tilt spring.
8. Reverse procedure to install.

LOWER BEARING & STEERING COLUMN JACKET

1. Remove steering wheel as outlined in "Electrical" section of "XLR" chassis chapter.
2. Remove steering column as outlined in

1- NUT, HEX LOCKING (M14x1.5)
2- RING, RETAINING
3- COIL ASM, SIR
4- WASHER, WAVE
5- RING, RETAINING
6- LOCK, SHAFT
7- CAM ASM, T/SIG CANCEL
8- SPRING, UPPER BEARING
9- SCREW, BNDG HD CR RECESS
10- SCREW, RD WASH HD (M4.2x1.41)
11- ARM ASM, SIGNAL SWITCH
12- SWITCH ASM, TURN SIGNAL
13- SEAT, UPPER BRG INNER RACE
14- RACE, INNER
15- SCREW, PAN HD 6 LOBED SOC TAP
16- SWITCH ASM, BUZZER
18- SCREW, LOCK RETAINING
19- COVER ASM, LOCK HOUSING
20- LOCK CYLINDER SET, STRG COL PASS KEY
21- ACTUATOR, DIMMER SWITCH ROD
22- PIN, SWITCH ACTUATOR PIVOT
23- SWITCH ASM, PIVOT & (PULSE)
24- BASE PLATE, COL HSG CVR END
25- CAP, COL HSG COVER END
26- PROTECTOR, WIRING
27- SCREW, FLT HD TAPPING
28- SHROUD, CONNECTOR
30- HOUSING ASM, STRG COLUMN
31- BEARING ASM
32- BOLT, LOCK
33- SPRING, LOCK BOLT
34- SHOE, STEERING WHEEL LOCK
35- SHOE, STEERING WHEEL LOCK
36- SHIELD, WIRE PROTECTOR
37- SHAFT, DRIVE
38- PIN, DOWEL
39- PIN, PIVOT
40- SPRING, SHOE
41- SPRING, RELEASE LEVER
42- PIN, RELEASE LEVER
43- LEVER, SHOE RELEASE
44- RACK, SWITCH ACTUATOR
45- SPRING, RACK PRELOAD
46- HOUSING, STRG COLUMN
47- SECTOR, SWITCH ACTUATOR

48- SCREW, HEX WASHER HEAD
50- GUIDE, SPRING
51- SPRING, WHEEL TILT
52- RETAINER, SPRING
55- SHAFT ASM, STEERING
56- SHAFT ASM, RACE & UPPER
57- SPHERE, CENTERING
58- SPRING, JOINT PRELOAD
59- SHAFT ASM, LOWER STEERING
61- SCREW, HEX WASHER HD TAPPING
62- SUPPORT ASM, STRG COL HSG
71- SHROUD, STRG COLUMN HSG
72- JACKET ASM, STRG COL
81- SWITCH ASM, COL LOCK & IGN
82- SCREW, WASH HD (#10-24X.25)
83- ACTUATOR ASM, IGNITION SWITCH
84- ROD, DIMMER SWITCH
85- NUT, HEXAGON (#10-24)
86- STUD, DIMR & IGN SW MTG
87- SWITCH ASM, DIMMER
91- BEARING ASM, ADAPTER &
93- SCREW, HEX WASHER HD TAP
94- SEAT, LOWER BEARING
95- SPRING, LOWER BEARING
96- RETAINER, LOWER SPRING
97- ADAPTER, STRG SENSOR
98- RETAINER, SENSOR
99- SEAL, STEERING SHAFT
100- BUSHING, SEAL RETAINING
101- SENSOR ASM, HI RES STRG WHL POSN
102- RETAINER, BEARING
103- SENSOR ASM, STRG WHL POSN
104- DAMPENER ASM, ROTATIONAL
105- HARNESS ASM, JUMPER

GC604970023600BX

Fig. 58 Exploded view of steering column (Part 2 of 2). DeVille, Eldorado & Seville w/console shift

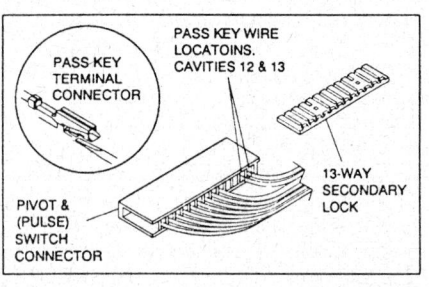

GC6049300112000X

Fig. 59 Pass key wire connection locations. DeVille, Eldorado & Seville

"Steering Column, Replace."

3. Remove turn signal and multifunction switch assembly, **Fig. 85.**
4. Remove wire harness assembly from steering column.
5. Remove telescope drive motor assembly and cable.
6. Remove tilt drive motor assembly and cable.
7. Remove control module Torx head screw from control module.
8. Slide control module from steering column.
9. Remove boot seal, steering shaft seal, sensor retainer, sensor locator and steering shaft position sensor.
10. Remove Torx screw from bottom of gearshift and tilt motor bracket, then the bracket.
11. Gently pry lower shield assembly off of steering column.
12. Remove steering column support assembly pivot pins using pivot pin remover tool No. J 21854-01, or equivalent.
13. Remove lead screw, then the tilt head assembly from steering column support assembly with steering shaft still attached.
14. Remove tilt head assembly from steering shaft assembly.

15. Mark race, upper shaft and lower steering shaft for assembly reference. Failure to assemble properly will cause steering wheel to be turned 180°.
16. Tilt upper shaft assembly 90° to steering shaft assembly and disengage.
17. Remove Torx screws from dampener.
18. Remove and discard support screws from steering column support.
19. Remove steering column support.
20. Reverse procedure to install.

INFLATABLE RESTRAINT STEERING WHEEL MODULE COIL CENTERING

1. Ensure wheels on vehicle are straight ahead, block tooth of steering shaft assembly is in 12 o'clock position and ignition switch assembly is in the LOCK position, **Figs. 86 through 89.**
2. If front of SIR coil has a centering window and back side has a spring service lock, **Fig. 86,** proceed as follows:
   a. Hold coil with face up.
   b. While depressing spring service lock, rotate coil hub clockwise until coil ribbon stops.
   c. Rotate coil hub slowly counterclockwise, until centering window

appears yellow and both arrows line up.
   d. Release spring service lock between locking tab.
   e. SIR coil is now centered.
   f. Align centered SIR coil with horn tower and slide onto steering shaft assembly.
3. If front of SIR coil has a centering window and the back side does not have spring service lock, **Fig. 87,** proceed as follows:
   a. Hold coil with face up.
   b. Rotate coil hub clockwise until coil ribbon stops.
   c. Rotate coil hub slowly counterclockwise until centering window appears yellow and both arrows line up.
   d. This is Center position.
   e. While holding coil hub in Center position, align coil with horn tower and slide coil onto steering shaft assembly.
4. If no centering window is present on front side of SIR coil, but a spring service lock is on back side, **Fig. 88,** proceed as follows:
   a. Hold coil with back side up.
   b. While depressing spring service lock, rotate coil hub in direction of arrow until coil ribbon stops.
   c. Still pressing spring service lock, rotate coil hub in opposite direction 2½ revolutions.
   d. Release spring service lock between locking tabs.
   e. SIR coil is now centered.
   f. Align centered coil with horn tower and slide coil onto steering shaft assembly.
5. If no centering window appears on front side of SIR coil and no spring service lock exists on back side, **Fig. 89,** proceed as follows:
   a. Hold coil with face up.
   b. Rotate coil hub in direction of arrow until coil ribbon stops.
   c. Rotate coil hub, slowly, counterclockwise, for 2½ revolutions.
   d. This is Center position.
   e. While maintaining coil hub in Center position, align coil with horn tower and slide coil onto steering shaft assembly.

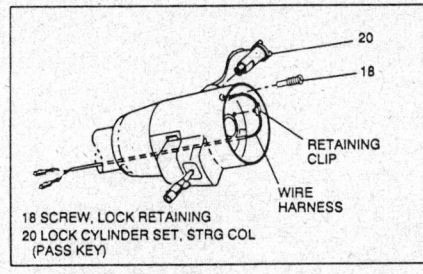

Fig. 60 Pass key wire installation. DeVille, Eldorado & Seville

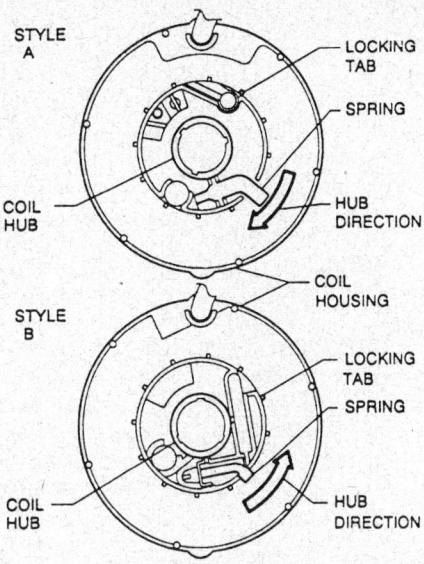

Fig. 61 Coil centering. DeVille, Eldorado & Seville

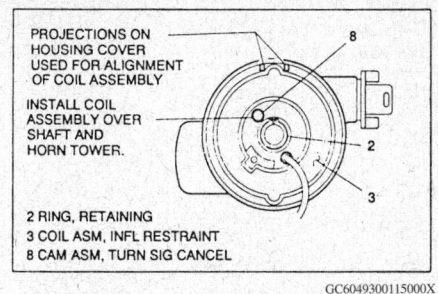

Fig. 62 Coil installation. DeVille, Eldorado & Seville

TECHNICAL SERVICE BULLETINS

Clunk Noise From Front Of Vehicle During Turning Maneuver/Steering Wheel Rotation

AURORA, BONNEVILLE, CAVALIER, GRAND PRIX, IMPALA, INTRIGUE, MONTE CARLO, REGAL, SEVILLE & SUNFIRE

On some of these models there may be a clunk type noise coming from the front of the vehicle during a turning maneuver. This condition may also be felt through the steering wheel when the vehicle is stationary and the wheel is rotated from steering stop to steering stop. Typically, the clunk noise will be heard once for every 180° of steering wheel rotation in either direction for on Cavalier and Sunfire models. However, some vehicles may only exhibit the noise once for every 360° of wheel rotation. On all other vehicles, this clunk noise will be noticed during low speed acceleration or deceleration, typically in light turns of the steering wheel.

This condition may be caused by inadequate lubrication of the steering intermediate shaft which results in a slip stick condition possibly resulting in the clunk noise.

This condition is commonly misdiagnosed as originating in the steering gear.

Do not replace following steering gear part Nos: 26063582, 26056808, 26031078, 26079915, 26055468, 26079917, 26079929, 26081813, 26080057, 26088612, 26086001, 26088334, 26088539, 26068964, 26058681, 26068967, 26088606, 26067451, 26087241, or 26087416.

Do not replace following intermediate shafts Nos: 10327501, 10327502, 10327553, 22680754, 22704392, 26050292, 26055042, 26073020, 26078302, 26079240, 26079787, or 26100571.

To correct this condition remove the in-termediate steering shaft from the vehicle and lubricate the shaft with a steering column shaft lubrication kit (P/N 26098237). as follows:

1. Remove steering intermediate shaft.
2. Fully extend intermediate shaft by pulling two shafts apart.
3. Apply grease supplied in lubrication kit in aluminum end of yoke opening. Direct syringe tip as deep as possible into yoke and dispense full content of syringe.
4. Install rubber stop plug from kit into yoke opening.
5. Secure rubber plug by swinging upper yoke 90°. One ear of yoke should press rubber plug in.
6. Collapse of intermediate shaft on suitable hard surface. Use pumping action when collapsing shaft. Collapse shaft as far as possible. **Ensure intermediate shaft is being pressed over ears of solid shaft.**
7. Remove rubber stopper plug from yoke end of shaft.
8. Slowly extend intermediate shaft apart.
9. Inspect intermediate shaft for minimum of .2 inch of grease on shaft splines. Repeat previous steps if less than .2 inch of grease is on shaft splines.
10. Stroke and extend intermediate shaft at least 15 times to completely lubricate internal surface of slip joint.
11. Install the intermediate shaft into vehicle.

Rubbing Noise From Steering Column

2001-02 DEVILLE

On some of these models there may be a rubbing noise coming from the lower part of the steering column.

This condition may be caused by the steering column intermediate shaft rubbing on the intermediate shaft seal at the base of the steering column.

To correct this condition inspect the steering column intermediate shaft seal, as follows:

1. Remove lefthand side instrument panel closeout/insulator panel.
2. Ensure top of intermediate steering shaft seal is properly positioned on black boot which is part of steering column. If seal is improperly positioned on this boot, it may be deformed and contact steering column intermediate shaft causing rubbing noise.
3. Position seal properly on steering column boot.
4. Inspect instrument panel wiring harnesses for contact with seal. Harness may push seal into contact with steering column intermediate shaft causing rubbing noise.
5. Position any wiring harnesses away from seal.
6. Inspect intermediate steering shaft seal for any type of damage or rub through. Replace damaged seal (P/N 25723408).

Clunk/Rattle Noise From Lower Steering Column Area When Traveling Over Road Bumps

2001-02 PARK AVENUE

On some of these models there may be a clunking or rattling noise from the lower steering column area that may be heard in the passenger compartment as the vehicle travels over bumps in the road.

This condition may be caused by clearance between the steering shaft and the inner race of the lower steering column shaft bearing.

To correct this condition replace the existing lower steering column shaft bearing (P/N 26100500), as follows:

1. Remove steering column.
2. Place steering column on clean flat surface.
3. Disconnect intermediate shaft by removing upper pinch bolt and nut.
4. Remove steering shaft seal and lower bearing retainer as a unit.

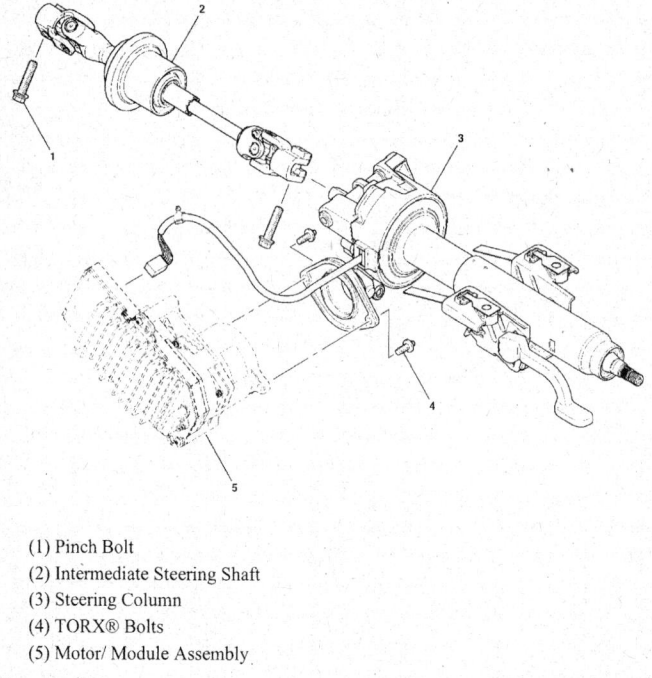

(1) Pinch Bolt
(2) Intermediate Steering Shaft
(3) Steering Column
(4) TORX® Bolts
(5) Motor/ Module Assembly

ARM0400000000044

Fig. 63 Exploded view of steering column. G6

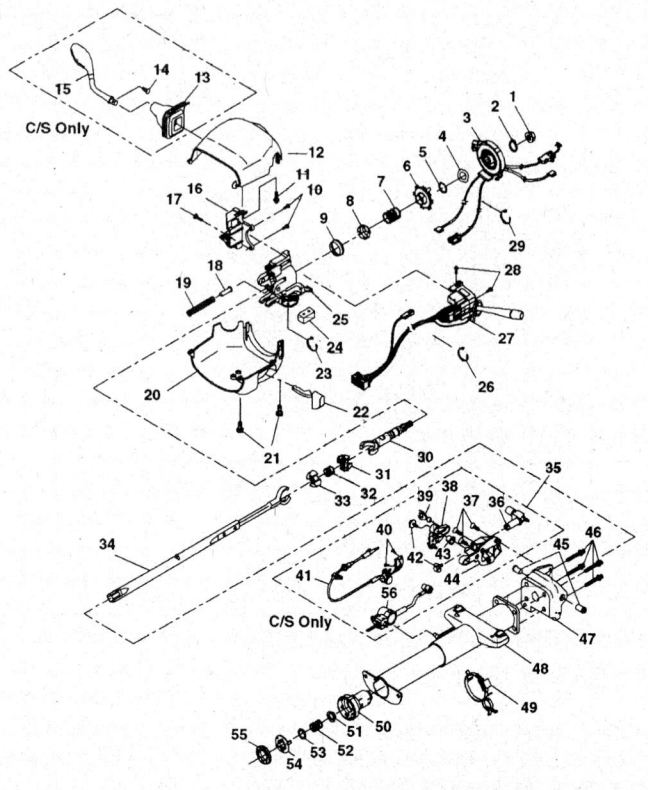

GC6040000291010X

Fig. 64 Exploded view of steering column (Part 1 of 2). Impala & Monte Carlo

5. Remove steering wheel position sensor assembly by inserting flat-bladed tool between sensor and steering shaft lower bearing, then gently prying.
6. Remove two lower spring retainers and bearing spring, then the lower bearing seat and lower steering column shaft bearing.
7. Install new steering shaft lower bearing.
8. Install steering wheel position sensor.
9. Install steering shaft seal and lower bearing retainer as a unit.
10. Connect intermediate shaft to steering column.
11. **Torque** upper pinch bolt and nut to 35 ft. lbs.
12. Install steering column.

2001-02 SEVILLE

On some of these models there may be a clunking or rattling noise from the lower steering column area that may be heard in the passenger compartment as the vehicle travels over bumps in the road.

This condition may be caused by clearance between the steering shaft and the inner race of the lower steering column shaft bearing.

To correct this condition replace the existing lower steering column shaft bearing (P/N 26100500) and install a new retainer/no back washer (P/N 07847029), as follows:

1. Disarm air bag system as outlined in "Air Bag System Precautions" in the front of this manual.
2. Turn steering wheel all way to right, then back to lefthand side slightly.
3. Lock steering column by installing steering column anti-rotation pin tool No. J-42640, or equivalent, into lower

steering column trim cover access hole.
4. Disconnect steering column electrical connectors.
5. Disconnecting steering column from intermediate shaft from inside vehicle by removing intermediate shaft upper pinch bolt and nut. If disconnecting steering column from the intermediate shaft from under vehicle, proceed as follows:
   a. Raise and support vehicle.
   b. Remove intermediate shaft lower pinch bolt and nut.
   c. Lower vehicle.
6. Remove lower and upper mounting nuts, then the steering column. Place column on flat surface.
7. Disconnect intermediate shaft by removing upper pinch bolt and nut.
8. Remove steering shaft seal and lower bearing retainer as a unit.
9. Remove steering wheel position sensor by inserting flat-bladed tool between sensor and steering shaft lower bearing, then gently prying.
10. **On models equipped with power tilt and telescoping steering columns,** remove retainer and wave washer. Discard washer.
11. **On models equipped with manual tilt steering columns,** proceed as follows:
    a. Remove retainer.
    b. Remove lower bearing spring and seat.
12. **On all models,** remove steering col-

umn jacket hole plug and lower bearing.
13. Install new steering shaft lower bearing.
14. Install steering column jacket hole plug.
15. Pull steering column shaft out until chamfer on shaft bottoms out against bearing.
16. **On models equipped with power tilt and telescoping steering columns,** install new retainer/no back washer with rounded side to bearing.
17. **On models equipped with manual tilt steering columns,** new retainer/ no back washer, lower bearing spring and seat are not required
18. **On all models,** install steering wheel position sensor.
19. Install steering shaft seal and steering shaft lower bearing retainer as a unit.
20. **If steering column was disconnected from under vehicle,** proceed as follows:
    a. Connect intermediate shaft to steering column.
    b. **Torque** upper pinch bolt and nut to 35 ft. lbs.
21. **On all models,** install steering column, lower and upper mounting nuts. **Torque** mounting nuts to 20 ft. lbs.
22. Connect steering column electrical connectors.
23. **If steering column was disconnected from inside vehicle,** proceed as follows:
    a. Connect intermediate shaft to steering column.

1. Hexagon Nut
2. Retaining Ring
3. SIR Coil Assembly
4. Wave Washer
5. Bearing Retainer
6. Turn Signal Cancel Cam Assembly
7. Upper Bearing Spring
8. Upper Bearing Inner Race Seat
9. Inner Race
10. Flat Head Screw
11. Pan Head Tapping Screw
12. Upper Shroud
13. Shift Lever Seal
14. Shift Lever Screw
15. Automatic Transmission Control Lever Assembly
16. Switch Mounting Bracket
17. Flat Head Screw
18. Spring Guide
19. Tilt Spring
20. Lower Shroud
21. TORX® Head Screw
22. Tilt Lever Assembly
23. Wire Harness Strap
24. Spacer
25. Steering Column Tilt Head
26. Wire Harness Strap
27. Turn Signal And Multifunction Switch Assembly
28. Pan Head Tapping Screw
29. Wire Harness Strap
30. Race And Upper Shaft Assembly
31. Centering Sphere
32. Joint Preload Spring

33. Centering Sphere
34. Lower Steering Shaft Assembly
35. Linear Shift Assembly
36. Shift Lever Clevis
37. Flat Head 6-Lobed Socket Tapping Screw
38. Cable Shift Cam Assembly
39. Ball and Actuator
40. Oval Head 6-Lobed Socket Tapping Screw
41. Park Lock Cable Assembly
42. Hex Flange Head Bolt
43. Cam Bushing
44. Gear Shift Lever Assembly Support Bracket
45. Pivot Pin
46. TORX® Head Screw
47. Steering Column Support Assembly
48. Steering Column Jacket Assembly
49. Wire Harness Strap
50. Adapter and Bearing Assembly
51. Lower Bearing Seat
52. Lower Bearing Spring
53. Lower Spring Retainer
54. Sensor Retainer
55. Steering Shaft Seal
56. Electrical (BTSI) Actuator

GC6040000291020X

Fig. 64 Exploded view of steering column (Part 2 of 2). Impala & Monte Carlo

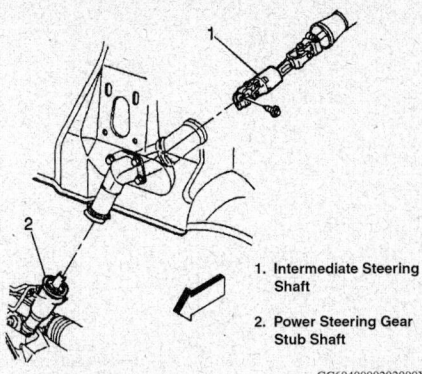

1. **Intermediate Steering Shaft**
2. **Power Steering Gear Stub Shaft**

GC6040000292000X

Fig. 65 Intermediate steering shaft replacement. Impala & Monte Carlo

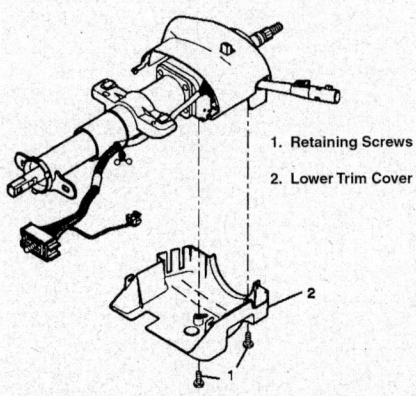

1. Retaining Screws
2. Lower Trim Cover

GC6040000293000X

Fig. 66 Steering column trim cover replacement (Lower). Impala & Monte Carlo

b. Install upper pinch bolt and nut.
c. **Torque** upper pinch bolt to 35 ft. lbs.
24. **If steering column was disconnected from under vehicle,** proceed as follows:
   a. Raise and support vehicle.
   b. Connect intermediate shaft to steering column.
   c. Install lower pinch bolt and nut.
   d. **Torque** lower pinch bolt to 35 ft. lbs.
   e. Lower vehicle.
25. **On all models,** install closeout/instrument panel insulator panel and knee bolster trim panel.
26. Remove locking pin from lower steering column trim cover access hole.
27. Arm air bag system.

Squeak Noise In Steering Column

2001 CATERA

On some of these models there may be a squeak noise coming from the steering column while turning the steering wheel. The noise is more noticeable with cold ambient temperatures.

This condition may be caused by a lack of lubricant at the lower steering column bearing. This causes the rubber lower bearing cage to become misaligned and allows the bearing cage to rub on the shaft.

To correct this condition, proceed as follows:

1. Disassemble steering column and remove lower steering column bearing.
2. Thoroughly clean old lubricant from lower bearing. using Scotchbrite pad, or equivalent, to restore bearing contact surface on steering column shaft.
3. Lubricate lower bearing thoroughly using Dielectric Silicone Grease (P/N 12345579), or equivalent.
4. Assemble column.

Noise/Clunk From Steering Column

2003 CTS

On some of these models built before VIN 30134433 there may be a clunk noise or loose feeling from the steering wheel/column that may be more noticeable while turning.

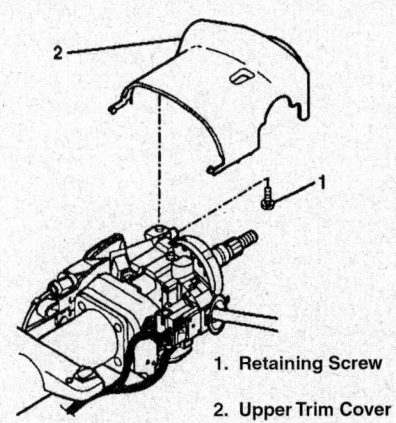

1. Retaining Screw
2. Upper Trim Cover

GC6040000294000X

Fig. 67 Steering column trim cover replacement (Upper). Impala & Monte Carlo

This condition may be caused by excessive play in the intermediate shaft.

To correct this condition replacement of the upper steering column intermediate shaft as follows:

1. Disarm air bag system zone 3 as outlined in "Air Bag System Precautions" in the front of this manual.
2. Turn steering wheel so that front wheels are pointing straight ahead, then turn ignition switch to OFF position. Remove key from ignition switch.
3. Lock steering column by installing steering column lock pin tool No. J-42640, or equivalent, into steering column access hole.
4. Raise and support vehicle.
5. Remove upper intermediate shaft to lower intermediate shaft bolt. Lower vehicle.
6. Remove knee bolster and steering column trim covers.
7. Disconnect steering column electrical connectors.

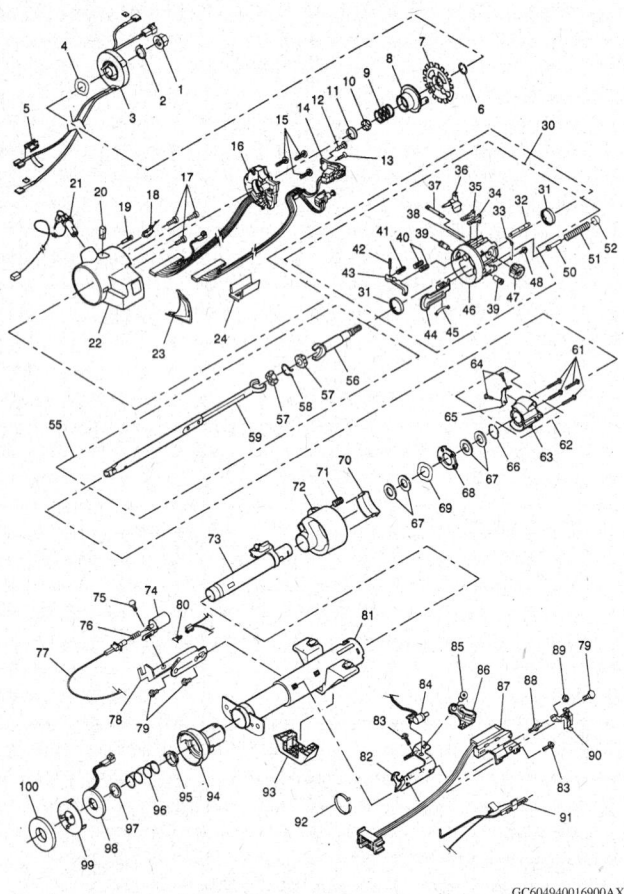

1-NUT, HEXAGON LOCKING (M14x1.5)
2-RING, RETAINING
3-COIL ASM, SIR
4-WASHER, WAVE
5-SHROUD, CONNECTOR
6-RING, RETAINING
7-LOCK, SHAFT
8-CAM ASM, T/SIG CANCEL
9-SPRING, UPPER BEARING
10-SEAT, UPPER BRG INNER RACE
11-RACE, INNER
12-SCREW, RD WASH HD (M4.2X1.41)
13-SCREW, FLAT HEAD
14-SW ASM, PIVOT & (PULSE-DIMMER)
15-SCREW, BNDG HD CR RECESS
16-SWITCH ASM, TURN SIGNAL
17-SCREW, PAN HD 6-LOBED SOC TAP
18-SWITCH ASM, BUZZER
19-SCREW, LOCK RETAINING
20-KNOB, HAZARD WARNING SW
21-LOCK CYLINDER SET, STRG COL
22-COVER & SLEEVE ASM, LOCK HSG
23-CAP, HSG COVER END
24-PROTECTOR, WIRING
30-HOUSING ASM, STRG COLUMN
31-BEARING ASM
32-BOLT ASM, SHAFT LOCK
33-SPRING, LOCK BOLT
34-SHOE, STEERING WHEEL LOCK
35-SHOE, STEERING WHEEL LOCK
36-SHIELD, PROTECTOR WIRE
37-SHAFT, DRIVE
38-PIN, DOWEL
39-PIN, PIVOT
40-SPRING, SHOE
41-SPRING, RELEASE LEVER
42-PIN, RELEASE LEVER
43-LEVER ASM, SHOE RELEASE
44-RACK, SWITCH ACTUATOR
45-SPRING, RACK PRELOAD
46-HOUSING, STRG COLUMN
47-SECTOR, SWITCH ACTUATOR
48-SCREW, HEX WASHER HEAD
50-GUIDE, SPRING
51-SPRING, WHEEL TILT
52-RETAINER, SPRING
55-SHAFT ASM, STEERING
56-SHAFT ASM, RACE & UPPER
57-SPHERE, CENTERING
58-SPRING, JOINT PRELOAD
59-SHAFT ASM, LOWER STEERING
61-SCREW, SUPPORT
62-SUPPORT ASM, STRG COL HSG
63-SUPPORT, STRG COL HSG
64-SCREW, OVL HD CROSS RECESS
65-GATE, SHIFT LEVER

66-RING, SHIFT TUBE RETAINING
67-WASHER, THRUST
68-PLATE, LOCK
69-WASHER, WAVE
70-PROTECTOR, SHIFT BOWL
71-SPRING, SHIFT LEVER
72-BOWL ASM, GEARSHIFT LEVER
73-TUBE ASM, SHIFT
74-SOLENOID ASM, INTERLOCK
75-SCREW, HEX WASHER HEAD
76-SPRING, BALL JOINT
77-CABLE-ASM, BTSI
78-BRACKET, SOLENOID ADAPTER
79-SCREW, HEX WASH HD (#10-24X0.25)
80-CONNECTOR, AXIAL POSN ASSUR
81-JACKET ASM, STRG COL
82-BRACKET ASM, STUD &
83-SCREW, TORX WASHER HEAD
84-SWITCH ASM, PARK POSITION
85-RETAINER, CAM
86-CAM ASM, CABLE SHIFT
87-SWITCH ASM, IGNITION
88-STUD, DIMR SW MOUNTING
89-NUT, HEXAGON (#10-24)
90-ADJUSTER ASM, PRNDL
91-ACTUATOR ASM, IGNITION SWITCH
92-STRAP, WIRE HARNESS
93-CAPSULE,STRG COL SUPPORT
94-BEARING ASM, ADAPTER &
95-SEAT, LOWER BEARING
96-SPRING, LOWER BEARING
97-RETAINER, LOWER SPRING
98-SENSOR ASM, STRG WHL SPD
99-RETAINER, SENSOR
100-SEAL, STEERING SHAFT

Service Kits

201-RACK SERV KIT, COL SECTOR &
    -INCLUDES: 11,31,33,44,47,48
202-SPRING SERV KIT, TILT COLUMN
    -INCLUDES: 10,11,39,50,51,52
203-COIL ASM SERV KIT, SIR
    -INCLUDES: 3,4,5
204-SPHERE SERV KIT, TILT COLUMN
    -INCLUDES: 57,58
205-GREASE SERV KIT, (SYNTHETIC)

GC604940016900AX

Fig. 68 Exploded view of tilt steering column (Part 1 of 2). Lumina w/column shift

GC604940016900BX

Fig. 68 Exploded view of tilt steering column (Part 2 of 2). Lumina w/column shift

8. Support steering column, then remove mounting nuts and steering column.
9. Remove upper intermediate shaft to steering column mounting bolt.
10. Remove upper intermediate shaft from steering column.
11. Replace new upper intermediate shaft (P/N 25749288) to steering column.
12. Install upper intermediate shaft to steering column bolt. **Torque** upper intermediate shaft to steering column retaining bolt to 35 ft. lbs.
13. Install steering column and mounting nuts. **Torque** mounting nuts to 18 ft. lbs.
14. Connect steering column electrical connectors.
15. Install steering column trim covers and knee bolster.
16. Raise and support vehicle.
17. Install upper intermediate shaft to lower intermediate shaft. **Torque** shaft bolt 37 ft. lbs., then lower vehicle.
18. Remove column lock tool and arm air bag system.

Reduced Power Steering Assist, Excessive Steering Effort, Rubbing, Excessive Noise in Passenger Compartment

2003 CENTURY, IMPALA, MONTE CARLO & REGAL

On some of these models there may be a reduced power steering, excessive steering effort, rubbing or excessive noise in the passenger compartment.

This condition may be caused by the intermediate shaft lower boot between the bulk head and the steering gear may be incorrectly installed and interfering with the intermediate shaft.

To correct this condition, proceed as follows:

1. Raise and support vehicle.
2. With ignition switch in ON position and engine off, have an assistant turn steering wheel from righthand to lefthand.
3. Grasp intermediate shaft boot with either hand and while steering wheel is being rotated, noting the following:
   a. There should be no contact felt between intermediate shaft boot and shaft.
   b. If no contact is felt continued steering inspection.
   c. If contact is felt, inspect lower intermediate shaft boot for proper installation and damage.

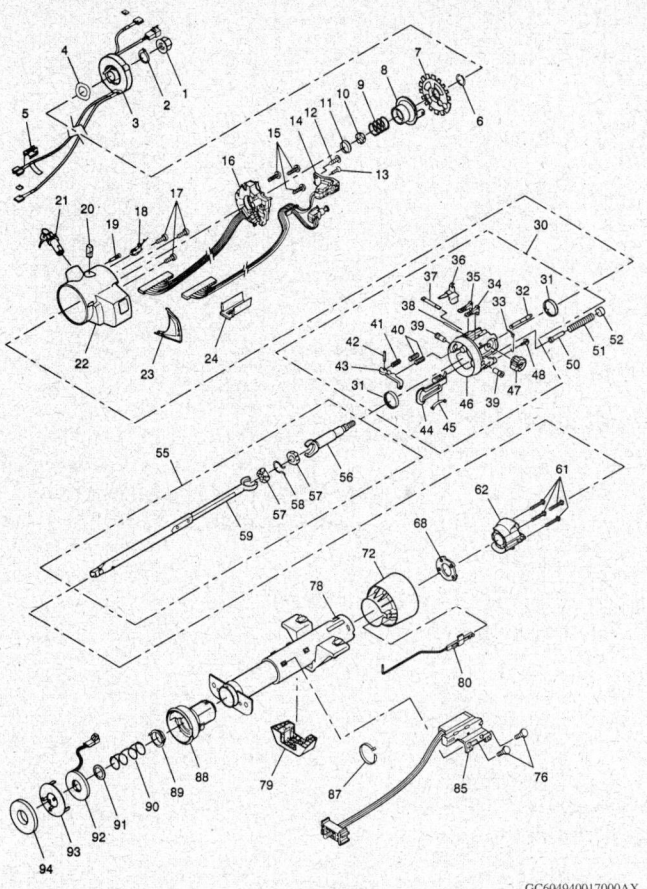

1-NUT, HEXAGON LOCKING (M14x1.5)
2-RING, RETAINING
3-COIL ASM, SIR
4-WASHER, WAVE
5-SHROUD, CONNECTOR
6-RING, RETAINING
7-LOCK, SHAFT
8-CAM ASM, T/SIG CANCEL
9-SPRING, UPPER BEARING
10-SEAT, UPPER BRG INNER RACE
11-RACE, INNER
12-SCREW, RD WASH HD (M4.2X1.41)
13-SCREW, FLAT HEAD
14-SW ASM, PIVOT & (PULSE-DIMMER)
15-SCREW, BNDG HD CR RECESS
16-SWITCH ASM, TURN SIGNAL
17-SCREW, PAN HD 6-LOBED SOC TAP
18-SWITCH ASM, BUZZER
19-SCREW, LOCK RETAINING
20-KNOB, HAZARD WARNING SW
21-LOCK CYLINDER SET, STRG COL
22-COVER & SLEEVE ASM, LOCK HSG
23-CAP, HSG COVER END
24-PROTECTOR, WIRING
30-HOUSING ASM, STRG COLUMN
31-BEARING ASM
32-BOLT ASM, SHAFT LOCK
33-SPRING, LOCK BOLT
34-SHOE, STEERING WHEEL LOCK
35-SHOE, STEERING WHEEL LOCK
36-SHIELD, PROTECTOR WIRE
37-SHAFT, DRIVE
38-PIN, DOWEL
39-PIN, PIVOT
40-SPRING, SHOE
41-SPRING, RELEASE LEVER
42-PIN, RELEASE LEVER
43-LEVER ASM, SHOE RELEASE
44-RACK, SWITCH ACTUATOR
45-SPRING, RACK PRELOAD
46-HOUSING, STRG COLUMN
47-SECTOR, SWITCH ACTUATOR
48-SCREW, HEX WASHER HEAD
50-GUIDE, SPRING
51-SPRING, TILT
52-RETAINER, SPRING
55-SHAFT ASM, STEERING
56-SHAFT ASM, RACE & UPPER
57-SPHERE, CENTERING
58-SPRING, JOINT PRELOAD

59-SHAFT ASM, LOWER STEERING
61-SCREW, SUPPORT
62-SUPPORT ASM, STRG COL HSG
68-PLATE, LOCK
72-SHROUD, STRG COL
76-SCREW, WASH HD (#10-24X0.25)
78-JACKET ASM, STRG COL
79-CAPSULE, STRG COL SUPPORT
80-ACTUATOR ASM, IGNITION SWITCH
85-SWITCH ASM, COLUMN LOCK & IGN
87-STRAP, WIRE HARNESS
88-BEARING ASM, ADAPTER &
89-SEAT, LOWER BEARING
90-SPRING, LOWER BEARING
91-RETAINER, LOWER SPRING
92-SENSOR ASM, STRG WHL SPD
93-RETAINER, SENSOR
94-SEAL, STEERING SHAFT

Service Kits

201-RACK SERV KIT, COL SECTOR &
   -INCLUDES: 11,31,33,44,47,48
202-SPRING SERV KIT, TILT COLUMN
   -INCLUDES: 10,11,39,50,51,52
203-COIL SERV KIT, INFL RESTRAINT
   -INCLUDES: 3,4,5
204-SPHERE SERV KIT, TILT COLUMN
   -INCLUDES: 57,58
205-GREASE SERV KIT, (SYNTHETIC)

GC604940017000AX

Fig. 69 Exploded view of tilt steering column (Part 1 of 2). Lumina w/floor shift

GC604940017000BX

Fig. 69 Exploded view of tilt steering column (Part 2 of 2). Lumina w/floor shift

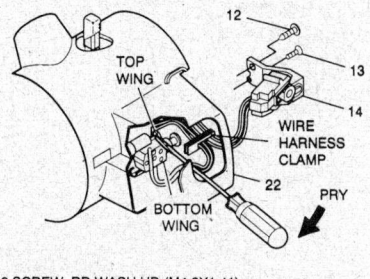

12 SCREW, RD WASH HD (M4.2X1.41)
13 SCREW, FLAT HEAD
14 SW ASM, PIVOT & (PULSE-DIMMER)
22 COVER & SLEEVE ASM, LOCK HSG

GC6049700239000X

Fig. 70 Pivot & pulse dimmer switch removal. Lumina

d. If boot is improperly installed with no damage to boot, correctly position boot.
e. If boot is improperly installed and damaged, proceed to next step.
4. Turn ignition switch to OFF position and remove key.
5. Raise and support vehicle, then remove lefthand front tire and wheel assembly.
6. Position boot to access to lower pinch bolt on intermediate steering shaft.

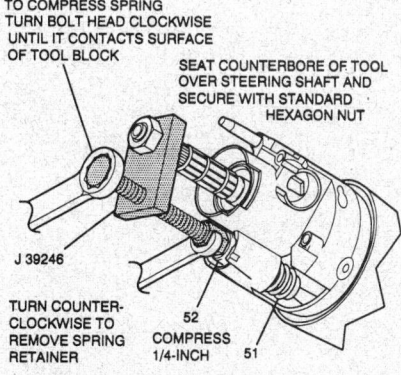

TO COMPRESS SPRING TURN BOLT HEAD CLOCKWISE UNTIL IT CONTACTS SURFACE OF TOOL BLOCK

SEAT COUNTERBORE OF TOOL OVER STEERING SHAFT AND SECURE WITH STANDARD HEXAGON NUT

J 39246

TURN COUNTER-CLOCKWISE TO REMOVE SPRING RETAINER

52 COMPRESS 1/4-INCH

51

51 SPRING, WHEEL TILT
52 RETAINER, SPRING

GC6049700247000X

Fig. 71 Tilt spring removal. Lumina

7. Remove lower pinch bolt from power steering gear stub shaft.
8. Remove intermediate steering shaft from power steering gear stub shaft.
9. Slide damaged lower boot out of upper boot and off intermediate shaft.
10. Install new lower intermediate shaft boot into upper boot (Buick P/N

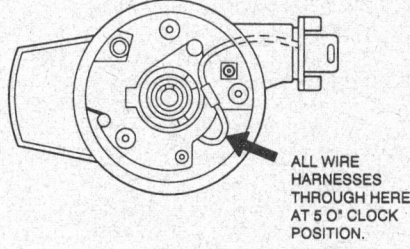

ALL WIRE HARNESSES THROUGH HERE AT 5 O' CLOCK POSITION.

GC6049700248000X

Fig. 72 Wire harness routing. Lumina

10403942   or   Chevrolet P/N 10430526).
11. Position intermediate steering shaft into place. Ensure intermediate shaft is correctly sealed on steering gear stub shaft.
12. Install lower pinch bolt to intermediate steering shaft at steering gear. **Torque** pinch bolt to 35 ft. lbs.
13. Install lower boot onto steering gear.
14. Ensure intermediate shaft is not contacting boot.
15. Install lefthand front tire and wheel assembly. Lower vehicle.

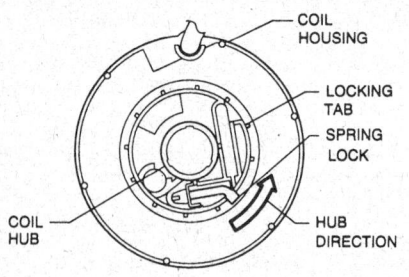

Fig. 73 Centering SIR coil. Lumina

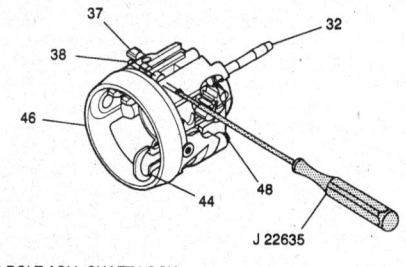

32 BOLT ASM, SHAFT LOCK
37 SHAFT, DRIVE
38 PIN, DOWEL
44 RACK, SWITCH ACTUATOR
46 HOUSING, STRG COLUMN
48 SCREW, HEX WASHER HEAD

GC6049700251000X

Fig. 74 Steering column housing. Lumina

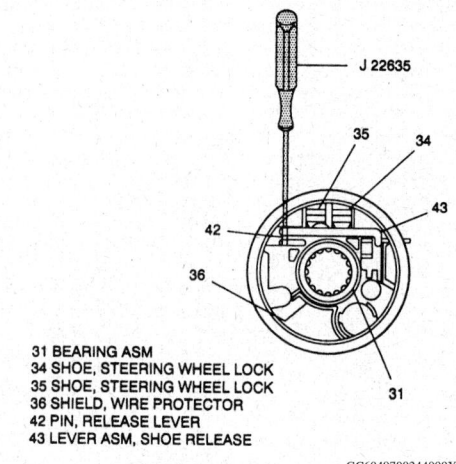

31 BEARING ASM
34 SHOE, STEERING WHEEL LOCK
35 SHOE, STEERING WHEEL LOCK
36 SHIELD, WIRE PROTECTOR
42 PIN, RELEASE LEVER
43 LEVER ASM, SHOE RELEASE

GC6049700244000X

Fig. 75 Lock housing cover components. Lumina

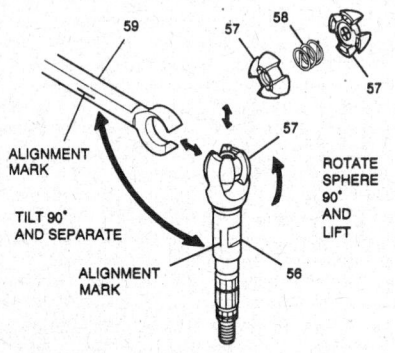

56 SHAFT ASM, RACE & UPPER
57 SPHERE, CENTERING
58 SPRING, JOINT PRELOAD
59 SHAFT ASM, LOWER STEERING

GC6049700245000X

Fig. 76 Steering shaft components. Lumina

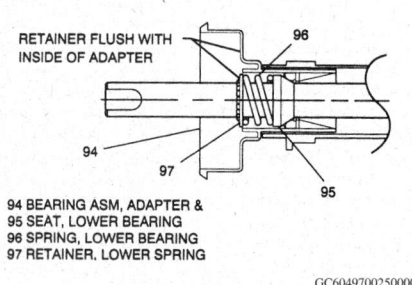

94 BEARING ASM, ADAPTER &
95 SEAT, LOWER BEARING
96 SPRING, LOWER BEARING
97 RETAINER, LOWER SPRING

GC6049700250000X

Fig. 78 Spring height measurement. Lumina

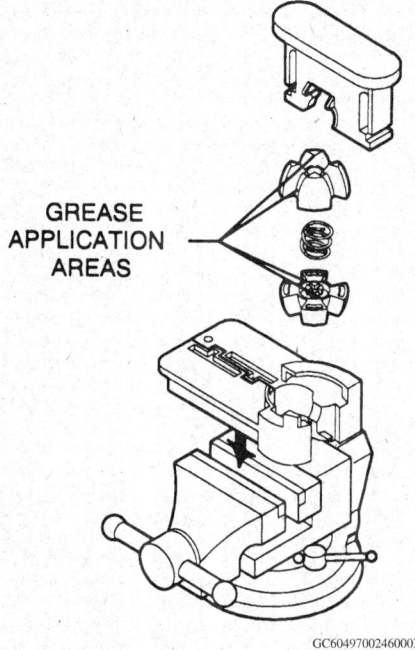

GC6049700246000X

Fig. 77 Centering sphere installation tool. Lumina

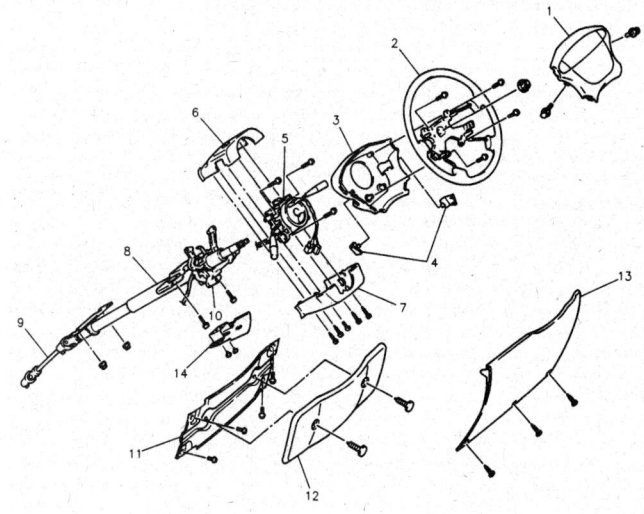

1 SIR INFLATOR MODULE
2 STEERING WHEEL
3 STEERING WHEEL LOWER COVER
4 STEERING WHEEL SIDE CAP
5 CONTACT COIL AND COMBINATION SWITCH ASSEMBLY
6 STEERING COLUMN UPPER COVER
7 STEERING COLUMN LOWER COVER
8 STEERING COLUMN ASSEMBLY
9 LOWER JOINT
10 STEERING LOCK ASSEMBLY
11 KNEE BOLSTER PANEL
12 KNEE BOLSTER ABSORBER
13 STEERING COLUMN HOLE COVER
14 KNEE PROTECTOR

GC6049500190000X

Fig. 79 Exploded view of steering column. Metro

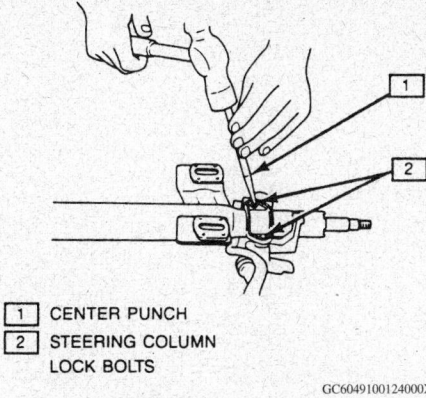

1 CENTER PUNCH
2 STEERING COLUMN
LOCK BOLTS

GC6049100124000X

Fig. 80 Steering column lock bolts removal. Metro

1-NUT,FLANGED PREVAIL TORQUE
2-COIL ASM, SIR
3-WASHER, WAVE
4-RING, RETAINER
5-SHIELD ASM, SHAFT LOCK
6-CAM ASM, T/SIG CANCEL
7-SPRING, UPPER BEARING
8-SEAT, UPPER BEARING INNER RACE
9-RACE, INNER
10-SHROUD, UPPER
11-BOLT ASM, LOCK
12-SPRING, LOCK BOLT
13-SCREW, PAN HD TAPPING
14-SCREW, TORX HEAD
15-ASM, LOCK MODULE
16-SEAL, SHIFT LEVER
17-LOCK CYL SET, STRG COLUMN
18-SCREW, TAPPING
19-SWITCH ASM, IGN & KEY ALARM
20-SPRING, TILT
21-GUIDE, SPRING
22-STRAP, WIRE HARNESS
24-SWITCH ASM, T/S & MULTIFUNCTION
25-CONTROL CODED KEY
26-TILT HEAD ASM, STRG COL
27-PROTECTOR, SHROUD
28-SHROUD, LOWER
29-STUD, SHROUD MOUNTING
30-RING, RETAINING
31-SCREW, SHIFT LEVER
32-LEVER ASM, A/TRNS CONTROL
33-LEVER ASM, TILT
34-SHAFT ASM, RACE & UPPER
35-SPHERE, CENTERING
36-SPRING, JOINT PRELOAD
37-SHAFT ASM, LOWER STRG
40-SHIFT ASM, LINEAR
41-CLEVIS, SHIFT LEVER
43-SCREW, FLAT HD 6-LOBED SOC TAP
44-CAM ASM, CABLE SHIFT
45-ACTUATOR ASM, BALL &
46-BOLT, HEX FLANGE HEAD
47-SCREW, OVAL HD 6-LOBED SOC TAP
48-CABLE ASM, PARK LOCK
49-BRACKET, G/S LEVER ASM SUPPORT
55-SCREW, TORX HEAD
56-PIN, PIVOT
57-SUPPORT ASM, STRG COL
58-JACKET ASM, STRG COL

59-SEAT, LOWER BEARING
60-BEARING ASM, ADAPTER &
61-ACTUATOR, ELECTRICAL (BTSI)
62-SPRING, LOWER BEARING
63-BUSHING, CAM
64-RETAINER, LOWER SPRING
65-RETAINER, SENSOR
66-SEAL, STEERING SHAFT
67-HARNESS ASM, JUMPER

GC604970023800BX

Fig. 81 Exploded view of steering column (Part 2 of 2). Park Avenue

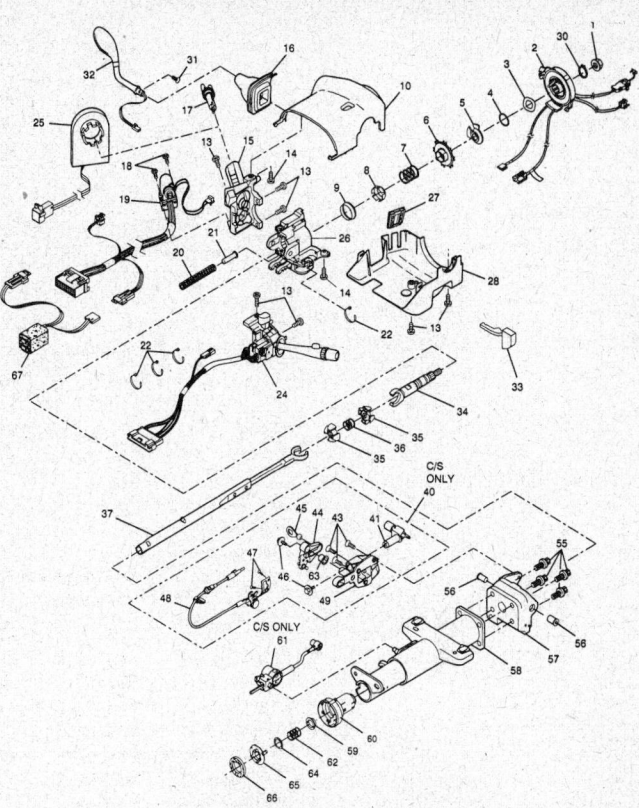

GC604970023800AX

Fig. 81 Exploded view of steering column (Part 1 of 2). Park Avenue

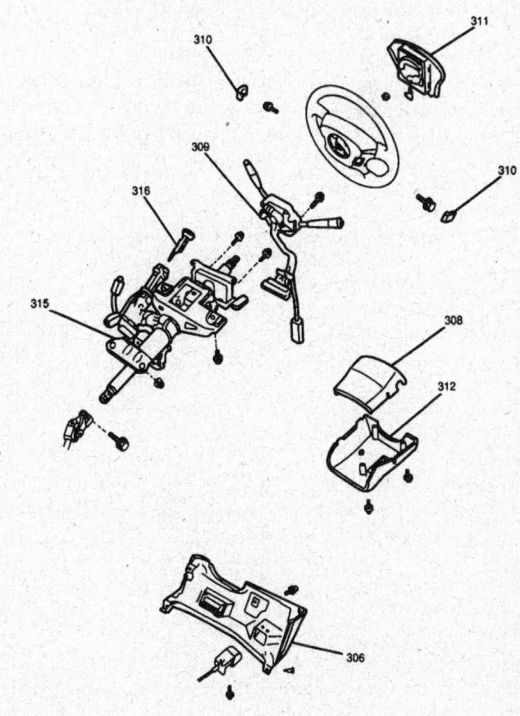

306 KNEE BOLSTER
308 UPPER STEERING COLUMN COVER
309 COMBINATION SWITCH
310 SIDE TRIM COVERS
311 INFLATOR MODULE
312 LOWER STEERING COLUMN COVER
315 STEERING COLUMN ASSEMBLY
316 IGNITION SWITCH

GC6049700237000X

Fig. 82 Exploded view of steering column. Prizm

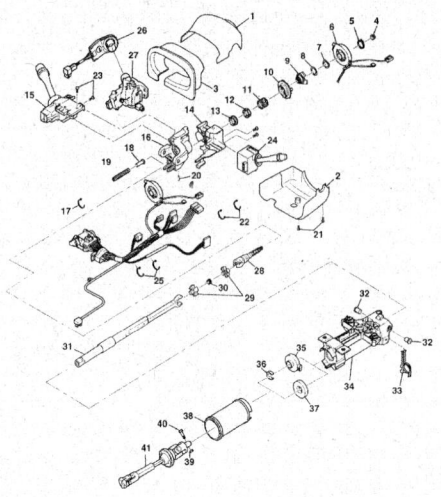

(1) Upper Trim Cover
(2) Lower Trim Cover
(3) Steering Column Closeout Trim
(4) Flanged Prevailing Torque Nut
(5) Retaining Ring
(6) SIR Coil
(7) Wave Washer
(8) Bearing Retainer
(9) Cam Orientation Plate
(10) Turn Signal Cancel Cam
(11) Upper Bearing Spring
(12) Upper Bearing Inner Race Seat
(13) Inner Race
(14) Switch Mounting Bracket
(15) Turn Signal and Multifunction Switch
(16) Steering Column Tilt Head Assembly
(17) Wire Strap
(18) Spring Guide
(19) Tilt Spring
(20) Pin
(21) Pan Head Tapping Screws

(22) Wire Straps
(23) Pan Head Tapping Screws
(24) Window Washer and Wiper Switch Assembly
(25) Wire Straps
(26) Theft Deterrent
(27) Ignition Lock Cylinder Case
(28) Race and Upper Shaft
(29) Centering Sphere
(30) Joint Preload Spring
(31) Lower Steering Shaft
(32) Pivot Pins
(33) Wire Strap
(34) Steering Column Jacket Assembly
(35) Steering Column Position Sensor
(36) Sensor Clip
(37) Sensor Seal
(38) Boot
(39) Bolt Retainer
(40) Pinch Bolt
(41) Intermediate Shaft Assembly

ARM0400000000043

Fig. 83 Exploded view of steering column. STS

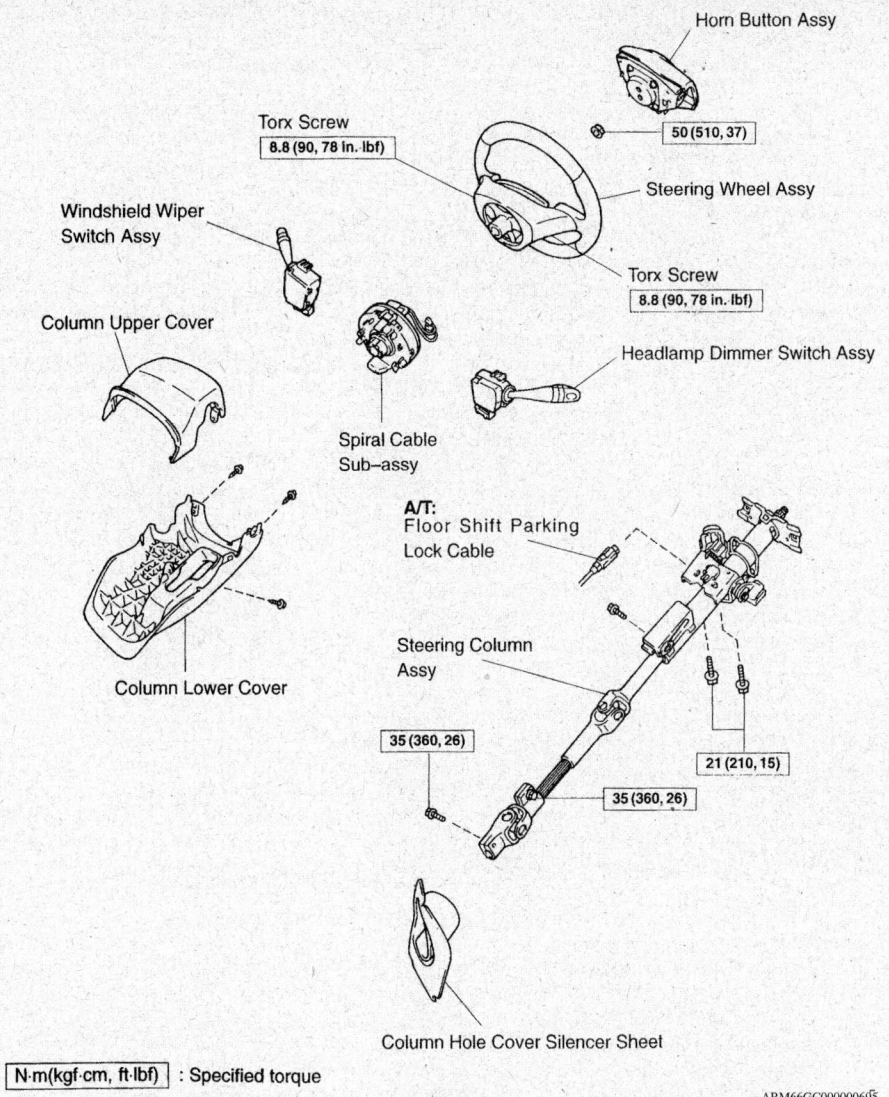

Horn Button Assy

Torx Screw
8.8 (90, 78 in. lbf)

50 (510, 37)

Steering Wheel Assy

Windshield Wiper
Switch Assy

Torx Screw
8.8 (90, 78 in. lbf)

Column Upper Cover

Headlamp Dimmer Switch Assy

Spiral Cable
Sub–assy

A/T:
Floor Shift Parking
Lock Cable

Steering Column
Assy

Column Lower Cover

35 (360, 26)

21 (210, 15)

35 (360, 26)

Column Hole Cover Silencer Sheet

N·m(kgf·cm, ft·lbf) : Specified torque

ARM66GC000000695

Fig. 84   Exploded view of steering column (Part 1 of 2). Vibe

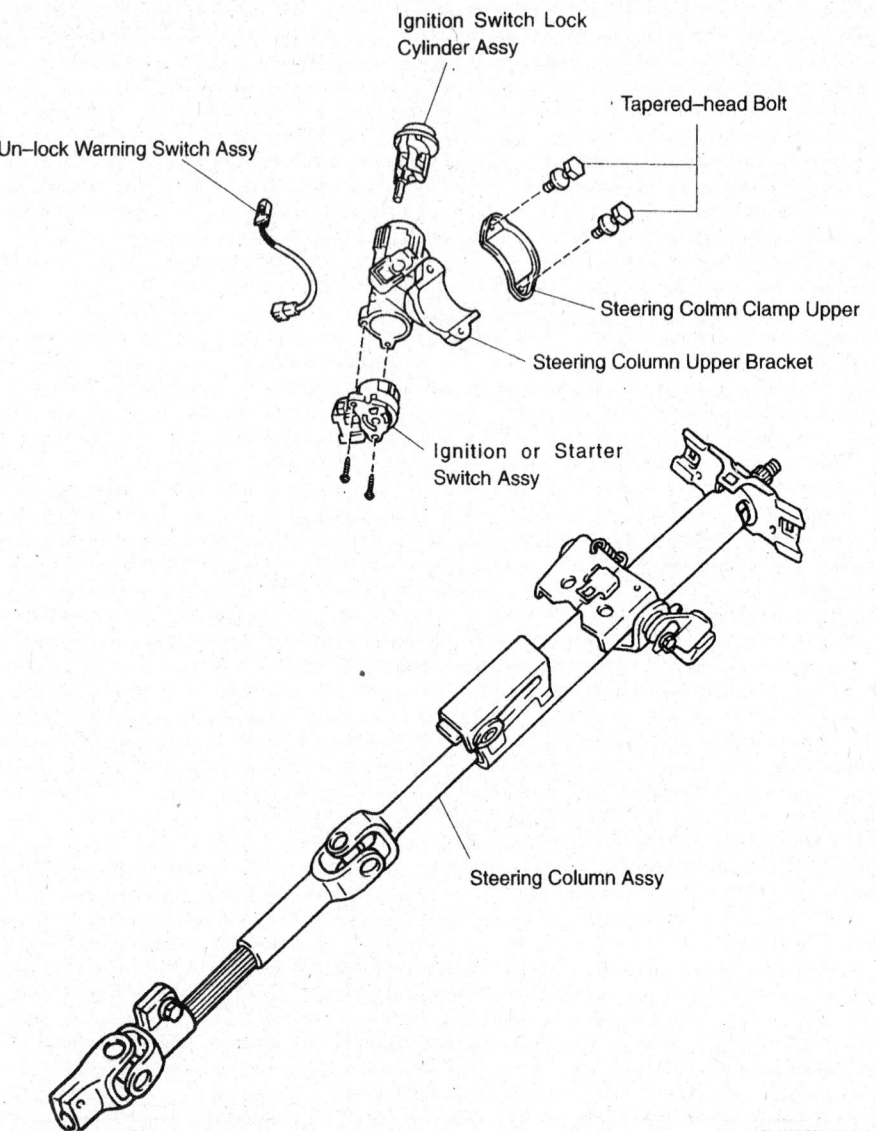

Ignition Switch Lock
Cylinder Assy

Un-lock Warning Switch Assy

Tapered-head Bolt

Steering Colmn Clamp Upper

Steering Column Upper Bracket

Ignition or Starter
Switch Assy

Steering Column Assy

ARM66GC000000696

Fig. 84 Exploded view of steering column (Part 2 of 2). Vibe

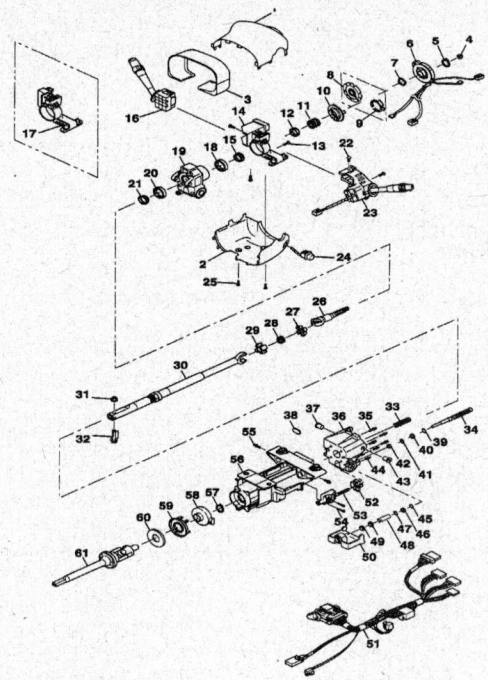

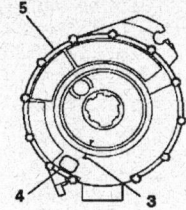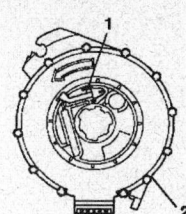

1-Spring service lock
2-Back side
3-Arrows
4-Centering window
5-Front side

ARM0300000000714

Fig. 86   SIR coil assembly. With centering window & spring service lock

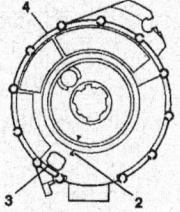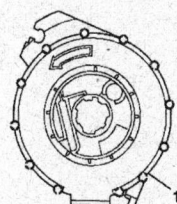

1-Back side
2-Arrows
3-Centering window
4-Front side

ARM0300000000715

Fig. 87   SIR coil assembly. With centering window & less spring service lock

(1) Upper Trim Cover (Kit)
(2) Lower Trim Cover (Kit)
(3) Steering Column Closeout Shroud
(4) Flanged Prevailing Torque Nut
(5) Retaing Ring
(6) Inflatable Restraint Steering Wheel Module Coil
(7) Wave Washer
(8) Shaft Lock Shield Assembly (Export)
(9) Cam Orientation Plate
(10) Turn Signal Cancel Cam Assembly
(11) Upper Bearing Spring
(12) Upper Bearing Inner Race Seat
(13) Pan Head Tapping Screw
(14) Switch Mounting Bracket
(15) Inner Race
(16) Washer Wiper Switch Assembly
(17) Switch Mounting Bracket
(18) Bearing Assembly
(19) Steering Column Tilt Head Assembly
(20) Bearing Assembly
(21) Inner Race
(22) Pan Head Tapping Screw
(23) Turn Signal and Multifunction Switch Assembly
(24) Power TNT Toggle Switch Assembly
(25) Pan Head Tapping Screw
(26) Race and Upper Shaft Assembly
(27) Centering Sphere (Kit)
(28) Joint Preload Spring (Kit)
(29) Centering Sphere (Kit)
(30) Lower Steering Shaft Assembly
(31) Bolt and Retainer Assembly

(32) Pinch Bolt
(33) Tilt Spring
(34) Lead Screw
(35) TORX Head Screw
(36) Tilt Support Assembly
(37) Pivot Pin
(38) Tilt Bumper
(39) Thrust Washer
(40) Thrust Bearing
(41) Thrust Washer
(42) Bearing Roller
(43) Pivot Pin
(44) TORX Head Screw
(45) Thrust Washer
(46) Thrust Bearing
(47) Thrust Washer
(48) Tilt Dampener Spacer
(49) Tilt Dampener Seal
(50) Lower Shield Assembly
(51) Steering Column Wiring Assembly
(52) Jacket Screw LH Telescoping Nut
(53) Jacket Screw Telescoping Actuator Assembly
(54) Pan Head Tapping Screw
(55) Pan Head Tapping Screw
(56) Telescoping Jacket Assembly
(57) Retaining Ring
(58) Steering Wheel Position Sensor
(59) Sensor Retainer
(60) Steering Shaft Seal
(61) Intermediate Steering Shaft Assembly

ARM0300000000713

Fig. 85   Exploded view of steering column. XLR

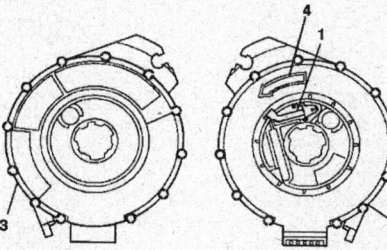

1-Spring service lock
2-Back side
3-Front side
4-Arrow

ARM0300000000716

Fig. 88   SIR coil assembly. Less centering window & w/spring service lock

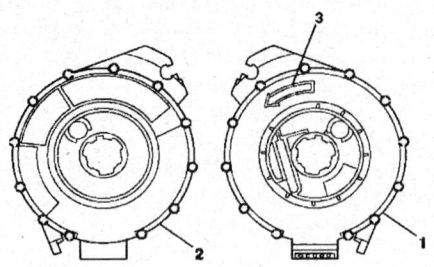

1-Back side
2-Front side
3-Arrow

ARM0300000000717

**Fig. 89 SIR coil assembly. Less
centering window & spring
service lock**

TIGHTENING SPECIFICATIONS

Year	Component	Torque/Ft. Lbs.
ALERO		
2001–04	Column Bracket Support	19
	Intermediate Shaft Pinch Bolt	16
	Steering Wheel	30
AURORA		
2001–03	Cable Support	89①
	Lower Cover	31①
	Upper Cover	13①
	Intermediate Shaft Pinch Bolt	35
	Intermediate Shaft Seal	21①
	Steering Wheel	30
	Support	20
	Switch Bracket	62①
	Wiring Harness Connector	71①
AVEO		
2005	Coupling Flange Pinch Bolt	16
	Ignition Switch Housing Sheer Bolts	97 ①
	Ignition Switch Retaining Screws	18①
	Lower Instrument Panel Trim Screws	27①
	Steering Wheel Nut	28
	Support Housing Screws	12
	Turn Signal Switch Housing Screws	27①
	Upper/Lower Steering Column Cover Screws	27①
BONNEVILLE & LESABRE		
2001–05	Cable Support Bracket Screws	26①
	Column Support Bolts	20
	Intermediate Shaft Pinch Bolt	35
	Intermediate Shaft Seal Screw	21①
	Multi-Function Switch Screws	62①
	Steering Column Trim Cover, Lower	31①
	Steering Column Trim Cover, Upper	13①
	Steering Column Wiring Harness Connector	71①
	Steering Wheel Nut	30
	Steering Wheel Rear Bezel	26①

Continued

TIGHTENING SPECIFICATIONS—Continued

Year	Component	Torque/Ft. Lbs.
CAMARO & FIREBIRD		
2001–02	Dimmer & Ignition Switch Bolts/Screws	35①
	Hazard Warning Switch Knob Bolt/Screw	6①
	Hydraulic Pump Fitting	55
	Hydraulic Pump Hose Fitting	21
	Ignition Switch	22①
	Inflatable Restraint Steering Wheel Mounting Plate Bolt/Screw	17①
	Intermediate Steering Shaft To Steering Column Bolt	35
	Intermediate Steering Shaft To Steering Gear Bolt	35
	Power Steering Gear Pipe Fitting Seat	21
	Radio Control Switch Bolt	17①
	Steering Column Bolts/Screws	14
	Steering Column Guide Bolt	18
	Steering Column Upper Support Nuts	18
	Steering Wheel Bolt/Screw	25①
	Steering Wheel Horn Switch Contact Plate Shoulder Bolt/Screw	25①
	Steering Wheel Nut	32
	Steering Wheel To Inflatable Restraint Steering Wheel Module Bolt	25①
	Steering Wheel To Steering Wheel Horn Switch Bolts/Screws	17①
CATERA		
2001	Connector	16
	Pass Key Lock Cylinder	22①
	Signal Switch Housing	35①
	Support Bracket, Rear	16
	Support Shear Bolt, Forward	15
	Support Strap, Forward	16
CAVALIER & SUNFIRE		
2001–05	Ignition Switch Screws	36①
	Lock Module Assembly Screws	61①
	Lower Pinch Bolt	30
	Multi-Function Switch Mounting Screws	36
	Steering Column Mounting Bolts	20
	Steering Column Trim Cover Screws	36①
	Steering Wheel Nut	27
	Upper Pinch Bolt	30
	Windshield Washer & Wiper Switch	36①
CENTURY, GRAND PRIX & REGAL		
2001–05	Column Cover, Lower	30①
	Column Cover, Upper	12①
	Mounting	18
	Park Lock Cable	58①
	Pinch Bolt	35
	Turn Signal Cam, Bolt	13
	Turn Signal Cam, Screws	84①

Continued

TIGHTENING SPECIFICATIONS—Continued

Year	Component	Torque/Ft. Lbs.
CORVETTE		
2001–04	Bracket	17
	Dimmer Switch	35①
	Lock Housing Cover	96①
	Pass Key Lock Cylinder	22①
	Pinch Bolt	35
	Support Plate	17
	Turn Signal Switch	30①
	Turn Signal Switch Arm	20①
CTS		
2003–05	Intermediate Shaft Bolts	37
	Lock Cylinder Case Screws	62①
	Multi-Function Switch Front Screw	62①
	Multi-Function Switch Top Screw	27①
	Steering Column Mounting Nuts	18
	Steering Column Trim Cover Lower Screws	31①
	Steering Column Trim Cover Upper Screw	13
	Steering Wheel Control Switch Upper Screws	20①
	Steering Wheel Nut	30
DEVILLE, ELDORADO, SEVILLE & STS		
2001–05	Cable Shift Cam	35①
	Gate	33①
	Interlock Solenoid Bracket	35①
	Lock	22①
	Lock Housing	80①
	Lower Bracket	12
	Pinch Bolt	35
	Support	20
	Turn Signal Switch	30①
	Turn Signal Switch Arm	20①
GRAND AM		
2001–05	Column Bracket Support	19
	Intermediate Shaft Pinch Bolt	16
	Steering Wheel	30
GTO		
2004	Ignition Switch Bolt	10.6①
	Steering Column Bolts	17
	Steering Column Nuts	17
	Steering Coupling to Steering Gear Pinion Nut and Bolt	20
	Steering Wheel Retaining Bolt	13
G6		
2005	EPS Motor to Steering Column Bolts	80①
	Intermediate Steering Shaft to Steering Column Pinch Bolt	36
	Intermediate Steering Shaft to Steering Gear Pinch Bolt	36
	Steering Wheel Nut	24

TIGHTENING SPECIFICATIONS—Continued

Year	Component	Torque/Ft. Lbs.
IMPALA		
2001–05	Cover, Lower Trim	31①
	Cover, Upper Trim	13①
	Mount	18
	Pinch Bolt	35
INTRIGUE		
2001–2003	Column Cover, Lower	30①
	Column Cover, Upper	12①
	Mounting	18
	Park Lock Cable	58①
	Pinch Bolt	35
	Turn Signal Cam, Screws	84①
	Turn Signal Cam, Bolt	13
ION		
2003–05	Ignition Lock Cylinder Case Shear Bolt	15
	Ignition Lock Cylinder Solenoid Screw	17①
	Ignition Switch Screws	17①
	Intermediate Shaft Pinch Bolt	25
	Multi-Function Switch Screw	17①
	Steering Column Mid Pivot Bolt	18
	Steering Column Mounting Bolt	18
	Steering Column Trim Cover Screws	17①
	Steering Column Upper Jacket Bolts	97①
	Steering Wheel Nut	31
L-SERIES		
2001–05	Intermediate Shaft Pinch Bolt	22
	Signal Switch Housing To Steering Column	14①
	Steering Column To I/P Support Beam	22
LUMINA		
2001	Cylinder Lock	22①
	Dimmer Switch	35①
	Mounting	18
	Pinch Bolt	35
	Turn Signal Switch	31①
MALIBU		
2001–05	Intermediate Shaft Pinch Bolt	16
	Steering Wheel	30
	Support Bracket	18
METRO		
2001	Mount	10
	Upper Pinch Bolt	18
MONTE CARLO		
2001–05	Cover, Lower Trim	31①
	Cover, Upper Trim	13①
	Mount	18
	Pinch Bolt	35
PARK AVENUE		
2001–05	Cover, Lower	60①
	Cover, Upper	13①
	Pinch Bolt	35
	Shift Lever, Bolt	14
	Shift Lever, Flat Head Tap Screw	84①
	Shift Lever, Oval Head Tap Screw	58①
	Support	20
	Wiring Harness Connector	72①

TIGHTENING SPECIFICATIONS—Continued

Year	Component	Torque/Ft. Lbs.
PRIZM		
2001–02	Knee Bolster	84①
	Mount	19
	Pinch Bolt	26
S-SERIES		
2001–02	Intermediate Shaft Pinch Bolt	
	Signal Switch Housing To Steering Column	14①
	Steering Column To I/P Support Beam	22
STS		
2005	Ignition Lock Cylinder Case Screws	62①
	Intermediate Shaft Bolts	22
	Intermediate Shaft to Steering Column Pinch Bolt	35
	Intermediate Shaft to Steering Gear Pinch Bolt	37
	Steering Column Mounting Nuts	18
	Steering Column Lower Cover Trim Screws	31①
	Steering Column Upper Cover Trim Screws	13①
	Steering Wheel Nut	30
	Turn Signal Multifunction Switch Screw Side	62①
	Turn Signal Multifunction Switch Screw Top	27①
	Upper Intermediate Shaft to Lower Intermediate Shaft Pinch Bolt	22
VIBE		
2003–05	Intermediate Steering Shaft Bolt	26
	Steering Column Bolts	16
	Steering Shaft Coupling Bolts	26
	Steering Wheel Nut	37
XLR		
2004–05	Column Support Bracket Nuts	17
	Dampener Screws	13①
	Intermediate Shaft to the Steering Column Pinch Bolt	35
	Steering Column Bottom Bracket Screw	26①
	Steering Column Support Screws	13
	Steering Wheel & Column Lower To Upper Intermediate Shaft Retaining Bolts	35
	Steering Wheel Nut	30
	Telescope Actuator Assembly Screws	44①

① — Inch lbs.

MANUAL STEERING GEARS

TABLE OF CONTENTS

Suzuki Rack & Pinion, Metro

INDEX

DESCRIPTION

The rack and pinion steering system consists of two main components: the rack and the pinion. The motion of turning the steering wheel is transferred to the pinion. The rotary motion of the pinion is then transferred through the pinion teeth which mesh with the rack teeth and, in turn, gives the rack linear motion. The linear motion is then transmitted through the inner and outer tie rods to the steering knuckles which turn the wheels.

STEERING GEAR SERVICE

Refer to **Fig. 1,** when servicing the steering gear.

Steering Rack

DISASSEMBLE

1. Mark position of outer tie rod end locknuts on inner tie rod threads.
2. Remove outer tie rod ends from inner tie rods.
3. Remove boot wires and clips, then slide boots toward tie rod end.
4. Unstake ball nut.
5. Remove inner tie rods from rack.
6. Clean dirt and grease from all steering gear components using a suitable solvent.
7. Remove pinion seal using socket tool No. J 34871-A, or equivalent.

INSPECTION

1. Inspect all components for damage and wear. Replace as required.

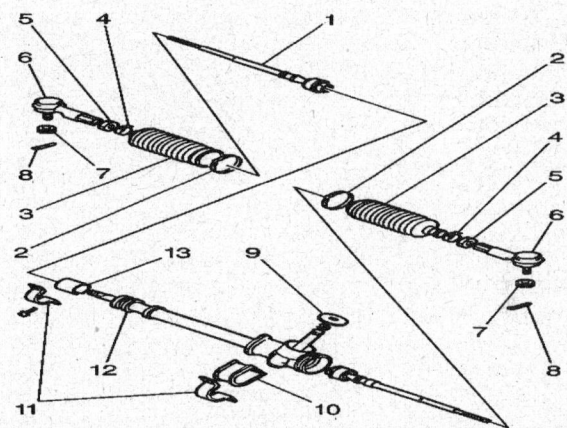

(1) Tie Rod
(2) Steering Gear Boot Clamp
(3) Steering Gear Boot
(4) Outer Boot Clamp
(5) Tie Rod End Locknut
(6) Tie Rod End
(7) Castle Nut
(8) Cotter Pin
(9) Steering Pinion Seal
(10) Steering Pinion Side Mount
(11) Steering Rack Mount Bracket
(12) Steering Rack Housing and Gear Case
(13) Steering Rack Side Mount

GC6030100057000X

Fig. 1 Exploded view of manual rack & pinion steering gear

2. Inspect pinion oil seal and rack boots for damage, tears or wear. Replace as required.
3. Measure pinion's resistance to rotation using a suitable torque wrench and socket tool No. J 34871-A, or equivalent. Resistance should be 9–13 inch lbs. Replace steering gear if resistance does not meet specifications.

ASSEMBLE

1. Coat inside of ball stud dust seal with chassis grease P/N 12377985, or equivalent.
2. Install seal to ball stud.
3. Install new inner tie rods to rack.
4. Stake each ball nut until flat spots are .95 inch apart, **Fig. 2.**
5. Coat inside of outer end of each boot with manual steering gear lubricant P/N 1052182, or equivalent.
6. Position boots on steering gear housing grooves and inner tie rods.
7. Install outer boot clamps.
8. Install a new inner boot clamp and secure using clamping tool No. J 22610, or equivalent.
9. Inspect all boots and ensure they are not twisted or improperly folded. Ensure boot clamps are secure.
10. Copy marks from old inner tie rods to new ones.
11. Install outer tie rod ends to inner tie rods. Ensure lock washer tabs are properly bent.

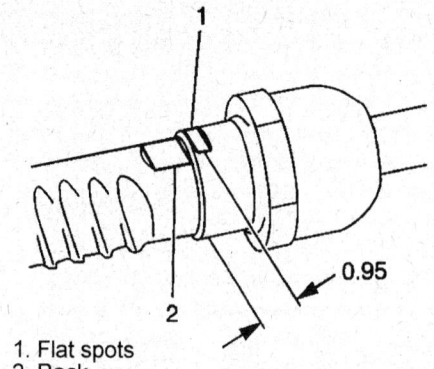

1. Flat spots
2. Rack

GC6030100058000X

Fig. 2 Ball nut staking

TIGHTENING SPECIFICATIONS

Component	Torque, Ft. Lbs.
Pinion Preload	9–13①
Adjuster Plug Locknut	70
Coupling To Column Pinch Bolt	18
Flange & Coupling Pinch Bolt	18
Outer Tie Rod Jam Nuts	32
Steering Gear Mounting Bracket Bolts	18
Steering Shaft Joint Bolts	18
Tie Rod Ball Nuts	51
Tie Rod End Castle Nuts & Locknuts	32

① — Inch lbs.

Saturn

INDEX

DESCRIPTION

The manual steering system is a rack and pinion design. The major components of the steering system are the steering wheel, steering column and shaft, intermediate shaft, manual steering gear, tie rods and steering knuckles.

When the steering wheel is turned, the steering shaft turns the intermediate shaft which turns the steering gear pinion. The pinion gear teeth mesh with the straight rack mating teeth inside the steering gear. Rotation of the pinion converts to a straight-line motion of the rack across the vehicle that moves the tie rods either left or right. This motion causes the steering knuckle to pivot either clockwise or counterclockwise, steering the front wheels.

TROUBLESHOOTING

Refer to **Fig. 1,** for manual steering system troubleshooting.

ADJUSTMENTS

BEARING PRELOAD

The following adjustment should be made with the front wheels raised and the steering wheel centered.

1. Loosen adjuster plug locknut on steering gear housing.
2. Turn adjuster plug clockwise until it bottoms in steering gear housing, **Fig. 2.**
3. **Torque** adjuster plug to 108 inch lbs.
4. Back adjuster plug off 50° (approximately one flat of nut).
5. **Torque** locknut to 52 ft. lbs., while holding adjuster plug.
6. Inspect steering wheel return following adjustment.

Complaint/Condition	Possible Cause(s)	Correction(s)
Hard Steering	Front tire(s) improperly inflated.	Inflate tire(s) correctly.
	Improperly adjusted, improperly lubricated, or damaged steering gear.	Adjust, lubricate (check for damaged boots), or replace steering gear.
	Worn or binding lower control arm ball stud(s).	Replace lower control arm(s).
	Worn or binding inner or outer tie rod end(s).	Replace inner or outer tie rod end(s).
	Worn or binding upper strut mount(s).	Replace mount(s).
	Worn or binding intermediate steering shaft joint(s).	Replace intermediate steering shaft.
	Binding within steering column or intermediate steering shaft joint.	Correct condition.
Poor return of steering wheel to center.	Front tire(s) improperly inflated.	Inflate tire(s) correctly.
	Improperly adjusted, lubricated, or damaged steering gear.	Adjust, lubricate (check for damaged boots), or replace steering gear.
	Worn or binding lower control arm ball stud(s).	Replace lower control arm(s).
	Worn or binding inner or outer tie rod end(s).	Replace inner or outer tie rod end(s).
	Worn or binding upper strut mount(s).	Replace mount(s).
	Worn or binding intermediate steering shaft joint(s).	Replace intermediate steering shaft.
	Binding within steering column or intermediate steering shaft boot.	Correct condition.
	Incorrect front wheel caster.	Perform alignment.
Excessive free play in steering.	Wheel bearing(s) worn.	Replace wheel bearing(s).
	Steering gear mounting bolt(s) loose.	Tighten bolt(s).
	Steering gear out of adjustment or worn.	Adjust or replace steering gear.
	Intermediate steering shaft joint(s) worn.	Replace intermediate steering shaft.
	Inner or outer steering tie rod(s) worn.	Replace tie rod(s).
	Lower control arm ball stud(s) worn.	Replace lower control arm(s).
	Front stabilizer shaft bushings worn.	Replace bushings.
Rattle and/or clunking noise in steering.	Inner or outer tie rod end(s) worn.	Replace tie rod end(s).
	Steering gear out of adjustment or worn.	Adjust or replace steering gear.
	Worn or loose steering gear right-hand bushing.	Repair or replace steering gear.
	Intermediate steering shaft joint(s) worn.	Replace intermediate steering shaft.
	Steering gear mounting bolt(s) loose.	Tighten bolt(s).
	Worn wheel bearing(s).	Replace wheel bearing(s).

G36030100001000X

Fig. 1 Steering system troubleshooting

STEERING GEAR SERVICE

The steering gear must be serviced as an assembly.

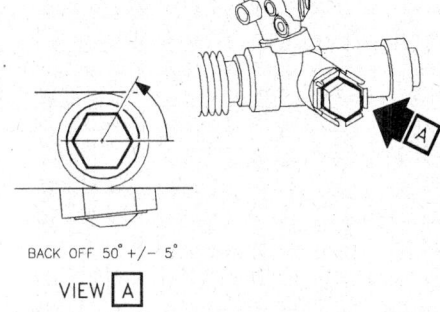

BACK OFF 50° +/− 5°

VIEW A

G36030100002000X

Fig. 2 Bearing preload adjustment

POWER STEERING

TABLE OF CONTENTS

Application Chart

Model	Year	Power Steering Type
BUICK		
Century	2001–05	Saginaw Rack & Pinion
LaCrosse	2005	Saginaw Rack & Pinion
LeSabre	2001–05	Saginaw Rack & Pinion
Park Avenue	2001–05	Saginaw Rack & Pinion
Regal	2001–04	Saginaw Rack & Pinion
CADILLAC		
Catera	2001	Saginaw Rotary Valve
CTS	2003–05	Saginaw Rack & Pinion
DeVille	2001–05	Saginaw Rack & Pinion
Eldorado	2001–02	Saginaw Rack & Pinion
Seville	2001–04	Saginaw Rack & Pinion
STS	2005	Saginaw Rack & Pinion
XLR	2004–05	Saginaw Rack & Pinion
CHEVROLET		
Aveo	2005	Saginaw Rack & Pinion
Camaro	2001–02	Saginaw Rack & Pinion
Cavalier	2001–05	Saginaw Rack & Pinion
Corvette	2001–05	Saginaw Rack & Pinion
Impala	2001–05	Saginaw Rack & Pinion
Lumina	2001	Saginaw Rack & Pinion
Malibu	2001–05	Saginaw Rack & Pinion
Metro	2001	Saginaw Rack & Pinion
Monte Carlo	2001–05	Saginaw Rack & Pinion
Prizm	2001–02	Toyota Rack & Pinion
OLDSMOBILE		
Alero	2001–04	Saginaw Rack & Pinion
Aurora	2001–03	Saginaw Rack & Pinion
Intrigue	2001–02	Saginaw Rack & Pinion
PONTIAC		
Bonneville	2001–05	Saginaw Rack & Pinion
Firebird	2001–02	Saginaw Rack & Pinion
Grand Am	2001–05	Saginaw Rack & Pinion
Grand Prix	2001–05	Saginaw Rack & Pinion
GTO	2004–05	Saginaw Rack & Pinion
G6	2005	Saginaw Rack & Pinion

Continued

POWER STEERING

Model	Year	Power Steering Type
PONTIAC		
Sunfire	2001–05	Saginaw Rack & Pinion
Vibe	2003–05	Toyota Rack & Pinion
SATURN		
ION	2003–05	Saginaw Rack & Pinion
L-Series	2001–05	Saginaw Rack & Pinion
S-Series	2001–02	Saturn Rack & Pinion

POWER STEERING PRESSURE SPECIFICATIONS

Model	Engine	High Flow Rate, GPM	Pressure Relief, PSI
Alero & Grand Am	2.2L & 2.4L	1.95–2.35	1300–1400
	3.4L	1.95–2.35	1400–1500
Aurora	3.5L & 4.0L	2.10–2.50	1700–1800
Aveo	1.6L	—	—
Bonneville, LeSabre & Park Avenue	3.8L	③	1350–1450
Camaro & Firebird	3.8L	2.40–2.80	1200–1300
	5.7L	2.70–3.10	1200–1300
Catera	3.0L	1.70–2.10	1400–1500
Cavalier & Sunfire	2.2L	1.95–2.35	1300–1400
	2.4L	1.95–2.35	1400–1500
Century, Grand Prix, Impala, Monte Carlo & Regal	3.1L	2.40–2.80	1200–1350
	3.4L	2.40–2.80	1200–1350
	3.8L	2.40–2.80	1200–1350 ④
Corvette	5.7L	2.40–2.80	1250–1350
CTS	3.2L	1.80–2.13	1400–1500
	3.6L	1.80–2.13	1640 1740
DeVille & Seville	4.6L	1.80–2.40	1700–1800
Eldorado	4.6L	2.10–2.50	1500–1600
GTO	5.7L	1.95–2.35	1100/1200
G6	3.5L	—	—
Intrigue	3.5L	2.40–2.80	1400–1500
ION	2.2L	1.70–2.10	1300–1400
LaCrosse	3.8L	2.40–2.80	1400
Lumina	3.1L	—	1000
L-Series	2.2L	1.70–2.10	1300–1400
	3.0L	1.70–2.10	1400–1500
Malibu	3.1L	1.95–2.35	1400–1500
Metro	1.0L & 1.3L	—	924
Prizm	1.8L	①	924–1076
S-Series	1.9L	—	—
STS	4.6L	2.84–3.24	1668/1770
Vibe	1.8L	1.27–1.64 ②	1059–1204
XLR	4.6L	2.40–2.80	1250–1350

GPM — Gallons Per Minute
① — At Idle, 1.71 GPM; at 3000 RPM, 1.20 GPM.
② — At 1500 RPM.
③ — 2001–02, 1.80–2.40 GPM; 2003–04, 1.90–2.40 GPM.
④ — 2004–05 Grand Prix, 1400–1500 RPM.

Power Steering Pumps

NOTE: On Air Bag Equipped Models, Refer To "Air Bag System Precautions" Located In The Front Of This Manual For System Disarming & Arming Procedures.

NOTE: Refer To "Computer Relearn Procedures" Located In The Front Of This Manual When Battery Power To The Computer Has Been Interrupted.

NOTE: Prior To Performing Any Service Operations Listed In This Section, Consult The "Technical Service Bulletins" Section For Related Information.

INDEX

DIAGNOSIS & TESTING

System Pressure Test

When performing system test procedures, power steering pressures can easily exceed 1000 psi. Extreme caution must be exercised when performing these tests to prevent personal injury.

Refer to "Power Steering Pressure Specifications" for specifications.

EXCEPT CATERA, METRO & PRIZM

1. Disconnect pressure hose at pump. Use suitable container to catch any fluid leakage.
2. Connect spare pressure hose to pump.
3. Connect pressure gauge tool kit No. J-44721, or equivalent test components, **Fig. 1.**
4. Open gauge valve.
5. Start engine and allow system to reach normal operating temperature.
6. Inspect and adjust fluid level.
7. When engine is at operating temperature, pressure reading should be as specified. If pressure is more than maximum specification, inspect hoses for restrictions.
8. **Do not leave valve fully closed for more than five seconds.**
9. Fully close valve three times, noting the following:
   a. Three readings should be within 50 psi., of each other.
   b. If pressure readings are at least minimum specified under and are

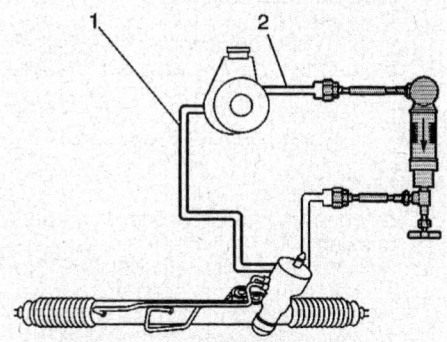

1) Powersteering return hose
2) Power steering pressure hose

GC6020100447000X

Fig. 1 Power steering pressure gauge connections. Except Catera & Metro

within 50 psi., of each other, pump is functioning properly.
   c. If pressure readings are at least minimum specified, but not within 50 psi., of each other, flow control valve is sticking and requires removal and cleaning. Burrs can be removed using crocus cloth.
10. If pressure readings are within specifications, leave valve open and turn steering wheel to both stops. If pressure at stops is not same as maximum pressure specified, steering gear is leaking internally.
11. Turn engine off and remove testing gauge and hoses.
12. Connect pressure hose and inspect fluid level.

CATERA

1. Disconnect power steering pump pressure hose from pump. Use suitable container to catch any fluid leakage.
2. Connect gauge tool No. J-5176-E and pressure tester adapter tool No. J-5176-5A, or equivalents, to pump, **Fig. 2.**
3. Connect pressure tester to power steering pressure hose using pressure test adapter tool No. J-5176-11A, or equivalent.
4. Open valve on pressure tester.
5. Bleed power steering system as outlined in "Power Steering System Service."
6. Start engine and allow it to reach normal operating temperature.
7. Pressure should be no more than 150 psi., with engine at idle and valve open. If pressure is more than specified, inspect as follows:
   a. Inspect hoses and pipes for restrictions or kinks.
   b. Inspect valve on steering gear inlet hose fitting for proper operation.
   c. Inspect valve on steering gear inlet hose fitting for restrictions.
8. **Do not leave valve fully closed for more than five seconds.**
9. Close valve on gauge three times, noting the following:
   a. Each reading should be at least 1600 psi., and be within 50 psi., of each other.
   b. If pressure readings are as specified and within 50 psi., of each other, pump is operating properly.
   c. If pressure readings are less than

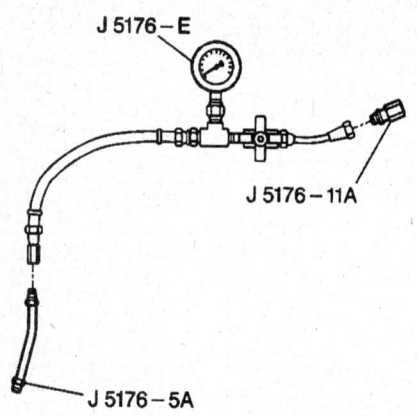

Fig. 2 Power steering pressure gauge connections. Catera

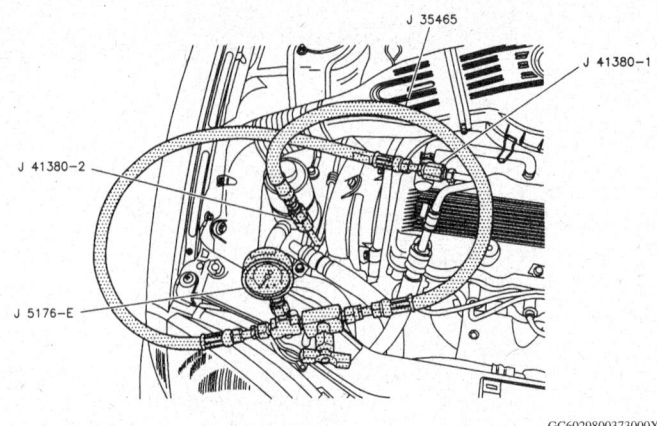

Fig. 3 Power steering pressure gauge connections. Metro

1600 psi., replace pump.

10. With valve in open position, turn steering wheel to both stops, noting the following:
    a. Pressure reading should be same as maximum pressure specified.
    b. If pressure is not as specified, steering gear is leaking internally.
11. Turn ignition to Off position and remove pressure test tools.
12. Connect pump pressure hose to pump.
13. **Torque** pressure hose fitting to 21 ft. lbs.
14. Bleed power steering system as outlined in "Power Steering System Service."

METRO

1. Remove mounting bolts and disconnect high pressure hose at pipe to core support.
2. Install pressure gauge tool No. J-5176-E, pressure tester adapter hose tool No. J-35465, and pressure tester adapter kit tool No. J-41380, or equivalents, as follows:
   a. Connect gauge side of pressure gauge to pressure hose from pump.
   b. Connect valve side of gauge to pressure line to rack, **Fig. 3**.
3. Bleed power steering system as outlined in "Power Steering System Bleed."
4. Start engine, then turn steering wheel from righthand and lefthand stops 2–3 times.
5. Ensure fluid level is at proper level.
6. Turn off engine and ensure fluid temperature is at least 176°F.
7. Start and run engine at idle.
8. Inspect pressure, noting the following:
   a. With valve open and engine idling, pressure reading should be no more than 142 psi.
   b. If pressure reading is more than 142 psi., inspect hoses for restrictions or control valve for damage.
9. **Do not leave valve closed for more than 10 seconds.** Inspect fluid pressure reading with valve closed, noting the following:
   a. If pressure reading is less than 825 psi., repair or replace power steering pump.
   b. If pressure gauge reading is more than 924 psi., possible cause is relief valve fault.
10. With engine idling and valve open, turn steering wheel to full right or left and read pressure, noting the following:
    a. Pressure should be no less than 825 psi., and no more than 924 psi.
    b. If reading is less than 825 psi., repair or replace rack and pinion.
    c. If reading is more than 924 psi., repair or replace relief valve.

PRIZM

1. Disconnect pressure line from gear housing.
2. Connect pressure gauge tool No. J-5176 and gauge adapter tool No. J-35465, or equivalents, to power steering system, **Fig. 1**.
3. Bleed power steering system as outlined in "Power Steering System Service."
4. Start engine and turn steering wheel from left to righthand stops 2–3 times.
5. Shut off engine and ensure fluid temperature is at least 176°F and reservoir is full.
6. Start engine and run at idle speed.
7. Inspect fluid pressure with valve on pressure gauge closed. **Do not keep valve closed for more than five seconds.**
8. If pressure is less than 924 psi., power steering pump is faulty. Repair or replace as required.
9. Open valve on power steering gear and record pressure reading at 1000 and 3000 RPM. If there is more than 71 psi., difference between 1000–3000 RPM inspections, repair or replace steering gear valve.

POWER STEERING SYSTEM SERVICE

Component Service

CB SERIES PUMP

DISASSEMBLE

1. Remove power steering pump from vehicle and outlined in "Front Suspension & Steering" section in appropriate chassis chapter.
2. Remove union fitting with O-ring and seal, **Fig. 4**.
3. Remove control valve and flow control spring.
4. Protect driveshaft with shim stock and remove driveshaft seal by cutting with small chisel. Discard seal.
5. Remove end cover retaining ring by inserting punch in access hole.
6. Push on driveshaft to assist in removing end cover, O-ring, pressure plate spring, pump ring, pump vanes and driveshaft subassembly.
7. Remove O-ring from housing.
8. Record orientation of pump ring holes and dowel pins for assembly alignment.
9. Remove dowel pins and driveshaft seal.
10. Remove pressure plate, pressure plate spring and O-ring from end cover.
11. Remove shaft retaining ring from driveshaft, pump rotor and thrust plate.

INSPECTION

1. Clean all components in clean power steering fluid, then dry thoroughly.
2. Inspect pump ring, vanes, thrust plate, pressure plate and driveshaft for scoring, pitting or chatter marks.

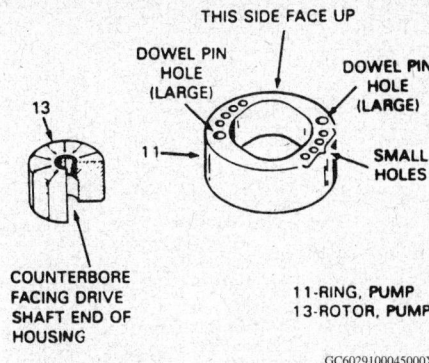

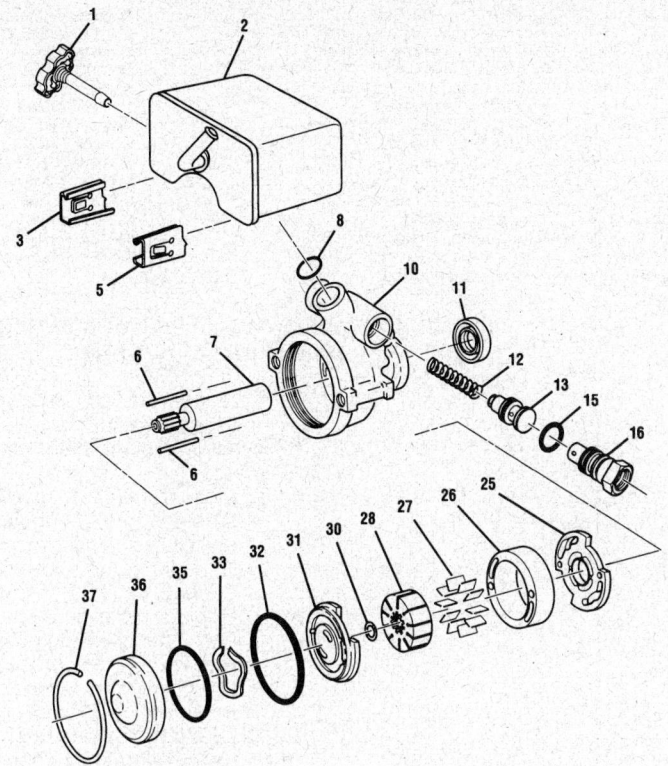

Fig. 5 Rotor and/or pump ring installation. CB series power steering pump

1 - CAPSTICK ASM, RESERVOIR
2 - RESERVOIR ASM, HYD PUMP (TYPICAL)
3 - CLIP, RESERVOIR RETAINING (LH)
5 - CLIP, RESERVOIR RETAINING (RH)
6 - PIN, PUMP RING DOWEL
7 - SHAFT, DRIVE
8 - SEAL, O-RING
10 - HOUSING ASM, HYD PUMP
11 - SEAL, DRIVE SHAFT
12 - SPRING, FLOW CONTROL
13 - VALVE ASM, CONTROL
15 - SEAL, O-RING
16 - FITTING, O-RING UNION
25 - PLATE, THRUST
26 - RING, PUMP
27 - VANE
28 - ROTOR, PUMP
30 - RING, SHAFT RETAINING
31 - PLATE, PRESSURE
32 - SEAL, O-RING
33 - SPRING, PRESSURE PLATE
35 - SEAL, O-RING
36 - COVER, END
37 - RING, RETAINING

GC6029700405000X

Fig. 4 Exploded view of CB series power steering pump

ASSEMBLE

1. Lubricate new driveshaft seal with power steering fluid and press seal into pump housing using seal installer tool No. J-7728, or equivalent.
2. Install pump ring dowel pins into housing.
3. Install thrust plate and pump rotor onto driveshaft, **Fig. 5.**
4. Install new shaft retaining ring onto driveshaft.
5. Install driveshaft subassembly into housing.
6. Install pump ring with holes positioned properly onto dowel pins in housing, **Fig. 5.**
7. Install vanes into pump rotor.
8. Lubricate new large O-ring with power steering fluid and install it into end cover.
9. Install pressure plate and spring.
10. Lubricate new small O-ring and install it into end cover.
11. Lubricate outer edge of end cover with power steering fluid and press it into housing.
12. Insert retaining ring into groove in housing with ring opening near access hole opening.

TC SERIES PUMP

Refer to **Fig. 6,** when servicing this power steering pump.

POWER STEERING SYSTEM BLEED

AURORA

1. Turn ignition switch to Off position.
2. Raise and support front of vehicle with tires clear ground.
3. Rotate steering wheel to full lefthand turn.
4. Fill power steering fluid reservoir to full cold level. Leave reservoir cap off.
5. Turn steering wheel lock-to-lock at least 40 times with engine stopped while an assistant inspects fluid level and condition. **Ensure fluid level remains at full cold level.**
6. If any bubbles appear, inspect for loose fluid line connections.

7. Start and idle engine, ensuring fluid is kept at proper level.
8. Install reservoir cap.
9. Turn steering wheel until front tires reach center position.
10. Lower vehicle and allow engine to idle for two minutes.
11. Turn steering wheel in both directions, ensuring it rotates smoothly and noiselessly.
12. Ensure fluid remains at proper level, has no bubbles, foam or discoloration and does not leak.
13. If bubbles, discoloration or foam appear in fluid, proceed as follows:
    a. Turn ignition switch to Off position.
    b. Wait two minutes, and inspect hose connections.
    c. Start and idle engine while maintaining fluid at proper level.
    d. Install reservoir cap.
    e. Turn steering wheel in both directions, ensuring it rotates smoothly and noiselessly.
    f. If fluid fault condition persists, inspect and replace return hose clamps and O-rings, pressure hose O-rings and gear cylinder line O-rings.
14. If pump groans or whines, idle engine and inspect for hose contact and interference with body, engine and frame.
15. If no hose contact or interference is found, proceed as follows:
    a. Stop engine and allow power steering system to cool off.
    b. Siphon fluid from reservoir using suitable suction device.
    c. Fill reservoir with cool, clean suitable power steering fluid.
    d. Install reservoir cap, then start engine and bring to operating temperature.
16. If noises persist, replace power steering pump and repeat bleeding procedure.

EXCEPT AURORA

STANDARD BLEEDING

Bleed power steering system after any component replacement, fluid line disconnection or in case of steering system noise. Bleed system to prevent pump damage, stop steering noise and to ensure proper system operation.

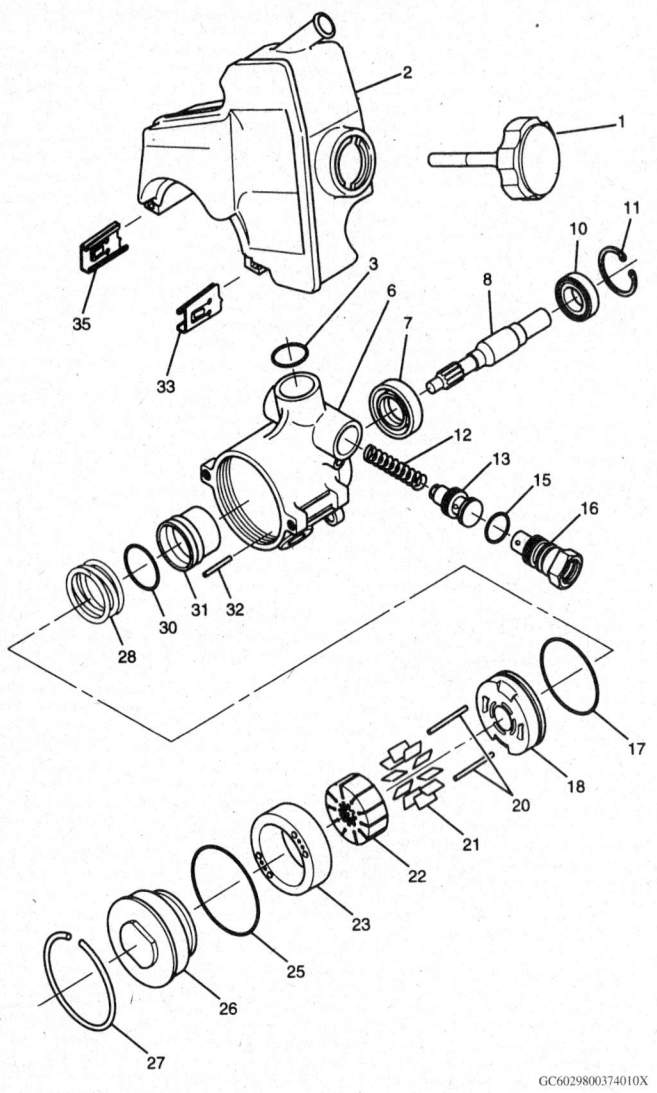

Key No.	Part Name
1	CAPSTICK ASM, RESERVOIR
2	RESERVOIR ASM, HYD PUMP
3	SEAL, O-RING
6	HOUSING ASM, HYD PUMP
7	SEAL, DRIVE SHAFT
8	SHAFT, DRIVE
10	BEARING ASM, BALL
11	RING, RETAINING
12	SPRING, FLOW CONTROL
13	VALVE ASM, CONTROL
15	SEAL, O-RING
16	FITTING, O-RING UNION
17	SEAL, O-RING
18	PLATE, PRESSURE

Key No.	Part Name
20	PIN, PUMP RING DOWEL (2)
21	VANE (10)
22	ROTOR, PUMP
23	RING, PUMP
25	SEAL, O-RING
26	PLATE ASM, THRUST
27	RING, THRUST PLATE RETAINING
28	SPRING, PRESSURE PLATE
30	SEAL, O-RING
31	SLEEVE ASM
32	PIN, DOWEL
33	CLIP, RESERVOIR RETAINING (RH)
35	CLIP, RESERVOIR RETAINING (LH)

GC6029800374020X

Fig. 6 Exploded view of power steering pump (Part 2 of 2). TC Series

5. If vacuum drops, repair or replace power steering pump.
6. If vacuum holds steady, proceed as follows:
   a. Inspect power steering fluid and ensure it is free of bubbles and is not discolored.
   b. Replace return hose clamps and O-rings.
   c. Replace pressure hose O-rings and reservoir to pump O-ring.
   d. Repeat bleeding procedure.
   e. Drive vehicle approximately 10 miles on smooth, flat surface to ensure power steering system reaches full operating temperature.

TECHNICAL SERVICE BULLETINS

Moan or Groan Noise While Turning Steering Wheel at Low Speeds

2001–04 L-SERIES

On some of these models equipped with 2.2L engine and automatic transaxle there may be moan or groan noise from the power steering system while turning the steering wheel at low vehicle speeds.

This condition may be caused by pressure pulses from the power steering pump may create resonance throughout the steering system.

To correct this condition install new tuned power steering pressure hose (P/N22714174), flush fluid and vacuum bleed steering system as follows:

1. Remove power steering reservoir cap.
2. Drain power steering fluid from reservoir using vacuum tool No. SA9180NE/J35555, or equivalent, with siphon cup.
3. Place suitable drain container under power steering hoses at steering gear.
4. Remove power steering pressure hose from steering gear.
5. Disconnect clip between power steering pressure and return hoses.
6. Remove power steering pressure hose. Record hose routing for installation alignment.
7. Position new tuned power steering

GC6029800374010X

Fig. 6 Exploded view of power steering pump (Part 1 of 2). TC Series

Inspect steering system before bleeding, looking for power steering lines touching frame, body or engine. Also inspect all hose connections for looseness or leaks.

1. Remove power steering pump reservoir cap.
2. Fill reservoir with proper fluid to full cold level.
3. Connect vacuum pump tool No. J-35555 and power steering bleeder adapter tool No. J-43485, or equivalents, to reservoir filler neck, **Fig. 7**.
4. Apply maximum vacuum of 20 inches and wait five minutes.
5. Inspect vacuum level after five minute. Vacuum typically will drop 2–3 inches. If vacuum does not remain steady, refer to "Special Bleeding."
6. Install reservoir cap, then start and idle engine.
7. Stop engine and inspect power steering fluid level.
8. Wait five minutes, then repeat previous two steps until fluid level has stabilized.
9. Start and idle engine, then turn steering wheel 180–360°F in both directions

five times. **Do not turn wheel all way to stops.**
10. Stop engine and inspect power steering fluid level.
11. Connect vacuum pump and power steering bleeder adapter to reservoir filler neck, **Fig. 7**.
12. Apply maximum vacuum of 20 inches and wait five minutes.
13. Inspect vacuum level after five minute. Vacuum typically will drop 2–3 inches. If vacuum does not remain steady, refer to "Special Bleeding."

SPECIAL BLEEDING

1. If vacuum continued to drop during bleeding procedure, remove power steering pressure and return hoses from power steering pump.
2. Install plugs from power steering bleeder adapter tool No. J-43485, or equivalents, into power steering pump pressure and return ports.
3. Connect vacuum pump and power steering bleeder adapter to reservoir filler neck, **Fig. 7**.
4. Apply maximum vacuum of 20 inches.

pressure hose following previously recorded route.

8. Hand start but do not tighten power steering pressure hose to steering gear and pump connections.
9. Hold fitting at gear end of pressure hose so that it does not contact (ground out) any other part of vehicle.
10. **Torque** hose connections to 20 ft. lbs.
11. Twist power steering pressure hose at pump end so hose is centered between brake master cylinder and heater hoses.
12. While holding power steering pressure hose in centered position, **torque** power steering pressure hose fitting to pump to 20 ft. lbs.
13. Attach clip between power steering pressure and return hoses.
14. Inspect power steering pressure hose routing to ensure there are no ground outs.
15. Fill power steering pump fluid reservoir with suitable power steering fluid.
16. Bleed power steering system as outlined in "Power Steering System Service."

Rattle/Knock Noise When Turning While Driving Slowly Over Rough Roads

2003 CAVALIER & SUNFIRE

On some of these models equipped with

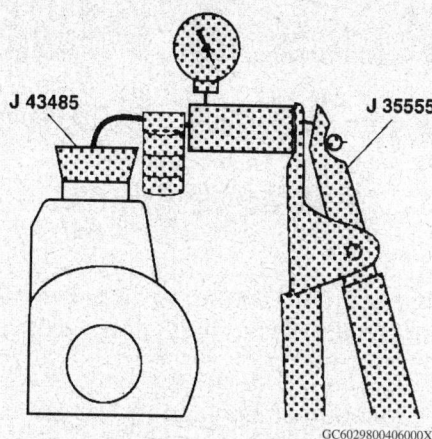

J 43485   J 35555

GC6029800406000X

Fig. 7   Power steering bleeder tool installation in reservoir

2.2L engine there may be a rattle/knocking noise when turning the steering wheel while driving slowly over bumps. This noise is often on a bumpy, hard-packed gravel surface while turning.

This condition may be caused by hydraulic noise within the steering rack.

To correct this condition, install a fluid restrictor (P/N 22592200) in power steering return line as follows:

1. Loosen two clamps and remove air cleaner intake tube.
2. Place suitable drain pan under power steering pump.
3. Remove clamp and power steering return hose from power steering pump.
4. Install fluid restrictor in fluid reservoir

return port. **Do not bend or distort inlet or outlet hoses.**

Momentary Reduction of Power Steering Assist On Initial Start Up With Low Ambient Temperatures

2002-03 ALERO, CAVALIER, GRAND AM & SUNFIRE

On some of these models equipped with 2.2L engine there may be a momentary reduction of power steering assist on initial start up with low ambient temperatures approximately 10°F. The system returns to full assist after the vehicle has run for a few seconds.

This condition may be caused by the power steering pump.

To correct this condition, replace the poser steering pump (P/N 26047567).

Do not replace steering gears Nos. 26073992, 26086616, 26068967, 26068964 and 26074935.

Saginaw Rack & Pinion Power Steering Gear Less Speed Sensitive Steering

NOTE: On Air Bag Equipped Models, Refer To "Air Bag System Precautions" Located In The Front Of This Manual For System Disarming & Arming Procedures.

NOTE: Refer To "Computer Relearn Procedures" Located In The Front Of This Manual When Battery Power To The Computer Has Been Interrupted.

INDEX

DESCRIPTION

Power Steering Gear

This power steering gear assembly incorporates an integral tube and housing containing a pinion shaft and steering rack. The tube and housing are joined by a plastic injection-bonding process. The pinion shaft is supported in the housing by thrust bearings and bushings. A bushing and bulkhead assembly supports the steering in the tube.

A rotary-type valve body is used to control the hydraulic steering assist. Fluid under pressure is directed to the gear housing and into the valve body. The valve body then directs fluid to the power cylinder.

A spool valve, connected to the stub shaft by a locating pin, rotates within the valve body. Fluid directional passages, machined into the spool valve, are aligned with fluid passages in the valve body as the spool valve rotates. Fluid is directed through these passages, into either side of the power cylinder through the externally mounted oil lines.

DIAGNOSIS & TESTING

External Leak Inspection

1. With engine off, wipe entire power steering system clean and dry.
2. Ensure fluid level is at proper level.
3. Start engine and turn steering wheel from stop-to-stop a few times. **Do not hold at stop for long period.**

4. Find and repair exact area of leak and repair as required, **Fig. 1.**

POWER STEERING SYSTEM SERVICE

Component Service

POWER STEERING GEAR, REPLACE

Refer to **Figs. 2 and 3,** for service procedures.

OUTER TIE ROD, REPLACE

1. Remove prevailing torque nut or cotter pin and hex slotted nut from outer tie rod, **Fig. 4.**
2. Loosen jam nut and remove outer tie rod from steering knuckle using steering linkage remover tool No. J-24319-01, or equivalent.
3. Remove outer from inner tie rod.
4. Reverse procedure to install, noting the following:
   a. **On all models except 2001 Century, Grand Prix and Regal, torque** hex slotted nut to 35 ft. lbs., with maximum of 52 ft. lbs., to install cotter pin. **Do not back off nut when installing cotter pin.**
   b. **On 2001 Century, Grand Prix and Regal models, torque** prevailing nut to tie rod end to 22 ft. lbs., then tighten an additional 120°.
   c. **On all models,** adjust toe by turning inner tie rod.
   d. **Torque** jam nut against outer tie rod to 50 ft. lbs.

INNER TIE ROD, REPLACE

Rack must be held during inner tie rod removal and installation.

REMOVAL

1. Remove rack and pinion.
2. Remove outer tie rod from inner tie rod, then rack and pinion boot.
3. Place wrench on flat of rack assembly and place wrench on flats of inner tie rod housing, **Fig. 5.**
4. Rotate housing counterclockwise until inner tie rod separates from rack.

INSTALLATION

1. Install inner tie rod on rack, **Fig. 6.**
2. Support rack and housing of inner tie rod and stake both sides of inner tie rod housing to flats on rack, **Fig. 7.**
3. Inspect both stakes by inserting .010 inch feeler gauge between rack and housing stake. **When properly staked, feeler gauge must not pass between rack and housing stakes.**
4. Slide shock damper over housing until it engages.
5. Install boot and rack outer tie rod, then the rack and pinion.

RACK BEARING PRELOAD

On all models except Century, Grand Prix and Regal, make adjustment with front wheels raised and steering wheel centered. Ensure steering wheel returns to center position after adjustment.

On Century, Grand Prix and Regal models, make adjustment with the steering rack assembly removed.

1. Loosen locknut, turn adjuster plug clockwise until it bottoms in housing,

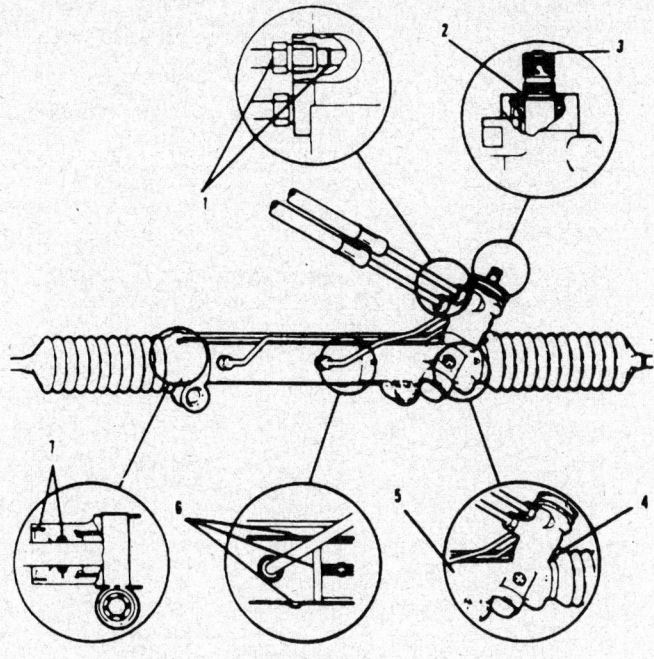

1 TIGHTEN FITTING TO 27 N m (20 LB FT) IF LEAKAGE PERSISTS, REPLACE
   O-RING SEAL IF LEAKAGE IS DUE TO DAMAGED THREADS, REPAIR FITTING
   NUT OR REPLACE LINE AS REQUIRED IF HOUSING THREADS ARE
   BADLY DAMAGED, REPLACE HOUSING

2 REPLACE DUST AND STUB SHAFT SEALS

3 IF LEAKAGE IS OBSERVED BETWEEN TORSION BAR AND STUB SHAFT,
   PARTIAL GEAR REPLACEMENT WILL BE REQUIRED

4 IF LEAKAGE IS OBSERVED AT DRIVER SIDE AND IS NOT AFFECTED BY THE
   DIRECTION OF TURN, PARTIAL GEAR REPLACEMENT WILL BE REQUIRED

5 IF LEAKAGE IS OBSERVED AT THE HOUSING END AND SPURTS WHEN
   BOTTOMED IN LEFT TURN, PARTIAL GEAR REPLACEMENT WILL
   BE REQUIRED

6 PARTIAL GEAR REPLACEMENT MAY BE REQUIRED

7 IF LEAKAGE IS OBSERVED AT PASSENGER SIDE, IT IS NECESSARY TO
   REPLACE WITH A PARTIAL GEAR ASSEMBLY.

GC6029700407000X

**Fig. 1 Power rack & pinion steering gear leak
diagnosis**

1 - NUT, HEXAGON SLOTTED	16 - ADAPTER, SEAL
2 - PIN, COTTER	23 - SEAL, O-RING
3 - SEAL, TIE ROD & END HSG	25 - LINE ASM, CYLINDER (RT)
5 - ROD ASM, OUTER TIE	26 - LINE ASM, CYLINDER (LT)
6 - FITTING, LUBRICATION	27 - BRACKET ASM, MOUNTING
7 - NUT, METRIC HEX (M14X1.5)	28 - GROMMET, MOUNTING
8 - CLAMP, TIE ROD END	30 - GEAR ASM, RACK & PINION (PARTIAL)
10 - BOOT, RACK & PINION	35 - TUBE, BREATHER
11 - CLAMP, SEAL RETAINING	38 - GASKET, MANIFOLD
12 - ROD ASM, INNER TIE	40 - MANIFOLD ASM, CONTROL VALVE &
13 - RING, SHOCK DAMPENER	41 - SCREW, PAN HD 6-LOBED SOC (M6X1)
15 - NUT, ADJUSTER PLUG LOCK	

GC6029600115000X

**Fig. 2 Exploded view of power rack & pinion
steering. Except Camaro & Firebird**

then back off 50–70°.

2. Tighten locknut while holding adjuster
   plug.

RACK & PINION BOOT & BREATHER TUBE, REPLACE

REMOVAL

1. Remove outer tie rod.
2. Remove hex jam nut from inner tie rod.
3. Remove tie rod end clamp. then remove and discard boot clamp using
   suitable side cutters, **Fig. 8.**
4. Mark I breather tube on housing position for installation alignment.
5. Removing tube, boot and breather
   tube.

INSTALLATION

1. Install new boot clamp onto boot.
2. Apply grease to inner tie rod or housing, **Fig. 9.**
3. Align and install breather tube.
4. Install boot onto housing until seated in
   housing groove tang.
5. Position boot clamp on boot and crimp.
6. Position tie rod end clamp on boot and

secure with pliers.

PINION SEAL, DUST SEAL & BEARING ANNULUS, REPLACE

REMOVAL

1. Remove rack and pinion steering.
2. Remove adjuster plug locknut from adjuster plug, **Fig. 10.**
3. Remove adjuster plug, spring and rack
   bearing.
4. Remove retaining ring from valve bore
   of housing and dust cover, **Fig. 11.**
5. Holding stub shaft, remove hex locknut
   from pinion and valve. **Stub shaft
   must be held to prevent damage to
   pinion teeth.**
6. Press on threaded end of pinion using
   an arbor press until it is possible to remove stub shaft, dust seal, stub shaft

seal and annulus bearing, **Fig. 12.**

INSTALLATION

1. While holding valve stub shaft, install
   hex locknut onto pinion. **Damage to
   pinion teeth will occur if stub shaft
   is not held.**
2. Install dust cover to gear.
3. Install stub shaft bearing annulus onto
   valve stub shaft.
4. Install seal protector tool No. J-29810,
   or equivalent, onto valve stub shaft.
5. Apply small amount of grease between
   seals, then install stub shaft seal and
   dust seal over protector and into gear.
6. Install retaining ring into groove in
   gear.
7. Lubricate stub shaft and dust seal area
   with grease.
8. Coat rack bearing, adjuster spring and
   adjuster plug with suitable lithium-
   base grease and install gear.

POWER STEERING

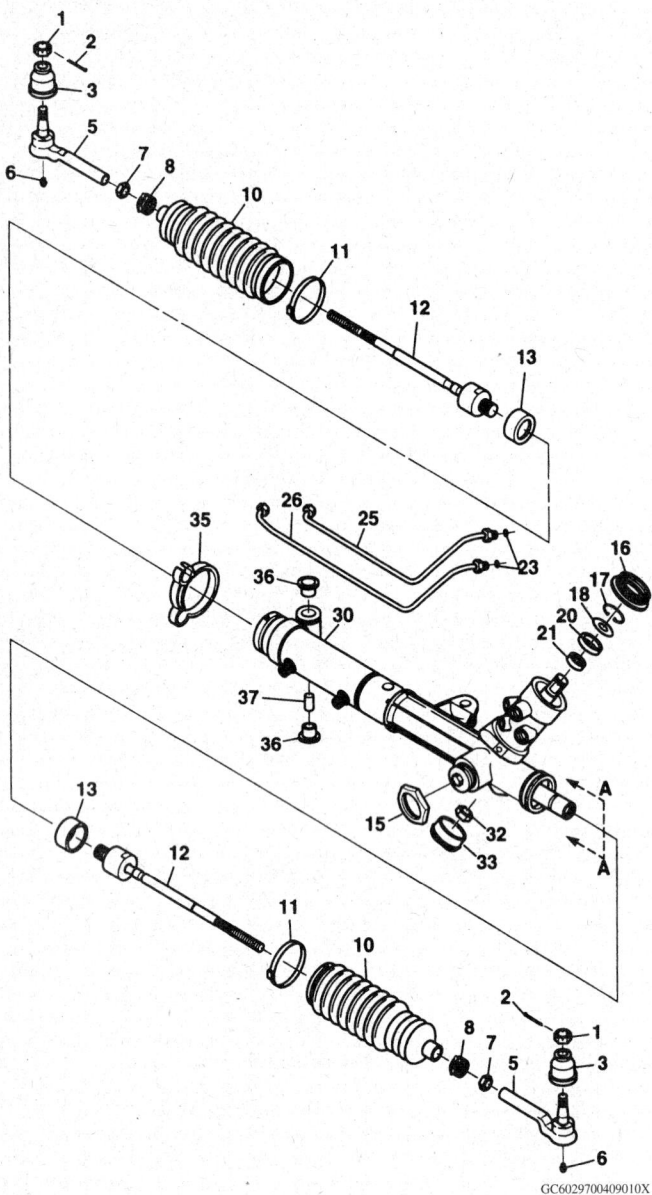

1 - NUT, HEXAGON SLOTTED
2 - PIN, COTTER
3 - SEAL, TIE ROD
5 - ROD ASM, OUTER TIE
6 - FITTING, LUBE (90 DEG ELBOW)
7 - NUT, METRIC HEX (M14 X 1.5)
8 - CLAMP, TIE ROD END
10 - BOOT, RACK & PINION
11 - CLAMP, SEAL RETAINING
12 - ROD ASM, INNER TIE
13 - RING, SHOCK DAMPENER
15 - NUT, ADJUSTER PLUG LOCK
16 - ADAPTER, SEAL

17 - RING, RETAINING
20 - SEAL, STUB SHAFT
21 - BEARING ANNULUS ASM, NEEDLE
23 - SEAL, O-RING (4.50 I.D.)
25 - LINE ASM, CYLINDER (RT)
26 - LINE ASM, CYLINDER (LT)
30 - GEAR ASM, RACK & PINION (PARTIAL)
32 - NUT, HEX LOCK
33 - COVER, DUST
35 - CLIP, PIPE
36 - BUSHING, STEERING GEAR
37 - SLEEVE, STEERING GEAR BUSHING

GC6029700409020X

Fig. 3 Exploded view of power rack & pinion steering (Part 2 of 2). Camaro & Firebird

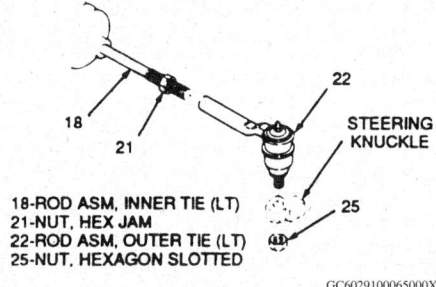

18-ROD ASM, INNER TIE (LT)
21-NUT, HEX JAM
22-ROD ASM, OUTER TIE (LT)
25-NUT, HEXAGON SLOTTED

GC6029100065000X

Fig. 4 Outer tie rod replacement

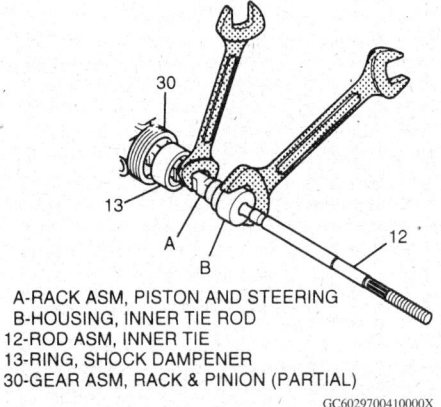

A-RACK ASM, PISTON AND STEERING
B-HOUSING, INNER TIE ROD
12-ROD ASM, INNER TIE
13-RING, SHOCK DAMPENER
30-GEAR ASM, RACK & PINION (PARTIAL)

GC6029700410000X

Fig. 5 Inner tie rod removal

GC6029700409010X

Fig. 3 Exploded view of power rack & pinion steering (Part 1 of 2). Camaro & Firebird

9. With rack centered in gear , turn adjuster plug clockwise until it bottoms in gear , then back off 50–70°.
10. Measure pinion rotational torque. Maximum preload torque should be 16 inch lbs.
11. Install adjuster plug locknut.
12. Tighten adjuster plug firmly against gear assembly while holding adjuster plug stationary.
13. Install rack and pinion.

POWER STEERING SYSTEM BLEED
STANDARD BLEEDING

Bleed power steering system after any component replacement, fluid line disconnection or in case of steering system noise. Bleed system to prevent pump damage, stop steering noise and to ensure proper system operation.

Inspect steering system before bleeding, looking for power steering lines touching frame, body or engine. Also inspect all hose connections for looseness or leaks.

1. Remove power steering pump reservoir cap.
2. Fill reservoir with proper fluid to full cold level.
3. Connect vacuum pump tool No. J-35555 and power steering bleeder adapter tool No. J-43485, or equivalents, to reservoir filler neck.
4. Apply maximum vacuum of 20 inches and wait five minutes.
5. Inspect vacuum level after five minute. Vacuum typically will drop 2–3 inches. If vacuum does not remain steady, refer to "Special Bleeding."
6. Install reservoir cap, then start and idle engine.
7. Stop engine and inspect power steering fluid level.

8. Wait five minutes, then repeat previous two steps until fluid level has stabilized.
9. Start and idle engine, then turn steering wheel 180–360° F in both directions five times. **Do not turn wheel all way to stops.**
10. Stop engine and inspect power steering fluid level.
11. Connect vacuum pump and power steering bleeder adapter to reservoir filler neck.
12. Apply maximum vacuum of 20 inches and wait five minutes.
13. Inspect vacuum level after five minute. Vacuum typically will drop 2–3 inches. If vacuum does not remain steady, refer to "Special Bleeding."

SPECIAL BLEEDING

1. If vacuum continued to drop during bleeding procedure, remove power steering pressure and return hoses from power steering pump.
2. Install plugs from power steering bleeder adapter tool No. J-43485, or equivalents, into power steering pump

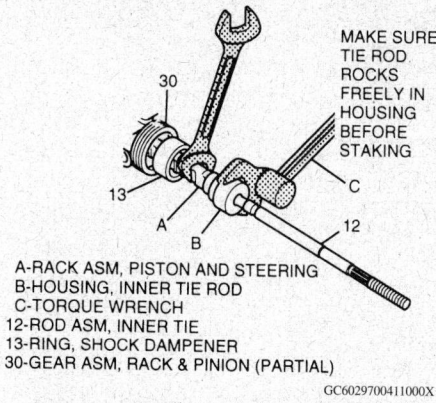

MAKE SURE TIE ROD ROCKS FREELY IN HOUSING BEFORE STAKING

A-RACK ASM, PISTON AND STEERING
B-HOUSING, INNER TIE ROD
C-TORQUE WRENCH
12-ROD ASM, INNER TIE
13-RING, SHOCK DAMPENER
30-GEAR ASM, RACK & PINION (PARTIAL)

GC6029700411000X

Fig. 6   Inner tie rod installation

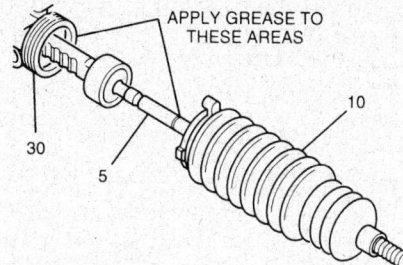

APPLY GREASE TO THESE AREAS

5-ROD ASM, INNER TIE
10-BOOT, RACK & PINION
30-GEAR ASM, RACK & PINION (PARTIAL)

GC6029700414000X

Fig. 9   Boot seal application

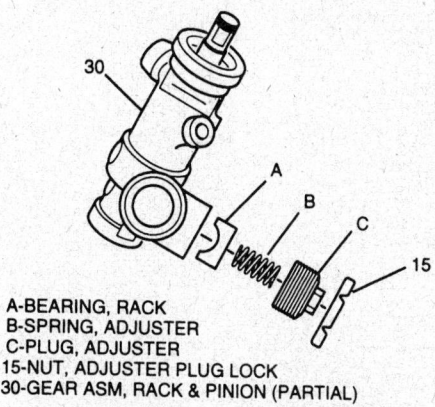

A-BEARING, RACK
B-SPRING, ADJUSTER
C-PLUG, ADJUSTER
15-NUT, ADJUSTER PLUG LOCK
30-GEAR ASM, RACK & PINION (PARTIAL)

GC6029700415000X

Fig. 10   Rack bearing removal

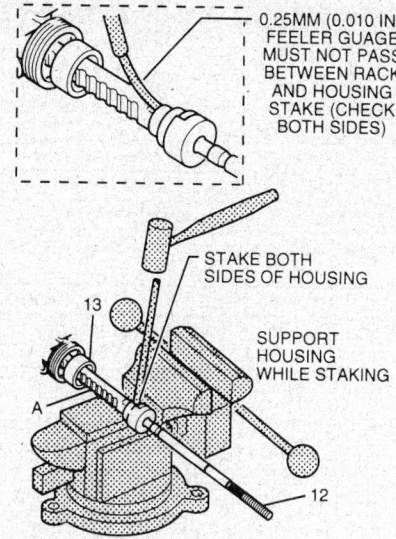

0.25MM (0.010 IN.) FEELER GUAGE MUST NOT PASS BETWEEN RACK AND HOUSING STAKE (CHECK BOTH SIDES)

STAKE BOTH SIDES OF HOUSING

SUPPORT HOUSING WHILE STAKING

A-RACK ASM, PISTON AND STEERING
12-ROD ASM, INNER TIE
13-RING, SHOCK DAMPENER

GC6029700412000X

Fig. 7   Inner tie rod staking procedure

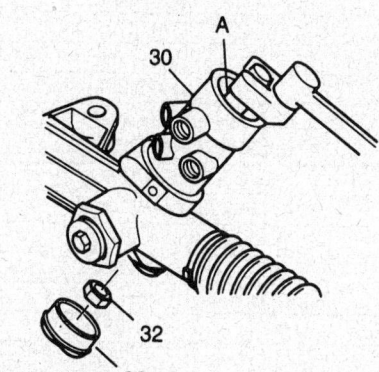

A-SHAFT, STUB
30-GEAR ASM, RACK & PINION (PARTIAL)
32-NUT, HEX LOCK
33-COVER, DUST

GC6029700416000X

Fig. 11   Retaining ring & locknut removal

e. Drive vehicle approximately 10 miles on smooth, flat surface to ensure power steering system reaches full operating temperature.

TECHNICAL SERVICE BULLETINS

Whistle Noise from Power Steering While Turning Left

2001-03 L-SERIES

On some of these models built before VIN 3Y521530 there may be a whistle noise while making slight left turns.

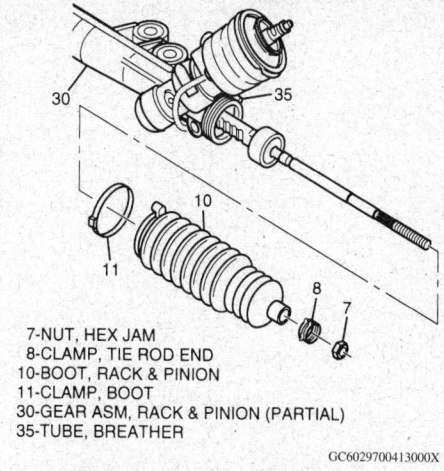

7-NUT, HEX JAM
8-CLAMP, TIE ROD END
10-BOOT, RACK & PINION
11-CLAMP, BOOT
30-GEAR ASM, RACK & PINION (PARTIAL)
35-TUBE, BREATHER

GC6029700413000X

Fig. 8   Boot replacement

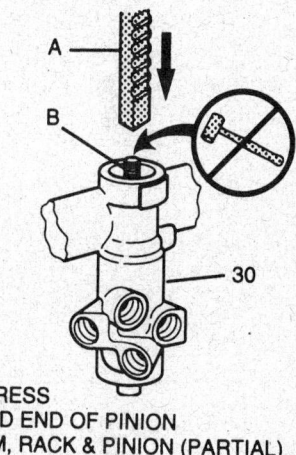

A-ARBOR PRESS
B-THREADED END OF PINION
30-GEAR ASM, RACK & PINION (PARTIAL)

GC6029700417000X

Fig. 12   Stub shaft, dust seal & stub shaft seal removal

This condition may be caused by the power steering gear.

To correct this condition install new steering gear (P/N 22708505) with internal modifications to correct the whistle noise.

pressure and return ports.

3. Connect vacuum pump and power steering bleeder adapter to reservoir filler neck.

4. Apply maximum vacuum of 20 inches.

5. If vacuum drops, repair or replace power steering pump.

6. If vacuum holds steady, proceed as follows:

   a. Inspect power steering fluid and ensure it is free of bubbles and is not discolored.

   b. Replace return hose clamps and O-rings.

   c. Replace pressure hose O-rings and reservoir to pump O-ring.

   d. Repeat bleeding procedure.

TIGHTENING SPECIFICATIONS

Year/ Model	Component	Torque/Ft. Lbs.
CTS		
2003–05	Intermediate Steering Shaft Pinch Bolt	35
	Power Steering Cooler Screws	48①
	Power Steering Cooler to Frame	80①
	Power Steering Lines to Power Steering Gear	22
	Power Steering Pressure Hose to Frame	80①
	Power Steering Pressure Hose to Power Steering Gear	80①
	Power Steering Pressure Line to Power Steering Pump	30
	Power Steering Pump	26
	Power Steering Reservoir, Lower	18
	Power Steering Reservoir, Upper	80①
	Power Steering Return & Pressure Hoses to Steering Gear	71①
	Power Steering Gear	70
	Tie Rod to Knuckle	52
CENTURY, GRAND PRIX, LUMINA, MONTE CARLO & REGAL		
2001–05	Adjuster Plug Locknut	55
	Inner Tie Rod Housing To Rack	74
	Tie Rod End Nut	22②
	Tie Rod Jam Nut	50
EXCEPT CENTURY, CTS, GRAND PRIX, IMPALA, LUMINA, MONTE CARLO & REGAL		
2001–05	Adjuster Plug Locknut	50
	Hex Locknut	22
	Hex Nut	50
	Hexagon Slotted Nut	35
	Inner Tie Rod Housing To Rack	70
	Tie Rod Jam Nut	50
IMPALA		
2001–05	Fluid Cooler Pipe	84①
	Inner Tie Rod	74
	Intermediate Shaft Pinch Bolt	35
	Steering Gear	59
	Steering Gear Cylinder Line Fitting	13
	Steering Gear Valve End Fitting	20
	Steering Pump	25
	Tie Rod End Nut	22②
	Tie Rod Jam Nut	50

① — Inch lbs.
② — Tighten an additional 120°.

Saginaw Rack & Pinion Power Steering Gear w/Speed Sensitive Steering

NOTE: On Air Bag Equipped Models, Refer To "Air Bag System Precautions" Located In The Front Of This Manual For System Disarming & Arming Procedures.

NOTE: Refer To "Computer Relearn Procedures" Located In The Front Of This Manual When Battery Power To The Computer Has Been Interrupted.

NOTE: "Electrical Symbol & Wire Color Code Identification" Located In The Front Of This Manual May Be Used As An Aid When Using Wiring Circuits Found In This Section.

NOTE: Prior To Performing Any Service Operations Listed In This Section, Consult The "Technical Service Bulletins" Section For Related Information.

INDEX

DESCRIPTION

Speed sensitive steering (Variable Effort or Magnasteer) varies the driver effort required to steer as vehicle speed changes. At low speeds, the system provides maximum power assist. At higher speeds, steering effort is increased to provide firmer steering and directional stability. Variable steering effort is accomplished by reducing power steering fluid flow from the pump as vehicle speed increases. When the vehicle is stationary, the system provides maximum flow. The speed sensitive steering system is made up of an Electronic Brake Control Module (EBCM) or Electronic Brake Traction Control Module (EBTCM), power steering fluid flow actuating device, steering wheel speed sensor, power rack and pinion and power steering pump.

Except for differences in valve machining, the design of the speed sensitive power rack and pinion steering is the same as for the non-speed sensitive power rack and pinion.

DIAGNOSIS & TESTING

Accessing Diagnostic Trouble Codes

Diagnostic Trouble Codes (DTCs) must be read using a suitably programmed scan tool. There are no provisions for flash code diagnostics.
1. Turn ignition switch to Off position.
2. Connect suitably programmed scan tool to Data Link Connector (DLC).
3. Turn ignition switch to On position.
4. Select scan tool's special functions.
5. Read and record DTCs.

Diagnostic Trouble Code Interpretation

Refer to **Fig. 1,** for Diagnostic Trouble Code (DTC) interpretation.

Wiring Diagrams

Refer to **Figs. 2 through 15,** for wiring diagrams.

Diagnostic Tests

Refer to **Figs. 16 through 37,** for diagnostic tests.

Clearing Diagnostic Trouble Codes

DTCs cannot be cleared by disconnecting EBTCM or battery cables. Follow the scan tool manufacturer's instructions to clear DTCs.

Power Steering

Code	Description
C0450	Steering Assist Control Actuator Circuit Fault
C0455	Steering Position Sensor Circuit Fault
C1241	Speed Sensitive Steering Circuit Fault
C1241	Magnasteer Fault
C1243	Steering Wheel Position Sensor Circuit Fault
C1273	Actuator Circuit Open Or Shorted To Ground
C1274	Actuator Circuit Shorted Or Solenoid Shorted
C1287	Steering Position Sensor Open Or Shorted Or Yaw Rate Sensor Data Mismatch
C1288	Yaw Rate Sensor Data Mismatch

Fig. 1 DTC interpretation

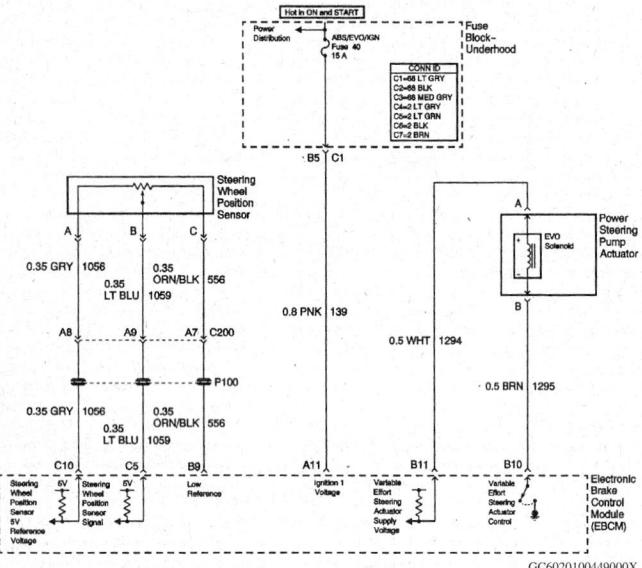

Fig. 3   Wiring diagram. 2002 Alero & Grand Am

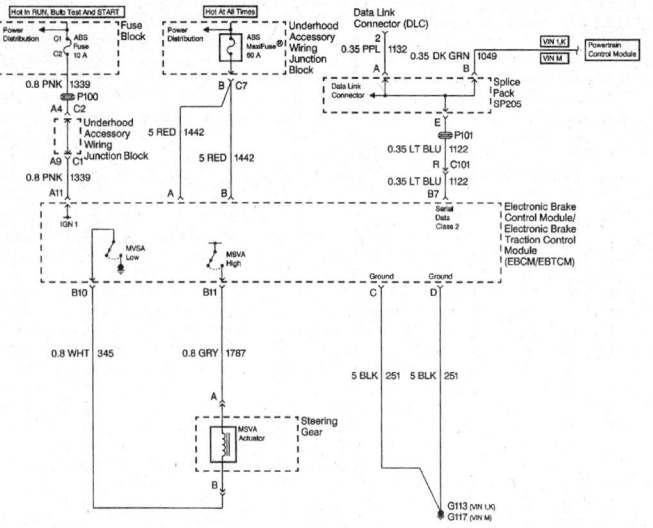

Fig. 5   Wiring diagram. 2001–02 Century & Regal

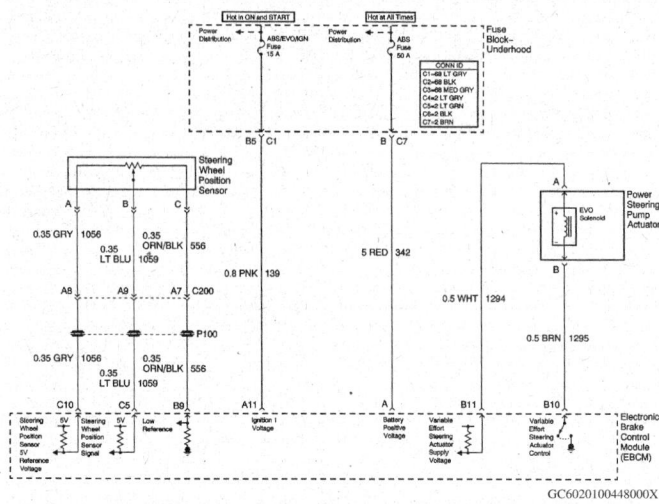

Fig. 2   Wiring diagram. 2001 Alero & Grand Am

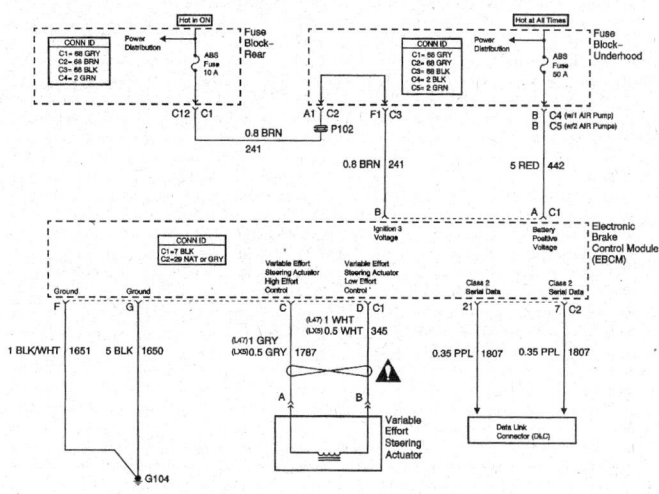

Fig. 4   Wiring diagram. Aurora

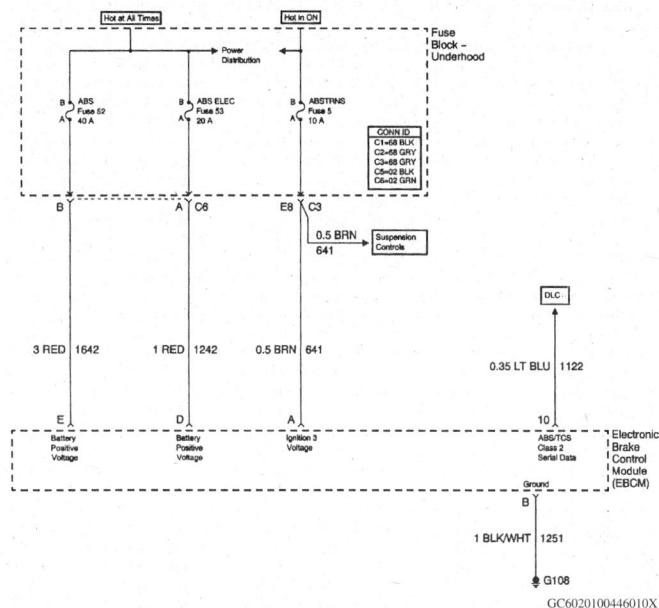

Fig. 6   Wiring diagram (Part 1 of 2). 2001–05 Corvette

SAGINAW RACK & PINION POWER STEERING GEAR W/SPEED SENSITIVE STEERING

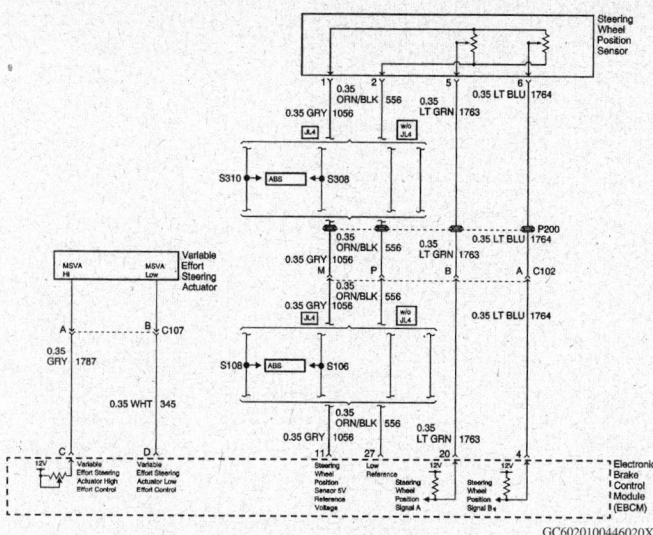

Fig. 6   Wiring diagram (Part 2 of 2). 2001–05 Corvette

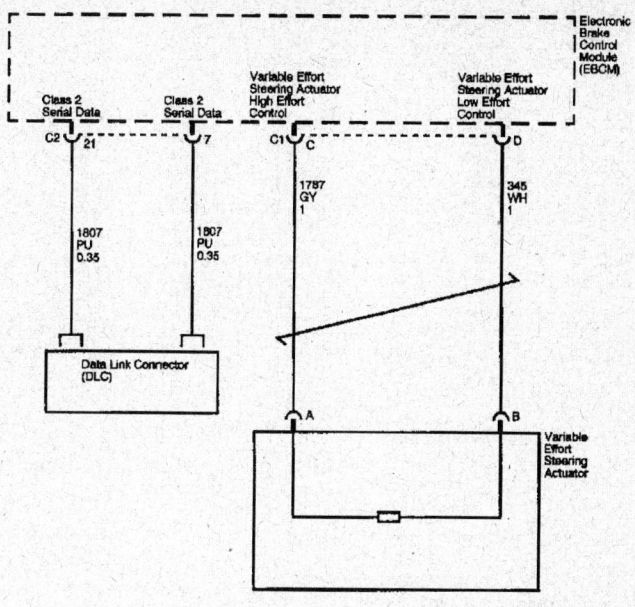

Fig. 7   Wiring diagram. 2003–05 CTS

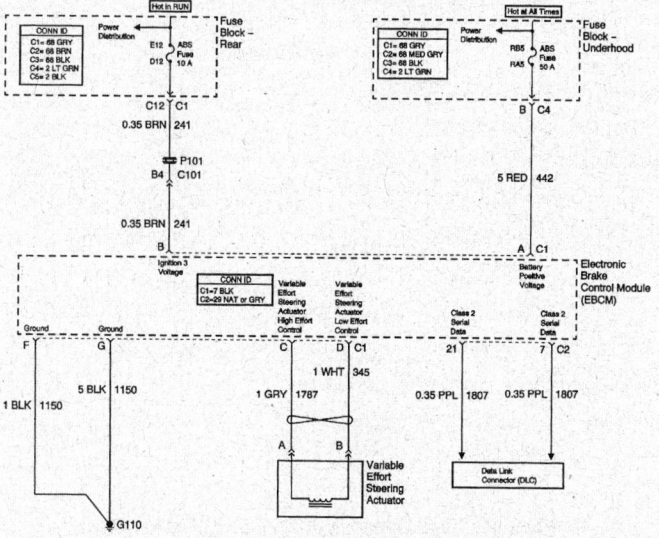

Fig. 8   Wiring diagram. DeVille & Seville

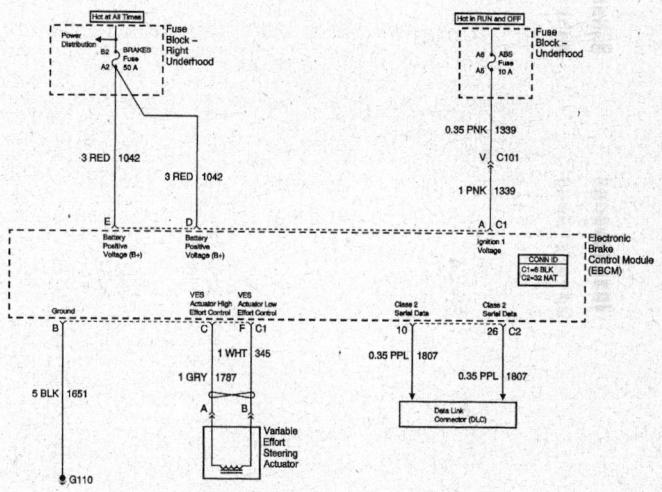

Fig. 9   Wiring diagram. Eldorado

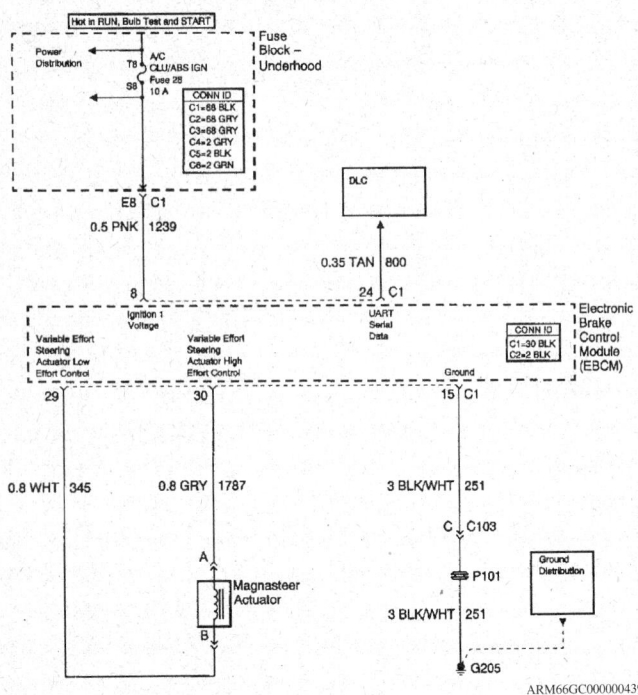

Fig. 10 Wiring diagram. 2001–05 Grand Prix

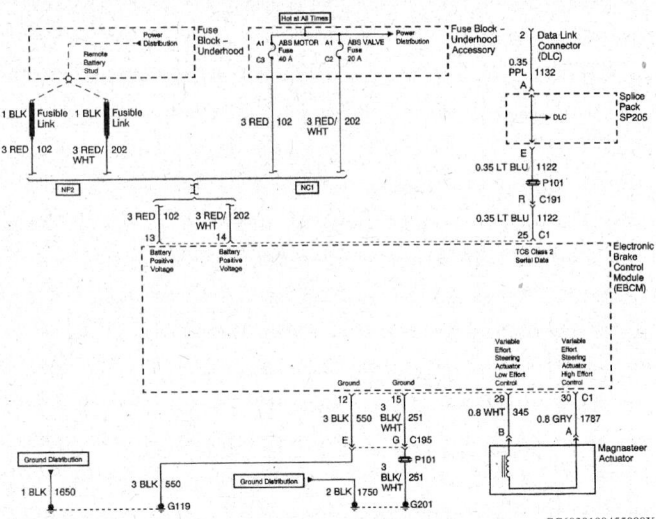

Fig. 11 Wiring diagram (Part 1 of 2). 2001 Intrigue

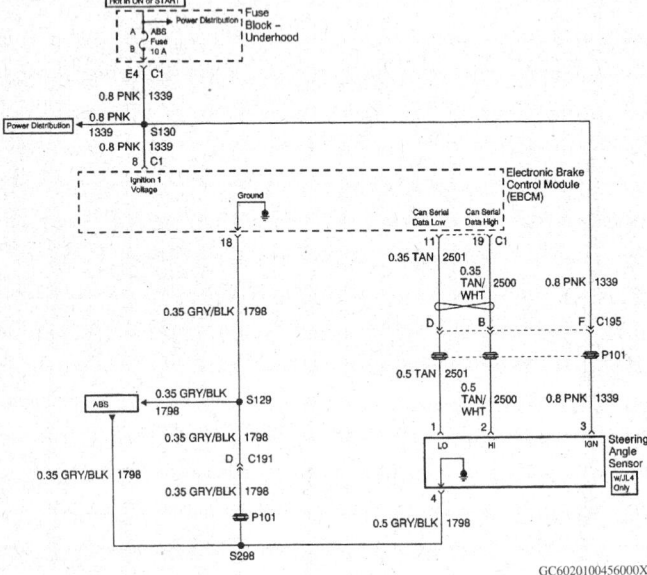

Fig. 11 Wiring diagram (Part 2 of 2). 2001 Intrigue

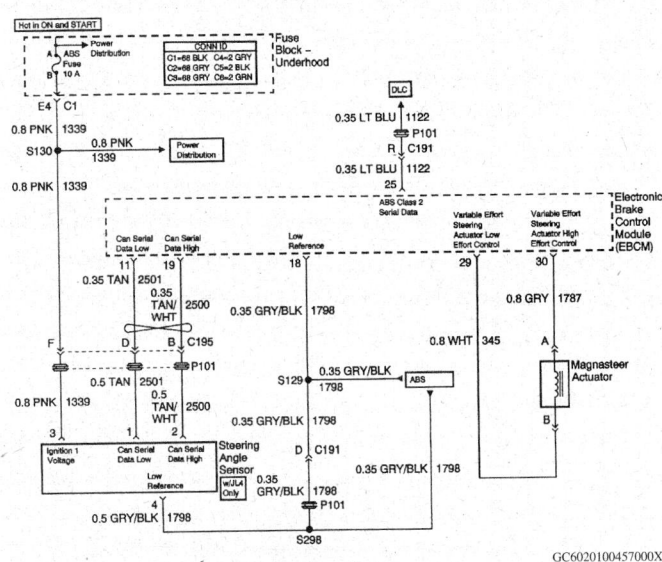

Fig. 12 Wiring diagram. 2002 Intrigue

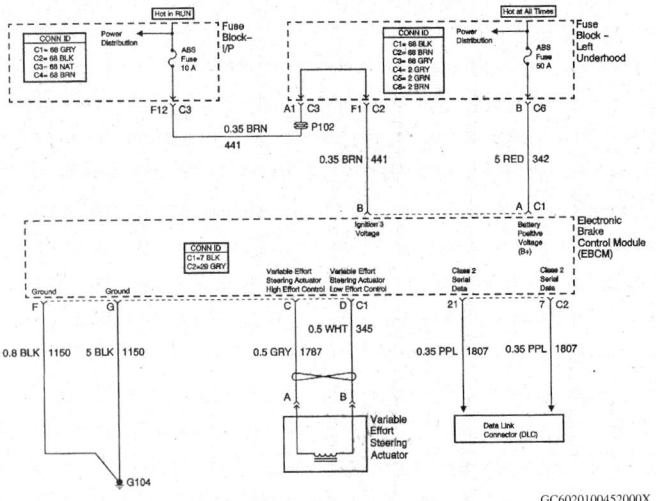

Fig. 13 Wiring diagram. Park Avenue

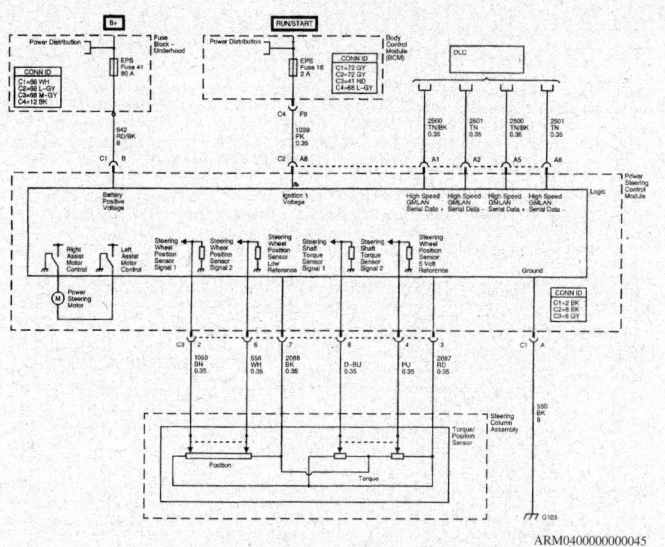

Fig. 14   Wiring diagram. Pontiac G6

ARM0400000000045

Fig. 15   Wiring diagram. STS

ARM0400000000046

DIAGNOSTIC CHART INDEX

Code	Description	Page No.	Fig. No.
ALERO & GRAND AM			
C1243	Steering Wheel Position Sensor Circuit Fault	25-29	33
C1273	Actuator Circuit Open Or Shorted To Ground	25-30	34
C1274	Actuator Circuit Shorted Or Solenoid Shorted	25-30	35
C1287	Yaw Rate Sensor Data Mismatch (2001)	25-31	36
	Steering Position Sensor Shorted Or Open (2002)	25-32	37
C1288	Yaw Rate Sensor Data Mismatch (2001)	25-31	36
AURORA			
—	Diagnostic System Inspection	25-18	16
C1241	Speed Sensitive Steering Circuit Fault	25-22	24
BONNEVILLE, LESABRE & PARK AVENUE			
—	Diagnostic System Inspection	25-18	16
C1241	Speed Sensitive Steering Circuit Fault (2001–02)	25-22	25
	Speed Sensitive Steering Circuit Fault (2003)	25-23	26
CENTURY & REGAL			
—	Variable Effort Steering System Inspection	25-18	17
C1241	Magnasteer Fault	25-25	29
CORVETTE			
C1241	Magnasteer Fault (2001)	25-24	27
	Magnasteer Fault (2002–05)	25-25	28
CTS			
—	Diagnostic System Check	25-18	18
C1241	Variable Effort Steering Actuator Circuit	25-28	32
DEVILLE, ELDORADO & SEVILLE			
—	Diagnostic System Inspection	25-18	16
C1241	Speed Sensitive Steering Circuit Fault (2001–02 DeVille & Seville)	25-26	30
	Magnasteer Fault (2001–02 Eldorado)	25-27	31
	Speed Sensitive Steering Circuit Fault (2003–05)	25-23	26
GRAND PRIX, INTRIGUE, STS & LACROSSE			
—	Variable Effort Steering System Inspection	25-18	17
C0450	Steering Assist Control Actuator Circuit Fault (2001)	25-18	19
	Steering Assist Control Actuator Circuit Fault (2002–05)	25-19	20
	Steering Assist Control Actuator Circuit Fault (2005) (STS)	25-20	21
C0450	Steering Assist Control Actuator Circuit Fault (LaCrosse)	25-20	22
C0455	Steering Position Sensor Circuit Fault (Intrigue)	25-21	23

Step	Action	Value (s)	Yes	No
1	Install a scan tool. Does the scan tool power up?	--	Go to Step 2	Tool Does Not Power Up in Data Link Communications
2	1. Start the engine. 2. Attempt to establish communications with the EBCM. Does the scan tool communicate with the EBCM?	--	Go to Step 3	Scan Tool Does Not Communicate with Class 2 Device
3	Select the Magna Steer display DTC function on the scan tool. Does the scan tool display any DRP/ABS/TCS/VSES (if equipped) DTCs?	--	Go to A Diagnostic System Check - ABS in Antilock Brake System	Go to Step 4
4	Select the Magna Steer display DTC function on the scan tool. Does the scan tool display DTC C1241?	--	Go to DTC C1241	Go to Power Steering

GC6010100020000X

Fig. 16 Diagnostic System Inspection. Aurora, Bonneville, DeVille, Eldorado, LeSabre, Park Avenue & Seville

Step	Action	Value (s)	Yes	No
1	Connect a scan tool to the Data Link Connector (DLC). Does the scan tool communicate with the electronic brake traction control module (EBCM/EBTCM)?	--	Go to Step 2	Go to Diagnostic System
2	Using the scan tool, inspect for DTC C1241 in the ABS Diagnostic Trouble Codes (DTC). Does the scan tool displays DTC C1241 as current or history DTC?	--	Go to DTC C1241 Magnasteer Malfunction	Go to Step 3
3	Does the scan tool read any other current or history ABS DTC(s)?	--	Go to Diagnostic Trouble Code (DTC) List	Go to Step 4
4	1. Start the engine. 2. Turn the steering wheel to the right. 3. Turn the steering wheel to the left. Does the steering wheel turn with little effort?	--	Go to Step 5	Diagnose Steering Effort Hard in One or Both Directions
5	1. Drive the vehicle. 2. While driving the vehicle perform several turns and listen for any unusual sounds. Are there any unusual noises (hissing, rattle, groaning, whining, or growling) heard from the vehicle when turning?	--	Diagnose Power Steering System Inspection or Power Steering Gear	System OK

GC6020100460000X

Fig. 17 Variable Effort Steering System Inspection. Century, Grand Prix, Intrigue & Regal

Test Description

The numbers below refer to the step numbers on the diagnostic table.

2. The lack of communication may be caused by a partial or a total malfunction of the circuit containing the class 2 serial data. The specified procedure will determine the particular condition.

3. Tests for other Electronic Brake Control Module (EBCM) controlled subsystem malfunctions that may use the same inputs as the Variable Effort Steering (VES) system.

4. The presence of DTCs which begin with "U" indicate some other module is not communicating. The specified procedure will collect all the available information before tests are performed.

5. Tests if the malfunction lies specifically in the VES system.

Step	Action	Yes	No
1	Install a scan tool. Does the scan tool turn on?	Go to Step 2	Inspect for power at Data Link connector
2	1. Turn ON the ignition, with the engine OFF. 2. Attempt to establish communication with the EBCM. Does the scan tool communicate with the EBCM?	Go to Step 3	Perform Data Link Communications inspection
3	Select the ABS Diagnostic Trouble Code(s) function on the scan tool. Does the scan tool display any DRP/ABS/TCS or VSES DTCs?	Go to Diagnostic System Check	Go to Step 4
4	Does the scan tool display any DTCs which begin with a "U"?	Go to Diagnostic Trouble Code (DTC) List	Go to Step 5
5	Does the scan tool display "DTC C1241?"	Go to Diagnostic Trouble Code (DTC)	System OK

ARM66GC000000446

Fig. 18 Diagnostic System Check. CTS

Circuit Description

The Magnetic Steering Variable Assist (MSVA), also known as MAGNASTEER® incorporates its controller into the electronic brake control module (EBCM). The EBCM controls the amount of current supplied to the MAGNASTEER® actuator based on input from the following components:
- The wheel speed sensors
- The steering wheel position sensor

Conditions for Setting the DTC

The MAGNASTEER® actuator or one or both of the MAGNASTEER® actuator circuit wires becomes open or shorted.

Action Taken When the DTC Sets
- A malfunction DTC is stored.
- No antilock brake system (ABS)/traction control system (TRAC OFF) indicators are turned ON.
- The MAGNASTEER® is disabled.
The ABS/TCS remains functional.

Conditions for Clearing the DTC

1. A history DTC will clear after 100 consecutive ignition cycles if the condition for the malfunction is no longer present.
2. You may use a scan tool in order to clear the DTC.

Diagnostic Aids

1. The following conditions may cause an intermittent malfunction to occur:
   - A poor connection
   - A rubbed-through wire insulation
   - A broken wire inside the insulation
2. Inspect the frequency of the malfunction by using the enhanced diagnostic function of the scan tool.
3. Inspect any circuitry that may cause the intermittent complaint for the following conditions:
   - Backed out terminals
   - Improper mating
   - Broken locks
   - Improperly formed terminals
   - Damaged terminals
   - Poor terminal to wiring connections
   - Physical damage to the wiring harness

Test Description

The numbers below refer to step numbers on the diagnostic table.

2. This step checks for an open or high resistance in the MAGNASTEER® circuit.
3. This step determines if the open or high resistance is in the MAGNASTEER® actuator, or the wiring harness.
16. This step checks if the MAGNASTEER® actuator is shorted to the steering gear case.

GC6019900025010X

Fig. 19 Code C0450: Steering Assist Control Actuator Circuit Fault (Part 1 of 4). 2001 Grand Prix & Intrigue

Step	Action	Value(s)	Yes	No
1	Was the Variable Effort Steering System Check performed?	—	Go to *Step 2*	Go to *Variable Effort Steering System Check*
2	1. Turn the ignition switch to the OFF position. 2. Disconnect the electronic brake control module (EBCM) harness connector. 3. Install the universal pinout box using the J 39700-530 cable adaptor to the EBCM harness connector only. 4. Use the DMM in order to measure the resistance between the following components: • The universal pinout box terminal 29 • Terminal 30 Is the resistance within the specified range?	1.6 - 3.1 Ω	Go to *Step 11*	Go to *Step 3*
3	1. Disconnect the two-way MAGNASTEER® actuator connector. 2. Using the DMM, measure the resistance between the following components: • MAGNASTEER® actuator pin A • MAGNASTEER® actuator pin B Is the resistance within the specified range?	1.6 - 3.1 Ω	Go to *Step 5*	Go to *Step 4*
4	Replace the MAGNASTEER® actuator. Is the repair complete?	—	Go to *Variable Effort Steering System Check*	—
5	Using the DMM, measure the resistance between the following components: • The universal pinout box terminal 29 • The MAGNASTEER® actuator harness connector terminal B Is the resistance within the specified range?	0–2 Ω	Go to *Step 7*	Go to *Step 6*
6	Repair the open or high resistance in CKT 345. Is the repair complete?	—	Go to *Variable Effort Steering System Check*	—
7	Using the DMM, measure the resistance between the following components: • The universal pinout box terminal 30 • The MAGNASTEER® actuator harness connector terminal A Is the resistance within the specified range?	0–2 Ω	Go to *Step 9*	Go to *Step 8*
8	Repair the open or high resistance in CKT 1787. Is the repair complete?	—	Go to *Variable Effort Steering System Check*	—
9	Using the DMM, measure the resistance between the following components: • The universal pinout box terminal 29 • The universal pinout box terminal 30 Is the resistance within the specified range?	OL (Infinite)	Go to *Step 22*	Go to *Step 10*
10	Repair the short between CKT 345 and CKT 1787. Is the repair complete?	—	Go to *Variable Effort Steering System Check*	—
11	Using the DMM, measure the resistance between the following components: • The universal pinout box terminal 15 • The universal pinout box terminal 29 Is the resistance within the specified range?	OL (Infinite)	Go to *Step 17*	Go to *Step 12*

GC6019900025020X

Fig. 19   Code C0450: Steering Assist Control Actuator Circuit Fault (Part 2 of 4). 2001 Grand Prix & Intrigue

Step	Action	Value(s)	Yes	No
22	1. Turn the ignition switch to the OFF position. **Important:** Damage or corrosion may result in an open or short with all of the connectors connected. 2. Inspect the EBCM harness connectors for the following conditions: • Damage • Corrosion **Important:** Damage or corrosion may result in an open or short with all of the connectors connected. 3. Inspect the two-way MAGNASTEER® actuator harness connector for the following conditions: • Damage • Corrosion Do the connectors exhibit signs of corrosion or damage?	—	Go to *Step 23*	Go to *Step 24*
23	1. Repair the damaged or corroded harness connectors in the EBCM. 2. Repair the damaged or corroded two-way MAGNASTEER® actuator harness connector. Is the repair complete?	—	Go to *Variable Effort Steering System Check*	—
24	1. Reconnect all of the connectors. 2. Test drive the vehicle to a speed greater than 40 km/h (25 mph). Did the DTC C0450 reset?	—	Go to *Step 25*	Go to *Variable Effort Steering System Check*
25	Replace the EBCM. Is the repair complete?	—	Go to *Variable Effort Steering System Check*	—

GC6019900025040X

Fig. 19   Code C0450: Steering Assist Control Actuator Circuit Fault (Part 4 of 4). 2001 Grand Prix & Intrigue

Step	Action	Value(s)	Yes	No
12	1. Disconnect the two-way MAGNASTEER® actuator connector. 2. Using the DMM, measure the resistance between the following components: • The universal pinout box terminal 15 • The universal pinout box terminal 29 Is the resistance within the specified range?	OL (Infinite)	Go to *Step 14*	Go to *Step 13*
13	Repair the short to ground in CKT 345. Is the repair complete?	—	Go to *Variable Effort Steering System Check*	—
14	Using the DMM, measure the resistance between the following components: • The universal pinout box terminal 15 • Terminal 30 Is the resistance within the specified range?	OL (Infinite)	Go to *Step 16*	Go to *Step 15*
15	Repair the short to ground in CKT 1787. Is the repair complete?	—	Go to *Variable Effort Steering System Check*	—
16	Using the DMM, measure the resistance between the following components: • The MAGNASTEER® actuator pin A • The steering gear case Is the resistance within the specified range?	OL (Infinite)	Go to *Step 22*	Go to *Step 4*
17	1. Turn the ignition switch to the ON position with the engine OFF. 2. Using the DMM, measure the voltage between the following components: • The universal pinout box terminal 15 • Terminal 29 Is the voltage within the specified range?	0–1 V	Go to *Step 22*	Go to *Step 18*
18	1. Disconnect the two-way MAGNASTEER® actuator connector. 2. Using the DMM, measure the voltage between the following components: • The universal pinout box terminal 15 • Terminal 29. Is the voltage within the specified range?	0–1 V	Go to *Step 20*	Go to *Step 19*
19	Repair the short to voltage in CKT 345. Is the repair complete?	—	Go to *Variable Effort Steering System Check*	—
20	Using the DMM, measure the voltage between the following components: • The universal pinout box terminal 15 • Terminal 30 Is the voltage within the specified range?	0–1 V	Go to *Step 22*	Go to *Step 21*
21	Repair the short to voltage in CKT 1787. Is the repair complete?	—	Go to *Variable Effort Steering System Check*	—

GC6019900025030X

Fig. 19   Code C0450: Steering Assist Control Actuator Circuit Fault (Part 3 of 4). 2001 Grand Prix & Intrigue

Step	Action	Value(s)	Yes	No
1	Did you perform the Variable Effort Steering Diagnostic System Check?	--	Go to Step 2	Perform Diagnostic System Check - Variable Effort Steering
2	1. Install a scan tool. 2. Turn the ignition ON, with the engine OFF. 3. With the scan tool, select the Diagnostic Trouble Codes (DTC) function. Does the scan tool indicate that DTC C0450 is a history DTC ?	--	Test for Intermittent and Poor Connections	Go to Step 3
3	1. Turn OFF the ignition. 2. Disconnect the VES actuator harness connector. 3. Measure the resistance of the VES actuator. Does the resistance measure within the specified range?	1.6-3.1 ohms	Go to Step 4	Go to Step 8
4	Test the High Effort Control circuit of the VES actuator for a short to ground. Did you find and correct the condition?	--	Go to Step 12	Go to Step 5
5	Test the High Effort Control circuit for an open or short to voltage. Did you find and correct the condition?	--	Go to Step 12	Go to Step 6
6	Test the Low Effort Control circuit for a short to ground. Did you find and correct the condition?	--	Go to Step 12	Go to Step 7
7	Test the Low Effort Control circuit for an open or short to voltage. Did you find and correct the condition?	--	Go to Step 12	Go to Step 9

GC6020100461010X

Fig. 20   Code C0450: Steering Assist Control Actuator Circuit Fault (Part 1 of 2). 2002–04 Grand Prix & Intrigue

Step	Action	Value(s)	Yes	No
8	Inspect for poor connections at the harness connector of the VES actuator. Did you find and correct the condition?	--	Go to Step 12	Go to Step 10
9	Inspect for poor connections at the harness connector of the EBCM. Did you find and correct the condition?	--	Go to Step 12	Go to Step 11
10	Replace the VES actuator. Did you complete the repair?	--	Go to Step 12	--
11	Replace the EBCM. Did you complete the repair?	--	Go to Step 12	--
12	1. Use the scan tool in order to clear the DTCs. 2. Operate the vehicle within the Conditions for Running the DTC. Does the DTC reset?	--	Go to Step 2	System OK

GC602010046l020X

Fig. 20   Code C0450: Steering Assist Control Actuator Circuit Fault (Part 2 of 2). 2002–04 Grand Prix & Intrigue

Step	Action	Values	Yes	No
1	Did you perform the Diagnostic System Check - Vehicle?	--	Go to Step 2	Go to Diagnostic System Check
2	1. Start the engine. 2. Observe the VES Actuator Commanded Current and VES Actuator Feedback Current Data parameters in the VES data list for the EBCM with a scan tool. Are the VES Actuator Commanded Current and VES Actuator Feedback Current parameters within 0.03 amps of each other and within the specified range?	0.9-1 amp	Go to Step 3	Go to Step 4
3	Select F2: VES Test with the scan tool. Does the scan tool indicate Test Passed?	--	Test for Intermittent Conditions and Poor Connections	Go to Step 4
4	1. Turn OFF the ignition. 2. Disconnect the variable effort steering (VES) actuator harness connector. 3. Measure the resistance of the VES actuator. Does the resistance measure within specified range?	5.7-7.2 ohms	Go to Step 5	Go to Step 12
5	Test the VES actuator and actuator harness for a short to ground. Was a short to ground located?	--	Go to Step 6	Go to Step 7

ARM0400000000047

Fig. 21   Code C0450: Steering Assist Control Actuator Circuit Fault. STS

Step	Action	Values	Yes	No
1	Did you perform the Diagnostic System Check - Vehicle?	--	Go to Step 2	Go to Diagnostic System Check
2	1. Start the engine. 2. With a scan tool, observe the VES Commanded Current and VES Feedback Current Data parameters in the VES data list for the EBCM. Does the scan tool display the VES Commanded and Feedback Current Data parameters are within 0.03 amps of each other and within specified range?	0.90-1.00 A	Go to Step 3	Go to Step 4
3	Using the scan tool, select F1 VES Test. Does the scan tool indicate Test Passed?	--	Test for Intermittent Conditions and Poor Connections	Go to Step 4
4	1. Turn OFF the ignition. 2. Disconnect the variable effort steering (VES) actuator harness connector. 3. Measure the resistance of the VES actuator. Does the resistance measure within specified range?	5-10 ohms	Go to Step 5	Go to Step 12
5	Test the VES actuator and actuator harness for a short to ground. Was a short to ground located?	--	Go to Step 6	Go to Step 7
6	Visually inspect the actuator harness for any cut, chaffed or damaged wires. Did you find and correct the condition?	--	Go to Step 15	Go to Step 14

ARM0400000000049

Fig. 22   Code C0450: Steering Assist Control Actuator Circuit Fault (Part 1 of 3). LaCrosse

Step	Action	Values	Yes	No
7	Test the control circuit of the VES actuator for a short to ground. Did you find and correct the condition?	--	Go to Step 15	Go to Step 8
8	Test the control circuit of the VES actuator for an open or short to voltage. Did you find and correct the condition?	--	Go to Step 15	Go to Step 9
9	Test the return circuit of the VES actuator for a short to ground. Did you find and correct the condition?	--	Go to Step 15	Go to Step 10

ARM0400000000050

Fig. 22   Code C0450: Steering Assist Control Actuator Circuit Fault (Part 2 of 3). LaCrosse

Step	Action	Value(s)	Yes	No
10	Test the return circuit of the VES actuator for an open or a short to voltage. Did you find and correct the condition?	—	Go to Step 15	Go to Step 11
11	Inspect for poor connections at the harness connector of the electronic brake control module (EBCM). Did you find and correct the condition?	—	Go to Step 15	Go to Step 13
12	Inspect for poor connections at the harness connector of the VES actuator. Did you find and correct the condition?	—	Go to Step 15	Go to Step 14
13	**Important** Always perform the setup procedure for the EBCM. 1. Replace the EBCM. 2. Perform the setup procedure for the EBCM. Did you complete the replacement?	—	Go to Step 15	—
14	Replace the VES actuator. Did you complete the replacement?	—	Go to Step 15	—
15	1. Clear the DTCs with the scan tool. 2. Operate the vehicle within the Conditions for Running the DTC. Does DTC C0450 reset?	—	Go to Step 2	System OK

ARM0400000000051

Fig. 22   Code C0450: Steering Assist Control Actuator Circuit Fault (Part 3 of 3). LaCrosse

Diagnostic Aids

The following are possible causes:
• The steering wheel was rotated with the steering gear disconnected.
• A malfunctioning steering wheel position sensor.
• A steering wheel position sensor circuit open.
• A steering wheel position sensor circuit shorted.
• A malfunctioning EBCM.

Perform an inspection of the wiring and of the connectors. Failure to carefully inspect the wiring and the connectors may result in misdiagnosis. Misdiagnosis causes part replacement with reappearance of the malfunction.

Test Description

The numbers below refer to the step numbers on the diagnostic table.
5. Re-centers the steering wheel position sensor.
11. Checks for an open in CKT 556.
12. Checks for a short to voltage in CKT 1059.
14. Checks for a short to ground in CKT 1059.
16. Checks for an open in CKT 1059.
18. Checks for a short to battery in CKT 1056.
20. Checks for an open in CKT 1056.
22. Checks for a short to ground in CKT 1056.

Step	Action	Value(s)	Yes	No
1	Was the Variable Effort Steering System Check performed?	—	Go to Step 2	Go to *Variable Effort Steering System Check*
2	1. Point the front wheels straight ahead. 2. Using a scan tool check the steering wheel position sensor analog voltage. Is the voltage within the range specified within the value(s) column?	2–3 V	Go to Step 4	Go to Step 3
3	Is the voltage in the range specified within the values(s) column?	0.15–4.84 V	Go to Step 5	Go to Step 9
4	Replace the EBCM. Is the repair complete?	—	Go to *Variable Effort Steering System Check*	—
5	1. Turn the ignition switch to the OFF position. 2. Disable the Supplemental Inflatable Restraint (SIR). 3. Remove the Inflatable Restraint Steering Wheel Module Coil. 4. Remove the Intermediate Steering Shaft. 5. Turn the ignition switch to the ON position, engine off. 6. Using a scan tool monitor the steering wheel position sensor analog voltage as you rotate the steering column shaft. 7. Turn the steering column shaft until the analog voltage is close to 2.5 volts. Does the analog voltage move smoothly to, or close to, 2.5 volts?	—	Go to Step 7	Go to Step 6
6	Replace the Steering Wheel Position Sensor. Is the replacement complete?	—	Go to *Variable Effort Steering System Check*	—

GC6019900026020X

Fig. 23   Code C0455: Steering Position Sensor Circuit Fault (Part 2 of 4). Intrigue

Circuit Description

The steering wheel position sensor provides the EBCM with an analog voltage reading from 0.15–4.84 V depending on the steering wheel angle. The EBCM uses the analog voltage for the centering routine. The EBCM runs a centering routine when the vehicle speed goes above 30 km/h (18 mph). When the vehicle reaches 30 km/h (18 mph), the EBCM monitors the steering wheel position sensor inputs (Analog voltage) to see if the steering wheel is moving. If the steering wheel is not moving for a set period of time then the EBCM assumes the vehicle is going in a straight line. At this point, the EBCM looks at the analog voltage signal and reads the voltage. This voltage, normally around 2.5 V, is then considered the center position and the digital degrees also become zero at the same time. This centering routine is necessary to compensate for wear in the steering and suspension. Wear in the steering and suspension can result in a change in the relationship between the steering wheel and the front wheels. By running the centering routine, the EBCM can compensate for these changes by changing the digital and analog center position.

Conditions for Setting the DTC
• The center position is +/-21.5° deviation from the previous nominal center point (0°) after the centering routine is complete.
• The steering wheel position sensor analog output voltage falls outside the 0.15–4.84 V range.

Action Taken When the DTC Sets
• Correct function of the steering wheel position sensor is incorrect and the EBCM stops using the sensor's data.
• MAGNASTEER® remains active using wheel speed data only.
• A malfunction DTC is stored.
• No ABS/TCS indicators are turned on and ABS/TCS remains active.

Conditions for Clearing the DTC
• Condition for DTC is no longer present and scan tool clear DTC function is used.
• 100 ignition cycles have passed with no DTCs detected.

GC6019900026010X

Fig. 23   Code C0455: Steering Position Sensor Circuit Fault (Part 1 of 4). Intrigue

Step	Action	Value(s)	Yes	No
7	1. Leave the steering column shaft centered at 2.5 volts. 2. Turn the ignition switch to the OFF position. 3. Install the Intermediate Steering Shaft. 4. Install the Inflatable Restraint Steering Wheel Module Coil. 5. Enable the SIR. Is the repair complete?	—	Go to Step 8	—
8	1. Turn the ignition switch to the ON position, engine off. 2. Using a scan tool, clear DTC C0455. 3. Drive vehicle above 30 km/h (18 mph) for several minutes in a straight line. 4. Using a scan tool check for DTC C0455. Did DTC C0455 set as a current DTC?	—	Go to Step 4	Go to *Variable Effort Steering System Check*
9	1. Turn the ignition switch to the OFF position. 2. Disconnect the EBCM. 3. Install the J 39700 universal pinout box using the J 39700-530 cable adapter to the EBCM harness connector and the EBCM. 4. Turn the ignition switch to the ON position, engine off. 5. Using a scan tool DMM, measure the voltage between ground and terminal 26 of J 39700. Is the voltage within the range specified in the value(s) column?	0.15–4.84 V	Go to Step 4	Go to Step 10
10	1. Turn the ignition switch to the OFF position. 2. Disconnect the steering wheel position sensor connector. 3. Turn the ignition switch to the ON position, engine off. 4. Using the J 39200 DMM, measure the voltage between ground and terminal 1 of the steering wheel position sensor harness connector. Is the voltage within the range specified in the value(s) column?	4.75–5.25 V	Go to Step 11	Go to Step 18
11	Using J 39200 DMM, measure the resistance between the steering wheel position sensor harness connector terminal 2 and a good ground. Is the resistance within the range specified in the value(s) column?	0–5 Ω	Go to Step 12	Go to Step 24
12	1. Turn the ignition switch to the ON position, engine off. 2. Using the J 39200 DMM, measure the voltage at terminal 6 of the steering wheel position sensor harness connector. Is the voltage above the value specified in the value(s) column?	1 V	Go to Step 13	Go to Step 14
13	Repair CKT 1059 for a short to voltage, being sure to check for a short to CKT 1056. Is the repair complete?	—	Go to *Variable Effort Steering System Check*	—
14	1. Turn the ignition switch to the OFF position. 2. Disconnect the J 39700-530 cable adapter from the EBCM leaving the J 39700-530 cable adapter connected to the EBCM harness connector. 3. Using the J 39200 DMM, measure the resistance between terminals 26 and 15 of J 39700. Is the resistance within the range specified within the value(s) column?	OL (infinite)	Go to Step 16	Go to Step 15

GC6019900026030X

Fig. 23   Code C0455: Steering Position Sensor Circuit Fault (Part 3 of 4). Intrigue

Step	Action	Value(s)	Yes	No
15	Repair CKT 1059 for a short to ground, being sure to check for a short to CKT 556. Is the repair complete?	—	Go to Variable Effort Steering System Check	—
16	1. Connect a jumper wire between terminals 26 and 18 of J 39700. 2. Using J 39200 DMM, measure the resistance between the steering wheel position sensors harness connector terminals 2 and 6. Is the resistance within the range specified within the value(s) column?	0–5 Ω	Go to Step 6	Go to Step 17
17	Repair CKT 1059 for an open or high resistance. Is the repair complete?	—	Go to Variable Effort Steering System Check	—
18	Using the J 39200 DMM, measure the voltage at terminal 1 of the steering wheel position sensor harness connector. Is the voltage above the value specified in the value(s) column?	5.25 V	Go to Step 19	Go to Step 20
19	Repair CKT 1056 for a short to battery. Is the repair complete?	—	Go to Variable Effort Steering System Check	—
20	1. Turn the ignition switch to the OFF position. 2. Disconnect the J 39700-530 cable adapter from the EBCM leaving the J 39700-530 cable adapter connected to the EBCM harness connector. 3. Connect a jumper wire between terminals 28 and 15 of J 39700. 4. Using J 39200 DMM, measure the resistance between the steering wheel position sensor harness connector terminal 1 and a good ground. Is the resistance within the range specified within the value(s) column?	0–5 Ω	Go to Step 22	Go to Step 21
21	Repair CKT 1056 for an open or high resistance. Is the repair complete?	—	Go to Variable Effort Steering System Check	—
22	1. Remove the jumper wire from J 39700. 2. Using J 39200 DMM, measure the resistance between the steering wheel position sensor harness connector terminal 1 and a good ground. Is the resistance within the range specified in the values column?	OL (infinite)	Go to Step 4	Go to Step 23
23	Repair CKT 1056 for a short to ground. Is the repair complete?	—	Go to Variable Effort Steering System Check	—
24	1. Turn the ignition switch to the OFF position. 2. Disconnect the J 39700-530 cable adapter from the EBCM leaving the J 39700-530 cable adapter connected to the EBCM harness connector. 3. Using the J 39200 DMM, measure the resistance between the J 39700 terminal 18 and terminal 2 of the steering wheel position sensor harness connector. Is the resistance within the range specified in the value(s) column?	0–5 Ω	Go to Step 4	Go to Step 25
25	Repair CKT 556 for an open or high resistance. Is the repair complete?	—	Go to Variable Effort Steering System Check	—

GC6019900026040X

Fig. 23 Code C0455: Steering Position Sensor Circuit Fault (Part 4 of 4). Intrigue

Step	Action	Value(s)	Yes	No
1	Did you perform the Variable Effort Steering Diagnostic System Check?	—	Go to Step 2	Diagnostic System Check -
2	1. Install a scan tool. 2. Start the engine. 3. With a scan tool, observe the MagnaSteer® Commanded Current and MagnaSteer® Feedback Current parameters in the MagnaSteer® data list. 4. Carefully test drive the vehicle so that the MagnaSteer® Commanded Current is greater than 826 mA. Does the scan tool indicate that the MagnaSteer® Feedback Current is greater than the specified value?	155 mA	Test for Intermittent and Poor Connections	Go to Step 3
3	1. Turn OFF the ignition. 2. Disconnect the variable effort steering actuator connector. 3. Measure the resistance across the variable effort steering actuator. Does the resistance measure within the specified range?	1.6–3.1 Ω	Go to Step 5	Go to Step 4
4	Test both variable effort steering actuator control circuits for a short to ground or short to voltage between the EBCM and the variable effort steering actuator pigtail connector. Did you find and correct the condition?	—	Go to Step 9	Go to Step 6
5	Inspect for poor connections at the harness connector of the variable effort steering actuator. Did you find and correct the condition?	—	Go to Step 9	Go to Step 7
6	Inspect for poor connections at the harness connector of the EBCM. Did you find and correct the condition?	—	Go to Step 9	Go to Step 8
7	Replace the variable effort steering actuator. Did you complete the repair?	—	Go to Step 9	—
8	**Important:** Perform the setup procedure for the EBCM. An unprogrammed EBCM will result in the following conditions: • Inoperative or poorly functioning DRP/ABS/TCS/VSES/VES/TIM (if equipped) • Set DTC C1248 EBCM Turned the Red Brake Warning Indicator On • Set DTC C1255 EBCM Internal Malfunction Replace the EBCM. Did you complete the repair?	—	Go to Step 9	—
9	1. Use the scan tool in order to clear the DTCs. 2. Operate the vehicle within the Conditions for Running the DTC as specified in the supporting text. Does the DTC reset?	—	Go to Step 2	System OK

ARM66GC000000441

Fig. 24 Code C1241: Speed Sensitive Steering Circuit Fault (Part 2 of 2). Aurora

Circuit Description

The EBCM controls a bi-directional magnetic rotary solenoid. The solenoid is in the steering gear. The solenoid adjusts the amount of power steering assist in order to achieve a given level of driver effort in turning the vehicle. The EBCM varies the steering assist by adjusting the current flow through the solenoid. The amount of steering assist adjusted for steering is dependent upon vehicle speed. As the vehicle speed increases, the following actions occur:

• The steering assist decreases.
• The driver effort increases.

As the vehicle speed decreases, the following actions occur:

• The steering assist increases.
• The driver effort decreases.

Conditions for Running the DTC

The EBCM performs 2 diagnostic tests for the VES circuits when the ignition voltage is between 10.5 volts and 17 volts. The numbers below corresponds to the numbers in Conditions for Setting the DTC.

1. Off State Test (Open Circuit Test) - When the ignition is first turned ON, the EBCM performs an open circuit test independent of vehicle speed or engine running.
2. On State Test (Open or Short Circuit Test) - If the Off State Test is passed, the EBCM runs the On State Test during VES operations. The VES operations occur during driving. The EBCM detects an open or short in the VES circuit by comparing the feedback current to the commanded current.

Conditions for Setting the DTC

The EBCM performs 2 different tests to detect a DTC condition. The numbers below correspond to the number in Conditions for Running the DTC.

1. The EBCM detects an open in the VES circuit.
2. The EBCM detects an open or short in the VES circuit when the feedback current is less than 155 mA while the absolute value of the commanded current is greater than 826 mA for 2.5 seconds.

Action Taken When the DTC Sets

The EBCM disables the variable effort steering (VES) for the duration of the ignition cycle.

Conditions for Clearing the DTC

• The condition for the DTC is no longer present (the DTC is not current) and you used the scan tool Clear DTC function.
• The EBCM automatically clears the history DTC when a current DTC is not detected in 100 consecutive drive cycles.

Diagnostic Aids

The vehicle may need to be driven to view non-zero values of the MagnaSteer® Commanded Current and MagnaSteer® Feedback Current on the scan tool.

Test Description

The numbers below refer to the step numbers on the diagnostic table.

2. This step uses the scan tool to check the MagnaSteer® Feedback Current parameter.
6. This step checks for an open in the variable effort steering actuator and circuit.

ARM66GC000000440

Fig. 24 Code C1241: Speed Sensitive Steering Circuit Fault (Part 1 of 2). Aurora

Circuit Description

The EBCM controls a bi-directional magnetic rotary solenoid. The solenoid is in the steering gear. The solenoid adjusts the amount of power steering assist in order to achieve a given level of driver effort in turning the vehicle. The EBCM varies the steering assist by adjusting the current flow through the solenoid. The amount of steering assist adjusted for steering is dependent upon vehicle speed. As the vehicle speed increases, the following actions occur:

• The steering assist decreases.
• The driver effort increases.

As the vehicle speed decreases, the following actions occur:

• The steering assist increases.
• The driver effort decreases.

Conditions for Running the DTC

The EBCM performs 2 diagnostic tests for the VES circuits when the ignition voltage is between 10.5 volts and 17 volts. The numbers below corresponds to the numbers in Conditions for Setting the DTC.

1. Off State Test (Open Circuit Test) - When the ignition is first turned ON, the EBCM performs an open circuit test independent of vehicle speed or engine running.
2. On State Test (Open or Short Circuit Test) - If the Off State Test is passed, the EBCM runs the On State Test during VES operations.

The VES operations occur during driving. The EBCM detects an open or short in the VES circuit by comparing the feedback current to the commanded current.

Conditions for Setting the DTC

The EBCM performs 2 different tests to detect a DTC condition. The numbers below correspond to the number in Conditions for Running the DTC.

1. The EBCM detects an open in the VES circuit.
2. The EBCM detects an open or short in the VES circuit when the feedback current is less than 155 mA while the absolute value of the commanded current is greater than 826 mA for 2.5 seconds.

Action Taken When the DTC Sets

The EBCM disables the variable effort steering (VES) for the duration of the ignition cycle.

Conditions for Clearing the DTC

• The condition for the DTC is no longer present (the DTC is not current) and you used the scan tool Clear DTC function.
• The EBCM automatically clears the history DTC when a current DTC is not detected in 100 consecutive drive cycles.

GC6010000021010X

Fig. 25 Code C1241: Speed Sensitive Steering Circuit Fault (Part 1 of 3). 2001–02 Bonneville, LeSabre & Park Avenue

Diagnostic Aids

The vehicle may need to be driven to view non-zero values of the Magna Steer Commanded Current and Magna Steer Feedback Current on the scan tool.

Test Description

The numbers below refer to the step numbers on the diagnostic table.

2. This step uses the scan tool to check the Magna Steer Feedback Current parameter.

6. This step checks for an open in the variable effort steering actuator and circuit.

Step	Action	Value(s)	Yes	No
1	Did you perform the Variable Effort Steering Diagnostic System Check?	—	Go to Step 2	Go to A Diagnostic System Check - Variable Effort Steering
2	1. Install a scan tool. 2. Start the engine. 3. With a scan tool, observe the Magna Steer Commanded Current and Magna Steer Feedback Current parameters in the Magna Steer data list. 4. Carefully test drive the vehicle so that the Magna Steer Commanded Current is greater than 826 mA. Does the scan tool indicate that the Magna Steer Feedback Current is greater than the specified value?	155 mA	Go to Intermittent	Go to Step 3
3	1. Turn OFF the ignition. 2. Disconnect the variable effort steering actuator connector. 3. Measure the resistance across the variable effort steering actuator. Does the resistance measure within the specified range?	1.6–3.1 Ω	Go to Step 5	Go to Step 4
4	Test both variable effort steering control circuits for a high resistance or an open between the variable effort steering actuator pigtail connector and the variable effort steering actuator. Did you find and correct the condition?	—	Go to Step 13	Go to Step 8
5	Test both variable effort steering control circuits for a short between the variable effort steering actuator pigtail connector and the variable effort steering actuator housing. Did you find and correct the condition?	—	Go to Step 13	Go to Step 6
6	1. Turn OFF the ignition. 2. Reconnect the variable effort steering actuator connector. **Important:** Removing battery voltage or ground from the EBCM will result in the following conditions. • Loss of the TIM learned tire inflation configuration parameters • Set DTC C1245 Low Tire Pressure Detected When the diagnosis is complete, inspect the tire pressures and perform the TIM reset. 3. Disconnect the EBCM harness connector. 4. Install the J 39700 universal pinout box using the J 39700-300 cable adapter to the EBCM harness connector only. 5. Measure the resistance at the J 39700 universal pinout box between the variable effort steering control circuits. Does the resistance measure within the specified range?	1.6–5 Ω	Go to Step 7	Go to Step 9

GC601000021020X

Fig. 25 Code C1241: Speed Sensitive Steering Circuit Fault (Part 2 of 3). 2001–02 Bonneville, LeSabre & Park Avenue

Circuit Description

The Variable Effort Steering (VES) system uses the Electronic Brake Control Module (EBCM) to command current from zero amps to positive three amps to an electromagnetic rotary actuator. The VES system uses the Antilock Brake System (ABS) wheel speed sensor inputs to determine vehicle speed. At low speeds, no current is commanded and steering is assisted by hydraulics only. At high speeds, A positive current is commanded to the VES actuator to create steering resistance. The EBCM monitors and compares commanded and feedback currents to detect malfunctions in the VES actuator or the circuits to the actuator.

Conditions for Running the DTC

• Ignition voltage between 10.5-17 volts
• Off state test -- initial ignition ON, no engine rpm, or vehicle speed present.
• On state test -- if off state test passes, engine rpm and vehicle speed present.

Condition for Setting the DTC

An open, short to ground, or short to voltage in the VES actuator, or the circuits to the actuator.

Action Taken When the DTC Sets

• A DTC C1241 is stored in memory.
• The DIC may display the SERVICE STEERING SYS warning message.
• The VES system is disabled.

Conditions for Clearing the DTC

• A current DTC will clear when the malfunction is no longer present.
• A history DTC will clear after 100 consecutive ignition cycles with no malfunction present.
• Using the scan tool

Diagnostic Aids

The vehicle needs to be driven to view the full commanded and feedback current ranges.

Test Description

The numbers below refer to the step numbers on the diagnostic table.

2. Tests if the commanded and feedback current parameters are in specified range in there active state.

3. Tests if the VES actuator resistance is within specified range.

ARM66GC000000442

Fig. 26 Code C1241: Speed Sensitive Steering Circuit Fault (Part 1 of 3). 2003–05 Bonneville, DeVille, Park Avenue & Seville

Step	Action	Value(s)	Yes	No
7	Test both variable effort steering control circuits for a short to ground or short to voltage between the EBCM and the variable effort steering actuator pigtail connector. Did you find and correct the condition?	—	Go to Step 13	Go to Step 12
8	Inspect for poor connections at the harness connector of the variable effort steering actuator. Did you find and correct the condition?	—	Go to Step 13	Go to Step 11
9	Inspect for poor connections at the harness connector of the EBCM. Did you find and correct the condition?	—	Go to Step 13	Go to Step 10
10	Test for and repair one of the following conditions in the suspect variable effort steering control circuit between the EBCM and the variable effort steering actuator pigtail connector. • An open • A high resistance • A short between the control circuits Refer to Wiring Repairs in Wiring System. Did you complete the repair?	—	Go to Step 13	—
11	Replace the variable effort steering actuator. Did you complete the repair?	—	Go to Step 13	—
12	**Important:** Perform the setup procedure for the EBCM. An unprogrammed EBCM will result in the following conditions: • Inoperative or poorly functioning DRP/ABS/TCS/VSES/VES/TIM (if equipped) • Set DTC C1248 EBCM Turned the Red Brake Warning Indicator On • Set DTC C1255m3 EBCM Internal Malfunction Replace the EBCM. Did you complete the repair?	—	Go to Step 13	—
13	1. Use the scan tool in order to clear the DTCs. 2. Operate the vehicle within the Conditions for Running the DTC as specified in the supporting text. Does the DTC reset?	—	Go to Step 2	System OK

GC601000021030X

Fig. 25 Code C1241: Speed Sensitive Steering Circuit Fault (Part 3 of 3). 2001–02 Bonneville, LeSabre & Park Avenue

Step	Action	Value(s)	Yes	No
1	Did you perform the Variable Effort Steering Diagnostic System Check?	--	Go to Step 2	Perform Diagnostic System Check - Variable Effort Steering
2	1. Install a scan tool. 2. Start the engine. 3. Test drive the vehicle at 64.3 km/h (40 mph). 4. With the scan tool, observe the Magna Steer Commanded current and the Magna Steer Feedback Current data parameters in the Magna Steer data list. Does the scan tool indicate that the Magna Steer Commanded and Feedback Current parameters are within .05 amps of each other and within the specified range?	0.60-0.87 amps	Test for Intermittent and Poor Connections	Go to Step 3
3	1. Turn OFF the ignition. 2. Disconnect the VES actuator harness connector. 3. Measure the resistance of the VES actuator. Does the resistance measure within the specified range?	1.6-3.1 ohms	Go to Step 4	Go to Step 8
4	Test the High Effort Control circuit of the VES actuator for a short to ground. Did you find and correct the condition?		Go to Step 12	Go to Step 5
5	Test the High Effort Control circuit of the VES actuator for an open or short to voltage. Did you find and correct the condition?		Go to Step 12	Go to Step 6
6	Test the Low Effort Control circuit of the VES actuator for a short to ground. Did you find and correct the condition?	--	Go to Step 12	Go to Step 7

ARM66GC000000443

Fig. 26 Code C1241: Speed Sensitive Steering Circuit Fault (Part 2 of 3). 2003–05 Bonneville, DeVille, Park Avenue & Seville

POWER STEERING

Step	Action	Value(s)	Yes	No
7	Test the Low Effort Control circuit of the VES actuator for an open or short to voltage. Did you find and correct the condition?		Go to Step 12	Go to Step 9
8	Inspect for poor connections at the harness connector of the VES actuator. Did you find and correct the condition?		Go to Step 12	Go to Step 10
9	Inspect for poor connections at the harness connector of the EBCM. Did you find and correct the condition?		Go to Step 12	Go to Step 11
10	Replace the variable effort steering actuator. Did you complete the repair?		Go to Step 12	--
11	**Important** Perform the setup procedure for the EBCM. An unprogrammed EBCM will result in the following conditions: • Inoperative or poorly functioning DRP/ABS/TCS/VSES/VES/TPM, if equipped • Set DTC C1248 • Set DTC C1255 Replace the EBCM. Did you complete the repair?		Go to Step 12	--
12	1. Use the scan tool in order to clear the DTCs. 2. Operate the vehicle within the Conditions for Running the DTC as specified in the supporting text. Does the DTC reset?		Go to Step 2	System OK

ARM66GC000000444

Fig. 26 Code C1241: Speed Sensitive Steering Circuit Fault (Part 3 of 3). 2003–05 Bonneville, DeVille, Park Avenue & Seville

Circuit Description

The Speed dependent Steering System (MAGNASTEER®) incorporates its controller into the EBCM. The EBCM controls the amount of current supplied to the MAGNASTEER® actuator based on input from the wheel speed sensors.

MAGNASTEER® 2 also uses inputs from the wheel speed sensors along with added input from the Steering Wheel Position Sensor.

Conditions for Setting the DTC

One or both of the MAGNASTEER® actuator circuit wires become open or shorted.

Action Taken When the DTC Sets

A malfunction DTC is stored. No ABS or Car Icon (TCS indicator) indicators are turned on but MAGNASTEER® is disabled. ABS/TCS remains functional.

Conditions for Clearing the DTC

- Condition for DTC is no longer present and scan tool clear DTC function is used.
- Fifty ignition cycles have passed with no DTC(s) detected.

Diagnostic Aids

- It is very important that a thorough inspection of the wiring and connectors be performed. Failure to carefully and fully inspect wiring and connectors may result in misdiagnosis, causing part replacement with reappearance of the malfunction.
- An intermittent malfunction can be caused by poor connections, broken insulation, or a wire that is broken inside the insulation.

Test Description

The numbers below refer to the step numbers on the diagnostic table.

2. This step uses the scan tool to check the Magna Steer Feedback Current parameter.

6. This step checks for an open in the variable effort steering actuator and circuit.

GC6020100466010X

Fig. 27 Code C1241: Magnasteer Fault (Part 1 of 3). 2001 Corvette

Step	Action	Value(s)	Yes	No
1	Did you perform the Variable Effort Steering Diagnostic System Check?	--	Go to Step 2	Perform System Check
2	1. Install a scan tool. 2. Start the engine. 3. With a scan tool, observe the MAGNASTEER® Commanded Current and MAGNASTEER® Feedback Current parameters in the MAGNASTEER® data list. 4. Carefully test drive the vehicle so that the MAGNASTEER® Commanded Current is greater than 826 mA. Does the scan tool indicate that the MAGNASTEER® Feedback Current is greater than the specified value?	155 mA	Repair Intermittent and Poor Connections	Go to Step 3
3	1. Turn OFF the ignition. 2. Disconnect the variable effort steering actuator connector. 3. Measure the resistance across the variable effort steering actuator. Does the resistance measure within the specified range?	1.6-3.1 ohms	Go to Step 4	Go to Step 5
4	Test both variable effort steering actuator control circuits for a short to ground, short to voltage, an or open between the EBCM and the variable effort steering actuator pigtail connector. Did you find and correct the condition?	--	Go to Step 9	Go to Step 6
5	Inspect for poor connections at the harness connector of the variable effort steering actuator. Did you find and correct the condition?	--	Go to Step 9	Go to Step 7
6	Inspect for poor connections at the harness connector of the EBCM. Did you find and correct the condition?	--	Go to Step 9	Go to Step 8

GC6020100466020X

Fig. 27 Code C1241: Magnasteer Fault (Part 2 of 3). 2001 Corvette

Step	Action	Value(s)	Yes	No
7	Replace the variable effort steering actuator. Did you complete the repair?	--	Go to Step 9	--
8	**Important** Perform the setup procedure for the EBCM. An unprogrammed EBCM will result in the following conditions: • Inoperative or poorly functioning DRP/ABS/TCS/VSES/VES (if equipped) • Set DTC C1248 EBCM Turned the Red Brake Warning Indicator On • Set DTC C1255 EBCM Internal Malfunction Replace the EBCM. Did you complete the repair?	--	Go to Step 9	--
9	1. Use the scan tool in order to clear the DTCs. 2. Operate the vehicle within the Conditions for Running the DTC as specified in the supporting text. Does the DTC reset?	--	Go to Step 2	System OK

GC6020100466030X

Fig. 27 Code C1241: Magnasteer Fault (Part 3 of 3). 2001 Corvette

Circuit Description

The Variable Effort Steering (VES) system uses the Electronic Brake Control Module (EBCM) to control current to a bi-directional electromagnetic rotary actuator. The EBCM commands current from negative two amps to positive three amps to the actuator. At low speeds, a negative current is commanded, which assists steering. At medium speeds, no current is commanded and steering is assisted by hydraulics only. At high speeds, a positive current is commanded, which creates steering resistance.

Conditions for running the DTC

- Ignition voltage between 10.5 and 17 volts
- Off state test - Initial ignition ON, no engine rpm or vehicle speed present.
- On state test - If off state test passes, engine rpm and vehicle speed present.

Conditions for Setting the DTC

An open, short to ground, or short to voltage in the VES actuator or the circuits to the actuator.

Action Taken When the DTC Sets

- A DTC C1241 is stored in memory
- The DIC may display the SERVICE STEERING SYS warning message.
- The VES system is disabled.

Conditions for Clearing the DTC

- A current DTC will clear when malfunction is no longer present.
- A history DTC will clear after 100 consecutive ignition cycles with no malfunction present.
- Using the scan tool

Diagnostic Aids

The vehicle needs to be driven to view full commanded and feedback current ranges on the scan tool.

GC6020100467010X

Fig. 28 Code C1241: Magnasteer Fault (Part 1 of 4). 2002–05 Corvette

Step	Action	Value(s)	Yes	No
1	Did you perform the Variable Effort Steering Diagnostic System Check?	--	Go to Step 2	Perform Diagnostic System Check - Variable Effort Steering
2	1. Install a scan tool. 2. Start the engine. 3. With the scan tool, observe the Magna Steer Commanded Current and the Magna Steer Feedback Current data parameters in the Magna Steer data list. Does the scan tool indicate that the Magna Steer Commanded and Magna Steer Feedback current parameters are within .05 amps of each other and within specified range?	-1.84 to -1.99 A	Repair Intermittent and Poor Connections	Go to Step 3
3	1. Turn OFF the ignition. 2. Disconnect the VES actuator harness connector. 3. Measure the resistance of the VES actuator. Does the resistance measure within the specified range?	1.6-3.1 ohms	Go to Step 4	Go to Step 8
4	Test the High Effort Control circuit of the VES actuator for a short to ground. Did you find and correct the condition?	--	Go to Step 12	Go to Step 5
5	Test the High Effort Control circuit of the VES actuator for an open or short to voltage. Did you find and correct the condition?	--	Go to Step 12	Go to Step 6
6	Test the Low Effort Control circuit of the VES actuator for a short to ground. Did you find and correct the condition?	--	Go to Step 12	Go to Step 7

GC6020100467030X

Fig. 28 Code C1241: Magnasteer Fault (Part 3 of 4). 2002–05 Corvette

Test Description

The numbers below refer to the step numbers on the diagnostic table.

2. Tests if the Commanded and Feedback current parameters are at the specified value in there active state.

3. Tests if the resistance of the VES actuator is in the specified range.

5. Tests the High Effort Control circuit for an open or short to voltage.

6. Tests the Low Effort Control circuit for a short to ground.

8. Tests for poor connections at the VES actuator harness connector.

11. Perform the setup procedure after EBCM replacement.

GC6020100467020X

Fig. 28 Code C1241: Magnasteer Fault (Part 2 of 4). 2002–05 Corvette

7	Test the Low Effort Control circuit of the VES actuator for an open or short to voltage Did you find and correct the condition?	-	Go to Step 12	Go to Step 9
8	Inspect for poor connections at the harness connector of the VES actuator. Did you find and correct the condition?	-	Go to Step 12	Go to Step 10
9	Inspect for poor connections at the harness connector of the EBCM. Did you find and correct the condition?	-	Go to Step 12	Go to Step 11
10	Replace the VES actuator. Did you complete the repair?	-	Go to Step 12	--
11	**Important** Perform the setup procedure for the EBCM. An unprogrammed EBCM will result in the following conditions: • Inoperative, or poorly functioning DRP/ABS/TCS/VSES/VES/TPM, if equipped, system. • Set DTC C1248 • Set DTC C1255 Replace the EBCM. Did you complete the repair?		Go to Step 12	--
12	1. Use the scan tool in order to clear the DTCs. 2. Operate the vehicle within the Conditions for Running the DTC as specified in the supporting text. Does the DTC reset?	-	Go to Step 2	System OK

GC6020100467040X

Fig. 28 Code C1241: Magnasteer Fault (Part 4 of 4). 2002–05 Corvette

Circuit Description

The Magnetic Steering Variable Assist (MSVA) system, also known as Magnasteer®, uses inputs from the ABS wheel speed sensors to determine the desired amount of power steering assist. The speed dependent Steering System is incorporated into the EBTCM. The EBTCM controls the amount of current supplied to the MSVA actuator based on inputs from the wheel speed sensors.

Conditions for Setting the DTC

DTC C1241 is set when the ignition voltage is between 17.0 and 10.5 volts, and either of the MSVA steering system actuator circuits (CKT 1787 or CKT 345) become open or shorted.

Action Taken When the DTC Sets

- A Malfunction DTC C1241 is stored within the EBTCM.
- The Antilock Brake System (ABS), Enhanced Traction Control (ETS), or the Traction Control System (TCS) indicator lamps are NOT illuminated.
- The MSVA system is disabled.
- The ABS/ETS/TCS remains functional.

Conditions for Clearing the DTC

1. A history DTC will clear after 100 consecutive ignition cycles if the condition for the malfunction is no longer present.
2. You may use a scan tool in order to clear the DTC.

Diagnostic Aids

- Possible causes for DTC C1241 to set are:
  - One or both MSVA circuits open.
  - One or both MSVA circuits short to battery.
  - One or both MSVA circuits short to ground.
- It is very important that a thorough inspection of the wiring and connectors be performed. Failure to carefully and fully inspect wiring and connectors may result in misdiagnosis, causing part replacement with reappearance of the malfunction.
- Inspect all of the circuitry that may cause the intermittent complaint for the following conditions:
  - Broken wire inside the insulation
  - Backed out terminals
  - Improper mating
  - Improperly formed terminals
  - Damaged terminals
  - Poor terminal to wiring connections
  - Physical damage to the wiring harness

GC6019900028010X

Fig. 29 Code C1241: Magnasteer Fault (Part 1 of 4). Century & Regal

Step	Action	Value(s)	Yes	No
1	Was the Variable Effort System (VES) Diagnostic System Check performed?	—	Go to Step 2	Go to Variable Effort Steering System Check
2	1. Turn the ignition switch to the OFF position. 2. Disconnect the EBTCM connector. 3. Install the J 39700 Universal Pinout Box using the J 39700-99 Cable Adaptor to the EBTCM harness connector only. 4. Using J 39200 DMM, measure the resistance between terminals B10 and B11 of J 39700 Universal Pinout Box. Is the resistance within the specified range?	1.6–3.1 Ω	Go to Step 11	Go to Step 3
3	1. Disconnect the two-way MSVA actuator connector. 2. Using the DMM, measure the resistance between terminal A and B of MSVA connector. Is the resistance within the specified range?	1.6–3.1 Ω	Go to Step 5	Go to Step 4
4	Replace the MSVA actuator. Is the repair complete?	—	Go to Variable Effort Steering System Check	—
5	1. Use the Universal Pinout box with the Cable Adaptor still connected to EBTCM harness only. 2. Use the DMM to measure the resistance between terminal B10 of the universal pinout box and the MSVA connector terminal B. Is the resistance within the specified range?	0–2 Ω	Go to Step 7	Go to Step 6
6	Repair open or high resistance in CKT 345. Is the repair complete?	—	Go to Variable Effort Steering System Check	—
7	Using the DMM, measure the resistance between terminal B11 of the universal pinout box and the MSVA connector terminal A. Is the resistance within the specified range?	0–2 Ω	Go to Step 9	Go to Step 8
8	Repair open or high resistance in CKT 1787. Is the repair complete?	—	Go to Variable Effort Steering System Check	—
9	1. MSVA connector still disconnected. 2. Use the DMM to measure the resistance between terminals B10 and B11 of the Universal Pinout Box. Is continuity present between the terminals B10 and B11 of the Universal Pinout Box?	—	Go to Step 10	Go to Step 20
10	Repair the short between CKT 345 and CKT 1787. Is the repair complete?	—	Go to Variable Effort Steering System Check	—
11	1. Disconnect the two-way MSVA actuator connector. 2. Using the DMM, measure the resistance between terminals B10 and D of the Universal Pinout Box. Is continuity present between the terminals B10 and D of the Universal Pinout Box?	—	Go to Step 12	Go to Step 13
12	Repair the short to ground in CKT 345. Is the repair complete?	—	Go to Variable Effort Steering System Check	—

GC6019900028020X

Fig. 29 Code C1241: Magnasteer Fault (Part 2 of 4). Century & Regal

Step	Action	Value(s)	Yes	No
13	Using the DMM, measure the resistance between terminals B11 and D of the Universal Pinout Box. Is continuity present between terminals B11 and D of the Universal Pinout Box?	—	Go to Step 14	Go to Step 15
14	Repair the short to ground in CKT 1787. Is the repair complete?	—	Go to Variable Effort Steering System Check	—
15	1. Using the DMM, measure the resistance between the MSVA actuator terminal A and the steering gear case. 2. Check for an internal short to ground inside the MSVA actuator. Is continuity present between the MSVA actuator terminal A and the steering gear case?	—	Go to Step 4	Go to Step 16
16	1. Disconnect the two-way MAGNASTEER® actuator connector. 2. Turn the ignition switch to the RUN position, engine off. 3. Connect the DMM between terminals B10 and D of the Universal Pinout Box. 4. Check for voltage at terminal B10 of the Universal Pinout Box. Is any voltage present at terminal B10 of the Universal Pinout Box?	—	Go to Step 17	Go to Step 18
17	1. Repair the short to voltage in CKT 345. 2. Inspect the variable effort steering system. Is the repair complete?	—	Go to Variable Effort Steering System Check	—
18	1. Ignition switch still in the RUN position, engine off. 2. Connect the DMM between terminals B11 and D of the Universal Pinout Box. 3. Check for voltage at terminal B11 of the Universal Pinout Box. Is any voltage present at terminal B11 of the Universal Pinout Box?	—	Go to Step 19	Go to Step 20
19	Repair the short to voltage in CKT 1787. Is the repair complete?	—	Go to Variable Effort Steering System Check	—
20	1. Turn the ignition switch to the OFF position. **Important:** Damage or corrosion may result in an open or short with all of the connectors connected. 2. Inspect the EBTCM harness connectors for the following conditions: • Damage • Corrosion **Important:** Damage or corrosion may result in an open or short with all of the connectors connected. 3. Inspect the two-way MSVA actuator harness connector for the following conditions: • Damage • Corrosion Do the connectors exhibit signs of corrosion or damage?	—	Go to Step 21	Go to Step 22

GC6019900028030X

Fig. 29 Code C1241: Magnasteer Fault (Part 3 of 4). Century & Regal

Step	Action	Value(s)	Yes	No
21	1. Repair the damaged or corroded harness connectors in the EBTCM. 2. Repair the damaged or corroded two-way MSVA actuator harness connector. 3. Inspect the variable effort steering system. Is the repair complete?	—	Go to Variable Effort Steering System Check	—
22	1. Reconnect all of the connectors. 2. Install the scan tool to the data link connector. 3. Select VES Data within the scan tool menus. 4. Start the engine and allow vehicle to idle in Park. 5. Monitor VES Actuator Commanded and VES Actuator Feedback. 6. Test drive vehicle while monitoring VES Actuator Commanded and VES Actuator Feedback signals. 7. Compare the values to those given below. • 0 km/h (0 mph) = 0 to -2 amps • 72 km/h (45 mph) = 0 amps • 72 km/h or higher (45 mph or higher) = 0 to 2 amps Does the VES Actuator Commanded and VES Actuator Feedback signals respond according to the given values?	—	Go to Step 4	Go to Step 23
23	1. Replace the EBTCM. 2. Inspect the variable effort steering system. Is the repair complete?	—	Go to Variable Effort Steering System Check	—

GC6019900028040X

Fig. 29 Code C1241: Magnasteer Fault (Part 4 of 4). Century & Regal

Circuit Description

The EBCM controls a bi-directional magnetic rotary solenoid. The solenoid is in the steering gear. The solenoid adjusts the amount of power steering assist in order to achieve a given level of driver effort in turning the vehicle. The EBCM varies the steering assist by adjusting the current flow through the solenoid. The amount of steering assist adjusted for steering is dependent upon vehicle speed. As the vehicle speed increases, the following actions occur:

• The steering assist decreases
• The driver effort increases.

As the vehicle speed decreases, the following actions occur:

• The steering assist increases
• The driver effort decreases.

Conditions for Running the DTC

The EBCM performs 2 diagnostic tests for the VES circuits when the ignition voltage is between 10.5 volts and 17 volts. The numbers below corresponds to the numbers in Conditions for Setting the DTC.

1. Off State Test (Open Circuit Test) - When the ignition is first turned ON, the EBCM performs an open circuit test independent of vehicle speed or engine running.

2. On State Test (Open or Short Circuit Test) - If the Off State Test is passed, the EBCM runs the On State Test during VES operations. The VES operations occur during driving. The EBCM detects an open or short in the VES circuit by comparing the feedback current to the commanded current.

GC6010000022010X

Fig. 30 Code C1241: Speed Sensitive Steering Circuit Fault (Part 1 of 3). 2001–05 DeVille & Seville

Conditions for Setting the DTC

The EBCM performs 2 different tests to detect a DTC condition. The numbers below correspond to the number in Conditions for Running the DTC.

1. The EBCM detects an open in the VES circuit.
2. The EBCM detects an open or short in the VES circuit when the feedback current is less than 155 mA while the absolute value of the commanded current is greater than 826 mA for 2.5 seconds.

Action Taken When the DTC Sets

- The EBCM disables the variable effort steering (VES) for the duration of the ignition cycle.
- The DIC displays the SERVICE STEERING SYS message.

Conditions for Clearing the DTC

- The condition for the DTC is no longer present (the DTC is not current) and you used the scan tool Clear DTC function.
- The condition for the DTC is no longer present (the DTC is not current) and you used the On-Board Diagnostics Clear DTC function.
- The EBCM automatically clears the history DTC when a current DTC is not detected in 100 consecutive drive cycles.

Diagnostic Aids

The vehicle may need to be driven to view non-zero values of the Magna Steer Commanded Current and Magna Steer Feedback Current on the scan tool.

Test Description

The numbers below refer to the step numbers on the diagnostic table.

2. This step uses the scan tool to check the Magna Steer Feedback Current parameter.
6. This step checks for an open in the variable effort steering actuator and circuit.

Step	Action	Value(s)	Yes	No
1	Did you perform the Variable Effort Steering Diagnostic System Check?	—	Go to Step 2	Go to A Diagnostic System Check - Variable Effort Steering
2	1. Install a scan tool. 2. Start the engine. 3. With a scan tool, observe the Magna Steer Commanded Current and Magna Steer Feedback Current parameters in the Magna Steer data list. 4. Carefully test drive the vehicle so that the Magna Steer Commanded Current is greater than 826 mA. Does the scan tool indicate that the Magna Steer Feedback Current is greater than the specified value?	155 mA	Go to Intermittent	Go to Step 3
3	1. Turn OFF the ignition. 2. Disconnect the variable effort steering actuator connector. 3. Measure the resistance across the variable effort steering actuator. Does the resistance measure within the specified range?	1.6–3.1 Ω	Go to Step 5	Go to Step 4
4	Test both variable effort steering control circuits for a high resistance or an open between the variable effort steering actuator pigtail connector and the variable effort steering actuator. Did you find and correct the condition?	—	Go to Step 13	Go to Step 8
5	Test both variable effort steering control circuits for a short between the variable effort steering actuator pigtail connector and the variable effort steering actuator housing. Did you find and correct the condition?	—	Go to Step 13	Go to Step 6

GC6010000022020X

Fig. 30 Code C1241: Speed Sensitive Steering Circuit Fault (Part 2 of 3). 2001–05 DeVille & Seville

Circuit Description

The EBCM controls a bi-directional magnetic rotary solenoid. The solenoid is in the steering gear. The solenoid adjusts the amount of power steering assist in order to achieve a given level of driver effort in turning the vehicle. The EBCM varies the steering assist by adjusting the current flow through the solenoid. The amount of steering assist adjusted for steering is dependent upon vehicle speed. As the vehicle speed increases, the following actions occur:

- The steering assist decreases
- The driver effort increases.

As the vehicle speed decreases, the following actions occur:

- The steering assist increases
- The driver effort decreases.

Conditions for Running the DTC

The ignition is ON.

Conditions for Setting the DTC

The EBCM detects an open or short in the VES circuit when the feedback current is less than 360 mA while the absolute value of the commanded current is greater than 826 mA for 2.5 seconds.

Action Taken When the DTC Sets

- The EBCM disables the variable effort steering (VES) for the duration of the ignition cycle.
- The DIC displays the SERVICE STEERING SYS message.

Conditions for Clearing the DTC

- The condition for the DTC is no longer present (the DTC is not current) and you used the scan tool Clear DTC function.
- The condition for the DTC is no longer present (the DTC is not current) and you used the On-Board Diagnostics Clear DTC function.
- The EBCM automatically clears the history DTC when a current DTC is not detected in 50 consecutive drive cycles.

Diagnostic Aids

The vehicle may need to be driven to view non-zero values of the Magna Steer Commanded Current and Magna Steer Feedback Current on the scan tool.

Test Description

The numbers below refer to the step numbers on the diagnostic table.

2. This step uses the scan tool to check the Magna Steer Feedback Current parameter.
6. This step checks for an open in the variable effort steering actuator and circuit.

GC6010000023010X

Fig. 31 Code C1241: Magnasteer Fault (Part 1 of 3). Eldorado

Step	Action	Value(s)	Yes	No
6	1. Turn OFF the ignition. 2. Reconnect the variable effort steering actuator connector. 3. Disconnect the EBCM harness connector. 4. Install the J 39700 universal pinout box using the J 39700-300 cable adapter to the EBCM harness connector only. 5. Measure the resistance at the J 39700 universal pinout box between the variable effort steering control circuits. Does the resistance measure within the specified range?	1.6–5 Ω	Go to Step 7	Go to Step 9
7	Test both variable effort steering control circuits for a short to ground or short to voltage between the EBCM and the variable effort steering actuator pigtail connector. Did you find and correct the condition?	—	Go to Step 13	Go to Step 12
8	Inspect for poor connections at the harness connector of the variable effort steering actuator. Did you find and correct the condition?	—	Go to Step 13	Go to Step 11
9	Inspect for poor connections at the harness connector of the EBCM. Did you find and correct the condition?	—	Go to Step 13	Go to Step 10
10	Test for and repair one of the following conditions in the suspect variable effort steering control circuit between the EBCM and the variable effort steering actuator pigtail connector. • An open • A high resistance • A short between the control circuits Did you complete the repair?	—	Go to Step 13	
11	Replace the variable effort steering actuator. Did you complete the repair?	—	Go to Step 13	
12	**Important:** Perform the setup procedure for the EBCM. An unprogrammed EBCM will result in the following conditions: • Inoperative or poorly functioning DRP/ABS/TCS/VSES/VES (if equipped) • Set DTC C1248 EBCM Turned the Red Brake Warning Indicator On • Set DTC C1255m3 EBCM Internal Malfunction Replace the EBCM. Did you complete the repair?	—	Go to Step 13	
13	1. Use the scan tool in order to clear the DTCs. 2. Operate the vehicle within the Conditions for Running the DTC as specified in the supporting text. Does the DTC reset?	—	Go to Step 2	System OK

GC6010000022030X

Fig. 30 Code C1241: Speed Sensitive Steering Circuit Fault (Part 3 of 3). 2001–05 DeVille & Seville

Step	Action	Value(s)	Yes	No
1	Did you perform the Variable Effort Steering Diagnostic System Check?	—	Go to Step 2	Go to A Diagnostic System Check - Variable Effort Steering
2	1. Install a scan tool. 2. Start the engine. 3. With the scan tool, observe the Magna Steer Commanded Current and Magna Steer Feedback Current parameters in the Delco/Bosch ABS/TCS ICCS (if equipped) data list. 4. Carefully test drive the vehicle so that the Magna Steer Commanded Current is greater than 826 mA. Does the scan tool indicate that the Magna Steer Feedback Current is greater than the specified value?	360 mA	Go to Testing for Intermittent and Poor Connections in Wiring Systems	Go to Step 3
3	1. Turn OFF the ignition. 2. Disconnect the variable effort steering actuator connector. 3. Measure the resistance across the variable effort steering actuator. Does the resistance measure within the specified range?	1.6–3.1 Ω	Go to Step 5	Go to Step 4
4	Test both variable effort steering control circuits for a high resistance or an open between the variable effort steering actuator pigtail connector and the variable effort steering actuator. Did you find and correct the condition?	—	Go to Step 13	Go to Step 8
5	Test both variable effort steering control circuits for a short between the variable effort steering actuator pigtail connector and the variable effort steering actuator housing. Refer to Circuit Testing and Wiring Repairs in Wiring System. Did you find and correct the condition?	—	Go to Step 13	Go to Step 6
6	1. Turn OFF the ignition. 2. Reconnect the variable effort steering actuator connector. 3. Disconnect the EBCM harness connector. 4. Install the J 39700 universal pinout box using the J 39700-25 cable adapter to the EBCM harness connector only. 5. Measure the resistance at the J 39700 universal pinout box between the variable effort steering control circuits. Does the resistance measure within the specified range?	1.6–5 Ω	Go to Step 7	Go to Step 9
7	Test both variable effort steering control circuits for a short to ground or short to voltage between the EBCM and the variable effort steering actuator pigtail connector. Did you find and correct the condition?	—	Go to Step 13	Go to Step 12
8	Inspect for poor connections at the harness connector of the variable effort steering actuator. Did you find and correct the condition?	—	Go to Step 13	Go to Step 11
9	Inspect for poor connections at the harness connector of the EBCM. Did you find and correct the condition?	—	Go to Step 13	Go to Step 10

GC6010000023020X

Fig. 31 Code C1241: Magnasteer Fault (Part 2 of 3). Eldorado

Step	Action	Value(s)	Yes	No
10	Test for and repair one of the following conditions in the suspect variable effort steering control circuit between the EBCM and the variable effort steering actuator pigtail connector. • An open • A high resistance • A short between the control circuits Did you complete the repair?	—	Go to *Step 13*	—
11	Replace the variable effort steering actuator. Did you complete the repair?	—	Go to *Step 13*	—
12	Replace the EBCM. Did you complete the repair?	—	Go to *Step 13*	—
13	1. Use the scan tool in order to clear the DTCs. 2. Operate the vehicle within the Conditions for Running the DTC as specified in the supporting text. Does the DTC reset?	—	Go to *Step 2*	System OK

GC6010000023030X

Fig. 31   Code C1241: Magnasteer Fault (Part 3 of 3). Eldorado

Step	Action	Values	Yes	No
1	Did you perform the Variable Effort Steering Diagnostic System Check?	--	Go to Step 2	Diagnostic System Check - Variable Effort Steering
2	1. Install a scan tool. 2. Start the engine. 3. With a scan tool, observe the VES Commanded Current and VES Feedback Current data parameters in the VES data list for the EBCM. Does the scan tool display the VES Commanded and Feedback current data parameters are within .03 amps of each other and within specified range?	Before VIN 01253 = 0.60 to 0.65 amps After VIN 01253 = .90 amps	Go to Step 3	Go to Step 4
3	Using the scan tool, select F2: VES Test. Does the scan tool indicate, Test Passed?	--	Test for Intermittent and Poor Connections	Go to Step 4
4	1. Turn OFF the ignition. 2. Disconnect the VES actuator harness connector. 3. Measure the resistance of the VES actuator. Does the resistance measure within specified range?	5.7-7.2 ohms	Go to Step 5	Go to Step 10
5	Test the control circuit of the VES actuator for a short to ground. Did you find and correct the condition?	--	Go to Step 13	Go to Step 6

ARM66GC000000448

Fig. 32   Code C1241: Variable Effort Steering Actuator Circuit (Part 2 of 3). CTS

Circuit Description

The Electronic Brake Control Module (EBCM) commands current from 0-1 amp to the VES actuator, depending on vehicle speed. At low speeds, 1 amp of current is commanded to the actuator and the actuator valve is in the retracted position. At high speeds, no current is commanded to the actuator and the valve moves closer to the power steering fluid orifice. The EBCM monitors and compares the commanded and feedback current parameters to detect malfunctions in the VES system.

Conditions for Running the DTC

- Ignition voltage between 10.5-17.0 volts
- Off state test - Initial ignition ON, no engine rpm or vehicle speed present.
- On state test - If off state test passes, engine rpm and vehicle speed present.

Conditions for Setting the DTC

AN open, short to ground or short to voltage in the VES actuator or the circuits to the actuator.

Action Taken When the DTC Sets

- A DTC C1241 is stored in memory.
- The DIC displays the SERVICE STEERING SYSTEM warning message.
- The VES system is disabled for the remainder of the ignition cycle.

Conditions for Clearing the DTC

- A current DTC will clear when the malfunction is no longer present.
- A history DTC will clear after 100 consecutive ignition cycles with the malfunction no longer present.
- Using a scan tool

Diagnostic Aids

The vehicle may need to be driven to view full VES Commanded and Feedback data parameters

Test Description

The numbers below refer to the step numbers on the diagnostic table.

2. Tests if the commanded and feedback current parameters are within specification in there active state

3. Perform the VES test located under Special Functions. This test may indicate if the VES actuator is mechanically bound.

ARM66GC000000447

Fig. 32   Code C1241: Variable Effort Steering Actuator Circuit (Part 1 of 3). CTS

Step	Action		Yes	No
6	Test the control circuit of the VES actuator for an open or short to voltage. Did you find and correct the condition?	-	Go to Step 13	Go to Step 7
7	Test the return circuit of the VES actuator for a short to ground. Did you find and correct the condition.	-	Go to Step 13	Go to Step 8
8	Test the return circuit of the VES actuator for an open or a short to voltage. Did you find and correct the condition?	-	Go to Step 13	Go to Step 9
9	Inspect for poor connections at the harness connector of the EBCM. Did you find and correct the condition?	-	Go to Step 13	Go to Step 11
10	Inspect for poor connections at the harness connector of the VES actuator. Did you find and correct the condition?	-	Go to Step 13	Go to Step 12
11	**Important** Always perform the setup procedure for the EBCM. 1. Replace the EBCM. 2. Perform the setup procedure for the EBCM. Did you complete the replacement?	-	Go to Step 13	--
12	Replace the VES actuator. Did you complete the replacement?	-	Go to Step 13	--
13	1. Use the scan tool in order to clear the DTCs. 2. Operate the vehicle within the Conditions for Running the DTC. Does the DTC reset?	-	Go to Step 2	System OK

ARM66GC000000449

Fig. 32   Code C1241: Variable Effort Steering Actuator Circuit (Part 3 of 3). CTS

Part 1

Step	Action	Value(s)	Yes	No
1	Was the ABS Diagnostic System Check performed?	—	Go to Step 2	Refer to Anti-Lock Brakes
2	1. Start the engine. 2. Using a scan tool, select DATA LIST and monitor the steering wheel sensor voltage while rotating the steering wheel from stop-to-stop. Is the voltage within the range specified?	0-.5V	Go to Step 5	Go to Step 3
3	Is the voltage from Step 2 within the range specified in the Value(s) column?	4.7-5V	Go to Step 14	Go to Step 4
4	Does the voltage from Step 2 vary?	—	Go to Step 21	Go to Step 1
5	1. Turn the ignition switch to the OFF position. 2. Disconnect the steering wheel position sensor. 3. Disconnect the ECBM harness connector. 4. Using the J 39200, measure the resistance between the ECBM harness connector terminals 17 and 5. Is the resistance within the range specified in the Value(s) column?	Infinite	Go to Step 6	Go to Step 29
6	Using the J 39200, measure the resistance between the ECBM harness connector terminals 1 and 5. Is the resistance within the range specified in the Value(s) column?	Infinite	Go to Step 7	Go to Step 30
7	Using the J 39200, measure the resistance between the ECBM harness connector terminal 17 and ground. Is the resistance within the range specified in the Value(s) column?	Infinite	Go to Step 8	Go to Step 31
8	Using the J 39200, measure the resistance between the ECBM harness connector terminal 1 and ground. Is the resistance within the range specified in the Value(s) column?	Infinite	Go to Step 9	Go to Step 32
9	Using the J 39200, measure the resistance between the ECBM harness connector terminal 1 and the steering wheel position sensor harness connector terminal A. Is the resistance within the range specified in the Value(s) column?	0-2 Ω	Go to Step 10	Go to Step 33
10	Using the J 39200, measure the resistance between the ECBM harness connector terminal 17 and the steering wheel position sensor harness connector terminal B. Is the resistance within the range specified in the Value(s) column?	0-2 Ω	Go to Step 11	Go to Step 34

GC6029800352010X

Fig. 33   Code C1243: Steering Wheel Position Sensor Circuit Fault (Part 1 of 5). Alero & Grand Am

Part 2

Step	Action	Value(s)	Yes	No
11	Inspect the ECBM harness connector terminals 1 and 17 and all steering wheel position sensor terminals for poor terminal contact. Is poor terminal contact evident?	—	Go to Step 35	Go to Step 12
12	1. Reconnect the ECBM harness connector. 2. Turn the ignition switch to the RUN position. 3. Using the J 39200, measure the voltage between the steering wheel position sensor harness connector terminals A and C. Is the voltage greater than the value listed in the Value(s) column?	4.0V	Go to Step 41	Go to Step 13
13	1. Turn the ignition switch to the OFF position. 2. Inspect CKTs 1056, 1059, and 556 for damage which may result in shorts between the circuits or shorts to ground. Repair damage if evident. 3. Reconnect all connectors. 4. Turn the ignition switch to the RUN position. Is DTC C1243 set as a current DTC?	—	Go to Step 42	Refer to Anti-Lock Brakes
14	1. Turn the ignition switch to the OFF position. 2. Disconnect steering wheel position sensor. 3. Turn the ignition switch to the RUN position. Does the scan tool display the steering wheel position sensor voltage within the range specified in the Value(s) column?	0-1V	Go to Step 15	Go to Step 16
15	Using the J 39200, measure the resistance between the steering wheel sensor harness connector terminal C and ground. Is the resistance within the range specified in the Value(s) column?	0-5 Ω	Go to Step 41	Go to Step 18
16	1. Turn the ignition switch to the OFF position. 2. Disconnect ECBM harness connector. 3. Turn the ignition switch to the RUN position. 4. Using the J 39200, measure the voltage between the ECBM harness connector terminal 17 and ground. Is the voltage within the range specified in the Value(s) column?	0-1V	Go to Step 17	Go to Step 38
17	1. Turn the ignition switch to the OFF position. 2. Inspect CKT 1059 for any damage which may result in a short to voltage with all connectors connected. Repair any damage if evident. 3. Reconnect all connectors. 4. Turn the ignition switch to the RUN position. Is DTC C1243 set as a current DTC?	—	Go to Step 42	Refer to Anti-Lock Brakes

GC6029800352020X

Fig. 33   Code C1243: Steering Wheel Position Sensor Circuit Fault (Part 2 of 5). Alero & Grand Am

Part 3

Step	Action	Value(s)	Yes	No
18	1. Turn the ignition switch to the OFF position. 2. Disconnect ECBM harness connector. 3. Using the J 39200, measure the resistance between the steering wheel position sensor harness connector terminal C and the ECBM harness connector terminal 5. Is the resistance within the range specified in the Value(s) column?	0-2 Ω	Go to Step 19	Go to Step 36
19	1. Turn the ignition switch to the RUN position. 2. Using the J 39200, measure the voltage between the ECBM harness connector terminal 5 and ground. Is the voltage within the range specified in the Value(s) column?	0-1V	Go to Step 20	Go to Step 37
20	1. Turn the ignition switch to the OFF position. 2. Inspect the ECBM harness connector and the steering wheel position sensor terminals for poor terminal contact, Replace any terminals with poor terminal contact. 3. Inspect all steering wheel position sensor circuits for damage which may result in a short to voltage or an open with all connectors connected. Repair damage if evident. 4. Reconnect all connectors. 5. Turn the ignition switch to the RUN position. Is DTC C1243 set as a current DTC?	—	Go to Step 42	Refer to "Diagnosis & Testing" in "Anti-lock Brakes"
21	1. Turn the ignition switch to the RUN position. 2. Using the J 39200, measure the voltage by backprobing between the steering wheel position sensor harness connector terminals A and C. Is the voltage within the range listed in the Value(s) column?	4.5-5.5V	Go to Step 22	Go to Step 23
22	1. Turn the ignition switch to the OFF position. 2. Disconnect the steering wheel position sensor. 3. Turn the ignition switch to the RUN position. 4. Using the J 39200, measure the voltage by backprobing between the steering wheel position sensor harness connector terminals A and C. Is the voltage within the range listed in the Value(s) column?	4.5-5.5V	Go to Step 27	Go to Step 41
23	1. Turn the ignition switch to the OFF position. 2. Disconnect the ECBM harness connector. 3. Disconnect the steering wheel position sensor harness connector. 4. Measure the resistance between the ECBM harness connector terminals 1 and 17. Is the resistance within the range specified in the Value(s) column?	Infinite	Go to Step 24	Go to Step 40

GC6029800352030X

Fig. 33   Code C1243: Steering Wheel Position Sensor Circuit Fault (Part 3 of 5). Alero & Grand Am

Part 4

Step	Action	Value(s)	Yes	No
24	Using the MIN/MAX function of the J 39200, measure the resistance between the steering wheel position sensor terminals A and B while rotating the steering wheel slowly from stop-to-stop. Is the resistance within the range specified in the Value(s) column?	390-12,000 Ω	Go to Step 25	Go to Step 41
25	1. Inspect CKTs 1056 and 1059 for damage which may result in a short between the two circuits with all connectors connected. Repair damage if evident. 2. Reconnect all connectors. 3. Being very careful not to move the steering wheel, turn the ignition switch to the RUN position. Is DTC C1243 set as a current DTC?	—	Go to Step 42	Go to Step 26
26	Turn the steering wheel slowly from stop-to-stop. Is DTC C1243 set as a current DTC?	—	Go to Step 41	Refer to Anti-Lock Brakes
27	1. Turn the ignition switch to the OFF position. 2. Disconnect the ECBM harness connector. 3. Turn the ignition switch to the RUN position. 4. Using the J 39200, measure the voltage between the ECBM harness connector terminal 1 and ground. Is the voltage within the the range listed in the Value(s) column?	4.5-5.5V	Go to Step 39	Go to Step 28
28	1. Turn the ignition switch to the OFF position. 2. Inspect CKT 1056 for any damage which may result in a short to voltage with all connectors connected. Repair damage if evident. 3. Reconnect all connectors. 4. Turn the ignition switch to the RUN position. Is DTC C1243 set as a current DTC?	—	Go to Step 42	Refer to Anti-Lock Brakes
29	Repair the short between CKTs 1059 and 556. Is the repair complete?	—	Refer to Anti-Lock Brakes	—
30	Repair the short between CKTs 1056 and 556. Is the repair complete?	—	Refer to Anti-Lock Brakes	—
31	Repair the short to ground in CKT 1059. Is the repair complete?	—	Refer to Anti-Lock Brakes	—
32	Repair the short to ground in CKT 1056. Is the repair complete?	—	Refer to Anti-Lock Brakes	—

GC6029800352040X

Fig. 33   Code C1243: Steering Wheel Position Sensor Circuit Fault (Part 4 of 5). Alero & Grand Am

Step	Action	Value(s)	Yes	No
33	Repair the open or high resistance in CKT 1056. Is the repair complete?	—	Refer to Anti-Lock Brakes	—
34	Repair the open or high resistance in CKT 1059. Is the repair complete?	—	Refer to Anti-Lock Brakes	—
35	Replace the terminals that exhibit poor contact. Is the repair complete?	—	Refer to Anti-Lock Brakes	—
36	Repair the open or high resistance in CKT 556. Is the repair complete?	—	Refer to Anti-Lock Brakes	—
37	Repair the short to voltage in CKT 556. Is the repair complete?	—	Refer to Anti-Lock Brakes	—
38	Repair the short to voltage in CKT 1059. Is the repair complete?	—	Refer to Anti-Lock Brakes	—
39	Repair the short to voltage in CKT 1056. Is the repair complete?	—	Refer to Anti-Lock Brakes	—
40	Repair the short between CKTs 1056 and 1059. Is the repair complete?	—	Refer to Anti-Lock Brakes	—
41	Replace the steering wheel position sensor. Is the repair complete?	—	Refer to Anti-Lock Brakes	—
42	Replace the ECBM. Is the repair complete?	—	Refer to Anti-Lock Brakes	—

GC6029800352050X

Fig. 33   Code C1243: Steering Wheel Position Sensor Circuit Fault (Part 5 of 5). Alero & Grand Am

Step	Action	Value(s)	Yes	No
9	1. Inspect the ECBM harness connector and the 2-way EVO actuator harness connector for poor terminal contact or corrosion. Replace any terminals with poor terminal contact or corrosion. 2. Inspect CKT 1295 for damage which may result in a short to ground or an open with all connectors connected. Repair the damage if evident. 3. Reconnect all connectors. 4. Turn the ignition switch to the RUN position. Is DTC C1273 set as a current DTC?	—	Check wiring circuit for damage or loose connections	Check wiring circuit for damage or loose connections
10	Repair the open or high resistance in CKT 1295. Is the repair complete?	—	Refer to ABS	—
11	Repair the short to ground in CKT 1295. Is the repair complete?	—	Refer to ABS	—
12	Repair the open or high resistance in CKT 1294/1633. Is the repair complete?	—	Refer to ABS	—
13	Repair short to ground in CKT 1633/1294 or 855. Is the repair complete?	—	Refer to ABS	—
14	Malfunction is intermittent.	—	Go to Diagnostic Aids	Go to Diagnostic Aids
15	Replace the EVO actuator. Is the repair complete?	—	Refer to ABS	—
16	Replace the ECBM. Is the repair complete?	—	Refer to ABS	—

GC6029800353020X

Fig. 34   Code C1273: Actuator Circuit Open Or Shorted To Ground (Part 2 of 2). Alero & Grand Am

Step	Action	Value(s)	Yes	No
1	Was the ABS Diagnostic System Check performed?	—	Go to Step 2	Refer to ABS
2	1. Turn the ignition switch to the RUN position. 2. Using the scan tool, select MISC. TESTS, select VES MANUAL CONTROL function, and command EVO actuator ON. Is the feedback current greater than the value listed in the Value(s) column?	100 mA	Go to Step 14	Go to Step 3
3	1. Turn the ignition switch to the OFF position. 2. Disconnect the ECBM harness connector. 3. Disconnect the 2-way EVO actuator connector. 4. Using the J 39200, measure the resistance between the 2-way EVO actuator harness connector terminal B and the ECBM harness connector terminal 18. Is the resistance within the range specified in the Value(s) column?	0-2 Ω	Go to Step 4	Go to Step 10
4	Using the J 39200, measure the resistance between the ECBM harness connector terminal 18 and ground. Is the resistance within the range specified in the Value(s) column?	Infinite	Go to Step 5	Go to Step 11
5	Using the J 39200, measure the resistance between the 2-way EVO actuator harness connector terminal A and the ECBM harness connector terminal C. Is the resistance within the range specified in the Value(s) column?	0-2 Ω	Go to Step 6	Go to Step 12
6	Using the J 39200, measure the resistance between the ECBM harness connector terminal C and ground. Is the resistance within the range specified in the Value(s) column?	Infinite	Go to Step 7	Go to Step 13
7	1. Reconnect the EVO actuator connector. 2. Using the J 39200, measure the resistance between the ECBM harness connector terminal 18 and ground. Is the resistance within the range specified in the Value(s) column?	Infinite	Go to Step 8	Go to Step 15
8	Using the J 39200, measure the resistance between the ECBM harness connector terminals 18 and C. Is the resistance within the range specified in the Value(s) column?	7-19 Ω	Go to Step 9	Go to Step 15

GC6029800353010X

Fig. 34   Code C1273: Actuator Circuit Open Or Shorted To Ground (Part 1 of 2). Alero & Grand Am

Step	Action	Value(s)	Yes	No
1	Was the ABS Diagnostic System Check performed?	—	Go to Step 2	Refer to ABS
2	1. Turn the ignition switch to the OFF position. 2. Disconnect the ECBM harness connector. 3. Turn the ignition switch to the RUN position. 4. Using the J 39200, measure the voltage between the ECBM harness connector terminal 18 and ground. Is the voltage within the range specified in the Value(s) column?	0-1V	Go to Step 3	Go to Step 6
3	1. Turn the ignition switch to the OFF position. 2. Using the J 39200, measure the resistance between the ECBM harness connector terminals 18 and C. Is the resistance within the range specified in the Value(s) column?	7-19 Ω	Go to Step 4	Go to Step 5
4	1. Inspect the ECBM harness connector and the 2-way EVO actuator harness connector for damage which may result in a short to voltage or an open with all connectors connected. Repair the damage if evident. 2. Reconnect all connectors. 3. Start the engine. Wait 10 seconds. Does DTC C1274 set as a current DTC?	—	Go to Step 10	Go to Step 8
5	1. Disconnect the 2-way EVO actuator connector. 2. Using the J 39200, measure the resistance between the ECBM harness connector terminals 18 and C. Is the resistance within the range specified in the Value(s) column?	Infinite	Go to Step 9	Go to Step 7
6	Repair the short to voltage in CKT 1295. Is the repair complete?	—	Refer to ABS	—
7	Repair the short between CKTs 1295 and 1294/1633. Is the repair complete?	—	Refer to ABS	—
8	Malfunction is intermittent.	—	—	—
9	Replace the EVO actuator. Is the repair complete?	—	Refer to ABS	—
10	Replace the ECBM. Is the repair complete?	—	Refer to ABS	—

GC6029800354000X

Fig. 35   Code C1274: Actuator Circuit Shorted Or Solenoid Shorted. Alero & Grand Am

Circuit Description

The vehicle stability enhancement system (VSES) is activated by the EBCM calculating the desired yaw rate and comparing it to the actual yaw rate input. The desired yaw rate is calculated from measured steering wheel position, vehicle speed, and lateral acceleration. The difference between the desired yaw rate and actual yaw rate is the yaw rate error, which is a measurement of oversteer or understeer. If the yaw rate error becomes too large, the EBCM will attempt to correct the vehicle's yaw motion by applying differential braking to the left or right front wheel.

The VSES activations generally occur during aggressive driving, in the turns or bumpy roads without much use of the accelerator pedal. When braking during VSES activation, the brake pedal will feel different than the ABS pedal pulsation. The brake pedal pulsates at a higher frequency during VSES activation.

The usable output voltage range for the lateral accelerometer and yaw rate sensors is 0.25-4.75 volts. The scan tool will report zero lateral acceleration or yaw rate as 2.5 volts with no sensor bias present. The sensor bias compensates for sensor mounting alignment errors, electronic signal errors, temperature changes, and manufacturing differences.

The steering wheel position sensor supplies 2 analog inputs, Phase A and Phase B, to the EBCM. The 2 input signals are approximately 90 degrees out of phase. By interpreting the relationship between the 2 inputs, the EBCM can determine the position of the steering wheel and the direction of steering wheel rotation.

Steer angle centering is the process by which the EBCM calibrates the steering sensor output so that the output reads zero when the steering wheel is centered. Using the yaw rate input, lateral accelerometer input, and wheel speed sensor inputs, the initial steering center position is calculated after driving greater than 10 km/h (6 mph) for more than 10 seconds in a straight line on a level surface.

Conditions for Running the DTC

The ignition is ON.

Conditions for Setting the DTC

C1287

One of the following conditions exists:

- The steering wheel position sensor is synchronized and the steer rate (speed that the steering wheel appears to be turning) is greater than 1100 degrees/second.
- The steer rate is less than 80 degrees/second and the difference in the phase angle between Phase A and Phase B is greater than 20 degrees.
- The 2 steering sensor signals (Phase A and Phase B) do not agree for 1 second. Under this condition, this DTC will set along with DTC C1281.

GC6020100464010X

Fig. 36   Codes C1287 & C1288: Yaw Rate Sensor Data Mismatch (Part 1 of 6). 2001 Alero & Grand Am

Step	Action	Value (s)	Yes	No
1	Did you perform the ABS Diagnostic System Check?	--	Go to Step 2	Perform Diagnostic System Check -
2	1. Install a scan tool. 2. Turn ON the ignition, with the engine OFF. 3. With the scan tool, perform the Steering Position Sensor Test. Did the SWPS pass the test?	--	Go to Diagnostic Aids	Go to Step 3
3	1. Turn OFF the ignition. 2. Disconnect the steering wheel position sensor (SWPS) connector. 3. Turn ON the ignition, with the engine OFF. 4. With the scan tool, observe the Dual Analog SWPS Input A parameter in the VSES data list. Does the scan tool indicate the Dual Analog SWPS Input A parameter is less than the specified value?	0.2 V	Go to Step 4	Go to Step 13
4	With the scan tool, observe the Dual Analog SWPS Input B parameter. Does the scan tool indicate the Dual Analog SWPS Input B parameter is less than the specified value?	0.2 V	Go to Step 5	Go to Step 14
5	1. Turn OFF the ignition. 2. Connect a 3 amp fused jumper wire between the 5 volt reference circuit of the steering wheel position sensor (SWPS) and the signal A circuit of the steering wheel position sensor (SWPS). 3. Turn ON the ignition, with the engine OFF. 4. With the scan tool, observe the Dual Analog SWPS Input A parameter. Does the scan tool indicate that the Dual Analog SWPS Input A parameter is greater than the specified value?	4.9 V	Go to Step 6	Go to Step 10

GC6020100464030X

Fig. 36   Code C1287 & C1288: Yaw Rate Sensor Data Mismatch (Part 3 of 6). 2001 Alero & Grand Am

C1288

One of the following conditions exists:

- Both Phase A and Phase B are greater than 4.9 volts for 1.6 seconds.
- Both Phase A and Phase B are less than 0.2 volts for 1.6 seconds.
- The difference in the changes in Phase A and Phase B is greater than 35.2 degrees for 9.76 milliseconds.

Action Taken When the DTC Sets

- The EBCM disables the VSES for the duration of the ignition cycle.
- The DIC displays the Service Stability System message.
- The ABS/TCS remains functional.

Conditions for Clearing the DTC

- The condition for the DTC is no longer present and you used the scan tool Clear DTC function.
- The EBCM automatically clears the history DTC when a current DTC is not detected in 100 consecutive drive cycles.

Diagnostic Aids

- During diagnosis, park the vehicle on a level surface.
- Check the vehicle for proper alignment. The car should not pull in either direction while driving straight on a level surface.
- Find out from the driver under what conditions the DTC was set (when the DIC displayed the Service Stability System message). This information will help to duplicate the failure.
- The Snapshot function on the scan tool can help find an intermittent DTC.

Test Description

The numbers below refer to the step numbers on the diagnostic table.

2. Perform the Steering Position Sensor Test in order to verify if the steering wheel position sensor (SWPS) is operating properly.

3. Tests for the proper operation of the steering wheel position signal A circuit in the low voltage range.

4. Tests for the proper operation of the steering wheel position signal B circuit in the low voltage range.

5. Tests for the proper operation of the steering wheel position signal A circuit in the high voltage range. If the fuse in the jumper opens when you perform this test, the signal circuit is shorted to ground.

6. Tests for the proper operation of the steering wheel position signal B circuit in the high voltage range. If the fuse in the jumper opens when you perform this test, the signal circuit is shorted to ground.

7. Tests for a short to voltage in the 5 volt reference circuit.

8. Tests for a high resistance or an open in the low reference circuit.

GC6020100464020X

Fig. 36   Code C1287 & C1288: Yaw Rate Sensor Data Mismatch (Part 2 of 6). 2001 Alero & Grand Am

Step	Action	Value (s)	Yes	No
6	1. Turn OFF the ignition. 2. Disconnect the fused jumper wire. 3. Connect a 3 amp fused jumper wire between the 5 volt reference circuit of the steering wheel position sensor (SWPS) and the signal B circuit of the steering wheel position sensor (SWPS). 4. Turn ON the ignition, with the engine OFF. 5. With the scan tool, observe the Dual Analog SWPS Input B parameter. Does the scan tool indicate that the Dual Analog SWPS Input B parameter is greater than the specified value?	4.9 V	Go to Step 7	Go to Step 10
7	1. Disconnect the fused jumper wire. 2. Measure the voltage between the 5 volt reference circuit of the steering wheel position sensor (SWPS) and the low reference circuit of the steering wheel position sensor (SWPS). Does the voltage measure less the specified value?	5 V	Go to Step 8	Go to Step 9
8	1. Turn OFF the ignition. 2. Disconnect the negative battery cable. 3. Measure the resistance from the low reference circuit of the steering wheel position sensor (SWPS) to a good ground. Does the resistance measure less than the specified value?	5 ohms	Go to Step 16	Go to Step 15
9	Test the 5 volt reference circuit of the steering wheel position sensor (SWPS) for a short to voltage. Did you find and correct the condition?	--	Go to Step 20	Go to Step 17
10	Test the 5 volt reference circuit of the steering wheel position sensor (SWPS) for the following conditions: - An open - A short to ground - A high resistance Did you find and correct the condition?	--	Go to Step 20	Go to Step 11
11	Test the signal A circuit of the steering wheel position sensor (SWPS) for the following conditions: - An open - A short to ground - A high resistance Did you find and correct the condition?	--	Go to Step 20	Go to Step 12

GC6020100464040X

Fig. 36   Code C1287 & C1288: Yaw Rate Sensor Data Mismatch (Part 4 of 6). 2001 Alero & Grand Am

12	Test the signal B circuit of the steering wheel position sensor (SWPS) for the following conditions: • An open • A short to ground • A high resistance Did you find and correct the condition?	- Go to Step 20	- Go to Step 17
13	Test the signal A circuit of the steering wheel position sensor (SWPS) for a short to voltage. Did you find and correct the condition?	- Go to Step 20	- Go to Step 17
14	Test the signal B circuit of the steering wheel position sensor (SWPS) for a short to voltage. Did you find and correct the condition?	- Go to Step 20	- Go to Step 17
15	**Important** Removing battery voltage or ground from the EBCM will result in the following conditions: ○ Loss of the TIM learned tire inflation configuration parameters in the EBCM ○ The EBCM sets DTC C1245 When the diagnosis is complete, inspect the tire pressures and perform the TIM reset when. 1. Disconnect the EBCM harness connector. 2. Install the J 39700 universal pinout box using the J 39700-300 cable adapter to the EBCM harness connector only. 3. Test the low reference circuit of the steering wheel position sensor (SWPS) for a high resistance or an open. Did you find and correct the condition?	- Go to Step 20	- Go to Step 17
16	Inspect for poor connections at the harness connector of the steering wheel position sensor (SWPS). Did you find and correct the condition?	- Go to Step 20	- Go to Step 18

GC6020100464050X

Fig. 36 Code C1287 & C1288: Yaw Rate Sensor Data Mismatch (Part 5 of 6). 2001 Alero & Grand Am

Circuit Description

The Steering Position Sensor is a 5 volt sensor that is used by the Variable Effort Steering (VES) system to detect rapid steering wheel movement. The valid voltage range of the sensor is 0.39-4.86 V. The signal circuit voltage will increase and decrease within the valid voltage range as the steering wheel is turned. The Electronic Brake Control Module (EBCM) monitors the signal voltage from the steering position sensor. If the EBCM detects rapid steering wheel movement, during abrupt driving maneuvers, less current is commanded to the VES actuator to provide full steering assists.

Conditions for Running the DTC

The ignition is on, and ignition voltage is between 10.5-17.0 volts.

Conditions for Setting the DTC

• The steering position sensor signal voltage is less than 0.39 V or greater than 4.89 V for more than 2 seconds.
• The steering position sensor signal voltage changes by more than 2.5 V within 0.02 seconds.

Action Taken When the DTC Sets

• A DTC C1287 is stored in memory.
• The VES system is disabled for the remainder of the ignition cycle.

Conditions for Clearing the DTC

• A current DTC will clear when the malfunction is no longer present.
• A history DTC will clear after 100 consecutive malfunction free ignition cycles.
• Using the scan tool

Test Description

The numbers below refer to the step numbers on the diagnostic table.

2. Tests if the sensor is with in the valid voltage range.

3. Tests for the proper operation of the signal circuit in the low voltage range.

4. Tests for the proper operation of the signal circuit in the high voltage range. If the fuse in the jumper opens when you perform this test, the signal circuit is shorted to ground.

5. Tests for a short to voltage in the 5 volt reference circuit.

6. Tests for a high resistance or an open in the low reference circuit.

15. Perform the setup procedure after EBCM replacement.

GC6020100463010X

Fig. 37 Code C1287: Steering Position Sensor Shorted Or Open (Part 1 of 4). 2002 Alero & Grand Am

17	Inspect for poor connections at the harness connector of the EBCM. Did you find and correct the condition?	- Go to Step 20	- Go to Step 19
18	Replace the steering wheel position sensor (SWPS). Did you complete the repair?	- Go to Step 20	- --
19	**Important** Perform the setup procedure for the EBCM. An unprogrammed EBCM will result in the following conditions: • Inoperative or poorly functioning system operations • The EBCM sets DTC C1248 and DTC C1255m3 Did you complete the repair?	- Go to Step 20	- --
20	1. Clear the DTCs using the scan tool. 2. Operate the vehicle within the Conditions for Running the DTC as specified in the supporting text. Does the DTC reset?	- Go to Step 2	- System OK

GC6020100464060X

Fig. 36 Code C1287 & C1288: Yaw Rate Sensor Data Mismatch (Part 6 of 6). 2001 Alero & Grand Am

Step	Action	Value(s)	Yes	No
1	Did you perform the Variable Effort Steering Diagnostic System Check?	--	Go to Step 2	Perform Diagnostic System Check - Variable Effort Steering
2	1. Install a scan tool. 2. Turn ON the ignition, with the engine OFF. 3. With the scan tool, observe the Steering Position Sensor data parameter in the VES data list. Does the scan tool indicate that the Steering Position Sensor data parameter is within the specified range?	0.39 V-4.86 V	Test for Intermittent and Poor Connections	Go to Step 3
3	1. Turn OFF the ignition. 2. Disconnect the steering position sensor harness connector. 3. Turn ON the ignition, with the engine OFF. 4. With a scan tool, observe the Steering Position Sensor data parameter. Does the scan tool indicate that the Steering Position Sensor data parameter is less than the specified value?	0.39 V	Go to Step 4	Go to Step 10
4	1. Turn OFF the ignition. 2. Connect a 3 amp fused jumper wire between the 5 volt reference circuit and the signal circuit of the steering position sensor harness connector. 3. Turn ON the ignition, with the engine OFF. 4. With a scan tool, observe the Steering Position Sensor data parameter. Does the scan tool indicate that the Steering Position Sensor data parameter is greater than the specified value?	4.86 V	Go to Step 5	Go to Step 8

GC6020100463020X

Fig. 37 Code C1287: Steering Position Sensor Shorted Or Open (Part 2 of 4). 2002 Alero & Grand Am

Step	Action	Value	Yes	No
5	1. Disconnect the fused jumper wire. 2. Measure the voltage between the 5 volt reference circuit and the low reference circuit of the steering position sensor harness connector. Does the voltage measure less than the specified value?	5 V	Go to Step 6	Go to Step 7
6	1. Turn OFF the ignition. 2. Disconnect the negative battery cable. 3. Measure the resistance from the low reference circuit of the steering position sensor to a good ground. Does the resistance measure less than the specified value?	5 ohms	Go to Step 12	Go to Step 11
7	Test the 5 volt reference circuit of the steering position sensor for a short to voltage. Did you find and correct the condition?	--	Go to Step 16	Go to Step 13
8	Test the 5 volt reference circuit of the steering position sensor for a short to ground, a high resistance, or an open. Did you find and correct the condition?	--	Go to Step 16	Go to Step 9
9	Test the signal circuit of the steering position sensor for a short to ground, a high resistance, or an open. Did you find and correct the condition?	--	Go to Step 16	Go to Step 13
10	Test the signal circuit of the steering position sensor for a short to voltage. Did you find and correct the condition?	--	Go to Step 16	Go to Step 13
11	1. Disconnect the EBCM. 2. Test the low reference circuit of the steering position sensor for a high resistance or an open. Did you find and correct the condition?	--	Go to Step 16	Go to Step 13

GC6020100463030X

Fig. 37 Code C1287: Steering Position Sensor Shorted Or Open (Part 3 of 4). 2002 Alero & Grand Am

Step	Action	Yes	No
12	Inspect for poor connections at the harness connector of the steering position sensor. Did you find and correct the condition?	Go to Step 16	Go to Step 14
13	Inspect for poor connections at the harness connector of the EBCM. Did you find and correct the condition?	Go to Step 16	Go to Step 15
14	Replace the steering position sensor. Did you complete the replacement?	Go to Step 16	--
15	**Important** Perform the set up procedure for the EBCM. Replace the EBCM. Did you complete the replacement?	Go to Step 16	
16	1. Use the scan tool in order to clear the DTCs. 2. Operate the vehicle within the Conditions for Running the DTC as specified in the supporting text. Does the DTC reset?	Go to Step 2	System OK

GC6020100463040X

Fig. 37 Code C1287: Steering Position Sensor Shorted Or Open (Part 4 of 4). 2002 Alero & Grand Am

1 - NUT, HEXAGON SLOTTED
2 - PIN, COTTER
3 - SEAL, TIE ROD
5 - ROD ASM, OUTER TIE
6 - FITTING, LUBRICATION
7 - NUT, HEX JAM
8 - CLAMP, TIE ROD END
10 - BOOT, RACK & PINION
11 - CLAMP, BOOT
12 - ROD ASM, INNER TIE
13 - RING, SHOCK DAMPENER
15 - NUT, ADJUSTER PLUG LOCK
23 - SEAL, O-RING
25 - LINE ASM, CYLINDER (RH)
26 - LINE ASM, CYLINDER (LH)
30 - GEAR ASM, RACK & PINION (PARTIAL)
33 - COVER, DUST (ADD)
35 - TUBE, BREATHER

GC6029500134020A

Fig. 38 Exploded view of power rack & pinion steering (Part 2 of 2). Aurora

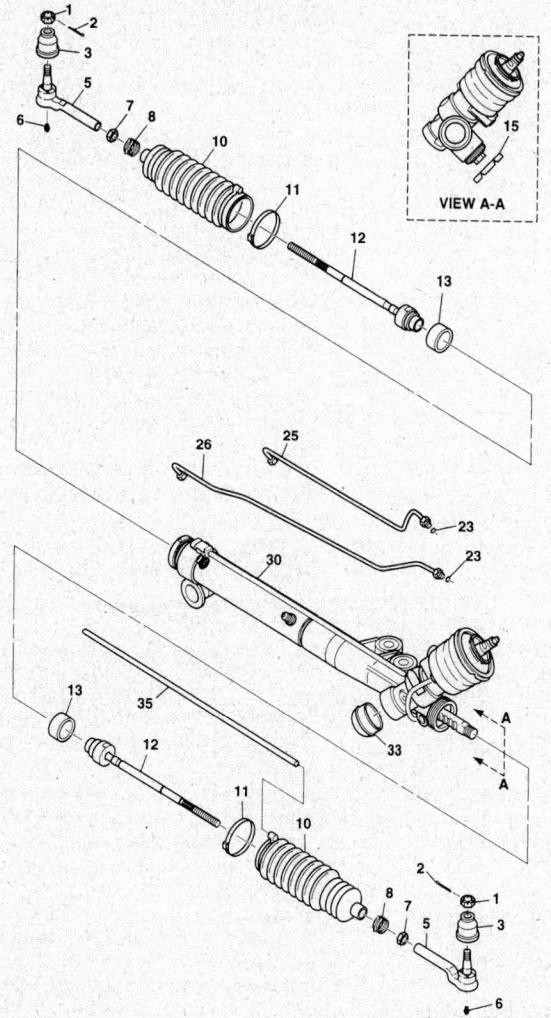

GC6029500134010A

Fig. 38 Exploded view of power rack & pinion steering (Part 1 of 2). Aurora

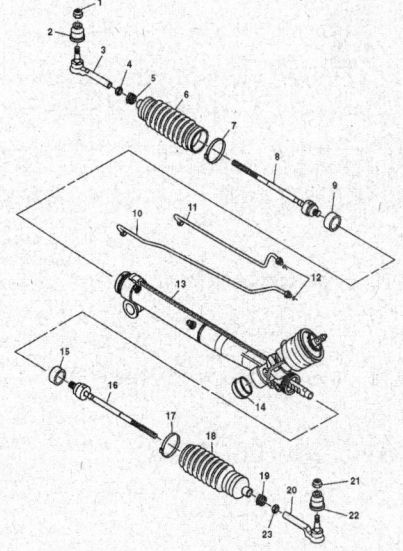

(1) Prevailing Torque Nut
(2) Tie Rod Seal
(3) Outer Tie Rod Assembly
(4) Hex Jam Nut
(5) Tie Rod End Clamp
(6) Rack and Pinion Boot
(7) Boot Clamp
(8) Inner Tie Rod Assembly
(9) Shock Dampener Ring
(10) Cylinder Line Assembly (LH)
(11) Cylinder Line Assembly (RH)
(12) O-ring Seal
(13) Rack and Pinion Gear Assembly (Partial)
(14) Dust Cover
(15) Shock Dampener Ring
(16) Inner Tie Rod Assembly
(17) Boot Clamp
(18) Rack and Pinion Boot
(19) Tie Rod End Clamp
(20) Outer Tie Rod Assembly
(21) Prevailing Torque Nut
(22) Tie Rod Seal
(23) Hex Jam Nut

GC6029800362000X

Fig. 39 Exploded view of power rack & pinion steering. Corvette & Intrigue

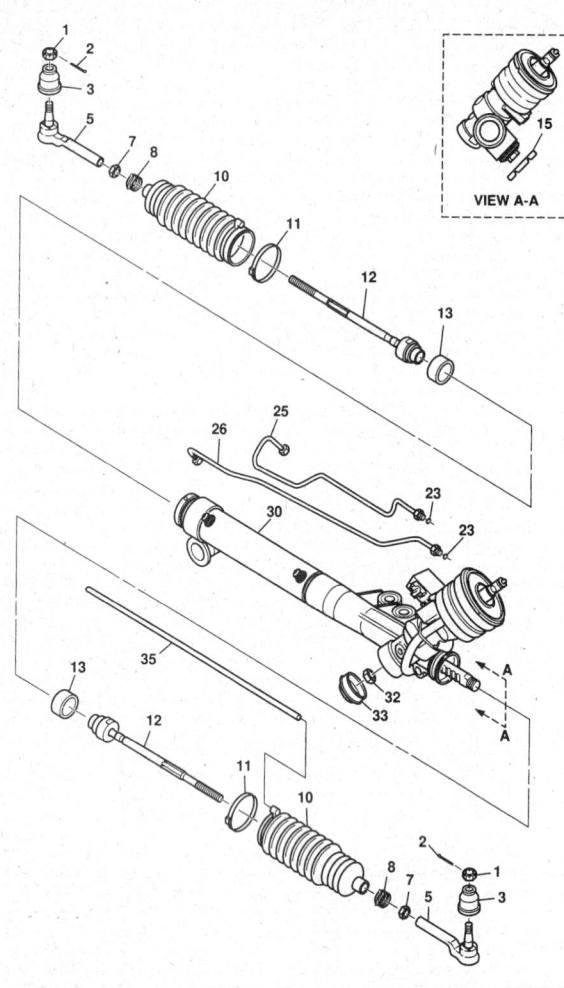

1 - NUT, HEXAGON SLOTTED	20 - SEAL, STUB SHAFT
2 - PIN, COTTER	21 - ANNULUS ASM, BEARING
3 - SEAL, TIE ROD	22 - PLUG ASM, O-RING
5 - ROD ASM, OUTER TIE	23 - SEAL, O-RING
7 - NUT, HEX JAM	25 - LINE ASM, CYLINDER (RH)
8 - CLAMP, TIE ROD END	26 - LINE ASM, CYLINDER (LH)
10 - BOOT, RACK & PINION	27 - BRACKET ASM, MOUNTING
11 - CLAMP, BOOT	28 - GROMMET, MOUNTING
12 - ROD ASM, INNER TIE	30 - GEAR ASM, RACK & PINION (PARTIAL)
13 - RING, SHOCK DAMPENER	32 - NUT, HEX LOCK
15 - NUT, ADJUSTER PLUG LOCK	33 - COVER, DUST
16 - ADAPTER, SEAL	35 - TUBE, BREATHER
17 - RING, RETAINING	

GC6029800386020X

Fig. 40 Exploded view of power rack & pinion steering (Part 2 of 2). DeVille, Eldorado & Seville

GC6029800386010X

Fig. 40 Exploded view of power rack & pinion steering (Part 1 of 2). DeVille, Eldorado & Seville

POWER STEERING SYSTEM SERVICE

Component Service

For procedures not covered in this section, refer to "Saginaw Rack & Pinion Power Steering Gear Less Speed Sensitive Steering."

POWER STEERING GEAR

Refer to **Figs. 38 through 41,** for exploded views of power steering gears.

EBCM

1. Disconnect EBCM from bracket using pressure tabs.
2. Disconnect EBCM electrical connectors.
3. Remove EBCM.
4. Reverse procedure to install.

VARIABLE EFFORT STEERING PROGRAMMING

Refer to **Figs. 42 and 43,** for variable effort steering programming procedures.

POWER STEERING SYSTEM BLEED

AURORA

1. Turn ignition switch to Off position.
2. Raise and support front of vehicle with tires clear ground.
3. Rotate steering wheel to full lefthand turn.
4. Fill power steering fluid reservoir to full cold level. Leave reservoir cap off.
5. Turn steering wheel lock-to-lock at least 40 times with engine stopped while an assistant inspects fluid level and condition. **Ensure fluid level remains at full cold level.**
6. If any bubbles appear, inspect for loose fluid line connections.
7. Start and idle engine, ensuring fluid is kept at proper level.
8. Install reservoir cap.
9. Turn steering wheel until front tires reach center position.
10. Lower vehicle and allow engine to idle for two minutes.
11. Turn steering wheel in both directions, ensuring it rotates smoothly and noiselessly.
12. Ensure fluid remains at proper level, has no bubbles, foam or discoloration and does not leak.
13. If bubbles, discoloration or foam appear in fluid, proceed as follows:
    a. Turn ignition switch to Off position.
    b. Wait two minutes, and inspect hose connections.
    c. Start and idle engine while maintaining fluid at proper level.
    d. Install reservoir cap.
    e. Turn steering wheel in both directions, ensuring it rotates smoothly and noiselessly.
    f. If fluid fault condition persists, inspect and replace return hose clamps and O-rings, pressure hose O-rings and gear cylinder line O-rings.
14. If pump groans or whines, idle engine and inspect for hose contact and interference with body, engine and frame.
15. If no hose contact or interference is found, proceed as follows:
    a. Stop engine and allow power steering system to cool off.
    b. Siphon fluid from reservoir using suitable suction device.
    c. Fill reservoir with cool, clean suitable power steering fluid.
    d. Install reservoir cap, then start engine and bring to operating temperature.
16. If noises persist, replace power steering pump and repeat bleeding procedure.

EXCEPT AURORA

STANDARD BLEEDING

Bleed power steering system after any component replacement, fluid line disconnection or in case of steering system noise. Bleed system to prevent pump damage, stop steering noise and to ensure proper system operation.

Inspect steering system before bleeding, looking for power steering lines touching frame, body or engine. Also inspect all hose connections for looseness or leaks.

1. Remove power steering pump reservoir cap.
2. Fill reservoir with proper fluid to full cold level.
3. Connect vacuum pump tool No. J-35555 and power steering bleeder adapter tool No. J-43485, or equivalents, to reservoir filler neck.
4. Apply maximum vacuum of 20 inches

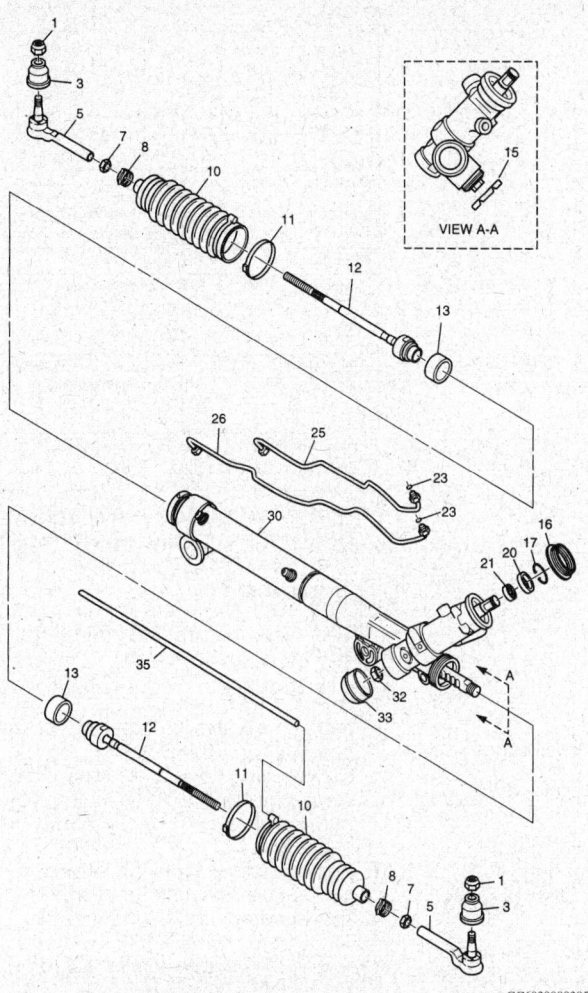

1 - NUT, HEX TORQUE PREVAILING
3 - SEAL, TIE ROD
5 - ROD ASM, OUTER TIE
7 - NUT, HEX JAM
8 - CLAMP, TIE ROD END
10 - BOOT, RACK & PINION
11 - CLAMP, BOOT
12 - ROD ASM, INNER TIE
13 - RING, SHOCK DAMPENER
15 - NUT, ADJUSTER PLUG LOCK
16 - ADAPTER, SEAL

17 - RING, RETAINING
20 - SEAL, STUB SHAFT
21 - ANNULUS BEARING ASM
23 - SEAL, O-RING
25 - LINE ASM, CYLINDER (RH)
26 - LINE ASM, CYLINDER (LH)
30 - GEAR ASM, RACK & PINION (PARTIAL)
32 - NUT, HEX LOCK
33 - COVER, DUST
35 - BREATHER TUBE

GC6029800385020X

Fig. 41 Exploded view of power rack & pinion steering (Part 2 of 2). Alero, Bonneville, Century, Grand Prix, LeSabre, Park Avenue, Regal & 2001 Grand Am

VIEW A-A

GC6029800385010X

Fig. 41 Exploded view of power rack & pinion steering (Part 1 of 2). Alero, Bonneville, Century, Grand Prix, LeSabre, Park Avenue, Regal & Grand Am

and wait five minutes.
5. Inspect vacuum level after five minute. Vacuum typically will drop 2–3 inches. If vacuum does not remain steady, refer to "Special Bleeding."
6. Install reservoir cap, then start and idle engine.
7. Stop engine and inspect power steering fluid level.
8. Wait five minutes, then repeat previous two steps until fluid level has stabilized.
9. Start and idle engine, then turn steering wheel 180–360° F in both directions five times. **Do not turn wheel all way to stops.**
10. Stop engine and inspect power steering fluid level.
11. Connect vacuum pump and power steering bleeder adapter to reservoir filler neck.
12. Apply maximum vacuum of 20 inches and wait five minutes.
13. Inspect vacuum level after five minute. Vacuum typically will drop 2–3 inches. If vacuum does not remain steady, refer to "Special Bleeding."

SPECIAL BLEEDING

1. If vacuum continued to drop during bleeding procedure, remove power steering pressure and return hoses from power steering pump.
2. Install plugs from power steering bleeder adapter tool No. J-43485, or equivalents, into power steering pump pressure and return ports.
3. Connect vacuum pump and power steering bleeder adapter to reservoir filler neck.
4. Apply maximum vacuum of 20 inches.
5. If vacuum drops, repair or replace power steering pump.
6. If vacuum holds steady, proceed as follows:
   a. Inspect power steering fluid and ensure it is free of bubbles and is not discolored.
   b. Replace return hose clamps and O-rings.
   c. Replace pressure hose O-rings and reservoir to pump O-ring.
   d. Repeat bleeding procedure.
   e. Drive vehicle approximately 10 miles on smooth, flat surface to ensure power steering system reach-

es full operating temperature.

TECHNICAL SERVICE BULLETINS

Power Steering Moan & Squawk

2001 PARK AVENUE

On these models equipped with the Gran Touring Performance Package Y56 there may be and audible moan/squawk noise during low speed turning maneuvers.

This condition may be caused by the power steering gear valve instability resulting in a pressure disturbance that creates an audible noise which is transferred through the vehicle structure.

To correct this condition, install a replacement steering gear (P/N 26098491), pressure hose (P/N 25739393) and clip bolt (P/N 10082184), as follows:
1. Install steering column lock pin tool No. J-42640, or equivalent.
2. Raise and support vehicle, then remove front tire and wheel assemblies.
3. Disconnect steering intermediate shaft at power steering gear.
4. Support rear of frame assembly, then remove four rear frame mounting bolts.
5. Remove two bolts and nut securing transaxle mount to frame assembly.
6. Remove outer tie rod to steering knuckle nuts and disconnect outer tie rod ends from steering knuckles using universal linkage puller tool No. J-24319-B, or equivalent.
7. Disconnect front stabilizer shaft end links and rotate shaft upward provide access to heat shield/steering gear.
8. Lower rear of frame assembly approximately two inches.
9. Remove mounting bolts, disconnect wiring harness clip and remove heat shield.
10. Disconnect steering gear wiring harness, then the power steering pressure and return hoses at steering gear.
11. Remove mounting bolts and steering gear.
12. Remove and discard existing power steering pressure hose clip from frame.
13. Disconnect, remove and discard

Step	Action	Scan Tool Display
1	1. Connect a scan tool to the data link connector (DLC). 2. Input the vehicle information and select Chassis.	• Delco Bosch ABS/TCS • Magna Steer
2	Select Magna Steer.	• Diagnostics • Recalibration
3	Select Recalibration.	• Magna Steer Recalibration Procedure - Ensure that the ignition is ON and the engine is OFF. • Press ENTER to Start.
4	Press ENTER.	Is the VIN correct?
5	Select YES.	Does the vehicle have Magna Steer RPO # <NV8 ?
6	Select YES.	Is the vehicle equipped with the Gran Touring Package RPO # <Y56 ?
7	Select YES.	Recal with the FACTORY STANDARD calibration
8	Select NO.	Select the calibration: • More firm • Factory calibration • Less firm
9	Select the desired response mode.	• Magna Steer Recalibration Procedure is complete. • Press EXIT in order to return to the menu.
10	Exit the scan tool.	Reprogramming is complete.

GC6029900427000X

Fig. 42 Variable effort steering programming. Aurora, Bonneville, LeSabre & Park Avenue

Action	Result
1. Install a Scan Tool. 2. Input the vehicle information and select Chassis.	• ABS/TCS/ICCS • Magna Steer
Select Magna Steer.	• Diagnostics • Recalibration
Select Recalibration.	Magna Steer Recalibration Procedure - Be sure Ignition is ON Engine OFF Press [ENTER] to Start
Press [ENTER].	Is VIN Correct?
Select YES.	Factory Standard Calibration Will Be Used For This VIN. Press [ENTER] to Start
Press [ENTER].	Magna Steer Recalibration Procedure is complete Press [EXIT] to Return to Menu.
Exit the scan tool.	Reprogramming is complete.

GC6019800016000X

Fig. 43 Variable effort steering programming. Eldorado & Seville

power steering pressure hose from power steering pump.

14. Install new power steering pressure hose and hand start fitting at pump.
15. Transfer outer tie rod ends from removed steering gear to new gear.
16. Install new steering gear. **Torque** mounting bolts to 48 ft. lbs.
17. Hand start power steering pressure and return hose fittings at steering gear.
18. Secure clip of new power steering pressure hose to frame with new bolt using hole in frame where previously removed clip was attached.
19. With clip positioned fore-aft, **torque** screw to 60 inch lbs.
20. **Torque** power steering pressure and return hose fittings to 20 ft. lbs.
21. Connect power steering wiring harness connector.
22. Position heat shield and install wiring harness clip to shield.
23. Install heat shield bolts and **torque** 80 inch lbs.
24. Raise frame into position and hand start mounting bolts. **Torque** mounting bolts to 141 ft. lbs.
25. Install outer tie rod ball joints to steering knuckles. **Torque** nuts to 33 ft. lbs.
26. Install transaxle mount bolts and nut. **Torque** mounting bolts and nut to 27 ft. lbs.
27. Rotate stabilizer shaft into position and install links. **Torque** to 11 ft. lbs.
28. Connect intermediate steering shaft to steering gear. **Torque** pinch bolt to 35 ft. lbs.
29. Install tire and wheel assemblies. **Torque** nuts to 100 ft. lbs.
30. Lower vehicle and remove steering column lock pin.
31. Bleed power steering system as outlined in "Power Steering System Service."
32. Inspect and adjust front toe.

Service Steering Message

2003-05 CTS

On some of these models there may be a Service Steering Message on the Driver's Information Center (DIC). Diagnostic Trouble Code (DTC) C0450 or C1241 may also be set.

This condition may be caused by an internal fault in the Variable Effort Steering (VES) solenoid.

To correct this condition, proceed as follows:

1. Raise and support vehicle, then remove lefthand front tire and wheel assembly.
2. Remove push-in retainers and front air deflector.
3. Clean dirt or debris from VES solenoid connector.
4. Disconnect VES solenoid harness retainers and electrical connector.
5. Measure resistance of VES actuator. noting the following:
   a. **On 2004–05 models,** if resistance is 5.7–7.2 ohms, continue with DTC C0450 diagnosis.
   b. **On 2003 models,** if resistance is 5.7–7.2 ohms, continue with DTC C1241 diagnosis.
   c. **On all models,** if resistance not is 5.7–7.2 ohms, proceed to next step.
6. Remove VES solenoid from the steering gear. **Do not replace complete steering gear**
7. Install new VES solenoid, (P/N 89047679) into steering gear.

Moan/Squawk Noise During Low Speed Turning

2001-02 AURORA

On some of these models built before 3.5L engine VIN 24131699 or 4.0L engine VIN 24100112 there may be an audible moan/squawk type noise heard during low speed turning maneuvers.

This condition may be caused by instability of the power steering gear valve. This may result in a pressure disturbance that creates an audible noise that is transferred through the vehicle structure.

To correct this condition, proceed as follows:

3.5L ENGINE

Install new power steering gear (P/N 26098941).

4.0L ENGINE

1. Install new power steering pressure hose (P/N25737839).
2. Secure new hose clip frame with new screw (P/N11515764), using hole in frame where existing clip had been installed.
3. Position clip in fore-aft direction with hoop of clip pointing forward.
4. **Torque** mounting 60 inch lbs.

Moan/Squawk Noise During Low Speed Turning Maneuvers

2001-02 DEVILLE & SEVILLE

On some of these models built before VIN 2U142766 there may be an audible moan/squawk type noise that is heard during low speed turning maneuvers.

This condition may be caused by the power steering gear valve instability resulting in a pressure disturbance which creates an audible noise that is transferred through the vehicle structure.

To correct this condition, proceed as follows:

1. **Only models with VINs 2U100085–2U142766 require new high pressure power steering hose.**
2. Install steering column lock pin J-42640, or equivalent.
3. **On DeVille models,** proceed as follows:
   a. Remove coolant recovery bottle mounting screw and two nuts.
   b. Rotate and secure coolant recovery bottle rearward to gain access to power steering pressure hose upper clamp.
4. **On all models,** remove power steering pressure hose upper clamp to engine mounting nut.

5. Disconnect power steering pressure hose at pump.
6. Raise and support vehicle, then remove front tire and wheel assemblies.
7. **On models equipped with Road Sensing Suspension (RSS),** disconnect height sensor links from LCA studs.
8. **On all models,** disconnect steering intermediate shaft at power steering gear.
9. Support rear of frame.
10. Remove four rear frame mounting bolts, then the two bolts and nuts securing transaxle mount to frame.
11. Remove outer tie rod to steering knuckle nuts.
12. Disconnect outer tie rod ends from steering knuckles using universal linkage puller No. J-24319-B, or equivalent.
13. Disconnect front stabilizer shaft end links, then rotate shaft upward to provide access to heat shield/steering gear.
14. Lower rear of frame assembly approximately two inches.
15. Remove heat shield mounting bolts.
16. Disconnect wiring harness clip and remove shield.
17. Disconnect steering gear wiring harness.
18. Disconnect power steering pressure and return hoses at steering gear.
19. Remove mounting bolts and steering gear.
20. Remove and discard existing clip and power steering pressure hose.
21. Install new power steering pressure hose (P/N 25737839).
22. Transfer outer tie rod ends from removed steering gear to new gear.
23. Install new steering gear and **torque** mounting bolts to 48 ft. lbs.
24. Secure new power steering pressure hose clip to frame with new bolt, using hole in frame where previously removed clip was attached.
25. Position clip fore-aft and **torque** it to 60 inch lbs.
26. Hand start power steering pressure and return hose fittings at steering gear. **Torque** hose fittings to 20 ft. lbs.
27. Connect power steering wiring harness connector.
28. Position heat shield and install wiring harness clip to shield.
29. **Torque** heat shield mounting bolts to 79 inch lbs.
30. Raise frame into position and hand start mounting bolts. **Torque** frame mounting bolts to 141 ft. lbs.
31. Install outer tie rod ball joints to steering knuckles. **Torque** nuts to 33 ft. lbs.
32. Install transaxle mount bolts and nut. **Torque** bolts and nuts to 37 ft. lbs.
33. Rotate stabilizer shaft into position and install shaft links. **Torque** links to 10 ft. lbs.
34. Connect intermediate steering shaft to steering gear. **Torque** pinch bolt to 35 ft. lbs.
35. **On models equipped with RSS,** connect height sensor links to LCA studs.
36. **On all models,** install tire and wheel assemblies. **Torque** nuts to 100 ft. lbs.
37. Lower vehicle and remove steering column lock pin.
38. Position upper clamp of pressure hose onto engine stud. **Torque** nut to 80 inch lbs.
39. Hand start pressure hose fitting at steering pump. **Torque** hose fitting to 20 ft. lbs.
40. **On DeVille models,** proceed as follows:
    a. Rotate coolant recovery bottle into position.
    b. Hand start screw and two nuts.
    c. **Torque** screw to 53 inch lbs.
41. **On all models,** bleed power steering system as outlined in "Power Steering System Service."

Power Steering System Moan/ Squawk

2001-02 BONNEVILLE SSEI

On some of these models built before VIN 24100674 there may be an audible moan/squawk type noise that is heard during a low speed turning maneuver.

This condition may be caused by power steering gear valve instability, resulting in a pressure disturbance which creates an audible noise that is transferred through the vehicle structure.

To correct this condition, replace the existing power steering gear with the new assembly (P/N 26098782).

Steering Vibration/ Shudder During Parking Maneuver

2001 BONNEVILLE, LESABRE & PARK AVENUE

On some of these models there may be a steering vibration, shudder or moan noise when steering during parking maneuvers on dry pavement.

This condition may be caused by the power steering press hose.

To correct this condition install a new

Model	Application	P/N
Less Magnasteer	Power Steering Pressure/Inlet Hydraulic Hose Assembly	26079288
	Power Steering Return/Outlet Hydraulic Hose Assembly	25727229
With Magnasteer	Power Steering Pressure/Inlet Hydraulic Hose Assembly	26079289
	Power Steering Return/Outlet Hydraulic Hose Assembly	25727230

Fig. 44   Power steering pressure hose application chart. 2001 Bonneville, LeSabre & Park Avenue

power steering pressure (inlet) hose assembly, **Fig. 44,** as follows:

1. Raise and support vehicle, then drain power steering fluid into suitable container.
2. Remove lefthand front tire and wheel assembly, then remove lefthand lower splash shield.
3. Remove lower radiator air deflector and power steering gear heat shield.
4. Disconnect power steering pressure and return hoses from power steering pump.
5. Remove retaining clips' mounting bolt/screws, then disconnect power steering pressure and return hoses from power steering gear.
6. Remove power steering pressure and return hose assemblies.
7. Drill two ¼ inch holes into top surface of lefthand engine frame crossmember. Both holes are to be approximately 1.5 inches rearward from front and rear control arm brackets horizontal flange edge.
8. Remove two rosebud clips from new hose assembly and install them into drilled holes.
9. Install new lefthand routed power steering return/outlet hose assembly as follows:
   a. From forward side of front engine mount, route pump end of hose to righthand side of vehicle, along righthand engine frame crossmember and up to steering pump.
   b. Route steering gear end of hose to lefthand side of vehicle, along lefthand engine frame crossmember and up to steering gear.
10. Install power steering pressure/inlet hose assembly.
11. Connect power steering pressure and return hoses to power steering pump and gear. **Torque** power steering pressure and return hoses to steering gear to 20 ft. lbs.
12. Install retaining clip' mounting bolt/screws. **Torque** mounting bolt/screws to 53 inch lbs.
13. Install power steering gear assembly heat shield, lower radiator air deflector and lefthand lower splash shield.
14. Install lefthand front tire and wheel assembly, then lower vehicle.
15. Fill and bleed power steering system as outlined in "Power Steering System Service."

Saginaw Rack & Pinion Power Steering Gear w/Electronic Power Steering

NOTE: On Air Bag Equipped Models, Refer To "Air Bag System Precautions" Located In The Front Of This Manual For System Disarming & Arming Procedures.

NOTE: Refer To "Computer Relearn Procedures" Located In The Front Of This Manual When Battery Power To The Computer Has Been Interrupted.

NOTE: "Electrical Symbol & Wire Color Code Identification" Located In The Front Of This Manual May Be Used As An Aid When Using Wiring Circuits Found In This Section.

INDEX

DESCRIPTION

This Electric Power Steering (EPS) system reduces the effort needed to steer vehicle. This system uses the Body Control Module (BCM), Power Steering Control Module (PSCM), torque sensor, discrete battery voltage supply circuit, EPS motor, class 2 serial data circuit, and the Instrument Panel Cluster (IPC) message center to perform system functions. The PSCM, torque sensor, nor the EPS motor are serviced separately from each other or from steering column. All EPS components diagnosed as faulting requires the steering column assembly to be replaced, also known as EPS assembly.

The PSCM uses a combination of torque sensor inputs, vehicle speed, calculated system temperature and steering calibration to determine amount of steering assist. When steering wheel is turned, the PSCM uses signal voltage from the torque sensor to detect the amount of torque being applied to steering column shaft and amount of current to command to the EPS motor. The PSCM receives a class 2 vehicle speed message from the Engine Control Module (ECM) to determine speed of vehicle. At lower speeds more assist is provided to make parking maneuvers easier. At higher speeds less assist is provided for more improved road feel and stability.

DIAGNOSIS & TESTING

Accessing Diagnostic Trouble Codes

Diagnostic Trouble Codes (DTCs) must be read using a suitably programmed scan tool. There are no provisions for flash code diagnostics.

1. Turn ignition switch to Off position.
2. Connect suitably programmed scan tool to Data Link Connector (DLC).
3. Turn ignition switch to On position.
4. Select scan tool's special functions.
5. Read and record DTCs.

Code	Description
C0000	No Vehicle Speed Message From ECM
C0475	EPS Motor Circuit Short Or Open
C0476	PSCM Detects High System Temperature
C0545	Torque Sensor Input Out Of Range
C0847	Ignition Voltage Circuit Shorted To Ground
C0848	Ignition Voltage Circuit Shorted To Voltage
C0896	EPS System Voltage Is 9–11 Volts
C0899	EPS System Voltage Is Less Than 8 Volts
C0900	EPS System Voltage Is More Than 17 Volts

Fig. 1 DTC interpretation

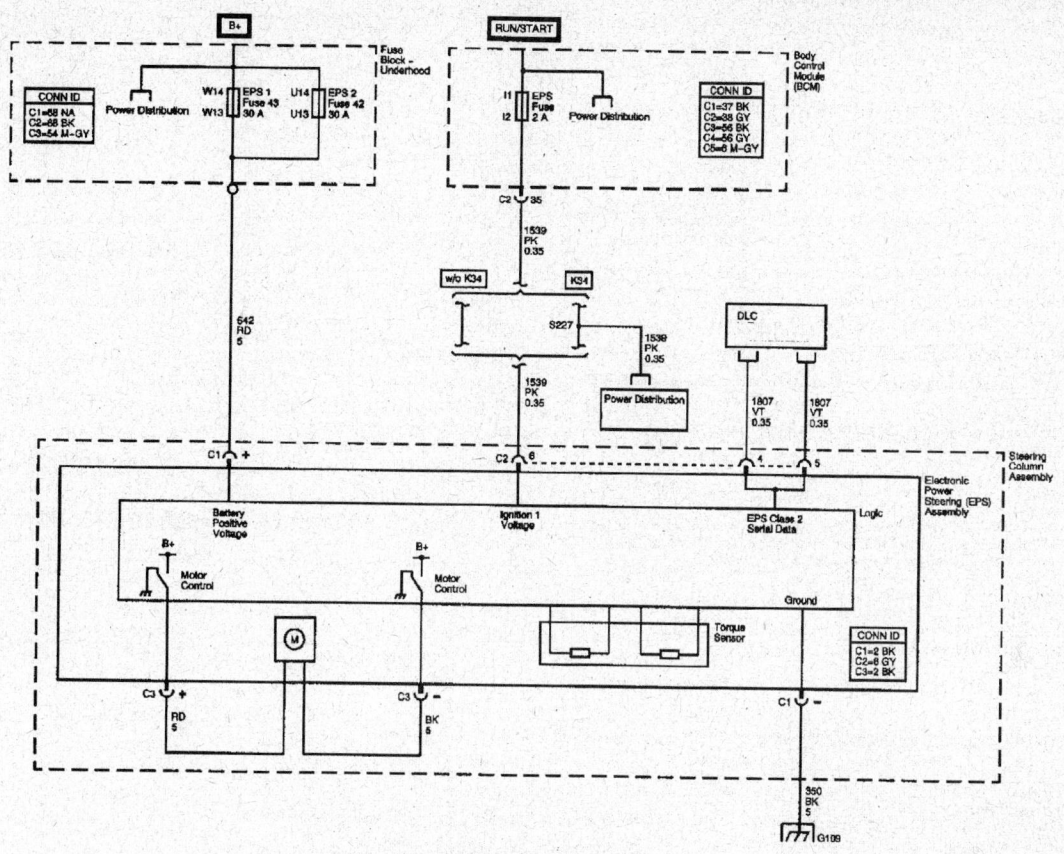

Fig. 2 Wiring diagram

ARM66GC000000450

Diagnostic Trouble Code Interpretation

Refer to **Fig. 1,** for Diagnostic Trouble Code (DTC) interpretation.

Wiring Diagrams

Refer to **Fig. 2,** for wiring diagrams.

Diagnostic Tests

Refer to **Figs. 3 through 12,** for diagnostic tests.

Clearing Diagnostic Trouble Codes

DTCs cannot be cleared by disconnecting EBTCM or battery cables. Follow the scan tool manufacturer's instructions to clear DTCs.

DIAGNOSTIC CHART INDEX

Code	Description	Page No.	Fig. No.
—	Diagnostic System Check	25-40	3
C0000	No Vehicle Speed Message From ECM	25-40	4
C0475	EPS Motor Circuit Short Or Open	25-40	5
C0476	PSCM Detects High System Temperature	25-41	6
C0545	Torque Sensor Input Out Of Range	25-41	7
C0847	Ignition Voltage Circuit Shorted To Ground	25-42	8
C0848	Ignition Voltage Circuit Shorted To Voltage	25-42	9
C0896	EPS System Voltage Is 9–11 Volts	25-43	10
C0899	EPS System Voltage Is Less Than 8 Volts	25-43	11
C0900	EPS System Voltage Is More Than 17 Volts	25-44	12

Step	Action	Value(s)	Yes	No
1	Install a scan tool. Does the scan tool turn on?	--	Go to Step 2	Scan Tool Does Not Power Up
2	1. Turn ON the ignition, with the engine OFF. 2. Attempt to establish communication with the Power Steering Control Module (PSCM). Does the scan tool communicate with the PSCM?	--	Go to Step 3	Scan Tool Does Not Communicate with Class 2 Device
3	Select the Diagnostic Trouble Codes (DTC) function on the scan tool. Does the scan tool display any DTCs that begin with a U?	--	Diagnostic Trouble Code (DTC)	Go to Step 4

ARM66GC000000451

Fig. 3   Diagnostic System Check (Part 1 of 2)

Circuit Description

The Power Steering Control Module (PSCM) receives a class 2 vehicle speed message from the Engine Control Module (ECM) via a class 2 serial data circuit. The PSCM uses this vehicle speed message, and other inputs, to determine the desired amount of steering assist.

Conditions for Running the DTC

- The ignition is ON.
- DTC U1300, U1301, or U2100 are not set.
- Vehicle speed is greater than 8.1 km/h (5 mph).

Conditions for Setting the DTC

The PSCM receives an invalid, or no vehicle speed message from the ECM.

Action Taken When the DTC Sets

- DTC C0000 is stored in memory.
- The IPC message center displays the PWR STR warning message.
- Steering assist level defaults to 120 km/h (74.5 mph) vehicle speed level of assist.

Conditions for Clearing the DTC

- A current DTC will clear on the next consecutive malfunction free ignition cycle.
- A history DTC will clear after 100 consecutive malfunction free ignition cycles.
- Using a scan tool

Test Description

2. tests for the presence of vehicle speed related DTCs in the control modules where the vehicle speed message originates.

ARM66GC000000453

Fig. 4   Code C0000: No Vehicle Speed Message From ECM (Part 1 of 2)

Circuit Description

The Power Steering Control Module (PSCM) continuously monitors the voltage and current levels being commanded to the Electric Power Steering (EPS) motor. The PSCM compares the desired and actual current levels to detect malfunctions in the EPS motor, or the circuits to the motor.

Conditions for Running the DTC

- The ignition is ON.
- No voltage DTCs are present.

Conditions for Setting the DTC

A short to ground, short to voltage, or an open in the EPS motor, or the circuits to the motor.

Action Taken When the DTC Sets

- A DTC C0475 is stored in memory.
- The IPC message center displays the PWR STR warning message.
- No steering assist is provided.

Conditions for Clearing the DTC

- A current DTC will clear on the next malfunction free ignition cycle.
- A history DTC will clear after 100 consecutive malfunction free ignition cycles.
- Using a scan tool

ARM66GC000000455

Fig. 5   Code C0475: EPS Motor Circuit Short Or Open (Part 1 of 2)

4	Does the scan tool display DTC C0550, or any DTCs that begin with a B?	--	Diagnostic Trouble Code (DTC)	Go to Step 5
5	Does the scan tool display any EPS DTCs?	--	Diagnostic Trouble Code (DTC)	Go to Step 6
6	1. Start the engine. 2. Turn the steering wheel 90° to the left, then 90° to the right, then return the steering wheel to center. 3. remove hands from steering wheel and ensure no force is being applied to the steering wheel. 4. Using the scan tool observe the Steering Shaft Torque data parameter in the EPS data list 2. Does the scan tool indicate that the Steering Shaft Torque data parameter is within the specified range?	< + or - 1 N·m (0.7 lb ft)	Power Steering System	Replace Steering Column

ARM66GC000000452

Fig. 3   Diagnostic System Check (Part 2 of 2)

Step	Action	Yes	No
1	Did you perform the Power Steering System Diagnostic System Check?	Go to Step 2	Go to Diagnostic System Check -
2	1. Install a scan tool. 2. Turn ON the ignition, with the engine OFF. 3. With the scan tool, select the Engine, or Transmission Diagnostic Trouble Codes (DTC) function in Powertrain. Does the scan tool indicate the presents of any ECM, or TCM DTCs?	Diagnostic Trouble Code (DTC)	Go to Step 3
3	1. Use the scan tool in order to clear the EPS DTCs 2. Operate the vehicle within the conditions for running the DTC. Does the DTC reset?	Go to Step 2	System OK

ARM66GC000000454

Fig. 4   Code C0000: No Vehicle Speed Message From ECM (Part 2 of 2)

Step	Action	Yes	No
1	Did you perform the Power Steering Diagnostic System Check?	Go to Step 2	Go to Diagnostic System Check
2	Inspect for poor connections at the EPS motor harness connector. Did you find and correct the condition?	Go to Step 6	Go to Step 3
3	Test the EPS motor control circuits for a short to ground or an open. Did you find and correct the condition?	Go to Step 6	Go to Step 4
4	Test the EPS motor control circuits for a short to voltage. Did you find and correct the condition?	Go to Step 6	Go to Step 5
5	Replace the EPS assembly. Did you complete the repair?	Go to Step 6	--
6	1. Use the scan tool in order to clear the DTCs. 2. Operate the vehicle within the Conditions for Running the DTC. Does the DTC reset?	Go to Step 2	System OK

ARM66GC000000456

Fig. 5   Code C0475: EPS Motor Circuit Short Or Open (Part 2 of 2)

Circuit Description

The Power Steering Control Module (PSCM) monitors the temperature of the Electric Power Steering (EPS) system. The PSCM uses voltage and current levels to calculate an estimated system temperature. If the PSCM detects a high system temperature event is occurring the amount of assist is reduced to lower the EPS system temperature to prevent system thermal damage.

Condition for Running the DTC

The ignition is ON.

Conditions for Setting the DTC

The PSCM detects a high system temperature.

Action Taken When the DTC Sets

- A DTC C0476 is stored in memory.
- Steering assist is reduced.

Conditions for Clearing the DTC

- A current DTC will clear when the EPS system temperature returns to normal.
- A history DTC will clear after 100 consecutive malfunction free ignition cycles.
- Using a scan tool

Diagnostic Aids

- DTC C0476 does not indicate that a malfunction has occurred. Rather that the PSCM had to limit current to the EPS motor to avoid system thermal damage.
- Inspect the under dash area around the EPS assembly. ensure that no other components have come in contact with the EPS assembly such as under dash insulation or other electrical components.
- Ensure that no steering components down stream of the EPS assembly, such as ball joints, tie rod ends, universal joints, or the steering rack and pinion are mechanically binding.

Test Description

The number below refer to the step number on the diagnostic table.

2. Tests if the high system temperature is system, or driving condition related.

ARM66GC000000457

Fig. 6 Code C0476: PSCM Detects High System Temperature (Part 1 of 2)

Circuit Description

The electric power steering (EPS) system uses a torque sensor to detect the amount of torque being applied to the steering column shaft when the steering wheel is turned. The power steering control module (PSCM) uses this sensor as it's main input in determining the amount of steering assist needed.

Condition for Running the DTC

The ignition, and the engine are ON.

Condition for Setting the DTC

- The PSCM's torque sensor input is greater than 20.70 N·m (15.2 lb ft) during a right turn.
- The PSCM's torque sensor input is less than -20.70 N·m (15.2 lb ft) during a left turn.
- The difference between the 2 torque sensor coils is greater than 2.4 N·m (1.7 lb ft).

Action Taken When the DTC Sets

- A DTC C0545 is stored in memory.
- The IPC message center displays the PWR STR warning message.
- No steering assist is provided.

Conditions for Clearing the DTC

- A current DTC will clear on the next malfunction free ignition cycle.
- A history DTC will clear after 100 consecutive malfunction free ignition cycles.
- Using a scan tool

Diagnostic Aids

The torque sensor is hard wired to the PSCM, thus no connector, or circuit testing can be performed. if an intermittent malfunction is suspected with the torque sensor, or the circuits to the torque sensor, replace the EPS assembly. The scan tool can be used to view the torque sensor value.

Test Description

The number below refers to the step number on the diagnostic table.

2. Tests the torque sensor in its active state.

ARM66GC000000459

Fig. 7 Code C0545: Torque Sensor Input Out Of Range (Part 1 of 2)

Step	Action	Yes	No
1	Did you perform the Power Steering Diagnostic System Check?	Go to Step 2	Go to Diagnostic System Check -
2	Since most occurrences of the DTC are caused by frequent static steering, such as parking maneuvers and high ambient temperatures, review the EPS system with the customer to determine the conditions under which the DTC set. Did steering conditions, or high ambient temperatures cause the DTC to set?	Go to Step 3	Go to Diagnostic Aids
3	1. Use the scan tool in order to clear the DTCs. 2. Operate the vehicle within the Conditions for Running the DTC. Does the DTC reset?	Go to Step 2	System OK

ARM66GC000000458

Fig. 6 Code C0476: PSCM Detects High System Temperature (Part 2 of 2)

Step	Action	Values	Yes	No
1	Did you perform the Power Steering Diagnostic System Check?		Go to Step 2	Go to Diagnostic System Check -
2	1. Install a scan tool 2. Start the engine. 3. With the scan tool, observe the Steering Shaft Torque data parameter in the EPS Data List 2. 4. Turn the steering wheel 90 degrees to the right and hold the steering wheel position. Does the scan tool indicate that the Steering Shaft Torque data parameter changes state wile turning the steering wheel and is less than the specified value?	20.70 N·m (15.2 lb ft)	Go to Diagnostic Aids	Go to Step 3
3	Replace the EPS assembly. Did you complete the repair?		Go to Step 4	--
4	1. Use the scan tool in order to clear the DTCs. 2. Operate the vehicle within the Conditions for Running the DTC. Does the DTC reset?		Go to Step 2	System OK

ARM66GC000000460

Fig. 7 Code C0545: Torque Sensor Input Out Of Range (Part 2 of 2)

Circuit Description

The Body Control Module (BCM) contains the 2 amp EPS fuse. This fuse and the ignition 1 voltage circuit supply ignition voltage to the Power Steering Control Module (PSCM). This ignition voltage is used to wake up the PSCM.

Conditions for Running the DTC

The ignition is ON.

Conditions for Setting the DTC

- The ignition 1 voltage circuit is shorted to ground or open.
- DTCs U1300 and U1301 are not set.

Action Taken When the DTC Sets

- DTC C0847 is stored in memory.
- The IPC message center displays the PWR STR warning message.
- The EPS system is disabled.

Conditions for Clearing the DTC

- A current DTC will clear when the malfunction is no longer present.
- A history DTC will clear after 100 consecutive malfunction free ignition cycles.
- Using a scan tool

Diagnostic Aids

The Ignition 1 voltage circuit supplies several other control modules with ignition voltage. Before preceding with the diagnostic table below, ensure no other control modules that use the ignition 1 circuit for their ignition voltage supply have any ignition voltage malfunctions present, such as the Sensing and Diagnostic Module (SDM), or the Cruise Control Module (CCM).

Test Description

The numbers below refer to the step numbers on the diagnostic table.

2. Tests if the malfunction is intermittent.

5. Tests if a short to ground exists in the ignition 1 voltage circuit, or in the PSCM.

ARM66GC000000461

Fig. 8   Code C0847: Ignition Voltage Circuit Shorted To Ground (Part 1 of 3)

Step	Action	Yes	No
1	Did you perform the Power Steering Diagnostic System Check?	Go to Step 2	Go to Diagnostic System Check -
2	1. Install a scan tool. 2. Turn ON the ignition, with the engine OFF. 3. With a scan tool, attempt to establish communication with the PSCM. Does the scan tool communicate with the PSCM?	Go to Diagnostic Aids	Go to Step 3
3	1. Turn OFF the ignition. 2. Inspect the 2 A EPS fuse for an open. Is the fuse open?	Go to Step 4	Go to Step 6
4	1. Replace the 2 A EPS fuse. 2. Turn ON the ignition, with the engine OFF. Does the fuse open?	Go to Step 5	Go to Diagnostic Aids
5	Test the ignition 1 voltage circuit of the PSCM for a short to ground. Did you find and correct the condition?	Go to Step 10	Go to Step 9

ARM66GC000000462

Fig. 8   Code C0847: Ignition Voltage Circuit Shorted To Ground (Part 2 of 3)

Step	Action	Yes	No
6	Test the ignition 1 voltage circuit of the PSCM for an open. Did you find and correct the condition?	Go to Step 10	Go to Step 7
7	Inspect for poor connections at the harness connector of the BCM. Did you find and correct the condition?	Go to Step 10	Go to Step 8
8	Inspect for poor connections at the harness connector of the PSCM. Did you find and correct the condition?	Go to Step 10	Go to Step 9
9	Replace the EPS assembly. Did you complete the replacement?	Go to Step 10	--
10	1. Use the scan tool in order to clear the DTCs. 2. Operate the vehicle within the Conditions for Running the DTC. Does the DTC reset?	Go to Step 2	System OK

ARM66GC000000463

Fig. 8   Code C0847: Ignition Voltage Circuit Shorted To Ground (Part 3 of 3)

Circuit Description

The Power Steering Control Module (PSCM) receives a class 2 power moding message from the Body Control Module (BCM) to determine the position of the ignition switch. After a power mode OFF message is received, the PSCM monitors the ignition 1 voltage circuit to detect if a short to voltage fault exists.

Conditions for Running the DTC

- The ignition is OFF.
- The class 2 power mode message indicates OFF.

Conditions for Setting the DTC

- The PSCM ignition 1 voltage circuit is shorted to voltage.
- DTCs U1300 and U1301 are not set.

Action Taken When the DTC Sets

- DTC C0848 is stored in memory.
- The IPC message center displays the PWR STR warning message.

Conditions for Clearing the MIL/DTC

- A current DTC will clear on the next consecutive malfunction free ignition cycle.
- A history DTC will clear after 100 consecutive malfunction free ignition cycles.
- Using a scan tool

Step	Action	Yes	No
1	Did you perform the Power Steering Diagnostic System Check?	Go to Step 2	Go to Diagnostic System Check
2	Test the ignition 1 voltage circuit for a short to voltage. Did you find and correct the condition?	Go to Step 3	Test for Intermittent and Poor Connections
3	1. Use the scan tool in order to clear the DTCs. 2. Operate the vehicle within the Conditions for Running the DTC. Does the DTC reset?	Go to Step 2	System OK

ARM66GC000000464

Fig. 9   Code C0848: Ignition Voltage Circuit Shorted To Voltage

Circuit Description

The Power Steering Control Module (PSCM) has a discrete battery positive voltage supply circuit. The PSCM monitors the voltage level on this circuit to ensure the Electric Power Steering (EPS) system has adequate voltage levels to perform the system functions.

Conditions for Running the DTC

The ignition is ON.

Conditions for Setting the DTC

EPS system battery voltage is 9–11 volts.

Action Taken When the DTC Sets

- DTC C0896 is stored in memory.
- The IPC message center displays the PWR STR warning message.
- Steering assist is reduced.

Conditions for Clearing the DTC

- A current DTC will clear when EPS system voltage is greater than 11 volts.
- A history DTC will clear after 100 consecutive ignition cycles with EPS system voltage greater than 11 volts.
- Using a scan tool

Diagnostic Aids

The scan tool can be used to view the number of times a low battery voltage incident has occurred.

Test Description

The number below refers to the step number on the diagnostic table.

2. Tests if the malfunction exists in the vehicles charging system.

3. Tests if the malfunction is intermittent.

ARM66GC000000465

Fig. 10   Code C0896: EPS System Voltage Is 9–11 Volts (Part 1 of 3)

Step	Action	Yes	No
6	Inspect for poor connections at the harness connector of the underhood fuse block stud terminal. Did you find and correct the condition?	Go to Step 10	Go to Step 7
7	Inspect for poor connections at the harness connector of the PSCM. Did you find and correct the condition?	Go to Step 10	Go to Step 8
8	Inspect for poor connections at the ground terminal G109. Did you find and correct the condition?	Go to Step 10	Go to Step 9
9	Replace the EPS assembly. Did you complete the replacement?	Go to Step 10	--
10	1. Use the scan tool in order to clear the DTCs. 2. Operate the vehicle within the Conditions for Running the DTC. Does the DTC reset?	Go to Step 2	System OK

ARM66GC000000467

Fig. 10   Code C0896: EPS System Voltage Is 9–11 Volts (Part 3 of 3)

Step	Action	Yes	No
1	Did you perform the Power Steering Diagnostic System Check?	Go to Step 2	Go to Diagnostic System Check
2	1. Install a scan tool. 2. Turn ON the ignition, with the engine OFF. 3. Turn ON the scan tool Does the scan tool power up and communicate with the Engine Control Module (ECM)?	Go to Step 3	Go to Diagnostic System Check
3	With the scan tool observe the Battery Voltage parameter in the EPS Data List 1. Does the scan tool display less than 8 Volts?	Go to Step 3	Go to Diagnostic Aids
4	Test the battery positive voltage circuit of the PSCM for a high resistance. Did you find and correct the condition?	Go to Step 10	Go to Step 5
5	Test the ground circuit of the PSCM for a high resistance. Did you find and correct the condition?	Go to Step 10	Go to Step 6

ARM66GC000000469

Fig. 11   Code C0899: EPS System Voltage Is Less Than 8 Volts (Part 2 of 3)

Step	Action	Yes	No
1	Did you perform the Power Steering Diagnostic System Check?	Go to Step 2	Go to Diagnostic System Check
2	1. Install a scan tool. 2. Turn ON the ignition, with the engine OFF. 3. With a scan tool, observe the Battery Voltage parameter in the ECM Data List. Does the scan tool display greater than 11 volts?	Go to Step 3	Go to Diagnostic System Check
3	With a scan tool, observe the Battery Voltage parameter in the EPS Data List 1. Does the scan tool display greater than 11 volts?	Go to Diagnostic Aids	Go to Step 4
4	Test the battery positive voltage circuit of the PSCM for a high resistance. Did you find and correct the condition?	Go to Step 10	Go to Step 5
5	Test the ground circuit of the PSCM for a high resistance. Did you find and correct the condition?	Go to Step 10	Go to Step 6

ARM66GC000000466

Fig. 10   Code C0896: EPS System Voltage Is 9–11 Volts (Part 2 of 3)

Circuit Description

The Power Steering Control Module (PSCM) has a discrete battery positive voltage supply circuit. The PSCM monitors the voltage level on this circuit to ensure the Electric Power Steering (EPS) system has adequate voltage levels to perform the system functions.

Conditions for Running the DTC

The ignition is ON.

Conditions for Setting the DTC

EPS system voltage is less than 8 volts

Action Taken When the DTC Sets

- DTC C0899 is stored in memory.
- The IPC message center displays the PWR STR warning message.
- No steering assist is provided.

Conditions for Clearing the DTC

- A current DTC will clear when EPS system voltage is greater than 8.65 volts.
- A history DTC will clear after 100 consecutive ignition cycles with the EPS system voltage greater than 8.65 volts.
- Using a scan tool

Diagnostic Aids

The scan tool can be used to view the number of times a low battery incident has occurred.

Test Description

The numbers below refer to the step numbers on the diagnostic table.

2. Tests if the malfunction exsists in the vehicles charging system.

3. Tests if the malfunction is in the EPS system.

ARM66GC000000468

Fig. 11   Code C0899: EPS System Voltage Is Less Than 8 Volts (Part 1 of 3)

Step	Action	Yes	No
6	Inspect for poor connections at the harness connector of the PSCM. Did you find and correct the condition?	Go to Step 10	Go to Step 7
7	Inspect for poor connections at the harness connector of the underhood fuse block stud terminal. Did you find and correct the condition?	Go to Step 10	Go to Step 8
8	Inspect for poor connections at the ground connector, G109. Did you find and correct the condition?	Go to Step 10	Go to Step 9
9	Replace the EPS assembly. Did you complete the replacement?	Go to Step 10	--
10	1. Use the scan tool in order to clear the DTCs. 2. Operate the vehicle within the Conditions for Running the DTC. Does the DTC reset?	Go to Step 2	System OK

ARM66GC000000470

Fig. 11   Code C0899: EPS System Voltage Is Less Than 8 Volts (Part 3 of 3)

Circuit Description

The Power Steering Control Module (PSCM) has a discrete battery voltage supply circuit. The PSCM monitors the voltage level on this circuit to protect itself against high voltage damage.

Conditions for Running the DTC

The ignition is ON.

Conditions for Setting the DTC

EPS system voltage is greater than 17 volts.

Action Taken When the DTC Sets

- DTC C0900 is stored in memory.
- The IPC message center displays the PWR STR warning message.
- The PSCM is disabled to protect itself.

Conditions for Clearing the MIL/DTC

- A current DTC will clear when the EPS system voltage returns to less than 15.5 volts.
- A history DTC will clear after 100 consecutive ignition cycles with the EPS system voltage less than 15.5 volts.
- Using a scan tool

Diagnostic Aids

Jump starting the vehicle can cause DTC C0900 to set.

ARM66GC000000471

Step	Action	Values	Yes	No
1	Did you perform the Power Steering Diagnostic System Check?	--	Go to Step 2	Go to Diagnostic System Check
2	1. Install a scan tool. 2. Turn ON the ignition, with the engine OFF. 3. With a scan tool, observe the Battery Voltage parameter in the Engine Control Module (ECM) data list. Does the scan tool display greater than the specified value?	17 V	Check Engine Electrical	Go to Step 3
3	Test the ground circuit of the PSCM for a high resistance. Did you find and correct the condition?		Go to Step 4	Go to Diagnostic Aids
4	1. Use the scan tool in order to clear the DTC. 2. Operate the vehicle within the conditions for running the DTC. Does the DTC reset?		Go to Step 2	System OK

ARM66GC000000472

Fig. 12 Code C0900: EPS System Voltage Is More Than 17 Volts (Part 1 of 2)

Fig. 12 Code C0900: EPS System Voltage Is More Than 17 Volts (Part 2 of 2)

POWER STEERING SYSTEM SERVICE

Component Service

POWER STEERING GEAR

The power steering gear on these models cannot be disassembled. Refer to the "Front Suspension & Steering" section of the "Saturn" chapter for power steering gear replacement procedure.

POWER STEERING SYSTEM BLEED

STANDARD BLEEDING

Bleed power steering system after any component replacement, fluid line disconnection or in case of steering system noise. Bleed system to prevent pump damage, stop steering noise and to ensure proper system operation.

Inspect steering system before bleeding, looking for power steering lines touching frame, body or engine. Also inspect all hose connections for looseness or leaks.

1. Remove power steering pump reservoir cap.
2. Fill reservoir with proper fluid to full cold level.
3. Connect vacuum pump tool No. J-35555 and power steering bleeder adapter tool No. J-43485, or equivalents, to reservoir filler neck.
4. Apply maximum vacuum of 20 inches and wait five minutes.
5. Inspect vacuum level after five minute. Vacuum typically will drop 2–3 inches. If vacuum does not remain steady, refer to "Special Bleeding."
6. Install reservoir cap, then start and idle engine.
7. Stop engine and inspect power steering fluid level.
8. Wait five minutes, then repeat previous two steps until fluid level has stabilized.
9. Start and idle engine, then turn steering wheel 180–360° F in both directions five times. **Do not turn wheel all way to stops.**
10. Stop engine and inspect power steering fluid level.
11. Connect vacuum pump and power steering bleeder adapter to reservoir filler neck.
12. Apply maximum vacuum of 20 inches and wait five minutes.
13. Inspect vacuum level after five minute. Vacuum typically will drop 2–3 inches.

If vacuum does not remain steady, refer to "Special Bleeding."

SPECIAL BLEEDING

1. If vacuum continued to drop during bleeding procedure, remove power steering pressure and return hoses from power steering pump.
2. Install plugs from power steering bleeder adapter tool No. J-43485, or equivalents, into power steering pump pressure and return ports.
3. Connect vacuum pump and power steering bleeder adapter to reservoir filler neck.
4. Apply maximum vacuum of 20 inches.
5. If vacuum drops, repair or replace power steering pump.
6. If vacuum holds steady, proceed as follows:
   a. Inspect power steering fluid and ensure it is free of bubbles and is not discolored.
   b. Replace return hose clamps and O-rings.
   c. Replace pressure hose O-rings and reservoir to pump O-ring.
   d. Repeat bleeding procedure.
   e. Drive vehicle approximately 10 miles on smooth, flat surface to ensure power steering system reaches full operating temperature.

Saginaw Rotary Valve Power Steering Gear

NOTE: On Air Bag Equipped Models, Refer To "Air Bag System Precautions" Located In The Front Of This Manual For System Disarming & Arming Procedures.

NOTE: Refer To "Computer Relearn Procedures" Located In The Front Of This Manual When Battery Power To The Computer Has Been Interrupted.

NOTE: "Electrical Symbol & Wire Color Code Identification" Located In The Front Of This Manual May Be Used As An Aid When Using Wiring Circuits Found In This Section.

INDEX

DESCRIPTION

The Saginaw rotary valve steering gear incorporates a recirculating ball system in which steel balls act as a rolling thread between a steering worm shaft and the rack piston.

Variable Effort Steering (VES) or Speed Sensitive Steering (SSS) is a power steering system varies the steering effort required to steer the vehicle at different speeds. At low speeds, the system provides maximum power assist. At higher speeds, increased steering effort will provide firmer steering (road feel) and direction stability. The power steering control module uses speed input from the Electronic Braking Traction Control Module (EBTCM) to control the power steering fluid flow control valve actuator. The power steering fluid flow control valve actuator utilizes a pintle valve to control fluid flow to the steering gear.

DIAGNOSIS & TESTING

Accessing Diagnostic Trouble Codes

Diagnostic Trouble Codes (DTCs) may

Code	Description
21	No Speed Signal
22	Solenoid Short To Ground/Open
23	Power Steering Control Module Fault

Fig. 1   DTC interpretation

be read using a suitably programmed scan tool. There are no provisions for flash code diagnostics.

1. Turn ignition switch to Off position.
2. Connect suitably programmed scan tool to Data Link Connector (DLC).
3. Turn ignition switch to On position.
4. Select scan tool's special functions.
5. Read and record DTCs.

Diagnostic Trouble Code Interpretation

Refer to **Fig. 1,** for Diagnostic Trouble Code (DTC) interpretation.

Wiring Diagrams

Refer to **Fig. 2,** for wiring diagrams.

Diagnostic Tests

Refer to **Fig. 3,** for system inspection and **Figs. 4 through 6,** for diagnostic tests.

Clearing Diagnostic Trouble Codes

DTCs cannot be cleared by disconnecting EBTCM or battery cables. Follow the scan tool manufacturer's instructions to clear DTCs.

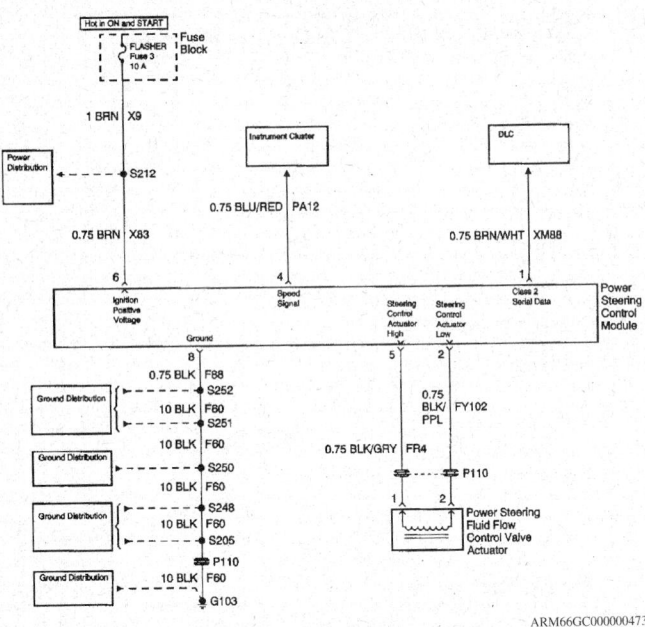

Fig. 2   Wiring diagram

ARM66GC000000473

Fig. 3   System Inspection

Step	Action	Value(s)	Yes	No
1	1. Prepare the vehicle for a road test. 2. Check the power steering fluid level. 3. Check the power steering belt tension. 4. Check the tire inflation. 5. Road test the vehicle using various parking maneuvers and a level stretch of highway. Does the steering force lessen when parking and require more force as the vehicle speed increases?	—	Go to Step 3	Go to Step 2
2	Was the problem found and repaired?	—	Go to Step 9	Go to Step 3
3	1. The procedure for reading DTCs is to use the scan tool. 2. When reading DTCs, follow the instructions that are supplied by the scan tool manufacturer. 3. Connect the scan tool to the data link connector (DLC). 4. Establish communication with the power steering control module. Does the scan tool communicate with the power steering control module?	—	Go to Step 5	Go to Step 4
4	ST Does Not Communicate with PS Control Module	—	—	—
5	Are there any current DTCs displayed?	—	Go to Step 6	Go to Step 7
6	1. If DTC 21 is present, refer to DTC 21. 2. If DTC 22 is present, refer to DTC 22. 3. If DTC 23 is present, refer to DTC 23. Go to the appropriate table to diagnose the DTC.	—	—	—
7	Are any history or intermittent codes displayed?	—	Go to Step 8	Go to Step 9
8	Locate and repair the problem. Was the intermittent problem found and repaired?	—	Go to Step 9	—
9	1. Connect all connectors and components that were disconnected. 2. Install the scan tool. 3. Check for any current or history or intermittent DTCs. Are there any current or history or intermittent DTCs present?	—	Go to Step 1	System OK

GC6029800380000X

Fig. 4   Code 21: No Speed Signal

Step	Action	Value(s)	Yes	No
1	Was the Variable Effort Steering System Check performed?	—	Go to Step 2	Check Speedometer
2	Does the speedometer operate properly?	—	Go to Step 3	Check Speedometer
3	1. Disconnect the power steering control module connector. 2. Raise the drive wheels. 3. Turn the ignition switch to the ON position. 4. Use the DMM, on the AC scale, to measure the voltage between terminals 4 and 8 of the power steering control module connector while rotating the LH rear wheel. Is the measured voltage within the specified value?	Greater than 1 VAC	Go to Step 5	Go to Step 4
4	1. Locate an open or a high resistance in circuit PA12. 2. Repair the open or the high resistance in circuit PA12. Is the repair complete?	—	Go to Step 6	—
5	Replace the power steering control module. Is the replacement complete?	—	Go to Step 6	—
6	1. Connect all connectors and components that were disconnected. 2. Road test the vehicle. 3. After road test, install the scan tool again. 4. Check for DTC 21. Is DTC 21 present?	—	Go to Step 1	System OK

GC6029800365000X

Fig. 5   Code 22: Solenoid Circuit Short To Ground/Open (Part 1 of 2)

Step	Action	Value(s)	Yes	No
1	Was the Variable Effort Steering System Check performed?	—	Go to Step 2	Refer to System Check
2	1. Connect the scan tool to the data link connector (DTC). 2. Check for a current DTC 22. Is a current DTC 22 displayed?	—	Go to Step 3	Go to Step 4
3	1. Remove the power steering control module (PSCM). 2. Use a DMM to measure the resistance across terminals 2 and 5 of the module connector. Is the measured resistance within the specified value?	7–8 Ω	Go to Step 6	Go to Step 7
4	Check for a history or an intermittent DTC 22. Is a history or an intermittent DTC 22 displayed?	—	Go to Step 5	Go to Step 6
5	1. Locate an intermittent in circuits FR4 and/or FY102. 2. Repair the intermittent in circuits FR4 and/or FY102. Is the repair complete?	—	Go to Step 10	—
6	1. Use the DMM to measure the resistance between terminal 2 of the PSCM connector and a known good ground. 2. Use the DMM to measure the resistance between terminal 5 of the PSCM connector and a known good ground. Is the measured resistance for both measurements within the specified value?	OL	Go to Step 8	Go to Step 9
7	1. Locate an open or a high resistance in circuits FR4 and/or FY102. 2. Repair the open or the high resistance in circuits FR4 and/or FY102. 3. Replace the power steering fluid flow control valve actuator if these circuits are OK. Is the repair or replacement complete?	—	Go to Step 10	—
8	1. Check power and ground circuits to the module. 2. Replace the power steering control module if power and ground is OK. Is the replacement complete?	—	Go to Step 10	—

GC6029800366010X

Fig. 5   Code 22: Solenoid Circuit Short To Ground/Open (Part 2 of 2)

Step	Action	Value(s)	Yes	No
9	1. If any continuity readings were observed, locate a short to ground in circuits FR4 and/or FY102. 2. Repair the short to ground in circuits FR4 and/or FY102. Is the repair complete?	—	Go to Step 10	—
10	1. Connect all connectors or components that were disconnected. 2. Road test the vehicle. 3. After the road test, install the scan tool again. 4. Check for DTC 22. Is DTC 22 displayed?	—	Go to Step 1	System OK

GC6029800366020X

Fig. 6   Code 23: Power Steering Control Module Fault

Step	Action	Value(s)	Yes	No
1	Was the Variable Effort Steering System Check performed?	—	Go to Step 2	Refer to System Check
2	1. Remove the power steering control module (PSCM). 2. Turn the ignition switch to the ON position. 3. Use a DMM to measure the voltage between terminal 6 of the PSCM connector and a known good ground. Is the measured voltage within the specified value?	B+	Go to Step 4	Go to Step 3
3	1. Locate an open or a high resistance in circuit X83. 2. Repair the open or the high resistance in circuit X83. Is the repair complete?	—	Go to Step 7	—
4	Use the DMM to measure the resistance between terminal 8 of the PSCM connector and a known good ground. Is the measured resistance within the specified value?	Less than 5 Ω	Go to Step 6	Go to Step 5
5	1. Locate an open or a high resistance in circuit F88. 2. Repair the open or the high resistance in circuit F88. Is the repair complete?	—	Go to Step 7	—
6	Replace the power steering control module. Effort Steering. Is the replacement complete?	—	Go to Step 7	—
7	1. Connect all of the connectors and components that were disconnected. 2. Road test the vehicle. 3. Install the scan tool after the road test. 4. Check for DTC 23. Is DTC 23 displayed?	—	Go to Step 1	System OK

GC6029800367000X

SAGINAW ROTARY VALVE POWER STEERING GEAR

POWER STEERING SYSTEM SERVICE

Component Service

POWER STEERING CONTROL MODULE

1. Twist self-locking screws to allow front of sound insulator to drop, **Fig. 7**.
2. Remove sound insulator.
3. Disconnect control module electrical connectors, **Fig. 8**.
4. Remove power steering control module.
5. Reverse procedure to install.

FLOW CONTROL VALVE ACTUATOR

1. Remove steering gear as outlined under "Front Suspension & Steering" in "Catera" chassis chapter.
2. Remove flow control valve actuator retaining screws, then the flow control valve actuator.
3. Reverse procedure to install.

POWER STEERING SYSTEM BLEED

STANDARD BLEEDING

Bleed power steering system after any component replacement, fluid line disconnection or in case of steering system noise. Bleed system to prevent pump damage, stop steering noise and to ensure proper system operation.

Inspect steering system before bleeding, looking for power steering lines touching frame, body or engine. Also inspect all hose connections for looseness or leaks.

1. Remove power steering pump reservoir cap.
2. Fill reservoir with proper fluid to full cold level.

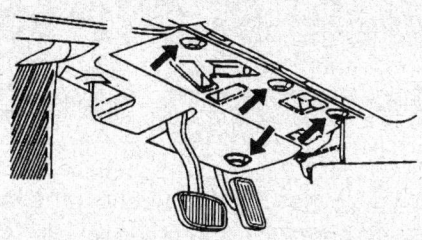

GC6029800368000X

Fig. 7 Sound insulator self-locking screws location

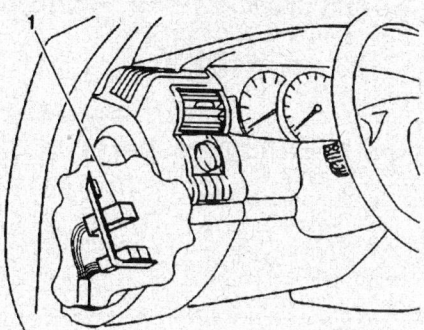

GC6029800369000X

Fig. 8 Power steering control module location

3. Connect vacuum pump tool No. J-35555 and power steering bleeder adapter tool No. J-43485, or equivalents, to reservoir filler neck.
4. Apply maximum vacuum of 20 inches and wait five minutes.
5. Inspect vacuum level after five minute. Vacuum typically will drop 2–3 inches. If vacuum does not remain steady, refer to "Special Bleeding."
6. Install reservoir cap, then start and idle engine.
7. Stop engine and inspect power steering fluid level.
8. Wait five minutes, then repeat previous two steps until fluid level has stabilized.
9. Start and idle engine, then turn steering wheel 180–360° F in both directions five times. **Do not turn wheel all way to stops.**
10. Stop engine and inspect power steering fluid level.
11. Connect vacuum pump and power steering bleeder adapter to reservoir filler neck.
12. Apply maximum vacuum of 20 inches and wait five minutes.
13. Inspect vacuum level after five minute. Vacuum typically will drop 2–3 inches. If vacuum does not remain steady, refer to "Special Bleeding."

SPECIAL BLEEDING

1. If vacuum continued to drop during bleeding procedure, remove power steering pressure and return hoses from power steering pump.
2. Install plugs from power steering bleeder adapter tool No. J-43485, or equivalents, into power steering pump pressure and return ports.
3. Connect vacuum pump and power steering bleeder adapter to reservoir filler neck.
4. Apply maximum vacuum of 20 inches.
5. If vacuum drops, repair or replace power steering pump.
6. If vacuum holds steady, proceed as follows:
   a. Inspect power steering fluid and ensure it is free of bubbles and is not discolored.
   b. Replace return hose clamps and O-rings.
   c. Replace pressure hose O-rings and reservoir to pump O-ring.
   d. Repeat bleeding procedure.
   e. Drive vehicle approximately 10 miles on smooth, flat surface to ensure power steering system reaches full operating temperature.

TIGHTENING SPECIFICATIONS

Year	Component	Torque/Ft. Lbs.
2001–05	Ball Stud	44①
	Flow Control Valve Actuator	27②
	Idler Arm	44
	Steering Gear	30
	Steering Gear Coupler	16
	Tie Rod Adjuster Clamp	11

① — Tighten an additional 52°.
② — Inch lbs.

Saturn Rack & Pinion Power Steering Gear

NOTE: On Air Bag Equipped Models, Refer To "Air Bag System Precautions" Located In The Front Of This Manual For System Disarming & Arming Procedures.

NOTE: Refer To "Computer Relearn Procedures" Located In The Front Of This Manual When Battery Power To The Computer Has Been Interrupted.

INDEX

DESCRIPTION

Steering System

The power steering system is a rack and pinion design featuring a constant flow or Electronic Variable Orifice (EVO) system. Models equipped with the DOHC engine utilize the EVO system while models equipped with the SOHC engine utilize the constant flow design.

Unlike conventional power steering systems, the EVO feature adjusts the amount of steering assist according to the speed of the vehicle, which is monitored by a vehicle speed sensor (VSS). This information is read electronically by the Powertrain Control Module (PCM), which commands the EVO actuator to control the power steering pump output flow.

At low speeds, where high levels of assist are desired, the EVO actuator is opened more widely, providing more flow to the steering gear and greater assist. At higher speeds, the actuator is closed further, providing less pump flow and less steering assist and improved road feeling. All of the additional flow of the pump that is not needed by the gear is allowed to return to the reservoir through a bypass.

EVO Actuator

The EVO actuator is a 10 ohm linear solenoid. The PCM controls the current to the high and low side of the actuator so current control is retained in the presence of any output fault condition.

The control of the actuator is accomplished by pulse width modulating (PWM) voltage to the actuator and monitoring the actual current flow. The PCM varies the PWM signal in order to make the actual current equal to the desired current.

COMPLAINT/CONDITION	POSSIBLE CAUSE(S)	CORRECTION(S)
Hard Steering	Front tire(s) improperly inflated.	Inflate tire(s) correctly.
	Improperly adjusted, improperly lubricated or damaged steering gear.	Adjust, lubricate (check for damaged boots), or replace steering gear.
	Worn or binding lower control arm ball stud(s).	Replace lower control arm(s).
	Worn or binding inner or outer tie rod(s).	Replace inner or outer tie rod end(s).
	Worn or binding upper strut mount(s).	Replace mount(s).
	Worn or binding intermediate shaft joint(s).	Replace intermediate shaft.
	Accessory drive belt loose.	Check accessory drive belt tension.
	Power steering fluid level low.	Add power steering fluid.
	Insufficient power steering pump pressure.	Repair or replace power steering pump.
	Faulty EVO actuator.	Replace EVO actuator.
	Restricted or leaking power steering hoses.	Replace hoses or tighten hose connections.
	High internal leakage in steering gear.	Replace steering gear.
	Excessive front wheel caster.	Perform alignment.
	Binding within steering column or intermediate shaft boot.	Correct condition.
Poor return of steering wheel to center.	Front tire(s) improperly inflated.	Inflate tire(s) correctly.
	Improperly adjusted, improperly lubricated, or binding steering gear.	Adjust, lubricate (check for damaged boots), or replace steering gear.
	Incorrect front wheel caster.	Perform alignment.
	Worn or binding inner or outer tie rod end(s).	Replace inner or outer tie rod end(s).
	Worn or binding upper strut mount(s).	Replace mount(s).
	Worn or binding intermediate shaft joint(s).	Replace intermediate shaft.
	Binding within steering column or intermediate shaft boot.	Correct condition.

G36029100001010A

Fig. 1 Power steering system troubleshooting
(Part 1 of 3)

TROUBLESHOOTING

Refer to **Fig. 1,** for power steering system troubleshooting.

DIAGNOSIS & TESTING

Hydraulic System Test

1. Disconnect high pressure line at steering gear and install power steering system tester tool No. SA9134C, or equivalent.
2. Open gate valve on power steering system tester.
3. Run engine until it has reached normal operating temperature. Replace any power steering fluid lost during tester installation.

COMPLAINT/CONDITION	POSSIBLE CAUSE(S)	CORRECTION(S)
Excessive free play in steering.	Wheel bearing(s) worn.	Replace wheel bearing(s).
	Steering gear mounting bolt(s) loose.	Tighten bolt(s).
	Steering gear out of adjustment or worn.	Adjust or replace steering gear.
	Worn inner or outer steering tie rod(s).	Replace tie rod(s).
	Lower control arm ball stud(s) worn.	Replace lower control arm(s).
	Front stabilizer bar bushings worn.	Replace bushings.
Rattle and/or clunking noise in steering	Inner or outer tie rod end(s) worn.	Replace inner or outer tie rod end(s).
	Steering gear out of adjustment or worn.	Adjust or replace steering gear.
	Intermediate shaft joint(s) worn.	Replace intermediate shaft.
	Steering gear mounting bolt(s) loose.	Tighten bolt(s).
	Worn wheel bearing(s).	Replace wheel bearing(s).
Momentary increase in steering effort when steering wheel is turned quickly with system at warm operating temperature.	High internal leakage in steering gear.	Replace steering gear.
	Low power steering fluid level.	Correct power steering fluid level.
	Insufficient pump pressure.	Repair or replace power steering pump.
	Damaged EVO actuator.	Replace actuator.
	EVO electrical circuit malfunction.	Correct condition.
Steering wheel surges or jerks when turning at low speeds.	Insufficient power steering pump pressure.	Repair or replace power steering pump.
	High internal leakage in steering gear.	Replace steering gear.
	Loose accessory drive belt.	Check accessory drive belt tension.
Insufficient system pressure — caused by pump.	Flow control valve stuck or inoperative.	Free or replace flow control valve.
	EVO system malfunction.	Refer to EVO system diagnosis.
	Pressure plate not flat against pump ring.	Correct condition.
	Worn pump ring.	Replace pump ring.
	Scored pressure plate, thrust plate, or rotor.	Replace components.
	Vane(s) sticking in rotor slot(s).	Clean rotor/vanes or replace component(s).
	Cracked or broken thrust or pressure plate.	Replace components.

G36029100001020A

Fig. 1   Power steering system troubleshooting (Part 2 of 3)

COMPLAINT/CONDITION	POSSIBLE CAUSE(S)	CORRECTION(S)
Insufficient system pressure — caused by steering gear.	Leaking steering gear piston seals or inner rack seal.	Replace steering gear.
Growling noise in power steering pump.	Excessive back pressure in hoses or steering gear caused by restriction.	Eliminate restriction.
	Scored pressure plate, thrust plate, or rotor.	Replace component(s)
	Worn pump ring.	Replace pump ring.
	Air in power steering fluid.	Add power steering fluid and bleed system.
	Pump mounting loose.	Tighten pump mounting.
Rattling noise in power steering pump.	Vane(s) sticking in rotor slot(s).	Clean rotor/vanes or replace component(s).
Swishing noise in power steering pump.	Damaged flow control valve.	Replace flow control valve.
Whining noise in power steering pump.	Pump shaft being scored.	Replace pump.

G36029100001030A

Fig. 1   Power steering system troubleshooting (Part 3 of 3)

8. Command EVO actuator to provide no assist using PDT. Record fluid flow rate as indicated on steering tester. Replace EVO actuator if flow rate is not between .4–.9 gallons per minute.

POWER STEERING SYSTEM SERVICE

Component Service

POWER STEERING PUMP OVERHAUL

DISASSEMBLE

1. Remove pump.
2. Remove retaining clips and reservoir.
3. Remove pump housing O-ring seal and pulley using puller tool No. SA9162C, or equivalent.
4. Remove three mounting bolts and bracket from pump.
5. Remove EVO actuator using removal tool No. SA9116C, or equivalent.
6. Remove flow control valve and spring.
7. Depress end cover using suitable C-clamp (one side on end cover, other on pump driveshaft), **Fig. 2.**
8. Insert piece of wood between C-clamp and pump driveshaft.
9. Place punch into pump housing access hole and remove retaining ring.
10. Push on driveshaft to assist in removing end cover.
11. Remove end cover, O-ring, pressure plate spring and pressure plate, **Fig. 3.**
12. Remove driveshaft with pump rotor, pump vanes, pump ring, thrust plate and shaft retaining ring.
13. Remove O-ring seal, two dowel pins and driveshaft seal from pump housing, **Fig. 4.**
14. Remove pressure plate, spring and O-ring from end cover.
15. Remove shaft retaining ring from driveshaft.
16. Remove pump rotor, pump vanes, pump ring and thrust plate from driveshaft, **Fig. 5.**
17. Separate pump rotor, vanes and ring.

INSPECTION

1. Clean all components with new power steering fluid.

4. Bleed power steering system as outlined in "Power Steering System Service."
5. With engine idling, record pressure and flow rate. If pressure reading is more than 150 psi., stop engine and inspect power steering lines for restrictions. **Do not turn steering wheel while performing this test.**
6. Slowly close gate valve until 700 psi., is indicated on power steering tester. Record pressure and flow rate.
7. Flow rate should not drop more than one gallon per minute from recorded flow rate.
8. If flow rate drops more than one gallon per minute, replace ring, rotor and vanes in pump. Also inspect pressure plate and thrust plates for wear.
9. Completely close and open gate valve three times. **Do not close gate valve for more than five seconds at a time.** Record fluid pressure each time valve is closed.
10. If all three readings are not within 50 psi., replace flow control valve.
11. With gate valve open, increase engine speed to 1600 RPM and record fluid pressure and flow rate. **Do not turn steering wheel.**
12. Flow rate should not vary more than one gallon per minute from previously recorded flow rate.
13. Ensure flow control valve moves freely

in pump housing. Inspect valve for burrs.
14. Turn steering wheel completely to left, then completely to right. Record fluid pressure and flow rate at each stop.
15. If flow rate is more than one gallon per minute, steering gear is leaking internally and must be replaced.

EVO Subsystem Test

1. Disconnect high pressure line at power steering pump and install power steering system tester tool No. SA9134C, or equivalent.
2. Connect Powertrain Diagnostic Tool (PDT) to ALDL diagnostic port. Follow tool manufacturer's instructions.
3. Open gate valve on steering system tester.
4. Run engine until normal operating temperature is reached. Replace any power steering fluid lost during tester installation.
5. Bleed power steering system as outlined in "Power Steering System Service."
6. Select EVO Subsystem Test using PDT tool in special test menu.
7. Command EVO actuator to provide full assist using PDT. Record power steering fluid flow rate as indicated on power steering system tester. Replace EVO actuator if flow rate is not between 2.35–2.85 gallons per minute.

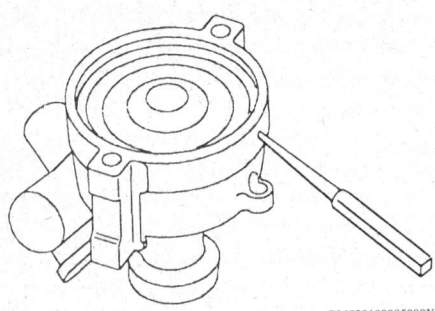

Fig. 2 Pump retaining ring removal

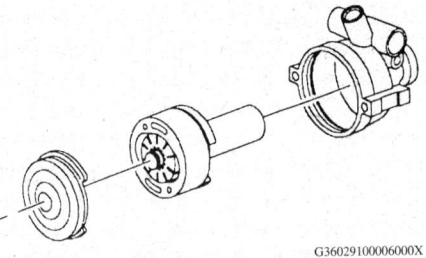

Fig. 3 Pump internal component removal

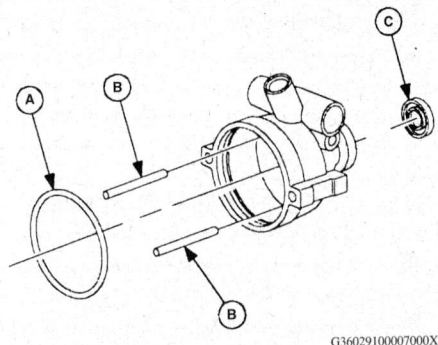

Fig. 4 Pump housing O-ring seal, dowel pins and driveshaft seal removal

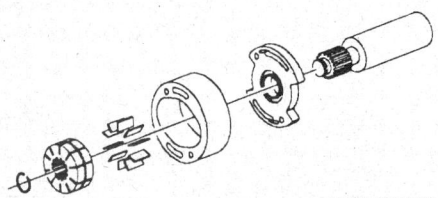

Fig. 5 Removing rotor, vanes, ring and thrust plate from driveshaft

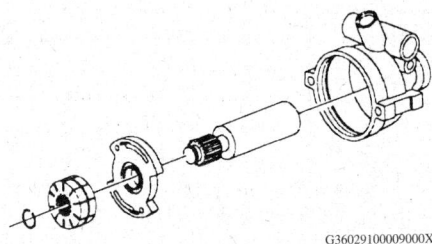

Fig. 6 Driveshaft/rotor/thrust plate assembly

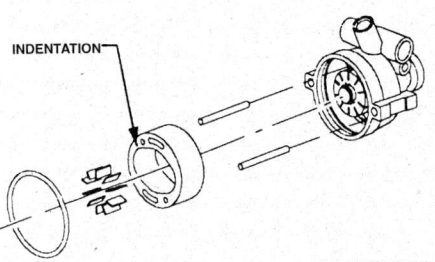

INDENTATION

Fig. 7 Pump ring dowel pins & pump ring assembly

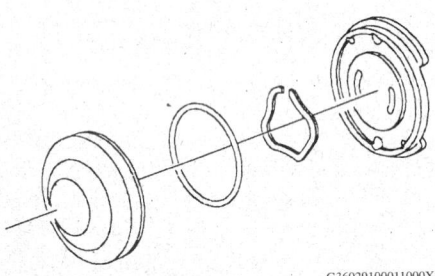

Fig. 8 Pressure plate assembly

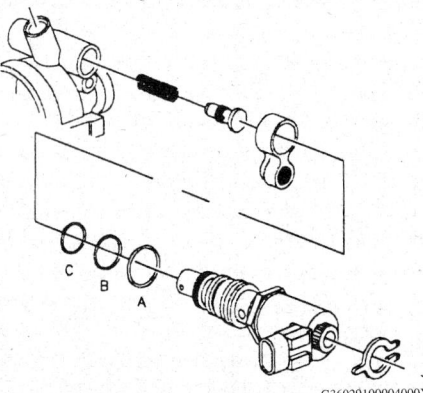

Fig. 9 EVO actuator O-ring locations

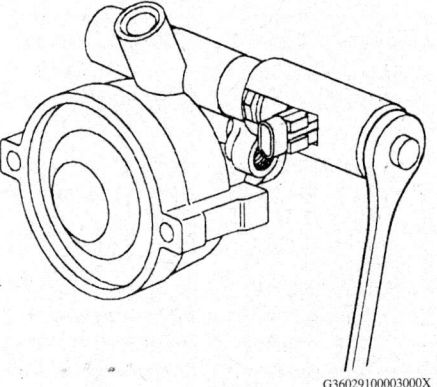

Fig. 10 EVO actuator replacement

2. Inspect pump ring, pump vanes, thrust plate and driveshaft for scoring, pitting or chatter marks.
3. Replace any damaged components. **Do not remove damage with abrasive cleaners.**
4. Wavy pattern on pump ring face will be present with low mileage and should not be mistaken for premature wear or damage.

ASSEMBLE

1. Lubricate driveshaft with new power steering fluid.
2. Install new driveshaft seal into pump housing using suitably-sized socket as driver.
3. Install thrust plate and pump rotor onto driveshaft.
4. Install driveshaft/rotor/thrust plate into housing, **Fig. 6.**
5. Install pump ring dowel pins into pump housing through thrust plate.
6. Install pump ring (with holes properly positioned onto dowel pins) into housing, **Fig. 7.**
7. Install pump ring with indentation facing up, **Fig. 7.**
8. Install vanes into pump rotor. Vanes may be installed in either direction.
9. Lubricate new pump housing O-ring with power steering fluid and install

into groove in housing.
10. Align pressure plate dowel holes with dowel pins and install plate into housing.
11. Position pressure plate spring against pressure plate.
12. Lubricate new end cover O-ring with power steering fluid and install onto end cover, **Fig. 8.**
13. Lubricate outer edge of end cover with power steering fluid and press it into pump housing.
14. Install retaining ring with opening near access hole into groove. Ensure ring is fully seated in housing groove.
15. Install three O-ring seals onto EVO actuator, **Fig. 9.**
16. Properly position EVO actuator and discharge fitting to pump , **Fig. 10.**
17. **Torque** EVO actuator using installation tool No. SA9116C, or equivalent, **Fig. 10.**
18. Install bracket onto power steering pump.
19. Install pump pulley using installation tool No. SA9162C, or equivalent.
20. Lubricate new reservoir O-ring with

power steering fluid and install onto reservoir.
21. Install reservoir into pump housing. Push reservoir straight into housing and install retaining clips.
22. Install pump on engine and bleed power steering system as outlined in "Power Steering System Service."

ELECTRONIC VARIABLE ORIFICE (EVO) ACTUATOR, REPLACE

1. Remove pump and disconnect EVO electrical connector locating clip.
2. Remove EVO actuator using socket removal tool No. SA91116C, or equivalent, **Fig. 10. Do not pivot socket tool during removal.**
3. Remove discharge fitting from actuator.

4. Remove three O-ring seals from actuator. Record size and location of O-ring seals.
5. Reverse procedure to install, noting the following:
   a. Install three O-ring seals onto EVO actuator, **Fig. 9.**
   b. Install pump and bleed power steering system as outlined in "Power Steering System Service."

POWER STEERING SYSTEM BLEED

1. Turn front wheels completely toward lefthand side, then turn ignition switch to Off position.
2. Raise and support vehicle until front tires clear ground.
3. Inspect reservoir fluid level. Add fluid if required.
4. Bleed system by turning wheels from side to side several times without contacting stops.

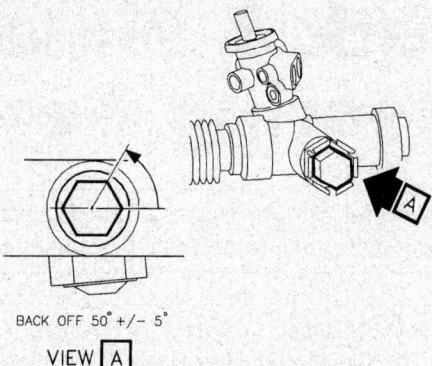

BACK OFF 50° +/− 5°

VIEW A

G36030100002000X

Fig. 11 Bearing preload adjustment

5. Start engine and inspect fluid level. Add fluid if required.
6. Return steering wheel to straight ahead position, lower front wheels and allow engine to idle for two to three minutes.
7. Road test vehicle to ensure steering functions normally and is free of noise.

Adjustments

STEERING GEAR BEARING PRELOAD

The following adjustment should be made with the front wheels raised and the steering wheel centered.
1. Loosen steering gear housing adjuster plug locknut.
2. Turn adjuster plug clockwise until it bottoms in steering gear housing, **Fig. 11.**
3. **Torque** adjuster plug to 108 inch lbs.
4. Back adjuster plug off 50° (approximately one flat of nut).
5. Inspect steering wheel return following adjustment.

TIGHTENING SPECIFICATIONS

Component	Torque/Ft. Lbs.
EVO Actuator	46
Power Steering Pump Bracket	28
Steering Gear Bearing Adjuster Plug	①
Steering Gear Bearing Locknut	52

① — Refer to "Adjustments" for tightening specifications and sequence.

Toyota Rack & Pinion Power Steering Gear

NOTE: On Air Bag Equipped Models, Refer To "Air Bag System Precautions" Located In The Front Of This Manual For System Disarming & Arming Procedures.

NOTE: Refer To "Computer Relearn Procedures" Located In The Front Of This Manual When Battery Power To The Computer Has Been Interrupted.

INDEX

DESCRIPTION

This steering system converts rotary motion to linear motion as follows: when the steering wheel is turned, rotary motion is transferred to the steering shaft, the shaft joint and rack pinion. The pinion teeth mesh with teeth on the rack and the rotary motion is transferred to the rack and changed to linear motion. The linear force is then transmitted through the tie rods to the steering knuckles which steer the front wheels.

POWER STEERING SYSTEM SERVICE

Component Service

STEERING GEAR

DISASSEMBLE

The power steering gear on these models cannot be disassembled. Power steering rack cannot be disassembled. Refer to "Front Suspension & Steering" sections in the appropriate chassis chapter for power steering gear replacement.

POWER STEERING SYSTEM BLEED

STANDARD BLEEDING

Bleed power steering system after any component replacement, fluid line disconnection or in case of steering system noise. Bleed system to prevent pump damage, stop steering noise and to ensure proper system operation.

Inspect steering system before bleeding, looking for power steering lines touching frame, body or engine. Also inspect all hose connections for looseness or leaks.

1. Remove power steering pump reservoir cap.
2. Fill reservoir with proper fluid to full cold level.
3. Connect vacuum pump tool No. J-35555 and power steering bleeder adapter tool No. J-43485, or equivalents, to reservoir filler neck.
4. Apply maximum vacuum of 20 inches and wait five minutes.
5. Inspect vacuum level after five minute. Vacuum typically will drop 2–3 inches. If vacuum does not remain steady, refer to "Special Bleeding."
6. Install reservoir cap, then start and idle engine.
7. Stop engine and inspect power steering fluid level.
8. Wait five minutes, then repeat previous two steps until fluid level has stabilized.
9. Start and idle engine, then turn steering wheel 180–360° F in both directions five times. **Do not turn wheel all way to stops.**
10. Stop engine and inspect power steering fluid level.
11. Connect vacuum pump and power steering bleeder adapter to reservoir filler neck.
12. Apply maximum vacuum of 20 inches and wait five minutes.
13. Inspect vacuum level after five minute. Vacuum typically will drop 2–3 inches. If vacuum does not remain steady, refer to "Special Bleeding."

SPECIAL BLEEDING

1. If vacuum continued to drop during bleeding procedure, remove power steering pressure and return hoses from power steering pump.
2. Install plugs from power steering bleeder adapter tool No. J-43485, or equivalents, into power steering pump pressure and return ports.
3. Connect vacuum pump and power steering bleeder adapter to reservoir filler neck.
4. Apply maximum vacuum of 20 inches.
5. If vacuum drops, repair or replace power steering pump.
6. If vacuum holds steady, proceed as follows:
   a. Inspect power steering fluid and ensure it is free of bubbles and is not discolored.
   b. Replace return hose clamps and O-rings.
   c. Replace pressure hose O-rings and reservoir to pump O-ring.
   d. Repeat bleeding procedure.
   e. Drive vehicle approximately 10 miles on smooth, flat surface to ensure power steering system reaches full operating temperature.

DISC BRAKES

NOTE: Refer To "Application Chart" To Determine Which Type Brakes Are Used On Vehicle Being Serviced.

TABLE OF CONTENTS

Application Chart

Model	Year	Front/Rear Brakes	Application
BUICK			
Century	2001–05	Front	AC Delco Single Piston
		Rear	AC Delco Single Piston
LeSabre	2001–05	Front	AC Delco Single Piston
Park Avenue	2001–05	Front	AC Delco Single Piston
		Rear	AC Delco Single Piston
Regal	2001–04	Front	AC Delco Single Piston
		Rear	AC Delco Single Piston
CADILLAC			
Catera	2001	Front	AC Delco Single Piston
		Rear	AC Delco Dual Piston
CTS	2003–05	Front	AC Delco Dual Piston
		Rear	AC Delco Single Piston
DeVille	2001–05	Front	AC Delco Single Piston
		Rear	AC Delco Single Piston
Eldorado	2001–02	Front	AC Delco Single Piston
		Rear	AC Delco Single Piston
Seville	2001–04	Front	AC Delco Single Piston
		Rear	AC Delco Single Piston
XLR	2004–05	Front	PBR Dual Piston
		Rear	PBR Single Piston
STS	2005	Front	A/C Delco Dual Piston
		Rear	A/C Delco Single Piston
CHEVROLET			
Aveo	2005	Front	A/C Delco Single Piston
Camaro	2001–02	Front	AC Delco Dual Piston
		Rear	PBR Single Piston
Cavalier	2001–05	Front	AC Delco Single Piston
Corvette	2001–05	Front	PBR Dual Piston
		Rear	PBR Single Piston

Continued

Model	Year	Front/Rear Brakes	Application
CHEVROLET			
Impala	2001–04	Front	AC Delco Single Piston
		Rear	AC Delco Single Piston
Lumina	2001	Front	AC Delco Single Piston
Malibu	2001–05	Front	AC Delco Single Piston
	2004–05	Rear	AC Delco Single Piston
Metro	2001	Front	Aisin-Seiki Single Piston
Monte Carlo	2001–05	Front	AC Delco Single Piston
		Rear	AC Delco Single Piston
Prizm	2001–02	Front	Toyota/GM Single Piston
OLDSMOBILE			
Alero	2001–04	Front	AC Delco Single Piston
		Rear	AC Delco Single Piston
Aurora	2001–03	Front	AC Delco Single Piston
		Rear	AC Delco Single Piston
Intrigue	2001–02	Front	AC Delco Single Piston
		Rear	AC Delco Single Piston
PONTIAC			
Bonneville	2001–05	Front	AC Delco Single Piston
Firebird	2001–02	Front	AC Delco Dual Piston
		Rear	PBR Single Piston
Grand Am	2001–05	Front	AC Delco Single Piston
		Rear	AC Delco Single Piston
Grand Prix	2001–05	Front	AC Delco Single Piston
		Rear	AC Delco Single Piston
G6	2005	Front	A/C Delco Single Piston
		Rear	A/C Delco Single Piston
GTO	2004–05	Front	A/C Delco Dual Piston
		Rear	A/C Delco Single Piston
Sunfire	2001–05	Front	AC Delco Single Piston
Vibe	2003–05	Front	Toyota/GM Single Piston
		Rear	Toyota/GM Single Piston
SATURN			
ION	2003–05	Front	Saturn
L-Series	2001–05	Front	Saturn
		Rear	Saturn
S-Series	2001–02	Front	Saturn
		Rear	Saturn

Aisin-Seiki Single Piston Front Disc Brake

NOTE: On Air Bag Equipped Models, Refer To "Air Bag System Precautions" Located In The Front Of This Manual For System Disarming & Arming Procedures.

NOTE: Refer To "Computer Relearn Procedures" Located In The Front Of This Manual When Battery Power To The Computer Has Been Interrupted.

INDEX

PRECAUTIONS

1. Keep grease and other foreign material off brake linings, caliper, surfaces of disc and external surfaces of hub.
2. Avoid deforming disc, and nicking or scratching brake linings.
3. Worn or damaged rubber piston seals should be replaced.
4. Ensure wheel removal and installation does not interfere with or damage caliper splash shield or bleed screws.
5. Front wheel bearing preload should be adjusted to specifications.
6. Ensure vehicle is centered on hoist before servicing any front end components to avoid bending or damaging disc splash shield on full left or right-hand wheel turns.
7. Before vehicle is moved after any brake service work, obtain a firm brake pedal.
8. Assembly bolts of two-piece caliper housings should not be disturbed unless caliper requires service.

DESCRIPTION

The single piston sliding caliper assembly is mounted to a support bracket by two slide pins, **Fig. 1**. The caliper assembly slides on the two mounting pins. Upon brake application, fluid pressure against the piston forces the inboard shoe and lining assembly against the inboard side of the disc. This action causes the caliper assembly to slide until the outboard lining comes into contact with the disc.

TROUBLESHOOTING

The most common cause of brake chatter on disc brakes is a variation in thickness of the disc. If roughness or vibration is encountered during highway operation or if pedal pulsation is experienced at low speeds, the disc may have excessive thickness variation. To inspect for this condition, measure the disc at 12 points with a micrometer at a radius approximately one inch from edge of disc. If thickness measurements vary by more than .0005 inch, the disc should be replaced with a new one.

Excessive lateral runout of braking disc may cause a piston knocking back, possibly creating increased pedal travel and vibration when brakes are applied.

Before inspecting the runout, the wheel bearings should be adjusted. The adjustment is very important and will be required at the completion of the test to prevent bearing failure. Adjust the wheel bearings as outlined in "Front Suspension & Steering" section of appropriate chassis chapter.

BRAKE SYSTEM BLEED

Refer to "Hydraulic Brake Systems" for manual and pressure bleeding procedures.

BRAKE PAD SERVICE

1. Remove approximately ⅔ of brake fluid from master cylinder.
2. Raise and support vehicle.
3. Mark front wheel and axle for installation alignment, then remove wheel and tire assembly.
4. Remove two caliper slide pins from bracket.
5. Disconnect caliper and support aside. Leave hydraulic lines connected.
6. Remove brake pads, shims, wear indicators and retainers.
7. Reverse procedure to install.

CALIPER SERVICE

Removal

1. Remove approximately ⅔ of brake fluid from master cylinder.
2. Raise and support vehicle.
3. Mark front wheel and axle for installation alignment, then remove wheel and tire assembly.
4. If caliper assembly is to be serviced, remove inlet fitting mounting bolt, copper washer and inlet fitting from caliper housing. Plug opening in inlet fitting. **Do not crimp brake hose.**
5. If only shoe and lining assemblies are to be replaced, do not disconnect brake line fitting from caliper.
6. Remove caliper slide pins and caliper. If only shoe and lining are to be replaced, suspend caliper from chassis. **Do not allow caliper to hang by brake hose.**
7. Remove shoe and lining.
8. Remove mounting bolts and bracket.
9. Remove slide pin boot from bracket.

Disassemble

1. Drain brake fluid from caliper into suitable container.
2. Apply clean shop towels to pad interior of caliper and remove piston by directing compressed air into caliper brake hose inlet hole, **Fig. 2.** Use just enough air pressure to ease piston out of bore. **Do not place fingers in front of piston.**
3. Remove dust boot from piston.
4. Remove piston seal from bore using small piece of wood or plastic. **Do not use metal tool to remove seal.**
5. Remove bleeder valve.

Inspection

1. Inspect piston for scoring, nicks, corrosion and wear.
2. Inspect caliper housing and seal groove for corrosion, nicks, scoring and excessive wear. Use crocus cloth

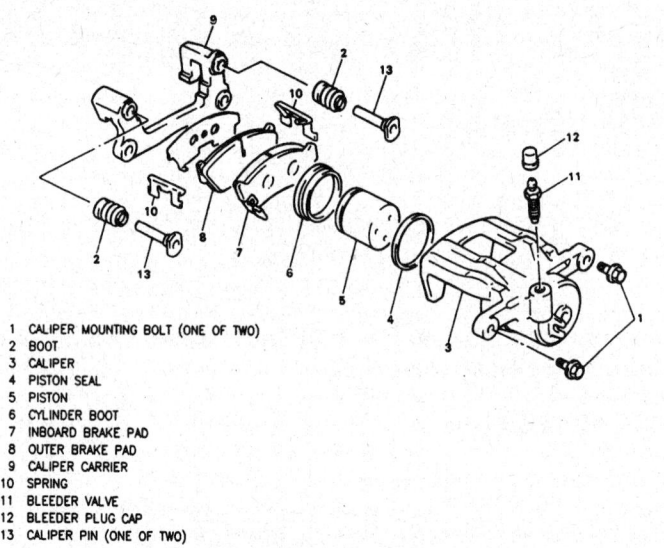

1 CALIPER MOUNTING BOLT (ONE OF TWO)
2 BOOT
3 CALIPER
4 PISTON SEAL
5 PISTON
6 CYLINDER BOOT
7 INBOARD BRAKE PAD
8 OUTER BRAKE PAD
9 CALIPER CARRIER
10 SPRING
11 BLEEDER VALVE
12 BLEEDER PLUG CAP
13 CALIPER PIN (ONE OF TWO)

GC4079700146000X

Fig. 1 Exploded view of disc brake caliper assembly

to polish away corrosion from housing bore.
3. Clean all components with denatured alcohol then dry with compressed air.
4. Blow out all passages in housing and bleeder valve.

Assemble

1. Apply suitable grease to piston seal and cylinder wall, then install seal. Ensure piston seal is not twisted.
2. Apply suitable grease to sliding portion of piston and install dust boot.
3. Insert edge of dust boot into boot groove and slowly force piston fully into cylinder.
4. Install bleeder valve.

Installation

1. Apply suitable grease to inner face of slide pin boot.
2. Install slide pin boot to bracket.
3. Install bracket and mounting bolts.
4. Install shoe and lining. Ensure wear indicators are located on trailing edge of

shoe during forward wheel rotation.
5. Install caliper to bracket.
6. Attach hose to caliper.
7. Install wheel and tire assembly, then lower vehicle.
8. Fill master cylinder to proper level and bleed brakes as outlined in "Hydraulic Brake Systems" chapter. **Before moving vehicle, pump brakes several times to ensure pedal is firm. Do not move vehicle until firm pedal is obtained.**

ROTOR
REPLACE
Removal

1. Remove approximately ⅔ of brake fluid from master cylinder.
2. Raise and support vehicle.
3. Mark front wheel and axle for installation alignment, then remove wheel and tire assembly.
4. If caliper assembly is to be serviced, remove inlet fitting mounting bolt, copper washer and inlet fitting from caliper

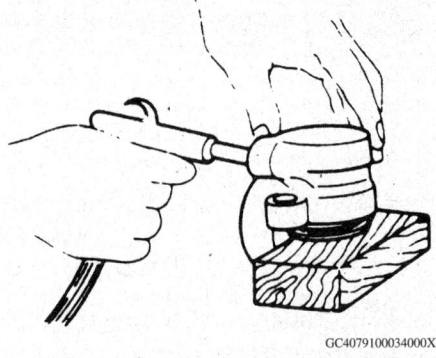

GC4079100034000X

Fig. 2 Caliper piston removal

housing. Plug opening in inlet fitting. **Do not crimp brake hose.**
5. If only shoe and lining assemblies are to be replaced, do not disconnect brake line fitting from caliper.
6. Remove caliper slide pins and caliper. If only shoe and lining are to be replaced, suspend caliper from chassis. **Do not allow caliper to hang by brake hose.**
7. Remove shoe and lining.
8. Remove mounting bolts and bracket.
9. Remove slide pin boot from bracket.
10. Remove rotor from wheel hub.

Installation

1. Install rotor.
2. Apply suitable grease to inner face of slide pin boot.
3. Install slide pin boot to bracket.
4. Install bracket and mounting bolts.
5. Install shoe and lining. Ensure wear indicators are located on trailing edge of shoe during forward wheel rotation.
6. Install caliper to bracket.
7. Attach hose to caliper.
8. Install wheel and tire assembly, then lower vehicle.
9. Fill master cylinder to proper level and bleed brakes as outlined in "Hydraulic Brake Systems" chapter. **Before moving vehicle, pump brakes several times to ensure pedal is firm. Do not move vehicle until firm pedal is obtained.**

DISC BRAKE SPECIFICATIONS
Rotor Specifications

Model	Year	Brake Lining Wear Limit, Inch	Nominal Thickness, Inch	Minimum Refinish Thickness, Inch	Discard Limit, Inch①	Thickness Variation Parallelism, Inch	Lateral Run Out (T.I.R.) Inch	Maximum Scoring Depth, Inch
Metro	2001	.0400	.6700	—	.5900	.0005	.0040	.0150

① — Discard thickness is stamped on rotor.

TIGHTENING SPECIFICATIONS

Year	Component	Torque/Ft. Lbs.
2001	Bleeder Valve	89①
	Brake Hose Union	17
	Brake Pipe Fittings	12
	Caliper	22
	Caliper Carrier	29–43

① — Inch lbs.

AC-Delco Dual Piston Front Disc Brake

NOTE: On Air Bag Equipped Models, Refer To "Air Bag System Precautions" Located In The Front Of This Manual For System Disarming & Arming Procedures.

NOTE: Refer To "Computer Relearn Procedures" Located In The Front Of This Manual When Battery Power To The Computer Has Been Interrupted.

INDEX

PRECAUTIONS

1. Keep grease and other foreign material off brake linings, caliper, surfaces of disc and external surfaces of hub.
2. Avoid deforming disc, and nicking or scratching brake linings.
3. Worn or damaged rubber piston seals should be replaced.
4. During removal and installation of a wheel assembly, ensure not to interfere with or damage caliper splash shield, or bleeder screw.
5. Front wheel bearings preload should be adjusted to specifications.
6. Ensure vehicle is centered on hoist before servicing any front end components to avoid bending or damaging disc splash shield on full left or right-hand wheel turns.
7. Before vehicle is moved after any brake service work, obtain a firm brake pedal.
8. Assembly bolts of two-piece caliper housings should not be disturbed unless caliper requires service.

DESCRIPTION

The dual piston sliding caliper is comprised of two interconnected bores and is attached to a mounting bracket with two mounting bolts, **Fig. 1.** Hydraulic pressure acting on the bottom of the caliper bores forces the pistons outward, enabling the caliper to slide inward, thereby clamping the brake shoes against the rotor.

TROUBLESHOOTING

The most common cause of brake chatter on disc brakes is a variation in disc thickness. If roughness or vibration is encountered during highway operation or if pedal pulsation is experienced at low speeds, the disc may have excessive thickness variation. To inspect for this condition, measure the disc at 12 points with a micrometer at a radius approximately one inch from edge of disc. If thickness measurements vary by more than .0005 inch, the disc should be replaced with a new one.

Excessive lateral runout of braking disc may cause a piston knocking back, possibly creating increased pedal travel and vibration when brakes are applied.

Before inspecting the runout, the wheel bearings should be adjusted. The adjustment is very important and will be required at the completion of the test to prevent bearing failure. Adjust the wheel bearings as outlined in "Front Suspension & Steering" section of appropriate chassis chapter.

BRAKE SYSTEM BLEED

Refer to "Hydraulic Brake Systems" for manual and pressure bleeding procedures.

BRAKE PAD SERVICE

1. Drain master cylinder fluid level to ⅓ full.
2. Raise and support vehicle, then remove front tire and wheel assemblies.
3. Mark wheel to hub and bearing relationship for installation alignment.
4. Push pistons back together into caliper bores using suitable C-clamp and block of wood.
5. **Do not disconnect brake line fitting from caliper.**
6. Remove two mounting bolts and caliper, then suspend caliper from chassis. **Do not allow caliper to hang by brake hose.**
7. Lift upward on outward retaining spring until it clears center lug and remove shoe.
8. Pull inboard shoe outward to disengage retainer springs from pistons and remove inboard shoe.
9. Reverse procedure to install, noting the following:

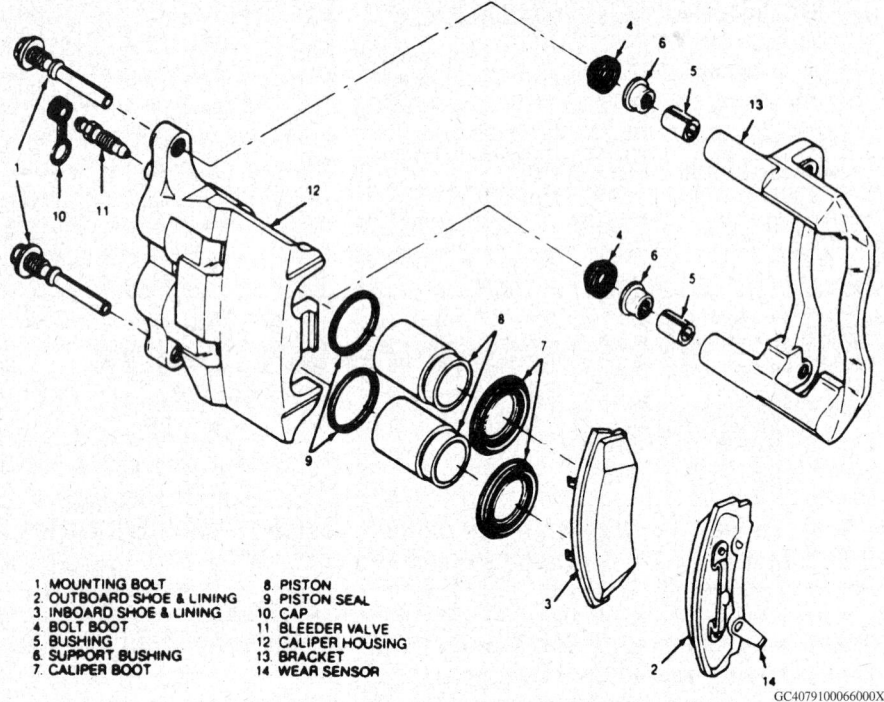

1. MOUNTING BOLT	8. PISTON
2. OUTBOARD SHOE & LINING	9. PISTON SEAL
3. INBOARD SHOE & LINING	10. CAP
4. BOLT BOOT	11. BLEEDER VALVE
5. BUSHING	12. CALIPER HOUSING
6. SUPPORT BUSHING	13. BRACKET
7. CALIPER BOOT	14. WEAR SENSOR

GC4079100066000X

Fig. 1 Exploded view of dual piston caliper

a. Install inboard shoe into caliper. Ensure retainer spring tangs are fully positioned into pistons.
b. Snap outboard shoe retaining spring over housing center lug and install outboard shoe into caliper.

CALIPER SERVICE
Removal

1. Drain master cylinder fluid level to ⅓ full.
2. Raise and support vehicle, then remove front tire and wheel assemblies.
3. Mark wheel to hub and bearing relationship for installation alignment.
4. Push pistons back together into caliper bores using suitable C-clamp and block of wood.
5. Remove mounting bolt, copper washer and inlet fitting. Plug opening in inlet fitting. **Do not crimp brake hose.**
6. Remove two mounting bolts and caliper.

Disassemble

1. Position shop towel in interior component of caliper, then slowly apply compressed air to inlet port and remove pistons. **One piston must be partially installed to facilitate removal of second piston. Pad or wooden spacer may be used to prevent complete removal of first piston.**
2. Remove piston boots from caliper bores, then pry piston seals from caliper bore grooves using suitable wooden or plastic tool. **Do not use metal tool to remove seal.**
3. Remove bleeder valve from caliper.

Inspection

1. Inspect piston for scoring, nicks, corrosion, and wear.
2. Inspect caliper housing and seal grooves for corrosion, nicks, scoring and excessive wear. Use crocus cloth to polish away corrosion from housing bore.
3. Clean all components with denatured alcohol and dry with compressed air.
4. Blow out all passages in housing and bleeder valve.

Mounting Bracket Service
REMOVAL

1. Drain master cylinder fluid level to ⅓ full.
2. Raise and support vehicle, then remove front tire and wheel assemblies.
3. Mark wheel to hub and bearing relationship for installation alignment.
4. Push pistons back together into caliper bores using suitable C-clamp and block of wood.
5. Remove mounting bolt, copper washer and inlet fitting. Plug opening in inlet fitting. **Do not crimp brake hose.**
6. Remove two mounting bolts and caliper.
7. Remove mounting bolts and mounting bracket.

BUSHING & BOOT REPLACEMENT

1. Remove bolt boots from support bushings.
2. Clamp bracket in suitable vise and pry support bushings from inner bushings

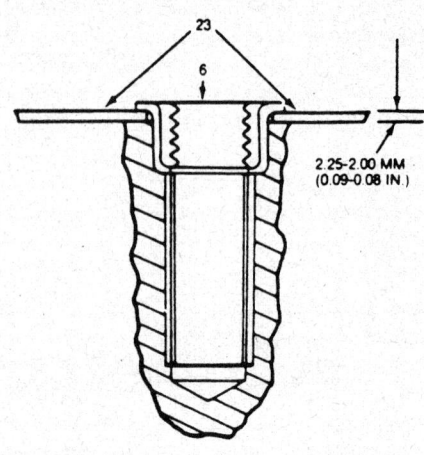

6. SUPPORT BUSHING
23. SHIM STOCK

GC4079100067000X

Fig. 2 Support bushing installation

in bracket ears with small screwdriver.
3. Pull inner bushings from mounting bracket ears using paper clip.
4. Lubricate inner bushings with silicone based grease and install bushings flush with bracket ears.
5. Position an .080–.090 inch thick shim stock on bracket ear face and drive support bushings into inner bushings, **Fig. 2.** Bushing should protrude .080–.090 inch above bracket ear face.
6. Snap new bolt boots over support bushing lip.

INSTALLATION

1. Coat mounting bracket mounting bolt threads with suitable Loctite sealant, or equivalent.
2. Align holes and install mounting bracket.

Assemble

1. Install bleeder valve.
2. Lubricate piston seals with clean brake fluid, then carefully install seals into caliper bore grooves. **Ensure seals are not twisted.**
3. Lubricate boots and install onto pistons, then push pistons fully into caliper bores.
4. Seat boots into caliper bores using boot seal installer tool No. J-36349, or equivalent.

Installation

1. Position caliper over rotor and onto mounting bracket.
2. Lubricate entire length of with silicone based grease and install mounting bolts.
3. Install fitting using new copper washer.
4. Install front wheels, fill master cylinder to proper level, and bleed brake.
5. Pump brake pedal several times to ensure it is firm. **Do not move vehicle until firm pedal is obtained.**

ROTOR
REPLACE

1. Raise and support vehicle, then remove tire and wheel assembly.
2. Drain master cylinder fluid level to ⅓ full.
3. Raise and support vehicle, then remove front tire and wheel assemblies.
4. Mark wheel to hub and bearing relationship for installation alignment.
5. Push pistons back together into caliper bores using suitable C-clamp and block of wood.
6. Remove mounting bolt, copper washer and inlet fitting. Plug opening in inlet fitting. **Do not crimp brake hose.**
7. Remove two mounting bolts and caliper.
8. Remove rotor from hub and bearing.
9. Reverse procedure to install.

DISC BRAKE SPECIFICATIONS
Rotor Specifications

Model	Year	Brake Lining Wear Limit, Inch	Nominal Thickness, Inch	Minimum Refinish Thickness, Inch	Discard Limit, Inch①	Thickness Variation Parallelism, Inch	Lateral Run Out (T.I.R.) Inch	Maximum Scoring Depth, Inch
Camaro & Firebird	2001–02	.0300	1.2600	1.2230	1.2090	.0010	.0020	.0590
CTS	2003–05	.0300	1.2670	1.2090	1.2090	.0010	.0020	.0590
GTO	2004–05	.0790	—	—	.9840	.0002	.0020	.0160
STS	2005	.0390	1.2670	1.2090	1.2090	.0010	.0020	.0590

① — Discard thickness is stamped on rotor.

TIGHTENING SPECIFICATIONS

Year	Component	Torque/Ft. Lbs.
CAMARO & FIREBIRD		
2001–02	Bleeder Valve	106①
	Caliper Guide Pin	23
	Caliper Mounting Bracket	74
	Hose (2000–01)	30
	Hose (2002)	41
	Wheel Lug Nut	100
CTS		
2003–05	Bleeder Valve	124①
	Caliper Bracket	96
	Caliper Pin	46
	Hose	37
	Pipe Fitting Tube	13
	Rotor	124①
GTO		
2004–05	Brake Caliper Bolt	63②
	Caliper Pin	24
	Hose	26
	Pipe Fitting Tube	12
STS		
2005	Bleeder Valve	124①
	Caliper Bracket	96
	Caliper Pin	46
	Hose	37
	Pipe Fitting Tube	13
	Rotor	124①

① — Inch lbs.
② — Then an additional 45°.

AC-Delco Single Piston Front Disc Brake

NOTE: On Air Bag Equipped Models, Refer To "Air Bag System Precautions" Located In The Front Of This Manual For System Disarming & Arming Procedures.

NOTE: Refer To "Computer Relearn Procedures" Located In The Front Of This Manual When Battery Power To The Computer Has Been Interrupted.

INDEX

PRECAUTIONS

1. Keep grease and other foreign material off brake linings, caliper, surfaces of disc and external surfaces of hub.
2. Avoid deforming disc, and nicking or scratching brake linings.
3. Worn or damaged rubber piston seals should be replaced.
4. During removal and installation of a wheel assembly, ensure not to interfere with or damage caliper splash shield, or bleeder screw.
5. Front wheel bearing preload should be adjusted to specifications.
6. Ensure vehicle is centered on hoist before servicing any front end components to avoid bending or damaging disc splash shield on full left or right-hand wheel turns.
7. Before vehicle is moved after any brake service work, ensure to obtain a firm brake pedal.
8. Assembly bolts of two-piece caliper housings should not be disturbed unless caliper requires service.

DESCRIPTION

The caliper has a single piston and is mounted to the support bracket by two mounting bolts, **Figs. 1 through 3.** The caliper assembly slides on the two mounting bolts. Upon brake application, fluid pressure against the piston forces the inboard shoe and lining assembly against the inboard side of the disc. This action causes the caliper assembly to slide until the outboard lining comes into contact with the disc. As pressure builds up the linings are pressed against the disc with increased force.

TROUBLESHOOTING

The most common cause of brake chatter on disc brakes is a variation in disc thick-

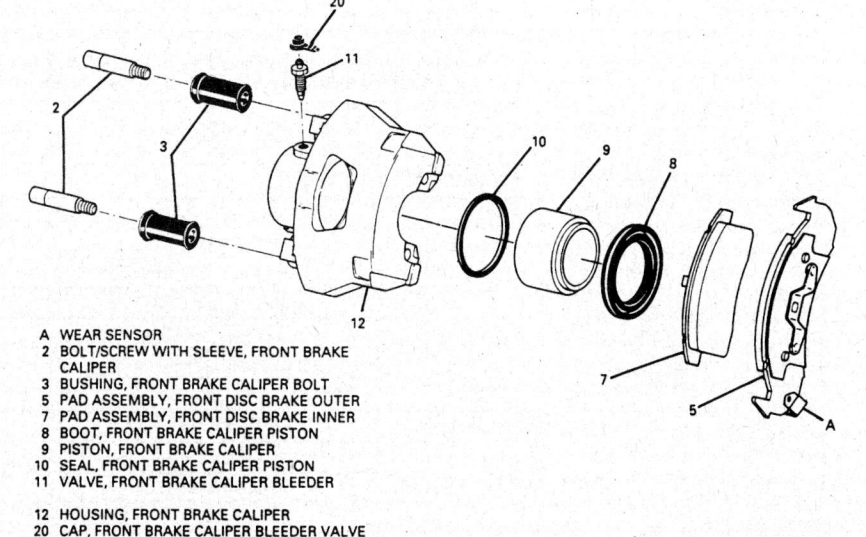

A   WEAR SENSOR
2   BOLT/SCREW WITH SLEEVE, FRONT BRAKE CALIPER
3   BUSHING, FRONT BRAKE CALIPER BOLT
5   PAD ASSEMBLY, FRONT DISC BRAKE OUTER
7   PAD ASSEMBLY, FRONT DISC BRAKE INNER
8   BOOT, FRONT BRAKE CALIPER PISTON
9   PISTON, FRONT BRAKE CALIPER
10 SEAL, FRONT BRAKE CALIPER PISTON
11 VALVE, FRONT BRAKE CALIPER BLEEDER

12 HOUSING, FRONT BRAKE CALIPER
20 CAP, FRONT BRAKE CALIPER BLEEDER VALVE

GC4079100054000X

Fig. 1   Exploded view of caliper. Alero, Cavalier, Grand Am & Sunfire

ness. If roughness or vibration is encountered during highway operation or if pedal pulsation is experienced at low speeds, the disc may have excessive thickness variation. To inspect for this condition, measure the disc at 12 points with a micrometer at a radius approximately one inch from edge of disc. If thickness measurements vary by more than .0005 inch, the disc should be replaced with a new one.

Excessive lateral runout of braking disc may cause a piston knocking back, possibly creating increased pedal travel and vibration when brakes are applied.

Before inspecting the runout, the wheel bearings should be adjusted. The adjustment is very important and will be required at the completion of the test to prevent bearing failure. Adjust the wheel bearings as outlined in "Front Suspension & Steering" section of appropriate chassis chapter.

BRAKE SYSTEM BLEED

Refer to "Hydraulic Brake Systems" for manual and pressure bleeding procedures.

BRAKE PAD SERVICE

1. Remove approximately ⅔ of brake fluid from master cylinder.
2. Raise and support front of vehicle, then remove wheel and tire assembly.
3. Push piston back into caliper bore using suitable C-clamp, **Fig. 4.**
4. **Do not disconnect brake line fitting from caliper.**
5. **On Catera models,** carefully separate sensor from inner brake pad by placing small screwdriver between lower section of sensor and brake pad, **Fig. 5.**
6. **On all models,** remove mounting bolts and caliper, then support aside, **Fig. 6.**

Do not allow caliper to hang from brake hose. If there signs of corrosion, replace bolts when installing caliper.

7. Remove brake pads and pad retainers from caliper bracket.
8. Reverse procedure to install.

CALIPER SERVICE

Replacement

1. Remove approximately ⅔ of brake fluid from master cylinder.
2. Raise and support front of vehicle, then remove wheel and tire assembly.
3. Push piston back into caliper bore using suitable C-clamp, **Fig. 4.**
4. Remove inlet fitting mounting bolt, copper washer and inlet fitting from caliper housing. Plug opening in inlet fitting. **Do not crimp brake hose.**
5. **On Catera models,** carefully separate sensor from inner brake pad by placing small screwdriver between lower section of sensor and brake pad, **Fig. 5.**
6. **On all models,** remove caliper mounting bolts and caliper, **Fig. 6.** If there are signs of corrosion, replace bolts when installing caliper assembly.
7. Reverse procedure to install.

Disassemble

1. Clean outside of caliper, then drain brake fluid from caliper into suitable container.
2. Place clean shop towels to pad caliper interior and remove piston by directing compressed air into caliper brake hose inlet hole, **Fig. 7.** Use just enough air pressure to ease piston out of bore. **Do not place fingers in front of piston.**
3. Remove dust boot from caliper bore using suitable screwdriver, **Fig. 8.**
4. Remove piston seal from bore using small piece of wood or plastic, **Do not use metal tool to remove seal.**
5. Remove bleeder valve.

Inspection

1. Inspect piston for scoring, nicks, corrosion, and wear and replace as needed.
2. Inspect caliper housing and seal groove for corrosion, nicks, scoring and excessive wear, then use crocus cloth to polish away corrosion from housing bore.
3. Clean all components with denatured alcohol and dry with compressed air.
4. Blow out all passages in housing and bleeder valve.

Assemble

1. Install bleeder valve.
2. Install piston seal and dust boot. Ensure to properly seat dust boot using installer tool No. J-36349, or equivalent, **Fig. 9.**
3. Install piston.

ROTOR
REPLACE

1. Remove approximately ⅔ of brake

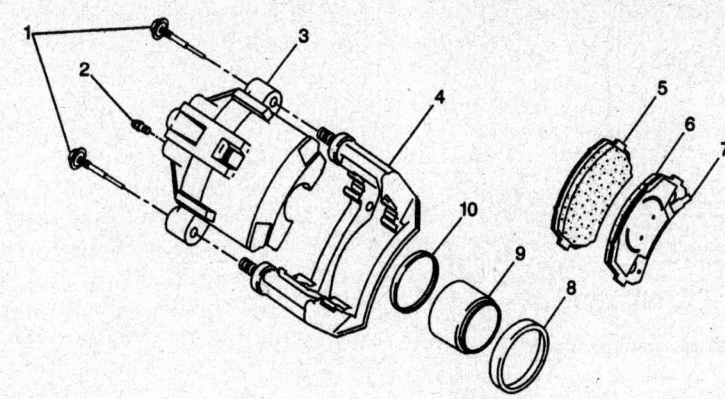

(1) Caliper Bolts
(2) Bleeder Valve
(3) Caliper Housing
(4) Caliper Bracket
(5) Inboard Pad
(6) Outboard Pad
(7) Wear Sensor
(8) Caliper Boot
(9) Piston
(10) Piston Seal

GC4079700137000X

Fig. 2 Exploded view of caliper. Aurora, Century, DeVille, Eldorado, Grand Prix, Intrigue, LeSabre, Regal & Seville

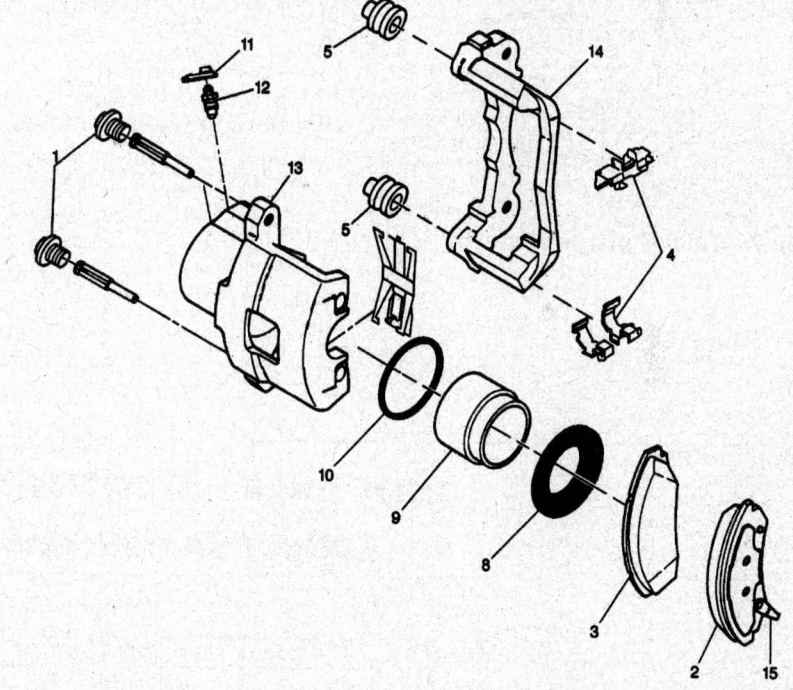

(1) Bolt and Slide Pin Assemblies
(2) Outboard Brake Pad
(3) Inboard Brake Pad
(4) Clips, Brake Pad
(5) Boot, Brake Pin Slide
(8) Seal, Brake Caliper Dust
(9) Piston, Brake Caliper
(10) Seal, Brake Caliper Piston
(11) Cap, Brake Bleeder Screw
(12) Screw, Brake Bleeder
(13) Caliper, Brake
(14) Bracket, Caliper to Knuckle
(15) Wear Sensor

GC4079700138000X

Fig. 3 Exploded view of caliper. Impala & Malibu

fluid from master cylinder.

2. Raise and support front of vehicle, then remove wheel and tire assembly.
3. Push piston back into caliper bore using suitable C-clamp, **Fig. 4.**
4. **Do not disconnect brake line fitting from caliper.**
5. **On Catera models,** carefully separate sensor from inner brake pad by placing small screwdriver between lower section of sensor and brake pad, **Fig. 5.**
6. **On all models,** remove mounting bolts and caliper, then support aside, **Fig. 6.** **Do not allow caliper to hang from brake hose.** If there signs of corrosion, replace bolts when installing caliper.
7. Remove mounting bolts and mounting bracket.
8. Remove rotor from hub and bearing.
9. Reverse procedure to install.

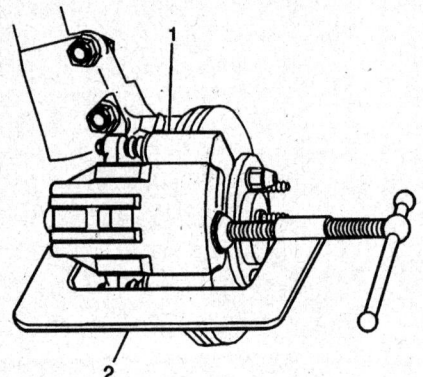

(1) Caliper
(2) C-Clamp

Fig. 4 Piston compression

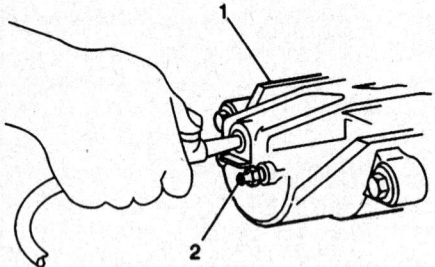

Fig. 7 Caliper piston removal

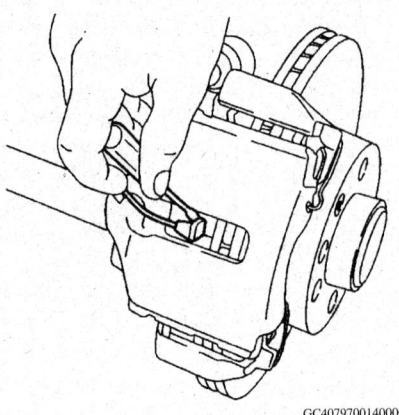

Fig. 5 Brake pad sensor removal. Catera

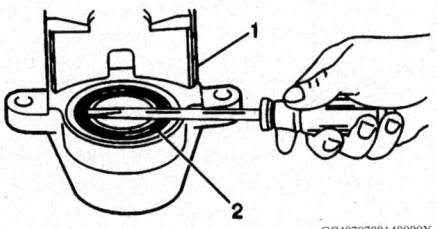

Fig. 8 Dust boot removal

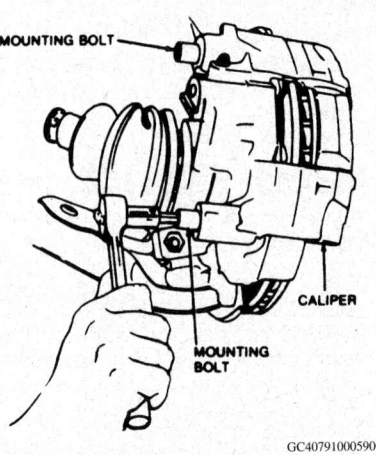

Fig. 6 Caliper mounting bolts replacement

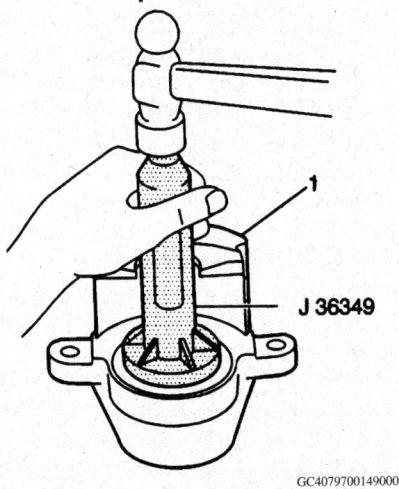

Fig. 9 Dust boot installation

DISC BRAKE SPECIFICATIONS
Caliper Specifications

Model	Year	Caliper Bore Dia. Inch
Aveo	2005	—
Alero & Grand Am	2001–05	2.36
Aurora	2001–03	2.52
Bonneville, LeSabre & Park Avenue	2001–05	2.52
Catera	2001	2.24
Cavalier & Sunfire	2001–05	2.24
Century, Grand Prix, Impala, Intrigue, Monte Carlo & Regal	2001–05	2.50
DeVille, Eldorado & Seville	2001–05	2.52
G6	2005	2.36
Malibu	2001–05	2.36

Rotor Specifications

Model	Year	Brake Lining Wear Limit, Inch	Nominal Thickness, Inch	Minimum Refinish Thickness, Inch	Discard Limit, Inch①	Thickness Variation Parallel-ism, Inch	Lateral Run Out (T.I.R.) Inch	Maximum Scoring Depth, Inch
Alero & Grand Am	2001–05	.0300	1.0310	.9800	.9720	.0010	.0015	.0590
Aurora	2001	.0300	1.2670	1.2240	1.2090	.0005	.0020	.0590
	2002–03	.0300	1.2670	1.2240	1.2090	.0010	.0020	.0590
Aveo	2005	.0280	.9450	—	.8660	.0040	.0040	.0160
Bonneville, LeSabre & Park Avenue	2001–05	.0300	1.2670	1.2240	1.2090	.0010	.0020	.0590
Catera	2001	.3150②	1.1020	1.0430	.9840	.0005	.0040	.0590
Cavalier & Sunfire	2001	.0300	.7860	.7390	.7360	.0010	.0030	.0590
	2002–05	.0300	.7860	.7390	.7360	.0010	.0020	.0590
Century, Grand Prix, Impala, Intrigue, Monte Carlo & Regal	2001	.0300	1.2700	1.2500	1.2100	.0005	.0030	.0590
	2002	.0300	1.2700	1.2500	1.2100	.0005	.0020	.0590
	2003–05	.0300	1.2700	1.2500⑧	1.2100	.0010	.0020	.0590
DeVille, Eldorado & Seville	2000–04	.0300	1.2670⑦	1.2240⑥	1.2090③	.0010⑤	.0020④	.0590
G6	2005	.0300	1.0230	.9060	.8980	.0010	.0020	.0590
Lumina	2001	.0300	1.0390	.9870	.9720	.0005	.0030	.0600
Malibu	2001–03	.0300	1.0310	.9800	.9720	.0010	.0015	.0590
	2004–05	—	1.0230	.9060	.8980	.0010	.0020	.0590

① — Discard thickness is stamped on rotor.
② — Includes backing plate.
③ — Heavy Duty, 1.4370 inches.
④ — Heavy Duty, .0030 inch.
⑤ — Heavy Duty, .0004 inch.
⑥ — Heavy Duty, 1.4570 inches.
⑦ — Heavy Duty, 1.4960 inches.
⑧ — 2004–05 Grand Prix, 1.2200 inches.

AC-DELCO SINGLE PISTON FRONT DISC BRAKE

TIGHTENING SPECIFICATIONS

Year	Component	Torque/Ft. Lbs.
ALERO & GRAND AM		
2001–05	Bleeder Valve	115①
	Caliper	23
	Caliper Bracket To Knuckle	85
	Hose	37
AURORA		
2001–03	Bleeder Valve	115①
	Caliper Bracket	137
	Caliper Pin	63
	Hose	32
	Pipe Fitting Tube	11
AVEO		
2005	Bleeder Valve	53①
	Caliper To Knuckle	70
	Hose	30
BONNEVILLE, LESABRE & PARK AVENUE		
2001–05	Bleeder Valve	115 ①
	Caliper	137
	Caliper Pin	63
	Hose	32
	Pipe Fitting Tube	11
CATERA		
2000–01	Bleeder Valve	80①
	Caliper	22
	Caliper Bracket	70②
	Hose	30
CAVALIER & SUNFIRE		
2001–05	Bleeder Valve	115①
	Caliper	38
	Hose	37
	Inlet Fitting	34
CENTURY, IMPALA, GRAND PRIX, MONTE CARLO & REGAL		
2001–05	Bleeder Valve	115①
	Caliper	70
	Caliper Bracket	133
	Hose	40
DEVILLE, ELDORADO & SEVILLE		
2001–05	Bleeder Valve	115①
	Caliper (Heavy Duty)	137
	Caliper (Less Heavy Duty)	181
	Caliper Pin (Heavy Duty)	83
	Caliper Pin (Less Heavy Duty)	63
	Hose	33
	Pipe Fitting	11
G6		
2005	Bleeder Valve	97①
	Caliper Pin	26
	Caliper Bracket	85
	Hose	37
LUMINA		
2001	Caliper	63
	Caliper Bracket	137

Continued

AC-DELCO SINGLE PISTON FRONT DISC BRAKE

TIGHTENING
SPECIFICATIONS—Continued

Year	Component	Torque/Ft. Lbs.
MALIBU		
2001–03	Bleeder Valve	115①
	Caliper	23
	Caliper Bracket	85
	Hose	37
2004–05	Bleeder Valve	97①
	Caliper Guide Pin	26
	Caliper Mounting Bracket	85
	Hose	37

① — Inch lbs.
② — Rotate an additional 37°.

PBR Dual Piston Front Disc Brake

NOTE: On Air Bag Equipped Models, Refer To "Air Bag System Precautions" Located In The Front Of This Manual For System Disarming & Arming Procedures.

NOTE: Refer To "Computer Relearn Procedures" Located In The Front Of This Manual When Battery Power To The Computer Has Been Interrupted.

INDEX

PRECAUTIONS

1. Keep grease and other foreign material off brake linings, caliper, surfaces of disc and external surfaces of hub.
2. Avoid deforming disc, and nicking or scratching brake linings.
3. Worn or damaged rubber piston seals should be replaced.
4. During removal and installation of a wheel assembly, ensure not to interfere with or damage caliper splash shield, or bleeder screw.
5. Front wheel bearings preload should be adjusted to specifications.
6. Ensure vehicle is centered on hoist before servicing any front end components to avoid bending or damaging disc splash shield on full left or right-hand wheel turns.
7. Before vehicle is moved after any brake service work, obtain a firm brake pedal.
8. Assembly bolts of two-piece caliper housings should not be disturbed unless caliper requires service.

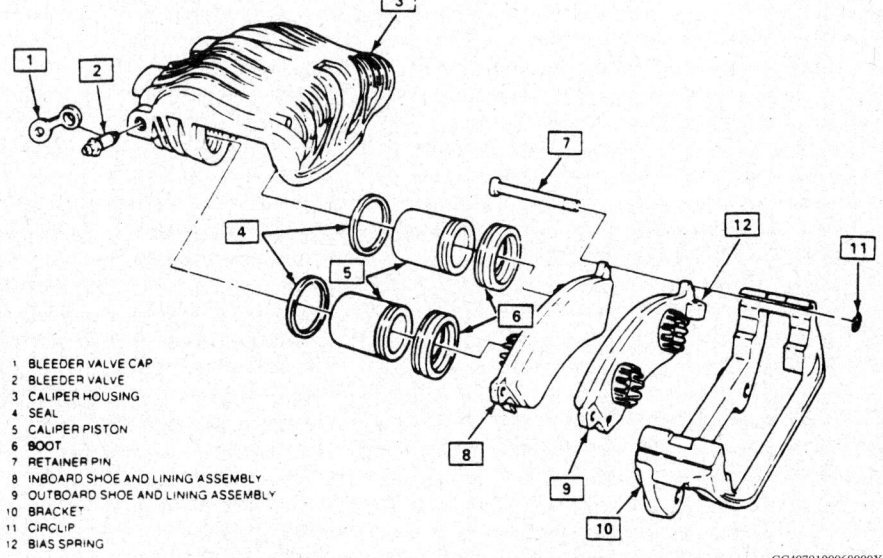

1. BLEEDER VALVE CAP
2. BLEEDER VALVE
3. CALIPER HOUSING
4. SEAL
5. CALIPER PISTON
6. BOOT
7. RETAINER PIN
8. INBOARD SHOE AND LINING ASSEMBLY
9. OUTBOARD SHOE AND LINING ASSEMBLY
10. BRACKET
11. CIRCLIP
12. BIAS SPRING

GC4079100068000X

Fig. 1 Exploded view of dual piston front caliper

DESCRIPTION

The front caliper consists of dual pistons and an aluminum housing which is suspended on the shoe and lining assemblies, **Fig. 1.** Hydraulic pressure, created by applying force to the brake pedal, acts equally against the pistons and the bottom of the caliper bores to move the pistons outward. This action slides the caliper inward, resulting in a clamping action on the brake rotor. This clamping action forces the linings against the rotor, creating the friction required to stop the vehicle.

TROUBLESHOOTING

The most common cause of brake chat-ter on disc brakes is a variation in disc thickness. If roughness or vibration is encountered during highway operation or if pedal pulsation is experienced at low speeds, the disc may have excessive thickness variation. To inspect for this condition, measure the disc at 12 points with a micrometer at a radius approximately one inch from edge of disc. If thickness measurements vary by more than .0005 inch, the disc should be replaced with a new one.

Excessive lateral runout of braking disc may cause a piston knocking back, possibly creating increased pedal travel and vibration when brakes are applied.

Before inspecting the runout, the wheel bearings should be adjusted. The adjust-ment is very important and will be required at the completion of the test to prevent bearing failure. Adjust the wheel bearings as outlined in "Front Suspension & Steering" section of appropriate chassis chapter.

BRAKE SYSTEM BLEED

Refer to "Hydraulic Brake Systems" for manual and pressure bleeding procedures.

BRAKE PAD SERVICE

Corvette

REMOVAL

1. Remove ⅔ of total brake fluid capacity

from master cylinder reservoir.

2. Raise and support vehicle, then remove tire and wheel assembly.
3. If caliper requires overhaul, remove inlet fitting mounting bolt, then disconnect inlet fitting from caliper housing.
4. Discard both gaskets, then plug openings in inlet fitting and caliper. **Do not crimp brake hose.**
5. Remove caliper guide pin bolts, then the caliper from rotor and caliper mounting bracket. If only shoe and linings require replacement, suspend caliper from upper control arm.
6. Position suitable pliers over caliper and center of inboard shoe and lining, then squeeze pliers to bottom pistons in caliper bores, **Fig. 2.**
7. Remove shoe and lining assemblies.

INSTALLATION

1. Install inboard shoe and lining.
2. Ensure tangs on shoe fully engage pistons. Shoe should be flush with piston.
3. Install outboard shoe and lining into caliper housing. Ensure insulators are fully seated into holes in outboard side of housing.
4. Ensure guiding surfaces on shoe and lining assemblies and mounting bracket are seated properly, then position caliper over rotor and onto mounting bracket.
5. Press caliper housing downward to compress bias springs, then install new retainer pin and circlip.
6. If caliper was overhauled, connect inlet fitting using new gaskets, then bleed brake system.
7. Install wheel and tire assembly, then lower vehicle.
8. Fill master cylinder to proper level, then pump brake pedal to bring pads into contact with brake rotor.

XLR

REMOVAL

1. Remove brake master cylinder reservoir fluid to midway between maximum-full point and minimum allowable level.
2. Raise and support vehicle, then remove tire and wheel assembly.
3. Install large C-clamp over caliper with ends against rear of body and outboard brake pad.
4. Tighten C-clamp evenly until caliper pistons are compressed into caliper bores enough to allow caliper to slide past brake rotor. Remove C-clamp.
5. Remove upper brake caliper guide pin bolt.
6. Pivot brake caliper downward and secure caliper aside. Ensure there is no tension on hydraulic brake flexible hose. **Do not disconnect hydraulic brake flexible hose from caliper.**
7. Remove brake pads.
8. Remove and inspect retainers.

INSTALLATION

1. Install large C-clamp over caliper with

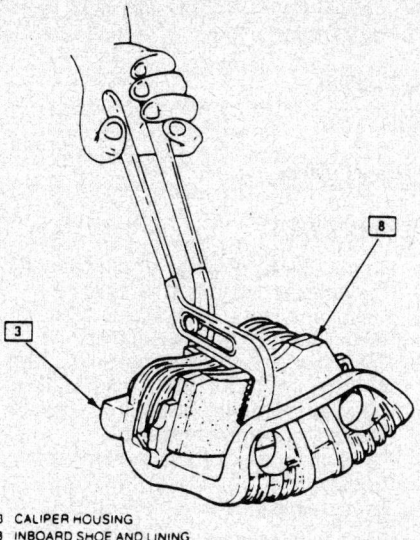

3 CALIPER HOUSING
8 INBOARD SHOE AND LINING

GC4079100069000X

Fig. 2 Piston retraction in caliper bores

ends against rear of body and old inboard brake pad or suitable wood block installed against pistons.
2. Tighten C-clamp evenly until pistons are compressed completely into bores. Remove C-clamp and old brake pad or wood block.
3. Install retainers and brake pad to bracket. Brake pad wear sensor, mounted on inboard brake pad, must be positioned so it is in trailing position during forward rotation of brake rotor.
4. Pivot brake caliper upward, over brake pads and into caliper bracket.
5. Install upper brake caliper guide pin bolt.
6. Install the tire and wheel assembly.
7. Lower vehicle.
8. With engine off, gradually apply brake pedal to approximately 2/3 of its travel distance. Slowly release brake pedal.
9. Wait 15 seconds, then repeat previous steps until firm brake pedal apply is obtained.
10. Fill brake master cylinder reservoir to proper level.

CALIPER SERVICE

Removal

CORVETTE

1. Remove 2/3 of total brake fluid capacity from master cylinder reservoir.
2. Raise and support vehicle, then remove tire and wheel assembly.
3. If caliper requires overhaul, remove inlet fitting mounting bolt, then disconnect inlet fitting from caliper housing.
4. Discard both gaskets, then plug openings in inlet fitting and caliper. **Do not crimp brake hose since this may damage hose's internal structure.**
5. Remove caliper guide pin bolts, then the caliper from rotor and caliper

mounting bracket. If only shoe and linings require replacement, suspend caliper from upper control arm to prevent damage to brake hose.

XLR

1. Remove brake master cylinder reservoir fluid to midway between maximum-full point and minimum allowable level.
2. Raise and support vehicle, then remove tire and wheel assembly.
3. Remove inlet fitting bolt and brake hose from caliper. Discard two copper brake hose gaskets.
4. Plug opening in caliper and brake hose.
5. Remove guide pin bolts and caliper from mounting bracket.

Disassemble

1. Pad caliper housing interior with suitable clean cloths.
2. Remove caliper pistons from bore by directing low pressure compressed air into bore through fluid inlet hole. Use just enough air to ease pistons out of bores. **Do not place finger in front of piston.**
3. Remove piston dust boot seals from caliper counterbores using suitable small wooden or plastic tool. Discard boot seals.
4. Remove bleeder valve and cap from caliper.

Inspection

1. Clean caliper piston bores, seal counterbores and pistons with denatured alcohol. **Do not use abrasives to clean pistons.**
2. Dry caliper piston bores, counterbores and pistons with non-lubricated, filtered compressed air.
3. Inspect caliper bores for cracks, scoring, pitting, excessive rust and/or excessive corrosion. If light rust or light corrosion are present, attempt to remove imperfection with fine emery paper.
4. Inspect pistons for cracks, scoring and/or damage to the chrome plating.

Assemble

1. Lubricate new piston seals with suitable DOT 3 brake fluid from clean, sealed brake fluid container.
2. Install lubricated, new piston seals into bores.
3. Install new piston dust boot seal over piston.
4. Install pistons into bores.
5. Install boots over pistons' ends so fold will face toward housing piston bore openings.
6. Seat boots into caliper bore grooves and slide pistons into bores.
7. Push pistons to bottom of caliper bores. Ensure boots are properly seated into piston and caliper bore grooves.

DISC BRAKES

8. Install caliper bleed screw and cap.

Installation
CORVETTE

1. Ensure guiding surfaces on shoe and lining assemblies and mounting bracket are seated properly, then position caliper over rotor and onto mounting bracket.
2. Press caliper housing downward to compress bias springs, then install new retainer pin and circlip.
3. If caliper was overhauled, connect inlet fitting using new gaskets, then bleed brake system as required.
4. Install wheel and tire assembly, then lower vehicle.
5. Fill master cylinder to proper level, then pump brake pedal to bring pads into contact with brake rotor.

XLR

1. Install caliper to mounting bracket.
2. Install guide pin bolts.
3. Remove plug from caliper opening and hose.
4. Install new copper brake hose gaskets and caliper inlet fitting bolt to brake hose.
5. Install hose and inlet fitting bolt to caliper.
6. Bleed hydraulic brake system.

7. Install tire and wheel assembly, then lower vehicle.

ROTOR
REPLACE

Corvette
REMOVAL

1. Remove ⅔ of total brake fluid capacity from master cylinder reservoir.
2. Raise and support vehicle, then remove tire and wheel assembly.
3. Remove caliper guide pin bolts, then the caliper from rotor and caliper mounting bracket. Suspend caliper from upper control arm.
4. Remove mounting bolts and mounting bracket.
5. Remove rotor from hub assembly.

INSTALLATION

1. Ensure guiding surfaces on shoe and lining assemblies and mounting bracket are seated properly, then position caliper over rotor and onto mounting bracket.
2. Press caliper housing downward to compress bias springs, then install new retainer pin and circlip.
3. Install wheel and tire assembly, then lower vehicle.

4. Fill master cylinder to proper level, then pump brake pedal to bring pads into contact with brake rotor.

XLR
REMOVAL

1. Raise and support vehicle, then remove tire and wheel assembly.
2. Install C-clamp over caliper of with ends against body rear and outboard disc brake pad.
3. Compress piston into bore just enough to allow caliper to slide away from rotor. Remove C-clamp.
4. Remove bracket bolts. **Do not disconnect brake flexible hose bolt.**
5. Remove caliper and mounting bracket, then support assembly aside. Ensure there is no tension on hydraulic brake flexible hose.
6. Mark brake rotor to wheel studs for installation alignment.
7. Remove brake rotor.

INSTALLATION

1. Install brake rotor to hub/axle flange.
2. Install caliper and bracket to suspension knuckle.
3. Install tire and wheel assembly, then lower vehicle.

DISC BRAKE SPECIFICATIONS
Rotor Specifications

Model	Year	Brake Lining Wear Limit, Inch	Nominal Thickness, Inch	Minimum Refinish Thickness, Inch	Discard Limit, Inch①	Thickness Variation Parallelism, Inch	Lateral Run Out (T.I.R.) Inch	Maximum Scoring Depth, Inch
Corvette	2001–04	.030	1.260	1.205	1.190	.001	.002	.059
	2005	.030	1.260	1.205	1.190	.001	.002	.059
XLR	2004–05	.030	1.260	1.205	1.190	—	.002	.059

① — Discard thickness is stamped on rotor.

TIGHTENING SPECIFICATIONS

Year	Component	Torque/Ft. Lbs.
2001–05	Bleeder Screw	106①
	Caliper Guide Pin	23
	Caliper Inlet Fitting	33
	Caliper Mounting Bracket	125
	Wheel Lug Nuts	100

① — Inch lbs.

PBR DUAL PISTON FRONT DISC BRAKE

AC-Delco Dual Piston Rear Disc Brake

NOTE: On Air Bag Equipped Models, Refer To "Air Bag System Precautions" Located In The Front Of This Manual For System Disarming & Arming Procedures.

NOTE: Refer To "Computer Relearn Procedures" Located In The Front Of This Manual When Battery Power To The Computer Has Been Interrupted.

INDEX

PRECAUTIONS

1. Keep grease and other foreign material off brake linings, caliper, surfaces of disc and external surfaces of hub.
2. Avoid deforming disc, and nicking or scratching brake linings.
3. If inspection reveals rubber piston seals are worn or damaged, they should be replaced.
4. During removal and installation of a wheel assembly, ensure not to interfere with or damage caliper splash shield, or bleeder screw.
5. Front wheel bearings preload should be adjusted to specifications.
6. Ensure vehicle is centered on hoist before servicing any front end components to avoid bending or damaging disc splash shield on full left or right-hand wheel turns.
7. Before vehicle is moved after any brake service work, ensure to obtain a firm brake pedal.
8. Assembly bolts of two-piece caliper housings should not be disturbed unless caliper requires service.

DESCRIPTION

The rear disc brake caliper contains opposing dual pistons in a two-piece cast iron housing which bolts directly to the mounting flange of the rear suspension lower trailing arm. Hydraulic pressure, created by applying force to the brake pedal, acts equally against all surfaces of both pistons and both piston bore cavity surfaces. The parking brake application is completely independent of the hydraulic braking system.

TROUBLESHOOTING

The most common cause of brake chat-

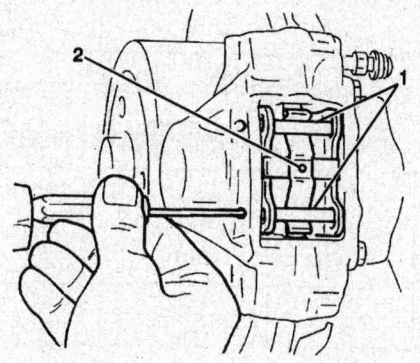

(1) Rear Brake Caliper Retaining Pins
(2) Rear Brake Caliper Spring Retainer

GC4079700141000X

Fig. 1 Rear brake pad removal. Catera

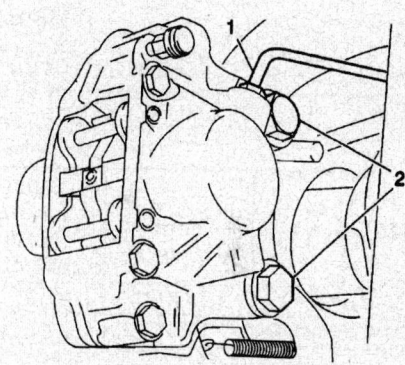

(1) Rear Brake Caliper Pipe
(2) Rear Brake Caliper Bolt

GC4079700142000X

Fig. 2 Caliper removal. Catera

ter on disc brakes is a variation in disc thickness. If roughness or vibration is encountered during highway operation or if pedal pulsation is experienced at low speeds, the disc may have excessive thickness variation. To inspect for this condition, measure the disc at 12 points with a micrometer at a radius approximately one inch from edge of disc. If thickness measurements vary by more than .0005 inch, the disc should be replaced with a new one.

Excessive lateral runout of braking disc may cause a piston knocking back, possibly creating increased pedal travel and vibration when brakes are applied.

Before inspecting the runout, the wheel bearings should be adjusted. The adjustment is very important and will be required

at the completion of the test to prevent bearing failure. Adjust the wheel bearings as outlined in "Front Suspension & Steering" section of appropriate chassis chapter.

BRAKE SYSTEM BLEED

Refer to "Hydraulic Brake Systems" for manual and pressure bleeding procedures.

BRAKE PAD SERVICE

1. Remove approximately ⅓ of brake fluid from master cylinder.
2. Raise and support vehicle, then remove wheel and tire assembly.
3. Pry between rotor and each brake pad to bottom each piston in its bore.

DISC BRAKES

4. Remove retaining pins and pads, **Fig. 1.**
5. Reverse procedure to install.

CALIPER SERVICE
Replacement

1. Remove approximately ⅓ of brake fluid from master cylinder.
2. Raise and support vehicle, then remove wheel and tire assembly.
3. Pry between rotor and each brake pad to bottom each piston in its bore.
4. Remove retaining pins and pads, **Fig. 1.**
5. Remove caliper pipe, **Fig. 2.**
6. Remove mounting bolts and caliper from rotor.
7. Reverse procedure to install.

Disassemble

1. Install piston retainer tool No. J-22429, or equivalent, opposite cylinder to be removed.
2. Remove piston by directing dry filtered compressed air into fluid channel port of caliper housing, then cover exposed bore with tool No. J-22429, or equivalent, and remove opposing piston using dry compressed air.
3. Remove piston seal from bore using small piece of wood or plastic. **Do not use metal tool to remove seal.**
4. Remove cap and caliper bleeder valve.

Assemble

1. Install new bleeder valve and cap, then the new piston seals lubricated with clean brake fluid.

2. Install dust boots lubricated with clean brake fluid onto pistons and pistons into caliper housing bores.
3. With pistons bottomed in bores, ensure outer edge of dust boots are around caliper housing embossments.

ROTOR
REPLACE

1. Remove approximately ⅓ of brake fluid from master cylinder.
2. Raise and support vehicle, then remove wheel and tire assembly.
3. Pry between rotor and each brake pad to bottom each piston in its bore.
4. Remove retaining pins and pads, **Fig. 1.**
5. Remove caliper pipe, **Fig. 2.**
6. Remove mounting bolts and caliper.
7. Remove rotor.
8. Reverse procedure to install.

DISC BRAKE SPECIFICATIONS
Caliper Specifications

Model	Year	Caliper Bore Dia. Inch
Catera	2001	1.57

Rotor Specifications

Model	Year	Brake Lining Wear Limit, Inch	Nominal Thickness, Inch	Minimum Refinish, Inch	Discard Thickness, Inch①	Variation (Parallelism), Inch	Lateral Run Out (T.I.R.) Inch	Maximum Scoring Depth, Inch
Solid Rotor	2001	—	.4720	.4330	.3930	.0005	.0040	.0590
Vented Rotor	2001	—	.7870	.7480	.7090	.0005	.0040	.0590

① — Discard thickness is stamped on rotor.

TIGHTENING SPECIFICATIONS

Year	Component	Torque/Ft. Lbs.
2001	Bleed Valve	71①
	Caliper	59
	Pipe Fitting	12
	Rotor	35①

① — Inch lbs.

AC-Delco Single Piston Rear Disc Brake

NOTE: On Air Bag Equipped Models, Refer To "Air Bag System Precautions" Located In The Front Of This Manual For System Disarming & Arming Procedures.

NOTE: Refer To "Computer Relearn Procedures" Located In The Front Of This Manual When Battery Power To The Computer Has Been Interrupted.

INDEX

PRECAUTIONS

1. Keep grease and other foreign material off brake linings, caliper, surfaces of disc and external surfaces of hub.
2. Avoid deforming disc, and nicking or scratching brake linings.
3. Worn or damaged rubber piston seals should be replaced.
4. During removal and installation of a wheel assembly, ensure not to interfere with or damage caliper splash shield, or bleeder screw.
5. Front wheel bearings preload should be adjusted to specifications.
6. Ensure vehicle is centered on hoist before servicing any front end components to avoid bending or damaging disc splash shield on full left or right-hand wheel turns.
7. Before vehicle is moved after any brake service work, ensure to obtain a firm brake pedal.
8. Assembly bolts of two-piece caliper housings should not be disturbed unless caliper requires service.

DESCRIPTION

On all models except Century, Grand Prix, Intrigue and Regal, the caliper assembly has a single bore and is mounted to the support bracket with two mounting bolt and sleeve assemblies, **Fig. 1.** Hydraulic pressure created by applying the brake pedal is converted by the caliper to a stopping force. This force acts equally against the piston and the bottom of the piston bore to move the piston outward and to slide the caliper inward resulting in a clamping ac-

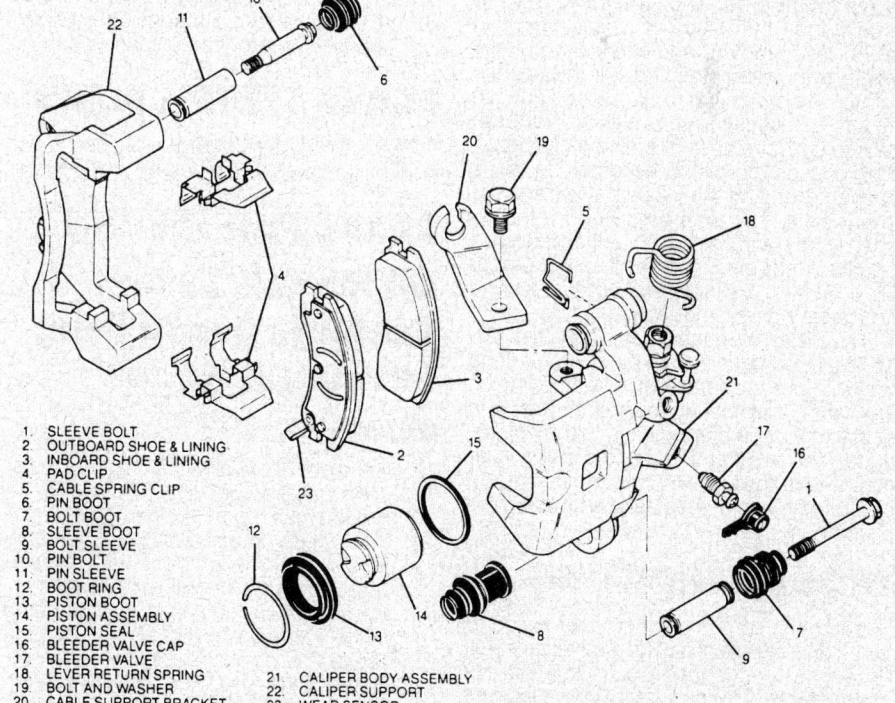

1. SLEEVE BOLT
2. OUTBOARD SHOE & LINING
3. INBOARD SHOE & LINING
4. PAD CLIP
5. CABLE SPRING CLIP
6. PIN BOOT
7. BOLT BOOT
8. SLEEVE BOOT
9. BOLT SLEEVE
10. PIN BOLT
11. PIN SLEEVE
12. BOOT RING
13. PISTON BOOT
14. PISTON ASSEMBLY
15. PISTON SEAL
16. BLEEDER VALVE CAP
17. BLEEDER VALVE
18. LEVER RETURN SPRING
19. BOLT AND WASHER
20. CABLE SUPPORT BRACKET
21. CALIPER BODY ASSEMBLY
22. CALIPER SUPPORT
23. WEAR SENSOR

GC4079100078000X

Fig. 1 Exploded view of rear disc brake caliper. All models except Century, Grand Prix, Intrigue & Regal

tion. This clamping action presses the linings against the rotor, creating friction to stop the vehicle.

On Century, Grand Prix, Intrigue and

Regal models, the caliper has a single piston, and is mounted to the support bracket by two mounting bolts, **Fig. 2.** The caliper assembly slides on the two mounting bolts.

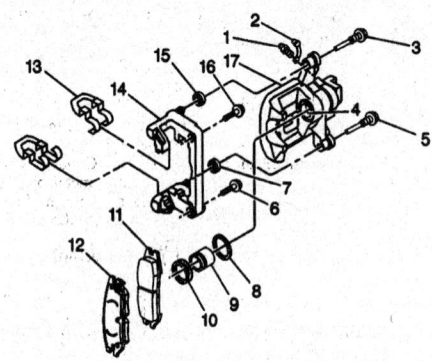

Fig. 2 Exploded view of rear caliper. Century, Grand Prix, Intrigue & Regal

(1) Valve, Caliper Bleeder
(2) Cap, Bleeder Valve
(3) Bolt, Caliper
(4) Caliper Bore
(5) Bolt, Caliper
(6) Bolt, Caliper Bracket
(7) Boot, Caliper
(8) Seal, Caliper Piston
(9) Piston, Caliper

(10) Boot, Caliper Piston
(11) Pad, Inner
(12) Pad, Outer
(13) Clips, Retainer
(14) Bracket, Caliper
(15) Boot, Caliper
(16) Bolt, Caliper Bracket
(17) Housing, Caliper

GC4079700143000X

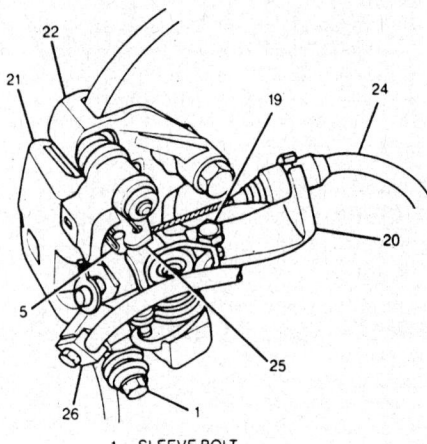

Fig. 3 Caliper assembly. All models except Century, Grand Prix, Intrigue & Regal

1	SLEEVE BOLT
5	CABLE SPRING CLIP
19	BOLT AND WASHER
20	CABLE SUPPORT BRACKET
21	CALIPER BODY ASSEMBLY
22	CALIPER SUPPORT
24	PARKING BRAKE CABLE
25	PARKING BRAKE LEVER
26	BRAKE HOSE

GC4079100079000X

Upon brake application, fluid pressure against the piston forces the inboard shoe and lining assembly against the inboard side of the disc. This action causes the caliper assembly to slide until the outboard lining comes into contact with the disc. As pressure builds up the linings are pressed against the disc with increased force.

On all models, when the parking brake is applied, the external caliper parking brake lever moves and rotates a spindle within the caliper housing. As the spindle rotates, a connecting rod is pushed against an internal adjusting screw which is threaded into a sleeve nut in the piston assembly. This causes the piston assembly to move outward bringing the inboard shoe and lining assembly against the rotor. As the inboard shoe and lining contacts the rotor, a reaction force causes the caliper housing to slide inward pressing the outboard shoe and lining against the rotor.

The piston assembly contains a self adjusting mechanism to keep the parking brake in proper adjustment. As the linings are worn, the piston moves through the seal to maintain proper lining to rotor clearance. The parking brake adjusts to proper clearances through an internal sleeve nut that rotates and moves as one unit with the piston.

TROUBLESHOOTING

The most common cause of brake chatter on disc brakes is a variation in disc thickness. If roughness or vibration is encountered during highway operation or if pedal pulsation is experienced at low speeds, the disc may have excessive thickness variation. To inspect for this condition, measure the disc at 12 points with a micrometer at a radius approximately one inch from edge of disc. If thickness measurements vary by more than .0005 inch, the disc should be replaced with a new one.

Excessive lateral runout of braking disc may cause a piston knocking back, possibly creating increased pedal travel and vibration when brakes are applied.

Before inspecting the runout, the wheel bearings should be adjusted. The adjustment is very important and will be required at the completion of the test to prevent bearing failure. Adjust the wheel bearings as outlined in "Front Suspension & Steering" section of appropriate chassis chapter.

BRAKE SYSTEM BLEED

Refer to "Hydraulic Brake Systems" for manual and pressure bleeding procedures.

BRAKE PAD SERVICE

All Models Except Century, Grand Prix, Intrigue & Regal

REMOVAL

1. Remove ⅔ of brake fluid from master cylinder reservoir.
2. Raise and support vehicle.
3. Mark wheel to axle flange relationship for installation alignment, then remove wheel and tire assembly.
4. Remove bolt and washer attaching cable support bracket to caliper, **Fig. 3.**
5. Remove sleeve bolt and pivot caliper, **Fig. 4. Do not completely remove caliper.**
6. Remove outboard and inboard shoe and linings, then two pad clips from caliper support.

INSTALLATION

1. Turn piston and thread it into caliper

assembly using suitable spanner-type tool in piston slots.
2. After bottoming piston, lift inner edge of boot next to piston and press out trapped air.
3. Ensure slots in end of piston are positioned properly, **Fig. 5.**
4. Install pad clips, outboard and inboard shoe and linings in caliper support. **Ensure wear sensor is on outboard shoe positioned downward at leading edge of rotor during forward wheel rotation.**
5. Pivot caliper over shoe and lining assemblies. **Do not damage piston boot on inboard shoe.**
6. Inspect pad clips. Use small screwdriver to seat or center pad clips on support abutments.
7. Install sleeve bolt.
8. Install cable support bracket.
9. Install wheels and tires, then lower vehicle.
10. Apply approximately 175 lbs., of force to brake pedal three times to seat shoe and linings against rotor.

Century, Grand Prix, Intrigue & Regal

1. Remove ⅔ of brake fluid from master cylinder reservoir.
2. Raise and support vehicle.
3. Mark wheel to axle flange relationship for installation alignment, then remove wheel and tire assembly.
4. Compress caliper piston enough for clearance using suitable C-clamp and remove upper caliper bolt.
5. Pivot caliper down. **Do not remove caliper.**
6. Remove brake pads and pad clips from caliper bracket.

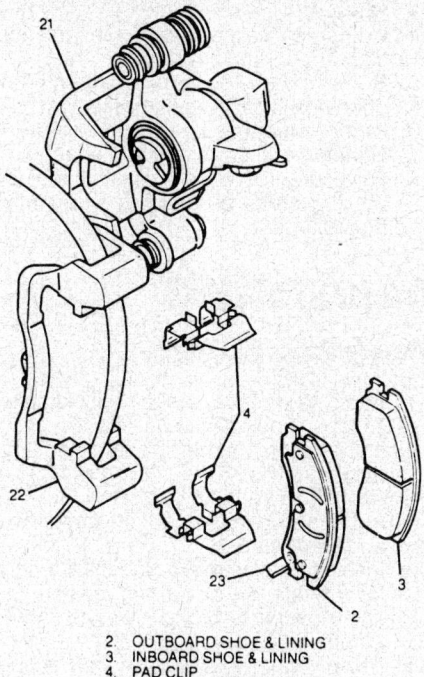

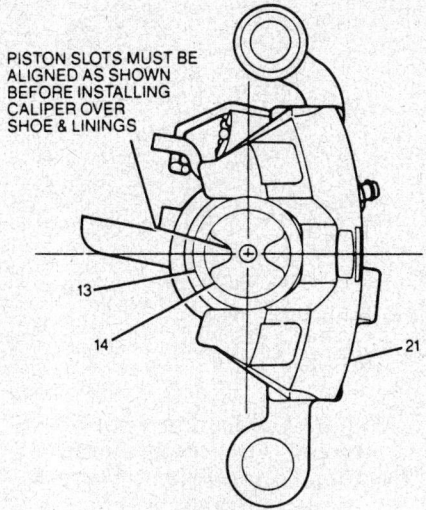

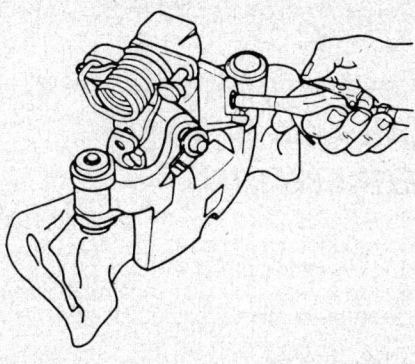

Fig. 6   Piston removal. All models except Century, Grand Prix, Intrigue & Regal

2. OUTBOARD SHOE & LINING
3. INBOARD SHOE & LINING
4. PAD CLIP
21. CALIPER BODY ASSEMBLY
22. CALIPER SUPPORT
23. WEAR SENSOR

GC4079100083000X

Fig. 4   Shoe & lining installation. All models except Century, Grand Prix, Intrigue & Regal

7. Reverse procedure to install.

CALIPER SERVICE

All Models Except Century, Grand Prix, Intrigue & Regal

REPLACEMENT

1. Raise and support vehicle.
2. Mark wheel to axle flange relationship for installation alignment, then remove wheel and tire assembly.
3. Remove brake hose from caliper. Plug openings in caliper and brake hose.
4. Lift able spring to free end of from lever, then disconnect parking brake cable from lever.
5. Remove cable support bracket mounting bolt and washer.
6. Remove sleeve bolt and caliper.
7. Reverse procedure to install, then bleed brakes.

DISASSEMBLE

1. Pad interior of caliper assembly with clean shop towel, then remove piston assembly using low pressure compressed air into caliper inlet hole, **Fig. 6. Do not place fingers in front of piston.**
2. Pry up one end of boot ring using small screwdriver, **Fig. 7.** Work boot ring out of caliper groove.

PISTON SLOTS MUST BE ALIGNED AS SHOWN BEFORE INSTALLING CALIPER OVER SHOE & LININGS

13. PISTON BOOT
14. PISTON ASSEMBLY
21. CALIPER BODY ASSEMBLY

GC4079100084000X

Fig. 5   Positioning piston slots. All models except Century, Grand Prix, Intrigue & Regal

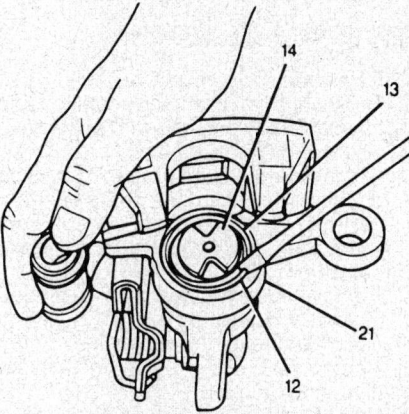

12. BOOT RING
13. PISTON BOOT
14. PISTON ASSEMBLY
21. CALIPER BODY ASSEMBLY

GC4079100081000X

Fig. 7   Boot ring removal. All models except Century, Grand Prix, Intrigue & Regal

3. Remove piston seal from caliper bore groove using small wooden or plastic tool.
4. Remove bleeder valve and cap.
5. If lever return spring replacement is required, remove it using screwdriver to disengage return spring from parking brake lever, then unhook spring from stopper pin, **Fig. 8.**
6. Remove pin boot and bolt, then the bolt and sleeve bolt from caliper.
7. Remove pin bolt and pin sleeve from caliper support.

INSPECTION

1. Clean all components in clean denatured alcohol, then dry with low pres-

sure compressed air.
2. Blow out passages in caliper and bleeder valve.
3. Inspect piston assembly for nicks, cracks, wear or corrosion.
4. Inspect piston bore for scoring, nicks, wear or corrosion. Use crocus cloth to polish out light corrosion. **Do not hone caliper bore.**
5. Inspect seal groove for nicks or burrs.
6. Inspect boots for cuts, tears or deterioration.
7. Inspect bolt sleeve and pin sleeve for corrosion or damage. **Do not polish away corrosion.**

ASSEMBLE

1. Lubricate pin sleeve with silicone grease, then install pin bolts and sleeve to caliper support.
2. Lubricate sleeve boot with silicone grease, then compress lip on sleeve boot and push it through caliper until lip emerges and seals on inboard face of caliper ear.
3. Lubricate push bolt sleeve with silicone grease, then push it in through lip end of boot until boot seats in sleeve groove at other end.
4. Install bolt boot onto caliper.
5. Install small end of pin boot over sleeve until boot seats in groove.
6. Position new lever return spring with hook end around stopper pin, then pry other end of spring over lever.
7. Install bleeder valve and cap.
8. Lubricate new piston seal with clean brake fluid and install in groove in caliper bore. Ensure seal is not twisted.
9. Install boot onto piston.
10. Lubricate piston with clean brake fluid.
11. Start piston assembly in by hand, then thread into bottom of caliper bore using spanner-type tool in slots in end of piston.
12. Ensure outside edge of piston boot is smoothly seated in counterbore.
13. Work boot ring into groove near open end of caliper bore. **Do not pinch piston boot between boot ring and caliper.**
14. Lift inner edge of boot next to piston

and press out trapped air. Ensure boot lays flat.

Century, Grand Prix, Intrigue & Regal

REPLACEMENT

1. Remove ⅔ of brake fluid from master cylinder reservoir.
2. Raise and support vehicle.
3. Mark wheel to axle flange relationship for installation alignment, then remove wheel and tire assembly.
4. Compress caliper piston enough for clearance using suitable C-clamp.
5. Remove brake hose from caliper. Plug openings in caliper and brake hose.
6. Remove mounting bolts and caliper.
7. Reverse procedure to install.

DISASSEMBLE

1. Pad interior of caliper assembly with clean shop towel, then remove piston using low pressure compressed air into caliper inlet hole. **Do not place fingers in front of piston.**
2. Pry up one end of boot ring and work boot ring out of caliper groove.
3. Remove piston seal from caliper bore groove.
4. Remove bleeder valve and cap.

INSPECT

1. Clean all components in clean denatured alcohol, then dry with low pressure compressed air.
2. Blow out passages in caliper and bleeder valve.
3. Inspect piston assembly for nicks, cracks, wear or corrosion.
4. Inspect piston bore for scoring, nicks, wear or corrosion. Use crocus cloth to polish out light corrosion. **Do not hone caliper bore.**
5. Inspect seal groove for nicks or burrs.
6. Inspect boots for cuts, tears or deterioration.

ASSEMBLE

1. Install bleeder valve and cap.
2. Install new lubricated piston seal into caliper bore grooves, then the piston boot onto piston.
3. Lubricate piston with clean brake fluid, then install piston and boot into bore of caliper.
4. Install piston ring. **Ensure outside edge of piston boot is seated smoothly in counterbore of caliper.**

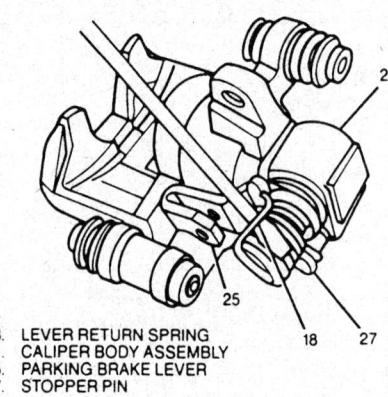

18. LEVER RETURN SPRING
21. CALIPER BODY ASSEMBLY
25. PARKING BRAKE LEVER
27. STOPPER PIN

GC4079100082000X

Fig. 8 Lever return spring removal. All models except Century, Grand Prix, Intrigue & Regal

ROTOR

REPLACE

All Models Except Century, Grand Prix, Intrigue & Regal

1. Raise and support vehicle.
2. Mark wheel to axle flange relationship for installation alignment, then remove wheel and tire assembly.
3. Remove brake hose from caliper. Plug openings in caliper and brake hose.
4. Lift able spring to free end of from lever, then disconnect parking brake cable from lever.
5. Remove cable support bracket mounting bolt and washer.
6. Remove sleeve bolt and caliper.
7. Remove mounting bolts and caliper mounting bracket.
8. Remove rotor from hub and bearing.
9. Reverse procedure to install. Adjust parking brake as outlined in "Adjustments."

Century, Grand Prix, Intrigue & Regal

1. Remove ⅔ of brake fluid from master cylinder reservoir.
2. Raise and support vehicle.
3. Mark wheel to axle flange relationship for installation alignment, then remove wheel and tire assembly.
4. Compress caliper piston enough for clearance using suitable C-clamp.
5. Remove brake hose from caliper. Plug openings in caliper and brake hose.
6. Remove mounting bolts and caliper.
7. Remove rotor from hub and bearing.
8. Reverse procedure to install. Adjust parking brake as outlined in "Adjustments."

ADJUSTMENTS

Parking Brake

1. Apply service brake with pedal force of 175 lbs., and release.
2. Fully apply parking brake using approximately 125 lbs., of force on final stroke and release.
3. Apply and release parking brake two additional times.
4. Inspect parking brake pedal assembly for full release by turning ignition On and observing brake warning lamp. Lamp should be off.
5. If brake warning lamp is on and parking brake appears to be fully released, operate manual pedal release lever and pull downward on front park brake cable to remove slack from pedal assembly.
6. Raise and support vehicle.
7. Inspect parking brake levers on rear calipers, noting the following:
   a. Levers should be against stops on caliper housing.
   b. If levers are not against stops, inspect for binding in rear brake cables and position levers against stops.
8. Tighten parking brake cable at adjuster until either left or righthand lever begins to move off of stop.
9. Loosen adjuster until lever which previously moved off the stop is again resting on the stop. **Both levers should be resting on caliper stops after completing this step.**
10. Operate parking brake several times to inspect adjustment.
11. Firm pedal feel should be obtained by pumping pedal less than one stroke.
12. Inspect left and righthand caliper levers. Both levers must be resting on stops after adjustment of parking brake.
13. Inspect operation of parking brake. If possible, place vehicle on grade and inspect parking brake holding ability.

DISC BRAKE SPECIFICATIONS
Caliper Specifications

Model	Year	Caliper Bore Dia. Inch
Alero, Grand Am & Malibu	2001–05	1.50
Aurora	2001–03	1.50
Century, Grand Prix, Impala, Intrigue, Monte Carlo & Regal	2001–05	1.50
CTS	2003–05	1.50
DeVille, Eldorado & Seville	2001–05	1.50
GTO	2004–05	—
G6	2005	1.50
Park Avenue	2001–05	1.50
STS	2005	—

Rotor Specifications

Model	Year	Nominal Thickness, Inch	Minimum Refinish Thickness, Inch	Discard Thickness, Inch	Thickness Variation, Inch[1]	Lateral Runout (T.I.R.), Inch	Maximum Scoring Depth, Inch
Alero & Grand Am	2001–05	.4330	.4170	.3540	.0010	.0015	.0590
Aurora	2001–03	.4330	.4040	.3540	.0010	.0020	.0590
Century, Impala, Intrigue, Monte Carlo & Regal	2001	.4300	.4100	.3500	.0005	.0030	.0590
	2002	.4300	.4100	.3500	.0005	.0020	.0590
	2003–05	.4300	.4200	.3500	.0010	.0020	.0590
CTS	2003–05	1.0200	.9440	.9440	.0010	.0020	.0590
DeVille, Eldorado & Seville	2001–02	.4330[3]	.3540[7]	.3540[7]	.0010[7]	.0020[2]	.0590
	2003–05	.4330[6]	.4040[5]	.3540[4]	.0010	.0020	.0590
Grand Prix	2001	.4300	.4100	.3500	.0005	.0030	.0590
	2002	.4300	.4100	.3500	.0005	.0020	.0590
	2003	.4300	.4200	.3500	.0010	.0020	.0590
	2004	.5500	.5100	.4900	.0010	.0020	.0590
GTO	2004	.0790	—	.5470	.0050	.0030	.0160
G6	2005	.5510	.4720	.4650	.0010	.0020	.0590
Malibu	2001–05	.5510	.4720	.4650	.0010	.0020	.0590
Park Avenue	2001–05	.4330	.4040	.3540	.0010	.0020	.0590
STS	2005	1.0230	.9440	.9440	.0010	.0020	.0590

[1] — Discard thickness is stamped on rotor.
[2] — Heavy Duty, .0004 inch.
[3] — Heavy Duty, .7870 inch.
[4] — Heavy Duty, 1.0830 inches.
[5] — Heavy Duty, 1.1020 inches.
[6] — Heavy Duty, 1.1420 inches
[7] — Heavy Duty, .7280 inch.

TIGHTENING SPECIFICATIONS

Year	Component	Torque/Ft. Lbs.
ALERO, GRAND AM & MALIBU		
2001–05	Bleeder Valve	98①
	Caliper	81
	Caliper Bracket	85
	Hose	37
AURORA		
2001–03	Caliper Bracket	94
	Caliper Pin	20
	Park Brake Cable Bracket	32
	Park Brake Cable Guide	18
CENTURY & REGAL		
2001–05	Caliper	32
	Caliper Bracket	85
	Rotor	25
	Hose	40
CTS		
2003–05	Caliper Bracket	88
	Caliper Pin	44
DEVILLE, ELDORADO & SEVILLE		
2001–05	Backing Plate	100
	Caliper Bracket (Heavy Duty)	181
	Caliper Bracket (Less Heavy Duty)	94
	Caliper Park Bake Cable Bracket	32
	Caliper Pin (Heavy Duty)	23
	Caliper Pin (Less Heavy Duty)	20
	Hose	33
	Park Brake Cable Guise	18
GRAND PRIX, IMPALA, INTRIGUE & MONTE CARLO		
2001–05	Caliper	32
	Caliper Bracket②	85
	Hose	40
GTO		
2004	Caliper Bracket	63
	Caliper Pin	24
	Hose	26
G6		
2005	Bleeder Valve	97①
	Caliper Pin	26
	Hose	37
PARK AVENUE		
2001–05	Caliper Bracket	94
	Caliper Pin	20
	Caliper Park Bake Cable Bracket	32
	Park Brake Cable Guide	18
STS		
2005	Bleeder Valve	124①
	Caliper Pin	46
	Hose	37

① — Inch lbs.
② — 2004–05 Grand Prix, 89 ft. lbs.

PBR Single Piston Rear Disc Brake

NOTE: On Air Bag Equipped Models, Refer To "Air Bag System Precautions" Located In The Front Of This Manual For System Disarming & Arming Procedures.

NOTE: Refer To "Computer Relearn Procedures" Located In The Front Of This Manual When Battery Power To The Computer Has Been Interrupted.

INDEX

PRECAUTIONS

1. Keep grease and other foreign material off brake linings, caliper, surfaces of disc and external surfaces of hub.
2. Avoid deforming disc, and nicking or scratching brake linings.
3. Worn or damaged rubber piston seals should be replaced.
4. During removal and installation of a wheel assembly, ensure not to interfere with or damage caliper splash shield, or bleeder screw.
5. Front wheel bearings preload should be adjusted to specifications.
6. Ensure vehicle is centered on hoist before servicing any front end components to avoid bending or damaging disc splash shield on full left or right-hand wheel turns.
7. Before vehicle is moved after any brake service work, obtain a firm brake pedal.
8. Assembly bolts of two-piece caliper housings should not be disturbed unless caliper requires service.

DESCRIPTION

The rear caliper consists of a single piston and an aluminum housing which is suspended in a mounting bracket through two slide pins, **Fig. 1.** Hydraulic pressure, created by applying force to the brake pedal, acts equally against the piston and the bottom of the caliper bore to move the piston outward. This action slides the caliper inward, resulting in a clamping action on the brake rotor. This clamping action forces the linings against the rotor, creating the friction required to stop the vehicle.

The parking brake mechanism on this caliper is completely independent of the hydraulic brake system. When the parking brake is applied, the lever on the caliper causes the pushrod, actuating collar and clamp rod assembly to move outward. This causes the caliper to move inward, mechanically forcing the linings against the rotor.

TROUBLESHOOTING

The most common cause of brake chatter on disc brakes is a variation in disc thickness. If roughness or vibration is encountered during highway operation or if pedal pulsation is experienced at low speeds, the disc may have excessive thickness variation. To inspect for this condition, measure the disc at 12 points with a micrometer at a radius approximately one inch from edge of disc. If thickness measurements vary by more than .0005 inch, the disc should be replaced with a new one.

Excessive lateral runout of braking disc may cause a piston knocking back, possibly creating increased pedal travel and vibration when brakes are applied.

Before inspecting the runout, the wheel bearings should be adjusted. The adjustment is very important and will be required at the completion of the test to prevent bearing failure. Adjust the wheel bearings as outlined in "Front Suspension & Steering" section of appropriate chassis chapter.

BRAKE SYSTEM BLEED

Refer to "Hydraulic Brake Systems" for manual and pressure bleeding procedures.

BRAKE PAD SERVICE

Camaro, Corvette & Firebird

REMOVAL

1. Remove ⅔ of total brake fluid capacity from master cylinder reservoir.
2. Raise and support vehicle, then remove tire and wheel assembly.
3. Install two wheel lug nuts to retain rotor in position.
4. Position one end of suitable C-clamp against inlet fitting bolt and other end against outboard shoe and lining.
5. Tighten clamp until piston fully bottoms in caliper bore, **Fig. 2.**
6. Remove upper guide pin bolt and discard.
7. Loosen lower guide pin bolt, then pivot caliper downward on lower guide pin bolt to expose shoe and lining assemblies.
8. Remove shoes and linings from mounting bracket.

INSTALLATION

1. Install outboard shoe and lining onto mounting bracket. Ensure insulator on shoe is positioned toward caliper housing.
2. Install inboard shoe and lining.
3. Ensure wear sensor is positioned nearest caliper piston. Sensor should be in trailing position when wheel is rotated in forward direction.
4. Pivot caliper into position over shoes and linings, noting the following:
   a. Ensure springs on outboard shoe do not protrude through inspection hole in housing.

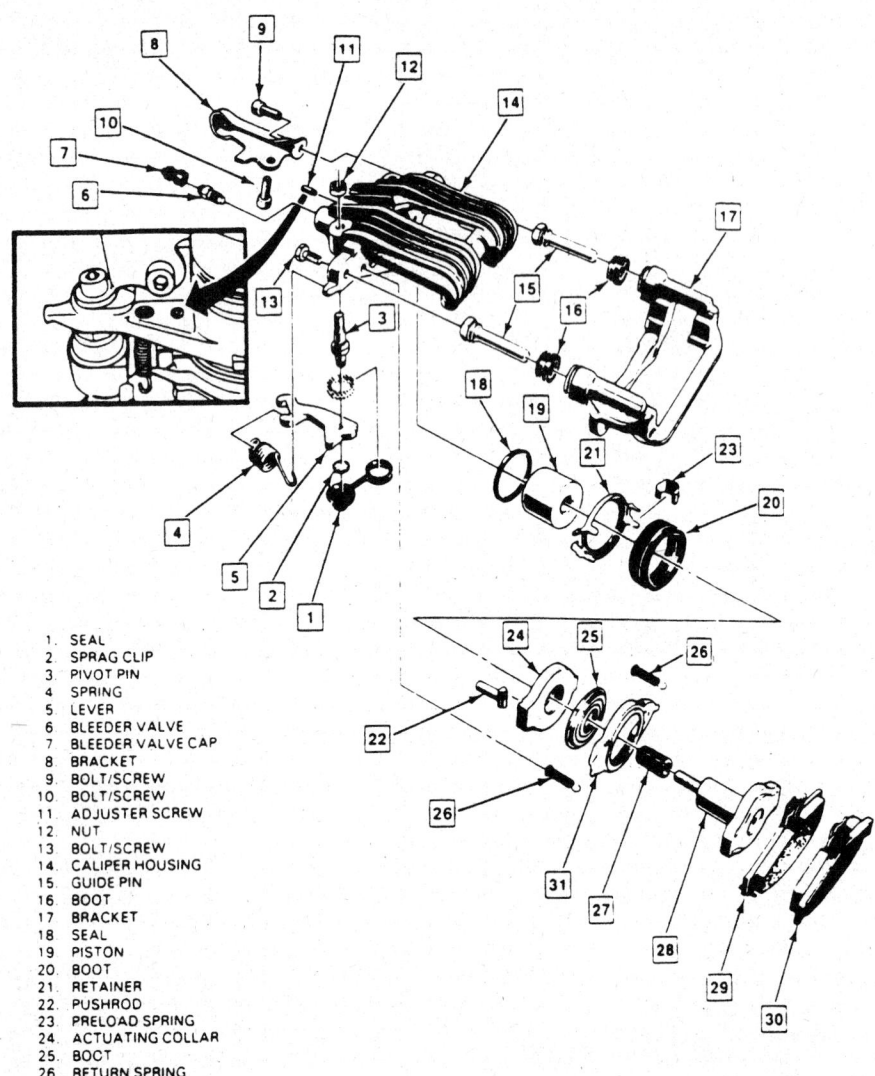

1. SEAL
2. SPRAG CLIP
3. PIVOT PIN
4. SPRING
5. LEVER
6. BLEEDER VALVE
7. BLEEDER VALVE CAP
8. BRACKET
9. BOLT/SCREW
10. BOLT/SCREW
11. ADJUSTER SCREW
12. NUT
13. BOLT/SCREW
14. CALIPER HOUSING
15. GUIDE PIN
16. BOOT
17. BRACKET
18. SEAL
19. PISTON
20. BOOT
21. RETAINER
22. PUSHROD
23. PRELOAD SPRING
24. ACTUATING COLLAR
25. BOOT
26. RETURN SPRING
27. BUSHING
28. CLAMP ROD
29. INBOARD SHOE AND LINING ASSEMBLY
30. OUTBOARD SHOE AND LINING ASSEMBLY
31. RETAINER

GC4079100094000X

Fig. 1   Typical exploded view of single piston rear caliper

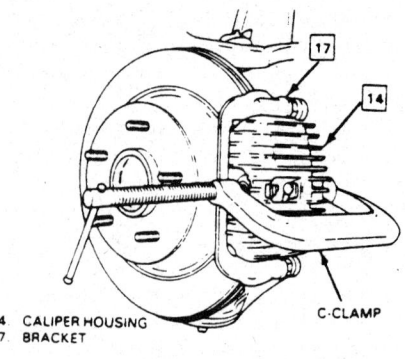

14   CALIPER HOUSING
17   BRACKET

GC4079100095000X

Fig. 2   Piston compression in caliper bore

b. If protrusion is evident, lift caliper housing and adjust position of outboard shoe and lining.
5. Install and tighten new upper guide pin bolt, then tighten lower bolt.
6. Fill master cylinder to proper level, then pump brake pedal to bring pads into contact with brake rotor.

XLR

REMOVAL

1. Remove brake master cylinder reservoir fluid to midway between maximum-full point and minimum allowable level.
2. Raise and support vehicle, then remove tire and wheel assembly.
3. Hand tighten wheel lug nut to stud to hold rotor to hub.
4. Install large C-clamp over caliper with ends against body rear and outboard brake pad.

5. Tighten C-clamp until caliper piston is compressed into bore enough to allow caliper to slide past brake rotor. Remove C-clamp.
6. Remove caliper guide pin bolts.
7. Remove brake caliper from bracket and support aside. Ensure there is no tension on hydraulic brake flexible hose. **Do not disconnect hydraulic brake flexible hose from caliper.**
8. Remove brake pads and retainers.

INSTALLATION

1. Install large C-clamp over caliper with ends against body rear and old inboard brake pad or suitable wood block installed against caliper piston.
2. Tighten C-clamp until piston is compressed completely into bore. Remove C-clamp and old brake pad or wood block.
3. Install brake pad retainers and brake pads to bracket. Brake pad wear sensor, mounted on inboard brake pad,

must be positioned so in trailing position during forward rotation of brake rotor.
4. Install caliper to bracket.
5. Install brake caliper guide pin bolts.
6. Install tire and wheel assembly, then lower vehicle.
7. With engine off, gradually apply brake pedal to approximately 2/3 travel distance. Slowly release pedal.
8. Wait 15 seconds, then repeat previous steps until firm brake pedal apply is obtained.
9. Fill brake master cylinder reservoir to proper level.

CALIPER SERVICE

Camaro, Corvette & Firebird

REPLACEMENT

1. Raise and support vehicle, then remove tire and wheel assembly.
2. If caliper requires overhaul, remove inlet fitting mounting bolt, then disconnect inlet fitting from caliper housing.
3. Discard two gaskets, then plug openings in inlet fitting and caliper.
4. Remove brake caliper guide pin bolts, then the caliper from rotor and mounting bracket.
5. Reverse procedure to install.

DISASSEMBLE

1. Remove two return springs from actuating collar, pull collar out of caliper housing.
2. Remove clamp rod and bushing. Discard bushing.
3. Bend back boot retainer tabs, then remove retainers, boots and pushrod from actuating collar.
4. Remove preload spring from retainer. Discard retainers and boots.
5. Pad interior of caliper assembly with clean shop towels, then remove piston by directing compressed air into caliper brake hose inlet hole. Use just enough air pressure to ease piston out of bore. **Do not place fingers in front of piston.**
6. Remove piston seal from bore using

small piece of wood or plastic. **Do not use metal tool to remove seal.**

7. Remove cap and bleeder valve.
8. Remove seal, sprag clip and lever from pivot pin. Discard sprag clip.
9. Clean all metal components with suitable solvent, then dry with compressed air.
10. Inspect parking brake lever components, piston, caliper bore and mounting bracket for scoring, excessive wear or corrosion.

ASSEMBLE

1. Lubricate piston sea with clean brake fluid, then install seal into caliper bore groove. Ensure seal is not twisted.
2. Lubricate caliper bore and piston with clean brake fluid.
3. Place piston into caliper bore, then push downward until fully bottomed in bore.
4. Lubricate actuating collar, then install pushrod, new boots and new retainers onto collar.
5. Clamp retainers firmly against collar, then bend tabs on retainer to hold assembly together.
6. Connect preload spring onto retainer.
7. Lubricate clamp rod, then slide rod through holes in boot and actuating collar. Ensure boot is firmly positioned against reaction plate on clamp rod.
8. Lubricate and install new compliance bushing onto clamp rod.
9. Lubricate grooved bead of inner boot, boot groove in caliper housing and actuating collar.
10. Push clamp rod to bottom of piston mating hole, then pull actuating collar and seat inner boot into boot groove in caliper housing.
11. Ensure pushrod is positioned in caliper housing hole, then install bleeder cap and valve.
12. If removed, install pivot pin and new nut onto caliper. Lubricate parking brake lever and pivot pin.
13. Install pivot pin seal, parking brake lever and new sprag clip.
14. Ensure teeth of sprag clip face away from lever and snap seal cap over pivot pin.
15. Install two collar return springs onto retainer. Ensure retainer enters springs at end of second coil.
16. Install adjustment screw into caliper housing until actuating collar is parallel to piston bore face of housing.
17. Lubricate guide pins with suitable grease and slide boots onto pins.
18. Fill boots with grease and install into mounting bracket. Ensure boots are properly positioned in grooves in pins and mounting bracket.
19. Install caliper and bleed brake system.

XLR
REMOVAL

1. Remove brake master cylinder reservoir fluid to midway between maximum-full point and minimum allowable level.
2. Raise and support vehicle, then re-

move tire and wheel assembly.
3. The brake caliper inlet fitting bolt and hose from caliper. Discard two copper brake hose gaskets.
4. Plug opening in brake caliper and brake hose.
5. Remove guide pin bolts and caliper from mounting bracket.

DISASSEMBLE

1. Pad caliper interior housing with suitable clean cloths.
2. Remove piston from caliper bore by directing low pressure compressed air into bore through fluid inlet hole. Use just enough air to ease pistons out of bores. **Do not place fingers in front of piston.**
3. Remove piston dust boot seal from seal counterbore using small wooden or plastic tool. Discard boot seal.
4. Remove and discard piston seal from caliper bore.
5. Remove bleeder valve and cap from caliper.

INSPECTION

1. Clean caliper piston bore, seal counterbore and piston with denatured alcohol. **Do not use abrasives to clean caliper piston.**
2. Dry piston bore, counterbore and piston with non-lubricated, filtered compressed air.
3. Inspect caliper bore for cracks, scoring, pitting, excessive rust and/or excessive corrosion. If light rust or light corrosion are present in caliper bore, attempt to remove imperfection with fine emery paper.
4. Inspect caliper piston for cracks, scoring and/or damage to chrome plating.

ASSEMBLE

1. Lubricate new piston seal with suitable DOT 3 brake fluid from clean, sealed brake fluid container.
2. Install lubricated, new piston seal into caliper bore and new piston dust boot seal over piston.
3. Install piston into caliper bore and boot over end of piston so fold will face toward housing piston bore opening.
4. Seat boot into bore groove and slide piston into bore.
5. Push piston to bottom of bore. Ensure boot is properly seated into piston and caliper bore grooves.
6. Install caliper bleed screw and cap.

INSTALLATION

1. Install brake caliper to mounting bracket.
2. Install guide pin bolts.
3. Remove plug from caliper opening and brake hose.
4. Install new copper brake hose gaskets and brake caliper inlet fitting bolt to brake hose.
5. Install brake hose and caliper inlet fitting bolt to caliper.
6. Bleed hydraulic brake system.
7. Install tire and wheel assembly, then lower vehicle.

ROTOR
REPLACE

Whenever the brake rotor has been separated from the hub/axle flange, any rust or contaminants should be cleaned from the hub/axle flange and the brake rotor mating surfaces.

Camaro, Corvette & Firebird

1. Raise and support vehicle, then remove tire and wheel assembly.
2. Remove guide pin bolts, and caliper.
3. Remove mounting bolts and mounting bracket.
4. Remove rotor from hub and bearing.
5. Reverse procedure to install.

XLR
REMOVAL

1. Raise and support vehicle, then remove tire and wheel assembly.
2. Disconnect park brake cable from apply lever.
3. Install C-clamp over caliper with ends against body rear and outboard disc brake pad.
4. Compress piston into bore just enough to allow caliper to slide away from rotor. Remove C-clamp.
5. Remove caliper bracket bolts. **Do not disconnect brake flexible hose bolt.**
6. Remove caliper and mounting bracket, then support aside. Ensure there is no tension on hydraulic brake flexible hose.
7. Mark brake rotor to wheel studs position for installation alignment.
8. Remove brake rotor. **Do not force rotor off.** If rotor is difficult to remove, ease it off by gently rotating it while pulling outward.

INSTALLATION

1. Connect park brake cable to lever.
2. Adjust clearance of park brake shoe to drum-in-hat portion of brake rotor.
3. Install brake rotor to hub/axle flange.
4. Install brake caliper and bracket a to suspension knuckle.
5. Install tire and wheel assembly, then lower vehicle.

ADJUSTMENTS
Parking Brake
CAMARO, CORVETTE & FIREBIRD

1. Release parking brake lever, then raise and support vehicle.
2. Remove rear wheels, then install lug nuts on two opposite wheel studs to hold brake rotor in position.
3. Back caliper pistons into bores.
4. Loosen parking brake cable adjusting nut until there is no tension on parking brake shoes.

DISC BRAKES

5. Turn each brake rotor until parking brake shoe star adjuster is visible through hole in rotor.
6. Adjusting one side at a time, tighten adjuster until rotor cannot be turned by hand, then back star wheel off 5–7 notches. **Adjust parking brake shoes by inserting suitable tool through hole in rotor. On driver's side, tighten adjuster by moving tool handle upward. On passenger's side, tighten adjuster by moving tool handle downward.**
7. Install rear wheels and pull parking lever up two notches.
8. Tighten cable adjusting nut at equalizer until there is drag on wheels.
9. Release parking brake lever and inspect adjustment. No drag should be felt when rotating wheels.

XLR

The park brake cables are tensioned automatically by cycling the park brake pedal three times.

DISC BRAKE SPECIFICATIONS
Rotor Specifications

Model	Year	Nominal Thickness, Inch	Minimum Refinish Thickness, Inch	Discard Thickness, Inch①	Thickness Variation (Parallelism), Inch	Lateral Runout (T.I.R.), Inch	Maximum Scoring Depth, Inch
Camaro & Firebird	2001–05	1.0200	.9800	.9650	.0010	.0020	.0590
Corvette	2001–05	1.0200	.9800	.9650	.0010	.0020	.0590
XLR	2004–05	1.0200	.9800	.9650	.0010	.0020	.0590

① — Discard thickness is stamped on rotor.

TIGHTENING SPECIFICATIONS

Year	Component	Torque/Ft. lbs.
2001–05	Bleed Screw	106①
	Caliper Guide Pin	23
	Caliper Inlet Fitting	33
	Caliper Mounting Bracket (Camaro & Firebird)	74
	Caliper Mounting Bracket (Corvette & XLR)	125
	Wheel Lug Nut	100

① — Inch lbs

Saturn

NOTE: On Air Bag Equipped Models, Refer To "Air Bag System Precautions" Located In The Front Of This Manual For System Disarming & Arming Procedures.

NOTE: Refer To "Computer Relearn Procedures" Located In The Front Of This Manual When Battery Power To The Computer Has Been Interrupted.

INDEX

BRAKE SYSTEM BLEED

Refer to "Hydraulic Brake Systems" for manual and pressure bleeding procedures.

BRAKE PAD SERVICE

Ion

1. Raise and support vehicle, then remove tire and wheel assemblies.
2. Tighten suitable C-clamp until piston is compressed into caliper bore. Remove C-clamp.
3. Remove brake caliper lower guide pin bolt.
4. Pivot caliper upward and support aside using suitable wire.
5. Remove brake pads from caliper, **Fig. 1.**
6. Reverse procedure to install, noting the following:
   a. Inspect brake components.
   b. Bleed brake system as outlined in "Brake System Bleed."

L-Series

FRONT

1. Raise and support vehicle, then remove front tire and wheel assemblies.
2. Pry off locking plate and remove brake pressure hose from strut.
3. Remove pad retainer spring, guide pins and caliper.
4. Remove inboard, and outboard brake pads from caliper.

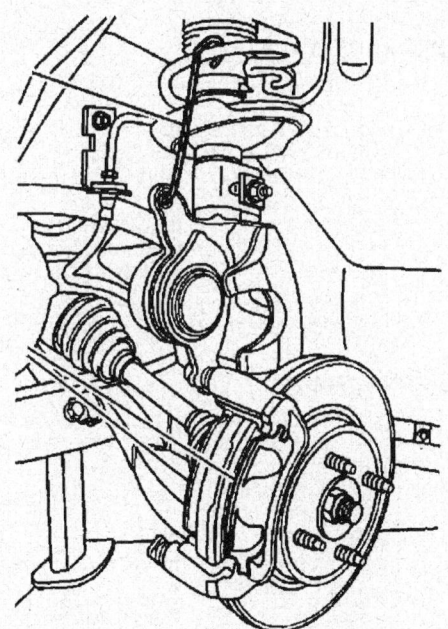

ARM66GC000000717

Fig. 1 Brake pad removal

5. Reverse procedure to install.

REAR

1. Raise and support vehicle, then remove rear tire and wheel assemblies.
2. Drive out brake pad retaining pins from outside to inside.
3. Remove pins, retaining spring and pads.

4. Reverse procedure to install.

S-Series

FRONT

1. Raise and support vehicle, then remove front tire and wheel assemblies.
2. Remove caliper lockpin.
3. Pivot caliper upward around guide pin.
4. Remove brake pads.
5. Remove two pad clips from caliper support.
6. Reverse procedure to install.

REAR

1. Raise and support vehicle, then remove tire and wheel assemblies.
2. Remove caliper lockpin and guide pin.
3. Remove caliper from support and suspend aside with suitable wire.
4. Remove brake pads and two pad clips from caliper support.
5. Reverse procedure to install.

CALIPER SERVICE

Ion

REPLACEMENT

1. Raise and support vehicle, then remove tire and wheel assemblies.
2. Install and tighten two wheel nuts opposite to retain rotor to hub.
3. Tighten suitable C-clamp to compress piston into caliper bore.

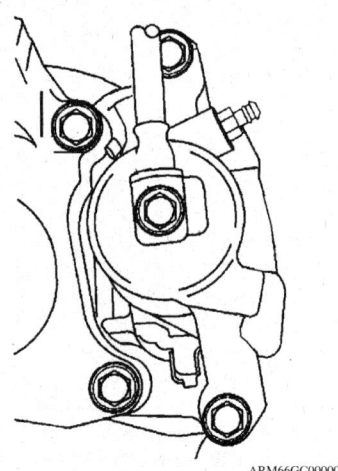

Fig. 2 Brake caliper hose removal. Ion

Fig. 3 Retaining ring removal. Ion

Fig. 5 Caliper piston installation. Ion

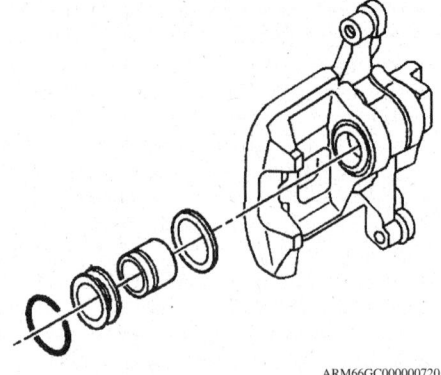

Fig. 4 Piston boot removal. Ion

4. Remove mounting bolt and brake hose from caliper, **Fig. 2.**
5. Remove and discard copper brake hose gaskets.
6. Cap opening in brake caliper and brake hose.
7. Remove guide pin bolts, caliper and bracket.
8. Reverse procedure to install.

DISASSEMBLE

1. Remove caliper piston from bore using compressed air through fluid inlet hole.
2. Remove retaining ring to dust boot of caliper housing, **Fig. 3.**
3. Remove piston boot seal from counterbore in caliper, then the piston seal using suitable piece of wood, **Fig. 4.**

ASSEMBLE

1. Lubricate new piston seal using suitable DOT 3 brake fluid and install seal into caliper bore.
2. Apply suitable DOT 3 brake fluid to surface area of caliper piston.
3. Install bottom half of caliper piston into caliper bore and dust boot seal over caliper piston, **Fig. 5.**
4. Compress caliper piston to caliper bore and seat piston boot into counterbore.
5. Install retaining ring and bleeder valve.
6. Install bleeder valve cap and caliper.

L-Series

FRONT

REPLACEMENT

1. Raise and support vehicle, then remove tire and wheel assemblies.
2. Remove brake hose from caliper and plug opening.
3. Remove brake pad retaining spring from caliper and caliper-to-bracket guide pins.
4. Remove caliper from support bracket and pads from caliper.
5. Reverse procedure to install.

DISASSEMBLE

1. Inspect guide pin sleeves and covers for damage.
2. Inspect boot for deterioration. If damaged, overhaul caliper.
3. Remove piston boot ring and boot using small screwdriver.
4. Pad caliper interior with suitable cushion and apply non-lubricated compressed air to caliper inlet hole to remove piston.
5. Remove piston seal, bleeder valve and cap.

INSPECTION

1. Clean all components in clean denatured alcohol, and dry with non-lubricated compressed air.
2. Blow out all caliper and bleeder valve passages.
3. Inspect piston for damage.
4. Inspect caliper bore for damage, noting the following:
   a. Slight corrosion may be removed using suitable crocus cloth.
   b. If damage is excessive, replace caliper.
   c. **Do not hone caliper bore.**
5. Inspect seal groove for damage.

ASSEMBLE

1. Install bleeder valve.
2. Lubricate piston seal using clean brake fluid and install. Ensure seal is not twisted.
3. Install lubricated piston boot to piston.
4. Install lubricated piston to body. Push piston to bottom of bore.
5. Install boot ring, noting the following:
   a. Ensure piston boot outer edge is

smoothly seated in counterbore.
   b. Work boot ring into groove near open end of caliper bore.
   c. **Do not pinch piston ring between boot ring and body.**
6. Lift piston boot inner edge to release trapped air, then install caliper and bleed brake system.

REAR

REPLACEMENT

1. Raise and support vehicle, then remove tire and wheel assemblies.
2. Drive out brake pad retaining pins from outside-to-inside, then remove pins, retaining spring and pads.
3. Remove brake pipe from caliper and plug opening.
4. Remove caliper to rear axle control arm fasteners and caliper.
5. Reverse procedure to install.

DISASSEMBLE

The rear caliper has a dual piston design. The caliper must not be completely disassembled. Disassemble only one piston at a time.
1. Carefully pry out piston boot clamp using small screwdriver and remove piston boot.
2. Pad caliper interior with suitable cushion and apply non-lubricated compressed air to caliper inlet hole to remove piston.
3. Remove piston seal, bleeder valve and cap.

INSPECTION

1. Clean all components in clean denatured alcohol and dry with non-lubricated compressed air.
2. Blow out all caliper and bleeder valve passages.
3. Inspect piston for damage.
4. Inspect caliper bore for damage, noting the following:
   a. Slight corrosion may be removed using suitable crocus cloth.
   b. If damage is excessive, replace caliper.
   c. **Do not hone caliper bore.**
5. Inspect seal groove for damage.

ASSEMBLE

1. Install bleeder valve and cap.
2. Lubricate piston seal using clean

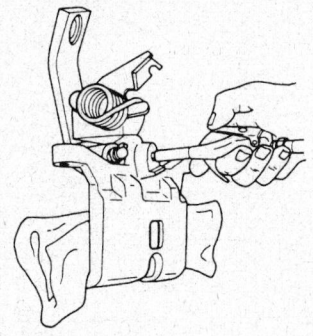

G34079100003000X

Fig. 6 Rear caliper piston removal. S-Series

brake fluid and install. Ensure seal is not twisted.
3. Install lubricated piston boot to piston.
4. Insert lubricated piston into body, then install caliper and bleed brake system.

S-Series

FRONT

REPLACEMENT

1. Raise and support vehicle, then remove tire and wheel assemblies.
2. Disconnect caliper brake fluid lines and plug opening.
3. Remove caliper lockpin, guide pin and pin boots.
4. Remove caliper from caliper support. **Do not damage pin boots.**
5. Remove brake pads.
6. Remove two pad clips from caliper support.
7. Reverse procedure to install.

DISASSEMBLE

1. Inspect lockpin and guide pin boots for damage.
2. Inspect piston boot and lockpin for damage.
3. Remove piston boot ring and boot using small screwdriver.
4. Pad caliper interior with suitable cushion and apply non-lubricated compressed air to caliper inlet hole to remove piston.
5. Remove piston seal, bleeder valve and cap.

INSPECTION

1. Clean all components in clean denatured alcohol and dry with non-lubricated compressed air.
2. Blow out all caliper and bleeder valve passages.
3. Inspect piston for damage.
4. Inspect caliper bore for damage. Slight corrosion may be removed using suitable crocus cloth. If damage is excessive, replace caliper. **Do not hone caliper bore.**
5. Inspect seal groove for damage.

ASSEMBLE

1. Install bleeder valve.
2. Lubricate piston seal using clean

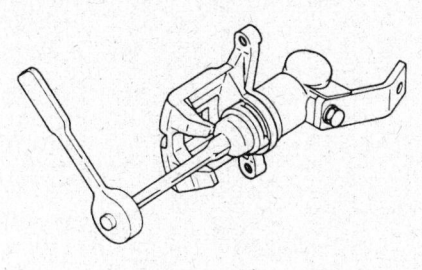

G34079100004000X

Fig. 7 Rear caliper piston installation. S-Series

brake fluid and install. Ensure seal is not twisted.
3. Install lubricated piston boot to piston.
4. Install lubricated piston to body, push piston to bottom of bore.
5. Install boot ring. Ensure piston boot outer edge is smoothly seated in counterbore.
6. Work boot ring into groove near open end of caliper bore. **Do not pinch piston ring between boot ring and body.**
7. Lift piston boot inner edge to release trapped air, then install caliper and bleed brake system.

REAR

REPLACEMENT

1. Raise and support vehicle, then remove tire and wheel assemblies.
2. Disconnect caliper brake fluid lines and plug opening.
3. Slip parking brake cable end from brake lever and remove cable outer housing using cable release tool No. SA9151BR, or equivalent.
4. Remove caliper lockpin and guide pin.
5. Remove caliper from caliper support. **Do not damage pin boots.**
6. Remove lockpin and guide pins from caliper support.
7. Reverse procedure to install.

DISASSEMBLE

1. Inspect lockpin and guide pin boots for damage.
2. Inspect piston boot and lockpin for damage.
3. Remove piston boot ring and boot using small screwdriver.
4. Pad caliper interior with suitable cushion, then apply non-lubricated compressed air to caliper inlet hole to remove piston, **Fig. 6.**
5. Remove piston seal, bleeder valve and cap.

INSPECTION

1. Clean all components in clean denatured alcohol and dry with non-lubricated compressed air.
2. Blow out all caliper and bleeder valve passages.
3. Inspect piston for damage.
4. Inspect caliper bore for damage. Slight

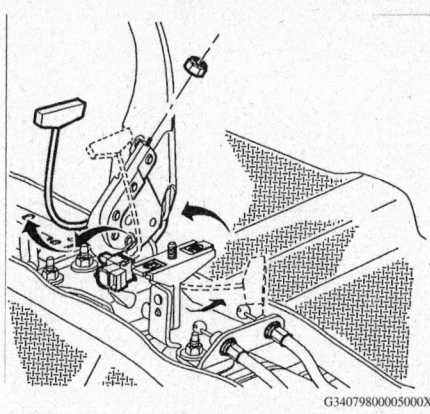

G34079800005000X

Fig. 8 Parking brake equalizer cable removal

corrosion may be removed using suitable crocus cloth. If damage is excessive, replace caliper. **Do not hone caliper bore.**
5. Inspect seal groove for damage.

ASSEMBLE

1. Install bleeder valve and cap.
2. Lubricate piston seal using clean brake fluid, then install, ensuring seal is not twisted.
3. Install lubricated piston boot to piston.
4. Install lubricated piston to body, push piston by hand, then install piston installation tool No. SA91110NE, or equivalent, to piston slots. Rotate piston clockwise to install, **Fig. 7.**
5. Install boot ring. Ensure piston boot outer edge is smoothly seated in counterbore.
6. Work boot ring into groove near open end of caliper bore. **Do not pinch piston ring between boot ring and body.**
7. Lift piston boot inner edge to release trapped air, then install caliper and bleed brake system.

ROTOR

REPLACE

Ion

1. Raise and support vehicle, then remove tire and wheel assembly.
2. Compress piston into caliper bore using suitable C-clamp to allow caliper pivot upward from brake pads.
3. Raise and support vehicle, then remove tire and wheel assemblies.
4. Install and tighten two wheel nuts opposite to retain rotor to hub.
5. Tighten suitable C-clamp to compress piston into caliper bore.
6. Remove mounting bolt and brake hose from caliper, **Fig. 2.**
7. Remove and discard copper brake hose gaskets.
8. Cap opening in brake caliper and brake hose.
9. Remove guide pin bolts, caliper and bracket.
10. Mark rotor to wheel studs for installation alignment and remove rotor.
11. Reverse procedure to install.

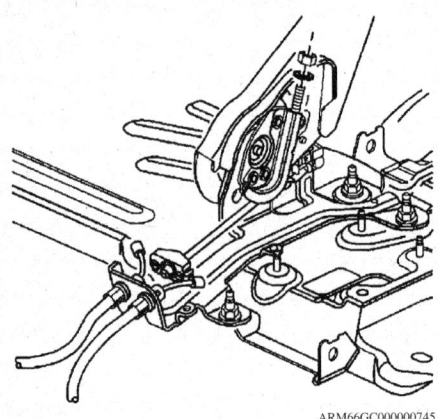

ARM66GC000000745

Fig. 9 Park brake cable removal. Ion

L-Series

1. Raise and support vehicle, then remove tire and wheel assembly.
2. Pry off locking plate and remove brake pressure hose from strut.
3. Remove caliper bracket to steering knuckle mounting bolts and suspend caliper aside.
4. Remove mounting screw and rotor.
5. Reverse procedure to install.

S-Series

1. Raise and support vehicle, then remove tire and wheel assembly.
2. Remove caliper support to knuckle bolts and suspend caliper from strut spring with wire.
3. Remove rotor.
4. Reverse procedure to install.

PARKING BRAKE SERVICE

Parking Brake Equalizer Cable, Replace

1. Remove center console as outlined in "Dash Panel Service" section of appropriate chassis chapter.
2. Remove adjuster nut and cables from equalizer, **Fig. 8.**
3. Place parking brake lever to highest position.
4. Lift equalizer cable over parking brake indicator switch and swing forward. Pull cable down and out of parking brake lever.
5. Reverse procedure to install. Adjust parking brake cable.

Parking Brake Cable, Replace

ION

FRONT

1. Raise park brake lever and unsnap park brake boot from console.

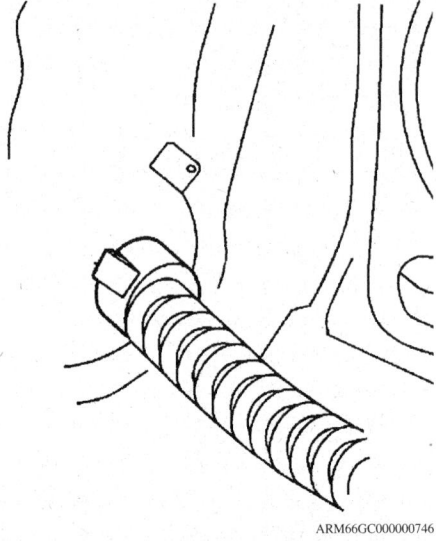

ARM66GC000000746

Fig. 10 Park brake cable retainer removal. Ion

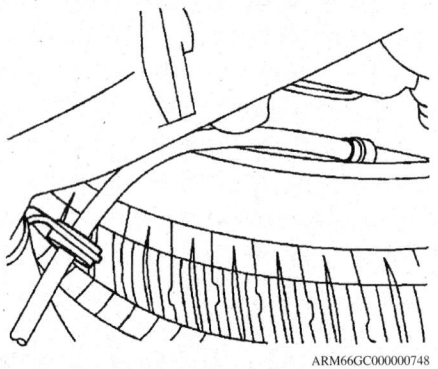

ARM66GC000000748

Fig. 12 Cable assembly removal. Ion

2. Lift up on rear of console compartment to release retaining fasteners.
3. Lift console compartment and push park brake boot through opening in compartment.
4. Slide console compartment over park brake lever.
5. Release park brake cable tension.
6. Remove park brake cable adjuster nut and washer, **Fig. 9.**
7. Disconnect rear park cables from front park brake cable equalizer, then remove front park brake cable by pulling rearward.
8. Reverse procedure to install. Adjust parking brake cable as outlined in "Adjustments."

REAR

1. Raise park brake lever and unsnap park brake boot from console.
2. Lift up on rear of console compartment to release retaining fasteners.
3. Lift console compartment and push park brake boot through opening in compartment.
4. Slide console compartment over park brake lever.
5. Release park brake cable tension.
6. Remove rear lower seat cushion.

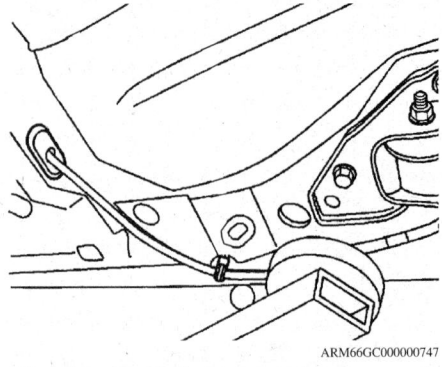

ARM66GC000000747

Fig. 11 Park brake cable removal. Ion

7. Release rear edge of carpet from retainers.
8. Place carpeting forward to access rear park brake cables.
9. With park brake lever released, remove rear brake cable from equalizer.
10. Release rear cable from retainer on park brake lever, then pass through grommet.
11. Raise and support vehicle.
12. Remove rear tire and wheel assembly.
13. Remove rear brake shoes as outlined in "Drum Brake" chapter.
14. Release park brake cable retainer from drum brake backing plate, **Fig. 10.**
15. Release rear cable to underbody retaining clip and park brake cable from clip, **Fig. 11.**
16. Release C-shaped retainer from park brake cable at bracket and remove cable, **Fig. 12.**
17. Reverse procedure to install. Adjust parking brake cable as outlined in "Adjustments."

L-SERIES

1. Release parking brake.
2. Remove parking brake boot by squeezing boot in sides while pulling upwards.
3. Loosen parking brake adjuster nut to provide ample slack in brake cable.
4. Raise and support vehicle, then disconnect exhaust resonator from exhaust manifold pipe.
5. Remove exhaust pipe to body insulator, then lower exhaust resonator pipe and muffler.
6. Remove exhaust heat shield and disconnect parking brake cable from rear parking brake cable. Discard clips.
7. Disconnect front parking brake cable from equalizer.
8. Remove cable body attachment points.
9. Reverse procedure to install. Adjust parking brake cable as outlined in "Adjustments."

S-SERIES

1. Remove center console as outlined in "Dash Panel Service" section of appropriate chassis chapter.
2. Loosen adjuster nut.
3. Remove parking brake cables from

equalizer and from parking brake base.

4. Remove rear seat bottom cushion, then pull carpet back.
5. Raise and support vehicle.
6. Remove parking brake cable grommet from floor pan.
7. Remove parking brake cable mounting brackets and tie strap.
8. Disconnect cable end from caliper.
9. Remove cable from bracket using parking brake release tool No. SA9151BR, or equivalent.
10. Reverse procedure to install. Adjust parking brake cable.

Parking Brake Shoes, Replace

1. Raise and support vehicle, then remove rear tire and wheel assemblies.
2. Remove rear caliper to rear axle control arm bolts and support caliper aside.
3. Remove mounting screw and rotor.
4. Remove return springs, parking brake shoes and hold-down retainers.
5. Remove parking brake shoes and adjuster.
6. Reverse procedure to install. Adjust parking brake as outlined in "Adjustments."

ADJUSTMENTS
Parking Brake
ION

1. Apply and release park brake several times. Ensure lever is released completely.

2. Turn ignition to On position and ensure red BRAKE lamp is not illuminated. If lamp is illuminated, verify following:
   a. Park brake lever is in released position and against stop.
   b. There is no slack in park brake cable.
3. Turn ignition to Off position.
4. Remove brake lever boot from console.
5. Pull boot away from console.
6. Loosen front park brake cable adjusting nut to end of front cable threaded rod.
7. Raise and support vehicle.
8. Adjust rear drum brakes as outlined in "Drum Brakes" chapter.
9. Ensure no brake shoe drag is present by rotating brake drums.
10. Install two wheel nuts to drums and lower vehicle.
11. Raise park brake lever six notched positions and install cable adjusting nut.
12. Tighten park brake cable adjusting nut.
13. Release park brake lever and ensure park brake is released.
14. If drums do not rotate freely, raise park brake lever three notched positions and rotate brake drum.
15. Righthand rear brake drum should not rotate forward or rearward and lefthand rear drum should not rotate in either direction.
16. Raise park brake lever one additional notched position and attempt to rotate brake drums.
17. Ensure left and righthand brake drums cannot be rotated. Raise vehicle.
18. Remove brake drum mounting bolts, then install tire and wheel assemblies.
19. Lower vehicle, position park brake lever boot to front console and release park brake lever.

L-SERIES

1. Remove parking brake boot by squeezing boot in sides while pulling upwards.
2. Raise and support vehicle, then remove rear tire and wheel assemblies.
3. Turn adjuster (through hole in front face of rotor) at rear rotor until brake disc locks. Turn back adjuster until disc just moves freely.
4. Pull parking brake lever to third click.
5. Tighten adjuster nut until heavy drag is felt at both rear wheels when turned by hand.
6. Apply and release parking brake several times. There should be no drag when lever is in rest position.
7. Pull lever to third click and ensure heavy drag exists at both rear wheels. Repeat procedure until proper adjustment is reached.

S-SERIES

1. Lift parking brake lever, then remove mounting screw and cover.
2. Raise and support vehicle.
3. Pull parking brake lever to first click.
4. Tighten adjuster nut until moderate drag is felt at both rear wheels when turned by hand.
5. Pull up on parking brake lever until twelfth or thirteenth click is heard. Repeat 3–4 times.
6. Ensure no drag exists when parking brake is in rest position.
7. Pull lever to first click and ensure moderate drag exists at both rear wheels. Repeat procedure until proper adjustment is reached.

DISC BRAKE SPECIFICATIONS
Caliper Specifications

Model	Year	Caliper Bore Dia. Inch
L-SERIES		
Front	2001–05	2.24
Rear	2001–05	1.38

DISC BRAKES

Rotor Specifications

Year	Front Disc Brake							Rear Disc Brake						
	Brake Lining Wear Limit, Inch	Rotor			Thickness Variation Parallelism Inch	Lateral Run-Out (T.I.R.) Inch	Maximum Scoring Depth, Inch	Brake Lining Wear Limit, Inch	Rotor			Thickness Variation Parallelism Inch	Lateral Run-Out (T.I.R.) Inch	Maximum Scoring Depth, Inch
		Thickness, Inch							Thickness, Inch					
		Nominal	Min. Re-finish	Discard Limit①					Nominal	Min. Re-finish	Discard Limit ①			
ION														
2003–05	.0390	.9330	.8960	.8700	.0010	.0020	.0590	—	—	—	—	—	—	—
L-SERIES														
2001–05	.0800	.9800	.9000	.8700	.0003	.0010	.0590	.0800	.3900	.3500	.3100	.0004	.0010	.0590
S-SERIES														
2001–02	.0800	.7100	.6330	.6250	.0005	.0024	.0590	.0800	.4400	.3700	.3500	.0005	.0024	.0590

① — Discard thickness is stamped on rotor.

TIGHTENING SPECIFICATIONS

Year	Component	Torque/Ft. Lbs.
ION		
2003–05	Bleeder Valve	97①
	Brake Caliper Guide Pin	25
	Brake Caliper Mounting Bracket	85
	Brake Hose To Brake Caliper	35
	Park Brake Cable Adjusting Nut	35①
	Park Brake Lever	18
	Park Brake Warning Lamp Switch	27①
L-SERIES		
2001–05	Bleed Valve, Front	71①
	Bleed Valve, Rear	53①
	Brake Hose To Brake Pipe	12
	Brake Hose To Brake Caliper	30
	Brake Pipe To Caliper	12
	Brake Lever To Floor	89①
	Caliper To Bracket Guide Pins	22
	Caliper To Rear Axle Control Arm	59
	Caliper To Steering Knuckle	70
	Exhaust Heat Shield	35①
	Wheel Lug Nuts	92②
	Wheel Speed Sensor To Knuckle	72①
S-SERIES		
2001–02	Backing Plate To Knuckle	63
	Bleed Valve, Front	97①
	Bleed Valve, Rear	66①
	Brake Hose To Caliper	36
	Brake Lever To Floor	23
	Brake Line To Brake Hose	18
	Brake Line To Master Cylinder	24
	Caliper Lock & Guide Pins	27
	Caliper Mount Bracket	81
	Caliper-To-Caliper Support	27
	Caliper To Knuckle	81
	Wheel Lug Nuts	103
	Wheel Speed Sensor	89①

① — Inch lbs.
② — For steel wheel & optional aluminum wheel w/large center cap,

install wheel cover or cap. With
socket, hand tighten five cap nuts

then, with wrench, tighten each cap
an additional 90°.

Toyota/GM Single Piston Caliper

NOTE: On Air Bag Equipped Models, Refer To "Air Bag System Precautions" Located In The Front Of This Manual For System Disarming & Arming Procedures.

NOTE: Refer To "Computer Relearn Procedures" Located In The Front Of This Manual When Battery Power To The Computer Has Been Interrupted.

INDEX

PRECAUTIONS

1. Keep grease and other foreign material off brake linings, caliper, surfaces of disc and external surfaces of hub.
2. Avoid deforming disc, and nicking or scratching brake linings.
3. Worn or damaged rubber piston seals should be replaced.
4. During removal and installation of a wheel assembly, ensure not to interfere with or damage caliper splash shield, or bleeder screw.
5. Front wheel bearing preload should be adjusted to specifications.
6. Ensure vehicle is centered on hoist before servicing any front end components to avoid bending or damaging disc splash shield on full left or right-hand wheel turns.
7. Before vehicle is moved after any brake service work, ensure to obtain a firm brake pedal.
8. Assembly bolts of two-piece caliper housings should not be disturbed unless caliper requires service.

DESCRIPTION

The caliper is a single bore design and is mounted to a carrier assembly, **Fig. 1.** Hydraulic pressure, created by applying the brake pedal, is converted by the caliper to a stopping force. This force acts equally against the piston and bottom of caliper bore to move the piston outward and to slide the caliper inward, resulting in a clamping action on the rotor. The clamping action forces the linings against the rotor, creating friction required to stop the vehicle.

TROUBLESHOOTING

The most common cause of brake chatter on disc brakes is a variation in disc thickness. If roughness or vibration is encountered during highway operation or if pedal pulsation is experienced at low speeds, the disc may have excessive thickness variation. To inspect for this condition, measure the disc at 12 points with a micrometer at a radius approximately one inch from edge of disc. If thickness measurements vary by more than .0005 inch, the disc should be replaced with a new one.

Excessive lateral runout of braking disc may cause a piston knocking back, possibly creating increased pedal travel and vibration when brakes are applied.

Before inspecting the runout, the wheel bearings should be adjusted. The adjustment is very important and will be required at the completion of the test to prevent bearing failure. Adjust the wheel bearings as outlined in "Front Suspension & Steering" section of appropriate chassis chapter.

BRAKE SYSTEM BLEED

Refer to "Hydraulic Brake Systems" for manual and pressure bleeding procedures.

BRAKE PAD SERVICE

Removal

Replace brake pads on one wheel at a time to prevent opposite side caliper piston from being forced out of bore.
1. Siphon ⅔ of brake fluid from master cylinder.

2. Raise and support vehicle, then remove tire and wheel assemblies.
3. Install two wheel lug nuts to retain rotor and remove caliper mounting bolts.
4. Remove union nut securing brake hose to caliper and drain fluid into suitable container. **If caliper is only being removed for brake pad replacement, do not disconnect brake hose.**
5. Compress piston and remove caliper. If brake hose remains connected, suspend caliper aside. **Do not support caliper with brake hose.**
6. Remove anti-rattle clips and brake pads, **Fig. 2.**
7. Remove pad wear indicator plates and anti-squeal shims.
8. Remove support plates.

Installation

1. Install new support plates on caliper mounting bracket.
2. Install new wear indicators and anti-squeal shims on each pad, then position pads in caliper mounting bracket. **Ensure a wear indicator arrow is pointing in rotating direction of rotor.**
3. Install anti-rattle springs.
4. Seat piston in caliper bore, then install caliper and mounting bolts.
5. Fill master cylinder and bleed brakes.
6. Seat piston in caliper bore. **Do not damage piston.**
7. Ensure support plates and anti-rattle springs are properly positioned, then mount caliper over rotor onto mounting bracket, **Fig. 3.**

8. Install caliper mounting bolts.
9. Install brake hose and mounting bolts using new copper gaskets.
10. Fill master cylinder and bleed brake system as outlined in "Hydraulic Brake Systems" chapter.

CALIPER SERVICE

Removal

1. Siphon ⅔ of brake fluid from master cylinder.
2. Raise and support vehicle, then remove tire and wheel assemblies.
3. Install two wheel lug nuts to retain rotor and remove caliper mounting bolts.
4. Remove union nut securing brake hose to caliper and drain fluid into suitable container. **If caliper is only being removed for brake pad replacement, do not disconnect brake hose.**
5. Compress piston and remove caliper. If brake hose remains connected, suspend caliper aside. **Do not support caliper with brake hose.**

Disassemble

1. Remove two caliper slide bushings, four dust boots and spacer collars, **Fig. 1.**
2. Pry out caliper dust boot retaining ring and remove dust boot.
3. Place clean shop towels in caliper web and apply compressed air to caliper fluid inlet to force piston from bore. **Keep fingers clear of caliper web when removing piston. Use only enough air pressure to ease piston out of bore.**
4. Remove piston seal from caliper bore. **Do not mar machined surface of caliper.**
5. Remove bleeder valve.

Inspection

1. Clean components with alcohol and wipe dry with clean, lint free shop towels.
2. Blow out caliper and fluid passages with clean, filtered compressed air.
3. Inspect caliper and piston for damage, distortion, excessive wear and pitting.

Assemble

1. Apply lithium soap base glycol grease to components, **Fig. 4.**
2. Install piston seal in caliper. Ensure seal is squarely seated in groove.
3. Press piston into bore. Ensure piston enters bore straight.
4. Seat piston dust boot in caliper groove and install retaining ring.
5. Install two collars and four slide bushing dust boots, rotating boots as they are pressed in to ensure they are fully seated.
6. Install slide bushings through dust boots. Ensure boots remain seated in caliper grooves.

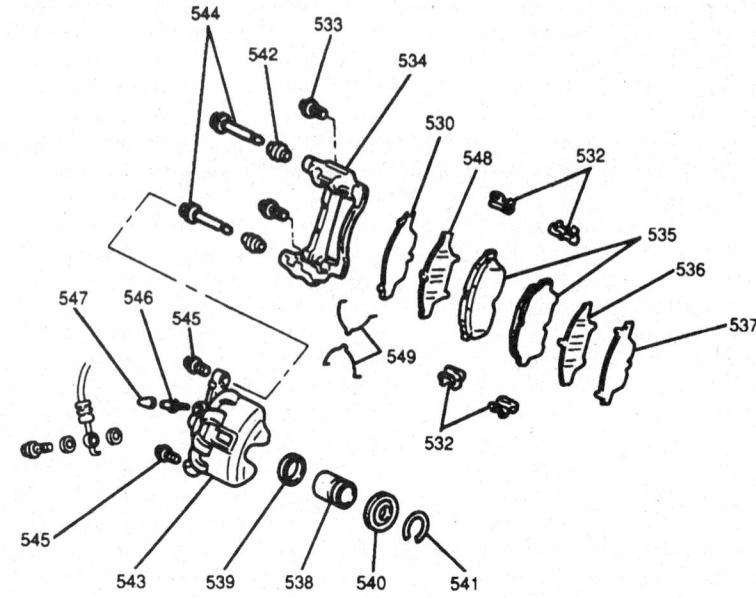

530 ANTI-SQUEAL SHIM (INBOARD)	540 PISTON BOOT
532 ANTI-RATTLE SPRINGS	541 CALIPER SET RING
533 CALIPER CARRIER BOLTS	542 DUST BOOTS
534 CALIPER CARRIER	543 CALIPER HOUSING
535 BRAKE PADS	544 SLIDE PINS
536 ANTI-SQUEAL SHIM (INNER OUTBOARD)	545 CALIPER MOUNTING BOLTS
537 ANTI-SQUEAL SHIM (OUTBOARD)	546 BLEEDER SCREW
538 PISTON	547 CAP
539 PISTON SEAL	548 ANTI-SQUEAL SHIM (INNER INBOARD)
	549 ANTI-SQUEAL SPRINGS

GC4079700151000X

Fig. 1 Exploded view of brake caliper

Installation

1. Seat piston in caliper bore. **Do not damage piston.**
2. Ensure support plates and anti-rattle springs are properly positioned, then mount caliper over rotor onto mounting bracket, **Fig. 3.**
3. Install caliper mounting bolts.
4. Install brake hose and mounting bolts using new copper gaskets.
5. Fill master cylinder and bleed brake system as outlined in "Hydraulic Brake Systems" chapter.

ROTOR

REPLACE

Removal

1. Siphon ⅔ of brake fluid from master cylinder.
2. Raise and support vehicle, then remove tire and wheel assemblies.
3. Install two wheel lug nuts to retain rotor and remove caliper mounting bolts.
4. Remove union nut securing brake hose to caliper and drain fluid into suitable container. **Do not disconnect brake hose.**
5. Compress piston and remove caliper. If brake hose remains connected, suspend caliper aside. **Do not support caliper with brake hose.**
6. Remove anti-rattle springs from caliper carrier.
7. Remove mounting bolts and caliper carrier.
8. Remove brake rotor from wheel hub. If rotor cannot be removed by hand, install two 8 MM bolts into rotor. Tightening bolts will force rotor off wheel hub.
9. Reverse procedure to install.

Installation

1. Install brake rotor.
2. Install mounting bolts and caliper carrier.
3. Install anti-rattle springs from caliper carrier.
4. Seat piston in caliper bore. **Do not damage piston.**
5. Ensure support plates and anti-rattle springs are properly positioned, then mount caliper over rotor onto mounting bracket, **Fig. 3.**
6. Install caliper mounting bolts.
7. Install brake hose and mounting bolts using new copper gaskets.
8. Fill master cylinder and bleed brake system as outlined in "Hydraulic Brake Systems" chapter.

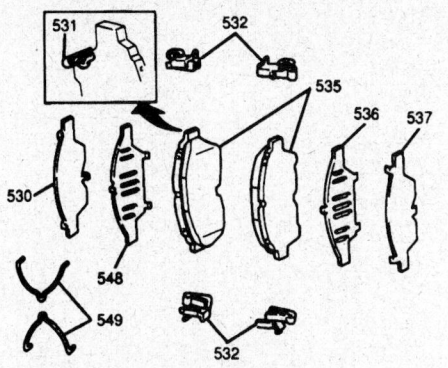

530 ANTI-SQUEAL SHIM (INBOARD)
531 PAD WEAR INDICATOR PLATE
532 ANTI-RATTLE SPRINGS
535 BRAKE PADS
536 ANTI-SQUEAL SHIM (INNER OUTBOARD)
537 ANTI-SQUEAL SHIM (OUTBOARD)
548 ANTI-SQUEAL SHIM (INNER INBOARD)
549 ANTI-SQUEAL SPRINGS

GC4079700150000X

Fig. 2 Brake pad assembly

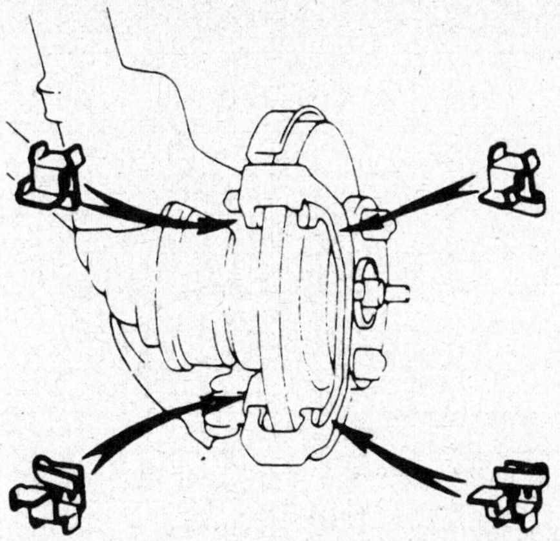

GC40791000099000X

Fig. 3 Caliper support installation

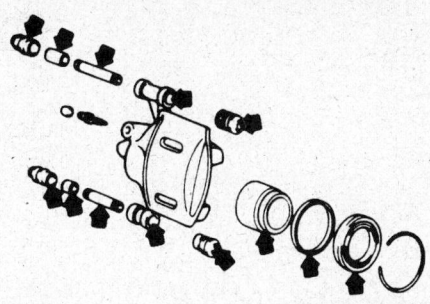

GC4079100103000X

Fig. 4 Caliper piston installation

DISC BRAKE SPECIFICATIONS
Rotor Specifications

Year	Front Disc Brake							Rear Disc Brake						
	Brake Lining Wear Limit, Inch	Rotor			Thickness Variation Parallelism Inch	Lateral Run-Out (T.I.R.) Inch	Maximum Scoring Depth, Inch	Brake Lining Wear Limit, Inch	Rotor			Thickness Variation Parallelism Inch	Lateral Run-Out (T.I.R.) Inch	Maximum Scoring Depth, Inch
		Thickness, Inch							Thickness, Inch					
		Nominal	Min. Refinish	Discard Limit①					Nominal	Min. Refinish	Discard Limit①			
PRIZM														
2001–02	.0390	.8660	—	.7870	.0005	.0020	.0150	—	—	—	—	—	—	—
VIBE														
2003–05	.0390	.9840	.9060	.9060	.0010	.0020	.0590	.0390	.3540	.2950	.2950	.0010	.0060	.0590

① — Discard thickness is stamped on rotor.

TIGHTENING SPECIFICATIONS

Year	Component	Torque/Ft. Lbs.
PRIZM		
2001–02	ABS Wheel Speed Sensor	69①
	Bleeder Valve	74①
	Brake Hose Union	22
	Caliper	25
	Caliper Bracket	65
VIBE		
2003–05	Bleeder Valve	73①
	Brake Hose To Caliper Fitting	21
	Caliper, Front	25
	Caliper, Rear	34
	Caliper Bracket	79
	Front Disc Brake Splash Shield	73①

① — Inch lbs.

DRUM BRAKES

TABLE OF CONTENTS

Alero, Century, Grand Am, Lumina, Malibu & Vibe

NOTE: On Air Bag Equipped Models, Refer To "Air Bag System Precautions" Located In The Front Of This Manual For System Disarming & Arming Procedures.

NOTE: Refer To "Computer Relearn Procedures" Located In The Front Of This Manual When Battery Power To The Computer Has Been Interrupted.

INDEX

DESCRIPTION

A single spring holds both shoe and lining to the backing plate and acts as a retractor spring for the shoe and lining assemblies, **Fig. 1.**

PRECAUTIONS

When working on or around brake assemblies, care must be taken to prevent breathing asbestos dust, as many manufacturers incorporate asbestos fibers in the production of brake linings. During routine service operations the amount of asbestos dust from brake lining wear is at a low level because of a chemical breakdown during use and a few precautions will minimize exposure.

1. Do not sand or grind brake linings unless suitable local exhaust ventilation equipment is used to prevent excessive asbestos exposure.
2. Wear suitable respirator approved for asbestos dust use during repair procedures.
3. When cleaning brake dust from brake components, use vacuum cleaner with highly efficient filter system. If suitable vacuum cleaner is not available, use water soaked rag. **Do not use compressed air or dry brush to clean brake components.**
4. Keep work area clean.
5. Properly dispose of rags and vacuum cleaner bags by placing them in plastic bags.
6. Do not smoke or eat while working on brake systems. **Never use gasoline, kerosene, alcohol, motor oil, transmission fluid, or any fluid containing mineral oil to clean brake system components. These fluids will damage rubber caps and seals. If system contamination is suspected, inspect brake fluid in reservoir for dirt, discoloration, or separation (breakdown) of brake fluid into distinct layers. Drain fluid into suitable container and flush hydraulic system with clean brake fluid if contamination is suspected.**

INSPECTION

1. If any components are of doubtful strength or quality because of heat discoloration, or are worn, replace them.
2. Inspect wheel cylinder dust boots for signs of excessive wear or damage. If any leakage is apparent replace wheel cylinder.
3. Clean dirt and/or rust from brake drum, backing plate and other components. **Do not use compressed air or dry brush to clean brake components. Many brake components contain asbestos fibers which, if inhaled, can cause serious injury. Clean brake components with water soaked rag or suitable vacuum cleaner to minimize airborne dust.**

Brake Drums

Any time the brake drums are removed for brake service, the braking surface diameter should be inspected with suitable brake drum micrometer at several points to determine if they are within the safe oversize limit stamped on the brake drum outer surface. If the braking surface diameter exceeds specifications, the drum must be replaced. If the braking surface diameter is within specifications, drums should be cleaned and inspected for cracks, scores, deep grooves, taper, out-of-round and heat

DRUM BRAKES

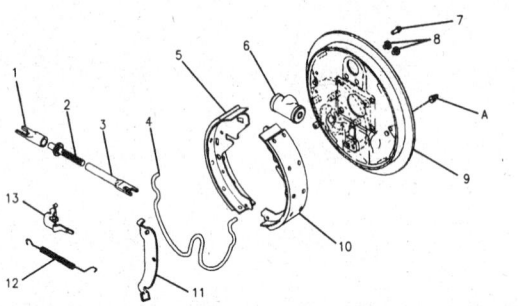

A	ACCESS HOLE PLUG. NOT PART OF ASM. SERVICE ONLY ITEM.	4	RETRACTOR SPRING	9	BACKING PLATE	
1	ADJUSTER SOCKET	5	ADJUSTER SHOE AND LINING	10	PARK BRAKE SHOE AND LINING	
2	ADJUSTER SCREW	6	WHEEL CYLINDER	11	PARK BRAKE LEVER	
3	PIVOT NUT	7	BLEEDER VALVE	12	ACTUATOR SPRING	
		8	BOLT	13	ADJUSTER ACTUATOR	

GC4089700048000X

Fig. 1 Brake drum assembly

spotting. If drums are cracked or heat spotted, they must be replaced. Minor scores should be removed with sandpaper. Grooves and large scores can only be removed by machining with special equipment, as long as the braking surface is within specifications stamped on brake drum outer surface. Any brake drum sufficiently out-of-round to cause vehicle vibration or noise while braking or showing taper should also be machined, removing only enough stock to true up the brake drum.

After a brake drum is machined, wipe the braking surface diameter with a denatured alcohol soaked cloth. If one brake drum is machined, the other should also be machined to the same diameter to maintain equal braking forces.

Brake Linings & Springs

Inspect brake linings for excessive wear, damage, oil, grease or brake fluid contamination. If any of the these conditions exists, brake linings should be replaced. Do not attempt to replace only one set of brake shoes. they should be replaced as an axle set only to maintain equal braking forces. Examine brake shoe webbing, hold-down and return springs for signs of overheating indicated by a slight blue color. If any component exhibits overheating signs, replace hold-down and return springs with new ones. Overheated springs lose their pull and could cause brake linings to wear out prematurely. Inspect springs for sags, bends and external damage and replace as required.

Inspect hold-down retainers and pins for bends, rust and corrosion. If any of these are found, replace as required.

Backing Plate

Inspect backing plate shoe contact surface for grooves that may restrict shoe movement and cannot be removed by lightly sanding with emery cloth or other suitable abrasive. If backing plate exhibits

these condition, it should be replaced. Also inspect for signs of cracks, warpage and excessive rust, indicating need for replacement.

Adjuster Mechanism

Inspect components for rust, corrosion, bends and fatigue. Replace as required. **On adjuster mechanism equipped with adjuster cable,** inspect cable for kinks, fraying or elongation of eyelet and replace as required.

Parking Brake Cable

Inspect parking brake cable end for kinks, fraying and elongation and replace as required. Use a small hose clamp to compress clamp where it enters backing plate to remove.

BRAKE SERVICE
Removal

1. Raise and support vehicle.
2. Mark relationship of wheel to axle, then remove wheel and tire assembly.
3. Remove brake drum. If drum is difficult to remove, proceed as follows:
   a. Ensure parking brake is released.
   b. Back off parking brake cable adjustment.
   c. Remove access hole plug from backing plate, insert screwdriver through hole and push parking brake lever off its stop.
   d. Insert punch through hole in splash shield, tap on punch to loosen drum and remove drum, **Fig. 2.**
4. Remove actuator spring using brake tool No. J-38400, or equivalent, to pry loop end of spring from adjuster actuator, **Fig. 3. Do not over stretch spring.**
5. Remove end of retractor spring from adjuster shoe and lining assembly, **Fig. 4. Keep finger away from retractor spring.**

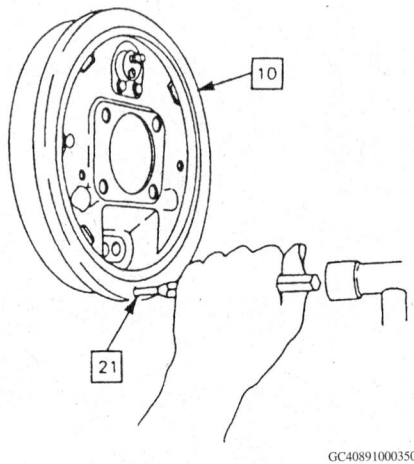

GC4089100035000X

Fig. 2 Loosening drum through splash shield

6. Remove adjuster shoe, lining, actuator and screw.
7. Remove park brake lever from shoe assembly. Do not remove parking brake cable from lever unless parking brake lever is being replaced.
8. Remove retractor spring from park brake shoe and lining.
9. Pry end of retractor spring toward axle using suitable brake tool until it snaps off shoe web onto backing plate. Remove park brake shoe.

Installation

1. Lubricate raised shoe pads on backing plate, anchor surfaces on backing plate and adjuster screw threads using brake lubricant No. 1052196, or equivalent.
2. Install retractor spring by hooking center spring section under tab on anchor.
3. Place shoe on backing plate.
4. Pull end of retractor spring up to rest on web of brake shoe using brake tool No. J-38400, or equivalent, **Fig. 5.**
5. Pull end of retractor spring over until it locks into slot of brake shoe, **Fig. 6.**
6. Install park brake lever.
7. Place shoe on backing plate.
8. Pull end of retractor spring up to rest on web of brake shoe using suitable brake tool.
9. Pull end of retractor spring over until if locks into slot of brake shoe.
10. Install adjuster actuator by spreading shoes using suitable brake tool and move actuator into place, **Fig. 7.**
11. Install actuator spring.
12. Adjust brakes using suitable adjustment tool. Shoes' outer diameter should be .050 inch less than inside diameter of each drum.
13. Install drums, wheels and tires.

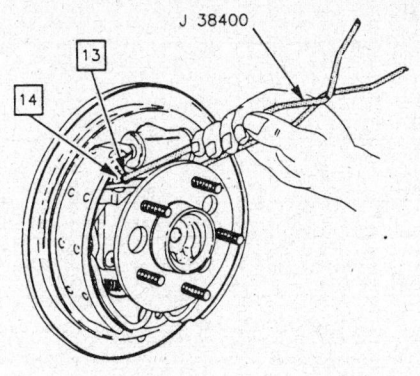

| 13 | ACTUATOR SPRING |
| 14 | ADJUSTER ACTUATOR |

GC4089100036000X

Fig. 3 Actuator spring removal

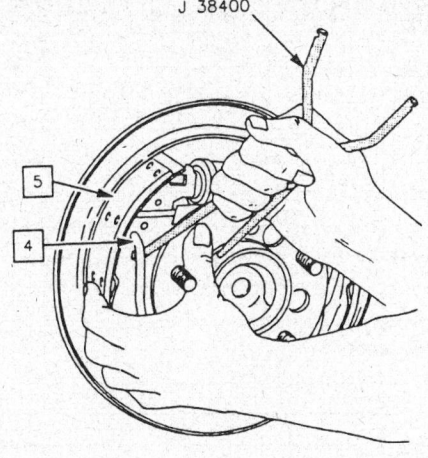

| 4 | RETRACTOR SPRING |
| 5 | ADJUSTER SHOE LINING |

GC4089100037000X

Fig. 4 Retractor spring disengagement

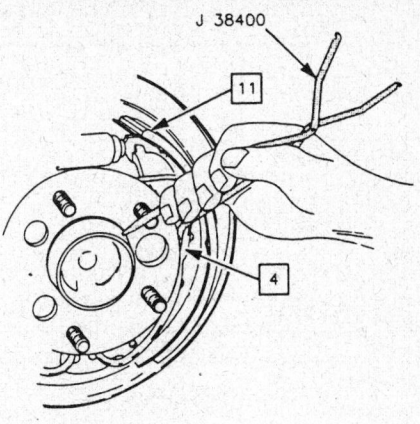

| 4 | RETRACTOR SPRING |
| 11 | PARK BRAKE SHOE AND LINING |

GC4089100038000X

Fig. 5 Spring end installation onto shoe web

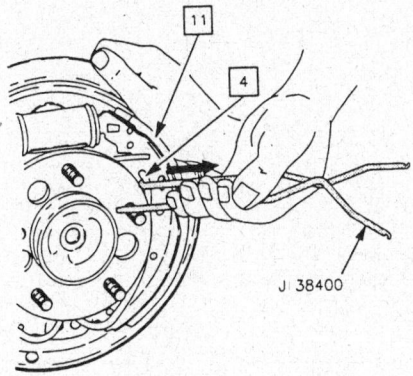

| 4 | RETRACTOR SPRING |
| 11 | PARK BRAKE SHOE AND LINING |

GC4089100039000X

Fig. 6 Spring end installation into shoe slot

ADJUSTMENTS

Service Brake

1. Raise and support vehicle.
2. Mark relationship of wheel to axle, then remove wheel and tire assembly.
3. Remove brake drum. If drum is difficult to remove, proceed as follows:
   a. Ensure parking brake is released.
   b. Back off parking brake cable adjustment.
   c. Remove access hole plug from backing plate, insert screwdriver through hole and push parking brake lever off its stop.
   d. Insert punch through hole in splash shield, tap on punch to loosen drum and remove drum.
4. Measure inside diameter of drum using tool Nos. J-21177-A or J-22364-01, or equivalents.
5. Adjust by turning star wheel adjuster.

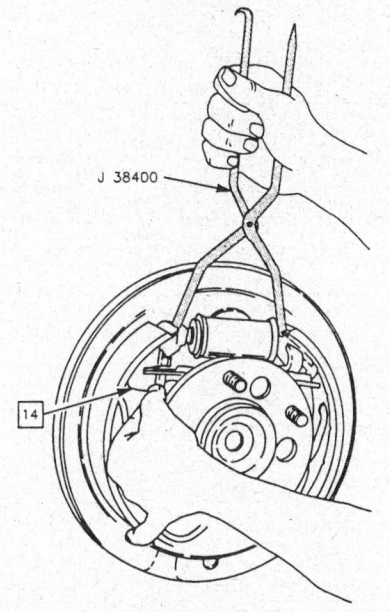

| 14 | ADJUSTER ACTUATOR |

GC4089100040000X

Fig. 7 Shoe spreading to install adjuster actuator

Lining diameter should be .050 inch less than inside diameter of each drum.

6. Install drums, wheels and tires.
7. Lower vehicle and tighten wheel lug nuts.

Parking Brake

1. Adjust brakes as outlined in "Service Brake."
2. Apply and release parking brake five times to six clicks.
3. Ensure pedal is fully released by turning ignition On. Brake warning lamp

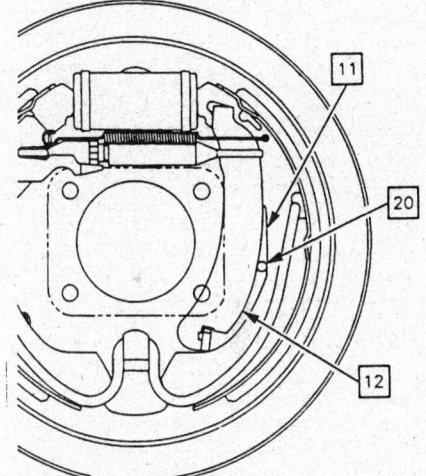

11	PARK BRAKE SHOE AND LINING
12	PARK BRAKE LEVER
20	1/8 INCH DRILL

GC4089100041000X

Fig. 8 Parking brake adjustment

should be off.
4. If brake warning lamp is lit, operate pedal release lever and pull downward on front parking brake cable.
5. Raise and support vehicle, then remove access hole plug.
6. Adjust cable until 1/8 inch drill bit can be inserted through access hole into space between shoe web and park lever, **Fig. 8.** Proper adjustment lets 1/8 inch drill bit fit in space but not 1/4 inch bit.
7. Release brake and ensure wheels rotate freely.
8. Replace access hole plug and lower vehicle.

DRUM BRAKES

DRUM BRAKE SPECIFICATIONS

| Model | Year | Lining Wear Limit, Inch② | Inside Diameter, Inches | | | Runout Limit, Inch | Allowable Scoring, Inch |
			Nominal	Maximum Refinish	Discard Limit①		
BUICK							
Century	2001–03	.030	8.863	8.909	8.920	.006	.059
CHEVROLET							
Lumina	2001	.030	8.863	8.909	8.920	.006	.059
Malibu	2001–05	.030	8.868	8.889	8.909	.004	.059
OLDSMOBILE							
Alero	2001–04	.030	8.868	8.889	8.909	.004	.059
PONTIAC							
Grand Am	2001–05	.030	8.868	8.889	8.909	.004	.059
Vibe	2003–05	.039	9.000	9.039	9.039	.002	.039

① — Discard Limit is stamped on drum. ② — Above rivet head or shoe. Original equipment type brake linings.

TIGHTENING SPECIFICATIONS

Year	Component	Torque/ Ft. Lbs.
2001–05	Wheel Cylinder Bleeder Screw (Alero & Grand Am)	115①
	Wheel Cylinder Bleeder Screw (Century, Lumina & Malibu)	62①
	Wheel Cylinder Line Fitting	11
	Wheel Cylinder To Backing Plate	108①
	Wheel Lug Nuts	100

① — Inch lbs.

Cavalier, Sunfire & Cobalt

NOTE: On Air Bag Equipped Models, Refer To "Air Bag System Precautions" Located In The Front Of This Manual For System Disarming & Arming Procedures.

NOTE: Refer To "Computer Relearn Procedures" Located In The Front Of This Manual When Battery Power To The Computer Has Been Interrupted.

INDEX

PRECAUTIONS

When working on or around brake assemblies, care must be taken to prevent breathing asbestos dust, as many manufacturers incorporate asbestos fibers in the production of brake linings. During routine service operations the amount of asbestos dust from brake lining wear is at a low level because of a chemical breakdown during use and a few precautions will minimize exposure.

1. Do not sand or grind brake linings unless suitable local exhaust ventilation equipment is used to prevent excessive asbestos exposure.
2. Wear suitable respirator approved for asbestos dust use during repair procedures.
3. When cleaning brake dust from brake components, use vacuum cleaner with highly efficient filter system. If suitable vacuum cleaner is not available, use water soaked rag. **Do not use compressed air or dry brush to clean brake components.**
4. Keep work area clean.
5. Properly dispose of rags and vacuum cleaner bags by placing them in plastic bags.
6. Do not smoke or eat while working on brake systems. **Never use gasoline, kerosene, alcohol, motor oil, transmission fluid, or any fluid containing mineral oil to clean brake system components.**
7. If system contamination is suspected, inspect brake fluid in reservoir for dirt, discoloration, or separation (breakdown). Drain fluid into suitable container and flush hydraulic system with clean brake fluid.

INSPECTION

1. Inspect components for damage or wear. Replace as required.
2. Inspect wheel cylinder boots for tears, cuts or heat damage. Replace as required.
3. Remove wheel cylinder links. If fluid spills from boot center hole, replace wheel cylinder.
4. Light fluid coatings on piston within cylinder is considered normal.
5. Inspect backing plate for evidence of axle seal leakage. If leakage exists, refer to individual vehicle chapters for axle seal replacement procedures.
6. Inspect backing plate mounting bolts and ensure they are tight.
7. Clean rust and dirt from shoe contact surface on backing plate using fine emery cloth or other suitable abrasive.

Brake Drums

Any time the brake drums are removed for brake service, the braking surface diameter should be inspected with suitable brake drum micrometer at several points to determine if they are within the safe oversize limit stamped on the brake drum outer surface. If the braking surface diameter exceeds specifications, the drum must be replaced. If the braking surface diameter is within specifications, drums should be cleaned and inspected for cracks, scores, deep grooves, taper, out-of-round and heat spotting. If drums are cracked or heat spotted, they must be replaced. Minor scores should be removed with sandpaper. Grooves and large scores can only be removed by machining with special equipment, as long as the braking surface is within specifications stamped on brake drum outer surface. Any brake drum sufficiently out-of-round to cause vehicle vibration or noise while braking or showing taper should also be machined, removing only enough stock to true up the brake drum.

After a brake drum is machined, wipe the braking surface diameter with a denatured alcohol soaked cloth. If one brake drum is machined, the other should also be machined to the same diameter to maintain equal braking forces.

Brake Linings & Springs

Inspect brake linings for excessive wear, damage, oil, grease or brake fluid contamination. If any of the these conditions exists, brake linings should be replaced. Do not attempt to replace only one set of brake shoes; they should be replaced as an axle set only to maintain equal braking forces. Examine brake shoe webbing, hold-down and return springs for signs of overheating indicated by a slight blue color. If any component exhibits overheating signs, replace hold-down and return springs with new ones. Overheated springs lose their pull and could cause brake linings to wear out prematurely. Inspect springs for sags, bends and external damage and replace as required.

Inspect hold-down retainers and pins for bends, rust and corrosion. If any of these are found, replace as required.

Backing Plate

Inspect backing plate shoe contact surface for grooves that may restrict shoe movement and cannot be removed by lightly sanding with emery cloth or other suitable abrasive. If backing plate exhibits these condition, it should be replaced. Also inspect for signs of cracks, warpage and excessive rust, indicating need for replacement.

Adjuster Mechanism

Inspect components for rust, corrosion, bends and fatigue. Replace as required. **On adjuster mechanism equipped with adjuster cable,** inspect cable for kinks, fraying or elongation of eyelet and replace as required.

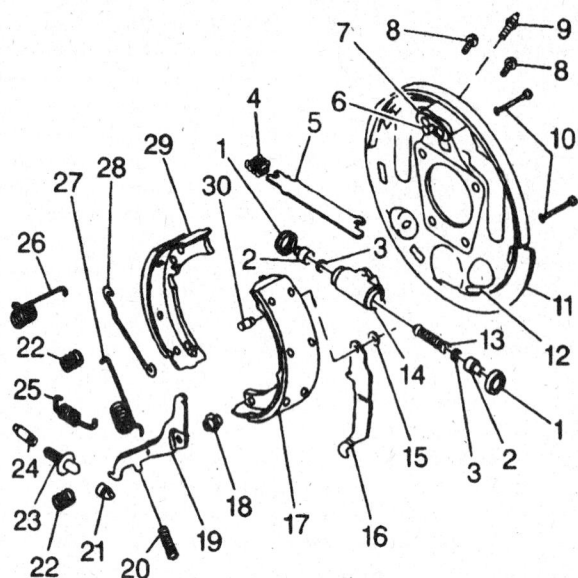

Fig. 1 Drum brake assembly

1. Boot
2. Piston
3. Seal
4. Strut Spring
5. Strut
6. Shoe Retainer
7. Anchor Pin
8. Bolt
9. Bleeder Screw
10. Hold down Pins
11. Backing Plate
12. Shoe Contact Points
13. Piston Spring
14. Cylinder
15. Reatainer Ring
16. Parking Brake Lever
17. Secondary Shoe
18. Sleeve
19. Actuator Lever
20. Return Spring
21. Socket
22. Hold Down Spring
23. Star Wheel
24. Pivot Nut
25. Adjuster Spring
26. Return Spring

GC4089700045000X

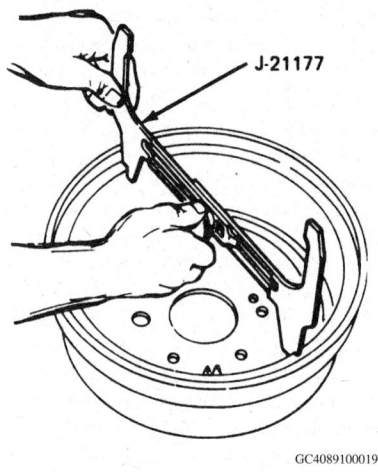

GC4089100019000X

Fig. 2 Brake drum measurement

Parking Brake Cable

Inspect parking brake cable end for kinks, fraying and elongation and replace as required. Use a small hose clamp to compress clamp where it enters backing plate to remove it.

BRAKE SERVICE

Removal

1. Raise and support rear of vehicle, then remove tire and wheel assembly.
2. Mark drum and axle hub, then remove brake drum. If brake lining is dragging on brake drum, back off brake adjustment by rotating adjustment screw. **If brake drum is rusted or corroded to axle flange and cannot be removed, lightly tap axle flange to drum mounting surface with suitable hammer.**
3. Unhook primary and secondary return springs using brake spring removal and installation tool Nos. J-8049 or J-29840, or equivalents, **Fig. 1.** Observe location of brake components being removed to aid during installation.
4. Remove brake hold-down springs with suitable tool.

5. Lift actuating lever, then unhook and remove actuating link from anchor pin.
6. Remove actuating lever(s) and return spring.
7. Spread shoes apart and remove parking brake strut and spring.
8. Disconnect parking brake cable from lever and remove brake shoes from backing plate.
9. Separate brake shoes by removing adjusting screw and spring, then unhook parking brake lever from shoe assembly.
10. Clean dirt from brake drum, backing plate and other components. **Do not use compressed air or dry brush to clean brake components. Clean brake components with water soaked rag or suitable vacuum cleaner to minimize airborne dust.**

Installation

1. Lubricate parking brake lever fulcrum with suitable brake lubricant and attach lever to brake shoe. Ensure lever operates smoothly.
2. Connect brake shoes with adjusting screw spring and position adjusting screw. **Ensure adjusting screw star wheel does not contact adjusting screw spring. Ensure righthand thread adjusting screw is installed**

on lefthand side of vehicle and lefthand thread adjusting screw is installed on righthand side of vehicle. Ensure star wheel lines up with adjusting hole in backing plate.
3. Lubricate backing plate shoe contact surfaces with suitable brake lubricant and area where parking brake cable contacts backing plate.
4. Install brake shoes on backing plate while engaging wheel cylinder links (if equipped) with shoe webbing. **Primary shoe (short lining) faces towards front of vehicle. End without strut spring should engage parking brake lever and secondary shoe. End with strut spring should engage primary shoe.**
5. Connect parking brake cable to parking brake lever.
6. Install actuating levers, actuating link and return spring.
7. Install hold-down springs with suitable tool.
8. Install primary and secondary shoe return springs using suitable brake spring pliers.
9. Measure inside diameter using suitable brake drum to shoe gauge.
10. Adjust brake shoes to dimension obtained on outside portion of gauge.
11. Install brake drum, wheel and tire assembly.
12. If any hydraulic connections have been opened, bleed brake system.
13. Adjust parking brake.
14. Inspect hydraulic lines and connections for leaks.
15. Inspect and adjust master cylinder fluid level.
16. Inspect brake pedal for proper feel and return.
17. Lower vehicle and road test. **Do not severely apply brakes immediately after installation of new brake linings or permanent damage may occur to linings, and/or brake drums may become scored. Brakes must be used moderately during first several hundred miles of operation to ensure proper burnishing of linings.**

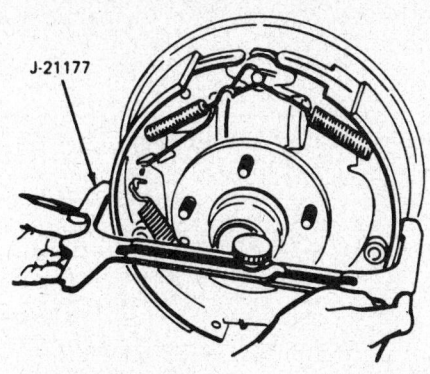

GC4089100018000X

Fig. 3 Brake shoe measurement

ADJUSTMENTS

These brakes have self-adjusting shoe mechanisms that ensure proper lining-to-drum clearances at all times. The automatic adjusters operate only when the brakes are applied as the vehicle is moving rearward.

An initial adjustment is required after the brake shoes have been relined or replaced, or when the length of the adjusting screw has been changed during service operations.

Frequent usage of an automatic transmission forward range to halt reverse vehicle motion may prevent the automatic adjusters from functioning, thereby inducing low pedal heights. Should low pedal heights be encountered, it is recommended that numerous forward and reverse stops be made until satisfactory pedal height is obtained. **If a low pedal condition cannot be corrected by making numerous reverse stops (provided the hydraulic system is free of air) it indicates that the self-adjusting mechanism is not functioning. It will be required to remove the brake drum, clean, free up and lubricate the adjusting mechanism. Then adjust the brakes as follows, ensuring the parking brake is fully released.**

Service Brake

Brake adjustment cannot be performed with the drums installed. The following procedure is mandatory after new linings are installed, or when the length of the brake shoe adjusting screw has been changed.

1. With brake drums removed, position caliper to inside diameter of drum and tighten clamp screw, **Fig. 2.**
2. Position brake shoe end of caliper tool over brake shoes, **Fig. 3.**
3. Rotate gauge slightly around shoes to ensure gauge contacts linings at largest diameter.
4. Adjust brake shoes until outside diameter is .030 inch less than drum's inside diameter. **If brake shoe must be**

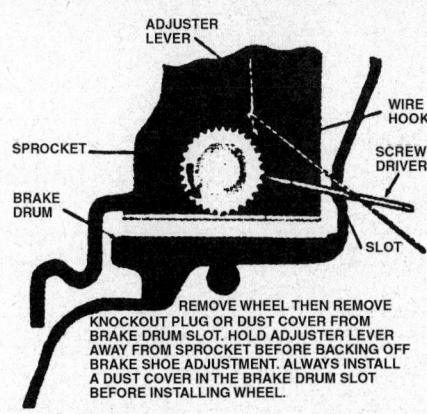

GC4089100013000X

Fig. 4 Brake shoe adjustment

backed off, hold adjuster lever away from adjuster screw, **Fig. 4.**

Parking Brake

On these brake systems, no adjustment is required. These models have a self-adjusting parking brake system and it should not be adjusted or modified in any way.

Fully applying and releasing the parking brake 4–6 times the system will perform its self-adjustment procedure.

DRUM BRAKE SPECIFICATIONS

| Model | Year | Lining Wear Limit, Inch② | Inside Diameter, Inches | | | Runout Limit, Inch | Allowable Scoring, Inch |
			Nominal	Maximum Refinish	Discard Limit①		
Cavalier & Sunfire	2001–03	.030	7.884	7.914	7.929	.006	.059
	2004–05	.030	9.055–9.065	9.075	9.094	.004	.059
Cobalt	2005	.020	9.055–9.065	9.075	9.094	.004	.059

① — Discard Limit is stamped on drum.   ② — Above rivet head or shoe. Original equipment type brake linings.

TIGHTENING SPECIFICATIONS

Year	Component	Torque/ Ft. Lbs.
2001–05	Wheel Cylinder Bleeder Screw	60①
	Wheel Cylinder Line Fitting	18
	Wheel Cylinder To Backing Plate	15
	Wheel Lug Nuts	②

① — Inch lbs.
② — Tighten lug nuts in star sequence in increments of 20 ft. lbs. until final torque of 100 ft. lbs., is reached.

Aveo

NOTE: On Air Bag Equipped Models, Refer To "Air Bag System Precautions" Located In The Front Of This Manual For System Disarming & Arming Procedures.

NOTE: Refer To "Computer Relearn Procedures" Located In The Front Of This Manual When Battery Power To The Computer Has Been Interrupted.

INDEX

PRECAUTIONS

When working on or around brake assemblies, care must be taken to prevent breathing asbestos dust, as many manufacturers incorporate asbestos fibers in the production of brake linings. During routine service operations the amount of asbestos dust from brake lining wear is at a low level because of a chemical breakdown during use and a few precautions will minimize exposure.

1. Do not sand or grind brake linings unless suitable local exhaust ventilation equipment is used to prevent excessive asbestos exposure.
2. Wear suitable respirator approved for asbestos dust use during repair procedures.
3. When cleaning brake dust from brake components, use vacuum cleaner with highly efficient filter system. If suitable vacuum cleaner is not available, use water soaked rag. **Do not use compressed air or dry brush to clean brake components.**
4. Keep work area clean.
5. Properly dispose of rags and vacuum cleaner bags by placing them in plastic bags.
6. Do not smoke or eat while working on brake systems. **Never use gasoline, kerosene, alcohol, motor oil, transmission fluid, or any fluid containing mineral oil to clean brake system components. These fluids will damage rubber caps and seals. If system contamination is suspected, inspect brake fluid in reservoir for dirt, discoloration, or separation (breakdown) of brake fluid into distinct layers. Drain fluid into suitable container and flush hydraulic system with clean brake fluid if contamination is suspected.**

INSPECTION

1. If any components are of doubtful strength or quality because of heat discoloration, or are worn, replace them.
2. Inspect wheel cylinder dust boots for signs of excessive wear or damage. If any leakage is apparent replace or rebuild wheel cylinder.
3. Clean dirt and/or rust from brake drum, backing plate and other components. **Do not use compressed air or dry brush to clean brake components. Many brake components contain asbestos fibers which, if inhaled, can cause serious injury. Clean brake components with water soaked rag or suitable vacuum cleaner to minimize airborne dust.**

Brake Drums

Any time the brake drums are removed for brake service, the braking surface diameter should be inspected with suitable brake drum micrometer at several points to determine if they are within the safe oversize limit stamped on the brake drum outer surface. If the braking surface diameter exceeds specifications, the drum must be replaced. If the braking surface diameter is within specifications, drums should be cleaned and inspected for cracks, scores, deep grooves, taper, out-of-round and heat spotting. If drums are cracked or heat spotted, they must be replaced. Minor scores should be removed with sandpaper. Grooves and large scores can only be removed by machining with special equipment, as long as the braking surface is within specifications stamped on brake drum outer surface. Any brake drum sufficiently out-of-round to cause vehicle vibration or noise while braking or showing taper should also be machined, removing only enough stock to true up the brake drum.

After a brake drum is machined, wipe the braking surface diameter with a denatured alcohol soaked cloth. If one brake drum is machined, the other should also be machined to the same diameter to maintain equal braking forces.

Brake Linings & Springs

Inspect brake linings for excessive wear, damage, oil, grease or brake fluid contamination. If any of the these conditions exists, brake linings should be replaced. Do not attempt to replace only one set of brake shoes. They should be replaced as an axle set only to maintain equal braking forces. Examine brake shoe webbing, hold-down and return springs for signs of overheating indicated by a slight blue color. If any component exhibits overheating signs, replace hold-down and return springs with new ones. Overheated springs lose their pull and could cause brake linings to wear out prematurely. Inspect springs for sags, bends and external damage and replace as required.

Inspect hold-down retainers and pins for bends, rust and corrosion. If any of these are found, replace as required.

Backing Plate

Inspect backing plate shoe contact surface for grooves that may restrict shoe movement and cannot be removed by lightly sanding with emery cloth or other suitable abrasive. If backing plate exhibits these condition, it should be replaced. Also inspect for signs of cracks, warpage and excessive rust, indicating need for replacement.

Adjuster Mechanism

Inspect components for rust, corrosion, bends and fatigue. Replace as required. **On adjuster mechanism equipped with adjuster cable,** inspect cable for kinks, fraying or elongation of eyelet and replace as required.

Parking Brake Cable

Inspect parking brake cable end for kinks, fraying and elongation and replace as required. Use a small hose clamp to compress clamp where it enters backing plate to remove.

BRAKE SERVICE

Removal

1. Raise and support vehicle, then remove tire and wheel assembly.
2. Remove lock ring and caulking nut from spindle, then remove brake drum. If drum is difficult to remove, proceed as follows:
   a. Ensure parking brake is released.
   b. Back off parking brake cable adjustment.
3. Loosen leading shoe hold down return spring.
4. Disconnect upper link of connecting link spring on leading shoe to release tension on upper return spring.
5. Remove upper return spring and adjuster.
6. Disconnect trailing shoe and lining assembly hold down return spring, then the trailing shoe and lining assembly.
7. Remove lower return spring.

Installation

1. Clean and grease adjuster assembly.
2. Install trailing shoe and lining assembly with hold down spring, washer and pin.
3. Verify parking brake cable routing and attach to shoe lever.
4. Install lower return spring on shoe. Do not overstretch spring.
5. Position leading shoe and adjuster assembly against backing plate, then attach lower return spring to leading shoe.
6. Install adjuster assembly, then turn adjuster in as far as possible.
7. Position spring clip toward the backing plate.
8. Install leading shoe with hold down spring.
9. Install leading shoe upper link spring connection.
10. Install upper return spring from spring connection link to brake shoe. Do not overstretch spring.
11. Ensure adjuster assembly nut is drawn to the stop, then adjust rear brakes.
12. Install brake drum, then adjust park brake.

ADJUSTMENTS

Service Brake

1. Raise and support vehicle, then remove tire and wheel assembly.

2. Remove brake drum.
3. Turn adjuster nut until sufficient amount of drag occurs on brake drum.
4. Place parking brake lever stops against edge of shoe web.
5. Install brake drum, then apply brake pedal at least 10 times. Ensure there is no clicking sound from either brake drum.
6. Adjust parking brake.

Parking Brake

1. Ensure parking brake is released, then raise and support vehicle.
2. Inspect parking brake cables for free movement.
3. Lower vehicle.
4. Remove plastic caps that cover parking brake hood to tunnel bracket screws access holes.
5. Remove parking brake console hood to tunnel bracket retaining screws.
6. Raise console hood to access parking brake lever assembly and adjustment nut.
7. Partially raise and support vehicle.
8. Turn adjustment nut on lever assembly until wheels are hard to turn.
9. Loosen nut until rear wheels are just free to turn.
10. Lower vehicle.
11. Install parking brake hood console and plastic caps on access holes.

DRUM BRAKE SPECIFICATIONS

| Model | Year | Lining Wear Limit, Inch② | Inside Diameter, Inches | | | Runout Limit, Inch | Allowable Scoring, Inch |
			Nominal	Maximum Refinish	Discard Limit①		
Aveo	2004–05	.020	—	—	7.91	—	—

TIGHTENING SPECIFICATIONS

Year	Component	Torque/ Ft. Lbs.
2004–05	Brake Line	12
	Brake Wheel Hub/Backing Plate to Rear Axle Nuts	21
	Drum Caulking Nut	148
	Wheel Cylinder to Backing Plate Bolt	71①

① — Inch lbs.

Metro

NOTE: On Air Bag Equipped Models, Refer To "Air Bag System Precautions" Located In The Front Of This Manual For System Disarming & Arming Procedures.

NOTE: Refer To "Computer Relearn Procedures" Located In The Front Of This Manual When Battery Power To The Computer Has Been Interrupted.

INDEX

PRECAUTIONS

When working on or around brake assemblies, care must be taken to prevent breathing asbestos dust, as many manufacturers incorporate asbestos fibers in the production of brake linings. During routine service operations the amount of asbestos dust from brake lining wear is at a low level because of a chemical breakdown during use and a few precautions will minimize exposure.

1. Do not sand or grind brake linings unless suitable local exhaust ventilation equipment is used to prevent excessive asbestos exposure.
2. Wear suitable respirator approved for asbestos dust use during repair procedures.
3. When cleaning brake dust from brake components, use vacuum cleaner with highly efficient filter system. If suitable vacuum cleaner is not available, use water soaked rag. **Do not use compressed air or dry brush to clean brake components.**
4. Keep work area clean.
5. Properly dispose of rags and vacuum cleaner bags by placing them in plastic bags.
6. Do not smoke or eat while working on brake systems. **Never use gasoline, kerosene, alcohol, motor oil, transmission fluid, or any fluid containing mineral oil to clean brake system components. These fluids will damage rubber caps and seals. If system contamination is suspected, inspect brake fluid in reservoir for dirt, discoloration, or separation (breakdown) of brake fluid into distinct layers. Drain fluid into suitable container and flush hydraulic system with clean brake fluid if contamination is suspected.**

INSPECTION

1. If any components are of doubtful

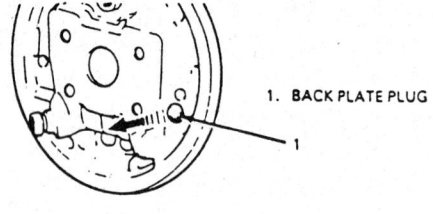

1. BACK PLATE PLUG

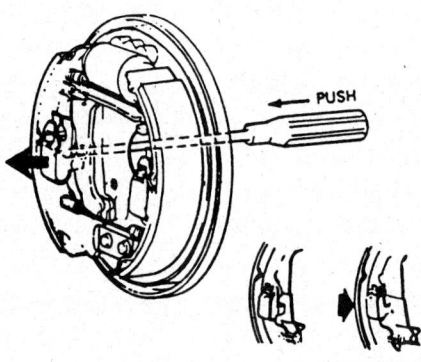

PUSH

GC4089100029000X

Fig. 1 Backing plate plug removal

strength or quality because of heat discoloration, or are worn, replace them.
2. Inspect wheel cylinder dust boots for signs of excessive wear or damage. If any leakage is apparent replace or rebuild wheel cylinder.
3. Clean dirt and/or rust from brake drum, backing plate and other components. **Do not use compressed air or dry brush to clean brake components. Many brake components contain asbestos fibers which, if inhaled, can cause serious injury. Clean brake components with water soaked rag or suitable vacuum cleaner to minimize airborne dust.**

Brake Drums

Any time the brake drums are removed

for brake service, the braking surface diameter should be inspected with suitable brake drum micrometer at several points to determine if they are within the safe oversize limit stamped on the brake drum outer surface. If the braking surface diameter exceeds specifications, the drum must be replaced. If the braking surface diameter is within specifications, drums should be cleaned and inspected for cracks, scores, deep grooves, taper, out-of-round and heat spotting. If drums are cracked or heat spotted, they must be replaced. Minor scores should be removed with sandpaper. Grooves and large scores can only be removed by machining with special equipment, as long as the braking surface is within specifications stamped on brake drum outer surface. Any brake drum sufficiently out-of-round to cause vehicle vibration or noise while braking or showing taper should also be machined, removing only enough stock to true up the brake drum.

After a brake drum is machined, wipe the braking surface diameter with a denatured alcohol soaked cloth. If one brake drum is machined, the other should also be machined to the same diameter to maintain equal braking forces.

Brake Linings & Springs

Inspect brake linings for excessive wear, damage, oil, grease or brake fluid contamination. If any of the these conditions exists, brake linings should be replaced. Do not attempt to replace only one set of brake shoes. They should be replaced as an axle set only to maintain equal braking forces. Examine brake shoe webbing, hold-down and return springs for signs of overheating indicated by a slight blue color. If any component exhibits overheating signs, replace hold-down and return springs with new ones. Overheated springs lose their pull and could cause brake linings to wear out

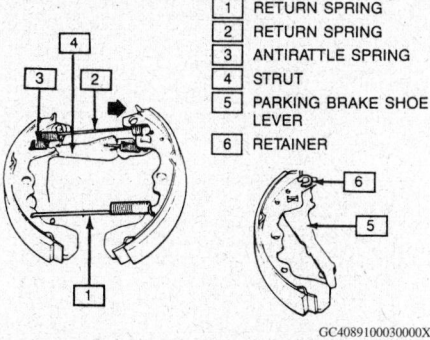

1 RETURN SPRING
2 RETURN SPRING
3 ANTIRATTLE SPRING
4 STRUT
5 PARKING BRAKE SHOE LEVER
6 RETAINER

GC4089100030000X

Fig. 2 Brake shoe return spring

prematurely. Inspect springs for sags, bends and external damage and replace as required.

Inspect hold-down retainers and pins for bends, rust and corrosion. If any of these are found, replace as required.

Backing Plate

Inspect backing plate shoe contact surface for grooves that may restrict shoe movement and cannot be removed by lightly sanding with emery cloth or other suitable abrasive. If backing plate exhibits these condition, it should be replaced. Also inspect for signs of cracks, warpage and excessive rust, indicating need for replacement.

Adjuster Mechanism

Inspect components for rust, corrosion, bends and fatigue. Replace as required. **On adjuster mechanism equipped with adjuster cable,** inspect cable for kinks, fraying or elongation of eyelet and replace as required.

Parking Brake Cable

Inspect parking brake cable end for kinks, fraying and elongation and replace as required. Use a small hose clamp to compress clamp where it enters backing plate to remove.

BRAKE SERVICE
Removal

1. Raise and support vehicle.
2. Remove spindle cap by hammering lightly at three points around cap.
3. Remove cotter pin or unfasten staked portion of nut, then remove castle nut and washer.
4. Loosen parking brake cable adjusting nuts.
5. Remove backing plate plug, **Fig. 1.**

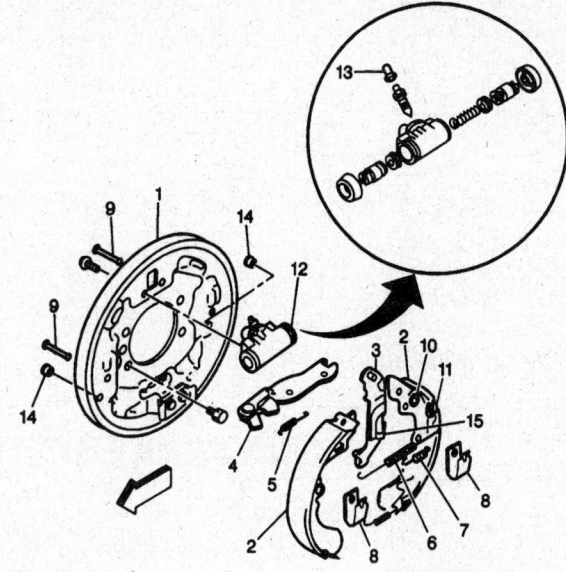

(1) Backing Plate
(2) Shoe
(3) Parking Brake Shoe Lever
(4) Adjuster
(5) Adjuster Spring
(6) Shoe Return Spring
(7) Spring
(8) Shoe Hold Down Spring
(9) Shoe Hold Down Pin
(10) Shim
(11) C-Clip
(12) Wheel Cylinder
(13) Bleeder Cap
(14) Plug

GC4089700047000X

Fig. 3 Rear brake unit assembly

6. Insert screwdriver into plug hole until it contacts shoe hold-down spring and push.
7. **On models equipped with ABS,** install and tighten two 8 mm bolts into drum to remove drum from hub.
8. **On models equipped less ABS,** pull off brake drum using slide hammer tool No. J-2619-01 and brake drum remover tool No. J-34866, or equivalents.
9. **On all models,** remove brake shoe hold-down springs by turning hold-down pins.
10. Disconnect parking brake cable from parking brake shoe lever and remove brake shoes.
11. Remove spring in and pull primary shoe, then disconnect strut and return spring, **Fig. 2.**
12. Disconnect return spring from shoe.
13. Disconnect parking brake shoe lever from shoe.

Installation

1. Apply white lithium grease part No. 1050109, or equivalent, to backing plate brake shoe contact points and to anchor plate brake shoe contact points.
2. Assemble brake shoes, levers and springs, **Fig. 3.**
3. Push shoe hold-down springs down into place. Turn hold-down pins to en-

gage springs.
4. To minimize dimension A-A, push strut towards backplate while pushing out on shoe, **Fig. 4.**
5. Position tab of spring clip behind parking brake lever.
6. Install brake drum and tighten castle nut.
7. Install cotter pin, spindle cap and wheel.
8. Depress brake pedal several times to obtain proper drum to shoe clearance and adjust parking brake.
9. Ensure brake drums do not drag.
10. Lower vehicle and test brake operation.

ADJUSTMENTS
Service Brake

Adjustment is accomplished automatically by applying brake pedal 3–5 times with 66 lbs. of pressure. Brake pedal should be cycled 3–5 times when replacement components are installed to ensure proper adjustment.

Parking Brake

1. Adjusted so lever comes up 3–6 notches with 44 ft. lbs. of pull applied.
2. Adjust travel by loosening adjustment nuts, **Fig. 5.**

DRUM BRAKES

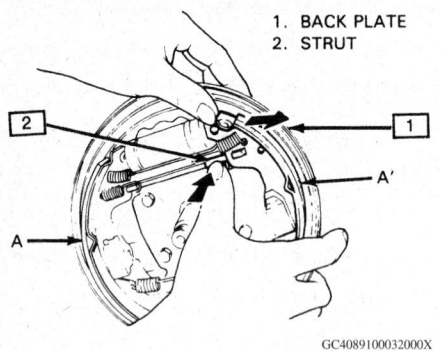

1. BACK PLATE
2. STRUT

GC4089100032000X

Fig. 4   Brake lining installation

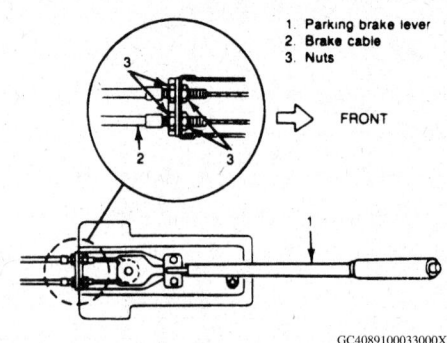

1. Parking brake lever
2. Brake cable
3. Nuts

FRONT

GC4089100033000X

Fig. 5   Parking brake adjustment

DRUM BRAKE SPECIFICATIONS

Model	Year	Lining Wear Limit, Inch②	Inside Diameter, Inches			Runout Limit, Inch	Out Of Round, Inch②
			Nominal	Maximum Refinish	Discard Limit①		
Metro Four-Door	2001	.040	—	—	7.950	.0016	.0004
Metro Two-Door	2001	.040	—	—	7.160	.0016	.0004

① — Discard Limit is stamped on drum.   ② — Above rivet head or shoe. Original equipment type brake linings.

TIGHTENING SPECIFICATIONS

Year	Component	Torque/ Ft. Lbs.
2001	Backing Plate	17
	Bleeder Valve	89①
	Brake Fluid Pipe	12
	Hub Spindle Nut	58–87
	Wheel Lug Nuts	44

① — Inch lbs.

Prizm

NOTE: On Air Bag Equipped Models, Refer To "Air Bag System Precautions" Located In The Front Of This Manual For System Disarming & Arming Procedures.

NOTE: Refer To "Computer Relearn Procedures" Located In The Front Of This Manual When Battery Power To The Computer Has Been Interrupted.

INDEX

PRECAUTIONS

When working on or around brake assemblies, care must be taken to prevent breathing asbestos dust, as many manufacturers incorporate asbestos fibers in the production of brake linings. During routine service operations the amount of asbestos dust from brake lining wear is at a low level because of a chemical breakdown during use and a few precautions will minimize exposure.

1. Do not sand or grind brake linings unless suitable local exhaust ventilation equipment is used to prevent excessive asbestos exposure.
2. Wear suitable respirator approved for asbestos dust use during repair procedures.
3. When cleaning brake dust from brake components, use vacuum cleaner with highly efficient filter system. If suitable vacuum cleaner is not available, use water soaked rag. **Do not use compressed air or dry brush to clean brake components.**
4. Keep work area clean.
5. Properly dispose of rags and vacuum cleaner bags by placing them in plastic bags.
6. Do not smoke or eat while working on brake systems. **Never use gasoline, kerosene, alcohol, motor oil, transmission fluid, or any fluid containing mineral oil to clean brake system components. These fluids will damage rubber caps and seals. If system contamination is suspected, inspect brake fluid in reservoir for dirt, discoloration, or separation (breakdown) of brake fluid into distinct layers. Drain fluid into suitable container and flush hydraulic system with clean brake fluid if contamination is suspected.**

INSPECTION

1. Inspect brake drum, shoes, strut, auto adjuster lever, springs and backing plate for wear, distortion, cracks or other abnormal conditions.
2. If any components are of doubtful strength or quality because of damage, heat discoloration, stress or wear, replace them.
3. Measure Inside Diameter and brake shoe lining thickness.
4. Inspect lining and drum for proper contact.

Brake Drums

Any time the brake drums are removed for brake service, the braking surface diameter should be inspected with suitable brake drum micrometer at several points to determine if they are within the safe oversize limit stamped on the brake drum outer surface. If the braking surface diameter exceeds specifications, the drum must be replaced. If the braking surface diameter is within specifications, drums should be cleaned and inspected for cracks, scores, deep grooves, taper, out-of-round and heat spotting. If drums are cracked or heat spotted, they must be replaced. Minor scores should be removed with sandpaper. Grooves and large scores can only be removed by machining with special equipment, as long as the braking surface is within specifications stamped on brake drum outer surface. Any brake drum sufficiently out-of-round to cause vehicle vibration or noise while braking or showing taper should also be machined, removing only enough stock to true up the brake drum.

After a brake drum is machined, wipe the braking surface diameter with a denatured alcohol soaked cloth. If one brake drum is machined, the other should also be machined to the same diameter to maintain equal braking forces.

Brake Linings & Springs

Inspect brake linings for excessive wear, damage, oil, grease or brake fluid contamination. If any of the these conditions exists, brake linings should be replaced. Do not attempt to replace only one set of brake shoes; they should be replaced as an axle set only to maintain equal braking forces. Examine brake shoe webbing, hold-down and return springs for signs of overheating indicated by a slight blue color. If any component exhibits overheating signs, replace hold-down and return springs with new ones. Overheated springs lose their pull and could cause brake linings to wear out prematurely. Inspect springs for sags, bends and external damage and replace as required.

Inspect hold-down retainers and pins for bends, rust and corrosion. If any of these are found, replace as required.

Backing Plate

Inspect backing plate shoe contact surface for grooves that may restrict shoe movement and cannot be removed by lightly sanding with emery cloth or other suitable abrasive. If backing plate exhibits these condition, it should be replaced. Also inspect for signs of cracks, warpage and excessive rust, indicating need for replacement.

Adjuster Mechanism

Inspect components for rust, corrosion, bends and fatigue. Replace as required. On adjuster mechanism equipped with adjuster cable, inspect cable for kinks, fraying or elongation of eyelet and replace as required.

Parking Brake Cable

Inspect parking brake cable end for kinks, fraying and elongation and replace as required. Use a small hose clamp to compress clamp where it enters backing plate to remove.

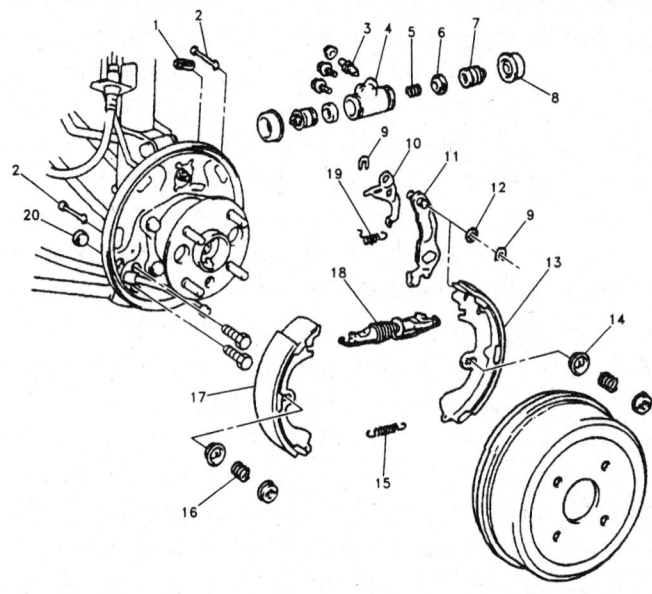

Fig. 1   Drum brake assembly

(1) Plug
(2) Pin
(3) Bleeder Valve
(4) Wheel Cylinder
(5) Spring
(6) Cup
(7) Piston
(8) Boot
(9) C-Clip
(10) Automatic Adjuster Lever
(11) Parking Brake Lever
(12) Shim
(13) Rear Shoe Lining
(14) Shoe Hold-Down
(15) Anchor Spring
(16) Shoe Hold-Down Spring
(17) Front Shoe Lining
(18) Adjuster
(19) Automatic Adjuster Lever Spring
(20) Inspection Hole Plug

GC4089700046000X

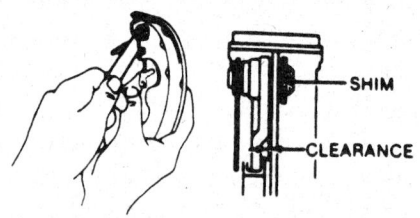

SHIM THICKNESS	
THICKNESS	THICKNESS
0.2 MM (0.008 IN.)	0.5 MM (0.020 IN.)
0.3 MM (0.012 IN.)	0.6 MM (0.024 IN.)
0.4 MM (0.016 IN.)	0.9 MM (0.035 IN.)

GC4089100025000X

Fig. 2   Lever to shoe clearance inspection

BRAKE SERVICE

Removal

1. Raise and support vehicle.
2. Mark relationship of wheel to axle, then remove wheel and tire assembly.
3. Remove brake drum. If drum is difficult to remove, proceed as follows:
   a. Insert screwdriver through hole in backing plate.
   b. Hold automatic adjusting lever away from adjusting bolt.
   c. Reduce brake shoe adjustment, using second screwdriver.
4. Remove return spring, **Fig. 1.**
5. Remove hold-down spring, retainers and pin retaining front shoe.
6. Disconnect anchor spring and remove front shoe.
7. Remove anchor spring.
8. Remove hold-down spring, retainers and pin retaining rear shoe.
9. Disconnect parking brake cable from anchor plate using screwdriver.
10. Disconnect parking brake cable from lever using suitable pliers and remove rear shoe together with strut.
11. Remove adjusting lever spring and strut together with return spring.
12. Remove parking brake lever and automatic adjusting lever from rear shoe by prying out C washer and removing shims and levers.
13. Clean dirt from brake drum, backing plate and other components. **Do not use compressed air or dry brush to clean brake components. Clean brake components with water soaked rag or suitable vacuum cleaner to minimize airborne dust.**

Installation

1. Apply white lithium grease part No. 1050109, or equivalent, to backing plate brake shoe contact points, anchor plate brake shoe contact points, strut and adjusting bolt contact points and strut, and brake shoe contact points.
2. Temporarily install levers and shim with new C washer.
3. Measure clearance between shoe and lever, **Fig. 2.**
4. If clearance is not 0–.0138 inch, adjust by installing replacement shim.
5. Stake C washer using suitable pliers.
6. Set strut and return spring in place on rear shoe and install adjusting lever spring.
7. Connect parking brake cable to lever using suitable pliers.
8. Pass parking brake cable through notch in anchor plate.
9. Set rear shoe in place with end of shoe inserted in wheel cylinder and other end in anchor plate.
10. Install hold-down spring, retainers and pin.
11. Install anchor spring between front and rear shoes.
12. Set front shoe in place with end of shoe inserted in wheel cylinder and strut in place.
13. Install hold-down spring, retainers and pin.
14. Connect return spring.
15. Move parking brake lever of rear shoe back and forth. Ensure adjusting bolt turns. If bolt does not turn, inspect brakes for improper installation.
16. Adjust strut length to shortest possible distance.
17. Install brake drum.
18. Pull parking brake lever all way up until clicking sound can no longer be heard.
19. Inspect clearance between brake shoes and drum
20. Remove drum and measure inside diameter and diameter of brake shoes.
21. If clearance is not .024 inch, inspect parking brake system.
22. Install brake drum and wheel and tire assembly.
23. Fill master cylinder and bleed brake system.
24. Inspect for fluid leakage.

ADJUSTMENTS

Service Brake

Adjustment is accomplished automatically by pulling the parking brake lever all the way up until a clicking sound can no longer be heard.

Parking Brake

1. Ensure parking brake lever travel is proper by pulling parking brake lever all way up and counting number of clicks.
2. Parking brake lever travel should be 4–7 clicks. If not, remove console, loosen locknut and turn adjusting nut until proper travel is achieved.

DRUM BRAKE SPECIFICATIONS

Model	Year	Lining Wear Limit, Inch②	Inside Diameter, Inches			Runout Limit, Inch	Out Of Round, Inch②
			Nominal	Maximum Refinish	Discard Limit①		
Prizm	2001–02	.039	7.870	—	7.913	.0016	.0004

① — Discard Limit is stamped on drum.

② — Above rivet head or shoe. Original equipment type brake linings.

TIGHTENING SPECIFICATIONS

Year	Component	Torque/ Ft. Lbs.
2001–02	Brake Line To Wheel Cylinder Fitting	11
	Hub	59
	Wheel Cylinder	89①
	Wheel Cylinder Bleeder Screw	72①
	Wheel Lug Nuts	76

① — Inch lbs.

Saturn

NOTE: On Air Bag Equipped Models, Refer To "Air Bag System Precautions" Located In The Front Of This Manual For System Disarming & Arming Procedures.

NOTE: Refer To "Computer Relearn Procedures" Located In The Front Of This Manual When Battery Power To The Computer Has Been Interrupted.

INDEX

INSPECTION

1. Release parking brake.
2. Raise and support vehicle.
3. Remove rear wheels and tires.
4. Remove brake drum. **Do not pry against brake backing plate.**
5. Inspect adjuster assembly, ensuring screw threads turn smoothly into nut over full threaded length.
6. Inspect wheel cylinder for damage, leakage or seizure.

BRAKE SERVICE

1. Release parking brake.
2. Raise and support vehicle.
3. Remove rear wheels.
4. Remove brake drum. **Do not pry against brake backing plate.**
5. Remove lower return spring, **Fig. 1.**
6. Remove adjuster spring.
7. Remove leading brake shoe hold-down, spring and pin.

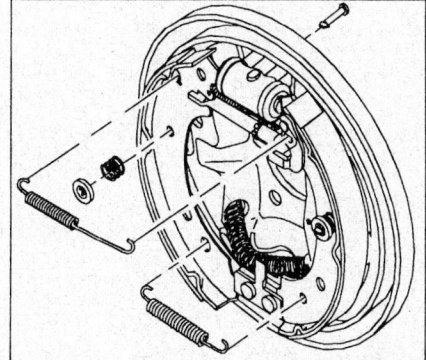

G34089100001000X

Fig. 1 Rear brake assembly

8. Remove adjuster assembly and lever. If difficult, pull leading shoe toward front of vehicle and or turn star wheel on adjuster to shorten length.
9. Twist shoe from upper return spring engagement to remove.
10. Remove parking brake shoe upper return spring.
11. Remove park brake shoe hold-down cup, spring and pin.
12. Push park brake lever into cable spring to remove park brake cable from lever.
13. Remove park brake lever retainer and wave washer and separate from park brake shoe.
14. Reverse procedure to install, noting the following:
    a. Lubricate adjuster assembly, adjuster lever surface, backing plate at shoe contact pads and park brake lever pin and brake shoe web contact surface.
    b. Measure drum inner and brake shoe assembly outer diameters using brake drum clearance tool No. SA91109NE, or equivalent.
    c. Adjust brake adjuster to obtain

DRUM BRAKES

measurement .050 inch less than drum inner diameter.

ADJUSTMENTS

Parking Brake

Refer to "Adjustments" in "Disc Brakes" chapter for parking brake adjustment.

DRUM BRAKE SPECIFICATIONS

Model	Year	Lining Wear Limit, Inch②	Inside Diameter, Inches			Runout Limit, Inch	Allowable Scoring, Inch
			Nominal	Maximum Refinish	Discard Limit①		
ION	2003–05	.020	9.055–9.065	9.075	9.094	.004	.059
L-Series	2001–03	.080	9.050	9.080	9.090	.002	.040
S-Series	2001–02	.040	7.870	7.900	7.930	.006	—

① — Discard Limit is stamped on drum. ② — Above rivet head or shoe. Original equipment type brake linings.

TIGHTENING SPECIFICATIONS

Year	Component	Torque/ Ft. Lbs.
2001–05	Backing Plate To Knuckle	63
	Bleed Valve	66①
	Brake Line To Brake Hose	18
	Brake Line To Wheel Cylinder	36
	Brake Pipe To Union	14
	Wheel Cylinder To Backing Plate	84①
	Wheel Lug Nuts (ION)	100
	Wheel Lug Nuts (L-Series)	92②
	Wheel Lug Nuts (S-Series)	103

① — Inch lbs.
② — For steel wheel & optional aluminum wheel w/large center cap, install wheel cover or cap. With socket, hand tighten five cap nuts. With wrench, tighten each cap an additional 90°.

HYDRAULIC BRAKE SYSTEMS

NOTE: On Air Bag Equipped Models, Refer To "Air Bag System Precautions" Located In The Front Of This Manual For System Disarming & Arming Procedures.

NOTE: Refer To "Computer Relearn Procedures" Located In The Front Of This Manual When Battery Power To The Computer Has Been Interrupted.

INDEX

DESCRIPTION

Front & Rear Split System

When the brake pedal is depressed, both the primary (front brake) and the secondary (rear brake) master cylinder pistons are moved simultaneously to exert hydraulic fluid pressure on their respective systems.

If the rear brake system fails, initial brake pedal movement will cause the unrestricted secondary piston to bottom in the master cylinder bore. Primary piston movement will displace hydraulic fluid in the primary section of the master cylinder to actuate the front brake system.

If the front brake system fails, initial brake pedal movement will cause the unrestricted primary piston to bottom out against the secondary piston. Continued downward movement of the brake pedal moves the secondary piston to displace hydraulic fluid in the rear brake system to actuate the rear brakes.

Diagonally Split System

This system operates on the same principle as conventional front and rear split systems, using primary and secondary master cylinders which move simultaneously to exert hydraulic pressure on their respective systems. The hydraulic brake lines on this system, however, have been diagonally split front to rear (lefthand front to righthand rear and righthand front to lefthand rear) in place of separate lines to the front and rear wheels.

In the event of a system failure, the remaining non-failed system will do all the braking on one front wheel and one rear wheel, maintaining 50% of the total braking force.

Components

WARNING LAMP

The warning lamp should illuminate when the ignition switch is in the start position and turn off when the switch returns to run. If the brake lamp remains on after the ignition returns to run, inspect fluid level in master cylinder reservoir and inspect parking brake. If the warning lamp does not turn on during cranking, inspect for faulty bulb or blown fuse.

FLUID LEVEL SENSOR

This sensor, mounted on the master cylinder, will activate the brake warning lamp if a low brake fluid level is detected. The lamp will turn off once the fluid level is corrected.

BRAKE WARNING LAMP SWITCHES

As pressure falls in one system, the other system's normal pressure forces the piston to the inoperative side, contacting the switch terminal, causing the warning lamp on the instrument panel to glow.

The switch is mounted directly in the master cylinder assembly. Whenever there is a specified differential pressure, the switch piston will activate the brake failure warning switch and cause the brake warning lamp to glow.

COMBINATION VALVE

The combination valve is a metering valve, failure warning switch, and a proportioner in one assembly and is used on disc brake applications. The metering valve delays front disc braking until the rear drum brake shoes contact the drum. The failure warning switch is actuated in event of front or rear brake system failure, in turn activating a dash warning lamp. The proportioner balances front to rear braking action during rapid deceleration.

METERING VALVE

When the brakes are not applied, the metering valve permits the brake fluid to flow through the valve allowing the fluid to expand and contract with temperature changes.

When the brakes are initially applied, the metering valve stem moves to the left, preventing fluid to flow through the valve to the front disc brakes. This is accomplished by the smooth end of the metering valve stem contacting the metering valve seal lip at 4–30 psi. The metering valve spring holds the retainer against the seal until a predetermined pressure is produced at the valve

Complaint/Condition	Possible Cause(s)	Correction(s)
Pedal Feel		
Excessive Pedal Travel	Air in brake system.	Bleed brake system.
	Front or rear brakes not adjusting to lining wear.	Check adjuster mechanism and replace or repair as needed.
	Leaking wheel cylinder or caliper piston seal.	Replace wheel cylinder or overhaul caliper
	Leaking at brake line or hose connections.	Tighten connection. Replace line or hose.
	Internal master cylinder seal leak.	Overhaul or replace master cylinder.
	Uneven lining wear or damaged lining.	Replace lining.
	Rotor or drum out of specifications (i.e. rotor too thin, parallelism, out of round, bell shaped etc.).	Replace rotor, or drum.
	Improper vacuum booster to master cylinder length.	Replace booster and pushrod.
Pedal Creeps Down	Internal master cylinder seal leak or defective master cylinder bore.	Repair or replace master cylinder.
	Leaking wheel cylinder or caliper piston seal.	Replace wheel cylinder or overhaul caliper
	Leaking at brake line or hose connections.	Tighten connection. Replace lines or hose.
	Damaged vacuum booster check valve or grommet.	Replace check valve and grommet.
Pedal Pulses	Rotor or drum out of specifications (i.e. lateral runout, parallelism, out of round, bell shaped etc.).	Replace or turn rotor or drum.
	Worn out linings or linings wearing unevenly.	Replace linings.
	Wheel bearings worn.	Replace wheel bearing.
	Damaged suspension, knuckle or axle.	Replace defective parts.

G34099100003010X

Fig. 1 Brake system troubleshooting chart (Part 1 of 6). Saturn

Complaint/Condition	Possible Cause(s)	Correction(s)
Excessive Pedal Effort	Leaking or damaged vacuum booster (i.e. cut diaphragm, restricted vacuum hose, damaged vacuum check valve, cracked power piston, restricted air passages)	Replace booster.
	Worn out brake linings (glazed)	Replace linings.
	Damage to braking surface of rotor or drum.	Replace rotor or drum.
	Crimped brake line or collapsed brake hose.	Replace line or hose.
	Engine out of specifications.	Check engine to specification.
Pedal Goes to the Floor	Low fluid level, large amount of air in system.	Bleed brake system.
	Broken brake line or brake hose.	Replace line or hose.
	Cut, torn or nicked master cylinder secondary seals.	Repair or replace master cylinder.
	Brake pedal not connected to push rod.	Check connection and repair.
	Wheel cylinder or caliper piston falls out.	Check assembly and repair.

G34099100003020X

Fig. 1 Brake system troubleshooting chart (Part 2 of 6). Saturn

inlet port which overcomes the spring pressure and permits hydraulic pressure to actuate the front disc brakes. The increased pressure into the valve is metered through the valve seal, to the front disc brakes, producing an increased force on the diaphragm. The diaphragm then pulls the pin, in turn pulling the retainer, and reduces the spring pressure on the metering valve seal. Eventually, the pressure reaches a point at which the spring is pulled away by the diaphragm pin and retainer, leaving the metering valve unrestricted, permitting full pressure to pass through the metering valve.

FAILURE WARNING SWITCH

If the rear brake system fails, the front system pressure forces the switch piston to the right. The switch pin is then forced up into the switch, completing the electrical circuit and activates the dash warning lamp.

When repairs are made and pressure returns to the system, the piston moves to the left, resetting the switch. The detent on the piston requires approximately 100–450 psi to permit full reset of the piston. In event of front brake system failure, the piston moves to the left and the same sequence of events is followed as for rear system failure except the piston resets to the right.

PROPORTIONING OR PRESSURE CONTROL VALVE

During rapid deceleration, a portion of vehicle weight is transferred to the front wheels. This resultant loss of weight at rear wheels must be compensated for to avoid early rear wheel skid. The proportioner or pressure control valve reduces rear brake system pressure, delaying rear wheel skid. When the proportioner or pressure control valve is incorporated in the combination valve assembly, pressure developed within the valve acts against the large end of the piston, overcoming the spring pressure, moving the piston left. The piston then contacts the stem seat and restricts line pressure through the valve.

During normal braking operation, the proportioner or pressure control valve is not functional. Brake fluid flows into the proportioner or pressure control valve between the piston center hole and the valve stem, through the stop plate and to the rear brakes. Spring pressure loads the piston during normal braking, causing it to rest against the stop plate.

On diagonally split brake systems, two proportioners or pressure control valves are used. One controls the lefthand rear brake, the other the righthand rear brake. The proportioners or pressure control valves are installed in the master cylinder rear brake outlet ports.

BRAKE DISTRIBUTION VALVE & SWITCH

This switch assembly is used on some diagonally split brake systems and Corvette four-wheel disc brake systems. It is connected to the outlet ports of the master cylinder and to the brake warning lamp and warns the driver if either the primary or secondary brake system has failed.

When hydraulic pressure is equal in both primary and secondary brake systems, the switch remains centered. If pressure fails in one of the systems, the piston moves toward the inoperative side. The shoulder of the piston contacts the switch terminal, providing a ground and lighting the warning lamp.

TROUBLESHOOTING

When troubleshooting the hydraulic brake system, perform the following inspections.

Master Cylinder Internal Fluid Leakage Check

Start engine and depress the brake pedal. If the pedal gradually falls under constant pressure, the hydraulic system may be leaking. Raise the vehicle on a lift and inspect all tubing lines and backing plates for signs of leakage. It may be required to lift or remove the carpeting or floor mats to inspect for booster or master cylinder leakage.

Road Test

When testing brakes, ensure the road is level and dry. Test brakes at both light and heavy pedal pressure. Do not lock up brakes or slide tires during a brake test.

Inspect the tires on the vehicle before performing a brake test. Tires should be equally inflated, identical in size and with equal tread pattern. Excessive camber and caster will cause the brakes to pull. An overloaded vehicle will also brake erratically.

Saturn

When troubleshooting the hydraulic brake system, perform the following inspections. If a fault still exists within the system, refer to the brake system diagnosis chart and the troubleshooting chart, **Fig. 1**.

DIAGNOSIS & TESTING

Refer to **Fig. 2**, for diagnosis chart.

Complaint/Condition	Possible Cause(s)	Correction(s)
Noise		
Squeal/Scrape While Not Braking	Worn linings, sensor scraping on rotor (normal).	Replace linings.
	Loose drum brake component (spring, lever, adjuster, etc.).	Check drum brake and repair.
	Loose front suspension attachments.	Tighten attachments or replace.
	Caliper interference with rotor.	Check clearance and repair.
	Bent or cracked suspension parts.	Replace components.
	Drum or rotor contacting backing plate or dust shield.	Check clearance and repair.
Squeal/Scrape While Braking	Linings worn out, shoe contacting drum or rotor.	Replace linings.
	Lack of lubrication on backing plate or on adjuster screw.	Lubricate backing plate or adjuster screw.
	Lack of lubrication on caliper sliding surfaces.	Lubricate.
	Lack of lubrication on brake pedal attachments.	Lubricate.
	Damage to insulator between disc brake shoe and caliper piston.	Replace insulator and pads as needed.
	Hot spots or worn surface on drum or rotor.	Replace rotor or drum.
	Weak hold down springs or worn drum brake components.	Replace drum brake springs.
Chatters/Rattles	Hot spots or worn surface on drum or rotor.	Replace drum or rotor.
	Rotor or drum out of specifications (i.e. lateral runout, parallelism, out of round, bell shaped, etc.).	Replace or turn rotor or drum.
	Lining contaminated with foreign substances.	Replace linings.
	Linings wearing unevenly.	Replace linings.
	Bent or loose brake shoes.	Replace show and linings.
	Weak or broken retractor springs.	Replace drum brake springs.
	Loose brake cable, brake line, or ABS wiring.	Check cable or line connection and tighten or replace as needed.
Groans (at/near stop)	Linings worn out.	Replace linings.
	Incorrect or damaged lining material.	Replace linings.
	Hot spots or worn surface on drum or rotor.	Replace drum or rotor.
	Cracked or bent knuckle or suspension parts.	Replace suspension component.
	Loose suspension.	Tighten suspension or replace.

G34099100003030X

Fig. 1 Brake system troubleshooting chart (Part 3 of 6). Saturn

Complaint/Condition	Possible Cause(s)	Correction(s)
Performance		
Brake Pull Left/Right	Caliper pistons sticking.	Overhaul caliper and replace piston.
	Loose wheel bearings or suspension attachments.	Replace wheel bearings or tighten suspension attachments.
	Worn suspension components.	Replace suspension components.
	Loose steering or steering gear.	Repair or replace steering components.
	Uneven wear on tires, tires not properly inflated or incorrect tires for vehicle.	Check tire and replace if necessary.
	Uneven worn linings.	Replace linings.
	Front suspension out of line.	Align suspension.
	Restricted brake line or hose.	Replace line or hose.
Brakes Grab	Contaminated brake linings.	Replace linings.
	Damage to braking surface of rotors or drums.	Replace rotors or drums.
	Rotor or drum out of specifications (i.e. lateral runout, parallelism, out of round, bell shaped, etc.).	Replace or turn rotor or drum.
	Damaged vacuum booster.	Replace booster.
Brakes Drag	Caliper pistons stuck.	Overhaul caliper and replace piston.
	Corroded caliper bolts. Caliper will not retract.	Replace bolts and bolt boots.
	Compensating port or bypass hole in master cylinder clogged.	Clean master cylinder and rebuild.
	Worn or damaged drum brake return springs.	Replace drum brake springs.
	Contaminated or improper brake fluid, rubber seals are swollen.	Flush brake system and replace all rubber parts including hoses.
	Parking brake not releasing.	Check cable and cable attachments.
	Self-adjusters over adjusting for lining wear.	Overhaul or replace adjusters.
	Improper vacuum booster push rod length.	Gage booster push rod and replace if needed.
Brake Action Uneven (Front – Rear)	Uneven wear on tires, tires improperly inflated or incorrect tires installed.	Check tires and replace if needed.
	Proportioning valve not functioning properly.	Replace master cylinder.
	Linings wearing unevenly front to rear.	Replace linings.
	Fluid leak in system.	Check system for leaks and repair or replace components.
	Hot spots or worn surface on drum or rotor.	Replace drum or rotor.

G34099100003040X

Fig. 1 Brake system troubleshooting chart (Part 4 of 6). Saturn

COMPONENT REPLACEMENT

Master Cylinder

ALL MODELS EXCEPT SATURN

1. **On Vibe models,** remove air filer hose clamp and hose from throttle body.
2. **On all models,** disconnect fluid level sensor retainer and electrical connector.
3. Drain master cylinder reservoir brake fluid into suitable container.
4. Plug hose.
5. Disconnect master cylinder brake pipes. Plug open pipes.
6. Remove mounting nuts and master cylinder.
7. Remove reservoir, as required.
8. Reverse procedure to install. Bleed hydraulic system as outlined in "Brake System Bleed."

SATURN

ION

1. Remove underhood electrical center cover.
2. Remove Connector Position Assurance (CPA) connector from brake fluid level sensor, **Fig. 3.**
3. Remove underhood battery positive terminal mounting bolt, then disconnect cables from electrical center and EPS cable from underhood center, **Fig. 4.**
4. Remove engine wiring harness retainer at engine control module.
5. Disconnect electrical connector from ECM and remove ECM from bracket setting aside.
6. **On models equipped with automatic transmissions,** remove Transmission Control Module (TCM), **Fig. 5.**
7. **On all models,** remove EPS cable retainer form underhood center and forward lamp harness retainer from ECM tray.
8. Remove surge tank clip from center bracket, then the underhood electrical center bracket and underhood electrical center from underhood.
9. Remove surge tank hose and electrical center bracket, **Fig. 6.**
10. Remove master cylinder reservoir assembly as outlined in "Fluid Reservoir."
11. Remove brake pipes from master cylinder. Cover pipe fittings to prevent contamination.
12. Remove mounting nuts and master cylinder, **Fig. 7.**
13. Reverse procedure to install. Bleed brake system as outlined in "Brake System Bleed."

L & S-SERIES

1. Remove brake fluid level sensor electrical connector.
2. Remove master cylinder brake line fitting nuts. **Plug open lines and fittings.**
3. Remove mounting nuts and master cylinder.
4. Reverse procedure to install.

Fluid Reservoir

ION

1. Remove underhood electrical center cover.
2. Disconnect CPA electrical connector from brake fluid level sensor.
3. Remove brake fluid from master cylinder reservoir and discard as required.
4. Remove reservoir mounting bolts, then the reservoir clutch hose from master cylinder fitting.
5. Plug brake hose and cover brake master cylinder.
6. Remove reservoir clutch hose and reservoir.
7. Reverse procedure to install. Bleed hydraulic brake system as outlined in "Brake System Bleed."

L-SERIES

1. Remove master cylinder as outlined in "Component Replacement."
2. Unclip hold down clamps and remove reservoir by pulling upward.
3. Reverse procedure to install.

S-SERIES

1. Remove master cylinder as outlined in

Complaint/Condition	Possible Cause(s)	Correction(s)
Brakes Slow to Release	Caliper piston sticking.	Overhaul caliper and replace piston.
	Corroded caliper bolts. Caliper will not retract.	Replace bolts and bolt boots.
	Contaminated or improper brake fluid, rubber seals are swollen.	Flush brake system and replace all rubber parts including hoses.
	Worn caliper piston seals.	Overhaul calipers.
	Worn or damaged drum brake return springs.	Replace drum brake springs.
	Worn or damaged master cylinder seals.	Overhaul master cylinder.
	Damage to mechanical action of brake pedal.	Check pedal and repair or replace.
Slow Response/Excessive Stopping Distance	Rotor not turned to proper surface finish.	Check rotor surface finish and turn rotor or replace.
	Linings not adjusting properly, damaged self-adjusters or worn piston seal.	Overhaul drum brake or caliper.
	Caliper pistons sticking.	Overhaul caliper and replace piston.
	Worn or glazed linings.	Replace linings.
	Proportioning valve not functioning properly.	Replace master cylinder.
Odor	Linings over heated.	
	Lining contaminated with foreign substances.	Replace lining.
Poor Fuel Economy	Linings over heated.	
	Egg shaped drum or bent rotor/knuckle.	Replace drum, rotor or knuckle.

G34099100003050X

Fig. 1 Brake system troubleshooting chart (Part 5 of 6). Saturn

Complaint/Condition	Possible Cause(s)	Correction(s)
Telltale		
Red (Brake) Telltale On	Park brake on.	Release park brake.
	Low brake fluid level in master cylinder (check for leaks).	Fill reservoir. Check for leaks.
	Improperly adjusted park brake switch.	Check park brake switch connection and adjustment.
	Damaged park brake switch or switch circuit.	Replace switch or repair circuit.
	Antilock brake system (ABS) problem	Refer to ABS
Amber (ABS) Telltale On (Solid/Flashing)	Refer to ABS	
Parking Brake		
Does Not Hold	Park brake not adjusted properly.	Adjust park brake.
	Brakes not adjusting properly.	Check brake adjusters and repair or replace as needed.
	Linings worn out.	Replace linings.
	Linings contaminated with foreign material.	Replace linings.
	Cable disconnected from lever.	Connect cable.
	Lever bent or loose.	Replace lever.
	Cable slipping.	Replace cable.
Does Not Release	Park brake cables binding.	Check cable and cable attachments.
	Release lever broken or binding.	Replace park brake lever.
Parking Brake Lever Hard to Apply	Lack of lubrication on apply mechanism.	Lubricate apply mechanism.
	Park brake cables binding.	Check cables and cable attachments.

G34099100003060X

Fig. 1 Brake system troubleshooting chart (Part 6 of 6). Saturn

"Component Replacement."
2. Wipe reservoir cap clean, remove cap and inspect reservoir cap and diaphragm for cuts, nicks or deformation.
3. Drain reservoir brake fluid into suitable container.
4. **On models equipped with anti-lock brakes,** remove modulator and motor pack.
5. **On all models,** remove brake fluid level sensor.
6. Place master cylinder in suitable vice. **Do not clamp on master cylinder body.**
7. Drive out spring pins using suitable ⅛ inch punch, **Fig. 8.**
8. Pull reservoir out of cylinder body and remove reservoir bayonets' O-rings, **Fig. 9.**
9. Clean reservoir with clean denatured alcohol and inspect for cracks or deformation.
10. Reverse procedure to install. Install new O-rings.

COMPONENT SERVICE

Master Cylinder Overhaul

EXCEPT AURORA, BONNEVILLE, CORVETTE, CTS, LESABRE, PARK AVENUE, SATURN, VIBE, XLR, COBALT,

DISASSEMBLE

Refer to **Figs. 10 and 11,** when performing the following procedures.
1. Disconnect and plug hydraulic lines.
2. Remove mounting nuts and master cylinder.
3. Remove reservoir cover and diaphragm. Discard old brake fluid.
4. Inspect cover and diaphragm.
5. Remove fluid level switch.
6. **On models equipped with compact master cylinder,** remove proportioner valve, **Fig. 11.**
7. **On all models,** depress primary piston and remove lock ring.
8. Plug primary fluid outlet (outlet nearest to cowl when master cylinder is installed), then remove primary and secondary pistons by applying compressed air into secondary fluid outlet.
9. Remove secondary piston spring retainer and seals.
10. Remove secondary piston spring retainer and seals.
11. Clamp the flange on the master cylinder body in a vise, then remove fluid reservoir, **Figs. 12 and 13.**
12. Remove reservoir grommets.
13. Inspect master cylinder bore for corrosion. **Do not use abrasive material on master cylinder bore.**

ASSEMBLE

Clean all components not included in repair kit with suitable brake fluid. **Do not dry with compressed air.** Lubricate all rubber components with clean brake fluid prior to installation.
1. Lubricate new reservoir grommets with suitable silicone brake lube.
2. Press grommets into master cylinder body. Ensure grommets are properly seated.
3. Lay reservoir upside down on flat, hard surface.
4. Press master cylinder body onto reservoir using rocking motion.
5. Install new seals on secondary piston and spring retainer.
6. Install spring and secondary piston into cylinder.
7. Install primary piston.
8. Depress primary piston into cylinder and install lock ring.
9. Install fluid level switch, if equipped.
10. **On models equipped with compact master cylinder,** install proportioner valve, **Fig. 11.**
11. **On all models,** install diaphragm into reservoir cover and cover onto reservoir.
12. Install master cylinder and bleed brake system.

AURORA, BONNEVILLE, ION, LESABRE & PARK AVENUE

These master cylinders are not serviceable. Master cylinder must be replaced as a complete unit. **Do not attempt to overhaul the master cylinder.**

AVEO

1. Disconnect electrical connector from reservoir.
2. Disconnect brake lines from master cylinder.
3. Plug brake line openings to prevent fluid loss and contamination.
4. Remove power booster attaching nuts.
5. Remove master cylinder assembly.
6. Remove brake fluid reservoir.
7. Remove seal ring from cylinder bore.
8. Remove retaining ring from cylinder body using suitable flat bladed tool. Discard ring.
9. Remove primary piston.
10. Carefully remove secondary piston assembly and spring from master cylinder bore.
11. Reverse procedure to install, noting the following:

Step	Action	Yes	No
1	Were you sent here from a Brake Symptom Table?	Go to Step 2	Diagnostic Starting Point -
2	Inspect and adjust the brake fluid level in the brake master cylinder. Was the brake fluid level low?	Go to Step 3	Go to Step 4

3	1. Inspect the brake fluid for the following conditions which indicate brake fluid contamination:
	  ○ Fluid separation indicates two types of fluid are present
	    ■ A swirled appearance indicates an oil-based substance
	    ■ A layered appearance indicates a silicone-based substance
	  ○ Fluid discoloration
	    ■ A cloudy appearance indicates moisture
	    ■ A dark appearance or suspended particles in the fluid indicates dirt, rust, corrosion, or brake dust
	2. Inspect the master cylinder reservoir cap diaphragm and the reservoir-to-master cylinder grommets for swelling. Swelling indicates fluid contamination.
	
	Do any of the above conditions exist?
		Go to Step 5	Go to Step 6

4	1. Inspect the brake fluid for the following conditions which indicate brake fluid contamination:
	  ○ Fluid separation indicates two types of fluid are present
	    ■ A swirled appearance indicates an oil-based substance
	    ■ A layered appearance indicates a silicone-based substance
	  ○ Fluid discoloration
	    ■ A cloudy appearance indicates moisture
	    ■ A dark appearance or suspended particles in the fluid indicates dirt, rust, corrosion, or brake dust
	2. Inspect the master cylinder reservoir cap diaphragm and the reservoir-to-master cylinder grommets for swelling. Swelling indicates fluid contamination.
	
	Do any of the above conditions exist?
		Go to Step 5	Go to Step 12

ARM66GC000000749

Fig. 2 Hydraulic brake system diagnosis chart (Part 1 of 4)

> a. Clean all parts with clean brake fluid, then dry with compressed air.
> b. Replace all rubber parts and retaining rings.
> c. Lubricate master cylinder bore with clean brake fluid.

CORVETTE

1. Remove reservoir cap and diaphragm.
2. Drain fluid into suitable container.
3. Remove master cylinder prime pipe clamp and prime pipe.
4. Remove mounting screw and reservoir, **Fig. 14.**
5. Remove reservoir O-rings.
6. Slightly depress piston and remove retaining ring using suitable retaining ring pliers.
7. Invert cylinder so reservoir wells face downward.
8. Depress primary and secondary pistons until fully bottomed in bore using suitable brass rod or wooden dowel. Secondary stop pin should fall freely from cylinder.
9. Gently bump open end of cylinder body against suitable wood piece to dislodge primary piston. Remove primary piston.
10. Gently bump open end of cylinder body against suitable wood piece to dislodge secondary piston and center valve. Remove secondary piston. **Do not remove or disturb screw which retains primary spring to secondary piston.**
11. Remove secondary return spring.
12. Remove secondary piston spring retainer using suitable small screwdriver to lift crimp and allow retainer to slide off piston, **Fig. 15.**
13. Remove secondary piston center valve plunger and spring.
14. Remove primary piston seal retainer using suitable sharp knife or razor blade to cut and remove plastic retaining cup retaining ring, **Fig. 16.**
15. Remove recuperating guide.
16. Remove pistons' rubber seals, **Figs. 17 and 18. Do not damage any piston surfaces, particularly areas where seals seat.**
17. Remove pressure differential switch. **Do not disassemble spring or probe.**
18. Remove end plug and O-ring. **Do not lose small electrical bias spring located just inside end plug.**
19. Remove warning switch. **Keep warning switch and probe together as an assembly.**
20. Remove end plug, O-ring and electrical bias spring.
21. Gently tap cylinder body against suitable wood piece to dislodge proportioning valve spool.
22. Remove proportioning valve spool including O-ring and spacer. **Do not disassemble proportioning valve.**
23. Proportioning valve is lubricated with special grease. **Do not use cleaning solution to clean it or components included in repair kit.** Clean other components in suitable denatured alcohol. Dry components and passages within cylinder using filtered compressed air.
24. Reverse procedure to assemble. Ensure seals and components are lubricated with clean brake fluid.

CTS

1. Remove master cylinder as outlined in "Master Cylinder, Replace."
2. Place mounting flange into suitable vise so piston is accessible.
3. Ensure outside area of master cylinder is clean of dirt and debris.
4. Remove reservoir cap and diaphragm.
5. Remove fluid level sensor and drain master cylinder reservoir brake fluid into suitable container.
6. Remove retaining pins and reservoir from master cylinder.
7. Remove seals from master cylinder reservoir.
8. Remove piston retainer using suitable tool.
9. Remove piston from cylinder bore.
10. Plug cylinder inlet ports and rear outlet port, then apply low pressure compressed air into front outlet port to remove secondary piston assembly.
11. Reverse procedure to install.

Step	Action	Yes	No

5	1. Flush the hydraulic brake system. Refer to Hydraulic Brake System Flushing.
	2. If the brake fluid WAS contaminated with an oil-based or a silicone-based fluid, complete the following steps and refer to the following procedures:
	  A. Remove ALL of the brake system components that utilize rubber seals or linings.
	  B. Clean out the hydraulic brake pipes and the reservoir using denatured alcohol, or equivalent.
	  C. Dry the brake pipes and the reservoir using non-lubricated, filtered air.
	3. If the brake fluid was NOT contaminated with an oil-based fluid, but WAS contaminated with moisture, dirt, rust, corrosion, or brake dust, replace the brake master cylinder reservoir cap diaphragm. The diaphragm may have allowed moisture or dirt to enter the system.
	4. Refill and bleed the hydraulic brake system. Refer to Hydraulic Brake System Bleeding.
	
	Did you complete the operation and any required repairs and/or replacements?
		Go to Step 9	--

6	1. Inspect the following hydraulic brake system components for external fluid leaks. Repair or replace any of the components found to be leaking brake fluid.
	
	2. If you repaired or replaced any of the brake system components listed, bleed the hydraulic brake system.
	  While bleeding the hydraulic brake system, observe for the following conditions:
	  ○ The presence of air in the system at a bleeder valve location other than at the repair location, except if the brake master cylinder was replaced
	  ○ An unrestricted and even flow of brake fluid per axle during the bleeding procedure
	
	Did you find and correct a condition?
		Go to Step 7	Go to Step 12

7	Was air in the system at a bleeder valve location other than at the repair location, except if the brake master cylinder was replaced?	Go to Step 19	Go to Step 8
8	Was the flow of brake fluid unrestricted and even per axle during the bleeding procedure?	Go to Step 9	Go to Step 10

ARM66GC000000750

Fig. 2 Hydraulic brake system diagnosis chart (Part 2 of 4)

Step	Action	Yes	No
9	Inspect the hydraulic function of the brake calipers and wheel cylinders, if equipped, for proper operation. Do the brake calipers and wheel cylinders, if equipped, operate properly?	Go to Step 21	Go to Step 14
10	Was the flow of brake fluid restricted or uneven through front axle hydraulic components during the bleeding procedure?	Go to Step 13	Go to Step 11
11	Was the flow of brake fluid restricted or uneven through rear axle hydraulic components during the bleeding procedure?	Go to Step 17	--
12	Inspect the hydraulic function of the brake calipers and wheel cylinders, if equipped, for proper operation. Do the brake calipers and wheel cylinders, if equipped, operate properly?	Go to Step 15	Go to Step 13
13	Use the following procedure in order to determine if the brake caliper is restricting the flow of brake fluid and/or not operating properly: 1. Raise and support the vehicle. 2. Remove the tire and wheel assemblies. 3. Open the suspected caliper bleeder valve. 4. Using a large C-clamp, compress the caliper piston and observe for an unrestricted flow of brake fluid and for free movement of the caliper piston. 5. Close the caliper bleeder valve. Was the flow of brake fluid unrestricted and did the caliper piston move freely?	Go to Step 17	Go to Step 14
14	Repair or replace any brake caliper or wheel cylinder, if equipped, that was not operating properly. Did you complete the repair and/or replacement?	Go to Step 21	--
15	Bleed the hydraulic brake system. Observe the condition and the flow of the brake fluid. Was air in the system?	Go to Step 19	Go to Step 16
16	Was the flow of brake fluid unrestricted and even per axle during the bleeding procedure?	Go to Step 21	Go to Step 17
17	1. Inspect the brake pipes and flexible brake hoses for signs of a fluid restriction; such as being bent, kinked, pinched or damaged. 2. Replace any of the hydraulic brake pipes and/or flexible brake hoses found to be bent, kinked, pinched or damaged. 3. If none of the hydraulic brake pipes or flexible brake hoses were visibly bent, kinked, pinched or damaged, replace the hydraulic brake flex hose at the restricted location. Did you find and correct a condition?	Go to Step 21	Go to Step 18

ARM66GC000000751

Fig. 2 Hydraulic brake system diagnosis chart (Part 3 of 4)

Step	Action	Yes	No
18	Replace the proportioning valve. Did you complete the replacement?	Go to Step 21	--
19	1. Inspect the hydraulic brake system components for brake fluid seepage at a seal and/or fitting location, which may have drawn air into the system. 2. Inspect the hydraulic brake system components for evidence of a recent repair, which may have introduced air into the system. 3. Repair or replace any of the components found to be installed incorrectly or seeping brake fluid. Did you find and correct a condition?	Go to Step 21	Go to Step 20
20	1. Inspect the brake master cylinder for internal fluid leaks. 2. Repair or replace the brake master cylinder if it is found to be leaking brake fluid internally. Did you find and correct a condition?	Go to Step 21	Symptom
21	Install or connect components that were removed or disconnected during diagnosis. Did you complete the operation?	Hydraulic Brake System OK	Symptom

ARM66GC000000752

Fig. 2 Hydraulic brake system diagnosis chart (Part 4 of 4)

5. Remove plate, cylinder cup, O-ring, piston guide and primary piston assembly from master cylinder.
6. Remove secondary piston using suitable hammer to tap cylinder flange against blocks.
7. Inspect components for wear and damage, replace as required.
8. Reverse procedure to install. Bleed brake system as outlined in "Brake System Bleed."

LACROSSE, STS & XLR

DISASSEMBLE

1. Remove master cylinder as outlined in "Component Replacement."
2. Secure master cylinder mounting flange in suitable bench vise so primary piston rear is accessible.
3. Clean outside of master cylinder reservoir, then remove reservoir cap and diaphragm.
4. Replace cap and diaphragm if cut or cracked, nicked or deformed.
5. Secure master cylinder in suitable vise. **Do not clamp master cylinder body, secure only at flange.**
6. Remove brake fluid level sensor by depressing tab with suitable nose pliers and pressing sensor through reservoir.
7. Tap out reservoir retaining pins.
8. Remove reservoir and seals.
9. Depress primary piston using smooth, round-ended tool and remove piston retainer.
10. Remove primary piston from cylinder bore.
11. Plug cylinder inlet and rear outlet ports.
12. Apply low pressure, non-lubricated, filtered air into front outlet port and remove secondary piston with primary and secondary seals, and return spring.
13. Discard primary piston assembly, piston retainer, seals and retainer from secondary piston.

ASSEMBLE

1. Clean interior and exterior of master cylinder, secondary piston and return spring in denatured alcohol, or equivalent.
2. Inspect the master cylinder bore, inlet

L & S-SERIES

DISASSEMBLE

1. Remove master cylinder as outlined in "Component Replacement."
2. Wipe reservoir cap clean, remove cap and inspect reservoir cap and diaphragm for cuts, nicks or deformation.
3. Drain reservoir brake fluid into suitable container.
4. **On models equipped with anti-lock brakes,** remove modulator and motor pack.
5. **On all models,** remove brake fluid level sensor.
6. Remove reservoir as outlined in "Component Replacement."
7. While depressing master cylinder piston, remove retainer clip, **Fig. 19.**
8. Apply low pressure non-lubricated compressed air into upper brake fluid output port, **Fig. 20.**
9. Clean components with clean denatured alcohol. Dry with unlubricated, low pressure compressed air. Blow out cylinder body passages.
10. Inspect pistons and seals for nicks, cuts, cracks, wear or corrosion.
11. Inspect master cylinder bore for scoring or corrosion. If cylinder bore is damaged, replace master cylinder. **Do not hone master cylinder bore.**

ASSEMBLE

1. Lubricate secondary seal and master cylinder bore with clean brake fluid.
2. Install spring and secondary piston into master cylinder bore, **Fig. 21.**
3. Lubricate primary seal and master cylinder bore with clean brake fluid.
4. Install primary piston into master cylinder bore.
5. While depressing master cylinder piston, install retainer clip.
6. Install reservoir as outlined in "Component Replacement."
7. Install brake fluid level sensor.
8. **On models equipped with anti-lock brakes,** install modulator and motor pack.
9. **On all models,** install master cylinder as outlined in "Component Replacement."

VIBE

1. Remove master cylinder from vehicle as outlined in "Master Cylinder, Replace."
2. Remove master cylinder bore O-ring and two attaching rubber grommets.
3. Secure master cylinder into suitable vise, then remove piston stopper bolt and gasket.
4. Remove snap ring pushing piston into master cylinder.

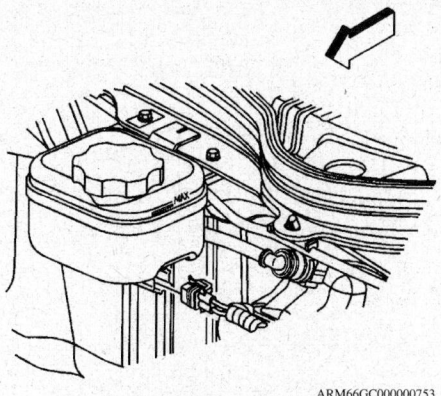

Fig. 3   CPA connector replacement. ION

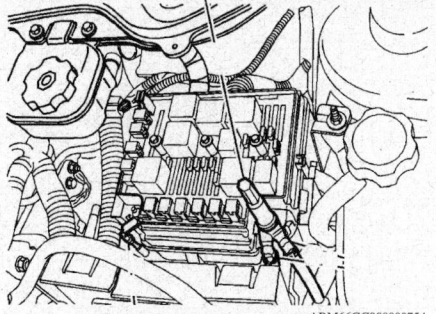

Fig. 4   Electrical connector replacement. ION

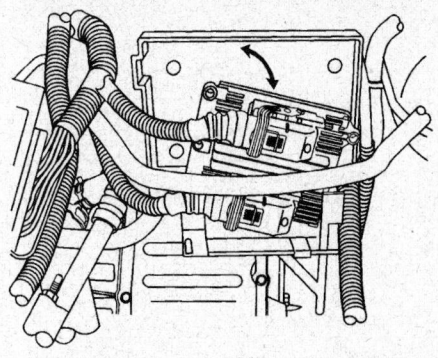

Fig. 5   TCM replacement. ION

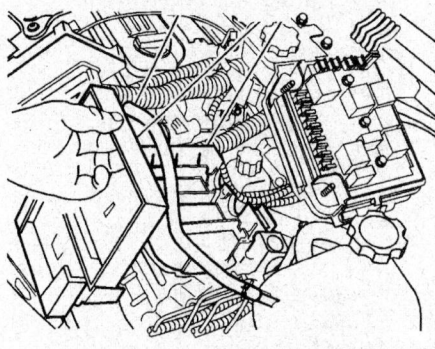

Fig. 6   Surge tank bracket replacement. ION

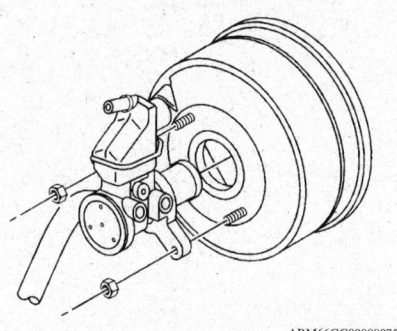

Fig. 7   Master cylinder replacement. ION

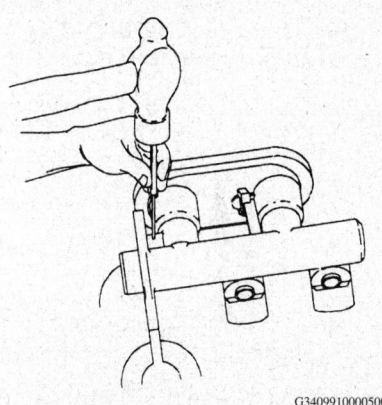

Fig. 8   Master cylinder reservoir spring pin replacement. S-Series

and outlet ports, secondary piston and return spring for cracks, scoring, pitting, and/or corrosion.

3. Dry master cylinder and components with non-lubricated, filtered air.
4. Lubricate master cylinder bore, secondary piston, return spring and components with suitable DOT-3 brake fluid.
5. Assemble lubricated, new primary seal, retainer and new secondary seal onto secondary piston.
6. Install lubricated return spring and secondary piston assembly into cylinder bore.
7. Install lubricated, new primary piston assembly into cylinder bore.
8. Depress primary piston using smooth, round-ended tool, and install new piston retainer.
9. Install lubricated reservoir seals. Ensure they are fully seated.
10. Install reservoir by pressing reservoir straight down on master cylinder until pin holes are aligned.
11. Tap reservoir retaining pins into place.
12. Place brake fluid level sensor into reservoir and press into place.
13. Install reservoir cap and diaphragm.

Wheel Cylinder Overhaul

DISASSEMBLE

1. Raise and support vehicle.

2. Remove wheel, drum and brake shoes.
3. Disconnect hydraulic line at wheel cylinder. **Do not pull metal line away from cylinder.** Line will separate from cylinder when cylinder is moved away from brake backing plate.
4. Remove mounting screws and wheel cylinder.
5. Remove boots, pistons, springs and cups, **Fig. 22.**

ASSEMBLE

1. Clean components with suitable brake fluid.
2. Inspect cylinder bore. Scored bore may be honed as long as diameter is not increased by more than .005 inch.
3. Ensure hands are clean before proceeding.
4. Lubricate cylinder wall and rubber cups with suitable brake fluid.
5. Install springs, cups, pistons and boots.
6. Wipe end of hydraulic line to remove any foreign matter and place wheel cylinder in position.
7. Enter tubing into cylinder and start threads on fitting.
8. Secure cylinder to backing plate and complete tightening of tubing fitting.
9. Install brake shoes, drum and wheel.
10. Bleed brake system and adjust brakes.

BRAKE SYSTEM BLEED

Brake fluid is corrosive to painted surfaces. Care must be taken not to allow brake fluid to come in contact with painted surfaces on vehicle.

When bleeding the brake system, always bleed righthand rear wheel circuit first, followed by the lefthand front, lefthand rear and, finally, righthand front.

Manual

Pressure bleeding is recommended for all hydraulic systems. However, if a pressure bleeder is unavailable, use the following procedure. **Brake fluid damages painted surfaces. Immediately clean any spilled fluid.**

1. Remove vacuum reserve by pumping brakes several times with engine off.
2. Fill master cylinder reservoir with clean brake fluid. **Do not let reservoir fall below half full during bleeding procedure.**
3. If required, bleed master cylinder as follows:
   a. Loosen master cylinder forward brake line connection until fluid flows from reservoir, then tighten brake line.
   b. Have assistant to slowly depress brake pedal one time and hold.
   c. Loosen front brake line connection and purge air from cylinder.
   d. Tighten connection and slowly release brake pedal.
   e. Wait 15 seconds, then repeat previous steps until all air is purged.
   f. Bleed rearward brake line connection by repeating previous steps.
4. Loosen and tighten bleeder valves at all four wheels.

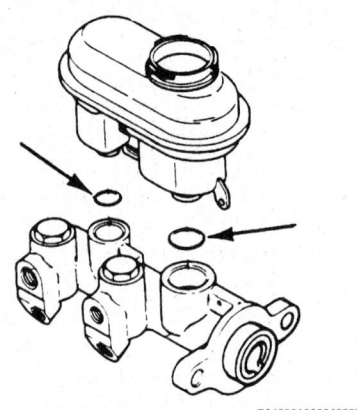

Fig. 9 Reservoir & O-ring replacement. S-Series

5. Bleed calipers or wheel cylinders in sequence outlined in "Bleed Sequence."
6. Place one end of transparent tube over bleeder valve and submerge other end into transparent container filled with clean brake fluid.
7. Have assistant slowly depress brake pedal one time and hold.
8. Loosen bleeder valve and purge air from wheel cylinder or caliper. Tighten bleeder screw and slowly release pedal.
9. Wait 15 seconds and repeat previous steps until all air is bled from system.

Pressure

1. Loosen and tighten bleeder valves at all four wheels.
2. Install suitable bleeder adapter to master cylinder using diaphragm type pressure bleeder.
3. Charge bleeder ball to 20–25 psi.
4. Connect pressure bleeder line to adapter.
5. Open line valve on pressure bleeder and depress bleed-off valve on adapter until small amount of brake fluid is released.
6. Raise and support vehicle.
7. Bleed calipers or wheel cylinders in sequence as outlined in "Bleed Sequence."
8. Place one end of transparent tube over bleeder valve and submerge other end into transparent container filled with clean brake fluid.
9. Open bleeder valve ½–¾ turn and allow fluid to flow into container until all air is purged from line.

Bleed Sequence

On models equipped with front & rear split system, righthand rear-lefthand rear-righthand front-lefthand front; if pressure bleeding, bleed front brakes together and rear brakes together.

On models equipped with diagonally split system, righthand rear-lefthand front-lefthand rear-righthand front.

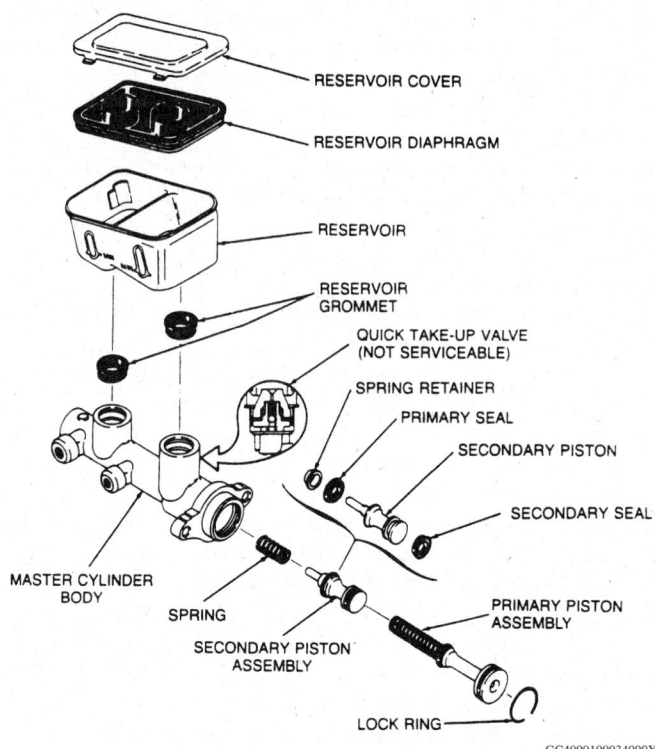

Fig. 10 Dual master cylinder assembly. Except Aurora, Bonneville, Corvette, CTS, LeSabre, Park Avenue, Saturn, Vibe & XLR

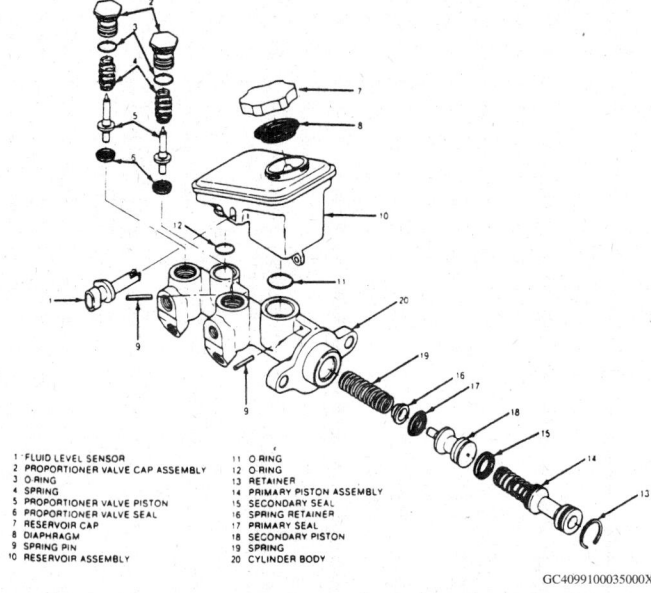

1 FLUID LEVEL SENSOR	11 O RING
2 PROPORTIONER VALVE CAP ASSEMBLY	12 O-RING
3 O-RING	13 RETAINER
4 SPRING	14 PRIMARY PISTON ASSEMBLY
5 PROPORTIONER VALVE PISTON	15 SECONDARY SEAL
6 PROPORTIONER VALVE SEAL	16 SPRING RETAINER
7 RESERVOIR CAP	17 PRIMARY SEAL
8 DIAPHRAGM	18 SECONDARY PISTON
9 SPRING PIN	19 SPRING
10 RESERVOIR ASSEMBLY	20 CYLINDER BODY

Fig. 11 Compact master cylinder assembly. Except Aurora, Bonneville, Corvette, CTS, LeSabre, Park Avenue, Saturn, Vibe & XLR

HYDRAULIC BRAKE SYSTEM FLUSH

If brake fluid is old, rusty or contaminated or whenever new components are installed in hydraulic system, the system must be flushed. Bleed brakes, allowing at least one quart of clean brake fluid to pass through system. Any rubber components in hydraulic system which were exposed to contaminated fluid must be replaced.

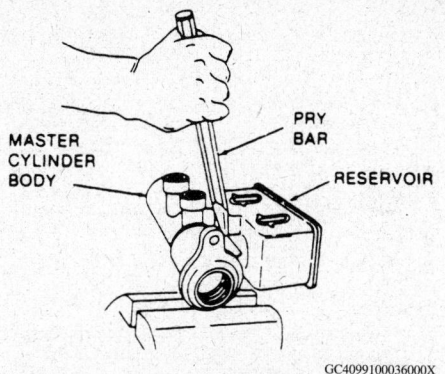

GC4099100036000X

Fig. 12 Master cylinder reservoir replacement. Composite type less retaining pins

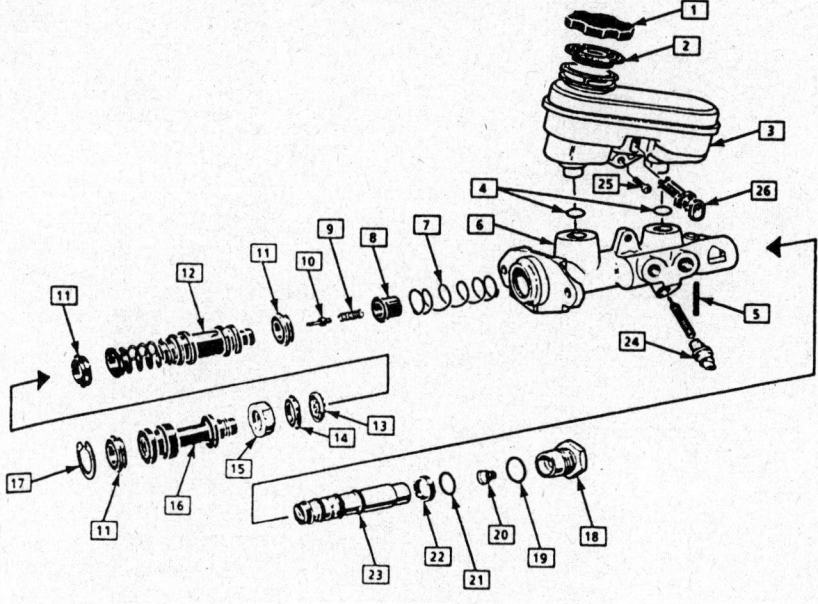

ARM66GC000000300

Fig. 13 Master cylinder reservoir replacement. Composite type w/retaining pins

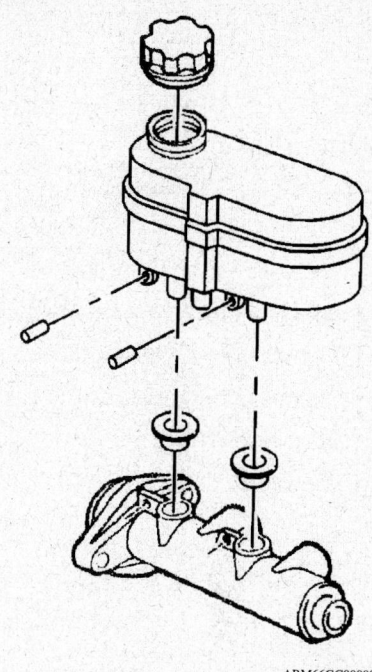

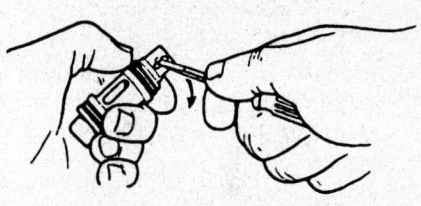

GC4099200038000X

Fig. 15 Lifting crimp on secondary spring retainer replacement. Corvette

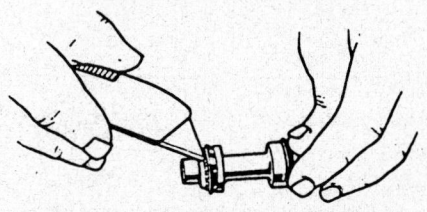

GC4099200039000X

Fig. 16 Seal retainer cutting. Corvette

1	RESERVOIR CAP	14	RECUPERATING TYPE CUP SEAL
2	RESERVOIR CAP DIAPHRAGM	15	RECUPERATING GUIDE
3	RESERVOIR BODY	16	PRIMARY PISTON
4	RESERVOIR 'O' RING	17	RETAINING RING
5	SECONDARY PISTON STOP PIN	18	ENG PLUG
6	CYLINDER BODY	19	END PLUG 'O' RING
7	SECONDARY RETURN SPRING	20	ELECTRICAL BIAS SPRING
8	SECONDARY SPRING RETAINER	21	PROPORTIONING VALVE O-RING
9	CENTER VALVE SPRING	22	PROPORTIONING VALVE SPACER
10	CENTER VALVE PLUNGER	23	PROPORTIONING VALVE/PRESSURE DIFFERENTIAL ASSEMBLY
11	'L' TYPE CUP SEAL	24	PRESSURE DIFFERENTIAL WARNING SWITCH ASSEMBLY
12	SECONDARY PISTON ASSEMBLY	25	RESERVOIR RETAINER SCREW
13	PRIMARY CUP RETAINING RING	26	FLUID LEVEL SWITCH ASSEMBLY

GC4099200037000X

Fig. 14 Composite master cylinder replacement. Corvette

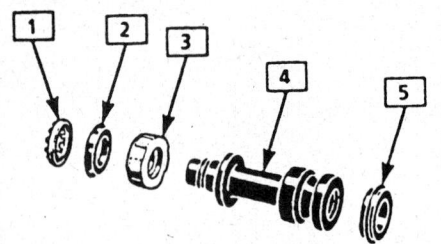

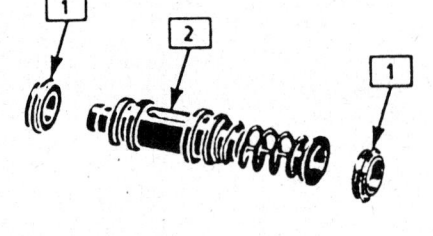

1	PRIMARY CUP RETAINING RING
2	RECUPERATING TYPE CUP SEAL
3	RECUPERATING GUIDE
4	PRIMARY PISTON
5	'L' TYPE CUP SEAL

GC4099200040000X

Fig. 17 Primary piston components. Corvette

| 1 | 'L' TYPE CUP SEAL |
| 2 | SECONDARY PISTON ASSEMBLY |

GC4099200041000X

Fig. 18 Secondary piston components. Corvette

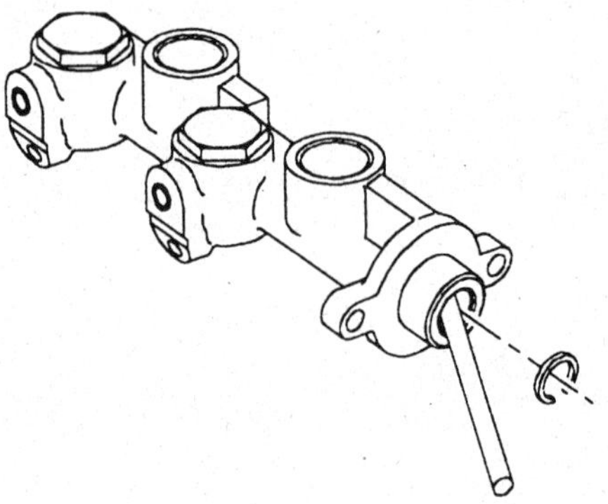

G34099100007000X

Fig. 19 Master cylinder retainer clip replacement. L & S-Series

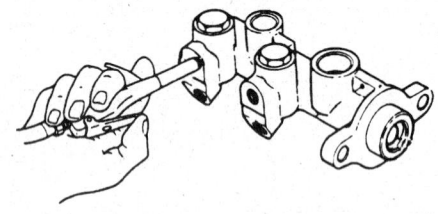

G34099100008000X

Fig. 20 Master cylinder piston replacement. L & S-Series

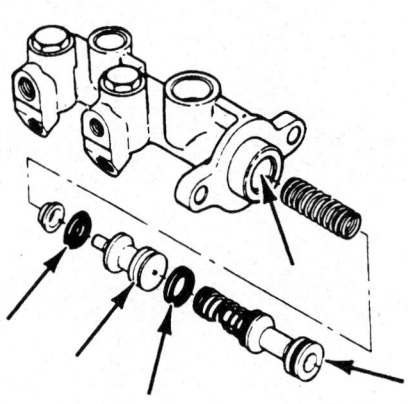

G34099100009000X

Fig. 21 Exploded view of master cylinder. L & S-Series

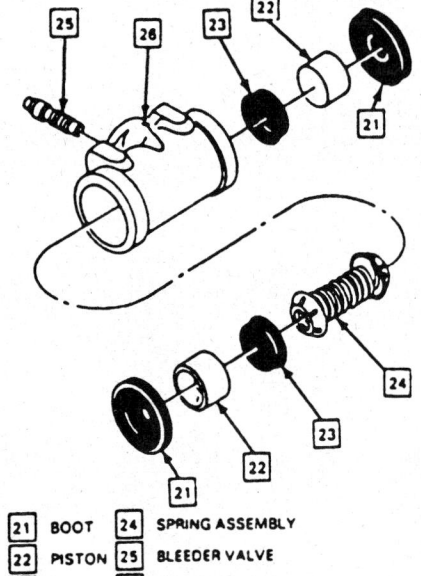

21	BOOT	24	SPRING ASSEMBLY
22	PISTON	25	BLEEDER VALVE
23	SEAL	26	CYLINDER BODY

GC4099100042000X

Fig. 22 Exploded view of wheel cylinder

HYDRAULIC BRAKE SYSTEM SPECIFICATIONS

Model	Year	Master Cylinder Bore Dia., Inch	Front Caliper Bore Dia., Inch	Rear Caliper Bore Dia., Inch	Wheel Cylinder Bore Dia., Inch
BUICK					
Century	2001–05	1.000	2.500	1.500	.874
LeSabre	2001–05	1.000④	2.500	1.500	—
LaCrosse	2005	1.000	2.500	1.500	—
Park Avenue	2001–05	1.000④	2.500	1.500	—
Regal	2001–04	1.000	2.500	1.500	—
CADILLAC					
Catera	2001	①	2.244	1.574	—
CTS	2003–05	—	1.780	1.780	—
DeVille	2001–05	1.000	2.500	1.500	—
Eldorado	2001–02	1.000	2.500	1.500	—
Seville	2001–04	1.000	2.520	1.500	.937
STS	2005	—	1.77	1.90	—
CHEVROLET/GEO					
Aveo	2004–05	0.87	2.12	2.12	0.81

Continued

HYDRAULIC BRAKE SYSTEM SPECIFICATIONS—Continued

Model	Year	Master Cylinder Bore Dia., Inch	Front Caliper Bore Dia., Inch	Rear Caliper Bore Dia., Inch	Wheel Cylinder Bore Dia., Inch
CHEVROLET/GEO					
Camaro	2001–02	1.000	2.500	1.595	.810
Cavalier	2001–05	.874	2.244	—	.689
Cobalt	2005	—	—	—	—
Corvette	2001–05	.930	1.500③	1.590	—
Impala	2001–05	—	—	—	—
Lumina	2001	.945	1.654	—	.874
Malibu	2001–05	1.000	2.362	—	.874
Metro	2001	.810	1.889	—	.685
Monte Carlo	2001–05	.945	1.654	—	.874
Prizm	2001–02	②	2.128	—	.688
OLDSMOBILE					
Alero	2001–04	1.000	2.360	1.500	.874
Aurora	2001–03	1.000④	2.500	1.50	—
Intrigue	2001–02	1.000	2.500	1.500	—
PONTIAC					
Bonneville	2001–05	1.000④	2.500	1.500	—
Firebird	2001–02	1.000	2.500	1.595	.810
G6	2005	1.000	2.362	—	.874
Grand Am	2001–05	1.000	2.360	1.500	.874
Grand Prix	2001–05	1.000	2.500	1.500	—
GTO	2004	—	—	—	—
Sunfire	200–05	.874	2.244	—	.689
Vibe	2003–05	—	—	—	—
SATURN					
ION	2003–05	—	—	—	—
L-Series	2001–05	—	2.24	1.38	—
S-Series	2001–04	.870	2.01	1.25	.750

① — Primary piston, .960 inch; secondary piston, .812 inch.

② — Less ABS, .812 inch; w/ABS, .875 inch.

③ — Dual piston caliper.

④ — Master cylinder cannot be overhauled.

TIGHTENING SPECIFICATIONS

Year	Component	Torque Ft. Lbs.
ALERO, CENTURY, GRAND PRIX, INTRIGUE, LACROSSE, LUMINA, MONTE CARLO & REGAL		
2001–05	Brake Hose Caliper	40
	Brake Pedal	30
	Brake Pedal Bracket, Lower	16
	Brake Pedal Bracket, Upper	18
	Brake Pedal Reinforcement Bracket	37
	Brake Pipe Fitting To Hose Drum	20
	Brake Pipe Fitting To Tube	11
	Front Brake Caliper Bleeder Screw	115①
	Master Cylinder	18
	Proportioning Valve Caps	20
	Rear Wheel Cylinder Bleeder Screw	62①

Continued

TIGHTENING
SPECIFICATIONS—Continued

Year	Component	Torque Ft. Lbs.
AURORA, BONNEVILLE, LESABRE, PARK AVENUE & LACROSSE		
2001–05	Booster To Pedal Bracket	15
	Bracket To Rear Drum Plate	80①
	Brake Hose Bracket	13
	Brake Hose To Caliper	33
	Brake Pedal Bracket	18
	Brake Pipe Fittings To Master Cylinder Tube	24
	Brake Pipe Fitting To Tube	11
	Brake Pipe To Proportioner	11
	Caliper Bleeder Valve	115①
	Master Cylinder	20
	Proportioner Valve To Brake Pipe Fitting	11
	Wheel Cylinder Bleeder Valve	88①
CAMARO & FIREBIRD		
2001–02	Battery Ground	11
	Brake Pedal	15
	Brake Pedal Bracket	18
	Brake Pedal Pivot	40
	Front Brake Hose Clip	115①
	Front Brake Hose Fitting	32
	Master Cylinder	21
	Master Cylinder Tube	24
	Rear Brake Center Hose Fitting	15
	Rear Brake Front Pipe To Rear Brake Center Hose	11
	Rear Brake Hose Fitting	32
	Rear Brake Pipe To Rear Brake Center Hose	18
	Rear Brake Pipe To Rear Brake Hose	13
CATERA		
2001	Bleeder Valve	71①
	Brake Pedal Bracket	15
	Brake Pipe Fittings	12
	Front Brake Hose	30
	Master Cylinder	16
	Power Brake Booster Support Bracket	13
	Power Brake Booster Vacuum Hose	13
	Power Steering Reservoir Bracket	62①
	Union Pipe Fitting	12
CAVALIER, CUTLASS, G6, GRAND AM, MALIBU & SUNFIRE		
2001–05	ABS Modulator Bleeder Valve	80
	Booster To Pedal Bracket	20
	Brake Hose To Caliper	32
	Brake Line Fitting At In-Line Proportioning Valve w/ABS	20
	Brake Pedal To Bracket	20
	Brake Pipe Tube	17
	Brake Pipe To Master Cylinder	17
	Caliper	38
	Caliper Bleeder Screw	115①
	Master Cylinder Booster	20
	Proportioner Valve Caps	20
	Vacuum Brake Booster To Brake Pedal	20
	Wheel Cylinder Bleeder Screw	62①
	Wheel Cylinder To Backing Plate	15

Continued

TIGHTENING
SPECIFICATIONS—Continued

Year	Component	Torque Ft. Lbs.
CORVETTE		
2001–05	Battery Ground	11
	Brake Booster	15
	Brake Caliper Bleed Screw	106①
	Brake Caliper Inlet Fitting	30
	Brake Pedal Pivot	21
	Brake Pipe To Brake Valve	13
	Brake Pipe To Flexible Brake Hose Tube	13
	Brake Pipe To Master Cylinder Tube	18
	Master Cylinder	21
	Telescoping Column Motor Mounting Bracket	62①
	Vacuum Booster To Brake Bracket	15
CTS		
2003–05	Brake Hose To Caliper	30
	Brake Master Cylinder	18
	Brake Pedal To Cowl	11
	Brake Pedal To Instrument Panel Carrier Mounting Studs	18
	Brake Pipe Fitting	11
	Brake Pipe Fitting At Master Cylinder	24
	Intermediate Brake Hose Assembly	89①
DEVILLE, ELDORADO & SEVILLE		
2001–05	Brake Booster	20
	Brake Caliper Bleed Screw	110①
	Brake Caliper Inlet Fitting	33
	Brake Hose Bracket	10
	Brake Pipe Fittings At Master Cylinder Tube	24
	Brake Pipe Fittings To Tube	11
	Engine Oil Cooler Line Retaining Bracket	53①
	Hydraulic Brake Booster	21
	Hydraulic Pump	80①
	Master Cylinder	20
	Park Brake Cable Bracket To Caliper	32
	Pedal To Booster	22
	Pedal To Cowl	12
	Proportioner Valve To Brake Pipe Fittings	11
ION		
2003–05	Brake Hose To Caliper	35
	Brake Master Cylinder	15
	Brake Master Cylinder Auxiliary Reservoir	89①
	Brake Pedal Bracket To Steering Column Bracket	18
	Brake Pipe Fitting At Front Brake Hose	14
	Brake Pipe Fittings At Master Cylinder	14
	Brake Pipe Fitting At Proportioning Valve Assembly	14
	Brake Pipe Fitting At Rear Brake Hose	14
	Cooling System Surge Tank	89①
	Electric Power Steering Cable	89①
	Front Brake Hose Bracket	18
	Proportioning Valve Assembly Bracket	18
	Proportioning Valve Assembly	18
	Underhood Electrical Center Bracket	18
	Underhood Electrical Center Bracket	89①
	Underhood Positive Battery Lug	11
	Vacuum Brake Booster	18

Continued

TIGHTENING
SPECIFICATIONS—Continued

Year	Component	Torque Ft. Lbs.
L-SERIES		
2001–05	Brake Pipe To Master Cylinder Nuts	12
	Caliper Bleed Valves	71①
	Cylinder To Brake Booster Nuts	25
	Proportioning Valve	12
	Rear Brake Hose	12
	Rear Crossover	12
METRO & PRIZM		
2001–02	Booster Assembly Mounting Nuts	115①
	Brake Fluid & Fuel Pipe Guard Plate Nut	10
	Brake Pedal Shaft	17
	Brake Pipe Fitting	12
	Caliper Bolt	17
	Master Cylinder Brake Pipe Flare Nut	12
	Master Cylinder Mounting Nuts	115①
	Piston Stopper Bolt	89①
	Push Rod Clevis Locknut	18
	Stop Lamp Switch Locknut	71①
S-SERIES		
2001–02	Brake Hose To Caliper/Wheel Cylinder	36
	Brake Pipes To Brake Hoses	18
	Brake Pipes To Master Cylinder	24
	Brake Pipes To Union	14
	Front Bleeder Valve	97①
	Master Cylinder To Brake Booster	20
	Rear Bleeder Valve	66①
STS		
2005	Brake Hose to Caliper Bolt	37
	Mater Cylinder Mounting Nuts	18
	Brake Pipe Fittings at Master Cylinder	28
	Brake Pipe Fitting –Tube	13
VIBE		
2003–05	Bleeder Valve	74①
	Brake Hose Bracket	21
	Bracket Hose To Bracket Pipe Fitting	11
	Brake Hose To Caliper Fitting	21
	Brake Pedal Bracket & Vacuum Booster	112①
	Brake Pedal Shaft	27
	Brake Pipe Flare	11
	Cruise Control Actuator Bracket	31
	Master Cylinder	110①
	Master Cylinder Piston Stopper	88①
	Proportioning Valve	48①
	Vacuum Booster Push Rod Nut	19

① — Inch lbs.

POWER BRAKE UNITS

NOTE: On Air Bag Equipped Models, Refer To "Air Bag System Precautions" Located In The Front Of This Manual For System Disarming & Arming Procedures.

NOTE: Refer To "Computer Relearn Procedures" Located In The Front Of This Manual When Battery Power To The Computer Has Been Interrupted.

INDEX

APPLICATION CHART

Model	Power Brake Type
Except Metro, Prizm & Vibe	AC-Delco Tandem Diaphragm
Metro	AC-Delco Single Diaphragm
Prizm & Vibe	Toyota/GM Single Diaphragm

PRECAUTIONS

1. After disassembling power brake unit, soak metal components in solvent.
2. Use only alcohol on components containing rubber. After components have been thoroughly cleaned and rinsed in solvent, they should be washed again in clean alcohol before assembly.
3. Use compressed air to blow dirt and cleaning fluid from recesses and internal passages.
4. Always use all components furnished in repair kit.
5. **Use extreme caution when disassembling power assist mechanisms. If internal spring tension is suddenly released it could cause damage or personal injury.**
6. **Cadillac CTS and XLR brake boosters are not serviceable and should be replaced as an assembly.**

DESCRIPTION

AC-Delco Tandem Diaphragm Type

This unit utilizes a vacuum power chamber, consisting of a front and rear shell, housing divider, front and rear diaphragm, plate assemblies, hydraulic pushrod and a diaphragm return spring, **Fig. 1.**

In normal operating mode, with service brakes in released position, the booster operates with vacuum on both sides of its diaphragms. When brakes are applied, air at atmospheric pressure is admitted to one side of each diaphragm to provide power assist. When the service brake is released, atmospheric air is shut off from one side of each diaphragm. The air is then drawn from the booster through the vacuum check valve to the vacuum source.

AC-Delco Single Diaphragm Type

The AC-Delco power booster assembly is located along the bulkhead in the left-hand side engine compartment, between the brake pedal and master cylinder, **Fig. 2.** It is designed to take advantage of the vacuum produced by the engine. The applied force created when brake pedal is applied is mechanically increased with assistance of engine vacuum.

Toyota/GM Single Diaphragm Type

The Toyota/GM single diaphragm type booster assembly is located between the master cylinder and brake pedal, **Fig. 3.** When the brake pedal is depressed, the force is transmitted to the master cylinder piston through the valve operating rod, booster air valve, reaction disc and piston rod. The force of the booster piston is de-veloped because of the pressure difference between the front and rear chambers.

TROUBLESHOOTING

Brakes Grab

1. Contaminated, worn or faulty brake linings.
2. Drum or brake rotor out-of-round.
3. Faulty brake booster.

Hard Pedal/Brakes Inefficient

1. Contaminated, glazed or faulty brake linings.
2. Frozen caliper piston.
3. Faulty vacuum pump, or leak in booster vacuum supply system.
4. Faulty brake booster.

Slow Or No Release

1. Faulty pushrod adjustment.
2. Bind in linkage.

ADJUSTMENTS

Brake Pedal

TOYOTA/GM SINGLE DIAPHRAGM TYPE

1. With engine running and brake pedal

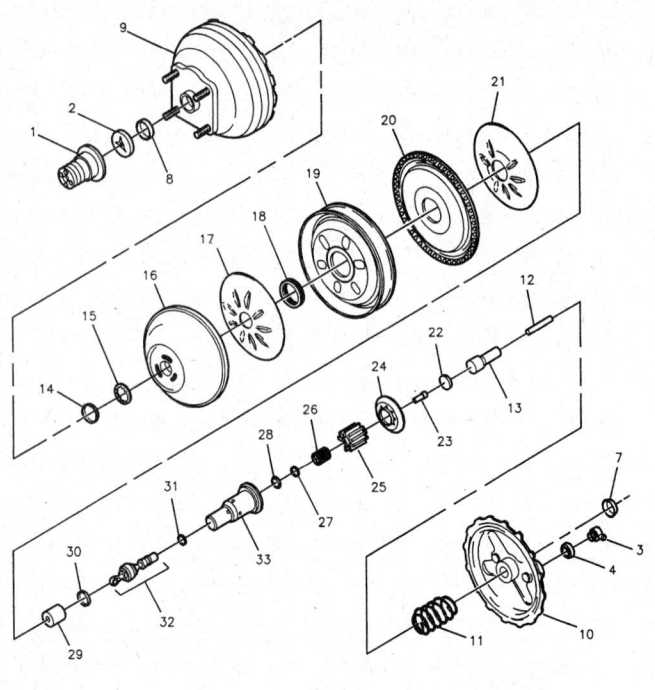

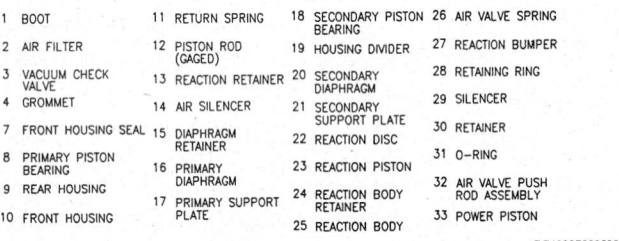

1	BOOT	11	RETURN SPRING	18	SECONDARY PISTON BEARING
2	AIR FILTER	12	PISTON ROD (GAGED)	19	HOUSING DIVIDER
3	VACUUM CHECK VALVE	13	REACTION RETAINER	20	SECONDARY DIAPHRAGM
4	GROMMET	14	AIR SILENCER	21	SECONDARY SUPPORT PLATE
7	FRONT HOUSING SEAL	15	DIAPHRAGM RETAINER	22	REACTION DISC
8	PRIMARY PISTON BEARING	16	PRIMARY DIAPHRAGM	23	REACTION PISTON
9	REAR HOUSING	17	PRIMARY SUPPORT PLATE	24	REACTION BODY RETAINER
10	FRONT HOUSING			25	REACTION BODY
				26	AIR VALVE SPRING
				27	REACTION BUMPER
				28	RETAINING RING
				29	SILENCER
				30	RETAINER
				31	O-RING
				32	AIR VALVE PUSH ROD ASSEMBLY
				33	POWER PISTON

GC4099700059000X

Fig. 1   Exploded view of AC-Delco tandem diaphragm booster

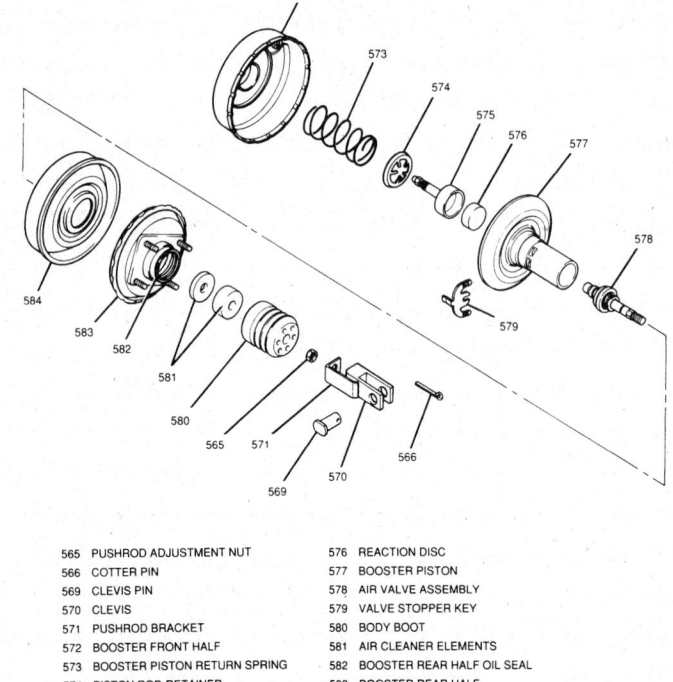

565	PUSHROD ADJUSTMENT NUT	576	REACTION DISC
566	COTTER PIN	577	BOOSTER PISTON
569	CLEVIS PIN	578	AIR VALVE ASSEMBLY
570	CLEVIS	579	VALVE STOPPER KEY
571	PUSHROD BRACKET	580	BODY BOOT
572	BOOSTER FRONT HALF	581	AIR CLEANER ELEMENTS
573	BOOSTER PISTON RETURN SPRING	582	BOOSTER REAR HALF OIL SEAL
574	PISTON ROD RETAINER	583	BOOSTER REAR HALF
575	PISTON ROD	584	DIAPHRAGM

GC4099400052000A

Fig. 2   Exploded view of AC-Delco single diaphragm booster

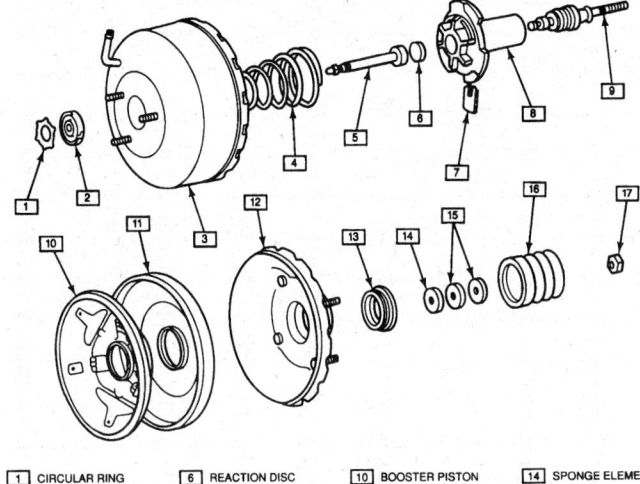

1	CIRCULAR RING	6	REACTION DISC	10	BOOSTER PISTON	14	SPONGE ELEMENT
2	BODY SEAL	7	STOPPER KEY	11	DIAPHRAGM	15	FELT ELEMENT
3	FRONT BODY	8	VALVE BODY	12	REAR BODY	16	BOOT
4	DIAPHRAGM SPRING	9	OPERATING ROD	13	BODY SEAL	17	NUT
5	PUSH ROD						

GC4099100050000A

Fig. 3   Exploded view of Toyota/GM brake booster

in rest position, measure distance between face of pedal and floor mat.

2. Distance should be 5.850–6.244 inches.

3. If distance is not as specified, adjust pedal height as follows:
   a. Remove lefthand lower instrument panel trim section and air duct.
   b. Loosen stop lamp switch sufficiently to access pedal adjustment.
   c. Loosen locknut and rotate pedal pushrod as required to obtain specified pedal height. Tighten locknut.
   d. Adjust brake lamp switch position so plunger lightly contacts pedal stopper and brake lamps are off when pedal is released.
   e. Inspect pedal free travel.

4. With engine stopped, depress brake pedal several times to ensure there is no vacuum pressure in booster.

5. Release pedal and press pedal down until beginning of resistance is felt. Measure pedal travel. **Pedal free travel is amount brake booster air valve is moved by pedal pushrod.**

6. If pedal travel is not .12–.24 inch, adjust pedal freeplay as follows:
   a. Adjust pedal free travel by loosening locknut and rotating pedal pushrod.
   b. Ensure brake lamp switch and

pedal height are properly adjusted.
   c. Start engine and confirm free travel still exists.
   d. Inspect pedal reserve distance.

7. Release parking brake and start engine.

8. Depress brake pedal with applied force of 110 lbs., and measure distance from face of pedal to floor mat.

9. Pedal reserve distance should not be more than 3.35 inches.

10. If pedal reserve distance does not meet specifications, inspect and repair

brake system as needed.

Pushrod

Proper adjustment of the master cylinder pushrod is required to ensure proper operation of the power brake system. A pushrod that is too long will cause the master cylinder piston to close off the compensating port, preventing hydraulic pressure from being released and resulting in brake drag. A pushrod that is too short will cause excessive brake pedal travel and cause groaning

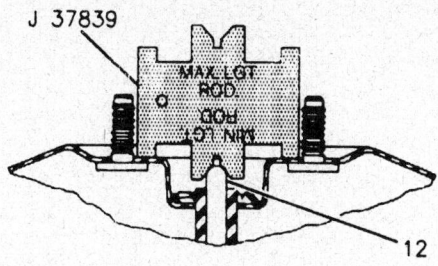

12 OUTPUT BUTTON / ROD

GC4099700063000X

Fig. 4   Master cylinder measurement. AC-Delco tandem diaphragm type

noises to come from the booster when the brakes are applied. A properly adjusted pushrod that remains assembled to the booster with which it was matched during production should not require service adjustment. However, if the booster, master cylinder or pushrod are serviced, the pushrod may require adjustment.

There are two methods that can be used to inspect for proper pushrod length and installation. These are the gauge method and air method. Usually, if the power unit pushrod requires adjustment, use the power unit repair kit gauge. The gauge measures from the end of the pushrod to the power unit shell.

GAUGE METHOD

AC-DELCO TANDEM DIAPHRAGM TYPE

The master cylinder pushrod length is fixed and is usually only inspected after the unit has been overhauled. This procedure can be performed with the unit removed from the vehicle if a suitable vacuum source is available.

1. Assemble booster unit and install pushrod. Ensure pushrod is fully seated.
2. Apply 20 inches or maximum engine vacuum to booster.
3. Position gauge tool No. J-37839, or equivalent, over pushrod, **Fig. 4**.
4. Replace booster if output button length is not within gauge limits.
5. Install power unit and inspect adjustment.
6. Ensure master cylinder compensating port is open with engine running and brake pedal released.

AC-DELCO & TOYOTA/GM SINGLE DIAPHRAGM TYPES

The length of the booster piston rod is adjusted to provide specified clearance between the piston rod end and master cylinder piston. Before making an adjustment, push piston rod several times to ensure reaction disc is in place. Ensure gasket is installed to master cylinder and keep inside of booster at atmospheric pressure.

1. Place booster pin rod gauge tool No. J-39567, or equivalent, on master cylinder and push pin until it contacts piston, **Fig. 5**.

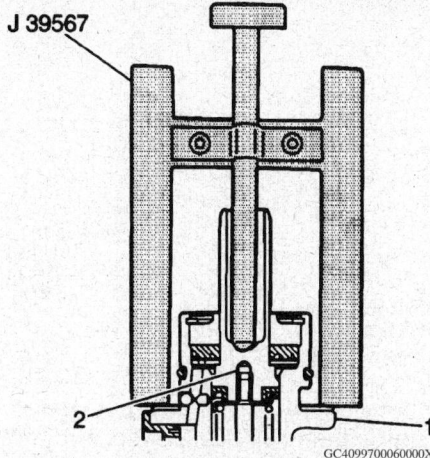

GC4099700060000X

Fig. 5   Master cylinder adjustment tool. AC-Delco & Toyota/GM single diaphragm type

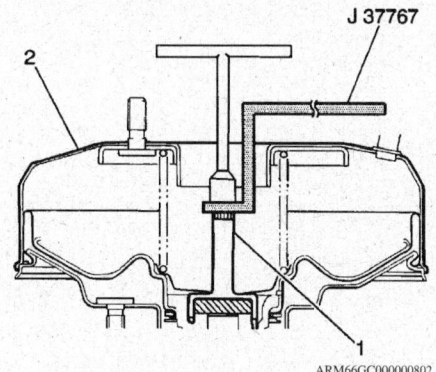

ARM66GC000000802

Fig. 7   Booster piston rod adjustment tool. AC-Delco & Toyota/GM single diaphragm type

2. Turn tool upside down and place it on booster. Adjust booster piston rod length until rod end contacts pin head.
3. Adjust clearance by turning adjusting bolt of piston rod, **Fig. 6**.
4. There should be no clearance between booster piston rod and gauge tool.
5. If measurement is not within specifications, use tool No J-37767, or equivalent, to hold brake booster piston rod, to adjustment nut clearance to specifications, **Fig. 7**.
6. **On Metro models,** adjust pushrod clevis length to 3.92–3.96 inches, **Fig. 8**. **Torque** locknut to 18 ft. lbs.

AIR METHOD

1. Ensure master cylinder mounting nuts are tight.
2. Remove master cylinder filler cap.
3. With brake released, force compressed air into hydraulic outlet of master cylinder. **Regulate air pressure to value of approximately 5 psi to prevent spraying brake fluid from master cylinder.**
4. If air passes through compensating port, which is smaller of two holes in bottom of master cylinder reservoir, adjustment is satisfactory.

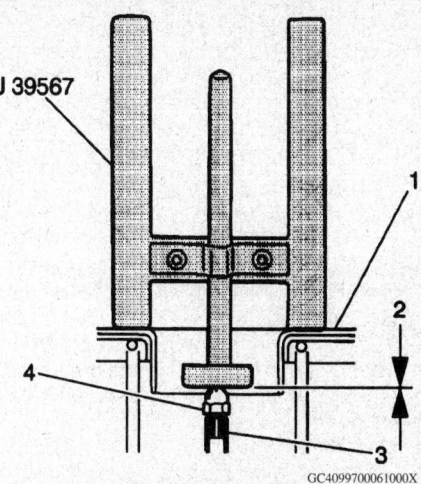

GC4099700061000X

Fig. 6   Booster piston rod adjustment. AC-Delco & Toyota/GM single diaphragm type

5. If air does not flow through compensating port, adjust pushrod as required, either by means of adjustment screw (if provided) or by adding shims between master cylinder and power unit shell until air flows freely.
6. Connect brake lines and bleed system.

GENERAL SERVICE

Two basic types of power assist mechanisms are used: vacuum assist diaphragm assemblies, which use engine vacuum or, in some cases vacuum pressure developed by an external vacuum pump. The second type is a hydraulic pressure assist mechanism, which use pressure developed by an external pump (usually the power steering pump). Both systems act to increase the force exerted on the master cylinder piston by the operator. This in turn increases the hydraulic pressure delivered to the wheel cylinders while decreasing driver effort required to obtain acceptable stopping performance.

Vacuum assist units are similar in operation and get their energy by opposing engine vacuum to atmospheric pressure. A piston and cylinder, flexible diaphragm (bellows) utilize this energy to provide brake assistance. The fundamental difference between these types of vacuum assist systems lies simply in how the diaphragm within the power unit is suspended when the brakes are not applied.

In order to properly diagnose vacuum assist system faults it is important to know whether the diaphragm within a power unit is air suspended or vacuum suspended. Air-suspended units are under atmospheric pressure until the brakes are applied. Engine vacuum is then admitted, causing the piston or diaphragm to move (or the bellows to collapse). Vacuum-suspended types are balanced with engine vacuum until the brake pedal is depressed, allowing atmospheric pressure to unbalance the unit and apply force to the brake system.

Regardless of whether the brakes are vacuum or hydraulically assisted, certain general service procedures apply. Only specified, clean brake fluid should be used in brake systems. On hydro-boost systems, use of the specified hydraulic fluid in the boost circuit is essential to proper system operation. Care must be taken not to mix the fluids of the two separate operating circuits.

POWER BRAKE UNIT SERVICE

Hydro–boost brake boosters are not serviceable and should be replaced as an assembly.

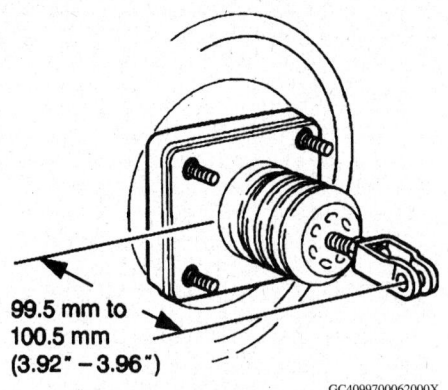

99.5 mm to
100.5 mm
(3.92″ – 3.96″)

GC4099700062000X

Fig. 8 Pushrod clevis length adjustment. AC-Delco diaphragm type

FRONT WHEEL DRIVE AXLES

NOTE: On Air Bag Equipped Models, Refer To "Air Bag System Precautions" Located In The Front Of This Manual For System Disarming & Arming Procedures.

NOTE: Refer To "Computer Relearn Procedures" Located In The Front Of This Manual When Battery Power To The Computer Has Been Interrupted.

INDEX

PRECAUTIONS

Battery Ground Cable

Prior to service, disconnect battery ground cable and isolate as required.

Joint Protection

On models equipped with tripod joints on inboard axles, care must be taken not to overextend joints.

On models equipped with ball type constant velocity inboard joints, install inner drive joint seal protector tool No. J34754 and axle boot protector tool No. J28712, or equivalents.

On models equipped with tripod inboard joints, install axle boot seal protector tool No. J28712, and tool No. J33162, or equivalents.

DESCRIPTION

Front wheel drive systems consist of an inner and outer constant velocity joint connected by an axle shaft, **Figs. 1 through 9.**

The inner joint is completely flexible, and can move in and out. The outer joint is also flexible, but cannot move in and out.

TROUBLESHOOTING

Click Noise In Turns

A click noise occurring during turns may be caused by a worn or damaged wheel drive shaft outer joint. This click is caused by wear and/or damage to the constant velocity joint bearings and/or races. Commonly, this damage or wear is caused by the loss of lubricating grease from the constant velocity joint and the entry of foreign material or contaminates.

1. Carefully inspect wheel drive shaft seals for cuts, tears or other damage which may allow lubricating grease to escape.
2. If inspection reveals no visual evidence of wear or damage, it may be necessary to remove wheel drive shaft from vehicle and manipulate outer joint manually.
3. Any binding or impeded movement of

joint may indicate damage which could contribute to concern.

Clunk When Accelerating from Coast

A clunk noise occurring when accelerating from coast or a standing start may be caused by a worn or damaged wheel drive shaft inner joint. The common cause of wheel drive shaft inner joint damage is the loss of lubricating grease and/or the presence of foreign material and contaminates in the joint. This usually occurs as a result of a torn or damaged inner joint seal.

1. Carefully inspect wheel drive shaft seal for cuts, tears or other damage that may allow loss of lubricating grease and/or entry of contaminates.
2. If inspection reveals no visual evidence of wear or damage, it may be necessary to remove wheel drive shaft from vehicle and manipulate inner joint manually.
3. **Do not allow joint to separate from**

wheel drive shaft bar.

4. Any binding or impeded movement of joint may indicate damage which could contribute to concern.

Clunk Noise When Accelerating During Turns

A clunk noise that occurs while accelerating during turns may be caused by wear and/or damage to the inboard and the outboard joints in combination. The loss of lubricant and/or the presence of contaminates can cause damage to the internal components of the joints.

1. Carefully inspect joint seals for cuts, tears or other damage.
2. If inspection reveals no visual evidence of wear or damage, it may be necessary to remove wheel drive shaft from vehicle and manipulate joints manually.
3. **Do not allow joints to separate from wheel drive shaft bar.**
4. Any binding or impeded movement of joints may indicate damage which could contribute to concern.

DRIVESHAFT
REPLACE

Alero & Grand Am

1. Raise and support vehicle, then remove tire and wheel assembly.
2. Disconnect tie rod from knuckle.
3. Prevent rotor from turning by inserting suitable drift into caliper and rotor, then remove axle shaft nut.
4. Disconnect stabilizer link and separate lower control arm ball joint from steering knuckle.
5. Remove hub and bearing using front hub spindle remover tool No. J28733-B, or equivalent.
6. Separate drive axle from transaxle using axle shaft remover tool No. J33008 and slide hammer tool J2619-01, or equivalents. **Do not overextend drive axle.**
7. Remove drive axle.
8. Reverse procedure to install. **On 2003–04 models,** there two style axles nuts with different tightening specifications, **Figs. 10 and 11.**

Aurora, Bonneville, DeVille, Eldorado, LeSabre, Park Avenue & Seville
REMOVAL

1. Raise and support vehicle, then remove tire and wheel assemblies.
2. Loosen or remove stabilizer shaft link.
3. Remove ball joint cotter pin and nut.
4. Loosen ball joint from steering knuckle

using ball joint separator tool No. J43828, or equivalent.
5. Separate ball joint from steering knuckle using suitable pry bar between suspension support and lower control arm.
6. Prevent rotor from turning by inserting suitable drift or screwdriver into caliper and rotor, then remove hub nut.
7. Disconnect axle from hub using front hub spindle remover tool No. J28733-B, or equivalent.
8. Position strut and knuckle rearward.
9. Remove drive axle from transaxle using axle shaft remover tool No. J33008 and slide hammer tool No. J2619-01, or equivalents. **Do not overextend drive axle.**

INSTALLATION

1. Inspect tripot housing at transmission seal surface for corrosion. Remove corrosion by sanding sealing surface with 320 grit emery cloth.
2. Lubricate tripot housing surface with suitable transmission fluid.
3. Push axle into transaxle. Ensure drive axle is seated by grasping inner joint housing and pulling. **Do not pull on drive axle shaft.**
4. Install drive axle into transaxle by placing suitable screwdriver into groove on joint housing and tapping until axle is seated.
5. Insert drive axle into hub and bearing, then install new hub nut.
6. Prevent rotor from turning by inserting suitable drift or screwdriver into caliper and rotor, then tighten axle nut.
7. Attach ball joint to knuckle.
8. Install stabilizer shaft link.
9. Install wheels and lower vehicle.

Aveo

1. Raise and support vehicle, then remove tire and wheel assemblies.
2. Remove mounting nuts and bolts, then the engine under cover.
3. Remove and discard axle shaft caulking nut.
4. Remove lower ball joint nut and separate steering knuckle from lower ball joint using ball joint remover tool No. KM-507-C, or equivalent.
5. Remove tie rod nut and separate tie rod end using lower ball joint using ball joint remover tool.
6. Remove mounting bolts and rear mounting bracket.
7. Remove damping block connection mounting nut and bolt.
8. Push drive axle shaft from wheel hub.
9. Place suitable drain pan below transaxle to catch escaping fluid.
10. Remove drive axle from transaxle using axle shaft remover tool No. KM-460-B, or equivalent.
11. Cap transaxle drive opening.
12. Reverse procedure to install, noting the following:
    a. **Do not damage seals.**
    b. Loosely install new axle shaft caulking nut.
    c. Loosely install wheel lug nuts.
    d. Lower vehicle to floor.

e. Tighten wheel lugs nuts,
f. Install and tighten axle shaft caulking nut.
g. Peen caulking nut with suitable punch and hammer until nut is locked into place on axle shaft hub.

Cavalier & Sunfire

1. Raise and support vehicle, then remove wheel and tire assembly.
2. Remove tie rod end to steering knuckle retaining nut, then disconnect tie rod end from steering knuckle.
3. Prevent rotor from turning by inserting suitable drift or punch into caliper and rotor, then remove drive axle nut and washer.
4. Remove ball joint cotter pin and nut, then separate joint from steering knuckle using ball joint separator tool No. J38892, or equivalent.
5. Disconnect ABS sensor wire.
6. Disconnect stabilizer link and separate joint using suitable ball joint separator.
7. Disconnect axle from hub and bearing using front hub spindle tool No. J28733-A, or equivalent.
8. Separate hub and bearing from axle.
9. Move strut and knuckle rearward.
10. Remove inner joint from transaxle using axle remover tool No. J33008, drive axle removal extension tool No. J29794 and slide hammer tool No. J2619-01, or equivalents.
11. Reverse procedure to install.

Century, Grand Prix, Impala, Intrigue, Lumina, Monte Carlo & Regal

1. Raise and support vehicle, then remove tire and wheel assembly.
2. Remove stabilizer link.
3. Prevent rotor from turning by inserting suitable drift or flat-bladed tool into caliper and rotor, then remove drive axle nut.
4. Disconnect tie rod from steering knuckle.
5. Disconnect ball joint from steering knuckle using ball joint/stud separator tool No. J41820, or equivalent.
6. **On righthand drive axle,** separate drive axle from transaxle using axle shaft tool No. J3308, extension tool No. J29794 and puller tool No. J2619-01, or equivalents.
7. **On lefthand side drive axle,** use frame for leverage and separate drive axle from transaxle using suitable screwdriver or pry bar in inner joint groove.
8. **On all drive axles,** reverse procedure to install, noting the following:
    a. Install axle seal protector tool No. J37292-A, or equivalent, to righthand side of transaxle so it can be pulled out after drive axle is installed.
    b. Install new axle nut.

G6 & Malibu MAXX

1. Raise and support vehicle, then remove tire and wheel assembly.
2. Remove front wheel drive shaft nut.
3. Loosen outer tie rod inner tie rod jam nut.
4. Remove outer tie rod to steering knuckle prevailing nut. Discard nut.
5. Separate tie rod from steering knuckle using tie rod separator tool No. J24319-B, or equivalent. **Do not free ball stud by using pickle fork or wedge-type tool.**
6. Remove outer from inner tie rod.
7. **On models equipped with 3.5L engine,** proceed as follows:
   a. If removing lefthand drive shaft, remove side transmission mount as outlined under "Engine Mount, Replace" in "3.5L Engine" section of "G6 & Malibu MAXX" chapter.
   b. If removing righthand drive shaft, remove engine mount as outlined under "Engine Mount, Replace" in "3.5L Engine" section of "G6 & Malibu MAXX" chapter.
8. **On all models,** remove front and rear lower control arm bushing to frame bolts and nuts.
9. Mark orientation of lower control arm ball stud to steering knuckle pinch bolt for installation alignment.
10. Remove pinch bolt and discard.
11. Separate ball stud from steering knuckle.
12. Separate front wheel drive axle from shaft bearing using hub spindle remover tool No. J42129, or equivalent.
13. Partially installed to protect nut threads.
14. Remove wheel drive shaft from transaxle.
15. Separate axle from transaxle using axle shaft remover tool No. J33008-A, axle shaft remover extension tool No. J29794 and slide hammer tool No. J2619-01, or equivalents.
16. Reverse procedure to install, noting the following:
   a. Tighten lower control arm nuts with vehicle at proper Z trim height. Refer to "Vehicle Ride Height" in "Wheel Alignment" section of "G6 & Malibu MAXX" chapter.
   b. Install new ball stud to steering knuckle pinch bolt.
   c. **Torque** ball stud to steering knuckle pinch nut to 37 ft. lbs.
   d. Reverse nut ¾ turn.
   e. **Torque** nut to 37 ft. lbs.
   f. Final tighten an additional 40°.
   g. Tighten nuts and bolts with front suspension loaded using suitable jackstand.
   h. **Torque** front and rear bushing to frame bolts to 37 ft. lbs.
   i. Tighten bushing bolts an additional 90°.

ION

1. Raise and support vehicle, then remove tire and wheel assemblies.
2. Remove stabilizer link as outlined under "Front Suspension & Steering" in "Ion" chapter.
3. Remove driveshaft mounting nut and secure brake rotor using suitable flat bladed tool to prevent rotor from turning, **Fig. 12.**
4. Disconnect outer tie rod from knuckle as outlined under "Front Suspension & Steering" in "ION" chapter.
5. Remove wheel speed sensor electrical connector from sensor and secure away from ball joint.
6. Remove ball joint as outlined under "Front Suspension & Steering" in "ION" chapter.
7. Remove driveshaft from transaxle using tool Nos. J45341 and SA9173G, or equivalents, **Fig. 13.**
8. Remove axle shaft from transaxle.
9. Reverse procedure to install.

L-Series
REMOVAL

1. Depress brake pedal, then remove cotter pin and drive axle nut. Discard cotter pin and nut.
2. Raise and support vehicle, then remove tire and wheel assembly.
3. Remove tie rod end torque prevailing nut. Discard nut.
4. Separate tie rod end from steering knuckle using removal tool No. SA91100-C, or equivalent. **Do not use wedge type tool to separate joint.**
5. Remove lower control arm to steering knuckle bolt and nut, then separate lower control arm from steering knuckle.
6. Pull outer end of drive axle out of wheel hub while pulling knuckle/strut away. If it is difficult to separate axle from hub, tap on end of drive axle shaft using suitable wood block and hammer.
7. Support or suspend drive axle using mechanics wire.
8. Place suitable container under transaxle to catch fluid spillage.
9. Remove drive axle by prying axle out of transaxle using suitable pry bar. **Do not contact transaxle oil seal.**

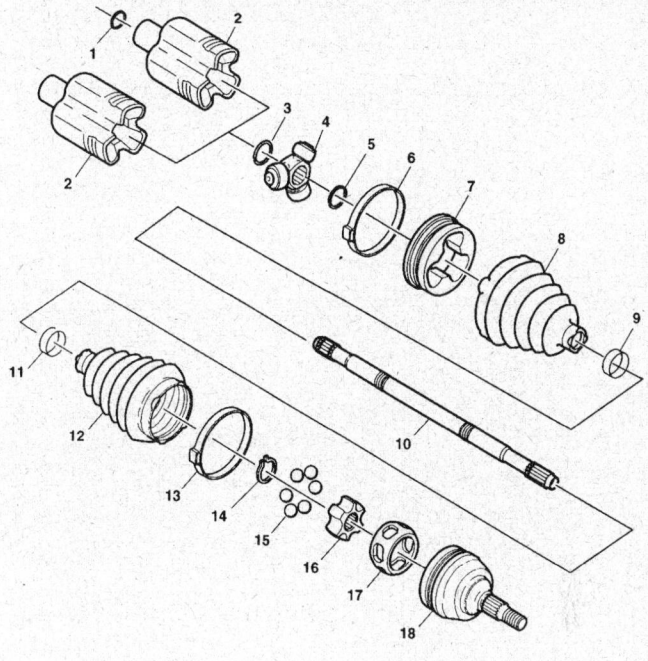

(1) Retaining Ring
(2) Retainer and Housing Assembly
(3) Shaft Retaining Ring
(4) Tripot Spider Assembly
(5) Spacer Ring
(6) Boot Retaining Clamp
(7) Tripot Trilobal Bushing
(8) Halfshaft Inboard Boot
(9) Swage Ring
(10) Halfshaft Bar
(11) Swage Ring
(12) Halfshaft Outboard Boot
(13) Boot Retaining Clamp
(14) Race Retaining Ring
(15) Chrome Alloy Ball
(16) CV Joint Inner Race
(17) CV Joint Cage
(18) CV Joint Outer Race

GC3039900339000X

Fig. 1 Exploded view of front drive axle. All models except Aveo, Cavalier, Metro, Prizm, Sunfire, Saturn & Vibe

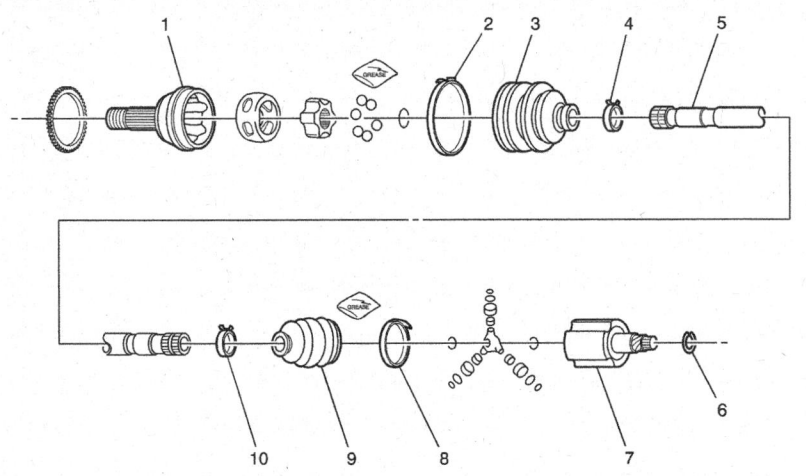

1. C/V Joint
2. Seal Retaining Clamp
3. Drive Axle Outboard Seal
4. Seal Retaining Clamp
5. Axle Shaft
6. Snap Ring
7. Tripot Housing
8. Seal Retaining Clamp
9. Drive Axle Inboard Seal
10. Seal Retaining Clamp

ARM0400000001364

Fig. 2   Exploded view of front drive axle. Aveo w/automatic transaxle

10. Remove and discard shaft retaining rings.

INSTALLATION

1. Install new retaining ring.
2. **On models equipped with automatic transaxle,** apply output shaft lubricant No. 7847638, or equivalent, to output shaft splines.
3. **On models equipped with manual transaxle,** install transaxle seal protector tool No. SA91112-T, or equivalent.
4. **On all models,** insert drive axle into transaxle.
5. After drive axle splines have passed transaxle oil seal, remove seal protector.
6. Fully seat drive axle into transaxle. **Do not tighten now.**
7. Insert drive axle outer end into wheel hub, then the hub washer and new nut.
8. Install lower control arm ball stud into steering knuckle.
9. Install tie rod end into steering knuckle.
10. Fully seat tie rod end using installer tool No. J44015, or equivalent, then install new nut.
11. **Torque** axle shaft nut to 85 ft. lbs.
12. Loosen nut until it turns freely by hand.
13. **Torque** shaft nut to 15 ft. lbs.
14. Tighten nut an additional 90° and align cotter pin slot.
15. Install new cotter pin.
16. Install wheels.
17. Lower vehicle from hoist.
18. **Torque** axle shaft to hub nut to 74–118 ft. lbs.
19. Release nut until it is free to turn by hand.
20. **Torque** axle shaft-to-hub nut 15 ft. lbs.
21. Final tighten nut an additional 90°.

LaCrosse

1. Raise and support vehicle, then remove tire and wheel assembly.
2. Remove mounting bolt and nut, then the stabilizer shaft link.
3. Prevent rotor from turning by Inserting suitable drift or flat-bladed tool into caliper and rotor, then remove front wheel drive shaft nut .
4. Remove prevailing torque nut from outer tie rod.
5. Loosen jam nut on inner tie rod.
6. Remove outer tie rod from steering knuckle using universal steering linkage puller tool No. J24319-B, or equivalent. **Do not attempt to disconnect steering linkage joint by driving wedge between joint and attached part.**
7. Remove outer from inner tie rod assembly.
8. Separate ball stud from steering knuckle by rotating nut counterclockwise and using ball joint/stud separator tool No. J41820, or equivalent.
9. Separate front wheel drive axle from shaft bearing using hub spindle remover tool No. J42129, or equivalent. Partially installed not to protect threads.
10. Remove drive axle from transaxle using axle shaft remover tools Nos. J33008-A. J29794, J29794 and J2619-01, or equivalents.
11. Reverse procedure to install,

Malibu

1. Raise and support vehicle, then remove wheel and tire assembly.
2. Disconnect steering knuckle tie rod.
3. Prevent rotor from turning by inserting

suitable drift or punch into caliper and rotor, then remove drive axle nut and washer.
4. Disconnect stabilizer link.
5. Remove ball joint cotter pin and nut, then separate ball joint from knuckle using ball joint separator tool No. J38892, or equivalent.
6. Disconnect axle from hub and bearing using front hub spindle tool No. J28733, or equivalent.
7. Remove righthand axle using axle shaft remover tool No. J3308 and slide hammer tool No. J2619-01, or equivalents.
8. Remove lefthand axle by separating shaft from transaxle using suitable flat-bladed screwdriver in tripod joint groove.
9. Reverse procedure to install. Reverse procedure to install. **On 2003–04 models,** there two style axles nuts with different tightening specifications, **Figs. 10 and 11.**

Metro

1. Raise and support vehicle, then remove tire and wheel assembly.
2. Remove mounting bolts and ABS speed sensor.
3. Unstake and remove driveshaft nut and washer.
4. Remove ball stud bolt and separate control arm from steering knuckle.
5. **On models equipped with manual transaxle,** separate righthand axle from intermediate shaft bearing by tapping gently using suitable plastic mallet.
6. **On all models,** separate lefthand driveshaft from transaxle by prying gently using suitable large screwdriver, **Fig. 14.**
7. Remove drive axle from steering knuckle.
8. Reverse procedure to install. Push drive axle into transaxle by hand until snap ring is seated in spline.

Prizm

1. Raise and support vehicle, then remove tire and wheel assembly.
2. Remove mounting bolts and splash shield.
3. **On models equipped with ABS,** remove mounting bolt and ABS speed sensor from steering knuckle.
4. **On all models,** remove cotter pin and lock cap.
5. Prevent rotor from turning by inserting suitable drift through caliper opening into rotor, then remove wheel drive shaft hub nut and washer.
6. Remove tie rod end cotter pin and nut.
7. Separate tie rod end from steering knuckle using steering linkage and tie rod puller tool No. J24319-B, or equivalent.
8. Remove mounting bolt, nuts and ball joint from control arm.
9. Remove drive axle outer joint from steering knuckle. **Do not overextend drive axle. Do not damage ABS components.**

10. Remove drive axle inner joint by gently prying away from transaxle using suitable pry bar, **Fig. 14.**
11. Inspect boots, joints, front wheel bearing oil seals and wheel drive shaft oil seal at transaxle for damage or wear.
12. Reverse procedure to install, noting the following:
    a. Lubricate wheel drive shaft splines and seal surfaces.
    b. Use only enough force to seat inner joint into transaxle.
    c. Ensure joint snap ring is seated in transaxle by grasping inner joint housing and pulling outward.
    d. Install new cotter pins.

S-Series

REMOVAL

1. Depress brake pedal and loosen drive axle nut.
2. Raise and support vehicle, then remove wheel and tire assembly.
3. **On lefthand side drive axle,** proceed as follows:
    a. Remove front and rear splash shields
    b. Drain transaxle fluid into suitable container.
4. **On righthand side drive axle,** remove front and rear splash shields.
5. **On all drive axles,** remove drive axle nut and washer, **Fig. 15.** Discard nut.
6. Remove lower control arm to steering knuckle cotter pin. Discard cotter pin.
7. Loosen lower control arm to steering knuckle castle nut until top is even with ball stud top. **Do not remove castle nut now.**
8. Separate lower control arm from steering knuckle using removal tool No. SA9132-S, or equivalent, **Fig. 16. Do not use wedge type tool to separate joint. Do not damage ABS speed sensor ring.**
9. Remove outer tie rod cotter pin and torque prevailing nut. Discard nut.
10. Separate tie rod end from steering knuckle using removal tool No. SA91100-C, or equivalent, **Fig. 17. Do not use wedge type tool to separate joint.**
11. Remove lower control arm to steering knuckle castle nut.
12. Separate lower control arm ball stud from steering knuckle by prying down at cradle and tension strut locations with suitable long pry bar, **Fig. 18.**
13. Pull steering knuckle away from ball stud.
14. Pull outer end of drive axle out of wheel hub while pulling knuckle/strut away. If it is difficult to separate axle from hub, tap on end of drive axle shaft using suitable wood block and hammer, **Fig. 19.**
15. Support or suspend drive axle using mechanics wire.
16. Remove righthand drive axle by tapping axle from intermediate using suitable hammer and wood block, **Fig. 20.**
17. Remove lefthand drive axle from transaxle by prying axle with suitable large screwdriver, **Fig. 21. Do not contact**

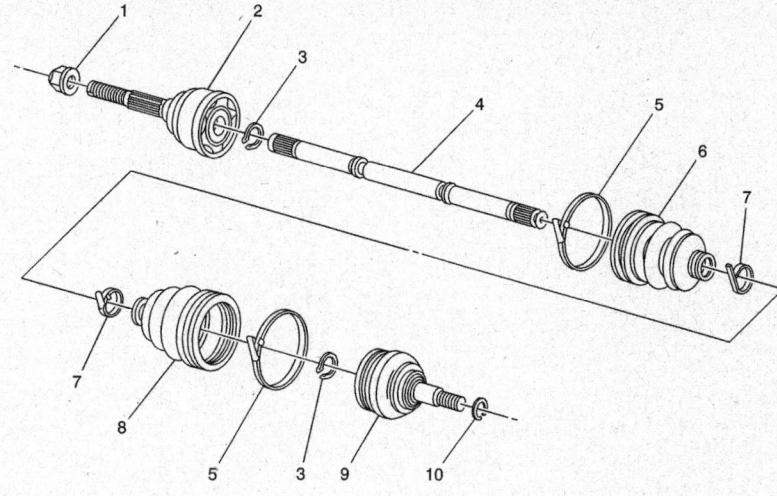

1. Caulking Nut
2. C/V Joint
3. Race Retaining Ring
4. Axle Shaft
5. Seal Retaining Clamp
6. Drive Axle Outboard Seal
7. Seal Retaining Clamp
8. Drive Axle Inboard Seal
9. Cross Groove Joint
10. Retaining Ring

ARM0400000001365

Fig. 3 Exploded view of front drive axle. Aveo w/manual transaxle

transaxle oil seal.

INSTALLATION

1. **On lefthand side drive axle,** proceed as follows:
    a. Install transaxle seal protector tool No. SA91112-T, or equivalent, **Fig. 22.**
    b. Insert drive axle into transaxle.
    c. After drive axle splines have safely passed transaxle oil seal, remove seal protector.
    d. Fully seat drive axle into transaxle.
2. **On righthand side drive axle,** insert drive axle inner end onto intermediate driveshaft outer end and push firmly to engage retaining ring.
3. **On all drive axles,** insert drive axle outer end into wheel hub. **Do not install drive axle hub washer and nut now.**
4. Install lower control arm ball stud into steering knuckle, then the ball stud castle nut. **Do not tighten nut now.**
5. Install tie rod end into steering knuckle.
6. Fully seat tie rod end using installer tool No. J44015, or equivalent, then tighten new nut.
7. Tighten ball joint stud castle nut and install new cotter pin.
8. Install axle to hub washer and new nut.
9. Install front inner fender splash shield.
10. Install wheels and lug nuts.

Vibe

1. Raise and support vehicle using suitable lift, then remove tire and wheel assemblies.
2. Remove engine splash shields.
3. Remove driveshaft locknut, then the

wheel speed sensor wire and brake hose retainer from strut assembly.
4. Remove mounting bolt and wheel speed sensor from steering knuckle, **Fig. 23.**
5. Remove outer tie rod as outlined under "Front Suspension & Steering" in "Vibe" chapter.
6. Remove lower ball joint from steering knuckle as outlined under "Front Suspension & Steering" in "Vibe" chapter.
7. Remove wheel drive shaft from wheel hub and bearing using suitable hammer.
8. Remove axle shaft from transaxle.
9. **On models equipped with AWD,** proceed as follows:
    a. Drain transaxle and transfer case into suitable container.
    b. Remove bearing lock bolt and snap ring using suitable pliers, **Fig. 24.**
10. **On all models,** remove driveshaft and retaining ring.
11. Reverse procedure to install.

DRIVESHAFT SERVICE

All Models Except Aveo, Cavalier, Metro, Prizm, Sunfire, Saturn & Vibe

INNER JOINT & BOOT

DISASSEMBLE

When the halfshaft is removed for any

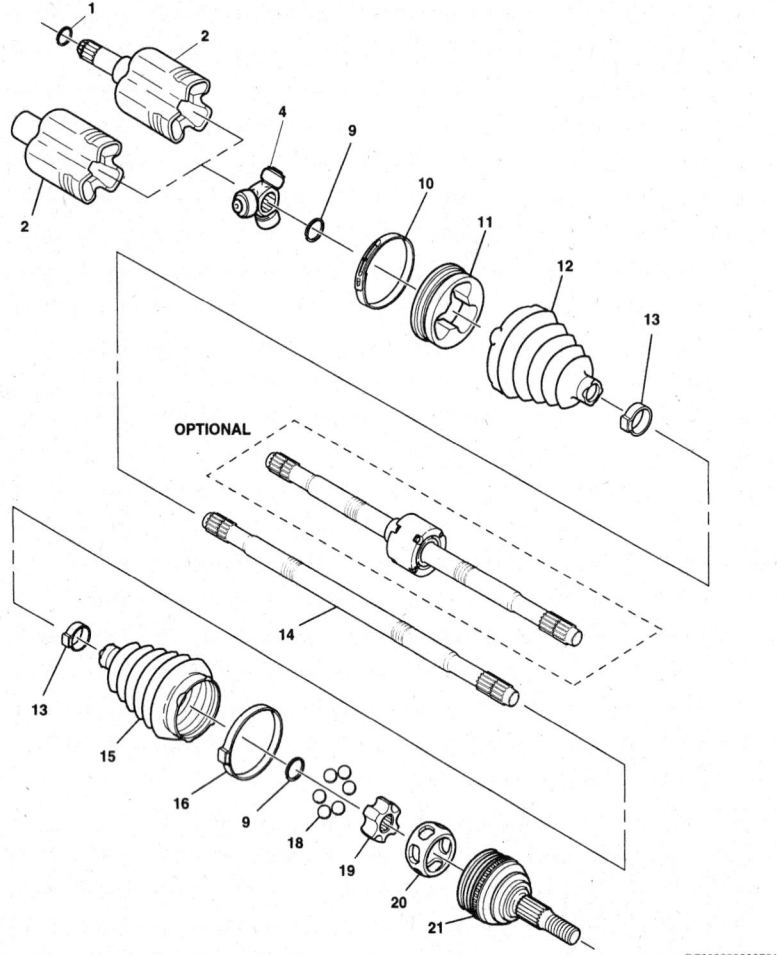

Fig. 4   Exploded view of front drive axle (Part 1 of 2). Cavalier & Sunfire

reason, the transmission sealing surface (tripod male/female shank of CV) should be inspected for corrosion. If corrosion is present, surface should be cleaned using crocus cloth or suitable equivalent.

1. Cut through swage ring using suitable hand grinder. **Do not damage tripod housing.**
2. Remove large boot retaining clamp from tripod joint using suitable side cutter. Discard clamp.
3. Separate inboard boot from trilobal tripod bushing at large diameter.
4. Slide boot away from joint along shaft.
5. Remove housing from tripod joint spider and shaft.
6. Remove trilobal tripod bushing from housing.
7. Spread spacer ring using snap ring pliers No. J8059, or equivalent.
8. Slide spacer ring and tripod joint spider backward on shaft.
9. Remove retaining ring from shaft groove.
10. Slide tripod joint spider assembly off shaft.
11. Clean tripot balls and needle rollers with suitable solvent. Dry thoroughly.
12. Inspect tripot joint spider, housing, trilobal tripod bushing and needle rollers for damage or wear. Replace as required.

ASSEMBLE

1. Place new small clamp onto joint boot small end.
2. Slide boot and clamp onto shaft.
3. Position boot small end into groove.
4. Swage ring using swage tool No. J41048, or equivalent.
5. Install retaining ring using snap ring pliers tool No. J8059, or equivalent, **Fig. 25.**
6. Ensure counterbored face on joint spider faces toward end of shaft.
7. Slide tripot joint spider toward spacer ring as far as it will go. Ensure trilobal tripot bushing is flush with housing face.
8. Place half of kit provided grease in inboard boot. Use remaining grease to pack housing.
9. Install trilobal bushing to housing.
10. Position larger new boot retaining clamp on inboard boot and slide housing over spider.
11. Slide inboard boot large diameter with clamp in place over outside of trilobal tripod bushing and locate lip in groove.
12. Ensure shaft inboard boot is not dimpled, stretched out or out of shape. Correct using thin, flat, blunt tool between to equalize pressure and shape by hand.

13. Align inboard boot, tripot housing and large retaining clamp.
14. Ensure boot is positioned properly.
15. Tighten clamp using eared clamp tool No. J35910, or equivalent, suitable breaker bar and torque wrench, **Fig. 26.**

OUTER JOINT & BOOT

DISASSEMBLE

1. Remove large and small boot retaining clamps from CV joint using suitable side cutter. Discard clamps.
2. Separate outboard boot from CV joint outer race at large diameter and slide boot away form joint, **Fig. 27.**
3. Wipe grease from CV joint inner race face.
4. Spread retaining ring race ears using snap ring pliers No. J8059, or equivalent, and remove CV joint and boot.
5. Tap CV joint cage using suitable brass drift and hammer until it is tilted enough to remove first chrome alloy ball.
6. Tilt cage in opposite direction to remove opposing ball.
7. Repeat until six balls are removed.
8. Position CV joint cage and inner race 90° to outer race centerline, and align joint cage windows with outer race lands.
9. Remove CV joint cage and inner race from outer race.
10. Rotate CV joint inner race 90° to CV joint cage centerline with inner race lands aligned with CV joint cage windows.
11. Remove inner race by pivoting into cage window.
12. Clean inner and outer races, CV joint cage and balls using suitable solvent. Dry thoroughly.

ASSEMBLE

1. Install new boot swage ring onto neck. **Do not swage now.**
2. Slide outboard boot onto shaft and position neck in groove.
3. Swage boot swage ring using swage tool No. J41048, or equivalent.
4. Lightly coat inner and outer race ball grooves with kit provided grease.
5. Hold inner race at a 90° angle to cage centerline, align inner race lands with cage windows, then install inner race into cage.
6. Hold cage and inner race at a 90° angle to outer race centerline, then align cage windows with outer race lands. Ensure inner race retaining ring side faces halfshaft.
7. Install cage and inner race into outer race.
8. Install first chrome ball, then tilt cage in opposite direction and install opposing ball. Repeat until all balls are in place.
9. Place approximately half of remaining kit provided grease inside outboard boot. Use remaining grease to pack CV joint.
10. Push CV joint onto shaft until retaining ring is seated in groove. Ensure boot is not dimpled, stretched out or out of shape. Correct by equalizing pressure and shaping by hand.

Key No.   **Part Name**
1 - RING, RETAINING
2 - HOUSING ASM, RETAINER &
4 - SPIDER, TRIPOT JOINT
9 - RING, RETAINING
10 - CLAMP, SEAL RETAINING
11 - BUSHING, TRILOBAL TRIPOT
12 - SEAL, DRIVE AXLE INBOARD
13 - CLAMP, SEAL RETAINING

Key No.   **Part Name**
14 - SHAFT, AXLE (RH SHOWN, LH SIMILAR)
15 - SEAL, DRIVE AXLE OUTBOARD
16 - CLAMP, SEAL RETAINING
18 - BALL, CHROME ALLOY
19 - RACE, C/V JOINT INNER
20 - CAGE, C/V JOINT
21 - RACE, C/V JOINT OUTER

GC303000033701BX

Fig. 4 Exploded view of front drive axle (Part 2 of 2). Cavalier & Sunfire

11. Slide large diameter of outboard boot with retaining clamp over outside CV joint outer race, locate lip in groove.
12. Crimp boot retaining clamp using seal clamp tool No. J35910, or equivalent, and suitable breaker bar. Ensure gap is .012 inch.

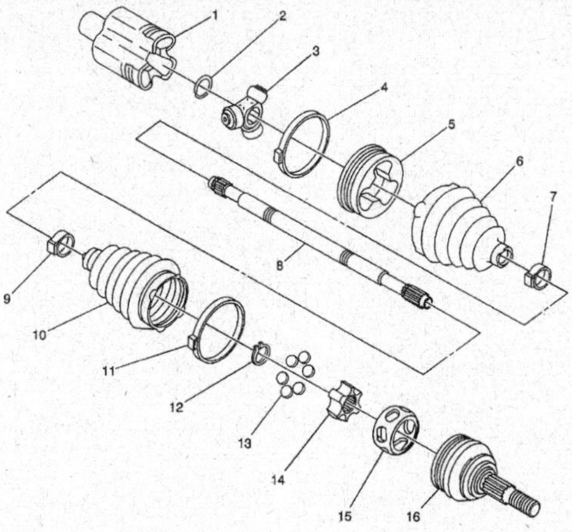

Aveo

AUTOMATIC

INNER JOINT & BOOT

Disassemble

1. Remove and discard large and small seal retaining clamps using seal retaining clamp tool No. J35566, or equivalent.
2. Separate joint housing from boot.
3. Degrease tripot.
4. Remove shaft retaining ring using snap ring pliers tool No. J8059, or equivalent.
5. Remove retaining ring, then the tripot and tripot joint from axle shaft.
6. Remove tripot joint seal from axle shaft.

Assemble

1. Install new small seal retaining clamp onto seal.
2. Install seal onto axle shaft.
3. Install shaft retaining ring onto axle shaft using suitable snap ring pliers.
4. Fill tripot housing with 6.9–7.6 ounces of suitable grease.
5. Pack tripot with 6.9–7.6 ounces of suitable grease.
6. Install boot to joint housing.
7. Install new large seal retaining clamp.
8. Crimp large and small seal retaining clamps using suitable seal retaining clamp tool.

OUTER JOINT & BOOT

The outer joint is designed to be replaced as a one piece unit. Do not attempt to disassemble or service the outer joint.

Disassemble

1. Remove and discard large and small seal retaining clamps using seal clamp pliers tool No. J35566, or equivalent.
2. Degrease joint.
3. Spread snap ring using snap ring pliers tool No. J8059, or equivalent, then remove outer joint and axle shaft

Assemble

1. Install seal onto axle shaft.
2. Spread snap ring using suitable snap

ring pliers , then remove outer joint and axle shaft.
3. Fill joint seal with 3.9–4.6 ounces of suitable grease.
4. Pack joint with 3.9–4.6 ounces of suitable grease.
5. Install new large and small seal retaining clamps.
6. Crimp clamps using suitable seal clamp pliers.

MANUAL

INNER JOINT & BOOT

The ball retainer is stacked in position and is not serviceable.

Disassemble

1. Remove and discard large and small seal retaining clamps using seal retaining clamp tool No. J35566, or equivalent.
2. Degrease joint.
3. Remove shaft retaining ring using snap ring pliers tool No. J8059 , or equivalent.
4. Remove axle shaft from joint.
5. Remove seal from joint.

Assemble

1. Install new small seal retaining clamp onto seal. Do not crimp.
2. Install seal and joint onto shaft.
3. Install shaft retaining ring using suitable snap ring pliers.
4. Fill joint with 4.2–4.9 ounces of suitable grease.
5. Pack tripot with 4.2–4.9 ounces of suitable grease.
6. Install new large seal retaining clamp.
7. Crimp new large and small seal retaining clamps using suitable seal clamp pliers.

OUTER JOINT & BOOT

The outer joint is designed to be re-

(1) Retainer and Housing Assembly
(2) Retaining Ring
(3) Tripot Joint Spider Assembly
(4) Boot Retaining Clamp
(5) Tripot Trilobal Bushing
(6) Inboard Boot
(7) Boot Retaining Clamp
(8) Axle Shaft
(9) Boot Retaining Clamp
(10) Outboard Boot
(11) Boot Retaining Clamp
(12) Race Retaining Ring
(13) Chrome Alloy Ball
(14) CV Joint Inner Race
(15) CV Joint Cage
(16) CV Joint Outer Race

ARM66GC000000768

Fig. 5 Exploded view of front drive axle. ION

placed as a one piece unit. Do not attempt to disassemble or service the outer joint.
The ball retainer is stacked in position and is not serviceable.

Disassemble

1. Remove and discard large and small seal retaining clamps.
2. Degrease joint.
3. Remove shaft retaining ring using snap ring pliers tool No. J8059, or equivalent.
4. Remove axle shaft from joint.
5. Remove cross groove joint seal from joint.
6. Remove and discard large and small seal retaining clips.
7. Degrease joint.
8. Remove seal from joint.

Assemble

1. Install seal onto axle shaft.
2. Fill joint seal with 3.9–4.6 ounces of suitable grease.
3. Pack joint with 3.9–4.6 ounces of suitable grease.
4. Install new large and small seal retaining clamps.
5. Crimp new clamps with suitable seal clamp pliers.
6. Install new small seal retaining clamp onto cross groove joint seal. Do not crimp.
7. Install seal onto and joint onto axle shaft.
8. Install shaft retaining ring using suitable snap ring pliers.
9. Fill joint assembly with 4.2–4.9 ounces of suitable grease.
10. Pack tripot 4.2–4.9 ounces of suitable grease.
11. Install new large seal retaining clamp.
12. Crimp clamps suitable seal clamp pliers.

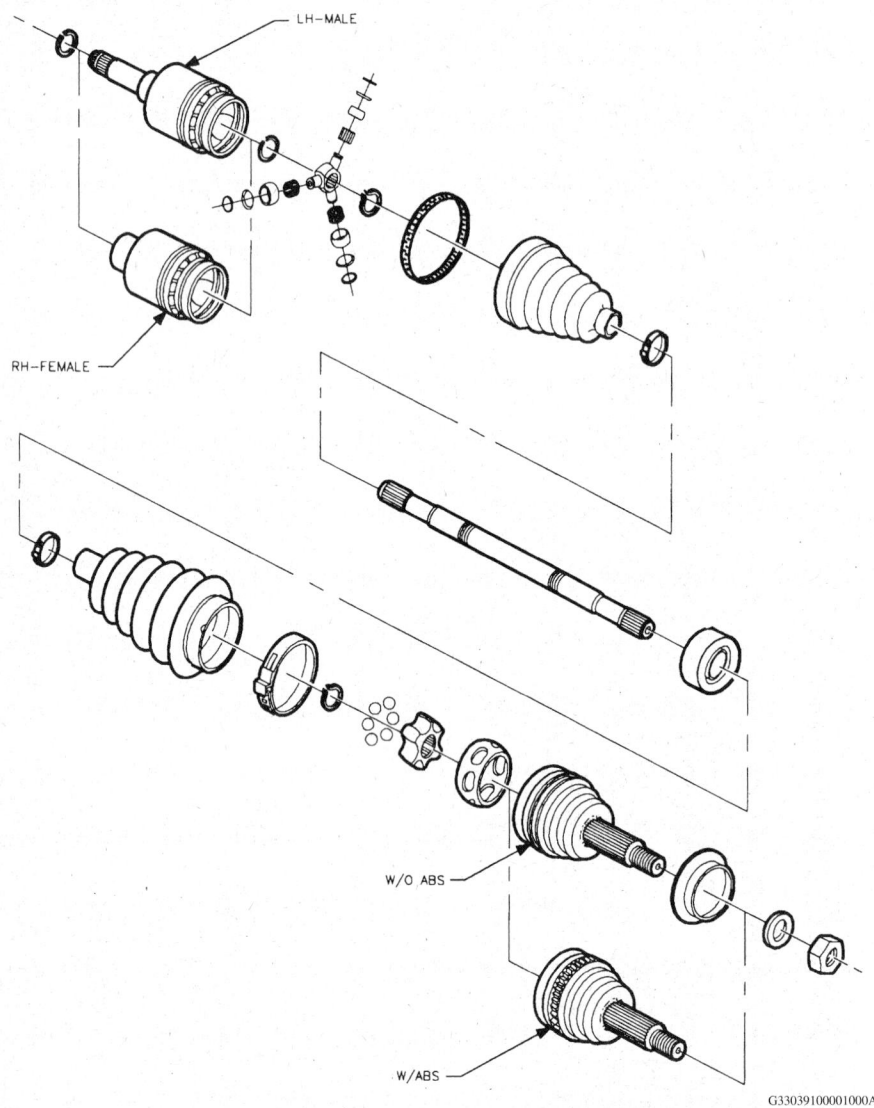

Fig. 6 Exploded view of front drive axle. L & S-Series

Cavalier & Sunfire

INNER JOINT & BOOT

DISASSEMBLE

1. **On models equipped with 2.4L engines,** if transaxle stub shaft disengages from transaxle during halfshaft tripod removal, separate shaft from tripod housing as follows:
   a. Remove and discard stub shaft snap ring.
   b. Remove shaft from tripot using stub shaft removal tool No. J38868 and impact slide hammer tool No. J6125-1B, or equivalents, **Fig. 28.**
   c. Install new snap rings onto stub shaft.
   d. Install stub axle into transaxle.
2. **On all models,** remove inboard boot small and large retaining clamps. Discard clamps.
3. Separate large diameter of inboard boot from trilobal tripot bushing.
4. Slide boot away from joint along halfshaft.
5. Remove spacer ring using snap ring pliers tool No. J8309-A, or equivalent, **Fig. 29.** Discard spacer ring.
6. Remove tripod spider using suitable brass drift and hammer, **Fig. 30.**
7. Remove spacer ring from halfshaft shoulder using snap ring pliers tool No. J8309-A, or equivalent.
8. Remove trilobal tripot bushing.
9. Clean tripod balls, needle rollers and housing with suitable solvent. Dry thoroughly.
10. Remove axle shaft boot.
11. Inspect inboard boot, spider, housing, trilobal tripot bushing, tripot balls, needle rollers and retaining ring for wear or damage.

ASSEMBLE

1. Install new small boot retaining clamp on boot neck. **Do not crimp now.**
2. Clean axle shaft using wire brush to remove rust from boot grooves.
3. Slide tripod boot onto halfshaft passing CV end boot grooves. Ensure spacer ring is next to halfshaft shoulder.
4. Install tripot spider.
5. Place axle assembly onto suitable arbor press with tripod spider on press plate and CV joint under press head, **Fig. 31.**
6. Lower arbor press head onto CV joint until tripod spider is next to spacer ring. **Do not exceed 4000 lbs. pressure.**
7. Remove axle assembly from arbor press.
8. Place new spacer ring in halfshaft end groove.
9. Slide tripod boot onto halfshaft groove.
10. Crimp small boot retaining clamp using seal clamp tool No. J35910, or equivalent.
11. Place approximately one quarter of kit provided grease in boot. Use remaining grease to Pack housing.
12. Install trilobal tripot bushing to housing. Ensure bushing is flush with housing face.
13. Slide housing over spider on halfshaft.
14. Position large boot retaining clamp around inboard boot.
15. Engage inboard boot.
16. Boot must not be dimpled, stretched or out of shape. Correct by equalizing pressure and shape using suitable thin, flat, blunt tool and hand.
17. Position joint properly, **Fig. 32.**
18. Ensure halfshaft inboard boot, housing and large clamp are aligned.
19. Latch boot retaining strap using seal clamp tool No. J35566, or equivalent.

OUTER JOINT & BOOT

DISASSEMBLE

1. Remove large and small CV boot retaining clamps using suitable side cutters, discard clamps.
2. Separate large diameter of boot from CV joint and slide away from joint along axle shaft.
3. Wipe grease away from inner CV joint race face.
4. Place reference mark on halfshaft, then measure and record distance between reference mark and CV joint inner race face for assembly reference.
5. Clamp axle into suitable vise.
6. Remove CV joint using CV puller tool No. J41398 and slide hammer tool No. J2619-01, or equivalents, **Fig. 33.**
7. Remove and discard retaining ring.
8. Remove CV joint boot.
9. Gently tap CV joint cage using suitable brass drift and hammer until it is tilted enough to remove first chrome ball, then tilt in opposite direction and remove ball. Repeat until all six balls are removed.
10. Position cage and inner race at a 90° angle to outer race centerline, then align cage windows with outer race lands.
11. Remove cage and inner race from outer race.
12. Remove inner race from cage by rotating inner race upward.

13. Clean inner and outer race assemblies, cage and balls with suitable solvent. Dry thoroughly.
14. Inspect for unusual war, cracks or damage.

ASSEMBLE

1. Lightly coat inner and outer race ball grooves with kit provided grease.
2. Hold inner race at a 90° angle to cage centerline and align inner race lands with cage windows, then insert race into cage.
3. Hold cage and inner race at a 90° angle to outer race centerline, then align cage windows with outer race lands. Ensure inner race retaining ring side faces outer race.
4. Install cage and inner race into outer race.
5. Tilt cage by gently tapping with suitable brass drift and hammer, then install first chrome ball. Repeat until all six balls are installed.
6. Pack CV joint with approximately half of kit provided grease.
7. Install new small retaining ring on CV boot neck. **Do not crimp now.**
8. Remove rust from CV boot mounting grooves with suitable wire brush.
9. Slide CV joint boot onto drive axle shaft far enough to expose reference mark made during disassembly.
10. Position large retaining clamp around CV joint boot.
11. Place new retaining ring in inner race.
12. While supporting tripot, place halfshaft assembly onto suitable arbor press with CV assembly under press head.
13. Lower arbor press head onto CV joint assembly until press cannot move any further, to ensure retaining ring engages into inner race. **Do not exceed 4000 lbs. of press load.**
14. Place neck of CV joint boot into seal groove on drive axle shaft.
15. Measure distance between reference mark and CV joint inner race. If distance is not within .039 inch of distance recorded during disassembly, repeat previous steps 13 and 14.
16. Place CV joint boot neck into halfshaft boot groove. Ensure clamp is positioned correctly.
17. Crimp small retaining clamp using seal clamp tool No. J35910, or equivalent, suitable breaker bar and torque wrench.
18. Ensure gap dimension is .085 inch.
19. Place remaining kit provided grease inside boot.
20. Measure approximately $^{11}/_{16}$ inch up from CV outer joint bottom edge and slide large diameter of boot with clamp in place over outside of CV joint, **Fig. 34.**
21. Boot must not be dimpled, stretched or out of shape. Correct by equalizing pressure and shaping by hand.
22. Crimp large clamp using seal clamp tool No. J35910, or equivalent, suitable breaker bar and torque wrench.
23. Ensure clamp gap is .102 inch.

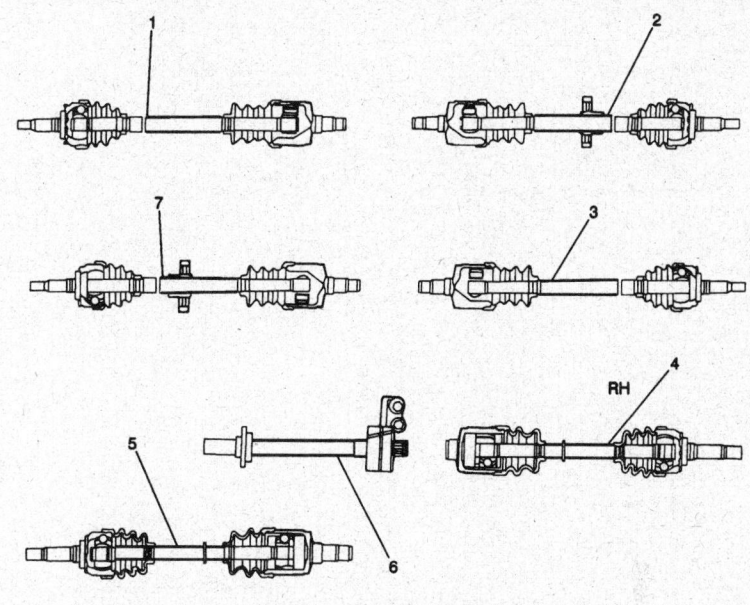

(1) Left Drive Axle Shaft (Automatic Transaxle)
(2) Right Drive Axle Shaft (Automatic Transaxle)
(3) Right Drive Axle Shaft (Manual Transaxle 1.0 L Vehicles Only)
(4) Right Drive Axle Shaft (Manual Transaxle 1.3 L Vehicles Only)
(5) Left Drive Axle Shaft (Manual Transaxle 1.3 L Vehicles Only)
(6) Right Inner Drive Axle Shaft Support Arbor (Manual Transaxle)
(7) Left Drive Axle Shaft (Manual Transaxle 1.0 L Vehicles Only)

GC3039900340000X

Fig. 7   Cutaway view of front drive axle. Metro

ION

INNER JOINT & SEAL

DISASSEMBLE

1. Remove small boot retaining clamp from axle shaft using suitable side cutter, then the earless clamp. Discard components.
2. Remove larger boot retaining clamp from joint using suitable side cutters and separate inboard boot from bushing at larger diameter.
3. Remove boot sliding along axle shaft.
4. Remove housing from joint spider and retaining ring from axle shaft, then slide assembly from axle shaft.
5. Degrease entire assemble allowing to dry, then inspect components for wear and damage.

ASSEMBLE

1. Install small boot clamp to inboard boot, then slide boot onto axle shaft, and secure into position using suitable crimp pliers **Fig. 35.**
2. Ensure end gap does not exceed .118 inch. Repeat procedure if not with specifications.
3. Install spider assembly until seated to shoulder, then the retaining ring into axle shaft groove, **Fig. 36.**
4. Install bushing to housing. Ensure bushing is seated flat against face of housing.
5. Install larger clamp on boot and slide onto axle shaft.
6. Install large diameter inboard boot with clamp in place over outside of bushing and clamp boot ring into place using suitable pliers, **Figs. 37 and 38.**

OUTER JOINT & SEAL

DISASSEMBLE

1. Remove retaining clamp and boot from CV joint using suitable side cutter.
2. Remove small clamp and boot from axle shaft using suitable hammer and flat bladed tool.
3. Separate boot from CV joint outer race, slide joint along bar and remove grease from CV joint inner race.
4. Remove CV joint using suitable hammer to tap on CV joint, then the boot from bar.
5. Tilt cage to remove first ball using suitable drift and hammer, **Fig. 39.** Tilt in opposite direction to remove remaining balls.
6. Secure CV joint cage and inner race at 90°, **Fig. 40.**
7. Remove CV joint cage and inner race from CV joint outer race.
8. Rotate CV joint 90° then pivot inner race into cage and remove inner race, **Fig. 41.**
9. Clean components thoroughly using suitable solvent and allow to dry.

ASSEMBLE

1. Install clamp to boot neck. **Do not crimp now.** Slide boot onto axle shaft

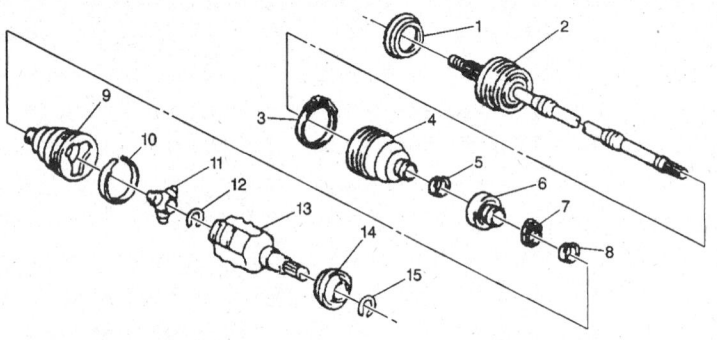

(1) Outer Joint Seal
(2) Outer Joint
(3) Outer Boot Clamp
(4) Outer Boot
(5) Outer Boot Clamp
(6) Damper (RH Shaft Only)
(7) Damper Clamp
(8) Inner Boot Clamp

(9) Inner Boot
(10) Inner Boot Clamp
(11) Tripot Joint
(12) Snap Ring
(13) Inner Joint Housing
(14) Inner Joint Seal
(15) Snap Ring

GC3039900341000X

Fig. 8 Exploded view of front drive axle. Prizm

and place both into groove on bar, **Fig. 42.**

2. Crimp boot clamp using tool no SA9203-C, or equivalent. Ensure end gap is not more than .118 inch.
3. Place grease on ball grooves of inner and outer race.
4. Install inner race into cage. Ensure retaining ring side of inner race faces axle shaft.
5. Install cage and inner race into outer race, then the first ball. Continue until all balls are installed.
6. Pack inside of boot and CV joint using suitable grease and push CV joint onto bar until seated into groove, **Fig. 43.**
7. Install boot with clamp over CV joint outer race and crimp clamp using suitable pliers.
8. Ensure end gap is not more than .118 inch.

L- & S-Series

DISASSEMBLE

1. Clamp axle shaft in suitable soft metal or wood vise.
2. If deflector ring is damaged, remove from CV outer race using suitable brass drift and hammer, **Fig. 44.**
3. Disengage large and small boot clamps outer band from inner band at retainer peg using suitable hammer and chisel or flat-bladed screwdriver.
4. Separate large diameter of boot from CV joint race, then slide boot away from joint along axle shaft.
5. Wipe excess grease from CV inner race face.
6. Remove race retaining ring with suitable snap ring pliers, **Fig. 45.**
7. Remove CV joint from axle shaft, then the boot.
8. **On models equipped with dynamic damper,** if shaft or damper is being replaced, remove damper using suitable arbor press.

9. **On all models,** tap cage enough to remove first ball using suitable brass drift, **Fig. 46.** Remove remaining balls in similar manner.
10. Pivot cage and inner race at a 90° angle to outer race centerline, then align cage windows with outer race lands.
11. Remove cage and inner race.
12. Rotate inner race upward and out of cage.
13. Thoroughly clean and dry CV joint parts.
14. Cut tripot boot retaining clamp using suitable side cutters. Discard clamp.
15. Remove endless clamp using suitable small bladed screwdriver. Discard clamp.
16. Separate boot from large diameter of tripot housing, then slide boot along axle shaft away from joint.
17. Wipe excess grease from tripot spider face and inside tripot housing.
18. Remove tripot housing from spider and shaft, **Fig. 47.**
19. Spread spacer ring using snap ring tool No. SA9198-C, or equivalent, then slide spacer ring and tripot spider back on axle, **Fig. 48.**
20. Remove spider retaining ring and slide spider off shaft. **Handle tripot spider with care. Tripot balls and needle rollers may separate from spider trunnions.**
21. Remove boot and thoroughly degrease housing. Allow to dry.

INSPECTION

1. Inspect tripot joint components for wear, cracks and damage.
2. Clean shaft.
3. Remove rust from shaft mounting groove with suitable wire brush.

ASSEMBLE

1. Install small retaining clamp on boot neck. **Do not crimp now.**

2. Slide boot onto shaft and position neck into groove.
3. Crimp boot retaining clamp using axle clamp installer tool No. SA9203-C, or equivalent, **Fig. 49.**
4. Ensure clamp is positioned correctly.
5. Measure clamp end gap and crimp, as required.
6. Install spacer ring beyond second groove.
7. Slide tripot spider past retaining groove. Ensure tripot counterbored surface faces end of shaft.
8. Install retaining ring using C/V joint snap ring pliers tool No. SA9198-C, or equivalent.
9. Slide tripot spider toward shaft end and seat spacer ring into groove.
10. Pack approximately half of kit provided grease inside boot. Use remaining grease to pack tripot housing.
11. Install kit provided convolute retainer over boot.
12. Position retaining clamp around large diameter of boot, then slide housing over tripot spider.
13. Slide large diameter of boot over tripot housing and position lip into housing groove.
14. Ensure boot is not dimpled, stretched or out of shape. Adjust by hand with suitable thin, flat, blunt tool.
15. Ensure tripot is installed to proper length, **Fig. 50.**
16. Install large boot retaining clamp and crimp with boot clamp installer tool No. SA9161-C, or equivalent, **Fig. 51.**
17. **If replacing or installing damper,** proceed as follows:
   a. Clean shaft thoroughly.
   b. Mark damper installation point 7.95 inches from shaft outboard end with masking tape.
   c. Lubricate shaft with suitable liquid detergent (dishwashing detergent).
   d. Place shaft in suitable brass-jaw vice and start damper on by hand.
   e. Work damper onto shaft by twisting back and forth.
   f. Align damper inboard edge with tape.
   g. Remove tape.
   h. Secure damper by crimping clamp with axle boot clamp installer tool No. SA9164-C, or equivalent, to an .085 inch gap.
18. Lightly coat inner and outer race grooves with suitable grease.
19. Insert and rotate inner race into cage.
20. Install cage and inner race into outer race, align cage windows with outer race lines.
21. Install balls, use suitable brass drift to rotate and position cage and inner race.
22. Install inner race retaining ring.
23. Pack joint with service kit provided grease.
24. Install small retaining clamp on boot new. **Do not crimp now.**
25. Slide boot onto shaft, position neck into groove.
26. Crimp retaining clamp using axle clamp installer tool No. SA9203-C, or equivalent, **Fig. 52.**
27. Ensure clamp is positioned properly

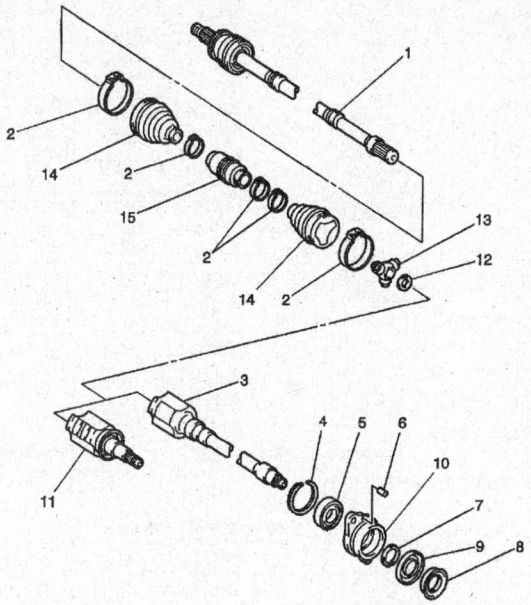

(1) Outboard Joint Shaft
(2) Boot Clamp
(3) RH Inboard Shaft
(4) Large Snap Ring
(5) Bearing
(6) Straight Pin
(7) Small Snap Ring
(8) Dust Cover
(9) Drive Shaft Dust Cover
(10) Bearing Case
(11) LH Inboard Shaft

(12) Snap Ring
(13) Tripod
(14) Boot
(15) Dynamic Damper

ARM66GC000000758

Fig. 9 Exploded view of front drive axle. Vibe

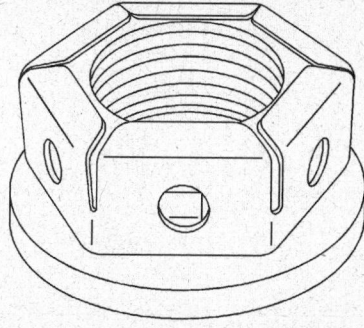

ARM0400000001362

Fig. 10 Type one drive axle nut. 2003–05 Alero, Grand Am & Malibu

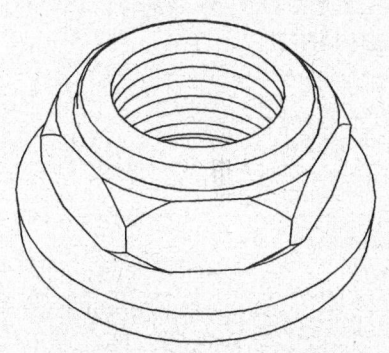

ARM0400000001363

Fig. 11 Type two drive axle nut. 2003–05 Alero, Grand Am & Malibu

around entire circumference.
28. Pack approximately half of kit provided grease inside boot. Use remaining grease to pack CV.
29. Position large retaining clamp around boot. Ensure inner race retaining ring side faces axle shaft.
30. Push CV joint onto shaft until retaining ring seats into groove.
31. Slide large diameter of boot over outside of CV joint race, position lip into housing groove.
32. Ensure boot is not dimpled, stretched or out of shape. Adjust by hand with suitable thin, flat, blunt tool.
33. Crimp retaining clamp using axle clamp installer tool No. SA9203-C, or equivalent, **Fig. 53.**
34. Ensure clamp is positioned properly.
35. Position deflecting ring at CV joint outer race.
36. Tighten nut until deflector bottoms against CV outer race shoulder using M20 x 1.0 mm nut and axle deflector ring installer tool No. SA9160-C, or equivalent, **Fig. 54.**

Metro

INNER JOINT & BOOT

DISASSEMBLE

1. Place index marks on inner joint and shaft for assembly reference.
2. Remove inner and outer boot bands, then slide boot back, **Fig. 55.**
3. Remove inner housing from tripod spider.
4. Place index mark on tripot joint spider and shaft for assembly reference.
5. Remove snap ring and spider.
6. Remove boot.

INSPECTION

1. Clean inner boot and tripot joint spider with clean, dry, solvent-free cloth. **Do not clean boots or tripot joint with solvent.**
2. Inspect boot for damage or wear.
3. Inspect tripot joint spider for excessive wear or damage.

ASSEMBLE

1. Install boot onto shaft and inner band onto boot.
2. Install tripot joint spider, align refer-

ence marks and secure with snap ring.
3. Pack inner joint housing with 2.8–3.5 oz. of kit provided grease.
4. Install inner housing onto spider.
5. Install inner band onto boot.
6. Inspect boots for distortion or dents. Correct by pulling boot outward.

OUTER JOINT & BOOT

Replace joint as an assembly. If boot is removed, pack with approximately 2.1–2.8 ounces of kit provided grease.

DISASSEMBLE

1. Place index mark on outer joint and shaft for assembly reference.
2. Remove outer and inner boot bands, **Fig. 56.**
3. Remove snap ring and outer housing.
4. Remove roller ball guide snap ring.
5. Place index mark on roller ball guide and shaft for assembly reference.
6. Remove roller guide, balls and cage.
7. Remove boot.

INSPECTION

1. Clean boot with clean, dry, solvent-free cloth.
2. **Do not clean boots in solvent.**
3. Clean joint components with solvent and dry thoroughly.
4. Inspect boot for damage and wear.
5. Inspect joint components for excessive wear or damage.

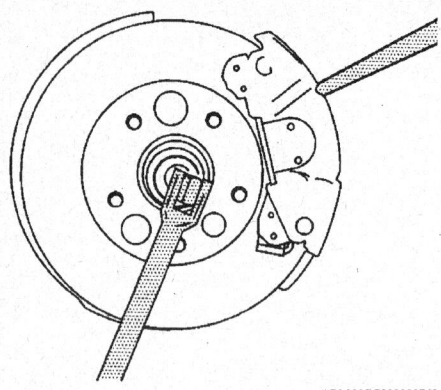

Fig. 12 Driveshaft nut removal. Ion

ASSEMBLE

1. Install boot and outer band.
2. Align marks made during disassemble procedure.
3. Install roller ball guide, balls and cage with smaller diameter facing boot.
4. Install snap ring.
5. Pack joint with 1–1.4 ounces of kit provided grease.
6. Fill outer housing with remaining grease.
7. Install outer joint housing onto joint and align reference mark.
8. Install snap ring and outer boot band.
9. Inspect boots for distortion or dents. Correct by pulling boot outward.

Prizm

INNER JOINT & BOOT

DISASSEMBLE

1. Secure axle assembly in suitable soft-jawed vise.
2. Remove large side inner joint boot clamp by drawing clamp hooks together using seal clamp tool No. J35566, or equivalent, **Fig. 57.**
3. Remove small side inner joint boot clamp using suitable pliers.
4. Slide boot towards center of drive axle.
5. Place index marks on inner joint housing and drive axle shaft for assembly reference.
6. Remove inner joint housing from tripot joint spider.
7. Place index marks on tripot joint spider and drive shaft for assembly reference.
8. Remove drive axle snap ring.
9. Remove tripot joint using suitable brass drift and hammer. Place drift on tripot body, not roller.
10. Remove inner boot, then the inner joint housing seal using bearing puller tool No. J22912-01, or equivalent, and suitable press.

INSPECTION

1. Clean tripot spider and boots using clean, dry, solvent-free rag. **Do not wash tripot joint spider or boots in solvent or degreaser.**
2. Inspect tripot joint for excessive wear or damage.

Fig. 13 Driveshaft & transaxle separation. Ion

3. Inspect wheel side joint for excessive wear or damage.
4. Inspect boots for excessive wear or damage.
5. Inspect righthand shaft dynamic dampener for damage or distortion.

ASSEMBLE

1. If damper was removed, proceed as follows:
   a. Install damper on righthand shaft.
   b. Position damper into shaft groove.
   c. Damper centerline should be 16.862–17.098 inches from outer joint.
   d. Crimp damper clamp using service boot clamp tool No. J22610, or equivalent.
2. Install inner joint seal using suitable press.
3. Install inner joint housing boot and clamps. **Do not crimp clamps now.**
4. Align tripot joint and shaft index marks. **Ensure tripot joint beveled splines are away from transaxle.**
5. Install tripot joint and snap ring.
6. Pack inner joint housing with approximately 5.8–6.4 ounces of kit provided grease.
7. Align index marks and install outer housing onto tripot joint.
8. Install inner joint boot and clamps. **Do not crimp clamps now.**
9. Measure drive shaft length to ensure boots are not stretched or excessively contracted when wheel drive axle is at its standard length, **Fig. 58.** Measurements are plus or minus .197 inch.
10. Ensure boots are not distorted or dented. Correct by pulling boot out. **Do not pull out on differential side joint.**
11. Crimp clamps using seal clamp tool No. J35566, or equivalent.

OUTER JOINT & BOOT

DISASSEMBLE

1. Remove boot retaining clamps, **Fig. 57.**
2. Slide boot toward center of shaft.
3. Place index marks on outer joint and shaft for assembly reference.
4. Remove outer joint from shaft while expanding shaft snap ring. **Do not damage ABS components.**
5. Secure axle in suitable soft-jawed vise.
6. Remove outer joint seal.

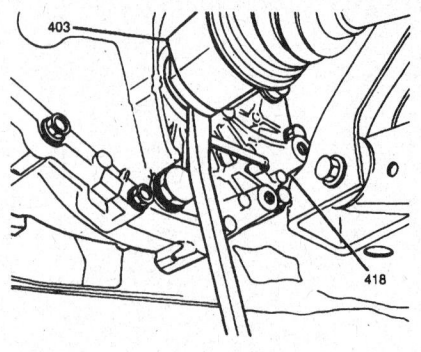

403 DIFFERENTIAL-SIDE JOINT HOUSING
418 TRANSAXLE ASSEMBLY

Fig. 14 Inner joint removal. Metro & Prizm

INSPECTION

1. Clean boots using clean, dry, solvent-free cloth. **Do not clean boots in solvent.**
2. Inspect boot for damage or wear.
3. Inspect joint for excessive wear or damage. Replace joint as necessary. **Do not disassemble outer joint.**
4. Inspect righthand dynamic dampener for damage or distortion.

ASSEMBLE

1. Install outer joint seal using suitable sleeve and press.
2. If damper was removed, replace as described under "Inner Joint & Boot."
3. Install outer boot and clamps. **Do not crimp clamps now.**
4. Align outer joint and shaft index marks.
5. Slide outer joint onto shaft by expanding snap ring. Ensure snap ring is securely seated in groove.
6. Pack outer joint with approximately 5.8–6.4 ounces of kit provide green grease.
7. Measure drive axle length as described under "Inner Joint & Boot."
8. Ensure boots are not distorted or dented. Correct by pulling boot out. **Do not pull out on joint.**
9. Crimp small and large boot clamps using keystone clamp pliers tool No. J22610, or equivalent.

Vibe

INNER JOINT & SEAL

DISASSEMBLE

1. Remove small seal clamp from driveshaft using suitable side cutters, then the large seal clamp from tripod joint.
2. Separate driveshaft outboard seal from tripod bushing and slide seal from joint along driveshaft.
3. Remove housing from tripod joint and driveshaft.
4. Place matching marks on tripod spider and driveshaft, **Fig. 59.**
5. Remove snap ring and joint from driveshaft using suitable hammer, **Fig. 60.**
6. Remove inboard joint boot from driveshaft.

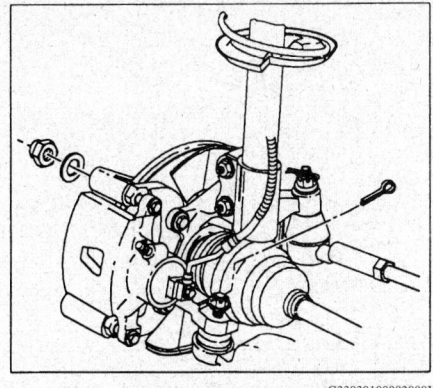

Fig. 15 Driveshaft nut & washer replacement. S-Series

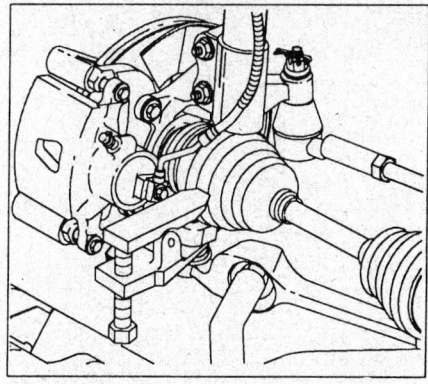

Fig. 16 Lower ball joint separation. S-Series

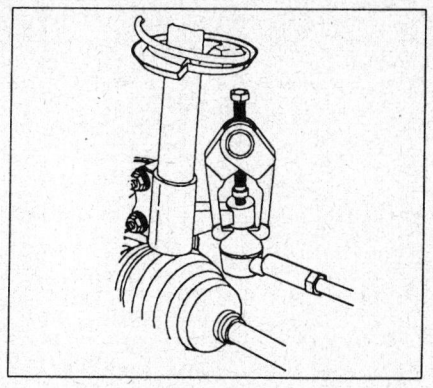

Fig. 17 Outer tie rod end separation. S-Series

7. Remove dynamic damper from right-hand driveshaft.
8. Remove joint seal from driveshaft.
9. Remove bearing from shaft using suitable press, **Fig. 61**.

ASSEMBLE

1. Install bearing using suitable press.
2. Install boots and clamps, placing vinyl tape over splined area.
3. Install dynamic damper to righthand side driveshaft.
4. Install outboard joint. Ensure alignment marks are referenced.
5. Install snap ring, then pack outboard and inboard joint and boot using 4.8–5.5 ounces of suitable grease.
6. Align matching marks on inboard and outboard joint shaft, then temporarily install boot to inboard joint and boots into grooves on driveshaft.
7. **On models equipped with FWD,** ensure that righthand driveshaft length is 33.201–33.595 inches and lefthand driveshaft length is 22.728–23.122 inches, **Fig. 62**.
8. **On models equipped with AWD,** ensure righthand driveshaft length is 33.661–34.055 inches and lefthand driveshaft length is 22.319–22.713 inches, **Fig. 63**.
9. **On all models,** ensure small seal is crimped using suitable shaft seal pliers.
10. Install retaining ring to driveshaft bar. Ensure 60° offset between inner and outer tripod spiders is maintained.
11. Install spider to driveshaft bar and compressing retaining ring using suitable flat bladed tool. Ensure component engagement attempting to pull free from each other.
12. Install driveshaft assembly in sequence, **Fig. 64**. Place half of grease to outboard seal and pack housing using remaining half of grease from service kit.
13. Install outboard seal over outside of tripod bushing and secure lip of seal in groove, **Fig. 65**.
14. Ensure driveshaft outboard seal, housing and large seal retaining clamp are aligned, then secure large retaining clamp.
15. Distribute grease throughout bearings.

INTERMEDIATE SHAFT
REPLACE

All Models Except Metro & Saturn

1. Raise and support vehicle, then remove righthand tire and wheel assembly.
2. Protect outer joint from sharp edges with suitable shop towels.
3. Remove stabilizer shaft from righthand control arm.
4. Remove righthand ball joint from knuckle.
5. Remove drive axle from intermediate shaft as outlined under "Driveshaft, Replace."
6. Remove intermediate driveshaft support bracket to engine mounting bolts.
7. Remove intermediate shaft from transaxle.
8. Reverse procedure to install. Coat splines of intermediate shaft with suitable chassis grease.

ION

1. Raise and support vehicle, then remove righthand tire and wheel assembly.
2. Remove nut and disconnect stabilizer shaft link.
3. Remove mounting nut and disconnect outer tie rod from steering knuckle. **Do not loosen tie rod adjustment jamb nut.**
4. Rotate steering knuckle to access wheel drive shaft inner joint.
5. Separate wheel drive shaft from intermediate drive shaft using rear wheel drive shaft removal tool No. J45341 and slide hammer tool No. SA9173G, or equivalents.
6. Position and support wheel drive shaft from intermediate drive shaft.
7. Disconnect Vehicle Speed Sensor (VSS) electrical connector.
8. Remove rear or lefthand intermediate drive shaft bracket-to-engine block bolts and VSS with bracket.
9. Remove remaining intermediate shaft

bracket-to-engine block bolt.
10. Remove intermediate drive shaft. **Do not damage transaxle output shaft seal.**
11. Reverse procedure to install, noting the following:
    a. Protect axle seal with axle seal protector tool No. SA91112T, or equivalent.
    b. **Do not tighten intermediate drive shaft bracket-to-engine block bolts** until VSS and bracket are installed.
    c. Tighten bracket-to-engine block bolts, beginning with upper bolt. into transaxle output shaft seal.
    d. Apply very small amount of grease No. 1051344, or equivalent, to wheel drive shaft inner joint splines.
    e. **Torque** new outer tie rod nut to 15 ft. lbs.
    f. Then tighten nut an additional 180°.

Metro

1. Remove righthand drive axle as outlined under "Driveshaft, Replace."
2. Remove intermediate shaft support bearing mounting bolts.
3. Remove intermediate shaft.
4. Reverse procedure to install.

L & S Series

REMOVAL

1. Remove righthand driveshaft as outlined under "Driveshaft, Replace."
2. **On models equipped with DOHC engine,** proceed as follows:
    a. Loosen intake manifold to intermediate axle shaft support bracket top mounting bolt. **Do not remove.**
    b. Remove intake manifold to intermediate axle shaft support bracket lower mounting bolt.
    c. Position intake manifold to intermediate axle shaft support bracket aside to provide clearance.
    d. Tighten intake manifold bracket mounting bolts to hold bracket in position.

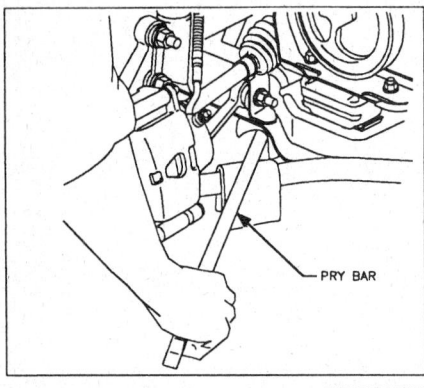

Fig. 18 Lower ball joint separation from steering knuckle. S-Series

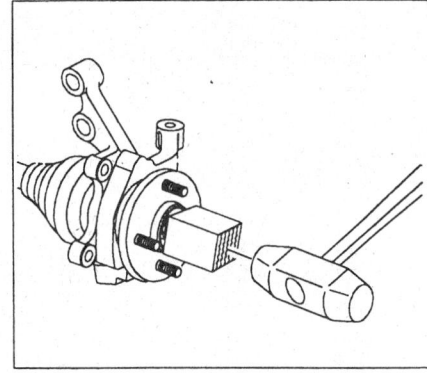

Fig. 19 Axle separation from hub. S-Series

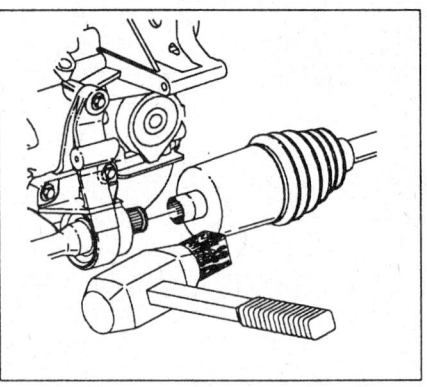

Fig. 20 Righthand drive axle removal. S-Series

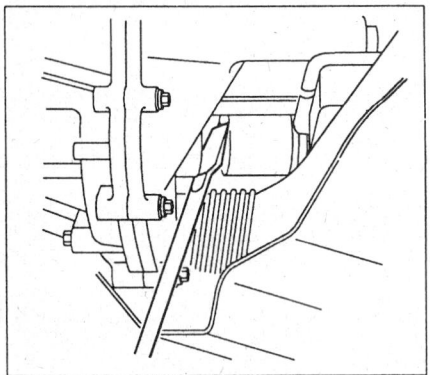

Fig. 21 Lefthand drive axle removal. S-Series

3. **On all models,** remove support bracket to engine block mounting bolt and intermediate axle shaft.

INSTALLATION

A new inner tripot joint must be installed whenever a new intermediate axle shaft is installed.

1. Install transaxle seal protector tool No. SA91112-T, or equivalent, **Fig. 22.**
2. Install intermediate driveshaft into transaxle. **Do not contact oil seal with shaft splines.**
3. After intermediate driveshaft splines have safely passed transaxle oil seal, remove seal protector.
4. Fully seat intermediate driveshaft into transaxle.
5. **On models equipped with DOHC engine,** proceed as follows:
   a. Install lower support bracket to engine block mounting bolts. **Do not tighten now.**
   b. Loosen support bracket to intake manifold mounting bolt and align holes.
   c. Tighten support bracket to intake manifold mounting bolts.
6. **On models equipped with SOHC engine,** install shaft support to engine block mounting bolts. **Do not tighten now.**
7. **On all models,** tighten support bracket to engine block mounting bolts.

INTERMEDIATE SHAFT SERVICE

All Models Except Metro, Prizm, Saturn & Vibe

DISASSEMBLE

1. Remove retaining ring and lip seal, **Fig. 66.**
2. Press shaft from bearing by positioning split plate tool No. J22912-1, or equivalent, behind inner slinger.
3. Remove retainer from support screws.
4. Press bearing from support using joint seal installer tool No. J23694, or equivalent.

ASSEMBLE

1. Press bearing into support using suitable press arbor plate across bearing.
2. Press inner slinger on shaft using split plate tool No. J22912-1, or equivalent.
3. Install retainer over shaft.
4. Place support with bearing on press arbor plate and press shaft into bearing until bearing inner race contacts shaft chamfer. **Do not press bearing beyond where chamfer begins on shaft.**
5. Press outer slinger on shaft using split plate.
6. Apply suitable RTV sealer to outer slinger and shaft joint.
7. Install lip seal using seal installer tool No. J34115, or equivalent.
8. Install retaining ring.
9. Install retainer to support.

Metro

DISASSEMBLE

1. Support intermediate shaft bearing arbor in suitable vise.
2. Remove outer bearing seal using oil seal remover tool No. J26941 and slide hammer tool No. J23907, or equivalents, **Fig. 67.**
3. Remove righthand driveshaft snap ring, **Fig. 68.**
4. Press righthand driveshaft from bear-

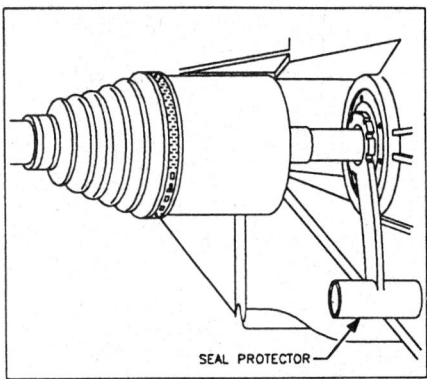

Fig. 22 Transaxle seal protector installed. S-Series

ing using side bearing remover tool No. J28888-D, or equivalent.
5. Remove inner bearing seal using oil seal remover tool and slide hammer.
6. Remove retaining clip and intermediate shaft

INSPECTION

1. Inspect intermediate shaft bearing for excessive wear or damage.
2. Inspect intermediate shaft bearing inner and outer seal for excessive wear or damage.

ASSEMBLE

1. Apply suitable wheel bearing lubricant to intermediate shaft bearing inner seal lip.
2. Install inner seal by tapping evenly using suitable plastic mallet. **Ensure seal is installed with garter spring facing out.**
3. Install righthand drive shaft into intermediate shaft into bearing using suitable hydraulic press.
4. Mount drive axle and bearing in suitable vice.
5. Install righthand driveshaft snap ring.
6. Apply wheel bearing lubricant part No. 1051344, or equivalent, to intermediate shaft bearing outer seal lip.
7. Install outer seal using oil seal installer tool No. J37751, or equivalent. **Ensure seal is installed with garter spring facing out.**

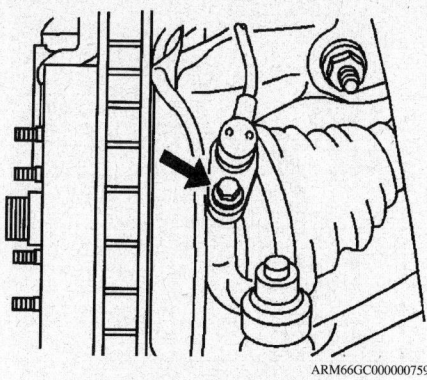

ARM66GC000000759

Fig. 23 Wheel speed sensor replacement. Vibe

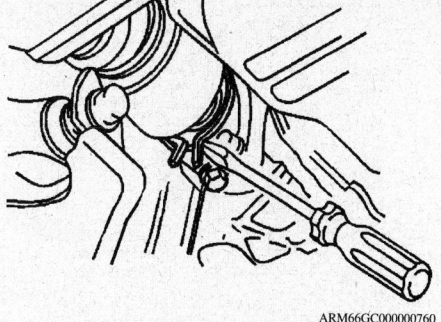

ARM66GC000000760

Fig. 24 Snap ring & lock bolt removal. Vibe

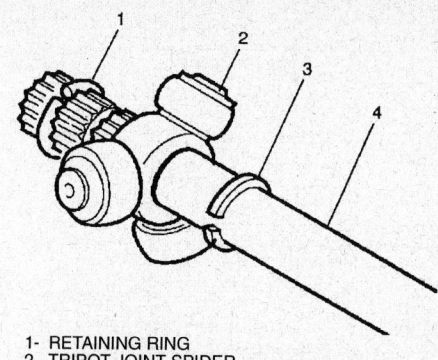

1- RETAINING RING
2- TRIPOT JOINT SPIDER
3- SPACER RING
4- HALFSHAFT BAR

GC3039900401000X

Fig. 25 Inner tripod joint assemble. All models except Cavalier, Metro, Prizm, Sunfire, Saturn & Vibe

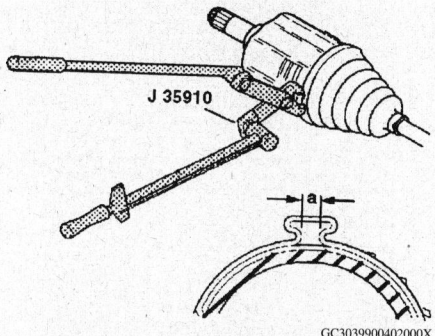

J 35910

GC3039900402000X

Fig. 26 Inner tripod joint alignment. All models except Cavalier, Metro, Prizm, Sunfire, Saturn & Vibe

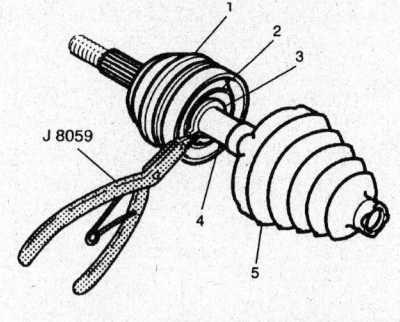

J 8059

GC3039900318000X

Fig. 27 Outer CV joint disassemble. All models except Cavalier, Metro, Prizm, Sunfire, Saturn & Vibe

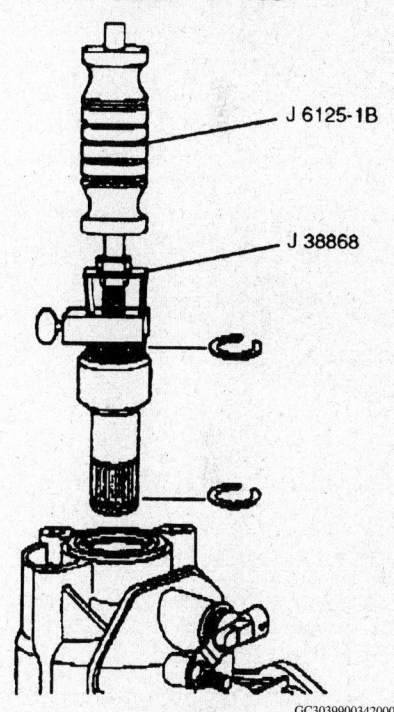

J 6125-1B

J 38868

GC3039900342000X

Fig. 28 Stub shaft removal. Cavalier & Sunfire

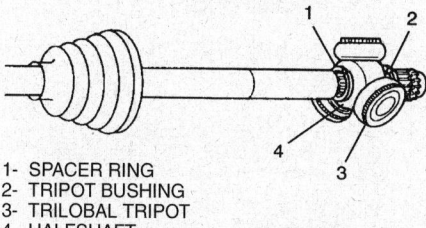

1- SPACER RING
2- TRIPOT BUSHING
3- TRILOBAL TRIPOT
4- HALFSHAFT

GC3039900404000X

Fig. 29 Inner tripod joint replacement. Cavalier & Sunfire

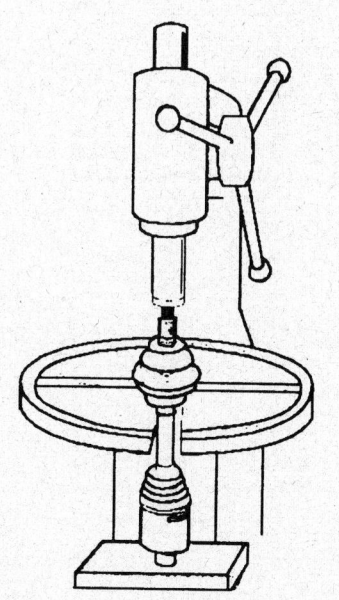

GC3039900349000X

Fig. 31 Driveshaft position in arbor press. Cavalier & Sunfire

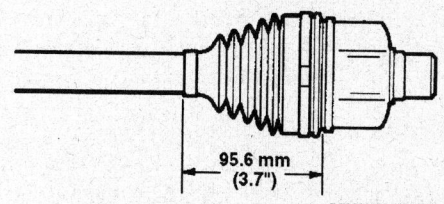

95.6 mm
(3.7")

GC3030000350020X

Fig. 32 Joint assembly dimension. Cavalier & Sunfire

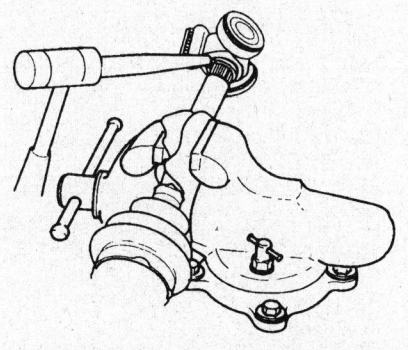

GC3039900348000X

Fig. 30 Tripod spider removal. Cavalier & Sunfire

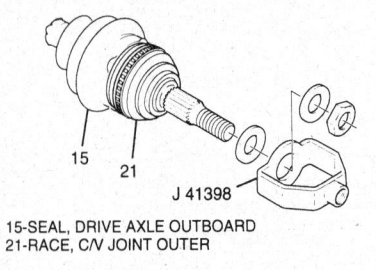

15-SEAL, DRIVE AXLE OUTBOARD
21-RACE, C/V JOINT OUTER

GC3039900354000X

Fig. 33 Outer CV joint removal. Cavalier & Sunfire

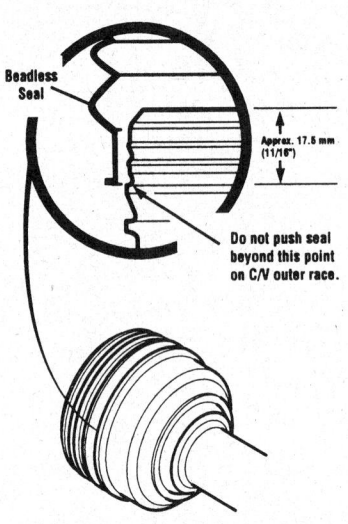

Beadless Seal

Approx. 17.5 mm (11/16")

Do not push seal beyond this point on C/V outer race.

GC3039900356000X

Fig. 34 CV outer joint installation measurement. Cavalier & Sunfire

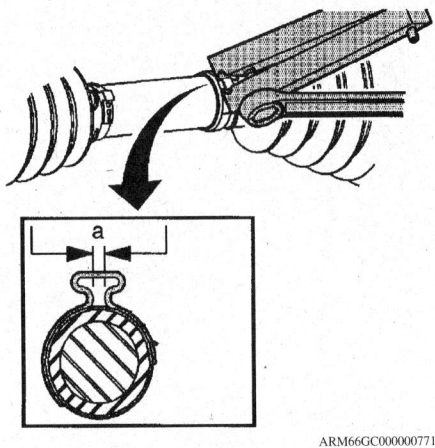

a

ARM66GC000000771

Fig. 35 Retaining clamp installation. ION

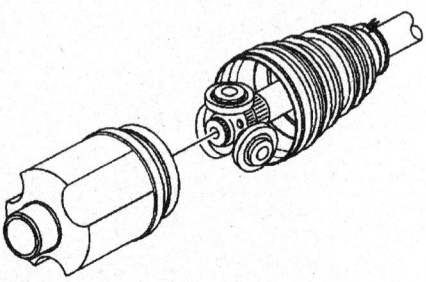

ARM66GC000000772

Fig. 36 Joint spider installation. ION

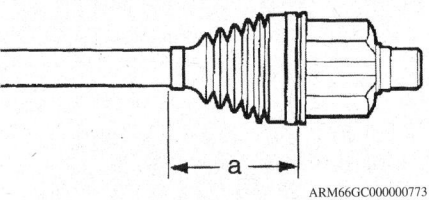

a

ARM66GC000000773

Fig. 37 Boot installation. ION

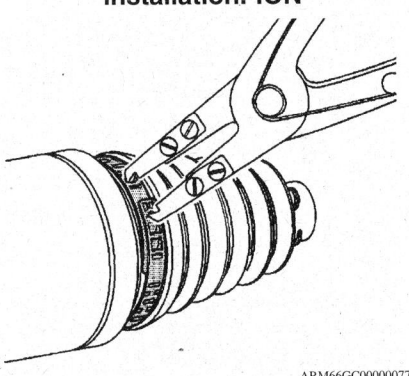

ARM66GC000000774

Fig. 38 Clamp crimp locations. ION

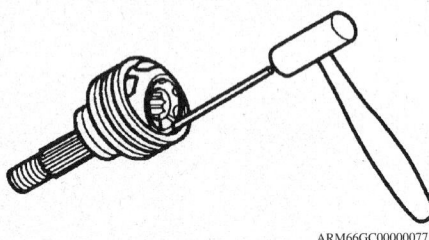

ARM66GC000000775

Fig. 39 CV joint ball removal. ION

ARM66GC000000776

Fig. 40 CV joint cage & inner race alignment. ION

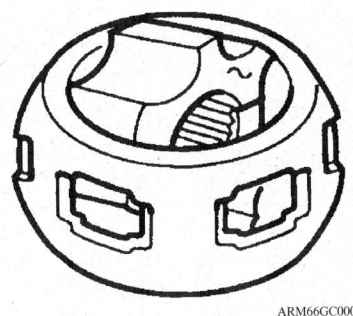

ARM66GC000000777

Fig. 41 CV joint inner race removal. ION

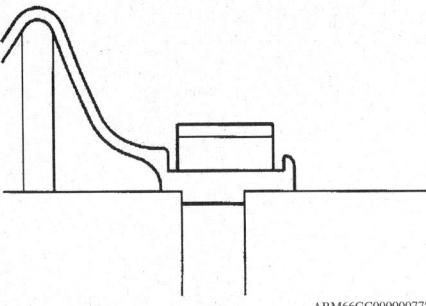

ARM66GC000000778

Fig. 42 Retaining boot & clamp installation. ION

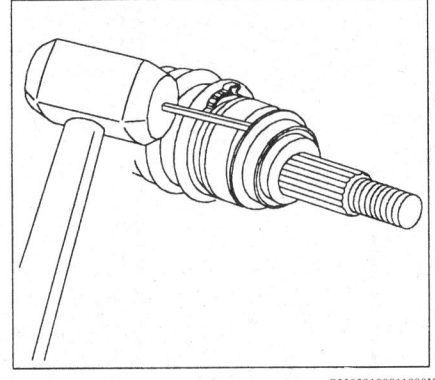

G33039100011000X

Fig. 44 Deflector ring removal. L & S-Series

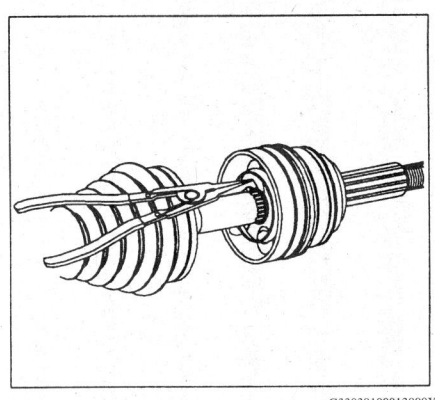

G33039100013000X

Fig. 45 Race retaining ring removal. L & S-Series

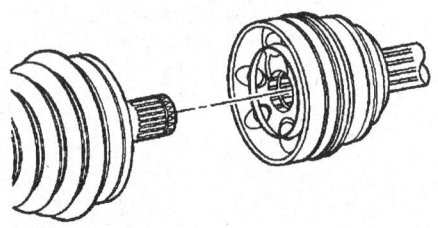

ARM66GC000000779

Fig. 43 CV joint installation. ION

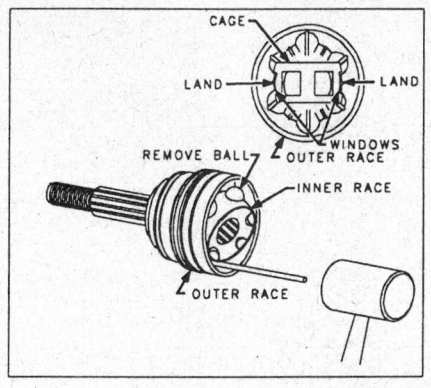

Fig. 46 CV joint ball removal. L & S-Series

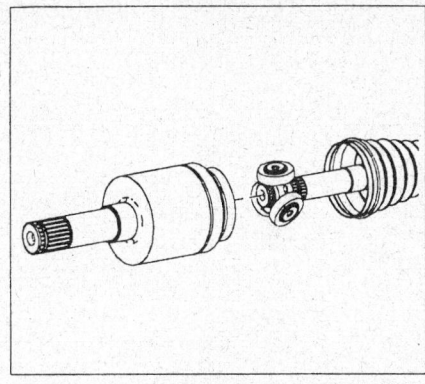

Fig. 47 Tripot housing removal. L & S-Series

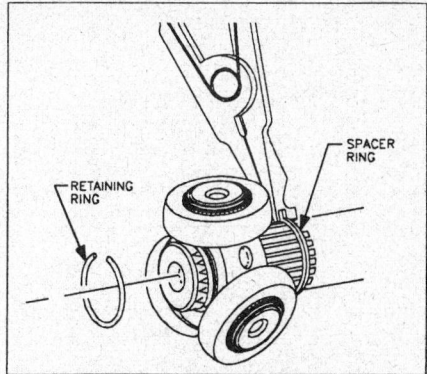

Fig. 48 Spider retaining ring removal. L & S-Series

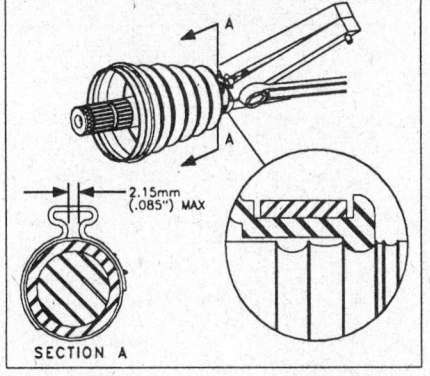

Fig. 49 Small tripot retaining ring crimp. L & S-Series

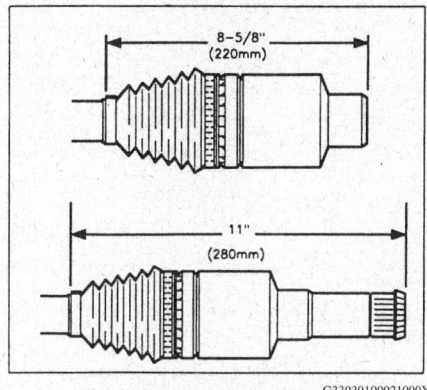

Fig. 50 Tripot assembly dimension. L & S-Series

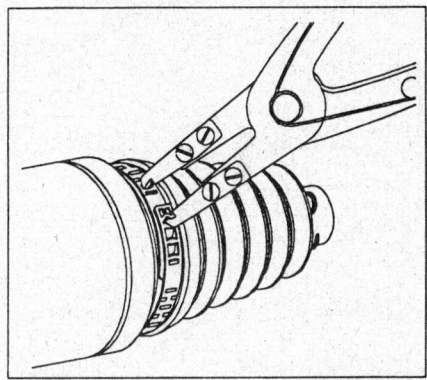

Fig. 51 Tripot large retaining clamp installation. L & S-Series

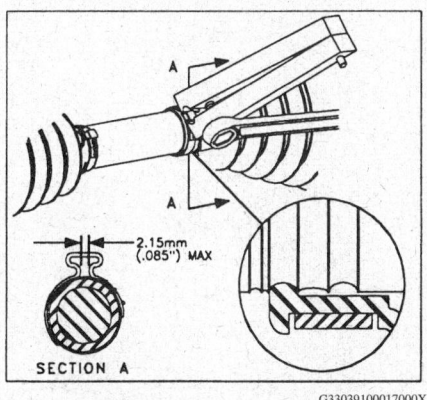

Fig. 52 Small CV joint retaining clamp installation. L & S-Series

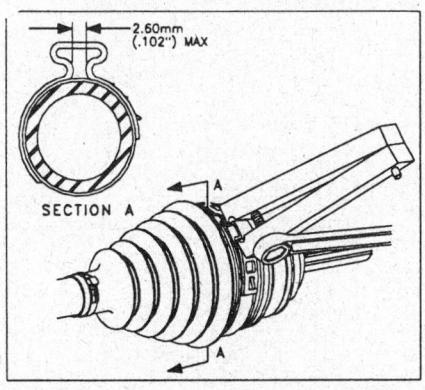

Fig. 53 Large CV joint retaining clamp crimp. L & S-Series

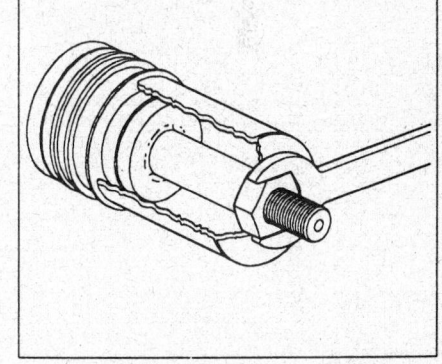

Fig. 54 Deflector ring installation. L & S-Series

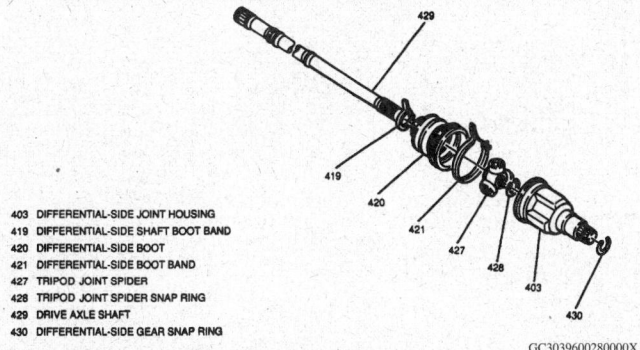

403 DIFFERENTIAL-SIDE JOINT HOUSING
419 DIFFERENTIAL-SIDE SHAFT BOOT BAND
420 DIFFERENTIAL-SIDE BOOT
421 DIFFERENTIAL-SIDE BOOT BAND
427 TRIPOD JOINT SPIDER
428 TRIPOD JOINT SPIDER SNAP RING
429 DRIVE AXLE SHAFT
430 DIFFERENTIAL-SIDE GEAR SNAP RING

Fig. 55 Exploded view of tripod inner joint. Metro

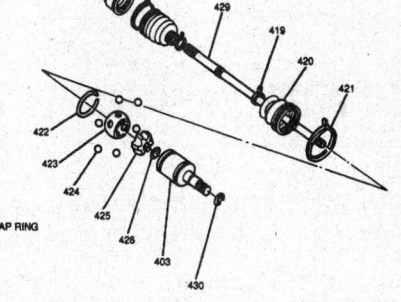

403 DIFFERENTIAL-SIDE JOINT HOUSING
419 DIFFERENTIAL-SIDE SHAFT BOOT BAND
420 DIFFERENTIAL-SIDE BOOT
421 DIFFERENTIAL-SIDE BOOT BAND
422 DIFFERENTIAL-SIDE JOINT HOUSING SNAP RING
423 ROLLER CAGE
424 ROLLER BALL
425 ROLLER BALL GUIDE
426 ROLLER BALL GUIDE SNAP RING
429 DRIVE AXLE SHAFT
430 DIFFERENTIAL-SIDE GEAR SNAP RING

Fig. 56 Exploded view of outer joint. Metro

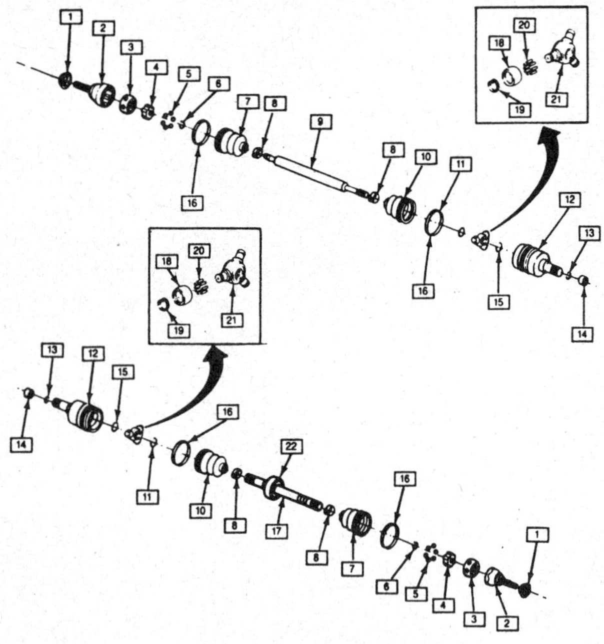

1	DEFLECTOR RING
2	CONSTANT VELOCITY JOINT OUTER RACE
3	CASE
4	CONSTANT VELOCITY JOINT INNER RACE
5	BALLS
6	AXLE SHAFT SNAP RING
7	OUTBOARD BOOT
8	SMALL BOOT CLAMP
9	RIGHT HAND DRIVE AXLE SHAFT
10	TRIPOD BOOT
11	AXLE SHAFT RETAINING RING
12	TRIPOD JOINT HOUSING
13	AXLE SHAFT RETAINING PINS
14	DRIVE AXLE DUST COVER
15	AXLE SHAFT SNAP RING
16	LARGE BOOT CLAMPS
17	LEFT HAND DRIVE AXLE SHAFT
18	TRIPOD JOINT BALL
19	TRIPOD JOINT BALL AND BEARING RETAINER
20	TRIPOD JOINT NEEDLE BEARINGS
21	TRIPOD JOINT SPIDER
22	DRIVE AXLE DAMPENER

GC3039100201000X

Fig. 57   Exploded view of front drive axle. Prizm

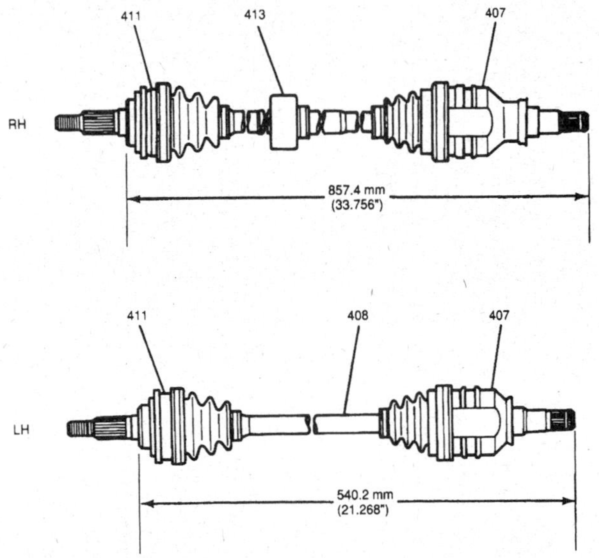

407   DIFFERENTIAL-SIDE JOINT HOUSING
408   DRIVE AXLE SHAFT
411   WHEEL-SIDE JOINT
413   DYNAMIC DAMPENER

GC3039400281000X

Fig. 58   Axle standard length. Prizm

ARM66GC000000761

Fig. 59   Driveshaft & tripod reference locations. Vibe

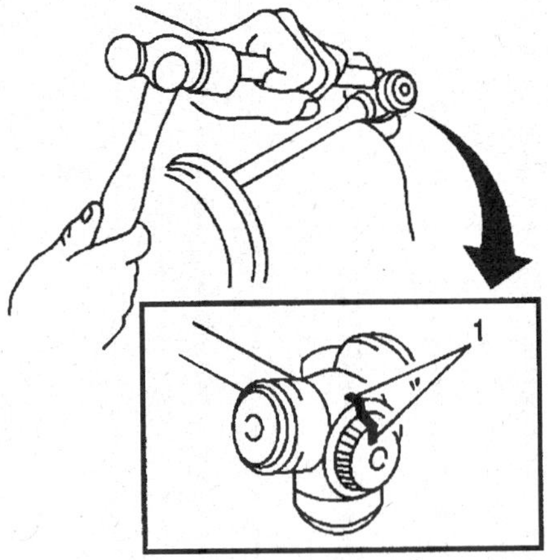

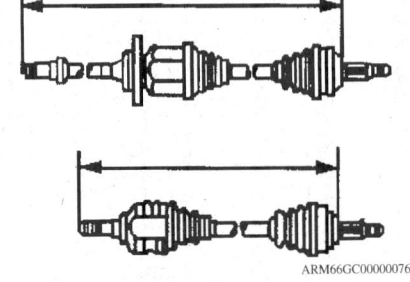

ARM66GC000000762

Fig. 60   Joint removal. Vibe

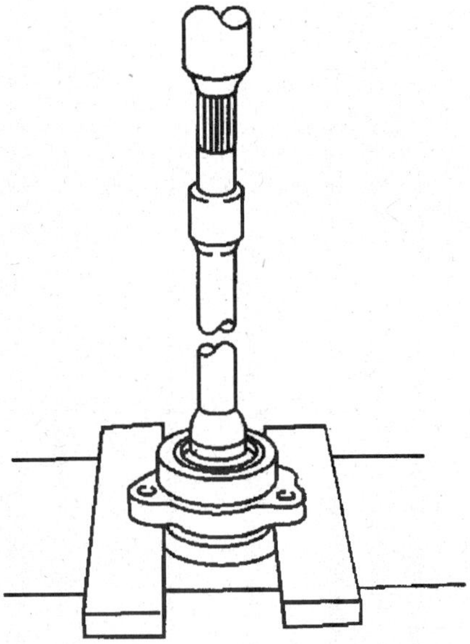

ARM66GC000000763

Fig. 61   Bearing removal. Vibe

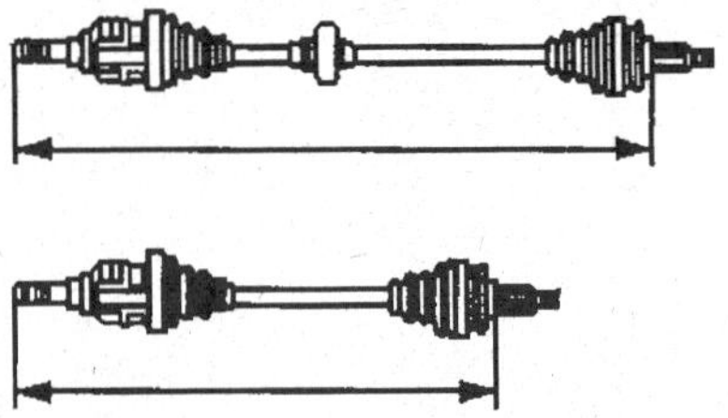

ARM66GC000000764

Fig. 62   Driveshaft measurement. Vibe w/FWD

ARM66GC000000765

Fig. 63   Driveshaft measurement. Vibe w/AWD

ARM66GC000000766

Fig. 64   Driveshaft assembly. Vibe

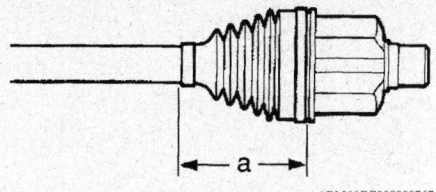

Fig. 65 Outboard seal installation. Vibe

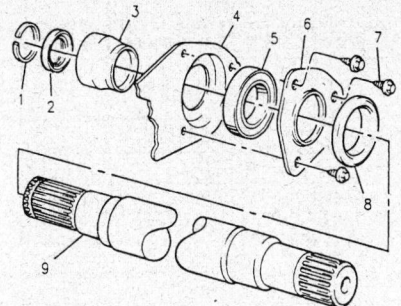

1 RETAINING RING
2 LIP SEAL
3 OUTER SLINGER
4 SUPPORT
5 BEARING
6 RETAINER
7 SCREW
8 INNER SLINGER
9 SHAFT

GC3039100203000X

Fig. 66 Exploded view of intermediate shaft. All models except Metro, Prizm, Saturn & Vibe

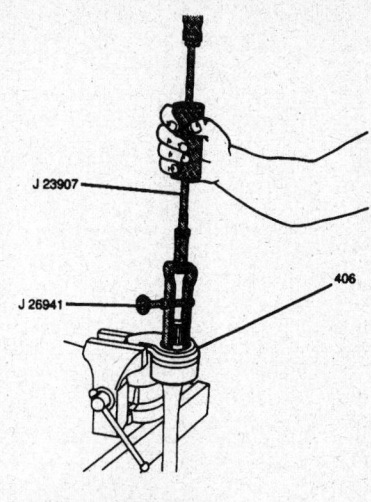

406 CENTER SUPPORT BEARING ARBOR (SEDAN MODEL)

GC3039600276000X

Fig. 67 Intermediate driveshaft support seal removal. Metro

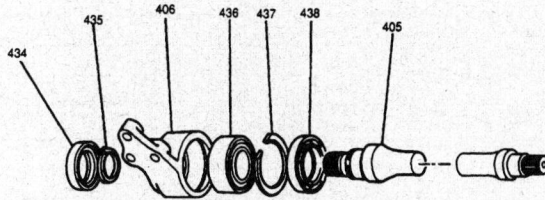

405 RIGHT INNER DRIVE AXLE (SEDAN MODEL)	436 CENTER SUPPORT BEARING (SEDAN MODEL)
406 CENTER SUPPORT BEARING ARBOR (SEDAN MODEL)	437 CENTER SUPPORT BEARING RETAINING RING (SEDAN MODEL)
434 CENTER SUPPORT BEARING OUTER SEAL (SEDAN MODEL)	438 CENTER SUPPORT BEARING INNER SEAL (SEDAN MODEL)
435 RIGHT INNER DRIVE AXLE SNAP RING (SEDAN MODEL)	

GC3039600277000X

Fig. 68 Exploded view of intermediate driveshaft support. Metro

TIGHTENING SPECIFICATIONS

Year	Component	Torque/Ft. Lbs.
ALERO, GRAND AM & MALIBU		
2001–05	Axle Nut	284⑥
	Ball Joint To Steering Knuckle	41
	CV Joint Large Boot Clamp	130
	CV Joint Small Boot Clamp	100
	Stabilizer Link	22
	Tie Rod To Knuckle	15③
	Wheel Lug Nuts	100
AURORA		
2001–03	Axle Nut	118
	Ball Joint To Steering Knuckle	50
	CV Joint Boot Clamp	130
	Stabilizer Link	13
	Wheel Lug Nuts	100
AVEO		
2004–05	Axle Shaft	221
	Damping Block Connection	59
	Engine Under Cover	31①
	Lower Ball Joint	37
	Rear Mounting Bracket	44
	Tie Rod	33
	Wheel Lug Nut	88
BONNEVILLE, LESABRE & PARK AVENUE		
2001–05	Axle Nut	118
	Ball Joint To Steering Knuckle	50
	CV Joint Boot Clamp	130
	Stabilizer Shaft Bracket	35
	Stabilizer Shaft Link	13
	Wheel Lug Nuts	100
CAVALIER & SUNFIRE		
2001–05	ABS Speed Sensor	107①
	Axle Nut	148
	Ball Joint To Knuckle	50③
	CV Joint Large Boot Clamp	130
	CV Joint Small Boot Clamp	100
	Stabilizer Link	13
	Wheel Lug Nuts	100
CENTURY, GRAND PRIX, IMPALA, INTRIGUE, MONTE CARLO & REGAL		
2001–05	Axle Nut	118
	Ball Joint To Steering Knuckle	15⑤
	CV Joint Large Boot Clamp	130
	CV Joint Small Boot Clamp	100
	Stabilizer Shaft Bracket	35
	Stabilizer Link	17
	Wheel Lug Nuts	100
DEVILLE		
2001–05	Axle Nut	⑦
	Ball Joint To Steering Knuckle Nut	37
	CV Joint Boot Clamp	130
	Stabilizer Bracket To Frame	33
	Stabilizer Link	41
	Wheel Lug Nuts	100

Continued

TIGHTENING
SPECIFICATIONS—Continued

Year	Component	Torque/Ft. Lbs.
ELDORADO		
2001–02	Axle Nut	118
	Ball Joint To Steering Knuckle Nut	37
	CV Joint Boot Clamp	130
	Stabilizer Bracket To Frame	33
	Stabilizer Link	41
	Wheel Lug Nuts	100
G6 & MALIBU MAXX		
2004–05	Axle Nut	59
	Lower Control Arm Bushing	⑧
	Steering Knuckle Ball Stud	⑧
	Tie Rod Ball Stud	44
	Wheel Lug Nut	100
ION		
2003–05	Driveshaft Wheel Nut	81
	Intermediate Drive Shaft Bracket-to-Engine Block	37
	Outer Tie Rod	⑨
	Stabilizer Shaft Link.	63
	Vehicle Speed Sensor	89①
L-SERIES		
2001–04	Axle Nut	②
	Ball Joint Stud Castle Nut	55
	Lower Control Arm Ball Stud	75
	Tie Rod End To Steering Knuckle	44
	Wheel Lugs Nuts	92
LACROSSE		
2005	Control Arm Ball Stud	50
	Drive Axle Seal Clamp	128
	Front Wheel Drive Shaft Nut	118
	Outer Tie Rod	34
	Stabilizer Shaft Link	17
LUMINA		
2001	Axle Nut	159
	Ball Joint To Steering Knuckle	63
	CV Joint Large Boot Clamp	130
	CV Joint Small Boot Clamp	100
	Stabilizer Link	17
	Stabilizer Shaft Bracket	35
	Wheel Lug Nuts	100
METRO		
2001	ABS Speed Sensor	71①
	Axle Nut	129
	Ball Stud	44
	Intermediate Shaft Bearing Support	44
	Transaxle Drain	21
	Wheel Bearing Support	40
	Wheel Lug Nuts	44

TIGHTENING
SPECIFICATIONS—Continued

Year	Component	Torque/Ft. Lbs.
PRIZM		
2001–02	ABS Speed Sensor	71①
	Axle Nut	166
	Ball Joint-To-Lower Control Arm	105
	Splash Shield	71①
	Tie Rod End	36
	Wheel Lug Nuts	76
S-SERIES		
2001–02	Axle Nut	148
	Ball Joint Stud Castle Nut	55
	Intermediate Shaft Bracket	22
	Intermediate Shaft Support Bracket-To-Engine Block	40
	Intermediate Shaft Support Bracket-To-Intake Manifold	71①
	Tie Rod End To Steering Knuckle	33
	Wheel Lug Nuts	103
SEVILLE		
2001–04	Axle Nut	118
	Ball Joint To Steering Knuckle Nut	88①④
	CV Joint Boot Clamp	130
	Stabilizer Bracket To Frame	33
	Stabilizer Link	41
	Wheel Lug Nuts	100
VIBE		
2003–05	ABS Speed Sensor Retaining Bolt	71①
	Ball Joint To Control Arm Bolts & Nuts	66
	Drive Axle Nut	159
	Splash Shield	71①
	Tie Rod End Nut	36
	Wheel Lug Nuts	76

① — Inch lbs.
② — Refer to "Driveshaft, Replace" for tightening procedure.
③ — Tighten an additional 180°.
④ — Tighten an additional 150°.
⑤ — Tighten an additional 120°.
⑥ — Type one, 284 ft. lbs; Type two, 173 ft. lbs.
⑦ — Soft Ride (FE1) & Sport suspension (FE3), 118 ft. lbs,; Heavy duty suspension (FE7), 170 ft. lbs.
⑧ — Refer to "Driveshaft, Replace" for tightening procedure.
⑨ — Refer to "Intermediate Shaft, Replace" for tightening procedure.

DRIVE AXLES

NOTE: On Air Bag Equipped Models, Refer To "Air Bag System Precautions" Located In The Front Of This Manual For System Disarming & Arming Procedures.

NOTE: Refer To "Computer Relearn Procedures" Located In The Front Of This Manual When Battery Power To The Computer Has Been Interrupted.

INDEX

APPLICATION CHART

Model	Gear Ratio	Ring Gear Diameter, Inch
Camaro & Firebird	2.73	7.625
	3.08	7.625
	3.23	7.625
	3.42	7.625
Catera	3.90	7.401
Corvette	2.73	①
	3.15	①
	3.42	①
CTS	3.23	7.625
	3.42	7.625
	3.73	7.625
	3.91	7.625
GTO	3.46	—
STS	3.23	7.625
	3.73	7.625
	3.91	7.625
XLR	2.93	8.000

① — 2001–04, 7.625–inch; 2005, 8-inch.

IDENTIFICATION
Camaro & Firebird

Axle identification numbers can be found stamped on the righthand front section of the axle shaft housing, **Fig. 1.** Production option codes are also located on the service components identification label.

Corvette, CTS, STS & XLR

Axle identification numbers can be found on a tag, located on the side of the differential carrier, **Figs. 2 through 5.**

DESCRIPTION
Camaro & Firebird

The standard rear axle is a semi-floating hypoid rear axle. When the vehicle turns a corner, the differential allows the outer rear wheel to turn faster than inner wheel. The inner wheel, turning slower with respect to the outer wheel, slows its side differential pinion gear. The differential pinion gears roll around the slowed side differential pinion gear, driving the other differential pinion gear and wheel at a faster pace.

Models equipped with the standard axle and Anti-Lock Brakes (ABS), a single rear wheel speed sensor is located on the differential carrier behind the ring gear. A wheel speed sensor mounts on the top of the axle housing opposite the reluctor wheel.

The limited slip rear axle differential found on Camaro and Firebird models is the Zexel Torsen differential. Unlike previous limited slip differentials, the Torsen assembly does not utilize cone clutches, but rather a system of close tolerance gears. With normal operation, both tires and wheels rotate at equal speeds while vehicle is being driven straight ahead. An equal driving force is delivered to each wheel during straight ahead driving. When turning a corner, the inside wheel requires extra driving force. This unequal driving force results in a compensation of inside and outside axles by differential.

All rear axle components of vehicles with limited slip rear axle are interchangeable with those equipped with the standard rear axle, except for the differential case. The differential case is non-serviceable and must be replaced as a unit.

On models equipped with limited slip axles, Anti-Lock Brakes (ABS) and Traction Control system (TCS), rear wheel speed sensors are mounted on the axle shafts behind the axle flange. Reluctor wheels are integral with the axle shafts and are not serviced separately. The entire axle must be replaced if reluctor wheel replacement is required.

Corvette

The splined output shaft of the transmission drives the pinion, which in turn, rotates the ring gear and differential case assembly. The limited slip differential distributes

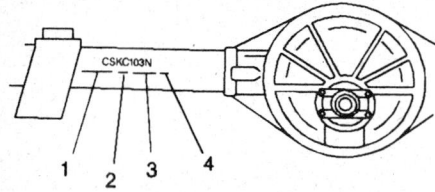

Fig. 1 Axle identification. Camaro & Firebird

torque/power to the rear wheels via individual axle shaft assemblies. The limited-slip differential is of a conventional separator plate and friction disc type design. The differential housing, side covers, pinion housing, and differential case halves are constructed of cast aluminum. The internal components incorporate a hypoid gear set, ring and pinion, carrier assembly, and pinion housing assembly. The pinion is supported in a pinion housing by tapered roller bearings. The pinion is positioned rearward of the ring gear centerline. Pinion position, ring gear position, and carrier bearing preload are determined by shimming procedures.

Each ring gear has specific setup dimensions, A1 and A2 values, stamped onto the side area of the gear. The A1 and A2 values are unique to each ring gear/pinion and are determined during the manufacturers gear/pinion noise and vibration setup and testing. The vehicle speed sensor reluctor ring is incorporated into the outside area of the ring gear. The vehicle speed sensor detects the rotational pulses produced by the reluctor ring and send the signal to the Vehicle Control Module (VCM). The differential assembly is available in three gear ratios. The 3.42 ratio axle is used in all manual transmission applications. The 2.73 ratio axle is standard equipment for automatic transmission applications with an optional 3.15 ratio axle available.

Some 2005 models have a differential lubricant pump and cooler. Oil is pulled from the sump through an external oil pipe into the pump. Oil is pumped through an external oil pipe to the cooler. The oil is cooled by dissipating heat with transmission oil returning from radiator mounted cooler.

CTS & STS

The differential housing, side cover and pinion housing are constructed of cast aluminum. The internal components incorporate a hypoid gear set, ring and pinion, carrier assembly and pinion housing assembly. The pinion is supported in a pinion housing by tapered roller bearings. The pinion is positioned forward of the ring gear centerline. All models have a 7 5/8- inch ring gear. Each ring gear has specific setup dimensions, A1 and A2 values, stamped onto the side area of the gear. The A1 and A2 values are unique to each ring gear/pinion and are determined during the manufacturers gear/pinion noise and vibration setup and testing. Pinion position, ring gear position and carrier bearing preload are determined by shimming procedures

GTO

The differential assembly, is a four pinion type limited slip differential final drive assembly mounted to an independent rear suspension. The differential is mounted directly to the crossmember which is rubber mounted to the underbody. The differential case and drive pinion are mounted in opposed taper roller bearing in the carrier. Differential case side bearing preload adjustment is provided by screw adjusters in the sides of the case. Pinion bearing preload is provided by a collapsible spacer. Torque is transferred from the propeller shaft to the differential via the pinion flange which is splined to the hypoid pinion. The torque is then transferred from the pinon through the ring gear, differential case, differential pinion cross shafts, differential pinions, side gears, and then via splines to the inner axle shafts and the drive shafts.

The limited slip differential performs the same functions as the conventual type differential. However, should the opposite wheel begin to spin, it transfers driving force to the wheel with traction. The differential case houses a cone type clutch pack that is an integral part of the side gears. The four pinion type limited slip differential has three pre-load springs inclosed in the center pinion cross shaft. The limited slip differential directs the major driving force to the wheel with greater amount of traction, but will not interfere with steering characteristics of differential action. The partial locking action, due to the spring load on the cones, is automatically increased by the inherent separating forces between the side gears and pinion, which progressively increases the resistance in the differential as applied torque is increased.

When the rear wheels are under extremely unbalanced conditions, such as one wheel on dry road and the other in mud or snow, with a standard differential, wheel spin easily occurs if over acceleration is attempted. However, with a limited slip differential, when the tendency for wheel spin occurs friction generated inside the case transfers driving force to the non-spinning wheel. In the event of continued spinning, a whirring sound from the over-running cones is produced, but this condition/sound does not indicate a failure of the unit.

XLR

The vehicle is powered by 4.6L engine. Motion is transferred from the engine crankshaft/flywheel through the driveline support, propeller shaft, assembly to the 5L50-E automatic transmission. The splined output shaft of the transmission drives the pinion, which in turn, rotates the ring gear and differential case assembly. The limited slip differential distributes torque/power to the rear wheels via individual axle shaft assemblies. The limited-slip differential is of a conventional separator plate and friction disc type design.

The differential housing, side covers, pinion housing, and differential case halves are constructed of cast aluminum. The in-

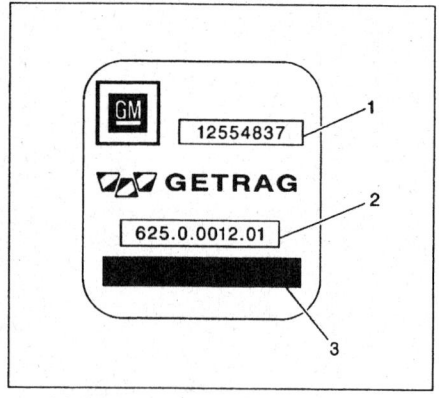

(1) GM Part Number
(2) Getrag Part Number
(3) Serial Number

Available Axle Ratios

GM P/N	Axle Ratio	Transmission
12551769	342	Manual
12554837	273 (Base)	Automatic
12556313	315 (Optional)	Automatic

GC3039700290000X

Fig. 2 Axle identification. Corvette

ternal components incorporate a hypoid gear set, ring and pinion, carrier assembly, and pinion housing assembly. The pinion is supported in a pinion housing by tapered roller bearings.

The pinion is positioned rearward of the ring gear centerline. Pinion position, ring gear position, and carrier bearing preload are determined by shimming procedures.

All models have an 8-inch ring gear. Each ring gear has specific setup dimensions, A1 and A2 values, stamped onto the side area of the gear. The A1 and A2 values are unique to each ring gear/pinion and are determined during the manufacturers gear/pinion noise and vibration setup and testing.

The differential assembly is available in one gear ratio. The 2.93 ratio axle is standard equipment for automatic transmissions.

TROUBLESHOOTING

Preliminary Inspections

Before the rear axle is to be serviced, ensure the source of the problem is the rear axle itself and not originating in other sources such as noise from the tires, road surface, engine, transmission, wheel bearings, muffler or body components. Perform the following procedures to inspect for other sources that could be mistaken for axle noise:

1. Ensure rear axle lubricant is at proper level and type, then select level asphalt road to reduce tire and body noise.
2. After vehicle has been driven far enough to warm lubricant, record speed noise occurs.

(1) Ratio
(2) GM Part Number
(3) Getrag Part Number
(4) Serial Number

Available Axle Ratios

Axle Ratio	Drive/Engine	Flange Size
3:23	RWD/3.6L V6	105 mm
3:42	RWD/3.2L V6	96 mm
3:42	RWD/2.8L V6	105 mm
3:73	RWD/5.7L V8	86 mm
3:91	RWD/2.6L V6	96 mm

ARM0400000001025

Fig. 3   Axle identification. CTS

(1) Ratio
(2) GM Part Number
(3) Getrag Part Number
(4) Serial Number

Available Axle Ratios

Axle Ratio	Drive/Engine	Flange Size
3:23	RWD/4.6L V8	105 mm
3:23	AWD/4.6L V8	96 mm
3:73	RWD/3.6L V6	105 mm
3:91	AWD/3.6L V6	96 mm

ARM0400000001041

Fig. 4   Axle identification. STS

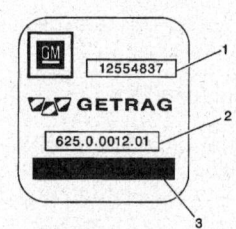

(1) GM Part Number
(2) Getrag Part Number
(3) Serial Number

Available Axle Ratios

GM P/N	Axle Ratio	Transmission
12566925	2.93 - Standard	Automatic

ARM0300000000362

Fig. 5   Axle identification. XLR

Checks	Action
Excessive pinion to ring gear backlash	Adjust the pinion to ring gear backlash.
Worn pinion and ring gear	Replace the pinion and the ring gear.
Worn pinion bearings	Replace the pinion bearings.
Loose pinion bearings	Adjust the pinion bearings preload.
Excessive pinion end play	Adjust the pinion end play.
Worn differential bearings	Replace the differential bearings.
Loose differential bearings	Adjust the differential bearing preload.
Excessive ring gear runout	Replace the ring gear.
Low oil level	Fill the fluid level to specifications with the proper lubricant.
Wrong or poor grade oil	Drain and refill the system with the proper lubricant.
Bent axle housing	Replace the axle housing.

ARM0400000001026

Fig. 6   Noisy In Drive. Camaro & Firebird

3. Stop vehicle.
4. With vehicle in neutral run engine slowly through RPM range that noise occurred to determine if noise was caused by exhaust or powertrain.
5. Inspect for tire noise by temporarily inflating all tires to approximately 50 psi for test purposes only.
6. Drive vehicle on level asphalt road and observe if change in noise occurs compared to noise while tires are inflated at normal pressure.
7. After test is completed ensure tires are inflated to manufacturer's specifications.
8. Inspect front and rear wheel bearings by lightly applying brakes while keeping vehicle speed steady. If the noise diminishes, inspect front and rear wheel bearings by jacking up front wheels, then spinning or shaking them to determine if bearings are loose.
9. With vehicle jacked up, inspect for metal to metal contact: between spring and opening in frame; upper and lower control arm bushings, and frame and axle housing brackets. Ensure there is no metal to metal contact between floor of body and frame.

Diagnosis
CAMARO & FIREBIRD

Refer to **Figs. 6 through 10** for rear axle noise diagnosis.

CATERA

Refer to **Fig. 11** for differential noise diagnosis.

CORVETTE, CTS, STS & XLR

Refer to **Figs. 12 through 16** for differential noise diagnosis.

GTO

Refer to **Figs. 17 through 21** for differential noise diagnosis.

DISASSEMBLE
Differential
CAMARO & FIREBIRD
DRUM BRAKES

1. Remove axle housing drain plug or rear cover and drain fluid into suitable container, **Fig. 22.**
2. Remove rear axle assembly as outlined under "Rear Axle & Suspension" in "Camaro & Firebird" chapter.
3. Remove rear brake pipe assemblies from rear brake cylinders and disconnect center hose assembly from junction block.
4. Remove rear brake assemblies from housing, then the rear axle shaft bearings and seals.
5. Remove rear backing plates, then the differential case and drive pinion gear.

DISC BRAKES

A shim may be installed between the rear brake caliper mounting plate and axle shaft tube flange on housing. This shim centers the rear brake caliper and pads over the brake rotor, ensuring even brake pad assembly pressure during braking. This shim may have to be changed when the housing is replaced.

1. Remove axle housing drain plug or rear cover and drain fluid into suitable container.

Checks	Action
Worn pinion and ring gear	Adjust or replace the pinion and the ring gear.
Insufficient pinion and ring gear backlash	Adjust the pinion and the ring gear backlash.

ARM0400000001027

Fig. 7   Noisy When Coasting. Camaro & Firebird

Checks	Action
Warped ring gear	Replace the ring gear.
Loose differential case bolts	Tighten differential case bolts to specifications.

ARM0400000001028

Fig. 8   Intermitten Noise. Camaro & Firebird

Checks	Action
Flat spot on the pinion or the ring gear teeth	Replace the pinion and the ring gear.
Flat spot on the pinion bearing	Replace the bearing.
Worn pinion splines	Replace the pinion.
Worn axle shaft dowel holes	Replace the axle shaft.
Worn hub studs	Replace the wheel studs.
Bent axle shaft	Replace the axle shaft.

ARM0400000001029

Fig. 9   Constant Noise. Camaro & Firebird

Checks	Action
Worn differential pinion gears	Replace the pinion gears.
Worn axle shaft splines	Replace the axle shaft.

ARM0400000001030

Fig. 10   Noisy On Turns. Camaro & Firebird

2. Remove rear axle assembly as outlined under "Rear Axle & Suspension" in "Camaro & Firebird" chapter.
3. Remove rear brake pipe assemblies from rear brake hose junction block and junction block from housing.
4. Remove rear brake pipe and hose assemblies from housing.
5. Remove brake shaft bearing assemblies and seals, then the caliper anchor brackets and mounting plates.
6. Remove shim.
7. Remove differential case and drive pinion gear.

CATERA

1. Remove rear axle assembly as outlined under "Rear Axle & Suspension" in "Catera" chapter.
2. Mount differential into holding fixture tool No. J-3289-20, or equivalent.
3. Remove mounting bolts and rear axle housing cover.
4. Remove drive axle seals using suitable prybar.
5. Install side bearing preload clamp plate tool No. J-42143, or equivalent, using rear axle housing cover bolts, onto righthand side of rear axle housing cover, **Fig. 23.**
6. Install side bearing preload clamp plate tool No. J-42143, or equivalent, onto righthand differential side bearing outer race. Tighten clamp only enough to relieve significant amount of bearing preload from snap ring.
7. Tighten clamp onto side bearing preload clamp tool No. J-42149, or equivalent.
8. Rotate rear axle differential adjuster ring so that ring opening is accessible using suitable hammer and drift.
9. Remove adjuster snap ring from righthand bearing cover. using suitable heavy duty snap ring pliers.
10. Remove side bearing preload clamp tool and side bearing preload clamp plate tool from rear axle housing.
11. Remove adjuster ring from lefthand side of rear axle housing.
12. Drive out righthand differential side bearing outer race from cover opening

of differential using suitable rubber-faced mallet and piece of wood. Inspect differential side bearing seal on outer race for damage.
13. Lightly tap carrier through righthand side bearing bore using suitable rubber mallet and piece of wood to drive lefthand side differential bearing outer race out of housing. Inspect differential side bearing seal on outer race for damage.
14. Remove differential carrier from rear axle housing.
15. Remove drive pinion from differential carrier using suitable rubber mallet.
16. Remove drive pinion seal from differential carrier, then drive pinion outer bearing from bearing bore.
17. Remove drive pinion gear inner bearing from pinion gear.
18. Remove pinion bearing outer races from rear axle housing.

CORVETTE & XLR

1. Remove rear axle assembly as outlined under "Rear Axle & Suspension" in "Corvette" or "XLR" chapter.
2. **On models equipped with automatic transmission,** remove differential carrier seal plate from front of differential carrier housing, then O-ring. Discard O-ring.
3. **On all models,** remove differential carrier mount.
4. Remove fill plug washer and fill tag.
5. Remove drain plug, allowing fluid to drain into suitable container.
6. Remove mounting bolt and vehicle speed sensor.
7. Remove mounting bolts, righthand side differential carrier cover and O-ring seal, **Fig. 24.** Discard O-ring.
8. Install two 10 mm nuts onto righthand side transmission mounting stud and remove stud from block.
9. Remove mounting bolts and righthand side transmission stud mount from differential carrier.
10. Remove righthand side output shaft snap ring.
11. Remove differential case assembly from differential carrier using differen-

tial housing lifting tool No. J-42155, or equivalent.
12. Remove differential carrier cover bolts, then rear cover and O-ring seal. Discard O-ring.
13. Remove pinion cartridge bolts.
14. Heat differential carrier around pinion cartridge using heat gun tool No. J-25070, or equivalent.
15. Remove pinion cartridge from differential carrier by threading two long bolts into pinion cartridge.
16. Remove pinion cartridge O-ring seal. Discard O-ring.
17. Remove pinion cartridge shim pack from differential carrier. **Tag shim pack to indicate its installation position.**
18. Remove lefthand side differential carrier cover bolts, then the cover and O-ring. Discard O-ring.

CTS & STS

1. Remove bearing carrier bolts from pinion housing, **Fig. 25.**
2. Heat around pinion housing to ease pinion removal using suitable heat gun.
3. Place two bolts in jackscrew holes, then tighten bolts equally to push out pinion assembly.
4. Remove pinion housing assembly, shims and O-ring seal from differential housing. **Tag shims for reference during assembly.**
5. Remove nine housing side cover bolts.
6. Remove housing side cover from housing using pry tabs.
7. Remove O-ring seal from cover.
8. Remove differential carrier from housing.
9. Remove axle oil seal from housing side cover.
10. Install bearing race remover tool No. J-42194, or equivalent, into bearing race, **Fig. 26.**
11. Place side cover on suitable press, then using pinion bearing race installer tool No. J-5590, or equivalent, press out bearing race and shim. **Tag shim and race for reference during assembly.**
12. Remove axle oil seal from housing.
13. Install bearing race remover tool No. J-42194, or equivalent, behind bearing race, **Fig. 27.**
14. Place housing on suitable press, then using pinion bearing race installer tool

Condition	Cause
Noise is the same in drive or coast.	• Road noise. • Tire noise. • Front wheel bearing noise. • Rear wheel bearing noise. • Incorrect driveline angles.
Noise changes on a different type of road.	1. Road noise. 2. Tire noise.
Noise tone is lower as the vehicle speed is lowered.	Tire noise.
Noise is produced with the vehicle standing and driving.	• Engine noise. • Automatic transmission noise.
Vibration	• Unbalanced propeller shaft. • Damaged propeller shaft. • Tire unbalance. • Worn universal joint in the propeller shaft. • Incorrect driveline angles.
A knock or a click approximately every two revolutions of the rear wheel.	Rear wheel bearing.
Noise is most pronounced on turns.	• Rear wheel bearing. • Worn rear tie rod ends.
A continuous low pitch whirring or scraping noise starting at a relatively low speed.	Differential drive pinion gear inner or outer bearing noise.
Drive noise, coast noise, or float noise.	Differential ring gear and differential drive pinion gear noise.
Clunk on acceleration or deceleration	• A worn differential drive pinion gear or differential side gear hub counterbore worn oversize. • A worn universal joint on propeller shaft.
Groan in forward or reverse	• Wrong axle lubricant in axle. • Differential drive pinion gear bearing worn.
Clunk or knock on rough road operation.	Worn rear tie rod ends.

GC3039700298000A

Fig. 11 Differential noise diagnosis. Catera

No. J-5590, or equivalent, press out bearing and race. **Tag shim and race for reference during assembly.**

Drive Pinion

CAMARO & FIREBIRD

1. Scribe reference mark between drive pinion and driveshaft yoke.
2. Hold yoke with suitable tool, then remove pinion nut and yoke. **Replace yoke if it shows wear in seal-to-flange contacting surface.**
3. Install pinion removal tool No. J-22536, or equivalent, to end of pinion shaft, then using suitable hammer, tap pinion shaft out of pinion housing. **Apply heavy hand pressure onto tool to keep outer drive pinion gear bearing seated. Hold gear end of pinion shaft when removing to prevent it from falling from axle housing. Remove and discard pinion nut and collapsible spacer.**
4. Remove front and rear bearing races from pinion housing using drift positioned in race slots and hammer.
5. Remove rear pinion bearing using arbor press and adapters. Measure and record thickness of shim found under rear bearing.

CATERA

1. Inspect differential drive pinion gear inner and outer bearing preload.
2. Shake differential drive pinion gear inner and outer bearing to inspect for drive pinion gear looseness if there is no preload reading.
3. Remove differential drive pinion flange.
4. Drive pinion gear from differential

housing using suitable rubber-faced dead blow hammer.
5. Remove pinion gear bearing spacer from pinion gear.
6. Remove pinion gear inner bearing from drive pinion gear.

CORVETTE & XLR

1. Unstake drive pinion nut from drive pinion using suitable punch.
2. Remove drive pinion nut from drive pinion using spanner wrench tool No. J-42163 and pinion gear holder tool No. J-42164, or equivalents.
3. Remove drive pinion bearing using hydraulic press, V-blocks and side gear compressor tool No. J-42162, or equivalent. Discard bearing and spacer. **Drive pinion bearings and spacer must be replaced as a set.**
4. Remove front drive pinion bearing from drive pinion using hydraulic press, side gear compressor tool No. J-42162 and front pinion bearing remover tool No. J-42166, or equivalents. Discard bearing.
5. Remove front drive pinion bearing inner race from drive pinion housing using hydraulic press and bearing race remover tool No. J-42194, or equivalent. Discard bearing race.
6. Remove rear drive pinion bearing outer race from drive pinion housing using hydraulic press and bearing race remover tool No. J-42194, or equivalent. Discard bearing race.

CTS & STS

1. Remove pinion flange nut from pinion shaft using holding tool No. J-45012, or equivalent.
2. Remove pinion flange from shaft.

GTO

1. Drain rear axle lubricant into suitable container.
2. Center punch alignment marks on pinion flange, nut and end for assembly alignment.
3. Measure and record pinion shaft rotational torque.
4. Remove pinion flange nut and pinion flange using flange holding tool No. DT-47735, or equivalent.
5. Remove pinion seal using suitable seal puller

Ring Gear & Differential Housing

CATERA

1. Clamp differential carrier in soft jawed vise.
2. Remove ring gear bolts.
3. Separate gear from differential carrier using suitable dead blow hammer and brass drift.
4. Drive out pinion shaft from side of carrier at machined recession in shaft using suitable drift and hammer.
5. Remove pinion gear shaft retaining ring from differential carrier.
6. Clamp counterpiece of pinion side gear alignment tool No. J-42178, or equivalent, in suitable vise.
7. Place carrier onto counterpiece with ring gear flange towards bottom, facing up.
8. Attach ½ inch drive ratchet to drive shaft pinion gear, **Fig. 28.**
9. Rotate pinion gears and accompanying washer from installed position using ratchet while holding differential carrier.
10. Remove shims from differential carrier.

SUBASSEMBLY SERVICE

Standard Differential

1. If side carrier bearings are to be replaced, remove bearings using suitable bearing puller.
2. Remove differential pinion shaft lock bolt and pinion shaft.
3. Remove differential pinions and thrust washers, side gears and side gear thrust washers. Record installation position for assembly. Keep thrust washers with respective gears.
4. Remove bolts, ring gear and driving ring gear from case using drift and hammer. Ring gear bolts have lefthand hand threads. **Do not pry between ring gear and case.**
5. Inspect components as outlined in "Cleaning & Inspection."
6. Lubricate all components with specified gear lubricant prior to assembly.
7. Install thrust washers on side gears and mount side gears in case.
8. Position one differential pinion less thrust washer between side gears and

Cause	Correction
Important Inspect for the proper gear oil levels prior to performing system diagnosis.	
Transmission noise	Repair or replace as required.
Driveline assembly noise	Repair or replace as required.
Worn axle shaft constant velocity joints	Replace the constant velocity joints as required.
Worn, loose, or damaged axle mount and/or bracket	Repair or replace the axle mount and/or bracket as required.
Bearing noise within the differential assembly	A grinding or roar type noise will increase or decrease relative to the vehicle speed. 1. Inspect for the proper fluid level. Fill as required. 2. If the noise continues, repair or replace the unit as required.
Gear set whine noise within the differential assembly	A whine type noise will increase or decrease relative to the vehicle speed, approximately 31-37 km/h (50-60 mph). Typical causes of a gear set whine type noise may include incorrect backlash and/or pinion depth adjustment or worn or scored gear set teeth. 1. Inspect for the proper fluid level. Fill as required. 2. Repair or replace the unit as required.

ARM0400000001035

Fig. 12 Noisy In Drive. Corvette, CTS, STS & XLR

Cause	Correction
Important Inspect for the proper gear oil levels prior to performing system diagnosis. Refer to Lubricant Level Inspection - Rear Drive Axle.	
Worn axle shaft constant velocity joints	Replace the constant velocity joints as required.
Worn, loose, or damaged axle mount and/or bracket	Repair or replace the axle mount and/or bracket as required.
Bearing noise within the differential assembly	A grinding or roar type noise will increase or decrease relative to the vehicle speed. 1. Inspect for the proper fluid level. Fill as required. 2. If the noise continues, repair or replace the unit as required.
Gear set whine noise within the differential assembly	A whine type noise will increase or decrease relative to the vehicle speed, approximately 31-37 km/h (50-60 mph). Typical causes of a gear set whine type noise may include incorrect backlash and/or pinion depth adjustment or worn or scored gear set teeth. 1. Inspect for the proper fluid level. Fill as required. 2. Repair or replace the unit as required.

ARM0400000001034

Fig. 13 Noisy When Coasting. Corvette, CTS, STS & XLR

rotate gears until pinion is directly opposite case loading opening.

9. Install other pinion with pinion shaft holes aligned, then rotate side gears and ensure pinions align with shaft openings in case.
10. When pinions are properly aligned, rotate pinions toward loading opening just enough and install thrust washer .
11. Align pinions with shaft opening in case, insert pinion shaft through case and install new lock bolt. **Do not tighten lock bolt now.**
12. Ensure ring gear and case mating surfaces are clean and free from burrs.
13. Mount gear on case, install two new mounting bolts at opposite sides of gear and alternately tighten bolts to draw gear on case.
14. Install remaining new ring gear bolts hand tight and ensure gear is squarely seated on case. **Do not use old bolts.**
15. Alternately **torque** ring gear bolts to 89 ft. lbs.
16. Press side bearings onto case. If using previously installed bearings, ensure they are installed in original positions.

Limited Slip

CAMARO & FIREBIRD

On these models the limited slip differential cannot be serviced separately. If damaged, the differential must be replaced as a unit.

1. Remove case side bearings using tool No. J-22888-20A, or equivalent.
2. Remove all but two opposite ring gear mounting bolts. Loosen two remaining bolts.
3. Loosen ring gear by tapping on bolts, then remove ring gear from differential.

CORVETTE & XLR

1. Remove ring gear to differential case mounting bolts.
2. Separate ring gear from differential case using brass punch and hammer.
3. Remove righthand differential case

side bearing from case using hydraulic press with righthand side differential bearing remover tool No. J-42159 and side gear compressor tool No. J-42162, or equivalents. Discard bearing.

4. Remove differential case bolts and separate righthand differential case from lefthand differential case.
5. Remove lefthand output shaft from differential case.
6. Remove lefthand clutch pack from differential case.
7. Keep plates and discs in specific order in which they were removed.
8. Inspect clutch plates and discs. If any plate or disc shows wear or scoring, replace complete pack.
9. Tag clutch pack to indicate installation position.
10. Remove lefthand differential case side bearing using hydraulic press with suitable V-blocks and side gear compressor tool No. J-42162, or equivalent.
11. Remove C-clip and lefthand output shaft from side gear.
12. Remove cross pin from righthand differential using hydraulic press and side gear compressor tool.
13. Record spider gears positions for installation alignment.
14. Remove spider gears from righthand differential case.
15. Remove righthand output shaft and side gear from differential case.
16. Remove righthand clutch pack from differential case, noting the following:
17. Keep plates and discs in specific order in which they were removed.
18. Inspect clutch plates and discs. If any plate or disc shows wear or scoring, replace complete pack.
19. Tag clutch pack to indicate its installation position.

CLEANING & INSPECTION

1. Clean components in solvent and blow

dry with compressed air.
2. Keep all components in order to ensure proper assembly.
3. Do not use brush when cleaning bearings.
4. Do not spin dry bearings.
5. Lightly lubricate components after cleaning.
6. Inspect gears for cracks, chipped teeth, wear and scoring and damaged bearing or mounting surfaces. Replace gears that are damaged or excessively worn. **Ring gear and pinion must be replaced as an assembly.**
7. Inspect differential case for cracks, damage, worn side gear bores and scored bearing surfaces.
8. Inspect housing for scored bearing mount surfaces, cracks and distortion.
9. Inspect bearing rollers and races for pitting, scoring, overheating and damage.
10. Mate bearing with race and inspect operation.
11. Replace bearings that are damaged, excessively worn or that fail to operate smoothly.
12. Mount differential case along with side bearings and ring gear in housing and measure runout with side bearings adjusted for zero preload and dial indicator positioned against machined edge of ring gear.
13. If runout exceeds .003 inch and gear cannot be positioned to eliminate runout, ring gear and/or case should be replaced.

ADJUSTMENTS

Differential Side Bearing Preload

CAMARO & FIREBIRD

On these models, side bearing preload should be set before pinion is installed. If pinion is installed, remove ring gear.

Cause	Correction
Important	
Inspect for the proper gear oil levels prior to performing system diagnosis.	
Worn, loose, or damaged axle mount and/or bracket	Repair or replace the axle mount and/or bracket as required.
Incorrect gear oil	Replace with the correct gear oil and friction modifier additive.

ARM0400000001033

Fig. 14   Intermittent Noise. Corvette, CTS, STS & XLR

Cause	Correction
Important	
• Inspect for the proper gear oil levels prior to performing system diagnosis.	
• Operate the vehicle turning in tight circles in both left and right directions. A chatter type concern may indicate an incorrect type gear oil, lack of the friction modifier additive, or worn friction discs and/or plates.	
Worn or loose rear axle mount and/or bracket	Repair or replace as required.
Worn axle shaft constant velocity joints	Replace the constant velocity joints as required.
Worn wheel bearings	Replace the wheel bearings as required.
Incorrect gear oil	Drain and fill to the proper level with the correct gear oil and friction modifier additive. Adding friction modifier to the existing fluid without draining will not correct this condition.
Worn clutch plates	Replace the friction discs and plates as required.

ARM0400000001031

Fig. 16   Noisy On Turns. Corvette, CTS, STS & XLR

Cause	Correction
Important	
Inspect for the proper gear oil levels prior to performing system diagnosis.	
Low gear oil levels	Faulty oil seals or other type leaks may contribute to lower than required fluid levels. Fill to the proper level with the correct gear oil and friction modifier additive.
Worn, loose, or damaged axle mount and/or bracket	Repair or replace the axle mount and/or bracket as required.
Bearing noise within the differential assembly	A grinding or roar type noise will increase or decrease relative to the vehicle speed. 1. Inspect for the proper fluid level. Fill as required. 2. If the noise continues, repair or replace the unit as required.
Gear set whine noise within the differential assembly	A whine type noise will increase or decrease relative to the vehicle speed, approximately 31-37 km/h (50-60 mph). Typical causes of a gear set whine type noise may include incorrect backlash and/or pinion depth adjustment or worn or scored gear set teeth. 1. Inspect for the proper fluid level. Fill as required. 2. Repair or replace the unit as required.

ARM0400000001032

Fig. 15   Constant Noise. Corvette, CTS, STS & XLR

Inspect	Causes
Rear Axle Lubricant	Low lubricant level contamination

ARM0400000001036

Fig. 17   Noisy In Drive. GTO

1. Ensure bearing bores in housing and bearing caps are clean and free from burrs.
2. Measure production shims or service spacer and shim packs removed during disassembly to determine approximate thickness of shims required for installation. **Do not use cast iron production shims more than once. If service spacers and shims were previously installed, they can be used again.**
3. In addition to .170 inch service spacers for each side, select service shim thickness required based on measurements made in previous step, **Fig. 29.**
4. Place outer races over side bearings, mount differential assembly in housing and insert service spacer between each bearing race and housing with chamfered edge against housing.
5. Install lefthand bearing cap to retain case assembly and tighten bolts hand tight so that case can be moved while inspecting adjustments. **Bearing cap bolt can be installed in lower righthand bearing cap hole to prevent case from dropping while performing shim adjustments.**
6. Select one or two shims totaling thickness previously calculated, then insert them between righthand bearing cap and service spacer.
7. Insert progressively larger feeler gauges between shim and service spacer until noticeable increase in drag can be felt, pushing gauge down until it contacts housing bore to obtain proper reading. Work case in and out and to left to insert feeler gauges. **Rotate case while inserting gauges to ensure even readings.**
8. Gauge used just before additional drag is felt is proper thickness to obtain zero preload.
9. Remove bearing cap, case assembly service spacers and shim pack.
10. Select two service shims of approximate equal thickness whose total thickness is equal to thickness of shims previously installed plus thickness of feeler gauge used to obtain zero preload.
11. Final preload is not added until backlash has been adjusted.

CATERA

1. Install side bearing preload clamp tool No. J-42143, or equivalent, onto rear axle housing cover surfaces, **Fig. 23.** Tighten cover bolts until fully seated.
2. Install side bearing preload clamp plate tool No. J-42149, or equivalent, between side bearing race and side bearing clamp tool.
3. Install dial indicator tool No. J-8001, or equivalent, onto side bearing clamp tool No. J-42143, or equivalent, with indicator button resting on ring gear surface.
4. Install differential carrier with bearing races into rear axle housing.
5. Install lefthand adjuster ring using suitable heavy duty snap ring pliers.
6. Install snap rings of various thickness until there is no movement of differential carrier indicated by dial indicator.
7. Add an additional .005 inch shim to each side in adjuster ring thickness. Total preload should be .010 inch.

8. If it is required to vary adjuster ring thickness once side bearing preload has been established, maintain same total thickness between two snap rings to maintain preload. For example, if it was required that .002 inch be removed from lefthand side adjuster ring thickness to properly establish backlash, .002 inch must be added to righthand side adjuster ring thickness.
9. Measure differential carrier rotating torque using differential side bearing alignment kit tool No. J-42178, or equivalent, and suitable inch pound torque wrench. With bearing lubricated, rotating torque should be 4.5–6.5 inch lbs.

CORVETTE & XLR

1. Place depth gauge tool No. J-42168-7, or equivalent, onto flat of gauge block tool No. J-42168-2, or equivalent, **Fig. 30.**
2. Place depth gauge tool plunger tip against bottom of differential carrier bearing bore. Tighten setscrew to lock plunger into place.
3. Install gauge block tool No. J-42168-6, or equivalent, onto gauge plate tool No. J-42168-5, or equivalent, with proper gear step closest to the outer edge.
4. Install gauge plate tool into suitable vise, **Fig. 31.**
5. Mount ring gear and case assembly onto gauge plate tool. Ensure lefthand side bearing seats in lefthand side bearing race.
6. Place depth gauge tool No. J-42168-7, or equivalent, onto back face of ring gear.
7. Measure distance between depth gauge tool and block.

Inspect	Causes
Wheels or Tires	Imbalance or improper inflation
Front Wheel Bearings	Wear or damage
Propeller Shaft	Excessive drive line angle
Ring and Pinion Gears	• Incorrect backlash • Incorrect pinion depth • Wear or damage

ARM0400000001037

Fig. 18 Noisy When Coasting. GTO

Inspect	Causes
Wheels and Tires	Imbalance or improper inflation
Rear Axle Shafts	Excessive end play
Pinion Shaft or Pinion Bearing	Wear or damage
Differential Case Side Gear Hub	Worn, oversized or damage
Universal Joint	Wear or damage

ARM0400000001038

Fig. 19 Intermitten Noise. GTO

Inspect	Causes
Pinion Bearings	Wear or damage

ARM0400000001039

Fig. 20 Constant Noise. GTO

Inspect	Causes
Differential Side Gears and Pinion Gears	• Wear or damage • Excessive backlash

ARM0400000001040

Fig. 21 Noisy On Turns, GTO

8. Determine proper shim thickness, then tag lefthand side bearing shim pack for assembly as follows:
   a. Ring gear value stamping is in millimeters.
   b. If ring gear has a zero (0) stamping, measured value is shim thickness.
   c. If ring gear has plus (+) or minus (–) value stamped on it, add or subtract that value from feeler gauge reading to calculate shim thickness.
9. Remove gauge block tools from differential housing.
10. Install righthand side cover bearing race using suitable hydraulic press and race installer tool No. J-42172, or equivalent, **Fig. 32.**
11. Install lefthand side bearing race and shim pack into differential housing using suitable hydraulic press and race installer tool.
12. Place differential carrier onto ring gear holder tool No. J-42173, or equivalent.
13. Install ring gear and case into differential carrier using differential case lifting tool No. J-42155, or equivalent.
14. Install righthand side differential carrier cover and bolts. **Torque** mounting bolts to 18 ft. lbs.
15. Position suitable dial indicator onto end of righthand axle shaft, **Fig. 33.**
16. Grip output shaft, then move it up and down to measure total travel, **Fig. 34.**
17. Add .004 inch to measurement from previous step. This is righthand side outer bearing race shim pack size.
18. Remove righthand side differential carrier cover and bolts.
19. Remove righthand side outer bearing race using hydraulic press and bearing race remover tool No. J-42194, or equivalent.
20. Install righthand side outer bearing race and shim pack.
21. Install bearing race using hydraulic press and race installer tool No. J-42172, or equivalent.
22. Install lefthand side output shaft bearing into cover using hydraulic press and bearing installer tool No. J-42157, or equivalent.
23. Install lefthand side axle seal into cover using seal installer tool No. J-36797, or equivalent.
24. Remove ring gear and case from differential housing using differential case lifting tool No. J-42155, or equivalent.

Drive Pinion Depth

CAMARO & FIREBIRD

1. Install pinion bearing races in housing using suitable driver.
2. Lubricate pinion bearings and install bearings in races.
3. Assemble gauge plate onto preload stud, **Fig. 35.**
4. Hold pinion bearings in position, insert stud through rear bearing and pilot and front bearing and pilot.
5. Install and tighten mounting nut snug.
6. Rotate tool to ensure bearings are properly seated.
7. Hold preload stud and tighten nut until 20 inch lbs. of torque is required to rotate stud. **Tighten nut in small increments, measuring rotating torque after each adjustment.**
8. Mount side bearing discs on arbor, using step for disc that corresponds to base of housing.
9. Mount arbor and plunger assembly in housing, ensuring side bearing discs are properly seated.
10. Install bearing caps and **torque** cap bolts to 55 ft. lbs., **Fig. 36.**
11. Mount dial indicator on arbor stud with indicator contact button bearing against top of arbor plunger.
12. Preload indicator ½ inch against plunger and secure to arbor mounting stud in position.
13. Place arbor plunger on gauge plate, rotating plate so plunger rests directly on button corresponding to ring gear size.
14. Slowly rock plunger rod back and forth across button while observing dial indicator.
15. At point on button where indicator registers greatest deflection, zero dial indicator. **Perform previous two steps several times to ensure proper setting.**
16. Once verified zero reading is obtained, swing plunger aside until it is clear of gauge plate button and record dial indicator reading. **Indicator reads required pinion depth shim thickness for nominal pinion.**
17. Record dial indicator's reading at pointer position. This will indicate proper drive pinion gear shim to install. As an example, if pointer moved .067 inch

counterclockwise to reading of .033 inch, this equals .033 inch shim thickness.
18. Remove gauging tools and pinion bearings from housing, recording installation position of bearings.

CATERA

1. When replacing differential ring and pinion set, ensure replacement drive pinion gear has markings on gear face, **Fig. 37.**
2. Markings indicate adjustments needed to shim thickness as for gear production tolerances.
3. Inspect value (+22 = .22 mm) is deep drive pinion should be installed relative to drive pinion zero line. Compare this value with value stamped on original pinion gear to determine which size shim should be installed.
4. Pairing value (2628) is stamped on pinion gear and ring gear. This marking identifies matched gear set.
5. Underline value does not come into play during service.

CORVETTE & XLR

1. Install gauge cylinder tool No. J-42168-1 and gauge block tool No. J-42168-2, or equivalents, into differential housing in lefthand side bearing race location, **Fig. 38.**
2. Measure distance between tip of gauge cylinder tool No. J-42168-1 and gauge block tool No. J-42168-2, or equivalents. **If pinion gear has plus (+) or minus (–) number stamped on end, shim thickness must be adjusted by that amount.**
3. Subtract measured value from .10826 inch. Value of .10826 inch is shim thickness required if pinion has zero stamped on end.
4. Remove gauge cylinder and gauge block tools from carrier.

ASSEMBLE

Differential

CAMARO & FIREBIRD

1. Ensure pinion depth and bearing preload are properly adjusted, as outlined in "Adjustments."

2. Install differential case assembly and selected side bearing shims as outlined in "Adjustments."

3. Install bearing caps and **torque** cap bolts to 55 ft. lbs.

4. Rotate assembly to ensure bearings are properly seated.

5. Mount dial indicator on housing with plunger bearing against tooth on ring gear, **Fig. 39.**

6. Use small contact button on indicator plunger so that contact can be made at heel end of tooth and position dial indicator with plunger inline with gear rotation and perpendicular to gear tooth.

7. Hold pinion stationary, then rock ring gear back and forth while reading backlash on indicator.

8. Measure backlash at three evenly spaced positions around ring gear and record readings. **If backlash varies by more than .002 inch at any position, inspect ring gear installation and runout.**

9. If backlash is not within specifications, remove differential case assembly and bearing shims. Keep shims in order.

10. Backlash is adjusted by increasing thickness of one shim while decreasing thickness of opposite side shim by same to maintain proper side bearing preload. Select shims to adjust backlash as follows:
   a. If backlash is excessive, increase thickness of shim on gear tooth side and decrease thickness of shim on opposite side by same amount.
   b. If backlash is less than specified, decrease thickness of shim on gear tooth side while increasing thickness of opposite shim by same amount.
   c. **Each .002 inch change in shim thickness alters backlash by .001 inch.**

11. Install differential assembly, shims and bearing caps. **Torque** bearing cap bolts to 55 ft. lbs.

12. Inspect and adjust backlash.

13. If side bearing preload was set to zero during side bearing preload adjustment, proceed as follows:
   a. Remove both bearing caps and shim packs, keeping shim packs in respective lefthand or righthand positions.
   b. Select lefthand side differential preload shim from specifications chart, then insert shim between lefthand bearing race and spacer.
   c. Install lefthand bearing cap with bolts hand tight.
   d. Select righthand side differential preload shim from specifications chart and insert shim between righthand bearing race and spacer using suitable soft faced hammer.
   e. Install righthand bearing cap. **Torque** cap bolts to 55 ft. lbs.

14. Ensure ring gear teeth are clean and free from oil, then coat both drive and coast side of each tooth with marking compound.

15. Apply braking force to load ring gear, then rotate driveshaft yoke with

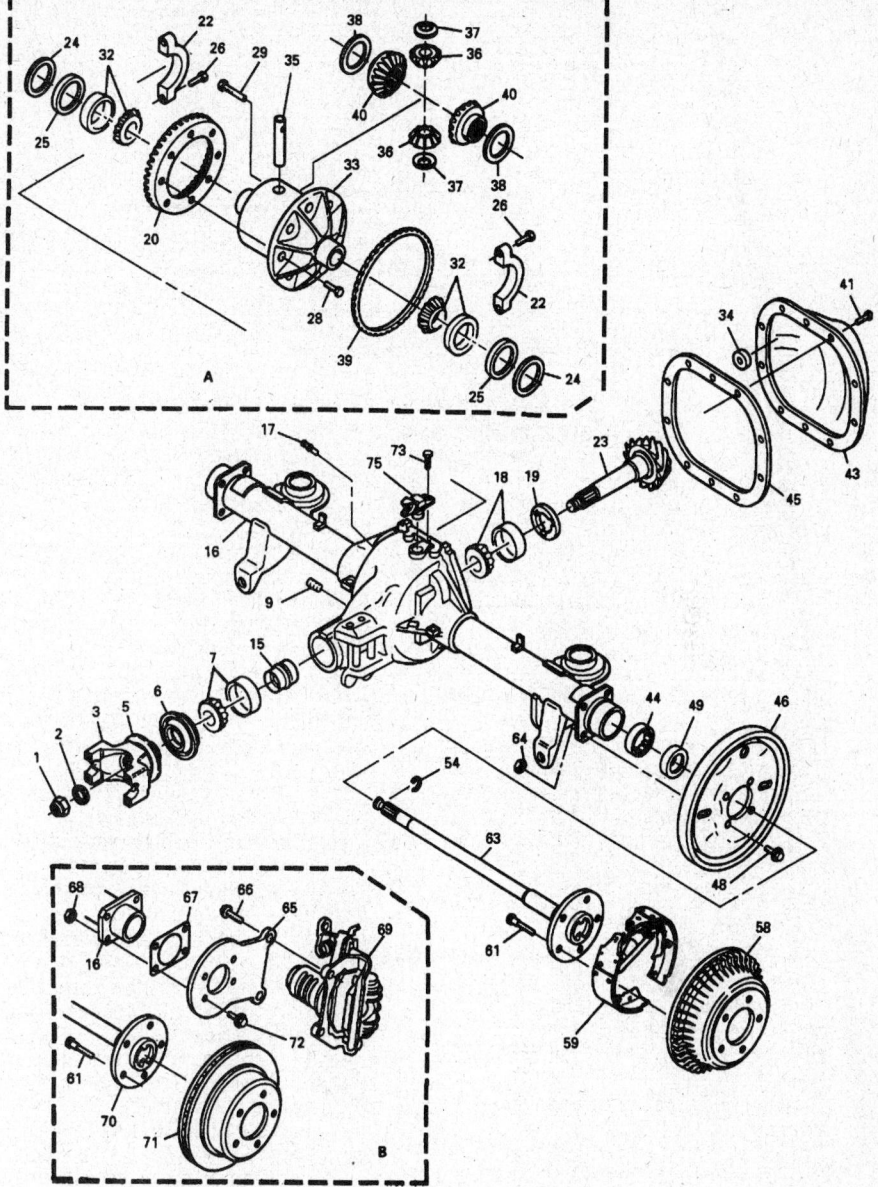

Fig. 22 Exploded view of standard rear axle (Part 1 of 2). Camaro & Firebird

wrench so ring gear rotates one full revolution in each direction. **Excessive gear rotation is not recommended.**

16. Compare gear tooth pattern and correct assembly adjustments, **Fig. 40.**

17. When proper gear tooth contact pattern has been obtained, clean marking compound from gears.

18. Install axles and driveshaft as outlined under "Rear Axle & Suspension" in "Camaro & Firebird" chassis chapter.

19. Install rear cover using RTV, or new gasket, **Torque** cover bolts to 22 ft. lbs.

20. Install fluid drain plug and **torque** to 26 ft. lbs

21. Fill rear axle with suitable lubricant.

22. **On models equipped with limited slip differential,** add limited slip additive No. 1052358, or equivalent, to rear axle lubricant.

CATERA

1. Place differential carrier on differential side and pinion alignment tool No. J-42178, or equivalent, **Fig. 41.**

2. Install counterpiece of alignment tool into opposing differential carrier bore.

3. Install new pinion gear retaining ring onto differential carrier.

4. Coat pinion gears and shims with rear axle lubricant.

5. Install thicker shim with notches around outer edge toward carrier.

6. Install thinner conical washer toward differential side gear.

7. Place shims on differential side gears.

8. Place differential side gears with previously installed shims into carrier and onto both pieces of alignment tool No.

DRIVE AXLES

A DIFFERENTIAL
B OPTIONAL DISC BRAKE
1 NUT, DIFFERENTIAL DRIVE PINION GEAR
2 WASHER, DIFFERENTIAL DRIVE PINION GEAR
3 YOKE, DIFFERENTIAL DRIVE PINION GEAR
5 DEFLECTOR, DIFFERENTIAL DRIVE PINION GEAR DIRT
6 SEAL, DIFFERENTIAL DRIVE PINION GEAR
7 BEARING, DIFFERENTIAL DRIVE PINION GEAR OUTER
9 PLUG, REAR AXLE HOUSING DRAIN
15 SPACER, DIFFERENTIAL DRIVE PINION GEAR BEARING
16 HOUSING, REAR AXLE
17 VENT, REAR AXLE
18 BEARING, DIFFERENTIAL DRIVE PINION GEAR INNER
19 SHIM, DIFFERENTIAL DRIVE PINION GEAR
20 GEAR, DIFFERENTIAL RING
22 CAP, DIFFERENTIAL CARRIER BEARING
23 GEAR, DIFFERENTIAL DRIVE PINION
24 SHIM, DIFFERENTIAL BEARING
25 SPACER, DIFFERENTIAL BEARING
26 BOLT/SCREW, DIFFERENTIAL BEARING CAP
28 BOLT/SCREW, DIFFERENTIAL RING GEAR
29 BOLT/SCREW, DIFFERENTIAL PINION GEAR SHAFT LOCK
32 BEARING, DIFFERENTIAL
33 CASE, DIFFERENTIAL
34 MAGNET, REAR AXLE HOUSING CHIP COLLECTING
35 SHAFT, DIFFERENTIAL PINION GEAR

36 GEAR, DIFFERENTIAL PINION
37 WASHER, DIFFERENTIAL PINION GEAR THRUST
38 WASHER, DIFFERENTIAL SIDE GEAR THRUST
39 WHEEL, REAR WHEEL SPEED SENSOR RELUCTOR
40 GEAR, DIFFERENTIAL SIDE
41 BOLT/SCREW, REAR AXLE HOUSING
43 COVER, REAR AXLE HOUSING
44 BEARING, REAR AXLE SHAFT
45 GASKET, REAR AXLE HOUSING COVER
46 PLATE, REAR BRAKE BACKING
48 BOLT/SCREW, REAR BRAKE BACKING
49 SEAL, REAR AXLE SHAFT BEARING
54 LOCK, REAR AXLE SHAFT
58 DRUM, REAR BRAKE
59 BRAKE, REAR
61 BOLT/SCREW, REAR WHEEL
63 SHAFT REAR AXLE (DRUM BRAKE ASSEMBLIES)
64 NUT, REAR BRAKE BACKING PLATE
65 PLATE, REAR BRAKE CALIPER MOUNTING
66 BOLT/SCREW, CALIPER MOUNTING
67 SHAM, AXLE TUBE FLANGE
68 NUT, REAR BRAKE CALIPER MOUNTING PLATE
69 CALIPER, REAR BRAKE
70 SHAFT, REAR AXLE (DISC BRAKE ASSEMBLIES)
71 ROTOR, REAR BRAKE
72 BOLT/SCREW, REAR BRAKE BACKING PLATE
73 BOLT/SCREW, SENSOR PLUG MOUNTING
75 SENSOR, WHEEL SPEED

GC3039400285020X

Fig. 22 Exploded view of standard rear axle (Part 2 of 2). Camaro & Firebird

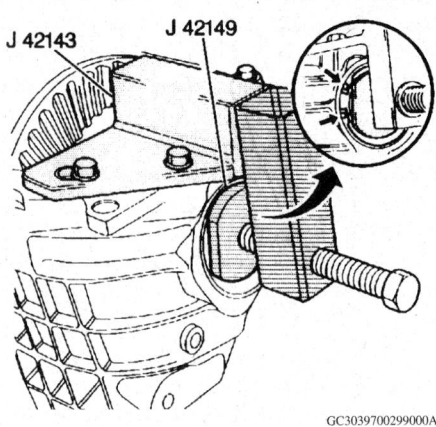

GC3039700299000A

Fig. 23 Preload clamp tool installation. Catera

J-42178, or equivalent.
9. Coat pinion gears and conical washers with rear axle lubricant.
10. Engage pinion gears and conical washers with side gears. Align gears and washers so they are exactly opposite each other in carrier window.
11. Move pinion gear conical washers forward in intended rotational direction to start or lead pinion gears into mounting position.
12. Rotate alignment tool using ratchet to draw pinion gears into position. **Ensure conical gears also move into position.** To assist washers into position use suitable small drift and hammer.
13. Drive rear axle gear shaft into carrier bore using suitable dead blow hammer.
14. Attach torque wrench to alignment tool No. J-42178, or equivalent, and measure rotating torque. Measurement should be 11–22 ft. lbs.
15. Heat ring gear to 212°F. **Do not overheat.**
16. Aligning bolt holes and install ring gear onto carrier.
17. **Torque** new ring gear bolts to 85 ft. lbs., in sequence, **Fig. 42.**
18. Lubricate carrier side bearings and carrier bearing surface.
19. Press side bearing onto carrier using suitable press.
20. Install inner and outer pinion bearing outer races into housing.
21. Install drive pinion gear inner bearing onto drive pinion gear.
22. Install drive pinion seal into differential.
23. Install drive pinion, then carrier into rear axle housing.
24. Drive axle seals into bearing cups using drive axle seal driver tool No. J-26234, or equivalent.
25. Install rear axle cover and **torque** mounting bolts to 44 ft. lbs.

CORVETTE & XLR

1. Install righthand clutch pack into differential case. Install steel plates and friction discs alternately, thicker friction washer, concave washer, then steel washer.
2. Install righthand output shaft and spider gears into differential case.
3. Install cross pin into differential case

using hydraulic press and side gear compressor tool No. J-42162, or equivalent.
4. Install lefthand output shaft into side gear, and C-clip onto shaft.
5. Install lefthand differential case side bearing using bearing installer tool No. J-42160, or equivalent.
6. Install lefthand clutch pack into differential case. Install steel plates and friction discs alternately, thicker friction washer, concave washer, then steel washer.
7. Install lefthand output shaft and side gear into differential case.
8. Install lefthand differential case to righthand differential case.
9. **Torque** differential case bolts, to 41 ft. lbs.
10. Install ring gear onto differential case.
11. Install ring gear bolts using ring gear holder tool No. J-42173, or equivalent, to support differential case. **Torque** bolts to 144 ft. lbs.
12. Install righthand differential case side bearing using bearing installer tool No. J-42160, or equivalent.
13. Install gauge block tool No. J-42168-2 and plug tool No. J-42168-12, or equivalents, into drive pinion location of differential carrier.
14. Place depth gauge tool No. J-42168-7, or equivalent, onto flat end of gauge block tool No. J-42168-2, or equivalent, **Fig. 30.**
15. Place tip of plunger on depth gauge tool No. J-42168-7, or equivalent, against bottom of bearing bore in differential carrier. Tighten set screw to lock plunger in place.
16. Install gauge block tool No. J-42168-6, or equivalent, onto gauge plate tool No. J-42168-5, or equivalent, with proper gear step closest to outer edge.
17. Place ring gear and case assembly onto gauge plate tool No. J-42168-5, or equivalent, **Fig. 31.**
18. Remove depth gauge tool No. J-42168-7, or equivalent. If ring gear has plus (+) or minus (–) stamped on the side the shim thickness must be adjusted by that amount.
19. Measure distance between plunger tip of depth gauge tool No. J-42168-7 and gauge block tool No. J-42168-6, or equivalents, **Fig. 31.** This distance is

shim thickness required if ring gear has zero stamped on side.
20. Remove gauge block and plug tools.
21. Install lefthand side shim pack into housing.
22. Install lefthand side outer bearing race into carrier using bearing race installer tool No. J-42172, or equivalent.
23. Install output shaft bearing into lefthand differential carrier cover using hydraulic press and output shaft bearing installer tool No. J-42157, or equivalent.
24. Install new output shaft oil seal into lefthand differential carrier cover using seal installer tool No. J-36797, or equivalent.
25. Install new O-ring seal into lefthand cover. **Torque** cover mounting bolts to 18 ft. lbs.
26. Place differential carrier on rear gear holder tool No. J-42173, or equivalent.
27. Install ring gear and case assembly into differential carrier using differential case lifting tool No. J-42155, or equivalent.
28. Install righthand side differential carrier cover and **torque** mounting bolts to 18 ft. lbs.
29. Position measuring tool No. J-8001, or equivalent, onto end of righthand axle shaft, **Fig. 33.**
30. Move output shaft up and down and measure total travel. To obtain proper size shim, add .004 inch to total travel measurement.
31. Remove righthand side outer bearing race using hydraulic press and bearing race remover tool No. J-42194, or equivalent.
32. Install righthand side shim pack into differential carrier cover.
33. Install righthand side outer bearing race using hydraulic press and bearing race installer tool No. J-42172, or equivalent.
34. Install righthand side output shaft bearing using hydraulic press and bearing installer tool No. J-42157, or equivalent.
35. Install righthand side output shaft oil seal into carrier cover using seal installer tool No. J-36797, or equivalent.
36. Remove ring gear and case assembly

from differential carrier using differential case lifting tool No. J-42155, or equivalent.

37. Install lefthand side carrier cover with new O-ring. **Torque** cover mounting bolts to 18 ft. lbs.

38. Install drive pinion shim pack onto pinion cartridge.

39. Lubricate new pinion cartridge O-ring seal with clean engine oil, and install into groove on pinion cartridge.

40. Heat differential carrier around drive pinion cartridge opening using heat gun tool No. J-25070, or equivalent, and install drive pinion cartridge into differential carrier.

41. **Torque** drive pinion cartridge bolts to 41 ft. lbs.

42. Measure pinion rotating torque using torque wrench and pinion gear holder tool No. J-42164, or equivalent. Measurement should not be more than 22 inch lbs.

43. Install rear differential cover, magnet and O-ring . **Torque** rear cover mounting bolts to 89 inch lbs.

44. Install differential case assembly into carrier using differential case lifting tool No. J-42155, or equivalent.

45. Install C-clip onto righthand output shaft.

46. Install righthand side transmission stud mount and **torque** mounting bolts to 89 inch lbs.

47. **Torque** righthand side transmission mounting stud to 31 ft. lbs.

48. Install righthand side differential carrier cover and O-ring. **Torque** mounting bolts to 18 ft. lbs.

49. Install vehicle speed sensor and **torque** mounting bolt to 89 inch lbs.

50. **Torque** axle lubricant drain plug to 26 ft. lbs.

51. Fill differential with synthetic axle lubricant part No. 12378261 and limited slip additive part No. 1052358, or equivalent.

52. Install axle lubricant fill tag and washer. **Torque** plug to 26 ft. lbs.

Drive Pinion

CAMARO & FIREBIRD

1. Install selected shim onto pinion shaft, lubricate rear pinion bearing with specified axle lubricant and press rear bearing onto pinion using suitable spacers.

2. Install new collapsible spacer onto pinion shaft, and insert pinion assembly into housing.

3. Lubricate front pinion bearing, install bearing into housing and tap bearing over pinion shaft with drift while assistant holds pinion in place. Old pinion nut and large washer can be used to seat front bearing on pinion. **Do not collapse spacer.**

4. Install new pinion seal in housing and coat seal lips with grease.

5. Mount driveshaft yoke on pinion shaft and lightly tapping yoke until several pinion shaft threads protrude from yoke.

6. Coat rear of pinion washer with suitable sealer, then install washer and new pinion nut.

7. Hold driveshaft yoke with suitable tool, then alternately tighten pinion nut and rotate pinion until endplay is reduced to zero.

8. Measure pinion bearing preload using suitable torque wrench.

9. Nut should be further tightened only slightly and preload should be inspected after each tightening.

10. Exceeding preload specifications will compress collapsible spacer too far and require installation of new spacer.

11. Set preload at 15–30 inch lbs., on new inner and outer bearing assemblies or 10–15 inch lbs., on used assemblies.

12. Rotate drive pinion several times to ensure inner and outer baring assemblies have been seated, then measure preload, again. If preload has been reduced by rotating drive pinion gear, set preload to specifications.

CATERA

1. Lubricate differential drive pinion gear outer bearing with suitable axle lubricant.

2. Install drive pinion gear outer bearing outer race into housing using drive handle tool No. J-8092 and outer race installer tool No. J-42147, or equivalents.

3. Install drive pinion gear outer bearing and pinion seal.

4. Install pinion shim into housing.

5. Install inner bearing race into housing using driver handle tool No. J-8092 and pinion bearing race installer tool No. J-8608, or equivalents.

6. Lubricate differential drive pinion gear inner bearing and drive pinion gear shaft with rear axle lubricant.

7. Install differential drive pinion gear inner bearing onto drive pinion gear.

8. Install pinion seal and drive pinion gear into housing.

9. Install drive pinion gear inner bearing onto drive pinion gear.

10. Install pinion gear bearing spacer onto drive pinion gear.

11. Install drive pinion gear into rear axle housing and set pinion depth.

12. Install drive pinion seal, noting the following:

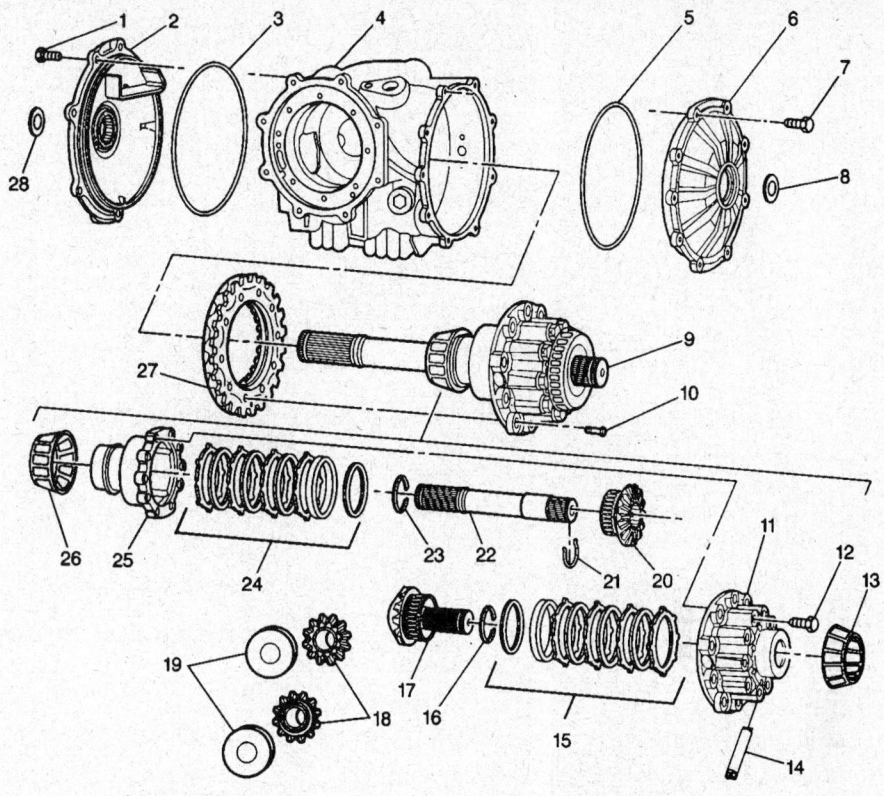

(1) Bolt
(2) Left Side Cover
(3) O-Ring Seal
(4) ifferential Carrier
(5) O-Ring Seal
(6) Right Side Cover
(7) Bolt
(8) Output Shaft Oil Seal
(9) Differential Case Assembly
(10) Bolt
(11) Right Side Differential Case
(12) Bolt
(13) Bearing
(14) Pin
(15) Clutch Pack
(16) C-Clip
(17) Right Output Gear and Shaft
(18) Side Gears
(19) Side Gear Washers
(20) Left Output Gear
(21) C-Clip
(22) Left Output Shaft
(23) C-Clip
(24) Clutch Pack

GC3039700363000X

Fig. 24 Exploded view of differential assembly. Corvette & XLR

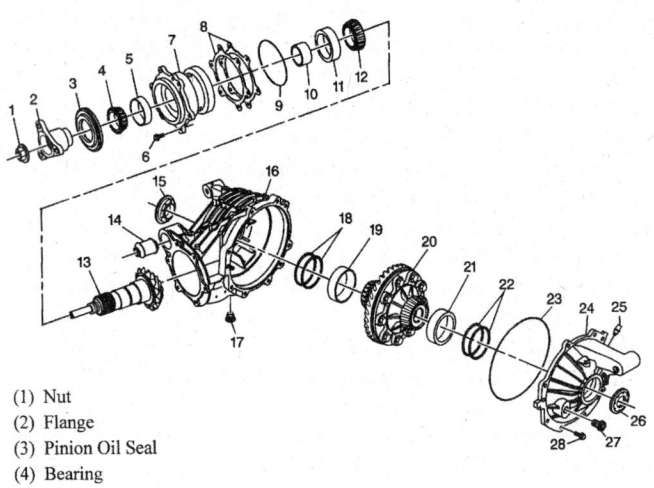

(1) Nut
(2) Flange
(3) Pinion Oil Seal
(4) Bearing
(5) Race
(6) Bolt
(7) Housing
(8) Shim
(9) O-Ring Seal
(10) Sleeve
(11) Race
(12) Bearing
(13) Pinion Gear
(14) Mount Bushing
(15) Axle Oil Seal
(16) Differential Housing

ARM66GC000000809

Fig. 25   Exploded view of differential assembly (Part 1 of 2). CTS & STS

a. Preload specification is being approached when no further endplay is detected and when holder will no longer pivot freely as drive pinion gear is rotated.
b. **Do not tighten further until preload is inspected.**
c. Tighten nut while inspecting preload after each tightening.
d. Exceeding preload specifications will compress collapsible spacer too far and new spacer will be required.
13. Hold pinion flange, then tighten nut until endplay begins to disappear while intermittently rotating drive pinion gear to seat inner and outer bearings.
14. **On new bearings,** set preload to 9–15 inch lbs.
15. **On used bearings,** set preload to 8–11 inch lbs.
16. Rotate drive pinion gear several times to ensure inner and outer bearings have been seated.
17. Measure and adjust preload.

CORVETTE & XLR

Drive pinion bearings and spacer must be replaced as a set.
1. Install front drive pinion bearing inner race into drive pinion housing using hydraulic press and bearing race installer tool No. J-42172, or equivalent.
2. Install rear drive pinion bearing outer race into drive pinion housing using hydraulic press and bearing race installer tool No. J-42170, or equivalent.

3. Install front pinion bearing onto drive pinion using hydraulic press, pinion bearing installer tool No. J-42160 and pinion gear holder tool No. J-42164, or equivalents.
4. Install drive pinion and bearing into drive pinion housing.
5. Install drive pinion bearing spacer onto drive pinion.
6. Install rear drive pinion bearing onto drive pinion using hydraulic press, pinion bearing installer tool No. J-42160 and pinion gear holder tool No. J-42164, or equivalents.
7. Install drive pinion nut and **torque** to 392 ft. lbs., using a ¾ inch torque wrench, spanner wrench tool No. J-42163 and pinion gear holder tool No. J-42164, or equivalents.
8. Stake areas of drive pinion nut into two notches in end of drive pinion.

GTO

1. Coat pinion shaft splines with suitable gear oil.
2. Lubricate seal with suitable gear oil.
3. Install new pinion shaft seal until it is flush with differential housing, using pinion seal installer tool No. DT-46853, or equivalent.
4. Install pinion flange on to shaft aligning punch marks.
5. Install pinion flange holding tool No. DT-47735, or equivalent, on pinion flange.
6. Apply thread locking compound to pinion shaft threads.

(17) Drain Plug
(18) Shim
(19) Race
(20) Differential Assembly
(21) Race
(22) Shim
(23) O-Ring Seal
(24) Housing Cover
(25) Vent
(26) Axle Seal
(27) Fill Plug
(28) Bolt

ARM66GC000000810

Fig. 25   Exploded view of differential assembly (Part 2 of 2). CTS & STS

7. Tighten pinion nut until three punch marks are aligned. **Do not overtighten pinion nut.**
8. Tighten nut to position no more than 5° past punch marks.

Ring Gear & Differential Housing

CATERA

1. Clamp pinion alignment tool No. J-42178, or equivalent, into vise.
2. Place differential carrier onto special tool with ring gear flange facing downward.
3. Place counterpiece of pinion alignment tool into opposing differential carrier bore.
4. Install new differential pinion gear retaining ring into carrier.
5. Install shims on side gears, placing thicker shim toward carrier and thinner washer toward side gear.
6. Place side gears with shims into carrier and onto pinion alignment tool.
7. Engage pinion gears and washers. Ensure they are opposite each other.
8. Move pinion gear washers forward in intended rotational direction, leading pinion gears into position.
9. Rotate pinion alignment tool to draw pinion gears into position.
10. Drive pinion gear shaft into carrier bore and through pinion gears and washers.
11. Attach torque wrench to pinion alignment tool and inspect rotational torque. Rotational torque should be 11–22 ft. lbs.
12. Heat ring gear to 212°F and install onto differential carrier. Ensure all bolt holes are aligned.
13. Torque ring gear bolts to 85 ft. lbs., in sequence, **Fig. 42.**

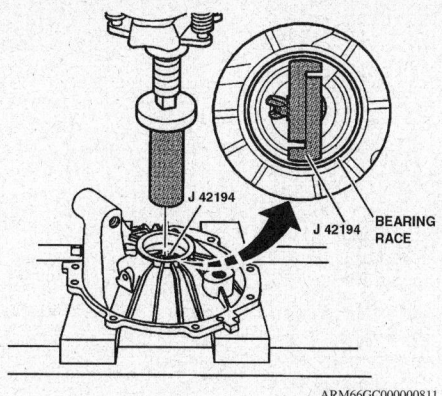

Fig. 26   Side cover bearing race removal. CTS & STS

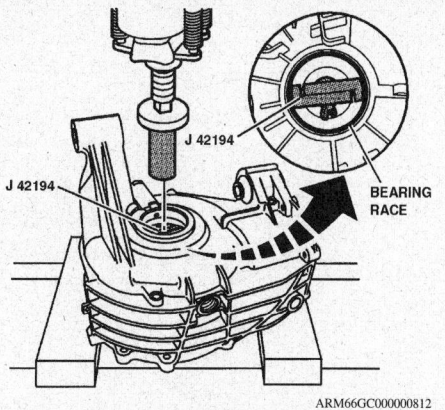

Fig. 27   Housing bearing race removal. CTS & STS

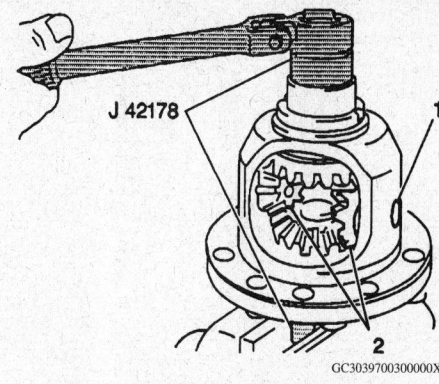

Fig. 28   Pinion & side gear removal. Catera

4.32 mm (0.170") SERVICE DIFFERENTIAL BEARING SPACER	
TOTAL THICKNESS OF BOTH PRODUCTION DIFFERENTIAL BEARING SHIMS REMOVED	TOTAL THICKNESS OF SERVICE DIFFERENTIAL BEARING SHIMS TO BE USED AS A STARTING POINT
10.57 mm (0.416")	1.52 mm (0.060")
10.92 mm (0.430")	1.78 mm (0.070")
11.18 mm (0.440")	2.03 mm (0.080")
11.43 mm (0.450")	2.29 mm (0.090")
11.68 mm (0.460")	2.54 mm (0.100")
11.94 mm (0.470")	2.79 mm (0.110")
12.19 mm (0.480")	3.05 mm (0.120")
12.45 mm (0.490")	3.30 mm (0.130")
12.70 mm (0.500")	3.56 mm (0.140")
12.95 mm (0.510")	3.81 mm (0.150")
13.21 mm (0.520")	4.06 mm (0.160")
13.46 mm (0.530")	4.32 mm (0.170")
13.97 mm (0.550")	4.83 mm (0.190")

Fig. 29   Service shim thickness chart

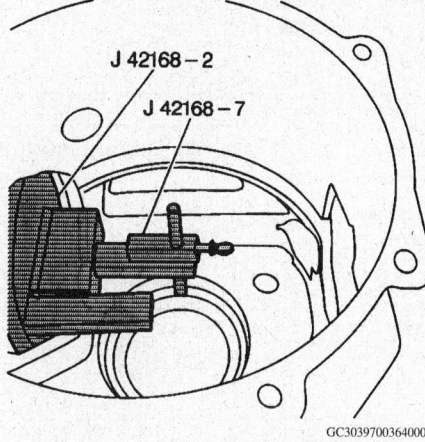

Fig. 30   Depth gauge & block setup. Corvette & XLR

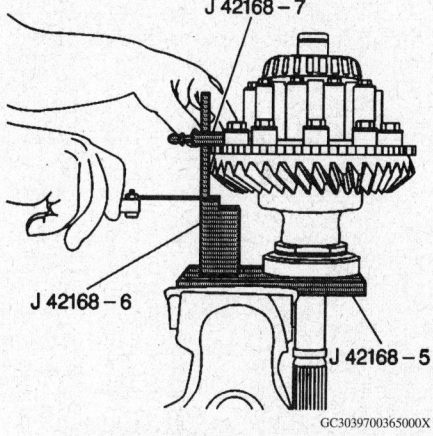

Fig. 31   Gauge plate tool installation in vise. Corvette & XLR

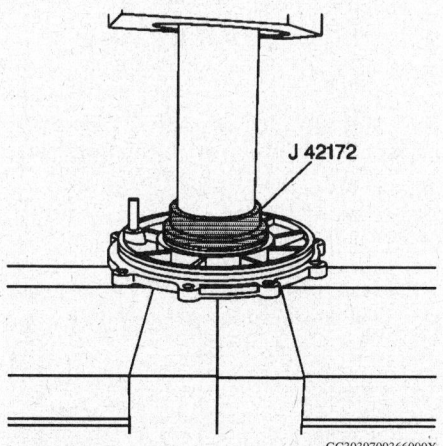

Fig. 32   Righthand side cover bearing race installation. Corvette & XLR

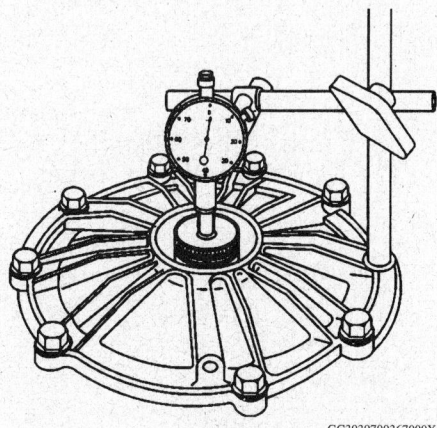

Fig. 33   Dial indicator installation onto righthand axle shaft. Corvette & XLR

Fig. 34   Output shaft total travel measurement. Corvette & XLR

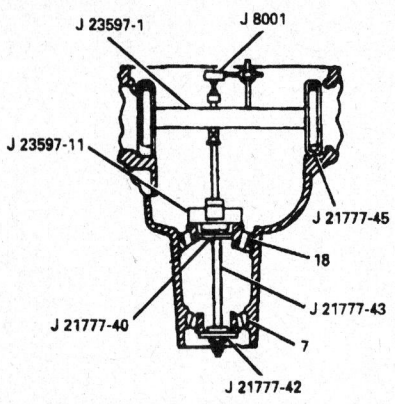

7 BEARING, DIFFERENTIAL DRIVE PINION GEAR OUTER
18 BEARING, DIFFERENTIAL DRIVE PINION GEAR INNER

GC3039700361000X

Fig. 35 Pinion gauge tool installation. Camaro & Firebird

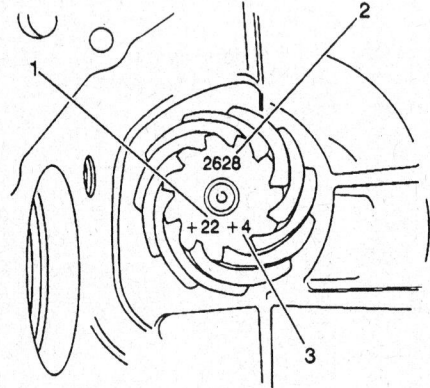

1. CHECK VALUE
2. PAIRING VALUE
3. UNDERLINE VALUE

GC3039700301000X

Fig. 37 Drive pinion gear face adjustment markings. Catera

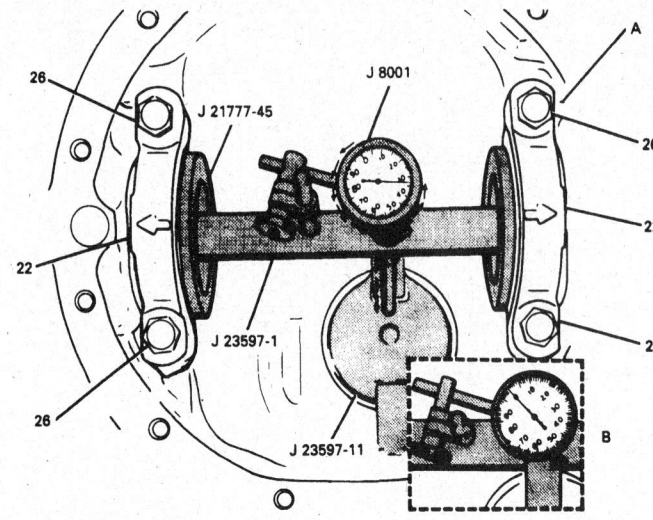

A OFF GAGE BLOCK
B ON GAGE BLOCK
22 CAP, DIFFERENTIAL CARRIER BEARING
26 BOLT/SCREW, DIFFERENTIAL CARRIER BEARING CAP

GC3039700362000X

Fig. 36 Pinion depth inspection. Camaro & Firebird

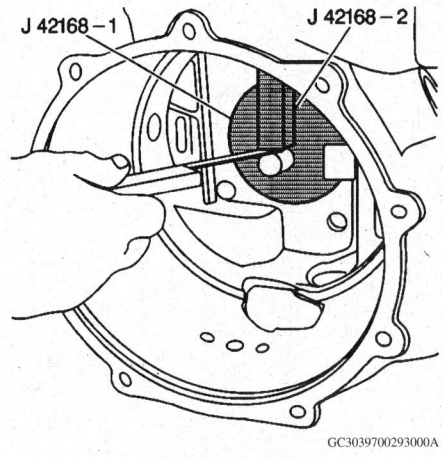

GC3039700293000A

Fig. 38 Pinion depth measurement. Corvette & XLR

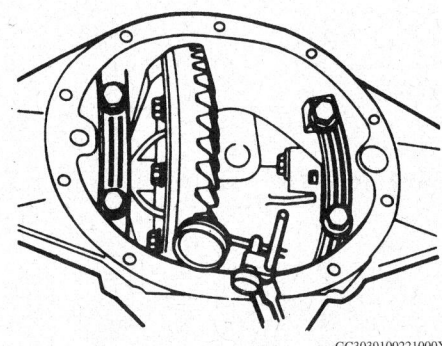

GC3039100221000X

Fig. 39 Ring gear & pinion backlash inspection. Camaro & Firebird

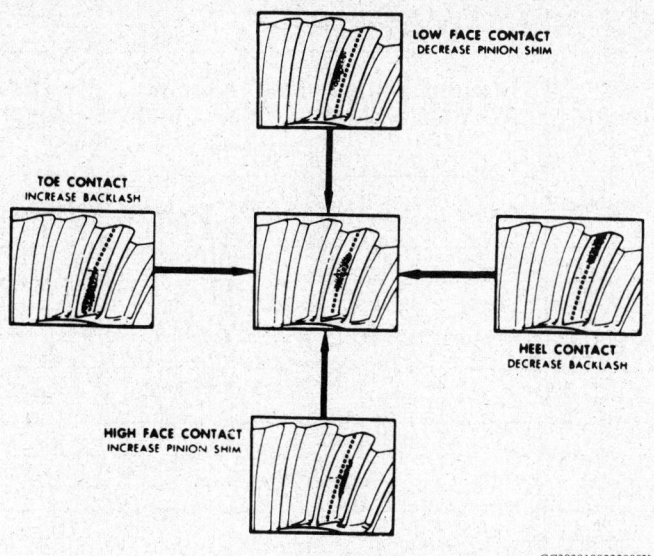

Fig. 40 Gear tooth contact pattern inspection.
Camaro & Firebird

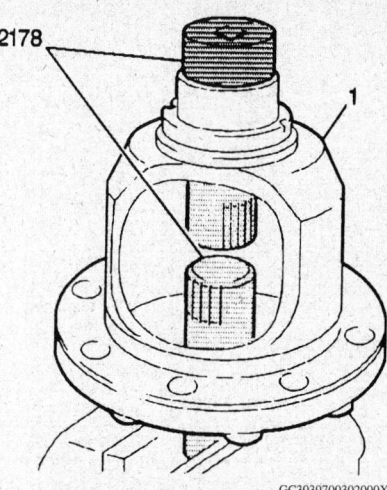

Fig. 41 Differential carrier
alignment. Catera

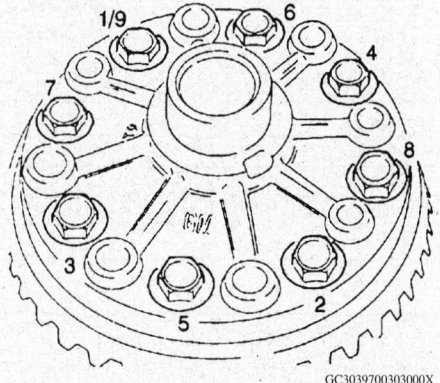

Fig. 42 Ring gear bolt tightening
sequence. Catera

DRIVE AXLE SPECIFICATIONS

Year	Ratio	Ring Gear Back-lash, Inch	Pinion Flange Rota-tional Torque, Inch Lbs.	Ring Gear/ Pinion Nominal Value, Inch		Pinion Bearing Preload, Inch Lbs.		Total Assembly Preload, Inch Lbs.		Differential Bearings, Inch Lbs.	
				A1	A2	New	Used	New	Used	Used	New
CAMARO & FIREBIRD											
2001–02	All	.0050– .0090	—	—	—	15–30	10–15	32–55	16–28	—	—
CATERA											
2001	3.90	.0040– .0080	—	—	—	9–15	8–11	—	—	4.5–6.5①	4.5–6.5①
CORVETTE											
2001–05	2.73	.0067– .0082	12–25	4.055	2.93	②	②	②	②	②	②
	3.15–3.42	.0067– .0082	12–25	4.055	2.58	②	②	②	②	②	②
CTS											
2003–05	3.23	.009–.014	22–35	4.37	2.50	②	②	②	②	②	②
	3.42	.009–.014	22–35	4.37	2.50	②	②	②	②	②	②
	3.73	.008–.013	22–35	4.37	2.50	②	②	②	②	②	②
GTO											
2004	3.46	—	2–4	—	—	—	—	—	—	—	—
STS											
2005	3.23	③	22–35	4.37	2.50	②	②	②	②	②	②
	3.73	.007–.012	22–35	4.37	2.50	②	②	②	②	②	②
	3.91	.010–.016	22–35	4.37	2.50	②	②	②	②	②	②
XLR											
2004	2.94	.0067– .0082	12–25	4.055	2.93	②	②	②	②	②	②
2005	2.94	.0063– .0102	12–25	4.055	2.93	②	②	②	②	②	②

① — Differential assembly preload, inch lbs., Without pinion gear in housing.

② — Adjustment is determined by markings on ring gear & pinion set.

③ — 4.6L engine w/AWD, .008–.013 inch; 4.6L engine w/RWD, .009–.014 inch.

ENGINE REBUILDING SPECIFICATIONS

NOTE: For Engine Tightening Specifications, Refer To The Engine Section In The Appropriate Chassis Chapter Of This Manual.

INDEX

CYLINDER HEAD, VALVE GUIDE & VALVE SEATS

All Measurements Given In Inches Unless Otherwise Specified

Engine (VIN①)	Year	Cylinder Head Warpage Limit	Cylinder Head Height/ Thickness	Valve Guides — Inside Diameter	Valve Guides — Stem To Guide Clearance Intake	Valve Guides — Stem To Guide Clearance Exhaust	Seat Angle, Deg.	Valve Seats — Seat Width Intake	Valve Seats — Seat Width Exhaust	Run-out
1.0L (6)	2001	.0020	—	.2165–.2170	.0008–.0027	.0018–.0035	45.00	.0512–.0590	.0512–.0590	.0310
1.3L (2)	2001	.0020	—	.2159–.2169	.0002–.0027	.0012–.0035	45.00	.0433–.0512	.0433–.0512	.0310
1.8L (L)	2003–05	.0080	—	.2169–.2177	.0010–.0039	.0011–.0039	45.00	.1300	.1300	—
1.8L (8)	2001–02	.0080	—	.2169–.2177	.0010–.0031	.0012–.0039	45.00	.0300–.0490	.0300–.0490	—
	2003–05	.0080	—	.2169–.2177	.0010–.0039	.0011–.0039	45.00	.1300	.1300	—
1.9L DOHC (7)	2001–02	③	—	.2364–.2390	.0010–.0040	.0010–.0040	44.50–45.50	.0394–.0653	.0512–.0756	—
1.9L SOHC (8 & 9)	2001–02	③	4.4440–4.4540	.2751–.2780	.0020–.0040	.0015–.0050	44.50–45.00	.0394–.0630	.0512–.0750	—
2.0L (P)	2005	.0040	—	.2362–.2367	.0012–.0022	.0020–.0026	—	—	—	—
2.2L DOHC (F)	2002–05	.0040	—	.2362–.2367	.0012–.0022	.0020–.0026	45.00	—	—	.0020
2.2L OHV (4 & 5)	2001–02	.0030	—	.2750–.2760	.0007–.0020	.0014–.0029	45.00	.1100	.1380	.0014
2.4L (T)	2001–02	.0030	—	.2348–.2358	.0010–.0027	.0010–.0027	45.00	.0370–.0748	.0370–.0748	.0011
3.0L (R)	2001–05	⑤	5.2720–5.2800	.2362–.2367	.0012–.0022	.0016–.0026	45.00	.0394–.0551	.0551–.0709	—
3.1L (J)	2001–02	.0100	—	—	.0010–.0027	.0010–.0027	45.00	.0610–.0710	.0670–.0790	.0010
	2003–05	②	—	.3150	.0010–.0027	.0010–.0027	46.00	.0610–.0710	.0670–.0790	.0015
3.2L (N)	2003–04	④	—	—	.0012–.0024	.0016–.0028	89.50	.0394–.0551	.0051–.0708	.0020
3.4L (E)	2001–02	.0100	—	—	.0010–.0027	.0010–.0027	46.00	.0610–.0710	.0670–.0790	.0020
	2003–05	②	—	.3150	.0010–.0027	.0010–.0027	46.00	.0610–.0710	.0670–.0790	.0015
3.5L (H)	2001–02	.0080	—	.2350–.2358	.0010–.0030	.0010–.0030	45.75	.0165–.0322	.0511–.0668	.0014
3.5L (8)	2004–05	⑥	—	.3150	.0010–.0027	.0010–.0027	46.00	.0610–.0710	.0607–.0790	—
3.6L (7)	2004–05	.0020	—	.2362–.2370	.0010–.0026	.0014–.0030	45.00	.0394–.5510	.0551–.0709	.0020
3.8L (K, 1, 2 & 4)	2001–05	.0040	4.0745–4.1015	.3150–.3158	.0012–.0028	.0014–.0029	45.00	.0600–.0800	.0900–.1100	.0020
4.0L (C)	2001–03	.0079	5.3540	.2350–.2358	.0011–.0043	.0020–.0047	45.75	.0165–.0323	.0512–.0669	.0020
4.6L (A, Y & 9)	2001–05	.0039	5.3540	.2350–.2358	.0011–.0043	.0020–.0047	45.75	.0165–.0323	.0512–.0669	.0020
5.7L (G & S)	2001–05	.0030	4.7320	—	.0010–.0037	.0010–.0037	46.00	.0400	.0700	.0020
6.0L (U)	2005	.0080	—	—	.0010–.0037	.0010–.0037	46.00	.0400	.0700	.0020

① — The eighth digit of Vehicle Identification Number (VIN) denotes engine code.

② — .003 inch per 6.000 inches.

③ — Longitudinal deck, .0028–.0040 inch; transverse deck, .0012–.0020 inch.

④ — .001 inch per 3.917 inches.

⑤ — .002 inch per 3.937 inches.

⑥ — .0019 inch per 6 inches.

VALVE SPRINGS

All Measurements Given In Inches Unless Otherwise Specified

Engine (VIN①)	Year	Free Length	Installed Height	Seated Pressure, Lbs. @ Inches	Comp. Pressure, Lbs. @ Inches	Out Of Square Limit
1.0L (6)	2001	1.6142–1.6649	1.2800	41.2–51.8 @ 1.2800	—	.079
1.3L (2)	2001	1.4043–1.4500	1.2400	20.5–27.5 @ 1.2400	—	.079
1.8L (8)	2001–02	1.8070	1.3230	35.7–39.5 @ 1.3230	—	.063
	2003–05	②	—	—	—	.063
1.8L (L)	2003–05	②	—	—	—	.063
1.9L DOHC (7)	2001–02	1.5600	1.2210	42.0–48.0 @ 1.2210	99.0–109.0 @ .8740	.100
1.9L SOHC (8 & 9)	2001–02	1.8898–1.9134	1.6100	76.0–87.0 @ 1.6100	202.0–211.0 @ 1.2800	.100
2.0L (P)	2005	—	—	55.1–60.9 @ 1.275	118.0–129.3 @ 1.279	—
2.2L DOHC (F)	2002–05	1.5430	1.2795	55.1–60.9 @ 1.2795	118.0–129.3 @ 1.2795	—
2.2L OHV (4 & 5)	2001–02	1.9100	1.6000	72.8–81.2 @ 1.6000	201.0–215.0 @ 1.1750	—
2.4L (T)	2001–02	—	.9840–1.0283	50.0–55.0 @ 1.4370	122.0–133.0 @ 1.0622	—
3.0L (R)	2001–05	—	1.3380	56.6 @ 1.3380	—	—
3.1L (J)	2001–04	1.8900	1.7010	75.0 @ 1.7010	230.0 @ 1.2600	—
3.2L (N)	2003–04	1.6500	1.3400	61.0 @ 1.3400	147.0 @ .9450	—
3.4L (E)	2001–05	1.8900	1.7010	75.0 @ 1.7010	230.0 @ 1.2600	—
3.5L (H)	2001–02	1.6059–1.7201	1.3780	47.5–52.5 @ 1.3780	130.2–141.9 @ .9670	—
3.5L (8)	2004–05	1.91	1.7400	77.0 @ 1.7400	234 @ 1.299	—
3.6L (7)	2004–05	1.6555–1.7657	1.3779	56.0–61.0 @ 1.3779	136.0–147.0 @ .9449	—
3.8L (K, 1, 2 & 4)	2001–05	1.9600	1.6900–1.7500	75.0 @ 1.7200	228.0 @ 1.2770	—
4.0L (C)	2001–03	1.6059–1.7201	1.3780	47.5–52.5 @ 1.3780	130.2–141.9 @ .9650	—
4.6L (A, Y & 9)	2001–05	1.6059–1.7201	1.3780	47.5–52.5 @ 1.3780	130.2–141.9 @ .9650	—
5.7L (G & S)	2001–05	2.0800	1.8000	76.0 @ 1.8000	220.0 @ 1.3200	—
6.0L (U)	2005	2.08	1.800	76.0 @ 1.800	220.0 @ 1.3200	—

① — The eighth digit of Vehicle Identification Number (VIN) denotes engine code.

② — Intake, 1.830 inches; exhaust, 1.831 inches.

VALVES

All Measurements Given In Inches Unless Otherwise Specified

Engine (VIN①)	Year	Stem Diameter		Valve Lash, Cold		Face Angle	Margin
		Intake	Exhaust	Intake	Exhaust		
1.0L (6)	2001	.2148–.2157	.2142–.2148	⑥	⑥	45.00	④
1.3L (2)	2001	.2152–.2157	.2142–.2148	.0050–.0070	.0090–.0110	45.00	—
1.8L (8)	2001–02	.2154–.2159	.2152–.2157	.0060–.0100	.0100–.0140	45.00	—
	2003–05	.2150–.2155	.2143–.2153	.0059–.0098	.0098–.0138	45.00	—
1.8L (L)	2003–05	.2150–.2155	.2143–.2153	.0031–.0071	.0087–.0126	45.00	—
1.9L DOHC (7)	2001–02	.2742–.2763	.2336–.2349	.0010–.0040	.0015–.0050	45.00–45.50°	③
1.9L SOHC (8 & 9)	2001–02	.2730–.2741	.2720–.2740	.0010–.0025	.0015–.0032	44.75–45.50°	②
2.0L (P)	2005	.2344–.2355	.2337–.2343	⑥	⑥	—	—
2.2L DOHC (F)	2002–05	.2344–.2355	.2337–.2343	⑥	⑥	45.00	—
2.2L OHV (4 & 5)	2001–02	—	—	—	—	45.00	⑤
2.4L (T)	2001–02	.2326–.2334	.2326–.2334	—	—	45.00	.0098
3.0L (R)	2001–05	.2344–.2350	.2341–.2346	—	—	45.00	—
3.1L (J)	2001–02	.3137–.3142	.3128–.3136	⑧	⑧	45.00	—
	2003–05	.3137–.3142	.3128–.3136	—	—	46.00	⑦
3.2L (N)	2003–04	.2345–.2350	.2341–.2346	—	—	89.50	—
3.4L (E)	2001–05	—	—	⑥	⑥	45.00	⑦
3.5L (H)	2001–02	.2331–.2339	.2331–.2339	⑥	⑥	45.00	⑨
3.5L (8)	2004–05			⑥	⑥	45.00	—
3.6L (7)	2004–05	.2344–.2352	.2341–.2348	⑥	⑥	44.25	—
3.8L (K, 1, 2 & 4)	2001–04	.3129–.3136	.3129–.3136	⑥	⑥	46.00	.0250
4.0L (C)	2001–03	.2331–.2339	.2331–.2339	⑥	⑥	45.00	.0421
4.6L (A, Y & 9)	2001–05	.2331–.2339	.2331–.2339	⑥	⑥	45.00	—
5.7L (G & S)	2001–05	.3130–.3144	.3130–.3144	⑥	⑥	45.00	.0500
6.0L (U)	2005	.3130–.3144	.3130–.3144	⑥	⑥	45.00	

① — The eighth digit of Vehicle Identification Number (VIN) denotes engine code.

② — Intake, .0350–.0496 inch; exhaust, .0390–.0559 inch.

③ — Intake, .035 inch; Exhaust, .039 inch

④ — Intake, .020 inch; exhaust, .027 inch.

⑤ — Intake, .048–.058 inch; exhaust, .073–.083 inch.

⑥ — Hydraulic lifters, zero lash.

⑦ — Intake, .083 inch; exhaust, .106 inch.

⑧ — Zero lash plus 1 1/2 turns.

⑨ — Intake, .0354 inch; exhaust, .0432 inch.

CAMSHAFT
All Measurements Given In Inches Unless Otherwise Specified

Engine (VIN①)	Year	Camshaft Journal Diameter	Maximum Journal Runout	Camshaft Bearing Clearance	Camshaft Endplay	Lifter Bore Diameter	Lifter Diameter	Lifter To Bore Clearance
1.0L (6)	2001	⑤	.0039	.0008–.0047	—	1.2205–1.2214	1.2188–1.2194	.0010–.0059
1.3L (2)	2001	1.1024–1.1031	.0039	.0016–.0047	—	—	—	—
1.8L (8)	2001–02	.9035–.9041	.0012	.0014–.0039	.0016–.0043	—	1.2191–1.2195	.0009–.0031
	2003–05	②	.0012	.0014–.0039	.0016–.0059	—	—	
1.8L (L)	2003–05	②	.0012	.0014–.0039	.0016–.0059	—	—	—
1.9L DOHC (7)	2001–02	1.0608–1.0626	.0030–.0047	.0021–.0050	.0020–.0180	.4371–.4744	.4672–.4728	.0003–.0024
1.9L SOHC (8 & 9)	2001–02	1.7470–1.7490	.0020–.0028	.0020–.0054	.0028–.0098	.8434–.8445	.8417–.8427	.0007–.0028
2.0L (P)	2005	1.0604–1.0614	—	—	.0016–.0057	.4730–.4739	—	—
2.2L DOHC (F)	2002–05	1.0604–1.0614	.0010	.0016–.0034	.0016–.0057	.4730–.4739	.4719–.4724	.0005–.0020
2.2L OHV (4 & 5)	2001–02	1.8680–1.8690	.0010	.0005–.0035	—	—	—	—
2.4L (T)	2001–02	④	—	.0019–.0043	.0009–.0088	1.298–1.299	1.297–1.298	.0006–.0023
3.0L (R)	2001–05	1.0990–1.1010	.0023	.0015–.0020	.0016–.0057	—	1.2976–1.282	.0010–.0030
3.1L (J)	2001–02	1.8680–1.8690	.0010	.0010–.0039	.0010	—	—	—
	2003–05	1.8680–1.8690	.0012	.0020–.0040	.0020	—	.8420–.8427	.0005–.0027
3.2L (N)	2003–04	1.1000–1.1008	.0015	.0035	—	—	—	—
3.4L (E)	2001–05	1.8680–1.8690	.0010	.0010–.0039	—	.8430–.8440	—	—
3.5L (H)	2001–02	1.0610–1.0620	.0020	.0016–.0033	—	.4727–.4736	.4716–.4721	.0014–.0016
3.5L (8)	2004–05	1.8680–1.8690	.0010	—	—	—	—	—
3.6L (7)	2004–05	③	.0002	.0016–.0033	.0018–.0085	.4728–.4736	.4719–.4724	.0015–.0016
3.8L (K, 1, 2 & 4)	2001–05	1.8478–1.8492	.00025	.0016–.0047	—	.8435–.8445	.8420–.8430	
4.0L (C)	2001–03	1.0610–1.0619	.0020	.0016–.0035	.0050–.0087	.4730–.4739	.4719–.4724	.0015–.0016
4.6L (A, Y & 9)	2001–05	1.0610–1.0619	.0020	.0016–.0035	.0050–.0087	.4730–.4739	.4719–.4724	.0015–.0016
5.7L (G & S)	2001–05	2.1640–2.1660	.0010	—	.0010–.0120	.8430–.8440	—	—
6.0L (U)	2005	2.164–2,166	.0010	—	.0020	.8430–.8440	—	—

① — The eighth digit of Vehicle Identification Number (VIN) denotes engine code.

② — Journal No. 1, 1.3563–1.3569 inches; journals Nos. 2–5, 1.1003–1.1010 inches.

③ — Journal No. 1, 1.3754–1.3764 inches; journals Nos. 2–4, 1.0605–1.0614 inches.

④ — Journal No. 1, 1.5720–1.5728 inches; journal Nos. 2–5, 1.3751–1.3760 inches.

⑤ — Journal No. 1, 1.0220–1.0228 inches; journal Nos. 2 & 3, 1.1795–1.1803 inches.

CRANKSHAFT, BEARINGS & RODS
All Measurements Given In Inches Unless Otherwise Specified

Engine (VIN①)	Year	Crankshaft					Bearing Clearance		Connecting Rod Side Clearance
		Main Bearing Journal Diameter	Connecting Rod Journal Diameter	Max. Out of Round	Max. Taper	Crankshaft Endplay	Main Bearings	Connecting Rod Bearings	
1.0L (6)	2001	③	1.65290–1.6535	.00040	.00040	.0044–.0122	.0008–.0023	.0012–.0031	.0039–.0078
1.3L (2)	2001	③	1.65290–1.6535	.00040	.00040	.0023	.0008–.0023	.0008–.0031	.0039–.0137

Continued

CRANKSHAFT, BEARINGS & RODS—Continued
All Measurements Given In Inches Unless Otherwise Specified

Engine (VIN①)	Year	Crankshaft					Bearing Clearance		Con-necting Rod Side Clearance
		Main Bearing Journal Diameter	Con-necting Rod Journal Diameter	Max. Out of Round	Max. Taper	Crank-shaft Endplay	Main Bear-ings	Con-necting Rod Bearings	
1.8L (L)	2003–05	1.8892–1.8898	1.7713–1.7717	.00080	.00080	.0016–.0118	.0008–.0118	.0011–.0031	.0063–.0138
1.8L (8)	2001–02	1.8892–1.8898	1.73200–1.7328	.00080	.00080	.0016–.0118	.0006–.0020	.0011–.0031	.0063–.0157
	2003–05	1.88932–1.8898	1.73197–1.73228	.00080	.00080	.0016–.0118	.0008–.0118	.0011–.0031	.0063–.0138
1.9L (7, 8 & 9)	2001–02	2.2437–2.2444	1.8500–1.8508	.00040	.00040	.0020–.0098	.0002–.0022	.0001–.0022	—
2.0L (P)	2005	2.2045–2.2050	1.9291–1.9297	—	—	.0012–.0150	.0012–.0026	.0011–.0027	.0028–.0146
2.2L DOHC (F)	2002–04	2.2045–2.2050	1.92910–1.92970	—	—	.0012–.0150	.0012–.0026	.0011–.0027	.0028–.0146
2.2L OHV (4 & 5)	2001–02	2.3945–2.4954	1.9983–1.99994	.00019	.00019	.0020–.0070	.0006–.0019	.0010–.0031	.0039–.0149
2.4L (T)	2001–02	2.3622–2.3631	1.88870–1.8897	.00020	.00030	.0034–.0095	.0004–.0023	.0004–.0026	.0059–.0177
3.0L (R)	2001–05	2.6763–2.6770	1.92700–1.92800	.00120	—	.0004–.0300	.0006–.0017	.0005–.0024	.0027–.0110
3.1L (J)	2001–02	2.6473–2.6483	1.99870–1.99940	.00020	.00020	.0024–.0083	.0008–.0025	.0007–.0170	.0100–.0150
	2003–05	2.6473–2.6483	1.99870–1.99940	.00020	.00020	.0024–.0083	②	.0007–.0170	.0100–.0150
3.2L (N)	2003–04	2.676–2.667	2.6764–2.6770	.00119	.00119	.0039–.00795	.0006–.0017	.0008–.0024	.0027–.0110
3.4L (E)	2001–05	2.6473–2.6483	1.99870–1.9994	.00020	.00020	.0024–.0083	②	.0007–.0024	.0070–.0170
3.5L (H)	2001–02	2.7550–2.7560	2.18290–2.1835	.00016	.00015	.0050–.0200	.0006–.0021	.0009–.0025	.0040–.0130
3.5L (8)	2004–05	2.6473–2.6483	2.248–2.249	.00020	.00030	.0024–.0083	.0008–.0025	.0007–.0170	.0080–.0090
3.6L (7)	2004–05	2.6768–2.6775	2.2044–2.2050	.00020	.00020	.0039–.0130	.0004–.0024	.0013	.01590
3.8L (K, 1, 2 & 4)	2001–05	2.4988–2.4998	2.24870–2.2499	.00025	.00035	.0030–.0110	④	.0005–.0026	.0040–.0200
4.0L (C)	2001–03	2.5335–2.5341	2.21390–2.1245	.00020	.00020	.0020–.0197	.0006–.0025	.0010–.0030	.0079–.0197
4.6L (A, Y & 9)	2001–05	2.5335–2.5341	2.12390–2.1245	.00020	.00020	.0020–.0197	.0006–.0025	.0010–.0030	.0079–.0197
5.7L (G & S)	2001–05	2.5580–2.559	2.0987–2.0999	.000118–.00031	.00039–.00780	.0015–.0078	.0008–.0025	.0009–.0030	.0043–.0200
6.0L (U)	2005	2.558–2.559	2.0987–2.0999	.000118–.00030	.00040–.000780	.0010	.008–.0025	.0009–.003	.00433–.02

① — The eighth digit of Vehicle Identification Number (VIN) denotes engine code.

② — Except No. 3, .0008–.0025 inch; No. 3, .0012–.0030 inch.

③ — No. 1, 1.7714–1.7716 inches; No. 2, 1.7712–1.7714 inches & No. 3, 1.7710–1.7712 inches.

④ — No. 1, .0070–.0016 inch; Nos. 2–4, .0009–.0018 inch.

BALANCE SHAFT

All Measurements Given In Inches, Unless Otherwise Specified.

Engine Liter (VIN①)	Year	Bearing Bore Diameter	Bearing Journal Diameter	Bearing Clearance	Bushing Journal Diameter	Bushing Clearance	End Play
2.0L (P)	2005	④	.7474–.7882	.0013–.0040	1.4458–1.4466	.0013–.0040	.0020–.0118
2.2L DOHC (F)	2001–05	1.6535–1.6542	.7874–.7882	.0012–.0025	1.4458–1.4466	.0013–.0040	.0020–.0118
2.4L (T)	2001–02	1.3001–1.1801	1.1791–1.1801	.0017–.0044	—	—	.0073–.0179
3.5L (H)	2001–02	1.9995–2.0005	—	.0006–.0030	—	—	—
3.8L (K, 1, 2 & 4)	2001–04	②	1.4994–1.5002	③	—	—	0–.0067

DOHC — Dual Overhead Cams.
① — Eighth digit of Vehicle Identification Number (Vehicle Identification Number (VIN) denotes engine code.
② — Front, 2.0462–2.0472 inches; rear, 1.8735–1.8745 inches.
③ — Front, 0–.001 inch; rear, 2001–02, .0005–.0043 inch, 2003–05, .0005–.0048 inch.
④ — Inside carrier, .7894–.7899 inch; outside carrier, 1.6562–1.6534 inches.

PISTONS, PINS & RINGS

All Measurements Given In Inches Unless Otherwise Specified

Engine (VIN①)	Year	Piston Diameter	Piston Clearance	Piston Pin Diameter⑨	Piston Pin To Piston Clearance	Ring End Gap Comp. Top	Ring End Gap Comp. 2nd	Ring End Gap Oil	Ring Side Clear. Comp. Top	Ring Side Clear. Comp. 2nd	Ring Side Clear. Oil
1.0L (6)	2001	2.9122–2.9130	.0008–.0015	—	—	.0079–.0276	.0079–.0276	.0079–.0708	.0012–.0027	.0008–.0023	.0008–.0023
1.3L (2)	2001	⑧	.0008–.0015	.7479–.7480	.0001–.0020	.0059–.0275	.0059–.0275	.0079–.0669	.0014–.0027	.0014–.0027	.0008–.0023
1.8L (8)	2001–02	3.1073–3.1077	.0026–.0039	.7876–.7879	②	.0098–.0413	.0138–.0472	.0059–.0413	.0012–.0028	.0012–.0028	—
1.8L (8)	2003–05	3.2274–3.2281	.0003–.0039	—	—	.0098–.0413	.0138–.0472	.0059–.0413	.0009–.0028	.0012–.0028	—
1.8L (L)	2003–05	3.2274–3.2281	.0003–.0039	—	—	.0098–.0413	.0138–.0472	.0059–.0413	.0009–.0028	.0012–.0028	—
1.9L (7, 8 & 9)	2001–02	3.2270–3.2280⑱	0–.0028	.7676–.7678	.0001–.0005	.0071–.0177	.0138–.0256	.0039–.0256	—	—	—
2.0L (P)	2005	3.3845–3.3851⑰	.0004–.0016	.7872–.7874	.0001–.0005	.0080–.0160	.0140–.0220	.010–.030	.0015–.0031	.0012–.0027	.0035–.0042
2.2L DOHC (F)	2002–05	3.3845–3.3851⑰	.0004–.0016	.7872–.7874	.0001–.0005	.0080–.0160	.0140–.0220	.0100–.0300	.0461–.0469	.0579–.0587	.0035–.0042
2.2L OHV (4 & 5)	2001–02	—	.0022–.0034⑲	.8001–.8002	.0003–.0006	.0100–.0200	.0012–.0177	.0100–.0300	.0020–.0035	.0016–.0031	.0005–.0087
2.4L (T)	2001–02	3.5404–3.5420⑯	.0010–.0031	.8659–.8661	.0001–.0004	.0060–.0120	.0098–.0157	.0098–.0299	.0016–.0031	.0012–.0028	—
3.0L (R)	2001–05	3.3834–3.3854	.0010–.0018	.8267	.0001–.0003	.0118–.0196	—	.0157–.0551	.0008–.0015	—	.0004–.0012
3.1L (J)	2001–02	3.5029–3.5040	.0013–.0027	.9052–.9054	.0004–.0008	.0060–.0140	.0197–.0280	.0098–.0500	.002–.0033	.002–.0035	.0080
3.1L (J)	2003–05	3.503–3.504	.0003–.0018	—	—	.0060–.0140	.0197–.0280	.0090–.0400	.002–.0033	.002–.0035	.0028–.0037
3.2L (N)	2003–04	3.4425–3.4445	.0010–.0018	.8264–.8268	.0004–.0006	.0118–.0196	—	.0158–.0551	.00079–.0024	—	.00079–.0024
3.4L (E)	2001	3.6209–3.6216⑭	.0010–.0027	.9052–.9054	.0004–.0008	.0060–.0140	.0197–.0280	.0098–.0500	.002–.0033	.002–.0035	.0080
3.4L (E)	2002	⑬	⑪	.9052–.9054	.0003–.0006	.0080–.0190	.0213–.0339	.0120–.0350	.0020–.0034	.0020–.0035	.0018–.0079
3.4L (E)	2003–05	⑩	⑦	.9053–.9054	.0001–.0006	.0060–.0140	.0188–.0291	.0098–.0303	.0020–.033	.0020–.0031	.0028–.0037
3.5L (H)	2001–02	3.5210–3.5220	.0010–.0025	.8265–.8267	.0001–.0006	.0100–.0160	.0140–.0200	.0100–.0300	.0016–.0037	.0016–.0037	⑫
3.5L (8)	2004–05	3.699–3.701	-.00101–.0030	.9447–.9448	.0003–.0006	.0070–.0150	.0190–.0290	.0100–.0290	.001–.003	.002–.003	.0040

Continued

PISTONS, PINS & RINGS—Continued
All Measurements Given In Inches Unless Otherwise Specified

Engine (VIN①)	Year	Piston Diameter	Piston Clearance	Piston Pin Diameter⑨	Piston Pin To Piston Clearance	Piston Ring End Gap			Piston Ring Side Clearance		
						Comp.		Oil	Comp.		Oil
						Top	2nd		Top	2nd	
3.6L (7)	2004–05	3.6990–3.6998	.0010–.0021	.9448–.9449	.0002–.0005	.0059–.0118	.0110–.0189	.0098–.0295	.0012–.0026	.0002–.0013	.0083–.0155
3.8L (K & 2)	2001–05	3.7969–3.7991	.0004–.0036	.8659–.8661	.00008–.00051	.0100–.0180	.0230–.0330	.0100–.0300	.0013–.0031	.0013–.0031	.0009–.0079
3.8L (1 & 4)	2001–05	3.7966–3.8003	.0008–.0039	⑮	.00061–.00026	.0100–.0180	.0230–.0330	.0100–.0300	.0013–.0031	.0013–.0031	.0009–.0079
4.0L (C)	2001–02	3.4243–3.4237	—	.8266–.8268	.0001–.0005	.0098–.0157	.0020–.0138	.0098–.0299	.0016–.0037	.0016–.0037	⑫
	2003	3.4235–3.4241⑳	.0000–.0020	.9053–.9055	.0001–.0005	.0098–.0157	.0020–.0138	.0098–.0299	.0016–.0037	.0016–.0037	⑫
4.6L (A, Y & 9)	2001–02	3.6597–3.6603	.0008–.0020	.8269–.8271	.0001–.0005	.0098–.0157	.0138–.0020	.0098–.0299	.0016–.0037	.0016–.0037	⑫
	2003–05	3.6597–3.6603⑳	.0008–.0020	.9056–.9058	.0001–.0005	.0098–.0157	.0138–.0196	.0098–.0299	.0016–.0037	.0016–.0037	⑫
5.7L (G & S)	2001–05	④	③	⑤	⑥	.0090–.0196	.0173–.0300	.0070–.0320	.00157–.00330	.0020–.0034	-.0003–.0069
6.0L (U)	2005	4.0000–4.0010㉑	㉒	.9430	.00027–.00086	.0080–.0160	.0150–.0270	.0090–.0310	.0012–.0040	.0014–.0031	.0005–.0079

① — The eighth digit of Vehicle Identification Number (VIN) denotes engine code.

② — Interference Fit.

③ — Non-coated, .0005–.0019 inch; coated, .0005–.0029 inch.

④ — Non-coated, 3.8964–3.897 inches; coated (measure over coating), 3.897–3.899 inches.

⑤ — 2001–2004, first design, .9447–.9448 inch; 2004, second design & 2005, .943 inch.

⑥ — 2001–2004, first design, .0004–.0008 inch; 2004, second design & 2005, .00008–.00040 inch.

⑦ — Cylinders Nos. 1–4, .0006–.0036 inch; Cylinders Nos. 5 & 6, -.0003–.0036 inch.

⑧ — Stamp No. 1, 2.9126–2.9130 inches; No. 2, 2.9120–2.9126 inches in diameter.

⑨ — Pistons & pins are matched set & should be replaced as an assembly.

⑩ — Cylinders Nos. 1–4, 3.619–3.622 inches; Cylinders Nos. 5 & 6, 3.619–3.623 inches.

⑪ — Non-coated, .0006–.0033 inch; Grafal coated, .00031–.0035 inch.

⑫ — Zero clearance; side sealing ring.

⑬ — Measure 1.9685 inches from top of piston: Non-coated, 3.620–3.621 inches; Grafal coated, 3.6217–3.6232 inches.

⑭ — Measure .51 inch below centerline of piston pin bore.

⑮ — VIN 1, .90531–.90551 inch; VIN 4, .8659–.8661 inch.

⑯ — Measured 1.8898 inches from top of piston.

⑰ — Measured .5708 inch from bottom of piston.

⑱ — Measured .20 inch from bottom of piston.

⑲ — Measured 1.6811 inches from top of piston

⑳ — Measured 1.6353 inches from top of piston.

㉑ — Measured over skirt coating.

㉒ — Production, .0009–.0012 inch; Service limit w/skirt coating worn off, .00094–.0031 inch.

CYLINDER BLOCK
All Measurements Given In Inches Unless Otherwise Specified

Engine (VIN①)	Year	Cylinder Bore Diameter	Cylinder Bore Taper Max.	Cylinder Bore Out of Round Max.
1.0L (6)	2001	2.9193	.0040	.0040
1.3L (2)	2001	2.9196	.0039	.0039
1.8L (L)	2003–05	3.1102–3.1107	—	—
1.8L (8)	2001–02	3.1102–3.1110	.0039	.0039
	2003–05	3.1102–3.1107	—	—
1.9L (7, 8 & 9)	2001–02	③	.0020	.0020
2.0L (P)	2005	3.3855–3.3861	.0004	.0004
2.2L DOHC (F)	2002–05	3.3855–3.3861	.0004	.0004
2.2L OHV (4 & 5)	2001–02	3.5036–3.5043	.0005	.0005
2.4L (T)	2001–02	3.5430–3.5435	.0003	.0004
3.0L (R)	2001–05	3.3848–3.3868	.0003	.0026
3.1L (J)	2001–02	3.5046–3.5053	.0005	.0008
	2003–05	3.5046–3.5056	.0010	.0010
3.2L (N)	2003–04	3.4439–3.4459	.0003	.0026

Continued

CYLINDER BLOCK—Continued
All Measurements Given In Inches Unless Otherwise Specified

Engine (VIN①)	Year	Cylinder Bore Diameter	Cylinder Bore Taper Max.	Cylinder Bore Out of Round Max.
3.4L (E)	2001	3.6228–3.6235	.0004	.0003
	2002	3.6228–3.6235	.0010	.00035
	2003–05	3.6220–3.6230	.0010	.0010
3.5L (H)	2001–02	3.5230②	.0040	.0040
3.5L (8)	2004–05	3.700–3.701	.0010	.0010
3.6L (7)	2004–05	3.7005–3.7011	—	.0005
3.8L (K, 1, 2 & 4)	2001–05	3.8000	.0010	.0010
4.0L (C)	2001–03	3.4249–3.4255②	.0039	.0039
4.6L (A, Y & 9)	2001–05	3.6611–3.6617②	.0039	.0039
5.7L (G & S)	2001–05	3.8970–3.8980	.0007	.0002
6.0L (U)	2005	4.0007–4.0017	—	.0002

① — The eighth digit of Vehicle Identification Number (VIN) denotes engine code.

② — Measure 1.610 inch below deck surface.

③ — Cylinder Nos. 1–3, 3.2280–3.2297 inches; cylinder No. 4, 3.2283–3.2301 inches.

OIL PUMP
All Measurements Given In Inches Unless Otherwise Specified

Engine (VIN①)	Year	Gear Backlash	Gear To Body Clearance	Gear Endplay	Gear Pocket Depth	Gear Pocket Diameter	Pump Gear Thickness	Pump Gear Diameter	Relief Valve To Body Clearance
1.0L (6)	2001	—	.0122	.0059	—	—	—	—	—
1.3L (2)	2001	—	.0122	.0059	—	—	—	—	—
1.8L (L)	2003–05	.0024–.0138	.0012–.0062	.0049–.0128	—	—	—	—	—
1.8L (8)	2001–02	.0138	.0118	.0059	—	—	—	—	—
	2003–05	.0024–.0138	.0012–.0062	.0049–.0128	—	—	—	—	—
1.9L (7, 8 & 9)	2001–02	.0060–.0110	.0016–.0050	.0060	—	—	—	—	—
2.0L (U)	2005	—	—	—	—	—	—	—	—
2.2L DOHC (F)	2002–05	.0120	.0030	.0060	.5510	—	—	—	—
2.2L OHV (4 & 5)	2001–02	.0091–.0201	.0010–.0040	.0020–.0070	1.1950–1.1980	1.5030–1.5060	.6727–.6731	1.4980–1.5000	.0015–.0035
2.4L (T)	2001–02	.0029–.0055	.0019–.0059	.0059	.6023–.6043	1.7730–1.7750	.5994–.6003	—	—
3.0L (R)②	2001–05	.0110	③	.0060	—	—	—	—	—
3.1L (J)	2001–02	.0037–.0077	.0010–.0030	.0020–.0050	1.2020–1.2040	1.5030–1.5050	1.1990–1.2000	1.4980–1.5000	.0015–.0035
	2003–05	.0037–.0077	—	—	1.2020–1.2040	1.5030–1.5050	—	1.498–1.5000	.0015–.0035
3.2L (N)	2003–04	—	—	.0026	—	—	—	—	—
3.4L (E)	2001–05	.0037–.0077	.0010–.0030	.0020–.0050	1.2020–1.2040	1.5030–1.5050	1.1990–1.2000	1.4980–1.5000	.0015–.0035
3.5L (H)②	2001–02	—	—	—	—	—	—	—	—
3.5L (8)	2004–05	.0037–.0077	—	—	1.2020–1.2040	1.5030–1.5050	—	1.4980–1.5000	.0015–.0035
3.6L (7)	2004–05	.0030–.0071	.0039–.0091	.0016–.0051	.6128–.6142	3.4360–3.4380	.6107–.6117	3.4289–3.4321	.0018–.0043
3.8L (K, 1, 2 & 4)	2001–05	.0060	.0080–.0150	.0010–.0035	.4610–.4625	3.5080–3.5120	—	—	.0015–.0030
4.0L (C)②	2001–03	—	—	—	—	—	—	—	—
4.6L (Y & 9)②	2001–05	—	—	—	—	—	—	—	—
6.0L (U)②	2005	—	—	—	—	—	—	—	—

① — The eighth digit of Vehicle Identification Number (VIN) denotes engine code.

② — Pump components are not serviced separately. If any component is damaged or worn, pump should be replaced.

③ — Inner gear to housing, .003 inch; outer gear to housing, .004 inch.

MANUAL INFORMATION LOCATOR

Front Wheel Drive Models

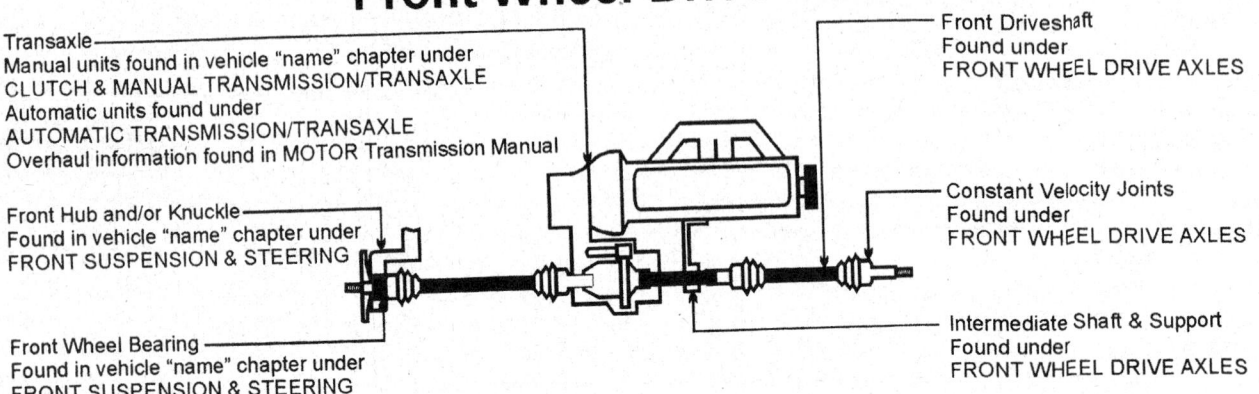

Transaxle
Manual units found in vehicle "name" chapter under
CLUTCH & MANUAL TRANSMISSION/TRANSAXLE
Automatic units found under
AUTOMATIC TRANSMISSION/TRANSAXLE
Overhaul information found in MOTOR Transmission Manual

Front Hub and/or Knuckle
Found in vehicle "name" chapter under
FRONT SUSPENSION & STEERING

Front Wheel Bearing
Found in vehicle "name" chapter under
FRONT SUSPENSION & STEERING

Front Driveshaft
Found under
FRONT WHEEL DRIVE AXLES

Constant Velocity Joints
Found under
FRONT WHEEL DRIVE AXLES

Intermediate Shaft & Support
Found under
FRONT WHEEL DRIVE AXLES

All Wheel Drive Models

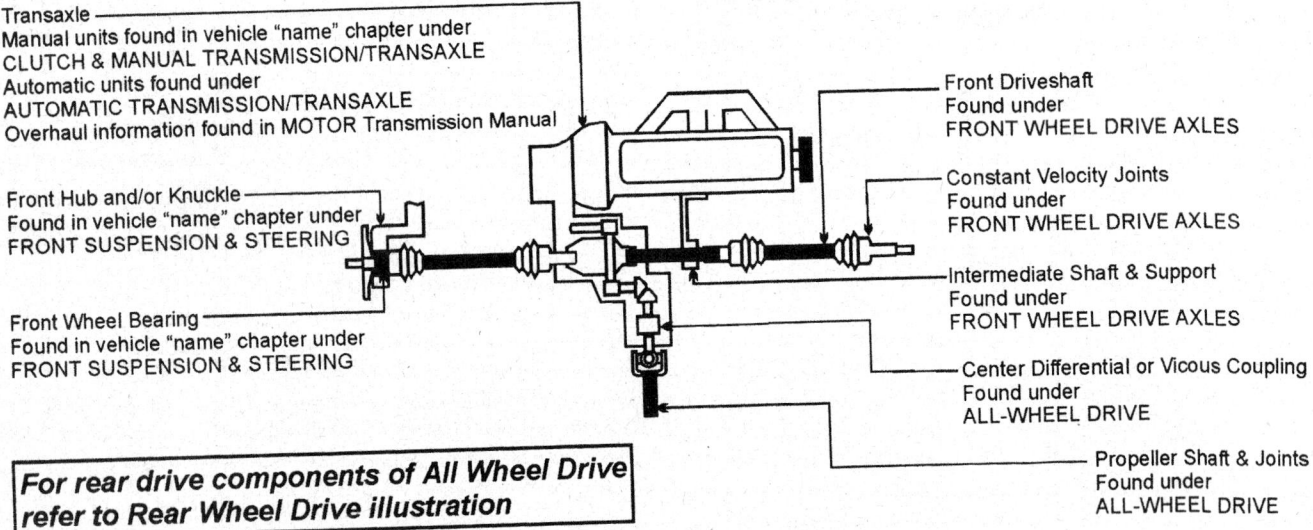

Transaxle
Manual units found in vehicle "name" chapter under
CLUTCH & MANUAL TRANSMISSION/TRANSAXLE
Automatic units found under
AUTOMATIC TRANSMISSION/TRANSAXLE
Overhaul information found in MOTOR Transmission Manual

Front Hub and/or Knuckle
Found in vehicle "name" chapter under
FRONT SUSPENSION & STEERING

Front Wheel Bearing
Found in vehicle "name" chapter under
FRONT SUSPENSION & STEERING

Front Driveshaft
Found under
FRONT WHEEL DRIVE AXLES

Constant Velocity Joints
Found under
FRONT WHEEL DRIVE AXLES

Intermediate Shaft & Support
Found under
FRONT WHEEL DRIVE AXLES

Center Differential or Vicous Coupling
Found under
ALL-WHEEL DRIVE

Propeller Shaft & Joints
Found under
ALL-WHEEL DRIVE

For rear drive components of All Wheel Drive refer to Rear Wheel Drive illustration

Rear Wheel Drive Models

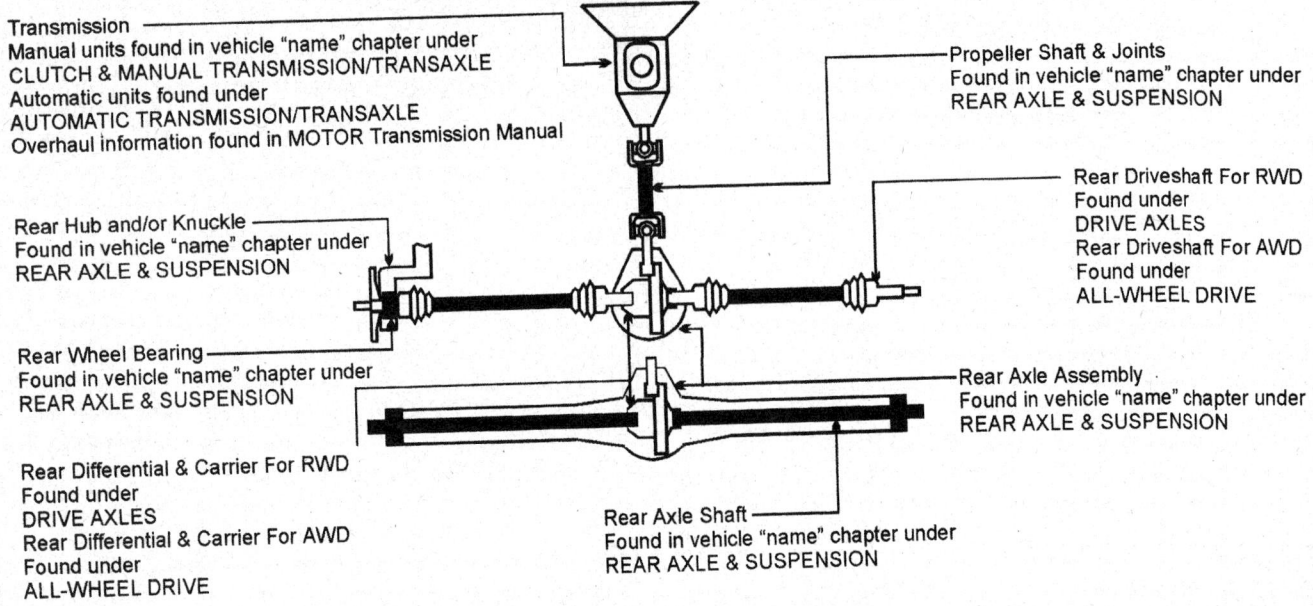

Transmission
Manual units found in vehicle "name" chapter under
CLUTCH & MANUAL TRANSMISSION/TRANSAXLE
Automatic units found under
AUTOMATIC TRANSMISSION/TRANSAXLE
Overhaul information found in MOTOR Transmission Manual

Rear Hub and/or Knuckle
Found in vehicle "name" chapter under
REAR AXLE & SUSPENSION

Rear Wheel Bearing
Found in vehicle "name" chapter under
REAR AXLE & SUSPENSION

Rear Differential & Carrier For RWD
Found under
DRIVE AXLES
Rear Differential & Carrier For AWD
Found under
ALL-WHEEL DRIVE

Propeller Shaft & Joints
Found in vehicle "name" chapter under
REAR AXLE & SUSPENSION

Rear Driveshaft For RWD
Found under
DRIVE AXLES
Rear Driveshaft For AWD
Found under
ALL-WHEEL DRIVE

Rear Axle Assembly
Found in vehicle "name" chapter under
REAR AXLE & SUSPENSION

Rear Axle Shaft
Found in vehicle "name" chapter under
REAR AXLE & SUSPENSION

DECIMAL & MILLIMETER EQUIVALENTS

Inch	Inch	mm
1/64	.015625	.397
1/32	.03125	.794
3/64	.046875	1.191
1/16	.0625	1.587
5/64	.078125	1.984
3/32	.09375	2.381
7/64	.109375	2.778
1/8	.125	3.175
9/64	.140625	3.572
5/32	.15625	3.969
11/64	.17185	4.366
3/16	.1875	4.762
13/64	.203125	5.159
7/32	.21875	5.556
15/64	.234375	5.953
1/4	.25	6.350
17/64	.265626	6.747
9/32	.28125	7.144
19/64	.296875	7.541
5/16	.3125	7.937
21/64	.328125	8.334
11/32	.34375	8.731

Inch	Inch	mm
23/64	.359375	9.128
3/8	.375	9.525
25/64	.390625	9.922
13/32	.40625	10.319
27/64	.421875	10.716
7/16	.4375	11.113
29/64	.453125	11.509
15/32	.46875	11.906
31/64	.484375	12.303
1/2	.5	12.700
33/64	.515625	13.097
17/32	.53125	13.494
35/64	.546875	13.890
9/16	.5625	14.287
37/64	.578125	14.684
19/32	.59375	15.081
39/64	.609375	15.478
5/8	.625	15.875
41/64	.640625	16.272
21/32	.65625	16.669
43/64	.671875	17.065

Inch	Inch	mm
11/16	.6875	17.462
45/64	.703125	17.859
23/32	.71875	18.265
47/64	.734375	18.653
3/4	.75	19.505
49/64	.765625	19.447
25/32	.78125	19.884
51/64	.796875	20.240
13/16	.8125	20.637
53/64	.828125	21.034
27/32	.84375	21.431
55/64	.859375	21.828
7/8	.875	22.225
57/64	.890625	22.622
29/32	.90625	23.019
59/64	.921875	23.415
15/16	.9375	23.812
61/64	.953125	24.209
31/32	.96875	24.606
63/64	.984375	25.003
1	1	25.400

Special Service Tools

Throughout this manual references are made to and illustrations may depict the use of special tools required to perform certain jobs. These special tools can generally be ordered through the dealers of the make vehicle being serviced. It is also suggested that you check with local automotive supply firms as they also supply tools manufactured by other firms that will assist in the performance of these jobs. The vehicle manufacturers special tools are supplied by:

Chrysler Corporation . . . . Miller Special Tools
OTC Division
28635 Mound Rd.
Warren, Michigan   48092-3499

Ford Motor Company . . . . SPX Corporation, OTC
Attn: Ford Rotunda
28635 Mound Rd.
Warren, Michigan 48092-3499

General Motors Corporation . . . . Kent-Moore
SPX Corporation
28635 Mound Rd.
Warren, Michigan 48092-3499

MANUAL INFORMATION LOCATOR

Operation/Subject/Topic	Auto Repair Manual, Vol. 1	Auto Repair Manual, Vol. 2	Domestic Engine Performance & Driveability Manual
Active Suspension System	—	X	—
Air Bags	—	X	—
Air Bag System Precautions	X	X	X
Air Conditioning	X	—	—
AIR Systems	—	—	X
All-Wheel Drive Systems	X	—	—
Alternator Specifications	X	—	—
Alternator Systems	X	—	—
Anti-Lock Brake Systems	—	X	—
Automatic Seat Belts	—	X	—
Axle Shaft Service	X	—	—
Back-Up Light Switch, Replace	X	—	—
Balance Shaft Service	X	—	—
Ball Joint Service	X	—	—
Belt Tension Data	X	—	—
Blower Motor, Replace	X	—	—
Brake Booster Service	X	—	—
Brake Service	X	—	—
Camber Adjustment	X	—	—
Camshaft Service	X	—	—
Capacity Data	X	—	—
Caster Adjustment	X	—	—
Catalytic Converters	—	—	X
Coil Pack, Replace	X	—	X
Coil Spring, Replace	X	—	—
Compression Check	X	—	X
Compression Pressures	X	—	X
Computer Relearn Procedures	X	X	X
Computerized Engine Control Systems	—	—	X
Control Arm Service	X	—	—
Cooling System Bleed	X	—	—
Cooling System Data	X	—	—
Crankshaft Pulley, Replace	X	—	—
Crankshaft Rear Oil Seal Service	X	—	—
Cruise Control Systems	—	X	—
Cylinder Block Specifications	X	—	—
Cylinder Head Service	X	—	—
Cylinder Head Specifications	X	—	—
Cylinder Head, Replace	X	—	—
Cylinder Liner, Replace	X	—	—
Dash Panel Service	—	X	—
Differential Service	X	—	—
Dimmer Switch, Replace	X	—	—
Disc Brake Service	X	—	—
Distributor Service	—	—	X
Distributor, Replace	X	—	X
Distributorless Ignition Systems	—	—	X
Drive Axle Service	X	—	—
Drive Belt Tension Data	X	—	—
Drum Brake Service	X	—	—
EGR System	—	—	X
Electric Engine Cooling Fans	X	—	—
Electric Fuel Pumps	X	—	X
Electrical Symbol Identification	X	X	X
Electronic Fuel Injection	—	—	X
Electronic Ignition	—	—	X
Electronic Instrumentation	—	—	X
Electronic Level Controls	—	X	—
Emission Control Application Charts	—	—	X
Emission Controls	—	—	X
Emission Vacuum Hose Routings	—	—	X
Engine Compartment Reference Diagrams	—	—	X

Operation/Subject/Topic	Auto Repair Manual, Vol. 1	Auto Repair Manual, Vol. 2	Domestic Engine Performance & Driveability Manual
Engine Cooling Fans	X	—	—
Engine Control Module, Replace	—	—	X
Engine Control Unit, Replace	—	—	X
Engine Front Cover Service	X	—	—
Engine Mounts, Replace	X	—	—
Engine Oil Seal Service	X	—	—
Engine Rebuilding Specifications	X	—	—
Engine Repairs	X	—	—
Engine Sensor Location	—	—	X
Engine Sensor Replacement	—	—	X
Engine Sensor Specifications	—	—	X
Engine System Identification Charts	—	—	X
Engine Tightening Specifications	X	—	—
Engine, Replace	X	—	—
Evaporator Core, Replace	X	—	—
Exhaust Gas Recirculation (EGR) Systems	—	—	X
Exhaust Manifold, Replace	X	—	—
Fast Idle Speed Adjustment	—	—	X
Federal Air Quality Standards	—	—	X
Flasher Location	X	—	—
Front Drive Axle Service	X	—	—
Front Wheel Alignment	X	—	—
Fuel Control System Identification	—	—	X
Fuel Filter, Replace	X	—	—
Fuel Injection Systems	—	—	X
Fuel Injector Cleaning Procedures	—	—	X
Fuel Injector, Replace	—	—	X
Fuel Pump Pressure Specifications	X	—	X
Fuel Pump Pressure Test	—	—	X
Fuel Pump Relay Location	X	—	X
Fuel Pump Replacement	X	—	X
Fuse Panel Location	X	—	—
General Engine Specifications	X	—	—
Headlight Switch, Replace	X	—	—
Heated Air Cleaners	—	—	X
Heater Core, Replace	X	—	—
Hub & Bearing Assembly Service	X	—	—
Hydraulic Brake System Service	X	—	—
Hydraulic Engine Cooling Fans	X	—	—
Hydraulic Valve Lifter Service	X	—	—
Idle Mixture Adjustments	—	—	X
Idle Speed Adjustments	—	—	X
Ignition Lock, Replace	X	—	—
Ignition Switch, Replace	X	—	—
Ignition System Application	—	—	X
Ignition Timing Procedures	—	—	X
Instrument Cluster, Replace	X	—	—
Intake Manifold, Replace	X	—	—
Intermittent Malfunction Computer Diagnosis	—	—	X
Knock Sensor, Replace	—	—	X
Leaf Spring, Replace	X	—	—
Lift Point Illustrations	X	X	—
Locking Differential Service	X	—	—
Locking Hub Service	X	—	—
Lower Ball Joint, Replace	X	—	—
Lower Control Arm Service	X	—	—
Lubricant Data	X	—	—
MacPherson Strut Service	X	—	—
Main & Rod Bearing Specifications	X	—	—
Maintenance & Warning Lamp Reset Procedures	X	X	X